Anonymous

Book of Mormon.

Deseret Alphabet

Anonymous

Book of Mormon.
Deseret Alphabet

ISBN/EAN: 9783337298166

Printed in Europe, USA, Canada, Australia, Japan

Cover: Foto ©Lupo / pixelio.de

More available books at **www.hansebooks.com**

Anonymous

Book of Mormon.
Deseret Alphabet

ISBN/EAN: 9783337298166

Printed in Europe, USA, Canada, Australia, Japan

Cover: Foto ©Lupo / pixelio.de

More available books at **www.hansebooks.com**

𐐜
𐐒𐐋𐐗 𐐉𐐚 𐐣𐐃𐐡𐐣𐐊𐐤:

𐐰𐑌 𐐰𐐿𐐵𐑌𐐻 𐑉𐐮𐐻𐑌 𐐺𐐴

𐐜 𐐐𐐈𐐤𐐔 𐐉𐐚 𐐣𐐃𐐡𐐣𐐊𐐤,

𐐊𐐑𐐉𐐤

𐐑𐐢𐐁𐐓𐐝 𐐓𐐁𐐗𐐤 𐐙𐐡𐐉𐐣 𐐜 𐐑𐐢𐐁𐐓𐐝 𐐉𐐚 𐐤𐐀𐐙𐐌.

𐐐𐐶𐐯𐑉𐑁𐐫𐑉, 𐐮𐐻 𐐮𐑆 𐐰𐑌 𐐰𐐺𐑉𐐮𐐾𐑋𐐯𐑌𐐻 𐐱𐑂 𐑄 𐑉𐐯𐐿𐐲𐑉𐐼 𐐱𐑂 𐑄 𐐹𐐨𐐹𐑊 𐐱𐑂 𐐤𐐨𐑁𐐴, 𐐰𐑌𐐼 𐐫𐑊𐑅𐐬 𐐱𐑂 𐑄 𐐢𐐩𐑋𐐰𐑌𐐴𐐻𐑅; 𐑉𐐮𐐻𐑌 𐐻𐐭 𐑄 𐐢𐐩𐑋𐐰𐑌𐐴𐐻𐑅, 𐐸𐐭 𐐪𐑉 𐐲 𐑉𐐯𐑋𐑌𐐲𐑌𐐻 𐐱𐑂 𐑄 𐐸𐐵𐑅 𐐱𐑂 𐐆𐑆𐑉𐐨𐐯𐑊; 𐐰𐑌𐐼 𐐫𐑊𐑅𐐬 𐐻𐐭 𐐖𐐭 𐐰𐑌𐐼 𐐖𐐯𐑌𐐻𐐴𐑊: 𐑉𐐮𐐻𐑌 𐐺𐐴 𐐶𐐩 𐐱𐑂 𐐿𐐲𐑋𐐰𐑌𐐼𐑋𐐯𐑌𐐻, 𐐰𐑌𐐼 𐐫𐑊𐑅𐐬 𐐺𐐴 𐑄 𐑅𐐹𐐮𐑉𐐮𐐻 𐐱𐑂 𐐹𐑉𐐱𐑁𐐯𐑅𐐨 𐐰𐑌𐐼 𐐱𐑂 𐑉𐐯𐑂𐐯𐑊𐐩𐑇𐐲𐑌. 𐐡𐐮𐐻𐑌 𐐰𐑌𐐼 𐑅𐐨𐑊𐐼 𐐲𐐹, 𐐰𐑌𐐼 𐐸𐐮𐐼 𐐲𐐹 𐐲𐑌𐐻𐐭 𐑄 𐐢𐐫𐑉𐐼, 𐑄𐐰𐐻 𐑄𐐩 𐑋𐐴𐐻 𐑌𐐱𐐻 𐐺 𐐼𐐨𐑅𐐻𐑉𐐱𐐮𐐼; 𐐻𐐭 𐐿𐐲𐑋 𐑁𐐬𐑉𐑃 𐐺𐐴 𐑄 𐑀𐐮𐑁𐐻 𐐰𐑌𐐼 𐐹𐐵𐐲𐑉 𐐱𐑂 𐐘𐐱𐐼 𐐲𐑌𐐻𐐭 𐑄 𐐮𐑌𐐻𐐲𐑉𐐹𐑉𐐯𐐻𐐩𐑇𐐲𐑌 𐑄𐐯𐑉𐐱𐑂: 𐑅𐐨𐑊𐐼 𐐺𐐴 𐑄 𐐸𐐰𐑌𐐼 𐐱𐑂 𐐣𐐫𐑉𐐬𐑌𐐴, 𐐰𐑌𐐼 𐐸𐐮𐐼 𐐲𐐹 𐐲𐑌𐐻𐐭 𐑄 𐐢𐐫𐑉𐐼, 𐐻𐐭 𐐿𐐲𐑋 𐑁𐐬𐑉𐑃 𐐮𐑌 𐐼𐐭 𐐻𐐴𐑋, 𐐺𐐴 𐑄 𐐶𐐩 𐐱𐑂 𐐖𐐯𐑌𐐻𐐴𐑊; 𐑄 𐐮𐑌𐐻𐐲𐑉𐐹𐑉𐐯𐐻𐐩𐑇𐐲𐑌 𐑄𐐯𐑉𐐱𐑂 𐐺𐐴 𐑄 𐑀𐐮𐑁𐐻 𐐱𐑂 𐐘𐐱𐐼:

𐐈𐑌 𐐰𐐺𐑉𐐮𐐾𐑋𐐯𐑌𐐻 𐐻𐐩𐐿𐑌 𐑁𐑉𐐱𐑋 𐑄 𐐒𐐳𐐿 𐐱𐑂 𐐀𐑃𐐲𐑉 𐐫𐑊𐑅𐐬; 𐐸𐐶𐐮𐐽 𐐮𐑆 𐐲 𐑉𐐯𐐿𐐲𐑉𐐼 𐐱𐑂 𐑄 𐐹𐐨𐐹𐑊 𐐱𐑂 𐐖𐐯𐑉𐐲𐐼; 𐐸𐐭 𐐶𐐲𐑉 𐑅𐐿𐐰𐐻𐐲𐑉𐐼 𐐰𐐻 𐑄 𐐻𐐴𐑋 𐑄 𐐢𐐫𐑉𐐼 𐐿𐐱𐑌𐑁𐐵𐑌𐐼𐐲𐐼 𐑄 𐑊𐐰𐑍𐑀𐐶𐐩𐐾 𐐱𐑂 𐑄 𐐹𐐨𐐹𐑊, 𐐸𐐶𐐯𐑌 𐑄𐐩 𐐶𐐲𐑉 𐐺𐐮𐑊𐐼𐐮𐑍 𐐲 𐐻𐐵𐐲𐑉 𐐻𐐭 𐑀𐐯𐐻 𐐻𐐭 𐐸𐐯𐑂𐑌; 𐐸𐐶𐐮𐐽 𐐮𐑆 𐐻𐐭 𐑇𐐬 𐐲𐑌𐐻𐐭 𐑄 𐑉𐐯𐑋𐑌𐐲𐑌𐐻 𐐱𐑂 𐑄 𐐸𐐵𐑅 𐐱𐑂 𐐆𐑆𐑉𐐨𐐯𐑊 𐐸𐐶𐐱𐐻 𐑀𐑉𐐩𐐻 𐑃𐐮𐑍𐑆 𐑄 𐐢𐐫𐑉𐐼 𐐸𐐰𐑃 𐐼𐐲𐑌 𐑁𐐫𐑉 𐑄𐐯𐑉 𐑁𐐪𐑄𐐲𐑉𐑆; 𐐰𐑌𐐼 𐑄𐐰𐐻 𐑄𐐩 𐑋𐐩 𐑌𐐬 𐑄 𐐿𐐲𐑂𐐯𐑌𐐲𐑌𐐻𐑅 𐐱𐑂 𐑄 𐐢𐐫𐑉𐐼, 𐑄𐐰𐐻 𐑄𐐩 𐐪𐑉 𐑌𐐱𐐻 𐐿𐐰𐑅𐐻 𐐫𐑁 𐑁𐐫𐑉𐐯𐑂𐐲𐑉; 𐐰𐑌𐐼 𐐫𐑊𐑅𐐬 𐐻𐐭 𐑄 𐐿𐐱𐑌𐑂𐐮𐑌𐑅𐐮𐑍 𐐱𐑂 𐑄 𐐖𐐭 𐐰𐑌𐐼 𐐖𐐯𐑌𐐻𐐴𐑊 𐑄𐐰𐐻 𐐖𐐨𐑆𐐲𐑅 𐐮𐑆 𐑄 𐐗𐑉𐐴𐑅𐐻, 𐑄 𐐀𐐻𐐲𐑉𐑌𐐲𐑊 𐐘𐐱𐐼, 𐑋𐐰𐑌𐐮𐑁𐐯𐑅𐐻𐐮𐑍 𐐸𐐮𐑋𐑅𐐯𐑊𐑁 𐐲𐑌𐐻𐐭 𐐫𐑊 𐑌𐐩𐑇𐐲𐑌𐑆. 𐐈𐑌𐐼 𐑌𐐵 𐐮𐑁 𐑄𐐯𐑉 𐐪𐑉 𐑁𐐫𐑊𐐻𐑅, 𐑄𐐩 𐐪𐑉 𐑄 𐑋𐐮𐑅𐐻𐐩𐐿𐑅 𐐱𐑂 𐑋𐐯𐑌; 𐐸𐐶𐐯𐑉𐑁𐐫𐑉, 𐐿𐐱𐑌𐐼𐐯𐑋 𐑌𐐱𐐻 𐑄 𐑃𐐮𐑍𐑆 𐐱𐑂 𐐘𐐱𐐼, 𐑄𐐰𐐻 𐐷𐐨 𐑋𐐩 𐐺 𐑁𐐵𐑌𐐼 𐑅𐐹𐐱𐐻𐑊𐐯𐑅 𐐰𐐻 𐑄 𐐾𐐲𐐾𐑋𐐯𐑌𐐻-𐑅𐐨𐐻 𐐱𐑂 𐐗𐑉𐐴𐑅𐐻.

𐐣𐐃𐐡𐐄𐐤𐐌.

𐐓𐐡𐐈𐐤𐐝𐐢𐐁𐐓𐐇𐐔 𐐒𐐌 𐐖𐐄𐐞𐐇𐐙 𐐝𐐣𐐆𐐛, 𐐖𐐊𐐤.

NEW YORK:
PUBLISHED FOR THE DESERET UNIVERSITY
BY RUSSELL BROS.
1869.

𐐜 𐐓𐐯𐑅𐐻𐐮𐑋𐐬𐑌𐐨 𐐲𐑂 𐐛𐑉𐐨 𐐎𐐮𐐻𐑌𐐯𐑅𐐯𐑆.

𐐒 𐐮𐐻 𐑌𐐬𐑌 𐐲𐑌𐐻𐐭 𐐫𐑊 𐑌𐐩𐑇𐐲𐑌𐑆, 𐐿𐐮𐑌𐐼𐑉𐐯𐐼𐑆, 𐐻𐐲𐑍𐑆, 𐐰𐑌𐐼 𐐹𐐨𐐹𐑊, 𐐲𐑌𐐻𐐭 𐐸𐐭𐑋 𐑄𐐮𐑅 𐐶𐐲𐑉𐐿 𐑇𐐰𐑊 𐐿𐐲𐑋, 𐑄𐐰𐐻 𐐶𐐨, 𐑃𐑉𐐭 𐑄 𐑀𐑉𐐩𐑅 𐐲𐑂 𐐘𐐪𐐼 𐑄 𐐙𐐪𐑄𐐲𐑉, 𐐰𐑌𐐼 𐐵𐑉 𐐢𐐫𐑉𐐼 𐐖𐐨𐑆𐐲𐑅 𐐗𐑉𐐴𐑅𐐻, 𐐸𐐰𐑂 𐑅𐐨𐑌 𐑄 𐐹𐑊𐐩𐐻𐑅 𐐸𐐶𐐮𐐽 𐐿𐐪𐑌𐐻𐐩𐑌 𐑄𐐮𐑅 𐑉𐐯𐐿𐐲𐑉𐐼, 𐐸𐐶𐐮𐐽 𐐮𐑆 𐐲 𐑉𐐯𐐿𐐲𐑉𐐼 𐐲𐑂 𐑄 𐐹𐐨𐐹𐑊 𐐲𐑂 𐐤𐐨𐑁𐐴, 𐐰𐑌𐐼 𐐫𐑊𐑅𐐬 𐐲𐑂 𐑄 𐐢𐐩𐑋𐐲𐑌𐐴𐐻𐑅, 𐑄𐐯𐑉 𐐺𐑉𐐯𐑄𐑉𐐯𐑌, 𐐰𐑌𐐼 𐐫𐑊𐑅𐐬 𐐲𐑂 𐑄 𐐹𐐨𐐹𐑊 𐐲𐑂 𐐖𐐩𐑉𐐯𐐼, 𐐸𐐭 𐐿𐐩𐑋 𐑁𐑉𐐪𐑋 𐑄 𐐻𐐵𐐲𐑉 𐐲𐑂 𐐸𐐶𐐮𐐽 𐐸𐐰𐑃 𐐺𐐮𐑌 𐑅𐐹𐐬𐐿𐐲𐑌; 𐐰𐑌𐐼 𐐶𐐨 𐐫𐑊𐑅𐐬 𐑌𐐬 𐑄𐐰𐐻 𐑄𐐩 𐐸𐐰𐑂 𐐺𐐮𐑌 𐐻𐑉𐐰𐑌𐑅𐑊𐐩𐐻𐐯𐐼 𐐺𐐴 𐑄 𐑀𐐮𐑁𐐻 𐐰𐑌𐐼 𐐹𐐵𐐲𐑉 𐐲𐑂 𐐘𐐪𐐼, 𐑁𐐫𐑉 𐐸𐐮𐑆 𐑂𐑎𐑅 𐐸𐐰𐑃 𐐼𐐨𐐿𐑊𐐩𐑉𐐼 𐐮𐐻 𐐲𐑌𐐻𐐭 𐐲𐑅; 𐐸𐐶𐐯𐑉𐑁𐐫𐑉 𐐶𐐨 𐑌𐐬 𐐲𐑂 𐐲 𐑇𐐭𐑉𐐯𐐻𐐨 𐑄𐐰𐐻 𐑄 𐐶𐐲𐑉𐐿 𐐮𐑆 𐐻𐑉𐐭. 𐐈𐑌𐐼 𐐶𐐨 𐐫𐑊𐑅𐐬 𐐻𐐯𐑅𐐻𐐮𐑁𐐴 𐑄𐐰𐐻 𐐶𐐨 𐐸𐐰𐑂 𐑅𐐨𐑌 𐑄 𐐯𐑌𐑀𐑉𐐩𐑂𐐮𐑍𐑆 𐐸𐐶𐐮𐐽 𐐪𐑉 𐐲𐐹𐐪𐑌 𐑄 𐐹𐑊𐐩𐐻𐑅; 𐐰𐑌𐐼 𐑄𐐩 𐐸𐐰𐑂 𐐺𐐮𐑌 𐑇𐐬𐑌 𐐲𐑌𐐻𐐭 𐐲𐑅 𐐺𐐴 𐑄 𐐹𐐵𐐲𐑉 𐐲𐑂 𐐘𐐪𐐼, 𐐰𐑌𐐼 𐑌𐐪𐐻 𐐲𐑂 𐑋𐐰𐑌. 𐐈𐑌𐐼 𐐶𐐨 𐐼𐐨𐐿𐑊𐐩𐑉 𐐶𐐮𐑄 𐐶𐐲𐑉𐐼𐑆 𐐲𐑂 𐑅𐐬𐐺𐐲𐑉𐑌𐐯𐑅, 𐑄𐐰𐐻 𐐰𐑌 𐐩𐑌𐐾𐐯𐑊 𐐲𐑂 𐐘𐐪𐐼 𐐿𐐩𐑋 𐐼𐐵𐑌 𐑁𐑉𐐪𐑋 𐐸𐐯𐑂𐐲𐑌, 𐐰𐑌𐐼 𐐸𐐨 𐐺𐑉𐐫𐐻 𐐰𐑌𐐼 𐑊𐐩𐐼 𐐺𐐨𐑁𐐫𐑉 𐐵𐑉 𐐴𐑆, 𐑄𐐰𐐻 𐐶𐐨 𐐺𐐨𐐸𐐯𐑊𐐼 𐐰𐑌𐐼 𐑅𐐫 𐑄 𐐹𐑊𐐩𐐻𐑅 𐐰𐑌𐐼 𐑄 𐐯𐑌𐑀𐑉𐐩𐑂𐐮𐑍𐑆 𐑄𐐯𐑉𐐪𐑌; 𐐰𐑌𐐼 𐐶𐐨 𐑌𐐬 𐑄𐐰𐐻 𐐮𐐻 𐐮𐑆 𐐺𐐴 𐑄 𐑀𐑉𐐩𐑅 𐐲𐑂 𐐘𐐪𐐼 𐑄 𐐙𐐪𐑄𐐲𐑉, 𐐰𐑌𐐼 𐐵𐑉 𐐢𐐫𐑉𐐼 𐐖𐐨𐑆𐐲𐑅 𐐗𐑉𐐴𐑅𐐻, 𐑄𐐰𐐻 𐐶𐐨 𐐺𐐨𐐸𐐯𐑊𐐼 𐐰𐑌𐐼 𐐺𐐯𐑉 𐑉𐐯𐐿𐐲𐑉𐐼 𐑄𐐰𐐻 𐑄𐐨𐑆 𐑃𐐮𐑍𐑆 𐐪𐑉 𐐻𐑉𐐭; 𐐰𐑌𐐼 𐐮𐐻 𐐮𐑆 𐑋𐐪𐑉𐑂𐐯𐑊𐐲𐑅 𐐮𐑌 𐐵𐑉 𐐴𐑆, 𐑌𐐯𐑂𐐲𐑉𐑄𐐯𐑊𐐯𐑅 𐑄 𐑂𐑎𐑅 𐐲𐑂 𐑄 𐐢𐐫𐑉𐐼 𐐿𐐪𐑋𐐰𐑌𐐼𐐯𐐼 𐐲𐑅 𐑄𐐰𐐻 𐐶𐐨 𐑇𐐳𐐼 𐐺𐐯𐑉 𐑉𐐯𐐿𐐲𐑉𐐼 𐐲𐑂 𐐮𐐻; 𐐸𐐶𐐯𐑉𐑁𐐫𐑉, 𐐻𐐭 𐐺 𐐬𐐺𐐨𐐼𐐨𐐯𐑌𐐻 𐐲𐑌𐐻𐐭 𐑄 𐐿𐐪𐑋𐐰𐑌𐐼𐑋𐐯𐑌𐐻𐑅 𐐲𐑂 𐐘𐐪𐐼, 𐐶𐐨 𐐺𐐯𐑉 𐐻𐐯𐑅𐐻𐐮𐑋𐐬𐑌𐐨 𐐲𐑂 𐑄𐐨𐑆 𐑃𐐮𐑍𐑆. 𐐈𐑌𐐼 𐐶𐐨 𐑌𐐬 𐑄𐐰𐐻 𐐮𐑁 𐐶𐐨 𐐪𐑉 𐑁𐐩𐑃𐑁𐐳𐑊 𐐮𐑌 𐐗𐑉𐐴𐑅𐐻, 𐐶𐐨 𐑇𐐰𐑊 𐑉𐐮𐐼 𐐵𐑉 𐑀𐐪𐑉𐑋𐐯𐑌𐐻𐑅 𐐲𐑂 𐑄 𐐺𐑊𐐲𐐼 𐐲𐑂 𐐫𐑊 𐑋𐐯𐑌, 𐐰𐑌𐐼 𐐺 𐑁𐐵𐑌𐐼 𐑅𐐹𐐪𐐻𐑊𐐯𐑅 𐐺𐐨𐑁𐐫𐑉 𐑄 𐐾𐐲𐐾𐑋𐐯𐑌𐐻-𐑅𐐨𐐻 𐐲𐑂 𐐗𐑉𐐴𐑅𐐻, 𐐰𐑌𐐼 𐑇𐐰𐑊 𐐼𐐶𐐯𐑊 𐐶𐐮𐑄 𐐸𐐮𐑋 𐐨𐐻𐐲𐑉𐑌𐐰𐑊𐐨 𐐮𐑌 𐑄 𐐸𐐯𐑂𐐲𐑌𐑆. 𐐈𐑌𐐼 𐑄 𐐪𐑌𐐲𐑉 𐐺 𐐻𐐭 𐑄 𐐙𐐪𐑄𐐲𐑉, 𐐰𐑌𐐼 𐐻𐐭 𐑄 𐐝𐐲𐑌, 𐐰𐑌𐐼 𐐻𐐭 𐑄 𐐐𐐬𐑊𐐨 𐐘𐐬𐑅𐐻, 𐐸𐐶𐐮𐐽 𐐮𐑆 𐐶𐐲𐑌 𐐘𐐪𐐼. 𐐁𐑋𐐯𐑌.

𐐉𐑊𐐮𐑂𐐲𐑉 𐐗𐐵𐐼𐐲𐑉𐐨,
𐐔𐐩𐑂𐐮𐐼 𐐐𐐶𐐮𐐻𐑋𐐲𐑉,
𐐣𐐪𐑉𐐻𐐮𐑌 𐐐𐐪𐑉𐐮𐑅.

𐐈𐑌𐐼 𐐃𐑊𐑅𐐬 𐑄 𐐓𐐯𐑅𐐻𐐮𐑋𐐬𐑌𐐨 𐐲𐑂 𐐁𐐻 𐐎𐐮𐐻𐑌𐐯𐑅𐐯𐑆.

𐐒 𐐮𐐻 𐑌𐐬𐑌 𐐲𐑌𐐻𐐭 𐐫𐑊 𐑌𐐩𐑇𐐲𐑌𐑆, 𐐿𐐮𐑌𐐼𐑉𐐯𐐼𐑆, 𐐻𐐲𐑍𐑆, 𐐰𐑌𐐼 𐐹𐐨𐐹𐑊, 𐐲𐑌𐐻𐐭 𐐸𐐭𐑋 𐑄𐐮𐑅 𐐶𐐲𐑉𐐿 𐑇𐐰𐑊 𐐿𐐲𐑋, 𐑄𐐰𐐻 𐐖𐐬𐑆𐐯𐑁 𐐝𐑋𐐮𐑃, 𐐖𐐭𐑌., 𐑄 𐐻𐑉𐐰𐑌𐑅𐑊𐐩𐐻𐐲𐑉 𐐲𐑂 𐑄𐐮𐑅 𐐶𐐲𐑉𐐿, 𐐸𐐰𐑆 𐑇𐐬𐑌 𐐲𐑌𐐻𐐭 𐐲𐑅 𐑄 𐐹𐑊𐐩𐐻𐑅 𐐲𐑂 𐐸𐐶𐐮𐐽 𐐸𐐰𐑃 𐐺𐐮𐑌 𐑅𐐹𐐬𐐿𐐲𐑌, 𐐸𐐶𐐮𐐽 𐐸𐐰𐑂 𐑄 𐐲𐐹𐐨𐑉𐐲𐑌𐑅 𐐲𐑂 𐑀𐐬𐑊𐐼; 𐐰𐑌𐐼 𐐰𐑆 𐑋𐐯𐑌𐐨 𐐲𐑂 𐑄 𐑊𐐨𐑂𐑆 𐐰𐑆 𐑄 𐑅𐐯𐐼 𐐝𐑋𐐮𐑃 𐐸𐐰𐑆 𐐻𐑉𐐰𐑌𐑅𐑊𐐩𐐻𐐯𐐼, 𐐶𐐨 𐐼𐐮𐐼 𐐸𐐰𐑌𐐼𐑊 𐐶𐐮𐑄 𐐵𐑉 𐐸𐐰𐑌𐐼𐑆; 𐐰𐑌𐐼 𐐶𐐨 𐐫𐑊𐑅𐐬 𐑅𐐫 𐑄 𐐯𐑌𐑀𐑉𐐩𐑂𐐮𐑍𐑆 𐑄𐐯𐑉𐐪𐑌, 𐐫𐑊 𐐲𐑂 𐐸𐐶𐐮𐐽 𐐸𐐰𐑆 𐑄 𐐲𐐹𐐨𐑉𐐲𐑌𐑅 𐐲𐑂 𐐩𐑌𐑇𐐯𐑌𐐻 𐐶𐐲𐑉𐐿, 𐐰𐑌𐐼 𐐲𐑂 𐐿𐐷𐐭𐑉𐐨𐐲𐑅 𐐶𐐲𐑉𐐿𐑋𐐰𐑌𐑇𐐮𐐹. 𐐈𐑌𐐼 𐑄𐐮𐑅 𐐶𐐨 𐐺𐐯𐑉 𐑉𐐯𐐿𐐲𐑉𐐼 𐐶𐐮𐑄 𐐶𐐲𐑉𐐼𐑆 𐐲𐑂 𐑅𐐬𐐺𐐲𐑉𐑌𐐯𐑅, 𐑄𐐰𐐻 𐑄 𐑅𐐯𐐼 𐐝𐑋𐐮𐑃 𐐸𐐰𐑆 𐑇𐐬𐑌 𐐲𐑌𐐻𐐭 𐐲𐑅, 𐑁𐐫𐑉 𐐶𐐨 𐐸𐐰𐑂 𐑅𐐨𐑌 𐐰𐑌𐐼 𐐸𐐯𐑁𐐻𐐯𐐼, 𐐰𐑌𐐼 𐑌𐐬 𐐲𐑂 𐐲 𐑇𐐭𐑉𐐯𐐻𐐨 𐑄𐐰𐐻 𐑄 𐑅𐐯𐐼 𐐝𐑋𐐮𐑃 𐐸𐐰𐑆 𐑀𐐪𐐻 𐑄 𐐹𐑊𐐩𐐻𐑅 𐐲𐑂 𐐸𐐶𐐮𐐽 𐐶𐐨 𐐸𐐰𐑂 𐑅𐐹𐐬𐐿𐐲𐑌. 𐐈𐑌𐐼 𐐶𐐨 𐑀𐐮𐑂 𐐵𐑉 𐑌𐐩𐑋𐑆 𐐲𐑌𐐻𐐭 𐑄 𐐶𐐲𐑉𐑊𐐼, 𐐻𐐭 𐐶𐐮𐐻𐑌𐐯𐑅 𐐲𐑌𐐻𐐭 𐑄 𐐶𐐲𐑉𐑊𐐼 𐑄𐐰𐐻 𐐸𐐶𐐮𐐽 𐐶𐐨 𐐸𐐰𐑂 𐑅𐐨𐑌; 𐐰𐑌𐐼 𐐶𐐨 𐑊𐐴 𐑌𐐪𐐻, 𐐘𐐪𐐼 𐐺𐐯𐑉𐐮𐑍 𐐶𐐮𐐻𐑌𐐯𐑅 𐐲𐑂 𐐮𐐻.

𐐗𐑉𐐮𐑅𐐽𐐲𐑌 𐐐𐐶𐐮𐐻𐑋𐐲𐑉,
𐐖𐐩𐐿𐐲𐐺 𐐐𐐶𐐮𐐻𐑋𐐲𐑉,
𐐑𐐨𐐻𐐲𐑉 𐐐𐐶𐐮𐐻𐑋𐐲𐑉, 𐐖𐐭𐑌.,
𐐖𐐪𐑌 𐐐𐐶𐐮𐐻𐑋𐐲𐑉,

𐐐𐐴𐑉𐐲𐑋 𐐑𐐩𐐾,
𐐖𐐬𐑆𐐯𐑁 𐐝𐑋𐐮𐑃, 𐐝𐐨𐑌.,
𐐐𐐴𐑉𐐲𐑋 𐐝𐑋𐐮𐑃,
𐐝𐐰𐑋𐐷𐐭𐐯𐑊 𐐐. 𐐝𐑋𐐮𐑃.

𐐗𐐲𐑌𐐻𐐲𐑌𐐻𐑅.

𐐜 𐐒𐐳𐐿 𐐱𐑂 𐐣𐐫𐑉𐑋𐐲𐑌.

𐐜 𐐙𐐲𐑉𐑅𐐻 𐐒𐐳𐐿 𐐱𐑂 𐐤𐐨𐑁𐐴:

𐐐𐐮𐑆 𐐡𐐩𐑌 𐐰𐑌𐐼 𐐣𐐮𐑌𐐮𐑅𐐻𐑉𐐨.

𐐕𐐰𐐹𐐻𐐲𐑉 I.

𐐈𐑌 𐐰𐐿𐐵𐑌𐐻 𐐱𐑂 𐐢𐐨𐐸𐐴 𐐰𐑌𐐼 𐐸𐐮𐑆 𐐶𐐴𐑁 𐐝𐐩𐑉𐐴𐐲, 𐐰𐑌𐐼 𐐸𐐮𐑆 𐑁𐐬𐑉 𐑅𐐲𐑌𐑆, 𐐺𐐨𐐮𐑍 𐐿𐐫𐑊𐐼, (𐐺𐐨𐑀𐐮𐑌𐐮𐑍 𐐰𐐻 𐑄 𐐯𐑊𐐼𐐯𐑅𐐻,) 𐐢𐐩𐑋𐐲𐑌, 𐐢𐐯𐑋𐐷𐐭𐐯𐑊, 𐐝𐐰𐑋, 𐐰𐑌𐐼 𐐤𐐨𐑁𐐴. 𐐜 𐐢𐐫𐑉𐐼 𐐶𐐫𐑉𐑌𐑆 𐐢𐐨𐐸𐐴 𐐻𐐭 𐐼𐐨𐐹𐐪𐑉𐐻 𐐵𐐻 𐐱𐑂 𐑄 𐑊𐐰𐑌𐐼 𐐱𐑂 𐐖𐐨𐑉𐐭𐑅𐐲𐑊𐐯𐑋, 𐐺𐐨𐐿𐐫𐑆 𐐸𐐨 𐐹𐑉𐐱𐑁𐐯𐑅𐐴𐐯𐑃 𐐲𐑌𐐻𐐭 𐑄 𐐹𐐨𐐹𐑊 𐐿𐐲𐑌𐑅𐐲𐑉𐑌𐐮𐑍 𐑄𐐩𐑉 𐐮𐑌𐐮𐐿𐐶𐐮𐐻𐐨; 𐐰𐑌𐐼 𐑄𐐩 𐑅𐐨𐐿 𐐻𐐭 𐐼𐐨𐑅𐐻𐑉𐐱𐐮 𐐸𐐮𐑆 𐑊𐐴𐑁. 𐐐𐐨 𐐻𐐩𐐿𐐯𐑃 𐑃𐑉𐐨 𐐼𐐩𐑆' 𐐾𐐲𐑉𐑌𐐨 𐐮𐑌𐐻𐐭 𐑄 𐐶𐐮𐑊𐐼𐐲𐑉𐑌𐐯𐑅 𐐶𐐮𐑄 𐐸𐐮𐑆 𐑁𐐰𐑋𐐮𐑊𐐨. 𐐤𐐨𐑁𐐴 𐐻𐐩𐐿𐐯𐑃 𐐸𐐮𐑆 𐐺𐑉𐐯𐑄𐑉𐐯𐑌 𐐰𐑌𐐼 𐑉𐐨𐐻𐐲𐑉𐑌𐐯𐑃 𐐻𐐭 𐑄 𐑊𐐰𐑌𐐼 𐐱𐑂 𐐖𐐨𐑉𐐭𐑅𐐲𐑊𐐯𐑋 𐐰𐑁𐐻𐐲𐑉 𐑄 𐑉𐐯𐐿𐐲𐑉𐐼 𐐱𐑂 𐑄 𐐖𐐭𐑆. 𐐜 𐐰𐐿𐐵𐑌𐐻 𐐱𐑂 𐑄𐐩𐑉 𐑅𐐲𐑁𐐲𐑉𐐮𐑍𐑆. 𐐜𐐩 𐐻𐐩𐐿 𐑄 𐐼𐐫𐐻𐐲𐑉𐑆 𐐱𐑂 𐐆𐑇𐑋𐐩𐐲𐑊 𐐻𐐭 𐐶𐐴𐑁. 𐐜𐐩 𐐻𐐩𐐿 𐑄𐐩𐑉 𐑁𐐰𐑋𐐮𐑊𐐨𐑆 𐐰𐑌𐐼 𐐼𐐨𐐹𐐪𐑉𐐻 𐐮𐑌𐐻𐐭 𐑄 𐐶𐐮𐑊𐐼𐐲𐑉𐑌𐐯𐑅. 𐐜𐐩𐑉 𐑅𐐲𐑁𐐲𐑉𐐮𐑍𐑆 𐐰𐑌𐐼 𐐰𐑁𐑊𐐮𐐿𐑇𐐲𐑌𐑆 𐐮𐑌 𐑄 𐐶𐐮𐑊𐐼𐐲𐑉𐑌𐐯𐑅. 𐐜 𐐿𐐬𐑉𐑅 𐐱𐑂 𐑄𐐩𐑉 𐐻𐑉𐐰𐑂𐐯𐑊𐑆. 𐐜𐐩 𐐿𐐲𐑋 𐐻𐐭 𐑄 𐑊𐐪𐑉𐐾 𐐶𐐫𐐻𐐲𐑉𐑆. 𐐤𐐨𐑁𐐴'𐑆 𐐺𐑉𐐯𐑄𐑉𐐯𐑌 𐑉𐐯𐐺𐐯𐑊𐐯𐑃 𐐲𐑀𐐯𐑌𐑅𐐻 𐐸𐐮𐑋. 𐐐𐐨 𐐿𐐱𐑌𐑁𐐵𐑌𐐼𐐯𐑃 𐑄𐐯𐑋, 𐐰𐑌𐐼 𐐺𐐮𐑊𐐼𐐯𐑃 𐐲 𐑇𐐮𐐹. 𐐜𐐩 𐐿𐐫𐑊 𐑄 𐐹𐑊𐐩𐑅 𐐒𐐵𐑌𐐻𐐨𐑁𐐳𐑊. 𐐜𐐩 𐐿𐑉𐐱𐑅 𐑄 𐑊𐐪𐑉𐐾 𐐶𐐫𐐻𐐲𐑉𐑆 𐐮𐑌𐐻𐐭 𐑄 𐐹𐑉𐐱𐑋𐐮𐑅𐐻 𐑊𐐰𐑌𐐼, 𐐯𐐻𐐽. 𐐜𐐮𐑅 𐐮𐑆 𐐰𐐿𐐫𐑉𐐼𐐮𐑍 𐐻𐐭 𐑄 𐐰𐐿𐐵𐑌𐐻 𐐱𐑂 𐐤𐐨𐑁𐐴; 𐐫𐑉 𐐮𐑌 𐐲𐑄𐐲𐑉 𐐶𐐲𐑉𐐼𐑆, 𐐌, 𐐤𐐨𐑁𐐴, 𐑉𐐬𐐻 𐑄𐐮𐑅 𐑉𐐯𐐿𐐲𐑉𐐼.

1. 𐐌, 𐐤𐐨𐑁𐐴, 𐐸𐐰𐑂𐐮𐑍 𐐺𐐨𐑌 𐐺𐐫𐑉𐑌 𐐱𐑂 𐑀𐐳𐐼𐑊𐐨 𐐹𐐯𐑉𐐲𐑌𐐻𐑅, 𐑄𐐯𐑉𐑁𐐬𐑉 𐐌 𐐶𐐲𐑆 𐐻𐐫𐐻 𐑅𐐲𐑋𐐶𐐱𐐻 𐐮𐑌 𐐫𐑊 𐑄 𐑊𐐲𐑉𐑌𐐮𐑍 𐐱𐑂 𐑋𐐴 𐑁𐐪𐑄𐐲𐑉; 𐐰𐑌𐐼 𐐸𐐰𐑂𐐮𐑍 𐑅𐐨𐑌 𐑋𐐰𐑌𐐨 𐐰𐑁𐑊𐐮𐐿𐑇𐐲𐑌𐑆 𐐮𐑌 𐑄 𐐿𐐬𐑉𐑅 𐐱𐑂 𐑋𐐴 𐐼𐐩𐑆—𐑌𐐯𐑂𐐲𐑉𐑄𐐯𐑊𐐯𐑅, 𐐸𐐰𐑂𐐮𐑍 𐐺𐐨𐑌 𐐸𐐴𐑊𐐨 𐑁𐐩𐑂𐐲𐑉𐐼 𐐱𐑂 𐑄 𐐢𐐫𐑉𐐼 𐐮𐑌 𐐫𐑊 𐑋𐐴 𐐼𐐩𐑆; 𐐷𐐯, 𐐸𐐰𐑂𐐮𐑍 𐐸𐐰𐐼 𐐲 𐑀𐑉𐐩𐐻 𐑌𐐱𐑊𐐯𐐾 𐐱𐑂 𐑄 𐑀𐐳𐐼𐑌𐐯𐑅 𐐰𐑌𐐼 𐑄 𐑋𐐮𐑅𐐻𐐲𐑉𐐨𐑆 𐐱𐑂 𐐘𐐱𐐼, 𐑄𐐯𐑉𐑁𐐬𐑉 𐐌 𐑋𐐩𐐿 𐐲 𐑉𐐯𐐿𐐲𐑉𐐼 𐐱𐑂 𐑋𐐴 𐐹𐑉𐐱𐑅𐐨𐐼𐐨𐑍𐑆 𐐮𐑌 𐑋𐐴 𐐼𐐩𐑆; 𐐷𐐯, 𐐌 𐑋𐐩𐐿 𐐲 𐑉𐐯𐐿𐐲𐑉𐐼 𐐮𐑌 𐑄 𐑊𐐰𐑍𐑀𐐶𐐮𐐾 𐐱𐑂 𐑋𐐴 𐑁𐐪𐑄𐐲𐑉, 𐐸𐐶𐐮𐐽 𐐿𐐲𐑌𐑅𐐮𐑅𐐻𐑅 𐐱𐑂 𐑄 𐑊𐐲𐑉𐑌𐐮𐑍 𐐱𐑂 𐑄 𐐖𐐭𐑆, 𐐰𐑌𐐼 𐑄 𐑊𐐰𐑍𐑀𐐶𐐮𐐾 𐐱𐑂 𐑄 𐐀𐐾𐐮𐐹𐑇𐐲𐑌𐑆. 𐐈𐑌𐐼 𐐌 𐑌𐐬 𐑄𐐰𐐻 𐑄 𐑉𐐯𐐿𐐲𐑉𐐼 𐐸𐐶𐐮𐐽 𐐌 𐑋𐐩𐐿 𐐮𐑆 𐐻𐑉𐐭; 𐐰𐑌𐐼 𐐌 𐑋𐐩𐐿 𐐮𐐻 𐐶𐐮𐑄 𐑋𐐴𐑌 𐐬𐑌 𐐸𐐰𐑌𐐼; 𐐰𐑌𐐼 𐐌 𐑋𐐩𐐿 𐐮𐐻 𐐰𐐿𐐫𐑉𐐼𐐮𐑍 𐐻𐐭 𐑋𐐴 𐑌𐐱𐑊𐐯𐐾.

2. 𐐙𐐫𐑉 𐐮𐐻 𐐿𐐩𐑋 𐐻𐐭 𐐹𐐰𐑅 𐐮𐑌 𐑄 𐐿𐐲𐑋𐐯𐑌𐑅𐑋𐐯𐑌𐐻 𐐱𐑂 𐑄 𐑁𐐲𐑉𐑅𐐻 𐐷𐐨𐑉 𐐱𐑂 𐑄 𐑉𐐩𐑌 𐐱𐑂 𐐞𐐯𐐼𐐯𐐿𐐴𐐲, 𐐿𐐮𐑍 𐐱𐑂 𐐖𐐭𐐼𐐲; (𐑋𐐴 𐑁𐐪𐑄𐐲𐑉 𐐢𐐨𐐸𐐴, 𐐸𐐰𐑂𐐮𐑍 𐐼𐐶𐐯𐑊𐐻 𐐰𐐻 𐐖𐐨𐑉𐐭𐑅𐐲𐑊𐐯𐑋 𐐮𐑌 𐐫𐑊 𐐸𐐮𐑆 𐐼𐐩𐑆;) 𐐰𐑌𐐼 𐐮𐑌 𐑄𐐰𐐻 𐑅𐐩𐑋 𐐷𐐨𐑉 𐑄𐐯𐑉 𐐿𐐩𐑋 𐑋𐐰𐑌𐐨 𐐹𐑉𐐱𐑁𐐯𐐻𐑅, 𐐹𐑉𐐱𐑁𐐯𐑅𐐴𐐮𐑍 𐐲𐑌𐐻𐐭 𐑄 𐐹𐐨𐐹𐑊 𐑄𐐰𐐻 𐑄𐐩 𐑋𐐲𐑅𐐻 𐑉𐐯𐐹𐐯𐑌𐐻, 𐐫𐑉 𐑄 𐑀𐑉𐐩𐐻 𐑅𐐮𐐻𐐨, 𐐖𐐨𐑉𐐭𐑅𐐲𐑊𐐯𐑋, 𐑋𐐲𐑅𐐻 𐐺𐐨 𐐼𐐨𐑅𐐻𐑉𐐱𐐮𐐼. 𐐐𐐶𐐯𐑉𐑁𐐬𐑉 𐐮𐐻 𐐿𐐩𐑋 𐐻𐐭 𐐹𐐰𐑅 𐑄𐐰𐐻 𐑋𐐴 𐑁𐐪𐑄𐐲𐑉 𐐢𐐨𐐸𐐴, 𐐰𐑆 𐐸𐐨 𐐶𐐯𐑌𐐻 𐑁𐐬𐑉𐑃, 𐐹𐑉𐐩𐐼 𐐲𐑌𐐻𐐭 𐑄 𐐢𐐫𐑉𐐼, 𐐷𐐯, 𐐨𐑂𐐲𐑌 𐐶𐐮𐑄 𐐫𐑊 𐐸𐐮𐑆 𐐸𐐪𐑉𐐻, 𐐮𐑌 𐐺𐐨𐐸𐐪𐑁 𐐱𐑂 𐐸𐐮𐑆 𐐹𐐨𐐹𐑊.

3. 𐐈𐑌𐐼 𐐮𐐻 𐐿𐐩𐑋 𐐻𐐭 𐐹𐐰𐑅, 𐐰𐑆 𐐸𐐨 𐐹𐑉𐐩𐐼 𐐲𐑌𐐻𐐭 𐑄 𐐢𐐫𐑉𐐼, 𐑄𐐯𐑉 𐐿𐐩𐑋 𐐲 𐐹𐐮𐑊𐐲𐑉 𐐱𐑂 𐑁𐐴𐑉 𐐰𐑌𐐼 𐐼𐐶𐐯𐑊𐐻 𐐲𐐹𐐱𐑌 𐐲 𐑉𐐱𐐿 𐐺𐐨𐑁𐐬𐑉 𐐸𐐮𐑋; 𐐰𐑌𐐼 𐐸𐐨 𐑅𐐫 𐐰𐑌𐐼 𐐸𐐲𐑉𐐼 𐑋𐐲𐐽; 𐐰𐑌𐐼 𐐺𐐨𐐿𐐫𐑆 𐐱𐑂 𐑄 𐑃𐐮𐑍𐑆 𐐸𐐶𐐮𐐽 𐐸𐐨 𐑅𐐫 𐐰𐑌𐐼 𐐸𐐲𐑉𐐼, 𐐸𐐨 𐐼𐐮𐐼 𐐿𐐶𐐩𐐿 𐐰𐑌𐐼 𐐻𐑉𐐯𐑋𐐺𐑊 𐐯𐐿𐑅𐐨𐐼𐐮𐑍𐑊𐐨.

4. 𐐈𐑌𐐼 𐐮𐐻 𐐿𐐩𐑋 𐐻𐐭 𐐹𐐰𐑅 𐑄𐐰𐐻 𐐸𐐨 𐑉𐐨𐐻𐐲𐑉𐑌𐐼 𐐻𐐭 𐐸𐐮𐑆 𐐬𐑌 𐐸𐐵𐑅 𐐰𐐻 𐐖𐐯𐑉𐐭𐑅𐐲𐑊𐐯𐑋; 𐐰𐑌𐐼 𐐸𐐨 𐐿𐐰𐑅𐐻 𐐸𐐮𐑋𐑅𐐯𐑊𐑁 𐐲𐐹𐐱𐑌 𐐸𐐮𐑆 𐐺𐐯𐐼, 𐐺𐐨𐐮𐑍 𐐬𐑂𐐲𐑉𐐿𐐲𐑋 𐐶𐐮𐑄 𐑄 𐐝𐐹𐐮𐑉𐐮𐐻 𐐰𐑌𐐼 𐑄 𐑃𐐮𐑍𐑆 𐐸𐐶𐐮𐐽 𐐸𐐨 𐐸𐐰𐐼 𐑅𐐨𐑌; 𐐰𐑌𐐼 𐐺𐐨𐐮𐑍 𐑄𐐲𐑅 𐐬𐑂𐐲𐑉𐐿𐐲𐑋 𐐶𐐮𐑄 𐑄 𐐝𐐹𐐮𐑉𐐮𐐻, 𐐸𐐨 𐐶𐐱𐑆 𐐿𐐰𐑉𐐮𐐼 𐐰𐐶𐐩 𐐮𐑌 𐐲 𐑂𐐮𐑈𐐲𐑌, 𐐨𐑂𐐲𐑌 𐑄𐐰𐐻 𐐸𐐨 𐑅𐐫 𐑄 𐐸𐐯𐑂𐐲𐑌𐑆 𐐬𐐹𐐲𐑌, 𐐰𐑌𐐼 𐐸𐐨 𐑃𐐫𐐻 𐐸𐐨 𐑅𐐫 𐐘𐐱𐐼 𐑅𐐮𐐻𐐮𐑍 𐐲𐐹𐐱𐑌 𐐸𐐮𐑆 𐑃𐑉𐐬𐑌, 𐑅𐐲𐑉𐐵𐑌𐐼𐐯𐐼 𐐶𐐮𐑄 𐑌𐐲𐑋𐐺𐐲𐑉𐑊𐐯𐑅 𐐿𐐱𐑍𐐿𐐬𐑉𐑅𐐯𐑆 𐐱𐑂 𐐩𐑌𐐾𐐯𐑊𐑆, 𐐮𐑌 𐑄 𐐰𐐻𐐮𐐻𐐷𐐭𐐼 𐐱𐑂 𐑅𐐮𐑍𐐮𐑍 𐐰𐑌𐐼 𐐹𐑉𐐩𐑆𐐮𐑍 𐑄𐐩𐑉 𐐘𐐱𐐼.

5. 𐐈𐑌𐐼 𐐮𐐻 𐐿𐐩𐑋 𐐻𐐭 𐐹𐐰𐑅 𐑄𐐰𐐻 𐐸𐐨 𐑅𐐫 𐐶𐐲𐑌 𐐼𐐨𐑅𐐯𐑌𐐼𐐮𐑍 𐐵𐐻 𐐱𐑂 𐑄 𐑋𐐮𐐼𐑅𐐻 𐐱𐑂 𐐸𐐯𐑂𐐲𐑌, 𐐰𐑌𐐼 𐐸𐐨 𐐺𐐨𐐸𐐯𐑊𐐼 𐑄𐐰𐐻 𐐸𐐮𐑆 𐑊𐐲𐑅𐐻𐐲𐑉 𐐶𐐱𐑆 𐐲𐐺𐐲𐑂 𐑄𐐰𐐻 𐐱𐑂 𐑄 𐑅𐐲𐑌 𐐰𐐻 𐑌𐐭𐑌-𐐼𐐩; 𐐰𐑌𐐼 𐐸𐐨 𐐫𐑊𐑅𐐬 𐑅𐐫 𐐻𐐶𐐯𐑊𐑂 𐐲𐑄𐐲𐑉𐑆 𐑁𐐱𐑊𐐬𐐮𐑍 𐐸𐐮𐑋, 𐐰𐑌𐐼 𐑄𐐩𐑉 𐐺𐑉𐐴𐐻𐑌𐐯𐑅 𐐼𐐮𐐼 𐐯𐐿𐑅𐐨𐐼 𐑄𐐰𐐻 𐐱𐑂 𐑄 𐑅𐐻𐐪𐑉𐑆 𐐮𐑌 𐑄 𐑁𐐲𐑉𐑋𐐲𐑋𐐯𐑌𐐻; 𐐰𐑌𐐼 𐑄𐐩 𐐿𐐩𐑋 𐐼𐐵𐑌 𐐰𐑌𐐼 𐐶𐐯𐑌𐐻 𐑁𐐬𐑉𐑃 𐐲𐐹𐐱𐑌 𐑄 𐑁𐐩𐑅 𐐱𐑂 𐑄 𐐲𐑉𐑃; 𐐰𐑌𐐼 𐑄 𐑁𐐲𐑉𐑅𐐻 𐐿𐐩𐑋 𐐰𐑌𐐼 𐑅𐐻𐐳𐐼 𐐺𐐨𐑁𐐬𐑉 𐑋𐐴 𐑁𐐪𐑄𐐲𐑉, 𐐰𐑌𐐼 𐑀𐐩𐑂 𐐲𐑌𐐻𐐭 𐐸𐐮𐑋 𐐲 𐐺𐐳𐐿, 𐐰𐑌𐐼 𐐺𐐰𐐼 𐐸𐐮𐑋 𐑄𐐰𐐻 𐐸𐐨 𐑇𐐳𐐼 𐑉𐐨𐐼.

6. 𐐈𐑌𐐼 𐐮𐐻 𐐿𐐩𐑋 𐐻𐐭 𐐹𐐰𐑅 𐑄𐐰𐐻 𐐰𐑆 𐐸𐐨 𐑉𐐯𐐼, 𐐸𐐨 𐐶𐐱𐑆 𐑁𐐮𐑊𐐼 𐐶𐐮𐑄 𐑄 𐐝𐐹𐐮𐑉𐐮𐐻 𐐱𐑂 𐑄 𐐢𐐫𐑉𐐼, 𐐰𐑌𐐼 𐐸𐐨 𐑉𐐯𐐼, 𐑅𐐩𐐮𐑍, 𐐎𐐬, 𐐶𐐬 𐐲𐑌𐐻𐐭 𐐖𐐯𐑉𐐭𐑅𐐲𐑊𐐯𐑋! 𐑁𐐫𐑉 𐐌 𐐸𐐰𐑂 𐑅𐐨𐑌 𐑄𐐴𐑌 𐐲𐐺𐐱𐑋𐐮𐑌𐐩𐑇𐐲𐑌𐑆; 𐐷𐐩, 𐐰𐑌𐐼 𐑋𐐯𐑌𐐨 𐑃𐐮𐑍𐑆 𐐼𐐮𐐼 𐑋𐐴 𐑁𐐪𐑄𐐲𐑉 𐑉𐐨𐐼 𐐿𐐱𐑌𐑅𐐲𐑉𐑌𐐮𐑍 𐐖𐐯𐑉𐐭𐑅𐐲𐑊𐐯𐑋—𐑄𐐰𐐻 𐐮𐐻 𐑇𐐳𐐼 𐐺𐐨 𐐼𐐨𐑅𐐻𐑉𐑎𐐼, 𐐰𐑌𐐼 𐑄 𐐮𐑌𐐸𐐰𐐺𐐮𐐻𐐰𐑌𐐻𐑅 𐑄𐐯𐑉𐐱𐑂; 𐑋𐐯𐑌𐐨 𐑇𐐳𐐼 𐐹𐐯𐑉𐐮𐑇 𐐺𐐴 𐑄 𐑅𐐬𐑉𐐼, 𐐰𐑌𐐼 𐑋𐐯𐑌𐐨 𐑇𐐳𐐼 𐐺𐐨 𐐿𐐰𐑉𐐮𐐼 𐐰𐐶𐐩 𐐿𐐰𐐹𐐻𐐮𐑂 𐐮𐑌𐐻𐐭 𐐒𐐰𐐺𐐮𐑊𐐱𐑌.

7. 𐐈𐑌𐐼 𐐮𐐻 𐐿𐐩𐑋 𐐻𐐭 𐐹𐐰𐑅 𐑄𐐰𐐻 𐐸𐐶𐐯𐑌 𐑋𐐴 𐑁𐐪𐑄𐐲𐑉 𐐸𐐰𐐼 𐑉𐐯𐐼 𐐰𐑌𐐼 𐑅𐐨𐑌 𐑋𐐯𐑌𐐨 𐑀𐑉𐐩𐐻 𐐰𐑌𐐼 𐑋𐐪𐑉𐑂𐐯𐑊𐐲𐑅 𐑃𐐮𐑍𐑆, 𐐸𐐨 𐐼𐐮𐐼 𐐯𐐿𐑅𐐿𐑊𐐩𐑋 𐑋𐐯𐑌𐐨 𐑃𐐮𐑍𐑆 𐐲𐑌𐐻𐐭 𐑄 𐐢𐐫𐑉𐐼; 𐑅𐐲𐐽 𐐰𐑆 𐐘𐑉𐐩𐐻 𐐰𐑌𐐼 𐑋𐐪𐑉𐑂𐐯𐑊𐐲𐑅 𐐪𐑉 𐑄𐐴 𐐶𐐲𐑉𐐿𐑅, O 𐐢𐐫𐑉𐐼 𐐘𐐱𐐼 𐐉𐑊𐑋𐐴𐐻𐐨! 𐐜𐐴 𐑃𐑉𐐬𐑌 𐐮𐑆 𐐸𐐴 𐐮𐑌 𐑄 𐐸𐐯𐑂𐐲𐑌𐑆, 𐐰𐑌𐐼 𐑄𐐴 𐐹𐐵𐐲𐑉, 𐐰𐑌𐐼 𐑀𐐳𐐼𐑌𐐯𐑅, 𐐰𐑌𐐼 𐑋𐐲𐑉𐑅𐐨 𐐪𐑉 𐐬𐑂𐐲𐑉 𐐫𐑊 𐑄 𐐮𐑌𐐸𐐰𐐺𐐮𐐻𐐰𐑌𐐻𐑅 𐐱𐑂 𐑄 𐐲𐑉𐑃; 𐐰𐑌𐐼 𐐺𐐨𐐿𐐫𐑆 𐑄𐐵 𐐪𐑉𐐻 𐑋𐐲𐑉𐑅𐐮𐑁𐐳𐑊, 𐑄𐐵 𐐶𐐮𐑊𐐻 𐑌𐐱𐐻 𐑅𐐲𐑁𐐲𐑉 𐑄𐐬𐑆 𐐸𐐭 𐐿𐐲𐑋 𐐲𐑌𐐻𐐭 𐑄𐐨 𐑄𐐰𐐻 𐑄𐐩 𐑇𐐰𐑊 𐐹𐐯𐑉𐐮𐑇! 𐐈𐑌𐐼 𐐪𐑁𐐻𐐲𐑉 𐑄𐐮𐑅 𐑋𐐰𐑌𐐲𐑉 𐐶𐐱𐑆 𐑄 𐑊𐐰𐑍𐑀𐐶𐐩𐐾 𐐱𐑂 𐑋𐐴 𐑁𐐪𐑄𐐲𐑉 𐐮𐑌 𐑄 𐐹𐑉𐐩𐑆𐐮𐑍 𐐱𐑂 𐐸𐐮𐑆 𐐘𐐱𐐼; 𐑁𐐫𐑉 𐐸𐐮𐑆 𐑅𐐬𐑊 𐐼𐐮𐐼 𐑉𐐨𐐾𐑎𐑅, 𐐰𐑌𐐼 𐐸𐐮𐑆 𐐸𐐬𐑊 𐐸𐐪𐑉𐐻 𐐶𐐱𐑆 𐑁𐐮𐑊𐐼, 𐐺𐐨𐐿𐐫𐑆 𐐱𐑂 𐑄 𐑃𐐮𐑍𐑆 𐐸𐐶𐐮𐐽 𐐸𐐨 𐐸𐐰𐐼 𐑅𐐨𐑌; 𐐷𐐩, 𐐸𐐶𐐮𐐽 𐑄 𐐢𐐫𐑉𐐼 𐐸𐐰𐐼 𐑇𐐬𐑌 𐐲𐑌𐐻𐐭 𐐸𐐮𐑋. 𐐈𐑌𐐼 𐑌𐐵 𐐌, 𐐤𐐨𐑁𐐴, 𐐼𐐭 𐑌𐐱𐐻 𐑋𐐩𐐿 𐐲 𐑁𐐳𐑊 𐐰𐐿𐐵𐑌𐐻 𐐱𐑂 𐑄 𐑃𐐮𐑍𐑆 𐐸𐐶𐐮𐐽 𐑋𐐴 𐑁𐐪𐑄𐐲𐑉 𐐸𐐰𐑃 𐑉𐐮𐐻𐑌, 𐑁𐐫𐑉 𐐸𐐨 𐐸𐐰𐑃 𐑉𐐮𐐻𐑌 𐑋𐐯𐑌𐐨 𐑃𐐮𐑍𐑆 𐐸𐐶𐐮𐐽 𐐸𐐨 𐑅𐐫 𐐮𐑌 𐑂𐐮𐑈𐐲𐑌𐑆 𐐰𐑌𐐼 𐐮𐑌 𐐼𐑉𐐨𐑋𐑆; 𐐰𐑌𐐼 𐐸𐐨 𐐫𐑊𐑅𐐬 𐐸𐐰𐑃 𐑉𐐮𐐻𐑌 𐑋𐐯𐑌𐐨 𐑃𐐮𐑍𐑆 𐐸𐐶𐐮𐐽 𐐸𐐨 𐐹𐑉𐐱𐑁𐐯𐑅𐐴𐐼 𐐰𐑌𐐼 𐑅𐐹𐐩𐐿 𐐲𐑌𐐻𐐭 𐐸𐐮𐑆 𐐽𐐮𐑊𐐼𐑉𐐯𐑌, 𐐱𐑂 𐐸𐐶𐐮𐐽 𐐌 𐑇𐐰𐑊 𐑌𐐱𐐻 𐑋𐐩𐐿 𐐲 𐑁𐐳𐑊 𐐰𐐿𐐵𐑌𐐻; 𐐺𐐲𐐻 𐐌 𐑇𐐰𐑊 𐑋𐐩𐐿 𐐰𐑌 𐐰𐐿𐐵𐑌𐐻 𐐱𐑂 𐑋𐐴 𐐹𐑉𐐬𐑅𐐨𐐼𐐮𐑍𐑆 𐐮𐑌 𐑋𐐴 𐐼𐐩𐑆. 𐐒𐐨𐐸𐐬𐑊𐐼, 𐐌 𐑋𐐩𐐿 𐐰𐑌 𐐲𐐺𐑉𐐮𐐾𐑋𐐯𐑌𐐻 𐐱𐑂 𐑄 𐑉𐐯𐐿𐐲𐑉𐐼 𐐱𐑂 𐑋𐐴 𐑁𐐪𐑄𐐲𐑉, 𐐲𐐹𐐱𐑌 𐐹𐑊𐐩𐐻𐑅 𐐸𐐶𐐮𐐽 𐐌 𐐸𐐰𐑂 𐑋𐐩𐐼 𐐶𐐮𐑄 𐑋𐐴𐑌 𐐬𐑌 𐐸𐐰𐑌𐐼𐑆; 𐐸𐐶𐐯𐑉𐑁𐐬𐑉, 𐐪𐑁𐐻𐐲𐑉 𐐌 𐐸𐐰𐑂 𐐲𐐺𐑉𐐮𐐾𐐼 𐑄 𐑉𐐯𐐿𐐲𐑉𐐼 𐐱𐑂 𐑋𐐴 𐑁𐐪𐑄𐐲𐑉, 𐑄𐐯𐑌 𐐶𐐮𐑊 𐐌 𐑋𐐩𐐿 𐐰𐑌 𐐰𐐿𐐵𐑌𐐻 𐐱𐑂 𐑋𐐴𐑌 𐐬𐑌 𐑊𐐴𐑁.

8. 𐐜𐐯𐑉𐑁𐐬𐑉, 𐐌 𐐶𐐳𐐼 𐑄𐐰𐐻 𐐷𐐨 𐑇𐐳𐐼 𐑌𐐬, 𐑄𐐰𐐻 𐐪𐑁𐐻𐐲𐑉 𐑄 𐐢𐐫𐑉𐐼 𐐸𐐰𐐼 𐑇𐐬𐑌 𐑅𐐬 𐑋𐐯𐑌𐐨 𐑋𐐪𐑉𐑂𐐯𐑊𐐲𐑅 𐑃𐐮𐑍𐑆 𐐲𐑌𐐻𐐭 𐑋𐐴 𐑁𐐪𐑄𐐲𐑉, 𐐢𐐨𐐸𐐴, 𐐷𐐩, 𐐿𐐱𐑌𐑅𐐲𐑉𐑌𐐮𐑍 𐑄 𐐼𐐨𐑅𐐻𐑉𐐲𐐿𐑇𐐲𐑌 𐐱𐑂 𐐖𐐯𐑉𐐭𐑅𐐲𐑊𐐯𐑋, 𐐺𐐨𐐸𐐬𐑊𐐼, 𐐸𐐨 𐐶𐐯𐑌𐐻 𐑁𐐬𐑉𐑃 𐐲𐑋𐐲𐑍 𐑄 𐐹𐐨𐐹𐑊, 𐐰𐑌𐐼 𐐺𐐨𐑀𐐰𐑌 𐐻𐐭 𐐹𐑉𐐱𐑁𐐯𐑅𐐴 𐐰𐑌𐐼 𐐻𐐭 𐐼𐐨𐐿𐑊𐐩𐑉 𐐲𐑌𐐻𐐭 𐑄𐐯𐑋 𐐿𐐱𐑌𐑅𐐲𐑉𐑌𐐮𐑍 𐑄 𐑃𐐮𐑍𐑆 𐐸𐐶𐐮𐐽 𐐸𐐨 𐐸𐐰𐐼 𐐺𐐬𐑃 𐑅𐐨𐑌 𐐰𐑌𐐼 𐐸𐐲𐑉𐐼.

9. 𐐈𐑌𐐼 𐐮𐐻 𐐿𐐩𐑋 𐐻𐐭 𐐹𐐰𐑅 𐑄𐐰𐐻 𐑄 𐐖𐐭𐑆 𐐼𐐮𐐼 𐑋𐐱𐐿 𐐸𐐮𐑋 𐐺𐐨𐐿𐐫𐑆 𐐱𐑂 𐑄 𐑃𐐮𐑍𐑆 𐐸𐐶𐐮𐐽 𐐸𐐨 𐐻𐐯𐑅𐐻𐐮𐑁𐐴𐐼 𐐱𐑂 𐑄𐐯𐑋; 𐑁𐐫𐑉 𐐸𐐨 𐐻𐑉𐐭𐑊𐐨 𐐻𐐯𐑅𐐻𐐮𐑁𐐴𐐼 𐐱𐑂 𐑄𐐩𐑉 𐐶𐐮𐐿𐐯𐐼𐑌𐐯𐑅 𐐰𐑌𐐼 𐑄𐐩𐑉 𐐲𐐺𐐱𐑋𐐮𐑌𐐩𐑇𐐲𐑌𐑆; 𐐰𐑌𐐼 𐐸𐐨 𐐻𐐯𐑅𐐻𐐮𐑁𐐴𐐼 𐑄𐐰𐐻 𐑄 𐑃𐐮𐑍𐑆 𐐸𐐶𐐮𐐽 𐐸𐐨 𐑅𐐫 𐐰𐑌𐐼 𐐸𐐲𐑉𐐼, 𐐰𐑌𐐼 𐐫𐑊𐑅𐐬 𐑄 𐑃𐐮𐑍𐑆 𐐸𐐶𐐮𐐽 𐐸𐐨 𐑉𐐯𐐼 𐐮𐑌 𐑄

𐐺𐐳𐐿, 𐑋𐐰𐑌𐐮𐑁𐐯𐑅𐐻𐐮𐐼 𐐹𐑊𐐩𐑌𐑊𐐨 𐐱𐑂 𐑄 𐐿𐐲𐑋𐐮𐑍 𐐱𐑂 𐐲 𐐣𐐯𐑅𐐴𐐲, 𐐰𐑌𐐼 𐐫𐑊𐑅𐐬 𐑄 𐑉𐐨𐐼𐐯𐑋𐑇𐐲𐑌 𐐱𐑂 𐑄 𐐶𐐲𐑉𐑊𐐼.

10. 𐐈𐑌𐐼 𐐸𐐶𐐯𐑌 𐑄 𐐖𐐭𐑆 𐐸𐐲𐑉𐐼 𐑄𐐨𐑆 𐑃𐐮𐑍𐑆, 𐑄𐐩 𐐶𐐲𐑉 𐐰𐑍𐑀𐑉𐐨 𐐶𐐮𐑄 𐐸𐐮𐑋; 𐐷𐐩, 𐐨𐑂𐐲𐑌 𐐰𐑆 𐐶𐐮𐑄 𐑄 𐐹𐑉𐐱𐑁𐐯𐐻𐑅 𐐱𐑂 𐐬𐑊𐐼, 𐐸𐐭𐑋 𐑄𐐩 𐐸𐐰𐐼 𐐿𐐰𐑅𐐻 𐐵𐐻, 𐐰𐑌𐐼 𐑅𐐻𐐬𐑌𐐼, 𐐰𐑌𐐼 𐑅𐑊𐐩𐑌; 𐐰𐑌𐐼 𐑄𐐩 𐐫𐑊𐑅𐐬 𐑅𐐫𐐻 𐐸𐐮𐑆 𐑊𐐴𐑁, 𐑄𐐰𐐻 𐑄𐐩 𐑋𐐴𐐻 𐐻𐐩𐐿 𐐮𐐻 𐐲𐐶𐐩. 𐐒𐐲𐐻 𐐺𐐨𐐸𐐬𐑊𐐼, 𐐌, 𐐤𐐨𐑁𐐴, 𐐶𐐮𐑊 𐑇𐐬 𐐲𐑌𐐻𐐭 𐐷𐐭 𐑄𐐰𐐻 𐑄 𐐻𐐯𐑌𐐼𐐲𐑉 𐑋𐐲𐑉𐑅𐐨𐑆 𐐱𐑂 𐑄 𐐢𐐫𐑉𐐼 𐐪𐑉 𐐬𐑂𐐲𐑉 𐐫𐑊 𐑄𐐬𐑆 𐐸𐐭𐑋 𐐸𐐨 𐐸𐐰𐑃 𐐽𐐬𐑆𐐲𐑌, 𐐺𐐨𐐿𐐫𐑆 𐐱𐑂 𐑄𐐯𐑉 𐑁𐐩𐑃, 𐐻𐐭 𐑋𐐩𐐿 𐑄𐐯𐑋 𐑋𐐴𐐻𐐨 𐐨𐑂𐐲𐑌 𐐲𐑌𐐻𐐭 𐑄 𐐹𐐵𐐲𐑉 𐐱𐑂 𐐼𐐮𐑊𐐮𐑂𐐲𐑉𐐲𐑌𐑅.

11. 𐐙𐐫𐑉 𐐺𐐨𐐸𐐬𐑊𐐼 𐐮𐐻 𐐿𐐩𐑋 𐐻𐐭 𐐹𐐰𐑅 𐑄𐐰𐐻 𐑄 𐐢𐐫𐑉𐐼 𐑅𐐹𐐩𐐿 𐐲𐑌𐐻𐐭 𐑋𐐴 𐑁𐐪𐑄𐐲𐑉, 𐐷𐐩, 𐐨𐑂𐐲𐑌 𐐮𐑌 𐐲 𐐼𐑉𐐨𐑋, 𐐰𐑌𐐼 𐑅𐐯𐐼 𐐲𐑌𐐻𐐭 𐐸𐐮𐑋, 𐐒𐑊𐐯𐑅𐐯𐐼 𐐪𐑉𐐻 𐑄𐐵 𐐢𐐨𐐸𐐴, 𐐺𐐨𐐿𐐫𐑆 𐐱𐑂 𐑄 𐑃𐐮𐑍𐑆 𐐸𐐶𐐮𐐽 𐑄𐐵 𐐸𐐰𐑅𐐻 𐐼𐐲𐑌; 𐐰𐑌𐐼 𐐺𐐨𐐿𐐫𐑆 𐑄𐐵 𐐸𐐰𐑅𐐻 𐐺𐐨𐑌 𐑁𐐩𐑃𐑁𐐳𐑊 𐐰𐑌𐐼 𐐼𐐨𐐿𐑊𐐯𐑉𐐼 𐐲𐑌𐐻𐐭 𐑄𐐮𐑅 𐐹𐐨𐐹𐐲𐑊 𐑄 𐑃𐐮𐑍𐑆 𐐸𐐶𐐮𐐽 𐐌 𐐿𐐲𐑋𐐰𐑌𐐼𐐯𐐼 𐑄𐐨, 𐐺𐐨𐐸𐐬𐑊𐐼 𐑄𐐩 𐑅𐐨𐐿 𐐻𐐭 𐐻𐐩𐐿 𐐲𐐶𐐩 𐑄𐐴 𐑊𐐴𐑁.

12. 𐐈𐑌𐐼 𐐮𐐻 𐐿𐐩𐑋 𐐻𐐭 𐐹𐐰𐑅 𐑄𐐰𐐻 𐑄 𐐢𐐫𐑉𐐼 𐐿𐐲𐑋𐐰𐑌𐐼𐐯𐐼 𐑋𐐴 𐑁𐐪𐑄𐐲𐑉, 𐐨𐑂𐐲𐑌 𐐮𐑌 𐐲 𐐼𐑉𐐨𐑋, 𐑄𐐰𐐻 𐐸𐐨 𐑇𐐳𐐼 𐐻𐐩𐐿 𐐸𐐮𐑆 𐑁𐐰𐑋𐐮𐑊𐐨 𐐰𐑌𐐼 𐐼𐐨𐐹𐐪𐑉𐐻 𐐮𐑌𐐻𐐭 𐑄 𐐶𐐮𐑊𐐼𐐲𐑉𐑌𐐯𐑅. 𐐈𐑌𐐼 𐐮𐐻 𐐿𐐩𐑋 𐐻𐐭 𐐹𐐰𐑅 𐑄𐐰𐐻 𐐸𐐨 𐐶𐐱𐑆 𐐬𐐺𐐨𐐼𐐨𐐲𐑌𐐻 𐐲𐑌𐐻𐐭 𐑄 𐐶𐐲𐑉𐐼 𐐱𐑂 𐑄 𐐢𐐫𐑉𐐼, 𐐸𐐶𐐯𐑉𐑁𐐫𐑉 𐐸𐐨 𐐼𐐮𐐼 𐐰𐑆 𐑄 𐐢𐐫𐑉𐐼 𐐿𐐲𐑋𐐰𐑌𐐼𐐯𐐼 𐐸𐐮𐑋.

13. 𐐈𐑌𐐼 𐐮𐐻 𐐿𐐩𐑋 𐐻𐐭 𐐹𐐰𐑅 𐑄𐐰𐐻 𐐸𐐨 𐐼𐐨𐐹𐐪𐑉𐐻𐐯𐐼 𐐮𐑌𐐻𐐭 𐑄 𐐶𐐮𐑊𐐼𐐲𐑉𐑌𐐯𐑅. 𐐈𐑌𐐼 𐐸𐐨 𐑊𐐯𐑁𐐻 𐐸𐐮𐑆 𐐸𐐵𐑅 𐐰𐑌𐐼 𐑄 𐑊𐐰𐑌𐐼 𐐱𐑂 𐐸𐐮𐑆 𐐮𐑌𐐸𐐯𐑉𐐮𐐻𐐲𐑌𐑅, 𐐰𐑌𐐼 𐐸𐐮𐑆 𐑀𐐬𐑊𐐼, 𐐰𐑌𐐼 𐐸𐐮𐑆 𐑅𐐮𐑊𐑂𐐲𐑉, 𐐰𐑌𐐼 𐐸𐐮𐑆 𐐹𐑉𐐯𐑇𐐲𐑅 𐑃𐐮𐑍𐑆, 𐐰𐑌𐐼 𐐻𐐳𐐿 𐑌𐐲𐑃𐐮𐑍 𐐶𐐮𐑄 𐐸𐐮𐑋, 𐑅𐐩𐑂 𐐮𐐻 𐐶𐐲𐑉 𐐸𐐮𐑆 𐑁𐐰𐑋𐐮𐑊𐐨, 𐐰𐑌𐐼 𐐹𐑉𐐬𐑂𐐮𐑈𐐲𐑌𐑆, 𐐰𐑌𐐼 𐐻𐐯𐑌𐐻𐑅, 𐐰𐑌𐐼 𐐼𐐨𐐹𐐪𐑉𐐻𐐯𐐼 𐐮𐑌𐐻𐐭 𐑄 𐐶𐐮𐑊𐐼𐐲𐑉𐑌𐐯𐑅; 𐐰𐑌𐐼 𐐸𐐨 𐐿𐐩𐑋 𐐼𐐵𐑌 𐐺𐐴 𐑄 𐐺𐐫𐑉𐐼𐐲𐑉𐑆 𐑌𐐨𐑉 𐑄 𐑇𐐬𐑉 𐐱𐑂 𐑄 𐐡𐐯𐐼 𐐝𐐨; 𐐰𐑌𐐼 𐐸𐐨 𐐻𐑉𐐰𐑂𐐯𐑊𐐼 𐐮𐑌 𐑄 𐐶𐐮𐑊𐐼𐐲𐑉𐑌𐐯𐑅 𐐮𐑌 𐑄 𐐺𐐫𐑉𐐼𐐲𐑉𐑆 𐐸𐐶𐐮𐐽 𐐪𐑉 𐑌𐐨𐑉𐐲𐑉 𐑄 𐐡𐐯𐐼 𐐝𐐨; 𐐰𐑌𐐼 𐐸𐐨 𐐼𐐮𐐼 𐐻𐑉𐐰𐑂𐐯𐑊 𐐮𐑌 𐑄 𐐶𐐮𐑊𐐼𐐲𐑉𐑌𐐯𐑅 𐐶𐐮𐑄 𐐸𐐮𐑆 𐑁𐐰𐑋𐐮𐑊𐐨 𐐸𐐶𐐮𐐽 𐐿𐐱𐑌𐑅𐐮𐑅𐐻𐐯𐐼 𐐱𐑂 𐑋𐐴 𐑋𐐲𐑄𐐲𐑉, 𐐝𐐪𐑉𐐴𐐲, 𐐰𐑌𐐼 𐑋𐐴 𐐯𐑊𐐼𐐲𐑉 𐐺𐑉𐐲𐑄𐐲𐑉𐑆, 𐐸𐐭 𐐶𐐲𐑉 𐐢𐐩𐑋𐐲𐑌, 𐐢𐐯𐑋𐐷𐐭𐐯𐑊, 𐐰𐑌𐐼 𐐝𐐰𐑋.

14. 𐐈𐑌𐐼 𐐮𐐻 𐐿𐐩𐑋 𐐻𐐭 𐐹𐐰𐑅 𐑄𐐰𐐻 𐐸𐐶𐐯𐑌 𐐸𐐨 𐐸𐐰𐐼 𐐻𐑉𐐰𐑂𐐯𐑊𐐼 𐑃𐑉𐐨 𐐼𐐩𐑆 𐐮𐑌 𐑄 𐐶𐐮𐑊𐐼𐐲𐑉𐑌𐐯𐑅, 𐐸𐐨 𐐹𐐮𐐽𐐻 𐐸𐐮𐑆 𐐻𐐯𐑌𐐻 𐐮𐑌 𐐲 𐑂𐐰𐑊𐐨 𐐺𐐴 𐑄 𐑅𐐴𐐼 𐐱𐑂 𐐲 𐑉𐐮𐑂𐐲𐑉 𐐱𐑂 𐐶𐐫𐐻𐐲𐑉. 𐐈𐑌𐐼 𐐮𐐻 𐐿𐐩𐑋 𐐻𐐭 𐐹𐐰𐑅 𐑄𐐰𐐻 𐐸𐐨 𐐺𐐮𐑊𐐻 𐐰𐑌 𐐫𐑊𐐻𐐲𐑉 𐐱𐑂 𐑅𐐻𐐬𐑌𐑆, 𐐰𐑌𐐼 𐑋𐐩𐐼 𐐰𐑌 𐐱𐑁𐐲𐑉𐐮𐑍 𐐲𐑌𐐻𐐭 𐑄 𐐢𐐫𐑉𐐼, 𐐰𐑌𐐼 𐑀𐐩𐑂 𐑃𐐰𐑍𐐿𐑅 𐐲𐑌𐐻𐐭 𐑄 𐐢𐐫𐑉𐐼 𐐵𐑉 𐐘𐐱𐐼. 𐐈𐑌𐐼 𐐮𐐻 𐐿𐐩𐑋 𐐻𐐭 𐐹𐐰𐑅 𐑄𐐰𐐻 𐐸𐐨 𐐿𐐫𐑊𐐼 𐑄 𐑌𐐩𐑋 𐐱𐑂 𐑄 𐑉𐐮𐑂𐐲𐑉 𐐢𐐩𐑋𐐲𐑌, 𐐰𐑌𐐼 𐐮𐐻 𐐯𐑋𐐹𐐻𐐮𐐼 𐐮𐑌𐐻𐐭 𐑄 𐐡𐐯𐐼 𐐝𐐨; 𐐰𐑌𐐼 𐑄 𐑂𐐰𐑊𐐨 𐐶𐐱𐑆 𐐮𐑌 𐑄 𐐺𐐫𐑉𐐼𐐲𐑉𐑆 𐑌𐐨𐑉 𐑄 𐑋𐐵𐑃 𐑄𐐯𐑉𐐱𐑂.

15. 𐐈𐑌𐐼 𐐸𐐶𐐯𐑌 𐑋𐐴 𐑁𐐪𐑄𐐲𐑉 𐑅𐐫 𐑄𐐰𐐻 𐑄 𐐶𐐫𐐻𐐲𐑉𐑆 𐐱𐑂 𐑄 𐑉𐐮𐑂𐐲𐑉 𐐯𐑋𐐹𐐻𐐮𐐼 𐐮𐑌𐐻𐐭 𐑄 𐑁𐐵𐑌𐐻𐐲𐑌 𐐱𐑂 𐑄 𐐡𐐯𐐼 𐐝𐐨, 𐐸𐐨 𐑅𐐹𐐩𐐿 𐐲𐑌𐐻𐐭 𐐢𐐩𐑋𐐲𐑌, 𐑅𐐩𐐮𐑍, 𐐄 𐑄𐐰𐐻 𐑄𐐵 𐑋𐐴𐐻𐐯𐑅𐐻 𐐺𐐨 𐑊𐐴𐐿 𐐲𐑌𐐻𐐭 𐑄𐐮𐑅 𐑉𐐮𐑂𐐲𐑉, 𐐿𐐲𐑌𐐻𐐮𐑌𐐷𐐭𐐲𐑊𐐨 𐑉𐐲𐑌𐐮𐑍 𐐮𐑌𐐻𐐭 𐑄 𐑁𐐵𐑌𐐻𐐲𐑌 𐐱𐑂 𐐫𐑊 𐑉𐐴𐐽𐐲𐑅𐑌𐐯𐑅. 𐐈𐑌𐐼 𐐸𐐨 𐐫𐑊𐑅𐐬 𐑅𐐹𐐩𐐿 𐐲𐑌𐐻𐐭 𐐢𐐯𐑋𐐷𐐭𐐯𐑊: 𐐄 𐑄𐐰𐐻 𐑄𐐵 𐑋𐐴𐐻𐐯𐑅𐐻 𐐺𐐨 𐑊𐐴𐐿 𐐲𐑌𐐻𐐭 𐑄𐐮𐑅 𐑂𐐰𐑊𐐨, 𐑁𐐲𐑉𐑋, 𐐰𐑌𐐼 𐑅𐐻𐐯𐐼𐑁𐐰𐑅𐐻, 𐐰𐑌𐐼 𐐮𐑋𐐭𐑂𐐲𐐺𐐲𐑊 𐐮𐑌 𐐿𐐨𐐹𐐮𐑍 𐑄 𐐿𐐲𐑋𐐰𐑌𐐼𐑋𐐯𐑌𐐻𐑅 𐐱𐑂 𐑄 𐐢𐐫𐑉𐐼. 𐐤𐐵 𐑄𐐮𐑅 𐐸𐐨 𐑅𐐹𐐩𐐿 𐐺𐐨𐐿𐐫𐑆 𐐱𐑂 𐑄 𐑅𐐻𐐮𐑁𐑌𐐯𐐿𐐯𐐼𐑌𐐯𐑅 𐐱𐑂 𐐢𐐩𐑋𐐲𐑌 𐐰𐑌𐐼 𐐢𐐯𐑋𐐷𐐭𐐯𐑊; 𐑁𐐫𐑉 𐐺𐐨𐐸𐐬𐑊𐐼 𐑄𐐩 𐐼𐐮𐐼 𐑋𐐲𐑉𐑋𐐲𐑉 𐐮𐑌 𐑋𐐯𐑌𐐨 𐑃𐐮𐑍𐑆 𐐲𐑀𐐯𐑌𐑅𐐻 𐑄𐐯𐑉 𐑁𐐪𐑄𐐲𐑉, 𐐺𐐨𐐿𐐫𐑆 𐐸𐐨 𐐶𐐱𐑆 𐐲 𐑂𐐮𐑈𐐲𐑌𐐯𐑉𐐨 𐑋𐐰𐑌, 𐐰𐑌𐐼 𐐸𐐰𐐼 𐑊𐐯𐐼 𐑄𐐯𐑋 𐐵𐐻 𐐱𐑂 𐑄 𐑊𐐰𐑌𐐼 𐐱𐑂 𐐖𐐯𐑉𐐭𐑅𐐲𐑊𐐯𐑋, 𐐻𐐭 𐑊𐐨𐑂 𐑄 𐑊𐐰𐑌𐐼 𐐱𐑂 𐑄𐐯𐑉 𐐮𐑌𐐸𐐯𐑉𐐮𐐻𐐲𐑌𐑅, 𐐰𐑌𐐼 𐑄𐐯𐑉 𐑀𐐬𐑊𐐼, 𐐰𐑌𐐼 𐑄𐐯𐑉 𐑅𐐮𐑊𐑂𐐲𐑉, 𐐰𐑌𐐼 𐑄𐐯𐑉 𐐹𐑉𐐯𐑇𐐲𐑅 𐑃𐐮𐑍𐑆, 𐐻𐐭 𐐹𐐯𐑉𐐮𐑇 𐐮𐑌 𐑄 𐐶𐐮𐑊𐐼𐐲𐑉𐑌𐐯𐑅. 𐐈𐑌𐐼 𐑄𐐮𐑅 𐑄𐐩 𐑅𐐯𐐼 𐐸𐐨 𐐸𐐰𐐼 𐐼𐐲𐑌 𐐺𐐨𐐿𐐫𐑆 𐐱𐑂 𐑄 𐑁𐐭𐑊𐐮𐑇 𐐮𐑋𐐰𐐾𐐮𐑌𐐩𐑇𐐲𐑌𐑆 𐐱𐑂 𐐸𐐮𐑆 𐐸𐐪𐑉𐐻. 𐐈𐑌𐐼 𐑄𐐲𐑅 𐐢𐐩𐑋𐐲𐑌 𐐰𐑌𐐼 𐐢𐐯𐑋𐐷𐐭𐐯𐑊, 𐐺𐐨𐐮𐑍 𐑄 𐐯𐑊𐐼𐐯𐑅𐐻, 𐐼𐐮𐐼 𐑋𐐲𐑉𐑋𐐲𐑉 𐐲𐑀𐐯𐑌𐑅𐐻 𐑄𐐯𐑉 𐑁𐐪𐑄𐐲𐑉. 𐐈𐑌𐐼 𐑄𐐩 𐐼𐐮𐐼 𐑋𐐲𐑉𐑋𐐲𐑉 𐐺𐐨𐐿𐐫𐑆 𐑄𐐩 𐑌𐐭 𐑌𐐱𐐻 𐑄 𐐼𐐨𐑊𐐮𐑍𐑆 𐐱𐑂 𐑄𐐰𐐻 𐐘𐐱𐐼 𐐸𐐭 𐐸𐐰𐐼 𐐿𐑉𐐨𐐩𐐻𐐯𐐼 𐑄𐐯𐑋. 𐐤𐐨𐑄𐐲𐑉 𐐼𐐮𐐼 𐑄𐐩 𐐺𐐨𐑊𐐨𐑂 𐑄𐐰𐐻 𐐖𐐯𐑉𐐭𐑅𐐲𐑊𐐯𐑋, 𐑄𐐰𐐻 𐑀𐑉𐐩𐐻 𐑅𐐮𐐻𐐨, 𐐿𐐳𐐼 𐐺𐐨 𐐼𐐨𐑅𐐻𐑉𐐶𐐮𐐼 𐐰𐐿𐐫𐑉𐐼𐐮𐑍 𐐻𐐭 𐑄 𐐶𐐲𐑉𐐼𐑆 𐐱𐑂 𐑄 𐐹𐑉𐐱𐑁𐐯𐐻𐑅. 𐐈𐑌𐐼 𐑄𐐩 𐐶𐐲𐑉 𐑊𐐴𐐿 𐐲𐑌𐐻𐐭 𐑄 𐐖𐐭𐑆 𐐸𐐭 𐐶𐐲𐑉 𐐰𐐻 𐐖𐐯𐑉𐐭𐑅𐐲𐑊𐐯𐑋, 𐐸𐐭 𐑅𐐫𐐻 𐐻𐐭 𐐻𐐩𐐿 𐐲𐐶𐐩 𐑄 𐑊𐐴𐑁 𐐱𐑂 𐑋𐐴 𐑁𐐪𐑄𐐲𐑉.

16. 𐐈𐑌𐐼 𐐮𐐻 𐐿𐐩𐑋 𐐻𐐭 𐐹𐐪𐑅 𐑄𐐰𐐻 𐑋𐐴 𐑁𐐪𐑄𐐲𐑉 𐐼𐐮𐐼 𐑅𐐹𐐨𐐿 𐐲𐑌𐐻𐐭 𐑄𐐯𐑋 𐐮𐑌 𐑄 𐑂𐐰𐑊𐐨 𐐱𐑂 𐐢𐐯𐑋-𐐷𐐭𐐯𐑊, 𐐶𐐮𐑄 𐐹𐐵𐐲𐑉, 𐐺𐐨𐐮𐑍 𐑁𐐮𐑊𐐼 𐐶𐐮𐑄 𐑄 𐐝𐐹𐐮𐑉𐐮𐐻, 𐐲𐑌𐐻𐐮𐑊 𐑄𐐩𐑉 𐑁𐑉𐐩𐑋𐑆 𐐼𐐮𐐼 𐑇𐐩𐐿 𐐺𐐨𐑁𐐬𐑉 𐐸𐐮𐑋. 𐐈𐑌𐐼 𐐸𐐨 𐐼𐐮𐐼 𐐿𐐱𐑌𐑁𐐵𐑌𐐼 𐑄𐐯𐑋, 𐑄𐐰𐐻 𐑄𐐩 𐐼𐐲𐑉𐑅𐐻 𐑌𐐱𐐻 𐐲𐐻𐐲𐑉 𐐲𐑀𐐯𐑌𐑅𐐻 𐐸𐐮𐑋; 𐐸𐐶𐐩𐑉𐑁𐐬𐑉, 𐑄𐐩 𐐼𐐮𐐼 𐐰𐑆 𐐸𐐨 𐐿𐐲𐑋𐐪𐑌𐐼𐐯𐐼 𐑄𐐯𐑋. 𐐈𐑌𐐼 𐑋𐐴 𐑁𐐪𐑄𐐲𐑉 𐐼𐐶𐐯𐑊𐐻 𐐮𐑌 𐐩 𐐻𐐯𐑌𐐻.

17. 𐐈𐑌𐐼 𐐮𐐻 𐐿𐐩𐑋 𐐻𐐭 𐐹𐐪𐑅 𐑄𐐰𐐻 𐐌, 𐐤𐐨𐑁𐐴, 𐐺𐐨𐐮𐑍 𐐯𐐿𐑅𐐨𐐼𐐮𐑍𐑊𐐨 𐐷𐐲𐑍, 𐑌𐐯𐑂𐐲𐑉𐑄𐐲𐑊𐐯𐑅 𐐺𐐨𐐮𐑍 𐑊𐐪𐑉𐐾 𐐮𐑌 𐑅𐐻𐐰𐐽𐐲𐑉, 𐐰𐑌𐐼 𐐫𐑊𐑅𐐬 𐐸𐐰𐑂𐐮𐑍 𐑀𐑉𐐩𐐻 𐐼𐐨𐑆𐐴𐑉𐑆 𐐻𐐭 𐑌𐐬 𐐱𐑂 𐑄 𐑋𐐮𐑅𐐻𐐲𐑉𐐨𐑆 𐐱𐑂 𐐘𐐱𐐼, 𐐸𐐶𐐩𐑉𐑁𐐬𐑉 𐐌 𐐼𐐮𐐼 𐐿𐑉𐐴 𐐲𐑌𐐻𐐭 𐑄 𐐢𐐫𐑉𐐼; 𐐰𐑌𐐼 𐐺𐐨𐐸𐐬𐑊𐐼 𐐸𐐨 𐐼𐐮𐐼 𐑂𐐮𐑆𐐮𐐻 𐑋𐐨, 𐐰𐑌𐐼 𐐼𐐮𐐼 𐑅𐐱𐑁𐐲𐑌 𐑋𐐴 𐐸𐐪𐑉𐐻 𐑄𐐰𐐻 𐐌 𐐼𐐮𐐼 𐐺𐐨𐑊𐐨𐑂 𐐫𐑊 𐑄 𐐶𐐲𐑉𐐼𐑆 𐐸𐐶𐐮𐐽 𐐸𐐰𐐼 𐐺𐐨𐑌 𐑅𐐹𐐬𐐿𐐲𐑌 𐐺𐐴 𐑋𐐴 𐑁𐐪𐑄𐐲𐑉; 𐐸𐐶𐐩𐑉𐑁𐐬𐑉 𐐌 𐐼𐐮𐐼 𐑌𐐱𐐻 𐑉𐐨𐐺𐐯𐑊 𐐲𐑀𐐯𐑌𐑅𐐻 𐐸𐐮𐑋 𐑊𐐴𐐿 𐐲𐑌𐐻𐐭 𐑋𐐴 𐐺𐑉𐐲𐑄𐐲𐑉𐑆. 𐐈𐑌𐐼 𐐌 𐑅𐐹𐐩𐐿 𐐲𐑌𐐻𐐭 𐐝𐐰𐑋, 𐑋𐐩𐐿𐐮𐑍 𐑌𐐬𐑌 𐐲𐑌𐐻𐐭 𐐸𐐮𐑋 𐑄 𐑃𐐮𐑍𐑆 𐐸𐐶𐐮𐐽 𐑄 𐐢𐐫𐑉𐐼 𐐸𐐰𐐼 𐑋𐐰𐑌𐐮𐑁𐐯𐑅𐐻𐐯𐐼 𐐲𐑌𐐻𐐭 𐑋𐐨 𐐺𐐴 𐐸𐐮𐑆 𐐐𐐬𐑊𐐨 𐐝𐐹𐐮𐑉𐐮𐐻.

18. 𐐈𐑌𐐼 𐐮𐐻 𐐿𐐩𐑋 𐐻𐐭 𐐹𐐪𐑅 𐑄𐐰𐐻 𐐸𐐨 𐐺𐐨𐑊𐐨𐑂𐐼 𐐮𐑌 𐑋𐐴 𐐶𐐲𐑉𐐼𐑆; 𐐺𐐲𐐻 𐐺𐐨𐐸𐐬𐑊𐐼 𐐢𐐩𐑋𐐲𐑌 𐐰𐑌𐐼 𐐢𐐯𐑋𐐷𐐭𐐯𐑊 𐐶𐐳𐐼 𐑌𐐱𐐻 𐐸𐐲𐑉𐐿𐐲𐑌 𐐲𐑌𐐻𐐭 𐑋𐐴 𐐶𐐲𐑉𐐼𐑆: 𐐰𐑌𐐼 𐐺𐐨𐐮𐑍 𐑀𐑉𐐨𐑂𐐼 𐐺𐐨𐐿𐐫𐑆 𐐱𐑂 𐑄 𐐸𐐪𐑉𐐼𐑌𐐯𐑅 𐐱𐑂 𐑄𐐩𐑉 𐐸𐐪𐑉𐐻𐑅, 𐐌 𐐿𐑉𐐴𐐼 𐐲𐑌𐐻𐐭 𐑄 𐐢𐐫𐑉𐐼 𐑁𐐫𐑉 𐑄𐐯𐑋.

19. 𐐈𐑌𐐼 𐐮𐐻 𐐿𐐩𐑋 𐐻𐐭 𐐹𐐪𐑅 𐑄𐐰𐐻 𐑄 𐐢𐐫𐑉𐐼 𐑅𐐹𐐩𐐿 𐐲𐑌𐐻𐐭 𐑋𐐨, 𐑅𐐩𐐮𐑍, 𐐒𐑊𐐯𐑅𐐯𐐼 𐐪𐑉𐐻 𐑄𐐵, 𐐤𐐨𐑁𐐴, 𐐺𐐨𐐿𐐫𐑆 𐐱𐑂 𐑄𐐴 𐑁𐐩𐑃, 𐑁𐐫𐑉 𐑄𐐵 𐐸𐐰𐑅𐐻 𐑅𐐫𐐻 𐑋𐐨 𐐼𐐮𐑊𐐮𐐾𐐯𐑌𐐻𐑊𐐨, 𐐶𐐮𐑄 𐑊𐐬𐑊𐐨𐑌𐐯𐑅 𐐱𐑂 𐐸𐐪𐑉𐐻. 𐐈𐑌𐐼 𐐮𐑌𐐰𐑆𐑋𐐲𐐽 𐐰𐑆 𐐷𐐨 𐑇𐐰𐑊 𐐿𐐨𐐹 𐑋𐐴 𐐿𐐲𐑋𐐪𐑌𐐼𐑋𐐯𐑌𐐻𐑅, 𐐷𐐨 𐑇𐐰𐑊 𐐹𐑉𐐱𐑅𐐹𐐲𐑉, 𐐰𐑌𐐼 𐑇𐐰𐑊 𐐺𐐨 𐑊𐐯𐐼 𐐻𐐭 𐐩 𐑊𐐰𐑌𐐼 𐐱𐑂 𐐹𐑉𐐱𐑋𐐮𐑅; 𐐷𐐩, 𐐨𐑂𐐯𐑌 𐐩 𐑊𐐰𐑌𐐼 𐐸𐐶𐐮𐐽 𐐌 𐐸𐐰𐑂 𐐹𐑉𐐨𐐹𐐩𐑉𐐼 𐑁𐐫𐑉 𐐷𐐭; 𐐷𐐩, 𐐩 𐑊𐐰𐑌𐐼 𐐸𐐶𐐮𐐽 𐐮𐑆 𐐽𐐱𐐮𐑅 𐐲𐐺𐐲𐑂 𐐫𐑊 𐐲𐑄𐐲𐑉 𐑊𐐰𐑌𐐼𐑆. 𐐈𐑌𐐼 𐐮𐑌𐐰𐑆𐑋𐐲𐐽 𐐰𐑆 𐑄𐐴 𐐺𐑉𐐯𐑄𐑉𐐯𐑌 𐑇𐐰𐑊 𐑉𐐨𐐺𐐯𐑊 𐐲𐑀𐐯𐑌𐑅𐐻 𐑄𐐨, 𐑄𐐩 𐑇𐐰𐑊 𐐺𐐨 𐐿𐐲𐐻 𐐫𐑁 𐑁𐑉𐐱𐑋 𐑄 𐐹𐑉𐐯𐑆𐐯𐑌𐑅 𐐱𐑂 𐑄 𐐢𐐫𐑉𐐼. 𐐈𐑌𐐼 𐐮𐑌𐐰𐑆𐑋𐐲𐐽 𐐰𐑆 𐑄𐐵 𐑇𐐰𐑊𐐻 𐐿𐐨𐐹 𐑋𐐴 𐐿𐐲𐑋𐐪𐑌𐐼𐑋𐐯𐑌𐐻𐑅, 𐑄𐐵 𐑇𐐰𐑊𐐻 𐐺𐐨 𐑋𐐩𐐼 𐐩 𐑉𐐭𐑊𐐲𐑉 𐐰𐑌𐐼 𐐩 𐐻𐐨𐐽𐐲𐑉 𐐬𐑂𐐲𐑉 𐑄𐐴 𐐺𐑉𐐯𐑄𐑉𐐯𐑌. 𐐙𐐫𐑉 𐐺𐐨𐐸𐐬𐑊𐐼, 𐐮𐑌 𐑄𐐰𐐻 𐐼𐐩 𐑄𐐰𐐻 𐑄𐐩 𐑇𐐰𐑊 𐑉𐐨𐐺𐐯𐑊 𐐲𐑀𐐯𐑌𐑅𐐻 𐑋𐐨, 𐐌 𐐶𐐮𐑊 𐐿𐐲𐑉𐑅 𐑄𐐯𐑋 𐐨𐑂𐐯𐑌 𐐶𐐮𐑄 𐐩 𐑅𐐬𐑉 𐐿𐐲𐑉𐑅, 𐐰𐑌𐐼 𐑄𐐩 𐑇𐐰𐑊 𐐸𐐰𐑂 𐑌𐐬 𐐹𐐵𐐲𐑉 𐐬𐑂𐐲𐑉 𐑄𐐴 𐑅𐐨𐐼, 𐐯𐐿𐑅𐐯𐐹𐐻 𐑄𐐩 𐑇𐐰𐑊 𐑉𐐨𐐺𐐯𐑊 𐐲𐑀𐐯𐑌𐑅𐐻 𐑋𐐨 𐐫𐑊𐑅𐐬. 𐐈𐑌𐐼 𐐮𐑁 𐐮𐐻 𐑅𐐬 𐐺𐐨 𐑄𐐰𐐻 𐑄𐐩 𐑉𐐨𐐺𐐯𐑊 𐐲𐑀𐐯𐑌𐑅𐐻 𐑋𐐨, 𐑄𐐩 𐑇𐐰𐑊 𐐺𐐨 𐐩 𐑅𐐿𐐲𐑉𐐾 𐐲𐑌𐐻𐐭 𐑄𐐴 𐑅𐐨𐐼, 𐐻𐐭 𐑅𐐻𐐲𐑉 𐑄𐐯𐑋 𐐲𐐹 𐐮𐑌 𐑄 𐐶𐐩𐑆 𐐱𐑂 𐑉𐐨𐑋𐐯𐑋𐐺𐑉𐐲𐑌𐑅.

20. 𐐈𐑌𐐼 𐐮𐐻 𐐿𐐩𐑋 𐐻𐐭 𐐹𐐪𐑅 𐑄𐐰𐐻 𐐌, 𐐤𐐨𐑁𐐴, 𐑉𐐨𐐻𐐲𐑉𐑌𐐼 𐑁𐑉𐐱𐑋 𐑅𐐹𐐨𐐿𐐮𐑍 𐐶𐐮𐑄 𐑄 𐐢𐐫𐑉𐐼, 𐐻𐐭 𐑄 𐐻𐐯𐑌𐐻 𐐱𐑂 𐑋𐐴 𐑁𐐪𐑄𐐲𐑉. 𐐈𐑌𐐼 𐐮𐐻 𐐿𐐩𐑋 𐐻𐐭 𐐹𐐪𐑅 𐑄𐐰𐐻 𐐸𐐨 𐑅𐐹𐐩𐐿 𐐲𐑌𐐻𐐭 𐑋𐐨, 𐑅𐐩𐐮𐑍, 𐐒𐐨𐐸𐐬𐑊𐐼 𐐌 𐐸𐐰𐑂 𐐼𐑉𐐨𐑋𐐼 𐐩 𐐼𐑉𐐨𐑋, 𐐮𐑌 𐑄 𐐸𐐶𐐮𐐽 𐑄 𐐢𐐫𐑉𐐼 𐐸𐐰𐑃 𐐿𐐲𐑋𐐪𐑌𐐼𐐯𐐼 𐑋𐐨 𐑄𐐰𐐻 𐑄𐐵 𐐰𐑌𐐼 𐑄𐐴 𐐺𐑉𐐯𐑄𐑉𐐯𐑌 𐑇𐐰𐑊 𐑉𐐨𐐻𐐲𐑉𐑌 𐐻𐐭 𐐖𐐭𐑉𐐭𐑅𐐲𐑊𐐯𐑋. 𐐙𐐫𐑉 𐐺𐐨𐐸𐐬𐑊𐐼, 𐐢𐐩𐐺𐐲𐑌 𐐸𐐰𐑃 𐑄 𐑉𐐯𐐿𐐲𐑉𐐼 𐐱𐑂 𐑄 𐐖𐐭𐑆, 𐐰𐑌𐐼 𐐫𐑊𐑅𐐬 𐐩 𐐾𐐨𐑌𐐨𐐰𐑊𐐲𐐾𐐨 𐐱𐑂 𐑄𐐴 𐑁𐐬𐑉𐑁𐐪𐑄𐐲𐑉𐑆, 𐐰𐑌𐐼 𐑄𐐩 𐐪𐑉 𐐯𐑌𐑀𐑉𐐩𐑂𐐲𐑌 𐐲𐐹𐐱𐑌 𐐹𐑊𐐩𐐻𐑅 𐐱𐑂 𐐺𐑉𐐪𐑅. 𐐐𐐶𐐩𐑉𐑁𐐬𐑉, 𐑄 𐐢𐐫𐑉𐐼 𐐸𐐰𐑃 𐐿𐐲𐑋𐐪𐑌𐐼𐐯𐐼 𐑋𐐨 𐑄𐐰𐐻 𐑄𐐵 𐐰𐑌𐐼 𐑄𐐴 𐐺𐑉𐐲𐑄𐐲𐑉𐑆 𐑇𐐳𐐼 𐑀𐐬 𐐲𐑌𐐻𐐭 𐑄 𐐸𐐵𐑅 𐐱𐑂 𐐢𐐩𐐺𐐲𐑌, 𐐰𐑌𐐼 𐑅𐐨𐐿 𐑄 𐑉𐐯𐐿𐐲𐑉𐐼𐑆, 𐐰𐑌𐐼 𐐺𐑉𐐮𐑍 𐑄𐐯𐑋 𐐼𐐵𐑌 𐐸𐐮𐑄𐐲𐑉 𐐮𐑌𐐻𐐭 𐑄 𐐶𐐮𐑊𐐼𐐲𐑉𐑌𐐯𐑅. 𐐈𐑌𐐼 𐑌𐐵, 𐐺𐐨𐐸𐐬𐑊𐐼 𐑄𐐴 𐐺𐑉𐐲𐑄𐐲𐑉𐑆 𐑋𐐲𐑉𐑋𐐲𐑉, 𐑅𐐩𐐮𐑍, 𐐮𐐻 𐐮𐑆 𐐩 𐐸𐐪𐑉𐐼 𐑃𐐮𐑍 𐐸𐐶𐐮𐐽 𐐌 𐐸𐐰𐑂 𐑉𐐨𐐿𐐶𐐴𐑉𐐼 𐐱𐑂 𐑄𐐯𐑋; 𐐺𐐲𐐻 𐐺𐐨𐐸𐐬𐑊𐐼 𐐌 𐐸𐐰𐑂 𐑌𐐱𐐻 𐑉𐐨𐐿𐐶𐐴𐑉𐐼 𐐮𐐻 𐐱𐑂 𐑄𐐯𐑋; 𐐺𐐲𐐻 𐐮𐐻 𐐮𐑆 𐐩 𐐿𐐲𐑋𐐪𐑌𐐼𐑋𐐯𐑌𐐻 𐐱𐑂 𐑄 𐐢𐐫𐑉𐐼. 𐐜𐐩𐑉𐑁𐐬𐑉 𐑀𐐬, 𐑋𐐴 𐑅𐐲𐑌, 𐐰𐑌𐐼 𐑄𐐵 𐑇𐐰𐑊𐐻 𐐺𐐨 𐑁𐐩𐑂𐐲𐑉𐐼 𐐱𐑂 𐑄 𐐢𐐫𐑉𐐼, 𐐺𐐨𐐿𐐫𐑆 𐑄𐐵 𐐸𐐰𐑅𐐻 𐑌𐐱𐐻 𐑋𐐲𐑉𐑋𐐲𐑉𐐼.

21. 𐐈𐑌𐐼 𐐮𐐻 𐐿𐐩𐑋 𐐻𐐭 𐐹𐐪𐑅 𐑄𐐰𐐻 𐐌, 𐐤𐐨𐑁𐐴, 𐑅𐐯𐐼 𐐲𐑌𐐻𐐭 𐑋𐐴 𐑁𐐪𐑄𐐲𐑉, 𐐌 𐐶𐐮𐑊 𐑀𐐬 𐐰𐑌𐐼 𐐼𐐭 𐑄 𐑃𐐮𐑍𐑆 𐐸𐐶𐐮𐐽 𐑄 𐐢𐐫𐑉𐐼 𐐸𐐰𐑃 𐐿𐐲𐑋𐐪𐑌𐐼𐐯𐐼, 𐑁𐐫𐑉 𐐌 𐑌𐐬 𐑄𐐰𐐻 𐑄 𐐢𐐫𐑉𐐼 𐑀𐐮𐑂𐐯𐑃 𐑌𐐬 𐐿𐐲𐑋𐐪𐑌𐐼𐑋𐐯𐑌𐐻𐑅 𐐲𐑌𐐻𐐭 𐑄 𐐽𐐮𐑊𐐼𐑉𐐯𐑌 𐐱𐑂 𐑋𐐯𐑌, 𐑅𐐩𐑂 𐐸𐐨 𐑇𐐰𐑊 𐐹𐑉𐐨𐐹𐐩𐑉 𐐩 𐐶𐐩 𐑁𐐫𐑉 𐑄𐐯𐑋 𐑄𐐰𐐻 𐑄𐐩 𐑋𐐩 𐐰𐐿𐐱𐑋𐐹𐑊𐐮𐑇 𐑄 𐑃𐐮𐑍 𐐸𐐶𐐮𐐽 𐐸𐐨 𐐿𐐲𐑋𐐪𐑌𐐼𐐯𐑃 𐑄𐐯𐑋.

22. 𐐈𐑌𐐼 𐐮𐐻 𐐿𐐩𐑋 𐐻𐐭 𐐹𐐰𐑅 𐑄𐐰𐐻 𐐸𐐶𐐯𐑌 𐑋𐐴 𐑁𐐪𐑄𐐲𐑉 𐐸𐐰𐐼 𐐸𐐲𐑉𐐼 𐑄𐐨𐑆 𐐶𐐲𐑉𐐼𐑆, 𐐸𐐨 𐐶𐐱𐑆 𐐯𐐿𐑅𐐨𐐼𐐮𐑍 𐑀𐑊𐐰𐐼, 𐑁𐐫𐑉 𐐸𐐨 𐑌𐐭 𐑄𐐰𐐻 𐐴 𐐸𐐰𐐼 𐐺𐐮𐑌 𐐺𐑊𐐯𐑅𐐯𐐼 𐐲𐑂 𐑄 𐐢𐐫𐑉𐐼. 𐐈𐑌𐐼 𐐌, 𐐤𐐨𐑁𐐴, 𐐰𐑌𐐼 𐑋𐐴 𐐺𐑉𐐯𐑄𐑉𐐯𐑌 𐐻𐐳𐐿 𐐵𐑉 𐐾𐐲𐑉𐑌𐐨 𐐮𐑌 𐑄 𐐶𐐮𐑊𐐼𐐲𐑉𐑌𐐯𐑅 𐐶𐐮𐑄 𐐵𐑉 𐐻𐐯𐑌𐐻𐑅, 𐐻𐐭 𐑀𐐬 𐐲𐐹 𐐻𐐭 𐑄 𐑊𐐰𐑌𐐼 𐐲𐑂 𐐖𐐭𐑉𐐭𐑅𐐲𐑊𐐯𐑋.

23. 𐐈𐑌𐐼 𐐮𐐻 𐐿𐐩𐑋 𐐻𐐭 𐐹𐐰𐑅 𐑄𐐰𐐻 𐐸𐐶𐐯𐑌 𐐶𐐨 𐐸𐐰𐐼 𐑀𐐱𐑌 𐐲𐐹 𐐻𐐭 𐑄 𐑊𐐰𐑌𐐼 𐐲𐑂 𐐖𐐭𐑉𐐭𐑅𐐲𐑊𐐯𐑋, 𐐌 𐐰𐑌𐐼 𐑋𐐴 𐐺𐑉𐐯𐑄𐑉𐐯𐑌 𐐼𐐮𐐼 𐐿𐐱𐑌𐑅𐐲𐑊𐐻 𐐶𐐲𐑌 𐐶𐐮𐑄 𐐰𐑌𐐲𐑄𐐲𐑉; 𐐰𐑌𐐼 𐐶𐐨 𐐿𐐰𐑅𐐻 𐑊𐐱𐐻𐑅 𐐸𐐭 𐐲𐑂 𐐲𐑅 𐑇𐐳𐐼 𐑀𐐬 𐐮𐑌 𐐲𐑌𐐻𐐭 𐑄 𐐸𐐵𐑅 𐐲𐑂 𐐢𐐩𐐺𐐲𐑌. 𐐈𐑌𐐼 𐐮𐐻 𐐿𐐩𐑋 𐐻𐐭 𐐹𐐰𐑅 𐑄𐐰𐐻 𐑄 𐑊𐐱𐐻 𐑁𐐯𐑊 𐐲𐐹𐐱𐑌 𐐢𐐩𐑋𐐲𐑌; 𐐰𐑌𐐼 𐐢𐐩𐑋𐐲𐑌 𐐶𐐯𐑌𐐻 𐐮𐑌 𐐲𐑌𐐻𐐭 𐑄 𐐸𐐵𐑅 𐐲𐑂 𐐢𐐩𐐺𐐲𐑌, 𐐰𐑌𐐼 𐐸𐐨 𐐻𐐫𐐿𐐻 𐐶𐐮𐑄 𐐸𐐮𐑋 𐐰𐑆 𐐸𐐨 𐑅𐐰𐐻 𐐮𐑌 𐐸𐐮𐑆 𐐸𐐵𐑅. 𐐈𐑌𐐼 𐐸𐐨 𐐼𐐨𐑆𐐴𐑉𐐼 𐐲𐑂 𐐢𐐩𐐺𐐲𐑌 𐑄 𐑉𐐯𐐿𐐫𐑉𐐼𐑆 𐐸𐐶𐐮𐐽 𐐶𐐲𐑉 𐐯𐑌𐑀𐑉𐐩𐑂𐑌 𐐲𐐹𐐱𐑌 𐑄 𐐹𐑊𐐩𐐻𐑅 𐐲𐑂 𐐺𐑉𐐰𐑅, 𐐸𐐶𐐮𐐽 𐐿𐐱𐑌𐐻𐐩𐑌𐐼 𐑄 𐑀𐐯𐑌𐐨𐐰𐑊𐐲𐐾𐐨 𐐲𐑂 𐑋𐐴 𐑁𐐪𐑄𐐲𐑉.

24. 𐐈𐑌𐐼 𐐺𐐨𐐸𐐬𐑊𐐼, 𐐮𐐻 𐐿𐐩𐑋 𐐻𐐭 𐐹𐐰𐑅 𐑄𐐰𐐻 𐐢𐐩𐐺𐐲𐑌 𐐶𐐱𐑆 𐐰𐑍𐑀𐑉𐐨, 𐐰𐑌𐐼 𐑃𐑉𐐲𐑅𐐻 𐐸𐐮𐑋 𐐵𐐻 𐑁𐑉𐐱𐑋 𐐸𐐮𐑆 𐐹𐑉𐐯𐑆𐐯𐑌𐑅; 𐐰𐑌𐐼 𐐸𐐨 𐐶𐐳𐐼 𐑌𐐱𐐻 𐑄𐐰𐐻 𐐸𐐨 𐑇𐐳𐐼 𐐸𐐰𐑂 𐑄 𐑉𐐯𐐿𐐫𐑉𐐼𐑆. 𐐐𐐶𐐩𐑉𐑁𐐫𐑉 𐐸𐐨 𐑅𐐯𐐼 𐐲𐑌𐐻𐐭 𐐸𐐮𐑋, 𐐒𐐨𐐸𐐬𐑊𐐼 𐑄𐐵 𐐪𐑉𐐻 𐐩 𐑉𐐱𐐺𐐲𐑉, 𐐰𐑌𐐼 𐐌 𐐶𐐮𐑊 𐑅𐑊𐐩 𐑄𐐨. 𐐒𐐲𐐻 𐐢𐐩𐑋𐐲𐑌 𐑁𐑊𐐯𐐼 𐐵𐐻 𐐲𐑂 𐐸𐐮𐑆 𐐹𐑉𐐯𐑆𐐯𐑌𐑅, 𐐰𐑌𐐼 𐐻𐐬𐑊𐐼 𐑄 𐑃𐐮𐑍𐑆 𐐸𐐶𐐮𐐽 𐐢𐐩𐐺𐐲𐑌 𐐸𐐰𐐼 𐐼𐐲𐑌 𐐲𐑌𐐻𐐭 𐐲𐑅. 𐐈𐑌𐐼 𐐶𐐨 𐐺𐐨𐑀𐐰𐑌 𐐻𐐭 𐐺𐐨 𐐯𐐿𐑅𐐨𐐼𐐮𐑍 𐑅𐐱𐑉𐐬𐑁𐐳𐑊, 𐐰𐑌𐐼 𐑋𐐴 𐐺𐑉𐐯𐑄𐑉𐐯𐑌 𐐶𐐲𐑉 𐐰𐐺𐐵𐐻 𐐻𐐭 𐑉𐐨𐐻𐐲𐑉𐑌 𐐲𐑌𐐻𐐭 𐑋𐐴 𐑁𐐪𐑄𐐲𐑉 𐐮𐑌 𐑄 𐐶𐐮𐑊𐐼𐐲𐑉𐑌𐐯𐑅. 𐐒𐐲𐐻 𐐺𐐨𐐸𐐬𐑊𐐼 𐐌 𐑅𐐯𐐼 𐐲𐑌𐐻𐐭 𐑄𐐯𐑋, 𐑄𐐰𐐻 𐐰𐑆 𐑄 𐐢𐐫𐑉𐐼 𐑊𐐮𐑂𐐯𐑃, 𐐰𐑌𐐼 𐐰𐑆 𐐶𐐨 𐑊𐐮𐑂, 𐐶𐐨 𐐶𐐮𐑊 𐑌𐐱𐐻 𐑀𐐬 𐐼𐐵𐑌 𐐲𐑌𐐻𐐭 𐐵𐑉 𐑁𐐪𐑄𐐲𐑉 𐐮𐑌 𐑄 𐐶𐐮𐑊𐐼𐐲𐑉𐑌𐐯𐑅, 𐐲𐑌𐐻𐐮𐑊 𐐶𐐨 𐐸𐐰𐑂 𐐰𐐿𐐱𐑋𐐹𐑊𐐮𐑇𐐻 𐑄 𐑃𐐮𐑍 𐐸𐐶𐐮𐐽 𐑄 𐐢𐐫𐑉𐐼 𐐸𐐰𐑃 𐐿𐐱𐑋𐐰𐑌𐐼𐐯𐐼 𐐲𐑅. 𐐐𐐶𐐩𐑉𐑁𐐫𐑉 𐑊𐐯𐐻 𐐲𐑅 𐐺𐐨 𐑁𐐩𐑃𐑁𐐳𐑊 𐐮𐑌 𐐿𐐨𐐹𐐮𐑍 𐑄 𐐿𐐱𐑋𐐰𐑌𐐼𐑋𐐯𐑌𐐻𐑅 𐐲𐑂 𐑄 𐐢𐐫𐑉𐐼; 𐑄𐐩𐑉𐑁𐐫𐑉 𐑊𐐯𐐻 𐐲𐑅 𐑀𐐬 𐐼𐐵𐑌 𐐻𐐭 𐑄 𐑊𐐰𐑌𐐼 𐐲𐑂 𐐵𐑉 𐑁𐐪𐑄𐐲𐑉𐑆 𐐮𐑌𐐸𐐯𐑉𐐮𐐻𐐰𐑌𐑅, 𐑁𐐫𐑉 𐐺𐐨𐐸𐐬𐑊𐐼 𐐸𐐨 𐑊𐐯𐑁𐐻 𐑀𐐬𐑊𐐼 𐐰𐑌𐐼 𐑅𐐮𐑊𐑂𐐲𐑉, 𐐰𐑌𐐼 𐐫𐑊 𐑋𐐰𐑌𐐲𐑉 𐐲𐑂 𐑉𐐮𐐽𐐯𐑆. 𐐈𐑌𐐼 𐐫𐑊 𐑄𐐮𐑅 𐐸𐐨 𐐸𐐰𐑃 𐐼𐐲𐑌 𐐺𐐨𐐿𐐫𐑆 𐐲𐑂 𐑄 𐐿𐐱𐑋𐐰𐑌𐐼𐑋𐐯𐑌𐐻𐑅 𐐲𐑂 𐑄 𐐢𐐫𐑉𐐼: 𐑁𐐫𐑉 𐐸𐐨 𐑌𐐭 𐑄𐐰𐐻 𐐖𐐭𐑉𐐭𐑅𐐲𐑊𐐯𐑋 𐑋𐐲𐑅𐐻 𐐺𐐨 𐐼𐐨𐑅𐐻𐑉𐑎𐐼, 𐐺𐐨𐐿𐐫𐑆 𐐲𐑂 𐑄 𐐶𐐮𐐿𐐯𐐼𐑌𐐯𐑅 𐐲𐑂 𐑄 𐐹𐐨𐐹𐑊.

25. 𐐙𐐫𐑉 𐐺𐐨𐐸𐐬𐑊𐐼 𐑄𐐩 𐐸𐐰𐑂 𐑉𐐨𐐾𐐯𐐿𐐻𐐯𐐼 𐑄 𐐶𐐲𐑉𐐼𐑆 𐐲𐑂 𐑄 𐐹𐑉𐐱𐑁𐐯𐐻𐑅. 𐐐𐐶𐐩𐑉𐑁𐐫𐑉, 𐐮𐑁 𐑋𐐴 𐑁𐐪𐑄𐐲𐑉 𐑇𐐳𐐼 𐐼𐐶𐐯𐑊 𐐮𐑌 𐑄 𐑊𐐰𐑌𐐼 𐐪𐑁𐐻𐐲𐑉 𐐸𐐨 𐐸𐐰𐑃 𐐺𐐮𐑌 𐐿𐐱𐑋𐐰𐑌𐐼𐐯𐐼 𐐻𐐭 𐑁𐑊𐐨 𐐵𐐻 𐐲𐑂 𐑄 𐑊𐐰𐑌𐐼, 𐐺𐐨𐐸𐐬𐑊𐐼 𐐸𐐨 𐐶𐐳𐐼 𐐫𐑊𐑅𐐬 𐐹𐐯𐑉𐐮𐑇. 𐐐𐐶𐐩𐑉𐑁𐐫𐑉 𐐮𐐻 𐑋𐐲𐑅𐐻 𐑌𐐨𐐼𐑆 𐐺𐐨 𐑄𐐰𐐻 𐐸𐐨 𐑁𐑊𐐨 𐐵𐐻 𐐲𐑂 𐑄 𐑊𐐰𐑌𐐼. 𐐈𐑌𐐼 𐐺𐐨𐐸𐐬𐑊𐐼, 𐐮𐐻 𐐮𐑆 𐐶𐐮𐑆𐐼𐐲𐑋 𐐮𐑌 𐐘𐐱𐐼 𐑄𐐰𐐻 𐐶𐐨 𐑇𐐳𐐼 𐐱𐐺𐐻𐐩𐑌 𐑄𐐨𐑆 𐑉𐐯𐐿𐐫𐑉𐐼𐑆, 𐑄𐐰𐐻 𐐶𐐨 𐑋𐐩 𐐹𐑉𐐨𐑆𐐲𐑉𐑂 𐐲𐑌𐐻𐐭 𐐵𐑉 𐐽𐐮𐑊𐐼𐑉𐐯𐑌 𐑄 𐑊𐐰𐑍𐑀𐐶𐐯𐐾 𐐲𐑂 𐐵𐑉 𐑁𐐪𐑄𐐲𐑉𐑆; 𐐰𐑌𐐼 𐐫𐑊𐑅𐐬 𐑄𐐰𐐻 𐐶𐐨 𐑋𐐩 𐐹𐑉𐐨𐑆𐐲𐑉𐑂 𐐲𐑌𐐻𐐭 𐑄𐐯𐑋 𐑄 𐐶𐐲𐑉𐐼𐑆 𐐸𐐶𐐮𐐽 𐐸𐐰𐑂 𐐺𐐮𐑌 𐑅𐐹𐐬𐐿𐑌 𐐺𐐴 𐑄 𐑋𐐵𐑃 𐐲𐑂 𐐫𐑊 𐑄 𐐸𐐬𐑊𐐨 𐐹𐑉𐐱𐑁𐐯𐐻𐑅, 𐐸𐐶𐐮𐐽 𐐸𐐰𐑂 𐐺𐐮𐑌 𐐼𐐨𐑊𐐮𐑂𐐲𐑉𐐼 𐐲𐑌𐐻𐐭 𐑄𐐯𐑋 𐐺𐐴 𐑄 𐐝𐐹𐐮𐑉𐐮𐐻 𐐰𐑌𐐼 𐐹𐐵𐐲𐑉 𐐲𐑂 𐐘𐐱𐐼, 𐑅𐐮𐑌𐑅 𐑄 𐐶𐐲𐑉𐑊𐐼 𐐺𐐨𐑀𐐰𐑌, 𐐨𐑂𐑌 𐐼𐐵𐑌 𐐲𐑌𐐻𐐭 𐑄𐐮𐑅 𐐹𐑉𐐯𐑆𐐯𐑌𐐻 𐐻𐐴𐑋.

26. 𐐈𐑌𐐼 𐐮𐐻 𐐿𐐩𐑋 𐐻𐐭 𐐹𐐰𐑅 𐑄𐐰𐐻 𐐪𐑁𐐻𐐲𐑉 𐑄𐐮𐑅 𐑋𐐰𐑌𐐲𐑉 𐐲𐑂 𐑊𐐰𐑍𐑀𐐶𐐯𐐾 𐐼𐐮𐐼 𐐌 𐐹𐐲𐑉𐑅𐐶𐐩𐐼 𐑋𐐴 𐐺𐑉𐐯𐑄𐑉𐐯𐑌, 𐑄𐐰𐐻 𐑄𐐩 𐑋𐐴𐐻 𐐺𐐨 𐑁𐐩𐑃𐑁𐐳𐑊 𐐮𐑌 𐐿𐐨𐐹𐐮𐑍 𐑄 𐐿𐐱𐑋𐐰𐑌𐐼𐑋𐐯𐑌𐐻𐑅 𐐲𐑂 𐐘𐐱𐐼. 𐐈𐑌𐐼 𐐮𐐻 𐐿𐐩𐑋 𐐻𐐭 𐐹𐐰𐑅 𐑄𐐰𐐻 𐐶𐐨 𐐶𐐯𐑌𐐻 𐐼𐐵𐑌 𐐻𐐭 𐑄 𐑊𐐰𐑌𐐼 𐐲𐑂 𐐵𐑉 𐐮𐑌𐐸𐐯𐑉𐐮𐐻𐐰𐑌𐑅, 𐐰𐑌𐐼 𐐶𐐨 𐐼𐐮𐐼 𐑀𐐰𐑄𐐲𐑉 𐐻𐐭𐑀𐐯𐑄𐐲𐑉 𐐵𐑉 𐑀𐐬𐑊𐐼, 𐐰𐑌𐐼 𐐵𐑉 𐑅𐐮𐑊𐑂𐐲𐑉, 𐐰𐑌𐐼 𐐵𐑉 𐐹𐑉𐐯𐑇𐐲𐑅 𐑃𐐮𐑍𐑆. 𐐈𐑌𐐼 𐐪𐑁𐐻𐐲𐑉 𐐶𐐨 𐐸𐐰𐐼 𐑀𐐰𐑄𐐲𐑉𐐼 𐑄𐐨𐑆 𐑃𐐮𐑍𐑆 𐐻𐐭𐑀𐐯𐑄𐐲𐑉, 𐐶𐐨 𐐶𐐯𐑌𐐻 𐐲𐐹 𐐲𐑀𐐯𐑌 𐐲𐑌𐐻𐐭 𐑄 𐐸𐐵𐑅 𐐲𐑂 𐐢𐐩𐐺𐐲𐑌.

27. 𐐈𐑌𐐼 𐐮𐐻 𐐿𐐩𐑋 𐐻𐐭 𐐹𐐰𐑅 𐑄𐐰𐐻 𐐶𐐨 𐐶𐐯𐑌𐐻 𐐮𐑌 𐐲𐑌𐐻𐐭 𐐢𐐩𐐺𐐲𐑌, 𐐰𐑌𐐼 𐐼𐐨𐑆𐐴𐑉𐐼 𐐸𐐮𐑋 𐑄𐐰𐐻 𐐸𐐨 𐐶𐐳𐐼 𐑀𐐮𐑂 𐐲𐑌𐐻𐐭 𐐲𐑅 𐑄 𐑉𐐯𐐿𐐫𐑉𐐼𐑆 𐐸𐐶𐐮𐐽 𐐶𐐲𐑉 𐐯𐑌𐑀𐑉𐐩𐑂𐑌 𐐲𐐹𐐱𐑌 𐑄 𐐹𐑊𐐩𐐻𐑅 𐐲𐑂 𐐺𐑉𐐰𐑅, 𐑁𐐫𐑉 𐐸𐐶𐐮𐐽 𐐶𐐨 𐐶𐐳𐐼 𐑀𐐮𐑂 𐐲𐑌𐐻𐐭 𐐸𐐮𐑋 𐐵𐑉 𐑀𐐬𐑊𐐼, 𐐰𐑌𐐼 𐐵𐑉 𐑅𐐮𐑊𐑂𐐲𐑉, 𐐰𐑌𐐼 𐐫𐑊 𐐵𐑉 𐐹𐑉𐐯𐑇𐐲𐑅 𐑃𐐮𐑍𐑆.

28. 𐐈𐑌𐐼 𐐮𐐻 𐐿𐐩𐑋 𐐻𐐭 𐐹𐐰𐑅 𐑄𐐰𐐻 𐐸𐐶𐐯𐑌 𐐢𐐩𐐺𐐲𐑌 𐑅𐐫 𐐵𐑉 𐐹𐑉𐐱𐐹𐐲𐑉𐐻𐐨, 𐐰𐑌𐐼 𐑄𐐰𐐻 𐐮𐐻 𐐶𐐱𐑆 𐐯𐐿𐑅𐐨𐐼𐐮𐑍 𐑀𐑉𐐩𐐻, 𐐸𐐨 𐐼𐐮𐐼 𐑊𐐲𐑅𐐻 𐐪𐑁𐐻𐐲𐑉 𐐮𐐻, 𐐮𐑌𐑅𐐬𐑋𐐲𐐽 𐑄𐐰𐐻 𐐸𐐨 𐑃𐑉𐐲𐑅𐐻 𐐲𐑅 𐐵𐐻, 𐐰𐑌𐐼 𐑅𐐯𐑌𐐻 𐐸𐐮𐑆 𐑅𐐲𐑉-

𐑂𐐲𐑌𐐻𐑅 𐐻𐐭 𐑅𐑊𐐩 𐐲𐑅, 𐑄𐐰𐐻 𐐸𐐨 𐑋𐐴𐐻 𐐱𐐺𐐻𐐩𐑌 𐐵𐑉 𐐹𐑉𐐱𐐹𐐲𐑉𐐻𐐨. 𐐈𐑌𐐼 𐐮𐐻 𐐿𐐩𐑋 𐐻𐐭 𐐹𐐰𐑅 𐑄𐐰𐐻 𐐶𐐨 𐐼𐐮𐐼 𐑁𐑊𐐨 𐐺𐐨𐑁𐐬𐑉 𐑄 𐑅𐐲𐑉𐑂𐐲𐑌𐐻𐑅 𐐱𐑂 𐐢𐐩𐐺𐐲𐑌, 𐐰𐑌𐐼 𐐶𐐨 𐐶𐐲𐑉 𐐬𐐺𐑊𐐴𐐾𐐼 𐐻𐐭 𐑊𐐨𐑂 𐐺𐐨𐐸𐐴𐑌𐐼 𐐵𐑉 𐐹𐑉𐐱𐐹𐐲𐑉𐐻𐐨, 𐐰𐑌𐐼 𐐮𐐻 𐑁𐐯𐑊 𐐮𐑌𐐻𐐭 𐑄 𐐸𐐰𐑌𐐼𐑆 𐐱𐑂 𐐢𐐩𐐺𐐲𐑌.

29. 𐐈𐑌𐐼 𐐮𐐻 𐐿𐐩𐑋 𐐻𐐭 𐐹𐐰𐑅 𐑄𐐰𐐻 𐐶𐐨 𐑁𐑊𐐯𐐼 𐐮𐑌𐐻𐐭 𐑄 𐐶𐐮𐑊𐐼𐐲𐑉𐑌𐐯𐑅, 𐐰𐑌𐐼 𐑄 𐑅𐐲𐑉𐑂𐐲𐑌𐐻𐑅 𐐱𐑂 𐐢𐐩𐐺𐐲𐑌 𐐼𐐮𐐼 𐑌𐐱𐐻 𐐬𐑂𐐲𐑉𐐻𐐩𐐿 𐐲𐑅, 𐐰𐑌𐐼 𐐶𐐨 𐐸𐐮𐐼 𐐵𐑉𐑅𐐯𐑊𐑂𐑆 𐐮𐑌 𐑄 𐐿𐐰𐑂𐐮𐐻𐐨 𐐱𐑂 𐐩 𐑉𐐱𐐿. 𐐈𐑌𐐼 𐐮𐐻 𐐿𐐩𐑋 𐐻𐐭 𐐹𐐰𐑅 𐑄𐐰𐐻 𐐢𐐩𐑋𐐲𐑌 𐐶𐐱𐑆 𐐰𐑍𐑀𐑉𐐨 𐐶𐐮𐑄 𐑋𐐨, 𐐰𐑌𐐼 𐐫𐑊𐑅𐐬 𐐶𐐮𐑄 𐑋𐐴 𐑁𐐪𐑄𐐲𐑉; 𐐰𐑌𐐼 𐐫𐑊𐑅𐐬 𐐶𐐱𐑆 𐐢𐐯𐑋𐐷𐐭𐐯𐑊; 𐑁𐐫𐑉 𐐸𐐨 𐐸𐐪𐑉𐐿𐐲𐑌𐐼 𐐲𐑌𐐻𐐭 𐑄 𐐶𐐲𐑉𐐼𐑆 𐐱𐑂 𐐢𐐩𐑋𐐲𐑌. 𐐐𐐶𐐯𐑉𐑁𐐫𐑉 𐐢𐐩𐑋𐐲𐑌 𐐰𐑌𐐼 𐐢𐐯𐑋𐐷𐐭𐐯𐑊 𐐼𐐮𐐼 𐑅𐐹𐐨𐐿 𐑋𐐯𐑌𐐨 𐐸𐐪𐑉𐐼 𐐶𐐲𐑉𐐼𐑆 𐐲𐑌𐐻𐐭 𐐲𐑅, 𐑄𐐩𐑉 𐐷𐐲𐑍𐑀𐐲𐑉 𐐺𐑉𐐲𐑄𐐲𐑉𐑆, 𐐰𐑌𐐼 𐑄𐐩 𐐼𐐮𐐼 𐑅𐑋𐐴𐐻 𐐲𐑅 𐐨𐑂𐐲𐑌 𐐶𐐮𐑄 𐐩 𐑉𐐱𐐼.

30. 𐐈𐑌𐐼 𐐮𐐻 𐐿𐐩𐑋 𐐻𐐭 𐐹𐐰𐑅 𐐰𐑆 𐑄𐐩 𐑅𐑋𐐬𐐻 𐐲𐑅 𐐶𐐮𐑄 𐐩 𐑉𐐱𐐼, 𐐺𐐨𐐸𐐬𐑊𐐼 𐐰𐑌 𐐩𐑌𐐾𐐯𐑊 𐐱𐑂 𐑄 𐐢𐐫𐑉𐐼 𐐿𐐩𐑋 𐐰𐑌𐐼 𐑅𐐻𐐳𐐼 𐐺𐐨𐑁𐐬𐑉 𐑄𐐯𐑋, 𐐰𐑌𐐼 𐐸𐐨 𐑅𐐹𐐩𐐿 𐐲𐑌𐐻𐐭 𐑄𐐯𐑋, 𐑅𐐩𐐮𐑍, 𐐐𐐶𐐴 𐐼𐐭 𐐷𐐨 𐑅𐑋𐐴𐐻 𐐷𐐭𐑉 𐐷𐐲𐑍𐑀𐐲𐑉 𐐺𐑉𐐲𐑄𐐲𐑉 𐐶𐐮𐑄 𐐩 𐑉𐐱𐐼? 𐐤𐐬 𐐷𐐨 𐑌𐐱𐐻 𐑄𐐰𐐻 𐑄 𐐢𐐫𐑉𐐼 𐐸𐐰𐑃 𐐽𐐬𐑆𐐲𐑌 𐐸𐐮𐑋 𐐻𐐭 𐐺𐐨 𐐩 𐑉𐐭𐑊𐐲𐑉 𐐬𐑂𐐲𐑉 𐐷𐐭, 𐐰𐑌𐐼 𐑄𐐮𐑅 𐐺𐐨𐐿𐐫𐑆 𐐱𐑂 𐐷𐐭𐑉 𐐮𐑌𐐮𐐿𐐶𐐮𐐻𐐨𐑆? 𐐒𐐨𐐸𐐬𐑊𐐼 𐐷𐐨 𐑇𐐰𐑊 𐑀𐐬 𐐲𐐹 𐐻𐐭 𐐖𐐨𐑉𐐭𐑅𐐲𐑊𐐯𐑋 𐐲𐑀𐐯𐑌, 𐐰𐑌𐐼 𐑄 𐐢𐐫𐑉𐐼 𐐶𐐮𐑊 𐐼𐐨𐑊𐐮𐑂𐐲𐑉 𐐢𐐩𐐺𐐲𐑌 𐐮𐑌𐐻𐐭 𐐷𐐭𐑉 𐐸𐐰𐑌𐐼𐑆. 𐐈𐑌𐐼 𐐰𐑁𐐻𐐲𐑉 𐑄 𐐩𐑌𐐾𐐯𐑊 𐐸𐐰𐐼 𐑅𐐹𐐬𐐿𐐲𐑌 𐐲𐑌𐐻𐐭 𐐲𐑅, 𐐸𐐨 𐐼𐐨𐐹𐐪𐑉𐐻𐐯𐐼. 𐐈𐑌𐐼 𐐰𐑁𐐻𐐲𐑉 𐑄 𐐩𐑌𐐾𐐯𐑊 𐐸𐐰𐐼 𐐼𐐨𐐹𐐪𐑉𐐻𐐯𐐼, 𐐢𐐩𐑋𐐲𐑌 𐐰𐑌𐐼 𐐢𐐯𐑋𐐷𐐭𐐯𐑊 𐐲𐑀𐐯𐑌 𐐺𐐨𐑀𐐰𐑌 𐐻𐐭 𐑋𐐲𐑉𐑋𐐲𐑉, 𐑅𐐩𐐮𐑍, 𐐐𐐵 𐐮𐑆 𐐮𐐻 𐐹𐐱𐑅𐐮𐐺𐑊 𐑄𐐰𐐻 𐑄 𐐢𐐫𐑉𐐼 𐐶𐐮𐑊 𐐼𐐨𐑊𐐮𐑂𐐲𐑉 𐐢𐐩𐐺𐐲𐑌 𐐮𐑌𐐻𐐭 𐐵𐑉 𐐸𐐰𐑌𐐼𐑆? 𐐒𐐨𐐸𐐬𐑊𐐼, 𐐸𐐨 𐐮𐑆 𐐩 𐑋𐐴𐐻𐐨 𐑋𐐰𐑌, 𐐰𐑌𐐼 𐐸𐐨 𐐿𐐰𐑌 𐐿𐐱𐑋𐐰𐑌𐐼 𐑁𐐮𐑁𐐻𐐨, 𐐷𐐩, 𐐨𐑂𐐲𐑌 𐐸𐐨 𐐿𐐰𐑌 𐑅𐑊𐐩 𐑁𐐮𐑁𐐻𐐨; 𐑄𐐯𐑌 𐐸𐐶𐐴 𐑌𐐱𐐻 𐐲𐑅?

31. 𐐈𐑌𐐼 𐐮𐐻 𐐿𐐩𐑋 𐐻𐐭 𐐹𐐰𐑅 𐑄𐐰𐐻 𐐌 𐑅𐐹𐐩𐐿 𐐲𐑌𐐻𐐭 𐑋𐐴 𐐺𐑉𐐯𐑄𐑉𐐯𐑌, 𐑅𐐩𐐮𐑍, 𐐢𐐯𐐻 𐐲𐑅 𐑀𐐬 𐐲𐐹 𐐲𐑀𐐯𐑌 𐐲𐑌𐐻𐐭 𐐖𐐨𐑉𐐭𐑅𐐲𐑊𐐯𐑋, 𐐰𐑌𐐼 𐑊𐐯𐐻 𐐲𐑅 𐐺𐐨 𐑁𐐩𐑃𐑁𐐳𐑊 𐐮𐑌 𐐿𐐨𐐹𐐮𐑍 𐑄 𐐿𐐱𐑋𐐰𐑌𐐼𐑋𐐯𐑌𐐻𐑅 𐐱𐑂 𐑄 𐐢𐐫𐑉𐐼; 𐑁𐐫𐑉 𐐺𐐨𐐸𐐬𐑊𐐼 𐐸𐐨 𐐮𐑆 𐑋𐐴𐐻𐐨𐐲𐑉 𐑄𐐰𐑌 𐐫𐑊 𐑄 𐐲𐑉𐑃, 𐑄𐐯𐑌 𐐸𐐶𐐴 𐑌𐐱𐐻 𐑋𐐴𐐻𐐨𐐲𐑉 𐑄𐐰𐑌 𐐢𐐩𐐺𐐲𐑌 𐐰𐑌𐐼 𐐸𐐮𐑆 𐑁𐐮𐑁𐐻𐐨, 𐐷𐐩, 𐐫𐑉 𐐨𐑂𐐲𐑌 𐑄𐐰𐑌 𐐸𐐮𐑆 𐐻𐐯𐑌𐑆 𐐱𐑂 𐑃𐐵𐑆𐐲𐑌𐐼𐑆. 𐐜𐐯𐑉𐑁𐐫𐑉, 𐑊𐐯𐐻 𐐲𐑅 𐑀𐐬 𐐲𐐹; 𐑊𐐯𐐻 𐐲𐑅 𐐺𐐨 𐑅𐐻𐑉𐐱𐑍 𐑊𐐴𐐿 𐐲𐑌𐐻𐐭 𐐣𐐬𐑆𐐯𐑆; 𐑁𐐫𐑉 𐐸𐐨 𐐻𐑉𐐭𐑊𐐨 𐑅𐐹𐐩𐐿 𐐲𐑌𐐻𐐭 𐑄 𐐶𐐫𐐻𐐲𐑉𐑆 𐐱𐑂 𐑄 𐐡𐐯𐐼 𐐝𐐨, 𐐰𐑌𐐼 𐑄𐐩 𐐼𐐮𐑂𐐴𐐼𐐯𐐼 𐐸𐐮𐑄𐐲𐑉 𐐰𐑌𐐼 𐑄𐐮𐑄𐐲𐑉, 𐐰𐑌𐐼 𐐵𐑉 𐑁𐐪𐑄𐐲𐑉𐑆 𐐿𐐩𐑋 𐑃𐑉𐐭, 𐐵𐐻 𐐱𐑂 𐐿𐐰𐐹𐐻𐐮𐑂𐐮𐐻𐐨, 𐐱𐑌 𐐼𐑉𐐴 𐑀𐑉𐐵𐑌𐐼, 𐐰𐑌𐐼 𐑄 𐐪𐑉𐑋𐐨𐑆 𐐱𐑂 𐐑𐐩𐑉𐐬 𐐼𐐮𐐼 𐑁𐐱𐑊𐐬, 𐐰𐑌𐐼 𐐶𐐲𐑉 𐐼𐑉𐐵𐑌𐐼 𐐮𐑌 𐑄 𐐶𐐫𐐻𐐲𐑉𐑆 𐐱𐑂 𐑄 𐐡𐐯𐐼 𐐝𐐨. 𐐤𐐵 𐐺𐐨𐐸𐐬𐑊𐐼 𐐷𐐨 𐑌𐐬 𐑄𐐰𐐻 𐑄𐐮𐑅 𐐮𐑆 𐐻𐑉𐐭; 𐐰𐑌𐐼 𐐷𐐨 𐐫𐑊𐑅𐐬 𐑌𐐬 𐑄𐐰𐐻 𐐰𐑌 𐐩𐑌𐐾𐐯𐑊 𐐸𐐰𐑃 𐑅𐐹𐐬𐐿𐐲𐑌 𐐲𐑌𐐻𐐭 𐐷𐐭, 𐐸𐐶𐐯𐑉𐑁𐐫𐑉 𐐿𐐰𐑌 𐐷𐐨 𐐼𐐵𐐻? 𐐢𐐯𐐻 𐐲𐑅 𐑀𐐬 𐐲𐐹; 𐑄 𐐢𐐫𐑉𐐼 𐐮𐑆 𐐩𐐺𐑊 𐐻𐐭 𐐼𐐨𐑊𐐮𐑂𐐲𐑉 𐐲𐑅, 𐐨𐑂𐐲𐑌 𐐰𐑆 𐐵𐑉 𐑁𐐪𐑄𐐲𐑉𐑆, 𐐰𐑌𐐼 𐐻𐐭 𐐼𐐨𐑅𐐻𐑉𐑎 𐐢𐐩𐐺𐐲𐑌, 𐐨𐑂𐐲𐑌 𐐰𐑆 𐑄 𐐀𐐾𐐮𐐹𐑇𐐲𐑌𐑆.

32. 𐐤𐐵 𐐸𐐶𐐯𐑌 𐐌 𐐸𐐰𐐼 𐑅𐐹𐐬𐐿𐐲𐑌 𐑄𐐨𐑆 𐐶𐐲𐑉𐐼𐑆, 𐑄𐐩 𐐶𐐲𐑉 𐐷𐐯𐐻 𐑉𐐫𐑃, 𐐰𐑌𐐼 𐐼𐐮𐐼 𐑅𐐻𐐮𐑊 𐐿𐐱𐑌𐐻𐐮𐑌𐐷𐐭 𐐻𐐭 𐑋𐐲𐑉𐑋𐐲𐑉; 𐑌𐐯𐑂𐐲𐑉𐑄𐐲𐑊𐐯𐑅 𐑄𐐩 𐐼𐐮𐐼 𐑁𐐱𐑊𐐬 𐑋𐐨 𐐲𐐹 𐐲𐑌𐐻𐐮𐑊 𐐶𐐨 𐐿𐐩𐑋 𐐶𐐮𐑄𐐵𐐻 𐑄 𐐶𐐫𐑊𐑆 𐐱𐑂 𐐖𐐨𐑉𐐭𐑅𐐲𐑊𐐯𐑋. 𐐈𐑌𐐼 𐐮𐐻 𐐶𐐱𐑆 𐐺𐐴 𐑌𐐴𐐻: 𐐰𐑌𐐼 𐐌 𐐿𐐫𐑆𐐼 𐑄𐐰𐐻 𐑄𐐩 𐑇𐐳𐐼 𐐸𐐴𐐼 𐑄𐐯𐑋𐑅𐐯𐑊𐑂𐑆 𐐶𐐮𐑄𐐵𐐻 𐑄 𐐶𐐫𐑊𐑆. 𐐈𐑌𐐼 𐐰𐑁𐐻𐐲𐑉 𐑄𐐩 𐐸𐐰𐐼 𐐸𐐮𐐼 𐑄𐐯𐑋𐑅𐐯𐑊𐑂𐑆, 𐐌, 𐐤𐐨𐑁𐐴, 𐐿𐑉𐐯𐐹𐐻 𐐮𐑌𐐻𐐭 𐑄 𐑅𐐮𐐻𐐨 𐐰𐑌𐐼 𐐶𐐯𐑌𐐻 𐑁𐐬𐑉𐑃 𐐻𐐬𐐲𐑉𐐼𐑆 𐑄 𐐸𐐵𐑅 𐐱𐑂 𐐢𐐩𐐺𐐲𐑌. 𐐈𐑌𐐼 𐐌 𐐶𐐱𐑆 𐑊𐐯𐐼 𐐺𐐴 𐑄 𐐝𐐹𐐮𐑉𐐮𐐻, 𐑌𐐱𐐻 𐑌𐐬𐐮𐑍 𐐺𐐨𐑁𐐬𐑉𐐸𐐰𐑌𐐼 𐑄 𐑃𐐮𐑍𐑆 𐐸𐐶𐐮𐐽 𐐌 𐑇𐐳𐐼 𐐼𐐭. 𐐤𐐯𐑂𐐲𐑉𐑄𐐲𐑊𐐯𐑅 𐐌 𐐶𐐯𐑌𐐻 𐑁𐐬𐑉𐑃, 𐐰𐑌𐐼 𐐰𐑆 𐐌 𐐿𐐩𐑋 𐑌𐐨𐑉 𐐲𐑌𐐻𐐭 𐑄 𐐸𐐵𐑅 𐐱𐑂 𐐢𐐩𐐺𐐲𐑌, 𐐌 𐐺𐐨𐐸𐐯𐑊𐐼 𐐩 𐑋𐐰𐑌, 𐐰𐑌𐐼 𐐸𐐨 𐐸𐐰𐐼 𐑁𐐫𐑊𐐲𐑌 𐐻𐐭 𐑄 𐐲𐑉𐑃 𐐺𐐨𐑁𐐬𐑉 𐑋𐐨, 𐑁𐐫𐑉 𐐸𐐨 𐐶𐐱𐑆 𐐼𐑉𐐲𐑍𐐿𐐲𐑌 𐐶𐐮𐑄 𐐶𐐴𐑌. 𐐈𐑌𐐼 𐐸𐐶𐐯𐑌 𐐌 𐐿𐐩𐑋 𐐻𐐭 𐐸𐐮𐑋, 𐐌 𐑁𐐵𐑌𐐼 𐑄𐐰𐐻 𐐮𐐻 𐐶𐐱𐑆 𐐢𐐩𐐺𐐲𐑌. 𐐈𐑌𐐼 𐐌 𐐺𐐨𐐸𐐯𐑊𐐼 𐐸𐐮𐑆 𐑅𐐬𐑉𐐼, 𐐰𐑌𐐼 𐐌 𐐼𐑉𐐭 𐐮𐐻 𐑁𐐬𐑉𐑃 𐑁𐑉𐐱𐑋 𐑄 𐑇𐐨𐑃 𐑄𐐯𐑉𐐱𐑂; 𐐰𐑌𐐼 𐑄 𐐸𐐮𐑊𐐻 𐑄𐐯𐑉𐐱𐑂 𐐶𐐱𐑆 𐐱𐑂 𐐹𐐷𐐭𐑉 𐑀𐐬𐑊𐐼, 𐐰𐑌𐐼 𐑄 𐐶𐐲𐑉𐐿𐑋𐐰𐑌𐑇𐐮𐐹 𐑄𐐯𐑉𐐱𐑂 𐐶𐐱𐑆 𐐯𐐿𐑅𐐨𐐼𐐮𐑍𐑊𐐨 𐑁𐐴𐑌, 𐐰𐑌𐐼 𐐌 𐑅𐐫 𐑄𐐰𐐻 𐑄 𐐺𐑊𐐩𐐼 𐑄𐐯𐑉𐐱𐑂 𐐶𐐱𐑆 𐐱𐑂 𐑄 𐑋𐐬𐑅𐐻 𐐹𐑉𐐯𐑇𐐲𐑅 𐑅𐐻𐐨𐑊.

33. 𐐈𐑌𐐼 𐐮𐐻 𐐿𐐩𐑋 𐐻𐐭 𐐹𐐪𐑅 𐑄𐐰𐐻 𐐌 𐐶𐐱𐑆 𐐿𐐲𐑌𐑅𐐻𐑉𐐩𐑌𐐼 𐐺𐐴 𐑄 𐐝𐐹𐐮𐑉𐐮𐐻 𐑄𐐰𐐻 𐐌 𐑇𐐳𐐼 𐐿𐐮𐑊 𐐢𐐩𐐺𐐲𐑌: 𐐺𐐲𐐻 𐐌 𐑅𐐯𐐼 𐐮𐑌 𐑋𐐴 𐐸𐐪𐑉𐐻, 𐑌𐐯𐑂𐐲𐑉 𐐰𐐻 𐐯𐑌𐐮 𐐻𐐴𐑋 𐐸𐐰𐑂 𐐌 𐑇𐐯𐐼 𐑄 𐐺𐑊𐐲𐐼 𐐱𐑂 𐑋𐐰𐑌, 𐐰𐑌𐐼 𐐌 𐑇𐑉𐐲𐑍𐐿 𐐰𐑌𐐼 𐐶𐐳𐐼 𐑄𐐰𐐻 𐐌 𐑋𐐴𐐻 𐑌𐐱𐐻 𐑅𐑊𐐩 𐐸𐐮𐑋. 𐐈𐑌𐐼 𐑄 𐐝𐐹𐐮𐑉𐐮𐐻 𐑅𐐯𐐼 𐐲𐑌𐐻𐐭 𐑋𐐨 𐐰𐑀𐐯𐑌, 𐐒𐐨𐐸𐐬𐑊𐐼 𐑄 𐐢𐐫𐑉𐐼 𐐸𐐰𐑃 𐐼𐐨𐑊𐐮𐑂𐐲𐑉𐐼 𐐸𐐮𐑋 𐐮𐑌𐐻𐐭 𐑄𐐴 𐐸𐐰𐑌𐐼𐑆; 𐐏𐐩, 𐐰𐑌𐐼 𐐌 𐐫𐑊𐑅𐐬 𐑌𐐷𐐭 𐑄𐐰𐐻 𐐸𐐨 𐐸𐐰𐐼 𐑅𐐫𐐻 𐐻𐐭 𐐻𐐩𐐿 𐐰𐐶𐐩 𐑋𐐴𐑌 𐐬𐑌 𐑊𐐴𐑁; 𐐏𐐩, 𐐰𐑌𐐼 𐐸𐐨 𐐶𐐳𐐼 𐑌𐐱𐐻 𐐸𐐪𐑉𐐿𐐯𐑌 𐐲𐑌𐐻𐐭 𐑄 𐐿𐐲𐑋𐐰𐑌𐐼𐑋𐐯𐑌𐐻𐑅 𐐱𐑂 𐑄 𐐢𐐫𐑉𐐼; 𐐰𐑌𐐼 𐐸𐐨 𐐫𐑊𐑅𐐬 𐐸𐐰𐐼 𐐻𐐩𐐿𐐯𐑌 𐐰𐐶𐐩 𐐵𐑉 𐐹𐑉𐐱𐐹𐐲𐑉𐐻𐐮.

34. 𐐈𐑌𐐼 𐐮𐐻 𐐿𐐩𐑋 𐐻𐐭 𐐹𐐪𐑅 𐑄𐐰𐐻 𐑄 𐐝𐐹𐐮𐑉𐐮𐐻 𐑅𐐯𐐼 𐐲𐑌𐐻𐐭 𐑋𐐨 𐐰𐑀𐐯𐑌, 𐐝𐑊𐐩 𐐸𐐮𐑋, 𐑁𐐫𐑉 𐑄 𐐢𐐫𐑉𐐼 𐐸𐐰𐑃 𐐼𐐨𐑊𐐮𐑂𐐲𐑉𐐼 𐐸𐐮𐑋 𐐮𐑌𐐻𐐭 𐑄𐐴 𐐸𐐰𐑌𐐼𐑆. 𐐒𐐨𐐸𐐬𐑊𐐼 𐑄 𐐢𐐫𐑉𐐼 𐑅𐑊𐐩𐐯𐑃 𐑄 𐐶𐐮𐐿𐐯𐐼 𐐻𐐭 𐐺𐑉𐐮𐑍 𐑁𐐫𐑉𐑃 𐐸𐐮𐑆 𐑉𐐴𐐽𐐲𐑅 𐐹𐐲𐑉𐐹𐐲𐑅𐐯𐑆. 𐐆𐐻 𐐮𐑆 𐐺𐐯𐐻𐐲𐑉 𐑄𐐰𐐻 𐐶𐐲𐑌 𐑋𐐰𐑌 𐑇𐐳𐐼 𐐹𐐯𐑉𐐮𐑇, 𐑄𐐰𐑌 𐑄𐐰𐐻 𐐪 𐑌𐐩𐑇𐐲𐑌 𐑇𐐳𐐼 𐐼𐐶𐐮𐑌𐐼𐑊 𐐰𐑌𐐼 𐐹𐐯𐑉𐐮𐑇 𐐮𐑌 𐐲𐑌𐐺𐐨𐑊𐐨𐑁.

35. 𐐈𐑌𐐼 𐑌𐐵, 𐐸𐐶𐐯𐑌 𐐌, 𐐤𐐨𐑁𐐴, 𐐸𐐰𐐼 𐐸𐐲𐑉𐐼 𐑄𐐨𐑆 𐐶𐐲𐑉𐐼𐑆, 𐐌 𐑉𐐨𐑋𐐯𐑋𐐺𐐲𐑉𐐼 𐑄 𐐶𐐲𐑉𐐼𐑆 𐐱𐑂 𐑄 𐐢𐐫𐑉𐐼 𐐸𐐶𐐮𐐽 𐐸𐐨 𐑅𐐹𐐩𐐿 𐐲𐑌𐐻𐐭 𐑋𐐨 𐐮𐑌 𐑄 𐐶𐐮𐑊𐐼𐐲𐑉𐑌𐐯𐑅, 𐑅𐐩𐐮𐑍, 𐑄𐐰𐐻 𐐮𐑌𐐰𐑆𐑋𐐲𐐽 𐐰𐑆 𐑄𐐴 𐑅𐐨𐐼 𐑇𐐰𐑊 𐐿𐐨𐐹 𐑋𐐴 𐐿𐐲𐑋𐐰𐑌𐐼𐑋𐐯𐑌𐐻𐑅, 𐑄𐐩 𐑇𐐰𐑊 𐐹𐑉𐐱𐑅𐐹𐐲𐑉 𐐮𐑌 𐑄 𐑊𐐰𐑌𐐼 𐐱𐑂 𐐹𐑉𐐱𐑋𐐮𐑅. 𐐏𐐩, 𐐰𐑌𐐼 𐐌 𐐫𐑊𐑅𐐬 𐑃𐐫𐐻 𐑄𐐰𐐻 𐑄𐐩 𐐿𐐳𐐼 𐑌𐐱𐐻 𐐿𐐨𐐹 𐑄 𐐿𐐲𐑋𐐰𐑌𐐼𐑋𐐯𐑌𐐻𐑅 𐐱𐑂 𐑄 𐐢𐐫𐑉𐐼 𐐰𐐿𐐫𐑉𐐼𐐮𐑍 𐐻𐐭 𐑄 𐑊𐐫 𐐱𐑂 𐐣𐐬𐑆𐐯𐑆, 𐑅𐐩𐑂 𐑄𐐩 𐑇𐐳𐐼 𐐸𐐰𐑂 𐑄 𐑊𐐫. 𐐈𐑌𐐼 𐐌 𐐫𐑊𐑅𐐬 𐑌𐐷𐐭 𐑄𐐰𐐻 𐑄 𐑊𐐫 𐐶𐐱𐑆 𐐯𐑌𐑀𐑉𐐩𐑂𐐯𐑌 𐐲𐐹𐐱𐑌 𐑄 𐐹𐑊𐐩𐐻𐑅 𐐱𐑂 𐐺𐑉𐐪𐑅. 𐐈𐑌𐐼 𐐰𐑀𐐯𐑌, 𐐌 𐑌𐐷𐐭 𐑄𐐰𐐻 𐑄 𐐢𐐫𐑉𐐼 𐐸𐐰𐐼 𐐼𐐨𐑊𐐮𐑂𐐲𐑉𐐼 𐐢𐐩𐐺𐐲𐑌 𐐮𐑌𐐻𐐭 𐑋𐐴 𐐸𐐰𐑌𐐼𐑆 𐑁𐐫𐑉 𐑄𐐮𐑅·𐐿𐐫𐑆, 𐑄𐐰𐐻 𐐌 𐑋𐐴𐐻 𐐱𐐺𐐻𐐩𐑌 𐑄 𐑉𐐯𐐿𐐲𐑉𐐼𐑆 𐐰𐐿𐐫𐑉𐐼𐐮𐑍 𐐻𐐭 𐐸𐐮𐑆 𐐿𐐲𐑋𐐰𐑌𐐼𐑋𐐯𐑌𐐻𐑅. 𐐜𐐯𐑉𐑁𐐫𐑉 𐐌 𐐼𐐮𐐼 𐐬𐐺𐐩 𐑄 𐑂𐑎𐑅 𐐱𐑂 𐑄 𐐝𐐹𐐮𐑉𐐮𐐻, 𐐰𐑌𐐼 𐐻𐐳𐐿 𐐢𐐩𐐺𐐲𐑌 𐐺𐐴 𐑄 𐐸𐐩𐑉 𐐱𐑂 𐑄 𐐸𐐯𐐼, 𐐰𐑌𐐼 𐐌 𐑅𐑋𐐬𐐻 𐐱𐑁 𐐸𐐮𐑆 𐐸𐐯𐐼 𐐶𐐮𐑄 𐐸𐐮𐑆 𐐬𐑌 𐑅𐐬𐑉𐐼.

36. 𐐈𐑌𐐼 𐐪𐑁𐐻𐐲𐑉 𐐌 𐐸𐐰𐐼 𐑅𐑋𐐮𐐻𐐲𐑌 𐐱𐑁 𐐸𐐮𐑆 𐐸𐐯𐐼 𐐶𐐮𐑄 𐐸𐐮𐑆 𐐬𐑌 𐑅𐐬𐑉𐐼, 𐐌 𐐻𐐳𐐿 𐑄 𐑀𐐪𐑉𐑋𐐯𐑌𐐻𐑅 𐐱𐑂 𐐢𐐩𐐺𐐲𐑌 𐐰𐑌𐐼 𐐹𐐳𐐻 𐑄𐐯𐑋 𐐲𐐹𐐱𐑌 𐑋𐐴𐑌 𐐬𐑌 𐐺𐐱𐐼𐐮; 𐐏𐐩, 𐐨𐑂𐐲𐑌 𐐯𐑂𐐲𐑉𐐮 𐐸𐐶𐐮𐐻; 𐐰𐑌𐐼 𐐌 𐐼𐐮𐐼 𐑀𐐲𐑉𐐼 𐐱𐑌 𐐸𐐮𐑆 𐐪𐑉𐑋𐐲𐑉 𐐰𐐺𐐵𐐻 𐑋𐐴 𐑊𐑎𐑌𐑆. 𐐈𐑌𐐼 𐐪𐑁𐐻𐐲𐑉 𐐌 𐐸𐐰𐐼 𐐼𐐲𐑌 𐑄𐐮𐑅, 𐐌 𐐶𐐯𐑌𐐻 𐑁𐐫𐑉𐑃 𐐲𐑌𐐻𐐭 𐑄 𐐻𐑉𐐯𐑈𐐲𐑉𐐮 𐐱𐑂 𐐢𐐩𐐺𐐲𐑌. 𐐈𐑌𐐼 𐐰𐑆 𐐌 𐐶𐐯𐑌𐐻 𐑁𐐫𐑉𐑃 𐐻𐐬𐑉𐐲𐑉𐐼𐑆 𐑄 𐐻𐑉𐐯𐑈𐐲𐑉𐐮 𐐱𐑂 𐐢𐐩𐐺𐐲𐑌, 𐐺𐐨𐐸𐐬𐑊𐐼, 𐐌 𐑅𐐫 𐑄 𐑅𐐲𐑉𐑂𐐲𐑌𐐻 𐐱𐑂 𐐢𐐩𐐺𐐲𐑌 𐐸𐐭 𐐸𐐰𐐼 𐑄 𐐿𐐨𐑆 𐐱𐑂 𐑄 𐐻𐑉𐐯𐑈𐐲𐑉𐐮. 𐐈𐑌𐐼 𐐌 𐐿𐐲𐑋𐐰𐑌𐐼𐐯𐐼 𐐸𐐮𐑋 𐐮𐑌 𐑄 𐑂𐑎𐑅 𐐱𐑂 𐐢𐐩𐐺𐐲𐑌, 𐑄𐐰𐐻 𐐸𐐨 𐑇𐐳𐐼 𐑀𐐬 𐐶𐐮𐑄 𐑋𐐨 𐐮𐑌𐐻𐐭 𐑄 𐐻𐑉𐐯𐑈𐐲𐑉𐐮; 𐐰𐑌𐐼 𐐸𐐨 𐑅𐐲𐐹𐐬𐑆𐐼 𐑋𐐨 𐐻𐐭 𐐺 𐐸𐐮𐑆 𐑋𐐪𐑅𐐻𐐲𐑉 𐐢𐐩𐐺𐐲𐑌, 𐑁𐐫𐑉 𐐸𐐨 𐐺𐐨𐐸𐐯𐑊𐐼 𐑄 𐑀𐐪𐑉𐑋𐐯𐑌𐐻𐑅 𐐰𐑌𐐼 𐐫𐑊𐑅𐐬 𐑄 𐑅𐐬𐑉𐐼 𐑀𐐲𐑉𐐼𐐯𐐼 𐐰𐐺𐐵𐐻 𐑋𐐴 𐑊𐑎𐑌𐑆. 𐐈𐑌𐐼 𐐸𐐨 𐑅𐐹𐐩𐐿 𐐲𐑌𐐻𐐭 𐑋𐐨 𐐿𐐲𐑌𐑅𐐲𐑉𐑌𐐮𐑍 𐑄 𐐯𐑊𐐼𐐲𐑉𐑆 𐐱𐑂 𐑄 𐐖𐐭𐑆, 𐐸𐐨 𐑌𐐬𐐮𐑍 𐑄𐐰𐐻 𐐸𐐮𐑆 𐑋𐐪𐑅𐐻𐐲𐑉 𐐢𐐩𐐺𐐲𐑌 𐐸𐐰𐐼 𐐺𐐮𐑌 𐐵𐐻 𐐺𐐴 𐑌𐐴𐐻 𐐰𐑋𐐲𐑍 𐑄𐐯𐑋. 𐐈𐑌𐐼 𐐌 𐑅𐐹𐐩𐐿 𐐲𐑌𐐻𐐭 𐐸𐐮𐑋 𐐰𐑆 𐐮𐑁 𐐮𐐻 𐐸𐐰𐐼 𐐺𐐮𐑌 𐐢𐐩𐐺𐐲𐑌. 𐐈𐑌𐐼 𐐌 𐐫𐑊𐑅𐐬 𐑅𐐹𐐩𐐿 𐐲𐑌𐐻𐐭 𐐸𐐮𐑋 𐑄𐐰𐐻 𐐌 𐑇𐐳𐐼 𐐿𐐰𐑉𐐮 𐑄 𐐯𐑌𐑀𐑉𐐩𐑂𐐮𐑍𐑆 𐐸𐐶𐐮𐐽 𐐶𐐲𐑉 𐐲𐐹𐐱𐑌 𐑄 𐐹𐑊𐐩𐐻𐑅 𐐱𐑂 𐐺𐑉𐐪𐑅, 𐐻𐐭 𐑋𐐴 𐐯𐑊𐐼𐐲𐑉 𐐺𐑉𐐯𐑄𐑉𐐯𐑌, 𐐸𐐭 𐐶𐐲𐑉 𐐶𐐮𐑄𐐵𐐻 𐑄 𐐶𐐫𐑊𐑆. 𐐈𐑌𐐼 𐐌 𐐫𐑊𐑅𐐬 𐐺𐐰𐐼 𐐸𐐮𐑋 𐑄𐐰𐐻 𐐸𐐨 𐑇𐐳𐐼 𐑁𐐱𐑊𐐬 𐑋𐐨. 𐐈𐑌𐐼 𐐸𐐨, 𐑅𐐲𐐹𐐬𐑆𐐮𐑍 𐑄𐐰𐐻 𐐌 𐑅𐐹𐐩𐐿 𐐱𐑂 𐑄 𐐺𐑉𐐯𐑄𐑉𐐯𐑌 𐐱𐑂 𐑄 𐐕𐐲𐑉𐐽, 𐐰𐑌𐐼 𐑄𐐰𐐻 𐐌 𐐶𐐱𐑆 𐐻𐑉𐐭𐑊𐐮 𐑄𐐰𐐻 𐐢𐐩𐐺𐐲𐑌 𐐸𐐭𐑋 𐐌 𐐸𐐰𐐼 𐑅𐑊𐐩𐑌, 𐐸𐐶𐐯𐑉𐑁𐐫𐑉 𐐸𐐨 𐐼𐐮𐐼 𐑁𐐱𐑊𐐬 𐑋𐐨. 𐐈𐑌𐐼 𐐸𐐨 𐑅𐐹𐐩𐐿 𐐲𐑌𐐻𐐭 𐑋𐐨 𐑋𐐯𐑌𐐮 𐐻𐐴𐑋𐑆 𐐿𐐲𐑌𐑅𐐲𐑉𐑌𐐮𐑍 𐑄 𐐯𐑊𐐼𐐲𐑉𐑆 𐐱𐑂 𐑄 𐐖𐐭𐑆, 𐐰𐑆 𐐌 𐐶𐐯𐑌𐐻 𐑁𐐫𐑉𐑃 𐐲𐑌𐐻𐐭 𐑋𐐴 𐐺𐑉𐐯𐑄𐑉𐐯𐑌, 𐐸𐐭 𐐶𐐲𐑉 𐐶𐐮𐑄𐐵𐐻 𐑄 𐐶𐐫𐑊𐑆.

37. 𐐈𐑌𐐼 𐐮𐐻 𐐿𐐩𐑋 𐐻𐐭 𐐹𐐪𐑅 𐑄𐐰𐐻 𐐸𐐶𐐯𐑌 𐐢𐐩𐑋𐐲𐑌 𐑅𐐫 𐑋𐐨, 𐐸𐐨 𐐶𐐱𐑆 𐐯𐐿𐑅𐐨𐐼𐐮𐑍𐑊𐐮 𐑁𐑉𐐴𐐻𐐲𐑌𐐼, 𐐰𐑌𐐼 𐐫𐑊𐑅𐐬 𐐢𐐯𐑋𐐷𐐭𐐯𐑊 𐐰𐑌𐐼 𐐝𐐰𐑋. 𐐈𐑌𐐼 𐑄𐐩 𐑁𐑊𐐯𐐼 𐑁𐑉𐐱𐑋 𐐺𐐨𐑁𐐬𐑉 𐑋𐐴 𐐹𐑉𐐯𐑆𐐯𐑌𐑅; 𐑁𐐫𐑉 𐑄𐐩 𐑅𐐲𐐹𐐬𐑆𐐼 𐐮𐐻 𐐶𐐱𐑆 𐐢𐐩𐐺𐐲𐑌, 𐐰𐑌𐐼 𐑄𐐰𐐻 𐐸𐐨 𐐸𐐰𐐼 𐑅𐑊𐐩𐑌 𐑋𐐨, 𐐰𐑌𐐼 𐐸𐐰𐐼 𐑅𐐫𐐻 𐐻𐐭 𐐻𐐩𐐿 𐐰𐐶𐐩 𐑄𐐩𐑉 𐑊𐐴𐑂𐑆 𐐫𐑊𐑅𐐬.

38. 𐐈𐑌𐐼 𐐮𐐻 𐐿𐐩𐑋 𐐻𐐭 𐐹𐐪𐑅 𐑄𐐰𐐻 𐐌 𐐿𐐫𐑊𐐼 𐐪𐑁𐐻𐐲𐑉 𐑄𐐯𐑋, 𐐰𐑌𐐼 𐑄𐐩 𐐼𐐮𐐼 𐐸𐐨𐑉 𐑋𐐨; 𐐸𐐶𐐯𐑉𐑁𐐫𐑉 𐑄𐐩 𐐼𐐮𐐼 𐑅𐐨𐑅 𐐻𐐭 𐑁𐑊𐐨 𐑁𐑉𐐱𐑋 𐑋𐐴 𐐹𐑉𐐯𐑆𐐯𐑌𐑅; 𐐰𐑌𐐼 𐐮𐐻 𐐿𐐩𐑋 𐐻𐐭 𐐹𐐪𐑅 𐑄𐐰𐐻 𐐸𐐶𐐯𐑌 𐑄 𐑅𐐲𐑉𐑂𐐲𐑌𐐻 𐐱𐑂

𐐢𐐩𐐺𐐲𐑌 𐐺𐐨𐐸𐐯𐑊𐐼 𐑋𐐴 𐐺𐑉𐐯𐑄𐑉𐐯𐑌, 𐐸𐐨 𐐺𐐨𐑀𐐰𐑌 𐐻𐐭 𐐻𐑉𐐯𐑋𐐺𐑊, 𐐰𐑌𐐼 𐐶𐐱𐑆 𐐲𐐺𐐵𐐻 𐐻𐐭 𐑁𐑊𐐨 𐑁𐑉𐐱𐑋 𐐺𐐨𐑁𐐬𐑉 𐑋𐐨, 𐐰𐑌𐐼 𐑉𐐨𐐻𐐲𐑉𐑌 𐐻𐐭 𐑄 𐑅𐐮𐐻𐐨 𐐱𐑂 𐐖𐐯𐑉𐐭𐑅𐐲𐑊𐐯𐑋.

39. 𐐈𐑌𐐼 𐑌𐐵, 𐐌, 𐐤𐐨𐑁𐐴, 𐐺𐐨𐐮𐑍 𐐲 𐑋𐐰𐑌 𐑊𐐪𐑉𐐾 𐐮𐑌 𐑅𐐻𐐰𐐻𐐷𐐭𐑉, 𐐰𐑌𐐼 𐐫𐑊𐑅𐐬 𐐸𐐰𐑂𐐮𐑍 𐑉𐐨𐑅𐐨𐑂𐐼 𐑋𐐲𐐽 𐑅𐐻𐑉𐐯𐑍𐑃 𐐱𐑂 𐑄 𐐢𐐫𐑉𐐼, 𐑄𐐯𐑉𐑁𐐬𐑉 𐐌 𐐼𐐮𐐼 𐑅𐐨𐑆 𐐲𐐹𐐱𐑌 𐑄 𐑅𐐲𐑉𐑂𐐲𐑌𐐻 𐐱𐑂 𐐢𐐩𐐺𐐲𐑌, 𐐰𐑌𐐼 𐐸𐐯𐑊𐐼 𐐸𐐮𐑋 𐑄𐐰𐐻 𐐸𐐨 𐑇𐐳𐐼 𐑌𐐱𐐻 𐑁𐑊𐐨.

40. 𐐈𐑌𐐼 𐐮𐐻 𐐿𐐩𐑋 𐐻𐐭 𐐹𐐰𐑅 𐑄𐐰𐐻 𐐌 𐑅𐐹𐐩𐐿 𐐶𐐮𐑄 𐐸𐐮𐑋, 𐑄𐐰𐐻 𐐮𐑁 𐐸𐐨 𐐶𐐳𐐼 𐐸𐐲𐑉𐐿𐐲𐑌 𐐲𐑌𐐻𐐭 𐑋𐐴 𐐶𐐲𐑉𐐼𐑆, 𐐰𐑆 𐑄 𐐢𐐫𐑉𐐼 𐑊𐐮𐑂𐐯𐑃, 𐐰𐑌𐐼 𐐰𐑆 𐐌 𐑊𐐮𐑂, 𐐨𐑂𐐯𐑌 𐑅𐐬 𐑄𐐰𐐻 𐐮𐑁 𐐸𐐨 𐐶𐐳𐐼 𐐸𐐲𐑉𐐿𐐲𐑌 𐐲𐑌𐐻𐐭 𐐵𐑉 𐐶𐐲𐑉𐐼𐑆, 𐐶𐐨 𐐶𐐳𐐼 𐑅𐐹𐐩𐑉 𐐸𐐮𐑆 𐑊𐐴𐑁. 𐐈𐑌𐐼 𐐌 𐑅𐐹𐐩𐐿 𐐲𐑌𐐻𐐭 𐐸𐐮𐑋, 𐐨𐑂𐐯𐑌 𐐶𐐮𐑄 𐐰𐑌 𐐬𐑃, 𐑄𐐰𐐻 𐐸𐐨 𐑌𐐨𐐼 𐑌𐐱𐐻 𐑁𐐨𐑉; 𐑄𐐰𐐻 𐐸𐐨 𐑇𐐳𐐼 𐐺𐐨 𐐲 𐑁𐑉𐐨 𐑋𐐰𐑌 𐑊𐐴𐐿 𐐲𐑌𐐻𐐭 𐐲𐑅, 𐐮𐑁 𐐸𐐨 𐐶𐐳𐐼 𐑀𐐬 𐐼𐐵𐑌 𐐮𐑌 𐑄 𐐶𐐮𐑊𐐼𐐲𐑉𐑌𐐯𐑅 𐐶𐐮𐑄 𐐲𐑅. 𐐈𐑌𐐼 𐐌 𐐫𐑊𐑅𐐬 𐑅𐐹𐐩𐐿 𐐲𐑌𐐻𐐭 𐐸𐐮𐑋, 𐑅𐐩𐐮𐑍, 𐐟𐐭𐑉𐑊𐐨 𐑄 𐐢𐐫𐑉𐐼 𐐸𐐰𐑃 𐐿𐐲𐑋𐐰𐑌𐐼𐐯𐐼 𐐲𐑅 𐐻𐐭 𐐼𐐭 𐑄𐐮𐑅 𐑃𐐮𐑍; 𐐰𐑌𐐼 𐑇𐐰𐑊 𐐶𐐨 𐑌𐐱𐐻 𐐺𐐨 𐐼𐐮𐑊𐐮𐐾𐐯𐑌𐐻 𐐮𐑌 𐐿𐐨𐐹𐐮𐑍 𐑄 𐐿𐐲𐑋𐐰𐑌𐐼𐑋𐐯𐑌𐐻𐑅 𐐱𐑂 𐑄 𐐢𐐫𐑉𐐼? 𐐜𐐯𐑉𐑁𐐬𐑉, 𐐮𐑁 𐑄𐐵 𐐶𐐮𐑊𐐻 𐑀𐐬 𐐼𐐵𐑌 𐐮𐑌𐐻𐐭 𐑄 𐐶𐐮𐑊𐐼𐐲𐑉𐑌𐐯𐑅 𐐻𐐭 𐑋𐐴 𐑁𐐪𐑄𐐲𐑉, 𐑄𐐵 𐑇𐐰𐑊𐐻 𐐸𐐰𐑂 𐐹𐑊𐐩𐑅 𐐶𐐮𐑄 𐐲𐑅.

41. 𐐈𐑌𐐼 𐐮𐐻 𐐿𐐩𐑋 𐐻𐐭 𐐹𐐰𐑅 𐑄𐐰𐐻 𐐞𐐬𐑉𐐲𐑋 𐐼𐐮𐐼 𐐻𐐩𐐿 𐐿𐐲𐑉𐐲𐐾 𐐰𐐻 𐑄 𐐶𐐲𐑉𐐼𐑆 𐐸𐐶𐐮𐐽 𐐌 𐑅𐐹𐐩𐐿. 𐐤𐐵 𐐞𐐬𐑉𐐲𐑋 𐐶𐐱𐑆 𐑄 𐑌𐐩𐑋 𐐱𐑂 𐑄 𐑅𐐲𐑉𐑂𐐲𐑌𐐻; 𐐰𐑌𐐼 𐐸𐐨 𐐹𐑉𐐱𐑋𐐮𐑅𐐻 𐑄𐐰𐐻 𐐸𐐨 𐐶𐐳𐐼 𐑀𐐬 𐐼𐐵𐑌 𐐮𐑌𐐻𐐭 𐑄 𐐶𐐮𐑊𐐼𐐲𐑉𐑌𐐯𐑅 𐐲𐑌𐐻𐐭 𐐵𐑉 𐑁𐐪𐑄𐐲𐑉. 𐐈𐑌𐐼 𐐸𐐨 𐐫𐑊𐑅𐐬 𐑋𐐩𐐼 𐐰𐑌 𐐬𐑃 𐐲𐑌𐐻𐐭 𐐲𐑅, 𐑄𐐰𐐻 𐐸𐐨 𐐶𐐳𐐼 𐐻𐐰𐑉𐐨 𐐶𐐮𐑄 𐐲𐑅 𐑁𐑉𐐱𐑋 𐑄𐐰𐐻 𐐻𐐴𐑋 𐑁𐐬𐑉𐑃. 𐐤𐐵 𐐶𐐨 𐐶𐐲𐑉 𐐼𐐨𐑆𐐴𐑉𐐲𐑅 𐑄𐐰𐐻 𐐸𐐨 𐑇𐐳𐐼 𐐻𐐰𐑉𐐨 𐐶𐐮𐑄 𐐲𐑅 𐑁𐐫𐑉 𐑄𐐮𐑅 𐐿𐐫𐑆, 𐑄𐐰𐐻 𐑄 𐐖𐐭𐑆 𐑋𐐴𐐻 𐑌𐐱𐐻 𐑌𐐬 𐐿𐐲𐑌𐑅𐐲𐑉𐑌𐐮𐑍 𐐵𐑉 𐑁𐑊𐐴𐐻 𐐮𐑌𐐻𐐭 𐑄 𐐶𐐮𐑊𐐼𐐲𐑉𐑌𐐯𐑅, 𐑊𐐯𐑅𐐻 𐑄𐐩 𐑇𐐳𐐼 𐐹𐐲𐑉𐑅𐐷𐐭 𐐲𐑅 𐐰𐑌𐐼 𐐼𐐨𐑅𐐻𐑉𐐱𐐮 𐐲𐑅.

42. 𐐈𐑌𐐼 𐐮𐐻 𐐿𐐩𐑋 𐐻𐐭 𐐹𐐰𐑅 𐑄𐐰𐐻 𐐸𐐶𐐯𐑌 𐐞𐐬𐑉𐐲𐑋 𐐸𐐰𐐼 𐑋𐐩𐐼 𐐰𐑌 𐐬𐑃 𐐲𐑌𐐻𐐭 𐐲𐑅, 𐐵𐑉 𐑁𐐨𐑉𐑆 𐐼𐐮𐐼 𐑅𐐨𐑅 𐐿𐐲𐑌𐑅𐐲𐑉𐑌𐐮𐑍 𐐸𐐮𐑋. 𐐈𐑌𐐼 𐐮𐐻 𐐿𐐩𐑋 𐐻𐐭 𐐹𐐰𐑅 𐑄𐐰𐐻 𐐶𐐨 𐐻𐐳𐐿 𐑄 𐐹𐑊𐐩𐐻𐑅 𐐱𐑂 𐐺𐑉𐐰𐑅 𐐰𐑌𐐼 𐑄 𐑅𐐲𐑉𐑂𐐲𐑌𐐻 𐐱𐑂 𐐢𐐩𐐺𐐲𐑌, 𐐰𐑌𐐼 𐐼𐐨𐐹𐐪𐑉𐐻𐐯𐐼 𐐮𐑌𐐻𐐭 𐑄 𐐶𐐮𐑊𐐼𐐲𐑉𐑌𐐯𐑅, 𐐰𐑌𐐼 𐐾𐐲𐑉𐑌𐐨𐐼 𐐲𐑌𐐻𐐭 𐑄 𐐻𐐯𐑌𐐻 𐐱𐑂 𐐵𐑉 𐑁𐐪𐑄𐐲𐑉.

43. 𐐈𐑌𐐼 𐐮𐐻 𐐿𐐩𐑋 𐐻𐐭 𐐹𐐰𐑅 𐑄𐐰𐐻 𐐰𐑁𐐻𐐲𐑉 𐐶𐐨 𐐸𐐰𐐼 𐐿𐐲𐑋 𐐼𐐵𐑌 𐐮𐑌𐐻𐐭 𐑄 𐐶𐐮𐑊𐐼𐐲𐑉𐑌𐐯𐑅 𐐲𐑌𐐻𐐭 𐐵𐑉 𐑁𐐪𐑄𐐲𐑉, 𐐺𐐨𐐸𐐬𐑊𐐼 𐐸𐐨 𐐶𐐱𐑆 𐑁𐐮𐑊𐐼 𐐶𐐮𐑄 𐐾𐐱𐐮, 𐐰𐑌𐐼 𐐫𐑊𐑅𐐬 𐑋𐐴 𐑋𐐲𐑄𐐲𐑉, 𐐝𐐲𐑉𐐴𐐲, 𐐶𐐱𐑆 𐐯𐐿𐑅𐐨𐐼𐐮𐑍𐑊𐐨 𐑀𐑊𐐰𐐼, 𐑁𐐫𐑉 𐑇𐐨 𐐻𐑉𐐭𐑊𐐨 𐐸𐐰𐐼 𐑋𐐬𐑉𐑌𐐼 𐐺𐐨𐐿𐐫𐑆 𐐱𐑂 𐐲𐑅; 𐑁𐐫𐑉 𐑇𐐨 𐐸𐐰𐐼 𐑅𐐲𐐹𐐬𐑆𐐼 𐑄𐐰𐐻 𐐶𐐨 𐐸𐐰𐐼 𐐹𐐯𐑉𐐮𐑇𐐻 𐐮𐑌 𐑄 𐐶𐐮𐑊𐐼𐐲𐑉𐑌𐐯𐑅; 𐐰𐑌𐐼 𐑇𐐨 𐐫𐑊𐑅𐐬 𐐸𐐰𐐼 𐐿𐐲𐑋𐐹𐑊𐐩𐑌𐐼 𐐲𐑀𐐯𐑌𐑅𐐻 𐑋𐐴 𐑁𐐪𐑄𐐲𐑉, 𐐻𐐯𐑊𐐮𐑍 𐐸𐐮𐑋 𐑄𐐰𐐻 𐐸𐐨 𐐶𐐱𐑆 𐐲 𐑂𐐮𐑈𐐲𐑌𐐯𐑉𐐨 𐑋𐐰𐑌; 𐑅𐐩𐐮𐑍, 𐐒𐐨𐐸𐐬𐑊𐐼 𐑄𐐵 𐐸𐐰𐑅𐐻 𐑊𐐯𐐼 𐐲𐑅 𐑁𐐬𐑉𐑃 𐑁𐑉𐐱𐑋 𐑄 𐑊𐐰𐑌𐐼 𐐱𐑂 𐐵𐑉 𐐮𐑌𐐸𐐯𐑉𐐮𐐻𐐲𐑌𐑅, 𐐰𐑌𐐼 𐑋𐐴 𐑅𐐲𐑌𐑆 𐐪𐑉 𐑌𐐬 𐑋𐐬𐑉, 𐐰𐑌𐐼 𐐶𐐨 𐐹𐐯𐑉𐐮𐑇 𐐮𐑌 𐑄 𐐶𐐮𐑊𐐼𐐲𐑉𐑌𐐯𐑅. 𐐈𐑌𐐼 𐐰𐑁𐐻𐐲𐑉 𐑄𐐮𐑅 𐑋𐐰𐑌𐐲𐑉 𐐱𐑂 𐑊𐐰𐑍𐑀𐐶𐐩𐐾 𐐸𐐰𐐼 𐑋𐐴 𐑋𐐲𐑄𐐲𐑉 𐐿𐐲𐑋𐐹𐑊𐐩𐑌𐐼 𐐲𐑀𐐯𐑌𐑅𐐻 𐑋𐐴 𐑁𐐪𐑄𐐲𐑉.

44. 𐐈𐑌𐐼 𐐮𐐻 𐐸𐐰𐐼 𐐿𐐲𐑋 𐐻𐐭 𐐹𐐰𐑅 𐑄𐐰𐐻 𐑋𐐴 𐑁𐐪𐑄𐐲𐑉 𐑅𐐹𐐩𐐿 𐐲𐑌𐐻𐐭 𐐸𐐲𐑉, 𐑅𐐩𐐮𐑍, 𐐌 𐑌𐐬 𐑄𐐰𐐻 𐐌 𐐰𐑋 𐐲 𐑂𐐮𐑈𐐲𐑌𐐯𐑉𐐨 𐑋𐐰𐑌; 𐑁𐐫𐑉 𐐮𐑁 𐐌 𐐸𐐰𐐼 𐑌𐐱𐐻 𐑅𐐨𐑌 𐑄 𐑃𐐮𐑍𐑆 𐐱𐑂 𐐘𐐱𐐼 𐐮𐑌 𐐲 𐑂𐐮𐑈𐐲𐑌, 𐐌 𐑇𐐳𐐼 𐑌𐐱𐐻 𐐸𐐰𐑂 𐑌𐐬𐑌 𐑄 𐑀𐐳𐐼𐑌𐐯𐑅 𐐱𐑂 𐐘𐐱𐐼, 𐐺𐐲𐐻 𐐸𐐰𐐼 𐐻𐐰𐑉𐐨𐐼 𐐰𐐻 𐐖𐐯𐑉𐐭𐑅𐐲𐑊𐐯𐑋, 𐐰𐑌𐐼 𐐸𐐰𐐼 𐐹𐐯𐑉𐐮𐑇𐐻 𐐶𐐮𐑄 𐑋𐐴 𐐺𐑉𐐯𐑄𐑉𐐯𐑌. 𐐒𐐲𐐻 𐐺𐐨𐐸𐐬𐑊𐐼, 𐐌 𐐸𐐰𐑂 𐐱𐐺𐐻𐐩𐑌𐐼 𐐲 𐑊𐐰𐑌𐐼 𐐱𐑂 𐐹𐑉𐐱𐑋𐐮𐑅, 𐐮𐑌 𐑄 𐐸𐐶𐐮𐐽 𐑃𐐮𐑍𐑆 𐐌 𐐼𐐭 𐑉𐐨𐐾𐐱𐐮𐑅; 𐐷𐐩, 𐐰𐑌𐐼 𐐌 𐑌𐐬 𐑄𐐰𐐻 𐑄 𐐢𐐫𐑉𐐼 𐐶𐐮𐑊 𐐼𐐨𐑊𐐮𐑂𐐲𐑉 𐑋𐐴 𐑅𐐲𐑌𐑆 𐐵𐐻 𐐱𐑂 𐑄 𐐸𐐰𐑌𐐼𐑆 𐐱𐑂 𐐢𐐩𐐺𐐲𐑌, 𐐰𐑌𐐼 𐐺𐑉𐐮𐑍 𐑄𐐯𐑋 𐐼𐐵𐑌 𐐲𐑀𐐯𐑌 𐐲𐑌𐐻𐐭 𐐲𐑅 𐐮𐑌 𐑄 𐐶𐐮𐑊𐐼𐐲𐑉𐑌𐐯𐑅. 𐐈𐑌𐐼 𐐰𐑁𐐻𐐲𐑉 𐑄𐐮𐑅 𐑋𐐰𐑌𐐲𐑉 𐐱𐑂 𐑊𐐰𐑌-𐑀𐐶𐐩𐐾 𐐼𐐮𐐼 𐑋𐐴 𐑁𐐪𐑄𐐲𐑉, 𐐢𐐨𐐸𐐴, 𐐿𐐲𐑋𐑁𐐲𐑉𐐻 𐑋𐐴 𐑋𐐲𐑄𐐲𐑉, 𐐝𐐲𐑉𐐴𐐲, 𐐿𐐲𐑌𐑅𐐲𐑉𐑌𐐮𐑍 𐐲𐑅, 𐐸𐐶𐐴𐑊 𐐶𐐨 𐐾𐐲𐑉-𐑌𐐨𐐼 𐐮𐑌 𐑄 𐐶𐐮𐑊𐐼𐐲𐑉𐑌𐐯𐑅 𐐲𐐹 𐐻𐐭 𐑄 𐑊𐐰𐑌𐐼 𐐱𐑂 𐐖𐐯𐑉𐐭𐑅𐐲𐑊𐐯𐑋, 𐐻𐐭 𐐱𐐺𐐻𐐩𐑌 𐑄 𐑉𐐯𐐿𐐲𐑉𐐼 𐐱𐑂 𐑄 𐐖𐐭𐑆.

45. 𐐈𐑌𐐼 𐐸𐐶𐐯𐑌 𐐶𐐨 𐐸𐐰𐐼 𐑉𐐨𐐻𐐲𐑉𐑌𐐼 𐐻𐐭 𐑄 𐐻𐐯𐑌𐐻 𐐱𐑂 𐑋𐐴 𐑁𐐪𐑄𐐲𐑉, 𐐺𐐨𐐸𐐬𐑊𐐼 𐑄𐐩𐑉 𐐾𐐱𐐮 𐐶𐐱𐑆 𐑁𐐳𐑊, 𐐰𐑌𐐼 𐑋𐐴 𐑋𐐲𐑄𐐲𐑉 𐐶𐐱𐑆 𐐿𐐲𐑋𐑁𐐲𐑉𐐻𐐯𐐼; 𐐰𐑌𐐼 𐑇𐐨 𐑅𐐹𐐩𐐿, 𐑅𐐩𐐮𐑍, 𐐤𐐵 𐐌 𐑌𐐬 𐐱𐑂 𐐲 𐑇𐐭𐑉𐐻𐐨 𐑄𐐰𐐻

𐑄 𐐢𐐫𐑉𐐼 𐐸𐐰𐑃 𐐿𐐱𐑋𐐰𐑌𐐼𐐯𐐼 𐑋𐐴 𐐸𐐲𐑆𐐺𐐲𐑌𐐼 𐐻𐐭 𐑁𐑊𐐨 𐐮𐑌𐐻𐐭 𐑄 𐐶𐐮𐑊𐐼𐐲𐑉𐑌𐐯𐑅; 𐐷𐐩, 𐐰𐑌𐐼 𐐌 𐐫𐑊𐑅𐐬 𐑌𐐬 𐐱𐑂 𐐲 𐑇𐐭𐑉𐐻𐐨 𐑄𐐰𐐻 𐑄 𐐢𐐫𐑉𐐼 𐐸𐐰𐑃 𐐹𐑉𐐬𐐻𐐯𐐿𐐻𐐯𐐼 𐑋𐐴 𐑅𐐲𐑌𐑆, 𐐰𐑌𐐼 𐐼𐐯𐑊𐐮𐑂𐐲𐑉𐐼 𐑄𐐯𐑋 𐐵𐐻 𐐱𐑂 𐑄 𐐸𐐰𐑌𐐼𐑆 𐐱𐑂 𐐢𐐩𐐺𐐰𐑌, 𐐰𐑌𐐼 𐑀𐐮𐑂𐑌 𐑄𐐯𐑋 𐐹𐐵𐑉 𐐸𐐶𐐯𐑉𐐺𐐴 𐑄𐐩 𐐿𐐳𐐼 𐐰𐐿𐐱𐑋𐐹𐑊𐐮𐑇 𐑄 𐑃𐐮𐑍 𐐸𐐶𐐮𐐽 𐑄 𐐢𐐫𐑉𐐼 𐐸𐐰𐑃 𐐿𐐱𐑋𐐰𐑌𐐼𐐯𐐼 𐑄𐐯𐑋. 𐐈𐑌𐐼 𐐰𐑁𐐻𐐲𐑉 𐑄𐐮𐑅 𐑋𐐰𐑌𐐲𐑉 𐐱𐑂 𐑊𐐰𐑍𐑀𐐶𐐯𐐾 𐐼𐐮𐐼 𐑇𐐨 𐑅𐐹𐐨𐐿.

46. 𐐈𐑌𐐼 𐐮𐐻 𐐿𐐩𐑋 𐐻𐐭 𐐹𐐰𐑅 𐑄𐐰𐐻 𐑄𐐩 𐐼𐐮𐐼 𐑉𐐨𐐾𐐫𐐮𐑅 𐐯𐐿𐑅𐐨𐐼𐐮𐑍𐑊𐐨, 𐐰𐑌𐐼 𐐼𐐮𐐼 𐐫𐑁𐐲𐑉 𐑅𐐰𐐿𐑉𐐮𐑁𐐴𐑅 𐐰𐑌𐐼 𐐺𐐲𐑉𐑌𐐻 𐐫𐑁𐐲𐑉𐐮𐑍𐑆 𐐲𐑌𐐻𐐭 𐑄 𐐢𐐫𐑉𐐼; 𐐰𐑌𐐼 𐑄𐐩 𐑀𐐩𐑂 𐑃𐐰𐑍𐐿𐑅 𐐲𐑌𐐻𐐭 𐑄 𐐘𐐱𐐼 𐐱𐑂 𐐆𐑆𐑉𐐩𐐯𐑊. 𐐈𐑌𐐼 𐐰𐑁𐐻𐐲𐑉 𐑄𐐩 𐐸𐐰𐐼 𐑀𐐮𐑂𐑌 𐑃𐐰𐑍𐐿𐑅 𐐲𐑌𐐻𐐭 𐑄 𐐘𐐱𐐼 𐐱𐑂 𐐆𐑆𐑉𐐩𐐯𐑊, 𐑋𐐴 𐑁𐐪𐑄𐐲𐑉, 𐐢𐐨𐐸𐐴, 𐐻𐐳𐐿 𐑄 𐑉𐐯𐐿𐐫𐑉𐐼𐑆 𐐸𐐶𐐮𐐽 𐐶𐐲𐑉 𐐯𐑌𐑀𐑉𐐩𐑂𐐯𐑌 𐐲𐐹𐐱𐑌 𐑄 𐐹𐑊𐐩𐐻𐑅 𐐱𐑂 𐐺𐑉𐐰𐑅, 𐐰𐑌𐐼 𐐸𐐨 𐐼𐐮𐐼 𐑅𐐲𐑉𐐽 𐑄𐐯𐑋 𐑁𐑉𐐱𐑋 𐑄 𐐺𐐨𐑀𐐮𐑌𐐮𐑍. 𐐈𐑌𐐼 𐐸𐐨 𐐺𐐨𐐸𐐯𐑊𐐼 𐑄𐐰𐐻 𐑄𐐩 𐐼𐐮𐐼 𐐿𐐱𐑌𐐻𐐩𐑌 𐑄 𐑁𐐴𐑂 𐐺𐐳𐐿𐑅 𐐱𐑂 𐐣𐐬𐑆𐐯𐑆, 𐐸𐐶𐐮𐐽 𐑀𐐩𐑂 𐐰𐑌 𐐰𐐿𐐵𐑌𐐻 𐐱𐑂 𐑄 𐐿𐑉𐐨𐐩𐑇𐐲𐑌 𐐱𐑂 𐑄 𐐶𐐲𐑉𐑊𐐼, 𐐰𐑌𐐼 𐐫𐑊𐑅𐐬 𐐱𐑂 𐐁𐐼𐐲𐑋 𐐰𐑌𐐼 𐐀𐑂, 𐐸𐐭 𐐶𐐲𐑉 𐐵𐑉 𐑁𐐲𐑉𐑅𐐻 𐐹𐐯𐑉𐐯𐑌𐐻𐑅; 𐐰𐑌𐐼 𐐫𐑊𐑅𐐬 𐐲 𐑉𐐯𐐿𐐫𐑉𐐼 𐐱𐑂 𐑄 𐐖𐐭𐑆 𐑁𐑉𐐱𐑋 𐑄 𐐺𐐨𐑀𐐮𐑌𐐮𐑍, 𐐀𐑂𐐯𐑌 𐐼𐐵𐑌 𐐻𐐭 𐑄 𐐿𐐱𐑋𐐯𐑌𐑅𐑋𐐯𐑌𐐻 𐐱𐑂 𐑄 𐑉𐐩𐑌 𐐱𐑂 𐐞𐐯𐐼𐐯𐐿𐐴𐐲, 𐐿𐐮𐑍 𐐱𐑂 𐐖𐐭𐐼𐐲; 𐐰𐑌𐐼 𐐫𐑊𐑅𐐬 𐑄 𐐹𐑉𐐱𐑁𐐯𐑅𐐨𐑆 𐐱𐑂 𐑄 𐐸𐐬𐑊𐐨 𐐹𐑉𐐱𐑁𐐯𐐻𐑅, 𐑁𐑉𐐱𐑋 𐑄 𐐺𐐨𐑀𐐮𐑌𐐮𐑍, 𐐀𐑂𐐯𐑌 𐐼𐐵𐑌 𐐻𐐭 𐑄 𐐿𐐱𐑋𐐯𐑌𐑅𐑋𐐯𐑌𐐻 𐐱𐑂 𐑄 𐑉𐐩𐑌 𐐱𐑂 𐐞𐐯𐐼𐐯𐐿𐐴𐐲; 𐐰𐑌𐐼 𐐫𐑊𐑅𐐬 𐑋𐐯𐑌𐐨 𐐹𐑉𐐱𐑁𐐯𐑅𐐨𐑆 𐐸𐐶𐐮𐐽 𐐸𐐰𐑂 𐐺𐐮𐑌 𐑅𐐹𐐬𐐿𐐲𐑌 𐐺𐐴 𐑄 𐑋𐐵𐑃 𐐱𐑂 𐐖𐐯𐑉𐐯𐑋𐐴𐐲.

47. 𐐈𐑌𐐼 𐐮𐐻 𐐿𐐩𐑋 𐐻𐐭 𐐹𐐰𐑅 𐑄𐐰𐐻 𐑋𐐴 𐑁𐐪𐑄𐐲𐑉, 𐐢𐐨𐐸𐐴, 𐐫𐑊𐑅𐐬 𐑁𐐵𐑌𐐼 𐐲𐐹𐐱𐑌 𐑄 𐐹𐑊𐐩𐐻𐑅 𐐱𐑂 𐐺𐑉𐐰𐑅 𐐲 𐐾𐐨𐑌𐐨𐐰𐑊𐐱𐐾𐐨 𐐱𐑂 𐐸𐐮𐑆 𐑁𐐪𐑄𐐲𐑉𐑆; 𐐸𐐶𐐯𐑉𐑁𐐬𐑉 𐐸𐐨 𐑌𐐭 𐑄𐐰𐐻 𐐸𐐨 𐐶𐐱𐑆 𐐲 𐐼𐐨𐑅𐐯𐑌𐐼𐐰𐑌𐐻 𐐱𐑂 𐐖𐐬𐑆𐐯𐑁; 𐐷𐐩, 𐐀𐑂𐐯𐑌 𐑄𐐰𐐻 𐐖𐐬𐑆𐐯𐑁 𐐸𐐭 𐐶𐐱𐑆 𐑄 𐑅𐐲𐑌 𐐱𐑂 𐐖𐐩𐐿𐐲𐐺, 𐐸𐐭 𐐶𐐱𐑆 𐑅𐐬𐑊𐐼 𐐮𐑌𐐻𐐭 𐐀𐐾𐐮𐐹𐐻, 𐐰𐑌𐐼 𐐸𐐭 𐐶𐐱𐑆 𐐹𐑉𐐨𐑆𐐲𐑉𐑂𐐼 𐐺𐐴 𐑄 𐐸𐐰𐑌𐐼 𐐱𐑂 𐑄 𐐢𐐫𐑉𐐼, 𐑄𐐰𐐻 𐐸𐐨 𐑋𐐴𐐻 𐐹𐑉𐐨𐑆𐐲𐑉𐑂 𐐸𐐮𐑆 𐑁𐐪𐑄𐐲𐑉 𐐖𐐩𐐿𐐲𐐺 𐐰𐑌𐐼 𐐫𐑊 𐐸𐐮𐑆 𐐸𐐵𐑅𐐸𐐬𐑊𐐼 𐑁𐑉𐐱𐑋 𐐹𐐯𐑉𐐮𐑇𐐮𐑍 𐐶𐐮𐑄 𐑁𐐰𐑋𐐮𐑌. 𐐈𐑌𐐼 𐑄𐐩 𐐶𐐲𐑉 𐐫𐑊𐑅𐐬 𐑊𐐯𐐼 𐐵𐐻 𐐱𐑂 𐐿𐐰𐐹𐐻𐐮𐑂𐐮𐐻𐐨 𐐰𐑌𐐼 𐐵𐐻 𐐱𐑂 𐑄 𐑊𐐰𐑌𐐼 𐐱𐑂 𐐀𐐾𐐮𐐹𐐻, 𐐺𐐴 𐑄𐐰𐐻 𐑅𐐩𐑋 𐐘𐐱𐐼 𐐸𐐭 𐐸𐐰𐐼 𐐹𐑉𐐨𐑆𐐲𐑉𐑂𐐼 𐑄𐐯𐑋. 𐐈𐑌𐐼 𐑄𐐲𐑅 𐑋𐐴 𐑁𐐪𐑄𐐲𐑉, 𐐢𐐨𐐸𐐴, 𐐼𐐮𐐼 𐐼𐐮𐑅𐐿𐐲𐑂𐐲𐑉 𐑄 𐐾𐐨𐑌𐐨𐐰𐑊𐐱𐐾𐐨 𐐱𐑂 𐐸𐐮𐑆 𐑁𐐪𐑄𐐲𐑉𐑆. 𐐈𐑌𐐼 𐐢𐐩𐐺𐐰𐑌 𐐫𐑊𐑅𐐬 𐐶𐐱𐑆 𐐲 𐐼𐐨𐑅𐐯𐑌𐐼𐐰𐑌𐐻 𐐱𐑂 𐐖𐐬𐑆𐐯𐑁, 𐐸𐐶𐐯𐑉𐑁𐐬𐑉 𐐸𐐨 𐐰𐑌𐐼 𐐸𐐮𐑆 𐑁𐐪𐑄𐐲𐑉𐑆 𐐸𐐰𐐼 𐐿𐐯𐐹𐐻 𐑄 𐑉𐐯𐐿𐐫𐑉𐐼𐑆.

48. 𐐈𐑌𐐼 𐑌𐐵 𐐸𐐶𐐯𐑌 𐑋𐐴 𐑁𐐪𐑄𐐲𐑉 𐑅𐐫 𐐫𐑊 𐑄𐐨𐑆 𐑃𐐮𐑍𐑆, 𐐸𐐨 𐐶𐐱𐑆 𐑁𐐮𐑊𐐼 𐐶𐐮𐑄 𐑄 𐐝𐐹𐐮𐑉𐐮𐐻, 𐐰𐑌𐐼 𐐺𐐨𐑀𐐰𐑌 𐐻𐐭 𐐹𐑉𐐱𐑁𐐯𐑅𐐴 𐐿𐐱𐑌𐑅𐐲𐑉𐑌𐐮𐑍 𐐸𐐮𐑆 𐑅𐐨𐐼; 𐑄𐐰𐐻 𐑄𐐨𐑆 𐐹𐑊𐐩𐐻𐑅 𐐱𐑂 𐐺𐑉𐐰𐑅 𐑇𐐳𐐼 𐑀𐐬 𐑁𐐬𐑉𐑃 𐐲𐑌𐐻𐐭 𐐫𐑊 𐑌𐐩𐑇𐐲𐑌𐑆, 𐐿𐐮𐑌𐐼𐑉𐐯𐐼𐑆, 𐐻𐐲𐑍𐑆, 𐐰𐑌𐐼 𐐹𐐨𐐹𐑊 𐐸𐐭 𐐶𐐲𐑉 𐐱𐑂 𐐸𐐮𐑆 𐑅𐐨𐐼. 𐐐𐐶𐐯𐑉𐑁𐐬𐑉, 𐐸𐐨 𐑅𐐯𐐼 𐑄𐐰𐐻 𐑄𐐨𐑆 𐐹𐑊𐐩𐐻𐑅 𐐱𐑂 𐐺𐑉𐐰𐑅 𐑇𐐳𐐼 𐑌𐐯𐑂𐐲𐑉 𐐹𐐯𐑉𐐮𐑇; 𐑌𐐨𐑄𐐲𐑉 𐑇𐐳𐐼 𐑄𐐩 𐐺𐐨 𐐼𐐮𐑋𐐼 𐐯𐑌𐐨 𐑋𐐬𐑉 𐐺𐐴 𐐻𐐴𐑋. 𐐈𐑌𐐼 𐐸𐐨 𐐹𐑉𐐱𐑁𐐯𐑅𐐴𐐼 𐑋𐐯𐑌𐐨 𐑃𐐮𐑍𐑆 𐐿𐐱𐑌𐑅𐐲𐑉𐑌𐐮𐑍 𐐸𐐮𐑆 𐑅𐐨𐐼.

49. 𐐈𐑌𐐼 𐐮𐐻 𐐿𐐩𐑋 𐐻𐐭 𐐹𐐰𐑅 𐑄𐐰𐐻 𐑄𐐲𐑅 𐑁𐐪𐑉 𐐌 𐐰𐑌𐐼 𐑋𐐴 𐑁𐐪𐑄𐐲𐑉 𐐸𐐰𐐼 𐐿𐐯𐐹𐐻 𐑄 𐐿𐐱𐑋𐐰𐑌𐐼𐑋𐐯𐑌𐐻𐑅 𐐸𐐶𐐯𐑉𐐶𐐮𐑄 𐑄 𐐢𐐫𐑉𐐼 𐐸𐐰𐐼 𐐿𐐱𐑋𐐰𐑌𐐼𐐯𐐼 𐐲𐑅. 𐐈𐑌𐐼 𐐶𐐨 𐐸𐐰𐐼 𐐱𐐺𐐻𐐩𐑌𐐼 𐑄 𐑉𐐯𐐿𐐫𐑉𐐼𐑆 𐐸𐐶𐐮𐐽 𐑄 𐐢𐐫𐑉𐐼 𐐸𐐰𐐼 𐐿𐐱𐑋𐐰𐑌𐐼𐐯𐐼 𐐲𐑅, 𐐰𐑌𐐼 𐑅𐐲𐑉𐐽𐐻 𐑄𐐯𐑋, 𐐰𐑌𐐼 𐑁𐐵𐑌𐐼 𐑄𐐰𐐻 𐑄𐐩 𐐶𐐲𐑉 𐐼𐐨𐑆𐐴𐑉𐐲𐐺𐑊; 𐐷𐐩, 𐐀𐑂𐐯𐑌 𐐱𐑂 𐑀𐑉𐐩𐐻 𐐶𐐲𐑉𐑃 𐐲𐑌𐐻𐐭 𐐲𐑅, 𐐮𐑌𐑅𐐬𐑋𐐲𐐽 𐑄𐐰𐐻 𐐶𐐨 𐐿𐐳𐐼 𐐹𐑉𐐨𐑆𐐲𐑉𐑂 𐑄 𐐿𐐱𐑋𐐰𐑌𐐼𐑋𐐯𐑌𐐻𐑅 𐐱𐑂 𐑄 𐐢𐐫𐑉𐐼 𐐲𐑌𐐻𐐭 𐐵𐑉 𐐽𐐮𐑊𐐼𐑉𐐯𐑌. 𐐐𐐶𐐯𐑉𐑁𐐬𐑉 𐐮𐐻 𐐶𐐱𐑆 𐐶𐐮𐑆𐐼𐐲𐑋 𐐮𐑌 𐑄 𐐢𐐫𐑉𐐼 𐑄𐐰𐐻 𐐶𐐨 𐑇𐐳𐐼 𐐿𐐰𐑉𐐨 𐑄𐐯𐑋 𐐶𐐮𐑄 𐐲𐑅 𐐰𐑆 𐐶𐐨 𐐾𐐲𐑉𐑌𐐨𐐼 𐐮𐑌 𐑄 𐐶𐐮𐑊𐐼𐐲𐑉𐑌𐐯𐑅 𐐻𐐬𐑉𐐼𐑆 𐑄 𐑊𐐰𐑌𐐼 𐐱𐑂 𐐹𐑉𐐱𐑋𐐮𐑅.

𐐕𐐈𐐑𐐓𐐊𐐡 II.

1. 𐐈𐑌𐐼 𐑌𐐵 𐐌, 𐐤𐐨𐑁𐐴, 𐐼𐐭 𐑌𐐱𐐻 𐑀𐐮𐑂 𐑄 𐐾𐐨𐑌𐐨𐐰𐑊𐐱𐐾𐐨 𐐱𐑂 𐑋𐐴 𐑁𐐪𐑄𐐲𐑉𐑆 𐐮𐑌 𐑄𐐮𐑅 𐐹𐐪𐑉𐐻 𐐱𐑂 𐑋𐐴 𐑉𐐯𐐿𐐫𐑉𐐼; 𐑌𐐨𐑄𐐲𐑉 𐐰𐐻 𐐯𐑌𐐨 𐐻𐐴𐑋 𐑇𐐰𐑊 𐐌 𐑀𐐮𐑂 𐐮𐐻 𐐰𐑁𐐻𐐲𐑉 𐐲𐐹𐐱𐑌 𐑄𐐨𐑆 𐐹𐑊𐐩𐐻𐑅 𐐸𐐶𐐮𐐽 𐐌 𐐰𐑋 𐑉𐐴𐐻𐐮𐑍; 𐑁𐐫𐑉 𐐮𐐻 𐐮𐑆 𐑀𐐮𐑂𐑌 𐐮𐑌 𐑄 𐑉𐐯𐐿𐐫𐑉𐐼 𐐸𐐶𐐮𐐽 𐐸𐐰𐑆 𐐺𐐮𐑌 𐐿𐐯𐐹𐐻 𐐺𐐴 𐑋𐐴 𐑁𐐪𐑄𐐲𐑉; 𐐸𐐶𐐯𐑉𐑁𐐬𐑉 𐐌

𐐼𐐭 𐑌𐐱𐐻 𐑉𐐴𐐻 𐐮𐐻 𐐮𐑌 𐑄𐐮𐑅 𐐶𐐲𐑉𐐿. 𐐙𐐫𐑉 𐐮𐐻 𐑅𐐲𐑁𐐴𐑅𐐯𐑃 𐑋𐐨 𐐻𐐭 𐑅𐐩, 𐑄𐐰𐐻 𐐶𐐨 𐐪𐑉 𐐼𐐯𐑅𐐯𐑌𐐼𐐰𐑌𐐻𐑅 𐐱𐑂 𐐖𐐬𐑆𐐯𐑁. 𐐈𐑌𐐼 𐐮𐐻 𐑋𐐰𐐻𐐲𐑉𐐯𐑃 𐑌𐐱𐐻 𐐻𐐭 𐑋𐐨 𐑄𐐰𐐻 𐐌 𐐰𐑋 𐐹𐐪𐑉𐐻𐐮𐐿𐐷𐐭𐑊𐐲𐑉 𐐻𐐭 𐑀𐐮𐑂 𐐲 𐑁𐐳𐑊 𐐰𐐿𐐵𐑌𐐻 𐐱𐑂 𐐫𐑊 𐑄 𐑃𐐮𐑍𐑆 𐐱𐑂 𐑋𐐴 𐑁𐐪𐑄𐐲𐑉, 𐑁𐐫𐑉 𐑄𐐩 𐐿𐐰𐑌𐐱𐐻 𐐺𐐨 𐑉𐐮𐐻𐐲𐑌 𐐲𐐹𐐱𐑌 𐑄𐐨𐑆 𐐹𐑊𐐩𐐻𐑅, 𐑁𐐫𐑉 𐐌 𐐼𐐯𐑆𐐴𐑉 𐑄 𐑉𐐭𐑋 𐑄𐐰𐐻 𐐌 𐑋𐐩 𐑉𐐴𐐻 𐐱𐑂 𐑄 𐑃𐐮𐑍𐑆 𐐱𐑂 𐐘𐐱𐐼. 𐐙𐐫𐑉 𐑄 𐑁𐐳𐑊𐑌𐐯𐑅 𐐱𐑂 𐑋𐐴𐑌 𐐮𐑌𐐻𐐯𐑌𐐻 𐐮𐑆, 𐑄𐐰𐐻 𐐌 𐑋𐐩 𐐹𐐲𐑉𐑅𐐶𐐩𐐼 𐑋𐐯𐑌 𐐻𐐭 𐐿𐐲𐑋 𐐲𐑌𐐻𐐭 𐑄 𐐘𐐱𐐼 𐐱𐑂 𐐁𐐺𐑉𐐲𐐸𐐰𐑋, 𐐰𐑌𐐼 𐑄 𐐘𐐱𐐼 𐐱𐑂 𐐌𐑆𐐰𐐿, 𐐰𐑌𐐼 𐑄 𐐘𐐱𐐼 𐐱𐑂 𐐖𐐩𐐿𐐲𐐺, 𐐰𐑌𐐼 𐐺𐐨 𐑅𐐩𐑂𐐼. 𐐐𐐶𐐯𐑉𐑁𐐫𐑉, 𐑄 𐑃𐐮𐑍𐑆 𐐸𐐶𐐮𐐽 𐐪𐑉 𐐹𐑊𐐨𐑆𐐮𐑍 𐐲𐑌𐐻𐐭 𐑄 𐐶𐐲𐑉𐑊𐐼, 𐐌 𐐼𐐭 𐑌𐐱𐐻 𐑉𐐴𐐻, 𐐺𐐲𐐻 𐑄 𐑃𐐮𐑍𐑆 𐐸𐐶𐐮𐐽 𐐪𐑉 𐐹𐑊𐐨𐑆𐐮𐑍 𐐲𐑌𐐻𐐭 𐐘𐐱𐐼, 𐐰𐑌𐐼 𐐲𐑌𐐻𐐭 𐑄𐐬𐑆 𐐸𐐭 𐐪𐑉 𐑌𐐱𐐻 𐐱𐑂 𐑄 𐐶𐐲𐑉𐑊𐐼. 𐐐𐐶𐐯𐑉𐑁𐐫𐑉, 𐐌 𐑇𐐰𐑊 𐑀𐐮𐑂 𐐿𐐱𐑋𐐰𐑌𐐼𐑋𐐯𐑌𐐻 𐐲𐑌𐐻𐐭 𐑋𐐴 𐑅𐐨𐐼, 𐑄𐐰𐐻 𐑄𐐩 𐑇𐐰𐑊 𐑌𐐱𐐻 𐐱𐐿𐐷𐐭𐐹𐐴 𐑄𐐨𐑆 𐐹𐑊𐐩𐐻𐑅 𐐶𐐮𐑄 𐑃𐐮𐑍𐑆 𐐸𐐶𐐮𐐽 𐐪𐑉 𐑌𐐱𐐻 𐐱𐑂 𐐶𐐲𐑉𐑃 𐐲𐑌𐐻𐐭 𐑄 𐐽𐐮𐑊𐐼𐑉𐐯𐑌 𐐱𐑂 𐑋𐐯𐑌.

2. 𐐈𐑌𐐼 𐑌𐐵 𐐌 𐐶𐐳𐐼 𐑄𐐰𐐻 𐐷𐐨 𐑋𐐴𐐻 𐑌𐐬, 𐑄𐐰𐐻 𐐰𐑁𐐻𐐲𐑉 𐑋𐐴 𐑁𐐪𐑄𐐲𐑉, 𐐢𐐨𐐸𐐴, 𐐸𐐰𐐼 𐑋𐐩𐐼 𐐰𐑌 𐐯𐑌𐐼 𐐱𐑂 𐐹𐑉𐐱𐑁𐐯𐑅𐐴𐐮𐑍 𐐿𐐱𐑌𐑅𐐲𐑉𐑌𐐮𐑍 𐐸𐐮𐑆 𐑅𐐨𐐼, 𐐮𐐻 𐐿𐐩𐑋 𐐻𐐭 𐐹𐐰𐑅 𐑄𐐰𐐻 𐑄 𐐢𐐫𐑉𐐼 𐑅𐐹𐐩𐐿 𐐲𐑌𐐻𐐭 𐐸𐐮𐑋 𐐲𐑀𐐯𐑌, 𐑅𐐩𐐮𐑍, 𐑄𐐰𐐻 𐐮𐐻 𐐶𐐱𐑆 𐑌𐐱𐐻 𐑋𐐨𐐻 𐑁𐐫𐑉 𐐸𐐮𐑋, 𐐢𐐨𐐸𐐴, 𐑄𐐰𐐻 𐐸𐐨 𐑇𐐳𐐼 𐐻𐐩𐐿 𐐸𐐮𐑆 𐑁𐐰𐑋𐐮𐑊𐐨 𐐮𐑌𐐻𐐭 𐑄 𐐶𐐮𐑊𐐼𐐲𐑉𐑌𐐯𐑅 𐐲𐑊𐐬𐑌; 𐐺𐐲𐐻 𐑄𐐰𐐻 𐐸𐐮𐑆 𐑅𐐲𐑌𐑆 𐑇𐐳𐐼 𐐻𐐩𐐿 𐐼𐐫𐐻𐐲𐑉𐑆 𐐻𐐭 𐐶𐐴𐑁, 𐑄𐐰𐐻 𐑄𐐩 𐑋𐐴𐐻 𐑉𐐩𐑆 𐐲𐐹 𐑅𐐨𐐼 𐐲𐑌𐐻𐐭 𐑄 𐐢𐐫𐑉𐐼 𐐮𐑌 𐑄 𐑊𐐰𐑌𐐼 𐐱𐑂 𐐹𐑉𐐱𐑋𐐮𐑅.

3. 𐐈𐑌𐐼 𐐮𐐻 𐐿𐐩𐑋 𐐻𐐭 𐐹𐐰𐑅 𐑄𐐰𐐻 𐑄 𐐢𐐫𐑉𐐼 𐐿𐐱𐑋𐐰𐑌𐐼𐐯𐐼 𐐸𐐮𐑋 𐑄𐐰𐐻 𐐌, 𐐤𐐨𐑁𐐴, 𐐰𐑌𐐼 𐑋𐐴 𐐺𐑉𐐯𐑄𐑉𐐯𐑌, 𐑇𐐳𐐼 𐐲𐑀𐐯𐑌 𐑉𐐨𐐻𐐲𐑉𐑌 𐐲𐑌𐐻𐐭 𐑄 𐑊𐐰𐑌𐐼 𐐱𐑂 𐐖𐐭𐑉𐐭𐑅𐐲𐑊𐐯𐑋, 𐐰𐑌𐐼 𐐺𐑉𐐮𐑍 𐐼𐐵𐑌 𐐆𐑇𐑋𐐩𐐯𐑊 𐐰𐑌𐐼 𐐸𐐮𐑆 𐑁𐐰𐑋𐐮𐑊𐐨 𐐮𐑌𐐻𐐭 𐑄 𐐶𐐮𐑊𐐼𐐲𐑉𐑌𐐯𐑅.

4. 𐐈𐑌𐐼 𐐮𐐻 𐐿𐐩𐑋 𐐻𐐭 𐐹𐐰𐑅 𐑄𐐰𐐻 𐐌, 𐐤𐐨𐑁𐐴, 𐐼𐐮𐐼 𐐲𐑀𐐯𐑌, 𐐶𐐮𐑄 𐑋𐐴 𐐺𐑉𐐯𐑄𐑉𐐯𐑌, 𐑀𐐬 𐑁𐐬𐑉𐑃 𐐮𐑌𐐻𐐭 𐑄 𐐶𐐮𐑊𐐼𐐲𐑉𐑌𐐯𐑅 𐐻𐐭 𐑀𐐬 𐐲𐐹 𐐻𐐭 𐐖𐐭𐑉𐐭𐑅𐐲𐑊𐐯𐑋. 𐐈𐑌𐐼 𐐮𐐻 𐐿𐐩𐑋 𐐻𐐭 𐐹𐐰𐑅 𐑄𐐰𐐻 𐐶𐐨 𐐶𐐯𐑌𐐻 𐐲𐐹 𐐲𐑌𐐻𐐭 𐑄 𐐸𐐵𐑅 𐐱𐑂 𐐆𐑇𐑋𐐩𐐯𐑊, 𐐰𐑌𐐼 𐐶𐐨 𐐼𐐮𐐼 𐑀𐐩𐑌 𐑁𐐩𐑂𐐲𐑉 𐐮𐑌 𐑄 𐑅𐐴𐐻 𐐱𐑂 𐐆𐑇𐑋𐐩𐐯𐑊, 𐐮𐑌𐑅𐐬𐑋𐐲𐐽 𐑄𐐰𐐻 𐐶𐐨 𐐼𐐮𐐼 𐑅𐐹𐐨𐐿 𐐲𐑌𐐻𐐭 𐐸𐐮𐑋 𐑄 𐐶𐐲𐑉𐐼𐑆 𐐱𐑂 𐑄 𐐢𐐫𐑉𐐼.

5. 𐐈𐑌𐐼 𐐮𐐻 𐐿𐐩𐑋 𐐻𐐭 𐐹𐐰𐑅 𐑄𐐰𐐻 𐑄 𐐢𐐫𐑉𐐼 𐐼𐐮𐐼 𐑅𐐱𐑁𐐲𐑌 𐑄 𐐸𐐪𐑉𐐻 𐐱𐑂 𐐆𐑇𐑋𐐩𐐯𐑊, 𐐰𐑌𐐼 𐐫𐑊𐑅𐐬 𐐸𐐮𐑆 𐐸𐐵𐑅𐐸𐐬𐑊𐐼, 𐐮𐑌𐑅𐐬𐑋𐐲𐐽 𐑄𐐰𐐻 𐑄𐐩 𐐻𐐳𐐿 𐑄𐐩𐑉 𐐾𐐲𐑉𐑌𐐨 𐐶𐐮𐑄 𐐲𐑅 𐐼𐐵𐑌 𐐮𐑌𐐻𐐭 𐑄 𐐶𐐮𐑊𐐼𐐲𐑉𐑌𐐯𐑅 𐐻𐐭 𐑄 𐐻𐐯𐑌𐐻 𐐱𐑂 𐐵𐑉 𐑁𐐪𐑄𐐲𐑉. 𐐈𐑌𐐼 𐐮𐐻 𐐿𐐩𐑋 𐐻𐐭 𐐹𐐰𐑅 𐑄𐐰𐐻 𐐰𐑆 𐐶𐐨 𐐾𐐲𐑉𐑌𐐨𐐼 𐐮𐑌 𐑄 𐐶𐐮𐑊𐐼𐐲𐑉𐑌𐐯𐑅, 𐐺𐐨𐐸𐐬𐑊𐐼 𐐢𐐩𐑋𐐲𐑌 𐐰𐑌𐐼 𐐢𐐯𐑋𐐷𐐭𐐯𐑊, 𐐰𐑌𐐼 𐐻𐐭 𐐱𐑂 𐑄 𐐼𐐫𐐻𐐲𐑉𐑆 𐐱𐑂 𐐆𐑇𐑋𐐩𐐯𐑊, 𐐰𐑌𐐼 𐑄 𐐻𐐭 𐑅𐐲𐑌𐑆 𐐱𐑂 𐐆𐑇𐑋𐐩𐐯𐑊 𐐰𐑌𐐼 𐑄𐐩𐑉 𐑁𐐰𐑋𐐮𐑊𐐨𐑆, 𐐼𐐮𐐼 𐑉𐐨𐐺𐐯𐑊 𐐲𐑀𐐯𐑌𐑅𐐻 𐐲𐑅; 𐐷𐐩, 𐐲𐑀𐐯𐑌𐑅𐐻 𐑋𐐨, 𐐤𐐨𐑁𐐴, 𐐰𐑌𐐼 𐐝𐐰𐑋, 𐐰𐑌𐐼 𐑄𐐩𐑉 𐑁𐐪𐑄𐐲𐑉, 𐐆𐑇𐑋𐐩𐐯𐑊, 𐐰𐑌𐐼 𐐸𐐮𐑆 𐐶𐐴𐑁, 𐐰𐑌𐐼 𐐸𐐮𐑆 𐑃𐑉𐐨 𐐲𐑄𐐲𐑉 𐐼𐐫𐐻𐐲𐑉𐑆.

6. 𐐈𐑌𐐼 𐐮𐐻 𐐿𐐩𐑋 𐐻𐐭 𐐹𐐰𐑅 𐐮𐑌 𐑄 𐐸𐐶𐐮𐐽 𐑉𐐨𐐺𐐯𐑊𐐷𐐲𐑌, 𐑄𐐩 𐐶𐐲𐑉 𐐼𐐯𐑆𐐴𐑉𐐲𐑅 𐐻𐐭 𐑉𐐨𐐻𐐲𐑉𐑌 𐐲𐑌𐐻𐐭 𐑄 𐑊𐐰𐑌𐐼 𐐱𐑂 𐐖𐐭𐑉𐐭𐑅𐐲𐑊𐐯𐑋. 𐐈𐑌𐐼 𐑌𐐵 𐐌, 𐐤𐐨𐑁𐐴, 𐐺𐐨𐐮𐑍 𐑀𐑉𐐨𐑂𐐼 𐑁𐐫𐑉 𐑄 𐐸𐐪𐑉𐐼𐑌𐐯𐑅 𐐱𐑂 𐑄𐐩𐑉 𐐸𐐪𐑉𐐻𐑅, 𐑄𐐯𐑉𐑁𐐫𐑉 𐐌 𐑅𐐹𐐩𐐿 𐐲𐑌𐐻𐐭 𐑄𐐯𐑋, 𐑅𐐩𐐮𐑍, 𐐷𐐩, 𐐨𐑂𐐯𐑌 𐐲𐑌𐐻𐐭 𐐢𐐩𐑋𐐲𐑌, 𐐰𐑌𐐼 𐐲𐑌𐐻𐐭 𐐢𐐯𐑋𐐷𐐭𐐯𐑊, 𐐒𐐨𐐸𐐬𐑊𐐼 𐐷𐐨 𐐪𐑉 𐑋𐐴𐑌 𐐯𐑊𐐼𐐲𐑉 𐐺𐑉𐐯𐑄𐑉𐐯𐑌, 𐐰𐑌𐐼 𐐸𐐵 𐐮𐑆 𐐮𐐻 𐑄𐐰𐐻 𐐷𐐨 𐐪𐑉 𐑅𐐬 𐐸𐐪𐑉𐐼 𐐮𐑌 𐐷𐐭𐑉 𐐸𐐪𐑉𐐻𐑅, 𐐰𐑌𐐼 𐑅𐐬 𐐺𐑊𐐴𐑌𐐼 𐐮𐑌 𐐷𐐭𐑉 𐑋𐐴𐑌𐐼𐑆, 𐑄𐐰𐐻 𐐷𐐨 𐐸𐐰𐑂 𐑌𐐨𐐼 𐑄𐐰𐐻 𐐌, 𐐷𐐭𐑉 𐐷𐐲𐑍𐑀𐐲𐑉 𐐺𐑉𐐲𐑄𐐲𐑉, 𐑇𐐳𐐼 𐑅𐐹𐐨𐐿 𐐲𐑌𐐻𐐭 𐐷𐐭, 𐐷𐐩, 𐐰𐑌𐐼 𐑅𐐯𐐻 𐐰𐑌 𐐯𐑀𐑆𐐰𐑋𐐹𐑊 𐑁𐐫𐑉 𐐷𐐭? 𐐐𐐵 𐐮𐑆 𐐮𐐻 𐑄𐐰𐐻 𐐷𐐨 𐐸𐐰𐑂 𐑌𐐱𐐻 𐐸𐐪𐑉𐐿𐐲𐑌𐐼 𐐲𐑌𐐻𐐭 𐑄 𐐶𐐲𐑉𐐼 𐐱𐑂 𐑄 𐐢𐐫𐑉𐐼? 𐐐𐐵 𐐮𐑆 𐐮𐐻 𐑄𐐰𐐻 𐐷𐐨 𐐸𐐰𐑂 𐑁𐐫𐑉𐑀𐐱𐐻𐐲𐑌 𐑄𐐰𐐻 𐐷𐐨 𐐸𐐰𐑂 𐑅𐐨𐑌 𐐰𐑌 𐐩𐑌𐐾𐐯𐑊 𐐱𐑂 𐑄 𐐢𐐫𐑉𐐼? 𐐖𐐩, 𐐰𐑌𐐼 𐐸𐐵 𐐮𐑆 𐐮𐐻 𐑄𐐰𐐻 𐐷𐐨 𐐸𐐰𐑂 𐑁𐐫𐑉𐑀𐐱𐐻𐐲𐑌 𐐸𐐶𐐱𐐻 𐑀𐑉𐐩𐐻 𐑃𐐮𐑍𐑆 𐑄 𐐢𐐫𐑉𐐼 𐐸𐐰𐑃 𐐼𐐲𐑌 𐑁𐐫𐑉 𐐲𐑅, 𐐮𐑌 𐐼𐐯𐑊𐐮𐑂𐐲𐑉𐐮𐑍 𐐲𐑅 𐐵𐐻 𐐱𐑂 𐑄 𐐸𐐰𐑌𐐼𐑆 𐐱𐑂 𐐢𐐩𐐺𐐲𐑌, 𐐰𐑌𐐼 𐐫𐑊𐑅𐐬 𐑄𐐰𐐻 𐐶𐐨 𐑇𐐳𐐼 𐐱𐐺𐐻𐐩𐑌 𐑄 𐑉𐐯𐐿𐐲𐑉𐐼? 𐐖𐐩, 𐐰𐑌𐐼 𐐸𐐵 𐐮𐑆 𐐮𐐻 𐑄𐐰𐐻 𐐷𐐨 𐐸𐐰𐑂 𐑁𐐫𐑉𐑀𐐱𐐻𐐲𐑌 𐑄𐐰𐐻 𐑄 𐐢𐐫𐑉𐐼 𐐮𐑆 𐐩𐐺𐑊 𐐻𐐭 𐐼𐐭 𐐫𐑊 𐑃𐐮𐑍𐑆 𐐰𐐿𐐫𐑉𐐼𐐮𐑍 𐐻𐐭 𐐸𐐮𐑆 𐐶𐐮𐑊, 𐑁𐐫𐑉 𐑄 𐐽𐐮𐑊𐐼𐑉𐐯𐑌 𐐱𐑂 𐑋𐐯𐑌, 𐐮𐑁 𐐮𐐻 𐑅𐐬 𐐺𐐨 𐑄𐐰𐐻 𐑄𐐩 𐐯𐐿𐑅𐐲𐑉𐑅𐐴𐑆 𐑁𐐩𐑃 𐐮𐑌 𐐸𐐮𐑋; 𐐸𐐶𐐯𐑉𐑁𐐫𐑉 𐑊𐐯𐐻 𐐲𐑅 𐐺𐐨 𐑁𐐩𐑃𐑁𐐳𐑊 𐐻𐐭 𐐸𐐮𐑋. 𐐈𐑌𐐼 𐐮𐑁 𐐮𐐻 𐑅𐐬 𐐺𐐨 𐑄𐐰𐐻 𐐶𐐨 𐐪𐑉 𐑁𐐩𐑃𐑁𐐳𐑊 𐐻𐐭 𐐸𐐮𐑋, 𐐶𐐨 𐑇𐐰𐑊 𐐱𐐺𐐻𐐩𐑌 𐑄 𐑊𐐰𐑌𐐼 𐐱𐑂 𐐹𐑉𐐱𐑋𐐮𐑅; 𐐰𐑌𐐼 𐐷𐐨 𐑇𐐰𐑊 𐑌𐐬 𐐰𐐻 𐑅𐐲𐑋

𐑁𐐧𐐻𐐷𐐭𐑉 𐐹𐐨𐑉𐐮𐐲𐐼, 𐑄𐐰𐐻 𐑄 𐐶𐐲𐑉𐐼 𐐲𐑂 𐑄 𐐢𐐫𐑉𐐼 𐑇𐐰𐑊 𐐺 𐑁𐐳𐑊𐑁𐐮𐑊𐐼 𐐿𐐲𐑌𐑅𐐲𐑉𐑌𐐮𐑍 𐑄 𐐼𐐨𐑅𐐻𐑉𐐲𐐿𐑇𐐲𐑌 𐐲𐑂 𐐖𐐨𐑉𐐭𐑅𐐲𐑊𐐲𐑋; 𐑁𐐫𐑉 𐐫𐑊 𐑃𐐮𐑍𐑆 𐐸𐐶𐐮𐐽 𐑄 𐐢𐐫𐑉𐐼 𐐸𐐰𐑃 𐑅𐐹𐐬𐐿𐐲𐑌 𐐿𐐲𐑌𐑅𐐲𐑉𐑌𐐮𐑍 𐑄 𐐼𐐨𐑅𐐻𐑉𐐲𐐿𐑇𐐲𐑌 𐐲𐑂 𐐖𐐨𐑉𐐭𐑅𐐲𐑊𐐲𐑋, 𐑋𐐲𐑅𐐻 𐐺 𐑁𐐳𐑊𐑁𐐮𐑊𐐼. 𐐙𐐫𐑉 𐐺𐐨𐐸𐐬𐑊𐐼, 𐑄 𐐝𐐹𐐮𐑉𐐮𐐻 𐐲𐑂 𐑄 𐐢𐐫𐑉𐐼 𐑅𐐨𐑅𐐲𐑃 𐑅𐐭𐑌 𐐻𐐭 𐑅𐐻𐑉𐐴𐑂 𐐶𐐮𐑄 𐑄𐐯𐑋; 𐑁𐐫𐑉 𐐺𐐨𐐸𐐬𐑊𐐼, 𐑄𐐩 𐐸𐐰𐑂 𐑉𐐨𐐾𐐯𐐿𐐻𐐯𐐼 𐑄 𐐹𐑉𐐱𐑁𐐯𐐻𐑅, 𐐰𐑌𐐼 𐐖𐐯𐑉𐐨𐑋𐐴𐐲 𐐸𐐰𐑂 𐑄𐐩 𐐿𐐰𐑅𐐻 𐐮𐑌𐐻𐐭 𐐹𐑉𐐮𐑆𐐲𐑌. 𐐈𐑌𐐼 𐑄𐐩 𐐸𐐰𐑂 𐑅𐐫𐐻 𐐻𐐭 𐐻𐐩𐐿 𐐰𐐶𐐩 𐑄 𐑊𐐴𐑁 𐐲𐑂 𐑋𐐴 𐑁𐐪𐑄𐐲𐑉, 𐐮𐑌𐑅𐐬𐑋𐐲𐐽 𐑄𐐰𐐻 𐑄𐐩 𐐸𐐰𐑂 𐐼𐑉𐐮𐑂𐑌 𐐸𐐮𐑋 𐐵𐐻 𐐲𐑂 𐑄 𐑊𐐰𐑌𐐼.

7. 𐐤𐐵 𐐺𐐨𐐸𐐬𐑊𐐼, 𐐌 𐑅𐐩 𐐲𐑌𐐻𐐭 𐐷𐐭, 𐑄𐐰𐐻 𐐮𐑁 𐐷 𐐶𐐮𐑊 𐑉𐐨𐐻𐐲𐑉𐑌 𐐲𐑌𐐻𐐭 𐐖𐐨𐑉𐐭𐑅𐐲𐑊𐐲𐑋, 𐐷 𐑇𐐰𐑊 𐐫𐑊𐑅𐐬 𐐹𐐯𐑉𐐮𐑇 𐐶𐐮𐑄 𐑄𐐯𐑋. 𐐈𐑌𐐼 𐑌𐐵, 𐐮𐑁 𐐷 𐐸𐐰𐑂 𐐽𐐦𐑅, 𐑀𐐬 𐐲𐐹 𐐻𐐭 𐑄 𐑊𐐰𐑌𐐼, 𐐰𐑌𐐼 𐑉𐐨𐑋𐐯𐑋𐐺𐐲𐑉 𐑄 𐐶𐐲𐑉𐐼𐑆 𐐸𐐶𐐮𐐽 𐐌 𐑅𐐹𐐨𐐿 𐐲𐑌𐐻𐐭 𐐷𐐭, 𐑄𐐰𐐻 𐐮𐑁 𐐷 𐑀𐐬 𐐷 𐐶𐐮𐑊 𐐫𐑊𐑅𐐬 𐐹𐐯𐑉𐐮𐑇; 𐑁𐐫𐑉 𐑄𐐲𐑅 𐑄 𐐝𐐹𐐮𐑉𐐮𐐻 𐐲𐑂 𐑄 𐐢𐐫𐑉𐐼 𐐿𐐲𐑌𐑅𐐻𐑉𐐩𐑌𐐯𐑃 𐑋𐐨 𐑄𐐰𐐻 𐐌 𐑇𐐳𐐼 𐑅𐐹𐐨𐐿.

8. 𐐈𐑌𐐼 𐐮𐐻 𐐿𐐩𐑋 𐐻𐐭 𐐹𐐰𐑅 𐑄𐐰𐐻 𐐸𐐶𐐯𐑌 𐐌, 𐐤𐐨𐑁𐐴, 𐐸𐐰𐐼 𐑅𐐹𐐬𐐿𐑌 𐑄𐐨𐑆 𐐶𐐲𐑉𐐼𐑆 𐐲𐑌𐐻𐐭 𐑋𐐴 𐐺𐑉𐐯𐑄𐑉𐐯𐑌, 𐑄𐐩 𐐶𐐲𐑉 𐐰𐑍𐑀𐑉𐐨 𐐶𐐮𐑄 𐑋𐐨. 𐐈𐑌𐐼 𐐮𐐻 𐐿𐐩𐑋 𐐻𐐭 𐐹𐐰𐑅 𐑄𐐰𐐻 𐑄𐐩 𐐼𐐮𐐼 𐑊𐐩 𐑄𐐩𐑉 𐐸𐐰𐑌𐐼𐑆 𐐲𐐹𐐱𐑌 𐑋𐐨—𐑁𐐫𐑉 𐐺𐐨𐐸𐐬𐑊𐐼, 𐑄𐐩 𐐶𐐲𐑉 𐐯𐐿𐑅𐐨𐐼𐐮𐑍 𐑉𐐫𐑃—𐐰𐑌𐐼 𐑄𐐩 𐐼𐐮𐐼 𐐺𐐴𐑌𐐼 𐑋𐐨 𐐶𐐮𐑄 𐐿𐐫𐑉𐐼𐑆, 𐑁𐐫𐑉 𐑄𐐩 𐑅𐐫𐐻 𐐻𐐭 𐐻𐐩𐐿 𐐰𐐶𐐩 𐑋𐐴 𐑊𐐴𐑁, 𐑄𐐰𐐻 𐑄𐐩 𐑋𐐴𐐻 𐑊𐐨𐑂 𐑋𐐨 𐐮𐑌 𐑄 𐐶𐐮𐑊𐐼𐐲𐑉𐑌𐐯𐑅 𐐻𐐭 𐐺 𐐼𐐨𐑂𐐵𐑉𐐼 𐐺𐐴 𐐶𐐴𐑊𐐼 𐐺𐐨𐑅𐐻𐑅.

9. 𐐒𐐲𐐻 𐐮𐐻 𐐿𐐩𐑋 𐐻𐐭 𐐹𐐰𐑅 𐑄𐐰𐐻 𐐌 𐐹𐑉𐐩𐐼 𐐲𐑌𐐻𐐭 𐑄 𐐢𐐫𐑉𐐼, 𐑅𐐩𐐮𐑍, 𐐄 𐐢𐐫𐑉𐐼, 𐐰𐐿𐐫𐑉𐐼𐐮𐑍 𐐻𐐭 𐑋𐐴 𐑁𐐩𐑃 𐐸𐐶𐐮𐐽 𐐮𐑆 𐐮𐑌 𐑄, 𐐶𐐮𐑊𐐻 𐑄𐐵 𐐼𐐨𐑊𐐮𐑂𐐲𐑉 𐑋𐐨 𐑁𐑉𐐱𐑋 𐑄 𐐸𐐰𐑌𐐼𐑆 𐐲𐑂 𐑋𐐴 𐐺𐑉𐐯𐑄𐑉𐐯𐑌; 𐐷𐐩, 𐐨𐑂𐑌 𐑀𐐮𐑂 𐑋𐐨 𐑅𐐻𐑉𐐯𐑍𐑃 𐑄𐐰𐐻 𐐌 𐑋𐐩 𐐺𐐲𐑉𐑅𐐻 𐑄𐐨𐑆 𐐺𐐰𐑌𐐼𐑆 𐐶𐐮𐑄 𐐸𐐶𐐮𐐽 𐐌 𐐰𐑋 𐐺𐐵𐑌𐐼.

10. 𐐈𐑌𐐼 𐐮𐐻 𐐿𐐩𐑋 𐐻𐐭 𐐹𐐰𐑅 𐑄𐐰𐐻 𐐸𐐶𐐯𐑌 𐐌 𐐸𐐰𐐼 𐑅𐐯𐐼 𐑄𐐨𐑆 𐐶𐐲𐑉𐐼𐑆, 𐐺𐐨𐐸𐐬𐑊𐐼, 𐑄 𐐺𐐰𐑌𐐼𐑆 𐐶𐐲𐑉 𐑊𐐭𐑅𐐻 𐑁𐑉𐐱𐑋 𐐱𐑁 𐑋𐐴 𐐸𐐰𐑌𐐼𐑆 𐐰𐑌𐐼 𐑁𐐨𐐻, 𐐰𐑌𐐼 𐐌 𐑅𐐻𐐳𐐼 𐐺𐐨𐑁𐐬𐑉 𐑋𐐴 𐐺𐑉𐐯𐑄𐑉𐐯𐑌, 𐐰𐑌𐐼 𐐌 𐑅𐐹𐐩𐐿 𐐲𐑌𐐻𐐭 𐑄𐐯𐑋 𐐰𐑀𐐯𐑌.

11. 𐐈𐑌𐐼 𐐮𐐻 𐐿𐐩𐑋 𐐻𐐭 𐐹𐐰𐑅 𐑄𐐰𐐻 𐑄𐐩 𐐶𐐲𐑉 𐐰𐑍𐑀𐑉𐐨 𐐶𐐮𐑄 𐑋𐐨 𐐰𐑀𐐯𐑌, 𐐰𐑌𐐼 𐑅𐐫𐐻 𐐻𐐭 𐑊𐐩 𐐸𐐰𐑌𐐼𐑆 𐐲𐐹𐐱𐑌 𐑋𐐨; 𐐺𐐲𐐻 𐐺𐐨𐐸𐐬𐑊𐐼, 𐐶𐐲𐑌 𐐲𐑂 𐑄 𐐼𐐫𐐻𐐲𐑉𐑆 𐐲𐑂 𐐆𐑇𐑋𐐩𐐯𐑊, 𐐷𐐩, 𐐰𐑌𐐼 𐐫𐑊𐑅𐐬 𐐸𐐲𐑉 𐑋𐐲𐑄𐐲𐑉, 𐐰𐑌𐐼 𐐶𐐲𐑌 𐐲𐑂 𐑄 𐑅𐐲𐑌𐑆 𐐲𐑂 𐐆𐑇𐑋𐐩𐐯𐑊, 𐐼𐐮𐐼 𐐹𐑊𐐨𐐼 𐐶𐐮𐑄 𐑋𐐴 𐐺𐑉𐐯𐑄𐑉𐐯𐑌, 𐐮𐑌𐑅𐐬𐑋𐐲𐐽 𐑄𐐰𐐻 𐑄𐐩 𐐼𐐮𐐼 𐑅𐐱𐑁𐑌 𐑄𐐩𐑉 𐐸𐐪𐑉𐐻𐑅; 𐐰𐑌𐐼 𐑄𐐩 𐐼𐐮𐐼 𐑅𐐨𐑅 𐑅𐐻𐑉𐐴𐑂𐐮𐑍 𐐻𐐭 𐐻𐐩𐐿 𐐰𐐶𐐩 𐑋𐐴 𐑊𐐴𐑁.

12. 𐐈𐑌𐐼 𐐮𐐻 𐐿𐐩𐑋 𐐻𐐭 𐐹𐐰𐑅 𐑄𐐰𐐻 𐑄𐐩 𐐶𐐲𐑉 𐑅𐐱𐑉𐐬𐑁𐐳𐑊, 𐐺𐐨𐐿𐐫𐑆 𐐲𐑂 𐑄𐐩𐑉 𐐶𐐮𐐿𐐯𐐼𐑌𐐯𐑅, 𐐮𐑌𐑅𐐬-𐑋𐐲𐐽 𐑄𐐰𐐻 𐑄𐐩 𐐼𐐮𐐼 𐐺𐐵 𐐼𐐵𐑌 𐐺𐐨𐑁𐐬𐑉 𐑋𐐨, 𐐰𐑌𐐼 𐐼𐐮𐐼 𐐹𐑊𐐨𐐼 𐐶𐐮𐑄 𐑋𐐨, 𐑄𐐰𐐻 𐐌 𐐶𐐳𐐼 𐑁𐐲𐑉𐑀𐐮𐑂 𐑄𐐯𐑋 𐐲𐑂 𐑄 𐑃𐐮𐑍 𐑄𐐰𐐻 𐑄𐐩 𐐸𐐰𐐼 𐐼𐐲𐑌 𐐰𐑀𐐯𐑌𐑅𐐻 𐑋𐐨.

13. 𐐈𐑌𐐼 𐐮𐐻 𐐿𐐩𐑋 𐐻𐐭 𐐹𐐰𐑅 𐑄𐐰𐐻 𐐌 𐐼𐐮𐐼 𐑁𐑉𐐰𐑍𐐿𐑊𐐨 𐑁𐐲𐑉𐑀𐐮𐑂 𐑄𐐯𐑋 𐐫𐑊 𐑄𐐰𐐻 𐑄𐐩 𐐸𐐰𐐼 𐐼𐐲𐑌, 𐐰𐑌𐐼 𐐌 𐐼𐐮𐐼 𐐯𐑀𐑆𐐫𐑉𐐻 𐑄𐐯𐑋 𐑄𐐰𐐻 𐑄𐐩 𐐶𐐳𐐼 𐐹𐑉𐐩 𐐲𐑌𐐻𐐭 𐑄 𐐢𐐫𐑉𐐼 𐑄𐐩𐑉 𐐘𐐱𐐼 𐑁𐐫𐑉 𐑁𐐲𐑉𐑀𐐮𐑂𐑌𐐯𐑅. 𐐈𐑌𐐼 𐐮𐐻 𐐿𐐩𐑋 𐐻𐐭 𐐹𐐰𐑅 𐑄𐐰𐐻 𐑄𐐩 𐐼𐐮𐐼 𐑅𐐬. 𐐈𐑌𐐼 𐐰𐑁𐐻𐐲𐑉 𐑄𐐩 𐐸𐐰𐐼 𐐼𐐲𐑌 𐐹𐑉𐐩𐐮𐑍 𐐲𐑌𐐻𐐭 𐑄 𐐢𐐫𐑉𐐼, 𐐶𐐨 𐐼𐐮𐐼 𐐰𐑀𐐯𐑌 𐐻𐑉𐐰𐑂𐐯𐑊 𐐱𐑌 𐐵𐑉 𐐾𐐲𐑉𐑌𐐨 𐐻𐐬𐐲𐑉𐐼𐑆 𐑄 𐐻𐐯𐑌𐐻 𐐲𐑂 𐐵𐑉 𐑁𐐪𐑄𐐲𐑉.

14. 𐐈𐑌𐐼 𐐮𐐻 𐐿𐐩𐑋 𐐻𐐭 𐐹𐐰𐑅 𐑄𐐰𐐻 𐐶𐐨 𐐼𐐮𐐼 𐐿𐐲𐑋 𐐼𐐵𐑌 𐐲𐑌𐐻𐐭 𐑄 𐐻𐐯𐑌𐐻 𐐲𐑂 𐐵𐑉 𐑁𐐪𐑄𐐲𐑉. 𐐈𐑌𐐼 𐐰𐑁𐐻𐐲𐑉 𐐌 𐐰𐑌𐐼 𐑋𐐴 𐐺𐑉𐐯𐑄𐑉𐐯𐑌, 𐐰𐑌𐐼 𐐫𐑊 𐑄 𐐸𐐵𐑅 𐐲𐑂 𐐆𐑇𐑋𐐩𐐯𐑊, 𐐸𐐰𐐼 𐐿𐐲𐑋 𐐼𐐵𐑌 𐐲𐑌𐐻𐐭 𐑄 𐐻𐐯𐑌𐐻 𐐲𐑂 𐑋𐐴 𐑁𐐪𐑄𐐲𐑉, 𐑄𐐩 𐐼𐐮𐐼 𐑀𐐮𐑂 𐑃𐐰𐑍𐐿𐑅 𐐲𐑌𐐻𐐭 𐑄 𐐢𐐫𐑉𐐼 𐑄𐐩𐑉 𐐘𐐱𐐼; 𐐰𐑌𐐼 𐑄𐐩 𐐼𐐮𐐼 𐐱𐑁𐐲𐑉 𐑅𐐰𐐿𐑉𐐮𐑁𐐴𐑆 𐐰𐑌𐐼 𐐺𐐲𐑉𐑌𐐻 𐐱𐑁𐐲𐑉𐐮𐑍𐑆 𐐲𐑌𐐻𐐭 𐐸𐐮𐑋.

15. 𐐈𐑌𐐼 𐐮𐐻 𐐿𐐩𐑋 𐐻𐐭 𐐹𐐰𐑅 𐑄𐐰𐐻 𐐶𐐨 𐐸𐐰𐐼 𐑀𐐰𐑄𐐲𐑉𐐼 𐐻𐐳𐑀𐐯𐑄𐐲𐑉 𐐫𐑊 𐑋𐐰𐑌𐐲𐑉 𐐲𐑂 𐑅𐐨𐐼𐑆 𐐲𐑂 𐐯𐑂𐐲𐑉𐐨 𐐿𐐴𐑌𐐼, 𐐺𐐬𐑃 𐐲𐑂 𐑀𐑉𐐩𐑌 𐐲𐑂 𐐯𐑂𐐲𐑉𐐨 𐐿𐐴𐑌𐐼, 𐐰𐑌𐐼 𐐫𐑊𐑅𐐬 𐐲𐑂 𐑄 𐑅𐐨𐐼𐑆 𐐲𐑂 𐑁𐑉𐐭𐐻 𐐲𐑂 𐐯𐑂𐐲𐑉𐐨 𐐿𐐴𐑌𐐼. 𐐈𐑌𐐼 𐐮𐐻 𐐿𐐩𐑋 𐐻𐐭 𐐹𐐰𐑅 𐑄𐐰𐐻 𐐸𐐶𐐴𐑊 𐑋𐐴 𐑁𐐪𐑄𐐲𐑉 𐐻𐐰𐑉𐐨𐐼 𐐮𐑌 𐑄 𐐶𐐮𐑊𐐼𐐲𐑉𐑌𐐯𐑅, 𐐸𐐨 𐑅𐐹𐐩𐐿

𐐲𐑌𐐻𐐭 𐑋𐐨, 𐐷𐐩, 𐐺𐐨𐐸𐐬𐑊𐐼, 𐐌 𐐸𐐰𐑂 𐐼𐑉𐐨𐑋𐐼 𐐲 𐐼𐑉𐐨𐑋; 𐐫𐑉, 𐐮𐑌 𐐲𐑄𐐲𐑉 𐐶𐐲𐑉𐐼𐑆, 𐐌 𐐸𐐰𐑂 𐑅𐐨𐑌 𐐲 𐑂𐐮𐑈𐐲𐑌. 𐐈𐑌𐐼 𐐺𐐨𐐸𐐬𐑊𐐼, 𐐺𐐨𐐿𐐫𐑆 𐐱𐑂 𐑄 𐑃𐐮𐑍 𐐸𐐶𐐮𐐽 𐐌 𐐸𐐰𐑂 𐑅𐐨𐑌, 𐐌 𐐸𐐰𐑂 𐑉𐐨𐑆𐐲𐑌 𐐻𐐭 𐑉𐐨𐐾𐑎𐑅 𐐮𐑌 𐑄 𐐢𐐫𐑉𐐼 𐐺𐐨𐐿𐐫𐑆 𐐱𐑂 𐐤𐐨𐑁𐐴 𐐰𐑌𐐼 𐐫𐑊𐑅𐐬 𐐱𐑂 𐐝𐐰𐑋; 𐑁𐐫𐑉 𐐌 𐐸𐐰𐑂 𐑉𐐨𐑆𐐲𐑌 𐐻𐐭 𐑅𐐲𐐹𐐬𐑆 𐑄𐐰𐐻 𐑄𐐩, 𐐰𐑌𐐼 𐐫𐑊𐑅𐐬 𐑋𐐯𐑌𐐨 𐐱𐑂 𐑄𐐩𐑉 𐑅𐐨𐐼, 𐐶𐐮𐑊 𐐺𐐨 𐑅𐐩𐑂𐐼. 𐐒𐐲𐐻 𐐺𐐨𐐸𐐬𐑊𐐼, 𐐢𐐩𐑋𐐲𐑌 𐐰𐑌𐐼 𐐢𐐯𐑋𐐷𐐭𐐯𐑊, 𐐌 𐑁𐐨𐑉 𐐯𐐿𐑅𐐨𐐼𐐮𐑍𐑊𐐨 𐐺𐐨𐐿𐐫𐑆 𐐱𐑂 𐐷𐐭; 𐑁𐐫𐑉 𐐺𐐨𐐸𐐬𐑊𐐼, 𐑋𐐨𐑃𐐫𐐻 𐐌 𐑅𐐫 𐐮𐑌 𐑋𐐴 𐐼𐑉𐐨𐑋, 𐐲 𐐼𐐪𐑉𐐿 𐐰𐑌𐐼 𐐼𐑉𐐨𐑉𐐨 𐐶𐐮𐑊𐐼𐐲𐑉𐑌𐐯𐑅.

16. 𐐈𐑌𐐼 𐐮𐐻 𐐿𐐩𐑋 𐐻𐐭 𐐹𐐰𐑅 𐑄𐐰𐐻 𐐌 𐑅𐐫 𐐲 𐑋𐐰𐑌, 𐐰𐑌𐐼 𐐸𐐨 𐐶𐐱𐑆 𐐼𐑉𐐯𐑅𐐻 𐐮𐑌 𐐲 𐐸𐐶𐐴𐐻 𐑉𐐬𐐺: 𐐰𐑌𐐼 𐐸𐐨 𐐿𐐩𐑋 𐐰𐑌𐐼 𐑅𐐻𐐳𐐼 𐐺𐐨𐑁𐐬𐑉 𐑋𐐨. 𐐈𐑌𐐼 𐐮𐐻 𐐿𐐩𐑋 𐐻𐐭 𐐹𐐰𐑅 𐑄𐐰𐐻 𐐸𐐨 𐑅𐐹𐐩𐐿 𐐲𐑌𐐻𐐭 𐑋𐐨, 𐐰𐑌𐐼 𐐺𐐰𐐼 𐑋𐐨 𐑁𐐱𐑊𐐬 𐐸𐐮𐑋. 𐐈𐑌𐐼 𐐮𐐻 𐐿𐐩𐑋 𐐻𐐭 𐐹𐐰𐑅 𐑄𐐰𐐻 𐐰𐑆 𐐌 𐑁𐐱𐑊𐐬𐐼 𐐸𐐮𐑋, 𐐌 𐐺𐐨𐐸𐐯𐑊𐐼 𐑋𐐴𐑅𐐯𐑊𐑁 𐑄𐐰𐐻 𐐌 𐐶𐐱𐑆 𐐮𐑌 𐐲 𐐼𐐪𐑉𐐿 𐐰𐑌𐐼 𐐼𐑉𐐨𐑉𐐨 𐐶𐐩𐑅𐐻. 𐐈𐑌𐐼 𐐰𐑁𐐻𐐲𐑉 𐐌 𐐸𐐰𐐼 𐐻𐑉𐐰𐑂𐐯𐑊𐐼 𐑁𐐫𐑉 𐑄 𐑅𐐹𐐩𐑅 𐐱𐑂 𐑋𐐯𐑌𐐨 𐐵𐐲𐑉𐑆 𐐮𐑌 𐐼𐐪𐑉𐐿𐑌𐐯𐑅, 𐐌 𐐺𐐨𐑀𐐰𐑌 𐐻𐐭 𐐹𐑉𐐩 𐐲𐑌𐐻𐐭 𐑄 𐐢𐐫𐑉𐐼, 𐑄𐐰𐐻 𐐸𐐨 𐐶𐐳𐐼 𐐸𐐰𐑂 𐑋𐐲𐑉𐑅𐐨 𐐱𐑌 𐑋𐐨, 𐐰𐐿𐐫𐑉𐐼𐐮𐑍 𐐻𐐭 𐑄 𐑋𐐲𐑊𐐻𐐮𐐻𐐷𐐭𐐼 𐐱𐑂 𐐸𐐮𐑆 𐐻𐐯𐑌𐐼𐐲𐑉 𐑋𐐲𐑉𐑅𐐨𐑆.

17. 𐐈𐑌𐐼 𐐮𐐻 𐐿𐐩𐑋 𐐻𐐭 𐐹𐐰𐑅 𐐰𐑁𐐻𐐲𐑉 𐐌 𐐸𐐰𐐼 𐐹𐑉𐐩𐐼 𐐲𐑌𐐻𐐭 𐑄 𐐢𐐫𐑉𐐼, 𐐌 𐐺𐐨𐐸𐐯𐑊𐐼 𐐲 𐑊𐐪𐑉𐐾 𐐰𐑌𐐼 𐑅𐐹𐐩𐑇𐐲𐑅 𐑁𐐨𐑊𐐼. 𐐈𐑌𐐼 𐐮𐐻 𐐿𐐩𐑋 𐐻𐐭 𐐹𐐰𐑅 𐑄𐐰𐐻 𐐌 𐐺𐐨𐐸𐐯𐑊𐐼 𐐲 𐐻𐑉𐐨, 𐐸𐐭𐑆 𐑁𐑉𐐭𐐻 𐐶𐐱𐑆 𐐼𐐨𐑆𐐴𐑉𐐲𐐺𐑊 𐐻𐐭 𐑋𐐩𐐿 𐐶𐐲𐑌 𐐸𐐰𐐹𐐨.

18. 𐐈𐑌𐐼 𐐮𐐻 𐐿𐐩𐑋 𐐻𐐭 𐐹𐐰𐑅 𐑄𐐰𐐻 𐐌 𐐼𐐮𐐼 𐑀𐐬 𐑁𐐬𐑉𐑃, 𐐰𐑌𐐼 𐐹𐐪𐑉𐐻𐐩𐐿 𐐱𐑂 𐑄 𐑁𐑉𐐭𐐻 𐑄𐐩𐑉𐐱𐑂, 𐐰𐑌𐐼 𐐌 𐐺𐐨𐐸𐐯𐑊𐐼 𐑄𐐰𐐻 𐐮𐐻 𐐶𐐱𐑆 𐑋𐐬𐑅𐐻 𐑅𐐶𐐨𐐻 𐐲𐐺𐐲𐑂 𐐫𐑊 𐑄𐐰𐐻 𐐌 𐐯𐑂𐐲𐑉 𐐺𐐨𐑁𐐬𐑉 𐐻𐐩𐑅𐐻𐐯𐐼. 𐐏𐐩, 𐐰𐑌𐐼 𐐌 𐐺𐐨𐐸𐐯𐑊𐐼 𐑄𐐰𐐻 𐑄 𐑁𐑉𐐭𐐻 𐑄𐐩𐑉𐐱𐑂 𐐶𐐱𐑆 𐐸𐐶𐐴𐐻 𐐻𐐭 𐐯𐐿𐑅𐐨𐐼 𐐫𐑊 𐑄 𐐸𐐶𐐴𐐻𐑌𐐯𐑅 𐑄𐐰𐐻 𐐌 𐐸𐐰𐐼 𐐯𐑂𐐲𐑉 𐑅𐐨𐑌. 𐐈𐑌𐐼 𐐰𐑆 𐐌 𐐹𐐪𐑉𐐻𐐳𐐿 𐐱𐑂 𐑄 𐑁𐑉𐐭𐐻 𐑄𐐩𐑉𐐱𐑂, 𐐮𐐻 𐑁𐐮𐑊𐐼 𐑋𐐴 𐑅𐐬𐑊 𐐶𐐮𐑄 𐐯𐐿𐑅𐐨𐐼𐐮𐑍 𐑀𐑉𐐩𐐻 𐐾𐑎; 𐐸𐐶𐐩𐑉𐑁𐐬𐑉, 𐐌 𐐺𐐨𐑀𐐰𐑌 𐐻𐐭 𐐺𐐨 𐐼𐐨𐑆𐐴𐑉𐐲𐑅 𐑄𐐰𐐻 𐑋𐐴 𐑁𐐰𐑋𐐮𐑊𐐨 𐑇𐐳𐐼 𐐹𐐪𐑉𐐻𐐩𐐿 𐐱𐑂 𐐮𐐻 𐐫𐑊𐑅𐐬; 𐑁𐐫𐑉 𐐌 𐑌𐐭 𐑄𐐰𐐻 𐐮𐐻 𐐶𐐱𐑆 𐐼𐐨𐑆𐐴𐑉𐐲𐐺𐑊 𐐲𐐺𐐲𐑂 𐐫𐑊 𐐲𐑄𐐲𐑉 𐑁𐑉𐐭𐐻. 𐐈𐑌𐐼 𐐰𐑆 𐐌 𐐿𐐰𐑅𐐻 𐑋𐐴 𐐴𐑆 𐑉𐐵𐑌𐐼 𐐲𐐺𐐵𐐻, 𐑄𐐰𐐻 𐐹𐐲𐑉𐐸𐐰𐐹𐑅 𐐌 𐑋𐐴𐐻 𐐼𐐮𐑅𐐿𐐲𐑂𐐲𐑉 𐑋𐐴 𐑁𐐰𐑋𐐮𐑊𐐨 𐐫𐑊𐑅𐐬, 𐐌 𐐺𐐨𐐸𐐯𐑊𐐼 𐐲 𐑉𐐮𐑂𐐲𐑉 𐐱𐑂 𐐶𐐫𐐻𐐲𐑉; 𐐰𐑌𐐼 𐐮𐐻 𐑉𐐰𐑌 𐐲𐑊𐐱𐑍, 𐐰𐑌𐐼 𐐮𐐻 𐐶𐐱𐑆 𐑌𐐨𐑉 𐑄 𐐻𐑉𐐨 𐐱𐑂 𐐸𐐶𐐮𐐽 𐐌 𐐶𐐱𐑆 𐐹𐐪𐑉𐐻𐐩𐐿𐐮𐑍 𐑄 𐑁𐑉𐐭𐐻. 𐐈𐑌𐐼 𐐌 𐑊𐐳𐐿𐐻 𐐻𐐭 𐐺𐐨𐐸𐐬𐑊𐐼 𐑁𐑉𐐱𐑋 𐐸𐐶𐐯𐑌𐑅 𐐮𐐻 𐐿𐐩𐑋; 𐐰𐑌𐐼 𐐌 𐑅𐐫 𐑄 𐐸𐐯𐐼 𐑄𐐩𐑉𐐱𐑂 𐐲 𐑊𐐮𐐻𐑊 𐐶𐐩 𐐫𐑁; 𐐰𐑌𐐼 𐐰𐐻 𐑄 𐐸𐐯𐐼 𐑄𐐩𐑉𐐱𐑂, 𐐌 𐐺𐐨𐐸𐐯𐑊𐐼 𐐷𐐭𐑉 𐑋𐐲𐑄𐐲𐑉, 𐐝𐐯𐑉𐐴𐐲, 𐐰𐑌𐐼 𐐝𐐰𐑋, 𐐰𐑌𐐼 𐐤𐐨𐑁𐐴; 𐐰𐑌𐐼 𐑄𐐩 𐑅𐐻𐐳𐐼 𐐰𐑆 𐐮𐑁 𐑄𐐩 𐑌𐐭 𐑌𐐱𐐻 𐐸𐐶𐐮𐑄𐐲𐑉 𐑄𐐩 𐑇𐐳𐐼 𐑀𐐬.

19. 𐐈𐑌𐐼 𐐮𐐻 𐐿𐐩𐑋 𐐻𐐭 𐐹𐐰𐑅 𐑄𐐰𐐻 𐐌 𐐺𐐯𐐿𐐲𐑌𐐼 𐐲𐑌𐐻𐐭 𐑄𐐯𐑋; 𐐰𐑌𐐼 𐐌 𐐫𐑊𐑅𐐬 𐐼𐐮𐐼 𐑅𐐩 𐐲𐑌𐐻𐐭 𐑄𐐯𐑋 𐐶𐐮𐑄 𐐲 𐑊𐐵𐐼 𐑂𐑎𐑅 𐑄𐐰𐐻 𐑄𐐩 𐑇𐐳𐐼 𐐿𐐲𐑋 𐐲𐑌𐐻𐐭 𐑋𐐨, 𐐰𐑌𐐼 𐐹𐐪𐑉𐐻𐐩𐐿 𐐱𐑂 𐑄 𐑁𐑉𐐭𐐻 𐐸𐐶𐐮𐐽 𐐶𐐱𐑆 𐐼𐐨𐑆𐐴𐑉𐐲𐐺𐑊 𐐲𐐺𐐲𐑂 𐐫𐑊 𐐲𐑄𐐲𐑉 𐑁𐑉𐐭𐐻.

20. 𐐈𐑌𐐼 𐐮𐐻 𐐿𐐩𐑋 𐐻𐐭 𐐹𐐰𐑅 𐑄𐐰𐐻 𐑄𐐩 𐐼𐐮𐐼 𐐿𐐲𐑋 𐐲𐑌𐐻𐐭 𐑋𐐨, 𐐰𐑌𐐼 𐐹𐐪𐑉𐐻𐐩𐐿 𐐱𐑂 𐑄 𐑁𐑉𐐭𐐻 𐐫𐑊𐑅𐐬. 𐐈𐑌𐐼 𐐮𐐻 𐐿𐐩𐑋 𐐻𐐭 𐐹𐐰𐑅 𐑄𐐰𐐻 𐐌 𐐶𐐱𐑆 𐐼𐐨𐑆𐐴𐑉𐐲𐑅 𐑄𐐰𐐻 𐐢𐐩𐑋𐐲𐑌 𐐰𐑌𐐼 𐐢𐐯𐑋𐐷𐐭𐐯𐑊 𐑇𐐳𐐼 𐐿𐐲𐑋 𐐰𐑌𐐼 𐐹𐐪𐑉𐐻𐐩𐐿 𐐱𐑂 𐑄 𐑁𐑉𐐭𐐻 𐐫𐑊𐑅𐐬; 𐐸𐐶𐐩𐑉𐑁𐐬𐑉 𐐌 𐐿𐐰𐑅𐐻 𐑋𐐴𐑌 𐐴𐑆 𐐻𐐬𐑉𐐼𐑆 𐑄 𐐸𐐯𐐼 𐐱𐑂 𐑄 𐑉𐐮𐑂𐐲𐑉, 𐑄𐐰𐐻 𐐹𐐲𐑉𐐸𐐰𐐹𐑅 𐐌 𐑋𐐴𐐻 𐑅𐐨 𐑄𐐯𐑋.

21. 𐐈𐑌𐐼 𐐮𐐻 𐐿𐐩𐑋 𐐻𐐭 𐐹𐐰𐑅 𐑄𐐰𐐻 𐐌 𐑅𐐫 𐑄𐐯𐑋, 𐐺𐐲𐐻 𐑄𐐩 𐐶𐐳𐐼 𐑌𐐱𐐻 𐐿𐐲𐑋 𐐲𐑌𐐻𐐭 𐑋𐐨. 𐐈𐑌𐐼 𐐌 𐐺𐐨𐐸𐐯𐑊𐐼 𐐲 𐑉𐐱𐐼 𐐱𐑂 𐐴𐐲𐑉𐑌, 𐐰𐑌𐐼 𐐮𐐻 𐐯𐐿𐑅𐐻𐐯𐑌𐐼𐐯𐐼 𐐲𐑊𐐱𐑍 𐑄 𐐺𐐰𐑍𐐿 𐐱𐑂 𐑄 𐑉𐐮𐑂𐐲𐑉, 𐐰𐑌𐐼 𐑊𐐯𐐼 𐐻𐐭 𐑄 𐐻𐑉𐐨 𐐺𐐴 𐐸𐐶𐐮𐐽 𐐌 𐑅𐐻𐐳𐐼. 𐐈𐑌𐐼 𐐌 𐐫𐑊𐑅𐐬 𐐺𐐨𐐸𐐯𐑊𐐼 𐐲 𐑅𐐻𐑉𐐩𐐻 𐐰𐑌𐐼 𐑌𐐰𐑉𐐬 𐐹𐐪𐑃, 𐐸𐐶𐐮𐐽 𐐿𐐩𐑋 𐐲𐑊𐐱𐑍 𐐺𐐴 𐑄 𐑉𐐱𐐼 𐐱𐑂 𐐴𐐲𐑉𐑌, 𐐨𐑂𐐲𐑌 𐐻𐐭 𐑄 𐐻𐑉𐐨 𐐺𐐴 𐐸𐐶𐐮𐐽 𐐌 𐑅𐐻𐐳𐐼; 𐐰𐑌𐐼 𐐮𐐻 𐐫𐑊𐑅𐐬 𐑊𐐯𐐼 𐐺𐐴 𐑄 𐐸𐐯𐐼 𐐱𐑂 𐑄 𐑁𐐵𐑌𐐻𐐲𐑌 𐐲𐑌𐐻𐐭 𐐲 𐑊𐐪𐑉𐐾 𐐰𐑌𐐼 𐑅𐐹𐐩𐑇𐐲𐑅 𐑁𐐨𐑊𐐼, 𐐰𐑆 𐐮𐑁 𐐮𐐻 𐐸𐐰𐐼 𐐺𐐮𐑌 𐐲 𐐶𐐲𐑉𐑊𐐼; 𐐰𐑌𐐼 𐐌 𐑅𐐫 𐑌𐐲𐑋𐐺𐐲𐑉𐑊𐐯𐑅 𐐿𐐱𐑍𐐿𐐬𐑉𐑅𐐯𐑆 𐐱𐑂 𐐹𐐨𐐹𐑊; 𐑋𐐯𐑌𐐨 𐐱𐑂 𐐸𐐭𐑋 𐐶𐐲𐑉 𐐹𐑉𐐯𐑅𐐮𐑍 𐑁𐐫𐑉𐐶𐐲𐑉𐐼, 𐑄𐐰𐐻 𐑄𐐩 𐑋𐐴𐐻 𐐱𐐺𐐻𐐩𐑌 𐑄 𐐹𐐪𐑃 𐐸𐐶𐐮𐐽 𐑊𐐯𐐼 𐐲𐑌𐐻𐐭 𐑄 𐐻𐑉𐐨 𐐺𐐴 𐐸𐐶𐐮𐐽 𐐌 𐑅𐐻𐐳𐐼.

22. 𐐈𐑌𐐼 𐐮𐐻 𐐿𐐩𐑋 𐐻𐐭 𐐹𐐪𐑅 𐑄𐐰𐐻 𐑄𐐩 𐐼𐐮𐐼 𐐿𐐲𐑋 𐑁𐐫𐑉𐑃, 𐐰𐑌𐐼 𐐿𐐲𐑋𐐯𐑌𐑅 𐐮𐑌 𐑄 𐐹𐐪𐑃 𐐸𐐶𐐮𐐽 𐑊𐐯𐐼 𐐻𐐭 𐑄 𐐻𐑉𐐨. 𐐈𐑌𐐼 𐐮𐐻 𐐿𐐩𐑋 𐐻𐐭 𐐹𐐪𐑅 𐑄𐐰𐐻 𐑄𐐩𐑉 𐐰𐑉𐐬𐑆 𐐩 𐑋𐐮𐑅𐐻 𐐱𐑂 𐐼𐐪𐑉𐐿𐑌𐐯𐑅; 𐐷𐐩, 𐐨𐑂𐐯𐑌 𐐰𐑌 𐐯𐐿𐑅𐐨𐐼𐐮𐑍𐑊𐐨 𐑀𐑉𐐩𐐻 𐑋𐐮𐑅𐐻 𐐱𐑂 𐐼𐐪𐑉𐐿𐑌𐐯𐑅, 𐐮𐑌𐑅𐐬𐑋𐐲𐐽 𐑄𐐰𐐻 𐑄𐐩 𐐸𐐭 𐐸𐐰𐐼 𐐿𐐲𐑋𐐯𐑌𐑅𐐻 𐐮𐑌 𐑄 𐐹𐐪𐑃 𐐼𐐮𐐼 𐑊𐐭𐑆 𐑄𐐩𐑉 𐐶𐐩, 𐑄𐐰𐐻 𐑄𐐩 𐐶𐐱𐑌𐐼𐐲𐑉𐐼 𐐱𐑁 𐐰𐑌𐐼 𐐶𐐲𐑉 𐑊𐐱𐑅𐐻.

23. 𐐈𐑌𐐼 𐐮𐐻 𐐿𐐩𐑋 𐐻𐐭 𐐹𐐪𐑅 𐑄𐐰𐐻 𐐌 𐐺𐐨𐐸𐐯𐑊𐐼 𐐲𐑄𐐲𐑉𐑆 𐐹𐑉𐐯𐑅𐐮𐑍 𐑁𐐫𐑉𐐶𐐲𐑉𐐼, 𐐰𐑌𐐼 𐑄𐐩 𐐿𐐩𐑋 𐑁𐐫𐑉𐑃 𐐰𐑌𐐼 𐐿𐐫𐐻 𐐸𐐬𐑊𐐼 𐐱𐑂 𐑄 𐐯𐑌𐐼 𐐱𐑂 𐑄 𐑉𐐬𐐼 𐐱𐑂 𐐴𐐲𐑉𐑌; 𐐰𐑌𐐼 𐑄𐐩 𐐼𐐮𐐼 𐐹𐑉𐐯𐑅 𐑁𐐫𐑉𐐶𐐲𐑉𐐼 𐑃𐑉𐐭 𐑄 𐑋𐐮𐑅𐐻 𐐱𐑂 𐐼𐐪𐑉𐐿𐑌𐐯𐑅, 𐐿𐑊𐐮𐑍𐐮𐑍 𐐻𐐭 𐑄 𐑉𐐬𐐼 𐐱𐑂 𐐴𐐲𐑉𐑌, 𐐨𐑂𐐯𐑌 𐐲𐑌𐐻𐐮𐑊 𐑄𐐩 𐐼𐐮𐐼 𐐿𐐲𐑋 𐑁𐐫𐑉𐑃 𐐰𐑌𐐼 𐐹𐐪𐑉𐐻𐐩𐐿 𐐱𐑂 𐑄 𐑁𐑉𐐭𐐻 𐐱𐑂 𐑄 𐐻𐑉𐐨. 𐐈𐑌𐐼 𐐪𐑁𐐻𐐲𐑉 𐑄𐐩 𐐸𐐰𐐼 𐐹𐐪𐑉𐐻𐐩𐐿𐑌 𐐱𐑂 𐑄 𐑁𐑉𐐭𐐻 𐐱𐑂 𐑄 𐐻𐑉𐐨, 𐑄𐐩 𐐼𐐮𐐼 𐐿𐐪𐑅𐐻 𐑄𐐩𐑉 𐐴𐑆 𐐰𐐺𐐵𐐻 𐐰𐑆 𐐮𐑁 𐑄𐐩 𐐶𐐲𐑉 𐐰𐑇𐐩𐑋𐐼. 𐐈𐑌𐐼 𐐌 𐐫𐑊𐑅𐐬 𐐿𐐪𐑅𐐻 𐑋𐐴 𐐴𐑆 𐑉𐐵𐑌𐐼 𐐰𐐺𐐵𐐻, 𐐰𐑌𐐼 𐐺𐐨𐐸𐐯𐑊𐐼, 𐐱𐑌 𐑄 𐐲𐑄𐐲𐑉 𐑅𐐴𐐼 𐐱𐑂 𐑄 𐑉𐐮𐑂𐐲𐑉 𐐱𐑂 𐐶𐐫𐐻𐐲𐑉, 𐐩 𐑀𐑉𐐩𐐻 𐐰𐑌𐐼 𐑅𐐹𐐩𐑇𐐲𐑅 𐐺𐐮𐑊𐐼𐐮𐑍, 𐐰𐑌𐐼 𐐮𐐻 𐑅𐐻𐐳𐐼 𐐰𐑆 𐐮𐐻 𐐶𐐲𐑉 𐐮𐑌 𐑄 𐐩𐑉, 𐐸𐐴 𐐰𐐺𐐲𐑂 𐑄 𐐲𐑉𐑃; 𐐰𐑌𐐼 𐐮𐐻 𐐶𐐱𐑆 𐑁𐐮𐑊𐐼 𐐶𐐮𐑄 𐐹𐐨𐐹𐑊, 𐐺𐐬𐑃 𐐬𐑊𐐼 𐐰𐑌𐐼 𐐷𐐲𐑍, 𐐺𐐬𐑃 𐑋𐐩𐑊 𐐰𐑌𐐼 𐑁𐐨𐑋𐐩𐑊; 𐐰𐑌𐐼 𐑄𐐩𐑉 𐑋𐐰𐑌𐐲𐑉 𐐱𐑂 𐐼𐑉𐐯𐑅 𐐶𐐱𐑆 𐐯𐐿𐑅𐐨𐐼𐐮𐑍𐑊𐐨 𐑁𐐴𐑌; 𐐰𐑌𐐼 𐑄𐐩 𐐶𐐲𐑉 𐐮𐑌 𐑄 𐐰𐐻𐐮𐐻𐐷𐐭𐐼 𐐱𐑂 𐑋𐐱𐐿𐐮𐑍 𐐰𐑌𐐼 𐐹𐑎𐑌𐐻𐐮𐑍 𐑄𐐩𐑉 𐑁𐐮𐑍𐑀𐐲𐑉𐑆 𐐻𐐬𐑉𐐼𐑆 𐑄𐐬𐑆 𐐸𐐭 𐐸𐐰𐐼 𐐿𐐲𐑋 𐐰𐐻, 𐐰𐑌𐐼 𐐶𐐲𐑉 𐐹𐐪𐑉𐐻𐐩𐐿𐐮𐑍 𐐱𐑂 𐑄 𐑁𐑉𐐭𐐻. 𐐈𐑌𐐼 𐐪𐑁𐐻𐐲𐑉 𐑄𐐩 𐐸𐐰𐐼 𐐻𐐩𐑅𐐻𐐯𐐼 𐐱𐑂 𐑄 𐑁𐑉𐐭𐐻 𐑄𐐩 𐐶𐐲𐑉 𐐰𐑇𐐩𐑋𐐼, 𐐺𐐨𐐿𐐫𐑆 𐐱𐑂 𐑄𐐬𐑆 𐑄𐐰𐐻 𐐶𐐲𐑉 𐑅𐐿𐐱𐑁𐐮𐑍 𐐰𐐻 𐑄𐐯𐑋; 𐐰𐑌𐐼 𐑄𐐩 𐑁𐐯𐑊 𐐰𐐶𐐩 𐐮𐑌𐐻𐐭 𐑁𐐲𐑉𐐺𐐮𐐼𐑌 𐐹𐐪𐑄𐑆, 𐐰𐑌𐐼 𐐶𐐲𐑉 𐑊𐐱𐑅𐐻.

24. 𐐈𐑌𐐼 𐑌𐐵 𐐌, 𐐤𐐨𐑁𐐴, 𐐼𐐭 𐑌𐐱𐐻 𐑅𐐹𐐨𐐿 𐐫𐑊 𐑄 𐐶𐐲𐑉𐐼𐑆 𐐱𐑂 𐑋𐐴 𐑁𐐪𐑄𐐲𐑉. 𐐒𐐲𐐻, 𐐻𐐭 𐐺 𐑇𐐫𐑉𐐻 𐐮𐑌 𐑉𐐴𐐻𐐮𐑍, 𐐒𐐨𐐸𐐬𐑊𐐼, 𐐸𐐨 𐑅𐐫 𐐲𐑄𐐲𐑉 𐑋𐐲𐑊𐐻𐐮𐐻𐐷𐐭𐐼𐑆 𐐹𐑉𐐯𐑅𐐮𐑍 𐑁𐐫𐑉𐐶𐐲𐑉𐐼; 𐐰𐑌𐐼 𐑄𐐩 𐐿𐐩𐑋 𐐰𐑌𐐼 𐐿𐐫𐐻 𐐸𐐬𐑊𐐼 𐐱𐑂 𐑄 𐐯𐑌𐐼 𐐱𐑂 𐑄 𐑉𐐬𐐼 𐐱𐑂 𐐴𐐲𐑉𐑌; 𐐰𐑌𐐼 𐑄𐐩 𐐼𐐮𐐼 𐐹𐑉𐐯𐑅 𐑄𐐩𐑉 𐐶𐐩 𐑁𐐫𐑉𐐶𐐲𐑉𐐼, 𐐿𐐲𐑌𐐻𐐮𐑌𐐷𐐭𐐲𐑊𐐨 𐐸𐐬𐑊𐐼𐐮𐑍 𐑁𐐪𐑅𐐻 𐐻𐐭 𐑄 𐑉𐐬𐐼 𐐱𐑂 𐐴𐐲𐑉𐑌, 𐐲𐑌𐐻𐐮𐑊 𐑄𐐩 𐐿𐐩𐑋 𐑁𐐫𐑉𐑃 𐐰𐑌𐐼 𐑁𐐯𐑊 𐐼𐐵𐑌 𐐰𐑌𐐼 𐐹𐐪𐑉𐐻𐐳𐐿 𐐱𐑂 𐑄 𐑁𐑉𐐭𐐻 𐐱𐑂 𐑄 𐐻𐑉𐐨. 𐐈𐑌𐐼 𐐸𐐨 𐐫𐑊𐑅𐐬 𐑅𐐫 𐐲𐑄𐐲𐑉 𐑋𐐲𐑊𐐻𐐮𐐻𐐷𐐭𐐼𐑆 𐑁𐐨𐑊𐐮𐑍 𐑄𐐩𐑉 𐐶𐐩 𐐻𐐬𐑉𐐼𐑆 𐑄𐐰𐐻 𐑀𐑉𐐩𐐻 𐐰𐑌𐐼 𐑅𐐹𐐩𐑇𐐲𐑅 𐐺𐐮𐑊𐐼𐐮𐑍.

25. 𐐈𐑌𐐼 𐐮𐐻 𐐿𐐩𐑋 𐐻𐐭 𐐹𐐪𐑅 𐑄𐐰𐐻 𐑋𐐯𐑌𐐨 𐐶𐐲𐑉 𐐼𐑉𐐵𐑌𐐼 𐐮𐑌 𐑄 𐐼𐐯𐐹𐑃𐑅 𐐱𐑂 𐑄 𐑁𐐵𐑌𐐻𐐮𐑌; 𐐰𐑌𐐼 𐑋𐐯𐑌𐐨 𐐶𐐲𐑉 𐑊𐐱𐑅𐐻 𐑁𐑉𐐱𐑋 𐐸𐐮𐑆 𐑂𐐷𐐭, 𐐶𐐱𐑌𐐼𐐲𐑉𐐮𐑍 𐐮𐑌 𐑅𐐻𐑉𐐩𐑌𐐾 𐑉𐐬𐐼𐑆. 𐐈𐑌𐐼 𐑀𐑉𐐩𐐻 𐐶𐐱𐑆 𐑄 𐑋𐐲𐑊𐐻𐐮𐐻𐐷𐐭𐐼 𐑄𐐰𐐻 𐐼𐐮𐐼 𐐯𐑌𐐻𐐲𐑉 𐐮𐑌𐐻𐐭 𐑄𐐰𐐻 𐑅𐐻𐑉𐐩𐑌𐐾 𐐺𐐮𐑊𐐼𐐮𐑍. 𐐈𐑌𐐼 𐐪𐑁𐐻𐐲𐑉 𐑄𐐩 𐐼𐐮𐐼 𐐯𐑌𐐻𐐲𐑉 𐐮𐑌𐐻𐐭 𐑄𐐰𐐻 𐐺𐐮𐑊𐐼𐐮𐑍, 𐑄𐐩 𐐼𐐮𐐼 𐐹𐑎𐑌𐐻 𐑄 𐑁𐐮𐑍𐑀𐐲𐑉 𐐱𐑂 𐑅𐐿𐐫𐑉𐑌 𐐰𐐻 𐑋𐐨, 𐐰𐑌𐐼 𐑄𐐬𐑆 𐑄𐐰𐐻 𐐶𐐲𐑉 𐐹𐐪𐑉𐐻𐐩𐐿𐐮𐑍 𐐱𐑂 𐑄 𐑁𐑉𐐭𐐻 𐐫𐑊𐑅𐐬; 𐐒𐐲𐐻 𐐶𐐨 𐐸𐐨𐐼𐐯𐐼 𐑄𐐯𐑋 𐑌𐐱𐐻. 𐐜𐐨𐑆 𐐪𐑉 𐑄 𐐶𐐲𐑉𐐼𐑆 𐐱𐑂 𐑋𐐴 𐑁𐐪𐑄𐐲𐑉: 𐑁𐐫𐑉 𐐰𐑆 𐑋𐐯𐑌𐐨 𐐰𐑆 𐐸𐐨𐐼𐐯𐐼 𐑄𐐯𐑋 𐐸𐐰𐐼 𐑁𐐫𐑊𐑌 𐐰𐐶𐐩. 𐐈𐑌𐐼 𐐢𐐩𐑋𐐲𐑌 𐐰𐑌𐐼 𐐢𐐯𐑋𐐷𐐭𐐯𐑊 𐐹𐐪𐑉𐐻𐐳𐐿 𐑌𐐱𐐻 𐐱𐑂 𐑄 𐑁𐑉𐐭𐐻, 𐑅𐐯𐐼 𐑋𐐴 𐑁𐐪𐑄𐐲𐑉.

26. 𐐈𐑌𐐼 𐐮𐐻 𐐿𐐩𐑋 𐐻𐐭 𐐹𐐪𐑅 𐐪𐑁𐐻𐐲𐑉 𐑋𐐴 𐑁𐐪𐑄𐐲𐑉 𐐸𐐰𐐼 𐑅𐐹𐐬𐐿𐐲𐑌 𐐫𐑊 𐑄 𐐶𐐲𐑉𐐼𐑆 𐐱𐑂 𐐸𐐮𐑆 𐐼𐑉𐐨𐑋 𐐫𐑉 𐑂𐐮𐑈𐐲𐑌, 𐐸𐐶𐐮𐐽 𐐶𐐲𐑉 𐑋𐐯𐑌𐐨, 𐐸𐐨 𐑅𐐯𐐼 𐐲𐑌𐐻𐐭 𐐲𐑅, 𐐺𐐨𐐿𐐫𐑆 𐐱𐑂 𐑄𐐨𐑆 𐑃𐐮𐑍𐑆 𐐸𐐶𐐮𐐽 𐐸𐐨 𐑅𐐫 𐐮𐑌 𐐩 𐑂𐐮𐑈𐐲𐑌, 𐐸𐐨 𐐯𐐿𐑅𐐨𐐼𐐮𐑍𐑊𐐨 𐑁𐐨𐑉𐐼 𐑁𐐫𐑉 𐐢𐐩𐑋𐐲𐑌 𐐰𐑌𐐼 𐐢𐐯𐑋𐐷𐐭𐐯𐑊; 𐐷𐐩, 𐐸𐐨 𐑁𐐨𐑉𐐼 𐑊𐐯𐑅𐐻 𐑄𐐩 𐑇𐐳𐐼 𐐺𐐨 𐐿𐐪𐑅𐐻 𐐫𐑁 𐑁𐑉𐐱𐑋 𐑄 𐐹𐑉𐐯𐑆𐐯𐑌𐑅 𐐱𐑂 𐑄 𐐢𐐫𐑉𐐼: 𐐰𐑌𐐼 𐐸𐐨 𐐼𐐮𐐼 𐐯𐑀𐑆𐐫𐑉𐐻 𐑄𐐯𐑋 𐑄𐐯𐑌 𐐶𐐮𐑄 𐐫𐑊 𐑄 𐑁𐐨𐑊𐐮𐑍 𐐱𐑂 𐐩 𐐻𐐯𐑌𐐼𐐲𐑉 𐐹𐐩𐑉𐐯𐑌𐐻, 𐑄𐐰𐐻 𐑄𐐩 𐐶𐐳𐐼 𐐸𐐪𐑉𐐿𐐲𐑌 𐐻𐐭 𐐸𐐮𐑆 𐐶𐐲𐑉𐐼𐑆, 𐑄𐐰𐐻 𐐹𐐲𐑉𐐸𐐰𐐹𐑅 𐑄 𐐢𐐫𐑉𐐼 𐐶𐐳𐐼 𐐺𐐨 𐑋𐐲𐑉𐑅𐐮𐑁𐐳𐑊 𐐻𐐭 𐑄𐐯𐑋, 𐐰𐑌𐐼 𐑌𐐱𐐻 𐐿𐐪𐑅𐐻 𐑄𐐯𐑋 𐐫𐑁; 𐐷𐐩, 𐑋𐐴 𐑁𐐪𐑄𐐲𐑉 𐐼𐐮𐐼 𐐹𐑉𐐨𐐽 𐐲𐑌𐐻𐐭 𐑄𐐯𐑋.

27. 𐐈𐑌𐐼 𐐪𐑁𐐻𐐲𐑉 𐐸𐐨 𐐸𐐰𐐼 𐐹𐑉𐐨𐐽𐐻 𐐲𐑌𐐻𐐭 𐑄𐐯𐑋, 𐐰𐑌𐐼 𐐫𐑊𐑅𐐬 𐐹𐑉𐐱𐑁𐐯𐑅𐐴𐐼 𐐲𐑌𐐻𐐭 𐑄𐐯𐑋 𐐱𐑂 𐑋𐐯𐑌𐐨 𐑃𐐮𐑍𐑆, 𐐸𐐨 𐐺𐐰𐐼 𐑄𐐯𐑋 𐐻𐐭 𐐿𐐨𐐹 𐑄 𐐿𐐲𐑋𐐰𐑌𐐼𐑋𐐯𐑌𐐻𐑅 𐐱𐑂 𐑄 𐐢𐐫𐑉𐐼; 𐐰𐑌𐐼 𐐸𐐨 𐐼𐐮𐐼 𐑅𐐨𐑅 𐑅𐐹𐐨𐐿𐐮𐑍 𐐲𐑌𐐻𐐭 𐑄𐐯𐑋. 𐐈𐑌𐐼 𐐫𐑊 𐑄𐐨𐑆 𐑃𐐮𐑍𐑆 𐐼𐐮𐐼 𐑋𐐴 𐑁𐐪𐑄𐐲𐑉 𐑅𐐨, 𐐰𐑌𐐼 𐐸𐐨𐑉, 𐐰𐑌𐐼 𐑅𐐹𐐨𐐿, 𐐰𐑆 𐐸𐐨 𐐼𐐶𐐯𐑊𐐻 𐐮𐑌 𐐩 𐐻𐐯𐑌𐐻, 𐐮𐑌 𐑄 𐑂𐐰𐑊𐐨 𐐱𐑂 𐐢𐐯𐑋𐐷𐐭𐐯𐑊; 𐐰𐑌𐐼 𐐫𐑊𐑅𐐬 𐐩 𐑀𐑉𐐩𐐻 𐑋𐐯𐑌𐐨 𐑋𐐬𐑉 𐑃𐐮𐑍𐑆, 𐐸𐐶𐐮𐐽 𐐿𐐰𐑌𐐱𐐻 𐐺𐐨 𐑉𐐮𐐻𐐲𐑌 𐐲𐐹𐐱𐑌 𐑄𐐨𐑆 𐐹𐑊𐐩𐐻𐑅. 𐐈𐑌𐐼 𐑌𐐵, 𐐰𐑆 𐐌 𐐸𐐰𐑂 𐑅𐐹𐐬𐐿𐐲𐑌 𐐿𐐲𐑌𐑅𐐲𐑉𐑌𐐮𐑍 𐑄𐐨𐑆 𐐹𐑊𐐩𐐻𐑅, 𐐺𐐨𐐸𐐬𐑊𐐼

𐑄𐐩 𐐪𐑉 𐑌𐐱𐐻 𐑄 𐐹𐑊𐐩𐐻𐑅 𐐲𐐹𐐱𐑌 𐐸𐐶𐐮𐐽 𐐌 𐑋𐐩𐐿 𐐲 𐑁𐐳𐑊 𐐲𐐿𐐵𐑌𐐻 𐐲𐑂 𐑄 𐐸𐐮𐑅𐐻𐐬𐑉𐐨 𐐲𐑂 𐑋𐐴 𐐹𐐨𐐹𐑊; 𐑁𐐫𐑉 𐑄 𐐹𐑊𐐩𐐻𐑅 𐐲𐐹𐐱𐑌 𐐸𐐶𐐮𐐽 𐐌 𐑋𐐩𐐿 𐐲 𐑁𐐳𐑊 𐐲𐐿𐐵𐑌𐐻 𐐲𐑂 𐑋𐐴 𐐹𐐨𐐹𐑊 𐐌 𐐸𐐰𐑂 𐑀𐐮𐑂𐐲𐑌 𐑄 𐑌𐐩𐑋 𐐲𐑂 𐐤𐐨𐑁𐐴; 𐐸𐐶𐐯𐑉𐑁𐐬𐑉 𐑄𐐩 𐐪𐑉 𐐿𐐫𐑊𐐼 𐑄 𐐹𐑊𐐩𐐻𐑅 𐐲𐑂 𐐤𐐨𐑁𐐴, 𐐰𐑁𐐻𐐲𐑉 𐑋𐐴𐑌 𐐬𐑌 𐑌𐐩𐑋; 𐐰𐑌𐐼 𐑄𐐨𐑆 𐐹𐑊𐐩𐐻𐑅 𐐫𐑊𐑅𐐬 𐐪𐑉 𐐿𐐫𐑊𐐼 𐑄 𐐹𐑊𐐩𐐻𐑅 𐐲𐑂 𐐤𐐨𐑁𐐴.

28. 𐐤𐐯𐑂𐐲𐑉𐑄𐐲𐑊𐐯𐑅, 𐐌 𐐸𐐰𐑂 𐑉𐐨𐑅𐐨𐑂𐐼 𐐲 𐐿𐐱𐑋𐐰𐑌𐐼𐑋𐐲𐑌𐐻 𐐲𐑂 𐑄 𐐢𐐫𐑉𐐼, 𐑄𐐰𐐻 𐐌 𐑇𐐳𐐼 𐑋𐐩𐐿 𐑄𐐨𐑆 𐐹𐑊𐐩𐐻𐑅, 𐑁𐐫𐑉 𐑄 𐑅𐐹𐐯𐑇𐐲𐑊 𐐹𐐲𐑉𐐹𐐲𐑅 𐑄𐐰𐐻 𐑄𐐯𐑉 𐑇𐐳𐐼 𐐺𐐨 𐐰𐑌 𐐲𐐿𐐵𐑌𐐻 𐐯𐑌𐑀𐑉𐐩𐑂𐐲𐑌 𐐲𐑂 𐑄 𐑋𐐮𐑌𐐮𐑅𐐻𐑉𐐨 𐐲𐑂 𐑋𐐴 𐐹𐐨𐐹𐑊. 𐐊𐐹𐐱𐑌 𐑄 𐐲𐑄𐐲𐑉 𐐹𐑊𐐩𐐻𐑅 𐑇𐐳𐐼 𐐺𐐨 𐐯𐑌𐑀𐑉𐐩𐑂𐐲𐑌 𐐰𐑌 𐐲𐐿𐐵𐑌𐐻 𐐲𐑂 𐑄 𐑉𐐩𐑌 𐐲𐑂 𐑄 𐐿𐐮𐑍𐑆, 𐐰𐑌𐐼 𐑄 𐐶𐐫𐑉𐑆 𐐰𐑌𐐼 𐐿𐐱𐑌𐐻𐐯𐑌𐑇𐐲𐑌𐑆 𐐲𐑂 𐑋𐐴 𐐹𐐨𐐹𐑊; 𐐸𐐶𐐯𐑉𐑁𐐬𐑉 𐑄𐐨𐑆 𐐹𐑊𐐩𐐻𐑅 𐐪𐑉 𐑁𐐫𐑉 𐑄 𐑋𐐬𐑉 𐐹𐐪𐑉𐐻 𐐲𐑂 𐑄 𐑋𐐮𐑌𐐮𐑅𐐻𐑉𐐨; 𐐰𐑌𐐼 𐑄 𐐲𐑄𐐲𐑉 𐐹𐑊𐐩𐐻𐑅 𐐪𐑉 𐑁𐐫𐑉 𐑄 𐑋𐐬𐑉 𐐹𐐪𐑉𐐻 𐐲𐑂 𐑄 𐑉𐐩𐑌 𐐲𐑂 𐑄 𐐿𐐮𐑍𐑆, 𐐰𐑌𐐼 𐑄 𐐶𐐫𐑉𐑆 𐐰𐑌𐐼 𐐿𐐱𐑌𐐻𐐯𐑌𐑇𐐲𐑌𐑆 𐐲𐑂 𐑋𐐴 𐐹𐐨𐐹𐑊.—𐐐𐐶𐐯𐑉𐑁𐐬𐑉 𐑄 𐐢𐐫𐑉𐐼 𐐸𐐰𐑃 𐐿𐐱𐑋𐐰𐑌𐐼𐐲𐐼 𐑋𐐨 𐐻𐐭 𐑋𐐩𐐿 𐑄𐐨𐑆 𐐹𐑊𐐩𐐻𐑅 𐑁𐐫𐑉 𐐲 𐐶𐐴𐑆 𐐹𐐲𐑉𐐹𐐲𐑅 𐐮𐑌 𐐸𐐮𐑋; 𐐸𐐶𐐮𐐽 𐐹𐐲𐑉𐐹𐐲𐑅 𐐌 𐑌𐐬 𐑌𐐱𐐻. 𐐒𐐲𐐻 𐑄 𐐢𐐫𐑉𐐼 𐑌𐐬𐐯𐑃 𐐫𐑊 𐑃𐐮𐑍𐑆 𐑁𐑉𐐱𐑋 𐑄 𐐺𐐨𐑀𐐮𐑌𐐮𐑍; 𐐸𐐶𐐯𐑉𐑁𐐬𐑉, 𐐸𐐨 𐐹𐑉𐐨𐐹𐐯𐑉𐐯𐑃 𐐲 𐐶𐐩 𐐻𐐭 𐐲𐐿𐐱𐑋𐐹𐑊𐐮𐑇 𐐫𐑊 𐐸𐐮𐑆 𐐶𐐲𐑉𐐿𐑅 𐐲𐑋𐐲𐑍 𐑄 𐐽𐐮𐑊𐐼𐑉𐐯𐑌 𐐲𐑂 𐑋𐐯𐑌; 𐑁𐐫𐑉 𐐺𐐨𐐸𐐬𐑊𐐼, 𐐸𐐨 𐐸𐐰𐑃 𐐫𐑊 𐐹𐐵𐐲𐑉 𐐲𐑌𐐻𐐭 𐑄 𐑁𐐳𐑊𐑁𐐮𐑊𐐮𐑍 𐐲𐑂 𐐫𐑊 𐐸𐐮𐑆 𐐶𐐲𐑉𐐼𐑆. 𐐈𐑌𐐼 𐑄𐐲𐑅 𐐮𐐻 𐐮𐑆. 𐐁𐑋𐐯𐑌.

𐐕𐐰𐐹𐐻𐐲𐑉 III.

1. 𐐈𐑌𐐼 𐑌𐐵 𐐌, 𐐤𐐨𐑁𐐴, 𐐹𐑉𐐬𐑅𐐨𐐼 𐐻𐐭 𐑀𐐮𐑂 𐐰𐑌 𐐲𐐿𐐵𐑌𐐻 𐐲𐐹𐐱𐑌 𐑄𐐨𐑆 𐐹𐑊𐐩𐐻𐑅 𐐲𐑂 𐑋𐐴 𐐹𐑉𐐬𐑅𐐨𐐼𐐮𐑍𐑆, 𐐰𐑌𐐼 𐑋𐐴 𐑉𐐩𐑌 𐐰𐑌𐐼 𐑋𐐮𐑌𐐮𐑅𐐻𐑉𐐨; 𐐸𐐶𐐯𐑉𐑁𐐬𐑉, 𐐻𐐭 𐐹𐑉𐐬𐑅𐐨𐐼 𐐶𐐮𐑄 𐑋𐐴𐑌 𐐲𐐿𐐵𐑌𐐻, 𐐌 𐑋𐐲𐑅𐐻 𐑅𐐹𐐨𐐿 𐑅𐐲𐑋𐐶𐐱𐐻 𐐲𐑂 𐑄 𐑃𐐮𐑍𐑆 𐐲𐑂 𐑋𐐴 𐑁𐐪𐑄𐐲𐑉, 𐐰𐑌𐐼 𐐫𐑊𐑅𐐬 𐐲𐑂 𐑋𐐴 𐐺𐑉𐐯𐑄𐑉𐐯𐑌.

2. 𐐙𐐫𐑉 𐐺𐐨𐐸𐐬𐑊𐐼, 𐐮𐐻 𐐿𐐩𐑋 𐐻𐐭 𐐹𐐰𐑅 𐑄𐐰𐐻 𐐰𐑁𐐻𐐲𐑉 𐑋𐐴 𐑁𐐪𐑄𐐲𐑉 𐐸𐐰𐐼 𐑋𐐩𐐼 𐐰𐑌 𐐯𐑌𐐼 𐐲𐑂 𐑅𐐹𐐨𐐿𐐮𐑍 𐑄 𐐶𐐲𐑉𐐼𐑆 𐐲𐑂 𐐸𐐮𐑆 𐐼𐑉𐐨𐑋, 𐐰𐑌𐐼 𐐫𐑊𐑅𐐬 𐐲𐑂 𐐯𐑀𐑆𐐫𐑉𐐻𐐮𐑍 𐑄𐐯𐑋 𐐻𐐭 𐐫𐑊 𐐼𐐮𐑊𐐮𐐖𐐯𐑌𐑅, 𐐸𐐨 𐑅𐐹𐐩𐐿 𐐲𐑌𐐻𐐭 𐑄𐐯𐑋 𐐿𐐱𐑌𐑅𐐲𐑉𐑌𐐮𐑍 𐑄 𐐖𐐭𐑆, 𐑄𐐰𐐻 𐐰𐑁𐐻𐐲𐑉 𐑄𐐩 𐑇𐐳𐐼 𐐺𐐨 𐐼𐐨𐑅𐐻𐑉𐐱𐐮𐐼, 𐐨𐑂𐐲𐑌 𐑄𐐰𐐻 𐑀𐑉𐐩𐐻 𐑅𐐮𐐻𐐨 𐐖𐐯𐑉𐐭𐑅𐐲𐑊𐐯𐑋, 𐐰𐑌𐐼 𐑋𐐯𐑌𐐨 𐐺𐐨 𐐿𐐰𐑉𐐨𐐼 𐐲𐐶𐐩 𐐿𐐰𐐹𐐻𐐮𐑂 𐐮𐑌𐐻𐐭 𐐒𐐰𐐺𐐮𐑊𐐱𐑌, 𐐰𐐿𐐫𐑉𐐼𐐮𐑍 𐐻𐐭 𐑄 𐐬𐑌 𐐼𐐭 𐐻𐐴𐑋 𐐲𐑂 𐑄 𐐢𐐫𐑉𐐼, 𐑄𐐩 𐑇𐐳𐐼 𐑉𐐨𐐻𐐲𐑉𐑌 𐐲𐑀𐐯𐑌; 𐐷𐐩, 𐐨𐑂𐐲𐑌 𐐺𐐨 𐐺𐑉𐐫𐐻 𐐺𐐰𐐿 𐐵𐐻 𐐲𐑂 𐐿𐐰𐐹𐐻𐐮𐑂𐐮𐐻𐐨; 𐐰𐑌𐐼 𐐰𐑁𐐻𐐲𐑉 𐑄𐐩 𐑇𐐳𐐼 𐐺𐐨 𐐺𐑉𐐫𐐻 𐐺𐐰𐐿 𐐵𐐻 𐐲𐑂 𐐿𐐰𐐹𐐻𐐮𐑂𐐮𐐻𐐨, 𐑄𐐩 𐑇𐐳𐐼 𐐹𐐲𐑆𐐯𐑅 𐐲𐑀𐐯𐑌 𐑄 𐑊𐐰𐑌𐐼 𐐲𐑂 𐑄𐐯𐑉 𐐮𐑌𐐸𐐯𐑉𐐮𐐻𐐲𐑌𐑅.

3. 𐐏𐐩, 𐐨𐑂𐐲𐑌 𐑅𐐮𐐿𐑅 𐐸𐐲𐑌𐐼𐑉𐐯𐐼 𐐷𐐨𐑉𐑆 𐑁𐑉𐐱𐑋 𐑄 𐐻𐐴𐑋 𐑄𐐰𐐻 𐑋𐐴 𐑁𐐪𐑄𐐲𐑉 𐑊𐐯𐑁𐐻 𐐖𐐯𐑉𐐭𐑅𐐲𐑊𐐯𐑋, 𐐲 𐐹𐑉𐐱𐑁𐐯𐐻 𐐶𐐳𐐼 𐑄 𐐢𐐫𐑉𐐼 𐐘𐐱𐐼 𐑉𐐩𐑆 𐐲𐐹 𐐲𐑋𐐲𐑍 𐑄 𐐖𐐭𐑆; 𐐨𐑂𐐲𐑌 𐐲 𐐣𐐯𐑅𐐴𐐲; 𐐫𐑉, 𐐮𐑌 𐐲𐑄𐐲𐑉 𐐶𐐲𐑉𐐼𐑆, 𐐲 𐐝𐐩𐑂𐐷𐐲𐑉 𐐲𐑂 𐑄 𐐶𐐲𐑉𐑊𐐼. 𐐈𐑌𐐼 𐐸𐐨 𐐫𐑊𐑅𐐬 𐑅𐐹𐐩𐐿 𐐿𐐱𐑌𐑅𐐲𐑉𐑌𐐮𐑍 𐑄 𐐹𐑉𐐱𐑁𐐯𐐻𐑅, 𐐸𐐵 𐑀𐑉𐐩𐐻 𐐲 𐑌𐐲𐑋𐐺𐐲𐑉 𐐸𐐰𐐼 𐐻𐐯𐑅𐐻𐐮𐑁𐐴𐐼 𐐲𐑂 𐑄𐐨𐑆 𐑃𐐮𐑍𐑆, 𐐿𐐱𐑌𐑅𐐲𐑉𐑌𐐮𐑍 𐑄𐐮𐑅 𐐣𐐯𐑅𐐴𐐲, 𐐲𐑂 𐐸𐐭𐑋 𐐸𐐨 𐐸𐐰𐐼 𐑅𐐹𐐬𐐿𐐲𐑌, 𐐫𐑉 𐑄𐐮𐑅 𐐡𐐨𐐼𐐨𐑋𐐲𐑉 𐐲𐑂 𐑄 𐐶𐐲𐑉𐑊𐐼. 𐐐𐐶𐐯𐑉𐑁𐐬𐑉, 𐐫𐑊 𐑋𐐰𐑌𐐿𐐴𐑌𐐼 𐐶𐐲𐑉 𐐮𐑌 𐐲 𐑊𐐱𐑅𐐻 𐐰𐑌𐐼 𐐮𐑌 𐐲 𐑁𐐫𐑊𐐲𐑌 𐑅𐐻𐐩𐐻, 𐐰𐑌𐐼 𐐯𐑂𐐲𐑉 𐐶𐐳𐐼 𐐺𐐨, 𐑅𐐩𐑂 𐑄𐐩 𐑇𐐳𐐼 𐑉𐐨𐑊𐐴 𐐱𐑌 𐑄𐐮𐑅 𐐡𐐨𐐼𐐨𐑋𐐲𐑉.

4. 𐐈𐑌𐐼 𐐸𐐨 𐑅𐐹𐐩𐐿 𐐫𐑊𐑅𐐬 𐐿𐐱𐑌𐑅𐐲𐑉𐑌𐐮𐑍 𐐲 𐐹𐑉𐐱𐑁𐐯𐐻 𐐸𐐭 𐑇𐐳𐐼 𐐿𐐲𐑋 𐐺𐐨𐑁𐐬𐑉 𐑄 𐐣𐐯𐑅𐐴𐐲, 𐐻𐐭 𐐹𐑉𐐨𐐹𐐯𐑉 𐑄 𐐶𐐩 𐐲𐑂 𐑄 𐐢𐐫𐑉𐐼; 𐐷𐐩, 𐐨𐑂𐐲𐑌 𐐸𐐨 𐑇𐐳𐐼 𐑀𐐬 𐑁𐐬𐑉𐑃 𐐰𐑌𐐼 𐐿𐑉𐐴 𐐮𐑌 𐑄 𐐶𐐮𐑊𐐼𐐲𐑉𐑌𐐯𐑅, 𐐑𐑉𐐨𐐹𐐯𐑉 𐐷𐐨 𐑄 𐐶𐐩 𐐲𐑂 𐑄 𐐢𐐫𐑉𐐼, 𐐰𐑌𐐼 𐑋𐐩𐐿 𐐸𐐮𐑆 𐐹𐐪𐑃𐑅 𐑅𐐻𐑉𐐩𐐻; 𐑁𐐫𐑉 𐑄𐐯𐑉 𐑅𐐻𐐰𐑌𐐼𐐯𐑃 𐐶𐐲𐑌 𐐲𐑋𐐲𐑍 𐐷𐐭 𐐸𐐭𐑋 𐐷𐐨 𐑌𐐬 𐑌𐐱𐐻; 𐐰𐑌𐐼 𐐸𐐨 𐐮𐑆 𐑋𐐴𐐻𐐨𐐲𐑉 𐑄𐐰𐑌 𐐌, 𐐸𐐭𐑆 𐑇𐐭'𐑆 𐑊𐐰𐐽𐐯𐐻 𐐌 𐐰𐑋 𐑌𐐱𐐻 𐐶𐐲𐑉𐑄𐐨 𐐻𐐭 𐐲𐑌𐑊𐐭𐑆. 𐐈𐑌𐐼 𐑋𐐲𐐽 𐑅𐐹𐐩𐐿 𐑋𐐴 𐑁𐐪𐑄𐐲𐑉 𐐿𐐱𐑌𐑅𐐲𐑉𐑌𐐮𐑍 𐑄𐐮𐑅 𐑃𐐮𐑍.

5. 𐐈𐑌𐐼 𐑋𐐴 𐑁𐐪𐑄𐐲𐑉 𐑅𐐯𐐼 𐐸𐐨 𐑇𐐳𐐼 𐐺𐐰𐐹𐐻𐐴𐑆 𐐮𐑌 𐐒𐐯𐑃𐐰𐐺𐐲𐑉𐐲, 𐐺𐐨𐐷𐐱𐑌𐐼 𐐖𐐫𐑉𐐼𐐲𐑌; 𐐰𐑌𐐼 𐐸𐐨 𐐫𐑊𐑅𐐬 𐑅𐐯𐐼 𐐸𐐨 𐑇𐐳𐐼 𐐺𐐰𐐹𐐻𐐴𐑆 𐐶𐐮𐑄 𐐶𐐫𐐻𐐲𐑉; 𐐨𐑂𐐲𐑌 𐑄𐐰𐐻 𐐸𐐨 𐑇𐐳𐐼 𐐺𐐰𐐹𐐻𐐴𐑆 𐑄 𐐣𐐯𐑅𐐴𐐲 𐐶𐐮𐑄

𐐶𐐲𐑉𐑊𐐼. 𐐈𐑌𐐼 𐐰𐑁𐐻𐐲𐑉 𐐸𐐨 𐐸𐐰𐐼 𐐺𐐰𐐹𐐻𐐴𐑆𐐼 𐑄 𐑋𐐯𐑅𐐴𐐲 𐐶𐐮𐑄 𐐶𐐫𐐻𐐲𐑉, 𐐸𐐨 𐑇𐐳𐐼 𐐺𐐨𐐸𐐬𐑊𐐼 𐐰𐑌𐐼 𐐺𐐩𐑉 𐑉𐐯𐐿𐐲𐑉𐐼, 𐑄𐐰𐐻 𐐸𐐨 𐐸𐐰𐐼 𐐺𐐰𐐹𐐻𐐴𐑆𐐼 𐑄 𐐢𐐰𐑋 𐐱𐑂 𐐘𐐱𐐼, 𐐸𐐭 𐑇𐐳𐐼 𐐻𐐩𐐿 𐐰𐐶𐐩 𐑄 𐑅𐐮𐑌𐑆 𐐱𐑂 𐑄 𐐶𐐲𐑉𐑊𐐼.

6. 𐐈𐑌𐐼 𐐮𐐻 𐐿𐐩𐑋 𐐻𐐭 𐐹𐐰𐑅 𐐰𐑁𐐻𐐲𐑉 𐑋𐐴 𐑁𐐪𐑄𐐲𐑉 𐐸𐐰𐐼 𐑅𐐹𐐬𐐿𐐲𐑌 𐑄𐐨𐑆 𐐶𐐲𐑉𐐼𐑆, 𐐸𐐨 𐑅𐐹𐐩𐐿 𐐲𐑌𐐻𐐭 𐑋𐐴 𐐺𐑉𐐯𐑄𐑉𐐯𐑌 𐐿𐐱𐑌𐑅𐐲𐑉𐑌𐐮𐑍 𐑄 𐑀𐐱𐑅𐐹𐐯𐑊 𐐸𐐶𐐮𐐽 𐑇𐐳𐐼 𐐺𐐨 𐐹𐑉𐐨𐐽𐐻 𐐲𐑋𐐲𐑍 𐑄 𐐖𐐭𐑆; 𐐰𐑌𐐼 𐐫𐑊𐑅𐐬 𐐿𐐱𐑌𐑅𐐲𐑉𐑌𐐮𐑍 𐑄 𐐼𐐶𐐮𐑌𐐼𐑊𐐮𐑍 𐐱𐑂 𐑄 𐐖𐐭𐑆 𐐮𐑌 𐐲𐑌𐐺𐐨𐑊𐐨𐑁. 𐐈𐑌𐐼 𐐰𐑁𐐻𐐲𐑉 𐑄𐐩 𐐸𐐰𐐼 𐑅𐑊𐐩𐑌 𐑄 𐑋𐐯𐑅𐐴𐐲, 𐐸𐐭 𐑇𐐳𐐼 𐐿𐐲𐑋, 𐐰𐑌𐐼 𐐰𐑁𐐻𐐲𐑉 𐐸𐐨 𐐸𐐰𐐼 𐐺𐐮𐑌 𐑅𐑊𐐩𐑌, 𐐸𐐨 𐑇𐐳𐐼 𐑉𐐴𐑆 𐑁𐑉𐐱𐑋 𐑄 𐐼𐐯𐐼, 𐐰𐑌𐐼 𐑇𐐳𐐼 𐑋𐐩𐐿 𐐸𐐮𐑋𐑅𐐯𐑊𐑁 𐑋𐐰𐑌𐐮𐑁𐐯𐑅𐐻, 𐐺𐐴 𐑄 𐐐𐐬𐑊𐐨 𐐘𐐬𐑅𐐻, 𐐲𐑌𐐻𐐭 𐑄 𐐖𐐯𐑌𐐻𐐴𐑊𐑆.

7. 𐐏𐐩, 𐐨𐑂𐐲𐑌 𐑋𐐴 𐑁𐐪𐑄𐐲𐑉 𐑅𐐹𐐩𐐿 𐑋𐐲𐐽 𐐿𐐱𐑌𐑅𐐲𐑉𐑌𐐮𐑍 𐑄 𐐖𐐯𐑌𐐻𐐴𐑊𐑆, 𐐰𐑌𐐼 𐐫𐑊𐑅𐐬 𐐿𐐱𐑌𐑅𐐲𐑉𐑌𐐮𐑍 𐑄 𐐸𐐵𐑅 𐐱𐑂 𐐆𐑆𐑉𐐩𐐯𐑊, 𐑄𐐰𐐻 𐑄𐐩 𐑇𐐳𐐼 𐐺𐐨 𐐿𐐱𐑋𐐹𐐩𐑉𐐼 𐑊𐐴𐐿 𐐲𐑌𐐻𐐭 𐐰𐑌 𐐱𐑊𐐮𐑂-𐐻𐑉𐐨, 𐐸𐐭𐑆 𐐺𐑉𐐰𐑌𐐽𐐯𐑆 𐑇𐐳𐐼 𐐺𐐨 𐐺𐑉𐐬𐐿𐐲𐑌 𐐫𐑁, 𐐰𐑌𐐼 𐑇𐐳𐐼 𐐺𐐨 𐑅𐐿𐐰𐐻𐐲𐑉𐐼 𐐲𐐹𐐱𐑌 𐐫𐑊 𐑄 𐑁𐐩𐑅 𐐱𐑂 𐑄 𐐲𐑉𐑃. 𐐐𐐶𐐯𐑉𐑁𐐬𐑉, 𐐸𐐨 𐑅𐐯𐐼 𐐮𐐻 𐑋𐐲𐑅𐐻 𐑌𐐨𐐼𐑆 𐐺𐐨 𐑄𐐰𐐻 𐐶𐐨 𐑇𐐳𐐼 𐐺𐐨 𐑊𐐯𐐼 𐐶𐐮𐑄 𐐶𐐲𐑌 𐐰𐐿𐐫𐑉𐐼 𐐮𐑌𐐻𐐭 𐑄 𐑊𐐰𐑌𐐼 𐐱𐑂 𐐹𐑉𐐱𐑋𐐮𐑅, 𐐲𐑌𐐻𐐭 𐑄 𐑁𐐳𐑊𐑁𐐮𐑊𐐮𐑍 𐐱𐑂 𐑄 𐐶𐐲𐑉𐐼 𐐱𐑂 𐑄 𐐢𐐫𐑉𐐼, 𐑄𐐰𐐻 𐐶𐐨 𐑇𐐳𐐼 𐐺𐐨 𐑅𐐿𐐰𐐻𐐲𐑉𐐼 𐐲𐐹𐐱𐑌 𐐫𐑊 𐑄 𐑁𐐩𐑅 𐐱𐑂 𐑄 𐐲𐑉𐑃. 𐐈𐑌𐐼 𐐰𐑁𐐻𐐲𐑉 𐑄 𐐸𐐵𐑅 𐐱𐑂 𐐆𐑆𐑉𐐩𐐯𐑊 𐑇𐐳𐐼 𐐺𐐨 𐑅𐐿𐐰𐐻𐐲𐑉𐐼, 𐑄𐐩 𐑇𐐳𐐼 𐐺𐐨 𐑀𐐰𐑄𐐲𐑉𐐼 𐐻𐐳𐑀𐐯𐑄𐐲𐑉 𐐲𐑀𐐯𐑌; 𐐫𐑉, 𐐮𐑌 𐑁𐐴𐑌, 𐐰𐑁𐐻𐐲𐑉 𐑄 𐐖𐐯𐑌𐐻𐐴𐑊𐑆 𐐸𐐰𐐼 𐑉𐐨𐑅𐐨𐑂𐐼 𐑄 𐑁𐐳𐑊𐑌𐐯𐑅 𐐱𐑂 𐑄 𐐘𐐱𐑅𐐹𐐯𐑊, 𐑄 𐑌𐐰𐐽𐐲𐑉𐐲𐑊 𐐺𐑉𐐰𐑌𐐽𐐯𐑆 𐐱𐑂 𐑄 𐐱𐑊𐐮𐑂-𐐻𐑉𐐨, 𐐫𐑉 𐑄 𐑉𐐯𐑋𐑌𐐰𐑌𐐻𐑅 𐐱𐑂 𐑄 𐐸𐐵𐑅 𐐱𐑂 𐐆𐑆𐑉𐐩𐐯𐑊, 𐑇𐐳𐐼 𐐺𐐨 𐑀𐑉𐐰𐑁𐐻𐐯𐐼 𐐮𐑌, 𐐫𐑉 𐐿𐐲𐑋 𐐻𐐭 𐑄 𐑌𐐱𐑊𐐯𐐾 𐐱𐑂 𐑄 𐐻𐑉𐐭 𐑋𐐯𐑅𐐴𐐲, 𐑄𐐩𐑉 𐐢𐐫𐑉𐐼 𐐰𐑌𐐼 𐑄𐐩𐑉 𐐡𐐨𐐼𐐨𐑋𐐲𐑉. 𐐈𐑌𐐼 𐐰𐑁𐐻𐐲𐑉 𐑄𐐮𐑅 𐑋𐐰𐑌𐐲𐑉 𐐱𐑂 𐑊𐐰𐑍𐑀𐐶𐐩𐐾 𐐼𐐮𐐼 𐑋𐐴 𐑁𐐪𐑄𐐲𐑉 𐐹𐑉𐐱𐑁𐐯𐑅𐐴 𐐰𐑌𐐼 𐑅𐐹𐐨𐐿 𐐲𐑌𐐻𐐭 𐑋𐐴 𐐺𐑉𐐯𐑄𐑉𐐯𐑌; 𐐰𐑌𐐼 𐐫𐑊𐑅𐐬 𐑋𐐯𐑌𐐨 𐑋𐐬𐑉 𐑃𐐮𐑍𐑆, 𐐸𐐶𐐮𐐽 𐐌 𐐼𐐭 𐑌𐐱𐐻 𐑉𐐴𐐻 𐐮𐑌 𐑄𐐮𐑅 𐐺𐐳𐐿; 𐑁𐐫𐑉 𐐌 𐐸𐐰𐑂 𐑉𐐮𐐻𐐲𐑌 𐐰𐑆 𐑋𐐯𐑌𐐨 𐐱𐑂 𐑄𐐯𐑋 𐐰𐑆 𐐶𐐲𐑉 𐐯𐐿𐑅𐐹𐐨𐐼𐐨𐐯𐑌𐐻 𐑁𐐫𐑉 𐑋𐐨 𐐮𐑌 𐑋𐐴𐑌 𐐲𐑄𐐲𐑉 𐐺𐐳𐐿. 𐐈𐑌𐐼 𐐫𐑊 𐑄𐐨𐑆 𐑃𐐮𐑍𐑆, 𐐱𐑂 𐐸𐐶𐐮𐐽 𐐌 𐐸𐐰𐑂 𐑅𐐹𐐬𐐿𐐲𐑌, 𐐶𐐲𐑉 𐐼𐐲𐑌 𐐰𐑆 𐑋𐐴 𐑁𐐪𐑄𐐲𐑉 𐐼𐐶𐐯𐑊𐐻 𐐮𐑌 𐐲 𐐻𐐯𐑌𐐻, 𐐮𐑌 𐑄 𐑂𐐰𐑊𐐨 𐐱𐑂 𐐢𐐯𐑋𐐷𐐭𐐯𐑊.

8. 𐐈𐑌𐐼 𐐮𐐻 𐐿𐐩𐑋 𐐻𐐭 𐐹𐐰𐑅 𐐰𐑁𐐻𐐲𐑉 𐐌, 𐐤𐐨𐑁𐐴, 𐐸𐐰𐑂𐐮𐑍 𐐸𐐲𐑉𐐼 𐐫𐑊 𐑄 𐐶𐐲𐑉𐐼𐑆 𐐱𐑂 𐑋𐐴 𐑁𐐪𐑄𐐲𐑉, 𐐿𐐱𐑌𐑅𐐲𐑉𐑌𐐮𐑍 𐑄 𐑃𐐮𐑍𐑆 𐐸𐐶𐐮𐐽 𐐸𐐨 𐑅𐐫 𐐮𐑌 𐐲 𐑂𐐮𐑈𐐲𐑌; 𐐰𐑌𐐼 𐐫𐑊𐑅𐐬 𐑄 𐑃𐐮𐑍𐑆 𐐸𐐶𐐮𐐽 𐐸𐐨 𐑅𐐹𐐩𐐿 𐐺𐐴 𐑄 𐐹𐐵𐐲𐑉 𐐱𐑂 𐑄 𐐐𐐬𐑊𐐨 𐐘𐐬𐑅𐐻; 𐐸𐐶𐐮𐐽 𐐹𐐵𐐲𐑉 𐐸𐐨 𐑉𐐨𐑅𐐨𐑂𐐼 𐐺𐐴 𐑁𐐩𐑃 𐐱𐑌 𐑄 𐐝𐐲𐑌 𐐱𐑂 𐐘𐐱𐐼; 𐐰𐑌𐐼 𐑄 𐐝𐐲𐑌 𐐱𐑂 𐐘𐐱𐐼 𐐶𐐱𐑆 𐑄 𐑋𐐯𐑅𐐴𐐲 𐐸𐐭 𐑇𐐳𐐼 𐐿𐐲𐑋; 𐐌, 𐐤𐐨𐑁𐐴, 𐐶𐐱𐑆 𐐼𐐯𐑆𐐴𐑉𐐲𐑅 𐐫𐑊𐑅𐐬, 𐑄𐐰𐐻 𐐌 𐑋𐐴𐐻 𐑅𐐨, 𐐰𐑌𐐼 𐐸𐐨𐑉, 𐐰𐑌𐐼 𐑌𐐬 𐐱𐑂 𐑄𐐨𐑆 𐑃𐐮𐑍𐑆, 𐐺𐐴 𐑄 𐐹𐐵𐐲𐑉 𐐱𐑂 𐑄 𐐐𐐬𐑊𐐨 𐐘𐐬𐑅𐐻, 𐐸𐐶𐐮𐐽 𐐮𐑆 𐑄 𐑀𐐮𐑁𐐻 𐐱𐑂 𐐘𐐱𐐼 𐐲𐑌𐐻𐐭 𐐫𐑊 𐑄𐐬𐑆 𐐸𐐭 𐐼𐐮𐑊𐐮𐐾𐐯𐑌𐐻𐑊𐐨 𐑅𐐨𐐿 𐐸𐐮𐑋, 𐐰𐑆 𐐶𐐯𐑊 𐐮𐑌 𐐻𐐴𐑋𐑆 𐐱𐑂 𐐬𐑊𐐼 𐐰𐑆 𐐮𐑌 𐑄 𐐻𐐴𐑋 𐑄𐐰𐐻 𐐸𐐨 𐑇𐐳𐐼 𐑋𐐰𐑌𐐮𐑁𐐯𐑅𐐻 𐐸𐐮𐑋𐑅𐐯𐑊𐑁 𐐲𐑌𐐻𐐭 𐑄 𐐽𐐮𐑊𐐼𐑉𐐯𐑌 𐐱𐑂 𐑋𐐯𐑌; 𐑁𐐫𐑉 𐐸𐐨 𐐮𐑆 𐑄 𐑅𐐩𐑋 𐐷𐐯𐑅𐐻𐐲𐑉𐐼𐐩, 𐐻𐐭-𐐼𐐩, 𐐰𐑌𐐼 𐑁𐐫𐑉𐐯𐑂𐐲𐑉; 𐐰𐑌𐐼 𐑄 𐐶𐐩 𐐮𐑆 𐐹𐑉𐐨𐐹𐐩𐑉𐐼 𐑁𐐫𐑉 𐐫𐑊 𐑋𐐯𐑌 𐑁𐑉𐐱𐑋 𐑄 𐑁𐐵𐑌𐐼𐐩𐑇𐐲𐑌 𐐱𐑂 𐑄 𐐶𐐲𐑉𐑊𐐼, 𐐮𐑁 𐐮𐐻 𐑅𐐬 𐐺𐐨 𐑄𐐰𐐻 𐑄𐐩 𐑉𐐨𐐹𐐯𐑌𐐻 𐐰𐑌𐐼 𐐿𐐲𐑋 𐐲𐑌𐐻𐐭 𐐸𐐮𐑋; 𐑁𐐫𐑉 𐐸𐐨 𐑄𐐰𐐻 𐐼𐐮𐑊𐐮𐐾𐐯𐑌𐐻𐑊𐐨 𐑅𐐨𐐿𐐯𐑃 𐑇𐐰𐑊 𐑁𐐴𐑌𐐼; 𐐰𐑌𐐼 𐑄 𐑋𐐮𐑅𐐻𐐲𐑉𐐨𐑆 𐐱𐑂 𐐘𐐱𐐼 𐑇𐐰𐑊 𐐺𐐨 𐐲𐑌𐑁𐐬𐑊𐐼𐐯𐐼 𐐲𐑌𐐻𐐭 𐑄𐐯𐑋, 𐐺𐐴 𐑄 𐐹𐐵𐐲𐑉 𐐱𐑂 𐑄 𐐐𐐬𐑊𐐨 𐐘𐐬𐑅𐐻, 𐐰𐑆 𐐶𐐯𐑊 𐐮𐑌 𐑄𐐨𐑆 𐐻𐐴𐑋𐑆 𐐰𐑆 𐐮𐑌 𐐻𐐴𐑋𐑆 𐐱𐑂 𐐬𐑊𐐼, 𐐰𐑌𐐼 𐐰𐑆 𐐶𐐯𐑊 𐐮𐑌 𐐻𐐴𐑋𐑆 𐐱𐑂 𐐬𐑊𐐼 𐐰𐑆 𐐮𐑌 𐐻𐐴𐑋𐑆 𐐻𐐭 𐐿𐐲𐑋; 𐐸𐐶𐐯𐑉𐑁𐐬𐑉 𐑄 𐐿𐐬𐑉𐑅 𐐱𐑂 𐑄 𐐢𐐫𐑉𐐼 𐐮𐑆 𐐶𐐲𐑌 𐐨𐐻𐐲𐑉𐑌𐐲𐑊 𐑉𐐵𐑌𐐼. 𐐜𐐯𐑉𐑁𐐬𐑉 𐑉𐐨𐑋𐐯𐑋𐐺𐐲𐑉, 𐐄 𐑋𐐰𐑌, 𐑁𐐫𐑉 𐐫𐑊 𐑄𐐴 𐐼𐐭𐐮𐑍𐑆 𐑄𐐵 𐑇𐐰𐑊𐐻 𐐺𐐨 𐐺𐑉𐐫𐐻 𐐮𐑌𐐻𐐭 𐐾𐐲𐐾𐑋𐐯𐑌𐐻. 𐐐𐐶𐐯𐑉𐑁𐐬𐑉 𐐮𐑁 𐐷𐐨 𐐸𐐰𐑂 𐑅𐐫𐐻 𐐻𐐭 𐐼𐐭 𐐶𐐮𐐿𐐯𐐼𐑊𐐨 𐐮𐑌 𐑄 𐐼𐐩𐑆 𐐱𐑂 𐐷𐐳𐑉 𐐹𐑉𐐬𐐺𐐩𐑇𐐲𐑌, 𐑄𐐯𐑌 𐐷𐐨 𐐪𐑉 𐑁𐐵𐑌𐐼 𐐲𐑌𐐿𐑊𐐨𐑌 𐐺𐐨𐑁𐐬𐑉 𐑄 𐐾𐐲𐐾𐑋𐐯𐑌𐐻-𐑅𐐨𐐻 𐐱𐑂 𐐘𐐱𐐼; 𐐰𐑌𐐼 𐑌𐐬 𐐲𐑌𐐿𐑊𐐨𐑌 𐑃𐐮𐑍 𐐿𐐰𐑌 𐐼𐐶𐐯𐑊 𐐶𐐮𐑄 𐐘𐐱𐐼; 𐐸𐐶𐐯𐑉𐑁𐐬𐑉 𐐷𐐨 𐑋𐐲𐑅𐐻 𐐺𐐨 𐐿𐐰𐑅𐐻 𐐫𐑁 𐑁𐐫𐑉𐐯𐑂𐐲𐑉. 𐐈𐑌𐐼 𐑄 𐐐𐐬𐑊𐐨 𐐘𐐬𐑅𐐻 𐑀𐐮𐑂𐐯𐑃 𐐫𐑃𐐱𐑉𐐮𐐻𐐨 𐑄𐐰𐐻 𐐌 𐑇𐐳𐐼 𐑅𐐹𐐨𐐿 𐑄𐐨𐑆 𐑃𐐮𐑍𐑆, 𐐰𐑌𐐼 𐐼𐐨𐑌𐐴 𐑄𐐯𐑋 𐑌𐐱𐐻.

9. 𐐙𐐫𐑉 𐐮𐐻 𐐿𐐩𐑋 𐐻𐐭 𐐹𐐰𐑅 𐐰𐑁𐐻𐐲𐑉 𐐌 𐐸𐐰𐐼 𐐼𐐯𐑆𐐴𐑉𐐼 𐐻𐐭 𐑌𐐬 𐑄 𐑃𐐮𐑍𐑆 𐑄𐐰𐐻 𐑋𐐴 𐑁𐐪𐑄𐐲𐑉 𐐸𐐰𐐼

𐑅𐐨𐑌, 𐐰𐑌𐐼 𐐺𐐮𐑊𐐨𐑂𐐮𐑍 𐑄𐐰𐐻 𐑄 𐐢𐐫𐑉𐐼 𐐶𐐱𐑆 𐐩𐐺𐑊 𐐻𐐭 𐑋𐐩𐐿 𐑄𐐯𐑋 𐑌𐐬𐑌 𐐲𐑌𐐻𐐭 𐑋𐐨, 𐐰𐑆 𐐴 𐑅𐐰𐐻 𐐹𐐱𐑌𐐼𐐲𐑉𐐮𐑍 𐐮𐑌 𐑋𐐴𐑌 𐐸𐐪𐑉𐐻, 𐐴 𐐶𐐱𐑆 𐐿𐐫𐐻 𐐲𐐶𐐩 𐐮𐑌 𐑄 𐐝𐐹𐐮𐑉𐐮𐐻 𐐱𐑂 𐑄 𐐢𐐫𐑉𐐼, 𐐷𐐩, 𐐮𐑌𐐻𐐭 𐐰𐑌 𐐯𐐿𐑅𐐨𐐼𐐮𐑍𐑊𐐨 𐐸𐐴 𐑋𐐵𐑌𐐻𐐲𐑌, 𐐸𐐶𐐮𐐽 𐐴 𐑌𐐯𐑂𐐲𐑉 𐐸𐐰𐐼 𐐺𐐨𐑁𐐬𐑉 𐑅𐐨𐑌, 𐐰𐑌𐐼 𐐲𐐹𐐱𐑌 𐐸𐐶𐐮𐐽 𐐴 𐑌𐐯𐑂𐐲𐑉 𐐸𐐰𐐼 𐐺𐐨𐑁𐐬𐑉 𐑅𐐯𐐻 𐑋𐐴 𐑁𐐳𐐻. 𐐈𐑌𐐼 𐑄 𐐝𐐹𐐮𐑉𐐮𐐻 𐑅𐐯𐐼 𐐲𐑌𐐻𐐭 𐑋𐐨, 𐐒𐐨𐐸𐐬𐑊𐐼, 𐐸𐐶𐐱𐐻 𐐼𐐨𐑆𐐴𐑉𐐯𐑅𐐻 𐑄𐐵? 𐐈𐑌𐐼 𐐴 𐑅𐐯𐐼, 𐐴 𐐼𐐨𐑆𐐴𐑉 𐐻𐐭 𐐺𐐨𐐸𐐬𐑊𐐼 𐑄 𐑃𐐮𐑍𐑆 𐐸𐐶𐐮𐐽 𐑋𐐴 𐑁𐐪𐑄𐐲𐑉 𐑅𐐫. 𐐈𐑌𐐼 𐑄 𐐝𐐹𐐮𐑉𐐮𐐻 𐑅𐐯𐐼 𐐲𐑌𐐻𐐭 𐑋𐐨, 𐐒𐐨𐑊𐐨𐑂𐐯𐑅𐐻 𐑄𐐵 𐑄𐐰𐐻 𐑄𐐴 𐑁𐐪𐑄𐐲𐑉 𐑅𐐫 𐑄 𐐻𐑉𐐨 𐐱𐑂 𐐸𐐶𐐮𐐽 𐐸𐐨 𐐸𐐰𐑃 𐑅𐐹𐐬𐐿𐐲𐑌? 𐐈𐑌𐐼 𐐴 𐑅𐐯𐐼, 𐐏𐐩, 𐑄𐐵 𐑌𐐬𐐯𐑅𐐻 𐑄𐐰𐐻 𐐴 𐐺𐐨𐑊𐐨𐑂 𐐫𐑊 𐑄 𐐶𐐲𐑉𐐼𐑆 𐐱𐑂 𐑋𐐴 𐑁𐐪𐑄𐐲𐑉.

10. 𐐈𐑌𐐼 𐐸𐐶𐐯𐑌 𐐴 𐐸𐐰𐐼 𐑅𐐹𐐬𐐿𐐲𐑌 𐑄𐐨𐑆 𐐶𐐲𐑉𐐼𐑆, 𐑄 𐐝𐐹𐐮𐑉𐐮𐐻 𐐿𐑉𐐴𐐼 𐐶𐐮𐑄 𐐲 𐑊𐐵𐐼 𐑂𐑎𐑅, 𐑅𐐩𐐮𐑍, 𐐐𐐬𐑆𐐰𐑌𐐲 𐐻𐐭 𐑄 𐐢𐐫𐑉𐐼, 𐑄 𐑋𐐬𐑅𐐻 𐐸𐐴 𐐘𐐱𐐼; 𐑁𐐫𐑉 𐐸𐐨 𐐮𐑆 𐐘𐐱𐐼 𐐬𐑂𐐲𐑉 𐐫𐑊 𐑄 𐐲𐑉𐑃, 𐐷𐐩, 𐐨𐑂𐐲𐑌 𐐲𐐺𐐲𐑂 𐐫𐑊: 𐐰𐑌𐐼 𐐺𐑊𐐯𐑅𐐯𐐼 𐐪𐑉𐐻 𐑄𐐵, 𐐤𐐨𐑁𐐴, 𐐺𐐨𐐿𐐫𐑆 𐑄𐐵 𐐺𐐨𐑊𐐨𐑂𐐯𐑅𐐻 𐐮𐑌 𐑄 𐐝𐐲𐑌 𐐱𐑂 𐑄 𐑋𐐬𐑅𐐻 𐐸𐐴 𐐘𐐱𐐼; 𐐸𐐶𐐩𐑉𐑁𐐫𐑉 𐑄𐐵 𐑇𐐰𐑊𐐻 𐐺𐐨𐐸𐐬𐑊𐐼 𐑄 𐑃𐐮𐑍𐑆 𐐸𐐶𐐮𐐽 𐑄𐐵 𐐸𐐰𐑅𐐻 𐐼𐐨𐑆𐐴𐑉𐐼. 𐐈𐑌𐐼 𐐺𐐨𐐸𐐬𐑊𐐼 𐑄𐐮𐑅 𐑃𐐮𐑍 𐑇𐐰𐑊 𐐺𐐨 𐑀𐐮𐑂𐐲𐑌 𐐲𐑌𐐻𐐭 𐑄𐐨 𐑁𐐫𐑉 𐐲 𐑅𐐴𐑌, 𐑄𐐰𐐻 𐐰𐑁𐐻𐐲𐑉 𐑄𐐵 𐐸𐐰𐑅𐐻 𐐺𐐨𐐸𐐯𐑊𐐼 𐑄 𐐻𐑉𐐨 𐐸𐐶𐐮𐐽 𐐺𐐬𐑉 𐑄 𐑁𐑉𐐭𐐻 𐐸𐐶𐐮𐐽 𐑄𐐴 𐑁𐐪𐑄𐐲𐑉 𐐻𐐩𐑅𐐻𐐯𐐼, 𐑄𐐵 𐑇𐐰𐑊𐐻 𐐫𐑊𐑅𐐬 𐐺𐐨𐐸𐐬𐑊𐐼 𐐲 𐑋𐐰𐑌 𐐼𐐨𐑅𐐯𐑌𐐼𐐮𐑍 𐐵𐐻 𐐱𐑂 𐐸𐐯𐑂𐐲𐑌, 𐐰𐑌𐐼 𐐸𐐮𐑋 𐑇𐐰𐑊 𐐷𐐨 𐐶𐐮𐐻𐑌𐐯𐑅; 𐐰𐑌𐐼 𐐰𐑁𐐻𐐲𐑉 𐐷𐐨 𐐸𐐰𐑂 𐐶𐐮𐐻𐑌𐐯𐑅𐐻 𐐸𐐮𐑋, 𐐷𐐨 𐑇𐐰𐑊 𐐺𐐩𐑉 𐑉𐐯𐐿𐐲𐑉𐐼 𐑄𐐰𐐻 𐐮𐐻 𐐮𐑆 𐑄 𐐝𐐲𐑌 𐐱𐑂 𐐘𐐱𐐼.

11. 𐐈𐑌𐐼 𐐮𐐻 𐐿𐐩𐑋 𐐻𐐭 𐐹𐐰𐑅 𐑄𐐰𐐻 𐑄 𐐝𐐹𐐮𐑉𐐮𐐻 𐑅𐐯𐐼 𐐲𐑌𐐻𐐭 𐑋𐐨, 𐐢𐐳𐐿! 𐐰𐑌𐐼 𐐴 𐑊𐐳𐐿𐐻 𐐰𐑌𐐼 𐐺𐐨𐐸𐐯𐑊𐐼 𐐲 𐐻𐑉𐐨; 𐐰𐑌𐐼 𐐮𐐻 𐐶𐐱𐑆 𐑊𐐴𐐿 𐐲𐑌𐐻𐐭 𐑄 𐐻𐑉𐐨 𐐸𐐶𐐮𐐽 𐑋𐐴 𐑁𐐪𐑄𐐲𐑉 𐐸𐐰𐐼 𐑅𐐨𐑌; 𐐰𐑌𐐼 𐑄 𐐺𐐧𐐻𐐨 𐑄𐐩𐑉𐐱𐑂 𐐶𐐱𐑆 𐑁𐐪𐑉 𐐺𐐨𐐷𐐱𐑌𐐼, 𐐷𐐩, 𐐯𐐿𐑅𐐨𐐼𐐮𐑍 𐐱𐑂 𐐫𐑊 𐐺𐐧𐐻𐐨; 𐐰𐑌𐐼 𐑄 𐐸𐐶𐐴𐐻𐑌𐐯𐑅 𐑄𐐩𐑉𐐱𐑂 𐐼𐐮𐐼 𐐯𐐿𐑅𐐨𐐼 𐑄 𐐸𐐶𐐴𐐻𐑌𐐯𐑅 𐐱𐑂 𐑄 𐐼𐑉𐐮𐑂𐐲𐑌 𐑅𐑌𐐬.

12. 𐐈𐑌𐐼 𐐮𐐻 𐐿𐐩𐑋 𐐻𐐭 𐐹𐐰𐑅 𐐰𐑁𐐻𐐲𐑉 𐐴 𐐸𐐰𐐼 𐑅𐐨𐑌 𐑄 𐐻𐑉𐐨, 𐐴 𐑅𐐯𐐼 𐐲𐑌𐐻𐐭 𐑄 𐐝𐐹𐐮𐑉𐐮𐐻, 𐐴 𐐺𐐨𐐸𐐬𐑊𐐼 𐑄𐐵 𐐸𐐰𐑅𐐻 𐑇𐐬𐑌 𐐲𐑌𐐻𐐭 𐑋𐐨 𐑄 𐐻𐑉𐐨 𐐸𐐶𐐮𐐽 𐐮𐑆 𐐹𐑉𐐯𐑇𐐲𐑅 𐐲𐐺𐐲𐑂 𐐫𐑊. 𐐈𐑌𐐼 𐐸𐐨 𐑅𐐯𐐼 𐐲𐑌𐐻𐐭 𐑋𐐨, 𐐐𐐶𐐱𐐻 𐐼𐐨𐑆𐐴𐑉𐐯𐑅𐐻 𐑄𐐵? 𐐈𐑌𐐼 𐐴 𐑅𐐯𐐼 𐐲𐑌𐐻𐐭 𐐸𐐮𐑋, 𐐓𐐭 𐑌𐐬 𐑄 𐐮𐑌𐐻𐐲𐑉𐐹𐑉𐐨𐐻𐐩𐑇𐐲𐑌 𐑄𐐩𐑉𐐱𐑂; 𐑁𐐫𐑉 𐐴 𐑅𐐹𐐩𐐿 𐐲𐑌𐐻𐐭 𐐸𐐮𐑋 𐐰𐑆 𐐲 𐑋𐐰𐑌 𐑅𐐹𐐨𐐿𐐯𐑃; 𐑁𐐫𐑉 𐐴 𐐺𐐨𐐸𐐯𐑊𐐼 𐑄𐐰𐐻 𐐸𐐨 𐐶𐐱𐑆 𐐮𐑌 𐑄 𐑁𐐫𐑉𐑋 𐐱𐑂 𐐲 𐑋𐐰𐑌; 𐐷𐐯𐐻 𐑌𐐯𐑂𐐲𐑉𐑄𐐲𐑊𐐯𐑅, 𐐴 𐑌𐐭 𐑄𐐰𐐻 𐐮𐐻 𐐶𐐱𐑆 𐑄 𐐝𐐹𐐮𐑉𐐮𐐻 𐐱𐑂 𐑄 𐐢𐐫𐑉𐐼; 𐐰𐑌𐐼 𐐸𐐨 𐑅𐐹𐐩𐐿 𐐲𐑌𐐻𐐭 𐑋𐐨 𐐰𐑆 𐐲 𐑋𐐰𐑌 𐑅𐐹𐐨𐐿𐐯𐑃 𐐶𐐮𐑃 𐐰𐑌𐐲𐑄𐐲𐑉.

13. 𐐈𐑌𐐼 𐐮𐐻 𐐿𐐩𐑋 𐐻𐐭 𐐹𐐰𐑅 𐑄𐐰𐐻 𐐸𐐨 𐑅𐐯𐐼 𐐲𐑌𐐻𐐭 𐑋𐐨, 𐐢𐐳𐐿! 𐐰𐑌𐐼 𐐴 𐑊𐐳𐐿𐐻 𐐰𐑆 𐐮𐑁 𐐻𐐭 𐑊𐐳𐐿 𐐲𐐹𐐱𐑌 𐐸𐐮𐑋, 𐐰𐑌𐐼 𐐴 𐑅𐐫 𐐸𐐮𐑋 𐑌𐐱𐐻; 𐑁𐐫𐑉 𐐸𐐨 𐐸𐐰𐐼 𐑀𐐱𐑌 𐑁𐑉𐐱𐑋 𐐺𐐨𐑁𐐬𐑉 𐑋𐐴 𐐹𐑉𐐯𐑆𐐯𐑌𐑅.

14. 𐐈𐑌𐐼 𐐮𐐻 𐐿𐐩𐑋 𐐻𐐭 𐐹𐐰𐑅 𐑄𐐰𐐻 𐐴 𐑊𐐳𐐿𐐻 𐐰𐑌𐐼 𐐺𐐨𐐸𐐯𐑊𐐼 𐑄 𐑀𐑉𐐩𐐻 𐑅𐐮𐐻𐐨 𐐱𐑂 𐐖𐐯𐑉𐐭𐑅𐐲𐑊𐐯𐑋, 𐐰𐑌𐐼 𐐫𐑊𐑅𐐬 𐐲𐑄𐐲𐑉 𐑅𐐮𐐻𐐨𐑆. 𐐈𐑌𐐼 𐐴 𐐺𐐨𐐸𐐯𐑊𐐼 𐑄 𐑅𐐮𐐻𐐨 𐐱𐑂 𐐤𐐰𐑆𐐲𐑉𐐯𐑃; 𐐰𐑌𐐼 𐐮𐑌 𐑄 𐑅𐐮𐐻𐐨 𐐱𐑂 𐐤𐐰𐑆𐐲𐑉𐐯𐑃 𐐴 𐐺𐐨𐐸𐐯𐑊𐐼 𐐲 𐑂𐐲𐑉𐐾𐐮𐑌, 𐐰𐑌𐐼 𐑇𐐨 𐐶𐐱𐑆 𐐯𐐿𐑅𐐨𐐼𐐮𐑍𐑊𐐨 𐑁𐐩𐑉 𐐰𐑌𐐼 𐐸𐐶𐐴𐐻.

15. 𐐈𐑌𐐼 𐐮𐐻 𐐿𐐩𐑋 𐐻𐐭 𐐹𐐰𐑅 𐑄𐐰𐐻 𐐴 𐑅𐐫 𐑄 𐐸𐐯𐑂𐐲𐑌𐑆 𐐬𐐹𐐲𐑌; 𐐰𐑌𐐼 𐐰𐑌 𐐩𐑌𐐾𐐯𐑊 𐐿𐐩𐑋 𐐼𐐵𐑌 𐐰𐑌𐐼 𐑅𐐻𐐳𐐼 𐐺𐐨𐑁𐐬𐑉 𐑋𐐨; 𐐰𐑌𐐼 𐐸𐐨 𐑅𐐯𐐼 𐐲𐑌𐐻𐐭 𐑋𐐨, 𐐤𐐨𐑁𐐴, 𐐸𐐶𐐱𐐻 𐐺𐐨𐐸𐐬𐑊𐐼𐐯𐑅𐐻 𐑄𐐵? 𐐈𐑌𐐼 𐐴 𐑅𐐯𐐼 𐐲𐑌𐐻𐐭 𐐸𐐮𐑋, 𐐊 𐑂𐐲𐑉𐐾𐐮𐑌, 𐑋𐐬𐑅𐐻 𐐺𐐧𐐻𐐨𐑁𐐳𐑊 𐐰𐑌𐐼 𐑁𐐩𐑉 𐐲𐐺𐐲𐑂 𐐫𐑊 𐐲𐑄𐐲𐑉 𐑂𐐲𐑉𐐾𐐮𐑌𐑆. 𐐈𐑌𐐼 𐐸𐐨 𐑅𐐯𐐼 𐐲𐑌𐐻𐐭 𐑋𐐨, 𐐤𐐬𐐯𐑅𐐻 𐑄𐐵 𐑄 𐐿𐐱𐑌𐐼𐐨𐑅𐐯𐑌𐑇𐐲𐑌 𐐱𐑂 𐐘𐐱𐐼? 𐐈𐑌𐐼 𐐴 𐑅𐐯𐐼 𐐲𐑌𐐻𐐭 𐐸𐐮𐑋, 𐐴 𐑌𐐬 𐑄𐐰𐐻 𐐸𐐨 𐑊𐐲𐑂𐐯𐑃 𐐸𐐮𐑆 𐐽𐐮𐑊𐐼𐑉𐐯𐑌; 𐑌𐐯𐑂𐐲𐑉𐑄𐐲𐑊𐐯𐑅, 𐐴 𐐼𐐭 𐑌𐐱𐐻 𐑌𐐬 𐑄 𐑋𐐨𐑌𐐮𐑍 𐐱𐑂 𐐫𐑊 𐑃𐐮𐑍𐑆. 𐐈𐑌𐐼 𐐸𐐨 𐑅𐐯𐐼 𐐲𐑌𐐻𐐭 𐑋𐐨, 𐐒𐐨𐐸𐐬𐑊𐐼, 𐑄 𐑂𐐲𐑉𐐾𐐮𐑌 𐐸𐐭𐑋 𐑄𐐵 𐑅𐐨𐐯𐑅𐐻, 𐐮𐑆 𐑄 𐑋𐐲𐑄𐐲𐑉 𐐱𐑂 𐑄 𐐝𐐲𐑌 𐐱𐑂 𐐘𐐱𐐼, 𐐰𐑁𐐻𐐲𐑉 𐑄 𐑋𐐰𐑌𐐲𐑉 𐐱𐑂 𐑄 𐑁𐑊𐐯𐑇.

16. 𐐈𐑌𐐼 𐐮𐐻 𐐿𐐩𐑋 𐐻𐐭 𐐹𐐰𐑅 𐑄𐐰𐐻 𐐴 𐐺𐐨𐐸𐐯𐑊𐐼 𐑄𐐰𐐻 𐑇𐐨 𐐶𐐱𐑆 𐐿𐐰𐑉𐐨𐐼 𐐲𐐶𐐩 𐐮𐑌 𐑄 𐐝𐐹𐐮𐑉𐐮𐐻; 𐐰𐑌𐐼 𐐰𐑁𐐻𐐲𐑉 𐑇𐐨 𐐸𐐰𐐼 𐐺𐐮𐑌 𐐿𐐰𐑉𐐨𐐼 𐐲𐐶𐐩 𐐮𐑌 𐑄 𐐝𐐹𐐮𐑉𐐮𐐻 𐑁𐐫𐑉 𐑄 𐑅𐐹𐐩𐑅 𐐱𐑂 𐐲 𐐻𐐴𐑋, 𐑄 𐐩𐑌𐐾𐐯𐑊 𐑅𐐹𐐩𐐿 𐐲𐑌𐐻𐐭 𐑋𐐨, 𐑅𐐩𐐮𐑍, 𐐢𐐳𐐿! 𐐈𐑌𐐼 𐐴 𐑊𐐳𐐿𐐻 𐐰𐑌𐐼 𐐺𐐨𐐸𐐯𐑊𐐼 𐑄 𐑂𐐲𐑉𐐾𐐮𐑌 𐐲𐑀𐐯𐑌, 𐐺𐐩𐑉𐐮𐑍 𐐲

𐐽𐐴𐑊𐐼 𐐮𐑌 𐐸𐐲𐑉 𐐪𐑉𐑋𐑆. 𐐈𐑌𐐼 𐑄 𐐩𐑌𐐾𐐯𐑊 𐑅𐐯𐐼 𐐲𐑌𐐻𐐭 𐑋𐐨, 𐐒𐐨𐐸𐐬𐑊𐐼 𐑄 𐐢𐐰𐑋 𐐲𐑂 𐐘𐐱𐐼, 𐐷𐐩, 𐐨𐑂𐐲𐑌 𐑄 𐐝𐐲𐑌 𐐲𐑂 𐑄 𐐀𐐻𐐲𐑉𐑌𐐲𐑊 𐐙𐐪𐑄𐐲𐑉! 𐐤𐐬𐐯𐑅𐐻 𐑄𐐵 𐑄 𐑋𐐨𐑌𐐮𐑍 𐐲𐑂 𐑄 𐐻𐑉𐐨 𐐸𐐶𐐮𐐽 𐑄𐐴 𐑁𐐪𐑄𐐲𐑉 𐑅𐐫? 𐐈𐑌𐐼 𐐌 𐐰𐑌𐑅𐐲𐑉𐐼 𐐸𐐮𐑋, 𐑅𐐩𐐮𐑍, 𐐏𐐩, 𐐮𐐻 𐐮𐑆 𐑄 𐑊𐐲𐑂 𐐲𐑂 𐐘𐐱𐐼, 𐐸𐐶𐐮𐐽 𐑇𐐯𐐼𐐯𐑃 𐐮𐐻𐑅𐐯𐑊𐑁 𐐲𐐺𐑉𐐫𐐼 𐐮𐑌 𐑄 𐐸𐐪𐑉𐐻𐑅 𐐲𐑂 𐑄 𐐽𐐮𐑊𐐼𐑉𐐯𐑌 𐐲𐑂 𐑋𐐯𐑌; 𐐸𐐶𐐯𐑉𐑁𐐬𐑉, 𐐮𐐻 𐐮𐑆 𐑄 𐑋𐐬𐑅𐐻 𐐼𐐯𐑆𐐴𐑉𐐲𐐺𐑊 𐐲𐐺𐐲𐑂 𐐫𐑊 𐑃𐐮𐑍𐑆. 𐐈𐑌𐐼 𐐸𐐨 𐑅𐐹𐐩𐐿 𐐲𐑌𐐻𐐭 𐑋𐐨, 𐑅𐐩𐐮𐑍, 𐐏𐐩, 𐐰𐑌𐐼 𐑄 𐑋𐐬𐑅𐐻 𐐾𐐱𐐲𐑅 𐐻𐐭 𐑄 𐑅𐐬𐑊. 𐐈𐑌𐐼 𐐰𐑁𐐻𐐲𐑉 𐐸𐐨 𐐸𐐰𐐼 𐑅𐐯𐐼 𐑄𐐨𐑆 𐐶𐐲𐑉𐐼𐑆, 𐐸𐐨 𐑅𐐯𐐼 𐐲𐑌𐐻𐐭 𐑋𐐨, 𐐢𐐳𐐿! 𐐈𐑌𐐼 𐐌 𐑊𐐳𐐿𐐻, 𐐰𐑌𐐼 𐐌 𐐺𐐨𐐸𐐯𐑊𐐼 𐑄 𐐝𐐲𐑌 𐐲𐑂 𐐘𐐱𐐼 𐑀𐐬𐐮𐑍 𐑁𐐬𐑉𐑃 𐐲𐑋𐐲𐑍 𐑄 𐐽𐐮𐑊𐐼𐑉𐐯𐑌 𐐲𐑂 𐑋𐐯𐑌; 𐐰𐑌𐐼 𐐌 𐑅𐐫 𐑋𐐯𐑌𐐨 𐑁𐐫𐑊 𐐼𐐵𐑌 𐐰𐐻 𐐸𐐮𐑆 𐑁𐐨𐐻 𐐰𐑌𐐼 𐐶𐐲𐑉𐑇𐐮𐐹 𐐸𐐮𐑋.

17. 𐐈𐑌𐐼 𐐮𐐻 𐐿𐐩𐑋 𐐻𐐭 𐐹𐐰𐑅 𐑄𐐰𐐻 𐐌 𐐺𐐨𐐸𐐯𐑊𐐼 𐑄𐐰𐐻 𐑄 𐑉𐐱𐐼 𐐲𐑂 𐐴𐐲𐑉𐑌, 𐐸𐐶𐐮𐐽 𐑋𐐴 𐑁𐐪𐑄𐐲𐑉 𐐸𐐰𐐼 𐑅𐐨𐑌, 𐐶𐐱𐑆 𐑄 𐐶𐐲𐑉𐐼 𐐲𐑂 𐐘𐐱𐐼, 𐐸𐐶𐐮𐐽 𐑊𐐯𐐼 𐐻𐐭 𐑄 𐑁𐐵𐑌𐐻𐐩𐑌 𐐲𐑂 𐑊𐐮𐑂𐐮𐑍 𐐶𐐫𐐻𐐲𐑉𐑆, 𐐫𐑉 𐐻𐐭 𐑄 𐐻𐑉𐐨 𐐲𐑂 𐑊𐐴𐑁; 𐐸𐐶𐐮𐐽 𐐶𐐫𐐻𐐲𐑉𐑆 𐐪𐑉 𐐩 𐑉𐐯𐐹𐑉𐐨𐑆𐐯𐑌𐐻𐐩𐑇𐐲𐑌 𐐲𐑂 𐑄 𐑊𐐲𐑂 𐐲𐑂 𐐘𐐱𐐼; 𐐰𐑌𐐼 𐐌 𐐫𐑊𐑅𐐬 𐐺𐐨𐐸𐐯𐑊𐐼 𐑄𐐰𐐻 𐑄 𐐻𐑉𐐨 𐐲𐑂 𐑊𐐴𐑁 𐐶𐐱𐑆 𐐩 𐑉𐐯𐐹𐑉𐐨𐑆𐐯𐑌𐐻𐐩𐑇𐐲𐑌 𐐲𐑂 𐑄 𐑊𐐲𐑂 𐐲𐑂 𐐘𐐱𐐼. 𐐈𐑌𐐼 𐑄 𐐩𐑌𐐾𐐯𐑊 𐑅𐐯𐐼 𐐲𐑌𐐻𐐭 𐑋𐐨 𐐲𐑀𐐯𐑌, 𐐢𐐳𐐿 𐐰𐑌𐐼 𐐺𐐨𐐸𐐬𐑊𐐼 𐑄 𐐿𐐱𐑌𐐼𐐨𐑅𐐯𐑌𐑇𐐲𐑌 𐐲𐑂 𐐘𐐱𐐼! 𐐈𐑌𐐼 𐐌 𐑊𐐳𐐿𐐻 𐐰𐑌𐐼 𐐺𐐨𐐸𐐯𐑊𐐼 𐑄 𐐡𐐨𐐼𐐨𐑋𐐲𐑉 𐐲𐑂 𐑄 𐐶𐐲𐑉𐑊𐐼, 𐐲𐑂 𐐸𐐭𐑋 𐑋𐐴 𐑁𐐪𐑄𐐲𐑉 𐐸𐐰𐐼 𐑅𐐹𐐬𐐿𐐲𐑌; 𐐰𐑌𐐼 𐐌 𐐫𐑊𐑅𐐬 𐐺𐐨𐐸𐐯𐑊𐐼 𐑄 𐐹𐑉𐐱𐑁𐐯𐐻 𐐸𐐭 𐑇𐐳𐐼 𐐹𐑉𐐨𐐹𐐩𐑉 𐑄 𐐶𐐩 𐐺𐐨𐑁𐐬𐑉 𐐸𐐮𐑋. 𐐈𐑌𐐼 𐑄 𐐢𐐰𐑋 𐐲𐑂 𐐘𐐱𐐼 𐐶𐐯𐑌𐐻 𐑁𐐬𐑉𐑃 𐐰𐑌𐐼 𐐶𐐱𐑆 𐐺𐐰𐐹𐐻𐐴𐑆𐐼 𐐲𐑂 𐐸𐐮𐑋; 𐐰𐑌𐐼 𐐰𐑁𐐻𐐲𐑉 𐐸𐐨 𐐶𐐱𐑆 𐐺𐐰𐐹𐐻𐐴𐑆𐐼, 𐐌 𐐺𐐨𐐸𐐯𐑊𐐼 𐑄 𐐸𐐯𐑂𐐲𐑌𐑆 𐐬𐐹𐐲𐑌, 𐐰𐑌𐐼 𐑄 𐐐𐐬𐑊𐐨 𐐘𐐬𐑅𐐻 𐐿𐐲𐑋 𐐼𐐵𐑌 𐐵𐐻 𐐲𐑂 𐐸𐐯𐑂𐐲𐑌 𐐰𐑌𐐼 𐐲𐐺𐐴𐐼 𐐲𐐹𐐱𐑌 𐐸𐐮𐑋 𐐮𐑌 𐑄 𐑁𐐫𐑉𐑋 𐐲𐑂 𐐩 𐐼𐐲𐑂. 𐐈𐑌𐐼 𐐌 𐐺𐐨𐐸𐐯𐑊𐐼 𐑄𐐰𐐻 𐐸𐐨 𐐶𐐯𐑌𐐻 𐑁𐐬𐑉𐑃 𐑋𐐮𐑌𐐮𐑅𐐻𐐲𐑉𐐮𐑍 𐐲𐑌𐐻𐐭 𐑄 𐐹𐐨𐐹𐑊, 𐐮𐑌 𐐹𐐵𐐲𐑉 𐐰𐑌𐐼 𐑀𐑉𐐩𐐻 𐑀𐑊𐐬𐑉𐐨; 𐐰𐑌𐐼 𐑄 𐑋𐐲𐑊𐐻𐐮𐐻𐐭𐐼𐑆 𐐶𐐲𐑉 𐑀𐐰𐑄𐐲𐑉𐐼 𐐻𐐭𐑀𐐯𐑄𐐲𐑉 𐐻𐐭 𐐸𐐨𐑉 𐐸𐐮𐑋; 𐐰𐑌𐐼 𐐌 𐐺𐐨𐐸𐐯𐑊𐐼 𐑄𐐰𐐻 𐑄𐐩 𐐿𐐰𐑅𐐻 𐐸𐐮𐑋 𐐵𐐻 𐑁𐑉𐐱𐑋 𐐲𐑋𐐲𐑍 𐑄𐐯𐑋. 𐐈𐑌𐐼 𐐌 𐐫𐑊𐑅𐐬 𐐺𐐨𐐸𐐯𐑊𐐼 𐐻𐐶𐐯𐑊𐑂 𐐲𐑄𐐲𐑉𐑆 𐑁𐐱𐑊𐐬𐐮𐑍 𐐸𐐮𐑋.

18. 𐐈𐑌𐐼 𐐮𐐻 𐐿𐐩𐑋 𐐻𐐭 𐐹𐐰𐑅 𐑄𐐰𐐻 𐑄𐐩 𐐶𐐲𐑉 𐐿𐐰𐑉𐐨𐐼 𐐲𐐶𐐩 𐐮𐑌 𐑄 𐐝𐐹𐐮𐑉𐐮𐐻, 𐑁𐑉𐐱𐑋 𐐺𐐨𐑁𐐬𐑉 𐑋𐐴 𐑁𐐩𐑅, 𐐰𐑌𐐼 𐐌 𐑅𐐫 𐑄𐐯𐑋 𐑌𐐱𐐻. 𐐈𐑌𐐼 𐐮𐐻 𐐿𐐩𐑋 𐐻𐐭 𐐹𐐰𐑅 𐑄𐐰𐐻 𐑄 𐐩𐑌𐐾𐐯𐑊 𐑅𐐹𐐩𐐿 𐐲𐑌𐐻𐐭 𐑋𐐨 𐐲𐑀𐐯𐑌, 𐑅𐐩𐐮𐑍, 𐐢𐐳𐐿! 𐐈𐑌𐐼 𐐌 𐑊𐐳𐐿𐐻, 𐐰𐑌𐐼 𐐌 𐐺𐐨𐐸𐐯𐑊𐐼 𐑄 𐐸𐐯𐑂𐐲𐑌𐑆 𐐬𐐹𐐲𐑌 𐐲𐑀𐐯𐑌, 𐐰𐑌𐐼 𐐌 𐑅𐐫 𐐩𐑌𐐾𐐯𐑊𐑆 𐐼𐐨𐑅𐐯𐑌𐐼𐐮𐑍 𐐲𐐹𐐱𐑌 𐑄 𐐽𐐮𐑊𐐼𐑉𐐯𐑌 𐐲𐑂 𐑋𐐯𐑌; 𐐰𐑌𐐼 𐑄𐐩 𐐼𐐮𐐼 𐑋𐐮𐑌𐐮𐑅𐐻𐐲𐑉 𐐲𐑌𐐻𐐭 𐑄𐐯𐑋. 𐐈𐑌𐐼 𐐸𐐨 𐑅𐐹𐐩𐐿 𐐲𐑌𐐻𐐭 𐑋𐐨 𐐲𐑀𐐯𐑌, 𐑅𐐩𐐮𐑍, 𐐢𐐳𐐿! 𐐈𐑌𐐼 𐐌 𐑊𐐳𐐿𐐻, 𐐰𐑌𐐼 𐐌 𐐺𐐨𐐸𐐯𐑊𐐼 𐑄 𐐢𐐰𐑋 𐐲𐑂 𐐘𐐱𐐼 𐑀𐐬𐐮𐑍 𐑁𐐬𐑉𐑃 𐐲𐑋𐐲𐑍 𐑄 𐐽𐐮𐑊𐐼𐑉𐐯𐑌 𐐲𐑂 𐑋𐐯𐑌. 𐐈𐑌𐐼 𐐌 𐐺𐐨𐐸𐐯𐑊𐐼 𐑋𐐲𐑊𐐻𐐮𐐻𐐭𐐼𐑆 𐐲𐑂 𐐹𐐨𐐹𐑊 𐐸𐐭 𐐶𐐲𐑉 𐑅𐐮𐐿, 𐐰𐑌𐐼 𐐸𐐭 𐐶𐐲𐑉 𐐲𐑁𐑊𐐮𐐿𐐻𐐯𐐼 𐐶𐐮𐑄 𐐫𐑊 𐑋𐐰𐑌𐐲𐑉 𐐲𐑂 𐐼𐐮𐑆𐐨𐑆𐐯𐑆, 𐐰𐑌𐐼 𐐶𐐮𐑄 𐐼𐐯𐑂𐐮𐑊𐑆 𐐰𐑌𐐼 𐐲𐑌𐐿𐑊𐐨𐑌 𐑅𐐹𐐮𐑉𐐮𐐻𐑅; 𐐰𐑌𐐼 𐑄 𐐩𐑌𐐾𐐯𐑊 𐑅𐐹𐐩𐐿 𐐰𐑌𐐼 𐑇𐐬𐐼 𐐫𐑊 𐑄𐐨𐑆 𐑃𐐮𐑍𐑆 𐐲𐑌𐐻𐐭 𐑋𐐨. 𐐈𐑌𐐼 𐑄𐐩 𐐶𐐲𐑉 𐐸𐐨𐑊𐐼 𐐺𐐴 𐑄 𐐹𐐵𐐲𐑉 𐐲𐑂 𐑄 𐐢𐐰𐑋 𐐲𐑂 𐐘𐐱𐐼; 𐐰𐑌𐐼 𐑄 𐐼𐐯𐑂𐐮𐑊𐑆 𐐰𐑌𐐼 𐑄 𐐲𐑌𐐿𐑊𐐨𐑌 𐑅𐐹𐐮𐑉𐐮𐐻𐑅 𐐶𐐲𐑉 𐐿𐐰𐑅𐐻 𐐵𐐻.

19. 𐐈𐑌𐐼 𐐮𐐻 𐐿𐐩𐑋 𐐻𐐭 𐐹𐐰𐑅 𐑄𐐰𐐻 𐑄 𐐩𐑌𐐾𐐯𐑊 𐑅𐐹𐐩𐐿 𐐲𐑌𐐻𐐭 𐑋𐐨 𐐲𐑀𐐯𐑌, 𐑅𐐩𐐮𐑍, 𐐢𐐳𐐿! 𐐈𐑌𐐼 𐐌 𐑊𐐳𐐿𐐻, 𐐰𐑌𐐼 𐐺𐐨𐐸𐐯𐑊𐐼 𐑄 𐐢𐐰𐑋 𐐲𐑂 𐐘𐐱𐐼, 𐑄𐐰𐐻 𐐸𐐨 𐐶𐐱𐑆 𐐻𐐩𐐿𐐲𐑌 𐐺𐐴 𐑄 𐐹𐐨𐐹𐑊; 𐐷𐐩, 𐑄 𐐝𐐲𐑌 𐐲𐑂 𐑄 𐐯𐑂𐐲𐑉𐑊𐐰𐑅𐐻𐐮𐑍 𐐘𐐱𐐼 𐐶𐐱𐑆 𐐾𐐲𐐾𐐼 𐐲𐑂 𐑄 𐐶𐐲𐑉𐑊𐐼; 𐐰𐑌𐐼 𐐌 𐑅𐐫 𐐰𐑌𐐼 𐐺𐐩𐑉 𐑉𐐯𐐿𐐲𐑉𐐼. 𐐈𐑌𐐼 𐐌, 𐐤𐐨𐑁𐐴, 𐑅𐐫 𐑄𐐰𐐻 𐐸𐐨 𐐶𐐱𐑆 𐑊𐐮𐑁𐐻𐐯𐐼 𐐲𐐹 𐐲𐐹𐐱𐑌 𐑄 𐐿𐑉𐐫𐑅, 𐐰𐑌𐐼 𐑅𐑊𐐩𐑌 𐑁𐐫𐑉 𐑄 𐑅𐐮𐑌𐑆 𐐲𐑂 𐑄 𐐶𐐲𐑉𐑊𐐼. 𐐈𐑌𐐼 𐐰𐑁𐐻𐐲𐑉 𐐸𐐨 𐐶𐐱𐑆 𐑅𐑊𐐩𐑌, 𐐌 𐑅𐐫 𐑄 𐑋𐐲𐑊𐐻𐐮𐐻𐐭𐐼𐑆 𐐲𐑂 𐑄 𐐲𐑉𐑃, 𐑄𐐰𐐻 𐑄𐐩 𐐶𐐲𐑉 𐑀𐐰𐑄𐐲𐑉𐐼 𐐻𐐭𐑀𐐯𐑄𐐲𐑉 𐐻𐐭 𐑁𐐴𐐻 𐐲𐑀𐐯𐑌𐑅𐐻 𐑄 𐐲𐐹𐐱𐑅𐑊𐑆 𐐲𐑂 𐑄 𐐢𐐰𐑋; 𐑁𐐫𐑉 𐑄𐐲𐑅 𐐶𐐲𐑉 𐑄 𐐻𐐶𐐯𐑊𐑂 𐐿𐐫𐑊𐐼 𐐺𐐴 𐑄 𐐩𐑌𐐾𐐯𐑊 𐐲𐑂 𐑄 𐐢𐐫𐑉𐐼. 𐐈𐑌𐐼 𐑄 𐑋𐐲𐑊𐐻𐐮𐐻𐐭𐐼 𐐲𐑂 𐑄 𐐲𐑉𐑃 𐐶𐐱𐑆 𐑀𐐰𐑄𐐲𐑉𐐼 𐐻𐐭𐑀𐐯𐑄𐐲𐑉; 𐐰𐑌𐐼 𐐌 𐐺𐐨𐐸𐐯𐑊𐐼 𐑄𐐰𐐻 𐑄𐐩 𐐶𐐲𐑉 𐐮𐑌 𐐩 𐑊𐐪𐑉𐐾 𐐰𐑌𐐼 𐑅𐐹𐐩𐑇𐐲𐑅 𐐺𐐮𐑊𐐼𐐮𐑍, 𐑊𐐴𐐿 𐐲𐑌𐐻𐐭 𐑄 𐐺𐐮𐑊𐐼𐐮𐑍 𐐸𐐶𐐮𐐽 𐑋𐐴 𐑁𐐪𐑄𐐲𐑉 𐑅𐐫! 𐐈𐑌𐐼 𐑄 𐐩𐑌𐐾𐐯𐑊 𐐲𐑂 𐑄 𐐢𐐫𐑉𐐼 𐑅𐐹𐐩𐐿 𐐲𐑌𐐻𐐭 𐑋𐐨 𐐲𐑀𐐯𐑌, 𐑅𐐩𐐮𐑍, 𐐒𐐨𐐸𐐬𐑊𐐼 𐑄 𐐶𐐲𐑉𐑊𐐼 𐐰𐑌𐐼 𐑄 𐐶𐐮𐑆𐐼𐐲𐑋 𐑄𐐯𐑉𐐱𐑂; 𐐷𐐩, 𐐺𐐨𐐸𐐬𐑊𐐼 𐑄 𐐸𐐵𐑅 𐐲𐑂 𐐆𐑆𐑉𐐩𐐯𐑊 𐐸𐐰𐑃 𐑀𐐰𐑄𐐲𐑉𐐼 𐐻𐐭𐑀𐐯𐑄𐐲𐑉 𐐻𐐭 𐑁𐐴𐐻 𐐲𐑀𐐯𐑌𐑅𐐻 𐑄 𐐻𐐶𐐯𐑊𐑂 𐐲𐐹𐐱𐑅𐑊𐑆 𐐲𐑂 𐑄 𐐢𐐰𐑋.

20. 𐐈𐑌𐐼 𐐮𐐻 𐐿𐐩𐑋 𐐻𐐭 𐐹𐐰𐑅 𐑄𐐰𐐻 𐐌 𐑅𐐫 𐐰𐑌𐐼 𐐺𐐯𐑉 𐑉𐐯𐐿𐐫𐑉𐐼 𐑄𐐰𐐻 𐑄 𐑀𐑉𐐩𐐻 𐐰𐑌𐐼 𐑅𐐹𐐩𐑇𐐲𐑅 𐐺𐐮𐑊𐐼𐐮𐑍 𐐶𐐱𐑆 𐑄 𐐹𐑉𐐴𐐼 𐐱𐑂 𐑄 𐐶𐐲𐑉𐑊𐐼: 𐐰𐑌𐐼 𐐮𐐻 𐑁𐐯𐑊; 𐐰𐑌𐐼 𐑄 𐑁𐐫𐑊 𐑄𐐩𐑉𐐱𐑂 𐐶𐐱𐑆 𐐯𐐿𐑅𐐨𐐼𐐮𐑍 𐑀𐑉𐐩𐐻. 𐐈𐑌𐐼 𐑄 𐐩𐑌𐐾𐐯𐑊 𐐱𐑂 𐑄 𐐢𐐫𐑉𐐼 𐑅𐐹𐐩𐐿 𐐲𐑌𐐻𐐭 𐑋𐐨 𐐲𐑀𐐯𐑌, 𐑅𐐩𐐮𐑍, 𐐜𐐲𐑅 𐑇𐐰𐑊 𐐺 𐑄 𐐼𐐯𐑅𐐻𐑉𐐲𐐿𐑇𐐲𐑌 𐐱𐑂 𐐫𐑊 𐑌𐐩𐑇𐐲𐑌𐑆, 𐐿𐐮𐑌𐐼𐑉𐐯𐐼𐑆, 𐐻𐐲𐑍𐑆, 𐐰𐑌𐐼 𐐹𐐨𐐹𐑊, 𐑄𐐰𐐻 𐑇𐐰𐑊 𐑁𐐴𐐻 𐐲𐑀𐐯𐑌𐑅𐐻 𐑄 𐐻𐐶𐐯𐑊𐑂 𐐲𐐹𐐱𐑅𐑊𐑆 𐐱𐑂 𐑄 𐐢𐐰𐑋.

21. 𐐈𐑌𐐼 𐐮𐐻 𐐿𐐩𐑋 𐐻𐐭 𐐹𐐰𐑅 𐑄𐐰𐐻 𐑄 𐐩𐑌𐐾𐐯𐑊 𐑅𐐯𐐼 𐐲𐑌𐐻𐐭 𐑋𐐨, 𐐢𐐳𐐿, 𐐰𐑌𐐼 𐐺𐐨𐐸𐐬𐑊𐐼 𐑄𐐴 𐑅𐐨𐐼, 𐐰𐑌𐐼 𐐫𐑊𐑅𐐬 𐑄 𐑅𐐨𐐼 𐐱𐑂 𐑄𐐴 𐐺𐑉𐐯𐑄𐑉𐐯𐑌! 𐐈𐑌𐐼 𐐌 𐑊𐐳𐐿𐐻 𐐰𐑌𐐼 𐐺𐐨𐐸𐐯𐑊𐐼 𐑄 𐑊𐐰𐑌𐐼 𐐱𐑂 𐐹𐑉𐐱𐑋-𐐮𐑅; 𐐰𐑌𐐼 𐐌 𐐺𐐨𐐸𐐯𐑊𐐼 𐑋𐐲𐑊𐐻𐐮𐐻𐐷𐐭𐐼𐑆 𐐱𐑂 𐐹𐐨𐐹𐑊, 𐐷𐐩, 𐐨𐑂𐑌 𐐰𐑆 𐐮𐐻 𐐶𐐯𐑉 𐐮𐑌 𐑌𐐲𐑋𐐺𐐲𐑉, 𐐰𐑆 𐑋𐐯𐑌𐐮 𐐰𐑆 𐑄 𐑅𐐰𐑌𐐼 𐐱𐑂 𐑄 𐑅𐐨.

22. 𐐈𐑌𐐼 𐐮𐐻 𐐿𐐩𐑋 𐐻𐐭 𐐹𐐰𐑅 𐑄𐐰𐐻 𐐌 𐐺𐐨𐐸𐐯𐑊𐐼 𐑋𐐲𐑊𐐻𐐮𐐻𐐷𐐭𐐼𐑆 𐑀𐐰𐑄𐐲𐑉𐐼 𐐻𐐭𐑀𐐯𐑄𐐲𐑉 𐐻𐐭 𐐺𐐰𐐻𐑊, 𐐶𐐲𐑌 𐐲𐑀𐐯𐑌𐑅𐐻 𐑄 𐐲𐑄𐐲𐑉; 𐐰𐑌𐐼 𐐌 𐐺𐐨𐐸𐐯𐑊𐐼 𐐶𐐫𐑉𐑆, 𐐰𐑌𐐼 𐑉𐐭𐑋𐐲𐑉𐑆 𐐱𐑂 𐐶𐐫𐑉𐑆, 𐐰𐑌𐐼 𐑀𐑉𐐩𐐻 𐑅𐑊𐐫𐐻𐐲𐑉𐑆 𐐶𐐮𐑄 𐑄 𐑅𐐫𐑉𐐼 𐐲𐑋𐐲𐑍 𐑋𐐴 𐐹𐐨𐐹𐑊.

23. 𐐈𐑌𐐼 𐐮𐐻 𐐿𐐩𐑋 𐐻𐐭 𐐹𐐰𐑅 𐑄𐐰𐐻 𐐌 𐐺𐐨𐐸𐐯𐑊𐐼 𐑋𐐯𐑌𐐮 𐐾𐐯𐑌𐐲𐑉𐐩𐑇𐐲𐑌𐑆 𐐹𐐰𐑅 𐐲𐐶𐐩, 𐐰𐑁𐐻𐐲𐑉 𐑄 𐑋𐐰𐑌𐐲𐑉 𐐱𐑂 𐐶𐐫𐑉𐑆 𐐰𐑌𐐼 𐐿𐐱𐑌𐐻𐐯𐑌𐑇𐐲𐑌𐑆 𐐮𐑌 𐑄 𐑊𐐰𐑌𐐼; 𐐰𐑌𐐼 𐐌 𐐺𐐨𐐸𐐯𐑊𐐼 𐑋𐐯𐑌𐐮 𐑅𐐮𐐻𐐮𐑆, 𐐷𐐩, 𐐨𐑂𐑌 𐑄𐐰𐐻 𐐌 𐐼𐐮𐐼 𐑌𐐱𐐻 𐑌𐐲𐑋𐐺𐐲𐑉 𐑄𐐯𐑋.

24. 𐐈𐑌𐐼 𐐮𐐻 𐐿𐐩𐑋 𐐻𐐭 𐐹𐐰𐑅 𐑄𐐰𐐻 𐐌 𐑅𐐫 𐐲 𐑋𐐮𐑅𐐻 𐐱𐑂 𐐼𐐪𐑉𐐿𐑌𐐯𐑅 𐐱𐑌 𐑄 𐑁𐐩𐑅 𐐱𐑂 𐑄 𐑊𐐰𐑌𐐼 𐐱𐑂 𐐹𐑉𐐱𐑋𐐮𐑅; 𐐰𐑌𐐼 𐐌 𐑅𐐫 𐑊𐐴𐐻𐑌𐐮𐑍𐑆, 𐐰𐑌𐐼 𐐌 𐐸𐐲𐑉𐐼 𐑃𐐲𐑌𐐼𐐲𐑉𐐮𐑍𐑆, 𐐰𐑌𐐼 𐐲𐑉𐑃𐐿𐐶𐐩𐐿𐑅, 𐐰𐑌𐐼 𐐫𐑊 𐑋𐐰𐑌𐐲𐑉 𐐱𐑂 𐐻𐐷𐐭𐑋𐐲𐑊𐐻𐐷𐐭𐐲𐑅 𐑌𐐱𐐮𐑆𐐯𐑆; 𐐰𐑌𐐼 𐐌 𐑅𐐫 𐑄 𐐲𐑉𐑃 𐐰𐑌𐐼 𐑄 𐑉𐐱𐐿𐑅 𐑄𐐰𐐻 𐑄𐐩 𐑉𐐯𐑌𐐻; 𐐰𐑌𐐼 𐐌 𐑅𐐫 𐑋𐐵𐑌𐐻𐐮𐑌𐑆 𐐻𐐲𐑋𐐺𐑊𐐮𐑍 𐐮𐑌𐐻𐐭 𐐹𐐨𐑅𐐯𐑆; 𐐰𐑌𐐼 𐐌 𐑅𐐫 𐑄 𐐹𐑊𐐩𐑌𐑆 𐐱𐑂 𐑄 𐐲𐑉𐑃, 𐑄𐐰𐐻 𐑄𐐩 𐐶𐐲𐑉 𐐺𐑉𐐬𐐿𐑌 𐐲𐐹; 𐐰𐑌𐐼 𐐌 𐑅𐐫 𐑋𐐯𐑌𐐮 𐑅𐐮𐐻𐐮𐑆, 𐑄𐐰𐐻 𐑄𐐩 𐐶𐐲𐑉 𐑅𐐲𐑍𐐿; 𐐰𐑌𐐼 𐐌 𐑅𐐫 𐑋𐐯𐑌𐐮 𐑄𐐰𐐻 𐑄𐐩 𐐶𐐲𐑉 𐐺𐐲𐑉𐑌𐐼 𐐶𐐮𐑄 𐑁𐐴𐑉; 𐐰𐑌𐐼 𐐌 𐑅𐐫 𐑋𐐯𐑌𐐮 𐑄𐐰𐐻 𐐼𐐮𐐼 𐐻𐐲𐑋𐐺𐑊 𐐻𐐭 𐑄 𐐲𐑉𐑃, 𐐺𐐨𐐿𐐫𐑆 𐐱𐑂 𐑄 𐐿𐐶𐐩𐐿𐐮𐑍 𐑄𐐩𐑉𐐱𐑂.

25. 𐐈𐑌𐐼 𐐮𐐻 𐐿𐐩𐑋 𐐻𐐭 𐐹𐐰𐑅 𐐰𐑁𐐻𐐲𐑉 𐐌 𐑅𐐫 𐑄𐐨𐑆 𐑃𐐮𐑍𐑆, 𐐌 𐑅𐐫 𐑄 𐑂𐐩𐐹𐐲𐑉 𐐱𐑂 𐐼𐐪𐑉𐐿𐑌𐐯𐑅, 𐑄𐐰𐐻 𐐮𐐻 𐐹𐐰𐑅𐐻 𐑁𐑉𐐱𐑋 𐐱𐑁 𐑄 𐑁𐐩𐑅 𐐱𐑂 𐑄 𐐲𐑉𐑃; 𐐰𐑌𐐼 𐐺𐐨𐐸𐐬𐑊𐐼 𐐌 𐑅𐐫 𐑋𐐲𐑊𐐻𐐮𐐻𐐷𐐭𐐼𐑆 𐐸𐐭 𐐸𐐰𐐼 𐑁𐐫𐑊𐑌, 𐐺𐐨𐐿𐐫𐑆 𐐱𐑂 𐑄 𐑀𐑉𐐩𐐻 𐐰𐑌𐐼 𐐻𐐯𐑉𐐮𐐺𐑊 𐐾𐐲𐐾𐑋𐐯𐑌𐐻𐑅 𐐱𐑂 𐑄 𐐢𐐫𐑉𐐼. 𐐈𐑌𐐼 𐐌 𐑅𐐫 𐑄 𐐸𐐯𐑂𐐯𐑌𐑆 𐐬𐐹𐑌, 𐐰𐑌𐐼 𐑄 𐐢𐐰𐑋 𐐱𐑂 𐐘𐐱𐐼 𐐼𐐨𐑅𐐯𐑌𐐼𐐮𐑍 𐐵𐐻 𐐱𐑂 𐐸𐐯𐑂𐑌; 𐐰𐑌𐐼 𐐸𐐨 𐐿𐐩𐑋 𐐼𐐵𐑌 𐐰𐑌𐐼 𐑇𐐬𐐼 𐐸𐐮𐑋𐑅𐐯𐑊𐑁 𐐲𐑌𐐻𐐭 𐑄𐐯𐑋. 𐐈𐑌𐐼 𐐌 𐐫𐑊𐑅𐐬 𐑅𐐫 𐐰𐑌𐐼 𐐺𐐯𐑉 𐑉𐐯𐐿𐐫𐑉𐐼, 𐑄𐐰𐐻 𐑄 𐐐𐐬𐑊𐐨 𐐘𐐬𐑅𐐻 𐑁𐐯𐑊 𐐲𐐹𐐱𐑌 𐐻𐐶𐐯𐑊𐑂 𐐲𐑄𐐲𐑉𐑆; 𐐰𐑌𐐼 𐑄𐐩 𐐶𐐲𐑉 𐐫𐑉𐐼𐐩𐑌𐐼 𐐱𐑂 𐐘𐐱𐐼, 𐐰𐑌𐐼 𐐽𐐬𐑆𐑌.

26. 𐐈𐑌𐐼 𐑄 𐐩𐑌𐐾𐐯𐑊 𐑅𐐹𐐩𐐿 𐐲𐑌𐐻𐐭 𐑋𐐨, 𐑅𐐩𐐮𐑍, 𐐒𐐨𐐸𐐬𐑊𐐼 𐑄 𐐻𐐶𐐯𐑊𐑂 𐐼𐐮𐑅𐐴𐐹𐑊𐑆 𐐱𐑂 𐑄 𐐢𐐰𐑋, 𐐸𐐭 𐐪𐑉 𐐽𐐬𐑆𐑌 𐐻𐐭 𐑋𐐮𐑌𐐮𐑅𐐻𐐲𐑉 𐐲𐑌𐐻𐐭 𐑄𐐴 𐑅𐐨𐐼. 𐐈𐑌𐐼 𐐸𐐨 𐑅𐐯𐐼 𐐲𐑌𐐻𐐭 𐑋𐐨, 𐐜𐐵 𐑉𐐨𐑋𐐯𐑋𐐺𐐲𐑉𐐯𐑅𐐻 𐑄 𐐻𐐶𐐯𐑊𐑂 𐐲𐐹𐐱𐑅𐑊𐑆 𐐱𐑂 𐑄 𐐢𐐰𐑋? 𐐒𐐨𐐸𐐬𐑊𐐼 𐑄𐐩 𐐪𐑉 𐑄𐐩 𐐸𐐭 𐑇𐐰𐑊 𐐾𐐲𐐾 𐑄 𐐻𐐶𐐯𐑊𐑂 𐐻𐑉𐐴𐐺𐑆 𐐱𐑂 𐐆𐑆-𐑉𐐩𐐯𐑊; 𐐸𐐶𐐯𐑉𐑁𐐫𐑉 𐑄 𐐻𐐶𐐯𐑊𐑂 𐑋𐐮𐑌𐐮𐑅𐐻𐐲𐑉𐑆 𐐱𐑂 𐑄𐐴 𐑅𐐨𐐼 𐑇𐐰𐑊 𐐺 𐐾𐐲𐐾𐐼 𐐱𐑂 𐑄𐐯𐑋; 𐑁𐐫𐑉 𐐷 𐐪𐑉 𐐱𐑂 𐑄 𐐸𐐵𐑅 𐐱𐑂 𐐆𐑆𐑉𐐩𐐯𐑊; 𐐰𐑌𐐼 𐑄𐐨𐑆 𐐻𐐶𐐯𐑊𐑂 𐑋𐐮𐑌𐐮𐑅𐐻𐐲𐑉𐑆 𐐸𐐭𐑋 𐑄𐐵 𐐺𐐨𐐸𐐬𐑊𐐼𐐯𐑅𐐻, 𐑇𐐰𐑊 𐐾𐐲𐐾 𐑄𐐴 𐑅𐐨𐐼. 𐐈𐑌𐐼 𐐺𐐨𐐸𐐬𐑊𐐼 𐑄𐐩 𐐪𐑉 𐑉𐐴𐐽𐐲𐑅 𐑁𐐫𐑉𐐯𐑂𐐲𐑉; 𐑁𐐫𐑉 𐐺𐐨𐐿𐐫𐑆 𐐱𐑂 𐑄𐐩𐑉 𐑁𐐩𐑃 𐐮𐑌 𐑄 𐐢𐐰𐑋 𐐱𐑂 𐐘𐐱𐐼, 𐑄𐐩𐑉 𐑀𐐪𐑉𐑋𐐯𐑌𐐻𐑅 𐐪𐑉 𐑋𐐩𐐼 𐐸𐐶𐐴𐐻 𐐮𐑌 𐐸𐐮𐑆 𐐺𐑊𐐲𐐼.

27. 𐐈𐑌𐐼 𐑄 𐐩𐑌𐐾𐐯𐑊 𐑅𐐯𐐼 𐐲𐑌𐐻𐐭 𐑋𐐨, 𐐢𐐳𐐿! 𐐈𐑌𐐼 𐐌 𐑊𐐳𐐿𐐻, 𐐰𐑌𐐼 𐐺𐐨𐐸𐐯𐑊𐐼 𐑃𐑉𐐨 𐐾𐐯𐑌𐐲𐑉𐐩-𐑇𐐲𐑌𐑆 𐐹𐐰𐑅 𐐲𐐶𐐩 𐐮𐑌 𐑉𐐴𐐽𐐲𐑅𐑌𐐯𐑅; 𐐰𐑌𐐼 𐑄𐐩𐑉 𐑀𐐪𐑉𐑋𐐯𐑌𐐻𐑅 𐐶𐐲𐑉 𐐸𐐶𐐴𐐻, 𐐨𐑂𐑌 𐑊𐐴𐐿 𐐲𐑌𐐻𐐭 𐑄 𐐢𐐰𐑋 𐐱𐑂 𐐘𐐱𐐼. 𐐈𐑌𐐼 𐑄 𐐩𐑌𐐾𐐯𐑊 𐑅𐐯𐐼 𐐲𐑌𐐻𐐭 𐑋𐐨, 𐐜𐐨𐑆 𐐪𐑉 𐑋𐐩𐐼 𐐸𐐶𐐴𐐻 𐐮𐑌 𐑄 𐐺𐑊𐐲𐐼 𐐱𐑂 𐑄 𐐢𐐰𐑋, 𐐺𐐨-𐐿𐐫𐑆 𐐱𐑂 𐑄𐐩𐑉 𐑁𐐩𐑃 𐐮𐑌 𐐸𐐮𐑋. 𐐈𐑌𐐼 𐐌, 𐐤𐐀𐑁𐐴, 𐐫𐑊𐑅𐐬 𐑅𐐫 𐑋𐐯𐑌𐐮 𐐱𐑂 𐑄 𐑁𐐬𐑉𐑃 𐐾𐐯𐑌𐐲𐑉𐐩𐑇𐐲𐑌 𐐸𐐭 𐐹𐐰𐑅𐐻 𐐲𐐶𐐩 𐐮𐑌 𐑉𐐴𐐽𐐲𐑅𐑌𐐯𐑅.

28. 𐐈𐑌𐐼 𐐮𐐻 𐐿𐐩𐑋 𐐻𐐭 𐐹𐐰𐑅, 𐑄𐐰𐐻 𐐌 𐑅𐐫 𐑄 𐑋𐐲𐑊𐐻𐐮𐐻𐐷𐐭𐐼𐑆 𐐱𐑂 𐑄 𐐲𐑉𐑃 𐑀𐐰𐑄𐐲𐑉𐐼 𐐻𐐭𐑀𐐯𐑄𐐲𐑉.

𐐰𐑌𐐼 𐑄 𐐩𐑌𐐾𐐯𐑊 𐑅𐐯𐐼 𐐲𐑌𐐻𐐭 𐑋𐐨, 𐐺𐐨𐐸𐐬𐑊𐐼 𐑄𐐴 𐑅𐐨𐐼, 𐐰𐑌𐐼 𐐫𐑊𐑅𐐬 𐑄 𐑅𐐨𐐼 𐐱𐑂 𐑄𐐴 𐐺𐑉𐐯𐑄𐑉𐐯𐑌! 𐐰𐑌𐐼 𐐮𐐻 𐐿𐐩𐑋 𐐻𐐭 𐐹𐐰𐑅 𐑄𐐰𐐻 𐐴 𐑊𐐳𐐿𐐻 𐐰𐑌𐐼 𐐺𐐨𐐸𐐯𐑊𐐼 𐑄 𐐹𐐨𐐹𐑊 𐐱𐑂 𐑋𐐴 𐑅𐐨𐐼 𐑀𐐰𐑄𐐯𐑉𐐼 𐐻𐐳𐑀𐐯𐑄𐐯𐑉 𐐮𐑌 𐑋𐐲𐑊𐐻𐐮𐐻𐐷𐐭𐐼𐑆 𐐰𐑀𐐯𐑌𐑅𐐻 𐑄 𐑅𐐨𐐼 𐐱𐑂 𐑋𐐴 𐐺𐑉𐐯𐑄𐑉𐐯𐑌; 𐐰𐑌𐐼 𐑄𐐩 𐐶𐐲𐑉 𐑀𐐰𐑄𐐯𐑉𐐼 𐐻𐐳𐑀𐐯𐑄𐐯𐑉 𐐻𐐭 𐐺𐐰𐐻𐑊.

29. 𐐰𐑌𐐼 𐑄 𐐩𐑌𐐾𐐯𐑊 𐑅𐐹𐐩𐐿 𐐲𐑌𐐻𐐭 𐑋𐐨, 𐑅𐐩𐐮𐑍, 𐐺𐐨𐐸𐐬𐑊𐐼 𐑄 𐑁𐐵𐑌𐐻𐐮𐑌 𐐱𐑂 𐑁𐐮𐑊𐑃𐐨 𐐶𐐫𐐻𐐲𐑉 𐐸𐐶𐐮𐐽 𐑄𐐴 𐑁𐐪𐑄𐐲𐑉 𐑅𐐫; 𐐷𐐩, 𐐨𐑂𐐯𐑌 𐑄 𐑉𐐮𐑂𐐲𐑉 𐐱𐑂 𐐸𐐶𐐮𐐽 𐐸𐐨 𐑅𐐹𐐩𐐿; 𐐰𐑌𐐼 𐑄 𐐼𐐯𐐹𐑃𐑅 𐑄𐐩𐑉𐐱𐑂 𐐪𐑉 𐑄 𐐼𐐯𐐹𐑃𐑅 𐐱𐑂 𐐸𐐯𐑊; 𐐰𐑌𐐼 𐑄 𐑋𐐮𐑅𐐻𐑅 𐐱𐑂 𐐼𐐪𐑉𐐿𐑌𐐯𐑅 𐐪𐑉 𐑄 𐐻𐐯𐑋𐐹𐐻𐐩𐑇𐐲𐑌𐑆 𐐱𐑂 𐑄 𐐼𐐯𐑂𐐮𐑊, 𐐸𐐶𐐮𐐽 𐐺𐑊𐐴𐑌𐐼𐐯𐑃 𐑄 𐐴𐑆, 𐐰𐑌𐐼 𐐸𐐪𐑉𐐼𐐯𐑌𐐯𐑃 𐑄 𐐸𐐪𐑉𐐻𐑅 𐐱𐑂 𐑄 𐐽𐐮𐑊𐐼𐑉𐐯𐑌 𐐱𐑂 𐑋𐐯𐑌, 𐐰𐑌𐐼 𐑊𐐨𐐼𐐯𐑃 𐑄𐐯𐑋 𐐰𐐶𐐩 𐐮𐑌𐐻𐐭 𐐺𐑉𐐫𐐼 𐑉𐐬𐐼𐑆, 𐑄𐐰𐐻 𐑄𐐩 𐐹𐐯𐑉𐐮𐑇 𐐰𐑌𐐼 𐐪𐑉 𐑊𐐫𐑅𐐻; 𐐰𐑌𐐼 𐑄 𐑊𐐪𐑉𐐾 𐐰𐑌𐐼 𐑅𐐹𐐩𐑇𐐲𐑅 𐐺𐐮𐑊𐐼𐐮𐑍 𐐸𐐶𐐮𐐽 𐑄𐐴 𐑁𐐪𐑄𐐲𐑉 𐑅𐐫 𐐮𐑆 𐑂𐐩𐑌 𐐮𐑋𐐰𐐾𐐮𐑌𐐩𐑇𐐲𐑌𐑆 𐐰𐑌𐐼 𐑄 𐐹𐑉𐐴𐐼 𐐱𐑂 𐑄 𐐽𐐮𐑊𐐼𐑉𐐯𐑌 𐐱𐑂 𐑋𐐯𐑌. 𐐰𐑌𐐼 𐐪 𐑀𐑉𐐩𐐻 𐐰𐑌𐐼 𐐪 𐐻𐐯𐑉𐐮𐐺𐑊 𐑀𐐲𐑊𐑁 𐐼𐐮𐑂𐐴𐐼𐐯𐑃 𐑄𐐯𐑋; 𐐷𐐩, 𐐨𐑂𐐯𐑌 𐑄 𐐶𐐲𐑉𐐼 𐐱𐑂 𐑄 𐐾𐐲𐑅𐐻𐐮𐑅 𐐱𐑂 𐑄 𐐨𐐻𐐲𐑉𐑌𐐲𐑊 𐐘𐐱𐐼, 𐐰𐑌𐐼 𐑄 𐑋𐐯𐑅𐐴𐐰 𐐸𐐭 𐐮𐑆 𐑄 𐑊𐐰𐑋 𐐱𐑂 𐐘𐐱𐐼, 𐐱𐑂 𐐸𐐭𐑋 𐑄 𐐸𐐬𐑊𐐨 𐐘𐐬𐑅𐐻 𐐺𐐩𐑉𐐯𐑃 𐑉𐐯𐐿𐐲𐑉𐐼, 𐑁𐑉𐐱𐑋 𐑄 𐐺𐐨𐑀𐐮𐑌𐐮𐑍 𐐱𐑂 𐑄 𐐶𐐲𐑉𐑊𐐼 𐐲𐑌𐐻𐐮𐑊 𐑄𐐮𐑅 𐐻𐐴𐑋, 𐐰𐑌𐐼 𐑁𐑉𐐱𐑋 𐑄𐐮𐑅 𐐻𐐴𐑋 𐐸𐐯𐑌𐑅𐑁𐐬𐑉𐑃 𐐰𐑌𐐼 𐑁𐐫𐑉 𐐯𐑂𐐲𐑉. 𐐰𐑌𐐼 𐐸𐐶𐐴𐑊 𐑄 𐐩𐑌𐐾𐐯𐑊 𐑅𐐹𐐩𐐿 𐑄𐐨𐑆 𐐶𐐲𐑉𐐼𐑆, 𐐴 𐐺𐐨𐐸𐐯𐑊𐐼 𐐰𐑌𐐼 𐑅𐐫 𐑄𐐰𐐻 𐑄 𐑅𐐨𐐼 𐐱𐑂 𐑋𐐴 𐐺𐑉𐐯𐑄𐑉𐐯𐑌 𐐼𐐮𐐼 𐐿𐐱𐑌𐐻𐐯𐑌𐐼 𐐰𐑀𐐯𐑌𐑅𐐻 𐑋𐐴 𐑅𐐨𐐼, 𐐰𐐿𐐫𐑉𐐼𐐮𐑍 𐐻𐐭 𐑄 𐐶𐐲𐑉𐐼 𐐱𐑂 𐑄 𐐩𐑌𐐾𐐯𐑊; 𐐰𐑌𐐼 𐐺𐐨𐐿𐐫𐑆 𐐱𐑂 𐑄 𐐹𐑉𐐴𐐼 𐐱𐑂 𐑋𐐴 𐑅𐐨𐐼, 𐐰𐑌𐐼 𐑄 𐐻𐐯𐑋𐐹𐐻𐐩𐑇𐐲𐑌𐑆 𐐱𐑂 𐑄 𐐼𐐯𐑂𐐮𐑊, 𐐴 𐐺𐐨𐐸𐐯𐑊𐐼 𐑄𐐰𐐻 𐑄 𐑅𐐨𐐼 𐐱𐑂 𐑋𐐴 𐐺𐑉𐐯𐑄𐑉𐐯𐑌 𐐼𐐮𐐼 𐐬𐑂𐐲𐑉𐐹𐐵𐐲𐑉 𐑄 𐐹𐐨𐐹𐑊 𐐱𐑂 𐑋𐐴 𐑅𐐨𐐼.

30. 𐐰𐑌𐐼 𐐮𐐻 𐐿𐐩𐑋 𐐻𐐭 𐐹𐐰𐑅 𐑄𐐰𐐻 𐐴 𐐺𐐨𐐸𐐯𐑊𐐼 𐐰𐑌𐐼 𐑅𐐫 𐑄 𐐹𐐨𐐹𐑊 𐐱𐑂 𐑄 𐑅𐐨𐐼 𐐱𐑂 𐑋𐐴 𐐺𐑉𐐯𐑄𐑉𐐯𐑌, 𐑄𐐰𐐻 𐑄𐐩 𐐸𐐰𐐼 𐐬𐑂𐐲𐑉𐐿𐐲𐑋 𐑋𐐴 𐑅𐐨𐐼; 𐐰𐑌𐐼 𐑄𐐩 𐐶𐐯𐑌𐐻 𐑁𐐬𐑉𐑃 𐐮𐑌 𐑋𐐲𐑊𐐻𐐮𐐻𐐷𐐭𐐼𐑆 𐐲𐐹𐐱𐑌 𐑄 𐑁𐐩𐑅 𐐱𐑂 𐑄 𐑊𐐰𐑌𐐼. 𐐰𐑌𐐼 𐐴 𐑅𐐫 𐑄𐐯𐑋 𐑀𐐰𐑄𐐯𐑉𐐼 𐐻𐐳𐑀𐐯𐑄𐐯𐑉 𐐮𐑌 𐑋𐐲𐑊𐐻𐐮𐐻𐐷𐐭𐐼𐑆; 𐐰𐑌𐐼 𐐴 𐑅𐐫 𐐶𐐫𐑉𐑆 𐐰𐑌𐐼 𐑉𐐭𐑋𐐲𐑉𐑆 𐐱𐑂 𐐶𐐫𐑉𐑆 𐐰𐑋𐐲𐑍 𐑄𐐯𐑋; 𐐰𐑌𐐼 𐐮𐑌 𐐶𐐫𐑉𐑆 𐐰𐑌𐐼 𐑉𐐭𐑋𐐲𐑉𐑆 𐐱𐑂 𐐶𐐫𐑉𐑆, 𐐴 𐑅𐐫 𐑋𐐯𐑌𐐨 𐐾𐐯𐑌𐐲𐑉𐐩𐑇𐐲𐑌𐑆 𐐹𐐰𐑅 𐐰𐐶𐐩. 𐐰𐑌𐐼 𐑄 𐐩𐑌𐐾𐐯𐑊 𐑅𐐯𐐼 𐐲𐑌𐐻𐐭 𐑋𐐨, 𐐺𐐨𐐸𐐬𐑊𐐼 𐑄𐐨𐑆 𐑇𐐰𐑊 𐐼𐐶𐐮𐑌𐐼𐑊 𐐮𐑌 𐐲𐑌𐐺𐐨𐑊𐐨𐑁.

31. 𐐰𐑌𐐼 𐐮𐐻 𐐿𐐩𐑋 𐐻𐐭 𐐹𐐰𐑅 𐑄𐐰𐐻 𐐴 𐐺𐐨𐐸𐐯𐑊𐐼 𐐪𐑁𐐻𐐲𐑉 𐑄𐐩 𐐸𐐰𐐼 𐐼𐐶𐐮𐑌𐐼𐑊𐐼 𐐮𐑌 𐐲𐑌𐐺𐐨𐑊𐐨𐑁, 𐑄𐐩 𐐺𐐨𐐿𐐩𐑋 𐐪 𐐼𐐪𐑉𐐿, 𐐰𐑌𐐼 𐑊𐐬𐑄𐑅𐐲𐑋, 𐐰𐑌𐐼 𐐪 𐑁𐐮𐑊𐑃𐐨 𐐹𐐨𐐹𐑊, 𐑁𐐳𐑊 𐐱𐑂 𐐴𐐼𐑊𐑌𐐯𐑅 𐐰𐑌𐐼 𐐫𐑊 𐑋𐐰𐑌𐐲𐑉 𐐱𐑂 𐐰𐐺𐐱𐑋𐐮𐑌𐐩𐑇𐐲𐑌𐑆.

32. 𐐰𐑌𐐼 𐐮𐐻 𐐿𐐩𐑋 𐐻𐐭 𐐹𐐰𐑅 𐑄𐐰𐐻 𐑄 𐐩𐑌𐐾𐐯𐑊 𐑅𐐹𐐩𐐿 𐐲𐑌𐐻𐐭 𐑋𐐨, 𐑅𐐩𐐮𐑍, 𐑊𐐳𐐿! 𐐰𐑌𐐼 𐐴 𐑊𐐳𐐿𐐻 𐐰𐑌𐐼 𐐺𐐨𐐸𐐯𐑊𐐼 𐑋𐐯𐑌𐐨 𐑌𐐩𐑇𐐲𐑌𐑆 𐐰𐑌𐐼 𐐿𐐮𐑍𐐼𐐲𐑋𐑆. 𐐰𐑌𐐼 𐑄 𐐩𐑌𐐾𐐯𐑊 𐑅𐐯𐐼 𐐲𐑌𐐻𐐭 𐑋𐐨, 𐐐𐐶𐐱𐐻 𐐺𐐨𐐸𐐬𐑊𐐼𐐯𐑅𐐻 𐑄𐐵? 𐐰𐑌𐐼 𐐴 𐑅𐐯𐐼, 𐐴 𐐺𐐨𐐸𐐬𐑊𐐼 𐑋𐐯𐑌𐐨 𐑌𐐩𐑇𐐲𐑌𐑆 𐐰𐑌𐐼 𐐿𐐮𐑍𐐼𐐲𐑋𐑆. 𐐰𐑌𐐼 𐐸𐐨 𐑅𐐯𐐼 𐐲𐑌𐐻𐐭 𐑋𐐨, 𐑄𐐨𐑆 𐐪𐑉 𐑄 𐑌𐐩𐑇𐐲𐑌𐑆 𐐰𐑌𐐼 𐐿𐐮𐑍𐐼𐐲𐑋𐑆 𐐱𐑂 𐑄 𐐖𐐯𐑌𐐻𐐴𐑊𐑆.

33. 𐐰𐑌𐐼 𐐮𐐻 𐐿𐐩𐑋 𐐻𐐭 𐐹𐐰𐑅 𐑄𐐰𐐻 𐐴 𐑅𐐫 𐐰𐑋𐐲𐑍 𐑄 𐑌𐐩𐑇𐐲𐑌𐑆 𐐱𐑂 𐑄 𐐖𐐯𐑌𐐻𐐴𐑊𐑆 𐑄 𐑁𐐫𐑉𐑋𐐩𐑇𐐲𐑌 𐐱𐑂 𐐪 𐑀𐑉𐐩𐐻 𐐽𐐲𐑉𐐽. 𐐰𐑌𐐼 𐑄 𐐩𐑌𐐾𐐯𐑊 𐑅𐐯𐐼 𐐲𐑌𐐻𐐭 𐑋𐐨, 𐐺𐐨𐐸𐐬𐑊𐐼 𐑄 𐑁𐐫𐑉𐑋𐐩𐑇𐐲𐑌 𐐱𐑂 𐐪 𐐽𐐲𐑉𐐽, 𐐸𐐶𐐮𐐽 𐐮𐑆 𐑋𐐬𐑅𐐻 𐐰𐐺𐐱𐑋𐐮𐑌𐐰𐐺𐑊 𐐰𐐺𐐲𐑂 𐐫𐑊 𐐲𐑄𐐲𐑉 𐐽𐐲𐑉𐐽𐐯𐑆, 𐐸𐐶𐐮𐐽 𐑅𐑊𐐩𐐯𐑃 𐑄 𐑅𐐩𐑌𐐻𐑅 𐐱𐑂 𐐘𐐱𐐼, 𐐷𐐩, 𐐰𐑌𐐼 𐐻𐐫𐑉𐐽𐐲𐑉𐐯𐑃 𐑄𐐯𐑋 𐐰𐑌𐐼 𐐺𐐴𐑌𐐼𐐯𐑃 𐑄𐐯𐑋 𐐼𐐵𐑌, 𐐰𐑌𐐼 𐐷𐐬𐐿𐐯𐑃 𐑄𐐯𐑋 𐐶𐐮𐑄 𐐪 𐐷𐐬𐐿 𐐱𐑂 𐐴𐐲𐑉𐑌, 𐐰𐑌𐐼 𐐺𐑉𐐮𐑍𐐯𐑃 𐑄𐐯𐑋 𐐼𐐵𐑌 𐐮𐑌𐐻𐐭 𐐿𐐰𐐹𐐻𐐮𐑂𐐮𐐻𐐨.

34. 𐐰𐑌𐐼 𐐮𐐻 𐐿𐐩𐑋 𐐻𐐭 𐐹𐐰𐑅 𐑄𐐰𐐻 𐐴 𐐺𐐨𐐸𐐯𐑊𐐼 𐑄𐐮𐑅 𐑀𐑉𐐩𐐻 𐐰𐑌𐐼 𐐰𐐺𐐱𐑋𐐮𐑌𐐰𐐺𐑊 𐐽𐐲𐑉𐐽; 𐐰𐑌𐐼 𐐴 𐑅𐐫 𐑄 𐐼𐐯𐑂𐐮𐑊 𐑄𐐰𐐻 𐐸𐐨 𐐶𐐱𐑆 𐑄 𐑁𐐵𐑌𐐼𐐩𐑇𐐲𐑌 𐐱𐑂 𐐮𐐻. 𐐰𐑌𐐼 𐐴 𐐫𐑊𐑅𐐬 𐑅𐐫 𐑀𐐬𐑊𐐼, 𐐰𐑌𐐼 𐑅𐐮𐑊𐑂𐐲𐑉, 𐐰𐑌𐐼 𐑅𐐮𐑊𐐿𐑅, 𐐰𐑌𐐼 𐑅𐐿𐐪𐑉𐑊𐐯𐐻𐑅, 𐐰𐑌𐐼 𐑁𐐴𐑌-𐐻𐐶𐐴𐑌𐐼 𐑊𐐮𐑌𐐯𐑌, 𐐰𐑌𐐼 𐐫𐑊 𐑋𐐰𐑌𐐲𐑉 𐐱𐑂 𐐹𐑉𐐯𐑇𐐲𐑅 𐐿𐑊𐐬𐑄𐐮𐑍; 𐐰𐑌𐐼 𐐴 𐑅𐐫 𐑋𐐯𐑌𐐨 𐐸𐐪𐑉𐑊𐐲𐐻𐑅. 𐐰𐑌𐐼 𐑄 𐐩𐑌𐐾𐐯𐑊 𐑅𐐹𐐩𐐿 𐐲𐑌𐐻𐐭 𐑋𐐨, 𐑅𐐩𐐮𐑍, 𐐒𐐨𐐸𐐬𐑊𐐼 𐑄 𐑀𐐬𐑊𐐼, 𐐰𐑌𐐼 𐑄 𐑅𐐮𐑊𐑂𐐲𐑉, 𐐰𐑌𐐼 𐑄 𐑅𐐮𐑊𐐿𐑅, 𐐰𐑌𐐼 𐑄 𐑅𐐿𐐪𐑉𐑊𐐯𐐻𐑅, 𐐰𐑌𐐼 𐑄 𐑁𐐴𐑌-𐐻𐐶𐐴𐑌𐐼 𐑊𐐮𐑌𐐯𐑌, 𐐰𐑌𐐼 𐑄 𐐹𐑉𐐯-

𐑇𐐲𐑅 𐐿𐑊𐐬𐑄𐐮𐑍, 𐐰𐑌𐐼 𐑄 𐐸𐐪𐑉𐑊𐐲𐐻𐑅, 𐐪𐑉 𐑄 𐐼𐐨𐑆𐐴𐑉𐑆 𐐱𐑂 𐑄𐐮𐑅 𐑀𐑉𐐩𐐻 𐐰𐑌𐐼 𐐲𐐺𐐱𐑋𐐮𐑌𐐲𐐺𐑊 𐐽𐐲𐑉𐐽: 𐐰𐑌𐐼 𐐫𐑊𐑅𐐬 𐑁𐐫𐑉 𐑄 𐐹𐑉𐐩𐑆 𐐱𐑂 𐑄 𐐶𐐲𐑉𐑊𐐼, 𐐼𐐭 𐑄𐐩 𐐼𐐯𐑅𐐻𐑉𐐱𐐮 𐑄 𐑅𐐩𐑌𐐻𐑅 𐐱𐑂 𐐘𐐪𐐼, 𐐰𐑌𐐼 𐐺𐑉𐐮𐑍 𐑄𐐯𐑋 𐐼𐐵𐑌 𐐮𐑌𐐻𐐭 𐐿𐐰𐐹𐐻𐐮𐑂𐐮𐐻𐐨.

35. 𐐰𐑌𐐼 𐐮𐐻 𐐿𐐩𐑋 𐐻𐐭 𐐹𐐰𐑅 𐑄𐐰𐐻 𐐌 𐑊𐐳𐐿𐐻 𐐰𐑌𐐼 𐐺𐐨𐐸𐐯𐑊𐐼 𐑋𐐯𐑌𐐨 𐐶𐐫𐐻𐐲𐑉𐑆; 𐐰𐑌𐐼 𐑄𐐩 𐐼𐐮𐑂𐐴𐐼𐐯𐐼 𐑄 𐐖𐐯𐑌𐐻𐐴𐑊𐑆 𐑁𐑉𐐱𐑋 𐑄 𐑅𐐨𐐼 𐐱𐑂 𐑋𐐴 𐐺𐑉𐐯𐑄𐑉𐐯𐑌. 𐐰𐑌𐐼 𐐮𐐻 𐐿𐐩𐑋 𐐻𐐭 𐐹𐐰𐑅 𐑄𐐰𐐻 𐑄 𐐩𐑌𐐾𐐯𐑊 𐑅𐐯𐐼 𐐲𐑌𐐻𐐭 𐑋𐐨, 𐐒𐐨𐐸𐐬𐑊𐐼 𐑄 𐑉𐐪𐑃 𐐱𐑂 𐐘𐐪𐐼 𐐮𐑆 𐐲𐐹𐐪𐑌 𐑄 𐑅𐐨𐐼 𐐱𐑂 𐑄𐐴 𐐺𐑉𐐯𐑄𐑉𐐯𐑌! 𐐰𐑌𐐼 𐐌 𐑊𐐳𐐿𐐻 𐐰𐑌𐐼 𐐺𐐨𐐸𐐯𐑊𐐼 𐐲 𐑋𐐰𐑌 𐐲𐑋𐐲𐑍 𐑄 𐐖𐐯𐑌𐐻𐐴𐑊𐑆, 𐐸𐐭 𐐶𐐱𐑆 𐑅𐐯𐐹𐐲𐑉𐐩𐐻𐐯𐐼 𐑁𐑉𐐱𐑋 𐑄 𐑅𐐨𐐼 𐐱𐑂 𐑋𐐴 𐐺𐑉𐐯𐑄𐑉𐐯𐑌 𐐺𐐴 𐑄 𐑋𐐯𐑌𐐨 𐐶𐐫𐐻𐐲𐑉𐑆; 𐐰𐑌𐐼 𐐌 𐐺𐐨𐐸𐐯𐑊𐐼 𐑄 𐐝𐐹𐐮𐑉𐐮𐐻 𐐱𐑂 𐐘𐐪𐐼, 𐑄𐐰𐐻 𐐮𐐻 𐐿𐐩𐑋 𐐼𐐵𐑌 𐐰𐑌𐐼 𐑉𐐫𐐻 𐐲𐐹𐐪𐑌 𐑄 𐑋𐐰𐑌; 𐐰𐑌𐐼 𐐸𐐨 𐐶𐐯𐑌𐐻 𐑁𐐬𐑉𐑃 𐐲𐐹𐐪𐑌 𐑄 𐑋𐐯𐑌𐐨 𐐶𐐫𐐻𐐲𐑉𐑆, 𐐨𐑂𐐯𐑌 𐐲𐑌𐐻𐐭 𐑄 𐑅𐐨𐐼 𐐱𐑂 𐑋𐐴 𐐺𐑉𐐯𐑄𐑉𐐯𐑌, 𐐸𐐭 𐐶𐐲𐑉 𐐮𐑌 𐑄 𐐹𐑉𐐱𐑋𐐮𐑅𐐻 𐑊𐐰𐑌𐐼.

36. 𐐰𐑌𐐼 𐐮𐐻 𐐿𐐩𐑋 𐐻𐐭 𐐹𐐰𐑅 𐑄𐐰𐐻 𐐌 𐐺𐐨𐐸𐐯𐑊𐐼 𐑄 𐐝𐐹𐐮𐑉𐐮𐐻 𐐱𐑂 𐐘𐐪𐐼, 𐑄𐐰𐐻 𐐮𐐻 𐑉𐐫𐐻 𐐲𐐹𐐪𐑌 𐐲𐑄𐐲𐑉 𐐖𐐯𐑌𐐻𐐴𐑊𐑆; 𐐰𐑌𐐼 𐑄𐐩 𐐶𐐯𐑌𐐻 𐑁𐐬𐑉𐑃 𐐵𐐻 𐐱𐑂 𐐿𐐰𐐹𐐻𐐮𐑂𐐮𐐻𐐨 𐐲𐐹𐐪𐑌 𐑄 𐑋𐐯𐑌𐐨 𐐶𐐫𐐻𐐲𐑉𐑆.

37. 𐐰𐑌𐐼 𐐮𐐻 𐐿𐐩𐑋 𐐻𐐭 𐐹𐐰𐑅 𐑄𐐰𐐻 𐐌 𐐺𐐨𐐸𐐯𐑊𐐼 𐑋𐐯𐑌𐐨 𐑋𐐲𐑊𐐻𐐨𐐻𐐭𐐼𐑆 𐐱𐑂 𐑄 𐐖𐐯𐑌𐐻𐐴𐑊𐑆 𐐲𐐹𐐪𐑌 𐑄 𐑊𐐰𐑌𐐼 𐐱𐑂 𐐹𐑉𐐱𐑋𐐮𐑅; 𐐰𐑌𐐼 𐐌 𐐺𐐨𐐸𐐯𐑊𐐼 𐑄 𐑉𐐪𐑃 𐐱𐑂 𐐘𐐪𐐼, 𐑄𐐰𐐻 𐐮𐐻 𐐶𐐱𐑆 𐐲𐐹𐐪𐑌 𐑄 𐑅𐐨𐐼 𐐱𐑂 𐑋𐐴 𐐺𐑉𐐯𐑄𐑉𐐯𐑌; 𐐰𐑌𐐼 𐑄𐐩 𐐶𐐲𐑉 𐑅𐐿𐐰𐐻𐐲𐑉𐐼 𐐺𐐨𐑁𐐬𐑉 𐑄 𐐖𐐯𐑌𐐻𐐴𐑊𐑆, 𐐰𐑌𐐼 𐐶𐐲𐑉 𐑅𐑋𐐮𐐻𐑌. 𐐰𐑌𐐼 𐐌 𐐺𐐨𐐸𐐯𐑊𐐼 𐑄 𐐝𐐹𐐮𐑉𐐮𐐻 𐐱𐑂 𐑄 𐐢𐐫𐑉𐐼, 𐑄𐐰𐐻 𐐮𐐻 𐐶𐐱𐑆 𐐲𐐹𐐪𐑌 𐑄 𐐖𐐯𐑌𐐻𐐴𐑊𐑆; 𐑄𐐰𐐻 𐑄𐐩 𐐼𐐮𐐼 𐐹𐑉𐐱𐑅𐐹𐐲𐑉, 𐐰𐑌𐐼 𐐱𐐺𐐻𐐩𐑌 𐑄 𐑊𐐰𐑌𐐼 𐑁𐐫𐑉 𐑄𐐩𐑉 𐐮𐑌𐐸𐐯𐑉𐐮𐐻𐐰𐑌𐑅; 𐐰𐑌𐐼 𐐌 𐐺𐐨𐐸𐐯𐑊𐐼 𐑄𐐰𐐻 𐑄𐐩 𐐶𐐲𐑉 𐐸𐐶𐐴𐐻, 𐐰𐑌𐐼 𐐯𐐿𐑅𐐨𐐼𐐮𐑍𐑊𐐨 𐑁𐐩𐑉 𐐰𐑌𐐼 𐐺𐐧𐐻𐐮𐑁𐐳𐑊, 𐑊𐐴𐐿 𐐲𐑌𐐻𐐭 𐑋𐐴 𐐹𐐨𐐹𐑊 𐐺𐐨𐑁𐐬𐑉 𐑄𐐩 𐐶𐐲𐑉 𐑅𐑊𐐩𐑌.

38. 𐐰𐑌𐐼 𐐮𐐻 𐐿𐐩𐑋 𐐻𐐭 𐐹𐐰𐑅 𐑄𐐰𐐻 𐐌, 𐐤𐐨𐑁𐐴, 𐐺𐐨𐐸𐐯𐑊𐐼 𐑄𐐰𐐻 𐑄 𐐖𐐯𐑌𐐻𐐴𐑊𐑆 𐐸𐐭 𐐸𐐰𐐼 𐑀𐐪𐑌 𐑁𐐬𐑉𐑃 𐐵𐐻 𐐱𐑂 𐐿𐐰𐐹𐐻𐐮𐑂𐐮𐐻𐐨, 𐐼𐐮𐐼 𐐸𐐲𐑋𐐺𐑊 𐑄𐐯𐑋𐑅𐐯𐑊𐑂𐑆 𐐺𐐨𐑁𐐬𐑉 𐑄 𐐢𐐫𐑉𐐼; 𐐰𐑌𐐼 𐑄 𐐹𐐵𐐲𐑉 𐐱𐑂 𐑄 𐐢𐐫𐑉𐐼 𐐶𐐱𐑆 𐐶𐐮𐑄 𐑄𐐯𐑋; 𐐰𐑌𐐼 𐐌 𐐺𐐨𐐸𐐯𐑊𐐼 𐑄𐐰𐐻 𐑄𐐩𐑉 𐑋𐐲𐑄𐐲𐑉 𐐖𐐯𐑌𐐻𐐴𐑊𐑆 𐐶𐐲𐑉 𐑀𐐰𐑄𐐲𐑉𐐼 𐐻𐐳𐑀𐐯𐑄𐐲𐑉 𐐲𐐹𐐪𐑌 𐑄 𐐶𐐫𐐻𐐲𐑉𐑆, 𐐰𐑌𐐼 𐐲𐐹𐐪𐑌 𐑄 𐑊𐐰𐑌𐐼 𐐫𐑊𐑅𐐬, 𐐻𐐭 𐐺𐐰𐐻𐑊 𐐲𐑀𐐯𐑌𐑅𐐻 𐑄𐐯𐑋; 𐐰𐑌𐐼 𐐌 𐐺𐐨𐐸𐐯𐑊𐐼 𐑄𐐰𐐻 𐑄 𐐹𐐵𐐲𐑉 𐐱𐑂 𐐘𐐪𐐼 𐐶𐐱𐑆 𐐶𐐮𐑄 𐑄𐐯𐑋, 𐐰𐑌𐐼 𐐫𐑊𐑅𐐬 𐑄𐐰𐐻 𐑄 𐑉𐐪𐑃 𐐱𐑂 𐐘𐐪𐐼 𐐶𐐱𐑆 𐐲𐐹𐐪𐑌 𐐫𐑊 𐑄𐐬𐑆 𐑄𐐰𐐻 𐐶𐐲𐑉 𐑀𐐰𐑄𐐲𐑉𐐼 𐐻𐐳𐑀𐐯𐑄𐐲𐑉 𐐲𐑀𐐯𐑌𐑅𐐻 𐑄𐐯𐑋 𐐻𐐭 𐐺𐐰𐐻𐑊. 𐐰𐑌𐐼 𐐌, 𐐤𐐨𐑁𐐴, 𐐺𐐨𐐸𐐯𐑊𐐼 𐑄𐐰𐐻 𐑄 𐐖𐐯𐑌𐐻𐐴𐑊𐑆 𐑄𐐰𐐻 𐐸𐐰𐐼 𐑀𐐪𐑌 𐐵𐐻 𐐱𐑂 𐐿𐐰𐐹𐐻𐐮𐑂𐐮𐐻𐐨 𐐶𐐲𐑉 𐐼𐐯𐑊𐐮𐑂𐐲𐑉𐐼 𐐺𐐴 𐑄 𐐹𐐵𐐲𐑉 𐐱𐑂 𐐘𐐪𐐼 𐐵𐐻 𐐱𐑂 𐑄 𐐸𐐰𐑌𐐼𐑆 𐐱𐑂 𐐫𐑊 𐐲𐑄𐐲𐑉 𐑌𐐩𐑇𐐲𐑌𐑆.

39. 𐐰𐑌𐐼 𐐮𐐻 𐐿𐐩𐑋 𐐻𐐭 𐐹𐐰𐑅 𐑄𐐰𐐻 𐐌, 𐐤𐐨𐑁𐐴, 𐐺𐐨𐐸𐐯𐑊𐐼 𐑄𐐰𐐻 𐑄𐐩 𐐼𐐮𐐼 𐐹𐑉𐐱𐑅𐐹𐐲𐑉 𐐮𐑌 𐑄 𐑊𐐰𐑌𐐼; 𐐰𐑌𐐼 𐐌 𐐺𐐨𐐸𐐯𐑊𐐼 𐐲 𐐺𐐳𐐿, 𐐰𐑌𐐼 𐐮𐐻 𐐶𐐱𐑆 𐐿𐐰𐑉𐐨𐐼 𐑁𐐬𐑉𐑃 𐐲𐑋𐐲𐑍 𐑄𐐯𐑋. 𐐰𐑌𐐼 𐑄 𐐩𐑌𐐾𐐯𐑊 𐑅𐐯𐐼 𐐲𐑌𐐻𐐭 𐑋𐐨, 𐐤𐐬𐐯𐑅𐐻 𐑄𐐵 𐑄 𐑋𐐨𐑌𐐮𐑍 𐐱𐑂 𐑄 𐐺𐐳𐐿? 𐐰𐑌𐐼 𐐌 𐑅𐐯𐐼 𐐲𐑌𐐻𐐭 𐐸𐐮𐑋, 𐐌 𐑌𐐬 𐑌𐐪𐐻. 𐐰𐑌𐐼 𐐸𐐨 𐑅𐐯𐐼, 𐐒𐐨𐐸𐐬𐑊𐐼 𐐮𐐻 𐐹𐑉𐐬𐑅𐐨𐐼𐐯𐑃 𐐵𐐻 𐐱𐑂 𐑄 𐑋𐐵𐑃 𐐱𐑂 𐐲 𐐖𐐭: 𐐰𐑌𐐼 𐐌, 𐐤𐐨𐑁𐐴, 𐐺𐐨𐐸𐐯𐑊𐐼 𐐮𐐻; 𐐰𐑌𐐼 𐐸𐐨 𐑅𐐯𐐼 𐐲𐑌𐐻𐐭 𐑋𐐨, 𐐜 𐐺𐐳𐐿 𐑄𐐰𐐻 𐑄𐐵 𐐺𐐨𐐸𐐬𐑊𐐼𐐯𐑅𐐻, 𐐮𐑆 𐐲 𐑉𐐯𐐿𐐲𐑉𐐼 𐐱𐑂 𐑄 𐐖𐐭𐑆, 𐐸𐐶𐐮𐐽 𐐿𐐪𐑌𐐻𐐩𐑌𐑆 𐑄 𐐿𐐲𐑂𐐯𐑌𐐰𐑌𐐻𐑅 𐐱𐑂 𐑄 𐐢𐐫𐑉𐐼 𐐸𐐶𐐮𐐽 𐐸𐐨 𐐸𐐰𐑃 𐑋𐐩𐐼 𐐲𐑌𐐻𐐭 𐑄 𐐸𐐵𐑅 𐐱𐑂 𐐆𐑆𐑉𐐩𐐯𐑊; 𐐰𐑌𐐼 𐐮𐐻 𐐫𐑊𐑅𐐬 𐐿𐐪𐑌𐐻𐐩𐑌𐐯𐑃 𐑋𐐯𐑌𐐨 𐐱𐑂 𐑄 𐐹𐑉𐐪𐑁𐐯𐑅𐐴𐑆 𐐱𐑂 𐑄 𐐸𐐬𐑊𐐨 𐐹𐑉𐐪𐑁𐐯𐐻𐑅; 𐐰𐑌𐐼 𐐮𐐻 𐐮𐑆 𐐲 𐑉𐐯𐐿𐐲𐑉𐐼 𐑊𐐴𐐿 𐐲𐑌𐐻𐐭 𐑄 𐐯𐑌𐑀𐑉𐐩𐑂𐐮𐑍𐑆 𐐸𐐶𐐮𐐽 𐐪𐑉 𐐲𐐹𐐪𐑌 𐑄 𐐹𐑊𐐩𐐻𐑅 𐐱𐑂 𐐺𐑉𐐰𐑅, 𐑅𐐩𐑂 𐑄𐐯𐑉 𐐪𐑉 𐑌𐐪𐐻 𐑅𐐬 𐑋𐐯𐑌𐐨; 𐑌𐐯𐑂𐐲𐑉𐑄𐐲𐑊𐐯𐑅, 𐑄𐐩 𐐿𐐪𐑌𐐻𐐩𐑌 𐑄 𐐿𐐲𐑂𐐯𐑌𐐰𐑌𐐻𐑅 𐐱𐑂 𐑄 𐐢𐐫𐑉𐐼, 𐐸𐐶𐐮𐐽 𐐸𐐨 𐐸𐐰𐑃 𐑋𐐩𐐼 𐐲𐑌𐐻𐐭 𐑄 𐐸𐐵𐑅 𐐱𐑂 𐐆𐑆𐑉𐐩𐐯𐑊; 𐐸𐐶𐐯𐑉𐑁𐐬𐑉, 𐑄𐐩 𐐪𐑉 𐐱𐑂 𐑀𐑉𐐩𐐻 𐐶𐐲𐑉𐑃 𐐲𐑌𐐻𐐭 𐑄 𐐖𐐯𐑌𐐻𐐴𐑊𐑆.

40. 𐐰𐑌𐐼 𐑄 𐐩𐑌𐐾𐐯𐑊 𐐱𐑂 𐑄 𐐢𐐫𐑉𐐼 𐑅𐐯𐐼 𐐲𐑌𐐻𐐭 𐑋𐐨, 𐐜𐐵 𐐸𐐰𐑅𐐻 𐐺𐐨𐐸𐐯𐑊𐐼 𐑄𐐰𐐻 𐑄 𐐺𐐳𐐿 𐐹𐑉𐐬𐑅𐐨𐐼𐐯𐐼 𐑁𐐬𐑉𐑃 𐑁𐑉𐐱𐑋 𐑄 𐑋𐐵𐑃 𐐱𐑂 𐐲 𐐖𐐭; 𐐰𐑌𐐼 𐐸𐐶𐐯𐑌 𐐮𐐻 𐐹𐑉𐐬𐑅𐐨𐐼𐐯𐐼 𐑁𐐬𐑉𐑃 𐑁𐑉𐐱𐑋 𐑄 𐑋𐐵𐑃 𐐱𐑂 𐐲 𐐖𐐭, 𐐮𐐻 𐐿𐐪𐑌𐐻𐐩𐑌𐐼 𐑄 𐐹𐑊𐐩𐑌𐑌𐐯𐑅 𐐱𐑂 𐑄 𐑀𐐪𐑅𐐹𐐯𐑊 𐐱𐑂 𐑄 𐐢𐐫𐑉𐐼, 𐐱𐑂 𐐸𐐭𐑋 𐑄 𐐻𐐶𐐯𐑊𐑂 𐐰𐐹𐐪𐑅𐑊𐑆 𐐺𐐩𐑉 𐑉𐐯𐐿𐐲𐑉𐐼; 𐐰𐑌𐐼 𐑄𐐩 𐐺𐐩𐑉 𐑉𐐯𐐿𐐲𐑉𐐼 𐐰𐐿𐐫𐑉𐐼𐐮𐑍 𐐻𐐭 𐑄 𐐻𐑉𐐭𐑃 𐐸𐐶𐐮𐐽 𐐮𐑆 𐐮𐑌 𐑄 𐐢𐐰𐑋 𐐱𐑂 𐐘𐐪𐐼;

𐐐𐐶𐐯𐑉𐑁𐐫𐑉, 𐑄𐐨𐑆 𐑃𐐮𐑍𐑆 𐑀𐐬 𐑁𐐫𐑉𐑃 𐑁𐑉𐐱𐑋 𐑄 𐐖𐐭𐑆 𐐮𐑌 𐐹𐐷𐐭𐑉𐐮𐐻𐐨, 𐐲𐑌𐐻𐐭 𐑄 𐐖𐐯𐑌𐐻𐐴𐑊𐑆, 𐐰𐐿𐐫𐑉𐐼𐐮𐑍 𐐻𐐭 𐑄 𐐻𐑉𐐭𐑃 𐐸𐐶𐐮𐐽 𐐮𐑆 𐐮𐑌 𐐘𐐱𐐼; 𐐰𐑌𐐼 𐐪𐑁𐐻𐐲𐑉 𐑄𐐩 𐑀𐐬 𐑁𐐫𐑉𐑃 𐐺𐐴 𐑄 𐐸𐐰𐑌𐐼 𐐱𐑂 𐑄 𐐻𐐶𐐯𐑊𐑂 𐐰𐐹𐐱𐑅𐑊𐑆 𐐱𐑂 𐑄 𐐢𐐰𐑋, 𐑁𐑉𐐱𐑋 𐑄 𐐖𐐭𐑆 𐐲𐑌𐐻𐐭 𐑄 𐐖𐐯𐑌𐐻𐐴𐑊𐑆, 𐑄𐐵 𐑅𐐨𐐲𐑅𐐻 𐑄 𐑁𐐫𐑉𐑋𐐩𐑇𐐲𐑌 𐐱𐑂 𐑄𐐰𐐻 𐑀𐑉𐐩𐐻 𐐰𐑌𐐼 𐐲𐐺𐐱𐑋𐐮𐑌𐐲𐐺𐑊 𐐽𐐲𐑉𐐽, 𐐸𐐶𐐮𐐽 𐐮𐑆 𐑋𐐬𐑅𐐻 𐐲𐐺𐐱𐑋𐐮𐑌𐐲𐐺𐑊 𐐲𐐺𐐲𐑂 𐐫𐑊 𐐲𐑄𐐲𐑉 𐐽𐐲𐑉𐐽𐐯𐑆; 𐑁𐐫𐑉 𐐺𐐨𐐸𐐬𐑊𐐼, 𐑄𐐩 𐐸𐐰𐑂 𐐻𐐩𐐿𐑌 𐐰𐐶𐐩 𐑁𐑉𐐱𐑋 𐑄 𐑀𐐱𐑅𐐹𐐯𐑊 𐐱𐑂 𐑄 𐐢𐐰𐑋, 𐑋𐐯𐑌𐐨 𐐹𐐪𐑉𐐻𐑅 𐐸𐐶𐐮𐐽 𐐪𐑉 𐐹𐑊𐐩𐑌 𐐰𐑌𐐼 𐑋𐐬𐑅𐐻 𐐹𐑉𐐯𐑇𐐲𐑅; 𐐰𐑌𐐼 𐐫𐑊𐑅𐐬 𐑋𐐯𐑌𐐨 𐐿𐐲𐑂𐐯𐑌𐐰𐑌𐐻𐑅 𐐱𐑂 𐑄 𐐢𐐫𐑉𐐼 𐐸𐐰𐑂 𐑄𐐩 𐐻𐐩𐐿𐑌 𐐰𐐶𐐩; 𐐰𐑌𐐼 𐐫𐑊 𐑄𐐮𐑅 𐐸𐐰𐑂 𐑄𐐩 𐐼𐐲𐑌, 𐑄𐐰𐐻 𐑄𐐩 𐑋𐐴𐐻 𐐹𐐲𐑉𐑂𐐲𐑉𐐻 𐑄 𐑉𐐴𐐻 𐐶𐐩𐑆 𐐱𐑂 𐑄 𐐢𐐫𐑉𐐼, 𐑄𐐰𐐻 𐑄𐐩 𐑋𐐴𐐻 𐐺𐑊𐐴𐑌𐐼 𐑄 𐐴𐑆, 𐐰𐑌𐐼 𐐸𐐪𐑉𐐼𐑌 𐑄 𐐸𐐪𐑉𐐻𐑅 𐐱𐑂 𐑄 𐐽𐐮𐑊𐐼𐑉𐐯𐑌 𐐱𐑂 𐑋𐐯𐑌; 𐐸𐐶𐐯𐑉𐑁𐐫𐑉, 𐑄𐐵 𐑅𐐨𐐲𐑅𐐻 𐑄𐐰𐐻 𐐪𐑁𐐻𐐲𐑉 𐑄 𐐺𐐳𐐿 𐐸𐐰𐑃 𐑀𐐫𐑌 𐑁𐐫𐑉𐑃 𐑃𐑉𐐭 𐑄 𐐸𐐰𐑌𐐼𐑆 𐐱𐑂 𐑄 𐑀𐑉𐐩𐐻 𐐰𐑌𐐼 𐐲𐐺𐐱𐑋𐐮𐑌𐐲𐐺𐑊 𐐽𐐲𐑉𐐽, 𐑄𐐰𐐻 𐑄𐐯𐑉 𐐪𐑉 𐑋𐐯𐑌𐐨 𐐹𐑊𐐩𐑌 𐐰𐑌𐐼 𐐹𐑉𐐯𐑇𐐲𐑅 𐑃𐐮𐑍𐑆 𐐻𐐩𐐿𐑌 𐐰𐐶𐐩 𐑁𐑉𐐱𐑋 𐑄 𐐺𐐳𐐿, 𐐸𐐶𐐮𐐽 𐐮𐑆 𐑄 𐐺𐐳𐐿 𐐱𐑂 𐑄 𐐢𐐰𐑋 𐐱𐑂 𐐘𐐱𐐼; 𐐰𐑌𐐼 𐐪𐑁𐐻𐐲𐑉 𐑄𐐨𐑆 𐐹𐑊𐐩𐑌 𐐰𐑌𐐼 𐐹𐑉𐐯𐑇𐐲𐑅 𐑃𐐮𐑍𐑆 𐐶𐐲𐑉 𐐻𐐩𐐿𐑌 𐐰𐐶𐐩, 𐐮𐐻 𐑀𐐬𐐯𐑃 𐑁𐐫𐑉𐑃 𐐲𐑌𐐻𐐭 𐐫𐑊 𐑄 𐑌𐐩𐑇𐐲𐑌𐑆 𐐱𐑂 𐑄 𐐖𐐯𐑌𐐻𐐴𐑊𐑆; 𐐰𐑌𐐼 𐐪𐑁𐐻𐐲𐑉 𐐮𐐻 𐑀𐐬𐐯𐑃 𐑁𐐫𐑉𐑃 𐐲𐑌𐐻𐐭 𐐫𐑊 𐑄 𐑌𐐩𐑇𐐲𐑌𐑆 𐐱𐑂 𐑄 𐐖𐐯𐑌𐐻𐐴𐑊𐑆, 𐐷𐐩, 𐐨𐑂𐑌 𐐰𐐿𐑉𐐱𐑅 𐑄 𐑋𐐯𐑌𐐨 𐐶𐐫𐐻𐐲𐑉𐑆 𐐸𐐶𐐮𐐽 𐑄𐐵 𐐸𐐰𐑅𐐻 𐑅𐐨𐑌 𐐶𐐮𐑄 𐑄 𐐖𐐯𐑌𐐻𐐴𐑊𐑆 𐐸𐐶𐐮𐐽 𐐸𐐰𐑂 𐑀𐐫𐑌 𐑁𐐫𐑉𐑃 𐐵𐐻 𐐱𐑂 𐐿𐐰𐐹𐐻𐐮𐑂𐐮𐐻𐐨, 𐑄𐐵 𐑅𐐨𐐲𐑅𐐻, 𐐺𐐨𐐿𐐫𐑆 𐐱𐑂 𐑄 𐑋𐐯𐑌𐐨 𐐹𐑊𐐩𐑌 𐐰𐑌𐐼 𐐹𐑉𐐯𐑇𐐲𐑅 𐑃𐐮𐑍𐑆 𐐸𐐶𐐮𐐽 𐐸𐐰𐑂 𐐺𐐮𐑌 𐐻𐐩𐐿𐑌 𐐵𐐻 𐐱𐑂 𐑄 𐐺𐐳𐐿, 𐐸𐐶𐐮𐐽 𐐶𐐲𐑉 𐐹𐑊𐐩𐑌 𐐲𐑌𐐻𐐭 𐑄 𐐲𐑌𐐼𐐲𐑉𐑅𐐻𐐰𐑌𐐼𐐮𐑍 𐐱𐑂 𐑄 𐐽𐐮𐑊𐐼𐑉𐐯𐑌 𐐱𐑂 𐑋𐐯𐑌, 𐐰𐐿𐐫𐑉𐐼𐐮𐑍 𐐻𐐭 𐑄 𐐹𐑊𐐩𐑌𐑌𐐯𐑅 𐐸𐐶𐐮𐐽 𐐮𐑆 𐐮𐑌 𐑄 𐐢𐐰𐑋 𐐱𐑂 𐐘𐐱𐐼; 𐐺𐐨𐐿𐐫𐑆 𐐱𐑂 𐑄𐐨𐑆 𐑃𐐮𐑍𐑆 𐐸𐐶𐐮𐐽 𐐪𐑉 𐐻𐐩𐐿𐑌 𐐰𐐶𐐩 𐐵𐐻 𐐱𐑂 𐑄 𐑀𐐱𐑅𐐹𐐯𐑊 𐐱𐑂 𐑄 𐐢𐐰𐑋, 𐐰𐑌 𐐯𐐿𐑅𐐨𐐼𐐮𐑍 𐑀𐑉𐐩𐐻 𐑋𐐯𐑌𐐨 𐐼𐐭 𐑅𐐻𐐲𐑋𐐺𐑊, 𐐷𐐩, 𐐮𐑌𐑅𐐬𐑋𐐲𐐽 𐑄𐐰𐐻 𐐝𐐩𐐻𐐲𐑌 𐐸𐐰𐑃 𐑀𐑉𐐩𐐻 𐐹𐐵𐐲𐑉 𐐬𐑂𐐲𐑉 𐑄𐐯𐑋; 𐑌𐐯𐑂𐐲𐑉𐑄𐐲𐑊𐐯𐑅, 𐑄𐐵 𐐺𐐨𐐸𐐬𐑊𐐼𐐯𐑅𐐻 𐑄𐐰𐐻 𐑄 𐐖𐐯𐑌𐐻𐐴𐑊𐑆 𐐸𐐶𐐮𐐽 𐐸𐐰𐑂 𐑀𐐫𐑌 𐑁𐐫𐑉𐑃 𐐵𐐻 𐐱𐑂 𐐿𐐰𐐹𐐻𐐮𐑂𐐮𐐻𐐨, 𐐰𐑌𐐼 𐐸𐐰𐑂 𐐺𐐮𐑌 𐑊𐐮𐑁𐐻𐐯𐐼 𐐲𐐹 𐐺𐐴 𐑄 𐐹𐐵𐐲𐑉 𐐱𐑂 𐐘𐐱𐐼 𐐲𐐺𐐲𐑂 𐐫𐑊 𐐲𐑄𐐲𐑉 𐑌𐐩𐑇𐐲𐑌𐑆 𐐲𐐹𐐱𐑌 𐑄 𐑁𐐩𐑅 𐐱𐑂 𐑄 𐑊𐐰𐑌𐐼 𐐸𐐶𐐮𐐽 𐐮𐑆 𐐽𐐦𐑅 𐐲𐐺𐐲𐑂 𐐫𐑊 𐐲𐑄𐐲𐑉 𐑊𐐰𐑌𐐼𐑆, 𐐸𐐶𐐮𐐽 𐐮𐑆 𐑄 𐑊𐐰𐑌𐐼 𐑄𐐰𐐻 𐑄 𐐢𐐫𐑉𐐼 𐐘𐐱𐐼 𐐸𐐰𐑃 𐐿𐐲𐑂𐐯𐑌𐐰𐑌𐐻𐐯𐐼 𐐶𐐮𐑄 𐑄𐐴 𐑁𐐪𐑄𐐲𐑉 𐑄𐐰𐐻 𐐸𐐮𐑆 𐑅𐐨𐐼 𐑇𐐳𐐼 𐐸𐐰𐑂 𐑁𐐫𐑉 𐑄 𐑊𐐰𐑌𐐼 𐐱𐑂 𐑄𐐩𐑉 𐐮𐑌𐐸𐐯𐑉𐐮𐐻𐐰𐑌𐑅; 𐐸𐐶𐐯𐑉𐑁𐐫𐑉, 𐑄𐐵 𐑅𐐨𐐲𐑅𐐻 𐑄𐐰𐐻 𐑄 𐐢𐐫𐑉𐐼 𐐘𐐱𐐼 𐐶𐐮𐑊 𐑌𐐱𐐻 𐑅𐐲𐑁𐐲𐑉 𐑄𐐰𐐻 𐑄 𐐖𐐯𐑌𐐻𐐴𐑊𐑆 𐐶𐐮𐑊 𐐲𐐻𐐲𐑉𐑊𐐨 𐐼𐐯𐑅𐐻𐑉𐐱𐐴 𐑄 𐑋𐐮𐐿𐑅𐐽𐐲𐑉 𐐱𐑂 𐑄𐐴 𐑅𐐨𐐼, 𐐸𐐶𐐮𐐽 𐐮𐑆 𐐲𐑋𐐲𐑍 𐑄𐐴 𐐺𐑉𐐯𐑄𐑉𐐯𐑌; 𐑌𐐨𐑄𐐲𐑉 𐐶𐐮𐑊 𐐸𐐨 𐑅𐐲𐑁𐐲𐑉 𐑄𐐰𐐻 𐑄 𐐖𐐯𐑌𐐻𐐴𐑊𐑆 𐑇𐐰𐑊 𐐼𐐯𐑅𐐻𐑉𐐱𐐴 𐑄 𐑅𐐨𐐼 𐐱𐑂 𐑄𐐴 𐐺𐑉𐐯𐑄𐑉𐐯𐑌; 𐑌𐐨𐑄𐐲𐑉 𐐶𐐮𐑊 𐑄 𐐢𐐫𐑉𐐼 𐐘𐐱𐐼 𐑅𐐲𐑁𐐲𐑉 𐑄𐐰𐐻 𐑄 𐐖𐐯𐑌𐐻𐐴𐑊𐑆 𐑇𐐰𐑊 𐑁𐐫𐑉𐐯𐑂𐐲𐑉 𐑉𐐨𐑋𐐩𐑌 𐐮𐑌 𐑄𐐰𐐻 𐑅𐐻𐐩𐐻 𐐱𐑂 𐐫𐑁𐐳𐑊 𐐺𐑊𐐴𐑌𐐼𐑌𐐯𐑅, 𐐸𐐶𐐮𐐽 𐑄𐐵 𐐺𐐨𐐸𐐬𐑊𐐼𐐯𐑅𐐻 𐑄𐐩 𐐪𐑉 𐐮𐑌, 𐐺𐐨𐐿𐐫𐑆 𐐱𐑂 𐑄 𐐹𐑊𐐩𐑌 𐐰𐑌𐐼 𐑋𐐬𐑅𐐻 𐐹𐑉𐐯𐑇𐐲𐑅 𐐹𐐪𐑉𐐻𐑅 𐐱𐑂 𐑄 𐑀𐐱𐑅𐐹𐐯𐑊 𐐱𐑂 𐑄 𐐢𐐰𐑋 𐐸𐐶𐐮𐐽 𐐸𐐰𐑂 𐐺𐐮𐑌 𐐿𐐯𐐹𐐻 𐐺𐐰𐐿 𐐺𐐴 𐑄𐐰𐐻 𐐲𐐺𐐱𐑋𐐮𐑌𐐲𐐺𐑊 𐐽𐐲𐑉𐐽, 𐐸𐐭𐑆 𐑁𐐫𐑉𐑋𐐩𐑇𐐲𐑌 𐑄𐐵 𐐸𐐰𐑅𐐻 𐑅𐐨𐑌. 𐐐𐐶𐐯𐑉𐑁𐐫𐑉, 𐑅𐐯𐑃 𐑄 𐐢𐐰𐑋 𐐱𐑂 𐐘𐐱𐐼, 𐐌 𐐶𐐮𐑊 𐐺𐐨 𐑋𐐲𐑉𐑅𐐮𐑁𐐳𐑊 𐐲𐑌𐐻𐐭 𐑄 𐐖𐐯𐑌𐐻𐐴𐑊𐑆, 𐐲𐑌𐐻𐐭 𐑄 𐑂𐐮𐑆𐐮𐐻𐐮𐑍 𐐱𐑂 𐑄 𐑉𐐯𐑋𐑌𐐰𐑌𐐻 𐐱𐑂 𐑄 𐐸𐐵𐑅 𐐱𐑂 𐐌𐑆𐑉𐐩𐐯𐑊 𐐮𐑌 𐑀𐑉𐐩𐐻 𐐾𐐲𐐾𐑋𐐯𐑌𐐻.

41. 𐐈𐑌𐐼 𐐮𐐻 𐐿𐐩𐑋 𐐻𐐭 𐐹𐐰𐑅 𐑄𐐰𐐻 𐑄 𐐩𐑌𐐾𐐯𐑊 𐐱𐑂 𐑄 𐐢𐐫𐑉𐐼 𐑅𐐹𐐩𐐿 𐐲𐑌𐐻𐐭 𐑋𐐨, 𐑅𐐩𐐮𐑍, 𐐒𐐨𐐸𐐬𐑊𐐼, 𐑅𐐯𐑃 𐑄 𐐢𐐰𐑋 𐐱𐑂 𐐘𐐱𐐼, 𐐪𐑁𐐻𐐲𐑉 𐐌 𐐸𐐰𐑂 𐑂𐐮𐑆𐐮𐐻𐐯𐐼 𐑄 𐑉𐐯𐑋𐑌𐐰𐑌𐐻 𐐱𐑂 𐑄 𐐸𐐵𐑅 𐐱𐑂 𐐌𐑆𐑉𐐩𐐯𐑊, 𐐰𐑌𐐼 𐑄𐐮𐑅 𐑉𐐯𐑋𐑌𐐰𐑌𐐻 𐐱𐑂 𐐸𐐭𐑋 𐐌 𐑅𐐹𐐨𐐿, 𐐮𐑆 𐑄 𐑅𐐨𐐼 𐐱𐑂 𐑄𐐴 𐑁𐐪𐑄𐐲𐑉; 𐐸𐐶𐐯𐑉𐑁𐐫𐑉, 𐐪𐑁𐐻𐐲𐑉 𐐌 𐐸𐐰𐑂 𐑂𐐮𐑆𐐮𐐻𐐯𐐼 𐑄𐐯𐑋 𐐮𐑌 𐐾𐐲𐐾𐑋𐐯𐑌𐐻, 𐐰𐑌𐐼 𐑅𐑋𐐮𐐻𐑌 𐑄𐐯𐑋 𐐺𐐴 𐑄 𐐸𐐰𐑌𐐼 𐐱𐑂 𐑄 𐐖𐐯𐑌𐐻𐐴𐑊𐑆; 𐐰𐑌𐐼 𐐪𐑁𐐻𐐲𐑉 𐑄 𐐖𐐯𐑌𐐻𐐴𐑊𐑆 𐐼𐐭 𐑅𐐻𐐲𐑋𐐺𐑊 𐐯𐐿𐑅𐐨𐐼𐐮𐑍𐑊𐐨, 𐐺𐐨𐐿𐐫𐑆 𐐱𐑂 𐑄 𐑋𐐬𐑅𐐻 𐐹𐑊𐐩𐑌 𐐰𐑌𐐼 𐐹𐑉𐐯𐑇𐐲𐑅 𐐹𐐪𐑉𐐻𐑅 𐐱𐑂 𐑄 𐑀𐐱𐑅𐐹𐐯𐑊 𐐱𐑂 𐑄 𐐢𐐰𐑋 𐐸𐐶𐐮𐐽 𐐸𐐰𐑂 𐐺𐐮𐑌 𐐿𐐯𐐹𐐻 𐐺𐐰𐐿 𐐺𐐴 𐑄𐐰𐐻 𐐲𐐺𐐱𐑋𐐮𐑌𐐲𐐺𐑊 𐐽𐐲𐑉𐐽, 𐐸𐐶𐐮𐐽 𐐮𐑆 𐑄 𐑋𐐲𐑄𐐲𐑉 𐐱𐑂 𐐸𐐪𐑉𐑊𐐲𐐻𐑅, 𐑅𐐯𐑃 𐑄 𐐢𐐰𐑋; 𐐌 𐐶𐐮𐑊 𐐺𐐨 𐑋𐐲𐑉𐑅𐐮𐑁𐐳𐑊 𐐲𐑌𐐻𐐭 𐑄 𐐖𐐯𐑌𐐻𐐴𐑊𐑆 𐐮𐑌 𐑄𐐰𐐻 𐐼𐐩, 𐐮𐑌𐑅𐐬𐑋𐐲𐐽 𐑄𐐰𐐻 𐐌 𐐶𐐮𐑊 𐐺𐑉𐐮𐑍 𐑁𐐫𐑉𐑃 𐐲𐑌𐐻𐐭 𐑄𐐯𐑋 𐐮𐑌 𐑋𐐴𐑌 𐐬𐑌 𐐹𐐵𐐲𐑉, 𐑋𐐲𐐽 𐐱𐑂 𐑋𐐴 𐑀𐐱𐑅𐐹𐐯𐑊, 𐐸𐐶𐐮𐐽 𐑇𐐰𐑊 𐐺𐐨 𐐹𐑊𐐩𐑌 𐐰𐑌𐐼 𐐹𐑉𐐯𐑇𐐲𐑅, 𐑅𐐯𐑃 𐑄 𐐢𐐰𐑋; 𐑁𐐫𐑉 𐐺𐐨𐐸𐐬𐑊𐐼, 𐑅𐐯𐑃 𐑄 𐐢𐐰𐑋, 𐐌 𐐶𐐮𐑊 𐑋𐐰𐑌𐐮𐑁𐐯𐑅𐐻 𐑋𐐴𐑅𐐯𐑊𐑁 𐐲𐑌𐐻𐐭 𐑄𐐴 𐑅𐐨𐐼, 𐑄𐐰𐐻 𐑄𐐩 𐑇𐐰𐑊 𐑉𐐴𐐻 𐑋𐐯𐑌𐐨 𐑃𐐮𐑍𐑆 𐐸𐐶𐐮𐐽 𐐌 𐑇𐐰𐑊 𐑋𐐮𐑌𐐮𐑅𐐻𐐲𐑉 𐐲𐑌𐐻𐐭 𐑄𐐯𐑋, 𐐸𐐶𐐮𐐽 𐑇𐐰𐑊 𐐺𐐨 𐐹𐑊𐐩𐑌 𐐰𐑌𐐼 𐐹𐑉𐐯𐑇𐐲𐑅; 𐐰𐑌𐐼 𐐪𐑁𐐻𐐲𐑉 𐑄𐐴 𐑅𐐨𐐼 𐑇𐐰𐑊 𐐺𐐨 𐐼𐐯𐑅𐐻𐑉𐐱𐐴𐐯𐐼, 𐐰𐑌𐐼 𐐼𐐶𐐮𐑌𐐼𐑊 𐐮𐑌

𐐲𐑌𐐺𐐨𐑊𐐨𐑁, 𐐰𐑌𐐼 𐐫𐑊𐑅𐐬 𐑄 𐑅𐐨𐐼 𐐱𐑂 𐑄𐐴 𐐺𐑉𐐯𐑄𐑉𐐯𐑌; 𐐺𐐨𐐸𐐬𐑊𐐼, 𐑄𐐨𐑆 𐑃𐐮𐑍𐑆 𐑇𐐰𐑊 𐐺 𐐸𐐮𐐼 𐐲𐐹, 𐐻𐐭 𐐿𐐲𐑋 𐑁𐐬𐑉𐑃 𐐲𐑌𐐻𐐭 𐑄 𐐖𐐯𐑌𐐻𐐴𐑊𐑆, 𐐺𐐴 𐑄 𐑀𐐮𐑁𐐻 𐐰𐑌𐐼 𐐹𐐵𐑉 𐐱𐑂 𐑄 𐐢𐐰𐑋; 𐐰𐑌𐐼 𐐮𐑌 𐑄𐐯𐑋 𐑇𐐰𐑊 𐐺 𐑉𐐮𐐻𐑌 𐑋𐐴 𐑀𐐱𐑅𐐹𐐯𐑊, 𐑅𐐯𐑃 𐑄 𐐢𐐰𐑋, 𐐰𐑌𐐼 𐑋𐐴 𐑉𐐱𐐿 𐐰𐑌𐐼 𐑋𐐴 𐑅𐐰𐑊𐑂𐐩𐑇𐐲𐑌; 𐐰𐑌𐐼 𐐺𐑊𐐯𐑅𐐯𐐼 𐐪𐑉 𐑄𐐩 𐐸𐐭 𐑇𐐰𐑊 𐑅𐐨𐐿 𐐻𐐭 𐐺𐑉𐐮𐑍 𐑁𐐬𐑉𐑃 𐑋𐐴 𐐞𐐴𐐲𐑌 𐐰𐐻 𐑄𐐰𐐻 𐐼𐐩, 𐑁𐐬𐑉 𐑄𐐩 𐑇𐐰𐑊 𐐸𐐰𐑂 𐑄 𐑀𐐮𐑁𐐻 𐐰𐑌𐐼 𐑄 𐐹𐐵𐑉 𐐱𐑂 𐑄 𐐐𐐬𐑊𐐮 𐐘𐐬𐑅𐐻: 𐐰𐑌𐐼 𐐮𐑁 𐑄𐐩 𐐯𐑌𐐼𐐷𐐭𐑉 𐐲𐑌𐐻𐐭 𐑄 𐐯𐑌𐐼, 𐑄𐐩 𐑇𐐰𐑊 𐐺 𐑊𐐮𐑁𐐻𐐯𐐼 𐐲𐐹 𐐰𐐻 𐑄 𐑊𐐰𐑅𐐻 𐐼𐐩, 𐐰𐑌𐐼 𐑇𐐰𐑊 𐐺 𐑅𐐩𐑂𐐼 𐐮𐑌 𐑄 𐐯𐑂𐐯𐑉𐑊𐐰𐑅𐐻𐐮𐑍 𐐿𐐮𐑍𐐼𐐲𐑋 𐐱𐑂 𐑄 𐐢𐐰𐑋; 𐐰𐑌𐐼 𐐸𐐭𐑅𐐬 𐑇𐐰𐑊 𐐹𐐲𐐺𐑊𐐮𐑇 𐐹𐐨𐑅, 𐐷𐐩, 𐐻𐐴𐐼𐐮𐑍𐑆 𐐱𐑂 𐑀𐑉𐐩𐐻 𐐾𐑎, 𐐸𐐵 𐐺𐑏𐐻𐐮𐑁𐐳𐑊 𐐲𐐹𐐱𐑌 𐑄 𐑋𐐵𐑌𐐻𐐮𐑌𐑆 𐑇𐐰𐑊 𐑄𐐩 𐐺.

42. 𐐰𐑌𐐼 𐐮𐐻 𐐿𐐩𐑋 𐐻𐐭 𐐹𐐪𐑅 𐑄𐐰𐐻 𐐌 𐐺𐐨𐐸𐐯𐑊𐐼 𐑄 𐑉𐐯𐑋𐑌𐐰𐑌𐐻 𐐱𐑂 𐑄 𐑅𐐨𐐼 𐐱𐑂 𐑋𐐴 𐐺𐑉𐐯𐑄𐑉𐐯𐑌, 𐐰𐑌𐐼 𐐫𐑊𐑅𐐬 𐑄 𐐺𐐳𐐿 𐐱𐑂 𐑄 𐐢𐐰𐑋 𐐱𐑂 𐐘𐐱𐐼, 𐐸𐐶𐐮𐐽 𐐸𐐰𐐼 𐐹𐑉𐐬𐑅𐐨𐐼𐐯𐐼 𐑁𐐬𐑉𐑃 𐑁𐑉𐐱𐑋 𐑄 𐑋𐐵𐑃 𐐱𐑂 𐐲 𐐖𐐷𐐭, 𐑄𐐰𐐻 𐐮𐐻 𐐿𐐩𐑋 𐑁𐐬𐑉𐑃 𐑁𐑉𐐱𐑋 𐑄 𐐖𐐯𐑌𐐻𐐴𐑊𐑆, 𐐲𐑌𐐻𐐭 𐑄 𐑉𐐯𐑋𐑌𐐰𐑌𐐻 𐐱𐑂 𐑄 𐑅𐐨𐐼 𐐱𐑂 𐑋𐐴 𐐺𐑉𐐯𐑄𐑉𐐯𐑌, 𐐰𐑌𐐼 𐐪𐑁𐐻𐑉 𐐮𐐻 𐐸𐐰𐐼 𐐿𐐲𐑋 𐑁𐐬𐑉𐑃 𐐲𐑌𐐻𐐭 𐑄𐐯𐑋, 𐐌 𐐺𐐨𐐸𐐯𐑊𐐼 𐐲𐑄𐑉 𐐺𐐳𐐿𐑅, 𐐸𐐶𐐮𐐽 𐐿𐐩𐑋 𐑁𐐬𐑉𐑃 𐐺𐐴 𐑄 𐐹𐐵𐑉 𐐱𐑂 𐑄 𐐢𐐰𐑋, 𐑁𐑉𐐱𐑋 𐑄 𐐖𐐯𐑌𐐻𐐴𐑊𐑆 𐐲𐑌𐐻𐐭 𐑄𐐯𐑋, 𐐲𐑌𐐻𐐭 𐑄 𐐿𐐱𐑌𐑂𐐮𐑌𐑅𐐮𐑍 𐐱𐑂 𐑄 𐐖𐐯𐑌𐐻𐐴𐑊𐑆, 𐐰𐑌𐐼 𐑄 𐑉𐐯𐑋𐑌𐐰𐑌𐐻 𐐱𐑂 𐑄 𐑅𐐨𐐼 𐐱𐑂 𐑋𐐴 𐐺𐑉𐐯𐑄𐑉𐐯𐑌, 𐐰𐑌𐐼 𐐫𐑊𐑅𐐬 𐑄 𐐖𐐷𐐭𐑆, 𐐸𐐭 𐐶𐐯𐑉 𐑅𐐿𐐰𐐻𐐲𐑉𐐼 𐐲𐐹𐐱𐑌 𐐫𐑊 𐑄 𐑁𐐩𐑅 𐐱𐑂 𐑄 𐐲𐑉𐑃, 𐑄𐐰𐐻 𐑄 𐑉𐐯𐐿𐐫𐑉𐐼𐑆 𐐱𐑂 𐑄 𐐹𐑉𐐱𐑁𐐯𐐻𐑅 𐐰𐑌𐐼 𐐱𐑂 𐑄 𐐻𐐶𐐯𐑊𐑂 𐐰𐐹𐐱𐑅𐐲𐑊𐑆 𐐱𐑂 𐑄 𐐢𐐰𐑋 𐐪𐑉 𐐻𐑉𐐭.

43. 𐐰𐑌𐐼 𐑄 𐐩𐑌𐐾𐐯𐑊 𐑅𐐹𐐩𐐿 𐐲𐑌𐐻𐐭 𐑋𐐨, 𐑅𐐩𐐮𐑍, 𐑄𐐨𐑆 𐑊𐐰𐑅𐐻 𐑉𐐯𐐿𐐫𐑉𐐼𐑆 𐐸𐐶𐐮𐐽 𐑄𐐵 𐐸𐐰𐑅𐐻 𐑅𐐨𐑌 𐐲𐑋𐐲𐑍 𐑄 𐐖𐐯𐑌𐐻𐐴𐑊𐑆 𐑇𐐰𐑊 𐐯𐑅𐐻𐐰𐐺𐑊𐐮𐑇 𐑄 𐐻𐑉𐐭𐑃 𐐱𐑂 𐑄 𐑁𐐲𐑉𐑅𐐻, 𐐸𐐶𐐮𐐽 𐐪𐑉 𐐱𐑂 𐑄 𐐻𐐶𐐯𐑊𐑂 𐐰𐐹𐐱𐑅𐐲𐑊𐑆 𐐱𐑂 𐑄 𐐢𐐰𐑋, 𐐰𐑌𐐼 𐑇𐐰𐑊 𐑋𐐩𐐿 𐑌𐐬𐑌 𐑄 𐐹𐑊𐐩𐑌 𐐰𐑌𐐼 𐐹𐑉𐐯𐑇𐐲𐑅 𐑃𐐮𐑍𐑆 𐐸𐐶𐐮𐐽 𐐸𐐰𐑂 𐐺𐐮𐑌 𐐻𐐩𐐿𐐯𐑌 𐐲𐐶𐐩 𐑁𐑉𐐱𐑋 𐑄𐐯𐑋; 𐐰𐑌𐐼 𐑇𐐰𐑊 𐑋𐐩𐐿 𐑌𐐬𐑌 𐐻𐐭 𐐫𐑊 𐐿𐐮𐑌𐐼𐑉𐐯𐐼𐑆, 𐐻𐐲𐑍𐑆, 𐐰𐑌𐐼 𐐹𐐨𐐹𐑊, 𐑄𐐰𐐻 𐑄 𐐢𐐰𐑋 𐐱𐑂 𐐘𐐱𐐼 𐐮𐑆 𐑄 𐐝𐐲𐑌 𐐱𐑂 𐑄 𐐀𐐻𐐲𐑉𐑌𐐰𐑊 𐐙𐐪𐑄𐐲𐑉, 𐐰𐑌𐐼 𐑄 𐐝𐐩𐑂𐐷𐐲𐑉 𐐱𐑂 𐑄 𐐶𐐲𐑉𐑊𐐼; 𐐰𐑌𐐼 𐑄𐐰𐐻 𐐫𐑊 𐑋𐐯𐑌 𐑋𐐲𐑅𐐻 𐐿𐐲𐑋 𐐲𐑌𐐻𐐭 𐐸𐐮𐑋, 𐐫𐑉 𐑄𐐩 𐐿𐐰𐑌𐐱𐐻 𐐺 𐑅𐐩𐑂𐐼; 𐐰𐑌𐐼 𐑄𐐩 𐑋𐐲𐑅𐐻 𐐿𐐲𐑋 𐐰𐐿𐐫𐑉𐐼𐐮𐑍 𐐻𐐭 𐑄 𐐶𐐲𐑉𐐼𐑆 𐐸𐐶𐐮𐐽 𐑇𐐰𐑊 𐐺 𐐯𐑅𐐻𐐰𐐺𐑊𐐮𐑇𐐻 𐐺𐐴 𐑄 𐑋𐐵𐑃 𐐱𐑂 𐑄 𐐢𐐰𐑋: 𐐰𐑌𐐼 𐑄 𐐶𐐲𐑉𐐼𐑆 𐐱𐑂 𐑄 𐐢𐐰𐑋 𐑇𐐰𐑊 𐐺 𐑋𐐩𐐼 𐑌𐐬𐑌 𐐮𐑌 𐑄 𐑉𐐯𐐿𐐫𐑉𐐼𐑆 𐐱𐑂 𐑄𐐴 𐑅𐐨𐐼, 𐐰𐑆 𐐶𐐯𐑊 𐐰𐑆 𐐮𐑌 𐑄 𐑉𐐯𐐿𐐫𐑉𐐼𐑆 𐐱𐑂 𐑄 𐐻𐐶𐐯𐑊𐑂 𐐰𐐹𐐱𐑅𐐲𐑊𐑆 𐐱𐑂 𐑄 𐐢𐐰𐑋; 𐐸𐐶𐐩𐑉𐑁𐐬𐑉, 𐑄𐐩 𐐺𐐬𐑃 𐑇𐐰𐑊 𐐺 𐐯𐑅𐐻𐐰𐐺𐑊𐐮𐑇𐐻 𐐮𐑌 𐐶𐐲𐑌; 𐑁𐐬𐑉 𐑄𐐩𐑉 𐐮𐑆 𐐶𐐲𐑌 𐐘𐐱𐐼 𐐰𐑌𐐼 𐐶𐐲𐑌 𐐟𐐯𐐹𐐲𐑉𐐼 𐐬𐑂𐐲𐑉 𐐫𐑊 𐑄 𐐲𐑉𐑃; 𐐰𐑌𐐼 𐑄 𐐻𐐴𐑋 𐐿𐐲𐑋𐐯𐑃 𐑄𐐰𐐻 𐐸𐐨 𐑇𐐰𐑊 𐑋𐐰𐑌𐐮𐑁𐐯𐑅𐐻 𐐸𐐮𐑋𐑅𐐯𐑊𐑁 𐐲𐑌𐐻𐐭 𐐫𐑊 𐑌𐐩𐑇𐐲𐑌𐑆, 𐐺𐐬𐑃 𐐲𐑌𐐻𐐭 𐑄 𐐖𐐷𐐭𐑆, 𐐰𐑌𐐼 𐐫𐑊𐑅𐐬 𐐲𐑌𐐻𐐭 𐑄 𐐖𐐯𐑌𐐻𐐴𐑊𐑆; 𐐰𐑌𐐼 𐐪𐑁𐐻𐑉 𐐸𐐨 𐐸𐐰𐑆 𐑋𐐰𐑌𐐮𐑁𐐯𐑅𐐻𐐯𐐼 𐐸𐐮𐑋𐑅𐐯𐑊𐑁 𐐲𐑌𐐻𐐭 𐑄 𐐖𐐷𐐭𐑆, 𐐰𐑌𐐼 𐐫𐑊𐑅𐐬 𐐲𐑌𐐻𐐭 𐑄 𐐖𐐯𐑌𐐻𐐴𐑊𐑆, 𐑄𐐯𐑌 𐐸𐐨 𐑇𐐰𐑊 𐑋𐐰𐑌𐐮𐑁𐐯𐑅𐐻 𐐸𐐮𐑋𐑅𐐯𐑊𐑁 𐐲𐑌𐐻𐐭 𐑄 𐐖𐐯𐑌𐐻𐐴𐑊𐑆, 𐐰𐑌𐐼 𐐫𐑊𐑅𐐬 𐐲𐑌𐐻𐐭 𐑄 𐐖𐐷𐐭𐑆, 𐐰𐑌𐐼 𐑄 𐑊𐐰𐑅𐐻 𐑇𐐰𐑊 𐐺 𐑁𐐲𐑉𐑅𐐻, 𐐰𐑌𐐼 𐑄 𐑁𐐲𐑉𐑅𐐻 𐑇𐐰𐑊 𐐺 𐑊𐐰𐑅𐐻.

44. 𐐰𐑌𐐼 𐐮𐐻 𐑇𐐰𐑊 𐐿𐐲𐑋 𐐻𐐭 𐐹𐐪𐑅, 𐑄𐐰𐐻 𐐮𐑁 𐑄 𐐖𐐯𐑌𐐻𐐴𐑊𐑆 𐑇𐐰𐑊 𐐸𐐪𐑉𐐿𐐯𐑌 𐐲𐑌𐐻𐐭 𐑄 𐐢𐐰𐑋 𐐱𐑂 𐐘𐐱𐐼 𐐮𐑌 𐑄𐐰𐐻 𐐼𐐩 𐑄𐐰𐐻 𐐸𐐨 𐑇𐐰𐑊 𐑋𐐰𐑌𐐮𐑁𐐯𐑅𐐻 𐐸𐐮𐑋𐑅𐐯𐑊𐑁 𐐲𐑌𐐻𐐭 𐑄𐐯𐑋 𐐮𐑌 𐐶𐐲𐑉𐐼, 𐐰𐑌𐐼 𐐫𐑊𐑅𐐬 𐐮𐑌 𐐹𐐵𐑉, 𐐮𐑌 𐑂𐐯𐑉𐐨 𐐼𐐨𐐼 𐐲𐑌𐐻𐐭 𐑄 𐐻𐐩𐐿𐐮𐑍 𐐲𐐶𐐩 𐐱𐑂 𐑄𐐩𐑉 𐑅𐐻𐐲𐑋𐐺𐑊𐐮𐑍 𐐺𐑊𐐱𐐿𐑅, 𐐰𐑌𐐼 𐐮𐑁 𐑄𐐩 𐐸𐐪𐑉𐐼𐐯𐑌 𐑌𐐱𐐻 𐑄𐐩𐑉 𐐸𐐪𐑉𐐻𐑅 𐐰𐑀𐐯𐑌𐑅𐐻 𐑄 𐐢𐐰𐑋 𐐱𐑂 𐐘𐐱𐐼, 𐑄𐐩 𐑇𐐰𐑊 𐐺 𐑌𐐲𐑋𐐺𐐲𐑉𐐼 𐐲𐑋𐐲𐑍 𐑄 𐑅𐐨𐐼 𐐱𐑂 𐑄𐐴 𐑁𐐪𐑄𐐲𐑉; 𐐷𐐩, 𐑄𐐩 𐑇𐐰𐑊 𐐺 𐑌𐐲𐑋𐐺𐐲𐑉𐐼 𐐲𐑋𐐲𐑍 𐑄 𐐸𐐵𐑅 𐐱𐑂 𐐆𐑆𐑉𐐩𐐯𐑊; 𐐰𐑌𐐼 𐑄𐐩 𐑇𐐰𐑊 𐐺 𐐲 𐐺𐑊𐐯𐑅𐐻 𐐹𐐨𐐹𐑊 𐐲𐐹𐐱𐑌 𐑄 𐐹𐑉𐐱𐑋𐐮𐑅𐐻 𐑊𐐰𐑌𐐼 𐑁𐐬𐑉𐐯𐑂𐐲𐑉: 𐑄𐐩 𐑇𐐰𐑊 𐐺 𐑌𐐬 𐑋𐐬𐑉 𐐺𐑉𐐫𐐻 𐐼𐐵𐑌 𐐮𐑌𐐻𐐭 𐐿𐐰𐐹𐐻𐐮𐑂𐐮𐐻𐐨; 𐐰𐑌𐐼 𐑄 𐐸𐐵𐑅 𐐱𐑂 𐐆𐑆𐑉𐐩𐐯𐑊 𐑇𐐰𐑊 𐑌𐐬 𐑋𐐬𐑉 𐐺 𐐿𐐱𐑌𐑁𐐵𐑌𐐼𐐯𐐼; 𐐰𐑌𐐼 𐑄𐐰𐐻 𐑀𐑉𐐩𐐻 𐐹𐐮𐐻 𐐸𐐶𐐮𐐽 𐐸𐐰𐑃 𐐺𐐮𐑌 𐐼𐐮𐑀𐐯𐐼 𐑁𐐬𐑉 𐑄𐐯𐑋, 𐐺𐐴 𐑄𐐰𐐻 𐑀𐑉𐐩𐐻 𐐰𐑌𐐼 𐐰𐐺𐐱𐑋𐐮𐑌𐐰𐐺𐑊 𐐽𐐲𐑉𐐽, 𐐸𐐶𐐮𐐽 𐐶𐐱𐑆 𐑁𐐵𐑌𐐼𐐯𐐼 𐐺𐐴 𐑄 𐐼𐐯𐑂𐐮𐑊 𐐰𐑌𐐼 𐐸𐐮𐑆 𐐽𐐮𐑊𐐼𐑉𐐯𐑌, 𐑄𐐰𐐻 𐐸𐐨 𐑋𐐴𐐻 𐑊𐐨𐐼 𐐲𐐶𐐩 𐑄 𐑅𐐬𐑊𐑆 𐐱𐑂 𐑋𐐯𐑌 𐐼𐐵𐑌 𐐻𐐭 𐐸𐐯𐑊; 𐐷𐐩, 𐑄𐐰𐐻 𐑀𐑉𐐩𐐻 𐐹𐐮𐐻 𐐸𐐶𐐮𐐽 𐐸𐐰𐑃 𐐺𐐮𐑌 𐐼𐐮𐑀𐐯𐐼 𐑁𐐬𐑉 𐑄 𐐼𐐨𐑅𐐻𐑉𐐲𐐿𐑇𐐲𐑌 𐐱𐑂 𐑋𐐯𐑌, 𐑇𐐰𐑊 𐐺 𐑁𐐮𐑊𐐼 𐐺𐐴 𐑄𐐬𐑆 𐐸𐐭 𐐼𐐮𐑀𐐯𐐼 𐐮𐐻, 𐐲𐑌𐐻𐐭 𐑄𐐩𐑉 𐐲𐐻𐐲𐑉 𐐼𐐨𐑅𐐻𐑉𐐲𐐿𐑇𐐲𐑌, 𐑅𐐯𐑃 𐑄 𐐢𐐰𐑋 𐐱𐑂 𐐘𐐱𐐼; 𐑌𐐱𐐻 𐑄 𐐼𐐨𐑅𐐻𐑉𐐲𐐿𐑇𐐲𐑌 𐐱𐑂 𐑄 𐑅𐐬𐑊, 𐑅𐐩𐑂 𐐮𐐻 𐐺 𐑄 𐐿𐐰𐑅𐐻𐐮𐑍 𐐱𐑂 𐐮𐐻 𐐮𐑌𐐻𐐭 𐑄𐐰𐐻 𐐸𐐯𐑊 𐐸𐐶𐐮𐐽 𐐸𐐰𐑃 𐑌𐐬 𐐯𐑌𐐼; 𐑁𐐬𐑉 𐐺𐐨𐐸𐐬𐑊𐐼,

𐑄𐐮𐑅 𐐮𐑆 𐐰𐐿𐐫𐑉𐐼𐐮𐑍 𐐻𐐭 𐑄 𐐿𐐰𐐹𐐻𐐮𐑂𐐮𐐻𐐨 𐐱𐑂 𐑄 𐐼𐐯𐑂𐑊, 𐐰𐑌𐐼 𐐫𐑊𐑅𐐬 𐐰𐐿𐐫𐑉𐐼𐐮𐑍 𐐻𐐭 𐑄 𐐾𐐲𐑅𐐻𐐮𐑅 𐐱𐑂 𐐘𐐱𐐼, 𐐲𐐹𐐱𐑌 𐐫𐑊 𐑄𐐬𐑆 𐐸𐐭 𐐶𐐮𐑊 𐐶𐐲𐑉𐐿 𐐶𐐮𐐿𐐯𐐼𐑌𐐯𐑅 𐐰𐑌𐐼 𐐰𐐺𐐱𐑋𐐮𐑌𐐩𐑇𐐲𐑌 𐐺𐐨𐑁𐐬𐑉 𐐸𐐮𐑋.

45. 𐐈𐑌𐐼 𐐮𐐻 𐐿𐐩𐑋 𐐻𐐭 𐐹𐐪𐑅 𐑄𐐰𐐻 𐑄 𐐩𐑌𐐾𐐯𐑊 𐑅𐐹𐐩𐐿 𐐲𐑌𐐻𐐭 𐑋𐐨, 𐐤𐐨𐑁𐐴, 𐑅𐐩𐐮𐑍, 𐐜𐐵 𐐸𐐰𐑅𐐻 𐐺𐐨𐐸𐐯𐑊𐐼 𐑄𐐰𐐻 𐐮𐑁 𐑄 𐐖𐐯𐑌𐐻𐐴𐑊𐑆 𐑉𐐨𐐹𐐯𐑌𐐻, 𐐮𐐻 𐑇𐐰𐑊 𐐺 𐐶𐐯𐑊 𐐶𐐮𐑄 𐑄𐐯𐑋; 𐐰𐑌𐐼 𐑄𐐵 𐐫𐑊𐑅𐐬 𐑌𐐬𐐯𐑅𐐻 𐐿𐐲𐑌𐑅𐐲𐑉𐑌𐐮𐑍 𐑄 𐐿𐐲𐑂𐐯𐑌𐐲𐑌𐐻𐑅 𐐱𐑂 𐑄 𐐢𐐫𐑉𐐼 𐐲𐑌𐐻𐐭 𐑄 𐐸𐐵𐑅 𐐱𐑂 𐐆𐑆𐑉𐐩𐐯𐑊; 𐐰𐑌𐐼 𐑄𐐵 𐐫𐑊𐑅𐐬 𐐸𐐰𐑅𐐻 𐐸𐐲𐑉𐐼, 𐑄𐐰𐐻 𐐸𐐭𐑅𐐬 𐑉𐐨𐐹𐐯𐑌𐐻𐐯𐑃 𐑌𐐱𐐻, 𐑋𐐲𐑅𐐻 𐐹𐐯𐑉𐐮𐑇; 𐑄𐐩𐑉𐑁𐐬𐑉, 𐐶𐐬, 𐐺 𐐲𐑌𐐻𐐭 𐑄 𐐖𐐯𐑌𐐻𐐴𐑊𐑆, 𐐮𐑁 𐐮𐐻 𐑅𐐬 𐐺 𐑄𐐰𐐻 𐑄𐐩 𐐸𐐪𐑉𐐼𐑌 𐑄𐐩𐑉 𐐸𐐪𐑉𐐻𐑅 𐐰𐑀𐐯𐑌𐑅𐐻 𐑄 𐐢𐐰𐑋 𐐱𐑂 𐐘𐐱𐐼; 𐑁𐐫𐑉 𐑄 𐐻𐐴𐑋 𐐿𐐲𐑋𐐯𐑃, 𐑅𐐯𐑃 𐑄 𐐢𐐰𐑋 𐐱𐑂 𐐘𐐱𐐼 𐑄𐐰𐐻 𐐴 𐐶𐐮𐑊 𐐶𐐲𐑉𐐿 𐐲 𐑀𐑉𐐩𐐻 𐐰𐑌𐐼 𐐲 𐑋𐐪𐑉𐑂𐐯𐑊𐐲𐑅 𐐶𐐲𐑉𐐿 𐐲𐑋𐐲𐑍 𐑄 𐐽𐐮𐑊𐐼𐑉𐐯𐑌 𐐱𐑂 𐑋𐐯𐑌; 𐐲 𐐶𐐲𐑉𐐿 𐐸𐐶𐐮𐐽 𐑇𐐰𐑊 𐐺 𐐯𐑂𐐲𐑉𐑊𐐪𐑅𐐻𐐮𐑍, 𐐨𐑄𐐲𐑉 𐐱𐑌 𐑄 𐐶𐐲𐑌 𐐸𐐰𐑌𐐼 𐐫𐑉 𐐱𐑌 𐑄 𐐲𐑄𐐲𐑉: 𐐨𐑄𐐲𐑉 𐐻𐐭 𐑄 𐐿𐐲𐑌𐑂𐐮𐑌𐑅𐐮𐑍 𐐱𐑂 𐑄𐐯𐑋 𐐲𐑌𐐻𐐭 𐐹𐐨𐑅 𐐰𐑌𐐼 𐑊𐐴𐑁 𐐨𐐻𐐲𐑉𐑌𐐲𐑊, 𐐫𐑉 𐐲𐑌𐐻𐐭 𐑄 𐐼𐐨𐑊𐐮𐑂𐐲𐑉𐐲𐑌𐑅 𐐱𐑂 𐑄𐐯𐑋 𐐻𐐭 𐑄 𐐸𐐪𐑉𐐼𐑌𐐯𐑅 𐐱𐑂 𐑄𐐩𐑉 𐐸𐐪𐑉𐐻𐑅 𐐰𐑌𐐼 𐑄 𐐺𐑊𐐴𐑌𐐼𐑌𐐯𐑅 𐐱𐑂 𐑄𐐩𐑉 𐑋𐐴𐑌𐐼𐑆, 𐐲𐑌𐐻𐐭 𐑄𐐩𐑉 𐐺𐐨𐐮𐑍 𐐺𐑉𐐫𐐻 𐐼𐐵𐑌 𐐮𐑌𐐻𐐭 𐐿𐐰𐐹𐐻𐐮𐑂𐐮𐐻𐐨, 𐐰𐑌𐐼 𐐫𐑊𐑅𐐬 𐐮𐑌𐐻𐐭 𐐼𐐯𐑅𐐻𐑉𐐲𐐿𐑇𐐲𐑌, 𐐺𐐬𐑃 𐐻𐐯𐑋𐐹𐐬𐑉𐐲𐑊𐐨 𐐰𐑌𐐼 𐑅𐐹𐐮𐑉𐐮𐐽𐐮𐐭𐐲𐑊𐐨, 𐐰𐐿𐐫𐑉𐐼𐐮𐑍 𐐻𐐭 𐑄 𐐿𐐰𐐹𐐻𐐮𐑂𐐮𐐻𐐨 𐐱𐑂 𐑄 𐐼𐐯𐑂𐑊, 𐐱𐑂 𐐸𐐶𐐮𐐽 𐐴 𐐸𐐰𐑂 𐑅𐐹𐐬𐐿𐑌.

46. 𐐈𐑌𐐼 𐐮𐐻 𐐿𐐩𐑋 𐐻𐐭 𐐹𐐪𐑅 𐑄𐐰𐐻 𐐸𐐶𐐯𐑌 𐑄 𐐩𐑌𐐾𐐯𐑊 𐐸𐐰𐐼 𐑅𐐹𐐬𐐿𐑌 𐑄𐐨𐑆 𐐶𐐲𐑉𐐼𐑆, 𐐸𐐨 𐑅𐐯𐐼 𐐲𐑌𐐻𐐭 𐑋𐐨, 𐐡𐐨𐑋𐐯𐑋𐐺𐐲𐑉𐐯𐑅𐐻 𐑄𐐵 𐑄 𐐿𐐲𐑂𐐯𐑌𐐲𐑌𐐻𐑅 𐐱𐑂 𐑄 𐐙𐐪𐑄𐐲𐑉 𐐲𐑌𐐻𐐭 𐑄 𐐸𐐵𐑅 𐐱𐑂 𐐆𐑆𐑉𐐩𐐯𐑊? 𐐌 𐑅𐐯𐐼 𐐲𐑌𐐻𐐭 𐐸𐐮𐑋, 𐐏𐐩. 𐐈𐑌𐐼 𐐮𐐻 𐐿𐐩𐑋 𐐻𐐭 𐐹𐐪𐑅 𐑄𐐰𐐻 𐐸𐐨 𐑅𐐯𐐼 𐐲𐑌𐐻𐐭 𐑋𐐨, 𐐢𐐳𐐿, 𐐰𐑌𐐼 𐐺𐐨𐐸𐐬𐑊𐐼 𐑄𐐰𐐻 𐑀𐑉𐐩𐐻 𐐰𐑌𐐼 𐐰𐐺𐐱𐑋𐐮𐑌𐐰𐐺𐑊 𐐽𐐲𐑉𐐽, 𐐸𐐶𐐮𐐽 𐐮𐑆 𐑄 𐑋𐐲𐑄𐐲𐑉 𐐱𐑂 𐐰𐐺𐐱𐑋𐐮𐑌𐐩𐑇𐐲𐑌𐑆, 𐐸𐐭𐑆 𐑁𐐵𐑌𐐼𐐩𐑇𐐲𐑌 𐐮𐑆 𐑄 𐐼𐐯𐑂𐑊. 𐐈𐑌𐐼 𐐸𐐨 𐑅𐐯𐐼 𐐲𐑌𐐻𐐭 𐑋𐐨, 𐐒𐐨𐐸𐐬𐑊𐐼 𐑄𐐩𐑉 𐐪𐑉, 𐑅𐐩𐑂 𐐻𐐭 𐐽𐐲𐑉𐐽𐐯𐑆 𐐬𐑌𐑊𐐨; 𐑄 𐐶𐐲𐑌 𐐮𐑆 𐑄 𐐕𐐲𐑉𐐽 𐐱𐑂 𐑄 𐐢𐐰𐑋 𐐱𐑂 𐐘𐐱𐐼, 𐐰𐑌𐐼 𐑄 𐐲𐑄𐐲𐑉 𐐮𐑆 𐑄 𐐽𐐲𐑉𐐽 𐐱𐑂 𐑄 𐐼𐐯𐑂𐑊; 𐐸𐐶𐐩𐑉𐑁𐐬𐑉, 𐐸𐐭𐑅𐐬 𐐺𐐨𐑊𐐱𐑍𐐯𐑃 𐑌𐐱𐐻 𐐻𐐭 𐑄 𐐕𐐲𐑉𐐽 𐐱𐑂 𐑄 𐐢𐐰𐑋 𐐱𐑂 𐐘𐐱𐐼, 𐐺𐐨𐑊𐐱𐑍𐐯𐑃 𐐻𐐭 𐑄𐐰𐐻 𐑀𐑉𐐩𐐻 𐐽𐐲𐑉𐐽, 𐐸𐐶𐐮𐐽 𐐮𐑆 𐑄 𐑋𐐲𐑄𐐲𐑉 𐐱𐑂 𐐰𐐺𐐱𐑋𐐮𐑌𐐩𐑇𐐲𐑌𐑆; 𐐰𐑌𐐼 𐑇𐐨 𐐮𐑆 𐑄 𐐸𐐬𐑉 𐐱𐑂 𐐫𐑊 𐑄 𐐲𐑉𐑃.

47. 𐐈𐑌𐐼 𐐮𐐻 𐐿𐐩𐑋 𐐻𐐭 𐐹𐐪𐑅 𐑄𐐰𐐻 𐐴 𐑊𐐳𐐿𐐻 𐐰𐑌𐐼 𐐺𐐨𐐸𐐯𐑊𐐼 𐑄 𐐸𐐬𐑉 𐐱𐑂 𐐫𐑊 𐑄 𐐲𐑉𐑃, 𐐰𐑌𐐼 𐑇𐐨 𐑅𐐰𐐻 𐐲𐐹𐐱𐑌 𐑋𐐯𐑌𐐨 𐐶𐐫𐐻𐐲𐑉𐑆; 𐐰𐑌𐐼 𐑇𐐨 𐐸𐐰𐐼 𐐼𐐬𐑋𐐮𐑌𐐷𐐲𐑌 𐐬𐑂𐐲𐑉 𐐫𐑊 𐑄 𐐲𐑉𐑃, 𐐲𐑋𐐲𐑍 𐐫𐑊 𐑌𐐩𐑇𐐲𐑌𐑆, 𐐿𐐮𐑌𐐼𐑉𐐯𐐼𐑆, 𐐻𐐲𐑍𐑆, 𐐰𐑌𐐼 𐐹𐐨𐐹𐑊.

48. 𐐈𐑌𐐼 𐐮𐐻 𐐿𐐩𐑋 𐐻𐐭 𐐹𐐪𐑅 𐑄𐐰𐐻 𐐴 𐐺𐐨𐐸𐐯𐑊𐐼 𐑄 𐐕𐐲𐑉𐐽 𐐱𐑂 𐑄 𐐢𐐰𐑋 𐐱𐑂 𐐘𐐱𐐼, 𐐰𐑌𐐼 𐐮𐐻𐑅 𐑌𐐲𐑋-𐐺𐐲𐑉𐑆 𐐶𐐲𐑉 𐑁𐐮𐐭, 𐐺𐐨𐐿𐐱𐑆 𐐱𐑂 𐑄 𐐶𐐮𐐿𐐯𐐼𐑌𐐯𐑅 𐐰𐑌𐐼 𐐰𐐺𐐱𐑋𐐮𐑌𐐩𐑇𐐲𐑌𐑆 𐐱𐑂 𐑄 𐐸𐐬𐑉 𐐸𐐭 𐑅𐐰𐐻 𐐲𐐹𐐱𐑌 𐑋𐐯𐑌𐐨 𐐶𐐫𐐻𐐲𐑉𐑆; 𐑌𐐯𐑂𐐲𐑉𐑄𐐯𐑊𐐯𐑅, 𐐴 𐐺𐐨𐐸𐐯𐑊𐐼 𐑄𐐰𐐻 𐑄 𐐕𐐲𐑉𐐽 𐐱𐑂 𐑄 𐐢𐐰𐑋, 𐐸𐐭 𐐶𐐲𐑉 𐑄 𐑅𐐩𐑌𐐻𐑅 𐐱𐑂 𐐘𐐱𐐼, 𐐶𐐲𐑉 𐐫𐑊𐑅𐐬 𐐲𐐹𐐱𐑌 𐐫𐑊 𐑄 𐑁𐐩𐑅 𐐱𐑂 𐑄 𐐲𐑉𐑃; 𐐰𐑌𐐼 𐑄𐐩𐑉 𐐼𐐬𐑋𐐮𐑌𐐷𐐲𐑌𐑆 𐐲𐐹𐐱𐑌 𐑄 𐑁𐐩𐑅 𐐱𐑂 𐑄 𐐲𐑉𐑃 𐐶𐐲𐑉 𐑅𐑋𐐫𐑊, 𐐺𐐨𐐿𐐱𐑆 𐐱𐑂 𐑄 𐐶𐐮𐐿𐐯𐐼𐑌𐐯𐑅 𐐱𐑂 𐑄 𐑀𐑉𐐩𐐻 𐐸𐐬𐑉 𐐸𐐭𐑋 𐐴 𐑅𐐫.

49. 𐐈𐑌𐐼 𐐮𐐻 𐐿𐐩𐑋 𐐻𐐭 𐐹𐐪𐑅 𐑄𐐰𐐻 𐐴 𐐺𐐨𐐸𐐯𐑊𐐼 𐑄𐐰𐐻 𐑄 𐑀𐑉𐐩𐐻 𐑋𐐲𐑄𐐲𐑉 𐐱𐑂 𐐰𐐺𐐱𐑋𐐮𐑌𐐩𐑇𐐲𐑌𐑆 𐐼𐐮𐐼 𐑀𐐰𐑄𐐲𐑉 𐐻𐐭𐑀𐐯𐑄𐐲𐑉 𐑋𐐲𐑊𐐻𐐮𐐻𐐷𐐭𐐼𐑆 𐐲𐐹𐐱𐑌 𐑄 𐑁𐐩𐑅 𐐱𐑂 𐐫𐑊 𐑄 𐐲𐑉𐑃, 𐐲𐑋𐐲𐑍 𐐫𐑊 𐑄 𐑌𐐩𐑇𐐲𐑌𐑆 𐐱𐑂 𐑄 𐐖𐐯𐑌-𐐻𐐴𐑊𐑆, 𐐻𐐭 𐑁𐐴𐐻 𐐰𐑀𐐯𐑌𐑅𐐻 𐑄 𐐢𐐰𐑋 𐐱𐑂 𐐘𐐱𐐼.

50. 𐐈𐑌𐐼 𐐮𐐻 𐐿𐐩𐑋 𐐻𐐭 𐐹𐐪𐑅 𐑄𐐰𐐻 𐐴, 𐐤𐐨𐑁𐐴, 𐐺𐐨𐐸𐐯𐑊𐐼 𐑄 𐐹𐐵𐑉 𐐱𐑂 𐑄 𐐢𐐰𐑋 𐐱𐑂 𐐘𐐱𐐼, 𐑄𐐰𐐻 𐐮𐐻 𐐼𐐨𐑅𐐯𐑌𐐼𐐯𐐼 𐐲𐐹𐐱𐑌 𐑄 𐑅𐐩𐑌𐐻𐑅 𐐱𐑂 𐑄 𐐕𐐲𐑉𐐽 𐐱𐑂 𐑄 𐐢𐐰𐑋, 𐐰𐑌𐐼 𐐲𐐹𐐱𐑌 𐑄 𐐿𐐲𐑂𐐯𐑌𐐲𐑌𐐻 𐐹𐐨𐐹𐑊 𐐱𐑂 𐑄 𐐢𐐫𐑉𐐼, 𐐸𐐭 𐐶𐐲𐑉 𐑅𐐿𐐰𐐻𐐲𐑉𐐼 𐐲𐐹𐐱𐑌 𐐫𐑊 𐑄 𐑁𐐩𐑅 𐐱𐑂 𐑄 𐐲𐑉𐑃; 𐐰𐑌𐐼 𐑄𐐩 𐐶𐐲𐑉 𐐪𐑉𐑋𐐼 𐐶𐐮𐑄 𐑉𐐴𐐽𐐲𐑅𐑌𐐯𐑅 𐐰𐑌𐐼 𐐶𐐮𐑄 𐑄 𐐹𐐵𐑉 𐐱𐑂 𐐘𐐱𐐼 𐐮𐑌 𐑀𐑉𐐩𐐻 𐑀𐑊𐐬𐑉𐐨.

51. 𐐈𐑌𐐼 𐐮𐐻 𐐿𐐩𐑋 𐐻𐐭 𐐹𐐪𐑅 𐑄𐐰𐐻 𐐴 𐐺𐐨𐐸𐐯𐑊𐐼 𐑄𐐰𐐻 𐑄 𐑉𐐰𐑃 𐐱𐑂 𐐘𐐱𐐼 𐐶𐐱𐑆 𐐹𐐬𐑉𐐼 𐐵𐐻 𐐲𐐹𐐱𐑌 𐑄 𐑀𐑉𐐩𐐻 𐐰𐑌𐐼 𐐰𐐺𐐱𐑋𐐮𐑌𐐰𐐺𐑊 𐐽𐐲𐑉𐐽, 𐐮𐑌𐑅𐐬𐑋𐐲𐐽 𐑄𐐰𐐻 𐑄𐐩𐑉 𐐶𐐲𐑉 𐐶𐐫𐑉𐑆 𐐰𐑌𐐼 𐑉𐐭𐑋𐐲𐑉𐑆 𐐱𐑂 𐐶𐐫𐑉𐑆 𐐲𐑋𐐲𐑍 𐐫𐑊 𐑄 𐑌𐐩𐑇𐐲𐑌𐑆 𐐰𐑌𐐼 𐐿𐐮𐑌𐐼𐑉𐐯𐐼𐑆 𐐱𐑂 𐑄 𐐲𐑉𐑃, 𐐰𐑌𐐼 𐐰𐑆 𐑄𐐩𐑉 𐐺𐐨𐑀𐐰𐑌 𐐻𐐭 𐐺 𐐶𐐫𐑉𐑆 𐐰𐑌𐐼 𐑉𐐭𐑋𐐲𐑉𐑆

𐐱𐑂 𐐶𐐫𐑉𐑆 𐐰𐑋𐐲𐑍 𐐫𐑊 𐑄 𐑌𐐩𐑇𐐲𐑌𐑆 𐐸𐐶𐐮𐐽 𐐺𐐨𐑊𐐱𐑍𐐼 𐐻𐐭 𐑄 𐑋𐐲𐑄𐐲𐑉 𐐱𐑂 𐐲𐐺𐐱𐑋𐐮𐑌𐐩𐑇𐐲𐑌𐑆, 𐑄 𐐩𐑌𐐾𐐯𐑊 𐑅𐐹𐐩𐐿 𐐲𐑌𐐻𐐭 𐑋𐐨, 𐑅𐐩𐐮𐑍, 𐐒𐐨𐐸𐐬𐑊𐐼 𐑄 𐑉𐐪𐑃 𐐱𐑂 𐐘𐐱𐐼 𐐮𐑆 𐐲𐐹𐐱𐑌 𐑄 𐑋𐐲𐑄𐐲𐑉 𐐱𐑂 𐐸𐐪𐑉𐑊𐐲𐐻𐑅; 𐐰𐑌𐐼 𐐺𐐨𐐸𐐬𐑊𐐼 𐑄𐐵 𐑅𐐨𐐯𐑅𐐻 𐐫𐑊 𐑄𐐨𐑆 𐑃𐐮𐑍𐑆: 𐐰𐑌𐐼 𐐸𐐶𐐯𐑌 𐑄 𐐼𐐩 𐐿𐐲𐑋𐐯𐑃 𐑄𐐰𐐻 𐑄 𐑉𐐪𐑃 𐐱𐑂 𐐘𐐱𐐼 𐐮𐑆 𐐹𐐬𐑉𐐼 𐐵𐐻 𐐲𐐹𐐱𐑌 𐑄 𐑋𐐲𐑄𐐲𐑉 𐐱𐑂 𐐸𐐪𐑉𐑊𐐲𐐻𐑅, 𐐸𐐶𐐮𐐽 𐐮𐑆 𐑄 𐑀𐑉𐐩𐐻 𐐰𐑌𐐼 𐐲𐐺𐐱𐑋𐐮𐑌𐐲𐐺𐑊 𐐽𐐲𐑉𐐽 𐐱𐑂 𐐫𐑊 𐑄 𐐲𐑉𐑃, 𐐸𐐭𐑆 𐑁𐐵𐑌𐐼𐐲𐑉 𐐮𐑆 𐑄 𐐼𐐯𐑂𐐮𐑊, 𐑄𐐯𐑌, 𐐰𐐻 𐑄𐐰𐐻 𐐼𐐩, 𐑄 𐐶𐐲𐑉𐐿 𐐱𐑂 𐑄 𐐙𐐪𐑄𐐲𐑉 𐑇𐐰𐑊 𐐿𐐱𐑋𐐯𐑌𐑅, 𐐮𐑌 𐐹𐑉𐐨𐐹𐐩𐑉𐐮𐑍 𐑄 𐐶𐐩 𐑁𐐫𐑉 𐑄 𐑁𐐳𐑊𐑁𐐮𐑊𐐮𐑍 𐐱𐑂 𐐸𐐮𐑆 𐐿𐐲𐑂𐐯𐑌𐐲𐑌𐐻𐑅, 𐐸𐐶𐐮𐐽 𐐸𐐨 𐐸𐐰𐑃 𐑋𐐩𐐼 𐐻𐐭 𐐸𐐮𐑆 𐐹𐐨𐐹𐑊, 𐐸𐐭 𐐪𐑉 𐐱𐑂 𐑄 𐐸𐐵𐑅 𐐱𐑂 𐐆𐑆𐑉𐐩𐐯𐑊.

52. 𐐈𐑌𐐼 𐐮𐐻 𐐿𐐩𐑋 𐐻𐐭 𐐹𐐰𐑅 𐑄𐐰𐐻 𐑄 𐐩𐑌𐐾𐐯𐑊 𐑅𐐹𐐩𐐿 𐐲𐑌𐐻𐐭 𐑋𐐨, 𐑅𐐩𐐮𐑍, 𐐢𐐳𐐿! 𐐈𐑌𐐼 𐐌 𐑊𐐳𐐿𐐻 𐐰𐑌𐐼 𐐺𐐨𐐸𐐯𐑊𐐼 𐐩 𐑋𐐰𐑌, 𐐰𐑌𐐼 𐐸𐐨 𐐶𐐱𐑆 𐐼𐑉𐐯𐑅𐐻 𐐮𐑌 𐐩 𐐸𐐶𐐴𐐻 𐑉𐐬𐐺; 𐐰𐑌𐐼 𐑄 𐐩𐑌𐐾𐐯𐑊 𐑅𐐯𐐼 𐐲𐑌𐐻𐐭 𐑋𐐨, 𐐒𐐨𐐸𐐬𐑊𐐼 𐐶𐐲𐑌 𐐱𐑂 𐑄 𐐻𐐶𐐯𐑊𐑂 𐐰𐐹𐐱𐑅𐐲𐑊𐑆 𐐱𐑂 𐑄 𐐢𐐰𐑋! 𐐒𐐨𐐸𐐬𐑊𐐼 𐐸𐐨 𐑇𐐰𐑊 𐑅𐐨 𐐰𐑌𐐼 𐑉𐐴𐐻 𐑄 𐑉𐐨𐑋𐐩𐑌𐐼𐐲𐑉 𐐱𐑂 𐑄𐐨𐑆 𐑃𐐮𐑍𐑆; 𐐷𐐩, 𐐰𐑌𐐼 𐐫𐑊𐑅𐐬 𐑋𐐯𐑌𐐨 𐑃𐐮𐑍𐑆 𐐸𐐶𐐮𐐽 𐐸𐐰𐑂 𐐺𐐮𐑌: 𐐰𐑌𐐼 𐐸𐐨 𐑇𐐰𐑊 𐐫𐑊𐑅𐐬 𐑉𐐴𐐻 𐐿𐐱𐑌𐑅𐐲𐑉𐑌𐐮𐑍 𐑄 𐐯𐑌𐐼 𐐱𐑂 𐑄 𐐶𐐲𐑉𐑊𐐼; 𐐸𐐶𐐯𐑉𐑁𐐫𐑉 𐑄 𐑃𐐮𐑍𐑆 𐐸𐐶𐐮𐐽 𐐸𐐨 𐑇𐐰𐑊 𐑉𐐴𐐻 𐐪𐑉 𐐾𐐲𐑅𐐻 𐐰𐑌𐐼 𐐻𐑉𐐭; 𐐰𐑌𐐼 𐐺𐐨𐐸𐐬𐑊𐐼 𐑄𐐩 𐐪𐑉 𐑉𐐮𐐻𐐲𐑌 𐐮𐑌 𐑄 𐐺𐐳𐐿 𐐸𐐶𐐮𐐽 𐑄𐐵 𐐺𐐨𐐸𐐯𐑊𐐼𐐯𐑅𐐻 𐐹𐑉𐐬𐑅𐐨𐐼𐐮𐑍 𐐵𐐻 𐐱𐑂 𐑄 𐑋𐐵𐑃 𐐱𐑂 𐑄 𐐖𐐭; 𐐰𐑌𐐼 𐐰𐐻 𐑄 𐐻𐐴𐑋 𐑄𐐩 𐐹𐑉𐐬𐑅𐐨𐐼𐐯𐐼 𐐵𐐻 𐐱𐑂 𐑄 𐑋𐐵𐑃 𐐱𐑂 𐑄 𐐖𐐭, 𐐫𐑉, 𐐰𐐻 𐑄 𐐻𐐴𐑋 𐑄 𐐺𐐳𐐿 𐐹𐑉𐐬𐑅𐐨𐐼𐐯𐐼 𐐵𐐻 𐐱𐑂 𐑄 𐑋𐐵𐑃 𐐱𐑂 𐑄 𐐖𐐭, 𐑄 𐑃𐐮𐑍𐑆 𐐸𐐶𐐮𐐽 𐐶𐐲𐑉 𐑉𐐮𐐻𐐲𐑌 𐐶𐐲𐑉 𐐹𐑊𐐩𐑌, 𐐰𐑌𐐼 𐐹𐐷𐐭𐑉, 𐐰𐑌𐐼 𐑋𐐬𐑅𐐻 𐐹𐑉𐐯𐑇𐐲𐑅, 𐐰𐑌𐐼 𐐨𐑆𐐨 𐐻𐐭 𐑄 𐐲𐑌𐐼𐐲𐑉𐑅𐐻𐐰𐑌𐐼𐐮𐑍 𐐱𐑂 𐐫𐑊 𐑋𐐯𐑌. 𐐈𐑌𐐼 𐐺𐐨𐐸𐐬𐑊𐐼, 𐑄 𐑃𐐮𐑍𐑆 𐐸𐐶𐐮𐐽 𐑄𐐮𐑅 𐐰𐐹𐐱𐑅𐐲𐑊 𐐱𐑂 𐑄 𐐢𐐰𐑋 𐑇𐐰𐑊 𐑉𐐴𐐻, 𐐪𐑉 𐑋𐐯𐑌𐐨 𐑃𐐮𐑍𐑆 𐐸𐐶𐐮𐐽 𐑄𐐵 𐐸𐐰𐑅𐐻 𐑅𐐨𐑌; 𐐰𐑌𐐼 𐐺𐐨𐐸𐐬𐑊𐐼, 𐑄 𐑉𐐨𐑋𐐩𐑌𐐼𐐲𐑉 𐑇𐐰𐑊𐐻 𐑄𐐵 𐑅𐐨; 𐐺𐐲𐐻 𐑄 𐑃𐐮𐑍𐑆 𐐸𐐶𐐮𐐽 𐑄𐐵 𐑇𐐰𐑊𐐻 𐑅𐐨 𐐸𐐨𐑉𐐰𐑁𐐻𐐲𐑉, 𐑄𐐵 𐑇𐐰𐑊𐐻 𐑌𐐱𐐻 𐑉𐐴𐐻; 𐑁𐐫𐑉 𐑄 𐐢𐐫𐑉𐐼 𐐘𐐱𐐼 𐐸𐐰𐑃 𐐫𐑉𐐼𐐩𐑌𐐼 𐑄 𐐰𐐹𐐱𐑅𐐲𐑊 𐐱𐑂 𐑄 𐐢𐐰𐑋 𐐱𐑂 𐐘𐐱𐐼, 𐑄𐐰𐐻 𐐸𐐨 𐑇𐐳𐐼 𐑉𐐴𐐻 𐑄𐐯𐑋. 𐐈𐑌𐐼 𐐫𐑊𐑅𐐬 𐐲𐑄𐐲𐑉𐑆 𐐸𐐭 𐐸𐐰𐑂 𐐺𐐮𐑌, 𐐻𐐭 𐑄𐐯𐑋 𐐸𐐰𐑃 𐐸𐐨 𐑇𐐬𐑌 𐐫𐑊 𐑃𐐮𐑍𐑆, 𐐰𐑌𐐼 𐑄𐐩 𐐸𐐰𐑂 𐑉𐐮𐐻𐐲𐑌 𐑄𐐯𐑋; 𐐰𐑌𐐼 𐑄𐐩 𐐪𐑉 𐑅𐐨𐑊𐐼 𐐲𐐹 𐐻𐐭 𐐿𐐲𐑋 𐑁𐐬𐑉𐑃 𐐮𐑌 𐑄𐐯𐑉 𐐹𐐷𐐭𐑉𐐮𐐻𐐨, 𐐰𐐿𐐫𐑉𐐼𐐮𐑍 𐐻𐐭 𐑄 𐐻𐑉𐐭𐑃 𐐸𐐶𐐮𐐽 𐐮𐑆 𐐮𐑌 𐑄 𐐢𐐰𐑋, 𐐮𐑌 𐑄 𐐬𐑌 𐐼𐐷𐐭 𐐻𐐴𐑋 𐐱𐑂 𐑄 𐐢𐐫𐑉𐐼, 𐐲𐑌𐐻𐐭 𐑄 𐐸𐐵𐑅 𐐱𐑂 𐐆𐑆𐑉𐐩𐐯𐑊.

53. 𐐈𐑌𐐼 𐐌, 𐐤𐐀𐐙𐐌, 𐐸𐐲𐑉𐐼 𐐰𐑌𐐼 𐐺𐐯𐑉 𐑉𐐯𐐿𐐲𐑉𐐼, 𐑄𐐰𐐻 𐑄 𐑌𐐩𐑋 𐐱𐑂 𐑄 𐐰𐐹𐐱𐑅𐐲𐑊 𐐱𐑂 𐑄 𐐢𐐰𐑋 𐐶𐐱𐑆 𐐖𐐱𐑌, 𐐰𐐿𐐫𐑉𐐼𐐮𐑍 𐐻𐐭 𐑄 𐐶𐐲𐑉𐐼 𐐱𐑂 𐑄 𐐩𐑌𐐾𐐯𐑊. 𐐈𐑌𐐼 𐐺𐐨𐐸𐐬𐑊𐐼, 𐐌, 𐐤𐐀𐐙𐐌, 𐐰𐑋 𐑁𐐫𐑉𐐺𐐮𐐼𐐲𐑌 𐑄𐐰𐐻 𐐌 𐑇𐐳𐐼 𐑉𐐴𐐻 𐑄 𐑉𐐨𐑋𐐩𐑌𐐼𐐲𐑉 𐐱𐑂 𐑄 𐑃𐐮𐑍𐑆 𐐸𐐶𐐮𐐽 𐐌 𐑅𐐫 𐐰𐑌𐐼 𐐸𐐲𐑉𐐼; 𐐸𐐶𐐯𐑉𐑁𐐫𐑉 𐑄 𐑃𐐮𐑍𐑆 𐐸𐐶𐐮𐐽 𐐌 𐐸𐐰𐑂 𐑉𐐮𐐻𐐲𐑌 𐑅𐐲𐑁𐐴𐑅𐐯𐑃 𐑋𐐨; 𐐰𐑌𐐼 𐐌 𐐸𐐰𐑂 𐑉𐐮𐐻𐐲𐑌 𐐺𐐲𐐻 𐐩 𐑅𐑋𐐫𐑊 𐐹𐐪𐑉𐐻 𐐱𐑂 𐑄 𐑃𐐮𐑍𐑆 𐐸𐐶𐐮𐐽 𐐌 𐑅𐐫. 𐐈𐑌𐐼 𐐌 𐐺𐐯𐑉 𐑉𐐯𐐿𐐲𐑉𐐼, 𐑄𐐰𐐻 𐐌 𐑅𐐫 𐑄 𐑃𐐮𐑍𐑆 𐐸𐐶𐐮𐐽 𐑋𐐴 𐑁𐐪𐑄𐐲𐑉 𐑅𐐫, 𐐰𐑌𐐼 𐑄 𐐩𐑌𐐾𐐯𐑊 𐐱𐑂 𐑄 𐐢𐐫𐑉𐐼 𐐼𐐮𐐼 𐑋𐐩𐐿 𐑄𐐯𐑋 𐑌𐐬𐑌 𐐲𐑌𐐻𐐭 𐑋𐐨. 𐐈𐑌𐐼 𐑌𐐵 𐐌 𐑋𐐩𐐿 𐐰𐑌 𐐯𐑌𐐼 𐐱𐑂 𐑅𐐹𐐨𐐿𐐮𐑍 𐐿𐐱𐑌𐑅𐐲𐑉𐑌𐐮𐑍 𐑄 𐑃𐐮𐑍𐑆 𐐸𐐶𐐮𐐽 𐐌 𐑅𐐫, 𐐸𐐶𐐴𐑊 𐐌 𐐶𐐱𐑆 𐐿𐐰𐑉𐐨𐐼 𐐲𐐶𐐩 𐐮𐑌 𐑄 𐑅𐐹𐐮𐑉𐐮𐐻: 𐐰𐑌𐐼 𐐮𐑁 𐐫𐑊 𐑄 𐑃𐐮𐑍𐑆 𐐸𐐶𐐮𐐽 𐐌 𐑅𐐫 𐐪𐑉 𐑌𐐱𐐻 𐑉𐐮𐐻𐐲𐑌, 𐑄 𐑃𐐮𐑍𐑆 𐐸𐐶𐐮𐐽 𐐌 𐐸𐐰𐑂 𐑉𐐮𐐻𐐲𐑌 𐐪𐑉 𐐻𐑉𐐭. 𐐈𐑌𐐼 𐑄𐐲𐑅 𐐮𐐻 𐐮𐑆. 𐐁𐑋𐐯𐑌.

𐐗𐐈𐐑𐐓𐐊𐐡 IV.

1. 𐐈𐑌𐐼 𐐮𐐻 𐐿𐐩𐑋 𐐻𐐭 𐐹𐐰𐑅 𐑄𐐰𐐻 𐐰𐑁𐐻𐐲𐑉 𐐌, 𐐤𐐀𐐙𐐌, 𐐸𐐰𐐼 𐐺𐐨𐑌 𐐿𐐰𐑉𐐨𐐼 𐐲𐐶𐐩 𐐮𐑌 𐑄 𐑅𐐹𐐮𐑉𐐮𐐻, 𐐰𐑌𐐼 𐑅𐐨𐑌 𐐫𐑊 𐑄𐐨𐑆 𐑃𐐮𐑍𐑆, 𐐌 𐑉𐐨𐐻𐐲𐑉𐑌𐐼 𐐻𐐭 𐑄 𐐻𐐯𐑌𐐻 𐐱𐑂 𐑋𐐴 𐑁𐐪𐑄𐐲𐑉. 𐐈𐑌𐐼 𐐮𐐻 𐐿𐐩𐑋 𐐻𐐭 𐐹𐐰𐑅 𐑄𐐰𐐻 𐐌 𐐺𐐨𐐸𐐯𐑊𐐼 𐑋𐐴 𐐺𐑉𐐲𐑄𐐲𐑉𐑆, 𐐰𐑌𐐼 𐑄𐐩 𐐶𐐲𐑉 𐐼𐐮𐑅𐐹𐐷𐐭𐐻𐐮𐑍 𐐶𐐲𐑌 𐐶𐐮𐑄 𐐲𐑌𐐲𐑄𐐲𐑉, 𐐿𐐱𐑌𐑅𐐲𐑉𐑌𐐮𐑍 𐑄 𐑃𐐮𐑍𐑆 𐐸𐐶𐐮𐐽 𐑋𐐴 𐑁𐐪𐑄𐐲𐑉 𐐸𐐰𐐼 𐑅𐐹𐐬𐐿𐐲𐑌 𐐲𐑌𐐻𐐭 𐑄𐐯𐑋; 𐑁𐐫𐑉 𐐸𐐨 𐐻𐑉𐐭𐑊𐐨 𐑅𐐹𐐩𐐿 𐑋𐐯𐑌𐐨 𐑀𐑉𐐩𐐻 𐑃𐐮𐑍𐑆 𐐲𐑌𐐻𐐭 𐑄𐐯𐑋, 𐐸𐐶𐐮𐐽 𐐶𐐲𐑉 𐐸𐐪𐑉𐐼 𐐻𐐭 𐐺𐐨 𐐲𐑌𐐼𐐲𐑉𐑅𐐻𐐳𐐼, 𐑅𐐩𐑂 𐐩 𐑋𐐰𐑌 𐑇𐐳𐐼 𐐮𐑌𐐿𐐶𐐴𐑉 𐐲𐑂 𐑄 𐐢𐐫𐑉𐐼; 𐐰𐑌𐐼 𐑄𐐩 𐐺𐐨𐐮𐑍 𐐸𐐪𐑉𐐼 𐐮𐑌 𐑄𐐯𐑉 𐐸𐐪𐑉𐐻𐑅, 𐑄𐐯𐑉𐑁𐐫𐑉 𐑄𐐩 𐐼𐐮𐐼 𐑌𐐱𐐻 𐑊𐐳𐐿 𐐲𐑌𐐻𐐭 𐑄 𐐢𐐫𐑉𐐼 𐐰𐑆 𐑄𐐩

𐐫𐐻. 𐐈𐑌𐐼 𐑌𐐵 𐐌, 𐐤𐐨𐑁𐐴, 𐐶𐐱𐑆 𐑀𐑉𐐨𐑂𐐼 𐐺𐐨𐐿𐐫𐑆 𐐱𐑂 𐑄 𐐸𐐪𐑉𐐼𐑌𐐯𐑅 𐐱𐑂 𐑄𐐩𐑉 𐐸𐐪𐑉𐐻𐑅, 𐐰𐑌𐐼 𐐫𐑊𐑅𐐬, 𐐺𐐨𐐿𐐫𐑆 𐐱𐑂 𐑄 𐑃𐐮𐑍𐑆 𐐸𐐶𐐮𐐽 𐐌 𐐸𐐰𐐼 𐑅𐐨𐑌, 𐐰𐑌𐐼 𐑌𐐷𐐭 𐑄𐐩 𐑋𐐲𐑅𐐻 𐐲𐑌𐐰𐑂𐐱𐐮𐐼𐐰𐐺𐑊𐐮 𐐿𐐲𐑋 𐐻𐐭 𐐹𐐰𐑅, 𐐺𐐨𐐿𐐫𐑆 𐐱𐑂 𐑄 𐑀𐑉𐐩𐐻 𐐶𐐮𐐿𐐯𐐼𐑌𐐯𐑅 𐐱𐑂 𐑄 𐐽𐐮𐑊𐐼𐑉𐐯𐑌 𐐱𐑂 𐑋𐐯𐑌. 𐐈𐑌𐐼 𐐮𐐻 𐐿𐐩𐑋 𐐻𐐭 𐐹𐐰𐑅 𐑄𐐰𐐻 𐐌 𐐶𐐱𐑆 𐐬𐑂𐐲𐑉𐐿𐐲𐑋 𐐺𐐨𐐿𐐫𐑆 𐐱𐑂 𐑋𐐴 𐐰𐑁𐑊𐐮𐐿𐑇𐐲𐑌𐑆, 𐑁𐐫𐑉 𐐌 𐐿𐐲𐑌𐑅𐐮𐐼𐐲𐑉𐐼 𐑄𐐰𐐻 𐑋𐐴𐑌 𐐰𐑁𐑊𐐮𐐿𐑇𐐲𐑌𐑆 𐐶𐐲𐑉 𐑀𐑉𐐩𐐻 𐐲𐐺𐐲𐑂 𐐫𐑊, 𐐺𐐨𐐿𐐫𐑆 𐐱𐑂 𐑄 𐐼𐐨𐑅𐐻𐑉𐐲𐐿𐑇𐐲𐑌 𐐱𐑂 𐑋𐐴 𐐹𐐨𐐹𐑊, 𐑁𐐫𐑉 𐐌 𐐸𐐰𐐼 𐐺𐐨𐐸𐐯𐑊𐐼 𐑄𐐩𐑉 𐑁𐐫𐑊.

2. 𐐈𐑌𐐼 𐐮𐐻 𐐿𐐩𐑋 𐐻𐐭 𐐹𐐰𐑅 𐑄𐐰𐐻 𐐰𐑁𐐻𐐲𐑉 𐐌 𐐸𐐰𐐼 𐑉𐐨𐑅𐐨𐑂𐐼 𐑅𐐻𐑉𐐯𐑍𐑃 𐐌 𐑅𐐹𐐩𐐿 𐐲𐑌𐐻𐐭 𐑋𐐴 𐐺𐑉𐐲𐑄𐐲𐑉𐑌, 𐐼𐐨𐑆𐐴𐑉𐐮𐑍 𐐻𐐭 𐑌𐐬 𐐱𐑂 𐑄𐐯𐑋 𐑄 𐐿𐐫𐑆 𐐱𐑂 𐑄𐐩𐑉 𐐼𐐮𐑅𐐹𐐷𐐭𐐻𐐩𐑇𐐲𐑌𐑆. 𐐈𐑌𐐼 𐑄𐐩 𐑅𐐯𐐼, 𐐒𐐨𐐸𐐬𐑊𐐼, 𐐶𐐨 𐐿𐐰𐑌𐐱𐐻 𐐲𐑌𐐼𐐲𐑉𐑅𐐻𐐰𐑌𐐼 𐑄 𐐶𐐲𐑉𐐼𐑆 𐐸𐐶𐐮𐐽 𐐵𐑉 𐑁𐐪𐑄𐐲𐑉 𐐸𐐰𐑃 𐑅𐐹𐐬𐐿𐐲𐑌 𐐿𐐲𐑌𐑅𐐲𐑉𐑌𐐮𐑍 𐑄 𐑌𐐰𐐽𐐲𐑉𐐲𐑊 𐐺𐑉𐐰𐑌𐐽𐐯𐑆 𐐱𐑂 𐑄 𐐱𐑊𐐮𐑂-𐐻𐑉𐐨, 𐐰𐑌𐐼 𐐫𐑊𐑅𐐬, 𐐿𐐲𐑌𐑅𐐲𐑉𐑌𐐮𐑍 𐑄 𐐖𐐯𐑌𐐻𐐴𐑊𐑆. 𐐈𐑌𐐼 𐐌 𐑅𐐯𐐼 𐐲𐑌𐐻𐐭 𐑄𐐯𐑋, 𐐐𐐰𐑂 𐐷𐐨 𐐮𐑌𐐿𐐶𐐴𐑉𐐼 𐐱𐑂 𐑄 𐐢𐐫𐑉𐐼? 𐐈𐑌𐐼 𐑄𐐩 𐑅𐐯𐐼 𐐲𐑌𐐻𐐭 𐑋𐐨, 𐐎𐐨 𐐸𐐰𐑂 𐑌𐐱𐐻; 𐑁𐐫𐑉 𐑄 𐐢𐐫𐑉𐐼 𐑋𐐩𐐿𐐯𐑃 𐑌𐐬 𐑅𐐲𐐽 𐑃𐐮𐑍 𐑌𐐬𐑌 𐐲𐑌𐐻𐐭 𐐲𐑅. 𐐒𐐨𐐸𐐬𐑊𐐼, 𐐌 𐑅𐐯𐐼 𐐲𐑌𐐻𐐭 𐑄𐐯𐑋, 𐐐𐐵 𐐮𐑆 𐐮𐐻 𐑄𐐰𐐻 𐐷𐐨 𐐼𐐭 𐑌𐐱𐐻 𐐿𐐨𐐹 𐑄 𐐿𐐱𐑋𐐰𐑌𐐼𐑋𐐯𐑌𐐻𐑅 𐐱𐑂 𐑄 𐐢𐐫𐑉𐐼? 𐐐𐐵 𐐮𐑆 𐐮𐐻 𐑄𐐰𐐻 𐐷𐐨 𐐶𐐮𐑊 𐐹𐐯𐑉𐐮𐑇, 𐐺𐐨𐐿𐐫𐑆 𐐱𐑂 𐑄 𐐸𐐪𐑉𐐼𐑌𐐯𐑅 𐐱𐑂 𐐷𐐬𐑉 𐐸𐐪𐑉𐐻𐑅? 𐐔𐐭 𐐷𐐨 𐑌𐐱𐐻 𐑉𐐨𐑋𐐯𐑋𐐺𐐲𐑉 𐑄 𐑃𐐮𐑍𐑆 𐐸𐐶𐐮𐐽 𐑄 𐐢𐐫𐑉𐐼 𐐸𐐰𐑃 𐑅𐐯𐐼, 𐐆𐑁 𐐷𐐨 𐐶𐐮𐑊 𐑌𐐱𐐻 𐐸𐐪𐑉𐐼𐑌 𐐷𐐬𐑉 𐐸𐐪𐑉𐐻𐑅, 𐐰𐑌𐐼 𐐰𐑅𐐿 𐑋𐐨 𐐮𐑌 𐑁𐐩𐑃, 𐐺𐐨𐑊𐐨𐑂𐐮𐑍 𐑄𐐰𐐻 𐐷𐐨 𐑇𐐰𐑊 𐑉𐐨𐑅𐐨𐑂, 𐐶𐐮𐑄 𐐼𐐮𐑊𐐮𐐾𐐯𐑌𐑅 𐐮𐑌 𐐿𐐨𐐹𐐮𐑍 𐑋𐐴 𐐿𐐱𐑋𐐰𐑌𐐼𐑋𐐯𐑌𐐻𐑅, 𐑇𐐳𐑉𐑊𐐨 𐑄𐐨𐑆 𐑃𐐮𐑍𐑆 𐑇𐐰𐑊 𐐺 𐑋𐐩𐐼 𐑌𐐬𐑌 𐐲𐑌𐐻𐐭 𐐷𐐭?

3. 𐐒𐐨𐐸𐐬𐑊𐐼, 𐐌 𐑅𐐩 𐐲𐑌𐐻𐐭 𐐷𐐭, 𐑄𐐰𐐻 𐑄 𐐸𐐵𐑅 𐐱𐑂 𐐆𐑆𐑉𐐩𐐯𐑊 𐐶𐐱𐑆 𐐿𐐲𐑋𐐹𐐩𐑉𐐼 𐐲𐑌𐐻𐐭 𐐰𐑌 𐐱𐑊𐐮𐑂-𐐻𐑉𐐨, 𐐺𐐴 𐑄 𐐝𐐹𐐮𐑉𐐮𐐻 𐐱𐑂 𐑄 𐐢𐐫𐑉𐐼 𐐸𐐶𐐮𐐽 𐐶𐐱𐑆 𐐮𐑌 𐐵𐑉 𐑁𐐪𐑄𐐲𐑉; 𐐰𐑌𐐼 𐐺𐐨𐐸𐐬𐑊𐐼 𐐪𐑉 𐐶𐐨 𐑌𐐱𐐻 𐐺𐑉𐐬𐐿𐐲𐑌 𐐫𐑁 𐑁𐑉𐐱𐑋 𐑄 𐐸𐐵𐑅 𐐱𐑂 𐐆𐑆𐑉𐐩𐐯𐑊? 𐐰𐑌𐐼 𐐪𐑉 𐐶𐐨 𐑌𐐱𐐻 𐐲 𐐺𐑉𐐰𐑌𐐽 𐐱𐑂 𐑄 𐐸𐐵𐑅 𐐱𐑂 𐐆𐑆𐑉𐐩𐐯𐑊? 𐐈𐑌𐐼 𐑌𐐵, 𐑄 𐑃𐐮𐑍 𐐸𐐶𐐮𐐽 𐐵𐑉 𐑁𐐪𐑄𐐲𐑉 𐑋𐐨𐑌𐐯𐑃 𐐿𐐲𐑌𐑅𐐲𐑉𐑌𐐮𐑍 𐑄 𐑀𐑉𐐰𐑁𐐻𐐮𐑍 𐐮𐑌 𐐱𐑂 𐑄 𐑌𐐰𐐽𐐲𐑉𐐲𐑊 𐐺𐑉𐐰𐑌𐐽𐐯𐑆 𐑃𐑉𐐭 𐑄 𐑁𐐳𐑊𐑌𐐯𐑅 𐐱𐑂 𐑄 𐐖𐐯𐑌𐐻𐐴𐑊𐑆, 𐐮𐑆, 𐑄𐐰𐐻 𐐮𐑌 𐑄 𐑊𐐰𐐻𐐲𐑉 𐐼𐐩𐑆, 𐐸𐐶𐐯𐑌 𐐵𐑉 𐑅𐐨𐐼 𐑇𐐰𐑊 𐐸𐐰𐑂 𐐼𐐶𐐮𐑌𐐼𐑊𐐼 𐐮𐑌 𐐲𐑌𐐺𐐨𐑊𐐨𐑁, 𐐷𐐩, 𐑁𐐫𐑉 𐑄 𐑅𐐹𐐩𐑅 𐐱𐑂 𐑋𐐯𐑌𐐨 𐐷𐐨𐑉𐑆, 𐐰𐑌𐐼 𐑋𐐯𐑌𐐨 𐐾𐐯𐑌𐐲𐑉𐐩𐑇𐐲𐑌𐑆 𐐰𐑁𐐻𐐲𐑉 𐑄 𐐣𐐯𐑅𐐴𐐲 𐑇𐐰𐑊 𐐺 𐑋𐐰𐑌𐐮𐑁𐐯𐑅𐐻𐐯𐐼 𐐮𐑌 𐐺𐐱𐐼𐐨 𐐲𐑌𐐻𐐭 𐑄 𐐽𐐮𐑊𐐼𐑉𐐯𐑌 𐐱𐑂 𐑋𐐯𐑌, 𐑄𐐯𐑌 𐑇𐐰𐑊 𐑄 𐑁𐐳𐑊𐑌𐐯𐑅 𐐱𐑂 𐑄 𐑀𐐱𐑅𐐹𐐯𐑊 𐐱𐑂 𐑄 𐐣𐐯𐑅𐐴𐐲 𐐿𐐲𐑋 𐐲𐑌𐐻𐐭 𐑄 𐐖𐐯𐑌𐐻𐐴𐑊𐑆, 𐐰𐑌𐐼 𐑁𐑉𐐱𐑋 𐑄 𐐖𐐯𐑌𐐻𐐴𐑊𐑆 𐐲𐑌𐐻𐐭 𐑄 𐑉𐐯𐑋𐑌𐐰𐑌𐐻 𐐱𐑂 𐐵𐑉 𐑅𐐨𐐼: 𐐰𐑌𐐼 𐐰𐐻 𐑄𐐰𐐻 𐐼𐐩 𐑇𐐰𐑊 𐑄 𐑉𐐯𐑋𐑌𐐰𐑌𐐻 𐐱𐑂 𐐵𐑉 𐑅𐐨𐐼 𐑌𐐬 𐑄𐐰𐐻 𐑄𐐩 𐐪𐑉 𐐱𐑂 𐑄 𐐸𐐵𐑅 𐐱𐑂 𐐆𐑆𐑉𐐩𐐯𐑊, 𐐰𐑌𐐼 𐑄𐐰𐐻 𐑄𐐩 𐐪𐑉 𐑄 𐐿𐐲𐑂𐐯𐑌𐐰𐑌𐐻 𐐹𐐨𐐹𐑊 𐐱𐑂 𐑄 𐐢𐐫𐑉𐐼; 𐐰𐑌𐐼 𐑄𐐯𐑌 𐑇𐐰𐑊 𐑄𐐩 𐑌𐐬 𐐰𐑌𐐼 𐐿𐐲𐑋 𐐻𐐭 𐑄 𐑌𐐱𐑊𐐯𐐾 𐐱𐑂 𐑄𐐩𐑉 𐑁𐐬𐑉𐑁𐐪𐑄𐐲𐑉𐑆, 𐐰𐑌𐐼 𐐫𐑊𐑅𐐬 𐐻𐐭 𐑄 𐑌𐐱𐑊𐐯𐐾 𐐱𐑂 𐑄 𐑀𐐱𐑅𐐹𐐯𐑊 𐐱𐑂 𐑄𐐩𐑉 𐐡𐐨𐐼𐐨𐑋𐐲𐑉, 𐐸𐐶𐐮𐐽 𐐶𐐱𐑆 𐑋𐐮𐑌𐐮𐑅𐐻𐐲𐑉𐐼 𐐲𐑌𐐻𐐭 𐑄𐐩𐑉 𐑁𐐪𐑄𐐲𐑉𐑆 𐐺𐐴 𐐸𐐮𐑋; 𐐸𐐶𐐯𐑉𐑁𐐬𐑉 𐑄𐐩 𐑇𐐰𐑊 𐐿𐐲𐑋 𐐻𐐭 𐑄 𐑌𐐱𐑊𐐯𐐾 𐐱𐑂 𐑄𐐩𐑉 𐐡𐐨𐐼𐐨𐑋𐐲𐑉 𐐰𐑌𐐼 𐑄 𐑂𐐯𐑉𐐨 𐐹𐐱𐐮𐑌𐐻𐑅 𐐱𐑂 𐐸𐐮𐑆 𐐼𐐱𐐿𐐻𐑉𐐮𐑌, 𐑄𐐰𐐻 𐑄𐐩 𐑋𐐩 𐑌𐐬 𐐸𐐵 𐐻𐐭 𐐿𐐲𐑋 𐐲𐑌𐐻𐐭 𐐸𐐮𐑋 𐐰𐑌𐐼 𐐺 𐑅𐐩𐑂𐐼. 𐐈𐑌𐐼 𐑄𐐯𐑌 𐐰𐐻 𐑄𐐰𐐻 𐐼𐐩, 𐐶𐐮𐑊 𐑄𐐩 𐑌𐐱𐐻 𐑉𐐨𐐾𐐱𐐮𐑅 𐐰𐑌𐐼 𐑀𐐮𐑂 𐐹𐑉𐐩𐑆 𐐲𐑌𐐻𐐭 𐑄𐐩𐑉 𐐯𐑂𐐲𐑉𐑊𐐰𐑅𐐻𐐮𐑍 𐐘𐐱𐐼, 𐑄𐐩𐑉 𐑉𐐱𐐿 𐐰𐑌𐐼 𐑄𐐩𐑉 𐑅𐐰𐑊𐑂𐐩𐑇𐐲𐑌? 𐐏𐐩, 𐐰𐐻 𐑄𐐰𐐻 𐐼𐐩, 𐐶𐐮𐑊 𐑄𐐩 𐑌𐐱𐐻 𐑉𐐨𐑅𐐨𐑂 𐑄 𐑅𐐻𐑉𐐯𐑍𐑃 𐐰𐑌𐐼 𐑌𐐲𐑉𐐮𐑇𐑋𐐯𐑌𐐻 𐑁𐑉𐐱𐑋 𐑄 𐐻𐑉𐐭 𐑂𐐴𐑌? 𐐏𐐩, 𐐶𐐮𐑊 𐑄𐐩 𐑌𐐱𐐻 𐐿𐐲𐑋 𐐲𐑌𐐻𐐭 𐑄 𐐻𐑉𐐭 𐑁𐐬𐑊𐐼 𐐱𐑂 𐐘𐐱𐐼? 𐐒𐐨𐐸𐐬𐑊𐐼, 𐐌 𐑅𐐩 𐐲𐑌𐐻𐐭 𐐷𐐭: 𐐏𐐩, 𐑄𐐩 𐑇𐐰𐑊 𐐺 𐑉𐐨𐑋𐐯𐑋𐐺𐐲𐑉𐐼 𐐲𐑀𐐯𐑌 𐐲𐑋𐐲𐑍 𐑄 𐐸𐐵𐑅 𐐱𐑂 𐐆𐑆𐑉𐐩𐐯𐑊; 𐑄𐐩 𐑇𐐰𐑊 𐐺 𐑀𐑉𐐰𐑁𐐻𐐯𐐼 𐐮𐑌, 𐐺𐐨𐐮𐑍 𐐲 𐑌𐐰𐐽𐐲𐑉𐐲𐑊 𐐺𐑉𐐰𐑌𐐽 𐐱𐑂 𐑄 𐐱𐑊𐐮𐑂-𐐻𐑉𐐨, 𐐮𐑌𐐻𐐭 𐑄 𐐻𐑉𐐭 𐐱𐑊𐐮𐑂-𐐻𐑉𐐨; 𐐰𐑌𐐼 𐑄𐐮𐑅 𐐮𐑆 𐐸𐐶𐐱𐐻 𐐵𐑉 𐑁𐐪𐑄𐐲𐑉 𐑋𐐨𐑌𐐯𐑃; 𐐰𐑌𐐼 𐐸𐐨 𐑋𐐨𐑌𐐯𐑃 𐑄𐐰𐐻 𐐮𐐻 𐐶𐐮𐑊 𐑌𐐱𐐻 𐐿𐐲𐑋 𐐻𐐭 𐐹𐐰𐑅 𐐲𐑌𐐻𐐮𐑊 𐐰𐑁𐐻𐐲𐑉 𐑄𐐩 𐐪𐑉 𐑅𐐿𐐰𐐻𐐲𐑉𐐼 𐐺𐐴 𐑄 𐐖𐐯𐑌𐐻𐐴𐑊𐑆; 𐐰𐑌𐐼 𐐸𐐨 𐑋𐐨𐑌𐐯𐑃 𐑄𐐰𐐻 𐐮𐐻 𐑇𐐰𐑊 𐐿𐐲𐑋 𐐺𐐴 𐐶𐐩 𐐱𐑂 𐑄 𐐖𐐯𐑌𐐻𐐴𐑊𐑆, 𐑄𐐰𐐻 𐑄 𐐢𐐫𐑉𐐼 𐑋𐐩 𐑇𐐬 𐐸𐐮𐑆 𐐹𐐵𐐲𐑉 𐐲𐑌𐐻𐐭 𐑄 𐐖𐐯𐑌𐐻𐐴𐑊𐑆, 𐑁𐐫𐑉 𐑄 𐑂𐐯𐑉𐐨 𐐿𐐫𐑆 𐑄𐐰𐐻 𐐸𐐨 𐑇𐐰𐑊 𐐺 𐑉𐐨𐐾𐐯𐐿𐐻𐐯𐐼 𐐱𐑂 𐑄 𐐖𐐭𐑆, 𐐫𐑉 𐐱𐑂 𐑄 𐐸𐐵𐑅 𐐱𐑂 𐐆𐑆𐑉𐐩𐐯𐑊; 𐐸𐐶𐐯𐑉𐑁𐐬𐑉 𐐵𐑉 𐑁𐐪𐑄𐐲𐑉 𐐸𐐰𐑃 𐑌𐐱𐐻 𐑅𐐹𐐬𐐿𐐲𐑌 𐐱𐑂 𐐵𐑉 𐑅𐐨𐐼 𐐲𐑊𐐬𐑌, 𐐺𐐲𐐻 𐐫𐑊𐑅𐐬 𐐱𐑂 𐐫𐑊 𐑄 𐐸𐐵𐑅 𐐱𐑂 𐐆𐑆𐑉𐐩𐐯𐑊, 𐐹𐐱𐐮𐑌𐐻𐐮𐑍 𐐻𐐭 𐑄 𐐿𐐲𐑂𐐯𐑌𐐰𐑌𐐻 𐐸𐐶𐐮𐐽 𐑇𐐳𐐼 𐐺

𐑁𐐳𐑊𐑁𐐮𐑊𐐼 𐐮𐑌 𐑄 𐑊𐐰𐐻𐐲𐑉 𐐼𐐩𐑆; 𐐸𐐶𐐮𐐽 𐐿𐐲𐑂𐐯𐑌𐐲𐑌𐐻 𐑄 𐐢𐐫𐑉𐐼 𐑋𐐩𐐼 𐐻𐐭 𐐵𐑉 𐑁𐐪𐑄𐐲𐑉 𐐁𐐺𐑉𐐲𐐸𐐰𐑋, 𐑅𐐩𐐮𐑍, 𐐮𐑌 𐑄𐐴 𐑅𐐨𐐼 𐑇𐐰𐑊 𐐫𐑊 𐑄 𐐿𐐮𐑌𐐼𐑉𐐯𐐼𐑆 𐐱𐑂 𐑄 𐐲𐑉𐑃 𐐺 𐐺𐑊𐐯𐑅𐐻.

4. 𐐈𐑌𐐼 𐐮𐐻 𐐿𐐩𐑋 𐐻𐐭 𐐹𐐪𐑅 𐑄𐐰𐐻 𐐌, 𐐤𐐨𐑁𐐴, 𐑅𐐹𐐩𐐿 𐑋𐐲𐐽 𐐲𐑌𐐻𐐭 𐑄𐐯𐑋 𐐿𐐱𐑌𐑅𐐲𐑉𐑌𐐮𐑍 𐑄𐐨𐑆 𐑃𐐮𐑍𐑆; 𐐷𐐩, 𐐌 𐑅𐐹𐐩𐐿 𐐲𐑌𐐻𐐭 𐑄𐐯𐑋 𐐿𐐱𐑌𐑅𐐲𐑉𐑌𐐮𐑍 𐑄 𐑉𐐯𐑅𐐻𐐬𐑉𐐩𐑇𐐲𐑌 𐐱𐑂 𐑄 𐐖𐐭𐑆, 𐐮𐑌 𐑄 𐑊𐐰𐐻𐐲𐑉 𐐼𐐩𐑆; 𐐰𐑌𐐼 𐐌 𐐼𐐮𐐼 𐑉𐐨𐐸𐐲𐑉𐑅 𐐲𐑌𐐻𐐭 𐑄𐐯𐑋 𐑄 𐐶𐐲𐑉𐐼𐑆 𐐱𐑂 𐐌𐑆𐐩𐐷𐐲 𐐸𐐭 𐑅𐐹𐐩𐐿 𐐿𐐱𐑌𐑅𐐲𐑉𐑌𐐮𐑍 𐑄 𐑉𐐯𐑅𐐻𐐬𐑉𐐩𐑇𐐲𐑌 𐐱𐑂 𐑄 𐐖𐐭𐑆, 𐐫𐑉 𐐱𐑂 𐑄 𐐸𐐵𐑅 𐐱𐑂 𐐆𐑆𐑉𐐨𐐯𐑊; 𐐰𐑌𐐼 𐐪𐑁𐐻𐐲𐑉 𐑄𐐩 𐐶𐐲𐑉 𐑉𐐯𐑅𐐻𐐬𐑉𐐼, 𐑄𐐩 𐑇𐐳𐐼 𐑌𐐬 𐑋𐐬𐑉 𐐺 𐐿𐐱𐑌𐑁𐐵𐑌𐐼𐐯𐐼, 𐑌𐐨𐑄𐐲𐑉 𐑇𐐳𐐼 𐑄𐐩 𐐺 𐑅𐐿𐐰𐐻𐐲𐑉𐐼 𐐲𐑀𐐯𐑌. 𐐈𐑌𐐼 𐐮𐐻 𐐿𐐩𐑋 𐐻𐐭 𐐹𐐪𐑅 𐑄𐐰𐐻 𐐌 𐐼𐐮𐐼 𐑅𐐹𐐨𐐿 𐑋𐐯𐑌𐐨 𐐶𐐲𐑉𐐼𐑆 𐐲𐑌𐐻𐐭 𐑋𐐴 𐐺𐑉𐐯𐑄𐑉𐐯𐑌, 𐑄𐐰𐐻 𐑄𐐩 𐐶𐐲𐑉 𐐹𐐰𐑅𐐮𐑁𐐴𐐼, 𐐰𐑌𐐼 𐐼𐐮𐐼 𐐸𐐲𐑋𐐺𐑊 𐑄𐐯𐑋𐑅𐐯𐑊𐑂𐑆 𐐺𐐨𐑁𐐬𐑉 𐑄 𐐢𐐫𐑉𐐼.

5. 𐐈𐑌𐐼 𐐮𐐻 𐐿𐐩𐑋 𐐻𐐭 𐐹𐐪𐑅 𐑄𐐰𐐻 𐑄𐐩 𐐼𐐮𐐼 𐑅𐐹𐐨𐐿 𐐲𐑌𐐻𐐭 𐑋𐐨 𐐲𐑀𐐯𐑌, 𐑅𐐩𐐮𐑍, 𐐐𐐶𐐱𐐻 𐑋𐐨𐑌𐐯𐑃 𐑄𐐮𐑅 𐑃𐐮𐑍 𐐸𐐶𐐮𐐽 𐐵𐑉 𐑁𐐪𐑄𐐲𐑉 𐑅𐐫 𐐮𐑌 𐐲 𐐼𐑉𐐨𐑋? 𐐐𐐶𐐱𐐻 𐑋𐐨𐑌𐐯𐑃 𐑄 𐐻𐑉𐐨 𐐸𐐶𐐮𐐽 𐐸𐐨 𐑅𐐫? 𐐈𐑌𐐼 𐐌 𐑅𐐯𐐼 𐐲𐑌𐐻𐐭 𐑄𐐯𐑋, 𐐮𐐻 𐐶𐐱𐑆 𐐲 𐑉𐐯𐐹𐑉𐐯𐑆𐐯𐑌𐐻𐐩𐑇𐐲𐑌 𐐱𐑂 𐑄 𐐻𐑉𐐨 𐐱𐑂 𐑊𐐴𐑁. 𐐈𐑌𐐼 𐑄𐐩 𐑅𐐯𐐼 𐐲𐑌𐐻𐐭 𐑋𐐨, 𐐐𐐶𐐱𐐻 𐑋𐐨𐑌𐐯𐑃 𐑄 𐑉𐐱𐐼 𐐱𐑂 𐐴𐐲𐑉𐑌 𐐸𐐶𐐮𐐽 𐐵𐑉 𐑁𐐪𐑄𐐲𐑉 𐑅𐐫, 𐑄𐐰𐐻 𐑊𐐯𐐼 𐐻𐐭 𐑄 𐐻𐑉𐐨? 𐐈𐑌𐐼 𐐌 𐑅𐐯𐐼 𐐲𐑌𐐻𐐭 𐑄𐐯𐑋, 𐑄𐐰𐐻 𐐮𐐻 𐐶𐐱𐑆 𐑄 𐐶𐐲𐑉𐐼 𐐱𐑂 𐐘𐐱𐐼; 𐐰𐑌𐐼 𐐸𐐭𐑅𐐬 𐐶𐐳𐐼 𐐸𐐪𐑉𐐿𐐯𐑌 𐐲𐑌𐐻𐐭 𐑄 𐐶𐐲𐑉𐐼 𐐱𐑂 𐐘𐐱𐐼, 𐐰𐑌𐐼 𐐶𐐳𐐼 𐐸𐐬𐑊𐐼 𐑁𐐪𐑅𐐻 𐐲𐑌𐐻𐐭 𐐮𐐻, 𐑄𐐩 𐐶𐐳𐐼 𐑌𐐯𐑂𐐲𐑉 𐐹𐐯𐑉𐐮𐑇; 𐑌𐐨𐑄𐐲𐑉 𐐿𐐳𐐼 𐑄 𐐻𐐯𐑋𐐻𐐩𐑇𐐲𐑌𐑆 𐐰𐑌𐐼 𐑄 𐑁𐐴𐑉𐐨 𐐼𐐪𐑉𐐻𐑅 𐐱𐑂 𐑄 𐐰𐐼𐑂𐐲𐑉𐑅𐐯𐑉𐐨 𐐬𐑂𐐲𐑉𐐹𐐵𐐲𐑉 𐑄𐐯𐑋 𐐲𐑌𐐻𐐭 𐐺𐑊𐐴𐑌𐐼𐑌𐐯𐑅, 𐐻𐐭 𐑊𐐨𐐼 𐑄𐐯𐑋 𐐲𐐶𐐩 𐐻𐐭 𐐼𐐯𐑅𐐻𐑉𐐲𐐿𐑇𐐲𐑌. 𐐐𐐶𐐯𐑉𐑁𐐬𐑉, 𐐌, 𐐤𐐨𐑁𐐴, 𐐼𐐮𐐼 𐐯𐑀𐑆𐐫𐑉𐐻 𐑄𐐯𐑋 𐐻𐐭 𐑀𐐮𐑂 𐐸𐐨𐐼 𐐲𐑌𐐻𐐭 𐑄 𐐶𐐲𐑉𐐼 𐐱𐑂 𐑄 𐐢𐐫𐑉𐐼; 𐐷𐐩, 𐐌 𐐼𐐮𐐼 𐐯𐑀𐑆𐐫𐑉𐐻 𐑄𐐯𐑋 𐐶𐐮𐑄 𐐫𐑊 𐑄 𐐯𐑌𐐲𐑉𐐾𐐨𐑆 𐐱𐑂 𐑋𐐴 𐑅𐐬𐑊, 𐐰𐑌𐐼 𐐶𐐮𐑄 𐐫𐑊 𐑄 𐑁𐐰𐐿𐐲𐑊𐐻𐐨 𐐸𐐶𐐮𐐽 𐐌 𐐹𐐱𐑆𐐯𐑅𐐻, 𐑄𐐰𐐻 𐑄𐐩 𐐶𐐳𐐼 𐑀𐐮𐑂 𐐸𐐨𐐼 𐐻𐐭 𐑄 𐐶𐐲𐑉𐐼 𐐱𐑂 𐐘𐐱𐐼, 𐐰𐑌𐐼 𐑉𐐨𐑋𐐯𐑋𐐺𐐲𐑉 𐐻𐐭 𐐿𐐨𐐹 𐐸𐐮𐑆 𐐿𐐱𐑋𐐰𐑌𐐼𐑋𐐯𐑌𐐻𐑅 𐐫𐑊𐐶𐐩𐑆 𐐮𐑌 𐐫𐑊 𐑃𐐮𐑍𐑆. 𐐈𐑌𐐼 𐑄𐐩 𐑅𐐯𐐼 𐐲𐑌𐐻𐐭 𐑋𐐨, 𐐐𐐶𐐱𐐻 𐑋𐐨𐑌𐐯𐑃 𐑄 𐑉𐐮𐑂𐐲𐑉 𐐱𐑂 𐐶𐐫𐐻𐐲𐑉 𐐸𐐶𐐮𐐽 𐐵𐑉 𐑁𐐪𐑄𐐲𐑉 𐑅𐐫? 𐐈𐑌𐐼 𐐌 𐑅𐐯𐐼 𐐲𐑌𐐻𐐭 𐑄𐐯𐑋, 𐑄𐐰𐐻 𐑄 𐐶𐐫𐐻𐐲𐑉 𐐸𐐶𐐮𐐽 𐑋𐐴 𐑁𐐪𐑄𐐲𐑉 𐑅𐐫 𐐶𐐱𐑆 𐑁𐐮𐑊𐑃𐐨𐑌𐐯𐑅; 𐐰𐑌𐐼 𐑅𐐬 𐑋𐐲𐐽 𐐶𐐱𐑆 𐐸𐐮𐑆 𐑋𐐴𐑌𐐼 𐑅𐐶𐐱𐑊𐐬𐐼 𐐲𐐹 𐐮𐑌 𐐲𐑄𐐲𐑉 𐑃𐐮𐑍𐑆, 𐑄𐐰𐐻 𐐸𐐨 𐐺𐐨𐐸𐐯𐑊𐐼 𐑌𐐱𐐻 𐑄 𐑁𐐮𐑊𐑃𐐨𐑌𐐯𐑅 𐐱𐑂 𐑄 𐐶𐐫𐐻𐐲𐑉; 𐐰𐑌𐐼 𐐌 𐑅𐐯𐐼 𐐲𐑌𐐻𐐭 𐑄𐐯𐑋, 𐑄𐐰𐐻 𐐮𐐻 𐐶𐐱𐑆 𐐰𐑌 𐐫𐑁𐐳𐑊 𐑀𐐲𐑊𐑁, 𐐸𐐶𐐮𐐽 𐑅𐐯𐐹𐐲𐑉𐐩𐐻𐐯𐐼 𐑄 𐐶𐐮𐐿𐐯𐐼 𐑁𐑉𐐱𐑋 𐑄 𐐻𐑉𐐨 𐐱𐑂 𐑊𐐴𐑁, 𐐰𐑌𐐼 𐐫𐑊𐑅𐐬 𐑁𐑉𐐱𐑋 𐑄 𐑅𐐩𐑌𐐻𐑅 𐐱𐑂 𐐘𐐱𐐼. 𐐈𐑌𐐼 𐐌 𐑅𐐯𐐼 𐐲𐑌𐐻𐐭 𐑄𐐯𐑋, 𐑄𐐰𐐻 𐐮𐐻 𐐶𐐱𐑆 𐐲 𐑉𐐯𐐹𐑉𐐯𐑆𐐯𐑌𐐻𐐩𐑇𐐲𐑌 𐐱𐑂 𐑄𐐰𐐻 𐐫𐑁𐐳𐑊 𐐸𐐯𐑊, 𐐸𐐶𐐮𐐽 𐑄 𐐩𐑌𐐾𐐯𐑊 𐑅𐐯𐐼 𐐲𐑌𐐻𐐭 𐑋𐐨 𐐶𐐱𐑆 𐐹𐑉𐐨𐐹𐐩𐑉𐐼 𐑁𐐫𐑉 𐑄 𐐶𐐮𐐿𐐯𐐼. 𐐈𐑌𐐼 𐐌 𐑅𐐯𐐼 𐐲𐑌𐐻𐐭 𐑄𐐯𐑋, 𐑄𐐰𐐻 𐐵𐑉 𐑁𐐪𐑄𐐲𐑉 𐐫𐑊𐑅𐐬 𐑅𐐫 𐑄𐐰𐐻 𐑄 𐐾𐐲𐑅𐐻𐐮𐑅 𐐱𐑂 𐐘𐐱𐐼 𐐼𐐮𐐼 𐐫𐑊𐑅𐐬 𐐼𐐮𐑂𐐴𐐼 𐑄 𐐶𐐮𐐿𐐯𐐼 𐑁𐑉𐐱𐑋 𐑄 𐑉𐐴𐐽𐐲𐑅; 𐐰𐑌𐐼 𐑄 𐐺𐑉𐐴𐐻𐑌𐐯𐑅 𐑄𐐩𐑉𐐱𐑂 𐐶𐐱𐑆 𐑊𐐴𐐿 𐐲𐑌𐐻𐐭 𐑄 𐐺𐑉𐐴𐐻𐑌𐐯𐑅 𐐱𐑂 𐐲 𐑁𐑊𐐩𐑋𐐮𐑍 𐑁𐐴𐑉, 𐐸𐐶𐐮𐐽 𐐰𐑅𐐯𐑌𐐼𐐯𐑃 𐐲𐐹 𐐲𐑌𐐻𐐭 𐐘𐐱𐐼 𐑁𐐫𐑉 𐐯𐑂𐐲𐑉 𐐰𐑌𐐼 𐐯𐑂𐐲𐑉, 𐐰𐑌𐐼 𐐸𐐰𐑃 𐑌𐐬 𐐯𐑌𐐼.

6. 𐐈𐑌𐐼 𐑄𐐩 𐑅𐐯𐐼 𐐲𐑌𐐻𐐭 𐑋𐐨, 𐐼𐐲𐑃 𐑄𐐮𐑅 𐑃𐐮𐑍 𐑋𐐨𐑌 𐑄 𐐻𐐫𐑉𐑋𐐯𐑌𐐻 𐐱𐑂 𐑄 𐐺𐐱𐐼𐐨 𐐮𐑌 𐑄 𐐼𐐩𐑆 𐐱𐑂 𐐹𐑉𐐬𐐺𐐩𐑇𐐲𐑌, 𐐫𐑉 𐐼𐐲𐑃 𐐮𐐻 𐑋𐐨𐑌 𐑄 𐑁𐐴𐑌𐐲𐑊 𐑅𐐻𐐩𐐻 𐐱𐑂 𐑄 𐑅𐐬𐑊 𐐪𐑁𐐻𐐲𐑉 𐑄 𐐼𐐯𐑃 𐐱𐑂 𐑄 𐐻𐐯𐑋𐐹𐐬𐑉𐐲𐑊 𐐺𐐱𐐼𐐨? 𐐃𐑉, 𐐼𐐲𐑃 𐐮𐐻 𐑅𐐹𐐨𐐿 𐐱𐑂 𐑄 𐑃𐐮𐑍𐑆 𐐸𐐶𐐮𐐽 𐐪𐑉 𐐻𐐯𐑋𐐹𐐬𐑉𐐲𐑊? 𐐈𐑌𐐼 𐐮𐐻 𐐿𐐩𐑋 𐐻𐐭 𐐹𐐪𐑅 𐑄𐐰𐐻 𐐌 𐑅𐐯𐐼 𐐲𐑌𐐻𐐭 𐑄𐐯𐑋, 𐑄𐐰𐐻 𐐮𐐻 𐐶𐐱𐑆 𐐲 𐑉𐐯𐐹𐑉𐐯𐑆𐐯𐑌𐐻𐐩𐑇𐐲𐑌 𐐱𐑂 𐑃𐐮𐑍𐑆 𐐺𐐬𐑃 𐐻𐐯𐑋𐐹𐐬𐑉𐐲𐑊 𐐰𐑌𐐼 𐑅𐐹𐐮𐑉𐐮𐐻𐐷𐐭𐐲𐑊; 𐑁𐐫𐑉 𐑄 𐐼𐐩 𐑇𐐳𐐼 𐐿𐐲𐑋 𐑄𐐰𐐻 𐑄𐐩 𐑋𐐲𐑅𐐻 𐐺 𐐾𐐲𐐾𐐼 𐐱𐑂 𐑄𐐩𐑉 𐐶𐐲𐑉𐐿𐑅, 𐐷𐐩, 𐐨𐑂𐐯𐑌 𐑄 𐐶𐐲𐑉𐐿𐑅 𐐸𐐶𐐮𐐽 𐐶𐐲𐑉 𐐼𐐲𐑌 𐐺𐐴 𐑄 𐐻𐐯𐑋𐐹𐐬𐑉𐐲𐑊 𐐺𐐱𐐼𐐨 𐐮𐑌 𐑄𐐩𐑉 𐐼𐐩𐑆 𐐱𐑂 𐐹𐑉𐐬𐐺𐐩𐑇𐐲𐑌; 𐐸𐐶𐐯𐑉𐑁𐐬𐑉 𐐮𐑁 𐑄𐐩 𐑇𐐳𐐼 𐐼𐐴 𐐮𐑌 𐑄𐐩𐑉 𐐶𐐮𐐿𐐯𐐼𐑌𐐯𐑅 𐑄𐐩 𐑋𐐲𐑅𐐻 𐐺 𐐿𐐪𐑅𐐻 𐐫𐑁 𐐫𐑊𐑅𐐬, 𐐰𐑆 𐐻𐐭 𐑄 𐑃𐐮𐑍𐑆 𐐸𐐶𐐮𐐽 𐐪𐑉 𐑅𐐹𐐮𐑉𐐮𐐻𐐷𐐭𐐲𐑊, 𐐸𐐶𐐮𐐽 𐐪𐑉 𐐹𐐲𐑉𐐻𐐩𐑌𐐮𐑍 𐐻𐐭 𐑉𐐴𐐽𐐲𐑅𐑌𐐯𐑅; 𐐸𐐶𐐯𐑉𐑁𐐬𐑉, 𐑄𐐩 𐑋𐐲𐑅𐐻 𐐺 𐐺𐑉𐐫𐐻 𐐻𐐭 𐑅𐐻𐐰𐑌𐐼 𐐺𐐨𐑁𐐬𐑉 𐐘𐐱𐐼, 𐐻𐐭 𐐺 𐐾𐐲𐐾𐐼 𐐱𐑂 𐑄𐐩𐑉 𐐶𐐲𐑉𐐿𐑅; 𐐰𐑌𐐼 𐐮𐑁 𐑄𐐩𐑉 𐐶𐐲𐑉𐐿𐑅 𐐸𐐰𐑂 𐐺𐐮𐑌 𐑁𐐮𐑊𐑃𐐨𐑌𐐯𐑅, 𐑄𐐩 𐑋𐐲𐑅𐐻 𐑌𐐨𐐼𐑆 𐐺 𐑁𐐮𐑊𐑃𐐨: 𐐰𐑌𐐼 𐐮𐑁 𐑄𐐩 𐐺 𐑁𐐮𐑊𐑃𐐨, 𐐮𐐻 𐑋𐐲𐑅𐐻 𐑌𐐨𐐼𐑆 𐐺 𐑄𐐰𐐻 𐑄𐐩 𐐿𐐰𐑌𐐱𐐻 𐐼𐐶𐐯𐑊 𐐮𐑌 𐑄 𐐿𐐮𐑍𐐼𐐲𐑋 𐐱𐑂 𐐘𐐱𐐼; 𐐮𐑁 𐑅𐐬, 𐑄 𐐿𐐮𐑍𐐼𐐲𐑋 𐐱𐑂 𐐘𐐱𐐼 𐑋𐐲𐑅𐐻 𐐺 𐑁𐐮𐑊𐑃𐐨 𐐫𐑊𐑅𐐬. 𐐒𐐲𐐻 𐐺𐐨𐐸𐐬𐑊𐐼, 𐐌

𐑅𐐩 𐐲𐑌𐐻𐐭 𐐷𐐭, 𐑄 𐐿𐐮𐑍𐐼𐐲𐑋 𐐱𐑂 𐐘𐐱𐐼 𐐮𐑆 𐑌𐐱𐐻 𐑁𐐮𐑊𐑃𐐨, 𐐰𐑌𐐼 𐑄𐐯𐑉 𐐿𐐰𐑌𐐱𐐻 𐐯𐑌𐐨 𐐲𐑌𐐿𐑊𐐨𐑌 𐑃𐐮𐑍 𐐯𐑌𐐻𐐲𐑉 𐐮𐑌𐐻𐐭 𐑄 𐐿𐐮𐑍𐐼𐐲𐑋 𐐱𐑂 𐐘𐐱𐐼: 𐐸𐐶𐐯𐑉𐑁𐐬𐑉 𐑄𐐯𐑉 𐑋𐐲𐑅𐐻 𐑌𐐨𐐼𐑆 𐐺𐐨 𐐩 𐐹𐑊𐐩𐑅 𐐱𐑂 𐑁𐐮𐑊𐑃𐐨𐑌𐐯𐑅 𐐹𐑉𐐨𐐹𐐯𐑉𐐼 𐑁𐐫𐑉 𐑄𐐰𐐻 𐐸𐐶𐐮𐐽 𐐮𐑆 𐑁𐐮𐑊𐑃𐐨. 𐐈𐑌𐐼 𐑄𐐯𐑉 𐐮𐑆 𐐩 𐐹𐑊𐐩𐑅 𐐹𐑉𐐨𐐹𐐯𐑉𐐼, 𐐷𐐩, 𐐨𐑂𐐲𐑌 𐑄𐐰𐐻 𐐫𐑁𐐳𐑊 𐐸𐐯𐑊 𐐱𐑂 𐐸𐐶𐐮𐐽 𐐌 𐐸𐐰𐑂 𐑅𐐹𐐬𐐿𐐲𐑌, 𐐰𐑌𐐼 𐑄 𐐼𐐯𐑂𐐮𐑊 𐐮𐑆 𐑄 𐐹𐑉𐐯𐐹𐐲𐑉𐐩𐐻𐐲𐑉 𐐱𐑂 𐐮𐐻; 𐐸𐐶𐐯𐑉𐑁𐐬𐑉 𐑄 𐑁𐐴𐑌𐐲𐑊 𐑅𐐻𐐩𐐻 𐐱𐑂 𐑄 𐑅𐐬𐑊𐑆 𐐱𐑂 𐑋𐐯𐑌 𐐮𐑆 𐐻𐐭 𐐼𐐶𐐯𐑊 𐐮𐑌 𐑄 𐐿𐐮𐑍𐐼𐐲𐑋 𐐱𐑂 𐐘𐐱𐐼, 𐐫𐑉 𐐻𐐭 𐐺𐐨 𐐿𐐰𐑅𐐻 𐐵𐐻 𐐺𐐨𐐿𐐫𐑆 𐐱𐑂 𐑄𐐰𐐻 𐐾𐐲𐑅𐐻𐐮𐑅 𐐱𐑂 𐐸𐐶𐐮𐐽 𐐌 𐐸𐐰𐑂 𐑅𐐹𐐬𐐿𐐲𐑌; 𐐸𐐶𐐯𐑉𐑁𐐬𐑉, 𐑄 𐐶𐐮𐐿𐐲𐐼 𐐪𐑉 𐑉𐐨𐐾𐐯𐐿𐐻𐐲𐐼 𐑁𐑉𐐱𐑋 𐑄 𐑉𐐴𐐽𐐲𐑅, 𐐰𐑌𐐼 𐐫𐑊𐑅𐐬 𐑁𐑉𐐱𐑋 𐑄𐐰𐐻 𐐻𐑉𐐨 𐐱𐑂 𐑊𐐴𐑁, 𐐸𐐭𐑆 𐑁𐑉𐐭𐐻 𐐮𐑆 𐑋𐐬𐑅𐐻 𐐹𐑉𐐯𐑇𐐲𐑅 𐐰𐑌𐐼 𐑋𐐬𐑅𐐻 𐐼𐐯𐑆𐐴𐑉𐐲𐐺𐑊 𐐲𐐺𐐲𐑂 𐐫𐑊 𐐲𐑄𐐲𐑉 𐑁𐑉𐐭𐐻𐑅; 𐐷𐐩, 𐐰𐑌𐐼 𐐮𐐻 𐐮𐑆 𐑄 𐑀𐑉𐐩𐐻𐐯𐑅𐐻 𐐱𐑂 𐐫𐑊 𐑄 𐑀𐐮𐑁𐐻𐑅 𐐱𐑂 𐐘𐐱𐐼. 𐐈𐑌𐐼 𐑄𐐲𐑅 𐐌 𐑅𐐹𐐩𐐿 𐐲𐑌𐐻𐐭 𐑋𐐴 𐐺𐑉𐐯𐑄𐑉𐐯𐑌. 𐐁𐑋𐐯𐑌.

𐐕𐐈𐐑𐐓𐐊𐐡 V.

1. 𐐈𐑌𐐼 𐑌𐐵 𐐮𐐻 𐐿𐐩𐑋 𐐻𐐭 𐐹𐐰𐑅 𐑄𐐰𐐻 𐐰𐑁𐐻𐐲𐑉 𐐌, 𐐤𐐨𐑁𐐴, 𐐸𐐰𐐼 𐑋𐐩𐐼 𐐰𐑌 𐐯𐑌𐐼 𐐱𐑂 𐑅𐐹𐐨𐐿𐐮𐑍 𐐻𐐭 𐑋𐐴 𐐺𐑉𐐯𐑄𐑉𐐯𐑌, 𐐺𐐨𐐸𐐬𐑊𐐼 𐑄𐐩 𐑅𐐯𐐼 𐐲𐑌𐐻𐐭 𐑋𐐨, 𐐜𐐵 𐐸𐐰𐑅𐐻 𐐼𐐯𐐿𐑊𐐯𐑉𐐼 𐐲𐑌𐐻𐐭 𐐲𐑅 𐐸𐐪𐑉𐐼 𐑃𐐮𐑍𐑆, 𐑋𐐬𐑉 𐑄𐐰𐑌 𐐶𐐨 𐐪𐑉 𐐩𐐺𐐲𐑊 𐐻𐐭 𐐺𐐯𐑉.

2. 𐐈𐑌𐐼 𐐮𐐻 𐐿𐐩𐑋 𐐻𐐭 𐐹𐐰𐑅 𐑄𐐰𐐻 𐐌 𐑅𐐯𐐼 𐐲𐑌𐐻𐐭 𐑄𐐯𐑋, 𐑄𐐰𐐻 𐐌 𐑌𐐭 𐑄𐐰𐐻 𐐌 𐐸𐐰𐐼 𐑅𐐹𐐬𐐿𐐲𐑌 𐐸𐐪𐑉𐐼 𐑃𐐮𐑍𐑆 𐐲𐑀𐐯𐑌𐑅𐐻 𐑄 𐐶𐐮𐐿𐐲𐐼, 𐐲𐐿𐐫𐑉𐐼𐐮𐑍 𐐻𐐭 𐑄 𐐻𐑉𐐭𐑃; 𐐰𐑌𐐼 𐑄 𐑉𐐴𐐽𐐲𐑅 𐐸𐐰𐑂 𐐌 𐐾𐐲𐑅𐐻𐐮𐑁𐐴𐐼, 𐐰𐑌𐐼 𐐻𐐯𐑅𐐻𐐮𐑁𐐴𐐼 𐑄𐐰𐐻 𐑄𐐩 𐑇𐐳𐐼 𐐺𐐨 𐑊𐐮𐑁𐐻𐐲𐐼 𐐲𐐹 𐐰𐐻 𐑄 𐑊𐐰𐑅𐐻 𐐼𐐩; 𐐸𐐶𐐯𐑉𐑁𐐬𐑉, 𐑄 𐑀𐐮𐑊𐐻𐐨 𐐻𐐩𐐿𐐯𐑃 𐑄 𐐻𐑉𐐭𐑃 𐐻𐐭 𐐺𐐨 𐐸𐐪𐑉𐐼, 𐑁𐐫𐑉 𐐮𐐻 𐐿𐐲𐐻𐐯𐑃 𐑄𐐯𐑋 𐐻𐐭 𐑄 𐑂𐐯𐑉𐐨 𐑅𐐯𐑌𐐻𐐲𐑉. 𐐈𐑌𐐼 𐑌𐐵, 𐑋𐐴 𐐺𐑉𐐯𐑄𐑉𐐯𐑌, 𐐮𐑁 𐐷𐐨 𐐶𐐯𐑉 𐑉𐐴𐐽𐐲𐑅, 𐐰𐑌𐐼 𐐶𐐯𐑉 𐐶𐐮𐑊𐐮𐑍 𐐻𐐭 𐐸𐐪𐑉𐐿𐐲𐑌 𐐻𐐭 𐑄 𐐻𐑉𐐭𐑃, 𐐰𐑌𐐼 𐑀𐐮𐑂 𐐸𐐨𐐼 𐐲𐑌𐐻𐐭 𐐮𐐻, 𐑄𐐰𐐻 𐐷𐐨 𐑋𐐴𐐻 𐐶𐐫𐐿 𐐲𐐹𐑉𐐴𐐻𐑊𐐨 𐐺𐐨𐑁𐐫𐑉 𐐘𐐱𐐼, 𐑄𐐯𐑌 𐐷𐐨 𐐶𐐳𐐼 𐑌𐐱𐐻 𐑋𐐲𐑉𐑋𐐲𐑉 𐐺𐐨𐐿𐐫𐑆 𐐱𐑂 𐑄 𐐻𐑉𐐭𐑃, 𐐰𐑌𐐼 𐑅𐐩, 𐐜𐐵 𐑅𐐹𐐨𐐿𐐯𐑅𐐻 𐐸𐐪𐑉𐐼 𐑃𐐮𐑍𐑆 𐐲𐑀𐐯𐑌𐑅𐐻 𐐲𐑅. 𐐈𐑌𐐼 𐐮𐐻 𐐿𐐩𐑋 𐐻𐐭 𐐹𐐰𐑅 𐑄𐐰𐐻 𐐌, 𐐤𐐨𐑁𐐴, 𐐼𐐮𐐼 𐐯𐐿𐑅𐐱𐑉𐐻 𐑋𐐴 𐐺𐑉𐐯𐑄𐑉𐐯𐑌 𐐶𐐮𐑄 𐐫𐑊 𐐼𐐮𐑊𐐮𐐾𐐯𐑌𐑅 𐐻𐐭 𐐿𐐨𐐹 𐑄 𐐿𐐲𐑋𐐰𐑌𐐼𐑋𐐯𐑌𐐻𐑅 𐐱𐑂 𐑄 𐐢𐐫𐑉𐐼. 𐐈𐑌𐐼 𐐮𐐻 𐐿𐐩𐑋 𐐻𐐭 𐐹𐐰𐑅 𐑄𐐰𐐻 𐑄𐐩 𐐼𐐮𐐼 𐐸𐐲𐑋𐐺𐑊 𐑄𐐯𐑋𐑅𐐯𐑊𐑂𐑆 𐐺𐐨𐑁𐐫𐑉 𐑄 𐐢𐐫𐑉𐐼; 𐐮𐑌𐑅𐐬𐑋𐐲𐐽 𐑄𐐰𐐻 𐐌 𐐸𐐰𐐼 𐐾𐑎 𐐰𐑌𐐼 𐑀𐑉𐐩𐐻 𐐸𐐬𐐹𐑅 𐐱𐑂 𐑄𐐯𐑋, 𐑄𐐰𐐻 𐑄𐐩 𐐶𐐳𐐼 𐐶𐐫𐐿 𐐮𐑌 𐑄 𐐹𐐰𐑃𐑅 𐐱𐑂 𐑉𐐴𐐽𐐲𐑅𐑌𐐯𐑅. 𐐤𐐵, 𐐫𐑊 𐑄𐐨𐑆 𐑃𐐮𐑍𐑆 𐐶𐐯𐑉 𐑅𐐯𐐼 𐐰𐑌𐐼 𐐼𐐲𐑌, 𐐰𐑆 𐑋𐐴 𐑁𐐪𐑄𐐲𐑉 𐐼𐐶𐐯𐑊𐐻 𐐮𐑌 𐐩 𐐻𐐯𐑌𐐻 𐐮𐑌 𐑄 𐑂𐐰𐑊𐐨 𐐸𐐶𐐮𐐽 𐐸𐐨 𐐿𐐫𐑊𐐲𐐼 𐐢𐐯𐑋𐐷𐐭𐐯𐑊.

3. 𐐈𐑌𐐼 𐐮𐐻 𐐿𐐩𐑋 𐐻𐐭 𐐹𐐰𐑅 𐑄𐐰𐐻 𐐌, 𐐤𐐨𐑁𐐴, 𐐻𐐳𐐿 𐐶𐐲𐑌 𐐱𐑂 𐑄 𐐼𐐫𐐻𐐲𐑉𐑆 𐐱𐑂 𐐆𐑇𐑋𐐩𐐯𐑊 𐐻𐐭 𐐶𐐴𐑁; 𐐰𐑌𐐼 𐐫𐑊𐑅𐐬 𐑋𐐴 𐐺𐑉𐐯𐑄𐑉𐐯𐑌 𐐻𐐳𐐿 𐐱𐑂 𐑄 𐐼𐐫𐐻𐐲𐑉𐑆 𐐱𐑂 𐐆𐑇𐑋𐐩𐐯𐑊 𐐻𐐭 𐐶𐐴𐑁; 𐐰𐑌𐐼 𐐫𐑊𐑅𐐬 𐐞𐐬𐑉𐐲𐑋 𐐻𐐳𐐿 𐑄 𐐯𐑊𐐼𐐯𐑅𐐻 𐐼𐐫𐐻𐐲𐑉 𐐱𐑂 𐐆𐑇𐑋𐐩𐐯𐑊 𐐻𐐭 𐐶𐐴𐑁. 𐐈𐑌𐐼 𐑄𐐲𐑅 𐑋𐐴 𐑁𐐪𐑄𐐲𐑉 𐐸𐐰𐐼 𐑁𐐳𐑊𐑁𐐮𐑊𐐼 𐐫𐑊 𐑄 𐐿𐐲𐑋𐐰𐑌𐐼𐑋𐐯𐑌𐐻𐑅 𐐱𐑂 𐑄 𐐢𐐫𐑉𐐼 𐐸𐐶𐐮𐐽 𐐸𐐰𐐼 𐐺𐐨𐑌 𐑀𐐮𐑂𐐲𐑌 𐐲𐑌𐐻𐐭 𐐸𐐮𐑋. 𐐈𐑌𐐼 𐐫𐑊𐑅𐐬 𐐌, 𐐤𐐨𐑁𐐴, 𐐸𐐰𐐼 𐐺𐐨𐑌 𐐺𐑊𐐯𐑅𐐲𐐼 𐐱𐑂 𐑄 𐐢𐐫𐑉𐐼 𐐯𐐿𐑅𐐨𐐼𐐮𐑍𐑊𐐨.

4. 𐐈𐑌𐐼 𐐮𐐻 𐐿𐐩𐑋 𐐻𐐭 𐐹𐐰𐑅 𐑄𐐰𐐻 𐑄 𐑂𐑎𐑅 𐐱𐑂 𐑄 𐐢𐐫𐑉𐐼 𐑅𐐹𐐩𐐿 𐐲𐑌𐐻𐐭 𐑋𐐴 𐑁𐐪𐑄𐐲𐑉 𐐺𐐴 𐑌𐐴𐐻, 𐐰𐑌𐐼 𐐿𐐲𐑋𐐰𐑌𐐼𐐲𐐼 𐐸𐐮𐑋 𐑄𐐰𐐻 𐐱𐑌 𐑄 𐑋𐐱𐑉𐐬 𐐸𐐨 𐑇𐐳𐐼 𐐻𐐩𐐿 𐐸𐐮𐑆 𐐾𐐲𐑉𐑌𐐨 𐐮𐑌𐐻𐐭 𐑄 𐐶𐐮𐑊𐐼𐐲𐑉𐑌𐐯𐑅. 𐐈𐑌𐐼 𐐮𐐻 𐐿𐐩𐑋 𐐻𐐭 𐐹𐐰𐑅 𐑄𐐰𐐻 𐐰𐑆 𐑋𐐴 𐑁𐐪𐑄𐐲𐑉 𐐲𐑉𐐬𐑆 𐐮𐑌 𐑄 𐑋𐐫𐑉𐑌𐐮𐑍, 𐐰𐑌𐐼 𐐶𐐯𐑌𐐻 𐑁𐐬𐑉𐑃 𐐻𐐭 𐑄 𐐻𐐯𐑌𐐻 𐐼𐐬𐑉, 𐐻𐐭 𐐸𐐮𐑆 𐑀𐑉𐐩𐐻 𐐲𐑅𐐻𐐱𐑌𐐮𐑇𐑋𐐯𐑌𐐻, 𐐸𐐨 𐐺𐐨𐐸𐐯𐑊𐐼 𐐲𐐹𐐱𐑌 𐑄 𐑀𐑉𐐵𐑌𐐼 𐐩 𐑉𐐵𐑌𐐼 𐐺𐐫𐑊 𐐱𐑂 𐐿𐐷𐐭𐑉𐐨𐐲𐑅 𐐶𐐲𐑉𐐿𐑋𐐲𐑌𐑇𐐮𐐹; 𐐰𐑌𐐼 𐐮𐐻 𐐶𐐱𐑆 𐐱𐑂 𐑁𐐴𐑌 𐐺𐑉𐐰𐑅. 𐐈𐑌𐐼 𐐶𐐮𐑄𐐮𐑌 𐑄 𐐺𐐫𐑊 𐐶𐐯𐑉 𐐻𐐭 𐑅𐐹𐐮𐑌𐐼𐐲𐑊𐑆: 𐐰𐑌𐐼 𐑄 𐐶𐐲𐑌 𐐹𐑎𐑌𐐻𐐲𐐼 𐑄 𐐶𐐩 𐐸𐐶𐐮𐑄𐐲𐑉 𐐶𐐨 𐑇𐐳𐐼 𐑀𐐬 𐐮𐑌𐐻𐐭 𐑄 𐐶𐐮𐑊𐐼𐐲𐑉𐑌𐐯𐑅.

5. 𐐈𐑌𐐼 𐐮𐐻 𐐿𐐩𐑋 𐐻𐐭 𐐹𐐰𐑅 𐑄𐐰𐐻 𐐶𐐨 𐐼𐐮𐐼 𐑀𐐰𐑄𐐲𐑉 𐐻𐐭𐑀𐐯𐑄𐐲𐑉 𐐸𐐶𐐱𐐻𐑅𐐬𐐯𐑂𐐲𐑉 𐑃𐐮𐑍𐑆 𐐶𐐨 𐑇𐐳𐐼 𐐿𐐰𐑉𐐨 𐐮𐑌𐐻𐐭 𐑄 𐐶𐐮𐑊𐐼𐐲𐑉𐑌𐐯𐑅, 𐐰𐑌𐐼 𐐫𐑊 𐑄 𐑉𐐨𐑋𐐩𐑌𐐼𐐲𐑉 𐐱𐑂 𐐵𐑉 𐐹𐑉𐐬𐑂𐐮𐑈𐐲𐑌𐑆 𐐸𐐶𐐮𐐽 𐑄 𐐢𐐫𐑉𐐼 𐐸𐐰𐐼

𐑀𐐮𐑂𐑌 𐐲𐑌𐐻𐐭 𐐲𐑅; 𐐰𐑌𐐼 𐐶𐐨 𐐼𐐮𐐼 𐐻𐐩𐐿 𐑅𐐨𐐼 𐐱𐑂 𐐯𐑂𐐲𐑉𐐨 𐐿𐐴𐑌𐐼 𐑄𐐰𐐻 𐐶𐐨 𐑋𐐴𐐻 𐐿𐐰𐑉𐐨 𐐮𐑌𐐻𐐭 𐑄 𐐶𐐮𐑊𐐼𐐲𐑉𐑌𐐯𐑅.

6. 𐐰𐑌𐐼 𐐮𐐻 𐐿𐐩𐑋 𐐻𐐭 𐐹𐐰𐑅 𐑄𐐰𐐻 𐐶𐐨 𐐼𐐮𐐼 𐐻𐐩𐐿 𐐵𐑉 𐐻𐐯𐑌𐐻𐑅, 𐐰𐑌𐐼 𐐼𐐨𐐹𐐪𐑉𐐻 𐐮𐑌𐐻𐐭 𐑄 𐐶𐐮𐑊𐐼𐐲𐑉𐑌𐐯𐑅 𐐲𐐿𐑉𐐫𐑅 𐑄 𐑉𐐮𐑂𐐲𐑉 𐐢𐐩𐑋𐐲𐑌. 𐐰𐑌𐐼 𐐮𐐻 𐐿𐐩𐑋 𐐻𐐭 𐐹𐐰𐑅 𐑄𐐰𐐻 𐐶𐐨 𐐻𐑉𐐰𐑂𐐯𐑊𐐼 𐑁𐐫𐑉 𐑄 𐑅𐐹𐐩𐑅 𐐱𐑂 𐑁𐐬𐑉 𐐼𐐩𐑆, 𐑌𐐨𐑉𐑊𐐨 𐐲 𐑅𐐵𐑃, 𐑅𐐵𐑃𐐨𐑅𐐻 𐐼𐐴𐑉𐐯𐐿𐑇𐐲𐑌, 𐐰𐑌𐐼 𐐶𐐨 𐐼𐐮𐐼 𐐹𐐮𐐽 𐐵𐑉 𐐻𐐯𐑌𐐻𐑅 𐐲𐑀𐐯𐑌; 𐐰𐑌𐐼 𐐶𐐨 𐐼𐐮𐐼 𐐿𐐫𐑊 𐑄 𐑌𐐩𐑋 𐐱𐑂 𐑄 𐐹𐑊𐐩𐑅 𐐟𐐩𐑆𐐲𐑉.

7. 𐐰𐑌𐐼 𐐮𐐻 𐐿𐐩𐑋 𐐻𐐭 𐐹𐐰𐑅 𐑄𐐰𐐻 𐐶𐐨 𐐼𐐮𐐼 𐐻𐐩𐐿 𐐵𐑉 𐐺𐐬𐑆 𐐰𐑌𐐼 𐐵𐑉 𐐰𐑉𐐬𐑆, 𐐰𐑌𐐼 𐑀𐐬 𐑁𐐫𐑉𐑃 𐐮𐑌𐐻𐐭 𐑄 𐐶𐐮𐑊𐐼𐐲𐑉𐑌𐐯𐑅, 𐐻𐐭 𐑅𐑊𐐩 𐑁𐐭𐐼 𐑁𐐫𐑉 𐐵𐑉 𐑁𐐰𐑋𐐮𐑊𐐨𐑆; 𐐰𐑌𐐼 𐐰𐑁𐐻𐐲𐑉 𐐶𐐨 𐐸𐐰𐐼 𐑅𐑊𐐩𐑌 𐑁𐐭𐐼 𐑁𐐫𐑉 𐐵𐑉 𐑁𐐰𐑋𐐮𐑊𐐨𐑆, 𐐶𐐨 𐐼𐐮𐐼 𐑉𐐨𐐻𐐲𐑉𐑌 𐐲𐑀𐐯𐑌 𐐻𐐭 𐐵𐑉 𐑁𐐰𐑋𐐮𐑊𐐨𐑆 𐐮𐑌 𐑄 𐐶𐐮𐑊𐐼𐐲𐑉𐑌𐐯𐑅, 𐐻𐐭 𐑄 𐐹𐑊𐐩𐑅 𐐱𐑂 𐐟𐐩𐑆𐐲𐑉. 𐐰𐑌𐐼 𐐶𐐨 𐐼𐐮𐐼 𐑀𐐬 𐑁𐐫𐑉𐑃 𐐲𐑀𐐯𐑌 𐐮𐑌 𐑄 𐐶𐐮𐑊𐐼𐐲𐑉𐑌𐐯𐑅, 𐑁𐐱𐑊𐐬𐐮𐑍 𐑄 𐑅𐐩𐑋 𐐼𐐴𐑉𐐯𐐿𐑇𐐲𐑌, 𐐿𐐨𐐹𐐮𐑍 𐐮𐑌 𐑄 𐑋𐐬𐑅𐐻 𐑁𐐲𐑉𐐻𐐮𐑊 𐐹𐐪𐑉𐐻𐑅 𐐱𐑂 𐑄 𐐶𐐮𐑊𐐼𐐲𐑉𐑌𐐯𐑅, 𐐸𐐶𐐮𐐽 𐐶𐐲𐑉 𐐮𐑌 𐑄 𐐺𐐫𐑉𐐼𐐲𐑉𐑆 𐑌𐐨𐑉 𐑄 𐐡𐐯𐐼 𐐝𐐨. 𐐰𐑌𐐼 𐐮𐐻 𐐿𐐩𐑋 𐐻𐐭 𐐹𐐰𐑅 𐑄𐐰𐐻 𐐶𐐨 𐐼𐐮𐐼 𐐻𐑉𐐰𐑂𐐯𐑊 𐑁𐐫𐑉 𐑄 𐑅𐐹𐐩𐑅 𐐱𐑂 𐑋𐐯𐑌𐐨 𐐼𐐩𐑆, 𐑅𐑊𐐩𐐮𐑍 𐑁𐐭𐐼 𐐺𐐴 𐑄 𐐶𐐩, 𐐶𐐮𐑄 𐐵𐑉 𐐺𐐬𐑆 𐐰𐑌𐐼 𐐵𐑉 𐐰𐑉𐐬𐑆 𐐰𐑌𐐼 𐐵𐑉 𐑅𐐻𐐬𐑌𐑆 𐐰𐑌𐐼 𐐵𐑉 𐑅𐑊𐐮𐑍𐑆; 𐐰𐑌𐐼 𐐶𐐨 𐐼𐐮𐐼 𐑁𐐱𐑊𐐬 𐑄 𐐼𐐴𐑉𐐯𐐿𐑇𐐲𐑌𐑆 𐐱𐑂 𐑄 𐐺𐐫𐑊, 𐐸𐐶𐐮𐐽 𐑊𐐯𐐼 𐐲𐑅 𐐮𐑌 𐑄 𐑋𐐬𐑉 𐑁𐐲𐑉𐐻𐐮𐑊 𐐹𐐪𐑉𐐻𐑅 𐐱𐑂 𐑄 𐐶𐐮𐑊𐐼𐐲𐑉𐑌𐐯𐑅. 𐐰𐑌𐐼 𐐰𐑁𐐻𐐲𐑉 𐐶𐐨 𐐸𐐰𐐼 𐐻𐑉𐐰𐑂𐐯𐑊𐐼 𐑁𐐫𐑉 𐑄 𐑅𐐹𐐩𐑅 𐐱𐑂 𐑋𐐯𐑌𐐨 𐐼𐐩𐑆, 𐐶𐐨 𐐼𐐮𐐼 𐐹𐐮𐐽 𐐵𐑉 𐐻𐐯𐑌𐐻𐑅 𐑁𐐫𐑉 𐑄 𐑅𐐹𐐩𐑅 𐐱𐑂 𐐲 𐐻𐐴𐑋, 𐑄𐐰𐐻 𐐶𐐨 𐑋𐐴𐐻 𐐲𐑀𐐯𐑌 𐑉𐐯𐑅𐐻 𐐵𐑉𐑅𐐯𐑊𐑂𐑆, 𐐰𐑌𐐼 𐐱𐐺𐐻𐐩𐑌 𐑁𐐭𐐼 𐑁𐐫𐑉 𐐵𐑉 𐑁𐐰𐑋𐐮𐑊𐐨𐑆.

8. 𐐰𐑌𐐼 𐐮𐐻 𐐿𐐩𐑋 𐐻𐐭 𐐹𐐰𐑅 𐑄𐐰𐐻 𐐰𐑆 𐐌, 𐐤𐐨𐑁𐐴, 𐐶𐐯𐑌𐐻 𐑁𐐫𐑉𐑃 𐐻𐐭 𐑅𐑊𐐩 𐑁𐐭𐐼, 𐐺𐐨𐐸𐐬𐑊𐐼, 𐐌 𐐼𐐮𐐼 𐐺𐑉𐐩𐐿 𐑋𐐴 𐐺𐐬, 𐐸𐐶𐐮𐐽 𐐶𐐱𐑆 𐑋𐐩𐐼 𐐱𐑂 𐑁𐐴𐑌 𐑅𐐻𐐨𐑊: 𐐰𐑌𐐼 𐐰𐑁𐐻𐐲𐑉 𐐌 𐐼𐐮𐐼 𐐺𐑉𐐩𐐿 𐑋𐐴 𐐺𐐬, 𐐺𐐨𐐸𐐬𐑊𐐼, 𐑋𐐴 𐐺𐑉𐐯𐑄𐑉𐐯𐑌 𐐶𐐲𐑉 𐐰𐑍𐑀𐑉𐐨 𐐶𐐮𐑄 𐑋𐐨, 𐐺𐐨𐐿𐐫𐑆 𐐱𐑂 𐑄 𐑊𐐫𐑅 𐐱𐑂 𐑋𐐴 𐐺𐐬, 𐑁𐐫𐑉 𐐶𐐨 𐐼𐐮𐐼 𐐱𐐺𐐻𐐩𐑌 𐑌𐐬 𐑁𐐭𐐼. 𐐰𐑌𐐼 𐐮𐐻 𐐿𐐩𐑋 𐐻𐐭 𐐹𐐰𐑅 𐑄𐐰𐐻 𐐶𐐨 𐐼𐐮𐐼 𐑉𐐨𐐻𐐲𐑉𐑌 𐐶𐐮𐑄𐐵𐐻 𐑁𐐭𐐼 𐐻𐐭 𐐵𐑉 𐑁𐐰𐑋𐐮𐑊𐐨𐑆. 𐐰𐑌𐐼 𐐺𐐨𐐮𐑍 𐑋𐐲𐐽 𐑁𐐰𐐻𐐨𐑀𐐼, 𐐺𐐨𐐿𐐫𐑆 𐐱𐑂 𐑄𐐩𐑉 𐐾𐐲𐑉𐑌𐐨𐐮𐑍, 𐑄𐐩 𐐼𐐮𐐼 𐑅𐐲𐑁𐐲𐑉 𐑋𐐲𐐽 𐑁𐐫𐑉 𐑄 𐐶𐐱𐑌𐐻 𐐱𐑂 𐑁𐐭𐐼.

9. 𐐰𐑌𐐼 𐐮𐐻 𐐿𐐩𐑋 𐐻𐐭 𐐹𐐰𐑅 𐑄𐐰𐐻 𐐢𐐩𐑋𐐲𐑌 𐐰𐑌𐐼 𐐢𐐯𐑋𐐷𐐭𐐯𐑊, 𐐰𐑌𐐼 𐑄 𐑅𐐲𐑌𐑆 𐐱𐑂 𐐌𐑇𐑋𐐩𐐯𐑊, 𐐼𐐮𐐼 𐐺𐐨𐑀𐐮𐑌 𐐻𐐭 𐑋𐐲𐑉𐑋𐐲𐑉 𐐯𐐿𐑅𐐨𐐼𐐮𐑍𐑊𐐨, 𐐺𐐨𐐿𐐫𐑆 𐐱𐑂 𐑄𐐩𐑉 𐑅𐐲𐑁𐐲𐑉𐐮𐑍𐑆 𐐰𐑌𐐼 𐐰𐑁𐑊𐐮𐐿𐑇𐐲𐑌𐑆 𐐮𐑌 𐑄 𐐶𐐮𐑊𐐼𐐲𐑉𐑌𐐯𐑅: 𐐰𐑌𐐼 𐐫𐑊𐑅𐐬 𐑋𐐴 𐑁𐐪𐑄𐐲𐑉 𐐺𐐨𐑀𐐰𐑌 𐐻𐐭 𐑋𐐲𐑉𐑋𐐲𐑉 𐐰𐑀𐐯𐑌𐑅𐐻 𐑄 𐐢𐐫𐑉𐐼 𐐸𐐮𐑆 𐐘𐐱𐐼; 𐐷𐐩, 𐐰𐑌𐐼 𐑄𐐩 𐐶𐐲𐑉 𐐫𐑊 𐐯𐐿𐑅𐐨𐐼𐐮𐑍𐑊𐐨 𐑅𐐱𐑉𐐬𐑁𐐳𐑊, 𐐨𐑂𐐲𐑌 𐑄𐐰𐐻 𐑄𐐩 𐐼𐐮𐐼 𐑋𐐲𐑉𐑋𐐲𐑉 𐐰𐑀𐐯𐑌𐑅𐐻 𐑄 𐐢𐐫𐑉𐐼.

10. 𐑌𐐵 𐐮𐐻 𐐿𐐩𐑋 𐐻𐐭 𐐹𐐰𐑅 𐑄𐐰𐐻 𐐌, 𐐤𐐨𐑁𐐴, 𐐸𐐰𐑂𐐮𐑍 𐐺𐐨𐑌 𐐰𐑁𐑊𐐮𐐿𐐻𐐲𐐼 𐐶𐐮𐑄 𐑋𐐴 𐐺𐑉𐐯𐑄𐑉𐐯𐑌 𐐺𐐨𐐿𐐫𐑆 𐐱𐑂 𐑄 𐑊𐐫𐑅 𐐱𐑂 𐑋𐐴 𐐺𐐬; 𐐰𐑌𐐼 𐑄𐐩𐑉 𐐺𐐬𐑆 𐐸𐐰𐑂𐐮𐑍 𐑊𐐫𐑅𐐻 𐑄𐐩𐑉 𐑅𐐹𐑉𐐮𐑍𐑆, 𐐮𐐻 𐐺𐐨𐑀𐐰𐑌 𐐻𐐭 𐐺𐐨 𐐯𐐿𐑅𐐨𐐼𐐮𐑍𐑊𐐨 𐐼𐐮𐑁𐐮𐐿𐐲𐑊𐐻, 𐐷𐐩, 𐐮𐑌𐑅𐐬𐑋𐐲𐐽 𐑄𐐰𐐻 𐐶𐐨 𐐿𐐳𐐼 𐐱𐐺𐐻𐐩𐑌 𐑌𐐬 𐑁𐐭𐐼. 𐐰𐑌𐐼 𐐮𐐻 𐐿𐐩𐑋 𐐻𐐭 𐐹𐐰𐑅 𐑄𐐰𐐻 𐐌, 𐐤𐐨𐑁𐐴, 𐐼𐐮𐐼 𐑅𐐹𐐨𐐿 𐑋𐐲𐐽 𐐲𐑌𐐻𐐭 𐑋𐐴 𐐺𐑉𐐯𐑄𐑉𐐯𐑌, 𐐺𐐨𐐿𐐫𐑆 𐑄𐐩 𐐸𐐰𐐼 𐐸𐐪𐑉𐐼𐐲𐑌𐐼 𐑄𐐩𐑉 𐐸𐐪𐑉𐐻𐑅 𐐲𐑀𐐯𐑌, 𐐨𐑂𐐲𐑌 𐐲𐑌𐐻𐐭 𐐿𐐱𐑋𐐹𐑊𐐩𐑌𐐮𐑍 𐐰𐑀𐐯𐑌𐑅𐐻 𐑄 𐐢𐐫𐑉𐐼 𐑄𐐩𐑉 𐐘𐐱𐐼. 𐐰𐑌𐐼 𐐮𐐻 𐐿𐐩𐑋 𐐻𐐭 𐐹𐐰𐑅 𐑄𐐰𐐻 𐐌, 𐐤𐐨𐑁𐐴, 𐐼𐐮𐐼 𐑋𐐩𐐿 𐐵𐐻 𐐱𐑂 𐐶𐐳𐐼 𐐩 𐐺𐐬, 𐐰𐑌𐐼 𐐵𐐻 𐐱𐑂 𐐲 𐑅𐐻𐑉𐐩𐐻 𐑅𐐻𐐮𐐿, 𐐰𐑌 𐐰𐑉𐐬: 𐐸𐐶𐐯𐑉𐑁𐐫𐑉, 𐐌 𐐼𐐮𐐼 𐐪𐑉𐑋 𐑋𐐴𐑅𐐯𐑊𐑁 𐐶𐐮𐑄 𐐲 𐐺𐐬 𐐰𐑌𐐼 𐐰𐑌 𐐰𐑉𐐬, 𐐶𐐮𐑄 𐐩 𐑅𐑊𐐮𐑍 𐐰𐑌𐐼 𐐶𐐮𐑄 𐑅𐐻𐐬𐑌𐑆. 𐐰𐑌𐐼 𐐌 𐑅𐐯𐐼 𐐲𐑌𐐻𐐭 𐑋𐐴 𐑁𐐪𐑄𐐲𐑉, 𐐐𐐶𐐮𐑄𐐲𐑉 𐑇𐐰𐑊 𐐌 𐑀𐐬 𐐻𐐭 𐐱𐐺𐐻𐐩𐑌 𐑁𐐭𐐼? 𐐰𐑌𐐼 𐐮𐐻 𐐿𐐩𐑋 𐐻𐐭 𐐹𐐰𐑅 𐑄𐐰𐐻 𐐸𐐨 𐐼𐐮𐐼 𐐮𐑌𐐿𐐶𐐴𐑉 𐐱𐑂 𐑄 𐐢𐐫𐑉𐐼, 𐑁𐐫𐑉 𐑄𐐩 𐐸𐐰𐐼 𐐸𐐲𐑋𐐺𐑊𐐼 𐑄𐐯𐑋𐑅𐐯𐑊𐑂𐑆, 𐐺𐐨𐐿𐐫𐑆 𐐱𐑂 𐑋𐐴 𐐶𐐲𐑉𐐼𐑆; 𐑁𐐫𐑉 𐐌 𐐼𐐮𐐼 𐑅𐐩 𐑋𐐯𐑌𐐨 𐑃𐐮𐑍𐑆 𐐲𐑌𐐻𐐭 𐑄𐐯𐑋 𐐮𐑌 𐑄 𐐯𐑌𐐲𐑉𐐾𐐨 𐐱𐑂 𐑋𐐴 𐑅𐐬𐑊.

11. 𐐰𐑌𐐼 𐐮𐐻 𐐿𐐩𐑋 𐐻𐐭 𐐹𐐰𐑅 𐑄𐐰𐐻 𐑄 𐑂𐐱𐐮𐑅 𐐱𐑂 𐑄 𐐢𐐫𐑉𐐼 𐐿𐐩𐑋 𐐲𐑌𐐻𐐭 𐑋𐐴 𐑁𐐪𐑄𐐲𐑉; 𐐰𐑌𐐼 𐐸𐐨 𐐶𐐱𐑆 𐐻𐑉𐐭𐑊𐐨 𐐽𐐩𐑅𐑌𐐼 𐐺𐐨𐐿𐐫𐑆 𐐱𐑂 𐐸𐐮𐑆 𐑋𐐲𐑉𐑋𐐲𐑉𐐮𐑍 𐐰𐑀𐐯𐑌𐑅𐐻 𐑄 𐐢𐐫𐑉𐐼, 𐐮𐑌𐑅𐐬𐑋𐐲𐐽 𐑄𐐰𐐻 𐐸𐐨 𐐶𐐱𐑆 𐐺𐑉𐐫𐐻 𐐼𐐵𐑌 𐐮𐑌𐐻𐐭 𐑄 𐐼𐐯𐐹𐑃𐑅 𐐱𐑂 𐑅𐐱𐑉𐐬. 𐐰𐑌𐐼 𐐮𐐻 𐐿𐐩𐑋 𐐻𐐭 𐐹𐐰𐑅 𐑄𐐰𐐻 𐑄 𐑂𐐱𐐮𐑅 𐐱𐑂 𐑄 𐐢𐐫𐑉𐐼 𐑅𐐯𐐼 𐐲𐑌𐐻𐐭 𐐸𐐮𐑋, 𐐢𐐳𐐿 𐐲𐐹𐐱𐑌 𐑄 𐐺𐐫𐑊, 𐐰𐑌𐐼 𐐺𐐨𐐸𐐬𐑊𐐼 𐑄 𐑃𐐮𐑍𐑆 𐐸𐐶𐐮𐐽 𐐪𐑉 𐑉𐐮𐐻𐑌. 𐐰𐑌𐐼 𐐮𐐻 𐐿𐐩𐑋 𐐻𐐭 𐐹𐐰𐑅 𐑄𐐰𐐻 𐐸𐐶𐐯𐑌 𐑋𐐴 𐑁𐐪𐑄𐐲𐑉 𐐺𐐨𐐸𐐯𐑊𐐼 𐑄 𐑃𐐮𐑍𐑆 𐐸𐐶𐐮𐐽 𐐶𐐲𐑉 𐑉𐐮𐐻𐑌 𐐲𐐹𐐱𐑌 𐑄 𐐺𐐫𐑊, 𐐸𐐨 𐐼𐐮𐐼 𐑁𐐨𐑉 𐐰𐑌𐐼 𐐻𐑉𐐯𐑋𐐺𐑊 𐐯𐐿𐑅𐐨𐐼𐐮𐑍𐑊𐐨, 𐐰𐑌𐐼 𐐫𐑊𐑅𐐬 𐑋𐐴 𐐺𐑉𐐯𐑄𐑉𐐯𐑌, 𐐰𐑌𐐼 𐑄 𐑅𐐲𐑌𐑆 𐐱𐑂 𐐌𐑇𐑋𐐩𐐯𐑊 𐐰𐑌𐐼 𐐵𐑉 𐐶𐐴𐑂𐑆.

12. 𐐈𐑌𐐼 𐐮𐐻 𐐿𐐩𐑋 𐐻𐐭 𐐹𐐰𐑅 𐑄𐐰𐐻 𐐌, 𐐤𐐨𐑁𐐴, 𐐺𐐨𐐸𐐯𐑊𐐼 𐑄 𐐹𐐱𐐮𐑌𐐻𐐲𐑉𐑆 𐐸𐐶𐐮𐐽 𐐶𐐲𐑉 𐐮𐑌 𐑄 𐐺𐐫𐑊, 𐑄𐐰𐐻 𐑄𐐩 𐐼𐐮𐐼 𐐶𐐲𐑉𐐿 𐐰𐐿𐐫𐑉𐐼𐐮𐑍 𐐻𐐭 𐑄 𐑁𐐩𐑃, 𐐰𐑌𐐼 𐐼𐐮𐑊𐐮𐐾𐐯𐑌𐑅, 𐐰𐑌𐐼 𐐸𐐨𐐼 𐐸𐐶𐐮𐐽 𐐶𐐨 𐐼𐐮𐐼 𐑀𐐮𐑂 𐐲𐑌𐐻𐐭 𐑄𐐯𐑋. 𐐈𐑌𐐼 𐑄𐐯𐑉 𐐶𐐱𐑆 𐐫𐑊𐑅𐐬 𐑉𐐮𐐻𐑌 𐐲𐐹𐐱𐑌 𐑄𐐯𐑋, 𐐩 𐑌𐐷𐐭 𐑉𐐴𐐻𐐮𐑍, 𐐸𐐶𐐮𐐽 𐐶𐐱𐑆 𐐹𐑊𐐩𐑌 𐐻𐐭 𐐺𐐨 𐑉𐐯𐐼, 𐐸𐐶𐐮𐐽 𐐼𐐮𐐼 𐑀𐐮𐑂 𐐲𐑅 𐐲𐑌𐐼𐐲𐑉𐑅𐐻𐐰𐑌𐐼𐐮𐑍 𐐿𐐱𐑌𐑅𐐲𐑉𐑌𐐮𐑍 𐑄 𐐶𐐩𐑆 𐐱𐑂 𐑄 𐐢𐐫𐑉𐐼; 𐐰𐑌𐐼 𐐮𐐻 𐐶𐐱𐑆 𐑉𐐮𐐻𐑌 𐐰𐑌𐐼 𐐽𐐩𐑌𐐾𐐼 𐑁𐑉𐐱𐑋 𐐻𐐴𐑋 𐐻𐐭 𐐻𐐴𐑋, 𐐰𐐿𐐫𐑉𐐼𐐮𐑍 𐐻𐐭 𐑄 𐑁𐐩𐑃 𐐰𐑌𐐼 𐐼𐐮𐑊𐐮𐐾𐐯𐑌𐑅 𐐸𐐶𐐮𐐽 𐐶𐐨 𐑀𐐩𐑂 𐐲𐑌𐐻𐐭 𐐮𐐻; 𐐰𐑌𐐼 𐑄𐐲𐑅 𐐶𐐨 𐑅𐐨 𐑄𐐰𐐻, 𐐺𐐴 𐑅𐑋𐐫𐑊 𐑋𐐨𐑌𐑆, 𐑄 𐐢𐐫𐑉𐐼 𐐿𐐰𐑌 𐐺𐑉𐐮𐑍 𐐲𐐺𐐵𐐻 𐑀𐑉𐐩𐐻 𐑃𐐮𐑍𐑆.

13. 𐐈𐑌𐐼 𐐮𐐻 𐐿𐐩𐑋 𐐻𐐭 𐐹𐐰𐑅 𐑄𐐰𐐻 𐐌, 𐐤𐐨𐑁𐐴, 𐐼𐐮𐐼 𐑀𐐬 𐑁𐐬𐑉𐑃 𐐲𐐹 𐐮𐑌𐐻𐐭 𐑄 𐐻𐐱𐐹 𐐱𐑂 𐑄 𐑋𐐵𐑌𐐻𐐮𐑌, 𐐰𐐿𐐫𐑉𐐼𐐮𐑍 𐐻𐐭 𐑄 𐐼𐐴𐑉𐐯𐐿𐑇𐐲𐑌𐑆 𐐸𐐶𐐮𐐽 𐐶𐐲𐑉 𐑀𐐮𐑂𐑌 𐐲𐐹𐐱𐑌 𐑄 𐐺𐐫𐑊. 𐐈𐑌𐐼 𐐮𐐻 𐐿𐐩𐑋 𐐻𐐭 𐐹𐐰𐑅 𐑄𐐰𐐻 𐐌 𐐼𐐮𐐼 𐑅𐑊𐐩 𐐶𐐴𐑊𐐼 𐐺𐐨𐑅𐐻𐑅, 𐐮𐑌𐑅𐐬𐑋𐐲𐐽 𐑄𐐰𐐻 𐐌 𐐼𐐮𐐼 𐐱𐐺𐐻𐐩𐑌 𐑁𐐭𐐼 𐑁𐐫𐑉 𐐵𐑉 𐑁𐐰𐑋𐐮𐑊𐐮𐑆. 𐐈𐑌𐐼 𐐮𐐻 𐐿𐐩𐑋 𐐻𐐭 𐐹𐐰𐑅 𐑄𐐰𐐻 𐐌 𐐼𐐮𐐼 𐑉𐐨𐐻𐐲𐑉𐑌 𐐻𐐭 𐐵𐑉 𐐻𐐯𐑌𐐻𐑅, 𐐺𐐩𐑉𐐮𐑍 𐑄 𐐺𐐨𐑅𐐻𐑅 𐐸𐐶𐐮𐐽 𐐌 𐐸𐐰𐐼 𐑅𐑊𐐩𐑌; 𐐰𐑌𐐼 𐑌𐐵, 𐐸𐐶𐐯𐑌 𐑄𐐩 𐐺𐐨𐐸𐐯𐑊𐐼 𐑄𐐰𐐻 𐐌 𐐸𐐰𐐼 𐐱𐐺𐐻𐐩𐑌𐐼 𐑁𐐭𐐼, 𐐸𐐵 𐑀𐑉𐐩𐐻 𐐶𐐱𐑆 𐑄𐐯𐑉 𐐾𐐦. 𐐈𐑌𐐼 𐐮𐐻 𐐿𐐩𐑋 𐐻𐐭 𐐹𐐰𐑅 𐑄𐐰𐐻 𐑄𐐩 𐐼𐐮𐐼 𐐸𐐲𐑋𐐺𐑊 𐑄𐐯𐑋𐑅𐐯𐑊𐑂𐑆 𐐺𐐨𐑁𐐬𐑉 𐑄 𐐢𐐫𐑉𐐼, 𐐰𐑌𐐼 𐐼𐐮𐐼 𐑀𐐮𐑂 𐑃𐐰𐑍𐐿𐑅 𐐲𐑌𐐻𐐭 𐐸𐐮𐑋.

14. 𐐈𐑌𐐼 𐐮𐐻 𐐿𐐩𐑋 𐐻𐐭 𐐹𐐰𐑅 𐑄𐐰𐐻 𐐶𐐨 𐐼𐐮𐐼 𐐰𐑀𐐯𐑌 𐐻𐐩𐐿 𐐵𐑉 𐐾𐐲𐑉𐑌𐐨, 𐐻𐑉𐐰𐑂𐐯𐑊𐐮𐑍 𐑌𐐨𐑉𐑊𐐨 𐑄 𐑅𐐩𐑋 𐐿𐐬𐑉𐑅 𐐰𐑆 𐐮𐑌 𐑄 𐐺𐐨𐑀𐐮𐑌𐐮𐑍: 𐐰𐑌𐐼 𐐰𐑁𐐻𐐲𐑉 𐐶𐐨 𐐸𐐰𐐼 𐐻𐑉𐐰𐑂𐐯𐑊𐐼 𐑁𐐫𐑉 𐑄 𐑅𐐹𐐩𐑅 𐐱𐑂 𐑋𐐯𐑌𐐨 𐐼𐐩𐑆, 𐐶𐐨 𐐼𐐮𐐼 𐐹𐐮𐐽 𐐵𐑉 𐐻𐐯𐑌𐐻𐑅 𐐰𐑀𐐯𐑌, 𐑄𐐰𐐻 𐐶𐐨 𐑋𐐴𐐻 𐐻𐐰𐑉𐐨 𐑁𐐫𐑉 𐑄 𐑅𐐹𐐩𐑅 𐐱𐑂 𐐩 𐐻𐐴𐑋.

15. 𐐈𐑌𐐼 𐐮𐐻 𐐿𐐩𐑋 𐐻𐐭 𐐹𐐰𐑅 𐑄𐐰𐐻 𐐆𐑇𐑋𐐩𐐯𐑊 𐐼𐐴𐐼, 𐐰𐑌𐐼 𐐶𐐱𐑆 𐐺𐐯𐑉𐐨𐐼 𐐮𐑌 𐑄 𐐹𐑊𐐩𐑅 𐐸𐐶𐐮𐐽 𐐶𐐱𐑆 𐐿𐐫𐑊𐐼 𐐤𐐩𐐸𐐱𐑋. 𐐈𐑌𐐼 𐐮𐐻 𐐿𐐩𐑋 𐐻𐐭 𐐹𐐰𐑅 𐑄𐐰𐐻 𐑄 𐐼𐐫𐐻𐐲𐑉𐑆 𐐱𐑂 𐐆𐑇𐑋𐐩𐐯𐑊 𐐼𐐮𐐼 𐑋𐐬𐑉𐑌 𐐯𐐿𐑅𐐨𐐼𐐮𐑍𐑊𐐨, 𐐺𐐨𐐿𐐫𐑆 𐐱𐑂 𐑄 𐑊𐐫𐑅 𐐱𐑂 𐑄𐐯𐑉 𐑁𐐪𐑄𐐲𐑉, 𐐰𐑌𐐼 𐐺𐐨𐐿𐐫𐑆 𐐱𐑂 𐑄𐐯𐑉 𐐰𐑁𐑊𐐮𐐿𐑇𐐲𐑌𐑆 𐐮𐑌 𐑄 𐐶𐐮𐑊𐐼𐐲𐑉𐑌𐐯𐑅; 𐐰𐑌𐐼 𐑄𐐩 𐐼𐐮𐐼 𐑋𐐲𐑉𐑋𐐲𐑉 𐐰𐑀𐐯𐑌𐑅𐐻 𐑋𐐴 𐑁𐐪𐑄𐐲𐑉, 𐐺𐐨𐐿𐐫𐑆 𐐸𐐨 𐐸𐐰𐐼 𐐺𐑉𐐫𐐻 𐑄𐐯𐑋 𐐵𐐻 𐐱𐑂 𐑄 𐑊𐐰𐑌𐐼 𐐱𐑂 𐐖𐐲𐑉𐐭𐑅𐐲𐑊𐐯𐑋, 𐑅𐐩𐐮𐑍, 𐐍𐑉 𐑁𐐪𐑄𐐲𐑉 𐐮𐑆 𐐼𐐯𐐼; 𐐷𐐩, 𐐰𐑌𐐼 𐐶𐐨 𐐸𐐰𐑂 𐐶𐐱𐑌𐐼𐐲𐑉𐐼 𐑋𐐲𐐽 𐐮𐑌 𐑄 𐐶𐐮𐑊𐐼𐐲𐑉𐑌𐐯𐑅, 𐐰𐑌𐐼 𐐶𐐨 𐐸𐐰𐑂 𐑅𐐲𐑁𐐲𐑉𐐼 𐑋𐐲𐐽 𐐰𐑁𐑊𐐮𐐿𐑇𐐲𐑌, 𐐸𐐲𐑍𐑀𐐲𐑉, 𐑃𐐲𐑉𐑅𐐻, 𐐰𐑌𐐼 𐑁𐐰𐐻𐐨𐑀; 𐐰𐑌𐐼 𐐰𐑁𐐻𐐲𐑉 𐐫𐑊 𐑄𐐨𐑆 𐑅𐐲𐑁𐐲𐑉𐐮𐑍𐑆, 𐐶𐐨 𐑋𐐲𐑅𐐻 𐐹𐐯𐑉𐐮𐑇 𐐮𐑌 𐑄 𐐶𐐮𐑊𐐼𐐲𐑉𐑌𐐯𐑅 𐐶𐐮𐑄 𐐸𐐲𐑍𐑀𐐲𐑉. 𐐈𐑌𐐼 𐑄𐐲𐑅 𐑄𐐩 𐐼𐐮𐐼 𐑋𐐲𐑉𐑋𐐲𐑉 𐐰𐑀𐐯𐑌𐑅𐐻 𐑋𐐴 𐑁𐐪𐑄𐐲𐑉, 𐐰𐑌𐐼 𐐫𐑊𐑅𐐬 𐐰𐑀𐐯𐑌𐑅𐐻 𐑋𐐨; 𐐰𐑌𐐼 𐑄𐐩 𐐶𐐲𐑉 𐐼𐐨𐑆𐐴𐑉𐐲𐑅 𐐻𐐭 𐑉𐐨𐐻𐐲𐑉𐑌 𐐰𐑀𐐯𐑌 𐐻𐐭 𐐖𐐲𐑉𐐭𐑅𐐲𐑊𐐯𐑋. 𐐈𐑌𐐼 𐐢𐐩𐑋𐐲𐑌 𐑅𐐯𐐼 𐐲𐑌𐐻𐐭 𐐢𐐯𐑋𐐷𐐭𐐯𐑊, 𐐰𐑌𐐼 𐐫𐑊𐑅𐐬 𐐲𐑌𐐻𐐭 𐑄 𐑅𐐲𐑌𐑆 𐐱𐑂 𐐆𐑇𐑋𐐩𐐯𐑊, 𐐒𐐨𐐸𐐬𐑊𐐼, 𐑊𐐯𐐻 𐐲𐑅 𐑅𐑊𐐩 𐐵𐑉 𐑁𐐪𐑄𐐲𐑉, 𐐰𐑌𐐼 𐐫𐑊𐑅𐐬 𐐵𐑉 𐐺𐑉𐐲𐑄𐐲𐑉 𐐤𐐨𐑁𐐴, 𐐸𐐭 𐐸𐐰𐑆 𐐻𐐩𐐿𐑌 𐐮𐐻 𐐲𐐹𐐱𐑌 𐐸𐐮𐑋 𐐻𐐭 𐐺𐐨 𐐵𐑉 𐑉𐐭𐑊𐐲𐑉 𐐰𐑌𐐼 𐐵𐑉 𐐻𐐨𐐽𐐲𐑉, 𐐸𐐭 𐐪𐑉 𐐸𐐮𐑆 𐐯𐑊𐐼𐐲𐑉 𐐺𐑉𐐯𐑄𐑉𐐯𐑌: 𐐤𐐵, 𐐸𐐨 𐑅𐐯𐑆 𐑄𐐰𐐻 𐑄 𐐢𐐫𐑉𐐼 𐐸𐐰𐑆 𐐻𐐫𐐿𐐻 𐐶𐐮𐑄 𐐸𐐮𐑋, 𐐰𐑌𐐼 𐐫𐑊𐑅𐐬 𐑄𐐰𐐻 𐐩𐑌𐐾𐐯𐑊𐑆 𐐸𐐰𐑂 𐑋𐐮𐑌𐐮𐑅𐐻𐐲𐑉𐐼 𐐲𐑌𐐻𐐭 𐐸𐐮𐑋. 𐐒𐐲𐐻 𐐺𐐨𐐸𐐬𐑊𐐼, 𐐶𐐨 𐑌𐐬 𐑄𐐰𐐻 𐐸𐐨 𐑊𐐴𐑆 𐐲𐑌𐐻𐐭 𐐲𐑅; 𐐰𐑌𐐼 𐐸𐐨 𐐻𐐯𐑊𐑆 𐐲𐑅 𐑄𐐨𐑆 𐑃𐐮𐑍𐑆, 𐐰𐑌𐐼 𐐸𐐨 𐐶𐐲𐑉𐐿𐐯𐑃 𐑋𐐯𐑌𐐨 𐑃𐐮𐑍𐑆 𐐺𐐴 𐐸𐐮𐑆 𐐿𐐲𐑌𐐮𐑍 𐐪𐑉𐐻𐑅, 𐑄𐐰𐐻 𐐸𐐨 𐑋𐐩 𐐼𐐨𐑅𐐨𐑂 𐐵𐑉 𐐴𐑆, 𐑃𐐮𐑍𐐿𐐮𐑍, 𐐹𐐲𐑉𐐸𐐰𐐹𐑅, 𐑄𐐰𐐻 𐐸𐐨 𐑋𐐩 𐑊𐐨𐐼 𐐲𐑅 𐐰𐐶𐐩 𐐮𐑌𐐻𐐭 𐑅𐐲𐑋 𐑅𐐻𐑉𐐩𐑌𐐾 𐐶𐐮𐑊𐐼𐐲𐑉𐑌𐐯𐑅; 𐐰𐑌𐐼 𐐰𐑁𐐻𐐲𐑉 𐐸𐐨 𐐸𐐰𐑆 𐑊𐐯𐐼 𐐲𐑅 𐐰𐐶𐐩, 𐐸𐐨 𐐸𐐰𐑆 𐑃𐐫𐐻 𐐻𐐭 𐑋𐐩𐐿 𐐸𐐮𐑋𐑅𐐯𐑊𐑁 𐐩 𐐿𐐮𐑍 𐐰𐑌𐐼 𐐩 𐑉𐐭𐑊𐐲𐑉 𐐬𐑂𐐲𐑉 𐐲𐑅, 𐑄𐐰𐐻 𐐸𐐨 𐑋𐐩 𐐼𐐭 𐐶𐐮𐑄 𐐲𐑅 𐐰𐐿𐐫𐑉𐐼𐐮𐑍 𐐻𐐭 𐐸𐐮𐑆 𐐶𐐮𐑊 𐐰𐑌𐐼 𐐹𐑊𐐯𐑈𐐲𐑉. 𐐈𐑌𐐼 𐐰𐑁𐐻𐐲𐑉 𐑄𐐮𐑅 𐑋𐐰𐑌𐐲𐑉 𐐼𐐮𐐼 𐑋𐐴 𐐺𐑉𐐲𐑄𐐲𐑉 𐐢𐐩𐑋𐐲𐑌 𐑅𐐻𐐲𐑉 𐐲𐐹 𐑄𐐯𐑉 𐐸𐐪𐑉𐐻𐑅 𐐻𐐭 𐐰𐑍𐑀𐐲𐑉.

16. 𐐈𐑌𐐼 𐐮𐐻 𐐿𐐩𐑋 𐐻𐐭 𐐹𐐰𐑅 𐑄𐐰𐐻 𐑄 𐐢𐐫𐑉𐐼 𐐶𐐱𐑆 𐐶𐐮𐑄 𐐲𐑅, 𐐷𐐩, 𐐨𐑂𐐲𐑌 𐑄 𐑂𐐦𐑅 𐐱𐑂 𐑄 𐐢𐐫𐑉𐐼 𐐿𐐩𐑋 𐐰𐑌𐐼 𐐼𐐮𐐼 𐑅𐐹𐐨𐐿 𐑋𐐯𐑌𐐨 𐐶𐐲𐑉𐐼𐑆 𐐲𐑌𐐻𐐭 𐑄𐐯𐑋, 𐐰𐑌𐐼 𐐼𐐮𐐼 𐐽𐐩𐑅𐑌 𐑄𐐯𐑋 𐐯𐐿𐑅𐐨𐐼𐐮𐑍𐑊𐐨; 𐐰𐑌𐐼 𐐰𐑁𐐻𐐲𐑉 𐑄𐐩 𐐶𐐲𐑉 𐐽𐐩𐑅𐑌𐐼 𐐺𐐴 𐑄 𐑂𐐦𐑅 𐐱𐑂 𐑄 𐐢𐐫𐑉𐐼, 𐑄𐐩 𐐼𐐮𐐼 𐐻𐐲𐑉𐑌 𐐰𐐶𐐩 𐑄𐐯𐑉 𐐰𐑍𐑀𐐲𐑉, 𐐰𐑌𐐼 𐐼𐐮𐐼 𐑉𐐨𐐹𐐯𐑌𐐻 𐐱𐑂 𐑄𐐯𐑉 𐑅𐐮𐑌𐑆, 𐐮𐑌𐑅𐐬𐑋𐐲𐐽 𐑄𐐰𐐻 𐑄 𐐢𐐫𐑉𐐼 𐐼𐐮𐐼 𐐺𐑊𐐯𐑅 𐐲𐑅 𐐰𐑀𐐯𐑌 𐐶𐐮𐑄 𐑁𐐭𐐼, 𐑄𐐰𐐻 𐐶𐐨 𐐼𐐮𐐼 𐑌𐐱𐐻 𐐹𐐯𐑉𐐮𐑇.

17. 𐐈𐑌𐐼 𐐮𐐻 𐐿𐐩𐑋 𐐻𐐭 𐐹𐐰𐑅 𐑄𐐰𐐻 𐐶𐐨 𐐼𐐮𐐼 𐐰𐑀𐐯𐑌 𐐻𐐩𐐿 𐐵𐑉 𐐾𐐲𐑉𐑌𐐨 𐐮𐑌 𐑄 𐐶𐐮𐑊𐐼𐐲𐑉𐑌𐐯𐑅; 𐐰𐑌𐐼 𐐶𐐨 𐐼𐐮𐐼 𐐻𐑉𐐰𐑂𐐯𐑊 𐑌𐐨𐑉𐑊𐐨 𐐨𐑅𐐻𐐶𐐲𐑉𐐼, 𐑁𐑉𐐱𐑋 𐑄𐐰𐐻 𐐻𐐴𐑋 𐑁𐐬𐑉𐑃. 𐐈𐑌𐐼 𐐶𐐨 𐐼𐐮𐐼 𐐻𐑉𐐰𐑂𐐯𐑊 𐐰𐑌𐐼 𐐶𐐩𐐼

𐑃𐑉𐐭 𐑋𐐲𐐽 𐐰𐑁𐑊𐐮𐐿𐑇𐐲𐑌 𐐮𐑌 𐑄 𐐶𐐮𐑊𐐼𐐲𐑉𐑌𐐯𐑅; 𐐰𐑌𐐼 𐐵𐑉 𐐶𐐮𐑋𐐮𐑌 𐐼𐐮𐐼 𐐺𐐯𐑉 𐐽𐐮𐑊𐐼𐑉𐐯𐑌 𐐮𐑌 𐑄 𐐶𐐮𐑊𐐼𐐲𐑉𐑌𐐯𐑅. 𐐈𐑌𐐼 𐑅𐐬 𐑀𐑉𐐩𐐻 𐐶𐐲𐑉 𐑄 𐐺𐑊𐐯𐑅𐐮𐑍𐑆 𐐲𐑂 𐑄 𐐢𐐫𐑉𐐼 𐐲𐐹𐐱𐑌 𐐲𐑅, 𐑄𐐰𐐻 𐐸𐐶𐐴𐑊 𐐶𐐨 𐐼𐐮𐐼 𐑊𐐮𐑂 𐐲𐐹𐐱𐑌 𐑉𐐫 𐑋𐐨𐐻 𐐮𐑌 𐑄 𐐶𐐮𐑊𐐼𐐲𐑉𐑌𐐯𐑅, 𐐵𐑉 𐐶𐐮𐑋𐐮𐑌 𐐼𐐮𐐼 𐑀𐐮𐑂 𐐹𐑊𐐯𐑌𐐻𐐮 𐐲𐑂 𐑅𐐲𐐿 𐑁𐐫𐑉 𐑄𐐯𐑉 𐐽𐐮𐑊𐐼𐑉𐐯𐑌, 𐐰𐑌𐐼 𐐶𐐲𐑉 𐑅𐐻𐑉𐐱𐑍, 𐐷𐐩, 𐐨𐑂𐐲𐑌 𐑊𐐴𐐿 𐐲𐑌𐐻𐐭 𐑄 𐑋𐐯𐑌; 𐐰𐑌𐐼 𐑄𐐩 𐐺𐐨𐑀𐐰𐑌 𐐻𐐭 𐐺𐐯𐑉 𐑄𐐯𐑉 𐐾𐐲𐑉𐑌𐐨𐐮𐑍𐑆 𐐶𐐮𐑄𐐵𐐻 𐑋𐐲𐑉𐑋𐐲𐑉𐐮𐑍𐑆. 𐐈𐑌𐐼 𐑄𐐲𐑅 𐐶𐐨 𐑅𐐨 𐑄𐐰𐐻 𐑄 𐐿𐐲𐑋𐐰𐑌𐐼𐑋𐐯𐑌𐐻𐑅 𐐲𐑂 𐐘𐐱𐐼 𐑋𐐲𐑅𐐻 𐐺 𐑁𐐳𐑊𐑁𐐮𐑊𐐼. 𐐈𐑌𐐼 𐐮𐑁 𐐮𐐻 𐑅𐐬 𐐺 𐑄𐐰𐐻 𐑄 𐐽𐐮𐑊𐐼𐑉𐐯𐑌 𐐲𐑂 𐑋𐐯𐑌 𐐿𐐨𐐹 𐑄 𐐿𐐲𐑋𐐰𐑌𐐼𐑋𐐯𐑌𐐻𐑅 𐐲𐑂 𐐘𐐱𐐼, 𐐸𐐨 𐐼𐐲𐑃 𐑌𐐲𐑉𐐮𐑇 𐑄𐐯𐑋, 𐐰𐑌𐐼 𐑅𐐻𐑉𐐯𐑍𐑃𐐯𐑌 𐑄𐐯𐑋, 𐐰𐑌𐐼 𐐹𐑉𐐬𐑂𐐴𐐼 𐑋𐐨𐑌𐑆 𐐸𐐶𐐯𐑉𐐺𐐴 𐑄𐐩 𐐿𐐰𐑌 𐐰𐐿𐐱𐑋𐐹𐑊𐐮𐑇 𐑄 𐑃𐐮𐑍 𐐸𐐶𐐮𐐽 𐐸𐐨 𐐸𐐰𐑆 𐐿𐐲𐑋𐐰𐑌𐐼𐐯𐐼 𐑄𐐯𐑋; 𐐸𐐶𐐯𐑉𐑁𐐫𐑉, 𐐸𐐨 𐐼𐐮𐐼 𐐹𐑉𐐬𐑂𐐴𐐼 𐑋𐐨𐑌𐑆 𐑁𐐫𐑉 𐐲𐑅 𐐸𐐶𐐴𐑊 𐐶𐐨 𐐼𐐮𐐼 𐑅𐐬𐐾𐐲𐑉𐑌 𐐮𐑌 𐑄 𐐶𐐮𐑊𐐼𐐲𐑉𐑌𐐯𐑅. 𐐈𐑌𐐼 𐐶𐐨 𐐼𐐮𐐼 𐑅𐐬𐐾𐐲𐑉𐑌 𐑁𐐫𐑉 𐑄 𐑅𐐹𐐩𐑅 𐐲𐑂 𐑋𐐯𐑌𐐨 𐐷𐐨𐑉𐑆, 𐐷𐐩, 𐐨𐑂𐐲𐑌 𐐩𐐻 𐐷𐐨𐑉𐑆 𐐮𐑌 𐑄 𐐶𐐮𐑊𐐼𐐲𐑉𐑌𐐯𐑅. 𐐈𐑌𐐼 𐐶𐐨 𐐼𐐮𐐼 𐐿𐐲𐑋 𐐻𐐭 𐑄 𐑊𐐰𐑌𐐼 𐐸𐐶𐐮𐐽 𐐶𐐨 𐐿𐐫𐑊𐐼 𐐒𐐵𐑌𐐻𐐮𐑁𐐳𐑊, 𐐺𐐨𐐿𐐫𐑆 𐐲𐑂 𐐮𐐻𐑅 𐑋𐐲𐐽 𐑁𐑉𐐭𐐻 𐐰𐑌𐐼 𐐫𐑊𐑅𐐬 𐐶𐐴𐑊𐐼 𐐸𐐲𐑌𐐨; 𐐰𐑌𐐼 𐐫𐑊 𐑄𐐨𐑆 𐑃𐐮𐑍𐑆 𐐶𐐲𐑉 𐐹𐑉𐐨𐐹𐐩𐑉𐐼 𐐲𐑂 𐑄 𐐢𐐫𐑉𐐼, 𐑄𐐰𐐻 𐐶𐐨 𐑋𐐴𐐻 𐑌𐐱𐐻 𐐹𐐯𐑉𐐮𐑇. 𐐈𐑌𐐼 𐐶𐐨 𐐺𐐨𐐸𐐯𐑊𐐼 𐑄 𐑅𐐨, 𐐸𐐶𐐮𐐽 𐐶𐐨 𐐿𐐫𐑊𐐼 𐐀𐑉𐐨𐐰𐑌𐐻𐐲𐑋, 𐐸𐐶𐐮𐐽 𐐺𐐨𐐮𐑍 𐐮𐑌𐐻𐐲𐑉𐐹𐑉𐐯𐐻𐐯𐐼, 𐐮𐑆, 𐑋𐐯𐑌𐐨 𐐶𐐫𐐻𐐲𐑉𐑆.

18. 𐐈𐑌𐐼 𐐮𐐻 𐐿𐐩𐑋 𐐻𐐭 𐐹𐐰𐑅 𐑄𐐰𐐻 𐐶𐐨 𐐼𐐮𐐼 𐐹𐐮𐐽 𐐵𐑉 𐐻𐐯𐑌𐐻𐑅 𐐺𐐴 𐑄 𐑅𐐨-𐑇𐐬𐑉; 𐐰𐑌𐐼 𐑌𐐱𐐻𐐶𐐮𐑄𐑅𐐻𐐰𐑌𐐼𐐮𐑍 𐐶𐐨 𐐸𐐰𐐼 𐑅𐐲𐑁𐐲𐑉𐐼 𐑋𐐯𐑌𐐨 𐐰𐑁𐑊𐐮𐐿𐑇𐐲𐑌𐑆 𐐰𐑌𐐼 𐑋𐐲𐐽 𐐼𐐮𐑁𐐮𐐿𐐲𐑊𐐻𐐨, 𐐷𐐩, 𐐨𐑂𐐲𐑌 𐑅𐐬 𐑋𐐲𐐽 𐑄𐐰𐐻 𐐶𐐨 𐐿𐐰𐑌𐐱𐐻 𐑉𐐴𐐻 𐑄𐐯𐑋 𐐫𐑊, 𐐶𐐨 𐐶𐐲𐑉 𐐯𐐿𐑅𐐨𐐼𐐮𐑍𐑊𐐨 𐑉𐐨𐐾𐐱𐐮𐑅𐐻 𐐸𐐶𐐯𐑌 𐐶𐐨 𐐿𐐩𐑋 𐐻𐐭 𐑄 𐑅𐐨-𐑇𐐬𐑉; 𐐰𐑌𐐼 𐐶𐐨 𐐿𐐫𐑊𐐼 𐑄 𐐹𐑊𐐩𐑅 𐐒𐐵𐑌𐐻𐐮𐑁𐐳𐑊, 𐐺𐐨𐐿𐐫𐑆 𐐲𐑂 𐐮𐐻𐑅 𐑋𐐲𐐽 𐑁𐑉𐐭𐐻.

19. 𐐈𐑌𐐼 𐐮𐐻 𐐿𐐩𐑋 𐐻𐐭 𐐹𐐰𐑅 𐑄𐐰𐐻 𐐰𐑁𐐻𐐲𐑉 𐐌, 𐐤𐐨𐑁𐐴, 𐐸𐐰𐐼 𐐺𐐮𐑌 𐐮𐑌 𐑄 𐑊𐐰𐑌𐐼 𐐲𐑂 𐐒𐐵𐑌𐐻𐐮𐑁𐐳𐑊 𐑁𐐫𐑉 𐑄 𐑅𐐹𐐩𐑅 𐐲𐑂 𐑋𐐯𐑌𐐨 𐐼𐐩𐑆, 𐑄 𐑂𐑎𐑅 𐐲𐑂 𐑄 𐐢𐐫𐑉𐐼 𐐿𐐩𐑋 𐐲𐑌𐐻𐐭 𐑋𐐨, 𐑅𐐩𐐮𐑍, 𐐊𐑉𐐴𐑆, 𐐰𐑌𐐼 𐑀𐐯𐐻 𐑄 𐐮𐑌𐐻𐐭 𐑄 𐑋𐐵𐑌𐐻𐐲𐑌. 𐐈𐑌𐐼 𐐮𐐻 𐐿𐐩𐑋 𐐻𐐭 𐐹𐐰𐑅 𐑄𐐰𐐻 𐐌 𐐲𐑉𐐬𐑆 𐐰𐑌𐐼 𐐶𐐯𐑌𐐻 𐐲𐐹 𐐮𐑌𐐻𐐭 𐑄 𐑋𐐵𐑌𐐻𐐲𐑌, 𐐰𐑌𐐼 𐐿𐑉𐐴𐐼 𐐲𐑌𐐻𐐭 𐑄 𐐢𐐫𐑉𐐼.

20. 𐐈𐑌𐐼 𐐮𐐻 𐐿𐐩𐑋 𐐻𐐭 𐐹𐐰𐑅 𐑄𐐰𐐻 𐑄 𐐢𐐫𐑉𐐼 𐑅𐐹𐐩𐐿 𐐲𐑌𐐻𐐭 𐑋𐐨, 𐑅𐐩𐐮𐑍, 𐐜𐐵 𐑇𐐰𐑊𐐻 𐐿𐐱𐑌𐑅𐐻𐑉𐐲𐐿𐐻 𐐲 𐑇𐐮𐐹, 𐐰𐑁𐐻𐐲𐑉 𐑄 𐑋𐐰𐑌𐐲𐑉 𐐸𐐶𐐮𐐽 𐐌 𐑇𐐰𐑊 𐑇𐐬 𐑄, 𐑄𐐰𐐻 𐐌 𐑋𐐩 𐐿𐐰𐑉𐐨 𐑄𐐴 𐐹𐐨𐐹𐑊 𐐲𐐿𐑉𐐱𐑅 𐑄𐐨𐑆 𐐶𐐫𐐻𐐲𐑉𐑆. 𐐈𐑌𐐼 𐐌 𐑅𐐯𐐼, 𐐢𐐫𐑉𐐼, 𐐸𐐶𐐮𐑄𐐲𐑉 𐑇𐐰𐑊 𐐌 𐑀𐐬 𐑄𐐰𐐻 𐐌 𐑋𐐩 𐑁𐐴𐑌𐐼 𐐬𐑉 𐐻𐐭 𐑋𐐬𐑊𐐻𐐲𐑌, 𐑄𐐰𐐻 𐐌 𐑋𐐩 𐑋𐐩𐐿 𐐻𐐭𐑊𐑆 𐐻𐐭 𐐿𐐱𐑌𐑅𐐻𐑉𐐲𐐿𐐻 𐑄 𐑇𐐮𐐹 𐐰𐑁𐐻𐐲𐑉 𐑄 𐑋𐐰𐑌𐐲𐑉 𐐸𐐶𐐮𐐽 𐑄𐐵 𐐸𐐰𐑅𐐻 𐑇𐐬𐑌 𐐲𐑌𐐻𐐭 𐑋𐐨? 𐐈𐑌𐐼 𐐮𐐻 𐐿𐐩𐑋 𐐻𐐭 𐐹𐐰𐑅 𐑄𐐰𐐻 𐑄 𐐢𐐫𐑉𐐼 𐐻𐐬𐑊𐐼 𐑋𐐨 𐐸𐐶𐐮𐑄𐐲𐑉 𐐌 𐑇𐐳𐐼 𐑀𐐬 𐐻𐐭 𐑁𐐴𐑌𐐼 𐐬𐑉, 𐑄𐐰𐐻 𐐌 𐑋𐐴𐐻 𐑋𐐩𐐿 𐐻𐐭𐑊𐑆.

21. 𐐈𐑌𐐼 𐐮𐐻 𐐿𐐩𐑋 𐐻𐐭 𐐹𐐰𐑅 𐑄𐐰𐐻 𐐌, 𐐤𐐨𐑁𐐴, 𐐼𐐮𐐼 𐑋𐐩𐐿 𐐲 𐐺𐐯𐑊𐐬𐑆 𐐸𐐶𐐯𐑉𐐶𐐮𐑄 𐐻𐐭 𐐺𐑊𐐬 𐑄 𐑁𐐴𐑉, 𐐲𐑂 𐑄 𐑅𐐿𐐮𐑌𐑆 𐐲𐑂 𐐺𐐨𐑅𐐻𐑅; 𐐰𐑌𐐼 𐐰𐑁𐐻𐐲𐑉 𐐌 𐐸𐐰𐐼 𐑋𐐩𐐼 𐐲 𐐺𐐯𐑊𐐬𐑆, 𐑄𐐰𐐻 𐐌 𐑋𐐴𐐻 𐐸𐐰𐑂 𐐸𐐶𐐯𐑉𐐶𐐮𐑄 𐐻𐐭 𐐺𐑊𐐬 𐑄 𐑁𐐴𐑉, 𐐌 𐐼𐐮𐐼 𐑅𐑋𐐴𐐻 𐐻𐐭 𐑅𐐻𐐬𐑌𐑆 𐐻𐐭𐑀𐐯𐑄𐐲𐑉 𐑄𐐰𐐻 𐐌 𐑋𐐴𐐻 𐑋𐐩𐐿 𐑁𐐴𐑉: 𐑁𐐫𐑉 𐑄 𐐢𐐫𐑉𐐼 𐐸𐐰𐐼 𐑌𐐱𐐻 𐐸𐐮𐑄𐐲𐑉𐐻𐐭 𐑅𐐲𐑁𐐲𐑉𐐼 𐑄𐐰𐐻 𐐶𐐨 𐑇𐐳𐐼 𐑋𐐩𐐿 𐑋𐐲𐐽 𐑁𐐴𐑉, 𐐰𐑆 𐐶𐐨 𐐾𐐲𐑉𐑌𐐨𐐼 𐐮𐑌 𐑄 𐐶𐐮𐑊𐐼𐐲𐑉𐑌𐐯𐑅; 𐑁𐐫𐑉 𐐸𐐨 𐑅𐐯𐐼, 𐐌 𐐶𐐮𐑊 𐑋𐐩𐐿 𐑄𐐴 𐑁𐐭𐐼 𐐺𐐨𐐿𐐲𐑋 𐑅𐐶𐐨𐐻, 𐑄𐐰𐐻 𐐷 𐐿𐐳𐐿 𐐮𐐻 𐑌𐐱𐐻; 𐐰𐑌𐐼 𐐌 𐐶𐐮𐑊 𐐫𐑊𐑅𐐬 𐐺 𐐷𐐫𐑉 𐑊𐐴𐐻 𐐮𐑌 𐑄 𐐶𐐮𐑊𐐼𐐲𐑉𐑌𐐯𐑅; 𐐰𐑌𐐼 𐐌 𐐶𐐮𐑊 𐐹𐑉𐐨𐐹𐐩𐑉 𐑄 𐐶𐐩 𐐺𐐨𐑁𐐬𐑉 𐐷𐐭, 𐐮𐑁 𐐮𐐻 𐑅𐐬 𐐺 𐑄𐐰𐐻 𐐷 𐑇𐐰𐑊 𐐿𐐨𐐹 𐑋𐐴 𐐿𐐲𐑋𐐰𐑌𐐼𐑋𐐯𐑌𐐻𐑅; 𐐸𐐶𐐯𐑉𐑁𐐫𐑉, 𐐮𐑌𐐰𐑆𐑋𐐲𐐽 𐐰𐑆 𐐷 𐑇𐐰𐑊 𐐿𐐨𐐹 𐑋𐐴 𐐿𐐲𐑋𐐰𐑌𐐼𐑋𐐯𐑌𐐻𐑅 𐐷 𐑇𐐰𐑊 𐐺 𐑊𐐯𐐼 𐐻𐐬𐑉𐐼𐑆 𐑄 𐐹𐑉𐐱𐑋𐐮𐑅𐐻 𐑊𐐰𐑌𐐼; 𐐰𐑌𐐼 𐐷 𐑇𐐰𐑊 𐑌𐐬 𐑄𐐰𐐻 𐐮𐐻 𐐮𐑆 𐐺𐐴 𐑋𐐨 𐑄𐐰𐐻 𐐷 𐐪𐑉 𐑊𐐯𐐼. 𐐏𐐩, 𐐰𐑌𐐼 𐑄 𐐢𐐫𐑉𐐼 𐑅𐐯𐐼 𐐫𐑊𐑅𐐬, 𐑄𐐰𐐻 𐐰𐑁𐐻𐐲𐑉 𐐷 𐐸𐐰𐑂 𐐰𐑉𐐴𐑂𐐼 𐐮𐑌 𐑄 𐐹𐑉𐐱𐑋𐐮𐑅𐐻 𐑊𐐰𐑌𐐼, 𐐷 𐑇𐐰𐑊 𐑌𐐬 𐑄𐐰𐐻 𐐌, 𐑄 𐐢𐐫𐑉𐐼, 𐐰𐑋 𐐘𐐱𐐼; 𐐰𐑌𐐼 𐑄𐐰𐐻 𐐌, 𐑄 𐐢𐐫𐑉𐐼, 𐐼𐐮𐐼 𐐼𐐮𐑊𐐮𐑂𐐲𐑉 𐐷𐐭 𐑁𐑉𐐱𐑋 𐐼𐐯𐑅𐐻𐑉𐐲𐐿𐑇𐐲𐑌; 𐐷𐐩, 𐑄𐐰𐐻 𐐌 𐐼𐐮𐐼 𐐺𐑉𐐮𐑍 𐐷𐐭 𐐵𐐻 𐐲𐑂 𐑄 𐑊𐐰𐑌𐐼 𐐲𐑂 𐐖𐐯𐑉𐐭𐑅𐐲𐑊𐐯𐑋. 𐐐𐐶𐐯𐑉𐑁𐐫𐑉, 𐐌, 𐐤𐐨𐑁𐐴, 𐐼𐐮𐐼 𐑅𐐻𐑉𐐴𐑂 𐐻𐐭 𐐿𐐨𐐹 𐑄 𐐿𐐲𐑋𐐰𐑌𐐼𐑋𐐯𐑌𐐻𐑅 𐐲𐑂 𐑄 𐐢𐐫𐑉𐐼, 𐐰𐑌𐐼 𐐌 𐐼𐐮𐐼 𐐯𐑀𐑆𐐫𐑉𐐻 𐑋𐐴 𐐺𐑉𐐯𐑄𐑉𐐯𐑌 𐐻𐐭 𐑁𐐩𐑃𐑁𐐳𐑊𐑌𐐯𐑅 𐐰𐑌𐐼 𐐼𐐮𐑊𐐮𐐾𐐯𐑌𐑅.

22. 𐐈𐑌𐐼 𐐮𐐻 𐐿𐐩𐑋 𐐻𐐭 𐐹𐐰𐑅 𐑄𐐰𐐻 𐐌 𐐼𐐮𐐼 𐑋𐐩𐐿 𐐻𐐭𐑊𐑆 𐐱𐑂 𐑄 𐐬𐑉 𐐸𐐶𐐮𐐽 𐐌 𐐼𐐮𐐼 𐑋𐐬𐑊𐐻𐐲𐑌 𐐵𐐻 𐐱𐑂 𐑄 𐑉𐐱𐐿. 𐐈𐑌𐐼 𐐸𐐶𐐯𐑌 𐑋𐐴 𐐺𐑉𐐯𐑄𐑉𐐯𐑌 𐑅𐐫 𐑄𐐰𐐻 𐐌 𐐶𐐱𐑆 𐐰𐐺𐐵𐐻 𐐻𐐭 𐐺𐐮𐑊𐐼 𐐩 𐑇𐐮𐐹, 𐑄𐐩 𐐺𐐨𐑀𐐰𐑌 𐐻𐐭 𐑋𐐲𐑉𐑋𐐲𐑉 𐐰𐑀𐐯𐑌𐑅𐐻 𐑋𐐨, 𐑅𐐩𐐮𐑍, 𐐍𐑉 𐐺𐑉𐐲𐑄𐐲𐑉 𐐮𐑆 𐐩 𐑁𐐭𐑊, 𐑁𐐫𐑉 𐐸𐐨 𐑃𐐮𐑍𐐿𐐯𐑃 𐑄𐐰𐐻 𐐸𐐨 𐐿𐐰𐑌 𐐺𐐮𐑊𐐼 𐐩 𐑇𐐮𐐹; 𐐷𐐩, 𐐰𐑌𐐼 𐐸𐐨 𐐫𐑊𐑅𐐬 𐑃𐐮𐑍𐐿𐐯𐑃 𐑄𐐰𐐻 𐐸𐐨 𐐿𐐰𐑌 𐐿𐑉𐐱𐑅 𐑄𐐨𐑆 𐑀𐑉𐐩𐐻 𐐶𐐫𐐻𐐲𐑉𐑆. 𐐈𐑌𐐼 𐑄𐐲𐑅 𐑋𐐴 𐐺𐑉𐐯𐑄𐑉𐐯𐑌 𐐼𐐮𐐼 𐐿𐐱𐑋𐐹𐑊𐐩𐑌 𐐰𐑀𐐯𐑌𐑅𐐻 𐑋𐐨, 𐐰𐑌𐐼 𐐶𐐲𐑉 𐐼𐐯𐑆𐐴𐑉𐐲𐑅 𐑄𐐰𐐻 𐑄𐐩 𐑋𐐴𐐻 𐑌𐐱𐐻 𐑊𐐩𐐺𐐲𐑉, 𐑁𐐫𐑉 𐑄𐐩 𐐼𐐮𐐼 𐑌𐐱𐐻 𐐺𐐨𐑊𐐨𐑂 𐑄𐐰𐐻 𐐌 𐐿𐐳𐐼 𐐺𐐮𐑊𐐼 𐐩 𐑇𐐮𐐹; 𐑌𐐨𐑄𐐲𐑉 𐐶𐐳𐐼 𐑄𐐩 𐐺𐐨𐑊𐐨𐑂 𐑄𐐰𐐻 𐐌 𐐶𐐱𐑆 𐐮𐑌𐑅𐐻𐑉𐐲𐐿𐐻𐐯𐐼 𐐱𐑂 𐑄 𐐢𐐫𐑉𐐼.

23. 𐐈𐑌𐐼 𐑌𐐵 𐐮𐐻 𐐿𐐩𐑋 𐐻𐐭 𐐹𐐰𐑅 𐑄𐐰𐐻 𐐌, 𐐤𐐨𐑁𐐴, 𐐶𐐱𐑆 𐐯𐐿𐑅𐐨𐐼𐐮𐑍𐑊𐐨 𐑅𐐱𐑉𐐬𐑁𐐳𐑊 𐐺𐐨𐐿𐐫𐑆 𐐱𐑂 𐑄 𐐸𐐪𐑉𐐼𐑌𐐯𐑅 𐐱𐑂 𐑄𐐯𐑉 𐐸𐐪𐑉𐐻𐑅; 𐐰𐑌𐐼 𐑌𐐵 𐐸𐐶𐐯𐑌 𐑄𐐩 𐑅𐐫 𐑄𐐰𐐻 𐐌 𐐺𐐨𐑀𐐰𐑌 𐐻𐐭 𐐺𐐨 𐑅𐐱𐑉𐐬𐑁𐐳𐑊, 𐑄𐐩 𐐶𐐲𐑉 𐑀𐑊𐐰𐐼 𐐮𐑌 𐑄𐐯𐑉 𐐸𐐪𐑉𐐻𐑅, 𐐮𐑌𐑅𐐬𐑋𐐲𐐽 𐑄𐐰𐐻 𐑄𐐩 𐐼𐐮𐐼 𐑉𐐨𐐾𐑎𐑅 𐐬𐑂𐐲𐑉 𐑋𐐨, 𐑅𐐩𐐮𐑍, 𐐎𐐨 𐑌𐐭 𐑄𐐰𐐻 𐐷𐐨 𐐿𐐳𐐼 𐑌𐐱𐐻 𐐿𐐱𐑌𐑅𐐻𐑉𐐲𐐿𐐻 𐐩 𐑇𐐮𐐹, 𐑁𐐫𐑉 𐐶𐐨 𐑌𐐭 𐑄𐐰𐐻 𐐷𐐨 𐐶𐐲𐑉 𐑊𐐰𐐿𐐮𐑍 𐐮𐑌 𐐾𐐲𐐾𐑋𐐯𐑌𐐻; 𐐸𐐶𐐯𐑉𐑁𐐬𐑉, 𐑄𐐵 𐐿𐐰𐑌𐑅𐐻 𐑌𐐱𐐻 𐐰𐐿𐐱𐑋𐐹𐑊𐐮𐑇 𐑅𐐬 𐑀𐑉𐐩𐐻 𐐩 𐐶𐐲𐑉𐐿; 𐐰𐑌𐐼 𐑄𐐵 𐐪𐑉𐐻 𐑊𐐴𐐿 𐐲𐑌𐐻𐐭 𐐵𐑉 𐑁𐐪𐑄𐐲𐑉, 𐑊𐐯𐐼 𐐰𐐶𐐩 𐐺𐐴 𐑄 𐑁𐐭𐑊𐐮𐑇 𐐮𐑋𐐰𐐾𐐮𐑌𐐩𐑇𐐲𐑌𐑆 𐐱𐑂 𐐸𐐮𐑆 𐐸𐐪𐑉𐐻; 𐐷𐐩, 𐐸𐐨 𐐸𐐰𐑃 𐑊𐐯𐐼 𐐲𐑅 𐐵𐐻 𐐱𐑂 𐑄 𐑊𐐰𐑌𐐼 𐐱𐑂 𐐖𐐭𐑉𐐭𐑅𐐲𐑊𐐯𐑋, 𐐰𐑌𐐼 𐐶𐐨 𐐸𐐰𐑂 𐐶𐐱𐑌𐐼𐐲𐑉𐐼 𐐮𐑌 𐑄 𐐶𐐮𐑊𐐼𐐲𐑉𐑌𐐯𐑅 𐑁𐐫𐑉 𐑄𐐨𐑆 𐑋𐐯𐑌𐐨 𐐷𐐨𐑉𐑆; 𐐰𐑌𐐼 𐐵𐑉 𐐶𐐮𐑋𐐯𐑌 𐐸𐐰𐑂 𐐻𐑎𐑊𐐼, 𐐺𐐨𐐮𐑍 𐐺𐐮𐑀 𐐶𐐮𐑄 𐐽𐐴𐑊𐐼; 𐐰𐑌𐐼 𐑄𐐩 𐐸𐐰𐑂 𐐺𐐬𐑉𐑌 𐐽𐐮𐑊𐐼𐑉𐐯𐑌 𐐮𐑌 𐑄 𐐶𐐮𐑊𐐼𐐲𐑉𐑌𐐯𐑅, 𐐰𐑌𐐼 𐑅𐐲𐑁𐐲𐑉𐐼 𐐫𐑊 𐑃𐐮𐑍𐑆, 𐑅𐐩𐑂 𐐮𐐻 𐐶𐐲𐑉 𐐼𐐯𐑃; 𐐰𐑌𐐼 𐐮𐐻 𐐶𐐳𐐼 𐐸𐐰𐑂 𐐺𐐮𐑌 𐐺𐐯𐐻𐐲𐑉 𐑄𐐰𐐻 𐑄𐐩 𐐸𐐰𐐼 𐐼𐐴𐐼 𐐺𐐨𐑁𐐬𐑉 𐑄𐐩 𐐿𐐩𐑋 𐐵𐐻 𐐱𐑂 𐐖𐐭𐑉𐐭𐑅𐐲𐑊𐐯𐑋, 𐑄𐐰𐑌 𐐻𐐭 𐐸𐐰𐑂 𐑅𐐲𐑁𐐲𐑉𐐼 𐑄𐐨𐑆 𐐰𐑁𐑊𐐮𐐿𐑇𐐲𐑌𐑆. 𐐒𐐨𐐸𐐬𐑊𐐼, 𐑄𐐨𐑆 𐑋𐐯𐑌𐐨 𐐷𐐨𐑉𐑆 𐐶𐐨 𐐸𐐰𐑂 𐑅𐐲𐑁𐐲𐑉𐐼 𐐮𐑌 𐑄 𐐶𐐮𐑊𐐼𐐲𐑉𐑌𐐯𐑅, 𐐸𐐶𐐮𐐽 𐐻𐐴𐑋 𐐶𐐨 𐑋𐐴𐐻 𐐸𐐰𐑂 𐐯𐑌𐐾𐑎𐐼 𐐵𐑉 𐐹𐐱𐑆𐐯𐑇𐐲𐑌𐑆 𐐰𐑌𐐼 𐑄 𐑊𐐰𐑌𐐼 𐐱𐑂 𐐵𐑉 𐐮𐑌𐐸𐐯𐑉𐐮𐐻𐐰𐑌𐑅; 𐐷𐐩, 𐐰𐑌𐐼 𐐶𐐨 𐑋𐐴𐐻 𐐸𐐰𐑂 𐐺𐐮𐑌 𐐸𐐰𐐹𐐨. 𐐈𐑌𐐼 𐐶𐐨 𐑌𐐬 𐑄𐐰𐐻 𐑄 𐐹𐐨𐐹𐐲𐑊 𐐸𐐭 𐐶𐐲𐑉 𐐮𐑌 𐑄 𐑊𐐰𐑌𐐼 𐐱𐑂 𐐖𐐭𐑉𐐭𐑅𐐲𐑊𐐯𐑋 𐐶𐐲𐑉 𐐩 𐑉𐐴𐐽𐐲𐑅 𐐹𐐨𐐹𐐲𐑊; 𐑁𐐫𐑉 𐑄𐐩 𐐿𐐯𐐹𐐻 𐑄 𐑅𐐻𐐰𐐽𐐭𐐻𐑅 𐐰𐑌𐐼 𐐾𐐲𐐾𐑋𐐯𐑌𐐻𐑅 𐐱𐑂 𐑄 𐐢𐐫𐑉𐐼, 𐐰𐑌𐐼 𐐫𐑊 𐐸𐐮𐑆 𐐿𐐱𐑋𐐰𐑌𐐼𐑋𐐯𐑌𐐻𐑅, 𐐰𐐿𐐫𐑉𐐼𐐮𐑍 𐐻𐐭 𐑄 𐑊𐐫 𐐱𐑂 𐐣𐐬𐑆𐐯𐑆; 𐐸𐐶𐐯𐑉𐑁𐐬𐑉, 𐐶𐐨 𐑌𐐬 𐑄𐐰𐐻 𐑄𐐩 𐐪𐑉 𐐩 𐑉𐐴𐐽𐐲𐑅 𐐹𐐨𐐹𐐲𐑊; 𐐰𐑌𐐼 𐐵𐑉 𐑁𐐪𐑄𐐲𐑉 𐐸𐐰𐑃 𐐾𐐲𐐾𐐼 𐑄𐐯𐑋, 𐐰𐑌𐐼 𐐸𐐰𐑃 𐑊𐐯𐐼 𐐲𐑅 𐐰𐐶𐐩 𐐺𐐨𐐿𐐫𐑆 𐐶𐐨 𐐶𐐳𐐼 𐐸𐐪𐑉𐐿𐐯𐑌 𐐲𐑌𐐻𐐭 𐐸𐐮𐑆 𐐶𐐲𐑉𐐼𐑆; 𐐷𐐩, 𐐰𐑌𐐼 𐐵𐑉 𐐺𐑉𐐲𐑄𐐲𐑉 𐐮𐑆 𐑊𐐴𐐿 𐐲𐑌𐐻𐐭 𐐸𐐮𐑋. 𐐈𐑌𐐼 𐐰𐑁𐐻𐐲𐑉 𐑄𐐮𐑅 𐑋𐐰𐑌𐐲𐑉 𐐱𐑂 𐑊𐐰𐑍𐑀𐐶𐐩𐐾 𐐼𐐮𐐼 𐑋𐐴 𐐺𐑉𐐯𐑄𐑉𐐯𐑌 𐑋𐐲𐑉𐑋𐐲𐑉 𐐰𐑌𐐼 𐐿𐐱𐑋𐐹𐑊𐐩𐑌 𐐰𐑀𐐯𐑌𐑅𐐻 𐐲𐑅.

24. 𐐈𐑌𐐼 𐐮𐐻 𐐿𐐩𐑋 𐐻𐐭 𐐹𐐰𐑅 𐑄𐐰𐐻 𐐌, 𐐤𐐨𐑁𐐴, 𐑅𐐹𐐩𐐿 𐐲𐑌𐐻𐐭 𐑄𐐯𐑋, 𐑅𐐩𐐮𐑍, 𐐔𐐭 𐐷𐐨 𐐺𐐨𐑊𐐨𐑂 𐑄𐐰𐐻 𐐵𐑉 𐑁𐐪𐑄𐐲𐑉𐑆, 𐐸𐐭 𐐶𐐲𐑉 𐑄 𐐽𐐮𐑊𐐼𐑉𐐯𐑌 𐐱𐑂 𐐆𐑆𐑉𐐩𐐯𐑊, 𐐶𐐳𐐼 𐐸𐐰𐑂 𐐺𐐮𐑌 𐑊𐐯𐐼 𐐰𐐶𐐩 𐐵𐐻 𐐱𐑂 𐑄 𐐸𐐰𐑌𐐼𐑆 𐐱𐑂 𐑄 𐐀𐐾𐐮𐐹𐑇𐐲𐑌𐑆, 𐐮𐑁 𐑄𐐩 𐐸𐐰𐐼 𐑌𐐱𐐻 𐐸𐐪𐑉𐐿𐐯𐑌𐐼 𐐲𐑌𐐻𐐭 𐑄 𐐶𐐲𐑉𐐼𐑆 𐐱𐑂 𐑄 𐐢𐐫𐑉𐐼? 𐐏𐐩, 𐐼𐐭 𐐷𐐨 𐑅𐐲𐐹𐐬𐑆 𐑄𐐰𐐻 𐑄𐐩 𐐶𐐳𐐼 𐐸𐐰𐑂 𐐺𐐮𐑌 𐑊𐐯𐐼 𐐵𐐻 𐐱𐑂 𐐺𐐱𐑌𐐼𐐩𐐾, 𐐮𐑁 𐑄 𐐢𐐫𐑉𐐼 𐐸𐐰𐐼 𐑌𐐱𐐻 𐐿𐐱𐑋𐐰𐑌𐐼𐐯𐐼 𐐣𐐬𐑆𐐯𐑆 𐑄𐐰𐐻 𐐸𐐨 𐑇𐐳𐐼 𐑊𐐨𐐼 𐑄𐐯𐑋 𐐵𐐻 𐐱𐑂 𐐺𐐱𐑌𐐼𐐩𐐾? 𐐤𐐵, 𐐷𐐨 𐑌𐐬 𐑄𐐰𐐻 𐑄 𐐽𐐮𐑊𐐼𐑉𐐯𐑌 𐐱𐑂 𐐆𐑆𐑉𐐩𐐯𐑊 𐐶𐐲𐑉 𐐮𐑌 𐐺𐐱𐑌𐐼𐐩𐐾; 𐐰𐑌𐐼 𐐷𐐨 𐑌𐐬 𐑄𐐰𐐻 𐑄𐐩 𐐶𐐲𐑉 𐑊𐐩𐐼𐐯𐑌 𐐶𐐮𐑄 𐐻𐐰𐑅𐐿𐑅, 𐐸𐐶𐐮𐐽 𐐶𐐲𐑉 𐑀𐑉𐐨𐑂𐐲𐑅 𐐻𐐭 𐐺𐐨 𐐺𐐬𐑉𐑌; 𐐸𐐶𐐯𐑉𐑁𐐬𐑉, 𐐷𐐨 𐑌𐐬 𐑄𐐰𐐻 𐐮𐐻 𐑋𐐲𐑅𐐻 𐑌𐐨𐐼𐑆 𐐺𐐨 𐐩 𐑀𐐳𐐼 𐑃𐐮𐑍 𐑁𐐫𐑉 𐑄𐐯𐑋, 𐑄𐐰𐐻 𐑄𐐩 𐑇𐐳𐐼 𐐺𐐨 𐐺𐑉𐐫𐐻 𐐵𐐻 𐐱𐑂 𐐺𐐱𐑌𐐼𐐩𐐾. 𐐤𐐵, 𐐷𐐨 𐑌𐐬 𐑄𐐰𐐻 𐐣𐐬𐑆𐐯𐑆 𐐶𐐱𐑆 𐐿𐐱𐑋𐐰𐑌𐐼𐐯𐐼 𐐱𐑂 𐑄 𐐢𐐫𐑉𐐼 𐐻𐐭 𐐼𐐭 𐑄𐐰𐐻 𐑀𐑉𐐩𐐻 𐐶𐐲𐑉𐐿; 𐐰𐑌𐐼 𐐷𐐨 𐑌𐐬 𐑄𐐰𐐻 𐐺𐐴 𐐸𐐮𐑆 𐐶𐐲𐑉𐐼 𐑄 𐐶𐐫𐐻𐐲𐑉𐑆 𐐱𐑂 𐑄 𐐡𐐯𐐼 𐐝𐐨 𐐶𐐲𐑉 𐐼𐐮𐑂𐐴𐐼𐐯𐐼 𐐸𐐮𐑄𐐲𐑉 𐐰𐑌𐐼 𐑄𐐮𐑄𐐲𐑉, 𐐰𐑌𐐼 𐑄𐐩 𐐹𐐰𐑅𐐻 𐑃𐑉𐐭 𐐱𐑌 𐐼𐑉𐐴 𐑀𐑉𐐵𐑌𐐼. 𐐒𐐲𐐻 𐐷𐐨 𐑌𐐬 𐑄𐐰𐐻 𐑄 𐐀𐐾𐐮𐐹𐑇𐐲𐑌𐑆 𐐶𐐲𐑉 𐐼𐑉𐐵𐑌𐐼 𐐮𐑌 𐑄 𐐡𐐯𐐼 𐐝𐐨, 𐐸𐐭 𐐶𐐲𐑉 𐑄 𐐪𐑉𐑋𐐨𐑆 𐐱𐑂 𐐙𐐩𐑉𐐬; 𐐰𐑌𐐼 𐐷𐐨 𐐫𐑊𐑅𐐬 𐑌𐐬 𐑄𐐰𐐻 𐑄𐐩 𐐶𐐲𐑉 𐑁𐐯𐐼 𐐶𐐮𐑄 𐑋𐐰𐑌𐐰 𐐮𐑌 𐑄 𐐶𐐮𐑊𐐼𐐲𐑉𐑌𐐯𐑅; 𐐷𐐩, 𐐰𐑌𐐼 𐐷𐐨 𐐫𐑊𐑅𐐬 𐑌𐐬 𐑄𐐰𐐻 𐐣𐐬𐑆𐐯𐑆, 𐐺𐐴 𐐸𐐮𐑆 𐐶𐐲𐑉𐐼 𐐰𐐿𐐫𐑉𐐼𐐮𐑍 𐐻𐐭 𐑄 𐐹𐐵𐐲𐑉 𐐱𐑂 𐐘𐐱𐐼 𐐸𐐶𐐮𐐽 𐐶𐐱𐑆 𐐮𐑌 𐐸𐐮𐑋, 𐑅𐑋𐐬𐐻 𐑄 𐑉𐐱𐐿, 𐐰𐑌𐐼 𐑄𐐯𐑉 𐐿𐐩𐑋 𐑁𐐬𐑉𐑃 𐐶𐐫𐐻𐐲𐑉, 𐑄𐐰𐐻 𐑄 𐐽𐐮𐑊𐐼𐑉𐐯𐑌 𐐱𐑂 𐐆𐑆𐑉𐐩𐐯𐑊 𐑋𐐴𐐻 𐐿𐐶𐐯𐑌𐐽 𐑄𐐯𐑉 𐑃𐐲𐑉𐑅𐐻; 𐐰𐑌𐐼 𐑌𐐱𐐻𐐶𐐮𐑄𐑅𐐻𐐰𐑌𐐼𐐮𐑍 𐑄𐐩 𐐺𐐨𐐮𐑍 𐑊𐐯𐐼, 𐑄 𐐢𐐫𐑉𐐼 𐑄𐐯𐑉 𐐘𐐱𐐼, 𐑄𐐯𐑉 𐐡𐐨𐐼𐐨𐑋𐐲𐑉, 𐑀𐐬𐐮𐑍 𐐺𐐨𐑁𐐬𐑉 𐑄𐐯𐑋, 𐑊𐐨𐐼𐐮𐑍 𐑄𐐯𐑋 𐐺𐐴 𐐼𐐩 𐐰𐑌𐐼 𐑀𐐮𐑂𐐮𐑍 𐑊𐐴𐐻 𐐲𐑌𐐻𐐭 𐑄𐐯𐑋 𐐺𐐴 𐑌𐐴𐐻, 𐐰𐑌𐐼

𐐼𐐭𐐮𐑍 𐐫𐑊 𐑃𐐮𐑍𐑆 𐑁𐐫𐑉 𐑄𐐯𐑋 𐐸𐐶𐐮𐐽 𐐶𐐲𐑉 𐐯𐐿𐑅𐐹𐐨𐐼𐐨𐐯𐑌𐐻 𐑁𐐫𐑉 𐑋𐐰𐑌 𐐻𐐭 𐑉𐐨𐑅𐐨𐑂, 𐑄𐐩 𐐸𐐪𐑉𐐼𐑌𐐼 𐑄𐐯𐑉 𐐸𐐪𐑉𐐻𐑅, 𐐰𐑌𐐼 𐐺𐑊𐐴𐑌𐐼𐐯𐐼 𐑄𐐯𐑉 𐑋𐐴𐑌𐐼𐑆, 𐐰𐑌𐐼 𐑉𐐨𐑂𐐴𐑊𐐼 𐐰𐑀𐐯𐑌𐑅𐐻 𐐣𐐬𐑆𐐯𐑆 𐐰𐑌𐐼 𐐰𐑀𐐯𐑌𐑅𐐻 𐑄 𐐻𐑉𐐭 𐐰𐑌𐐼 𐑊𐐮𐑂𐐮𐑍 𐐘𐐱𐐼.

25. 𐐈𐑌𐐼 𐐮𐐻 𐐿𐐩𐑋 𐐻𐐭 𐐹𐐰𐑅 𐑄𐐰𐐻 𐐰𐐿𐐫𐑉𐐼𐐮𐑍 𐐻𐐭 𐐸𐐮𐑆 𐐶𐐲𐑉𐐼, 𐐸𐐨 𐐼𐐮𐐼 𐐼𐐯𐑅𐐻𐑉𐐫𐐮 𐑄𐐯𐑋; 𐐰𐑌𐐼 𐐰𐐿𐐫𐑉𐐼𐐮𐑍 𐐻𐐭 𐐸𐐮𐑆 𐐶𐐲𐑉𐐼, 𐐸𐐨 𐐼𐐮𐐼 𐑊𐐨𐐼 𐑄𐐯𐑋; 𐐰𐑌𐐼 𐐰𐐿𐐫𐑉𐐼𐐮𐑍 𐐻𐐭 𐐸𐐮𐑆 𐐶𐐲𐑉𐐼 𐐸𐐨 𐐼𐐮𐐼 𐐼𐐭 𐐫𐑊 𐑃𐐮𐑍𐑆 𐑁𐐫𐑉 𐑄𐐯𐑋: 𐐰𐑌𐐼 𐑄𐐯𐑉 𐐶𐐱𐑆 𐑌𐐱𐐻 𐐯𐑌𐐨 𐑃𐐮𐑍 𐐼𐐲𐑌, 𐑅𐐩𐑂 𐐮𐐻 𐐶𐐲𐑉 𐐺𐐴 𐐸𐐮𐑆 𐐶𐐲𐑉𐐼. 𐐈𐑌𐐼 𐐰𐑁𐐻𐐲𐑉 𐑄𐐩 𐐸𐐰𐐼 𐐿𐑉𐐫𐑅𐐻 𐑄 𐑉𐐮𐑂𐐲𐑉 𐐖𐐫𐑉𐐼𐐲𐑌, 𐐸𐐨 𐐼𐐮𐐼 𐑋𐐩𐐿 𐑄𐐯𐑋 𐑋𐐴𐐻𐐨 𐐲𐑌𐐻𐐭 𐑄 𐐼𐑉𐐴𐑂𐐮𐑍 𐐵𐐻 𐐱𐑂 𐑄 𐐽𐐮𐑊𐐼𐑉𐐯𐑌 𐐱𐑂 𐑄 𐑊𐐰𐑌𐐼, 𐐷𐐩, 𐐲𐑌𐐻𐐭 𐑄 𐑅𐐿𐐰𐐻𐐲𐑉𐐮𐑍 𐑄𐐯𐑋 𐐻𐐭 𐐼𐐯𐑅𐐻𐑉𐐲𐐿𐑇𐐲𐑌. 𐐈𐑌𐐼 𐑌𐐵 𐐼𐐭 𐐷 𐑅𐐲𐐹𐐬𐑆 𐑄𐐰𐐻 𐑄 𐐽𐐮𐑊𐐼𐑉𐐯𐑌 𐐱𐑂 𐑄𐐮𐑅 𐑊𐐰𐑌𐐼, 𐐸𐐭 𐐶𐐲𐑉 𐐮𐑌 𐑄 𐑊𐐰𐑌𐐼 𐐱𐑂 𐐹𐑉𐐱𐑋𐐮𐑅, 𐐸𐐭 𐐶𐐲𐑉 𐐼𐑉𐐮𐑂𐐲𐑌 𐐵𐐻 𐐺𐐴 𐐵𐑉 𐑁𐐪𐑄𐐲𐑉𐑆, 𐐼𐐭 𐐷 𐑅𐐲𐐹𐐬𐑆 𐑄𐐰𐐻 𐑄𐐩 𐐶𐐲𐑉 𐑉𐐴𐐽𐐲𐑅? 𐐒𐐨𐐸𐐬𐑊𐐼, 𐐌 𐑅𐐩 𐐲𐑌𐐻𐐭 𐐷𐐭, 𐑌𐐩. 𐐔𐐭 𐐷 𐑅𐐲𐐹𐐬𐑆 𐑄𐐰𐐻 𐐵𐑉 𐑁𐐪𐑄𐐲𐑉𐑆 𐐶𐐳𐐼 𐐸𐐰𐑂 𐐺𐐮𐑌 𐑋𐐬𐑉 𐐽𐐫𐐮𐑅 𐑄𐐰𐑌 𐑄𐐩, 𐐮𐑁 𐑄𐐩 𐐸𐐰𐐼 𐐺𐐮𐑌 𐑉𐐴𐐽𐐲𐑅? 𐐌 𐑅𐐩 𐐲𐑌𐐻𐐭 𐐷𐐭, 𐑌𐐩; 𐐺𐐨𐐸𐐬𐑊𐐼, 𐑄 𐐢𐐫𐑉𐐼 𐐯𐑅𐐻𐐨𐑋𐐯𐑃 𐐫𐑊 𐑁𐑊𐐯𐑇 𐐮𐑌 𐐶𐐲𐑌: 𐐸𐐨 𐑄𐐰𐐻 𐐮𐑆 𐑉𐐴𐐽𐐲𐑅 𐐮𐑆 𐑁𐐩𐑂𐐲𐑉𐐼 𐐱𐑂 𐐘𐐱𐐼. 𐐒𐐲𐐻 𐐺𐐨𐐸𐐬𐑊𐐼, 𐑄𐐮𐑅 𐐹𐐨𐐹𐑊 𐐸𐐰𐐼 𐑉𐐨𐐾𐐯𐐿𐐻𐐯𐐼 𐐯𐑂𐐲𐑉𐐨 𐐶𐐲𐑉𐐼 𐐱𐑂 𐐘𐐱𐐼, 𐐰𐑌𐐼 𐑄𐐩 𐐶𐐲𐑉 𐑉𐐴𐐹 𐐮𐑌 𐐮𐑌𐐮𐐿𐐶𐐮𐐻𐐨; 𐐰𐑌𐐼 𐑄 𐑁𐐳𐑊𐑌𐐯𐑅 𐐱𐑂 𐑄 𐑉𐐪𐑃 𐐱𐑂 𐐘𐐱𐐼 𐐶𐐱𐑆 𐐲𐐹𐐱𐑌 𐑄𐐯𐑋; 𐐰𐑌𐐼 𐑄 𐐢𐐫𐑉𐐼 𐐼𐐮𐐼 𐐿𐐲𐑉𐑅 𐑄 𐑊𐐰𐑌𐐼 𐐰𐑀𐐯𐑌𐑅𐐻 𐑄𐐯𐑋, 𐐰𐑌𐐼 𐐺𐑊𐐯𐑅 𐐮𐐻 𐐲𐑌𐐻𐐭 𐐵𐑉 𐑁𐐪𐑄𐐲𐑉𐑆; 𐐷𐐩, 𐐸𐐨 𐐼𐐮𐐼 𐐿𐐲𐑉𐑅 𐐮𐐻 𐐰𐑀𐐯𐑌𐑅𐐻 𐑄𐐯𐑋 𐐲𐑌𐐻𐐭 𐑄𐐯𐑉 𐐼𐐯𐑅𐐻𐑉𐐲𐐿𐑇𐐲𐑌; 𐐰𐑌𐐼 𐐸𐐨 𐐼𐐮𐐼 𐐺𐑊𐐯𐑅 𐐮𐐻 𐐲𐑌𐐻𐐭 𐐵𐑉 𐑁𐐪𐑄𐐲𐑉𐑆, 𐐲𐑌𐐻𐐭 𐑄𐐯𐑉 𐐱𐐺𐐻𐐩𐑌𐐮𐑍 𐐹𐐵𐑉 𐐬𐑂𐐲𐑉 𐐮𐐻. 𐐒𐐨𐐸𐐬𐑊𐐼, 𐑄 𐐢𐐫𐑉𐐼 𐐸𐐰𐑃 𐐿𐑉𐐨𐐩𐐻𐐯𐐼 𐑄 𐐲𐑉𐑃 𐑄𐐰𐐻 𐐮𐐻 𐑇𐐳𐐼 𐐺 𐐮𐑌𐐸𐐰𐐺𐐮𐐻𐐯𐐼: 𐐰𐑌𐐼 𐐸𐐨 𐐸𐐰𐑃 𐐿𐑉𐐨𐐩𐐻𐐯𐐼 𐐸𐐮𐑆 𐐽𐐮𐑊𐐼𐑉𐐯𐑌, 𐑄𐐰𐐻 𐑄𐐩 𐑇𐐳𐐼 𐐹𐐲𐑆𐐯𐑅 𐐮𐐻. 𐐈𐑌𐐼 𐐸𐐨 𐑉𐐩𐑆𐐯𐑃 𐐲𐐹 𐐲 𐑉𐐴𐐽𐐲𐑅 𐑌𐐩𐑇𐐲𐑌, 𐐰𐑌𐐼 𐐼𐐯𐑅𐐻𐑉𐐫𐐮𐐯𐑃 𐑄 𐑌𐐩𐑇𐐲𐑌𐑆 𐐱𐑂 𐑄 𐐶𐐮𐐿𐐯𐐼. 𐐈𐑌𐐼 𐐸𐐨 𐑊𐐨𐐼𐐯𐑃 𐐰𐐶𐐩 𐑄 𐑉𐐴𐐽𐐲𐑅 𐐮𐑌𐐻𐐭 𐐹𐑉𐐯𐑇𐐲𐑅 𐑊𐐰𐑌𐐼𐑆, 𐐰𐑌𐐼 𐑄 𐐶𐐮𐐿𐐯𐐼 𐐸𐐨 𐐼𐐯𐑅𐐻𐑉𐐫𐐮𐐯𐑃, 𐐰𐑌𐐼 𐐿𐐲𐑉𐑅𐐯𐑃 𐑄 𐑊𐐰𐑌𐐼 𐐲𐑌𐐻𐐭 𐑄𐐯𐑋 𐑁𐐫𐑉 𐑄𐐯𐑉 𐑅𐐩𐐿𐑅. 𐐐𐐨 𐑉𐐭𐑊𐐯𐑃 𐐸𐐴 𐐮𐑌 𐑄 𐐸𐐯𐑂𐐯𐑌𐑆, 𐑁𐐫𐑉 𐐮𐐻 𐐮𐑆 𐐸𐐮𐑆 𐑃𐑉𐐬𐑌, 𐐰𐑌𐐼 𐑄𐐮𐑅 𐐲𐑉𐑃 𐐮𐑆 𐐸𐐮𐑆 𐑁𐐳𐐻𐑅𐐻𐐭𐑊. 𐐈𐑌𐐼 𐐸𐐨 𐑊𐐲𐑂𐐯𐑃 𐑄𐐬𐑆 𐐸𐐭 𐐶𐐮𐑊 𐐸𐐰𐑂 𐐸𐐮𐑋 𐐻𐐭 𐐺 𐑄𐐯𐑉 𐐘𐐱𐐼. 𐐒𐐨𐐸𐐬𐑊𐐼, 𐐸𐐨 𐑊𐐲𐑂𐐼 𐐵𐑉 𐑁𐐪𐑄𐐲𐑉𐑆! 𐐰𐑌𐐼 𐐸𐐨 𐐿𐐲𐑂𐐯𐑌𐐲𐑌𐐻𐐯𐐼 𐐶𐐮𐑄 𐑄𐐯𐑋, 𐐷𐐩, 𐐨𐑂𐑌 𐐁𐐺𐑉𐐲𐐸𐐰𐑋, 𐐌𐑆𐐲𐐿, 𐐰𐑌𐐼 𐐖𐐩𐐿𐐲𐐺: 𐐰𐑌𐐼 𐐸𐐨 𐑉𐐨𐑋𐐯𐑋𐐺𐐲𐑉𐐼 𐑄 𐐿𐐲𐑂𐐯𐑌𐐲𐑌𐐻𐑅 𐐸𐐶𐐮𐐽 𐐸𐐨 𐐸𐐰𐐼 𐑋𐐩𐐼; 𐐸𐐶𐐯𐑉𐑁𐐫𐑉, 𐐸𐐨 𐐼𐐮𐐼 𐐺𐑉𐐮𐑍 𐑄𐐯𐑋 𐐵𐐻 𐐱𐑂 𐑄 𐑊𐐰𐑌𐐼 𐐱𐑂 𐐀𐐾𐐮𐐹𐐻, 𐐰𐑌𐐼 𐐸𐐨 𐐼𐐮𐐼 𐑅𐐻𐑉𐐩𐐻𐑌 𐑄𐐯𐑋 𐐮𐑌 𐑄 𐐶𐐮𐑊𐐼𐐲𐑉𐑌𐐯𐑅 𐐶𐐮𐑄 𐐸𐐮𐑆 𐑉𐐱𐐼, 𐑁𐐫𐑉 𐑄𐐩 𐐸𐐪𐑉𐐼𐑌𐐼 𐑄𐐯𐑉 𐐸𐐪𐑉𐐻𐑅, 𐐨𐑂𐑌 𐐰𐑆 𐐷 𐐸𐐰𐑂; 𐐰𐑌𐐼 𐑄 𐐢𐐫𐑉𐐼 𐑅𐐻𐑉𐐩𐐻𐑌𐐼 𐑄𐐯𐑋 𐐺𐐨𐐿𐐫𐑆 𐐱𐑂 𐑄𐐯𐑉 𐐮𐑌𐐮𐐿𐐶𐐮𐐻𐐨. 𐐐𐐨 𐑅𐐯𐑌𐐻 𐑁𐐴𐐲𐑉𐐨-𐑁𐑊𐐴𐐮𐑍 𐑅𐐲𐑉𐐹𐐯𐑌𐐻𐑅 𐐰𐑋𐐲𐑍 𐑄𐐯𐑋; 𐐰𐑌𐐼 𐐰𐑁𐐻𐐲𐑉 𐑄𐐩 𐐶𐐲𐑉 𐐺𐐮𐐻𐑌, 𐐸𐐨 𐐹𐑉𐐨𐐹𐐩𐑉𐐼 𐐲 𐐶𐐩 𐑄𐐰𐐻 𐑄𐐩 𐑋𐐴𐐻 𐐺 𐐸𐐨𐑊𐐼: 𐐰𐑌𐐼 𐑄 𐑊𐐩𐐺𐐲𐑉 𐐸𐐶𐐮𐐽 𐑄𐐩 𐐸𐐰𐐼 𐐻𐐭 𐐹𐐲𐑉𐑁𐐫𐑉𐑋, 𐐶𐐱𐑆 𐐻𐐭 𐑊𐐳𐐿; 𐐰𐑌𐐼 𐐺𐐨𐐿𐐫𐑆 𐐱𐑂 𐑄 𐑅𐐮𐑋𐐹𐑊𐑌𐐯𐑅 𐐱𐑂 𐑄 𐐶𐐩, 𐐫𐑉 𐑄 𐐨𐑆𐐮𐑌𐐯𐑅 𐐱𐑂 𐐮𐐻, 𐑄𐐯𐑉 𐐶𐐲𐑉 𐑋𐐯𐑌𐐨 𐐸𐐭 𐐹𐐯𐑉𐐮𐑇𐐻. 𐐈𐑌𐐼 𐑄𐐩 𐐼𐐮𐐼 𐐸𐐪𐑉𐐼𐑌 𐑄𐐯𐑉 𐐸𐐪𐑉𐐻𐑅 𐑁𐑉𐐱𐑋 𐐻𐐴𐑋 𐐻𐐭 𐐻𐐴𐑋, 𐐰𐑌𐐼 𐑄𐐩 𐐼𐐮𐐼 𐑉𐐨𐑂𐐴𐑊 𐐰𐑀𐐯𐑌𐑅𐐻 𐐣𐐬𐑆𐐯𐑆, 𐐰𐑌𐐼 𐐫𐑊𐑅𐐬 𐐰𐑀𐐯𐑌𐑅𐐻 𐐘𐐱𐐼; 𐑌𐐯𐑂𐐲𐑉𐑄𐐲𐑊𐐯𐑅, 𐐷 𐑌𐐬 𐑄𐐰𐐻 𐑄𐐩 𐐶𐐲𐑉 𐑊𐐯𐐼 𐑁𐐫𐑉𐑃 𐐺𐐴 𐐸𐐮𐑆 𐑋𐐰𐐽𐑊𐐯𐑅 𐐹𐐵𐑉 𐐮𐑌𐐻𐐭 𐑄 𐑊𐐰𐑌𐐼 𐐱𐑂 𐐹𐑉𐐱𐑋𐐮𐑅.

26. 𐐈𐑌𐐼 𐑌𐐵, 𐐰𐑁𐐻𐐲𐑉 𐐫𐑊 𐑄𐐨𐑆 𐑃𐐮𐑍𐑆, 𐑄 𐐻𐐴𐑋 𐐸𐐰𐑆 𐐿𐐲𐑋 𐑄𐐰𐐻 𐑄𐐩 𐐸𐐰𐑂 𐐺𐐨𐐿𐐲𐑋 𐐶𐐮𐐿𐐯𐐼, 𐐷𐐩, 𐑌𐐨𐑉𐑊𐐨 𐐲𐑌𐐻𐐭 𐑉𐐴𐐹𐑌𐐯𐑅; 𐐰𐑌𐐼 𐐌 𐑌𐐬 𐑌𐐱𐐻, 𐐺𐐲𐐻 𐑄𐐩 𐐪𐑉 𐐰𐐻 𐑄𐐮𐑅 𐐼𐐩 𐐰𐐺𐐵𐐻 𐐻𐐭 𐐺 𐐼𐐯𐑅𐐻𐑉𐐫𐐮𐐼; 𐑁𐐫𐑉 𐐌 𐑌𐐬 𐑄𐐰𐐻 𐑄 𐐼𐐩 𐑋𐐲𐑅𐐻 𐑇𐐳𐑉𐑊𐐨 𐐿𐐲𐑋, 𐑄𐐰𐐻 𐑄𐐩 𐑋𐐲𐑅𐐻 𐐺 𐐼𐐯𐑅𐐻𐑉𐐫𐐮𐐼, 𐑅𐐩𐑂 𐐲 𐑁𐐷𐐭 𐐬𐑌𐑊𐐨, 𐐸𐐭 𐑇𐐰𐑊 𐐺 𐑊𐐯𐐼 𐐰𐐶𐐩 𐐮𐑌𐐻𐐭 𐐿𐐰𐐹𐐻𐐮𐑂𐐮𐐻𐐨; 𐐸𐐶𐐯𐑉𐑁𐐫𐑉, 𐑄 𐐢𐐫𐑉𐐼 𐐿𐐲𐑋𐐰𐑌𐐼𐐯𐐼 𐑋𐐴 𐑁𐐪𐑄𐐲𐑉 𐑄𐐰𐐻 𐐸𐐨 𐑇𐐳𐐼 𐐼𐐨𐐹𐐪𐑉𐐻 𐐮𐑌𐐻𐐭 𐑄 𐐶𐐮𐑊𐐼𐐲𐑉𐑌𐐯𐑅; 𐐰𐑌𐐼 𐑄 𐐖𐐭𐑆 𐐫𐑊𐑅𐐬 𐑅𐐫𐐻 𐐻𐐭 𐐻𐐩𐐿 𐐰𐐶𐐩 𐐸𐐮𐑆 𐑊𐐴𐑁; 𐐷𐐩, 𐐰𐑌𐐼 𐐷 𐐫𐑊𐑅𐐬 𐐸𐐰𐑂 𐑅𐐫𐐻 𐐻𐐭 𐐻𐐩𐐿 𐐰𐐶𐐩 𐐸𐐮𐑆 𐑊𐐴𐑁; 𐐸𐐶𐐯𐑉𐑁𐐫𐑉, 𐐷 𐐪𐑉 𐑋𐐲𐑉𐐼𐐲𐑉𐐲𐑉𐑆 𐐮𐑌 𐐷𐐬𐑉 𐐸𐐪𐑉𐐻𐑅, 𐐰𐑌𐐼 𐐷 𐐪𐑉 𐑊𐐴𐐿 𐐲𐑌𐐻𐐭 𐑄𐐯𐑋. 𐐏 𐐪𐑉 𐑅𐐶𐐮𐑁𐐻 𐐻𐐭 𐐼𐐭 𐐮𐑌𐐮𐐿𐐶𐐮𐐻𐐨, 𐐺𐐲𐐻 𐑅𐑊𐐬 𐐻𐐭 𐑉𐐨-

𐑋𐐯𐑋𐐺𐐲𐑉 𐑄 𐐢𐐫𐑉𐐼 𐐷𐐫𐑉 𐐘𐐱𐐼. 𐐏 𐐸𐐰𐑂 𐑅𐐨𐑌 𐐰𐑌 𐐩𐑌𐐾𐐯𐑊, 𐐰𐑌𐐼 𐐸𐐨 𐑅𐐹𐐩𐐿 𐐲𐑌𐐻𐐭 𐐷𐐭; 𐐷𐐩, 𐐷 𐐸𐐰𐑂 𐐸𐐲𐑉𐐼 𐐸𐐮𐑆 𐑂𐐱𐐮𐑅 𐑁𐑉𐐱𐑋 𐐻𐐴𐑋 𐐻𐐭 𐐻𐐴𐑋; 𐐰𐑌𐐼 𐐸𐐨 𐐸𐐰𐑃 𐑅𐐹𐐬𐐿𐑌 𐐲𐑌𐐻𐐭 𐐷𐐭 𐐮𐑌 𐐰 𐑅𐐻𐐮𐑊 𐑅𐑋𐐫𐑊 𐑂𐐱𐐮𐑅, 𐐺𐐲𐐻 𐐷 𐐶𐐲𐑉 𐐹𐐪𐑅𐐻 𐑁𐐨𐑊𐐮𐑍, 𐑄𐐰𐐻 𐐷 𐐿𐐳𐐼 𐑌𐐱𐐻 𐑁𐐨𐑊 𐐸𐐮𐑆 𐐶𐐲𐑉𐐼𐑆; 𐐸𐐶𐐯𐑉𐑁𐐫𐑉, 𐐸𐐨 𐐸𐐰𐑆 𐑅𐐹𐐬𐐿𐑌 𐐲𐑌𐐻𐐭 𐐷𐐭 𐑊𐐴𐐿 𐐲𐑌𐐻𐐭 𐑄 𐑂𐐱𐐮𐑅 𐐱𐑂 𐑃𐐲𐑌𐐼𐐲𐑉, 𐐸𐐶𐐮𐐽 𐐼𐐮𐐼 𐐿𐐫𐑆 𐑄 𐐲𐑉𐑃 𐐻𐐭 𐑇𐐩𐐿 𐐰𐑆 𐐮𐑁 𐐮𐐻 𐐶𐐲𐑉 𐐻𐐭 𐐼𐐮𐑂𐐴𐐼 𐐰𐑅𐐲𐑌𐐼𐐲𐑉. 𐐈𐑌𐐼 𐐷 𐐫𐑊𐑅𐐬 𐑌𐐬, 𐑄𐐰𐐻 𐐺𐐴 𐑄 𐐹𐐵𐑉 𐐱𐑂 𐐸𐐮𐑆 𐐫𐑊𐑋𐐴𐐻𐐮 𐐶𐐲𐑉𐐼, 𐐸𐐨 𐐿𐐰𐑌 𐐿𐐫𐑆 𐑄 𐐲𐑉𐑃 𐑄𐐰𐐻 𐐮𐐻 𐑇𐐰𐑊 𐐹𐐪𐑅 𐐰𐐶𐐩; 𐐷𐐩, 𐐰𐑌𐐼 𐐷 𐑌𐐬 𐑄𐐰𐐻 𐐺𐐴 𐐸𐐮𐑆 𐐶𐐲𐑉𐐼, 𐐸𐐨 𐐿𐐰𐑌 𐐿𐐫𐑆 𐑄 𐑉𐐲𐑁 𐐹𐑊𐐩𐑅𐐯𐑆 𐐻𐐭 𐐺 𐑋𐐩𐐼 𐑅𐑋𐐭𐑄, 𐐰𐑌𐐼 𐑅𐑋𐐭𐑄 𐐹𐑊𐐩𐑅𐐯𐑆 𐑇𐐰𐑊 𐐺 𐐺𐑉𐐬𐐿𐑌 𐐲𐐹. 𐐄, 𐑄𐐯𐑌, 𐐸𐐶𐐴 𐐮𐑆 𐐮𐐻, 𐑄𐐰𐐻 𐐷 𐐿𐐰𐑌 𐐺 𐑅𐐬 𐐸𐐪𐑉𐐼 𐐮𐑌 𐐷𐐫𐑉 𐐸𐐪𐑉𐐻𐑅? 𐐒𐐨𐐸𐐬𐑊𐐼, 𐑋𐐴 𐑅𐐬𐑊 𐐮𐑆 𐑉𐐯𐑌𐐻 𐐶𐐮𐑄 𐐰𐑍𐑀𐐶𐐮𐑇 𐐺𐐨𐐿𐐫𐑆 𐐱𐑂 𐐷𐐭, 𐐰𐑌𐐼 𐑋𐐴 𐐸𐐪𐑉𐐻 𐐮𐑆 𐐹𐐩𐑌𐐼: 𐐌 𐑁𐐨𐑉 𐑊𐐯𐑅𐐻 𐐷 𐑇𐐰𐑊 𐐺 𐐿𐐪𐑅𐐻 𐐱𐑁 𐑁𐐫𐑉 𐐯𐑂𐐲𐑉. 𐐒𐐨𐐸𐐬𐑊𐐼, 𐐌 𐐰𐑋 𐑁𐐳𐑊 𐐱𐑂 𐑄 𐐝𐐹𐐮𐑉𐐮𐐻 𐐱𐑂 𐐘𐐱𐐼, 𐐮𐑌𐑅𐐬𐑋𐐲𐐽 𐑄𐐰𐐻 𐑋𐐴 𐑁𐑉𐐩𐑋 𐐸𐐰𐑆 𐑌𐐬 𐑅𐐻𐑉𐐯𐑍𐑃.

27. 𐐈𐑌𐐼 𐑌𐐵 𐐮𐐻 𐐿𐐩𐑋 𐐻𐐭 𐐹𐐪𐑅 𐑄𐐰𐐻 𐐸𐐶𐐯𐑌 𐐌 𐐸𐐰𐐼 𐑅𐐹𐐬𐐿𐑌 𐑄𐐨𐑆 𐐶𐐲𐑉𐐼𐑆, 𐑄𐐩 𐐶𐐲𐑉 𐐰𐑍𐑀𐑉𐐨 𐐶𐐮𐑄 𐑋𐐨, 𐐰𐑌𐐼 𐐶𐐲𐑉 𐐼𐐨𐑆𐐴𐑉𐐲𐑅 𐐻𐐭 𐑃𐑉𐐬 𐑋𐐨 𐐮𐑌𐐻𐐭 𐑄 𐐼𐐯𐐹𐑃𐑅 𐐱𐑂 𐑄 𐑅𐐨; 𐐰𐑌𐐼 𐐰𐑆 𐑄𐐩 𐐿𐐩𐑋 𐑁𐐫𐑉𐑃 𐐻𐐭 𐑊𐐩 𐑄𐐩𐑉 𐐸𐐰𐑌𐐼𐑆 𐐲𐐹𐐱𐑌 𐑋𐐨, 𐐌 𐑅𐐹𐐩𐐿 𐐲𐑌𐐻𐐭 𐑄𐐯𐑋, 𐑅𐐩𐐮𐑍, 𐐮𐑌 𐑄 𐑌𐐩𐑋 𐐱𐑂 𐑄 𐐃𐑊𐑋𐐴𐐻𐐮 𐐘𐐱𐐼, 𐐌 𐐿𐐲𐑋𐐰𐑌𐐼 𐐷𐐭 𐑄𐐰𐐻 𐐷 𐐻𐐲𐐽 𐑋𐐨 𐑌𐐱𐐻, 𐑁𐐫𐑉 𐐌 𐐰𐑋 𐑁𐐮𐑊𐐼 𐐶𐐮𐑄 𐑄 𐐹𐐵𐑉 𐐱𐑂 𐐘𐐱𐐼, 𐐨𐑂𐐯𐑌 𐐲𐑌𐐻𐐭 𐑄 𐐿𐐲𐑌𐑅𐐮𐐭𐑋𐐮𐑍 𐐱𐑂 𐑋𐐴 𐑁𐑊𐐯𐑇; 𐐰𐑌𐐼 𐐸𐐭𐑅𐐬 𐑇𐐰𐑊 𐑊𐐩 𐐸𐐮𐑆 𐐸𐐰𐑌𐐼𐑆 𐐲𐐹𐐱𐑌 𐑋𐐨, 𐑇𐐰𐑊 𐐶𐐮𐑄𐐲𐑉 𐐨𐑂𐐯𐑌 𐐰𐑆 𐐰 𐐼𐑉𐐴𐐼 𐑉𐐨𐐼; 𐐰𐑌𐐼 𐐸𐐨 𐑇𐐰𐑊 𐐺 𐐰𐑆 𐑌𐐫𐐻 𐐺𐐨𐑁𐐬𐑉 𐑄 𐐹𐐵𐑉 𐐱𐑂 𐐘𐐱𐐼, 𐑁𐐫𐑉 𐐘𐐱𐐼 𐑇𐐰𐑊 𐑅𐑋𐐴𐐻 𐐸𐐮𐑋.

28. 𐐈𐑌𐐼 𐐮𐐻 𐐿𐐩𐑋 𐐻𐐭 𐐹𐐪𐑅 𐑄𐐰𐐻 𐐌, 𐐤𐐨𐑁𐐴, 𐑅𐐯𐐼 𐐲𐑌𐐻𐐭 𐑄𐐯𐑋, 𐑄𐐰𐐻 𐑄𐐩 𐑇𐐳𐐼 𐑋𐐲𐑉𐑋𐐲𐑉 𐑌𐐬 𐑋𐐬𐑉 𐐰𐑀𐐯𐑌𐑅𐐻 𐑄𐐩𐑉 𐑁𐐪𐑄𐐲𐑉; 𐑌𐐨𐑄𐐲𐑉 𐑇𐐳𐐼 𐑄𐐩 𐐶𐐮𐑄𐐸𐐬𐑊𐐼 𐑄𐐩𐑉 𐑊𐐩𐐺𐐲𐑉 𐑁𐑉𐐱𐑋 𐑋𐐨, 𐑁𐐫𐑉 𐐘𐐱𐐼 𐐸𐐰𐐼 𐐿𐐲𐑋𐐰𐑌𐐼𐐯𐐼 𐑋𐐨 𐑄𐐰𐐻 𐐌 𐑇𐐳𐐼 𐐺𐐮𐑊𐐼 𐐰 𐑇𐐮𐐹.

29. 𐐈𐑌𐐼 𐐌 𐑅𐐯𐐼 𐐲𐑌𐐻𐐭 𐑄𐐯𐑋, 𐐆𐑁 𐐘𐐱𐐼 𐐸𐐰𐐼 𐐿𐐲𐑋𐐰𐑌𐐼𐐯𐐼 𐑋𐐨 𐐻𐐭 𐐼𐐭 𐐫𐑊 𐑃𐐮𐑍𐑆, 𐐌 𐐿𐐳𐐼 𐐼𐐭 𐑄𐐯𐑋. 𐐆𐑁 𐐸𐐨 𐑇𐐳𐐼 𐐿𐐲𐑋𐐰𐑌𐐼 𐑋𐐨 𐑄𐐰𐐻 𐐌 𐑇𐐳𐐼 𐑅𐐩 𐐲𐑌𐐻𐐭 𐑄𐐮𐑅 𐐶𐐫𐐻𐐲𐑉, 𐐺 𐑄𐐵 𐐲𐑉𐑃, 𐐮𐐻 𐑇𐐳𐐼 𐐺 𐐲𐑉𐑃; 𐐰𐑌𐐼 𐐮𐑁 𐐌 𐑇𐐳𐐼 𐑅𐐩 𐐮𐐻, 𐐮𐐻 𐐶𐐳𐐼 𐐺 𐐼𐐲𐑌. 𐐈𐑌𐐼 𐑌𐐵, 𐐮𐑁 𐑄 𐐢𐐫𐑉𐐼 𐐸𐐰𐑆 𐑅𐐲𐐽 𐑀𐑉𐐩𐐻 𐐹𐐵𐑉, 𐐰𐑌𐐼 𐐸𐐰𐑆 𐑉𐐫𐐻 𐑅𐐬 𐑋𐐯𐑌𐐮 𐑋𐐮𐑉𐐰𐐿𐑊𐑆 𐐰𐑋𐐲𐑍 𐑄 𐐽𐐮𐑊𐐼𐑉𐐯𐑌 𐐱𐑂 𐑋𐐯𐑌, 𐐸𐐵 𐐮𐑆 𐐮𐐻 𐑄𐐰𐐻 𐐸𐐨 𐐿𐐰𐑌𐐱𐐻 𐐮𐑌𐑅𐐻𐑉𐐲𐐿𐐻 𐑋𐐨, 𐑄𐐰𐐻 𐐌 𐑇𐐳𐐼 𐐺𐐮𐑊𐐼 𐐰 𐑇𐐮𐐹?

30. 𐐈𐑌𐐼 𐐮𐐻 𐐿𐐩𐑋 𐐻𐐭 𐐹𐐪𐑅 𐑄𐐰𐐻 𐐌, 𐐤𐐨𐑁𐐴, 𐑅𐐯𐐼 𐑋𐐯𐑌𐐮 𐑃𐐮𐑍𐑆 𐐲𐑌𐐻𐐭 𐑋𐐴 𐐺𐑉𐐯𐑄𐑉𐐯𐑌, 𐐮𐑌𐑅𐐬𐑋𐐲𐐽 𐑄𐐰𐐻 𐑄𐐩 𐐶𐐲𐑉 𐐿𐐱𐑌𐑁𐐵𐑌𐐼𐐯𐐼, 𐐰𐑌𐐼 𐐿𐐳𐐼 𐑌𐐱𐐻 𐐿𐐱𐑌𐐻𐐯𐑌𐐼 𐐰𐑀𐐯𐑌𐑅𐐻 𐑋𐐨; 𐑌𐐨𐑄𐐲𐑉 𐐼𐐲𐑉𐑅𐐻 𐑄𐐩 𐑊𐐩 𐑄𐐩𐑉 𐐸𐐰𐑌𐐼𐑆 𐐲𐐹𐐱𐑌 𐑋𐐨, 𐑌𐐫𐑉 𐐻𐐲𐐽 𐑋𐐨 𐐶𐐮𐑄 𐑄𐐩𐑉 𐑁𐐮𐑍𐑀𐐲𐑉𐑆, 𐐨𐑂𐐯𐑌 𐑁𐐫𐑉 𐑄 𐑅𐐹𐐩𐑅 𐐱𐑂 𐑋𐐯𐑌𐐮 𐐼𐐩𐑆, 𐑌𐐵 𐑄𐐩 𐐼𐐲𐑉𐑅𐐻 𐑌𐐱𐐻 𐐼𐐭 𐑄𐐮𐑅, 𐑊𐐯𐑅𐐻 𐑄𐐩 𐑇𐐳𐐼 𐐶𐐮𐑄𐐲𐑉 𐐺𐐨𐑁𐐬𐑉 𐑋𐐨, 𐑅𐐬 𐐹𐐵𐑉𐑁𐐳𐑊 𐐶𐐱𐑆 𐑄 𐐝𐐹𐐮𐑉𐐮𐐻 𐐱𐑂 𐐘𐐱𐐼; 𐐰𐑌𐐼 𐑄𐐲𐑅 𐐮𐐻 𐐸𐐰𐐼 𐑉𐐫𐐻 𐐲𐐹𐐱𐑌 𐑄𐐯𐑋.

31. 𐐈𐑌𐐼 𐐮𐐻 𐐿𐐩𐑋 𐐻𐐭 𐐹𐐪𐑅 𐑄𐐰𐐻 𐑄 𐐢𐐫𐑉𐐼 𐑅𐐯𐐼 𐐲𐑌𐐻𐐭 𐑋𐐨, 𐐝𐐻𐑉𐐯𐐽 𐑁𐐫𐑉𐑃 𐑄𐐴𐑌 𐐸𐐰𐑌𐐼 𐐰𐑀𐐯𐑌 𐐲𐑌𐐻𐐭 𐑄𐐴 𐐺𐑉𐐯𐑄𐑉𐐯𐑌, 𐐰𐑌𐐼 𐑄𐐩 𐑇𐐰𐑊 𐑌𐐱𐐻 𐐶𐐮𐑄𐐲𐑉 𐐺𐐨𐑁𐐬𐑉 𐑄𐐨, 𐐺𐐲𐐻 𐐌 𐐶𐐮𐑊 𐑇𐐱𐐿 𐑄𐐯𐑋, 𐑅𐐯𐑃 𐑄 𐐢𐐫𐑉𐐼, 𐐰𐑌𐐼 𐑄𐐮𐑅 𐐶𐐮𐑊 𐐌 𐐼𐐭, 𐑄𐐰𐐻 𐑄𐐩 𐑋𐐩 𐑌𐐬 𐑄𐐰𐐻 𐐌 𐐰𐑋 𐑄 𐐢𐐫𐑉𐐼 𐑄𐐩𐑉 𐐘𐐱𐐼. 𐐈𐑌𐐼 𐐮𐐻 𐐿𐐩𐑋 𐐻𐐭 𐐹𐐪𐑅 𐑄𐐰𐐻 𐐌 𐑅𐐻𐑉𐐯𐐽𐐻 𐑁𐐫𐑉𐑃 𐑋𐐴 𐐸𐐰𐑌𐐼 𐐲𐑌𐐻𐐭 𐑋𐐴 𐐺𐑉𐐯𐑄𐑉𐐯𐑌, 𐐰𐑌𐐼 𐑄𐐩 𐐼𐐮𐐼 𐑌𐐱𐐻 𐐶𐐮𐑄𐐲𐑉 𐐺𐐨𐑁𐐬𐑉 𐑋𐐨; 𐐺𐐲𐐻 𐑄 𐐢𐐫𐑉𐐼 𐐼𐐮𐐼 𐑇𐐩𐐿 𐑄𐐯𐑋, 𐐨𐑂𐐯𐑌 𐐰𐐿𐐫𐑉𐐼𐐮𐑍 𐐻𐐭 𐑄 𐐶𐐲𐑉𐐼 𐐸𐐶𐐮𐐽 𐐸𐐨 𐐸𐐰𐐼 𐑅𐐹𐐬𐐿𐑌. 𐐈𐑌𐐼 𐑌𐐵, 𐑄𐐩 𐑅𐐯𐐼, 𐐎𐐨 𐑌𐐬 𐐱𐑂 𐐰 𐑇𐐭𐑉𐐮𐐻𐐮 𐑄𐐰𐐻 𐑄 𐐢𐐫𐑉𐐼 𐐮𐑆 𐐶𐐮𐑄 𐑄𐐨, 𐑁𐐫𐑉 𐐶𐐨 𐑌𐐬 𐑄𐐰𐐻 𐐮𐐻 𐐮𐑆 𐑄 𐐹𐐵𐑉 𐐱𐑂 𐑄 𐐢𐐫𐑉𐐼 𐑄𐐰𐐻 𐐸𐐰𐑆 𐑇𐐩𐐿𐑌 𐐲𐑅. 𐐈𐑌𐐼 𐑄𐐩 𐑁𐐯𐑊 𐐼𐐵𐑌 𐐺𐐨𐑁𐐬𐑉 𐑋𐐨, 𐐰𐑌𐐼 𐐶𐐲𐑉 𐐰𐐺𐐵𐐻 𐐻𐐭 𐐶𐐲𐑉𐑇𐐮𐐹 𐑋𐐨, 𐐺𐐲𐐻 𐐌 𐐶𐐳𐐼 𐑌𐐱𐐻 𐑅𐐲𐑁𐐲𐑉 𐑄𐐯𐑋, 𐑅𐐩𐐮𐑍, 𐐌 𐐰𐑋 𐑄𐐴 𐐺𐑉𐐲𐑄𐐲𐑉, 𐐷𐐩, 𐐨𐑂𐐯𐑌 𐑄𐐴 𐐷𐐲𐑍𐑀𐐲𐑉 𐐺𐑉𐐲𐑄𐐲𐑉; 𐐸𐐶𐐯𐑉𐑁𐐫𐑉 𐐶𐐲𐑉𐑇𐐮𐐹 𐑄 𐐢𐐫𐑉𐐼 𐑄𐐴 𐐘𐐱𐐼, 𐐰𐑌𐐼 𐐱𐑌𐐲𐑉 𐑄𐐴 𐑁𐐪𐑄𐐲𐑉 𐐰𐑌𐐼 𐑄𐐴 𐑋𐐲𐑄𐐲𐑉, 𐑄𐐰𐐻 𐑄𐐴 𐐼𐐩𐑆 𐑋𐐩 𐐺 𐑊𐐱𐑍 𐐮𐑌 𐑄 𐑊𐐰𐑌𐐼 𐐸𐐶𐐮𐐽 𐑄 𐐢𐐫𐑉𐐼 𐑄𐐴 𐐘𐐱𐐼 𐑇𐐰𐑊 𐑀𐐮𐑂 𐑄𐐨.

32. 𐐈𐑌𐐼 𐐮𐐻 𐐿𐐩𐑋 𐐻𐐭 𐐹𐐰𐑅 𐑄𐐰𐐻 𐑄𐐩 𐐼𐐮𐐼 𐐶𐐲𐑉𐑇𐐮𐐹 𐑄 𐐢𐐫𐑉𐐼, 𐐰𐑌𐐼 𐐼𐐮𐐼 𐑀𐐬 𐑁𐐬𐑉𐑃 𐐶𐐮𐑄 𐑋𐐨; 𐐰𐑌𐐼 𐐶𐐨 𐐼𐐮𐐼 𐐶𐐲𐑉𐐿 𐐻𐐮𐑋𐐺𐐲𐑉𐑆 𐐱𐑂 𐐿𐐷𐐭𐑉𐐨𐐲𐑅 𐐶𐐲𐑉𐐿𐑋𐐰𐑌𐑇𐐮𐐹. 𐐈𐑌𐐼 𐑄 𐐢𐐫𐑉𐐼 𐐼𐐮𐐼 𐑇𐐬 𐑋𐐨 𐑁𐑉𐐲𐑋 𐐻𐐴𐑋 𐐻𐐭 𐐻𐐴𐑋 𐐰𐑁𐐻𐐲𐑉 𐐸𐐶𐐱𐐻 𐑋𐐰𐑌𐐲𐑉 𐐌 𐑇𐐳𐐼 𐐶𐐲𐑉𐐿 𐑄 𐐻𐐮𐑋𐐺𐐲𐑉𐑆 𐐱𐑂 𐑄 𐑇𐐮𐐹. 𐐤𐐵 𐐌, 𐐤𐐀𐑁𐐴, 𐐼𐐮𐐼 𐑌𐐱𐐻 𐐶𐐲𐑉𐐿 𐑄 𐐻𐐮𐑋𐐺𐐲𐑉𐑆 𐐰𐑁𐐻𐐲𐑉 𐑄 𐑋𐐰𐑌𐐲𐑉 𐐸𐐶𐐮𐐽 𐐶𐐱𐑆 𐑊𐐲𐑉𐑌𐐼 𐐺𐐴 𐑋𐐯𐑌, 𐑌𐐨𐑄𐐲𐑉 𐐼𐐮𐐼 𐐌 𐐺𐐮𐑊𐐼 𐑄 𐑇𐐮𐐹 𐐰𐑁𐐻𐐲𐑉 𐑄 𐑋𐐰𐑌𐐲𐑉 𐐱𐑂 𐑋𐐯𐑌; 𐐺𐐲𐐻 𐐌 𐐼𐐮𐐼 𐐺𐐮𐑊𐐼 𐐮𐐻 𐐰𐑁𐐻𐐲𐑉 𐑄 𐑋𐐰𐑌𐐲𐑉 𐐸𐐶𐐮𐐽 𐑄 𐐢𐐫𐑉𐐼 𐐸𐐰𐐼 𐑇𐐬𐑌 𐐲𐑌𐐻𐐭 𐑋𐐨; 𐐸𐐶𐐯𐑉𐑁𐐬𐑉, 𐐮𐐻 𐐶𐐱𐑆 𐑌𐐱𐐻 𐐰𐑁𐐻𐐲𐑉 𐑄 𐑋𐐰𐑌𐐲𐑉 𐐱𐑂 𐑋𐐯𐑌.

33. 𐐈𐑌𐐼 𐐌, 𐐤𐐀𐑁𐐴, 𐐼𐐮𐐼 𐑀𐐬 𐐮𐑌𐐻𐐭 𐑄 𐑋𐐵𐑌𐐻 𐐫𐑁𐐲𐑌, 𐐰𐑌𐐼 𐐌 𐐼𐐮𐐼 𐐹𐑉𐐩 𐐫𐑁𐐲𐑌 𐐲𐑌𐐻𐐭 𐑄 𐐢𐐫𐑉𐐼; 𐐸𐐶𐐯𐑉𐑁𐐬𐑉 𐑄 𐐢𐐫𐑉𐐼 𐑇𐐬𐐼 𐐲𐑌𐐻𐐭 𐑋𐐨 𐑀𐑉𐐩𐐻 𐑃𐐮𐑍𐑆.

34. 𐐈𐑌𐐼 𐐮𐐻 𐐿𐐩𐑋 𐐻𐐭 𐐹𐐰𐑅 𐑄𐐰𐐻 𐐰𐑁𐐻𐐲𐑉 𐐌 𐐸𐐰𐐼 𐑁𐐮𐑌𐐮𐑇𐐻 𐑄 𐑇𐐮𐐹, 𐐰𐐿𐐫𐑉𐐼𐐮𐑍 𐐻𐐭 𐑄 𐐶𐐲𐑉𐐼 𐐱𐑂 𐑄 𐐢𐐫𐑉𐐼, 𐑋𐐴 𐐺𐑉𐐯𐑄𐑉𐐯𐑌 𐐺𐐨𐐸𐐯𐑊𐐼 𐑄𐐰𐐻 𐐮𐐻 𐐶𐐱𐑆 𐑀𐐳𐐼, 𐐰𐑌𐐼 𐑄𐐰𐐻 𐑄 𐐶𐐲𐑉𐐿𐑋𐐰𐑌𐑇𐐮𐐹 𐑄𐐯𐑉𐐱𐑂 𐐶𐐱𐑆 𐐯𐐿𐑅𐐨𐐼𐐨𐑍𐑊𐐨 𐑁𐐴𐑌; 𐐸𐐶𐐯𐑉𐑁𐐬𐑉 𐑄𐐩 𐐼𐐮𐐼 𐐸𐐲𐑋𐐺𐑊 𐑄𐐯𐑋𐑅𐐯𐑊𐑂𐑆 𐐲𐑀𐐯𐑌 𐐺𐐨𐑁𐐬𐑉 𐑄 𐐢𐐫𐑉𐐼.

35. 𐐈𐑌𐐼 𐐮𐐻 𐐿𐐩𐑋 𐐻𐐭 𐐹𐐰𐑅 𐑄𐐰𐐻 𐑄 𐑂𐐱𐐮𐑅 𐐱𐑂 𐑄 𐐢𐐫𐑉𐐼 𐐿𐐩𐑋 𐐲𐑌𐐻𐐭 𐑋𐐴 𐑁𐐪𐑄𐐲𐑉, 𐑄𐐰𐐻 𐐶𐐨 𐑇𐐳𐐼 𐐲𐑉𐐴𐑆 𐐰𐑌𐐼 𐑀𐐬 𐐼𐐵𐑌 𐐮𐑌𐐻𐐭 𐑄 𐑇𐐮𐐹. 𐐈𐑌𐐼 𐐮𐐻 𐐿𐐩𐑋 𐐻𐐭 𐐹𐐰𐑅 𐑄𐐰𐐻 𐐱𐑌 𐑄 𐑋𐐱𐑉𐐬, 𐐰𐑁𐐻𐐲𐑉 𐐶𐐨 𐐸𐐰𐐼 𐐹𐑉𐐨𐐹𐐯𐑉𐐼 𐐫𐑊 𐑃𐐮𐑍𐑆, 𐑋𐐲𐐽 𐑁𐑉𐐭𐐻𐑅 𐐰𐑌𐐼 𐑋𐐨𐐻 𐑁𐑉𐐱𐑋 𐑄 𐐶𐐮𐑊𐐼𐐲𐑉𐑌𐐯𐑅, 𐐰𐑌𐐼 𐐸𐐲𐑌𐐨 𐐮𐑌 𐐰𐐺𐐲𐑌𐐼𐐲𐑌𐑅, 𐐰𐑌𐐼 𐐹𐑉𐐱𐑂𐐮𐑈𐐲𐑌𐑆 𐐰𐐿𐐫𐑉𐐼𐐮𐑍 𐐻𐐭 𐑄𐐰𐐻 𐐸𐐶𐐮𐐽 𐑄 𐐢𐐫𐑉𐐼 𐐸𐐰𐐼 𐐿𐐱𐑋𐐰𐑌𐐼𐐯𐐼 𐐲𐑅, 𐐶𐐨 𐐼𐐮𐐼 𐑀𐐬 𐐼𐐵𐑌 𐐮𐑌𐐻𐐭 𐑄 𐑇𐐮𐐹, 𐐶𐐮𐑄 𐐫𐑊 𐐵𐐲𐑉 𐑊𐐬𐐼𐐮𐑍 𐐰𐑌𐐼 𐐵𐐲𐑉 𐑅𐐨𐐼𐑆, 𐐰𐑌𐐼 𐐸𐐶𐐱𐐻𐑅𐐬𐐯𐑂𐐲𐑉 𐑃𐐮𐑍 𐐶𐐨 𐐸𐐰𐐼 𐐺𐑉𐐫𐐻 𐐶𐐮𐑄 𐐲𐑅, 𐐯𐑂𐐲𐑉𐐨 𐐶𐐲𐑌 𐐰𐐿𐐫𐑉𐐼𐐮𐑍 𐐻𐐭 𐐸𐐮𐑆 𐐩𐐾; 𐐸𐐶𐐯𐑉𐑁𐐬𐑉, 𐐶𐐨 𐐼𐐮𐐼 𐐫𐑊 𐑀𐐬 𐐼𐐵𐑌 𐐮𐑌𐐻𐐭 𐑄 𐑇𐐮𐐹, 𐐶𐐮𐑄 𐐵𐐲𐑉 𐐶𐐴𐑂𐑆 𐐰𐑌𐐼 𐐵𐐲𐑉 𐐽𐐮𐑊𐐼𐑉𐐯𐑌.

36. 𐐈𐑌𐐼 𐑌𐐵, 𐑋𐐴 𐑁𐐪𐑄𐐲𐑉 𐐸𐐰𐐼 𐐺𐐨𐑀𐐰𐐻 𐐻𐐭 𐑅𐐲𐑌𐑆 𐐮𐑌 𐑄 𐐶𐐮𐑊𐐼𐐲𐑉𐑌𐐯𐑅; 𐑄 𐐯𐑊𐐼𐐲𐑉 𐐶𐐱𐑆 𐐿𐐫𐑊𐐼 𐐖𐐩𐐿𐐲𐐺 𐐰𐑌𐐼 𐑄 𐐷𐐲𐑍𐐲𐑉 𐐖𐐬𐑆𐐯𐑁. 𐐈𐑌𐐼 𐐮𐐻 𐐿𐐩𐑋 𐐻𐐭 𐐹𐐰𐑅 𐐰𐑁𐐻𐐲𐑉 𐐶𐐨 𐐸𐐰𐐼 𐐫𐑊 𐑀𐐱𐑌 𐐼𐐵𐑌 𐐮𐑌𐐻𐐭 𐑄 𐑇𐐮𐐹, 𐐰𐑌𐐼 𐐸𐐰𐐼 𐐻𐐩𐐿𐐲𐑌 𐐶𐐮𐑄 𐐲𐑅 𐐵𐐲𐑉 𐐹𐑉𐐱𐑂𐐮𐑈𐐲𐑌𐑆 𐐰𐑌𐐼 𐑃𐐮𐑍𐑆 𐐸𐐶𐐮𐐽 𐐸𐐰𐐼 𐐺𐐮𐑌 𐐿𐐱𐑋𐐰𐑌𐐼𐐯𐐼 𐐲𐑅, 𐐶𐐨 𐐼𐐮𐐼 𐐹𐐳𐐻 𐑁𐐬𐑉𐑃 𐐮𐑌𐐻𐐭 𐑄 𐑅𐐨, 𐐰𐑌𐐼 𐐶𐐲𐑉 𐐼𐑉𐐮𐑂𐑌 𐑁𐐬𐑉𐑃 𐐺𐐨𐑁𐐬𐑉 𐑄 𐐶𐐮𐑌𐐼 𐐻𐐫𐑉𐐼𐑆 𐑄 𐐹𐑉𐐱𐑋𐐮𐑅𐐻 𐑊𐐰𐑌𐐼; 𐐰𐑌𐐼 𐐰𐑁𐐻𐐲𐑉 𐐶𐐨 𐐸𐐰𐐼 𐐺𐐮𐑌 𐐼𐑉𐐮𐑂𐑌 𐑁𐐬𐑉𐑃 𐐺𐐨𐑁𐐬𐑉 𐑄 𐐶𐐮𐑌𐐼 𐑁𐐫𐑉 𐑄 𐑅𐐹𐐩𐑅 𐐱𐑂 𐑋𐐯𐑌𐐨 𐐼𐐩𐑆, 𐐺𐐨𐐸𐐯𐑊𐐼, 𐑋𐐴 𐐺𐑉𐐯𐑄𐑉𐐯𐑌 𐐰𐑌𐐼 𐑄 𐑅𐐲𐑌𐑆 𐐱𐑂 𐐆𐑇𐑋𐐩𐐯𐑊, 𐐰𐑌𐐼 𐐫𐑊𐑅𐐬 𐑄𐐩𐑉 𐐶𐐴𐑂𐑆, 𐐺𐐨𐑀𐐰𐑌 𐐻𐐭 𐑋𐐩𐐿 𐑄𐐯𐑋𐑅𐐯𐑊𐑂𐑆 𐑋𐐯𐑉𐐨, 𐐮𐑌𐑅𐐬𐑋𐐲𐐽 𐑄𐐰𐐻 𐑄𐐩 𐐺𐐨𐑀𐐰𐑌 𐐻𐐭 𐐼𐐰𐑌𐑅 𐐰𐑌𐐼 𐐻𐐭 𐑅𐐮𐑍, 𐐰𐑌𐐼 𐐻𐐭 𐑅𐐹𐐨𐐿 𐐶𐐮𐑄 𐑋𐐲𐐽 𐑉𐐭𐐼𐑌𐐯𐑅, 𐐷𐐩, 𐐨𐑂𐐲𐑌 𐑄𐐰𐐻 𐑄𐐩 𐐼𐐮𐐼 𐑁𐐫𐑉𐑀𐐯𐐻 𐐺𐐴 𐐸𐐶𐐱𐐻 𐐹𐐵𐐲𐑉 𐑄𐐩 𐐸𐐰𐐼 𐐺𐐮𐑌 𐐺𐑉𐐫𐐻 𐑄𐐮𐑄𐐲𐑉; 𐐷𐐩, 𐑄𐐩 𐐶𐐲𐑉 𐑊𐐮𐑁𐐻𐐯𐐼 𐐲𐐹 𐐲𐑌𐐻𐐭 𐐯𐐿𐑅𐐨𐐼𐐨𐑍 𐑉𐐭𐐼𐑌𐐯𐑅. 𐐈𐑌𐐼 𐐌, 𐐤𐐀𐑁𐐴, 𐐺𐐨𐑀𐐰𐑌 𐐻𐐭 𐑁𐐨𐑉 𐐯𐐿𐑅𐐨𐐼𐐨𐑍𐑊𐐨, 𐑊𐐯𐑅𐐻 𐑄 𐐢𐐫𐑉𐐼 𐑇𐐳𐐼 𐐺𐐨 𐐰𐑍𐑀𐑉𐐨 𐐶𐐮𐑄 𐐲𐑅, 𐐰𐑌𐐼 𐑅𐑋𐐴𐐻 𐐲𐑅, 𐐺𐐨𐐿𐐫𐑆 𐐱𐑂 𐐵𐐲𐑉 𐐮𐑌𐐮𐐿𐐶𐐮𐐻𐐨, 𐑄𐐰𐐻 𐐶𐐨 𐑇𐐳𐐼 𐐺𐐨 𐑅𐐶𐐱𐑊𐐬𐐼 𐐲𐐹 𐐮𐑌 𐑄 𐐼𐐯𐐹𐑃𐑅 𐐱𐑂 𐑄 𐑅𐐨; 𐐸𐐶𐐯𐑉𐑁𐐬𐑉 𐐌, 𐐤𐐀𐑁𐐴, 𐐺𐐨𐑀𐐰𐑌 𐐻𐐭 𐑅𐐹𐐨𐐿 𐐻𐐭 𐑄𐐯𐑋 𐐶𐐮𐑄 𐑋𐐲𐐽 𐑅𐐬𐐺𐐲𐑉𐑌𐐯𐑅; 𐐺𐐲𐐻 𐐺𐐨𐐸𐐯𐑊𐐼 𐑄𐐩 𐐶𐐲𐑉 𐐰𐑍𐑀𐑉𐐨 𐐶𐐮𐑄 𐑋𐐨, 𐑅𐐩𐐮𐑍, 𐐎𐐨 𐐶𐐮𐑊 𐑌𐐱𐐻 𐑄𐐰𐐻 𐐵𐐲𐑉 𐐷𐐲𐑍𐐲𐑉 𐐺𐑉𐐲𐑄𐐲𐑉 𐑇𐐰𐑊 𐐺𐐨 𐐩 𐑉𐐭𐑊𐐲𐑉 𐐬𐑂𐐲𐑉 𐐲𐑅.

37. 𐐈𐑌𐐼 𐐮𐐻 𐐿𐐩𐑋 𐐻𐐭 𐐹𐐰𐑅 𐑄𐐰𐐻 𐐢𐐩𐑋𐐲𐑌 𐐰𐑌𐐼 𐐢𐐯𐑋𐐷𐐭𐐯𐑊 𐐼𐐮𐐼 𐐻𐐩𐐿 𐑋𐐨 𐐰𐑌𐐼 𐐺𐐴𐑌𐐼 𐑋𐐨 𐐶𐐮𐑄 𐐿𐐫𐑉𐐼𐑆, 𐐰𐑌𐐼 𐑄𐐩 𐐼𐐮𐐼 𐐻𐑉𐐨𐐻 𐑋𐐨 𐐶𐐮𐑄 𐑋𐐲𐐽 𐐸𐐪𐑉𐑇𐑌𐐯𐑅; 𐑌𐐯𐑂𐐲𐑉𐑄𐐯𐑊𐐯𐑅 𐑄 𐐢𐐫𐑉𐐼 𐐼𐐮𐐼 𐑅𐐲𐑁𐐲𐑉 𐐮𐐻, 𐑄𐐰𐐻 𐐸𐐨 𐑋𐐴𐐻 𐑇𐐬 𐑁𐐬𐑉𐑃 𐐸𐐮𐑆 𐐹𐐵𐐲𐑉, 𐐲𐑌𐐻𐐭 𐑄 𐑁𐐳𐑊𐑁𐐮𐑊𐐮𐑍 𐐱𐑂 𐐸𐐮𐑆 𐐶𐐲𐑉𐐼, 𐐸𐐶𐐮𐐽 𐐸𐐨 𐐸𐐰𐐼 𐑅𐐹𐐬𐐿𐐲𐑌 𐐿𐐲𐑌𐑅𐐲𐑉𐑌𐐮𐑍 𐑄 𐐶𐐮𐐿𐐯𐐼.

38. 𐐈𐑌𐐼 𐐮𐐻 𐐿𐐩𐑋 𐐻𐐭 𐐹𐐰𐑅 𐑄𐐰𐐻 𐐰𐑁𐐻𐐲𐑉 𐑄𐐩 𐐸𐐰𐐼 𐐺𐐵𐑌𐐼 𐑋𐐨, 𐐮𐑌𐑅𐐬𐑋𐐲𐐽 𐑄𐐰𐐻 𐐌 𐐿𐐳𐐼 𐑌𐐱𐐻 𐑋𐐭𐑂, 𐑄 𐐿𐐲𐑋𐐹𐐲𐑅, 𐐸𐐶𐐮𐐽 𐐸𐐰𐐼 𐐺𐐮𐑌 𐐹𐑉𐐨𐐹𐐯𐑉𐐼 𐐱𐑂 𐑄 𐐢𐐫𐑉𐐼, 𐐼𐐮𐐼 𐑅𐐨𐑅 𐐻𐐭 𐐶𐐲𐑉𐐿; 𐐸𐐶𐐯𐑉𐑁𐐬𐑉, 𐑄𐐩 𐑌𐐬 𐑌𐐱𐐻 𐐸𐐶𐐮𐑄𐐲𐑉 𐑄𐐩 𐑇𐐳𐐼 𐑅𐐻𐐨𐑉 𐑄 𐑇𐐮𐐹, 𐐮𐑌𐑅𐐬𐑋𐐲𐐽 𐑄𐐰𐐻 𐑄𐐯𐑉 𐐲𐑉𐐬𐑆 𐐩 𐑀𐑉𐐩𐐻 𐑅𐐻𐐫𐑉𐑋, 𐐷𐐩, 𐐩 𐑀𐑉𐐩𐐻 𐐰𐑌𐐼 𐐻𐐯𐑉𐐲𐐺𐑊 𐐻𐐯𐑋𐐹𐐯𐑅𐐻, 𐐰𐑌𐐼 𐐶𐐨 𐐶𐐲𐑉 𐐼𐑉𐐮𐑂𐑌 𐐺𐐰𐐿 𐐲𐐹𐐱𐑌 𐑄 𐐶𐐫𐐻𐐲𐑉𐑆 𐑁𐐫𐑉 𐑄 𐑅𐐹𐐩𐑅 𐐱𐑂 𐑃𐑉𐐨 𐐼𐐩𐑆; 𐐰𐑌𐐼 𐑄𐐩 𐐺𐐨𐑀𐐰𐑌 𐐻𐐭 𐐺𐐨 𐑁𐑉𐐴𐐻𐑌𐐼 𐐯𐐿𐑅𐐨𐐼𐐨𐑍𐑊𐐨, 𐑊𐐯𐑅𐐻 𐑄𐐩 𐑇𐐳𐐼 𐐺𐐨 𐐼𐑉𐐵𐑌𐐼 𐐮𐑌 𐑄 𐑅𐐨;

𐑌𐐯𐑂𐐲𐑉𐑄𐐲𐑊𐐯𐑅 𐑄𐐩 𐐼𐐮𐐼 𐑌𐐱𐐻 𐑊𐐭𐑅 𐑋𐐨. 𐐈𐑌𐐼 𐐱𐑌 𐑄 𐑁𐐬𐑉𐑃 𐐼𐐩, 𐐸𐐶𐐮𐐽 𐐶𐐨 𐐸𐐰𐐼 𐐺𐐮𐑌 𐐼𐑉𐐮𐑂𐐲𐑌 𐐺𐐰𐐿, 𐑄 𐐻𐐯𐑋𐐹𐐯𐑅𐐻 𐐺𐐨𐑀𐐰𐑌 𐐻𐐭 𐐺𐐨 𐐯𐐿𐑅𐐨𐐼𐐮𐑍𐑊𐐨 𐑅𐐬𐑉.

39. 𐐈𐑌𐐼 𐐮𐐻 𐐿𐐩𐑋 𐐻𐐭 𐐹𐐰𐑅 𐑄𐐰𐐻 𐐶𐐨 𐐶𐐲𐑉 𐐲𐐺𐐵𐐻 𐐻𐐭 𐐺𐐨 𐑅𐐶𐐱𐑊𐐬𐐼 𐐲𐐹 𐐮𐑌 𐑄 𐐼𐐯𐐹𐑃𐑅 𐐱𐑂 𐑄 𐑅𐐨. 𐐈𐑌𐐼 𐐰𐑁𐐻𐐲𐑉 𐐶𐐨 𐐸𐐰𐐼 𐐺𐐮𐑌 𐐼𐑉𐐮𐑂𐐲𐑌 𐐺𐐰𐐿 𐐲𐐹𐐱𐑌 𐑄 𐐶𐐫𐐻𐐲𐑉𐑆 𐑁𐐫𐑉 𐑄 𐑅𐐹𐐩𐑅 𐐱𐑂 𐑁𐐬𐑉 𐐼𐐩𐑆, 𐑋𐐴 𐐺𐑉𐐯𐑄𐑉𐐯𐑌 𐐺𐐨𐑀𐐰𐑌 𐐻𐐭 𐑅𐐨 𐑄𐐰𐐻 𐑄 𐐾𐐲𐐾𐑋𐐯𐑌𐐻𐑅 𐐱𐑂 𐐘𐐱𐐼 𐐶𐐲𐑉 𐐲𐐹𐐱𐑌 𐑄𐐯𐑋, 𐐰𐑌𐐼 𐑄𐐰𐐻 𐑄𐐩 𐑋𐐲𐑅𐐻 𐐹𐐯𐑉𐐮𐑇 𐑅𐐩𐑂 𐑄𐐰𐐻 𐑄𐐩 𐑇𐐳𐐼 𐑉𐐨𐐹𐐯𐑌𐐻 𐐱𐑂 𐑄𐐩𐑉 𐐮𐑌𐐮𐐿𐐶𐐮𐐻𐐨𐑆; 𐐸𐐶𐐯𐑉𐑁𐐬𐑉 𐑄𐐩 𐐿𐐩𐑋 𐐲𐑌𐐻𐐭 𐑋𐐨, 𐐰𐑌𐐼 𐑊𐐭𐑅𐐻 𐑄 𐐺𐐰𐑌𐐼𐑆 𐐸𐐶𐐮𐐽 𐐶𐐲𐑉 𐐲𐐹𐐱𐑌 𐑋𐐴 𐑉𐐮𐑅𐐻𐑅, 𐐰𐑌𐐼 𐐺𐐨𐐸𐐬𐑊𐐼 𐑄𐐩 𐐸𐐰𐐼 𐑅𐐶𐐬𐑊𐐲𐑌 𐐯𐐿𐑅𐐨𐐼𐐮𐑍𐑊𐐨; 𐐰𐑌𐐼 𐐫𐑊𐑅𐐬 𐑋𐐴𐑌 𐐰𐑍𐐿𐑊𐑆 𐐶𐐲𐑉 𐑋𐐲𐐽 𐑅𐐶𐐬𐑊𐐲𐑌, 𐐰𐑌𐐼 𐑀𐑉𐐩𐐻 𐐶𐐱𐑆 𐑄 𐑅𐐬𐑉𐑌𐐯𐑅 𐑄𐐯𐑉𐐱𐑂.

40. 𐐤𐐯𐑂𐐲𐑉𐑄𐐲𐑊𐐯𐑅 𐐌 𐐼𐐮𐐼 𐑊𐐳𐐿 𐐲𐑌𐐻𐐭 𐑋𐐴 𐐘𐐱𐐼, 𐐰𐑌𐐼 𐐌 𐐼𐐮𐐼 𐐹𐑉𐐩𐑆 𐐸𐐮𐑋 𐐫𐑊 𐑄 𐐼𐐩 𐑊𐐱𐑍; 𐐰𐑌𐐼 𐐌 𐐼𐐮𐐼 𐑌𐐱𐐻 𐑋𐐲𐑉𐑋𐐲𐑉 𐐲𐑀𐐯𐑌𐑅𐐻 𐑄 𐐢𐐫𐑉𐐼, 𐐺𐐨𐐿𐐫𐑆 𐐱𐑂 𐑋𐐴𐑌 𐐲𐑁𐑊𐐮𐐿𐑇𐐲𐑌𐑆.

41. 𐐤𐐵 𐑋𐐴 𐑁𐐪𐑄𐐲𐑉, 𐐢𐐨𐐸𐐴, 𐐸𐐰𐐼 𐑅𐐯𐐼 𐑋𐐯𐑌𐐨 𐑃𐐮𐑍𐑆 𐐲𐑌𐐻𐐭 𐑄𐐯𐑋, 𐐰𐑌𐐼 𐐫𐑊𐑅𐐬 𐐲𐑌𐐻𐐭 𐑄 𐑅𐐲𐑌𐑆 𐐱𐑂 𐐆𐑇𐑋𐐩𐐯𐑊; 𐐺𐐲𐐻 𐐺𐐨𐐸𐐬𐑊𐐼 𐑄𐐩 𐐼𐐮𐐼 𐐺𐑉𐐨𐑄 𐐵𐐻 𐑋𐐲𐐽 𐑃𐑉𐐯𐐻𐐲𐑌𐐮𐑍𐑆 𐐲𐑀𐐯𐑌𐑅𐐻 𐐯𐑌𐐨 𐐶𐐲𐑌 𐑄𐐰𐐻 𐑇𐐳𐐼 𐑅𐐹𐐨𐐿 𐑁𐐫𐑉 𐑋𐐨; 𐐰𐑌𐐼 𐑋𐐴 𐐹𐐯𐑉𐐯𐑌𐐻𐑅 𐐺𐐨𐐮𐑍 𐑅𐐻𐑉𐐮𐐿𐐲𐑌 𐐮𐑌 𐐷𐐨𐑉𐑆, 𐐰𐑌𐐼 𐐸𐐰𐑂𐐮𐑍 𐑅𐐲𐑁𐐲𐑉𐐼 𐑋𐐲𐐽 𐑀𐑉𐐨𐑁 𐐺𐐨𐐿𐐫𐑆 𐐱𐑂 𐑄𐐩𐑉 𐐽𐐮𐑊𐐼𐑉𐐯𐑌, 𐑄𐐩 𐐶𐐲𐑉 𐐺𐑉𐐫𐐻 𐐼𐐵𐑌, 𐐷𐐩, 𐐨𐑂𐐲𐑌 𐐲𐐹𐐱𐑌 𐑄𐐩𐑉 𐑅𐐮𐐿 𐐺𐐯𐐼𐑆. 𐐒𐐨𐐿𐐫𐑆 𐐱𐑂 𐑄𐐩𐑉 𐑀𐑉𐐨𐑁, 𐐰𐑌𐐼 𐑋𐐲𐐽 𐑅𐐱𐑉𐐬, 𐐰𐑌𐐼 𐑄 𐐮𐑌𐐮𐐿𐐶𐐮𐐻𐐨 𐐱𐑂 𐑋𐐴 𐐺𐑉𐐯𐑄𐑉𐐯𐑌, 𐑄𐐩 𐐶𐐲𐑉 𐐺𐑉𐐫𐐻 𐑌𐐨𐑉 𐐨𐑂𐐲𐑌 𐐻𐐭 𐐺𐐨 𐐿𐐰𐑉𐐨𐐼 𐐵𐐻 𐐱𐑂 𐑄𐐮𐑅 𐐻𐐴𐑋 𐐻𐐭 𐑋𐐨𐐻 𐑄𐐩𐑉 𐐘𐐱𐐼; 𐐷𐐩, 𐑄𐐩𐑉 𐑀𐑉𐐩 𐐸𐐩𐑉𐑆 𐐶𐐲𐑉 𐐲𐐺𐐵𐐻 𐐻𐐭 𐐺𐐨 𐐺𐑉𐐫𐐻 𐐼𐐵𐑌 𐐻𐐭 𐑊𐐴 𐑊𐐬 𐐮𐑌 𐑄 𐐼𐐲𐑅𐐻; 𐐷𐐩, 𐐨𐑂𐐲𐑌 𐑄𐐩 𐐶𐐲𐑉 𐑌𐐨𐑉 𐐻𐐭 𐐺𐐨 𐐿𐐰𐑅𐐻 𐐶𐐮𐑄 𐑅𐐱𐑉𐐬 𐐮𐑌𐐻𐐭 𐐲 𐐶𐐫𐐻𐐲𐑉𐐨 𐑀𐑉𐐩𐑂. 𐐈𐑌𐐼 𐐖𐐩𐐿𐐲𐐺 𐐰𐑌𐐼 𐐖𐐬𐑆𐐯𐑁 𐐫𐑊𐑅𐐬, 𐐺𐐨𐐮𐑍 𐐷𐐲𐑍, 𐐸𐐰𐑂𐐮𐑍 𐑌𐐨𐐼 𐐱𐑂 𐑋𐐲𐐽 𐑌𐐲𐑉𐐮𐑇𐑋𐐯𐑌𐐻, 𐐶𐐲𐑉 𐑀𐑉𐐨𐑂𐐼 𐐺𐐨𐐿𐐫𐑆 𐐱𐑂 𐑄 𐐲𐑁𐑊𐐮𐐿𐑇𐐲𐑌𐑆 𐐱𐑂 𐑄𐐩𐑉 𐑋𐐲𐑄𐐲𐑉; 𐐰𐑌𐐼 𐐫𐑊𐑅𐐬 𐑋𐐴 𐐶𐐴𐑁, 𐐶𐐮𐑄 𐐸𐐲𐑉 𐐻𐐨𐑉𐑆 𐐰𐑌𐐼 𐐹𐑉𐐩𐑉𐑆, 𐐰𐑌𐐼 𐐫𐑊𐑅𐐬 𐑋𐐴 𐐽𐐮𐑊𐐼𐑉𐐯𐑌, 𐐼𐐮𐐼 𐑌𐐱𐐻 𐑅𐐱𐑁𐐲𐑌 𐑄 𐐸𐐪𐑉𐐻𐑅 𐐱𐑂 𐑋𐐴 𐐺𐑉𐐯𐑄𐑉𐐯𐑌, 𐑄𐐰𐐻 𐑄𐐩 𐐶𐐳𐐼 𐑊𐐭𐑅 𐑋𐐨; 𐐰𐑌𐐼 𐑄𐐯𐑉 𐐶𐐱𐑆 𐑌𐐲𐑃𐐮𐑍 𐑅𐐩𐑂 𐐮𐐻 𐐶𐐲𐑉 𐑄 𐐹𐐵𐐲𐑉 𐐱𐑂 𐐘𐐱𐐼, 𐐸𐐶𐐮𐐽 𐑃𐑉𐐯𐐻𐐲𐑌𐐼 𐑄𐐯𐑋 𐐶𐐮𐑄 𐐼𐐨𐑅𐐻𐑉𐐲𐐿𐑇𐐲𐑌, 𐐿𐐳𐐼 𐑅𐐱𐑁𐐲𐑌 𐑄𐐩𐑉 𐐸𐐪𐑉𐐻𐑅; 𐐸𐐶𐐯𐑉𐑁𐐬𐑉 𐐸𐐶𐐯𐑌 𐑄𐐩 𐑅𐐫 𐑄𐐰𐐻 𐑄𐐩 𐐶𐐲𐑉 𐐲𐐺𐐵𐐻 𐐻𐐭 𐐺𐐨 𐑅𐐶𐐱𐑊𐐬𐐼 𐐲𐐹 𐐮𐑌 𐑄 𐐼𐐯𐐹𐑃𐑅 𐐱𐑂 𐑄 𐑅𐐨, 𐑄𐐩 𐑉𐐨𐐹𐐯𐑌𐐻𐐲𐐼 𐐱𐑂 𐑄 𐑃𐐮𐑍 𐐸𐐶𐐮𐐽 𐑄𐐩 𐐸𐐰𐐼 𐐼𐐲𐑌, 𐐮𐑌𐑅𐐬𐑋𐐲𐐽 𐑄𐐰𐐻 𐑄𐐩 𐑊𐐭𐑅𐐻 𐑋𐐨.

42. 𐐈𐑌𐐼 𐐮𐐻 𐐿𐐩𐑋 𐐻𐐭 𐐹𐐰𐑅 𐐰𐑁𐐻𐐲𐑉 𐑄𐐩 𐐸𐐰𐐼 𐑊𐐭𐑅𐐻 𐑋𐐨, 𐐺𐐨𐐸𐐬𐑊𐐼, 𐐌 𐐻𐐳𐐿 𐑄 𐐿𐐲𐑋𐐹𐐲𐑅, 𐐰𐑌𐐼 𐐮𐐻 𐐼𐐮𐐼 𐐶𐐲𐑉𐐿 𐐸𐐶𐐮𐑄𐐲𐑉 𐐌 𐐼𐐨𐑆𐐴𐑉𐐼 𐐮𐐻. 𐐈𐑌𐐼 𐐮𐐻 𐐿𐐩𐑋 𐐻𐐭 𐐹𐐰𐑅 𐑄𐐰𐐻 𐐌 𐐹𐑉𐐩𐐼 𐐲𐑌𐐻𐐭 𐑄 𐐢𐐫𐑉𐐼; 𐐰𐑌𐐼 𐐰𐑁𐐻𐐲𐑉 𐐌 𐐸𐐰𐐼 𐐹𐑉𐐩𐐼, 𐑄 𐐶𐐮𐑌𐐼𐑆 𐐼𐐮𐐼 𐑅𐐨𐑅, 𐐰𐑌𐐼 𐑄 𐑅𐐻𐐫𐑉𐑋 𐐼𐐮𐐼 𐑅𐐨𐑅, 𐐰𐑌𐐼 𐑄𐐯𐑉 𐐶𐐱𐑆 𐐲 𐑀𐑉𐐩𐐻 𐐿𐐪𐑋.

43. 𐐈𐑌𐐼 𐐮𐐻 𐐿𐐩𐑋 𐐻𐐭 𐐹𐐰𐑅 𐑄𐐰𐐻 𐐌, 𐐤𐐨𐑁𐐴, 𐐼𐐮𐐼 𐑀𐐴𐐼 𐑄 𐑇𐐮𐐹, 𐑄𐐰𐐻 𐐶𐐨 𐑅𐐩𐑊𐐼 𐐻𐐫𐑉𐐼𐑆 𐑄 𐐹𐑉𐐱𐑋𐐮𐑅𐐻 𐑊𐐰𐑌𐐼. 𐐈𐑌𐐼 𐐮𐐻 𐐿𐐩𐑋 𐐻𐐭 𐐹𐐰𐑅 𐑄𐐰𐐻 𐐰𐑁𐐻𐐲𐑉 𐐶𐐨 𐐸𐐰𐐼 𐑅𐐩𐑊𐐼 𐑁𐐫𐑉 𐑄 𐑅𐐹𐐩𐑅 𐐱𐑂 𐑋𐐯𐑌𐐨 𐐼𐐩𐑆, 𐐶𐐨 𐐼𐐮𐐼 𐐲𐑉𐐴𐑂 𐐻𐐭 𐑄 𐐹𐑉𐐱𐑋𐐮𐑅𐐻 𐑊𐐰𐑌𐐼; 𐐰𐑌𐐼 𐐶𐐨 𐐶𐐯𐑌𐐻 𐑁𐐬𐑉𐑃 𐐲𐐹𐐱𐑌 𐑄 𐑊𐐰𐑌𐐼, 𐐰𐑌𐐼 𐐼𐐮𐐼 𐐹𐐮𐐽 𐐵𐑉 𐐻𐐯𐑌𐐻𐑅; 𐐰𐑌𐐼 𐐶𐐨 𐐼𐐮𐐼 𐐿𐐫𐑊 𐐮𐐻 𐑄 𐐹𐑉𐐱𐑋𐐮𐑅𐐻 𐑊𐐰𐑌𐐼.

44. 𐐈𐑌𐐼 𐐮𐐻 𐐿𐐩𐑋 𐐻𐐭 𐐹𐐰𐑅 𐑄𐐰𐐻 𐐶𐐨 𐐼𐐮𐐼 𐐺𐐨𐑀𐐮𐑌 𐐻𐐭 𐐻𐐮𐑊 𐑄 𐐲𐑉𐑃, 𐐰𐑌𐐼 𐐶𐐨 𐐺𐐨𐑀𐐰𐑌 𐐻𐐭 𐐹𐑊𐐰𐑌𐐻 𐑅𐐨𐐼𐑆; 𐐷𐐩, 𐐶𐐨 𐐼𐐮𐐼 𐐹𐐳𐐻 𐐫𐑊 𐐵𐑉 𐑅𐐨𐐼𐑆 𐐮𐑌𐐻𐐭 𐑄 𐐲𐑉𐑃, 𐐸𐐶𐐮𐐽 𐐶𐐨 𐐸𐐰𐐼 𐐺𐑉𐐫𐐻 𐑁𐑉𐐱𐑋 𐑄 𐑊𐐰𐑌𐐼 𐐱𐑂 𐐖𐐨𐑉𐐭𐑅𐐲𐑊𐐲𐑋. 𐐈𐑌𐐼 𐐮𐐻 𐐿𐐩𐑋 𐐻𐐭 𐐹𐐰𐑅 𐑄𐐰𐐻 𐑄𐐩 𐐼𐐮𐐼 𐑀𐑉𐐬 𐐯𐐿𐑅𐐨𐐼𐐮𐑍𐑊𐐨; 𐐸𐐶𐐯𐑉𐑁𐐬𐑉 𐐶𐐨 𐐶𐐲𐑉 𐐺𐑊𐐯𐑅𐐻 𐐮𐑌 𐐲𐐺𐐲𐑌𐐼𐐲𐑌𐑅.

45. 𐐈𐑌𐐼 𐐮𐐻 𐐿𐐩𐑋 𐐻𐐭 𐐹𐐰𐑅 𐑄𐐰𐐻 𐐶𐐨 𐐼𐐮𐐼 𐑁𐐴𐑌𐐼 𐐲𐐹𐐱𐑌 𐑄 𐑊𐐰𐑌𐐼 𐐱𐑂 𐐹𐑉𐐱𐑋𐐮𐑅, 𐐰𐑆 𐐶𐐨 𐐾𐐲𐑉𐑌𐐨𐐼 𐐮𐑌 𐑄 𐐶𐐮𐑊𐐼𐐲𐑉𐑌𐐯𐑅, 𐑄𐐰𐐻 𐑄𐐯𐑉 𐐶𐐲𐑉 𐐺𐐨𐑅𐐻𐑅 𐐮𐑌 𐑄 𐑁𐐱𐑉𐐯𐑅𐐻𐑅 𐐱𐑂 𐐯𐑂𐐲𐑉𐐨 𐐿𐐴𐑌𐐼, 𐐺𐐬𐑃 𐑄 𐐿𐐵 𐐰𐑌𐐼 𐑄 𐐱𐐿𐑅, 𐐰𐑌𐐼 𐑄 𐐰𐑅 𐐰𐑌𐐼 𐑄 𐐸𐐫𐑉𐑅, 𐐰𐑌𐐼 𐑄 𐑀𐐬𐐻 𐐰𐑌𐐼 𐑄 𐐶𐐴𐑊𐐼 𐑀𐐬𐐻, 𐐰𐑌𐐼 𐐫𐑊 𐑋𐐰𐑌𐐲𐑉 𐐱𐑂 𐐶𐐴𐑊𐐼 𐐰𐑌𐐮𐑋𐐲𐑊𐑆, 𐐸𐐶𐐮𐐽 𐐶𐐲𐑉 𐑁𐐫𐑉 𐑄 𐐷𐐭𐑅 𐐱𐑂 𐑋𐐯𐑌. 𐐈𐑌𐐼 𐐶𐐨 𐐼𐐮𐐼 𐑁𐐴𐑌𐐼 𐐫𐑊 𐑋𐐰𐑌𐐲𐑉 𐐱𐑂 𐐬𐑉, 𐐺𐐬𐑃 𐐱𐑂 𐑀𐐬𐑊𐐼, 𐐰𐑌𐐼 𐐱𐑂 𐑅𐐮𐑊𐑂𐐲𐑉, 𐐰𐑌𐐼 𐐱𐑂 𐐿𐐱𐐹𐐲𐑉.

46. 𐐈𐑌𐐼 𐐮𐐻 𐐿𐐩𐑋 𐐻𐐭 𐐹𐐰𐑅 𐑄𐐰𐐻 𐑄 𐐢𐐫𐑉𐐼 𐐿𐐲𐑋𐐰𐑌𐐼𐐯𐐼 𐑋𐐨, 𐐸𐐶𐐯𐑉𐑁𐐬𐑉 𐐌 𐐼𐐮𐐼 𐑋𐐩𐐿 𐐹𐑊𐐩𐐻𐑅 𐐲𐑂 𐐬𐑉, 𐑄𐐰𐐻 𐐌 𐑋𐐴𐐻 𐐯𐑌𐑀𐑉𐐩𐑂𐐯𐑌 𐐲𐐹𐐱𐑌 𐑄𐐯𐑋 𐑄 𐑉𐐯𐐿𐐫𐑉𐐼 𐐲𐑂 𐑋𐐴 𐐹𐐨𐐹𐑊. 𐐈𐑌𐐼 𐐲𐐹𐐱𐑌 𐑄 𐐹𐑊𐐩𐐻𐑅 𐐸𐐶𐐮𐐽 𐐌 𐑋𐐩𐐼 𐐌 𐐼𐐮𐐼 𐐯𐑌𐑀𐑉𐐩𐑂𐐯𐑌 𐑄 𐑉𐐯𐐿𐐫𐑉𐐼 𐐲𐑂 𐑋𐐴 𐑁𐐪𐑄𐐲𐑉, 𐐰𐑌𐐼 𐐫𐑊𐑅𐐬 𐐵𐑉 𐐾𐐲𐑉𐑌𐐨𐐮𐑍𐑆 𐐮𐑌 𐑄 𐐶𐐮𐑊𐐼𐐲𐑉𐑌𐐯𐑅, 𐐰𐑌𐐼 𐑄 𐐹𐑉𐐱𐑁𐐯𐑅𐐨𐑆 𐐲𐑂 𐑋𐐴 𐑁𐐪𐑄𐐲𐑉: 𐐰𐑌𐐼 𐐫𐑊𐑅𐐬 𐑋𐐯𐑌𐐨 𐐲𐑂 𐑋𐐴𐑌 𐐬𐑌 𐐹𐑉𐐱𐑁𐐯𐑅𐐨𐑆 𐐸𐐰𐑂 𐐌 𐐯𐑌𐑀𐑉𐐩𐑂𐐯𐑌 𐐲𐐹𐐱𐑌 𐑄𐐯𐑋. 𐐈𐑌𐐼 𐐌 𐑌𐐷𐐭 𐑌𐐱𐐻 𐐰𐐻 𐑄 𐐻𐐴𐑋 𐐸𐐶𐐯𐑌 𐐌 𐑋𐐩𐐼 𐑄𐐯𐑋 𐑄𐐰𐐻 𐐌 𐑇𐐳𐐼 𐐺𐐨 𐐿𐐲𐑋𐐰𐑌𐐼𐐯𐐼 𐐲𐑂 𐑄 𐐢𐐫𐑉𐐼 𐐻𐐭 𐑋𐐩𐐿 𐑄𐐨𐑆 𐐹𐑊𐐩𐐻𐑅: 𐐸𐐶𐐯𐑉𐑁𐐬𐑉 𐑄 𐑉𐐯𐐿𐐫𐑉𐐼 𐐲𐑂 𐑋𐐴 𐑁𐐪𐑄𐐲𐑉, 𐐰𐑌𐐼 𐑄 𐐾𐐨𐑌𐐨𐐰𐑊𐐬𐐾𐐨 𐐲𐑂 𐐸𐐮𐑆 𐑁𐐪𐑄𐐲𐑉𐑆, 𐐰𐑌𐐼 𐑄 𐑋𐐬𐑉 𐐹𐐪𐑉𐐻 𐐲𐑂 𐐫𐑊 𐐵𐑉 𐐹𐑉𐐬𐑅𐐨𐐼𐐮𐑍𐑆 𐐮𐑌 𐑄 𐐶𐐮𐑊𐐼𐐲𐑉𐑌𐐯𐑅, 𐐪𐑉 𐐯𐑌𐑀𐑉𐐩𐑂𐐯𐑌 𐐲𐐹𐐱𐑌 𐑄𐐬𐑆 𐑁𐐲𐑉𐑅𐐻 𐐹𐑊𐐩𐐻𐑅 𐐲𐑂 𐐸𐐶𐐮𐐽 𐐌 𐐸𐐰𐑂 𐑅𐐹𐐬𐐿𐐲𐑌; 𐐸𐐶𐐯𐑉𐑁𐐬𐑉 𐑄 𐑃𐐮𐑍𐑆 𐐸𐐶𐐮𐐽 𐐻𐑉𐐰𐑌𐑅𐐹𐐴𐑉𐐼 𐐺𐐨𐑁𐐬𐑉 𐐌 𐑋𐐩𐐼 𐑄𐐨𐑆 𐐹𐑊𐐩𐐻𐑅 𐐪𐑉, 𐐲𐑂 𐐲 𐐻𐑉𐐭𐑃, 𐑋𐐬𐑉 𐐹𐐲𐑉𐐻𐐮𐐿𐐷𐐭𐑊𐐲𐑉𐑊𐐨 𐑋𐐩𐐼 𐑋𐐯𐑌𐑇𐐲𐑌 𐐲𐐹𐐱𐑌 𐑄 𐑁𐐲𐑉𐑅𐐻 𐐹𐑊𐐩𐐻𐑅.

47. 𐐈𐑌𐐼 𐐰𐑁𐐻𐐲𐑉 𐐌 𐐸𐐰𐐼 𐑋𐐩𐐼 𐑄𐐨𐑆 𐐹𐑊𐐩𐐻𐑅 𐐺𐐴 𐐶𐐩 𐐲𐑂 𐐿𐐲𐑋𐐰𐑌𐐼𐑋𐐯𐑌𐐻, 𐐌, 𐐤𐐨𐑁𐐴, 𐑉𐐨𐑅𐐨𐑂𐐼 𐐲 𐐿𐐲𐑋𐐰𐑌𐐼𐑋𐐯𐑌𐐻 𐑄𐐰𐐻 𐑄 𐑋𐐮𐑌𐐮𐑅𐐻𐑉𐐨 𐐰𐑌𐐼 𐑄 𐐹𐑉𐐱𐑁𐐯𐑅𐐨𐑆, 𐑄 𐑋𐐬𐑉 𐐹𐑊𐐩𐑌 𐐰𐑌𐐼 𐐹𐑉𐐯𐑇𐐲𐑅 𐐹𐐪𐑉𐐻𐑅 𐐲𐑂 𐑄𐐯𐑋, 𐑇𐐳𐐼 𐐺𐐨 𐑉𐐮𐐻𐑌 𐐲𐐹𐐱𐑌 𐑄𐐨𐑆 𐐹𐑊𐐩𐐻𐑅; 𐐰𐑌𐐼 𐑄𐐰𐐻 𐑄 𐑃𐐮𐑍𐑆 𐐸𐐶𐐮𐐽 𐐶𐐲𐑉 𐑉𐐮𐐻𐑌, 𐑇𐐳𐐼 𐐺𐐨 𐐿𐐯𐐹𐐻 𐑁𐐬𐑉 𐑄 𐐮𐑌𐑅𐐻𐑉𐐲𐐿𐑇𐐲𐑌 𐐲𐑂 𐑋𐐴 𐐹𐐨𐐹𐑊, 𐐸𐐭 𐑇𐐳𐐼 𐐹𐐲𐑆𐐯𐑅 𐑄 𐑊𐐰𐑌𐐼, 𐐰𐑌𐐼 𐐫𐑊𐑅𐐬 𐑁𐐬𐑉 𐐲𐑄𐐲𐑉 𐐶𐐴𐑆 𐐹𐐲𐑉𐐹𐐲𐑅𐐯𐑆, 𐐸𐐶𐐮𐐽 𐐹𐐲𐑉𐐹𐐲𐑅𐐯𐑆 𐐪𐑉 𐑌𐐬𐑌 𐐲𐑌𐐻𐐭 𐑄 𐐢𐐫𐑉𐐼; 𐐸𐐶𐐯𐑉𐑁𐐬𐑉, 𐐌, 𐐤𐐨𐑁𐐴, 𐐼𐐮𐐼 𐑋𐐩𐐿 𐐲 𐑉𐐯𐐿𐐫𐑉𐐼 𐐲𐐹𐐱𐑌 𐑄 𐐲𐑄𐐲𐑉 𐐹𐑊𐐩𐐻𐑅, 𐐸𐐶𐐮𐐽 𐑀𐐮𐑂𐑆 𐐰𐑌 𐐰𐐿𐐵𐑌𐐻, 𐐫𐑉 𐐸𐐶𐐮𐐽 𐑀𐐮𐑂𐑆 𐐲 𐑀𐑉𐐩𐐻𐐲𐑉 𐐰𐐿𐐵𐑌𐐻 𐐲𐑂 𐑄 𐐶𐐫𐑉𐑆, 𐐰𐑌𐐼 𐐿𐐱𐑌𐐻𐐯𐑌𐑇𐐲𐑌𐑆, 𐐰𐑌𐐼 𐐼𐐨𐑅𐐻𐑉𐐲𐐿𐑇𐐲𐑌𐑆 𐐲𐑂 𐑋𐐴 𐐹𐐨𐐹𐑊. 𐐈𐑌𐐼 𐑄𐐮𐑅 𐐸𐐰𐑂 𐐌 𐐼𐐲𐑌, 𐐰𐑌𐐼 𐐿𐐲𐑋𐐰𐑌𐐼𐐯𐐼 𐑋𐐴 𐐹𐐨𐐹𐑊 𐐸𐐶𐐱𐐻 𐑄𐐩 𐑇𐐳𐐼 𐐼𐐭 𐐰𐑁𐐻𐐲𐑉 𐐌 𐐶𐐲𐑆 𐑀𐐱𐑌; 𐐰𐑌𐐼 𐑄𐐰𐐻 𐑄𐐨𐑆 𐐹𐑊𐐩𐐻𐑅 𐑇𐐳𐐼 𐐺𐐨 𐐸𐐰𐑌𐐼𐐯𐐼 𐐼𐐵𐑌 𐑁𐑉𐐱𐑋 𐐶𐐲𐑌 𐐾𐐯𐑌𐐲𐑉𐐩𐑇𐐲𐑌 𐐻𐐭 𐐰𐑌𐐲𐑄𐐲𐑉, 𐐫𐑉 𐑁𐑉𐐱𐑋 𐐶𐐲𐑌 𐐹𐑉𐐱𐑁𐐯𐐻 𐐻𐐭 𐐰𐑌𐐲𐑄𐐲𐑉, 𐐲𐑌𐐻𐐮𐑊 𐑁𐐲𐑉𐑄𐐲𐑉 𐐿𐐲𐑋𐐰𐑌𐐼𐑋𐐯𐑌𐐻𐑅 𐐲𐑂 𐑄 𐐢𐐫𐑉𐐼. 𐐈𐑌𐐼 𐐰𐑌 𐐰𐐿𐐵𐑌𐐻 𐐲𐑂 𐑋𐐴 𐑋𐐩𐐿𐐮𐑍 𐑄𐐨𐑆 𐐹𐑊𐐩𐐻𐑅 𐑇𐐰𐑊 𐐺𐐨 𐑀𐐮𐑂𐐲𐑌 𐐸𐐨𐑉𐐰𐑁𐐻𐐲𐑉; 𐐰𐑌𐐼 𐑄𐐯𐑌, 𐐺𐐨𐐸𐐬𐑊𐐼, 𐐌 𐐹𐑉𐐬𐑅𐐨𐐼 𐐰𐐿𐐫𐑉𐐼𐐮𐑍 𐐻𐐭 𐑄𐐰𐐻 𐐸𐐶𐐮𐐽 𐐌 𐐸𐐰𐑂 𐑅𐐹𐐬𐐿𐐲𐑌; 𐐰𐑌𐐼 𐑄𐐮𐑅 𐐌 𐐼𐐭 𐑄𐐰𐐻 𐑄 𐑋𐐬𐑉 𐑅𐐩𐐿𐑉𐐯𐐼 𐑃𐐮𐑍𐑆 𐑋𐐩 𐐺𐐨 𐐿𐐯𐐹𐐻 𐑁𐐬𐑉 𐑄 𐑌𐐱𐑊𐐯𐐾 𐐲𐑂 𐑋𐐴 𐐹𐐨𐐹𐑊. 𐐤𐐯𐑂𐐲𐑉𐑄𐐯𐑊𐐯𐑅, 𐐌 𐐼𐐭 𐑌𐐱𐐻 𐑉𐐴𐐻 𐐯𐑌𐐨𐑃𐐮𐑍 𐐲𐐹𐐱𐑌 𐐹𐑊𐐩𐐻𐑅, 𐑅𐐩𐑂 𐐮𐐻 𐐺𐐨 𐑄𐐰𐐻 𐐌 𐑃𐐮𐑍𐐿 𐐮𐐻 𐐺𐐨 𐑅𐐩𐐿𐑉𐐯𐐼. 𐐈𐑌𐐼 𐑌𐐵, 𐐮𐑁 𐐌 𐐼𐐭 𐐲𐑉, 𐐨𐑂𐐲𐑌 𐐼𐐮𐐼 𐑄𐐩 𐐲𐑉 𐐲𐑂 𐐬𐑊𐐼; 𐑌𐐱𐐻 𐑄𐐰𐐻 𐐌 𐐶𐐳𐐼 𐐯𐐿𐑅𐐿𐐷𐐭𐑆 𐑋𐐴𐑅𐐯𐑊𐑁 𐐺𐐨𐐿𐐫𐑆 𐐲𐑂 𐐲𐑄𐐲𐑉 𐑋𐐯𐑌, 𐐺𐐲𐐻 𐐺𐐨𐐿𐐫𐑆 𐐲𐑂 𐑄 𐐶𐐨𐐿𐑌𐐯𐑅 𐐸𐐶𐐮𐐽 𐐮𐑆 𐐮𐑌 𐑋𐐨, 𐐰𐐿𐐫𐑉𐐼𐐮𐑍 𐐻𐐭 𐑄 𐑁𐑊𐐯𐑇, 𐐌 𐐶𐐳𐐼 𐐯𐐿𐑅𐐿𐐷𐐭𐑆 𐑋𐐴𐑅𐐯𐑊𐑁. 𐐙𐐬𐑉 𐑄 𐑃𐐮𐑍𐑆 𐐸𐐶𐐮𐐽 𐑅𐐲𐑋 𐑋𐐯𐑌 𐐯𐑅𐐻𐐨𐑋 𐐻𐐭 𐐺𐐨 𐐲𐑂 𐑀𐑉𐐩𐐻 𐐶𐐲𐑉𐑃, 𐐺𐐬𐑃 𐐻𐐭 𐑄 𐐺𐐱𐐼𐐨 𐐰𐑌𐐼 𐑅𐐬𐑊, 𐐲𐑄𐐲𐑉𐑆 𐑅𐐯𐐻 𐐰𐐻 𐑌𐐫𐐻 𐐰𐑌𐐼 𐐻𐑉𐐰𐑋𐐹𐑊 𐐲𐑌𐐼𐐲𐑉 𐑄𐐩𐑉 𐑁𐐨𐐻. 𐐏𐐩, 𐐨𐑂𐐲𐑌 𐑄 𐑂𐐯𐑉𐐨 𐐘𐐱𐐼 𐐲𐑂 𐐆𐑆𐑉𐐩𐐯𐑊, 𐐼𐐭 𐑋𐐯𐑌 𐐻𐑉𐐰𐑋𐐹𐑊 𐐲𐑌𐐼𐐲𐑉 𐑄𐐩𐑉 𐑁𐐨𐐻; 𐐌 𐑅𐐩, 𐐻𐑉𐐰𐑋𐐹𐑊 𐐲𐑌𐐼𐐲𐑉 𐑄𐐩𐑉 𐑁𐐨𐐻, 𐐺𐐲𐐻 𐐌 𐐶𐐳𐐼 𐑅𐐹𐐨𐐿 𐐮𐑌 𐐲𐑄𐐲𐑉 𐐶𐐲𐑉𐐼𐑆; 𐑄𐐩 𐑅𐐯𐐻 𐐸𐐮𐑋 𐐰𐐻 𐑌𐐫𐐻, 𐐰𐑌𐐼 𐐸𐐪𐑉𐐿𐐲𐑌 𐑌𐐱𐐻 𐐻𐐭 𐑄 𐑂𐑎𐑅 𐐲𐑂 𐐸𐐮𐑆 𐐿𐐵𐑌𐑅𐐯𐑊𐑆. 𐐈𐑌𐐼 𐐺𐐨𐐸𐐬𐑊𐐼 𐐸𐐨 𐐿𐐲𐑋𐐯𐑃, 𐐰𐐿𐐫𐑉𐐼𐐮𐑍 𐐻𐐭 𐑄 𐐶𐐲𐑉𐐼𐑆 𐐲𐑂 𐑄 𐐩𐑌𐐾𐐯𐑊, 𐐮𐑌 𐑅𐐮𐐿𐑅 𐐸𐐲𐑌𐐼𐑉𐐯𐐼 𐐷𐐨𐑉𐑆 𐑁𐑉𐐱𐑋 𐑄 𐐻𐐴𐑋 𐑋𐐴 𐑁𐐪𐑄𐐲𐑉 𐑊𐐯𐑁𐐻 𐐖𐐯𐑉𐐭𐑅𐐲𐑊𐐯𐑋. 𐐈𐑌𐐼 𐑄 𐐶𐐲𐑉𐑊𐐼, 𐐺𐐨𐐿𐐫𐑆 𐐲𐑂 𐑄𐐩𐑉 𐐮𐑌𐐮𐐿𐐶𐐮𐐻𐐨, 𐑇𐐰𐑊 𐐾𐐲𐐾 𐐸𐐮𐑋 𐐻𐐭 𐐺𐐨 𐐲 𐑃𐐮𐑍 𐐲𐑂 𐑌𐐫𐐻; 𐐸𐐶𐐯𐑉𐑁𐐬𐑉 𐑄𐐩 𐑅𐐿𐐲𐑉𐐾 𐐸𐐮𐑋, 𐐰𐑌𐐼 𐐸𐐨 𐑅𐐲𐑁𐐲𐑉𐐯𐑃 𐐮𐐻; 𐐰𐑌𐐼 𐑄𐐩 𐑅𐑋𐐴𐐻 𐐸𐐮𐑋, 𐐰𐑌𐐼 𐐸𐐨 𐑅𐐲𐑁𐐲𐑉𐐯𐑃 𐐮𐐻. 𐐏𐐩, 𐑄𐐩 𐑅𐐹𐐮𐐻 𐐲𐐹𐐱𐑌 𐐸𐐮𐑋, 𐐰𐑌𐐼 𐐸𐐨 𐑅𐐲𐑁𐐲𐑉𐐯𐑃 𐐮𐐻, 𐐺𐐨𐐿𐐫𐑆 𐐲𐑂 𐐸𐐮𐑆 𐑊𐐲𐑂𐐮𐑍 𐐿𐐴𐑌𐐼𐑌𐐯𐑅 𐐰𐑌𐐼 𐐸𐐮𐑆 𐑊𐐫𐑍 𐑅𐐲𐑁𐐲𐑉𐐮𐑍 𐐻𐐬𐐲𐑉𐐼𐑆 𐑄 𐐽𐐮𐑊𐐼𐑉𐐯𐑌 𐐲𐑂 𐑋𐐯𐑌. 𐐈𐑌𐐼 𐑄 𐐘𐐱𐐼 𐐲𐑂 𐐵𐑉 𐑁𐐪𐑄𐐲𐑉𐑆, 𐐸𐐭 𐐶𐐲𐑉 𐑊𐐯𐐼 𐐵𐐻 𐐲𐑂 𐐀𐐾𐐮𐐹𐐻, 𐐵𐐻 𐐲𐑂 𐐺𐐱𐑌𐐼𐐩𐐾, 𐐰𐑌𐐼 𐐫𐑊𐑅𐐬 𐐶𐐲𐑉 𐐹𐑉𐐯𐑆𐐲𐑉𐑂𐐼 𐐮𐑌 𐑄 𐐶𐐮𐑊𐐼𐐲𐑉𐑌𐐯𐑅 𐐺𐐴 𐐸𐐮𐑋; 𐐷𐐩, 𐑄 𐐘𐐱𐐼 𐐲𐑂 𐐁𐐺𐑉𐐲𐐸𐐰𐑋, 𐐰𐑌𐐼 𐐲𐑂 𐐌𐑆𐐲𐐿, 𐐰𐑌𐐼 𐑄 𐐘𐐱𐐼 𐐲𐑂 𐐖𐐩𐐿𐐲𐐺, 𐐷𐐨𐑊𐐼𐐯𐑃 𐐸𐐮𐑋𐑅𐐯𐑊𐑁, 𐐰𐐿𐐫𐑉𐐼𐐮𐑍 𐐻𐐭 𐑄 𐐶𐐲𐑉𐐼𐑆 𐐲𐑂 𐑄 𐐩𐑌𐐾𐐯𐑊, 𐐰𐑆 𐐲 𐑋𐐰𐑌, 𐐮𐑌𐐻𐐭 𐑄 𐐸𐐰𐑌𐐼𐑆 𐐲𐑂 𐐶𐐮𐐿𐐯𐐼 𐑋𐐯𐑌, 𐐻𐐭 𐐺𐐨 𐑊𐐮𐑁𐐻𐐯𐐼 𐐲𐐹, 𐐰𐐿𐐫𐑉𐐼𐐮𐑍 𐐻𐐭 𐑄 𐐶𐐲𐑉𐐼𐑆 𐐲𐑂 𐐞𐐨𐑌𐐱𐐿, 𐐰𐑌𐐼 𐐻𐐭 𐐺𐐨 𐐿𐑉𐐭𐑅𐐮𐑁𐐴𐐼, 𐐰𐐿𐐫𐑉𐐼𐐮𐑍 𐐻𐐭 𐑄 𐐶𐐲𐑉𐐼𐑆 𐐲𐑂 𐐤𐐨𐐲𐑋, 𐐰𐑌𐐼 𐐻𐐭 𐐺𐐨 𐐺𐐯𐑉𐐨𐐼 𐐮𐑌 𐐲 𐑅𐐯𐐹𐐲𐑊𐐿𐐲𐑉, 𐐰𐐿𐐫𐑉𐐼𐐮𐑍 𐐻𐐭 𐑄 𐐶𐐲𐑉𐐼𐑆 𐐲𐑂 𐐞𐐨𐑌𐐱𐑅, 𐐸𐐶𐐮𐐽 𐐸𐐨 𐑅𐐹𐐩𐐿 𐐿𐐱𐑌𐑅𐐲𐑉𐑌𐐮𐑍 𐑄 𐑃𐑉𐐨 𐐼𐐩𐑆 𐐲𐑂 𐐼𐐪𐑉𐐿𐑌𐐯𐑅, 𐐸𐐶𐐮𐐽 𐑇𐐳𐐼 𐐺𐐨 𐐲 𐑅𐐴𐑌 𐑀𐐮𐑂𐐲𐑌 𐐲𐑂 𐐸𐐮𐑆 𐐼𐐯𐑃, 𐐲𐑌𐐻𐐭 𐑄𐐬𐑆 𐐸𐐭 𐑇𐐳𐐼 𐐮𐑌𐐸𐐰𐐺𐐮𐐻 𐑄 𐐴𐑊𐑆 𐐲𐑂 𐑄 𐑅𐐨; 𐑋𐐬𐑉 𐐯𐑅𐐹𐐯𐑇𐐲𐑊𐐨 𐑀𐐮𐑂𐐲𐑌 𐐲𐑌𐐻𐐭 𐑄𐐬𐑆 𐐸𐐭 𐐪𐑉 𐐲𐑂 𐑄 𐐸𐐵𐑅 𐐲𐑂 𐐆𐑆𐑉𐐩𐐯𐑊.

48. 𐐙𐐫𐑉 𐑄𐐲𐑅 𐑅𐐹𐐩𐐿 𐑄 𐐹𐑉𐐱𐑁𐐯𐐻, 𐑄 𐐢𐐫𐑉𐐼 𐐘𐐱𐐼 𐑇𐐳𐑉𐑊𐐨 𐑇𐐰𐑊 𐑂𐐮𐑆𐐮𐐻 𐐫𐑊 𐑄 𐐸𐐵𐑅 𐐱𐑂 𐐆𐑆𐑉𐐩𐐯𐑊 𐐰𐐻 𐑄𐐰𐐻 𐐼𐐩: 𐑅𐐲𐑋 𐐶𐐮𐑄 𐐸𐐮𐑆 𐑂𐑎𐑅, 𐐺𐐨𐐿𐐫𐑆 𐐱𐑂 𐑄𐐩𐑉 𐑉𐐴𐐽𐐲𐑅𐑌𐐯𐑅, 𐐲𐑌𐐻𐐭 𐑄𐐩𐑉 𐑀𐑉𐐩𐐻 𐐾𐑎 𐐰𐑌𐐼 𐑅𐐰𐑊𐑂𐐩𐑇𐐲𐑌, 𐐰𐑌𐐼 𐐲𐑄𐐲𐑉𐑆 𐐶𐐮𐑄 𐑄 𐑃𐐲𐑌𐐼𐐲𐑉𐐮𐑍𐑆 𐐰𐑌𐐼 𐑄 𐑊𐐴𐐻𐑌𐐮𐑍𐑆 𐐱𐑂 𐐸𐐮𐑆 𐐹𐐵𐐲𐑉, 𐐺𐐴 𐐻𐐯𐑋𐐹𐐯𐑅𐐻𐑅, 𐐺𐐴 𐑁𐐴𐑉, 𐐰𐑌𐐼 𐐺𐐴 𐑅𐑋𐐬𐐿, 𐐰𐑌𐐼 𐑂𐐩𐐹𐐲𐑉 𐐱𐑂 𐐼𐐪𐑉𐐿𐑌𐐯𐑅, 𐐰𐑌𐐼 𐐺𐐴 𐑄 𐐬𐐹𐐲𐑌𐐮𐑍 𐐱𐑂 𐑄 𐐲𐑉𐑃, 𐐰𐑌𐐼 𐐺𐐴 𐑋𐐵𐑌𐐻𐐩𐑌𐑆 𐐸𐐶𐐮𐐽 𐑇𐐰𐑊 𐐺𐐨 𐐿𐐰𐑉𐐨𐐼 𐐲𐐹; 𐐰𐑌𐐼 𐐫𐑊 𐑄𐐨𐑆 𐑃𐐮𐑍𐑆 𐑋𐐲𐑅𐐻 𐑇𐐳𐑉𐑊𐐨 𐐿𐐲𐑋, 𐑅𐐯𐑃 𐑄 𐐹𐑉𐐱𐑁𐐯𐐻 𐐞𐐨𐑌𐐱𐑅. 𐐈𐑌𐐼 𐑄 𐑉𐐱𐐿𐑅 𐐱𐑂 𐑄 𐐲𐑉𐑃 𐑋𐐲𐑅𐐻 𐑉𐐯𐑌𐐼; 𐐰𐑌𐐼 𐐺𐐨𐐿𐐫𐑆 𐐱𐑂 𐑄 𐑀𐑉𐐬𐑌𐐮𐑍𐑆 𐐱𐑂 𐑄 𐐲𐑉𐑃, 𐑋𐐯𐑌𐐨 𐐱𐑂 𐑄 𐐿𐐮𐑍𐑆 𐐱𐑂 𐑄 𐐴𐑊𐑆 𐐱𐑂 𐑄 𐑅𐐨 𐑇𐐰𐑊 𐐺𐐨 𐑉𐐫𐐻 𐐲𐐹𐐱𐑌 𐐺𐐴 𐑄 𐐝𐐹𐐮𐑉𐐮𐐻 𐐱𐑂 𐐘𐐱𐐼, 𐐻𐐭 𐐯𐐿𐑅𐐿𐑊𐐩𐑋, 𐑄 𐐘𐐱𐐼 𐐱𐑂 𐑌𐐩𐐽𐐲𐑉 𐑅𐐲𐑁𐐲𐑉𐑆. 𐐈𐑌𐐼 𐐰𐑆 𐑁𐐫𐑉 𐑄𐐬𐑆 𐐸𐐭 𐐪𐑉 𐐰𐐻 𐐖𐐯𐑉𐐭𐑅𐐲𐑊𐐯𐑋, 𐑅𐐯𐑃 𐑄 𐐹𐑉𐐱𐑁𐐯𐐻, 𐑄𐐩 𐑇𐐰𐑊 𐐺𐐨 𐑅𐐿𐐲𐑉𐐾𐐼 𐐺𐐴 𐐫𐑊 𐐹𐐨𐐹𐐲𐑊, 𐐺𐐨𐐿𐐫𐑆 𐑄𐐩 𐐿𐑉𐐭𐑅𐐮𐑁𐐴 𐑄 𐐘𐐱𐐼 𐐱𐑂 𐐆𐑆𐑉𐐩𐐯𐑊, 𐐰𐑌𐐼 𐐻𐐲𐑉𐑌 𐑄𐐩𐑉 𐐸𐐪𐑉𐐻𐑅 𐐲𐑅𐐴𐐼, 𐑉𐐨𐐾𐐯𐐿𐐻𐐮𐑍 𐑅𐐴𐑌𐑆 𐐰𐑌𐐼 𐐶𐐲𐑌𐐼𐐲𐑉𐑆, 𐐰𐑌𐐼 𐑄 𐐹𐐵𐐲𐑉 𐐰𐑌𐐼 𐑀𐑊𐐬𐑉𐐨 𐐱𐑂 𐑄 𐐘𐐱𐐼 𐐱𐑂 𐐆𐑆𐑉𐐩𐐯𐑊; 𐐰𐑌𐐼 𐐺𐐨𐐿𐐫𐑆 𐑄𐐩 𐐻𐐲𐑉𐑌 𐑄𐐩𐑉 𐐸𐐪𐑉𐐻𐑅 𐐲𐑅𐐴𐐼, 𐑅𐐯𐑃 𐑄 𐐹𐑉𐐱𐑁𐐯𐐻, 𐐰𐑌𐐼 𐐸𐐰𐑂 𐐼𐐯𐑅𐐹𐐴𐑆𐐼 𐑄 𐐐𐐬𐑊𐐨 𐐎𐐲𐑌 𐐱𐑂 𐐆𐑆𐑉𐐩𐐯𐑊, 𐑄𐐩 𐑇𐐰𐑊 𐐶𐐱𐑌𐐼𐐲𐑉 𐐮𐑌 𐑄 𐑁𐑊𐐯𐑇, 𐐰𐑌𐐼 𐐹𐐯𐑉𐐮𐑇, 𐐰𐑌𐐼 𐐺𐐨𐐿𐐲𐑋 𐐲 𐐸𐐮𐑅 𐐰𐑌𐐼 𐐲 𐐺𐐴-𐐶𐐲𐑉𐐼, 𐐰𐑌𐐼 𐐺𐐨 𐐸𐐩𐐻𐐯𐐼 𐐲𐑋𐐲𐑍 𐐫𐑊 𐑌𐐩𐑇𐐲𐑌𐑆; 𐑌𐐯𐑂𐐲𐑉𐑄𐐯𐑊𐐯𐑅, 𐐸𐐶𐐯𐑌 𐑄𐐰𐐻 𐐼𐐩 𐐿𐐲𐑋𐐯𐑃, 𐑅𐐯𐑃 𐑄 𐐹𐑉𐐱𐑁𐐯𐐻, 𐑄𐐰𐐻 𐑄𐐩 𐑌𐐬 𐑋𐐬𐑉 𐐻𐐲𐑉𐑌 𐐲𐑅𐐴𐐼 𐑄𐐩𐑉 𐐸𐐪𐑉𐐻𐑅 𐐲𐑀𐐯𐑌𐑅𐐻 𐑄 𐐐𐐬𐑊𐐨 𐐎𐐲𐑌 𐐱𐑂 𐐆𐑆𐑉𐐩𐐯𐑊, 𐑄𐐯𐑌 𐐶𐐮𐑊 𐐸𐐨 𐑉𐐨𐑋𐐯𐑋𐐺𐐲𐑉 𐑄 𐐿𐐲𐑂𐐯𐑌𐐰𐑌𐐻𐑅 𐐸𐐶𐐮𐐽 𐐸𐐨 𐑋𐐩𐐼 𐐻𐐭 𐑄𐐩𐑉 𐑁𐐪𐑄𐐲𐑉𐑆; 𐐷𐐩, 𐑄𐐯𐑌 𐐶𐐮𐑊 𐐸𐐨 𐑉𐐨𐑋𐐯𐑋𐐺𐐲𐑉 𐑄 𐐴𐑊𐑆 𐐱𐑂 𐑄 𐑅𐐨; 𐐷𐐩, 𐐰𐑌𐐼 𐐫𐑊 𐑄 𐐹𐐨𐐹𐐲𐑊 𐐸𐐭 𐐪𐑉 𐐱𐑂 𐑄 𐐸𐐵𐑅 𐐱𐑂 𐐆𐑆𐑉𐐩𐐯𐑊, 𐐶𐐮𐑊 𐐌 𐑀𐐰𐑄𐐲𐑉 𐐮𐑌, 𐑅𐐯𐑃 𐑄 𐐢𐐫𐑉𐐼, 𐐰𐐿𐐫𐑉𐐼𐐮𐑍 𐐻𐐭 𐑄 𐐶𐐲𐑉𐐼𐑆 𐐱𐑂 𐑄 𐐹𐑉𐐱𐑁𐐯𐐻 𐐞𐐨𐑌𐐱𐑅, 𐑁𐑉𐐱𐑋 𐑄 𐑁𐐬𐑉 𐐿𐐶𐐫𐑉𐐻𐐲𐑉𐑆 𐐱𐑂 𐑄 𐐲𐑉𐑃; 𐐷𐐩, 𐐰𐑌𐐼 𐐫𐑊 𐑄 𐐲𐑉𐑃 𐑇𐐰𐑊 𐑅𐐨 𐑄 𐑅𐐰𐑊𐑂𐐩𐑇𐐲𐑌 𐐱𐑂 𐑄 𐐢𐐫𐑉𐐼, 𐑅𐐯𐑃 𐑄 𐐹𐑉𐐱𐑁𐐯𐐻; 𐐯𐑂𐐲𐑉𐐨 𐑌𐐩𐑇𐐲𐑌, 𐐿𐐮𐑌𐐼𐑉𐐯𐐼, 𐐻𐐲𐑍, 𐐰𐑌𐐼 𐐹𐐨𐐹𐐲𐑊, 𐑇𐐰𐑊 𐐺𐐨 𐐺𐑊𐐯𐑅𐐯𐐼.

49. 𐐈𐑌𐐼 𐐌, 𐐤𐐨𐑁𐐴, 𐐸𐐰𐑂 𐑉𐐮𐐻𐑌 𐑄𐐨𐑆 𐑃𐐮𐑍𐑆 𐐲𐑌𐐻𐐭 𐑋𐐴 𐐹𐐨𐐹𐐲𐑊, 𐑄𐐰𐐻 𐐹𐐲𐑉𐐸𐐰𐐹𐑅 𐐌 𐑋𐐴𐐻 𐐹𐐲𐑉𐑅𐐶𐐩𐐼 𐑄𐐯𐑋 𐑄𐐰𐐻 𐑄𐐩 𐐶𐐳𐐼 𐑉𐐨𐑋𐐯𐑋𐐺𐐲𐑉 𐑄 𐐢𐐫𐑉𐐼 𐑄𐐩𐑉 𐐡𐐨𐐼𐐨𐑋𐐲𐑉; 𐐸𐐶𐐯𐑉𐑁𐐫𐑉, 𐐌 𐑅𐐹𐐨𐐿 𐐲𐑌𐐻𐐭 𐐫𐑊 𐑄 𐐸𐐵𐑅 𐐱𐑂 𐐆𐑆𐑉𐐩𐐯𐑊, 𐐮𐑁 𐐮𐐻 𐑅𐐬 𐐺𐐨 𐑄𐐰𐐻 𐑄𐐩 𐑇𐐳𐐼 𐐱𐐺𐐻𐐩𐑌 𐑄𐐨𐑆 𐑃𐐮𐑍𐑆. 𐐙𐐫𐑉 𐐺𐐨𐐸𐐬𐑊𐐼, 𐐌 𐐸𐐰𐑂 𐐶𐐲𐑉𐐿𐐮𐑍𐑆 𐐮𐑌 𐑄 𐑅𐐹𐐮𐑉𐐮𐐻, 𐐸𐐶𐐮𐐽 𐐼𐐲𐑃 𐐶𐐨𐑉𐐨 𐑋𐐨, 𐐨𐑂𐐲𐑌 𐑄𐐰𐐻 𐐫𐑊 𐑋𐐴 𐐾𐑎𐑌𐐻𐑅 𐐪𐑉 𐐶𐐨𐐿, 𐑁𐐫𐑉 𐑄𐐬𐑆 𐐸𐐭 𐐪𐑉 𐐰𐐻 𐐖𐐯𐑉𐐭𐑅𐐲𐑊𐐯𐑋; 𐑁𐐫𐑉 𐐸𐐰𐐼 𐑌𐐱𐐻 𐑄 𐐢𐐫𐑉𐐼 𐐺𐐮𐑌 𐑋𐐲𐑉𐑅𐐮𐑁𐐳𐑊, 𐐻𐐭 𐑇𐐬 𐐲𐑌𐐻𐐭 𐑋𐐨 𐐿𐐱𐑌𐑅𐐲𐑉𐑌𐐮𐑍 𐑄𐐯𐑋, 𐐨𐑂𐐲𐑌 𐐰𐑆 𐐸𐐨 𐐸𐐰𐐼 𐐹𐑉𐐱𐑁𐐯𐐻𐑅 𐐱𐑂 𐐬𐑊𐐼, 𐐌 𐑇𐐳𐐼 𐐸𐐰𐑂 𐐹𐐯𐑉𐐮𐑇𐐻 𐐫𐑊𐑅𐐬. 𐐈𐑌𐐼 𐐸𐐨 𐑇𐐳𐑉𐑊𐐨 𐐼𐐮𐐼 𐑇𐐬 𐐲𐑌𐐻𐐭 𐑄 𐐹𐑉𐐱𐑁𐐯𐐻𐑅 𐐱𐑂 𐐬𐑊𐐼 𐐫𐑊 𐑃𐐮𐑍𐑆 𐐿𐐱𐑌𐑅𐐲𐑉𐑌𐐮𐑍 𐑄𐐯𐑋; 𐐰𐑌𐐼 𐐫𐑊𐑅𐐬 𐐸𐐨 𐐼𐐮𐐼 𐑇𐐬 𐐲𐑌𐐻𐐭 𐑋𐐯𐑌𐐨 𐐿𐐱𐑌𐑅𐐲𐑉𐑌𐐮𐑍 𐐲𐑅; 𐐸𐐶𐐯𐑉𐑁𐐫𐑉 𐐮𐐻 𐑋𐐲𐑅𐐻 𐑌𐐨𐐼𐑆 𐐺𐐨 𐑄𐐰𐐻 𐐶𐐨 𐑌𐐬 𐐿𐐱𐑌𐑅𐐲𐑉𐑌𐐮𐑍 𐑄𐐯𐑋, 𐑁𐐫𐑉 𐑄𐐩 𐐪𐑉 𐑉𐐮𐐻𐑌 𐐲𐐹𐐱𐑌 𐑄 𐐹𐑊𐐩𐐻𐑅 𐐱𐑂 𐐺𐑉𐐰𐑅.

𐐕𐐈𐐑𐐓𐐊𐐡 VI.

1. 𐐤𐐵 𐐮𐐻 𐐿𐐩𐑋 𐐻𐐭 𐐹𐐰𐑅 𐑄𐐰𐐻 𐐌, 𐐤𐐨𐑁𐐴, 𐐼𐐮𐐼 𐐻𐐨𐐽 𐑋𐐴 𐐺𐑉𐐯𐑄𐑉𐐯𐑌 𐑄𐐨𐑆 𐑃𐐮𐑍𐑆; 𐐰𐑌𐐼 𐐮𐐻 𐐿𐐩𐑋 𐐻𐐭 𐐹𐐰𐑅 𐑄𐐰𐐻 𐐌 𐐼𐐮𐐼 𐑉𐐨𐐼 𐑋𐐯𐑌𐐨 𐑃𐐮𐑍𐑆 𐐻𐐭 𐑄𐐯𐑋, 𐐸𐐶𐐮𐐽 𐐶𐐲𐑉 𐐯𐑌𐑀𐑉𐐩𐑂𐐯𐑌 𐐲𐐹𐐱𐑌 𐑄 𐐹𐑊𐐩𐐻𐑅 𐐱𐑂 𐐺𐑉𐐰𐑅, 𐑄𐐰𐐻 𐑄𐐩 𐑋𐐴𐐻 𐑌𐐬 𐐿𐐱𐑌𐑅𐐲𐑉𐑌𐐮𐑍 𐑄 𐐼𐐭𐐮𐑍𐑆 𐐱𐑂 𐑄 𐐢𐐫𐑉𐐼 𐐮𐑌 𐐲𐑄𐐲𐑉 𐑊𐐰𐑌𐐼𐑆, 𐐲𐑋𐐲𐑍 𐐹𐐨𐐹𐐲𐑊 𐐱𐑂 𐐬𐑊𐐼. 𐐈𐑌𐐼 𐐌 𐐼𐐮𐐼 𐑉𐐨𐐼 𐑋𐐯𐑌𐐨 𐑃𐐮𐑍𐑆 𐐲𐑌𐐻𐐭 𐑄𐐯𐑋 𐐸𐐶𐐮𐐽 𐐶𐐲𐑉 𐐯𐑌𐑀𐑉𐐩𐑂𐐯𐑌 𐐮𐑌 𐑄 𐐺𐐳𐐿𐑅 𐐱𐑂 𐐣𐐬𐑆𐐯𐑆; 𐐺𐐲𐐻 𐑄𐐰𐐻 𐐌 𐑋𐐴𐐻 𐑋𐐬𐑉 𐑁𐐳𐑊𐐨 𐐹𐐲𐑉𐑅𐐶𐐩𐐼 𐑄𐐯𐑋 𐐻𐐭 𐐺𐐨𐑊𐐨𐑂 𐐮𐑌 𐑄 𐐢𐐫𐑉𐐼 𐑄𐐩𐑉 𐐡𐐨𐐼𐐨𐑋𐐲𐑉, 𐐌 𐐼𐐮𐐼 𐑉𐐨𐐼 𐐲𐑌𐐻𐐭 𐑄𐐯𐑋 𐑄𐐰𐐻 𐐸𐐶𐐮𐐽 𐐶𐐱𐑆 𐑉𐐮𐐻𐑌 𐐺𐐴 𐑄 𐐹𐑉𐐱𐑁𐐯𐐻 𐐌𐑆𐐩𐐲; 𐑁𐐫𐑉 𐐌 𐐼𐐮𐐼 𐑊𐐴𐐿𐐲𐑌 𐐫𐑊 𐑅𐐿𐑉𐐮𐐹𐐽𐐲𐑉𐑆 𐐲𐑌𐐻𐐭 𐐲𐑅, 𐑄𐐰𐐻 𐐮𐐻 𐑋𐐴𐐻 𐐺𐐨 𐑁𐐫𐑉 𐐵𐑉 𐐹𐑉𐐱𐑁𐐮𐐻 𐐰𐑌𐐼 𐑊𐐲𐑉𐑌𐐮𐑍. 𐐐𐐶𐐯𐑉𐑁𐐫𐑉 𐐌 𐑅𐐹𐐩𐐿 𐐲𐑌𐐻𐐭

𐑄𐐯𐑋, 𐑅𐐩𐐮𐑍, 𐐐𐐨𐑉 𐐷 𐑄 𐐶𐐲𐑉𐐼𐑆 𐐱𐑂 𐑄 𐐹𐑉𐐱𐑁𐐯𐐻, 𐐷 𐐸𐐭 𐐪𐑉 𐐲 𐑉𐐯𐑋𐑌𐐲𐑌𐐻 𐐱𐑂 𐑄 𐐸𐐵𐑅 𐐱𐑂 𐐆𐑆𐑉𐐩𐐯𐑊, 𐐲 𐐺𐑉𐐰𐑌𐐽 𐐸𐐭 𐐸𐐰𐑂 𐐺𐐮𐑌 𐐺𐑉𐐬𐐿𐐲𐑌 𐐫𐑁; 𐐸𐐨𐑉 𐐷 𐑄 𐐶𐐲𐑉𐐼𐑆 𐐱𐑂 𐑄 𐐹𐑉𐐱𐑁𐐯𐐻, 𐐸𐐶𐐮𐐽 𐐶𐐲𐑉 𐑉𐐮𐐻𐑌 𐐲𐑌𐐻𐐭 𐐫𐑊 𐑄 𐐸𐐵𐑅 𐐱𐑂 𐐆𐑆𐑉𐐩𐐯𐑊, 𐐰𐑌𐐼 𐑊𐐴𐐿𐐲𐑌 𐑄𐐯𐑋 𐐲𐑌𐐻𐐭 𐐷𐐭𐑉𐑅𐐯𐑊𐑂𐑆, 𐑄𐐰𐐻 𐐷 𐑋𐐩 𐐸𐐰𐑂 𐐸𐐬𐐹 𐐰𐑆 𐐶𐐯𐑊 𐐰𐑆 𐐷𐐭𐑉 𐐺𐑉𐐯𐑄𐑉𐐯𐑌 𐑁𐑉𐐱𐑋 𐐸𐐭𐑋 𐐷 𐐸𐐰𐑂 𐐺𐐮𐑌 𐐺𐑉𐐬𐐿𐐲𐑌 𐐫𐑁; 𐑁𐐫𐑉 𐐰𐑁𐐻𐐲𐑉 𐑄𐐮𐑅 𐑋𐐰𐑌𐐲𐑉 𐐸𐐰𐑆 𐑄 𐐹𐑉𐐱𐑁𐐯𐐻 𐑉𐐮𐐻𐑌—𐐐𐐪𐑉𐐿𐐲𐑌 𐐰𐑌𐐼 𐐸𐐨𐑉 𐑄𐐮𐑅, O 𐐸𐐵𐑅 𐐱𐑂 𐐖𐐩𐐿𐐲𐐺, 𐐸𐐭 𐐪𐑉 𐐿𐐫𐑊𐐼 𐐺𐐴 𐑄 𐑌𐐩𐑋 𐐱𐑂 𐐆𐑆𐑉𐐩𐐯𐑊, 𐐰𐑌𐐼 𐐪𐑉 𐐿𐐲𐑋 𐑁𐐬𐑉𐑃 𐐵𐐻 𐐱𐑂 𐑄 𐐶𐐫𐐻𐐲𐑉𐑆 𐐱𐑂 𐐖𐐭𐐼𐐲, 𐐸𐐭 𐑅𐐶𐐩𐑉 𐐺𐐴 𐑄 𐑌𐐩𐑋 𐐱𐑂 𐑄 𐐢𐐫𐑉𐐼, 𐐰𐑌𐐼 𐑋𐐩𐐿 𐑋𐐯𐑌𐑇𐐲𐑌 𐐱𐑂 𐑄 𐐘𐐱𐐼 𐐱𐑂 𐐆𐑆𐑉𐐩𐐯𐑊, 𐐷𐐯𐐻 𐑄𐐩 𐑅𐐶𐐩𐑉 𐑌𐐱𐐻 𐐮𐑌 𐐻𐑉𐐭𐑃 𐑌𐐫𐑉 𐐮𐑌 𐑉𐐴𐐽𐐲𐑅𐑌𐐯𐑅; 𐑌𐐯𐑂𐐲𐑉𐑄𐐲𐑊𐐯𐑅 𐑄𐐩 𐐿𐐫𐑊 𐑄𐐯𐑋𐑅𐐯𐑊𐑂𐑆 𐐱𐑂 𐑄 𐐸𐐬𐑊𐐨 𐑅𐐮𐐻𐐨, 𐐺𐐲𐐻 𐑄𐐩 𐐼𐐭 𐑌𐐱𐐻 𐑅𐐻𐐩 𐑄𐐯𐑋𐑅𐐯𐑊𐑂𐑆 𐐲𐐹𐐱𐑌 𐑄 𐐘𐐱𐐼 𐐱𐑂 𐐆𐑆𐑉𐐩𐐯𐑊, 𐐸𐐭 𐐮𐑆 𐑄 𐐢𐐫𐑉𐐼 𐐱𐑂 𐐐𐐬𐑅𐐻𐑅; 𐐷𐐩, 𐑄 𐐢𐐫𐑉𐐼 𐐱𐑂 𐐐𐐬𐑅𐐻𐑅 𐐮𐑆 𐐸𐐮𐑆 𐑌𐐩𐑋. 𐐒𐐨𐐸𐐬𐑊𐐼 𐐌 𐐸𐐰𐑂 𐐼𐐯𐐿𐑊𐐩𐑉𐐼 𐑄 𐑁𐐫𐑉𐑋𐐲𐑉 𐑃𐐮𐑍𐑆 𐑁𐑉𐐱𐑋 𐑄 𐐺𐐨𐑀𐐮𐑌𐐮𐑍; 𐐰𐑌𐐼 𐑄𐐩 𐐶𐐯𐑌𐐻 𐑁𐐬𐑉𐑃 𐐵𐐻 𐐱𐑂 𐑋𐐴 𐑋𐐵𐑃, 𐐰𐑌𐐼 𐐌 𐑇𐐬𐐼 𐑄𐐯𐑋. 𐐌 𐐼𐐮𐐼 𐑇𐐬 𐑄𐐯𐑋 𐑅𐐲𐐼𐐲𐑌𐑊𐐨, 𐐰𐑌𐐼 𐐌 𐐼𐐮𐐼 𐐮𐐻 𐐺𐐨𐐿𐐫𐑆 𐐌 𐑌𐐭 𐑄𐐰𐐻 𐑄𐐵 𐐪𐑉𐐻 𐐱𐐺𐑅𐐻𐐮𐑌𐐩𐐻, 𐐰𐑌𐐼 𐑄𐐴 𐑌𐐯𐐿 𐐮𐑆 𐐰𐑌 𐐴𐐲𐑉𐑌 𐑅𐐮𐑌𐐷𐐭, 𐐰𐑌𐐼 𐑄𐐴 𐐺𐑉𐐵 𐐺𐑉𐐰𐑅; 𐐰𐑌𐐼 𐐌 𐐸𐐰𐑂, 𐐨𐑂𐐲𐑌 𐑁𐑉𐐱𐑋 𐑄 𐐺𐐨𐑀𐐮𐑌𐐮𐑍 𐐼𐐯𐐿𐑊𐐩𐑉𐐼 𐐻𐐭 𐑄𐐨, 𐐺𐐨𐑁𐐬𐑉 𐐮𐐻 𐐿𐐩𐑋 𐐻𐐭 𐐹𐐰𐑅 𐐌 𐑇𐐬𐐼 𐑄𐐯𐑋 𐑄𐐨; 𐐰𐑌𐐼 𐐌 𐑇𐐬𐐼 𐑄𐐯𐑋 𐑁𐐫𐑉 𐑁𐐨𐑉 𐑊𐐯𐑅𐐻 𐑄𐐵 𐑇𐐳𐐼𐑅𐐻 𐑅𐐩, 𐐣𐐴𐑌 𐐴𐐼𐐲𐑊 𐐸𐐰𐑃 𐐼𐐲𐑌 𐑄𐐯𐑋, 𐐰𐑌𐐼 𐑋𐐴 𐑀𐑉𐐩𐑂𐐲𐑌 𐐮𐑋𐐲𐐾, 𐐰𐑌𐐼 𐑋𐐴 𐑋𐐬𐑊𐐻𐐲𐑌 𐐮𐑋𐐲𐐾 𐐸𐐰𐑃 𐐿𐐲𐑋𐐰𐑌𐐼𐐯𐐼 𐑄𐐯𐑋. 𐐜𐐵 𐐸𐐰𐑅𐐻 𐑅𐐨𐑌 𐐰𐑌𐐼 𐐸𐐲𐑉𐐼 𐐫𐑊 𐑄𐐮𐑅; 𐐰𐑌𐐼 𐐶𐐮𐑊 𐐷 𐑌𐐱𐐻 𐐼𐐯𐐿𐑊𐐩𐑉 𐑄𐐯𐑋? 𐐰𐑌𐐼 𐑄𐐰𐐻 𐐌 𐐸𐐰𐑂 𐑇𐐬𐐼 𐑄𐐨 𐑌𐐭 𐑃𐐮𐑍𐑆 𐑁𐑉𐐱𐑋 𐑄𐐮𐑅 𐐻𐐴𐑋, 𐐨𐑂𐐲𐑌 𐐸𐐮𐐼𐐲𐑌 𐑃𐐮𐑍𐑆, 𐐰𐑌𐐼 𐑄𐐵 𐐼𐐮𐐼𐑅𐐻 𐑌𐐱𐐻 𐑌𐐬 𐑄𐐯𐑋; 𐐜𐐩 𐐪𐑉 𐐿𐑉𐐨𐐩𐐻𐐯𐐼 𐑌𐐵, 𐐰𐑌𐐼 𐑌𐐱𐐻 𐑁𐑉𐐱𐑋 𐑄 𐐺𐐨𐑀𐐮𐑌𐐮𐑍; 𐐨𐑂𐐲𐑌 𐐺𐐨𐑁𐐬𐑉 𐑄 𐐼𐐩 𐐸𐐶𐐯𐑌 𐑄𐐵 𐐸𐐲𐑉𐐼𐐯𐑅𐐻 𐑄𐐯𐑋 𐑌𐐱𐐻 𐑄𐐩 𐐶𐐲𐑉 𐐼𐐯𐐿𐑊𐐩𐑉𐐼 𐐲𐑌𐐻𐐭 𐑄𐐨, 𐑊𐐯𐑅𐐻 𐑄𐐵 𐑇𐐳𐐼𐑅𐐻 𐑅𐐩, 𐐒𐐨𐐸𐐬𐑊𐐼 𐐌 𐑌𐐭 𐑄𐐯𐑋. 𐐏𐐩, 𐐰𐑌𐐼 𐑄𐐵 𐐸𐐲𐑉𐐼𐐯𐑅𐐻 𐑌𐐱𐐻; 𐐷𐐩, 𐑄𐐵 𐑌𐐭𐐯𐑅𐐻 𐑌𐐱𐐻; 𐐷𐐩, 𐑁𐑉𐐱𐑋 𐑄𐐰𐐻 𐐻𐐴𐑋 𐑄𐐴𐑌 𐐨𐑉 𐐶𐐱𐑆 𐑌𐐱𐐻 𐐬𐐹𐐲𐑌𐐼; 𐑁𐐫𐑉 𐐌 𐑌𐐭 𐑄𐐰𐐻 𐑄𐐵 𐐶𐐳𐐼𐑅𐐻 𐐼𐐨𐑊 𐑂𐐯𐑉𐐨 𐐻𐑉𐐯𐐽𐐲𐑉𐐲𐑅𐑊𐐨, 𐐰𐑌𐐼 𐐶𐐱𐑅𐐻 𐐿𐐫𐑊𐐼 𐐲 𐐻𐑉𐐰𐑌𐑅𐑀𐑉𐐯𐑅𐐲𐑉 𐑁𐑉𐐱𐑋 𐑄 𐐶𐐭𐑋.

2. 𐐤𐐯𐑂𐐲𐑉𐑄𐐲𐑊𐐯𐑅, 𐑁𐐫𐑉 𐑋𐐴 𐑌𐐩𐑋'𐑆 𐑅𐐩𐐿 𐐶𐐮𐑊 𐐌 𐐼𐐨𐑁𐐲𐑉 𐑋𐐴𐑌 𐐰𐑍𐑀𐐲𐑉, 𐐰𐑌𐐼 𐑁𐐫𐑉 𐑋𐐴 𐐹𐑉𐐩𐑆 𐐶𐐮𐑊 𐐌 𐑉𐐨𐑁𐑉𐐩𐑌 𐑁𐑉𐐱𐑋 𐑄𐐨, 𐑄𐐰𐐻 𐐌 𐐿𐐲𐐻 𐑄𐐨 𐑌𐐱𐐻 𐐫𐑁; 𐑁𐐫𐑉, 𐐺𐐨𐐸𐐬𐑊𐐼, 𐐌 𐐸𐐰𐑂 𐑉𐐨𐑁𐐴𐑌𐐼 𐑄𐐨, 𐐌 𐐸𐐰𐑂 𐐽𐐬𐑆𐐲𐑌 𐑄𐐨 𐐮𐑌 𐑄 𐑁𐐲𐑉𐑌𐐲𐑅 𐐱𐑂 𐐰𐑁𐑊𐐮𐐿𐑇𐐲𐑌. 𐐙𐐫𐑉 𐑋𐐴𐑌 𐐬𐑌 𐑅𐐩𐐿, 𐐷𐐩, 𐑁𐐫𐑉 𐑋𐐴𐑌 𐐬𐑌 𐑅𐐩𐐿 𐐶𐐮𐑊 𐐌 𐐼𐐭 𐑄𐐮𐑅; 𐑁𐐫𐑉 𐐌 𐐶𐐮𐑊 𐑌𐐱𐐻 𐑅𐐲𐑁𐐲𐑉 𐑋𐐴 𐑌𐐩𐑋 𐐻𐐭 𐐺𐐨 𐐹𐐱𐑊𐐭𐐻𐐯𐐼, 𐐰𐑌𐐼 𐐌 𐐶𐐮𐑊 𐑌𐐱𐐻 𐑀𐐮𐑂 𐑋𐐴 𐑀𐑊𐐬𐑉𐐨 𐐲𐑌𐐻𐐭 𐐰𐑌𐐲𐑄𐐲𐑉.

3. 𐐐𐐪𐑉𐐿𐐲𐑌 𐐲𐑌𐐻𐐭 𐑋𐐨, O 𐐖𐐩𐐿𐐲𐐺, 𐐰𐑌𐐼 𐐆𐑆𐑉𐐩𐐯𐑊 𐑋𐐴 𐐿𐐫𐑊𐐼; 𐑁𐐫𐑉 𐐌 𐐰𐑋 𐐸𐐨; 𐐌 𐐰𐑋 𐑄 𐑁𐐲𐑉𐑅𐐻, 𐐰𐑌𐐼 𐐌 𐐰𐑋 𐐫𐑊𐑅𐐬 𐑄 𐑊𐐰𐑅𐐻. 𐐣𐐴𐑌 𐐸𐐰𐑌𐐼 𐐸𐐰𐑃 𐐫𐑊𐑅𐐬 𐑊𐐩𐐼 𐑄 𐑁𐐵𐑌𐐼𐐩𐑇𐐲𐑌 𐐱𐑂 𐑄 𐐲𐑉𐑃, 𐐰𐑌𐐼 𐑋𐐴 𐑉𐐴𐐻 𐐸𐐰𐑌𐐼 𐐸𐐰𐑃 𐑅𐐹𐐰𐑌𐐼 𐑄 𐐸𐐯𐑂𐐲𐑌𐑆. 𐐌 𐐿𐐫𐑊 𐐲𐑌𐐻𐐭 𐑄𐐯𐑋, 𐐰𐑌𐐼 𐑄𐐩 𐑅𐐻𐐰𐑌𐐼 𐐲𐐹 𐐻𐐳𐑀𐐯𐑄𐐲𐑉. 𐐃𐑊 𐐷, 𐐲𐑅𐐯𐑋𐐺𐑊 𐐷𐐭𐑉𐑅𐐯𐑊𐑂𐑆, 𐐰𐑌𐐼 𐐸𐐨𐑉; 𐐸𐐭 𐐲𐑋𐐲𐑍 𐑄𐐯𐑋 𐐸𐐰𐑃 𐐼𐐯𐐿𐑊𐐩𐑉𐐼 𐑄𐐨𐑆 𐑃𐐮𐑍𐑆 𐐲𐑌𐐻𐐭 𐑄𐐯𐑋? 𐐜 𐐢𐐫𐑉𐐼 𐐸𐐰𐑃 𐑊𐐲𐑂𐐼 𐐸𐐮𐑋; 𐐷𐐩, 𐐰𐑌𐐼 𐐸𐐨 𐐶𐐮𐑊 𐑁𐐳𐑊𐑁𐐮𐑊 𐐸𐐮𐑆 𐐶𐐲𐑉𐐼 𐐸𐐶𐐮𐐽 𐐸𐐨 𐐸𐐰𐑃 𐐼𐐯𐐿𐑊𐐩𐑉𐐼 𐐺𐐴 𐑄𐐯𐑋; 𐐰𐑌𐐼 𐐸𐐨 𐐶𐐮𐑊 𐐼𐐭 𐐸𐐮𐑆 𐐹𐑊𐐯𐑈𐐲𐑉 𐐱𐑌 𐐒𐐰𐐺𐐮𐑊𐐱𐑌, 𐐰𐑌𐐼 𐐸𐐮𐑆 𐐪𐑉𐑋 𐑇𐐰𐑊 𐐿𐐲𐑋 𐐲𐐹𐐱𐑌 𐑄 𐐗𐐰𐑊𐐼𐐨𐐲𐑌𐑆. 𐐃𐑊𐑅𐐬, 𐑅𐐯𐑃 𐑄 𐐢𐐫𐑉𐐼; 𐐌 𐑄 𐐢𐐫𐑉𐐼, 𐐷𐐩, 𐐌 𐐸𐐰𐑂 𐑅𐐹𐐬𐐿𐐲𐑌; 𐐷𐐩, 𐐌 𐐸𐐰𐑂 𐐿𐐫𐑊𐐼 𐐸𐐮𐑋 𐐻𐐭 𐐼𐐯𐐿𐑊𐐩𐑉, 𐐌 𐐸𐐰𐑂 𐐺𐑉𐐫𐐻 𐐸𐐮𐑋, 𐐰𐑌𐐼 𐐸𐐨 𐑇𐐰𐑊 𐑋𐐩𐐿 𐐸𐐮𐑆 𐐶𐐩 𐐹𐑉𐐱𐑅𐐹𐐲𐑉𐐲𐑅.

4. 𐐗𐐲𐑋 𐐷 𐑌𐐨𐑉 𐐲𐑌𐐻𐐭 𐑋𐐨; 𐐌 𐐸𐐰𐑂 𐑌𐐱𐐻 𐑅𐐹𐐬𐐿𐐲𐑌 𐐮𐑌 𐑅𐐨𐐿𐑉𐐯𐐻; 𐑁𐑉𐐱𐑋 𐑄 𐐺𐐨𐑀𐐮𐑌𐐮𐑍; 𐑁𐑉𐐱𐑋 𐑄 𐐻𐐴𐑋 𐑄𐐰𐐻 𐐮𐐻 𐐶𐐱𐑆 𐐼𐐯𐐿𐑊𐐩𐑉𐐼 𐐸𐐰𐑂 𐐌 𐑅𐐹𐐬𐐿𐐲𐑌; 𐐰𐑌𐐼 𐑄 𐐢𐐫𐑉𐐼 𐐘𐐱𐐼, 𐐰𐑌𐐼 𐐸𐐮𐑆 𐐝𐐹𐐮𐑉𐐮𐐻, 𐐸𐐰𐑃 𐑅𐐯𐑌𐐻 𐑋𐐨. 𐐈𐑌𐐼 𐑄𐐲𐑅 𐑅𐐯𐑃 𐑄 𐐢𐐫𐑉𐐼, 𐑄𐐴 𐐡𐐨𐐼𐐨𐑋𐐲𐑉, 𐑄 𐐐𐐬𐑊𐐨 𐐎𐐲𐑌 𐐱𐑂 𐐆𐑆𐑉𐐩𐐯𐑊; 𐐌 𐐸𐐰𐑂 𐑅𐐯𐑌𐐻 𐐸𐐮𐑋, 𐑄 𐐢𐐫𐑉𐐼 𐑄𐐴 𐐘𐐱𐐼 𐐸𐐭 𐐻𐐨𐐽𐐯𐑃 𐑄𐐨 𐐻𐐭 𐐹𐑉𐐱𐑁𐐮𐐻, 𐐸𐐭 𐑊𐐨𐐼𐐯𐑃 𐑄𐐨 𐐺𐐴 𐑄 𐐶𐐩 𐑄𐐵 𐑇𐐳𐐼𐑅𐐻 𐑀𐐬, 𐐸𐐰𐑃 𐐼𐐲𐑌 𐐮𐐻. O 𐑄𐐰𐐻 𐑄𐐵 𐐸𐐰𐐼𐑅𐐻 𐐸𐐪𐑉𐐿𐐲𐑌𐐼 𐐻𐐭 𐑋𐐴 𐐿𐐲𐑋𐐰𐑌𐐼𐑋𐐯𐑌𐐻𐑅! 𐑄𐐯𐑌 𐐸𐐰𐐼 𐑄𐐴 𐐹𐐨𐑅

𐐺𐐮𐑌 𐐰𐑆 𐐩 𐑉𐐮𐑂𐐲𐑉, 𐐰𐑌𐐼 𐑄𐐴 𐑉𐐴𐐽𐐲𐑅𐑌𐐯𐑅 𐐰𐑆 𐑄 𐐶𐐩𐑂𐑆 𐐱𐑂 𐑄 𐑅𐐨; 𐑄𐐴 𐑅𐐨𐐼 𐐫𐑊𐑅𐐬 𐐸𐐰𐐼 𐐺𐐮𐑌 𐐰𐑆 𐑄 𐑅𐐰𐑌𐐼; 𐑄 𐐱𐑁𐑅𐐹𐑉𐐮𐑍 𐐱𐑂 𐑄𐐴 𐐺𐐵𐐯𐑊𐑆 𐑊𐐴𐐿 𐑄 𐑀𐑉𐐰𐑂𐐯𐑊 𐑄𐐩𐑉𐐱𐑂; 𐐸𐐮𐑆 𐑌𐐩𐑋 𐑇𐐳𐐼 𐑌𐐱𐐻 𐐸𐐰𐑂 𐐺𐐮𐑌 𐐿𐐲𐐻 𐐱𐑁 𐑌𐐫𐑉 𐐼𐐨𐑅𐐻𐑉𐐱𐐮𐐼 𐑁𐑉𐐱𐑋 𐐺𐐨𐑁𐐬𐑉 𐑋𐐨.

5. 𐐘𐐬 𐐷 𐑁𐐫𐑉𐑃 𐐱𐑂 𐐒𐐰𐐺𐐮𐑊𐐲𐑌, 𐑁𐑊𐐨 𐐷 𐑁𐑉𐐱𐑋 𐑄 𐐗𐐰𐑊𐐼𐐨𐐲𐑌𐑆, 𐐶𐐮𐑄 𐑄 𐑂𐐱𐐮𐑅 𐐱𐑂 𐑅𐐮𐑍𐐮𐑍 𐐼𐐨𐐿𐑊𐐩𐑉 𐐷, 𐐻𐐯𐑊 𐑄𐐮𐑅, 𐐲𐐻𐐲𐑉 𐐻𐐭 𐑄 𐐯𐑌𐐼 𐐱𐑂 𐑄 𐐲𐑉𐑃; 𐑅𐐩 𐐷, 𐑄 𐐢𐐫𐑉𐐼 𐐸𐐰𐑃 𐑉𐐨𐐼𐐨𐑋𐐼 𐐸𐐮𐑆 𐑅𐐲𐑉𐑂𐐲𐑌𐐻 𐐖𐐩𐐿𐐲𐐺. 𐐈𐑌𐐼 𐑄𐐩 𐑃𐐲𐑉𐑅𐐻𐐯𐐼 𐑌𐐱𐐻; 𐐸𐐨 𐑊𐐯𐐼 𐑄𐐯𐑋 𐑃𐑉𐐭 𐑄 𐐼𐐯𐑆𐐲𐑉𐐻𐑅; 𐐸𐐨 𐐿𐐫𐑆𐐼 𐑄 𐐶𐐫𐐻𐐲𐑉𐑆 𐐻𐐭 𐑁𐑊𐐬 𐐵𐐻 𐐱𐑂 𐑄 𐑉𐐱𐐿 𐑁𐐫𐑉 𐑄𐐯𐑋; 𐐸𐐨 𐐿𐑊𐐩𐑂 𐑄 𐑉𐐱𐐿 𐐫𐑊𐑅𐐬, 𐐰𐑌𐐼 𐑄 𐐶𐐫𐐻𐐲𐑉𐑆 𐑀𐐲𐑇𐐻 𐐵𐐻. 𐐈𐑌𐐼 𐑌𐐱𐐻𐐶𐐮𐑄𐑅𐐻𐐰𐑌𐐼𐐮𐑍 𐐸𐐨 𐐸𐐰𐑃 𐐼𐐲𐑌 𐐫𐑊 𐑄𐐮𐑅, 𐐰𐑌𐐼 𐑀𐑉𐐩𐐻𐐲𐑉 𐐫𐑊𐑅𐐬, 𐑄𐐩𐑉 𐐮𐑆 𐑌𐐬 𐐹𐐨𐑅, 𐑅𐐯𐑃 𐑄 𐐢𐐫𐑉𐐼 𐐲𐑌𐐻𐐭 𐑄 𐐶𐐮𐐿𐐯𐐼.

6. 𐐈𐑌𐐼 𐐰𐑀𐐯𐑌: 𐐐𐐪𐑉𐐿𐐲𐑌, 𐐄 𐐷 𐐸𐐵𐑅 𐐱𐑂 𐐆𐑆𐑉𐐩𐐯𐑊, 𐐫𐑊 𐐷 𐑄𐐰𐐻 𐐪𐑉 𐐺𐑉𐐬𐐿𐐲𐑌 𐐱𐑁 𐐰𐑌𐐼 𐐪𐑉 𐐼𐑉𐐮𐑂𐐲𐑌 𐐵𐐻 𐐺𐐨𐐿𐐫𐑆 𐐱𐑂 𐑄 𐐶𐐮𐐿𐐯𐐼𐑌𐐯𐑅 𐐱𐑂 𐑄 𐐹𐐰𐑅𐐻𐐲𐑉𐑆 𐐱𐑂 𐑋𐐴 𐐹𐐨𐐹𐑊; 𐐷𐐩, 𐐫𐑊 𐐷 𐑄𐐰𐐻 𐐪𐑉 𐐺𐑉𐐬𐐿𐐲𐑌 𐐱𐑁, 𐑄𐐰𐐻 𐐪𐑉 𐑅𐐿𐐰𐐻𐐲𐑉𐐼 𐐰𐐺𐑉𐐫𐐼, 𐐸𐐭 𐐪𐑉 𐐱𐑂 𐑋𐐴 𐐹𐐨𐐹𐑊, 𐐄 𐐸𐐵𐑅 𐐱𐑂 𐐆𐑆𐑉𐐩𐐯𐑊. 𐐢𐐮𐑅𐐲𐑌, 𐐄 𐐴𐑊𐑆, 𐐲𐑌𐐻𐐭 𐑋𐐨, 𐐰𐑌𐐼 𐐸𐐪𐑉𐐿𐐲𐑌 𐐷 𐐹𐐨𐐹𐑊 𐑁𐑉𐐱𐑋 𐑁𐐪𐑉; 𐑄 𐐢𐐫𐑉𐐼 𐐸𐐰𐑃 𐐿𐐫𐑊𐐼 𐑋𐐨 𐑁𐑉𐐱𐑋 𐑄 𐐶𐐭𐑋; 𐑁𐑉𐐱𐑋 𐑄 𐐺𐐵𐐯𐑊𐑆 𐐱𐑂 𐑋𐐴 𐑋𐐲𐑄𐐲𐑉 𐐸𐐰𐑃 𐐸𐐨 𐑋𐐩𐐼 𐑋𐐯𐑌𐑇𐐲𐑌 𐐱𐑂 𐑋𐐴 𐑌𐐩𐑋. 𐐈𐑌𐐼 𐐸𐐨 𐐸𐐰𐑃 𐑋𐐩𐐼 𐑋𐐴 𐑋𐐵𐑃 𐑊𐐴𐐿 𐐩 𐑇𐐪𐑉𐐹 𐑅𐐬𐑉𐐼; 𐐮𐑌 𐑄 𐑇𐐰𐐼𐐬 𐐱𐑂 𐐸𐐮𐑆 𐐸𐐰𐑌𐐼 𐐸𐐰𐑃 𐐸𐐨 𐐸𐐮𐐼 𐑋𐐨; 𐐰𐑌𐐼 𐑋𐐩𐐼 𐑋𐐨 𐐩 𐐹𐐱𐑊𐐮𐑇𐐻 𐑇𐐰𐑁𐐻; 𐐮𐑌 𐐸𐐮𐑆 𐐿𐐶𐐮𐑂𐐲𐑉 𐐸𐐰𐑃 𐐸𐐨 𐐸𐐮𐐼 𐑋𐐨; 𐐰𐑌𐐼 𐑅𐐯𐐼 𐐲𐑌𐐻𐐭 𐑋𐐨, 𐐜𐐵 𐐪𐑉𐐻 𐑋𐐴 𐑅𐐲𐑉𐑂𐐲𐑌𐐻, 𐐄 𐐆𐑆𐑉𐐩𐐯𐑊, 𐐮𐑌 𐐸𐐭𐑋 𐐌 𐐶𐐮𐑊 𐐺𐐨 𐑀𐑊𐐬𐑉𐐮𐑁𐐴𐐼. 𐐜𐐯𐑌 𐐌 𐑅𐐯𐐼, 𐐌 𐐸𐐰𐑂 𐑊𐐩𐐺𐐲𐑉𐐼 𐐮𐑌 𐑂𐐩𐑌, 𐐌 𐐸𐐰𐑂 𐑅𐐹𐐯𐑌𐐻 𐑋𐐴 𐑅𐐻𐑉𐐯𐑍𐑃 𐑁𐐫𐑉 𐑌𐐫𐐻 𐐰𐑌𐐼 𐐮𐑌 𐑂𐐩𐑌; 𐑇𐐭𐑉𐑊𐐨 𐑋𐐴 𐐾𐐲𐐼𐐾𐑋𐐯𐑌𐐻 𐐮𐑆 𐐶𐐮𐑄 𐑄 𐐢𐐫𐑉𐐼, 𐐰𐑌𐐼 𐑋𐐴 𐐶𐐲𐑉𐐿 𐐶𐐮𐑄 𐑋𐐴 𐐘𐐱𐐼.

7. 𐐈𐑌𐐼 𐑌𐐵, 𐑅𐐯𐑃 𐑄 𐐢𐐫𐑉𐐼, 𐑄𐐰𐐻 𐑁𐐫𐑉𐑋𐐼 𐑋𐐨 𐑁𐑉𐐱𐑋 𐑄 𐐶𐐭𐑋 𐑄𐐰𐐻 𐐌 𐑇𐐳𐐼 𐐺𐐨 𐐸𐐮𐑆 𐑅𐐲𐑉𐑂𐐲𐑌𐐻, 𐐻𐐭 𐐺𐑉𐐮𐑍 𐐖𐐩𐐿𐐲𐐺 𐐰𐑀𐐯𐑌 𐐻𐐭 𐐸𐐮𐑋: 𐐜𐐬 𐐆𐑆𐑉𐐩𐐯𐑊 𐐺𐐨 𐑌𐐱𐐻 𐑀𐐰𐑄𐐲𐑉𐐼, 𐐷𐐯𐐻 𐑇𐐰𐑊 𐐌 𐐺𐐨 𐑀𐑊𐐬𐑉𐐨𐐲𐑅 𐐮𐑌 𐑄 𐐴𐑆 𐐱𐑂 𐑄 𐐢𐐫𐑉𐐼, 𐐰𐑌𐐼 𐑋𐐴 𐐘𐐱𐐼 𐑇𐐰𐑊 𐐺𐐨 𐑋𐐴 𐑅𐐻𐑉𐐯𐑍𐑃. 𐐈𐑌𐐼 𐐸𐐨 𐑅𐐯𐐼, 𐐆𐐻 𐐮𐑆 𐐩 𐑊𐐴𐐻 𐑃𐐮𐑍 𐑄𐐰𐐻 𐑄𐐵 𐑇𐐳𐐼𐑅𐐻 𐐺𐐨 𐑋𐐴 𐑅𐐲𐑉𐑂𐐲𐑌𐐻 𐐻𐐭 𐑉𐐩𐑆 𐐲𐐹 𐑄 𐐻𐑉𐐴𐐺𐑆 𐐱𐑂 𐐖𐐩𐐿𐐲𐐺, 𐐰𐑌𐐼 𐐻𐐭 𐑉𐐨𐑅𐐻𐐬𐑉 𐑄 𐐹𐑉𐐨𐑆𐐲𐑉𐑂𐐼 𐐱𐑂 𐐆𐑆𐑉𐐩𐐯𐑊. 𐐌 𐐶𐐮𐑊 𐐫𐑊𐑅𐐬 𐑀𐐮𐑂 𐑄 𐑁𐐫𐑉 𐐩 𐑊𐐴𐐻 𐐻𐐭 𐑄 𐐖𐐯𐑌𐐻𐐴𐑊𐑆, 𐑄𐐰𐐻 𐑄𐐵 𐑋𐐩𐐯𐑅𐐻 𐐺𐐨 𐑋𐐴 𐑅𐐰𐑊𐑂𐐩𐑇𐐲𐑌 𐐲𐑌𐐻𐐭 𐑄 𐐯𐑌𐐼𐑆 𐐱𐑂 𐑄 𐐲𐑉𐑃. 𐐜𐐲𐑅 𐑅𐐯𐑃 𐑄 𐐢𐐫𐑉𐐼, 𐑄 𐐡𐐨𐐼𐐨𐑋𐐲𐑉 𐐱𐑂 𐐆𐑆𐑉𐐩𐐯𐑊, 𐐸𐐮𐑆 𐐐𐐬𐑊𐐨 𐐎𐐲𐑌, 𐐻𐐭 𐐸𐐮𐑋 𐐸𐐭𐑋 𐑋𐐰𐑌 𐐼𐐨𐑅𐐹𐐴𐑆𐐯𐑃, 𐐻𐐭 𐐸𐐮𐑋 𐐸𐐭𐑋 𐑄 𐑌𐐩𐑇𐐲𐑌𐑆 𐐰𐐺𐐸𐐫𐑉𐐯𐑃, 𐐻𐐭 𐑅𐐲𐑉𐑂𐐲𐑌𐐻 𐐱𐑂 𐑉𐐭𐑊𐐲𐑉𐑆: 𐐗𐐮𐑍𐑆 𐑇𐐰𐑊 𐑅𐐨 𐐰𐑌𐐼 𐐲𐑉𐐴𐑆, 𐐹𐑉𐐮𐑌𐑅𐐯𐑆 𐐫𐑊𐑅𐐬 𐑇𐐰𐑊 𐐶𐐲𐑉𐑇𐐮𐐹, 𐐺𐐨𐐿𐐫𐑆 𐐱𐑂 𐑄 𐐢𐐫𐑉𐐼 𐑄𐐰𐐻 𐐮𐑆 𐑁𐐩𐑃𐑁𐐳𐑊. 𐐜𐐲𐑅 𐑅𐐯𐑃 𐑄 𐐢𐐫𐑉𐐼, 𐐆𐑌 𐐰𐑌 𐐰𐐿𐑅𐐯𐐹𐐻𐐲𐐺𐑊 𐐻𐐴𐑋 𐐸𐐰𐑂 𐐌 𐐸𐐲𐑉𐐼 𐑄, 𐐄 𐐴𐑊𐑆 𐐱𐑂 𐑄 𐑅𐐨, 𐐰𐑌𐐼 𐐮𐑌 𐐩 𐐼𐐩 𐐱𐑂 𐑅𐐰𐑊𐑂𐐩𐑇𐐲𐑌 𐐸𐐰𐑂 𐐌 𐐸𐐯𐑊𐐹𐐻 𐑄; 𐐰𐑌𐐼 𐐌 𐐶𐐮𐑊 𐐹𐑉𐐨𐑆𐐲𐑉𐑂 𐑄, 𐐰𐑌𐐼 𐑀𐐮𐑂 𐑄 𐑋𐐴 𐑅𐐲𐑉𐑂𐐲𐑌𐐻 𐑁𐐫𐑉 𐐩 𐐿𐐲𐑂𐐯𐑌𐐲𐑌𐐻 𐐱𐑂 𐑄 𐐹𐐨𐐹𐑊, 𐐻𐐭 𐐯𐑅𐐻𐐰𐐺𐑊𐐮𐑇 𐑄 𐐲𐑉𐑃, 𐐻𐐭 𐐿𐐫𐑆 𐐻𐐭 𐐮𐑌𐐸𐐯𐑉𐐮𐐻 𐑄 𐐼𐐯𐑅𐐬𐑊𐐯𐐻 𐐸𐐯𐑉𐐮𐐻𐐯𐐾𐐯𐑆; 𐑄𐐰𐐻 𐑄𐐵 𐑋𐐩𐐯𐑅𐐻 𐑅𐐩 𐐻𐐭 𐑄 𐐹𐑉𐐮𐑆𐐲𐑌𐐲𐑉𐑆, 𐐘𐐬 𐑁𐐫𐑉𐑃; 𐐻𐐭 𐑄𐐯𐑋 𐑄𐐰𐐻 𐑅𐐮𐐻 𐐮𐑌 𐐼𐐪𐑉𐐿𐑌𐐯𐑅, 𐐟𐐬 𐐷𐐭𐑉𐑅𐐯𐑊𐑂𐑆. 𐐜𐐩 𐑇𐐰𐑊 𐑁𐐨𐐼 𐐮𐑌 𐑄 𐐶𐐩𐑆, 𐐰𐑌𐐼 𐑄𐐩𐑉 𐐹𐐰𐑅𐐽𐐲𐑉𐑆 𐑇𐐰𐑊 𐐺𐐨 𐐮𐑌 𐐫𐑊 𐐸𐐴 𐐹𐑊𐐩𐑅𐐯𐑆. 𐐜𐐩 𐑇𐐰𐑊 𐑌𐐱𐐻 𐐸𐐲𐑍𐑀𐐲𐑉 𐑌𐐫𐑉 𐑃𐐲𐑉𐑅𐐻, 𐑌𐐨𐑄𐐲𐑉 𐑇𐐰𐑊 𐑄 𐐸𐐨𐐻 𐑌𐐫𐑉 𐑄 𐑅𐐲𐑌 𐑅𐑋𐐴𐐻 𐑄𐐯𐑋; 𐑁𐐫𐑉 𐐸𐐨 𐑄𐐰𐐻 𐐸𐐰𐑃 𐑋𐐲𐑉𐑅𐐨 𐐱𐑌 𐑄𐐯𐑋 𐑇𐐰𐑊 𐑊𐐨𐐼 𐑄𐐯𐑋, 𐐨𐑂𐐲𐑌 𐐺𐐴 𐑄 𐑅𐐹𐑉𐐮𐑍𐑆 𐐱𐑂 𐐶𐐫𐐻𐐲𐑉 𐑇𐐰𐑊 𐐸𐐨 𐑀𐐴𐐼 𐑄𐐯𐑋. 𐐈𐑌𐐼 𐐌 𐐶𐐮𐑊 𐑋𐐩𐐿 𐐫𐑊 𐑋𐐴 𐑋𐐵𐑌𐐻𐐮𐑍𐑆 𐐩 𐐶𐐩, 𐐰𐑌𐐼 𐑋𐐴 𐐸𐐴𐐶𐐩𐑆 𐑇𐐰𐑊 𐐺𐐨 𐐯𐑀𐑆𐐫𐑊𐐻𐐯𐐼. 𐐈𐑌𐐼 𐑄𐐯𐑌, 𐐄 𐐸𐐵𐑅 𐐱𐑂 𐐆𐑆𐑉𐐩𐐯𐑊, 𐐺𐐨𐐸𐐬𐑊𐐼, 𐑄𐐨𐑆 𐑇𐐰𐑊 𐐿𐐲𐑋 𐑁𐑉𐐱𐑋 𐑁𐐪𐑉; 𐐰𐑌𐐼 𐑊𐐬, 𐑄𐐨𐑆 𐑁𐑉𐐱𐑋 𐑄 𐑌𐐫𐑉𐑃 𐐰𐑌𐐼 𐑁𐑉𐐱𐑋 𐑄 𐐶𐐯𐑅𐐻; 𐐰𐑌𐐼 𐑄𐐨𐑆 𐑁𐑉𐐱𐑋 𐑄 𐑊𐐰𐑌𐐼 𐐱𐑂 𐐝𐐴𐑌𐐮𐑋.

8. 𐐝𐐮𐑍, 𐐄 𐐸𐐯𐑂𐐲𐑌𐑆; 𐐰𐑌𐐼 𐐺𐐨 𐐾𐐱𐐮𐑁𐐳𐑊, 𐐄 𐐲𐑉𐑃; 𐑁𐐫𐑉 𐑄 𐑁𐐨𐐻 𐐱𐑂 𐑄𐐬𐑆 𐐸𐐭 𐐪𐑉 𐐮𐑌 𐑄 𐐨𐑅𐐻 𐑇𐐰𐑊 𐐺𐐨 𐐯𐑅𐐻𐐰𐐺𐑊𐐮𐑇𐐻; 𐐰𐑌𐐼 𐐺𐑉𐐩𐐿 𐑁𐐫𐑉𐑃 𐐮𐑌𐐻𐐭 𐑅𐐮𐑍𐐮𐑍, 𐐄 𐑋𐐵𐑌𐐻𐐮𐑍𐑆; 𐑁𐐫𐑉 𐑄𐐩 𐑇𐐰𐑊 𐐺𐐨 𐑅𐑋𐐮𐐻𐐲𐑌 𐑌𐐬 𐑋𐐫𐑉; 𐑁𐐫𐑉 𐑄 𐐢𐐫𐑉𐐼 𐐸𐐰𐑃 𐐿𐐲𐑋𐑁𐐲𐑉𐐻𐐯𐐼 𐐸𐐮𐑆 𐐹𐐨𐐹𐑊, 𐐰𐑌𐐼 𐐶𐐮𐑊 𐐸𐐰𐑂 𐑋𐐲𐑉𐑅𐐨 𐐲𐐹𐐱𐑌 𐐸𐐮𐑆 𐐰𐑁𐑊𐐮𐐿𐐻𐐯𐐼.

𐐒𐐲𐐻, 𐐺𐐨𐐸𐐬𐑊𐐼, 𐐞𐐴𐐲𐑌 𐐸𐐰𐑃 𐑅𐐯𐐼, 𐑄 𐐢𐐫𐑉𐐼 𐐸𐐰𐑃 𐑁𐐲𐑉𐑅𐐩𐐿𐑌 𐑋𐐨, 𐐰𐑌𐐼 𐑋𐐴 𐐢𐐫𐑉𐐼 𐐸𐐰𐑃 𐑁𐐲𐑉𐑀𐐱𐐻𐑌 𐑋𐐨; 𐐺𐐲𐐻 𐐸𐐨 𐐶𐐮𐑊 𐑇𐐬 𐑄𐐰𐐻 𐐸𐐨 𐐸𐐰𐑃 𐑌𐐱𐐻. 𐐙𐐫𐑉 𐐿𐐰𐑌 𐐩 𐐶𐐳𐑋𐐲𐑌 𐑁𐐲𐑉𐑀𐐯𐐻 𐐸𐐲𐑉 𐑅𐐲𐐿𐐮𐑍 𐐽𐐴𐑊𐐼, 𐑄𐐰𐐻 𐑇𐐨 𐑇𐐳𐐼 𐑌𐐱𐐻 𐐸𐐰𐑂 𐐿𐐲𐑋𐐹𐐰𐑇𐐲𐑌 𐐱𐑌 𐑄 𐑅𐐲𐑌 𐐱𐑂 𐐸𐐲𐑉 𐐶𐐭𐑋? 𐐏𐐩, 𐑄𐐩 𐑋𐐩 𐑁𐐲𐑉𐑀𐐯𐐻, 𐐷𐐯𐐻 𐐶𐐮𐑊 𐐌 𐑌𐐱𐐻 𐑁𐐲𐑉𐑀𐐯𐐻 𐑄, 𐐄 𐐸𐐵𐑅 𐐱𐑂 𐐆𐑆𐑉𐐩𐐯𐑊. 𐐒𐐨𐐸𐐬𐑊𐐼, 𐐌 𐐸𐐰𐑂 𐑀𐑉𐐩𐑂𐐯𐑌 𐑄 𐐲𐐹𐐱𐑌 𐑄 𐐹𐐪𐑋𐑆 𐐱𐑂 𐑋𐐴 𐐸𐐰𐑌𐐼𐑆; 𐑄𐐴 𐐶𐐫𐑊𐑆 𐐪𐑉 𐐿𐐲𐑌𐐻𐐮𐑌𐐷𐐭𐐲𐑊𐐨 𐐺𐐨𐑁𐐬𐑉 𐑋𐐨. 𐐜𐐴 𐐽𐐮𐑊𐐼𐑉𐐯𐑌 𐑇𐐰𐑊 𐑋𐐩𐐿 𐐸𐐩𐑅𐐻 𐐰𐑀𐐯𐑌𐑅𐐻 𐑄𐐴 𐐼𐐨𐑅𐐻𐑉𐐱𐐮𐐲𐑉𐑆; 𐐰𐑌𐐼 𐑄𐐩 𐑄𐐰𐐻 𐑋𐐩𐐼 𐑄 𐐶𐐩𐑅𐐻, 𐑇𐐰𐑊 𐑀𐐬 𐑁𐐫𐑉𐑃 𐐱𐑂 𐑄.

9. 𐐢𐐮𐑁𐐻 𐐲𐐹 𐑄𐐴𐑌 𐐴𐑆 𐑉𐐵𐑌𐐼 𐐰𐐺𐐵𐐻 𐐰𐑌𐐼 𐐺𐐨𐐸𐐬𐑊𐐼; 𐐫𐑊 𐑄𐐨𐑆 𐑀𐐰𐑄𐐲𐑉 𐑄𐐯𐑋𐑅𐐯𐑊𐑂𐑆 𐐻𐐳𐑀𐐯𐑄𐐲𐑉, 𐐰𐑌𐐼 𐑄𐐩 𐑇𐐰𐑊 𐐿𐐲𐑋 𐐻𐐭 𐑄. 𐐈𐑌𐐼 𐐰𐑆 𐐌 𐑊𐐮𐑂, 𐑅𐐯𐑃 𐑄 𐐢𐐫𐑉𐐼, 𐑄𐐵 𐑇𐐰𐑊𐐻 𐑇𐐭𐑉𐑊𐐨 𐐿𐑊𐐬𐑄 𐑄 𐐶𐐮𐑄 𐑄𐐯𐑋 𐐫𐑊, 𐐰𐑆 𐐶𐐮𐑄 𐐰𐑌 𐐫𐑉𐑌𐐰𐑋𐐯𐑌𐐻, 𐐰𐑌𐐼 𐐺𐐴𐑌𐐼 𐑄𐐯𐑋 𐐱𐑌 𐐨𐑂𐑌 𐐰𐑆 𐐩 𐐺𐑉𐐴𐐼. 𐐙𐐫𐑉 𐑄𐐴 𐐶𐐩𐑅𐐻 𐐰𐑌𐐼 𐑄𐐴 𐐼𐐯𐑅𐐬𐑊𐐩𐐻 𐐹𐑊𐐩𐑅𐐯𐑆, 𐐰𐑌𐐼 𐑄 𐑊𐐰𐑌𐐼 𐐱𐑂 𐑄𐐴 𐐼𐐨𐑅𐐻𐑉𐐲𐐿𐑇𐐲𐑌, 𐑇𐐰𐑊 𐐨𐑂𐑌 𐑌𐐵 𐐺𐐨 𐐻𐐭 𐑌𐐰𐑉𐐬 𐐺𐐴 𐑉𐐨𐑆𐑌 𐐱𐑂 𐑄 𐐮𐑌𐐸𐐰𐐺𐐮𐐻𐐲𐑌𐐻𐑅; 𐐰𐑌𐐼 𐑄𐐩 𐑄𐐰𐐻 𐑅𐐶𐐱𐑊𐐬𐐼 𐑄 𐐲𐐹 𐑇𐐰𐑊 𐐺𐐨 𐑁𐐪𐑉 𐐰𐐶𐐩. 𐐜 𐐽𐐮𐑊𐐼𐑉𐐯𐑌 𐐸𐐭𐑋 𐑄𐐵 𐑇𐐰𐑊𐐻 𐐸𐐰𐑂, 𐐰𐑁𐐻𐐲𐑉 𐑄𐐵 𐐸𐐰𐑅𐐻 𐑊𐐱𐑅𐐻 𐑄 𐑁𐐲𐑉𐑅𐐻, 𐑇𐐰𐑊 𐐰𐑀𐐯𐑌 𐐮𐑌 𐑄𐐴𐑌 𐐨𐑉𐑆 𐑅𐐩, 𐑄 𐐹𐑊𐐩𐑅 𐐮𐑆 𐐻𐐭 𐑅𐐻𐑉𐐩𐐻 𐑁𐐫𐑉 𐑋𐐨; 𐑀𐐮𐑂 𐐹𐑊𐐩𐑅 𐐻𐐭 𐑋𐐨 𐑄𐐰𐐻 𐐌 𐑋𐐩 𐐼𐐶𐐯𐑊. 𐐜𐐯𐑌 𐑇𐐰𐑊𐐻 𐑄𐐵 𐑅𐐩 𐐮𐑌 𐑄𐐴𐑌 𐐸𐐪𐑉𐐻, 𐐸𐐭 𐐸𐐰𐑃 𐐺𐐨𐑀𐐱𐐻𐑌 𐑋𐐨 𐑄𐐨𐑆, 𐑅𐐨𐐮𐑍 𐐌 𐐸𐐰𐑂 𐑊𐐱𐑅𐐻 𐑋𐐴 𐐽𐐮𐑊𐐼𐑉𐐯𐑌, 𐐰𐑌𐐼 𐐰𐑋 𐐼𐐯𐑅𐐬𐑊𐐩𐐻, 𐐩 𐐿𐐰𐐹𐐻𐐮𐑂, 𐐰𐑌𐐼 𐑉𐐨𐑋𐐭𐑂𐐮𐑍 𐐻𐐭 𐐰𐑌𐐼 𐑁𐑉𐐬? 𐐈𐑌𐐼 𐐸𐐭 𐐸𐐰𐑃 𐐺𐑉𐐫𐐻 𐐲𐐹 𐑄𐐨𐑆? 𐐒𐐨𐐸𐐬𐑊𐐼, 𐐌 𐐶𐐱𐑆 𐑊𐐯𐑁𐐻 𐐰𐑊𐐬𐑌: 𐑄𐐨𐑆, 𐐸𐐶𐐩𐑉 𐐸𐐰𐑂 𐑄𐐩 𐐺𐐮𐑌? 𐐜𐐲𐑅 𐑅𐐯𐑃 𐑄 𐐢𐐫𐑉𐐼 𐐘𐐱𐐼, 𐐺𐐨𐐸𐐬𐑊𐐼 𐐌 𐐶𐐮𐑊 𐑊𐐮𐑁𐐻 𐐲𐐹 𐑋𐐴𐑌 𐐸𐐰𐑌𐐼 𐐻𐐭 𐑄 𐐖𐐯𐑌𐐻𐐴𐑊𐑆, 𐐰𐑌𐐼 𐑅𐐯𐐻 𐐲𐐹 𐑋𐐴 𐑅𐐻𐐰𐑌𐐼𐐲𐑉𐐼 𐐻𐐭 𐑄 𐐹𐐨𐐹𐑊; 𐐰𐑌𐐼 𐑄𐐩 𐑇𐐰𐑊 𐐺𐑉𐐮𐑍 𐑄𐐴 𐑅𐐲𐑌𐑆 𐐮𐑌 𐑄𐐩𐑉 𐐪𐑉𐑋𐑆, 𐐰𐑌𐐼 𐑄𐐴 𐐼𐐫𐐻𐐲𐑉𐑆 𐑇𐐰𐑊 𐐺𐐨 𐐿𐐰𐑉𐐮𐐼 𐐲𐐹𐐱𐑌 𐑄𐐩𐑉 𐑇𐐬𐑊𐐼𐐲𐑉𐑆. 𐐈𐑌𐐼 𐐿𐐮𐑍𐑆 𐑇𐐰𐑊 𐐺𐐨 𐑄𐐴 𐑌𐐲𐑉𐑅𐐮𐑍 𐑁𐐪𐑄𐐲𐑉𐑆, 𐐰𐑌𐐼 𐑄𐐩𐑉 𐐿𐐶𐐨𐑌𐑆 𐑄𐐴 𐑌𐐲𐑉𐑅𐐮𐑍 𐑋𐐲𐑄𐐲𐑉𐑆; 𐑄𐐩 𐑇𐐰𐑊 𐐺𐐵 𐐼𐐵𐑌 𐐻𐐭 𐑄 𐐶𐐮𐑄 𐑄𐐩𐑉 𐑁𐐩𐑅 𐐻𐐭𐐲𐑉𐐼𐑆 𐑄 𐐲𐑉𐑃, 𐐰𐑌𐐼 𐑊𐐮𐐿 𐐲𐐹 𐑄 𐐼𐐲𐑅𐐻 𐐱𐑂 𐑄𐐴 𐑁𐐨𐐻; 𐐰𐑌𐐼 𐑄𐐵 𐑇𐐰𐑊𐐻 𐑌𐐬 𐑄𐐰𐐻 𐐌 𐐰𐑋 𐑄 𐐢𐐫𐑉𐐼; 𐑁𐐫𐑉 𐑄𐐩 𐑇𐐰𐑊 𐑌𐐱𐐻 𐐺𐐨 𐐰𐑇𐐩𐑋𐐼 𐑄𐐰𐐻 𐐶𐐩𐐻 𐑁𐐫𐑉 𐑋𐐨. 𐐙𐐫𐑉 𐑇𐐰𐑊 𐑄 𐐹𐑉𐐩 𐐺𐐨 𐐻𐐩𐐿𐑌 𐑁𐑉𐐱𐑋 𐑄 𐑋𐐴𐐻𐐨, 𐐫𐑉 𐑄 𐑊𐐫𐑁𐐳𐑊 𐐿𐐰𐐹𐐻𐐮𐑂𐑆 𐐼𐐨𐑊𐐮𐑂𐐲𐑉𐐼? 𐐒𐐲𐐻 𐑄𐐲𐑅 𐑅𐐯𐑃 𐑄 𐐢𐐫𐑉𐐼, 𐐨𐑂𐑌 𐑄 𐐿𐐰𐐹𐐻𐐮𐑂𐑆 𐐱𐑂 𐑄 𐑋𐐴𐐻𐐨 𐑇𐐰𐑊 𐐺𐐨 𐐻𐐩𐐿𐑌 𐐰𐐶𐐩, 𐐰𐑌𐐼 𐑄 𐐹𐑉𐐩 𐐱𐑂 𐑄 𐐻𐐯𐑉𐐮𐐺𐑊 𐑇𐐰𐑊 𐐺𐐨 𐐼𐐨𐑊𐐮𐑂𐐲𐑉𐐼; 𐑁𐐫𐑉 𐐌 𐐶𐐮𐑊 𐐿𐐲𐑌𐐻𐐯𐑌𐐼 𐐶𐐮𐑄 𐐸𐐮𐑋 𐑄𐐰𐐻 𐐿𐐲𐑌𐐻𐐯𐑌𐐼𐐯𐑃 𐐶𐐮𐑄 𐑄, 𐐰𐑌𐐼 𐐌 𐐶𐐮𐑊 𐑅𐐩𐑂 𐑄𐐴 𐐽𐐮𐑊𐐼𐑉𐐯𐑌. 𐐈𐑌𐐼 𐐌 𐐶𐐮𐑊 𐑁𐐨𐐼 𐑄𐐯𐑋 𐑄𐐰𐐻 𐐲𐐹𐑉𐐯𐑅 𐑄 𐐶𐐮𐑄 𐑄𐐩𐑉 𐐬𐑌 𐑁𐑊𐐯𐑇; 𐑄𐐩 𐑇𐐰𐑊 𐐺𐐨 𐐼𐑉𐐲𐑍𐐿𐑌 𐐶𐐮𐑄 𐑄𐐩𐑉 𐐬𐑌 𐐺𐑊𐐲𐐼 𐐰𐑆 𐐶𐐮𐑄 𐑅𐐶𐐨𐐻 𐐶𐐴𐑌; 𐐰𐑌𐐼 𐐫𐑊 𐑁𐑊𐐯𐑇 𐑇𐐰𐑊 𐑌𐐬 𐑄𐐰𐐻 𐐌 𐑄 𐐢𐐫𐑉𐐼 𐐰𐑋 𐑄𐐴 𐐝𐐩𐑂𐐷𐐲𐑉 𐐰𐑌𐐼 𐑄𐐴 𐐡𐐨𐐼𐐨𐑋𐐲𐑉, 𐑄 𐐣𐐴𐐻𐐨 𐐎𐐲𐑌 𐐱𐑂 𐐖𐐩𐐿𐐲𐐺.

𐐕𐐰𐐹𐐻𐐲𐑉 VII.

1. 𐐈𐑌𐐼 𐑌𐐵 𐐮𐐻 𐐿𐐩𐑋 𐐻𐐭 𐐹𐐰𐑅 𐑄𐐰𐐻 𐐰𐑁𐐻𐐲𐑉 𐐌, 𐐤𐐨𐑁𐐴, 𐐸𐐰𐐼 𐑉𐐯𐐼 𐑄𐐨𐑆 𐑃𐐮𐑍𐑆 𐐸𐐶𐐮𐐽 𐐶𐐲𐑉 𐐯𐑌𐑀𐑉𐐩𐑂𐑌 𐐲𐐹𐐱𐑌 𐑄 𐐹𐑊𐐩𐐻𐑅 𐐱𐑂 𐐺𐑉𐐰𐑅, 𐑋𐐴 𐐺𐑉𐐯𐑄𐑉𐐯𐑌 𐐿𐐩𐑋 𐐲𐑌𐐻𐐭 𐑋𐐨, 𐐰𐑌𐐼 𐑅𐐯𐐼 𐐲𐑌𐐻𐐭 𐑋𐐨, 𐐸𐐶𐐱𐐻 𐑋𐐨𐑌𐐯𐑃 𐑄𐐨𐑆 𐑃𐐮𐑍𐑆 𐐸𐐶𐐮𐐽 𐐷𐐨 𐐸𐐰𐑂 𐑉𐐯𐐼? 𐐒𐐨𐐸𐐬𐑊𐐼 𐐪𐑉 𐑄𐐩 𐐻𐐭 𐐺𐐨 𐐲𐑌𐐼𐐲𐑉𐑅𐐻𐐳𐐼 𐐰𐐿𐐫𐑉𐐼𐐮𐑍 𐐻𐐭 𐑃𐐮𐑍𐑆 𐐸𐐶𐐮𐐽 𐐪𐑉 𐑅𐐹𐐮𐑉𐐮𐐻𐐷𐐭𐐲𐑊, 𐐸𐐶𐐮𐐽 𐑇𐐰𐑊 𐐿𐐲𐑋 𐐻𐐭 𐐹𐐰𐑅 𐐰𐐿𐐫𐑉𐐼𐐮𐑍 𐐻𐐭 𐑄 𐑅𐐹𐐮𐑉𐐮𐐻 𐐰𐑌𐐼 𐑌𐐱𐐻 𐑄 𐑁𐑊𐐯𐑇? 𐐈𐑌𐐼 𐐌, 𐐤𐐨𐑁𐐴, 𐑅𐐯𐐼 𐐲𐑌𐐻𐐭 𐑄𐐯𐑋, 𐐒𐐨𐐸𐐬𐑊𐐼, 𐑄𐐩 𐐶𐐲𐑉 𐑋𐐰𐑌𐐮𐑁𐐯𐑅𐐻 𐐲𐑌𐐻𐐭 𐑄 𐐹𐑉𐐱𐑁𐐯𐐻, 𐐺𐐴 𐑄 𐑂𐐦𐑅 𐐱𐑂 𐑄 𐐝𐐹𐐮𐑉𐐮𐐻; 𐑁𐐫𐑉 𐐺𐐴 𐑄 𐐝𐐹𐐮𐑉𐐮𐐻 𐐪𐑉 𐐫𐑊 𐑃𐐮𐑍𐑆 𐑋𐐩𐐼 𐑌𐐬𐑌 𐐲𐑌𐐻𐐭 𐑄 𐐹𐑉𐐱𐑁𐐯𐐻𐑅, 𐐸𐐶𐐮𐐽 𐑇𐐰𐑊 𐐿𐐲𐑋 𐐲𐐹𐐱𐑌 𐑄 𐐽𐐮𐑊𐐼𐑉𐐯𐑌 𐐱𐑂 𐑋𐐯𐑌 𐐰𐐿𐐫𐑉𐐼𐐮𐑍 𐐻𐐭 𐑄 𐑁𐑊𐐯𐑇. 𐐐𐐶𐐩𐑉𐑁𐐫𐑉, 𐑄 𐑃𐐮𐑍𐑆 𐐱𐑂 𐐸𐐶𐐮𐐽 𐐌 𐐸𐐰𐑂 𐑉𐐯𐐼 𐐪𐑉 𐑃𐐮𐑍𐑆 𐐹𐐲𐑉𐐻𐐩𐑌𐐮𐑍 𐐻𐐭 𐑃𐐮𐑍𐑆 𐐺𐐬𐑃 𐐻𐐯𐑋𐐹𐐬𐑉𐐲𐑊 𐐰𐑌𐐼 𐑅𐐹𐐮𐑉𐐮𐐻𐐷𐐭𐐲𐑊; 𐑁𐐫𐑉 𐐮𐐻 𐐰𐐹𐐨𐑉𐑆 𐑄𐐰𐐻 𐑄 𐐸𐐵𐑅 𐐱𐑂 𐐆𐑆𐑉𐐩𐐯𐑊, 𐑅𐐭𐑌𐐲𐑉 𐐫𐑉 𐑊𐐩𐐻𐐲𐑉, 𐐶𐐮𐑊 𐐺𐐨 𐑅𐐿𐐰𐐻𐐲𐑉𐐼 𐐲𐐹𐐱𐑌

𐐫𐑊 𐑄 𐑁𐐩𐑅 𐐱𐑂 𐑄 𐐲𐑉𐑃, 𐐰𐑌𐐼 𐐫𐑊𐑅𐐬 𐐲𐑋𐐲𐑍 𐐫𐑊 𐑌𐐩𐑇𐐲𐑌𐑆, 𐐰𐑌𐐼 𐐺𐐨𐐸𐐬𐑊𐐼, 𐑄𐐯𐑉 𐐪𐑉 𐑋𐐯𐑌𐐨 𐐸𐐭 𐐪𐑉 𐐫𐑊𐑉𐐯𐐼𐐨 𐑊𐐱𐑅𐐻 𐑁𐑉𐐱𐑋 𐑄 𐑌𐐱𐑊𐐲𐐾 𐐱𐑂 𐑄𐐬𐑆 𐐸𐐭 𐐪𐑉 𐐰𐐻 𐐖𐐲𐑉𐐭𐑅𐐲𐑊𐐲𐑋. 𐐏𐐩, 𐑄 𐑋𐐫𐑉 𐐹𐐪𐑉𐐻 𐐱𐑂 𐐫𐑊 𐑄 𐐻𐑉𐐴𐐺𐑆 𐐸𐐰𐑂 𐐺𐐨𐑌 𐑊𐐯𐐼 𐐲𐐶𐐩; 𐐰𐑌𐐼 𐑄𐐩 𐐪𐑉 𐑅𐐿𐐰𐐻𐐲𐑉𐐼 𐐻𐐭 𐐰𐑌𐐼 𐑁𐑉𐐬 𐐲𐐹𐐪𐑌 𐑄 𐐴𐑊𐑆 𐐱𐑂 𐑄 𐑅𐐨; 𐐰𐑌𐐼 𐐸𐐶𐐮𐑄𐐲𐑉 𐑄𐐩 𐐪𐑉, 𐑌𐐲𐑌 𐐱𐑂 𐐲𐑅 𐑌𐐬𐐯𐑃, 𐑅𐐩𐑂 𐑄𐐰𐐻 𐐶𐐨 𐑌𐐬 𐑄𐐰𐐻 𐑄𐐩 𐐸𐐰𐑂 𐐺𐐨𐑌 𐑊𐐯𐐼 𐐲𐐶𐐩. 𐐈𐑌𐐼 𐑅𐐮𐑌𐑅 𐑄𐐩 𐐸𐐰𐑂 𐐺𐐨𐑌 𐑊𐐯𐐼 𐐲𐐶𐐩, 𐑄𐐨𐑆 𐑃𐐮𐑍𐑆 𐐸𐐰𐑂 𐐺𐐨𐑌 𐐹𐑉𐐱𐑁𐐯𐑅𐐴𐑆𐐼 𐐿𐐱𐑌𐑅𐐲𐑉𐑌𐐮𐑍 𐑄𐐲𐑋, 𐐰𐑌𐐼 𐐫𐑊𐑅𐐬 𐐿𐐱𐑌𐑅𐐲𐑉𐑌𐐮𐑍 𐐫𐑊 𐑄𐐬𐑆 𐐸𐐭 𐑇𐐰𐑊 𐐸𐐨𐑉𐐰𐑁𐐻𐐲𐑉 𐐺𐐨 𐑅𐐿𐐰𐐻𐐲𐑉𐐼 𐐰𐑌𐐼 𐐺𐐨 𐐿𐐱𐑌𐑁𐐵𐑌𐐼𐐲𐐼, 𐐺𐐨𐐿𐐫𐑆 𐐱𐑂 𐑄 𐐐𐐬𐑊𐐨 𐐎𐐲𐑌 𐐱𐑂 𐐀𐑆𐑉𐐩𐐲𐑊; 𐑁𐐫𐑉 𐐲𐑀𐐯𐑌𐑅𐐻 𐐸𐐮𐑋 𐐶𐐮𐑊 𐑄𐐩 𐐸𐐪𐑉𐐼𐐲𐑌 𐑄𐐯𐑉 𐐸𐐪𐑉𐐻𐑅; 𐐸𐐶𐐯𐑉𐑁𐐫𐑉, 𐑄𐐩 𐑇𐐰𐑊 𐐺𐐨 𐑅𐐿𐐰𐐻𐐲𐑉𐐼 𐐲𐑋𐐲𐑍 𐐫𐑊 𐑌𐐩𐑇𐐲𐑌𐑆, 𐐰𐑌𐐼 𐑇𐐰𐑊 𐐺𐐨 𐐸𐐩𐐻𐐲𐐼 𐐱𐑂 𐐫𐑊 𐑋𐐯𐑌. 𐐤𐐯𐑂𐐲𐑉𐑄𐐲𐑊𐐯𐑅, 𐐰𐑁𐐻𐐲𐑉 𐑄𐐩 𐑇𐐰𐑊 𐐺𐐨 𐑌𐐲𐑉𐑅𐐻 𐐺𐐴 𐑄 𐐖𐐯𐑌𐐻𐐴𐑊𐑆, 𐐰𐑌𐐼 𐑄 𐐢𐐫𐑉𐐼 𐐸𐐰𐑆 𐑊𐐮𐑁𐐻𐐲𐐼 𐐲𐐹 𐐸𐐮𐑆 𐐸𐐰𐑌𐐼 𐐲𐐹𐐪𐑌 𐑄 𐐖𐐯𐑌𐐻𐐴𐑊𐑆, 𐐰𐑌𐐼 𐑅𐐯𐐻 𐑄𐐯𐑋 𐐲𐐹 𐑁𐐫𐑉 𐐩 𐑅𐐻𐐰𐑌𐐼𐐲𐑉𐐼, 𐐰𐑌𐐼 𐑄𐐯𐑉 𐐽𐐮𐑊𐐼𐑉𐐲𐑌 𐑇𐐰𐑊 𐐺𐐨 𐐿𐐰𐑉𐐨𐐼 𐐮𐑌 𐑄𐐯𐑉 𐐪𐑉𐑋𐑆, 𐐰𐑌𐐼 𐑄𐐯𐑉 𐐼𐐫𐐻𐐲𐑉𐑆 𐑇𐐰𐑊 𐐺𐐨 𐐿𐐰𐑉𐐨𐐼 𐐲𐐹𐐪𐑌 𐑄𐐯𐑉 𐑇𐐬𐑊𐐼𐐲𐑉𐑆, 𐐺𐐨𐐸𐐬𐑊𐐼 𐑄𐐨𐑆 𐑃𐐮𐑍𐑆 𐐱𐑂 𐐸𐐶𐐮𐐽 𐐪𐑉 𐑅𐐹𐐬𐐿𐐲𐑌 𐐪𐑉 𐐻𐐯𐑋𐐹𐐲𐑉𐐲𐑊; 𐑁𐐫𐑉 𐑄𐐲𐑅 𐐪𐑉 𐑄 𐐿𐐲𐑂𐐯𐑌𐐲𐑌𐐻𐑅 𐐱𐑂 𐑄 𐐢𐐫𐑉𐐼 𐐶𐐮𐑄 𐐵𐑉 𐑁𐐪𐑄𐐲𐑉𐑆; 𐐰𐑌𐐼 𐐮𐐻 𐑋𐐨𐑌𐐯𐑃 𐐲𐑅 𐐮𐑌 𐑄 𐐼𐐩𐑆 𐐻𐐭 𐐿𐐲𐑋, 𐐰𐑌𐐼 𐐫𐑊𐑅𐐬 𐐫𐑊 𐐵𐑉 𐐺𐑉𐐯𐑄𐑉𐐯𐑌 𐐸𐐭 𐐪𐑉 𐐱𐑂 𐑄 𐐸𐐵𐑅 𐐱𐑂 𐐀𐑆𐑉𐐩𐐲𐑊. 𐐈𐑌𐐼 𐐮𐐻 𐑋𐐨𐑌𐐯𐑃 𐑄𐐰𐐻 𐑄 𐐻𐐴𐑋 𐐿𐐲𐑋𐐯𐑃 𐑄𐐰𐐻 𐐰𐑁𐐻𐐲𐑉 𐐫𐑊 𐑄 𐐸𐐵𐑅 𐐱𐑂 𐐀𐑆𐑉𐐩𐐲𐑊 𐐸𐐰𐑂 𐐺𐐨𐑌 𐑅𐐿𐐰𐐻𐐲𐑉𐐼 𐐰𐑌𐐼 𐐿𐐱𐑌𐑁𐐵𐑌𐐼𐐲𐐼, 𐑄𐐰𐐻 𐑄 𐐢𐐫𐑉𐐼 𐐘𐐱𐐼 𐐶𐐮𐑊 𐑉𐐩𐑆 𐐲𐐹 𐐩 𐑋𐐴𐐻𐐨 𐑌𐐩𐑇𐐲𐑌 𐐲𐑋𐐲𐑍 𐑄 𐐖𐐯𐑌𐐻𐐴𐑊𐑆, 𐐷𐐩, 𐐨𐑂𐑌 𐐲𐐹𐐪𐑌 𐑄 𐑁𐐩𐑅 𐐱𐑂 𐑄𐐮𐑅 𐑊𐐰𐑌𐐼; 𐐰𐑌𐐼 𐐺𐐴 𐑄𐐯𐑋 𐑇𐐰𐑊 𐐵𐑉 𐑅𐐨𐐼 𐐺𐐨 𐑅𐐿𐐰𐐻𐐲𐑉𐐼.

2. 𐐈𐑌𐐼 𐐰𐑁𐐻𐐲𐑉 𐐵𐑉 𐑅𐐨𐐼 𐐮𐑆 𐑅𐐿𐐰𐐻𐐲𐑉𐐼, 𐑄 𐐢𐐫𐑉𐐼 𐐘𐐱𐐼 𐐶𐐮𐑊 𐐹𐑉𐐬𐑅𐐨𐐼 𐐻𐐭 𐐼𐐭 𐐩 𐑋𐐪𐑉𐑂𐐯𐑊𐐲𐑅 𐐶𐐲𐑉𐐿 𐐲𐑋𐐲𐑍 𐑄 𐐖𐐯𐑌𐐻𐐴𐑊𐑆, 𐐸𐐶𐐮𐐽 𐑇𐐰𐑊 𐐺𐐨 𐐱𐑂 𐑀𐑉𐐩𐐻 𐐶𐐲𐑉𐑃 𐐲𐑌𐐻𐐭 𐐵𐑉 𐑅𐐨𐐼; 𐐸𐐶𐐯𐑉𐑁𐐫𐑉, 𐐮𐐻 𐐮𐑆 𐑊𐐴𐐿𐐲𐑌𐐼 𐐲𐑌𐐻𐐭 𐑄𐐯𐑉 𐐺𐐨𐐮𐑍 𐑌𐐲𐑉𐐮𐑇𐐻 𐐺𐐴 𐑄 𐐖𐐯𐑌𐐻𐐴𐑊𐑆 𐐰𐑌𐐼 𐐺𐐨𐐮𐑍 𐐿𐐰𐑉𐐨𐐼 𐐮𐑌 𐑄𐐯𐑉 𐐪𐑉𐑋𐑆 𐐰𐑌𐐼 𐐲𐐹𐐪𐑌 𐑄𐐯𐑉 𐑇𐐬𐑊𐐼𐐲𐑉𐑆. 𐐈𐑌𐐼 𐐮𐐻 𐑇𐐰𐑊 𐐫𐑊𐑅𐐬 𐐺𐐨 𐐱𐑂 𐐶𐐲𐑉𐑃 𐐲𐑌𐐻𐐭 𐑄 𐐖𐐯𐑌𐐻𐐴𐑊𐑆; 𐐰𐑌𐐼 𐑌𐐱𐐻 𐐬𐑌𐑊𐐨 𐐲𐑌𐐻𐐭 𐑄 𐐖𐐯𐑌𐐻𐐴𐑊𐑆, 𐐺𐐲𐐻 𐐲𐑌𐐻𐐭 𐐫𐑊 𐑄 𐐸𐐵𐑅 𐐱𐑂 𐐀𐑆𐑉𐐩𐐲𐑊, 𐐲𐑌𐐻𐐭 𐑄 𐑋𐐩𐐿𐐮𐑍 𐑌𐐬𐑌 𐐱𐑂 𐑄 𐐿𐐲𐑂𐐯𐑌𐐲𐑌𐐻𐑅 𐐱𐑂 𐑄 𐐙𐐪𐑄𐐲𐑉 𐐱𐑂 𐐸𐐯𐑂𐐲𐑌 𐐲𐑌𐐻𐐭 𐐁𐐺𐑉𐐲𐐸𐐰𐑋, 𐑅𐐩𐐮𐑍, 𐐆𐑌 𐑄𐐴 𐑅𐐨𐐼 𐑇𐐰𐑊 𐐫𐑊 𐑄 𐐿𐐮𐑌𐐼𐑉𐐲𐐼𐑆 𐐱𐑂 𐑄 𐐲𐑉𐑃 𐐺𐐨 𐐺𐑊𐐯𐑅𐐻; 𐐰𐑌𐐼 𐐌 𐐶𐐳𐐼, 𐑋𐐴 𐐺𐑉𐐯𐑄𐑉𐐯𐑌, 𐑄𐐰𐐻 𐐷𐐨 𐑇𐐳𐐼 𐑌𐐬 𐑄𐐰𐐻 𐐫𐑊 𐑄 𐐿𐐮𐑌𐐼𐑉𐐲𐐼𐑆 𐐱𐑂 𐑄 𐐲𐑉𐑃 𐐿𐐰𐑌𐐱𐐻 𐐺𐐨 𐐺𐑊𐐯𐑅𐐻, 𐐲𐑌𐑊𐐯𐑅 𐐸𐐨 𐑇𐐰𐑊 𐑋𐐩𐐿 𐐺𐐯𐑉 𐐸𐐮𐑆 𐐪𐑉𐑋 𐐮𐑌 𐑄 𐐴𐑆 𐐱𐑂 𐑄 𐑌𐐩𐑇𐐲𐑌𐑆. 𐐐𐐶𐐯𐑉𐑁𐐫𐑉, 𐑄 𐐢𐐫𐑉𐐼 𐐘𐐱𐐼 𐐶𐐮𐑊 𐐹𐑉𐐬𐑅𐐨𐐼 𐐻𐐭 𐑋𐐩𐐿 𐐺𐐯𐑉 𐐸𐐮𐑆 𐐪𐑉𐑋 𐐮𐑌 𐑄 𐐴𐑆 𐐱𐑂 𐐫𐑊 𐑄 𐑌𐐩𐑇𐐲𐑌𐑆, 𐐮𐑌 𐐺𐑉𐐮𐑍𐐮𐑍 𐐲𐐺𐐵𐐻 𐐸𐐮𐑆 𐐿𐐲𐑂𐐯𐑌𐐲𐑌𐐻𐑅 𐐰𐑌𐐼 𐐸𐐮𐑆 𐐘𐐱𐑅𐐹𐐲𐑊, 𐐲𐑌𐐻𐐭 𐑄𐐬𐑆 𐐸𐐭 𐐪𐑉 𐐱𐑂 𐑄 𐐸𐐵𐑅 𐐱𐑂 𐐀𐑆𐑉𐐩𐐲𐑊. 𐐐𐐶𐐯𐑉𐑁𐐫𐑉, 𐐸𐐨 𐐶𐐮𐑊 𐐺𐑉𐐮𐑍 𐑄𐐯𐑋 𐐲𐑀𐐯𐑌 𐐵𐐻 𐐱𐑂 𐐿𐐰𐐹𐐻𐐮𐑂𐐮𐐻𐐨, 𐐰𐑌𐐼 𐑄𐐩 𐑇𐐰𐑊 𐐺𐐨 𐑀𐐰𐑄𐐲𐑉𐐼 𐐻𐐭𐑀𐐯𐑄𐐲𐑉 𐐻𐐭 𐑄 𐑊𐐰𐑌𐐼𐑆 𐐱𐑂 𐑄𐐯𐑉 𐐮𐑌𐐸𐐯𐑉𐐮𐐻𐐲𐑌𐑅; 𐐰𐑌𐐼 𐑄𐐩 𐑇𐐰𐑊 𐐺𐐨 𐐺𐑉𐐱𐐻 𐐵𐐻 𐐱𐑂 𐐱𐐺𐑅𐐿𐐷𐐭𐑉𐐮𐐻𐐨, 𐐰𐑌𐐼 𐐵𐐻 𐐱𐑂 𐐼𐐪𐑉𐐿𐑌𐐯𐑅; 𐐰𐑌𐐼 𐑄𐐩 𐑇𐐰𐑊 𐑌𐐬 𐑄𐐰𐐻 𐑄 𐐢𐐫𐑉𐐼 𐐮𐑆 𐑄𐐯𐑉 𐐝𐐩𐑂𐐷𐐲𐑉 𐐰𐑌𐐼 𐑄𐐯𐑉 𐐡𐐨𐐼𐐨𐑋𐐲𐑉, 𐑄 𐐣𐐴𐐻𐐨 𐐎𐐲𐑌 𐐱𐑂 𐐀𐑆𐑉𐐩𐐲𐑊. 𐐈𐑌𐐼 𐑄 𐐺𐑊𐐲𐐼 𐐱𐑂 𐑄𐐰𐐻 𐑀𐑉𐐩𐐻 𐐰𐑌𐐼 𐐲𐐺𐐱𐑋𐐮𐑌𐐲𐐺𐑊 𐐽𐐲𐑉𐐽, 𐐸𐐶𐐮𐐽 𐐮𐑆 𐑄 𐐸𐐫𐑉 𐐱𐑂 𐐫𐑊 𐑄 𐐲𐑉𐑃, 𐑇𐐰𐑊 𐐻𐐲𐑉𐑌 𐐲𐐹𐐪𐑌 𐑄𐐯𐑉 𐐬𐑌 𐐸𐐯𐐼𐑆; 𐑁𐐫𐑉 𐑄𐐩 𐑇𐐰𐑊 𐐶𐐫𐑉 𐐲𐑋𐐲𐑍 𐑄𐐯𐑋𐑅𐐯𐑊𐑂𐑆, 𐐰𐑌𐐼 𐑄 𐑅𐐫𐑉𐐼 𐐱𐑂 𐑄𐐯𐑉 𐐬𐑌 𐐸𐐰𐑌𐐼𐑆 𐑇𐐰𐑊 𐑁𐐫𐑊 𐐲𐐹𐐪𐑌 𐑄𐐯𐑉 𐐬𐑌 𐐸𐐯𐐼𐑆, 𐐰𐑌𐐼 𐑄𐐩 𐑇𐐰𐑊 𐐺𐐨 𐐼𐑉𐐲𐑍𐐿𐐲𐑌 𐐶𐐮𐑄 𐑄𐐯𐑉 𐐬𐑌 𐐺𐑊𐐲𐐼. 𐐈𐑌𐐼 𐐯𐑂𐑉𐐨 𐑌𐐩𐑇𐐲𐑌 𐐸𐐶𐐮𐐽 𐑇𐐰𐑊 𐐶𐐫𐑉 𐐲𐑀𐐯𐑌𐑅𐐻 𐑄𐐨, 𐐄 𐐸𐐵𐑅 𐐱𐑂 𐐀𐑆𐑉𐐩𐐲𐑊, 𐑇𐐰𐑊 𐐺𐐨 𐐻𐐲𐑉𐑌𐐼 𐐶𐐲𐑌 𐐲𐑀𐐯𐑌𐑅𐐻 𐐲𐑌𐐲𐑄𐐲𐑉, 𐐰𐑌𐐼 𐑄𐐩 𐑇𐐰𐑊 𐑁𐐫𐑊 𐐮𐑌𐐻𐐭 𐑄 𐐹𐐮𐐻 𐐸𐐶𐐮𐐽 𐑄𐐩 𐐼𐐮𐑀𐐼 𐐻𐐭 𐐯𐑌𐑅𐑌𐐩𐑉 𐑄 𐐹𐐨𐐹𐑊 𐐱𐑂 𐑄 𐐢𐐫𐑉𐐼.

3. 𐐈𐑌𐐼 𐐫𐑊 𐑄𐐰𐐻 𐑁𐐴𐐻 𐐲𐑀𐐯𐑌𐑅𐐻 𐐞𐐴𐐲𐑌 𐑇𐐰𐑊 𐐺𐐨 𐐼𐐮𐑅𐐻𐑉𐐱𐐮𐐼, 𐐰𐑌𐐼 𐑄𐐰𐐻 𐑀𐑉𐐩𐐻 𐐸𐐫𐑉, 𐐸𐐭 𐐸𐐰𐑃 𐐹𐐲𐑉𐑂𐐲𐑉𐐻𐐲𐐼 𐑄 𐑉𐐴𐐻 𐐶𐐩𐑆 𐐱𐑂 𐑄 𐐢𐐫𐑉𐐼, 𐐷𐐩, 𐑄𐐰𐐻 𐑀𐑉𐐩𐐻 𐐰𐑌𐐼 𐐲𐐺𐐱𐑋𐐮𐑌𐐲𐐺𐑊 𐐽𐐲𐑉𐐽 𐑇𐐰𐑊 𐐻𐐲𐑋𐐺𐑊 𐐻𐐭 𐑄 𐐼𐐲𐑅𐐻, 𐐰𐑌𐐼 𐑀𐑉𐐩𐐻 𐑇𐐰𐑊 𐐺𐐨 𐑄 𐑁𐐫𐑊 𐐱𐑂 𐐮𐐻. 𐐙𐐫𐑉 𐐺𐐨𐐸𐐬𐑊𐐼, 𐑅𐐯𐑆 𐑄 𐐹𐑉𐐱𐑁𐐯𐐻, 𐑄 𐐻𐐴𐑋 𐐿𐐲𐑋𐐯𐑃 𐑅𐐹𐐨𐐼𐐮𐑊𐐨, 𐑄𐐰𐐻 𐐝𐐩𐐻𐐲𐑌 𐑇𐐰𐑊 𐐸𐐰𐑂 𐑌𐐬 𐑋𐐫𐑉 𐐹𐐵𐐲𐑉 𐐬𐑂𐐲𐑉 𐑄 𐐸𐐪𐑉𐐻𐑅 𐐱𐑂 𐑄 𐐽𐐮𐑊𐐼𐑉𐐲𐑌 𐐱𐑂

𐑋𐐯𐑌; 𐑁𐐫𐑉 𐑄 𐐼𐐩 𐑅𐐭𐑌 𐐿𐐲𐑋𐐯𐑃 𐑄𐐰𐐻 𐐫𐑊 𐑄 𐐹𐑉𐐵𐐼 𐐰𐑌𐐼 𐑄𐐩 𐐸𐐭 𐐼𐐭 𐐶𐐮𐐿𐐯𐐼𐑊𐐨, 𐑇𐐰𐑊 𐐺𐐨 𐐰𐑆 𐑅𐐻𐐲𐐺𐐲𐑊; 𐐰𐑌𐐼 𐑄 𐐼𐐩 𐐿𐐲𐑋𐐯𐑃 𐑄𐐰𐐻 𐑄𐐩 𐑋𐐲𐑅𐐻 𐐺𐐨 𐐺𐐲𐑉𐑌𐐼. 𐐙𐐫𐑉 𐑄 𐐻𐐴𐑋 𐑅𐐭𐑌 𐐿𐐲𐑋𐐯𐑃 𐑄𐐰𐐻 𐑄 𐑁𐐳𐑊𐑌𐐯𐑅 𐐱𐑂 𐑄 𐑉𐐪𐑃 𐐱𐑂 𐐘𐐱𐐼 𐑇𐐰𐑊 𐐺𐐨 𐐹𐐬𐑉𐐼 𐐵𐐻 𐐲𐐹𐐱𐑌 𐐫𐑊 𐑄 𐐽𐐮𐑊𐐼𐑉𐐯𐑌 𐐱𐑂 𐑋𐐯𐑌; 𐑁𐐫𐑉 𐐸𐐨 𐐶𐐮𐑊 𐑌𐐱𐐻 𐑅𐐲𐑁𐐲𐑉 𐑄𐐰𐐻 𐑄 𐐶𐐮𐐿𐐯𐐼 𐑇𐐰𐑊 𐐼𐐯𐑅𐐻𐑉𐐱𐐴 𐑄 𐑉𐐴𐐽𐐲𐑅. 𐐐𐐶𐐯𐑉𐑁𐐫𐑉, 𐐸𐐨 𐐶𐐮𐑊 𐐹𐑉𐐨𐑆𐐲𐑉𐑂 𐑄 𐑉𐐴𐐽𐐲𐑅 𐐺𐐴 𐐸𐐮𐑆 𐐹𐐵𐐲𐑉, 𐐨𐑂𐐲𐑌 𐐮𐑁 𐐮𐐻 𐑅𐐬 𐐺𐐨 𐑄𐐰𐐻 𐑄 𐑁𐐳𐑊𐑌𐐯𐑅 𐐱𐑂 𐐸𐐮𐑆 𐑉𐐪𐑃 𐑋𐐲𐑅𐐻 𐐿𐐲𐑋, 𐐰𐑌𐐼 𐑄 𐑉𐐴𐐽𐐲𐑅 𐐺𐐨 𐐹𐑉𐐨𐑆𐐲𐑉𐑂𐐼, 𐐨𐑂𐐲𐑌 𐐲𐑌𐐻𐐭 𐑄 𐐼𐐯𐑅𐐻𐑉𐐲𐐿𐑇𐐲𐑌 𐐱𐑂 𐑄𐐩𐑉 𐐯𐑌𐐯𐑋𐐨𐑆 𐐺𐐴 𐑁𐐴𐑉. 𐐐𐐶𐐯𐑉𐑁𐐫𐑉, 𐑄 𐑉𐐴𐐽𐐲𐑅 𐑌𐐨𐐼 𐑌𐐱𐐻 𐑁𐐨𐑉; 𐑁𐐫𐑉 𐑄𐐲𐑅 𐑅𐐯𐑃 𐑄 𐐹𐑉𐐱𐑁𐐯𐐻, 𐑄𐐩 𐑇𐐰𐑊 𐐺𐐨 𐑅𐐩𐑂𐐼, 𐐨𐑂𐐲𐑌 𐐮𐑁 𐐮𐐻 𐑅𐐬 𐐺𐐨 𐐰𐑆 𐐺𐐴 𐑁𐐴𐑉. 𐐒𐐨𐐸𐐬𐑊𐐼, 𐑋𐐴 𐐺𐑉𐐯𐑄𐑉𐐯𐑌, 𐐌 𐑅𐐩 𐐲𐑌𐐻𐐭 𐐷𐐭, 𐑄𐐰𐐻 𐑄𐐨𐑆 𐑃𐐮𐑍𐑆 𐑋𐐲𐑅𐐻 𐑇𐐫𐑉𐐻𐑊𐐨 𐐿𐐲𐑋; 𐐷𐐩, 𐐨𐑂𐐲𐑌 𐐺𐑊𐐲𐐼, 𐐰𐑌𐐼 𐑁𐐴𐑉, 𐐰𐑌𐐼 𐑂𐐩𐐹𐐲𐑉 𐐱𐑂 𐑅𐑋𐐬𐐿 𐑋𐐲𐑅𐐻 𐐿𐐲𐑋; 𐐰𐑌𐐼 𐐮𐐻 𐑋𐐲𐑅𐐻 𐑌𐐨𐐼𐑆 𐐺𐐨 𐐲𐐹𐐱𐑌 𐑄 𐑁𐐩𐑅 𐐱𐑂 𐑄𐐮𐑅 𐐲𐑉𐑃; 𐐰𐑌𐐼 𐐮𐐻 𐐿𐐲𐑋𐐯𐑃 𐐲𐑌𐐻𐐭 𐑋𐐯𐑌 𐐰𐐿𐐫𐑉𐐼𐐮𐑍 𐐻𐐭 𐑄 𐑁𐑊𐐯𐑇, 𐐮𐑁 𐐮𐐻 𐑅𐐬 𐐺𐐨 𐑄𐐰𐐻 𐑄𐐩 𐐶𐐮𐑊 𐐸𐐪𐑉𐐼𐐯𐑌 𐑄𐐩𐑉 𐐸𐐪𐑉𐐻𐑅 𐐰𐑀𐐯𐑌𐑅𐐻 𐑄 𐐐𐐬𐑊𐐨 𐐎𐐲𐑌 𐐱𐑂 𐐆𐑆𐑉𐐩𐐯𐑊; 𐑁𐐫𐑉 𐐺𐐨𐐸𐐬𐑊𐐼, 𐑄 𐑉𐐴𐐽𐐲𐑅 𐑇𐐰𐑊 𐑌𐐱𐐻 𐐹𐐯𐑉𐐮𐑇; 𐑁𐐫𐑉 𐑄 𐐻𐐴𐑋 𐑇𐐭𐑉𐑊𐐨 𐑋𐐲𐑅𐐻 𐐿𐐲𐑋 𐑄𐐰𐐻 𐐫𐑊 𐑄𐐩 𐐸𐐭 𐑁𐐴𐐻 𐐰𐑀𐐯𐑌𐑅𐐻 𐐞𐐴𐐲𐑌 𐑇𐐰𐑊 𐐺𐐨 𐐿𐐲𐐻 𐐫𐑁. 𐐈𐑌𐐼 𐑄 𐐢𐐫𐑉𐐼 𐐶𐐮𐑊 𐑇𐐭𐑉𐑊𐐨 𐐹𐑉𐐨𐐹𐐩𐑉 𐐲 𐐶𐐩 𐑁𐐫𐑉 𐐸𐐮𐑆 𐐹𐐨𐐹𐑊, 𐐲𐑌𐐻𐐭 𐑄 𐑁𐐳𐑊𐑁𐐮𐑊𐐮𐑍 𐐱𐑂 𐑄 𐐶𐐲𐑉𐐼𐑆 𐐱𐑂 𐐣𐐬𐑆𐐯𐑆, 𐐸𐐶𐐮𐐽 𐐸𐐨 𐑅𐐹𐐩𐐿, 𐑅𐐩𐐮𐑍: 𐐀 𐐹𐑉𐐱𐑁𐐯𐐻 𐑇𐐰𐑊 𐑄 𐐢𐐫𐑉𐐼 𐐷𐐭𐑉 𐐘𐐱𐐼 𐑉𐐩𐑆 𐐲𐐹 𐐲𐑌𐐻𐐭 𐐷𐐭, 𐑊𐐴𐐿 𐐲𐑌𐐻𐐭 𐑋𐐨; 𐐸𐐮𐑋 𐑇𐐰𐑊 𐐷𐐨 𐐸𐐨𐑉 𐐮𐑌 𐐫𐑊 𐑃𐐮𐑍𐑆 𐐸𐐶𐐱𐐻𐑅𐐬𐐯𐑂𐐲𐑉 𐐸𐐨 𐑇𐐰𐑊 𐑅𐐩 𐐲𐑌𐐻𐐭 𐐷𐐭. 𐐈𐑌𐐼 𐐮𐐻 𐑇𐐰𐑊 𐐿𐐲𐑋 𐐻𐐭 𐐹𐐰𐑅 𐑄𐐰𐐻 𐐫𐑊 𐑄𐐬𐑆 𐐸𐐭 𐐶𐐮𐑊 𐑌𐐱𐐻 𐐸𐐨𐑉 𐑄𐐰𐐻 𐐹𐑉𐐱𐑁𐐯𐐻, 𐑇𐐰𐑊 𐐺𐐨 𐐿𐐲𐐻 𐐫𐑁 𐑁𐑉𐐱𐑋 𐐰𐑋𐐲𐑍 𐑄 𐐹𐐨𐐹𐑊.

4. 𐐈𐑌𐐼 𐑌𐐵 𐐌, 𐐤𐐨𐑁𐐴, 𐐼𐐨𐐿𐑊𐐩𐑉 𐐲𐑌𐐻𐐭 𐐷𐐭, 𐑄𐐰𐐻 𐑄𐐮𐑅 𐐹𐑉𐐱𐑁𐐯𐐻 𐐱𐑂 𐐸𐐭𐑋 𐐣𐐬𐑆𐐯𐑆 𐑅𐐹𐐩𐐿, 𐐶𐐱𐑆 𐑄 𐐐𐐬𐑊𐐨 𐐎𐐲𐑌 𐐱𐑂 𐐆𐑆𐑉𐐩𐐯𐑊; 𐐸𐐶𐐯𐑉𐑁𐐫𐑉, 𐐸𐐨 𐑇𐐰𐑊 𐐯𐐿𐑅𐐯𐐿𐐷𐐭𐐻 𐐾𐐲𐐾𐑋𐐯𐑌𐐻 𐐮𐑌 𐑉𐐴𐐽𐐲𐑅𐑌𐐯𐑅; 𐐰𐑌𐐼 𐑄 𐑉𐐴𐐽𐐲𐑅 𐑌𐐨𐐼 𐑌𐐱𐐻 𐑁𐐨𐑉, 𐑁𐐫𐑉 𐑄𐐩 𐐪𐑉 𐑄𐐬𐑆 𐐸𐐭 𐑇𐐰𐑊 𐑌𐐱𐐻 𐐺𐐨 𐐿𐐱𐑌𐑁𐐵𐑌𐐼𐐯𐐼. 𐐒𐐲𐐻 𐐮𐐻 𐐮𐑆 𐑄 𐐿𐐮𐑍𐐼𐐲𐑋 𐐱𐑂 𐑄 𐐼𐐯𐑂𐐮𐑊, 𐐸𐐶𐐮𐐽 𐑇𐐰𐑊 𐐺𐐨 𐐺𐐮𐑊𐐻 𐐲𐐹 𐐰𐑋𐐲𐑍 𐑄 𐐽𐐮𐑊𐐼𐑉𐐯𐑌 𐐱𐑂 𐑋𐐯𐑌, 𐐸𐐶𐐮𐐽 𐐿𐐮𐑍𐐼𐐲𐑋 𐐮𐑆 𐐯𐑅𐐻𐐰𐐺𐑊𐐮𐑇𐐻 𐐰𐑋𐐲𐑍 𐑄𐐯𐑋 𐐸𐐶𐐮𐐽 𐐪𐑉 𐐮𐑌 𐑄 𐑁𐑊𐐯𐑇; 𐑁𐐫𐑉 𐑄 𐐻𐐴𐑋 𐑅𐐹𐐨𐐼𐐮𐑊𐐨 𐑇𐐰𐑊 𐐿𐐲𐑋, 𐑄𐐰𐐻 𐐫𐑊 𐐽𐐲𐑉𐐽𐐯𐑆 𐐸𐐶𐐮𐐽 𐐪𐑉 𐐺𐐮𐑊𐐻 𐐲𐐹 𐐻𐐭 𐑀𐐯𐐻 𐑀𐐩𐑌, 𐐰𐑌𐐼 𐐫𐑊 𐑄𐐬𐑆 𐐸𐐭 𐐪𐑉 𐐺𐐮𐑊𐐻 𐐲𐐹 𐐻𐐭 𐑀𐐯𐐻 𐐹𐐵𐐲𐑉 𐐬𐑂𐐲𐑉 𐑄 𐑁𐑊𐐯𐑇, 𐐰𐑌𐐼 𐑄𐐬𐑆 𐐸𐐭 𐐪𐑉 𐐺𐐮𐑊𐐻 𐐲𐐹 𐐻𐐭 𐐺𐐨𐐿𐐲𐑋 𐐹𐐱𐐹𐐷𐐭𐑊𐐲𐑉 𐐮𐑌 𐑄 𐐴𐑆 𐐱𐑂 𐑄 𐐶𐐲𐑉𐑊𐐼, 𐐰𐑌𐐼 𐑄𐐬𐑆 𐐸𐐭 𐑅𐐨𐐿 𐑄 𐑊𐐲𐑅𐐻𐑅 𐐱𐑂 𐑄 𐑁𐑊𐐯𐑇 𐐰𐑌𐐼 𐑄 𐑃𐐮𐑍𐑆 𐐱𐑂 𐑄 𐐶𐐲𐑉𐑊𐐼, 𐐰𐑌𐐼 𐐻𐐭 𐐼𐐭 𐐫𐑊 𐑋𐐰𐑌𐐲𐑉 𐐱𐑂 𐐮𐑌𐐮𐐿𐐶𐐮𐐻𐐨; 𐐷𐐩, 𐐮𐑌 𐑁𐐴𐑌, 𐐫𐑊 𐑄𐐬𐑆 𐐸𐐭 𐐺𐐨𐑊𐐱𐑍 𐐻𐐭 𐑄 𐐿𐐮𐑍𐐼𐐲𐑋 𐐱𐑂 𐑄 𐐼𐐯𐑂𐐮𐑊, 𐐪𐑉 𐑄𐐩 𐐸𐐭 𐑌𐐨𐐼 𐑁𐐨𐑉, 𐐰𐑌𐐼 𐐻𐑉𐐯𐑋𐐺𐑊, 𐐰𐑌𐐼 𐐿𐐶𐐩𐐿; 𐑄𐐩 𐐪𐑉 𐑄𐐬𐑆 𐐸𐐭 𐑋𐐲𐑅𐐻 𐐺𐐨 𐐺𐑉𐐫𐐻 𐑊𐐬 𐐮𐑌 𐑄 𐐼𐐲𐑅𐐻; 𐑄𐐩 𐐪𐑉 𐑄𐐬𐑆 𐐸𐐭 𐑋𐐲𐑅𐐻 𐐺𐐨 𐐿𐐱𐑌𐑅𐐭𐑋𐐼 𐐰𐑆 𐑅𐐻𐐲𐐺𐐲𐑊; 𐐰𐑌𐐼 𐑄𐐮𐑅 𐐮𐑆 𐐰𐐿𐐫𐑉𐐼𐐮𐑍 𐐻𐐭 𐑄 𐐶𐐲𐑉𐐼𐑆 𐐱𐑂 𐑄 𐐹𐑉𐐱𐑁𐐯𐐻. 𐐈𐑌𐐼 𐑄 𐐻𐐴𐑋 𐐿𐐲𐑋𐐯𐑃 𐑅𐐹𐐨𐐼𐐮𐑊𐐨, 𐑄𐐰𐐻 𐑄 𐑉𐐴𐐽𐐲𐑅 𐑋𐐲𐑅𐐻 𐐺𐐨 𐑊𐐯𐐼 𐐲𐐹 𐐰𐑆 𐐿𐐪𐑂𐑆 𐐱𐑂 𐑄 𐑅𐐻𐐫𐑊, 𐐰𐑌𐐼 𐑄 𐐐𐐬𐑊𐐨 𐐎𐐲𐑌 𐐱𐑂 𐐆𐑆𐑉𐐩𐐯𐑊 𐑋𐐲𐑅𐐻 𐑉𐐩𐑌 𐐮𐑌 𐐼𐐬𐑋𐐮𐑌𐐷𐐲𐑌, 𐐰𐑌𐐼 𐑋𐐴𐐻, 𐐰𐑌𐐼 𐐹𐐵𐐲𐑉, 𐐰𐑌𐐼 𐑀𐑉𐐩𐐻 𐑀𐑊𐐬𐑉𐐨. 𐐈𐑌𐐼 𐐸𐐨 𐑀𐐰𐑄𐐲𐑉𐐯𐑃 𐐸𐐮𐑆 𐐽𐐮𐑊𐐼𐑉𐐯𐑌 𐑁𐑉𐐱𐑋 𐑄 𐑁𐐬𐑉 𐐿𐐶𐐫𐑉𐐻𐐲𐑉𐑆 𐐱𐑂 𐑄 𐐲𐑉𐑃; 𐐰𐑌𐐼 𐐸𐐨 𐑌𐐲𐑋𐐺𐐲𐑉𐐯𐑃 𐐸𐐮𐑆 𐑇𐐨𐐹, 𐐰𐑌𐐼 𐑄𐐩 𐑌𐐬 𐐸𐐮𐑋; 𐐰𐑌𐐼 𐑄𐐩𐑉 𐑇𐐰𐑊 𐐺𐐨 𐐶𐐲𐑌 𐑁𐐬𐑊𐐼 𐐰𐑌𐐼 𐐶𐐲𐑌 𐑇𐐯𐐹𐐲𐑉𐐼; 𐐰𐑌𐐼 𐐸𐐨 𐑇𐐰𐑊 𐑁𐐨𐐼 𐐸𐐮𐑆 𐑇𐐨𐐹, 𐐰𐑌𐐼 𐐮𐑌 𐐸𐐮𐑋 𐑄𐐩 𐑇𐐰𐑊 𐑁𐐴𐑌𐐼 𐐹𐐪𐑅𐐽𐐲𐑉. 𐐈𐑌𐐼 𐐺𐐨𐐿𐐫𐑆 𐐱𐑂 𐑄 𐑉𐐴𐐽𐐲𐑅𐑌𐐯𐑅 𐐱𐑂 𐐸𐐮𐑆 𐐹𐐨𐐹𐑊, 𐐝𐐩𐐻𐐲𐑌 𐐸𐐰𐑆 𐑌𐐬 𐐹𐐵𐐲𐑉; 𐐸𐐶𐐯𐑉𐑁𐐫𐑉, 𐐸𐐨 𐐿𐐰𐑌𐐱𐐻 𐐺𐐨 𐑊𐐭𐑅𐐻 𐑁𐐫𐑉 𐑄 𐑅𐐹𐐩𐑅 𐐱𐑂 𐑋𐐯𐑌𐐨 𐐷𐐨𐑉𐑆; 𐑁𐐫𐑉 𐐸𐐨 𐐸𐐰𐑃 𐑌𐐬 𐐹𐐵𐐲𐑉 𐐬𐑂𐐲𐑉 𐑄 𐐸𐐪𐑉𐐻𐑅 𐐱𐑂 𐑄 𐐹𐐨𐐹𐑊, 𐑁𐐫𐑉 𐑄𐐩 𐐼𐐶𐐯𐑊 𐐮𐑌 𐑉𐐴𐐽𐐲𐑅𐑌𐐯𐑅, 𐐰𐑌𐐼 𐑄 𐐐𐐬𐑊𐐨 𐐎𐐲𐑌 𐐱𐑂 𐐆𐑆𐑉𐐩𐐯𐑊 𐑉𐐩𐑌𐐯𐑃. 𐐈𐑌𐐼 𐑌𐐵 𐐺𐐨𐐸𐐬𐑊𐐼, 𐐌, 𐐤𐐨𐑁𐐴, 𐑅𐐩 𐐲𐑌𐐻𐐭 𐐷𐐭, 𐑄𐐰𐐻 𐐫𐑊 𐑄𐐨𐑆 𐑃𐐮𐑍𐑆 𐑋𐐲𐑅𐐻 𐐿𐐲𐑋 𐐰𐐿𐐫𐑉𐐼𐐮𐑍 𐐻𐐭 𐑄 𐑁𐑊𐐯𐑇. 𐐒𐐲𐐻 𐐺𐐨𐐸𐐬𐑊𐐼, 𐐫𐑊 𐑌𐐩𐑇𐐲𐑌𐑆, 𐐿𐐮𐑌𐐼𐑉𐐯𐐼𐑆, 𐐻𐐲𐑍𐑆, 𐐰𐑌𐐼 𐐹𐐨𐐹𐑊, 𐑇𐐰𐑊 𐐼𐐶𐐯𐑊 𐑅𐐩𐑁𐑊𐐨 𐐮𐑌 𐑄 𐐐𐐬𐑊𐐨 𐐎𐐲𐑌 𐐱𐑂 𐐆𐑆𐑉𐐩𐐯𐑊, 𐐮𐑁 𐐮𐐻 𐑅𐐬 𐐺𐐨 𐑄𐐰𐐻 𐑄𐐩 𐐶𐐮𐑊 𐑉𐐨𐐹𐐯𐑌𐐻.

5. 𐐈𐑌𐐼 𐑌𐐵 𐐌, 𐐤𐐨𐑁𐐴, 𐑋𐐩𐐿 𐐰𐑌 𐐯𐑌𐐼; 𐑁𐐫𐑉 𐐌 𐐼𐐲𐑉𐑅𐐻 𐑌𐐱𐐻 𐑅𐐹𐐨𐐿 𐑁𐐲𐑉𐑄𐐲𐑉 𐐰𐑆 𐐷𐐯𐐻,

𐐿𐐪𐑌𐑅𐐲𐑉𐑌𐐮𐑍 𐑄𐐨𐑆 𐑃𐐮𐑍𐑆. 𐐐𐐶𐐯𐑉𐑁𐐬𐑉, 𐑋𐐴 𐐺𐑉𐐯𐑄𐑉𐐯𐑌, 𐐌 𐐶𐐳𐐼 𐑄𐐰𐐻 𐐷 𐑇𐐳𐐼 𐐿𐐪𐑌𐑅𐐮𐐼𐐲𐑉 𐑄𐐰𐐻 𐑄 𐑃𐐮𐑍𐑆 𐐸𐐶𐐮𐐽 𐐸𐐰𐑂 𐐺𐐨𐑌 𐑉𐐮𐐻𐑌 𐐲𐐹𐐱𐑌 𐑄 𐐹𐑊𐐩𐐻𐑅 𐐱𐑂 𐐺𐑉𐐰𐑅 𐐪𐑉 𐐻𐑉𐐭; 𐐰𐑌𐐼 𐑄𐐩 𐐻𐐯𐑅𐐻𐐮𐑁𐐴 𐑄𐐰𐐻 𐐲 𐑋𐐰𐑌 𐑋𐐲𐑅𐐻 𐐺𐐨 𐐬𐐺𐐨𐐼𐐨𐐲𐑌𐐻 𐐻𐐭 𐑄 𐐿𐐲𐑋𐐰𐑌𐐼𐑋𐐯𐑌𐐻𐑅 𐐱𐑂 𐐘𐐱𐐼. 𐐐𐐶𐐯𐑉𐑁𐐬𐑉, 𐐷 𐑌𐐨𐐼 𐑌𐐱𐐻 𐑅𐐲𐐹𐐬𐑆 𐑄𐐰𐐻 𐐌 𐐰𐑌𐐼 𐑋𐐴 𐑁𐐪𐑄𐐲𐑉 𐐪𐑉 𐑄 𐐬𐑌𐑊𐐨 𐐶𐐲𐑌𐑆 𐑄𐐰𐐻 𐐸𐐰𐑂 𐐻𐐯𐑅𐐻𐐮𐑁𐐴𐐼, 𐐰𐑌𐐼 𐐫𐑊𐑅𐐬 𐐻𐐫𐐻 𐑄𐐯𐑋. 𐐐𐐶𐐯𐑉𐑁𐐬𐑉, 𐐮𐑁 𐐷 𐑇𐐰𐑊 𐐺𐐨 𐐬𐐺𐐨𐐼𐐨𐐲𐑌𐐻 𐐻𐐭 𐑄 𐐿𐐲𐑋𐐰𐑌𐐼𐑋𐐯𐑌𐐻𐑅, 𐐰𐑌𐐼 𐐯𐑌𐐼𐐷𐐭𐑉 𐐻𐐭 𐑄 𐐯𐑌𐐼, 𐐷 𐑇𐐰𐑊 𐐺𐐨 𐑅𐐩𐑂𐐼 𐐰𐐻 𐑄 𐑊𐐰𐑅𐐻 𐐼𐐩. 𐐈𐑌𐐼 𐑄𐐲𐑅 𐐮𐐻 𐐮𐑆. 𐐁𐑋𐐯𐑌.

𐐜 𐐝𐐯𐐿𐐲𐑌𐐼 𐐒𐐳𐐿 𐐱𐑂 𐐤𐐀𐑁𐐴.

𐐗𐐰𐐹𐐻𐐲𐑉 I.

𐐈𐑌 𐐰𐐿𐐵𐑌𐐻 𐐱𐑂 𐑄 𐐼𐐯𐑃 𐐱𐑂 𐐢𐐀𐐸𐐴. 𐐤𐐀𐑁𐐴'𐑆 𐐺𐑉𐐯𐑄𐑉𐐯𐑌 𐑉𐐨𐐺𐐯𐑊 𐐰𐑀𐐯𐑌𐑅𐐻 𐐸𐐮𐑋. 𐐜 𐐢𐐫𐑉𐐼 𐐶𐐫𐑉𐑌𐑆 𐐤𐐀𐑁𐐴 𐐻𐐭 𐐼𐐨𐐹𐐪𐑉𐐻 𐐮𐑌𐐻𐐭 𐑄 𐐶𐐮𐑊𐐼𐐲𐑉𐑌𐐯𐑅. 𐐐𐐮𐑆 𐐾𐐲𐑉𐑌𐐨𐐮𐑍𐑆 𐐮𐑌 𐑄 𐐶𐐮𐑊𐐼𐐲𐑉𐑌𐐯𐑅, 𐐯𐐻𐑅.

1. 𐐈𐑌𐐼 𐑌𐐵 𐐮𐐻 𐐿𐐩𐑋 𐐻𐐭 𐐹𐐪𐑅 𐐰𐑁𐐻𐐲𐑉 𐐌, 𐐤𐐀𐑁𐐴, 𐐸𐐰𐐼 𐑋𐐩𐐼 𐐰𐑌 𐐯𐑌𐐼 𐐱𐑂 𐐻𐐨𐐽𐐮𐑍 𐑋𐐴 𐐺𐑉𐐯𐑄𐑉𐐯𐑌, 𐐵𐑉 𐑁𐐪𐑄𐐲𐑉 𐐢𐐀𐐸𐐴, 𐐫𐑊𐑅𐐬 𐑅𐐹𐐩𐐿 𐑋𐐯𐑌𐐨 𐑃𐐮𐑍𐑆 𐐲𐑌𐐻𐐭 𐑄𐐯𐑋, 𐐸𐐵 𐑀𐑉𐐩𐐻 𐑃𐐮𐑍𐑆 𐑄 𐐢𐐫𐑉𐐼 𐐸𐐰𐐼 𐐼𐐲𐑌 𐑁𐐫𐑉 𐑄𐐯𐑋, 𐐮𐑌 𐐺𐑉𐐮𐑍𐐮𐑍 𐑄𐐯𐑋 𐐵𐐻 𐐱𐑂 𐑄 𐑊𐐰𐑌𐐼 𐐱𐑂 𐐖𐐯𐑉𐐭𐑅𐐲𐑊𐐯𐑋. 𐐈𐑌𐐼 𐐸𐐨 𐑅𐐹𐐩𐐿 𐐲𐑌𐐻𐐭 𐑄𐐯𐑋 𐐿𐐱𐑌𐑅𐐲𐑉𐑌𐐮𐑍 𐑄𐐩𐑉 𐑉𐐨𐐺𐐯𐑊𐐷𐐲𐑌𐑆 𐐲𐐹𐐱𐑌 𐑄 𐐶𐐫𐐻𐐲𐑉𐑆, 𐐰𐑌𐐼 𐑄 𐑋𐐲𐑉𐑅𐐨𐑆 𐐱𐑂 𐐘𐐱𐐼 𐐮𐑌 𐑅𐐹𐐩𐑉𐐮𐑍 𐑄𐐩𐑉 𐑊𐐴𐑂𐑆, 𐑄𐐰𐐻 𐑄𐐩 𐐶𐐲𐑉 𐑌𐐱𐐻 𐑅𐐶𐐱𐑊𐐬𐐼 𐐲𐐹 𐐮𐑌 𐑄 𐑅𐐨. 𐐈𐑌𐐼 𐐸𐐨 𐐫𐑊𐑅𐐬 𐑅𐐹𐐩𐐿 𐐲𐑌𐐻𐐭 𐑄𐐯𐑋 𐐿𐐱𐑌𐑅𐐲𐑉𐑌𐐮𐑍 𐑄 𐑊𐐰𐑌𐐼 𐐱𐑂 𐐹𐑉𐐱𐑋𐐮𐑅, 𐐸𐐶𐐮𐐽 𐑄𐐩 𐐸𐐰𐐼 𐐱𐐺𐐻𐐩𐑌𐐼: 𐐸𐐵 𐑋𐐲𐑉𐑅𐐮𐑁𐐳𐑊 𐑄 𐐢𐐫𐑉𐐼 𐐸𐐰𐐼 𐐺𐐨𐑌 𐐮𐑌 𐐶𐐫𐑉𐑌𐐮𐑍 𐐲𐑅 𐑄𐐰𐐻 𐐶𐐨 𐑇𐐳𐐼 𐑁𐑊𐐨 𐐵𐐻 𐐱𐑂 𐑄 𐑊𐐰𐑌𐐼 𐐱𐑂 𐐖𐐯𐑉𐐭𐑅𐐲𐑊𐐯𐑋. 𐐙𐐫𐑉, 𐐺𐐨𐐸𐐬𐑊𐐼, 𐑅𐐯𐐼 𐐸𐐨, 𐐌 𐐸𐐰𐑂 𐑅𐐨𐑌 𐐩 𐑂𐐮𐑈𐐲𐑌, 𐐮𐑌 𐐸𐐶𐐮𐐽 𐐌 𐑌𐐬 𐑄𐐰𐐻 𐐖𐐯𐑉𐐭𐑅𐐲𐑊𐐯𐑋 𐐮𐑆 𐐼𐐨𐑅𐐻𐑉𐐱𐐮𐐼; 𐐰𐑌𐐼 𐐸𐐰𐐼 𐐶𐐨 𐑉𐐨𐑋𐐩𐑌𐐼 𐐮𐑌 𐐖𐐯𐑉𐐭𐑅𐐲𐑊𐐯𐑋, 𐐶𐐨 𐑇𐐳𐐼 𐐫𐑊𐑅𐐬 𐐸𐐰𐑂 𐐹𐐯𐑉𐐮𐑇𐐻. 𐐒𐐲𐐻, 𐑅𐐯𐐼 𐐸𐐨, 𐑌𐐱𐐻𐐶𐐮𐑄𐑅𐐻𐐰𐑌𐐼𐐮𐑍 𐐵𐑉 𐐰𐑁𐑊𐐮𐐿𐑇𐐲𐑌𐑆, 𐐶𐐨 𐐸𐐰𐑂 𐐱𐐺𐐻𐐩𐑌𐐼 𐐩 𐑊𐐰𐑌𐐼 𐐱𐑂 𐐹𐑉𐐱𐑋𐐮𐑅, 𐐩 𐑊𐐰𐑌𐐼 𐐸𐐶𐐮𐐽 𐐮𐑆 𐐽𐐱𐐮𐑅 𐐰𐐺𐐲𐑂 𐐫𐑊 𐐲𐑄𐐲𐑉 𐑊𐐰𐑌𐐼𐑆; 𐐩 𐑊𐐰𐑌𐐼 𐐸𐐶𐐮𐐽 𐑄 𐐢𐐫𐑉𐐼 𐐘𐐱𐐼 𐐸𐐰𐑃 𐐿𐐲𐑂𐐯𐑌𐐰𐑌𐐻𐐯𐐼 𐐶𐐮𐑄 𐑋𐐨 𐑇𐐳𐐼 𐐺 𐐩 𐑊𐐰𐑌𐐼 𐑁𐐫𐑉 𐑄 𐐮𐑌𐐸𐐯𐑉𐐮𐐻𐐲𐑌𐑅 𐐱𐑂 𐑋𐐴 𐑅𐐨𐐼. 𐐏𐐩, 𐑄 𐐢𐐫𐑉𐐼 𐐸𐐰𐑃 𐐿𐐲𐑂𐐯𐑌𐐰𐑌𐐻𐐯𐐼 𐑄𐐮𐑅 𐑊𐐰𐑌𐐼 𐐲𐑌𐐻𐐭 𐑋𐐨, 𐐰𐑌𐐼 𐐻𐐭 𐑋𐐴 𐐽𐐮𐑊𐐼𐑉𐐯𐑌 𐑁𐐫𐑉 𐐯𐑂𐐲𐑉; 𐐰𐑌𐐼 𐐫𐑊𐑅𐐬 𐐫𐑊 𐑄𐐬𐑆 𐐸𐐭 𐑇𐐳𐐼 𐐺 𐑊𐐯𐐼 𐐵𐐻 𐐱𐑂 𐐲𐑄𐐲𐑉 𐐿𐐲𐑌𐐻𐑉𐐨𐑆 𐐺𐐴 𐑄 𐐸𐐰𐑌𐐼 𐐱𐑂 𐑄 𐐢𐐫𐑉𐐼. 𐐐𐐶𐐯𐑉𐑁𐐫𐑉, 𐐌, 𐐢𐐀𐐸𐐴, 𐐹𐑉𐐱𐑁𐐯𐑅𐐴 𐐰𐐿𐐫𐑉𐐼𐐮𐑍 𐐻𐐭 𐑄 𐐶𐐲𐑉𐐿𐐮𐑍𐑆 𐐱𐑂 𐑄 𐐝𐐹𐐮𐑉𐐮𐐻 𐐸𐐶𐐮𐐽 𐐮𐑆 𐐮𐑌 𐑋𐐨, 𐑄𐐰𐐻 𐑄𐐯𐑉 𐑇𐐰𐑊 𐑌𐐲𐑌 𐐿𐐲𐑋 𐐮𐑌𐐻𐐭 𐑄𐐮𐑅 𐑊𐐰𐑌𐐼, 𐑅𐐩𐑂 𐑄𐐩 𐑇𐐰𐑊 𐐺 𐐺𐑉𐐫𐐻 𐐺𐐴 𐑄 𐐸𐐰𐑌𐐼 𐐱𐑂 𐑄 𐐢𐐫𐑉𐐼. 𐐐𐐶𐐯𐑉𐑁𐐫𐑉 𐑄𐐮𐑅 𐑊𐐰𐑌𐐼 𐐮𐑆 𐐿𐐱𐑌𐑅𐐨𐐿𐑉𐐩𐐻𐐯𐐼 𐐲𐑌𐐻𐐭 𐐸𐐮𐑋 𐐸𐐭𐑋 𐐸𐐨 𐑇𐐰𐑊 𐐺𐑉𐐮𐑍. 𐐈𐑌𐐼 𐐮𐑁 𐐮𐐻 𐑅𐐬 𐐺 𐑄𐐰𐐻 𐑄𐐩 𐑇𐐰𐑊 𐑅𐐲𐑉𐑂 𐐸𐐮𐑋 𐐰𐐿𐐫𐑉𐐼𐐮𐑍 𐐻𐐭 𐑄 𐐿𐐱𐑋𐐰𐑌𐐼𐑋𐐯𐑌𐐻𐑅 𐐸𐐶𐐮𐐽 𐐸𐐨 𐐸𐐰𐑃 𐑀𐐮𐑂𐐲𐑌, 𐐮𐐻 𐑇𐐰𐑊 𐐺 𐐩 𐑊𐐰𐑌𐐼 𐐱𐑂 𐑊𐐮𐐺𐐲𐑉𐐻𐐨 𐐲𐑌𐐻𐐭 𐑄𐐯𐑋; 𐐸𐐶𐐯𐑉𐑁𐐫𐑉, 𐑄𐐩 𐑇𐐰𐑊 𐑌𐐯𐑂𐐲𐑉 𐐺 𐐺𐑉𐐫𐐻 𐐼𐐵𐑌 𐐮𐑌𐐻𐐭 𐐿𐐰𐐹𐐻𐐮𐑂𐐮𐐻𐐨; 𐐮𐑁 𐑅𐐬, 𐐮𐐻 𐑇𐐰𐑊 𐐺 𐐺𐐨𐐿𐐫𐑆 𐐱𐑂 𐐮𐑌𐐮𐐿𐐶𐐮𐐻𐐨; 𐑁𐐫𐑉 𐐮𐑁 𐐮𐑌𐐮𐐿𐐶𐐮𐐻𐐨 𐑇𐐰𐑊 𐐰𐐺𐐵𐑌𐐼, 𐐿𐐲𐑉𐑅𐐻 𐑇𐐰𐑊 𐐺 𐑄 𐑊𐐰𐑌𐐼 𐑁𐐫𐑉 𐑄𐐩𐑉 𐑅𐐩𐐿𐑅; 𐐺𐐲𐐻 𐐲𐑌𐐻𐐭 𐑄 𐑉𐐴𐐻𐐷𐐲𐑅 𐐮𐐻 𐑇𐐰𐑊 𐐺 𐐺𐑊𐐯𐑅𐐻 𐑁𐐫𐑉 𐐯𐑂𐐲𐑉.

2. 𐐈𐑌𐐼 𐐺𐐨𐐸𐐬𐑊𐐼, 𐐮𐐻 𐐮𐑆 𐐶𐐮𐑆𐐼𐐲𐑋 𐑄𐐰𐐻 𐑄𐐮𐑅 𐑊𐐰𐑌𐐼 𐑇𐐳𐐼 𐐺 𐐿𐐯𐐹𐐻 𐐰𐑆 𐐷𐐯𐐻 𐑁𐑉𐐱𐑋 𐑄 𐑌𐐱𐑊𐐯𐐾 𐐱𐑂 𐐲𐑄𐐲𐑉 𐑌𐐩𐑇𐐲𐑌𐑆; 𐑁𐐫𐑉 𐐺𐐨𐐸𐐬𐑊𐐼, 𐑋𐐯𐑌𐐨 𐑌𐐩𐑇𐐲𐑌𐑆 𐐶𐐳𐐼 𐐬𐑂𐐲𐑉𐑉𐐲𐑌 𐑄 𐑊𐐰𐑌𐐼, 𐑄𐐰𐐻 𐑄𐐯𐑉 𐐶𐐳𐐼 𐐺 𐑌𐐬 𐐹𐑊𐐩𐑅 𐑁𐐫𐑉 𐐰𐑌 𐐮𐑌𐐸𐐯𐑉𐐮𐐻𐐲𐑌𐑅. 𐐐𐐶𐐯𐑉𐑁𐐫𐑉, 𐐌, 𐐢𐐀𐐸𐐴, 𐐸𐐰𐑂 𐐱𐐺𐐻𐐩𐑌𐐼 𐐩 𐐹𐑉𐐱𐑋𐐮𐑅, 𐑄𐐰𐐻 𐐮𐑌𐐰𐑆𐑋𐐲𐐽 𐐰𐑆 𐑄𐐬𐑆 𐐸𐐭𐑋 𐑄 𐐢𐐫𐑉𐐼 𐐘𐐱𐐼 𐑇𐐰𐑊 𐐺𐑉𐐮𐑍 𐐵𐐻 𐐱𐑂 𐑄 𐑊𐐰𐑌𐐼 𐐱𐑂 𐐖𐐯𐑉𐐭𐑅𐐲𐑊𐐯𐑋 𐑇𐐰𐑊 𐐿𐐨𐐹 𐐸𐐮𐑆 𐐿𐐱𐑋𐐰𐑌𐐼𐑋𐐯𐑌𐐻𐑅, 𐑄𐐩 𐑇𐐰𐑊 𐐹𐑉𐐱𐑅𐐹𐐲𐑉 𐐲𐐹𐐱𐑌 𐑄 𐑁𐐩𐑅 𐐱𐑂 𐑄𐐮𐑅 𐑊𐐰𐑌𐐼; 𐐰𐑌𐐼 𐑄𐐩 𐑇𐐰𐑊 𐐺 𐐿𐐯𐐹𐐻 𐑁𐑉𐐱𐑋 𐐫𐑊 𐐲𐑄𐐲𐑉 𐑌𐐩𐑇𐐲𐑌𐑆, 𐑄𐐰𐐻 𐑄𐐩 𐑋𐐩 𐐹𐐲𐑆𐐯𐑅 𐑄𐐮𐑅 𐑊𐐰𐑌𐐼 𐐲𐑌𐐻𐐭 𐑄𐐯𐑋𐑅𐐯𐑊𐑂𐑆. 𐐈𐑌𐐼 𐐮𐑁 𐐮𐐻 𐑅𐐬 𐐺 𐑄𐐰𐐻 𐑄𐐩 𐑇𐐰𐑊 𐐿𐐨𐐹 𐐸𐐮𐑆 𐐿𐐱𐑋𐐰𐑌𐐼𐑋𐐯𐑌𐐻𐑅, 𐑄𐐩 𐑇𐐰𐑊 𐐺 𐐺𐑊𐐯𐑅𐐻 𐐲𐐹𐐱𐑌 𐑄 𐑁𐐩𐑅 𐐱𐑂 𐑄𐐮𐑅 𐑊𐐰𐑌𐐼, 𐐰𐑌𐐼 𐑄𐐯𐑉 𐑇𐐰𐑊 𐐺 𐑌𐐲𐑌 𐐻𐐭 𐑋𐐬𐑊𐐯𐑅𐐻 𐑄𐐯𐑋, 𐑌𐐫𐑉 𐐻𐐭 𐐻𐐩𐐿 𐐰𐐶𐐩 𐑄 𐑊𐐰𐑌𐐼 𐐱𐑂 𐑄𐐩𐑉 𐐮𐑌𐐸𐐯𐑉𐐮𐐻𐐲𐑌𐑅; 𐐰𐑌𐐼

𐑄𐐩 𐑖𐐰𐑊 𐐼𐐶𐐯𐑊 𐑅𐐩𐑁𐑊𐐨 𐑁𐐫𐑉 𐐯𐑂𐐲𐑉. 𐐒𐐲𐐻 𐐺𐐨𐐸𐐬𐑊𐐼, 𐐸𐐶𐐯𐑌 𐑄 𐐻𐐴𐑋 𐐿𐐲𐑋𐐯𐑃 𐑄𐐰𐐻 𐑄𐐩 𐑖𐐰𐑊 𐐼𐐶𐐮𐑌𐐼𐑊 𐐮𐑌 𐐲𐑌𐐺𐐨𐑊𐐨𐑁, 𐐰𐑁𐐻𐐲𐑉 𐑄𐐩 𐐸𐐰𐑂 𐑉𐐨𐑅𐐨𐑂𐐼 𐑅𐐬 𐑀𐑉𐐩𐐻 𐐺𐑊𐐯𐑅𐐮𐑍𐑆 𐑁𐑉𐐱𐑋 𐑄 𐐸𐐰𐑌𐐼 𐐱𐑂 𐑄 𐐢𐐫𐑉𐐼; 𐐸𐐰𐑂𐐮𐑍 𐐲 𐑌𐐱𐑊𐐯𐐾 𐐱𐑂 𐑄 𐐿𐑉𐐨𐐩𐑇𐐲𐑌 𐐱𐑂 𐑄 𐐲𐑉𐑃, 𐐰𐑌𐐼 𐐫𐑊 𐑋𐐯𐑌, 𐑌𐐬𐐮𐑍 𐑄 𐑀𐑉𐐩𐐻 𐐰𐑌𐐼 𐑋𐐪𐑉𐑂𐐯𐑊𐐲𐑅 𐐶𐐲𐑉𐐿𐑅 𐐱𐑂 𐑄 𐐢𐐫𐑉𐐼 𐑁𐑉𐐱𐑋 𐑄 𐐿𐑉𐐨𐐩𐑇𐐲𐑌 𐐱𐑂 𐑄 𐐶𐐲𐑉𐑊𐐼; 𐐸𐐰𐑂𐐮𐑍 𐐹𐐵𐐲𐑉 𐑀𐐮𐑂𐑌 𐑄𐐯𐑋 𐐻𐐭 𐐼𐐭 𐐫𐑊 𐑃𐐮𐑍𐑆 𐐺𐐴 𐑁𐐩𐑃; 𐐸𐐰𐑂𐐮𐑍 𐐫𐑊 𐑄 𐐿𐐱𐑋𐐰𐑌𐐼𐑋𐐯𐑌𐐻𐑅 𐑁𐑉𐐱𐑋 𐑄 𐐺𐐨𐑀𐐮𐑌𐐮𐑍, 𐐰𐑌𐐼 𐐸𐐰𐑂𐐮𐑍 𐐺𐐮𐑌 𐐺𐑉𐐫𐐻 𐐺𐐴 𐐸𐐮𐑆 𐐮𐑌𐑁𐐮𐑌𐐮𐐻 𐑀𐐳𐐼𐑌𐐯𐑅 𐐮𐑌𐐻𐐭 𐑄𐐮𐑅 𐐹𐑉𐐯𐑇𐐲𐑅 𐑊𐐰𐑌𐐼 𐐱𐑂 𐐹𐑉𐐱𐑋𐐮𐑅; 𐐺𐐨𐐸𐐬𐑊𐐼, 𐐴 𐑅𐐩, 𐐮𐑁 𐑄 𐐼𐐩 𐑖𐐰𐑊 𐐿𐐲𐑋 𐑄𐐰𐐻 𐑄𐐩 𐐶𐐮𐑊 𐑉𐐨𐐾𐐯𐐿𐐻 𐑄 𐐐𐐬𐑊𐐨 𐐎𐐲𐑌 𐐱𐑂 𐐀𐑆𐑉𐐩𐐯𐑊, 𐑄 𐐻𐑉𐐭 𐐣𐐯𐑅𐐴𐐲, 𐑄𐐩𐑉 𐐡𐐨𐐼𐐨𐑋𐐲𐑉 𐐰𐑌𐐼 𐑄𐐩𐑉 𐐘𐐱𐐼, 𐐺𐐨𐐸𐐬𐑊𐐼 𐑄 𐐾𐐲𐐾𐑋𐐯𐑌𐐻𐑅 𐐱𐑂 𐐸𐐮𐑋 𐑄𐐰𐐻 𐐮𐑆 𐐾𐐲𐑅𐐻 𐑖𐐰𐑊 𐑉𐐯𐑅𐐻 𐐲𐐹𐐱𐑌 𐑄𐐯𐑋; 𐐷𐐩, 𐐸𐐨 𐐶𐐮𐑊 𐐺𐑉𐐮𐑍 𐐲𐑄𐐲𐑉 𐑌𐐩𐑇𐐲𐑌𐑆 𐐲𐑌𐐻𐐭 𐑄𐐯𐑋, 𐐰𐑌𐐼 𐐸𐐨 𐐶𐐮𐑊 𐑀𐐮𐑂 𐐲𐑌𐐻𐐭 𐑄𐐯𐑋 𐐹𐐵𐐲𐑉, 𐐰𐑌𐐼 𐐸𐐨 𐐶𐐮𐑊 𐐻𐐩𐐿 𐐲𐐶𐐩 𐑁𐑉𐐱𐑋 𐑄𐐯𐑋 𐑄 𐑊𐐰𐑌𐐼𐑆 𐐱𐑂 𐑄𐐩𐑉 𐐹𐐲𐑆𐐯𐑇𐐲𐑌𐑆; 𐐰𐑌𐐼 𐐸𐐨 𐐶𐐮𐑊 𐐿𐐫𐑆 𐑄𐐯𐑋 𐐻𐐭 𐐺 𐑅𐐿𐐰𐐻𐐲𐑉𐐼 𐐰𐑌𐐼 𐑅𐑋𐐮𐐻𐑌. 𐐏𐐩, 𐐰𐑆 𐐶𐐲𐑌 𐐾𐐯𐑌𐐲𐑉𐐩𐑇𐐲𐑌 𐐹𐐰𐑅𐐯𐑃 𐐻𐐭 𐐲𐑌𐐲𐑄𐐲𐑉, 𐑄𐐩𐑉 𐑖𐐰𐑊 𐐺 𐐺𐑊𐐲𐐼𐑖𐐯𐐼𐑆, 𐐰𐑌𐐼 𐑀𐑉𐐩𐐻 𐑂𐐮𐑆𐐮𐐻𐐩𐑇𐐲𐑌𐑆 𐐲𐑋𐐲𐑍 𐑄𐐯𐑋; 𐐸𐐶𐐩𐑉𐑁𐐫𐑉, 𐑋𐐴 𐑅𐐲𐑌𐑆, 𐐴 𐐶𐐳𐐼 𐑄𐐰𐐻 𐐷 𐐶𐐳𐐼 𐑉𐐨𐑋𐐯𐑋𐐺𐐲𐑉; 𐐷𐐩, 𐐴 𐐶𐐳𐐼 𐑄𐐰𐐻 𐐷 𐐶𐐳𐐼 𐐸𐐲𐑉𐐿𐑌 𐐲𐑌𐐻𐐭 𐑋𐐴 𐐶𐐲𐑉𐐼𐑆.

3. 𐐄 𐑄𐐰𐐻 𐐷 𐐶𐐳𐐼 𐐰𐐶𐐩𐐿; 𐐰𐐶𐐩𐐿 𐑁𐑉𐐱𐑋 𐐲 𐐼𐐨𐐹 𐑅𐑊𐐨𐐹, 𐐷𐐩, 𐐨𐑂𐐲𐑌 𐑁𐑉𐐱𐑋 𐑄 𐑅𐑊𐐨𐐹 𐐱𐑂 𐐸𐐯𐑊, 𐐰𐑌𐐼 𐑖𐐩𐐿 𐐫𐑁 𐑄 𐐫𐑁𐐳𐑊 𐐽𐐩𐑌𐑆 𐐺𐐴 𐐸𐐶𐐮𐐽 𐐷 𐐪𐑉 𐐺𐐵𐑌𐐼, 𐐸𐐶𐐮𐐽 𐐪𐑉 𐑄 𐐽𐐩𐑌𐑆 𐐸𐐶𐐮𐐽 𐐺𐐴𐑌𐐼 𐑄 𐐽𐐮𐑊𐐼𐑉𐐯𐑌 𐐱𐑂 𐑋𐐯𐑌, 𐑄𐐰𐐻 𐑄𐐩 𐐪𐑉 𐐿𐐰𐑉𐐨𐐼 𐐲𐐶𐐩 𐐿𐐰𐐹𐐻𐐮𐑂 𐐼𐐵𐑌 𐐻𐐭 𐑄 𐐨𐐻𐐲𐑉𐑌𐐲𐑊 𐑀𐐲𐑊𐑁 𐐱𐑂 𐑋𐐮𐑆𐐲𐑉𐐨 𐐰𐑌𐐼 𐐶𐐬! 𐐈𐐶𐐩𐐿! 𐐰𐑌𐐼 𐐲𐑉𐐴𐑆 𐑁𐑉𐐱𐑋 𐑄 𐐼𐐲𐑅𐐻, 𐐰𐑌𐐼 𐐸𐐨𐑉 𐑄 𐐶𐐲𐑉𐐼𐑆 𐐱𐑂 𐐲 𐐻𐑉𐐯𐑋𐐺𐑊𐐮𐑍 𐐹𐐩𐑉𐐯𐑌𐐻, 𐐸𐐭𐑆 𐑊𐐮𐑋𐑆 𐐷 𐑋𐐲𐑅𐐻 𐑅𐐭𐑌 𐑊𐐩 𐐼𐐵𐑌 𐐮𐑌 𐑄 𐐿𐐬𐑊𐐼 𐐰𐑌𐐼 𐑅𐐴𐑊𐐯𐑌𐐻 𐑀𐑉𐐩𐑂, 𐑁𐑉𐐱𐑋 𐐸𐐶𐐯𐑌𐑅 𐑌𐐬 𐐻𐑉𐐰𐑂𐐯𐑊𐐲𐑉 𐐿𐐰𐑌 𐑉𐐨𐐻𐐲𐑉𐑌; 𐐲 𐑁𐑏 𐑋𐐫𐑉 𐐼𐐩𐑆, 𐐰𐑌𐐼 𐐴 𐑀𐐬 𐑄 𐐶𐐩 𐐱𐑂 𐐫𐑊 𐑄 𐐲𐑉𐑃. 𐐒𐐲𐐻 𐐺𐐨𐐸𐐬𐑊𐐼, 𐑄 𐐢𐐫𐑉𐐼 𐐸𐐰𐑃 𐑉𐐨𐐼𐐨𐑋𐐼 𐑋𐐴 𐑅𐐬𐑊 𐑁𐑉𐐱𐑋 𐐸𐐯𐑊; 𐐴 𐐸𐐰𐑂 𐐺𐐨𐐸𐐯𐑊𐐼 𐐸𐐮𐑆 𐑀𐑊𐐬𐑉𐐨, 𐐰𐑌𐐼 𐐴 𐐰𐑋 𐐯𐑌𐑅𐐲𐑉𐐿𐐲𐑊𐐼 𐐲𐐺𐐵𐐻 𐐨𐐻𐐲𐑉𐑌𐐲𐑊𐐨 𐐮𐑌 𐑄 𐐪𐑉𐑋𐑆 𐐱𐑂 𐐸𐐮𐑆 𐑊𐐲𐑂. 𐐈𐑌𐐼 𐐴 𐐼𐐨𐑆𐐴𐑉 𐑄𐐰𐐻 𐐷 𐑖𐐳𐐼 𐑉𐐨𐑋𐐯𐑋𐐺𐐲𐑉 𐐻𐐭 𐐱𐐺𐑆𐐲𐑉𐑂 𐑄 𐑅𐐻𐐰𐐽𐐭𐐻𐑅 𐐰𐑌𐐼 𐑄 𐐾𐐲𐐾𐑋𐐯𐑌𐐻𐑅 𐐱𐑂 𐑄 𐐢𐐫𐑉𐐼; 𐐺𐐨𐐸𐐬𐑊𐐼, 𐑄𐐮𐑅 𐐸𐐰𐑃 𐐺𐐮𐑌 𐑄 𐐰𐑍𐑆𐐴𐐲𐐻𐐨 𐐱𐑂 𐑋𐐴 𐑅𐐬𐑊 𐑁𐑉𐐱𐑋 𐑄 𐐺𐐨𐑀𐐮𐑌𐐮𐑍. 𐐣𐐴 𐐸𐐪𐑉𐐻 𐐸𐐰𐑃 𐐺𐐮𐑌 𐐶𐐩𐐼 𐐼𐐵𐑌 𐐶𐐮𐑄 𐑅𐐱𐑉𐐬 𐑁𐑉𐐱𐑋 𐐻𐐴𐑋 𐐻𐐭 𐐻𐐴𐑋, 𐑁𐐫𐑉 𐐴 𐐸𐐰𐑂 𐑁𐐨𐑉𐐼, 𐑊𐐯𐑅𐐻 𐑁𐐫𐑉 𐑄 𐐸𐐪𐑉𐐼𐑌𐐯𐑅 𐐱𐑂 𐐷𐐫𐑉 𐐸𐐪𐑉𐐻𐑅, 𐑄 𐐢𐐫𐑉𐐼 𐐷𐐫𐑉 𐐘𐐱𐐼 𐑖𐐳𐐼 𐐿𐐲𐑋 𐐵𐐻 𐐮𐑌 𐑄 𐑁𐐳𐑊𐑌𐐯𐑅 𐐱𐑂 𐐸𐐮𐑆 𐑉𐐪𐑃 𐐲𐐹𐐱𐑌 𐐷𐐭, 𐑄𐐰𐐻 𐐷 𐐺 𐐿𐐲𐐻 𐐫𐑁 𐐰𐑌𐐼 𐐼𐐨𐑅𐐻𐑉𐐱𐐮𐐼 𐑁𐐫𐑉 𐐯𐑂𐐲𐑉; 𐐫𐑉 𐑄𐐰𐐻 𐐲 𐐿𐐲𐑉𐑅𐐮𐑍 𐑖𐐳𐐼 𐐿𐐲𐑋 𐐲𐐹𐐱𐑌 𐐷𐐭 𐑁𐐫𐑉 𐑄 𐑅𐐹𐐩𐑅 𐐱𐑂 𐑋𐐯𐑌𐐨 𐐾𐐯𐑌𐐲𐑉𐐩𐑇𐐲𐑌𐑆; 𐐰𐑌𐐼 𐐷 𐐪𐑉 𐑂𐐮𐑆𐐮𐐻𐐯𐐼 𐐺𐐴 𐑅𐐫𐑉𐐼, 𐐰𐑌𐐼 𐐺𐐴 𐑁𐐰𐑋𐐮𐑌, 𐐰𐑌𐐼 𐐪𐑉 𐐸𐐩𐐻𐐯𐐼, 𐐰𐑌𐐼 𐐪𐑉 𐑊𐐯𐐼 𐐰𐐿𐐫𐑉𐐼𐐮𐑍 𐐻𐐭 𐑄 𐐶𐐮𐑊 𐐰𐑌𐐼 𐐿𐐰𐐹𐐻𐐮𐑂𐐮𐐻𐐨 𐐱𐑂 𐑄 𐐼𐐯𐑂𐐲𐑊.

4. 𐐄 𐑋𐐴 𐑅𐐲𐑌𐑆, 𐑄𐐰𐐻 𐑄𐐨𐑆 𐑃𐐮𐑍𐑆 𐑋𐐴𐐻 𐑌𐐱𐐻 𐐿𐐲𐑋 𐐲𐐹𐐱𐑌 𐐷𐐭, 𐐺𐐲𐐻 𐑄𐐰𐐻 𐐷 𐑋𐐴𐐻 𐐺 𐐲 𐐽𐐱𐐮𐑅 𐐰𐑌𐐼 𐐲 𐑁𐐩𐑂𐐲𐑉𐐼 𐐹𐐨𐐹𐑊 𐐱𐑂 𐑄 𐐢𐐫𐑉𐐼. 𐐒𐐲𐐻 𐐺𐐨𐐸𐐬𐑊𐐼, 𐐸𐐮𐑆 𐐶𐐮𐑊 𐐺 𐐼𐐲𐑌; 𐑁𐐫𐑉 𐐸𐐮𐑆 𐐶𐐩𐑆 𐐪𐑉 𐑉𐐴𐐽𐐲𐑅𐑌𐐯𐑅 𐑁𐐫𐑉 𐐯𐑂𐐲𐑉; 𐐰𐑌𐐼 𐐸𐐨 𐐸𐐰𐑃 𐑅𐐯𐐼, 𐑄𐐰𐐻 𐐮𐑌𐐰𐑆𐑋𐐲𐐽 𐐰𐑆 𐐷 𐑖𐐰𐑊 𐐿𐐨𐐹 𐑋𐐴 𐐿𐐱𐑋𐐰𐑌𐐼𐑋𐐯𐑌𐐻𐑅, 𐐷 𐑖𐐰𐑊 𐐹𐑉𐐱𐑅𐐹𐐲𐑉 𐐮𐑌 𐑄 𐑊𐐰𐑌𐐼; 𐐺𐐲𐐻 𐐮𐑌𐐰𐑆𐑋𐐲𐐽 𐐰𐑆 𐐷 𐐶𐐮𐑊 𐑌𐐱𐐻 𐐿𐐨𐐹 𐑋𐐴 𐐿𐐱𐑋𐐰𐑌𐐼𐑋𐐯𐑌𐐻𐑅, 𐐷 𐑖𐐰𐑊 𐐺 𐐿𐐲𐐻 𐐫𐑁 𐑁𐑉𐐱𐑋 𐑋𐐴 𐐹𐑉𐐯𐑆𐐯𐑌𐑅. 𐐈𐑌𐐼 𐑌𐐵 𐑄𐐰𐐻 𐑋𐐴 𐑅𐐬𐑊 𐑋𐐴𐐻 𐐸𐐰𐑂 𐐾𐐱𐐮 𐐮𐑌 𐐷𐐭, 𐐰𐑌𐐼 𐑄𐐰𐐻 𐑋𐐴 𐐸𐐪𐑉𐐻 𐑋𐐴𐐻 𐑊𐐨𐑂 𐑄𐐮𐑅 𐐶𐐲𐑉𐑊𐐼 𐐶𐐮𐑄 𐑀𐑊𐐰𐐼𐑌𐐯𐑅 𐐺𐐨𐐿𐐫𐑆 𐐱𐑂 𐐷𐐭, 𐑄𐐰𐐻 𐐴 𐑋𐐴𐐻 𐑌𐐱𐐻 𐐺 𐐺𐑉𐐫𐐻 𐐼𐐵𐑌 𐐶𐐮𐑄 𐑀𐑉𐐨𐑁 𐐰𐑌𐐼 𐑅𐐱𐑉𐐬 𐐻𐐭 𐑄 𐑀𐑉𐐩𐑂, 𐐲𐑉𐐴𐑆 𐑁𐑉𐐱𐑋 𐑄 𐐼𐐲𐑅𐐻, 𐑋𐐴 𐑅𐐲𐑌𐑆, 𐐰𐑌𐐼 𐐺 𐑋𐐯𐑌, 𐐰𐑌𐐼 𐐺 𐐼𐐨𐐻𐐲𐑉𐑋𐐮𐑌𐐼 𐐮𐑌 𐐶𐐲𐑌 𐑋𐐴𐑌𐐼, 𐐰𐑌𐐼 𐐮𐑌 𐐶𐐲𐑌 𐐸𐐪𐑉𐐻, 𐐷𐐭𐑌𐐴𐐻𐐯𐐼 𐐮𐑌 𐐫𐑊 𐑃𐐮𐑍𐑆, 𐑄𐐰𐐻 𐐷 𐑋𐐩 𐑌𐐱𐐻 𐐿𐐲𐑋 𐐼𐐵𐑌 𐐮𐑌𐐻𐐭 𐐿𐐰𐐹𐐻𐐮𐑂𐐮𐐻𐐨; 𐑄𐐰𐐻 𐐷 𐑋𐐩 𐑌𐐱𐐻 𐐺 𐐿𐐲𐑉𐑅𐐯𐐼 𐐶𐐮𐑄 𐐲 𐑅𐐬𐑉 𐐿𐐲𐑉𐑅𐐮𐑍; 𐐰𐑌𐐼 𐐫𐑊𐑅𐐬, 𐑄𐐰𐐻 𐐷 𐑋𐐩 𐑌𐐱𐐻 𐐮𐑌𐐿𐐲𐑉 𐑄 𐐼𐐮𐑅𐐹𐑊𐐯𐑈𐐲𐑉 𐐱𐑂 𐐲 𐐾𐐲𐑅𐐻 𐐘𐐱𐐼 𐐲𐐹𐐱𐑌 𐐷𐐭, 𐐲𐑌𐐻𐐭 𐑄 𐐼𐐨𐑅𐐻𐑉𐐲𐐿𐑇𐐲𐑌, 𐐷𐐩, 𐑄 𐐨𐐻𐐲𐑉𐑌𐐲𐑊 𐐼𐐨𐑅𐐻𐑉𐐲𐐿𐑇𐐲𐑌 𐐱𐑂 𐐺𐐬𐑃 𐑅𐐬𐑊 𐐰𐑌𐐼 𐐺𐐱𐐼𐐨. 𐐈𐐶𐐩𐐿, 𐑋𐐴 𐑅𐐲𐑌𐑆; 𐐹𐐳𐐻 𐐱𐑌 𐑄 𐐪𐑉𐑋𐐲𐑉 𐐱𐑂 𐑉𐐴𐐽𐐲𐑅𐑌𐐯𐑅. 𐐟𐐩𐐿 𐐫𐑁 𐑄 𐐽𐐩𐑌𐑆 𐐶𐐮𐑄 𐐸𐐶𐐮𐐽 𐐷 𐐪𐑉 𐐺𐐵𐑌𐐼, 𐐰𐑌𐐼 𐐿𐐲𐑋 𐑁𐐫𐑉𐑃 𐐵𐐻 𐐱𐑂 𐐱𐐺𐑅𐐿𐐷𐐭𐑉𐐮𐐻𐐨, 𐐰𐑌𐐼 𐐲𐑉𐐴𐑆 𐑁𐑉𐐱𐑋 𐑄 𐐼𐐲𐑅𐐻. 𐐡𐐨𐐺𐐯𐑊 𐑌𐐬 𐑋𐐫𐑉 𐐲𐑀𐐯𐑌𐑅𐐻 𐐷𐐫𐑉 𐐺𐑉𐐯𐑄𐑉𐐯𐑌, 𐐸𐐭𐑆 𐑂𐐷𐐭𐑆 𐐸𐐰𐑂 𐐺𐐮𐑌 𐑀𐑊𐐬𐑉𐐨𐐲𐑅, 𐐰𐑌𐐼 𐐸𐐭 𐐸𐐰𐑂 𐐿𐐯𐐹𐐻 𐑄 𐐿𐐱𐑋𐐰𐑌𐐼𐑋𐐯𐑌𐐻𐑅 𐑁𐑉𐐱𐑋 𐑄 𐐻𐐴𐑋 𐑄𐐰𐐻 𐐶𐐨 𐑊𐐯𐑁𐐻 𐐖𐐲𐑉𐐭𐑅𐐲𐑊𐐯𐑋;

𐐰𐑌𐐼 𐐸𐐭 𐐸𐐰𐑃 𐐺𐐨𐑌 𐐰𐑌 𐐮𐑌𐑅𐐻𐑉𐐭𐑋𐐯𐑌𐐻 𐐮𐑌 𐑄 𐐸𐐰𐑌𐐼𐑆 𐐱𐑂 𐐘𐐱𐐼, 𐐮𐑌 𐐺𐑉𐐮𐑍𐐮𐑍 𐐲𐑅 𐑁𐐫𐑉𐑃 𐐮𐑌𐐻𐐭 𐑄 𐑊𐐰𐑌𐐼 𐐱𐑂 𐐹𐑉𐐱𐑋𐐮𐑅; 𐑁𐐫𐑉 𐐶𐐲𐑉 𐐮𐐻 𐑌𐐱𐐻 𐑁𐐫𐑉 𐐸𐐮𐑋, 𐐶𐐨 𐑋𐐲𐑅𐐻 𐐸𐐰𐑂 𐐹𐐯𐑉𐐮𐑇𐐻 𐐶𐐮𐑃 𐐸𐐲𐑍𐑀𐐲𐑉 𐐮𐑌 𐑄 𐐶𐐮𐑊𐐼𐐲𐑉𐑌𐐯𐑅; 𐑌𐐯𐑂𐐲𐑉𐑄𐐲𐑊𐐯𐑅, 𐐷𐐨 𐑅𐐫𐐻 𐐻𐐭 𐐻𐐩𐐿 𐐲𐐶𐐩 𐐸𐐮𐑆 𐑊𐐴𐑁; 𐐷𐐩, 𐐰𐑌𐐼 𐐸𐐨 𐐸𐐰𐑃 𐑅𐐲𐑁𐐲𐑉𐐼 𐑋𐐲𐐽 𐑅𐐱𐑉𐐬 𐐺𐐨𐐿𐐫𐑆 𐐱𐑂 𐐷𐐭. 𐐈𐑌𐐼 𐐌 𐐯𐐿𐑅𐐨𐐼𐐮𐑍𐑊𐐨 𐑁𐐨𐑉 𐐰𐑌𐐼 𐐻𐑉𐐯𐑋𐐺𐑊 𐐺𐐨𐐿𐐫𐑆 𐐱𐑂 𐐷𐐭, 𐑊𐐯𐑅𐐻 𐐸𐐨 𐑇𐐰𐑊 𐑅𐐲𐑁𐐲𐑉 𐐲𐑀𐐯𐑌; 𐑁𐐫𐑉 𐐺𐐨𐐸𐐬𐑊𐐼, 𐐷𐐨 𐐸𐐰𐑂 𐐰𐐿𐐷𐐭𐑆𐐼 𐐸𐐮𐑋 𐑄𐐰𐐻 𐐸𐐨 𐑅𐐫𐐻 𐐹𐐵𐐲𐑉 𐐰𐑌𐐼 𐐫𐑃𐐱𐑉𐐮𐐻𐐨 𐐬𐑂𐐲𐑉 𐐷𐐭; 𐐺𐐲𐐻 𐐌 𐑌𐐬 𐑄𐐰𐐻 𐐸𐐨 𐐸𐐰𐑃 𐑌𐐱𐐻 𐑅𐐫𐐻 𐑁𐐫𐑉 𐐹𐐵𐐲𐑉 𐑌𐐫𐑉 𐐫𐑃𐐱𐑉𐐮𐐻𐐨 𐐬𐑂𐐲𐑉 𐐷𐐭; 𐐺𐐲𐐻 𐐸𐐨 𐐸𐐰𐑃 𐑅𐐫𐐻 𐑄 𐑀𐑊𐐬𐑉𐐨 𐐱𐑂 𐐘𐐱𐐼, 𐐰𐑌𐐼 𐐷𐐭𐑉 𐐬𐑌 𐐨𐐻𐐲𐑉𐑌𐐲𐑊 𐐶𐐯𐑊𐑁𐐩𐑉. 𐐈𐑌𐐼 𐐷𐐨 𐐸𐐰𐑂 𐑋𐐲𐑉𐑋𐐲𐑉𐐼 𐐺𐐨𐐿𐐫𐑆 𐐸𐐨 𐐸𐐰𐑃 𐐺𐐨𐑌 𐐹𐑊𐐩𐑌 𐐲𐑌𐐻𐐭 𐐷𐐭. 𐐏𐐨 𐑅𐐩 𐑄𐐰𐐻 𐐸𐐨 𐐸𐐰𐑃 𐐷𐐭𐑆𐐼 𐑇𐐪𐑉𐐹𐑌𐐯𐑅; 𐐷𐐨 𐑅𐐩 𐑄𐐰𐐻 𐐸𐐨 𐐸𐐰𐑃 𐐺𐐨𐑌 𐐰𐑍𐑀𐑉𐐨 𐐶𐐮𐑃 𐐷𐐭; 𐐺𐐲𐐻 𐐺𐐨𐐸𐐬𐑊𐐼, 𐐸𐐮𐑆 𐑇𐐪𐑉𐐹𐑌𐐯𐑅 𐐶𐐱𐑆 𐑄 𐑇𐐪𐑉𐐹𐑌𐐯𐑅 𐐱𐑂 𐑄 𐐹𐐵𐐲𐑉 𐐱𐑂 𐑄 𐐶𐐲𐑉𐐼 𐐱𐑂 𐐘𐐱𐐼, 𐐸𐐶𐐮𐐽 𐐶𐐱𐑆 𐐮𐑌 𐐸𐐮𐑋; 𐐰𐑌𐐼 𐑄𐐰𐐻 𐐸𐐶𐐮𐐽 𐐷𐐨 𐐿𐐫𐑊 𐐰𐑍𐑀𐐲𐑉 𐐶𐐱𐑆 𐑄 𐐻𐑉𐐭𐑃, 𐐰𐐿𐐫𐑉𐐼𐐮𐑍 𐐻𐐭 𐑄𐐰𐐻 𐐸𐐶𐐮𐐽 𐐮𐑆 𐐮𐑌 𐐘𐐱𐐼, 𐐸𐐶𐐮𐐽 𐐸𐐨 𐐿𐐳𐐼 𐑌𐐱𐐻 𐑉𐐨𐑅𐐻𐑉𐐩𐑌, 𐑋𐐰𐑌𐐮𐑁𐐯𐑅𐐻𐐮𐑍 𐐺𐐬𐑊𐐼𐑊𐐨 𐐿𐐱𐑌𐑅𐐲𐑉𐑌𐐮𐑍 𐐷𐐭𐑉 𐐮𐑌𐐮𐐿𐐶𐐮𐐻𐐨𐑆. 𐐈𐑌𐐼 𐐮𐐻 𐑋𐐲𐑅𐐻 𐑌𐐨𐐼𐑆 𐐺𐐨 𐑄𐐰𐐻 𐑄 𐐹𐐵𐐲𐑉 𐐱𐑂 𐐘𐐱𐐼 𐑋𐐲𐑅𐐻 𐐺𐐨 𐐶𐐮𐑃 𐐸𐐮𐑋, 𐐨𐑂𐐲𐑌 𐐲𐑌𐐻𐐭 𐐸𐐮𐑆 𐐿𐐱𐑋𐐰𐑌𐐼𐐮𐑍 𐐷𐐭 𐑄𐐰𐐻 𐐷𐐨 𐑋𐐲𐑅𐐻 𐐬𐐺𐐩. 𐐒𐐲𐐻 𐐺𐐨𐐸𐐬𐑊𐐼, 𐐮𐐻 𐐶𐐱𐑆 𐑌𐐱𐐻 𐐸𐐨, 𐐺𐐲𐐻 𐐮𐐻 𐐶𐐱𐑆 𐑄 𐐝𐐹𐐮𐑉𐐮𐐻 𐐱𐑂 𐑄 𐐢𐐫𐑉𐐼 𐐸𐐶𐐮𐐽 𐐶𐐱𐑆 𐐮𐑌 𐐸𐐮𐑋, 𐐸𐐶𐐮𐐽 𐐬𐐹𐐲𐑌𐐼 𐐸𐐮𐑆 𐑋𐐵𐑃 𐐻𐐭 𐐲𐐻𐐲𐑉𐐰𐑌𐑅, 𐑄𐐰𐐻 𐐸𐐨 𐐿𐐳𐐼 𐑌𐐱𐐻 𐑇𐐲𐐻 𐐮𐐻.

5. 𐐈𐑌𐐼 𐑌𐐵, 𐑋𐐴 𐑅𐐲𐑌 𐐢𐐩𐑋𐐰𐑌, 𐐰𐑌𐐼 𐐫𐑊𐑅𐐬 𐐢𐐯𐑋𐐷𐐭𐐯𐑊 𐐰𐑌𐐼 𐐝𐐰𐑋, 𐐰𐑌𐐼 𐐫𐑊𐑅𐐬 𐑋𐐴 𐑅𐐲𐑌𐑆 𐐸𐐭 𐐪𐑉 𐑄 𐑅𐐲𐑌𐑆 𐐱𐑂 𐐆𐑇𐑋𐐩𐐯𐑊, 𐐺𐐨𐐸𐐬𐑊𐐼, 𐐮𐑁 𐐷𐐨 𐐶𐐮𐑊 𐐸𐐪𐑉𐐿𐐲𐑌 𐐲𐑌𐐻𐐭 𐑄 𐑂𐑎𐑅 𐐱𐑂 𐐤𐐨𐑁𐐴, 𐐷𐐨 𐑇𐐰𐑊 𐑌𐐱𐐻 𐐹𐐯𐑉𐐮𐑇. 𐐈𐑌𐐼 𐐮𐑁 𐐷𐐨 𐐶𐐮𐑊 𐐸𐐪𐑉𐐿𐐲𐑌 𐐲𐑌𐐻𐐭 𐐸𐐮𐑋, 𐐌 𐑊𐐨𐑂 𐐲𐑌𐐻𐐭 𐐷𐐭 𐐲 𐐺𐑊𐐯𐑅𐐮𐑍, 𐐷𐐩, 𐐨𐑂𐐲𐑌 𐑋𐐴 𐑁𐐲𐑉𐑅𐐻 𐐺𐑊𐐯𐑅𐐮𐑍. 𐐒𐐲𐐻 𐐮𐑁 𐐷𐐨 𐐶𐐮𐑊 𐑌𐐱𐐻 𐐸𐐪𐑉𐐿𐐲𐑌 𐐲𐑌𐐻𐐭 𐐸𐐮𐑋, 𐐌 𐐻𐐩𐐿 𐐲𐐶𐐩 𐑋𐐴 𐑁𐐲𐑉𐑅𐐻 𐐺𐑊𐐯𐑅𐐮𐑍, 𐐷𐐩, 𐐨𐑂𐐲𐑌 𐑋𐐴 𐐺𐑊𐐯𐑅𐐮𐑍, 𐐰𐑌𐐼 𐐮𐐻 𐑇𐐰𐑊 𐑉𐐯𐑅𐐻 𐐲𐐹𐐱𐑌 𐐸𐐮𐑋. 𐐈𐑌𐐼 𐑌𐐵, 𐐞𐐬𐑉𐐲𐑋, 𐐌 𐑅𐐹𐐨𐐿 𐐲𐑌𐐻𐐭 𐐷𐐭: 𐐒𐐨𐐸𐐬𐑊𐐼, 𐑄𐐵 𐐪𐑉𐐻 𐑄 𐑅𐐲𐑉𐑂𐐲𐑌𐐻 𐐱𐑂 𐐢𐐩𐐺𐐲𐑌; 𐑌𐐯𐑂𐐲𐑉𐑄𐐲𐑊𐐯𐑅, 𐑄𐐵 𐐸𐐰𐑅𐐻 𐐺𐐨𐑌 𐐺𐑉𐐫𐐻 𐐵𐐻 𐐱𐑂 𐑄 𐑊𐐰𐑌𐐼 𐐱𐑂 𐐖𐐯𐑉𐐭𐑅𐐲𐑊𐐯𐑋, 𐐰𐑌𐐼 𐐌 𐑌𐐬 𐑄𐐰𐐻 𐑄𐐵 𐐪𐑉𐐻 𐐲 𐐻𐑉𐐭 𐑁𐑉𐐯𐑌𐐼 𐐲𐑌𐐻𐐭 𐑋𐐴 𐑅𐐲𐑌 𐐤𐐨𐑁𐐴, 𐑁𐐫𐑉𐐯𐑂𐐲𐑉. 𐐐𐐶𐐯𐑉𐑁𐐫𐑉, 𐐺𐐨𐐿𐐫𐑆 𐑄𐐵 𐐸𐐰𐑅𐐻 𐐺𐐨𐑌 𐑁𐐩𐑃𐑁𐐳𐑊 𐑄𐐴 𐑅𐐨𐐼 𐑇𐐰𐑊 𐐺𐐨 𐐺𐑊𐐯𐑅𐐯𐐼 𐐶𐐮𐑃 𐐸𐐮𐑆 𐑅𐐨𐐼, 𐑄𐐰𐐻 𐑄𐐩 𐐼𐐶𐐯𐑊 𐐮𐑌 𐐹𐑉𐐱𐑅𐐹𐐯𐑉𐐮𐐻𐐨 𐑊𐐱𐑍 𐐲𐐹𐐱𐑌 𐑄 𐑁𐐩𐑅 𐐱𐑂 𐑄𐐮𐑅 𐑊𐐰𐑌𐐼; 𐐰𐑌𐐼 𐑌𐐲𐑃𐐮𐑍, 𐑅𐐩𐑂 𐐮𐐻 𐑇𐐰𐑊 𐐺𐐨 𐐮𐑌𐐮𐐿𐐶𐐮𐐻𐐨 𐐲𐑋𐐲𐑍 𐑄𐐯𐑋, 𐑇𐐰𐑊 𐐸𐐪𐑉𐑋 𐐫𐑉 𐐼𐐮𐑅𐐻𐐲𐑉𐐺 𐑄𐐩𐑉 𐐹𐑉𐐱𐑅𐐹𐐯𐑉𐐮𐐻𐐨 𐐲𐐹𐐱𐑌 𐑄 𐑁𐐩𐑅 𐐱𐑂 𐑄𐐮𐑅 𐑊𐐰𐑌𐐼 𐑁𐐫𐑉𐐯𐑂𐐲𐑉. 𐐐𐐶𐐯𐑉𐑁𐐫𐑉, 𐐮𐑁 𐐷𐐨 𐑇𐐰𐑊 𐐿𐐨𐐹 𐑄 𐐿𐐱𐑋𐐰𐑌𐐼𐑋𐐯𐑌𐐻𐑅 𐐱𐑂 𐑄 𐐢𐐫𐑉𐐼, 𐑄 𐐢𐐫𐑉𐐼 𐐸𐐰𐑃 𐐿𐐱𐑌𐑅𐐯𐐿𐑉𐐩𐐻𐐯𐐼 𐑄𐐮𐑅 𐑊𐐰𐑌𐐼 𐑁𐐫𐑉 𐑄 𐑅𐐯𐐿𐐷𐐭𐑉𐐮𐐻𐐨 𐐱𐑂 𐑄𐐴 𐑅𐐨𐐼 𐐶𐐮𐑃 𐑄 𐑅𐐨𐐼 𐐱𐑂 𐑋𐐴 𐑅𐐲𐑌. 𐐈𐑌𐐼 𐑌𐐵, 𐐖𐐩𐐿𐐲𐐺, 𐐌 𐑅𐐹𐐨𐐿 𐐲𐑌𐐻𐐭 𐐷𐐭: 𐐜𐐵 𐐪𐑉𐐻 𐑋𐐴 𐑁𐐲𐑉𐑅𐐻-𐐺𐐫𐑉𐑌 𐐮𐑌 𐑄 𐐼𐐩𐑆 𐐱𐑂 𐑋𐐴 𐐻𐑉𐐮𐐺𐐷𐐭𐑊𐐩𐑇𐐲𐑌 𐐮𐑌 𐑄 𐐶𐐮𐑊𐐼𐐲𐑉𐑌𐐯𐑅. 𐐈𐑌𐐼 𐐺𐐨𐐸𐐬𐑊𐐼, 𐐮𐑌 𐑄𐐴 𐐽𐐴𐑊𐐼𐐸𐐳𐐼 𐑄𐐵 𐐸𐐰𐑅𐐻 𐑅𐐲𐑁𐐲𐑉𐐼 𐐰𐑁𐑊𐐮𐐿𐑇𐐲𐑌𐑆 𐐰𐑌𐐼 𐑋𐐲𐐽 𐑅𐐱𐑉𐐬, 𐐺𐐨𐐿𐐫𐑆 𐐱𐑂 𐑄 𐑉𐐭𐐼𐑌𐐯𐑅 𐐱𐑂 𐑄𐐴 𐐺𐑉𐐯𐑄𐑉𐐯𐑌. 𐐤𐐯𐑂𐐲𐑉𐑄𐐲𐑊𐐯𐑅, 𐐖𐐩𐐿𐐲𐐺, 𐑋𐐴 𐑁𐐲𐑉𐑅𐐻-𐐺𐐫𐑉𐑌 𐐮𐑌 𐑄 𐐶𐐮𐑊𐐼𐐲𐑉𐑌𐐯𐑅, 𐑄𐐵 𐑌𐐬𐐯𐑅𐐻 𐑄 𐑀𐑉𐐩𐐻𐑌𐐯𐑅 𐐱𐑂 𐐘𐐱𐐼; 𐐰𐑌𐐼 𐐸𐐨 𐑇𐐰𐑊 𐐿𐐱𐑌𐑅𐐯𐐿𐑉𐐩𐐻 𐑄𐐴𐑌 𐐰𐑁𐑊𐐮𐐿𐑇𐐲𐑌𐑆 𐑁𐐫𐑉 𐑄𐐴 𐑀𐐩𐑌. 𐐐𐐶𐐯𐑉𐑁𐐫𐑉, 𐑄𐐴 𐑅𐐬𐑊 𐑇𐐰𐑊 𐐺𐐨 𐐺𐑊𐐯𐑅𐐯𐐼, 𐐰𐑌𐐼 𐑄𐐵 𐑇𐐰𐑊𐐻 𐐼𐐶𐐯𐑊 𐑅𐐩𐑁𐑊𐐨 𐐶𐐮𐑃 𐑄𐐴 𐐺𐑉𐐲𐑄𐐲𐑉, 𐐤𐐨𐑁𐐴; 𐐰𐑌𐐼 𐑄𐐴 𐐼𐐩𐑆 𐑇𐐰𐑊 𐐺𐐨 𐑅𐐹𐐯𐑌𐐻 𐐮𐑌 𐑄 𐑅𐐲𐑉𐑂𐐮𐑅 𐐱𐑂 𐑄𐐴 𐐘𐐱𐐼. 𐐐𐐶𐐯𐑉𐑁𐐫𐑉, 𐐌 𐑌𐐬 𐑄𐐰𐐻 𐑄𐐵 𐐪𐑉𐐻 𐑉𐐨𐐼𐐨𐑋𐐼, 𐐺𐐨𐐿𐐫𐑆 𐐱𐑂 𐑄 𐑉𐐴𐐽𐐲𐑅𐑌𐐯𐑅 𐐱𐑂 𐑄𐐴 𐐡𐐨𐐼𐐨𐑋𐐲𐑉; 𐑁𐐫𐑉 𐑄𐐵 𐐸𐐰𐑅𐐻 𐐺𐐨𐐸𐐯𐑊𐐼 𐑄𐐰𐐻 𐐮𐑌 𐑄 𐑁𐐳𐑊𐑌𐐯𐑅 𐐱𐑂 𐐻𐐴𐑋 𐐸𐐨 𐐿𐐲𐑋𐐯𐑃 𐐻𐐭 𐐺𐑉𐐮𐑍 𐑅𐐰𐑊𐑂𐐩𐑇𐐲𐑌 𐐲𐑌𐐻𐐭 𐑋𐐯𐑌. 𐐈𐑌𐐼 𐑄𐐵 𐐸𐐰𐑅𐐻 𐐺𐐨𐐸𐐯𐑊𐐼 𐐮𐑌 𐑄𐐴 𐐷𐐭𐑃 𐐸𐐮𐑆 𐑀𐑊𐐬𐑉𐐨; 𐐸𐐶𐐯𐑉𐑁𐐫𐑉, 𐑄𐐵 𐐪𐑉𐐻 𐐺𐑊𐐯𐑅𐐯𐐼 𐐨𐑂𐐲𐑌 𐐰𐑆 𐑄𐐩 𐐲𐑌𐐻𐐭 𐐸𐐭𐑋 𐐸𐐨 𐑇𐐰𐑊 𐑋𐐮𐑌𐐮𐑅𐐻𐐲𐑉 𐐮𐑌 𐑄 𐑁𐑊𐐯𐑇; 𐑁𐐫𐑉 𐑄 𐐝𐐹𐐮𐑉𐐮𐐻 𐐮𐑆 𐑄 𐑅𐐩𐑋, 𐐷𐐯𐑅𐐻𐐲𐑉𐐼𐐩, 𐐻𐐭-𐐼𐐩, 𐐰𐑌𐐼 𐑁𐐫𐑉𐐯𐑂𐐲𐑉. 𐐈𐑌𐐼 𐑄 𐐶𐐩 𐐮𐑆 𐐹𐑉𐐨𐐹𐐩𐑉𐐼 𐑁𐑉𐐱𐑋 𐑄 𐑁𐐫𐑊 𐐱𐑂 𐑋𐐰𐑌, 𐐰𐑌𐐼 𐑅𐐰𐑊𐑂𐐩𐑇𐐲𐑌 𐐮𐑆 𐑁𐑉𐐨. 𐐈𐑌𐐼 𐑋𐐯𐑌 𐐪𐑉 𐐮𐑌𐑅𐐻𐑉𐐲𐐿𐐻𐐯𐐼 𐑅𐐲𐑁𐐮𐑇𐐯𐑌𐐻𐑊𐐨, 𐑄𐐰𐐻 𐑄𐐩 𐑌𐐬 𐑀𐐳𐐼 𐑁𐑉𐐱𐑋 𐐨𐑂𐐲𐑊. 𐐈𐑌𐐼 𐑄 𐑊𐐫 𐐮𐑆 𐑀𐐮𐑂𐐲𐑌 𐐲𐑌𐐻𐐭 𐑋𐐯𐑌. 𐐈𐑌𐐼 𐐺𐐴 𐑄 𐑊𐐫 𐑌𐐬 𐑁𐑊𐐯𐑇 𐐮𐑆 𐐾𐐲𐑅𐐻𐐮𐑁𐐴𐐼; 𐐫𐑉, 𐐺𐐴 𐑄 𐑊𐐫, 𐑋𐐯𐑌 𐐪𐑉 𐐿𐐲𐐻 𐐫𐑁. 𐐏𐐩, 𐐺𐐴 𐑄 𐐻𐐯𐑋𐐹𐐬𐑉𐐲𐑊 𐑊𐐫, 𐑄𐐩 𐐶𐐲𐑉 𐐿𐐲𐐻

𐑋𐐯𐑌; 𐐰𐑌𐐼 𐐫𐑊𐑅𐐬 𐐺𐐴 𐑄 𐑅𐐹𐐮𐑉𐐮𐐻𐐷𐐭𐐲𐑊 𐑊𐐫 𐑄𐐩 𐐹𐐯𐑉𐐮𐑇 𐑁𐑉𐐱𐑋 𐑄𐐰𐐻 𐐸𐐶𐐮𐐽 𐐮𐑆 𐑀𐐳𐐼, 𐐰𐑌𐐼 𐐺𐐨𐐿𐐲𐑋 𐑋𐐮𐑆𐐲𐑉𐐲𐐺𐑊 𐑁𐐫𐑉𐐯𐑂𐐲𐑉. 𐐐𐐶𐐯𐑉𐑁𐐬𐑉, 𐑉𐐨𐐼𐐯𐑋𐑇𐐲𐑌 𐐿𐐲𐑋𐐯𐑃 𐐮𐑌 𐐰𐑌𐐼 𐑃𐑉𐐭 𐑄 𐐐𐐬𐑊𐐨 𐐣𐐯𐑅𐐴𐐲; 𐑁𐐫𐑉 𐐸𐐨 𐐮𐑆 𐑁𐐳𐑊 𐐱𐑂 𐑀𐑉𐐩𐑅 𐐰𐑌𐐼 𐐻𐑉𐐭𐑃.

6. 𐐒𐐨𐐸𐐬𐑊𐐼, 𐐸𐐨 𐐱𐑁𐐲𐑉𐐯𐑃 𐐸𐐮𐑋𐑅𐐯𐑊𐑁 𐐩 𐑅𐐰𐐿𐑉𐐮𐑁𐐴𐑅 𐑁𐐫𐑉 𐑅𐐮𐑌, 𐐻𐐭 𐐰𐑌𐑅𐐲𐑉 𐑄 𐐯𐑌𐐼𐑆 𐐱𐑂 𐑄 𐑊𐐫, 𐐲𐑌𐐻𐐭 𐐫𐑊 𐑄𐐬𐑆 𐐸𐐭 𐐸𐐰𐑂 𐐩 𐐺𐑉𐐬𐐿𐐲𐑌 𐐸𐐪𐑉𐐻 𐐰𐑌𐐼 𐐩 𐐿𐐱𐑌𐐻𐑉𐐴𐐻 𐑅𐐹𐐮𐑉𐐮𐐻; 𐐰𐑌𐐼 𐐲𐑌𐐻𐐭 𐑌𐐲𐑌 𐐯𐑊𐑅 𐐿𐐰𐑌 𐑄 𐐯𐑌𐐼𐑆 𐐱𐑂 𐑄 𐑊𐐫 𐐺𐐨 𐐰𐑌𐑅𐐲𐑉𐐼. 𐐐𐐶𐐯𐑉𐑁𐐬𐑉, 𐐸𐐵 𐑀𐑉𐐩𐐻 𐑄 𐐮𐑋𐐹𐐫𐑉𐐻𐐰𐑌𐑅 𐐻𐐭 𐑋𐐩𐐿 𐑄𐐨𐑆 𐑃𐐮𐑍𐑆 𐑌𐐬𐑌 𐐲𐑌𐐻𐐭 𐑄 𐐮𐑌𐐸𐐰𐐺𐐮𐐻𐐰𐑌𐐻𐑅 𐐱𐑂 𐑄 𐐲𐑉𐑃, 𐑄𐐰𐐻 𐑄𐐩 𐑋𐐩 𐑌𐐬 𐑄𐐰𐐻 𐑄𐐯𐑉 𐐮𐑆 𐑌𐐬 𐑁𐑊𐐯𐑇 𐑄𐐰𐐻 𐐿𐐰𐑌 𐐼𐐶𐐯𐑊 𐐮𐑌 𐑄 𐐹𐑉𐐯𐑆𐐯𐑌𐑅 𐐱𐑂 𐐘𐐱𐐼, 𐑅𐐩𐑂 𐐮𐐻 𐐺𐐨 𐑃𐑉𐐭 𐑄 𐑋𐐯𐑉𐐮𐐻𐑅, 𐐰𐑌𐐼 𐑋𐐲𐑉𐑅𐐨, 𐐰𐑌𐐼 𐑀𐑉𐐩𐑅 𐐱𐑂 𐑄 𐐐𐐬𐑊𐐨 𐐣𐐯𐑅𐐴𐐲, 𐐸𐐭 𐑊𐐩𐐯𐑃 𐐼𐐵𐑌 𐐸𐐮𐑆 𐑊𐐴𐑁 𐐰𐐿𐐫𐑉𐐼𐐮𐑍 𐐻𐐭 𐑄 𐑁𐑊𐐯𐑇, 𐐰𐑌𐐼 𐐻𐐩𐐿𐐯𐑃 𐐮𐐻 𐐰𐑀𐐯𐑌 𐐺𐐴 𐑄 𐐹𐐵𐐲𐑉 𐐱𐑂 𐑄 𐐝𐐹𐐮𐑉𐐮𐐻, 𐑄𐐰𐐻 𐐸𐐨 𐑋𐐩 𐐺𐑉𐐮𐑍 𐐻𐐭 𐐹𐐰𐑅 𐑄 𐑉𐐯𐑆𐐲𐑉𐐯𐐿𐑇𐐲𐑌 𐐱𐑂 𐑄 𐐼𐐯𐐼, 𐐺𐐨𐐮𐑍 𐑄 𐑁𐐲𐑉𐑅𐐻 𐑄𐐰𐐻 𐑇𐐳𐐼 𐑉𐐴𐑆. 𐐐𐐶𐐯𐑉𐑁𐐬𐑉, 𐐸𐐨 𐐮𐑆 𐑄 𐑁𐐲𐑉𐑅𐐻 𐑁𐑉𐐭𐐻𐑅 𐐲𐑌𐐻𐐭 𐐘𐐱𐐼, 𐐮𐑌𐐰𐑆𐑋𐐲𐐽 𐐰𐑆 𐐸𐐨 𐑇𐐰𐑊 𐑋𐐩𐐿 𐐮𐑌𐐻𐐲𐑉𐑅𐐯𐑇𐐲𐑌 𐑁𐐫𐑉 𐐫𐑊 𐑄 𐐽𐐮𐑊𐐼𐑉𐐯𐑌 𐐱𐑂 𐑋𐐯𐑌; 𐐰𐑌𐐼 𐑄𐐩 𐑄𐐰𐐻 𐐺𐐨𐑊𐐨𐑂 𐐮𐑌 𐐸𐐮𐑋 𐑇𐐰𐑊 𐐺𐐨 𐑅𐐩𐑂𐐼. 𐐈𐑌𐐼 𐐺𐐨𐐿𐐫𐑆 𐐱𐑂 𐑄 𐐮𐑌𐐻𐐲𐑉𐑅𐐯𐑇𐐲𐑌 𐑁𐐫𐑉 𐐫𐑊, 𐐫𐑊 𐑋𐐯𐑌 𐐿𐐲𐑋 𐐲𐑌𐐻𐐭 𐐘𐐱𐐼; 𐐸𐐶𐐯𐑉𐑁𐐬𐑉, 𐑄𐐩 𐑅𐐻𐐰𐑌𐐼 𐐮𐑌 𐑄 𐐹𐑉𐐯𐑆𐐯𐑌𐑅 𐐱𐑂 𐐸𐐮𐑋, 𐐻𐐭 𐐺𐐨 𐐾𐐲𐐾𐐼 𐐱𐑂 𐐸𐐮𐑋, 𐐰𐐿𐐫𐑉𐐼𐐮𐑍 𐐻𐐭 𐑄 𐐻𐑉𐐭𐑃 𐐰𐑌𐐼 𐐸𐐬𐑊𐐨𐑌𐐯𐑅 𐐸𐐶𐐮𐐽 𐐮𐑆 𐐮𐑌 𐐸𐐮𐑋. 𐐐𐐶𐐯𐑉𐑁𐐬𐑉, 𐑄 𐐯𐑌𐐼𐑆 𐐱𐑂 𐑄 𐑊𐐫 𐐸𐐶𐐮𐐽 𐑄 𐐐𐐬𐑊𐐨 𐐎𐐲𐑌 𐐸𐐰𐑃 𐑀𐐮𐑂𐐯𐑌, 𐐲𐑌𐐻𐐭 𐑄 𐐮𐑌𐑁𐑊𐐮𐐿𐐻𐐮𐑍 𐐱𐑂 𐑄 𐐹𐐲𐑌𐐮𐑇𐑋𐐯𐑌𐐻 𐐸𐐶𐐮𐐽 𐐮𐑆 𐐰𐑁𐐮𐐿𐑅𐐻, 𐐸𐐶𐐮𐐽 𐐹𐐲𐑌𐐮𐑇𐑋𐐯𐑌𐐻 𐑄𐐰𐐻 𐐮𐑆 𐐰𐑁𐐮𐐿𐑅𐐻 𐐮𐑆 𐐮𐑌 𐐱𐐹𐐬𐑆𐐮𐑇𐐲𐑌 𐐻𐐭 𐑄𐐰𐐻 𐐱𐑂 𐑄 𐐸𐐰𐐹𐐨𐑌𐐯𐑅 𐐸𐐶𐐮𐐽 𐐮𐑆 𐐰𐑁𐐮𐐿𐑅𐐻, 𐐻𐐭 𐐰𐑌𐑅𐐲𐑉 𐑄 𐐯𐑌𐐼𐑆 𐐱𐑂 𐑄 𐐰𐐻𐐬𐑌𐑋𐐯𐑌𐐻; 𐑁𐐫𐑉 𐐮𐐻 𐑋𐐲𐑅𐐻 𐑌𐐨𐐼𐑆 𐐺𐐨, 𐑄𐐰𐐻 𐑄𐐯𐑉 𐐮𐑆 𐐰𐑌 𐐱𐐹𐐬𐑆𐐮𐑇𐐲𐑌 𐐮𐑌 𐐫𐑊 𐑃𐐮𐑍𐑆. 𐐇𐑁 𐑌𐐱𐐻 𐑅𐐬, 𐑋𐐴 𐑁𐐲𐑉𐑅𐐻 𐐺𐐫𐑉𐑌 𐐮𐑌 𐑄 𐐶𐐮𐑊𐐼𐐲𐑉𐑌𐐯𐑅, 𐑉𐐴𐐽𐐲𐑅𐑌𐐯𐑅 𐐿𐐳𐐼 𐑌𐐱𐐻 𐐺𐐨 𐐺𐑉𐐫𐐻 𐐻𐐭 𐐹𐐰𐑅; 𐑌𐐨𐑄𐐲𐑉 𐐶𐐮𐐿𐐯𐐼𐑌𐐯𐑅; 𐑌𐐨𐑄𐐲𐑉 𐐸𐐬𐑊𐐨𐑌𐐯𐑅 𐑌𐐫𐑉 𐑋𐐮𐑆𐐲𐑉𐐨; 𐑌𐐨𐑄𐐲𐑉 𐑀𐐳𐐼 𐑌𐐫𐑉 𐐺𐐰𐐼. 𐐐𐐶𐐯𐑉𐑁𐐬𐑉, 𐐫𐑊 𐑃𐐮𐑍𐑆 𐑋𐐲𐑅𐐻 𐑌𐐨𐐼𐑆 𐐺𐐨 𐐩 𐐿𐐱𐑋𐐹𐐵𐑌𐐼 𐐮𐑌 𐐶𐐲𐑌; 𐐸𐐶𐐯𐑉𐑁𐐬𐑉, 𐐮𐑁 𐐮𐐻 𐑇𐐳𐐼 𐐺𐐨 𐐶𐐲𐑌 𐐺𐐱𐐼𐐨 𐐮𐐻 𐑋𐐲𐑅𐐻 𐑌𐐨𐐼𐑆 𐑉𐐨𐑋𐐩𐑌 𐐰𐑆 𐐼𐐯𐐼, 𐐸𐐰𐑂𐐮𐑍 𐑌𐐬 𐑊𐐴𐑁, 𐑌𐐨𐑄𐐲𐑉 𐐼𐐯𐑃 𐑌𐐫𐑉 𐐿𐐫𐑉𐐲𐐹𐑇𐐲𐑌, 𐐸𐐰𐐹𐐨𐑌𐐯𐑅 𐑌𐐫𐑉 𐑋𐐮𐑆𐐲𐑉𐐨, 𐑌𐐨𐑄𐐲𐑉 𐑅𐐯𐑌𐑅 𐑌𐐫𐑉 𐐮𐑌𐑅𐐯𐑌𐑅𐐮𐐺𐐮𐑊𐐮𐐻𐐨. 𐐐𐐶𐐯𐑉𐑁𐐬𐑉, 𐐮𐐻 𐑋𐐲𐑅𐐻 𐑌𐐨𐐼𐑆 𐐸𐐰𐑂 𐐺𐐨𐑌 𐐿𐑉𐐨𐐩𐐻𐐯𐐼 𐑁𐐫𐑉 𐐩 𐑃𐐮𐑍 𐐱𐑂 𐑌𐐫𐐻; 𐐸𐐶𐐯𐑉𐑁𐐬𐑉, 𐑄𐐯𐑉 𐐶𐐳𐐼 𐐸𐐰𐑂 𐐺𐐨𐑌 𐑌𐐬 𐐹𐐲𐑉𐐹𐐲𐑅 𐐮𐑌 𐑄 𐐯𐑌𐐼 𐐱𐑂 𐐮𐐻𐑅 𐐿𐑉𐐨𐐩𐑇𐐲𐑌. 𐐐𐐶𐐯𐑉𐑁𐐬𐑉, 𐑄𐐮𐑅 𐑃𐐮𐑍 𐑋𐐲𐑅𐐻 𐑌𐐨𐐼𐑆 𐐼𐐯𐑅𐐻𐑉𐐱𐐮 𐑄 𐐶𐐮𐑆𐐼𐐲𐑋 𐐱𐑂 𐐘𐐱𐐼, 𐐰𐑌𐐼 𐐸𐐮𐑆 𐐨𐐻𐐲𐑉𐑌𐐲𐑊 𐐹𐐲𐑉𐐹𐐲𐑅𐐯𐑆; 𐐰𐑌𐐼 𐐫𐑊𐑅𐐬, 𐑄 𐐹𐐵𐐲𐑉, 𐐰𐑌𐐼 𐑄 𐑋𐐲𐑉𐑅𐐨, 𐐰𐑌𐐼 𐑄 𐐾𐐲𐑅𐐻𐐮𐑅 𐐱𐑂 𐐘𐐱𐐼. 𐐈𐑌𐐼 𐐮𐑁 𐐷𐐨 𐑇𐐰𐑊 𐑅𐐩 𐑄𐐯𐑉 𐐮𐑆 𐑌𐐬 𐑊𐐫, 𐐷𐐨 𐑇𐐰𐑊 𐐫𐑊𐑅𐐬 𐑅𐐩 𐑄𐐯𐑉 𐐮𐑆 𐑌𐐬 𐑅𐐮𐑌. 𐐇𐑁 𐐷𐐨 𐑇𐐰𐑊 𐑅𐐩 𐑄𐐯𐑉 𐐮𐑆 𐑌𐐬 𐑅𐐮𐑌, 𐐷𐐨 𐑇𐐰𐑊 𐐫𐑊𐑅𐐬 𐑅𐐩 𐑄𐐯𐑉 𐐮𐑆 𐑌𐐬 𐑉𐐴𐐽𐐲𐑅𐑌𐐯𐑅. 𐐈𐑌𐐼 𐐮𐑁 𐑄𐐯𐑉 𐐺𐐨 𐑌𐐬 𐑉𐐴𐐽𐐲𐑅𐑌𐐯𐑅, 𐑄𐐯𐑉 𐐺𐐨 𐑌𐐬 𐐸𐐰𐐹𐐨𐑌𐐯𐑅. 𐐈𐑌𐐼 𐐮𐑁 𐑄𐐯𐑉 𐐺𐐨 𐑌𐐬 𐑉𐐴𐐽𐐲𐑅𐑌𐐯𐑅 𐑌𐐫𐑉 𐐸𐐰𐐹𐐨𐑌𐐯𐑅, 𐑄𐐯𐑉 𐐺𐐨 𐑌𐐬 𐐹𐐲𐑌𐐮𐑇𐑋𐐯𐑌𐐻 𐑌𐐫𐑉 𐑋𐐮𐑆𐐲𐑉𐐨. 𐐈𐑌𐐼 𐐮𐑁 𐑄𐐨𐑆 𐑃𐐮𐑍𐑆 𐐪𐑉 𐑌𐐱𐐻, 𐑄𐐯𐑉 𐐮𐑆 𐑌𐐬 𐐘𐐱𐐼. 𐐇𐑁 𐑄𐐯𐑉 𐐮𐑆 𐑌𐐬 𐐘𐐱𐐼, 𐐶𐐨 𐐪𐑉 𐑌𐐱𐐻, 𐑌𐐨𐑄𐐲𐑉 𐑄 𐐲𐑉𐑃; 𐑁𐐫𐑉 𐑄𐐯𐑉 𐐿𐐳𐐼 𐐸𐐰𐑂 𐐺𐐨𐑌 𐑌𐐬 𐐿𐑉𐐨𐐩𐑇𐐲𐑌 𐐱𐑂 𐑃𐐮𐑍𐑆, 𐑌𐐨𐑄𐐲𐑉 𐐻𐐭 𐐰𐐿𐐻 𐑌𐐫𐑉 𐐻𐐭 𐐺𐐨 𐐰𐐿𐐻𐐯𐐼 𐐲𐐹𐐱𐑌; 𐐸𐐶𐐯𐑉𐑁𐐬𐑉, 𐐫𐑊 𐑃𐐮𐑍𐑆 𐑋𐐲𐑅𐐻 𐐸𐐰𐑂 𐑂𐐰𐑌𐐮𐑇𐐼 𐐰𐐶𐐩.

7. 𐐈𐑌𐐼 𐑌𐐵, 𐑋𐐴 𐑅𐐲𐑌𐑆, 𐐌 𐑅𐐹𐐨𐐿 𐐲𐑌𐐻𐐭 𐐷𐐭 𐑄𐐨𐑆 𐑃𐐮𐑍𐑆, 𐑁𐐫𐑉 𐐷𐐫𐑉 𐐹𐑉𐐱𐑁𐐮𐐻 𐐰𐑌𐐼 𐑊𐐲𐑉𐑌𐐮𐑍; 𐑁𐐫𐑉 𐑄𐐯𐑉 𐐮𐑆 𐐩 𐐘𐐱𐐼, 𐐰𐑌𐐼 𐐸𐐨 𐐸𐐰𐑃 𐐿𐑉𐐨𐐩𐐻𐐯𐐼 𐐫𐑊 𐑃𐐮𐑍𐑆, 𐐺𐐬𐑃 𐑄 𐐸𐐯𐑂𐐯𐑌𐑆 𐐰𐑌𐐼 𐑄 𐐲𐑉𐑃, 𐐰𐑌𐐼 𐐫𐑊 𐑃𐐮𐑍𐑆 𐑄𐐰𐐻 𐐮𐑌 𐑄𐐯𐑋 𐐪𐑉; 𐐺𐐬𐑃 𐑃𐐮𐑍𐑆 𐐻𐐭 𐐰𐐿𐐻, 𐐰𐑌𐐼 𐑃𐐮𐑍𐑆 𐐻𐐭 𐐺𐐨 𐐰𐐿𐐻𐐯𐐼 𐐲𐐹𐐱𐑌; 𐐰𐑌𐐼 𐐻𐐭 𐐺𐑉𐐮𐑍 𐐰𐐺𐐵𐐻 𐐸𐐮𐑆 𐐨𐐻𐐲𐑉𐑌𐐲𐑊 𐐹𐐲𐑉𐐹𐐲𐑅𐐯𐑆 𐐮𐑌 𐑄 𐐯𐑌𐐼 𐐱𐑂 𐑋𐐰𐑌, 𐐰𐑁𐐻𐐲𐑉 𐐸𐐨 𐐸𐐰𐐼 𐐿𐑉𐐨𐐩𐐻𐐯𐐼 𐐵𐑉 𐑁𐐲𐑉𐑅𐐻 𐐹𐐯𐑉𐐯𐑌𐐻𐑅, 𐐰𐑌𐐼 𐑄 𐐺𐐨𐑅𐐻𐑅 𐐱𐑂 𐑄 𐑁𐐨𐑊𐐼, 𐐰𐑌𐐼 𐑄 𐑁𐐵𐑊𐑆 𐐱𐑂 𐑄 𐐯𐑉, 𐐰𐑌𐐼, 𐐮𐑌 𐑁𐐴𐑌, 𐐫𐑊 𐑃𐐮𐑍𐑆 𐐸𐐶𐐮𐐽 𐐪𐑉 𐐿𐑉𐐨𐐩𐐻𐐯𐐼, 𐐮𐐻 𐑋𐐲𐑅𐐻 𐑌𐐨𐐼𐑆 𐐺𐐨 𐑄𐐰𐐻 𐑄𐐯𐑉 𐐶𐐱𐑆 𐐰𐑌 𐐱𐐹𐐬𐑆𐐮𐑇𐐲𐑌; 𐐨𐑂𐐯𐑌 𐑄 𐑁𐐫𐑉𐐺𐐮𐐼𐐯𐑌 𐑁𐑉𐐭𐐻 𐐮𐑌 𐐱𐐹𐐬𐑆𐐮𐑇𐐲𐑌 𐐻𐐭 𐑄 𐐻𐑉𐐨 𐐱𐑂 𐑊𐐴𐑁; 𐑄 𐐶𐐲𐑌 𐐺𐐨𐐮𐑍 𐑅𐐶𐐨𐐻 𐐰𐑌𐐼 𐑄 𐐲𐑄𐐲𐑉 𐐺𐐮𐐻𐐲𐑉; 𐐸𐐶𐐯𐑉𐑁𐐬𐑉, 𐑄 𐐢𐐫𐑉𐐼 𐐘𐐱𐐼 𐑀𐐩𐑂 𐐲𐑌𐐻𐐭 𐑋𐐰𐑌 𐑄𐐰𐐻 𐐸𐐨 𐑇𐐳𐐼 𐐰𐐿𐐻 𐑁𐐫𐑉 𐐸𐐮𐑋𐑅𐐯𐑊𐑁. 𐐐𐐶𐐯𐑉𐑁𐐬𐑉 𐑋𐐰𐑌 𐐿𐐳𐐼 𐑌𐐱𐐻 𐐰𐐿𐐻 𐑁𐐫𐑉 𐐸𐐮𐑋𐑅𐐯𐑊𐑁, 𐑅𐐩𐑂 𐐮𐐻 𐑇𐐳𐐼 𐐺𐐨 𐑄𐐰𐐻 𐐸𐐨 𐐶𐐱𐑆 𐐯𐑌𐐻𐐴𐑅𐐻 𐐺𐐴 𐑄 𐐶𐐲𐑌 𐐫𐑉 𐑄 𐐲𐑄𐐲𐑉.

8. 𐐈𐑌𐐼 𐐌, 𐐢𐐨𐐸𐐴, 𐐰𐐿𐐫𐑉𐐼𐐮𐑍 𐐻𐐭 𐑄 𐑃𐐮𐑍𐑆 𐐸𐐶𐐮𐐽 𐐌 𐐸𐐰𐑂 𐑉𐐯𐐼, 𐑋𐐲𐑅𐐻 𐑌𐐨𐐼𐑆 𐑅𐐲𐐹𐐬𐑆 𐑄𐐰𐐻 𐐰𐑌 𐐩𐑌𐐾𐐯𐑊 𐐱𐑂 𐐘𐐱𐐼, 𐐰𐐿𐐫𐑉𐐼𐐮𐑍 𐐻𐐭 𐑄𐐰𐐻 𐐸𐐶𐐮𐐽 𐐮𐑆 𐑉𐐮𐐻𐑌, 𐐸𐐰𐐼 𐑁𐐫𐑊𐑌 𐑁𐑉𐐱𐑋 𐐸𐐯𐑂𐑌; 𐐸𐐶𐐯𐑉𐑁𐐬𐑉, 𐐸𐐨 𐐺𐐨𐐿𐐩𐑋 𐐲 𐐼𐐯𐑂𐑊, 𐐸𐐰𐑂𐐮𐑍 𐑅𐐫𐐻 𐑄𐐰𐐻 𐐸𐐶𐐮𐐽 𐐶𐐱𐑆 𐐨𐑂𐑊 𐐺𐐨𐑁𐐬𐑉 𐐘𐐱𐐼. 𐐈𐑌𐐼 𐐺𐐨𐐿𐐫𐑆 𐐸𐐨 𐐸𐐰𐐼 𐑁𐐫𐑊𐑌 𐑁𐑉𐐱𐑋 𐐸𐐯𐑂𐑌, 𐐰𐑌𐐼 𐐸𐐰𐐼 𐐺𐐨𐐿𐐲𐑋 𐑋𐐮𐑆𐐲𐑉𐐲𐐺𐑊 𐑁𐐫𐑉 𐐯𐑂𐐲𐑉, 𐐸𐐨 𐑅𐐫𐐻 𐐫𐑊𐑅𐐬 𐑄 𐑋𐐮𐑆𐐲𐑉𐐨 𐐱𐑂 𐐫𐑊 𐑋𐐰𐑌𐐿𐐴𐑌𐐼. 𐐐𐐶𐐯𐑉𐑁𐐬𐑉, 𐐸𐐨 𐑅𐐯𐐼 𐐲𐑌𐐻𐐭 𐐀𐑂, 𐐷𐐩, 𐐨𐑂𐑌 𐑄𐐰𐐻 𐐬𐑊𐐼 𐑅𐐲𐑉𐐹𐐯𐑌𐐻, 𐐸𐐭 𐐮𐑆 𐑄 𐐼𐐯𐑂𐑊, 𐐸𐐭 𐐮𐑆 𐑄 𐑁𐐪𐑄𐐲𐑉 𐐱𐑂 𐐫𐑊 𐑊𐐴𐑆; 𐐸𐐶𐐯𐑉𐑁𐐬𐑉 𐐸𐐨 𐑅𐐯𐐼, 𐐑𐐪𐑉𐐻𐐩𐐿 𐐱𐑂 𐑄 𐑁𐐫𐑉𐐺𐐮𐐼𐑌 𐑁𐑉𐐭𐐻, 𐐰𐑌𐐼 𐐷𐐨 𐑇𐐰𐑊 𐑌𐐱𐐻 𐐼𐐴, 𐐺𐐲𐐻 𐐷𐐨 𐑇𐐰𐑊 𐐺 𐐰𐑆 𐐘𐐱𐐼, 𐑌𐐬𐐮𐑍 𐑀𐐳𐐼 𐐰𐑌𐐼 𐐨𐑂𐑊. 𐐈𐑌𐐼 𐐰𐑁𐐻𐐲𐑉 𐐈𐐼𐐲𐑋 𐐰𐑌𐐼 𐐀𐑂 𐐸𐐰𐐼 𐐹𐐪𐑉𐐻𐐩𐐿𐑌 𐐱𐑂 𐑄 𐑁𐐫𐑉𐐺𐐮𐐼𐑌 𐑁𐑉𐐭𐐻, 𐑄𐐩 𐐶𐐲𐑉 𐐼𐑉𐐮𐑂𐑌 𐐵𐐻 𐐱𐑂 𐑄 𐑀𐐪𐑉𐐼𐑌 𐐱𐑂 𐐀𐐼𐑌 𐐻𐐭 𐐻𐐮𐑊 𐑄 𐐲𐑉𐑃. 𐐈𐑌𐐼 𐑄𐐩 𐐸𐐰𐑂 𐐺𐑉𐐫𐐻 𐑁𐐬𐑉𐑃 𐐽𐐮𐑊𐐼𐑉𐐯𐑌; 𐐷𐐩, 𐐨𐑂𐑌 𐑄 𐑁𐐰𐑋𐐮𐑊𐐨 𐐱𐑂 𐐫𐑊 𐑄 𐐲𐑉𐑃. 𐐈𐑌𐐼 𐑄 𐐼𐐩𐑆 𐐱𐑂 𐑄 𐐽𐐮𐑊𐐼𐑉𐐯𐑌 𐐱𐑂 𐑋𐐯𐑌 𐐶𐐲𐑉 𐐹𐑉𐐬𐑊𐐱𐑍𐐼, 𐐰𐐿𐐫𐑉𐐼𐐮𐑍 𐐻𐐭 𐑄 𐐶𐐮𐑊 𐐱𐑂 𐐘𐐱𐐼, 𐑄𐐰𐐻 𐑄𐐩 𐑋𐐴𐐻 𐑉𐐨𐐹𐐯𐑌𐐻 𐐸𐐶𐐴𐑊 𐐮𐑌 𐑄 𐑁𐑊𐐯𐑇; 𐐸𐐶𐐯𐑉𐑁𐐬𐑉, 𐑄𐐩𐑉 𐑅𐐻𐐩𐐻 𐐺𐐨𐐿𐐩𐑋 𐐲 𐑅𐐻𐐩𐐻 𐐱𐑂 𐐹𐑉𐐬𐐺𐐩𐑇𐐲𐑌, 𐐰𐑌𐐼 𐑄𐐩𐑉 𐐻𐐴𐑋 𐐶𐐱𐑆 𐑊𐐯𐑍𐑃𐑌𐐼, 𐐰𐐿𐐫𐑉𐐼𐐮𐑍 𐐻𐐭 𐑄 𐐿𐐱𐑋𐐰𐑌𐐼𐑋𐐯𐑌𐐻𐑅 𐐸𐐶𐐮𐐽 𐑄 𐐢𐐫𐑉𐐼 𐐘𐐱𐐼 𐑀𐐩𐑂 𐐲𐑌𐐻𐐭 𐑄 𐐽𐐮𐑊𐐼𐑉𐐯𐑌 𐐱𐑂 𐑋𐐯𐑌. 𐐙𐐫𐑉 𐐸𐐨 𐑀𐐩𐑂 𐐿𐐱𐑋𐐰𐑌𐐼𐑋𐐯𐑌𐐻 𐑄𐐰𐐻 𐐫𐑊 𐑋𐐯𐑌 𐑋𐐲𐑅𐐻 𐑉𐐨𐐹𐐯𐑌𐐻, 𐑁𐐫𐑉 𐐸𐐨 𐑇𐐬𐐼 𐐲𐑌𐐻𐐭 𐐫𐑊 𐑋𐐯𐑌 𐑄𐐰𐐻 𐑄𐐩 𐐶𐐲𐑉 𐑊𐐫𐑅𐐻, 𐐺𐐨𐐿𐐫𐑆 𐐱𐑂 𐑄 𐐻𐑉𐐰𐑌𐑆𐑀𐑉𐐯𐑇𐐲𐑌 𐐱𐑂 𐑄𐐩𐑉 𐐹𐐩𐑉𐐯𐑌𐐻𐑅. 𐐈𐑌𐐼 𐑌𐐵, 𐐺𐐨𐐸𐐬𐑊𐐼, 𐐮𐑁 𐐈𐐼𐐲𐑋 𐐸𐐰𐐼 𐑌𐐱𐐻 𐐻𐑉𐐰𐑌𐑆𐑀𐑉𐐯𐑅𐐻, 𐐸𐐨 𐐶𐐳𐐼 𐑌𐐱𐐻 𐐸𐐰𐑂 𐑁𐐫𐑊𐑌; 𐐺𐐲𐐻 𐐸𐐨 𐐶𐐳𐐼 𐐸𐐰𐑂 𐑉𐐨𐑋𐐩𐑌𐐼 𐐮𐑌 𐑄 𐑀𐐪𐑉𐐼𐑌 𐐱𐑂 𐐀𐐼𐑌. 𐐈𐑌𐐼 𐐫𐑊 𐑃𐐮𐑍𐑆 𐐸𐐶𐐮𐐽 𐐶𐐲𐑉 𐐿𐑉𐐨𐐩𐐻𐐯𐐼, 𐑋𐐲𐑅𐐻 𐐸𐐰𐑂 𐑉𐐨𐑋𐐩𐑌𐐼 𐐮𐑌 𐑄 𐑅𐐩𐑋 𐑅𐐻𐐩𐐻 𐐸𐐶𐐮𐐽 𐑄𐐩 𐐶𐐲𐑉, 𐐰𐑁𐐻𐐲𐑉 𐑄𐐩 𐐶𐐲𐑉 𐐿𐑉𐐨𐐩𐐻𐐯𐐼; 𐐰𐑌𐐼 𐑄𐐩 𐑋𐐲𐑅𐐻 𐐸𐐰𐑂 𐑉𐐨𐑋𐐩𐑌𐐼 𐑁𐐫𐑉 𐐯𐑂𐐲𐑉, 𐐰𐑌𐐼 𐐸𐐰𐐼 𐑌𐐬 𐐯𐑌𐐼. 𐐈𐑌𐐼 𐑄𐐩 𐐶𐐳𐐼 𐐸𐐰𐑂 𐐸𐐰𐐼 𐑌𐐬 𐐽𐐮𐑊𐐼𐑉𐐯𐑌; 𐐸𐐶𐐯𐑉𐑁𐐬𐑉, 𐑄𐐩 𐐶𐐳𐐼 𐐸𐐰𐑂 𐑉𐐨𐑋𐐩𐑌𐐼 𐐮𐑌 𐐲 𐑅𐐻𐐩𐐻 𐐱𐑂 𐐮𐑌𐐬𐑅𐐯𐑌𐑅, 𐐸𐐰𐑂𐐮𐑍 𐑌𐐬 𐐾𐐫𐐮, 𐑁𐐫𐑉 𐑄𐐩 𐑌𐐭 𐑌𐐬 𐑋𐐮𐑆𐐲𐑉𐐨; 𐐼𐐭𐐮𐑍 𐑌𐐬 𐑀𐐳𐐼, 𐑁𐐫𐑉 𐑄𐐩 𐑌𐐭 𐑌𐐬 𐑅𐐮𐑌. 𐐒𐐲𐐻 𐐺𐐨𐐸𐐬𐑊𐐼, 𐐫𐑊 𐑃𐐮𐑍𐑆 𐐸𐐰𐑂 𐐺𐐮𐑌 𐐼𐐲𐑌 𐐮𐑌 𐑄 𐐶𐐮𐑆𐐼𐐲𐑋 𐐱𐑂 𐐸𐐮𐑋 𐐸𐐭 𐑌𐐬𐐯𐑃 𐐫𐑊 𐑃𐐮𐑍𐑆. 𐐈𐐼𐐲𐑋 𐑁𐐯𐑊 𐑄𐐰𐐻 𐑋𐐯𐑌 𐑋𐐴𐐻 𐐺; 𐐰𐑌𐐼 𐑋𐐯𐑌 𐐪𐑉, 𐑄𐐰𐐻 𐑄𐐩 𐑋𐐴𐐻 𐐸𐐰𐑂 𐐾𐐫𐐮. 𐐈𐑌𐐼 𐑄 𐐣𐐯𐑅𐐴𐐲 𐐿𐐲𐑋𐐯𐑃 𐐮𐑌 𐑄 𐑁𐐳𐑊𐑌𐐯𐑅 𐐱𐑂 𐐻𐐴𐑋, 𐑄𐐰𐐻 𐐸𐐨 𐑋𐐩 𐑉𐐨𐐼𐐨𐑋 𐑄 𐐽𐐮𐑊𐐼𐑉𐐯𐑌 𐐱𐑂 𐑋𐐯𐑌 𐑁𐑉𐐱𐑋 𐑄 𐑁𐐫𐑊. 𐐈𐑌𐐼 𐐺𐐨𐐿𐐫𐑆 𐑄𐐰𐐻 𐑄𐐩 𐐪𐑉 𐑉𐐨𐐼𐐨𐑋𐐼 𐑁𐑉𐐱𐑋 𐑄 𐑁𐐫𐑊, 𐑄𐐩 𐐸𐐰𐑂 𐐺𐐨𐐿𐐲𐑋 𐑁𐑉𐐨 𐑁𐐫𐑉 𐐯𐑂𐐲𐑉, 𐑌𐐬𐐮𐑍 𐑀𐐳𐐼 𐑁𐑉𐐱𐑋 𐐨𐑂𐑊; 𐐻𐐭 𐐰𐐿𐐻 𐑁𐐫𐑉 𐑄𐐯𐑋𐑅𐐯𐑊𐑂𐑆, 𐐰𐑌𐐼 𐑌𐐱𐐻 𐐻𐐭 𐐺 𐐰𐐿𐐻𐐯𐐼 𐐲𐐹𐐱𐑌, 𐑅𐐩𐑂 𐐮𐐻 𐐺 𐐺𐐴 𐑄 𐐹𐐲𐑌𐐮𐑇𐑋𐐯𐑌𐐻 𐐱𐑂 𐑄 𐑊𐐫 𐐰𐐻 𐑄 𐑀𐑉𐐩𐐻 𐐰𐑌𐐼 𐑊𐐰𐑅𐐻 𐐼𐐩, 𐐰𐐿𐐫𐑉𐐼𐐮𐑍 𐐻𐐭 𐑄 𐐿𐐱𐑋𐐰𐑌𐐼𐑋𐐯𐑌𐐻𐑅 𐐸𐐶𐐮𐐽 𐐘𐐱𐐼 𐐸𐐰𐑃 𐑀𐐮𐑂𐑌. 𐐐𐐶𐐯𐑉𐑁𐐬𐑉, 𐑋𐐯𐑌 𐐪𐑉 𐑁𐑉𐐨 𐐰𐐿𐐫𐑉𐐼𐐮𐑍 𐐻𐐭 𐑄 𐑁𐑊𐐯𐑇; 𐐰𐑌𐐼 𐐫𐑊 𐑃𐐮𐑍𐑆 𐐪𐑉 𐑀𐐮𐑂𐑌 𐑄𐐯𐑋 𐐸𐐶𐐮𐐽 𐐪𐑉 𐐯𐐿𐑅𐐹𐐨𐐼𐐨𐐯𐑌𐐻 𐐲𐑌𐐻𐐭 𐑋𐐰𐑌. 𐐈𐑌𐐼 𐑄𐐩 𐐪𐑉 𐑁𐑉𐐨 𐐻𐐭 𐐽𐐭𐑆 𐑊𐐮𐐺𐐲𐑉𐐻𐐨 𐐰𐑌𐐼 𐐨𐐻𐐲𐑉𐑌𐐲𐑊 𐑊𐐴𐑁, 𐑃𐑉𐐭 𐑄 𐑀𐑉𐐩𐐻 𐑋𐐨𐐼𐐨𐐩𐑇𐐲𐑌 𐐱𐑂 𐐫𐑊 𐑋𐐯𐑌, 𐐫𐑉 𐐻𐐭 𐐽𐐭𐑆 𐐿𐐰𐐹𐐻𐐮𐑂𐐮𐐻𐐨 𐐰𐑌𐐼 𐐼𐐯𐑃, 𐐰𐐿𐐫𐑉𐐼𐐮𐑍 𐐻𐐭 𐑄 𐐿𐐰𐐹𐐻𐐮𐑂𐐮𐐻𐐨 𐐰𐑌𐐼 𐐹𐐵𐐲𐑉 𐐱𐑂 𐑄 𐐼𐐯𐑂𐑊; 𐑁𐐫𐑉 𐐸𐐨 𐑅𐐨𐐿𐐯𐑃 𐑄𐐰𐐻 𐐫𐑊 𐑋𐐯𐑌 𐑋𐐴𐐻 𐐺 𐑋𐐮𐑆𐐲𐑉𐐲𐐺𐑊 𐑊𐐴𐐿 𐐲𐑌𐐻𐐭 𐐸𐐮𐑋𐑅𐐯𐑊𐑁.

9. 𐐈𐑌𐐼 𐑌𐐵, 𐑋𐐴 𐑅𐐲𐑌𐑆, 𐐌 𐐶𐐳𐐼 𐑄𐐰𐐻 𐐷𐐨 𐑇𐐳𐐼 𐑊𐐳𐐿 𐐻𐐭 𐑄 𐑀𐑉𐐩𐐻 𐐣𐐨𐐼𐐨𐐩𐐻𐐲𐑉, 𐐰𐑌𐐼 𐐸𐐲𐑉𐐿𐑌 𐐲𐑌𐐻𐐭 𐐸𐐮𐑆 𐑀𐑉𐐩𐐻 𐐿𐐱𐑋𐐰𐑌𐐼𐑋𐐯𐑌𐐻𐑅; 𐐰𐑌𐐼 𐐺 𐑁𐐩𐑃𐑁𐐳𐑊 𐐲𐑌𐐻𐐭 𐐸𐐮𐑆 𐐶𐐲𐑉𐐼𐑆, 𐐰𐑌𐐼 𐐽𐐭𐑆 𐐨𐐻𐐲𐑉𐑌𐐲𐑊 𐑊𐐴𐑁, 𐐰𐐿𐐫𐑉𐐼𐐮𐑍 𐐻𐐭 𐑄 𐐶𐐮𐑊 𐐱𐑂 𐐸𐐮𐑆 𐐐𐐬𐑊𐐨 𐐝𐐹𐐮𐑉𐐮𐐻, 𐐰𐑌𐐼 𐑌𐐱𐐻 𐐽𐐭𐑆 𐐨𐐻𐐲𐑉𐑌𐐲𐑊 𐐼𐐯𐑃, 𐐰𐐿𐐫𐑉𐐼𐐮𐑍 𐐻𐐭 𐑄 𐐶𐐮𐑊 𐐱𐑂 𐑄 𐑁𐑊𐐯𐑇 𐐰𐑌𐐼 𐑄 𐐨𐑂𐑊 𐐸𐐶𐐮𐐽 𐐮𐑆 𐑄𐐯𐑉𐐮𐑌, 𐐸𐐶𐐮𐐽 𐑀𐐮𐑂𐐯𐑃 𐑄 𐑅𐐹𐐮𐑉𐐮𐐻 𐐱𐑂 𐑄 𐐼𐐯𐑂𐑊 𐐹𐐵𐐲𐑉 𐐻𐐭 𐐿𐐰𐐹𐐻𐐮𐑂𐐩𐐻, 𐐻𐐭 𐐺𐑉𐐮𐑍 𐐷𐐭 𐐼𐐵𐑌 𐐻𐐭 𐐸𐐯𐑊, 𐑄𐐰𐐻 𐐸𐐨 𐑋𐐩 𐑉𐐩𐑌 𐐬𐑂𐐲𐑉 𐐷𐐭 𐐮𐑌 𐐸𐐮𐑆 𐐬𐑌 𐐿𐐮𐑍𐐼𐐲𐑋.

10. 𐐌 𐐸𐐰𐑂 𐑅𐐹𐐬𐐿𐑌 𐑄𐐨𐑆 𐑁𐐷𐐭 𐐶𐐲𐑉𐐼𐑆 𐐲𐑌𐐻𐐭 𐐷𐐭 𐐫𐑊, 𐑋𐐴 𐑅𐐲𐑌𐑆, 𐐮𐑌 𐑄 𐑊𐐰𐑅𐐻 𐐼𐐩𐑆 𐐱𐑂 𐑋𐐴 𐐹𐑉𐐬𐐺𐐩𐑇𐐲𐑌; 𐐰𐑌𐐼 𐐌 𐐸𐐰𐑂 𐐽𐐬𐑆𐑌 𐑄 𐑀𐐳𐐼 𐐹𐐪𐑉𐐻, 𐐰𐐿𐐫𐑉𐐼𐐮𐑍 𐐻𐐭 𐑄 𐐶𐐲𐑉𐐼𐑆 𐐱𐑂 𐑄 𐐹𐑉𐐱𐑁𐐯𐐻. 𐐈𐑌𐐼 𐐌 𐐸𐐰𐑂 𐑌𐐲𐑌 𐐲𐑄𐐲𐑉 𐐱𐐺𐐾𐐯𐐿𐐻, 𐑅𐐩𐑂 𐐮𐐻 𐐺 𐑄 𐐯𐑂𐐲𐑉𐑊𐐰𐑅𐐻𐐮𐑍 𐐶𐐯𐑊𐑁𐐯𐑉 𐐱𐑂 𐐷𐐭𐑉 𐑅𐐬𐑊𐑆. 𐐁𐑋𐐯𐑌.

𐐕𐐈𐐑𐐓𐐊𐐡 II.

1. 𐐈𐑌𐐼 𐑌𐐵 𐐌 𐑅𐐹𐐨𐐿 𐐲𐑌𐐻𐐭 𐐷𐐭, 𐐖𐐬𐑆𐐯𐑁, 𐑋𐐴 𐑊𐐪𐑅𐐻 𐐺𐐫𐑉𐑌. 𐐜𐐵 𐐶𐐱𐑆𐐻 𐐺𐐫𐑉𐑌 𐐮𐑌 𐑄 𐐶𐐮𐑊𐐼𐐲𐑉𐑌𐐯𐑅 𐐱𐑂 𐑋𐐴𐑌 𐐰𐑁𐑊𐐮𐐿𐑇𐐲𐑌𐑆; 𐐷𐐩, 𐐮𐑌 𐑄 𐐼𐐩𐑆 𐐱𐑂 𐑋𐐴 𐑀𐑉𐐩𐐻𐐯𐑅𐐻 𐑅𐐱𐑉𐐬 𐐼𐐮𐐼 𐑄𐐴 𐑋𐐲𐑄𐐲𐑉 𐐺𐐯𐑉 𐑄𐐨. 𐐈𐑌𐐼 𐑋𐐩 𐑄 𐐢𐐫𐑉𐐼 𐐿𐐱𐑌𐑅𐐯𐐿𐑉𐐩𐐻 𐐫𐑊𐑅𐐬 𐐲𐑌𐐻𐐭 𐑄𐐨 𐑄𐐮𐑅 𐑊𐐰𐑌𐐼, 𐐸𐐶𐐮𐐽 𐐮𐑆 𐐰 𐑋𐐬𐑅𐐻 𐐹𐑉𐐯𐑇𐐲𐑅 𐑊𐐰𐑌𐐼, 𐑁𐐫𐑉 𐑄𐐴𐑌 𐐮𐑌𐐸𐐯𐑉𐐮𐐻𐐲𐑌𐑅 𐐰𐑌𐐼 𐑄 𐐮𐑌𐐸𐐯𐑉𐐮𐐻𐐲𐑌𐑅 𐐱𐑂 𐑄𐐴 𐑅𐐨𐐼 𐐶𐐮𐑄 𐑄𐐴 𐐺𐑉𐐯𐑄𐑉𐐯𐑌, 𐑁𐐫𐑉 𐑄𐐴 𐑅𐐨𐐿𐐷𐐭𐑉𐐮𐐻𐐨 𐑁𐐫𐑉𐐯𐑂𐐲𐑉, 𐐮𐑁 𐐮𐐻 𐑅𐐬 𐐺𐐨 𐑄𐐰𐐻 𐐷𐐨 𐑇𐐰𐑊 𐐿𐐨𐐹 𐑄 𐐿𐐱𐑋𐐰𐑌𐐼𐑋𐐯𐑌𐐻𐑅 𐐱𐑂 𐑄 𐐐𐐬𐑊𐐨 𐐎𐐲𐑌 𐐱𐑂 𐐆𐑆𐑉𐐩𐐯𐑊. 𐐈𐑌𐐼 𐑌𐐵 𐐖𐐬𐑆𐐯𐑁, 𐑋𐐴 𐑊𐐪𐑅𐐻 𐐺𐐫𐑉𐑌, 𐐸𐐭𐑋 𐐌 𐐸𐐰𐑂 𐐺𐑉𐐫𐐻 𐐵𐐻 𐐱𐑂 𐑄 𐐶𐐮𐑊𐐼𐐲𐑉𐑌𐐯𐑅 𐐱𐑂 𐑋𐐴𐑌 𐐰𐑁𐑊𐐮𐐿𐑇𐐲𐑌𐑆, 𐑋𐐩 𐑄 𐐢𐐫𐑉𐐼 𐐺𐑊𐐯𐑅 𐑄𐐨 𐑁𐐫𐑉𐐯𐑂𐐲𐑉, 𐑁𐐫𐑉 𐑄𐐴 𐑅𐐨𐐼 𐑇𐐰𐑊 𐑌𐐱𐐻 𐐲𐐻𐐲𐑉𐑊𐐨 𐐺𐐨 𐐼𐐯𐑅𐐻𐑉𐑎𐐼. 𐐙𐐫𐑉 𐐺𐐨𐐸𐐬𐑊𐐼, 𐑄𐐵 𐐪𐑉𐐻 𐑄 𐑁𐑉𐐭𐐻 𐐱𐑂 𐑋𐐴 𐑊𐑎𐑌𐑆; 𐐰𐑌𐐼 𐐌 𐐰𐑋 𐐰 𐐼𐐯𐑅𐐯𐑌𐐼𐐰𐑌𐐻 𐐱𐑂 𐐖𐐬𐑆𐐯𐑁, 𐐸𐐭 𐐶𐐱𐑆 𐐿𐐰𐑉𐐨𐐼 𐐿𐐰𐐹𐐻𐐮𐑂 𐐮𐑌𐐻𐐭 𐐀𐐾𐐮𐐹𐐻. 𐐈𐑌𐐼 𐑀𐑉𐐩𐐻 𐐶𐐲𐑉 𐑄 𐐿𐐲𐑂𐐯𐑌𐐰𐑌𐐻𐑅 𐐱𐑂 𐑄 𐐢𐐫𐑉𐐼, 𐐸𐐶𐐮𐐽 𐐸𐐨 𐑋𐐩𐐼 𐐲𐑌𐐻𐐭 𐐖𐐬𐑆𐐯𐑁; 𐐸𐐶𐐯𐑉𐑁𐐫𐑉, 𐐖𐐬𐑆𐐯𐑁 𐐻𐑉𐐭𐑊𐐨 𐑅𐐫 𐐵𐑉 𐐼𐐩. 𐐈𐑌𐐼 𐐸𐐨 𐐱𐐺𐐻𐐩𐑌𐐼 𐐰 𐐹𐑉𐐱𐑋𐐮𐑅 𐐱𐑂 𐑄 𐐢𐐫𐑉𐐼, 𐑄𐐰𐐻 𐐵𐐻 𐐱𐑂 𐑄 𐑁𐑉𐐭𐐻 𐐱𐑂 𐐸𐐮𐑆 𐑊𐑎𐑌𐑆 𐑄 𐐢𐐫𐑉𐐼 𐐘𐐱𐐼 𐐶𐐳𐐼 𐑉𐐩𐑆 𐐲𐐹 𐐰 𐑉𐐴𐐽𐐲𐑅 𐐺𐑉𐐰𐑌𐐽 𐐲𐑌𐐻𐐭 𐑄 𐐸𐐵𐑅 𐐱𐑂 𐐆𐑆𐑉𐐩𐐯𐑊; 𐑌𐐱𐐻 𐑄 𐐣𐐯𐑅𐐴𐐲, 𐐺𐐲𐐻 𐐰 𐐺𐑉𐐰𐑌𐐽 𐐸𐐶𐐮𐐽 𐐶𐐱𐑆 𐐻𐐭 𐐺𐐨 𐐺𐑉𐐬𐐿𐐯𐑌 𐐫𐑁; 𐑌𐐯𐑂𐐲𐑉𐑄𐐯𐑊𐐯𐑅, 𐐻𐐭 𐐺𐐨 𐑉𐐨𐑋𐐯𐑋𐐺𐐲𐑉𐐼 𐐮𐑌 𐑄 𐐿𐐲𐑂𐐯𐑌𐐰𐑌𐐻𐑅 𐐱𐑂 𐑄 𐐢𐐫𐑉𐐼, 𐑄𐐰𐐻 𐑄 𐐣𐐯𐑅𐐴𐐲 𐑇𐐳𐐼 𐐺𐐨 𐑋𐐩𐐼 𐑋𐐰𐑌𐐮𐑁𐐯𐑅𐐻 𐐲𐑌𐐻𐐭 𐑄𐐯𐑋 𐐮𐑌 𐑄 𐑊𐐰𐐻𐐲𐑉 𐐼𐐩𐑆, 𐐮𐑌 𐑄 𐑅𐐹𐐮𐑉𐐮𐐻 𐐱𐑂 𐐹𐐵𐐲𐑉, 𐐲𐑌𐐻𐐭 𐑄 𐐺𐑉𐐮𐑍𐐮𐑍 𐐱𐑂 𐑄𐐯𐑋 𐐵𐐻 𐐱𐑂 𐐼𐐪𐑉𐐿𐑌𐐯𐑅 𐐲𐑌𐐻𐐭 𐑊𐐴𐐻; 𐐷𐐩, 𐐵𐐻 𐐱𐑂 𐐸𐐮𐐼 𐐼𐐪𐑉𐐿𐑌𐐯𐑅 𐐰𐑌𐐼 𐐵𐐻 𐐱𐑂 𐐿𐐰𐐹𐐻𐐮𐑂𐐮𐐻𐐨 𐐲𐑌𐐻𐐭 𐑁𐑉𐐨𐐼𐐲𐑋.

2. 𐐙𐐫𐑉 𐐖𐐬𐑆𐐯𐑁 𐐻𐑉𐐭𐑊𐐨 𐐻𐐯𐑅𐐻𐐮𐑁𐐴𐐲𐐼, 𐑅𐐩𐐮𐑍: 𐐌 𐑅𐐨𐐲𐑉 𐑇𐐰𐑊 𐑄 𐐢𐐫𐑉𐐼 𐑋𐐴 𐐘𐐱𐐼 𐑉𐐩𐑆 𐐲𐐹, 𐐸𐐭 𐑇𐐰𐑊 𐐺𐐨 𐐰 𐐽𐑎𐑅 𐑅𐐨𐐲𐑉 𐐲𐑌𐐻𐐭 𐑄 𐑁𐑉𐐭𐐻 𐐱𐑂 𐑋𐐴 𐑊𐑎𐑌𐑆. 𐐏𐐩, 𐐖𐐬𐑆𐐯𐑁 𐐻𐑉𐐭𐑊𐐨 𐑅𐐯𐐼, 𐑄𐐲𐑅 𐑅𐐯𐑃 𐑄 𐐢𐐫𐑉𐐼 𐐲𐑌𐐻𐐭 𐑋𐐨: 𐐌 𐐽𐑎𐑅 𐑅𐐨𐐲𐑉 𐐶𐐮𐑊 𐐌 𐑉𐐩𐑆 𐐲𐐹 𐐵𐐻 𐐱𐑂 𐑄 𐑁𐑉𐐭𐐻 𐐱𐑂 𐑄𐐴 𐑊𐑎𐑌𐑆; 𐐰𐑌𐐼 𐐸𐐨 𐑇𐐰𐑊 𐐺𐐨 𐐯𐑅𐐻𐐨𐑋𐐼 𐐸𐐴𐑊𐐨 𐐲𐑋𐐲𐑍 𐑄 𐑁𐑉𐐭𐐻 𐐱𐑂 𐑄𐐴 𐑊𐑎𐑌𐑆. 𐐈𐑌𐐼 𐐲𐑌𐐻𐐭 𐐸𐐮𐑋 𐐶𐐮𐑊 𐐌 𐑀𐐮𐑂 𐐿𐐱𐑋𐐰𐑌𐐼𐑋𐐯𐑌𐐻 𐑄𐐰𐐻 𐐸𐐨 𐑇𐐰𐑊 𐐼𐐭 𐐰 𐐶𐐲𐑉𐐿 𐑁𐐫𐑉 𐑄 𐑁𐑉𐐭𐐻 𐐱𐑂 𐑄𐐴 𐑊𐑎𐑌𐑆, 𐐸𐐮𐑆 𐐺𐑉𐐯𐑄𐑉𐐯𐑌, 𐐸𐐶𐐮𐐽 𐑇𐐰𐑊 𐐺𐐨 𐐱𐑂 𐑀𐑉𐐩𐐻 𐐶𐐲𐑉𐑃 𐐲𐑌𐐻𐐭 𐑄𐐯𐑋, 𐐨𐑂𐐯𐑌 𐐻𐐭 𐑄 𐐺𐑉𐐮𐑍𐐮𐑍 𐐱𐑂 𐑄𐐯𐑋 𐐻𐐭 𐑄 𐑌𐐱𐑊𐐯𐐾 𐐱𐑂 𐑄 𐐿𐐲𐑂𐐯𐑌𐐰𐑌𐐻𐑅 𐐸𐐶𐐮𐐽 𐐌 𐐸𐐰𐑂 𐑋𐐩𐐼 𐐶𐐮𐑄 𐑄𐐴 𐑁𐐪𐑄𐐲𐑉𐑆. 𐐈𐑌𐐼 𐐌 𐐶𐐮𐑊 𐑀𐐮𐑂 𐐲𐑌𐐻𐐭 𐐸𐐮𐑋 𐐰 𐐿𐐱𐑋𐐰𐑌𐐼𐑋𐐯𐑌𐐻, 𐑄𐐰𐐻 𐐸𐐨 𐑇𐐰𐑊 𐐼𐐭 𐑌𐐲𐑌 𐐲𐑄𐐲𐑉 𐐶𐐲𐑉𐐿, 𐑅𐐩𐑂 𐑄 𐐶𐐲𐑉𐐿 𐐸𐐶𐐮𐐽 𐐌 𐑇𐐰𐑊 𐐿𐐱𐑋𐐰𐑌𐐼 𐐸𐐮𐑋. 𐐈𐑌𐐼 𐐌 𐐶𐐮𐑊 𐑋𐐩𐐿 𐐸𐐮𐑋 𐑀𐑉𐐩𐐻 𐐮𐑌 𐑋𐐴𐑌 𐐴𐑆; 𐑁𐐫𐑉 𐐸𐐨 𐑇𐐰𐑊 𐐼𐐭 𐑋𐐴 𐐶𐐲𐑉𐐿. 𐐈𐑌𐐼 𐐸𐐨 𐑇𐐰𐑊 𐐺𐐨 𐑀𐑉𐐩𐐻 𐑊𐐴𐐿 𐐲𐑌𐐻𐐭 𐐣𐐬𐑆𐐯𐑆, 𐐸𐐭𐑋 𐐌 𐐸𐐰𐑂 𐑅𐐯𐐼 𐐌 𐐶𐐳𐐼 𐑉𐐩𐑆 𐐲𐐹 𐐲𐑌𐐻𐐭 𐐷𐐭, 𐐻𐐭 𐐼𐐯𐑊𐐮𐑂𐐲𐑉 𐑋𐐴 𐐹𐐨𐐹𐑊, 𐐄 𐐸𐐵𐑅 𐐱𐑂 𐐆𐑆𐑉𐐩𐐯𐑊. 𐐈𐑌𐐼 𐐣𐐬𐑆𐐯𐑆 𐐶𐐮𐑊 𐐌 𐑉𐐩𐑆 𐐲𐐹, 𐐻𐐭 𐐼𐐯𐑊𐐮𐑂𐐲𐑉 𐑄𐐴 𐐹𐐨𐐹𐑊 𐐵𐐻 𐐱𐑂 𐑄 𐑊𐐰𐑌𐐼 𐐱𐑂 𐐀𐐾𐐮𐐹𐐻. 𐐒𐐲𐐻 𐐰 𐑅𐐨𐐲𐑉 𐐶𐐮𐑊 𐐌 𐑉𐐩𐑆 𐐲𐐹 𐐵𐐻 𐐱𐑂 𐑄 𐑁𐑉𐐭𐐻 𐐱𐑂 𐑄𐐴 𐑊𐑎𐑌𐑆; 𐐰𐑌𐐼 𐐲𐑌𐐻𐐭 𐐸𐐮𐑋 𐐶𐐮𐑊 𐐌 𐑀𐐮𐑂 𐐹𐐵𐐲𐑉 𐐻𐐭 𐐺𐑉𐐮𐑍 𐑁𐐬𐑉𐑃 𐑋𐐴 𐐶𐐲𐑉𐐼 𐐲𐑌𐐻𐐭 𐑄 𐑅𐐨𐐼 𐐱𐑂 𐑄𐐴 𐑊𐑎𐑌𐑆; 𐐰𐑌𐐼 𐑌𐐱𐐻 𐐻𐐭 𐑄 𐐺𐑉𐐮𐑍𐐮𐑍 𐑁𐐬𐑉𐑃 𐑋𐐴 𐐶𐐲𐑉𐐼 𐐬𐑌𐑊𐐨, 𐑅𐐯𐑃 𐑄 𐐢𐐫𐑉𐐼, 𐐺𐐲𐐻 𐐻𐐭 𐑄 𐐿𐐱𐑌𐑂𐐮𐑌𐑅𐐮𐑍 𐑄𐐯𐑋 𐐱𐑂 𐑋𐐴 𐐶𐐲𐑉𐐼, 𐐸𐐶𐐮𐐽 𐑇𐐰𐑊 𐐸𐐰𐑂 𐐫𐑊𐑉𐐯𐐼𐐨 𐑀𐐱𐑌 𐑁𐐬𐑉𐑃 𐐲𐑋𐐲𐑍 𐑄𐐯𐑋. 𐐐𐐶𐐯𐑉𐑁𐐫𐑉, 𐑄 𐑁𐑉𐐭𐐻 𐐱𐑂 𐑄𐐴 𐑊𐑎𐑌𐑆 𐑇𐐰𐑊 𐑉𐐴𐐻; 𐐰𐑌𐐼 𐑄 𐑁𐑉𐐭𐐻 𐐱𐑂 𐑄 𐑊𐑎𐑌𐑆 𐐱𐑂 𐐖𐐭𐐼𐐲 𐑇𐐰𐑊 𐑉𐐴𐐻; 𐐰𐑌𐐼 𐑄𐐰𐐻 𐐸𐐶𐐮𐐽 𐑇𐐰𐑊 𐐺𐐨 𐑉𐐮𐐻𐐯𐑌 𐐺𐐴 𐑄 𐑁𐑉𐐭𐐻 𐐱𐑂 𐑄𐐴 𐑊𐑎𐑌𐑆, 𐐰𐑌𐐼 𐐫𐑊𐑅𐐬 𐑄𐐰𐐻 𐐸𐐶𐐮𐐽 𐑇𐐰𐑊 𐐺𐐨 𐑉𐐮𐐻𐐯𐑌 𐐺𐐴 𐑄 𐑁𐑉𐐭𐐻 𐐱𐑂 𐑄 𐑊𐑎𐑌𐑆 𐐱𐑂 𐐖𐐭𐐼𐐲, 𐑇𐐰𐑊 𐑀𐑉𐐬 𐐻𐐭𐑀𐐯𐑄𐐲𐑉, 𐐲𐑌𐐻𐐭 𐑄 𐐿𐐱𐑌𐑁𐐵𐑌𐐼𐐮𐑍 𐐱𐑂 𐑁𐐫𐑊𐑅 𐐼𐐱𐐿𐐻𐑉𐐮𐑌𐑆, 𐐰𐑌𐐼 𐑊𐐩𐐮𐑍 𐐼𐐵𐑌 𐐱𐑂 𐐿𐐱𐑌𐐻𐐯𐑌𐑇𐐲𐑌𐑆, 𐐰𐑌𐐼 𐐯𐑅𐐻𐐰𐐺𐑊𐐮𐑇𐐮𐑍 𐐹𐐨𐑅 𐐲𐑋𐐲𐑍 𐑄 𐑁𐑉𐐭𐐻 𐐱𐑂 𐑄𐐴 𐑊𐑎𐑌𐑆, 𐐰𐑌𐐼 𐐺𐑉𐐮𐑍𐐮𐑍 𐑄𐐯𐑋 𐐻𐐭 𐑄 𐑌𐐱𐑊𐐯𐐾 𐐱𐑂 𐑄𐐯𐑉 𐑁𐐪𐑄𐐲𐑉𐑆 𐐮𐑌 𐑄 𐑊𐐰𐐻𐐲𐑉 𐐼𐐩𐑆; 𐐰𐑌𐐼 𐐫𐑊𐑅𐐬 𐐻𐐭 𐑄 𐑌𐐱𐑊𐐯𐐾 𐐱𐑂 𐑋𐐴 𐐿𐐲𐑂𐐯𐑌𐐰𐑌𐐻𐑅, 𐑅𐐯𐑃 𐑄 𐐢𐐫𐑉𐐼. 𐐈𐑌𐐼 𐐵𐐻 𐐱𐑂 𐐶𐐨𐐿𐑌𐐯𐑅 𐐸𐐨 𐑇𐐰𐑊 𐐺𐐨 𐑋𐐩𐐼 𐑅𐐻𐑉𐐱𐑍, 𐐮𐑌 𐑄𐐰𐐻 𐐼𐐩 𐐸𐐶𐐯𐑌 𐑋𐐴 𐐶𐐲𐑉𐐿 𐑇𐐰𐑊 𐐿𐐱𐑋𐐯𐑌𐑅 𐐲𐑋𐐲𐑍 𐐫𐑊 𐑋𐐴 𐐹𐐨𐐹𐑊, 𐐲𐑌𐐻𐐭 𐑄 𐑉𐐯𐑅𐐻𐐬𐑉𐐮𐑍 𐑄𐐨, 𐐄 𐐸𐐵𐑅 𐐱𐑂 𐐆𐑆𐑉𐐩𐐯𐑊, 𐑅𐐯𐑃 𐑄 𐐢𐐫𐑉𐐼.

3. 𐐈𐑌𐐼 𐑄𐐲𐑅 𐐹𐑉𐐱𐑁𐐯𐑅𐐴𐐼 𐐖𐐬𐑆𐐯𐑁, 𐑅𐐩𐐮𐑍: 𐐒𐐨𐐸𐐬𐑊𐐼, 𐑄𐐰𐐻 𐑅𐐨𐑉 𐐶𐐮𐑊 𐑄 𐐢𐐫𐑉𐐼 𐐺𐑊𐐯𐑅; 𐐰𐑌𐐼 𐑄𐐩 𐑄𐐰𐐻 𐑅𐐨𐐿 𐐻𐐭 𐐼𐐨𐑅𐐻𐑉𐑎 𐐸𐐮𐑋 𐑇𐐰𐑊 𐐺𐐨 𐐿𐐱𐑌𐑁𐐵𐑌𐐼𐐯𐐼; 𐑁𐐫𐑉 𐑄𐐮𐑅 𐐹𐑉𐐱𐑋𐐮𐑅, 𐐶𐐮𐐽 𐐌 𐐸𐐰𐑂 𐐱𐐺𐐻𐐩𐑌𐐼 𐐲𐑂 𐑄 𐐢𐐫𐑉𐐼, 𐐲𐑂 𐑄 𐑁𐑉𐐭𐐻 𐐲𐑂 𐑋𐐴 𐑊𐑎𐑌𐑆, 𐑇𐐰𐑊 𐐺𐐨 𐑁𐐳𐑊𐑁𐐮𐑊𐐼. 𐐒𐐨𐐸𐐬𐑊𐐼, 𐐌 𐐰𐑋 𐑇𐐭𐑉 𐐲𐑂 𐑄 𐑁𐐳𐑊𐑁𐐮𐑊𐐮𐑍 𐐲𐑂 𐑄𐐮𐑅 𐐹𐑉𐐱𐑋𐐮𐑅. 𐐈𐑌𐐼 𐐸𐐮𐑆 𐑌𐐩𐑋 𐑇𐐰𐑊 𐐺𐐨 𐐿𐐫𐑊𐐼 𐐪𐑁𐐻𐐲𐑉 𐑋𐐨: 𐐰𐑌𐐼 𐐮𐐻 𐑇𐐰𐑊 𐐺𐐨 𐐪𐑁𐐻𐐲𐑉 𐑄 𐑌𐐩𐑋 𐐲𐑂 𐐸𐐮𐑆 𐑁𐐪𐑄𐐲𐑉. 𐐈𐑌𐐼 𐐸𐐨 𐑇𐐰𐑊 𐐺𐐨 𐑊𐐴𐐿 𐐲𐑌𐐻𐐭 𐑋𐐨; 𐑁𐐫𐑉 𐑄 𐑃𐐮𐑍 𐐶𐐮𐐽 𐑄 𐐢𐐫𐑉𐐼 𐑇𐐰𐑊 𐐺𐑉𐐮𐑍 𐑁𐐬𐑉𐑃 𐐺𐐴 𐐸𐐮𐑆 𐐸𐐰𐑌𐐼, 𐐺𐐴 𐑄 𐐹𐐵𐐲𐑉 𐐲𐑂 𐑄 𐐢𐐫𐑉𐐼, 𐑇𐐰𐑊 𐐺𐑉𐐮𐑍 𐑋𐐴 𐐹𐐨𐐹𐑊 𐐲𐑌𐐻𐐭 𐑅𐐰𐑊𐑂𐐩𐑇𐐲𐑌; 𐐏𐐩, 𐑄𐐲𐑅, 𐐹𐑉𐐱𐑁𐐯𐑅𐐴𐐼 𐐖𐐬𐑆𐐯𐑁, 𐐌 𐐰𐑋 𐑇𐐭𐑉 𐐲𐑂 𐑄𐐮𐑅 𐑃𐐮𐑍, 𐐨𐑂𐐲𐑌 𐐰𐑆 𐐌 𐐰𐑋 𐑇𐐭𐑉 𐐲𐑂 𐑄 𐐹𐑉𐐱𐑋𐐮𐑅 𐐲𐑂 𐐣𐐬𐑆𐐯𐑆; 𐑁𐐫𐑉 𐑄 𐐢𐐫𐑉𐐼 𐐸𐐰𐑃 𐑅𐐯𐐼 𐐲𐑌𐐻𐐭 𐑋𐐨, 𐐌 𐐶𐐮𐑊 𐐹𐑉𐐨𐑆𐐲𐑉𐑂 𐑄𐐴 𐑅𐐨𐐼 𐑁𐐫𐑉𐐯𐑂𐐲𐑉. 𐐈𐑌𐐼 𐑄 𐐢𐐫𐑉𐐼 𐐸𐐰𐑃 𐑅𐐯𐐼, 𐐌 𐐶𐐮𐑊 𐑉𐐩𐑆 𐐲𐐹 𐐲 𐐣𐐬𐑆𐐯𐑆; 𐐰𐑌𐐼 𐐌 𐐶𐐮𐑊 𐑀𐐮𐑂 𐐹𐐵𐐲𐑉 𐐲𐑌𐐻𐐭 𐐸𐐮𐑋 𐐮𐑌 𐐲 𐑉𐐱𐐼; 𐐰𐑌𐐼 𐐌 𐐶𐐮𐑊 𐑀𐐮𐑂 𐐾𐐲𐐾𐑋𐐯𐑌𐐻 𐐲𐑌𐐻𐐭 𐐸𐐮𐑋 𐐮𐑌 𐑉𐐴𐐻𐐮𐑍. 𐐏𐐯𐐻 𐐌 𐐶𐐮𐑊 𐑌𐐱𐐻 𐑊𐐭𐑅 𐐸𐐮𐑆 𐐻𐐲𐑍, 𐑄𐐰𐐻 𐐸𐐨 𐑇𐐰𐑊 𐑅𐐹𐐨𐐿 𐑋𐐲𐐽, 𐑁𐐫𐑉 𐐌 𐐶𐐮𐑊 𐑌𐐱𐐻 𐑋𐐩𐐿 𐐸𐐮𐑋 𐑋𐐴𐐻𐐨 𐐮𐑌 𐑅𐐹𐐨𐐿𐐮𐑍. 𐐒𐐲𐐻 𐐌 𐐶𐐮𐑊 𐑉𐐴𐐻 𐐲𐑌𐐻𐐭 𐐸𐐮𐑋 𐑋𐐴 𐑊𐐫, 𐐺𐐴 𐑄 𐑁𐐮𐑍𐑀𐐲𐑉 𐐲𐑂 𐑋𐐴𐑌 𐐬𐑌 𐐸𐐰𐑌𐐼; 𐐰𐑌𐐼 𐐌 𐐶𐐮𐑊 𐑋𐐩𐐿 𐐲 𐑅𐐹𐐬𐐿𐑅𐑋𐐰𐑌 𐑁𐐫𐑉 𐐸𐐮𐑋. 𐐈𐑌𐐼 𐑄 𐐢𐐫𐑉𐐼 𐑅𐐯𐐼 𐐲𐑌𐐻𐐭 𐑋𐐨 𐐫𐑊𐑅𐐬, 𐐌 𐐶𐐮𐑊 𐑉𐐩𐑆 𐐲𐐹 𐐲𐑌𐐻𐐭 𐑄 𐑁𐑉𐐭𐐻 𐐲𐑂 𐑄𐐴 𐑊𐑎𐑌𐑆; 𐐰𐑌𐐼 𐐌 𐐶𐐮𐑊 𐑋𐐩𐐿 𐑁𐐫𐑉 𐐸𐐮𐑋 𐐲 𐑅𐐹𐐬𐐿𐑅𐑋𐐰𐑌. 𐐈𐑌𐐼 𐐌, 𐐺𐐨𐐸𐐬𐑊𐐼, 𐐌 𐐶𐐮𐑊 𐑀𐐮𐑂 𐐲𐑌𐐻𐐭 𐐸𐐮𐑋 𐑄𐐰𐐻 𐐸𐐨 𐑇𐐰𐑊 𐑉𐐴𐐻 𐑄 𐑉𐐴𐐻𐐮𐑍 𐐲𐑂 𐑄 𐑁𐑉𐐭𐐻 𐐲𐑂 𐑄𐐴 𐑊𐑎𐑌𐑆, 𐐲𐑌𐐻𐐭 𐑄 𐑁𐑉𐐭𐐻 𐐲𐑂 𐑄𐐴 𐑊𐑎𐑌𐑆; 𐐰𐑌𐐼 𐑄 𐑅𐐹𐐬𐐿𐑅𐑋𐐰𐑌 𐐲𐑂 𐑄𐐴 𐑊𐑎𐑌𐑆 𐑇𐐰𐑊 𐐼𐐨𐐿𐑊𐐩𐑉 𐐮𐐻. 𐐈𐑌𐐼 𐑄 𐐶𐐲𐑉𐐼𐑆 𐐶𐐮𐐽 𐐸𐐨 𐑇𐐰𐑊 𐑉𐐴𐐻, 𐑇𐐰𐑊 𐐺𐐨 𐑄 𐐶𐐲𐑉𐐼𐑆 𐐶𐐮𐐽 𐐪𐑉 𐐯𐐿𐑅𐐹𐐨𐐼𐐨𐐯𐑌𐐻 𐐮𐑌 𐑋𐐴 𐐶𐐮𐑆𐐼𐐲𐑋 𐑇𐐳𐐼 𐑀𐐬 𐑁𐐬𐑉𐑃 𐐲𐑌𐐻𐐭 𐑄 𐑁𐑉𐐭𐐻 𐐲𐑂 𐑄𐐴 𐑊𐑎𐑌𐑆. 𐐈𐑌𐐼 𐐮𐐻 𐑇𐐰𐑊 𐐺𐐨 𐐰𐑆 𐐮𐑁 𐑄 𐑁𐑉𐐭𐐻 𐐲𐑂 𐑄𐐴 𐑊𐑎𐑌𐑆 𐐸𐐰𐐼 𐐿𐑉𐐴𐐼 𐐲𐑌𐐻𐐭 𐑄𐐯𐑋 𐑁𐑉𐐱𐑋 𐑄 𐐼𐐲𐑅𐐻; 𐑁𐐫𐑉 𐐌 𐑌𐐬 𐑄𐐩𐑉 𐑁𐐩𐑃. 𐐈𐑌𐐼 𐑄𐐩 𐑇𐐰𐑊 𐐿𐑉𐐴 𐑁𐑉𐐱𐑋 𐑄 𐐼𐐲𐑅𐐻; 𐐷𐐩, 𐐨𐑂𐐲𐑌 𐑉𐐨𐐹𐐯𐑌𐐻𐐰𐑌𐑅 𐐲𐑌𐐻𐐭 𐑄𐐩𐑉 𐐺𐑉𐐯𐑄𐑉𐐯𐑌, 𐐨𐑂𐐲𐑌 𐐪𐑁𐐻𐐲𐑉 𐑋𐐯𐑌𐐨 𐐾𐐯𐑌𐐲𐑉𐐩𐑇𐐲𐑌𐑆 𐐸𐐰𐑂 𐑀𐐱𐑌 𐐺𐐴 𐑄𐐯𐑋. 𐐈𐑌𐐼 𐐮𐐻 𐑇𐐰𐑊 𐐿𐐲𐑋 𐐻𐐭 𐐹𐐰𐑅, 𐑄𐐰𐐻 𐑄𐐩𐑉 𐐿𐑉𐐴 𐑇𐐰𐑊 𐑀𐐬, 𐐨𐑂𐐲𐑌 𐐰𐐿𐐫𐑉𐐼𐐮𐑍 𐐻𐐭 𐑄 𐑅𐐮𐑋𐐹𐑊𐑌𐐯𐑅 𐐲𐑂 𐑄𐐩𐑉 𐐶𐐲𐑉𐐼𐑆. 𐐒𐐨𐐿𐐫𐑆 𐐲𐑂 𐑄𐐩𐑉 𐑁𐐩𐑃, 𐑄𐐩𐑉 𐐶𐐲𐑉𐐼𐑆 𐑇𐐰𐑊 𐐹𐑉𐐬𐑅𐐨𐐼 𐑁𐐬𐑉𐑃 𐐵𐐻 𐐲𐑂 𐑋𐐴 𐑋𐐵𐑃 𐐲𐑌𐐻𐐭 𐑄𐐩𐑉 𐐺𐑉𐐯𐑄𐑉𐐯𐑌, 𐐸𐐭 𐐪𐑉 𐑄 𐑁𐑉𐐭𐐻 𐐲𐑂 𐑄𐐴 𐑊𐑎𐑌𐑆; 𐐰𐑌𐐼 𐑄 𐐶𐐨𐐿𐑌𐐯𐑅 𐐲𐑂 𐑄𐐩𐑉 𐐶𐐲𐑉𐐼𐑆 𐐶𐐮𐑊 𐐌 𐑋𐐩𐐿 𐑅𐐻𐑉𐐱𐑍 𐐮𐑌 𐑄𐐩𐑉 𐑁𐐩𐑃, 𐐲𐑌𐐻𐐭 𐑄 𐑉𐐨𐑋𐐯𐑋𐐺𐐲𐑉𐐮𐑍 𐐲𐑂 𐑋𐐴 𐐿𐐲𐑂𐐯𐑌𐐰𐑌𐐻 𐐶𐐮𐐽 𐐌 𐑋𐐩𐐼 𐐲𐑌𐐻𐐭 𐑄𐐴 𐑁𐐪𐑄𐐲𐑉𐑆.

4. 𐐈𐑌𐐼 𐑌𐐵, 𐐺𐐨𐐸𐐬𐑊𐐼, 𐑋𐐴 𐑅𐐲𐑌 𐐖𐐬𐑆𐐯𐑁, 𐐪𐑁𐐻𐐲𐑉 𐑄𐐮𐑅 𐑋𐐰𐑌𐐲𐑉 𐐼𐐮𐐼 𐑋𐐴 𐑁𐐪𐑄𐐲𐑉 𐐲𐑂 𐐬𐑊𐐼 𐐹𐑉𐐱𐑁𐐯𐑅𐐴. 𐐐𐐶𐐯𐑉𐑁𐐫𐑉, 𐐺𐐨𐐿𐐫𐑆 𐐲𐑂 𐑄𐐮𐑅 𐐿𐐲𐑂𐐯𐑌𐐰𐑌𐐻 𐑄𐐵 𐐪𐑉𐐻 𐐺𐑊𐐯𐑅𐐯𐐼: 𐑁𐐫𐑉 𐑄𐐴 𐑅𐐨𐐼 𐑇𐐰𐑊 𐑌𐐱𐐻 𐐺𐐨 𐐼𐐨𐑅𐐻𐑉𐑎𐐼, 𐑁𐐫𐑉 𐑄𐐩 𐑇𐐰𐑊 𐐸𐐪𐑉𐐿𐐲𐑌 𐐲𐑌𐐻𐐭 𐑄 𐐶𐐲𐑉𐐼𐑆 𐐲𐑂 𐑄 𐐒𐐳𐐿. 𐐈𐑌𐐼 𐑄𐐯𐑉 𐑇𐐰𐑊 𐑉𐐴𐑆 𐐲𐐹 𐐶𐐲𐑌 𐑋𐐴𐐻𐐨 𐐲𐑋𐐲𐑍 𐑄𐐯𐑋, 𐐸𐐭 𐑇𐐰𐑊 𐐼𐐭 𐑋𐐲𐐽 𐑀𐐳𐐼, 𐐺𐐬𐑃 𐐮𐑌 𐐶𐐲𐑉𐐼 𐐰𐑌𐐼 𐐮𐑌 𐐼𐐨𐐼, 𐐺𐐨𐐮𐑍 𐐰𐑌 𐐮𐑌𐑅𐐻𐑉𐐭𐑋𐐯𐑌𐐻 𐐮𐑌 𐑄 𐐸𐐰𐑌𐐼𐑆 𐐲𐑂 𐐘𐐱𐐼, 𐐶𐐮𐑄 𐐯𐐿𐑅𐐨𐐼𐐮𐑍 𐑁𐐩𐑃, 𐐻𐐭 𐐶𐐲𐑉𐐿 𐑋𐐴𐐻𐐨 𐐶𐐲𐑌𐐼𐐲𐑉𐑆, 𐐰𐑌𐐼 𐐼𐐭 𐑄𐐰𐐻 𐑃𐐮𐑍 𐐶𐐮𐐽 𐐮𐑆 𐑀𐑉𐐩𐐻 𐐮𐑌 𐑄 𐑅𐐴𐐻 𐐲𐑂 𐐘𐐱𐐼, 𐐲𐑌𐐻𐐭 𐑄 𐐺𐑉𐐮𐑍𐐮𐑍 𐐻𐐭 𐐹𐐰𐑅 𐑋𐐲𐐽 𐑉𐐯𐑅𐐻𐐬𐑉𐐩𐑇𐐲𐑌 𐐲𐑌𐐻𐐭 𐑄 𐐸𐐵𐑅 𐐲𐑂 𐐆𐑆𐑉𐐩𐐯𐑊, 𐐰𐑌𐐼 𐐲𐑌𐐻𐐭 𐑄 𐑅𐐨𐐼 𐐲𐑂 𐑄𐐴 𐐺𐑉𐐯𐑄𐑉𐐯𐑌. 𐐈𐑌𐐼 𐑌𐐵, 𐐺𐑊𐐯𐑅𐐯𐐼 𐐪𐑉𐐻 𐑄𐐵, 𐐖𐐬𐑆𐐯𐑁. 𐐒𐐨𐐸𐐬𐑊𐐼, 𐑄𐐵 𐐪𐑉𐐻 𐑊𐐮𐐻𐑊; 𐐸𐐶𐐯𐑉𐑁𐐫𐑉 𐐸𐐪𐑉𐐿𐐲𐑌 𐐲𐑌𐐻𐐭 𐑄 𐐶𐐲𐑉𐐼𐑆 𐐲𐑂 𐑄𐐴 𐐺𐑉𐐲𐑄𐐲𐑉 𐐤𐐨𐑁𐐴, 𐐰𐑌𐐼 𐐮𐐻 𐑇𐐰𐑊 𐐺𐐨 𐐼𐐲𐑌 𐐲𐑌𐐻𐐭 𐑄𐐨, 𐐨𐑂𐐲𐑌 𐐰𐐿𐐫𐑉𐐼𐐮𐑍 𐐻𐐭 𐑄 𐐶𐐲𐑉𐐼𐑆 𐐶𐐮𐐽 𐐌 𐐸𐐰𐑂 𐑅𐐹𐐬𐐿𐐲𐑌. 𐐡𐐨𐑋𐐯𐑋𐐺𐐲𐑉 𐑄 𐐶𐐲𐑉𐐼𐑆 𐐲𐑂 𐑄𐐴 𐐼𐐴𐐮𐑍 𐑁𐐪𐑄𐐲𐑉. 𐐁𐑋𐐯𐑌.

𐐕𐐈𐐑𐐓𐐊𐐡 III.

1. 𐐈𐑌𐐼 𐑌𐐵, 𐐌, 𐐤𐐨𐑁𐐴, 𐑅𐐹𐐨𐐿 𐐿𐐱𐑌𐑅𐐲𐑉𐑌𐐮𐑍 𐑄 𐐹𐑉𐐱𐑁𐐯𐑅𐐨𐑆 𐐲𐑂 𐐶𐐮𐐽 𐑋𐐴 𐑁𐐪𐑄𐐲𐑉 𐐸𐐰𐑃 𐑅𐐹𐐬𐐿𐐲𐑌, 𐐿𐐱𐑌𐑅𐐲𐑉𐑌𐐮𐑍 𐐖𐐬𐑆𐐯𐑁, 𐐸𐐭 𐐶𐐱𐑆 𐐿𐐰𐑉𐐨𐐼 𐐮𐑌𐐻𐐭 𐐀𐐾𐐮𐐹𐐻: 𐑁𐐫𐑉 𐐺𐐨𐐸𐐬𐑊𐐼, 𐐸𐐨 𐐻𐑉𐐭𐑊𐐨 𐐹𐑉𐐱𐑁𐐯𐑅𐐴𐐼 𐐿𐐱𐑌𐑅𐐲𐑉𐑌𐐮𐑍 𐐫𐑊 𐐸𐐮𐑆 𐑅𐐨𐐼. 𐐈𐑌𐐼 𐑄 𐐹𐑉𐐱𐑁𐐯𐑅𐐨𐑆 𐐶𐐮𐐽 𐐸𐐨 𐑉𐐬𐐻, 𐑄𐐯𐑉 𐐪𐑉 𐑌𐐱𐐻 𐑋𐐯𐑌𐐨

𐑉𐐮𐐻𐐲𐑌. 𐐈𐑌𐐼 𐐸𐐨 𐐹𐑉𐐱𐑁𐐯𐑅𐐴𐐼 𐐿𐐱𐑌𐑅𐐲𐑉𐑌𐐮𐑍 𐐲𐑅, 𐐰𐑌𐐼 𐐵𐑉 𐑁𐐷𐐭𐐽𐐲𐑉 𐐾𐐯𐑌𐐲𐑉𐐩𐑇𐐲𐑌𐑆; 𐐰𐑌𐐼 𐑄𐐩 𐐪𐑉 𐑉𐐮𐐻𐐲𐑌 𐐲𐐹𐐱𐑌 𐑄 𐐹𐑊𐐩𐐻𐑅 𐐱𐑂 𐐺𐑉𐐰𐑅. 𐐐𐐶𐐯𐑉𐑁𐐬𐑉, 𐐰𐑁𐐻𐐲𐑉 𐑋𐐴 𐑁𐐪𐑄𐐲𐑉 𐐸𐐰𐐼 𐑋𐐩𐐼 𐐰𐑌 𐐯𐑌𐐼 𐐱𐑂 𐑅𐐹𐐨𐐿𐐮𐑍 𐐿𐐱𐑌𐑅𐐲𐑉𐑌𐐮𐑍 𐑄 𐐹𐑉𐐱𐑁𐐯𐑅𐐨𐑆 𐐱𐑂 𐐖𐐬𐑆𐐯𐑁, 𐐸𐐨 𐐿𐐫𐑊𐐼 𐑄 𐐽𐐮𐑊𐐼𐑉𐐯𐑌 𐐱𐑂 𐐢𐐩𐑋𐐲𐑌, 𐐸𐐮𐑆 𐑅𐐲𐑌𐑆 𐐰𐑌𐐼 𐐸𐐮𐑆 𐐼𐐫𐐻𐐲𐑉𐑆, 𐐰𐑌𐐼 𐑅𐐯𐐼 𐐲𐑌𐐻𐐭 𐑄𐐯𐑋, 𐐒𐐨𐐸𐐬𐑊𐐼, 𐑋𐐴 𐑅𐐲𐑌𐑆, 𐐰𐑌𐐼 𐑋𐐴 𐐼𐐫𐐻𐐲𐑉𐑆, 𐐸𐐭 𐐪𐑉 𐑄 𐑅𐐲𐑌𐑆 𐐰𐑌𐐼 𐑄 𐐼𐐫𐐻𐐲𐑉𐑆 𐐱𐑂 𐑋𐐴 𐑁𐐲𐑉𐑅𐐻-𐐺𐐫𐑉𐑌, 𐐌 𐐶𐐳𐐼 𐑄𐐰𐐻 𐐷𐐨 𐑇𐐳𐐼 𐑀𐐮𐑂 𐐨𐑉 𐐲𐑌𐐻𐐭 𐑋𐐴 𐐶𐐲𐑉𐐼𐑆; 𐑁𐐫𐑉 𐑄 𐐢𐐫𐑉𐐼 𐐘𐐱𐐼 𐐸𐐰𐑃 𐑅𐐯𐐼, 𐑄𐐰𐐻 𐐮𐑌𐐰𐑆𐑋𐐲𐐽 𐐰𐑆 𐐷𐐨 𐑇𐐰𐑊 𐐿𐐨𐐹 𐑋𐐴 𐐿𐐱𐑋𐐰𐑌𐐼𐑋𐐯𐑌𐐻𐑅, 𐐷𐐨 𐑇𐐰𐑊 𐐹𐑉𐐱𐑅𐐹𐐲𐑉 𐐮𐑌 𐑄 𐑊𐐰𐑌𐐼; 𐐰𐑌𐐼 𐐮𐑌𐐰𐑆𐑋𐐲𐐽 𐐰𐑆 𐐷𐐨 𐐶𐐮𐑊 𐑌𐐱𐐻 𐐿𐐨𐐹 𐑋𐐴 𐐿𐐱𐑋𐐰𐑌𐐼𐑋𐐯𐑌𐐻𐑅, 𐐷𐐨 𐑇𐐰𐑊 𐐺𐐨 𐐿𐐲𐐻 𐐱𐑁 𐑁𐑉𐐱𐑋 𐑋𐐴 𐐹𐑉𐐯𐑆𐐯𐑌𐑅. 𐐒𐐲𐐻 𐐺𐐨𐐸𐐬𐑊𐐼, 𐑋𐐴 𐑅𐐲𐑌𐑆 𐐰𐑌𐐼 𐑋𐐴 𐐼𐐫𐐻𐐲𐑉𐑆, 𐐌 𐐿𐐰𐑌𐐱𐐻 𐑀𐐬 𐐼𐐵𐑌 𐐻𐐭 𐑋𐐴 𐑀𐑉𐐩𐑂 𐑅𐐩𐑂 𐐌 𐑇𐐳𐐼 𐑊𐐨𐑂 𐐰 𐐺𐑊𐐯𐑅𐐮𐑍 𐐲𐐹𐐱𐑌 𐐷𐐭; 𐑁𐐫𐑉 𐐺𐐨𐐸𐐬𐑊𐐼, 𐐌 𐑌𐐬 𐑄𐐰𐐻 𐐮𐑁 𐐷𐐨 𐐪𐑉 𐐺𐑉𐐫𐐻 𐐲𐐹 𐐮𐑌 𐑄 𐐶𐐩 𐐷𐐨 𐑇𐐳𐐼 𐑀𐐬, 𐐷𐐨 𐐶𐐮𐑊 𐑌𐐱𐐻 𐐼𐐨𐐹𐐪𐑉𐐻 𐑁𐑉𐐱𐑋 𐐮𐐻. 𐐐𐐶𐐯𐑉𐑁𐐬𐑉, 𐐮𐑁 𐐷𐐨 𐐪𐑉 𐐿𐐲𐑉𐑅𐐻, 𐐺𐐨𐐸𐐬𐑊𐐼, 𐐌 𐑊𐐨𐑂 𐑋𐐴 𐐺𐑊𐐯𐑅𐐮𐑍 𐐲𐐹𐐱𐑌 𐐷𐐭, 𐑄𐐰𐐻 𐑄 𐐿𐐲𐑉𐑅𐐮𐑍 𐑋𐐩 𐐺𐐨 𐐻𐐩𐐿𐐲𐑌 𐑁𐑉𐐱𐑋 𐐷𐐭, 𐐰𐑌𐐼 𐐺𐐨 𐐰𐑌𐑅𐐲𐑉𐐼 𐐲𐐹𐐱𐑌 𐑄 𐐸𐐯𐐼𐑆 𐐱𐑂 𐐷𐐵𐑉 𐐹𐐩𐑉𐐯𐑌𐐻𐑅. 𐐐𐐶𐐯𐑉𐑁𐐬𐑉, 𐐺𐐨𐐿𐐫𐑆 𐐱𐑂 𐑋𐐴 𐐺𐑊𐐯𐑅𐐮𐑍, 𐑄 𐐢𐐫𐑉𐐼 𐐘𐐱𐐼 𐐶𐐮𐑊 𐑌𐐱𐐻 𐑅𐐲𐑁𐐲𐑉 𐑄𐐰𐐻 𐐷𐐨 𐑇𐐰𐑊 𐐹𐐯𐑉𐐮𐑇; 𐐸𐐶𐐯𐑉𐑁𐐬𐑉 𐐸𐐨 𐐶𐐮𐑊 𐐺𐐨 𐑋𐐲𐑉𐑅𐐮𐑁𐐳𐑊 𐐲𐑌𐐻𐐭 𐐷𐐭, 𐐰𐑌𐐼 𐐲𐑌𐐻𐐭 𐐷𐐵𐑉 𐑅𐐨𐐼 𐑁𐐫𐑉 𐐯𐑂𐐲𐑉.

2. 𐐈𐑌𐐼 𐐮𐐻 𐐿𐐩𐑋 𐐻𐐭 𐐹𐐰𐑅 𐑄𐐰𐐻 𐐰𐑁𐐻𐐲𐑉 𐑋𐐴 𐑁𐐪𐑄𐐲𐑉 𐐸𐐰𐐼 𐑋𐐩𐐼 𐐰𐑌 𐐯𐑌𐐼 𐐱𐑂 𐑅𐐹𐐨𐐿𐐮𐑍 𐐻𐐭 𐑄 𐑅𐐲𐑌𐑆 𐐰𐑌𐐼 𐐼𐐫𐐻𐐲𐑉𐑆 𐐱𐑂 𐐢𐐩𐑋𐐲𐑌, 𐐸𐐨 𐐿𐐫𐑆𐐼 𐑄 𐑅𐐲𐑌𐑆 𐐰𐑌𐐼 𐐼𐐫𐐻𐐲𐑉𐑆 𐐱𐑂 𐐢𐐯𐑋𐐷𐐭𐐯𐑊 𐐻𐐭 𐐺𐐨 𐐺𐑉𐐫𐐻 𐐺𐐨𐑁𐐬𐑉 𐐸𐐮𐑋. 𐐈𐑌𐐼 𐐸𐐨 𐑅𐐹𐐩𐐿 𐐲𐑌𐐻𐐭 𐑄𐐯𐑋, 𐑅𐐩𐐮𐑍: 𐐒𐐨𐐸𐐬𐑊𐐼, 𐑋𐐴 𐑅𐐲𐑌𐑆 𐐰𐑌𐐼 𐑋𐐴 𐐼𐐫𐐻𐐲𐑉𐑆, 𐐸𐐭 𐐪𐑉 𐑄 𐑅𐐲𐑌𐑆 𐐰𐑌𐐼 𐑄 𐐼𐐫𐐻𐐲𐑉𐑆 𐐱𐑂 𐑋𐐴 𐑅𐐯𐐿𐐲𐑌𐐼 𐑅𐐲𐑌; 𐐺𐐨𐐸𐐬𐑊𐐼, 𐐌 𐑊𐐨𐑂 𐐲𐑌𐐻𐐭 𐐷𐐭 𐑄 𐑅𐐩𐑋 𐐺𐑊𐐯𐑅𐐮𐑍 𐐸𐐶𐐮𐐽 𐐌 𐑊𐐯𐑁𐐻 𐐲𐑌𐐻𐐭 𐑄 𐑅𐐲𐑌𐑆 𐐰𐑌𐐼 𐐼𐐫𐐻𐐲𐑉𐑆 𐐱𐑂 𐐢𐐩𐑋𐐲𐑌; 𐐸𐐶𐐯𐑉𐑁𐐬𐑉, 𐑄𐐵 𐑇𐐰𐑊𐐻 𐑌𐐱𐐻 𐐲𐐻𐐲𐑉𐑊𐐨 𐐺𐐨 𐐼𐐯𐑅𐐻𐑉𐐱𐐮𐐼; 𐐺𐐲𐐻 𐐮𐑌 𐑄 𐐯𐑌𐐼 𐑄𐐴 𐑅𐐨𐐼 𐑇𐐰𐑊 𐐺𐐨 𐐺𐑊𐐯𐑅𐐯𐐼.

3. 𐐈𐑌𐐼 𐐮𐐻 𐐿𐐩𐑋 𐐻𐐭 𐐹𐐰𐑅 𐑄𐐰𐐻 𐐸𐐶𐐯𐑌 𐑋𐐴 𐑁𐐪𐑄𐐲𐑉 𐐸𐐰𐐼 𐑋𐐩𐐼 𐐰𐑌 𐐯𐑌𐐼 𐐱𐑂 𐑅𐐹𐐨𐐿𐐮𐑍 𐐲𐑌𐐻𐐭 𐑄𐐯𐑋, 𐐺𐐨𐐸𐐬𐑊𐐼, 𐐸𐐨 𐑅𐐹𐐩𐐿 𐐲𐑌𐐻𐐭 𐑄 𐑅𐐲𐑌𐑆 𐐱𐑂 𐐆𐑇𐑋𐐩𐐯𐑊, 𐐷𐐩, 𐐰𐑌𐐼 𐐨𐑂𐐲𐑌 𐐫𐑊 𐐸𐐮𐑆 𐐸𐐵𐑅𐐸𐐬𐑊𐐼. 𐐈𐑌𐐼 𐐰𐑁𐐻𐐲𐑉 𐐸𐐨 𐐸𐐰𐐼 𐑋𐐩𐐼 𐐰𐑌 𐐯𐑌𐐼 𐐱𐑂 𐑅𐐹𐐨𐐿𐐮𐑍 𐐲𐑌𐐻𐐭 𐑄𐐯𐑋, 𐐸𐐨 𐑅𐐹𐐩𐐿 𐐲𐑌𐐻𐐭 𐐝𐐰𐑋, 𐑅𐐩𐐮𐑍: 𐐒𐑊𐐯𐑅𐐯𐐼 𐐪𐑉𐐻 𐑄𐐵, 𐐰𐑌𐐼 𐑄𐐴 𐑅𐐨𐐼; 𐑁𐐫𐑉 𐑄𐐵 𐑇𐐰𐑊𐐻 𐐮𐑌𐐸𐐯𐑉𐐮𐐻 𐑄 𐑊𐐰𐑌𐐼, 𐑊𐐴𐐿 𐐲𐑌𐐻𐐭 𐑄𐐴 𐐺𐑉𐐲𐑄𐐲𐑉 𐐤𐐨𐑁𐐴. 𐐈𐑌𐐼 𐑄𐐴 𐑅𐐨𐐼 𐑇𐐰𐑊 𐐺𐐨 𐑌𐐲𐑋𐐺𐐲𐑉𐐼 𐐶𐐮𐑄 𐐸𐐮𐑆 𐑅𐐨𐐼; 𐐰𐑌𐐼 𐑄𐐵 𐑇𐐰𐑊𐐻 𐐺𐐨 𐐨𐑂𐐲𐑌 𐑊𐐴𐐿 𐐲𐑌𐐻𐐭 𐑄𐐴 𐐺𐑉𐐲𐑄𐐲𐑉, 𐐰𐑌𐐼 𐑄𐐴 𐑅𐐨𐐼 𐑊𐐴𐐿 𐐲𐑌𐐻𐐭 𐐸𐐮𐑆 𐑅𐐨𐐼; 𐐰𐑌𐐼 𐑄𐐵 𐑇𐐰𐑊𐐻 𐐺𐐨 𐐺𐑊𐐯𐑅𐐻 𐐮𐑌 𐐫𐑊 𐑄𐐴 𐐼𐐩𐑆.

4. 𐐈𐑌𐐼 𐐮𐐻 𐐿𐐩𐑋 𐐻𐐭 𐐹𐐰𐑅 𐐰𐑁𐐻𐐲𐑉 𐑋𐐴 𐑁𐐪𐑄𐐲𐑉 𐐢𐐨𐐸𐐴 𐐸𐐰𐐼 𐑅𐐹𐐬𐐿𐐲𐑌 𐐲𐑌𐐻𐐭 𐐫𐑊 𐐸𐐮𐑆 𐐸𐐵𐑅𐐸𐐬𐑊𐐼, 𐐰𐐿𐐫𐑉𐐼𐐮𐑍 𐐻𐐭 𐑄 𐑁𐐨𐑊𐐮𐑍𐑆 𐐱𐑂 𐐸𐐮𐑆 𐐸𐐪𐑉𐐻 𐐰𐑌𐐼 𐑄 𐐝𐐹𐐮𐑉𐐮𐐻 𐐱𐑂 𐑄 𐐢𐐫𐑉𐐼 𐐸𐐶𐐮𐐽 𐐶𐐱𐑆 𐐮𐑌 𐐸𐐮𐑋, 𐐸𐐨 𐐶𐐰𐐿𐑅𐐻 𐐬𐑊𐐼. 𐐈𐑌𐐼 𐐮𐐻 𐐿𐐩𐑋 𐐻𐐭 𐐹𐐰𐑅 𐑄𐐰𐐻 𐐸𐐨 𐐼𐐴𐐼, 𐐰𐑌𐐼 𐐶𐐱𐑆 𐐺𐐯𐑉𐐨𐐼.

5. 𐐈𐑌𐐼 𐐮𐐻 𐐿𐐩𐑋 𐐻𐐭 𐐹𐐰𐑅 𐑄𐐰𐐻 𐑌𐐱𐐻 𐑋𐐯𐑌𐐨 𐐼𐐩𐑆 𐐰𐑁𐐻𐐲𐑉 𐐸𐐮𐑆 𐐼𐐯𐑃, 𐐢𐐩𐑋𐐲𐑌 𐐰𐑌𐐼 𐐢𐐯𐑋𐐷𐐭𐐯𐑊, 𐐰𐑌𐐼 𐑄 𐑅𐐲𐑌𐑆 𐐱𐑂 𐐆𐑇𐑋𐐩𐐯𐑊, 𐐶𐐲𐑉 𐐰𐑍𐑀𐑉𐐮 𐐶𐐮𐑄 𐑋𐐨 𐐺𐐨𐐿𐐫𐑆 𐐱𐑂 𐑄 𐐰𐐼𐑋𐐬𐑌𐐮𐑇𐐲𐑌𐑆 𐐱𐑂 𐑄 𐐢𐐫𐑉𐐼; 𐑁𐐫𐑉 𐐌, 𐐤𐐨𐑁𐐴, 𐐶𐐱𐑆 𐐿𐐱𐑌𐑅𐐻𐑉𐐩𐑌𐐼 𐐻𐐭 𐑅𐐹𐐨𐐿 𐐲𐑌𐐻𐐭 𐑄𐐯𐑋, 𐐰𐐿𐐫𐑉𐐼𐐮𐑍 𐐻𐐭 𐐸𐐮𐑆 𐐶𐐲𐑉𐐼: 𐑁𐐫𐑉 𐐌 𐐸𐐰𐐼 𐑅𐐹𐐬𐐿𐐲𐑌 𐑋𐐯𐑌𐐨 𐑃𐐮𐑍𐑆 𐐲𐑌𐐻𐐭 𐑄𐐯𐑋, 𐐰𐑌𐐼 𐐫𐑊𐑅𐐬 𐑋𐐴 𐑁𐐪𐑄𐐲𐑉, 𐐺𐐨𐑁𐐬𐑉 𐐸𐐮𐑆 𐐼𐐯𐑃; 𐑋𐐯𐑌𐐨 𐐱𐑂 𐐸𐐶𐐮𐐽 𐑅𐐩𐐮𐑍𐑆 𐐪𐑉 𐑉𐐮𐐻𐐲𐑌 𐐲𐐹𐐱𐑌 𐑋𐐴𐑌 𐐲𐑄𐐲𐑉 𐐹𐑊𐐩𐐻𐑅; 𐑁𐐫𐑉 𐐰 𐑋𐐬𐑉 𐐸𐐮𐑅𐐻𐐲𐑉𐐨 𐐹𐐪𐑉𐐻 𐐪𐑉 𐑉𐐮𐐻𐐲𐑌 𐐲𐐹𐐱𐑌 𐑋𐐴𐑌 𐐲𐑄𐐲𐑉 𐐹𐑊𐐩𐐻𐑅. 𐐈𐑌𐐼 𐐲𐐹𐐱𐑌 𐑄𐐨𐑆 𐐌 𐑉𐐴𐐻 𐑄 𐑃𐐮𐑍𐑆 𐐱𐑂 𐑋𐐴 𐑅𐐬𐑊, 𐐰𐑌𐐼 𐑋𐐯𐑌𐐨 𐐱𐑂 𐑄 𐑅𐐿𐑉𐐮𐐹𐐽𐐲𐑉𐑆 𐐸𐐶𐐮𐐽 𐐪𐑉 𐐯𐑌𐑀𐑉𐐩𐑂𐐲𐑌 𐐲𐐹𐐱𐑌 𐑄 𐐹𐑊𐐩𐐻𐑅 𐐱𐑂 𐐺𐑉𐐰𐑅. 𐐙𐐫𐑉 𐑋𐐴 𐑅𐐬𐑊 𐐼𐐨𐑊𐐴𐐻𐐯𐑃 𐐮𐑌 𐑄 𐑅𐐿𐑉𐐮𐐹𐐽𐐲𐑉𐑆, 𐐰𐑌𐐼 𐑋𐐴 𐐸𐐪𐑉𐐻 𐐹𐐱𐑌𐐼𐐲𐑉𐐯𐑃 𐑄𐐯𐑋, 𐐰𐑌𐐼 𐑉𐐴𐐻𐐯𐑃 𐑄𐐯𐑋 𐑁𐐫𐑉 𐑄 𐑊𐐲𐑉𐑌𐐮𐑍 𐐰𐑌𐐼 𐑄 𐐹𐑉𐐱𐑁𐐮𐐻 𐐱𐑂 𐑋𐐴 𐐽𐐮𐑊𐐼𐑉𐐯𐑌. 𐐒𐐨𐐸𐐬𐑊𐐼, 𐑋𐐴 𐑅𐐬𐑊 𐐼𐐨𐑊𐐴𐐻𐐯𐑃 𐐮𐑌 𐑄 𐑃𐐮𐑍𐑆 𐐱𐑂 𐑄 𐐢𐐫𐑉𐐼; 𐐰𐑌𐐼 𐑋𐐴 𐐸𐐪𐑉𐐻 𐐹𐐱𐑌𐐼𐐲𐑉𐐯𐑃 𐐿𐐱𐑌𐐻𐐮𐑌𐐷𐐭𐐰𐑊𐐨 𐐲𐐹𐐱𐑌 𐑄 𐑃𐐮𐑍𐑆 𐐸𐐶𐐮𐐽 𐐌 𐐸𐐰𐑂 𐑅𐐨𐑌 𐐰𐑌𐐼 𐐸𐐲𐑉𐐼. 𐐤𐐯𐑂𐐲𐑉𐑄𐐯𐑊𐐯𐑅, 𐑌𐐱𐐻𐐶𐐮𐑃𐑅𐐻𐐰𐑌𐐼𐐮𐑍 𐑄 𐑀𐑉𐐩𐐻 𐑀𐐳𐐼𐑌𐐯𐑅 𐐱𐑂 𐑄 𐐢𐐫𐑉𐐼, 𐐮𐑌 𐑇𐐬𐐮𐑍 𐑋𐐨 𐐸𐐮𐑆 𐑀𐑉𐐩𐐻 𐐰𐑌𐐼 𐑋𐐪𐑉𐑂𐐯𐑊𐐲𐑅 𐐶𐐲𐑉𐐿𐑅, 𐑋𐐴

𐐸𐐪𐑉𐐻 𐐯𐐿𐑅𐐿𐑊𐐩𐑋𐐯𐑃, 𐐄 𐑉𐐯𐐽𐐯𐐼 𐑋𐐰𐑌 𐑄𐐰𐐻 𐐌 𐐰𐑋; 𐐏𐐩, 𐑋𐐴 𐐸𐐪𐑉𐐻 𐑅𐐱𐑉𐐬𐐯𐑃 𐐺𐐨𐐿𐐫𐑆 𐐱𐑂 𐑋𐐴 𐑁𐑊𐐯𐑇. 𐐣𐐴 𐑅𐐬𐑊 𐑀𐑉𐐨𐑂𐐯𐑃 𐐺𐐨𐐿𐐫𐑆 𐐱𐑂 𐑋𐐴𐑌 𐐮𐑌𐐮𐐿𐐶𐐮𐐻𐐮𐑆. 𐐌 𐐰𐑋 𐐯𐑌𐐿𐐲𐑋𐐹𐐲𐑅𐐻 𐐲𐐺𐐵𐐻 𐐺𐐨𐐿𐐫𐑆 𐐱𐑂 𐑄 𐐻𐐯𐑋𐐻𐐩𐑇𐐲𐑌𐑆 𐐰𐑌𐐼 𐑄 𐑅𐐮𐑌𐑆 𐐸𐐶𐐮𐐽 𐐼𐐭 𐑅𐐬 𐐨𐑆𐐮𐑊𐐨 𐐺𐐨𐑅𐐯𐐻 𐑋𐐨. 𐐈𐑌𐐼 𐐸𐐶𐐯𐑌 𐐌 𐐼𐐨𐑆𐐴𐑉 𐐻𐐭 𐑉𐐨𐐾𐐦𐑅, 𐑋𐐴 𐐸𐐪𐑉𐐻 𐑀𐑉𐐬𐑌𐐯𐑃 𐐺𐐨𐐿𐐫𐑆 𐐱𐑂 𐑋𐐴 𐑅𐐮𐑌𐑆; 𐑌𐐯𐑂𐐲𐑉𐑄𐐯𐑊𐐯𐑅, 𐐌 𐑌𐐬 𐐮𐑌 𐐸𐐭𐑋 𐐌 𐐸𐐰𐑂 𐐻𐑉𐐲𐑅𐐻𐐯𐐼. 𐐣𐐴 𐐘𐐱𐐼 𐐸𐐰𐑃 𐐺𐐮𐑌 𐑋𐐴 𐑅𐐲𐐹𐐬𐑉𐐻; 𐐸𐐨 𐐸𐐰𐑃 𐑊𐐯𐐼 𐑋𐐨 𐑃𐑉𐐭 𐑋𐐴𐑌 𐐰𐑁𐑊𐐮𐐿𐑇𐐲𐑌𐑆 𐐮𐑌 𐑄 𐐶𐐮𐑊𐐼𐐲𐑉𐑌𐐯𐑅; 𐐰𐑌𐐼 𐐸𐐨 𐐸𐐰𐑃 𐐹𐑉𐐨𐑆𐐲𐑉𐑂𐐼 𐑋𐐨 𐐲𐐹𐐱𐑌 𐑄 𐐶𐐫𐐻𐐲𐑉𐑆 𐐱𐑂 𐑄 𐑀𐑉𐐩𐐻 𐐼𐐨𐐹. 𐐐𐐨 𐐸𐐰𐑃 𐑁𐐮𐑊𐐼 𐑋𐐨 𐐶𐐮𐑄 𐐸𐐮𐑆 𐑊𐐲𐑂, 𐐨𐑂𐐲𐑌 𐐲𐑌𐐻𐐭 𐑄 𐐿𐐱𐑌𐑅𐐭𐑋𐐮𐑍 𐐱𐑂 𐑋𐐴 𐑁𐑊𐐯𐑇. 𐐐𐐨 𐐸𐐰𐑃 𐐿𐐱𐑌𐑁𐐵𐑌𐐼𐐯𐐼 𐑋𐐴𐑌 𐐯𐑌𐐯𐑋𐐨𐑆, 𐐲𐑌𐐻𐐭 𐑄 𐐿𐐫𐑆𐐮𐑍 𐐱𐑂 𐑄𐐯𐑋 𐐻𐐭 𐐿𐐶𐐩𐐿 𐐺𐐨𐑁𐐬𐑉 𐑋𐐨. 𐐒𐐨𐐸𐐬𐑊𐐼, 𐐸𐐨 𐐸𐐰𐑃 𐐸𐐲𐑉𐐼 𐑋𐐴 𐐿𐑉𐐴 𐐺𐐴 𐐼𐐩, 𐐰𐑌𐐼 𐐸𐐨 𐐸𐐰𐑃 𐑀𐐮𐑂𐐲𐑌 𐑋𐐨 𐑌𐐱𐑊𐐯𐐾 𐐺𐐴 𐑂𐐮𐑈𐐲𐑌𐑆 𐐮𐑌 𐑄 𐑌𐐴𐐻-𐐻𐐴𐑋. 𐐈𐑌𐐼 𐐺𐐴 𐐼𐐩 𐐸𐐰𐑂 𐐌 𐐶𐐰𐐿𐑅𐐻 𐐺𐐬𐑊𐐼 𐐮𐑌 𐑋𐐴𐐻𐐨 𐐹𐑉𐐩𐑉 𐐺𐐨𐑁𐐬𐑉 𐐸𐐮𐑋; 𐐷𐐩, 𐑋𐐴 𐑂𐐦𐑅 𐐸𐐰𐑂 𐐌 𐑅𐐯𐑌𐐻 𐐲𐐹 𐐱𐑌 𐐸𐐴; 𐐰𐑌𐐼 𐐩𐑌𐐾𐐯𐑊𐑆 𐐿𐐩𐑋 𐐼𐐵𐑌 𐐰𐑌𐐼 𐑋𐐮𐑌𐐮𐑅𐐻𐐲𐑉𐐼 𐐲𐑌𐐻𐐭 𐑋𐐨. 𐐈𐑌𐐼 𐐲𐐹𐐱𐑌 𐑄 𐐶𐐮𐑍𐑆 𐐱𐑂 𐐸𐐮𐑆 𐐝𐐹𐐮𐑉𐐮𐐻 𐐸𐐰𐑃 𐑋𐐴 𐐺𐐱𐐼𐐨 𐐺𐐮𐑌 𐐿𐐰𐑉𐐨𐐼 𐐲𐐶𐐩 𐐲𐐹𐐱𐑌 𐐯𐐿𐑅𐐨𐐼𐐮𐑍𐑊𐐨 𐐸𐐴 𐑋𐐵𐑌𐐻𐐩𐑌𐑆. 𐐈𐑌𐐼 𐑋𐐴𐑌 𐐴𐑆 𐐸𐐰𐑂 𐐺𐐨𐐸𐐯𐑊𐐼 𐑀𐑉𐐩𐐻 𐑃𐐮𐑍𐑆; 𐐷𐐩, 𐐨𐑂𐐲𐑌 𐐻𐐭 𐑀𐑉𐐩𐐻 𐑁𐐫𐑉 𐑋𐐰𐑌; 𐑄𐐯𐑉𐑁𐐬𐑉 𐐌 𐐶𐐱𐑆 𐐺𐐮𐐼𐐲𐑌 𐑄𐐰𐐻 𐐌 𐑇𐐳𐐼 𐑌𐐱𐐻 𐑉𐐴𐐻 𐑄𐐯𐑋. 𐐄 𐑄𐐯𐑌, 𐐮𐑁 𐐌 𐐸𐐰𐑂 𐑅𐐨𐑌 𐑅𐐬 𐑀𐑉𐐩𐐻 𐑃𐐮𐑍𐑆, 𐐮𐑁 𐑄 𐐢𐐫𐑉𐐼 𐐮𐑌 𐐸𐐮𐑆 𐐿𐐱𐑌𐐼𐐯𐑅𐐯𐑌𐑇𐐲𐑌 𐐲𐑌𐐻𐐭 𐑄 𐐽𐐮𐑊𐐼𐑉𐐯𐑌 𐐱𐑂 𐑋𐐯𐑌, 𐐸𐐰𐑃 𐑂𐐮𐑆𐐮𐐻𐐯𐐼 𐑋𐐯𐑌 𐐮𐑌 𐑅𐐬 𐑋𐐲𐐽 𐑋𐐲𐑉𐑅𐐨, 𐐸𐐶𐐴 𐑇𐐳𐐼 𐑋𐐴 𐐸𐐪𐑉𐐻 𐐶𐐨𐐹, 𐐰𐑌𐐼 𐑋𐐴 𐑅𐐬𐑊 𐑊𐐮𐑍𐑀𐐲𐑉 𐐮𐑌 𐑄 𐑂𐐰𐑊𐐨 𐐱𐑂 𐑅𐐱𐑉𐐬, 𐐰𐑌𐐼 𐑋𐐴 𐑁𐑊𐐯𐑇 𐐶𐐩𐑅𐐻 𐐲𐐶𐐩, 𐐰𐑌𐐼 𐑋𐐴 𐑅𐐻𐑉𐐯𐑍𐑃 𐑅𐑊𐐰𐐿𐐲𐑌, 𐐺𐐨𐐿𐐫𐑆 𐐱𐑂 𐑋𐐴𐑌 𐐰𐑁𐑊𐐮𐐿𐑇𐐲𐑌𐑆? 𐐈𐑌𐐼 𐐸𐐶𐐴 𐑇𐐳𐐼 𐐌 𐐷𐐨𐑊𐐼 𐐻𐐭 𐑅𐐮𐑌, 𐐺𐐨𐐿𐐫𐑆 𐐱𐑂 𐑋𐐴 𐑁𐑊𐐯𐑇? 𐐏𐐩, 𐐸𐐶𐐴 𐑇𐐳𐐼 𐐌 𐑀𐐮𐑂 𐐶𐐩 𐐻𐐭 𐐻𐐯𐑋𐐻𐐩𐑇𐐲𐑌𐑆, 𐑄𐐰𐐻 𐑄 𐐨𐑂𐐲𐑊 𐐶𐐲𐑌 𐐸𐐰𐑂 𐐹𐑊𐐩𐑅 𐐮𐑌 𐑋𐐴 𐐸𐐪𐑉𐐻, 𐐻𐐭 𐐼𐐯𐑅𐐻𐑉𐐦 𐑋𐐴 𐐹𐐨𐑅 𐐰𐑌𐐼 𐐰𐑁𐑊𐐮𐐿𐐻 𐑋𐐴 𐑅𐐬𐑊? 𐐐𐐶𐐴 𐐰𐑋 𐐌 𐐰𐑍𐑀𐑉𐐨 𐐺𐐨𐐿𐐫𐑆 𐐱𐑂 𐑋𐐴𐑌 𐐯𐑌𐐯𐑋𐐨?

6. 𐐊𐐶𐐩𐐿, 𐑋𐐴 𐑅𐐬𐑊! 𐐤𐐬 𐑊𐐱𐑍𐑀𐐲𐑉 𐐼𐑉𐐭𐐹 𐐮𐑌 𐑅𐐮𐑌. 𐐡𐐨𐐾𐐦𐑅, 𐐄 𐑋𐐴 𐐸𐐪𐑉𐐻, 𐐰𐑌𐐼 𐑀𐐮𐑂 𐐹𐑊𐐩𐑅 𐑌𐐬 𐑋𐐬𐑉 𐑁𐐫𐑉 𐑄 𐐯𐑌𐐯𐑋𐐨 𐐱𐑂 𐑋𐐴 𐑅𐐬𐑊. 𐐔𐐭 𐑌𐐱𐐻 𐐰𐑍𐑀𐐲𐑉 𐐲𐑀𐐯𐑌 𐐺𐐨𐐿𐐫𐑆 𐐱𐑂 𐑋𐐴𐑌 𐐯𐑌𐐯𐑋𐐨𐑆. 𐐔𐐭 𐑌𐐱𐐻 𐑅𐑊𐐰𐐿𐐲𐑌 𐑋𐐴 𐑅𐐻𐑉𐐯𐑍𐑃, 𐐺𐐨𐐿𐐫𐑆 𐐱𐑂 𐑋𐐴𐑌 𐐰𐑁𐑊𐐮𐐿𐑇𐐲𐑌𐑆. 𐐡𐐨𐐾𐐦𐑅, 𐐄 𐑋𐐴 𐐸𐐪𐑉𐐻, 𐐰𐑌𐐼 𐐿𐑉𐐴 𐐲𐑌𐐻𐐭 𐑄 𐐢𐐫𐑉𐐼, 𐐰𐑌𐐼 𐑅𐐩, 𐐄 𐐢𐐫𐑉𐐼, 𐐌 𐐶𐐮𐑊 𐐹𐑉𐐩𐑆 𐑄𐐨 𐑁𐐫𐑉𐐯𐑂𐐲𐑉; 𐐷𐐩, 𐑋𐐴 𐑅𐐬𐑊 𐐶𐐮𐑊 𐑉𐐨𐐾𐐦𐑅 𐐮𐑌 𐑄𐐨, 𐑋𐐴 𐐘𐐱𐐼, 𐐰𐑌𐐼 𐑄 𐑉𐐱𐐿 𐐱𐑂 𐑋𐐴 𐑅𐐰𐑊𐑂𐐩𐑇𐐲𐑌. 𐐄 𐐢𐐫𐑉𐐼, 𐐶𐐮𐑊𐐻 𐑄𐐵 𐑉𐐨𐐼𐐨𐑋 𐑋𐐴 𐑅𐐬𐑊? 𐐎𐐮𐑊𐐻 𐑄𐐵 𐐼𐐨𐑊𐐮𐑂𐐲𐑉 𐑋𐐨 𐐵𐐻 𐐱𐑂 𐑄 𐐸𐐰𐑌𐐼𐑆 𐐱𐑂 𐑋𐐴𐑌 𐐯𐑌𐐯𐑋𐐨𐑆? 𐐎𐐮𐑊𐐻 𐑄𐐵 𐑋𐐩𐐿 𐑋𐐨 𐑄𐐰𐐻 𐐌 𐑋𐐩 𐑇𐐩𐐿 𐐰𐐻 𐑄 𐐰𐐹𐐨𐑉𐐲𐑌𐑅 𐐱𐑂 𐑅𐐮𐑌? 𐐣𐐩 𐑄 𐑀𐐩𐐻𐑅 𐐱𐑂 𐐸𐐯𐑊 𐐺𐐨 𐑇𐐲𐐻 𐐿𐐱𐑌𐐻𐐮𐑌𐐷𐐭𐐰𐑊𐐨 𐐺𐐨𐑁𐐬𐑉 𐑋𐐨, 𐐺𐐨𐐿𐐫𐑆 𐑄𐐰𐐻 𐑋𐐴 𐐸𐐪𐑉𐐻 𐐮𐑆 𐐺𐑉𐐬𐐿𐐲𐑌 𐐰𐑌𐐼 𐑋𐐴 𐑅𐐹𐐮𐑉𐐮𐐻 𐐮𐑆 𐐿𐐱𐑌𐐻𐑉𐐴𐐻? 𐐄 𐐢𐐫𐑉𐐼, 𐐶𐐮𐑊𐐻 𐑄𐐵 𐑌𐐱𐐻 𐑇𐐲𐐻 𐑄 𐑀𐐩𐐻𐑅 𐐱𐑂 𐑄𐐴 𐑉𐐴𐐽𐐲𐑅𐑌𐐯𐑅 𐐺𐐨𐑁𐐬𐑉 𐑋𐐨, 𐑄𐐰𐐻 𐐌 𐑋𐐩 𐐶𐐫𐐿 𐐮𐑌 𐑄 𐐹𐐪𐑃 𐐱𐑂 𐑄 𐑊𐐬 𐑂𐐰𐑊𐐨, 𐑄𐐰𐐻 𐐌 𐑋𐐩 𐐺𐐨 𐑅𐐻𐑉𐐮𐐿𐐻 𐐮𐑌 𐑄 𐐹𐑊𐐩𐑌 𐑉𐐬𐐼? 𐐄 𐐢𐐫𐑉𐐼, 𐐶𐐮𐑊𐐻 𐑄𐐵 𐐯𐑌𐑅𐐲𐑉𐐿𐐲𐑊 𐑋𐐨 𐐲𐑉𐐵𐑌𐐼 𐐮𐑌 𐑄 𐑉𐐬𐐺 𐐱𐑂 𐑄𐐴 𐑉𐐴𐐽𐐲𐑅𐑌𐐯𐑅? 𐐄 𐐢𐐫𐑉𐐼, 𐐶𐐮𐑊𐐻 𐑄𐐵 𐑋𐐩𐐿 𐐲 𐐶𐐩 𐑁𐐫𐑉 𐑋𐐴𐑌 𐐯𐑅𐐿𐐩𐐹 𐐺𐐨𐑁𐐬𐑉 𐑋𐐴𐑌 𐐯𐑌𐐯𐑋𐐨𐑆? 𐐎𐐮𐑊𐐻 𐑄𐐵 𐑋𐐩𐐿 𐑋𐐴 𐐹𐐪𐑃 𐑅𐐻𐑉𐐩𐐻 𐐺𐐨𐑁𐐬𐑉 𐑋𐐨? 𐐎𐐮𐑊𐐻 𐑄𐐵 𐑌𐐱𐐻 𐐹𐑊𐐩𐑅 𐐲 𐑅𐐻𐐲𐑋𐐺𐑊𐐮𐑍 𐐺𐑊𐐱𐐿 𐐮𐑌 𐑋𐐴 𐐶𐐩? 𐐒𐐲𐐻 𐑄𐐰𐐻 𐑄𐐵 𐐶𐐳𐐼𐑅𐐻 𐐿𐑊𐐨𐑉 𐑋𐐴 𐐶𐐩 𐐺𐐨𐑁𐐬𐑉 𐑋𐐨, 𐐰𐑌𐐼 𐐸𐐯𐐾 𐑌𐐱𐐻 𐐲𐐹 𐑋𐐴 𐐶𐐩, 𐐺𐐲𐐻 𐑄 𐐶𐐩𐑆 𐐱𐑂 𐑋𐐴𐑌 𐐯𐑌𐐯𐑋𐐨. 𐐄 𐐢𐐫𐑉𐐼, 𐐌 𐐸𐐰𐑂 𐐻𐑉𐐲𐑅𐐻𐐯𐐼 𐐮𐑌 𐑄𐐨, 𐐰𐑌𐐼 𐐌 𐐶𐐮𐑊 𐐻𐑉𐐲𐑅𐐻 𐐮𐑌 𐑄𐐨 𐑁𐐫𐑉𐐯𐑂𐐲𐑉. 𐐌 𐐶𐐮𐑊 𐑌𐐱𐐻 𐐹𐐳𐐻 𐑋𐐴 𐐻𐑉𐐲𐑅𐐻 𐐮𐑌 𐑄 𐐪𐑉𐑋 𐐱𐑂 𐑁𐑊𐐯𐑇; 𐑁𐐫𐑉 𐐌 𐑌𐐬 𐑄𐐰𐐻 𐐿𐐲𐑉𐑅𐐯𐐼 𐐮𐑆 𐐸𐐨 𐑄𐐰𐐻 𐐹𐐳𐐻𐐯𐑃 𐐸𐐮𐑆 𐐻𐑉𐐲𐑅𐐻 𐐮𐑌 𐑄 𐐪𐑉𐑋 𐐱𐑂 𐑁𐑊𐐯𐑇. 𐐏𐐩, 𐐿𐐲𐑉𐑅𐐯𐐼 𐐮𐑆 𐐸𐐨 𐑄𐐰𐐻 𐐹𐐳𐐻𐐯𐑃 𐐸𐐮𐑆 𐐻𐑉𐐲𐑅𐐻 𐐮𐑌 𐑋𐐰𐑌, 𐐫𐑉 𐑋𐐩𐐿𐐯𐑃 𐑁𐑊𐐯𐑇 𐐸𐐮𐑆 𐐪𐑉𐑋. 𐐏𐐩, 𐐌 𐑌𐐬 𐑄𐐰𐐻 𐐘𐐱𐐼 𐐶𐐮𐑊 𐑀𐐮𐑂 𐑊𐐮𐐺𐐲𐑉𐐲𐑊𐐨 𐐻𐐭 𐐸𐐮𐑋 𐑄𐐰𐐻 𐐰𐑅𐐿𐐯𐑃. 𐐏𐐩, 𐑋𐐴 𐐘𐐱𐐼 𐐶𐐮𐑊 𐑀𐐮𐑂 𐑋𐐨, 𐐮𐑁 𐐌 𐐰𐑅𐐿 𐑌𐐱𐐻 𐐲𐑋𐐮𐑅; 𐑄𐐯𐑉𐑁𐐬𐑉 𐐌 𐐶𐐮𐑊 𐑊𐐮𐑁𐐻 𐐲𐐹 𐑋𐐴 𐑂𐐦𐑅 𐐲𐑌𐐻𐐭 𐑄𐐨; 𐐷𐐩, 𐐌 𐐶𐐮𐑊 𐐿𐑉𐐴 𐐲𐑌𐐻𐐭 𐑄𐐨, 𐑋𐐴 𐐘𐐱𐐼, 𐑄 𐑉𐐱𐐿 𐐱𐑂 𐑋𐐴 𐑉𐐴𐐽𐐲𐑅𐑌𐐯𐑅. 𐐒𐐨𐐸𐐬𐑊𐐼, 𐑋𐐴 𐑂𐐦𐑅 𐑇𐐰𐑊 𐑁𐐫𐑉𐐯𐑂𐐲𐑉 𐐰𐑅𐐯𐑌𐐼 𐐲𐐹 𐐲𐑌𐐻𐐭 𐑄𐐨, 𐑋𐐴 𐑉𐐱𐐿 𐐰𐑌𐐼 𐑋𐐴𐑌 𐐯𐑂𐐲𐑉𐑊𐐰𐑅𐐻𐐮𐑍 𐐘𐐱𐐼. 𐐁𐑋𐐯𐑌.

𐐗𐐈𐐑𐐓𐐊𐐡 IV.

1. 𐐒𐐨𐐸𐐬𐑊𐐼, 𐐮𐐻 𐐿𐐩𐑋 𐐻𐐭 𐐹𐐰𐑅 𐑄𐐰𐐻 𐐌, 𐐤𐐨𐑁𐐴, 𐐼𐐮𐐼 𐐿𐑉𐐴 𐑋𐐲𐐽 𐐲𐑌𐐻𐐭 𐑄 𐐢𐐫𐑉𐐼 𐑋𐐴 𐐘𐐱𐐼, 𐐺𐐨𐐿𐐫𐑆 𐐲𐑂 𐑄 𐐰𐑍𐑀𐐲𐑉 𐐲𐑂 𐑋𐐴 𐐺𐑉𐐯𐑄𐑉𐐯𐑌. 𐐒𐐲𐐻 𐐺𐐨𐐸𐐬𐑊𐐼, 𐑄𐐩𐑉 𐐰𐑍𐑀𐐲𐑉 𐐼𐐮𐐼 𐐮𐑌𐐿𐑉𐐨𐑅 𐐰𐑀𐐯𐑌𐑅𐐻 𐑋𐐨; 𐐮𐑌𐑅𐐬𐑋𐐲𐐽 𐑄𐐰𐐻 𐑄𐐩 𐐼𐐮𐐼 𐑅𐐨𐐿 𐐻𐐭 𐐻𐐩𐐿 𐐰𐐶𐐩 𐑋𐐴 𐑊𐐴𐑁. 𐐏𐐩, 𐑄𐐩 𐐼𐐮𐐼 𐑋𐐲𐑉𐑋𐐲𐑉 𐐰𐑀𐐯𐑌𐑅𐐻 𐑋𐐨, 𐑅𐐩𐐮𐑍: 𐐍𐑉 𐐷𐐲𐑍𐑀𐐲𐑉 𐐺𐑉𐐲𐑄𐐲𐑉 𐑃𐐮𐑍𐐿𐑅 𐐻𐐭 𐑉𐐭𐑊 𐐬𐑂𐐲𐑉 𐐲𐑅; 𐐰𐑌𐐼 𐐶𐐨 𐐸𐐰𐑂 𐐸𐐰𐐼 𐑋𐐲𐐽 𐐻𐑉𐐴𐐲𐑊 𐐺𐐨𐐿𐐫𐑆 𐐲𐑂 𐐸𐐮𐑋; 𐐸𐐶𐐩𐑉𐑁𐐬𐑉, 𐑌𐐵 𐑊𐐯𐐻 𐐲𐑅 𐑅𐑊𐐩 𐐸𐐮𐑋, 𐑄𐐰𐐻 𐐶𐐨 𐑋𐐩 𐑌𐐱𐐻 𐐺𐐨 𐐰𐑁𐑊𐐮𐐿𐐻𐐯𐐼 𐑋𐐬𐑉 𐐺𐐨𐐿𐐫𐑆 𐐲𐑂 𐐸𐐮𐑆 𐐶𐐲𐑉𐐼𐑆. 𐐙𐐫𐑉 𐐺𐐨𐐸𐐬𐑊𐐼, 𐐶𐐨 𐐶𐐮𐑊 𐑌𐐱𐐻 𐐸𐐰𐑂 𐐸𐐮𐑋 𐐻𐐭 𐐺𐐨 𐐵𐑉 𐑉𐐭𐑊𐐲𐑉; 𐑁𐐫𐑉 𐐮𐐻 𐐺𐐨𐑊𐐫𐑍𐑆 𐐲𐑌𐐻𐐭 𐐲𐑅, 𐐸𐐭 𐐪𐑉 𐑄 𐐯𐑊𐐼𐐲𐑉 𐐺𐑉𐐯𐑄𐑉𐐯𐑌, 𐐻𐐭 𐑉𐐭𐑊 𐐬𐑂𐐲𐑉 𐑄𐐮𐑅 𐐹𐐨𐐹𐑊. 𐐤𐐵 𐐌 𐐼𐐭 𐑌𐐱𐐻 𐑉𐐴𐐻 𐐲𐐹𐐱𐑌 𐑄𐐨𐑆 𐐹𐑊𐐩𐐻𐑅 𐐫𐑊 𐑄 𐐶𐐲𐑉𐐼𐑆 𐐸𐐶𐐮𐐽 𐑄𐐩 𐑋𐐲𐑉𐑋𐐲𐑉𐐼 𐐰𐑀𐐯𐑌𐑅𐐻 𐑋𐐨. 𐐒𐐲𐐻 𐐮𐐻 𐑅𐐲𐑁𐐴𐑅𐐯𐑃 𐑋𐐨 𐐻𐐭 𐑅𐐩, 𐑄𐐰𐐻 𐑄𐐩 𐐼𐐮𐐼 𐑅𐐨𐐿 𐐻𐐭 𐐻𐐩𐐿 𐐰𐐶𐐩 𐑋𐐴 𐑊𐐴𐑁.

2. 𐐈𐑌𐐼 𐐮𐐻 𐐿𐐩𐑋 𐐻𐐭 𐐹𐐰𐑅 𐑄𐐰𐐻 𐑄 𐐢𐐫𐑉𐐼 𐐼𐐮𐐼 𐐶𐐫𐑉𐑌 𐑋𐐨, 𐑄𐐰𐐻 𐐌, 𐐤𐐨𐑁𐐴, 𐑇𐐳𐐼 𐐼𐐨𐐹𐐪𐑉𐐻 𐑁𐑉𐐱𐑋 𐑄𐐯𐑋, 𐐰𐑌𐐼 𐑁𐑊𐐨 𐐮𐑌𐐻𐐭 𐑄 𐐶𐐮𐑊𐐼𐐲𐑉𐑌𐐯𐑅, 𐐰𐑌𐐼 𐐫𐑊 𐑄𐐬𐑆 𐐸𐐭 𐐶𐐳𐐼 𐑀𐐬 𐐶𐐮𐑄 𐑋𐐨. 𐐐𐐶𐐩𐑉𐑁𐐬𐑉, 𐐮𐐻 𐐿𐐩𐑋 𐐻𐐭 𐐹𐐰𐑅 𐑄𐐰𐐻 𐐌, 𐐤𐐨𐑁𐐴, 𐐼𐐮𐐼 𐐻𐐩𐐿 𐑋𐐴 𐑁𐐰𐑋𐐮𐑊𐐮, 𐐰𐑌𐐼 𐐫𐑊𐑅𐐬 𐐞𐐬𐑉𐐰𐑋 𐐰𐑌𐐼 𐐸𐐮𐑆 𐑁𐐰𐑋𐐮𐑊𐐮, 𐐰𐑌𐐼 𐐝𐐰𐑋, 𐑋𐐴𐑌 𐐯𐑊𐐼𐐲𐑉 𐐺𐑉𐐲𐑄𐐲𐑉, 𐐰𐑌𐐼 𐐸𐐮𐑆 𐑁𐐰𐑋𐐮𐑊𐐮, 𐐰𐑌𐐼 𐐖𐐩𐐿𐐲𐐺 𐐰𐑌𐐼 𐐖𐐬𐑆𐐯𐑁, 𐑋𐐴 𐐷𐐲𐑍𐑀𐐲𐑉 𐐺𐑉𐐯𐑄𐑉𐐯𐑌, 𐐰𐑌𐐼 𐐫𐑊𐑅𐐬 𐑋𐐴 𐑅𐐮𐑅𐐻𐐲𐑉𐑆, 𐐰𐑌𐐼 𐐫𐑊 𐑄𐐬𐑆 𐐸𐐭 𐐶𐐳𐐼 𐑀𐐬 𐐶𐐮𐑄 𐑋𐐨. 𐐈𐑌𐐼 𐐫𐑊 𐑄𐐬𐑆 𐐸𐐭 𐐶𐐳𐐼 𐑀𐐬 𐐶𐐮𐑄 𐑋𐐨 𐐶𐐲𐑉 𐑄𐐬𐑆 𐐸𐐭 𐐺𐐨𐑊𐐨𐑂𐐼 𐐮𐑌 𐑄 𐐶𐐫𐑉𐑌𐐮𐑍𐑆 𐐰𐑌𐐼 𐑄 𐑉𐐯𐑂𐐯𐑊𐐩𐑇𐐲𐑌𐑆 𐐲𐑂 𐐘𐐱𐐼; 𐐸𐐶𐐩𐑉𐑁𐐬𐑉 𐑄𐐩 𐐼𐐮𐐼 𐐸𐐪𐑉𐐿𐐯𐑌 𐐲𐑌𐐻𐐭 𐑋𐐴 𐐶𐐲𐑉𐐼𐑆. 𐐈𐑌𐐼 𐐶𐐨 𐐼𐐮𐐼 𐐻𐐩𐐿 𐐵𐑉 𐐻𐐯𐑌𐐻𐑅 𐐰𐑌𐐼 𐐸𐐶𐐱𐐻𐑅𐐬-𐐯𐑂𐐲𐑉 𐑃𐐮𐑍𐑆 𐐶𐐲𐑉 𐐹𐐱𐑅𐐮𐐺𐑊 𐑁𐐫𐑉 𐐲𐑅, 𐐰𐑌𐐼 𐐼𐐮𐐼 𐐾𐐲𐑉𐑌𐐨 𐐮𐑌 𐑄 𐐶𐐮𐑊𐐼𐐲𐑉𐑌𐐯𐑅 𐑁𐐫𐑉 𐑄 𐑅𐐹𐐩𐑅 𐐲𐑂 𐑋𐐯𐑌𐐨 𐐼𐐩𐑆. 𐐈𐑌𐐼 𐐰𐑁𐐻𐐲𐑉 𐐶𐐨 𐐸𐐰𐐼 𐐾𐐲𐑉𐑌𐐨𐐼 𐑁𐐫𐑉 𐑄 𐑅𐐹𐐩𐑅 𐐲𐑂 𐑋𐐯𐑌𐐨 𐐼𐐩𐑆, 𐐶𐐨 𐐼𐐮𐐼 𐐹𐐮𐐽 𐐵𐑉 𐐻𐐯𐑌𐐻𐑅. 𐐈𐑌𐐼 𐑋𐐴 𐐹𐐨𐐹𐑊 𐐶𐐳𐐼 𐑄𐐰𐐻 𐐶𐐨 𐑇𐐳𐐼 𐐿𐐫𐑊 𐑄 𐑌𐐩𐑋 𐐲𐑂 𐑄 𐐹𐑊𐐩𐑅 𐐤𐐨𐑁𐐴; 𐐸𐐶𐐩𐑉𐑁𐐬𐑉 𐐶𐐨 𐐼𐐮𐐼 𐐿𐐫𐑊 𐐮𐐻 𐐤𐐨𐑁𐐴. 𐐈𐑌𐐼 𐐫𐑊 𐑄𐐬𐑆 𐐸𐐭 𐐶𐐲𐑉 𐐶𐐮𐑄 𐑋𐐨, 𐐼𐐮𐐼 𐐻𐐩𐐿 𐐲𐐹𐐱𐑌 𐑄𐐯𐑋 𐐻𐐭 𐐿𐐫𐑊 𐑄𐐯𐑋𐑅𐐯𐑊𐑂𐑆 𐑄 𐐹𐐨𐐹𐑊 𐐲𐑂 𐐤𐐨𐑁𐐴. 𐐈𐑌𐐼 𐐶𐐨 𐐼𐐮𐐼 𐐱𐐺𐑆𐐲𐑉𐑂 𐐻𐐭 𐐿𐐨𐐹 𐑄 𐐾𐐲𐐾𐑋𐐯𐑌𐐻𐑅, 𐐰𐑌𐐼 𐑄 𐑅𐐻𐐰𐐻𐐧𐐻𐑅, 𐐰𐑌𐐼 𐑄 𐐿𐐱𐑋𐐰𐑌𐐼𐑋𐐯𐑌𐐻𐑅 𐐲𐑂 𐑄 𐐢𐐫𐑉𐐼 𐐮𐑌 𐐫𐑊 𐑃𐐮𐑍𐑆, 𐐰𐐿𐐫𐑉𐐼𐐮𐑍 𐐻𐐭 𐑄 𐑊𐐫 𐐲𐑂 𐐣𐐬𐑆𐐯𐑆. 𐐈𐑌𐐼 𐑄 𐐢𐐫𐑉𐐼 𐐶𐐱𐑆 𐐶𐐮𐑄 𐐲𐑅; 𐐰𐑌𐐼 𐐶𐐨 𐐼𐐮𐐼 𐐹𐑉𐐱𐑅𐐹𐐲𐑉 𐐯𐐿𐑅𐐨𐐼𐐮𐑍𐑊𐐨; 𐑁𐐫𐑉 𐐶𐐨 𐐼𐐮𐐼 𐑅𐐬 𐑅𐐨𐐼, 𐐰𐑌𐐼 𐐶𐐨 𐐼𐐮𐐼 𐑉𐐨𐐹 𐐰𐑀𐐯𐑌 𐐮𐑌 𐐰𐐺𐐲𐑌𐐼𐐰𐑌𐑅. 𐐈𐑌𐐼 𐐶𐐨 𐐺𐐨𐑀𐐰𐑌 𐐻𐐭 𐑉𐐩𐑆 𐑁𐑊𐐱𐐿𐑅, 𐐰𐑌𐐼 𐐸𐐲𐑉𐐼𐑆, 𐐰𐑌𐐼 𐐰𐑌𐐮𐑋𐐲𐑊𐑆 𐐲𐑂 𐐯𐑂𐐲𐑉𐐨 𐐿𐐴𐑌𐐼. 𐐈𐑌𐐼 𐐌, 𐐤𐐨𐑁𐐴, 𐐸𐐰𐐼 𐐫𐑊𐑅𐐬 𐐺𐑉𐐫𐐻 𐑄 𐑉𐐯𐐿𐐲𐑉𐐼𐑆 𐐸𐐶𐐮𐐽 𐐶𐐲𐑉 𐐯𐑌𐑀𐑉𐐩𐑂𐐯𐑌 𐐲𐐹𐐱𐑌 𐑄 𐐹𐑊𐐩𐐻𐑅 𐐲𐑂 𐐺𐑉𐐰𐑅; 𐐰𐑌𐐼 𐐫𐑊𐑅𐐬 𐑄 𐐺𐐫𐑊, 𐐫𐑉 𐐿𐐲𐑋𐐹𐐲𐑅, 𐐸𐐶𐐮𐐽 𐐶𐐱𐑆 𐐹𐑉𐐨𐐹𐐩𐑉𐐼 𐑁𐐫𐑉 𐑋𐐴 𐑁𐐪𐑄𐐲𐑉, 𐐺𐐴 𐑄 𐐸𐐰𐑌𐐼 𐐲𐑂 𐑄 𐐢𐐫𐑉𐐼, 𐐰𐐿𐐫𐑉𐐼𐐮𐑍 𐐻𐐭 𐑄𐐰𐐻 𐐸𐐶𐐮𐐽 𐐮𐑆 𐑉𐐮𐐻𐐯𐑌.

3. 𐐈𐑌𐐼 𐐮𐐻 𐐿𐐩𐑋 𐐻𐐭 𐐹𐐰𐑅 𐑄𐐰𐐻 𐐶𐐨 𐐺𐐨𐑀𐐰𐑌 𐐻𐐭 𐐹𐑉𐐱𐑅𐐹𐐲𐑉 𐐯𐐿𐑅𐐨𐐼𐐮𐑍𐑊𐐨, 𐐰𐑌𐐼 𐐻𐐭 𐑋𐐲𐑊𐐻𐐮𐐹𐑊𐐴 𐐮𐑌 𐑄 𐑊𐐰𐑌𐐼. 𐐈𐑌𐐼 𐐌, 𐐤𐐨𐑁𐐴, 𐐼𐐮𐐼 𐐻𐐩𐐿 𐑄 𐑅𐐬𐑉𐐼 𐐲𐑂 𐐢𐐩𐐺𐐲𐑌, 𐐰𐑌𐐼 𐐰𐑁𐐻𐐲𐑉 𐑄 𐑋𐐰𐑌𐐲𐑉 𐐲𐑂 𐐮𐐻, 𐐼𐐮𐐼 𐑋𐐩𐐿 𐑋𐐯𐑌𐐨 𐑅𐐬𐑉𐐼𐑆, 𐑊𐐯𐑅𐐻 𐐺𐐴 𐐯𐑌𐐨 𐑋𐐨𐑌𐑆 𐑄 𐐹𐐨𐐹𐑊 𐐸𐐭 𐐶𐐲𐑉 𐑌𐐵 𐐿𐐫𐑊𐐼 𐐢𐐩𐑋𐐲𐑌𐐴𐐻𐑅 𐑇𐐳𐐼 𐐿𐐲𐑋 𐐲𐐹𐐱𐑌 𐐲𐑅 𐐰𐑌𐐼 𐐼𐐯𐑅𐐻𐑉𐐦 𐐲𐑅; 𐑁𐐫𐑉 𐐌 𐑌𐐧 𐑄𐐩𐑉 𐐸𐐩𐐻𐑉𐐯𐐼 𐐻𐐬𐑉𐐼𐑆 𐑋𐐨 𐐰𐑌𐐼 𐑋𐐴 𐐽𐐮𐑊𐐼𐑉𐐯𐑌, 𐐰𐑌𐐼 𐑄𐐬𐑆 𐐸𐐭 𐐶𐐲𐑉 𐐿𐐫𐑊𐐼 𐑋𐐴 𐐹𐐨𐐹𐑊. 𐐈𐑌𐐼 𐐌 𐐼𐐮𐐼 𐐻𐐨𐐽 𐑋𐐴 𐐹𐐨𐐹𐑊 𐐻𐐭 𐐺𐐮𐑊𐐼 𐐺𐐮𐑊𐐼𐐮𐑍𐑆; 𐐰𐑌𐐼 𐐻𐐭 𐐶𐐲𐑉𐐿 𐐮𐑌 𐐫𐑊 𐑋𐐰𐑌𐐲𐑉 𐐲𐑂 𐐶𐐳𐐼, 𐐰𐑌𐐼 𐐲𐑂 𐐴𐐲𐑉𐑌, 𐐰𐑌𐐼 𐐲𐑂 𐐿𐐱𐐹𐐲𐑉, 𐐰𐑌𐐼 𐐲𐑂 𐐺𐑉𐐰𐑅, 𐐰𐑌𐐼 𐐲𐑂 𐑅𐐻𐐨𐑊, 𐐰𐑌𐐼 𐐲𐑂 𐑀𐐬𐑊𐐼, 𐐰𐑌𐐼 𐐲𐑂 𐑅𐐮𐑊𐑂𐐲𐑉, 𐐰𐑌𐐼 𐐲𐑂 𐐹𐑉𐐯𐑇𐐲𐑅 𐐬𐑉𐑆, 𐐸𐐶𐐮𐐽 𐐶𐐲𐑉 𐐮𐑌 𐑀𐑉𐐩𐐻 𐐰𐐺𐐲𐑌-𐐼𐐰𐑌𐑅. 𐐈𐑌𐐼 𐐌, 𐐤𐐨𐑁𐐴, 𐐼𐐮𐐼 𐐺𐐮𐑊𐐼 𐐰 𐐻𐐯𐑋𐐹𐑊; 𐐰𐑌𐐼 𐐌 𐐼𐐮𐐼 𐐿𐐱𐑌𐑅𐐻𐑉𐐲𐐿𐐻 𐐮𐐻 𐐰𐑁𐐻𐐲𐑉 𐑄 𐑋𐐰𐑌𐐲𐑉 𐐲𐑂 𐑄 𐐻𐐯𐑋𐐹𐑊 𐐲𐑂 𐐝𐐱𐑊𐐬𐑋𐐲𐑌, 𐑅𐐩𐑂 𐐮𐐻 𐐶𐐲𐑉 𐑌𐐱𐐻 𐐺𐐮𐑊𐐻 𐐲𐑂 𐑅𐐬 𐑋𐐯𐑌𐐨 𐐹𐑉𐐯𐑇𐐲𐑅 𐑃𐐮𐑍𐑆; 𐑁𐐫𐑉 𐑄𐐩 𐐶𐐲𐑉 𐑌𐐱𐐻 𐐻𐐭 𐐺𐐨 𐑁𐐵𐑌𐐼 𐐲𐐹𐐱𐑌 𐑄 𐑊𐐰𐑌𐐼; 𐐸𐐶𐐩𐑉𐑁𐐬𐑉 𐐮𐐻 𐐿𐐳𐐼 𐑌𐐱𐐻 𐐺𐐨 𐐺𐐮𐑊𐐻 𐑊𐐴𐐿 𐐲𐑌𐐻𐐭 𐐝𐐱𐑊𐐬𐑋𐐲𐑌'𐑆 𐐻𐐯𐑋𐐹𐑊. 𐐒𐐲𐐻 𐑄 𐑋𐐰𐑌𐐲𐑉 𐐲𐑂 𐑄 𐐿𐐱𐑌𐑅𐐻𐑉𐐲𐐿𐑇𐐲𐑌 𐐶𐐱𐑆 𐑊𐐴𐐿 𐐲𐑌𐐻𐐭 𐑄 𐐻𐐯𐑋𐐹𐑊 𐐲𐑂 𐐝𐐱𐑊𐐬𐑋𐐲𐑌; 𐐰𐑌𐐼 𐑄 𐐶𐐲𐑉𐐿𐑋𐐰𐑌𐑇𐐮𐐹 𐑄𐐩𐑉𐐱𐑂 𐐶𐐱𐑆 𐐯𐐿𐑅𐐨𐐼𐐮𐑍𐑊𐐨 𐑁𐐴𐑌.

4. 𐐈𐑌𐐼 𐐮𐐻 𐐿𐐩𐑋 𐐻𐐭 𐐹𐐪𐑅 𐑄𐐰𐐻 𐐌, 𐐤𐐨𐑁𐐴, 𐐼𐐮𐐼 𐐿𐐫𐑆 𐑋𐐴 𐐹𐐨𐐹𐑊 𐐻𐐭 𐐺𐐨 𐐮𐑌𐐼𐐲𐑅𐐻𐑉𐐨𐐲𐑅, 𐐰𐑌𐐼 𐐻𐐭 𐑊𐐩𐐺𐐲𐑉 𐐶𐐮𐑄 𐑄𐐩𐑉 𐐸𐐰𐑌𐐼𐑆. 𐐈𐑌𐐼 𐐮𐐻 𐐿𐐩𐑋 𐐻𐐭 𐐹𐐪𐑅 𐑄𐐰𐐻 𐑄𐐩 𐐶𐐳𐐼 𐑄𐐰𐐻 𐐌 𐑇𐐳𐐼 𐐺𐐨 𐑄𐐩𐑉 𐐿𐐮𐑍. 𐐒𐐲𐐻 𐐌, 𐐤𐐨𐑁𐐴, 𐐶𐐱𐑆 𐐼𐐯𐑆𐐴𐑉𐐲𐑅 𐑄𐐰𐐻 𐑄𐐩 𐑇𐐳𐐼 𐐸𐐰𐑂 𐑌𐐬 𐐿𐐮𐑍; 𐑌𐐯𐑂𐐲𐑉𐑄𐐲𐑊𐐯𐑅, 𐐌 𐐼𐐮𐐼 𐑁𐐫𐑉 𐑄𐐯𐑋 𐐰𐐿𐐫𐑉𐐼𐐮𐑍 𐐻𐐭 𐑄𐐰𐐻 𐐸𐐶𐐮𐐽 𐐶𐐱𐑆 𐐮𐑌 𐑋𐐴 𐐹𐐵𐐲𐑉. 𐐈𐑌𐐼 𐐺𐐨𐐸𐐬𐑊𐐼, 𐑄 𐐶𐐲𐑉𐐼𐑆 𐐱𐑂 𐑄 𐐢𐐫𐑉𐐼 𐐸𐐰𐐼 𐐺𐐮𐑌 𐑁𐐳𐑊𐑁𐐮𐑊𐐼 𐐲𐑌𐐻𐐭 𐑋𐐴 𐐺𐑉𐐯𐑄𐑉𐐯𐑌, 𐐸𐐶𐐮𐐽 𐐸𐐨 𐑅𐐹𐐩𐐿 𐐿𐐱𐑌𐑅𐐲𐑉𐑌𐐮𐑍 𐑄𐐯𐑋, 𐑄𐐰𐐻 𐐌 𐑇𐐳𐐼 𐐺𐐨 𐑄𐐩𐑉 𐑉𐐭𐑊𐐲𐑉 𐐰𐑌𐐼 𐑄𐐩𐑉 𐐻𐐨𐐽𐐲𐑉; 𐐸𐐶𐐯𐑉𐑁𐐬𐑉, 𐐌 𐐸𐐰𐐼 𐐺𐐮𐑌 𐑄𐐩𐑉 𐑉𐐭𐑊𐐲𐑉 𐐰𐑌𐐼 𐑄𐐩𐑉 𐐻𐐨𐐽𐐲𐑉, 𐐰𐐿𐐫𐑉𐐼𐐮𐑍 𐐻𐐭 𐑄 𐐿𐐱𐑋𐐰𐑌𐐼𐑋𐐯𐑌𐐻𐑅 𐐱𐑂 𐑄 𐐢𐐫𐑉𐐼, 𐐲𐑌𐐻𐐮𐑊 𐑄 𐐻𐐴𐑋 𐑄𐐩 𐑅𐐫𐐻 𐐻𐐭 𐐻𐐩𐐿 𐐰𐐶𐐩 𐑋𐐴 𐑊𐐴𐑁. 𐐐𐐶𐐯𐑉𐑁𐐬𐑉, 𐑄 𐐶𐐲𐑉𐐼 𐐱𐑂 𐑄 𐐢𐐫𐑉𐐼 𐐶𐐱𐑆 𐑁𐐳𐑊𐑁𐐮𐑊𐐼 𐐸𐐶𐐮𐐽 𐐸𐐨 𐑅𐐹𐐩𐐿 𐐲𐑌𐐻𐐭 𐑋𐐨, 𐑅𐐩𐐮𐑍: 𐐆𐑌𐐰𐑆𐑋𐐲𐐽 𐐰𐑆 𐑄𐐩 𐐶𐐮𐑊 𐑌𐐱𐐻 𐐸𐐪𐑉𐐿𐐲𐑌 𐐲𐑌𐐻𐐭 𐑄𐐴 𐐶𐐲𐑉𐐼𐑆, 𐑄𐐩 𐑇𐐰𐑊 𐐺𐐨 𐐿𐐲𐐻 𐐱𐑁 𐑁𐑉𐐱𐑋 𐑄 𐐹𐑉𐐯𐑆𐐯𐑌𐑅 𐐱𐑂 𐑄 𐐢𐐫𐑉𐐼. 𐐈𐑌𐐼 𐐺𐐨𐐸𐐬𐑊𐐼, 𐑄𐐩 𐐶𐐲𐑉 𐐿𐐲𐐻 𐐱𐑁 𐑁𐑉𐐱𐑋 𐐸𐐮𐑆 𐐹𐑉𐐯𐑆𐐯𐑌𐑅. 𐐈𐑌𐐼 𐐸𐐨 𐐸𐐰𐐼 𐐿𐐫𐑆𐐼 𐑄 𐐿𐐲𐑉𐑅𐐮𐑍 𐐻𐐭 𐐿𐐲𐑋 𐐲𐐹𐐱𐑌 𐑄𐐯𐑋, 𐐷𐐩, 𐐨𐑂𐐲𐑌 𐐰 𐑅𐐬𐑉 𐐿𐐲𐑉𐑅𐐮𐑍, 𐐺𐐨𐐿𐐫𐑆 𐐱𐑂 𐑄𐐩𐑉 𐐮𐑌𐐮𐐿𐐶𐐮𐐻𐐨. 𐐙𐐫𐑉 𐐺𐐨𐐸𐐬𐑊𐐼, 𐑄𐐩 𐐸𐐰𐐼 𐐸𐐪𐑉𐐼𐐲𐑌𐐼 𐑄𐐩𐑉 𐐸𐐪𐑉𐐻𐑅 𐐰𐑀𐐯𐑌𐑅𐐻 𐐸𐐮𐑋, 𐑄𐐰𐐻 𐑄𐐩 𐐸𐐰𐐼 𐐺𐐨𐐿𐐲𐑋 𐑊𐐴𐐿 𐐲𐑌𐐻𐐭 𐐰 𐑁𐑊𐐮𐑌𐐻; 𐐸𐐶𐐯𐑉𐑁𐐬𐑉, 𐐰𐑆 𐑄𐐩 𐐶𐐲𐑉 𐐸𐐶𐐴𐐻 𐐰𐑌𐐼 𐐯𐐿𐑅𐐨𐐼𐐮𐑍𐑊𐐨 𐑁𐐩𐑉 𐐰𐑌𐐼 𐐼𐐨𐑊𐐴𐐻𐑅𐐲𐑋, 𐑄𐐰𐐻 𐑄𐐩 𐑋𐐴𐐻 𐑌𐐱𐐻 𐐺𐐨 𐐯𐑌𐐻𐐴𐑅𐐮𐑍 𐐲𐑌𐐻𐐭 𐑋𐐴 𐐹𐐨𐐹𐑊, 𐑄 𐐢𐐫𐑉𐐼 𐐘𐐱𐐼 𐐼𐐮𐐼 𐐿𐐫𐑆 𐐰 𐑅𐐿𐐮𐑌 𐐱𐑂 𐐺𐑊𐐰𐐿𐑌𐐯𐑅 𐐻𐐭 𐐿𐐲𐑋 𐐲𐐹𐐱𐑌 𐑄𐐯𐑋. 𐐈𐑌𐐼 𐑄𐐲𐑅 𐑅𐐯𐑃 𐑄 𐐢𐐫𐑉𐐼 𐐘𐐱𐐼, 𐐌 𐐶𐐮𐑊 𐐿𐐫𐑆 𐑄𐐰𐐻 𐑄𐐩 𐑇𐐰𐑊 𐐺𐐨 𐑊𐐬𐑄𐑅𐐲𐑋 𐐲𐑌𐐻𐐭 𐑄𐐴 𐐹𐐨𐐹𐑊, 𐑅𐐩𐑂 𐑄𐐩 𐑇𐐰𐑊 𐑉𐐨𐐹𐐯𐑌𐐻 𐐱𐑂 𐑄𐐩𐑉 𐐮𐑌𐐮𐐿𐐶𐐮𐐻𐐨𐑆. 𐐈𐑌𐐼 𐐿𐐲𐑉𐑅𐐯𐐼 𐑇𐐰𐑊 𐐺𐐨 𐑄 𐑅𐐨𐐼 𐐱𐑂 𐐸𐐮𐑋 𐑄𐐰𐐻 𐑋𐐮𐐿𐑅𐐯𐑃 𐐶𐐮𐑄 𐑄𐐩𐑉 𐑅𐐨𐐼; 𐑁𐐫𐑉 𐑄𐐩 𐑇𐐰𐑊 𐐺𐐨 𐐿𐐲𐑉𐑅𐐯𐐼 𐐨𐑂𐐲𐑌 𐐶𐐮𐑄 𐑄 𐑅𐐩𐑋 𐐿𐐲𐑉𐑅𐐮𐑍. 𐐈𐑌𐐼 𐑄 𐐢𐐫𐑉𐐼 𐑅𐐹𐐩𐐿 𐐮𐐻, 𐐰𐑌𐐼 𐐮𐐻 𐐶𐐱𐑆 𐐼𐐲𐑌. 𐐈𐑌𐐼 𐐺𐐨𐐿𐐫𐑆 𐐱𐑂 𐑄𐐩𐑉 𐐿𐐲𐑉𐑅𐐮𐑍 𐐸𐐶𐐮𐐽 𐐶𐐱𐑆 𐐲𐐹𐐱𐑌 𐑄𐐯𐑋, 𐑄𐐩 𐐼𐐮𐐼 𐐺𐐨𐐿𐐲𐑋 𐐰𐑌 𐐴𐐼𐑊 𐐹𐐨𐐹𐑊, 𐑁𐐳𐑊 𐐱𐑂 𐑋𐐮𐑅𐐽𐐮𐑁 𐐰𐑌𐐼 𐑅𐐲𐐻𐑊𐐻𐐨, 𐐰𐑌𐐼 𐐼𐐮𐐼 𐑅𐐨𐐿 𐐮𐑌 𐑄 𐐶𐐮𐑊𐐼𐐲𐑉𐑌𐐯𐑅 𐑁𐐫𐑉 𐐺𐐨𐑅𐐻𐑅 𐐱𐑂 𐐹𐑉𐐩. 𐐈𐑌𐐼 𐑄 𐐢𐐫𐑉𐐼 𐐘𐐱𐐼 𐑅𐐯𐐼 𐐲𐑌𐐻𐐭 𐑋𐐨, 𐐜𐐩 𐑇𐐰𐑊 𐐺𐐨 𐐰 𐑅𐐿𐐲𐑉𐑈 𐐲𐑌𐐻𐐭 𐑄𐐴 𐐹𐐨𐐹𐑊, 𐐻𐐭 𐑅𐐻𐐲𐑉 𐑄𐐯𐑋 𐐲𐐹 𐐮𐑌 𐑉𐐨𐑋𐐯𐑋𐐺𐑉𐐲𐑌𐑅 𐐱𐑂 𐑋𐐨; 𐐰𐑌𐐼 𐐮𐑌𐐰𐑆𐑋𐐲𐐽 𐐰𐑆 𐑄𐐩 𐐶𐐮𐑊 𐑌𐐱𐐻 𐑉𐐨𐑋𐐯𐑋𐐺𐐲𐑉 𐑋𐐨, 𐐰𐑌𐐼 𐐸𐐪𐑉𐐿𐐲𐑌 𐐲𐑌𐐻𐐭 𐑋𐐴 𐐶𐐲𐑉𐐼𐑆, 𐑄𐐩 𐑇𐐰𐑊 𐑅𐐿𐐲𐑉𐑈 𐑄𐐯𐑋 𐐨𐑂𐐲𐑌 𐐲𐑌𐐻𐐭 𐐼𐐨𐑅𐐻𐑉𐐲𐐿𐑇𐐲𐑌.

5. 𐐈𐑌𐐼 𐐮𐐻 𐐿𐐩𐑋 𐐻𐐭 𐐹𐐪𐑅 𐑄𐐰𐐻 𐐌, 𐐤𐐨𐑁𐐴, 𐐼𐐮𐐼 𐐿𐐱𐑌𐑅𐐨𐐿𐑉𐐩𐐻 𐐖𐐩𐐿𐐲𐐺 𐐰𐑌𐐼 𐐖𐐬𐑆𐐯𐑁, 𐑄𐐰𐐻 𐑄𐐩 𐑇𐐳𐐼 𐐺𐐨 𐐹𐑉𐐨𐑅𐐻𐑅 𐐰𐑌𐐼 𐐻𐐨𐐽𐐲𐑉𐑆 𐐬𐑂𐐲𐑉 𐑄 𐑊𐐰𐑌𐐼 𐐱𐑂 𐑋𐐴 𐐹𐐨𐐹𐑊. 𐐈𐑌𐐼 𐐮𐐻 𐐿𐐩𐑋 𐐻𐐭 𐐹𐐪𐑅 𐑄𐐰𐐻 𐐶𐐨 𐑊𐐮𐑂𐐼 𐐰𐑁𐐻𐐲𐑉 𐑄 𐑋𐐰𐑌𐐲𐑉 𐐱𐑂 𐐸𐐰𐐹𐐨𐑌𐐯𐑅. 𐐈𐑌𐐼 𐑃𐐲𐑉𐐻𐐨 𐐷𐐨𐑉𐑆 𐐸𐐰𐐼 𐐹𐐪𐑅𐐻 𐐰𐐶𐐩 𐑁𐑉𐐱𐑋 𐑄 𐐻𐐴𐑋 𐐶𐐨 𐑊𐐯𐑁𐐻 𐐖𐐯𐑉𐐭𐑅𐐲𐑊𐐯𐑋. 𐐈𐑌𐐼 𐐌, 𐐤𐐨𐑁𐐴, 𐐸𐐰𐐼 𐐿𐐯𐐹𐐻 𐑄 𐑉𐐯𐐿𐐲𐑉𐐼𐑆 𐐲𐐹𐐱𐑌 𐑋𐐴 𐐹𐑊𐐩𐐻𐑅, 𐐸𐐶𐐮𐐽 𐐌 𐐸𐐰𐐼 𐑋𐐩𐐼, 𐐱𐑂 𐑋𐐴 𐐹𐐨𐐹𐑊 𐑄𐐲𐑅 𐑁𐐪𐑉.

6. 𐐈𐑌𐐼 𐐮𐐻 𐐿𐐩𐑋 𐐻𐐭 𐐹𐐪𐑅 𐑄𐐰𐐻 𐑄 𐐢𐐫𐑉𐐼 𐐘𐐱𐐼 𐑅𐐯𐐼 𐐲𐑌𐐻𐐭 𐑋𐐨, 𐐣𐐩𐐿 𐐲𐑄𐐲𐑉 𐐹𐑊𐐩𐐻𐑅; 𐐰𐑌𐐼 𐑄𐐵 𐑇𐐰𐑊𐐻 𐐯𐑌𐑀𐑉𐐩𐑂𐐲𐑌 𐑋𐐯𐑌𐐨 𐑃𐐮𐑍𐑆 𐐲𐐹𐐱𐑌 𐑄𐐯𐑋 𐐸𐐶𐐮𐐽 𐐪𐑉 𐑀𐐳𐐼 𐐮𐑌 𐑋𐐴 𐑅𐐴𐐻, 𐑁𐐫𐑉 𐑄 𐐹𐑉𐐱𐑁𐐮𐐻 𐐱𐑂 𐑄𐐴 𐐹𐐨𐐹𐑊. 𐐐𐐶𐐯𐑉𐑁𐐬𐑉, 𐐌, 𐐤𐐨𐑁𐐴, 𐐻𐐭 𐐺𐐨 𐐬𐐺𐐨𐐼𐐨𐐯𐑌𐐻 𐐻𐐭 𐑄 𐐿𐐱𐑋𐐰𐑌𐐼𐑋𐐯𐑌𐐻𐑅 𐐱𐑂 𐑄 𐐢𐐫𐑉𐐼, 𐐶𐐯𐑌𐐻 𐐰𐑌𐐼 𐑋𐐩𐐼 𐑄𐐨𐑆 𐐹𐑊𐐩𐐻𐑅 𐐲𐐹𐐱𐑌 𐐸𐐶𐐮𐐽 𐐌 𐐸𐐰𐑂 𐐯𐑌𐑀𐑉𐐩𐑂𐐲𐑌 𐑄𐐨𐑆 𐑃𐐮𐑍𐑆. 𐐈𐑌𐐼 𐐌 𐐯𐑌𐑀𐑉𐐩𐑂𐐼 𐑄𐐰𐐻 𐐸𐐶𐐮𐐽 𐐮𐑆 𐐹𐑊𐐨𐑆𐐮𐑍 𐐲𐑌𐐻𐐭 𐐘𐐱𐐼. 𐐈𐑌𐐼 𐐮𐑁 𐑋𐐴 𐐹𐐨𐐹𐑊 𐐪𐑉 𐐹𐑊𐐨𐑆𐐼 𐐶𐐮𐑄 𐑄 𐑃𐐮𐑍𐑆 𐐱𐑂 𐐘𐐱𐐼, 𐑄𐐩 𐐶𐐮𐑊 𐐺𐐨 𐐹𐑊𐐨𐑆𐐼 𐐶𐐮𐑄 𐑋𐐴𐑌 𐐯𐑌𐑀𐑉𐐩𐑂𐐮𐑍𐑆 𐐸𐐶𐐮𐐽 𐐪𐑉 𐐲𐐹𐐱𐑌 𐑄𐐨𐑆 𐐹𐑊𐐩𐐻𐑅. 𐐈𐑌𐐼 𐐮𐑁 𐑋𐐴 𐐹𐐨𐐹𐑊 𐐼𐐯𐑆𐐴𐑉 𐐻𐐭 𐑌𐐬 𐑄 𐑋𐐬𐑉 𐐹𐐲𐑉𐐻𐐮𐐿𐐷𐐭𐑊𐐲𐑉 𐐹𐐪𐑉𐐻 𐐱𐑂 𐑄 𐐸𐐮𐑅𐐻𐐲𐑉𐐨 𐐱𐑂 𐑋𐐴 𐐹𐐨𐐹𐑊, 𐑄𐐩 𐑋𐐲𐑅𐐻 𐑅𐐲𐑉𐐽 𐑋𐐴𐑌 𐐲𐑄𐐲𐑉 𐐹𐑊𐐩𐐻𐑅. 𐐈𐑌𐐼 𐐮𐐻 𐑅𐐲𐑁𐐴𐑅𐐯𐑃 𐑋𐐨 𐐻𐐭 𐑅𐐩 𐑄𐐰𐐻 𐑁𐐫𐑉𐐻𐐨 𐐷𐐨𐑉𐑆 𐐸𐐰𐐼 𐐹𐐪𐑅𐐻 𐐰𐐶𐐩, 𐐰𐑌𐐼 𐐶𐐨 𐐸𐐰𐐼 𐐫𐑊𐑉𐐯𐐼𐐨 𐐸𐐰𐐼 𐐶𐐫𐑉𐑆 𐐰𐑌𐐼 𐐿𐐱𐑌𐐻𐐯𐑌𐑇𐐲𐑌𐑆 𐐶𐐮𐑄 𐐵𐑉 𐐺𐑉𐐯𐑄𐑉𐐯𐑌.

𐐕𐐰𐐹𐐻𐐲𐑉 V.

1. 𐐜 𐐶𐐲𐑉𐐼𐑆 𐐲𐑂 𐐖𐐩𐐿𐐲𐐺, 𐑄 𐐺𐑉𐐲𐑄𐐲𐑉 𐐲𐑂 𐐤𐐨𐑁𐐴, 𐐸𐐶𐐮𐐽 𐐸𐐨 𐑅𐐹𐐩𐐿 𐐲𐑌𐐻𐐭 𐑄 𐐹𐐨𐐹𐑊 𐐲𐑂 𐐤𐐨𐑁𐐴: 𐐒𐐨𐐸𐐬𐑊𐐼, 𐑋𐐴 𐐺𐐨𐑊𐐲𐑂𐐯𐐼 𐐺𐑉𐐯𐑄𐑉𐐯𐑌, 𐐌 𐐖𐐩𐐿𐐲𐐺, 𐐸𐐰𐑂𐐮𐑍 𐐺𐐨𐑌 𐐿𐐫𐑊𐐼 𐐲𐑂 𐐘𐐱𐐼, 𐐰𐑌𐐼 𐐫𐑉𐐼𐐩𐑌𐐼 𐐰𐑁𐐻𐐲𐑉 𐑄 𐑋𐐰𐑌𐐲𐑉 𐐲𐑂 𐐸𐐮𐑆 𐐸𐐬𐑊𐐨 𐐫𐑉𐐼𐐲𐑉, 𐐰𐑌𐐼 𐐸𐐰𐑂𐐮𐑍 𐐺𐐨𐑌 𐐿𐐱𐑌𐑅𐐯𐐿𐑉𐐩𐐻𐐯𐐼 𐐺𐐴 𐑋𐐴 𐐺𐑉𐐲𐑄𐐲𐑉 𐐤𐐨𐑁𐐴, 𐐲𐑌𐐻𐐭 𐐸𐐭𐑋 𐐷𐐨 𐑊𐐳𐐿 𐑆 𐐩 𐐿𐐮𐑍 𐐫𐑉 𐐩 𐐹𐑉𐐬𐐻𐐯𐐿𐐻𐐲𐑉, 𐐰𐑌𐐼 𐐱𐑌 𐐸𐐭𐑋 𐐷𐐨 𐐼𐐨𐐹𐐯𐑌𐐼 𐑁𐐫𐑉 𐑅𐐩𐑁𐐻𐐨, 𐐺𐐨𐐸𐐬𐑊𐐼 𐐷𐐨 𐑌𐐬 𐑄𐐰𐐻 𐐌 𐐸𐐰𐑂 𐑅𐐹𐐬𐐿𐑌 𐐲𐑌𐐻𐐭 𐐷𐐭 𐐯𐐿𐑅𐐨𐐼𐐮𐑍 𐑋𐐯𐑌𐐨 𐑃𐐮𐑍𐑆; 𐑌𐐯𐑂𐐲𐑉𐑄𐐲𐑊𐐯𐑅, 𐐌 𐑅𐐹𐐨𐐿 𐐲𐑌𐐻𐐭 𐐷𐐭 𐐲𐑀𐐯𐑌; 𐑁𐐫𐑉 𐐌 𐐰𐑋 𐐼𐐨𐑆𐐴𐑉𐐲𐑅 𐑁𐐫𐑉 𐑄 𐐶𐐯𐑊𐑁𐐩𐑉 𐐲𐑂 𐐷𐐬𐑉 𐑅𐐬𐑊𐑆. 𐐏𐐩, 𐑋𐐴𐑌 𐐰𐑍𐑆𐐴𐐯𐐻𐐨 𐐮𐑆 𐑀𐑉𐐩𐐻 𐑁𐐫𐑉 𐐷𐐭; 𐐰𐑌𐐼 𐐷𐐨 𐐷𐐬𐑉𐑅𐐯𐑊𐑂𐑆 𐑌𐐬 𐑄𐐰𐐻 𐐮𐐻 𐐯𐑂𐐲𐑉 𐐸𐐰𐑆 𐐺𐐨𐑌. 𐐙𐐫𐑉 𐐌 𐐸𐐰𐑂 𐐯𐑀𐑆𐐫𐑉𐐻𐐯𐐼 𐐷𐐭 𐐶𐐮𐑄 𐐫𐑊 𐐼𐐮𐑊𐐮𐐾𐐯𐑌𐑅; 𐐰𐑌𐐼 𐐌 𐐸𐐰𐑂 𐐻𐐫𐐻 𐐷𐐭 𐑄 𐐶𐐲𐑉𐐼𐑆 𐐲𐑂 𐑋𐐴 𐑁𐐪𐑄𐐲𐑉; 𐐰𐑌𐐼 𐐌 𐐸𐐰𐑂 𐑅𐐹𐐬𐐿𐑌 𐐲𐑌𐐻𐐭 𐐷𐐭 𐐿𐐱𐑌𐑅𐐲𐑉𐑌𐐮𐑍 𐐫𐑊 𐑃𐐮𐑍𐑆 𐐸𐐶𐐮𐐽 𐐪𐑉 𐑉𐐴𐐻𐑌, 𐑁𐑉𐐱𐑋 𐑄 𐐿𐑉𐐨𐐩𐑇𐐲𐑌 𐐲𐑂 𐑄 𐐶𐐲𐑉𐑊𐐼.

2. 𐐈𐑌𐐼 𐑌𐐵, 𐐺𐐨𐐸𐐬𐑊𐐼, 𐐌 𐐶𐐳𐐼 𐑅𐐹𐐨𐐿 𐐲𐑌𐐻𐐭 𐐷𐐭 𐐿𐐱𐑌𐑅𐐲𐑉𐑌𐐮𐑍 𐑃𐐮𐑍𐑆 𐐸𐐶𐐮𐐽 𐐪𐑉, 𐐰𐑌𐐼 𐐸𐐶𐐮𐐽 𐐪𐑉 𐐻𐐭 𐐿𐐲𐑋; 𐐸𐐶𐐯𐑉𐑁𐐫𐑉, 𐐌 𐐶𐐮𐑊 𐑉𐐨𐐼 𐐷𐐭 𐑄 𐐶𐐲𐑉𐐼𐑆 𐐲𐑂 𐐌𐑆𐐩𐐲. 𐐈𐑌𐐼 𐑄𐐩 𐐪𐑉 𐑄 𐐶𐐲𐑉𐐼𐑆 𐐸𐐶𐐮𐐽 𐑋𐐴 𐐺𐑉𐐲𐑄𐐲𐑉 𐐸𐐰𐑆 𐐼𐐨𐑆𐐴𐑉𐐼 𐑄𐐰𐐻 𐐌 𐑇𐐳𐐼 𐑅𐐹𐐨𐐿 𐐲𐑌𐐻𐐭 𐐷𐐭. 𐐈𐑌𐐼 𐐌 𐑅𐐹𐐨𐐿 𐐲𐑌𐐻𐐭 𐐷𐐭 𐑁𐐫𐑉 𐐷𐐬𐑉 𐑅𐐩𐐿𐑅, 𐑄𐐰𐐻 𐐷𐐨 𐑋𐐩 𐑊𐐲𐑉𐑌 𐐰𐑌𐐼 𐑀𐑊𐐬𐑉𐐮𐑁𐐴 𐑄 𐑌𐐩𐑋 𐐲𐑂 𐐷𐐬𐑉 𐐘𐐱𐐼. 𐐈𐑌𐐼 𐑌𐐵, 𐑄 𐐶𐐲𐑉𐐼𐑆 𐐸𐐶𐐮𐐽 𐐌 𐑇𐐰𐑊 𐑉𐐨𐐼 𐐪𐑉 𐑄𐐩 𐐸𐐶𐐮𐐽 𐐌𐑆𐐩𐐲 𐑅𐐹𐐰𐐿 𐐿𐐱𐑌𐑅𐐲𐑉𐑌𐐮𐑍 𐐫𐑊 𐑄 𐐸𐐵𐑅 𐐲𐑂 𐐆𐑆𐑉𐐩𐐯𐑊; 𐐸𐐶𐐯𐑉𐑁𐐫𐑉, 𐑄𐐩 𐑋𐐩 𐐺𐐨 𐑊𐐴𐐿𐑌𐐯𐐼 𐐲𐑌𐐻𐐭 𐐷𐐭, 𐑁𐐫𐑉 𐐷𐐨 𐐪𐑉 𐐲𐑂 𐑄 𐐸𐐵𐑅 𐐲𐑂 𐐆𐑆𐑉𐐩𐐯𐑊. 𐐈𐑌𐐼 𐑄𐐯𐑉 𐐪𐑉 𐑋𐐯𐑌𐐨 𐑃𐐮𐑍𐑆 𐐸𐐶𐐮𐐽 𐐸𐐰𐑂 𐐺𐐨𐑌 𐑅𐐹𐐬𐐿𐑌 𐐺𐐴 𐐌𐑆𐐩𐐲, 𐐸𐐶𐐮𐐽 𐑋𐐩 𐐺𐐨 𐑊𐐴𐐿𐑌𐐯𐐼 𐐲𐑌𐐻𐐭 𐐷𐐭, 𐐺𐐨𐐿𐐫𐑆 𐐷𐐨 𐐪𐑉 𐐲𐑂 𐑄 𐐸𐐵𐑅 𐐲𐑂 𐐆𐑆𐑉𐐩𐐯𐑊.

3. 𐐈𐑌𐐼 𐑌𐐵, 𐑄𐐨𐑆 𐐪𐑉 𐑄 𐐶𐐲𐑉𐐼𐑆: 𐐜𐐲𐑅 𐑅𐐯𐑃 𐑄 𐐢𐐫𐑉𐐼 𐐘𐐱𐐼: 𐐒𐐨𐐸𐐬𐑊𐐼, 𐐌 𐐶𐐮𐑊 𐑊𐐮𐑁𐐻 𐐲𐐹 𐑋𐐴𐑌 𐐸𐐰𐑌𐐼 𐐻𐐭 𐑄 𐐖𐐯𐑌𐐻𐐴𐑊𐑆, 𐐰𐑌𐐼 𐑅𐐯𐐻 𐐲𐐹 𐑋𐐴 𐑅𐐻𐐰𐑌𐐼𐐲𐑉𐐼 𐐻𐐭 𐑄 𐐹𐐨𐐹𐑊; 𐐰𐑌𐐼 𐑄𐐩 𐑇𐐰𐑊 𐐺𐑉𐐮𐑍 𐑄𐐴 𐑅𐐲𐑌𐑆 𐐮𐑌 𐑄𐐯𐑉 𐐪𐑉𐑋𐑆, 𐐰𐑌𐐼 𐑄𐐴 𐐼𐐫𐐻𐐲𐑉𐑆 𐑇𐐰𐑊 𐐺𐐨 𐐿𐐰𐑉𐐨𐐼 𐐲𐐹𐐱𐑌 𐑄𐐯𐑉 𐑇𐐬𐑊𐐼𐐲𐑉𐑆. 𐐈𐑌𐐼 𐐿𐐮𐑍𐑆 𐑇𐐰𐑊 𐐺𐐨 𐑄𐐴 𐑌𐐲𐑉𐑅𐐮𐑍 𐑁𐐪𐑄𐐲𐑉𐑆, 𐐰𐑌𐐼 𐑄𐐯𐑉 𐐿𐐶𐐨𐑌𐑆 𐑄𐐴 𐑌𐐲𐑉𐑅𐐮𐑍 𐑋𐐲𐑄𐐲𐑉𐑆; 𐑄𐐩 𐑇𐐰𐑊 𐐺𐐵 𐐼𐐵𐑌 𐐻𐐭 𐑄𐐨 𐐶𐐮𐑄 𐑄𐐯𐑉 𐑁𐐩𐑅𐐯𐑆 𐐻𐐭𐐶𐐫𐑉𐐼𐑆 𐑄 𐐲𐑉𐑃, 𐐰𐑌𐐼 𐑊𐐮𐐿 𐐲𐐹 𐑄 𐐼𐐲𐑅𐐻 𐐲𐑂 𐑄𐐴 𐑁𐐨𐐻; 𐐰𐑌𐐼 𐑄𐐵 𐑇𐐰𐑊𐐻 𐑌𐐬 𐑄𐐰𐐻 𐐌 𐐰𐑋 𐑄 𐐢𐐫𐑉𐐼; 𐑁𐐫𐑉 𐑄𐐩 𐑇𐐰𐑊 𐑌𐐱𐐻 𐐺𐐨 𐐲𐑇𐐩𐑋𐐼 𐑄𐐰𐐻 𐐶𐐩𐐻 𐑁𐐫𐑉 𐑋𐐨.

4. 𐐈𐑌𐐼 𐑌𐐵 𐐌, 𐐖𐐩𐐿𐐲𐐺, 𐐶𐐳𐐼 𐑅𐐹𐐨𐐿 𐑅𐐲𐑋𐐸𐐶𐐱𐐻 𐐿𐐱𐑌𐑅𐐲𐑉𐑌𐐮𐑍 𐑄𐐨𐑆 𐐶𐐲𐑉𐐼𐑆: 𐐙𐐫𐑉 𐐺𐐨𐐸𐐬𐑊𐐼, 𐑄 𐐢𐐫𐑉𐐼 𐐸𐐰𐑆 𐑇𐐬𐑌 𐑋𐐨 𐑄𐐰𐐻 𐑄𐐬𐑆 𐐸𐐭 𐐶𐐲𐑉 𐐰𐐻 𐐖𐐯𐑉𐐭𐑅𐐲𐑊𐐯𐑋, 𐑁𐑉𐐱𐑋 𐐸𐐶𐐯𐑌𐑅 𐐶𐐨 𐐿𐐩𐑋, 𐐸𐐰𐑂 𐐺𐐨𐑌 𐑅𐑊𐐩𐑌 𐐰𐑌𐐼 𐐿𐐰𐑉𐐨𐐼 𐐲𐐶𐐩 𐐿𐐰𐐹𐐻𐐮𐑂; 𐑌𐐯𐑂𐐲𐑉𐑄𐐲𐑊𐐯𐑅, 𐑄 𐐢𐐫𐑉𐐼 𐐸𐐰𐑆 𐑇𐐬𐑌 𐐲𐑌𐐻𐐭 𐑋𐐨 𐑄𐐰𐐻 𐑄𐐩 𐑇𐐳𐐼 𐑉𐐨𐐻𐐲𐑉𐑌 𐐲𐑀𐐯𐑌. 𐐈𐑌𐐼 𐐸𐐨 𐐫𐑊𐑅𐐬 𐐸𐐰𐑆 𐑇𐐬𐑌 𐐲𐑌𐐻𐐭 𐑋𐐨 𐑄𐐰𐐻 𐑄 𐐢𐐫𐑉𐐼 𐐘𐐱𐐼, 𐑄 𐐐𐐬𐑊𐐨 𐐎𐐲𐑌 𐐲𐑂 𐐆𐑆𐑉𐐩𐐯𐑊, 𐑇𐐳𐐼 𐑋𐐰𐑌𐐮𐑁𐐯𐑅𐐻 𐐸𐐮𐑋𐑅𐐯𐑊𐑁 𐐲𐑌𐐻𐐭 𐑄𐐯𐑋 𐐮𐑌 𐑄 𐑁𐑊𐐯𐑇; 𐐰𐑌𐐼 𐐰𐑁𐐻𐐲𐑉 𐐸𐐨 𐑇𐐳𐐼 𐑋𐐰𐑌𐐮𐑁𐐯𐑅𐐻 𐐸𐐮𐑋𐑅𐐯𐑊𐑁, 𐑄𐐩 𐑇𐐳𐐼 𐑅𐐿𐐬𐑉𐐾 𐐸𐐮𐑋 𐐰𐑌𐐼 𐐿𐑉𐐭𐑅𐐮𐑁𐐴 𐐸𐐮𐑋, 𐐰𐐿𐐫𐑉𐐼𐐮𐑍 𐐻𐐭 𐑄 𐐶𐐲𐑉𐐼𐑆 𐐲𐑂 𐑄 𐐩𐑌𐐾𐐯𐑊, 𐐸𐐭 𐑅𐐹𐐰𐐿 𐐮𐐻 𐐲𐑌𐐻𐐭 𐑋𐐨. 𐐈𐑌𐐼 𐐰𐑁𐐻𐐲𐑉 𐑄𐐩 𐐸𐐰𐑂 𐐸𐐪𐑉𐐼𐑌𐐯𐐼 𐑄𐐯𐑉 𐐸𐐪𐑉𐐻𐑅 𐐰𐑌𐐼 𐑅𐐻𐐮𐑁𐑌𐐯𐐼 𐑄𐐯𐑉 𐑌𐐯𐐿𐑅 𐐲𐑀𐐯𐑌𐑅𐐻 𐑄 𐐐𐐬𐑊𐐨 𐐎𐐲𐑌 𐐲𐑂 𐐆𐑆𐑉𐐩𐐯𐑊, 𐐺𐐨𐐸𐐬𐑊𐐼 𐑄 𐐾𐐲𐐾𐑋𐐯𐑌𐐻𐑅 𐐲𐑂 𐑄 𐐐𐐬𐑊𐐨 𐐎𐐲𐑌 𐐲𐑂 𐐆𐑆𐑉𐐩𐐯𐑊 𐑇𐐰𐑊 𐐿𐐲𐑋 𐐲𐐹𐐱𐑌 𐑄𐐯𐑋. 𐐈𐑌𐐼 𐑄 𐐼𐐩 𐐿𐐲𐑋𐐯𐑃 𐑄𐐰𐐻 𐑄𐐩 𐑇𐐰𐑊 𐐺𐐨 𐑅𐑋𐐮𐐻𐑌 𐐰𐑌𐐼 𐐰𐑁𐑊𐐮𐐿𐐻𐐯𐐼. 𐐐𐐶𐐯𐑉𐑁𐐫𐑉, 𐐰𐑁𐐻𐐲𐑉 𐑄𐐩 𐐪𐑉 𐐼𐑉𐐮𐑂𐑌 𐐻𐐭 𐐰𐑌𐐼 𐑁𐑉𐐬, 𐑁𐐫𐑉 𐑄𐐲𐑅 𐑅𐐯𐑃 𐑄 𐐩𐑌𐐾𐐯𐑊, 𐑋𐐯𐑌𐐨 𐑇𐐰𐑊 𐐺𐐨 𐐰𐑁𐑊𐐮𐐿𐐻𐐯𐐼 𐐮𐑌 𐑄 𐑁𐑊𐐯𐑇, 𐐰𐑌𐐼 𐑇𐐰𐑊 𐑌𐐱𐐻 𐐺𐐨 𐑅𐐲𐑁𐐲𐑉𐐼 𐐻𐐭 𐐹𐐯𐑉𐐮𐑇, 𐐺𐐨𐐿𐐫𐑆 𐐲𐑂 𐑄 𐐹𐑉𐐩𐐲𐑉𐑆 𐐲𐑂 𐑄 𐑁𐐩𐑃𐑁𐐳𐑊; 𐑄𐐩 𐑇𐐰𐑊 𐐺𐐨 𐑅𐐿𐐰𐐻𐐲𐑉𐐼, 𐐰𐑌𐐼 𐑅𐑋𐐮𐐻𐑌, 𐐰𐑌𐐼 𐐸𐐩𐐻𐐯𐐼; 𐑌𐐯𐑂𐐲𐑉𐑄𐐲𐑊𐐯𐑅, 𐑄 𐐢𐐫𐑉𐐼 𐐶𐐮𐑊 𐐺𐐨 𐑋𐐲𐑉𐑅𐐮𐑁𐐳𐑊 𐐲𐑌𐐻𐐭 𐑄𐐯𐑋, 𐑄𐐰𐐻 𐐸𐐶𐐯𐑌 𐑄𐐩 𐑇𐐰𐑊 𐐿𐐲𐑋 𐐻𐐭 𐑄 𐑌𐐱𐑊𐐯𐐾 𐐲𐑂 𐑄𐐯𐑉 𐐡𐐨𐐼𐐨𐑋𐐲𐑉, 𐑄𐐩 𐑇𐐰𐑊 𐐺𐐨 𐑀𐐰𐑄𐐲𐑉𐐼 𐐻𐐭𐑀𐐯𐑄𐐲𐑉 𐐲𐑀𐐯𐑌 𐐻𐐭 𐑄 𐑊𐐰𐑌𐐼𐑆 𐐲𐑂 𐑄𐐯𐑉 𐐮𐑌𐐸𐐯𐑉𐐮𐐻𐐲𐑌𐑅.

5. 𐐈𐑌𐐼 𐐺𐑊𐐯𐑅𐐯𐐼 𐐪𐑉 𐑄 𐐖𐐯𐑌𐐻𐐴𐑊𐑆, 𐑄𐐩 𐐱𐑂 𐐸𐐭𐑋 𐑄 𐐹𐑉𐐱𐑁𐐯𐐻 𐐸𐐰𐑆 𐑉𐐮𐐻𐑌; 𐑁𐐫𐑉 𐐺𐐨𐐸𐐬𐑊𐐼, 𐐮𐑁 𐐮𐐻 𐑅𐐬 𐐺 𐑄𐐰𐐻 𐑄𐐩 𐑇𐐰𐑊 𐑉𐐨𐐹𐐯𐑌𐐻 𐐰𐑌𐐼 𐑁𐐴𐐻 𐑌𐐱𐐻 𐐰𐑀𐐯𐑌𐑅𐐻 𐐞𐐴𐐲𐑌, 𐐰𐑌𐐼 𐐼𐐭 𐑌𐐱𐐻 𐐷𐐭𐑌𐐴𐐻 𐑄𐐯𐑋𐑅𐐯𐑊𐑂𐑆 𐐻𐐭 𐑄𐐰𐐻 𐑀𐑉𐐩𐐻 𐐰𐑌𐐼 𐐰𐐺𐐱𐑋𐐮𐑌𐐰𐐺𐑊 𐐽𐐲𐑉𐐽, 𐑄𐐩 𐑇𐐰𐑊 𐐺 𐑅𐐩𐑂𐐼; 𐑁𐐫𐑉 𐑄 𐐢𐐫𐑉𐐼 𐐘𐐱𐐼 𐐶𐐮𐑊 𐑁𐐳𐑊𐑁𐐮𐑊 𐐸𐐮𐑆 𐐿𐐲𐑂𐐯𐑌𐐰𐑌𐐻𐑅 𐐸𐐶𐐮𐐽 𐐸𐐨 𐐸𐐰𐑆 𐑋𐐩𐐼 𐐲𐑌𐐻𐐭 𐐸𐐮𐑆 𐐽𐐮𐑊𐐼𐑉𐐯𐑌; 𐐰𐑌𐐼 𐑁𐐫𐑉 𐑄𐐮𐑅 𐐿𐐫𐑆 𐑄 𐐹𐑉𐐱𐑁𐐯𐐻 𐐸𐐰𐑆 𐑉𐐮𐐻𐑌 𐑄𐐨𐑆 𐑃𐐮𐑍𐑆. 𐐐𐐶𐐯𐑉𐑁𐐫𐑉, 𐑄𐐩 𐑄𐐰𐐻 𐑁𐐴𐐻 𐐰𐑀𐐯𐑌𐑅𐐻 𐐞𐐴𐐲𐑌 𐐰𐑌𐐼 𐑄 𐐿𐐲𐑂𐐯𐑌𐐲𐑌𐐻 𐐹𐐨𐐹𐑊 𐐱𐑂 𐑄 𐐢𐐫𐑉𐐼, 𐑇𐐰𐑊 𐑊𐐮𐐿 𐐲𐐹 𐑄 𐐼𐐲𐑅𐐻 𐐱𐑂 𐑄𐐩𐑉 𐑁𐐨𐐻; 𐐰𐑌𐐼 𐑄 𐐹𐐨𐐹𐑊 𐐱𐑂 𐑄 𐐢𐐫𐑉𐐼 𐑇𐐰𐑊 𐑌𐐱𐐻 𐐺 𐐰𐑇𐐩𐑋𐐼. 𐐙𐐫𐑉 𐑄 𐐹𐐨𐐹𐑊 𐐱𐑂 𐑄 𐐢𐐫𐑉𐐼 𐐪𐑉 𐑄𐐩 𐐸𐐭 𐐶𐐩𐐻 𐑁𐐫𐑉 𐐸𐐮𐑋; 𐑁𐐫𐑉 𐑄𐐩 𐑅𐐻𐐮𐑊 𐐶𐐩𐐻 𐑁𐐫𐑉 𐑄 𐐿𐐲𐑋𐐮𐑍 𐐱𐑂 𐑄 𐐣𐐯𐑅𐐴𐐲. 𐐈𐑌𐐼 𐐺𐐨𐐸𐐬𐑊𐐼, 𐐰𐐿𐐫𐑉𐐼𐐮𐑍 𐐻𐐭 𐑄 𐐶𐐲𐑉𐐼𐑆 𐐱𐑂 𐑄 𐐹𐑉𐐱𐑁𐐯𐐻, 𐑄 𐐣𐐯𐑅𐐴𐐲 𐐶𐐮𐑊 𐑅𐐯𐐻 𐐸𐐮𐑋𐑅𐐯𐑊𐑁 𐐰𐑀𐐯𐑌 𐑄 𐑅𐐯𐐿𐐲𐑌𐐼 𐐻𐐴𐑋 𐐻𐐭 𐑉𐐨𐐿𐐲𐑂𐐲𐑉 𐑄𐐯𐑋; 𐐸𐐶𐐯𐑉𐑁𐐫𐑉, 𐐸𐐨 𐐶𐐮𐑊 𐑋𐐰𐑌𐐮𐑁𐐯𐑅𐐻 𐐸𐐮𐑋𐑅𐐯𐑊𐑁 𐐲𐑌𐐻𐐭 𐑄𐐯𐑋 𐐮𐑌 𐐹𐐵𐑉 𐐰𐑌𐐼 𐑀𐑉𐐩𐐻 𐑀𐑊𐐬𐑉𐐨, 𐐲𐑌𐐻𐐭 𐑄 𐐼𐐯𐑅𐐻𐑉𐐲𐐿𐑇𐐲𐑌 𐐱𐑂 𐑄𐐩𐑉 𐐯𐑌𐐯𐑋𐐨𐑆, 𐐸𐐶𐐯𐑌 𐑄𐐰𐐻 𐐼𐐩 𐐿𐐲𐑋𐐯𐑃 𐐸𐐶𐐯𐑌 𐑄𐐩 𐑇𐐰𐑊 𐐺𐐨𐑊𐐨𐑂 𐐮𐑌 𐐸𐐮𐑋; 𐐰𐑌𐐼 𐑌𐐲𐑌 𐐶𐐮𐑊 𐐸𐐨 𐐼𐐯𐑅𐐻𐑉𐑎 𐑄𐐰𐐻 𐐺𐐨𐑊𐐨𐑂 𐐮𐑌 𐐸𐐮𐑋. 𐐈𐑌𐐼 𐑄𐐩 𐑄𐐰𐐻 𐐺𐐨𐑊𐐨𐑂 𐑌𐐱𐐻 𐐮𐑌 𐐸𐐮𐑋 𐑇𐐰𐑊 𐐺 𐐼𐐯𐑅𐐻𐑉𐑎𐐼, 𐐺𐐬𐑃 𐐺𐐴 𐑁𐐴𐑉, 𐐰𐑌𐐼 𐐺𐐴 𐐻𐐯𐑋𐐹𐐯𐑅𐐻, 𐐰𐑌𐐼 𐐺𐐴 𐐲𐑉𐑃𐐿𐐶𐐩𐐿𐑅, 𐐰𐑌𐐼 𐐺𐐴 𐐺𐑊𐐲𐐼𐑇𐐯𐐼𐑆, 𐐰𐑌𐐼 𐐺𐐴 𐐹𐐯𐑅𐐻𐐮𐑊𐐯𐑌𐑅, 𐐰𐑌𐐼 𐐺𐐴 𐑁𐐰𐑋𐐮𐑌. 𐐈𐑌𐐼 𐑄𐐩 𐑇𐐰𐑊 𐑌𐐬 𐑄𐐰𐐻 𐑄 𐐢𐐫𐑉𐐼 𐐮𐑆 𐐘𐐱𐐼, 𐑄 𐐐𐐬𐑊𐐨 𐐎𐐲𐑌 𐐱𐑂 𐐆𐑆𐑉𐐩𐐯𐑊; 𐑁𐐫𐑉 𐑇𐐰𐑊 𐑄 𐐹𐑉𐐩 𐐺 𐐻𐐩𐐿𐑌 𐑁𐑉𐐱𐑋 𐑄 𐑋𐐴𐐻𐐨, 𐐫𐑉 𐑄 𐑊𐐫𐑁𐐳𐑊 𐐿𐐰𐐹𐐻𐐮𐑂 𐐼𐐯𐑊𐐮𐑂𐐲𐑉𐐼? 𐐒𐐲𐐻 𐑄𐐲𐑅 𐑅𐐯𐑃 𐑄 𐐢𐐫𐑉𐐼: 𐐀𐑂𐑌 𐑄 𐐿𐐰𐐹𐐻𐐮𐑂𐑆 𐐱𐑂 𐑄 𐑋𐐴𐐻𐐨 𐑇𐐰𐑊 𐐺 𐐻𐐩𐐿𐑌 𐐰𐐶𐐩, 𐐰𐑌𐐼 𐑄 𐐹𐑉𐐩 𐐱𐑂 𐑄 𐐻𐐯𐑉𐐮𐐺𐑊 𐑇𐐰𐑊 𐐺 𐐼𐐯𐑊𐐮𐑂𐐲𐑉𐐼; 𐑁𐐫𐑉 𐑄 𐐣𐐴𐐻𐐨 𐐘𐐱𐐼 𐑇𐐰𐑊 𐐼𐐯𐑊𐐮𐑂𐐲𐑉 𐐸𐐮𐑆 𐐿𐐲𐑂𐐯𐑌𐐲𐑌𐐻 𐐹𐐨𐐹𐑊. 𐐙𐐫𐑉 𐑄𐐲𐑅 𐑅𐐯𐑃 𐑄 𐐢𐐫𐑉𐐼; 𐐌 𐐶𐐮𐑊 𐐿𐐲𐑌𐐻𐐯𐑌𐐼 𐐶𐐮𐑄 𐑄𐐯𐑋 𐑄𐐰𐐻 𐐿𐐲𐑌𐐻𐐯𐑌𐐼𐐯𐑃 𐐶𐐮𐑄 𐑄, 𐐰𐑌𐐼 𐐌 𐐶𐐮𐑊 𐑁𐐨𐐼 𐑄𐐯𐑋 𐑄𐐰𐐻 𐐱𐐹𐑉𐐯𐑅 𐑄, 𐐶𐐮𐑄 𐑄𐐩𐑉 𐐬𐑌 𐑁𐑊𐐯𐑇; 𐐰𐑌𐐼 𐑄𐐩 𐑇𐐰𐑊 𐐺 𐐼𐑉𐐲𐑍𐐿𐑌 𐐶𐐮𐑄 𐑄𐐩𐑉 𐐬𐑌 𐐺𐑊𐐲𐐼, 𐐰𐑆 𐐶𐐮𐑄 𐑅𐐶𐐨𐐻 𐐶𐐴𐑌; 𐐰𐑌𐐼 𐐫𐑊 𐑁𐑊𐐯𐑇 𐑇𐐰𐑊 𐑌𐐬 𐑄𐐰𐐻 𐐌 𐑄 𐐢𐐫𐑉𐐼 𐐰𐑋 𐑄𐐴 𐐝𐐩𐑂𐐷𐐲𐑉 𐐰𐑌𐐼 𐑄𐐴 𐐡𐐨𐐼𐐨𐑋𐐲𐑉, 𐑄 𐐣𐐴𐐻𐐨 𐐎𐐲𐑌 𐐱𐑂 𐐖𐐩𐐿𐐲𐐺. 𐐏𐐩, 𐑁𐐫𐑉 𐑄𐐲𐑅 𐑅𐐯𐑃 𐑄 𐐢𐐫𐑉𐐼: 𐐐𐐰𐑂 𐐌 𐐹𐐳𐐻 𐑄 𐐰𐐶𐐩, 𐐫𐑉 𐐸𐐰𐑂 𐐌 𐐿𐐰𐑅𐐻 𐑄 𐐱𐑁 𐑁𐐫𐑉 𐐯𐑂𐐲𐑉? 𐐙𐐫𐑉 𐑄𐐲𐑅 𐑅𐐯𐑃 𐑄 𐐢𐐫𐑉𐐼: 𐐐𐐶𐐯𐑉 𐐮𐑆 𐑄 𐐺𐐮𐑊 𐐱𐑂 𐐷𐐫𐑉 𐑋𐐲𐑄𐐲𐑉'𐑆 𐐼𐐮𐑂𐐬𐑉𐑅𐑋𐐯𐑌𐐻? 𐐓𐐭 𐐸𐐭𐑋 𐐸𐐰𐑂 𐐌 𐐹𐐳𐐻 𐑄 𐐰𐐶𐐩, 𐐫𐑉 𐐻𐐭 𐐸𐐶𐐮𐐽 𐐱𐑂 𐑋𐐴 𐐿𐑉𐐯𐐼𐐮𐐻𐐲𐑉𐑆 𐐸𐐰𐑂 𐐌 𐑅𐐬𐑊𐐼 𐐷𐐭? 𐐏𐐩, 𐐻𐐭 𐐸𐐭𐑋 𐐸𐐰𐑂 𐐌 𐑅𐐬𐑊𐐼 𐐷𐐭? 𐐒𐐨𐐸𐐬𐑊𐐼, 𐑁𐐫𐑉 𐐷𐐫𐑉 𐐮𐑌𐐮𐐿𐐶𐐮𐐻𐐨𐑆 𐐸𐐰𐑂 𐐷 𐑅𐐬𐑊𐐼 𐐷𐐫𐑉𐑅𐐯𐑊𐑂𐑆, 𐐰𐑌𐐼 𐑁𐐫𐑉 𐐷𐐫𐑉 𐐻𐑉𐐰𐑌𐑅𐑀𐑉𐐯𐑇𐐲𐑌𐑆 𐐮𐑆 𐐷𐐫𐑉 𐑋𐐲𐑄𐐲𐑉 𐐹𐐳𐐻 𐐰𐐶𐐩; 𐐸𐐶𐐯𐑉𐑁𐐫𐑉, 𐐸𐐶𐐯𐑌 𐐌 𐐿𐐩𐑋, 𐑄𐐩𐑉 𐐶𐐱𐑆 𐑌𐐬 𐑋𐐰𐑌; 𐐸𐐶𐐯𐑌 𐐌 𐐿𐐫𐑊𐐼, 𐐷𐐩, 𐑄𐐩𐑉 𐐶𐐱𐑆 𐑌𐐲𐑌 𐐻𐐭 𐐰𐑌𐑅𐐲𐑉.

6. 𐐄 𐐸𐐵𐑅 𐐱𐑂 𐐆𐑆𐑉𐐩𐐯𐑊, 𐐮𐑆 𐑋𐐴 𐐸𐐰𐑌𐐼 𐑇𐐫𐑉𐐻𐑌𐐼 𐐰𐐻 𐐫𐑊 𐑄𐐰𐐻 𐐮𐐻 𐐿𐐰𐑌𐐱𐐻 𐑉𐐨𐐼𐐨𐑋, 𐐫𐑉 𐐸𐐰𐑂 𐐌 𐑌𐐬 𐐹𐐵𐑉 𐐻𐐭 𐐼𐐯𐑊𐐮𐑂𐐲𐑉? 𐐒𐐨𐐸𐐬𐑊𐐼 𐐰𐐻 𐑋𐐴 𐑉𐐨𐐺𐐷𐐭𐐿 𐐌 𐐼𐑉𐐴 𐐲𐐹 𐑄 𐑅𐐨, 𐐌 𐑋𐐩𐐿 𐑄𐐩𐑉 𐑉𐐮𐑂𐐲𐑉𐑆 𐐲 𐐶𐐮𐑊𐐼𐐲𐑉𐑌𐐯𐑅 𐐰𐑌𐐼 𐑄𐐩𐑉 𐑁𐐮𐑇 𐐻𐐭 𐑅𐐻𐐮𐑍𐐿, 𐐺𐐨𐐿𐐫𐑆 𐑄 𐐶𐐫𐐻𐐲𐑉𐑆 𐐪𐑉 𐐼𐑉𐐴𐐼 𐐲𐐹; 𐐰𐑌𐐼 𐑄𐐩 𐐼𐐴 𐐺𐐨𐐿𐐫𐑆 𐐱𐑂 𐑃𐐲𐑉𐑅𐐻. 𐐌 𐐿𐑊𐐬𐑄 𐑄 𐐸𐐯𐑂𐑌𐑆 𐐶𐐮𐑄 𐐺𐑊𐐰𐐿𐑌𐐯𐑅, 𐐰𐑌𐐼 𐐌 𐑋𐐩𐐿 𐑅𐐰𐐿𐐿𐑊𐐫𐑃 𐑄𐐩𐑉 𐐿𐐲𐑂𐐲𐑉𐐮𐑍. 𐐜 𐐢𐐫𐑉𐐼 𐐘𐐱𐐼 𐐸𐐰𐑃 𐑀𐐮𐑂𐑌 𐑋𐐨 𐑄 𐐻𐐲𐑍 𐐱𐑂 𐑄 𐑊𐐲𐑉𐑌𐐼, 𐑄𐐰𐐻 𐐌 𐑇𐐳𐐼 𐑌𐐬 𐐸𐐵 𐐻𐐭 𐑅𐐹𐐨𐐿 𐐲 𐐶𐐲𐑉𐐼 𐐮𐑌 𐑅𐐨𐑆𐑌 𐐲𐑌𐐻𐐭 𐑄, 𐐄 𐐸𐐵𐑅 𐐱𐑂 𐐆𐑆𐑉𐐩𐐯𐑊. 𐐐𐐶𐐯𐑌 𐐷 𐐪𐑉 𐐶𐐨𐑉𐐨, 𐐸𐐨 𐐶𐐩𐐿𐐯𐑃 𐑋𐐫𐑉𐑌𐐮𐑍 𐐺𐐴 𐑋𐐫𐑉𐑌𐐮𐑍. 𐐐𐐨 𐐶𐐩𐐿𐐯𐑃 𐑋𐐴𐑌 𐐨𐑉 𐐻𐐭 𐐸𐐨𐑉 𐐰𐑆 𐑄 𐑊𐐲𐑉𐑌𐐼. 𐐜 𐐢𐐫𐑉𐐼 𐐘𐐱𐐼 𐐸𐐰𐑃 𐐬𐐹𐑌𐐼 𐑋𐐴𐑌 𐐨𐑉, 𐐰𐑌𐐼 𐐌 𐐶𐐱𐑆 𐑌𐐱𐐻 𐑉𐐨𐐺𐐯𐑊𐐷𐐲𐑅, 𐑌𐐨𐑄𐐲𐑉 𐐻𐐲𐑉𐑌𐐼 𐐰𐐶𐐩 𐐺𐐰𐐿. 𐐌 𐑀𐐩𐑂 𐑋𐐴 𐐺𐐰𐐿 𐐻𐐭 𐑄 𐑅𐑋𐐴𐐻𐐲𐑉, 𐐰𐑌𐐼 𐑋𐐴 𐐽𐐨𐐿𐑅 𐐻𐐭 𐑄𐐯𐑋 𐑄𐐰𐐻 𐐹𐑊𐐲𐐿𐐻 𐐱𐑁 𐑄 𐐸𐐩𐑉. 𐐌 𐐸𐐮𐐼 𐑌𐐱𐐻 𐑋𐐴 𐑁𐐩𐑅 𐑁𐑉𐐱𐑋 𐑇𐐩𐑋 𐐰𐑌𐐼 𐑅𐐹𐐮𐐻𐐮𐑍, 𐑁𐐫𐑉 𐑄 𐐢𐐫𐑉𐐼 𐐘𐐱𐐼 𐐶𐐮𐑊 𐐸𐐯𐑊𐐹 𐑋𐐨; 𐑄𐐩𐑉𐑁𐐫𐑉 𐑇𐐰𐑊 𐐌 𐑌𐐱𐐻 𐐺 𐐿𐐱𐑌𐑁𐐵𐑌𐐼𐐯𐐼. 𐐜𐐩𐑉𐑁𐐫𐑉 𐐸𐐰𐑂 𐐌 𐑅𐐯𐐻 𐑋𐐴 𐑁𐐩𐑅 𐑊𐐴𐐿 𐐲 𐑁𐑊𐐮𐑌𐐻, 𐐰𐑌𐐼 𐐌 𐑌𐐬 𐑄𐐰𐐻 𐐌 𐑇𐐰𐑊 𐑌𐐱𐐻 𐐺 𐐰𐑇𐐩𐑋𐐼; 𐐰𐑌𐐼 𐑄 𐐢𐐫𐑉𐐼 𐐮𐑆 𐑌𐐨𐑉, 𐐰𐑌𐐼 𐐸𐐨 𐐾𐐲𐑅𐐻𐐮𐑁𐐴𐐯𐑃 𐑋𐐨. 𐐐𐐭 𐐶𐐮𐑊 𐐿𐐲𐑌𐐻𐐯𐑌𐐼 𐐶𐐮𐑄 𐑋𐐨? 𐐢𐐯𐐻 𐐲𐑅 𐑅𐐻𐐰𐑌𐐼 𐐻𐐭𐑀𐐯𐑄𐐲𐑉. 𐐐𐐭 𐐮𐑆 𐑋𐐴𐑌 𐐰𐐼𐑂𐐲𐑉𐑅𐐯𐑉𐐨? 𐐢𐐯𐐻 𐐸𐐮𐑋 𐐿𐐲𐑋 𐑌𐐨𐑉 𐑋𐐨, 𐐰𐑌𐐼 𐐌 𐐶𐐮𐑊 𐑅𐑋𐐴𐐻 𐐸𐐮𐑋 𐐶𐐮𐑄 𐑄 𐑅𐐻𐑉𐐯𐑍𐑃 𐐱𐑂 𐑋𐐴 𐑋𐐵𐑃. 𐐙𐐫𐑉 𐑄 𐐢𐐫𐑉𐐼 𐐘𐐱𐐼 𐐶𐐮𐑊 𐐸𐐯𐑊𐐹 𐑋𐐨. 𐐈𐑌𐐼 𐐫𐑊 𐑄𐐩 𐐸𐐭 𐑇𐐰𐑊

𐐿𐐱𐑌𐐼𐐯𐑋 𐑋𐐨, 𐐺𐐨𐐸𐐬𐑊𐐼, 𐐫𐑊 𐑄𐐩 𐑇𐐰𐑊 𐐶𐐰𐐿𐑅 𐐬𐑊𐐼 𐐰𐑆 𐐲 𐑀𐐪𐑉𐑋𐐯𐑌𐐻, 𐐰𐑌𐐼 𐑄 𐑋𐐫𐑃 𐑇𐐰𐑊 𐐨𐐻 𐑄𐐯𐑋 𐐲𐐹.

7. 𐐐𐐭 𐐮𐑆 𐐰𐑋𐐲𐑍 𐐷𐐭 𐑄𐐰𐐻 𐑁𐐨𐑉𐐯𐑃 𐑄 𐐢𐐫𐑉𐐼; 𐑄𐐰𐐻 𐐬𐐺𐐩𐐯𐑃 𐑄 𐑂𐐦𐑅 𐐱𐑂 𐐸𐐮𐑆 𐑅𐐲𐑉𐑂𐐰𐑌𐐻; 𐑄𐐰𐐻 𐐶𐐫𐐿𐐯𐑃 𐐮𐑌 𐐼𐐪𐑉𐐿𐑌𐐯𐑅, 𐐰𐑌𐐼 𐐸𐐰𐑃 𐑌𐐬 𐑊𐐴𐐻? 𐐒𐐨𐐸𐐬𐑊𐐼 𐐫𐑊 𐐷𐐨 𐑄𐐰𐐻 𐐿𐐮𐑌𐐼𐑊 𐑁𐐴𐑉, 𐑄𐐰𐐻 𐐿𐐲𐑋𐐹𐐲𐑅 𐐷𐐭𐑉𐑅𐐯𐑊𐑂𐑆 𐐲𐐺𐐵𐐻 𐐶𐐮𐑄 𐑅𐐹𐐪𐑉𐐿𐑅, 𐐶𐐫𐐿 𐐮𐑌 𐑄 𐑊𐐴𐐻 𐐱𐑂 𐐷𐐭𐑉 𐑁𐐴𐑉, 𐐰𐑌𐐼 𐐮𐑌 𐑄 𐑅𐐹𐐪𐑉𐐿𐑅 𐐸𐐶𐐮𐐽 𐐷𐐨 𐐸𐐰𐑂 𐐿𐐮𐑌𐐼𐑊𐐼. 𐐜𐐮𐑅 𐑇𐐰𐑊 𐐷𐐨 𐐸𐐰𐑂 𐐱𐑂 𐑋𐐴𐑌 𐐸𐐰𐑌𐐼: 𐐷𐐨 𐑇𐐰𐑊 𐑊𐐴 𐐼𐐵𐑌 𐐮𐑌 𐑅𐐱𐑉𐐬. 𐐐𐐪𐑉𐐿𐑌 𐐲𐑌𐐻𐐭 𐑋𐐨, 𐐷𐐨 𐑄𐐰𐐻 𐑁𐐱𐑊𐐬 𐐰𐑁𐐻𐐲𐑉 𐑉𐐴𐐽𐐲𐑅𐑌𐐯𐑅: 𐑊𐐳𐐿 𐐲𐑌𐐻𐐭 𐑄 𐑉𐐱𐐿 𐑁𐑉𐐱𐑋 𐐸𐐶𐐯𐑌𐑅 𐐷𐐨 𐐪𐑉 𐐸𐑏𐑌, 𐐰𐑌𐐼 𐐻𐐭 𐑄 𐐸𐐬𐑊 𐐱𐑂 𐑄 𐐹𐐮𐐻 𐑁𐑉𐐱𐑋 𐐸𐐶𐐯𐑌𐑅 𐐷𐐨 𐐪𐑉 𐐼𐐮𐑀𐐼. 𐐢𐐳𐐿 𐐲𐑌𐐻𐐭 𐐁𐐺𐑉𐐲𐐸𐐰𐑋, 𐐷𐐭𐑉 𐑁𐐪𐑄𐐲𐑉, 𐐰𐑌𐐼 𐐲𐑌𐐻𐐭 𐐝𐐩𐑉𐐲, 𐑇𐐨 𐑄𐐰𐐻 𐐺𐐩𐑉 𐐷𐐭; 𐑁𐐫𐑉 𐐌 𐐿𐐫𐑊𐐼 𐐸𐐮𐑋 𐐲𐑊𐐬𐑌, 𐐰𐑌𐐼 𐐺𐑊𐐯𐑅𐐻 𐐸𐐮𐑋. 𐐙𐐫𐑉 𐑄 𐐢𐐫𐑉𐐼 𐑇𐐰𐑊 𐐿𐐲𐑋𐑁𐐲𐑉𐐻 𐐞𐐴𐐲𐑌, 𐐸𐐨 𐐶𐐮𐑊 𐐿𐐲𐑋𐑁𐐲𐑉𐐻 𐐫𐑊 𐐸𐐲𐑉 𐐶𐐩𐑅𐐻 𐐹𐑊𐐩𐑅𐐯𐑆; 𐐰𐑌𐐼 𐐸𐐨 𐐶𐐮𐑊 𐑋𐐩𐐿 𐐸𐐲𐑉 𐐶𐐮𐑊𐐼𐐲𐑉𐑌𐐯𐑅 𐑊𐐴𐐿 𐐀𐐼𐐯𐑌, 𐐰𐑌𐐼 𐐸𐐲𐑉 𐐼𐐯𐑆𐐲𐑉𐐻 𐑊𐐴𐐿 𐑄 𐑀𐐪𐑉𐐼𐑌 𐐱𐑂 𐑄 𐐢𐐫𐑉𐐼. 𐐖𐐦 𐐰𐑌𐐼 𐑀𐑊𐐰𐐼𐑌𐐯𐑅 𐑇𐐰𐑊 𐐺𐐨 𐑁𐐵𐑌𐐼 𐑄𐐯𐑉𐐮𐑌, 𐑃𐐰𐑍𐐿𐑅𐑀𐐮𐑂𐐮𐑍 𐐰𐑌𐐼 𐑄 𐑂𐐦𐑅 𐐱𐑂 𐑋𐐯𐑊𐐲𐐼𐐨. 𐐐𐐪𐑉𐐿𐑌 𐐲𐑌𐐻𐐭 𐑋𐐨, 𐑋𐐴 𐐹𐐨𐐹𐑊; 𐐰𐑌𐐼 𐑀𐐮𐑂 𐐨𐑉 𐐲𐑌𐐻𐐭 𐑋𐐨, 𐐄 𐑋𐐴 𐑌𐐩𐑇𐐲𐑌; 𐑁𐐫𐑉 𐐲 𐑊𐐫 𐑇𐐰𐑊 𐐹𐑉𐐬𐑅𐐨𐐼 𐑁𐑉𐐱𐑋 𐑋𐐨, 𐐰𐑌𐐼 𐐌 𐐶𐐮𐑊 𐑋𐐩𐐿 𐑋𐐴 𐐾𐐲𐐾𐑋𐐯𐑌𐐻 𐐻𐐭 𐑉𐐯𐑅𐐻 𐑁𐐫𐑉 𐐲 𐑊𐐴𐐻 𐑁𐐫𐑉 𐑄 𐐹𐐨𐐹𐑊. 𐐣𐐴 𐑉𐐴𐐽𐐲𐑅𐑌𐐯𐑅 𐐮𐑆 𐑌𐐨𐑉; 𐑋𐐴 𐑅𐐰𐑊𐑂𐐩𐑇𐐲𐑌 𐐮𐑆 𐑀𐐱𐑌 𐑁𐐫𐑉𐑃, 𐐰𐑌𐐼 𐑋𐐴𐑌 𐐪𐑉𐑋 𐑇𐐰𐑊 𐐾𐐲𐐾 𐑄 𐐹𐐨𐐹𐑊. 𐐜 𐐴𐑊𐑆 𐑇𐐰𐑊 𐐶𐐩𐐻 𐐲𐐹𐐱𐑌 𐑋𐐨, 𐐰𐑌𐐼 𐐱𐑌 𐑋𐐴𐑌 𐐪𐑉𐑋 𐑇𐐰𐑊 𐑄𐐩 𐐻𐑉𐐲𐑅𐐻. 𐐢𐐮𐑁𐐻 𐐲𐐹 𐐷𐐭𐑉 𐐴𐑆 𐐻𐐭 𐑄 𐐸𐐯𐑂𐑌𐑆, 𐐰𐑌𐐼 𐑊𐐳𐐿 𐐲𐐹𐐱𐑌 𐑄 𐐲𐑉𐑃 𐐺𐐨𐑌𐐨𐑃; 𐑁𐐫𐑉 𐑄 𐐸𐐯𐑂𐑌𐑆 𐑇𐐰𐑊 𐑂𐐰𐑌𐐮𐑇 𐐲𐐶𐐩 𐑊𐐴𐐿 𐑅𐑋𐐬𐐿, 𐐰𐑌𐐼 𐑄 𐐲𐑉𐑃 𐑇𐐰𐑊 𐐶𐐰𐐿𐑅 𐐬𐑊𐐼 𐑊𐐴𐐿 𐐲 𐑀𐐪𐑉𐑋𐐯𐑌𐐻; 𐐰𐑌𐐼 𐑄𐐩 𐑄𐐰𐐻 𐐼𐐶𐐯𐑊 𐑄𐐯𐑉𐐮𐑌, 𐑇𐐰𐑊 𐐼𐐴 𐐮𐑌 𐑊𐐴𐐿 𐑋𐐰𐑌𐐲𐑉. 𐐒𐐲𐐻 𐑋𐐴 𐑅𐐰𐑊𐑂𐐩𐑇𐐲𐑌 𐑇𐐰𐑊 𐐺𐐨 𐑁𐐫𐑉 𐐯𐑂𐐲𐑉, 𐐰𐑌𐐼 𐑋𐐴 𐑉𐐴𐐽𐐲𐑅𐑌𐐯𐑅 𐑇𐐰𐑊 𐑌𐐱𐐻 𐐺𐐨 𐐲𐐺𐐱𐑊𐐮𐑇𐐻.

8. 𐐐𐐪𐑉𐐿𐑌 𐐲𐑌𐐻𐐭 𐑋𐐨, 𐐷𐐨 𐑄𐐰𐐻 𐑌𐐬 𐑉𐐴𐐽𐐲𐑅𐑌𐐯𐑅, 𐑄 𐐹𐐨𐐹𐑊 𐐮𐑌 𐐸𐐭𐑆 𐐸𐐪𐑉𐐻 𐐌 𐐸𐐰𐑂 𐑉𐐮𐐻𐑌 𐑋𐐴 𐑊𐐫; 𐑁𐐨𐑉 𐐷𐐨 𐑌𐐱𐐻 𐑄 𐑉𐐨𐐹𐑉𐐬𐐽 𐐱𐑂 𐑋𐐯𐑌, 𐑌𐐨𐑄𐐲𐑉 𐐺𐐨 𐐷𐐨 𐐲𐑁𐑉𐐩𐐼 𐐱𐑂 𐑄𐐩𐑉 𐑉𐐨𐑂𐐴𐑊𐐮𐑍𐑆; 𐑁𐐫𐑉 𐑄 𐑋𐐫𐑃 𐑇𐐰𐑊 𐐨𐐻 𐑄𐐯𐑋 𐐲𐐹 𐑊𐐴𐐿 𐐲 𐑀𐐪𐑉𐑋𐐯𐑌𐐻, 𐐰𐑌𐐼 𐑄 𐐶𐐲𐑉𐑋 𐑇𐐰𐑊 𐐨𐐻 𐑄𐐯𐑋 𐑊𐐴𐐿 𐐶𐐳𐑊. 𐐒𐐲𐐻 𐑋𐐴 𐑉𐐴𐐽𐐲𐑅𐑌𐐯𐑅 𐑇𐐰𐑊 𐐺𐐨 𐑁𐐫𐑉 𐐯𐑂𐐲𐑉; 𐐰𐑌𐐼 𐑋𐐴 𐑅𐐰𐑊𐑂𐐩𐑇𐐲𐑌 𐑁𐑉𐐱𐑋 𐐾𐐯𐑌𐐲𐑉𐐩𐑇𐐲𐑌 𐐻𐐭 𐐾𐐯𐑌𐐲𐑉𐐩𐑇𐐲𐑌.

9. 𐐊𐐶𐐩𐐿, 𐐲𐐶𐐩𐐿! 𐐑𐐳𐐻 𐐱𐑌 𐑅𐐻𐑉𐐯𐑍𐑃, 𐐄 𐐪𐑉𐑋 𐐱𐑂 𐑄 𐐢𐐫𐑉𐐼; 𐐲𐐶𐐩𐐿 𐐰𐑆 𐐮𐑌 𐑄 𐐩𐑌𐑇𐐯𐑌𐐻 𐐼𐐩𐑆. 𐐂𐑉𐐻 𐑄𐐵 𐑌𐐱𐐻 𐐸𐐨 𐑄𐐰𐐻 𐐸𐐰𐑃 𐐿𐐲𐐻 𐐡𐐩𐐸𐐰𐐺, 𐐰𐑌𐐼 𐐶𐐭𐑌𐐼𐐯𐐼 𐑄 𐐼𐑉𐐰𐑀𐐲𐑌? 𐐂𐑉𐐻 𐑄𐐵 𐑌𐐱𐐻 𐐸𐐨 𐐸𐐭 𐐸𐐰𐑃 𐐼𐑉𐐴𐐼 𐑄 𐑅𐐨, 𐑄 𐐶𐐫𐐻𐐲𐑉𐑆 𐐱𐑂 𐑄 𐑀𐑉𐐩𐐻 𐐼𐐨𐐹; 𐑄𐐰𐐻 𐐸𐐰𐑃 𐑋𐐩𐐼 𐑄 𐐼𐐯𐐹𐑃𐑅 𐐱𐑂 𐑄 𐑅𐐨 𐐲 𐐶𐐩 𐑁𐐫𐑉 𐑄 𐑉𐐰𐑌𐑅𐐲𐑋𐐼 𐐻𐐭 𐐹𐐰𐑅 𐐬𐑂𐐲𐑉? 𐐜𐐯𐑉𐑁𐐫𐑉, 𐑄 𐑉𐐨𐐼𐐨𐑋𐐼 𐐱𐑂 𐑄 𐐢𐐫𐑉𐐼 𐑇𐐰𐑊 𐑉𐐨𐐻𐐲𐑉𐑌, 𐐰𐑌𐐼 𐐿𐐲𐑋 𐐶𐐮𐑄 𐑅𐐮𐑍𐐮𐑍 𐐲𐑌𐐻𐐭 𐐞𐐴𐐲𐑌; 𐐰𐑌𐐼 𐐯𐑂𐐲𐑉𐑊𐐰𐑅𐐻𐐮𐑍 𐐾𐐦 𐐰𐑌𐐼 𐐸𐐬𐑊𐐨𐑌𐐯𐑅 𐑇𐐰𐑊 𐐺𐐨 𐐲𐐹𐐱𐑌 𐑄𐐩𐑉 𐐸𐐯𐐼𐑆; 𐐰𐑌𐐼 𐑄𐐩 𐑇𐐰𐑊 𐐱𐐺𐐻𐐩𐑌 𐑀𐑊𐐰𐐼𐑌𐐯𐑅 𐐰𐑌𐐼 𐐾𐐦; 𐑅𐐱𐑉𐐬 𐐰𐑌𐐼 𐑋𐐬𐑉𐑌𐐮𐑍 𐑇𐐰𐑊 𐑁𐑊𐐨 𐐲𐐶𐐩. 𐐌 𐐰𐑋 𐐸𐐨; 𐐷𐐩, 𐐌 𐐰𐑋 𐐸𐐨 𐑄𐐰𐐻 𐐿𐐲𐑋𐑁𐐲𐑉𐐻𐐯𐑃 𐐷𐐭. 𐐒𐐨𐐸𐐬𐑊𐐼, 𐐸𐐭 𐐪𐑉𐐻 𐑄𐐵, 𐑄𐐰𐐻 𐑄𐐵 𐑇𐐳𐐼𐑅𐐻 𐐺𐐨 𐐲𐑁𐑉𐐩𐐼 𐐱𐑂 𐑋𐐰𐑌, 𐐸𐐭 𐑇𐐰𐑊 𐐼𐐴; 𐐰𐑌𐐼 𐐱𐑂 𐑄 𐑅𐐲𐑌 𐐱𐑂 𐑋𐐰𐑌, 𐐸𐐭 𐑇𐐰𐑊 𐐺𐐨 𐑋𐐩𐐼 𐑊𐐴𐐿 𐐲𐑌𐐻𐐭 𐑀𐑉𐐰𐑅; 𐐰𐑌𐐼 𐑁𐐫𐑉𐑀𐐯𐐻𐐯𐑅𐐻 𐑄 𐐢𐐫𐑉𐐼 𐑄𐐴 𐐣𐐩𐐿𐐲𐑉, 𐑄𐐰𐐻 𐐸𐐰𐑃 𐑅𐐻𐑉𐐯𐐽𐐻 𐑁𐐫𐑉𐑃 𐑄 𐐸𐐯𐑂𐑌𐑆, 𐐰𐑌𐐼 𐑊𐐩𐐼 𐑄 𐑁𐐵𐑌𐐼𐐩𐑇𐐲𐑌𐑆 𐐱𐑂 𐑄 𐐲𐑉𐑃; 𐐰𐑌𐐼 𐐸𐐰𐑅𐐻 𐑁𐐨𐑉𐐼 𐐿𐐱𐑌𐐻𐐮𐑌𐑏𐐰𐑊𐐨 𐐯𐑂𐑉𐐨 𐐼𐐩, 𐐺𐐨𐐿𐐫𐑆 𐐱𐑂 𐑄 𐑁𐑏𐑉𐐨 𐐱𐑂 𐑄 𐐱𐐹𐑉𐐯𐑅𐐲𐑉, 𐐰𐑆 𐐮𐑁 𐐸𐐨 𐐶𐐲𐑉 𐑉𐐯𐐼𐐨 𐐻𐐭 𐐼𐐯𐑅𐐻𐑉𐐦? 𐐈𐑌𐐼 𐐸𐐶𐐩𐑉 𐐮𐑆 𐑄 𐑁𐑏𐑉𐐨 𐐱𐑂 𐑄 𐐱𐐹𐑉𐐯𐑅𐐲𐑉? 𐐜 𐐿𐐰𐐹𐐻𐐮𐑂 𐐯𐐿𐑅𐐴𐑊 𐐸𐐩𐑅𐑌𐐯𐑃, 𐑄𐐰𐐻 𐐸𐐨 𐑋𐐩 𐐺𐐨 𐑊𐐭𐑅𐐻, 𐐰𐑌𐐼 𐑄𐐰𐐻 𐐸𐐨 𐑇𐐳𐐼 𐑌𐐱𐐻 𐐼𐐴 𐐮𐑌 𐑄 𐐹𐐮𐐻, 𐑌𐐫𐑉 𐑄𐐰𐐻 𐐸𐐮𐑆 𐐺𐑉𐐯𐐼 𐑇𐐳𐐼 𐑁𐐩𐑊. 𐐒𐐲𐐻 𐐌 𐐰𐑋 𐑄 𐐢𐐫𐑉𐐼 𐑄𐐴 𐐘𐐱𐐼, 𐐸𐐭𐑆 𐐶𐐩𐑂𐑆 𐑉𐐬𐑉𐐼; 𐑄 𐐢𐐫𐑉𐐼 𐐱𐑂 𐐐𐐬𐑅𐐻𐑅 𐐮𐑆 𐑋𐐴 𐑌𐐩𐑋. 𐐈𐑌𐐼 𐐌 𐐸𐐰𐑂 𐐹𐐳𐐻 𐑋𐐴 𐐶𐐲𐑉𐐼𐑆 𐐮𐑌 𐑄𐐴 𐑋𐐵𐑃, 𐐰𐑌𐐼 𐐸𐐰𐑂 𐐿𐐲𐑂𐐲𐑉𐐼 𐑄𐐨 𐐮𐑌 𐑄 𐑇𐐰𐐼𐐬 𐐱𐑂 𐑋𐐴𐑌 𐐸𐐰𐑌𐐼, 𐑄𐐰𐐻 𐐌 𐑋𐐩 𐐹𐑊𐐰𐑌𐐻 𐑄 𐐸𐐯𐑂𐑌𐑆 𐐰𐑌𐐼 𐑊𐐩 𐑄 𐑁𐐵𐑌𐐼𐐩𐑇𐐲𐑌𐑆 𐐱𐑂 𐑄 𐐲𐑉𐑃, 𐐰𐑌𐐼 𐑅𐐩 𐐲𐑌𐐻𐐭 𐐞𐐴𐐲𐑌, 𐐒𐐨𐐸𐐬𐑊𐐼, 𐑄𐐵 𐐪𐑉𐐻 𐑋𐐴 𐐹𐐨𐐹𐑊. 𐐊𐐶𐐩𐐿, 𐐲𐐶𐐩𐐿, 𐑅𐐻𐐰𐑌𐐼 𐐲𐐹, 𐐄 𐐖𐐯𐑉𐐭𐑅𐐲𐑊𐐯𐑋, 𐐸𐐶𐐮𐐽 𐐸𐐰𐑅𐐻 𐐼𐑉𐐲𐑍𐐿 𐐰𐐻 𐑄 𐐸𐐰𐑌𐐼 𐐱𐑂 𐑄 𐐢𐐫𐑉𐐼 𐑄 𐐿𐐲𐐹 𐐱𐑂 𐐸𐐮𐑆 𐑁𐑏𐑉𐐨; 𐑄𐐵 𐐸𐐰𐑅𐐻 𐐼𐑉𐐲𐑍𐐿𐑌 𐑄

𐐼𐑉𐐯𐑀𐑆 𐐱𐑂 𐑄 𐐿𐐲𐐹 𐐱𐑂 𐐻𐑉𐐯𐑋𐐺𐑊𐐮𐑍 𐑉𐐲𐑍 𐐵𐐻; 𐐰𐑌𐐼 𐑌𐐲𐑌 𐐻𐐭 𐑀𐐴𐐼 𐐸𐐲𐑉 𐐲𐑋𐐲𐑍 𐐫𐑊 𐑄 𐑅𐐲𐑌𐑆 𐑇𐐨 𐐸𐐰𐑃 𐐺𐑉𐐫𐐻 𐑁𐐬𐑉𐑃; 𐑌𐐨𐑄𐐲𐑉 𐑄𐐰𐐻 𐐻𐐩𐐿𐐯𐑃 𐐸𐐲𐑉 𐐺𐐴 𐑄 𐐸𐐰𐑌𐐼, 𐐱𐑂 𐐫𐑊 𐑄 𐑅𐐲𐑌𐑆 𐑇𐐨 𐐸𐐰𐑃 𐐺𐑉𐐫𐐻 𐐲𐐹. 𐐜𐐨𐑆 𐐻𐐭 𐑅𐐲𐑌𐑆 𐐪𐑉 𐐿𐐲𐑋 𐐲𐑌𐐻𐐭 𐑄; 𐐸𐐭 𐑇𐐰𐑊 𐐺𐐨 𐑅𐐱𐑉𐐨 𐑁𐐫𐑉 𐑄: 𐑄𐐴 𐐼𐐯𐑅𐐬𐑊𐐩𐑇𐐲𐑌 𐐰𐑌𐐼 𐐼𐐯𐑅𐐻𐑉𐐲𐐿𐑇𐐲𐑌, 𐐰𐑌𐐼 𐑄 𐑁𐐰𐑋𐐮𐑌 𐐰𐑌𐐼 𐑄 𐑅𐐬𐑉𐐼: 𐐰𐑌𐐼 𐐺𐐴 𐐸𐐭𐑋 𐑇𐐰𐑊 𐐌 𐐿𐐲𐑋𐑁𐐲𐑉𐐻 𐑄? 𐐜𐐴 𐑅𐐲𐑌𐑆 𐐸𐐰𐑂 𐑁𐐩𐑌𐐻𐐯𐐼, 𐑅𐐩𐑂 𐑄𐐨𐑆 𐐻𐐭; 𐑄𐐩 𐑊𐐴 𐐰𐐻 𐑄 𐐸𐐯𐐼 𐐱𐑂 𐐫𐑊 𐑄 𐑅𐐻𐑉𐐨𐐻𐑅, 𐐰𐑆 𐐰 𐐶𐐴𐑊𐐼 𐐺𐐳𐑊 𐐮𐑌 𐐰 𐑌𐐯𐐻; 𐑄𐐩 𐐪𐑉 𐑁𐐳𐑊 𐐱𐑂 𐑄 𐑁𐑏𐑉𐐨 𐐱𐑂 𐑄 𐐢𐐫𐑉𐐼, 𐑄 𐑉𐐨𐐺𐑏𐐿 𐐱𐑂 𐑄𐐴 𐐘𐐱𐐼.

10. 𐐜𐐯𐑉𐑁𐐬𐑉 𐐸𐐨𐑉 𐑌𐐵 𐑄𐐮𐑅, 𐑄𐐵 𐐰𐑁𐑊𐐮𐐿𐐻𐐯𐐼, 𐐰𐑌𐐼 𐐼𐑉𐐲𐑍𐐿𐐲𐑌, 𐐰𐑌𐐼 𐑌𐐱𐐻 𐐶𐐮𐑄 𐐶𐐴𐑌; 𐑄𐐲𐑅 𐑅𐐯𐑃 𐑄𐐴 𐐢𐐫𐑉𐐼, 𐑄 𐐢𐐫𐑉𐐼 𐐰𐑌𐐼 𐑄𐐴 𐐘𐐱𐐼 𐐹𐑊𐐨𐐼𐐯𐑃 𐑄 𐐿𐐫𐑆 𐐱𐑂 𐐸𐐮𐑆 𐐹𐐨𐐹𐑊; 𐐺𐐨𐐸𐐬𐑊𐐼 𐐌 𐐸𐐰𐑂 𐐻𐐩𐐿𐐲𐑌 𐐵𐐻 𐐱𐑂 𐑄𐐴𐑌 𐐸𐐰𐑌𐐼 𐑄 𐐿𐐲𐐹 𐐱𐑂 𐐻𐑉𐐯𐑋𐐺𐑊𐐮𐑍, 𐑄 𐐼𐑉𐐯𐑀𐑆 𐐱𐑂 𐑄 𐐿𐐲𐐹 𐐱𐑂 𐑋𐐴 𐑁𐑏𐑉𐐨; 𐑄𐐵 𐑇𐐰𐑊𐐻 𐑌𐐬 𐑋𐐬𐑉 𐐼𐑉𐐮𐑍𐐿 𐐮𐐻 𐐲𐑀𐐯𐑌. 𐐒𐐲𐐻 𐐌 𐐶𐐮𐑊 𐐹𐐳𐐻 𐐮𐐻 𐐮𐑌𐐻𐐭 𐑄 𐐸𐐰𐑌𐐼 𐐱𐑂 𐑄𐐯𐑋 𐑄𐐰𐐻 𐐰𐑁𐑊𐐮𐐿𐐻 𐑄; 𐐸𐐭 𐐸𐐰𐑂 𐑅𐐯𐐼 𐐻𐐭 𐑄𐐴 𐑅𐐬𐑊, 𐐒𐐵 𐐼𐐵𐑌, 𐑄𐐰𐐻 𐐶𐐨 𐑋𐐩 𐑀𐐬 𐐬𐑂𐐲𐑉: 𐐰𐑌𐐼 𐑄𐐵 𐐸𐐰𐑅𐐻 𐑊𐐩𐐼 𐑄𐐴 𐐺𐐱𐐼𐐨 𐐰𐑆 𐑄 𐑀𐑉𐐵𐑌𐐼, 𐐰𐑌𐐼 𐐰𐑆 𐑄 𐑅𐐻𐑉𐐨𐐻 𐐻𐐭 𐑄𐐯𐑋 𐑄𐐰𐐻 𐐶𐐯𐑌𐐻 𐐬𐑂𐐲𐑉.

11. 𐐊𐐶𐐩𐐿, 𐐲𐐶𐐩𐐿, 𐐹𐐳𐐻 𐐱𐑌 𐑄𐐴 𐑅𐐻𐑉𐐯𐑍𐑃, 𐐄 𐐞𐐴𐐲𐑌; 𐐹𐐳𐐻 𐐱𐑌 𐑄𐐴 𐐺𐑏𐐻𐐮𐑁𐐳𐑊 𐑀𐐪𐑉𐑋𐐯𐑌𐐻𐑅, 𐐄 𐐖𐐭𐑉𐐭𐑅𐐲𐑊𐐯𐑋, 𐑄 𐐸𐐬𐑊𐐨 𐑅𐐮𐐻𐐨; 𐑁𐐫𐑉 𐐸𐐯𐑌𐑅𐑁𐐬𐑉𐑃 𐑄𐐯𐑉 𐑇𐐰𐑊 𐑌𐐬 𐑋𐐬𐑉 𐐿𐐲𐑋 𐐮𐑌𐐻𐐭 𐑄, 𐑄 𐐲𐑌𐑅𐐲𐑉-𐐿𐐲𐑋𐑅𐐴𐑆𐐼 𐐰𐑌𐐼 𐑄 𐐲𐑌𐐿𐑊𐐨𐑌. 𐐟𐐩𐐿 𐑄𐐴𐑅𐐯𐑊𐑁 𐑁𐑉𐐱𐑋 𐑄 𐐼𐐲𐑅𐐻; 𐐲𐑉𐐴𐑆, 𐑅𐐮𐐻 𐐼𐐵𐑌, 𐐄 𐐖𐐭𐑉𐐭𐑅𐐲𐑊𐐯𐑋; 𐑊𐐭𐑅 𐑄𐐴𐑅𐐯𐑊𐑁 𐑁𐑉𐐱𐑋 𐑄 𐐺𐐰𐑌𐐼𐑆 𐐱𐑂 𐑄𐐴 𐑌𐐯𐐿, 𐐄 𐐿𐐰𐐹𐐻𐐮𐑂 𐐼𐐫𐐻𐐲𐑉 𐐱𐑂 𐐞𐐴𐐲𐑌.

𐐕𐐰𐐹𐐻𐐲𐑉 VI.

1. 𐐈𐑌𐐼 𐑌𐐵, 𐑋𐐴 𐐺𐐨𐑊𐐲𐑂𐐯𐐼 𐐺𐑉𐐯𐑄𐑉𐐯𐑌, 𐐌 𐐸𐐰𐑂 𐑉𐐯𐐼 𐑄𐐨𐑆 𐑃𐐮𐑍𐑆 𐑄𐐰𐐻 𐐷𐐨 𐑋𐐴𐐻 𐑌𐐬 𐐿𐐱𐑌𐑅𐐲𐑉𐑌𐐮𐑍 𐑄 𐐿𐐲𐑂𐐯𐑌𐐰𐑌𐐻𐑅 𐐱𐑂 𐑄 𐐢𐐫𐑉𐐼; 𐑄𐐰𐐻 𐐸𐐨 𐐸𐐰𐑆 𐐿𐐲𐑂𐐯𐑌𐐰𐑌𐐻𐐯𐐼 𐐶𐐮𐑄 𐐫𐑊 𐑄 𐐸𐐵𐑅 𐐱𐑂 𐐆𐑆𐑉𐐩𐐯𐑊; 𐑄𐐰𐐻 𐐸𐐨 𐐸𐐰𐑆 𐑅𐐹𐐬𐐿𐐲𐑌 𐐲𐑌𐐻𐐭 𐑄 𐐖𐐭𐑆, 𐐺𐐴 𐑄 𐑋𐐵𐑃 𐐱𐑂 𐐸𐐮𐑆 𐐸𐐬𐑊𐐨 𐐹𐑉𐐱𐑁𐐯𐐻𐑅, 𐐨𐑂𐐲𐑌 𐑁𐑉𐐱𐑋 𐑄 𐐺𐐨𐑀𐐮𐑌𐐮𐑍 𐐼𐐵𐑌, 𐑁𐑉𐐱𐑋 𐐾𐐯𐑌𐐲𐑉𐐩𐑇𐐲𐑌 𐐻𐐭 𐐾𐐯𐑌𐐲𐑉𐐩𐑇𐐲𐑌, 𐐲𐑌𐐻𐐮𐑊 𐑄 𐐻𐐴𐑋 𐐿𐐲𐑋𐑆 𐑄𐐰𐐻 𐑄𐐩 𐑇𐐰𐑊 𐐺𐐨 𐑉𐐨𐑅𐐻𐐬𐑉𐐼 𐐻𐐭 𐑄 𐐻𐑉𐐭 𐐕𐐲𐑉𐐽 𐐰𐑌𐐼 𐑁𐐬𐑊𐐼 𐐱𐑂 𐐘𐐱𐐼; 𐐸𐐶𐐯𐑌 𐑄𐐩 𐑇𐐰𐑊 𐐺𐐨 𐑀𐐰𐑄𐐲𐑉𐐼 𐐸𐐬𐑋 𐐻𐐭 𐑄 𐑊𐐰𐑌𐐼𐑆 𐐱𐑂 𐑄𐐯𐑉 𐐮𐑌𐐸𐐯𐑉𐐮𐐻𐐲𐑌𐑅, 𐐰𐑌𐐼 𐑇𐐰𐑊 𐐺𐐨 𐐯𐑅𐐻𐐰𐐺𐑊𐐮𐑇𐐻 𐐮𐑌 𐐫𐑊 𐑄𐐯𐑉 𐑊𐐰𐑌𐐼𐑆 𐐱𐑂 𐐹𐑉𐐱𐑋𐐮𐑅.

2. 𐐒𐐨𐐸𐐬𐑊𐐼, 𐑋𐐴 𐐺𐐨𐑊𐐲𐑂𐐯𐐼 𐐺𐑉𐐯𐑄𐑉𐐯𐑌, 𐐌 𐑅𐐹𐐨𐐿 𐐲𐑌𐐻𐐭 𐐷𐐭 𐑄𐐨𐑆 𐑃𐐮𐑍𐑆 𐑄𐐰𐐻 𐐷𐐨 𐑋𐐩 𐑉𐐨-𐐾𐐱𐐮𐑅, 𐐰𐑌𐐼 𐑊𐐮𐑁𐐻 𐐲𐐹 𐐷𐐬𐑉 𐐸𐐯𐐼𐑆 𐑁𐐫𐑉𐐯𐑂𐐲𐑉, 𐐺𐐨𐐿𐐫𐑆 𐐱𐑂 𐑄 𐐺𐑊𐐯𐑅𐐮𐑍𐑆 𐐸𐐶𐐮𐐽 𐑄 𐐢𐐫𐑉𐐼 𐐘𐐱𐐼 𐑇𐐰𐑊 𐐺𐐨𐑅𐐻𐐬 𐐲𐐹𐐱𐑌 𐐷𐐬𐑉 𐐕𐐮𐑊𐐼𐑉𐐯𐑌. 𐐙𐐫𐑉 𐐌 𐑌𐐬 𐑄𐐰𐐻 𐐷𐐨 𐐸𐐰𐑂 𐑅𐐲𐑉𐐽𐐻 𐑋𐐲𐐽, 𐑋𐐯𐑌𐐨 𐐱𐑂 𐐷𐐭, 𐐻𐐭 𐑌𐐬 𐐱𐑂 𐑃𐐮𐑍𐑆 𐐻𐐭 𐐿𐐲𐑋; 𐐸𐐶𐐯𐑉𐑁𐐬𐑉 𐐌 𐑌𐐬 𐑄𐐰𐐻 𐐷𐐨 𐑌𐐬 𐑄𐐰𐐻 𐐪𐑉 𐑁𐑊𐐯𐑇 𐑋𐐲𐑅𐐻 𐐶𐐩𐑅𐐻 𐐲𐐶𐐩 𐐰𐑌𐐼 𐐼𐐴; 𐑌𐐯𐑂𐐲𐑉𐑄𐐲𐑊𐐯𐑅, 𐐮𐑌 𐐪𐑉 𐐺𐐱𐐼𐐨𐑆 𐐶𐐨 𐑇𐐰𐑊 𐑅𐐨 𐐘𐐱𐐼. 𐐏𐐩, 𐐌 𐑌𐐬 𐑄𐐰𐐻 𐐷𐐨 𐑌𐐬 𐑄𐐰𐐻 𐐮𐑌 𐑄 𐐺𐐱𐐼𐐨 𐐸𐐨 𐑇𐐰𐑊 𐑇𐐬 𐐸𐐮𐑋𐑅𐐯𐑊𐑁 𐐲𐑌𐐻𐐭 𐑄𐐬𐑆 𐐰𐐻 𐐖𐐭𐑉𐐭𐑅𐐲𐑊𐐯𐑋, 𐑁𐑉𐐱𐑋 𐐸𐐶𐐯𐑌𐑅 𐐶𐐨 𐐿𐐩𐑋; 𐑁𐐫𐑉 𐐮𐐻 𐐮𐑆 𐐯𐐿𐑅-𐐹𐐨𐐼𐐨𐐯𐑌𐐻 𐑄𐐰𐐻 𐐮𐐻 𐑇𐐳𐐼 𐐺𐐨 𐐲𐑋𐐲𐑍 𐑄𐐯𐑋; 𐑁𐐫𐑉 𐐮𐐻 𐐺𐐨𐐸𐐭𐑂𐐯𐑃 𐑄 𐑀𐑉𐐩𐐻 𐐗𐑉𐐨𐐩𐐻𐐲𐑉 𐑄𐐰𐐻 𐐸𐐨 𐑅𐐲𐑁𐐲𐑉𐐯𐑃 𐐸𐐮𐑋𐑅𐐯𐑊𐑁 𐐻𐐭 𐐺𐐨𐐿𐐲𐑋 𐑅𐐲𐐺𐐾𐐯𐐿𐐻 𐐲𐑌𐐻𐐭 𐑋𐐰𐑌 𐐮𐑌 𐑄 𐑁𐑊𐐯𐑇, 𐐰𐑌𐐼 𐐼𐐴 𐑁𐐫𐑉 𐐫𐑊 𐑋𐐯𐑌, 𐑄𐐰𐐻 𐐫𐑊 𐑋𐐯𐑌 𐑋𐐴𐐻 𐐺𐐨𐐿𐐲𐑋 𐑅𐐲𐐺𐐾𐐯𐐿𐐻 𐐲𐑌𐐻𐐭 𐐸𐐮𐑋. 𐐙𐐫𐑉 𐐰𐑆 𐐼𐐯𐑃 𐐸𐐰𐑃 𐐹𐐰𐑅𐐻 𐐲𐐹𐐱𐑌 𐐫𐑊 𐑋𐐯𐑌, 𐐻𐐭 𐑁𐐳𐑊𐑁𐐮𐑊 𐑄 𐑋𐐲𐑉𐑅𐐮𐑁𐐳𐑊 𐐹𐑊𐐰𐑌 𐐱𐑂 𐑄 𐑀𐑉𐐩𐐻 𐐗𐑉𐐨𐐩𐐻𐐲𐑉, 𐑄𐐯𐑉 𐑋𐐲𐑅𐐻 𐑌𐐨𐐼𐑆 𐐺𐐨 𐐰 𐐹𐐵𐐲𐑉 𐐱𐑂 𐑉𐐯𐑆𐐲𐑉𐐯𐐿𐑇𐐲𐑌, 𐐰𐑌𐐼 𐑄 𐑉𐐯𐑆𐐲𐑉𐐯𐐿𐑇𐐲𐑌 𐑋𐐲𐑅𐐻 𐑌𐐨𐐼𐑆 𐐿𐐲𐑋 𐐲𐑌𐐻𐐭 𐑋𐐰𐑌 𐐺𐐴 𐑉𐐨𐑆𐐲𐑌 𐐱𐑂 𐑄 𐑁𐐫𐑊; 𐐰𐑌𐐼 𐑄 𐑁𐐫𐑊 𐐿𐐩𐑋 𐐺𐐴 𐑉𐐨𐑆𐐲𐑌 𐐱𐑂 𐐻𐑉𐐰𐑌𐑆𐑀𐑉𐐯𐑇𐐲𐑌; 𐐰𐑌𐐼 𐐺𐐨𐐿𐐫𐑆 𐑋𐐰𐑌 𐐺𐐨𐐿𐐩𐑋 𐑁𐐫𐑊𐐯𐑌, 𐑄𐐩 𐐶𐐲𐑉 𐐿𐐲𐐻 𐐱𐑁 𐑁𐑉𐐱𐑋 𐑄 𐐹𐑉𐐯𐑆𐐯𐑌𐑅 𐐱𐑂 𐑄 𐐢𐐫𐑉𐐼; 𐐸𐐶𐐯𐑉𐑁𐐬𐑉 𐐮𐐻 𐑋𐐲𐑅𐐻 𐑌𐐨𐐼𐑆 𐐺𐐨 𐐰𐑌 𐐮𐑌𐑁𐐮𐑌𐐮𐐻 𐐰𐐻𐐬𐑌𐑋𐐯𐑌𐐻; 𐑅𐐩𐑂 𐐮𐐻 𐑇𐐳𐐼 𐐺𐐨 𐐰𐑌 𐐮𐑌𐑁𐐮𐑌𐐮𐐻 𐐰𐐻𐐬𐑌𐑋𐐯𐑌𐐻, 𐑄𐐮𐑅 𐐿𐐫𐑉𐐲𐐹𐑇𐐲𐑌 𐐿𐐳𐐼 𐑌𐐱𐐻 𐐹𐐳𐐻 𐐱𐑌 𐐮𐑌𐐿𐐫𐑉𐐲𐐹𐑇𐐲𐑌. 𐐐𐐶𐐯𐑉𐑁𐐬𐑉, 𐑄 𐑁𐐲𐑉𐑅𐐻 𐐾𐐲𐐾𐑋𐐯𐑌𐐻 𐐸𐐶𐐮𐐽 𐐿𐐩𐑋 𐐲𐐹𐐱𐑌 𐑋𐐰𐑌 𐑋𐐲𐑅𐐻 𐑌𐐨𐐼𐑆 𐐸𐐰𐑂 𐑉𐐨𐑋𐐩𐑌𐐼 𐐻𐐭 𐐰𐑌 𐐯𐑌𐐼𐑊𐐯𐑅 𐐼𐐭𐑉𐐩𐑇𐐲𐑌. 𐐈𐑌𐐼 𐐮𐑁 𐑅𐐬,

𐑄𐐮𐑅 𐑁𐑊𐐯𐑇 𐑋𐐲𐑅𐐻 𐐸𐐰𐑂 𐑊𐐩𐐼 𐐼𐐵𐑌 𐐻𐐭 𐑉𐐱𐐻 𐐰𐑌𐐼 𐐻𐐭 𐐿𐑉𐐲𐑋𐐺𐑊 𐐻𐐭 𐐮𐐻𐑅 𐑋𐐲𐑄𐐲𐑉 𐐲𐑉𐑃, 𐐻𐐭 𐑉𐐴𐑆 𐑌𐐬 𐑋𐐬𐑉.

3. 𐐄 𐑄 𐐶𐐮𐑆𐐼𐐲𐑋 𐐱𐑂 𐐘𐐱𐐼! 𐐸𐐮𐑆 𐑋𐐲𐑉𐑅𐐨 𐐰𐑌𐐼 𐑀𐑉𐐩𐑅! 𐐙𐐫𐑉 𐐺𐐨𐐸𐐬𐑊𐐼, 𐐮𐑁 𐑄 𐑁𐑊𐐯𐑇 𐑇𐐳𐐼 𐑉𐐴𐑆 𐑌𐐬 𐑋𐐬𐑉, 𐐵𐑉 𐑅𐐹𐐮𐑉𐐮𐐻𐑅 𐑋𐐲𐑅𐐻 𐐺𐐨𐐿𐐲𐑋 𐑅𐐲𐐺𐐾𐐯𐐿𐐻 𐐻𐐭 𐑄𐐰𐐻 𐐩𐑌𐐾𐐯𐑊 𐐸𐐭 𐑁𐐯𐑊 𐑁𐑉𐐲𐑋 𐐺𐐨𐑁𐐬𐑉 𐑄 𐐹𐑉𐐯𐑆𐐯𐑌𐑅 𐐱𐑂 𐑄 𐐀𐐻𐐲𐑉𐑌𐐲𐑊 𐐘𐐱𐐼, 𐐰𐑌𐐼 𐐺𐐨𐐿𐐩𐑋 𐑄 𐐼𐐯𐑂𐐲𐑊, 𐐻𐐭 𐑉𐐴𐑆 𐑌𐐬 𐑋𐐬𐑉. 𐐈𐑌𐐼 𐐵𐑉 𐑅𐐹𐐮𐑉𐐮𐐻𐑅 𐑋𐐲𐑅𐐻 𐐸𐐰𐑂 𐐺𐐨𐐿𐐲𐑋 𐑊𐐴𐐿 𐐲𐑌𐐻𐐭 𐐸𐐮𐑋, 𐐰𐑌𐐼 𐐶𐐨 𐐺𐐨𐐿𐐲𐑋 𐐼𐐯𐑂𐐲𐑊𐑆, 𐐩𐑌𐐾𐐯𐑊𐑆 𐐻𐐭 𐐩 𐐼𐐯𐑂𐐲𐑊, 𐐻𐐭 𐐺𐐨 𐑇𐐲𐐻 𐐵𐐻 𐑁𐑉𐐲𐑋 𐑄 𐐹𐑉𐐯𐑆𐐯𐑌𐑅 𐐱𐑂 𐐵𐑉 𐐘𐐱𐐼, 𐐰𐑌𐐼 𐐻𐐭 𐑉𐐨𐑋𐐩𐑌 𐐶𐐮𐑄 𐑄 𐑁𐐪𐑄𐐲𐑉 𐐱𐑂 𐑊𐐴𐑆, 𐐮𐑌 𐑋𐐮𐑆𐐲𐑉𐐨, 𐑊𐐴𐐿 𐐲𐑌𐐻𐐭 𐐸𐐮𐑋𐑅𐐯𐑊𐑁; 𐐷𐐩, 𐐻𐐭 𐑄𐐰𐐻 𐐺𐐨𐐮𐑍 𐐸𐐭 𐐺𐐨𐑀𐐴𐑊𐐼 𐐵𐑉 𐑁𐐲𐑉𐑅𐐻 𐐹𐐩𐑉𐐯𐑌𐐻𐑅; 𐐸𐐭 𐐻𐑉𐐰𐑌𐑅𐑁𐐫𐑉𐑋𐐯𐑃 𐐸𐐮𐑋𐑅𐐯𐑊𐑁 𐑌𐐴 𐐲𐑌𐐻𐐭 𐐰𐑌 𐐩𐑌𐐾𐐯𐑊 𐐱𐑂 𐑊𐐴𐐻, 𐐰𐑌𐐼 𐑅𐐻𐐲𐑉𐐯𐑃 𐐲𐐹 𐑄 𐐽𐐮𐑊𐐼𐑉𐐯𐑌 𐐱𐑂 𐑋𐐯𐑌 𐐲𐑌𐐻𐐭 𐑅𐐨𐐿𐑉𐐯𐐻 𐐿𐐱𐑋𐐺𐐮𐑌𐐩𐑇𐐲𐑌𐑆 𐐱𐑂 𐑋𐐲𐑉𐐼𐐲𐑉 𐐰𐑌𐐼 𐐫𐑊 𐑋𐐰𐑌𐐲𐑉 𐐱𐑂 𐑅𐐨𐐿𐑉𐐯𐐻 𐐶𐐲𐑉𐐿𐑅 𐐱𐑂 𐐼𐐪𐑉𐐿𐑌𐐯𐑅.

4. 𐐄 𐐸𐐵 𐑀𐑉𐐩𐐻 𐑄 𐑀𐐳𐐼𐑌𐐯𐑅 𐐱𐑂 𐐵𐑉 𐐘𐐱𐐼, 𐐸𐐭 𐐹𐑉𐐨𐐹𐐩𐑉𐐯𐑃 𐐩 𐐶𐐩 𐑁𐐫𐑉 𐐵𐑉 𐐯𐑅𐐿𐐩𐐹 𐑁𐑉𐐲𐑋 𐑄 𐑀𐑉𐐰𐑅𐐹 𐐱𐑂 𐑄𐐮𐑅 𐐫𐑁𐐳𐑊 𐑋𐐱𐑌𐑅𐐻𐐲𐑉; 𐐷𐐩, 𐑄𐐰𐐻 𐑋𐐱𐑌𐑅𐐻𐐲𐑉, 𐐼𐐯𐑃 𐐰𐑌𐐼 𐐸𐐯𐑊, 𐐸𐐶𐐮𐐽 𐐌 𐐿𐐫𐑊 𐑄 𐐼𐐯𐑃 𐐱𐑂 𐑄 𐐺𐐱𐐼𐐨, 𐐰𐑌𐐼 𐐫𐑊𐑅𐐬 𐑄 𐐼𐐯𐑃 𐐱𐑂 𐑄 𐑅𐐹𐐮𐑉𐐮𐐻. 𐐈𐑌𐐼 𐐺𐐨𐐿𐐫𐑆 𐐱𐑂 𐑄 𐐶𐐩 𐐱𐑂 𐐼𐐨𐑊𐐮𐑂𐐲𐑉𐐰𐑌𐑅 𐐱𐑂 𐐵𐑉 𐐘𐐱𐐼, 𐑄 𐐐𐐬𐑊𐐨 𐐎𐐲𐑌 𐐱𐑂 𐐀𐑆𐑉𐐩𐐯𐑊, 𐑄𐐮𐑅 𐐼𐐯𐑃 𐐱𐑂 𐐸𐐶𐐮𐐽 𐐌 𐐸𐐰𐑂 𐑅𐐹𐐬𐐿𐐯𐑌, 𐐸𐐶𐐮𐐽 𐐮𐑆 𐑄 𐐻𐐯𐑋𐐹𐐬𐑉𐐲𐑊, 𐑇𐐰𐑊 𐐼𐐨𐑊𐐮𐑂𐐲𐑉 𐐲𐐹 𐐮𐐻𐑅 𐐼𐐯𐐼; 𐐸𐐶𐐮𐐽 𐐼𐐯𐑃 𐐮𐑆 𐑄 𐑀𐑉𐐩𐑂. 𐐈𐑌𐐼 𐑄𐐮𐑅 𐐼𐐯𐑃 𐐱𐑂 𐐸𐐶𐐮𐐽 𐐌 𐐸𐐰𐑂 𐑅𐐹𐐬𐐿𐐯𐑌, 𐐸𐐶𐐮𐐽 𐐮𐑆 𐑄 𐑅𐐹𐐮𐑉𐐮𐐻𐐷𐐭𐐲𐑊 𐐼𐐯𐑃, 𐑇𐐰𐑊 𐐼𐐨𐑊𐐮𐑂𐐲𐑉 𐐲𐐹 𐐮𐐻𐑅 𐐼𐐯𐐼; 𐐸𐐶𐐮𐐽 𐑅𐐹𐐮𐑉𐐮𐐻𐐷𐐭𐐲𐑊 𐐼𐐯𐑃 𐐮𐑆 𐐸𐐯𐑊; 𐐸𐐶𐐯𐑉𐑁𐐬𐑉, 𐐼𐐯𐑃 𐐰𐑌𐐼 𐐸𐐯𐑊 𐑋𐐲𐑅𐐻 𐐼𐐨𐑊𐐮𐑂𐐲𐑉 𐐲𐐹 𐑄𐐩𐑉 𐐼𐐯𐐼, 𐐰𐑌𐐼 𐐸𐐯𐑊 𐑋𐐲𐑅𐐻 𐐼𐐨𐑊𐐮𐑂𐐲𐑉 𐐲𐐹 𐐮𐐻𐑅 𐐿𐐰𐐹𐐻𐐮𐑂 𐑅𐐹𐐮𐑉𐐮𐐻𐑅, 𐐰𐑌𐐼 𐑄 𐑀𐑉𐐩𐑂 𐑋𐐲𐑅𐐻 𐐼𐐨𐑊𐐮𐑂𐐲𐑉 𐐲𐐹 𐐮𐐻𐑅 𐐿𐐰𐐹𐐻𐐮𐑂 𐐺𐐱𐐼𐐨𐑆, 𐐰𐑌𐐼 𐑄 𐐺𐐱𐐼𐐨𐑆 𐐰𐑌𐐼 𐑄 𐑅𐐹𐐮𐑉𐐮𐐻𐑅 𐐱𐑂 𐑋𐐯𐑌 𐐶𐐮𐑊 𐐺𐐨 𐑉𐐨𐑅𐐻𐐬𐑉𐐼 𐐶𐐲𐑌 𐐻𐐭 𐑄 𐐲𐑄𐐲𐑉; 𐐰𐑌𐐼 𐐮𐐻 𐐮𐑆 𐐺𐐴 𐑄 𐐹𐐵𐐲𐑉 𐐱𐑂 𐑄 𐑉𐐯𐑆𐐲𐑉𐐯𐐿𐑇𐐲𐑌 𐐱𐑂 𐑄 𐐐𐐬𐑊𐐨 𐐎𐐲𐑌 𐐱𐑂 𐐀𐑆𐑉𐐩𐐯𐑊.

5. 𐐄 𐐸𐐵 𐑀𐑉𐐩𐐻 𐑄 𐐹𐑊𐐰𐑌 𐐱𐑂 𐐵𐑉 𐐘𐐱𐐼! 𐐙𐐫𐑉 𐐱𐑌 𐑄 𐐲𐑄𐐲𐑉 𐐸𐐰𐑌𐐼, 𐑄 𐐹𐐰𐑉𐐲𐐼𐐴𐑅 𐐱𐑂 𐐘𐐱𐐼 𐑋𐐲𐑅𐐻 𐐼𐐨𐑊𐐮𐑂𐐲𐑉 𐐲𐐹 𐑄 𐑅𐐹𐐮𐑉𐐮𐐻𐑅 𐐱𐑂 𐑄 𐑉𐐴𐐽𐐲𐑅, 𐐰𐑌𐐼 𐑄 𐑀𐑉𐐩𐑂 𐐼𐐨𐑊𐐮𐑂𐐲𐑉 𐐲𐐹 𐑄 𐐺𐐱𐐼𐐨 𐐱𐑂 𐑄 𐑉𐐴𐐽𐐲𐑅; 𐐰𐑌𐐼 𐑄 𐑅𐐹𐐮𐑉𐐮𐐻 𐐰𐑌𐐼 𐑄 𐐺𐐱𐐼𐐨 𐐮𐑆 𐑉𐐨𐑅𐐻𐐬𐑉𐐼 𐐻𐐭 𐐮𐐻𐑅𐐯𐑊𐑁 𐐲𐑀𐐯𐑌, 𐐰𐑌𐐼 𐐫𐑊 𐑋𐐯𐑌 𐐺𐐨𐐿𐐲𐑋 𐐮𐑌𐐿𐐱𐑉𐐲𐐹𐐻𐐮𐐺𐑊, 𐐰𐑌𐐼 𐐮𐑋𐐫𐑉𐐻𐐲𐑊, 𐐰𐑌𐐼 𐑄𐐩 𐐪𐑉 𐑊𐐮𐑂𐐮𐑍 𐑅𐐬𐑊𐑆, 𐐸𐐰𐑂𐐮𐑍 𐐩 𐐹𐐲𐑉𐑁𐐯𐐿𐐻 𐑌𐐱𐑊𐐯𐐾 𐑊𐐴𐐿 𐐲𐑅 𐐮𐑌 𐑄 𐑁𐑊𐐯𐑇; 𐑅𐐩𐑂 𐐮𐐻 𐐺𐐨 𐑄𐐰𐐻 𐐵𐑉 𐑌𐐱𐑊𐐯𐐾 𐑇𐐰𐑊 𐐺𐐨 𐐹𐐲𐑉𐑁𐐯𐐿𐐻; 𐐸𐐶𐐯𐑉𐑁𐐬𐑉, 𐐶𐐨 𐑇𐐰𐑊 𐐸𐐰𐑂 𐐩 𐐹𐐲𐑉𐑁𐐯𐐿𐐻 𐑌𐐱𐑊𐐯𐐾 𐐱𐑂 𐐫𐑊 𐐵𐑉 𐑀𐐮𐑊𐐻, 𐐰𐑌𐐼 𐐵𐑉 𐐲𐑌𐐿𐑊𐐨𐑌𐑌𐐯𐑅, 𐐰𐑌𐐼 𐐵𐑉 𐑌𐐩𐐿𐐯𐐼𐑌𐐯𐑅; 𐐰𐑌𐐼 𐑄 𐑉𐐴𐐽𐐲𐑅 𐑇𐐰𐑊 𐐸𐐰𐑂 𐐩 𐐹𐐲𐑉𐑁𐐯𐐿𐐻 𐑌𐐱𐑊𐐯𐐾 𐐱𐑂 𐑄𐐩𐑉 𐐯𐑌𐐾𐑎𐑋𐐯𐑌𐐻, 𐐰𐑌𐐼 𐑄𐐩𐑉 𐑉𐐴𐐽𐐲𐑅𐑌𐐯𐑅, 𐐺𐐨𐐮𐑍 𐐿𐑊𐐬𐑄𐐼 𐐶𐐮𐑄 𐐹𐑏𐑉𐐮𐐻𐐨, 𐐷𐐩, 𐐨𐑂𐑌 𐐶𐐮𐑄 𐑄 𐑉𐐬𐐺 𐐱𐑂 𐑉𐐴𐐽𐐲𐑅𐑌𐐯𐑅.

6. 𐐈𐑌𐐼 𐐮𐐻 𐑇𐐰𐑊 𐐿𐐲𐑋 𐐻𐐭 𐐹𐐰𐑅, 𐑄𐐰𐐻 𐐸𐐶𐐯𐑌 𐐫𐑊 𐑋𐐯𐑌 𐑇𐐰𐑊 𐐸𐐰𐑂 𐐹𐐰𐑅𐐻 𐑁𐑉𐐲𐑋 𐑄𐐮𐑅 𐑁𐐲𐑉𐑅𐐻 𐐼𐐯𐑃 𐐲𐑌𐐻𐐭 𐑊𐐴𐑁, 𐐮𐑌𐑅𐐬𐑋𐐲𐐽 𐐰𐑆 𐑄𐐩 𐐸𐐰𐑂 𐐺𐐨𐐿𐐲𐑋 𐐮𐑋𐐫𐑉𐐻𐐲𐑊, 𐑄𐐩 𐑋𐐲𐑅𐐻 𐐰𐐹𐐨𐑉 𐐺𐐨𐑁𐐬𐑉 𐑄 𐐾𐐲𐐾𐑋𐐯𐑌𐐻 𐑅𐐨𐐻 𐐱𐑂 𐑄 𐐐𐐬𐑊𐐨 𐐎𐐲𐑌 𐐱𐑂 𐐀𐑆𐑉𐐩𐐯𐑊; 𐐰𐑌𐐼 𐑄𐐯𐑌 𐐿𐐲𐑋𐐯𐑃 𐑄 𐐾𐐲𐐾𐑋𐐯𐑌𐐻, 𐐰𐑌𐐼 𐑄𐐯𐑌 𐑋𐐲𐑅𐐻 𐑄𐐩 𐐺𐐨 𐐾𐐲𐐾𐐼 𐐰𐐿𐐫𐑉𐐼𐐮𐑍 𐐻𐐭 𐑄 𐐸𐐬𐑊𐐨 𐐾𐐲𐐾𐑋𐐯𐑌𐐻 𐐱𐑂 𐐘𐐱𐐼. 𐐈𐑌𐐼 𐐰𐑇𐐭𐑉𐐯𐐼𐑊𐐨, 𐐰𐑆 𐑄 𐐢𐐫𐑉𐐼 𐑊𐐮𐑂𐐯𐑃, 𐑁𐐫𐑉 𐑄 𐐢𐐫𐑉𐐼 𐐘𐐱𐐼 𐐸𐐰𐑃 𐑅𐐹𐐬𐐿𐐯𐑌 𐐮𐐻, 𐐰𐑌𐐼 𐐮𐐻 𐐮𐑆 𐐸𐐮𐑆 𐐨𐐻𐐲𐑉𐑌𐐲𐑊 𐐶𐐲𐑉𐐼, 𐐸𐐶𐐮𐐽 𐐿𐐰𐑌𐐱𐐻 𐐹𐐰𐑅 𐐲𐐶𐐩, 𐑄𐐰𐐻 𐑄𐐩 𐐸𐐭 𐐪𐑉 𐑉𐐴𐐽𐐲𐑅, 𐑇𐐰𐑊 𐐺𐐨 𐑉𐐴𐐽𐐲𐑅 𐑅𐐻𐐮𐑊, 𐐰𐑌𐐼 𐑄𐐩 𐐸𐐭 𐐪𐑉 𐑁𐐮𐑊𐑃𐐨, 𐑇𐐰𐑊 𐐺𐐨 𐑁𐐮𐑊𐑃𐐨 𐑅𐐻𐐮𐑊; 𐐸𐐶𐐯𐑉𐑁𐐬𐑉, 𐑄𐐩 𐐸𐐭 𐐪𐑉 𐑁𐐮𐑊𐑃𐐨 𐐪𐑉 𐑄 𐐼𐐯𐑂𐐲𐑊 𐐰𐑌𐐼 𐐸𐐮𐑆 𐐩𐑌𐐾𐐯𐑊𐑆; 𐐰𐑌𐐼 𐑄𐐩 𐑇𐐰𐑊 𐑀𐐬 𐐲𐐶𐐩 𐐮𐑌𐐻𐐭 𐐯𐑂𐐲𐑉𐑊𐐰𐑅𐐻𐐮𐑍 𐑁𐐴𐑉, 𐐹𐑉𐐨𐐹𐐩𐑉𐐼 𐑁𐐫𐑉 𐑄𐐯𐑋; 𐐰𐑌𐐼 𐑄𐐩𐑉 𐐻𐐫𐑉𐑋𐐯𐑌𐐻 𐐮𐑆 𐐰𐑆 𐐩 𐑊𐐩𐐿 𐐱𐑂 𐑁𐐴𐑉 𐐰𐑌𐐼 𐐺𐑉𐐮𐑋𐑅𐐻𐐬𐑌, 𐐸𐐭𐑆 𐑁𐑊𐐩𐑋 𐐰𐑅𐐯𐑌𐐼𐐯𐑃 𐐲𐐹 𐑁𐐫𐑉 𐐯𐑂𐐲𐑉 𐐰𐑌𐐼 𐐯𐑂𐐲𐑉, 𐐰𐑌𐐼 𐐸𐐰𐑆 𐑌𐐬 𐐯𐑌𐐼.

7. 𐐄 𐑄 𐑀𐑉𐐩𐐻𐑌𐐯𐑅 𐐰𐑌𐐼 𐑄 𐐾𐐲𐑅𐐻𐐮𐑅 𐐱𐑂 𐐵𐑉 𐐘𐐱𐐼! 𐐙𐐫𐑉 𐐸𐐨 𐐯𐐿𐑅𐐯𐐿𐐷𐐭𐐻𐐯𐑃 𐐫𐑊 𐐸𐐮𐑆 𐐶𐐲𐑉𐐼𐑆, 𐐰𐑌𐐼 𐑄𐐩 𐐸𐐰𐑂 𐑀𐐫𐑌 𐑁𐐬𐑉𐑃 𐐵𐐻 𐐱𐑂 𐐸𐐮𐑆 𐑋𐐵𐑃, 𐐰𐑌𐐼 𐐸𐐮𐑆 𐑊𐐫 𐑋𐐲𐑅𐐻 𐐺𐐨 𐑁𐐳𐑊𐑁𐐮𐑊𐐼. 𐐒𐐲𐐻, 𐐺𐐨𐐸𐐬𐑊𐐼, 𐑄 𐑉𐐴𐐽𐐲𐑅, 𐑄 𐑅𐐩𐑌𐐻𐑅 𐐱𐑂 𐑄 𐐐𐐬𐑊𐐨 𐐎𐐲𐑌 𐐱𐑂 𐐀𐑆𐑉𐐩𐐯𐑊, 𐑄𐐩 𐐸𐐭 𐐸𐐰𐑂 𐐺𐐨𐑊𐐨𐑂𐐼 𐐮𐑌 𐑄 𐐐𐐬𐑊𐐨 𐐎𐐲𐑌 𐐱𐑂 𐐀𐑆𐑉𐐩𐐯𐑊, 𐑄𐐩 𐐸𐐭 𐐸𐐰𐑂 𐐯𐑌𐐼𐐷𐐭𐑉𐐼 𐑄 𐐿𐑉𐐫𐑅𐐯𐑆 𐐱𐑂 𐑄 𐐶𐐲𐑉𐑊𐐼, 𐐰𐑌𐐼 𐐼𐐨𐑅𐐹𐐴𐑆𐐼 𐑄

𐑇𐐩𐑋 𐐱𐑂 𐐮𐐻; 𐑄𐐩 𐑇𐐰𐑊 𐐮𐑌𐐸𐐯𐑉𐐮𐐻 𐑄 𐐿𐐮𐑍𐐼𐐲𐑋 𐐱𐑂 𐐘𐐪𐐼; 𐐸𐐶𐐮𐐽 𐐶𐐱𐑆 𐐹𐑉𐐨𐐹𐐩𐑉𐐼 𐑁𐐫𐑉 𐑄𐐯𐑋 𐑁𐑉𐐱𐑋 𐑄 𐑁𐐵𐑌𐐼𐐩𐑇𐐲𐑌 𐐱𐑂 𐑄 𐐶𐐲𐑉𐑊𐐼, 𐐰𐑌𐐼 𐑄𐐩𐑉 𐐾𐐦 𐑇𐐰𐑊 𐐺 𐑁𐐳𐑊 𐑁𐐫𐑉 𐐯𐑂𐐯𐑉.

8. 𐐄 𐑄 𐑀𐑉𐐩𐐻𐑌𐐯𐑅 𐐱𐑂 𐑄 𐑋𐐲𐑉𐑅𐐨 𐐱𐑂 𐐵𐑉 𐐘𐐪𐐼, 𐑄 𐐐𐐬𐑊𐐨 𐐎𐐲𐑌 𐐱𐑂 𐐆𐑆𐑉𐐩𐐯𐑊! 𐐙𐐫𐑉 𐐸𐐨 𐐼𐐯𐑊𐐮𐑂𐐯𐑉𐐯𐑃 𐐸𐐮𐑆 𐑅𐐩𐑌𐐻𐑅 𐑁𐑉𐐱𐑋 𐑄𐐰𐐻 𐐫𐑁𐐳𐑊 𐑋𐐱𐑌𐑅𐐻𐐲𐑉 𐑄 𐐼𐐯𐑂𐑊, 𐐰𐑌𐐼 𐐼𐐯𐑃, 𐐰𐑌𐐼 𐐸𐐯𐑊, 𐐰𐑌𐐼 𐑄𐐰𐐻 𐑊𐐩𐐿 𐐱𐑂 𐑁𐐴𐑉 𐐰𐑌𐐼 𐐺𐑉𐐮𐑋𐑅𐐻𐐬𐑌, 𐐸𐐶𐐮𐐽 𐐮𐑆 𐐯𐑌𐐼𐑊𐐯𐑅 𐐻𐐫𐑉𐑋𐐯𐑌𐐻.

9. 𐐄 𐐸𐐵 𐑀𐑉𐐩𐐻 𐑄 𐐸𐐬𐑊𐐨𐑌𐐯𐑅 𐐱𐑂 𐐵𐑉 𐐘𐐪𐐼! 𐐙𐐫𐑉 𐐸𐐨 𐑌𐐬𐐯𐑃 𐐫𐑊 𐑃𐐮𐑍𐑆, 𐐰𐑌𐐼 𐑄𐐩𐑉 𐐮𐑆 𐑌𐐱𐐻 𐐯𐑌𐐨 𐑃𐐮𐑍, 𐑅𐐩𐑂 𐐸𐐨 𐑌𐐬𐑆 𐐮𐐻. 𐐈𐑌𐐼 𐐸𐐨 𐐿𐐲𐑋𐐯𐑃 𐐮𐑌𐐻𐐭 𐑄 𐐶𐐲𐑉𐑊𐐼 𐑄𐐰𐐻 𐐸𐐨 𐑋𐐩 𐑅𐐩𐑂 𐐫𐑊 𐑋𐐯𐑌, 𐐮𐑁 𐑄𐐩 𐐶𐐮𐑊 𐐸𐐪𐑉𐐿𐐯𐑌 𐐲𐑌𐐻𐐭 𐐸𐐮𐑆 𐑂𐐦𐑅; 𐑁𐐫𐑉 𐐺𐐨𐐸𐐬𐑊𐐼 𐐸𐐨 𐑅𐐲𐑁𐐲𐑉𐐯𐑃 𐑄 𐐹𐐩𐑌𐑆 𐐱𐑂 𐐫𐑊 𐑋𐐯𐑌; 𐐷𐐩, 𐑄 𐐹𐐩𐑌𐑆 𐐱𐑂 𐐯𐑂𐐲𐑉𐐨 𐑊𐐮𐑂𐐮𐑍 𐐿𐑉𐐨𐐽𐐲𐑉, 𐐺𐐬𐑃 𐑋𐐯𐑌, 𐐶𐐮𐑋𐐯𐑌, 𐐰𐑌𐐼 𐐽𐐮𐑊𐐼𐑉𐐯𐑌, 𐐸𐐭 𐐺𐐨𐑊𐐱𐑍 𐐻𐐭 𐑄 𐑁𐐰𐑋𐐮𐑊𐐨 𐐱𐑂 𐐈𐐼𐐲𐑋. 𐐈𐑌𐐼 𐐸𐐨 𐑅𐐲𐑁𐐲𐑉𐐯𐑃 𐑄𐐮𐑅, 𐑄𐐰𐐻 𐑄 𐑉𐐯𐑆𐐲𐑉𐐯𐐿𐑇𐐲𐑌 𐑋𐐴𐐻 𐐹𐐰𐑅 𐐲𐐹𐐱𐑌 𐐫𐑊 𐑋𐐯𐑌, 𐑄𐐰𐐻 𐐫𐑊 𐑋𐐴𐐻 𐑅𐐻𐐰𐑌𐐼 𐐺𐐨𐑁𐐫𐑉 𐐸𐐮𐑋 𐐰𐐻 𐑄 𐑀𐑉𐐩𐐻 𐐰𐑌𐐼 𐐾𐐲𐐾𐑋𐐯𐑌𐐻 𐐼𐐩. 𐐈𐑌𐐼 𐐸𐐨 𐐿𐐱𐑋𐐰𐑌𐐼𐐯𐑃 𐐫𐑊 𐑋𐐯𐑌 𐑄𐐰𐐻 𐑄𐐩 𐑋𐐲𐑅𐐻 𐑉𐐨𐐹𐐯𐑌𐐻, 𐐰𐑌𐐼 𐐺 𐐺𐐰𐐹𐐻𐐴𐑆𐐼 𐐮𐑌 𐐸𐐮𐑆 𐑌𐐩𐑋, 𐐸𐐰𐑂𐐮𐑍 𐐹𐐲𐑉𐑁𐐯𐐿𐐻 𐑁𐐩𐑃 𐐮𐑌 𐑄 𐐐𐐬𐑊𐐨 𐐎𐐲𐑌 𐐱𐑂 𐐆𐑆𐑉𐐩𐐯𐑊, 𐐫𐑉 𐑄𐐩 𐐿𐐰𐑌𐐱𐐻 𐐺 𐑅𐐩𐑂𐐼 𐐮𐑌 𐑄 𐐿𐐮𐑍𐐼𐐲𐑋 𐐱𐑂 𐐘𐐪𐐼. 𐐈𐑌𐐼 𐐮𐑁 𐑄𐐩 𐐶𐐮𐑊 𐑌𐐱𐐻 𐑉𐐨𐐹𐐯𐑌𐐻 𐐰𐑌𐐼 𐐺𐐨𐑊𐐨𐑂 𐐮𐑌 𐐸𐐮𐑆 𐑌𐐩𐑋, 𐐰𐑌𐐼 𐐺 𐐺𐐰𐐹𐐻𐐴𐑆𐐼 𐐮𐑌 𐐸𐐮𐑆 𐑌𐐩𐑋, 𐐰𐑌𐐼 𐐯𐑌𐐼𐐷𐐭𐑉 𐐻𐐭 𐑄 𐐯𐑌𐐼, 𐑄𐐩 𐑋𐐲𐑅𐐻 𐐺 𐐼𐐰𐑋𐐼; 𐑁𐐫𐑉 𐑄 𐐢𐐫𐑉𐐼 𐐘𐐪𐐼, 𐑄 𐐐𐐬𐑊𐐨 𐐎𐐲𐑌 𐐱𐑂 𐐆𐑆𐑉𐐩𐐯𐑊, 𐐸𐐰𐑆 𐑅𐐹𐐬𐐿𐐯𐑌 𐐮𐐻; 𐐸𐐶𐐯𐑉𐑁𐐫𐑉 𐐸𐐨 𐐸𐐰𐑆 𐑀𐐮𐑂𐐯𐑌 𐐰 𐑊𐐫; 𐐰𐑌𐐼 𐐸𐐶𐐯𐑉 𐑄𐐩𐑉 𐐮𐑆 𐑌𐐬 𐑊𐐫 𐑀𐐮𐑂𐐯𐑌, 𐑄𐐩𐑉 𐐮𐑆 𐑌𐐬 𐐹𐐲𐑌𐐮𐑇𐑋𐐯𐑌𐐻; 𐐰𐑌𐐼 𐐸𐐶𐐯𐑉 𐑄𐐩𐑉 𐐮𐑆 𐑌𐐬 𐐹𐐲𐑌𐐮𐑇𐑋𐐯𐑌𐐻, 𐑄𐐩𐑉 𐐮𐑆 𐑌𐐬 𐐿𐐱𐑌𐐼𐐯𐑋𐑌𐐩𐑇𐐲𐑌; 𐐰𐑌𐐼 𐐸𐐶𐐯𐑉 𐑄𐐩𐑉 𐐮𐑆 𐑌𐐬 𐐿𐐱𐑌𐐼𐐯𐑋𐑌𐐩𐑇𐐲𐑌, 𐑄 𐑋𐐲𐑉𐑅𐐨𐑆 𐐱𐑂 𐑄 𐐐𐐬𐑊𐐨 𐐎𐐲𐑌 𐐱𐑂 𐐆𐑆𐑉𐐩𐐯𐑊 𐐸𐐰𐑂 𐐿𐑊𐐩𐑋 𐐲𐐹𐐱𐑌 𐑄𐐯𐑋, 𐐺𐐨𐐿𐐫𐑆 𐐱𐑂 𐑄 𐐰𐐻𐐬𐑌𐑋𐐯𐑌𐐻; 𐑁𐐫𐑉 𐑄𐐩 𐐪𐑉 𐐼𐐯𐑊𐐮𐑂𐐯𐑉𐐼 𐐺𐐴 𐑄 𐐹𐐵𐑉 𐐱𐑂 𐐸𐐮𐑋; 𐑁𐐫𐑉 𐑄 𐐰𐐻𐐬𐑌𐑋𐐯𐑌𐐻 𐑅𐐰𐐻𐐮𐑅𐑁𐐴𐐯𐑃 𐑄 𐐼𐐨𐑋𐐰𐑌𐐼𐑆 𐐱𐑂 𐐸𐐮𐑆 𐐾𐐲𐑅𐐻𐐮𐑅 𐐲𐐹𐐱𐑌 𐐫𐑊 𐑄𐐬𐑆 𐐸𐐭 𐐸𐐰𐑂 𐑌𐐱𐐻 𐑄 𐑊𐐫 𐑀𐐮𐑂𐐯𐑌 𐐻𐐭 𐑄𐐯𐑋, 𐑄𐐰𐐻 𐑄𐐩 𐐪𐑉 𐐼𐐯𐑊𐐮𐑂𐐯𐑉𐐼 𐑁𐑉𐐱𐑋 𐑄𐐰𐐻 𐐫𐑁𐐳𐑊 𐑋𐐱𐑌𐑅𐐻𐐲𐑉, 𐐼𐐯𐑃 𐐰𐑌𐐼 𐐸𐐯𐑊, 𐐰𐑌𐐼 𐑄 𐐼𐐯𐑂𐑊, 𐐰𐑌𐐼 𐑄 𐑊𐐩𐐿 𐐱𐑂 𐑁𐐴𐑉 𐐰𐑌𐐼 𐐺𐑉𐐮𐑋𐑅𐐻𐐬𐑌, 𐐸𐐶𐐮𐐽 𐐮𐑆 𐐯𐑌𐐼𐑊𐐯𐑅 𐐻𐐫𐑉𐑋𐐯𐑌𐐻; 𐐰𐑌𐐼 𐑄𐐩 𐐪𐑉 𐑉𐐨𐑅𐐻𐐬𐑉𐐼 𐐻𐐭 𐑄𐐰𐐻 𐐘𐐪𐐼 𐐸𐐭 𐑀𐐩𐑂 𐑄𐐯𐑋 𐐺𐑉𐐯𐑃, 𐐸𐐶𐐮𐐽 𐐮𐑆 𐑄 𐐐𐐬𐑊𐐨 𐐎𐐲𐑌 𐐱𐑂 𐐆𐑆𐑉𐐩𐐯𐑊.

10. 𐐒𐐲𐐻 𐐶𐐬 𐐲𐑌𐐻𐐭 𐐸𐐮𐑋 𐑄𐐰𐐻 𐐸𐐰𐑆 𐑄 𐑊𐐫 𐑀𐐮𐑂𐐯𐑌: 𐐷𐐩, 𐑄𐐰𐐻 𐐸𐐰𐑆 𐐫𐑊 𐑄 𐐿𐐱𐑋𐐰𐑌𐐼𐑋𐐯𐑌𐐻𐑅 𐐱𐑂 𐐘𐐪𐐼, 𐑊𐐴𐐿 𐐲𐑌𐐻𐐭 𐐲𐑅, 𐐰𐑌𐐼 𐑄𐐰𐐻 𐐻𐑉𐐰𐑌𐑅𐑀𐑉𐐯𐑅𐐯𐑃 𐑄𐐯𐑋, 𐐰𐑌𐐼 𐑄𐐰𐐻 𐐶𐐩𐑅𐐻𐐯𐑃 𐑄 𐐼𐐩𐑆 𐐱𐑂 𐐸𐐮𐑆 𐐹𐑉𐐬𐐺𐐩𐑇𐐲𐑌, 𐑁𐐫𐑉 𐐫𐑁𐐳𐑊 𐐮𐑆 𐐸𐐮𐑆 𐑅𐐻𐐩𐐻!

11. 𐐄 𐑄𐐰𐐻 𐐿𐐲𐑌𐐮𐑍 𐐹𐑊𐐰𐑌 𐐱𐑂 𐑄 𐐨𐑂𐑊 𐐎𐐲𐑌! 𐐄 𐑄 𐑂𐐩𐑌𐑌𐐯𐑅. 𐐰𐑌𐐼 𐑄 𐑁𐑉𐐩𐑊𐐻𐐨𐑆, 𐐰𐑌𐐼 𐑁𐐭𐑊𐐮𐑇𐑌𐐯𐑅 𐐱𐑂 𐑋𐐯𐑌! 𐐐𐐶𐐯𐑌 𐑄𐐩 𐐪𐑉 𐑊𐐲𐑉𐑌𐐯𐐼, 𐑄𐐩 𐑃𐐮𐑍𐐿 𐑄𐐩 𐐪𐑉 𐐶𐐴𐑆, 𐐰𐑌𐐼 𐑄𐐩 𐐸𐐪𐑉𐐿𐐯𐑌 𐑌𐐱𐐻 𐐲𐑌𐐻𐐭 𐑄 𐐿𐐵𐑌𐑅𐐯𐑊 𐐱𐑂 𐐘𐐪𐐼, 𐑁𐐫𐑉 𐑄𐐩 𐑅𐐯𐐻 𐐮𐐻 𐐲𐑅𐐴𐐼, 𐑅𐐲𐐹𐐬𐑆𐐮𐑍 𐑄𐐩 𐑌𐐬 𐐱𐑂 𐑄𐐯𐑋𐑅𐐯𐑊𐑂𐑆,—𐐸𐐶𐐯𐑉𐑁𐐫𐑉, 𐑄𐐩𐑉 𐐶𐐮𐑆𐐼𐐲𐑋 𐐮𐑆 𐑁𐐭𐑊𐐮𐑇𐑌𐐯𐑅, 𐐰𐑌𐐼 𐐮𐐻 𐐹𐑉𐐱𐑁𐐮𐐻𐐯𐑃 𐑄𐐯𐑋 𐑌𐐱𐐻. 𐐈𐑌𐐼 𐑄𐐩 𐑇𐐰𐑊 𐐹𐐯𐑉𐐮𐑇.

12. 𐐒𐐲𐐻 𐐻𐐭 𐐺 𐑊𐐲𐑉𐑌𐐯𐐼 𐐮𐑆 𐑀𐐳𐐼, 𐐮𐑁 𐑄𐐩 𐐸𐐪𐑉𐐿𐐯𐑌 𐐲𐑌𐐻𐐭 𐑄 𐐿𐐵𐑌𐑅𐐯𐑊𐑆 𐐱𐑂 𐐘𐐪𐐼. 𐐒𐐲𐐻 𐐶𐐬 𐐲𐑌𐐻𐐭 𐑄 𐑉𐐮𐐽, 𐐸𐐭 𐐪𐑉 𐑉𐐮𐐽 𐐰𐑆 𐐻𐐭 𐑄 𐑃𐐮𐑍𐑆 𐐱𐑂 𐑄 𐐶𐐲𐑉𐑊𐐼. 𐐙𐐫𐑉 𐐺𐐨𐐿𐐫𐑆 𐑄𐐩 𐐪𐑉 𐑉𐐮𐐽, 𐑄𐐩 𐐼𐐯𐑅𐐹𐐴𐑆 𐑄 𐐹𐐭𐑉, 𐐰𐑌𐐼 𐑄𐐩 𐐹𐐲𐑉𐑅𐐨𐐿𐐷𐐭𐐻 𐑄 𐑋𐐨𐐿, 𐐰𐑌𐐼 𐑄𐐩𐑉 𐐸𐐪𐑉𐐻𐑅 𐐪𐑉 𐐲𐐹𐐱𐑌 𐑄𐐩𐑉 𐐻𐑉𐐯𐑈𐐲𐑉𐑆; 𐐸𐐶𐐯𐑉𐑁𐐫𐑉 𐑄𐐩𐑉 𐐻𐑉𐐯𐑈𐐲𐑉 𐐮𐑆 𐑄𐐩𐑉 𐐘𐐪𐐼. 𐐈𐑌𐐼 𐐺𐐨𐐸𐐬𐑊𐐼, 𐑄𐐩𐑉 𐐻𐑉𐐯𐑈𐐲𐑉 𐑇𐐰𐑊 𐐹𐐯𐑉𐐮𐑇 𐐶𐐮𐑃 𐑄𐐯𐑋 𐐫𐑊𐑅𐐬. 𐐈𐑌𐐼 𐐶𐐬 𐐲𐑌𐐻𐐭 𐑄 𐐼𐐯𐑁, 𐑄𐐰𐐻 𐐶𐐮𐑊 𐑌𐐱𐐻 𐐸𐐨𐑉; 𐑁𐐫𐑉 𐑄𐐩 𐑇𐐰𐑊 𐐹𐐯𐑉𐐮𐑇. 𐐎𐐬 𐐲𐑌𐐻𐐭 𐑄 𐐺𐑊𐐴𐑌𐐼, 𐑄𐐰𐐻 𐐶𐐮𐑊 𐑌𐐱𐐻 𐑅𐐨; 𐑁𐐫𐑉 𐑄𐐩 𐑇𐐰𐑊 𐐹𐐯𐑉𐐮𐑇 𐐫𐑊𐑅𐐬. 𐐎𐐬 𐐲𐑌𐐻𐐭 𐑄 𐐲𐑌𐑅𐐲𐑉𐐿𐐲𐑋𐑅𐐴𐑆𐐼 𐐱𐑂 𐐸𐐪𐑉𐐻; 𐑁𐐫𐑉 𐐰 𐑌𐐱𐑊𐐯𐐾 𐐱𐑂 𐑄𐐩𐑉 𐐮𐑌𐐮𐐿𐐶𐐮𐐻𐐨𐑆 𐑇𐐰𐑊 𐑅𐑋𐐴𐐻 𐑄𐐯𐑋 𐐰𐐻 𐑄 𐑊𐐰𐑅𐐻 𐐼𐐩. 𐐎𐐬 𐐲𐑌𐐻𐐭 𐑄 𐑊𐐴𐐲𐑉; 𐑁𐐫𐑉 𐐸𐐨 𐑇𐐰𐑊 𐐺 𐑃𐑉𐐲𐑅𐐻 𐐼𐐵𐑌 𐐻𐐭 𐐸𐐯𐑊. 𐐎𐐬 𐐲𐑌𐐻𐐭 𐑄 𐑋𐐲𐑉𐐼𐐲𐑉𐐲𐑉, 𐐸𐐭 𐐼𐐯𐑊𐐮𐐺𐐲𐑉𐐩𐐻𐑊𐐨 𐐿𐐮𐑊𐐯𐑃; 𐑁𐐫𐑉 𐐸𐐨 𐑇𐐰𐑊 𐐼𐐴. 𐐎𐐬 𐐲𐑌𐐻𐐭 𐑄𐐯𐑋 𐐸𐐭 𐐿𐐱𐑋𐐮𐐻 𐐸𐐬𐑉𐐼𐐲𐑋𐑆; 𐑁𐐫𐑉 𐑄𐐩 𐑇𐐰𐑊 𐐺 𐑃𐑉𐐲𐑅𐐻 𐐼𐐵𐑌 𐐻𐐭 𐐸𐐯𐑊. 𐐏𐐩, 𐐶𐐬 𐐲𐑌𐐻𐐭 𐑄𐐬𐑆 𐑄𐐰𐐻

𐐶𐐲𐑉𐑇𐐮𐐹 𐐴𐐼𐐲𐑊𐑆; 𐑁𐐫𐑉 𐑄 𐐼𐐯𐑂𐐮𐑊 𐐱𐑂 𐐫𐑊 𐐼𐐯𐑂𐐮𐑊𐑆 𐐼𐐨𐑊𐐴𐐻𐐯𐑃 𐐮𐑌 𐑄𐐯𐑋. 𐐈𐑌𐐼, 𐐮𐑌 𐑁𐐴𐑌, 𐐶𐐬 𐐲𐑌𐐻𐐭 𐐫𐑊 𐑄𐐬𐑆 𐐸𐐭 𐐼𐐴 𐐮𐑌 𐑄𐐩𐑉 𐑅𐐮𐑌𐑆; 𐑁𐐫𐑉 𐑄𐐩 𐑇𐐰𐑊 𐑉𐐨𐐻𐐲𐑉𐑌 𐐻𐐭 𐐘𐐱𐐼, 𐐰𐑌𐐼 𐐺𐐨𐐸𐐬𐑊𐐼 𐐸𐐮𐑆 𐑁𐐩𐑅, 𐐰𐑌𐐼 𐑉𐐨𐑋𐐩𐑌 𐐮𐑌 𐑄𐐩𐑉 𐑅𐐮𐑌𐑆.

13. 𐐄, 𐑋𐐴 𐐺𐐨𐑊𐐲𐑂𐐯𐐼 𐐺𐑉𐐯𐑄𐑉𐐯𐑌, 𐑉𐐨𐑋𐐯𐑋𐐺𐐲𐑉 𐑄 𐐫𐑁𐐳𐑊𐑌𐐯𐑅 𐐮𐑌 𐐻𐑉𐐰𐑌𐑅𐑀𐑉𐐯𐑅𐐮𐑍 𐐲𐑀𐐯𐑌𐑅𐐻 𐑄𐐰𐐻 𐐸𐐬𐑊𐐨 𐐘𐐱𐐼, 𐐰𐑌𐐼 𐐫𐑊𐑅𐐬 𐑄 𐐫𐑁𐐳𐑊𐑌𐐯𐑅 𐐱𐑂 𐐷𐐨𐑊𐐼𐐮𐑍 𐐻𐐭 𐑄 𐐯𐑌𐐻𐐴𐑅𐐮𐑍𐑆 𐐱𐑂 𐑄𐐰𐐻 𐐿𐐲𐑌𐐮𐑍 𐐶𐐲𐑌. 𐐡𐐨𐑋𐐯𐑋𐐺𐐲𐑉 𐐻𐐭 𐐺𐐨 𐐿𐐪𐑉𐑌𐐲𐑊-𐑋𐐴𐑌𐐼𐐯𐐼 𐐮𐑆 𐐼𐐯𐑃, 𐐰𐑌𐐼 𐐻𐐭 𐐺𐐨 𐑅𐐹𐐮𐑉𐐮𐐻𐐷𐐳𐐲𐑊-𐑋𐐴𐑌𐐼𐐯𐐼 𐐮𐑆 𐑊𐐴𐑁 𐐨𐐻𐐲𐑉𐑌𐐲𐑊.

14. 𐐄, 𐑋𐐴 𐐺𐐨𐑊𐐲𐑂𐐯𐐼 𐐺𐑉𐐯𐑄𐑉𐐯𐑌, 𐑀𐐮𐑂 𐐨𐑉 𐐻𐐭 𐑋𐐴 𐐶𐐲𐑉𐐼𐑆. 𐐡𐐨𐑋𐐯𐑋𐐺𐐲𐑉 𐑄 𐑀𐑉𐐩𐐻𐑌𐐯𐑅 𐐱𐑂 𐑄 𐐸𐐬𐑊𐐨 𐐎𐐲𐑌 𐐱𐑂 𐐆𐑆𐑉𐐩𐐯𐑊. 𐐔𐐭 𐑌𐐱𐐻 𐑅𐐩 𐑄𐐰𐐻 𐐌 𐐸𐐰𐑂 𐑅𐐹𐐬𐐿𐑌 𐐸𐐪𐑉𐐼 𐑃𐐮𐑍𐑆 𐐲𐑀𐐯𐑌𐑅𐐻 𐐷𐐭; 𐑁𐐫𐑉 𐐮𐑁 𐐷𐐨 𐐼𐐭, 𐐷𐐨 𐐶𐐮𐑊 𐑉𐐨𐑂𐐴𐑊 𐐲𐑀𐐯𐑌𐑅𐐻 𐑄 𐐻𐑉𐐭𐑃; 𐑁𐐫𐑉 𐐌 𐐸𐐰𐑂 𐑅𐐹𐐬𐐿𐑌 𐑄 𐐶𐐲𐑉𐐼𐑆 𐐱𐑂 𐐷𐐬𐑉 𐐣𐐩𐐿𐐲𐑉. 𐐌 𐑌𐐬 𐑄𐐰𐐻 𐑄 𐐶𐐲𐑉𐐼𐑆 𐐱𐑂 𐐻𐑉𐐭𐑃 𐐪𐑉 𐐸𐐪𐑉𐐼 𐐲𐑀𐐯𐑌𐑅𐐻 𐐫𐑊 𐐲𐑌𐐿𐑊𐐨𐑌𐑌𐐯𐑅; 𐐺𐐲𐐻 𐑄 𐑉𐐴𐐽𐐲𐑅 𐑁𐐨𐑉 𐑄𐐯𐑋 𐑌𐐱𐐻, 𐑁𐐫𐑉 𐑄𐐩 𐑊𐐲𐑂 𐑄 𐐻𐑉𐐭𐑃 𐐰𐑌𐐼 𐐪𐑉 𐑌𐐱𐐻 𐑇𐐩𐐿𐑌.

15. 𐐄 𐑄𐐯𐑌, 𐑋𐐴 𐐺𐐨𐑊𐐲𐑂𐐯𐐼 𐐺𐑉𐐯𐑄𐑉𐐯𐑌, 𐐿𐐲𐑋 𐐲𐑌𐐻𐐭 𐑄 𐐢𐐫𐑉𐐼, 𐑄 𐐸𐐬𐑊𐐨 𐐎𐐲𐑌. 𐐡𐐨𐑋𐐯𐑋𐐺𐐲𐑉 𐑄𐐰𐐻 𐐸𐐮𐑆 𐐹𐐪𐑃𐑅 𐐪𐑉 𐑉𐐴𐐽𐐲𐑅. 𐐒𐐨𐐸𐐬𐑊𐐼, 𐑄 𐐶𐐩 𐑁𐐫𐑉 𐑋𐐰𐑌 𐐮𐑆 𐑌𐐰𐑉𐐬, 𐐺𐐲𐐻 𐐮𐐻 𐑊𐐴𐐯𐑃 𐐮𐑌 𐐩 𐑅𐐻𐑉𐐩𐐻 𐐿𐐬𐑉𐑅 𐐺𐐨𐑁𐐬𐑉 𐐸𐐮𐑋, 𐐰𐑌𐐼 𐑄 𐐿𐐨𐐹𐐲𐑉 𐐱𐑂 𐑄 𐑀𐐩𐐻 𐐮𐑆 𐑄 𐐸𐐬𐑊𐐨 𐐎𐐲𐑌 𐐱𐑂 𐐆𐑆𐑉𐐩𐐯𐑊; 𐐰𐑌𐐼 𐐸𐐨 𐐯𐑋𐐹𐑊𐐱𐐨𐐯𐑃 𐑌𐐬 𐑅𐐲𐑉𐑂𐐲𐑌𐐻 𐑄𐐩𐑉; 𐐰𐑌𐐼 𐑄𐐩𐑉 𐐮𐑆 𐑌𐐲𐑌 𐐲𐑄𐐲𐑉 𐐶𐐩 𐑅𐐩𐑂 𐐮𐐻 𐐺𐐨 𐐺𐐴 𐑄 𐑀𐐩𐐻; 𐑁𐐫𐑉 𐐸𐐨 𐐿𐐰𐑌𐐱𐐻 𐐺𐐨 𐐼𐐨𐑅𐐨𐑂𐐼, 𐑁𐐫𐑉 𐑄 𐐢𐐫𐑉𐐼 𐐘𐐱𐐼 𐐮𐑆 𐐸𐐮𐑆 𐑌𐐩𐑋. 𐐈𐑌𐐼 𐐸𐐭𐑅𐐬 𐑌𐐱𐐿𐐯𐑃, 𐐻𐐭 𐐸𐐮𐑋 𐐶𐐮𐑊 𐐸𐐨 𐐬𐐹𐑌; 𐐰𐑌𐐼 𐑄 𐐶𐐴𐑆, 𐐰𐑌𐐼 𐑄 𐑊𐐲𐑉𐑌𐐯𐐼, 𐐰𐑌𐐼 𐑄𐐩 𐑄𐐰𐐻 𐐪𐑉 𐑉𐐮𐐽, 𐐸𐐭 𐐪𐑉 𐐹𐐲𐑁𐐻 𐐲𐐹 𐐮𐑌 𐑄 𐐹𐑉𐐴𐐼 𐐱𐑂 𐑄𐐩𐑉 𐑊𐐲𐑉𐑌𐐮𐑍, 𐐰𐑌𐐼 𐑄𐐩𐑉 𐐶𐐮𐑆𐐼𐐲𐑋, 𐐰𐑌𐐼 𐑄𐐩𐑉 𐑉𐐮𐐽𐐯𐑆; 𐐷𐐩, 𐑄𐐩 𐐪𐑉 𐑄𐐩, 𐐸𐐭𐑋 𐐸𐐨 𐐼𐐯𐑅𐐹𐐴𐑆𐐯𐑃; 𐐰𐑌𐐼 𐑅𐐩𐑂 𐑄𐐩 𐑇𐐰𐑊 𐐿𐐰𐑅𐐻 𐑄𐐨𐑆 𐑃𐐮𐑍𐑆 𐐲𐐶𐐩, 𐐰𐑌𐐼 𐐿𐐱𐑌𐑅𐐮𐐼𐐲𐑉 𐑄𐐯𐑋𐑅𐐯𐑊𐑂𐑆 𐑁𐐭𐑊𐑆 𐐺𐐨𐑁𐐬𐑉 𐐘𐐱𐐼, 𐐰𐑌𐐼 𐐿𐐲𐑋 𐐼𐐵𐑌 𐐮𐑌 𐑄 𐐼𐐯𐐹𐑃𐑅 𐐱𐑂 𐐸𐐷𐐭𐑋𐐮𐑊𐐮𐐻𐐨, 𐐸𐐨 𐐶𐐮𐑊 𐑌𐐱𐐻 𐐬𐐹𐑌 𐐲𐑌𐐻𐐭 𐑄𐐯𐑋. 𐐒𐐲𐐻 𐑄 𐑃𐐮𐑍𐑆 𐐱𐑂 𐑄 𐐶𐐴𐑆 𐐰𐑌𐐼 𐑄 𐐹𐑉𐐭𐐼𐐯𐑌𐐻 𐑇𐐰𐑊 𐐺𐐨 𐐸𐐮𐐼 𐑁𐑉𐐲𐑋 𐑄𐐯𐑋 𐑁𐐫𐑉𐐯𐑂𐐲𐑉; 𐐷𐐩, 𐑄𐐰𐐻 𐐸𐐰𐐹𐐨𐑌𐐯𐑅 𐐸𐐶𐐮𐐽 𐐮𐑆 𐐹𐑉𐐨𐐹𐐩𐑉𐐼 𐑁𐐫𐑉 𐑄 𐑅𐐩𐑌𐐻𐑅. 𐐄 𐑋𐐴 𐐺𐐨𐑊𐐲𐑂𐐯𐐼 𐐺𐑉𐐯𐑄𐑉𐐯𐑌, 𐑉𐐨𐑋𐐯𐑋𐐺𐐲𐑉 𐑋𐐴 𐐶𐐲𐑉𐐼𐑆: 𐐒𐐨𐐸𐐬𐑊𐐼, 𐐌 𐐻𐐩𐐿 𐐫𐑁 𐑋𐐴 𐑀𐐪𐑉𐑋𐐯𐑌𐐻𐑅, 𐐰𐑌𐐼 𐐌 𐑇𐐩𐐿 𐑄𐐯𐑋 𐐺𐐨𐑁𐐬𐑉 𐐷𐐭: 𐐌 𐐹𐑉𐐩 𐑄 𐐘𐐱𐐼 𐐱𐑂 𐑋𐐴 𐑅𐐰𐑊𐑂𐐩𐑇𐐲𐑌 𐑄𐐰𐐻 𐐸𐐨 𐑂𐐷𐐭 𐑋𐐨 𐐶𐐮𐑄 𐐸𐐮𐑆 𐐫𐑊-𐑅𐐲𐑉𐐽𐐮𐑍 𐐴; 𐐸𐐶𐐯𐑉𐑁𐐬𐑉, 𐐷𐐨 𐑇𐐰𐑊 𐑌𐐬 𐐰𐐻 𐑄 𐑊𐐰𐑅𐐻 𐐼𐐩, 𐐸𐐶𐐯𐑌 𐐫𐑊 𐑋𐐯𐑌 𐑇𐐰𐑊 𐐺𐐨 𐐾𐐲𐐾𐐼 𐐱𐑂 𐑄𐐩𐑉 𐐶𐐲𐑉𐐿𐑅, 𐑄𐐰𐐻 𐑄 𐐘𐐱𐐼 𐐱𐑂 𐐆𐑆𐑉𐐩𐐯𐑊 𐐼𐐮𐐼 𐐶𐐮𐐻𐑌𐐯𐑅 𐑄𐐰𐐻 𐐌 𐑇𐐳𐐿 𐐷𐐬𐑉 𐐮𐑌𐐮𐐿𐐶𐐮𐐻𐐨𐑆 𐑁𐑉𐐲𐑋 𐑋𐐴 𐑅𐐬𐑊, 𐐰𐑌𐐼 𐑄𐐰𐐻 𐐌 𐑅𐐻𐐰𐑌𐐼 𐐶𐐮𐑄 𐐺𐑉𐐴𐐻𐑌𐐯𐑅 𐐺𐐨𐑁𐐬𐑉 𐐸𐐮𐑋, 𐐰𐑌𐐼 𐐰𐑋 𐑉𐐮𐐼 𐐱𐑂 𐐷𐐬𐑉 𐐺𐑊𐐲𐐼.

16. 𐐄 𐑋𐐴 𐐺𐐨𐑊𐐲𐑂𐐯𐐼 𐐺𐑉𐐯𐑄𐑉𐐯𐑌, 𐐻𐐲𐑉𐑌 𐐲𐐶𐐩 𐑁𐑉𐐲𐑋 𐐷𐐬𐑉 𐑅𐐮𐑌𐑆; 𐑇𐐩𐐿 𐐫𐑁 𐑄 𐐽𐐩𐑌𐑆 𐐱𐑂 𐐸𐐮𐑋 𐑄𐐰𐐻 𐐶𐐳𐐼 𐐺𐐴𐑌𐐼 𐐷𐐭 𐑁𐐪𐑅𐐻; 𐐿𐐲𐑋 𐐲𐑌𐐻𐐭 𐑄𐐰𐐻 𐐘𐐱𐐼 𐐸𐐭 𐐮𐑆 𐑄 𐑉𐐱𐐿 𐐱𐑂 𐐷𐐬𐑉 𐑅𐐰𐑊𐑂𐐩𐑇𐐲𐑌. 𐐑𐑉𐐨𐐹𐐩𐑉 𐐷𐐬𐑉 𐑅𐐬𐑊𐑆 𐑁𐐫𐑉 𐑄𐐰𐐻 𐑀𐑊𐐬𐑉𐐨𐐲𐑅 𐐼𐐩, 𐐸𐐶𐐯𐑌 𐐾𐐲𐑅𐐻𐐮𐑅 𐑇𐐰𐑊 𐐺𐐨 𐐰𐐼𐑋𐐮𐑌𐐮𐑅𐐻𐐲𐑉𐐼 𐐲𐑌𐐻𐐭 𐑄 𐑉𐐴𐐽𐐲𐑅; 𐐨𐑂𐐯𐑌 𐑄 𐐼𐐩 𐐱𐑂 𐐾𐐲𐐾𐑋𐐯𐑌𐐻, 𐑄𐐰𐐻 𐐷𐐨 𐑋𐐩 𐑌𐐱𐐻 𐑇𐑉𐐮𐑍𐐿 𐐶𐐮𐑄 𐐫𐑁𐐳𐑊 𐑁𐐨𐑉; 𐑄𐐰𐐻 𐐷𐐨 𐑋𐐩 𐑌𐐱𐐻 𐑉𐐨𐑋𐐯𐑋𐐺𐐲𐑉 𐐷𐐬𐑉 𐐫𐑁𐐳𐑊 𐑀𐐮𐑊𐐻 𐐮𐑌 𐐹𐐲𐑉𐑁𐐯𐐿𐐻𐑌𐐯𐑅, 𐐰𐑌𐐼 𐐺𐐨 𐐿𐐲𐑌𐑅𐐻𐑉𐐩𐑌𐐼 𐐻𐐭 𐐯𐐿𐑅𐐿𐑊𐐩𐑋, 𐐸𐐬𐑊𐐨, 𐐸𐐬𐑊𐐨 𐐪𐑉 𐑄𐐴 𐐾𐐲𐐾𐑋𐐯𐑌𐐻𐑅, 𐐄 𐐢𐐫𐑉𐐼 𐐘𐐱𐐼 𐐉𐑊𐑋𐐴𐐻𐐨. 𐐒𐐲𐐻 𐐌 𐑌𐐬 𐑋𐐴 𐑀𐐮𐑊𐐻; 𐐌 𐐻𐑉𐐰𐑌𐑅𐑀𐑉𐐯𐑅𐐻 𐑄𐐴 𐑊𐐫, 𐐰𐑌𐐼 𐑋𐐴 𐐻𐑉𐐰𐑌𐑅𐑀𐑉𐐯𐑇𐐲𐑌𐑆 𐐪𐑉 𐑋𐐴𐑌; 𐐰𐑌𐐼 𐑄 𐐼𐐯𐑂𐐮𐑊 𐐸𐐰𐑃 𐐱𐐺𐐻𐐩𐑌𐐼 𐑋𐐨, 𐑄𐐰𐐻 𐐌 𐐰𐑋 𐐩 𐐹𐑉𐐩 𐐻𐐭 𐐸𐐮𐑆 𐐫𐑁𐐳𐑊 𐑋𐐮𐑆𐐲𐑉𐐨. 𐐒𐐲𐐻 𐐺𐐨𐐸𐐬𐑊𐐼, 𐑋𐐴 𐐺𐑉𐐯𐑄𐑉𐐯𐑌, 𐐮𐑆 𐐮𐐻 𐐯𐐿𐑅𐐹𐐨𐐼𐐨𐐯𐑌𐐻 𐑄𐐰𐐻 𐐌 𐑇𐐳𐐼 𐐲𐐶𐐩𐐿 𐐷𐐭 𐐻𐐭 𐐰𐑌 𐐫𐑁𐐳𐑊 𐑉𐐨𐐰𐑊𐐮𐐻𐐨 𐐱𐑂 𐑄𐐨𐑆 𐑃𐐮𐑍𐑆? 𐐎𐐳𐐼 𐐌 𐐸𐐰𐑉𐐬 𐐲𐐹 𐐷𐐬𐑉 𐑅𐐬𐑊𐑆, 𐐮𐑁 𐐷𐐬𐑉 𐑋𐐴𐑌𐐼𐑆 𐐶𐐲𐑉 𐐹𐐷𐐭𐑉? 𐐎𐐳𐐼 𐐌 𐐺𐐨 𐐹𐑊𐐩𐑌 𐐲𐑌𐐻𐐭 𐐷𐐭 𐐲𐐿𐐫𐑉𐐼𐐮𐑍 𐐻𐐭 𐑄 𐐹𐑊𐐩𐑌𐑌𐐯𐑅 𐐱𐑂 𐑄 𐐻𐑉𐐭𐑃, 𐐮𐑁 𐐷𐐨 𐐶𐐲𐑉 𐑁𐑉𐐨𐐼 𐑁𐑉𐐲𐑋 𐑅𐐮𐑌? 𐐒𐐨𐐸𐐬𐑊𐐼, 𐐮𐑁 𐐷𐐨 𐐶𐐲𐑉 𐐸𐐬𐑊𐐨, 𐐌 𐐶𐐳𐐼 𐑅𐐹𐐨𐐿 𐐲𐑌𐐻𐐭 𐐷𐐭 𐐱𐑂 𐐸𐐬𐑊𐐨𐑌𐐯𐑅; 𐐺𐐲𐐻 𐐰𐑆 𐐷𐐨 𐐪𐑉 𐑌𐐱𐐻 𐐸𐐬𐑊𐐨, 𐐰𐑌𐐼 𐐷𐐨 𐑊𐐳𐐿 𐐲𐐹𐐱𐑌 𐑋𐐨 𐐰𐑆 𐐩 𐐻𐐨𐐽𐐲𐑉, 𐐮𐐻 𐑋𐐲𐑅𐐻 𐑌𐐨𐐼𐑆 𐐺𐐨 𐐯𐐿𐑅𐐹𐐨𐐼𐐨𐐯𐑌𐐻 𐑄𐐰𐐻 𐐌 𐐻𐐨𐐽 𐐷𐐭 𐑄 𐐿𐐱𐑌𐑅𐐨𐐿𐐶𐐯𐑌𐑅𐐯𐑆 𐐱𐑂 𐑅𐐮𐑌. 𐐒𐐨𐐸𐐬𐑊𐐼, 𐑋𐐴 𐑅𐐬𐑊 𐐰𐐺𐐸𐐫𐑉-

𐐲𐑃 𐑅𐐮𐑌, 𐐰𐑌𐐼 𐑋𐐴 𐐸𐐪𐑉𐐻 𐐼𐐨𐑊𐐴𐐻𐐲𐑃 𐐮𐑌 𐑉𐐴𐐽𐐲𐑅𐑌𐐯𐑅; 𐐰𐑌𐐼 𐐴 𐐶𐐮𐑊 𐐹𐑉𐐩𐑆 𐑄 𐐸𐐬𐑊𐐨 𐑌𐐩𐑋 𐐱𐑂 𐑋𐐴 𐐘𐐱𐐼. 𐐗𐐲𐑋, 𐑋𐐴 𐐺𐑉𐐯𐑄𐑉𐐯𐑌, 𐐯𐑂𐐯𐑉𐐨 𐐶𐐲𐑌 𐑄𐐰𐐻 𐑃𐐲𐑉𐑅𐐻𐐯𐑃, 𐐿𐐲𐑋 𐐷𐐨 𐐻𐐭 𐑄 𐐶𐐫𐐻𐐲𐑉𐑆; 𐐰𐑌𐐼 𐐸𐐨 𐑄𐐰𐐻 𐐸𐐰𐑃 𐑌𐐬 𐑋𐐲𐑌𐐨, 𐐿𐐲𐑋 𐐺𐐴 𐐰𐑌𐐼 𐐨𐐻; 𐐷𐐩, 𐐿𐐲𐑋 𐐺𐐴 𐐶𐐴𐑌 𐐰𐑌𐐼 𐑋𐐮𐑊𐐿 𐐶𐐮𐑄𐐵𐐻 𐑋𐐲𐑌𐐨 𐐰𐑌𐐼 𐐶𐐮𐑄𐐵𐐻 𐐹𐑉𐐴𐑅. 𐐐𐐶𐐯𐑉𐑁𐐫𐑉, 𐐼𐐭 𐑌𐐱𐐻 𐑅𐐹𐐯𐑌𐐼 𐑋𐐲𐑌𐐨 𐑁𐐫𐑉 𐑄𐐰𐐻 𐐸𐐶𐐮𐐽 𐐮𐑆 𐐱𐑂 𐑌𐐬 𐐶𐐲𐑉𐑃, 𐑌𐐫𐑉 𐐷𐐭𐑉 𐑊𐐩𐐺𐐲𐑉 𐑁𐐫𐑉 𐑄𐐰𐐻 𐐸𐐶𐐮𐐽 𐐿𐐰𐑌𐐱𐐻 𐑅𐐰𐐻𐐮𐑅𐑁𐐴. 𐐐𐐪𐑉𐐿𐐲𐑌 𐐼𐐮𐑊𐐮𐐾𐐯𐑌𐐻𐑊𐐨 𐐲𐑌𐐻𐐭 𐑋𐐨, 𐐰𐑌𐐼 𐑉𐐨𐑋𐐯𐑋𐐺𐐲𐑉 𐑄 𐐶𐐲𐑉𐐼𐑆 𐐸𐐶𐐮𐐽 𐐴 𐐸𐐰𐑂 𐑅𐐹𐐬𐐿𐐲𐑌; 𐐰𐑌𐐼 𐐿𐐲𐑋 𐐲𐑌𐐻𐐭 𐑄 𐐐𐐬𐑊𐐨 𐐎𐐲𐑌 𐐱𐑂 𐐆𐑆𐑉𐐩𐐯𐑊, 𐐰𐑌𐐼 𐑁𐐨𐑅𐐻 𐐲𐐹𐐱𐑌 𐑄𐐰𐐻 𐐸𐐶𐐮𐐽 𐐹𐐯𐑉𐐮𐑇𐐯𐑃 𐑌𐐱𐐻, 𐑌𐐨𐑄𐐲𐑉 𐐿𐐰𐑌 𐐺𐐨 𐐿𐐫𐑉𐐲𐐹𐐻𐐯𐐼, 𐐰𐑌𐐼 𐑊𐐯𐐻 𐐷𐐭𐑉 𐑅𐐬𐑊 𐐼𐐨𐑊𐐴𐐻 𐐮𐑌 𐑁𐐰𐐻𐑌𐐯𐑅. 𐐒𐐨𐐸𐐬𐑊𐐼, 𐑋𐐴 𐐺𐐨𐑊𐐲𐑂𐐯𐐼 𐐺𐑉𐐯𐑄𐑉𐐯𐑌, 𐑉𐐨𐑋𐐯𐑋𐐺𐐲𐑉 𐑄 𐐶𐐲𐑉𐐼𐑆 𐐱𐑂 𐐷𐐭𐑉 𐐘𐐱𐐼; 𐐹𐑉𐐩 𐐲𐑌𐐻𐐭 𐐸𐐮𐑋 𐐿𐐲𐑌𐐻𐐮𐑌𐐷𐐭𐐲𐑊𐐨 𐐺𐐴 𐐼𐐩, 𐐰𐑌𐐼 𐑀𐐮𐑂 𐑃𐐰𐑍𐐿𐑅 𐐲𐑌𐐻𐐭 𐐸𐐮𐑆 𐐸𐐬𐑊𐐨 𐑌𐐩𐑋 𐐺𐐴 𐑌𐐴𐐻. 𐐢𐐯𐐻 𐐷𐐭𐑉 𐐸𐐪𐑉𐐻𐑅 𐑉𐐨𐐾𐐱𐐮𐑅, 𐐰𐑌𐐼 𐐺𐐨𐐸𐐬𐑊𐐼 𐐸𐐵 𐑀𐑉𐐩𐐻 𐑄 𐐿𐐲𐑂𐐯𐑌𐐰𐑌𐐻𐑅 𐐱𐑂 𐑄 𐐢𐐫𐑉𐐼, 𐐰𐑌𐐼 𐐸𐐵 𐑀𐑉𐐩𐐻 𐐸𐐮𐑆 𐐿𐐱𐑌𐐼𐐯𐑅𐐯𐑌𐑇𐐲𐑌𐑆 𐐲𐑌𐐻𐐭 𐑄 𐐽𐐮𐑊𐐼𐑉𐐯𐑌 𐐱𐑂 𐑋𐐯𐑌; 𐐰𐑌𐐼 𐐺𐐨𐐿𐐱𐑆 𐐱𐑂 𐐸𐐮𐑆 𐑀𐑉𐐩𐐻𐑌𐐯𐑅, 𐐰𐑌𐐼 𐐸𐐮𐑆 𐑀𐑉𐐩𐑅 𐐰𐑌𐐼 𐑋𐐲𐑉𐑅𐐨, 𐐸𐐨 𐐸𐐰𐑆 𐐹𐑉𐐱𐑋𐐮𐑅𐐻 𐐲𐑌𐐻𐐭 𐐲𐑅 𐑄𐐰𐐻 𐐵𐑉 𐑅𐐨𐐼 𐑇𐐰𐑊 𐑌𐐱𐐻 𐐲𐐻𐐲𐑉𐑊𐐨 𐐺𐐨 𐐼𐐯𐑅𐐻𐑉𐐶𐐼, 𐐰𐐿𐐫𐑉𐐼𐐮𐑍 𐐻𐐭 𐑄 𐑁𐑊𐐯𐑇, 𐐺𐐲𐐻 𐑄𐐰𐐻 𐐸𐐨 𐐶𐐳𐐼 𐐹𐑉𐐨𐑆𐐲𐑉𐑂 𐑄𐐯𐑋; 𐐰𐑌𐐼 𐐮𐑌 𐑁𐐷𐐭𐐽𐐲𐑉 𐐾𐐯𐑌𐐲𐑉𐐩𐑇𐐲𐑌𐑆 𐑄𐐩 𐑇𐐰𐑊 𐐺𐐨𐐿𐐲𐑋 𐐩 𐑉𐐴𐐽𐐲𐑅 𐐺𐑉𐐰𐑌𐐽 𐐲𐑌𐐻𐐭 𐑄 𐐸𐐵𐑅 𐐱𐑂 𐐆𐑆𐑉𐐩𐐯𐑊.

17. 𐐈𐑌𐐼 𐑌𐐵, 𐑋𐐴 𐐺𐑉𐐯𐑄𐑉𐐯𐑌, 𐐴 𐐶𐐳𐐼 𐑅𐐹𐐨𐐿 𐐲𐑌𐐻𐐭 𐐷𐐭 𐑋𐐫𐑉; 𐐺𐐲𐐻 𐐱𐑌 𐑄 𐑋𐐫𐑉𐐬 𐐴 𐐶𐐮𐑊 𐐼𐐨𐐿𐑊𐐩𐑉 𐐲𐑌𐐻𐐭 𐐷𐐭 𐑄 𐑉𐐨𐑋𐐩𐑌𐐼𐐲𐑉 𐐱𐑂 𐑋𐐴 𐐶𐐲𐑉𐐼𐑆. 𐐁𐑋𐐯𐑌.

𐐕𐐰𐐹𐐻𐐲𐑉 VII.

1. 𐐈𐑌𐐼 𐑌𐐵 𐐴, 𐐖𐐩𐐿𐐲𐐺, 𐑅𐐹𐐨𐐿 𐐲𐑌𐐻𐐭 𐐷𐐭 𐐲𐑀𐐯𐑌, 𐑋𐐴 𐐺𐐨𐑊𐐲𐑂𐐯𐐼 𐐺𐑉𐐯𐑄𐑉𐐯𐑌, 𐐿𐐱𐑌𐑅𐐲𐑉𐑌𐐮𐑍 𐑄𐐮𐑅 𐑉𐐴𐐽𐐲𐑅 𐐺𐑉𐐰𐑌𐐽 𐐱𐑂 𐐸𐐶𐐮𐐽 𐐴 𐐸𐐰𐑂 𐑅𐐹𐐬𐐿𐐲𐑌. 𐐙𐐫𐑉 𐐺𐐨𐐸𐐬𐑊𐐼, 𐑄 𐐹𐑉𐐱𐑋𐐮𐑅𐐯𐑆 𐐸𐐶𐐮𐐽 𐐶𐐨 𐐸𐐰𐑂 𐐱𐐺𐐻𐐩𐑌𐐼, 𐐪𐑉 𐐹𐑉𐐱𐑋𐐮𐑅𐐯𐑆 𐐲𐑌𐐻𐐭 𐐲𐑅 𐐰𐐿𐐫𐑉𐐼𐐮𐑍 𐐻𐐭 𐑄 𐑁𐑊𐐯𐑇; 𐐸𐐶𐐯𐑉𐑁𐐫𐑉, 𐐰𐑆 𐐮𐐻 𐐸𐐰𐑆 𐐺𐐨𐑌 𐑇𐐬𐑌 𐐲𐑌𐐻𐐭 𐑋𐐨 𐑄𐐰𐐻 𐑋𐐯𐑌𐐨 𐐱𐑂 𐐵𐑉 𐐽𐐮𐑊𐐼𐑉𐐯𐑌 𐑇𐐰𐑊 𐐹𐐯𐑉𐐮𐑇 𐐮𐑌 𐑄 𐑁𐑊𐐯𐑇 𐐺𐐨𐐿𐐱𐑆 𐐱𐑂 𐐲𐑌𐐺𐐨𐑊𐐨𐑁, 𐑌𐐯𐑂𐐲𐑉𐑄𐐯𐑊𐐯𐑅, 𐐘𐐱𐐼 𐐶𐐮𐑊 𐐺𐐨 𐑋𐐲𐑉𐑅𐐮𐑁𐐳𐑊 𐐲𐑌𐐻𐐭 𐑋𐐯𐑌𐐨; 𐐰𐑌𐐼 𐐵𐑉 𐐽𐐮𐑊𐐼𐑉𐐯𐑌 𐑇𐐰𐑊 𐐺𐐨 𐑉𐐨𐑅𐐻𐐬𐑉𐐼, 𐑄𐐰𐐻 𐑄𐐩 𐑋𐐩 𐐿𐐲𐑋 𐐻𐐭 𐑄𐐰𐐻 𐐸𐐶𐐮𐐽 𐐶𐐮𐑊 𐑀𐐮𐑂 𐑄𐐯𐑋 𐑄 𐐻𐑉𐐭 𐑌𐐱𐑊𐐯𐐾 𐐱𐑂 𐑄𐐩𐑉 𐐡𐐨𐐼𐐨𐑋𐐲𐑉. 𐐐𐐶𐐯𐑉𐑁𐐫𐑉, 𐐰𐑆 𐐴 𐑅𐐯𐐼 𐐲𐑌𐐻𐐭 𐐷𐐭, 𐐮𐐻 𐑋𐐲𐑅𐐻 𐑌𐐨𐐼𐑆 𐐺𐐨 𐐯𐐿𐑅𐐹𐐨𐐼𐐨𐐲𐑌𐐻 𐑄𐐰𐐻 𐐗𐑉𐐴𐑅𐐻, (𐑁𐐫𐑉 𐐮𐑌 𐑄 𐑊𐐰𐑅𐐻 𐑌𐐴𐐻 𐑄 𐐁𐑌𐐾𐐯𐑊 𐑅𐐹𐐩𐐿 𐐲𐑌𐐻𐐭 𐑋𐐨 𐑄𐐰𐐻 𐑄𐐮𐑅 𐑇𐐳𐐼 𐐺𐐨 𐐸𐐮𐑆 𐑌𐐩𐑋,) 𐑇𐐳𐐼 𐐿𐐲𐑋 𐐲𐑋𐐲𐑍 𐑄 𐐖𐐭𐑆, 𐐲𐑋𐐲𐑍 𐑄𐐬𐑆 𐐸𐐭 𐐪𐑉 𐑄 𐑋𐐫𐑉 𐐶𐐮𐐿𐐯𐐼 𐐹𐐪𐑉𐐻 𐐱𐑂 𐑄 𐐶𐐲𐑉𐑊𐐼; 𐐰𐑌𐐼 𐑄𐐩 𐑇𐐰𐑊 𐐿𐑉𐐭𐑅𐐮𐑁𐐴 𐐸𐐮𐑋: 𐑁𐐫𐑉 𐑄𐐲𐑅 𐐮𐐻 𐐺𐐨𐐸𐐭𐑂𐐯𐑃 𐐵𐑉 𐐘𐐱𐐼; 𐐰𐑌𐐼 𐑄𐐩𐑉 𐐮𐑆 𐑌𐐲𐑌 𐐲𐑄𐐲𐑉 𐑌𐐩𐑇𐐲𐑌 𐐱𐑌 𐐲𐑉𐑃 𐑄𐐰𐐻 𐐶𐐳𐐼 𐐿𐑉𐐭𐑅𐐮𐑁𐐴 𐑄𐐩𐑉 𐐘𐐱𐐼. 𐐙𐐫𐑉 𐑇𐐳𐐼 𐑄 𐑋𐐴𐐻𐐨 𐑋𐐮𐑉𐐲𐐿𐐲𐑊𐑆 𐐺𐐨 𐑉𐐫𐐻 𐐲𐑋𐐲𐑍 𐐲𐑄𐐲𐑉 𐑌𐐩𐑇𐐲𐑌𐑆, 𐑄𐐩 𐐶𐐳𐐼 𐑉𐐨𐐹𐐯𐑌𐐻, 𐐰𐑌𐐼 𐑌𐐬 𐑄𐐰𐐻 𐐸𐐨 𐐺𐐨 𐑄𐐩𐑉 𐐘𐐱𐐼; 𐐺𐐲𐐻 𐐺𐐨𐐿𐐱𐑆 𐐱𐑂 𐐹𐑉𐐨𐑅𐐻𐐿𐑉𐐰𐑁𐐻𐑅 𐐰𐑌𐐼 𐐮𐑌𐐮𐐿𐐶𐐮𐐻𐐨𐑆, 𐑄𐐩 𐐰𐐻 𐐖𐐯𐑉𐐭𐑅𐐲𐑊𐐯𐑋 𐐶𐐮𐑊 𐑅𐐻𐐮𐑁𐑌 𐑄𐐩𐑉 𐑌𐐯𐐿𐑅 𐐲𐑀𐐯𐑌𐑅𐐻 𐐸𐐮𐑋, 𐑄𐐰𐐻 𐐸𐐨 𐐺𐐨 𐐿𐑉𐐭𐑅𐐮𐑁𐐴𐐼. 𐐐𐐶𐐯𐑉𐑁𐐫𐑉, 𐐺𐐨𐐿𐐱𐑆 𐐱𐑂 𐑄𐐩𐑉 𐐮𐑌𐐮𐐿𐐶𐐮𐐻𐐨𐑆, 𐐼𐐯𐑅𐐻𐑉𐐲𐐿𐑇𐐲𐑌𐑆, 𐑁𐐰𐑋𐐮𐑌𐑆, 𐐹𐐯𐑅𐐻𐐮𐑊𐐯𐑌𐑅𐐯𐑆, 𐐰𐑌𐐼 𐐺𐑊𐐲𐐼𐑇𐐯𐐼, 𐑇𐐰𐑊 𐐿𐐲𐑋 𐐲𐐹𐐱𐑌 𐑄𐐯𐑋; 𐐰𐑌𐐼 𐑄𐐩 𐐸𐐭 𐑇𐐰𐑊 𐑌𐐱𐐻 𐐺𐐨 𐐼𐐯𐑅𐐻𐑉𐐶𐐼, 𐑇𐐰𐑊 𐐺𐐨 𐑅𐐿𐐰𐐻𐐲𐑉𐐼 𐐲𐑋𐐲𐑍 𐐫𐑊 𐑌𐐩𐑇𐐲𐑌𐑆.

2. 𐐒𐐲𐐻 𐐺𐐨𐐸𐐬𐑊𐐼, 𐑄𐐲𐑅 𐑅𐐯𐑃 𐑄 𐐢𐐫𐑉𐐼 𐐘𐐱𐐼: 𐐐𐐶𐐯𐑌 𐑄 𐐼𐐩 𐐿𐐲𐑋𐐯𐑃 𐑄𐐰𐐻 𐑄𐐩 𐑇𐐰𐑊 𐐺𐐨𐑊𐐨𐑂 𐐮𐑌 𐑋𐐨, 𐑄𐐰𐐻 𐐴 𐐰𐑋 𐐗𐑉𐐴𐑅𐐻, 𐑄𐐯𐑌 𐐸𐐰𐑂 𐐴 𐐿𐐲𐑂𐐯𐑌𐐰𐑌𐐻𐐯𐐼 𐐶𐐮𐑄 𐑄𐐩𐑉 𐑁𐐪𐑄𐐲𐑉𐑆 𐑄𐐰𐐻 𐑄𐐩 𐑇𐐰𐑊 𐐺𐐨 𐑉𐐨𐑅𐐻𐐬𐑉𐐼 𐐮𐑌 𐑄 𐑁𐑊𐐯𐑇, 𐐲𐐹𐐱𐑌 𐑄 𐐲𐑉𐑃, 𐐲𐑌𐐻𐐭 𐑄 𐑊𐐰𐑌𐐼𐑆 𐐱𐑂 𐑄𐐩𐑉 𐐮𐑌𐐸𐐯𐑉𐐮𐐻𐐲𐑌𐑅𐐯𐑆. 𐐈𐑌𐐼 𐐮𐐻 𐑇𐐰𐑊 𐐿𐐲𐑋 𐐻𐐭 𐐹𐐰𐑅 𐑄𐐰𐐻 𐑄𐐩 𐑇𐐰𐑊 𐐺𐐨 𐑀𐐰𐑄𐐲𐑉𐐼 𐐮𐑌 𐑁𐑉𐐱𐑋 𐑄𐐩𐑉 𐑊𐐱𐑍 𐐼𐐮𐑅𐐹𐐲𐑉𐑇𐐲𐑌, 𐑁𐑉𐐱𐑋 𐑄 𐐴𐑊𐑆 𐐱𐑂 𐑄 𐑅𐐨, 𐐰𐑌𐐼 𐑁𐑉𐐱𐑋 𐑄 𐑁𐐬𐑉 𐐹𐐪𐑉𐐻𐑅 𐐱𐑂 𐑄 𐐲𐑉𐑃; 𐐰𐑌𐐼 𐑄 𐑌𐐩𐑇𐐲𐑌𐑆 𐐱𐑂 𐑄 𐐘𐐯𐑌𐐻𐐴𐑊𐑆 𐑇𐐰𐑊 𐐺𐐨 𐑀𐑉𐐩𐐻 𐐮𐑌 𐑄 𐐴𐑆 𐐱𐑂 𐑋𐐨, 𐑅𐐯𐑃 𐐘𐐱𐐼, 𐐮𐑌 𐐿𐐰𐑉𐐨𐐮𐑍 𐑄𐐯𐑋 𐑁𐐬𐑉𐑃 𐐻𐐭 𐑄 𐑊𐐰𐑌𐐼𐑆 𐐱𐑂 𐑄𐐩𐑉 𐐮𐑌𐐸𐐯𐑉𐐮𐐻-

𐐻𐐲𐑌𐑅. 𐐏𐐩, 𐑄 𐐿𐐮𐑍𐑆 𐐱𐑂 𐑄 𐐖𐐯𐑌𐐻𐐴𐑊𐑆 𐑇𐐰𐑊 𐐺 𐑌𐐲𐑉𐑅𐐮𐑍 𐑁𐐪𐑄𐐲𐑉𐑆 𐐲𐑌𐐻𐐭 𐑄𐐯𐑋, 𐐰𐑌𐐼 𐑄𐐯𐑉 𐐿𐐶𐐨𐑌𐑆 𐑇𐐰𐑊 𐐺𐐨𐐿𐐲𐑋 𐑌𐐲𐑉𐑅𐐮𐑍 𐑋𐐲𐑄𐐲𐑉𐑆; 𐐸𐐶𐐯𐑉𐑁𐐫𐑉, 𐑄 𐐹𐑉𐐱𐑋𐐮𐑅𐐯𐑆 𐐱𐑂 𐑄 𐐢𐐫𐑉𐐼 𐐪𐑉 𐑀𐑉𐐩𐐻 𐐲𐑌𐐻𐐭 𐑄 𐐖𐐯𐑌𐐻𐐴𐑊𐑆, 𐑁𐐫𐑉 𐐸𐐨 𐐸𐐰𐑃 𐑅𐐹𐐬𐐿𐐲𐑌 𐐮𐐻, 𐐰𐑌𐐼 𐐸𐐭 𐐿𐐰𐑌 𐐼𐐮𐑅𐐹𐐷𐐭𐐻? 𐐒𐐲𐐻 𐐺𐐨𐐸𐐬𐑊𐐼, 𐑄𐐮𐑅 𐑊𐐰𐑌𐐼, 𐑅𐐯𐐼 𐐘𐐱𐐼, 𐑇𐐰𐑊 𐐺 𐐩 𐑊𐐰𐑌𐐼 𐐱𐑂 𐑄𐐴𐑌 𐐮𐑌𐐸𐐯𐑉𐐮𐐻𐐲𐑌𐑅, 𐐰𐑌𐐼 𐑄 𐐖𐐯𐑌𐐻𐐴𐑊𐑆 𐑇𐐰𐑊 𐐺 𐐺𐑊𐐯𐑅𐐻 𐐲𐐹𐐱𐑌 𐑄 𐑊𐐰𐑌𐐼. 𐐈𐑌𐐼 𐑄𐐮𐑅 𐑊𐐰𐑌𐐼 𐑇𐐰𐑊 𐐺 𐐩 𐑊𐐰𐑌𐐼 𐐱𐑂 𐑊𐐮𐐺𐐲𐑉𐐻𐐨 𐐲𐑌𐐻𐐭 𐑄 𐐖𐐯𐑌𐐻𐐴𐑊𐑆, 𐐰𐑌𐐼 𐑄𐐯𐑉 𐑇𐐰𐑊 𐐺 𐑌𐐬 𐐿𐐮𐑍𐑆 𐐲𐐹𐐱𐑌 𐑄 𐑊𐐰𐑌𐐼, 𐐸𐐭 𐑇𐐰𐑊 𐑉𐐩𐑆 𐐲𐐹 𐐲𐑌𐐻𐐭 𐑄 𐐖𐐯𐑌𐐻𐐴𐑊𐑆; 𐐰𐑌𐐼 𐐌 𐐶𐐮𐑊 𐑁𐐫𐑉𐐻𐐮𐑁𐐴 𐑄𐐮𐑅 𐑊𐐰𐑌𐐼 𐐲𐑀𐐯𐑌𐑅𐐻 𐐫𐑊 𐐲𐑄𐐲𐑉 𐑌𐐩𐑇𐐲𐑌𐑆, 𐐰𐑌𐐼 𐐸𐐨 𐑄𐐰𐐻 𐑁𐐴𐐻𐐯𐑃 𐐲𐑀𐐯𐑌𐑅𐐻 𐐞𐐴𐐲𐑌 𐑇𐐰𐑊 𐐹𐐯𐑉𐐮𐑇, 𐑅𐐯𐑃 𐐘𐐱𐐼; 𐑁𐐫𐑉 𐐸𐐨 𐑄𐐰𐐻 𐑉𐐩𐑆𐐯𐑃 𐐲𐐹 𐐩 𐐿𐐮𐑍 𐐲𐑀𐐯𐑌𐑅𐐻 𐑋𐐨 𐑇𐐰𐑊 𐐹𐐯𐑉𐐮𐑇, 𐑁𐐫𐑉 𐐌, 𐑄 𐐢𐐫𐑉𐐼, 𐑄 𐐿𐐮𐑍 𐐱𐑂 𐐸𐐯𐑂𐐲𐑌, 𐐶𐐮𐑊 𐐺 𐑄𐐯𐑉 𐐿𐐮𐑍, 𐐰𐑌𐐼 𐐌 𐐶𐐮𐑊 𐐺 𐐩 𐑊𐐴𐐻 𐐲𐑌𐐻𐐭 𐑄𐐯𐑋 𐑁𐐫𐑉𐐯𐑂𐐲𐑉 𐑄𐐰𐐻 𐐸𐐨𐑉 𐑋𐐴 𐐶𐐲𐑉𐐼𐑆. 𐐐𐐶𐐯𐑉𐑁𐐫𐑉, 𐑁𐐫𐑉 𐑄𐐮𐑅 𐐿𐐫𐑆, 𐑄𐐰𐐻 𐑋𐐴 𐐿𐐲𐑂𐐯𐑌𐐰𐑌𐐻𐑅 𐑋𐐩 𐐺 𐑁𐐳𐑊𐑁𐐮𐑊𐐼 𐐸𐐶𐐮𐐽 𐐌 𐐸𐐰𐑂 𐑋𐐩𐐼 𐐲𐑌𐐻𐐭 𐑄 𐐽𐐮𐑊𐐼𐑉𐐯𐑌 𐐱𐑂 𐑋𐐯𐑌, 𐑄𐐰𐐻 𐐌 𐐶𐐮𐑊 𐐼𐐭 𐐲𐑌𐐻𐐭 𐑄𐐯𐑋 𐐸𐐶𐐴𐑊 𐑄𐐩 𐐪𐑉 𐐮𐑌 𐑄 𐑁𐑊𐐯𐑇, 𐐌 𐑋𐐲𐑅𐐻 𐑌𐐨𐐼𐑆 𐐼𐐯𐑅𐐻𐑉𐐱𐐦 𐑄 𐑅𐐨𐐿𐑉𐐯𐐻 𐐶𐐲𐑉𐐿𐑅 𐐱𐑂 𐐼𐐪𐑉𐐿𐑌𐐯𐑅, 𐐰𐑌𐐼 𐐱𐑂 𐑋𐐲𐑉𐐼𐐲𐑉𐑆, 𐐰𐑌𐐼 𐐱𐑂 𐐲𐐺𐐱𐑋𐐮𐑌𐐩𐑇𐐲𐑌𐑆; 𐐸𐐶𐐯𐑉𐑁𐐫𐑉, 𐐸𐐨 𐑄𐐰𐐻 𐑁𐐴𐐻𐐯𐑃 𐐲𐑀𐐯𐑌𐑅𐐻 𐐞𐐴𐐲𐑌, 𐐺𐐬𐑃 𐐖𐐭 𐐰𐑌𐐼 𐐖𐐯𐑌𐐻𐐴𐑊, 𐐺𐐬𐑃 𐐺𐐱𐑌𐐼 𐐰𐑌𐐼 𐑁𐑉𐐨, 𐐺𐐬𐑃 𐑋𐐩𐑊 𐐰𐑌𐐼 𐑁𐐨𐑋𐐩𐑊, 𐑇𐐰𐑊 𐐹𐐯𐑉𐐮𐑇: 𐑁𐐫𐑉 𐑄𐐩 𐐪𐑉 𐑄𐐩 𐐸𐐭 𐐪𐑉 𐑄 𐐸𐐬𐑉 𐐱𐑂 𐐫𐑊 𐑄 𐐲𐑉𐑃; 𐑁𐐫𐑉 𐑄𐐩 𐐸𐐭 𐐪𐑉 𐑌𐐱𐐻 𐑁𐐫𐑉 𐑋𐐨 𐐪𐑉 𐐲𐑀𐐯𐑌𐑅𐐻 𐑋𐐨 𐑅𐐯𐑃 𐐵𐑉 𐐘𐐱𐐼. 𐐙𐐫𐑉 𐐌 𐐶𐐮𐑊 𐑁𐐳𐑊𐑁𐐮𐑊 𐑋𐐴 𐐹𐑉𐐱𐑋𐐮𐑅𐐯𐑆 𐐸𐐶𐐮𐐽 𐐌 𐐸𐐰𐑂 𐑋𐐩𐐼 𐐲𐑌𐐻𐐭 𐑄 𐐽𐐮𐑊𐐼𐑉𐐯𐑌 𐐱𐑂 𐑋𐐯𐑌, 𐑄𐐰𐐻 𐐌 𐐶𐐮𐑊 𐐼𐐭 𐐲𐑌𐐻𐐭 𐑄𐐯𐑋 𐐸𐐶𐐴𐑊 𐑄𐐩 𐐪𐑉 𐐮𐑌 𐑄 𐑁𐑊𐐯𐑇: 𐐸𐐶𐐯𐑉𐑁𐐫𐑉, 𐑋𐐴 𐐺𐐨𐑊𐐲𐑂𐐯𐐼 𐐺𐑉𐐯𐑄𐑉𐐯𐑌, 𐑄𐐲𐑅 𐑅𐐯𐑃 𐐵𐑉 𐐘𐐱𐐼, 𐐌 𐐶𐐮𐑊 𐐰𐑁𐑊𐐮𐐿𐐻 𐑄𐐴 𐑅𐐨𐐼 𐐺𐐴 𐑄 𐐸𐐰𐑌𐐼 𐐱𐑂 𐑄 𐐖𐐯𐑌𐐻𐐴𐑊𐑆; 𐑌𐐯𐑂𐐲𐑉𐑄𐐯𐑊𐐯𐑅 𐐌 𐐶𐐮𐑊 𐑅𐐱𐑁𐐲𐑌 𐑄 𐐸𐐪𐑉𐐻𐑅 𐐱𐑂 𐑄 𐐖𐐯𐑌𐐻𐐴𐑊𐑆, 𐑄𐐰𐐻 𐑄𐐩 𐑇𐐰𐑊 𐐺 𐑊𐐴𐐿 𐐲𐑌𐐻𐐭 𐐩 𐑁𐐪𐑄𐐲𐑉 𐐻𐐭 𐑄𐐯𐑋; 𐐸𐐶𐐯𐑉𐑁𐐫𐑉 𐑄 𐐖𐐯𐑌𐐻𐐴𐑊𐑆 𐑇𐐰𐑊 𐐺 𐐺𐑊𐐯𐑅𐐻 𐐰𐑌𐐼 𐑌𐐲𐑋𐐺𐐲𐑉𐐼 𐐲𐑋𐐲𐑍 𐑄 𐐸𐐵𐑅 𐐱𐑂 𐐆𐑆𐑉𐐩𐐯𐑊. 𐐐𐐶𐐯𐑉𐑁𐐫𐑉, 𐐌 𐐶𐐮𐑊 𐐿𐐱𐑌𐑅𐐯𐐿𐑉𐐩𐐻 𐑄𐐮𐑅 𐑊𐐰𐑌𐐼 𐐲𐑌𐐻𐐭 𐑄𐐴 𐑅𐐨𐐼 𐐰𐑌𐐼 𐑄𐐩 𐐸𐐭 𐑇𐐰𐑊 𐐺 𐑌𐐲𐑋𐐺𐐲𐑉𐐼 𐐲𐑋𐐲𐑍 𐑄𐐴 𐑅𐐨𐐼, 𐑁𐐫𐑉𐐯𐑂𐐲𐑉, 𐑁𐐫𐑉 𐑄 𐑊𐐰𐑌𐐼 𐐱𐑂 𐑄𐐯𐑉 𐐮𐑌𐐸𐐯𐑉𐐮𐐻𐐲𐑌𐑅: 𐑁𐐫𐑉 𐐮𐐻 𐐮𐑆 𐐩 𐐽𐐦𐑅 𐑊𐐰𐑌𐐼, 𐑅𐐯𐑃 𐐘𐐱𐐼 𐐲𐑌𐐻𐐭 𐑋𐐨, 𐐲𐐺𐐲𐑂 𐐫𐑊 𐐲𐑄𐐲𐑉 𐑊𐐰𐑌𐐼𐑆, 𐐸𐐶𐐯𐑉𐑁𐐫𐑉 𐐌 𐐶𐐮𐑊 𐐸𐐰𐑂 𐐫𐑊 𐑋𐐯𐑌 𐑄𐐰𐐻 𐐼𐐶𐐯𐑊 𐑄𐐯𐑉𐐱𐑌 𐑄𐐰𐐻 𐑄𐐩 𐑇𐐰𐑊 𐐶𐐲𐑉𐑇𐐮𐐹 𐑋𐐨, 𐑅𐐯𐑃 𐐘𐐱𐐼.

3. 𐐈𐑌𐐼 𐑌𐐵, 𐑋𐐴 𐐺𐐨𐑊𐐲𐑂𐐯𐐼 𐐺𐑉𐐯𐑄𐑉𐐯𐑌, 𐑅𐐨𐐮𐑍 𐑄𐐰𐐻 𐐵𐑉 𐑋𐐲𐑉𐑅𐐮𐑁𐐳𐑊 𐐘𐐱𐐼 𐐸𐐰𐑆 𐑀𐐮𐑂𐐲𐑌 𐐲𐑅 𐑅𐐬 𐑀𐑉𐐩𐐻 𐑌𐐱𐑊𐐯𐐾 𐐿𐐱𐑌𐑅𐐲𐑉𐑌𐐮𐑍 𐑄𐐨𐑆 𐑃𐐮𐑍𐑆, 𐑊𐐯𐐻 𐐲𐑅 𐑉𐐨𐑋𐐯𐑋𐐺𐐲𐑉 𐐸𐐮𐑋, 𐐰𐑌𐐼 𐑊𐐩 𐐲𐑅𐐴𐐼 𐐵𐑉 𐑅𐐮𐑌𐑆, 𐐰𐑌𐐼 𐑌𐐱𐐻 𐐸𐐰𐑍 𐐼𐐵𐑌 𐐵𐑉 𐐸𐐯𐐼𐑆, 𐑁𐐫𐑉 𐐶𐐨 𐐪𐑉 𐑌𐐱𐐻 𐐿𐐰𐑅𐐻 𐐫𐑁; 𐑌𐐯𐑂𐐲𐑉𐑄𐐯𐑊𐐯𐑅 𐐶𐐨 𐐸𐐰𐑂 𐐺𐐮𐑌 𐐼𐑉𐐮𐑂𐐲𐑌 𐐵𐐻 𐐱𐑂 𐑄 𐑊𐐰𐑌𐐼 𐐱𐑂 𐐵𐑉 𐐮𐑌𐐸𐐯𐑉𐐮𐐻𐐲𐑌𐑅; 𐐺𐐲𐐻 𐐶𐐨 𐐸𐐰𐑂 𐐺𐐮𐑌 𐑊𐐯𐐼 𐐻𐐭 𐐩 𐐺𐐯𐐻𐐲𐑉 𐑊𐐰𐑌𐐼, 𐑁𐐫𐑉 𐑄 𐐢𐐫𐑉𐐼 𐐸𐐰𐑆 𐑋𐐩𐐼 𐑄 𐑅𐐨 𐐵𐑉 𐐹𐐰𐑃, 𐐰𐑌𐐼 𐐶𐐨 𐐪𐑉 𐐲𐐹𐐱𐑌 𐐰𐑌 𐐴𐑊 𐐱𐑂 𐑄 𐑅𐐨. 𐐒𐐲𐐻 𐑀𐑉𐐩𐐻 𐐪𐑉 𐑄 𐐹𐑉𐐱𐑋𐐮𐑅𐐯𐑆 𐐱𐑂 𐑄 𐐢𐐫𐑉𐐼 𐐲𐑌𐐻𐐭 𐑄𐐩 𐐸𐐭 𐐪𐑉 𐐲𐐹𐐱𐑌 𐑄 𐐴𐑊𐑆 𐐱𐑂 𐑄 𐑅𐐨; 𐐸𐐶𐐯𐑉𐑁𐐫𐑉 𐐰𐑆 𐐮𐐻 𐑅𐐯𐑆 𐐴𐑊𐑆, 𐑄𐐯𐑉 𐑋𐐲𐑅𐐻 𐑌𐐨𐐼𐑆 𐐺 𐑋𐐬𐑉 𐑄𐐰𐑌 𐑄𐐮𐑅, 𐐰𐑌𐐼 𐑄𐐩 𐐪𐑉 𐐮𐑌𐐸𐐰𐐺𐐮𐐻𐐯𐐼 𐐫𐑊𐑅𐐬 𐐺𐐴 𐐵𐑉 𐐺𐑉𐐯𐑄𐑉𐐯𐑌. 𐐙𐐫𐑉 𐐺𐐨𐐸𐐬𐑊𐐼, 𐑄 𐐢𐐫𐑉𐐼 𐐘𐐱𐐼 𐐸𐐰𐑆 𐑊𐐯𐐼 𐐲𐐶𐐩 𐑁𐑉𐐱𐑋 𐐻𐐴𐑋 𐐻𐐭 𐐻𐐴𐑋 𐑁𐑉𐐱𐑋 𐑄 𐐸𐐵𐑅 𐐱𐑂 𐐆𐑆𐑉𐐩𐐯𐑊, 𐐲𐐿𐐫𐑉𐐼𐐮𐑍 𐐻𐐭 𐐸𐐮𐑆 𐐶𐐮𐑊 𐐰𐑌𐐼 𐐹𐑊𐐯𐑈𐐲𐑉. 𐐈𐑌𐐼 𐑌𐐵 𐐺𐐨𐐸𐐬𐑊𐐼, 𐑄 𐐢𐐫𐑉𐐼 𐑉𐐨𐑋𐐯𐑋𐐺𐐲𐑉𐐯𐑃 𐐫𐑊 𐑄𐐩 𐐸𐐭 𐐸𐐰𐑂 𐐺𐐮𐑌 𐐺𐑉𐐬𐐿𐐲𐑌 𐐫𐑁, 𐐸𐐶𐐯𐑉𐑁𐐫𐑉 𐐸𐐨 𐑉𐐨𐑋𐐯𐑋𐐺𐐲𐑉𐐯𐑃 𐐲𐑅 𐐫𐑊𐑅𐐬; 𐑄𐐯𐑉𐑁𐐫𐑉 𐐽𐐨𐑉 𐐲𐐹 𐐷𐐭𐑉 𐐸𐐪𐑉𐐻𐑅, 𐐰𐑌𐐼 𐑉𐐨𐑋𐐯𐑋𐐺𐐲𐑉 𐑄𐐰𐐻 𐐷𐐨 𐐪𐑉 𐑁𐑉𐐨 𐐻𐐭 𐐰𐐿𐐻 𐑁𐐫𐑉 𐐷𐐭𐑉𐑅𐐯𐑊𐑂𐑆—𐐻𐐭 𐐽𐐭𐑆 𐑄 𐐶𐐩 𐐱𐑂 𐐯𐑂𐐲𐑉𐑊𐐰𐑅𐐻𐐮𐑍 𐐼𐐯𐑃, 𐐫𐑉 𐑄 𐐶𐐩 𐐱𐑂 𐐨𐐻𐐲𐑉𐑌𐐲𐑊 𐑊𐐴𐑁. 𐐐𐐶𐐯𐑉𐑁𐐫𐑉, 𐑋𐐴 𐐺𐐨𐑊𐐲𐑂𐐯𐐼 𐐺𐑉𐐯𐑄𐑉𐐯𐑌, 𐑉𐐯𐐿𐐱𐑌𐑅𐐴𐑊 𐐷𐐭𐑉𐑅𐐯𐑊𐑂𐑆 𐐻𐐭 𐑄 𐐶𐐮𐑊 𐐱𐑂 𐐘𐐱𐐼, 𐐰𐑌𐐼 𐑌𐐱𐐻 𐐻𐐭 𐑄 𐐶𐐮𐑊 𐐱𐑂 𐑄 𐐼𐐯𐑂𐐲𐑊 𐐰𐑌𐐼 𐑄 𐑁𐑊𐐯𐑇: 𐐰𐑌𐐼 𐑉𐐨𐑋𐐯𐑋𐐺𐐲𐑉 𐐰𐑁𐐻𐐲𐑉 𐐷𐐨 𐐪𐑉 𐑉𐐯𐐿𐐱𐑌𐑅𐐴𐑊𐐼 𐐲𐑌𐐻𐐭 𐐘𐐱𐐼, 𐑄𐐰𐐻 𐐮𐐻 𐐮𐑆 𐐬𐑌𐑊𐐨 𐐮𐑌 𐐰𐑌𐐼 𐑃𐑉𐐭 𐑄 𐑀𐑉𐐩𐑅 𐐱𐑂 𐐘𐐱𐐼 𐑄𐐰𐐻 𐐷𐐨 𐐪𐑉 𐑅𐐩𐑂𐐼. 𐐐𐐶𐐯𐑉𐑁𐐫𐑉, 𐑋𐐩 𐐘𐐱𐐼 𐑉𐐩𐑆 𐐷𐐭 𐑁𐑉𐐱𐑋 𐐼𐐯𐑃 𐐺𐐴 𐑄 𐐹𐐵𐐲𐑉 𐐱𐑂 𐑄 𐑉𐐯𐑆𐐲𐑉𐐯𐐿𐑇𐐲𐑌, 𐐰𐑌𐐼 𐐫𐑊𐑅𐐬 𐑁𐑉𐐱𐑋 𐐯𐑂𐐲𐑉𐑊𐐰𐑅𐐻𐐮𐑍 𐐼𐐯𐑃 𐐺𐐴 𐑄 𐐹𐐵𐐲𐑉 𐐱𐑂 𐑄 𐐲𐐻𐐬𐑌𐑋𐐯𐑌𐐻, 𐑄𐐰𐐻 𐐷𐐨 𐑋𐐩 𐐺 𐑉𐐨𐑅𐐨𐑂𐐼 𐐮𐑌𐐻𐐭 𐑄 𐐨𐐻𐐲𐑉𐑌𐐲𐑊 𐐿𐐮𐑍𐐼𐐲𐑋 𐐱𐑂 𐐘𐐱𐐼, 𐑄𐐰𐐻 𐐷𐐨 𐑋𐐩 𐐹𐑉𐐩𐑆 𐐸𐐮𐑋 𐑃𐑉𐐭 𐑀𐑉𐐩𐑅 𐐼𐐮𐑂𐐴𐑌. 𐐁𐑋𐐯𐑌.

𐐕𐐰𐐹𐐻𐐲𐑉 VIII.

1. 𐐈𐑌𐐼 𐑌𐐵 𐐖𐐩𐐿𐐲𐐺 𐑅𐐹𐐪𐐿 𐑋𐐯𐑌𐐨 𐑋𐐬𐑉 𐑃𐐮𐑍𐑆 𐐻𐐭 𐑋𐐴 𐐹𐐨𐐹𐑊 𐐰𐐻 𐑄𐐰𐐻 𐐻𐐴𐑋: 𐑌𐐯𐑂𐐲𐑉𐑄𐐲𐑊𐐯𐑅 𐐬𐑌𐑊𐐨 𐑄𐐨𐑆 𐑃𐐮𐑍𐑆 𐐸𐐰𐑂 𐐌 𐐿𐐫𐑆𐐼 𐐻𐐭 𐐺𐐨 𐑉𐐮𐐻𐑌, 𐑁𐐫𐑉 𐑄 𐑃𐐮𐑍𐑆 𐐸𐐶𐐮𐐽 𐐌 𐐸𐐰𐑂 𐑉𐐮𐐻𐑌 𐑅𐐲𐑁𐐴𐑅𐐯𐑃 𐑋𐐨.

2. 𐐈𐑌𐐼 𐑌𐐵 𐐌, 𐐤𐐨𐑁𐐴, 𐑉𐐴𐐻 𐑋𐐬𐑉 𐐱𐑂 𐑄 𐐶𐐲𐑉𐐼𐑆 𐐱𐑂 𐐌𐑆𐐩𐐲, 𐑁𐐫𐑉 𐑋𐐴 𐑅𐐬𐑊 𐐼𐐨𐑊𐐴𐐻𐐯𐑃 𐐮𐑌 𐐸𐐮𐑆 𐐶𐐲𐑉𐐼𐑆. 𐐙𐐫𐑉 𐐌 𐐶𐐮𐑊 𐑊𐐴𐐿𐐲𐑌 𐐸𐐮𐑆 𐐶𐐲𐑉𐐼𐑆 𐐲𐑌𐐻𐐭 𐑋𐐴 𐐹𐐨𐐹𐑊, 𐐰𐑌𐐼 𐐌 𐐶𐐮𐑊 𐑅𐐯𐑌𐐼 𐑄𐐯𐑋 𐑁𐐫𐑉𐑃 𐐲𐑌𐐻𐐭 𐐫𐑊 𐑋𐐴 𐐽𐐮𐑊𐐼𐑉𐐯𐑌, 𐑁𐐫𐑉 𐐸𐐨 𐑂𐐯𐑉𐐮𐑊𐐨 𐑅𐐫 𐑋𐐴 𐐡𐐨𐐼𐐨𐑋𐐲𐑉, 𐐨𐑂𐐲𐑌 𐐰𐑆 𐐌 𐐸𐐰𐑂 𐑅𐐨𐑌 𐐸𐐮𐑋. 𐐈𐑌𐐼 𐑋𐐴 𐐺𐑉𐐲𐑄𐐲𐑉 𐐖𐐩𐐿𐐲𐐺 𐐫𐑊𐑅𐐬 𐐸𐐰𐑆 𐑅𐐨𐑌 𐐸𐐮𐑋 𐐰𐑆 𐐌 𐐸𐐰𐑂 𐑅𐐨𐑌 𐐸𐐮𐑋: 𐐸𐐶𐐯𐑉𐑁𐐫𐑉 𐐌 𐐶𐐮𐑊 𐑅𐐯𐑌𐐼 𐑄𐐯𐑉 𐐶𐐲𐑉𐐼𐑆 𐑁𐐫𐑉𐑃 𐐲𐑌𐐻𐐭 𐑋𐐴 𐐽𐐮𐑊𐐼𐑉𐐯𐑌, 𐐻𐐭 𐐹𐑉𐐭𐑂 𐐲𐑌𐐻𐐭 𐑄𐐯𐑋 𐑄𐐰𐐻 𐑋𐐴 𐐶𐐲𐑉𐐼𐑆 𐐪𐑉 𐐻𐑉𐐭. 𐐐𐐶𐐯𐑉𐑁𐐫𐑉, 𐐺𐐴 𐑄 𐐶𐐲𐑉𐐼𐑆 𐐱𐑂 𐑃𐑉𐐨, 𐐘𐐱𐐼 𐐸𐐰𐑃 𐑅𐐯𐐼 𐐌 𐐶𐐮𐑊 𐐯𐑅𐐻𐐰𐐺𐑊𐐮𐑇 𐑋𐐴 𐐶𐐲𐑉𐐼. 𐐤𐐯𐑂𐐲𐑉𐑄𐐲𐑊𐐯𐑅, 𐐘𐐱𐐼 𐑅𐐯𐑌𐐼𐐯𐑃 𐑋𐐬𐑉 𐐶𐐮𐐻𐑌𐐯𐑅𐐯𐑆, 𐐰𐑌𐐼 𐐸𐐨 𐐹𐑉𐐭𐑂𐐯𐑃 𐐫𐑊 𐐸𐐮𐑆 𐐶𐐲𐑉𐐼𐑆. 𐐒𐐨𐐸𐐬𐑊𐐼, 𐑋𐐴 𐑅𐐬𐑊 𐐼𐐨𐑊𐐴𐐻𐐯𐑃 𐐮𐑌 𐐹𐑉𐐭𐑂𐐮𐑍 𐐲𐑌𐐻𐐭 𐑋𐐴 𐐹𐐨𐐹𐑊 𐑄 𐐻𐑉𐐭𐑃 𐐱𐑂 𐑄 𐐿𐐲𐑋𐐮𐑍 𐐱𐑂 𐐗𐑉𐐴𐑅𐐻: 𐑁𐐫𐑉, 𐑁𐐫𐑉 𐑄𐐮𐑅 𐐯𐑌𐐼 𐐸𐐰𐑃 𐑄 𐑊𐐫 𐐱𐑂 𐐣𐐬𐑆𐐯𐑆 𐐺𐐨𐑌 𐑀𐐮𐑂𐑌; 𐐰𐑌𐐼 𐐫𐑊 𐑃𐐮𐑍𐑆 𐐸𐐶𐐮𐐽 𐐸𐐰𐑂 𐐺𐐨𐑌 𐑀𐐮𐑂𐑌 𐐱𐑂 𐐘𐐱𐐼 𐑁𐑉𐐱𐑋 𐑄 𐐺𐐨𐑀𐐮𐑌𐐮𐑍 𐐱𐑂 𐑄 𐐶𐐲𐑉𐑊𐐼 𐐲𐑌𐐻𐐭 𐑋𐐰𐑌, 𐐪𐑉 𐑄 𐐻𐐮𐐹𐐮𐑁𐐴𐐮𐑍 𐐱𐑂 𐐸𐐮𐑋. 𐐈𐑌𐐼 𐐫𐑊𐑅𐐬 𐑋𐐴 𐑅𐐬𐑊 𐐼𐐨𐑊𐐴𐐻𐐯𐑃 𐐮𐑌 𐑄 𐐿𐐲𐑂𐐯𐑌𐐰𐑌𐐻𐑅 𐐱𐑂 𐑄 𐐢𐐫𐑉𐐼 𐐸𐐶𐐮𐐽 𐐸𐐨 𐐸𐐰𐑃 𐑋𐐩𐐼 𐐻𐐭 𐐵𐑉 𐑁𐐪𐑄𐐲𐑉𐑆; 𐐷𐐩, 𐑋𐐴 𐑅𐐬𐑊 𐐼𐐨𐑊𐐴𐐻𐐯𐑃 𐐮𐑌 𐐸𐐮𐑆 𐑀𐑉𐐩𐑅, 𐐰𐑌𐐼 𐐮𐑌 𐐸𐐮𐑆 𐐾𐐲𐑅𐐻𐐮𐑅, 𐐰𐑌𐐼 𐐹𐐵𐐲𐑉, 𐐰𐑌𐐼 𐑋𐐲𐑉𐑅𐐨 𐐮𐑌 𐑄 𐑀𐑉𐐩𐐻 𐐰𐑌𐐼 𐐨𐐻𐐲𐑉𐑌𐐲𐑊 𐐹𐑊𐐰𐑌 𐐱𐑂 𐐼𐐨𐑊𐐮𐑂𐐲𐑉𐐲𐑌𐑅 𐑁𐑉𐐱𐑋 𐐼𐐯𐑃. 𐐈𐑌𐐼 𐑋𐐴 𐑅𐐬𐑊 𐐼𐐨𐑊𐐴𐐻𐐯𐑃 𐐮𐑌 𐐹𐑉𐐭𐑂𐐮𐑍 𐐲𐑌𐐻𐐭 𐑋𐐴 𐐹𐐨𐐹𐑊 𐑄𐐰𐐻 𐑅𐐩𐑂 𐐗𐑉𐐴𐑅𐐻 𐑇𐐳𐐼 𐐿𐐲𐑋 𐐫𐑊 𐑋𐐯𐑌 𐑋𐐲𐑅𐐻 𐐹𐐯𐑉𐐮𐑇. 𐐙𐐫𐑉 𐐮𐑁 𐑄𐐯𐑉 𐐺𐐨 𐑌𐐬 𐐗𐑉𐐴𐑅𐐻, 𐑄𐐯𐑉 𐐺𐐨 𐑌𐐬 𐐘𐐱𐐼; 𐐰𐑌𐐼 𐐮𐑁 𐑄𐐯𐑉 𐐺𐐨 𐑌𐐬 𐐘𐐱𐐼 𐐶𐐨 𐐪𐑉 𐑌𐐱𐐻, 𐑁𐐫𐑉 𐑄𐐯𐑉 𐐿𐐳𐐼 𐐸𐐰𐑂 𐐺𐐨𐑌 𐑌𐐬 𐐿𐑉𐐨𐐩𐑇𐐲𐑌. 𐐒𐐲𐐻 𐑄𐐯𐑉 𐐮𐑆 𐐲 𐐘𐐱𐐼, 𐐰𐑌𐐼 𐐸𐐨 𐐮𐑆 𐐗𐑉𐐴𐑅𐐻, 𐐰𐑌𐐼 𐐸𐐨 𐐿𐐲𐑋𐐯𐑃 𐐮𐑌 𐑄 𐑁𐐳𐑊𐑌𐐯𐑅 𐐱𐑂 𐐸𐐮𐑆 𐐬𐑌 𐐻𐐴𐑋.

3. 𐐈𐑌𐐼 𐑌𐐵 𐐌 𐑉𐐴𐐻 𐑅𐐲𐑋 𐐱𐑂 𐑄 𐐶𐐲𐑉𐐼𐑆 𐐱𐑂 𐐌𐑆𐐩𐐲, 𐑄𐐰𐐻 𐐸𐐭𐑅𐐬 𐐱𐑂 𐑋𐐴 𐐹𐐨𐐹𐑊 𐑇𐐰𐑊 𐑅𐐨 𐑄𐐨𐑆 𐐶𐐲𐑉𐐼𐑆 𐑋𐐩 𐑊𐐮𐑁𐐻 𐐲𐐹 𐑄𐐯𐑉 𐐸𐐪𐑉𐐻𐑅 𐐰𐑌𐐼 𐑉𐐨𐐾𐐲𐐴𐑅 𐑁𐐫𐑉 𐐫𐑊 𐑋𐐯𐑌. 𐐤𐐵 𐑄𐐨𐑆 𐐪𐑉 𐑄 𐐶𐐲𐑉𐐼𐑆, 𐐰𐑌𐐼 𐐷𐐨 𐑋𐐩 𐑊𐐴𐐿𐐲𐑌 𐑄𐐯𐑋 𐐲𐑌𐐻𐐭 𐐷𐐭 𐐰𐑌𐐼 𐐲𐑌𐐻𐐭 𐐫𐑊 𐑋𐐯𐑌.

4. 𐐜 𐐶𐐲𐑉𐐼 𐑄𐐰𐐻 𐐌𐑆𐐩𐐲, 𐑄 𐑅𐐲𐑌 𐐱𐑂 𐐁𐑋𐐱𐑆, 𐑅𐐫, 𐐿𐐲𐑌𐑅𐐲𐑉𐑌𐐮𐑍 𐐖𐐭𐐼𐐲 𐐰𐑌𐐼 𐐖𐐯𐑉𐐭𐑅𐐲𐑊𐐯𐑋. 𐐈𐑌𐐼 𐐮𐐻 𐑇𐐰𐑊 𐐿𐐲𐑋 𐐻𐐭 𐐹𐐰𐑅 𐐮𐑌 𐑄 𐑊𐐰𐑅𐐻 𐐼𐐩𐑆, 𐐸𐐶𐐯𐑌 𐑄 𐑋𐐵𐑌𐐻𐐲𐑌 𐐱𐑂 𐑄 𐐢𐐫𐑉𐐼'𐑆 𐐸𐐵𐑅 𐑇𐐰𐑊 𐐺𐐨 𐐯𐑅𐐻𐐰𐐺𐑊𐐮𐑇𐐻 𐐮𐑌 𐑄 𐐻𐐱𐐹 𐐱𐑂 𐑄 𐑋𐐵𐑌𐐻𐐲𐑌𐑆, 𐐰𐑌𐐼 𐑇𐐰𐑊 𐐺𐐨 𐐯𐑀𐑆𐐪𐑊𐐻𐐯𐐼 𐐲𐐺𐐲𐑂 𐑄 𐐸𐐮𐑊𐑆, 𐐰𐑌𐐼 𐐫𐑊 𐑌𐐩𐑇𐐲𐑌𐑆 𐑇𐐰𐑊 𐑁𐑊𐐬 𐐲𐑌𐐻𐐭 𐐮𐐻. 𐐈𐑌𐐼 𐑋𐐯𐑌𐐨 𐐹𐐨𐐹𐑊 𐑇𐐰𐑊 𐑀𐐬 𐐰𐑌𐐼 𐑅𐐩, 𐐗𐐲𐑋 𐐷𐐨, 𐐰𐑌𐐼 𐑊𐐯𐐻 𐐲𐑅 𐑀𐐬 𐐲𐐹 𐐻𐐭 𐑄 𐑋𐐵𐑌𐐻𐐲𐑌 𐐱𐑂 𐑄 𐐢𐐫𐑉𐐼, 𐐻𐐭 𐑄 𐐸𐐵𐑅 𐐱𐑂 𐑄 𐐘𐐱𐐼 𐐱𐑂 𐐖𐐩𐐿𐐲𐐺; 𐐰𐑌𐐼 𐐸𐐨 𐐶𐐮𐑊 𐐻𐐨𐐽 𐐲𐑅 𐐱𐑂 𐐸𐐮𐑆 𐐶𐐩𐑆, 𐐰𐑌𐐼 𐐶𐐨 𐐶𐐮𐑊 𐐶𐐫𐐿 𐐮𐑌 𐐸𐐮𐑆 𐐹𐐪𐑃𐑅: 𐑁𐐫𐑉 𐐵𐐻 𐐱𐑂 𐐞𐐴𐐲𐑌 𐑇𐐰𐑊 𐑀𐐬 𐑁𐐫𐑉𐑃 𐑄 𐑊𐐫, 𐐰𐑌𐐼 𐑄 𐐶𐐲𐑉𐐼 𐐱𐑂 𐑄 𐐢𐐫𐑉𐐼 𐑁𐑉𐐱𐑋 𐐖𐐯𐑉𐐭𐑅𐐲𐑊𐐯𐑋. 𐐈𐑌𐐼 𐐸𐐨 𐑇𐐰𐑊 𐐾𐐲𐐾 𐐲𐑋𐐲𐑍 𐑄 𐑌𐐩𐑇𐐲𐑌𐑆, 𐐰𐑌𐐼 𐑇𐐰𐑊 𐑉𐐨𐐺𐐷𐐭𐐿 𐑋𐐯𐑌𐐨 𐐹𐐨𐐹𐑊: 𐐰𐑌𐐼 𐑄𐐩 𐑇𐐰𐑊 𐐺𐐨𐐻 𐑄𐐯𐑉 𐑅𐐫𐑉𐐼𐑆 𐐮𐑌𐐻𐐭 𐐹𐑊𐐵-𐑇𐐯𐑉𐑆, 𐐰𐑌𐐼 𐑄𐐯𐑉 𐑅𐐹𐐨𐑉𐑆 𐐮𐑌𐐻𐐭 𐐹𐑉𐐭𐑌𐐮𐑍-𐐸𐐳𐐿𐑅: 𐑌𐐩𐑇𐐲𐑌 𐑇𐐰𐑊 𐑌𐐱𐐻 𐑊𐐮𐑁𐐻 𐐲𐐹 𐑅𐐫𐑉𐐼 𐐲𐑀𐐯𐑌𐑅𐐻 𐑌𐐩𐑇𐐲𐑌, 𐑌𐐨𐑄𐐲𐑉 𐑇𐐰𐑊 𐑄𐐩 𐑊𐐲𐑉𐑌 𐐶𐐫𐑉 𐐯𐑌𐐨 𐑋𐐬𐑉. 𐐄 𐐸𐐵𐑅 𐐱𐑂 𐐖𐐩𐐿𐐲𐐺, 𐐿𐐲𐑋 𐐷𐐨 𐐰𐑌𐐼 𐑊𐐯𐐻 𐐲𐑅 𐐶𐐫𐐿 𐐮𐑌 𐑄 𐑊𐐴𐐻 𐐱𐑂 𐑄 𐐢𐐫𐑉𐐼; 𐐷𐐩, 𐐿𐐲𐑋, 𐑁𐐫𐑉 𐐷𐐨 𐐸𐐰𐑂 𐐫𐑊 𐑀𐐱𐑌 𐐲𐑅𐐻𐑉𐐩, 𐐯𐑂𐑉𐐨 𐐶𐐲𐑌 𐐻𐐭 𐐸𐐮𐑆 𐐶𐐮𐐿𐐯𐐼 𐐶𐐩𐑆.

5. 𐐜𐐯𐑉𐑁𐐫𐑉, 𐐄 𐐢𐐫𐑉𐐼, 𐑄𐐵 𐐸𐐰𐑅𐐻 𐑁𐐫𐑉𐑅𐐩𐐿𐐲𐑌 𐑄𐐴 𐐹𐐨𐐹𐑊, 𐑄 𐐸𐐵𐑅 𐐱𐑂 𐐖𐐩𐐿𐐲𐐺, 𐐺𐐨𐐿𐐫𐑆 𐑄𐐩 𐐺𐐨 𐑉𐐨𐐹𐑊𐐯𐑌𐐮𐑇𐐻 𐑁𐑉𐐱𐑋 𐑄 𐐨𐑅𐐻, 𐐰𐑌𐐼 𐐸𐐪𐑉𐐿𐐲𐑌 𐐲𐑌𐐻𐐭 𐑅𐐭𐑃-𐑅𐐩𐐲𐑉𐑆 𐑊𐐴𐐿 𐑄 𐐙𐐮𐑊𐐮𐑅𐐻𐐴𐑌𐑆, 𐐰𐑌𐐼 𐑄𐐩 𐐹𐑊𐐨𐑆 𐑄𐐯𐑋𐑅𐐯𐑊𐑂𐑆 𐐮𐑌 𐑄 𐐽𐐮𐑊𐐼𐑉𐐯𐑌 𐐱𐑂 𐑅𐐻𐑉𐐩𐑌𐐾𐐲𐑉𐑆. 𐐜𐐯𐑉 𐑊𐐰𐑌𐐼 𐐫𐑊𐑅𐐬 𐐮𐑆 𐑁𐐳𐑊 𐐱𐑂 𐑅𐐮𐑊𐑂𐐲𐑉 𐐰𐑌𐐼 𐑀𐐬𐑊𐐼, 𐑌𐐨𐑄𐐲𐑉 𐐮𐑆 𐑄𐐯𐑉 𐐯𐑌𐐨 𐐯𐑌𐐼 𐐱𐑂 𐑄𐐯𐑉 𐐻𐑉𐐯𐑈𐐲𐑉𐑆—𐑄𐐯𐑉 𐑊𐐰𐑌𐐼 𐐮𐑆 𐐫𐑊𐑅𐐬 𐑁𐐳𐑊 𐐱𐑂 𐐸𐐫𐑉𐑅𐐯𐑆, 𐑌𐐨𐑄𐐲𐑉 𐐮𐑆 𐑄𐐯𐑉 𐐯𐑌𐐨 𐐯𐑌𐐼 𐐱𐑂 𐑄𐐯𐑉 𐐽𐐰𐑉𐐨𐐲𐐻𐑅: 𐑄𐐯𐑉 𐑊𐐰𐑌𐐼 𐐮𐑆 𐐫𐑊𐑅𐐬 𐑁𐐳𐑊 𐐱𐑂 𐐴𐐼𐐲𐑊𐑆—𐑄𐐩

𐐶𐐲𐑉𐑇𐐮𐐹 𐑄 𐐶𐐲𐑉𐐿 𐐱𐑂 𐑄𐐯𐑉 𐐬𐑌 𐐸𐐰𐑌𐐼𐑆, 𐑄𐐰𐐻 𐐸𐐶𐐮𐐽 𐑄𐐯𐑉 𐐬𐑌 𐑁𐐮𐑍𐑀𐐲𐑉𐑆 𐐸𐐰𐑂 𐑋𐐩𐐼: 𐐰𐑌𐐼 𐑄 𐑋𐐨𐑌 𐑋𐐰𐑌 𐐺𐐵𐐯𐑃 𐑌𐐱𐐻 𐐼𐐵𐑌, 𐐰𐑌𐐼 𐑄 𐑀𐑉𐐩𐐻 𐑋𐐰𐑌 𐐸𐐲𐑋𐐺𐑊𐐯𐑃 𐐸𐐮𐑋𐑅𐐯𐑊𐑁 𐑌𐐱𐐻, 𐑄𐐯𐑉𐑁𐐬𐑉, 𐑁𐐫𐑉𐑀𐐮𐑂 𐐸𐐮𐑋 𐑌𐐱𐐻.

6. 𐐄 𐐷𐐨 𐐶𐐮𐐿𐐯𐐼 𐐶𐐲𐑌𐑆, 𐐯𐑌𐐻𐐲𐑉 𐐮𐑌𐐻𐐭 𐑄 𐑉𐐱𐐿, 𐐰𐑌𐐼 𐐸𐐴𐐼 𐑄𐐨 𐐮𐑌 𐑄 𐐼𐐲𐑅𐐻, 𐑁𐐫𐑉 𐑄 𐑁𐐨𐑉 𐐱𐑂 𐑄 𐐢𐐫𐑉𐐼 𐐰𐑌𐐼 𐑄 𐑀𐑊𐐬𐑉𐐨 𐐱𐑂 𐐸𐐮𐑆 𐑋𐐰𐐾𐐯𐑅𐐻𐐨 𐑇𐐰𐑊 𐑅𐑋𐐴𐐻 𐑄𐐨. 𐐈𐑌𐐼 𐐮𐐻 𐑇𐐰𐑊 𐐿𐐲𐑋 𐐻𐐭 𐐹𐐰𐑅 𐑄𐐰𐐻 𐑄 𐑊𐐱𐑁𐐻𐐨 𐑊𐐳𐐿𐑅 𐐱𐑂 𐑋𐐰𐑌 𐑇𐐰𐑊 𐐺𐐨 𐐸𐐲𐑋𐐺𐑊𐐼, 𐐰𐑌𐐼 𐑄 𐐸𐐫𐐻𐐨𐑌𐐯𐑅 𐐱𐑂 𐑋𐐯𐑌 𐑇𐐰𐑊 𐐺𐐨 𐐺𐐵𐐼 𐐼𐐵𐑌, 𐐰𐑌𐐼 𐑄 𐐢𐐫𐑉𐐼 𐐰𐑊𐐬𐑌 𐑇𐐰𐑊 𐐺𐐨 𐐯𐑀𐑆𐐫𐑊𐐻𐐯𐐼 𐐮𐑌 𐑄𐐰𐐻 𐐼𐐩. 𐐙𐐫𐑉 𐑄 𐐼𐐩 𐐱𐑂 𐑄 𐐢𐐫𐑉𐐼 𐐱𐑂 𐐐𐐬𐑅𐐻𐑅 𐑅𐐭𐑌 𐐿𐐲𐑋𐐯𐑃 𐐲𐐹𐐱𐑌 𐐫𐑊 𐑌𐐩𐑇𐐲𐑌𐑆; 𐐷𐐩, 𐐲𐐹𐐱𐑌 𐐯𐑂𐐲𐑉𐐨 𐐶𐐲𐑌; 𐐷𐐩, 𐐲𐐹𐐱𐑌 𐑄 𐐹𐑉𐐵𐐼 𐐰𐑌𐐼 𐑊𐐱𐑁𐐻𐐨, 𐐰𐑌𐐼 𐐲𐐹𐐱𐑌 𐐯𐑂𐐲𐑉𐐨 𐐶𐐲𐑌 𐐸𐐭 𐐮𐑆 𐑊𐐮𐑁𐐻𐐯𐐼 𐐲𐐹, 𐐰𐑌𐐼 𐐸𐐨 𐑇𐐰𐑊 𐐺𐐨 𐐺𐑉𐐫𐐻 𐑊𐐬; 𐐷𐐩, 𐐰𐑌𐐼 𐑄 𐐼𐐩 𐐱𐑂 𐑄 𐐢𐐫𐑉𐐼 𐑇𐐰𐑊 𐐿𐐲𐑋 𐐲𐐹𐐱𐑌 𐐫𐑊 𐑄 𐑅𐐨𐐼𐐲𐑉𐑆 𐐱𐑂 𐐢𐐯𐐺𐐲𐑌𐐲𐑌, 𐑁𐐫𐑉 𐑄𐐩 𐐪𐑉 𐐸𐐴 𐐰𐑌𐐼 𐑊𐐮𐑁𐐻𐐯𐐼 𐐲𐐹; 𐐰𐑌𐐼 𐐲𐐹𐐱𐑌 𐐫𐑊 𐑄 𐐬𐐿𐑅 𐐱𐑂 𐐒𐐩𐑇𐐲𐑌, 𐐰𐑌𐐼 𐐲𐐹𐐱𐑌 𐐫𐑊 𐑄 𐐸𐐴 𐑋𐐵𐑌𐐻𐐲𐑌𐑆, 𐐰𐑌𐐼 𐐲𐐹𐐱𐑌 𐐫𐑊 𐑄 𐐸𐐮𐑊𐑆, 𐐰𐑌𐐼 𐐲𐐹𐐱𐑌 𐐫𐑊 𐑄 𐑌𐐩𐑇𐐲𐑌𐑆 𐐸𐐶𐐮𐐽 𐐪𐑉 𐑊𐐮𐑁𐐻𐐯𐐼 𐐲𐐹, 𐐰𐑌𐐼 𐐲𐐹𐐱𐑌 𐐯𐑂𐐲𐑉𐐨 𐐹𐐨𐐹𐑊, 𐐰𐑌𐐼 𐐲𐐹𐐱𐑌 𐐯𐑂𐐲𐑉𐐨 𐐸𐐴 𐐻𐐵𐐲𐑉, 𐐰𐑌𐐼 𐐲𐐹𐐱𐑌 𐐯𐑂𐐲𐑉𐐨 𐑁𐐯𐑌𐑅𐐻 𐐶𐐫𐑊, 𐐰𐑌𐐼 𐐲𐐹𐐱𐑌 𐐫𐑊 𐑄 𐑇𐐮𐐹𐑅 𐐱𐑂 𐑄 𐑅𐐨, 𐐰𐑌𐐼 𐐲𐐹𐐱𐑌 𐐫𐑊 𐑄 𐑇𐐮𐐹𐑅 𐐱𐑂 𐐓𐐪𐑉𐑇𐐮𐑇, 𐐰𐑌𐐼 𐐲𐐹𐐱𐑌 𐐫𐑊 𐐹𐑊𐐯𐑆𐐲𐑌𐐻 𐐹𐐮𐐿𐐽𐐲𐑉𐑆. 𐐈𐑌𐐼 𐑄 𐑊𐐱𐑁𐐻𐐨𐑌𐐯𐑅 𐐱𐑂 𐑋𐐰𐑌 𐑇𐐰𐑊 𐐺𐐨 𐐺𐐵𐐼 𐐼𐐵𐑌, 𐐰𐑌𐐼 𐑄 𐐸𐐫𐐻𐐨𐑌𐐯𐑅 𐐱𐑂 𐑋𐐯𐑌 𐑇𐐰𐑊 𐐺𐐨 𐑋𐐩𐐼 𐑊𐐬; 𐐰𐑌𐐼 𐑄 𐐢𐐫𐑉𐐼 𐐰𐑊𐐬𐑌 𐑇𐐰𐑊 𐐺𐐨 𐐯𐑀𐑆𐐫𐑊𐐻𐐯𐐼 𐐮𐑌 𐑄𐐰𐐻 𐐼𐐩. 𐐈𐑌𐐼 𐑄 𐐴𐐼𐐲𐑊𐑆 𐐸𐐨 𐑇𐐰𐑊 𐐲𐐻𐐲𐑉𐑊𐐨 𐐰𐐺𐐱𐑊𐐮𐑇. 𐐈𐑌𐐼 𐑄𐐩 𐑇𐐰𐑊 𐑀𐐬 𐐮𐑌𐐻𐐭 𐑄 𐐸𐐬𐑊𐑆 𐐱𐑂 𐑄 𐑉𐐱𐐿𐑅, 𐐰𐑌𐐼 𐐮𐑌𐐻𐐭 𐑄 𐐿𐐩𐑂𐑆 𐐱𐑂 𐑄 𐐲𐑉𐑃, 𐑁𐐫𐑉 𐑄 𐑁𐐨𐑉 𐐱𐑂 𐑄 𐐢𐐫𐑉𐐼 𐑇𐐰𐑊 𐐿𐐲𐑋 𐐲𐐹𐐱𐑌 𐑄𐐯𐑋, 𐐰𐑌𐐼 𐑄 𐑀𐑊𐐬𐑉𐐨 𐐱𐑂 𐐸𐐮𐑆 𐑋𐐰𐐾𐐯𐑅𐐻𐐨 𐑇𐐰𐑊 𐑅𐑋𐐴𐐻 𐑄𐐯𐑋, 𐐸𐐶𐐯𐑌 𐐸𐐨 𐐲𐑉𐐴𐑆𐐯𐑃 𐐻𐐭 𐑇𐐩𐐿 𐐻𐐯𐑉𐐲𐐺𐑊𐐨 𐑄 𐐲𐑉𐑃. 𐐆𐑌 𐑄𐐰𐐻 𐐼𐐩 𐐩 𐑋𐐰𐑌 𐑇𐐰𐑊 𐐿𐐰𐑅𐐻 𐐸𐐮𐑆 𐐴𐐼𐐲𐑊𐑆 𐐱𐑂 𐑅𐐮𐑊𐑂𐐲𐑉, 𐐰𐑌𐐼 𐐸𐐮𐑆 𐐴𐐼𐐲𐑊𐑆 𐐱𐑂 𐑀𐐬𐑊𐐼, 𐐸𐐶𐐮𐐽 𐐸𐐨 𐐸𐐰𐑃 𐑋𐐩𐐼 𐑁𐐫𐑉 𐐸𐐮𐑋𐑅𐐯𐑊𐑁 𐐻𐐭 𐐶𐐲𐑉𐑇𐐮𐐹, 𐐻𐐭 𐑄 𐑋𐐬𐑊𐑆 𐐰𐑌𐐼 𐐻𐐭 𐑄 𐐺𐐰𐐻𐑅; 𐐻𐐭 𐑀𐐬 𐐮𐑌𐐻𐐭 𐑄 𐐿𐑊𐐯𐑁𐐻𐑅 𐐱𐑂 𐑄 𐑉𐐱𐐿𐑅, 𐐰𐑌𐐼 𐐮𐑌𐐻𐐭 𐑄 𐐻𐐱𐐹𐑅 𐐱𐑂 𐑄 𐑉𐐰𐑀𐐯𐐼 𐑉𐐱𐐿𐑅, 𐑁𐐫𐑉 𐑄 𐑁𐐨𐑉 𐐱𐑂 𐑄 𐐢𐐫𐑉𐐼 𐑇𐐰𐑊 𐐿𐐲𐑋 𐐲𐐹𐐱𐑌 𐑄𐐯𐑋, 𐐰𐑌𐐼 𐑄 𐑋𐐰𐐾𐐯𐑅𐐻𐐨 𐐱𐑂 𐐸𐐮𐑆 𐑀𐑊𐐬𐑉𐐨 𐑇𐐰𐑊 𐑅𐑋𐐴𐐻 𐑄𐐯𐑋, 𐐸𐐶𐐯𐑌 𐐸𐐨 𐐲𐑉𐐴𐑆𐐯𐑃 𐐻𐐭 𐑇𐐩𐐿 𐐻𐐯𐑉𐐲𐐺𐑊𐐨 𐑄 𐐲𐑉𐑃. 𐐝𐐨𐑅 𐐷𐐨 𐑁𐑉𐐱𐑋 𐑋𐐰𐑌, 𐐸𐐭𐑆 𐐺𐑉𐐯𐑃 𐐮𐑆 𐐮𐑌 𐐸𐐮𐑆 𐑌𐐱𐑅𐐻𐑉𐐮𐑊𐑆; 𐑁𐐫𐑉 𐐸𐐶𐐯𐑉𐐮𐑌 𐐮𐑆 𐐸𐐨 𐐻𐐭 𐐺𐐨 𐐰𐐿𐐵𐑌𐐻𐐯𐐼 𐐱𐑂?

7. 𐐙𐐫𐑉 𐐺𐐨𐐸𐐬𐑊𐐼, 𐑄 𐐢𐐫𐑉𐐼, 𐑄 𐐢𐐫𐑉𐐼 𐐱𐑂 𐐐𐐬𐑅𐐻𐑅, 𐐼𐐲𐑃 𐐻𐐩𐐿 𐐰𐐶𐐩 𐑁𐑉𐐱𐑋 𐐖𐐲𐑉𐐭𐑅𐐲𐑊𐐯𐑋, 𐐰𐑌𐐼 𐑁𐑉𐐱𐑋 𐐖𐐭𐐼𐐲, 𐑄 𐑅𐐻𐐩 𐐰𐑌𐐼 𐑄 𐑅𐐻𐐰𐑁, 𐑄 𐐸𐐬𐑊 𐑅𐐻𐐰𐑁 𐐱𐑂 𐐺𐑉𐐯𐐼, 𐐰𐑌𐐼 𐑄 𐐸𐐬𐑊 𐑅𐐻𐐩 𐐱𐑂 𐐶𐐫𐐻𐐲𐑉, 𐑄 𐑋𐐴𐐻𐐨 𐑋𐐰𐑌, 𐐰𐑌𐐼 𐑄 𐑋𐐰𐑌 𐐱𐑂 𐐶𐐫𐑉, 𐑄 𐐾𐐲𐐾, 𐐰𐑌𐐼 𐑄 𐐹𐑉𐐱𐑁𐐯𐐻, 𐐰𐑌𐐼 𐑄 𐐹𐑉𐐭𐐼𐐯𐑌𐐻, 𐐰𐑌𐐼 𐑄 𐐩𐑌𐑇𐐯𐑌𐐻, 𐑄 𐐿𐐰𐐹𐐻𐐮𐑌 𐐱𐑂 𐑁𐐮𐑁𐐻𐐨, 𐐰𐑌𐐼 𐑄 𐐱𐑌𐐲𐑉𐐲𐐺𐑊 𐑋𐐰𐑌, 𐐰𐑌𐐼 𐑄 𐐿𐐵𐑌𐑅𐐯𐑊𐐲𐑉, 𐐰𐑌𐐼 𐑄 𐐿𐐲𐑌𐐮𐑍 𐐪𐑉𐐻𐐮𐑁𐐮𐑅𐐲𐑉, 𐐰𐑌𐐼 𐑄 𐐯𐑊𐐬𐐿𐐶𐐯𐑌𐐻 𐐱𐑉𐐲𐐻𐐲𐑉. 𐐈𐑌𐐼 𐐌 𐐶𐐮𐑊 𐑀𐐮𐑂 𐐽𐐮𐑊𐐼𐑉𐐯𐑌 𐐲𐑌𐐻𐐭 𐑄𐐯𐑋 𐐻𐐭 𐐺𐐨 𐑄𐐯𐑉 𐐹𐑉𐐮𐑌𐑅𐐯𐑆, 𐐰𐑌𐐼 𐐺𐐩𐐺𐑆 𐑇𐐰𐑊 𐑉𐐭𐑊 𐐬𐑂𐐲𐑉 𐑄𐐯𐑋. 𐐈𐑌𐐼 𐑄 𐐹𐐨𐐹𐑊 𐑇𐐰𐑊 𐐺𐐨 𐐱𐐹𐑉𐐯𐑅𐐻, 𐐯𐑂𐐲𐑉𐐨 𐐶𐐲𐑌 𐐺𐐴 𐐰𐑌𐐲𐑄𐐲𐑉, 𐐰𐑌𐐼 𐐯𐑂𐐲𐑉𐐨 𐐶𐐲𐑌 𐐺𐐴 𐐸𐐮𐑆 𐑌𐐩𐐺𐐲𐑉; 𐑄 𐐽𐐴𐑊𐐼 𐑇𐐰𐑊 𐐺𐐨𐐸𐐩𐑂 𐐸𐐮𐑋𐑅𐐯𐑊𐑁 𐐹𐑉𐐵𐐼𐑊𐐨 𐐲𐑀𐐯𐑌𐑅𐐻 𐑄 𐐩𐑌𐑇𐐯𐑌𐐻, 𐐰𐑌𐐼 𐑄 𐐺𐐩𐑅 𐐲𐑀𐐯𐑌𐑅𐐻 𐑄 𐐱𐑌𐐲𐑉𐐲𐐺𐑊. 𐐐𐐶𐐯𐑌 𐐩 𐑋𐐰𐑌 𐑇𐐰𐑊 𐐻𐐩𐐿 𐐸𐐬𐑊𐐼 𐐱𐑂 𐐸𐐮𐑆 𐐺𐑉𐐲𐑄𐐲𐑉 𐐱𐑂 𐑄 𐐸𐐵𐑅 𐐱𐑂 𐐸𐐮𐑆 𐑁𐐪𐑄𐐲𐑉, 𐐰𐑌𐐼 𐑇𐐰𐑊 𐑅𐐩: 𐐜𐐵 𐐸𐐰𐑅𐐻 𐐿𐑊𐐬𐑄𐐮𐑍, 𐐺𐐨 𐑄𐐵 𐐵𐑉 𐑉𐐭𐑊𐐲𐑉, 𐐰𐑌𐐼 𐑊𐐯𐐻 𐑌𐐱𐐻 𐑄𐐮𐑅 𐑉𐐭𐐮𐑌 𐐿𐐲𐑋 𐐲𐑌𐐼𐐲𐑉 𐑄𐐴 𐐸𐐰𐑌𐐼 — 𐐆𐑌 𐑄𐐰𐐻 𐐼𐐩 𐑇𐐰𐑊 𐐸𐐨 𐑅𐐶𐐯𐑉, 𐑅𐐩𐐮𐑍, 𐐌 𐐶𐐮𐑊 𐑌𐐱𐐻 𐐺𐐨 𐐩 𐐸𐐨𐑊𐐲𐑉; 𐑁𐐫𐑉 𐐮𐑌 𐑋𐐴 𐐸𐐵𐑅 𐑄𐐯𐑉 𐐮𐑆 𐑌𐐨𐑄𐐲𐑉 𐐺𐑉𐐯𐐼 𐑌𐐫𐑉 𐐿𐑊𐐬𐑄𐐮𐑍; 𐑋𐐩𐐿 𐑋𐐨 𐑌𐐱𐐻 𐐩 𐑉𐐭𐑊𐐲𐑉 𐐱𐑂 𐑄 𐐹𐐨𐐹𐑊. 𐐙𐐫𐑉 𐐖𐐲𐑉𐐭𐑅𐐲𐑊𐐯𐑋 𐐮𐑆 𐑉𐐭𐐮𐑌𐐼, 𐐰𐑌𐐼 𐐖𐐭𐐼𐐲 𐐮𐑆 𐑁𐐫𐑊𐐲𐑌; 𐐺𐐨𐐿𐐫𐑆 𐑄𐐯𐑉 𐐻𐐲𐑍𐑆 𐐰𐑌𐐼 𐑄𐐯𐑉 𐐼𐐭𐐮𐑍𐑆 𐐸𐐰𐑂 𐐺𐐮𐑌 𐐲𐑀𐐯𐑌𐑅𐐻 𐑄 𐐢𐐫𐑉𐐼, 𐐻𐐭 𐐹𐑉𐐬𐑂𐐬𐐿 𐑄 𐐴𐑆 𐐱𐑂 𐐸𐐮𐑆 𐑀𐑊𐐬𐑉𐐨.

8. 𐐜 𐑇𐐬 𐐱𐑂 𐑄𐐯𐑉 𐐿𐐵𐑌𐐻𐐯𐑌𐐲𐑌𐑅 𐐼𐐲𐑃 𐐶𐐮𐐻𐑌𐐯𐑅 𐐲𐑀𐐯𐑌𐑅𐐻 𐑄𐐯𐑋, 𐐰𐑌𐐼 𐐼𐐲𐑃 𐐼𐐯𐐿𐑊𐐩𐑉 𐑄𐐯𐑉 𐑅𐐮𐑌 𐐻𐐭 𐐺𐐨 𐐨𐑂𐐲𐑌 𐐰𐑆 𐐝𐐱𐐼𐐲𐑋, 𐐰𐑌𐐼 𐑄𐐩 𐐿𐐰𐑌𐑌𐐱𐐻 𐐸𐐴𐐼 𐐮𐐻. 𐐎𐐬 𐐲𐑌𐐻𐐭 𐑄𐐯𐑉 𐑅𐐬𐑊𐑆! 𐐙𐐫𐑉 𐑄𐐩 𐐸𐐰𐑂 𐑉𐐨𐐶𐐫𐑉𐐼𐐯𐐼 𐐨𐑂𐐲𐑊 𐐲𐑌𐐻𐐭 𐑄𐐯𐑋𐑅𐐯𐑊𐑂𐑆. 𐐝𐐩 𐐲𐑌𐐻𐐭 𐑄 𐑉𐐴𐐽𐐲𐑅, 𐑄𐐰𐐻 𐐮𐐻 𐐮𐑆 𐐶𐐯𐑊 𐐶𐐮𐑄 𐑄𐐯𐑋; 𐑁𐐫𐑉 𐑄𐐩 𐑇𐐰𐑊 𐐨𐐻 𐑄 𐑁𐑉𐐭𐐻 𐐱𐑂 𐑄𐐯𐑉 𐐼𐐭𐐮𐑍𐑆. 𐐎𐐬 𐐲𐑌𐐻𐐭 𐑄 𐐶𐐮𐐿𐐯𐐼! 𐑁𐐫𐑉 𐑄𐐩 𐑇𐐰𐑊 𐐹𐐯𐑉𐐮𐑇; 𐑁𐐫𐑉 𐑄 𐑉𐐨𐐶𐐫𐑉𐐼 𐐱𐑂 𐑄𐐯𐑉 𐐸𐐰𐑌𐐼𐑆 𐑇𐐰𐑊 𐐺𐐨 𐐲𐐹𐐱𐑌 𐑄𐐯𐑋.

9. 𐐈𐑌𐐼 𐑋𐐴 𐐹𐐨𐐹𐑊, 𐐽𐐮𐑊𐐼𐑉𐐯𐑌 𐐪𐑉 𐑄𐐩𐑉 𐐱𐐹𐑉𐐯𐑅𐐲𐑉𐑆, 𐐰𐑌𐐼 𐐶𐐮𐑋𐐯𐑌 𐑉𐐭𐑊 𐐬𐑂𐐲𐑉 𐑄𐐯𐑋. 𐐄 𐑋𐐴 𐐹𐐨𐐹𐑊, 𐑄𐐩 𐐸𐐭 𐑊𐐨𐐼 𐑄, 𐐿𐐫𐑆 𐑄 𐐻𐐭 𐐯𐑉, 𐐰𐑌𐐼 𐐼𐐯𐑅𐐻𐑉𐑎 𐑄 𐐶𐐩 𐐱𐑂 𐑄𐐴 𐐹𐐪𐑃𐑅. 𐐜 𐐢𐐫𐑉𐐼 𐑅𐐻𐐰𐑌𐐼𐐯𐑃 𐐲𐐹 𐐻𐐭 𐐹𐑊𐐨𐐼, 𐐰𐑌𐐼 𐑅𐐻𐐰𐑌𐐼𐐯𐑃 𐐻𐐭 𐐾𐐲𐐾 𐑄 𐐹𐐨𐐹𐑊. 𐐜 𐐢𐐫𐑉𐐼 𐐶𐐮𐑊 𐐯𐑌𐐻𐐲𐑉 𐐮𐑌𐐻𐐭 𐐾𐐲𐐾𐑋𐐯𐑌𐐻 𐐶𐐮𐑃 𐑄 𐐩𐑌𐑇𐐯𐑌𐐻𐑅 𐐱𐑂 𐐸𐐮𐑆 𐐹𐐨𐐹𐑊, 𐐰𐑌𐐼 𐑄 𐐹𐑉𐐮𐑌𐑅𐐯𐑆 𐑄𐐩𐑉𐐱𐑂; 𐑁𐐫𐑉 𐐷𐐨 𐐸𐐰𐑂 𐐨𐐻𐑌 𐐲𐐹 𐑄 𐑂𐐮𐑌𐐷𐐲𐑉𐐼, 𐐰𐑌𐐼 𐑄 𐑅𐐹𐑎𐑊 𐐱𐑂 𐑄 𐐹𐐭𐑉 𐐮𐑌 𐐷𐐭𐑉 𐐸𐐵𐑆𐐯𐑆. 𐐐𐐶𐐱𐐻 𐑋𐐨𐑌 𐐷𐐨? 𐐏𐐨 𐐺𐐨𐐻 𐑋𐐴 𐐹𐐨𐐹𐑊 𐐻𐐭 𐐹𐐨𐑅𐐯𐑆, 𐐰𐑌𐐼 𐑀𐑉𐐴𐑌𐐼 𐑄 𐑁𐐩𐑅𐐯𐑆 𐐱𐑂 𐑄 𐐹𐐭𐑉, 𐑅𐐯𐑃 𐑄 𐐢𐐫𐑉𐐼 𐐘𐐱𐐼 𐐱𐑂 𐐐𐐬𐑅𐐻𐑅.

10. 𐐣𐐬𐑉𐐬𐑂𐐲𐑉, 𐑄 𐐢𐐫𐑉𐐼 𐑅𐐯𐑃, 𐐒𐐨𐐿𐐫𐑆 𐑄 𐐼𐐫𐐻𐐲𐑉𐑆 𐐱𐑂 𐐞𐐴𐐲𐑌 𐐪𐑉 𐐸𐐫𐐻𐐨, 𐐰𐑌𐐼 𐐶𐐫𐐿 𐐶𐐮𐑃 𐑅𐐻𐑉𐐯𐐽𐐻-𐑁𐐬𐑉𐑃 𐑌𐐯𐐿𐑅 𐐰𐑌𐐼 𐐶𐐱𐑌𐐻𐐲𐑌 𐐴𐑆, 𐐶𐐫𐐿𐐮𐑍 𐐰𐑌𐐼 𐑋𐐮𐑌𐑅𐐮𐑍 𐐰𐑆 𐑄𐐩 𐑀𐐬, 𐐰𐑌𐐼 𐑋𐐩𐐿𐐮𐑍 𐐲 𐐻𐐮𐑍𐐿𐑊𐐮𐑍 𐐶𐐮𐑃 𐑄𐐩𐑉 𐑁𐐨𐐻; 𐑄𐐯𐑉𐑁𐐬𐑉 𐑄 𐐢𐐫𐑉𐐼 𐐶𐐮𐑊 𐑅𐑋𐐴𐐻 𐐶𐐮𐑃 𐐲 𐑅𐐿𐐰𐐺 𐑄 𐐿𐑉𐐵𐑌 𐐱𐑂 𐑄 𐐸𐐯𐐼 𐐱𐑂 𐑄 𐐼𐐫𐐻𐐲𐑉𐑆 𐐱𐑂 𐐞𐐴𐐲𐑌, 𐐰𐑌𐐼 𐑄 𐐢𐐫𐑉𐐼 𐐶𐐮𐑊 𐐼𐐮𐑅𐐿𐐲𐑂𐐲𐑉 𐑄𐐩𐑉 𐑅𐐨𐐿𐑉𐐯𐐻 𐐹𐐪𐑉𐐻𐑅. 𐐆𐑌 𐑄𐐰𐐻 𐐼𐐩 𐑄 𐐢𐐫𐑉𐐼 𐐶𐐮𐑊 𐐻𐐩𐐿 𐐰𐐶𐐩 𐑄 𐐺𐑉𐐩𐑂𐐲𐑉𐐨 𐐱𐑂 𐑄𐐩𐑉 𐐻𐐮𐑍𐐿𐑊𐐮𐑍 𐐫𐑉𐑌𐐲𐑋𐐯𐑌𐐻𐑅, 𐐰𐑌𐐼 𐐿𐐫𐑊𐑆, 𐐰𐑌𐐼 𐑉𐐵𐑌𐐼 𐐻𐐴𐑉𐑆 𐑊𐐴𐐿 𐑄 𐑋𐐭𐑌; 𐑄 𐐽𐐩𐑌𐑆 𐐰𐑌𐐼 𐑄 𐐺𐑉𐐩𐑅𐑊𐐯𐐻𐑅, 𐐰𐑌𐐼 𐑄 𐑋𐐲𐑁𐑊𐐲𐑉𐑆; 𐑄 𐐺𐐱𐑌𐐯𐐻𐑅, 𐐰𐑌𐐼 𐑄 𐐫𐑉𐑌𐐲𐑋𐐯𐑌𐐻𐑅 𐐱𐑂 𐑄 𐑊𐐯𐑀𐑆, 𐐰𐑌𐐼 𐑄 𐐸𐐯𐐼𐐺𐐰𐑌𐐼𐑆, 𐐰𐑌𐐼 𐑄 𐐻𐐰𐐺𐑊𐐯𐐻𐑅, 𐐰𐑌𐐼 𐑄 𐐨𐑉-𐑉𐐮𐑍𐑆; 𐑄 𐑉𐐮𐑍𐑆, 𐐰𐑌𐐼 𐑌𐐬𐑆 𐐾𐐭𐐯𐑊𐑆; 𐑄 𐐽𐐩𐑌𐐾𐐲𐐺𐑊 𐑅𐐭𐐻𐑅 𐐱𐑂 𐐰𐐹𐐰𐑉𐐯𐑊, 𐐰𐑌𐐼 𐑄 𐑋𐐰𐑌𐐻𐑊𐑆, 𐐰𐑌𐐼 𐑄 𐐶𐐮𐑋𐐹𐑊𐑆, 𐐰𐑌𐐼 𐑄 𐐿𐑉𐐮𐑅𐐹𐐮𐑍-𐐹𐐮𐑌𐑆; 𐑄 𐑀𐑊𐐰𐑅𐐯𐑆, 𐐰𐑌𐐼 𐑄 𐑁𐐴𐑌 𐑊𐐮𐑌𐐯𐑌, 𐐰𐑌𐐼 𐐸𐐳𐐼𐑆, 𐐰𐑌𐐼 𐑄 𐑂𐐩𐑊𐑆.

11. 𐐈𐑌𐐼 𐐮𐐻 𐑇𐐰𐑊 𐐿𐐲𐑋 𐐻𐐭 𐐹𐐰𐑅, 𐐮𐑌𐑅𐐻𐐯𐐼 𐐱𐑂 𐑅𐐶𐐨𐐻 𐑅𐑋𐐯𐑊 𐑄𐐩𐑉 𐑇𐐰𐑊 𐐺𐐨 𐑅𐐻𐐮𐑍𐐿; 𐐰𐑌𐐼 𐐮𐑌𐑅𐐻𐐯𐐼 𐐱𐑂 𐐲 𐑀𐐲𐑉𐐼𐑊, 𐐲 𐑉𐐯𐑌𐐻; 𐐰𐑌𐐼 𐐮𐑌𐑅𐐻𐐯𐐼 𐐱𐑂 𐐶𐐯𐑊 𐑅𐐯𐐻 𐐸𐐩𐑉, 𐐺𐐫𐑊𐐼𐑌𐐯𐑅; 𐐰𐑌𐐼 𐐮𐑌𐑅𐐻𐐯𐐼 𐐱𐑂 𐐲 𐑅𐐻𐐲𐑋𐐲𐐽𐐲𐑉, 𐐲 𐑀𐐲𐑉𐐼𐐮𐑍 𐐱𐑂 𐑅𐐰𐐿𐐿𐑊𐐫𐑃; 𐐺𐐲𐑉𐑌𐐮𐑍 𐐮𐑌𐑅𐐻𐐯𐐼 𐐱𐑂 𐐺𐐧𐐻𐐨. 𐐜𐐴 𐑋𐐯𐑌 𐑇𐐰𐑊 𐑁𐐫𐑊 𐐺𐐴 𐑄 𐑅𐐬𐑉𐐼, 𐐰𐑌𐐼 𐑄𐐴 𐑋𐐴𐐻𐐨 𐐮𐑌 𐑄 𐐶𐐫𐑉. 𐐈𐑌𐐼 𐐸𐐲𐑉 𐑀𐐩𐐻𐑅 𐑇𐐰𐑊 𐑊𐐰𐑋𐐯𐑌𐐻 𐐰𐑌𐐼 𐑋𐐬𐑉𐑌; 𐐰𐑌𐐼 𐑇𐐨 𐑇𐐰𐑊 𐐺𐐨 𐐼𐐯𐑅𐐬𐑊𐐩𐐻, 𐐰𐑌𐐼 𐑇𐐰𐑊 𐑅𐐮𐐻 𐐲𐐹𐐱𐑌 𐑄 𐑀𐑉𐐵𐑌𐐼.

12. 𐐈𐑌𐐼 𐐮𐑌 𐑄𐐰𐐻 𐐼𐐩, 𐑅𐐯𐑂𐐯𐑌 𐐶𐐮𐑋𐐯𐑌 𐑇𐐰𐑊 𐐻𐐩𐐿 𐐸𐐬𐑊𐐼 𐐱𐑂 𐐶𐐲𐑌 𐑋𐐰𐑌, 𐑅𐐩𐐮𐑍, 𐐎𐐨 𐐶𐐮𐑊 𐐨𐐻 𐐵𐑉 𐐬𐑌 𐐺𐑉𐐯𐐼, 𐐰𐑌𐐼 𐐶𐐩𐑉 𐐵𐑉 𐐬𐑌 𐐰𐐹𐐰𐑉𐐯𐑊; 𐐬𐑌𐑊𐐨 𐑊𐐯𐐻 𐐲𐑅 𐐺𐐨 𐐿𐐫𐑊𐐼 𐐺𐐴 𐑄𐐴 𐑌𐐩𐑋 𐐻𐐭 𐐻𐐩𐐿 𐐰𐐶𐐩 𐐵𐑉 𐑉𐐨𐐹𐑉𐐬𐐽. 𐐆𐑌 𐑄𐐰𐐻 𐐼𐐩 𐑇𐐰𐑊 𐑄 𐐺𐑉𐐰𐑌𐐽 𐐱𐑂 𐑄 𐐢𐐫𐑉𐐼 𐐺𐐨 𐐺𐐧𐐻𐐨𐑁𐐳𐑊 𐐰𐑌𐐼 𐑀𐑊𐐬𐑉𐐨𐐲𐑅; 𐑄 𐑁𐑉𐐭𐐻 𐐱𐑂 𐑄 𐐲𐑉𐑃 𐐯𐐿𐑅𐐯𐑊𐐯𐑌𐐻 𐐰𐑌𐐼 𐐿𐐲𐑋𐑊𐐨 𐐻𐐭 𐑄𐐯𐑋 𐑄𐐰𐐻 𐐪𐑉 𐐯𐑅𐐿𐐩𐐹𐐻 𐐱𐑂 𐐆𐑆𐑉𐐩𐐯𐑊.

13. 𐐈𐑌𐐼 𐐮𐐻 𐑇𐐰𐑊 𐐿𐐲𐑋 𐐻𐐭 𐐹𐐰𐑅, 𐑄𐐩 𐑄𐐰𐐻 𐐪𐑉 𐑊𐐯𐑁𐐻 𐐮𐑌 𐐞𐐴𐐲𐑌, 𐐰𐑌𐐼 𐑉𐐨𐑋𐐩𐑌 𐐮𐑌 𐐖𐐯𐑉𐐭𐑅𐐰𐑊𐐯𐑋, 𐑇𐐰𐑊 𐐺𐐨 𐐿𐐫𐑊𐐼 𐐸𐐬𐑊𐐨, 𐐯𐑂𐐲𐑉𐐨 𐐶𐐲𐑌 𐑄𐐰𐐻 𐐮𐑆 𐑉𐐮𐐻𐑌 𐐰𐑋𐐲𐑍 𐑄 𐑊𐐮𐑂𐐮𐑍 𐐮𐑌 𐐖𐐯𐑉𐐭𐑅𐐰𐑊𐐯𐑋; 𐐸𐐶𐐯𐑌 𐑄 𐐢𐐫𐑉𐐼 𐑇𐐰𐑊 𐐸𐐰𐑂 𐐶𐐱𐑇𐐻 𐐰𐐶𐐩 𐑄 𐑁𐐮𐑊𐑃 𐐱𐑂 𐑄 𐐼𐐫𐐻𐐲𐑉𐑆 𐐱𐑂 𐐞𐐴𐐲𐑌, 𐐰𐑌𐐼 𐑇𐐰𐑊 𐐸𐐰𐑂 𐐹𐐲𐑉𐐾𐐼 𐑄 𐐺𐑊𐐲𐐼 𐐱𐑂 𐐖𐐯𐑉𐐭𐑅𐐰𐑊𐐯𐑋 𐑁𐑉𐐱𐑋 𐑄 𐑋𐐮𐐼𐑅𐐻 𐑄𐐩𐑉𐐱𐑂 𐐺𐐴 𐑄 𐑅𐐹𐐮𐑉𐐮𐐻 𐐱𐑂 𐐾𐐲𐐾𐑋𐐯𐑌𐐻 𐐰𐑌𐐼 𐐺𐐴 𐑄 𐑅𐐹𐐮𐑉𐐮𐐻 𐐱𐑂 𐐺𐐲𐑉𐑌𐐮𐑍. 𐐈𐑌𐐼 𐑄 𐐢𐐫𐑉𐐼 𐐶𐐮𐑊 𐐿𐑉𐐨𐐩𐐻 𐐲𐐹𐐱𐑌 𐐯𐑂𐐲𐑉𐐨 𐐼𐐶𐐯𐑊𐐮𐑍-𐐹𐑊𐐩𐑅 𐐱𐑂 𐑋𐐵𐑌𐐻 𐐞𐐴𐐲𐑌, 𐐰𐑌𐐼 𐐲𐐹𐐱𐑌 𐐸𐐲𐑉 𐐰𐑅𐐯𐑋𐐺𐑊𐐨𐑆, 𐐲 𐐿𐑊𐐵𐐼 𐐰𐑌𐐼 𐑅𐑋𐐬𐐿 𐐺𐐴 𐐼𐐩, 𐐰𐑌𐐼 𐑄 𐑇𐐴𐑌𐐮𐑍 𐐱𐑂 𐐲 𐑁𐑊𐐩𐑋𐐮𐑍 𐑁𐐴𐑉 𐐺𐐴 𐑌𐐴𐐻; 𐑁𐐫𐑉 𐐲𐐹𐐱𐑌 𐐫𐑊 𐑄 𐑀𐑊𐐬𐑉𐐨 𐐱𐑂 𐐞𐐴𐐲𐑌 𐑇𐐰𐑊 𐐺𐐨 𐐲 𐐼𐐨𐑁𐐯𐑌𐑅. 𐐈𐑌𐐼 𐑄𐐩𐑉 𐑇𐐰𐑊 𐐺𐐨 𐐲 𐐻𐐰𐐺𐐲𐑉𐑌𐐰𐐿𐑊 𐑁𐐫𐑉 𐐲 𐑇𐐰𐐼𐐬 𐐮𐑌 𐑄 𐐼𐐩-𐐻𐐴𐑋 𐑁𐑉𐐱𐑋 𐑄 𐐸𐐨𐐻, 𐐰𐑌𐐼 𐑁𐐫𐑉 𐐲 𐐹𐑊𐐩𐑅 𐐱𐑂 𐑉𐐯𐑁𐐷𐐭𐐾, 𐐰𐑌𐐼 𐐲 𐐿𐐲𐑂𐐲𐑉𐐻 𐑁𐑉𐐱𐑋 𐑅𐐻𐐫𐑉𐑋 𐐰𐑌𐐼 𐑁𐑉𐐱𐑋 𐑉𐐩𐑌.

14. 𐐈𐑌𐐼 𐑄𐐯𐑌 𐐶𐐮𐑊 𐐌 𐑅𐐮𐑍 𐐻𐐭 𐑋𐐴 𐐶𐐯𐑊-𐐺𐐨𐑊𐐲𐑂𐐯𐐼 𐐲 𐑅𐐫𐑍 𐐱𐑂 𐑋𐐴 𐐺𐐨𐑊𐐲𐑂𐐯𐐼, 𐐻𐐲𐐽𐐮𐑍 𐐸𐐮𐑆 𐑂𐐮𐑌𐐷𐐲𐑉𐐼. 𐐣𐐴 𐐶𐐯𐑊-𐐺𐐨𐑊𐐲𐑂𐐯𐐼 𐐸𐐰𐑃 𐐲 𐑂𐐮𐑌𐐷𐐲𐑉𐐼 𐐮𐑌 𐐲 𐑂𐐯𐑉𐐨 𐑁𐑉𐐭𐐻𐑁𐐳𐑊 𐐸𐐮𐑊; 𐐰𐑌𐐼 𐐸𐐨 𐑁𐐯𐑌𐑅𐐻 𐐮𐐻, 𐐰𐑌𐐼 𐑀𐐰𐑄𐐲𐑉𐐼 𐐵𐐻 𐑄 𐑅𐐻𐐬𐑌𐑆 𐑄𐐩𐑉𐐱𐑂, 𐐰𐑌𐐼 𐐹𐑊𐐰𐑌𐐻𐐯𐐼 𐐮𐐻 𐐶𐐮𐑃 𐑄 𐐽𐑎𐑅𐐯𐑅𐐻 𐑂𐐴𐑌, 𐐰𐑌𐐼 𐐺𐐮𐑊𐐻 𐐲 𐐻𐐵𐐲𐑉 𐐮𐑌 𐑄 𐑋𐐮𐐼𐑅𐐻 𐐱𐑂 𐐮𐐻, 𐐰𐑌𐐼 𐐫𐑊𐑅𐐬 𐑋𐐩𐐼 𐐲 𐐶𐐴𐑌-𐐹𐑉𐐯𐑅 𐑄𐐩𐑉𐐮𐑌; 𐐰𐑌𐐼 𐐸𐐨 𐑊𐐳𐐿𐐻 𐑄𐐰𐐻 𐐮𐐻 𐑇𐐳𐐼 𐐺𐑉𐐮𐑍 𐑁𐐬𐑉𐑃 𐑀𐑉𐐩𐐹𐑅, 𐐰𐑌𐐼 𐐮𐐻 𐐺𐑉𐐫𐐻 𐑁𐐬𐑉𐑃 𐐶𐐴𐑊𐐼 𐑀𐑉𐐩𐐹𐑅. 𐐈𐑌𐐼 𐑌𐐵, 𐐄 𐐮𐑌𐐸𐐰𐐺𐐮𐐻𐐰𐑌𐐻𐑅 𐐱𐑂 𐐖𐐯𐑉𐐭𐑅𐐰𐑊𐐯𐑋, 𐐰𐑌𐐼 𐑋𐐯𐑌 𐐱𐑂 𐐖𐐭𐐼𐐲, 𐐾𐐲𐐾, 𐐌 𐐹𐑉𐐩 𐐷𐐭, 𐐺𐐨𐐻𐐶𐐮𐐿𐑅𐐻 𐑋𐐨 𐐰𐑌𐐼 𐑋𐐴 𐑂𐐮𐑌𐐷𐐲𐑉𐐼. 𐐐𐐶𐐱𐐻 𐐿𐐳𐐼 𐐸𐐰𐑂 𐐺𐐮𐑌 𐐼𐐲𐑌 𐑋𐐬𐑉 𐐻𐐭 𐑋𐐴 𐑂𐐮𐑌𐐷𐐲𐑉𐐼, 𐑄𐐰𐐻 𐐌 𐐸𐐰𐑂 𐑌𐐱𐐻 𐐼𐐲𐑌 𐐮𐑌 𐐮𐐻? 𐐐𐐶𐐩𐑉𐑁𐐬𐑉, 𐐸𐐶𐐯𐑌 𐐌 𐑊𐐳𐐿𐐻 𐑄𐐰𐐻 𐐮𐐻 𐑇𐐳𐐼 𐐺𐑉𐐮𐑍 𐑁𐐬𐑉𐑃 𐑀𐑉𐐩𐐹𐑅, 𐐮𐐻 𐐺𐑉𐐫𐐻 𐑁𐐬𐑉𐑃 𐐶𐐴𐑊𐐼 𐑀𐑉𐐩𐐹𐑅. 𐐈𐑌𐐼 𐑌𐐵

𐑀𐐬 𐐻𐐭; 𐐌 𐐶𐐮𐑊 𐐻𐐯𐑊 𐐷𐐭 𐐸𐐶𐐱𐐻 𐐌 𐐶𐐮𐑊 𐐼𐐭 𐐻𐐭 𐑋𐐴 𐑂𐐮𐑌𐐷𐐲𐑉𐐼; 𐐌 𐐶𐐮𐑊 𐐻𐐩𐐿 𐐰𐐶𐐩 𐑄 𐐸𐐯𐐾 𐑄𐐩𐑉𐐱𐑂, 𐐰𐑌𐐼 𐐮𐐻 𐑇𐐰𐑊 𐐺 𐐨𐐻𐐲𐑌 𐐲𐐹; 𐐰𐑌𐐼 𐐌 𐐶𐐮𐑊 𐐺𐑉𐐩𐐿 𐐼𐐵𐑌 𐑄 𐐶𐐫𐑊 𐑄𐐩𐑉𐐱𐑂, 𐐰𐑌𐐼 𐐮𐐻 𐑇𐐰𐑊 𐐺 𐐻𐑉𐐱𐐼𐐲𐑌 𐐼𐐵𐑌; 𐐰𐑌𐐼 𐐌 𐐶𐐮𐑊 𐑊𐐩 𐐮𐐻 𐐶𐐩𐑅𐐻; 𐐮𐐻 𐑇𐐰𐑊 𐑌𐐱𐐻 𐐺 𐐹𐑉𐐭𐑌𐐼 𐑌𐐫𐑉 𐐼𐐮𐑀𐐼; 𐐺𐐲𐐻 𐑄𐐩𐑉 𐑇𐐰𐑊 𐐿𐐲𐑋 𐐲𐐹 𐐺𐑉𐐴𐐲𐑉𐑆 𐐰𐑌𐐼 𐑃𐐫𐑉𐑌𐑆; 𐐌 𐐶𐐮𐑊 𐐫𐑊𐑅𐐬 𐐿𐐱𐑋𐐰𐑌𐐼 𐑄 𐐿𐑊𐐵𐐼𐑆 𐑄𐐰𐐻 𐑄𐐩 𐑉𐐩𐑌 𐑌𐐬 𐑉𐐩𐑌 𐐲𐐹𐐱𐑌 𐐮𐐻. 𐐙𐐫𐑉 𐑄 𐑂𐐮𐑌𐐷𐐲𐑉𐐼 𐐲𐑂 𐑄 𐐢𐐫𐑉𐐼 𐐲𐑂 𐐐𐐬𐑅𐐻𐑅 𐐮𐑆 𐑄 𐐸𐐵𐑅 𐐲𐑂 𐐆𐑆𐑉𐐩𐐯𐑊, 𐐰𐑌𐐼 𐑄 𐑋𐐯𐑌 𐐲𐑂 𐐖𐐭𐐼𐐲 𐐸𐐮𐑆 𐐹𐑊𐐯𐑆𐐲𐑌𐐻 𐐹𐑊𐐰𐑌𐐻; 𐐰𐑌𐐼 𐐸𐐨 𐑊𐐳𐐿𐐻 𐑁𐐫𐑉 𐐾𐐲𐐾𐑋𐐯𐑌𐐻, 𐐰𐑌𐐼 𐐺𐐨𐐸𐐬𐑊𐐼 𐐱𐐹𐑉𐐯𐑇𐐲𐑌; 𐑁𐐫𐑉 𐑉𐐴𐐽𐐲𐑅𐑌𐐯𐑅, 𐐺𐐲𐐻 𐐺𐐨𐐸𐐬𐑊𐐼 𐐰 𐐿𐑉𐐴.

15. 𐐎𐐬 𐐲𐑌𐐻𐐭 𐑄𐐯𐑋 𐑄𐐰𐐻 𐐾𐑎𐑌 𐐸𐐵𐑅 𐐻𐐭 𐐸𐐵𐑅, 𐐻𐐮𐑊 𐑄𐐩𐑉 𐐿𐐰𐑌 𐐺 𐑌𐐬 𐐹𐑊𐐩𐑅, 𐑄𐐰𐐻 𐑄𐐩 𐑋𐐩 𐐺 𐐹𐑊𐐩𐑅𐐻 𐐰𐑊𐐬𐑌 𐐮𐑌 𐑄 𐑋𐐮𐐼𐑅𐐻 𐐲𐑂 𐑄 𐐲𐑉𐑃! 𐐆𐑌 𐑋𐐴𐑌 𐐨𐑉𐑆, 𐑅𐐯𐐼 𐑄 𐐢𐐫𐑉𐐼 𐐲𐑂 𐐐𐐬𐑅𐐻𐑅, 𐐲𐑂 𐐰 𐐻𐑉𐐭𐑃 𐑋𐐯𐑌𐐨 𐐸𐐵𐑆𐐯𐑆 𐑇𐐰𐑊 𐐺 𐐼𐐯𐑅𐐬𐑊𐐩𐐻, 𐐰𐑌𐐼 𐑀𐑉𐐩𐐻 𐐰𐑌𐐼 𐑁𐐩𐑉 𐑅𐐮𐐻𐐮𐑆 𐐶𐐮𐑄𐐵𐐻 𐐮𐑌𐐸𐐰𐐺𐐮𐐻𐐲𐑌𐐻. 𐐏𐐩, 𐐻𐐯𐑌 𐐩𐐿𐐲𐑉𐑆 𐐲𐑂 𐑂𐐮𐑌𐐷𐐲𐑉𐐼 𐑇𐐰𐑊 𐐷𐐨𐑊𐐼 𐐶𐐲𐑌 𐐺𐐪𐑃, 𐐰𐑌𐐼 𐑄 𐑅𐐨𐐼 𐐲𐑂 𐐰𐑌 𐐸𐐬𐑋𐐲𐑉 𐑇𐐰𐑊 𐐷𐐨𐑊𐐼 𐐰𐑌 𐐨𐑁𐐪.

16. 𐐎𐐬 𐐲𐑌𐐻𐐭 𐑄𐐯𐑋 𐑄𐐰𐐻 𐑉𐐴𐑆 𐐲𐐹 𐐲𐑉𐑊𐐨 𐐮𐑌 𐑄 𐑋𐐫𐑉𐑌𐐮𐑍, 𐑄𐐰𐐻 𐑄𐐩 𐑋𐐩 𐑁𐐱𐑊𐐬 𐑅𐐻𐑉𐐱𐑍 𐐼𐑉𐐮𐑍𐐿, 𐑄𐐰𐐻 𐐿𐐱𐑌𐐻𐐮𐑌𐐷𐐭 𐐲𐑌𐐻𐐮𐑊 𐑌𐐴𐐻, 𐐰𐑌𐐼 𐐶𐐴𐑌 𐐮𐑌𐑁𐑊𐐩𐑋 𐑄𐐯𐑋! 𐐈𐑌𐐼 𐑄 𐐸𐐪𐑉𐐹, 𐐰𐑌𐐼 𐑄 𐑂𐐴𐐲𐑊, 𐑄 𐐻𐐰𐐺𐑉𐐯𐐻, 𐐰𐑌𐐼 𐐹𐐴𐐹, 𐐰𐑌𐐼 𐐶𐐴𐑌 𐐪𐑉 𐐮𐑌 𐑄𐐩𐑉 𐑁𐐨𐑅𐐻𐑅; 𐐺𐐲𐐻 𐑄𐐩 𐑉𐐨𐑀𐐪𐑉𐐼 𐑌𐐱𐐻 𐑄 𐐶𐐲𐑉𐐿 𐐲𐑂 𐑄 𐐢𐐫𐑉𐐼, 𐑌𐐨𐑄𐐲𐑉 𐐿𐐱𐑌𐑅𐐮𐐼𐐲𐑉 𐑄 𐐱𐐹𐐲𐑉𐐩𐑇𐐲𐑌 𐐲𐑂 𐐸𐐮𐑆 𐐸𐐰𐑌𐐼𐑆.

17. 𐐜𐐯𐑉𐑁𐐫𐑉, 𐑋𐐴 𐐹𐐨𐐹𐑊 𐐪𐑉 𐑀𐐱𐑌 𐐮𐑌𐐻𐐭 𐐿𐐰𐐹𐐻𐐮𐑂𐐮𐐻𐐨, 𐐺𐐨𐐿𐐫𐑆 𐑄𐐩 𐐸𐐰𐑂 𐑌𐐬 𐑌𐐱𐑊𐐯𐐾; 𐐰𐑌𐐼 𐑄𐐩𐑉 𐐱𐑌𐐲𐑉𐐰𐐺𐑊 𐑋𐐯𐑌 𐐪𐑉 𐑁𐐰𐑋𐐮𐑇𐐻, 𐐰𐑌𐐼 𐑄𐐩𐑉 𐑋𐐲𐑊𐐻𐐮𐐻𐐷𐐭𐐼 𐐼𐑉𐐴𐐼 𐐲𐐹 𐐶𐐮𐑄 𐑃𐐲𐑉𐑅𐐻. 𐐜𐐯𐑉𐑁𐐫𐑉, 𐐸𐐯𐑊 𐐸𐐰𐑃 𐐯𐑌𐑊𐐪𐑉𐐾𐐼 𐐸𐐲𐑉𐑅𐐯𐑊𐑁, 𐐰𐑌𐐼 𐐬𐐹𐐲𐑌𐐼 𐐸𐐲𐑉 𐑋𐐵𐑃 𐐶𐐮𐑄𐐵𐐻 𐑋𐐯𐑈𐐲𐑉; 𐐰𐑌𐐼 𐑄𐐩𐑉 𐑀𐑊𐐬𐑉𐐨, 𐐰𐑌𐐼 𐑄𐐩𐑉 𐑋𐐲𐑊𐐻𐐮𐐻𐐷𐐭𐐼, 𐐰𐑌𐐼 𐑄𐐩𐑉 𐐹𐐱𐑋𐐹, 𐐰𐑌𐐼 𐐸𐐨 𐑄𐐰𐐻 𐑉𐐨𐐾𐑎𐑅𐐯𐑃, 𐑇𐐰𐑊 𐐼𐐯𐑅𐐯𐑌𐐼 𐐮𐑌𐐻𐐭 𐐮𐐻. 𐐈𐑌𐐼 𐑄 𐑋𐐨𐑌 𐑋𐐰𐑌 𐑇𐐰𐑊 𐐺 𐐺𐑉𐐫𐐻 𐐼𐐵𐑌, 𐐰𐑌𐐼 𐑄 𐑋𐐴𐐻𐐨 𐑋𐐰𐑌 𐑇𐐰𐑊 𐐺 𐐸𐐲𐑋𐐺𐑊𐐼, 𐐰𐑌𐐼 𐑄 𐐴𐑆 𐐲𐑂 𐑄 𐑊𐐱𐑁𐐻𐐨 𐑇𐐰𐑊 𐐺 𐐸𐐲𐑋𐐺𐑊𐐼; 𐐺𐐲𐐻 𐑄 𐐢𐐫𐑉𐐼 𐐲𐑂 𐐐𐐬𐑅𐐻𐑅 𐑇𐐰𐑊 𐐺 𐐯𐑀𐑆𐐫𐑊𐐻𐐯𐐼 𐐮𐑌 𐐾𐐲𐐾𐑋𐐯𐑌𐐻, 𐐰𐑌𐐼 𐐘𐐱𐐼 𐑄𐐰𐐻 𐐮𐑆 𐐸𐐬𐑊𐐨 𐑇𐐰𐑊 𐐺 𐑅𐐰𐑍𐐿𐐻𐐮𐑁𐐴𐐼 𐐮𐑌 𐑉𐐴𐐽𐐲𐑅𐑌𐐯𐑅. 𐐜𐐯𐑌 𐑇𐐰𐑊 𐑄 𐑊𐐰𐑋𐑆 𐑁𐐨𐐼 𐐰𐑁𐐻𐐲𐑉 𐑄𐐩𐑉 𐑋𐐰𐑌𐐲𐑉, 𐐰𐑌𐐼 𐑄 𐐶𐐩𐑅𐐻 𐐹𐑊𐐩𐑅𐐯𐑆 𐐲𐑂 𐑄 𐑁𐐰𐐻 𐐶𐐲𐑌𐑆 𐑇𐐰𐑊 𐑅𐐻𐑉𐐩𐑌𐐾𐐲𐑉𐑆 𐐨𐐻. 𐐎𐐬 𐐲𐑌𐐻𐐭 𐑄𐐯𐑋 𐑄𐐰𐐻 𐐼𐑉𐐫 𐐮𐑌𐐮𐐿𐐶𐐮𐐻𐐨 𐐶𐐮𐑄 𐐿𐐫𐑉𐐼𐑆 𐐲𐑂 𐑂𐐰𐑌𐐮𐐻𐐨, 𐐰𐑌𐐼 𐑅𐐮𐑌 𐐰𐑆 𐐮𐐻 𐐶𐐲𐑉 𐐶𐐮𐑄 𐐰 𐐿𐐪𐑉𐐻 𐑉𐐬𐐹; 𐑄𐐰𐐻 𐑅𐐩, 𐐢𐐯𐐻 𐐸𐐮𐑋 𐑋𐐩𐐿 𐑅𐐹𐐨𐐼, 𐐸𐐩𐑅𐐲𐑌 𐐸𐐮𐑆 𐐶𐐲𐑉𐐿, 𐑄𐐰𐐻 𐐶𐐨 𐑋𐐩 𐑅𐐨 𐐮𐐻; 𐐰𐑌𐐼 𐑊𐐯𐐻 𐑄 𐐿𐐵𐑌𐑅𐐯𐑊 𐐲𐑂 𐑄 𐐐𐐬𐑊𐐨 𐐎𐐲𐑌 𐐲𐑂 𐐆𐑆𐑉𐐩𐐯𐑊 𐐼𐑉𐐫 𐑌𐐴 𐐰𐑌𐐼 𐐿𐐲𐑋, 𐑄𐐰𐐻 𐐶𐐨 𐑋𐐩 𐑌𐐬 𐐮𐐻.

18. 𐐎𐐬 𐐲𐑌𐐻𐐭 𐑄𐐯𐑋 𐑄𐐰𐐻 𐐿𐐫𐑊 𐐨𐑂𐐮𐑊 𐑀𐐳𐐼, 𐐰𐑌𐐼 𐑀𐐳𐐼 𐐨𐑂𐐮𐑊; 𐑄𐐰𐐻 𐐹𐐳𐐻 𐐼𐐪𐑉𐐿𐑌𐐯𐑅 𐑁𐐫𐑉 𐑊𐐴𐐻, 𐐰𐑌𐐼 𐑊𐐴𐐻 𐑁𐐫𐑉 𐐼𐐪𐑉𐐿𐑌𐐯𐑅; 𐑄𐐰𐐻 𐐹𐐳𐐻 𐐺𐐮𐐻𐐲𐑉 𐑁𐐫𐑉 𐑅𐐶𐐨𐐻, 𐐰𐑌𐐼 𐑅𐐶𐐨𐐻 𐑁𐐫𐑉 𐐺𐐮𐐻𐐲𐑉! 𐐎𐐬 𐐲𐑌𐐻𐐭 𐑄 𐐶𐐴𐑆 𐐮𐑌 𐑄𐐩𐑉 𐐬𐑌 𐐴𐑆, 𐐰𐑌𐐼 𐐹𐑉𐐭𐐼𐐯𐑌𐐻 𐐮𐑌 𐑄𐐩𐑉 𐐬𐑌 𐑅𐐴𐐻! 𐐎𐐬 𐐲𐑌𐐻𐐭 𐑄 𐑋𐐴𐐻𐐨 𐐻𐐭 𐐼𐑉𐐮𐑍𐐿 𐐶𐐴𐑌, 𐐰𐑌𐐼 𐑋𐐯𐑌 𐐲𐑂 𐑅𐐻𐑉𐐯𐑍𐑃 𐐻𐐭 𐑋𐐮𐑍𐑀𐑊 𐑅𐐻𐑉𐐱𐑍 𐐼𐑉𐐮𐑍𐐿; 𐐸𐐭 𐐾𐐲𐑅𐐻𐐮𐑁𐐴 𐑄 𐐶𐐮𐐿𐐯𐐼 𐑁𐐫𐑉 𐑉𐐨𐐶𐐫𐑉𐐼, 𐐰𐑌𐐼 𐐻𐐩𐐿 𐐰𐐶𐐩 𐑄 𐑉𐐴𐐽𐐲𐑅𐑌𐐯𐑅 𐐲𐑂 𐑄 𐑉𐐴𐐽𐐲𐑅 𐑁𐑉𐐱𐑋 𐐸𐐮𐑋! 𐐜𐐯𐑉𐑁𐐫𐑉, 𐐰𐑆 𐑄 𐑁𐐴𐑉 𐐼𐐯𐑂𐐵𐑉𐐯𐑃 𐑄 𐑅𐐻𐐲𐐺𐑊, 𐐰𐑌𐐼 𐑄 𐑁𐑊𐐩𐑋 𐐿𐐱𐑌𐑅𐐷𐐭𐑋𐐯𐑃 𐑄 𐐽𐐰𐑁, 𐑄𐐩𐑉 𐑉𐐭𐐻 𐑇𐐰𐑊 𐐺 𐑉𐐱𐐻𐐲𐑌𐑌𐐯𐑅, 𐐰𐑌𐐼 𐑄𐐩𐑉 𐐺𐑊𐐱𐑅𐐲𐑋𐑆 𐑇𐐰𐑊 𐑀𐐬 𐐲𐐹 𐐰𐑆 𐐼𐐲𐑅𐐻; 𐐺𐐨𐐿𐐫𐑆 𐑄𐐩 𐐸𐐰𐑂 𐐿𐐰𐑅𐐻 𐐰𐐶𐐩 𐑄 𐑊𐐫 𐐲𐑂 𐑄 𐐢𐐫𐑉𐐼 𐐲𐑂 𐐐𐐬𐑅𐐻𐑅, 𐐰𐑌𐐼 𐐼𐐯𐑅𐐹𐐴𐑆𐐼 𐑄 𐐶𐐲𐑉𐐼 𐐲𐑂 𐑄 𐐐𐐬𐑊𐐨 𐐎𐐲𐑌 𐐲𐑂 𐐆𐑆𐑉𐐩𐐯𐑊. 𐐜𐐯𐑉𐑁𐐫𐑉 𐐮𐑆 𐑄 𐐰𐑍𐑀𐐲𐑉 𐐲𐑂 𐑄 𐐢𐐫𐑉𐐼 𐐿𐐮𐑌𐐼𐑊𐐼 𐐰𐑀𐐯𐑌𐑅𐐻 𐐸𐐮𐑆 𐐹𐐨𐐹𐑊, 𐐰𐑌𐐼 𐐸𐐨 𐐸𐐰𐑃 𐑅𐐻𐑉𐐯𐐽𐐻 𐑁𐐬𐑉𐑃 𐐸𐐮𐑆 𐐸𐐰𐑌𐐼 𐐰𐑀𐐯𐑌𐑅𐐻 𐑄𐐯𐑋, 𐐰𐑌𐐼 𐐸𐐰𐑃 𐑅𐑋𐐮𐐻𐐲𐑌 𐑄𐐯𐑋; 𐐰𐑌𐐼 𐑄 𐐸𐐮𐑊𐑆 𐐼𐐮𐐼 𐐻𐑉𐐯𐑋𐐺𐑊, 𐐰𐑌𐐼 𐑄𐐩𐑉 𐐿𐐪𐑉𐐿𐐰𐑅𐐯𐑆 𐐶𐐲𐑉 𐐻𐐫𐑉𐑌 𐐮𐑌 𐑄 𐑋𐐮𐐼𐑅𐐻 𐐲𐑂 𐑄 𐑅𐐻𐑉𐐨𐐻𐑅. 𐐙𐐫𐑉 𐐫𐑊 𐑄𐐮𐑅 𐐸𐐮𐑆 𐐰𐑍𐑀𐐲𐑉 𐐮𐑆 𐑌𐐱𐐻 𐐻𐐲𐑉𐑌𐐼 𐐰𐐶𐐩, 𐐺𐐲𐐻 𐐸𐐮𐑆 𐐸𐐰𐑌𐐼 𐐮𐑆 𐑅𐐻𐑉𐐯𐐽𐐻 𐐵𐐻 𐑅𐐻𐐮𐑊.

19. 𐐈𐑌𐐼 𐐸𐐨 𐐶𐐮𐑊 𐑊𐐮𐑁𐐻 𐐲𐐹 𐐰𐑌 𐐯𐑌𐑅𐐴𐑌 𐐻𐐭 𐑄 𐑌𐐩𐑇𐐲𐑌𐑆 𐑁𐑉𐐱𐑋 𐑁𐐪𐑉, 𐐰𐑌𐐼 𐐶𐐮𐑊 𐐸𐐮𐑅 𐐲𐑌𐐻𐐭 𐑄𐐯𐑋 𐑁𐑉𐐱𐑋 𐑄 𐐯𐑌𐐼 𐐲𐑂 𐑄 𐐲𐑉𐑃; 𐐰𐑌𐐼 𐐺𐐨𐐸𐐬𐑊𐐼, 𐑄𐐩 𐑇𐐰𐑊 𐐿𐐲𐑋 𐐶𐐮𐑄 𐑅𐐹𐐨𐐼 𐑅𐐶𐐮𐑁𐐻𐑊𐐨; 𐑌𐐲𐑌 𐑇𐐰𐑊 𐐺 𐐶𐐨𐑉𐐨 𐑌𐐫𐑉 𐑅𐐻𐐲𐑋𐐺𐑊 𐐰𐑋𐐲𐑍 𐑄𐐯𐑋; 𐑌𐐲𐑌 𐑇𐐰𐑊 𐑅𐑊𐐲𐑋𐐺𐐲𐑉 𐑌𐐫𐑉 𐑅𐑊𐐨𐐹; 𐑌𐐨𐑄𐐲𐑉 𐑇𐐰𐑊 𐑄 𐑀𐐲𐑉𐐼𐑊 𐐲𐑂

𐑄𐐩𐑉 𐑊𐐫𐐮𐑌𐑆 𐐺 𐑊𐐭𐑅𐐻, 𐑌𐐫𐑉 𐑄 𐑊𐐰𐐽𐐯𐐻 𐐱𐑂 𐑄𐐩𐑉 𐑇𐐭𐑆 𐐺 𐐺𐑉𐐬𐐿𐑌; 𐐸𐐭𐑆 𐐰𐑉𐐬𐑆 𐑇𐐰𐑊 𐐺 𐑇𐐪𐑉𐐹, 𐐰𐑌𐐼 𐐫𐑊 𐑄𐐩𐑉 𐐺𐐬𐑆 𐐺𐐯𐑌𐐻, 𐐰𐑌𐐼 𐑄𐐩𐑉 𐐸𐐫𐑉𐑅𐐯𐑆' 𐐸𐐭𐑁𐑅 𐑇𐐰𐑊 𐐺 𐐿𐐵𐑌𐐻𐐯𐐼 𐑊𐐴𐐿 𐑁𐑊𐐮𐑌𐐻, 𐐰𐑌𐐼 𐑄𐐩𐑉 𐐸𐐶𐐨𐑊𐑆 𐑊𐐴𐐿 𐐩 𐐸𐐶𐐲𐑉𐑊𐐶𐐮𐑌𐐼, 𐑄𐐩𐑉 𐑉𐐬𐑉𐐮𐑍 𐑊𐐴𐐿 𐐩 𐑊𐐴𐐲𐑌. 𐐜𐐩 𐑇𐐰𐑊 𐑉𐐬𐑉 𐑊𐐴𐐿 𐐷𐐲𐑍 𐑊𐐴𐐲𐑌𐑆; 𐐷𐐩, 𐑄𐐩 𐑇𐐰𐑊 𐑉𐐬𐑉, 𐐰𐑌𐐼 𐑊𐐩 𐐸𐐬𐑊𐐼 𐐱𐑂 𐑄 𐐹𐑉𐐩, 𐐰𐑌𐐼 𐑇𐐰𐑊 𐐿𐐰𐑉𐐨 𐐰𐐶𐐩 𐑅𐐩𐑁, 𐐰𐑌𐐼 𐑌𐐲𐑌 𐑇𐐰𐑊 𐐼𐐯𐑊𐐮𐑂𐐲𐑉. 𐐈𐑌𐐼 𐐮𐑌 𐑄𐐰𐐻 𐐼𐐩 𐑄𐐩 𐑇𐐰𐑊 𐑉𐐬𐑉 𐐰𐑀𐐯𐑌𐑅𐐻 𐑄𐐯𐑋 𐑊𐐴𐐿 𐑄 𐑉𐐬𐑉𐐮𐑍 𐐱𐑂 𐑄 𐑅𐐨; 𐐰𐑌𐐼 𐐮𐑁 𐑄𐐩 𐑊𐐳𐐿 𐐲𐑌𐐻𐐭 𐑄 𐑊𐐰𐑌𐐼, 𐐺𐐨𐐸𐐬𐑊𐐼, 𐐼𐐪𐑉𐐿𐑌𐐯𐑅 𐐰𐑌𐐼 𐑅𐐱𐑉𐐬, 𐐰𐑌𐐼 𐑄 𐑊𐐴𐐻 𐐮𐑆 𐐼𐐪𐑉𐐿𐐲𐑌𐐼 𐐮𐑌 𐑄 𐐸𐐯𐑂𐐲𐑌𐑆 𐑄𐐩𐑉𐐱𐑂.

𐐕𐐰𐐹𐐻𐐲𐑉 IX.

1. 𐐆𐑌 𐑄 𐐷𐐨𐑉 𐑄𐐰𐐻 𐐿𐐮𐑍 𐐊𐑆𐐴𐐲 𐐼𐐴𐐼, 𐐴 𐑅𐐫 𐐫𐑊𐑅𐐬 𐑄 𐐢𐐫𐑉𐐼 𐑅𐐮𐐻𐐮𐑍 𐐲𐐹𐐱𐑌 𐐩 𐑃𐑉𐐬𐑌, 𐐸𐐴 𐐰𐑌𐐼 𐑊𐐮𐑁𐐻𐐯𐐼 𐐲𐐹, 𐐰𐑌𐐼 𐐸𐐮𐑆 𐐻𐑉𐐩𐑌 𐑁𐐮𐑊𐐼 𐑄 𐐻𐐯𐑋𐐹𐑊. 𐐈𐐺𐐲𐑂 𐐮𐐻 𐑅𐐻𐐳𐐼 𐑄 𐑅𐐯𐑉𐐰𐑁𐐮𐑋; 𐐨𐐽 𐐶𐐲𐑌 𐐸𐐰𐐼 𐑅𐐮𐐿𐑅 𐐶𐐮𐑍𐑆; 𐐶𐐮𐑄 𐐻𐐶𐐩𐑌 𐐸𐐨 𐐿𐐲𐑂𐐲𐑉𐐼 𐐸𐐮𐑆 𐑁𐐩𐑅, 𐐰𐑌𐐼 𐐶𐐮𐑄 𐐻𐐶𐐩𐑌 𐐸𐐨 𐐿𐐲𐑂𐐲𐑉𐐼 𐐸𐐮𐑆 𐑁𐐨𐐻, 𐐰𐑌𐐼 𐐶𐐮𐑄 𐐻𐐶𐐩𐑌 𐐸𐐨 𐐼𐐮𐐼 𐑁𐑊𐐴. 𐐈𐑌𐐼 𐐶𐐲𐑌 𐐿𐑉𐐴𐐼 𐐲𐑌𐐻𐐭 𐐰𐑌𐐲𐑄𐐲𐑉, 𐐰𐑌𐐼 𐑅𐐯𐐼, 𐐐𐐬𐑊𐐨, 𐐸𐐬𐑊𐐨, 𐐸𐐬𐑊𐐨, 𐐮𐑆 𐑄 𐐢𐐫𐑉𐐼 𐐱𐑂 𐐐𐐬𐑅𐐻𐑅; 𐑄 𐐸𐐬𐑊 𐐲𐑉𐑃 𐐮𐑆 𐑁𐐳𐑊 𐐱𐑂 𐐸𐐮𐑆 𐑀𐑊𐐬𐑉𐐨. 𐐈𐑌𐐼 𐑄 𐐹𐐬𐑅𐐻𐑅 𐐱𐑂 𐑄 𐐼𐐬𐑉 𐑋𐐭𐑂𐐼 𐐰𐐻 𐑄 𐑂𐐱𐐮𐑅 𐐱𐑂 𐐸𐐮𐑋 𐑄𐐰𐐻 𐐿𐑉𐐴𐐼, 𐐰𐑌𐐼 𐑄 𐐸𐐵𐑅 𐐶𐐱𐑆 𐑁𐐮𐑊𐐼 𐐶𐐮𐑄 𐑅𐑋𐐬𐐿.

2. 𐐜𐐯𐑌 𐑅𐐯𐐼 𐐴, 𐐎𐐬 𐐮𐑆 𐐲𐑌𐐻𐐭 𐑋𐐨! 𐑁𐐫𐑉 𐐴 𐐰𐑋 𐐲𐑌𐐼𐐲𐑌; 𐐺𐐨𐐿𐐫𐑆 𐐴 𐐰𐑋 𐐩 𐑋𐐰𐑌 𐐱𐑂 𐐲𐑌𐐿𐑊𐐨𐑌 𐑊𐐮𐐹𐑅; 𐐰𐑌𐐼 𐐴 𐐼𐐶𐐯𐑊 𐐮𐑌 𐑄 𐑋𐐮𐐼𐑅𐐻 𐐱𐑂 𐐩 𐐹𐐨𐐹𐑊 𐐱𐑂 𐐲𐑌𐐿𐑊𐐨𐑌 𐑊𐐮𐐹𐑅; 𐑁𐐫𐑉 𐑋𐐴𐑌 𐐴𐑆 𐐸𐐰𐑂 𐑅𐐨𐑌 𐑄 𐐗𐐮𐑍, 𐑄 𐐢𐐫𐑉𐐼 𐐱𐑂 𐐐𐐬𐑅𐐻𐑅. 𐐜𐐯𐑌 𐑁𐑊𐐭 𐐶𐐲𐑌 𐐱𐑂 𐑄 𐑅𐐯𐑉𐐰𐑁𐐮𐑋 𐐲𐑌𐐻𐐭 𐑋𐐨, 𐐸𐐰𐑂𐐮𐑍 𐐩 𐑊𐐴𐑂 𐐿𐐬𐑊 𐐮𐑌 𐐸𐐮𐑆 𐐸𐐰𐑌𐐼, 𐐸𐐶𐐮𐐽 𐐸𐐨 𐐸𐐰𐐼 𐐻𐐩𐐿𐑌 𐐶𐐮𐑄 𐑄 𐐻𐐱𐑍𐑆 𐑁𐑉𐐱𐑋 𐐫𐑁 𐑄 𐐫𐑊𐐻𐐲𐑉; 𐐰𐑌𐐼 𐐸𐐨 𐑊𐐩𐐼 𐐮𐐻 𐐲𐐹𐐱𐑌 𐑋𐐴 𐑋𐐵𐑃, 𐐰𐑌𐐼 𐑅𐐯𐐼, 𐐢𐐬, 𐑄𐐮𐑅 𐐸𐐰𐑆 𐐻𐐲𐐽𐐻 𐑄𐐴 𐑊𐐮𐐹𐑅; 𐐰𐑌𐐼 𐑄𐐴𐑌 𐐮𐑌𐐮𐐿𐐶𐐮𐐻𐐨 𐐮𐑆 𐐻𐐩𐐿𐑌 𐐰𐐶𐐩, 𐐰𐑌𐐼 𐑄𐐴 𐑅𐐮𐑌 𐐹𐐲𐑉𐐾𐐼. 𐐃𐑊𐑅𐐬 𐐴 𐐸𐐲𐑉𐐼 𐑄 𐑂𐐱𐐮𐑅 𐐱𐑂 𐑄 𐐢𐐫𐑉𐐼, 𐑅𐐩𐐮𐑍, 𐐐𐐭𐑋 𐑇𐐰𐑊 𐐴 𐑅𐐯𐑌𐐼, 𐐰𐑌𐐼 𐐸𐐭 𐐶𐐮𐑊 𐑀𐐬 𐑁𐐫𐑉 𐐲𐑅? 𐐜𐐯𐑌 𐐴 𐑅𐐯𐐼, 𐐐𐐨𐑉 𐐰𐑋 𐐴; 𐑅𐐯𐑌𐐼 𐑋𐐨.

3. 𐐈𐑌𐐼 𐐸𐐨 𐑅𐐯𐐼, 𐐘𐐬, 𐐰𐑌𐐼 𐐻𐐯𐑊 𐑄𐐮𐑅 𐐹𐐨𐐹𐑊, 𐐸𐐨𐑉 𐐷𐐨 𐐮𐑌𐐼𐐨𐐼, 𐐺𐐲𐐻 𐑄𐐩 𐐲𐑌𐐼𐐲𐑉𐑅𐐻𐐳𐐼 𐑌𐐱𐐻; 𐐰𐑌𐐼 𐑅𐐨 𐐷𐐨 𐐮𐑌𐐼𐐨𐐼, 𐐺𐐲𐐻 𐑄𐐩 𐐹𐐲𐑉𐑅𐐨𐑂𐐼 𐑌𐐱𐐻. 𐐣𐐩𐐿 𐑄 𐐸𐐪𐑉𐐻 𐐱𐑂 𐑄𐐮𐑅 𐐹𐐨𐐹𐑊 𐑁𐐰𐐻, 𐐰𐑌𐐼 𐑋𐐩𐐿 𐑄𐐩𐑉 𐐨𐑉𐑆 𐐸𐐯𐑂𐐨, 𐐰𐑌𐐼 𐑇𐐲𐐻 𐑄𐐩𐑉 𐐴𐑆; 𐑊𐐯𐑅𐐻 𐑄𐐩 𐑅𐐨 𐐶𐐮𐑄 𐑄𐐩𐑉 𐐴𐑆, 𐐰𐑌𐐼 𐐸𐐨𐑉 𐐶𐐮𐑄 𐑄𐐩𐑉 𐐨𐑉𐑆, 𐐰𐑌𐐼 𐐲𐑌𐐼𐐲𐑉𐑅𐐻𐐰𐑌𐐼 𐐶𐐮𐑄 𐑄𐐩𐑉 𐐸𐐪𐑉𐐻, 𐐰𐑌𐐼 𐐺 𐐿𐐱𐑌𐑂𐐲𐑉𐐻𐐯𐐼 𐐰𐑌𐐼 𐐺 𐐸𐐨𐑊𐐼. 𐐜𐐯𐑌 𐑅𐐯𐐼 𐐴, 𐐢𐐫𐑉𐐼, 𐐸𐐵 𐑊𐐱𐑍? 𐐈𐑌𐐼 𐐸𐐨 𐑅𐐯𐐼, 𐐊𐑌𐐻𐐮𐑊 𐑄 𐑅𐐮𐐻𐐮𐑆 𐐺 𐐶𐐩𐑅𐐻𐐯𐐼 𐐶𐐮𐑄𐐵𐐻 𐐮𐑌𐐸𐐰𐐺𐐮𐐻𐐲𐑌𐐻, 𐐰𐑌𐐼 𐑄 𐐸𐐵𐑆𐐯𐑆 𐐶𐐮𐑄𐐵𐐻 𐑋𐐰𐑌, 𐐰𐑌𐐼 𐑄 𐑊𐐰𐑌𐐼 𐐺 𐐲𐐻𐐲𐑉𐑊𐐨 𐐼𐐯𐑅𐐬𐑊𐐩𐐻; 𐐰𐑌𐐼 𐑄 𐐢𐐫𐑉𐐼 𐐸𐐰𐑂 𐑉𐐨𐑋𐐭𐑂𐐼 𐑋𐐯𐑌 𐑁𐐪𐑉 𐐰𐐶𐐩, 𐑁𐐫𐑉 𐑄𐐩𐑉 𐑇𐐰𐑊 𐐺 𐐩 𐑀𐑉𐐩𐐻 𐑁𐐫𐑉𐑅𐐩𐐿𐐮𐑍 𐐮𐑌 𐑄 𐑋𐐮𐐼𐑅𐐻 𐐱𐑂 𐑄 𐑊𐐰𐑌𐐼.

4. 𐐒𐐲𐐻 𐐷𐐯𐐻 𐑄𐐩𐑉 𐑇𐐰𐑊 𐐺 𐐩 𐐻𐐯𐑌𐑃, 𐐰𐑌𐐼 𐑄𐐩 𐑇𐐰𐑊 𐑉𐐨𐐻𐐲𐑉𐑌, 𐐰𐑌𐐼 𐑇𐐰𐑊 𐐺 𐐨𐐻𐑌; 𐐰𐑆 𐐩 𐐻𐐨𐑊-𐐻𐑉𐐨, 𐐰𐑌𐐼 𐐰𐑆 𐐰𐑌 𐐬𐐿 𐐸𐐭𐑆 𐑅𐐲𐐺𐑅𐐻𐐰𐑌𐑅 𐐮𐑆 𐐮𐑌 𐑄𐐯𐑋 𐐸𐐶𐐯𐑌 𐑄𐐩 𐐿𐐰𐑅𐐻 𐑄𐐩𐑉 𐑊𐐨𐑂𐑆; 𐑅𐐬 𐑄 𐐸𐐬𐑊𐐨 𐑅𐐨𐐼 𐑇𐐰𐑊 𐐺 𐑄 𐑅𐐲𐐺𐑅𐐻𐐰𐑌𐑅 𐑄𐐩𐑉𐐱𐑂.

5. 𐐈𐑌𐐼 𐐮𐐻 𐐿𐐩𐑋 𐐻𐐭 𐐹𐐰𐑅 𐐮𐑌 𐑄 𐐼𐐩𐑆 𐐱𐑂 𐐁𐐸𐐰𐑆, 𐑄 𐑅𐐲𐑌 𐐱𐑂 𐐖𐐬𐑃𐐲𐑋, 𐑄 𐑅𐐲𐑌 𐐱𐑂 𐐊𐑆𐐴𐐲, 𐐿𐐮𐑍 𐐱𐑂 𐐖𐐭𐐼𐐲, 𐑄𐐰𐐻 𐐡𐐨𐑆𐐮𐑌, 𐐿𐐮𐑍 𐐱𐑂 𐐝𐐮𐑉𐐨𐐲, 𐐰𐑌𐐼 𐐑𐐨𐐿𐐲, 𐑄 𐑅𐐲𐑌 𐐱𐑂 𐐡𐐯𐑋𐐲𐑊𐐴𐐲, 𐐿𐐮𐑍 𐐱𐑂 𐐆𐑆𐑉𐐩𐐯𐑊, 𐐶𐐯𐑌𐐻 𐐲𐐹 𐐻𐐭𐐲𐑉𐐼𐑆 𐐖𐐯𐑉𐐭𐑅𐐲𐑊𐐯𐑋 𐐻𐐭 𐐶𐐫𐑉 𐐰𐑀𐐯𐑌𐑅𐐻 𐐮𐐻, 𐐺𐐲𐐻 𐐿𐐳𐐼 𐑌𐐱𐐻 𐐹𐑉𐐨𐑂𐐩𐑊 𐐰𐑀𐐯𐑌𐑅𐐻 𐐮𐐻. 𐐈𐑌𐐼 𐐮𐐻 𐐶𐐱𐑆 𐐻𐐬𐑊𐐼 𐑄 𐐸𐐵𐑅 𐐱𐑂 𐐔𐐩𐑂𐐮𐐼, 𐑅𐐩𐐮𐑍, 𐐝𐐮𐑉𐐨𐐲 𐐮𐑆 𐐿𐐱𐑌𐑁𐐯𐐼𐐲𐑉𐐩𐐻 𐐶𐐮𐑄 𐐀𐑁𐑉𐐩𐐮𐑋. 𐐈𐑌𐐼 𐐸𐐮𐑆 𐐸𐐪𐑉𐐻 𐐶𐐱𐑆 𐑋𐐭𐑂𐐼, 𐐰𐑌𐐼 𐑄 𐐸𐐪𐑉𐐻 𐐱𐑂 𐐸𐐮𐑆 𐐹𐐨𐐹𐑊, 𐐰𐑆 𐑄 𐐻𐑉𐐨𐑆 𐐱𐑂 𐑄 𐐶𐐳𐐼 𐐪𐑉 𐑋𐐭𐑂𐐼 𐐶𐐮𐑄 𐑄 𐐶𐐮𐑌𐐼. 𐐜𐐯𐑌 𐑅𐐯𐐼 𐑄 𐐢𐐫𐑉𐐼 𐐲𐑌𐐻𐐭 𐐌𐑆𐐩𐐲, 𐐘𐐬 𐑁𐐬𐑉𐑃 𐑌𐐵 𐐻𐐭 𐑋𐐨𐐻 𐐁𐐸𐐰𐑆, 𐑄𐐵, 𐐰𐑌𐐼 𐐟𐐨𐐲𐑉𐐾𐐰𐑇𐐲𐐺 𐑄𐐴 𐑅𐐲𐑌, 𐐰𐐻 𐑄 𐐯𐑌𐐼 𐐱𐑂 𐑄 𐐿𐐱𐑌𐐼𐐮𐐻 𐐱𐑂 𐑄 𐐲𐐹𐐲𐑉 𐐹𐐭𐑊 𐐮𐑌 𐑄 𐐸𐐴𐐶𐐩 𐐱𐑂 𐑄 𐑁𐐳𐑊𐐲𐑉'𐑆 𐑁𐐨𐑊𐐼; 𐐰𐑌𐐼 𐑅𐐩 𐐲𐑌𐐻𐐭 𐐸𐐮𐑋, 𐐓𐐩𐐿 𐐸𐐨𐐼, 𐐰𐑌𐐼 𐐺 𐐿𐐶𐐴𐐯𐐻; 𐑁𐐨𐑉 𐑌𐐱𐐻, 𐑌𐐨𐑄𐐲𐑉 𐐺

𐑁𐐩𐑌𐐻-𐐸𐐪𐑉𐐻𐐯𐐼 𐑁𐐫𐑉 𐑄 𐐻𐐭 𐐻𐐩𐑊𐑆 𐐱𐑂 𐑄𐐨𐑆 𐑅𐑋𐐬𐐿𐐮𐑍 𐑁𐐴𐑉-𐐺𐑉𐐰𐑌𐐼𐑆, 𐑁𐐫𐑉 𐑄 𐑁𐐨𐑉𐑅 𐐰𐑍𐑀𐐲𐑉 𐐱𐑂 𐐡𐐨𐑆𐐮𐑌 𐐶𐐮𐑄 𐐝𐐮𐑉𐐨𐐲, 𐐰𐑌𐐼 𐐱𐑂 𐑄 𐑅𐐲𐑌 𐐱𐑂 𐐡𐐯𐑋𐐲𐑊𐐴𐐲. 𐐒𐐨𐐿𐐫𐑆 𐐝𐐮𐑉𐐨𐐲, 𐐀𐑁𐑉𐐩𐐮𐑋, 𐐰𐑌𐐼 𐑄 𐑅𐐲𐑌 𐐱𐑂 𐐡𐐯𐑋𐐲𐑊𐐴𐐲, 𐐸𐐰𐑂 𐐻𐐩𐐿𐑌 𐐨𐑂𐑊 𐐿𐐵𐑌𐑅𐐯𐑊 𐐲𐑀𐐯𐑌𐑅𐐻 𐑄𐐨, 𐑅𐐩𐐮𐑍, 𐐢𐐯𐐻 𐐲𐑅 𐑀𐐬 𐐲𐐹 𐐲𐑀𐐯𐑌𐑅𐐻 𐐖𐐭𐐼𐐲 𐐰𐑌𐐼 𐑂𐐯𐐿𐑅 𐐮𐐻, 𐐰𐑌𐐼 𐑊𐐯𐐻 𐐲𐑅 𐑋𐐩𐐿 𐐲 𐐺𐑉𐐨𐐽 𐑄𐐯𐑉𐐮𐑌 𐑁𐐫𐑉 𐐲𐑅, 𐐰𐑌𐐼 𐑅𐐯𐐻 𐐲 𐐿𐐮𐑍 𐐮𐑌 𐑄 𐑋𐐮𐐼𐑅𐐻 𐐱𐑂 𐐮𐐻, 𐐷𐐩, 𐑄 𐑅𐐲𐑌 𐐱𐑂 𐐓𐐰𐐺𐐨𐐲𐑊; 𐑄𐐲𐑅 𐑅𐐯𐑃 𐑄 𐐢𐐫𐑉𐐼 𐐘𐐱𐐼, 𐐆𐐻 𐑇𐐰𐑊 𐑌𐐱𐐻 𐑅𐐻𐐰𐑌𐐼, 𐑌𐐨𐑄𐐲𐑉 𐑇𐐰𐑊 𐐮𐐻 𐐿𐐲𐑋 𐐻𐐭 𐐹𐐪𐑅. 𐐙𐐫𐑉 𐑄 𐐸𐐯𐐼 𐐱𐑂 𐐝𐐮𐑉𐐨𐐲 𐐮𐑆 𐐔𐐲𐑋𐐰𐑅𐐿𐐲𐑅, 𐐰𐑌𐐼 𐑄 𐐸𐐯𐐼 𐐱𐑂 𐐔𐐲𐑋𐐰𐑅𐐿𐐲𐑅, 𐐡𐐨𐑆𐐮𐑌; 𐐰𐑌𐐼 𐐶𐐮𐑄𐐮𐑌 𐑃𐑉𐐨𐑅𐐿𐐬𐑉 𐐰𐑌𐐼 𐑁𐐴𐑂 𐐷𐐨𐑉𐑆 𐑇𐐰𐑊 𐐀𐑁𐑉𐐩𐐮𐑋 𐐺𐐨 𐐺𐑉𐐬𐐿𐑌, 𐑄𐐰𐐻 𐐮𐐻 𐐺𐐨 𐑌𐐱𐐻 𐐲 𐐹𐐨𐐹𐑊. 𐐈𐑌𐐼 𐑄 𐐸𐐯𐐼 𐐱𐑂 𐐀𐑁𐑉𐐩𐐮𐑋 𐐮𐑆 𐐝𐐲𐑋𐐩𐑉𐐨𐐲, 𐐰𐑌𐐼 𐑄 𐐸𐐯𐐼 𐐱𐑂 𐐝𐐲𐑋𐐩𐑉𐐨𐐲 𐐮𐑆 𐐡𐐯𐑋𐐲𐑊𐐴𐐲'𐑆 𐑅𐐲𐑌. 𐐆𐑁 𐐷𐐨 𐐶𐐮𐑊 𐑌𐐱𐐻 𐐺𐐨𐑊𐐨𐑂, 𐑇𐐭𐑉𐑊𐐨 𐐷𐐨 𐑇𐐰𐑊 𐑌𐐱𐐻 𐐺𐐨 𐐯𐑅𐐻𐐰𐐺𐑊𐐮𐑇𐐻.

6. 𐐣𐐫𐑉𐐬𐑂𐐲𐑉, 𐑄 𐐢𐐫𐑉𐐼 𐑅𐐹𐐩𐐿 𐐲𐑀𐐯𐑌 𐐲𐑌𐐻𐐭 𐐁𐐸𐐰𐑆, 𐑅𐐩𐐮𐑍, 𐐈𐑅𐐿 𐑄𐐨 𐐲 𐑅𐐴𐑌 𐐱𐑂 𐑄 𐐢𐐫𐑉𐐼 𐑄𐐴 𐐘𐐱𐐼; 𐐰𐑅𐐿 𐐮𐐻 𐐨𐑄𐐲𐑉 𐐮𐑌 𐑄 𐐼𐐯𐐹𐑃𐑅, 𐐫𐑉 𐐮𐑌 𐑄 𐐸𐐴𐐻𐑅 𐐲𐐺𐐲𐑂. 𐐒𐐲𐐻 𐐁𐐸𐐰𐑆 𐑅𐐯𐐼, 𐐌 𐐶𐐮𐑊 𐑌𐐱𐐻 𐐰𐑅𐐿, 𐑌𐐨𐑄𐐲𐑉 𐐶𐐮𐑊 𐐌 𐐻𐐯𐑋𐐻 𐑄 𐐢𐐫𐑉𐐼. 𐐈𐑌𐐼 𐐸𐐨 𐑅𐐯𐐼: 𐐐𐐨𐑉 𐐷𐐨 𐑌𐐵, 𐐄 𐐸𐐵𐑅 𐐱𐑂 𐐔𐐩𐑂𐐮𐐼; 𐐮𐑆 𐐮𐐻 𐐲 𐑅𐑋𐐫𐑊 𐑃𐐮𐑍 𐑁𐐫𐑉 𐐷𐐭 𐐻𐐭 𐐶𐐨𐑉𐐨 𐑋𐐯𐑌, 𐐺𐐲𐐻 𐐶𐐮𐑊 𐐷𐐨 𐐶𐐨𐑉𐐨 𐑋𐐴 𐐘𐐱𐐼 𐐫𐑊𐑅𐐬? 𐐜𐐯𐑉𐑁𐐫𐑉, 𐑄 𐐢𐐫𐑉𐐼 𐐸𐐮𐑋𐑅𐐯𐑊𐑁 𐑇𐐰𐑊 𐑀𐐮𐑂 𐐷𐐭 𐐲 𐑅𐐴𐑌; 𐐒𐐨𐐸𐐬𐑊𐐼, 𐐲 𐑂𐐲𐑉𐐾𐐮𐑌 𐑇𐐰𐑊 𐐿𐐱𐑌𐑅𐐨𐑂, 𐐰𐑌𐐼 𐑇𐐰𐑊 𐐺𐐩𐑉 𐐲 𐑅𐐲𐑌, 𐐰𐑌𐐼 𐑇𐐰𐑊 𐐿𐐫𐑊 𐐸𐐮𐑆 𐑌𐐩𐑋 𐐆𐑋𐐰𐑌𐐷𐐭𐐯𐑊. 𐐒𐐲𐐻𐐲𐑉 𐐰𐑌𐐼 𐐸𐐲𐑌𐐨 𐑇𐐰𐑊 𐐸𐐨 𐐨𐐻, 𐑄𐐰𐐻 𐐸𐐨 𐑋𐐩 𐑌𐐬 𐐻𐐭 𐑉𐐯𐑁𐐷𐐭𐑆 𐑄 𐐨𐑂𐑊 𐐰𐑌𐐼 𐐻𐐭 𐐽𐐭𐑆 𐑄 𐑀𐐳𐐼. 𐐙𐐫𐑉 𐐺𐐨𐑁𐐬𐑉 𐑄 𐐽𐐴𐑊𐐼 𐑇𐐰𐑊 𐑌𐐬 𐐻𐐭 𐑉𐐯𐑁𐐷𐐭𐑆 𐑄 𐐨𐑂𐑊 𐐰𐑌𐐼 𐐽𐐭𐑆 𐑄 𐑀𐐳𐐼, 𐑄 𐑊𐐰𐑌𐐼 𐑄𐐰𐐻 𐑄𐐵 𐐰𐐺𐐸𐐫𐑉𐐯𐑅𐐻 𐑇𐐰𐑊 𐐺𐐨 𐑁𐐫𐑉𐑅𐐩𐐿𐑌 𐐱𐑂 𐐺𐐬𐑃 𐐸𐐲𐑉 𐐿𐐮𐑍𐑆.

7. 𐐜 𐐢𐐫𐑉𐐼 𐑇𐐰𐑊 𐐺𐑉𐐮𐑍 𐐲𐐹𐐱𐑌 𐑄𐐨, 𐐰𐑌𐐼 𐐲𐐹𐐱𐑌 𐑄𐐴 𐐹𐐨𐐹𐑊, 𐐰𐑌𐐼 𐐲𐐹𐐱𐑌 𐑄𐐴 𐑁𐐪𐑄𐐲𐑉'𐑆 𐐸𐐵𐑅, 𐐼𐐩𐑆 𐑄𐐰𐐻 𐑄𐐩 𐐸𐐰𐑂 𐑌𐐱𐐻 𐐿𐐲𐑋, 𐑁𐑉𐐱𐑋 𐑄 𐐼𐐩 𐑄𐐰𐐻 𐐀𐑁𐑉𐐩𐐮𐑋 𐐼𐐨𐐹𐐪𐑉𐐻𐐯𐐼 𐑁𐑉𐐱𐑋 𐐖𐐭𐐼𐐲, 𐑄 𐐿𐐮𐑍 𐐱𐑂 𐐈𐑅𐐮𐑉𐐨𐐲. 𐐈𐑌𐐼 𐐮𐐻 𐑇𐐰𐑊 𐐿𐐲𐑋 𐐻𐐭 𐐹𐐪𐑅 𐐮𐑌 𐑄𐐰𐐻 𐐼𐐩, 𐑄𐐰𐐻 𐑄 𐐢𐐫𐑉𐐼 𐑇𐐰𐑊 𐐸𐐮𐑅 𐑁𐐫𐑉 𐑄 𐑁𐑊𐐴 𐑄𐐰𐐻 𐐮𐑆 𐐮𐑌 𐑄 𐐲𐐻𐐲𐑉𐑋𐐬𐑅𐐻 𐐹𐐪𐑉𐐻 𐐱𐑂 𐐀𐐾𐐮𐐹𐐻, 𐐰𐑌𐐼 𐑁𐐫𐑉 𐑄 𐐺𐐨 𐑄𐐰𐐻 𐐮𐑆 𐐮𐑌 𐑄 𐑊𐐰𐑌𐐼 𐐱𐑂 𐐈𐑅𐐮𐑉𐐨𐐲. 𐐈𐑌𐐼 𐑄𐐩 𐑇𐐰𐑊 𐐿𐐲𐑋, 𐐰𐑌𐐼 𐑇𐐰𐑊 𐑉𐐯𐑅𐐻 𐐫𐑊 𐐱𐑂 𐑄𐐯𐑋 𐐮𐑌 𐑄 𐐼𐐯𐑅𐐬𐑊𐐩𐐻 𐑂𐐰𐑊𐐨𐑆, 𐐰𐑌𐐼 𐐮𐑌 𐑄 𐐸𐐬𐑊𐑆 𐐱𐑂 𐑄 𐑉𐐱𐐿𐑅, 𐐰𐑌𐐼 𐐲𐐹𐐱𐑌 𐐫𐑊 𐑃𐐫𐑉𐑌𐑆, 𐐰𐑌𐐼 𐐲𐐹𐐱𐑌 𐐫𐑊 𐐺𐐳𐑇𐐯𐑆. 𐐆𐑌 𐑄 𐑅𐐩𐑋 𐐼𐐩 𐑇𐐰𐑊 𐑄 𐐢𐐫𐑉𐐼 𐑇𐐩𐑂 𐐶𐐮𐑄 𐐲 𐑉𐐩𐑆𐐲𐑉 𐑄𐐰𐐻 𐐮𐑆 𐐸𐐴𐑉𐐼, 𐐺𐐴 𐑄𐐯𐑋 𐐺𐐨𐐷𐐱𐑌𐐼 𐑄 𐑉𐐮𐑂𐐲𐑉, 𐐺𐐴 𐑄 𐐿𐐮𐑍 𐐱𐑂 𐐈𐑅𐐮𐑉𐐨𐐲, 𐑄 𐐸𐐯𐐼, 𐐰𐑌𐐼 𐑄 𐐸𐐩𐑉 𐐱𐑂 𐑄 𐑁𐐨𐐻; 𐐰𐑌𐐼 𐐮𐐻 𐑇𐐰𐑊 𐐫𐑊𐑅𐐬 𐐿𐐱𐑌𐑅𐐭𐑋 𐑄 𐐺𐐨𐑉𐐼. 𐐈𐑌𐐼 𐐮𐐻 𐑇𐐰𐑊 𐐿𐐲𐑋 𐐻𐐭 𐐹𐐪𐑅 𐐮𐑌 𐑄𐐰𐐻 𐐼𐐩, 𐐲 𐑋𐐰𐑌 𐑇𐐰𐑊 𐑌𐐲𐑉𐐮𐑇 𐐲 𐐷𐐲𐑍 𐐿𐐵 𐐰𐑌𐐼 𐐻𐐭 𐑇𐐨𐐹; 𐐰𐑌𐐼 𐐮𐐻 𐑇𐐰𐑊 𐐿𐐲𐑋 𐐻𐐭 𐐹𐐪𐑅, 𐑁𐐫𐑉 𐑄 𐐲𐐺𐐲𐑌𐐼𐐲𐑌𐑅 𐐱𐑂 𐑋𐐮𐑊𐐿 𐑄𐐩 𐑇𐐰𐑊 𐑀𐐮𐑂 𐐸𐐨 𐑇𐐰𐑊 𐐨𐐻 𐐺𐐲𐐻𐐲𐑉: 𐑁𐐫𐑉 𐐺𐐲𐐻𐐲𐑉 𐐰𐑌𐐼 𐐸𐐲𐑌𐐨 𐑇𐐰𐑊 𐐯𐑂𐐲𐑉𐐨 𐐶𐐲𐑌 𐐨𐐻 𐑄𐐰𐐻 𐐮𐑆 𐑊𐐯𐑁𐐻 𐐮𐑌 𐑄 𐑊𐐰𐑌𐐼. 𐐈𐑌𐐼 𐐮𐐻 𐑇𐐰𐑊 𐐿𐐲𐑋 𐐻𐐭 𐐹𐐪𐑅 𐐮𐑌 𐑄𐐰𐐻 𐐼𐐩, 𐐯𐑂𐐲𐑉𐐨 𐐹𐑊𐐩𐑅 𐑇𐐰𐑊 𐐺𐐨, 𐐸𐐶𐐯𐑉 𐑄𐐯𐑉 𐐶𐐲𐑉 𐐲 𐑃𐐵𐑆𐐲𐑌𐐼 𐑂𐐴𐑌𐑆 𐐰𐐻 𐐲 𐑃𐐵𐑆𐐲𐑌𐐼 𐑅𐐮𐑊𐑂𐐲𐑉𐑊𐐮𐑍𐑆, 𐐸𐐶𐐮𐐽 𐑇𐐰𐑊 𐐺𐐨 𐑁𐐫𐑉 𐐺𐑉𐐴𐐲𐑉𐑆 𐐰𐑌𐐼 𐑃𐐫𐑉𐑌𐑆. 𐐎𐐮𐑄 𐐰𐑉𐐬𐑆 𐐰𐑌𐐼 𐐶𐐮𐑄 𐐺𐐬𐑆 𐑇𐐰𐑊 𐑋𐐯𐑌 𐐿𐐲𐑋 𐑄𐐮𐑄𐐲𐑉, 𐐺𐐨𐐿𐐫𐑆 𐐫𐑊 𐑄 𐑊𐐰𐑌𐐼 𐑇𐐰𐑊 𐐺𐐨𐐿𐐲𐑋 𐐺𐑉𐐴𐐲𐑉𐑆 𐐰𐑌𐐼 𐑃𐐫𐑉𐑌𐑆. 𐐈𐑌𐐼 𐐫𐑊 𐐸𐐮𐑊𐑆 𐑄𐐰𐐻 𐑇𐐰𐑊 𐐺𐐨 𐐼𐐮𐑀𐐯𐐼 𐐶𐐮𐑄 𐑄 𐑋𐐰𐐻𐐲𐐿, 𐑄𐐯𐑉 𐑇𐐰𐑊 𐑌𐐱𐐻 𐐿𐐲𐑋 𐑄𐐮𐑄𐐲𐑉 𐑄 𐑁𐐨𐑉 𐐱𐑂 𐐺𐑉𐐴𐐲𐑉𐑆 𐐰𐑌𐐼 𐑃𐐫𐑉𐑌𐑆; 𐐺𐐲𐐻 𐐮𐐻 𐑇𐐰𐑊 𐐺𐐨 𐑁𐐫𐑉 𐑄 𐑅𐐯𐑌𐐼𐐮𐑍 𐑁𐐫𐑉𐑃 𐐱𐑂 𐐱𐐿𐑅𐐯𐑌, 𐐰𐑌𐐼 𐑄 𐐻𐑉𐐯𐐼𐐮𐑍 𐐱𐑂 𐑊𐐯𐑅𐐲𐑉 𐐿𐐰𐐻𐑊.

8. 𐐣𐐫𐑉𐐬𐑂𐐲𐑉, 𐑄 𐐶𐐲𐑉𐐼 𐐱𐑂 𐑄 𐐢𐐫𐑉𐐼 𐑅𐐯𐐼 𐐲𐑌𐐻𐐭 𐑋𐐨, 𐐓𐐩𐐿 𐑄𐐨 𐐲 𐑀𐑉𐐩𐐻 𐑉𐐬𐑊, 𐐰𐑌𐐼 𐑉𐐴𐐻 𐐮𐑌 𐐮𐐻 𐐶𐐮𐑄 𐐲 𐑋𐐰𐑌'𐑆 𐐹𐐯𐑌, 𐐿𐐱𐑌𐑅𐐲𐑉𐑌𐐮𐑍 𐐣𐐩𐐸𐐲𐑉-𐑇𐐰𐑊𐐰𐑊-𐐸𐐰𐑇-𐐺𐐰𐑆. 𐐈𐑌𐐼 𐐌 𐐻𐐳𐐿 𐐲𐑌𐐻𐐭 𐑋𐐨 𐑁𐐩𐑃𐑁𐐳𐑊 𐐶𐐮𐐻𐑌𐐯𐑅𐐯𐑆 𐐻𐐭 𐑉𐐨𐐿𐐫𐑉𐐼, 𐐏𐐭𐑉𐐴𐐲 𐑄 𐐹𐑉𐐨𐑅𐐻, 𐐰𐑌𐐼 𐐞𐐯𐐿𐐲𐑉𐐴𐐲 𐑄 𐑅𐐲𐑌 𐐱𐑂 𐐖𐐯𐐺𐐯𐑉𐐯𐐿𐐴𐐲. 𐐈𐑌𐐼 𐐌 𐐶𐐯𐑌𐐻 𐐲𐑌𐐻𐐭 𐑄 𐐹𐑉𐐱𐑁𐐯𐐻𐐯𐑅; 𐐰𐑌𐐼 𐑇𐐨 𐐿𐐱𐑌𐑅𐐨𐑂𐐼 𐐰𐑌𐐼 𐐺𐐩𐑉 𐐲 𐑅𐐲𐑌. 𐐜𐐯𐑌 𐑅𐐯𐐼 𐑄 𐐢𐐫𐑉𐐼 𐐻𐐭 𐑋𐐨, 𐐗𐐫𐑊 𐐸𐐮𐑆 𐑌𐐩𐑋 𐐣𐐩𐐸𐐲𐑉-𐑇𐐰𐑊𐐰𐑊-𐐸𐐰𐑇-𐐺𐐰𐑆. 𐐙𐐫𐑉 𐐺𐐨𐐸𐐬𐑊𐐼, 𐑄 𐐽𐐴𐑊𐐼 𐑇𐐰𐑊 𐑌𐐱𐐻 𐐸𐐰𐑂 𐑌𐐱𐑊𐐯𐐾 𐐻𐐭 𐐿𐑉𐐴, 𐐣𐐴 𐑁𐐪𐑄𐐲𐑉, 𐐰𐑌𐐼 𐑋𐐴 𐑋𐐲𐑄𐐲𐑉, 𐐺𐐨𐑁𐐬𐑉 𐑄 𐑉𐐮𐐽𐐯𐑆 𐐱𐑂 𐐔𐐲𐑋𐐰𐑅𐐿𐐲𐑅 𐐰𐑌𐐼 𐑄 𐑅𐐹𐐱𐐮𐑊 𐐱𐑂 𐐝𐐲𐑋𐐩𐑉𐐨𐐲 𐑇𐐰𐑊 𐐺𐐨 𐐻𐐩𐐿𐑌 𐐲𐐶𐐩 𐐺𐐨𐑁𐐬𐑉 𐑄 𐐿𐐮𐑍 𐐱𐑂 𐐈𐑅𐐮𐑉𐐨𐐲.

9. 𐐜 𐐢𐐫𐑉𐐼 𐑅𐐹𐐰𐐿 𐐫𐑊𐑅𐐬 𐐲𐑌𐐻𐐭 𐑋𐐨 𐐲𐑀𐐯𐑌, 𐑅𐐩𐐮𐑍, 𐑁𐐬𐑉𐐰𐑆𐑋𐐲𐐽 𐐰𐑆 𐑄𐐮𐑅 𐐹𐐨𐐹𐑊 𐑉𐐯𐑁𐐷𐐭𐑆𐐯𐑃 𐑄 𐐶𐐫𐐻𐐲𐑉𐑆 𐐲𐑂 𐐟𐐴𐑊𐐬𐐰 𐑄𐐰𐐻 𐑀𐐬 𐑅𐐱𐑁𐐻𐑊𐐨, 𐐰𐑌𐐼 𐑉𐐨𐐾𐐱𐐮𐑅 𐐮𐑌 𐐡𐐯𐑆𐐮𐑌 𐐰𐑌𐐼 𐐡𐐯𐑋𐐲𐑊𐐴𐐲'𐑆 𐑅𐐲𐑌; 𐑌𐐵 𐑄𐐯𐑉𐑁𐐬𐑉, 𐐺𐐨𐐸𐐬𐑊𐐼, 𐑄 𐐢𐐫𐑉𐐼 𐐺𐑉𐐮𐑍𐐯𐑃 𐐲𐐹 𐐲𐐹𐐱𐑌 𐑄𐐯𐑋 𐑄 𐐶𐐫𐐻𐐲𐑉𐑆 𐐲𐑂 𐑄 𐑉𐐮𐑂𐐲𐑉, 𐑅𐐻𐑉𐐱𐑍 𐐰𐑌𐐼 𐑋𐐯𐑌𐐨, 𐐨𐑂𐐲𐑌 𐑄 𐐿𐐮𐑍 𐐲𐑂 𐐊𐑅𐐮𐑉𐐨𐐲, 𐐰𐑌𐐼 𐐫𐑊 𐐸𐐮𐑆 𐑀𐑊𐐬𐑉𐐨; 𐐰𐑌𐐼 𐐸𐐨 𐑇𐐰𐑊 𐐿𐐲𐑋 𐐲𐐹 𐐬𐑂𐐲𐑉 𐐫𐑊 𐐸𐐮𐑆 𐐽𐐰𐑌𐐯𐑊𐑆, 𐐰𐑌𐐼 𐑀𐐬 𐐬𐑂𐐲𐑉 𐐫𐑊 𐐸𐐮𐑆 𐐺𐐰𐑍𐐿𐑅; 𐐰𐑌𐐼 𐐸𐐨 𐑇𐐰𐑊 𐐹𐐰𐑅 𐑃𐑉𐐭 𐐖𐐭𐐼𐐲; 𐐸𐐨 𐑇𐐰𐑊 𐐬𐑂𐐲𐑉𐑁𐑊𐐬 𐐰𐑌𐐼 𐑀𐐬 𐐬𐑂𐐲𐑉, 𐐸𐐨 𐑇𐐰𐑊 𐑉𐐨𐐽 𐐨𐑂𐐲𐑌 𐐻𐐭 𐑄 𐑌𐐯𐐿; 𐐰𐑌𐐼 𐑄 𐑅𐐻𐑉𐐯𐐽𐐮𐑍 𐐬𐐻 𐐲𐑂 𐐸𐐮𐑆 𐐶𐐮𐑍𐑆 𐑇𐐰𐑊 𐑁𐐮𐑊 𐑄 𐐺𐑉𐐯𐐼𐑃 𐐲𐑂 𐑄𐐴 𐑊𐐰𐑌𐐼, 𐐄 𐐆𐑋𐐰𐑌𐐷𐐲𐐯𐑊.

10. 𐐈𐑅𐐬𐑇𐐨𐐩𐐻 𐐷𐐫𐑉𐑅𐐯𐑊𐑂𐑆, 𐐄 𐐷𐐨 𐐹𐐨𐐹𐑊, 𐐰𐑌𐐼 𐐷𐐨 𐑇𐐰𐑊 𐐺𐐨 𐐺𐑉𐐬𐐿𐐲𐑌 𐐮𐑌 𐐹𐐨𐑅𐐲𐑆, 𐐰𐑌𐐼 𐑀𐐮𐑂 𐐨𐑉 𐐫𐑊 𐐷𐐨 𐐲𐑂 𐑁𐐪𐑉 𐐿𐐲𐑌𐐻𐑉𐐨𐑆; 𐑀𐐲𐑉𐐼 𐐷𐐫𐑉𐑅𐐯𐑊𐑂𐑆, 𐐰𐑌𐐼 𐐷𐐨 𐑇𐐰𐑊 𐐺𐐨 𐐺𐑉𐐬𐐿𐐲𐑌 𐐮𐑌 𐐹𐐨𐑅𐐲𐑆; 𐑀𐐲𐑉𐐼 𐐷𐐫𐑉𐑅𐐯𐑊𐑂𐑆, 𐐰𐑌𐐼 𐐷𐐨 𐑇𐐰𐑊 𐐺𐐨 𐐺𐑉𐐬𐐿𐐲𐑌 𐐮𐑌 𐐹𐐨𐑅𐐲𐑆. 𐐓𐐩𐐿 𐐿𐐵𐑌𐑅𐐯𐑊 𐐻𐐭𐑀𐐯𐑄𐐲𐑉, 𐐰𐑌𐐼 𐐮𐐻 𐑇𐐰𐑊 𐐿𐐲𐑋 𐐻𐐭 𐑌𐐫𐐻; 𐑅𐐹𐐨𐐿 𐑄 𐐶𐐲𐑉𐐼, 𐐰𐑌𐐼 𐐮𐐻 𐑇𐐰𐑊 𐑌𐐱𐐻 𐑅𐐻𐐰𐑌𐐼; 𐑁𐐫𐑉 𐐘𐐱𐐼 𐐮𐑆 𐐶𐐮𐑄 𐐲𐑅.

11. 𐐙𐐫𐑉 𐑄 𐐢𐐫𐑉𐐼 𐑅𐐹𐐰𐐿 𐑄𐐲𐑅 𐐻𐐭 𐑋𐐨 𐐶𐐮𐑄 𐐲 𐑅𐐻𐑉𐐱𐑍 𐐸𐐰𐑌𐐼, 𐐰𐑌𐐼 𐐮𐑌𐑅𐐻𐑉𐐲𐐿𐐻𐐯𐐼 𐑋𐐨 𐑄𐐰𐐻 𐐌 𐑇𐐭𐐼 𐑌𐐱𐐻 𐐶𐐪𐐿 𐐮𐑌 𐑄 𐐶𐐩 𐐲𐑂 𐑄𐐮𐑅 𐐹𐐨𐐹𐑊, 𐑅𐐩𐐮𐑍, 𐑅𐐩 𐐷𐐨 𐑌𐐱𐐻, 𐐲 𐐿𐐲𐑌𐑁𐐯𐐼𐐲𐑉𐐩𐑅𐐨 𐐻𐐭 𐐫𐑊 𐐻𐐭 𐐸𐐭𐑋 𐑄𐐮𐑅 𐐹𐐨𐐹𐑊 𐑇𐐰𐑊 𐑅𐐩 𐐲 𐐿𐐲𐑌𐑁𐐯𐐼𐐲𐑉𐐩𐑅𐐨; 𐑌𐐴𐑄𐐲𐑉 𐑁𐐨𐑉 𐐷𐐨 𐑄𐐯𐑉 𐑁𐐨𐑉, 𐑌𐐫𐑉 𐐺𐐨 𐐰𐑁𐑉𐐩𐐼. 𐐝𐐰𐑍𐐿𐐻𐐮𐑁𐐴 𐑄 𐐢𐐫𐑉𐐼 𐐲𐑂 𐐐𐐬𐑅𐐻𐑅 𐐸𐐮𐑋𐑅𐐯𐑊𐑁, 𐐰𐑌𐐼 𐑊𐐯𐐻 𐐸𐐮𐑋 𐐺𐐨 𐐷𐐫𐑉 𐑁𐐨𐑉, 𐐰𐑌𐐼 𐑊𐐯𐐻 𐐸𐐮𐑋 𐐺𐐨 𐐷𐐫𐑉 𐐼𐑉𐐯𐐼. 𐐈𐑌𐐼 𐐸𐐨 𐑇𐐰𐑊 𐐺𐐨 𐑁𐐫𐑉 𐐲 𐑅𐐰𐑍𐐿𐐽𐐭𐐯𐑉𐐨; 𐐺𐐲𐐻 𐑁𐐫𐑉 𐐲 𐑅𐐻𐐬𐑌 𐐲𐑂 𐑅𐐻𐐲𐑋𐐺𐑊𐐮𐑍, 𐐰𐑌𐐼 𐑁𐐫𐑉 𐐲 𐑉𐐱𐐿 𐐲𐑂 𐐱𐑁𐐯𐑌𐑅 𐐻𐐭 𐐺𐐬𐑃 𐑄 𐐸𐐵𐑆𐐯𐑆 𐐲𐑂 𐐆𐑆𐑉𐐩𐐯𐑊, 𐑁𐐫𐑉 𐐲 𐑀𐐮𐑌 𐐰𐑌𐐼 𐐲 𐑅𐑌𐐯𐑉 𐐻𐐭 𐑄 𐐮𐑌𐐸𐐰𐐺𐐮𐐻𐐲𐑌𐐻𐑅 𐐲𐑂 𐐖𐐯𐑉𐐭𐑅𐐲𐑊𐐯𐑋. 𐐈𐑌𐐼 𐑋𐐯𐑌𐐨 𐐲𐑋𐐲𐑍 𐑄𐐯𐑋 𐑇𐐰𐑊 𐑅𐐻𐐲𐑋𐐺𐑊 𐐰𐑌𐐼 𐑁𐐫𐑊, 𐐰𐑌𐐼 𐐺𐐨 𐐺𐑉𐐬𐐿𐐲𐑌, 𐐰𐑌𐐼 𐐺𐐨 𐑅𐑌𐐯𐑉𐐼, 𐐰𐑌𐐼 𐐺𐐨 𐐻𐐩𐐿𐐲𐑌. 𐐒𐐴𐑌𐐼 𐐲𐐹 𐑄 𐐻𐐯𐑅𐐻𐐮𐑋𐐬𐑌𐐨, 𐑅𐐨𐑊 𐑄 𐑊𐐫 𐐲𐑋𐐲𐑍 𐑋𐐴 𐐼𐐮𐑅𐐴𐐹𐑊𐑆. 𐐈𐑌𐐼 𐐌 𐐶𐐮𐑊 𐐶𐐩𐐻 𐐲𐐹𐐱𐑌 𐑄 𐐢𐐫𐑉𐐼, 𐑄𐐰𐐻 𐐸𐐴𐐼𐐯𐑃 𐐸𐐮𐑆 𐑁𐐩𐑅 𐑁𐑉𐐱𐑋 𐑄 𐐸𐐵𐑅 𐐲𐑂 𐐖𐐩𐐿𐐲𐐺, 𐐰𐑌𐐼 𐐌 𐐶𐐮𐑊 𐑊𐐳𐐿 𐑁𐐫𐑉 𐐸𐐮𐑋. 𐐒𐐨𐐸𐐬𐑊𐐼, 𐐌 𐐰𐑌𐐼 𐑄 𐐽𐐮𐑊𐐼𐑉𐐯𐑌 𐐸𐐭𐑋 𐑄 𐐢𐐫𐑉𐐼 𐐸𐐰𐑆 𐑀𐐮𐑂𐐯𐑌 𐑋𐐨 𐐪𐑉 𐑁𐐫𐑉 𐑅𐐴𐑌𐑆 𐐰𐑌𐐼 𐑁𐐫𐑉 𐐶𐐲𐑌𐐼𐐲𐑉𐑆 𐐮𐑌 𐐆𐑆𐑉𐐩𐐯𐑊 𐑁𐑉𐐱𐑋 𐑄 𐐢𐐫𐑉𐐼 𐐲𐑂 𐐐𐐬𐑅𐐻𐑅, 𐑄𐐰𐐻 𐐼𐐶𐐯𐑊𐐯𐑃 𐐮𐑌 𐐣𐐵𐑌𐐻 𐐞𐐴𐐲𐑌.

12. 𐐈𐑌𐐼 𐐸𐐶𐐯𐑌 𐐷𐐨 𐑇𐐰𐑊 𐑅𐐩 𐐲𐑌𐐻𐐭 𐐷𐐭, 𐑅𐐨𐐿 𐐲𐑌𐐻𐐭 𐑄𐐯𐑋 𐑄𐐰𐐻 𐐸𐐰𐑂 𐑁𐐲𐑋𐐮𐑊𐐷𐐲𐑉 𐑅𐐹𐐮𐑉𐐮𐐻𐑅, 𐐰𐑌𐐼 𐐲𐑌𐐻𐐭 𐐶𐐮𐑆𐐲𐑉𐐼𐑆 𐑄𐐰𐐻 𐐹𐐨𐐹 𐐰𐑌𐐼 𐑋𐐲𐐻𐐲𐑉; 𐑇𐐳𐐼 𐑌𐐱𐐻 𐐲 𐐹𐐨𐐹𐑊 𐑅𐐨𐐿 𐐲𐑌𐐻𐐭 𐑄𐐯𐑉 𐐘𐐱𐐼? 𐑁𐐫𐑉 𐑄 𐑊𐐮𐑂𐐮𐑍 𐐻𐐭 𐐸𐐨𐑉 𐑁𐑉𐐱𐑋 𐑄 𐐼𐐯𐐼? 𐐻𐐭 𐑄 𐑊𐐫 𐐰𐑌𐐼 𐐻𐐭 𐑄 𐐻𐐯𐑅𐐻𐐮𐑋𐐬𐑌𐐨; 𐐰𐑌𐐼 𐐮𐑁 𐑄𐐩 𐑅𐐹𐐨𐐿 𐑌𐐱𐐻 𐐰𐐿𐐫𐑉𐐼𐐮𐑍 𐐻𐐭 𐑄𐐮𐑅 𐐶𐐲𐑉𐐼, 𐐮𐐻 𐐮𐑆 𐐺𐐨𐐿𐐫𐑆 𐑄𐐯𐑉 𐐮𐑆 𐑌𐐬 𐑊𐐴𐐻 𐐮𐑌 𐑄𐐯𐑋. 𐐈𐑌𐐼 𐑄𐐩 𐑇𐐰𐑊 𐐹𐐰𐑅 𐑃𐑉𐐭 𐐮𐐻 𐐸𐐪𐑉𐐼𐑊𐐨 𐐺𐐯𐑅𐐻𐐲𐐼 𐐰𐑌𐐼 𐐸𐐲𐑍𐑀𐑉𐐨, 𐐰𐑌𐐼 𐐮𐐻 𐑇𐐰𐑊 𐐿𐐲𐑋 𐐻𐐭 𐐹𐐰𐑅, 𐑄𐐰𐐻 𐐸𐐶𐐯𐑌 𐑄𐐩 𐑇𐐰𐑊 𐐺𐐨 𐐸𐐲𐑍𐑀𐑉𐐨, 𐑄𐐩 𐑇𐐰𐑊 𐑁𐑉𐐯𐐻 𐑄𐐯𐑋𐑅𐐯𐑊𐑂𐑆, 𐐰𐑌𐐼 𐐿𐐲𐑉𐑅 𐑄𐐯𐑉 𐐿𐐮𐑍 𐐰𐑌𐐼 𐑄𐐯𐑉 𐐘𐐱𐐼, 𐐰𐑌𐐼 𐑊𐐳𐐿 𐐲𐐹𐐶𐐲𐑉𐐼. 𐐈𐑌𐐼 𐑄𐐩 𐑇𐐰𐑊 𐑊𐐳𐐿 𐐲𐑌𐐻𐐭 𐑄 𐐲𐑉𐑃; 𐐰𐑌𐐼 𐐺𐐨𐐸𐐬𐑊𐐼 𐐻𐑉𐐲𐐺𐑊, 𐐰𐑌𐐼 𐐼𐐪𐑉𐐿𐑌𐐯𐑅, 𐐼𐐮𐑋𐑌𐐯𐑅 𐐲𐑂 𐐰𐑍𐑀𐐶𐐮𐑇, 𐐰𐑌𐐼 𐑇𐐰𐑊 𐐺𐐨 𐐼𐑉𐐮𐑂𐐲𐑌 𐐻𐐭 𐐼𐐪𐑉𐐿𐑌𐐯𐑅.

13. 𐐤𐐯𐑂𐐲𐑉𐑄𐐯𐑊𐐯𐑅 𐑄 𐐼𐐮𐑋𐑌𐐯𐑅 𐑇𐐰𐑊 𐑌𐐱𐐻 𐐺𐐨 𐑅𐐲𐐽 𐐰𐑆 𐐶𐐲𐑆 𐐮𐑌 𐐸𐐲𐑉 𐑂𐐯𐐿𐑅𐐩𐑇𐐲𐑌, 𐐸𐐶𐐯𐑌 𐐰𐐻 𐑁𐐲𐑉𐑅𐐻 𐐸𐐨 𐑊𐐴𐐻𐑊𐐨 𐐰𐑁𐑊𐐮𐐿𐐻𐐯𐐼 𐑄 𐑊𐐰𐑌𐐼 𐐲𐑂 𐐞𐐯𐐺𐐲𐑊𐐲𐑌, 𐐰𐑌𐐼 𐑄 𐑊𐐰𐑌𐐼 𐐲𐑂 𐐤𐐰𐑁𐑃𐐰𐑊𐐨, 𐐰𐑌𐐼 𐐰𐑁𐐻𐐲𐑉𐐶𐐲𐑉𐐼 𐐼𐐮𐐼 𐑋𐐬𐑉 𐑀𐑉𐐨𐑂𐐲𐑅𐑊𐐨 𐐰𐑁𐑊𐐮𐐿𐐻 𐐺𐐴 𐑄 𐐶𐐩 𐐲𐑂 𐑄 𐐡𐐯𐐼 𐐝𐐨 𐐺𐐨𐐷𐐱𐑌𐐼 𐐖𐐫𐑉𐐼𐐲𐑌 𐐮𐑌 𐐘𐐰𐑊𐐲𐑊𐐨 𐐲𐑂 𐑄 𐑌𐐩𐑇𐐲𐑌𐑆. 𐐜 𐐹𐐨𐐹𐑊 𐑄𐐰𐐻 𐐶𐐫𐐿𐐻 𐐮𐑌 𐐼𐐪𐑉𐐿𐑌𐐯𐑅 𐐸𐐰𐑂 𐑅𐐨𐑌 𐐲 𐑀𐑉𐐩𐐻 𐑊𐐴𐐻; 𐑄𐐩 𐑄𐐰𐐻 𐐼𐐶𐐯𐑊 𐐮𐑌 𐑄 𐑊𐐰𐑌𐐼 𐐲𐑂 𐑄 𐑇𐐰𐐼𐐬 𐐲𐑂 𐐼𐐯𐑃, 𐐲𐐹𐐱𐑌 𐑄𐐯𐑋 𐐸𐐰𐑆 𐑄 𐑊𐐴𐐻 𐑇𐐴𐑌𐐼. 𐐜𐐵 𐐸𐐰𐑅𐐻 𐑋𐐲𐑊𐐻𐐮𐐹𐑊𐐴𐐼 𐑄 𐑌𐐩𐑇𐐲𐑌, 𐐰𐑌𐐼 𐐮𐑍𐐿𐑉𐐨𐑅𐐻 𐑄 𐐾𐐱𐐮: 𐑄𐐩 𐐾𐐱𐐮 𐐺𐐨𐑁𐐬𐑉 𐑄𐐨 𐐰𐐿𐐫𐑉𐐼𐐮𐑍 𐐻𐐭 𐑄 𐐾𐐱𐐮 𐐮𐑌 𐐸𐐪𐑉𐑂𐐯𐑅𐐻, 𐐰𐑌𐐼 𐐰𐑆 𐑋𐐯𐑌 𐑉𐐨𐐾𐐱𐐮𐑅 𐐸𐐶𐐯𐑌 𐑄𐐩 𐐼𐐮𐑂𐐴𐐼 𐑄 𐑅𐐹𐐱𐐮𐑊. 𐐙𐐫𐑉 𐑄𐐵 𐐸𐐰𐑅𐐻 𐐺𐑉𐐬𐐿𐐲𐑌 𐑄 𐐷𐐬𐐿 𐐲𐑂 𐐸𐐮𐑆 𐐺𐐲𐑉𐐼𐐲𐑌, 𐐰𐑌𐐼 𐑄 𐑅𐐻𐐰𐑁 𐐲𐑂 𐐸𐐮𐑆 𐑇𐐬𐑊𐐼𐐲𐑉, 𐑄 𐑉𐐱𐐼 𐐲𐑂 𐐸𐐮𐑆 𐐱𐐹𐑉𐐯𐑅𐐲𐑉. 𐐙𐐫𐑉 𐐯𐑂𐐲𐑉𐐨 𐐺𐐰𐐻𐑊 𐐲𐑂 𐑄 𐐶𐐫𐑉𐐨𐐲𐑉 𐐶𐐮𐑄 𐐿𐐲𐑌𐑁𐐷𐐭𐑆𐐼 𐑌𐐱𐐮𐑆, 𐐰𐑌𐐼 𐑀𐐪𐑉𐑋𐐲𐑌𐐻𐑅 𐑉𐐬𐑊𐐼 𐐮𐑌 𐐺𐑊𐐲𐐼; 𐐺𐐲𐐻 𐑄𐐮𐑅 𐑇𐐰𐑊 𐐺𐐨 𐐶𐐮𐑄 𐐺𐐲𐑉𐑌𐐮𐑍 𐐰𐑌𐐼 𐑁𐐷𐐭𐐲𐑊 𐐲𐑂 𐑁𐐴𐑉. 𐐙𐐫𐑉 𐐲𐑌𐐻𐐭 𐐲𐑅 𐐲 𐐽𐐴𐑊𐐼 𐐮𐑆 𐐺𐐫𐑉𐑌, 𐐲𐑌𐐻𐐭 𐐲𐑅 𐐲 𐑅𐐲𐑌 𐐮𐑆

𐑀𐐮𐑂𐑌; 𐐰𐑌𐐼 𐑄 𐑀𐐲𐑂𐐲𐑉𐑌𐑋𐐲𐑌𐐻 𐑇𐐰𐑊 𐐺 𐐲𐐹𐐪𐑌 𐐸𐐮𐑆 𐑇𐐬𐑊𐐼𐐲𐑉; 𐐰𐑌𐐼 𐐸𐐮𐑆 𐑌𐐩𐑋 𐑇𐐰𐑊 𐐺 𐐿𐐫𐑊𐐼 𐐎𐐲𐑌𐐼𐐲𐑉𐑁𐐳𐑊, 𐐗𐐵𐑌𐑅𐐲𐑊𐐲𐑉. 𐐜 𐐣𐐴𐐻𐐨 𐐘𐐪𐐼, 𐐜 𐐇𐑂𐐲𐑉𐑊𐐰𐑅𐐻𐐮𐑍 𐐙𐐪𐑄𐐲𐑉, 𐐜 𐐑𐑉𐐮𐑌𐑅 𐐲𐑂 𐐑𐐨𐑅. 𐐊𐑂 𐑄 𐐮𐑌𐐿𐑉𐐨𐑅 𐐲𐑂 𐑀𐐲𐑂𐐲𐑉𐑌𐑋𐐲𐑌𐐻 𐐰𐑌𐐼 𐐹𐐨𐑅 𐑄𐐯𐑉 𐐮𐑆 𐑌𐐬 𐐯𐑌𐐼, 𐐲𐐹𐐪𐑌 𐑄 𐑃𐑉𐐬𐑌 𐐲𐑂 𐐔𐐩𐑂𐐮𐐼, 𐐰𐑌𐐼 𐐲𐐹𐐪𐑌 𐐸𐐮𐑆 𐐿𐐮𐑍𐐼𐐲𐑋 𐐻𐐭 𐐫𐑉𐐼𐐲𐑉 𐐮𐐻, 𐐰𐑌𐐼 𐐻𐐭 𐐯𐑅𐐻𐐰𐐺𐑊𐐮𐑇 𐐮𐐻 𐐶𐐮𐑄 𐐾𐐲𐐾𐑋𐐲𐑌𐐻 𐐰𐑌𐐼 𐐶𐐮𐑄 𐐾𐐲𐑅𐐻𐐮𐑅 𐑁𐑉𐐪𐑋 𐐸𐐯𐑌𐑅𐑁𐐫𐑉𐑃, 𐐨𐑂𐐲𐑌 𐑁𐐫𐑉 𐐯𐑂𐐲𐑉. 𐐜 𐑆𐐨𐑊 𐐲𐑂 𐑄 𐐢𐐫𐑉𐐼 𐐲𐑂 𐐐𐐬𐑅𐐻𐑅 𐐶𐐮𐑊 𐐹𐐲𐑉𐑁𐐫𐑉𐑋 𐑄𐐮𐑅.

14. 𐐜 𐐢𐐫𐑉𐐼 𐑅𐐯𐑌𐐻 𐐸𐐮𐑆 𐐶𐐲𐑉𐐼 𐐲𐑌𐐻𐐭 𐐖𐐩𐐿𐐲𐐺 𐐰𐑌𐐼 𐐮𐐻 𐐸𐐰𐑃 𐑊𐐴𐐻𐐯𐐼 𐐲𐐹𐐪𐑌 𐐆𐑆𐑉𐐩𐐯𐑊. 𐐈𐑌𐐼 𐐫𐑊 𐑄 𐐹𐐨𐐹𐑊 𐑇𐐰𐑊 𐑌𐐬, 𐐨𐑂𐐲𐑌 𐐀𐑁𐑉𐐩𐐮𐑋 𐐰𐑌𐐼 𐑄 𐐮𐑌𐐸𐐰𐐺𐐮𐐻𐐲𐑌𐐻𐑅 𐐲𐑂 𐐝𐐲𐑋𐐩𐑉𐐨𐐲, 𐑄𐐰𐐻 𐑅𐐩 𐐮𐑌 𐑄 𐐹𐑉𐐴𐐼 𐐰𐑌𐐼 𐑅𐐻𐐵𐐻𐑌𐐯𐑅 𐐲𐑂 𐐸𐐪𐑉𐐻, 𐑄 𐐺𐑉𐐮𐐿𐑅 𐐪𐑉 𐑁𐐫𐑊𐑌 𐐼𐐵𐑌, 𐐺𐐲𐐻 𐐶𐐨 𐐶𐐮𐑊 𐐺𐐮𐑊𐐼 𐐶𐐮𐑄 𐐸𐑏𐑌 𐑅𐐻𐐬𐑌𐑆; 𐑄 𐑅𐐮𐐿𐐲𐑋𐐬𐑉𐑆 𐐪𐑉 𐐿𐐲𐐻 𐐼𐐵𐑌, 𐐺𐐲𐐻 𐐶𐐨 𐐶𐐮𐑊 𐐽𐐩𐑌𐐾 𐑄𐐯𐑋 𐐮𐑌𐐻𐐭 𐑅𐐨𐐼𐐲𐑉𐑆. 𐐜𐐯𐑉𐑁𐐬𐑉 𐑄 𐐢𐐫𐑉𐐼 𐑇𐐰𐑊 𐑅𐐯𐐻 𐐲𐐹 𐑄 𐐰𐐼𐑂𐐲𐑉𐑅𐐯𐑉𐐨𐑆 𐐲𐑂 𐐡𐐨𐑆𐐮𐑌 𐐲𐑀𐐯𐑌𐑅𐐻 𐐸𐐮𐑋, 𐐰𐑌𐐼 𐐾𐑎𐑌 𐐸𐐮𐑆 𐐯𐑌𐐯𐑋𐐨𐑆 𐐻𐐭𐑀𐐯𐑄𐐲𐑉; 𐑄 𐐝𐐮𐑉𐐨𐐲𐑌𐑆 𐐺𐐨𐑁𐐬𐑉 𐐰𐑌𐐼 𐑄 𐐙𐐮𐑊𐐮𐑅𐐻𐐮𐑌𐑆 𐐺𐐨𐐸𐐴𐑌𐐼; 𐐰𐑌𐐼 𐑄𐐩 𐑇𐐰𐑊 𐐼𐐨𐑂𐐵𐑉 𐐆𐑆𐑉𐐩𐐯𐑊 𐐶𐐮𐑄 𐐬𐐹𐑌 𐑋𐐵𐑃. 𐐙𐐫𐑉 𐐫𐑊 𐑄𐐮𐑅 𐐸𐐮𐑆 𐐰𐑍𐑀𐐲𐑉 𐐮𐑆 𐑌𐐪𐐻 𐐻𐐲𐑉𐑌𐐼 𐐲𐐶𐐩, 𐐺𐐲𐐻 𐐸𐐮𐑆 𐐸𐐰𐑌𐐼 𐐮𐑆 𐑅𐐻𐑉𐐯𐐽𐐻 𐐵𐐻 𐑅𐐻𐐮𐑊.

15. 𐐙𐐫𐑉 𐑄 𐐹𐐨𐐹𐑊 𐐻𐐲𐑉𐑌𐐯𐑃 𐑌𐐪𐐻 𐐲𐑌𐐻𐐭 𐐸𐐮𐑋 𐑄𐐰𐐻 𐑅𐑋𐐴𐐻𐐯𐑃 𐑄𐐯𐑋, 𐑌𐐨𐑄𐐲𐑉 𐐼𐐭 𐑄𐐩 𐑅𐐨𐐿 𐑄 𐐢𐐫𐑉𐐼 𐐲𐑂 𐐐𐐬𐑅𐐻𐑅. 𐐜𐐯𐑉𐑁𐐬𐑉 𐐶𐐮𐑊 𐑄 𐐢𐐫𐑉𐐼 𐐿𐐲𐐻 𐐫𐑁 𐑁𐑉𐐪𐑋 𐐆𐑆𐑉𐐩𐐯𐑊 𐐸𐐯𐐼 𐐰𐑌𐐼 𐐻𐐩𐑊, 𐐺𐑉𐐰𐑌𐐽 𐐰𐑌𐐼 𐑉𐐲𐑇 𐐮𐑌 𐐶𐐲𐑌 𐐼𐐩. 𐐜 𐐩𐑌𐑇𐐯𐑌𐐻, 𐐸𐐨 𐐮𐑆 𐑄 𐐸𐐯𐐼; 𐐰𐑌𐐼 𐑄 𐐹𐑉𐐪𐑁𐐯𐐻 𐑄𐐰𐐻 𐐻𐐨𐐽𐐯𐑃 𐑊𐐴𐑆, 𐐸𐐨 𐐮𐑆 𐑄 𐐻𐐩𐑊. 𐐙𐐫𐑉 𐑄 𐑊𐐨𐐼𐐲𐑉𐑆 𐐲𐑂 𐑄𐐮𐑅 𐐹𐐨𐐹𐑊 𐐿𐐫𐑆 𐑄𐐯𐑋 𐐻𐐭 𐐲𐑉; 𐐰𐑌𐐼 𐑄𐐩 𐑄𐐰𐐻 𐐪𐑉 𐑊𐐯𐐼 𐐲𐑂 𐑄𐐯𐑋 𐐪𐑉 𐐼𐐨𐑅𐐻𐑉𐑎𐐼. 𐐜𐐯𐑉𐑁𐐬𐑉 𐑄 𐐢𐐫𐑉𐐼 𐑇𐐰𐑊 𐐸𐐰𐑂 𐑌𐐬 𐐾𐑎 𐐮𐑌 𐑄𐐯𐑉 𐐷𐐲𐑍 𐑋𐐯𐑌, 𐑌𐐨𐑄𐐲𐑉 𐑇𐐰𐑊 𐐸𐐰𐑂 𐑋𐐲𐑉𐑅𐐨 𐐪𐑌 𐑄𐐯𐑉 𐑁𐐪𐑄𐐲𐑉𐑊𐐯𐑅 𐐰𐑌𐐼 𐐶𐐮𐐼𐐬𐑆; 𐑁𐐫𐑉 𐐯𐑂𐐲𐑉𐐨 𐐶𐐲𐑌 𐐲𐑂 𐑄𐐯𐑋 𐐮𐑆 𐐲 𐐸𐐮𐐹𐐬𐐿𐑉𐐮𐐻 𐐰𐑌𐐼 𐐰𐑌 𐐨𐑂𐐮𐑊-𐐼𐐭𐐲𐑉, 𐐰𐑌𐐼 𐐯𐑂𐐲𐑉𐐨 𐑋𐐵𐑃 𐑅𐐹𐐨𐐿𐐯𐑃 𐑁𐐪𐑊𐐨. 𐐙𐐫𐑉 𐐫𐑊 𐑄𐐮𐑅 𐐸𐐮𐑆 𐐰𐑍𐑀𐐲𐑉 𐐮𐑆 𐑌𐐪𐐻 𐐻𐐲𐑉𐑌𐐼 𐐲𐐶𐐩, 𐐺𐐲𐐻 𐐸𐐮𐑆 𐐸𐐰𐑌𐐼 𐐮𐑆 𐑅𐐻𐑉𐐯𐐽𐐻 𐐵𐐻 𐑅𐐻𐐮𐑊.

16. 𐐙𐐫𐑉 𐐶𐐮𐐿𐐯𐐼𐑌𐐯𐑅 𐐺𐐲𐑉𐑌𐐯𐑃 𐐰𐑆 𐑄 𐑁𐐴𐑉; 𐐮𐐻 𐑇𐐰𐑊 𐐼𐐨𐑂𐐵𐑉 𐑄 𐐺𐑉𐐴𐐲𐑉𐑆 𐐰𐑌𐐼 𐑃𐐫𐑉𐑌𐑆, 𐐰𐑌𐐼 𐑇𐐰𐑊 𐐿𐐮𐑌𐐼𐑊 𐐮𐑌 𐑄 𐑃𐐮𐐿𐐯𐐻𐑅 𐐲𐑂 𐑄 𐑁𐐪𐑉𐐯𐑅𐐻𐑅, 𐐰𐑌𐐼 𐑄𐐩 𐑇𐐰𐑊 𐑋𐐵𐑌𐐻 𐐲𐐹 𐑊𐐴𐐿 𐑄 𐑊𐐮𐑁𐐻𐐮𐑍 𐐲𐐹 𐐲𐑂 𐑅𐑋𐐬𐐿. 𐐛𐑉𐐭 𐑄 𐑉𐐪𐑃 𐐲𐑂 𐑄 𐐢𐐫𐑉𐐼 𐐲𐑂 𐐐𐐬𐑅𐐻𐑅 𐐮𐑆 𐑄 𐑊𐐰𐑌𐐼 𐐼𐐪𐑉𐐿𐐲𐑌𐐼, 𐐰𐑌𐐼 𐑄 𐐹𐐨𐐹𐑊 𐑇𐐰𐑊 𐐺 𐐰𐑆 𐑄 𐑁𐑏𐐯𐑊 𐐲𐑂 𐑄 𐑁𐐴𐑉; 𐑌𐐬 𐑋𐐰𐑌 𐑇𐐰𐑊 𐑅𐐹𐐯𐑉 𐐸𐐮𐑆 𐐺𐑉𐐲𐑄𐐲𐑉. 𐐈𐑌𐐼 𐐸𐐨 𐑇𐐰𐑊 𐑅𐑌𐐰𐐽 𐐪𐑌 𐑄 𐑉𐐴𐐻 𐐸𐐰𐑌𐐼 𐐰𐑌𐐼 𐐺 𐐸𐐲𐑍𐑀𐑉𐐨; 𐐰𐑌𐐼 𐐸𐐨 𐑇𐐰𐑊 𐐨𐐻 𐐪𐑌 𐑄 𐑊𐐯𐑁𐐻 𐐸𐐰𐑌𐐼, 𐐰𐑌𐐼 𐑄𐐩 𐑇𐐰𐑊 𐑌𐐪𐐻 𐐺 𐑅𐐰𐐻𐐮𐑅𐑁𐐴𐐼; 𐑄𐐩 𐑇𐐰𐑊 𐐨𐐻 𐐯𐑂𐐲𐑉𐐨 𐑋𐐰𐑌 𐑄 𐑁𐑊𐐯𐑇 𐐲𐑂 𐐸𐐮𐑆 𐐬𐑌 𐐪𐑉𐑋: 𐐣𐐲𐑌𐐰𐑅𐐲, 𐐀𐑁𐑉𐐩𐐮𐑋; 𐐰𐑌𐐼 𐐀𐑁𐑉𐐩𐐮𐑋, 𐐣𐐲𐑌𐐰𐑅𐐲; 𐑄𐐩 𐐻𐐭𐑀𐐯𐑄𐐲𐑉 𐑇𐐰𐑊 𐐺 𐐲𐑀𐐯𐑌𐑅𐐻 𐐖𐐭𐐼𐐲. 𐐙𐐫𐑉 𐐫𐑊 𐑄𐐮𐑅 𐐸𐐮𐑆 𐐰𐑍𐑀𐐲𐑉 𐐮𐑆 𐑌𐐪𐐻 𐐻𐐲𐑉𐑌𐐼 𐐲𐐶𐐩, 𐐺𐐲𐐻 𐐸𐐮𐑆 𐐸𐐰𐑌𐐼 𐐮𐑆 𐑅𐐻𐑉𐐯𐐽𐐻 𐐵𐐻 𐑅𐐻𐐮𐑊.

17. 𐐎𐐬 𐐲𐑌𐐻𐐭 𐑄𐐯𐑋 𐑄𐐰𐐻 𐐼𐐨𐐿𐑉𐐨 𐐲𐑌𐑉𐐴𐐽𐐲𐑅 𐐼𐐨𐐿𐑉𐐨𐑆, 𐐰𐑌𐐼 𐑄𐐰𐐻 𐑉𐐴𐐻 𐑀𐑉𐐨𐑂𐐲𐑅𐑌𐐯𐑅 𐐸𐐶𐐮𐐽 𐑄𐐩 𐐸𐐰𐑂 𐐹𐑉𐐨𐑅𐐿𐑉𐐴𐐺𐐼; 𐐻𐐭 𐐻𐐲𐑉𐑌 𐐲𐐶𐐩 𐑄 𐑌𐐨𐐼𐐨 𐑁𐑉𐐪𐑋 𐐾𐐲𐐾𐑋𐐲𐑌𐐻, 𐐰𐑌𐐼 𐐻𐐭 𐐻𐐩𐐿 𐐲𐐶𐐩 𐑄 𐑉𐐴𐐻 𐑁𐑉𐐪𐑋 𐑄 𐐹𐐭𐑉 𐐲𐑂 𐑋𐐴 𐐹𐐨𐐹𐑊, 𐑄𐐰𐐻 𐐶𐐮𐐼𐐬𐑆 𐑋𐐩 𐐺 𐑄𐐯𐑉 𐐹𐑉𐐩, 𐐰𐑌𐐼 𐑄𐐰𐐻 𐑄𐐩 𐑋𐐩 𐑉𐐪𐐺 𐑄 𐑁𐐪𐑄𐐲𐑉𐑊𐐯𐑅! 𐐈𐑌𐐼 𐐸𐐶𐐪𐐻 𐐶𐐮𐑊 𐐷𐐨 𐐼𐐭 𐐮𐑌 𐑄 𐐼𐐩 𐐲𐑂 𐑂𐐮𐑆𐐮𐐻𐐩𐑇𐐲𐑌, 𐐰𐑌𐐼 𐐮𐑌 𐑄 𐐼𐐯𐑅𐐬𐑊𐐩𐑇𐐲𐑌 𐐸𐐶𐐮𐐽 𐑇𐐰𐑊 𐐿𐐲𐑋 𐑁𐑉𐐪𐑋 𐑁𐐪𐑉? 𐐓𐐭 𐐸𐐭𐑋 𐐶𐐮𐑊 𐐷𐐨 𐑁𐑊𐐨 𐑁𐐫𐑉 𐐸𐐯𐑊𐐹? 𐐈𐑌𐐼 𐐸𐐶𐐯𐑉 𐐶𐐮𐑊 𐐷𐐨 𐑊𐐨𐑂 𐐷𐐭𐑉 𐑀𐑊𐐬𐑉𐐨? 𐐎𐐮𐑄𐐵𐐻 𐑋𐐨 𐑄𐐩 𐑇𐐰𐑊 𐐺𐐵 𐐼𐐵𐑌 𐐲𐑌𐐼𐐲𐑉 𐑄 𐐹𐑉𐐮𐑆𐐲𐑌𐐲𐑉𐑆, 𐐰𐑌𐐼 𐑄𐐩 𐑇𐐰𐑊 𐑁𐐫𐑊 𐐲𐑌𐐼𐐲𐑉 𐑄 𐑅𐑊𐐩𐑌. 𐐙𐐫𐑉 𐐫𐑊 𐑄𐐮𐑅 𐐸𐐮𐑆 𐐰𐑍𐑀𐐲𐑉 𐐮𐑆 𐑌𐐪𐐻 𐐻𐐲𐑉𐑌𐐼 𐐲𐐶𐐩, 𐐺𐐲𐐻 𐐸𐐮𐑆 𐐸𐐰𐑌𐐼 𐐮𐑆 𐑅𐐻𐑉𐐯𐐽𐐻 𐐵𐐻 𐑅𐐻𐐮𐑊.

18. 𐐄 𐐈𐑅𐐮𐑉𐐨𐐲𐑌, 𐑄 𐑉𐐪𐐼 𐐲𐑂 𐑋𐐴𐑌 𐐰𐑍𐑀𐐲𐑉, 𐐰𐑌𐐼 𐑄 𐑅𐐻𐐰𐑁 𐐮𐑌 𐑄𐐯𐑉 𐐸𐐰𐑌𐐼 𐐮𐑆 𐑄𐐯𐑉 𐐮𐑌𐐼𐐮𐑀𐑌𐐩𐑇𐐲𐑌. 𐐌 𐐶𐐮𐑊 𐑅𐐯𐑌𐐼 𐐸𐐮𐑋 𐐲𐑀𐐯𐑌𐑅𐐻 𐐲 𐐸𐐮𐐹𐐬𐐿𐑉𐐮𐐻𐐮𐐿𐐲𐑊 𐑌𐐩𐑇𐐲𐑌, 𐐰𐑌𐐼 𐐲𐑀𐐯𐑌𐑅𐐻 𐑄 𐐹𐐨𐐹𐑊 𐐲𐑂 𐑋𐐴 𐑉𐐪𐑃 𐐶𐐮𐑊 𐐌 𐑀𐐮𐑂 𐐸𐐮𐑋 𐐲 𐐽𐐪𐑉𐐾 𐐻𐐭 𐐻𐐩𐐿 𐑄 𐑅𐐹𐑎𐑊, 𐐰𐑌𐐼 𐐻𐐭 𐐻𐐩𐐿 𐑄 𐐹𐑉𐐩, 𐐰𐑌𐐼 𐐻𐐭 𐐻𐑉𐐯𐐼 𐑄𐐯𐑋 𐐼𐐵𐑌 𐑊𐐴𐐿 𐑄 𐑋𐐴𐑉 𐐲𐑂 𐑄 𐑅𐐻𐑉𐐨𐐻𐑅. 𐐐𐐵𐐺𐐨𐐮𐐻 𐐸𐐨 𐑋𐐨𐑌𐐯𐑃 𐑌𐐪𐐻 𐑅𐐬, 𐑌𐐨𐑄𐐲𐑉 𐐼𐐲𐑃 𐐸𐐮𐑆 𐐸𐐪𐑉𐐻 𐑃𐐮𐑍𐐿 𐑅𐐬; 𐐺𐐲𐐻 𐐮𐑌 𐐸𐐮𐑆 𐐸𐐪𐑉𐐻 𐐮𐐻 𐐮𐑆 𐐻𐐭 𐐼𐐨𐑅𐐻𐑉𐑎 𐐰𐑌𐐼 𐐿𐐲𐐻 𐐫𐑁 𐑌𐐩𐑇𐐲𐑌𐑆 𐑌𐐪𐐻 𐐲 𐑁𐑏. 𐐙𐐫𐑉 𐐸𐐨 𐑅𐐯𐑃, 𐐂𐑉 𐑌𐐪𐐻 𐑋𐐴 𐐹𐑉𐐮𐑌𐑅𐐯𐑆 𐐫𐑊𐐻𐐭𐑀𐐯𐑄𐐲𐑉 𐐿𐐮𐑍𐑆? 𐐆𐑆 𐑌𐐪𐐻 𐐗𐐰𐑊𐑌𐐬 𐐰𐑆 𐐗𐐪𐑉𐐿𐐯𐑋𐐮𐑇?

𐐮𐑆 𐑌𐐱𐐻 𐐐𐐩𐑋𐐲𐑃 𐐰𐑆 𐐂𐑉𐐹𐐰𐐼? 𐐮𐑆 𐑌𐐱𐐻 𐐝𐐲𐑋𐐩𐑉𐐨𐐲 𐐰𐑆 𐐔𐐲𐑋𐐰𐑅𐐿𐐲𐑅? 𐐈𐑆 𐑋𐐴 𐐸𐐰𐑌𐐼 𐐸𐐰𐑃 𐑁𐐵𐑌𐐼𐐯𐐼 𐑄 𐐿𐐮𐑍𐐼𐐲𐑋𐑆 𐐱𐑂 𐑄 𐐴𐐼𐐲𐑊𐑆, 𐐰𐑌𐐼 𐐸𐐭𐑆 𐑀𐑉𐐩𐑂𐑌 𐐮𐑋𐐯𐐾𐐯𐑆 𐐼𐐮𐐼 𐐯𐐿𐑅𐐯𐑊 𐑄𐐯𐑋 𐐱𐑂 𐐖𐐯𐑉𐐭𐑅𐐲𐑊𐐯𐑋, 𐐰𐑌𐐼 𐐱𐑂 𐐝𐐲𐑋𐐩𐑉𐐨𐐲; 𐑇𐐰𐑊 𐐌 𐑌𐐱𐐻, 𐐰𐑆 𐐌 𐐸𐐰𐑂 𐐼𐐲𐑌 𐐲𐑌𐐻𐐭 𐐝𐐲𐑋𐐩𐑉𐐨𐐲 𐐰𐑌𐐼 𐐸𐐲𐑉 𐐴𐐼𐐲𐑊𐑆, 𐑅𐐬 𐐼𐐭 𐐻𐐭 𐐖𐐯𐑉𐐭𐑅𐐲𐑊𐐯𐑋 𐐰𐑌𐐼 𐐻𐐭 𐐸𐐲𐑉 𐐴𐐼𐐲𐑊𐑆? 𐐐𐐶𐐯𐑉𐑁𐐬𐑉 𐐮𐐻 𐑇𐐰𐑊 𐐿𐐲𐑋 𐐻𐐭 𐐹𐐰𐑅, 𐑄𐐰𐐻 𐐸𐐶𐐯𐑌 𐑄 𐐢𐐫𐑉𐐼 𐐸𐐰𐑃 𐐹𐐲𐑉𐑁𐐫𐑉𐑋𐐼 𐐸𐐮𐑆 𐐸𐐬𐑊 𐐶𐐲𐑉𐐿 𐐲𐐹𐐱𐑌 𐐣𐐵𐑌𐐻 𐐞𐐴𐐲𐑌 𐐰𐑌𐐼 𐐲𐐹𐐱𐑌 𐐖𐐯𐑉𐐭𐑅𐐲𐑊𐐯𐑋, 𐐌 𐐶𐐮𐑊 𐐹𐐲𐑌𐐮𐑇 𐑄 𐑁𐑉𐐭𐐻 𐐱𐑂 𐑄 𐑅𐐻𐐵𐐻 𐐸𐐪𐑉𐐻 𐐱𐑂 𐑄 𐐿𐐮𐑍 𐐱𐑂 𐐈𐑅𐐮𐑉𐐨𐐲, 𐐰𐑌𐐼 𐑄 𐑀𐑊𐐬𐑉𐐨 𐐱𐑂 𐐸𐐮𐑆 𐐸𐐴 𐑊𐐳𐐿𐑅. 𐐙𐐫𐑉 𐐸𐐨 𐑅𐐯𐑃, 𐐒𐐴 𐑄 𐑅𐐻𐑉𐐯𐑍𐑃 𐐱𐑂 𐑋𐐴 𐐸𐐰𐑌𐐼 𐐰𐑌𐐼 𐐺𐐴 𐑋𐐴 𐐶𐐮𐑆𐐼𐐲𐑋 𐐌 𐐸𐐰𐑂 𐐼𐐲𐑌 𐑄𐐨𐑆 𐑃𐐮𐑍𐑆; 𐑁𐐫𐑉 𐐌 𐐰𐑋 𐐹𐑉𐐭𐐼𐐯𐑌𐐻; 𐐰𐑌𐐼 𐐌 𐐸𐐰𐑂 𐑋𐐭𐑂𐐼 𐑄 𐐺𐐫𐑉𐐼𐐲𐑉𐑆 𐐱𐑂 𐑄 𐐹𐐨𐐹𐑊, 𐐰𐑌𐐼 𐐸𐐰𐑂 𐑉𐐱𐐺𐐼 𐑄𐐩𐑉 𐐻𐑉𐐯𐑈𐐲𐑉𐑆, 𐐰𐑌𐐼 𐐌 𐐸𐐰𐑂 𐐹𐐳𐐻 𐐼𐐵𐑌 𐑄 𐐮𐑌𐐸𐐰𐐺𐐮𐐻𐐲𐑌𐐻𐑅 𐑊𐐴𐐿 𐐰 𐑂𐐰𐑊𐐷𐐲𐑌𐐻 𐑋𐐰𐑌; 𐐰𐑌𐐼 𐑋𐐴 𐐸𐐰𐑌𐐼 𐐸𐐰𐑃 𐑁𐐵𐑌𐐼 𐐰𐑆 𐐰 𐑌𐐯𐑅𐐻 𐑄 𐑉𐐮𐐽𐐯𐑆 𐐱𐑂 𐑄 𐐹𐐨𐐹𐑊; 𐐰𐑌𐐼 𐐰𐑆 𐐶𐐲𐑌 𐑀𐐰𐑄𐐲𐑉𐐯𐑃 𐐯𐑀𐑆 𐑄𐐰𐐻 𐐪𐑉 𐑊𐐯𐑁𐐻 𐐸𐐰𐑂 𐐌 𐑀𐐰𐑄𐐲𐑉𐐼 𐐫𐑊 𐑄 𐐲𐑉𐑃; 𐐰𐑌𐐼 𐑄𐐩𐑉 𐐶𐐱𐑆 𐑌𐐲𐑌 𐑄𐐰𐐻 𐑋𐐭𐑂𐐼 𐑄 𐐶𐐮𐑍, 𐐫𐑉 𐐬𐐹𐑌𐐼 𐑄 𐑋𐐵𐑃, 𐐫𐑉 𐐹𐐨𐐹𐐻. 𐐟𐐰𐑊 𐑄 𐐰𐐿𐑅 𐐺𐐬𐑅𐐻 𐐮𐐻𐑅𐐯𐑊𐑁 𐐲𐑀𐐯𐑌𐑅𐐻 𐐸𐐮𐑋 𐑄𐐰𐐻 𐐸𐐷𐐭𐐯𐑃 𐑄𐐩𐑉𐐶𐐮𐑄? 𐐟𐐰𐑊 𐑄 𐑅𐐫 𐑋𐐰𐑀𐑌𐐮𐑁𐐴 𐐮𐐻𐑅𐐯𐑊𐑁 𐐲𐑀𐐯𐑌𐑅𐐻 𐐸𐐮𐑋 𐑄𐐰𐐻 𐑇𐐩𐐿𐐯𐑃 𐐮𐐻? 𐐈𐑆 𐐮𐑁 𐑄 𐑉𐐱𐐼 𐑇𐐳𐐼 𐑇𐐩𐐿 𐐮𐐻𐑅𐐯𐑊𐑁 𐐲𐑀𐐯𐑌𐑅𐐻 𐑄𐐯𐑋 𐑄𐐰𐐻 𐑊𐐮𐑁𐐻 𐐮𐐻 𐐲𐐹, 𐐫𐑉 𐐰𐑆 𐐮𐑁 𐑄 𐑅𐐻𐐰𐑁 𐑇𐐳𐐼 𐑊𐐮𐑁𐐻 𐐲𐐹 𐐮𐐻𐑅𐐯𐑊𐑁 𐐰𐑆 𐐮𐑁 𐐮𐐻 𐐶𐐲𐑉 𐑌𐐬 𐐶𐐳𐐼. 𐐜𐐩𐑉𐑁𐐬𐑉 𐑇𐐰𐑊 𐑄 𐐢𐐫𐑉𐐼, 𐑄 𐐢𐐫𐑉𐐼 𐐱𐑂 𐐐𐐬𐑅𐐻𐑅, 𐑅𐐯𐑌𐐼 𐐲𐑋𐐲𐑍 𐐸𐐮𐑆 𐑁𐐰𐐻 𐐶𐐲𐑌𐑆, 𐑊𐐨𐑌𐐯𐑅; 𐐰𐑌𐐼 𐐲𐑌𐐼𐐲𐑉 𐐸𐐮𐑆 𐑀𐑊𐐬𐑉𐐨 𐐸𐐨 𐑇𐐰𐑊 𐐿𐐮𐑌𐐼𐑊 𐐰 𐐺𐐲𐑉𐑌𐐮𐑍 𐑊𐐴𐐿 𐑄 𐐺𐐲𐑉𐑌𐐮𐑍 𐐱𐑂 𐐰 𐑁𐐴𐐲𐑉. 𐐈𐑌𐐼 𐑄 𐑊𐐴𐐻 𐐱𐑂 𐐆𐑆𐑉𐐩𐐯𐑊 𐑇𐐰𐑊 𐐺𐐨 𐑁𐐫𐑉 𐐰 𐑁𐐴𐐲𐑉, 𐐰𐑌𐐼 𐐸𐐮𐑆 𐐐𐐬𐑊𐐨 𐐎𐐲𐑌 𐑁𐐫𐑉 𐐰 𐑁𐑊𐐩𐑋, 𐐰𐑌𐐼 𐑇𐐰𐑊 𐐺𐐲𐑉𐑌 𐐰𐑌𐐼 𐑇𐐰𐑊 𐐼𐐨𐑂𐐵𐑉 𐐸𐐮𐑆 𐑃𐐫𐑉𐑌𐑆 𐐰𐑌𐐼 𐐸𐐮𐑆 𐐺𐑉𐐴𐐲𐑉𐑆 𐐮𐑌 𐐶𐐲𐑌 𐐼𐐩; 𐐰𐑌𐐼 𐑇𐐰𐑊 𐐿𐐱𐑌𐑅𐐭𐑋 𐑄 𐑀𐑊𐐬𐑉𐐨 𐐱𐑂 𐐸𐐮𐑆 𐑁𐐱𐑉𐐯𐑅𐐻, 𐐰𐑌𐐼 𐐱𐑂 𐐸𐐮𐑆 𐑁𐑉𐐭𐐻𐑁𐐳𐑊 𐑁𐐨𐑊𐐼, 𐐺𐐬𐑃 𐑅𐐬𐑊 𐐰𐑌𐐼 𐐺𐐱𐐼𐐨; 𐐰𐑌𐐼 𐑄𐐩 𐑇𐐰𐑊 𐐺𐐨 𐐰𐑆 𐐸𐐶𐐯𐑌 𐐰 𐑅𐐻𐐰𐑌𐐼𐐲𐑉𐐼-𐐺𐐩𐑉𐐲𐑉 𐑁𐐩𐑌𐐻𐐯𐑃. 𐐈𐑌𐐼 𐑄 𐑉𐐯𐑅𐐻 𐐱𐑂 𐑄 𐐻𐑉𐐨𐑆 𐐱𐑂 𐐸𐐮𐑆 𐑁𐐱𐑉𐐯𐑅𐐻 𐑇𐐰𐑊 𐐺𐐨 𐑁𐑏, 𐑄𐐰𐐻 𐐰 𐐽𐐴𐑊𐐼 𐑋𐐩 𐑉𐐴𐐻 𐑄𐐯𐑋.

19. 𐐈𐑌𐐼 𐐮𐐻 𐑇𐐰𐑊 𐐿𐐲𐑋 𐐻𐐭 𐐹𐐰𐑅 𐐮𐑌 𐑄𐐰𐐻 𐐼𐐩, 𐑄𐐰𐐻 𐑄 𐑉𐐯𐑋𐑌𐐲𐑌𐐻 𐐱𐑂 𐐆𐑆𐑉𐐩𐐯𐑊, 𐐰𐑌𐐼 𐑅𐐲𐐽 𐐰𐑆 𐐪𐑉 𐐯𐑅𐐿𐐩𐐹𐐻 𐐱𐑂 𐑄 𐐸𐐵𐑅 𐐱𐑂 𐐖𐐩𐐿𐐲𐐺, 𐑇𐐰𐑊 𐑌𐐬 𐑋𐐬𐑉 𐐲𐑀𐐯𐑌 𐑅𐐻𐐩 𐐲𐐹𐐱𐑌 𐐸𐐮𐑋 𐑄𐐰𐐻 𐑅𐑋𐐬𐐻 𐑄𐐯𐑋, 𐐺𐐲𐐻 𐑇𐐰𐑊 𐑅𐐻𐐩 𐐲𐐹𐐱𐑌 𐑄 𐐢𐐫𐑉𐐼, 𐑄 𐐐𐐬𐑊𐐨 𐐎𐐲𐑌 𐐱𐑂 𐐆𐑆𐑉𐐩𐐯𐑊, 𐐮𐑌 𐐻𐑉𐐭𐑃. 𐐜 𐑉𐐯𐑋𐑌𐐲𐑌𐐻 𐑇𐐰𐑊 𐑉𐐨𐐻𐐲𐑉𐑌, 𐐷𐐩, 𐐨𐑂𐐲𐑌 𐑄 𐑉𐐯𐑋𐑌𐐲𐑌𐐻 𐐱𐑂 𐐖𐐩𐐿𐐲𐐺, 𐐲𐑌𐐻𐐭 𐑄 𐑋𐐴𐐻𐐨 𐐘𐐱𐐼. 𐐙𐐫𐑉 𐑄𐐬 𐑄𐐴 𐐹𐐨𐐹𐑊 𐐆𐑆𐑉𐐩𐐯𐑊 𐐺𐐨 𐐰𐑆 𐑄 𐑅𐐰𐑌𐐼 𐐱𐑂 𐑄 𐑅𐐨, 𐐷𐐯𐐻 𐐰 𐑉𐐯𐑋𐑌𐐲𐑌𐐻 𐐱𐑂 𐑄𐐯𐑋 𐑇𐐰𐑊 𐑉𐐨𐐻𐐲𐑉𐑌; 𐑄 𐐿𐐱𐑌𐑅𐐲𐑋𐑇𐐲𐑌 𐐼𐐨𐐿𐑉𐐨𐐼 𐑇𐐰𐑊 𐐬𐑂𐐲𐑉𐑁𐑊𐐬 𐐶𐐮𐑄 𐑉𐐴𐐽𐐲𐑅𐑌𐐯𐑅. 𐐙𐐫𐑉 𐑄 𐐢𐐫𐑉𐐼 𐐘𐐱𐐼 𐐱𐑂 𐐐𐐬𐑅𐐻𐑅 𐑇𐐰𐑊 𐑋𐐩𐐿 𐐰 𐐿𐐱𐑌𐑅𐐲𐑋𐑇𐐲𐑌, 𐐨𐑂𐐲𐑌 𐐼𐐨𐐻𐐲𐑉𐑋𐐮𐑌𐐼 𐐮𐑌 𐐫𐑊 𐑄 𐑊𐐰𐑌𐐼.

20. 𐐜𐐩𐑉𐑁𐐬𐑉, 𐑄𐐲𐑅 𐑅𐐯𐑃 𐑄 𐐢𐐫𐑉𐐼 𐐘𐐱𐐼 𐐱𐑂 𐐐𐐬𐑅𐐻𐑅, O 𐑋𐐴 𐐹𐐨𐐹𐑊 𐑄𐐰𐐻 𐐼𐐶𐐯𐑊𐐯𐑅𐐻 𐐮𐑌 𐐞𐐴𐐲𐑌, 𐐺𐐨 𐑌𐐱𐐻 𐐲𐑁𐑉𐐩𐐼 𐐱𐑂 𐑄 𐐈𐑅𐐮𐑉𐐨𐐲𐑌; 𐐸𐐨 𐑇𐐰𐑊 𐑅𐑋𐐴𐐻 𐑄𐐨 𐐶𐐮𐑄 𐐰 𐑉𐐱𐐼, 𐐰𐑌𐐼 𐑇𐐰𐑊 𐑊𐐮𐑁𐐻 𐐲𐐹 𐐸𐐮𐑆 𐑅𐐻𐐰𐑁 𐐲𐑀𐐯𐑌𐑅𐐻 𐑄𐐨, 𐐰𐑁𐐻𐐲𐑉 𐑄 𐑋𐐰𐑌𐐲𐑉 𐐱𐑂 𐐀𐐾𐐮𐐹𐐻. 𐐙𐐫𐑉 𐐷𐐯𐐻 𐐰 𐑂𐐯𐑉𐐨 𐑊𐐮𐐻𐑊 𐐸𐐶𐐴𐑊, 𐐰𐑌𐐼 𐑄 𐐮𐑌𐐼𐐮𐑀𐑌𐐩𐑇𐐲𐑌 𐑇𐐰𐑊 𐑅𐐨𐑅, 𐐰𐑌𐐼 𐑋𐐴𐑌 𐐰𐑍𐑀𐐲𐑉 𐐮𐑌 𐑄𐐩𐑉 𐐼𐐨𐑅𐐻𐑉𐐲𐐿𐑇𐐲𐑌. 𐐈𐑌𐐼 𐑄 𐐢𐐫𐑉𐐼 𐐱𐑂 𐐐𐐬𐑅𐐻𐑅 𐑇𐐰𐑊 𐑅𐐻𐐲𐑉 𐐲𐐹 𐐰 𐑅𐐿𐐲𐑉𐐾 𐑁𐐫𐑉 𐐸𐐮𐑋 𐐰𐐿𐐫𐑉𐐼𐐮𐑍 𐐻𐐭 𐑄 𐑅𐑊𐐫𐐻𐐲𐑉 𐐱𐑂 𐐣𐐮𐐼𐐨𐐲𐑌 𐐰𐐻 𐑄 𐑉𐐱𐐿 𐐱𐑂 𐐄𐑉𐐯𐐺; 𐐰𐑌𐐼 𐐰𐑆 𐐸𐐮𐑆 𐑉𐐱𐐼 𐐶𐐱𐑆 𐐲𐐹𐐱𐑌 𐑄 𐑅𐐨, 𐑅𐐬 𐑇𐐰𐑊 𐐸𐐨 𐑊𐐮𐑁𐐻 𐐮𐐻 𐐲𐐹 𐐰𐑁𐐻𐐲𐑉 𐑄 𐑋𐐰𐑌𐐲𐑉 𐐱𐑂 𐐀𐐾𐐮𐐹𐐻. 𐐈𐑌𐐼 𐐮𐐻 𐑇𐐰𐑊 𐐿𐐲𐑋 𐐻𐐭 𐐹𐐰𐑅 𐐮𐑌 𐑄𐐰𐐻 𐐼𐐩, 𐑄𐐰𐐻 𐐸𐐮𐑆 𐐺𐐲𐑉𐐼𐑌 𐑇𐐰𐑊 𐐺𐐨 𐐻𐐩𐐿𐑌 𐐲𐐶𐐩 𐑁𐑉𐐱𐑋 𐐫𐑁 𐑄𐐴 𐑇𐐬𐑊𐐼𐐲𐑉, 𐐰𐑌𐐼 𐐸𐐮𐑆 𐐷𐐬𐐿 𐑁𐑉𐐱𐑋 𐐫𐑁 𐑄𐐴 𐑌𐐯𐐿, 𐐰𐑌𐐼 𐑄 𐐷𐐬𐐿 𐑇𐐰𐑊 𐐺𐐨 𐐼𐐨𐑅𐐻𐑉𐐱𐐮𐐼 𐐺𐐨𐐿𐐫𐑆 𐐱𐑂 𐑄 𐐲𐑌𐐱𐐮𐑌𐐻𐐮𐑍. 𐐐𐐨 𐐮𐑆 𐐿𐐲𐑋 𐐻𐐭 𐐁𐐴𐐲𐑃; 𐐸𐐨 𐐮𐑆 𐐹𐐰𐑅𐐻 𐐻𐐭 𐐣𐐮𐑀𐑉𐐱𐑌; 𐐰𐐻 𐐣𐐮𐐿𐑋𐐰𐑇 𐐸𐐨 𐐸𐐰𐑃 𐑊𐐩𐐼 𐐲𐐹 𐐸𐐮𐑆 𐐿𐐰𐑉𐐮𐐾𐐯𐑆; 𐑄𐐩 𐐪𐑉 𐑀𐐫𐑌 𐐬𐑂𐐲𐑉 𐑄 𐐹𐐰𐑅𐐯𐐾; 𐑄𐐩 𐐸𐐰𐑂 𐐻𐐩𐐿𐑌 𐐲𐐹 𐑄𐐩𐑉 𐑊𐐱𐐾𐐮𐑍 𐐰𐐻 𐐘𐐨𐐺𐐲; 𐐡𐐩𐑋𐐲𐑃 𐐮𐑆 𐐲𐑁𐑉𐐩𐐼; 𐐘𐐮𐐺𐐨𐐲 𐐱𐑂 𐐝𐐫𐑊 𐐮𐑆 𐑁𐑊𐐯𐐼. 𐐢𐐮𐑁𐐻 𐐲𐐹 𐑄 𐑂𐐱𐐮𐑅, O 𐐼𐐫𐐻𐐲𐑉 𐐱𐑂 𐐘𐐰𐑊𐐮𐑋; 𐐿𐐫𐑆 𐐮𐐻 𐐻𐐭 𐐺𐐨 𐐸𐐲𐑉𐐼 𐐲𐑌𐐻𐐭 𐐢𐐩𐐮𐑇, O 𐐹𐐭𐑉 𐐈𐑌𐐲𐑃𐐱𐑃. 𐐣𐐰𐐼𐑋𐐨𐑌𐐲 𐐮𐑆 𐑉𐐨𐑋𐐭𐑂𐐼; 𐑄 𐐮𐑌𐐸𐐰𐐺𐐮𐐻𐐲𐑌𐐻𐑅 𐐱𐑂 𐐘𐐯𐐺𐐮𐑋 𐑀𐐰𐑄𐐲𐑉 𐑄𐐯𐑋𐑅𐐯𐑊𐑂𐑆 𐐻𐐭 𐑁𐑊𐐨. 𐐈𐑆 𐐷𐐯𐐻 𐑇𐐰𐑊 𐐸𐐨 𐑉𐐨𐑋𐐩𐑌 𐐰𐐻 𐐤𐐱𐐺 𐑄𐐰𐐻 𐐼𐐩;

𐐸𐐨 𐑇𐐰𐑊 𐑇𐐩𐐿 𐐸𐐮𐑆 𐐸𐐰𐑌𐐼 𐐰𐑀𐐯𐑌𐑅𐐻 𐑄 𐑋𐐵𐑌𐐻 𐐱𐑂 𐑄 𐐼𐐫𐐻𐐲𐑉 𐐱𐑂 𐐞𐐴𐐲𐑌, 𐑄 𐐸𐐮𐑊 𐐱𐑂 𐐖𐐯𐑉𐐭𐑅𐐲𐑊𐐯𐑋. 𐐒𐐨𐐸𐐬𐑊𐐼, 𐑄 𐐢𐐫𐑉𐐼, 𐑄 𐐢𐐫𐑉𐐼 𐐱𐑂 𐐐𐐬𐑅𐐻𐑅 𐑇𐐰𐑊 𐑊𐐱𐐹 𐑄 𐐺𐐵 𐐶𐐮𐑄 𐐻𐐯𐑉𐐲𐑉; 𐐰𐑌𐐼 𐑄 𐐸𐐴 𐐶𐐲𐑌𐑆 𐐱𐑂 𐑅𐐻𐐰𐐻𐐷𐐭𐑉 𐑇𐐰𐑊 𐐺 𐐸𐐷𐐭𐑌 𐐼𐐵𐑌; 𐐰𐑌𐐼 𐑄 𐐸𐐫𐐻𐐨 𐑇𐐰𐑊 𐐺 𐐸𐐲𐑋𐐺𐑊𐐼. 𐐈𐑌𐐼 𐐸𐐨 𐑇𐐰𐑊 𐐿𐐲𐐻 𐐼𐐵𐑌 𐑄 𐑃𐐮𐐿𐐯𐐻𐑅 𐐱𐑂 𐑄 𐑁𐐫𐑉𐐯𐑅𐐻 𐐶𐐮𐑄 𐐴𐐲𐑉𐑌, 𐐰𐑌𐐼 𐐢𐐯𐐺𐐰𐑌𐐲𐑌 𐑇𐐰𐑊 𐑁𐐫𐑊 𐐺𐐴 𐐩 𐑋𐐴𐐻𐐨 𐐶𐐲𐑌.

21. 𐐈𐑌𐐼 𐑄𐐯𐑉 𐑇𐐰𐑊 𐐿𐐲𐑋 𐑁𐐬𐑉𐑃 𐐩 𐑉𐐱𐐼 𐐵𐐻 𐐱𐑂 𐑄 𐑅𐐻𐐯𐑋 𐐱𐑂 𐐖𐐯𐑅𐐨, 𐐰𐑌𐐼 𐐩 𐐺𐑉𐐰𐑌𐐽 𐑇𐐰𐑊 𐑀𐑉𐐬 𐐵𐐻 𐐱𐑂 𐐸𐐮𐑆 𐑉𐐭𐐻𐑅; 𐐰𐑌𐐼 𐑄 𐐝𐐹𐐮𐑉𐐮𐐻 𐐱𐑂 𐑄 𐐢𐐫𐑉𐐼 𐑇𐐰𐑊 𐑉𐐯𐑅𐐻 𐐲𐐹𐐱𐑌 𐐸𐐮𐑋, 𐑄 𐑅𐐹𐐮𐑉𐐮𐐻 𐐱𐑂 𐐶𐐮𐑆𐐼𐐲𐑋 𐐰𐑌𐐼 𐐲𐑌𐐼𐐯𐑉𐑅𐐻𐐰𐑌𐐼𐐮𐑍, 𐑄 𐑅𐐹𐐮𐑉𐐮𐐻 𐐱𐑂 𐐿𐐵𐑌𐑅𐐯𐑊 𐐰𐑌𐐼 𐑋𐐴𐐻, 𐑄 𐑅𐐹𐐮𐑉𐐮𐐻 𐐱𐑂 𐑌𐐱𐑊𐐯𐐾 𐐰𐑌𐐼 𐐱𐑂 𐑄 𐑁𐐨𐑉 𐐱𐑂 𐑄 𐐢𐐫𐑉𐐼; 𐐰𐑌𐐼 𐑇𐐰𐑊 𐑋𐐩𐐿 𐐸𐐮𐑋 𐐱𐑂 𐐿𐐶𐐮𐐿 𐐲𐑌𐐼𐐯𐑉𐑅𐐻𐐰𐑌𐐼𐐮𐑍 𐐮𐑌 𐑄 𐑁𐐨𐑉 𐐱𐑂 𐑄 𐐢𐐫𐑉𐐼: 𐐰𐑌𐐼 𐐸𐐨 𐑇𐐰𐑊 𐑌𐐱𐐻 𐐾𐐲𐐾 𐐰𐑁𐐻𐐲𐑉 𐑄 𐑅𐐴𐐻 𐐱𐑂 𐐸𐐮𐑆 𐐴𐑆, 𐑌𐐨𐑄𐐲𐑉 𐑉𐐨𐐹𐑉𐐭𐑂 𐐰𐑁𐐻𐐲𐑉 𐑄 𐐸𐐨𐑉𐐮𐑍 𐐱𐑂 𐐸𐐮𐑆 𐐨𐑉𐑆: 𐐺𐐲𐐻 𐐶𐐮𐑄 𐑉𐐴𐐽𐐲𐑅𐑌𐐯𐑅 𐑇𐐰𐑊 𐐸𐐨 𐐾𐐲𐐾 𐑄 𐐹𐐬𐑉, 𐐰𐑌𐐼 𐑉𐐨𐐹𐑉𐐭𐑂 𐐶𐐮𐑄 𐐯𐐿𐐶𐐮𐐻𐐨 𐑁𐐫𐑉 𐑄 𐑋𐐨𐐿 𐐱𐑂 𐑄 𐐲𐑉𐑃: 𐐰𐑌𐐼 𐐸𐐨 𐑇𐐰𐑊 𐑅𐑋𐐴𐐻 𐑄 𐐲𐑉𐑃 𐐶𐐮𐑄 𐑄 𐑉𐐱𐐼 𐐱𐑂 𐐸𐐮𐑆 𐑋𐐵𐑃, 𐐰𐑌𐐼 𐐶𐐮𐑄 𐑄 𐐺𐑉𐐯𐑃 𐐱𐑂 𐐸𐐮𐑆 𐑊𐐮𐐹𐑅 𐑇𐐰𐑊 𐐸𐐨 𐑅𐑊𐐩 𐑄 𐐶𐐮𐐿𐐯𐐼. 𐐈𐑌𐐼 𐑉𐐴𐐽𐐲𐑅𐑌𐐯𐑅 𐑇𐐰𐑊 𐐺 𐑄 𐑀𐐲𐑉𐐼𐐯𐑊 𐐱𐑂 𐐸𐐮𐑆 𐑊𐑎𐑌𐑆, 𐐰𐑌𐐼 𐑁𐐩𐑃𐑁𐐳𐑊𐑌𐐯𐑅 𐑄 𐑀𐐲𐑉𐐼𐐯𐑊 𐐱𐑂 𐐸𐐮𐑆 𐑉𐐩𐑌𐑆. 𐐜 𐐶𐐳𐑊𐑁 𐐫𐑊𐑅𐐬 𐑇𐐰𐑊 𐐼𐐶𐐯𐑊 𐐶𐐮𐑄 𐑄 𐑊𐐰𐑋, 𐐰𐑌𐐼 𐑄 𐑊𐐯𐐹𐐲𐑉𐐼 𐑇𐐰𐑊 𐑊𐐴 𐐼𐐵𐑌 𐐶𐐮𐑄 𐑄 𐐿𐐮𐐼; 𐐰𐑌𐐼 𐑄 𐐿𐐪𐑁 𐐰𐑌𐐼 𐑄 𐐷𐐲𐑍 𐑊𐐴𐐲𐑌 𐐰𐑌𐐼 𐑁𐐰𐐻𐑊𐐮𐑍 𐐻𐐳𐑀𐐯𐑄𐐲𐑉; 𐐰𐑌𐐼 𐐩 𐑊𐐮𐐻𐑊 𐐽𐐴𐑊𐐼 𐑇𐐰𐑊 𐑊𐐨𐐼 𐑄𐐯𐑋. 𐐈𐑌𐐼 𐑄 𐐿𐐵 𐐰𐑌𐐼 𐑄 𐐺𐐯𐑉 𐑇𐐰𐑊 𐑁𐐨𐐼; 𐑄𐐯𐑉 𐐷𐐲𐑍 𐐶𐐲𐑌𐑆 𐑇𐐰𐑊 𐑊𐐴 𐐼𐐵𐑌 𐐻𐐳𐑀𐐯𐑄𐐲𐑉; 𐐰𐑌𐐼 𐑄 𐑊𐐴𐐲𐑌 𐑇𐐰𐑊 𐐨𐐻 𐑅𐐻𐑉𐐫 𐑊𐐴𐐿 𐑄 𐐱𐐿𐑅. 𐐈𐑌𐐼 𐑄 𐑅𐐲𐐿𐐮𐑍 𐐽𐐴𐑊𐐼 𐑇𐐰𐑊 𐐹𐑊𐐩 𐐱𐑌 𐑄 𐐸𐐬𐑊 𐐱𐑂 𐑄 𐐰𐑅𐐹, 𐐰𐑌𐐼 𐑄 𐐶𐐨𐑌𐐼 𐐽𐐴𐑊𐐼 𐑇𐐰𐑊 𐐹𐐳𐐻 𐐸𐐮𐑆 𐐸𐐰𐑌𐐼 𐐱𐑌 𐑄 𐐿𐐱𐐿𐐰𐐻𐑉𐐴𐑅'𐑆 𐐼𐐯𐑌. 𐐜𐐩 𐑇𐐰𐑊 𐑌𐐱𐐻 𐐸𐐲𐑉𐐻 𐑌𐐫𐑉 𐐼𐐨𐑅𐐻𐑉𐐱𐐴 𐐮𐑌 𐐫𐑊 𐑋𐐴 𐐸𐐬𐑊𐐨 𐑋𐐵𐑌𐐻𐐮𐑌: 𐑁𐐫𐑉 𐑄 𐐲𐑉𐑃 𐑇𐐰𐑊 𐐺 𐑁𐐳𐑊 𐐱𐑂 𐑄 𐑌𐐱𐑊𐐯𐐾 𐐱𐑂 𐑄 𐐢𐐫𐑉𐐼, 𐐰𐑆 𐑄 𐐶𐐫𐐻𐐲𐑉𐑆 𐐿𐐲𐑂𐐲𐑉 𐑄 𐑅𐐨.

22. 𐐈𐑌𐐼 𐐮𐑌 𐑄𐐰𐐻 𐐼𐐩 𐑄𐐯𐑉 𐑇𐐰𐑊 𐐺 𐐩 𐑉𐐭𐐻 𐐱𐑂 𐐖𐐯𐑅𐐨, 𐐸𐐶𐐮𐐽 𐑇𐐰𐑊 𐑅𐐻𐐰𐑌𐐼 𐑁𐐫𐑉 𐐰𐑌 𐐯𐑌𐑅𐐴𐑌 𐐱𐑂 𐑄 𐐹𐐨𐐹𐑊; 𐐻𐐭 𐐮𐐻 𐑇𐐰𐑊 𐑄 𐐖𐐯𐑌𐐻𐐴𐑊𐑆 𐑅𐐨𐐿: 𐐰𐑌𐐼 𐐸𐐮𐑆 𐑉𐐯𐑅𐐻 𐑇𐐰𐑊 𐐺 𐑀𐑊𐐬𐑉𐐨𐐲𐑅. 𐐈𐑌𐐼 𐐮𐐻 𐑇𐐰𐑊 𐐿𐐲𐑋 𐐻𐐭 𐐹𐐰𐑅 𐐮𐑌 𐑄𐐰𐐻 𐐼𐐩, 𐑄𐐰𐐻 𐑄 𐐢𐐫𐑉𐐼 𐑇𐐰𐑊 𐑅𐐯𐐻 𐐸𐐮𐑆 𐐸𐐰𐑌𐐼 𐐰𐑀𐐯𐑌 𐑄 𐑅𐐯𐐿𐐲𐑌𐐼 𐐻𐐴𐑋 𐐻𐐭 𐑉𐐨𐐿𐐲𐑂𐐲𐑉 𐑄 𐑉𐐯𐑋𐑌𐐲𐑌𐐻 𐐱𐑂 𐐸𐐮𐑆 𐐹𐐨𐐹𐑊, 𐐸𐐶𐐮𐐽 𐑇𐐰𐑊 𐐺 𐑊𐐯𐑁𐐻, 𐑁𐑉𐐱𐑋 𐐈𐑅𐐮𐑉𐐨𐐲, 𐐰𐑌𐐼 𐑁𐑉𐐱𐑋 𐐀𐐾𐐮𐐹𐐻, 𐐰𐑌𐐼 𐑁𐑉𐐱𐑋 𐐑𐐰𐑃𐑉𐐱𐑅, 𐐰𐑌𐐼 𐑁𐑉𐐱𐑋 𐐗𐐲𐑇, 𐐰𐑌𐐼 𐑁𐑉𐐱𐑋 𐐀𐑊𐐲𐑋, 𐐰𐑌𐐼 𐑁𐑉𐐱𐑋 𐐡𐐴𐑌𐐪𐑉, 𐐰𐑌𐐼 𐑁𐑉𐐱𐑋 𐐐𐐩𐑋𐐰𐑃, 𐐰𐑌𐐼 𐑁𐑉𐐱𐑋 𐑄 𐐴𐑊𐐲𐑌𐐼𐑆 𐐱𐑂 𐑄 𐑅𐐨. 𐐈𐑌𐐼 𐐸𐐨 𐑇𐐰𐑊 𐑅𐐯𐐻 𐐲𐐹 𐐰𐑌 𐐯𐑌𐑅𐐴𐑌 𐑁𐐫𐑉 𐑄 𐑌𐐩𐑇𐐲𐑌𐑆, 𐐰𐑌𐐼 𐑇𐐰𐑊 𐐰𐑅𐐯𐑋𐐺𐑊 𐑄 𐐵𐐻𐐿𐐰𐑅𐐻𐑅 𐐱𐑂 𐐆𐑆𐑉𐐩𐐯𐑊, 𐐰𐑌𐐼 𐑀𐐰𐑄𐐲𐑉 𐐻𐐳𐑀𐐯𐑄𐐲𐑉 𐑄 𐐼𐐮𐑅𐐹𐐲𐑉𐑅𐐼 𐐱𐑂 𐐖𐐭𐐼𐐲 𐑁𐑉𐐱𐑋 𐑄 𐑁𐐬𐑉 𐐿𐐫𐑉𐑌𐐲𐑉𐑆 𐐱𐑂 𐑄 𐐲𐑉𐑃. 𐐜 𐐯𐑌𐑂𐐨 𐐫𐑊𐑅𐐬 𐐱𐑂 𐐀𐑁𐑉𐐩𐐮𐑋 𐑇𐐰𐑊 𐐼𐐨𐐹𐐪𐑉𐐻, 𐐰𐑌𐐼 𐑄 𐐰𐐼𐑂𐐲𐑉𐑅𐐯𐑉𐐨𐑆 𐐱𐑂 𐐖𐐭𐐼𐐲 𐑇𐐰𐑊 𐐺 𐐿𐐲𐐻 𐐱𐑁; 𐐀𐑁𐑉𐐩𐐮𐑋 𐑇𐐰𐑊 𐑌𐐱𐐻 𐐯𐑌𐑂𐐨 𐐖𐐭𐐼𐐲, 𐐰𐑌𐐼 𐐖𐐭𐐼𐐲 𐑇𐐰𐑊 𐑌𐐱𐐻 𐑂𐐯𐐿𐑅 𐐀𐑁𐑉𐐩𐐮𐑋. 𐐒𐐲𐐻 𐑄𐐩 𐑇𐐰𐑊 𐑁𐑊𐐴 𐐲𐐹𐐱𐑌 𐑄 𐑇𐐬𐑊𐐼𐐲𐑉𐑆 𐐱𐑂 𐑄 𐐙𐐮𐑊𐐮𐑅𐐻𐐮𐑌𐑆 𐐻𐐬𐑉𐐼𐑆 𐑄 𐐶𐐯𐑅𐐻; 𐑄𐐩 𐑇𐐰𐑊 𐑅𐐹𐑎𐑊 𐑄𐐯𐑋 𐐱𐑂 𐑄 𐐨𐑅𐐻 𐐻𐐳𐑀𐐯𐑄𐐲𐑉; 𐑄𐐩 𐑇𐐰𐑊 𐑊𐐩 𐑄𐐯𐑉 𐐸𐐰𐑌𐐼 𐐲𐐹𐐱𐑌 𐐀𐐼𐐲𐑋 𐐰𐑌𐐼 𐐣𐐬𐐰𐐺: 𐐰𐑌𐐼 𐑄 𐐽𐐮𐑊𐐼𐑉𐐯𐑌 𐐱𐑂 𐐊𐑋𐐲𐑌 𐑇𐐰𐑊 𐐬𐐺𐐩 𐑄𐐯𐑋. 𐐈𐑌𐐼 𐑄 𐐢𐐫𐑉𐐼 𐑇𐐰𐑊 𐐲𐐻𐐲𐑉𐑊𐐨 𐐼𐐨𐑅𐐻𐑉𐐱𐐴 𐑄 𐐻𐐲𐑍 𐐱𐑂 𐑄 𐐀𐐾𐐮𐐹𐑇𐐲𐑌 𐑅𐐨; 𐐰𐑌𐐼 𐐶𐐮𐑄 𐐸𐐮𐑆 𐑋𐐴𐐻𐐨 𐐶𐐮𐑌𐐼 𐐸𐐨 𐑇𐐰𐑊 𐑇𐐩𐐿 𐐸𐐮𐑆 𐐸𐐰𐑌𐐼 𐐬𐑂𐐲𐑉 𐑄 𐑉𐐮𐑂𐐲𐑉, 𐐰𐑌𐐼 𐑇𐐰𐑊 𐑅𐑋𐐴𐐻 𐐮𐐻 𐐮𐑌 𐑄 𐑅𐐯𐑂𐐲𐑌 𐑅𐐻𐑉𐐨𐑋𐑆, 𐐰𐑌𐐼 𐑋𐐩𐐿 𐑋𐐯𐑌 𐑀𐐬 𐐬𐑂𐐲𐑉 𐐼𐑉𐐴 𐑇𐐱𐐼. 𐐈𐑌𐐼 𐑄𐐯𐑉 𐑇𐐰𐑊 𐐺 𐐩 𐐸𐐴𐐶𐐩 𐑁𐐫𐑉 𐑄 𐑉𐐯𐑋𐑌𐐲𐑌𐐻 𐐱𐑂 𐐸𐐮𐑆 𐐹𐐨𐐹𐑊, 𐐸𐐶𐐮𐐽 𐑇𐐰𐑊 𐐺 𐑊𐐯𐑁𐐻, 𐑁𐑉𐐱𐑋 𐐈𐑅𐐮𐑉𐐨𐐲, 𐑊𐐴𐐿 𐐰𐑆 𐐮𐐻 𐐶𐐱𐑆 𐐻𐐭 𐐆𐑆𐑉𐐩𐐯𐑊 𐐮𐑌 𐑄 𐐼𐐩 𐑄𐐰𐐻 𐐸𐐨 𐐿𐐩𐑋 𐐲𐐹 𐐵𐐻 𐐱𐑂 𐑄 𐑊𐐰𐑌𐐼 𐐱𐑂 𐐀𐐾𐐮𐐹𐐻.

23. 𐐈𐑌𐐼 𐐮𐑌 𐑄𐐰𐐻 𐐼𐐩 𐑄𐐵 𐑇𐐰𐑊𐐻 𐑅𐐩, 𐐄 𐐢𐐫𐑉𐐼, 𐐌 𐐶𐐮𐑊 𐐹𐑉𐐩𐑆 𐑄𐐨: 𐑄𐐬 𐑄𐐵 𐐶𐐱𐑅𐐻 𐐰𐑍𐑀𐑉𐐨 𐐶𐐮𐑄 𐑋𐐨, 𐑄𐐴𐑌 𐐰𐑍𐑀𐐲𐑉 𐐮𐑆 𐐻𐐲𐑉𐑌𐐼 𐐰𐐶𐐩, 𐐰𐑌𐐼 𐑄𐐵 𐐿𐐲𐑋𐑁𐐲𐑉𐐻𐐯𐐼𐑅𐐻 𐑋𐐨. 𐐒𐐨𐐸𐐬𐑊𐐼, 𐐘𐐱𐐼 𐐮𐑆 𐑋𐐴 𐑅𐐰𐑊𐑂𐐩𐑇𐐲𐑌; 𐐌 𐐶𐐮𐑊 𐐻𐑉𐐲𐑅𐐻, 𐐰𐑌𐐼 𐑌𐐱𐐻 𐐺 𐐰𐑁𐑉𐐩𐐼: 𐑁𐐫𐑉 𐑄 𐐢𐐫𐑉𐐼, 𐐖𐐇𐐐𐐄𐐚𐐈, 𐐮𐑆 𐑋𐐴 𐑅𐐻𐑉𐐯𐑍𐑃 𐐰𐑌𐐼 𐑋𐐴 𐑅𐐱𐑍; 𐐸𐐨 𐐫𐑊𐑅𐐬 𐐸𐐰𐑆 𐐺𐐨𐐿𐐲𐑋 𐑋𐐴 𐑅𐐰𐑊𐑂𐐩𐑇𐐲𐑌. 𐐜𐐯𐑉𐑁𐐬𐑉, 𐐶𐐮𐑄 𐐖𐐱𐐴 𐑇𐐰𐑊 𐐷𐐨 𐐼𐑉𐐫 𐐶𐐫𐐻𐐲𐑉 𐐵𐐻 𐐱𐑂 𐑄 𐐶𐐯𐑊𐑆 𐐱𐑂 𐑅𐐰𐑊𐑂𐐩𐑇𐐲𐑌. 𐐈𐑌𐐼 𐐮𐑌 𐑄𐐰𐐻 𐐼𐐩 𐑇𐐰𐑊 𐐷𐐨 𐑅𐐩, 𐐑𐑉𐐩𐑆 𐑄 𐐢𐐫𐑉𐐼, 𐐿𐐫𐑊 𐐲𐐹𐐱𐑌 𐐸𐐮𐑆 𐑌𐐩𐑋, 𐐼𐐯𐐿𐑊𐐩𐑉 𐐸𐐮𐑆 𐐼𐐭𐐮𐑍𐑆 𐐲𐑋𐐲𐑍 𐑄 𐐹𐐨𐐹𐑊, 𐑋𐐩𐐿 𐑋𐐯𐑌𐑇𐐲𐑌 𐑄𐐰𐐻 𐐸𐐮𐑆

𐑌𐐩𐑋 𐐮𐑆 𐐯𐑀𐑆𐐫𐑊𐐻𐐯𐐼. 𐐝𐐮𐑍 𐐲𐑌𐐻𐐭 𐑄 𐐢𐐫𐑉𐐼; 𐑁𐐫𐑉 𐐸𐐨 𐐸𐐰𐑃 𐐼𐐲𐑌 𐐯𐐿𐑅𐐯𐑊𐐯𐑌𐐻 𐑃𐐮𐑍𐑆: 𐑄𐐮𐑅 𐐮𐑆 𐑌𐐬𐑌 𐐮𐑌 𐐫𐑊 𐑄 𐐲𐑉𐑃. 𐐗𐑉𐐴 𐐵𐐻 𐐰𐑌𐐼 𐑇𐐵𐐻, 𐑄𐐵 𐐮𐑌𐐸𐐰𐐺𐐮𐐻𐐲𐑌𐐻 𐐲𐑂 𐐞𐐴𐐲𐑌; 𐑁𐐫𐑉 𐑀𐑉𐐩𐐻 𐐮𐑆 𐑄 𐐐𐐬𐑊𐐨 𐐎𐐲𐑌 𐐲𐑂 𐐆𐑆𐑉𐐩𐐯𐑊 𐐮𐑌 𐑄 𐑋𐐮𐐼𐑅𐐻 𐐲𐑂 𐑄.

𐐕𐐰𐐹𐐻𐐲𐑉 X.

1. 𐐜 𐐺𐐲𐑉𐐼𐐲𐑌 𐐲𐑂 𐐒𐐰𐐺𐐮𐑊𐐲𐑌, 𐐸𐐶𐐮𐐽 𐐌𐑆𐐩𐐲 𐑄 𐑅𐐲𐑌 𐐲𐑂 𐐁𐑋𐐱𐑆 𐐼𐐮𐐼 𐑅𐐨. 𐐢𐐮𐑁𐐻 𐐷𐐨 𐐲𐐹 𐐩 𐐺𐐰𐑌𐐲𐑉 𐐲𐐹𐐱𐑌 𐑄 𐐸𐐴 𐑋𐐵𐑌𐐻𐐲𐑌, 𐐯𐑀𐑆𐐫𐑊𐐻 𐑄 𐑂𐐱𐐮𐑅 𐐲𐑌𐐻𐐭 𐑄𐐯𐑋, 𐑇𐐩𐐿 𐑄 𐐸𐐰𐑌𐐼, 𐑄𐐰𐐻 𐑄𐐩 𐑋𐐩 𐑀𐐬 𐐮𐑌𐐻𐐭 𐑄 𐑀𐐩𐐻𐑅 𐐲𐑂 𐑄 𐑌𐐬𐐺𐑊𐑆. 𐐌 𐐸𐐰𐑂 𐐿𐐲𐑋𐐰𐑌𐐼𐐯𐐼 𐑋𐐴 𐑅𐐰𐑍𐐿𐐻𐐮𐑁𐐴𐐼 𐐶𐐲𐑌𐑆, 𐐌 𐐸𐐰𐑂 𐐫𐑊𐑅𐐬 𐐿𐐫𐑊𐐼 𐑋𐐴 𐑋𐐴𐐻𐐨 𐐶𐐲𐑌𐑆, 𐑁𐐫𐑉 𐑋𐐴𐑌 𐐰𐑍𐑀𐐲𐑉 𐐮𐑆 𐑌𐐱𐐻 𐐲𐐹𐐱𐑌 𐑄𐐯𐑋 𐑄𐐰𐐻 𐑉𐐨𐐾𐐱𐐮𐑅 𐐮𐑌 𐑋𐐴 𐐸𐐴𐑌𐐯𐑅. 𐐜 𐑌𐐱𐐮𐑆 𐐲𐑂 𐑄 𐑋𐐲𐑊𐐻𐐮𐐻𐐧𐐼 𐐮𐑌 𐑄 𐑋𐐵𐑌𐐻𐐲𐑌𐑆 𐑊𐐴𐐿 𐐰𐑆 𐐲𐑂 𐐩 𐑀𐑉𐐩𐐻 𐐹𐐨𐐹𐑊: 𐐩 𐐻𐐭𐑋𐐲𐑊𐐽𐐭𐐲𐑅 𐑌𐐱𐐮𐑆 𐐲𐑂 𐑄 𐐿𐐮𐑍𐐼𐐲𐑋𐑆 𐐲𐑂 𐑌𐐩𐑇𐐲𐑌𐑆 𐑀𐐰𐑄𐐲𐑉𐐼 𐐻𐐭𐑀𐐯𐑄𐐲𐑉: 𐑄 𐐢𐐫𐑉𐐼 𐐲𐑂 𐐐𐐬𐑅𐐻𐑅 𐑋𐐲𐑅𐐻𐐲𐑉𐐯𐑃 𐑄 𐐸𐐬𐑅𐐻𐑅 𐐲𐑂 𐑄 𐐺𐐰𐐻𐑊. 𐐜𐐩 𐐿𐐲𐑋 𐑁𐑉𐐱𐑋 𐐩 𐑁𐐪𐑉 𐐿𐐲𐑌𐐻𐑉𐐨, 𐑁𐑉𐐱𐑋 𐑄 𐐯𐑌𐐼 𐐲𐑂 𐐸𐐯𐑂𐐲𐑌, 𐐷𐐩, 𐑄 𐐢𐐫𐑉𐐼, 𐐰𐑌𐐼 𐑄 𐐶𐐯𐐹𐐲𐑌𐑆 𐐲𐑂 𐐸𐐮𐑆 𐐮𐑌𐐼𐐮𐑀𐑌𐐩𐑇𐐲𐑌, 𐐻𐐭 𐐼𐐯𐑅𐐻𐑉𐐱𐐮 𐑄 𐐸𐐬𐑊 𐑊𐐰𐑌𐐼.

2. 𐐐𐐵𐑊 𐐷𐐨; 𐑁𐐫𐑉 𐑄 𐐼𐐩 𐐲𐑂 𐑄 𐐢𐐫𐑉𐐼 𐐮𐑆 𐐰𐐻 𐐸𐐰𐑌𐐼: 𐐮𐐻 𐑇𐐰𐑊 𐐿𐐲𐑋 𐐰𐑆 𐐩 𐐼𐐯𐑅𐐻𐑉𐐲𐐿𐑇𐐲𐑌 𐑁𐑉𐐱𐑋 𐑄 𐐄𐑊𐑋𐐴𐐻𐐨. 𐐜𐐯𐑉𐑁𐐫𐑉 𐑇𐐰𐑊 𐐫𐑊 𐐸𐐰𐑌𐐼𐑆 𐐺𐐨 𐑁𐐩𐑌𐐻, 𐐯𐑂𐐲𐑉𐐨 𐑋𐐰𐑌'𐑆 𐐸𐐪𐑉𐐻 𐑇𐐰𐑊 𐑋𐐯𐑊𐐻; 𐐰𐑌𐐼 𐑄𐐩 𐑇𐐰𐑊 𐐺𐐨 𐐰𐑁𐑉𐐩𐐼; 𐐹𐐰𐑍𐑆 𐐰𐑌𐐼 𐑅𐐱𐑉𐐬𐑆 𐑇𐐰𐑊 𐐻𐐩𐐿 𐐸𐐬𐑊𐐼 𐐲𐑂 𐑄𐐯𐑋; 𐑄𐐩 𐑇𐐰𐑊 𐐺𐐨 𐐰𐑋𐐩𐑆𐐼 𐐶𐐲𐑌 𐐰𐐻 𐐰𐑌𐐲𐑄𐐲𐑉; 𐑄𐐯𐑉 𐑁𐐩𐑅𐐯𐑆 𐑇𐐰𐑊 𐐺𐐨 𐐰𐑆 𐑁𐑊𐐩𐑋𐑆. 𐐒𐐨𐐸𐐬𐑊𐐼, 𐑄 𐐼𐐩 𐐲𐑂 𐑄 𐐢𐐫𐑉𐐼 𐐿𐐲𐑋𐐯𐑃, 𐐿𐑉𐐭𐐯𐑊 𐐺𐐬𐑃 𐐶𐐮𐑄 𐑉𐐪𐑃 𐐰𐑌𐐼 𐑁𐐨𐑉𐑅 𐐰𐑍𐑀𐐲𐑉, 𐐻𐐭 𐑊𐐩 𐑄 𐑊𐐰𐑌𐐼 𐐼𐐯𐑅𐐬𐑊𐐩𐐻: 𐐰𐑌𐐼 𐐸𐐨 𐑇𐐰𐑊 𐐼𐐯𐑅𐐻𐑉𐐱𐐮 𐑄 𐑅𐐮𐑌𐐲𐑉𐑆 𐑄𐐯𐑉𐐱𐑂 𐐵𐐻 𐐲𐑂 𐐮𐐻. 𐐙𐐫𐑉 𐑄 𐑅𐐻𐐪𐑉𐑆 𐐲𐑂 𐐸𐐯𐑂𐐲𐑌 𐐰𐑌𐐼 𐑄 𐐿𐐱𐑌𐑅𐐻𐐯𐑊𐐩𐑇𐐲𐑌𐑆 𐑄𐐯𐑉𐐱𐑂 𐑇𐐰𐑊 𐑌𐐱𐐻 𐑀𐐮𐑂 𐑄𐐯𐑉 𐑊𐐴𐐻; 𐑄 𐑅𐐲𐑌 𐑇𐐰𐑊 𐐺𐐨 𐐼𐐪𐑉𐐿𐐲𐑌𐐼 𐐮𐑌 𐐸𐐮𐑆 𐑀𐐬𐐮𐑍 𐑁𐐬𐑉𐑃, 𐐰𐑌𐐼 𐑄 𐑋𐐭𐑌 𐑇𐐰𐑊 𐑌𐐱𐐻 𐐿𐐫𐑆 𐐸𐐲𐑉 𐑊𐐴𐐻 𐐻𐐭 𐑇𐐴𐑌. 𐐈𐑌𐐼 𐐌 𐐶𐐮𐑊 𐐹𐐲𐑌𐐮𐑇 𐑄 𐐶𐐲𐑉𐑊𐐼 𐑁𐐫𐑉 𐐨𐑂𐐲𐑊, 𐐰𐑌𐐼 𐑄 𐐶𐐮𐐿𐐯𐐼 𐑁𐐫𐑉 𐑄𐐯𐑉 𐐮𐑌𐐮𐐿𐐶𐐮𐐻𐐨; 𐐌 𐐶𐐮𐑊 𐐿𐐫𐑆 𐑄 𐐰𐑉𐐬𐑀𐐲𐑌𐑅𐐨 𐐲𐑂 𐑄 𐐹𐑉𐐵𐐼 𐐻𐐭 𐑅𐐨𐑅, 𐐰𐑌𐐼 𐐶𐐮𐑊 𐑊𐐩 𐐼𐐵𐑌 𐑄 𐐸𐐫𐐻𐐨𐑌𐐯𐑅 𐐲𐑂 𐑄 𐐻𐐯𐑉𐐮𐐺𐑊. 𐐌 𐐶𐐮𐑊 𐑋𐐩𐐿 𐐩 𐑋𐐰𐑌 𐑋𐐬𐑉 𐐹𐑉𐐯𐑇𐐲𐑅 𐑄𐐰𐑌 𐑁𐐴𐑌 𐑀𐐬𐑊𐐼; 𐐨𐑂𐐲𐑌 𐐩 𐑋𐐰𐑌 𐑄𐐰𐑌 𐑄 𐑀𐐬𐑊𐐼𐐲𐑌 𐐶𐐯𐐾 𐐲𐑂 𐐄𐑁𐐲𐑉. 𐐜𐐯𐑉𐑁𐐫𐑉, 𐐌 𐐶𐐮𐑊 𐑇𐐩𐐿 𐑄 𐐸𐐯𐑂𐐲𐑌𐑆, 𐐰𐑌𐐼 𐑄 𐐲𐑉𐑃 𐑇𐐰𐑊 𐑉𐐨𐑋𐐭𐑂 𐐵𐐻 𐐲𐑂 𐐸𐐲𐑉 𐐹𐑊𐐩𐑅, 𐐮𐑌 𐑄 𐑉𐐪𐑃 𐐲𐑂 𐑄 𐐢𐐫𐑉𐐼 𐐲𐑂 𐐐𐐬𐑅𐐻𐑅, 𐐰𐑌𐐼 𐐮𐑌 𐑄 𐐼𐐩 𐐲𐑂 𐐸𐐮𐑆 𐑁𐐨𐑉𐑅 𐐰𐑍𐑀𐐲𐑉. 𐐈𐑌𐐼 𐐮𐐻 𐑇𐐰𐑊 𐐺𐐨 𐐰𐑆 𐑄 𐐽𐐩𐑅𐐻 𐑉𐐬, 𐐰𐑌𐐼 𐐰𐑆 𐐩 𐑇𐐨𐐹 𐑄𐐰𐐻 𐑌𐐬 𐑋𐐰𐑌 𐐻𐐩𐐿𐐯𐑃 𐐲𐐹; 𐐰𐑌𐐼 𐑄𐐩 𐑇𐐰𐑊 𐐯𐑂𐐲𐑉𐐨 𐑋𐐰𐑌 𐐻𐐲𐑉𐑌 𐐻𐐭 𐐸𐐮𐑆 𐐬𐑌 𐐹𐐨𐐹𐑊, 𐐰𐑌𐐼 𐑁𐑊𐐨 𐐯𐑂𐐲𐑉𐐨 𐐶𐐲𐑌 𐐮𐑌𐐻𐐭 𐐸𐐮𐑆 𐐬𐑌 𐑊𐐰𐑌𐐼. 𐐇𐑂𐐲𐑉𐐨 𐐶𐐲𐑌 𐑄𐐰𐐻 𐐮𐑆 𐐹𐑉𐐵𐐼 𐑇𐐰𐑊 𐐺𐐨 𐑃𐑉𐐲𐑅𐐻 𐑃𐑉𐐭; 𐐷𐐩, 𐐰𐑌𐐼 𐐯𐑂𐐲𐑉𐐨 𐐶𐐲𐑌 𐑄𐐰𐐻 𐐮𐑆 𐐾𐐱𐐮𐑌𐐼 𐐻𐐭 𐑄 𐐶𐐮𐐿𐐯𐐼, 𐑇𐐰𐑊 𐑁𐐫𐑊 𐐺𐐴 𐑄 𐑅𐐬𐑉𐐼. 𐐜𐐯𐑉 𐐽𐐮𐑊𐐼𐑉𐐯𐑌 𐐫𐑊𐑅𐐬 𐑇𐐰𐑊 𐐺𐐨 𐐼𐐰𐑇𐐻 𐐻𐐭 𐐹𐐨𐑅𐐯𐑆 𐐺𐐨𐑁𐐬𐑉 𐑄𐐯𐑉 𐐴𐑆; 𐑄𐐯𐑉 𐐸𐐵𐑆𐐯𐑆 𐑇𐐰𐑊 𐐺𐐨 𐑅𐐹𐐱𐐮𐑊𐐼, 𐐰𐑌𐐼 𐑄𐐯𐑉 𐐶𐐴𐑂𐑆 𐑉𐐰𐑂𐐮𐑇𐐻. 𐐒𐐨𐐸𐐬𐑊𐐼, 𐐌 𐐶𐐮𐑊 𐑅𐐻𐐲𐑉 𐐲𐐹 𐑄 𐐣𐐨𐐼𐑆 𐐰𐑀𐐯𐑌𐑅𐐻 𐑄𐐯𐑋, 𐐸𐐶𐐮𐐽 𐑇𐐰𐑊 𐑌𐐱𐐻 𐑉𐐨𐑀𐐪𐑉𐐼 𐑅𐐮𐑊𐑂𐐲𐑉 𐐰𐑌𐐼 𐑀𐐬𐑊𐐼, 𐑌𐐫𐑉 𐑇𐐰𐑊 𐑄𐐩 𐐼𐐨𐑊𐐴𐐻 𐐮𐑌 𐐮𐐻. 𐐜𐐯𐑉 𐐺𐐬𐑆 𐑇𐐰𐑊 𐐫𐑊𐑅𐐬 𐐼𐐰𐑇 𐑄 𐐷𐐲𐑍 𐑋𐐯𐑌 𐐻𐐭 𐐹𐐨𐑅𐐯𐑆; 𐐰𐑌𐐼 𐑄𐐩 𐑇𐐰𐑊 𐐸𐐰𐑂 𐑌𐐬 𐐹𐐮𐐻𐐨 𐐱𐑌 𐑄 𐑁𐑉𐐭𐐻 𐐲𐑂 𐑄 𐐶𐐭𐑋; 𐑄𐐯𐑉 𐐴𐑆 𐑇𐐰𐑊 𐑌𐐱𐐻 𐑅𐐹𐐯𐑉 𐐽𐐮𐑊𐐼𐑉𐐯𐑌.

3. 𐐈𐑌𐐼 𐐒𐐰𐐺𐐮𐑊𐐲𐑌, 𐑄 𐑀𐑊𐐬𐑉𐐨 𐐲𐑂 𐐿𐐮𐑍𐐼𐐲𐑋𐑆, 𐑄 𐐺𐐧𐐻𐐨 𐐲𐑂 𐑄 𐐗𐐰𐑊𐐼𐐨'𐑆 𐐯𐐿𐑅𐐯𐑊𐐯𐑌𐑅𐐨, 𐑇𐐰𐑊 𐐺𐐨 𐐰𐑆 𐐸𐐶𐐯𐑌 𐐘𐐱𐐼 𐐬𐑂𐐲𐑉𐑃𐑉𐐭 𐐝𐐱𐐼𐐲𐑋 𐐰𐑌𐐼 𐐘𐐬𐑋𐐱𐑉𐐲. 𐐆𐐻 𐑇𐐰𐑊 𐑌𐐯𐑂𐐲𐑉 𐐺𐐨 𐐮𐑌𐐸𐐰𐐺𐐮𐐻𐐯𐐼, 𐑌𐐨𐑄𐐲𐑉 𐑇𐐰𐑊 𐐮𐐻 𐐺𐐨 𐐼𐐶𐐯𐑊𐐻 𐐮𐑌 𐑁𐑉𐐱𐑋 𐑀𐐯𐑌𐐲𐑉𐐩𐑇𐐲𐑌 𐐻𐐭 𐑀𐐯𐑌𐐲𐑉𐐩𐑇𐐲𐑌: 𐑌𐐨𐑄𐐲𐑉 𐑇𐐰𐑊 𐑄 𐐂𐑉𐐩𐐺𐐨𐐲𐑌 𐐹𐐮𐐽 𐐻𐐯𐑌𐐻 𐑄𐐯𐑉; 𐑌𐐨𐑄𐐲𐑉 𐑇𐐰𐑊 𐑄 𐑇𐐯𐐹𐐲𐑉𐐼𐑆 𐑋𐐩𐐿 𐑄𐐯𐑉 𐑁𐐬𐑊𐐼 𐑄𐐯𐑉; 𐐺𐐲𐐻 𐐶𐐴𐑊𐐼 𐐺𐐨𐑅𐐻𐑅 𐐲𐑂 𐑄 𐐼𐐯𐑆𐐲𐑉𐐻 𐑇𐐰𐑊 𐑊𐐴 𐑄𐐯𐑉; 𐐰𐑌𐐼 𐑄𐐯𐑉 𐐸𐐵𐑆𐐯𐑆 𐑇𐐰𐑊 𐐺𐐨 𐑁𐐳𐑊 𐐲𐑂 𐐼𐐬𐑊𐑁𐐳𐑊 𐐿𐑉𐐨𐐽𐐲𐑉𐑆; 𐐰𐑌𐐼 𐐵𐑊𐑆 𐑇𐐰𐑊 𐐼𐐶𐐯𐑊 𐑄𐐯𐑉, 𐐰𐑌𐐼 𐑅𐐩𐐻𐐲𐑉𐑆 𐑇𐐰𐑊 𐐼𐐰𐑌𐑅 𐑄𐐯𐑉. 𐐈𐑌𐐼 𐑄 𐐶𐐴𐑊𐐼 𐐺𐐨𐑅𐐻𐑅 𐐲𐑂 𐑄 𐐴𐑊𐐲𐑌𐐼𐑆 𐑇𐐰𐑊 𐐿𐑉𐐴

𐐮𐑌 𐑄𐐩𐑉 𐐼𐐯𐑅𐐬𐑊𐐩𐐻 𐐸𐐵𐑆𐐯𐑆, 𐐰𐑌𐐼 𐐼𐑉𐐰𐑀𐐲𐑌𐑆 𐐮𐑌 𐑄𐐩𐑉 𐐹𐑊𐐯𐑆𐐲𐑌𐐻 𐐹𐐰𐑊𐐯𐑅𐐯𐑆: 𐐰𐑌𐐼 𐐸𐐲𐑉 𐐻𐐴𐑋 𐐮𐑆 𐑌𐐨𐑉 𐐻𐐭 𐐿𐐲𐑋, 𐐰𐑌𐐼 𐐸𐐲𐑉 𐐼𐐩 𐑇𐐰𐑊 𐑌𐐱𐐻 𐐺 𐐹𐑉𐐬𐑊𐐱𐑍𐐼. 𐐙𐐫𐑉 𐐌 𐐶𐐮𐑊 𐐼𐐨𐑅𐐻𐑉𐐦 𐐸𐐲𐑉 𐑅𐐹𐐨𐐼𐐮𐑊𐐮; 𐐷𐐩, 𐑁𐐫𐑉 𐐌 𐐶𐐮𐑊 𐐺 𐑋𐐲𐑉𐑅𐐮𐑁𐐳𐑊 𐐲𐑌𐐻𐐭 𐑋𐐴 𐐹𐐨𐐹𐑊; 𐐺𐐲𐐻 𐑄 𐐶𐐮𐐿𐐯𐐼 𐑇𐐰𐑊 𐐹𐐯𐑉𐐮𐑇.

4. 𐐙𐐫𐑉 𐑄 𐐢𐐫𐑉𐐼 𐐶𐐮𐑊 𐐸𐐰𐑂 𐑋𐐲𐑉𐑅𐐮 𐐱𐑌 𐐖𐐩𐐿𐐲𐐺, 𐐰𐑌𐐼 𐐶𐐮𐑊 𐐷𐐯𐐻 𐐽𐐭𐑆 𐐆𐑆𐑉𐐩𐐯𐑊, 𐐰𐑌𐐼 𐑅𐐯𐐻 𐑄𐐯𐑋 𐐮𐑌 𐑄𐐩𐑉 𐐬𐑌 𐑊𐐰𐑌𐐼: 𐐰𐑌𐐼 𐑄 𐑅𐐻𐑉𐐩𐑌𐐾𐐯𐑉𐑆 𐑇𐐰𐑊 𐐺 𐐾𐐦𐑌𐐼 𐐶𐐮𐑄 𐑄𐐯𐑋, 𐐰𐑌𐐼 𐑄𐐩 𐑇𐐰𐑊 𐐿𐑊𐐨𐑂 𐐻𐐭 𐑄 𐐸𐐵𐑅 𐐱𐑂 𐐖𐐩𐐿𐐲𐐺. 𐐈𐑌𐐼 𐑄 𐐹𐐨𐐹𐑊 𐑇𐐰𐑊 𐐻𐐩𐐿 𐑄𐐯𐑋, 𐐰𐑌𐐼 𐐺𐑉𐐮𐑍 𐑄𐐯𐑋 𐐻𐐭 𐑄𐐩𐑉 𐐹𐑊𐐩𐑅; 𐐷𐐩, 𐑁𐑉𐐱𐑋 𐑁𐐪𐑉 𐐲𐑌𐐻𐐭 𐑄 𐐯𐑌𐐼𐑆 𐐱𐑂 𐑄 𐐲𐑉𐑃: 𐐰𐑌𐐼 𐑄𐐩 𐑇𐐰𐑊 𐑉𐐨𐐻𐐲𐑉𐑌 𐐻𐐭 𐑄𐐩𐑉 𐑊𐐰𐑌𐐼𐑆 𐐱𐑂 𐐹𐑉𐐱𐑋𐐮𐑅. 𐐈𐑌𐐼 𐑄 𐐸𐐵𐑅 𐐱𐑂 𐐆𐑆𐑉𐐩𐐯𐑊 𐑇𐐰𐑊 𐐹𐐲𐑅𐐯𐑅 𐑄𐐯𐑋, 𐐰𐑌𐐼 𐑄 𐑊𐐰𐑌𐐼 𐐱𐑂 𐑄 𐐢𐐫𐑉𐐼 𐑇𐐰𐑊 𐐺 𐑁𐐫𐑉 𐑅𐐲𐑉𐑂𐐲𐑌𐐻𐑅 𐐰𐑌𐐼 𐐸𐐰𐑌𐐼𐑋𐐩𐐼𐑆; 𐐰𐑌𐐼 𐑄𐐩 𐑇𐐰𐑊 𐐻𐐩𐐿 𐑄𐐯𐑋 𐐿𐐰𐐹𐐻𐐮𐑂𐑆 𐐲𐑌𐐻𐐭 𐐸𐐭𐑋 𐑄𐐩 𐐶𐐲𐑉 𐐿𐐰𐐹𐐻𐐮𐑂𐑆; 𐐰𐑌𐐼 𐑄𐐩 𐑇𐐰𐑊 𐑉𐐭𐑊 𐐬𐑂𐐯𐑉 𐑄𐐩𐑉 𐐲𐐹𐑉𐐯𐑅𐐲𐑉𐑆. 𐐈𐑌𐐼 𐐮𐐻 𐑇𐐰𐑊 𐐿𐐲𐑋 𐐻𐐭 𐐹𐐰𐑅 𐐮𐑌 𐑄𐐰𐐻 𐐼𐐩 𐑄𐐰𐐻 𐑄 𐐢𐐫𐑉𐐼 𐑇𐐰𐑊 𐑀𐐮𐑂 𐑄 𐑉𐐯𐑅𐐻, 𐑁𐑉𐐱𐑋 𐑄𐐴 𐑅𐐱𐑉𐐬, 𐐰𐑌𐐼 𐑁𐑉𐐱𐑋 𐑄𐐴 𐑁𐐨𐑉, 𐐰𐑌𐐼 𐑁𐑉𐐱𐑋 𐑄 𐐸𐐪𐑉𐐼 𐐺𐐱𐑌𐐼𐐯𐐾 𐐸𐐶𐐩𐑉𐐮𐑌 𐑄𐐵 𐐶𐐱𐑅𐐻 𐑋𐐩𐐼 𐐻𐐭 𐑅𐐲𐑉𐑂.

5. 𐐈𐑌𐐼 𐐮𐐻 𐑇𐐰𐑊 𐐿𐐲𐑋 𐐻𐐭 𐐹𐐰𐑅 𐐮𐑌 𐑄𐐰𐐻 𐐼𐐩, 𐑄𐐰𐐻 𐑄𐐵 𐑇𐐰𐑊𐐻 𐐻𐐩𐐿 𐐲𐐹 𐑄𐐮𐑅 𐐹𐑉𐐱𐑂𐐲𐑉𐐺 𐐰𐑀𐐯𐑌𐑅𐐻 𐑄 𐐿𐐮𐑍 𐐱𐑂 𐐒𐐰𐐺𐐮𐑊𐐲𐑌, 𐐰𐑌𐐼 𐑅𐐩, 𐐸𐐵 𐐸𐐰𐑃 𐑄 𐐲𐐹𐑉𐐯𐑅𐐲𐑉 𐑅𐐨𐑅𐐻, 𐑄 𐑀𐐬𐑊𐐼𐑌 𐑅𐐮𐐻𐐮 𐑅𐐨𐑅𐐻! 𐐜 𐐢𐐫𐑉𐐼 𐐸𐐰𐑃 𐐺𐑉𐐬𐐿𐑌 𐑄 𐑅𐐻𐐰𐑁 𐐱𐑂 𐑄 𐐶𐐮𐐿𐐯𐐼, 𐑄 𐑅𐐯𐐹𐐻𐐲𐑉 𐐱𐑂 𐑄 𐑉𐐭𐑊𐐲𐑉𐑆. 𐐐𐐨 𐐸𐐭 𐑅𐑋𐐬𐐻 𐑄 𐐹𐐨𐐹𐑊 𐐮𐑌 𐑉𐐰𐑃 𐐶𐐮𐑄 𐐲 𐐿𐐲𐑌𐐻𐐮𐑌𐐷𐐭𐐲𐑊 𐑅𐐻𐑉𐐬𐐿, 𐐸𐐨 𐑄𐐰𐐻 𐑉𐐭𐑊𐐯𐐼 𐑄 𐑌𐐩𐑇𐐲𐑌𐑆 𐐮𐑌 𐐰𐑍𐑀𐐲𐑉, 𐐮𐑆 𐐹𐐲𐑉𐑅𐐨𐐿𐐷𐐭𐐻𐐯𐐼, 𐐰𐑌𐐼 𐑌𐐲𐑌 𐐸𐐮𐑌𐐼𐐲𐑉𐐯𐑃. 𐐜 𐐸𐐬𐑊 𐐲𐑉𐑃 𐐮𐑆 𐐰𐐻 𐑉𐐯𐑅𐐻, 𐐰𐑌𐐼 𐐮𐑆 𐐿𐐶𐐴𐐯𐐻: 𐑄𐐩 𐐺𐑉𐐩𐐿 𐑁𐐫𐑉𐑃 𐐮𐑌𐐻𐐭 𐑅𐐮𐑍𐐮𐑍. 𐐏𐐩, 𐑄 𐑁𐐲𐑉-𐐻𐑉𐐨𐑆 𐑉𐐨𐐾𐐦𐑅 𐐰𐐻 𐑄, 𐐰𐑌𐐼 𐐫𐑊𐑅𐐬 𐑄 𐑅𐐨𐐼𐐲𐑉𐑆 𐐱𐑂 𐐢𐐯𐐺𐐲𐑌𐐲𐑌, 𐑅𐐩𐐮𐑍, 𐑅𐐮𐑌𐑅 𐑄𐐵 𐐪𐑉𐐻 𐑊𐐩𐐼 𐐼𐐵𐑌, 𐑌𐐬 𐑁𐐯𐑊𐐲𐑉 𐐮𐑆 𐐿𐐲𐑋 𐐲𐐹 𐐰𐑀𐐯𐑌𐑅𐐻 𐐲𐑅. 𐐐𐐯𐑊 𐑁𐑉𐐱𐑋 𐐺𐐨𐑌𐐨𐑃 𐐮𐑆 𐑋𐐭𐑂𐐼 𐑁𐐫𐑉 𐑄 𐐻𐐭 𐑋𐐨𐐻 𐑄 𐐰𐐻 𐑄𐐴 𐐿𐐲𐑋𐐮𐑍: 𐐮𐐻 𐑅𐐻𐐲𐑉𐐯𐑃 𐐲𐐹 𐑄 𐐼𐐯𐐼 𐑁𐐫𐑉 𐑄, 𐐨𐑂𐑌 𐐫𐑊 𐑄 𐐽𐐨𐑁 𐐶𐐲𐑌𐑆 𐐱𐑂 𐑄 𐐲𐑉𐑃: 𐐮𐐻 𐐸𐐰𐑃 𐑉𐐩𐑆𐐼 𐐲𐐹 𐑁𐑉𐐱𐑋 𐑄𐐩𐑉 𐑃𐑉𐐬𐑌𐑆 𐐫𐑊 𐑄 𐐿𐐮𐑍𐑆 𐐱𐑂 𐑄 𐑌𐐩𐑇𐐲𐑌𐑆. 𐐃𐑊 𐑄𐐩 𐑇𐐰𐑊 𐑅𐐹𐐨𐐿 𐐰𐑌𐐼 𐑅𐐩 𐐲𐑌𐐻𐐭 𐑄, 𐐂𐑉𐐻 𐑄𐐵 𐐫𐑊𐑅𐐬 𐐺𐐨𐐿𐐲𐑋 𐐶𐐨𐐿 𐐰𐑆 𐐶𐐨? 𐐂𐑉𐐻 𐑄𐐵 𐐺𐐨𐐿𐐲𐑋 𐑊𐐴𐐿 𐐲𐑌𐐻𐐭 𐐲𐑅? 𐐜𐐴 𐐹𐐱𐑋𐐹 𐐮𐑆 𐐺𐑉𐐫𐐻 𐐼𐐵𐑌 𐐻𐐭 𐑄 𐑀𐑉𐐩𐑂; 𐑄 𐑌𐐦𐑆 𐐱𐑂 𐑄𐐴 𐑂𐐴𐐲𐑊𐑆 𐐮𐑆 𐑌𐐱𐐻 𐐸𐐲𐑉𐐼: 𐑄 𐐶𐐲𐑉𐑋 𐐮𐑆 𐑅𐐹𐑉𐐯𐐼 𐐲𐑌𐐼𐐲𐑉 𐑄, 𐐰𐑌𐐼 𐑄 𐐶𐐲𐑉𐑋𐑆 𐐿𐐲𐑂𐐲𐑉 𐑄. 𐐐𐐵 𐐪𐑉𐐻 𐑄𐐵 𐑁𐐫𐑊𐑌 𐑁𐑉𐐱𐑋 𐐸𐐯𐑂𐑌, 𐐄 𐐢𐐷𐐭𐑅𐐮𐑁𐐲𐑉, 𐑅𐐲𐑌 𐐱𐑂 𐑄 𐑋𐐫𐑉𐑌𐐮𐑍! 𐐂𐑉𐐻 𐑄𐐵 𐐿𐐲𐐻 𐐼𐐵𐑌 𐐻𐐭 𐑄 𐑀𐑉𐐵𐑌𐐼, 𐐸𐐶𐐮𐐽 𐐼𐐮𐐼 𐐶𐐨𐐿𐑌 𐑄 𐑌𐐩𐑇𐐲𐑌𐑆! 𐐙𐐫𐑉 𐑄𐐵 𐐸𐐰𐑅𐐻 𐑅𐐯𐐼 𐐮𐑌 𐑄𐐴 𐐸𐐪𐑉𐐻, 𐐌 𐐶𐐮𐑊 𐐰𐑅𐐯𐑌𐐼 𐐮𐑌𐐻𐐭 𐐸𐐯𐑂𐑌, 𐐌 𐐶𐐮𐑊 𐐯𐑀𐑆𐐫𐑊𐐻 𐑋𐐴 𐑃𐑉𐐬𐑌 𐐰𐐺𐐲𐑂 𐑄 𐑅𐐻𐐪𐑉𐑆 𐐱𐑂 𐐘𐐱𐐼: 𐐌 𐐶𐐮𐑊 𐑅𐐮𐐻 𐐫𐑊𐑅𐐬 𐐲𐐹𐐱𐑌 𐑄 𐑋𐐵𐑌𐐻 𐐱𐑂 𐑄 𐐿𐐱𐑌𐑀𐑉𐐨𐑀𐐩𐑇𐐲𐑌, 𐐮𐑌 𐑄 𐑅𐐴𐐼𐑆 𐐱𐑂 𐑄 𐑌𐐫𐑉𐑃; 𐐌 𐐶𐐮𐑊 𐐰𐑅𐐯𐑌𐐼 𐐰𐐺𐐲𐑂 𐑄 𐐸𐐴𐐻𐑅 𐐱𐑂 𐑄 𐐿𐑊𐐵𐐼𐑆: 𐐌 𐐶𐐮𐑊 𐐺 𐑊𐐴𐐿 𐑄 𐐣𐐬𐑅𐐻 𐐐𐐴. 𐐏𐐯𐐻 𐑄𐐵 𐑇𐐰𐑊𐐻 𐐺 𐐺𐑉𐐫𐐻 𐐼𐐵𐑌 𐐻𐐭 𐐸𐐯𐑊, 𐐻𐐭 𐑄 𐑅𐐴𐐼𐑆 𐐱𐑂 𐑄 𐐹𐐮𐐻. 𐐜𐐩 𐑄𐐰𐐻 𐑅𐐨 𐑄 𐑇𐐰𐑊 𐑌𐐰𐑉𐐬𐑊𐐮 𐑊𐐳𐐿 𐐲𐐹𐐱𐑌 𐑄, 𐐰𐑌𐐼 𐑇𐐰𐑊 𐐿𐐱𐑌𐑅𐐮𐐼𐐲𐑉 𐑄, 𐐰𐑌𐐼 𐑇𐐰𐑊 𐑅𐐩, 𐐆𐑆 𐑄𐐮𐑅 𐑄 𐑋𐐰𐑌 𐑄𐐰𐐻 𐑋𐐩𐐼 𐑄 𐐲𐑉𐑃 𐐻𐐭 𐐻𐑉𐐯𐑋𐐺𐑊, 𐑄𐐰𐐻 𐐼𐐮𐐼 𐑇𐐩𐐿 𐐿𐐮𐑍𐐼𐐲𐑋𐑆, 𐐰𐑌𐐼 𐑋𐐩𐐼 𐑄 𐐶𐐲𐑉𐑊𐐼 𐐰𐑆 𐐲 𐐶𐐮𐑊𐐼𐐲𐑉𐑌𐐯𐑅, 𐐰𐑌𐐼 𐐼𐐨𐑅𐐻𐑉𐐦𐐼 𐑄 𐑅𐐮𐐻𐐮𐑆 𐑄𐐩𐑉𐐱𐑂, 𐐰𐑌𐐼 𐐬𐐹𐐯𐑌𐐼 𐑌𐐱𐐻 𐑄 𐐸𐐵𐑅 𐐱𐑂 𐐸𐐮𐑆 𐐹𐑉𐐮𐑆𐐲𐑌𐐯𐑉𐑆? 𐐃𐑊 𐑄 𐐿𐐮𐑍𐑆 𐐱𐑂 𐑄 𐑌𐐩𐑇𐐲𐑌𐑆, 𐐷𐐩, 𐐫𐑊 𐐱𐑂 𐑄𐐯𐑋, 𐑊𐐴 𐐮𐑌 𐑀𐑊𐐬𐑉𐐮, 𐐯𐑂𐐯𐑉𐐮 𐐶𐐲𐑌 𐐱𐑂 𐑄𐐯𐑋 𐐮𐑌 𐐸𐐮𐑆 𐐬𐑌 𐐸𐐵𐑅. 𐐒𐐲𐐻 𐑄𐐵 𐐪𐑉𐐻 𐐿𐐰𐑅𐐻 𐐵𐐻 𐐱𐑂 𐑄𐐴 𐑀𐑉𐐩𐑂 𐑊𐐴𐐿 𐐰𐑌 𐐰𐐺𐐱𐑋𐐮𐑌𐐰𐐺𐑊 𐐺𐑉𐐰𐑌𐐽, 𐐰𐑌𐐼 𐑄 𐑉𐐯𐑋𐑌𐐲𐑌𐐻 𐐱𐑂 𐑄𐐬𐑆 𐑄𐐰𐐻 𐐪𐑉 𐑅𐑊𐐩𐑌, 𐑃𐑉𐐲𐑅𐐻 𐑃𐑉𐐭 𐐶𐐮𐑄 𐐲 𐑅𐐬𐑉𐐼, 𐑄𐐰𐐻 𐑀𐐬 𐐼𐐵𐑌 𐐻𐐭 𐑄 𐑅𐐻𐐬𐑌𐑆 𐐱𐑂 𐑄 𐐹𐐮𐐻; 𐐰𐑆 𐐲 𐐿𐐪𐑉𐐿𐐲𐑅 𐐻𐑉𐐱𐐼𐑌 𐐲𐑌𐐼𐐲𐑉 𐑁𐐨𐐻. 𐐜𐐵 𐑇𐐰𐑊𐐻 𐑌𐐱𐐻 𐐺 𐐾𐐦𐑌𐐼 𐐶𐐮𐑄 𐑄𐐯𐑋 𐐮𐑌 𐐺𐐯𐑉𐐮𐐲𐑊, 𐐺𐐨𐐿𐐫𐑆 𐑄𐐵 𐐸𐐰𐑅𐐻 𐐼𐐨𐑅𐐻𐑉𐐦𐐼 𐑄𐐴 𐑊𐐰𐑌𐐼, 𐐰𐑌𐐼 𐑅𐑊𐐩𐑌 𐑄𐐴 𐐹𐐨𐐹𐑊: 𐑄 𐑅𐐨𐐼 𐐱𐑂 𐐨𐑂𐑊-𐐼𐐭𐑉𐑆 𐑇𐐰𐑊 𐑌𐐯𐑂𐐲𐑉 𐐺 𐑉𐐨𐑌𐐵𐑌𐐼. 𐐑𐑉𐐨𐐹𐐩𐑉 𐑅𐑊𐐫𐐻𐐲𐑉 𐑁𐐫𐑉 𐐸𐐮𐑆 𐐽𐐮𐑊𐐼𐑉𐐯𐑌 𐑁𐐫𐑉 𐑄 𐐮𐑌𐐮𐐿𐐶𐐮𐐻𐐮𐑆 𐐱𐑂 𐑄𐐩𐑉 𐑁𐐪𐑄𐐲𐑉𐑆: 𐑄𐐰𐐻 𐑄𐐩 𐐼𐐭 𐑌𐐱𐐻 𐑉𐐴𐑆, 𐑌𐐫𐑉 𐐹𐐲𐑅𐐯𐑅 𐑄 𐑊𐐰𐑌𐐼, 𐑌𐐫𐑉 𐑁𐐮𐑊 𐑄 𐑁𐐩𐑅 𐐱𐑂 𐑄 𐐶𐐲𐑉𐑊𐐼 𐐶𐐮𐑄 𐑅𐐮𐐻𐐮𐑆. 𐐙𐐫𐑉 𐐌 𐐶𐐮𐑊 𐑉𐐴𐑆 𐐲𐐹 𐐰𐑀𐐯𐑌𐑅𐐻 𐑄𐐯𐑋, 𐑅𐐯𐑃 𐑄 𐐢𐐫𐑉𐐼 𐐱𐑂 𐐐𐐬𐑅𐐻𐑅, 𐐰𐑌𐐼 𐐿𐐲𐐻 𐐱𐑁 𐑁𐑉𐐱𐑋 𐐒𐐰𐐺𐐮𐑊𐐲𐑌 𐑄 𐑌𐐩𐑋, 𐐰𐑌𐐼 𐑉𐐯𐑋𐑌𐐲𐑌𐐻, 𐐰𐑌𐐼 𐑅𐐲𐑌, 𐐰𐑌𐐼 𐑌𐐯𐑁𐐷𐐭, 𐑅𐐯𐑃 𐑄 𐐢𐐫𐑉𐐼. 𐐌 𐐶𐐮𐑊 𐐫𐑊𐑅𐐬 𐑋𐐩𐐿 𐐮𐐻 𐐲 𐐹𐐲𐑆𐐯𐑇𐐲𐑌

𐑁𐐫𐑉 𐑄 𐐺𐐮𐐻𐐲𐑉𐑌, 𐐰𐑌𐐼 𐐹𐐭𐑊𐑆 𐐱𐑂 𐐶𐐫𐐻𐐲𐑉: 𐐰𐑌𐐼 𐐌 𐐶𐐮𐑊 𐑅𐐶𐐨𐐹 𐐮𐐻 𐐶𐐮𐑄 𐑄 𐐺𐐨𐑆𐐲𐑋 𐐱𐑂 𐐼𐐨𐑅𐐻𐑉𐐲𐐿𐑇𐐲𐑌, 𐑅𐐯𐑃 𐑄 𐐢𐐫𐑉𐐼 𐐱𐑂 𐐐𐐬𐑅𐐻𐑅.

6. 𐐜 𐐢𐐫𐑉𐐼 𐐱𐑂 𐐐𐐬𐑅𐐻𐑅 𐐸𐐰𐑃 𐑅𐐶𐐫𐑉𐑌, 𐑅𐐩𐐮𐑍, 𐑇𐐳𐑉𐑊𐐨 𐐰𐑆 𐐌 𐐸𐐰𐑂 𐑃𐐫𐐻, 𐑅𐐬 𐑇𐐰𐑊 𐐮𐐻 𐐿𐐲𐑋 𐐻𐐭 𐐹𐐰𐑅; 𐐰𐑌𐐼 𐐰𐑆 𐐌 𐐸𐐰𐑂 𐐹𐐲𐑉𐐹𐐲𐑅𐐻, 𐑅𐐬 𐑇𐐰𐑊 𐐮𐐻 𐑅𐐻𐐰𐑌𐐼: 𐑄𐐰𐐻 𐐌 𐐶𐐮𐑊 𐐺𐑉𐐮𐑍 𐑄 𐐈𐑅𐐮𐑉𐐨𐐲𐑌 𐐮𐑌 𐑋𐐴 𐑊𐐰𐑌𐐼, 𐐰𐑌𐐼 𐐲𐐹𐐱𐑌 𐑋𐐴 𐑋𐐵𐑌𐐻𐐩𐑌𐑆 𐐻𐑉𐐯𐐼 𐐸𐐮𐑋 𐐲𐑌𐐼𐐲𐑉 𐑁𐐳𐐻; 𐑄𐐯𐑌 𐑇𐐰𐑊 𐐸𐐮𐑆 𐐷𐐬𐐿 𐐼𐐨𐐹𐐪𐑉𐐻 𐑁𐑉𐐱𐑋 𐐱𐑁 𐑄𐐯𐑋, 𐐰𐑌𐐼 𐐸𐐮𐑆 𐐺𐐲𐑉𐐼𐐲𐑌 𐐼𐐨𐐹𐐪𐑉𐐻 𐑁𐑉𐐱𐑋 𐐱𐑁 𐑄𐐩𐑉 𐑇𐐬𐑊𐐼𐐲𐑉𐑆. 𐐜𐐮𐑅 𐐮𐑆 𐑄 𐐹𐐲𐑉𐐹𐐲𐑅 𐑄𐐰𐐻 𐐮𐑆 𐐹𐐲𐑉𐐹𐐲𐑅𐐻 𐐲𐐹𐐱𐑌 𐑄 𐐸𐐬𐑊 𐐲𐑉𐑃: 𐐰𐑌𐐼 𐑄𐐮𐑅 𐐮𐑆 𐑄 𐐸𐐰𐑌𐐼 𐑄𐐰𐐻 𐐮𐑆 𐑅𐐻𐑉𐐯𐐽𐐻 𐐵𐐻 𐐲𐐹𐐱𐑌 𐐫𐑊 𐑌𐐩𐑇𐐲𐑌𐑆. 𐐙𐐫𐑉 𐑄 𐐢𐐫𐑉𐐼 𐐱𐑂 𐐐𐐬𐑅𐐻𐑅 𐐸𐐰𐑃 𐐹𐐲𐑉𐐹𐐲𐑅𐐻, 𐐰𐑌𐐼 𐐸𐐭 𐑇𐐰𐑊 𐐼𐐮𐑅𐐰𐑌𐐲𐑊? 𐐈𐑌𐐼 𐐸𐐮𐑆 𐐸𐐰𐑌𐐼 𐐮𐑆 𐑅𐐻𐑉𐐯𐐽𐐻 𐐵𐐻, 𐐰𐑌𐐼 𐐸𐐭 𐑇𐐰𐑊 𐐻𐐲𐑉𐑌 𐐮𐐻 𐐺𐐰𐐿? 𐐆𐑌 𐑄 𐐷𐐨𐑉 𐑄𐐰𐐻 𐐿𐐮𐑍 𐐁𐐸𐐰𐑆 𐐼𐐴𐐼 𐐶𐐱𐑆 𐑄𐐮𐑅 𐐺𐐲𐑉𐐼𐐲𐑌.

7. 𐐡𐐨𐐾𐐱𐐮𐑅 𐑌𐐱𐐻 𐑄𐐵, 𐐸𐐬𐑊 𐐑𐐰𐑊𐐯𐑅𐐻𐐴𐑌𐐲, 𐐺𐐨𐐿𐐫𐑆 𐑄 𐑉𐐱𐐼 𐐱𐑂 𐐸𐐮𐑋 𐑄𐐰𐐻 𐑅𐑋𐐬𐐻 𐑄𐐨 𐐮𐑆 𐐺𐑉𐐬𐐿𐐲𐑌: 𐑁𐐫𐑉 𐐵𐐻 𐐱𐑂 𐑄 𐑅𐐲𐑉𐐹𐐲𐑌𐐻𐑅 𐑉𐐭𐐻 𐑇𐐰𐑊 𐐿𐐲𐑋 𐑁𐐫𐑉𐑃 𐐩 𐐿𐐱𐐿𐐰𐐻𐑉𐐮𐑅, 𐐰𐑌𐐼 𐐸𐐮𐑆 𐑁𐑉𐐭𐐻 𐑇𐐰𐑊 𐐺𐐨 𐐩 𐑁𐐴𐐲𐑉𐐨 𐑁𐑊𐐴𐐮𐑍 𐑅𐐲𐑉𐐹𐐲𐑌𐐻, 𐐰𐑌𐐼 𐑄 𐑁𐐲𐑉𐑅𐐻 𐐺𐐫𐑉𐑌 𐐱𐑂 𐑄 𐐹𐐭𐑉 𐑇𐐰𐑊 𐑁𐐨𐐼, 𐐰𐑌𐐼 𐑄 𐑌𐐨𐐼𐐨 𐑇𐐰𐑊 𐑊𐐴 𐐼𐐵𐑌 𐐮𐑌 𐑅𐐩𐑁𐐻𐐨: 𐐰𐑌𐐼 𐐌 𐐶𐐮𐑊 𐐿𐐮𐑊 𐑄𐐴 𐑉𐐭𐐻 𐐶𐐮𐑄 𐑁𐐰𐑋𐐮𐑌, 𐐰𐑌𐐼 𐐸𐐨 𐑇𐐰𐑊 𐑅𐑊𐐩 𐑄𐐴 𐑉𐐯𐑋𐑌𐐲𐑌𐐻. 𐐐𐐵𐑊, 𐐄 𐑀𐐩𐐻; 𐐿𐑉𐐴, 𐐄 𐑅𐐮𐐻𐐨; 𐑄𐐵, 𐐸𐐬𐑊 𐐑𐐰𐑊𐐯𐑅𐐻𐐴𐑌𐐲, 𐐪𐑉𐐻 𐐼𐐮𐑆𐐱𐑊𐑂𐐼: 𐑁𐐫𐑉 𐑄𐐩𐑉 𐑇𐐰𐑊 𐐿𐐲𐑋 𐑁𐑉𐐱𐑋 𐑄 𐑌𐐫𐑉𐑃 𐐩 𐑅𐑋𐐬𐐿, 𐐰𐑌𐐼 𐑌𐐲𐑌 𐑇𐐰𐑊 𐐺𐐨 𐐩𐑊𐐬𐑌 𐐮𐑌 𐐸𐐮𐑆 𐐰𐐹𐐱𐐮𐑌𐐻𐐯𐐼 𐐻𐐴𐑋𐑆. 𐐐𐐶𐐱𐐻 𐑇𐐰𐑊 𐑄𐐯𐑌 𐐰𐑌𐑅𐐲𐑉 𐑄 𐑋𐐯𐑅𐐯𐑌𐐾𐐲𐑉𐑆 𐐱𐑂 𐑄 𐑌𐐩𐑇𐐲𐑌𐑆? 𐐜𐐰𐐻 𐑄 𐐢𐐫𐑉𐐼 𐐸𐐰𐑃 𐑁𐐵𐑌𐐼𐐯𐐼 𐐞𐐴𐐲𐑌, 𐐰𐑌𐐼 𐑄 𐐹𐐭𐑉 𐐱𐑂 𐐸𐐮𐑆 𐐹𐐨𐐹𐑊 𐑇𐐰𐑊 𐐻𐑉𐐲𐑅𐐻 𐐮𐑌 𐐮𐐻.

𐐕𐐰𐐹𐐻𐐲𐑉 XI.

1. 𐐤𐐵 𐐌, 𐐤𐐨𐑁𐐴, 𐐼𐐭 𐑅𐐹𐐨𐐿 𐑅𐐲𐑋𐐸𐐶𐐱𐐻 𐐿𐐱𐑌𐑅𐐲𐑉𐑌𐐮𐑍 𐑄 𐐶𐐲𐑉𐐼𐑆 𐐸𐐶𐐮𐐽 𐐌 𐐸𐐰𐑂 𐑉𐐮𐐻𐐲𐑌, 𐐸𐐶𐐮𐐽 𐐸𐐰𐑂 𐐺𐐮𐑌 𐑅𐐹𐐬𐐿𐐲𐑌 𐐺𐐴 𐑄 𐑋𐐵𐑃 𐐱𐑂 𐐌𐑆𐐩𐐲. 𐐙𐐫𐑉 𐐺𐐨𐐸𐐬𐑊𐐼 𐐌𐑆𐐩𐐲 𐑅𐐹𐐩𐐿 𐑋𐐯𐑌𐐨 𐑃𐐮𐑍𐑆 𐐸𐐶𐐮𐐽 𐐶𐐲𐑉 𐐸𐐪𐑉𐐼 𐑁𐐫𐑉 𐑋𐐯𐑌𐐨 𐐱𐑂 𐑋𐐴 𐐹𐐨𐐹𐑊 𐐻𐐭 𐐲𐑌𐐼𐐲𐑉𐑅𐐻𐐰𐑌𐐼; 𐑁𐐫𐑉 𐑄𐐩 𐑌𐐬 𐑌𐐱𐐻 𐐿𐐱𐑌𐑅𐐲𐑉𐑌𐐮𐑍 𐑄 𐑋𐐰𐑌𐐲𐑉 𐐱𐑂 𐐹𐑉𐐱𐑁𐐯𐑅𐐴𐐮𐑍 𐐲𐑋𐐲𐑍 𐑄 𐐖𐐭𐑆. 𐐙𐐫𐑉 𐐌, 𐐤𐐨𐑁𐐴, 𐐸𐐰𐑂 𐑌𐐱𐐻 𐐻𐐫𐐻 𐑄𐐯𐑋 𐑋𐐯𐑌𐐨 𐑃𐐮𐑍𐑆 𐐿𐐱𐑌𐑅𐐲𐑉𐑌𐐮𐑍 𐑄 𐑋𐐰𐑌𐐲𐑉 𐐱𐑂 𐑄 𐐖𐐭𐑆; 𐑁𐐫𐑉 𐑄𐐩𐑉 𐐶𐐲𐑉𐐿𐑅 𐐶𐐲𐑉 𐐶𐐲𐑉𐐿𐑅 𐐱𐑂 𐐼𐐪𐑉𐐿𐑌𐐯𐑅, 𐐰𐑌𐐼 𐑄𐐩𐑉 𐐼𐐭𐐮𐑍𐑆 𐐶𐐲𐑉 𐐼𐐭𐐮𐑍𐑆 𐐱𐑂 𐐰𐐺𐐱𐑋𐐮𐑌𐐩𐑇𐐲𐑌𐑆. 𐐐𐐶𐐯𐑉𐑁𐐫𐑉, 𐐌 𐑉𐐴𐐻 𐐲𐑌𐐻𐐭 𐑋𐐴 𐐹𐐨𐐹𐑊, 𐐲𐑌𐐻𐐭 𐐫𐑊 𐑄𐐬𐑆 𐑄𐐰𐐻 𐑇𐐰𐑊 𐑉𐐨𐑅𐐨𐑂 𐐸𐐨𐑉𐐰𐑁𐐻𐐲𐑉 𐑄𐐨𐑆 𐑃𐐮𐑍𐑆 𐐸𐐶𐐮𐐽 𐐌 𐑉𐐴𐐻, 𐑄𐐰𐐻 𐑄𐐩 𐑋𐐩 𐑌𐐬 𐑄 𐐾𐐲𐐾𐑋𐐯𐑌𐐻𐑅 𐐱𐑂 𐐘𐐱𐐼, 𐑄𐐰𐐻 𐑄𐐩 𐐿𐐲𐑋 𐐲𐐹𐐱𐑌 𐐫𐑊 𐑌𐐩𐑇𐐲𐑌𐑆, 𐐰𐐿𐐫𐑉𐐼𐐮𐑍 𐐻𐐭 𐑄 𐐶𐐲𐑉𐐼 𐐸𐐶𐐮𐐽 𐐸𐐨 𐐸𐐰𐑃 𐑅𐐹𐐬𐐿𐐲𐑌. 𐐐𐐶𐐯𐑉𐑁𐐫𐑉, 𐐸𐐪𐑉𐐿𐐲𐑌, 𐐄 𐑋𐐴 𐐹𐐨𐐹𐑊, 𐐸𐐶𐐮𐐽 𐐪𐑉 𐐱𐑂 𐑄 𐐸𐐵𐑅 𐐱𐑂 𐐆𐑆𐑉𐐩𐐯𐑊, 𐐰𐑌𐐼 𐑀𐐮𐑂 𐐨𐑉 𐐲𐑌𐐻𐐭 𐑋𐐴 𐐶𐐲𐑉𐐼𐑆: 𐑁𐐫𐑉 𐐺𐐨𐐿𐐫𐑆 𐑄 𐐶𐐲𐑉𐐼𐑆 𐐱𐑂 𐐌𐑆𐐩𐐲 𐐪𐑉 𐑌𐐱𐐻 𐐹𐑊𐐩𐑌 𐐲𐑌𐐻𐐭 𐐷𐐭, 𐑌𐐯𐑂𐐲𐑉𐑄𐐲𐑊𐐯𐑅 𐑄𐐩 𐐪𐑉 𐐹𐑊𐐩𐑌 𐐲𐑌𐐻𐐭 𐐫𐑊 𐑄𐐬𐑆 𐑄𐐰𐐻 𐐪𐑉 𐑁𐐮𐑊𐐼 𐐶𐐮𐑄 𐑄 𐑅𐐹𐐮𐑉𐐮𐐻 𐐱𐑂 𐐹𐑉𐐱𐑁𐐯𐑅𐐨. 𐐒𐐲𐐻 𐐌 𐑀𐐮𐑂 𐐲𐑌𐐻𐐭 𐐷𐐭 𐐩 𐐹𐑉𐐱𐑁𐐯𐑅𐐨, 𐐰𐐿𐐫𐑉𐐼𐐮𐑍 𐐻𐐭 𐑄 𐑅𐐹𐐮𐑉𐐮𐐻 𐐸𐐶𐐮𐐽 𐐮𐑆 𐐮𐑌 𐑋𐐨; 𐐸𐐶𐐯𐑉𐑁𐐫𐑉 𐐌 𐑇𐐰𐑊 𐐹𐑉𐐱𐑁𐐯𐑅𐐴 𐐰𐐿𐐫𐑉𐐼𐐮𐑍 𐐻𐐭 𐑄 𐐹𐑊𐐩𐑌𐑌𐐯𐑅 𐐸𐐶𐐮𐐽 𐐸𐐰𐑃 𐐺𐐮𐑌 𐐶𐐮𐑄 𐑋𐐨 𐑁𐑉𐐱𐑋 𐑄 𐐻𐐴𐑋 𐑄𐐰𐐻 𐐌 𐐿𐐩𐑋 𐐵𐐻 𐑁𐑉𐐱𐑋 𐐖𐐨𐑉𐐭𐑅𐐲𐑊𐐯𐑋 𐐶𐐮𐑄 𐑋𐐴 𐑁𐐪𐑄𐐲𐑉: 𐑁𐐫𐑉 𐐺𐐨𐐸𐐬𐑊𐐼 𐑋𐐴 𐑅𐐬𐑊 𐐼𐐨𐑊𐐴𐐻𐐯𐑃 𐐮𐑌 𐐹𐑊𐐩𐑌𐑌𐐯𐑅 𐐲𐑌𐐻𐐭 𐑋𐐴 𐐹𐐨𐐹𐑊, 𐑄𐐰𐐻 𐑄𐐩 𐑋𐐩 𐑊𐐲𐑉𐑌; 𐐷𐐩, 𐐰𐑌𐐼 𐑋𐐴 𐑅𐐬𐑊 𐐼𐐨𐑊𐐴𐐻𐐯𐑃 𐐮𐑌 𐑄 𐐶𐐲𐑉𐐼𐑆 𐐱𐑂 𐐌𐑆𐐩𐐲, 𐑁𐐫𐑉 𐐌 𐐿𐐩𐑋 𐐵𐐻 𐑁𐑉𐐱𐑋 𐐖𐐨𐑉𐐭𐑅𐐲𐑊𐐯𐑋, 𐐰𐑌𐐼 𐑋𐐴𐑌 𐐴𐑆 𐐸𐐰𐑃 𐐺𐐨𐐸𐐯𐑊𐐼 𐑄 𐑃𐐮𐑍𐑆 𐐱𐑂 𐑄 𐐖𐐭𐑆, 𐐰𐑌𐐼 𐐌 𐑌𐐬 𐑄𐐰𐐻 𐑄 𐐖𐐭𐑆 𐐼𐐭 𐐲𐑌𐐼𐐲𐑉𐑅𐐻𐐰𐑌𐐼 𐑄 𐑃𐐮𐑍𐑆 𐐱𐑂 𐑄 𐐹𐑉𐐱𐑁𐐯𐐻𐑅, 𐐰𐑌𐐼 𐑄𐐩𐑉 𐐮𐑆 𐑌𐐲𐑌 𐐲𐑄𐐲𐑉 𐐹𐐨𐐹𐑊 𐑄𐐰𐐻 𐐲𐑌𐐼𐐲𐑉𐑅𐐻𐐰𐑌𐐼 𐑄 𐑃𐐮𐑍𐑆 𐐸𐐶𐐮𐐽 𐐶𐐲𐑉 𐑅𐐹𐐬𐐿𐐲𐑌 𐐲𐑌𐐻𐐭 𐑄 𐐖𐐭𐑆, 𐑊𐐴𐐿 𐐲𐑌𐐻𐐭 𐑄𐐯𐑋, 𐑅𐐩𐑂 𐐮𐐻 𐐺𐐨 𐑄𐐰𐐻 𐑄𐐩 𐐪𐑉 𐐻𐐫𐐻 𐐰𐑁𐐻𐐲𐑉 𐑄 𐑋𐐰𐑌𐐲𐑉 𐐱𐑂 𐑄 𐑃𐐮𐑍𐑆 𐐱𐑂 𐑄 𐐖𐐭𐑆. 𐐒𐐲𐐻 𐐒𐐨𐐸𐐬𐑊𐐼 𐐌, 𐐤𐐨𐑁𐐴, 𐐸𐐰𐑂 𐑌𐐱𐐻 𐐻𐐫𐐻 𐑋𐐴 𐐽𐐮𐑊𐐼𐑉𐐯𐑌 𐐰𐑁𐐻𐐲𐑉 𐑄 𐑋𐐰𐑌𐐲𐑉 𐐱𐑂 𐑄 𐐖𐐭𐑆; 𐐺𐐲𐐻 𐐺𐐨𐐸𐐬𐑊𐐼, 𐐌, 𐐱𐑂 𐑋𐐴𐑅𐐯𐑊𐑁, 𐐸𐐰𐑂 𐐼𐐶𐐯𐑊𐐻 𐐰𐐻 𐐖𐐨𐑉𐐭𐑅𐐲𐑊𐐯𐑋, 𐐸𐐶𐐯𐑉𐑁𐐫𐑉 𐐌 𐑌𐐬 𐐿𐐱𐑌𐑅𐐲𐑉𐑌𐐮𐑍 𐑄 𐑉𐐨𐐾𐐲𐑌𐑆 𐑉𐐵𐑌𐐼

𐐲𐐺𐐵𐐻; 𐐰𐑌𐐼 𐐌 𐐸𐐰𐑂 𐑋𐐩𐐼 𐑋𐐯𐑌𐑇𐐲𐑌 𐐲𐑌𐐻𐐭 𐑋𐐴 𐐽𐐮𐑊𐐼𐑉𐐯𐑌 𐐿𐐱𐑌𐑅𐐲𐑉𐑌𐐮𐑍 𐑄 𐐾𐐲𐐾𐑋𐐯𐑌𐐻𐑅 𐐱𐑂 𐐘𐐱𐐼, 𐐸𐐶𐐮𐐽 𐐸𐐰𐑃 𐐿𐐲𐑋 𐐻𐐭 𐐹𐐰𐑅 𐐲𐑋𐐲𐑍 𐑄 𐐖𐐭𐑆, 𐐲𐑌𐐻𐐭 𐑋𐐴 𐐽𐐮𐑊𐐼𐑉𐐯𐑌, 𐐰𐐿𐐫𐑉𐐼𐐮𐑍 𐐻𐐭 𐐫𐑊 𐑄𐐰𐐻 𐐸𐐶𐐮𐐽 𐐌𐑆𐐩𐐲 𐐸𐐰𐑃 𐑅𐐹𐐬𐐿𐐲𐑌, 𐐰𐑌𐐼 𐐌 𐐼𐐭 𐑌𐐱𐐻 𐑉𐐴𐐻 𐑄𐐯𐑋.

2. 𐐒𐐲𐐻 𐐺𐐨𐐸𐐬𐑊𐐼, 𐐌 𐐹𐑉𐐬𐑅𐐨𐐼 𐐶𐐮𐑄 𐑋𐐴𐑌 𐐬𐑌 𐐹𐑉𐐱𐑁𐐯𐑅𐐨, 𐐰𐐿𐐫𐑉𐐼𐐮𐑍 𐐻𐐭 𐑋𐐴 𐐹𐑊𐐩𐑌𐑌𐐯𐑅; 𐐮𐑌 𐑄 𐐸𐐶𐐮𐐽 𐐌 𐑌𐐬 𐑄𐐰𐐻 𐑌𐐬 𐑋𐐰𐑌 𐐿𐐰𐑌 𐐲𐑉; 𐑌𐐯𐑂𐐲𐑉𐑄𐐲𐑊𐐯𐑅, 𐐮𐑌 𐑄 𐐼𐐩𐑆 𐑄𐐰𐐻 𐑄 𐐹𐑉𐐱𐑁𐐯𐑅𐐨𐑆 𐐱𐑂 𐐌𐑆𐐩𐐲 𐑇𐐰𐑊 𐐺𐐨 𐑁𐐳𐑊𐑁𐐮𐑊𐐼, 𐑋𐐯𐑌 𐑇𐐰𐑊 𐑌𐐬 𐐱𐑂 𐐰 𐑇𐐭𐑉𐐯𐐻𐐨, 𐐰𐐻 𐑄 𐐻𐐴𐑋𐑆 𐐸𐐶𐐯𐑌 𐑄𐐩 𐑇𐐰𐑊 𐐿𐐲𐑋 𐐻𐐭 𐐹𐐰𐑅; 𐐸𐐶𐐯𐑉𐑁𐐬𐑉, 𐑄𐐩 𐐪𐑉 𐐱𐑂 𐐶𐐲𐑉𐑃 𐐲𐑌𐐻𐐭 𐑄 𐐽𐐮𐑊𐐼𐑉𐐯𐑌 𐐱𐑂 𐑋𐐯𐑌, 𐐰𐑌𐐼 𐐸𐐨 𐑄𐐰𐐻 𐑅𐐲𐐹𐐬𐑆𐐯𐑃 𐑄𐐰𐐻 𐑄𐐩 𐐪𐑉 𐑌𐐱𐐻, 𐐲𐑌𐐻𐐭 𐑄𐐯𐑋 𐐶𐐮𐑊 𐐌 𐑅𐐹𐐨𐐿 𐐹𐐪𐑉𐐻𐐮𐐿𐐷𐐭𐑊𐐲𐑉𐑊𐐨, 𐐰𐑌𐐼 𐐿𐐱𐑌𐑁𐐴𐑌 𐑄 𐐶𐐲𐑉𐐼𐑆 𐐲𐑌𐐻𐐭 𐑋𐐴𐑌 𐐬𐑌 𐐹𐐨𐐹𐑊; 𐑁𐐫𐑉 𐐌 𐑌𐐬 𐑄𐐰𐐻 𐑄𐐩 𐑇𐐰𐑊 𐐺𐐨 𐐱𐑂 𐑀𐑉𐐩𐐻 𐐶𐐲𐑉𐑃 𐐲𐑌𐐻𐐭 𐑄𐐯𐑋 𐐮𐑌 𐑄 𐑊𐐰𐑅𐐻 𐐼𐐩𐑆: 𐑁𐐫𐑉 𐐮𐑌 𐑄𐐰𐐻 𐐼𐐩 𐑇𐐰𐑊 𐑄𐐩 𐐲𐑌𐐼𐐲𐑉𐑅𐐻𐐰𐑌𐐼 𐑄𐐯𐑋; 𐐸𐐶𐐯𐑉𐑁𐐬𐑉, 𐑁𐐫𐑉 𐑄𐐩𐑉 𐑀𐐳𐐼 𐐸𐐰𐑂 𐐌 𐑉𐐮𐐻𐐲𐑌 𐑄𐐯𐑋. 𐐈𐑌𐐼 𐐰𐑆 𐐶𐐲𐑌 𐐾𐐯𐑌𐐲𐑉𐐩𐑇𐐲𐑌 𐐸𐐰𐑃 𐐺𐐮𐑌 𐐼𐐯𐑅𐐻𐑉𐑎𐐼 𐐲𐑋𐐲𐑍 𐑄 𐐖𐐭𐑆 𐐺𐐨𐐿𐐫𐑆 𐐱𐑂 𐐮𐑌𐐮𐐿𐐶𐐮𐐻𐐨, 𐐨𐑂𐐲𐑌 𐑅𐐬 𐐸𐐰𐑂 𐑄𐐩 𐐺𐐮𐑌 𐐼𐐯𐑅𐐻𐑉𐑎𐐼 𐑁𐑉𐐱𐑋 𐐾𐐯𐑌𐐲𐑉𐐩𐑇𐐲𐑌 𐐻𐐭 𐐾𐐯𐑌𐐲𐑉𐐩𐑇𐐲𐑌, 𐐰𐐿𐐫𐑉𐐼𐐮𐑍 𐐻𐐭 𐑄𐐩𐑉 𐐮𐑌𐐮𐐿𐐶𐐮𐐻𐐨𐑆; 𐐰𐑌𐐼 𐑌𐐯𐑂𐐲𐑉 𐐸𐐰𐑃 𐐯𐑌𐐨 𐐱𐑂 𐑄𐐯𐑋 𐐺𐐮𐑌 𐐼𐐯𐑅𐐻𐑉𐑎𐐼, 𐑅𐐩𐑂 𐐮𐐻 𐐶𐐲𐑉 𐑁𐐬𐑉𐐻𐐬𐑊𐐼 𐑄𐐯𐑋 𐐺𐐴 𐑄 𐐹𐑉𐐱𐑁𐐯𐐻𐑅 𐐱𐑂 𐑄 𐐢𐐫𐑉𐐼. 𐐐𐐶𐐯𐑉𐑁𐐬𐑉, 𐐮𐐻 𐐸𐐰𐑃 𐐺𐐮𐑌 𐐻𐐬𐑊𐐼 𐑄𐐯𐑋 𐐿𐐱𐑌𐑅𐐲𐑉𐑌𐐮𐑍 𐑄 𐐼𐐯𐑅𐐻𐑉𐐲𐐿𐑇𐐲𐑌 𐐸𐐶𐐮𐐽 𐑇𐐳𐐼 𐐿𐐲𐑋 𐐲𐐹𐐱𐑌 𐑄𐐯𐑋, 𐐮𐑋𐐨𐐼𐐨𐐲𐐻𐑊𐐨 𐐰𐑁𐐻𐐲𐑉 𐑋𐐴 𐑁𐐪𐑄𐐲𐑉 𐑊𐐯𐑁𐐻 𐐖𐐲𐑉𐐭𐑅𐐲𐑊𐐯𐑋; 𐑌𐐯𐑂𐐲𐑉𐑄𐐲𐑊𐐯𐑅, 𐑄𐐩 𐐸𐐪𐑉𐐼𐐲𐑌𐐼 𐑄𐐩𐑉 𐐸𐐪𐑉𐐻𐑅; 𐐰𐑌𐐼 𐐰𐐿𐐫𐑉𐐼𐐮𐑍 𐐻𐐭 𐑋𐐴 𐐹𐑉𐐱𐑁𐐯𐑅𐐨, 𐑄𐐩 𐐸𐐰𐑂 𐐺𐐮𐑌 𐐼𐐯𐑅𐐻𐑉𐑎𐐼, 𐑅𐐩𐑂 𐐮𐐻 𐐺𐐨 𐑄𐐬𐑆 𐐸𐐶𐐮𐐽 𐐪𐑉 𐐿𐐰𐑉𐐨𐐼 𐐲𐐶𐐩 𐐿𐐰𐐹𐐻𐐮𐑂 𐐮𐑌𐐻𐐭 𐐒𐐰𐐺𐐮𐑊𐐱𐑌. 𐐈𐑌𐐼 𐑌𐐵 𐑄𐐮𐑅 𐐌 𐑅𐐹𐐨𐐿 𐐺𐐨𐐿𐐫𐑆 𐐱𐑂 𐑄 𐑅𐐹𐐮𐑉𐐮𐐻 𐐸𐐶𐐮𐐽 𐐮𐑆 𐐮𐑌 𐑋𐐨. 𐐈𐑌𐐼 𐑌𐐱𐐻𐐶𐐮𐑄𐑅𐐻𐐰𐑌𐐼𐐮𐑍 𐑄𐐩 𐐸𐐰𐑂 𐐺𐐮𐑌 𐐿𐐰𐑉𐐨𐐼 𐐲𐐶𐐩, 𐑄𐐩 𐑇𐐰𐑊 𐑉𐐨𐐻𐐲𐑉𐑌 𐐲𐑀𐐯𐑌, 𐐰𐑌𐐼 𐐹𐐱𐑆𐐯𐑅 𐑄 𐑊𐐰𐑌𐐼 𐐱𐑂 𐐖𐐲𐑉𐐭𐑅𐐲𐑊𐐯𐑋; 𐐸𐐶𐐯𐑉𐑁𐐬𐑉, 𐑄𐐩 𐑇𐐰𐑊 𐐺𐐨 𐑉𐐨𐑅𐐻𐐬𐑉𐐼 𐐲𐑀𐐯𐑌 𐐻𐐭 𐑄 𐑊𐐰𐑌𐐼 𐐱𐑂 𐑄𐐩𐑉 𐐮𐑌𐐸𐐯𐑉𐐮𐐻𐐰𐑌𐑅. 𐐒𐐲𐐻, 𐐺𐐨𐐸𐐬𐑊𐐼, 𐑄𐐩 𐑇𐐰𐑊 𐐸𐐰𐑂 𐐶𐐫𐑉𐑆, 𐐰𐑌𐐼 𐑉𐐭𐑋𐐲𐑉𐑆 𐐱𐑂 𐐶𐐫𐑉𐑆; 𐐰𐑌𐐼 𐐸𐐶𐐯𐑌 𐑄 𐐼𐐩 𐐿𐐲𐑋𐐯𐑃 𐑄𐐰𐐻 𐑄 𐐄𐑌𐑊𐐨 𐐒𐐨𐑀𐐱𐐻𐐲𐑌 𐐱𐑂 𐑄 𐐙𐐪𐑄𐐲𐑉, 𐐷𐐩, 𐐨𐑂𐐲𐑌 𐑄 𐐙𐐪𐑄𐐲𐑉 𐐱𐑂 𐐸𐐯𐑂𐐲𐑌 𐐰𐑌𐐼 𐐱𐑂 𐐲𐑉𐑃, 𐑇𐐰𐑊 𐑋𐐰𐑌𐐮𐑁𐐯𐑅𐐻 𐐸𐐮𐑋𐑅𐐯𐑊𐑁 𐐲𐑌𐐻𐐭 𐑄𐐯𐑋 𐐮𐑌 𐑄 𐑁𐑊𐐯𐑇, 𐐺𐐨𐐸𐐬𐑊𐐼, 𐑄𐐩 𐐶𐐮𐑊 𐑉𐐨𐐾𐐯𐐿𐐻 𐐸𐐮𐑋, 𐐺𐐨𐐿𐐫𐑆 𐐱𐑂 𐑄𐐩𐑉 𐐮𐑌𐐮𐐿𐐶𐐮𐐻𐐨𐑆, 𐐰𐑌𐐼 𐑄 𐐸𐐪𐑉𐐼𐑌𐐯𐑅 𐐱𐑂 𐑄𐐩𐑉 𐐸𐐪𐑉𐐻𐑅, 𐐰𐑌𐐼 𐑄 𐑅𐐻𐐮𐑁𐑌𐐯𐑅 𐐱𐑂 𐑄𐐩𐑉 𐑌𐐯𐐿𐑅. 𐐒𐐨𐐸𐐬𐑊𐐼, 𐑄𐐩 𐐶𐐮𐑊 𐐿𐑉𐐭𐑅𐐮𐑁𐐴 𐐸𐐮𐑋; 𐐰𐑌𐐼 𐐰𐑁𐐻𐐲𐑉 𐐸𐐨 𐐮𐑆 𐑊𐐩𐐼 𐐮𐑌 𐐰 𐑅𐐯𐐹𐐲𐑊𐐿𐐲𐑉 𐑁𐐫𐑉 𐑄 𐑅𐐹𐐩𐑅 𐐱𐑂 𐑃𐑉𐐨 𐐼𐐩𐑆, 𐐸𐐨 𐑇𐐰𐑊 𐑉𐐴𐑆 𐑁𐑉𐐱𐑋 𐑄 𐐼𐐯𐐼, 𐐶𐐮𐑄 𐐸𐐨𐑊𐐮𐑍 𐐮𐑌 𐐸𐐮𐑆 𐐶𐐮𐑍𐑆, 𐐰𐑌𐐼 𐐫𐑊 𐑄𐐩 𐑄𐐰𐐻 𐑇𐐰𐑊 𐐺𐐨𐑊𐐨𐑂 𐐱𐑌 𐐸𐐮𐑆 𐑌𐐩𐑋, 𐑇𐐰𐑊 𐐺𐐨 𐑅𐐩𐑂𐐼 𐐮𐑌 𐑄 𐐿𐐮𐑍𐐼𐐲𐑋 𐐱𐑂 𐐘𐐱𐐼: 𐐸𐐶𐐯𐑉𐑁𐐬𐑉, 𐑋𐐴 𐑅𐐬𐑊 𐐼𐐨𐑊𐐴𐐻𐐯𐑃 𐐻𐐭 𐐹𐑉𐐱𐑁𐐯𐑅𐐴 𐐿𐐱𐑌𐑅𐐲𐑉𐑌𐐮𐑍 𐐸𐐮𐑋, 𐑁𐐫𐑉 𐐌 𐐸𐐰𐑂 𐑅𐐨𐑌 𐐸𐐮𐑆 𐐼𐐩, 𐐰𐑌𐐼 𐑋𐐴 𐐸𐐪𐑉𐐻 𐐼𐐲𐑃 𐑋𐐰𐑀𐑌𐐮𐑁𐐴 𐐸𐐮𐑆 𐐸𐐬𐑊𐐨 𐑌𐐩𐑋.

3. 𐐈𐑌𐐼 𐐺𐐨𐐸𐐬𐑊𐐼 𐐮𐐻 𐑇𐐰𐑊 𐐿𐐲𐑋 𐐻𐐭 𐐹𐐰𐑅 𐑄𐐰𐐻 𐐰𐑁𐐻𐐲𐑉 𐑄 𐐣𐐯𐑅𐐴𐐲 𐐸𐐰𐑃 𐑉𐐮𐑆𐐲𐑌 𐑁𐑉𐐱𐑋 𐑄 𐐼𐐯𐐼, 𐐰𐑌𐐼 𐐸𐐰𐑃 𐑋𐐰𐑌𐐮𐑁𐐯𐑅𐐻𐐯𐐼 𐐸𐐮𐑋𐑅𐐯𐑊𐑁 𐐲𐑌𐐻𐐭 𐐸𐐮𐑆 𐐹𐐨𐐹𐑊, 𐐲𐑌𐐻𐐭 𐐰𐑆 𐑋𐐯𐑌𐐨 𐐰𐑆 𐐶𐐮𐑊 𐐺𐐨𐑊𐐨𐑂 𐐱𐑌 𐐸𐐮𐑆 𐑌𐐩𐑋, 𐐺𐐨𐐸𐐬𐑊𐐼 𐐖𐐲𐑉𐐭𐑅𐐲𐑊𐐯𐑋 𐑇𐐰𐑊 𐐺𐐨 𐐼𐐯𐑅𐐻𐑉𐑎𐐼 𐐲𐑀𐐯𐑌: 𐑁𐐫𐑉 𐐶𐐬 𐐲𐑌𐐻𐐭 𐑄𐐯𐑋 𐑄𐐰𐐻 𐑁𐐴𐐻 𐐲𐑀𐐯𐑌𐑅𐐻 𐐘𐐱𐐼 𐐰𐑌𐐼 𐑄 𐐹𐐨𐐹𐑊 𐐱𐑂 𐐸𐐮𐑆 𐐕𐐲𐑉𐐽. 𐐐𐐶𐐯𐑉𐑁𐐬𐑉, 𐑄 𐐖𐐭𐑆 𐑇𐐰𐑊 𐐺𐐨 𐑅𐐿𐐰𐐻𐐲𐑉𐐼 𐐲𐑋𐐲𐑍 𐐫𐑊 𐑌𐐩𐑇𐐲𐑌𐑆; 𐐷𐐩, 𐐰𐑌𐐼 𐐫𐑊𐑅𐐬 𐐒𐐰𐐺𐐮𐑊𐐱𐑌 𐑇𐐰𐑊 𐐺𐐨 𐐼𐐯𐑅𐐻𐑉𐑎𐐼; 𐐸𐐶𐐯𐑉𐑁𐐬𐑉 𐑄 𐐖𐐭𐑆 𐑇𐐰𐑊 𐐺𐐨 𐑅𐐿𐐰𐐻𐐲𐑉𐐼 𐐺𐐴 𐐲𐑄𐐲𐑉 𐑌𐐩𐑇𐐲𐑌𐑆; 𐐰𐑌𐐼 𐐰𐑁𐐻𐐲𐑉 𐑄𐐩 𐐸𐐰𐑂 𐐺𐐮𐑌 𐑅𐐿𐐰𐐻𐐲𐑉𐐼, 𐐰𐑌𐐼 𐑄 𐐢𐐫𐑉𐐼 𐐘𐐱𐐼 𐐸𐐰𐑃 𐑅𐐿𐐲𐑉𐐾𐐼 𐑄𐐯𐑋 𐐺𐐴 𐐲𐑄𐐲𐑉 𐑌𐐩𐑇𐐲𐑌𐑆, 𐑁𐐫𐑉 𐑄 𐑅𐐹𐐩𐑅 𐐱𐑂 𐑋𐐯𐑌𐐨 𐐾𐐯𐑌𐐲𐑉𐐩𐑇𐐲𐑌𐑆, 𐐷𐐩, 𐐨𐑂𐐲𐑌 𐐼𐐵𐑌 𐑁𐑉𐐱𐑋 𐐾𐐯𐑌𐐲𐑉𐐩𐑇𐐲𐑌 𐐻𐐭 𐐾𐐯𐑌𐐲𐑉𐐩𐑇𐐲𐑌, 𐐲𐑌𐐻𐐮𐑊 𐑄𐐩 𐑇𐐰𐑊 𐐺𐐨 𐐹𐐲𐑉𐑅𐐶𐐩𐐼𐐯𐐼 𐐻𐐭 𐐺𐐨𐑊𐐨𐑂 𐐮𐑌 𐐗𐑉𐐴𐑅𐐻, 𐑄 𐐝𐐲𐑌 𐐱𐑂 𐐘𐐱𐐼, 𐐰𐑌𐐼 𐑄 𐐰𐐻𐐬𐑌𐑋𐐯𐑌𐐻, 𐐸𐐶𐐮𐐽 𐐮𐑆 𐐮𐑌𐑁𐐮𐑌𐐮𐐻 𐑁𐐫𐑉 𐐫𐑊 𐑋𐐰𐑌𐐿𐐴𐑌𐐼; 𐐰𐑌𐐼 𐐸𐐶𐐯𐑌 𐑄𐐰𐐻 𐐼𐐩 𐑇𐐰𐑊 𐐿𐐲𐑋, 𐑄𐐰𐐻 𐑄𐐩 𐑇𐐰𐑊 𐐺𐐨𐑊𐐨𐑂 𐐮𐑌 𐐗𐑉𐐴𐑅𐐻, 𐐰𐑌𐐼 𐐶𐐲𐑉𐑇𐐮𐐹 𐑄 𐐙𐐪𐑄𐐲𐑉 𐐮𐑌 𐐸𐐮𐑆 𐑌𐐩𐑋, 𐐶𐐮𐑄 𐐹𐐷𐐭𐑉 𐐸𐐪𐑉𐐻𐑅 𐐰𐑌𐐼 𐐿𐑊𐐨𐑌 𐐸𐐰𐑌𐐼𐑆, 𐐰𐑌𐐼 𐑊𐐳𐐿 𐑌𐐱𐐻 𐑁𐐫𐑉𐐶𐐲𐑉𐐼 𐐯𐑌𐐨 𐑋𐐬𐑉 𐑁𐐫𐑉 𐐲𐑌𐐲𐑄𐐲𐑉 𐐣𐐯𐑅𐐴𐐲, 𐑄𐐯𐑌, 𐐰𐐻 𐑄𐐰𐐻 𐐻𐐴𐑋, 𐑄 𐐼𐐩 𐐶𐐮𐑊 𐐿𐐲𐑋 𐑄𐐰𐐻 𐐮𐐻 𐑋𐐲𐑅𐐻 𐑌𐐨𐐼𐑆 𐐺𐐨 𐐯𐐿𐑅𐐹𐐨𐐼𐐨𐐲𐑌𐐻 𐑄𐐰𐐻 𐑄𐐩 𐑇𐐳𐐼 𐐺𐐨𐑊𐐨𐑂 𐑄𐐨𐑆 𐑃𐐮𐑍𐑆. 𐐈𐑌𐐼 𐑄 𐐢𐐫𐑉𐐼 𐐶𐐮𐑊 𐑅𐐯𐐻 𐐸𐐮𐑆 𐐸𐐰𐑌𐐼 𐐲𐑀𐐯𐑌 𐑄 𐑅𐐯𐐿𐐲𐑌𐐼 𐐻𐐴𐑋 𐐻𐐭 𐑉𐐨𐑅𐐻𐐬𐑉 𐐸𐐮𐑆 𐐹𐐨𐐹𐑊 𐑁𐑉𐐱𐑋 𐑄𐐩𐑉 𐑊𐐱𐑅𐐻 𐐰𐑌𐐼 𐑁𐐫𐑊𐐲𐑌 𐑅𐐻𐐩𐐻. 𐐐𐐶𐐯𐑉𐑁𐐬𐑉, 𐐸𐐨 𐐶𐐮𐑊 𐐹𐑉𐐬𐑅𐐨𐐼 𐐻𐐭 𐐼𐐭 𐐰 𐑋𐐪𐑉𐑂𐐯𐑊𐐲𐑅 𐐶𐐲𐑉𐐿 𐐰𐑌𐐼 𐐰 𐐶𐐲𐑌𐐼𐐲𐑉 𐐲𐑋𐐲𐑍 𐑄 𐐽𐐮𐑊𐐼𐑉𐐯𐑌 𐐱𐑂 𐑋𐐯𐑌.

4. 𐐐𐐶𐐯𐑉𐑁𐐬𐑉, 𐐸𐐨 𐑖𐐰𐑊 𐐺𐑉𐐮𐑍 𐑁𐐫𐑉𐑃 𐐸𐐮𐑆 𐐶𐐲𐑉𐐼𐑆 𐐲𐑌𐐻𐐭 𐑄𐐯𐑋, 𐐸𐐶𐐮𐐽 𐐶𐐲𐑉𐐼𐑆 𐑖𐐰𐑊 𐐾𐐲𐐾 𐑄𐐯𐑋
𐐰𐐻 𐑄 𐑊𐐰𐑅𐐻 𐐼𐐩, 𐑁𐐫𐑉 𐑄𐐩 𐑖𐐰𐑊 𐐺𐐨 𐑀𐐮𐑂𐐲𐑌 𐑄𐐯𐑋 𐑁𐐫𐑉 𐑄 𐐹𐐲𐑉𐐹𐐲𐑅 𐐱𐑂 𐐿𐐱𐑌𐑂𐐮𐑌𐑅𐐮𐑍 𐑄𐐯𐑋 𐐱𐑂 𐑄 𐐻𐑉𐐭
𐐣𐐯𐑅𐐴𐐲, 𐐸𐐭 𐐶𐐱𐑆 𐑉𐐨𐐾𐐯𐐿𐐻𐐲𐐼 𐐺𐐴 𐑄𐐯𐑋; 𐐰𐑌𐐼 𐐲𐑌𐐻𐐭 𐑄 𐐿𐐱𐑌𐑂𐐮𐑌𐑅𐐮𐑍 𐐱𐑂 𐑄𐐯𐑋 𐑄𐐰𐐻 𐑄𐐩 𐑌𐐨𐐼 𐑌𐐱𐐻
𐑊𐐳𐐿 𐑁𐐫𐑉𐐶𐐲𐑉𐐼 𐐯𐑌𐐨 𐑋𐐫𐑉 𐑁𐐫𐑉 𐐰 𐐣𐐯𐑅𐐴𐐲 𐐻𐐭 𐐿𐐲𐑋, 𐑁𐐫𐑉 𐑄𐐯𐑉 𐑖𐐳𐐼 𐑌𐐱𐐻 𐐯𐑌𐐨 𐐿𐐲𐑋, 𐑅𐐩𐑂 𐐮𐐻 𐑖𐐳𐐼
𐐺𐐨 𐐰 𐑁𐐫𐑊𐑅 𐐣𐐯𐑅𐐴𐐲, 𐐸𐐶𐐮𐐽 𐑖𐐳𐐼 𐐼𐐨𐑅𐐨𐑂 𐑄 𐐹𐐨𐐹𐑊: 𐑁𐐫𐑉 𐑄𐐯𐑉 𐐮𐑆 𐑅𐐩𐑂 𐐶𐐲𐑌 𐐣𐐯𐑅𐐴𐐲 𐑅𐐹𐐬𐐿𐐲𐑌 𐐱𐑂
𐐺𐐴 𐑄 𐐹𐑉𐐱𐑁𐐯𐐻𐑅, 𐐰𐑌𐐼 𐑄𐐰𐐻 𐐣𐐯𐑅𐐴𐐲 𐐮𐑆 𐐸𐐨 𐐸𐐭 𐑖𐐳𐐼 𐐺𐐨 𐑉𐐨𐐾𐐯𐐿𐐻𐐲𐐼 𐐱𐑂 𐑄 𐐖𐐭𐑆. 𐐙𐐫𐑉 𐐰𐐿𐐫𐑉𐐼𐐮𐑍
𐐻𐐭 𐑄 𐐶𐐲𐑉𐐼𐑆 𐐱𐑂 𐑄 𐐹𐑉𐐱𐑁𐐯𐐻𐑅, 𐑄 𐐣𐐯𐑅𐐴𐐲 𐐿𐐲𐑋𐐯𐑃 𐐮𐑌 𐑅𐐮𐐿𐑅 𐐸𐐲𐑌𐐼𐑉𐐲𐐼 𐐷𐐨𐑉𐑆 𐑁𐑉𐐲𐑋 𐑄 𐐻𐐴𐑋 𐑄𐐰𐐻
𐑋𐐴 𐑁𐐱𐑄𐐲𐑉 𐑊𐐯𐑁𐐻 𐐖𐐲𐑉𐐭𐑅𐐲𐑊𐐯𐑋; 𐐰𐑌𐐼 𐐰𐐿𐐫𐑉𐐼𐐮𐑍 𐐻𐐭 𐑄 𐐶𐐲𐑉𐐼𐑆 𐐱𐑂 𐑄 𐐹𐑉𐐱𐑁𐐯𐐻𐑅, 𐐰𐑌𐐼 𐐫𐑊𐑅𐐬 𐑄
𐐶𐐲𐑉𐐼 𐐱𐑂 𐑄 𐐩𐑌𐐾𐐲𐑊 𐐱𐑂 𐐘𐐱𐐼, 𐐸𐐮𐑆 𐑌𐐩𐑋 𐑖𐐰𐑊 𐐺𐐨 𐐖𐐨𐑆𐐲𐑅 𐐗𐑉𐐴𐑅𐐻, 𐑄 𐐝𐐲𐑌 𐐱𐑂 𐐘𐐱𐐼.

5. 𐐰𐑌𐐼 𐑌𐐵, 𐑋𐐴 𐐺𐑉𐐯𐑄𐑉𐐯𐑌, 𐐌 𐐸𐐰𐑂 𐑅𐐹𐐬𐐿𐐲𐑌 𐐹𐑊𐐩𐑌𐑊𐐨 𐑄𐐰𐐻 𐐷𐐨 𐐿𐐰𐑌𐐱𐐻 𐐲𐑉: 𐐰𐑌𐐼 𐐰𐑆 𐑄 𐐢𐐫𐑉𐐼
𐐘𐐱𐐼 𐑊𐐮𐑂𐐯𐑃 𐑄𐐰𐐻 𐐺𐑉𐐱𐐻 𐐆𐑆𐑉𐐩𐐯𐑊 𐐲𐐹 𐐵𐐻 𐐱𐑂 𐑄 𐑊𐐰𐑌𐐼 𐐱𐑂 𐐀𐐾𐐮𐐹𐐻, 𐐰𐑌𐐼 𐑀𐐩𐑂 𐐲𐑌𐐻𐐭 𐐣𐐬𐑆𐐯𐑆
𐐹𐐵𐐲𐑉 𐑄𐐰𐐻 𐐸𐐨 𐑖𐐳𐐼 𐐸𐐨𐑊 𐑄 𐑌𐐩𐑖𐐲𐑌𐑆, 𐐰𐑁𐐻𐐲𐑉 𐑄𐐩 𐐸𐐰𐐼 𐐺𐐨𐑌 𐐺𐐮𐐻𐐲𐑌 𐐺𐐴 𐑄 𐐹𐐱𐐮𐑆𐐲𐑌𐐲𐑅 𐑅𐐲𐑉𐐹𐐲𐑌𐐻𐑅,
𐐮𐑁 𐑄𐐩 𐐶𐐳𐐼 𐐿𐐰𐑅𐐻 𐑄𐐯𐑉 𐐴𐑆 𐐲𐑌𐐻𐐭 𐑄 𐑅𐐲𐑉𐐹𐐲𐑌𐐻 𐐸𐐶𐐮𐐽 𐐸𐐨 𐐼𐐮𐐼 𐑉𐐩𐑆 𐐲𐐹 𐐺𐐨𐑁𐐬𐑉 𐑄𐐯𐑋, 𐐰𐑌𐐼
𐐫𐑊𐑅𐐬 𐑀𐐩𐑂 𐐸𐐮𐑋 𐐹𐐵𐐲𐑉 𐑄𐐰𐐻 𐐸𐐨 𐑖𐐳𐐼 𐑅𐑋𐐴𐐻 𐑄 𐑉𐐱𐐿, 𐐰𐑌𐐼 𐑄 𐐶𐐫𐐻𐐲𐑉 𐑖𐐳𐐼 𐐿𐐲𐑋 𐑁𐐬𐑉𐑃; 𐐷𐐩, 𐐺𐐨𐐸𐐬𐑊𐐼 𐐌 𐑅𐐩 𐐲𐑌𐐻𐐭 𐐷𐐭, 𐑄𐐰𐐻 𐐰𐑆 𐑄𐐨𐑆 𐑃𐐮𐑍𐑆 𐐪𐑉 𐐻𐑉𐐭, 𐐰𐑌𐐼 𐐰𐑆 𐑄 𐐢𐐫𐑉𐐼 𐐘𐐱𐐼 𐑊𐐮𐑂𐐯𐑃, 𐑄𐐯𐑉 𐐮𐑆
𐑌𐐲𐑌 𐐲𐑄𐐲𐑉 𐑌𐐩𐑋 𐑀𐐮𐑂𐐲𐑌 𐐲𐑌𐐼𐐲𐑉 𐐸𐐯𐑂𐐲𐑌 𐑅𐐩𐑂 𐐮𐐻 𐐺𐐨 𐑄𐐮𐑅 𐐖𐐨𐑆𐐲𐑅 𐐗𐑉𐐴𐑅𐐻 𐐱𐑂 𐐸𐐶𐐮𐐽 𐐌 𐐸𐐰𐑂 𐑅𐐹𐐬𐐿𐐲𐑌,
𐐸𐐶𐐯𐑉𐐺𐐴 𐑋𐐰𐑌 𐐿𐐰𐑌 𐐺𐐨 𐑅𐐩𐑂𐐼.

6. 𐐐𐐶𐐯𐑉𐑁𐐬𐑉, 𐑁𐐫𐑉 𐑄𐐮𐑅 𐐿𐐫𐑆 𐐸𐐰𐑃 𐑄 𐐢𐐫𐑉𐐼 𐐘𐐱𐐼 𐐹𐑉𐐱𐑋𐐮𐑅𐐼 𐐲𐑌𐐻𐐭 𐑋𐐨 𐑄𐐰𐐻 𐑄𐐨𐑆 𐑃𐐮𐑍𐑆
𐐸𐐶𐐮𐐽 𐐌 𐑉𐐴𐐻, 𐑖𐐰𐑊 𐐺𐐨 𐐿𐐯𐐹𐐻 𐐰𐑌𐐼 𐐹𐑉𐐨𐑆𐐲𐑉𐑂𐐼, 𐐰𐑌𐐼 𐐸𐐰𐑌𐐼𐐲𐐼 𐐼𐐵𐑌 𐐲𐑌𐐻𐐭 𐑋𐐴 𐑅𐐨𐐼, 𐑁𐑉𐐲𐑋 𐐾𐐯𐑌𐐲𐑉𐐩𐑖𐐲𐑌 𐐻𐐭 𐐾𐐯𐑌𐐲𐑉𐐩𐑖𐐲𐑌, 𐑄𐐰𐐻 𐑄 𐐹𐑉𐐱𐑋𐐮𐑅 𐑋𐐩 𐐺𐐨 𐑁𐐳𐑊𐑁𐐮𐑊𐐼 𐐲𐑌𐐻𐐭 𐐖𐐬𐑆𐐯𐑁, 𐑄𐐰𐐻 𐐸𐐮𐑆 𐑅𐐨𐐼 𐑖𐐳𐐼
𐑌𐐯𐑂𐐲𐑉 𐐹𐐯𐑉𐐮𐑖 𐐰𐑆 𐑊𐐱𐑍 𐐰𐑆 𐑄 𐐲𐑉𐑃 𐑖𐐳𐐼 𐑅𐐻𐐰𐑌𐐼. 𐐐𐐶𐐯𐑉𐑁𐐬𐑉, 𐑄𐐨𐑆 𐑃𐐮𐑍𐑆 𐑖𐐰𐑊 𐑀𐐬 𐑁𐑉𐐲𐑋
𐐾𐐯𐑌𐐲𐑉𐐩𐑖𐐲𐑌 𐐻𐐭 𐐾𐐯𐑌𐐲𐑉𐐩𐑖𐐲𐑌 𐐰𐑆 𐑊𐐱𐑍 𐐰𐑆 𐑄 𐐲𐑉𐑃 𐑖𐐰𐑊 𐑅𐐻𐐰𐑌𐐼; 𐐰𐑌𐐼 𐑄𐐩 𐑖𐐰𐑊 𐑀𐐬 𐐰𐐿𐐫𐑉𐐼𐐮𐑍
𐐻𐐭 𐑄 𐐶𐐮𐑊 𐐰𐑌𐐼 𐐹𐑊𐐯𐑈𐐲𐑉 𐐱𐑂 𐐘𐐱𐐼; 𐐰𐑌𐐼 𐑄 𐑌𐐩𐑖𐐲𐑌𐑆 𐐸𐐭 𐑖𐐰𐑊 𐐹𐐲𐑆𐐯𐑅 𐑄𐐯𐑋, 𐑖𐐰𐑊 𐐺𐐨 𐐾𐐲𐐾𐐼
𐐱𐑂 𐑄𐐯𐑋 𐐰𐐿𐐫𐑉𐐼𐐮𐑍 𐐻𐐭 𐑄 𐐶𐐲𐑉𐐼𐑆 𐐸𐐶𐐮𐐽 𐐪𐑉 𐑉𐐮𐐻𐐲𐑌. 𐐙𐐫𐑉 𐐶𐐨 𐑊𐐩𐐺𐐲𐑉 𐐼𐐮𐑊𐐮𐐾𐐲𐑌𐐻𐑊𐐨 𐐻𐐭 𐑉𐐴𐐻, 𐐻𐐭
𐐹𐐲𐑉𐑅𐐶𐐩𐐼 𐐵𐑉 𐐽𐐮𐑊𐐼𐑉𐐲𐑌, 𐐰𐑌𐐼 𐐫𐑊𐑅𐐬 𐐵𐑉 𐐺𐑉𐐯𐑄𐑉𐐯𐑌, 𐐻𐐭 𐐺𐐨𐑊𐐨𐑂 𐐮𐑌 𐐗𐑉𐐴𐑅𐐻, 𐐰𐑌𐐼 𐐻𐐭 𐐺𐐨 𐑉𐐯𐐿𐐲𐑌𐑅𐐴𐑊𐐼 𐐻𐐭 𐐘𐐱𐐼; 𐑁𐐫𐑉 𐐶𐐨 𐑌𐐬 𐑄𐐰𐐻 𐐮𐐻 𐐮𐑆 𐐺𐐴 𐑀𐑉𐐩𐑅 𐑄𐐰𐐻 𐐶𐐨 𐐪𐑉 𐑅𐐩𐑂𐐼, 𐐰𐑁𐐻𐐲𐑉 𐐫𐑊 𐐶𐐨
𐐿𐐰𐑌 𐐼𐐭.

7. 𐐰𐑌𐐼 𐑌𐐱𐐻𐐶𐐮𐑃𐑅𐐻𐐰𐑌𐐼𐐮𐑍 𐐶𐐨 𐐺𐐨𐑊𐐨𐑂 𐐮𐑌 𐐗𐑉𐐴𐑅𐐻, 𐐶𐐨 𐐿𐐨𐐹 𐑄 𐑊𐐫 𐐱𐑂 𐐣𐐬𐑆𐐯𐑆, 𐐰𐑌𐐼 𐑊𐐳𐐿
𐑁𐐫𐑉𐐶𐐲𐑉𐐼 𐐶𐐮𐑃 𐑅𐐻𐐯𐐼𐑁𐐰𐑅𐐻𐑌𐐯𐑅 𐐲𐑌𐐻𐐭 𐐗𐑉𐐴𐑅𐐻, 𐐲𐑌𐐻𐐮𐑊 𐑄 𐑊𐐫 𐑖𐐰𐑊 𐐺𐐨 𐑁𐐳𐑊𐑁𐐮𐑊𐐼; 𐑁𐐫𐑉, 𐑁𐐫𐑉 𐑄𐐮𐑅
𐐯𐑌𐐼 𐐶𐐱𐑆 𐑄 𐑊𐐫 𐑀𐐮𐑂𐐲𐑌; 𐐸𐐶𐐯𐑉𐑁𐐬𐑉 𐑄 𐑊𐐫 𐐸𐐰𐑃 𐐺𐐨𐐿𐐲𐑋 𐐼𐐯𐐼 𐐲𐑌𐐻𐐭 𐐲𐑅, 𐐰𐑌𐐼 𐐶𐐨 𐐪𐑉 𐑋𐐩𐐼 𐐰𐑊𐐴𐑂
𐐮𐑌 𐐗𐑉𐐴𐑅𐐻, 𐐺𐐨𐐿𐐫𐑆 𐐱𐑂 𐐵𐑉 𐑁𐐩𐑃; 𐐷𐐯𐐻 𐐶𐐨 𐐿𐐨𐐹 𐑄 𐑊𐐫 𐐺𐐨𐐿𐐫𐑆 𐐱𐑂 𐑄 𐐿𐐱𐑋𐐰𐑌𐐼𐑋𐐯𐑌𐐻𐑅; 𐐰𐑌𐐼
𐐶𐐨 𐐻𐐫𐐿 𐐱𐑂 𐐗𐑉𐐴𐑅𐐻, 𐐶𐐨 𐑉𐐨𐐾𐐱𐐮𐑅 𐐮𐑌 𐐗𐑉𐐴𐑅𐐻, 𐐶𐐨 𐐹𐑉𐐨𐐽 𐐱𐑂 𐐗𐑉𐐴𐑅𐐻, 𐐶𐐨 𐐹𐑉𐐱𐑁𐐯𐑅𐐴 𐐱𐑂
𐐗𐑉𐐴𐑅𐐻, 𐐰𐑌𐐼 𐐶𐐨 𐑉𐐴𐐻 𐐰𐐿𐐫𐑉𐐼𐐮𐑍 𐐻𐐭 𐐵𐑉 𐐹𐑉𐐱𐑁𐐯𐑅𐐨𐑆, 𐑄𐐰𐐻 𐐵𐑉 𐐽𐐮𐑊𐐼𐑉𐐲𐑌 𐑋𐐩 𐑌𐐬 𐐻𐐭 𐐸𐐶𐐲𐐻
𐑅𐐬𐑉𐑅 𐑄𐐩 𐑋𐐩 𐑊𐐳𐐿 𐑁𐐫𐑉 𐐰 𐑉𐐨𐑋𐐮𐑖𐐲𐑌 𐐱𐑂 𐑄𐐯𐑉 𐑅𐐮𐑌𐑆. 𐐐𐐶𐐯𐑉𐑁𐐬𐑉, 𐐶𐐨 𐑅𐐹𐐨𐐿 𐐿𐐱𐑌𐑅𐐲𐑉𐑌𐐮𐑍 𐑄
𐑊𐐫, 𐑄𐐰𐐻 𐐵𐑉 𐐽𐐮𐑊𐐼𐑉𐐲𐑌 𐑋𐐩 𐑌𐐬 𐑄 𐐼𐐯𐐼𐑌𐐯𐑅 𐐱𐑂 𐑄 𐑊𐐫; 𐐰𐑌𐐼 𐑄𐐩, 𐐺𐐴 𐑌𐐬𐐮𐑍 𐑄 𐐼𐐯𐐼𐑌𐐯𐑅 𐐱𐑂 𐑄
𐑊𐐫, 𐑋𐐩 𐑊𐐳𐐿 𐑁𐐫𐑉𐐶𐐲𐑉𐐼 𐐲𐑌𐐻𐐭 𐑄𐐰𐐻 𐑊𐐴𐑁 𐐸𐐶𐐮𐐽 𐐮𐑆 𐐮𐑌 𐐗𐑉𐐴𐑅𐐻, 𐐰𐑌𐐼 𐑌𐐬 𐑁𐐫𐑉 𐐸𐐶𐐲𐐻 𐐯𐑌𐐼 𐑄
𐑊𐐫 𐐶𐐱𐑆 𐑀𐐮𐑂𐐲𐑌. 𐐰𐑌𐐼 𐐰𐑁𐐻𐐲𐑉 𐑄 𐑊𐐫 𐐮𐑆 𐑁𐐳𐑊𐑁𐐮𐑊𐐼 𐐮𐑌 𐐗𐑉𐐴𐑅𐐻, 𐑄𐐰𐐻 𐑄𐐩 𐑌𐐨𐐼 𐑌𐐱𐐻 𐐸𐐪𐑉𐐼𐐲𐑌 𐑄𐐯𐑉
𐐸𐐪𐑉𐐻𐑅 𐐲𐑀𐐯𐑌𐑅𐐻 𐐸𐐮𐑋, 𐐸𐐶𐐯𐑌 𐑄 𐑊𐐫 𐐫𐐻 𐐻𐐭 𐐺𐐨 𐐼𐐲𐑌 𐐲𐐶𐐩.

8. 𐐰𐑌𐐼 𐑌𐐵 𐐺𐐨𐐸𐐬𐑊𐐼, 𐑋𐐴 𐐹𐐨𐐹𐑊, 𐐷𐐨 𐐪𐑉 𐐰 𐑅𐐻𐐮𐑁𐑌𐐯𐐿𐐻 𐐹𐐨𐐹𐑊: 𐐸𐐶𐐯𐑉𐑁𐐬𐑉, 𐐌 𐐸𐐰𐑂 𐑅𐐹𐐬𐐿𐐲𐑌
𐐹𐑊𐐩𐑌𐑊𐐨 𐐲𐑌𐐻𐐭 𐐷𐐭, 𐑄𐐰𐐻 𐐷𐐨 𐐿𐐰𐑌𐐱𐐻 𐑋𐐮𐑅𐐲𐑌𐐼𐐲𐑉𐑅𐐻𐐰𐑌𐐼. 𐐰𐑌𐐼 𐑄 𐐶𐐲𐑉𐐼𐑆 𐐸𐐶𐐮𐐽 𐐌 𐐸𐐰𐑂 𐑅𐐹𐐬𐐿𐐲𐑌,
𐑖𐐰𐑊 𐑅𐐻𐐰𐑌𐐼 𐐰𐑆 𐐰 𐐻𐐯𐑅𐐻𐐮𐑋𐐬𐑌𐐨 𐐲𐑀𐐯𐑌𐑅𐐻 𐐷𐐭: 𐑁𐐫𐑉 𐑄𐐩 𐐪𐑉 𐑅𐐲𐑁𐐮𐑖𐐲𐑌𐐻 𐐻𐐭 𐐻𐐨𐐽 𐐯𐑌𐐨 𐑋𐐰𐑌 𐑄

𐑉𐐴𐐻 𐐶𐐩: 𐑁𐐫𐑉 𐑄 𐑉𐐴𐐻 𐐶𐐩 𐐮𐑆 𐐻𐐭 𐐺𐐨𐑊𐐨𐑂 𐐮𐑌 𐐗𐑉𐐴𐑅𐐻 𐐰𐑌𐐼 𐐼𐐨𐑌𐐴 𐐸𐐮𐑋 𐑌𐐱𐐻; 𐑁𐐫𐑉 𐐺𐐴 𐐼𐐨𐑌𐐴𐐮𐑍 𐐸𐐮𐑋, 𐐷 𐐫𐑊𐑅𐐬 𐐼𐐨𐑌𐐴 𐑄 𐐹𐑉𐐱𐑁𐐯𐐻𐑅 𐐰𐑌𐐼 𐑄 𐑊𐐫.

9. 𐐈𐑌𐐼 𐑌𐐵 𐐺𐐨𐐸𐐬𐑊𐐼 𐐌 𐑅𐐩 𐐲𐑌𐐻𐐭 𐐷𐐭, 𐑄𐐰𐐻 𐑄 𐑉𐐴𐐻 𐐶𐐩 𐐮𐑆 𐐻𐐭 𐐺𐐨𐑊𐐨𐑂 𐐮𐑌 𐐗𐑉𐐴𐑅𐐻, 𐐰𐑌𐐼 𐐼𐐨𐑌𐐴 𐐸𐐮𐑋 𐑌𐐱𐐻; 𐐰𐑌𐐼 𐐗𐑉𐐴𐑅𐐻 𐐮𐑆 𐑄 𐐐𐐬𐑊𐐨 𐐎𐐲𐑌 𐐲𐑂 𐐆𐑆𐑉𐐩𐐯𐑊: 𐐸𐐶𐐯𐑉𐑁𐐫𐑉 𐐷 𐑋𐐲𐑅𐐻 𐐺𐐵 𐐼𐐵𐑌 𐐺𐐨𐑁𐐫𐑉 𐐸𐐮𐑋, 𐐰𐑌𐐼 𐐶𐐲𐑉𐑇𐐮𐐹 𐐸𐐮𐑋 𐐶𐐮𐑄 𐐫𐑊 𐐷𐐬𐑉 𐑋𐐴𐐻, 𐑋𐐴𐑌𐐼, 𐐰𐑌𐐼 𐑅𐐻𐑉𐐯𐑍𐑃, 𐐰𐑌𐐼 𐐷𐐬𐑉 𐐸𐐬𐑊 𐑅𐐬𐑊; 𐐰𐑌𐐼 𐐮𐑁 𐐷 𐐼𐐭 𐑄𐐮𐑅 𐐷 𐑇𐐰𐑊 𐐮𐑌 𐑌𐐬 𐐶𐐴𐑆 𐐺 𐐿𐐰𐑅𐐻 𐐵𐐻. 𐐈𐑌𐐼, 𐐮𐑌𐐰𐑆𐑋𐐲𐐽 𐐰𐑆 𐐮𐐻 𐑇𐐰𐑊 𐐺 𐐯𐐿𐑅𐐹𐐨𐐼𐐮𐐲𐑌𐐻, 𐐷 𐑋𐐲𐑅𐐻 𐐿𐐨𐐹 𐑄 𐐹𐐲𐑉𐑁𐐫𐑉𐑋𐐲𐑌𐑅𐐯𐑆 𐐰𐑌𐐼 𐐫𐑉𐐼𐐮𐑌𐐲𐑌𐑅𐐯𐑆 𐐲𐑂 𐐘𐐱𐐼, 𐐲𐑌𐐻𐐮𐑊 𐑄 𐑊𐐫 𐑇𐐰𐑊 𐐺 𐑁𐐳𐑊𐑁𐐮𐑊𐐼 𐐸𐐶𐐮𐐽 𐐶𐐲𐑆 𐑀𐐮𐑂𐑌 𐐲𐑌𐐻𐐭 𐐣𐐬𐑆𐐯𐑆.

10. 𐐈𐑌𐐼 𐐰𐑁𐐻𐐲𐑉 𐐗𐑉𐐴𐑅𐐻 𐑇𐐰𐑊 𐐸𐐰𐑂 𐑉𐐮𐑆𐑌 𐑁𐑉𐐱𐑋 𐑄 𐐼𐐯𐐼, 𐐸𐐨 𐑇𐐰𐑊 𐑇𐐬 𐐸𐐮𐑋𐑅𐐯𐑊𐑁 𐐲𐑌𐐻𐐭 𐐷𐐭, 𐑋𐐴 𐐽𐐮𐑊𐐼𐑉𐐯𐑌, 𐐰𐑌𐐼 𐑋𐐴 𐐺𐐨𐑊𐐲𐑂𐐯𐐼 𐐺𐑉𐐯𐑄𐑉𐐯𐑌; 𐐰𐑌𐐼 𐑄 𐐶𐐲𐑉𐐼𐑆 𐐸𐐶𐐮𐐽 𐐸𐐨 𐑇𐐰𐑊 𐑅𐐹𐐨𐐿 𐐲𐑌𐐻𐐭 𐐷𐐭 𐑇𐐰𐑊 𐐺 𐑄 𐑊𐐫 𐐸𐐶𐐮𐐽 𐐷 𐑇𐐰𐑊 𐐼𐐭. 𐐙𐐫𐑉 𐐺𐐨𐐸𐐬𐑊𐐼, 𐐌 𐑅𐐩 𐐲𐑌𐐻𐐭 𐐷𐐭, 𐑄𐐰𐐻 𐐌 𐐸𐐰𐑂 𐐺𐐨𐐸𐐯𐑊𐐼 𐑄𐐰𐐻 𐑋𐐯𐑌𐐨 𐐾𐐯𐑌𐐲𐑉𐐩𐑇𐐲𐑌𐑆 𐑇𐐰𐑊 𐐹𐐰𐑅 𐐲𐐶𐐩, 𐐰𐑌𐐼 𐑄𐐩𐑉 𐑇𐐰𐑊 𐐺 𐑀𐑉𐐩𐐻 𐐶𐐫𐑉𐑆 𐐰𐑌𐐼 𐐿𐐲𐑌𐐻𐐯𐑌𐑇𐐲𐑌𐑆 𐐲𐑋𐐲𐑍 𐑋𐐴 𐐹𐐨𐐹𐑊. 𐐈𐑌𐐼 𐐰𐑁𐐻𐐲𐑉 𐑄 𐐣𐐯𐑅𐐴𐐲 𐑇𐐰𐑊 𐐿𐐲𐑋, 𐑄𐐩𐑉 𐑇𐐰𐑊 𐐺 𐑅𐐴𐑌𐑆 𐑀𐐮𐑂𐑌 𐐲𐑌𐐻𐐭 𐑋𐐴 𐐹𐐨𐐹𐑊 𐐲𐑂 𐐸𐐮𐑆 𐐺𐐲𐑉𐑃, 𐐰𐑌𐐼 𐐫𐑊𐑅𐐬 𐐲𐑂 𐐸𐐮𐑆 𐐼𐐯𐑃 𐐰𐑌𐐼 𐑉𐐯𐑆𐐲𐑉𐐯𐐿𐑇𐐲𐑌; 𐐰𐑌𐐼 𐑀𐑉𐐩𐐻 𐐰𐑌𐐼 𐐻𐐯𐑉𐐮𐐺𐑊 𐑇𐐰𐑊 𐑄𐐰𐐻 𐐼𐐩 𐐺 𐐲𐑌𐐻𐐭 𐑄 𐐶𐐮𐐿𐐯𐐼; 𐑁𐐫𐑉 𐑄𐐩 𐑇𐐰𐑊 𐐹𐐯𐑉𐐮𐑇; 𐐰𐑌𐐼 𐑄𐐩 𐐹𐐯𐑉𐐮𐑇 𐐺𐐨𐐿𐐫𐑆 𐑄𐐩 𐐿𐐰𐑅𐐻 𐐵𐐻 𐑄 𐐹𐑉𐐱𐑁𐐯𐐻𐑅, 𐐰𐑌𐐼 𐑄 𐑅𐐩𐑌𐐻𐑅, 𐐰𐑌𐐼 𐑅𐐻𐐬𐑌 𐑄𐐯𐑋, 𐐰𐑌𐐼 𐑅𐑊𐐩 𐑄𐐯𐑋: 𐐸𐐶𐐯𐑉𐑁𐐫𐑉 𐑄 𐐿𐑉𐐴 𐐲𐑂 𐑄 𐐺𐑊𐐲𐐼 𐐲𐑂 𐑄 𐑅𐐩𐑌𐐻𐑅 𐑇𐐰𐑊 𐐰𐑅𐐯𐑌𐐼 𐐲𐐹 𐐻𐐭 𐐘𐐱𐐼 𐑁𐑉𐐱𐑋 𐑄 𐑀𐑉𐐵𐑌𐐼 𐐰𐑀𐐯𐑌𐑅𐐻 𐑄𐐯𐑋. 𐐐𐐶𐐯𐑉𐑁𐐫𐑉 𐐫𐑊 𐑄𐐬𐑆 𐐸𐐭 𐐪𐑉 𐐹𐑉𐐵𐐼, 𐐰𐑌𐐼 𐑄𐐰𐐻 𐐼𐐭 𐐶𐐮𐐿𐐯𐐼𐑊𐐨, 𐑄 𐐼𐐩 𐑄𐐰𐐻 𐐿𐐲𐑋𐐯𐑃 𐑇𐐰𐑊 𐐺𐐲𐑉𐑌 𐑄𐐯𐑋 𐐲𐐹, 𐑅𐐯𐑃 𐑄 𐐢𐐫𐑉𐐼 𐐲𐑂 𐐐𐐬𐑅𐐻𐑅, 𐑁𐐫𐑉 𐑄𐐩 𐑇𐐰𐑊 𐐺 𐐰𐑆 𐑅𐐻𐐲𐐺𐑊; 𐐰𐑌𐐼 𐑄𐐩 𐑄𐐰𐐻 𐐿𐐮𐑊 𐑄 𐐹𐑉𐐱𐑁𐐯𐐻𐑅, 𐐰𐑌𐐼 𐑄 𐑅𐐩𐑌𐐻𐑅, 𐑄 𐐼𐐯𐐹𐑃𐑅 𐐲𐑂 𐑄 𐐲𐑉𐑃 𐑇𐐰𐑊 𐑅𐐶𐐱𐑊𐐬 𐑄𐐯𐑋 𐐲𐐹, 𐑅𐐯𐑃 𐑄 𐐢𐐫𐑉𐐼 𐐲𐑂 𐐐𐐬𐑅𐐻𐑅; 𐐰𐑌𐐼 𐑋𐐵𐑌𐐻𐐮𐑌𐑆 𐑇𐐰𐑊 𐐿𐐲𐑂𐐲𐑉 𐑄𐐯𐑋, 𐐰𐑌𐐼 𐐸𐐶𐐲𐑉𐑊𐐶𐐮𐑌𐐼𐑆 𐑇𐐰𐑊 𐐿𐐰𐑉𐐨 𐑄𐐯𐑋 𐐲𐐶𐐩, 𐐰𐑌𐐼 𐐺𐐮𐑊𐐼𐐮𐑍𐑆 𐑇𐐰𐑊 𐑁𐐫𐑊 𐐲𐐹𐐱𐑌 𐑄𐐯𐑋, 𐐰𐑌𐐼 𐐿𐑉𐐲𐑇 𐑄𐐯𐑋 𐐻𐐭 𐐹𐐨𐑅𐐯𐑆 𐐰𐑌𐐼 𐑀𐑉𐐴𐑌𐐼 𐑄𐐯𐑋 𐐻𐐭 𐐹𐐵𐐼𐐲𐑉; 𐐰𐑌𐐼 𐑄𐐩 𐑇𐐰𐑊 𐐺 𐑂𐐮𐑆𐐮𐐻𐐯𐐼 𐐶𐐮𐑄 𐑃𐐲𐑌𐐼𐐲𐑉𐐮𐑍𐑆, 𐐰𐑌𐐼 𐑊𐐴𐐻𐑌𐐮𐑍𐑆, 𐐰𐑌𐐼 𐐲𐑉𐑃𐐿𐐶𐐩𐐿𐑅, 𐐰𐑌𐐼 𐐫𐑊 𐑋𐐰𐑌𐐲𐑉 𐐲𐑂 𐐼𐐨𐑅𐐻𐑉𐐲𐐿𐑇𐐲𐑌𐑆, 𐑁𐐫𐑉 𐑄 𐑁𐐴𐑉 𐐲𐑂 𐑄 𐐰𐑍𐑀𐐲𐑉 𐐲𐑂 𐑄 𐐢𐐫𐑉𐐼 𐑇𐐰𐑊 𐐺 𐐿𐐮𐑌𐐼𐑊𐐼 𐐰𐑀𐐯𐑌𐑅𐐻 𐑄𐐯𐑋, 𐐰𐑌𐐼 𐑄𐐩 𐑇𐐰𐑊 𐐺 𐐰𐑆 𐑅𐐻𐐲𐐺𐑊, 𐐰𐑌𐐼 𐑄 𐐼𐐩 𐑄𐐰𐐻 𐐿𐐲𐑋𐐯𐑃 𐑇𐐰𐑊 𐐿𐐲𐑌𐑅𐐭𐑋 𐑄𐐯𐑋, 𐑅𐐯𐑃 𐑄 𐐢𐐫𐑉𐐼 𐐲𐑂 𐐐𐐬𐑅𐐻𐑅.

11. 𐐄 𐑄 𐐹𐐩𐑌, 𐐰𐑌𐐼 𐑄 𐐰𐑍𐑀𐐶𐐮𐑇 𐐲𐑂 𐑋𐐴 𐑅𐐬𐑊 𐑁𐐫𐑉 𐑄 𐑊𐐫𐑅 𐐲𐑂 𐑄 𐑅𐑊𐐩𐑌 𐐲𐑂 𐑋𐐴 𐐹𐐨𐐹𐑊! 𐐙𐐫𐑉 𐐌, 𐐤𐐨𐑁𐐴, 𐐸𐐰𐑂 𐑅𐐨𐑌 𐐮𐐻, 𐐰𐑌𐐼 𐐮𐐻 𐐶𐐯𐑊 𐑌𐐴 𐐿𐐲𐑌𐑅𐐭𐑋𐐯𐑃 𐑋𐐨 𐐺𐐨𐑁𐐫𐑉 𐑄 𐐹𐑉𐐯𐑆𐐯𐑌𐑅 𐐲𐑂 𐑄 𐐢𐐫𐑉𐐼; 𐐺𐐲𐐻 𐐌 𐑋𐐲𐑅𐐻 𐐿𐑉𐐴 𐐲𐑌𐐻𐐭 𐑋𐐴 𐐘𐐱𐐼, 𐑄𐐴 𐐶𐐩𐑆 𐐪𐑉 𐐾𐐲𐑅𐐻. 𐐒𐐲𐐻 𐐺𐐨𐐸𐐬𐑊𐐼, 𐑄 𐑉𐐴𐐽𐐲𐑅, 𐑄𐐰𐐻 𐐸𐐪𐑉𐐿𐑌 𐐲𐑌𐐻𐐭 𐑄 𐐶𐐲𐑉𐐼𐑆 𐐲𐑂 𐑄 𐐹𐑉𐐱𐑁𐐯𐐻𐑅, 𐐰𐑌𐐼 𐐼𐐨𐑅𐐻𐑉𐐱𐐨 𐑄𐐯𐑋 𐑌𐐱𐐻, 𐐺𐐲𐐻 𐑊𐐳𐐿 𐑁𐐫𐑉𐐶𐐲𐑉𐐼 𐐲𐑌𐐻𐐭 𐐗𐑉𐐴𐑅𐐻 𐐶𐐮𐑄 𐑅𐐻𐐯𐐼𐑁𐐰𐑅𐐻𐑌𐐯𐑅 𐑁𐐫𐑉 𐑄 𐑅𐐴𐑌𐑆 𐐸𐐶𐐮𐐽 𐐪𐑉 𐑀𐐮𐑂𐑌, 𐑌𐐱𐐻𐐶𐐮𐑄𐑅𐐻𐐰𐑌𐐼𐐮𐑍 𐐫𐑊 𐐹𐐲𐑉𐑅𐐨𐐿𐐷𐐭𐑇𐐲𐑌𐑆; 𐐺𐐨𐐸𐐬𐑊𐐼 𐑄𐐩 𐐪𐑉 𐑄𐐩 𐐸𐐶𐐮𐐽 𐑇𐐰𐑊 𐑌𐐱𐐻 𐐹𐐯𐑉𐐮𐑇. 𐐒𐐲𐐻 𐑄 𐐝𐐲𐑌 𐐲𐑂 𐑉𐐴𐐽𐐲𐑅𐑌𐐯𐑅 𐑇𐐰𐑊 𐐲𐐹𐐨𐑉 𐐲𐑌𐐻𐐭 𐑄𐐯𐑋; 𐐰𐑌𐐼 𐐸𐐨 𐑇𐐰𐑊 𐐸𐐨𐑊 𐑄𐐯𐑋, 𐐰𐑌𐐼 𐑄𐐩 𐑇𐐰𐑊 𐐸𐐰𐑂 𐐹𐐨𐑅 𐐶𐐮𐑄 𐐸𐐮𐑋, 𐐲𐑌𐐻𐐮𐑊 𐑃𐑉𐐨 𐐾𐐯𐑌𐐲𐑉𐐩𐑇𐐲𐑌𐑆 𐑇𐐰𐑊 𐐸𐐰𐑂 𐐹𐐰𐑅𐐻 𐐲𐐶𐐩, 𐐰𐑌𐐼 𐑋𐐯𐑌𐐨 𐐲𐑂 𐑄 𐑁𐐬𐑉𐑃 𐐾𐐯𐑌𐐲𐑉𐐩𐑇𐐲𐑌 𐑇𐐰𐑊 𐐸𐐰𐑂 𐐹𐐰𐑅𐐻 𐐲𐐶𐐩 𐐮𐑌 𐑉𐐴𐐽𐐲𐑅𐑌𐐯𐑅. 𐐈𐑌𐐼 𐐸𐐶𐐯𐑌 𐑄𐐨𐑆 𐑃𐐮𐑍𐑆 𐐸𐐰𐑂 𐐹𐐰𐑅𐐻 𐐲𐐶𐐩, 𐐰 𐑅𐐹𐐨𐐼𐐨 𐐼𐐨𐑅𐐻𐑉𐐲𐐿𐑇𐐲𐑌 𐐿𐐲𐑋𐐯𐑃 𐐲𐑌𐐻𐐭 𐑋𐐴 𐐹𐐨𐐹𐑊; 𐑁𐐫𐑉, 𐑌𐐱𐐻𐐶𐐮𐑄𐑅𐐻𐐰𐑌𐐼𐐮𐑍 𐑄 𐐹𐐩𐑌𐑆 𐐲𐑂 𐑋𐐴 𐑅𐐬𐑊, 𐐌 𐐸𐐰𐑂 𐑅𐐨𐑌 𐐮𐐻; 𐐸𐐶𐐯𐑉𐑁𐐫𐑉, 𐐌 𐑌𐐬 𐑄𐐰𐐻 𐐮𐐻 𐑇𐐰𐑊 𐐿𐐲𐑋 𐐻𐐭 𐐹𐐰𐑅; 𐐰𐑌𐐼 𐑄𐐩 𐑅𐐯𐑊 𐑄𐐯𐑋𐑅𐐯𐑊𐑂𐑆 𐑁𐐫𐑉 𐑌𐐫𐐻: 𐑁𐐫𐑉, 𐑁𐐫𐑉 𐑄 𐑉𐐨𐐶𐐫𐑉𐐼 𐐲𐑂 𐑄𐐩𐑉 𐐹𐑉𐐴𐐼, 𐐰𐑌𐐼 𐑄𐐩𐑉 𐑁𐐭𐑊𐐮𐑇𐑌𐐯𐑅, 𐑄𐐩 𐑇𐐰𐑊 𐑉𐐨𐐹 𐐼𐐨𐑅𐐻𐑉𐐲𐐿𐑇𐐲𐑌; 𐑁𐐫𐑉 𐐺𐐨𐐿𐐫𐑆 𐑄𐐩 𐐷𐐨𐑊𐐼 𐐲𐑌𐐻𐐭 𐑄 𐐼𐐯𐑂𐑊, 𐐰𐑌𐐼 𐐽𐐭𐑆 𐐶𐐲𐑉𐐿𐑅 𐐲𐑂 𐐼𐐪𐑉𐐿𐑌𐐯𐑅 𐑉𐐰𐑄𐐲𐑉 𐑄𐐰𐑌 𐑊𐐴𐐻: 𐑄𐐯𐑉𐑁𐐫𐑉 𐑄𐐩 𐑋𐐲𐑅𐐻 𐑀𐐬 𐐼𐐵𐑌 𐐻𐐭 𐐸𐐯𐑊, 𐑁𐐫𐑉 𐑄 𐐝𐐹𐐮𐑉𐐮𐐻 𐐲𐑂 𐑄 𐐢𐐫𐑉𐐼 𐐶𐐮𐑊 𐑌𐐱𐐻 𐐫𐑊𐐶𐐩𐑆 𐑅𐐻𐑉𐐴𐑂 𐐶𐐮𐑄 𐑋𐐰𐑌. 𐐈𐑌𐐼 𐐸𐐶𐐯𐑌 𐑄 𐐝𐐹𐐮𐑉𐐮𐐻 𐑅𐐨𐑅𐐯𐑃 𐐻𐐭 𐑅𐐻𐑉𐐴𐑂 𐐶𐐮𐑄 𐑋𐐰𐑌, 𐑄𐐯𐑌 𐐿𐐲𐑋𐐯𐑃 𐑅𐐹𐐨𐐼𐐨 𐐼𐐨𐑅𐐻𐑉𐐲𐐿𐑇𐐲𐑌, 𐐰𐑌𐐼 𐑄𐐮𐑅 𐑀𐑉𐐨𐑂𐐯𐑃 𐑋𐐴 𐑅𐐬𐑊.

12. 𐐈𐑌𐐼 𐐰𐑆 𐐌 𐑅𐐹𐐩𐐿 𐐿𐐱𐑌𐑅𐐲𐑉𐑌𐐮𐑍 𐑄 𐐿𐐱𐑌𐑂𐐮𐑌𐑅𐐮𐑍 𐐱𐑂 𐑄 𐐖𐐭𐑆, 𐑄𐐰𐐻 𐐖𐐨𐑆𐐲𐑅 𐐮𐑆 𐑄 𐑂𐐯𐑉𐐨 𐐗𐑉𐐴𐑅𐐻, 𐐮𐐻 𐑋𐐲𐑅𐐻 𐑌𐐨𐐼𐑆 𐐺𐐨 𐑄𐐰𐐻 𐑄 𐐖𐐯𐑌𐐻𐐴𐑊𐑆 𐐺𐐨 𐐿𐐱𐑌𐑂𐐮𐑌𐑅𐐻 𐐫𐑊𐑅𐐬 𐑄𐐰𐐻 𐐖𐐨𐑆𐐲𐑅 𐐮𐑆 𐑄 𐐗𐑉𐐴𐑅𐐻, 𐑄 𐐀𐐻𐐲𐑉𐑌𐐲𐑊 𐐘𐐱𐐼; 𐐰𐑌𐐼 𐑄𐐰𐐻 𐐸𐐨 𐑋𐐰𐑌𐐮𐑁𐐯𐑅𐐻𐐯𐑃 𐐸𐐮𐑋𐑅𐐯𐑊𐑁 𐐲𐑌𐐻𐐭 𐐫𐑊 𐑄𐐬𐑆 𐐸𐐭 𐐺𐐨𐑊𐐨𐑂 𐐮𐑌 𐐸𐐮𐑋, 𐐺𐐴 𐑄 𐐹𐐵𐐲𐑉 𐐱𐑂 𐑄 𐐐𐐬𐑊𐐨 𐐘𐐬𐑅𐐻; 𐐷𐐩, 𐐲𐑌𐐻𐐭 𐐯𐑂𐑉𐐨 𐑌𐐩𐑇𐐲𐑌, 𐐿𐐮𐑌𐐼𐑉𐐯𐐼, 𐐻𐐲𐑍, 𐐰𐑌𐐼 𐐹𐐨𐐹𐑊, 𐐶𐐲𐑉𐐿𐐮𐑍 𐑋𐐴𐐻𐐨 𐑋𐐮𐑉𐐲𐐿𐑊𐑆, 𐑅𐐴𐑌𐑆, 𐐰𐑌𐐼 𐐶𐐲𐑌𐐼𐐲𐑉𐑆, 𐐲𐑋𐐲𐑍 𐑄 𐐽𐐮𐑊𐐼𐑉𐐯𐑌 𐐱𐑂 𐑋𐐯𐑌, 𐐰𐐿𐐫𐑉𐐼𐐮𐑍 𐐻𐐭 𐑄𐐩𐑉 𐑁𐐩𐑃.

13. 𐐒𐐲𐐻 𐐺𐐨𐐸𐐬𐑊𐐼, 𐐌 𐐹𐑉𐐱𐑁𐐯𐑅𐐴 𐐲𐑌𐐻𐐭 𐐷𐐭 𐐿𐐱𐑌𐑅𐐲𐑉𐑌𐐮𐑍 𐑄 𐑊𐐰𐑅𐐻 𐐼𐐩𐑆; 𐐿𐐱𐑌𐑅𐐲𐑉𐑌𐐮𐑍 𐑄 𐐼𐐩𐑆 𐐸𐐶𐐯𐑌 𐑄 𐐢𐐫𐑉𐐼 𐐘𐐱𐐼 𐑇𐐰𐑊 𐐺𐑉𐐮𐑍 𐑄𐐨𐑆 𐑃𐐮𐑍𐑆 𐑁𐐬𐑉𐑃 𐐲𐑌𐐻𐐭 𐑄 𐐽𐐮𐑊𐐼𐑉𐐯𐑌 𐐱𐑂 𐑋𐐯𐑌. 𐐈𐑁𐐻𐐲𐑉 𐑋𐐴 𐑅𐐨𐐼 𐐰𐑌𐐼 𐑄 𐑅𐐨𐐼 𐐱𐑂 𐑋𐐴 𐐺𐑉𐐯𐑄𐑉𐐯𐑌 𐑇𐐰𐑊 𐐸𐐰𐑂 𐐼𐐶𐐮𐑌𐐼𐑊𐐼 𐐮𐑌 𐐲𐑌𐐺𐐨𐑊𐐨𐑁, 𐐰𐑌𐐼 𐑇𐐰𐑊 𐐸𐐰𐑂 𐐺𐐮𐑌 𐑅𐑋𐐮𐐻𐑌 𐐺𐐴 𐑄 𐐖𐐯𐑌𐐻𐐴𐑊𐑆; 𐐷𐐩, 𐐰𐑁𐐻𐐲𐑉 𐑄 𐐢𐐫𐑉𐐼 𐐘𐐱𐐼 𐑇𐐰𐑊 𐐸𐐰𐑂 𐐿𐐰𐑋𐐹𐐻 𐐲𐑀𐐯𐑌𐑅𐐻 𐑄𐐯𐑋 𐑉𐐵𐑌𐐼 𐐲𐐺𐐵𐐻, 𐐰𐑌𐐼 𐑇𐐰𐑊 𐐸𐐰𐑂 𐑊𐐩𐐼 𐑅𐐨𐐾 𐐲𐑀𐐯𐑌𐑅𐐻 𐑄𐐯𐑋 𐐶𐐮𐑄 𐐲 𐑋𐐵𐑌𐐻, 𐐰𐑌𐐼 𐑉𐐩𐑆𐐼 𐑁𐐬𐑉𐐻𐑅 𐐲𐑀𐐯𐑌𐑅𐐻 𐑄𐐯𐑋; 𐐰𐑌𐐼 𐐰𐑁𐐻𐐲𐑉 𐑄𐐩 𐑇𐐰𐑊 𐐸𐐰𐑂 𐐺𐐮𐑌 𐐺𐑉𐐫𐐻 𐐼𐐵𐑌 𐑊𐐬 𐐮𐑌 𐑄 𐐼𐐲𐑅𐐻, 𐐨𐑂𐐲𐑌 𐑄𐐰𐐻 𐑄𐐩 𐐪𐑉 𐑌𐐱𐐻, 𐐷𐐯𐐻 𐑄 𐐶𐐲𐑉𐐼𐑆 𐐱𐑂 𐑄 𐑉𐐴𐐽𐐲𐑅 𐑇𐐰𐑊 𐐺𐐨 𐑉𐐮𐐻𐑌, 𐐰𐑌𐐼 𐑄 𐐹𐑉𐐩𐐲𐑉𐑆 𐐱𐑂 𐑄 𐑁𐐩𐑃𐑁𐐳𐑊 𐑇𐐰𐑊 𐐺𐐨 𐐸𐐲𐑉𐐼, 𐐰𐑌𐐼 𐐫𐑊 𐑄𐐬𐑆 𐐸𐐭 𐐸𐐰𐑂 𐐼𐐶𐐮𐑌𐐼𐑊𐐼 𐐮𐑌 𐐲𐑌𐐺𐐨𐑊𐐨𐑁 𐑇𐐰𐑊 𐑌𐐱𐐻 𐐺𐐨 𐑁𐐫𐑉𐑀𐐱𐐻𐑌. 𐐙𐐫𐑉 𐑄𐐬𐑆 𐐸𐐭 𐑇𐐰𐑊 𐐺𐐨 𐐼𐐯𐑅𐐻𐑉𐑎𐐼 𐑇𐐰𐑊 𐑅𐐹𐐨𐐿 𐐲𐑌𐐻𐐭 𐑄𐐯𐑋 𐐵𐐻 𐐱𐑂 𐑄 𐑀𐑉𐐵𐑌𐐼, 𐐰𐑌𐐼 𐑄𐐩𐑉 𐑅𐐹𐐨𐐽 𐑇𐐰𐑊 𐐺𐐨 𐑊𐐬 𐐵𐐻 𐐱𐑂 𐑄 𐐼𐐲𐑅𐐻, 𐐰𐑌𐐼 𐑄𐐩𐑉 𐑂𐑎𐑅 𐑇𐐰𐑊 𐐺𐐨 𐐰𐑆 𐐶𐐲𐑌 𐑄𐐰𐐻 𐐸𐐰𐑃 𐐲 𐑁𐐲𐑋𐐮𐑊𐐷𐐲𐑉 𐑅𐐹𐐮𐑉𐐮𐐻; 𐑁𐐫𐑉 𐑄 𐐢𐐫𐑉𐐼 𐐘𐐱𐐼 𐐶𐐮𐑊 𐑀𐐮𐑂 𐐲𐑌𐐻𐐭 𐐸𐐮𐑋 𐐹𐐵𐐲𐑉, 𐑄𐐰𐐻 𐐸𐐨 𐑋𐐩 𐐸𐐶𐐮𐑅𐐹𐐲𐑉 𐐿𐐱𐑌𐑅𐐲𐑉𐑌𐐮𐑍 𐑄𐐯𐑋, 𐐨𐑂𐐲𐑌 𐐰𐑆 𐐮𐐻 𐐶𐐲𐑉 𐐵𐐻 𐐱𐑂 𐑄 𐑀𐑉𐐵𐑌𐐼; 𐐰𐑌𐐼 𐑄𐐩𐑉 𐑅𐐹𐐨𐐽 𐑇𐐰𐑊 𐐸𐐶𐐮𐑅𐐹𐐲𐑉 𐐵𐐻 𐐱𐑂 𐑄 𐐼𐐲𐑅𐐻. 𐐙𐐫𐑉 𐑄𐐲𐑅 𐑅𐐯𐑃 𐑄 𐐢𐐫𐑉𐐼 𐐘𐐱𐐼: 𐐜𐐩 𐑇𐐰𐑊 𐑉𐐴𐐻 𐑄 𐑃𐐮𐑍𐑆 𐐸𐐶𐐮𐐽 𐑇𐐰𐑊 𐐺𐐨 𐐼𐐲𐑌 𐐲𐑋𐐲𐑍 𐑄𐐯𐑋, 𐐰𐑌𐐼 𐑄𐐩 𐑇𐐰𐑊 𐐺𐐨 𐑉𐐮𐐻𐑌 𐐰𐑌𐐼 𐑅𐐨𐑊𐐼 𐐲𐐹 𐐮𐑌 𐐲 𐐺𐐳𐐿, 𐐰𐑌𐐼 𐑄𐐬𐑆 𐐸𐐭 𐐸𐐰𐑂 𐐼𐐶𐐮𐑌𐐼𐑊𐐼 𐐮𐑌 𐐲𐑌𐐺𐐨𐑊𐐨𐑁 𐑇𐐰𐑊 𐑌𐐱𐐻 𐐸𐐰𐑂 𐑄𐐯𐑋, 𐑁𐐫𐑉 𐑄𐐩 𐑅𐐨𐐿 𐐻𐐭 𐐼𐐯𐑅𐐻𐑉𐑎 𐑄 𐑃𐐮𐑍𐑆 𐐱𐑂 𐐘𐐱𐐼: 𐐸𐐶𐐩𐑉𐑁𐐬𐑉, 𐐰𐑆 𐑄𐐬𐑆 𐐸𐐭 𐐸𐐰𐑂 𐐺𐐮𐑌 𐐼𐐯𐑅𐐻𐑉𐑎𐐼 𐐸𐐰𐑂 𐐺𐐮𐑌 𐐼𐐯𐑅𐐻𐑉𐑎𐐼 𐑅𐐹𐐨𐐼𐐮𐑊𐐨; 𐐰𐑌𐐼 𐑄 𐑋𐐲𐑊𐐻𐐮𐐻𐐧𐐼 𐐱𐑂 𐑄𐐩𐑉 𐐻𐐯𐑉𐐲𐐺𐑊 𐐶𐐲𐑌𐑆 𐑇𐐰𐑊 𐐺𐐨 𐐰𐑆 𐐽𐐰𐑁 𐑄𐐰𐐻 𐐹𐐰𐑅𐐯𐑃 𐐲𐐶𐐩. 𐐏𐐩, 𐑄𐐲𐑅 𐑅𐐯𐑃 𐑄 𐐢𐐫𐑉𐐼 𐐘𐐱𐐼: 𐐆𐐻 𐑇𐐰𐑊 𐐺𐐨 𐐰𐐻 𐐰𐑌 𐐮𐑌𐑅𐐻𐐲𐑌𐐻, 𐑅𐐲𐐼𐑌𐑊𐐨.

14. 𐐈𐑌𐐼 𐐮𐐻 𐑇𐐰𐑊 𐐿𐐲𐑋 𐐻𐐭 𐐹𐐰𐑅 𐑄𐐰𐐻 𐑄𐐬𐑆 𐐸𐐭 𐐸𐐰𐑂 𐐼𐐶𐐮𐑌𐐼𐑊𐐼 𐐮𐑌 𐐲𐑌𐐺𐐨𐑊𐐨𐑁, 𐑇𐐰𐑊 𐐺𐐨 𐑅𐑋𐐮𐐻𐑌 𐐺𐐴 𐑄 𐐸𐐰𐑌𐐼 𐐱𐑂 𐑄 𐐖𐐯𐑌𐐻𐐴𐑊𐑆. 𐐈𐑌𐐼 𐑄 𐐖𐐯𐑌𐐻𐐴𐑊𐑆 𐐪𐑉 𐑊𐐮𐑁𐐻𐐯𐐼 𐐲𐐹 𐐮𐑌 𐑄 𐐹𐑉𐐴𐐼 𐐱𐑂 𐑄𐐩𐑉 𐐴𐑆, 𐐰𐑌𐐼 𐐸𐐰𐑂 𐑅𐐻𐐲𐑋𐐺𐑊𐐼, 𐐺𐐨𐐿𐐫𐑆 𐐱𐑂 𐑄 𐑀𐑉𐐩𐐻𐑌𐐯𐑅 𐐱𐑂 𐑄𐐩𐑉 𐑅𐐻𐐲𐑋𐐺𐑊𐐮𐑍 𐐺𐑊𐐱𐐿, 𐑄𐐰𐐻 𐑄𐐩 𐐸𐐰𐑂 𐐺𐐮𐑊𐐻 𐐲𐐹 𐑋𐐯𐑌𐐨 𐐽𐐲𐑉𐐽𐐯𐑆; 𐑌𐐯𐑂𐐲𐑉𐑄𐐲𐑊𐐯𐑅, 𐑄𐐩 𐐹𐐳𐐻 𐐼𐐵𐑌 𐑄 𐐹𐐵𐐲𐑉 𐐰𐑌𐐼 𐑋𐐮𐑉𐐲𐐿𐑊𐑆 𐐱𐑂 𐐘𐐱𐐼, 𐐰𐑌𐐼 𐐹𐑉𐐨𐐽 𐐲𐐹 𐐲𐑌𐐻𐐭 𐑄𐐯𐑋𐑅𐐯𐑊𐑂𐑆 𐑄𐐩𐑉 𐐬𐑌 𐐶𐐮𐑆𐐼𐐲𐑋, 𐐰𐑌𐐼 𐑄𐐩𐑉 𐐬𐑌 𐑊𐐲𐑉𐑌𐐮𐑍, 𐑄𐐰𐐻 𐑄𐐩 𐑋𐐩 𐑀𐐯𐐻 𐑀𐐩𐑌 𐐰𐑌𐐼 𐑀𐑉𐐴𐑌𐐼 𐐲𐐹𐐱𐑌 𐑄 𐑁𐐩𐑅 𐐱𐑂 𐑄 𐐹𐐭𐑉; 𐐰𐑌𐐼 𐑄𐐩𐑉 𐐪𐑉 𐑋𐐯𐑌𐐨 𐐽𐐲𐑉𐐽𐐯𐑆 𐐺𐐮𐑊𐐻 𐐲𐐹 𐐸𐐶𐐮𐐽 𐐿𐐫𐑆 𐐯𐑌𐑂𐐨𐐮𐑍𐑆, 𐐰𐑌𐐼 𐑅𐐻𐑉𐐴𐑁𐑅, 𐐰𐑌𐐼 𐑋𐐰𐑊𐐮𐑅; 𐐰𐑌𐐼 𐑄𐐩𐑉 𐐪𐑉 𐐫𐑊𐑅𐐬 𐑅𐐨𐐿𐑉𐐯𐐻 𐐿𐐱𐑋𐐺𐐮𐑌𐐩𐑇𐐲𐑌𐑆, 𐐨𐑂𐐲𐑌 𐐰𐑆 𐐮𐑌 𐐻𐐴𐑋𐑆 𐐱𐑂 𐐬𐑊𐐼, 𐐰𐐿𐐫𐑉𐐼𐐮𐑍 𐐻𐐭 𐑄 𐐿𐐱𐑋𐐺𐐮𐑌𐐩𐑇𐐲𐑌𐑆 𐐱𐑂 𐑄 𐐼𐐯𐑂𐑊, 𐑁𐐫𐑉 𐐸𐐨 𐐮𐑆 𐑄 𐑁𐐵𐑌𐐼𐐲𐑉 𐐱𐑂 𐐫𐑊 𐑄𐐨𐑆 𐑃𐐮𐑍𐑆; 𐐷𐐩, 𐑄 𐑁𐐵𐑌𐐼𐐲𐑉 𐐱𐑂 𐑋𐐲𐑉𐐼𐐲𐑉, 𐐰𐑌𐐼 𐐶𐐲𐑉𐐿𐑅 𐐱𐑂 𐐼𐐪𐑉𐐿𐑌𐐯𐑅; 𐐷𐐩, 𐐰𐑌𐐼 𐐸𐐨 𐑊𐐨𐐼𐐯𐑃 𐑄𐐯𐑋 𐐺𐐴 𐑄 𐑌𐐯𐐿 𐐶𐐮𐑄 𐐲 𐑁𐑊𐐰𐐿𐑅𐐲𐑌 𐐿𐐫𐑉𐐼, 𐐲𐑌𐐻𐐮𐑊 𐐸𐐨 𐐺𐐴𐑌𐐼𐐯𐑃 𐑄𐐯𐑋 𐐶𐐮𐑄 𐐸𐐮𐑆 𐑅𐐻𐑉𐐱𐑍 𐐿𐐫𐑉𐐼𐑆 𐑁𐐱𐑉𐐯𐑂𐐲𐑉.

15. 𐐙𐐫𐑉 𐐺𐐨𐐸𐐬𐑊𐐼, 𐑋𐐴 𐐺𐐨𐑊𐐲𐑂𐐯𐐼 𐐺𐑉𐐯𐑄𐑉𐐯𐑌, 𐐌 𐑅𐐩 𐐲𐑌𐐻𐐭 𐐷𐐭, 𐑄𐐰𐐻 𐑄 𐐢𐐫𐑉𐐼 𐐘𐐱𐐼 𐐶𐐲𐑉𐐿𐐯𐑃 𐑌𐐱𐐻 𐐮𐑌 𐐼𐐪𐑉𐐿𐑌𐐯𐑅. 𐐐𐐨 𐐼𐐭𐐯𐑃 𐑌𐐱𐐻 𐐯𐑌𐐨𐑃𐐮𐑍, 𐑅𐐩𐑂 𐐮𐐻 𐐺𐐨 𐑁𐐫𐑉 𐑄 𐐺𐐯𐑌𐐯𐑁𐐮𐐻 𐐱𐑂 𐑄 𐐶𐐲𐑉𐑊𐐼; 𐑁𐐫𐑉 𐐸𐐨 𐑊𐐲𐑂𐐯𐑃 𐑄 𐐶𐐲𐑉𐑊𐐼, 𐐨𐑂𐐲𐑌 𐑄𐐰𐐻 𐐸𐐨 𐑊𐐩𐐯𐑃 𐐼𐐵𐑌 𐐸𐐮𐑆 𐐬𐑌 𐑊𐐴𐑁, 𐑄𐐰𐐻 𐐸𐐨 𐑋𐐩 𐐼𐑉𐐫 𐐫𐑊 𐑋𐐯𐑌 𐐲𐑌𐐻𐐭 𐐸𐐮𐑋. 𐐐𐐶𐐩𐑉𐑁𐐬𐑉 𐐸𐐨 𐐿𐐱𐑋𐐰𐑌𐐼𐐯𐑃 𐑌𐐲𐑌 𐑄𐐰𐐻 𐑄𐐩 𐑇𐐰𐑊 𐑌𐐱𐐻 𐐹𐐪𐑉𐐻𐐩𐐿 𐐱𐑂 𐐸𐐮𐑆 𐑅𐐰𐑊𐑂𐐩𐑇𐐲𐑌. 𐐒𐐨𐐸𐐬𐑊𐐼, 𐐼𐐲𐑃 𐐸𐐨 𐐿𐑉𐐴 𐐲𐑌𐐻𐐭 𐐯𐑌𐐨, 𐑅𐐩𐐮𐑍, 𐐔𐐨𐐹𐐪𐑉𐐻 𐑁𐑉𐐱𐑋 𐑋𐐨? 𐐒𐐨𐐸𐐬𐑊𐐼, 𐐌 𐑅𐐩 𐐲𐑌𐐻𐐭 𐐷𐐭, 𐐤𐐩; 𐐺𐐲𐐻 𐐸𐐨 𐑅𐐯𐑃, 𐐗𐐲𐑋 𐐲𐑌𐐻𐐭 𐑋𐐨 𐐫𐑊 𐐷𐐨 𐐯𐑌𐐼𐑆 𐐱𐑂 𐑄 𐐲𐑉𐑃, 𐐺𐐴 𐑋𐐮𐑊𐐿 𐐰𐑌𐐼 𐐸𐐲𐑌𐐨, 𐐶𐐮𐑄𐐵𐐻 𐑋𐐲𐑌𐐨 𐐰𐑌𐐼 𐐶𐐮𐑄𐐵𐐻 𐐹𐑉𐐴𐑅. 𐐒𐐨𐐸𐐬𐑊𐐼, 𐐸𐐰𐑃 𐐸𐐨 𐐿𐐱𐑋𐐰𐑌𐐼𐐯𐐼 𐐯𐑌𐐨 𐑄𐐰𐐻 𐑄𐐩 𐑇𐐳𐐼 𐐼𐐨𐐹𐐪𐑉𐐻

𐐵𐐻 𐐱𐑂 𐑄 𐑅𐐮𐑌𐐲𐑀𐐱𐑀𐑆, 𐐫𐑉 𐐵𐐻 𐐱𐑂 𐑄 𐐸𐐵𐑆𐐯𐑆 𐐱𐑂 𐐶𐐲𐑉𐑇𐐮𐐹? 𐐒𐐨𐐸𐐬𐑊𐐼, 𐐌 𐑅𐐩 𐐲𐑌𐐻𐐭 𐐷𐐭, 𐑌𐐩. 𐐐𐐰𐑃 𐐸𐐨 𐐿𐐱𐑋𐐰𐑌𐐼𐐯𐐼 𐐯𐑌𐐨 𐑄𐐰𐐻 𐑄𐐩 𐑇𐐳𐐼 𐑌𐐱𐐻 𐐹𐐪𐑉𐐻𐐩𐐿 𐐱𐑂 𐐸𐐮𐑆 𐑅𐐰𐑊𐑂𐐩𐑇𐐲𐑌? 𐐒𐐨𐐸𐐬𐑊𐐼 𐐌 𐑅𐐩 𐐲𐑌𐐻𐐭 𐐷𐐭, 𐑌𐐩; 𐐺𐐲𐐻 𐐸𐐨 𐐸𐐰𐑃 𐑀𐐮𐑂𐐲𐑌 𐐮𐐻 𐑁𐑉𐐨 𐑁𐐫𐑉 𐐫𐑊 𐑋𐐯𐑌; 𐐰𐑌𐐼 𐐸𐐨 𐐸𐐰𐑃 𐐿𐐱𐑋𐐰𐑌𐐼𐐯𐐼 𐐸𐐮𐑆 𐐹𐐨𐐹𐑊 𐑄𐐰𐐻 𐑄𐐩 𐑇𐐳𐐼 𐐹𐐲𐑉𐑅𐐶𐐩𐐼 𐐫𐑊 𐑋𐐯𐑌 𐐻𐐭 𐑉𐐨𐐹𐐯𐑌𐐻𐐰𐑌𐑅. 𐐒𐐨𐐸𐐬𐑊𐐼, 𐐸𐐰𐑃 𐑄 𐐢𐐫𐑉𐐼 𐐿𐐱𐑋𐐰𐑌𐐼𐐯𐐼 𐐯𐑌𐐨 𐑄𐐰𐐻 𐑄𐐩 𐑇𐐳𐐼 𐑌𐐱𐐻 𐐹𐐪𐑉𐐻𐐩𐐿 𐐱𐑂 𐐸𐐮𐑆 𐑀𐐳𐐼𐑌𐐯𐑅? 𐐒𐐨𐐸𐐬𐑊𐐼 𐐌 𐑅𐐩 𐐲𐑌𐐻𐐭 𐐷𐐭, 𐑌𐐩; 𐐺𐐲𐐻 𐐫𐑊 𐑋𐐯𐑌 𐐪𐑉 𐐹𐑉𐐮𐑂𐐮𐑊𐐯𐑀𐐯𐐼 𐑄 𐐶𐐲𐑌 𐑊𐐴𐐿 𐐲𐑌𐐻𐐭 𐑄 𐐲𐑄𐐲𐑉, 𐐰𐑌𐐼 𐑌𐐲𐑌 𐐪𐑉 𐑁𐐫𐑉𐐺𐐮𐐼𐐲𐑌. 𐐐𐐨 𐐿𐐱𐑋𐐰𐑌𐐼𐐯𐑃 𐑄𐐰𐐻 𐑄𐐯𐑉 𐑇𐐰𐑊 𐐺𐐨 𐑌𐐬 𐐹𐑉𐐨𐑅𐐻-𐐿𐑉𐐰𐑁𐐻𐑅; 𐑁𐐫𐑉, 𐐺𐐨𐐸𐐬𐑊𐐼, 𐐹𐑉𐐨𐑅𐐻-𐐿𐑉𐐰𐑁𐐻𐑅 𐐪𐑉 𐑄𐐰𐐻 𐑋𐐯𐑌 𐐹𐑉𐐨𐐽 𐐰𐑌𐐼 𐑅𐐯𐐻 𐑄𐐯𐑋𐑅𐐯𐑊𐑂𐑆 𐐲𐐹 𐑁𐐫𐑉 𐐩 𐑊𐐴𐐻 𐐲𐑌𐐻𐐭 𐑄 𐐶𐐲𐑉𐑊𐐼, 𐑄𐐰𐐻 𐑄𐐩 𐑋𐐩 𐑀𐐯𐐻 𐑀𐐩𐑌, 𐐰𐑌𐐼 𐐹𐑉𐐩𐑆 𐐱𐑂 𐑄 𐐶𐐲𐑉𐑊𐐼; 𐐺𐐲𐐻 𐑄𐐩 𐑅𐐨𐐿 𐑌𐐱𐐻 𐑄 𐐶𐐯𐑊𐑁𐐯𐑉 𐐱𐑂 𐐞𐐴𐐲𐑌. 𐐒𐐨𐐸𐐬𐑊𐐼, 𐑄 𐐢𐐫𐑉𐐼 𐐸𐐰𐑃 𐑁𐐫𐑉𐐺𐐮𐐼𐐲𐑌 𐑄𐐮𐑅 𐑃𐐮𐑍; 𐐸𐐶𐐯𐑉𐑁𐐫𐑉, 𐑄 𐐢𐐫𐑉𐐼 𐐘𐐱𐐼 𐐸𐐰𐑃 𐑀𐐮𐑂𐐲𐑌 𐐩 𐐿𐐱𐑋𐐰𐑌𐐼𐑋𐐯𐑌𐐻, 𐑄𐐰𐐻 𐐫𐑊 𐑋𐐯𐑌 𐑇𐐳𐐼 𐐸𐐰𐑂 𐐽𐐰𐑉𐐮𐐻𐐨, 𐐸𐐶𐐮𐐽 𐐽𐐰𐑉𐐮𐐻𐐨 𐐮𐑆 𐑊𐐲𐑂. 𐐈𐑌𐐼 𐐯𐐿𐑅𐐯𐐹𐐻 𐑄𐐩 𐑇𐐳𐐼 𐐸𐐰𐑂 𐐽𐐰𐑉𐐮𐐻𐐨, 𐑄𐐩 𐐶𐐲𐑉 𐑌𐐲𐑃𐐮𐑍: 𐐸𐐶𐐯𐑉𐑁𐐫𐑉, 𐐮𐑁 𐑄𐐩 𐑇𐐳𐐼 𐐸𐐰𐑂 𐐽𐐰𐑉𐐮𐐻𐐨 𐑄𐐩 𐐶𐐳𐐼 𐑌𐐱𐐻 𐑅𐐲𐑁𐐲𐑉 𐑄 𐑊𐐩𐐺𐐲𐑉𐐲𐑉 𐐮𐑌 𐐞𐐴𐐲𐑌 𐐻𐐭 𐐹𐐯𐑉𐐮𐑇. 𐐒𐐲𐐻 𐑄 𐑊𐐩𐐺𐐲𐑉𐐲𐑉 𐐮𐑌 𐐞𐐴𐐲𐑌 𐑇𐐰𐑊 𐑊𐐩𐐺𐐲𐑉 𐑁𐐫𐑉 𐐞𐐴𐐲𐑌; 𐑁𐐫𐑉 𐐮𐑁 𐑄𐐩 𐑊𐐩𐐺𐐲𐑉 𐑁𐐫𐑉 𐑋𐐲𐑌𐐨, 𐑄𐐩 𐑇𐐰𐑊 𐐹𐐯𐑉𐐮𐑇.

16. 𐐈𐑌𐐼 𐐰𐑀𐐯𐑌, 𐑄 𐐢𐐫𐑉𐐼 𐐘𐐱𐐼 𐐸𐐰𐑃 𐐿𐐱𐑋𐐰𐑌𐐼𐐯𐐼 𐑄𐐰𐐻 𐑋𐐯𐑌 𐑇𐐳𐐼 𐑌𐐱𐐻 𐑋𐐲𐑉𐐼𐐲𐑉; 𐑄𐐰𐐻 𐑄𐐩 𐑇𐐳𐐼 𐑌𐐱𐐻 𐑊𐐴; 𐑄𐐰𐐻 𐑄𐐩 𐑇𐐳𐐼 𐑌𐐱𐐻 𐑅𐐻𐐨𐑊; 𐑄𐐰𐐻 𐑄𐐩 𐑇𐐳𐐼 𐑌𐐱𐐻 𐐻𐐩𐐿 𐑄 𐑌𐐩𐑋 𐐱𐑂 𐑄 𐐢𐐫𐑉𐐼 𐑄𐐯𐑉 𐐘𐐱𐐼 𐐮𐑌 𐑂𐐩𐑌; 𐑄𐐰𐐻 𐑄𐐩 𐑇𐐳𐐼 𐑌𐐱𐐻 𐐯𐑌𐑂𐐨; 𐑄𐐰𐐻 𐑄𐐩 𐑇𐐳𐐼 𐑌𐐱𐐻 𐐸𐐰𐑂 𐑋𐐰𐑊𐐮𐑅; 𐑄𐐰𐐻 𐑄𐐩 𐑇𐐳𐐼 𐑌𐐱𐐻 𐐿𐐱𐑌𐐻𐐯𐑌𐐼 𐐶𐐲𐑌 𐐶𐐮𐑄 𐐰𐑌𐐲𐑄𐐲𐑉; 𐑄𐐰𐐻 𐑄𐐩 𐑇𐐳𐐼 𐑌𐐱𐐻 𐐿𐐱𐑋𐐮𐐻 𐐸𐐬𐑉𐐼𐐲𐑋𐑆; 𐐰𐑌𐐼 𐑄𐐰𐐻 𐑄𐐩 𐑇𐐳𐐼 𐐼𐐭 𐑌𐐲𐑌 𐐱𐑂 𐑄𐐨𐑆 𐑃𐐮𐑍𐑆; 𐑁𐐫𐑉 𐐸𐐭𐑅𐐬 𐐼𐐭𐐯𐑃 𐑄𐐯𐑋 𐑇𐐰𐑊 𐐹𐐯𐑉𐐮𐑇; 𐑁𐐫𐑉 𐑌𐐲𐑌 𐐱𐑂 𐑄𐐨𐑆 𐐮𐑌𐐮𐐿𐐶𐐮𐐻𐐨𐑆 𐐿𐐲𐑋 𐐱𐑂 𐑄 𐐢𐐫𐑉𐐼; 𐑁𐐫𐑉 𐐸𐐨 𐐼𐐭𐐯𐑃 𐑄𐐰𐐻 𐐸𐐶𐐮𐐽 𐐮𐑆 𐑀𐐳𐐼 𐐰𐑋𐐲𐑍 𐑄 𐐽𐐮𐑊𐐼𐑉𐐯𐑌 𐐱𐑂 𐑋𐐯𐑌; 𐐰𐑌𐐼 𐐸𐐨 𐐼𐐭𐐯𐑃 𐑌𐐲𐑃𐐮𐑍 𐑅𐐩𐑂 𐐮𐐻 𐐺𐐨 𐐹𐑊𐐩𐑌 𐐲𐑌𐐻𐐭 𐑄 𐐽𐐮𐑊𐐼𐑉𐐯𐑌 𐐱𐑂 𐑋𐐯𐑌; 𐐰𐑌𐐼 𐐸𐐨 𐐮𐑌𐑂𐐴𐐻𐐯𐑃 𐑄𐐯𐑋 𐐫𐑊 𐐻𐐭 𐐿𐐲𐑋 𐐲𐑌𐐻𐐭 𐐸𐐮𐑋, 𐐰𐑌𐐼 𐐹𐐪𐑉𐐻𐐩𐐿 𐐱𐑂 𐐸𐐮𐑆 𐑀𐐳𐐼𐑌𐐯𐑅; 𐐰𐑌𐐼 𐐸𐐨 𐐼𐐨𐑌𐐴𐐯𐑃 𐑌𐐲𐑌 𐑄𐐰𐐻 𐐿𐐲𐑋 𐐲𐑌𐐻𐐭 𐐸𐐮𐑋, 𐐺𐑊𐐰𐐿 𐐰𐑌𐐼 𐐸𐐶𐐴𐐻, 𐐺𐐱𐑌𐐼 𐐰𐑌𐐼 𐑁𐑉𐐨, 𐑋𐐩𐑊 𐐰𐑌𐐼 𐑁𐐨𐑋𐐩𐑊; 𐐰𐑌𐐼 𐐸𐐨 𐑉𐐨𐑋𐐯𐑋𐐺𐐲𐑉𐐯𐑃 𐑄 𐐸𐐨𐑄𐐲𐑌, 𐐰𐑌𐐼 𐐫𐑊 𐐪𐑉 𐐰𐑊𐐴𐐿 𐐲𐑌𐐻𐐭 𐐘𐐱𐐼, 𐐺𐐬𐑃 𐐖𐐭 𐐰𐑌𐐼 𐐖𐐯𐑌𐐻𐐴𐑊. 𐐒𐐲𐐻, 𐐺𐐨𐐸𐐬𐑊𐐼, 𐐮𐑌 𐑄 𐑊𐐰𐑅𐐻 𐐼𐐩𐑆, 𐐫𐑉 𐐮𐑌 𐑄 𐐼𐐩𐑆 𐐱𐑂 𐑄 𐐖𐐯𐑌𐐻𐐴𐑊𐑆; 𐐷𐐩, 𐐺𐐨𐐸𐐬𐑊𐐼 𐐫𐑊 𐑄 𐑌𐐩𐑇𐐲𐑌𐑆 𐐱𐑂 𐑄 𐐖𐐯𐑌𐐻𐐴𐑊𐑆, 𐐰𐑌𐐼 𐐫𐑊𐑅𐐬 𐑄 𐐖𐐭𐑆, 𐐺𐐬𐑃 𐑄𐐬𐑆 𐐸𐐭 𐑇𐐰𐑊 𐐿𐐲𐑋 𐐲𐐹𐐱𐑌 𐑄𐐮𐑅 𐑊𐐰𐑌𐐼, 𐐰𐑌𐐼 𐑄𐐬𐑆 𐐸𐐭 𐑇𐐰𐑊 𐐺𐐨 𐐲𐐹𐐱𐑌 𐐲𐑄𐐲𐑉 𐑊𐐰𐑌𐐼𐑆; 𐐷𐐩, 𐐨𐑂𐐲𐑌 𐐲𐐹𐐱𐑌 𐐫𐑊 𐑄 𐑊𐐰𐑌𐐼𐑆 𐐱𐑂 𐑄 𐐲𐑉𐑃, 𐐺𐐨𐐸𐐬𐑊𐐼, 𐑄𐐩 𐐶𐐮𐑊 𐐺𐐨 𐐼𐑉𐐲𐑍𐐿𐐲𐑌 𐐶𐐮𐑃 𐐮𐑌𐐮𐐿𐐶𐐮𐐻𐐨, 𐐰𐑌𐐼 𐐫𐑊 𐑋𐐰𐑌𐐲𐑉 𐐱𐑂 𐐰𐐺𐐱𐑋𐐮𐑌𐐩𐑇𐐲𐑌𐑆; 𐐰𐑌𐐼 𐐸𐐶𐐯𐑌 𐑄𐐰𐐻 𐐼𐐩 𐑇𐐰𐑊 𐐿𐐲𐑋, 𐑄𐐩 𐑇𐐰𐑊 𐐺𐐨 𐑂𐐮𐑆𐐮𐐻𐐯𐐼 𐐱𐑂 𐑄 𐐢𐐫𐑉𐐼 𐐱𐑂 𐐐𐐬𐑅𐐻𐑅, 𐐶𐐮𐑃 𐑃𐐲𐑌𐐼𐐲𐑉 𐐰𐑌𐐼 𐐶𐐮𐑃 𐐲𐑉𐑃𐐿𐐶𐐩𐐿, 𐐰𐑌𐐼 𐐶𐐮𐑃 𐐩 𐑀𐑉𐐩𐐻 𐑌𐐱𐐮𐑆, 𐐰𐑌𐐼 𐐶𐐮𐑃 𐑅𐐻𐐫𐑉𐑋, 𐐰𐑌𐐼 𐐶𐐮𐑃 𐐻𐐯𐑋𐐹𐐯𐑅𐐻, 𐐰𐑌𐐼 𐐶𐐮𐑃 𐑄 𐑁𐑊𐐩𐑋 𐐱𐑂 𐐼𐐨𐑂𐐵𐑉𐐮𐑍 𐑁𐐴𐑉; 𐐰𐑌𐐼 𐐫𐑊 𐑄 𐑌𐐩𐑇𐐲𐑌𐑆 𐑄𐐰𐐻 𐑁𐐴𐐻 𐐰𐑀𐐯𐑌𐑅𐐻 𐐞𐐴𐐲𐑌, 𐐰𐑌𐐼 𐑄𐐰𐐻 𐐼𐐮𐑅𐐻𐑉𐐯𐑅 𐐸𐐲𐑉, 𐑇𐐰𐑊 𐐺𐐨 𐐰𐑆 𐐩 𐐼𐑉𐐨𐑋 𐐱𐑂 𐐩 𐑌𐐴𐐻 𐑂𐐮𐑈𐐲𐑌; 𐐷𐐩, 𐐮𐐻 𐑇𐐰𐑊 𐐺𐐨 𐐲𐑌𐐻𐐭 𐑄𐐯𐑋, 𐐨𐑂𐐲𐑌 𐐰𐑆 𐐲𐑌𐐻𐐭 𐐩 𐐸𐐲𐑍𐑀𐑉𐐨 𐑋𐐰𐑌 𐐸𐐶𐐮𐐽 𐐼𐑉𐐨𐑋𐐯𐑃, 𐐰𐑌𐐼 𐐺𐐨𐐸𐐬𐑊𐐼 𐐸𐐨 𐐨𐐻𐐯𐑃, 𐐺𐐲𐐻 𐐸𐐨 𐐰𐐶𐐩𐐿𐐯𐑃 𐐰𐑌𐐼 𐐸𐐮𐑆 𐑅𐐬𐑊 𐐮𐑆 𐐯𐑋𐐹𐐻𐐨; 𐐫𐑉 𐑊𐐴𐐿 𐐲𐑌𐐻𐐭 𐐩 𐑃𐐲𐑉𐑅𐐻𐐨 𐑋𐐰𐑌 𐐸𐐶𐐮𐐽 𐐼𐑉𐐨𐑋𐐯𐑃, 𐐰𐑌𐐼 𐐺𐐨𐐸𐐬𐑊𐐼 𐐸𐐨 𐐼𐑉𐐮𐑍𐐿𐐯𐑃, 𐐺𐐲𐐻 𐐸𐐨 𐐰𐐶𐐩𐐿𐐯𐑃, 𐐰𐑌𐐼 𐐺𐐨𐐸𐐬𐑊𐐼 𐐸𐐨 𐐮𐑆 𐑁𐐩𐑌𐐻, 𐐰𐑌𐐼 𐐸𐐮𐑆 𐑅𐐬𐑊 𐐸𐐰𐑃 𐐰𐐹𐐯𐐻𐐴𐐻: 𐐷𐐩, 𐐨𐑂𐐲𐑌 𐑅𐐬 𐑇𐐰𐑊 𐑄 𐑋𐐲𐑊𐐻𐐮𐐻𐐭𐐼 𐐱𐑂 𐐫𐑊 𐑄 𐑌𐐩𐑇𐐲𐑌𐑆 𐐺𐐨 𐑄𐐰𐐻 𐑁𐐴𐐻 𐐰𐑀𐐯𐑌𐑅𐐻 𐐣𐐵𐑌𐐻 𐐞𐐴𐐲𐑌: 𐑁𐐫𐑉 𐐺𐐨𐐸𐐬𐑊𐐼, 𐐫𐑊 𐐷𐐨 𐑄𐐰𐐻 𐐼𐐭 𐐮𐑌𐐮𐐿𐐶𐐮𐐻𐐨, 𐑅𐐻𐐩 𐐷𐐭𐑉𐑅𐐯𐑊𐑂𐑆 𐐰𐑌𐐼 𐐶𐐲𐑌𐐼𐐲𐑉, 𐑁𐐫𐑉 𐐷𐐨 𐑇𐐰𐑊 𐐿𐑉𐐴 𐐵𐐻, 𐐰𐑌𐐼 𐐿𐑉𐐴; 𐐷𐐩, 𐐷𐐨 𐑇𐐰𐑊 𐐺𐐨 𐐼𐑉𐐲𐑍𐐿𐐲𐑌, 𐐺𐐲𐐻 𐑌𐐱𐐻 𐐶𐐮𐑃 𐐶𐐴𐑌, 𐐷𐐨 𐑇𐐰𐑊 𐑅𐐻𐐰𐑀𐐲𐑉, 𐐺𐐲𐐻 𐑌𐐱𐐻 𐐶𐐮𐑃 𐑅𐐻𐑉𐐱𐑍 𐐼𐑉𐐮𐑍𐐿: 𐑁𐐫𐑉 𐐺𐐨𐐸𐐬𐑊𐐼, 𐑄 𐐢𐐫𐑉𐐼 𐐸𐐰𐑃 𐐹𐐬𐑉𐐼 𐐵𐐻 𐐲𐐹𐐱𐑌 𐐷𐐭 𐑄 𐑅𐐹𐐮𐑉𐐮𐐻 𐐱𐑂 𐐼𐐨𐐹 𐑅𐑊𐐨𐐹. 𐐙𐐫𐑉 𐐺𐐨𐐸𐐬𐑊𐐼, 𐐷𐐨 𐐸𐐰𐑂 𐐿𐑊𐐬𐑆𐐼 𐐷𐐭𐑉 𐐴𐑆, 𐐰𐑌𐐼 𐐷𐐨 𐐸𐐰𐑂 𐑉𐐨𐐾𐐯𐐿𐐻𐐯𐐼 𐑄 𐐹𐑉𐐱𐑁𐐯𐐻𐑅, 𐐰𐑌𐐼 𐐷𐐭𐑉 𐑉𐐭𐑊𐐲𐑉𐑆, 𐐰𐑌𐐼 𐑄 𐑅𐐨𐐲𐑉𐑆 𐐸𐐰𐑃 𐐸𐐨 𐐿𐐲𐑂𐐲𐑉𐐼 𐐺𐐨𐐿𐐫𐑆 𐐱𐑂 𐐷𐐭𐑉 𐐮𐑌𐐮𐐿𐐶𐐮𐐻𐐨.

17. 𐐈𐑌𐐼 𐐮𐐻 𐑇𐐰𐑊 𐐿𐐲𐑋 𐐻𐐭 𐐹𐐰𐑅 𐑄𐐰𐐻 𐑄 𐐢𐐫𐑉𐐼 𐐘𐐱𐐼 𐑇𐐰𐑊 𐐺𐑉𐐮𐑍 𐑁𐐬𐑉𐑃 𐐲𐑌𐐻𐐭 𐐷𐐭 𐑄 𐐶𐐲𐑉𐐼𐑆 𐐱𐑂 𐐩 𐐺𐐳𐐿, 𐐰𐑌𐐼 𐑄𐐩 𐑇𐐰𐑊 𐐺 𐑄 𐐶𐐲𐑉𐐼𐑆 𐐱𐑂 𐑄𐐯𐑋 𐐸𐐶𐐮𐐽 𐐸𐐰𐑂 𐑅𐑊𐐲𐑋𐐺𐐲𐑉𐐼. 𐐈𐑌𐐼 𐐺𐐨𐐸𐐬𐑊𐐼 𐑄 𐐺𐐳𐐿 𐑇𐐰𐑊 𐐺 𐑅𐐨𐑊𐐼: 𐐰𐑌𐐼 𐐮𐑌 𐑄 𐐺𐐳𐐿 𐑇𐐰𐑊 𐐺 𐐩 𐑉𐐯𐑂𐐯𐑊𐐩𐑇𐐲𐑌 𐑁𐑉𐐲𐑋 𐐘𐐱𐐼, 𐑁𐑉𐐲𐑋 𐑄 𐐺𐐨𐑀𐐮𐑌𐐮𐑍 𐐱𐑂 𐑄 𐐶𐐲𐑉𐑊𐐼 𐐻𐐭 𐑄 𐐯𐑌𐐼𐐮𐑍 𐑄𐐯𐑉𐐱𐑂. 𐐐𐐶𐐯𐑉𐑁𐐫𐑉, 𐐺𐐨𐐿𐐫𐑆 𐐱𐑂 𐑄 𐑃𐐮𐑍𐑆 𐐸𐐶𐐮𐐽 𐐪𐑉 𐑅𐐨𐑊𐐼 𐐲𐐹, 𐑄 𐑃𐐮𐑍𐑆 𐐸𐐶𐐮𐐽 𐐪𐑉 𐑅𐐨𐑊𐐼 𐑇𐐰𐑊 𐑌𐐱𐐻 𐐺 𐐼𐐨𐑊𐐮𐑂𐐲𐑉𐐼 𐐮𐑌 𐑄 𐐼𐐩 𐐱𐑂 𐑄 𐐶𐐮𐐿𐐯𐐼𐑌𐐯𐑅 𐐰𐑌𐐼 𐐲𐐺𐐱𐑋𐐮𐑌𐐩𐑇𐐲𐑌𐑆 𐐱𐑂 𐑄 𐐹𐐨𐐹𐑊. 𐐐𐐶𐐯𐑉𐑁𐐫𐑉 𐑄 𐐺𐐳𐐿 𐑇𐐰𐑊 𐐺 𐐿𐐯𐐹𐐻 𐑁𐑉𐐲𐑋 𐑄𐐯𐑋. 𐐒𐐲𐐻 𐑄 𐐺𐐳𐐿 𐑇𐐰𐑊 𐐺 𐐼𐐨𐑊𐐮𐑂𐐲𐑉𐐼 𐐲𐑌𐐻𐐭 𐐩 𐑋𐐰𐑌, 𐐰𐑌𐐼 𐐸𐐨 𐑇𐐰𐑊 𐐼𐐨𐑊𐐮𐑂𐐲𐑉 𐑄 𐐶𐐲𐑉𐐼𐑆 𐐱𐑂 𐑄 𐐺𐐳𐐿, 𐐸𐐶𐐮𐐽 𐐪𐑉 𐑄 𐐶𐐲𐑉𐐼𐑆 𐐱𐑂 𐑄𐐬𐑆 𐐸𐐭 𐐸𐐰𐑂 𐑅𐑊𐐲𐑋𐐺𐐲𐑉𐐼 𐐮𐑌 𐑄 𐐼𐐲𐑅𐐻; 𐐰𐑌𐐼 𐐸𐐨 𐑇𐐰𐑊 𐐼𐐨𐑊𐐮𐑂𐐲𐑉 𐑄𐐨𐑆 𐐶𐐲𐑉𐐼𐑆 𐐲𐑌𐐻𐐭 𐐰𐑌𐐲𐑄𐐲𐑉; 𐐺𐐲𐐻 𐑄 𐐶𐐲𐑉𐐼𐑆 𐐸𐐶𐐮𐐽 𐐪𐑉 𐑅𐐨𐑊𐐼 𐐸𐐨 𐑇𐐰𐑊 𐑌𐐱𐐻 𐐼𐐨𐑊𐐮𐑂𐐲𐑉, 𐑌𐐨𐑄𐐲𐑉 𐑇𐐰𐑊 𐐸𐐨 𐐼𐐨𐑊𐐮𐑂𐐲𐑉 𐑄 𐐺𐐳𐐿. 𐐙𐐫𐑉 𐑄 𐐺𐐳𐐿 𐑇𐐰𐑊 𐐺 𐑅𐐨𐑊𐐼 𐐺𐐴 𐑄 𐐹𐐵𐐲𐑉 𐐱𐑂 𐐘𐐱𐐼, 𐐰𐑌𐐼 𐑄 𐑉𐐯𐑂𐐯𐑊𐐩𐑇𐐲𐑌 𐐸𐐶𐐮𐐽 𐐶𐐱𐑆 𐑅𐐨𐑊𐐼 𐑇𐐰𐑊 𐐺 𐐿𐐯𐐹𐐻 𐐮𐑌 𐑄 𐐺𐐳𐐿 𐐲𐑌𐐻𐐮𐑊 𐑄 𐐬𐑌 𐐼𐐷𐐭 𐐻𐐴𐑋 𐐱𐑂 𐑄 𐐢𐐫𐑉𐐼, 𐑄𐐰𐐻 𐑄𐐩 𐑋𐐩 𐐿𐐲𐑋 𐑁𐐬𐑉𐑃: 𐑁𐐫𐑉 𐐺𐐨𐐸𐐬𐑊𐐼 𐑄𐐩 𐑉𐐨𐑂𐐨𐑊 𐐫𐑊 𐑃𐐮𐑍𐑆 𐑁𐑉𐐲𐑋 𐑄 𐑁𐐵𐑌𐐼𐐩𐑇𐐲𐑌 𐐱𐑂 𐑄 𐐶𐐲𐑉𐑊𐐼 𐐲𐑌𐐻𐐭 𐑄 𐐯𐑌𐐼 𐑄𐐯𐑉𐐱𐑂. 𐐈𐑌𐐼 𐑄 𐐼𐐩 𐐿𐐲𐑋𐐯𐑃 𐑄𐐰𐐻 𐑄 𐐶𐐲𐑉𐐼𐑆 𐐱𐑂 𐑄 𐐺𐐳𐐿 𐐸𐐶𐐮𐐽 𐐶𐐲𐑉 𐑅𐐨𐑊𐐼 𐑇𐐰𐑊 𐐺 𐑉𐐯𐐼 𐐲𐐹𐐱𐑌 𐑄 𐐸𐐵𐑅 𐐻𐐱𐐹𐑅; 𐐰𐑌𐐼 𐑄𐐩 𐑇𐐰𐑊 𐐺 𐑉𐐯𐐼 𐐺𐐴 𐑄 𐐹𐐵𐐲𐑉 𐐱𐑂 𐐗𐑉𐐴𐑅𐐻: 𐐰𐑌𐐼 𐐫𐑊 𐑃𐐮𐑍𐑆 𐑇𐐰𐑊 𐐺 𐑉𐐨𐑂𐐨𐑊𐐼 𐐲𐑌𐐻𐐭 𐑄 𐐽𐐮𐑊𐐼𐑉𐐯𐑌 𐐱𐑂 𐑋𐐯𐑌 𐐸𐐶𐐮𐐽 𐐯𐑂𐐲𐑉 𐐸𐐰𐑂 𐐺𐐮𐑌 𐐲𐑋𐐲𐑍 𐑄 𐐽𐐮𐑊𐐼𐑉𐐯𐑌 𐐱𐑂 𐑋𐐯𐑌, 𐐰𐑌𐐼 𐐸𐐶𐐮𐐽 𐐯𐑂𐐲𐑉 𐐶𐐮𐑊 𐐺, 𐐨𐑂𐐯𐑌 𐐲𐑌𐐻𐐭 𐑄 𐐯𐑌𐐼 𐐱𐑂 𐑄 𐐲𐑉𐑃. 𐐐𐐶𐐯𐑉𐑁𐐫𐑉, 𐐰𐐻 𐑄𐐰𐐻 𐐼𐐩 𐐸𐐶𐐯𐑌 𐑄 𐐺𐐳𐐿 𐑇𐐰𐑊 𐐺 𐐼𐐨𐑊𐐮𐑂𐐲𐑉𐐼 𐐲𐑌𐐻𐐭 𐑄 𐑋𐐰𐑌 𐐱𐑂 𐐸𐐭𐑋 𐐌 𐐸𐐰𐑂 𐑅𐐹𐐬𐐿𐐲𐑌, 𐑄 𐐺𐐳𐐿 𐑇𐐰𐑊 𐐺 𐐸𐐮𐐼 𐑁𐑉𐐲𐑋 𐑄 𐐴𐑆 𐐱𐑂 𐑄 𐐶𐐲𐑉𐑊𐐼, 𐑄𐐰𐐻 𐑄 𐐴𐑆 𐐱𐑂 𐑌𐐲𐑌 𐑇𐐰𐑊 𐐺𐐨𐐸𐐬𐑊𐐼 𐐮𐐻 𐑅𐐩𐑂 𐐮𐐻 𐐺 𐑄𐐰𐐻 𐑃𐑉𐐨 𐐶𐐮𐐻𐑌𐐯𐑅𐐯𐑆 𐑇𐐰𐑊 𐐺𐐨𐐸𐐬𐑊𐐼 𐐮𐐻, 𐐺𐐴 𐑄 𐐹𐐵𐐲𐑉 𐐱𐑂 𐐘𐐱𐐼, 𐐺𐐨𐑅𐐴𐐼𐑆 𐐸𐐮𐑋 𐐻𐐭 𐐸𐐭𐑋 𐑄 𐐺𐐳𐐿 𐑇𐐰𐑊 𐐺 𐐼𐐨𐑊𐐮𐑂𐐲𐑉𐐼; 𐐰𐑌𐐼 𐑄𐐩 𐑇𐐰𐑊 𐐻𐐯𐑅𐐻𐐮𐑁𐐴 𐐻𐐭 𐑄 𐐻𐑉𐐭𐑃 𐐱𐑂 𐑄 𐐺𐐳𐐿 𐐰𐑌𐐼 𐑄 𐑃𐐮𐑍𐑆 𐑄𐐯𐑉𐐮𐑌. 𐐈𐑌𐐼 𐑄𐐯𐑉 𐐮𐑆 𐑌𐐲𐑌 𐐲𐑄𐐲𐑉 𐐸𐐶𐐮𐐽 𐑇𐐰𐑊 𐑂𐐷𐐭 𐐮𐐻, 𐑅𐐩𐑂 𐐮𐐻 𐐺 𐐩 𐑁𐐷𐐭 𐐲𐐿𐐫𐑉𐐼𐐮𐑍 𐐻𐐭 𐑄 𐐶𐐮𐑊 𐐱𐑂 𐐘𐐱𐐼, 𐐻𐐭 𐐺𐐯𐑉 𐐻𐐯𐑅𐐻𐐮𐑋𐐬𐑌𐐨 𐐱𐑂 𐐸𐐮𐑆 𐐶𐐲𐑉𐐼 𐐲𐑌𐐻𐐭 𐑄 𐐽𐐮𐑊𐐼𐑉𐐯𐑌 𐐱𐑂 𐑋𐐯𐑌: 𐑁𐐫𐑉 𐑄 𐐢𐐫𐑉𐐼 𐐘𐐱𐐼 𐐸𐐰𐑃 𐑅𐐯𐐼 𐑄𐐰𐐻 𐑄 𐐶𐐲𐑉𐐼𐑆 𐐱𐑂 𐑄 𐑁𐐩𐑃𐑁𐐳𐑊 𐑇𐐳𐐼 𐑅𐐹𐐨𐐿 𐐰𐑆 𐐮𐑁 𐐮𐐻 𐐶𐐲𐑉 𐑁𐑉𐐲𐑋 𐑄 𐐼𐐯𐐼. 𐐐𐐶𐐯𐑉𐑁𐐫𐑉, 𐑄 𐐢𐐫𐑉𐐼 𐐘𐐱𐐼 𐐶𐐮𐑊 𐐹𐑉𐐬𐑅𐐨𐐼 𐐻𐐭 𐐺𐑉𐐮𐑍 𐑁𐐬𐑉𐑃 𐑄 𐐶𐐲𐑉𐐼𐑆 𐐱𐑂 𐑄 𐐺𐐳𐐿; 𐐰𐑌𐐼 𐐮𐑌 𐑄 𐑋𐐵𐑃 𐐱𐑂 𐐰𐑆 𐑋𐐯𐑌𐐨 𐐶𐐮𐐻𐑌𐐯𐑅𐐯𐑆 𐐰𐑆 𐑅𐐨𐑋𐐯𐑃 𐐸𐐮𐑋 𐑀𐐳𐐼, 𐐶𐐮𐑊 𐐸𐐨 𐐯𐑅𐐻𐐰𐐺𐑊𐐮𐑇 𐐸𐐮𐑆 𐐶𐐲𐑉𐐼; 𐐰𐑌𐐼 𐐶𐐬 𐐺 𐐲𐑌𐐻𐐭 𐐸𐐮𐑋 𐑄𐐰𐐻 𐑉𐐨𐐾𐐯𐐿𐐻𐐯𐑃 𐑄 𐐶𐐲𐑉𐐼 𐐱𐑂 𐐘𐐱𐐼.

18. 𐐒𐐲𐐻 𐐺𐐨𐐸𐐬𐑊𐐼 𐐮𐐻 𐑇𐐰𐑊 𐐿𐐲𐑋 𐐻𐐭 𐐹𐐰𐑅 𐑄𐐰𐐻 𐑄 𐐢𐐫𐑉𐐼 𐐘𐐱𐐼 𐑇𐐰𐑊 𐑅𐐩 𐐲𐑌𐐻𐐭 𐐸𐐮𐑋 𐐻𐐭 𐐸𐐭𐑋 𐐸𐐨 𐑇𐐰𐑊 𐐼𐐨𐑊𐐮𐑂𐐲𐑉 𐑄 𐐺𐐳𐐿, 𐐓𐐩𐐿 𐑄𐐨𐑆 𐐶𐐲𐑉𐐼𐑆 𐐸𐐶𐐮𐐽 𐐪𐑉 𐑌𐐱𐐻 𐑅𐐨𐑊𐐼 𐐰𐑌𐐼 𐐼𐐨𐑊𐐮𐑂𐐲𐑉 𐑄𐐯𐑋 𐐻𐐭 𐐰𐑌𐐲𐑄𐐲𐑉, 𐑄𐐰𐐻 𐐸𐐨 𐑋𐐩 𐑇𐐬 𐑄𐐯𐑋 𐐲𐑌𐐻𐐭 𐑄 𐑊𐐲𐑉𐑌𐐯𐐼, 𐑅𐐩𐐮𐑍, 𐐡𐐨𐐼 𐑄𐐮𐑅, 𐐌 𐐹𐑉𐐩 𐑄𐐨. 𐐈𐑌𐐼 𐑄 𐑊𐐲𐑉𐑌𐐯𐐼 𐑇𐐰𐑊 𐑅𐐩, 𐐒𐑉𐐮𐑍 𐐸𐐮𐑄𐐲𐑉 𐑄 𐐺𐐳𐐿, 𐐰𐑌𐐼 𐐌 𐐶𐐮𐑊 𐑉𐐨𐐼 𐑄𐐯𐑋: 𐐰𐑌𐐼 𐑌𐐵, 𐐺𐐨𐐿𐐫𐑆 𐐱𐑂 𐑄 𐑀𐑊𐐬𐑉𐐨 𐐱𐑂 𐑄 𐐶𐐲𐑉𐑊𐐼, 𐐰𐑌𐐼 𐐻𐐭 𐑀𐐯𐐻 𐑀𐐩𐑌 𐐶𐐮𐑊 𐑄𐐩 𐑅𐐩 𐑄𐐮𐑅, 𐐰𐑌𐐼 𐑌𐐱𐐻 𐑁𐐫𐑉 𐑄 𐑀𐑊𐐬𐑉𐐨 𐐱𐑂 𐐘𐐱𐐼. 𐐈𐑌𐐼 𐑄 𐑋𐐰𐑌 𐑇𐐰𐑊 𐑅𐐩, 𐐌 𐐿𐐰𐑌𐐱𐐻 𐐺𐑉𐐮𐑍 𐑄 𐐺𐐳𐐿, 𐑁𐐫𐑉 𐐮𐐻 𐐮𐑆 𐑅𐐨𐑊𐐼. 𐐜𐐯𐑌 𐑇𐐰𐑊 𐑄 𐑊𐐲𐑉𐑌𐐯𐐼 𐑅𐐩, 𐐌 𐐿𐐰𐑌𐐱𐐻 𐑉𐐨𐐼 𐐮𐐻. 𐐐𐐶𐐯𐑉𐑁𐐫𐑉 𐐮𐐻 𐑇𐐰𐑊 𐐿𐐲𐑋 𐐻𐐭 𐐹𐐰𐑅, 𐑄𐐰𐐻 𐑄 𐐢𐐫𐑉𐐼 𐐘𐐱𐐼 𐐶𐐮𐑊 𐐼𐐨𐑊𐐮𐑂𐐲𐑉 𐐲𐑀𐐯𐑌 𐑄 𐐺𐐳𐐿 𐐰𐑌𐐼 𐑄 𐐶𐐲𐑉𐐼𐑆 𐑄𐐯𐑉𐐱𐑂 𐐻𐐭 𐐸𐐮𐑋 𐑄𐐰𐐻 𐐮𐑆 𐑌𐐱𐐻 𐑊𐐲𐑉𐑌𐐯𐐼; 𐐰𐑌𐐼 𐑄 𐑋𐐰𐑌 𐑄𐐰𐐻 𐐮𐑆 𐑌𐐱𐐻 𐑊𐐲𐑉𐑌𐐯𐐼 𐑇𐐰𐑊 𐑅𐐩, 𐐌 𐐰𐑋 𐑌𐐱𐐻 𐑊𐐲𐑉𐑌𐐯𐐼. 𐐜𐐯𐑌 𐑇𐐰𐑊 𐑄 𐐢𐐫𐑉𐐼 𐐘𐐱𐐼 𐑅𐐩 𐐲𐑌𐐻𐐭 𐐸𐐮𐑋, 𐐜 𐑊𐐲𐑉𐑌𐐯𐐼 𐑇𐐰𐑊 𐑌𐐱𐐻 𐑉𐐨𐐼 𐑄𐐯𐑋, 𐑁𐐫𐑉 𐑄𐐩 𐐸𐐰𐑂 𐑉𐐨𐐾𐐯𐐿𐐻𐐯𐐼 𐑄𐐯𐑋, 𐐰𐑌𐐼 𐐌 𐐰𐑋 𐐩𐐺𐑊 𐐻𐐭 𐐼𐐭 𐑋𐐴𐑌 𐐬𐑌 𐐶𐐲𐑉𐐿; 𐐸𐐶𐐯𐑉𐑁𐐫𐑉 𐑄𐐵 𐑇𐐰𐑊𐐻 𐑉𐐨𐐼 𐑄 𐐶𐐲𐑉𐐼𐑆 𐐸𐐶𐐮𐐽 𐐌 𐑇𐐰𐑊 𐑀𐐮𐑂 𐐲𐑌𐐻𐐭 𐑄𐐨. 𐐓𐐲𐐽 𐑌𐐱𐐻 𐑄 𐑃𐐮𐑍𐑆 𐐸𐐶𐐮𐐽 𐐪𐑉 𐑅𐐨𐑊𐐼, 𐑁𐐫𐑉 𐐌 𐐶𐐮𐑊 𐐺𐑉𐐮𐑍 𐑄𐐯𐑋 𐑁𐐬𐑉𐑃 𐐮𐑌 𐑋𐐴𐑌 𐐬𐑌 𐐼𐐷𐐭 𐐻𐐴𐑋: 𐑁𐐫𐑉 𐐌 𐐶𐐮𐑊 𐑇𐐬 𐐲𐑌𐐻𐐭 𐑄 𐐽𐐮𐑊𐐼𐑉𐐯𐑌 𐐱𐑂 𐑋𐐯𐑌 𐑄𐐰𐐻 𐐌 𐐰𐑋 𐐩𐐺𐑊 𐐻𐐭 𐐼𐐭 𐑋𐐴𐑌 𐐬𐑌 𐐶𐐲𐑉𐐿. 𐐐𐐶𐐯𐑉𐑁𐐫𐑉, 𐐸𐐶𐐯𐑌 𐑄𐐵 𐐸𐐰𐑅𐐻 𐑉𐐯𐐼 𐑄 𐐶𐐲𐑉𐐼𐑆 𐐸𐐶𐐮𐐽 𐐌 𐐸𐐰𐑂 𐐿𐐲𐑋𐐰𐑌𐐼𐐯𐐼 𐑄𐐨, 𐐰𐑌𐐼 𐐱𐐺𐐻𐐩𐑌𐐼 𐑄 𐐶𐐮𐐻𐑌𐐯𐑅𐐯𐑆 𐐸𐐶𐐮𐐽 𐐌 𐐸𐐰𐑂 𐐹𐑉𐐱𐑋𐐮𐑅𐐻 𐐲𐑌𐐻𐐭 𐑄𐐨, 𐑄𐐯𐑌 𐑇𐐰𐑊𐐻 𐑄𐐵 𐑅𐐨𐑊 𐐲𐐹 𐑄 𐐺𐐳𐐿 𐐲𐑀𐐯𐑌, 𐐰𐑌𐐼 𐐸𐐴𐐼 𐐮𐐻 𐐲𐐹 𐐲𐑌𐐻𐐭 𐑋𐐨, 𐑄𐐰𐐻 𐐌 𐑋𐐩 𐐹𐑉𐐨𐑆𐐲𐑉𐑂 𐑄 𐐶𐐲𐑉𐐼𐑆 𐐸𐐶𐐮𐐽 𐑄𐐵 𐐸𐐰𐑅𐐻 𐑌𐐱𐐻 𐑉𐐯𐐼, 𐐲𐑌𐐻𐐮𐑊 𐐌 𐑇𐐰𐑊 𐑅𐐨 𐑁𐐮𐐻 𐐮𐑌 𐑋𐐴𐑌 𐐬𐑌 𐐶𐐮𐑆𐐼𐐲𐑋 𐐻𐐭 𐑉𐐨𐑂𐐨𐑊 𐐫𐑊 𐑃𐐮𐑍𐑆 𐐲𐑌𐐻𐐭 𐑄

𐐽𐐮𐑊𐐼𐑉𐐯𐑌 𐐱𐑂 𐑋𐐯𐑌. 𐐙𐐫𐑉 𐐺𐐨𐐸𐐬𐑊𐐼, 𐐌 𐐰𐑋 𐐘𐐱𐐼; 𐐰𐑌𐐼 𐐌 𐐰𐑋 𐐪 𐐘𐐱𐐼 𐐱𐑂 𐑋𐐮𐑉𐐲𐐿𐑊𐑆: 𐐰𐑌𐐼 𐐌 𐐶𐐮𐑊 𐑇𐐬 𐐲𐑌𐐻𐐭 𐑄 𐐶𐐲𐑉𐑊𐐼 𐑄𐐰𐐻 𐐌 𐐰𐑋 𐑄 𐑅𐐩𐑋 𐐷𐐯𐑅𐐻𐐯𐑉𐐼𐐩, 𐐻𐐳-𐐼𐐩, 𐐰𐑌𐐼 𐑁𐐫𐑉 𐐯𐑂𐐯𐑉; 𐐰𐑌𐐼 𐐌 𐐶𐐲𐑉𐐿 𐑌𐐪𐐻 𐐲𐑋𐐲𐑍 𐑄 𐐽𐐮𐑊𐐼𐑉𐐯𐑌 𐐱𐑂 𐑋𐐯𐑌, 𐑅𐐩𐑂 𐐮𐐻 𐐺 𐐰𐐿𐐫𐑉𐐼𐐮𐑍 𐐻𐐭 𐑄𐐩𐑉 𐑁𐐩𐑃.

19. 𐐈𐑌𐐼 𐐲𐑀𐐯𐑌 𐐮𐐻 𐑇𐐰𐑊 𐐿𐐲𐑋 𐐻𐐭 𐐹𐐪𐑅, 𐑄𐐰𐐻 𐑄 𐐢𐐫𐑉𐐼 𐑇𐐰𐑊 𐑅𐐩 𐐲𐑌𐐻𐐭 𐐸𐐮𐑋 𐑄𐐰𐐻 𐑇𐐰𐑊 𐑉𐐨𐐼 𐑄 𐐶𐐲𐑉𐐼𐑆 𐑄𐐰𐐻 𐑇𐐰𐑊 𐐺 𐐼𐐨𐑊𐐮𐑂𐐯𐑉𐐼 𐐸𐐮𐑋, 𐐙𐐫𐑉𐐰𐑆𐑋𐐲𐐽 𐐰𐑆 𐑄𐐮𐑅 𐐹𐐨𐐹𐑊 𐐼𐑉𐐫 𐑌𐐨𐑉 𐐲𐑌𐐻𐐭 𐑋𐐨 𐐶𐐮𐑄 𐑄𐐩𐑉 𐑋𐐵𐑃, 𐐰𐑌𐐼 𐐶𐐮𐑄 𐑄𐐩𐑉 𐑊𐐮𐐹𐑅 𐐼𐐭 𐐱𐑌𐐲𐑉 𐑋𐐨, 𐐺𐐲𐐻 𐐸𐐰𐑂 𐑉𐐨𐑋𐐭𐑂𐐼 𐑄𐐩𐑉 𐐸𐐪𐑉𐐻𐑅 𐑁𐐪𐑉 𐑁𐑉𐐱𐑋 𐑋𐐨, 𐐰𐑌𐐼 𐑄𐐩𐑉 𐑁𐐨𐑉 𐐻𐐬𐑉𐐼𐑆 𐑋𐐨 𐐮𐑆 𐐻𐐫𐐻 𐐺𐐴 𐑄 𐐹𐑉𐐨𐑅𐐯𐐹𐐻𐑅 𐐱𐑂 𐑋𐐯𐑌, 𐑄𐐩𐑉𐑁𐐫𐑉, 𐐌 𐐶𐐮𐑊 𐐹𐑉𐐬𐑅𐐨𐐼 𐐻𐐭 𐐼𐐭 𐐪 𐑋𐐪𐑉𐑂𐐯𐑊𐐲𐑅 𐐶𐐲𐑉𐐿 𐐲𐑋𐐲𐑍 𐑄𐐮𐑅 𐐹𐐨𐐹𐑊, 𐐷𐐩, 𐐪 𐑋𐐪𐑉𐑂𐐯𐑊𐐲𐑅 𐐶𐐲𐑉𐐿 𐐰𐑌𐐼 𐐪 𐐶𐐲𐑌𐐼𐐲𐑉: 𐑁𐐫𐑉 𐑄 𐐶𐐮𐑆𐐼𐐲𐑋 𐐱𐑂 𐑄𐐩𐑉 𐐶𐐴𐑆 𐐰𐑌𐐼 𐑊𐐲𐑉𐑌𐐼 𐑇𐐰𐑊 𐐹𐐯𐑉𐐮𐑇, 𐐰𐑌𐐼 𐑄 𐐲𐑌𐐼𐐲𐑉𐑅𐐻𐐰𐑌𐐼𐐮𐑍 𐐱𐑂 𐑄𐐩𐑉 𐐹𐑉𐐭𐐼𐐯𐑌𐐻 𐑇𐐰𐑊 𐐺 𐐸𐐮𐐼. 𐐈𐑌𐐼 𐐶𐐬 𐐲𐑌𐐻𐐭 𐑄𐐯𐑋 𐑄𐐰𐐻 𐑅𐐨𐐿 𐐼𐐨𐐹 𐐻𐐭 𐐸𐐴𐐼 𐑄𐐩𐑉 𐐿𐐵𐑌𐑅𐐯𐑊 𐑁𐑉𐐱𐑋 𐑄 𐐢𐐫𐑉𐐼. 𐐈𐑌𐐼 𐑄𐐩𐑉 𐐶𐐲𐑉𐐿𐑅 𐐪𐑉 𐐮𐑌 𐑄 𐐼𐐪𐑉𐐿; 𐐰𐑌𐐼 𐑄𐐩 𐑅𐐩, 𐐐𐐭 𐑅𐐨𐐯𐑃 𐐲𐑅, 𐐰𐑌𐐼 𐐸𐐭 𐑌𐐬𐐯𐑃 𐐲𐑅? 𐐈𐑌𐐼 𐑄𐐩 𐐫𐑊𐑅𐐬 𐑅𐐩, 𐐟𐐭𐑉𐑊𐐮, 𐐷𐐬𐑉 𐐻𐐲𐑉𐑌𐐮𐑍 𐐱𐑂 𐑃𐐮𐑍𐑆 𐐲𐐹𐑅𐐴𐐼 𐐼𐐵𐑌 𐑇𐐰𐑊 𐐺 𐐯𐑅𐐻𐐨𐑋𐐼 𐐰𐑆 𐑄 𐐹𐐱𐐻𐐲𐑉'𐑆 𐐿𐑊𐐩. 𐐒𐐲𐐻 𐐺𐐨𐐸𐐬𐑊𐐼, 𐐌 𐐶𐐮𐑊 𐑇𐐬 𐐲𐑌𐐻𐐭 𐑄𐐯𐑋, 𐑅𐐯𐑃 𐑄 𐐢𐐫𐑉𐐼 𐐱𐑂 𐐐𐐬𐑅𐐻𐑅, 𐑄𐐰𐐻 𐐌 𐑌𐐬 𐐫𐑊 𐑄𐐩𐑉 𐐶𐐲𐑉𐐿𐑅. 𐐙𐐫𐑉 𐑇𐐰𐑊 𐑄 𐐶𐐲𐑉𐐿 𐑅𐐩 𐐱𐑂 𐐸𐐮𐑋 𐑄𐐰𐐻 𐑋𐐩𐐼 𐐮𐐻, 𐐸𐐨 𐑋𐐩𐐼 𐑋𐐨 𐑌𐐪𐐻? 𐐉𐑉 𐑇𐐰𐑊 𐑄 𐑃𐐮𐑍 𐑁𐑉𐐩𐑋𐐼 𐑅𐐩 𐐱𐑂 𐐸𐐮𐑋 𐑄𐐰𐐻 𐑁𐑉𐐩𐑋𐐼 𐐮𐐻, 𐐸𐐨 𐐸𐐰𐐼 𐑌𐐬 𐐲𐑌𐐼𐐲𐑉𐑅𐐻𐐰𐑌𐐼𐐮𐑍? 𐐒𐐲𐐻 𐐺𐐨𐐸𐐬𐑊𐐼, 𐑅𐐯𐑃 𐑄 𐐢𐐫𐑉𐐼 𐐱𐑂 𐐐𐐬𐑅𐐻𐑅, 𐐌 𐐶𐐮𐑊 𐑇𐐬 𐐲𐑌𐐻𐐭 𐑄 𐐽𐐮𐑊𐐼𐑉𐐯𐑌 𐐱𐑂 𐑋𐐯𐑌 𐑄𐐰𐐻 𐐮𐐻 𐐮𐑆 𐐷𐐯𐐻 𐐪 𐑂𐐯𐑉𐐮 𐑊𐐮𐐻𐑊 𐐸𐐶𐐴𐑊 𐐰𐑌𐐼 𐐢𐐯𐐺𐐲𐑌𐐲𐑌 𐑇𐐰𐑊 𐐺 𐐻𐐲𐑉𐑌𐐼 𐐮𐑌𐐻𐐭 𐐪 𐑁𐑉𐐭𐐻𐑁𐐳𐑊 𐑁𐐨𐑊𐐼; 𐐰𐑌𐐼 𐑄 𐑁𐑉𐐭𐐻𐑁𐐳𐑊 𐑁𐐨𐑊𐐼 𐑇𐐰𐑊 𐐺 𐐯𐑅𐐻𐐨𐑋𐐼 𐐰𐑆 𐐪 𐑁𐐱𐑉𐐯𐑅𐐻. 𐐈𐑌𐐼 𐐮𐑌 𐑄𐐰𐐻 𐐼𐐩 𐑇𐐰𐑊 𐑄 𐐼𐐯𐑁 𐐸𐐨𐑉 𐑄 𐐶𐐲𐑉𐐼𐑆 𐐱𐑂 𐑄 𐐺𐐳𐐿, 𐐰𐑌𐐼 𐑄 𐐴𐑆 𐐱𐑂 𐑄 𐐺𐑊𐐴𐑌𐐼 𐑇𐐰𐑊 𐑅𐐨 𐐵𐐻 𐐱𐑂 𐐱𐐺𐑅𐐿𐐭𐑉𐐮𐐻𐐮 𐐰𐑌𐐼 𐐵𐐻 𐐱𐑂 𐐼𐐪𐑉𐐿𐑌𐐯𐑅, 𐐰𐑌𐐼 𐑄 𐑋𐐨𐐿 𐐫𐑊𐑅𐐬 𐑇𐐰𐑊 𐐮𐑌𐐿𐑉𐐨𐑅, 𐐰𐑌𐐼 𐑄𐐩𐑉 𐐾𐐱𐐮 𐑇𐐰𐑊 𐐺 𐐮𐑌 𐑄 𐐢𐐫𐑉𐐼, 𐐰𐑌𐐼 𐑄 𐐹𐐭𐑉 𐐲𐑋𐐲𐑍 𐑋𐐯𐑌 𐑇𐐰𐑊 𐑉𐐨𐐾𐐱𐐮𐑅 𐐮𐑌 𐑄 𐐐𐐬𐑊𐐮 𐐎𐐲𐑌 𐐱𐑂 𐐆𐑆𐑉𐐩𐐯𐑊. 𐐙𐐫𐑉 𐐰𐑇𐐭𐑉𐐯𐐼𐑊𐐮 𐐰𐑆 𐑄 𐐢𐐫𐑉𐐼 𐑊𐐮𐑂𐐯𐑃, 𐑄𐐩 𐑇𐐰𐑊 𐑅𐐨 𐑄𐐰𐐻 𐑄 𐐻𐐯𐑉𐐮𐐺𐑊 𐐶𐐲𐑌 𐐮𐑆 𐐺𐑉𐐫𐐻 𐐻𐐭 𐑌𐐫𐐻, 𐐰𐑌𐐼 𐑄 𐑅𐐿𐐫𐑉𐑌𐐲𐑉 𐐮𐑆 𐐿𐐲𐑌𐑅𐐮𐐭𐑋𐐼, 𐐰𐑌𐐼 𐐫𐑊 𐑄𐐰𐐻 𐐶𐐱𐐽 𐑁𐐫𐑉 𐐮𐑌𐐮𐐿𐐶𐐮𐐻𐐮 𐐪𐑉 𐐿𐐲𐐻 𐐱𐑁; 𐐰𐑌𐐼 𐑄𐐩 𐑄𐐰𐐻 𐑋𐐩𐐿 𐐪 𐑋𐐰𐑌 𐐰𐑌 𐐲𐑁𐐯𐑌𐐼𐐲𐑉 𐑁𐐫𐑉 𐐪 𐐶𐐲𐑉𐐼, 𐐰𐑌𐐼 𐑊𐐩 𐐪 𐑅𐑌𐐩𐑉 𐑁𐐫𐑉 𐐸𐐮𐑋 𐑄𐐰𐐻 𐑉𐐨𐐹𐑉𐐭𐑂𐐯𐑃 𐐮𐑌 𐑄 𐑀𐐩𐐻, 𐐰𐑌𐐼 𐐻𐐲𐑉𐑌 𐐲𐑅𐐴𐐼 𐑄 𐐾𐐲𐑅𐐻 𐑁𐐫𐑉 𐐪 𐑃𐐮𐑍 𐐱𐑂 𐑌𐐫𐐻. 𐐜𐐩𐑉𐑁𐐫𐑉 𐑄𐐲𐑅 𐑅𐐯𐑃 𐑄 𐐢𐐫𐑉𐐼, 𐐸𐐭 𐑉𐐨𐐼𐐨𐑋𐐼 𐐁𐐺𐑉𐐲𐐸𐐰𐑋, 𐐿𐐲𐑌𐑅𐐲𐑉𐑌𐐮𐑍 𐑄 𐐸𐐵𐑅 𐐱𐑂 𐐖𐐩𐐿𐐲𐐺, 𐐖𐐩𐐿𐐲𐐺 𐑇𐐰𐑊 𐑌𐐪𐐻 𐑌𐐵 𐐺 𐐲𐑇𐐩𐑋𐐼, 𐑌𐐨𐑄𐐲𐑉 𐑇𐐰𐑊 𐐸𐐮𐑆 𐑁𐐩𐑅 𐑌𐐵 𐐶𐐰𐐿𐑅 𐐹𐐩𐑊. 𐐒𐐲𐐻 𐐸𐐶𐐯𐑌 𐐸𐐨 𐑅𐐨𐐯𐑃 𐐸𐐮𐑆 𐐽𐐮𐑊𐐼𐑉𐐯𐑌, 𐑄 𐐶𐐲𐑉𐐿 𐐱𐑂 𐑋𐐴 𐐸𐐰𐑌𐐼𐑆, 𐐮𐑌 𐑄 𐑋𐐮𐐼𐑅𐐻 𐐱𐑂 𐐸𐐮𐑋, 𐑄𐐩 𐑇𐐰𐑊 𐑅𐐰𐑍𐐿𐐻𐐮𐑁𐐴 𐑋𐐴 𐑌𐐩𐑋, 𐐰𐑌𐐼 𐑅𐐰𐑍𐐿𐐻𐐮𐑁𐐴 𐑄 𐐐𐐬𐑊𐐮 𐐎𐐲𐑌 𐐱𐑂 𐐖𐐩𐐿𐐲𐐺, 𐐰𐑌𐐼 𐑇𐐰𐑊 𐑁𐐨𐑉 𐑄 𐐘𐐱𐐼 𐐱𐑂 𐐆𐑆𐑉𐐩𐐯𐑊. 𐐜𐐩 𐐫𐑊𐑅𐐬 𐑄𐐰𐐻 𐐲𐑉𐐼 𐐮𐑌 𐑅𐐹𐐮𐑉𐐮𐐻 𐑇𐐰𐑊 𐐿𐐲𐑋 𐐻𐐭 𐐲𐑌𐐼𐐲𐑉𐑅𐐻𐐰𐑌𐐼𐐮𐑍, 𐐰𐑌𐐼 𐑄𐐩 𐑄𐐰𐐻 𐑋𐐲𐑉𐑋𐐲𐑉𐐼 𐑇𐐰𐑊 𐑊𐐲𐑉𐑌 𐐼𐐱𐐿𐐻𐑉𐐮𐑌.

𐐕𐐰𐐹𐐻𐐲𐑉 XII.

1. 𐐈𐑌𐐼 𐑌𐐵, 𐐺𐐨𐐸𐐬𐑊𐐼, 𐑋𐐴 𐐺𐑉𐐯𐑄𐑉𐐯𐑌, 𐐌 𐐸𐐰𐑂 𐑅𐐹𐐬𐐿𐐲𐑌 𐐲𐑌𐐻𐐭 𐐷𐐭, 𐐰𐐿𐐫𐑉𐐼𐐮𐑍 𐐰𐑆 𐑄 𐐝𐐹𐐮𐑉𐐮𐐻 𐐸𐐰𐑃 𐐿𐐲𐑌𐑅𐐻𐑉𐐩𐑌𐐼 𐑋𐐨; 𐐸𐐶𐐩𐑉𐑁𐐫𐑉 𐐌 𐑌𐐬 𐑄𐐰𐐻 𐑄𐐩 𐑋𐐲𐑅𐐻 𐑇𐐭𐑉𐑊𐐮 𐐿𐐲𐑋 𐐻𐐭 𐐹𐐪𐑅. 𐐜 𐑃𐐮𐑍𐑆 𐐸𐐶𐐮𐐽 𐑇𐐰𐑊 𐐺 𐑉𐐮𐐻𐑌 𐐵𐐻 𐐱𐑂 𐑄 𐐺𐐳𐐿 𐑇𐐰𐑊 𐐺 𐐱𐑂 𐑀𐑉𐐩𐐻 𐐶𐐲𐑉𐑃 𐐲𐑌𐐻𐐭 𐑄 𐐽𐐮𐑊𐐼𐑉𐐯𐑌 𐐱𐑂 𐑋𐐯𐑌, 𐐰𐑌𐐼 𐐯𐑅𐐹𐐯𐑇𐐲𐑊𐐮 𐐲𐑌𐐻𐐭 𐐵𐑉 𐑅𐐨𐐼, 𐐸𐐶𐐮𐐽 𐐮𐑆 𐐪 𐑉𐐯𐑋𐑌𐐲𐑌𐐻 𐐱𐑂 𐑄 𐐸𐐵𐑅 𐐱𐑂 𐐆𐑆𐑉𐐩𐐯𐑊. 𐐙𐐫𐑉 𐐮𐐻 𐑇𐐰𐑊 𐐿𐐲𐑋 𐐻𐐭 𐐹𐐪𐑅 𐐮𐑌 𐑄𐐰𐐻 𐐼𐐩, 𐑄𐐰𐐻 𐑄 𐐽𐐲𐑉𐐽𐐯𐑆 𐐸𐐶𐐮𐐽 𐐪𐑉 𐐺𐐮𐑊𐐻 𐐲𐐹, 𐐰𐑌𐐼 𐑌𐐪𐐻 𐐲𐑌𐐻𐐭 𐑄 𐐢𐐫𐑉𐐼, 𐐸𐐶𐐯𐑌 𐑄 𐐶𐐲𐑌 𐑇𐐰𐑊 𐑅𐐩 𐐲𐑌𐐻𐐭 𐑄 𐐲𐑄𐐲𐑉, 𐐒𐐨𐐸𐐬𐑊𐐼 𐐌, 𐐌 𐐰𐑋 𐑄 𐐢𐐫𐑉𐐼'𐑆; 𐐰𐑌𐐼 𐑄 𐐲𐑄𐐲𐑉𐑆 𐑇𐐰𐑊 𐑅𐐩, 𐐌, 𐐌 𐐰𐑋 𐑄 𐐢𐐫𐑉𐐼'𐑆. 𐐈𐑌𐐼 𐑄𐐲𐑅 𐑇𐐰𐑊 𐐯𐑂𐐯𐑉𐐮 𐐶𐐲𐑌 𐑅𐐩 𐑄𐐰𐐻 𐐸𐐰𐑃 𐐺𐐮𐑊𐐻 𐐲𐐹 𐐽𐐲𐑉𐐽𐐯𐑆, 𐐰𐑌𐐼 𐑌𐐪𐐻 𐐲𐑌𐐻𐐭 𐑄 𐐢𐐫𐑉𐐼; 𐐰𐑌𐐼 𐑄𐐩 𐑇𐐰𐑊 𐐿𐐲𐑌𐐻𐐯𐑌𐐼 𐐶𐐲𐑌 𐐶𐐮𐑄 𐐲𐑌𐐲𐑄𐐲𐑉; 𐐰𐑌𐐼 𐑄𐐩𐑉 𐐹𐑉𐐨𐑅𐐻𐑅 𐑇𐐰𐑊 𐐿𐐲𐑌𐐻𐐯𐑌𐐼

𐐶𐐲𐑌 𐐶𐐮𐑄 𐐰𐑌𐐲𐑄𐐲𐑉, 𐐰𐑌𐐼 𐑄𐐩 𐑇𐐰𐑊 𐐻𐐨𐐽 𐐶𐐮𐑄 𐑄𐐩𐑉 𐑊𐐲𐑉𐑌𐐮𐑍, 𐐰𐑌𐐼 𐐼𐐨𐑌𐐴 𐑄 𐐐𐐬𐑊𐐨 𐐘𐐬𐑅𐐻, 𐐸𐐶𐐮𐐽 𐑀𐐮𐑂𐐯𐑃 𐐲𐐻𐐲𐑉𐐰𐑌𐑅. 𐐈𐑌𐐼 𐑄𐐩 𐐼𐐨𐑌𐐴 𐑄 𐐹𐐵𐐲𐑉 𐐲𐑂 𐐘𐐱𐐼, 𐑄 𐐐𐐬𐑊𐐨 𐐎𐐲𐑌 𐐲𐑂 𐐆𐑆𐑉𐐩𐐯𐑊; 𐐰𐑌𐐼 𐑄𐐩 𐑅𐐩 𐐲𐑌𐐻𐐭 𐑄 𐐹𐐨𐐹𐑊, 𐐐𐐪𐑉𐐿𐐯𐑌 𐐲𐑌𐐻𐐭 𐐲𐑅, 𐐰𐑌𐐼 𐐸𐐨𐑉 𐐷𐐨 𐐵𐐲𐑉 𐐹𐑉𐐨𐑅𐐯𐐹𐐻; 𐑁𐐫𐑉 𐐺𐐨𐐸𐐬𐑊𐐼 𐑄𐐯𐑉 𐐮𐑆 𐑌𐐬 𐐘𐐱𐐼 𐐻𐐭-𐐼𐐩, 𐑁𐐫𐑉 𐑄 𐐢𐐫𐑉𐐼 𐐰𐑌𐐼 𐑄 𐐡𐐯𐐼𐐨𐑋𐐲𐑉 𐐸𐐰𐑃 𐐼𐐲𐑌 𐐸𐐮𐑆 𐐶𐐲𐑉𐐿, 𐐰𐑌𐐼 𐐸𐐨 𐐸𐐰𐑃 𐑀𐐮𐑂𐐯𐑌 𐐸𐐮𐑆 𐐹𐐵𐐲𐑉 𐐲𐑌𐐻𐐭 𐑋𐐯𐑌. 𐐒𐐨𐐸𐐬𐑊𐐼, 𐐸𐐪𐑉𐐿𐐯𐑌 𐐷𐐨 𐐲𐑌𐐻𐐭 𐑋𐐴 𐐹𐑉𐐨𐑅𐐯𐐹𐐻; 𐐮𐑁 𐑄𐐩 𐑇𐐰𐑊 𐑅𐐩 𐑄𐐯𐑉 𐐮𐑆 𐐰 𐑋𐐮𐑉𐐲𐐿𐑊 𐑉𐐫𐐻 𐐺𐐴 𐑄 𐐸𐐰𐑌𐐼 𐐲𐑂 𐑄 𐐢𐐫𐑉𐐼, 𐐺𐐨𐑊𐐨𐑂 𐐮𐐻 𐑌𐐱𐐻; 𐑁𐐫𐑉 𐑄𐐮𐑅 𐐼𐐩 𐐸𐐨 𐐮𐑆 𐑌𐐱𐐻 𐐰 𐐘𐐱𐐼 𐐲𐑂 𐑋𐐮𐑉𐐲𐐿𐑊𐑆; 𐐸𐐨 𐐸𐐰𐑃 𐐼𐐲𐑌 𐐸𐐮𐑆 𐐶𐐲𐑉𐐿. 𐐏𐐩, 𐐰𐑌𐐼 𐑄𐐯𐑉 𐑇𐐰𐑊 𐐺𐐨 𐑋𐐯𐑌𐐨 𐐸𐐶𐐮𐐽 𐑇𐐰𐑊 𐑅𐐩, 𐐀𐐻, 𐐼𐑉𐐮𐑍𐐿, 𐐰𐑌𐐼 𐐺𐐨 𐑋𐐯𐑉𐐨, 𐑁𐐫𐑉 𐐻𐐭-𐑋𐐱𐑉𐐬 𐐶𐐨 𐐼𐐴; 𐐰𐑌𐐼 𐐮𐐻 𐑇𐐰𐑊 𐐺𐐨 𐐶𐐯𐑊 𐐶𐐮𐑄 𐐲𐑅. 𐐈𐑌𐐼 𐑄𐐯𐑉 𐑇𐐰𐑊 𐐫𐑊𐑅𐐬 𐐺𐐨 𐑋𐐯𐑌𐐨 𐐸𐐶𐐮𐐽 𐑇𐐰𐑊 𐑅𐐩, 𐐀𐐻, 𐐼𐑉𐐮𐑍𐐿, 𐐰𐑌𐐼 𐐺𐐨 𐑋𐐯𐑉𐐨; 𐑌𐐯𐑂𐐲𐑉𐑄𐐲𐑊𐐯𐑅, 𐑁𐐨𐑉 𐐘𐐱𐐼, 𐐸𐐨 𐐶𐐮𐑊 𐐾𐐲𐑅𐐻𐐮𐑁𐐴 𐐮𐑌 𐐿𐐱𐑋𐐮𐐻𐐮𐑍 𐐰 𐑊𐐮𐐻𐑊 𐑅𐐮𐑌; 𐐷𐐩, 𐑊𐐴 𐐰 𐑊𐐮𐐻𐑊, 𐐻𐐩𐐿 𐑄 𐐰𐐼𐑂𐐰𐑌𐐻𐐩𐐾 𐐲𐑂 𐐶𐐲𐑌 𐐺𐐨𐐿𐐫𐑆 𐐲𐑂 𐐸𐐮𐑆 𐐶𐐲𐑉𐐼𐑆, 𐐼𐐮𐑀 𐐰 𐐹𐐮𐐻 𐑁𐐫𐑉 𐑄𐐴 𐑌𐐩𐐺𐐲𐑉; 𐑄𐐯𐑉 𐐮𐑆 𐑌𐐬 𐐸𐐪𐑉𐑋 𐐮𐑌 𐑄𐐮𐑅. 𐐈𐑌𐐼 𐐼𐐭 𐐫𐑊 𐑄𐐨𐑆 𐑃𐐮𐑍𐑆, 𐑁𐐫𐑉 𐐻𐐭-𐑋𐐱𐑉𐐬 𐐶𐐨 𐐼𐐴; 𐐰𐑌𐐼 𐐮𐑁 𐐮𐐻 𐑅𐐬 𐐺𐐨 𐑄𐐰𐐻 𐐶𐐨 𐐪𐑉 𐑀𐐮𐑊𐐻𐐨, 𐐘𐐱𐐼 𐐶𐐮𐑊 𐐺𐐨𐐻 𐐲𐑅 𐐶𐐮𐑄 𐐰 𐑁𐑏 𐑅𐐻𐑉𐐴𐐹𐑅, 𐐰𐑌𐐼 𐐰𐐻 𐑊𐐰𐑅𐐻 𐐶𐐨 𐑇𐐰𐑊 𐐺𐐨 𐑅𐐩𐑂𐐼 𐐮𐑌 𐑄 𐐿𐐮𐑍𐐼𐐲𐑋 𐐲𐑂 𐐘𐐱𐐼. 𐐏𐐩, 𐐰𐑌𐐼 𐑄𐐯𐑉 𐑇𐐰𐑊 𐐺𐐨 𐑋𐐯𐑌𐐨 𐐸𐐶𐐮𐐽 𐑇𐐰𐑊 𐐻𐐨𐐽 𐐰𐑁𐐻𐐲𐑉 𐑄𐐮𐑅 𐑋𐐰𐑌𐐲𐑉, 𐑁𐐫𐑊𐑅, 𐐰𐑌𐐼 𐑂𐐩𐑌, 𐐰𐑌𐐼 𐑁𐐭𐑊𐐮𐑇 𐐼𐐱𐐿𐐻𐑉𐐮𐑌𐑆, 𐐰𐑌𐐼 𐑇𐐰𐑊 𐐺𐐨 𐐹𐐲𐑁𐐻 𐐲𐐹 𐐮𐑌 𐑄𐐩𐑉 𐐸𐐪𐑉𐐻𐑅, 𐐰𐑌𐐼 𐑇𐐰𐑊 𐑅𐐨𐐿 𐐼𐐨𐐹 𐐻𐐭 𐐸𐐴𐐼 𐑄𐐩𐑉 𐐿𐐵𐑌𐑅𐐯𐑊𐑆 𐑁𐑉𐐱𐑋 𐑄 𐐢𐐫𐑉𐐼; 𐐰𐑌𐐼 𐑄𐐩𐑉 𐐶𐐲𐑉𐐿𐑅 𐑇𐐰𐑊 𐐺𐐨 𐐮𐑌 𐑄 𐐼𐐪𐑉𐐿; 𐐰𐑌𐐼 𐑄 𐐺𐑊𐐲𐐼 𐐲𐑂 𐑄 𐑅𐐩𐑌𐐻𐑅 𐑇𐐰𐑊 𐐿𐑉𐐴 𐑁𐑉𐐱𐑋 𐑄 𐑀𐑉𐐵𐑌𐐼 𐐰𐑀𐐯𐑌𐑅𐐻 𐑄𐐯𐑋. 𐐏𐐩, 𐑄𐐩 𐐸𐐰𐑂 𐐫𐑊 𐑀𐐫𐑌 𐐵𐐻 𐐲𐑂 𐑄 𐐶𐐩; 𐑄𐐩 𐐸𐐰𐑂 𐐺𐐨𐐿𐐲𐑋 𐐿𐐫𐑉𐐲𐐹𐐻𐐯𐐼. 𐐒𐐨𐐿𐐫𐑆 𐐲𐑂 𐐹𐑉𐐴𐐼, 𐐰𐑌𐐼 𐐺𐐨𐐿𐐫𐑆 𐐲𐑂 𐑁𐐫𐑊𐑅 𐐻𐐨𐐽𐐲𐑉𐑆, 𐐰𐑌𐐼 𐑁𐐫𐑊𐑅 𐐼𐐱𐐿𐐻𐑉𐐮𐑌, 𐑄𐐩𐑉 𐐽𐐲𐑉𐐽𐐯𐑆 𐐸𐐰𐑂 𐐺𐐨𐐿𐐲𐑋 𐐿𐐫𐑉𐐲𐐹𐐻𐐯𐐼, 𐐰𐑌𐐼 𐑄𐐩𐑉 𐐽𐐲𐑉𐐽𐐯𐑆 𐐪𐑉 𐑊𐐮𐑁𐐻𐐯𐐼 𐐲𐐹; 𐐺𐐨𐐿𐐫𐑆 𐐲𐑂 𐐹𐑉𐐴𐐼 𐑄𐐩 𐐪𐑉 𐐹𐐲𐑁𐐻 𐐲𐐹. 𐐜𐐩 𐑉𐐱𐐺 𐑄 𐐹𐐭𐑉 𐐺𐐨𐐿𐐫𐑆 𐐲𐑂 𐑄𐐩𐑉 𐑁𐐴𐑌 𐑅𐐰𐑍𐐿𐐽𐐭𐐯𐑉𐐨𐑆; 𐑄𐐩 𐑉𐐱𐐺 𐑄 𐐹𐐭𐑉 𐐺𐐨𐐿𐐫𐑆 𐐲𐑂 𐑄𐐩𐑉 𐑁𐐴𐑌 𐐿𐑊𐐬𐑄𐐮𐑍; 𐐰𐑌𐐼 𐑄𐐩 𐐹𐐲𐑉𐑅𐐯𐐿𐐷𐐭𐐻 𐑄 𐑋𐐨𐐿, 𐐰𐑌𐐼 𐑄 𐐹𐐭𐑉 𐐮𐑌 𐐸𐐪𐑉𐐻, 𐐺𐐨𐐿𐐫𐑆 𐐮𐑌 𐑄𐐩𐑉 𐐹𐑉𐐴𐐼 𐑄𐐩 𐐪𐑉 𐐹𐐲𐑁𐐻 𐐲𐐹. 𐐜𐐩 𐐶𐐩𐑉 𐑅𐐻𐐮𐑁 𐑌𐐯𐐿𐑅 𐐰𐑌𐐼 𐐸𐐴 𐐸𐐯𐐼𐑆; 𐐷𐐩, 𐐰𐑌𐐼 𐐺𐐨𐐿𐐫𐑆 𐐲𐑂 𐐹𐑉𐐴𐐼, 𐐰𐑌𐐼 𐐶𐐮𐐿𐐯𐐼𐑌𐐯𐑅, 𐐰𐑌𐐼 𐐰𐐺𐐱𐑋𐐮𐑌𐐩𐑇𐐲𐑌𐑆, 𐐰𐑌𐐼 𐐸𐐬𐑉𐐼𐐲𐑋𐑆, 𐑄𐐩 𐐸𐐰𐑂 𐐫𐑊 𐑀𐐫𐑌 𐐰𐑅𐐻𐑉𐐩, 𐑅𐐩𐑂 𐐮𐐻 𐐺𐐨 𐐰 𐑁𐑏, 𐐸𐐭 𐐪𐑉 𐑄 𐐸𐐲𐑋𐐺𐑊 𐑁𐐱𐑊𐐬𐐲𐑉𐑆 𐐲𐑂 𐐗𐑉𐐴𐑅𐐻; 𐑌𐐯𐑂𐐲𐑉𐑄𐐲𐑊𐐯𐑅, 𐑄𐐩 𐐪𐑉 𐑊𐐯𐐼, 𐑄𐐰𐐻 𐐮𐑌 𐑋𐐯𐑌𐐨 𐐮𐑌𐑅𐐻𐐰𐑌𐑅𐐯𐑆 𐑄𐐩 𐐼𐐭 𐐲𐑉 𐐺𐐨𐐿𐐫𐑆 𐑄𐐩 𐐪𐑉 𐐻𐐫𐐻 𐐺𐐴 𐑄 𐐹𐑉𐐨𐑅𐐯𐐹𐐻𐑅 𐐲𐑂 𐑋𐐯𐑌.

2. 𐐄 𐑄 𐐶𐐴𐑆, 𐐰𐑌𐐼 𐑄 𐑊𐐲𐑉𐑌𐐯𐐼, 𐐰𐑌𐐼 𐑄 𐑉𐐮𐐽, 𐑄𐐰𐐻 𐐪𐑉 𐐹𐐲𐑁𐐻 𐐲𐐹 𐐮𐑌 𐑄 𐐹𐑉𐐴𐐼 𐐲𐑂 𐑄𐐩𐑉 𐐸𐐪𐑉𐐻𐑅, 𐐰𐑌𐐼 𐐫𐑊 𐑄𐐬𐑆 𐐸𐐭 𐐹𐑉𐐨𐐽 𐑁𐐫𐑊𐑅 𐐼𐐱𐐿𐐻𐑉𐐮𐑌𐑆, 𐐰𐑌𐐼 𐐫𐑊 𐑄𐐬𐑆 𐐸𐐭 𐐿𐐱𐑋𐐮𐐻 𐐸𐐬𐑉𐐼𐐲𐑋𐑆, 𐐰𐑌𐐼 𐐹𐐲𐑉𐑂𐐲𐑉𐐻 𐑄 𐑉𐐴𐐻 𐐶𐐩 𐐲𐑂 𐑄 𐐢𐐫𐑉𐐼; 𐐶𐐬, 𐐶𐐬, 𐐶𐐬 𐐺𐐨 𐐲𐑌𐐻𐐭 𐑄𐐯𐑋, 𐑅𐐯𐑃 𐑄 𐐢𐐫𐑉𐐼 𐐘𐐱𐐼 𐐃𐑊𐑋𐐴𐐻𐐨, 𐑁𐐫𐑉 𐑄𐐩 𐑇𐐰𐑊 𐐺𐐨 𐑃𐑉𐐲𐑅𐐻 𐐼𐐵𐑌 𐐻𐐭 𐐸𐐯𐑊.

3. 𐐎𐐬 𐐲𐑌𐐻𐐭 𐑄𐐯𐑋 𐑄𐐰𐐻 𐐻𐐲𐑉𐑌 𐐰𐑅𐐴𐐼 𐑄 𐐾𐐲𐑅𐐻 𐑁𐐫𐑉 𐐰 𐑃𐐮𐑍 𐐲𐑂 𐑌𐐫𐐻, 𐐰𐑌𐐼 𐑉𐐨𐑂𐐴𐑊 𐐰𐑀𐐯𐑌𐑅𐐻 𐑄𐐰𐐻 𐐸𐐶𐐮𐐽 𐐮𐑆 𐑀𐐳𐐼, 𐐰𐑌𐐼 𐑅𐐩 𐑄𐐰𐐻 𐐮𐐻 𐐮𐑆 𐐲𐑂 𐑌𐐬 𐐶𐐲𐑉𐑃; 𐑁𐐫𐑉 𐑄 𐐼𐐩 𐑇𐐰𐑊 𐐿𐐲𐑋 𐑄𐐰𐐻 𐑄 𐐢𐐫𐑉𐐼 𐐘𐐱𐐼 𐐶𐐮𐑊 𐑅𐐹𐐨𐐼𐐮𐑊𐐨 𐑂𐐮𐑆𐐮𐐻 𐑄 𐐮𐑌𐐸𐐰𐐺𐐮𐐻𐐰𐑌𐐻𐑅 𐐲𐑂 𐑄 𐐲𐑉𐑃; 𐐰𐑌𐐼 𐐮𐑌 𐑄𐐰𐐻 𐐼𐐩 𐑄𐐰𐐻 𐑄𐐩 𐐪𐑉 𐑁𐐳𐑊𐐨 𐑉𐐴𐐹 𐐮𐑌 𐐮𐑌𐐮𐐿𐐶𐐮𐐻𐐨, 𐑄𐐩 𐑇𐐰𐑊 𐐹𐐯𐑉𐐮𐑇. 𐐒𐐲𐐻 𐐺𐐨𐐸𐐬𐑊𐐼, 𐐮𐑁 𐑄 𐐮𐑌𐐸𐐰𐐺𐐮𐐻𐐰𐑌𐐻𐑅 𐐲𐑂 𐑄 𐐲𐑉𐑃 𐑇𐐰𐑊 𐑉𐐨𐐹𐐯𐑌𐐻 𐐲𐑂 𐑄𐐩𐑉 𐐶𐐮𐐿𐐯𐐼𐑌𐐯𐑅 𐐰𐑌𐐼 𐐰𐐺𐐱𐑋𐐮𐑌𐐩𐑇𐐲𐑌𐑆, 𐑄𐐩 𐑇𐐰𐑊 𐑌𐐱𐐻 𐐺𐐨 𐐼𐐯𐑅𐐻𐑉𐐦𐐼, 𐑅𐐯𐑃 𐑄 𐐢𐐫𐑉𐐼 𐐲𐑂 𐐐𐐬𐑅𐐻𐑅. 𐐒𐐲𐐻 𐐺𐐨𐐸𐐬𐑊𐐼, 𐑄𐐰𐐻 𐑀𐑉𐐩𐐻 𐐰𐑌𐐼 𐐰𐐺𐐱𐑋𐐮𐑌𐐰𐐺𐑊 𐐽𐐲𐑉𐐽, 𐑄 𐐸𐐬𐑉 𐐲𐑂 𐐫𐑊 𐑄 𐐲𐑉𐑃, 𐑋𐐲𐑅𐐻 𐐻𐐲𐑋𐐺𐑊 𐐻𐐭 𐑄 𐐲𐑉𐑃, 𐐰𐑌𐐼 𐑀𐑉𐐩𐐻 𐑋𐐲𐑅𐐻 𐐺𐐨 𐑄 𐑁𐐫𐑊 𐑄𐐯𐑉𐐱𐑂; 𐑁𐐫𐑉 𐑄 𐐿𐐮𐑍𐐼𐐲𐑋 𐐲𐑂 𐑄 𐐼𐐯𐑂𐐮𐑊 𐑋𐐲𐑅𐐻 𐑇𐐩𐐿, 𐐰𐑌𐐼 𐑄𐐩 𐐸𐐶𐐮𐐽 𐐺𐐨𐑊𐐫𐑍 𐐻𐐭 𐐮𐐻 𐑋𐐲𐑅𐐻 𐑌𐐨𐐼𐑆 𐐺𐐨 𐑅𐐻𐐲𐑉𐐼 𐐲𐐹 𐐲𐑌𐐻𐐭 𐑉𐐨𐐹𐐯𐑌𐐻𐐰𐑌𐑅, 𐐫𐑉 𐑄 𐐼𐐯𐑂𐐮𐑊 𐐶𐐮𐑊 𐑀𐑉𐐰𐑅𐐹 𐑄𐐯𐑋 𐐶𐐮𐑄 𐐸𐐮𐑆 𐐯𐑂𐐲𐑉𐑊𐐰𐑅𐐻𐐮𐑍 𐐽𐐩𐑌𐑆, 𐐰𐑌𐐼 𐑄𐐩 𐐺𐐨 𐑅𐐻𐐲𐑉𐐼 𐐲𐐹 𐐻𐐭 𐐰𐑍𐑀𐐲𐑉, 𐐰𐑌𐐼 𐐹𐐯𐑉𐐮𐑇; 𐑁𐐫𐑉 𐐺𐐨𐐸𐐬𐑊𐐼, 𐐰𐐻 𐑄𐐰𐐻 𐐼𐐩 𐑇𐐰𐑊 𐐸𐐨 𐑉𐐩𐐾 𐐮𐑌 𐑄 𐐸𐐪𐑉𐐻𐑅 𐐲𐑂 𐑄 𐐽𐐮𐑊𐐼𐑉𐐯𐑌 𐐲𐑂 𐑋𐐯𐑌, 𐐰𐑌𐐼 𐑅𐐻𐐲𐑉 𐑄𐐯𐑋 𐐲𐐹 𐐻𐐭 𐐰𐑍𐑀𐐲𐑉 𐐰𐑀𐐯𐑌𐑅𐐻 𐑄𐐰𐐻 𐐸𐐶𐐮𐐽 𐐮𐑆 𐑀𐐳𐐼; 𐐰𐑌𐐼 𐐲𐑄𐐲𐑉𐑆 𐐶𐐮𐑊 𐐸𐐨 𐐹𐐰𐑅𐐮𐑁𐐴, 𐐰𐑌𐐼 𐑊𐐲𐑊 𐑄𐐯𐑋 𐐰𐐶𐐩 𐐮𐑌𐐻𐐭 𐐿𐐪𐑉𐑌𐐰𐑊 𐑅𐐯𐐿𐐷𐐭𐑉𐐮𐐻𐐨, 𐑄𐐰𐐻 𐑄𐐩 𐐶𐐮𐑊 𐑅𐐩, 𐐃𐑊 𐐮𐑆 𐐶𐐯𐑊 𐐮𐑌 𐐞𐐴𐐲𐑌; 𐐷𐐩,

𐐞𐐴𐐲𐑌 𐐹𐑉𐐱𐑅𐐹𐐯𐑉𐐯𐑃, 𐐫𐑊 𐐮𐑆 𐐶𐐯𐑊; 𐐰𐑌𐐼 𐑄𐐲𐑅 𐑄 𐐼𐐯𐑂𐐮𐑊 𐐽𐐨𐐻𐐯𐑃 𐑄𐐩𐑉 𐑅𐐬𐑊𐑆, 𐐰𐑌𐐼 𐑊𐐨𐐼𐐯𐑃 𐑄𐐯𐑋 𐐲𐐶𐐩 𐐿𐐩𐑉𐑁𐐳𐑊𐐨 𐐼𐐵𐑌 𐐻𐐭 𐐸𐐯𐑊. 𐐈𐑌𐐼 𐐺𐐨𐐸𐐬𐑊𐐼, 𐐲𐑄𐐲𐑉𐑆 𐐸𐐨 𐑁𐑊𐐰𐐻𐐲𐑉𐐯𐑃 𐐲𐐶𐐩, 𐐰𐑌𐐼 𐐻𐐯𐑊𐐯𐑃 𐑄𐐯𐑋 𐑄𐐩𐑉 𐐮𐑆 𐑌𐐬 𐐸𐐯𐑊; 𐐰𐑌𐐼 𐐸𐐨 𐑅𐐯𐑃 𐐲𐑌𐐻𐐭 𐑄𐐯𐑋, 𐐌 𐐰𐑋 𐑌𐐬 𐐼𐐯𐑂𐐮𐑊, 𐑁𐐫𐑉 𐑄𐐩𐑉 𐐮𐑆 𐑌𐐲𐑌; 𐐰𐑌𐐼 𐑄𐐲𐑅 𐐸𐐨 𐐸𐐶𐐮𐑅𐐹𐐲𐑉𐐯𐑃 𐐮𐑌 𐑄𐐩𐑉 𐐨𐑉𐑆, 𐐲𐑌𐐻𐐮𐑊 𐐸𐐨 𐑀𐑉𐐰𐑅𐐹𐑅 𐑄𐐯𐑋 𐐶𐐮𐑄 𐐸𐐮𐑆 𐐫𐑁𐐳𐑊 𐐽𐐩𐑌𐑆, 𐑁𐑉𐐱𐑋 𐐸𐐶𐐯𐑌𐑅 𐑄𐐩𐑉 𐐮𐑆 𐑌𐐬 𐐼𐐯𐑊𐐮𐑂𐐲𐑉𐐰𐑌𐑅. 𐐏𐐩, 𐑄𐐩 𐐪𐑉 𐑀𐑉𐐰𐑅𐐹𐐻 𐐶𐐮𐑄 𐐼𐐯𐑃, 𐐰𐑌𐐼 𐐸𐐯𐑊; 𐐰𐑌𐐼 𐐼𐐯𐑃, 𐐰𐑌𐐼 𐐸𐐯𐑊, 𐐰𐑌𐐼 𐑄 𐐼𐐯𐑂𐐮𐑊, 𐐰𐑌𐐼 𐐫𐑊 𐑄𐐰𐐻 𐐸𐐰𐑂 𐐺𐐮𐑌 𐑅𐐨𐑆𐐼 𐑄𐐩𐑉𐐶𐐮𐑄, 𐑋𐐲𐑅𐐻 𐑅𐐻𐐰𐑌𐐼 𐐺𐐨𐑁𐐬𐑉 𐑄 𐑃𐑉𐐬𐑌 𐐱𐑂 𐐘𐐱𐐼, 𐐰𐑌𐐼 𐐺 𐐾𐐲𐐾𐐼 𐐰𐐿𐐫𐑉𐐼𐐮𐑍 𐐻𐐭 𐑄𐐩𐑉 𐐶𐐲𐑉𐐿𐑅, 𐑁𐑉𐐱𐑋 𐐸𐐶𐐯𐑌𐑅 𐑄𐐩 𐑋𐐲𐑅𐐻 𐑀𐐬 𐐮𐑌𐐻𐐭 𐑄 𐐹𐑊𐐩𐑅 𐐹𐑉𐐨𐐹𐐩𐑉𐐼 𐑁𐐫𐑉 𐑄𐐯𐑋, 𐐨𐑂𐐲𐑌 𐐩 𐑊𐐩𐐿 𐐱𐑂 𐑁𐐴𐑉 𐐰𐑌𐐼 𐐺𐑉𐐮𐑋𐑅𐐻𐐬𐑌, 𐐸𐐶𐐮𐐽 𐐮𐑆 𐐯𐑌𐐼𐑊𐐯𐑅 𐐻𐐫𐑉𐑋𐐯𐑌𐐻. 𐐜𐐩𐑉𐑁𐐬𐑉, 𐐶𐐬 𐐺 𐐲𐑌𐐻𐐭 𐐸𐐮𐑋 𐑄𐐰𐐻 𐐮𐑆 𐐰𐐻 𐐨𐑆 𐐮𐑌 𐐞𐐴𐐲𐑌. 𐐎𐐬 𐐺 𐐲𐑌𐐻𐐭 𐐸𐐮𐑋 𐑄𐐰𐐻 𐐿𐑉𐐴𐐯𐑃, 𐐋𐑊 𐐮𐑆 𐐶𐐯𐑊; 𐐏𐐩, 𐐶𐐬 𐐺 𐐲𐑌𐐻𐐭 𐐸𐐮𐑋 𐑄𐐰𐐻 𐐸𐐪𐑉𐐿𐐲𐑌𐐯𐑃 𐐲𐑌𐐻𐐭 𐑄 𐐹𐑉𐐨𐑅𐐯𐐹𐐻𐑅 𐐱𐑂 𐑋𐐯𐑌, 𐐰𐑌𐐼 𐐼𐐯𐑌𐐴𐐯𐑃 𐑄 𐐹𐐵𐐲𐑉 𐐱𐑂 𐐘𐐱𐐼, 𐐰𐑌𐐼 𐑄 𐑀𐐮𐑁𐐻 𐐱𐑂 𐑄 𐐐𐐬𐑊𐐨 𐐘𐐬𐑅𐐻. 𐐏𐐩, 𐐶𐐬 𐐺 𐐲𐑌𐐻𐐭 𐐸𐐮𐑋 𐑄𐐰𐐻 𐑅𐐯𐑃, 𐐎𐐨 𐐸𐐰𐑂 𐑉𐐨𐑅𐐨𐑂𐐼, 𐐰𐑌𐐼 𐐶𐐨 𐑌𐐨𐐼 𐑌𐐬 𐑋𐐬𐑉. 𐐈𐑌𐐼 𐐮𐑌 𐑁𐐴𐑌, 𐐶𐐬 𐐲𐑌𐐻𐐭 𐐫𐑊 𐑄𐐬𐑆 𐐸𐐭 𐐻𐑉𐐯𐑋𐐺𐑊, 𐐰𐑌𐐼 𐐪𐑉 𐐰𐑍𐑀𐑉𐐨 𐐺𐐨𐐿𐐫𐑆 𐐱𐑂 𐑄 𐐻𐑉𐐭𐑃 𐐱𐑂 𐐘𐐱𐐼. 𐐙𐐫𐑉 𐐺𐐨𐐸𐐬𐑊𐐼, 𐐸𐐨 𐑄𐐰𐐻 𐐮𐑆 𐐺𐐮𐑊𐐻 𐐲𐐹𐐱𐑌 𐑄 𐑉𐐱𐐿, 𐑉𐐨𐑅𐐨𐑂𐐯𐑃 𐐮𐐻 𐐶𐐮𐑄 𐑀𐑊𐐰𐐼𐑌𐐯𐑅; 𐐰𐑌𐐼 𐐸𐐨 𐑄𐐰𐐻 𐐮𐑆 𐐺𐐮𐑊𐐻 𐐲𐐹𐐱𐑌 𐐩 𐑅𐐰𐑌𐐼𐐨 𐑁𐐵𐑌𐐼𐐩𐑇𐐲𐑌, 𐐻𐑉𐐯𐑋𐐺𐑊𐐯𐑃 𐑊𐐯𐑅𐐻 𐐸𐐨 𐑇𐐰𐑊 𐑁𐐫𐑊.

4. 𐐎𐐬 𐐺 𐐲𐑌𐐻𐐭 𐐸𐐮𐑋 𐑄𐐰𐐻 𐑇𐐰𐑊 𐑅𐐩, 𐐎𐐨 𐐸𐐰𐑂 𐑉𐐨𐑅𐐨𐑂𐐼 𐑄 𐐶𐐲𐑉𐐼 𐐱𐑂 𐐘𐐱𐐼, 𐐰𐑌𐐼 𐐶𐐨 𐑌𐐨𐐼 𐑌𐐬 𐑋𐐬𐑉 𐐱𐑂 𐑄 𐐶𐐲𐑉𐐼 𐐱𐑂 𐐘𐐱𐐼, 𐑁𐐫𐑉 𐐶𐐨 𐐸𐐰𐑂 𐐨𐑌𐐲𐑁. 𐐙𐐫𐑉 𐐺𐐨𐐸𐐬𐑊𐐼, 𐑄𐐲𐑅 𐑅𐐯𐑃 𐑄 𐐢𐐫𐑉𐐼 𐐘𐐱𐐼; 𐐌 𐐶𐐮𐑊 𐑀𐐮𐑂 𐐲𐑌𐐻𐐭 𐑄 𐐽𐐮𐑊𐐼𐑉𐐯𐑌 𐐱𐑂 𐑋𐐯𐑌 𐑊𐐴𐑌 𐐲𐐹𐐱𐑌 𐑊𐐴𐑌, 𐐹𐑉𐐨𐑅𐐯𐐹𐐻 𐐲𐐹𐐱𐑌 𐐹𐑉𐐨𐑅𐐯𐐹𐐻, 𐐸𐐨𐑉 𐐩 𐑊𐐮𐐻𐑊 𐐰𐑌𐐼 𐑄𐐩𐑉 𐐩 𐑊𐐮𐐻𐑊; 𐐰𐑌𐐼 𐐺𐑊𐐯𐑅𐐯𐐼 𐐪𐑉 𐑄𐐬𐑆 𐐸𐐭 𐐸𐐪𐑉𐐿𐐲𐑌 𐐲𐑌𐐻𐐭 𐑋𐐴 𐐹𐑉𐐨𐑅𐐯𐐹𐐻𐑅, 𐐰𐑌𐐼 𐑊𐐯𐑌𐐼 𐐰𐑌 𐐨𐑉 𐐲𐑌𐐻𐐭 𐑋𐐴 𐐿𐐵𐑌𐑅𐐯𐑊, 𐑁𐐫𐑉 𐑄𐐩 𐑇𐐰𐑊 𐑊𐐲𐑉𐑌 𐐶𐐮𐑆𐐼𐐲𐑋; 𐑁𐐫𐑉 𐐲𐑌𐐻𐐭 𐐸𐐮𐑋 𐑄𐐰𐐻 𐑉𐐨𐑅𐐨𐑂𐐯𐑃, 𐐌 𐐶𐐮𐑊 𐑀𐐮𐑂 𐑋𐐬𐑉; 𐐰𐑌𐐼 𐑁𐑉𐐱𐑋 𐑄𐐯𐑋 𐑄𐐰𐐻 𐑇𐐰𐑊 𐑅𐐩, 𐐎𐐨 𐐸𐐰𐑂 𐐨𐑌𐐲𐑁, 𐑁𐑉𐐱𐑋 𐑄𐐯𐑋 𐑇𐐰𐑊 𐐺 𐐻𐐩𐐿𐑌 𐐲𐐶𐐩 𐐨𐑂𐐲𐑌 𐑄𐐰𐐻 𐐸𐐶𐐮𐐽 𐑄𐐩 𐐸𐐰𐑂. 𐐗𐐲𐑉𐑅𐐯𐐼 𐐮𐑆 𐐸𐐨 𐑄𐐰𐐻 𐐹𐐳𐐻𐐯𐑃 𐐸𐐮𐑆 𐐻𐑉𐐲𐑅𐐻 𐐮𐑌 𐑋𐐰𐑌, 𐐫𐑉 𐑋𐐩𐐿𐐯𐑃 𐑁𐑊𐐯𐑇 𐐸𐐮𐑆 𐐪𐑉𐑋, 𐐫𐑉 𐑇𐐰𐑊 𐐸𐐪𐑉𐐿𐐲𐑌 𐐲𐑌𐐻𐐭 𐑄 𐐹𐑉𐐨𐑅𐐯𐐹𐐻𐑅 𐐱𐑂 𐑋𐐯𐑌, 𐑅𐐩𐑂 𐑄𐐩𐑉 𐐹𐑉𐐨𐑅𐐯𐐹𐐻𐑅 𐑇𐐰𐑊 𐐺 𐑀𐐮𐑂𐑌 𐐺𐐴 𐑄 𐐹𐐵𐐲𐑉 𐐱𐑂 𐑄 𐐐𐐬𐑊𐐨 𐐘𐐬𐑅𐐻.

5. 𐐎𐐬 𐐺 𐐲𐑌𐐻𐐭 𐑄 𐐖𐐯𐑌𐐻𐐴𐑊𐑆, 𐑅𐐯𐑃 𐑄 𐐢𐐫𐑉𐐼 𐐘𐐱𐐼 𐐱𐑂 𐐐𐐬𐑅𐐻𐑅; 𐑁𐐫𐑉 𐑌𐐱𐐻𐐶𐐮𐑄𐑅𐐻𐐰𐑌𐐼𐐮𐑍 𐐌 𐑇𐐰𐑊 𐑊𐐯𐑍𐑃𐑌 𐐵𐐻 𐑋𐐴𐑌 𐐪𐑉𐑋 𐐲𐑌𐐻𐐭 𐑄𐐯𐑋 𐑁𐑉𐐱𐑋 𐐼𐐩 𐐻𐐭 𐐼𐐩, 𐑄𐐩 𐐶𐐮𐑊 𐐼𐐨𐑌𐐴 𐑋𐐨; 𐑌𐐯𐑂𐐲𐑉𐑄𐐯𐑊𐐯𐑅, 𐐌 𐐶𐐮𐑊 𐐺 𐑋𐐲𐑉𐑅𐐮𐑁𐐳𐑊 𐐲𐑌𐐻𐐭 𐑄𐐯𐑋, 𐑅𐐯𐑃 𐑄 𐐢𐐫𐑉𐐼 𐐘𐐱𐐼, 𐐮𐑁 𐑄𐐩 𐐶𐐮𐑊 𐑉𐐨𐐹𐐯𐑌𐐻 𐐰𐑌𐐼 𐐿𐐲𐑋 𐐲𐑌𐐻𐐭 𐑋𐐨; 𐑁𐐫𐑉 𐑋𐐴𐑌 𐐪𐑉𐑋 𐐮𐑆 𐑊𐐯𐑍𐑃𐑌𐐼 𐐵𐐻 𐐫𐑊 𐑄 𐐼𐐩 𐑊𐐱𐑍, 𐑅𐐯𐑃 𐑄 𐐢𐐫𐑉𐐼 𐐘𐐱𐐼 𐐱𐑂 𐐐𐐬𐑅𐐻𐑅.

6. 𐐒𐐲𐐻 𐐺𐐨𐐸𐐬𐑊𐐼, 𐑄𐐩𐑉 𐑇𐐰𐑊 𐐺 𐑋𐐯𐑌𐐨 𐐰𐐻 𐑄𐐰𐐻 𐐼𐐩, 𐐸𐐶𐐯𐑌 𐐌 𐑇𐐰𐑊 𐐹𐑉𐐬𐑅𐐨𐐼 𐐻𐐭 𐐼𐐭 𐐩 𐑋𐐪𐑉𐑂𐐯𐑊𐐲𐑅 𐐶𐐲𐑉𐐿 𐐰𐑋𐐲𐑍 𐑄𐐯𐑋, 𐑄𐐰𐐻 𐐌 𐑋𐐩 𐑉𐐨𐑋𐐯𐑋𐐺𐐲𐑉 𐑋𐐴 𐐿𐐲𐑂𐐯𐑌𐐰𐑌𐐻𐑅 𐐸𐐶𐐮𐐽 𐐌 𐐸𐐰𐑂 𐑋𐐩𐐼 𐐲𐑌𐐻𐐭 𐑄 𐐽𐐮𐑊𐐼𐑉𐐯𐑌 𐐱𐑂 𐑋𐐯𐑌, 𐑄𐐰𐐻 𐐌 𐑋𐐩 𐑅𐐯𐐻 𐑋𐐴 𐐸𐐰𐑌𐐼 𐐲𐑀𐐯𐑌 𐑄 𐑅𐐯𐐿𐐲𐑌𐐼 𐐻𐐴𐑋, 𐐻𐐭 𐑉𐐨𐐿𐐲𐑂𐐲𐑉 𐑋𐐴 𐐹𐐨𐐹𐑊, 𐐸𐐶𐐮𐐽 𐐪𐑉 𐐱𐑂 𐑄 𐐸𐐵𐑅 𐐱𐑂 𐐆𐑆𐑉𐐩𐐯𐑊; 𐐰𐑌𐐼 𐐫𐑊𐑅𐐬, 𐑄𐐰𐐻 𐐌 𐑋𐐩 𐑉𐐨𐑋𐐯𐑋𐐺𐐲𐑉 𐑄 𐐹𐑉𐐱𐑋𐐮𐑅𐐯𐑆 𐐸𐐶𐐮𐐽 𐐌 𐐸𐐰𐑂 𐑋𐐩𐐼 𐐲𐑌𐐻𐐭 𐑄𐐨, 𐐤𐐨𐑁𐐴, 𐐰𐑌𐐼 𐐫𐑊𐑅𐐬 𐐲𐑌𐐻𐐭 𐑄𐐴 𐑁𐐪𐑄𐐲𐑉, 𐑄𐐰𐐻 𐐌 𐐶𐐳𐐼 𐑉𐐨𐑋𐐯𐑋𐐺𐐲𐑉 𐐷𐐭𐑉 𐑅𐐨𐐼; 𐐰𐑌𐐼 𐑄𐐰𐐻 𐑄 𐐶𐐲𐑉𐐼𐑆 𐐱𐑂 𐐷𐐭𐑉 𐑅𐐨𐐼 𐑇𐐳𐐼 𐐹𐑉𐐬𐑅𐐨𐐼 𐑁𐐬𐑉𐑃 𐐵𐐻 𐐱𐑂 𐑋𐐴 𐑋𐐵𐑃 𐐲𐑌𐐻𐐭 𐐷𐐭𐑉 𐑅𐐨𐐼. 𐐈𐑌𐐼 𐑋𐐴 𐐶𐐲𐑉𐐼𐑆 𐑇𐐰𐑊 𐐸𐐮𐑅 𐑁𐐬𐑉𐑃 𐐲𐑌𐐻𐐭 𐑄 𐐯𐑌𐐼𐑆 𐐱𐑂 𐑄 𐐲𐑉𐑃, 𐑁𐐫𐑉 𐐩 𐑅𐐻𐐰𐑌𐐼𐐲𐑉𐐼 𐐲𐑌𐐻𐐭 𐑋𐐴 𐐹𐐨𐐹𐑊, 𐐸𐐶𐐮𐐽 𐐪𐑉 𐐱𐑂 𐑄 𐐸𐐵𐑅 𐐱𐑂 𐐆𐑆𐑉𐐩𐐯𐑊. 𐐈𐑌𐐼 𐐺𐐨𐐿𐐫𐑆 𐑋𐐴 𐐶𐐲𐑉𐐼𐑆 𐑇𐐰𐑊 𐐸𐐮𐑅 𐑁𐐬𐑉𐑃, 𐑋𐐯𐑌𐐨 𐐱𐑂 𐑄 𐐖𐐯𐑌𐐻𐐴𐑊𐑆 𐑇𐐰𐑊 𐑅𐐩, 𐐊 𐐒𐐴𐐺𐑊, 𐐩 𐐒𐐴𐐺𐑊, 𐐶𐐨 𐐸𐐰𐑂 𐑀𐐱𐐻 𐐩 𐐒𐐴𐐺𐑊, 𐐰𐑌𐐼 𐑄𐐩𐑉 𐐿𐐰𐑌𐐱𐐻 𐐺 𐐯𐑌𐐨 𐑋𐐬𐑉 𐐒𐐴𐐺𐑊. 𐐒𐐲𐐻 𐑄𐐲𐑅 𐑅𐐯𐑃 𐑄 𐐢𐐫𐑉𐐼 𐐘𐐱𐐼; 𐐄 𐑁𐐭𐑊𐑆, 𐑄𐐩 𐑇𐐰𐑊 𐐸𐐰𐑂 𐐩 𐐒𐐴𐐺𐑊; 𐐰𐑌𐐼 𐐮𐐻 𐑇𐐰𐑊 𐐹𐑉𐐬𐑅𐐨𐐼 𐑁𐐬𐑉𐑃 𐑁𐑉𐐱𐑋 𐑄 𐐖𐐭𐑆, 𐑋𐐴𐑌 𐐩𐑌𐑇𐐯𐑌𐐻 𐐿𐐲𐑂𐐯𐑌𐐰𐑌𐐻 𐐹𐐨𐐹𐑊. 𐐈𐑌𐐼 𐐸𐐶𐐱𐐻 𐑃𐐰𐑍𐐿 𐑄𐐩 𐑄 𐐖𐐭𐑆 𐑁𐐫𐑉 𐑄 𐐒𐐴𐐺𐑊 𐐸𐐶𐐮𐐽 𐑄𐐩 𐑉𐐨𐑅𐐨𐑂 𐑁𐑉𐐱𐑋 𐑄𐐯𐑋? 𐐏𐐩, 𐐸𐐶𐐱𐐻 𐐼𐐭 𐑄 𐐖𐐯𐑌𐐻𐐴𐑊𐑆 𐑋𐐨𐑌? 𐐔𐐭 𐑄𐐩 𐑉𐐨𐑋𐐯𐑋𐐺𐐲𐑉 𐑄 𐐻𐑉𐐰𐑂𐐩𐑊𐑆, 𐐰𐑌𐐼 𐑄 𐑊𐐩𐐺𐐲𐑉𐑆, 𐐰𐑌𐐼 𐑄 𐐹𐐩𐑌𐑆 𐐱𐑂 𐑄 𐐖𐐭𐑆, 𐐰𐑌𐐼 𐑄𐐩𐑉 𐐼𐐮𐑊𐐮𐐾𐐯𐑌𐑅 𐐲𐑌𐐻𐐭 𐑋𐐨, 𐐮𐑌 𐐺𐑉𐐮𐑍𐐮𐑍 𐑁𐐬𐑉𐑃 𐑅𐐰𐑊𐑂𐐩𐑇𐐲𐑌 𐐲𐑌𐐻𐐭 𐑄 𐐖𐐯𐑌𐐻𐐴𐑊𐑆?

7. 𐐄 𐐷 𐐖𐐯𐑌𐐻𐐴𐑊𐑆, 𐐸𐐰𐑂 𐐷 𐑉𐐯𐑋𐐯𐑋𐐺𐐲𐑉𐐼 𐑄 𐐖𐐭𐑆, 𐑋𐐴𐑌 𐐩𐑌𐑇𐐯𐑌𐐻 𐐿𐐲𐑂𐐯𐑌𐐰𐑌𐐻 𐐹𐐨𐐹𐑊? 𐐤𐐩; 𐐺𐐲𐐻 𐐷 𐐸𐐰𐑂 𐐿𐐲𐑉𐑅𐐯𐐼 𐑄𐐯𐑋, 𐐰𐑌𐐼 𐐸𐐰𐑂 𐐸𐐩𐐻𐐯𐐼 𐑄𐐯𐑋, 𐐰𐑌𐐼 𐐸𐐰𐑂 𐑌𐐱𐐻 𐑅𐐫𐐻 𐐻𐐭 𐑉𐐨𐐿𐐲𐑂𐐲𐑉 𐑄𐐯𐑋. 𐐒𐐲𐐻 𐐺𐐨𐐸𐐬𐑊𐐼, 𐐌 𐐶𐐮𐑊 𐑉𐐨𐐻𐐲𐑉𐑌 𐐫𐑊 𐑄𐐨𐑆 𐑃𐐮𐑍𐑆 𐐲𐐹𐐱𐑌 𐐷𐐭𐑉 𐐬𐑌 𐐸𐐯𐐼𐑆; 𐑁𐐫𐑉 𐐌 𐑄 𐐢𐐫𐑉𐐼 𐐸𐐰𐑂 𐑌𐐱𐐻 𐑁𐐫𐑉𐑀𐐱𐐻𐑌 𐑋𐐴 𐐹𐐨𐐹𐑊. 𐐛𐐵 𐑁𐐭𐑊, 𐑄𐐰𐐻 𐑇𐐰𐑊 𐑅𐐩: 𐐈 𐐒𐐴𐐺𐑊, 𐐶𐐨 𐐸𐐰𐑂 𐑀𐐱𐐻 𐐲 𐐒𐐴𐐺𐑊, 𐐰𐑌𐐼 𐐶𐐨 𐑌𐐨𐐼 𐑌𐐬 𐑋𐐫𐑉 𐐒𐐴𐐺𐑊. 𐐐𐐰𐑂 𐐷 𐐱𐐺𐐻𐐩𐑌𐐼 𐐲 𐐒𐐴𐐺𐑊, 𐑅𐐩𐑂 𐐮𐐻 𐐶𐐲𐑉 𐐺𐐴 𐑄 𐐖𐐭𐑆? 𐐤𐐬 𐐷 𐑌𐐱𐐻 𐑄𐐰𐐻 𐑄𐐯𐑉 𐐪𐑉 𐑋𐐫𐑉 𐑌𐐩𐑇𐐲𐑌𐑆 𐑄𐐰𐑌 𐐶𐐲𐑌? 𐐤𐐬 𐐷 𐑌𐐱𐐻 𐑄𐐰𐐻 𐐌 𐑄 𐐢𐐫𐑉𐐼 𐐷𐐭𐑉 𐐘𐐱𐐼 𐐸𐐰𐑂 𐐿𐑉𐐨𐐩𐐻𐐯𐐼 𐐫𐑊 𐑋𐐯𐑌, 𐐰𐑌𐐼 𐑄𐐰𐐻 𐐌 𐑉𐐨𐑋𐐯𐑋𐐺𐐲𐑉 𐑄𐐬𐑆 𐐸𐐭 𐐪𐑉 𐐲𐐹𐐱𐑌 𐑄 𐐴𐑊𐑆 𐐱𐑂 𐑄 𐑅𐐨; 𐐰𐑌𐐼 𐑄𐐰𐐻 𐐌 𐑉𐐭𐑊 𐐮𐑌 𐑄 𐐸𐐯𐑂𐐲𐑌𐑆 𐐲𐐺𐐲𐑂, 𐐰𐑌𐐼 𐐮𐑌 𐑄 𐐲𐑉𐑃 𐐺𐐨𐑌𐐨𐑃; 𐐰𐑌𐐼 𐐌 𐐺𐑉𐐮𐑍 𐑁𐐫𐑉𐑃 𐑋𐐴 𐐶𐐲𐑉𐐼 𐐲𐑌𐐻𐐭 𐑄 𐐽𐐮𐑊𐐼𐑉𐐯𐑌 𐐱𐑂 𐑋𐐯𐑌, 𐐷𐐩, 𐐨𐑂𐐯𐑌 𐐲𐐹𐐱𐑌 𐐫𐑊 𐑄 𐑌𐐩𐑇𐐲𐑌𐑆 𐐱𐑂 𐑄 𐐲𐑉𐑃? 𐐐𐐶𐐯𐑉𐑁𐐫𐑉, 𐑋𐐲𐑉𐑋𐐲𐑉 𐐷, 𐐺𐐨𐐿𐐫𐑆 𐑄𐐰𐐻 𐐷 𐑇𐐰𐑊 𐑉𐐨𐑅𐐨𐑂 𐑋𐐫𐑉 𐐱𐑂 𐑋𐐴 𐐶𐐲𐑉𐐼? 𐐤𐐬 𐐷 𐑌𐐱𐐻 𐑄𐐰𐐻 𐑄 𐐻𐐯𐑅𐐻𐐮𐑋𐐬𐑌𐐨 𐐱𐑂 𐐻𐐭 𐑌𐐩𐑇𐐲𐑌𐑆 𐐮𐑆 𐐲 𐐶𐐮𐐻𐑌𐐯𐑅 𐐲𐑌𐐻𐐭 𐐷𐐭 𐑄𐐰𐐻 𐐌 𐐰𐑋 𐐘𐐱𐐼, 𐑄𐐰𐐻 𐐌 𐑉𐐨𐑋𐐯𐑋𐐺𐐲𐑉 𐐶𐐲𐑌 𐑌𐐩𐑇𐐲𐑌 𐑊𐐴𐐿 𐐲𐑌𐐻𐐭 𐐰𐑌𐐲𐑄𐐲𐑉? 𐐐𐐶𐐯𐑉𐑁𐐫𐑉, 𐐌 𐑅𐐹𐐨𐐿 𐑄 𐑅𐐩𐑋 𐐶𐐲𐑉𐐼𐑆 𐐲𐑌𐐻𐐭 𐐶𐐲𐑌 𐑌𐐩𐑇𐐲𐑌 𐑊𐐴𐐿 𐐲𐑌𐐻𐐭 𐐰𐑌𐐲𐑄𐐲𐑉. 𐐈𐑌𐐼 𐐸𐐶𐐯𐑌 𐑄 𐐻𐐭 𐑌𐐩𐑇𐐲𐑌𐑆 𐑇𐐰𐑊 𐑉𐐲𐑌 𐐻𐐭𐑀𐐯𐑄𐐲𐑉, 𐑄 𐐻𐐯𐑅𐐻𐐮𐑋𐐬𐑌𐐨 𐐱𐑂 𐑄 𐐻𐐭 𐑌𐐩𐑇𐐲𐑌𐑆 𐑇𐐰𐑊 𐑉𐐲𐑌 𐐻𐐭𐑀𐐯𐑄𐐲𐑉 𐐫𐑊𐑅𐐬. 𐐈𐑌𐐼 𐐌 𐐼𐐭 𐑄𐐮𐑅 𐑄𐐰𐐻 𐐌 𐑋𐐩 𐐹𐑉𐐭𐑂 𐐲𐑌𐐻𐐭 𐑋𐐯𐑌𐐨, 𐑄𐐰𐐻 𐐌 𐐰𐑋 𐑄 𐑅𐐩𐑋 𐐷𐐯𐑅𐐻𐐲𐑉𐐼𐐩, 𐐻𐐭-𐐼𐐩, 𐐰𐑌𐐼 𐑁𐐫𐑉𐐯𐑂𐐲𐑉; 𐐰𐑌𐐼 𐑄𐐰𐐻 𐐌 𐑅𐐹𐐨𐐿 𐑁𐐫𐑉𐑃 𐑋𐐴 𐐶𐐲𐑉𐐼𐑆 𐐰𐐿𐐫𐑉𐐼𐐮𐑍 𐐻𐐭 𐑋𐐴𐑌 𐐬𐑌 𐐹𐑊𐐯𐑈𐐲𐑉. 𐐈𐑌𐐼 𐐺𐐨𐐿𐐫𐑆 𐑄𐐰𐐻 𐐌 𐐸𐐰𐑂 𐑅𐐹𐐬𐐿𐑌 𐐶𐐲𐑌 𐐶𐐲𐑉𐐼, 𐐷 𐑌𐐨𐐼 𐑌𐐱𐐻 𐑅𐐲𐐹𐐬𐑆 𐑄𐐰𐐻 𐐌 𐐿𐐰𐑌𐐱𐐻 𐑅𐐹𐐨𐐿 𐐰𐑌𐐲𐑄𐐲𐑉; 𐑁𐐫𐑉 𐑋𐐴 𐐶𐐲𐑉𐐿 𐐮𐑆 𐑌𐐱𐐻 𐐷𐐯𐐻 𐑁𐐮𐑌𐐮𐑇𐐻; 𐑌𐐨𐑄𐐲𐑉 𐑇𐐰𐑊 𐐮𐐻 𐐺𐐨 𐐲𐑌𐐻𐐮𐑊 𐑄 𐐯𐑌𐐼 𐐱𐑂 𐑋𐐰𐑌, 𐑌𐐨𐑄𐐲𐑉 𐑁𐑉𐐱𐑋 𐑄𐐰𐐻 𐐻𐐴𐑋 𐐸𐐯𐑌𐑅𐑁𐐫𐑉𐑃 𐐰𐑌𐐼 𐑁𐐫𐑉𐐯𐑂𐐲𐑉.

8. 𐐐𐐶𐐯𐑉𐑁𐐫𐑉, 𐐺𐐨𐐿𐐫𐑆 𐑄𐐰𐐻 𐐷 𐐸𐐰𐑂 𐐲 𐐒𐐴𐐺𐑊, 𐐷 𐑌𐐨𐐼 𐑌𐐱𐐻 𐑅𐐲𐐹𐐬𐑆 𐑄𐐰𐐻 𐐮𐐻 𐐿𐐱𐑌𐐻𐐩𐑌𐑆 𐐫𐑊 𐑋𐐴 𐐶𐐲𐑉𐐼𐑆; 𐑌𐐨𐑄𐐲𐑉 𐑌𐐨𐐼 𐐷 𐑅𐐲𐐹𐐬𐑆 𐑄𐐰𐐻 𐐌 𐐸𐐰𐑂 𐑌𐐱𐐻 𐐿𐐫𐑆𐐯𐐼 𐑋𐐫𐑉 𐐻𐐭 𐐺𐐨 𐑉𐐮𐐻𐑌: 𐑁𐐫𐑉 𐐌 𐐿𐐱𐑋𐐰𐑌𐐼 𐐫𐑊 𐑋𐐯𐑌, 𐐺𐐬𐑃 𐐮𐑌 𐑄 𐐨𐑅𐐻 𐐰𐑌𐐼 𐐮𐑌 𐑄 𐐶𐐯𐑅𐐻, 𐐰𐑌𐐼 𐐮𐑌 𐑄 𐑌𐐫𐑉𐑃, 𐐰𐑌𐐼 𐐮𐑌 𐑄 𐑅𐐵𐑃, 𐐰𐑌𐐼 𐐮𐑌 𐑄 𐐴𐑊𐐲𐑌𐐼𐑆 𐐱𐑂 𐑄 𐑅𐐨, 𐑄𐐰𐐻 𐑄𐐩 𐑇𐐰𐑊 𐑉𐐴𐐻 𐑄 𐐶𐐲𐑉𐐼𐑆 𐐸𐐶𐐮𐐽 𐐌 𐑅𐐹𐐨𐐿 𐐲𐑌𐐻𐐭 𐑄𐐯𐑋: 𐑁𐐫𐑉 𐐵𐐻 𐐱𐑂 𐑄 𐐺𐐳𐐿𐑅 𐐸𐐶𐐮𐐽 𐑇𐐰𐑊 𐐺𐐨 𐑉𐐮𐐻𐑌, 𐐌 𐐶𐐮𐑊 𐐖𐐲𐐾 𐑄 𐐶𐐲𐑉𐑊𐐼, 𐐯𐑂𐐲𐑉𐐨 𐑋𐐰𐑌 𐐰𐐿𐐫𐑉𐐼𐐮𐑍 𐐻𐐭 𐑄𐐯𐑉 𐐶𐐲𐑉𐐿𐑅, 𐐰𐐿𐐫𐑉𐐼𐐮𐑍 𐐻𐐭 𐑄𐐰𐐻 𐐸𐐶𐐮𐐽 𐐮𐑆 𐑉𐐮𐐻𐑌. 𐐙𐐫𐑉 𐐺𐐨𐐸𐐬𐑊𐐼, 𐐌 𐑇𐐰𐑊 𐑅𐐹𐐨𐐿 𐐲𐑌𐐻𐐭 𐑄 𐐖𐐭𐑆, 𐐰𐑌𐐼 𐑄𐐩 𐑇𐐰𐑊 𐑉𐐴𐐻 𐐮𐐻; 𐐰𐑌𐐼 𐐌 𐑇𐐰𐑊 𐐫𐑊𐑅𐐬 𐑅𐐹𐐨𐐿 𐐲𐑌𐐻𐐭 𐑄 𐐤𐐨𐑁𐐴𐐻𐑅, 𐐰𐑌𐐼 𐑄𐐩 𐑇𐐰𐑊 𐑉𐐴𐐻 𐐮𐐻; 𐐰𐑌𐐼 𐐌 𐑇𐐰𐑊 𐐫𐑊𐑅𐐬 𐑅𐐹𐐨𐐿 𐐲𐑌𐐻𐐭 𐑄 𐐲𐑄𐐲𐑉 𐐻𐑉𐐴𐐺𐑆 𐐱𐑂 𐑄 𐐸𐐵𐑅 𐐱𐑂 𐐆𐑆𐑉𐐩𐐯𐑊, 𐐸𐐶𐐮𐐽 𐐌 𐐸𐐰𐑂 𐑊𐐯𐐼 𐐲𐐶𐐩, 𐐰𐑌𐐼 𐑄𐐩 𐑇𐐰𐑊 𐑉𐐴𐐻 𐐮𐐻; 𐐰𐑌𐐼 𐐌 𐑇𐐰𐑊 𐐫𐑊𐑅𐐬 𐑅𐐹𐐨𐐿 𐐲𐑌𐐻𐐭 𐐫𐑊 𐑌𐐩𐑇𐐲𐑌𐑆 𐐱𐑂 𐑄 𐐲𐑉𐑃, 𐐰𐑌𐐼 𐑄𐐩 𐑇𐐰𐑊 𐑉𐐴𐐻 𐐮𐐻.

9. 𐐈𐑌𐐼 𐐮𐐻 𐑇𐐰𐑊 𐐿𐐲𐑋 𐐻𐐭 𐐹𐐰𐑅 𐑄𐐰𐐻 𐑄 𐐖𐐭𐑆 𐑇𐐰𐑊 𐐸𐐰𐑂 𐑄 𐐶𐐲𐑉𐐼𐑆 𐐱𐑂 𐑄 𐐤𐐨𐑁𐐴𐐻𐑅, 𐐰𐑌𐐼 𐑄 𐐤𐐨𐑁𐐴𐐻𐑅 𐑇𐐰𐑊 𐐸𐐰𐑂 𐑄 𐐶𐐲𐑉𐐼𐑆 𐐱𐑂 𐑄 𐐖𐐭𐑆, 𐐰𐑌𐐼 𐑄 𐐤𐐨𐑁𐐴𐐻𐑅 𐐰𐑌𐐼 𐑄 𐐖𐐭𐑆 𐑇𐐰𐑊 𐐸𐐰𐑂 𐑄 𐐶𐐲𐑉𐐼𐑆 𐐱𐑂 𐑄 𐑊𐐫𐑅𐐻 𐐻𐑉𐐴𐐺𐑆 𐐱𐑂 𐐆𐑆𐑉𐐩𐐯𐑊; 𐐰𐑌𐐼 𐑄 𐑊𐐫𐑅𐐻 𐐻𐑉𐐴𐐺𐑆 𐐱𐑂 𐐆𐑆𐑉𐐩𐐯𐑊 𐑇𐐰𐑊 𐐸𐐰𐑂 𐑄 𐐶𐐲𐑉𐐼𐑆 𐐱𐑂 𐑄 𐐤𐐨𐑁𐐴𐐻𐑅 𐐰𐑌𐐼 𐑄 𐐖𐐭𐑆.

10. 𐐈𐑌𐐼 𐐮𐐻 𐑇𐐰𐑊 𐐿𐐲𐑋 𐐻𐐭 𐐹𐐰𐑅 𐑄𐐰𐐻 𐑋𐐴 𐐹𐐨𐐹𐑊 𐐸𐐶𐐮𐐽 𐐪𐑉 𐐱𐑂 𐑄 𐐸𐐵𐑅 𐐱𐑂 𐐆𐑆𐑉𐐩𐐯𐑊, 𐑇𐐰𐑊 𐐺𐐨 𐑀𐐰𐑄𐐲𐑉𐐼 𐐸𐐬𐑋 𐐲𐑌𐐻𐐭 𐑄 𐑊𐐰𐑌𐐼𐑆 𐐱𐑂 𐑄𐐯𐑉 𐐹𐐱𐑆𐐯𐑇𐐲𐑌𐑆; 𐐰𐑌𐐼 𐑋𐐴 𐐶𐐲𐑉𐐼 𐐫𐑊𐑅𐐬 𐑇𐐰𐑊 𐐺𐐨 𐑀𐐰𐑄𐐲𐑉𐐼 𐐮𐑌 𐐶𐐲𐑌. 𐐈𐑌𐐼 𐐌 𐐶𐐮𐑊 𐑇𐐬 𐐲𐑌𐐻𐐭 𐑄𐐯𐑋 𐑄𐐰𐐻 𐑁𐐴𐐻 𐐲𐑀𐐩𐑌𐑅𐐻 𐑋𐐴 𐐶𐐲𐑉𐐼 𐐰𐑌𐐼 𐐲𐑀𐐩𐑌𐑅𐐻 𐑋𐐴 𐐹𐐨𐐹𐑊, 𐐸𐐭 𐐪𐑉 𐐱𐑂 𐑄 𐐸𐐵𐑅 𐐱𐑂 𐐆𐑆𐑉𐐩𐐯𐑊, 𐑄𐐰𐐻 𐐌 𐐰𐑋 𐐘𐐱𐐼, 𐐰𐑌𐐼 𐑄𐐰𐐻 𐐌 𐐿𐐲𐑂𐐯𐑌𐐰𐑌𐐻𐐯𐐼 𐐶𐐮𐑄 𐐁𐐺𐑉𐐲𐐸𐐰𐑋, 𐑄𐐰𐐻 𐐌 𐐶𐐳𐐼 𐑉𐐨𐑋𐐯𐑋𐐺𐐲𐑉 𐐸𐐮𐑆 𐑅𐐨𐐼 𐑁𐐫𐑉𐐯𐑂𐐲𐑉.

11. 𐐈𐑌𐐼 𐑌𐐵 𐐺𐐨𐐸𐐬𐑊𐐼, 𐑋𐐴 𐐺𐐨𐑊𐐲𐑂𐐯𐐼 𐐺𐑉𐐯𐑄𐑉𐐯𐑌, 𐐌 𐐶𐐳𐐼 𐑅𐐹𐐨𐐿 𐐲𐑌𐐻𐐭 𐐷𐐭: 𐑁𐐫𐑉 𐐌, 𐐤𐐨𐑁𐐴, 𐐶𐐳𐐼 𐑌𐐱𐐻 𐑅𐐲𐑁𐐲𐑉 𐑄𐐰𐐻 𐐷 𐑇𐐳𐐼 𐑅𐐲𐐹𐐬𐑆 𐑄𐐰𐐻 𐐷 𐐪𐑉 𐑋𐐫𐑉 𐑉𐐴𐐽𐐲𐑅 𐑄𐐰𐑌 𐑄 𐐖𐐯𐑌𐐻𐐴𐑊𐑆 𐑇𐐰𐑊 𐐺𐐨. 𐐙𐐫𐑉 𐐺𐐨𐐸𐐬𐑊𐐼, 𐐯𐐿𐑅𐐯𐐹𐐻 𐐷 𐑇𐐰𐑊 𐐿𐐨𐐹 𐑄 𐐿𐐱𐑋𐐰𐑌𐐼𐑋𐐯𐑌𐐻𐑅 𐐱𐑂 𐐘𐐱𐐼, 𐐷 𐑇𐐰𐑊 𐐫𐑊 𐑊𐐴𐐿𐐶𐐴𐑆 𐐹𐐲𐑉𐐮𐑇; 𐐰𐑌𐐼 𐐺𐐨𐐿𐐫𐑆 𐐱𐑂 𐑄 𐐶𐐲𐑉𐐼𐑆 𐐸𐐶𐐮𐐽 𐐸𐐰𐑂 𐐺𐐮𐑌 𐑅𐐹𐐬𐐿𐑌, 𐐷 𐑌𐐨𐐼 𐑌𐐱𐐻 𐑅𐐲𐐹𐐬𐑆 𐑄𐐰𐐻 𐑄 𐐖𐐯𐑌𐐻𐐴𐑊𐑆 𐐪𐑉 𐐲𐐻𐐲𐑉𐑊𐐨 𐐼𐐨𐑅𐐻𐑉𐐱𐐮𐐼. 𐐙𐐫𐑉 𐐺𐐨𐐸𐐬𐑊𐐼, 𐐌 𐑅𐐩 𐐲𐑌𐐻𐐭 𐐷𐐭, 𐑄𐐰𐐻 𐐰𐑆 𐑋𐐯𐑌𐐨 𐐱𐑂 𐑄 𐐖𐐯𐑌𐐻𐐴𐑊𐑆 𐐰𐑆 𐐶𐐮𐑊

𐑉𐐨𐐹𐐯𐑌𐐻, 𐐪𐑉 𐑄 𐐿𐐲𐑂𐐯𐑌𐐰𐑌𐐻 𐐹𐐨𐐹𐐲𐑊 𐐱𐑂 𐑄 𐐢𐐫𐑉𐐼; 𐐰𐑌𐐼 𐐰𐑆 𐑋𐐯𐑌𐐨 𐐱𐑂 𐑄 𐐖𐐭𐑆 𐐰𐑆 𐐶𐐮𐑊 𐑌𐐱𐐻 𐑉𐐨𐐹𐐯𐑌𐐻, 𐑇𐐰𐑊 𐐺 𐐿𐐪𐑅𐐻 𐐱𐑁; 𐑁𐐫𐑉 𐑄 𐐢𐐫𐑉𐐼 𐐿𐐲𐑂𐐯𐑌𐐰𐑌𐐻𐐯𐑃 𐐶𐐮𐑄 𐑌𐐲𐑌, 𐑅𐐩𐑂 𐐮𐐻 𐐺 𐐶𐐮𐑄 𐑄𐐯𐑋 𐑄𐐰𐐻 𐑉𐐨𐐹𐐯𐑌𐐻 𐐰𐑌𐐼 𐐺𐐨𐑊𐐨𐑂 𐐮𐑌 𐐸𐐮𐑆 𐐝𐐲𐑌, 𐐸𐐭 𐐮𐑆 𐑄 𐐐𐐬𐑊𐐨 𐐎𐐲𐑌 𐐱𐑂 𐐆𐑆𐑉𐐩𐐯𐑊.

12. 𐐈𐑌𐐼 𐑌𐐵, 𐐌 𐐶𐐳𐐼 𐐹𐑉𐐱𐑁𐐯𐑅𐐴 𐑅𐐲𐑋𐐸𐐶𐐱𐐻 𐑋𐐬𐑉 𐐿𐐱𐑌𐑅𐐲𐑉𐑌𐐮𐑍 𐑄 𐐖𐐭𐑆 𐐰𐑌𐐼 𐑄 𐐖𐐯𐑌𐐻𐐴𐑊𐑆. 𐐙𐐫𐑉 𐐰𐑁𐐻𐐲𐑉 𐑄 𐐺𐐳𐐿 𐐱𐑂 𐐸𐐶𐐮𐐽 𐐌 𐐸𐐰𐑂 𐑅𐐹𐐬𐐿𐐲𐑌 𐑇𐐰𐑊 𐐿𐐲𐑋 𐑁𐐬𐑉𐑃, 𐐰𐑌𐐼 𐐺 𐑉𐐮𐐻𐐲𐑌 𐐲𐑌𐐻𐐭 𐑄 𐐖𐐯𐑌𐐻𐐴𐑊𐑆, 𐐰𐑌𐐼 𐑅𐐨𐑊𐐼 𐐲𐐹 𐐰𐑀𐐯𐑌 𐐲𐑌𐐻𐐭 𐑄 𐐢𐐫𐑉𐐼, 𐑄𐐩𐑉 𐑇𐐰𐑊 𐐺 𐑋𐐯𐑌𐐨 𐐸𐐶𐐮𐐽 𐑇𐐰𐑊 𐐺𐐨𐑊𐐨𐑂 𐑄 𐐶𐐲𐑉𐐼𐑆 𐐸𐐶𐐮𐐽 𐐪𐑉 𐑉𐐮𐐻𐐲𐑌; 𐐰𐑌𐐼 𐑄𐐩 𐑇𐐰𐑊 𐐿𐐰𐑉𐐨 𐑄𐐯𐑋 𐑁𐐬𐑉𐑃 𐐲𐑌𐐻𐐭 𐑄 𐑉𐐯𐑋𐑌𐐰𐑌𐐻 𐐱𐑂 𐐵𐑉 𐑅𐐨𐐼. 𐐈𐑌𐐼 𐑄𐐯𐑌 𐑇𐐰𐑊 𐑄 𐑉𐐯𐑋𐑌𐐰𐑌𐐻 𐐱𐑂 𐐵𐑉 𐑅𐐨𐐼 𐑌𐐬 𐐿𐐱𐑌𐑅𐐲𐑉𐑌𐐮𐑍 𐐲𐑅, 𐐸𐐵 𐑄𐐰𐐻 𐐶𐐨 𐐿𐐩𐑋 𐐵𐐻 𐑁𐑉𐐱𐑋 𐐖𐐯𐑉𐐭𐑅𐐲𐑊𐐯𐑋, 𐐰𐑌𐐼 𐑄𐐰𐐻 𐑄𐐩 𐐪𐑉 𐐼𐐨𐑅𐐯𐑌𐐼𐐰𐑌𐐻𐑅 𐐱𐑂 𐑄 𐐖𐐭𐑆. 𐐈𐑌𐐼 𐑄 𐑀𐐱𐑅𐐹𐐯𐑊 𐐱𐑂 𐐖𐐨𐑆𐐲𐑅 𐐗𐑉𐐴𐑅𐐻 𐑇𐐰𐑊 𐐺 𐐼𐐨𐐿𐑊𐐩𐑉𐐼 𐐲𐑋𐐲𐑍 𐑄𐐯𐑋; 𐐸𐐶𐐩𐑉𐑁𐐬𐑉, 𐑄𐐩 𐑇𐐰𐑊 𐐺 𐑉𐐨𐑅𐐻𐐬𐑉𐐼 𐐲𐑌𐐻𐐭 𐑄 𐑌𐐱𐑊𐐯𐐾 𐐱𐑂 𐑄𐐩𐑉 𐑁𐐪𐑄𐐲𐑉𐑆, 𐐰𐑌𐐼 𐐫𐑊𐑅𐐬 𐐻𐐭 𐑄 𐑌𐐱𐑊𐐯𐐾 𐐱𐑂 𐐖𐐨𐑆𐐲𐑅 𐐗𐑉𐐴𐑅𐐻, 𐐸𐐶𐐮𐐽 𐐶𐐱𐑆 𐐸𐐰𐐼 𐐲𐑋𐐲𐑍 𐑄𐐩𐑉 𐑁𐐪𐑄𐐲𐑉𐑆. 𐐈𐑌𐐼 𐑄𐐯𐑌 𐑇𐐰𐑊 𐑄𐐩 𐑉𐐨𐐾𐐦𐑅; 𐑁𐐫𐑉 𐑄𐐩 𐑇𐐰𐑊 𐑌𐐬 𐑄𐐰𐐻 𐐮𐐻 𐐮𐑆 𐐲 𐐺𐑊𐐯𐑅𐐮𐑍 𐐲𐑌𐐻𐐭 𐑄𐐯𐑋 𐑁𐑉𐐱𐑋 𐑄 𐐸𐐰𐑌𐐼 𐐱𐑂 𐐘𐐱𐐼; 𐐰𐑌𐐼 𐑄𐐩𐑉 𐑅𐐿𐐩𐑊𐑆 𐐱𐑂 𐐼𐐪𐑉𐐿𐑌𐐯𐑅 𐑇𐐰𐑊 𐐺𐐨𐑀𐐮𐑌 𐐻𐐭 𐑁𐐫𐑊 𐑁𐑉𐐱𐑋 𐑄𐐩𐑉 𐐴𐑆; 𐐰𐑌𐐼 𐑋𐐯𐑌𐐨 𐐾𐐯𐑌𐐲𐑉𐐩𐑇𐐲𐑌𐑆 𐑇𐐰𐑊 𐑌𐐱𐐻 𐐹𐐪𐑅 𐐲𐐶𐐩 𐐲𐑋𐐲𐑍 𐑄𐐯𐑋, 𐑅𐐩𐑂 𐑄𐐩 𐑇𐐰𐑊 𐐺 𐐲 𐐸𐐶𐐴𐐻 𐐰𐑌𐐼 𐐲 𐐼𐐨𐑊𐐴𐐻𐑅𐐲𐑋 𐐹𐐨𐐹𐐲𐑊.

13. 𐐈𐑌𐐼 𐐮𐐻 𐑇𐐰𐑊 𐐿𐐲𐑋 𐐻𐐭 𐐹𐐪𐑅 𐑄𐐰𐐻 𐑄 𐐖𐐭𐑆 𐐸𐐶𐐮𐐽 𐐪𐑉 𐑅𐐿𐐰𐐻𐐲𐑉𐐼, 𐐫𐑊𐑅𐐬 𐑇𐐰𐑊 𐐺𐐨𐑀𐐮𐑌 𐐻𐐭 𐐺𐐨𐑊𐐨𐑂 𐐮𐑌 𐐗𐑉𐐴𐑅𐐻; 𐐰𐑌𐐼 𐑄𐐩 𐑇𐐰𐑊 𐐺𐐨𐑀𐐮𐑌 𐐻𐐭 𐑀𐐰𐑄𐐲𐑉 𐐮𐑌 𐐲𐐹𐐱𐑌 𐑄 𐑁𐐩𐑅 𐐱𐑂 𐑄 𐑊𐐰𐑌𐐼; 𐐰𐑌𐐼 𐐰𐑆 𐑋𐐯𐑌𐐨 𐐰𐑆 𐑇𐐰𐑊 𐐺𐐨𐑊𐐨𐑂 𐐮𐑌 𐐗𐑉𐐴𐑅𐐻, 𐑇𐐰𐑊 𐐫𐑊𐑅𐐬 𐐺𐐨𐐿𐐲𐑋 𐐲 𐐼𐐨𐑊𐐴𐐻𐑅𐐲𐑋 𐐹𐐨𐐹𐐲𐑊.

14. 𐐈𐑌𐐼 𐐮𐐻 𐑇𐐰𐑊 𐐿𐐲𐑋 𐐻𐐭 𐐹𐐪𐑅 𐑄𐐰𐐻 𐑄 𐐢𐐫𐑉𐐼 𐐘𐐱𐐼 𐑇𐐰𐑊 𐐿𐐱𐑋𐐯𐑌𐑅 𐐸𐐮𐑆 𐐶𐐲𐑉𐐿, 𐐲𐑋𐐲𐑍 𐐫𐑊 𐑌𐐩𐑇𐐲𐑌𐑆, 𐐿𐐮𐑌𐐼𐑉𐐯𐐼𐑆, 𐐻𐐲𐑍𐑆, 𐐰𐑌𐐼 𐐹𐐨𐐹𐐲𐑊, 𐐻𐐭 𐐺𐑉𐐮𐑍 𐐲𐐺𐐵𐐻 𐑄 𐑉𐐯𐑅𐐻𐐬𐑉𐐩𐑇𐐲𐑌 𐐱𐑂 𐐸𐐮𐑆 𐐹𐐨𐐹𐐲𐑊 𐐲𐐹𐐱𐑌 𐑄 𐐲𐑉𐑃. 𐐈𐑌𐐼 𐐶𐐮𐑄 𐑉𐐴𐐽𐐲𐑅𐑌𐐯𐑅 𐑇𐐰𐑊 𐑄 𐐢𐐫𐑉𐐼 𐐘𐐱𐐼 𐐾𐐲𐐾 𐑄 𐐹𐐭𐑉, 𐐰𐑌𐐼 𐑉𐐨𐐹𐑉𐐭𐑂 𐐶𐐮𐑄 𐐯𐐿𐐶𐐮𐐻𐐨 𐑁𐐫𐑉 𐑄 𐑋𐐨𐐿 𐐱𐑂 𐑄 𐐲𐑉𐑃. 𐐈𐑌𐐼 𐐸𐐨 𐑇𐐰𐑊 𐑅𐑋𐐴𐐻 𐑄 𐐲𐑉𐑃 𐐶𐐮𐑄 𐑄 𐑉𐐱𐐼 𐐱𐑂 𐐸𐐮𐑆 𐑋𐐵𐑃; 𐐰𐑌𐐼 𐐶𐐮𐑄 𐑄 𐐺𐑉𐐯𐑃 𐐱𐑂 𐐸𐐮𐑆 𐑊𐐮𐐹𐑅 𐑇𐐰𐑊 𐐸𐐨 𐑅𐑊𐐩 𐑄 𐐶𐐮𐐿𐐯𐐼. 𐐙𐐫𐑉 𐑄 𐐻𐐴𐑋 𐑅𐐹𐐨𐐼𐐮𐑊𐐨 𐐿𐐲𐑋𐐯𐑃 𐑄𐐰𐐻 𐑄 𐐢𐐫𐑉𐐼 𐐘𐐱𐐼 𐑇𐐰𐑊 𐐿𐐫𐑆 𐐲 𐑀𐑉𐐩𐐻 𐐼𐐮𐑂𐐮𐑈𐐲𐑌 𐐲𐑋𐐲𐑍 𐑄 𐐹𐐨𐐹𐐲𐑊, 𐐰𐑌𐐼 𐑄 𐐶𐐮𐐿𐐯𐐼 𐐶𐐮𐑊 𐐸𐐨 𐐼𐐨𐑅𐐻𐑉𐐦; 𐐰𐑌𐐼 𐐸𐐨 𐐶𐐮𐑊 𐑅𐐹𐐩𐑉 𐐸𐐮𐑆 𐐹𐐨𐐹𐐲𐑊, 𐐷𐐩, 𐐨𐑂𐐲𐑌 𐐮𐑁 𐐮𐐻 𐑅𐐬 𐐺 𐑄𐐰𐐻 𐐸𐐨 𐑋𐐲𐑅𐐻 𐐼𐐨𐑅𐐻𐑉𐐦 𐑄 𐐶𐐮𐐿𐐯𐐼 𐐺𐐴 𐑁𐐴𐑉. 𐐈𐑌𐐼 𐑉𐐴𐐽𐐲𐑅𐑌𐐯𐑅 𐑇𐐰𐑊 𐐺 𐑄 𐑀𐐲𐑉𐐼𐑊 𐐱𐑂 𐐸𐐮𐑆 𐑊𐐦𐑌𐑆, 𐐰𐑌𐐼 𐑁𐐩𐑃𐑁𐐳𐑊𐑌𐐯𐑅 𐑄 𐑀𐐲𐑉𐐼𐑊 𐐱𐑂 𐐸𐐮𐑆 𐑉𐐩𐑌𐑆. 𐐈𐑌𐐼 𐑄𐐯𐑌 𐑇𐐰𐑊 𐑄 𐐶𐐳𐑊𐑁 𐐼𐐶𐐯𐑊 𐐶𐐮𐑄 𐑄 𐑊𐐰𐑋; 𐐰𐑌𐐼 𐑄 𐑊𐐯𐐹𐐲𐑉𐐼 𐑇𐐰𐑊 𐑊𐐴 𐐼𐐵𐑌 𐐶𐐮𐑄 𐑄 𐐿𐐮𐐼; 𐐰𐑌𐐼 𐑄 𐐿𐐪𐑁, 𐐰𐑌𐐼 𐑄 𐐷𐐲𐑍 𐑊𐐴𐐲𐑌, 𐐰𐑌𐐼 𐑄 𐑁𐐰𐐻𐑊𐐮𐑍, 𐐻𐐭𐑀𐐯𐑄𐐲𐑉; 𐐰𐑌𐐼 𐐲 𐑊𐐮𐐻𐑊 𐐽𐐴𐑊𐐼 𐑇𐐰𐑊 𐑊𐐨𐐼 𐑄𐐯𐑋. 𐐈𐑌𐐼 𐑄 𐐿𐐵 𐐰𐑌𐐼 𐑄 𐐺𐐩𐑉 𐑇𐐰𐑊 𐑁𐐨𐐼; 𐑄𐐩𐑉 𐐷𐐲𐑍 𐐶𐐲𐑌𐑆 𐑇𐐰𐑊 𐑊𐐴 𐐼𐐵𐑌 𐐻𐐭𐑀𐐯𐑄𐐲𐑉; 𐐰𐑌𐐼 𐑄 𐑊𐐴𐐲𐑌 𐑇𐐰𐑊 𐐨𐐻 𐑅𐐻𐑉𐐫 𐑊𐐴𐐿 𐑄 𐐱𐐿𐑅. 𐐈𐑌𐐼 𐑄 𐑅𐐲𐐿𐐮𐑍 𐐽𐐴𐑊𐐼 𐑇𐐰𐑊 𐐹𐑊𐐩 𐐱𐑌 𐑄 𐐸𐐬𐑊 𐐱𐑂 𐑄 𐐰𐑅𐐹, 𐐰𐑌𐐼 𐑄 𐐶𐐨𐑌𐐼 𐐽𐐴𐑊𐐼 𐑇𐐰𐑊 𐐹𐐳𐐻 𐐸𐐮𐑆 𐐸𐐰𐑌𐐼 𐐱𐑌 𐑄 𐐿𐐱𐐿𐐰𐐻𐑉𐐮𐑅'𐐯𐑆 𐐼𐐯𐑌. 𐐜𐐩 𐑇𐐰𐑊 𐑌𐐱𐐻 𐐸𐐲𐑉𐐻 𐑌𐐫𐑉 𐐼𐐨𐑅𐐻𐑉𐐦 𐐮𐑌 𐐫𐑊 𐑋𐐴 𐐸𐐬𐑊𐐨 𐑋𐐵𐑌𐐻𐐯𐑌; 𐑁𐐫𐑉 𐑄 𐐲𐑉𐑃 𐑇𐐰𐑊 𐐺 𐑁𐐳𐑊 𐐱𐑂 𐑄 𐑌𐐱𐑊𐐯𐐾 𐐱𐑂 𐑄 𐐢𐐫𐑉𐐼, 𐐰𐑆 𐑄 𐐶𐐫𐐻𐐲𐑉𐑆 𐐿𐐲𐑂𐐲𐑉 𐑄 𐑅𐐨. 𐐐𐐶𐐩𐑉𐑁𐐬𐑉 𐑄 𐑃𐐮𐑍𐑆 𐐱𐑂 𐐫𐑊 𐑌𐐩𐑇𐐲𐑌𐑆 𐑇𐐰𐑊 𐐺 𐑋𐐩𐐼 𐑌𐐬𐑌; 𐐷𐐩, 𐐫𐑊 𐑃𐐮𐑍𐑆 𐑇𐐰𐑊 𐐺 𐑋𐐩𐐼 𐑌𐐬𐑌 𐐲𐑌𐐻𐐭 𐑄 𐐽𐐮𐑊𐐼𐑉𐐯𐑌 𐐱𐑂 𐑋𐐯𐑌. 𐐜𐐩𐑉 𐐮𐑆 𐑌𐐲𐑃𐐮𐑍 𐐸𐐶𐐮𐐽 𐐮𐑆 𐑅𐐨𐐿𐑉𐐯𐐻, 𐑅𐐩𐑂 𐐮𐐻 𐑇𐐰𐑊 𐐺 𐑉𐐨𐑂𐐨𐑊𐐼; 𐑄𐐩𐑉 𐐮𐑆 𐑌𐐬 𐐶𐐲𐑉𐐿 𐐱𐑂 𐐼𐐪𐑉𐐿𐑌𐐯𐑅, 𐑅𐐩𐑂 𐐮𐐻 𐑇𐐰𐑊 𐐺 𐑋𐐩𐐼 𐑋𐐰𐑌𐐮𐑁𐐯𐑅𐐻 𐐮𐑌 𐑄 𐑊𐐴𐐻; 𐐰𐑌𐐼 𐑄𐐩𐑉 𐐮𐑆 𐑌𐐲𐑃𐐮𐑍 𐐸𐐶𐐮𐐽 𐐮𐑆 𐑅𐐨𐑊𐐼 𐐲𐐹𐐱𐑌 𐑄 𐐲𐑉𐑃, 𐑅𐐩𐑂 𐐮𐐻 𐑇𐐰𐑊 𐐺 𐑊𐐭𐑅𐐻. 𐐐𐐶𐐩𐑉𐑁𐐬𐑉, 𐐫𐑊 𐑃𐐮𐑍𐑆 𐐸𐐶𐐮𐐽 𐐸𐐰𐑂 𐐺𐐮𐑌 𐑉𐐨𐑂𐐨𐑊𐐼 𐐲𐑌𐐻𐐭 𐑄 𐐽𐐮𐑊𐐼𐑉𐐯𐑌 𐐱𐑂 𐑋𐐯𐑌, 𐑇𐐰𐑊 𐐰𐐻 𐑄𐐰𐐻 𐐼𐐩 𐐺 𐑉𐐨𐑂𐐨𐑊𐐼; 𐐰𐑌𐐼 𐐝𐐩𐐻𐐲𐑌 𐑇𐐰𐑊 𐐸𐐰𐑂 𐐹𐐵𐐲𐑉 𐐬𐑂𐐲𐑉 𐑄 𐐸𐐪𐑉𐐻𐑅 𐐱𐑂 𐑄 𐐽𐐮𐑊𐐼𐑉𐐯𐑌 𐐱𐑂 𐑋𐐯𐑌 𐑌𐐬 𐑋𐐬𐑉, 𐑁𐐫𐑉 𐐲 𐑊𐐱𐑍 𐐻𐐴𐑋. 𐐈𐑌𐐼 𐑌𐐵, 𐑋𐐴 𐐺𐐨𐑊𐐲𐑂𐐯𐐼 𐐺𐑉𐐯𐑄𐑉𐐯𐑌, 𐐌 𐑋𐐩𐐿 𐐰𐑌 𐐯𐑌𐐼 𐐱𐑂 𐑋𐐴 𐑅𐐩𐐮𐑍𐑆.

𐐗𐐰𐐹𐐻𐐲𐑉 XIII.

1. 𐐈𐑌𐐼 𐑌𐐵 𐐌, 𐐤𐐨𐑁𐐴, 𐑋𐐩𐐿 𐐰𐑌 𐐯𐑌𐐼 𐐱𐑂 𐑋𐐴 𐐹𐑉𐐱𐑁𐐯𐑅𐐴𐐮𐑍 𐐲𐑌𐐻𐐭 𐐷𐐭, 𐑋𐐴 𐐺𐐮𐑊𐐲𐑂𐐯𐐼 𐐺𐑉𐐯𐑄𐑉𐐯𐑌. 𐐈𐑌𐐼 𐐌 𐐿𐐰𐑌𐐱𐐻 𐑉𐐴𐐻 𐐺𐐲𐐻 𐐲 𐑁𐐧 𐑃𐐮𐑍𐑆, 𐐸𐐶𐐮𐐽 𐐌 𐑌𐐬 𐑋𐐲𐑅𐐻 𐑇𐐭𐑉𐑊𐐨 𐐿𐐲𐑋 𐐻𐐭 𐐹𐐪𐑅: 𐑌𐐨𐑄𐐲𐑉 𐐿𐐰𐑌 𐐌 𐑉𐐴𐐻 𐐺𐐲𐐻 𐐲 𐑁𐐧 𐐱𐑂 𐑄 𐐶𐐲𐑉𐐼𐑆 𐐱𐑂 𐑋𐐴 𐐺𐑉𐐲𐑄𐐲𐑉 𐐖𐐩𐐿𐐲𐐺. 𐐐𐐶𐐯𐑉𐑁𐐬𐑉 𐑄 𐑃𐐮𐑍𐑆 𐐸𐐶𐐮𐐽 𐐌 𐐸𐐰𐑂 𐑉𐐮𐐻𐑌 𐑅𐐲𐑁𐐴𐑅𐐯𐑃 𐑋𐐨, 𐑅𐐩𐑂 𐐮𐐻 𐐺𐐨 𐐲 𐑁𐐧 𐐶𐐲𐑉𐐼𐑆 𐐸𐐶𐐮𐐽 𐐌 𐑋𐐲𐑅𐐻 𐑅𐐹𐐨𐐿, 𐐿𐐱𐑌𐑅𐐲𐑉𐑌𐐮𐑍 𐑄 𐐼𐐱𐐿𐐻𐑉𐐮𐑌 𐐱𐑂 𐐗𐑉𐐴𐑅𐐻; 𐐸𐐶𐐯𐑉𐑁𐐬𐑉 𐐌 𐑇𐐰𐑊 𐑅𐐹𐐨𐐿 𐐲𐑌𐐻𐐭 𐐷𐐭 𐐹𐑊𐐩𐑌𐑊𐐨, 𐐰𐐿𐐫𐑉𐐼𐐮𐑍 𐐻𐐭 𐑄 𐐹𐑊𐐩𐑌𐑌𐐯𐑅 𐐱𐑂 𐑋𐐴 𐐹𐑉𐐱𐑁𐐯𐑅𐐴𐐮𐑍. 𐐙𐐫𐑉 𐑋𐐴 𐑅𐐬𐑊 𐐼𐐨𐑊𐐴𐐻𐐯𐑃 𐐮𐑌 𐐹𐑊𐐩𐑌𐑌𐐯𐑅: 𐑁𐐫𐑉 𐐰𐑁𐐻𐐲𐑉 𐑄𐐮𐑅 𐑋𐐰𐑌𐐲𐑉 𐐼𐐲𐑃 𐑄 𐐢𐐫𐑉𐐼 𐐘𐐱𐐼 𐐶𐐲𐑉𐐿 𐐰𐑋𐐲𐑍 𐑄 𐐽𐐮𐑊𐐼𐑉𐐯𐑌 𐐱𐑂 𐑋𐐯𐑌. 𐐙𐐫𐑉 𐑄 𐐢𐐫𐑉𐐼 𐐘𐐱𐐼 𐑀𐐮𐑂𐐯𐑃 𐑊𐐴𐐻 𐐲𐑌𐐻𐐭 𐑄 𐐲𐑌𐐼𐐲𐑉𐑅𐐻𐐰𐑌𐐼𐐮𐑍: 𐑁𐐫𐑉 𐐸𐐨 𐑅𐐹𐐨𐐿𐐯𐑃 𐐲𐑌𐐻𐐭 𐑋𐐯𐑌 𐐰𐐿𐐫𐑉𐐼𐐮𐑍 𐐻𐐭 𐑄𐐩𐑉 𐑊𐐰𐑍𐑀𐐶𐐩𐑈, 𐐲𐑌𐐻𐐭 𐑄𐐩𐑉 𐐲𐑌𐐼𐐲𐑉𐑅𐐻𐐰𐑌𐐼𐐮𐑍. 𐐐𐐶𐐯𐑉𐑁𐐬𐑉 𐐌 𐐶𐐳𐐼 𐑄𐐰𐐻 𐐷𐐨 𐑇𐐳𐐼 𐑉𐐨𐑋𐐯𐑋𐐺𐐲𐑉 𐑄𐐰𐐻 𐐌 𐐸𐐰𐑂 𐑅𐐹𐐬𐐿𐐲𐑌 𐐲𐑌𐐻𐐭 𐐷𐐭, 𐐿𐐱𐑌𐑅𐐲𐑉𐑌𐐮𐑍 𐑄𐐰𐐻 𐐹𐑉𐐱𐑁𐐯𐐻 𐐸𐐶𐐮𐐽 𐑄 𐐢𐐫𐑉𐐼 𐑇𐐬𐐼 𐐲𐑌𐐻𐐭 𐑋𐐨, 𐑄𐐰𐐻 𐑇𐐳𐐼 𐐺𐐰𐐹𐐻𐐴𐑆 𐑄 𐐢𐐰𐑋 𐐱𐑂 𐐘𐐱𐐼, 𐐸𐐶𐐮𐐽 𐑇𐐳𐐼 𐐻𐐩𐐿 𐐰𐐶𐐩 𐑄 𐑅𐐮𐑌𐑆 𐐱𐑂 𐑄 𐐶𐐲𐑉𐑊𐐼.

2. 𐐈𐑌𐐼 𐑌𐐵 𐐮𐑁 𐑄 𐐢𐐰𐑋 𐐱𐑂 𐐘𐐱𐐼, 𐐸𐐨 𐐺𐐨𐐮𐑍 𐐸𐐬𐑊𐐨, 𐑇𐐳𐐼 𐐸𐐰𐑂 𐑌𐐨𐐼 𐐻𐐭 𐐺𐐨 𐐺𐐰𐐹𐐻𐐴𐑆𐐼 𐐺𐐴 𐐶𐐫𐐻𐐲𐑉, 𐐻𐐭 𐑁𐐳𐑊𐑁𐐮𐑊 𐐫𐑊 𐑉𐐴𐐽𐐲𐑅𐑌𐐯𐑅, 𐐄 𐑄𐐯𐑌, 𐐸𐐵 𐑋𐐲𐐽 𐑋𐐬𐑉 𐑌𐐨𐐼 𐐸𐐰𐑂 𐐶𐐨, 𐐺𐐨𐐮𐑍 𐐲𐑌𐐸𐐬𐑊𐐨, 𐐻𐐭 𐐺𐐨 𐐺𐐰𐐹𐐻𐐴𐑆𐐼, 𐐷𐐩, 𐐨𐑂𐐲𐑌 𐐺𐐴 𐐶𐐫𐐻𐐲𐑉. 𐐈𐑌𐐼 𐑌𐐵, 𐐌 𐐶𐐳𐐼 𐐰𐑅𐐿 𐐱𐑂 𐐷𐐭, 𐑋𐐴 𐐺𐐮𐑊𐐲𐑂𐐯𐐼 𐐺𐑉𐐯𐑄𐑉𐐯𐑌, 𐐸𐐶𐐯𐑉𐐮𐑌 𐑄 𐐢𐐰𐑋 𐐱𐑂 𐐘𐐱𐐼 𐐼𐐮𐐼 𐑁𐐳𐑊𐑁𐐮𐑊 𐐫𐑊 𐑉𐐴𐐽𐐲𐑅𐑌𐐯𐑅 𐐮𐑌 𐐺𐐨𐐮𐑍 𐐺𐐰𐐹𐐻𐐴𐑆𐐼 𐐺𐐴 𐐶𐐫𐐻𐐲𐑉? 𐐤𐐬 𐐷𐐨 𐑌𐐱𐐻 𐑄𐐰𐐻 𐐸𐐨 𐐶𐐱𐑆 𐐸𐐬𐑊𐐨? 𐐒𐐲𐐻 𐑌𐐱𐐻𐐶𐐮𐑃𐑅𐐻𐐰𐑌𐐼𐐮𐑍 𐐸𐐨 𐐺𐐨𐐮𐑍 𐐸𐐬𐑊𐐨, 𐐸𐐨 𐑇𐐬𐐯𐑃 𐐲𐑌𐐻𐐭 𐑄 𐐽𐐮𐑊𐐼𐑉𐐯𐑌 𐐱𐑂 𐑋𐐯𐑌, 𐑄𐐰𐐻 𐐰𐐿𐐫𐑉𐐼𐐮𐑍 𐐻𐐭 𐑄 𐑁𐑊𐐯𐑇, 𐐸𐐨 𐐸𐐲𐑋𐐺𐑊𐐯𐑃 𐐸𐐮𐑋𐑅𐐯𐑊𐑁 𐐺𐐨𐑁𐐬𐑉 𐑄 𐐙𐐪𐑄𐐲𐑉, 𐐰𐑌𐐼 𐐶𐐮𐐻𐑌𐐯𐑅𐐯𐑃 𐐲𐑌𐐻𐐭 𐑄 𐐙𐐪𐑄𐐲𐑉 𐑄𐐰𐐻 𐐸𐐨 𐐶𐐳𐐼 𐐺𐐨 𐐬𐐺𐐨𐐼𐐨𐐲𐑌𐐻 𐐲𐑌𐐻𐐭 𐐸𐐮𐑋 𐐮𐑌 𐐿𐐨𐐹𐐮𐑍 𐐸𐐮𐑆 𐐿𐐱𐑋𐐰𐑌𐐼𐑋𐐯𐑌𐐻𐑅; 𐐸𐐶𐐯𐑉𐑁𐐬𐑉, 𐐰𐑁𐐻𐐲𐑉 𐐸𐐨 𐐶𐐱𐑆 𐐺𐐰𐐹𐐻𐐴𐑆𐐼 𐐶𐐮𐑄 𐐶𐐫𐐻𐐲𐑉, 𐑄 𐐐𐐬𐑊𐐨 𐐘𐐬𐑅𐐻 𐐼𐐨𐑅𐐯𐑌𐐼𐐯𐐼 𐐲𐐹𐐱𐑌 𐐸𐐮𐑋 𐐮𐑌 𐑄 𐑁𐐫𐑉𐑋 𐐱𐑂 𐐲 𐐼𐐲𐑂. 𐐈𐑌𐐼 𐐰𐑀𐐯𐑌: 𐐮𐐻 𐑇𐐬𐐯𐑃 𐐲𐑌𐐻𐐭 𐑄 𐐽𐐮𐑊𐐼𐑉𐐯𐑌 𐐱𐑂 𐑋𐐯𐑌 𐑄 𐑅𐐻𐑉𐐩𐐻𐑌𐐯𐑅 𐐱𐑂 𐑄 𐐹𐐪𐑃, 𐐰𐑌𐐼 𐑄 𐑌𐐰𐑉𐐬𐑌𐐯𐑅 𐐱𐑂 𐑄 𐑀𐐩𐐻, 𐐺𐐴 𐐸𐐶𐐮𐐽 𐑄𐐩 𐑇𐐳𐐼 𐐯𐑌𐐻𐐲𐑉, 𐐸𐐨 𐐸𐐰𐑂𐐮𐑍 𐑅𐐯𐐻 𐑄 𐐯𐑀𐑆𐐰𐑋𐐹𐑊 𐐺𐐨𐑁𐐬𐑉 𐑄𐐯𐑋. 𐐈𐑌𐐼 𐐸𐐨 𐑅𐐯𐐼 𐐲𐑌𐐻𐐭 𐑄 𐐽𐐮𐑊𐐼𐑉𐐯𐑌 𐐱𐑂 𐑋𐐯𐑌, 𐐙𐐱𐑊𐐬 𐑄𐐵 𐑋𐐨. 𐐐𐐶𐐯𐑉𐑁𐐬𐑉, 𐑋𐐴 𐐺𐐮𐑊𐐲𐑂𐐯𐐼 𐐺𐑉𐐯𐑄𐑉𐐯𐑌, 𐐿𐐰𐑌 𐐶𐐨 𐑁𐐱𐑊𐐬 𐐖𐐨𐑆𐐲𐑅, 𐑅𐐩𐑂 𐐶𐐨 𐑇𐐰𐑊 𐐺𐐨 𐐶𐐮𐑊𐐮𐑍 𐐻𐐭 𐐿𐐨𐐹 𐑄 𐐿𐐱𐑋𐐰𐑌𐐼𐑋𐐯𐑌𐐻𐑅 𐐱𐑂 𐑄 𐐙𐐪𐑄𐐲𐑉? 𐐈𐑌𐐼 𐑄 𐐙𐐪𐑄𐐲𐑉 𐑅𐐯𐐼, 𐐡𐐨𐐹𐐯𐑌𐐻 𐐷𐐨, 𐑉𐐨𐐹𐐯𐑌𐐻 𐐷𐐨, 𐐰𐑌𐐼 𐐺𐐨 𐐺𐐰𐐹𐐻𐐴𐑆𐐼 𐐮𐑌 𐑄 𐑌𐐩𐑋 𐐱𐑂 𐑋𐐴 𐐺𐐮𐑊𐐲𐑂𐐯𐐼 𐐝𐐲𐑌. 𐐈𐑌𐐼 𐐫𐑊𐑅𐐬, 𐑄 𐑂𐐦𐑅 𐐱𐑂 𐑄 𐐝𐐲𐑌 𐐿𐐩𐑋 𐐲𐑌𐐻𐐭 𐑋𐐨, 𐑅𐐩𐐮𐑍, 𐐐𐐨 𐑄𐐰𐐻 𐐮𐑆 𐐺𐐰𐐹𐐻𐐴𐑆𐐼 𐐮𐑌 𐑋𐐴 𐑌𐐩𐑋, 𐐻𐐭 𐐸𐐮𐑋 𐐶𐐮𐑊 𐑄 𐐙𐐪𐑄𐐲𐑉 𐑀𐐮𐑂 𐑄 𐐐𐐬𐑊𐐨 𐐘𐐬𐑅𐐻, 𐑊𐐴𐐿 𐐲𐑌𐐻𐐭 𐑋𐐨; 𐐸𐐶𐐯𐑉𐑁𐐬𐑉 𐑁𐐱𐑊𐐬 𐑋𐐨, 𐐰𐑌𐐼 𐐼𐐭 𐑄 𐑃𐐮𐑍𐑆 𐐸𐐶𐐮𐐽 𐐷𐐨 𐐸𐐰𐑂 𐑅𐐨𐑌 𐑋𐐨 𐐼𐐭. 𐐐𐐶𐐯𐑉𐑁𐐬𐑉, 𐑋𐐴 𐐺𐐮𐑊𐐲𐑂𐐯𐐼 𐐺𐑉𐐯𐑄𐑉𐐯𐑌, 𐐌 𐑌𐐬 𐑄𐐰𐐻 𐐮𐑁 𐐷𐐨 𐑇𐐰𐑊 𐑁𐐱𐑊𐐬 𐑄 𐐝𐐲𐑌 𐐶𐐮𐑄 𐑁𐐳𐑊 𐐹𐐲𐑉𐐹𐐲𐑅 𐐱𐑂 𐐸𐐪𐑉𐐻, 𐐰𐐿𐐻𐐮𐑍 𐑌𐐬 𐐸𐐮𐐹𐐱𐐿𐑉𐐮𐑅𐐨, 𐐰𐑌𐐼 𐑌𐐬 𐐼𐐨𐑅𐐯𐐹𐑇𐐲𐑌 𐐺𐐨𐑁𐐬𐑉 𐐘𐐱𐐼, 𐐺𐐲𐐻 𐐶𐐮𐑄 𐑉𐐨𐐲𐑊 𐐮𐑌𐐻𐐯𐑌𐐻, 𐑉𐐨𐐹𐐯𐑌𐐻𐐮𐑍 𐐱𐑂 𐐷𐐭𐑉 𐑅𐐮𐑌𐑆, 𐐶𐐮𐐻𐑌𐐯𐑅𐐮𐑍 𐐲𐑌𐐻𐐭 𐑄 𐐙𐐪𐑄𐐲𐑉, 𐑄𐐰𐐻 𐐷𐐨 𐐪𐑉 𐐶𐐮𐑊𐐮𐑍 𐐻𐐭 𐐻𐐩𐐿 𐐲𐐹𐐱𐑌 𐐷𐐭 𐑄 𐑌𐐩𐑋 𐐱𐑂 𐐗𐑉𐐴𐑅𐐻, 𐐺𐐴 𐐺𐐰𐐹𐐻𐐮𐑆𐑋: 𐐷𐐩, 𐐺𐐴 𐑁𐐱𐑊𐐬𐐮𐑍 𐐷𐐭𐑉 𐐢𐐫𐑉𐐼 𐐰𐑌𐐼 𐐷𐐭𐑉 𐐝𐐩𐑂𐐷𐐲𐑉 𐐼𐐵𐑌 𐐮𐑌𐐻𐐭 𐑄 𐐶𐐫𐐻𐐲𐑉, 𐐰𐐿𐐫𐑉𐐼𐐮𐑍 𐐻𐐭 𐐸𐐮𐑆 𐐶𐐲𐑉𐐼; 𐐺𐐨𐐸𐐬𐑊𐐼 𐑄𐐯𐑌 𐑇𐐰𐑊 𐐷𐐨 𐑉𐐨𐑅𐐨𐑂 𐑄 𐐐𐐬𐑊𐐨 𐐘𐐬𐑅𐐻; 𐐷𐐩, 𐑄𐐯𐑌 𐐿𐐲𐑋𐐯𐑃 𐑄 𐐺𐐰𐐹𐐻𐐮𐑆𐑋 𐐱𐑂 𐑁𐐴𐑉 𐐰𐑌𐐼 𐐱𐑂 𐑄 𐐐𐐬𐑊𐐨 𐐘𐐬𐑅𐐻; 𐐰𐑌𐐼 𐑄𐐯𐑌 𐐿𐐰𐑌 𐐷𐐨 𐑅𐐹𐐨𐐿 𐐶𐐮𐑄 𐑄 𐐻𐐲𐑍 𐐱𐑂 𐐩𐑌𐑈𐐯𐑊𐑆, 𐐰𐑌𐐼 𐑇𐐵𐐻 𐐹𐑉𐐩𐑆𐐯𐑆 𐐲𐑌𐐻𐐭 𐑄 𐐐𐐬𐑊𐐨 𐐎𐐲𐑌 𐐱𐑂 𐐆𐑆𐑉𐐩𐐯𐑊.

3. 𐐒𐐲𐐻, 𐐺𐐨𐐸𐐬𐑊𐐼, 𐑋𐐴 𐐺𐐮𐑊𐐲𐑂𐐯𐐼 𐐺𐑉𐐯𐑄𐑉𐐯𐑌, 𐑄𐐲𐑅 𐐿𐐩𐑋 𐑄 𐑂𐐦𐑅 𐐱𐑂 𐑄 𐐝𐐲𐑌 𐐲𐑌𐐻𐐭 𐑋𐐨, 𐑅𐐩𐐮𐑍, 𐐈𐑁𐐻𐐲𐑉 𐐷𐐨 𐐸𐐰𐑂 𐑉𐐨𐐹𐐯𐑌𐐻𐐯𐐼 𐐱𐑂 𐐷𐐭𐑉 𐑅𐐮𐑌𐑆, 𐐰𐑌𐐼 𐐶𐐮𐐻𐑌𐐯𐑅𐐻 𐐲𐑌𐐻𐐭 𐑄 𐐙𐐪𐑄𐐲𐑉 𐑄𐐰𐐻 𐐷𐐨 𐐪𐑉 𐐶𐐮𐑊𐐮𐑍 𐐻𐐭 𐐿𐐨𐐹 𐑋𐐴 𐐿𐐱𐑋𐐰𐑌𐐼𐑋𐐯𐑌𐐻𐑅, 𐐺𐐴 𐑄 𐐺𐐰𐐹𐐻𐐮𐑆𐑋 𐐱𐑂 𐐶𐐫𐐻𐐲𐑉, 𐐰𐑌𐐼 𐐸𐐰𐑂 𐑉𐐨𐑅𐐨𐑂𐐼 𐑄 𐐺𐐰𐐹-

𐐻𐐮𐑆𐑋 𐐱𐑂 𐑁𐐴𐑉 𐐰𐑌𐐼 𐐱𐑂 𐑄 𐐐𐐬𐑊𐐮 𐐘𐐬𐑅𐐻, 𐐰𐑌𐐼 𐐿𐐰𐑌 𐑅𐐹𐐨𐐿 𐐶𐐮𐑄 𐐪 𐑌𐐮𐐭 𐐻𐐲𐑍, 𐐷𐐩, 𐐨𐑂𐑌 𐐶𐐮𐑄 𐑄 𐐻𐐲𐑍 𐐱𐑂 𐐁𐑌𐐾𐐯𐑊𐑆, 𐐰𐑌𐐼 𐐰𐑁𐐻𐐲𐑉 𐑄𐐮𐑅 𐑇𐐳𐐼 𐐼𐐨𐑌𐐴 𐑋𐐨, 𐐮𐐻 𐐶𐐳𐐼 𐐸𐐰𐑂 𐐺𐐮𐑌 𐐺𐐯𐐻𐐲𐑉 𐑁𐐫𐑉 𐐷𐐭, 𐑄𐐰𐐻 𐐷 𐐸𐐰𐐼 𐑌𐐱𐐻 𐑌𐐬𐑌 𐑋𐐨.

4. 𐐈𐑌𐐼 𐐌 𐐸𐐲𐑉𐐼 𐐪 𐑂𐐱𐐮𐑅 𐑁𐑉𐐱𐑋 𐑄 𐐙𐐪𐑄𐐲𐑉, 𐑅𐐩𐐮𐑍, 𐐏𐐩, 𐑄 𐐶𐐲𐑉𐐼𐑆 𐐱𐑂 𐑋𐐴 𐐒𐐨𐑊𐐲𐑂𐐯𐐼 𐐪𐑉 𐐻𐑉𐐭 𐐰𐑌𐐼 𐑁𐐩𐑃𐑁𐐳𐑊. 𐐐𐐨 𐑄𐐰𐐻 𐐯𐑌𐐼𐐷𐐭𐑉𐐯𐑃 𐐻𐐭 𐑄 𐐯𐑌𐐼, 𐑄 𐑅𐐩𐑋 𐑇𐐰𐑊 𐐺 𐑅𐐩𐑂𐐼. 𐐈𐑌𐐼 𐑌𐐵, 𐑋𐐴 𐐺𐐨𐑊𐐲𐑂𐐯𐐼 𐐺𐑉𐐯𐑄𐑉𐐯𐑌, 𐐌 𐑌𐐬 𐐺𐐴 𐑄𐐮𐑅, 𐑄𐐰𐐻 𐐲𐑌𐑊𐐯𐑅 𐐪 𐑋𐐰𐑌 𐑇𐐰𐑊 𐐯𐑌𐐼𐐷𐐭𐑉 𐐻𐐭 𐑄 𐐯𐑌𐐼, 𐐮𐑌 𐑁𐐱𐑊𐐬-𐐮𐑍 𐑄 𐐯𐑀𐑆𐐰𐑋𐐹𐑊 𐐱𐑂 𐑄 𐐝𐐲𐑌 𐐱𐑂 𐑄 𐑊𐐮𐑂𐐮𐑍 𐐘𐐱𐐼, 𐐸𐐨 𐐿𐐰𐑌𐐰𐐻 𐐺 𐑅𐐩𐑂𐐼; 𐐸𐐶𐐩𐑉𐑁𐐫𐑉, 𐐼𐐭 𐑄 𐑃𐐮𐑍𐑆 𐐸𐐶𐐮𐐽 𐐌 𐐸𐐰𐑂 𐐻𐐬𐑊𐐼 𐐷𐐭 𐐌 𐐸𐐰𐑂 𐑅𐐨𐑌, 𐑄𐐰𐐻 𐐷𐐫𐑉 𐐢𐐫𐑉𐐼 𐐰𐑌𐐼 𐐷𐐫𐑉 𐐡𐐨𐐼𐐨𐑋𐐲𐑉 𐑇𐐳𐐼 𐐼𐐭: 𐑁𐐫𐑉, 𐑁𐐫𐑉 𐑄𐐮𐑅 𐐿𐐫𐑆 𐐸𐐰𐑂 𐑄𐐩 𐐺𐐮𐑌 𐑇𐐬𐑌 𐐲𐑌𐐻𐐭 𐑋𐐨, 𐑄𐐰𐐻 𐐷 𐑋𐐴𐐻 𐑌𐐬 𐑄 𐑀𐐩𐐻 𐐺𐐴 𐐸𐐶𐐮𐐽 𐐷 𐑇𐐳𐐼 𐐯𐑌𐐻𐐲𐑉. 𐐙𐐫𐑉 𐑄 𐑀𐐩𐐻 𐐺𐐴 𐐸𐐶𐐮𐐽 𐐷 𐑇𐐳𐐼 𐐯𐑌𐐻𐐲𐑉, 𐐮𐑆 𐑉𐐨𐐹𐐯𐑌𐐻𐐰𐑌𐑅, 𐐰𐑌𐐼 𐐺𐐰𐐹𐐻𐐮𐑆𐑋 𐐺𐐴 𐐶𐐫𐐻𐐲𐑉; 𐐰𐑌𐐼 𐑄𐐯𐑌 𐐿𐐲𐑋𐐯𐑃 𐐪 𐑉𐐨𐑋𐐮𐑇𐐲𐑌 𐐱𐑂 𐐷𐐫𐑉 𐑅𐐮𐑌𐑆, 𐐺𐐴 𐑁𐐴𐑉 𐐰𐑌𐐼 𐐺𐐴 𐑄 𐐐𐐬𐑊𐐮 𐐘𐐬𐑅𐐻. 𐐈𐑌𐐼 𐑄𐐯𐑌 𐐪𐑉 𐐷 𐐮𐑌 𐑄𐐮𐑅 𐑅𐐻𐑉𐐩𐐻 𐐰𐑌𐐼 𐑌𐐰𐑉𐐬 𐐹𐐪𐑃 𐐸𐐶𐐮𐐽 𐑊𐐨𐐼𐑆 𐐻𐐭 𐐨𐐻𐐲𐑉𐑌𐐲𐑊 𐑊𐐴𐑁; 𐐷𐐩, 𐐷 𐐸𐐰𐑂 𐐯𐑌-𐐻𐐲𐑉𐐼 𐐮𐑌 𐐺𐐴 𐑄 𐑀𐐩𐐻: 𐐷 𐐸𐐰𐑂 𐐼𐐲𐑌 𐐰𐐿𐐫𐑉𐐼𐐮𐑍 𐐻𐐭 𐑄 𐐿𐐲𐑋𐐰𐑌𐐼𐑋𐐯𐑌𐐻𐑅 𐐱𐑂 𐑄 𐐙𐐪𐑄𐐲𐑉 𐐰𐑌𐐼 𐑄 𐐝𐐲𐑌; 𐐰𐑌𐐼 𐐷 𐐸𐐰𐑂 𐑉𐐨𐑅𐐨𐑂𐐼 𐑄 𐐐𐐬𐑊𐐮 𐐘𐐬𐑅𐐻, 𐐸𐐶𐐮𐐽 𐐶𐐮𐐻𐑌𐐯𐑅𐐯𐑆 𐐱𐑂 𐑄 𐐙𐐪𐑄𐐲𐑉 𐐰𐑌𐐼 𐑄 𐐝𐐲𐑌, 𐐲𐑌𐐻𐐭 𐑄 𐑁𐐳𐑊𐑁𐐮𐑊𐐮𐑍 𐐱𐑂 𐑄 𐐹𐑉𐐱𐑋𐐮𐑅 𐐸𐐶𐐮𐐽 𐐸𐐨 𐐸𐐰𐑃 𐑋𐐩𐐼, 𐑄𐐰𐐻 𐐮𐑁 𐐷 𐐯𐑌𐐻𐐲𐑉𐐼 𐐮𐑌 𐐺𐐴 𐑄 𐐶𐐩, 𐐷 𐑇𐐳𐐼 𐑉𐐨𐑅𐐨𐑂.

5. 𐐈𐑌𐐼 𐑌𐐵, 𐑋𐐴 𐐺𐐨𐑊𐐲𐑂𐐯𐐼 𐐺𐑉𐐯𐑄𐑉𐐯𐑌, 𐐰𐑁𐐻𐐲𐑉 𐐷 𐐸𐐰𐑂 𐑀𐐱𐐻𐑌 𐐮𐑌𐐻𐐭 𐑄𐐮𐑅 𐑅𐐻𐑉𐐩𐐻 𐐰𐑌𐐼 𐑌𐐰𐑉𐐬 𐐹𐐪𐑃, 𐐌 𐐶𐐳𐐼 𐐪𐑅𐐿, 𐐮𐑁 𐐫𐑊 𐐮𐑆 𐐼𐐲𐑌? 𐐒𐐨𐐸𐐬𐑊𐐼, 𐐌 𐑅𐐩 𐐲𐑌𐐻𐐭 𐐷𐐭, 𐐤𐐩; 𐑁𐐫𐑉 𐐷 𐐸𐐰𐑂 𐑌𐐱𐐻 𐐿𐐲𐑋 𐑄𐐲𐑅 𐑁𐐪𐑉, 𐑅𐐩𐑂 𐐮𐐻 𐐶𐐲𐑉 𐐺𐐴 𐑄 𐐶𐐲𐑉𐐼 𐐱𐑂 𐐗𐑉𐐴𐑅𐐻 𐐶𐐮𐑄 𐐲𐑌𐑇𐐩𐐿𐐯𐑌 𐑁𐐩𐑃 𐐮𐑌 𐐸𐐮𐑋, 𐑉𐐨𐑊𐐴𐐮𐑍 𐐸𐐬𐑊𐐮 𐐲𐐹𐐱𐑌 𐑄 𐑋𐐯𐑉𐐮𐐻𐑅 𐐱𐑂 𐐸𐐮𐑋 𐐸𐐭 𐐮𐑆 𐑋𐐴𐐻𐐮 𐐻𐐭 𐑅𐐩𐑂; 𐐸𐐶𐐩𐑉𐑁𐐫𐑉, 𐐷 𐑋𐐲𐑅𐐻 𐐹𐑉𐐯𐑅 𐑁𐐫𐑉𐐶𐐲𐑉𐐼 𐐶𐐮𐑄 𐐪 𐑅𐐻𐐯𐐼𐑁𐐰𐑅𐐻𐑌𐐯𐑅 𐐮𐑌 𐐗𐑉𐐴𐑅𐐻, 𐐸𐐰𐑂𐐮𐑍 𐐪 𐐹𐐲𐑉𐑁𐐯𐐿𐐻 𐐺𐑉𐐴𐐻𐑌𐐯𐑅 𐐱𐑂 𐐸𐐬𐐹, 𐐰𐑌𐐼 𐐪 𐑊𐐲𐑂 𐐱𐑂 𐐘𐐱𐐼 𐐰𐑌𐐼 𐐱𐑂 𐐫𐑊 𐑋𐐯𐑌. 𐐐𐐶𐐩𐑉𐑁𐐫𐑉, 𐐮𐑁 𐐷 𐑇𐐰𐑊 𐐹𐑉𐐯𐑅 𐑁𐐫𐑉𐐶𐐲𐑉𐐼, 𐑁𐐨𐑅𐐻𐐮𐑍 𐐲𐐹𐐱𐑌 𐑄 𐐶𐐲𐑉𐐼 𐐱𐑂 𐐗𐑉𐐴𐑅𐐻, 𐐰𐑌𐐼 𐐯𐑌𐐼𐐷𐐭𐑉 𐐻𐐭 𐑄 𐐯𐑌𐐼, 𐐺𐐨𐐸𐐬𐑊𐐼, 𐑄𐐲𐑅 𐑅𐐯𐑃 𐑄 𐐙𐐪𐑄𐐲𐑉, 𐐏 𐑇𐐰𐑊 𐐸𐐰𐑂 𐐨𐐻𐐲𐑉-𐑌𐐲𐑊 𐑊𐐴𐑁.

6. 𐐈𐑌𐐼 𐑌𐐵, 𐐺𐐨𐐸𐐬𐑊𐐼, 𐑋𐐴 𐐺𐐨𐑊𐐲𐑂𐐯𐐼 𐐺𐑉𐐯𐑄𐑉𐐯𐑌, 𐑄𐐮𐑅 𐐮𐑆 𐑄 𐐶𐐩; 𐐰𐑌𐐼 𐑄𐐩𐑉 𐐮𐑆 𐑌𐐲𐑌 𐐲𐑄𐐲𐑉 𐐶𐐩 𐑌𐐫𐑉 𐑌𐐩𐑋 𐑀𐐮𐑂𐑌 𐐲𐑌𐐼𐐲𐑉 𐐸𐐯𐑂𐑌, 𐐸𐐶𐐩𐑉𐐺𐐴 𐑋𐐰𐑌 𐐿𐐰𐑌 𐐺 𐑅𐐩𐑂𐐼 𐐮𐑌 𐑄 𐐿𐐮𐑍𐐼𐐲𐑋 𐐱𐑂 𐐘𐐱𐐼. 𐐈𐑌𐐼 𐑌𐐵, 𐐺𐐨𐐸𐐬𐑊𐐼 𐑄𐐮𐑅 𐐮𐑆 𐑄 𐐼𐐱𐐿𐐻𐑉𐐮𐑌 𐐱𐑂 𐐗𐑉𐐴𐑅𐐻, 𐐰𐑌𐐼 𐑄 𐐬𐑌𐑊𐐮 𐐰𐑌𐐼 𐐻𐑉𐐭 𐐼𐐱𐐿𐐻𐑉𐐮𐑌 𐐱𐑂 𐑄 𐐙𐐪𐑄𐐲𐑉, 𐐰𐑌𐐼 𐐱𐑂 𐑄 𐐝𐐲𐑌, 𐐰𐑌𐐼 𐐱𐑂 𐑄 𐐐𐐬𐑊𐐮 𐐘𐐬𐑅𐐻, 𐐸𐐶𐐮𐐽 𐐮𐑆 𐐶𐐲𐑌 𐐘𐐱𐐼, 𐐶𐐮𐑄𐐵𐐻 𐐯𐑌𐐼. 𐐁𐑋𐐯𐑌.

𐐕𐐈𐐑𐐓𐐊𐐡 XIV.

1. 𐐈𐑌𐐼 𐑌𐐵, 𐐺𐐨𐐸𐐬𐑊𐐼, 𐑋𐐴 𐐺𐐨𐑊𐐲𐑂𐐯𐐼 𐐺𐑉𐐯𐑄𐑉𐐯𐑌, 𐐌 𐑅𐐲𐐹𐐬𐑆 𐑄𐐰𐐻 𐐷 𐐹𐐱𐑌𐐼𐐲𐑉 𐑅𐐲𐑋𐐸𐐶𐐱𐐻 𐐮𐑌 𐐷𐐫𐑉 𐐸𐐪𐑉𐐻𐑅, 𐐿𐐱𐑌𐑅𐐲𐑉𐑌𐐮𐑍 𐑄𐐰𐐻 𐐸𐐶𐐮𐐽 𐐷 𐑇𐐳𐐼 𐐼𐐭, 𐐰𐑁𐐻𐐲𐑉 𐐷 𐐸𐐰𐑂 𐐯𐑌𐐻𐐲𐑉𐐼 𐐮𐑌 𐐺𐐴 𐑄 𐐶𐐩. 𐐒𐐲𐐻 𐐺𐐨𐐸𐐬𐑊𐐼, 𐐸𐐶𐐴 𐐼𐐭 𐐷 𐐹𐐱𐑌𐐼𐐲𐑉 𐑄𐐨𐑆 𐑃𐐮𐑍𐑆 𐐮𐑌 𐐷𐐫𐑉 𐐸𐐪𐑉𐐻𐑅? 𐐔𐐭 𐐷 𐑌𐐱𐐻 𐑉𐐨𐑋𐐯𐑋𐐺𐐲𐑉 𐑄𐐰𐐻 𐐌 𐑅𐐯𐐼 𐐲𐑌𐐻𐐭 𐐷𐐭, 𐑄𐐰𐐻 𐐰𐑁𐐻𐐲𐑉 𐐷 𐐸𐐰𐐼 𐑉𐐨𐑅𐐨𐑂𐐼 𐑄 𐐐𐐬𐑊𐐮 𐐘𐐬𐑅𐐻, 𐐷 𐐿𐐳𐐼 𐑅𐐹𐐨𐐿 𐐶𐐮𐑄 𐑄 𐐻𐐲𐑍 𐐱𐑂 𐐁𐑌𐐾𐐯𐑊𐑆? 𐐈𐑌𐐼 𐑌𐐵, 𐐸𐐵 𐐿𐐳𐐼 𐐷 𐑅𐐹𐐨𐐿 𐐶𐐮𐑄 𐑄 𐐻𐐲𐑍 𐐱𐑂 𐐁𐑌𐐾𐐯𐑊𐑆, 𐑅𐐩𐑂 𐐮𐐻 𐐶𐐲𐑉 𐐺𐐴 𐑄 𐐐𐐬𐑊𐐮 𐐘𐐬𐑅𐐻? 𐐁𐑌𐐾𐐯𐑊𐑆 𐑅𐐹𐐨𐐿 𐐺𐐴 𐑄 𐐹𐐵𐐲𐑉 𐐱𐑂 𐑄 𐐐𐐬𐑊𐐮 𐐘𐐬𐑅𐐻; 𐐸𐐶𐐩𐑉𐑁𐐫𐑉, 𐑄𐐩 𐑅𐐹𐐨𐐿 𐑄 𐐶𐐲𐑉𐐼𐑆 𐐱𐑂 𐐗𐑉𐐴𐑅𐐻. 𐐐𐐶𐐩𐑉𐑁𐐫𐑉, 𐐌 𐑅𐐯𐐼 𐐲𐑌𐐻𐐭 𐐷𐐭, 𐐙𐐨𐑅𐐻 𐐲𐐹𐐱𐑌 𐑄 𐐶𐐲𐑉𐐼𐑆 𐐱𐑂 𐐗𐑉𐐴𐑅𐐻: 𐑁𐐫𐑉 𐐺𐐨𐐸𐐬𐑊𐐼, 𐑄 𐐶𐐲𐑉𐐼𐑆 𐐱𐑂 𐐗𐑉𐐴𐑅𐐻 𐐶𐐮𐑊 𐐻𐐯𐑊 𐐷𐐭 𐐫𐑊 𐑃𐐮𐑍𐑆 𐐸𐐶𐐱𐐻 𐐷 𐑇𐐳𐐼 𐐼𐐭.

𐐸𐐶𐐯𐑉𐑁𐐬𐑉, 𐑌𐐵 𐐰𐑁𐐻𐐲𐑉 𐐌 𐐸𐐰𐑂 𐑅𐐹𐐬𐐿𐑌 𐑄𐐨𐑆 𐐶𐐲𐑉𐐼𐑆, 𐐮𐑁 𐐷 𐐿𐐰𐑌𐐱𐐻 𐐲𐑌𐐼𐐲𐑉𐑅𐐻𐐰𐑌𐐼 𐑄𐐯𐑋, 𐐮𐐻 𐐶𐐮𐑊 𐐺 𐐺𐐨𐐿𐐫𐑆 𐐷 𐐰𐑅𐐿 𐑌𐐱𐐻, 𐑌𐐨𐑄𐐲𐑉 𐐼𐐭 𐐷 𐑌𐐱𐐿; 𐐸𐐶𐐯𐑉𐑁𐐬𐑉, 𐐷 𐐪𐑉 𐑌𐐱𐐻 𐐺𐑉𐐫𐐻 𐐮𐑌𐐻𐐭 𐑄 𐑊𐐴𐐻, 𐐺𐐲𐐻 𐑋𐐲𐑅𐐻 𐐹𐐯𐑉𐐮𐑇 𐐮𐑌 𐑄 𐐼𐐪𐑉𐐿. 𐐙𐐬𐑉 𐐺𐐨𐐸𐐬𐑊𐐼, 𐐲𐑀𐐯𐑌 𐐌 𐑅𐐩 𐐲𐑌𐐻𐐭 𐐷𐐭, 𐑄𐐰𐐻 𐐮𐑁 𐐷 𐐶𐐮𐑊 𐐯𐑌𐐻𐐲𐑉 𐐮𐑌 𐐺𐐴 𐑄 𐐶𐐩, 𐐰𐑌𐐼 𐑉𐐨𐑅𐐨𐑂 𐑄 𐐐𐐬𐑊𐐨 𐐘𐐬𐑅𐐻, 𐐮𐐻 𐐶𐐮𐑊 𐑇𐐬 𐐲𐑌𐐻𐐭 𐐷𐐭 𐐫𐑊 𐑃𐐮𐑍𐑆 𐐸𐐶𐐱𐐻 𐐷 𐑇𐐳𐐼 𐐼𐐭. 𐐒𐐨𐐸𐐬𐑊𐐼, 𐑄𐐮𐑅 𐐮𐑆 𐑄 𐐼𐐱𐐿𐐻𐑉𐐮𐑌 𐐱𐑂 𐐗𐑉𐐴𐑅𐐻, 𐐰𐑌𐐼 𐑄𐐩𐑉 𐐶𐐮𐑊 𐐺 𐑌𐐬 𐑋𐐬𐑉 𐐼𐐱𐐿𐐻𐑉𐐮𐑌 𐑀𐐮𐑂𐐲𐑌, 𐐲𐑌𐐻𐐮𐑊 𐐰𐑁𐐻𐐲𐑉 𐐸𐐨 𐑇𐐰𐑊 𐑋𐐰𐑌𐐮𐑁𐐯𐑅𐐻 𐐸𐐮𐑋𐑅𐐯𐑊𐑁 𐐲𐑌𐐻𐐭 𐐷𐐭 𐐮𐑌 𐑄 𐑁𐑊𐐯𐑇. 𐐈𐑌𐐼 𐐸𐐶𐐯𐑌 𐐸𐐨 𐑇𐐰𐑊 𐑋𐐰𐑌𐐮𐑁𐐯𐑅𐐻 𐐸𐐮𐑋𐑅𐐯𐑊𐑁 𐐲𐑌𐐻𐐭 𐐷𐐭 𐐮𐑌 𐑄 𐑁𐑊𐐯𐑇, 𐑄 𐑃𐐮𐑍𐑆 𐐸𐐶𐐮𐐽 𐐸𐐨 𐑇𐐰𐑊 𐑅𐐩 𐐲𐑌𐐻𐐭 𐐷𐐭, 𐑇𐐰𐑊 𐐷 𐐱𐐺𐑆𐐲𐑉𐑂 𐐻𐐭 𐐼𐐭.

2. 𐐈𐑌𐐼 𐑌𐐵 𐐌, 𐐤𐐨𐑁𐐴, 𐐿𐐰𐑌𐐱𐐻 𐑅𐐩 𐑋𐐬𐑉; 𐑄 𐐝𐐹𐐮𐑉𐐮𐐻 𐑅𐐻𐐱𐐹𐐯𐑃 𐑋𐐴𐑌 𐐲𐐻𐐲𐑉𐐲𐑌𐑅, 𐐰𐑌𐐼 𐐌 𐐰𐑋 𐑊𐐯𐑁𐐻 𐐻𐐭 𐑋𐐬𐑉𐑌 𐐺𐐨𐐿𐐫𐑆 𐐱𐑂 𐑄 𐐲𐑌𐐺𐐨𐑊𐐨𐑁, 𐐰𐑌𐐼 𐑄 𐐶𐐮𐐿𐐯𐐼𐑌𐐯𐑅, 𐐰𐑌𐐼 𐑄 𐐮𐑀𐑌𐐬𐑉𐐲𐑌𐑅, 𐐰𐑌𐐼 𐑄 𐑅𐐻𐐮𐑁𐑌𐐯𐐿𐐯𐐼𐑌𐐯𐑅 𐐱𐑂 𐑋𐐯𐑌: 𐑁𐐬𐑉 𐑄𐐩 𐐶𐐮𐑊 𐑌𐐱𐐻 𐑅𐐲𐑉𐐽 𐑌𐐱𐑊𐐯𐐾, 𐑌𐐫𐑉 𐐲𐑌𐐼𐐲𐑉𐑅𐐻𐐰𐑌𐐼 𐑀𐑉𐐩𐐻 𐑌𐐱𐑊𐐯𐐾, 𐐸𐐶𐐯𐑌 𐐮𐐻 𐐮𐑆 𐑀𐐮𐑂𐐲𐑌 𐐲𐑌𐐻𐐭 𐑄𐐯𐑋 𐐮𐑌 𐐹𐑊𐐩𐑌𐑌𐐯𐑅, 𐐨𐑂𐐲𐑌 𐐰𐑆 𐐹𐑊𐐩𐑌 𐐰𐑆 𐐶𐐲𐑉𐐼 𐐿𐐰𐑌 𐐺.

3. 𐐈𐑌𐐼 𐑌𐐵 𐑋𐐴 𐐺𐐨𐑊𐐲𐑂𐐯𐐼 𐐺𐑉𐐯𐑄𐑉𐐯𐑌, 𐐌 𐐹𐐲𐑉𐑅𐐨𐑂 𐑄𐐰𐐻 𐐷 𐐹𐐱𐑌𐐼𐐲𐑉 𐑅𐐻𐐮𐑊 𐐮𐑌 𐐷𐐬𐑉 𐐸𐐪𐑉𐐻𐑅; 𐐰𐑌𐐼 𐐮𐐻 𐑀𐑉𐐨𐑂𐐯𐑃 𐑋𐐨 𐑄𐐰𐐻 𐐌 𐑋𐐲𐑅𐐻 𐑅𐐹𐐨𐐿 𐐿𐐱𐑌𐑅𐐲𐑉𐑌𐐮𐑍 𐑄𐐮𐑅 𐑃𐐮𐑍. 𐐙𐐬𐑉 𐐮𐑁 𐐷 𐐶𐐳𐐼 𐐸𐐪𐑉𐐿𐐲𐑌 𐐲𐑌𐐻𐐭 𐑄 𐐝𐐹𐐮𐑉𐐮𐐻 𐐸𐐶𐐮𐐽 𐐻𐐨𐐽𐐯𐑃 𐐲 𐑋𐐰𐑌 𐐻𐐭 𐐹𐑉𐐩, 𐐷 𐐶𐐳𐐼 𐑌𐐬 𐑄𐐰𐐻 𐐷 𐑋𐐲𐑅𐐻 𐐹𐑉𐐩: 𐑁𐐬𐑉 𐑄 𐐨𐑂𐑊 𐑅𐐹𐐮𐑉𐐮𐐻 𐐻𐐨𐐽𐐯𐑃 𐑌𐐱𐐻 𐐲 𐑋𐐰𐑌 𐐻𐐭 𐐹𐑉𐐩, 𐐺𐐲𐐻 𐐻𐐨𐐽𐐯𐑃 𐐸𐐮𐑋 𐑄𐐰𐐻 𐐸𐐨 𐑋𐐲𐑅𐐻 𐑌𐐱𐐻 𐐹𐑉𐐩. 𐐒𐐲𐐻 𐐺𐐨𐐸𐐬𐑊𐐼, 𐐌 𐑅𐐩 𐐲𐑌𐐻𐐭 𐐷𐐭, 𐑄𐐰𐐻 𐐷 𐑋𐐲𐑅𐐻 𐐹𐑉𐐩 𐐫𐑊𐐶𐐩𐑆, 𐐰𐑌𐐼 𐑌𐐱𐐻 𐑁𐐩𐑌𐐻; 𐑄𐐰𐐻 𐐷 𐑋𐐲𐑅𐐻 𐑌𐐱𐐻 𐐹𐐲𐑉𐑁𐐫𐑉𐑋 𐐯𐑌𐐨 𐑃𐐮𐑍 𐐲𐑌𐐻𐐭 𐑄 𐐢𐐫𐑉𐐼, 𐑅𐐩𐑂 𐐮𐑌 𐑄 𐑁𐐲𐑉𐑅𐐻 𐐹𐑊𐐩𐑅 𐐷 𐑇𐐰𐑊 𐐹𐑉𐐩 𐐲𐑌𐐻𐐭 𐑄 𐐙𐐪𐑄𐐲𐑉 𐐮𐑌 𐑄 𐑌𐐩𐑋 𐐱𐑂 𐐗𐑉𐐴𐑅𐐻, 𐑄𐐰𐐻 𐐸𐐨 𐐶𐐮𐑊 𐐿𐐱𐑌𐑅𐐯𐐿𐑉𐐩𐐻 𐑄𐐴 𐐹𐐲𐑉𐑁𐐫𐑉𐑋𐐲𐑌𐑅 𐐲𐑌𐐻𐐭 𐑄, 𐑄𐐰𐐻 𐑄𐐴 𐐹𐐲𐑉𐑁𐐫𐑉𐑋𐐲𐑌𐑅 𐑋𐐩 𐐺 𐑁𐐬𐑉 𐑄 𐐶𐐯𐑊𐑁𐐩𐑉 𐐱𐑂 𐑄𐐴 𐑅𐐬𐑊.

𐐕𐐰𐐹𐐻𐐲𐑉 XV.

1. 𐐈𐑌𐐼 𐑌𐐵, 𐐌, 𐐤𐐨𐑁𐐴, 𐐿𐐰𐑌𐐱𐐻 𐑉𐐴𐐻 𐐫𐑊 𐑄 𐑃𐐮𐑍𐑆 𐐸𐐶𐐮𐐽 𐐶𐐲𐑉 𐐻𐐫𐐻 𐐲𐑋𐐲𐑍 𐑋𐐴 𐐹𐐨𐐹𐑊; 𐑌𐐨𐑄𐐲𐑉 𐐰𐑋 𐐌 𐑋𐐴𐐻𐐨 𐐮𐑌 𐑉𐐴𐐻𐐮𐑍, 𐑊𐐴𐐿 𐐲𐑌𐐻𐐭 𐑅𐐹𐐨𐐿𐐮𐑍: 𐑁𐐬𐑉 𐐸𐐶𐐯𐑌 𐐲 𐑋𐐰𐑌 𐑅𐐹𐐨𐐿𐐯𐑃 𐐺𐐴 𐑄 𐐹𐐵𐑉 𐐱𐑂 𐑄 𐐐𐐬𐑊𐐨 𐐘𐐬𐑅𐐻, 𐑄 𐐹𐐵𐑉 𐐱𐑂 𐑄 𐐐𐐬𐑊𐐨 𐐘𐐬𐑅𐐻 𐐿𐐰𐑉𐐨𐐯𐑃 𐐮𐐻 𐐲𐑌𐐻𐐭 𐑄 𐐸𐐪𐑉𐐻𐑅 𐐱𐑂 𐑄 𐐽𐐮𐑊𐐼𐑉𐐯𐑌 𐐱𐑂 𐑋𐐯𐑌. 𐐒𐐲𐐻 𐐺𐐨𐐸𐐬𐑊𐐼, 𐑄𐐩𐑉 𐐪𐑉 𐑋𐐯𐑌𐐨 𐑄𐐰𐐻 𐐸𐐪𐑉𐐼𐐲𐑌 𐑄𐐩𐑉 𐐸𐐪𐑉𐐻𐑅 𐐲𐑀𐐯𐑌𐑅𐐻 𐑄 𐐐𐐬𐑊𐐨 𐐝𐐹𐐮𐑉𐐮𐐻, 𐑄𐐰𐐻 𐐮𐐻 𐐸𐐰𐑃 𐑌𐐬 𐐹𐑊𐐩𐑅 𐐮𐑌 𐑄𐐯𐑋; 𐐸𐐶𐐯𐑉𐑁𐐬𐑉, 𐑄𐐩 𐐿𐐰𐑅𐐻 𐑋𐐯𐑌𐐨 𐑃𐐮𐑍𐑆 𐐲𐐶𐐩 𐐸𐐶𐐮𐐽 𐐪𐑉 𐑉𐐮𐐻𐐲𐑌, 𐐰𐑌𐐼 𐐯𐑅𐐻𐐨𐑋 𐑄𐐯𐑋 𐐰𐑆 𐑃𐐮𐑍𐑆 𐐱𐑂 𐑌𐐫𐐻. 𐐒𐐲𐐻 𐐌, 𐐤𐐨𐑁𐐴, 𐐸𐐰𐑂 𐑉𐐮𐐻𐐲𐑌 𐐸𐐶𐐱𐐻 𐐌 𐐸𐐰𐑂 𐑉𐐮𐐻𐐲𐑌; 𐐰𐑌𐐼 𐐌 𐐯𐑅𐐻𐐨𐑋 𐐮𐐻 𐐰𐑆 𐐱𐑂 𐑀𐑉𐐩𐐻 𐐶𐐲𐑉𐑃, 𐐰𐑌𐐼 𐐯𐑅𐐹𐐯𐑇𐐲𐑊𐐨 𐐲𐑌𐐻𐐭 𐑋𐐴 𐐹𐐨𐐹𐑊. 𐐙𐐬𐑉 𐐌 𐐹𐑉𐐩 𐐿𐐱𐑌𐐻𐐮𐑌𐐷𐐭𐐲𐑊𐐨 𐑁𐐬𐑉 𐑄𐐯𐑋 𐐺𐐴 𐐼𐐩, 𐐰𐑌𐐼 𐑋𐐴𐑌 𐐴𐑆 𐐶𐐫𐐻𐐲𐑉 𐑋𐐴 𐐹𐐮𐑊𐐬 𐐺𐐴 𐑌𐐴𐐻, 𐐺𐐨𐐿𐐫𐑆 𐐱𐑂 𐑄𐐯𐑋; 𐐰𐑌𐐼 𐐌 𐐿𐑉𐐴 𐐲𐑌𐐻𐐭 𐑋𐐴 𐐘𐐱𐐼 𐐮𐑌 𐑁𐐩𐑃, 𐐰𐑌𐐼 𐐌 𐑌𐐬 𐑄𐐰𐐻 𐐸𐐨 𐐶𐐮𐑊 𐐸𐐨𐑉 𐑋𐐴 𐐿𐑉𐐴; 𐐰𐑌𐐼 𐐌 𐑌𐐬 𐑄𐐰𐐻 𐑄 𐐢𐐫𐑉𐐼 𐐘𐐱𐐼 𐐶𐐮𐑊 𐐿𐐱𐑌𐑅𐐯𐐿𐑉𐐩𐐻 𐑋𐐴 𐐹𐑉𐐩𐐲𐑉𐑆, 𐑁𐐬𐑉 𐑄 𐑀𐐩𐑌 𐐱𐑂 𐑋𐐴 𐐹𐐨𐐹𐑊. 𐐈𐑌𐐼 𐑄 𐐶𐐲𐑉𐐼𐑆 𐐸𐐶𐐮𐐽 𐐌 𐐸𐐰𐑂 𐑉𐐮𐐻𐐲𐑌 𐐮𐑌 𐐶𐐨𐐿𐑌𐐯𐑅 𐐶𐐮𐑊 𐐺 𐑋𐐩𐐼 𐑅𐐻𐑉𐐫𐑍 𐐲𐑌𐐻𐐭 𐑄𐐯𐑋; 𐑁𐐬𐑉 𐐮𐐻 𐐹𐐲𐑉𐑅𐐶𐐩𐐼𐐯𐑃 𐑄𐐯𐑋 𐐻𐐭 𐐼𐐭 𐑀𐐳𐐼; 𐐮𐐻 𐑋𐐩𐐿𐐯𐑃 𐑌𐐬𐑌 𐐲𐑌𐐻𐐭 𐑄𐐯𐑋 𐐱𐑂 𐑄𐐩𐑉 𐑁𐐪𐑄𐐲𐑉𐑆; 𐐰𐑌𐐼 𐐮𐐻 𐑅𐐹𐐨𐐿𐐯𐑃 𐐱𐑂 𐐖𐐨𐑆𐐲𐑅, 𐐰𐑌𐐼 𐐹𐐲𐑉𐑅𐐶𐐩𐐼𐐯𐑃 𐑄𐐯𐑋 𐐻𐐭 𐐺𐐨𐑊𐐨𐑂 𐐮𐑌 𐐸𐐮𐑋, 𐐰𐑌𐐼 𐐻𐐭 𐐯𐑌𐐼𐐷𐐭𐑉 𐐻𐐭 𐑄 𐐯𐑌𐐼, 𐐸𐐶𐐮𐐽 𐐮𐑆 𐑊𐐴𐑁 𐐨𐐻𐐲𐑉𐑌𐐲𐑊. 𐐈𐑌𐐼 𐐮𐐻 𐑅𐐹𐐨𐐿𐐯𐑃 𐐸𐐪𐑉𐑇𐑊𐐨 𐐲𐑀𐐯𐑌𐑅𐐻 𐑅𐐮𐑌, 𐐰𐐿𐐫𐑉𐐼𐐮𐑍 𐐻𐐭 𐑄 𐐹𐑊𐐩𐑌𐑌𐐯𐑅 𐐱𐑂 𐑄 𐐻𐑉𐐭𐑃; 𐐸𐐶𐐯𐑉𐑁𐐬𐑉, 𐑌𐐬 𐑋𐐰𐑌 𐐶𐐮𐑊 𐐺 𐐰𐑍𐑀𐑉𐐨 𐐰𐐻 𐑄 𐐶𐐲𐑉𐐼𐑆 𐐸𐐶𐐮𐐽 𐐌 𐐸𐐰𐑂 𐑉𐐮𐐻𐐲𐑌, 𐑅𐐩𐑂 𐐸𐐨 𐑇𐐰𐑊 𐐺 𐐱𐑂 𐑄 𐑅𐐹𐐮𐑉𐐮𐐻 𐐱𐑂 𐑄 𐐼𐐯𐑂𐐲𐑊. 𐐌 𐑀𐑊𐐬𐑉𐐨 𐐮𐑌 𐐹𐑊𐐩𐑌𐑌𐐯𐑅; 𐐌 𐑀𐑊𐐬𐑉𐐨 𐐮𐑌 𐐻𐑉𐐭𐑃; 𐐌 𐑀𐑊𐐬𐑉𐐨 𐐮𐑌 𐑋𐐴 𐐖𐐨𐑆𐐲𐑅, 𐑁𐐬𐑉 𐐸𐐨 𐐸𐐰𐑃 𐑉𐐨𐐼𐐨𐑋𐐼 𐑋𐐴 𐑅𐐬𐑊 𐑁𐑉𐐱𐑋 𐐸𐐯𐑊. 𐐌 𐐸𐐰𐑂 𐐽𐐰𐑉𐐮𐐻𐐨 𐑁𐐬𐑉 𐑋𐐴 𐐹𐐨𐐹𐑊, 𐐰𐑌𐐼 𐑀𐑉𐐩𐐻 𐑁𐐩𐑃 𐐮𐑌 𐐗𐑉𐐴𐑅𐐻, 𐑄𐐰𐐻

𐐌 𐑇𐐰𐑊 𐑋𐐨𐐻 𐑋𐐯𐑌𐐮 𐑅𐐬𐑊𐑆 𐑅𐐹𐐱𐐻𐑊𐐯𐑅 𐐰𐐻 𐐸𐐮𐑆 𐐾𐐲𐐾𐑋𐐯𐑌𐐻 𐑅𐐨𐐻. 𐐌 𐐸𐐰𐑂 𐐽𐐰𐑉𐐮𐐻𐐮 𐑁𐐫𐑉 𐑄 𐐖𐐮𐐭: 𐐌 𐑅𐐩 𐐖𐐮𐐭, 𐐺𐐨𐐿𐐫𐑆 𐐌 𐑋𐐨𐑌 𐑄𐐯𐑋 𐑁𐑉𐐱𐑋 𐐸𐐶𐐯𐑌𐑅 𐐌 𐐿𐐩𐑋. 𐐌 𐐫𐑊𐑅𐐬 𐐸𐐰𐑂 𐐽𐐰𐑉𐐮𐐻𐐮 𐑁𐐫𐑉 𐑄 𐐖𐐯𐑌𐐻𐐴𐑊𐑆. 𐐒𐐲𐐻 𐐺𐐨𐐸𐐬𐑊𐐼, 𐑁𐐫𐑉 𐑌𐐲𐑌 𐐱𐑂 𐑄𐐨𐑆 𐐿𐐰𐑌 𐐌 𐐸𐐬𐐹, 𐐯𐐿𐑅𐐯𐐹𐐻 𐑄𐐩 𐑇𐐰𐑊 𐐺 𐑉𐐯𐐿𐐲𐑌𐑅𐐴𐑊𐐼 𐐲𐑌𐐻𐐭 𐐗𐑉𐐴𐑅𐐻, 𐐰𐑌𐐼 𐐯𐑌𐐻𐐯𐑉 𐐮𐑌𐐻𐐭 𐑄 𐑌𐐰𐑉𐐬 𐑀𐐩𐐻, 𐐰𐑌𐐼 𐐶𐐫𐐿 𐐮𐑌 𐑄 𐑅𐐻𐑉𐐩𐐻 𐐹𐐪𐑃, 𐐸𐐶𐐮𐐽 𐑊𐐨𐐼𐑆 𐐻𐐭 𐑊𐐴𐑁, 𐐰𐑌𐐼 𐐿𐐲𐑌𐐻𐐮𐑌𐐷𐐭 𐐮𐑌 𐑄 𐐹𐐪𐑃 𐐲𐑌𐐻𐐮𐑊 𐑄 𐐯𐑌𐐼 𐐱𐑂 𐑄 𐐼𐐩 𐐱𐑂 𐐹𐑉𐐬𐐺𐐩𐑇𐐲𐑌.

2. 𐐈𐑌𐐼 𐑌𐐵, 𐑋𐐴 𐐺𐐨𐑊𐐲𐑂𐐯𐐼 𐐺𐑉𐐯𐑄𐑉𐐯𐑌, 𐐰𐑌𐐼 𐐫𐑊𐑅𐐬 𐐖𐐮𐐭, 𐐰𐑌𐐼 𐐫𐑊 𐐷 𐐯𐑌𐐼𐑆 𐐱𐑂 𐑄 𐐲𐑉𐑃 𐐸𐐲𐑉𐐿𐐲𐑌 𐐲𐑌𐐻𐐭 𐑄𐐨𐑆 𐐶𐐲𐑉𐐼𐑆, 𐐰𐑌𐐼 𐐺𐐨𐑊𐐨𐑂 𐐮𐑌 𐐗𐑉𐐴𐑅𐐻; 𐐰𐑌𐐼 𐐮𐑁 𐐷 𐐺𐐨𐑊𐐨𐑂 𐑌𐐱𐐻 𐐮𐑌 𐑄𐐨𐑆 𐐶𐐲𐑉𐐼𐑆, 𐐺𐐨𐑊𐐨𐑂 𐐮𐑌 𐐗𐑉𐐴𐑅𐐻. 𐐈𐑌𐐼 𐐮𐑁 𐐷 𐑇𐐰𐑊 𐐺𐐨𐑊𐐨𐑂 𐐮𐑌 𐐗𐑉𐐴𐑅𐐻, 𐐷 𐐶𐐮𐑊 𐐺𐐨𐑊𐐨𐑂 𐐮𐑌 𐑄𐐨𐑆 𐐶𐐲𐑉𐐼𐑆: 𐑁𐐫𐑉 𐑄𐐩 𐐪𐑉 𐑄 𐐶𐐲𐑉𐐼𐑆 𐐱𐑂 𐐗𐑉𐐴𐑅𐐻, 𐐰𐑌𐐼 𐐸𐐨 𐐸𐐰𐑃 𐑀𐐮𐑂𐐯𐑌 𐑄𐐯𐑋 𐐲𐑌𐐻𐐭 𐑋𐐨; 𐐰𐑌𐐼 𐑄𐐩 𐐻𐐨𐐽 𐐫𐑊 𐑋𐐯𐑌 𐑄𐐰𐐻 𐑄𐐩 𐑇𐐳𐐼 𐐼𐐭 𐑀𐐳𐐼. 𐐈𐑌𐐼 𐐮𐑁 𐑄𐐩 𐐪𐑉 𐑌𐐱𐐻 𐑄 𐐶𐐲𐑉𐐼𐑆 𐐱𐑂 𐐗𐑉𐐴𐑅𐐻, 𐐾𐐲𐐾 𐐷: 𐑁𐐫𐑉 𐐗𐑉𐐴𐑅𐐻 𐐶𐐮𐑊 𐑇𐐬 𐐲𐑌𐐻𐐭 𐐷𐐭, 𐐶𐐮𐑄 𐐹𐐵𐑉 𐐰𐑌𐐼 𐑀𐑉𐐩𐐻 𐑀𐑊𐐬𐑉𐐮, 𐑄𐐰𐐻 𐑄𐐩 𐐪𐑉 𐐸𐐮𐑆 𐐶𐐲𐑉𐐼𐑆, 𐐰𐐻 𐑄 𐑊𐐰𐑅𐐻 𐐼𐐩; 𐐰𐑌𐐼 𐐷𐐭 𐐰𐑌𐐼 𐐌 𐑇𐐰𐑊 𐑅𐐻𐐰𐑌𐐼 𐑁𐐩𐑅 𐐻𐐭 𐑁𐐩𐑅 𐐺𐐨𐑁𐐫𐑉 𐐸𐐮𐑆 𐐺𐐪𐑉; 𐐰𐑌𐐼 𐐷 𐑇𐐰𐑊 𐑌𐐬 𐑄𐐰𐐻 𐐌 𐐸𐐰𐑂 𐐺𐐮𐑌 𐐿𐐲𐑋𐐰𐑌𐐼𐐯𐐼 𐐱𐑂 𐐸𐐮𐑋 𐐻𐐭 𐑉𐐴𐐻 𐑄𐐨𐑆 𐑃𐐮𐑍𐑆, 𐑌𐐱𐐻𐐶𐐮𐑄𐑅𐐻𐐰𐑌𐐼𐐮𐑍 𐑋𐐴 𐐶𐐨𐐿𐑌𐐯𐑅: 𐐰𐑌𐐼 𐐌 𐐹𐑉𐐩 𐑄 𐐙𐐪𐑄𐐲𐑉 𐐮𐑌 𐑄 𐑌𐐩𐑋 𐐱𐑂 𐐗𐑉𐐴𐑅𐐻, 𐑄𐐰𐐻 𐑋𐐯𐑌𐐮 𐐱𐑂 𐐲𐑅, 𐐮𐑁 𐑌𐐱𐐻 𐐫𐑊, 𐑋𐐩 𐐺 𐑅𐐩𐑂𐐼 𐐮𐑌 𐐸𐐮𐑆 𐐿𐐮𐑍𐐼𐐲𐑋, 𐐰𐐻 𐑄𐐰𐐻 𐑀𐑉𐐩𐐻 𐐰𐑌𐐼 𐑊𐐰𐑅𐐻 𐐼𐐩.

3. 𐐈𐑌𐐼 𐑌𐐵, 𐑋𐐴 𐐺𐐨𐑊𐐲𐑂𐐯𐐼 𐐺𐑉𐐯𐑄𐑉𐐯𐑌, 𐐫𐑊 𐑄𐐬𐑆 𐐸𐐭 𐐪𐑉 𐐱𐑂 𐑄 𐐸𐐵𐑅 𐐱𐑂 𐐆𐑆𐑉𐐩𐐯𐑊, 𐐰𐑌𐐼 𐐫𐑊 𐐷 𐐯𐑌𐐼𐑆 𐐱𐑂 𐑄 𐐲𐑉𐑃, 𐐌 𐑅𐐹𐐨𐐿 𐐲𐑌𐐻𐐭 𐐷𐐭, 𐐰𐑆 𐑄 𐑂𐐱𐐮𐑅 𐐱𐑂 𐐶𐐲𐑌 𐐿𐑉𐐴𐐮𐑍 𐑁𐑉𐐱𐑋 𐑄 𐐼𐐲𐑅𐐻: 𐐙𐐩𐑉𐐶𐐯𐑊 𐐲𐑌𐐻𐐮𐑊 𐑄𐐰𐐻 𐑀𐑉𐐩𐐻 𐐼𐐩 𐑇𐐰𐑊 𐐿𐐲𐑋; 𐐰𐑌𐐼 𐐷𐐭 𐑄𐐰𐐻 𐐶𐐮𐑊 𐑌𐐱𐐻 𐐹𐐪𐑉𐐻𐐩𐐿 𐐱𐑂 𐑄 𐑀𐐳𐐼𐑌𐐯𐑅 𐐱𐑂 𐐘𐐱𐐼, 𐐰𐑌𐐼 𐑉𐐯𐑅𐐹𐐯𐐿𐐻 𐑄 𐐶𐐲𐑉𐐼𐑆 𐐱𐑂 𐑄 𐐖𐐮𐐭𐑆, 𐐰𐑌𐐼 𐐫𐑊𐑅𐐬 𐑋𐐴 𐐶𐐲𐑉𐐼𐑆, 𐐰𐑌𐐼 𐑄 𐐶𐐲𐑉𐐼𐑆 𐐸𐐶𐐮𐐽 𐑇𐐰𐑊 𐐹𐑉𐐬𐑅𐐨𐐼 𐑁𐐫𐑉𐑃 𐐱𐑂 𐑄 𐑋𐐵𐑃 𐐱𐑂 𐑄 𐐢𐐰𐑋 𐐱𐑂 𐐘𐐱𐐼, 𐐺𐐨𐐸𐐬𐑊𐐼, 𐐌 𐐺𐐮𐐼 𐐷𐐭 𐐰𐑌 𐐯𐑂𐐲𐑉𐑊𐐰𐑅𐐻𐐮𐑍 𐑁𐐩𐑉𐐶𐐯𐑊, 𐑁𐐫𐑉 𐑄𐐨𐑆 𐐶𐐲𐑉𐐼𐑆 𐑇𐐰𐑊 𐐿𐐲𐑌𐐼𐐯𐑋 𐐷𐐭 𐐰𐐻 𐑄 𐑊𐐰𐑅𐐻 𐐼𐐩: 𐑁𐐫𐑉 𐐸𐐶𐐱𐐻 𐐌 𐑅𐐨𐑊 𐐱𐑌 𐐲𐑉𐑃 𐑇𐐰𐑊 𐐺 𐐺𐑉𐐫𐐻 𐐰𐑀𐐯𐑌𐑅𐐻 𐐷𐐭 𐐰𐐻 𐑄 𐐾𐐲𐐾𐑋𐐯𐑌𐐻 𐐺𐐪𐑉; 𐑁𐐫𐑉 𐑄𐐲𐑅 𐐸𐐰𐑃 𐑄 𐐢𐐫𐑉𐐼 𐐿𐐲𐑋𐐰𐑌𐐼𐐯𐐼 𐑋𐐨, 𐐰𐑌𐐼 𐐌 𐑋𐐲𐑅𐐻 𐐬𐐺𐐩. 𐐁𐑋𐐯𐑌.

𐐜 𐐒𐐳𐐿 𐐱𐑂 𐐖𐐩𐐿𐐲𐐺,

𐐜 𐐒𐑉𐐲𐑄𐐲𐑉 𐐱𐑂 𐐤𐐨𐑁𐐴.

𐐕𐐰𐐹𐐻𐐲𐑉 I.

𐐜 𐐶𐐲𐑉𐐼𐑆 𐐱𐑂 𐐸𐐮𐑆 𐐹𐑉𐐨𐐽𐐮𐑍 𐐲𐑌𐐻𐐭 𐐸𐐮𐑆 𐐺𐑉𐐯𐑄𐑉𐐯𐑌. 𐐐𐐨 𐐿𐐱𐑌𐑁𐐵𐑌𐐼𐐯𐑃 𐐲 𐑋𐐰𐑌 𐐸𐐭 𐑅𐐨𐐿𐐯𐑃 𐐻𐐭 𐐬𐑂𐐲𐑉𐑃𐑉𐐬 𐑄 𐐼𐐱𐐿𐐻𐑉𐐮𐑌 𐐱𐑂 𐐗𐑉𐐴𐑅𐐻. 𐐊 𐑁𐑏 𐐶𐐲𐑉𐐼𐑆 𐐿𐐱𐑌𐑅𐐲𐑉𐑌𐐮𐑍 𐑄 𐐸𐐮𐑅𐐻𐐲𐑉𐐨 𐐱𐑂 𐑄 𐐹𐐨𐐹𐐲𐑊 𐐱𐑂 𐐤𐐨𐑁𐐴.

1. 𐐙𐐫𐑉 𐐺𐐨𐐸𐐬𐑊𐐼, 𐐮𐐻 𐐿𐐩𐑋 𐐻𐐭 𐐹𐐰𐑅 𐑄𐐰𐐻 𐑁𐐮𐑁𐐻𐐨 𐐰𐑌𐐼 𐑁𐐴𐑂 𐐷𐐨𐑉𐑆 𐐸𐐰𐐼 𐐹𐐰𐑅𐐻 𐐲𐐶𐐩 𐑁𐑉𐐱𐑋 𐑄 𐐻𐐴𐑋 𐑄𐐰𐐻 𐐢𐐨𐐸𐐴 𐑊𐐯𐑁𐐻 𐐖𐐯𐑉𐐭𐑅𐐲𐑊𐐯𐑋; 𐐸𐐶𐐯𐑉𐑁𐐬𐑉, 𐐤𐐨𐑁𐐴 𐑀𐐩𐑂 𐑋𐐨, 𐐖𐐩𐐿𐐲𐐺, 𐐲 𐐿𐐱𐑋𐐰𐑌𐐼𐑋𐐯𐑌𐐻 𐐿𐐱𐑌𐑅𐐲𐑉𐑌𐐮𐑍 𐑄 𐑅𐑋𐐫𐑊 𐐹𐑊𐐩𐐻𐑅, 𐐲𐐹𐐱𐑌 𐐸𐐶𐐮𐐽 𐑄𐐨𐑆 𐑃𐐮𐑍𐑆 𐐪𐑉 𐐯𐑌𐑀𐑉𐐩𐑂𐐲𐑌. 𐐈𐑌𐐼 𐐸𐐨 𐑀𐐩𐑂 𐑋𐐨, 𐐖𐐩𐐿𐐲𐐺, 𐐲 𐐿𐐱𐑋𐐰𐑌𐐼𐑋𐐯𐑌𐐻 𐑄𐐰𐐻 𐐴 𐑇𐐳𐐼 𐑉𐐴𐐻 𐐲𐐹𐐱𐑌 𐑄𐐨𐑆 𐐹𐑊𐐩𐐻𐑅 𐐲 𐑁𐑏 𐐱𐑂 𐑄 𐑃𐐮𐑍𐑆 𐐸𐐶𐐮𐐽 𐐴 𐐿𐐱𐑌𐑅𐐮𐐼𐐲𐑉𐐼 𐐻𐐭 𐐺𐐨 𐑋𐐬𐑅𐐻 𐐹𐑉𐐯𐑇𐐲𐑅; 𐑄𐐰𐐻 𐐴 𐑇𐐳𐐼 𐑌𐐱𐐻 𐐻𐐲𐐽, 𐑅𐐩𐑂 𐐮𐐻 𐐶𐐲𐑉 𐑊𐐴𐐻𐑊𐐨, 𐐿𐐱𐑌𐑅𐐲𐑉𐑌𐐮𐑍 𐑄 𐐸𐐮𐑅𐐻𐐲𐑉𐐨 𐐱𐑂 𐑄𐐮𐑅 𐐹𐐨𐐹𐐲𐑊 𐐸𐐶𐐮𐐽 𐐪𐑉 𐐿𐐫𐑊𐐼 𐑄 𐐹𐐨𐐹𐐲𐑊 𐐱𐑂 𐐤𐐨𐑁𐐴. 𐐙𐐫𐑉 𐐸𐐨 𐑅𐐯𐐼 𐑄𐐰𐐻 𐑄 𐐸𐐮𐑅𐐻𐐲𐑉𐐨 𐐱𐑂 𐐸𐐮𐑆 𐐹𐐨𐐹𐐲𐑊 𐑇𐐳𐐼 𐐺𐐨 𐐯𐑌𐑀𐑉𐐩𐑂𐐲𐑌 𐐲𐐹𐐱𐑌 𐐸𐐮𐑆 𐐲𐑄𐐲𐑉 𐐹𐑊𐐩𐐻𐑅, 𐐰𐑌𐐼 𐑄𐐰𐐻 𐐴 𐑇𐐳𐐼 𐐹𐑉𐐨𐑆𐐲𐑉𐑂 𐑄𐐨𐑆 𐐹𐑊𐐩𐐻𐑅 𐐰𐑌𐐼 𐐸𐐰𐑌𐐼 𐑄𐐯𐑋 𐐼𐐵𐑌 𐐲𐑌𐐻𐐭 𐑋𐐴 𐑅𐐨𐐼, 𐑁𐑉𐐱𐑋 𐐾𐐯𐑌𐐲𐑉𐐩𐑇𐐲𐑌 𐐻𐐭 𐐾𐐯𐑌𐐲𐑉𐐩𐑇𐐲𐑌. 𐐈𐑌𐐼 𐐮𐑁 𐑄𐐯𐑉 𐐶𐐲𐑉 𐐹𐑉𐐨𐐽𐐮𐑍 𐐸𐐶𐐮𐐽 𐐶𐐱𐑆 𐑅𐐩𐐿𐑉𐐯𐐼, 𐐫𐑉 𐑉𐐯𐑂𐐯𐑊𐐩𐑇𐐲𐑌 𐐸𐐶𐐮𐐽 𐐶𐐱𐑆 𐑀𐑉𐐩𐐻, 𐐫𐑉 𐐹𐑉𐐱𐑁𐐯𐑅𐐴𐐮𐑍, 𐑄𐐰𐐻 𐐴 𐑇𐐳𐐼 𐐯𐑌𐑀𐑉𐐩𐑂𐐲𐑌 𐑄 𐐸𐐯𐐼𐑆 𐐱𐑂 𐑄𐐯𐑋 𐐲𐐹𐐱𐑌 𐑄𐐨𐑆 𐐹𐑊𐐩𐐻𐑅, 𐐰𐑌𐐼 𐐻𐐲𐐽 𐐲𐐹𐐱𐑌 𐑄𐐯𐑋 𐐰𐑆 𐑋𐐲𐐽 𐐰𐑆 𐐮𐐻 𐐶𐐲𐑉 𐐹𐐱𐑅𐐮𐐺𐑊, 𐑁𐐫𐑉 𐐗𐑉𐐴𐑅𐐻'𐑅 𐑅𐐩𐐿, 𐐰𐑌𐐼 𐑁𐐫𐑉 𐑄 𐑅𐐩𐐿 𐐱𐑂 𐐵𐑉 𐐹𐐨𐐹𐐲𐑊; 𐑁𐐫𐑉 𐐺𐐨𐐿𐐫𐑆 𐐱𐑂 𐑁𐐩𐑃 𐐰𐑌𐐼 𐑀𐑉𐐩𐐻 𐐰𐑍𐑆𐐴𐐲𐐻𐐨 𐐮𐐻 𐐻𐑉𐐭𐑊𐐨 𐐸𐐰𐐼 𐐺𐐮𐑌 𐑋𐐩𐐼 𐑋𐐰𐑌𐐮𐑁𐐯𐑅𐐻 𐐲𐑌𐐻𐐭 𐐲𐑅 𐐿𐐱𐑌𐑅𐐲𐑉𐑌𐐮𐑍 𐐵𐑉 𐐹𐐨𐐹𐐲𐑊, 𐐸𐐶𐐱𐐻 𐑃𐐮𐑍𐑆 𐑇𐐳𐐼 𐐸𐐰𐐹𐐲𐑌 𐐲𐑌𐐻𐐭 𐑄𐐯𐑋. 𐐈𐑌𐐼 𐐶𐐨 𐐫𐑊𐑅𐐬 𐐸𐐰𐐼 𐑋𐐯𐑌𐐨 𐑉𐐯𐑂𐐯𐑊𐐩𐑇𐐲𐑌𐑆, 𐐰𐑌𐐼 𐑄 𐑅𐐹𐐮𐑉𐐮𐐻 𐐱𐑂 𐑋𐐲𐐽 𐐹𐑉𐐱𐑁𐐯𐑅𐐨; 𐐸𐐶𐐯𐑉𐑁𐐬𐑉, 𐐶𐐨 𐑌𐑏 𐐱𐑂 𐐗𐑉𐐴𐑅𐐻 𐐰𐑌𐐼 𐐸𐐮𐑆 𐐿𐐮𐑍𐐼𐐲𐑋, 𐐸𐐶𐐮𐐽 𐑇𐐳𐐼 𐐿𐐲𐑋. 𐐐𐐶𐐯𐑉𐑁𐐬𐑉, 𐐶𐐨 𐑊𐐩𐐺𐐲𐑉𐐼 𐐼𐐮𐑊𐐮𐐾𐐯𐑌𐐻𐑊𐐨 𐐲𐑋𐐲𐑍 𐐵𐑉 𐐹𐐨𐐹𐐲𐑊, 𐑄𐐰𐐻 𐐶𐐨 𐑋𐐴𐐻 𐐹𐐲𐑉𐑅𐐶𐐩𐐼 𐑄𐐯𐑋 𐐻𐐭 𐐿𐐲𐑋 𐐲𐑌𐐻𐐭 𐐗𐑉𐐴𐑅𐐻, 𐐰𐑌𐐼 𐐹𐐪𐑉𐐻𐐩𐐿 𐐱𐑂 𐑄 𐑀𐐳𐐼𐑌𐐯𐑅 𐐱𐑂 𐐘𐐱𐐼, 𐑄𐐰𐐻 𐑄𐐩 𐑋𐐴𐐻 𐐯𐑌𐐻𐐲𐑉 𐐮𐑌𐐻𐐭 𐐸𐐮𐑆 𐑉𐐯𐑅𐐻, 𐑊𐐯𐑅𐐻 𐐺𐐴 𐐯𐑌𐐨 𐑋𐐨𐑌𐑆 𐐸𐐨 𐑇𐐳𐐼 𐑅𐐶𐐯𐑉 𐐮𐑌 𐐸𐐮𐑆 𐑉𐐪𐑃 𐑄𐐩 𐑇𐐳𐐼 𐑌𐐱𐐻 𐐯𐑌𐐻𐐲𐑉 𐐮𐑌, 𐐰𐑆 𐐮𐑌 𐑄 𐐹𐑉𐐱𐑂𐐬𐐿𐐩𐑇𐐲𐑌 𐐮𐑌 𐑄 𐐼𐐩𐑆 𐐱𐑂 𐐻𐐯𐑋𐐻𐐩𐑇𐐲𐑌, 𐐸𐐶𐐴𐑊 𐑄 𐐽𐐮𐑊𐐼𐑉𐐯𐑌 𐐱𐑂 𐐆𐑆𐑉𐐩𐐯𐑊 𐐶𐐲𐑉 𐐮𐑌 𐑄 𐐶𐐮𐑊𐐼𐐲𐑉𐑌𐐯𐑅. 𐐐𐐶𐐯𐑉𐑁𐐬𐑉, 𐐶𐐨 𐐶𐐳𐐼 𐐻𐐭 𐐘𐐱𐐼 𐑄𐐰𐐻 𐐶𐐨 𐐿𐐳𐐼 𐐹𐐲𐑉𐑅𐐶𐐩𐐼 𐐫𐑊 𐑋𐐯𐑌 𐑌𐐱𐐻 𐐻𐐭 𐑉𐐯𐐺𐐯𐑊 𐐲𐑀𐐯𐑌𐑅𐐻 𐐘𐐱𐐼, 𐐻𐐭 𐐹𐑉𐐬𐑂𐐬𐐿 𐐸𐐮𐑋 𐐻𐐭 𐐰𐑍𐑀𐐲𐑉, 𐐺𐐲𐐻 𐑄𐐰𐐻 𐐫𐑊 𐑋𐐯𐑌 𐐶𐐳𐐼 𐐺𐐨𐑊𐐨𐑂 𐐮𐑌 𐐗𐑉𐐴𐑅𐐻, 𐐰𐑌𐐼 𐑂𐑏 𐐸𐐮𐑆 𐐼𐐯𐑃, 𐐰𐑌𐐼 𐑅𐐲𐑁𐐲𐑉 𐐸𐐮𐑆 𐐿𐑉𐐫𐑅 𐐰𐑌𐐼 𐐺𐐯𐑉 𐑄 𐑇𐐩𐑋 𐐱𐑂 𐑄 𐐶𐐲𐑉𐑊𐐼; 𐐸𐐶𐐯𐑉𐑁𐐬𐑉, 𐐴, 𐐖𐐩𐐿𐐲𐐺, 𐐻𐐩𐐿 𐐮𐐻 𐐲𐐹𐐱𐑌 𐑋𐐨 𐐻𐐭 𐑁𐐳𐑊𐑁𐐮𐑊 𐑄 𐐿𐐱𐑋𐐰𐑌𐐼𐑋𐐯𐑌𐐻 𐐱𐑂 𐑋𐐴 𐐺𐑉𐐲𐑄𐐲𐑉 𐐤𐐨𐑁𐐴.

2. 𐐤𐐵 𐐤𐐨𐑁𐐴 𐐺𐐨𐑀𐐰𐑌 𐐻𐐭 𐐺𐐨 𐐬𐑊𐐼, 𐐰𐑌𐐼 𐐸𐐨 𐑅𐐫 𐑄𐐰𐐻 𐐸𐐨 𐑋𐐲𐑅𐐻 𐑅𐐭𐑌 𐐼𐐴; 𐐸𐐶𐐯𐑉𐑁𐐬𐑉, 𐐸𐐨 𐐲𐑌𐐬𐐮𐑌𐐻𐐯𐐼 𐐲 𐑋𐐰𐑌 𐐻𐐭 𐐺𐐨 𐐲 𐐿𐐮𐑍 𐐰𐑌𐐼 𐐲 𐑉𐐭𐑊𐐲𐑉 𐐬𐑂𐐲𐑉 𐐸𐐮𐑆 𐐹𐐨𐐹𐐲𐑊 𐑌𐐵, 𐐰𐐿𐐫𐑉𐐼𐐮𐑍 𐐻𐐭 𐑄 𐑉𐐩𐑌𐑆 𐐱𐑂 𐑄 𐐿𐐮𐑍𐑆. 𐐜 𐐹𐐨𐐹𐐲𐑊 𐐸𐐰𐑂𐐮𐑍 𐑊𐐲𐑂𐐼 𐐤𐐨𐑁𐐴 𐐯𐐿𐑅𐐨𐐼𐐮𐑍𐑊𐐨, 𐐸𐐨 𐐸𐐰𐑂𐐮𐑍 𐐺𐐮𐑌 𐐲 𐑀𐑉𐐩𐐻 𐐹𐑉𐐬𐐻𐐯𐐿𐐻𐐲𐑉 𐑁𐐫𐑉 𐑄𐐯𐑋, 𐐸𐐰𐑂𐐮𐑍 𐐶𐐨𐑊𐐼𐐯𐐼 𐑄 𐑅𐐬𐑉𐐼 𐐱𐑂 𐐢𐐩𐐺𐐲𐑌 𐐮𐑌 𐑄𐐯𐑉 𐐼𐐨𐑁𐐯𐑌𐑅, 𐐰𐑌𐐼 𐐸𐐰𐑂𐐮𐑍 𐑊𐐩𐐺𐐲𐑉𐐼 𐐮𐑌 𐐫𐑊 𐐸𐐮𐑆

𐐼𐐩𐑆 𐑁𐐫𐑉 𐑄𐐩𐑉 𐐶𐐯𐑊𐑁𐐩𐑉; 𐐸𐐶𐐩𐑉𐑁𐐫𐑉, 𐑄 𐐹𐐨𐐹𐑊 𐐶𐐲𐑉 𐐼𐐨𐑆𐐴𐑉𐐲𐑅 𐐻𐐭 𐑉𐐨𐐻𐐩𐑌 𐐮𐑌 𐑉𐐨𐑋𐐯𐑋𐐺𐑉𐐲𐑌𐑅 𐐸𐐮𐑆 𐑌𐐩𐑋. 𐐈𐑌𐐼 𐐸𐐭𐑆𐐬 𐑇𐐳𐐼 𐑉𐐩𐑌 𐐮𐑌 𐐸𐐮𐑆 𐑅𐐻𐐯𐐼, 𐐶𐐲𐑉 𐐿𐐫𐑊𐐼 𐐺𐐴 𐑄 𐐹𐐨𐐹𐑊, 𐑅𐐯𐐿𐐲𐑌𐐼 𐐤𐐨𐑁𐐴, 𐐛𐐲𐑉𐐼 𐐤𐐨𐑁𐐴, 𐐯𐐻𐑅., 𐐰𐐿𐐫𐑉𐐼𐐮𐑍 𐐻𐐭 𐑄 𐑉𐐩𐑌𐑆 𐐱𐑂 𐑄 𐐿𐐮𐑍𐑆; 𐐰𐑌𐐼 𐑄𐐲𐑅 𐑄𐐩 𐐶𐐲𐑉 𐐿𐐫𐑊𐐼 𐐺𐐴 𐑄 𐐹𐐨𐐹𐑊, 𐑊𐐯𐐻 𐑄𐐯𐑋 𐐺𐐨 𐐱𐑂 𐐸𐐶𐐱𐐻𐐯𐑂𐐲𐑉 𐑌𐐩𐑋 𐑄𐐩 𐐶𐐳𐐼.

3. 𐐈𐑌𐐼 𐐮𐐻 𐐿𐐩𐑋 𐐻𐐭 𐐹𐐰𐑅 𐑄𐐰𐐻 𐐤𐐨𐑁𐐴 𐐼𐐴𐐼. 𐐤𐐵 𐑄 𐐹𐐨𐐹𐑊 𐐸𐐶𐐮𐐽 𐐶𐐲𐑉 𐑌𐐱𐐻 𐐢𐐩𐑋𐐲𐑌𐐴𐐻𐑅, 𐐶𐐲𐑉 𐐤𐐨𐑁𐐴𐐻𐑅; 𐑌𐐯𐑂𐐲𐑉𐑄𐐲𐑊𐐯𐑅, 𐑄𐐩 𐐶𐐲𐑉 𐐿𐐫𐑊𐐼 𐐤𐐨𐑁𐐴𐐻𐑅, 𐐖𐐩𐐿𐐲𐐺𐐴𐐻𐑅, 𐐖𐐬𐑆𐐯𐑁𐐴𐐻𐑅, 𐐞𐐬𐑉𐐲𐑋𐐴𐐻𐑅, 𐐢𐐩𐑋𐐲𐑌𐐴𐐻𐑅, 𐐢𐐯𐑋𐐷𐐭𐐯𐑊𐐴𐐻𐑅, 𐐰𐑌𐐼 𐐆𐑇𐑋𐐩𐐯𐑊𐐴𐐻𐑅. 𐐒𐐲𐐻 𐐌, 𐐖𐐩𐐿𐐲𐐺, 𐑇𐐰𐑊 𐑌𐐱𐐻 𐐸𐐨𐑉𐐰𐑁𐐻𐐲𐑉 𐐼𐐮𐑅𐐻𐐮𐑍𐑀𐐶𐐮𐑇 𐑄𐐯𐑋 𐐺𐐴 𐑄𐐨𐑆 𐑌𐐩𐑋𐑆, 𐐺𐐲𐐻 𐐌 𐑇𐐰𐑊 𐐿𐐫𐑊 𐑄𐐯𐑋 𐐢𐐩𐑋𐐲𐑌𐐴𐐻𐑅 𐑄𐐰𐐻 𐑅𐐨𐐿 𐐻𐐭 𐐼𐐯𐑅𐐻𐑉𐐱𐐶 𐑄 𐐹𐐨𐐹𐑊 𐐱𐑂 𐐤𐐨𐑁𐐴, 𐐰𐑌𐐼 𐑄𐐬𐑆 𐐸𐐭 𐐪𐑉 𐑁𐑉𐐯𐑌𐐼𐑊𐐨 𐐻𐐭 𐐤𐐨𐑁𐐴, 𐐌 𐑇𐐰𐑊 𐐿𐐫𐑊 𐐤𐐨𐑁𐐴𐐻𐑅, 𐐫𐑉 𐑄 𐐹𐐨𐐹𐑊 𐐱𐑂 𐐤𐐨𐑁𐐴, 𐐰𐐿𐐫𐑉𐐼𐐮𐑍 𐐻𐐭 𐑄 𐑉𐐩𐑌𐑆 𐐱𐑂 𐑄 𐐿𐐮𐑍𐑆.

4. 𐐈𐑌𐐼 𐑌𐐵 𐐮𐐻 𐐿𐐩𐑋 𐐻𐐭 𐐹𐐰𐑅 𐑄𐐰𐐻 𐑄 𐐹𐐨𐐹𐑊 𐐱𐑂 𐐤𐐨𐑁𐐴, 𐐲𐑌𐐼𐐲𐑉 𐑄 𐑉𐐩𐑌 𐐱𐑂 𐑄 𐑅𐐯𐐿𐐲𐑌𐐼 𐐿𐐮𐑍, 𐐺𐐨𐑀𐐰𐑌 𐐻𐐭 𐑀𐑉𐐬 𐐸𐐪𐑉𐐼 𐐮𐑌 𐑄𐐩𐑉 𐐸𐐪𐑉𐐻𐑅, 𐐰𐑌𐐼 𐐮𐑌𐐼𐐲𐑊𐐾 𐑄𐐯𐑋𐑅𐐯𐑊𐑂𐑆 𐑅𐐲𐑋𐐸𐐶𐐱𐐻 𐐮𐑌 𐐶𐐮𐐿𐐯𐐼 𐐹𐑉𐐰𐐿𐐻𐐮𐑅𐐯𐑆, 𐑅𐐲𐐽 𐐰𐑆 𐑊𐐴𐐿 𐐲𐑌𐐻𐐭 𐐔𐐩𐑂𐐮𐐼 𐐱𐑂 𐐬𐑊𐐼, 𐐼𐐯𐑆𐐴𐑉𐐮𐑍 𐑋𐐯𐑌𐐨 𐐶𐐴𐑂𐑆 𐐰𐑌𐐼 𐐿𐐱𐑍𐐿𐐷𐐭𐐺𐐴𐑌𐑆, 𐐰𐑌𐐼 𐐫𐑊𐑅𐐬 𐐝𐐱𐑊𐐲𐑋𐐲𐑌, 𐐸𐐮𐑆 𐑅𐐲𐑌: 𐐷𐐩, 𐐰𐑌𐐼 𐑄𐐩 𐐫𐑊𐑅𐐬 𐐺𐐨𐑀𐐰𐑌 𐐻𐐭 𐑅𐐲𐑉𐐽 𐑋𐐲𐐽 𐑀𐐬𐑊𐐼 𐐰𐑌𐐼 𐑅𐐮𐑊𐑂𐐲𐑉, 𐐰𐑌𐐼 𐐺𐐨𐑀𐐰𐑌 𐐻𐐭 𐐺𐐨 𐑊𐐮𐑁𐐻𐐲𐐼 𐐲𐐹 𐑅𐐲𐑋𐐸𐐶𐐱𐐻 𐐮𐑌 𐐹𐑉𐐴𐐼; 𐐸𐐶𐐩𐑉𐑁𐐫𐑉 𐐌, 𐐖𐐩𐐿𐐲𐐺, 𐑀𐐩𐑂 𐐲𐑌𐐻𐐭 𐑄𐐯𐑋 𐑄𐐨𐑆 𐐶𐐲𐑉𐐼𐑆 𐐰𐑆 𐐌 𐐻𐐫𐐻 𐑄𐐯𐑋 𐐮𐑌 𐑄 𐐻𐐯𐑋𐐹𐑊, 𐐸𐐰𐑂𐐮𐑍 𐑁𐐲𐑉𐑅𐐻 𐐱𐐺𐐻𐐩𐑌𐐼 𐑋𐐴𐑌 𐐯𐑉𐐲𐑌𐐼 𐑁𐑉𐐱𐑋 𐑄 𐐢𐐫𐑉𐐼. 𐐙𐐫𐑉 𐐌, 𐐖𐐩𐐿𐐲𐐺, 𐐰𐑌𐐼 𐑋𐐴 𐐺𐑉𐐲𐑄𐐲𐑉 𐐖𐐬𐑆𐐯𐑁, 𐐸𐐰𐐼 𐐺𐐨𐑌 𐐿𐐱𐑌𐑅𐐯𐐿𐑉𐐩𐐻𐐯𐐼 𐐹𐑉𐐨𐑅𐐻𐑅 𐐰𐑌𐐼 𐐻𐐨𐐽𐐲𐑉𐑆 𐐱𐑂 𐑄𐐮𐑅 𐐹𐐨𐐹𐑊, 𐐺𐐴 𐑄 𐐸𐐰𐑌𐐼 𐐱𐑂 𐐤𐐨𐑁𐐴. 𐐈𐑌𐐼 𐐶𐐨 𐐼𐐮𐐼 𐑋𐐰𐑀𐑌𐐮𐑁𐐴 𐐵𐑉 𐐱𐑁𐐮𐑅 𐐲𐑌𐐻𐐭 𐑄 𐐢𐐫𐑉𐐼, 𐐻𐐩𐐿𐐮𐑍 𐐲𐐹𐐱𐑌 𐐲𐑅 𐑄 𐑉𐐨𐑅𐐹𐐱𐑌𐑅𐐮𐐺𐐮𐑊𐐮𐐻𐐨, 𐐰𐑌𐑅𐐲𐑉𐐮𐑍 𐑄 𐑅𐐮𐑌𐑆 𐐱𐑂 𐑄 𐐹𐐨𐐹𐑊 𐐲𐐹𐐱𐑌 𐐵𐑉 𐐬𐑌 𐐸𐐯𐐼𐑆, 𐐮𐑁 𐐶𐐨 𐐼𐐮𐐼 𐑌𐐱𐐻 𐐻𐐨𐐽 𐑄𐐯𐑋 𐑄 𐐶𐐲𐑉𐐼 𐐱𐑂 𐐘𐐱𐐼 𐐶𐐮𐑄 𐐫𐑊 𐐼𐐮𐑊𐐮𐐾𐐯𐑌𐑅; 𐐸𐐶𐐩𐑉𐑁𐐫𐑉, 𐐺𐐴 𐑊𐐩𐐺𐐲𐑉𐐮𐑍 𐐶𐐮𐑄 𐐵𐑉 𐑋𐐴𐐻 𐑄𐐩𐑉 𐐺𐑊𐐲𐐼 𐑋𐐴𐐻 𐑌𐐱𐐻 𐐿𐐲𐑋 𐐲𐐹𐐱𐑌 𐐵𐑉 𐑀𐐪𐑉𐑋𐐲𐑌𐐻𐑅; 𐐲𐑄𐐲𐑉𐐶𐐴𐑆, 𐑄𐐩𐑉 𐐺𐑊𐐲𐐼 𐐶𐐳𐐼 𐐿𐐲𐑋 𐐲𐐹𐐱𐑌 𐐵𐑉 𐑀𐐪𐑉𐑋𐐲𐑌𐐻𐑅, 𐐰𐑌𐐼 𐐶𐐨 𐐶𐐳𐐼 𐑌𐐱𐐻 𐐺𐐨 𐑁𐐵𐑌𐐼 𐑅𐐹𐐱𐐻𐑊𐐯𐑅 𐐰𐐻 𐑄 𐑊𐐰𐑅𐐻 𐐼𐐩.

𐐕𐐈𐐑𐐓𐐊𐐡 II.

1. 𐐜 𐐶𐐲𐑉𐐼𐑆 𐐸𐐶𐐮𐐽 𐐖𐐩𐐿𐐲𐐺, 𐑄 𐐺𐑉𐐲𐑄𐐲𐑉 𐐱𐑂 𐐤𐐨𐑁𐐴, 𐑅𐐹𐐩𐐿 𐐲𐑌𐐻𐐭 𐑄 𐐹𐐨𐐹𐑊 𐐱𐑂 𐐤𐐨𐑁𐐴, 𐐰𐑁𐐻𐐲𐑉 𐑄 𐐼𐐯𐑃 𐐱𐑂 𐐤𐐨𐑁𐐴:—𐐤𐐵, 𐑋𐐴 𐐺𐐨𐑊𐐲𐑂𐐯𐐼 𐐺𐑉𐐯𐑄𐑉𐐯𐑌, 𐐌, 𐐖𐐩𐐿𐐲𐐺, 𐐰𐐿𐐫𐑉𐐼𐐮𐑍 𐐻𐐭 𐑄 𐑉𐐨𐑅𐐹𐐱𐑌𐑅𐐮𐐺𐐮𐑊𐐮𐐻𐐨 𐐸𐐶𐐮𐐽 𐐌 𐐰𐑋 𐐲𐑌𐐼𐐲𐑉 𐐻𐐭 𐐘𐐱𐐼, 𐐻𐐭 𐑋𐐰𐑀𐑌𐐮𐑁𐐴 𐑋𐐴𐑌 𐐱𐑁𐐮𐑅 𐐶𐐮𐑄 𐑅𐐬𐐺𐐲𐑉𐑌𐐯𐑅. 𐐈𐑌𐐼 𐑄𐐰𐐻 𐐌 𐑋𐐴𐐻 𐑉𐐮𐐼 𐑋𐐴 𐑀𐐪𐑉𐑋𐐲𐑌𐐻𐑅 𐐱𐑂 𐐷𐐫𐑉 𐑅𐐮𐑌𐑆, 𐐌 𐐿𐐲𐑋 𐐲𐐹 𐐮𐑌𐐻𐐭 𐑄 𐐻𐐯𐑋𐐹𐑊 𐑄𐐮𐑅 𐐼𐐩, 𐑄𐐰𐐻 𐐌 𐑋𐐴𐐻 𐐼𐐨𐐿𐑊𐐩𐑉 𐐲𐑌𐐻𐐭 𐐷𐐭 𐑄 𐐶𐐲𐑉𐐼 𐐱𐑂 𐐘𐐱𐐼; 𐐰𐑌𐐼 𐐷𐐨 𐐷𐐫𐑉𐑅𐐯𐑊𐑂𐑆 𐑌𐐬, 𐑄𐐰𐐻 𐐌 𐐸𐐰𐑂 𐐸𐐮𐑄𐐲𐑉𐐻𐐭 𐐺𐐨𐑌 𐐼𐐮𐑊𐐮𐐾𐐯𐑌𐐻 𐐮𐑌 𐑄 𐐱𐑁𐐮𐑅 𐐱𐑂 𐑋𐐴 𐐿𐐫𐑊𐐮𐑍; 𐐺𐐲𐐻 𐐌 𐑄𐐮𐑅 𐐼𐐩 𐐰𐑋 𐐶𐐩𐐼 𐐼𐐵𐑌 𐐶𐐮𐑄 𐑋𐐲𐐽 𐑋𐐬𐑉 𐐼𐐨𐑆𐐴𐑉 𐐰𐑌𐐼 𐐰𐑍𐑆𐐴𐐲𐐻𐐨 𐑁𐐫𐑉 𐑄 𐐶𐐯𐑊𐑁𐐩𐑉 𐐱𐑂 𐐷𐐫𐑉 𐑅𐐬𐑊𐑆 𐑄𐐰𐑌 𐐌 𐐸𐐰𐑂 𐐸𐐮𐑄𐐲𐑉𐐻𐐭 𐐺𐐨𐑌. 𐐙𐐫𐑉 𐐺𐐨𐐸𐐬𐑊𐐼, 𐐰𐑆 𐐷𐐯𐐻, 𐐷𐐨 𐐸𐐰𐑂 𐐺𐐨𐑌 𐐬𐐺𐐨𐐼𐐨𐐯𐑌𐐻 𐐲𐑌𐐻𐐭 𐑄 𐐶𐐲𐑉𐐼 𐐱𐑂 𐑄 𐐢𐐫𐑉𐐼, 𐐸𐐶𐐮𐐽 𐐌 𐐸𐐰𐑂 𐑀𐐮𐑂𐐲𐑌 𐐲𐑌𐐻𐐭 𐐷𐐭. 𐐒𐐲𐐻 𐐺𐐨𐐸𐐬𐑊𐐼, 𐐸𐐪𐑉𐐿𐐲𐑌 𐐷𐐨 𐐲𐑌𐐻𐐭 𐑋𐐨, 𐐰𐑌𐐼 𐑌𐐬 𐑄𐐰𐐻 𐐺𐐴 𐑄 𐐸𐐯𐑊𐐹 𐐱𐑂 𐑄 𐐫𐑊-𐐹𐐵𐐲𐑉𐑁𐐳𐑊 𐐗𐑉𐐨𐐩𐐻𐐲𐑉 𐐱𐑂 𐐸𐐯𐑂𐐲𐑌 𐐰𐑌𐐼 𐐲𐑉𐑃, 𐐌 𐐿𐐰𐑌 𐐻𐐯𐑊 𐐷𐐭 𐐿𐐱𐑌𐑅𐐲𐑉𐑌𐐮𐑍 𐐷𐐫𐑉 𐑃𐐫𐐻𐑅, 𐐸𐐵 𐑄𐐰𐐻 𐐷𐐨 𐐪𐑉 𐐺𐐨𐑀𐐮𐑌𐐮𐑍 𐐻𐐭 𐑊𐐩𐐺𐐲𐑉 𐐮𐑌 𐑅𐐮𐑌, 𐐸𐐶𐐮𐐽 𐑅𐐮𐑌 𐐰𐐹𐐨𐑉𐐯𐑃 𐑂𐐯𐑉𐐨 𐐰𐐺𐐱𐑋𐐮𐑌𐐲𐐺𐑊 𐐲𐑌𐐻𐐭 𐑋𐐨; 𐐷𐐩, 𐐰𐑌𐐼 𐐰𐐺𐐱𐑋𐐮𐑌𐐲𐐺𐑊 𐐲𐑌𐐻𐐭 𐐘𐐱𐐼; 𐐷𐐩, 𐐮𐐻 𐑀𐑉𐐨𐑂𐐯𐑃 𐑋𐐴 𐑅𐐬𐑊 𐐰𐑌𐐼 𐐿𐐫𐑆𐐯𐑃 𐑋𐐨 𐐻𐐭 𐑇𐑉𐐮𐑍𐐿 𐐶𐐮𐑄 𐑇𐐩𐑋 𐐺𐐨𐑁𐐬𐑉 𐑄 𐐹𐑉𐐯𐑆𐐯𐑌𐑅 𐐱𐑂 𐑋𐐴 𐐣𐐩𐐿𐐲𐑉, 𐑄𐐰𐐻 𐐌 𐑋𐐲𐑅𐐻 𐐻𐐯𐑅𐐻𐐮𐑁𐐴 𐐲𐑌𐐻𐐭 𐐷𐐭 𐐿𐐱𐑌𐑅𐐲𐑉𐑌𐐮𐑍 𐑄 𐐶𐐮𐐿𐐯𐐼𐑌𐐯𐑅 𐐱𐑂 𐐷𐐫𐑉 𐐸𐐪𐑉𐐻𐑅; 𐐰𐑌𐐼 𐐫𐑊𐑅𐐬 𐐮𐐻 𐑀𐑉𐐨𐑂𐐯𐑃 𐑋𐐨 𐑄𐐰𐐻 𐐌 𐑋𐐲𐑅𐐻 𐐷𐐭𐑆 𐑅𐐬 𐑋𐐲𐐽 𐐺𐐬𐑊𐐼𐑌𐐯𐑅 𐐱𐑂 𐑅𐐹𐐨𐐽 𐐿𐐱𐑌𐑅𐐲𐑉𐑌𐐮𐑍 𐐷𐐭, 𐐺𐐨𐑁𐐬𐑉 𐐷𐐫𐑉 𐐶𐐴𐑂𐑆 𐐰𐑌𐐼 𐐷𐐫𐑉 𐐽𐐮𐑊𐐼𐑉𐐯𐑌, 𐑋𐐯𐑌𐐨 𐐱𐑂 𐐸𐐭𐑆 𐑁𐐨𐑊𐐮𐑍𐑆 𐐪𐑉 𐐯𐐿𐑅𐐨𐐼𐐮𐑍𐑊𐐨 𐐻𐐯𐑌𐐼𐐲𐑉 𐐰𐑌𐐼

𐐽𐐩𐑅𐐻, 𐐰𐑌𐐼 𐐼𐐯𐑊𐐮𐐿𐐩𐐻 𐐺𐐨𐑁𐐬𐑉 𐐘𐐱𐐼, 𐐸𐐶𐐮𐐽 𐑃𐐮𐑍 𐐮𐑆 𐐹𐑊𐐨𐑆𐐮𐑍 𐐲𐑌𐐻𐐭 𐐘𐐱𐐼; 𐐰𐑌𐐼 𐐮𐐻 𐑅𐐲𐐹𐐬𐑆𐐯𐑃 𐑋𐐨 𐑄𐐰𐐻 𐑄𐐩 𐐸𐐰𐑂 𐐿𐐲𐑋 𐐲𐐹 𐐸𐐮𐑄𐐲𐑉 𐐻𐐭 𐐸𐐨𐑉 𐑄 𐐹𐑊𐐨𐑆𐐮𐑍 𐐶𐐲𐑉𐐼 𐐱𐑂 𐐘𐐱𐐼, 𐐷𐐩, 𐑄 𐐶𐐲𐑉𐐼 𐐸𐐶𐐮𐐽 𐐸𐐨𐑊𐐯𐑃 𐑄 𐐶𐐭𐑌𐐼𐐯𐐼 𐑅𐐬𐑊.

2. 𐐐𐐶𐐯𐑉𐑁𐐬𐑉, 𐐮𐐻 𐐺𐐲𐑉𐐼𐐯𐑌𐐯𐑃 𐑋𐐴 𐑅𐐬𐑊, 𐑄𐐰𐐻 𐐌 𐑇𐐳𐐼 𐐺𐐨 𐐿𐐱𐑌𐑅𐐻𐑉𐐩𐑌𐐼, 𐐺𐐨𐐿𐐫𐑆 𐐱𐑂 𐑄 𐑅𐐻𐑉𐐮𐐿𐐻 𐐿𐐱𐑋𐐰𐑌𐐼𐑋𐐯𐑌𐐻 𐐸𐐶𐐮𐐽 𐐌 𐐸𐐰𐑂 𐑉𐐨𐑅𐐨𐑂𐐼 𐑁𐑉𐐱𐑋 𐐘𐐱𐐼, 𐐻𐐭 𐐰𐐼𐑋𐐱𐑌𐐮𐑇 𐐷𐐭 𐐰𐐿𐐫𐑉𐐼𐐮𐑍 𐐻𐐭 𐐷𐐭𐑉 𐐿𐑉𐐴𐑋𐑆, 𐐻𐐭 𐐯𐑌𐑊𐐪𐑉𐐾 𐑄 𐐶𐐭𐑌𐐼𐑆 𐐱𐑂 𐑄𐐬𐑆 𐐸𐐭 𐐪𐑉 𐐫𐑊𐑉𐐯𐐼𐐨 𐐶𐐭𐑌𐐼𐐯𐐼, 𐐮𐑌𐑅𐐻𐐯𐐼 𐐱𐑂 𐐿𐐱𐑌𐑅𐐬𐑊𐐮𐑍 𐐰𐑌𐐼 𐐸𐐨𐑊𐐮𐑍 𐑄𐐩𐑉 𐐶𐐭𐑌𐐼𐑆; 𐐰𐑌𐐼 𐑄𐐬𐑆 𐐸𐐭 𐐸𐐰𐑂 𐑌𐐱𐐻 𐐺𐐮𐑌 𐐶𐐭𐑌𐐼𐐯𐐼, 𐐮𐑌𐑅𐐻𐐯𐐼 𐐱𐑂 𐑁𐐨𐑅𐐻𐐮𐑍 𐐲𐐹𐐱𐑌 𐑄 𐐹𐑊𐐨𐑆𐐮𐑍 𐐶𐐲𐑉𐐼 𐐱𐑂 𐐘𐐱𐐼, 𐐸𐐰𐑂 𐐼𐐰𐑀𐐲𐑉𐑆 𐐹𐑊𐐩𐑅𐐻 𐐻𐐭 𐐹𐐨𐑉𐑅 𐑄𐐩𐑉 𐑅𐐬𐑊𐑆, 𐐰𐑌𐐼 𐐶𐐭𐑌𐐼 𐑄𐐩𐑉 𐐼𐐯𐑊𐐮𐐿𐐩𐐻 𐑋𐐴𐑌𐐼𐑆. 𐐒𐐲𐐻, 𐑌𐐱𐐻𐐶𐐮𐑄𐑅𐐻𐐰𐑌𐐼𐐮𐑍 𐑄 𐑀𐑉𐐩𐐻𐑌𐐯𐑅 𐐱𐑂 𐑄 𐐻𐐰𐑅𐐿, 𐐌 𐑋𐐲𐑅𐐻 𐐼𐐭 𐐰𐐿𐐫𐑉𐐼𐐮𐑍 𐐻𐐭 𐑄 𐑅𐐻𐑉𐐮𐐿𐐻 𐐿𐐱𐑋𐐰𐑌𐐼𐑆 𐐱𐑂 𐐘𐐱𐐼, 𐐰𐑌𐐼 𐐻𐐯𐑊 𐐷𐐭 𐐿𐐱𐑌𐑅𐐲𐑉𐑌𐐮𐑍 𐐷𐐭𐑉 𐐶𐐮𐐿𐐯𐐼𐑌𐐯𐑅 𐐰𐑌𐐼 𐐰𐐺𐐱𐑋𐐮𐑌𐐩𐑇𐐲𐑌𐑆, 𐐮𐑌 𐑄 𐐹𐑉𐐯𐑆𐐯𐑌𐑅 𐐱𐑂 𐑄 𐐹𐐷𐐭𐑉 𐐮𐑌 𐐸𐐪𐑉𐐻, 𐐰𐑌𐐼 𐑄 𐐺𐑉𐐬𐐿𐐯𐑌 𐐸𐐪𐑉𐐻, 𐐰𐑌𐐼 𐐲𐑌𐐼𐐲𐑉 𐑄 𐑀𐑊𐐰𐑌𐑅 𐐱𐑂 𐑄 𐐹𐐨𐑉𐑅𐐮𐑍 𐐴 𐐱𐑂 𐑄 𐐈𐑊𐑋𐐴𐐻𐐨 𐐘𐐱𐐼.

3. 𐐐𐐶𐐯𐑉𐑁𐐬𐑉, 𐐌 𐑋𐐲𐑅𐐻 𐐻𐐯𐑊 𐐷𐐭 𐑄 𐐻𐑉𐐭𐑃 𐐰𐐿𐐫𐑉𐐼𐐮𐑍 𐐻𐐭 𐑄 𐐹𐑊𐐩𐑌𐑌𐐯𐑅 𐐱𐑂 𐑄 𐐶𐐲𐑉𐐼 𐐱𐑂 𐐘𐐱𐐼. 𐐙𐐫𐑉 𐐺𐐨𐐸𐐬𐑊𐐼, 𐐰𐑆 𐐌 𐐮𐑌𐐿𐐶𐐴𐑉𐐼 𐐱𐑂 𐑄 𐐢𐐫𐑉𐐼, 𐑄𐐲𐑅 𐐿𐐩𐑋 𐑄 𐐶𐐲𐑉𐐼 𐐲𐑌𐐻𐐭 𐑋𐐨, 𐑅𐐩𐐮𐑍, 𐐖𐐩𐐿𐐲𐐺, 𐑀𐐯𐐻 𐑄𐐵 𐐲𐐹 𐐮𐑌𐐻𐐭 𐑄 𐐻𐐯𐑋𐐹𐑊 𐐱𐑌 𐑄 𐑋𐐱𐑉𐐬, 𐐰𐑌𐐼 𐐼𐐨𐐿𐑊𐐩𐑉 𐑄 𐐶𐐲𐑉𐐼 𐐸𐐶𐐮𐐽 𐐌 𐑇𐐰𐑊 𐑀𐐮𐑂 𐑄𐐨 𐐲𐑌𐐻𐐭 𐑄𐐮𐑅 𐐹𐐨𐐹𐑊.

4. 𐐈𐑌𐐼 𐑌𐐵, 𐐺𐐨𐐸𐐬𐑊𐐼, 𐑋𐐴 𐐺𐑉𐐯𐑄𐑉𐐯𐑌, 𐑄𐐮𐑅 𐐮𐑆 𐑄 𐐶𐐲𐑉𐐼 𐐸𐐶𐐮𐐽 𐐌 𐐼𐐨𐐿𐑊𐐩𐑉 𐐲𐑌𐐻𐐭 𐐷𐐭, 𐑄𐐰𐐻 𐑋𐐯𐑌𐐨 𐐱𐑂 𐐷𐐭 𐐸𐐰𐑂 𐐺𐐨𐑀𐐲𐑌 𐐻𐐭 𐑅𐐲𐑉𐐽 𐑁𐐫𐑉 𐑀𐐬𐑊𐐼, 𐐰𐑌𐐼 𐑁𐐫𐑉 𐑅𐐮𐑊𐑂𐐲𐑉, 𐐰𐑌𐐼 𐑁𐐫𐑉 𐐫𐑊 𐑋𐐰𐑌𐐲𐑉 𐐱𐑂 𐐹𐑉𐐯𐑇𐐲𐑅 𐐬𐑉𐑆, 𐐮𐑌 𐑄 𐐸𐐶𐐮𐐽 𐑄𐐮𐑅 𐑊𐐰𐑌𐐼, 𐐸𐐶𐐮𐐽 𐐮𐑆 𐐩 𐑊𐐰𐑌𐐼 𐐱𐑂 𐐹𐑉𐐱𐑋𐐮𐑅 𐐲𐑌𐐻𐐭 𐐷𐐭, 𐐰𐑌𐐼 𐐻𐐭 𐐷𐐭𐑉 𐑅𐐨𐐼, 𐐼𐐲𐑃 𐐰𐐺𐐵𐑌𐐼 𐑋𐐬𐑅𐐻 𐐹𐑊𐐯𐑌𐐻𐐮𐑁𐐳𐑊𐐨. 𐐈𐑌𐐼 𐑄 𐐸𐐰𐑌𐐼 𐐱𐑂 𐐹𐑉𐐱𐑂𐐮𐐼𐐯𐑌𐑅 𐐸𐐰𐑃 𐑅𐑋𐐴𐑊𐐼 𐐲𐐹𐐱𐑌 𐐷𐐭 𐑋𐐬𐑅𐐻 𐐹𐑊𐐨𐑆𐐮𐑍𐑊𐐨, 𐑄𐐰𐐻 𐐷𐐭 𐐸𐐰𐑂 𐐱𐐺𐐻𐐩𐑌𐐼 𐑋𐐯𐑌𐐨 𐑉𐐮𐐽𐐯𐑆; 𐐰𐑌𐐼 𐐺𐐨𐐿𐐫𐑆 𐑅𐐲𐑋 𐐱𐑂 𐐷𐐭 𐐸𐐰𐑂 𐐱𐐺𐐻𐐩𐑌𐐼 𐑋𐐬𐑉 𐐰𐐺𐐲𐑌𐐼𐐰𐑌𐐻𐑊𐐨 𐑄𐐰𐑌 𐑄𐐰𐐻 𐐱𐑂 𐐷𐐭𐑉 𐐺𐑉𐐯𐑄𐑉𐐯𐑌, 𐐷𐐨 𐐪𐑉 𐑊𐐮𐑁𐐻𐐯𐐼 𐐲𐐹 𐐮𐑌 𐑄 𐐹𐑉𐐴𐐼 𐐱𐑂 𐐷𐐭𐑉 𐐸𐐪𐑉𐐻𐑅, 𐐰𐑌𐐼 𐐶𐐩𐑉 𐑅𐐻𐐮𐑁 𐑌𐐯𐐿𐑅 𐐰𐑌𐐼 𐐸𐐴 𐐸𐐯𐐼𐑆, 𐐺𐐨𐐿𐐫𐑆 𐐱𐑂 𐑄 𐐿𐐱𐑅𐐻𐑊𐐨𐑌𐐯𐑅 𐐱𐑂 𐐷𐐭𐑉 𐐰𐐹𐐰𐑉𐐯𐑊, 𐐰𐑌𐐼 𐐹𐐲𐑉𐑅𐐨𐐿𐐷𐐭𐐻 𐐷𐐭𐑉 𐐺𐑉𐐯𐑄𐑉𐐯𐑌 𐐺𐐨𐐿𐐫𐑆 𐐷𐐨 𐑅𐐲𐐹𐐬𐑆 𐑄𐐰𐐻 𐐷𐐨 𐐪𐑉 𐐺𐐯𐐻𐐲𐑉 𐑄𐐰𐑌 𐑄𐐩.

5. 𐐈𐑌𐐼 𐑌𐐵, 𐑋𐐴 𐐺𐑉𐐯𐑄𐑉𐐯𐑌, 𐐼𐐭 𐐷𐐨 𐑅𐐲𐐹𐐬𐑆 𐑄𐐰𐐻 𐐘𐐱𐐼 𐐾𐐲𐑅𐐻𐐮𐑁𐐴𐐯𐑃 𐐷𐐭 𐐮𐑌 𐑄𐐮𐑅 𐑃𐐮𐑍? 𐐒𐐨𐐸𐐬𐑊𐐼 𐐌 𐑅𐐩 𐐲𐑌𐐻𐐭 𐐷𐐭, 𐑌𐐩. 𐐒𐐲𐐻 𐐸𐐨 𐐿𐐱𐑌𐐼𐐯𐑋𐐯𐑃 𐐷𐐭, 𐐰𐑌𐐼 𐐮𐑁 𐐷𐐨 𐐹𐐲𐑉𐑅𐐮𐑅𐐻 𐐮𐑌 𐑄𐐨𐑆 𐑃𐐮𐑍𐑆, 𐐸𐐮𐑆 𐐾𐐲𐐾𐑋𐐯𐑌𐐻𐑅 𐑋𐐲𐑅𐐻 𐑅𐐹𐐨𐐼𐐮𐑊𐐨 𐐿𐐲𐑋 𐐲𐑌𐐻𐐭 𐐷𐐭. 𐐄 𐑄𐐰𐐻 𐐸𐐨 𐐶𐐳𐐼 𐑇𐐬 𐐷𐐭 𐑄𐐰𐐻 𐐸𐐨 𐐿𐐰𐑌 𐐹𐐨𐑉𐑅 𐐷𐐭, 𐐰𐑌𐐼 𐐶𐐮𐑄 𐐶𐐲𐑌 𐑀𐑊𐐰𐑌𐑅 𐐱𐑂 𐐸𐐮𐑆 𐐴 𐐸𐐨 𐐿𐐰𐑌 𐑅𐑋𐐴𐐻 𐐷𐐭 𐐻𐐭 𐑄 𐐼𐐲𐑅𐐻. 𐐄 𐑄𐐰𐐻 𐐸𐐨 𐐶𐐳𐐼 𐑉𐐮𐐼 𐐷𐐭 𐑁𐑉𐐱𐑋 𐑄𐐮𐑅 𐐮𐑌𐐮𐐿𐐶𐐮𐐻𐐨 𐐰𐑌𐐼 𐐰𐐺𐐱𐑋𐐮𐑌𐐩𐑇𐐲𐑌. 𐐈𐑌𐐼, 𐐄 𐑄𐐰𐐻 𐐷𐐨 𐐶𐐳𐐼 𐑊𐐮𐑅𐐯𐑌 𐐲𐑌𐐻𐐭 𐑄 𐐶𐐲𐑉𐐼 𐐱𐑂 𐐸𐐮𐑆 𐐿𐐱𐑋𐐰𐑌𐐼𐑆, 𐐰𐑌𐐼 𐑊𐐯𐐻 𐑌𐐱𐐻 𐑄𐐮𐑅 𐐹𐑉𐐴𐐼 𐐱𐑂 𐐷𐐭𐑉 𐐸𐐪𐑉𐐻𐑅 𐐼𐐨𐑅𐐻𐑉𐑎 𐐷𐐭𐑉 𐑅𐐬𐑊𐑆. 𐐛𐐮𐑍𐐿 𐐱𐑂 𐐷𐐭𐑉 𐐺𐑉𐐯𐑄𐑉𐐯𐑌 𐑊𐐴𐐿 𐐲𐑌𐐻𐐭 𐐷𐐭𐑉𐑅𐐯𐑊𐑂𐑆, 𐐰𐑌𐐼 𐐺𐐨 𐑁𐐲𐑋𐐮𐑊𐐷𐐲𐑉 𐐶𐐮𐑄 𐐫𐑊, 𐐰𐑌𐐼 𐑁𐑉𐐨 𐐶𐐮𐑄 𐐷𐐭𐑉 𐑅𐐲𐐺𐑅𐐻𐐰𐑌𐑅, 𐑄𐐰𐐻 𐑄𐐩 𐑋𐐩 𐐺𐐨 𐑉𐐮𐐽 𐑊𐐴𐐿 𐐲𐑌𐐻𐐭 𐐷𐐭. 𐐒𐐲𐐻 𐐺𐐨𐑁𐐬𐑉 𐐷𐐨 𐑅𐐨𐐿 𐑁𐐫𐑉 𐑉𐐮𐐽𐐯𐑆, 𐑅𐐨𐐿 𐐷𐐨 𐑁𐐫𐑉 𐑄 𐐿𐐮𐑍𐐼𐐲𐑋 𐐱𐑂 𐐘𐐱𐐼. 𐐈𐑌𐐼 𐐰𐑁𐐻𐐲𐑉 𐐷𐐨 𐐸𐐰𐑂 𐐱𐐺𐐻𐐩𐑌𐐼 𐐩 𐐸𐐬𐐹 𐐮𐑌 𐐗𐑉𐐴𐑅𐐻, 𐐷𐐨 𐑇𐐰𐑊 𐐱𐐺𐐻𐐩𐑌 𐑉𐐮𐐽𐐯𐑆, 𐐮𐑁 𐐷𐐨 𐑅𐐨𐐿 𐑄𐐯𐑋; 𐐰𐑌𐐼 𐐷𐐨 𐐶𐐮𐑊 𐑅𐐨𐐿 𐑄𐐯𐑋 𐑁𐐫𐑉 𐑄 𐐮𐑌𐐻𐐯𐑌𐐻 𐐻𐐭 𐐼𐐭 𐑀𐐳𐐼; 𐐻𐐭 𐐿𐑊𐐬𐑄 𐑄 𐑌𐐩𐐿𐐯𐐼, 𐐰𐑌𐐼 𐐻𐐭 𐑁𐐨𐐼 𐑄 𐐸𐐲𐑍𐑀𐑉𐐨, 𐐰𐑌𐐼 𐐻𐐭 𐑊𐐮𐐺𐐲𐑉𐐩𐐻 𐑄 𐐿𐐰𐐹𐐻𐐮𐑂, 𐐰𐑌𐐼 𐐰𐐼𐑋𐐮𐑌𐐮𐑅𐐻𐐲𐑉 𐑉𐐨𐑊𐐨𐑁 𐐻𐐭 𐑄 𐑅𐐮𐐿, 𐐰𐑌𐐼 𐑄 𐐰𐑁𐑊𐐮𐐿𐐻𐐯𐐼.

6. 𐐈𐑌𐐼 𐑌𐐵, 𐑋𐐴 𐐺𐑉𐐯𐑄𐑉𐐯𐑌, 𐐌 𐐸𐐰𐑂 𐑅𐐹𐐬𐐿𐐯𐑌 𐐲𐑌𐐻𐐭 𐐷𐐭 𐐿𐐱𐑌𐑅𐐲𐑉𐑌𐐮𐑍 𐐹𐑉𐐴𐐼; 𐐰𐑌𐐼 𐑄𐐬𐑆 𐐱𐑂 𐐷𐐭 𐐸𐐶𐐮𐐽 𐐸𐐰𐑂 𐐰𐑁𐑊𐐮𐐿𐐻𐐯𐐼 𐐷𐐭𐑉 𐑌𐐩𐐺𐐲𐑉 𐐰𐑌𐐼 𐐹𐐲𐑉𐑅𐐨𐐿𐐷𐐭𐐻𐐯𐐼 𐐸𐐮𐑋 𐐺𐐨𐐿𐐫𐑆 𐐷𐐨 𐐶𐐲𐑉 𐐹𐑉𐐵𐐼 𐐮𐑌 𐐷𐐭𐑉 𐐸𐐪𐑉𐐻𐑅, 𐐱𐑂 𐑄 𐑃𐐮𐑍𐑆 𐐸𐐶𐐮𐐽 𐐘𐐱𐐼 𐐸𐐰𐑃 𐑀𐐮𐑂𐐯𐑌 𐐷𐐭, 𐐸𐐶𐐱𐐻 𐑅𐐩 𐐷𐐨 𐐱𐑂 𐐮𐐻? 𐐔𐐭 𐐷𐐨 𐑌𐐱𐐻 𐑅𐐲𐐹𐐬𐑆 𐑄𐐰𐐻 𐑅𐐲𐐽 𐑃𐐮𐑍𐑆 𐐪𐑉 𐐰𐐺𐐱𐑋𐐮𐑌𐐲𐐺𐑊 𐐲𐑌𐐻𐐭 𐐸𐐮𐑋 𐐸𐐭 𐐿𐑉𐐨𐐩𐐻𐐯𐐼 𐐫𐑊 𐑁𐑊𐐯𐑇? 𐐈𐑌𐐼 𐑄 𐐶𐐲𐑌 𐐺𐐨𐐮𐑍 𐐮𐑆 𐐰𐑆 𐐹𐑉𐐯𐑇𐐲𐑅 𐐮𐑌 𐐸𐐮𐑆 𐑅𐐴𐐻 𐐰𐑆 𐑄 𐐲𐑄𐐲𐑉; 𐐰𐑌𐐼 𐐫𐑊 𐑁𐑊𐐯𐑇 𐐮𐑆 𐐱𐑂 𐑄 𐐼𐐲𐑅𐐻; 𐐰𐑌𐐼 𐑁𐐫𐑉 𐑄 𐑅𐐯𐑊𐑁-𐑅𐐩𐑋

𐐯𐑌𐐼 𐐸𐐰𐑃 𐐸𐐨 𐐿𐑉𐐨𐐩𐐻𐐯𐐼 𐑄𐐯𐑋, 𐑄𐐰𐐻 𐑄𐐩 𐑇𐐳𐐼 𐐿𐐨𐐹 𐐸𐐮𐑆 𐐿𐐱𐑋𐐰𐑌𐐼𐑋𐐯𐑌𐐻𐑅, 𐐰𐑌𐐼 𐑀𐑊𐐬𐑉𐐮𐑁𐐴 𐐸𐐮𐑋 𐑁𐐫𐑉𐐯𐑂𐐲𐑉. 𐐈𐑌𐐼 𐑌𐐵 𐐌 𐑋𐐩𐐿 𐐰𐑌 𐐯𐑌𐐼 𐐱𐑂 𐑅𐐹𐐨𐐿𐐮𐑍 𐐲𐑌𐐻𐐭 𐐷𐐭 𐐿𐐲𐑌𐑅𐐲𐑉𐑌𐐮𐑍 𐑄𐐮𐑅 𐐹𐑉𐐴𐐼. 𐐈𐑌𐐼 𐐶𐐲𐑉 𐐮𐐻 𐑌𐐱𐐻 𐑄𐐰𐐻 𐐌 𐑋𐐲𐑅𐐻 𐑅𐐹𐐨𐐿 𐐲𐑌𐐻𐐭 𐐷𐐭 𐐿𐐲𐑌𐑅𐐲𐑉𐑌𐐮𐑍 𐐰 𐑀𐑉𐐬𐑅𐐲𐑉 𐐿𐑉𐐴𐑋, 𐑋𐐴 𐐸𐐪𐑉𐐻 𐐶𐐳𐐼 𐑉𐐨𐐾𐐱𐐮𐑅 𐐯𐐿𐑅𐐨𐐼𐐮𐑍𐑊𐐨, 𐐺𐐨𐐿𐐫𐑆 𐐱𐑂 𐐷𐐭. 𐐒𐐲𐐻 𐑄 𐐶𐐲𐑉𐐼 𐐱𐑂 𐐘𐐱𐐼 𐐺𐐲𐑉𐐼𐐲𐑌𐑆 𐑋𐐨 𐐺𐐨𐐿𐐫𐑆 𐐱𐑂 𐐷𐐭𐑉 𐑀𐑉𐐬𐑅𐐲𐑉 𐐿𐑉𐐴𐑋𐑆. 𐐙𐐫𐑉 𐐺𐐨𐐸𐐬𐑊𐐼, 𐑄𐐲𐑅 𐑅𐐯𐑃 𐑄 𐐢𐐫𐑉𐐼, 𐑄𐐮𐑅 𐐹𐐨𐐹𐐲𐑊 𐐺𐐨𐑀𐐮𐑌 𐐻𐐭 𐐶𐐰𐐿𐑅 𐐮𐑌 𐐮𐑌𐐮𐐿𐐶𐐮𐐻𐐨; 𐑄𐐩 𐐲𐑌𐐼𐐲𐑉𐑅𐐻𐐰𐑌𐐼 𐑌𐐱𐐻 𐑄 𐑅𐐿𐑉𐐮𐐹𐐽𐐲𐑉𐑆; 𐑁𐐫𐑉 𐑄𐐩 𐑅𐐨𐐿 𐐻𐐭 𐐯𐐿𐑅𐐿𐐷𐐭𐑆 𐑄𐐯𐑋𐑅𐐯𐑊𐑂𐑆 𐐮𐑌 𐐿𐐲𐑋𐐮𐐻𐐮𐑍 𐐸𐐫𐑉𐐼𐐲𐑋𐑆, 𐐺𐐨𐐿𐐫𐑆 𐐱𐑂 𐑄 𐑃𐐮𐑍𐑆 𐐸𐐶𐐮𐐽 𐐶𐐲𐑉 𐑉𐐮𐐻𐐲𐑌 𐐿𐐲𐑌𐑅𐐲𐑉𐑌𐐮𐑍 𐐔𐐩𐑂𐐮𐐼, 𐐰𐑌𐐼 𐐝𐐱𐑊𐐬𐑋𐐲𐑌 𐐸𐐮𐑆 𐑅𐐲𐑌. 𐐒𐐨𐐸𐐬𐑊𐐼, 𐐔𐐩𐑂𐐮𐐼 𐐰𐑌𐐼 𐐝𐐱𐑊𐐬𐑋𐐲𐑌 𐐻𐑉𐐭𐑊𐐨 𐐸𐐰𐐼 𐑋𐐯𐑌𐐨 𐐶𐐴𐑂𐑆 𐐰𐑌𐐼 𐐿𐐱𐑍𐐿𐐷𐐭𐐺𐐴𐑌𐑆, 𐐸𐐶𐐮𐐽 𐑃𐐮𐑍 𐐶𐐱𐑆 𐐰𐐺𐐱𐑋𐐮𐑌𐐲𐐺𐐲𐑊 𐐺𐐨𐑁𐐫𐑉 𐑋𐐨, 𐑅𐐯𐑃 𐑄 𐐢𐐫𐑉𐐼; 𐐸𐐶𐐯𐑉𐑁𐐫𐑉, 𐑄𐐲𐑅 𐑅𐐯𐑃 𐑄 𐐢𐐫𐑉𐐼, 𐐌 𐐸𐐰𐑂 𐑊𐐯𐐼 𐑄𐐮𐑅 𐐹𐐨𐐹𐐲𐑊 𐑁𐐫𐑉𐑃 𐐵𐐻 𐐱𐑂 𐑄 𐑊𐐰𐑌𐐼 𐐱𐑂 𐐖𐐯𐑉𐐭𐑅𐐲𐑊𐐲𐑋, 𐐺𐐴 𐑄 𐐹𐐵𐐲𐑉 𐐱𐑂 𐑋𐐴𐑌 𐐪𐑉𐑋, 𐑄𐐰𐐻 𐐌 𐑋𐐴𐐻 𐑉𐐩𐑆 𐐲𐐹 𐐲𐑌𐐻𐐭 𐑋𐐨 𐐰 𐑉𐐴𐐽𐐲𐑅 𐐺𐑉𐐰𐑌𐐽 𐑁𐑉𐐱𐑋 𐑄 𐑁𐑉𐐭𐐻 𐐱𐑂 𐑄 𐑊𐐬𐐮𐑌𐑆 𐐱𐑂 𐐖𐐬𐑆𐐯𐑁. 𐐐𐐶𐐯𐑉𐑁𐐫𐑉, 𐐌 𐑄 𐐢𐐫𐑉𐐼 𐐘𐐱𐐼 𐐶𐐮𐑊 𐑌𐐱𐐻 𐑅𐐲𐑁𐐲𐑉 𐑄𐐰𐐻 𐑄𐐮𐑅 𐐹𐐨𐐹𐐲𐑊 𐑇𐐰𐑊 𐐼𐐭 𐑊𐐴𐐿 𐐲𐑌𐐻𐐭 𐑄𐐯𐑋 𐐱𐑂 𐐬𐑊𐐼. 𐐐𐐶𐐯𐑉𐑁𐐫𐑉, 𐑋𐐴 𐐺𐑉𐐯𐑄𐑉𐐯𐑌, 𐐸𐐨𐑉 𐑋𐐨, 𐐰𐑌𐐼 𐐸𐐲𐑉𐐿𐐲𐑌 𐐻𐐭 𐑄 𐐶𐐲𐑉𐐼 𐐱𐑂 𐑄 𐐢𐐫𐑉𐐼; 𐑁𐐫𐑉 𐑄𐐯𐑉 𐑇𐐰𐑊 𐑌𐐱𐐻 𐐯𐑌𐐨 𐑋𐐰𐑌 𐐰𐑋𐐲𐑍 𐐷𐐭 𐐸𐐰𐑂 𐑅𐐩𐑂 𐐮𐐻 𐐺𐐨 𐐶𐐲𐑌 𐐶𐐴𐑁; 𐐰𐑌𐐼 𐐿𐐱𐑍𐐿𐐷𐐭𐐺𐐴𐑌𐑆 𐐸𐐨 𐑇𐐰𐑊 𐐸𐐰𐑂 𐑌𐐲𐑌; 𐑁𐐫𐑉 𐐌, 𐑄 𐐢𐐫𐑉𐐼 𐐘𐐱𐐼, 𐐼𐐨𐑊𐐴𐐻𐐯𐑃 𐐮𐑌 𐑄 𐐽𐐰𐑅𐐻𐐮𐐻𐐨 𐐱𐑂 𐐶𐐮𐑋𐐯𐑌. 𐐈𐑌𐐼 𐐸𐐫𐑉𐐼𐐲𐑋𐑆 𐐪𐑉 𐐰𐑌 𐐰𐐺𐐱𐑋𐐮𐑌𐐩𐑇𐐲𐑌 𐐺𐐨𐑁𐐫𐑉 𐑋𐐨; 𐑄𐐲𐑅 𐑅𐐯𐑃 𐑄 𐐢𐐫𐑉𐐼 𐐱𐑂 𐐐𐐬𐑅𐐻𐑅. 𐐐𐐶𐐯𐑉𐑁𐐫𐑉, 𐑄𐐮𐑅 𐐹𐐨𐐹𐐲𐑊 𐑇𐐰𐑊 𐐿𐐨𐐹 𐑋𐐴 𐐿𐐱𐑋𐐰𐑌𐐼𐑋𐐯𐑌𐐻𐑅, 𐑅𐐯𐑃 𐑄 𐐢𐐫𐑉𐐼 𐐱𐑂 𐐐𐐬𐑅𐐻𐑅, 𐐫𐑉 𐐿𐐲𐑉𐑅𐐯𐐼 𐐺𐐨 𐑄 𐑊𐐰𐑌𐐼 𐑁𐐫𐑉 𐑄𐐯𐑉 𐑅𐐩𐐿𐑅. 𐐙𐐫𐑉 𐐮𐑁 𐐌 𐐶𐐮𐑊, 𐑅𐐯𐑃 𐑄 𐐢𐐫𐑉𐐼 𐐱𐑂 𐐐𐐬𐑅𐐻𐑅, 𐑉𐐩𐑆 𐐲𐐹 𐑅𐐨𐐼 𐐲𐑌𐐻𐐭 𐑋𐐨, 𐐌 𐐶𐐮𐑊 𐐿𐐱𐑋𐐰𐑌𐐼 𐑋𐐴 𐐹𐐨𐐹𐐲𐑊; 𐐲𐑄𐐲𐑉𐐶𐐴𐑆 𐑄𐐩 𐑇𐐰𐑊 𐐸𐐲𐑉𐐿𐐲𐑌 𐐲𐑌𐐻𐐭 𐑄𐐨𐑆 𐑃𐐮𐑍𐑆. 𐐙𐐫𐑉 𐐺𐐨𐐸𐐬𐑊𐐼, 𐐌, 𐑄 𐐢𐐫𐑉𐐼, 𐐸𐐰𐑂 𐑅𐐨𐑌 𐑄 𐑅𐐱𐑉𐐬 𐐰𐑌𐐼 𐐸𐐲𐑉𐐼 𐑄 𐑋𐐬𐑉𐑌𐐮𐑍 𐐱𐑂 𐑄 𐐼𐐫𐐻𐐲𐑉𐑆 𐐱𐑂 𐑋𐐴 𐐹𐐨𐐹𐐲𐑊 𐐮𐑌 𐑄 𐑊𐐰𐑌𐐼 𐐱𐑂 𐐖𐐯𐑉𐐭𐑅𐐲𐑊𐐲𐑋; 𐐷𐐩, 𐐰𐑌𐐼 𐐮𐑌 𐐫𐑊 𐑄 𐑊𐐰𐑌𐐼𐑆 𐐱𐑂 𐑋𐐴 𐐹𐐨𐐹𐐲𐑊, 𐐺𐐨𐐿𐐫𐑆 𐐱𐑂 𐑄 𐐶𐐮𐐿𐐯𐐼𐑌𐐯𐑅 𐐰𐑌𐐼 𐐰𐐺𐐱𐑋𐐮𐑌𐐩𐑇𐐲𐑌𐑆 𐐱𐑂 𐑄𐐯𐑉 𐐸𐐲𐑆𐐺𐐲𐑌𐐼𐑆. 𐐈𐑌𐐼 𐐌 𐐶𐐮𐑊 𐑌𐐱𐐻 𐑅𐐲𐑁𐐲𐑉, 𐑅𐐯𐑃 𐑄 𐐢𐐫𐑉𐐼 𐐱𐑂 𐐐𐐬𐑅𐐻𐑅, 𐑄𐐰𐐻 𐑄 𐐿𐑉𐐴𐑆 𐐱𐑂 𐑄 𐑁𐐯𐑉 𐐼𐐫𐐻𐐲𐑉𐑆 𐐱𐑂 𐑄𐐮𐑅 𐐹𐐨𐐹𐐲𐑊, 𐐸𐐶𐐮𐐽 𐐌 𐐸𐐰𐑂 𐑊𐐯𐐼 𐐵𐐻 𐐱𐑂 𐑄 𐑊𐐰𐑌𐐼 𐐱𐑂 𐐖𐐯𐑉𐐭𐑅𐐲𐑊𐐲𐑋, 𐑇𐐰𐑊 𐐿𐐲𐑋 𐐲𐐹 𐐲𐑌𐐻𐐭 𐑋𐐨, 𐐰𐑀𐐯𐑌𐑅𐐻 𐑄 𐑋𐐯𐑌 𐐱𐑂 𐑋𐐴 𐐹𐐨𐐹𐐲𐑊, 𐑅𐐯𐑃 𐑄 𐐢𐐫𐑉𐐼 𐐱𐑂 𐐐𐐬𐑅𐐻𐑅; 𐑁𐐫𐑉 𐑄𐐩 𐑇𐐰𐑊 𐑌𐐱𐐻 𐑊𐐨𐐼 𐐰𐐶𐐩 𐐿𐐰𐐹𐐻𐐮𐑂 𐑄 𐐼𐐫𐐻𐐲𐑉𐑆 𐐱𐑂 𐑋𐐴 𐐹𐐨𐐹𐐲𐑊, 𐐺𐐨𐐿𐐫𐑆 𐐱𐑂 𐑄𐐯𐑉 𐐻𐐯𐑌𐐼𐐲𐑉𐑌𐐯𐑅, 𐑅𐐩𐑂 𐐌 𐑇𐐰𐑊 𐑂𐐮𐑆𐐮𐐻 𐑄𐐯𐑋 𐐶𐐮𐑄 𐐰 𐑅𐐫𐑉 𐐿𐐲𐑉𐑅, 𐐨𐑂𐐲𐑌 𐐲𐑌𐐻𐐭 𐐼𐐯𐑅𐐻𐑉𐐲𐐿𐑇𐐲𐑌: 𐑁𐐫𐑉 𐑄𐐩 𐑇𐐰𐑊 𐑌𐐱𐐻 𐐿𐐱𐑋𐐮𐐻 𐐸𐐫𐑉𐐼𐐲𐑋𐑆, 𐑊𐐴𐐿 𐐲𐑌𐐻𐐭 𐑄𐐯𐑋 𐐱𐑂 𐐬𐑊𐐼, 𐑅𐐯𐑃 𐑄 𐐢𐐫𐑉𐐼 𐐱𐑂 𐐐𐐬𐑅𐐻𐑅.

7. 𐐈𐑌𐐼 𐑌𐐵, 𐐺𐐨𐐸𐐬𐑊𐐼, 𐑋𐐴 𐐺𐑉𐐯𐑄𐑉𐐯𐑌, 𐐷 𐑌𐐬 𐑄𐐰𐐻 𐑄𐐨𐑆 𐐿𐐱𐑋𐐰𐑌𐐼𐑋𐐯𐑌𐐻𐑅 𐐶𐐲𐑉 𐑀𐐮𐑂𐐲𐑌 𐐻𐐭 𐐪𐑉 𐑁𐐪𐑄𐐲𐑉 𐐢𐐨𐐸𐐴, 𐐸𐐶𐐯𐑉𐑁𐐫𐑉 𐐷 𐐸𐐰𐑂 𐑌𐐬𐑌 𐑄𐐯𐑋 𐐺𐐨𐑁𐐫𐑉; 𐐰𐑌𐐼 𐐷 𐐸𐐰𐑂 𐐿𐐲𐑋 𐐲𐑌𐐻𐐭 𐑀𐑉𐐩𐐻 𐐿𐐱𐑌𐐼𐐯𐑋𐑌𐐩𐑇𐐲𐑌; 𐑁𐐫𐑉 𐐷 𐐸𐐰𐑂 𐐼𐐲𐑌 𐑄𐐨𐑆 𐑃𐐮𐑍𐑆, 𐐸𐐶𐐮𐐽 𐐷 𐐫𐐻 𐑌𐐱𐐻 𐐻𐐭 𐐸𐐰𐑂 𐐼𐐲𐑌. 𐐒𐐨𐐸𐐬𐑊𐐼, 𐐷 𐐸𐐰𐑂 𐐼𐐲𐑌 𐑀𐑉𐐩𐐻𐐲𐑉 𐐮𐑌𐐮𐐿𐐶𐐮𐐻𐐨𐑆 𐑄𐐰𐑌 𐑄 𐐢𐐩𐑋𐐲𐑌𐐴𐐻𐑅, 𐐵𐑉 𐐺𐑉𐐯𐑄𐑉𐐯𐑌. 𐐏 𐐸𐐰𐑂 𐐺𐑉𐐬𐐿𐐲𐑌 𐑄 𐐸𐐪𐑉𐐻𐑅 𐐱𐑂 𐐷𐐭𐑉 𐐻𐐯𐑌𐐼𐐲𐑉 𐐶𐐴𐑂𐑆, 𐐰𐑌𐐼 𐑊𐐱𐑅𐐻 𐑄 𐐿𐐱𐑌𐑁𐐮𐐼𐐯𐑌𐑅 𐐱𐑂 𐐷𐐭𐑉 𐐽𐐮𐑊𐐼𐑉𐐯𐑌, 𐐺𐐨𐐿𐐫𐑆 𐐱𐑂 𐐷𐐭𐑉 𐐺𐐰𐐼 𐐯𐑀𐑆𐐰𐑋𐐹𐑊𐑆 𐐺𐐨𐑁𐐫𐑉 𐑄𐐯𐑋; 𐐰𐑌𐐼 𐑄 𐑅𐐱𐐺𐐮𐑍𐑆 𐐱𐑂 𐑄𐐯𐑉 𐐸𐐪𐑉𐐻𐑅 𐐰𐑅𐐯𐑌𐐼 𐐲𐐹 𐐻𐐭 𐐘𐐱𐐼 𐐰𐑀𐐯𐑌𐑅𐐻 𐐷𐐭. 𐐈𐑌𐐼 𐐺𐐨𐐿𐐫𐑆 𐐱𐑂 𐑄 𐑅𐐻𐑉𐐮𐐿𐐻𐑌𐐯𐑅 𐐱𐑂 𐑄 𐐶𐐲𐑉𐐼 𐐱𐑂 𐐘𐐱𐐼, 𐐸𐐶𐐮𐐽 𐐿𐐲𐑋𐐯𐑃 𐐼𐐵𐑌 𐐰𐑀𐐯𐑌𐑅𐐻 𐐷𐐭, 𐑋𐐯𐑌𐐨 𐐸𐐪𐑉𐐻𐑅 𐐼𐐴𐐼, 𐐹𐐨𐑉𐑅𐐻 𐐶𐐮𐑄 𐐼𐐨𐐹 𐐶𐐭𐑌𐐼𐑆.

8. 𐐒𐐲𐐻 𐐺𐐨𐐸𐐬𐑊𐐼, 𐐌, 𐐖𐐩𐐿𐐲𐐺, 𐐶𐐳𐐼 𐑅𐐹𐐨𐐿 𐐲𐑌𐐻𐐭 𐐷𐐭 𐑄𐐰𐐻 𐐪𐑉 𐐹𐐷𐐭𐑉 𐐮𐑌 𐐸𐐪𐑉𐐻. 𐐢𐐳𐐿 𐐲𐑌𐐻𐐭 𐐘𐐱𐐼 𐐶𐐮𐑄 𐑁𐐲𐑉𐑋𐑌𐐯𐑅 𐐱𐑂 𐑋𐐴𐑌𐐼, 𐐰𐑌𐐼 𐐹𐑉𐐩 𐐲𐑌𐐻𐐭 𐐸𐐮𐑋 𐐶𐐮𐑄 𐐯𐐿𐑅𐐨𐐼𐐮𐑍 𐑁𐐩𐑃, 𐐰𐑌𐐼 𐐸𐐨 𐐶𐐮𐑊 𐐿𐐱𐑌𐑅𐐬𐑊 𐐷𐐭 𐐮𐑌 𐐷𐐭𐑉 𐐰𐑁𐑊𐐮𐐿𐑇𐐲𐑌𐑆, 𐐰𐑌𐐼 𐐸𐐨 𐐶𐐮𐑊 𐐹𐑊𐐨𐐼 𐐷𐐭𐑉 𐐿𐐫𐑆, 𐐰𐑌𐐼 𐑅𐐯𐑌𐐼 𐐼𐐵𐑌 𐐾𐐲𐑅𐐻𐐮𐑅 𐐲𐐹𐐱𐑌 𐑄𐐬𐑆 𐐸𐐭 𐑅𐐨𐐿 𐐷𐐭𐑉 𐐼𐐯𐑅𐐻𐑉𐐲𐐿𐑇𐐲𐑌.

9. 𐐄 𐐫𐑊 𐐷 𐑄𐐰𐐻 𐐪𐑉 𐐹𐐷𐐭𐑉 𐐮𐑌 𐐸𐐪𐑉𐐻, 𐑊𐐮𐑁𐐻 𐐲𐐹 𐐷𐐭𐑉 𐐸𐐯𐐼𐑆 𐐰𐑌𐐼 𐑉𐐨𐑅𐐨𐑂 𐑄 𐐹𐑊𐐨𐑆𐐮𐑍 𐐶𐐲𐑉𐐼 𐐱𐑂 𐐘𐐱𐐼, 𐐰𐑌𐐼 𐑁𐐨𐑅𐐻 𐐲𐐹𐐱𐑌 𐐸𐐮𐑆 𐑊𐐲𐑂; 𐑁𐐫𐑉 𐐷 𐑋𐐩, 𐐮𐑁 𐐷𐐭𐑉 𐑋𐐴𐑌𐐼𐑆 𐐺𐐨 𐑁𐐲𐑉𐑋, 𐑁𐐫𐑉𐐯𐑂𐐲𐑉.

𐐒𐐲𐐻 𐐶𐐬, 𐐶𐐬, 𐐲𐑌𐐻𐐭 𐐷𐐭 𐑄𐐰𐐻 𐐪𐑉 𐑌𐐱𐐻 𐐹𐐷𐐭𐑉 𐐮𐑌 𐐸𐐪𐑉𐐻; 𐑄𐐰𐐻 𐐪𐑉 𐑁𐐮𐑊𐑃𐐨 𐑄𐐮𐑅 𐐼𐐩 𐐺𐐨𐑁𐐬𐑉 𐐘𐐱𐐼; 𐑁𐐫𐑉 𐐯𐐿𐑅𐐯𐐹𐐻 𐐷 𐑉𐐨𐐹𐐯𐑌𐐻, 𐑄 𐑊𐐰𐑌𐐼 𐐮𐑆 𐐿𐐲𐑉𐑅𐐻 𐑁𐐫𐑉 𐐷𐐭𐑉 𐑅𐐩𐐿𐑅; 𐐰𐑌𐐼 𐑄 𐐢𐐩𐑋𐐲𐑌𐐴𐐻𐑅 𐐸𐐶𐐮𐐽 𐐪𐑉 𐑌𐐱𐐻 𐑁𐐮𐑊𐑃𐐨 𐑊𐐴𐐿 𐐲𐑌𐐻𐐭 𐐷𐐭 (𐑌𐐯𐑂𐐯𐑉𐑄𐐯𐑊𐐯𐑅, 𐑄𐐩 𐐪𐑉 𐐿𐐲𐑉𐑅𐐻 𐐶𐐮𐑄 𐐪 𐑅𐐬𐑉 𐐿𐐲𐑉𐑅𐐮𐑍,) 𐑇𐐰𐑊 𐑅𐐿𐐲𐑉𐐾 𐐷𐐭 𐐨𐑂𐑌 𐐲𐑌𐐻𐐭 𐐼𐐯𐑅𐐻𐑉𐐲𐐿𐑇𐐲𐑌. 𐐈𐑌𐐼 𐑄 𐐻𐐴𐑋 𐑅𐐹𐐨𐐼𐐮𐑊𐐨 𐐿𐐲𐑋𐐯𐑃, 𐑄𐐰𐐻 𐐯𐐿𐑅𐐯𐐹𐐻 𐐷 𐑉𐐨𐐹𐐯𐑌𐐻, 𐑄𐐩 𐑇𐐰𐑊 𐐹𐐲𐑆𐐯𐑅 𐑄 𐑊𐐰𐑌𐐼 𐐱𐑂 𐐷𐐭𐑉 𐐮𐑌𐐸𐐯𐑉𐐮𐐻𐐲𐑌𐑅, 𐐰𐑌𐐼 𐑄 𐐢𐐫𐑉𐐼 𐐘𐐱𐐼 𐐶𐐮𐑊 𐑊𐐨𐐼 𐐰𐐶𐐩 𐑄 𐑉𐐴𐐽𐐲𐑅 𐐵𐐻 𐑁𐑉𐐱𐑋 𐐲𐑋𐐲𐑍 𐐷𐐭. 𐐒𐐨𐐸𐐬𐑊𐐼, 𐑄 𐐢𐐩𐑋𐐲𐑌𐐴𐐻𐑅 𐐷𐐭𐑉 𐐺𐑉𐐯𐑄𐑉𐐯𐑌, 𐐸𐐭𐑋 𐐷 𐐸𐐩𐐻, 𐐺𐐨𐐿𐐫𐑆 𐐱𐑂 𐑄𐐩𐑉 𐑁𐐮𐑊𐑃𐐮𐑌𐐯𐑅 𐐰𐑌𐐼 𐑄 𐐿𐐲𐑉𐑅𐐮𐑍 𐐸𐐶𐐮𐐽 𐐸𐐰𐑃 𐐿𐐲𐑋 𐐲𐐹𐐱𐑌 𐑄𐐩𐑉 𐑅𐐿𐐮𐑌𐑆, 𐐪𐑉 𐑋𐐬𐑉 𐑉𐐴𐐽𐐲𐑅 𐑄𐐰𐑌 𐐷𐐭; 𐑁𐐫𐑉 𐑄𐐩 𐐸𐐰𐑂 𐑌𐐱𐐻 𐑁𐐫𐑉𐑀𐐱𐐻𐑌 𐑄 𐐿𐐲𐑋𐐰𐑌𐐼𐑋𐐯𐑌𐐻 𐐱𐑂 𐑄 𐐢𐐫𐑉𐐼, 𐐸𐐶𐐮𐐽 𐐶𐐱𐑆 𐑀𐐮𐑂𐑌 𐐲𐑌𐐻𐐭 𐐵𐑉 𐑁𐐪𐑄𐐯𐑉𐑆, 𐑄𐐰𐐻 𐑄𐐩 𐑇𐐳𐐼 𐐸𐐰𐑂, 𐑅𐐩𐑂 𐐮𐐻 𐐶𐐲𐑉 𐐶𐐲𐑌 𐐶𐐴𐑁; 𐐰𐑌𐐼 𐐿𐐱𐑌𐐿𐐷𐐭𐐺𐐴𐑌𐑆 𐑄𐐩 𐑇𐐳𐐼 𐐸𐐰𐑂 𐑌𐐲𐑌; 𐐰𐑌𐐼 𐑄𐐩𐑉 𐑇𐐳𐐼 𐑌𐐱𐐻 𐐺 𐐸𐐬𐑉𐐼𐐲𐑋𐑆 𐐿𐐲𐑋𐐮𐐻𐐯𐐼 𐐲𐑋𐐲𐑍 𐑄𐐯𐑋. 𐐈𐑌𐐼 𐑌𐐵 𐑄𐐮𐑅 𐐿𐐲𐑋𐐰𐑌𐐼𐑋𐐯𐑌𐐻 𐑄𐐩 𐐲𐐺𐑆𐐲𐑉𐑂 𐐻𐐭 𐐿𐐨𐐹; 𐐸𐐶𐐯𐑉𐑁𐐬𐑉, 𐐺𐐨𐐿𐐫𐑆 𐐱𐑂 𐑄𐐮𐑅 𐐲𐐺𐑆𐐲𐑉𐑂𐐲𐑌𐑅, 𐐮𐑌 𐐿𐐨𐐹𐐮𐑍 𐑄𐐮𐑅 𐐿𐐲𐑋𐐰𐑌𐐼𐑋𐐯𐑌𐐻, 𐑄 𐐢𐐫𐑉𐐼 𐐘𐐱𐐼 𐐶𐐮𐑊 𐑌𐐱𐐻 𐐼𐐯𐑅𐐻𐑉𐐱𐐩 𐑄𐐯𐑋, 𐐺𐐲𐐻 𐐶𐐮𐑊 𐐺 𐑋𐐲𐑉𐑅𐐮𐑁𐐳𐑊 𐐲𐑌𐐻𐐭 𐑄𐐯𐑋; 𐐰𐑌𐐼 𐐶𐐲𐑌 𐐼𐐩 𐑄𐐩 𐑇𐐰𐑊 𐐺𐐨𐐿𐐲𐑋 𐐪 𐐺𐑊𐐯𐑅𐐯𐐼 𐐹𐐨𐐹𐑊. 𐐒𐐨𐐸𐐬𐑊𐐼, 𐑄𐐩𐑉 𐐸𐐲𐑆𐐺𐐲𐑌𐐼𐑆 𐑊𐐲𐑂 𐑄𐐩𐑉 𐐶𐐴𐑂𐑆, 𐐰𐑌𐐼 𐑄𐐩𐑉 𐐶𐐴𐑂𐑆 𐑊𐐲𐑂 𐑄𐐩𐑉 𐐸𐐲𐑆𐐺𐐲𐑌𐐼𐑆; 𐐰𐑌𐐼 𐑄𐐩𐑉 𐐸𐐲𐑆𐐺𐐲𐑌𐐼𐑆 𐐰𐑌𐐼 𐑄𐐩𐑉 𐐶𐐴𐑂𐑆 𐑊𐐲𐑂 𐑄𐐩𐑉 𐐽𐐮𐑊𐐼𐑉𐐯𐑌; 𐐰𐑌𐐼 𐑄𐐩𐑉 𐐲𐑌𐐺𐐨𐑊𐐨𐑁 𐐰𐑌𐐼 𐑄𐐩𐑉 𐐸𐐩𐐻𐑉𐐯𐐼 𐐻𐐬𐑉𐐼𐑆 𐐷𐐭, 𐐮𐑆 𐐺𐐨𐐿𐐫𐑆 𐐱𐑂 𐑄 𐐮𐑌𐐮𐐿𐐶𐐮𐐻𐐨 𐐱𐑂 𐑄𐐩𐑉 𐑁𐐪𐑄𐐯𐑉𐑆; 𐐸𐐶𐐯𐑉𐑁𐐬𐑉, 𐐸𐐵 𐑋𐐲𐐽 𐐺𐐯𐐻𐐯𐑉 𐐪𐑉 𐐷𐐭 𐑄𐐰𐑌 𐑄𐐩, 𐐮𐑌 𐑄 𐑅𐐴𐐻 𐐱𐑂 𐐷𐐭𐑉 𐑀𐑉𐐩𐐻 𐐗𐑉𐐨𐐩𐐻𐐲𐑉?

10. 𐐉 𐑋𐐴 𐐺𐑉𐐯𐑄𐑉𐐯𐑌, 𐐌 𐑁𐐨𐑉, 𐑄𐐰𐐻 𐐲𐑌𐑊𐐯𐑅 𐐷 𐑇𐐰𐑊 𐑉𐐨𐐹𐐯𐑌𐐻 𐐱𐑂 𐐷𐐭𐑉 𐑅𐐮𐑌𐑆, 𐑄𐐰𐐻 𐑄𐐩𐑉 𐑅𐐿𐐮𐑌𐑆 𐐶𐐮𐑊 𐐺 𐐸𐐶𐐴𐐻𐐯𐑉 𐑄𐐰𐑌 𐐷𐐭𐑉𐑆, 𐐸𐐶𐐯𐑌 𐐷 𐑇𐐰𐑊 𐐺 𐐺𐑉𐐫𐐻 𐐶𐐮𐑄 𐑄𐐯𐑋 𐐺𐐨𐑁𐐬𐑉 𐑄 𐑃𐑉𐐬𐑌 𐐱𐑂 𐐘𐐱𐐼. 𐐐𐐶𐐯𐑉𐑁𐐬𐑉, 𐐪 𐐿𐐲𐑋𐐰𐑌𐐼𐑋𐐯𐑌𐐻 𐐌 𐑀𐐮𐑂 𐐲𐑌𐐻𐐭 𐐷𐐭, 𐐸𐐶𐐮𐐽 𐐮𐑆 𐑄 𐐶𐐲𐑉𐐼 𐐱𐑂 𐐘𐐱𐐼, 𐑄𐐰𐐻 𐐷 𐑉𐐨𐑂𐐴𐑊 𐑌𐐬 𐑋𐐬𐑉 𐐰𐑀𐐯𐑌𐑅𐐻 𐑄𐐯𐑋, 𐐺𐐨𐐿𐐫𐑆 𐐱𐑂 𐑄 𐐼𐐪𐑉𐐿𐑌𐐯𐑅 𐐱𐑂 𐑄𐐩𐑉 𐑅𐐿𐐮𐑌𐑆; 𐑌𐐨𐑄𐐯𐑉 𐑇𐐰𐑊 𐐷 𐑉𐐨𐑂𐐴𐑊 𐐰𐑀𐐯𐑌𐑅𐐻 𐑄𐐯𐑋 𐐺𐐨𐐿𐐫𐑆 𐐱𐑂 𐑄𐐩𐑉 𐑁𐐮𐑊𐑃𐐮𐑌𐐯𐑅; 𐐺𐐲𐐻 𐐷 𐑇𐐰𐑊 𐑉𐐨𐑋𐐯𐑋𐐺𐐯𐑉 𐐷𐐭𐑉 𐐬𐑌 𐑁𐐮𐑊𐑃𐐮𐑌𐐯𐑅, 𐐰𐑌𐐼 𐑉𐐨𐑋𐐯𐑋𐐺𐐯𐑉 𐑄𐐰𐐻 𐑄𐐩𐑉 𐑁𐐮𐑊𐑃𐐮𐑌𐐯𐑅 𐐿𐐩𐑋 𐐺𐐨𐐿𐐫𐑆 𐐱𐑂 𐑄𐐩𐑉 𐑁𐐪𐑄𐐯𐑉𐑆. 𐐐𐐶𐐯𐑉𐑁𐐬𐑉, 𐐷 𐑇𐐰𐑊 𐑉𐐨𐑋𐐯𐑋𐐺𐐯𐑉 𐐷𐐭𐑉 𐐽𐐮𐑊𐐼𐑉𐐯𐑌, 𐐸𐐵 𐑄𐐰𐐻 𐐷 𐐸𐐰𐑂 𐑀𐑉𐐨𐑂𐐼 𐑄𐐩𐑉 𐐸𐐪𐑉𐐻𐑅 𐐺𐐨𐐿𐐫𐑆 𐐱𐑂 𐑄 𐐯𐑀𐑆𐐰𐑋𐐹𐑊 𐑄𐐰𐐻 𐐷 𐐸𐐰𐑂 𐑅𐐯𐐻 𐐺𐐨𐑁𐐬𐑉 𐑄𐐯𐑋; 𐐰𐑌𐐼 𐐫𐑊𐑅𐐬 𐑉𐐨𐑋𐐯𐑋𐐺𐐯𐑉 𐑄𐐰𐐻 𐐷 𐑋𐐩, 𐐺𐐨𐐿𐐫𐑆 𐐱𐑂 𐐷𐐭𐑉 𐑁𐐮𐑊𐑃𐐮𐑌𐐯𐑅, 𐐺𐑉𐐮𐑍 𐐷𐐭𐑉 𐐽𐐮𐑊𐐼𐑉𐐯𐑌 𐐲𐑌𐐻𐐭 𐐼𐐯𐑅𐐻𐑉𐐲𐐿𐑇𐐲𐑌, 𐐰𐑌𐐼 𐑄𐐩𐑉 𐑅𐐮𐑌𐑆 𐐺 𐐸𐐨𐐹𐐻 𐐲𐐹𐐱𐑌 𐐷𐐭𐑉 𐐸𐐯𐐼𐑆 𐐰𐐻 𐑄 𐑊𐐰𐑅𐐻 𐐼𐐩.

11. 𐐉 𐑋𐐴 𐐺𐑉𐐯𐑄𐑉𐐯𐑌, 𐐸𐐪𐑉𐐿𐑌 𐐲𐑌𐐻𐐭 𐑋𐐴 𐐶𐐲𐑉𐐼𐑆; 𐐲𐑉𐐵𐑆 𐑄 𐑁𐐰𐐿𐐲𐑊𐐻𐐮𐑆 𐐱𐑂 𐐷𐐭𐑉 𐑅𐐬𐑊𐑆; 𐑇𐐩𐐿 𐐷𐐭𐑉𐑅𐐯𐑊𐑂𐑆, 𐑄𐐰𐐻 𐐷 𐑋𐐩 𐐰𐐶𐐩𐐿 𐑁𐑉𐐱𐑋 𐑄 𐑅𐑊𐐲𐑋𐐺𐐯𐑉 𐐱𐑂 𐐼𐐯𐑃; 𐐰𐑌𐐼 𐑊𐐭𐑆 𐐷𐐭𐑉𐑅𐐯𐑊𐑂𐑆 𐑁𐑉𐐱𐑋 𐑄 𐐹𐐩𐑌𐑆 𐐱𐑂 𐐸𐐯𐑊, 𐑄𐐰𐐻 𐐷 𐑋𐐩 𐑌𐐱𐐻 𐐺𐐨𐐿𐐲𐑋 𐐩𐑌𐐾𐐯𐑊𐑆 𐐻𐐭 𐑄 𐐼𐐯𐑂𐐮𐑊, 𐐻𐐭 𐐺 𐐿𐐰𐑅𐐻 𐐮𐑌𐐻𐐭 𐑄𐐰𐐻 𐑊𐐩𐐿 𐐱𐑂 𐑁𐐴𐑉 𐐰𐑌𐐼 𐐺𐑉𐐮𐑋𐑅𐐻𐐬𐑌 𐐸𐐶𐐮𐐽 𐐮𐑆 𐑄 𐑅𐐯𐐿𐐲𐑌𐐼 𐐼𐐯𐑃. 𐐈𐑌𐐼 𐑌𐐵 𐐌, 𐐖𐐩𐐿𐐲𐐺, 𐑅𐐹𐐩𐐿 𐑋𐐯𐑌𐐨 𐑋𐐬𐑉 𐑃𐐮𐑍𐑆 𐐲𐑌𐐻𐐭 𐑄 𐐹𐐨𐐹𐑊 𐐱𐑂 𐐤𐐨𐑁𐐴, 𐐶𐐫𐑉𐑌𐐮𐑍 𐑄𐐯𐑋 𐐰𐑀𐐯𐑌𐑅𐐻 𐑁𐐫𐑉𐑌𐐮𐐿𐐩𐑇𐐲𐑌 𐐰𐑌𐐼 𐑊𐐰𐑅𐐮𐑂𐐨𐐲𐑅𐑌𐐯𐑅, 𐐰𐑌𐐼 𐐯𐑂𐐯𐑉𐐨 𐐿𐐴𐑌𐐼 𐐱𐑂 𐑅𐐮𐑌, 𐐻𐐯𐑊𐐮𐑍 𐑄𐐯𐑋 𐑄 𐐫𐑁𐐳𐑊 𐐿𐐱𐑌𐑅𐐨𐐿𐐶𐐯𐑌𐑅𐐯𐑆 𐐱𐑂 𐑄𐐯𐑋; 𐐰𐑌𐐼 𐐪 𐐸𐐲𐑌𐐼𐑉𐐯𐐼𐑃 𐐹𐐪𐑉𐐻 𐐱𐑂 𐑄 𐐹𐑉𐐬𐑅𐐨𐐼𐐮𐑍𐑆 𐐱𐑂 𐑄𐐮𐑅 𐐹𐐨𐐹𐑊, 𐐸𐐶𐐮𐐽 𐑌𐐵 𐐺𐐨𐑀𐐰𐑌 𐐻𐐭 𐐺 𐑌𐐭𐑋𐐯𐑉𐐲𐑅, 𐐿𐐰𐑌𐐱𐐻 𐐺 𐑉𐐮𐐻𐑌 𐐲𐐹𐐱𐑌 𐑄𐐨𐑆 𐐹𐑊𐐩𐐻𐑅; 𐐺𐐲𐐻 𐑋𐐯𐑌𐐨 𐐱𐑂 𐑄𐐩𐑉 𐐹𐑉𐐬𐑅𐐨𐐼𐐮𐑍𐑆 𐐪𐑉 𐑉𐐮𐐻𐑌 𐐲𐐹𐐱𐑌 𐑄 𐑊𐐪𐑉𐐾𐐯𐑉 𐐹𐑊𐐩𐐻𐑅, 𐐰𐑌𐐼 𐑄𐐩𐑉 𐐶𐐫𐑉𐑆, 𐐰𐑌𐐼 𐑄𐐩𐑉 𐐿𐐱𐑌𐐻𐐯𐑌𐑇𐐲𐑌𐑆, 𐐰𐑌𐐼 𐑄 𐑉𐐩𐑌𐑆 𐐱𐑂 𐑄𐐩𐑉 𐐿𐐮𐑍𐑆. 𐐜𐐨𐑆 𐐹𐑊𐐩𐐻𐑅 𐐪𐑉 𐐿𐐫𐑊𐐼 𐑄 𐐹𐑊𐐩𐐻𐑅 𐐱𐑂 𐐖𐐩𐐿𐐲𐐺, 𐐰𐑌𐐼 𐑄𐐩 𐐶𐐲𐑉 𐑋𐐩𐐼 𐐺𐐴 𐑄 𐐸𐐰𐑌𐐼 𐐱𐑂 𐐤𐐨𐑁𐐴. 𐐈𐑌𐐼 𐐌 𐑋𐐩𐐿 𐐰𐑌 𐐯𐑌𐐼 𐐱𐑂 𐑅𐐹𐐨𐐿𐐮𐑍 𐑄𐐨𐑆 𐐶𐐲𐑉𐐼𐑆.

𐐕𐐰𐐹𐐻𐐲𐑉 III.

1. 𐐤𐐵, 𐐺𐐨𐐸𐐬𐑊𐐼, 𐐮𐐻 𐐿𐐩𐑋 𐐻𐐭 𐐹𐐰𐑅 𐑄𐐰𐐻 𐐴, 𐐖𐐩𐐿𐐲𐐺, 𐐸𐐰𐑂𐐮𐑍 𐑋𐐮𐑌𐐮𐑅𐐻𐐲𐑉𐐼 𐑋𐐲𐐽 𐐲𐑌𐐻𐐭 𐑋𐐴 𐐹𐐨𐐹𐑊 𐐮𐑌 𐐶𐐲𐑉𐐼, (𐐰𐑌𐐼 𐐴 𐐿𐐰𐑌𐐱𐐻 𐑉𐐴𐐻 𐐺𐐲𐐻 𐐲 𐑊𐐮𐐻𐑊 𐐱𐑂 𐑋𐐴 𐐶𐐲𐑉𐐼𐑆, 𐐺𐐨𐐿𐐫𐑆 𐐱𐑂 𐑄 𐐼𐐮𐑁𐐮𐐿𐐲𐑊𐐻𐐨 𐐱𐑂 𐐯𐑌𐑀𐑉𐐩𐑂𐐮𐑍 𐐵𐑉 𐐶𐐲𐑉𐐼𐑆 𐐲𐐹𐐱𐑌 𐐹𐑊𐐩𐐻𐑅,) 𐐰𐑌𐐼 𐐶𐐨 𐑌𐐬 𐑄𐐰𐐻 𐑄 𐑃𐐮𐑍𐑆 𐐸𐐶𐐮𐐽 𐐶𐐨 𐑉𐐴𐐻 𐐲𐐹𐐱𐑌 𐐹𐑊𐐩𐐻𐑅 𐑋𐐲𐑅𐐻 𐑉𐐨𐑋𐐩𐑌; 𐐺𐐲𐐻 𐐸𐐶𐐱𐐻𐑅𐐯𐑂𐐲𐑉 𐑃𐐮𐑍𐑆 𐐶𐐨 𐑉𐐴𐐻 𐐲𐐹𐐱𐑌 𐐯𐑌𐐨 𐑃𐐮𐑍, 𐑅𐐩𐑂 𐐮𐐻 𐐺𐐨 𐐲𐐹𐐱𐑌 𐐹𐑊𐐩𐐻𐑅, 𐑋𐐲𐑅𐐻 𐐹𐐯𐑉𐐮𐑇 𐐰𐑌𐐼 𐑂𐐰𐑌𐐮𐑇 𐐲𐐶𐐩; 𐐺𐐲𐐻 𐐶𐐨 𐐿𐐰𐑌 𐑉𐐴𐐻 𐐲 𐑁𐐷𐐭 𐐶𐐲𐑉𐐼𐑆 𐐲𐐹𐐱𐑌 𐐹𐑊𐐩𐐻𐑅, 𐐸𐐶𐐮𐐽 𐐶𐐮𐑊 𐑀𐐮𐑂 𐐵𐑉 𐐽𐐮𐑊𐐼𐑉𐐯𐑌, 𐐰𐑌𐐼 𐐫𐑊𐑅𐐬 𐐵𐑉 𐐺𐐨𐑊𐐲𐑂𐐯𐐼 𐐺𐑉𐐯𐑄𐑉𐐯𐑌, 𐐲 𐑅𐑋𐐫𐑊 𐐼𐐨𐑀𐑉𐐨 𐐱𐑂 𐑌𐐱𐑊𐐯𐐾 𐐿𐐱𐑌𐑅𐐲𐑉𐑌𐐮𐑍 𐐲𐑅, 𐐫𐑉 𐐿𐐱𐑌𐑅𐐲𐑉𐑌𐐮𐑍 𐑄𐐯𐑉 𐑁𐐪𐑄𐐲𐑉𐑆. 𐐤𐐵 𐐮𐑌 𐑄𐐮𐑅 𐑃𐐮𐑍 𐐶𐐨 𐐼𐐭 𐑉𐐨𐐾𐑎𐑅; 𐐰𐑌𐐼 𐐶𐐨 𐑊𐐩𐐺𐐲𐑉 𐐼𐐮𐑊𐐮𐐾𐐯𐑌𐐻𐑊𐐨 𐐻𐐭 𐐯𐑌𐑀𐑉𐐩𐑂 𐑄𐐨𐑆 𐐶𐐲𐑉𐐼𐑆 𐐲𐐹𐐱𐑌 𐐹𐑊𐐩𐐻𐑅, 𐐸𐐬𐐹𐐮𐑍 𐑄𐐰𐐻 𐐵𐑉 𐐺𐐨𐑊𐐲𐑂𐐯𐐼 𐐺𐑉𐐯𐑄𐑉𐐯𐑌 𐐰𐑌𐐼 𐐵𐑉 𐐽𐐮𐑊𐐼𐑉𐐯𐑌 𐐶𐐮𐑊 𐑉𐐨𐑅𐐨𐑂 𐑄𐐯𐑋 𐐶𐐮𐑄 𐑃𐐰𐑍𐐿𐑁𐐳𐑊 𐐸𐐪𐑉𐐻𐑅, 𐐰𐑌𐐼 𐑊𐐳𐐿 𐐲𐐹𐐱𐑌 𐑄𐐯𐑋 𐑄𐐰𐐻 𐑄𐐩 𐑋𐐩 𐑊𐐲𐑉𐑌 𐐶𐐮𐑄 𐐾𐑎 𐐰𐑌𐐼 𐑌𐐱𐐻 𐐶𐐮𐑄 𐑅𐐱𐑉𐐬, 𐑌𐐨𐑄𐐲𐑉 𐐶𐐮𐑄 𐐿𐐱𐑌𐐻𐐯𐑋𐐹𐐻, 𐐿𐐱𐑌𐑅𐐲𐑉𐑌𐐮𐑍 𐑄𐐯𐑉 𐑁𐐲𐑉𐑅𐐻 𐐹𐐯𐑉𐐯𐑌𐐻𐑅: 𐑁𐐫𐑉, 𐑁𐐫𐑉 𐑄𐐮𐑅 𐐮𐑌𐐻𐐯𐑌𐐻 𐐸𐐰𐑂 𐐶𐐨 𐑉𐐮𐐻𐑌 𐑄𐐨𐑆 𐑃𐐮𐑍𐑆, 𐑄𐐰𐐻 𐑄𐐩 𐑋𐐩 𐑌𐐬 𐑄𐐰𐐻 𐐶𐐨 𐑌𐐭 𐐱𐑂 𐐗𐑉𐐴𐑅𐐻, 𐐰𐑌𐐼 𐐶𐐨 𐐸𐐰𐐼 𐐲 𐐸𐐬𐐹 𐐱𐑂 𐐸𐐮𐑆 𐑀𐑊𐐬𐑉𐐨 𐑋𐐯𐑌𐐨 𐐸𐐲𐑌𐐼𐑉𐐯𐐼 𐐷𐐨𐑉𐑆 𐐺𐐨𐑁𐐫𐑉 𐐸𐐮𐑆 𐐿𐐲𐑋𐐮𐑍; 𐐰𐑌𐐼 𐑌𐐱𐐻 𐐬𐑌𐑊𐐨 𐐶𐐨 𐐵𐑉𐑅𐐯𐑊𐑂𐑆 𐐸𐐰𐐼 𐐲 𐐸𐐬𐐹 𐐱𐑂 𐐸𐐮𐑆 𐑀𐑊𐐬𐑉𐐨, 𐐺𐐲𐐻 𐐫𐑊𐑅𐐬 𐐫𐑊 𐑄 𐐸𐐬𐑊𐐨 𐐹𐑉𐐱𐑁𐐯𐐻𐑅 𐐸𐐶𐐮𐐽 𐐶𐐲𐑉 𐐺𐐨𐑁𐐫𐑉 𐐲𐑅.

2. 𐐒𐐨𐐸𐐬𐑊𐐼, 𐑄𐐩 𐐺𐐨𐑊𐐨𐑂𐐼 𐐮𐑌 𐐗𐑉𐐴𐑅𐐻, 𐐰𐑌𐐼 𐐶𐐲𐑉𐑇𐐮𐐹𐐻 𐑄 𐐙𐐪𐑄𐐲𐑉 𐐮𐑌 𐐸𐐮𐑆 𐑌𐐩𐑋, 𐐰𐑌𐐼 𐐫𐑊𐑅𐐬 𐐶𐐨 𐐶𐐲𐑉𐑇𐐮𐐹 𐑄 𐐙𐐪𐑄𐐲𐑉 𐐮𐑌 𐐸𐐮𐑆 𐑌𐐩𐑋. 𐐈𐑌𐐼 𐑁𐐫𐑉 𐑄𐐮𐑅 𐐮𐑌𐐻𐐯𐑌𐐻 𐐶𐐨 𐐿𐐨𐐹 𐑄 𐑊𐐫 𐐱𐑂 𐐣𐐬𐑆𐐯𐑆, 𐐮𐐻 𐐹𐑎𐑌𐐻𐐮𐑍 𐐵𐑉 𐑅𐐬𐑊𐑆 𐐻𐐭 𐐸𐐮𐑋; 𐐰𐑌𐐼 𐑁𐐫𐑉 𐑄𐐮𐑅 𐐿𐐫𐑆 𐐮𐐻 𐐮𐑆 𐑅𐐰𐑍𐐿𐐻𐐮𐑁𐐴𐐼 𐐲𐑌𐐻𐐭 𐐲𐑅 𐑁𐐫𐑉 𐑉𐐴𐐽𐐲𐑅𐑌𐐯𐑅, 𐐨𐑂𐐯𐑌 𐐰𐑆 𐐮𐐻 𐐶𐐱𐑆 𐐰𐐿𐐵𐑌𐐻𐐯𐐼 𐐲𐑌𐐻𐐭 𐐁𐐺𐑉𐐲𐐸𐐰𐑋 𐐮𐑌 𐑄 𐐶𐐮𐑊𐐼𐐲𐑉𐑌𐐯𐑅, 𐐻𐐭 𐐺𐐨 𐐬𐐺𐐨𐐼𐐨𐐯𐑌𐐻 𐐲𐑌𐐻𐐭 𐑄 𐐿𐐱𐑋𐐰𐑌𐐼𐑆 𐐱𐑂 𐐘𐐱𐐼 𐐮𐑌 𐐱𐑁𐐲𐑉𐐮𐑍 𐐲𐐹 𐐸𐐮𐑆 𐑅𐐲𐑌 𐐌𐑆𐐲𐐿, 𐐸𐐶𐐮𐐽 𐐮𐑆 𐐲 𐑅𐐮𐑋𐐮𐑊𐐮𐐻𐐭𐐼 𐐱𐑂 𐐘𐐱𐐼 𐐰𐑌𐐼 𐐸𐐮𐑆 𐐄𐑌𐑊𐐨 𐐒𐐨𐑀𐐱𐐻𐑌 𐐝𐐲𐑌. 𐐐𐐶𐐯𐑉𐑁𐐫𐑉, 𐐶𐐨 𐑅𐐲𐑉𐐽 𐑄 𐐹𐑉𐐱𐑁𐐯𐐻𐑅, 𐐰𐑌𐐼 𐐶𐐨 𐐸𐐰𐑂 𐑋𐐯𐑌𐐨 𐑉𐐯𐑂𐐯𐑊𐐩𐑇𐐲𐑌𐑆, 𐐰𐑌𐐼 𐑄 𐑅𐐹𐐮𐑉𐐮𐐻 𐐱𐑂 𐐹𐑉𐐱𐑁𐐯𐑅𐐨; 𐐰𐑌𐐼 𐐸𐐰𐑂𐐮𐑍 𐐫𐑊 𐑄𐐨𐑆 𐐶𐐮𐐻𐑌𐐯𐑅𐐯𐑆 𐐶𐐨 𐐱𐐺𐐻𐐩𐑌 𐐲 𐐸𐐬𐐹, 𐐰𐑌𐐼 𐐵𐑉 𐑁𐐩𐑃 𐐺𐐨𐐿𐐲𐑋𐐯𐑃 𐐲𐑌𐑇𐐩𐐿𐑌, 𐐮𐑌𐑅𐐬𐑋𐐲𐐽 𐑄𐐰𐐻 𐐶𐐨 𐐻𐑉𐐭𐑊𐐨 𐐿𐐰𐑌 𐐿𐐱𐑋𐐰𐑌𐐼 𐐮𐑌 𐑄 𐑌𐐩𐑋 𐐱𐑂 𐐖𐐨𐑆𐐲𐑅, 𐐰𐑌𐐼 𐑄 𐑂𐐯𐑉𐐨 𐐻𐑉𐐨𐑆 𐐬𐐺𐐩 𐐲𐑅, 𐐫𐑉 𐑄 𐑋𐐵𐑌𐐻𐐯𐑌𐑆, 𐐫𐑉 𐑄 𐐶𐐩𐑂𐑆 𐐱𐑂 𐑄 𐑅𐐨; 𐑌𐐯𐑂𐐲𐑉𐑄𐐲𐑊𐐯𐑅, 𐑄 𐐢𐐫𐑉𐐼 𐐘𐐱𐐼 𐑇𐐬𐐯𐑃 𐐲𐑅 𐐵𐑉 𐐶𐐨𐐿𐑌𐐯𐑅, 𐑄𐐰𐐻 𐐶𐐨 𐑋𐐩 𐑌𐐬 𐑄𐐰𐐻 𐐮𐐻 𐐮𐑆 𐐺𐐴 𐐸𐐮𐑆 𐑀𐑉𐐩𐑅, 𐐰𐑌𐐼 𐐸𐐮𐑆 𐑀𐑉𐐩𐐻 𐐿𐐱𐑌𐐼𐐯𐑅𐐯𐑌𐑇𐐲𐑌𐑆 𐐲𐑌𐐻𐐭 𐑄 𐐽𐐮𐑊𐐼𐑉𐐯𐑌 𐐱𐑂 𐑋𐐯𐑌, 𐑄𐐰𐐻 𐐶𐐨 𐐸𐐰𐑂 𐐹𐐵𐐲𐑉 𐐻𐐭 𐐼𐐭 𐑄𐐨𐑆 𐑃𐐮𐑍𐑆.

3. 𐐒𐐨𐐸𐐬𐑊𐐼, 𐑀𐑉𐐩𐐻 𐐰𐑌𐐼 𐑋𐐪𐑉𐑂𐐯𐑊𐐲𐑅 𐐪𐑉 𐑄 𐐶𐐲𐑉𐐿𐑅 𐐱𐑂 𐑄 𐐢𐐫𐑉𐐼. 𐐐𐐵 𐐲𐑌𐑅𐐲𐑉𐐽𐐲𐐺𐑊 𐐪𐑉 𐑄 𐐼𐐯𐐹𐑃𐑅 𐐱𐑂 𐑄 𐑋𐐮𐑅𐐻𐐲𐑉𐐨𐑆 𐐱𐑂 𐐸𐐮𐑋; 𐐰𐑌𐐼 𐐮𐐻 𐐮𐑆 𐐮𐑋𐐹𐐱𐑅𐐮𐐺𐑊 𐑄𐐰𐐻 𐑋𐐰𐑌 𐑇𐐳𐐼 𐑁𐐴𐑌𐐼 𐐵𐐻 𐐫𐑊 𐐸𐐮𐑆 𐐶𐐩𐑆. 𐐈𐑌𐐼 𐑌𐐬 𐑋𐐰𐑌 𐑌𐐬𐐯𐑃 𐐱𐑂 𐐸𐐮𐑆 𐐶𐐩𐑆, 𐑅𐐩𐑂 𐐮𐐻 𐐺𐐨 𐑉𐐨𐑂𐐨𐑊𐐼 𐐲𐑌𐐻𐐭 𐐸𐐮𐑋; 𐐸𐐶𐐯𐑉𐑁𐐫𐑉, 𐐺𐑉𐐯𐑄𐑉𐐯𐑌, 𐐼𐐯𐑅𐐹𐐴𐑆 𐑌𐐱𐐻 𐑄 𐑉𐐯𐑂𐐯𐑊𐐩𐑇𐐲𐑌𐑆 𐐱𐑂 𐐘𐐱𐐼. 𐐙𐐫𐑉 𐐺𐐨𐐸𐐬𐑊𐐼, 𐐺𐐴 𐑄 𐐹𐐵𐐲𐑉 𐐱𐑂 𐐸𐐮𐑆 𐐶𐐲𐑉𐐼, 𐑋𐐰𐑌 𐐿𐐩𐑋 𐐲𐐹𐐱𐑌 𐑄 𐑁𐐩𐑅 𐐱𐑂 𐑄 𐐲𐑉𐑃! 𐐸𐐶𐐮𐐽 𐐲𐑉𐑃 𐐶𐐱𐑆 𐐿𐑉𐐨𐐩𐐻𐐯𐐼 𐐺𐐴 𐑄 𐐹𐐵𐐲𐑉 𐐱𐑂 𐐸𐐮𐑆 𐐶𐐲𐑉𐐼. 𐐐𐐶𐐯𐑉𐑁𐐫𐑉, 𐐮𐑁 𐐘𐐱𐐼 𐐺𐐨𐐮𐑍 𐐩𐐺𐑊 𐐻𐐭 𐑅𐐹𐐨𐐿, 𐐰𐑌𐐼 𐑄 𐐶𐐲𐑉𐑊𐐼 𐐶𐐱𐑆, 𐐰𐑌𐐼 𐐻𐐭 𐑅𐐹𐐨𐐿, 𐐰𐑌𐐼 𐑋𐐰𐑌 𐐶𐐱𐑆 𐐿𐑉𐐨𐐩𐐻𐐯𐐼, 𐐄 𐑄𐐯𐑌, 𐐸𐐶𐐴 𐑌𐐱𐐻 𐐩𐐺𐑊 𐐻𐐭 𐐿𐐱𐑋𐐰𐑌𐐼 𐑄 𐐲𐑉𐑃, 𐐫𐑉 𐑄 𐐶𐐲𐑉𐐿𐑋𐐰𐑌𐑇𐐮𐐹 𐐱𐑂 𐐸𐐮𐑆 𐐸𐐰𐑌𐐼𐑆 𐐲𐐹𐐱𐑌 𐑄 𐑁𐐩𐑅 𐐱𐑂 𐐮𐐻, 𐐰𐐿𐐫𐑉𐐼𐐮𐑍 𐐻𐐭 𐐸𐐮𐑆 𐐶𐐮𐑊 𐐰𐑌𐐼 𐐹𐑊𐐯𐑈𐐲𐑉? 𐐐𐐶𐐯𐑉𐑁𐐫𐑉, 𐐺𐑉𐐯𐑄𐑉𐐯𐑌, 𐑅𐐨𐐿 𐑌𐐱𐐻 𐐻𐐭 𐐿𐐵𐑌𐑅𐐯𐑊 𐑄 𐐢𐐫𐑉𐐼, 𐐺𐐲𐐻 𐐻𐐭 𐐻𐐩𐐿 𐐿𐐵𐑌𐑅𐐯𐑊 𐑁𐑉𐐱𐑋 𐐸𐐮𐑆 𐐸𐐰𐑌𐐼. 𐐙𐐫𐑉 𐐺𐐨𐐸𐐬𐑊𐐼, 𐐷𐐨 𐐷𐐫𐑉𐑅𐐯𐑊𐑂𐑆 𐑌𐐬 𐑄𐐰𐐻 𐐸𐐨 𐐿𐐵𐑌𐑅𐐯𐑊𐐯𐑃 𐐮𐑌 𐐶𐐮𐑆𐐼𐐲𐑋, 𐐰𐑌𐐼 𐐮𐑌 𐐾𐐲𐑅𐐻𐐮𐑅, 𐐰𐑌𐐼 𐐮𐑌 𐑀𐑉𐐩𐐻 𐑋𐐲𐑉𐑅𐐨, 𐐬𐑂𐐲𐑉 𐐫𐑊 𐐸𐐮𐑆 𐐶𐐲𐑉𐐿𐑅; 𐐸𐐶𐐯𐑉𐑁𐐫𐑉, 𐐺𐐨𐑊𐐲𐑂𐐯𐐼 𐐺𐑉𐐯𐑄𐑉𐐯𐑌, 𐐺𐐨 𐑉𐐯𐐿𐐲𐑌𐑅𐐴𐑊𐐼 𐐲𐑌𐐻𐐭 𐐸𐐮𐑋 𐑃𐑉𐐭 𐑄 𐐲𐐻𐐬𐑌𐑋𐐯𐑌𐐻 𐐱𐑂 𐐗𐑉𐐴𐑅𐐻, 𐐸𐐮𐑆 𐐄𐑌𐑊𐐨 𐐒𐐨𐑀𐐱𐐻𐑌 𐐝𐐲𐑌, 𐐰𐑌𐐼 𐐷𐐨 𐑋𐐩 𐐱𐐺𐐻𐐩𐑌 𐐲 𐑉𐐯𐑆𐐲𐑉𐐯𐐿𐑇𐐲𐑌,

𐐲𐐿𐐫𐑉𐐼𐐮𐑍 𐐻𐐭 𐑄 𐐹𐐵𐐲𐑉 𐐱𐑂 𐑄 𐑉𐐯𐑆𐐲𐑉𐐯𐐿𐑇𐐲𐑌 𐐸𐐶𐐮𐐽 𐐮𐑆 𐐮𐑌 𐐗𐑉𐐴𐑅𐐻, 𐐰𐑌𐐼 𐐺 𐐹𐑉𐐯𐑆𐐯𐑌𐐻𐐯𐐼 𐐰𐑆 𐑄 𐑁𐐲𐑉𐑅𐐻-𐑁𐑉𐐭𐐻𐑅 𐐱𐑂 𐐗𐑉𐐴𐑅𐐻 𐐲𐑌𐐻𐐭 𐐘𐐱𐐼, 𐐸𐐰𐑂𐐮𐑍 𐑁𐐩𐑃, 𐐰𐑌𐐼 𐐱𐐺𐐻𐐩𐑌𐐼 𐐲 𐑀𐐳𐐼 𐐸𐐬𐐹 𐐱𐑂 𐑀𐑊𐐬𐑉𐐨 𐐮𐑌 𐐸𐐮𐑋 𐐺𐐨𐑁𐐬𐑉 𐐸𐐨 𐑋𐐰𐑌𐐮𐑁𐐯𐑅𐐻𐐯𐑃 𐐸𐐮𐑋𐑅𐐯𐑊𐑁 𐐮𐑌 𐑄 𐑁𐑊𐐯𐑇.

4. 𐐈𐑌𐐼 𐑌𐐵, 𐐺𐐨𐑊𐐲𐑂𐐯𐐼, 𐑋𐐪𐑉𐑂𐐯𐑊 𐑌𐐱𐐻 𐑄𐐰𐐻 𐐌 𐐻𐐯𐑊 𐐷𐐭 𐑄𐐨𐑆 𐑃𐐮𐑍𐑆; 𐑁𐐫𐑉 𐐸𐐶𐐴 𐑌𐐱𐐻 𐑅𐐹𐐨𐐿 𐐱𐑂 𐑄 𐐲𐐻𐐬𐑌𐑋𐐯𐑌𐐻 𐐱𐑂 𐐗𐑉𐐴𐑅𐐻, 𐐰𐑌𐐼 𐐲𐐻𐐩𐑌 𐐻𐐭 𐐲 𐐹𐐲𐑉𐑁𐐯𐐿𐐻 𐑌𐐱𐑊𐐯𐐾 𐐱𐑂 𐐸𐐮𐑋, 𐐰𐑆 𐐻𐐭 𐐲𐐻𐐩𐑌 𐐻𐐭 𐑄 𐑌𐐱𐑊𐐯𐐾 𐐱𐑂 𐐲 𐑉𐐯𐑆𐐲𐑉𐐯𐐿𐑇𐐲𐑌 𐐰𐑌𐐼 𐑄 𐐶𐐲𐑉𐑊𐐼 𐐻𐐭 𐐿𐐲𐑋? 𐐒𐐨𐐸𐐬𐑊𐐼, 𐑋𐐴 𐐺𐑉𐐯𐑄𐑉𐐯𐑌, 𐐸𐐨 𐑄𐐰𐐻 𐐹𐑉𐐱𐑁𐐯𐑅𐐴𐐯𐑃, 𐑊𐐯𐐻 𐐸𐐮𐑋 𐐹𐑉𐐱𐑁𐐯𐑅𐐴 𐐻𐐭 𐑄 𐐲𐑌𐐼𐐲𐑉𐑅𐐻𐐰𐑌𐐼𐐮𐑍 𐐱𐑂 𐑋𐐯𐑌; 𐑁𐐫𐑉 𐑄 𐐝𐐹𐐮𐑉𐐮𐐻 𐑅𐐹𐐨𐐿𐐯𐑃 𐑄 𐐻𐑉𐐭𐑃 𐐰𐑌𐐼 𐑊𐐴𐐯𐑃 𐑌𐐱𐐻. 𐐐𐐶𐐯𐑉𐑁𐐫𐑉, 𐐮𐐻 𐑅𐐹𐐨𐐿𐐯𐑃 𐐱𐑂 𐑃𐐮𐑍𐑆 𐐰𐑆 𐑄𐐩 𐑉𐐨𐐲𐑊𐐨 𐐪𐑉, 𐐰𐑌𐐼 𐐱𐑂 𐑃𐐮𐑍𐑆 𐐰𐑆 𐑄𐐩 𐑉𐐨𐐲𐑊𐐨 𐐶𐐮𐑊 𐐺; 𐐸𐐶𐐯𐑉𐑁𐐫𐑉, 𐑄𐐨𐑆 𐑃𐐮𐑍𐑆 𐐪𐑉 𐑋𐐰𐑌𐐮𐑁𐐯𐑅𐐻𐐯𐐼 𐐲𐑌𐐻𐐭 𐐲𐑅 𐐹𐑊𐐩𐑌𐑊𐐨, 𐑁𐐫𐑉 𐑄 𐑅𐐰𐑊𐑂𐐩𐑇𐐲𐑌 𐐱𐑂 𐐪𐑉 𐑅𐐬𐑊𐑆. 𐐒𐐲𐐻 𐐺𐐨𐐸𐐬𐑊𐐼, 𐐶𐐨 𐐪𐑉 𐑌𐐱𐐻 𐐶𐐮𐐻𐑌𐐯𐑅𐐯𐑆 𐐲𐑊𐐬𐑌 𐐮𐑌 𐑄𐐨𐑆 𐑃𐐮𐑍𐑆; 𐑁𐐫𐑉 𐐘𐐱𐐼 𐐫𐑊𐑅𐐬 𐑅𐐹𐐩𐐿 𐑄𐐯𐑋 𐐲𐑌𐐻𐐭 𐐹𐑉𐐱𐑁𐐯𐐻𐑅 𐐱𐑂 𐐬𐑊𐐼.

5. 𐐒𐐲𐐻 𐐺𐐨𐐸𐐬𐑊𐐼, 𐑄 𐐖𐐭𐑆 𐐶𐐲𐑉 𐐲 𐑅𐐻𐐮𐑁𐑌𐐯𐐿𐐻 𐐹𐐨𐐹𐑊; 𐐰𐑌𐐼 𐑄𐐩 𐐼𐐯𐑅𐐹𐐴𐑆𐐼 𐑄 𐐶𐐲𐑉𐐼𐑆 𐐱𐑂 𐐹𐑊𐐩𐑌𐑌𐐯𐑅, 𐐰𐑌𐐼 𐐿𐐮𐑊𐐼 𐑄 𐐹𐑉𐐱𐑁𐐯𐐻𐑅, 𐐰𐑌𐐼 𐑅𐐫𐐻 𐑁𐐫𐑉 𐑃𐐮𐑍𐑆 𐑄𐐰𐐻 𐑄𐐩 𐐿𐐳𐐼 𐑌𐐱𐐻 𐐲𐑌𐐼𐐲𐑉𐑅𐐻𐐰𐑌𐐼. 𐐐𐐶𐐯𐑉𐑁𐐫𐑉, 𐐺𐐨𐐿𐐫𐑆 𐐱𐑂 𐑄𐐯𐑉 𐐺𐑊𐐴𐑌𐐼𐑌𐐯𐑅, 𐐸𐐶𐐮𐐽 𐐺𐑊𐐴𐑌𐐼𐑌𐐯𐑅 𐐿𐐩𐑋 𐐺𐐴 𐑊𐐳𐐿𐐮𐑍 𐐺𐐨𐐷𐐱𐑌𐐼 𐑄 𐑋𐐪𐑉𐐿, 𐑄𐐩 𐑋𐐲𐑅𐐻 𐑌𐐨𐐼𐑆 𐑁𐐫𐑊: 𐑁𐐫𐑉 𐐘𐐱𐐼 𐐸𐐰𐑃 𐐻𐐩𐐿𐐲𐑌 𐐲𐐶𐐩 𐐸𐐮𐑆 𐐹𐑊𐐩𐑌𐑌𐐯𐑅 𐑁𐑉𐐱𐑋 𐑄𐐯𐑋, 𐐰𐑌𐐼 𐐼𐐯𐑊𐐮𐑂𐐲𐑉𐐼 𐐲𐑌𐐻𐐭 𐑄𐐯𐑋 𐑋𐐯𐑌𐐨 𐑃𐐮𐑍𐑆 𐐸𐐶𐐮𐐽 𐑄𐐩 𐐿𐐰𐑌𐐱𐐻 𐐲𐑌𐐼𐐲𐑉𐑅𐐻𐐰𐑌𐐼, 𐐺𐐨𐐿𐐫𐑆 𐑄𐐩 𐐼𐐯𐑆𐐴𐑉𐐼 𐐮𐐻. 𐐈𐑌𐐼 𐐺𐐨𐐿𐐫𐑆 𐑄𐐩 𐐼𐐯𐑆𐐴𐑉𐐼 𐐮𐐻, 𐐘𐐱𐐼 𐐸𐐰𐑃 𐐼𐐲𐑌 𐐮𐐻, 𐑄𐐰𐐻 𐑄𐐩 𐑋𐐩 𐑅𐐻𐐲𐑋𐐺𐑊.

6. 𐐈𐑌𐐼 𐑌𐐵 𐐌, 𐐖𐐩𐐿𐐲𐐺, 𐐰𐑋 𐑊𐐯𐐼 𐐱𐑌 𐐺𐐴 𐑄 𐐝𐐹𐐮𐑉𐐮𐐻 𐐲𐑌𐐻𐐭 𐐹𐑉𐐱𐑁𐐯𐑅𐐴𐐮𐑍: 𐑁𐐫𐑉 𐐌 𐐹𐐲𐑉𐑅𐐨𐑂 𐐺𐐴 𐑄 𐐶𐐲𐑉𐐿𐐮𐑍𐑆 𐐱𐑂 𐑄 𐐝𐐹𐐮𐑉𐐮𐐻 𐐸𐐶𐐮𐐽 𐐮𐑆 𐐮𐑌 𐑋𐐨, 𐑄𐐰𐐻 𐐺𐐴 𐑄 𐑅𐐻𐐲𐑋𐐺𐑊𐐮𐑍 𐐱𐑂 𐑄 𐐖𐐭𐑆, 𐑄𐐩 𐐶𐐮𐑊 𐑉𐐨𐐾𐐯𐐿𐐻 𐑄 𐑅𐐻𐐬𐑌 𐐲𐐹𐐱𐑌 𐐸𐐶𐐮𐐽 𐑄𐐩 𐑋𐐴𐐻 𐐺𐐮𐑊𐐼, 𐐰𐑌𐐼 𐐸𐐰𐑂 𐑅𐐩𐑁 𐑁𐐵𐑌𐐼𐐩𐑇𐐲𐑌. 𐐒𐐲𐐻 𐐺𐐨𐐸𐐬𐑊𐐼, 𐐲𐐿𐐫𐑉𐐼𐐮𐑍 𐐻𐐭 𐑄 𐑅𐐿𐑉𐐮𐐹𐐽𐐲𐑉𐑆, 𐑄𐐮𐑅 𐑅𐐻𐐬𐑌 𐑇𐐰𐑊 𐐺𐐨𐐿𐐲𐑋 𐑄 𐑀𐑉𐐩𐐻, 𐐰𐑌𐐼 𐑄 𐑊𐐰𐑅𐐻, 𐐰𐑌𐐼 𐑄 𐐬𐑌𐑊𐐨 𐑇𐐳𐑉 𐑁𐐵𐑌𐐼𐐩𐑇𐐲𐑌, 𐐲𐐹𐐱𐑌 𐐸𐐶𐐮𐐽 𐑄 𐐖𐐭𐑆 𐐿𐐰𐑌 𐐺𐐮𐑊𐐼. 𐐈𐑌𐐼 𐑌𐐵, 𐑋𐐴 𐐺𐐨𐑊𐐲𐑂𐐯𐐼, 𐐸𐐵 𐐮𐑆 𐐮𐐻 𐐹𐐱𐑅𐐮𐐺𐑊 𐑄𐐰𐐻 𐑄𐐨𐑆, 𐐰𐑁𐐻𐐲𐑉 𐐸𐐰𐑂𐐮𐑍 𐑉𐐨𐐾𐐯𐐿𐐻𐐯𐐼 𐑄 𐑇𐐳𐑉 𐑁𐐵𐑌𐐼𐐩𐑇𐐲𐑌, 𐐿𐐰𐑌 𐐯𐑂𐐲𐑉 𐐺𐐮𐑊𐐼 𐐲𐐹𐐱𐑌 𐐮𐐻, 𐑄𐐰𐐻 𐐮𐐻 𐑋𐐩 𐐺𐐨𐐿𐐲𐑋 𐑄 𐐸𐐯𐐼 𐐱𐑂 𐑄𐐯𐑉 𐐿𐐫𐑉𐑌𐐲𐑉? 𐐒𐐨𐐸𐐬𐑊𐐼, 𐑋𐐴 𐐺𐐨𐑊𐐲𐑂𐐯𐐼 𐐺𐑉𐐯𐑄𐑉𐐯𐑌, 𐐌 𐐶𐐮𐑊 𐐲𐑌𐑁𐐬𐑊𐐼 𐑄𐐮𐑅 𐑋𐐮𐑅𐐻𐐲𐑉𐐨 𐐲𐑌𐐻𐐭 𐐷𐐭; 𐐮𐑁 𐐌 𐐼𐐭 𐑌𐐱𐐻, 𐐺𐐴 𐐯𐑌𐐨 𐑋𐐨𐑌𐑆, 𐑀𐐯𐐻 𐑇𐐩𐐿𐐲𐑌 𐑁𐑉𐐱𐑋 𐑋𐐴 𐑁𐐲𐑉𐑋𐑌𐐯𐑅 𐐮𐑌 𐑄 𐐝𐐹𐐮𐑉𐐮𐐻, 𐐰𐑌𐐼 𐑅𐐻𐐲𐑋𐐺𐑊 𐐺𐐨𐐿𐐫𐑆 𐐱𐑂 𐑋𐐴 𐐬𐑂𐐲𐑉 𐐰𐑍𐑆𐐴𐐯𐐻𐐨 𐑁𐐫𐑉 𐐷𐐭.

7. 𐐒𐐨𐐸𐐬𐑊𐐼, 𐑋𐐴 𐐺𐑉𐐯𐑄𐑉𐐯𐑌, 𐐼𐐭 𐐷𐐨 𐑌𐐱𐐻 𐑉𐐨𐑋𐐯𐑋𐐺𐐲𐑉 𐐻𐐭 𐐸𐐰𐑂 𐑉𐐯𐐼 𐑄 𐐶𐐲𐑉𐐼𐑆 𐐱𐑂 𐑄 𐐹𐑉𐐱𐑁𐐯𐐻 𐐞𐐨𐑌𐐲𐑅, 𐐸𐐶𐐮𐐽 𐑅𐐹𐐩𐐿 𐐲𐑌𐐻𐐭 𐑄 𐐸𐐵𐑅 𐐱𐑂 𐐆𐑆𐑉𐐩𐐯𐑊, 𐑅𐐩𐐮𐑍; 𐐐𐐲𐑉𐐿𐐲𐑌, 𐐄 𐐷𐐨 𐐸𐐵𐑅 𐐱𐑂 𐐆𐑆𐑉𐐩𐐯𐑊, 𐐰𐑌𐐼 𐐸𐐨𐑉 𐑄 𐐶𐐲𐑉𐐼𐑆 𐐱𐑂 𐑋𐐨, 𐐲 𐐹𐑉𐐱𐑁𐐯𐐻 𐐱𐑂 𐑄 𐐢𐐫𐑉𐐼; 𐑁𐐫𐑉 𐐺𐐨𐐸𐐬𐑊𐐼, 𐑄𐐲𐑅 𐑅𐐯𐑃 𐑄 𐐢𐐫𐑉𐐼, 𐐌 𐐶𐐮𐑊 𐑊𐐴𐐿𐐲𐑌 𐑄𐐨, 𐐄 𐐸𐐵𐑅 𐐱𐑂 𐐆𐑆𐑉𐐩𐐯𐑊, 𐑊𐐴𐐿 𐐲𐑌𐐻𐐭 𐐲 𐐻𐐩𐑋 𐐱𐑊𐐮𐑂 𐐻𐑉𐐨, 𐐸𐐶𐐮𐐽 𐐲 𐑋𐐰𐑌 𐐻𐐳𐐿 𐐰𐑌𐐼 𐑌𐐲𐑉𐐮𐑇𐐻 𐐮𐑌 𐐸𐐮𐑆 𐑂𐐮𐑌𐐷𐐲𐑉𐐼; 𐐰𐑌𐐼 𐐮𐐻 𐑀𐑉𐐭, 𐐰𐑌𐐼 𐐶𐐰𐐿𐑅𐐻 𐐬𐑊𐐼, 𐐰𐑌𐐼 𐐺𐐨𐑀𐐰𐑌 𐐻𐐭 𐐼𐐨𐐿𐐩. 𐐈𐑌𐐼 𐐮𐐻 𐐿𐐩𐑋 𐐻𐐭 𐐹𐐰𐑅 𐑄𐐰𐐻 𐑄 𐑋𐐰𐑅𐐻𐐲𐑉 𐐱𐑂 𐑄 𐑂𐐮𐑌𐐷𐐲𐑉𐐼 𐐶𐐯𐑌𐐻 𐑁𐐫𐑉𐑃, 𐐰𐑌𐐼 𐐸𐐨 𐑅𐐱 𐑄𐐰𐐻 𐐸𐐮𐑆 𐐱𐑊𐐮𐑂 𐐻𐑉𐐨 𐐺𐐨𐑀𐐰𐑌 𐐻𐐭 𐐼𐐨𐐿𐐩; 𐐰𐑌𐐼 𐐸𐐨 𐑅𐐯𐐼, 𐐌 𐐶𐐮𐑊 𐐹𐑉𐐭𐑌 𐐮𐐻, 𐐰𐑌𐐼 𐐼𐐮𐑀 𐐲𐐺𐐵𐐻 𐐮𐐻, 𐐰𐑌𐐼 𐑌𐐲𐑉𐐮𐑇 𐐮𐐻, 𐑄𐐰𐐻 𐐹𐐲𐑉𐐸𐐰𐐹𐑅 𐐮𐐻 𐑋𐐩 𐑇𐐭𐐻 𐑁𐐫𐑉𐑃 𐐷𐐲𐑍 𐐰𐑌𐐼 𐐻𐐯𐑌𐐼𐐲𐑉 𐐺𐑉𐐰𐑌𐐽𐐯𐑆, 𐐰𐑌𐐼 𐐮𐐻 𐐹𐐯𐑉𐐮𐑇 𐑌𐐱𐐻. 𐐈𐑌𐐼 𐐮𐐻 𐐿𐐩𐑋 𐐻𐐭 𐐹𐐰𐑅 𐑄𐐰𐐻 𐐸𐐨 𐐹𐑉𐐭𐑌𐐼 𐐮𐐻, 𐐰𐑌𐐼 𐐼𐐮𐑀𐐼 𐐲𐐺𐐵𐐻 𐐮𐐻, 𐐰𐑌𐐼 𐑌𐐲𐑉𐐮𐑇𐐻 𐐮𐐻 𐐲𐐿𐐫𐑉𐐼𐐮𐑍 𐐻𐐭 𐐸𐐮𐑆 𐐶𐐲𐑉𐐼. 𐐈𐑌𐐼 𐐮𐐻 𐐿𐐩𐑋 𐐻𐐭 𐐹𐐰𐑅 𐑄𐐰𐐻 𐐰𐑁𐐻𐐲𐑉 𐑋𐐯𐑌𐐨 𐐼𐐩𐑆, 𐐮𐐻 𐐺𐐨𐑀𐐰𐑌 𐐻𐐭 𐐹𐐳𐐻 𐑁𐐫𐑉𐑃 𐑅𐐲𐑋𐐸𐐶𐐱𐐻 𐐲 𐑊𐐮𐐻𐑊, 𐐷𐐲𐑍 𐐰𐑌𐐼 𐐻𐐯𐑌𐐼𐐲𐑉 𐐺𐑉𐐰𐑌𐐽𐐯𐑆; 𐐺𐐲𐐻 𐐺𐐨𐐸𐐬𐑊𐐼, 𐑄 𐑋𐐩𐑌 𐐻𐐱𐐹 𐑄𐐯𐑉𐐱𐑂 𐐺𐐨𐑀𐐰𐑌 𐐻𐐭 𐐹𐐯𐑉𐐮𐑇. 𐐈𐑌𐐼 𐐮𐐻 𐐿𐐩𐑋 𐐻𐐭 𐐹𐐰𐑅 𐑄𐐰𐐻 𐑄 𐑋𐐰𐑅𐐻𐐲𐑉 𐐱𐑂 𐑄 𐑂𐐮𐑌𐐷𐐲𐑉𐐼 𐑅𐐱 𐐮𐐻, 𐐰𐑌𐐼 𐐸𐐨 𐑅𐐯𐐼 𐐲𐑌𐐻𐐭 𐐸𐐮𐑆 𐑅𐐲𐑉𐑂𐐲𐑌𐐻, 𐐮𐐻 𐑀𐑉𐐨𐑂𐐯𐑃 𐑋𐐨 𐑄𐐰𐐻 𐐌 𐑇𐐳𐐼 𐑊𐐭𐑆 𐑄𐐮𐑅 𐐻𐑉𐐨; 𐐸𐐶𐐯𐑉𐑁𐐫𐑉, 𐑀𐐬 𐐰𐑌𐐼 𐐹𐑊𐐲𐐿 𐑄 𐐺𐑉𐐰𐑌𐐽𐐯𐑆 𐑁𐑉𐐱𐑋 𐐲 𐐶𐐴𐑊𐐼 𐐱𐑊𐐮𐑂 𐐻𐑉𐐨, 𐐰𐑌𐐼 𐐺𐑉𐐮𐑍 𐑄𐐯𐑋 𐐸𐐮𐑄𐐲𐑉 𐐲𐑌𐐻𐐭 𐑋𐐨, 𐐰𐑌𐐼 𐐶𐐨 𐐶𐐮𐑊 𐐹𐑊𐐲𐐿 𐐫𐑁 𐑄𐐬𐑆 𐑋𐐩𐑌 𐐺𐑉𐐰𐑌𐐽𐐯𐑆 𐐸𐐶𐐮𐐽 𐐪𐑉 𐐺𐐨𐑀𐐮𐑌𐐮𐑍 𐐻𐐭 𐐶𐐮𐑄𐐲𐑉 𐐲𐐶𐐩, 𐐰𐑌𐐼 𐐶𐐨 𐐶𐐮𐑊 𐐿𐐰𐑅𐐻 𐑄𐐯𐑋 𐐮𐑌𐐻𐐭 𐑄 𐑁𐐴𐑉, 𐑄𐐰𐐻 𐑄𐐩 𐑋𐐩 𐐺

𐐺𐐲𐑉𐑌𐐼. 𐐈𐑌𐐼 𐐺𐐮𐐸𐐬𐑊𐐼, 𐑅𐐯𐑃 𐑄 𐐢𐐫𐑉𐐼 𐐱𐑂 𐑄 𐑂𐐮𐑌𐐷𐐲𐑉𐐼, 𐐌 𐐻𐐩𐐿 𐐰𐐶𐐩 𐑋𐐯𐑌𐐨 𐐱𐑂 𐑄𐐨𐑆 𐐷𐐲𐑍 𐐰𐑌𐐼 𐐻𐐯𐑌𐐼𐐯𐑉 𐐺𐑉𐐰𐑌𐐽𐐯𐑆, 𐐰𐑌𐐼 𐐌 𐐶𐐮𐑊 𐑀𐑉𐐪𐑁𐐻 𐑄𐐯𐑋 𐐸𐐶𐐮𐑄𐐯𐑉𐑅𐐬𐐯𐑂𐐯𐑉 𐐌 𐐶𐐮𐑊; 𐐰𐑌𐐼 𐐮𐐻 𐑋𐐰𐐻𐐯𐑉𐐯𐑃 𐑌𐐱𐐻 𐑄𐐰𐐻 𐐮𐑁 𐐮𐐻 𐑅𐐬 𐐺, 𐑄𐐰𐐻 𐑄 𐑉𐐭𐐻 𐐱𐑂 𐑄𐐮𐑅 𐐻𐑉𐐨 𐐶𐐮𐑊 𐐹𐐯𐑉𐐮𐑇, 𐐌 𐑋𐐩 𐐹𐑉𐐨𐑆𐐲𐑉𐑂 𐑄 𐑁𐑉𐐭𐐻 𐑄𐐯𐑉𐐱𐑂 𐐲𐑌𐐻𐐭 𐑋𐐴𐑅𐐯𐑊𐑁; 𐐸𐐶𐐯𐑉𐑁𐐬𐑉, 𐐌 𐐶𐐮𐑊 𐐻𐐩𐐿 𐑄𐐨𐑆 𐐷𐐲𐑍 𐐰𐑌𐐼 𐐻𐐯𐑌𐐼𐐯𐑉 𐐺𐑉𐐰𐑌𐐽𐐯𐑆, 𐐰𐑌𐐼 𐐌 𐐶𐐮𐑊 𐑀𐑉𐐪𐑁𐐻 𐑄𐐯𐑋 𐐸𐐶𐐮𐑄𐐯𐑉𐑅𐐬𐐯𐑂𐐯𐑉 𐐌 𐐶𐐮𐑊. 𐐓𐐩𐐿 𐑄𐐵 𐑄 𐐺𐑉𐐰𐑌𐐽𐐯𐑆 𐐱𐑂 𐑄 𐐶𐐴𐑊𐐼 𐐱𐑊𐐮𐑂 𐐻𐑉𐐨, 𐐰𐑌𐐼 𐑀𐑉𐐪𐑁𐐻 𐑄𐐯𐑋 𐐮𐑌, 𐐮𐑌 𐑄 𐑅𐐻𐐯𐐼 𐑄𐐯𐑉𐐱𐑂; 𐐰𐑌𐐼 𐑄𐐨𐑆 𐐸𐐶𐐮𐐽 𐐌 𐐸𐐰𐑂 𐐹𐑊𐐲𐐿𐐻 𐐫𐑁, 𐐌 𐐶𐐮𐑊 𐐿𐐪𐑅𐐻 𐐮𐑌𐐻𐐭 𐑄 𐑁𐐴𐑉, 𐐰𐑌𐐼 𐐺𐐲𐑉𐑌 𐑄𐐯𐑋, 𐑄𐐰𐐻 𐑄𐐩 𐑋𐐩 𐑌𐐱𐐻 𐐿𐐲𐑋𐐺𐐯𐑉 𐑄 𐑀𐑉𐐵𐑌𐐼 𐐱𐑂 𐑋𐐴 𐑂𐐮𐑌𐐷𐐲𐑉𐐼.

8. 𐐈𐑌𐐼 𐐮𐐻 𐐿𐐩𐑋 𐐻𐐭 𐐹𐐪𐑅 𐑄𐐰𐐻 𐑄 𐑅𐐲𐑉𐑂𐐲𐑌𐐻 𐐱𐑂 𐑄 𐐢𐐫𐑉𐐼 𐐱𐑂 𐑄 𐑂𐐮𐑌𐐷𐐲𐑉𐐼, 𐐼𐐮𐐼 𐐰𐐿𐐫𐑉𐐼𐐮𐑍 𐐻𐐭 𐑄 𐐶𐐲𐑉𐐼 𐐱𐑂 𐑄 𐐢𐐫𐑉𐐼 𐐱𐑂 𐑄 𐑂𐐮𐑌𐐷𐐲𐑉𐐼, 𐐰𐑌𐐼 𐑀𐑉𐐪𐑁𐐻𐐯𐐼 𐐮𐑌 𐑄 𐐺𐑉𐐰𐑌𐐽𐐯𐑆 𐐱𐑂 𐑄 𐐶𐐴𐑊𐐼 𐐱𐑊𐐮𐑂 𐐻𐑉𐐨. 𐐈𐑌𐐼 𐑄 𐐢𐐫𐑉𐐼 𐐱𐑂 𐑄 𐑂𐐮𐑌𐐷𐐲𐑉𐐼 𐐿𐐫𐑆𐐼 𐑄𐐰𐐻 𐐮𐐻 𐑇𐐳𐐼 𐐺 𐐼𐐮𐑀𐐼 𐐰𐐺𐐵𐐻, 𐐰𐑌𐐼 𐐹𐑉𐐭𐑌𐐼, 𐐰𐑌𐐼 𐑌𐐲𐑉𐐮𐑇𐐻, 𐑅𐐩𐐮𐑍 𐐲𐑌𐐻𐐭 𐐸𐐮𐑆 𐑅𐐲𐑉𐑂𐐲𐑌𐐻, 𐐆𐐻 𐑀𐑉𐐨𐑂𐐯𐑃 𐑋𐐨 𐑄𐐰𐐻 𐐌 𐑇𐐳𐐼 𐑊𐐭𐑆 𐑄𐐮𐑅 𐐻𐑉𐐨; 𐐸𐐶𐐯𐑉𐑁𐐬𐑉, 𐑄𐐰𐐻 𐐹𐐲𐑉𐐸𐐰𐐹𐑅 𐐌 𐑋𐐴𐐻 𐐹𐑉𐐨𐑆𐐲𐑉𐑂 𐑄 𐑉𐐭𐐻𐑅 𐑄𐐯𐑉𐐱𐑂 𐑄𐐰𐐻 𐑄𐐩 𐐹𐐯𐑉𐐮𐑇 𐑌𐐱𐐻, 𐑄𐐰𐐻 𐐌 𐑋𐐴𐐻 𐐹𐑉𐐨𐑆𐐲𐑉𐑂 𐑄𐐯𐑋 𐐲𐑌𐐻𐐭 𐑋𐐴𐑅𐐯𐑊𐑁, 𐐌 𐐸𐐰𐑂 𐐼𐐲𐑌 𐑄𐐮𐑅 𐑃𐐮𐑍. 𐐐𐐶𐐯𐑉𐑁𐐬𐑉, 𐑀𐐬 𐑄𐐴 𐐶𐐩; 𐐶𐐱𐐽 𐑄 𐐻𐑉𐐨, 𐐰𐑌𐐼 𐑌𐐲𐑉𐐮𐑇 𐐮𐐻, 𐐰𐐿𐐫𐑉𐐼𐐮𐑍 𐐻𐐭 𐑋𐐴 𐐶𐐲𐑉𐐼𐑆. 𐐈𐑌𐐼 𐑄𐐨𐑆 𐐶𐐮𐑊 𐐌 𐐹𐑊𐐩𐑅 𐐮𐑌 𐑄 𐑌𐐯𐑄𐐲𐑉𐑋𐐬𐑅𐐻 𐐹𐐪𐑉𐐻 𐐱𐑂 𐑋𐐴 𐑂𐐮𐑌𐐷𐐲𐑉𐐼, 𐐸𐐶𐐮𐑄𐐯𐑉𐑅𐐬𐐯𐑂𐐯𐑉 𐐌 𐐶𐐮𐑊, 𐐮𐐻 𐑋𐐰𐐻𐐯𐑉𐐯𐑃 𐑌𐐱𐐻 𐐲𐑌𐐻𐐭 𐑄; 𐐰𐑌𐐼 𐐌 𐐼𐐭 𐐮𐐻 𐑄𐐰𐐻 𐐌 𐑋𐐩 𐐹𐑉𐐨𐑆𐐲𐑉𐑂 𐐲𐑌𐐻𐐭 𐑋𐐴𐑅𐐯𐑊𐑁 𐑄 𐑌𐐰𐐻𐐷𐐭𐑉𐐲𐑊 𐐺𐑉𐐰𐑌𐐽𐐯𐑆 𐐱𐑂 𐑄 𐐻𐑉𐐨; 𐐰𐑌𐐼 𐐫𐑊𐑅𐐬, 𐑄𐐰𐐻 𐐌 𐑋𐐩 𐑊𐐩 𐐲𐐹 𐑁𐑉𐐭𐐻 𐑄𐐯𐑉𐐱𐑂, 𐐰𐑀𐐯𐑌𐑅𐐻 𐑄 𐑅𐐨𐑆𐐲𐑌, 𐐲𐑌𐐻𐐭 𐑋𐐴𐑅𐐯𐑊𐑁: 𐑁𐐫𐑉 𐐮𐐻 𐑀𐑉𐐨𐑂𐐯𐑃 𐑋𐐨 𐑄𐐰𐐻 𐐌 𐑇𐐳𐐼 𐑊𐐭𐑆 𐑄𐐮𐑅 𐐻𐑉𐐨 𐐰𐑌𐐼 𐑄 𐑁𐑉𐐭𐐻 𐑄𐐯𐑉𐐱𐑂.

9. 𐐈𐑌𐐼 𐐮𐐻 𐐿𐐩𐑋 𐐻𐐭 𐐹𐐪𐑅 𐑄𐐰𐐻 𐑄 𐐢𐐫𐑉𐐼 𐐱𐑂 𐑄 𐑂𐐮𐑌𐐷𐐲𐑉𐐼 𐐶𐐯𐑌𐐻 𐑁𐐬𐑉𐑃, 𐐰𐑌𐐼 𐐸𐐮𐐼 𐑄 𐑌𐐰𐐻𐐷𐐭𐑉𐐲𐑊 𐐺𐑉𐐰𐑌𐐽𐐯𐑆 𐐱𐑂 𐑄 𐐻𐐩𐑋 𐐱𐑊𐐮𐑂 𐐻𐑉𐐨 𐐮𐑌 𐑄 𐑌𐐯𐑄𐐲𐑉𐑋𐐬𐑅𐐻 𐐹𐐪𐑉𐐻𐑅 𐐱𐑂 𐑄 𐑂𐐮𐑌𐐷𐐲𐑉𐐼; 𐑅𐐲𐑋 𐐮𐑌 𐐶𐐲𐑌, 𐐰𐑌𐐼 𐑅𐐲𐑋 𐐮𐑌 𐐰𐑌𐐲𐑄𐐯𐑉, 𐐰𐐿𐐫𐑉𐐼𐐮𐑍 𐐻𐐭 𐐸𐐮𐑆 𐐶𐐮𐑊 𐐰𐑌𐐼 𐐹𐑊𐐯𐑈𐐲𐑉. 𐐈𐑌𐐼 𐐮𐐻 𐐿𐐩𐑋 𐐻𐐭 𐐹𐐪𐑅 𐑄𐐰𐐻 𐐰 𐑊𐐱𐑍 𐐻𐐴𐑋 𐐹𐐪𐑅𐐻 𐐰𐐶𐐩, 𐐰𐑌𐐼 𐑄 𐐢𐐫𐑉𐐼 𐐱𐑂 𐑄 𐑂𐐮𐑌𐐷𐐲𐑉𐐼 𐑅𐐯𐐼 𐐲𐑌𐐻𐐭 𐐸𐐮𐑆 𐑅𐐲𐑉𐑂𐐲𐑌𐐻, 𐐗𐐲𐑋, 𐑊𐐯𐐻 𐐲𐑅 𐑀𐐬 𐐼𐐵𐑌 𐐮𐑌𐐻𐐭 𐑄 𐑂𐐮𐑌𐐷𐐲𐑉𐐼, 𐑄𐐰𐐻 𐐶𐐨 𐑋𐐩 𐑊𐐩𐐺𐐲𐑉 𐐮𐑌 𐑄 𐑂𐐮𐑌𐐷𐐲𐑉𐐼.

10. 𐐈𐑌𐐼 𐐮𐐻 𐐿𐐩𐑋 𐐻𐐭 𐐹𐐪𐑅 𐑄𐐰𐐻 𐑄 𐐢𐐫𐑉𐐼 𐐱𐑂 𐑄 𐑂𐐮𐑌𐐷𐐲𐑉𐐼, 𐐰𐑌𐐼 𐐫𐑊𐑅𐐬 𐑄 𐑅𐐲𐑉𐑂𐐲𐑌𐐻 𐐶𐐯𐑌𐐻 𐐼𐐵𐑌 𐐮𐑌𐐻𐐭 𐑄 𐑂𐐮𐑌𐐷𐐲𐑉𐐼 𐐻𐐭 𐑊𐐩𐐺𐐲𐑉. 𐐈𐑌𐐼 𐐮𐐻 𐐿𐐩𐑋 𐐻𐐭 𐐹𐐪𐑅 𐑄𐐰𐐻 𐑄 𐑅𐐲𐑉𐑂𐐲𐑌𐐻 𐑅𐐯𐐼 𐐲𐑌𐐻𐐭 𐐸𐐮𐑆 𐑋𐐪𐑅𐐻𐐯𐑉, 𐐒𐐮𐐸𐐬𐑊𐐼, 𐑊𐐳𐐿 𐐸𐐨𐑉; 𐐺𐐮𐐸𐐬𐑊𐐼 𐑄 𐐻𐑉𐐨. 𐐈𐑌𐐼 𐐮𐐻 𐐿𐐩𐑋 𐐻𐐭 𐐹𐐪𐑅 𐑄𐐰𐐻 𐑄 𐐢𐐫𐑉𐐼 𐐱𐑂 𐑄 𐑂𐐮𐑌𐐷𐐲𐑉𐐼 𐑊𐐳𐐿𐐻 𐐰𐑌𐐼 𐐺𐐨𐐸𐐯𐑊𐐼 𐑄 𐐻𐑉𐐨, 𐐮𐑌 𐑄 𐐸𐐶𐐮𐐽 𐑄 𐐶𐐴𐑊𐐼 𐐱𐑊𐐮𐑂 𐐺𐑉𐐰𐑌𐐽𐐯𐑆 𐐸𐐰𐐼 𐐺𐐮𐑌 𐑀𐑉𐐪𐑁𐐻𐐯𐐼; 𐐰𐑌𐐼 𐐮𐐻 𐐸𐐰𐐼 𐑅𐐹𐑉𐐲𐑍 𐑁𐐬𐑉𐑃, 𐐰𐑌𐐼 𐐺𐐮𐑀𐐲𐑌 𐐻𐐭 𐐺𐐩𐑉 𐑁𐑉𐐭𐐻. 𐐈𐑌𐐼 𐐸𐐨 𐐺𐐨𐐸𐐯𐑊𐐼 𐑄𐐰𐐻 𐐮𐐻 𐐶𐐱𐑆 𐑀𐐳𐐼; 𐐰𐑌𐐼 𐑄 𐑁𐑉𐐭𐐻 𐑄𐐯𐑉𐐱𐑂 𐐶𐐱𐑆 𐑊𐐴𐐿 𐐲𐑌𐐻𐐭 𐑄 𐑌𐐰𐐻𐐷𐐭𐑉𐐲𐑊 𐑁𐑉𐐭𐐻. 𐐈𐑌𐐼 𐐸𐐨 𐑅𐐯𐐼 𐐲𐑌𐐻𐐭 𐑄 𐑅𐐲𐑉𐑂𐐲𐑌𐐻, 𐐒𐐮𐐸𐐬𐑊𐐼, 𐑄 𐐺𐑉𐐰𐑌𐐽𐐯𐑆 𐐱𐑂 𐑄 𐐶𐐴𐑊𐐼 𐐻𐑉𐐨 𐐸𐐰𐑂 𐐻𐐩𐐿𐑌 𐐸𐐬𐑊𐐼 𐐱𐑂 𐑄 𐑋𐑎𐑅𐐻𐐷𐐭𐑉 𐐱𐑂 𐑄 𐑉𐐭𐐻 𐑄𐐯𐑉𐐱𐑂, 𐑄𐐰𐐻 𐑄 𐑉𐐭𐐻 𐑄𐐯𐑉𐐱𐑂 𐐸𐐰𐑃 𐐺𐑉𐐫𐐻 𐑁𐐬𐑉𐑃 𐑋𐐲𐐽 𐑅𐐻𐑉𐐯𐑍𐑃; 𐐰𐑌𐐼 𐐺𐐨𐐿𐐫𐑆 𐐱𐑂 𐑄 𐑋𐐲𐐽 𐑅𐐻𐑉𐐯𐑍𐑃 𐐱𐑂 𐑄 𐑉𐐭𐐻 𐑄𐐯𐑉𐐱𐑂, 𐑄 𐐶𐐴𐑊𐐼 𐐺𐑉𐐰𐑌𐐽𐐯𐑆 𐐸𐐰𐑂 𐐺𐑉𐐫𐐻 𐑁𐐬𐑉𐑃 𐐻𐐩𐑋 𐑁𐑉𐐭𐐻: 𐐤𐐵, 𐐮𐑁 𐐶𐐨 𐐸𐐰𐐼 𐑌𐐱𐐻 𐑀𐑉𐐪𐑁𐐻𐐯𐐼 𐐮𐑌 𐑄𐐨𐑆 𐐺𐑉𐐰𐑌𐐽𐐯𐑆, 𐑄 𐐻𐑉𐐨 𐑄𐐯𐑉𐐱𐑂 𐐶𐐳𐐼 𐐸𐐰𐑂 𐐹𐐯𐑉𐐮𐑇𐐻. 𐐈𐑌𐐼 𐑌𐐵, 𐐺𐐮𐐸𐐬𐑊𐐼, 𐐌 𐑇𐐰𐑊 𐑊𐐩 𐐲𐐹 𐑋𐐲𐐽 𐑁𐑉𐐭𐐻, 𐐸𐐶𐐮𐐽 𐑄 𐐻𐑉𐐨 𐑄𐐯𐑉𐐱𐑂 𐐸𐐰𐑃 𐐺𐑉𐐫𐐻 𐑁𐐬𐑉𐑃; 𐐰𐑌𐐼 𐑄 𐑁𐑉𐐭𐐻 𐑄𐐯𐑉𐐱𐑂 𐐌 𐑇𐐰𐑊 𐑊𐐩 𐐲𐐹, 𐐰𐑀𐐯𐑌𐑅𐐻 𐑄 𐑅𐐨𐑆𐐲𐑌, 𐐲𐑌𐐻𐐭 𐑋𐐴𐑌 𐐬𐑌 𐑅𐐯𐑊𐑁.

11. 𐐈𐑌𐐼 𐐮𐐻 𐐿𐐩𐑋 𐐻𐐭 𐐹𐐪𐑅 𐑄𐐰𐐻 𐑄 𐐢𐐫𐑉𐐼 𐐱𐑂 𐑄 𐑂𐐮𐑌𐐷𐐲𐑉𐐼 𐑅𐐯𐐼 𐐲𐑌𐐻𐐭 𐑄 𐑅𐐲𐑉𐑂𐐲𐑌𐐻, 𐐗𐐲𐑋, 𐑊𐐯𐐻 𐐲𐑅 𐑀𐐬 𐐻𐐭 𐑄 𐑌𐐯𐑄𐐲𐑉𐑋𐐬𐑅𐐻 𐐹𐐪𐑉𐐻 𐐱𐑂 𐑄 𐑂𐐮𐑌𐐷𐐲𐑉𐐼, 𐐰𐑌𐐼 𐐺𐐮𐐸𐐬𐑊𐐼 𐐮𐑁 𐑄 𐑌𐐰𐐻𐐷𐐭𐑉𐐲𐑊 𐐺𐑉𐐰𐑌𐐽𐐯𐑆 𐐱𐑂 𐑄 𐐻𐑉𐐨 𐐸𐐰𐑂 𐑌𐐱𐐻 𐐺𐑉𐐫𐐻 𐑁𐐬𐑉𐑃 𐑋𐐲𐐽 𐑁𐑉𐐭𐐻 𐐫𐑊𐑅𐐬, 𐑄𐐰𐐻 𐐌 𐑋𐐩 𐑊𐐩 𐐲𐐹 𐐱𐑂 𐑄 𐑁𐑉𐐭𐐻 𐑄𐐯𐑉𐐱𐑂, 𐐰𐑀𐐯𐑌𐑅𐐻 𐑄 𐑅𐐨𐑆𐐲𐑌, 𐐲𐑌𐐻𐐭 𐑋𐐴𐑌 𐐬𐑌 𐑅𐐯𐑊𐑁. 𐐈𐑌𐐼 𐐮𐐻 𐐿𐐩𐑋 𐐻𐐭 𐐹𐐪𐑅 𐑄𐐰𐐻 𐑄𐐩 𐐶𐐯𐑌𐐻 𐑁𐐬𐑉𐑃 𐐸𐐶𐐮𐑄𐐯𐑉 𐑄 𐑋𐐪𐑅𐐻𐐯𐑉 𐐸𐐰𐐼 𐐸𐐮𐐼 𐑄 𐑌𐐰𐐻𐐷𐐭𐑉𐐲𐑊 𐐺𐑉𐐰𐑌𐐽𐐯𐑆 𐐱𐑂 𐑄 𐐻𐑉𐐨, 𐐰𐑌𐐼 𐐸𐐨 𐑅𐐯𐐼 𐐲𐑌𐐻𐐭 𐑄 𐑅𐐲𐑉𐑂𐐲𐑌𐐻, 𐐒𐐮𐐸𐐬𐑊𐐼 𐑄𐐨𐑆: 𐐰𐑌𐐼 𐐸𐐨 𐐺𐐨𐐸𐐯𐑊𐐼 𐑄 𐑁𐐲𐑉𐑅𐐻, 𐑄𐐰𐐻 𐐮𐐻 𐐸𐐰𐐼 𐐺𐑉𐐫𐐻 𐑁𐐬𐑉𐑃 𐑋𐐲𐐽

𐑁𐑉𐐭𐐻; 𐐰𐑌𐐼 𐐸𐐨 𐐺𐐨𐐸𐐯𐑊𐐼 𐐫𐑊𐑅𐐬 𐑄𐐰𐐻 𐐮𐐻 𐐶𐐱𐑆 𐑀𐐳𐐼. 𐐈𐑌𐐼 𐐸𐐨 𐑅𐐯𐐼 𐐲𐑌𐐻𐐭 𐑄 𐑅𐐲𐑉𐑂𐐲𐑌𐐻, 𐐓𐐩𐐿 𐐱𐑂 𐑄 𐑁𐑉𐐭𐐻 𐑄𐐯𐑉𐐱𐑂, 𐐰𐑌𐐼 𐑊𐐩 𐐮𐐻 𐐲𐐹, 𐐰𐑀𐐯𐑌𐑅𐐻 𐑄 𐑅𐐨𐑆𐐲𐑌, 𐑄𐐰𐐻 𐐌 𐑋𐐩 𐐹𐑉𐐨𐑆𐐲𐑉𐑂 𐐮𐐻 𐐲𐑌𐐻𐐭 𐑋𐐴𐑌 𐐬𐑌 𐑅𐐯𐑊𐑁; 𐑁𐐫𐑉 𐐺𐐨𐐸𐐬𐑊𐐼, 𐑅𐐯𐐼 𐐸𐐨, 𐑄𐐮𐑅 𐑊𐐫𐑍 𐐻𐐴𐑋 𐐸𐐰𐑂 𐐌 𐑌𐐲𐑉𐐮𐑇𐐻 𐐮𐐻, 𐐰𐑌𐐼 𐐮𐐻 𐐸𐐰𐑃 𐐺𐑉𐐫𐐻 𐑁𐐫𐑉𐑃 𐑋𐐲𐐽 𐑁𐑉𐐭𐐻.

12. 𐐈𐑌𐐼 𐐮𐐻 𐐿𐐩𐑋 𐐻𐐭 𐐹𐐰𐑅 𐑄𐐰𐐻 𐑄 𐑅𐐲𐑉𐑂𐐲𐑌𐐻 𐑅𐐯𐐼 𐐲𐑌𐐻𐐭 𐐸𐐮𐑆 𐑋𐐰𐑅𐐻𐐲𐑉, 𐐐𐐵 𐐿𐐲𐑋𐐯𐑅𐐻 𐑄𐐵 𐐸𐐮𐑄𐐲𐑉 𐐻𐐭 𐐹𐑊𐐰𐑌𐐻 𐑄𐐮𐑅 𐐻𐑉𐐨, 𐐫𐑉 𐑄𐐮𐑅 𐐺𐑉𐐰𐑌𐐽 𐐱𐑂 𐑄 𐐻𐑉𐐨? 𐐙𐐫𐑉 𐐺𐐨𐐸𐐬𐑊𐐼, 𐐮𐐻 𐐶𐐱𐑆 𐑄 𐐹𐐭𐑉𐐯𐑅𐐻 𐑅𐐹𐐱𐐻 𐐮𐑌 𐐫𐑊 𐑄 𐑊𐐰𐑌𐐼 𐐱𐑂 𐑄𐐴 𐑂𐐮𐑌𐐷𐐲𐑉𐐼. 𐐈𐑌𐐼 𐑄 𐐢𐐫𐑉𐐼 𐐱𐑂 𐑄 𐑂𐐮𐑌𐐷𐐲𐑉𐐼 𐑅𐐯𐐼 𐐲𐑌𐐻𐐭 𐐸𐐮𐑋, 𐐗𐐵𐑌𐑅𐐯𐑊 𐑋𐐨 𐑌𐐱𐐻: 𐐌 𐑌𐐭 𐑄𐐰𐐻 𐐮𐐻 𐐶𐐱𐑆 𐐲 𐐹𐐭𐑉 𐑅𐐹𐐱𐐻 𐐱𐑂 𐑀𐑉𐐵𐑌𐐼; 𐐸𐐶𐐯𐑉𐑁𐐫𐑉, 𐐌 𐑅𐐯𐐼 𐐲𐑌𐐻𐐭 𐑄𐐨, 𐐌 𐐸𐐰𐑂 𐑌𐐲𐑉𐐮𐑇𐐻 𐐮𐐻 𐑄𐐮𐑅 𐑊𐐫𐑍 𐐻𐐴𐑋, 𐐰𐑌𐐼 𐑄𐐵 𐐺𐐨𐐸𐐬𐑊𐐼𐐯𐑅𐐻 𐑄𐐰𐐻 𐐮𐐻 𐐸𐐰𐑃 𐐺𐑉𐐫𐐻 𐑁𐐫𐑉𐑃 𐑋𐐲𐐽 𐑁𐑉𐐭𐐻.

13. 𐐈𐑌𐐼 𐐮𐐻 𐐿𐐩𐑋 𐐻𐐭 𐐹𐐰𐑅 𐑄𐐰𐐻 𐑄 𐐢𐐫𐑉𐐼 𐐱𐑂 𐑄 𐑂𐐮𐑌𐐷𐐲𐑉𐐼 𐑅𐐯𐐼 𐐲𐑌𐐻𐐭 𐐸𐐮𐑆 𐑅𐐲𐑉𐑂𐐲𐑌𐐻, 𐐢𐐳𐐿 𐐸𐐮𐑄𐐲𐑉; 𐐺𐐨𐐸𐐬𐑊𐐼 𐐌 𐐸𐐰𐑂 𐐹𐑊𐐰𐑌𐐻𐐯𐐼 𐐰𐑌𐐲𐑄𐐲𐑉 𐐺𐑉𐐰𐑌𐐽 𐐱𐑂 𐑄 𐐻𐑉𐐨 𐐫𐑊𐑅𐐬; 𐐰𐑌𐐼 𐑄𐐵 𐑌𐐬𐐯𐑅𐐻 𐑄𐐰𐐻 𐑄𐐮𐑅 𐑅𐐹𐐱𐐻 𐐱𐑂 𐑀𐑉𐐵𐑌𐐼 𐐶𐐱𐑆 𐐹𐐭𐑉𐐲𐑉 𐑄𐐰𐑌 𐑄 𐑁𐐲𐑉𐑅𐐻. 𐐒𐐲𐐻, 𐐺𐐨𐐸𐐬𐑊𐐼 𐑄 𐐻𐑉𐐨: 𐐌 𐐸𐐰𐑂 𐑌𐐲𐑉𐐮𐑇𐐻 𐐮𐐻 𐑄𐐮𐑅 𐑊𐐫𐑍 𐐻𐐴𐑋, 𐐰𐑌𐐼 𐐮𐐻 𐐸𐐰𐑃 𐐺𐑉𐐫𐐻 𐑁𐐫𐑉𐑃 𐑋𐐲𐐽 𐑁𐑉𐐭𐐻; 𐑄𐐯𐑉𐑁𐐫𐑉, 𐑀𐐰𐑄𐐲𐑉 𐐮𐐻, 𐐰𐑌𐐼 𐑊𐐩 𐐮𐐻 𐐲𐐹, 𐐰𐑀𐐯𐑌𐑅𐐻 𐑄 𐑅𐐨𐑆𐐲𐑌, 𐑄𐐰𐐻 𐐌 𐑋𐐩 𐐹𐑉𐐨𐑆𐐲𐑉𐑂 𐐮𐐻 𐐲𐑌𐐻𐐭 𐑋𐐴𐑌 𐐬𐑌 𐑅𐐯𐑊𐑁.

14. 𐐈𐑌𐐼 𐐮𐐻 𐐿𐐩𐑋 𐐻𐐭 𐐹𐐰𐑅 𐑄𐐰𐐻 𐑄 𐐢𐐫𐑉𐐼 𐐱𐑂 𐑄 𐑂𐐮𐑌𐐷𐐲𐑉𐐼 𐑅𐐯𐐼 𐐰𐑀𐐯𐑌 𐐲𐑌𐐻𐐭 𐐸𐐮𐑆 𐑅𐐲𐑉𐑂𐐲𐑌𐐻, 𐐢𐐳𐐿 𐐸𐐮𐑄𐐲𐑉, 𐐰𐑌𐐼 𐐺𐐨𐐸𐐬𐑊𐐼 𐐰𐑌𐐲𐑄𐐲𐑉 𐐺𐑉𐐰𐑌𐐽 𐐫𐑊𐑅𐐬, 𐐸𐐶𐐮𐐽 𐐌 𐐸𐐰𐑂 𐐹𐑊𐐰𐑌𐐻𐐯𐐼; 𐐺𐐨𐐸𐐬𐑊𐐼 𐑄𐐰𐐻 𐐌 𐐸𐐰𐑂 𐑌𐐲𐑉𐐮𐑇𐐻 𐐮𐐻 𐐫𐑊𐑅𐐬, 𐐰𐑌𐐼 𐐮𐐻 𐐸𐐰𐑃 𐐺𐑉𐐫𐐻 𐑁𐐫𐑉𐑃 𐑁𐑉𐐭𐐻. 𐐈𐑌𐐼 𐐸𐐨 𐑅𐐯𐐼 𐐲𐑌𐐻𐐭 𐑄 𐑅𐐲𐑉𐑂𐐲𐑌𐐻, 𐐢𐐳𐐿 𐐸𐐮𐑄𐐲𐑉 𐐰𐑌𐐼 𐐺𐐨𐐸𐐬𐑊𐐼 𐑄 𐑊𐐰𐑅𐐻: 𐐺𐐨𐐸𐐬𐑊𐐼, 𐑄𐐮𐑅 𐐸𐐰𐑂 𐐌 𐐹𐑊𐐰𐑌𐐻𐐯𐐼 𐐮𐑌 𐐲 𐑀𐐳𐐼 𐑅𐐹𐐱𐐻 𐐱𐑂 𐑀𐑉𐐵𐑌𐐼; 𐐰𐑌𐐼 𐐌 𐐸𐐰𐑂 𐑌𐐲𐑉𐐮𐑇𐐻 𐐮𐐻 𐑄𐐮𐑅 𐑊𐐫𐑍 𐐻𐐴𐑋, 𐐰𐑌𐐼 𐐬𐑌𐑊𐐨 𐐲 𐐹𐐪𐑉𐐻 𐐱𐑂 𐑄 𐐻𐑉𐐨 𐐸𐐰𐑃 𐐺𐑉𐐫𐐻 𐑁𐐫𐑉𐑃 𐐻𐐩𐑋 𐑁𐑉𐐭𐐻; 𐐰𐑌𐐼 𐑄 𐐲𐑄𐐲𐑉 𐐹𐐪𐑉𐐻 𐐱𐑂 𐑄 𐐻𐑉𐐨 𐐸𐐰𐑃 𐐺𐑉𐐫𐐻 𐑁𐐫𐑉𐑃 𐐶𐐴𐑊𐐼 𐑁𐑉𐐭𐐻; 𐐺𐐨𐐸𐐬𐑊𐐼, 𐐌 𐐸𐐰𐑂 𐑌𐐲𐑉𐐮𐑇𐐻 𐑄𐐮𐑅 𐐻𐑉𐐨 𐑊𐐴𐐿 𐐲𐑌𐐻𐐭 𐑄 𐐲𐑄𐐲𐑉𐑆.

15. 𐐈𐑌𐐼 𐐮𐐻 𐐿𐐩𐑋 𐐻𐐭 𐐹𐐰𐑅 𐑄𐐰𐐻 𐑄 𐐢𐐫𐑉𐐼 𐐱𐑂 𐑄 𐑂𐐮𐑌𐐷𐐲𐑉𐐼 𐑅𐐯𐐼 𐐲𐑌𐐻𐐭 𐑄 𐑅𐐲𐑉𐑂𐐲𐑌𐐻, 𐐑𐑊𐐲𐐿 𐐫𐑁 𐑄 𐐺𐑉𐐰𐑌𐐽𐐯𐑆 𐑄𐐰𐐻 𐐸𐐰𐑂 𐑌𐐱𐐻 𐐺𐑉𐐫𐐻 𐑁𐐫𐑉𐑃 𐑀𐐳𐐼 𐑁𐑉𐐭𐐻, 𐐰𐑌𐐼 𐐿𐐰𐑅𐐻 𐑄𐐯𐑋 𐐮𐑌𐐻𐐭 𐑄 𐑁𐐴𐐲𐑉. 𐐒𐐲𐐻 𐐺𐐨𐐸𐐬𐑊𐐼, 𐑄 𐑅𐐲𐑉𐑂𐐲𐑌𐐻 𐑅𐐯𐐼 𐐲𐑌𐐻𐐭 𐐸𐐮𐑋, 𐐢𐐯𐐻 𐐲𐑅 𐐹𐑉𐐭𐑌 𐐮𐐻, 𐐰𐑌𐐼 𐐼𐐮𐑀 𐐰𐐺𐐵𐐻 𐐮𐐻, 𐐰𐑌𐐼 𐑌𐐲𐑉𐐮𐑇 𐐮𐐻 𐐲 𐑊𐐮𐐻𐑊 𐑊𐐫𐑍𐑀𐐲𐑉, 𐑄𐐰𐐻 𐐹𐐲𐑉𐐸𐐰𐐹𐑅 𐐮𐐻 𐑋𐐩 𐐺𐑉𐐮𐑍 𐑁𐐫𐑉𐑃 𐑀𐐳𐐼 𐑁𐑉𐐭𐐻 𐐲𐑌𐐻𐐭 𐑄𐐨, 𐑄𐐰𐐻 𐑄𐐵 𐐿𐐰𐑌𐑅𐐻 𐑊𐐩 𐐮𐐻 𐐲𐐹 𐐰𐑀𐐯𐑌𐑅𐐻 𐑄 𐑅𐐨𐑆𐐲𐑌. 𐐈𐑌𐐼 𐐮𐐻 𐐿𐐩𐑋 𐐻𐐭 𐐹𐐰𐑅 𐑄𐐰𐐻 𐑄 𐐢𐐫𐑉𐐼 𐐱𐑂 𐑄 𐑂𐐮𐑌𐐷𐐲𐑉𐐼, 𐐰𐑌𐐼 𐑄 𐑅𐐲𐑉𐑂𐐲𐑌𐐻 𐐱𐑂 𐑄 𐐢𐐫𐑉𐐼 𐐱𐑂 𐑄 𐑂𐐮𐑌𐐷𐐲𐑉𐐼, 𐐼𐐮𐐼 𐑌𐐲𐑉𐐮𐑇 𐐫𐑊 𐑄 𐑁𐑉𐐭𐐻 𐐱𐑂 𐑄 𐑂𐐮𐑌𐐷𐐲𐑉𐐼.

16. 𐐈𐑌𐐼 𐐮𐐻 𐐿𐐩𐑋 𐐻𐐭 𐐹𐐰𐑅 𐑄𐐰𐐻 𐐲 𐑊𐐫𐑍 𐐻𐐴𐑋 𐐸𐐰𐐼 𐐹𐐰𐑅𐐻 𐐰𐐶𐐩, 𐐰𐑌𐐼 𐑄 𐐢𐐫𐑉𐐼 𐐱𐑂 𐑄 𐑂𐐮𐑌𐐷𐐲𐑉𐐼 𐑅𐐯𐐼 𐐲𐑌𐐻𐐭 𐐸𐐮𐑆 𐑅𐐲𐑉𐑂𐐲𐑌𐐻, 𐐗𐐲𐑋, 𐑊𐐯𐐻 𐐲𐑅 𐑀𐐬 𐐼𐐵𐑌 𐐮𐑌𐐻𐐭 𐑄 𐑂𐐮𐑌𐐷𐐲𐑉𐐼, 𐑄𐐰𐐻 𐐶𐐨 𐑋𐐩 𐑊𐐩𐐺𐐲𐑉 𐐰𐑀𐐯𐑌 𐐮𐑌 𐑄 𐑂𐐮𐑌𐐷𐐲𐑉𐐼. 𐐙𐐫𐑉 𐐺𐐨𐐸𐐬𐑊𐐼, 𐑄 𐐻𐐴𐑋 𐐼𐑉𐐫𐑆 𐑌𐐨𐑉, 𐐰𐑌𐐼 𐑄 𐐯𐑌𐐼 𐑅𐐭𐑌 𐐿𐐲𐑋𐐯𐑃; 𐐸𐐶𐐯𐑉𐑁𐐫𐑉, 𐐌 𐑋𐐲𐑅𐐻 𐑊𐐩 𐐲𐐹 𐑁𐑉𐐭𐐻, 𐐰𐑀𐐯𐑌𐑅𐐻 𐑄 𐑅𐐨𐑆𐐲𐑌, 𐐲𐑌𐐻𐐭 𐑋𐐴𐑌 𐐬𐑌 𐑅𐐯𐑊𐑁.

17. 𐐈𐑌𐐼 𐐮𐐻 𐐿𐐩𐑋 𐐻𐐭 𐐹𐐰𐑅 𐑄𐐰𐐻 𐑄 𐐢𐐫𐑉𐐼 𐐱𐑂 𐑄 𐑂𐐮𐑌𐐷𐐲𐑉𐐼, 𐐰𐑌𐐼 𐑄 𐑅𐐲𐑉𐑂𐐲𐑌𐐻, 𐐶𐐯𐑌𐐻 𐐼𐐵𐑌 𐐮𐑌𐐻𐐭 𐑄 𐑂𐐮𐑌𐐷𐐲𐑉𐐼: 𐐰𐑌𐐼 𐑄𐐩 𐐿𐐩𐑋 𐐻𐐭 𐑄 𐐻𐑉𐐨 𐐸𐐭𐑆 𐑌𐐰𐐽𐐲𐑉𐐲𐑊 𐐺𐑉𐐰𐑌𐐽𐐯𐑆 𐐸𐐰𐐼 𐐺𐐮𐑌 𐐺𐑉𐐬𐐿𐐲𐑌 𐐫𐑁, 𐐰𐑌𐐼 𐑄 𐐶𐐴𐑊𐐼 𐐺𐑉𐐰𐑌𐐽𐐯𐑆 𐐸𐐰𐐼 𐐺𐐮𐑌 𐑀𐑉𐐰𐑁𐐻𐐯𐐼 𐐮𐑌: 𐐰𐑌𐐼 𐐺𐐨𐐸𐐬𐑊𐐼 𐐫𐑊 𐑅𐐫𐑉𐐻𐑅 𐐱𐑂 𐑁𐑉𐐭𐐻 𐐼𐐮𐐼 𐐿𐐲𐑋𐐺𐐲𐑉 𐑄 𐐻𐑉𐐨.

18. 𐐈𐑌𐐼 𐐮𐐻 𐐿𐐩𐑋 𐐻𐐭 𐐹𐐰𐑅 𐑄𐐰𐐻 𐑄 𐐢𐐫𐑉𐐼 𐐱𐑂 𐑄 𐑂𐐮𐑌𐐷𐐲𐑉𐐼 𐐼𐐮𐐼 𐐻𐐩𐑅𐐻 𐐱𐑂 𐑄 𐑁𐑉𐐭𐐻, 𐐯𐑂𐐲𐑉𐐨 𐑅𐐫𐑉𐐻 𐐰𐐿𐐫𐑉𐐼𐐮𐑍 𐐻𐐭 𐐮𐐻𐑅 𐑌𐐲𐑋𐐺𐐲𐑉. 𐐈𐑌𐐼 𐑄 𐐢𐐫𐑉𐐼 𐐱𐑂 𐑄 𐑂𐐮𐑌𐐷𐐲𐑉𐐼 𐑅𐐯𐐼, 𐐒𐐨𐐸𐐬𐑊𐐼 𐑄𐐮𐑅 𐑊𐐫𐑍 𐐻𐐴𐑋 𐐸𐐰𐑂 𐐶𐐨 𐑌𐐲𐑉𐐮𐑇𐐻 𐑄𐐮𐑅 𐐻𐑉𐐨, 𐐰𐑌𐐼 𐐌 𐐸𐐰𐑂 𐑊𐐩𐐼 𐐲𐐹 𐐲𐑌𐐻𐐭 𐑋𐐴𐑅𐐯𐑊𐑁 𐐰𐑀𐐯𐑌𐑅𐐻 𐑄 𐑅𐐨𐑆𐐲𐑌, 𐑋𐐲𐐽 𐑁𐑉𐐭𐐻. 𐐒𐐲𐐻 𐐺𐐨𐐸𐐬𐑊𐐼, 𐑄𐐮𐑅 𐐻𐐴𐑋 𐐮𐐻 𐐸𐐰𐑃 𐐺𐑉𐐫𐐻 𐑁𐐫𐑉𐑃 𐑋𐐲𐐽 𐑁𐑉𐐭𐐻, 𐐰𐑌𐐼 𐑄𐐯𐑉 𐐮𐑆 𐑌𐐲𐑌 𐐱𐑂 𐐮𐐻 𐐸𐐶𐐮𐐽 𐐮𐑆 𐑀𐐳𐐼. 𐐈𐑌𐐼 𐐺𐐨𐐸𐐬𐑊𐐼 𐑄𐐯𐑉 𐐪𐑉 𐐫𐑊 𐐿𐐴𐑌𐐼𐑆 𐐱𐑂 𐐺𐐰𐐼 𐑁𐑉𐐭𐐻; 𐐰𐑌𐐼 𐐮𐐻 𐐹𐑉𐐱𐑁𐐮𐐻𐐯𐑃

𐑋𐐨 𐑌𐐲𐑃𐐮𐑍, 𐑌𐐱𐐻𐐶𐐮𐑃𐑅𐐻𐐰𐑌𐐼𐐮𐑍 𐐫𐑊 𐐵𐑉 𐑊𐐩𐐺𐐲𐑉: 𐐰𐑌𐐼 𐑌𐐵 𐐮𐐻 𐑀𐑉𐐨𐑂𐐯𐑃 𐑋𐐨 𐑄𐐰𐐻 𐐌 𐑇𐐳𐐼 𐑊𐐭𐑆 𐑄𐐮𐑅 𐐻𐑉𐐨. 𐐈𐑌𐐼 𐑄 𐐢𐐫𐑉𐐼 𐐲𐑂 𐑄 𐑂𐐴𐑌𐐷𐐲𐑉𐐼 𐑅𐐯𐐼 𐐲𐑌𐐻𐐭 𐑄 𐑅𐐲𐑉𐑂𐐲𐑌𐐻, 𐐐𐐶𐐱𐐻 𐑇𐐰𐑊 𐐶𐐨 𐐼𐐭 𐐲𐑌𐐻𐐭 𐑄 𐐻𐑉𐐨, 𐑄𐐰𐐻 𐐌 𐑋𐐩 𐐹𐑉𐐨𐑆𐐲𐑉𐑂 𐐲𐑀𐐯𐑌 𐑀𐐳𐐼 𐑁𐑉𐐭𐐻 𐑄𐐯𐑉𐐱𐑂 𐐲𐑌𐐻𐐭 𐑋𐐴𐑌 𐐬𐑌 𐑅𐐯𐑊𐑁? 𐐈𐑌𐐼 𐑄 𐑅𐐲𐑉𐑂𐐲𐑌𐐻 𐑅𐐯𐐼 𐐲𐑌𐐻𐐭 𐐸𐐮𐑆 𐑋𐐪𐑅𐐻𐐲𐑉, 𐐒𐐨𐐸𐐬𐑊𐐼, 𐐺𐐨𐐿𐐫𐑆 𐑄𐐵 𐐼𐐮𐐼𐑅𐐻 𐑀𐑉𐐪𐑁𐐻 𐐮𐑌 𐑄 𐐺𐑉𐐪𐑌𐐽𐐯𐑆 𐐲𐑂 𐑄 𐐶𐐴𐑊𐐼 𐐱𐑊𐐮𐑂 𐐻𐑉𐐨, 𐑄𐐩 𐐸𐐰𐑂 𐑌𐐲𐑉𐐮𐑇𐐻 𐑄 𐑉𐐭𐐻𐑅, 𐑄𐐰𐐻 𐑄𐐩 𐐪𐑉 𐐲𐑊𐐴𐑂, 𐐰𐑌𐐼 𐑄𐐩 𐐸𐐰𐑂 𐑌𐐱𐐻 𐐹𐐯𐑉𐐮𐑇𐐻; 𐐸𐐶𐐯𐑉𐑁𐐫𐑉 𐑄𐐵 𐐺𐐨𐐸𐐬𐑊𐐼𐐯𐑅𐐻 𐑄𐐰𐐻 𐑄𐐩 𐐪𐑉 𐐷𐐯𐐻 𐑀𐐳𐐼.

19. 𐐈𐑌𐐼 𐐮𐐻 𐐿𐐩𐑋 𐐻𐐭 𐐹𐐰𐑅 𐑄𐐰𐐻 𐑄 𐐢𐐫𐑉𐐼 𐐲𐑂 𐑄 𐑂𐐴𐑌𐐷𐐲𐑉𐐼 𐑅𐐯𐐼 𐐲𐑌𐐻𐐭 𐐸𐐮𐑆 𐑅𐐲𐑉𐑂𐐲𐑌𐐻, 𐐜 𐐻𐑉𐐨 𐐹𐑉𐐱𐑁𐐮𐐻𐐯𐑃 𐑋𐐨 𐑌𐐲𐑃𐐮𐑍; 𐐰𐑌𐐼 𐑄 𐑉𐐭𐐻𐑅 𐑄𐐯𐑉𐐱𐑂 𐐹𐑉𐐱𐑁𐐮𐐻 𐑋𐐨 𐑌𐐲𐑃𐐮𐑍 𐑅𐐬 𐑊𐐱𐑍 𐐰𐑆 𐐮𐐻 𐑇𐐰𐑊 𐐺𐑉𐐮𐑍 𐑁𐐫𐑉𐑃 𐐨𐑂𐐲𐑊 𐑁𐑉𐐭𐐻. 𐐤𐐯𐑂𐐲𐑉𐑄𐐲𐑊𐐯𐑅 𐐌 𐑌𐐬 𐑄𐐰𐐻 𐑄 𐑉𐐭𐐻𐑅 𐐪𐑉 𐑀𐐳𐐼; 𐐰𐑌𐐼 𐑁𐐫𐑉 𐑋𐐴𐑌 𐐬𐑌 𐐹𐐲𐑉𐐹𐐲𐑅 𐐌 𐐸𐐰𐑂 𐐹𐑉𐐨𐑆𐐲𐑉𐑂𐐼 𐑄𐐯𐑋; 𐐰𐑌𐐼 𐐺𐐨𐐿𐐫𐑆 𐐲𐑂 𐑄𐐩𐑉 𐑋𐐲𐐽 𐑅𐐻𐑉𐐯𐑍𐑃 𐑄𐐩 𐐸𐐰𐑂 𐐸𐐮𐑄𐐲𐑉𐐻𐐭 𐐺𐑉𐐫𐐻 𐑁𐐫𐑉𐑃, 𐑁𐑉𐐱𐑋 𐑄 𐐶𐐴𐑊𐐼 𐐺𐑉𐐪𐑌𐐽𐐯𐑆, 𐑀𐐳𐐼 𐑁𐑉𐐭𐐻. 𐐒𐐲𐐻 𐐺𐐨𐐸𐐬𐑊𐐼, 𐑄 𐐶𐐴𐑊𐐼 𐐺𐑉𐐪𐑌𐐽𐐯𐑆 𐐸𐐰𐑂 𐑀𐑉𐐬𐑌 𐐰𐑌𐐼 𐐸𐐰𐑂 𐐬𐑂𐐲𐑉𐑉𐐲𐑌 𐑄 𐑉𐐭𐐻𐑅 𐑄𐐯𐑉𐐱𐑂; 𐐰𐑌𐐼 𐐺𐐨𐐿𐐫𐑆 𐑄𐐰𐐻 𐑄 𐐶𐐴𐑊𐐼 𐐺𐑉𐐪𐑌𐐽𐐯𐑆 𐐸𐐰𐑂 𐐬𐑂𐐲𐑉𐐿𐐲𐑋 𐑄 𐑉𐐭𐐻𐑅 𐑄𐐯𐑉𐐱𐑂, 𐐮𐐻 𐐸𐐰𐑃 𐐺𐑉𐐫𐐻 𐑁𐐫𐑉𐑃 𐑋𐐲𐐽 𐐨𐑂𐐲𐑊 𐑁𐑉𐐭𐐻; 𐐰𐑌𐐼 𐐺𐐨𐐿𐐫𐑆 𐑄𐐰𐐻 𐐮𐐻 𐐸𐐰𐑃 𐐺𐑉𐐫𐐻 𐑁𐐫𐑉𐑃 𐑅𐐬 𐑋𐐲𐐽 𐐨𐑂𐐲𐑊 𐑁𐑉𐐭𐐻, 𐑄𐐵 𐐺𐐨𐐸𐐬𐑊𐐼𐐯𐑅𐐻 𐑄𐐰𐐻 𐐮𐐻 𐐺𐐨𐑀𐐮𐑌𐐯𐑃 𐐻𐐭 𐐹𐐯𐑉𐐮𐑇; 𐐰𐑌𐐼 𐐮𐐻 𐐶𐐮𐑊 𐑅𐐭𐑌 𐐺𐐨𐐿𐐲𐑋 𐑉𐐴𐐹𐐲𐑌𐐼, 𐑄𐐰𐐻 𐐮𐐻 𐑋𐐩 𐐺𐐨 𐐿𐐪𐑅𐐻 𐐮𐑌𐐻𐐭 𐑄 𐑁𐐴𐑉, 𐐯𐐿𐑅𐐯𐐹𐐻 𐐶𐐨 𐑇𐐳𐐼 𐐼𐐭 𐑅𐐲𐑋𐑃𐐮𐑍 𐑁𐐫𐑉 𐐮𐐻 𐐻𐐭 𐐹𐑉𐐨𐑆𐐲𐑉𐑂 𐐮𐐻.

20. 𐐈𐑌𐐼 𐐮𐐻 𐐿𐐩𐑋 𐐻𐐭 𐐹𐐰𐑅 𐑄𐐰𐐻 𐑄 𐐢𐐫𐑉𐐼 𐐲𐑂 𐑄 𐑂𐐴𐑌𐐷𐐲𐑉𐐼 𐑅𐐯𐐼 𐐲𐑌𐐻𐐭 𐐸𐐮𐑆 𐑅𐐲𐑉𐑂𐐲𐑌𐐻, 𐐢𐐯𐐻 𐐲𐑅 𐑀𐐬 𐐼𐐵𐑌 𐐮𐑌𐐻𐐭 𐑄 𐑌𐐯𐑄𐐲𐑉𐑋𐐬𐑅𐐻 𐐹𐐪𐑉𐐻𐑅 𐐲𐑂 𐑄 𐑂𐐴𐑌𐐷𐐲𐑉𐐼, 𐐰𐑌𐐼 𐐺𐐨𐐸𐐬𐑊𐐼 𐐮𐑁 𐑄 𐑌𐐰𐐽𐐲𐑉𐐲𐑊 𐐺𐑉𐐪𐑌𐐽𐐯𐑆 𐐸𐐰𐑂 𐐫𐑊𐑅𐐬 𐐺𐑉𐐫𐐻 𐑁𐐫𐑉𐑃 𐐨𐑂𐐲𐑊 𐑁𐑉𐐭𐐻. 𐐈𐑌𐐼 𐐮𐐻 𐐿𐐩𐑋 𐐻𐐭 𐐹𐐰𐑅 𐑄𐐰𐐻 𐑄𐐩 𐐶𐐯𐑌𐐻 𐐼𐐵𐑌 𐐮𐑌𐐻𐐭 𐑄 𐑌𐐯𐑄𐐲𐑉𐑋𐐬𐑅𐐻 𐐹𐐪𐑉𐐻𐑅 𐐲𐑂 𐑄 𐑂𐐴𐑌𐐷𐐲𐑉𐐼. 𐐈𐑌𐐼 𐐮𐐻 𐐿𐐩𐑋 𐐻𐐭 𐐹𐐰𐑅 𐑄𐐰𐐻 𐑄𐐩 𐐺𐐨𐐸𐐯𐑊𐐼 𐑄𐐰𐐻 𐑄 𐑁𐑉𐐭𐐻 𐐲𐑂 𐑄 𐑌𐐰𐐽𐐲𐑉𐐲𐑊 𐐺𐑉𐐪𐑌𐐽𐐯𐑆 𐐸𐐰𐐼 𐐺𐐨𐐿𐐲𐑋 𐐿𐐲𐑉𐐲𐐹𐐻 𐐫𐑊𐑅𐐬; 𐐷𐐩, 𐑄 𐑁𐐲𐑉𐑅𐐻, 𐐰𐑌𐐼 𐑄 𐑅𐐯𐐿𐐲𐑌𐐼, 𐐰𐑌𐐼 𐐫𐑊𐑅𐐬 𐑄 𐑊𐐪𐑅𐐻; 𐐰𐑌𐐼 𐑄𐐩 𐐸𐐰𐐼 𐐫𐑊 𐐺𐐨𐐿𐐲𐑋 𐐿𐐲𐑉𐐲𐐹𐐻. 𐐈𐑌𐐼 𐑄 𐐶𐐴𐑊𐐼 𐑁𐑉𐐭𐐻 𐐲𐑂 𐑄 𐑊𐐪𐑅𐐻 𐐸𐐰𐐼 𐐬𐑂𐐲𐑉𐐿𐐲𐑋 𐑄𐐰𐐻 𐐹𐐪𐑉𐐻 𐐲𐑂 𐑄 𐐻𐑉𐐨 𐐸𐐶𐐮𐐽 𐐺𐑉𐐫𐐻 𐑁𐐫𐑉𐑃 𐑀𐐳𐐼 𐑁𐑉𐐭𐐻, 𐐨𐑂𐐲𐑌 𐑄𐐰𐐻 𐑄 𐐺𐑉𐐪𐑌𐐽 𐐸𐐰𐐼 𐐶𐐮𐑄𐐲𐑉𐐼 𐐲𐐶𐐩 𐐰𐑌𐐼 𐐼𐐴𐐼.

21. 𐐈𐑌𐐼 𐐮𐐻 𐐿𐐩𐑋 𐐻𐐭 𐐹𐐰𐑅 𐑄𐐰𐐻 𐑄 𐐢𐐫𐑉𐐼 𐐲𐑂 𐑄 𐑂𐐴𐑌𐐷𐐲𐑉𐐼 𐐶𐐯𐐹𐐻, 𐐰𐑌𐐼 𐑅𐐯𐐼 𐐲𐑌𐐻𐐭 𐑄 𐑅𐐲𐑉𐑂𐐲𐑌𐐻, 𐐐𐐶𐐱𐐻 𐐿𐐳𐐼 𐐌 𐐸𐐰𐑂 𐐼𐐲𐑌 𐑋𐐬𐑉 𐑁𐐫𐑉 𐑋𐐴 𐑂𐐴𐑌𐐷𐐲𐑉𐐼? 𐐒𐐨𐐸𐐬𐑊𐐼, 𐐌 𐑌𐐭 𐑄𐐰𐐻 𐐫𐑊 𐑄 𐑁𐑉𐐭𐐻 𐐲𐑂 𐑄 𐑂𐐴𐑌𐐷𐐲𐑉𐐼, 𐑅𐐩𐑂 𐐮𐐻 𐐶𐐲𐑉 𐑄𐐨𐑆, 𐐸𐐰𐐼 𐐺𐐨𐐿𐐲𐑋 𐐿𐐲𐑉𐐲𐐹𐐻𐐯𐐼. 𐐈𐑌𐐼 𐑌𐐵 𐑄𐐨𐑆 𐐸𐐶𐐮𐐽 𐐸𐐰𐑂 𐐶𐐲𐑌𐑅 𐐺𐑉𐐫𐐻 𐑁𐐫𐑉𐑃 𐑀𐐳𐐼 𐑁𐑉𐐭𐐻, 𐐸𐐰𐑂 𐐫𐑊𐑅𐐬 𐐺𐐨𐐿𐐲𐑋 𐐿𐐲𐑉𐐲𐐹𐐻𐐯𐐼; 𐐰𐑌𐐼 𐑌𐐵 𐐫𐑊 𐑄 𐐻𐑉𐐨𐑆 𐐲𐑂 𐑋𐐴 𐑂𐐴𐑌𐐷𐐲𐑉𐐼 𐐪𐑉 𐑀𐐳𐐼 𐑁𐐫𐑉 𐑌𐐲𐑃𐐮𐑍, 𐑅𐐩𐑂 𐐮𐐻 𐐺𐐨 𐐻𐐭 𐐺𐐨 𐐸𐐷𐐭𐑌 𐐼𐐵𐑌 𐐰𐑌𐐼 𐐿𐐪𐑅𐐻 𐐮𐑌𐐻𐐭 𐑄 𐑁𐐴𐑉. 𐐈𐑌𐐼 𐐺𐐨𐐸𐐬𐑊𐐼 𐑄𐐮𐑅 𐑊𐐪𐑅𐐻, 𐐸𐐭𐑆 𐐺𐑉𐐪𐑌𐐽 𐐸𐐰𐑃 𐐶𐐮𐑄𐐲𐑉𐐼 𐐲𐐶𐐩, 𐐌 𐐼𐐮𐐼 𐐹𐑊𐐪𐑌𐐻 𐐮𐑌 𐐲 𐑀𐐳𐐼 𐑅𐐹𐐱𐐻 𐐲𐑂 𐑀𐑉𐐵𐑌𐐼; 𐐷𐐩, 𐐨𐑂𐐲𐑌 𐑄𐐰𐐻 𐐸𐐶𐐮𐐽 𐐶𐐱𐑆 𐐽𐑎𐑅 𐐲𐑌𐐻𐐭 𐑋𐐨 𐐲𐐺𐐲𐑂 𐐫𐑊 𐐲𐑄𐐲𐑉 𐐹𐐪𐑉𐐻𐑅 𐐲𐑂 𐑄 𐑊𐐰𐑌𐐼 𐐲𐑂 𐑋𐐴 𐑂𐐴𐑌𐐷𐐲𐑉𐐼. 𐐈𐑌𐐼 𐑄𐐵 𐐺𐐨𐐸𐐯𐑊𐐼𐐯𐑅𐐻 𐑄𐐰𐐻 𐐌 𐐫𐑊𐑅𐐬 𐐿𐐲𐐻 𐐼𐐵𐑌 𐑄𐐰𐐻 𐐸𐐶𐐮𐐽 𐐿𐐲𐑋𐐺𐐲𐑉𐐼 𐑄𐐮𐑅 𐑅𐐹𐐱𐐻 𐐲𐑂 𐑀𐑉𐐵𐑌𐐼, 𐑄𐐰𐐻 𐐌 𐑋𐐴𐐻 𐐹𐑊𐐪𐑌𐐻 𐑄𐐮𐑅 𐐻𐑉𐐨 𐐮𐑌 𐑄 𐑅𐐻𐐯𐐼 𐑄𐐯𐑉𐐱𐑂. 𐐈𐑌𐐼 𐑄𐐵 𐐺𐐨𐐸𐐯𐑊𐐼𐐯𐑅𐐻 𐑄𐐰𐐻 𐐲 𐐹𐐪𐑉𐐻 𐑄𐐯𐑉𐐱𐑂 𐐺𐑉𐐫𐐻 𐑁𐐫𐑉𐑃 𐑀𐐳𐐼 𐑁𐑉𐐭𐐻, 𐐰𐑌𐐼 𐐲 𐐹𐐪𐑉𐐻 𐑄𐐯𐑉𐐱𐑂 𐐺𐑉𐐫𐐻 𐑁𐐫𐑉𐑃 𐐶𐐴𐑊𐐼 𐑁𐑉𐐭𐐻; 𐐰𐑌𐐼 𐐺𐐨𐐿𐐫𐑆 𐐌 𐐹𐑊𐐲𐐿𐐻 𐑌𐐱𐐻 𐑄 𐐺𐑉𐐪𐑌𐐽𐐯𐑆 𐑄𐐯𐑉𐐱𐑂 𐐰𐑌𐐼 𐐿𐐪𐑅𐐻 𐑄𐐯𐑋 𐐮𐑌𐐻𐐭 𐑄 𐑁𐐴𐑉, 𐐺𐐨𐐸𐐬𐑊𐐼, 𐑄𐐩 𐐸𐐰𐑂 𐐬𐑂𐐲𐑉𐐿𐐲𐑋 𐑄 𐑀𐐳𐐼 𐐺𐑉𐐪𐑌𐐽 𐑄𐐰𐐻 𐐮𐐻 𐐸𐐰𐑃 𐐶𐐮𐑄𐐲𐑉𐐼 𐐲𐐶𐐩. 𐐈𐑌𐐼 𐑌𐐵, 𐐺𐐨𐐸𐐬𐑊𐐼, 𐑌𐐱𐐻𐐶𐐮𐑃𐑅𐐻𐐰𐑌𐐼𐐮𐑍 𐐫𐑊 𐑄 𐐿𐐩𐑉 𐐸𐐶𐐮𐐽 𐐶𐐨 𐐸𐐰𐑂 𐐻𐐩𐐿𐐲𐑌 𐐲𐑂 𐑋𐐴 𐑂𐐴𐑌𐐷𐐲𐑉𐐼, 𐑄 𐐻𐑉𐐨𐑆 𐑄𐐯𐑉𐐱𐑂 𐐸𐐰𐑂 𐐺𐐨𐐿𐐲𐑋 𐐿𐐲𐑉𐐲𐐹𐐻𐐯𐐼, 𐑄𐐰𐐻 𐑄𐐩 𐐺𐑉𐐮𐑍 𐑁𐐫𐑉𐑃 𐑌𐐬 𐑀𐐳𐐼 𐑁𐑉𐐭𐐻; 𐐰𐑌𐐼 𐑄𐐨𐑆 𐐌 𐐸𐐰𐐼 𐐸𐐬𐐹𐐻 𐐻𐐭 𐐹𐑉𐐨𐑆𐐲𐑉𐑂, 𐐻𐐭 𐐸𐐰𐑂 𐑊𐐩𐐼 𐐲𐐹 𐑁𐑉𐐭𐐻 𐑄𐐯𐑉𐐱𐑂 𐐲𐑀𐐯𐑌𐑅𐐻 𐑄 𐑅𐐨𐑆𐐲𐑌, 𐐲𐑌𐐻𐐭 𐑋𐐴𐑌 𐐬𐑌 𐑅𐐯𐑊𐑁. 𐐒𐐲𐐻, 𐐺𐐨𐐸𐐬𐑊𐐼, 𐑄𐐩 𐐸𐐰𐑂 𐐺𐐨𐐿𐐲𐑋 𐑊𐐴𐐿 𐐲𐑌𐐻𐐭 𐑄 𐐶𐐴𐑊𐐼 𐐱𐑊𐐮𐑂 𐐻𐑉𐐨, 𐐰𐑌𐐼 𐑄𐐩 𐐪𐑉 𐐲𐑂 𐑌𐐬 𐐶𐐲𐑉𐑃 𐐺𐐲𐐻 𐐻𐐭 𐐺𐐨 𐐸𐐷𐐭𐑌 𐐼𐐵𐑌 𐐰𐑌𐐼 𐐿𐐪𐑅𐐻 𐐮𐑌𐐻𐐭 𐑄 𐑁𐐴𐑉; 𐐰𐑌𐐼 𐐮𐐻 𐑀𐑉𐐨𐑂𐐯𐑃 𐑋𐐨 𐑄𐐰𐐻 𐐌 𐑇𐐳𐐼 𐑊𐐭𐑆 𐑄𐐯𐑋. 𐐒𐐲𐐻 𐐸𐐶𐐱𐐻 𐐿𐐳𐐼 𐐌

𐐸𐐰𐑂 𐐼𐐲𐑌 𐑋𐐫𐑉 𐐮𐑌 𐑋𐐴 𐑂𐐮𐑌𐐷𐐲𐑉𐐼? 𐐐𐐰𐑂 𐐌 𐑅𐑊𐐰𐐿𐑌𐐼 𐑋𐐴𐑌 𐐸𐐰𐑌𐐼, 𐑄𐐰𐐻 𐐌 𐐸𐐰𐑂 𐑌𐐱𐐻 𐑌𐐲𐑉𐐮𐑇𐐻 𐐮𐐻? 𐐤𐐩, 𐐌 𐐸𐐰𐑂 𐑌𐐲𐑉𐐮𐑇𐐻 𐐮𐐻, 𐐰𐑌𐐼 𐐌 𐐸𐐰𐑂 𐐼𐐮𐑀𐐼 𐐲𐐺𐐵𐐻 𐐮𐐻, 𐐰𐑌𐐼 𐐌 𐐸𐐰𐑂 𐐹𐑉𐐭𐑌𐐼 𐐮𐐻, 𐐰𐑌𐐼 𐐌 𐐸𐐰𐑂 𐐼𐐲𐑍𐐼 𐐮𐐻; 𐐰𐑌𐐼 𐐌 𐐸𐐰𐑂 𐑅𐐻𐑉𐐯𐐽𐐻 𐑁𐐫𐑉𐑃 𐑋𐐴𐑌 𐐸𐐰𐑌𐐼 𐐫𐑊𐑋𐐬𐑅𐐻 𐐫𐑊 𐑄 𐐼𐐩 𐑊𐐱𐑍, 𐐰𐑌𐐼 𐑄 𐐯𐑌𐐼 𐐼𐑉𐐫𐐯𐑃 𐑌𐐴. 𐐈𐑌𐐼 𐐮𐐻 𐑀𐑉𐐨𐑂𐐯𐑃 𐑋𐐨 𐑄𐐰𐐻 𐐌 𐑇𐐳𐐼 𐐸𐐷𐐭 𐐼𐐵𐑌 𐐫𐑊 𐑄 𐐻𐑉𐐨𐑆 𐐱𐑂 𐑋𐐴 𐑂𐐮𐑌𐐷𐐲𐑉𐐼, 𐐰𐑌𐐼 𐐿𐐰𐑅𐐻 𐑄𐐯𐑋 𐐮𐑌𐐻𐐭 𐑄 𐑁𐐴𐑉 𐑄𐐰𐐻 𐑄𐐩 𐑇𐐳𐐼 𐐺𐐨 𐐺𐐲𐑉𐑌𐐼. 𐐐𐐭 𐐮𐑆 𐐮𐐻 𐑄𐐰𐐻 𐐸𐐰𐑆 𐐿𐐫𐑉𐐲𐐹𐐻𐐯𐐼 𐑋𐐴 𐑂𐐮𐑌𐐷𐐲𐑉𐐼?

22. 𐐈𐑌𐐼 𐐮𐐻 𐐿𐐩𐑋 𐐻𐐭 𐐹𐐰𐑅 𐑄𐐰𐐻 𐑄 𐑅𐐲𐑉𐑂𐐲𐑌𐐻 𐑅𐐯𐐼 𐐲𐑌𐐻𐐭 𐐸𐐮𐑆 𐑋𐐰𐑅𐐻𐐲𐑉, 𐐮𐑆 𐐮𐐻 𐑌𐐱𐐻 𐑄 𐑊𐐱𐑁𐐻𐐨𐑌𐐯𐑅 𐐱𐑂 𐑄𐐴 𐑂𐐮𐑌𐐷𐐲𐑉𐐼? 𐐸𐐰𐑂 𐑌𐐱𐐻 𐑄 𐐺𐑉𐐰𐑌𐐽𐐯𐑆 𐑄𐐯𐑉𐐱𐑂 𐐬𐑂𐐲𐑉𐐿𐐲𐑋 𐑄 𐑉𐐭𐐻𐑅 𐐸𐐶𐐮𐐽 𐐪𐑉 𐑀𐐳𐐼? 𐐈𐑌𐐼 𐐺𐐨𐐿𐐫𐑆 𐑄 𐐺𐑉𐐰𐑌𐐽𐐯𐑆 𐐸𐐰𐑂 𐐬𐑂𐐲𐑉𐐿𐐲𐑋 𐑄 𐑉𐐭𐐻𐑅 𐑄𐐯𐑉𐐱𐑂, 𐐺𐐨𐐸𐐬𐑊𐐼 𐑄𐐩 𐑀𐑉𐐭 𐑁𐐰𐑅𐐻𐐲𐑉 𐑄𐐰𐑌 𐑄 𐑅𐐻𐑉𐐯𐑍𐑃 𐐱𐑂 𐑄 𐑉𐐭𐐻𐑅, 𐐻𐐩𐐿𐐮𐑍 𐑅𐐻𐑉𐐯𐑍𐑃 𐐲𐑌𐐻𐐭 𐑄𐐯𐑋𐑅𐐯𐑊𐑂𐑆. 𐐒𐐨𐐸𐐬𐑊𐐼, 𐐌 𐑅𐐩, 𐐮𐑆 𐑌𐐱𐐻 𐑄𐐮𐑅 𐑄 𐐿𐐫𐑆 𐑄𐐰𐐻 𐑄 𐐻𐑉𐐨𐑆 𐐱𐑂 𐑄𐐴 𐑂𐐮𐑌𐐷𐐲𐑉𐐼 𐐸𐐰𐑂 𐐺𐐨𐐿𐐲𐑋 𐐿𐐫𐑉𐐲𐐹𐐻𐐯𐐼?

23. 𐐈𐑌𐐼 𐐮𐐻 𐐿𐐩𐑋 𐐻𐐭 𐐹𐐰𐑅 𐑄𐐰𐐻 𐑄 𐐢𐐫𐑉𐐼 𐐱𐑂 𐑄 𐑂𐐮𐑌𐐷𐐲𐑉𐐼 𐑅𐐯𐐼 𐐲𐑌𐐻𐐭 𐑄 𐑅𐐲𐑉𐑂𐐲𐑌𐐻, 𐑊𐐯𐐻 𐐲𐑅 𐑀𐐬 𐐻𐐭 𐐰𐑌𐐼 𐐸𐐷𐐭 𐐼𐐵𐑌 𐑄 𐐻𐑉𐐨𐑆 𐐱𐑂 𐑄 𐑂𐐮𐑌𐐷𐐲𐑉𐐼, 𐐰𐑌𐐼 𐐿𐐰𐑅𐐻 𐑄𐐯𐑋 𐐮𐑌𐐻𐐭 𐑄 𐑁𐐴𐑉, 𐑄𐐰𐐻 𐑄𐐩 𐑇𐐰𐑊 𐑌𐐱𐐻 𐐿𐐲𐑋𐐺𐐲𐑉 𐑄 𐑀𐑉𐐵𐑌𐐼 𐐱𐑂 𐑋𐐴 𐑂𐐮𐑌𐐷𐐲𐑉𐐼, 𐑁𐐫𐑉 𐐌 𐐸𐐰𐑂 𐐼𐐲𐑌 𐐫𐑊; 𐐸𐐶𐐱𐐻 𐐿𐐳𐐼 𐐌 𐐸𐐰𐑂 𐐼𐐲𐑌 𐑋𐐫𐑉 𐑁𐐫𐑉 𐑋𐐴 𐑂𐐮𐑌𐐷𐐲𐑉𐐼? 𐐒𐐲𐐻, 𐐺𐐨𐐸𐐬𐑊𐐼, 𐑄 𐑅𐐲𐑉𐑂𐐲𐑌𐐻 𐑅𐐯𐐼 𐐲𐑌𐐻𐐭 𐑄 𐐢𐐫𐑉𐐼 𐐱𐑂 𐑄 𐑂𐐮𐑌𐐷𐐲𐑉𐐼, 𐑅𐐹𐐩𐑉 𐐮𐐻 𐐲 𐑊𐐮𐐻𐑊 𐑊𐐱𐑍𐑀𐐲𐑉. 𐐈𐑌𐐼 𐑄 𐐢𐐫𐑉𐐼 𐑅𐐯𐐼, 𐐷𐐩, 𐐌 𐐶𐐮𐑊 𐑅𐐹𐐩𐑉 𐐮𐐻 𐐲 𐑊𐐮𐐻𐑊 𐑊𐐱𐑍𐑀𐐲𐑉, 𐑁𐐫𐑉 𐐮𐐻 𐑀𐑉𐐨𐑂𐐯𐑃 𐑋𐐨 𐑄𐐰𐐻 𐐌 𐑇𐐳𐐼 𐑊𐐭𐑆 𐑄 𐐻𐑉𐐨𐑆 𐐱𐑂 𐑋𐐴 𐑂𐐮𐑌𐐷𐐲𐑉𐐼. 𐐐𐐶𐐯𐑉𐑁𐐬𐑉 𐑊𐐯𐐻 𐐲𐑅 𐐻𐐩𐐿 𐐱𐑂 𐑄 𐐺𐑉𐐰𐑌𐐽𐐯𐑆 𐐱𐑂 𐑄𐐨𐑆 𐐸𐐶𐐮𐐽 𐐌 𐐸𐐰𐑂 𐐹𐑊𐐰𐑌𐐻𐐯𐐼 𐐮𐑌 𐑄 𐑌𐐯𐑄𐐲𐑉𐑋𐐬𐑅𐐻 𐐹𐐪𐑉𐐻𐑅 𐐱𐑂 𐑋𐐴 𐑂𐐮𐑌𐐷𐐲𐑉𐐼, 𐐰𐑌𐐼 𐑊𐐯𐐻 𐐲𐑅 𐑀𐑉𐐰𐑁𐐻 𐑄𐐯𐑋 𐐮𐑌𐐻𐐭 𐑄 𐐻𐑉𐐨 𐑁𐑉𐐱𐑋 𐐸𐐶𐐯𐑌𐑅 𐑄𐐩 𐐿𐐩𐑋; 𐐰𐑌𐐼 𐑊𐐯𐐻 𐐲𐑅 𐐹𐑊𐐲𐐿 𐑁𐑉𐐱𐑋 𐑄 𐐻𐑉𐐨 𐑄𐐬𐑆 𐐺𐑉𐐰𐑌𐐽𐐯𐑆 𐐸𐐭𐑆 𐑁𐑉𐐭𐐻 𐐮𐑆 𐑋𐐬𐑅𐐻 𐐺𐐮𐐻𐐲𐑉, 𐐰𐑌𐐼 𐑀𐑉𐐰𐑁𐐻 𐐮𐑌 𐑄 𐑌𐐰𐐽𐐲𐑉𐐲𐑊 𐐺𐑉𐐰𐑌𐐽𐐯𐑆 𐐱𐑂 𐑄 𐐻𐑉𐐨 𐐮𐑌 𐑄 𐑅𐐻𐐯𐐼 𐑄𐐯𐑉𐐱𐑂. 𐐈𐑌𐐼 𐑄𐐮𐑅 𐐶𐐮𐑊 𐐌 𐐼𐐭, 𐑄𐐰𐐻 𐑄 𐐻𐑉𐐨 𐑋𐐩 𐑌𐐱𐐻 𐐹𐐯𐑉𐐮𐑇, 𐑄𐐰𐐻, 𐐹𐐲𐑉𐐸𐐰𐐹𐑅, 𐐌 𐑋𐐩 𐐹𐑉𐐨𐑆𐐲𐑉𐑂 𐐲𐑌𐐻𐐭 𐑋𐐴𐑅𐐯𐑊𐑁 𐑄 𐑉𐐭𐐻𐑅 𐑄𐐯𐑉𐐱𐑂 𐑁𐐫𐑉 𐑋𐐴𐑌 𐐬𐑌 𐐹𐐲𐑉𐐹𐐲𐑅. 𐐈𐑌𐐼, 𐐺𐐨𐐸𐐬𐑊𐐼, 𐑄 𐑉𐐭𐐻𐑅 𐐱𐑂 𐑄 𐑌𐐰𐐽𐐲𐑉𐐲𐑊 𐐺𐑉𐐰𐑌𐐽𐐯𐑆 𐐱𐑂 𐑄 𐐻𐑉𐐨 𐐸𐐶𐐮𐐽 𐐌 𐐹𐑊𐐰𐑌𐐻𐐯𐐼 𐐸𐐶𐐮𐑄𐐲𐑉𐑅𐐬𐐯𐑂𐐲𐑉 𐐌 𐐶𐐳𐐼 𐐪𐑉 𐐷𐐯𐐻 𐐲𐑊𐐴𐑂; 𐐸𐐶𐐯𐑉𐑁𐐬𐑉, 𐑄𐐰𐐻 𐐌 𐑋𐐩 𐐹𐑉𐐨𐑆𐐲𐑉𐑂 𐑄𐐯𐑋 𐐫𐑊𐑅𐐬 𐑁𐐫𐑉 𐑋𐐴𐑌 𐐬𐑌 𐐹𐐲𐑉𐐹𐐲𐑅, 𐐌 𐐶𐐮𐑊 𐐻𐐩𐐿 𐐱𐑂 𐑄 𐐺𐑉𐐰𐑌𐐽𐐯𐑆 𐐱𐑂 𐑄𐐮𐑅 𐐻𐑉𐐨, 𐐰𐑌𐐼 𐐌 𐐶𐐮𐑊 𐑀𐑉𐐰𐑁𐐻 𐑄𐐯𐑋 𐐮𐑌 𐐲𐑌𐐻𐐭 𐑄𐐯𐑋. 𐐏𐐩, 𐐌 𐐶𐐮𐑊 𐑀𐑉𐐰𐑁𐐻 𐐮𐑌 𐐲𐑌𐐻𐐭 𐑄𐐯𐑋 𐑄 𐐺𐑉𐐰𐑌𐐽𐐯𐑆 𐐱𐑂 𐑄𐐩𐑉 𐑋𐐲𐑄𐐲𐑉 𐐻𐑉𐐨, 𐑄𐐰𐐻 𐐌 𐑋𐐩 𐐹𐑉𐐨𐑆𐐲𐑉𐑂 𐑄 𐑉𐐭𐐻𐑅 𐐫𐑊𐑅𐐬 𐐲𐑌𐐻𐐭 𐑋𐐴𐑌 𐐬𐑌 𐑅𐐯𐑊𐑁, 𐑄𐐰𐐻 𐐸𐐶𐐯𐑌 𐑄𐐩 𐑇𐐰𐑊 𐐺𐐨 𐑅𐐲𐑁𐐮𐑇𐐯𐑌𐐻𐑊𐐨 𐑅𐐻𐑉𐐱𐑍, 𐐹𐐲𐑉𐐸𐐰𐐹𐑅 𐑄𐐩 𐑋𐐩 𐐺𐑉𐐮𐑍 𐑁𐐫𐑉𐑃 𐑀𐐳𐐼 𐑁𐑉𐐭𐐻 𐐲𐑌𐐻𐐭 𐑋𐐨, 𐐰𐑌𐐼 𐐌 𐑋𐐩 𐐷𐐯𐐻 𐐸𐐰𐑂 𐑀𐑊𐐬𐑉𐐨 𐐮𐑌 𐑄 𐑁𐑉𐐭𐐻 𐐱𐑂 𐑋𐐴 𐑂𐐮𐑌𐐷𐐲𐑉𐐼.

24. 𐐈𐑌𐐼 𐐮𐐻 𐐿𐐩𐑋 𐐻𐐭 𐐹𐐰𐑅 𐑄𐐰𐐻 𐑄𐐩 𐐻𐐳𐐿 𐑁𐑉𐐱𐑋 𐑄 𐑌𐐰𐐽𐐲𐑉𐐲𐑊 𐐻𐑉𐐨 𐐸𐐶𐐮𐐽 𐐸𐐰𐐼 𐐺𐐨𐐿𐐲𐑋 𐐶𐐴𐑊𐐼, 𐐰𐑌𐐼 𐑀𐑉𐐰𐑁𐐻𐐯𐐼 𐐮𐑌 𐐲𐑌𐐻𐐭 𐑄 𐑌𐐰𐐽𐐲𐑉𐐲𐑊 𐐻𐑉𐐨𐑆, 𐐸𐐶𐐮𐐽 𐐫𐑊𐑅𐐬 𐐸𐐰𐐼 𐐺𐐨𐐿𐐲𐑋 𐐶𐐴𐑊𐐼; 𐐰𐑌𐐼 𐑄𐐩 𐐫𐑊𐑅𐐬 𐐻𐐳𐐿 𐐱𐑂 𐑄 𐑌𐐰𐐽𐐲𐑉𐐲𐑊 𐐻𐑉𐐨𐑆 𐐸𐐶𐐮𐐽 𐐸𐐰𐐼 𐐺𐐨𐐿𐐲𐑋 𐐶𐐴𐑊𐐼, 𐐰𐑌𐐼 𐑀𐑉𐐰𐑁𐐻𐐯𐐼 𐐮𐑌𐐻𐐭 𐑄𐐩𐑉 𐑋𐐲𐑄𐐲𐑉 𐐻𐑉𐐨. 𐐈𐑌𐐼 𐑄 𐐢𐐫𐑉𐐼 𐐱𐑂 𐑄 𐑂𐐮𐑌𐐷𐐲𐑉𐐼 𐑅𐐯𐐼 𐐲𐑌𐐻𐐭 𐑄 𐑅𐐲𐑉𐑂𐐲𐑌𐐻, 𐐹𐑊𐐲𐐿 𐑌𐐱𐐻 𐑄 𐐶𐐴𐑊𐐼 𐐺𐑉𐐰𐑌𐐽𐐯𐑆 𐑁𐑉𐐱𐑋 𐑄 𐐻𐑉𐐨𐑆, 𐑅𐐩𐑂 𐐮𐐻 𐐺𐐨 𐑄𐐬𐑆 𐐸𐐶𐐮𐐽 𐐪𐑉 𐑋𐐬𐑅𐐻 𐐺𐐮𐐻𐐲𐑉; 𐐰𐑌𐐼 𐐮𐑌 𐑄𐐯𐑋 𐐷𐐨 𐑇𐐰𐑊 𐑀𐑉𐐰𐑁𐐻 𐐲𐐿𐐫𐑉𐐼𐐮𐑍 𐐻𐐭 𐑄𐐰𐐻 𐐸𐐶𐐮𐐽 𐐌 𐐸𐐰𐑂 𐑅𐐯𐐼. 𐐈𐑌𐐼 𐐶𐐨 𐐶𐐮𐑊 𐑌𐐲𐑉𐐮𐑇 𐐲𐑀𐐯𐑌 𐑄 𐐻𐑉𐐨𐑆 𐐱𐑂 𐑄 𐑂𐐮𐑌𐐷𐐲𐑉𐐼, 𐐰𐑌𐐼 𐐶𐐨 𐐶𐐮𐑊 𐐻𐑉𐐮𐑋 𐐲𐐹 𐑄 𐐺𐑉𐐰𐑌𐐽𐐯𐑆 𐑄𐐯𐑉𐐱𐑂; 𐐰𐑌𐐼 𐐶𐐨 𐐶𐐮𐑊 𐐹𐑊𐐲𐐿 𐑁𐑉𐐱𐑋 𐑄 𐐻𐑉𐐨𐑆 𐑄𐐬𐑆 𐐺𐑉𐐰𐑌𐐽𐐯𐑆 𐐸𐐶𐐮𐐽 𐐪𐑉 𐑉𐐴𐐹𐐲𐑌𐐼, 𐑄𐐰𐐻 𐑋𐐲𐑅𐐻 𐐹𐐯𐑉𐐮𐑇, 𐐰𐑌𐐼 𐐿𐐰𐑅𐐻 𐑄𐐯𐑋 𐐮𐑌𐐻𐐭 𐑄 𐑁𐐴𐑉. 𐐈𐑌𐐼 𐑄𐐮𐑅 𐐌 𐐼𐐭 𐑄𐐰𐐻, 𐐹𐐲𐑉𐐸𐐰𐐹𐑅, 𐑄 𐑉𐐭𐐻𐑅 𐑄𐐯𐑉𐐱𐑂 𐑋𐐩 𐐻𐐩𐐿 𐑅𐐻𐑉𐐯𐑍𐑃 𐐺𐐨𐐿𐐫𐑆 𐐱𐑂 𐑄𐐩𐑉 𐑀𐐳𐐼𐑌𐐯𐑅; 𐐰𐑌𐐼 𐐺𐐨𐐿𐐫𐑆 𐐱𐑂 𐑄 𐐽𐐩𐑌𐐾 𐐱𐑂 𐑄 𐐺𐑉𐐰𐑌𐐽𐐯𐑆, 𐑄𐐰𐐻 𐑄 𐑀𐐳𐐼 𐑋𐐩 𐐬𐑂𐐲𐑉𐐿𐐲𐑋 𐑄 𐐨𐑂𐐲𐑊; 𐐰𐑌𐐼 𐐺𐐨𐐿𐐫𐑆 𐑄𐐰𐐻 𐐌 𐐸𐐰𐑂 𐐹𐑉𐐨𐑆𐐲𐑉𐑂𐐼 𐑄 𐑌𐐰𐐽𐐲𐑉𐐲𐑊 𐐺𐑉𐐰𐑌𐐽𐐯𐑆 𐐰𐑌𐐼 𐑄 𐑉𐐭𐐻𐑅 𐑄𐐯𐑉𐐱𐑂, 𐐰𐑌𐐼 𐑄𐐰𐐻 𐐌 𐐸𐐰𐑂 𐑀𐑉𐐰𐑁𐐻𐐯𐐼 𐐮𐑌 𐑄 𐑌𐐰𐐽𐐲𐑉𐐲𐑊 𐐺𐑉𐐰𐑌𐐽𐐯𐑆 𐐲𐑀𐐯𐑌 𐐮𐑌𐐻𐐭 𐑄𐐩𐑉 𐑋𐐲𐑄𐐲𐑉 𐐻𐑉𐐨, 𐐰𐑌𐐼 𐐸𐐰𐑂 𐐹𐑉𐐨𐑆𐐲𐑉𐑂𐐼 𐑄 𐑉𐐭𐐻𐑅 𐐱𐑂 𐑄𐐩𐑉 𐑋𐐲𐑄𐐲𐑉 𐐻𐑉𐐨, 𐑄𐐰𐐻, 𐐹𐐲𐑉𐐸𐐰𐐹𐑅, 𐑄 𐐻𐑉𐐨𐑆 𐐱𐑂 𐑋𐐴 𐑂𐐮𐑌𐐷𐐲𐑉𐐼 𐑋𐐩 𐐺𐑉𐐮𐑍 𐑁𐐫𐑉𐑃 𐐲𐑀𐐯𐑌 𐑀𐐳𐐼 𐑁𐑉𐐭𐐻; 𐐰𐑌𐐼 𐑄𐐰𐐻

𐐌 𐑋𐐩 𐐸𐐰𐑂 𐐾𐐦 𐐲𐑀𐐯𐑌 𐐮𐑌 𐑄 𐑁𐑉𐐭𐐻 𐐱𐑂 𐑋𐐴 𐑂𐐴𐑌𐐷𐐲𐑉𐐼, 𐐰𐑌𐐼, 𐐹𐐲𐑉𐐸𐐰𐐹𐑅, 𐑄𐐰𐐻 𐐌 𐑋𐐩 𐑉𐐨𐐾𐐦𐑅 𐐯𐐿𐑅𐐨𐐼𐐮𐑍𐑊𐐨 𐑄𐐰𐐻 𐐌 𐐸𐐰𐑂 𐐹𐑉𐐨𐑆𐐲𐑉𐑂𐐼 𐑄 𐑉𐐭𐐻𐑅 𐐰𐑌𐐼 𐑄 𐐺𐑉𐐰𐑌𐐽𐐯𐑆 𐐱𐑂 𐑄 𐑁𐐲𐑉𐑅𐐻 𐑁𐑉𐐭𐐻.

25. 𐐐𐐶𐐯𐑉𐑁𐐬𐑉, 𐑀𐐬 𐐻𐐭, 𐐰𐑌𐐼 𐐿𐐫𐑊 𐑅𐐲𐑉𐑂𐐲𐑌𐐻𐑅, 𐑄𐐰𐐻 𐐶𐐨 𐑋𐐩 𐑊𐐩𐐺𐐲𐑉 𐐼𐐮𐑊𐐮𐐾𐐯𐑌𐐻𐑊𐐨 𐐶𐐮𐑄 𐐵𐑉 𐑋𐐴𐐻 𐐮𐑌 𐑄 𐑂𐐴𐑌𐐷𐐲𐑉𐐼, 𐑄𐐰𐐻 𐐶𐐨 𐑋𐐩 𐐹𐑉𐐨𐐹𐐩𐑉 𐑄 𐐶𐐩, 𐑄𐐰𐐻 𐐌 𐑋𐐩 𐐺𐑉𐐮𐑍 𐑁𐐬𐑉𐑃 𐐲𐑀𐐯𐑌 𐑄 𐑌𐐰𐐽𐐲𐑉𐐲𐑊 𐑁𐑉𐐭𐐻, 𐐸𐐶𐐮𐐽 𐑌𐐰𐐽𐐲𐑉𐐲𐑊 𐑁𐑉𐐭𐐻 𐐮𐑆 𐑀𐐳𐐼, 𐐰𐑌𐐼 𐑄 𐑋𐐬𐑅𐐻 𐐹𐑉𐐯𐑇𐐲𐑅 𐐲𐐺𐐲𐑂 𐐫𐑊 𐐲𐑄𐐲𐑉 𐑁𐑉𐐭𐐻. 𐐐𐐶𐐯𐑉𐑁𐐬𐑉, 𐑊𐐯𐐻 𐐲𐑅 𐑀𐐬 𐐻𐐭 𐐰𐑌𐐼 𐑊𐐩𐐺𐐲𐑉 𐐶𐐮𐑄 𐐵𐑉 𐑋𐐴𐐻 𐑄𐐮𐑅 𐑊𐐰𐑅𐐻 𐐻𐐴𐑋, 𐑁𐐫𐑉 𐐺𐐨𐐸𐐬𐑊𐐼 𐑄 𐐯𐑌𐐼 𐐼𐑉𐐫𐐯𐑃 𐑌𐐴, 𐐰𐑌𐐼 𐑄𐐮𐑅 𐐮𐑆 𐑁𐐫𐑉 𐑄 𐑊𐐰𐑅𐐻 𐐻𐐴𐑋 𐑄𐐰𐐻 𐐌 𐑇𐐰𐑊 𐐹𐑉𐐭𐑌 𐑋𐐴 𐑂𐐴𐑌𐐷𐐲𐑉𐐼. 𐐘𐑉𐐰𐑁𐐻 𐐮𐑌 𐑄 𐐺𐑉𐐰𐑌𐐽𐐯𐑆, 𐐺𐐨𐑀𐐮𐑌 𐐰𐐻 𐑄 𐑊𐐰𐑅𐐻 𐑄𐐰𐐻 𐑄𐐩 𐑋𐐩 𐐺𐐨 𐑁𐐲𐑉𐑅𐐻, 𐐰𐑌𐐼 𐑄𐐰𐐻 𐑄 𐑁𐐲𐑉𐑅𐐻 𐑋𐐩 𐐺𐐨 𐑊𐐰𐑅𐐻, 𐐰𐑌𐐼 𐐼𐐮𐑀 𐐲𐐺𐐵𐐻 𐑄 𐐻𐑉𐐨𐑆, 𐐺𐐬𐑃 𐐬𐑊𐐼 𐐰𐑌𐐼 𐐷𐐲𐑍, 𐑄 𐑁𐐲𐑉𐑅𐐻 𐐰𐑌𐐼 𐑄 𐑊𐐰𐑅𐐻, 𐐰𐑌𐐼 𐑄 𐑊𐐰𐑅𐐻 𐐰𐑌𐐼 𐑄 𐑁𐐲𐑉𐑅𐐻, 𐑄𐐰𐐻 𐐫𐑊 𐑋𐐩 𐐺𐐨 𐑌𐐲𐑉𐐮𐑇𐐻 𐐶𐐲𐑌𐑅 𐐲𐑀𐐯𐑌 𐑁𐐫𐑉 𐑄 𐑊𐐰𐑅𐐻 𐐻𐐴𐑋. 𐐐𐐶𐐯𐑉𐑁𐐬𐑉, 𐐼𐐮𐑀 𐐲𐐺𐐵𐐻 𐑄𐐯𐑋, 𐐰𐑌𐐼 𐐹𐑉𐐭𐑌 𐑄𐐯𐑋, 𐐰𐑌𐐼 𐐼𐐲𐑍 𐑄𐐯𐑋 𐐶𐐲𐑌𐑅 𐑋𐐬𐑉, 𐑁𐐫𐑉 𐑄 𐑊𐐰𐑅𐐻 𐐻𐐴𐑋, 𐑁𐐫𐑉 𐑄 𐐯𐑌𐐼 𐐼𐑉𐐫𐐯𐑃 𐑌𐐴. 𐐈𐑌𐐼 𐐮𐑁 𐐮𐐻 𐐺𐐨 𐑅𐐬 𐑄𐐰𐐻 𐑄𐐨𐑆 𐑊𐐰𐑅𐐻 𐑀𐑉𐐰𐑁𐐻𐑅 𐑇𐐰𐑊 𐑀𐑉𐐬, 𐐰𐑌𐐼 𐐺𐑉𐐮𐑍 𐑁𐐬𐑉𐑃 𐑄 𐑌𐐰𐐽𐐲𐑉𐐲𐑊 𐑁𐑉𐐭𐐻, 𐑄𐐯𐑌 𐑇𐐰𐑊 𐐷𐐨 𐐹𐑉𐐨𐐹𐐩𐑉 𐑄 𐐶𐐩 𐑁𐐫𐑉 𐑄𐐯𐑋, 𐑄𐐰𐐻 𐑄𐐩 𐑋𐐩 𐑀𐑉𐐬; 𐐰𐑌𐐼 𐐰𐑆 𐑄𐐩 𐐺𐐨𐑀𐐮𐑌 𐐻𐐭 𐑀𐑉𐐬, 𐐷𐐨 𐑇𐐰𐑊 𐐿𐑊𐐨𐑉 𐐲𐐶𐐩 𐑄 𐐺𐑉𐐰𐑌𐐽𐐯𐑆 𐐸𐐶𐐮𐐽 𐐺𐑉𐐮𐑍 𐑁𐐬𐑉𐑃 𐐺𐐮𐐻𐐲𐑉 𐑁𐑉𐐭𐐻, 𐐰𐐿𐐫𐑉𐐼𐐮𐑍 𐐻𐐭 𐑄 𐑅𐐻𐑉𐐯𐑍𐑃 𐐱𐑂 𐑄 𐑀𐐳𐐼 𐐰𐑌𐐼 𐑄 𐑅𐐴𐑆 𐑄𐐯𐑉𐐱𐑂; 𐐰𐑌𐐼 𐐷𐐨 𐑇𐐰𐑊 𐑌𐐱𐐻 𐐿𐑊𐐨𐑉 𐐲𐐶𐐩 𐑄 𐐺𐐰𐐼 𐑄𐐯𐑉𐐱𐑂 𐐫𐑊 𐐰𐐻 𐐶𐐲𐑌𐑅, 𐑊𐐯𐑅𐐻 𐑄 𐑉𐐭𐐻𐑅 𐑄𐐯𐑉𐐱𐑂 𐑇𐐳𐐼 𐐺𐐨 𐐻𐐭 𐑅𐐻𐑉𐐫𐑍 𐑁𐐫𐑉 𐑄 𐑀𐑉𐐰𐑁𐐻, 𐐰𐑌𐐼 𐑄 𐑀𐑉𐐰𐑁𐐻 𐑄𐐯𐑉𐐱𐑂 𐑇𐐰𐑊 𐐹𐐯𐑉𐐮𐑇, 𐐰𐑌𐐼 𐐌 𐑊𐐭𐑆 𐑄 𐐻𐑉𐐨𐑆 𐐱𐑂 𐑋𐐴 𐑂𐐴𐑌𐐷𐐲𐑉𐐼. 𐐙𐐫𐑉 𐐮𐐻 𐑀𐑉𐐨𐑂𐐯𐑃 𐑋𐐨 𐑄𐐰𐐻 𐐌 𐑇𐐳𐐼 𐑊𐐭𐑆 𐑄 𐐻𐑉𐐨𐑆 𐐱𐑂 𐑋𐐴 𐑂𐐴𐑌𐐷𐐲𐑉𐐼; 𐐸𐐶𐐯𐑉𐑁𐐬𐑉 𐐷𐐨 𐑇𐐰𐑊 𐐿𐑊𐐨𐑉 𐐲𐐶𐐩 𐑄 𐐺𐐰𐐼 𐐰𐐿𐐫𐑉𐐼𐐮𐑍 𐐰𐑆 𐑄 𐑀𐐳𐐼 𐑇𐐰𐑊 𐑀𐑉𐐬, 𐑄𐐰𐐻 𐑄 𐑉𐐭𐐻 𐐰𐑌𐐼 𐑄 𐐻𐐱𐐹 𐑋𐐩 𐐺𐐨 𐐨𐐿𐐶𐐲𐑊 𐐮𐑌 𐑅𐐻𐑉𐐯𐑍𐑃, 𐐲𐑌𐐻𐐮𐑊 𐑄 𐑀𐐳𐐼 𐑇𐐰𐑊 𐐬𐑂𐐲𐑉𐐿𐐲𐑋 𐑄 𐐺𐐰𐐼, 𐐰𐑌𐐼 𐑄 𐐺𐐰𐐼 𐐺𐐨 𐐸𐐧𐑌 𐐼𐐵𐑌 𐐰𐑌𐐼 𐐿𐐰𐑅𐐻 𐐮𐑌𐐻𐐭 𐑄 𐑁𐐴𐑉, 𐑄𐐰𐐻 𐑄𐐩 𐐿𐐲𐑋𐐺𐐲𐑉 𐑌𐐱𐐻 𐑄 𐑀𐑉𐐵𐑌𐐼 𐐱𐑂 𐑋𐐴 𐑂𐐴𐑌𐐷𐐲𐑉𐐼; 𐐰𐑌𐐼 𐑄𐐲𐑅 𐐶𐐮𐑊 𐐌 𐑅𐐶𐐨𐐹 𐐲𐐶𐐩 𐑄 𐐺𐐰𐐼 𐐵𐐻 𐐱𐑂 𐑋𐐴 𐑂𐐴𐑌𐐷𐐲𐑉𐐼; 𐐰𐑌𐐼 𐑄 𐐺𐑉𐐰𐑌𐐽𐐯𐑆 𐐱𐑂 𐑄 𐑌𐐰𐐽𐐲𐑉𐐲𐑊 𐐻𐑉𐐨 𐐶𐐮𐑊 𐐌 𐑀𐑉𐐰𐑁𐐻 𐐮𐑌 𐐲𐑀𐐯𐑌 𐐮𐑌𐐻𐐭 𐑄 𐑌𐐰𐐽𐐲𐑉𐐲𐑊 𐐻𐑉𐐨; 𐐰𐑌𐐼 𐑄 𐐺𐑉𐐰𐑌𐐽𐐯𐑆 𐐱𐑂 𐑄 𐑌𐐰𐐽𐐲𐑉𐐲𐑊 𐐻𐑉𐐨 𐐶𐐮𐑊 𐐌 𐑀𐑉𐐰𐑁𐐻 𐐮𐑌𐐻𐐭 𐑄 𐑌𐐰𐐽𐐲𐑉𐐲𐑊 𐐺𐑉𐐰𐑌𐐽𐐯𐑆 𐐱𐑂 𐑄 𐐻𐑉𐐨; 𐐰𐑌𐐼 𐑄𐐲𐑅 𐐶𐐮𐑊 𐐌 𐐺𐑉𐐮𐑍 𐑄𐐯𐑋 𐐻𐐭𐑀𐐯𐑄𐐲𐑉 𐐲𐑀𐐯𐑌, 𐑄𐐰𐐻 𐑄𐐩 𐑇𐐰𐑊 𐐺𐑉𐐮𐑍 𐑁𐐬𐑉𐑃 𐑄 𐑌𐐰𐐽𐐲𐑉𐐲𐑊 𐑁𐑉𐐭𐐻, 𐐰𐑌𐐼 𐑄𐐩 𐑇𐐰𐑊 𐐺𐐨 𐐶𐐲𐑌. 𐐈𐑌𐐼 𐑄 𐐺𐐰𐐼 𐑇𐐰𐑊 𐐺𐐨 𐐿𐐰𐑅𐐻 𐐲𐐶𐐩, 𐐷𐐩, 𐐨𐑂𐐲𐑌 𐐵𐐻 𐐱𐑂 𐐫𐑊 𐑄 𐑊𐐰𐑌𐐼 𐐱𐑂 𐑋𐐴 𐑂𐐴𐑌𐐷𐐲𐑉𐐼: 𐑁𐐫𐑉 𐐺𐐨𐐸𐐬𐑊𐐼, 𐐬𐑌𐑊𐐨 𐑄𐐮𐑅 𐐶𐐲𐑌𐑅 𐐶𐐮𐑊 𐐌 𐐹𐑉𐐭𐑌 𐑋𐐴 𐑂𐐴𐑌𐐷𐐲𐑉𐐼.

26. 𐐈𐑌𐐼 𐐮𐐻 𐐿𐐩𐑋 𐐻𐐭 𐐹𐐰𐑅 𐑄𐐰𐐻 𐑄 𐐢𐐫𐑉𐐼 𐐱𐑂 𐑄 𐑂𐐴𐑌𐐷𐐲𐑉𐐼 𐑅𐐯𐑌𐐻 𐐸𐐮𐑆 𐑅𐐲𐑉𐑂𐐲𐑌𐐻; 𐐰𐑌𐐼 𐑄 𐑅𐐲𐑉𐑂𐐲𐑌𐐻 𐐶𐐯𐑌𐐻 𐐰𐑌𐐼 𐐼𐐮𐐼 𐐰𐑆 𐑄 𐐢𐐫𐑉𐐼 𐐸𐐰𐐼 𐐿𐐱𐑋𐐰𐑌𐐼𐐯𐐼 𐐸𐐮𐑋, 𐐰𐑌𐐼 𐐺𐑉𐐫𐐻 𐐲𐑄𐐲𐑉 𐑅𐐲𐑉𐑂𐐲𐑌𐐻𐑅; 𐐰𐑌𐐼 𐑄𐐩 𐐶𐐲𐑉 𐑁𐐧. 𐐈𐑌𐐼 𐑄 𐐢𐐫𐑉𐐼 𐐱𐑂 𐑄 𐑂𐐴𐑌𐐷𐐲𐑉𐐼 𐑅𐐯𐐼 𐐲𐑌𐐻𐐭 𐑄𐐯𐑋, 𐐘𐐬 𐐻𐐭, 𐐰𐑌𐐼 𐑊𐐩𐐺𐐲𐑉 𐐮𐑌 𐑄 𐑂𐐴𐑌𐐷𐐲𐑉𐐼, 𐐶𐐮𐑄 𐐷𐐭𐑉 𐑋𐐴𐐻. 𐐙𐐫𐑉 𐐺𐐨𐐸𐐬𐑊𐐼, 𐑄𐐮𐑅 𐐮𐑆 𐑄 𐑊𐐰𐑅𐐻 𐐻𐐴𐑋 𐑄𐐰𐐻 𐐌 𐑇𐐰𐑊 𐑌𐐲𐑉𐐮𐑇 𐑋𐐴 𐑂𐐴𐑌𐐷𐐲𐑉𐐼: 𐑁𐐫𐑉 𐑄 𐐯𐑌𐐼 𐐮𐑆 𐑌𐐴 𐐰𐐻 𐐸𐐰𐑌𐐼, 𐐰𐑌𐐼 𐑄 𐑅𐐨𐑆𐐲𐑌 𐑅𐐹𐐨𐐼𐐮𐑊𐐨 𐐿𐐲𐑋𐐯𐑃; 𐐰𐑌𐐼 𐐮𐑁 𐐷𐐨 𐑊𐐩𐐺𐐲𐑉 𐐶𐐮𐑄 𐐷𐐭𐑉 𐑋𐐴𐐻 𐐶𐐮𐑄 𐑋𐐨, 𐐷𐐨 𐑇𐐰𐑊 𐐸𐐰𐑂 𐐾𐐦 𐐮𐑌 𐑄 𐑁𐑉𐐭𐐻 𐐸𐐶𐐮𐐽 𐐌 𐑇𐐰𐑊 𐑊𐐩 𐐲𐐹 𐐲𐑌𐐻𐐭 𐑋𐐴𐑅𐐯𐑊𐑁, 𐐲𐑀𐐯𐑌𐑅𐐻 𐑄 𐐻𐐴𐑋 𐐸𐐶𐐮𐐽 𐐶𐐮𐑊 𐑅𐐭𐑌 𐐿𐐲𐑋.

27. 𐐈𐑌𐐼 𐐮𐐻 𐐿𐐩𐑋 𐐻𐐭 𐐹𐐰𐑅 𐑄𐐰𐐻 𐑄 𐑅𐐲𐑉𐑂𐐲𐑌𐐻𐑅 𐐼𐐮𐐼 𐑀𐐬, 𐐰𐑌𐐼 𐑊𐐩𐐺𐐲𐑉 𐐶𐐮𐑄 𐑄𐐩𐑉 𐑋𐐴𐐻𐑅; 𐐰𐑌𐐼 𐑄 𐐢𐐫𐑉𐐼 𐐱𐑂 𐑄 𐑂𐐴𐑌𐐷𐐲𐑉𐐼 𐑊𐐩𐐺𐐲𐑉𐐼 𐐫𐑊𐑅𐐬 𐐶𐐮𐑄 𐑄𐐯𐑋: 𐐰𐑌𐐼 𐑄𐐩 𐐼𐐮𐐼 𐐬𐐺𐐩 𐑄 𐐿𐐱𐑋𐐰𐑌𐐼𐑋𐐯𐑌𐐻𐑅 𐐱𐑂 𐑄 𐐢𐐫𐑉𐐼 𐐱𐑂 𐑄 𐑂𐐴𐑌𐐷𐐲𐑉𐐼, 𐐮𐑌 𐐫𐑊 𐑃𐐮𐑍𐑆. 𐐈𐑌𐐼 𐑄𐐩𐑉 𐐺𐐨𐑀𐐰𐑌 𐐻𐐭 𐐺𐐨 𐑄 𐑌𐐰𐐽𐐲𐑉𐐲𐑊 𐑁𐑉𐐭𐐻 𐐲𐑀𐐯𐑌 𐐮𐑌 𐑄 𐑂𐐴𐑌𐐷𐐲𐑉𐐼; 𐐰𐑌𐐼 𐑄 𐑌𐐰𐐽𐐲𐑉𐐲𐑊 𐐺𐑉𐐰𐑌𐐽𐐯𐑆 𐐺𐐨𐑀𐐰𐑌 𐐻𐐭 𐑀𐑉𐐬 𐐰𐑌𐐼 𐑃𐑉𐐴𐑂 𐐯𐐿𐑅𐐨𐐼𐐮𐑍𐑊𐐨; 𐐰𐑌𐐼 𐑄 𐐶𐐴𐑊𐐼 𐐺𐑉𐐰𐑌𐐽𐐯𐑆 𐐺𐐨𐑀𐐰𐑌 𐐻𐐭 𐐺𐐨 𐐹𐑊𐐲𐐿𐐻 𐐫𐑁, 𐐰𐑌𐐼 𐐻𐐭 𐐺𐐨 𐐿𐐰𐑅𐐻 𐐲𐐶𐐩; 𐐰𐑌𐐼 𐑄𐐩 𐐼𐐮𐐼 𐐿𐐨𐐹 𐑄 𐑉𐐭𐐻 𐐰𐑌𐐼 𐑄 𐐻𐐱𐐹 𐑄𐐯𐑉𐐱𐑂 𐐨𐐿𐐶𐐲𐑊, 𐐰𐐿𐐫𐑉𐐼𐐮𐑍 𐐻𐐭 𐑄 𐑅𐐻𐑉𐐯𐑍𐑃 𐑄𐐯𐑉𐐱𐑂. 𐐈𐑌𐐼 𐑄𐐲𐑅 𐑄𐐩 𐑊𐐩𐐺𐐲𐑉𐐼, 𐐶𐐮𐑄 𐐫𐑊 𐐼𐐮𐑊𐐮𐐾𐐯𐑌𐑅, 𐐰𐐿𐐫𐑉𐐼𐐮𐑍 𐐻𐐭 𐑄 𐐿𐐱𐑋𐐰𐑌𐐼𐑋𐐯𐑌𐐻𐑅 𐐱𐑂 𐑄 𐐢𐐫𐑉𐐼 𐐱𐑂 𐑄 𐑂𐐴𐑌𐐷𐐲𐑉𐐼, 𐐨𐑂𐐲𐑌 𐐲𐑌𐐻𐐮𐑊 𐑄 𐐺𐐰𐐼 𐐸𐐰𐐼 𐐺𐐮𐑌 𐐿𐐰𐑅𐐻 𐐲𐐶𐐩 𐐵𐐻 𐐱𐑂 𐑄 𐑂𐐴𐑌𐐷𐐲𐑉𐐼, 𐐰𐑌𐐼 𐑄 𐐢𐐫𐑉𐐼 𐐸𐐰𐐼 𐐹𐑉𐐨𐑆𐐲𐑉𐑂𐐼 𐐲𐑌𐐻𐐭 𐐸𐐮𐑋𐑅𐐯𐑊𐑁, 𐑄𐐰𐐻 𐑄 𐐻𐑉𐐨𐑆 𐐸𐐰𐐼 𐐺𐐨𐐿𐐲𐑋 𐐲𐑀𐐯𐑌 𐑄 𐑌𐐰𐐽𐐲𐑉𐐲𐑊 𐑁𐑉𐐭𐐻; 𐐰𐑌𐐼 𐑄𐐩 𐐺𐐨𐐿𐐩𐑋 𐑊𐐴𐐿 𐐲𐑌𐐻𐐭

𐑄𐐩 𐐨𐐿𐐶𐐲𐑊; 𐐰𐑌𐐼 𐑄 𐑁𐑉𐐭𐐻𐑅 𐐶𐐲𐑉 𐐨𐐿𐐶𐐲𐑊; 𐐰𐑌𐐼 𐑄 𐐢𐐫𐑉𐐼 𐐱𐑂 𐑄 𐑂𐐮𐑌𐐷𐐲𐑉𐐼 𐐸𐐰𐐼 𐐹𐑉𐐨𐑆𐐲𐑉𐑂𐐼 𐐲𐑌𐐻𐐭 𐐸𐐮𐑋𐑅𐐯𐑊𐑁 𐑄 𐑌𐐰𐐽𐐲𐑉𐐲𐑊 𐑁𐑉𐐭𐐻, 𐐸𐐶𐐮𐐽 𐐶𐐱𐑆 𐑋𐐬𐑅𐐻 𐐹𐑉𐐯𐑇𐐲𐑅 𐐲𐑌𐐻𐐭 𐐸𐐮𐑋 𐑁𐑉𐐱𐑋 𐑄 𐐺𐐨𐑀𐐮𐑌𐐮𐑍.

28. 𐐰𐑌𐐼 𐐮𐐻 𐐿𐐩𐑋 𐐻𐐭 𐐹𐐰𐑅 𐑄𐐰𐐻 𐐸𐐶𐐯𐑌 𐑄 𐐢𐐫𐑉𐐼 𐐱𐑂 𐑄 𐑂𐐮𐑌𐐷𐐲𐑉𐐼 𐑅𐐫 𐑄𐐰𐐻 𐐸𐐮𐑆 𐑁𐑉𐐭𐐻 𐐶𐐱𐑆 𐑀𐐳𐐼, 𐐰𐑌𐐼 𐑄𐐰𐐻 𐐸𐐮𐑆 𐑂𐐮𐑌𐐷𐐲𐑉𐐼 𐐶𐐱𐑆 𐑌𐐬 𐑋𐐬𐑉 𐐿𐐱𐑉𐐲𐐹𐐻, 𐐸𐐨 𐐿𐐫𐑊𐐼 𐐲𐐹 𐐸𐐮𐑆 𐑅𐐲𐑉𐑂𐐰𐑌𐐻𐑅, 𐐰𐑌𐐼 𐑅𐐯𐐼 𐐲𐑌𐐻𐐭 𐑄𐐯𐑋, 𐐒𐐨𐐸𐐬𐑊𐐼, 𐑁𐐫𐑉 𐑄𐐮𐑅 𐑊𐐰𐑅𐐻 𐐻𐐴𐑋 𐐸𐐰𐑂 𐐶𐐨 𐑌𐐲𐑉𐐮𐑇𐐻 𐑋𐐴 𐑂𐐮𐑌𐐷𐐲𐑉𐐼; 𐐰𐑌𐐼 𐑄𐐵 𐐺𐐨𐐸𐐬𐑊𐐼𐐯𐑅𐐻 𐑄𐐰𐐻 𐐴 𐐸𐐰𐑂 𐐼𐐲𐑌 𐐰𐐿𐐫𐑉𐐼𐐮𐑍 𐐻𐐭 𐑋𐐴 𐐶𐐮𐑊; 𐐰𐑌𐐼 𐐴 𐐸𐐰𐑂 𐐹𐑉𐐨𐑆𐐲𐑉𐑂𐐼 𐑄 𐑌𐐰𐐽𐐲𐑉𐐲𐑊 𐑁𐑉𐐭𐐻, 𐑄𐐰𐐻 𐐮𐐻 𐐮𐑆 𐑀𐐳𐐼, 𐐨𐑂𐐲𐑌 𐑊𐐴𐐿 𐐰𐑆 𐐮𐐻 𐐶𐐱𐑆 𐐮𐑌 𐑄 𐐺𐐨𐑀𐐮𐑌𐐮𐑍; 𐐰𐑌𐐼 𐐺𐑊𐐯𐑅𐐯𐐼 𐐪𐑉𐐻 𐑄𐐵. 𐐙𐐫𐑉 𐐺𐐨𐐿𐐫𐑆 𐐷𐐨 𐐸𐐰𐑂 𐐺𐐮𐑌 𐐼𐐮𐑊𐐮𐐾𐐯𐑌𐐻 𐐮𐑌 𐑊𐐩𐐺𐐲𐑉𐐮𐑍 𐐶𐐮𐑄 𐑋𐐨 𐐮𐑌 𐑋𐐴 𐑂𐐮𐑌𐐷𐐲𐑉𐐼, 𐐰𐑌𐐼 𐐸𐐰𐑂 𐐿𐐯𐐹𐐻 𐑋𐐴 𐐿𐐱𐑋𐐰𐑌𐐼𐑋𐐯𐑌𐐻𐑅, 𐐰𐑌𐐼 𐐸𐐰𐑂 𐐺𐑉𐐫𐐻 𐐲𐑌𐐻𐐭 𐑋𐐨 𐐰𐑀𐐯𐑌 𐑄 𐑌𐐰𐐽𐐲𐑉𐐲𐑊 𐑁𐑉𐐭𐐻, 𐑄𐐰𐐻 𐑋𐐴 𐑂𐐮𐑌𐐷𐐲𐑉𐐼 𐐮𐑆 𐑌𐐬 𐑋𐐬𐑉 𐐿𐐱𐑉𐐲𐐹𐐻𐐯𐐼, 𐐰𐑌𐐼 𐑄 𐐺𐐰𐐼 𐐮𐑆 𐐿𐐰𐑅𐐻 𐐰𐐶𐐩, 𐐺𐐨𐐸𐐬𐑊𐐼 𐐷𐐨 𐑇𐐰𐑊 𐐸𐐰𐑂 𐐾𐑎 𐐶𐐮𐑄 𐑋𐐨, 𐐺𐐨𐐿𐐫𐑆 𐐱𐑂 𐑄 𐑁𐑉𐐭𐐻 𐐱𐑂 𐑋𐐴 𐑂𐐮𐑌𐐷𐐲𐑉𐐼. 𐐙𐐫𐑉 𐐺𐐨𐐸𐐬𐑊𐐼, 𐑁𐐫𐑉 𐐲 𐑊𐐱𐑍 𐐻𐐴𐑋 𐐶𐐮𐑊 𐐴 𐑊𐐩 𐐲𐐹 𐐱𐑂 𐑄 𐑁𐑉𐐭𐐻 𐐱𐑂 𐑋𐐴 𐑂𐐮𐑌𐐷𐐲𐑉𐐼 𐐲𐑌𐐻𐐭 𐑋𐐴𐑌 𐐬𐑌 𐑅𐐯𐑊𐑁, 𐐰𐑀𐐯𐑌𐑅𐐻 𐑄 𐑅𐐨𐑆𐐲𐑌, 𐐸𐐶𐐮𐐽 𐑅𐐹𐐨𐐼𐐮𐑊𐐨 𐐿𐐲𐑋𐐯𐑃; 𐐰𐑌𐐼 𐑁𐐫𐑉 𐑄 𐑊𐐰𐑅𐐻 𐐻𐐴𐑋 𐐸𐐰𐑂 𐐴 𐑌𐐲𐑉𐐮𐑇𐐻 𐑋𐐴 𐑂𐐮𐑌𐐷𐐲𐑉𐐼, 𐐰𐑌𐐼 𐐹𐑉𐐭𐑌𐐼 𐐮𐐻, 𐐰𐑌𐐼 𐐼𐐲𐑀 𐐰𐐺𐐵𐐻 𐐮𐐻, 𐐰𐑌𐐼 𐐼𐐲𐑍𐐼 𐐮𐐻; 𐐸𐐶𐐯𐑉𐑁𐐫𐑉, 𐐴 𐐶𐐮𐑊 𐑊𐐩 𐐲𐐹 𐐲𐑌𐐻𐐭 𐑋𐐴𐑌 𐐬𐑌 𐑅𐐯𐑊𐑁 𐐱𐑂 𐑄 𐑁𐑉𐐭𐐻, 𐑁𐐫𐑉 𐐲 𐑊𐐱𐑍 𐐻𐐴𐑋, 𐐰𐐿𐐫𐑉𐐼𐐮𐑍 𐐻𐐭 𐑄𐐰𐐻 𐐸𐐶𐐮𐐽 𐐴 𐐸𐐰𐑂 𐑅𐐹𐐬𐐿𐐲𐑌. 𐐰𐑌𐐼 𐐸𐐶𐐯𐑌 𐑄 𐐻𐐴𐑋 𐐿𐐲𐑋𐐯𐑃 𐑄𐐰𐐻 𐐨𐑂𐐲𐑊 𐑁𐑉𐐭𐐻 𐑇𐐰𐑊 𐐰𐑀𐐯𐑌 𐐿𐐲𐑋 𐐮𐑌𐐻𐐭 𐑋𐐴 𐑂𐐮𐑌𐐷𐐲𐑉𐐼, 𐑄𐐯𐑌 𐐶𐐮𐑊 𐐴 𐐿𐐫𐑆 𐑄 𐑀𐐳𐐼 𐐰𐑌𐐼 𐑄 𐐺𐐰𐐼 𐐻𐐭 𐐺𐐨 𐑀𐐰𐑄𐐲𐑉𐐼; 𐐰𐑌𐐼 𐑄 𐑀𐐳𐐼 𐐶𐐮𐑊 𐐴 𐐹𐑉𐐨𐑆𐐲𐑉𐑂 𐐲𐑌𐐻𐐭 𐑋𐐴𐑅𐐯𐑊𐑁; 𐐰𐑌𐐼 𐑄 𐐺𐐰𐐼 𐐶𐐮𐑊 𐐴 𐐿𐐰𐑅𐐻 𐐰𐐶𐐩 𐐮𐑌𐐻𐐭 𐐮𐐻𐑅 𐐬𐑌 𐐹𐑊𐐩𐑅. 𐐰𐑌𐐼 𐑄𐐯𐑌 𐐿𐐲𐑋𐐯𐑃 𐑄 𐑅𐐨𐑆𐐲𐑌 𐐰𐑌𐐼 𐑄 𐐯𐑌𐐼; 𐐰𐑌𐐼 𐑋𐐴 𐑂𐐮𐑌𐐷𐐲𐑉𐐼 𐐶𐐮𐑊 𐐴 𐐿𐐫𐑆 𐐻𐐭 𐐺𐐨 𐐺𐐲𐑉𐑌𐐼 𐐶𐐮𐑄 𐑁𐐴𐑉

𐐕𐐰𐐹𐐻𐐲𐑉 IV.

1. 𐐰𐑌𐐼 𐑌𐐵, 𐐺𐐨𐐸𐐬𐑊𐐼, 𐑋𐐴 𐐺𐑉𐐯𐑄𐑉𐐯𐑌, 𐐰𐑆 𐐴 𐑅𐐯𐐼 𐐲𐑌𐐻𐐭 𐐷𐐭 𐑄𐐰𐐻 𐐴 𐐶𐐳𐐼 𐐹𐑉𐐱𐑁𐐯𐑅𐐴, 𐐺𐐨-𐐸𐐬𐑊𐐼 𐑄𐐮𐑅 𐐮𐑆 𐑋𐐴 𐐹𐑉𐐱𐑁𐐯𐑅𐐨: 𐑄𐐰𐐻 𐑄 𐑃𐐮𐑍𐑆 𐐸𐐶𐐮𐐽 𐑄𐐮𐑅 𐐹𐑉𐐱𐑁𐐯𐐻 𐐞𐐨𐑌𐐱𐑅 𐑅𐐹𐐩𐐿, 𐐿𐐱𐑌𐑅𐐲𐑉𐑌𐐮𐑍 𐑄 𐐸𐐵𐑅 𐐱𐑂 𐐆𐑆𐑉𐐩𐐯𐑊, 𐐮𐑌 𐑄 𐐸𐐶𐐮𐐽 𐐸𐐨 𐑊𐐴𐐿𐐲𐑌𐐼 𐑄𐐯𐑋 𐐲𐑌𐐻𐐭 𐐲 𐐻𐐩𐑋 𐐱𐑊𐐮𐑂 𐐻𐑉𐐨, 𐑋𐐲𐑅𐐻 𐑇𐐭𐑉𐑊𐐨 𐐿𐐲𐑋 𐐻𐐭 𐐹𐐰𐑅. 𐐰𐑌𐐼 𐐮𐑌 𐑄 𐐼𐐩 𐑄𐐰𐐻 𐐸𐐨 𐑇𐐰𐑊 𐑅𐐯𐐻 𐐸𐐮𐑆 𐐸𐐰𐑌𐐼 𐐰𐑀𐐯𐑌 𐑄 𐑅𐐯𐐿𐐲𐑌𐐼 𐐻𐐴𐑋 𐐻𐐭 𐑉𐐨𐐿𐐲𐑂𐐲𐑉 𐐸𐐮𐑆 𐐹𐐨𐐹𐐲𐑊, 𐐮𐑆 𐑄 𐐼𐐩, 𐐷𐐩, 𐐨𐑂𐐲𐑌 𐑄 𐑊𐐰𐑅𐐻 𐐻𐐴𐑋, 𐑄𐐰𐐻 𐑄 𐑅𐐲𐑉𐑂𐐰𐑌𐐻𐑅 𐐱𐑂 𐑄 𐐢𐐫𐑉𐐼 𐑇𐐰𐑊 𐑀𐐬 𐑁𐐫𐑉𐑃 𐐮𐑌 𐐸𐐮𐑆 𐐹𐐵𐐲𐑉, 𐐻𐐭 𐑌𐐲𐑉𐐮𐑇 𐐰𐑌𐐼 𐐹𐑉𐐭𐑌 𐐸𐐮𐑆 𐑂𐐮𐑌𐐷𐐲𐑉𐐼; 𐐰𐑌𐐼 𐐰𐑁𐐻𐐲𐑉 𐑄𐐰𐐻 𐑄 𐐯𐑌𐐼 𐑅𐐭𐑌 𐐿𐐲𐑋𐐯𐑃. 𐐰𐑌𐐼 𐐸𐐵 𐐺𐑊𐐯𐑅𐐯𐐼 𐐪𐑉 𐑄𐐩 𐐸𐐭 𐐸𐐰𐑂 𐑊𐐩𐐺𐐲𐑉𐐼 𐐼𐐮𐑊𐐮𐐾𐐯𐑌𐐻𐑊𐐨 𐐮𐑌 𐐸𐐮𐑆 𐑂𐐮𐑌𐐷𐐲𐑉𐐼: 𐐰𐑌𐐼 𐐸𐐵 𐐿𐐲𐑉𐑅𐐯𐐼 𐐪𐑉 𐑄𐐩 𐐸𐐭 𐑇𐐰𐑊 𐐺𐐨 𐐿𐐰𐑅𐐻 𐐵𐐻 𐐮𐑌𐐻𐐭 𐑄𐐩𐑉 𐐬𐑌 𐐹𐑊𐐩𐑅! 𐐰𐑌𐐼 𐑄 𐐶𐐲𐑉𐑊𐐼 𐑇𐐰𐑊 𐐺𐐨 𐐺𐐲𐑉𐑌𐐼 𐐶𐐮𐑄 𐑁𐐴𐑉. 𐐰𐑌𐐼 𐐸𐐵 𐑋𐐲𐑉𐑅𐐮𐑁𐐳𐑊 𐐮𐑆 𐐵𐑉 𐐘𐐱𐐼 𐐲𐑌𐐻𐐭 𐐲𐑅: 𐑁𐐫𐑉 𐐸𐐨 𐑉𐐨𐑋𐐯𐑋𐐺𐐲𐑉𐐯𐑃 𐑄 𐐸𐐵𐑅 𐐱𐑂 𐐆𐑆𐑉𐐩𐐯𐑊, 𐐺𐐬𐑃 𐑉𐐭𐐻𐑅 𐐰𐑌𐐼 𐐺𐑉𐐰𐑌𐐽𐐯𐑆; 𐐰𐑌𐐼 𐐸𐐨 𐑅𐐻𐑉𐐯𐐽𐐯𐑆 𐑁𐐫𐑉𐑃 𐐸𐐮𐑆 𐐸𐐰𐑌𐐼𐑆 𐐲𐑌𐐻𐐭 𐑄𐐯𐑋, 𐐫𐑊 𐑄 𐐼𐐩 𐑊𐐱𐑍; 𐐰𐑌𐐼 𐑄𐐩 𐐪𐑉 𐐲 𐑅𐐻𐐮𐑁𐑌𐐯𐐿𐐻 𐐰𐑌𐐼 𐐲 𐑀𐐩𐑌𐑅𐐩𐐮𐑍 𐐹𐐨𐐹𐐲𐑊: 𐐺𐐲𐐻 𐐰𐑆 𐑋𐐯𐑌𐐨 𐐰𐑆 𐐶𐐮𐑊 𐑌𐐱𐐻 𐐸𐐪𐑉𐐼𐐲𐑌 𐑄𐐩𐑉 𐐸𐐪𐑉𐐻𐑅, 𐑇𐐰𐑊 𐐺𐐨 𐑅𐐩𐑂𐐼 𐐮𐑌 𐑄 𐐿𐐮𐑍𐐼𐐲𐑋 𐐱𐑂 𐐘𐐱𐐼. 𐐐𐐶𐐯𐑉𐑁𐐫𐑉, 𐑋𐐴 𐐺𐐨𐑊𐐲𐑂𐐯𐐼 𐐺𐑉𐐯𐑄𐑉𐐯𐑌, 𐐴 𐐺𐐨𐑅𐐨𐐽 𐐱𐑂 𐐷𐐭 𐐮𐑌 𐐶𐐲𐑉𐐼𐑆 𐐱𐑂 𐑅𐐬𐐺𐐲𐑉𐑌𐐯𐑅, 𐑄𐐰𐐻 𐐷𐐨 𐐶𐐳𐐼 𐑉𐐨𐐹𐐯𐑌𐐻, 𐐰𐑌𐐼 𐐿𐐲𐑋 𐐶𐐮𐑄 𐑁𐐳𐑊 𐐹𐐲𐑉𐐹𐐲𐑅 𐐱𐑂 𐐸𐐪𐑉𐐻, 𐐰𐑌𐐼 𐐿𐑊𐐨𐑂 𐐲𐑌𐐻𐐭 𐐘𐐱𐐼 𐐰𐑆 𐐸𐐨 𐐿𐑊𐐨𐑂𐐯𐑃 𐐲𐑌𐐻𐐭 𐐷𐐭. 𐐰𐑌𐐼 𐐸𐐶𐐴𐑊 𐐸𐐮𐑆 𐐪𐑉𐑋 𐐱𐑂 𐑋𐐲𐑉𐑅𐐨 𐐮𐑆 𐐯𐐿𐑅𐐻𐐯𐑌𐐼𐐯𐐼 𐐻𐐬𐑉𐐼𐑆 𐐷𐐭 𐐮𐑌 𐑄 𐑊𐐴𐐻 𐐱𐑂 𐑄 𐐼𐐩, 𐐸𐐪𐑉𐐼𐐲𐑌 𐑌𐐱𐐻 𐐷𐐭𐑉 𐐸𐐪𐑉𐐻𐑅. 𐐏𐐩, 𐐻𐐭-𐐼𐐩 𐐮𐑁 𐐷𐐨 𐐶𐐮𐑊 𐐸𐐨𐑉 𐐸𐐮𐑆 𐑂𐑎𐑅, 𐐸𐐪𐑉𐐼𐐲𐑌 𐑌𐐱𐐻 𐐷𐐭𐑉 𐐸𐐪𐑉𐐻𐑅: 𐑁𐐫𐑉 𐐸𐐶𐐴 𐐶𐐮𐑊 𐐷𐐨 𐐼𐐴? 𐐙𐐫𐑉 𐐺𐐨𐐸𐐬𐑊𐐼, 𐐰𐑁𐐻𐐲𐑉 𐐷𐐨 𐐸𐐰𐑂 𐐺𐐮𐑌 𐑌𐐲𐑉𐐮𐑇𐐻 𐐺𐐴 𐑄 𐑀𐐳𐐼 𐐶𐐲𐑉𐐼 𐐱𐑂 𐐘𐐱𐐼 𐐫𐑊 𐑄 𐐼𐐩 𐑊𐐱𐑍, 𐐶𐐮𐑊 𐐷𐐨 𐐺𐑉𐐮𐑍 𐑁𐐫𐑉𐑃 𐐨𐑂𐐲𐑊 𐑁𐑉𐐭𐐻, 𐑄𐐰𐐻 𐐷𐐨 𐑋𐐲𐑅𐐻 𐐺𐐨 𐐸𐐷𐐭𐑌 𐐼𐐵𐑌 𐐰𐑌𐐼 𐐿𐐰𐑅𐐻 𐐮𐑌𐐻𐐭 𐑄 𐑁𐐴𐑉? 𐐒𐐨𐐸𐐬𐑊𐐼, 𐐶𐐮𐑊 𐐷𐐨 𐑉𐐨𐐾𐐯𐐿𐐻 𐑄𐐨𐑆 𐐶𐐲𐑉𐐼𐑆? 𐐎𐐮𐑊 𐐷𐐨 𐑉𐐨𐐾𐐯𐐿𐐻 𐑄 𐐶𐐲𐑉𐐼𐑆 𐐱𐑂 𐑄 𐐹𐑉𐐱𐑁𐐯𐐻𐑅? 𐐰𐑌𐐼 𐐶𐐮𐑊 𐐷𐐨 𐑉𐐨𐐾𐐯𐐿𐐻 𐐫𐑊 𐑄 𐐶𐐲𐑉𐐼𐑆 𐐸𐐶𐐮𐐽 𐐸𐐰𐑂 𐐺𐐮𐑌 𐑅𐐹𐐬𐐿𐐲𐑌 𐐿𐐱𐑌𐑅𐐲𐑉𐑌𐐮𐑍 𐐗𐑉𐐴𐑅𐐻, 𐐰𐑁𐐻𐐲𐑉 𐑅𐐬 𐑋𐐯𐑌𐐨 𐐸𐐰𐑂 𐑅𐐹𐐬𐐿𐐲𐑌 𐐿𐐱𐑌𐑅𐐲𐑉𐑌𐐮𐑍

𐐸𐐮𐑋; 𐐰𐑌𐐼 𐐼𐐨𐑌𐐴 𐑄 𐑀𐐳𐐼 𐐶𐐲𐑉𐐼 𐐱𐑂 𐐗𐑉𐐴𐑅𐐻, 𐐰𐑌𐐼 𐑄 𐐹𐐵𐑉 𐐱𐑂 𐐘𐐱𐐼, 𐐰𐑌𐐼 𐑄 𐑀𐐮𐑁𐐻 𐐱𐑂 𐑄 𐐐𐐬𐑊𐐨 𐐘𐐬𐑅𐐻, 𐐰𐑌𐐼 𐐿𐐶𐐯𐑌𐐽 𐑄 𐐐𐐬𐑊𐐨 𐐝𐐹𐐮𐑉𐐮𐐻? 𐐈𐑌𐐼 𐑋𐐩𐐿 𐐲 𐑋𐐱𐐿 𐐱𐑂 𐑄 𐑀𐑉𐐩𐐻 𐐹𐑊𐐰𐑌 𐐱𐑂 𐑉𐐨𐐼𐐯𐑋𐐹𐑇𐐲𐑌, 𐐸𐐶𐐮𐐽 𐐸𐐰𐑃 𐐺𐐮𐑌 𐑊𐐩𐐼 𐑁𐐫𐑉 𐐷𐐭? 𐐤𐐬 𐐷 𐑌𐐱𐐻 𐑄𐐰𐐻 𐐮𐑁 𐐷 𐐶𐐮𐑊 𐐼𐐭 𐑄𐐨𐑆 𐑃𐐮𐑍𐑆, 𐑄𐐰𐐻 𐑄 𐐹𐐵𐑉 𐐱𐑂 𐑄 𐑉𐐨𐐼𐐯𐑋𐐹𐑇𐐲𐑌 𐐰𐑌𐐼 𐑄 𐑉𐐯𐑆𐐲𐑉𐐯𐐿𐑇𐐲𐑌 𐐸𐐶𐐮𐐽 𐐮𐑆 𐐮𐑌 𐐗𐑉𐐴𐑅𐐻, 𐐶𐐮𐑊 𐐺𐑉𐐮𐑍 𐐷𐐭 𐐻𐐭 𐑅𐐻𐐰𐑌𐐼 𐐶𐐮𐑄 𐑇𐐩𐑋 𐐰𐑌𐐼 𐐫𐑁𐐳𐑊 𐑀𐐮𐑊𐐻 𐐺𐐨𐑁𐐬𐑉 𐑄 𐐺𐐪𐑉 𐐱𐑂 𐐘𐐱𐐼? 𐐈𐑌𐐼 𐐰𐐿𐐫𐑉𐐼𐐮𐑍 𐐻𐐭 𐑄 𐐹𐐵𐑉 𐐱𐑂 𐐾𐐲𐑅𐐻𐐮𐑅; 𐑁𐐫𐑉 𐐾𐐲𐑅𐐻𐐮𐑅 𐐿𐐰𐑌𐐱𐐻 𐐺 𐐼𐐨𐑌𐐴𐐼, 𐐷 𐑋𐐲𐑅𐐻 𐑀𐐬 𐐰𐐶𐐩 𐐮𐑌𐐻𐐭 𐑄𐐰𐐻 𐑊𐐩𐐿 𐐱𐑂 𐑁𐐴𐑉 𐐰𐑌𐐼 𐐺𐑉𐐮𐑋𐑅𐐻𐐬𐑌, 𐐸𐐭𐑆 𐑁𐑊𐐩𐑋𐑆 𐐪𐑉 𐐲𐑌𐐿𐐶𐐯𐑌𐐽𐐰𐐺𐑊, 𐐰𐑌𐐼 𐐸𐐭𐑆 𐑅𐑋𐐬𐐿 𐐰𐑅𐐯𐑌𐐼𐐯𐑃 𐐲𐐹 𐑁𐐫𐑉 𐐯𐑂𐐲𐑉 𐐰𐑌𐐼 𐐯𐑂𐐲𐑉, 𐐸𐐶𐐮𐐽 𐑊𐐩𐐿 𐐱𐑂 𐑁𐐴𐑉 𐐰𐑌𐐼 𐐺𐑉𐐮𐑋𐑅𐐻𐐬𐑌 𐐮𐑆 𐐯𐑌𐐼𐑊𐐯𐑅 𐐻𐐫𐑉𐑋𐐯𐑌𐐻. 𐐄 𐑄𐐯𐑌, 𐑋𐐴 𐐺𐐨𐑊𐐲𐑂𐐯𐐼 𐐺𐑉𐐯𐑄𐑉𐐯𐑌, 𐑉𐐨𐐹𐐯𐑌𐐻 𐐷, 𐐰𐑌𐐼 𐐯𐑌𐐻𐐲𐑉 𐐮𐑌 𐐰𐐻 𐑄 𐑅𐐻𐑉𐐩𐐻 𐑀𐐩𐐻, 𐐰𐑌𐐼 𐐿𐐱𐑌𐐻𐐮𐑌𐐷𐐭 𐐮𐑌 𐑄 𐐶𐐩 𐐸𐐶𐐮𐐽 𐐮𐑆 𐑌𐐰𐑉𐐬, 𐐲𐑌𐐻𐐮𐑊 𐐷 𐑇𐐰𐑊 𐐱𐐺𐐻𐐩𐑌 𐐨𐐻𐐲𐑉𐑌𐐲𐑊 𐑊𐐴𐑁. 𐐄 𐐺 𐐶𐐴𐑆: 𐐸𐐶𐐱𐐻 𐐿𐐰𐑌 𐐴 𐑅𐐩 𐑋𐐫𐑉? 𐐙𐐴𐑌𐐲𐑊𐐨, 𐐴 𐐺𐐮𐐼 𐐷𐐭 𐑁𐐩𐑉𐐶𐐯𐑊, 𐐲𐑌𐐻𐐮𐑊 𐐴 𐑇𐐰𐑊 𐑋𐐨𐐻 𐐷𐐭 𐐺𐐨𐑁𐐬𐑉 𐑄 𐐹𐑊𐐨𐑆𐐮𐑍 𐐺𐐪𐑉 𐐱𐑂 𐐘𐐱𐐼, 𐐸𐐶𐐮𐐽 𐐺𐐪𐑉 𐑅𐐻𐑉𐐴𐐿𐐯𐑃 𐑄 𐐶𐐮𐐿𐐯𐐼 𐐶𐐮𐑄 𐐫𐑁𐐳𐑊 𐐼𐑉𐐯𐐼 𐐰𐑌𐐼 𐑁𐐨𐑉. 𐐁𐑋𐐯𐑌.

𐐕𐐈𐐑𐐓𐐊𐐡 V.

1. 𐐈𐑌𐐼 𐑌𐐵 𐐮𐐻 𐐿𐐩𐑋 𐐻𐐭 𐐹𐐪𐑅 𐐰𐑁𐐻𐐲𐑉 𐑅𐐲𐑋 𐐷𐐨𐑉𐑆 𐐸𐐰𐐼 𐐹𐐪𐑅𐐻 𐐰𐐶𐐩, 𐑄𐐯𐑉 𐐿𐐩𐑋 𐐲 𐑋𐐰𐑌 𐐲𐑋𐐲𐑍 𐑄 𐐹𐐨𐐹𐑊 𐐱𐑂 𐐤𐐨𐑁𐐴, 𐐸𐐭𐑆 𐑌𐐩𐑋 𐐶𐐱𐑆 𐐟𐐯𐑉𐐯𐑋. 𐐈𐑌𐐼 𐐮𐐻 𐐿𐐩𐑋 𐐻𐐭 𐐹𐐪𐑅 𐑄𐐰𐐻 𐐸𐐨 𐐺𐐨𐑀𐐰𐑌 𐐻𐐭 𐐹𐑉𐐨𐐽 𐐲𐑋𐐲𐑍 𐑄 𐐹𐐨𐐹𐑊, 𐐰𐑌𐐼 𐐻𐐭 𐐼𐐨𐐿𐑊𐐩𐑉 𐐲𐑌𐐻𐐭 𐑄𐐯𐑋 𐑄𐐰𐐻 𐑄𐐯𐑉 𐑇𐐳𐐼 𐐺 𐑌𐐬 𐐗𐑉𐐴𐑅𐐻. 𐐈𐑌𐐼 𐐸𐐨 𐐹𐑉𐐨𐐽𐐻 𐑋𐐯𐑌𐐨 𐑃𐐮𐑍𐑆 𐐸𐐶𐐮𐐽 𐐶𐐲𐑉 𐑁𐑊𐐰𐐻𐐲𐑉𐐮𐑍 𐐲𐑌𐐻𐐭 𐑄 𐐹𐐨𐐹𐑊; 𐐰𐑌𐐼 𐑄𐐮𐑅 𐐸𐐨 𐐼𐐮𐐼 𐑄𐐰𐐻 𐐸𐐨 𐑋𐐴𐐻 𐐬𐑂𐐲𐑉𐑃𐑉𐐬 𐑄 𐐼𐐱𐐿𐐻𐑉𐐮𐑌 𐐱𐑂 𐐗𐑉𐐴𐑅𐐻. 𐐈𐑌𐐼 𐐸𐐨 𐑊𐐩𐐺𐐲𐑉𐐼 𐐼𐐮𐑊𐐮𐐾𐐯𐑌𐐻𐑊𐐨 𐑄𐐰𐐻 𐐸𐐨 𐑋𐐴𐐻 𐑊𐐨𐐼 𐐰𐐶𐐩 𐑄 𐐸𐐪𐑉𐐻𐑅 𐐱𐑂 𐑄 𐐹𐐨𐐹𐑊, 𐐮𐑌𐑅𐐬𐑋𐐲𐐽 𐑄𐐰𐐻 𐐸𐐨 𐐼𐐮𐐼 𐑊𐐨𐐼 𐐰𐐶𐐩 𐑋𐐯𐑌𐐨 𐐸𐐪𐑉𐐻𐑅; 𐐰𐑌𐐼 𐐸𐐨 𐑌𐐬𐐮𐑍 𐑄𐐰𐐻 𐐴, 𐐖𐐩𐐿𐐲𐐺, 𐐸𐐰𐐼 𐑁𐐩𐑃 𐐮𐑌 𐐗𐑉𐐴𐑅𐐻 𐐸𐐭 𐑇𐐳𐐼 𐐿𐐲𐑋, 𐐸𐐨 𐑅𐐫𐐻 𐑋𐐲𐐽 𐐱𐐹𐐲𐑉𐐻𐐭𐑌𐐮𐐻𐐨 𐑄𐐰𐐻 𐐸𐐨 𐑋𐐴𐐻 𐐿𐐲𐑋 𐐲𐑌𐐻𐐭 𐑋𐐨. 𐐈𐑌𐐼 𐐸𐐨 𐐶𐐱𐑆 𐑊𐐲𐑉𐑌𐐯𐐼, 𐑄𐐰𐐻 𐐸𐐨 𐐸𐐰𐐼 𐐲 𐐹𐐲𐑉𐑁𐐯𐐿𐐻 𐑌𐐱𐑊𐐯𐐾 𐐱𐑂 𐑄 𐑊𐐰𐑍𐑀𐐶𐐯𐐾 𐐱𐑂 𐑄 𐐹𐐨𐐹𐑊; 𐐸𐐶𐐯𐑉𐑁𐐫𐑉, 𐐸𐐨 𐐿𐐳𐐼 𐐷𐐭𐑆 𐑋𐐲𐐽 𐑁𐑊𐐰𐐻𐐲𐑉𐐨, 𐐰𐑌𐐼 𐑋𐐲𐐽 𐐹𐐵𐑉 𐐱𐑂 𐑅𐐹𐐨𐐽, 𐐰𐐿𐐫𐑉𐐼𐐮𐑍 𐐻𐐭 𐑄 𐐹𐐵𐑉 𐐱𐑂 𐑄 𐐼𐐯𐑂𐐮𐑊. 𐐈𐑌𐐼 𐐸𐐨 𐐸𐐰𐐼 𐐸𐐬𐐹 𐐻𐐭 𐑇𐐩𐐿 𐑋𐐨 𐑁𐑉𐐱𐑋 𐑄 𐑁𐐩𐑃, 𐑌𐐱𐐻𐐶𐐮𐑄𐑅𐐻𐐰𐑌𐐼𐐮𐑍 𐑄 𐑋𐐯𐑌𐐨 𐑉𐐯𐑂𐐯𐑊𐐩𐑇𐐲𐑌𐑆 𐐰𐑌𐐼 𐑄 𐑋𐐯𐑌𐐨 𐑃𐐮𐑍𐑆 𐐸𐐶𐐮𐐽 𐐴 𐐸𐐰𐐼 𐑅𐐨𐑌 𐐿𐐱𐑌𐑅𐐲𐑉𐑌𐐮𐑍 𐑄𐐨𐑆 𐑃𐐮𐑍𐑆; 𐑁𐐫𐑉 𐐴 𐐻𐑉𐐭𐑊𐐨 𐐸𐐰𐐼 𐑅𐐨𐑌 𐐩𐑌𐐾𐐯𐑊𐑆, 𐐰𐑌𐐼 𐑄𐐩 𐐸𐐰𐐼 𐑋𐐮𐑌𐐮𐑅𐐻𐐲𐑉𐐼 𐐲𐑌𐐻𐐭 𐑋𐐨. 𐐈𐑌𐐼 𐐫𐑊𐑅𐐬, 𐐴 𐐸𐐰𐐼 𐐸𐐲𐑉𐐼 𐑄 𐑂𐑎𐑅 𐐱𐑂 𐑄 𐐢𐐫𐑉𐐼 𐑅𐐹𐐨𐐿𐐮𐑍 𐐲𐑌𐐻𐐭 𐑋𐐨 𐐮𐑌 𐑂𐐯𐑉𐐨 𐐶𐐲𐑉𐐼, 𐑁𐑉𐐱𐑋 𐐻𐐴𐑋 𐐻𐐭 𐐻𐐴𐑋; 𐐸𐐶𐐯𐑉𐑁𐐫𐑉, 𐐴 𐐿𐐳𐐼 𐑌𐐱𐐻 𐐺 𐑇𐐩𐐿𐑌.

2. 𐐈𐑌𐐼 𐐮𐐻 𐐿𐐩𐑋 𐐻𐐭 𐐹𐐪𐑅 𐑄𐐰𐐻 𐐸𐐨 𐐿𐐩𐑋 𐐲𐑌𐐻𐐭 𐑋𐐨; 𐐰𐑌𐐼 𐐱𐑌 𐑄𐐮𐑅 𐐶𐐴𐑆 𐐼𐐮𐐼 𐐸𐐨 𐑅𐐹𐐨𐐿 𐐲𐑌𐐻𐐭 𐑋𐐨, 𐑅𐐩𐐮𐑍: 𐐒𐑉𐐲𐑄𐐲𐑉 𐐖𐐩𐐿𐐲𐐺, 𐐴 𐐸𐐰𐑂 𐑅𐐫𐐻 𐑋𐐲𐐽 𐐱𐐹𐐲𐑉𐐻𐐭𐑌𐐮𐐻𐐨 𐑄𐐰𐐻 𐐴 𐑋𐐴𐐻 𐑅𐐹𐐨𐐿 𐐲𐑌𐐻𐐭 𐐷𐐭: 𐑁𐐫𐑉 𐐴 𐐸𐐰𐑂 𐐸𐐲𐑉𐐼 𐐰𐑌𐐼 𐐫𐑊𐑅𐐬 𐑌𐐬, 𐑄𐐰𐐻 𐑄𐐵 𐑀𐐬𐐯𐑅𐐻 𐐲𐐺𐐵𐐻 𐑋𐐲𐐽, 𐐹𐑉𐐨𐐽𐐮𐑍 𐑄𐐰𐐻 𐐸𐐶𐐮𐐽 𐐷 𐐿𐐫𐑊 𐑄 𐑀𐐱𐑅𐐹𐐯𐑊, 𐐫𐑉 𐑄 𐐼𐐱𐐿𐐻𐑉𐐮𐑌 𐐱𐑂 𐐗𐑉𐐴𐑅𐐻; 𐐰𐑌𐐼 𐐷 𐐸𐐰𐑂 𐑊𐐯𐐼 𐐰𐐶𐐩 𐑋𐐲𐐽 𐐱𐑂 𐑄𐐮𐑅 𐐹𐐨𐐹𐑊, 𐑄𐐰𐐻 𐑄𐐩 𐐹𐐲𐑉𐑂𐐲𐑉𐐻 𐑄 𐑉𐐴𐐻 𐐶𐐩 𐐱𐑂 𐐘𐐱𐐼, 𐐰𐑌𐐼 𐐿𐐨𐐹 𐑌𐐱𐐻 𐑄 𐑊𐐫 𐐱𐑂 𐐣𐐬𐑆𐐯𐑆, 𐐸𐐶𐐮𐐽 𐐮𐑆 𐑄 𐑉𐐴𐐻 𐐶𐐩; 𐐰𐑌𐐼 𐐿𐐱𐑌𐑂𐐲𐑉𐐻 𐑄 𐑊𐐫 𐐱𐑂 𐐣𐐬𐑆𐐯𐑆 𐐮𐑌𐐻𐐭 𐑄 𐐶𐐲𐑉𐑇𐐮𐐹 𐐱𐑂 𐐲 𐐺𐐨𐐮𐑍, 𐐸𐐶𐐮𐐽 𐐷 𐑅𐐩 𐑇𐐰𐑊 𐐿𐐲𐑋 𐑋𐐯𐑌𐐨 𐐸𐐲𐑌𐐼𐑉𐐯𐐼 𐐷𐐨𐑉𐑆 𐐸𐐯𐑌𐑅. 𐐈𐑌𐐼 𐑌𐐵 𐐺𐐨𐐸𐐬𐑊𐐼, 𐐴, 𐐟𐐯𐑉𐐯𐑋, 𐐼𐐨𐐿𐑊𐐩𐑉 𐐲𐑌𐐻𐐭 𐐷𐐭 𐑄𐐰𐐻 𐑄𐐮𐑅 𐐮𐑆 𐐺𐑊𐐰𐑅𐑁𐐲𐑋𐐨; 𐑁𐐫𐑉 𐑌𐐬 𐑋𐐰𐑌 𐑌𐐬𐐯𐑃 𐐱𐑂 𐑅𐐲𐐽 𐑃𐐮𐑍𐑆; 𐑁𐐫𐑉 𐐸𐐨 𐐿𐐰𐑌𐐱𐐻 𐐻𐐯𐑊 𐐱𐑂 𐑃𐐮𐑍𐑆 𐐻𐐭 𐐿𐐲𐑋. 𐐈𐑌𐐼 𐐰𐑁𐐻𐐲𐑉 𐑄𐐮𐑅 𐑋𐐰𐑌𐐲𐑉 𐐼𐐮𐐼 𐐟𐐯𐑉𐐯𐑋 𐐿𐐱𐑌𐐻𐐯𐑌𐐼 𐐲𐑀𐐯𐑌𐑅𐐻 𐑋𐐨. 𐐒𐐲𐐻 𐐺𐐨𐐸𐐬𐑊𐐼, 𐑄 𐐢𐐫𐑉𐐼 𐐘𐐱𐐼 𐐹𐐫𐑉𐐼 𐐮𐑌 𐐸𐐮𐑆 𐐝𐐹𐐮𐑉𐐮𐐻 𐐮𐑌𐐻𐐭 𐑋𐐴 𐑅𐐬𐑊, 𐐮𐑌𐑅𐐬𐑋𐐲𐐽 𐑄𐐰𐐻 𐐴 𐐼𐐮𐐼 𐐿𐐱𐑌𐑁𐐵𐑌𐐼 𐐸𐐮𐑋 𐐮𐑌 𐐫𐑊 𐐸𐐮𐑆 𐐶𐐲𐑉𐐼𐑆. 𐐈𐑌𐐼 𐐴 𐑅𐐯𐐼 𐐲𐑌𐐻𐐭 𐐸𐐮𐑋: 𐐔𐐨𐑌𐐴𐐯𐑅𐐻 𐑄𐐵 𐑄 𐐗𐑉𐐴𐑅𐐻 𐐸𐐭 𐑇𐐰𐑊 𐐿𐐲𐑋?

𐐰𐑌𐐼 𐐸𐐨 𐑅𐐯𐐼, 𐐮𐑁 𐑄𐐩𐑉 𐑇𐐳𐐼 𐐺𐐨 𐐩 𐐗𐑉𐐴𐑅𐐻, 𐐴 𐐶𐐳𐐼 𐑌𐐱𐐻 𐐼𐐨𐑌𐐴 𐐸𐐮𐑋; 𐐺𐐲𐐻 𐐴 𐑌𐐬 𐑄𐐰𐐻 𐑄𐐩𐑉 𐐮𐑆 𐑌𐐬 𐐗𐑉𐐴𐑅𐐻, 𐑌𐐨𐑄𐐲𐑉 𐐸𐐰𐑆 𐐺𐐮𐑌, 𐑌𐐫𐑉 𐐯𐑂𐐲𐑉 𐐶𐐮𐑊 𐐺𐐨. 𐐈𐑌𐐼 𐐴 𐑅𐐯𐐼 𐐲𐑌𐐻𐐭 𐐸𐐮𐑋, 𐐒𐐨𐑊𐐨𐑂𐐯𐑅𐐻 𐑄𐐵 𐑄 𐑅𐐿𐑉𐐮𐐹𐐽𐐲𐑉𐑆? 𐐈𐑌𐐼 𐐸𐐨 𐑅𐐯𐐼, 𐐏𐐩. 𐐈𐑌𐐼 𐐴 𐑅𐐯𐐼 𐐲𐑌𐐻𐐭 𐐸𐐮𐑋, 𐐜𐐯𐑌 𐐷𐐨 𐐼𐐭 𐑌𐐱𐐻 𐐲𐑌𐐼𐐲𐑉𐑅𐐻𐐰𐑌𐐼 𐑄𐐯𐑋; 𐑁𐐫𐑉 𐑄𐐩 𐐻𐑉𐐭𐑊𐐨 𐐻𐐯𐑅𐐻𐐮𐑁𐐴 𐐲𐑂 𐐗𐑉𐐴𐑅𐐻. 𐐒𐐨𐐸𐐬𐑊𐐼, 𐐴 𐑅𐐩 𐐲𐑌𐐻𐐭 𐐷𐐭, 𐑄𐐰𐐻 𐑌𐐲𐑌 𐐲𐑂 𐑄 𐐹𐑉𐐱𐑁𐐯𐐻𐑅 𐐸𐐰𐑂 𐑉𐐮𐐻𐑌, 𐑌𐐫𐑉 𐐹𐑉𐐱𐑁𐐯𐑅𐐴𐐼, 𐑅𐐩𐑂 𐑄𐐩 𐐸𐐰𐑂 𐑅𐐹𐐬𐐿𐑌 𐐿𐐱𐑌𐑅𐐲𐑉𐑌𐐮𐑍 𐑄𐐮𐑅 𐐗𐑉𐐴𐑅𐐻. 𐐈𐑌𐐼 𐑄𐐮𐑅 𐐮𐑆 𐑌𐐱𐐻 𐐫𐑊: 𐐮𐐻 𐐸𐐰𐑆 𐐺𐐮𐑌 𐑋𐐩𐐼 𐑋𐐰𐑌𐐮𐑁𐐯𐑅𐐻 𐐲𐑌𐐻𐐭 𐑋𐐨, 𐑁𐐫𐑉 𐐴 𐐸𐐰𐑂 𐐸𐐲𐑉𐐼 𐐰𐑌𐐼 𐑅𐐨𐑌; 𐐰𐑌𐐼 𐐮𐐻 𐐫𐑊𐑅𐐬 𐐸𐐰𐑆 𐐺𐐮𐑌 𐑋𐐩𐐼 𐑋𐐰𐑌𐐮𐑁𐐯𐑅𐐻 𐐲𐑌𐐻𐐭 𐑋𐐨 𐐺𐐴 𐑄 𐐹𐐵𐐲𐑉 𐐲𐑂 𐑄 𐐐𐐬𐑊𐐨 𐐘𐐬𐑅𐐻; 𐐸𐐶𐐩𐑉𐑁𐐫𐑉, 𐐴 𐑌𐐬 𐐮𐑁 𐑄𐐩𐑉 𐑇𐐳𐐼 𐐺𐐨 𐑌𐐬 𐐲𐐻𐐬𐑌𐑋𐐯𐑌𐐻 𐑋𐐩𐐼, 𐐫𐑊 𐑋𐐰𐑌𐐿𐐴𐑌𐐼 𐑋𐐲𐑅𐐻 𐐺𐐨 𐑊𐐫𐑅𐐻.

3. 𐐈𐑌𐐼 𐐮𐐻 𐐿𐐩𐑋 𐐻𐐭 𐐹𐐰𐑅 𐑄𐐰𐐻 𐐸𐐨 𐑅𐐯𐐼 𐐲𐑌𐐻𐐭 𐑋𐐨, 𐐟𐐬 𐑋𐐨 𐐩 𐑅𐐴𐑌 𐐺𐐴 𐑄𐐮𐑅 𐐹𐐵𐐲𐑉 𐐲𐑂 𐑄 𐐐𐐬𐑊𐐨 𐐘𐐬𐑅𐐻, 𐐮𐑌 𐑄 𐐸𐐶𐐮𐐽 𐐷𐐨 𐑌𐐬 𐑅𐐬 𐑋𐐲𐐽. 𐐈𐑌𐐼 𐐴 𐑅𐐯𐐼 𐐲𐑌𐐻𐐭 𐐸𐐮𐑋, 𐐐𐐶𐐱𐐻 𐐰𐑋 𐐴 𐑄𐐰𐐻 𐐴 𐑇𐐳𐐼 𐐻𐐯𐑋𐐻 𐐘𐐱𐐼 𐐻𐐭 𐑇𐐬 𐐲𐑌𐐻𐐭 𐑄𐐨 𐐩 𐑅𐐴𐑌 𐐮𐑌 𐑄 𐑃𐐮𐑍 𐐸𐐶𐐮𐐽 𐑄𐐵 𐑌𐐬𐐯𐑅𐐻 𐐻𐐭 𐐺𐐨 𐐻𐑉𐐭? 𐐏𐐯𐐻 𐑄𐐵 𐐶𐐮𐑊𐐻 𐐼𐐨𐑌𐐴 𐐮𐐻, 𐐺𐐨𐐿𐐫𐑆 𐑄𐐵 𐐪𐑉𐐻 𐐲𐑂 𐑄 𐐼𐐯𐑂𐐮𐑊. 𐐤𐐯𐑂𐐲𐑉𐑄𐐲𐑊𐐯𐑅, 𐑌𐐱𐐻 𐑋𐐴 𐐶𐐮𐑊 𐐺𐐨 𐐼𐐲𐑌; 𐐺𐐲𐐻 𐐮𐑁 𐐘𐐱𐐼 𐑇𐐰𐑊 𐑅𐑋𐐴𐐻 𐑄𐐨, 𐑊𐐯𐐻 𐑄𐐰𐐻 𐐺𐐨 𐐩 𐑅𐐴𐑌 𐐲𐑌𐐻𐐭 𐑄𐐨 𐑄𐐰𐐻 𐐸𐐨 𐐸𐐰𐑆 𐐹𐐵𐐲𐑉, 𐐺𐐬𐑃 𐐮𐑌 𐐸𐐯𐑂𐑌 𐐰𐑌𐐼 𐐮𐑌 𐐲𐑉𐑃; 𐐰𐑌𐐼 𐐫𐑊𐑅𐐬, 𐑄𐐰𐐻 𐐗𐑉𐐴𐑅𐐻 𐑇𐐰𐑊 𐐿𐐲𐑋. 𐐈𐑌𐐼 𐑄𐐴 𐐶𐐮𐑊, 𐐄 𐐢𐐫𐑉𐐼, 𐐺𐐨 𐐼𐐲𐑌, 𐐰𐑌𐐼 𐑌𐐱𐐻 𐑋𐐴𐑌.

4. 𐐈𐑌𐐼 𐐮𐐻 𐐿𐐩𐑋 𐐻𐐭 𐐹𐐰𐑅 𐑄𐐰𐐻 𐐸𐐶𐐯𐑌 𐐴, 𐐖𐐩𐐿𐐲𐐺, 𐐸𐐰𐐼 𐑅𐐹𐐬𐐿𐑌 𐑄𐐨𐑆 𐐶𐐲𐑉𐐼𐑆, 𐑄 𐐹𐐵𐐲𐑉 𐐲𐑂 𐑄 𐐢𐐫𐑉𐐼 𐐿𐐩𐑋 𐐲𐐹𐐱𐑌 𐐸𐐮𐑋, 𐐮𐑌𐑅𐐬𐑋𐐲𐐽 𐑄𐐰𐐻 𐐸𐐨 𐑁𐐯𐑊 𐐻𐐭 𐑄 𐐲𐑉𐑃. 𐐈𐑌𐐼 𐐮𐐻 𐐿𐐩𐑋 𐐻𐐭 𐐹𐐰𐑅 𐑄𐐰𐐻 𐐸𐐨 𐐶𐐱𐑆 𐑌𐐲𐑉𐐮𐑇𐐻 𐑁𐐫𐑉 𐑄 𐑅𐐹𐐩𐑅 𐐲𐑂 𐑋𐐯𐑌𐐨 𐐼𐐩𐑆. 𐐈𐑌𐐼 𐐮𐐻 𐐿𐐩𐑋 𐐻𐐭 𐐹𐐰𐑅 𐑄𐐰𐐻 𐐸𐐨 𐑅𐐯𐐼 𐐲𐑌𐐻𐐭 𐑄 𐐹𐐨𐐹𐑊, 𐐘𐐰𐑄𐐲𐑉 𐐻𐐭𐑀𐐯𐑄𐐲𐑉 𐐱𐑌 𐑄 𐑋𐐱𐑉𐐬, 𐑁𐐫𐑉 𐐴 𐑇𐐰𐑊 𐐼𐐴; 𐐸𐐶𐐩𐑉𐑁𐐫𐑉, 𐐴 𐐼𐐨𐑆𐐴𐑉 𐐻𐐭 𐑅𐐹𐐨𐐿 𐐲𐑌𐐻𐐭 𐑄 𐐹𐐨𐐹𐑊 𐐺𐐨𐑁𐐬𐑉 𐐴 𐑇𐐰𐑊 𐐼𐐴.

5. 𐐈𐑌𐐼 𐐮𐐻 𐐿𐐩𐑋 𐐻𐐭 𐐹𐐰𐑅 𐑄𐐰𐐻 𐐱𐑌 𐑄 𐑋𐐱𐑉𐐬 𐑄 𐑋𐐲𐑊𐐻𐐮𐐻𐐷𐐭𐐼 𐐶𐐲𐑉 𐑀𐐰𐑄𐐲𐑉𐐼 𐐻𐐭𐑀𐐯𐑄𐐲𐑉; 𐐰𐑌𐐼 𐐸𐐨 𐑅𐐹𐐩𐐿 𐐹𐑊𐐩𐑌𐑊𐐨 𐐲𐑌𐐻𐐭 𐑄𐐯𐑋, 𐐰𐑌𐐼 𐐼𐐨𐑌𐐴𐐼 𐑄 𐑃𐐮𐑍𐑆 𐐸𐐶𐐮𐐽 𐐸𐐨 𐐸𐐰𐐼 𐐻𐐫𐐻 𐑄𐐯𐑋; 𐐰𐑌𐐼 𐐿𐐱𐑌𐑁𐐯𐑅𐐻 𐑄 𐐗𐑉𐐴𐑅𐐻, 𐐰𐑌𐐼 𐑄 𐐹𐐵𐐲𐑉 𐐲𐑂 𐑄 𐐐𐐬𐑊𐐨 𐐘𐐬𐑅𐐻, 𐐰𐑌𐐼 𐑄 𐑋𐐮𐑌𐐮𐑅𐐻𐐲𐑉𐐮𐑍 𐐲𐑂 𐐩𐑌𐐾𐐯𐑊𐑆. 𐐈𐑌𐐼 𐐸𐐨 𐑅𐐹𐐩𐐿 𐐹𐑊𐐩𐑌𐑊𐐨 𐐲𐑌𐐻𐐭 𐑄𐐯𐑋, 𐑄𐐰𐐻 𐐸𐐨 𐐸𐐰𐐼 𐐺𐐮𐑌 𐐼𐐨𐑅𐐨𐑂𐐼 𐐺𐐴 𐑄 𐐹𐐵𐐲𐑉 𐐲𐑂 𐑄 𐐼𐐯𐑂𐐮𐑊. 𐐈𐑌𐐼 𐐸𐐨 𐑅𐐹𐐩𐐿 𐐲𐑂 𐐸𐐯𐑊, 𐐰𐑌𐐼 𐐲𐑂 𐐨𐐻𐐲𐑉𐑌𐐮𐐻𐐨, 𐐰𐑌𐐼 𐐲𐑂 𐐨𐐻𐐲𐑉𐑌𐐲𐑊 𐐹𐐲𐑌𐐮𐑇𐑋𐐯𐑌𐐻. 𐐈𐑌𐐼 𐐸𐐨 𐑅𐐯𐐼, 𐐴 𐑁𐐨𐑉 𐑊𐐯𐑅𐐻 𐐴 𐐸𐐰𐑂 𐐿𐐱𐑋𐐮𐐻𐐯𐐼 𐑄 𐐲𐑌𐐹𐐪𐑉𐐼𐐲𐑌𐐲𐐺𐑊 𐑅𐐮𐑌, 𐑁𐐫𐑉 𐐴 𐐸𐐰𐑂 𐑊𐐴𐐼 𐐲𐑌𐐻𐐭 𐐘𐐱𐐼: 𐑁𐐫𐑉 𐐴 𐐼𐐨𐑌𐐴𐐼 𐑄 𐐗𐑉𐐴𐑅𐐻, 𐐰𐑌𐐼 𐑅𐐯𐐼 𐑄𐐰𐐻 𐐴 𐐺𐐨𐑊𐐨𐑂𐐼 𐑄 𐑅𐐿𐑉𐐮𐐹𐐽𐐲𐑉𐑆; 𐐰𐑌𐐼 𐑄𐐩 𐐻𐑉𐐭𐑊𐐨 𐐻𐐯𐑅𐐻𐐮𐑁𐐴 𐐲𐑂 𐐸𐐮𐑋. 𐐈𐑌𐐼 𐐺𐐨𐐿𐐫𐑆 𐐴 𐐸𐐰𐑂 𐑄𐐲𐑅 𐑊𐐴𐐼 𐐲𐑌𐐻𐐭 𐐘𐐱𐐼, 𐐴 𐑀𐑉𐐩𐐻𐑊𐐨 𐑁𐐨𐑉 𐑊𐐯𐑅𐐻 𐑋𐐴 𐐿𐐩𐑅 𐑇𐐰𐑊 𐐺𐐨 𐐫𐑁𐐳𐑊; 𐐺𐐲𐐻 𐐴 𐐿𐐱𐑌𐑁𐐯𐑅 𐐲𐑌𐐻𐐭 𐐘𐐱𐐼.

6. 𐐈𐑌𐐼 𐐮𐐻 𐐿𐐩𐑋 𐐻𐐭 𐐹𐐰𐑅 𐑄𐐰𐐻 𐐸𐐶𐐯𐑌 𐐸𐐨 𐐸𐐰𐐼 𐑅𐐯𐐼 𐑄𐐨𐑆 𐐶𐐲𐑉𐐼𐑆, 𐐸𐐨 𐐿𐐳𐐼 𐑅𐐩 𐑌𐐬 𐑋𐐬𐑉, 𐐰𐑌𐐼 𐐸𐐨 𐑀𐐩𐑂 𐐲𐐹 𐑄 𐑀𐐬𐑅𐐻. 𐐈𐑌𐐼 𐐸𐐶𐐯𐑌 𐑄 𐑋𐐲𐑊𐐻𐐮𐐻𐐷𐐭𐐼 𐐸𐐰𐐼 𐐶𐐮𐐻𐑌𐐯𐑅𐐻 𐑄𐐰𐐻 𐐸𐐨 𐑅𐐹𐐩𐐿 𐑄𐐨𐑆 𐑃𐐮𐑍𐑆 𐐰𐑆 𐐸𐐨 𐐶𐐱𐑆 𐐲𐐺𐐵𐐻 𐐻𐐭 𐑀𐐮𐑂 𐐲𐐹 𐑄 𐑀𐐬𐑅𐐻, 𐑄𐐩 𐐶𐐲𐑉 𐐰𐑅𐐻𐐱𐑌𐐮𐑇𐐻 𐐯𐐿𐑅𐐨𐐼𐐮𐑍𐑊𐐨; 𐐮𐑌𐑅𐐬𐑋𐐲𐐽 𐑄𐐰𐐻 𐑄 𐐹𐐵𐐲𐑉 𐐲𐑂 𐐘𐐱𐐼 𐐿𐐩𐑋 𐐼𐐵𐑌 𐐲𐐹𐐱𐑌 𐑄𐐯𐑋, 𐐰𐑌𐐼 𐑄𐐩 𐐶𐐲𐑉 𐐬𐑂𐐲𐑉𐐿𐐲𐑋, 𐑄𐐰𐐻 𐑄𐐩 𐑁𐐯𐑊 𐐻𐐭 𐑄 𐐲𐑉𐑃. 𐐤𐐵, 𐑄𐐮𐑅 𐑃𐐮𐑍 𐐶𐐱𐑆 𐐹𐑊𐐨𐑆𐐮𐑍 𐐲𐑌𐐻𐐭 𐑋𐐨, 𐐖𐐩𐐿𐐲𐐺, 𐑁𐐫𐑉 𐐴 𐐸𐐰𐐼 𐑉𐐨𐐿𐐶𐐯𐑅𐐻𐐯𐐼 𐐮𐐻 𐐲𐑂 𐑋𐐴 𐐙𐐪𐑄𐐲𐑉 𐐸𐐭 𐐶𐐱𐑆 𐐮𐑌 𐐸𐐯𐑂𐑌: 𐑁𐐫𐑉 𐐸𐐨 𐐸𐐰𐐼 𐐸𐐲𐑉𐐼 𐑋𐐴 𐐿𐑉𐐴 𐐰𐑌𐐼 𐐰𐑌𐑅𐐲𐑉𐐼 𐑋𐐴 𐐹𐑉𐐩𐑉.

7. 𐐈𐑌𐐼 𐐮𐐻 𐐿𐐩𐑋 𐐻𐐭 𐐹𐐰𐑅 𐑄𐐰𐐻 𐐹𐐨𐑅 𐐰𐑌𐐼 𐑄 𐑊𐐲𐑂 𐐲𐑂 𐐘𐐱𐐼 𐐶𐐱𐑆 𐑉𐐨𐑅𐐻𐐬𐑉𐐼 𐐲𐑀𐐯𐑌 𐐲𐑋𐐲𐑍 𐑄 𐐹𐐨𐐹𐑊; 𐐰𐑌𐐼 𐑄𐐩 𐑅𐐲𐑉𐐽𐐻 𐑄 𐑅𐐿𐑉𐐮𐐹𐐽𐐲𐑉𐑆, 𐐰𐑌𐐼 𐐸𐐪𐑉𐐿𐑌𐐼 𐑌𐐬 𐑋𐐬𐑉 𐐻𐐭 𐑄 𐐶𐐲𐑉𐐼𐑆 𐐲𐑂 𐑄𐐮𐑅 𐐶𐐮𐐿𐐯𐐼 𐑋𐐰𐑌. 𐐈𐑌𐐼 𐐮𐐻 𐐿𐐩𐑋 𐐻𐐭 𐐹𐐰𐑅 𐑄𐐰𐐻 𐑋𐐯𐑌𐐨 𐑋𐐨𐑌𐑆 𐐶𐐲𐑉 𐐼𐐨𐑂𐐴𐑆𐐼 𐐻𐐭 𐑉𐐨𐐿𐑊𐐩𐑋 𐐰𐑌𐐼 𐑉𐐨𐑅𐐻𐐬𐑉 𐑄 𐐢𐐰𐑋𐐲𐑌𐐴𐐻𐑅 𐐻𐐭 𐑄 𐑌𐐱𐑊𐐯𐐾 𐐲𐑂 𐑄 𐐻𐑉𐐭𐑃; 𐐺𐐲𐐻 𐐮𐐻 𐐫𐑊 𐐶𐐱𐑆 𐑂𐐩𐑌, 𐑁𐐫𐑉 𐑄𐐩 𐐼𐐨𐑊𐐴𐐻𐐯𐐼 𐐮𐑌 𐐶𐐫𐑉𐑆 𐐰𐑌𐐼 𐐺𐑊𐐲𐐼𐑇𐐯𐐼, 𐐰𐑌𐐼 𐑄𐐩 𐐸𐐰𐐼 𐐰𐑌 𐐨𐐻𐐲𐑉𐑌𐐲𐑊 𐐸𐐩𐐻𐑉𐐯𐐼 𐐲𐑀𐐯𐑌𐑅𐐻 𐐲𐑅, 𐑄𐐩𐑉 𐐺𐑉𐐯𐑄𐑉𐐯𐑌. 𐐈𐑌𐐼 𐑄𐐩 𐑅𐐫𐐻 𐐺𐐴 𐑄 𐐹𐐵𐐲𐑉 𐐲𐑂 𐑄𐐩𐑉 𐐪𐑉𐑋𐑆 𐐻𐐭 𐐼𐐯𐑅𐐻𐑉𐐱𐐴 𐐲𐑅 𐐿𐐱𐑌𐐻𐐮𐑌𐐷𐐭𐐲𐑊𐐨; 𐐸𐐶𐐩𐑉𐑁𐐫𐑉, 𐑄 𐐹𐐨𐐹𐑊 𐐲𐑂 𐐤𐐨𐑁𐐴

𐐼𐐮𐐼 𐑁𐐫𐑉𐐻𐐮𐑁𐐴 𐐲𐑀𐐯𐑌𐑅𐐻 𐑄𐐯𐑋 𐐶𐐮𐑄 𐑄𐐩𐑉 𐐪𐑉𐑋𐑆, 𐐰𐑌𐐼 𐐶𐐮𐑄 𐐫𐑊 𐑄𐐩𐑉 𐑋𐐴𐐻, 𐐻𐑉𐐲𐑅𐐻𐐮𐑍 𐐮𐑌 𐑄 𐐘𐐱𐐼 𐐰𐑌𐐼 𐑉𐐱𐐿 𐐱𐑂 𐑄𐐩𐑉 𐑅𐐰𐑊𐑂𐐩𐑇𐐲𐑌; 𐐸𐐶𐐩𐑉𐑁𐐫𐑉, 𐑄𐐩 𐐺𐐨𐐿𐐩𐑋 𐐰𐑆 𐐷𐐯𐐻, 𐐿𐐱𐑍𐐿𐐲𐑉𐐲𐑉𐑆 𐐱𐑂 𐑄𐐩𐑉 𐐯𐑌𐐲𐑋𐐮𐑆.

8. 𐐈𐑌𐐼 𐐮𐐻 𐐿𐐩𐑋 𐐻𐐭 𐐹𐐪𐑅 𐑄𐐰𐐻 𐐌, 𐐖𐐩𐐿𐐲𐐺, 𐐺𐐨𐑀𐐰𐑌 𐐻𐐭 𐐺 𐐬𐑊𐐼; 𐐰𐑌𐐼 𐑄 𐑉𐐯𐐿𐐫𐑉𐐼 𐐱𐑂 𐑄𐐮𐑅 𐐹𐐨𐐹𐑊 𐐺𐐨𐐮𐑍 𐐿𐐯𐐹𐐻 𐐱𐑌 𐑄 𐐲𐑄𐐲𐑉 𐐹𐑊𐐩𐐻𐑅 𐐱𐑂 𐐤𐐨𐑁𐐴, 𐐸𐐶𐐩𐑉𐑁𐐫𐑉, 𐐌 𐐿𐐱𐑌𐐿𐑊𐐭𐐼 𐑄𐐮𐑅 𐑉𐐯𐐿𐐫𐑉𐐼, 𐐼𐐨𐐿𐑊𐐩𐑉𐐮𐑍 𐑄𐐰𐐻 𐐌 𐐸𐐰𐑂 𐑉𐐮𐐻𐑌 𐐰𐐿𐐫𐑉𐐼𐐮𐑍 𐐻𐐭 𐑄 𐐺𐐯𐑅𐐻 𐐱𐑂 𐑋𐐴 𐑌𐐱𐑊𐐯𐐾, 𐐺𐐴 𐑅𐐩𐐮𐑍, 𐑄𐐰𐐻 𐑄 𐐻𐐴𐑋 𐐹𐐰𐑅𐐻 𐐰𐐶𐐩 𐐶𐐮𐑄 𐐲𐑅, 𐐰𐑌𐐼 𐐫𐑊𐑅𐐬 𐐵𐑉 𐑊𐐴𐑂𐑆 𐐹𐐰𐑅𐐻 𐐰𐐶𐐩 𐑊𐐴𐐿 𐐰𐑆 𐐮𐐻 𐐶𐐲𐑉 𐐲𐑌𐐻𐐭 𐐲𐑅 𐐩 𐐼𐑉𐐨𐑋, 𐐶𐐨 𐐺𐐨𐐮𐑍 𐐩 𐑊𐐬𐑌𐑅𐐲𐑋 𐐰𐑌𐐼 𐐩 𐑅𐐱𐑊𐐯𐑋 𐐹𐐨𐐹𐑊, 𐐶𐐱𐑌𐐼𐐲𐑉𐐲𐑉𐑆, 𐐿𐐪𐑅𐐻 𐐵𐐻 𐑁𐑉𐐱𐑋 𐐖𐐯𐑉𐐭𐑅𐐰𐑊𐐯𐑋; 𐐺𐐫𐑉𐑌 𐐮𐑌 𐐻𐑉𐐮𐐺𐐷𐐭𐑊𐐩𐑇𐐲𐑌, 𐐮𐑌 𐐩 𐐶𐐮𐑊𐐼𐐲𐑉𐑌𐐯𐑅, 𐐰𐑌𐐼 𐐸𐐩𐐻𐐯𐐼 𐐱𐑂 𐐵𐑉 𐐺𐑉𐐯𐑄𐑉𐐯𐑌, 𐐸𐐶𐐮𐐽 𐐿𐐫𐑆𐐼 𐐶𐐫𐑉𐑆 𐐰𐑌𐐼 𐐿𐐱𐑌𐐻𐐯𐑌𐑇𐐲𐑌𐑆; 𐐸𐐶𐐩𐑉𐑁𐐫𐑉, 𐐶𐐨 𐐼𐐮𐐼 𐑋𐐬𐑉𐑌 𐐵𐐻 𐐵𐑉 𐐼𐐩𐑆.

9. 𐐈𐑌𐐼 𐐌, 𐐖𐐩𐐿𐐲𐐺, 𐑅𐐫 𐑄𐐰𐐻 𐐌 𐑋𐐲𐑅𐐻 𐑅𐐭𐑌 𐑀𐐬 𐐼𐐵𐑌 𐐻𐐭 𐑋𐐴 𐑀𐑉𐐩𐑂; 𐐸𐐶𐐩𐑉𐑁𐐫𐑉, 𐐌 𐑅𐐯𐐼 𐐲𐑌𐐻𐐭 𐑋𐐴 𐑅𐐲𐑌 𐐀𐑌𐐱𐑅, 𐐓𐐩𐐿 𐑄𐐨𐑆 𐐹𐑊𐐩𐐻𐑅. 𐐈𐑌𐐼 𐐌 𐐻𐐬𐑊𐐼 𐐸𐐮𐑋 𐑄 𐑃𐐮𐑍𐑆 𐐸𐐶𐐮𐐽 𐑋𐐴 𐐺𐑉𐐲𐑄𐐲𐑉 𐐤𐐨𐑁𐐴 𐐸𐐰𐐼 𐐿𐐱𐑋𐐰𐑌𐐼𐐯𐐼 𐑋𐐨, 𐐰𐑌𐐼 𐐸𐐨 𐐹𐑉𐐱𐑋𐐮𐑅𐐻 𐐬𐐺𐐨𐐼𐐨𐐯𐑌𐑅 𐐲𐑌𐐻𐐭 𐑄 𐐿𐐱𐑋𐐰𐑌𐐼𐑆. 𐐈𐑌𐐼 𐐌 𐑋𐐩𐐿 𐐰𐑌 𐐯𐑌𐐼 𐐱𐑂 𐑋𐐴 𐑉𐐴𐐻𐐮𐑍 𐐲𐐹𐐱𐑌 𐑄𐐨𐑆 𐐹𐑊𐐩𐐻𐑅, 𐐸𐐶𐐮𐐽 𐑉𐐴𐐻𐐮𐑍 𐐸𐐰𐑆 𐐺𐐮𐑌 𐑅𐑋𐐫𐑊; 𐐰𐑌𐐼 𐐻𐐭 𐑄 𐑉𐐨𐐼𐐲𐑉 𐐌 𐐺𐐮𐐼 𐑁𐐩𐑉𐐶𐐯𐑊, 𐐸𐐬𐐹𐐮𐑍 𐑄𐐰𐐻 𐑋𐐯𐑌𐐨 𐐱𐑂 𐑋𐐴 𐐺𐑉𐐯𐑄𐑉𐐯𐑌 𐑋𐐩 𐑉𐐨𐐼 𐑋𐐴 𐐶𐐲𐑉𐐼𐑆. 𐐒𐑉𐐯𐑄𐑉𐐯𐑌, 𐐲𐐼𐐷𐐭.

𐐜 𐐒𐐳𐐿 𐐱𐑂 𐐀𐑌𐐬𐑅.

𐐕𐐰𐐹𐐻𐐲𐑉 I.

1. 𐐒𐐨𐐸𐐬𐑊𐐼, 𐐮𐐻 𐐿𐐩𐑋 𐐻𐐭 𐐹𐐪𐑅 𐑄𐐰𐐻 𐐌, 𐐀𐑌𐐬𐑅, 𐑌𐐬𐐮𐑍 𐑋𐐴 𐑁𐐪𐑄𐐲𐑉 𐑄𐐰𐐻 𐐸𐐨 𐐶𐐱𐑆 𐐩 𐐾𐐲𐑅𐐻
𐑋𐐰𐑌: 𐑁𐐫𐑉 𐐸𐐨 𐐻𐐫𐐻 𐑋𐐨 𐐮𐑌 𐐸𐐮𐑆 𐑊𐐰𐑍𐑀𐐶𐐩𐐾, 𐐰𐑌𐐼 𐐫𐑊𐑅𐐬 𐐮𐑌 𐑄 𐑌𐐲𐑉𐐽𐐲𐑉 𐐰𐑌𐐼 𐐰𐐼𐑋𐐬𐑌𐐮𐑇𐐲𐑌 𐐱𐑂
𐑄 𐐢𐐫𐑉𐐼. 𐐈𐑌𐐼 𐐺𐑊𐐯𐑅𐐯𐐼 𐐺𐐨 𐑄 𐑌𐐩𐑋 𐐱𐑂 𐑋𐐴 𐐘𐐱𐐼 𐑁𐐫𐑉 𐐮𐐻. 𐐈𐑌𐐼 𐐌 𐐶𐐮𐑊 𐐻𐐯𐑊 𐐷𐐭 𐐱𐑂 𐑄
𐑉𐐯𐑅𐑊 𐐸𐐶𐐮𐐽 𐐌 𐐸𐐰𐐼 𐐺𐐨𐑁𐐬𐑉 𐐘𐐱𐐼, 𐐺𐐨𐑁𐐬𐑉 𐐌 𐑉𐐨𐑅𐐨𐑂𐐼 𐐩 𐑉𐐨𐑋𐐮𐑇𐐲𐑌 𐐱𐑂 𐑋𐐴 𐑅𐐮𐑌𐑆: 𐐺𐐨𐐸𐐬𐑊𐐼, 𐐌
𐐶𐐯𐑌𐐻 𐐻𐐭 𐐸𐐲𐑌𐐻 𐐺𐐨𐑅𐐻𐑅 𐐮𐑌 𐑄 𐑁𐐱𐑉𐐯𐑅𐐻𐑅; 𐐰𐑌𐐼 𐑄 𐐶𐐲𐑉𐐼𐑆 𐐸𐐶𐐮𐐽 𐐌 𐐸𐐰𐐼 𐐫𐑁𐑌 𐐸𐐲𐑉𐐼 𐑋𐐴 𐑁𐐪𐑄𐐲𐑉
𐑅𐐹𐐨𐐿 𐐿𐐱𐑌𐑅𐐲𐑉𐑌𐐮𐑍 𐐨𐐻𐐲𐑉𐑌𐐲𐑊 𐑊𐐴𐑁, 𐐰𐑌𐐼 𐑄 𐐾𐐱𐐮 𐐱𐑂 𐑄 𐑅𐐩𐑌𐐻𐑅, 𐑅𐐲𐑍𐐿 𐐼𐐨𐐹 𐐮𐑌𐐻𐐭 𐑋𐐴 𐐸𐐪𐑉𐐻.
𐐈𐑌𐐼 𐑋𐐴 𐑅𐐬𐑊 𐐸𐐲𐑍𐑀𐐲𐑉𐐼; 𐐰𐑌𐐼 𐐌 𐑌𐐨𐑊𐐼 𐐼𐐵𐑌 𐐺𐐨𐑁𐐬𐑉 𐑋𐐴 𐑋𐐩𐐿𐐲𐑉, 𐐰𐑌𐐼 𐐌 𐐿𐑉𐐴𐐼 𐐲𐑌𐐻𐐭 𐐸𐐮𐑋 𐐮𐑌
𐑋𐐴𐐻𐐨 𐐹𐑉𐐩𐑉 𐐰𐑌𐐼 𐑅𐐲𐐹𐑊𐐮𐐿𐐩𐑇𐐲𐑌 𐑁𐐫𐑉 𐑋𐐴𐑌 𐐬𐑌 𐑅𐐬𐑊; 𐐰𐑌𐐼 𐐫𐑊 𐑄 𐐼𐐩 𐑊𐐫𐑍 𐐼𐐮𐐼 𐐌 𐐿𐑉𐐴 𐐲𐑌𐐻𐐭 𐐸𐐮𐑋;
𐐏𐐩, 𐐰𐑌𐐼 𐐸𐐶𐐯𐑌 𐑄 𐑌𐐴𐐻 𐐿𐐩𐑋, 𐐌 𐐼𐐮𐐼 𐑅𐐻𐐮𐑊 𐑉𐐩𐑆 𐑋𐐴 𐑂𐐱𐐮𐑅 𐐸𐐴 𐑄𐐰𐐻 𐐮𐐻 𐑉𐐨𐐽𐐻 𐑄 𐐸𐐯𐑂𐑌𐑆. 𐐈𐑌𐐼
𐑄𐐩𐑉 𐐿𐐩𐑋 𐐩 𐑂𐐱𐐮𐑅 𐐲𐑌𐐻𐐭 𐑋𐐨, 𐑅𐐩𐐮𐑍, 𐐀𐑌𐐬𐑅, 𐑄𐐴 𐑅𐐮𐑌𐑆 𐐪𐑉 𐑁𐐫𐑉𐑀𐐮𐑂𐑌 𐑄𐐨, 𐐰𐑌𐐼 𐑄𐐵 𐑇𐐰𐑊𐐻 𐐺𐐨 𐐺𐑊𐐯𐑅𐐯𐐼.
𐐈𐑌𐐼 𐐌, 𐐀𐑌𐐬𐑅, 𐑌𐐭 𐑄𐐰𐐻 𐐘𐐱𐐼 𐐿𐐳𐐼 𐑌𐐱𐐻 𐑊𐐴, 𐐸𐐶𐐩𐑉𐑁𐐬𐑉, 𐑋𐐴 𐑀𐐮𐑊𐐻 𐐶𐐱𐑆 𐑅𐐶𐐯𐐹𐐻 𐐰𐐶𐐩. 𐐈𐑌𐐼
𐐌 𐑅𐐯𐐼, 𐐢𐐫𐑉𐐼, 𐐸𐐵 𐐮𐑆 𐐮𐐻 𐐼𐐲𐑌? 𐐈𐑌𐐼 𐐸𐐨 𐑅𐐯𐐼 𐐲𐑌𐐻𐐭 𐑋𐐨, 𐐒𐐨𐐿𐐫𐑆 𐐱𐑂 𐑄𐐴 𐑁𐐩𐑃 𐐮𐑌 𐐗𐑉𐐴𐑅𐐻,
𐐸𐐭𐑋 𐑄𐐵 𐐸𐐰𐑅𐐻 𐑌𐐯𐑂𐐲𐑉 𐐺𐐨𐑁𐐬𐑉 𐐸𐐲𐑉𐐼 𐑌𐐫𐑉 𐑅𐐨𐑌. 𐐈𐑌𐐼 𐑋𐐯𐑌𐐨 𐐷𐐨𐑉𐑆 𐐹𐐪𐑅 𐐰𐐶𐐩, 𐐺𐐨𐑁𐐬𐑉 𐐸𐐨 𐑇𐐰𐑊
𐑋𐐰𐑌𐐮𐑁𐐯𐑅𐐻 𐐸𐐮𐑋𐑅𐐯𐑊𐑁 𐐮𐑌 𐑄 𐑁𐑊𐐯𐑇; 𐐸𐐶𐐩𐑉𐑁𐐬𐑉, 𐑀𐐬 𐐻𐐭, 𐑄𐐴 𐑁𐐩𐑃 𐐸𐐰𐑃 𐑋𐐩𐐼 𐑄𐐨 𐐸𐐬𐑊.

2. 𐐤𐐵, 𐐮𐐻 𐐿𐐩𐑋 𐐻𐐭 𐐹𐐪𐑅, 𐑄𐐰𐐻 𐐸𐐶𐐯𐑌 𐐌 𐐸𐐰𐐼 𐐸𐐲𐑉𐐼 𐑄𐐨𐑆 𐐶𐐲𐑉𐐼𐑆, 𐐌 𐐺𐐨𐑀𐐰𐑌 𐐻𐐭 𐑁𐐨𐑊 𐐩
𐐼𐐨𐑆𐐴𐑉 𐑁𐐫𐑉 𐑄 𐐶𐐯𐑊𐑁𐐩𐑉 𐐱𐑂 𐑋𐐴 𐐺𐑉𐐯𐑄𐑉𐐯𐑌, 𐑄 𐐤𐐨𐑁𐐴𐐻𐑅; 𐐸𐐶𐐩𐑉𐑁𐐬𐑉, 𐐌 𐐼𐐮𐐼 𐐹𐐬𐑉 𐐵𐐻 𐑋𐐴 𐐸𐐬𐑊
𐑅𐐬𐑊 𐐲𐑌𐐻𐐭 𐐘𐐱𐐼 𐑁𐐫𐑉 𐑄𐐯𐑋. 𐐈𐑌𐐼 𐐸𐐶𐐴𐑊 𐐌 𐐶𐐱𐑆 𐑄𐐲𐑅 𐑅𐐻𐑉𐐲𐑀𐑊𐐮𐑍 𐐮𐑌 𐑄 𐑅𐐹𐐮𐑉𐐮𐐻, 𐐺𐐨𐐸𐐬𐑊𐐼, 𐑄 𐑂𐐱𐐮𐑅
𐐱𐑂 𐑄 𐐢𐐫𐑉𐐼 𐐿𐐩𐑋 𐐮𐑌𐐻𐐭 𐑋𐐴 𐑋𐐴𐑌𐐼 𐐰𐑀𐐯𐑌, 𐑅𐐩𐐮𐑍, 𐐌 𐐶𐐮𐑊 𐑂𐐮𐑆𐐮𐐻 𐑄𐐴 𐐺𐑉𐐯𐑄𐑉𐐯𐑌, 𐐰𐐿𐐫𐑉𐐼𐐮𐑍 𐐻𐐭
𐑄𐐩𐑉 𐐼𐐮𐑊𐐮𐐾𐐯𐑌𐑅 𐐮𐑌 𐐿𐐨𐐹𐐮𐑍 𐑋𐐴 𐐿𐐱𐑋𐐰𐑌𐐼𐑋𐐯𐑌𐐻𐑅. 𐐌 𐐸𐐰𐑂 𐑀𐐮𐑂𐑌 𐐲𐑌𐐻𐐭 𐑄𐐯𐑋 𐑄𐐮𐑅 𐑊𐐰𐑌𐐼; 𐐰𐑌𐐼
𐐮𐐻 𐐮𐑆 𐐩 𐐸𐐬𐑊𐐨 𐑊𐐰𐑌𐐼: 𐐰𐑌𐐼 𐐌 𐐿𐐲𐑉𐑅 𐐮𐐻 𐑌𐐱𐐻, 𐑅𐐩𐑂 𐐮𐐻 𐐺𐐨 𐑁𐐫𐑉 𐑄 𐐿𐐫𐑆 𐐱𐑂 𐐮𐑌𐐮𐐿𐐶𐐮𐐻𐐨; 𐐸𐐶𐐩𐑉𐑁𐐬𐑉,
𐐌 𐐶𐐮𐑊 𐑂𐐮𐑆𐐮𐐻 𐑄𐐴 𐐺𐑉𐐯𐑄𐑉𐐯𐑌, 𐐰𐐿𐐫𐑉𐐼𐐮𐑍 𐐰𐑆 𐐌 𐐸𐐰𐑂 𐑅𐐯𐐼; 𐐰𐑌𐐼 𐑄𐐩𐑉 𐐻𐑉𐐰𐑌𐑅𐑀𐑉𐐯𐑇𐐲𐑌𐑆 𐐶𐐮𐑊 𐐌
𐐺𐑉𐐮𐑍 𐐼𐐵𐑌 𐐶𐐮𐑄 𐑅𐐱𐑉𐐬 𐐲𐐹𐐱𐑌 𐑄𐐩𐑉 𐐬𐑌 𐐸𐐯𐐼𐑆. 𐐈𐑌𐐼 𐐰𐑁𐐻𐐲𐑉 𐐌, 𐐀𐑌𐐬𐑅, 𐐸𐐰𐐼 𐐸𐐲𐑉𐐼 𐑄𐐨𐑆
𐐶𐐲𐑉𐐼𐑆, 𐑋𐐴 𐑁𐐩𐑃 𐐺𐐨𐑀𐐰𐑌 𐐻𐐭 𐐺𐐨 𐐲𐑌𐑇𐐩𐐿𐐲𐑌 𐐮𐑌 𐑄 𐐢𐐫𐑉𐐼; 𐐰𐑌𐐼 𐐌 𐐹𐑉𐐩𐐼 𐐲𐑌𐐻𐐭 𐐸𐐮𐑋 𐐶𐐮𐑄 𐑋𐐯𐑌𐐨 𐑊𐐫𐑍
𐑅𐐻𐑉𐐲𐑀𐑊𐐮𐑍𐑆 𐑁𐐫𐑉 𐑋𐐴 𐐺𐑉𐐯𐑄𐑉𐐯𐑌, 𐑄 𐐢𐐰𐑋𐐲𐑌𐐴𐐻𐑅.

3. 𐐈𐑌𐐼 𐐮𐐻 𐐿𐐩𐑋 𐐻𐐭 𐐹𐐪𐑅, 𐑄𐐰𐐻 𐐰𐑁𐐻𐐲𐑉 𐐌 𐐸𐐰𐐼 𐐹𐑉𐐩𐐼 𐐰𐑌𐐼 𐑊𐐩𐐺𐐲𐑉𐐼 𐐶𐐮𐑄 𐐫𐑊 𐐼𐐮𐑊𐐮𐐾𐐯𐑌𐑅, 𐑄
𐐢𐐫𐑉𐐼 𐑅𐐯𐐼 𐐲𐑌𐐻𐐭 𐑋𐐨, 𐐌 𐐶𐐮𐑊 𐑀𐑉𐐰𐑌𐐻 𐐲𐑌𐐻𐐭 𐑄𐐨 𐐰𐐿𐐫𐑉𐐼𐐮𐑍 𐐻𐐭 𐑄𐐴 𐐼𐐨𐑆𐐴𐑉𐑆, 𐐺𐐨𐐿𐐫𐑆 𐐱𐑂 𐑄𐐴
𐑁𐐩𐑃. 𐐈𐑌𐐼 𐑌𐐵 𐐺𐐨𐐸𐐬𐑊𐐼, 𐑄𐐮𐑅 𐐶𐐱𐑆 𐑄 𐐼𐐨𐑆𐐴𐑉 𐐸𐐶𐐮𐐽 𐐌 𐐼𐐨𐑆𐐴𐑉𐐼 𐐱𐑂 𐐸𐐮𐑋: 𐑄𐐰𐐻 𐐮𐑁 𐐮𐐻 𐑇𐐳𐐼
𐑅𐐬 𐐺𐐨, 𐑄𐐰𐐻 𐑋𐐴 𐐹𐐨𐐹𐑊, 𐑄 𐐤𐐨𐑁𐐴𐐻𐑅, 𐑇𐐳𐐼 𐑁𐐫𐑊 𐐮𐑌𐐻𐐭 𐐻𐑉𐐰𐑌𐑅𐑀𐑉𐐯𐑇𐐲𐑌, 𐐰𐑌𐐼 𐐺𐐴 𐐯𐑌𐐨 𐑋𐐨𐑌𐑆
𐐺𐐨 𐐼𐐨𐑅𐐻𐑉𐐱𐐮𐐼, 𐐰𐑌𐐼 𐑄 𐐢𐐰𐑋𐐲𐑌𐐴𐐻𐑅 𐑇𐐳𐐼 𐑌𐐱𐐻 𐐺𐐨 𐐼𐐨𐑅𐐻𐑉𐐱𐐮𐐼, 𐑄𐐰𐐻 𐑄 𐐢𐐫𐑉𐐼 𐐘𐐱𐐼 𐐶𐐳𐐼 𐐹𐑉𐐨𐑆𐐲𐑉𐑂 𐐩 𐑉𐐯𐐿𐐲𐑉𐐼 𐐱𐑂 𐑋𐐴 𐐹𐐨𐐹𐑊, 𐑄 𐐤𐐨𐑁𐐴𐐻𐑅; 𐐨𐑂𐑌 𐐮𐑁 𐐮𐐻 𐑅𐐬 𐐺𐐨, 𐐺𐐴 𐑄 𐐹𐐵𐐲𐑉 𐐱𐑂 𐐸𐐮𐑆 𐐸𐐬𐑊𐐨 𐐪𐑉𐑋,
𐑄𐐰𐐻 𐐮𐐻 𐑋𐐴𐐻 𐐺𐐨 𐐺𐑉𐐫𐐻 𐑁𐐬𐑉𐑃 𐐰𐐻 𐑅𐐲𐑋 𐑁𐐷𐐭𐐽𐐲𐑉 𐐼𐐩 𐐲𐑌𐐻𐐭 𐑄 𐐢𐐰𐑋𐐲𐑌𐐴𐐻𐑅, 𐑄𐐰𐐻, 𐐹𐐲𐑉𐐸𐐰𐐹𐑅, 𐑄𐐩
𐑋𐐴𐐻 𐐺𐐨 𐐺𐑉𐐫𐐻 𐐲𐑌𐐻𐐭 𐑅𐐰𐑊𐑂𐐩𐑇𐐲𐑌: 𐑁𐐫𐑉 𐐰𐐻 𐑄 𐐹𐑉𐐯𐑆𐐯𐑌𐐻, 𐐵𐑉 𐑅𐐻𐑉𐐲𐑀𐑊𐐮𐑍𐑆 𐐶𐐲𐑉 𐑂𐐩𐑌 𐐮𐑌 𐑉𐐨𐑅𐐻𐐬𐑉𐐮𐑍
𐑄𐐯𐑋 𐐻𐐭 𐑄 𐐻𐑉𐐭 𐑁𐐩𐑃. 𐐈𐑌𐐼 𐑄𐐩 𐑅𐐶𐐬𐑉 𐐮𐑌 𐑄𐐩𐑉 𐑉𐐱𐑃 𐑄𐐰𐐻, 𐐮𐑁 𐐮𐐻 𐐶𐐲𐑉 𐐹𐐱𐑅𐐮𐐺𐑊, 𐑄𐐩 𐐶𐐳𐐼
𐐼𐐨𐑅𐐻𐑉𐐱𐐮 𐐵𐑉 𐑉𐐯𐐿𐐲𐑉𐐼𐑆 𐐰𐑌𐐼 𐐲𐑅; 𐐰𐑌𐐼, 𐐫𐑊𐑅𐐬, 𐐫𐑊 𐑄 𐐻𐑉𐐰𐐼𐐮𐑇𐐲𐑌𐑆 𐐱𐑂 𐐵𐑉 𐑁𐐪𐑄𐐲𐑉𐑆.

4. 𐐐𐐶𐐩𐑉𐑁𐐬𐑉, 𐐌 𐑌𐐬𐐮𐑍 𐑄𐐰𐐻 𐑄 𐐢𐐫𐑉𐐼 𐐘𐐱𐐼 𐐶𐐱𐑆 𐐩𐐺𐑊 𐐻𐐭 𐐹𐑉𐐨𐑆𐐲𐑉𐑂 𐐵𐑉 𐑉𐐯𐐿𐐲𐑉𐐼𐑆, 𐐌 𐐿𐑉𐐴𐐼 𐐲𐑌𐐻𐐭 𐐸𐐮𐑋 𐐿𐐲𐑌𐐻𐐮𐑌𐐷𐐭𐐰𐑊𐐨, 𐑁𐐫𐑉 𐐸𐐨 𐐸𐐰𐐼 𐑅𐐯𐐼 𐐲𐑌𐐻𐐭 𐑋𐐨, 𐐐𐐶𐐱𐐻𐑅𐐬𐐯𐑂𐐲𐑉 𐑃𐐮𐑍 𐐷𐐨 𐑇𐐰𐑊 𐐰𐑅𐐿 𐐮𐑌 𐑁𐐩𐑃, 𐐺𐐨𐑊𐐨𐑂𐐮𐑍 𐑄𐐰𐐻 𐐷𐐨 𐑇𐐰𐑊 𐑉𐐨𐑅𐐨𐑂 𐐮𐑌 𐑄 𐑌𐐩𐑋 𐐱𐑂 𐐗𐑉𐐴𐑅𐐻, 𐐷𐐨 𐑇𐐰𐑊 𐑉𐐨𐑅𐐨𐑂 𐐮𐐻. 𐐈𐑌𐐼 𐐌 𐐸𐐰𐐼 𐑁𐐩𐑃, 𐐰𐑌𐐼 𐐌 𐐼𐐮𐐼 𐐿𐑉𐐴 𐐲𐑌𐐻𐐭 𐐘𐐱𐐼 𐑄𐐰𐐻 𐐸𐐨 𐐶𐐳𐐼 𐐹𐑉𐐨𐑆𐐲𐑉𐑂 𐑄 𐑉𐐯𐐿𐐲𐑉𐐼𐑆; 𐐰𐑌𐐼 𐐸𐐨 𐐿𐐲𐑂𐐲𐑌𐐰𐑌𐐻𐐲𐐼 𐐶𐐮𐑃 𐑋𐐨 𐑄𐐰𐐻 𐐸𐐨 𐐶𐐳𐐼 𐐺𐑉𐐮𐑍 𐑄𐐯𐑋 𐑁𐐫𐑉𐑃 𐐲𐑌𐐻𐐭 𐑄 𐐢𐐰𐑋𐐲𐑌𐐴𐐻𐑅 𐐮𐑌 𐐸𐐮𐑆 𐐬𐑌 𐐼𐐭 𐐻𐐴𐑋. 𐐈𐑌𐐼 𐐌, 𐐀𐑌𐐲𐑅, 𐑌𐐭 𐐮𐐻 𐐶𐐳𐐼 𐐺𐐨 𐐰𐐿𐐫𐑉𐐼𐐮𐑍 𐐻𐐭 𐑄 𐐿𐐲𐑂𐐲𐑌𐐰𐑌𐐻 𐐸𐐶𐐮𐐽 𐐸𐐨 𐐸𐐰𐐼 𐑋𐐩𐐼; 𐐸𐐶𐐩𐑉𐑁𐐬𐑉 𐑋𐐴 𐑅𐐬𐑊 𐐼𐐮𐐼 𐑉𐐯𐑅𐐻. 𐐈𐑌𐐼 𐑄 𐐢𐐫𐑉𐐼 𐑅𐐯𐐼 𐐲𐑌𐐻𐐭 𐑋𐐨, 𐐜𐐴 𐑁𐐪𐑄𐐲𐑉𐑆 𐐸𐐰𐑂 𐐫𐑊𐑅𐐬 𐑉𐐨𐐿𐐶𐐴𐑉𐐼 𐐱𐑂 𐑋𐐨 𐑄𐐮𐑅 𐑃𐐮𐑍; 𐐰𐑌𐐼 𐐮𐐻 𐑇𐐰𐑊 𐐺𐐨 𐐼𐐲𐑌 𐐲𐑌𐐻𐐭 𐑄𐐯𐑋 𐐰𐐿𐐫𐑉𐐼𐐮𐑍 𐐻𐐭 𐑄𐐯𐑉 𐑁𐐩𐑃; 𐑁𐐫𐑉 𐑄𐐯𐑉 𐑁𐐩𐑃 𐐶𐐱𐑆 𐑊𐐴𐐿 𐐲𐑌𐐻𐐭 𐑄𐐴𐑌.

5. 𐐈𐑌𐐼 𐑌𐐵 𐐮𐐻 𐐿𐐩𐑋 𐐻𐐭 𐐹𐐰𐑅 𐑄𐐰𐐻 𐐌, 𐐀𐑌𐐲𐑅, 𐐶𐐯𐑌𐐻 𐐲𐐺𐐵𐐻 𐐲𐑋𐐲𐑍 𐑄 𐐹𐐨𐐹𐐲𐑊 𐐱𐑂 𐐤𐐨𐑁𐐴, 𐐹𐑉𐐱𐑁𐐯𐑅𐐴𐐮𐑍 𐐱𐑂 𐑃𐐮𐑍𐑆 𐐻𐐭 𐐿𐐲𐑋, 𐐰𐑌𐐼 𐐻𐐯𐑅𐐻𐐮𐑁𐐴𐐮𐑍 𐐱𐑂 𐑄 𐑃𐐮𐑍𐑆 𐐸𐐶𐐮𐐽 𐐌 𐐸𐐰𐐼 𐐸𐐲𐑉𐐼 𐐰𐑌𐐼 𐑅𐐨𐑌. 𐐈𐑌𐐼 𐐌 𐐺𐐩𐑉 𐑉𐐯𐐿𐐲𐑉𐐼 𐑄𐐰𐐻 𐑄 𐐹𐐨𐐹𐐲𐑊 𐐱𐑂 𐐤𐐨𐑁𐐴 𐐼𐐮𐐼 𐑅𐐨𐐿 𐐼𐐮𐑊𐐮𐐾𐐯𐑌𐐻𐑊𐐨 𐐻𐐭 𐑉𐐨𐑅𐐻𐐬𐑉 𐑄 𐐢𐐰𐑋𐐲𐑌𐐴𐐻𐑅 𐐲𐑌𐐻𐐭 𐑄 𐐻𐑉𐐭 𐑁𐐩𐑃 𐐮𐑌 𐐘𐐱𐐼. 𐐒𐐲𐐻 𐐵𐑉 𐑊𐐩𐐺𐐲𐑉𐑆 𐐶𐐲𐑉 𐑂𐐩𐑌; 𐑄𐐯𐑉 𐐸𐐩𐐻𐑉𐐯𐐼 𐐶𐐱𐑆 𐑁𐐮𐐿𐑅𐐻, 𐐰𐑌𐐼 𐑄𐐩 𐐶𐐲𐑉 𐑊𐐯𐐼 𐐺𐐴 𐑄𐐯𐑉 𐐨𐑂𐐲𐑊 𐑌𐐩𐐽𐐲𐑉 𐑄𐐰𐐻 𐑄𐐩 𐐺𐐨𐐿𐐩𐑋 𐐶𐐴𐑊𐐼, 𐐰𐑌𐐼 𐑁𐐯𐑉𐐬𐑇𐐲𐑅, 𐐰𐑌𐐼 𐐲 𐐺𐑊𐐲𐐼-𐑃𐐲𐑉𐑅𐐻𐐨 𐐹𐐨𐐹𐐲𐑊, 𐑁𐐳𐑊 𐐱𐑂 𐐴𐐼𐐱𐑊𐐲𐐻𐑉𐐨 𐐰𐑌𐐼 𐑁𐐮𐑊𐑃𐐨𐑌𐐯𐑅; 𐑁𐐨𐐼𐐮𐑍 𐐲𐐹𐐱𐑌 𐐺𐐨𐑅𐐻𐑅 𐐱𐑂 𐐹𐑉𐐩; 𐐼𐐶𐐯𐑊𐐮𐑍 𐐮𐑌 𐐻𐐯𐑌𐐻𐑅, 𐐰𐑌𐐼 𐐶𐐪𐑌𐐼𐐲𐑉𐐮𐑍 𐐲𐐺𐐵𐐻 𐐮𐑌 𐑄 𐐶𐐮𐑊𐐼𐐲𐑉𐑌𐐯𐑅 𐐶𐐮𐑄 𐐲 𐑇𐐫𐑉𐐻 𐑅𐐿𐐮𐑌 𐑀𐐲𐑉𐐼𐐲𐑊 𐐲𐐺𐐵𐐻 𐑄𐐯𐑉 𐑊𐐬𐑌𐑆, 𐐰𐑌𐐼 𐑄𐐯𐑉 𐐸𐐯𐐼𐑆 𐑇𐐩𐑂𐐲𐑌; 𐐰𐑌𐐼 𐑄𐐯𐑉 𐑅𐐿𐐮𐑊 𐐶𐐱𐑆 𐐮𐑌 𐑄 𐐺𐐬, 𐐰𐑌𐐼 𐐮𐑌 𐑄 𐑅𐐮𐑋𐐮𐐻𐐲𐑉, 𐐰𐑌𐐼 𐑄 𐐰𐐿𐑅. 𐐈𐑌𐐼 𐑋𐐯𐑌𐐨 𐐱𐑂 𐑄𐐯𐑋 𐐼𐐮𐐼 𐐨𐐻 𐑌𐐲𐑃𐐮𐑍 𐑅𐐩𐑂 𐐮𐐻 𐐶𐐱𐑆 𐑉𐐫 𐑋𐐨𐐻; 𐐰𐑌𐐼 𐑄𐐩 𐐶𐐲𐑉 𐐿𐐲𐑌𐐻𐐮𐑌𐐷𐐭𐐰𐑊𐐨 𐑅𐐨𐐿𐐮𐑍 𐐻𐐭 𐐼𐐨𐑅𐐻𐑉𐑎 𐐲𐑅.

6. 𐐈𐑌𐐼 𐐮𐐻 𐐿𐐩𐑋 𐐻𐐭 𐐹𐐰𐑅 𐑄𐐰𐐻 𐑄 𐐹𐐨𐐹𐐲𐑊 𐐱𐑂 𐐤𐐨𐑁𐐴 𐐼𐐮𐐼 𐐻𐐮𐑊 𐑄 𐑊𐐰𐑌𐐼, 𐐰𐑌𐐼 𐑉𐐩𐑆 𐐫𐑊 𐑋𐐰𐑌𐐲𐑉 𐐱𐑂 𐑀𐑉𐐩𐑌, 𐐰𐑌𐐼 𐐱𐑂 𐑁𐑉𐐭𐐻, 𐐰𐑌𐐼 𐑁𐑊𐐱𐐿𐑅 𐐱𐑂 𐐸𐐲𐑉𐐼𐑆, 𐐰𐑌𐐼 𐑁𐑊𐐱𐐿𐑅 𐐱𐑂 𐐫𐑊 𐑋𐐰𐑌𐐲𐑉 𐐱𐑂 𐐿𐐰𐐻𐐲𐑊 𐐱𐑂 𐐯𐑂𐐲𐑉𐐨 𐐿𐐴𐑌𐐼, 𐐰𐑌𐐼 𐑀𐐬𐐻𐑅, 𐐰𐑌𐐼 𐐶𐐴𐑊𐐼 𐑀𐐬𐐻𐑅, 𐐰𐑌𐐼 𐐫𐑊𐑅𐐬 𐑋𐐯𐑌𐐨 𐐸𐐫𐑉𐑅𐐯𐑆. 𐐈𐑌𐐼 𐑄𐐯𐑉 𐐶𐐲𐑉 𐐯𐐿𐑅𐐨𐐼𐐮𐑍𐑊𐐨 𐑋𐐯𐑌𐐨 𐐹𐑉𐐱𐑁𐐯𐐻𐑅 𐐲𐑋𐐲𐑍 𐐲𐑅. 𐐈𐑌𐐼 𐑄 𐐹𐐨𐐹𐐲𐑊 𐐶𐐲𐑉 𐐲 𐑅𐐻𐐮𐑁𐑌𐐯𐐿𐐻 𐐹𐐨𐐹𐐲𐑊, 𐐸𐐪𐑉𐐼 𐐻𐐭 𐐲𐑌𐐼𐐲𐑉𐑅𐐻𐐰𐑌𐐼. 𐐈𐑌𐐼 𐑄𐐯𐑉 𐐶𐐱𐑆 𐑌𐐲𐑃𐐮𐑍 𐑅𐐩𐑂 𐐮𐐻 𐐶𐐱𐑆 𐐯𐐿𐑅𐐨𐐼𐐮𐑍 𐐸𐐪𐑉𐑇𐑌𐐯𐑅, 𐐹𐑉𐐨𐐽𐐮𐑍 𐐰𐑌𐐼 𐐹𐑉𐐱𐑁𐐯𐑅𐐴𐐮𐑍 𐐱𐑂 𐐶𐐫𐑉𐑆, 𐐰𐑌𐐼 𐐿𐐱𐑌𐐻𐐯𐑌𐑇𐐲𐑌𐑆, 𐐰𐑌𐐼 𐐼𐐨𐑅𐐻𐑉𐐲𐐿𐑇𐐲𐑌𐑆, 𐐰𐑌𐐼 𐐿𐐲𐑌𐐻𐐮𐑌𐐷𐐭𐐰𐑊𐐨 𐑉𐐨𐑋𐐴𐑌𐐼𐐮𐑍 𐑄𐐯𐑋 𐐱𐑂 𐐼𐐯𐑃, 𐐰𐑌𐐼 𐑄 𐐼𐐷𐐭𐑉𐐩𐑇𐐲𐑌 𐐱𐑂 𐐨𐐻𐐲𐑉𐑌𐐮𐐻𐐨, 𐐰𐑌𐐼 𐑄 𐐾𐐲𐐾𐑋𐐯𐑌𐐻𐑅 𐐰𐑌𐐼 𐑄 𐐹𐐵𐐲𐑉 𐐱𐑂 𐐘𐐱𐐼, 𐐰𐑌𐐼 𐐫𐑊 𐑄𐐨𐑆 𐑃𐐮𐑍𐑆—𐑅𐐻𐐲𐑉𐐮𐑍 𐑄𐐯𐑋 𐐲𐐹 𐐿𐐲𐑌𐐻𐐮𐑌𐐷𐐭𐐰𐑊𐐨 𐐻𐐭 𐐿𐐨𐐹 𐑄𐐯𐑋 𐐮𐑌 𐑄 𐑁𐐨𐑉 𐐱𐑂 𐑄 𐐢𐐫𐑉𐐼. 𐐌 𐑅𐐩 𐑄𐐯𐑉 𐐶𐐱𐑆 𐑌𐐲𐑃𐐮𐑍 𐑇𐐫𐑉𐐻 𐐱𐑂 𐑄𐐨𐑆 𐑃𐐮𐑍𐑆, 𐐰𐑌𐐼 𐐯𐐿𐑅𐐨𐐼𐐮𐑍𐑊𐐨 𐑀𐑉𐐩𐐻 𐐹𐑊𐐩𐑌𐑌𐐯𐑅 𐐱𐑂 𐑅𐐹𐐨𐐽, 𐐶𐐳𐐼 𐐿𐐨𐐹 𐑄𐐯𐑋 𐑁𐑉𐐱𐑋 𐑀𐐬𐐮𐑍 𐐼𐐵𐑌 𐑅𐐹𐐨𐐼𐐮𐑊𐐨 𐐻𐐭 𐐼𐐨𐑅𐐻𐑉𐐲𐐿𐑇𐐲𐑌. 𐐈𐑌𐐼 𐐰𐑁𐐻𐐲𐑉 𐑄𐐮𐑅 𐑋𐐰𐑌𐐲𐑉 𐐼𐐭 𐐌 𐑉𐐴𐐻 𐐿𐐲𐑌𐑅𐐲𐑉𐑌𐐮𐑍 𐑄𐐯𐑋. 𐐈𐑌𐐼 𐐌 𐑅𐐫 𐐶𐐫𐑉𐑆 𐐺𐐨𐐻𐐶𐐨𐑌 𐑄 𐐤𐐨𐑁𐐴𐐻𐑅 𐐰𐑌𐐼 𐐢𐐰𐑋𐐲𐑌𐐴𐐻𐑅 𐐮𐑌 𐑄 𐐿𐐬𐑉𐑅 𐐱𐑂 𐑋𐐴 𐐼𐐩𐑆.

7. 𐐈𐑌𐐼 𐐮𐐻 𐐿𐐩𐑋 𐐻𐐭 𐐹𐐰𐑅 𐑄𐐰𐐻 𐐌 𐐺𐐨𐑀𐐰𐑌 𐐻𐐭 𐐺𐐨 𐐬𐑊𐐼, 𐐰𐑌𐐼 𐐰𐑌 𐐸𐐲𐑌𐐼𐑉𐐯𐐼 𐐰𐑌𐐼 𐑅𐐯𐑂𐐲𐑌𐐻𐐨 𐐰𐑌𐐼 𐑌𐐴𐑌 𐐷𐐨𐑉𐑆 𐐸𐐰𐐼 𐐹𐐰𐑅𐐻 𐐲𐐶𐐩 𐑁𐑉𐐱𐑋 𐑄 𐐻𐐴𐑋 𐑄𐐰𐐻 𐐵𐑉 𐑁𐐪𐑄𐐲𐑉 𐐢𐐨𐐸𐐴 𐑊𐐯𐑁𐐻 𐐖𐐲𐑉𐐭𐑅𐐲𐑊𐐲𐑋. 𐐈𐑌𐐼 𐐌 𐑅𐐫 𐑄𐐰𐐻 𐐌 𐑋𐐲𐑅𐐻 𐑅𐐭𐑌 𐑀𐐬 𐐼𐐵𐑌 𐐻𐐭 𐑋𐐴 𐑀𐑉𐐩𐑂, 𐐸𐐰𐑂𐐮𐑍 𐐺𐐨𐑌 𐑉𐐫𐐻 𐐲𐐹𐐱𐑌 𐐺𐐴 𐑄 𐐹𐐵𐐲𐑉 𐐱𐑂 𐐘𐐱𐐼 𐑄𐐰𐐻 𐐌 𐑋𐐲𐑅𐐻 𐐹𐑉𐐨𐐽 𐐰𐑌𐐼 𐐹𐑉𐐱𐑁𐐯𐑅𐐴 𐐲𐑌𐐻𐐭 𐑄𐐮𐑅 𐐹𐐨𐐹𐐲𐑊, 𐐰𐑌𐐼 𐐼𐐨𐐿𐑊𐐩𐑉 𐑄 𐐶𐐲𐑉𐐼 𐐰𐐿𐐫𐑉𐐼𐐮𐑍 𐐻𐐭 𐑄 𐐻𐑉𐐭𐑃 𐐸𐐶𐐮𐐽 𐐮𐑆 𐐮𐑌 𐐗𐑉𐐴𐑅𐐻. 𐐈𐑌𐐼 𐐌 𐐸𐐰𐑂 𐐼𐐨𐐿𐑊𐐩𐑉𐐼 𐐮𐐻 𐐮𐑌 𐐫𐑊 𐑋𐐴 𐐼𐐩𐑆, 𐐰𐑌𐐼 𐐸𐐰𐑂 𐑉𐐨𐐾𐑎𐑅𐐻 𐐮𐑌 𐐮𐐻 𐐲𐐺𐐲𐑂 𐑄𐐰𐐻 𐐱𐑂 𐑄 𐐶𐐲𐑉𐑊𐐼. 𐐈𐑌𐐼 𐐌 𐑅𐐭𐑌 𐑀𐐬 𐐻𐐭 𐑄 𐐹𐑊𐐩𐑅 𐐱𐑂 𐑋𐐴 𐑉𐐯𐑅𐐻, 𐐸𐐶𐐮𐐽 𐐮𐑆 𐐶𐐮𐑄 𐑋𐐴 𐐡𐐨𐐼𐐨𐑋𐐲𐑉; 𐑁𐐫𐑉 𐐌 𐑌𐐬 𐑄𐐰𐐻 𐐮𐑌 𐐸𐐮𐑋 𐐌 𐑇𐐰𐑊 𐑉𐐯𐑅𐐻. 𐐈𐑌𐐼 𐐌 𐑉𐐨𐐾𐑎𐑅 𐐮𐑌 𐑄 𐐼𐐩 𐐸𐐶𐐯𐑌 𐑋𐐴 𐑋𐐫𐑉𐐻𐐲𐑊 𐑇𐐰𐑊 𐐹𐐳𐐻 𐐱𐑌 𐐮𐑋𐐫𐑉𐐻𐐰𐑊𐐮𐐻𐐨, 𐐰𐑌𐐼 𐑇𐐰𐑊 𐑅𐐻𐐰𐑌𐐼 𐐺𐐨𐑁𐐬𐑉 𐐸𐐮𐑋; 𐑄𐐯𐑌 𐑇𐐰𐑊 𐐌 𐑅𐐨 𐐸𐐮𐑆 𐑁𐐩𐑅 𐐶𐐮𐑄 𐑊𐐯𐑈𐐲𐑉, 𐐰𐑌𐐼 𐐸𐐨 𐐶𐐮𐑊 𐑅𐐩 𐐲𐑌𐐻𐐭 𐑋𐐨, 𐐗𐐲𐑋 𐐲𐑌𐐻𐐭 𐑋𐐨, 𐐷𐐨 𐐺𐑊𐐯𐑅𐐯𐐼, 𐑄𐐯𐑉 𐐮𐑆 𐐲 𐐹𐑊𐐩𐑅 𐐹𐑉𐐨𐐹𐐯𐑉𐐼 𐑁𐐫𐑉 𐐷𐐭 𐐮𐑌 𐑄 𐑋𐐰𐑌𐑇𐐲𐑌𐑆 𐐱𐑂 𐑋𐐴 𐐙𐐪𐑄𐐲𐑉. 𐐈𐑋𐐯𐑌.

𐐜 𐐒𐐳𐐿 𐐲𐑂 𐐖𐐩𐑉𐐲𐑋.

𐐕𐐰𐐹𐐻𐐲𐑉 I.

1. 𐐤𐐵 𐐺𐐨𐐸𐐬𐑊𐐼, 𐐌, 𐐖𐐩𐑉𐐲𐑋, 𐑉𐐴𐐻 𐐲 𐑁𐐷𐐭 𐐶𐐲𐑉𐐼𐑆, 𐐰𐐿𐐫𐑉𐐼𐐮𐑍 𐐻𐐭 𐑄 𐐿𐐲𐑋𐐰𐑌𐐼𐑋𐐯𐑌𐐻 𐐲𐑂 𐑋𐐴 𐑁𐐪𐑄𐐲𐑉, 𐐀𐑌𐐲𐑅, 𐑄𐐰𐐻 𐐵𐑉 𐐾𐐨𐑌𐐨𐐰𐑊𐐲𐐾𐐨 𐑋𐐩 𐐺𐐨 𐐿𐐯𐐹𐐻. 𐐈𐑌𐐼 𐐰𐑆 𐑄𐐨𐑆 𐐹𐑊𐐩𐐻𐑅 𐐪𐑉 𐑅𐑋𐐫𐑊, 𐐰𐑌𐐼 𐐰𐑆 𐑄𐐨𐑆 𐑃𐐮𐑍𐑆 𐐪𐑉 𐑉𐐮𐐻𐐲𐑌 𐑁𐐫𐑉 𐑄 𐐮𐑌𐐻𐐯𐑌𐐻 𐐲𐑂 𐑄 𐐺𐐯𐑌𐐲𐑁𐐮𐐻 𐐲𐑂 𐐵𐑉 𐐺𐑉𐐯𐑃𐑉𐐯𐑌 𐑄 𐐢𐐩𐑋𐐲𐑌𐐴𐐻𐑅, 𐐸𐐶𐐯𐑉𐑁𐐫𐑉, 𐐮𐐻 𐑋𐐲𐑅𐐻 𐑌𐐨𐐼𐑆 𐐺𐐨 𐑄𐐰𐐻 𐐌 𐑉𐐴𐐻 𐐲 𐑊𐐮𐐻𐐲𐑊; 𐐺𐐲𐐻 𐐌 𐑇𐐰𐑊 𐑌𐐱𐐻 𐑉𐐴𐐻 𐑄 𐑃𐐮𐑍𐑆 𐐲𐑂 𐑋𐐴 𐐹𐑉𐐱𐑁𐐯𐑅𐐴𐐮𐑍, 𐑌𐐫𐑉 𐐲𐑂 𐑋𐐴 𐑉𐐯𐑂𐐯𐑊𐐩𐑇𐐲𐑌𐑆. 𐐙𐐫𐑉 𐐸𐐶𐐱𐐻 𐐿𐐳𐐼 𐐌 𐑉𐐴𐐻 𐑋𐐬𐑉 𐑄𐐰𐑌 𐑋𐐴 𐑁𐐪𐑄𐐲𐑉𐑆 𐐸𐐰𐑂 𐑉𐐮𐐻𐐲𐑌? 𐐙𐐫𐑉 𐐸𐐰𐑂 𐑌𐐱𐐻 𐑄𐐩 𐑉𐐯𐑂𐐨𐑊𐐼 𐑄 𐐹𐑊𐐰𐑌 𐐲𐑂 𐑅𐐰𐑊𐑂𐐩𐑇𐐲𐑌? 𐐌 𐑅𐐩 𐐲𐑌𐐻𐐭 𐐷𐐭, 𐐷𐐩; 𐐰𐑌𐐼 𐑄𐐮𐑅 𐑅𐐲𐑁𐐨𐑅𐐯𐑃 𐑋𐐨.

2. 𐐒𐐨𐐸𐐬𐑊𐐼, 𐐮𐐻 𐐮𐑆 𐐯𐐿𐑅𐐹𐐨𐐼𐐨𐐯𐑌𐐻 𐑄𐐰𐐻 𐑋𐐲𐐽 𐑇𐐳𐐼 𐐺𐐨 𐐼𐐲𐑌 𐐲𐑋𐐲𐑍 𐑄𐐮𐑅 𐐹𐐨𐐹𐐲𐑊, 𐐺𐐨𐐿𐐫𐑆 𐐲𐑂 𐑄 𐐸𐐪𐑉𐐼𐑌𐐯𐑅 𐐲𐑂 𐑄𐐩𐑉 𐐸𐐪𐑉𐐻𐑅, 𐐰𐑌𐐼 𐑄 𐐼𐐯𐑁𐑌𐐯𐑅 𐐲𐑂 𐑄𐐩𐑉 𐐨𐑉𐑆, 𐐰𐑌𐐼 𐑄 𐐺𐑊𐐴𐑌𐐼𐑌𐐯𐑅 𐐲𐑂 𐑄𐐩𐑉 𐑋𐐴𐑌𐐼𐑆, 𐐰𐑌𐐼 𐑄 𐑅𐐻𐐮𐑁𐑌𐐯𐑅 𐐲𐑂 𐑄𐐩𐑉 𐑌𐐯𐐿𐑅; 𐑌𐐯𐑂𐐲𐑉𐑄𐐲𐑊𐐯𐑅, 𐐘𐐱𐐼 𐐮𐑆 𐐯𐐿𐑅𐐨𐐼𐐮𐑍𐑊𐐨 𐑋𐐲𐑉𐑅𐐮𐑁𐐳𐑊 𐐲𐑌𐐻𐐭 𐑄𐐯𐑋, 𐐰𐑌𐐼 𐐸𐐰𐑆 𐑌𐐱𐐻 𐐰𐑆 𐐷𐐯𐐻 𐑅𐐶𐐯𐐹𐐻 𐑄𐐯𐑋 𐐫𐑁 𐑁𐑉𐐱𐑋 𐑄 𐑁𐐩𐑅 𐐲𐑂 𐑄 𐑊𐐰𐑌𐐼. 𐐈𐑌𐐼 𐑄𐐩𐑉 𐐪𐑉 𐑋𐐯𐑌𐐨 𐐲𐑋𐐲𐑍 𐐲𐑅 𐐸𐐭 𐐸𐐰𐑂 𐑋𐐯𐑌𐐨 𐑉𐐯𐑂𐐯𐑊𐐩𐑇𐐲𐑌𐑆, 𐑁𐐫𐑉 𐑄𐐩 𐐪𐑉 𐑌𐐱𐐻 𐐫𐑊 𐑅𐐻𐐮𐑁𐑌𐐯𐐿𐐻. 𐐈𐑌𐐼 𐐰𐑆 𐑋𐐯𐑌𐐨 𐐰𐑆 𐐪𐑉 𐑌𐐱𐐻 𐑅𐐻𐐮𐑁𐑌𐐯𐐿𐐻 𐐰𐑌𐐼 𐐸𐐰𐑂 𐑁𐐩𐑃, 𐐸𐐰𐑂 𐐿𐐲𐑋𐐷𐐭𐑌𐐷𐐲𐑌 𐐶𐐮𐑄 𐑄 𐐐𐐬𐑊𐐨 𐐝𐐹𐐮𐑉𐐮𐐻, 𐐸𐐶𐐮𐐽 𐑋𐐩𐐿𐐯𐑃 𐑋𐐰𐑌𐐮𐑁𐐯𐑅𐐻 𐐲𐑌𐐻𐐭 𐑄 𐐽𐐮𐑊𐐼𐑉𐐯𐑌 𐐲𐑂 𐑋𐐯𐑌, 𐐰𐐿𐐫𐑉𐐼𐐮𐑍 𐐻𐐭 𐑄𐐩𐑉 𐑁𐐩𐑃.

3. 𐐈𐑌𐐼 𐑌𐐵, 𐐺𐐨𐐸𐐬𐑊𐐼, 𐐻𐐭 𐐸𐐲𐑌𐐼𐑉𐐯𐐼 𐐷𐐨𐑉𐑆 𐐸𐐰𐐼 𐐹𐐰𐑅𐐻 𐐲𐐶𐐩, 𐐰𐑌𐐼 𐑄 𐐹𐐨𐐹𐐲𐑊 𐐲𐑂 𐐤𐐨𐑁𐐴 𐐸𐐰𐐼 𐐶𐐰𐐿𐑅𐐻 𐑅𐐻𐑉𐐱𐑍 𐐮𐑌 𐑄 𐑊𐐰𐑌𐐼. 𐐜𐐩 𐐲𐐺𐑆𐐲𐑉𐑂𐐼 𐐻𐐭 𐐿𐐨𐐹 𐑄 𐑊𐐫 𐐲𐑂 𐐣𐐬𐑆𐐯𐑆 𐐰𐑌𐐼 𐑄 𐑅𐐰𐐺𐐲𐑃 𐐼𐐩 𐐸𐐬𐑊𐐨 𐐲𐑌𐐻𐐭 𐑄 𐐢𐐫𐑉𐐼. 𐐈𐑌𐐼 𐑄𐐩 𐐹𐑉𐐬𐑁𐐩𐑌𐐼 𐑌𐐱𐐻; 𐑌𐐨𐑄𐐲𐑉 𐐼𐐮𐐼 𐑄𐐩 𐐺𐑊𐐰𐑅𐑁𐐨𐑋. 𐐈𐑌𐐼 𐑄 𐑊𐐫𐑆 𐐲𐑂 𐑄 𐑊𐐰𐑌𐐼 𐐶𐐲𐑉 𐐯𐐿𐑅𐐨𐐼𐐮𐑍𐑊𐐨 𐑅𐐻𐑉𐐮𐐿𐐻. 𐐈𐑌𐐼 𐑄𐐩 𐐶𐐲𐑉 𐑅𐐿𐐰𐐻𐐲𐑉𐐼 𐐲𐐹𐐱𐑌 𐑋𐐲𐐽 𐐲𐑂 𐑄 𐑁𐐩𐑅 𐐲𐑂 𐑄 𐑊𐐰𐑌𐐼; 𐐰𐑌𐐼 𐑄 𐐢𐐩𐑋𐐲𐑌𐐴𐐻𐑅 𐐫𐑊𐑅𐐬. 𐐈𐑌𐐼 𐑄𐐩 𐐶𐐲𐑉 𐐯𐐿𐑅𐐨𐐼𐐮𐑍𐑊𐐨 𐑋𐐬𐑉 𐑌𐐭𐑋𐐲𐑉𐐲𐑅 𐑄𐐰𐑌 𐐶𐐲𐑉 𐑄𐐩 𐐲𐑂 𐑄 𐐤𐐨𐑁𐐴𐐻𐑅; 𐐰𐑌𐐼 𐑄𐐩 𐑊𐐲𐑂𐐼 𐑋𐐲𐑉𐐼𐐲𐑉 𐐰𐑌𐐼 𐐶𐐳𐐼 𐐼𐑉𐐮𐑍𐐿 𐑄 𐐺𐑊𐐲𐐼 𐐲𐑂 𐐺𐐨𐑅𐐻𐑅.

4. 𐐈𐑌𐐼 𐐮𐐻 𐐿𐐩𐑋 𐐻𐐭 𐐹𐐰𐑅 𐑄𐐰𐐻 𐑄𐐩 𐐿𐐩𐑋 𐑋𐐯𐑌𐐨 𐐻𐐴𐑋𐑆 𐐲𐑀𐐯𐑌𐑅𐐻 𐐲𐑅, 𐑄 𐐤𐐨𐑁𐐴𐐻𐑅, 𐐻𐐭 𐐺𐐰𐐻𐐲𐑊. 𐐒𐐲𐐻 𐐵𐑉 𐐿𐐮𐑍𐑆 𐐰𐑌𐐼 𐐵𐑉 𐑊𐐨𐐼𐐲𐑉𐑆 𐐶𐐲𐑉 𐑋𐐴𐐻𐐨 𐑋𐐯𐑌 𐐮𐑌 𐑄 𐑁𐐩𐑃 𐐲𐑂 𐑄 𐐢𐐫𐑉𐐼; 𐐰𐑌𐐼 𐑄𐐩 𐐻𐐫𐐻 𐑄 𐐹𐐨𐐹𐐲𐑊 𐑄 𐐶𐐩𐑆 𐐲𐑂 𐑄 𐐢𐐫𐑉𐐼; 𐐸𐐶𐐯𐑉𐑁𐐫𐑉, 𐐶𐐨 𐐶𐐮𐑄𐑅𐐻𐐳𐐼 𐑄 𐐢𐐩𐑋𐐲𐑌𐐴𐐻𐑅, 𐐰𐑌𐐼 𐑅𐐶𐐯𐐹𐐻 𐑄𐐯𐑋 𐐲𐐶𐐩 𐐵𐐻 𐐲𐑂 𐐵𐑉 𐑊𐐰𐑌𐐼𐑆, 𐐰𐑌𐐼 𐐺𐐨𐑀𐐰𐑌 𐐻𐐭 𐑁𐐫𐑉𐐻𐐮𐑁𐐴 𐐵𐑉 𐑅𐐮𐐻𐐨𐑆, 𐐫𐑉 𐐸𐐶𐐱𐐻𐑅𐐬𐐯𐑂𐐲𐑉 𐐹𐑊𐐩𐑅 𐐲𐑂 𐐵𐑉 𐐮𐑌𐐸𐐯𐑉𐐮𐐻𐐲𐑌𐑅. 𐐈𐑌𐐼 𐐶𐐨 𐑋𐐲𐑊𐐻𐐮𐐹𐑊𐐴𐐼 𐐯𐐿𐑅𐐨𐐼𐐮𐑍𐑊𐐨, 𐐰𐑌𐐼 𐑅𐐹𐑉𐐯𐐼 𐐲𐐹𐐱𐑌 𐑄 𐑁𐐩𐑅 𐐲𐑂 𐑄 𐑊𐐰𐑌𐐼, 𐐰𐑌𐐼 𐐺𐐨𐐿𐐩𐑋 𐐯𐐿𐑅𐐨𐐼𐐮𐑍𐑊𐐨 𐑉𐐮𐐽 𐐮𐑌 𐑀𐐬𐑊𐐼, 𐐰𐑌𐐼 𐐮𐑌 𐑅𐐮𐑊𐑂𐐲𐑉, 𐐰𐑌𐐼 𐐮𐑌 𐐹𐑉𐐯𐑇𐐲𐑅 𐑃𐐮𐑍𐑆, 𐐰𐑌𐐼 𐐮𐑌 𐑁𐐴𐑌 𐐶𐐲𐑉𐐿𐑋𐐰𐑌𐑇𐐮𐐹 𐐲𐑂 𐐶𐐳𐐼, 𐐮𐑌 𐐺𐐮𐑊𐐼𐐮𐑍𐑆, 𐐰𐑌𐐼 𐐮𐑌 𐑋𐐲𐑇𐐨𐑌𐐲𐑉𐐨, 𐐰𐑌𐐼 𐐫𐑊𐑅𐐬 𐐮𐑌 𐐴𐐲𐑉𐑌 𐐰𐑌𐐼 𐐿𐐱𐐹𐐲𐑉, 𐐰𐑌𐐼 𐐺𐑉𐐰𐑅 𐐰𐑌𐐼 𐑅𐐻𐐨𐑊, 𐑋𐐩𐐿𐐮𐑍 𐐫𐑊 𐑋𐐰𐑌𐐲𐑉 𐐲𐑂 𐐻𐐭𐑊𐑆 𐐲𐑂 𐐯𐑂𐐲𐑉𐐨 𐐿𐐴𐑌𐐼 𐐻𐐭 𐐻𐐮𐑊 𐑄 𐑀𐑉𐐵𐑌𐐼, 𐐰𐑌𐐼 𐐶𐐯𐐹𐐲𐑌𐑆 𐐲𐑂 𐐶𐐫𐑉; 𐐷𐐩, 𐑄 𐑇𐐪𐑉𐐹 𐐹𐐱𐐮𐑌𐐻𐐲𐐼 𐐰𐑉𐐬, 𐐰𐑌𐐼 𐑄 𐐿𐐶𐐮𐑂𐐲𐑉, 𐐰𐑌𐐼 𐑄 𐐼𐐪𐑉𐐻, 𐐰𐑌𐐼 𐑄 𐐾𐐰𐑂𐐲𐑊𐐮𐑌, 𐐰𐑌𐐼 𐐫𐑊 𐐹𐑉𐐯𐐹𐐲𐑉𐐩𐑇𐐲𐑌𐑆 𐑁𐐫𐑉 𐐶𐐫𐑉; 𐐰𐑌𐐼 𐑄𐐲𐑅 𐐺𐐨𐐮𐑍 𐐹𐑉𐐯𐐹𐐩𐑉𐐼 𐐻𐐭 𐑋𐐨𐐻 𐑄 𐐢𐐩𐑋𐐲𐑌𐐴𐐻𐑅, 𐑄𐐩 𐐼𐐮𐐼 𐑌𐐱𐐻 𐐹𐑉𐐱𐑅𐐹𐐲𐑉 𐐲𐑀𐐯𐑌𐑅𐐻 𐐲𐑅. 𐐒𐐲𐐻 𐑄 𐐶𐐲𐑉𐐼 𐐲𐑂 𐑄 𐐢𐐫𐑉𐐼 𐐶𐐱𐑆 𐑂𐐯𐑉𐐮𐑁𐐴𐐼, 𐐸𐐶𐐮𐐽 𐐸𐐨

𐑅𐐹𐐩𐐿 𐐲𐑌𐐻𐐭 𐐵𐑉 𐑁𐐪𐑄𐐲𐑉𐑆, 𐑅𐐩𐐮𐑍, 𐐜𐐰𐐻 𐐮𐑌𐐰𐑆𐑋𐐲𐐽 𐐰𐑆 𐐷 𐐶𐐮𐑊 𐐿𐐨𐐹 𐑋𐐴 𐐿𐐲𐑋𐐰𐑌𐐼𐑋𐐲𐑌𐐻𐑅 𐐷 𐑇𐐰𐑊 𐐹𐑉𐐱𐑅𐐹𐐲𐑉 𐐮𐑌 𐑄 𐑊𐐰𐑌𐐼.

5. 𐐈𐑌𐐼 𐐮𐐻 𐐿𐐩𐑋 𐐻𐐭 𐐹𐐪𐑅 𐑄𐐰𐐻 𐑄 𐐹𐑉𐐱𐑁𐐯𐐻𐑅 𐐱𐑂 𐑄 𐐢𐐫𐑉𐐼 𐐼𐐮𐐼 𐑃𐑉𐐯𐐻𐑌 𐑄 𐐹𐐨𐐹𐑊 𐐱𐑂 𐐤𐐨𐑁𐐴, 𐐰𐐿𐐫𐑉𐐼𐐮𐑍 𐐻𐐭 𐑄 𐐶𐐲𐑉𐐼𐑆 𐐱𐑂 𐐘𐐱𐐼, 𐑄𐐰𐐻 𐐮𐑁 𐑄𐐩 𐐼𐐮𐐼 𐑌𐐱𐐻 𐐿𐐨𐐹 𐑄 𐐿𐐲𐑋𐐰𐑌𐐼𐑋𐐲𐑌𐐻𐑅, 𐐺𐐲𐐻 𐑇𐐳𐐼 𐑁𐐫𐑊 𐐮𐑌𐐻𐐭 𐐻𐑉𐐰𐑌𐑅𐑀𐑉𐐯𐑇𐐲𐑌, 𐑄𐐩 𐑇𐐳𐐼 𐐺 𐐼𐐮𐑅𐐻𐑉𐑎𐐼 𐑁𐑉𐐱𐑋 𐐱𐑁 𐑄 𐑁𐐩𐑅 𐐱𐑂 𐑄 𐑊𐐰𐑌𐐼; 𐐸𐐶𐐩𐑉𐑁𐐫𐑉, 𐑄 𐐹𐑉𐐱𐑁𐐯𐐻𐑅, 𐐰𐑌𐐼 𐑄 𐐹𐑉𐐨𐑅𐐻𐑅, 𐐰𐑌𐐼 𐑄 𐐻𐐨𐐽𐐲𐑉𐑆, 𐐼𐐮𐐼 𐑊𐐩𐐺𐐲𐑉 𐐼𐐮𐑊𐐮𐐾𐐯𐑌𐐻𐑊𐐮, 𐐯𐑀𐑆𐐫𐑉𐐻𐐮𐑍 𐐶𐐮𐑄 𐐫𐑊 𐑊𐐫𐑍 𐑅𐐲𐑁𐐲𐑉𐐮𐑍, 𐑄 𐐹𐐨𐐹𐑊 𐐻𐐭 𐐼𐐮𐑊𐐮𐐾𐐯𐑌𐑅; 𐐻𐐨𐐽𐐮𐑍 𐑄 𐑊𐐫 𐐱𐑂 𐐣𐐬𐑆𐐯𐑆, 𐐰𐑌𐐼 𐑄 𐐮𐑌𐐻𐐯𐑌𐐻 𐑁𐐫𐑉 𐐸𐐶𐐮𐐽 𐐮𐐻 𐐶𐐱𐑆 𐑀𐐮𐑂𐑌; 𐐹𐐲𐑉𐑅𐐶𐐩𐐼𐐮𐑍 𐑄𐐯𐑋 𐐻𐐭 𐑊𐐳𐐿 𐑁𐐫𐑉𐐶𐐲𐑉𐐼 𐐲𐑌𐐻𐐭 𐑄 𐐣𐐯𐑅𐐴𐐲, 𐐰𐑌𐐼 𐐺𐐨𐑊𐐨𐑂 𐐮𐑌 𐐸𐐮𐑋 𐐻𐐭 𐐿𐐲𐑋 𐐰𐑆 𐑄𐐬 𐐸𐐨 𐐫𐑊𐑉𐐯𐐼𐐮 𐐶𐐱𐑆. 𐐈𐑌𐐼 𐐰𐑁𐐻𐐲𐑉 𐑄𐐮𐑅 𐑋𐐰𐑌𐐲𐑉 𐐼𐐮𐐼 𐑄𐐩 𐐻𐐨𐐽 𐑄𐐯𐑋. 𐐈𐑌𐐼 𐐮𐐻 𐐿𐐩𐑋 𐐻𐐭 𐐹𐐪𐑅, 𐑄𐐰𐐻 𐐺𐐴 𐑅𐐬 𐐼𐐭𐐮𐑍 𐑄𐐩 𐐿𐐯𐐹𐐻 𐑄𐐯𐑋 𐑁𐑉𐐱𐑋 𐐺𐐨𐐮𐑍 𐐼𐐮𐑅𐐻𐑉𐑎𐐼 𐐲𐐹𐐱𐑌 𐑄 𐑁𐐩𐑅 𐐱𐑂 𐑄 𐑊𐐰𐑌𐐼: 𐑁𐐫𐑉 𐑄𐐩 𐐼𐐮𐐼 𐐹𐑉𐐮𐐿 𐑄𐐩𐑉 𐐸𐐪𐑉𐐻𐑅 𐐶𐐮𐑄 𐑄 𐐶𐐲𐑉𐐼, 𐐿𐐲𐑌𐐻𐐮𐑌𐐷𐐭𐐲𐑊𐐮 𐑅𐐻𐐲𐑉𐐮𐑍 𐑄𐐯𐑋 𐐲𐐹 𐐲𐑌𐐻𐐭 𐑉𐐨-𐐹𐐯𐑌𐐻𐐲𐑌𐑅.

6. 𐐈𐑌𐐼 𐐮𐐻 𐐿𐐩𐑋 𐐻𐐭 𐐹𐐪𐑅 𐑄𐐰𐐻 𐐻𐐭 𐐸𐐲𐑌𐐼𐑉𐐯𐐼 𐐰𐑌𐐼 𐑃𐐲𐑉𐐻𐐮 𐐰𐑌𐐼 𐐩𐐻 𐐷𐐨𐑉𐑆 𐐸𐐰𐐼 𐐹𐐪𐑅𐐻 𐐲𐐶𐐩, 𐐰𐑁𐐻𐐲𐑉 𐑄 𐑋𐐰𐑌𐐲𐑉 𐐱𐑂 𐐶𐐫𐑉𐑆, 𐐰𐑌𐐼 𐐿𐐲𐑌𐐻𐐯𐑌𐑇𐐲𐑌𐑆, 𐐰𐑌𐐼 𐐼𐐮𐑅𐐯𐑌𐑇𐐲𐑌𐑆, 𐑁𐐫𐑉 𐑄 𐑅𐐹𐐩𐑅 𐐱𐑂 𐑋𐐲𐐽 𐐱𐑂 𐑄 𐐻𐐴𐑋. 𐐈𐑌𐐼 𐐌, 𐐖𐐩𐑉𐐲𐑋, 𐐼𐐭 𐑌𐐱𐐻 𐑉𐐴𐐻 𐑋𐐫𐑉, 𐑁𐐫𐑉 𐑄 𐐹𐑊𐐩𐐻𐑅 𐐪𐑉 𐑅𐑋𐐫𐑊. 𐐒𐐲𐐻 𐐺𐐮𐐸𐐬𐑊𐐼, 𐑋𐐴 𐐺𐑉𐐯𐑄𐑉𐐯𐑌, 𐐷 𐐿𐐰𐑌 𐑀𐐬 𐐻𐐭 𐑄 𐐲𐑄𐐲𐑉 𐐹𐑊𐐩𐐻𐑅 𐐱𐑂 𐐤𐐨𐑁𐐴; 𐑁𐐫𐑉 𐐺𐐮𐐸𐐬𐑊𐐼, 𐐲𐐹𐐱𐑌 𐑄𐐯𐑋 𐑄 𐑉𐐯𐐿𐐫𐑉𐐼𐑆 𐐱𐑂 𐐵𐑉 𐐶𐐫𐑉𐑆 𐐪𐑉 𐐯𐑌𐑀𐑉𐐩𐑂𐑌, 𐐰𐐿𐐫𐑉𐐼𐐮𐑍 𐐻𐐭 𐑄 𐑉𐐴𐐻𐐮𐑍𐑆 𐐱𐑂 𐑄 𐐿𐐮𐑍𐑆, 𐐫𐑉 𐑄𐐬𐑆 𐐸𐐶𐐮𐐽 𐑄𐐩 𐐿𐐫𐑆𐐼 𐐻𐐭 𐐺 𐑉𐐮𐐻𐑌. 𐐈𐑌𐐼 𐐌 𐐼𐐮𐑊𐐮𐑂𐐲𐑉 𐑄𐐨𐑆 𐐹𐑊𐐩𐐻𐑅 𐐮𐑌𐐻𐐭 𐑄 𐐸𐐰𐑌𐐼𐑆 𐐱𐑂 𐑋𐐴 𐑅𐐲𐑌 𐐉𐑋𐑌𐐴, 𐑄𐐰𐐻 𐑄𐐩 𐑋𐐩 𐐺 𐐿𐐯𐐹𐐻 𐐰𐐿𐐫𐑉𐐼𐐮𐑍 𐐻𐐭 𐑄 𐐿𐐲𐑋𐐰𐑌𐐼𐑋𐐲𐑌𐐻𐑅 𐐱𐑂 𐑋𐐴 𐑁𐐪𐑄𐐲𐑉𐑆.

𐐜 𐐒𐐳𐐿 𐐱𐑂 𐐉𐑋𐑌𐐴.

𐐕𐐰𐐹𐐻𐐲𐑉 I.

1. 𐐒𐐨𐐸𐐬𐑊𐐼, 𐐮𐐻 𐐿𐐩𐑋 𐐻𐐭 𐐹𐐰𐑅 𐑄𐐰𐐻 𐐌, 𐐉𐑋𐑌𐐴, 𐐺𐐨𐐮𐑍 𐐿𐐱𐑋𐐰𐑌𐐼𐐯𐐼 𐐺𐐴 𐑋𐐴 𐑁𐐪𐑄𐐲𐑉, 𐐖𐐩𐑉𐐲𐑋, 𐑄𐐰𐐻 𐐌 𐑇𐐳𐐼 𐑉𐐴𐐻 𐑅𐐲𐑋𐐸𐐶𐐱𐐻 𐐲𐐹𐐱𐑌 𐑄𐐨𐑆 𐐹𐑊𐐩𐐻𐑅, 𐐻𐐭 𐐹𐑉𐐨𐑆𐐲𐑉𐑂 𐐵𐑉 𐐾𐐨𐑌𐐨𐐰𐑊𐐱𐐾𐐨; 𐐸𐐶𐐩𐑉𐑁𐐬𐑉, 𐐮𐑌 𐑋𐐴 𐐼𐐩𐑆, 𐐌 𐐶𐐳𐐼 𐑄𐐰𐐻 𐐷𐐨 𐑇𐐳𐐼 𐑌𐐬 𐑄𐐰𐐻 𐐌 𐑁𐐫𐐻 𐑋𐐲𐐽 𐐶𐐮𐑄 𐑄 𐑅𐐬𐑉𐐼 𐐻𐐭 𐐹𐑉𐐨𐑆𐐲𐑉𐑂 𐑋𐐴 𐐹𐐨𐐹𐑊, 𐑄 𐐤𐐨𐑁𐐴𐐻𐑅, 𐑁𐑉𐐱𐑋 𐑁𐐫𐑊𐐮𐑍 𐐮𐑌𐐻𐐭 𐑄 𐐸𐐰𐑌𐐼𐑆 𐐱𐑂 𐑄𐐩𐑉 𐐯𐑌𐐯𐑋𐐨𐑆, 𐑄 𐐢𐐩𐑋𐐲𐑌𐐴𐐻𐑅. 𐐒𐐲𐐻 𐐺𐐨𐐸𐐬𐑊𐐼, 𐐌, 𐐱𐑂 𐑋𐐴𐑅𐐯𐑊𐑁 𐐰𐑋 𐐲 𐐶𐐮𐐿𐐯𐐼 𐑋𐐰𐑌, 𐐰𐑌𐐼 𐐌 𐐸𐐰𐑂 𐑌𐐱𐐻 𐐿𐐯𐐹𐐻 𐑄 𐑅𐐻𐐰𐐻𐑏𐐻𐑅 𐐰𐑌𐐼 𐑄 𐐿𐐱𐑋𐐰𐑌𐐼𐑋𐐯𐑌𐐻𐑅 𐐱𐑂 𐑄 𐐢𐐫𐑉𐐼 𐐰𐑆 𐐌 𐐫𐐻 𐐻𐐭 𐐸𐐰𐑂 𐐼𐐲𐑌.

2. 𐐈𐑌𐐼 𐐮𐐻 𐐿𐐩𐑋 𐐻𐐭 𐐹𐐰𐑅 𐑄𐐰𐐻 𐐻𐐭 𐐸𐐲𐑌𐐼𐑉𐐯𐐼 𐐰𐑌𐐼 𐑅𐐯𐑂𐐲𐑌𐐻𐐨 𐐰𐑌𐐼 𐑅𐐮𐐿𐑅 𐐷𐐨𐑉𐑆 𐐸𐐰𐐼 𐐹𐐰𐑅𐐻 𐐲𐐶𐐩, 𐐰𐑌𐐼 𐐶𐐨 𐐸𐐰𐐼 𐑋𐐯𐑌𐐨 𐑅𐐨𐑆𐐲𐑌𐑆 𐐱𐑂 𐐹𐐨𐑅; 𐐰𐑌𐐼 𐐶𐐨 𐐸𐐰𐐼 𐑋𐐯𐑌𐐨 𐑅𐐨𐑆𐐲𐑌𐑆 𐐱𐑂 𐑅𐐨𐑉𐐨𐐲𐑅 𐐶𐐫𐑉 𐐰𐑌𐐼 𐐺𐑊𐐲𐐼𐑇𐐯𐐼. 𐐏𐐩, 𐐰𐑌𐐼 𐐮𐑌 𐑁𐐴𐑌, 𐐻𐐭 𐐸𐐲𐑌𐐼𐑉𐐯𐐼 𐐰𐑌𐐼 𐐩𐐻𐐨 𐐰𐑌𐐼 𐐻𐐭 𐐷𐐨𐑉𐑆 𐐸𐐰𐐼 𐐹𐐰𐑅𐐻 𐐲𐐶𐐩, 𐐰𐑌𐐼 𐐌 𐐸𐐰𐐼 𐐿𐐯𐐹𐐻 𐑄𐐨𐑆 𐐹𐑊𐐩𐐻𐑅 𐐰𐐿𐐫𐑉𐐼𐐮𐑍 𐐻𐐭 𐑄 𐐿𐐱𐑋𐐰𐑌𐐼𐑋𐐯𐑌𐐻𐑅 𐐱𐑂 𐑋𐐴 𐑁𐐪𐑄𐐲𐑉𐑆; 𐐰𐑌𐐼 𐐌 𐐿𐐱𐑌𐑁𐐲𐑉𐐼 𐑄𐐯𐑋 𐐲𐐹𐐱𐑌 𐑋𐐴 𐑅𐐲𐑌 𐐈𐑋𐐲𐑉𐐱𐑌. 𐐈𐑌𐐼 𐐌 𐑋𐐩𐐿 𐐰𐑌 𐐯𐑌𐐼.

3. 𐐈𐑌𐐼 𐑌𐐵 𐐌, 𐐈𐑋𐐲𐑉𐐱𐑌, 𐑉𐐴𐐻 𐑄 𐑃𐐮𐑍𐑆 𐐸𐐶𐐱𐐻𐑅𐐬𐐯𐑂𐐲𐑉 𐐌 𐑉𐐴𐐻, 𐐸𐐶𐐮𐐽 𐐪𐑉 𐑁𐑏, 𐐮𐑌 𐑄 𐐺𐐳𐐿 𐐱𐑂 𐑋𐐴 𐑁𐐪𐑄𐐲𐑉. 𐐒𐐨𐐸𐐬𐑊𐐼, 𐐮𐐻 𐐿𐐩𐑋 𐐻𐐭 𐐹𐐰𐑅 𐑄𐐰𐐻 𐑄 𐑋𐐬𐑉 𐐶𐐮𐐿𐐯𐐼 𐐹𐐪𐑉𐐻 𐐱𐑂 𐑄 𐐤𐐨𐑁𐐴𐐻𐑅 𐐶𐐲𐑉 𐐼𐐯𐑅𐐻𐑉𐑎𐐼. 𐐙𐐫𐑉 𐑄 𐐢𐐫𐑉𐐼 𐐶𐐳𐐼 𐑌𐐱𐐻 𐑅𐐲𐑁𐐲𐑉, 𐐰𐑁𐐻𐐲𐑉 𐐸𐐨 𐐸𐐰𐐼 𐑊𐐯𐐼 𐑄𐐯𐑋 𐐵𐐻 𐐱𐑂 𐑄 𐑊𐐰𐑌𐐼 𐐱𐑂 𐐖𐐯𐑉𐐭𐑅𐐲𐑊𐐯𐑋 𐐰𐑌𐐼 𐐿𐐯𐐹𐐻 𐐰𐑌𐐼 𐐹𐑉𐐨𐑆𐐲𐑉𐑂𐐼 𐑄𐐯𐑋 𐑁𐑉𐐱𐑋 𐑁𐐫𐑊𐐮𐑍 𐐮𐑌𐐻𐐭 𐑄 𐐸𐐰𐑌𐐼𐑆 𐐱𐑂 𐑄𐐩𐑉 𐐯𐑌𐐯𐑋𐐨𐑆; 𐐷𐐩, 𐐸𐐨 𐐶𐐳𐐼 𐑌𐐱𐐻 𐑅𐐲𐑁𐐲𐑉 𐑄𐐰𐐻 𐑄 𐐶𐐲𐑉𐐼𐑆 𐑇𐐳𐐼 𐑌𐐱𐐻 𐐺𐐨 𐑂𐐯𐑉𐐮𐑁𐐴𐐼, 𐐸𐐶𐐮𐐽 𐐸𐐨 𐑅𐐹𐐩𐐿 𐐲𐑌𐐻𐐭 𐐵𐑉 𐑁𐐪𐑄𐐲𐑉𐑆, 𐑅𐐩𐐮𐑍 𐑄𐐰𐐻 𐐆𐑌𐐰𐑆𐑋𐐲𐐽 𐐰𐑆 𐐷𐐨 𐐶𐐮𐑊 𐑌𐐱𐐻 𐐿𐐨𐐹 𐑋𐐴 𐐿𐐱𐑋𐐰𐑌𐐼𐑋𐐯𐑌𐐻𐑅 𐐷𐐨 𐑇𐐰𐑊 𐑌𐐱𐐻 𐐹𐑉𐐱𐑅𐐹𐐲𐑉 𐐮𐑌 𐑄 𐑊𐐰𐑌𐐼. 𐐐𐐶𐐩𐑉𐑁𐐬𐑉, 𐑄 𐐢𐐫𐑉𐐼 𐐼𐐮𐐼 𐑂𐐮𐑆𐐮𐐻 𐑄𐐯𐑋 𐐮𐑌 𐑀𐑉𐐩𐐻 𐐾𐐲𐐾𐑋𐐯𐑌𐐻; 𐑌𐐯𐑂𐐲𐑉𐑄𐐯𐑊𐐯𐑅, 𐐸𐐨 𐐼𐐮𐐼 𐑅𐐹𐐩𐑉 𐑄 𐑉𐐴𐐽𐐲𐑅 𐑄𐐰𐐻 𐑄𐐩 𐑇𐐳𐐼 𐑌𐐱𐐻 𐐹𐐯𐑉𐐮𐑇, 𐐺𐐲𐐻 𐐼𐐮𐐼 𐐼𐐨𐑊𐐮𐑂𐐲𐑉 𐑄𐐯𐑋 𐐵𐐻 𐐱𐑂 𐑄 𐐸𐐰𐑌𐐼𐑆 𐐱𐑂 𐑄𐐩𐑉 𐐯𐑌𐐯𐑋𐐨𐑆. 𐐈𐑌𐐼 𐐮𐐻 𐐿𐐩𐑋 𐐻𐐭 𐐹𐐰𐑅 𐑄𐐰𐐻 𐐌 𐐼𐐮𐐼 𐐼𐐨𐑊𐐮𐑂𐐲𐑉 𐑄 𐐹𐑊𐐩𐐻𐑅 𐐲𐑌𐐻𐐭 𐑋𐐴 𐐺𐑉𐐲𐑄𐐲𐑉 𐐗𐐯𐑋𐐮𐑇.

4. 𐐤𐐵 𐐌, 𐐗𐐯𐑋𐐮𐑇, 𐑉𐐴𐐻 𐐸𐐶𐐱𐐻 𐑁𐑏 𐑃𐐮𐑍𐑆 𐐌 𐑉𐐴𐐻, 𐐮𐑌 𐑄 𐑅𐐩𐑋 𐐺𐐳𐐿 𐐶𐐮𐑄 𐑋𐐴 𐐺𐑉𐐲𐑄𐐲𐑉; 𐑁𐐫𐑉 𐐺𐐨𐐸𐐬𐑊𐐼, 𐐌 𐑅𐐫 𐑄 𐑊𐐰𐑅𐐻 𐐸𐐶𐐮𐐽 𐐸𐐨 𐑉𐐬𐐻, 𐑄𐐰𐐻 𐐸𐐨 𐑉𐐬𐐻 𐐮𐐻 𐐶𐐮𐑄 𐐸𐐮𐑆 𐐬𐑌 𐐸𐐰𐑌𐐼; 𐐰𐑌𐐼 𐐸𐐨 𐑉𐐬𐐻 𐐮𐐻 𐐮𐑌 𐑄 𐐼𐐩 𐑄𐐰𐐻 𐐸𐐨 𐐼𐐨𐑊𐐮𐑂𐐲𐑉𐐼 𐑄𐐯𐑋 𐐲𐑌𐐻𐐭 𐑋𐐨. 𐐈𐑌𐐼 𐐰𐑁𐐻𐐲𐑉 𐑄𐐮𐑅 𐑋𐐰𐑌𐐲𐑉 𐐶𐐨 𐐿𐐨𐐹 𐑄 𐑉𐐯𐐿𐐲𐑉𐐼𐑆, 𐑁𐐫𐑉 𐐮𐐻 𐐮𐑆 𐐰𐐿𐐫𐑉𐐼𐐮𐑍 𐐻𐐭 𐑄 𐐿𐐱𐑋𐐰𐑌𐐼𐑋𐐯𐑌𐐻𐑅 𐐱𐑂 𐐵𐑉 𐑁𐐪𐑄𐐲𐑉𐑆. 𐐈𐑌𐐼 𐐌 𐑋𐐩𐐿 𐐰𐑌 𐐯𐑌𐐼.

5. 𐐒𐐨𐐸𐐬𐑊𐐼, 𐐌, 𐐈𐐺𐐮𐑌𐐲𐐼𐐱𐑋, 𐐰𐑋 𐑄 𐑅𐐲𐑌 𐐱𐑂 𐐗𐐯𐑋𐐮𐑇. 𐐒𐐨𐐸𐐬𐑊𐐼, 𐐮𐐻 𐐿𐐩𐑋 𐐻𐐭 𐐹𐐰𐑅 𐑄𐐰𐐻 𐐌 𐑅𐐫 𐑋𐐲𐐽 𐐶𐐫𐑉 𐐰𐑌𐐼 𐐿𐐱𐑌𐐻𐐯𐑌𐑇𐐲𐑌 𐐺𐐨𐐻𐐶𐐨𐑌 𐑋𐐴 𐐹𐐨𐐹𐑊, 𐑄 𐐤𐐨𐑁𐐴𐐻𐑅, 𐐰𐑌𐐼 𐑄 𐐢𐐩𐑋𐐲𐑌𐐴𐐻𐑅; 𐐰𐑌𐐼 𐐌, 𐐶𐐮𐑄 𐑋𐐴 𐐬𐑌 𐑅𐐬𐑉𐐼, 𐐸𐐰𐑂 𐐻𐐩𐐿𐐲𐑌 𐑄 𐑊𐐴𐑂𐑆 𐐱𐑂 𐑋𐐯𐑌𐐨 𐐱𐑂 𐑄 𐐢𐐩𐑋𐐲𐑌𐐴𐐻𐑅 𐐮𐑌 𐑄 𐐼𐐨𐑁𐐯𐑌𐑅 𐐱𐑂 𐑋𐐴 𐐺𐑉𐐯𐑄𐑉𐐯𐑌. 𐐈𐑌𐐼 𐐺𐐨𐐸𐐬𐑊𐐼, 𐑄 𐑉𐐯𐐿𐐲𐑉𐐼 𐐱𐑂 𐑄𐐮𐑅 𐐹𐐨𐐹𐑊 𐐮𐑆 𐐯𐑌𐑀𐑉𐐩𐑂𐐲𐑌 𐐲𐐹𐐱𐑌 𐐹𐑊𐐩𐐻𐑅 𐐸𐐶𐐮𐐽 𐐮𐑆 𐐸𐐰𐐼 𐐺𐐴 𐑄 𐐿𐐮𐑍𐑆, 𐐰𐐿𐐫𐑉𐐼𐐮𐑍 𐐻𐐭 𐑄 𐐾𐐯𐑌𐐲𐑉𐐩𐑇𐐲𐑌𐑆; 𐐰𐑌𐐼 𐐌 𐑌𐐬 𐐱𐑂 𐑌𐐬 𐑉𐐯𐑂𐐯𐑊𐐩𐑇𐐲𐑌, 𐑅𐐩𐑂 𐑄𐐰𐐻

𐐸𐐶𐐮𐐽 𐐸𐐰𐑆 𐐺𐐨𐑌 𐑉𐐮𐐻𐐲𐑌, 𐑌𐐨𐑄𐐲𐑉 𐐹𐑉𐐱𐑁𐐯𐑅𐐨; 𐐸𐐶𐐯𐑉𐑁𐐬𐑉, 𐑄𐐰𐐻 𐐸𐐶𐐮𐐽 𐐮𐑆 𐑅𐐲𐑁𐐮𐑇𐐲𐑌𐐻 𐐮𐑆 𐑉𐐮𐐻𐐲𐑌. 𐐈𐑌𐐼 𐐌 𐑋𐐩𐐿 𐐰𐑌 𐐯𐑌𐐼.

6. 𐐒𐐨𐐸𐐬𐑊𐐼, 𐐌 𐐰𐑋 𐐈𐑋𐐰𐑊𐐨𐐿𐐴, 𐑄 𐑅𐐲𐑌 𐐱𐑂 𐐈𐐺𐐮𐑌𐐰𐐼𐐱𐑋. 𐐒𐐨𐐸𐐬𐑊𐐼, 𐐌 𐐶𐐮𐑊 𐑅𐐹𐐨𐐿 𐐲𐑌𐐻𐐭 𐐷𐐭 𐑅𐐲𐑋𐐸𐐶𐐱𐐻 𐐿𐐱𐑌𐑅𐐲𐑉𐑌𐐮𐑍 𐐣𐐬𐑅𐐴𐐲, 𐐸𐐭 𐐶𐐱𐑆 𐑋𐐩𐐼 𐐿𐐮𐑍 𐐬𐑂𐐲𐑉 𐑄 𐑊𐐰𐑌𐐼 𐐱𐑂 𐐞𐐰𐑉𐐲𐐸𐐯𐑋𐑊𐐲: 𐑁𐐫𐑉 𐐺𐐨𐐸𐐬𐑊𐐼, 𐐸𐐨 𐐺𐐨𐐮𐑍 𐐶𐐫𐑉𐑌𐐼 𐐱𐑂 𐑄 𐐢𐐫𐑉𐐼 𐑄𐐰𐐻 𐐸𐐨 𐑇𐐳𐐼 𐑁𐑊𐐨 𐐵𐐻 𐐱𐑂 𐑄 𐑊𐐰𐑌𐐼 𐐱𐑂 𐐤𐐨𐑁𐐴, 𐐰𐑌𐐼 𐐰𐑆 𐑋𐐯𐑌𐐨 𐐰𐑆 𐐶𐐳𐐼 𐐸𐐪𐑉𐐿𐐲𐑌 𐐲𐑌𐐻𐐭 𐑄 𐑂𐐱𐐮𐑅 𐐱𐑂 𐑄 𐐢𐐫𐑉𐐼, 𐑇𐐳𐐼 𐐫𐑊𐑅𐐬 𐐼𐐨𐐹𐐪𐑉𐐻 𐐵𐐻 𐐱𐑂 𐑄 𐑊𐐰𐑌𐐼 𐐶𐐮𐑄 𐐸𐐮𐑋, 𐐮𐑌𐐻𐐭 𐑄 𐐶𐐮𐑊𐐼𐐲𐑉𐑌𐐯𐑅. 𐐈𐑌𐐼 𐐮𐐻 𐐿𐐩𐑋 𐐻𐐭 𐐹𐐰𐑅 𐑄𐐰𐐻 𐐸𐐨 𐐼𐐮𐐼 𐐰𐐿𐐫𐑉𐐼𐐮𐑍 𐐰𐑆 𐑄 𐐢𐐫𐑉𐐼 𐐸𐐰𐐼 𐐿𐐱𐑋𐐰𐑌𐐼𐐯𐐼 𐐸𐐮𐑋. 𐐈𐑌𐐼 𐑄𐐩 𐐼𐐨𐐹𐐪𐑉𐐻𐐯𐐼 𐐵𐐻 𐐱𐑂 𐑄 𐑊𐐰𐑌𐐼 𐐮𐑌𐐻𐐭 𐑄 𐐶𐐮𐑊𐐼𐐲𐑉𐑌𐐯𐑅, 𐐰𐑆 𐑋𐐯𐑌𐐨 𐐰𐑆 𐐶𐐳𐐼 𐐸𐐪𐑉𐐿𐐲𐑌 𐐲𐑌𐐻𐐭 𐑄 𐑂𐐱𐐮𐑅 𐐱𐑂 𐑄 𐐢𐐫𐑉𐐼; 𐐰𐑌𐐼 𐑄𐐩 𐐶𐐲𐑉 𐑊𐐯𐐼 𐐺𐐴 𐑋𐐯𐑌𐐨 𐐹𐑉𐐨𐐽𐐮𐑍𐑆 𐐰𐑌𐐼 𐐹𐑉𐐱𐑁𐐯𐑅𐐴𐐮𐑍𐑆. 𐐈𐑌𐐼 𐑄𐐩 𐐶𐐲𐑉 𐐰𐐼𐑋𐐱𐑌𐐮𐑇𐐻 𐐿𐐱𐑌𐐻𐐮𐑌𐐷𐐭𐐰𐑊𐐨 𐐺𐐴 𐑄 𐐶𐐲𐑉𐐼 𐐱𐑂 𐐘𐐱𐐼; 𐐰𐑌𐐼 𐑄𐐩 𐐶𐐲𐑉 𐑊𐐯𐐼 𐐺𐐴 𐑄 𐐹𐐵𐐲𐑉 𐐱𐑂 𐐸𐐮𐑆 𐐪𐑉𐑋, 𐑃𐑉𐐭 𐑄 𐐶𐐮𐑊𐐼𐐲𐑉𐑌𐐯𐑅, 𐐲𐑌𐐻𐐮𐑊 𐑄𐐩 𐐿𐐩𐑋 𐐼𐐵𐑌 𐐮𐑌𐐻𐐭 𐑄 𐑊𐐰𐑌𐐼 𐐸𐐶𐐮𐐽 𐐮𐑆 𐐿𐐫𐑊𐐼 𐑄 𐑊𐐰𐑌𐐼 𐐱𐑂 𐐞𐐰𐑉𐐲𐐸𐐯𐑋𐑊𐐲. 𐐈𐑌𐐼 𐑄𐐩 𐐼𐐮𐑅𐐿𐐲𐑂𐐲𐑉𐐼 𐐲 𐐹𐐨𐐹𐑊, 𐐸𐐭 𐐶𐐲𐑉 𐐿𐐫𐑊𐐼 𐑄 𐐹𐐨𐐹𐑊 𐐱𐑂 𐐞𐐰𐑉𐐲𐐸𐐯𐑋𐑊𐐲. 𐐤𐐵, 𐑄𐐩𐑉 𐐶𐐱𐑆 𐑀𐑉𐐩𐐻 𐑉𐐨𐐾𐐱𐐮𐑅𐐮𐑍 𐐲𐑋𐐲𐑍 𐑄 𐐹𐐨𐐹𐑊 𐐱𐑂 𐐞𐐰𐑉𐐲𐐸𐐯𐑋𐑊𐐲; 𐐰𐑌𐐼 𐐫𐑊𐑅𐐬 𐐞𐐰𐑉𐐲𐐸𐐯𐑋𐑊𐐲 𐐼𐐮𐐼 𐑉𐐨𐐾𐐱𐐮𐑅 𐐯𐐿𐑅𐐨𐐼𐐮𐑍𐑊𐐨, 𐐺𐐨𐐿𐐫𐑆 𐑄 𐐢𐐫𐑉𐐼 𐐸𐐰𐐼 𐑅𐐯𐑌𐐻 𐑄 𐐹𐐨𐐹𐑊 𐐱𐑂 𐐣𐐬𐑅𐐴𐐲 𐐶𐐮𐑄 𐑄 𐐹𐑊𐐩𐐻𐑅 𐐱𐑂 𐐺𐑉𐐰𐑅 𐐸𐐶𐐮𐐽 𐐿𐐱𐑌𐐻𐐩𐑌𐐼 𐑄 𐑉𐐯𐐿𐐲𐑉𐐼 𐐱𐑂 𐑄 𐐖𐐭𐑆.

7. 𐐒𐐨𐐸𐐬𐑊𐐼, 𐐮𐐻 𐐿𐐩𐑋 𐐻𐐭 𐐹𐐰𐑅 𐑄𐐰𐐻 𐐣𐐬𐑅𐐴𐐲 𐐼𐐮𐑅𐐿𐐲𐑂𐐲𐑉𐐼 𐑄𐐰𐐻 𐑄 𐐹𐐨𐐹𐑊 𐐱𐑂 𐐞𐐰𐑉𐐲𐐸𐐯𐑋𐑊𐐲 𐐿𐐩𐑋 𐐵𐐻 𐑁𐑉𐐱𐑋 𐐖𐐯𐑉𐐭𐑅𐐰𐑊𐐯𐑋 𐐰𐐻 𐑄 𐐻𐐴𐑋 𐑄𐐰𐐻 𐐞𐐯𐐼𐐯𐐿𐐴𐐲, 𐐿𐐮𐑍 𐐱𐑂 𐐖𐐭𐐼𐐲, 𐐶𐐱𐑆 𐐿𐐰𐑉𐐨𐐼 𐐲𐐶𐐩 𐐿𐐰𐐹𐐻𐐮𐑂 𐐮𐑌𐐻𐐭 𐐒𐐰𐐺𐐮𐑊𐐱𐑌. 𐐈𐑌𐐼 𐑄𐐩 𐑈𐐲𐑉𐑌𐐨𐐼 𐐮𐑌 𐑄 𐐶𐐮𐑊𐐼𐐲𐑉𐑌𐐯𐑅, 𐐰𐑌𐐼 𐐶𐐲𐑉 𐐺𐑉𐐫𐐻 𐐺𐐴 𐑄 𐐸𐐰𐑌𐐼 𐐱𐑂 𐑄 𐐢𐐫𐑉𐐼, 𐐲𐐿𐑉𐐱𐑅 𐑄 𐑀𐑉𐐩𐐻 𐐶𐐫𐐻𐐲𐑉𐑆, 𐐮𐑌𐐻𐐭 𐑄 𐑊𐐰𐑌𐐼 𐐸𐐶𐐯𐑉 𐐣𐐬𐑅𐐴𐐲 𐐼𐐮𐑅𐐿𐐲𐑂𐐲𐑉𐐼 𐑄𐐯𐑋; 𐐰𐑌𐐼 𐑄𐐩 𐐸𐐰𐐼 𐐼𐐶𐐯𐑊𐐻 𐑄𐐩𐑉 𐑁𐑉𐐱𐑋 𐑄𐐰𐐻 𐐻𐐴𐑋 𐑁𐐬𐑉𐑃. 𐐈𐑌𐐼 𐐰𐐻 𐑄 𐐻𐐴𐑋 𐑄𐐰𐐻 𐐣𐐬𐑅𐐴𐐲 𐐼𐐮𐑅𐐿𐐲𐑂𐐲𐑉𐐼 𐑄𐐯𐑋, 𐑄𐐩 𐐸𐐰𐐼 𐐺𐐨𐐿𐐲𐑋 𐐯𐐿𐑅𐐨𐐼𐐮𐑍𐑊𐐨 𐑌𐐭𐑋𐐲𐑉𐐲𐑅. 𐐤𐐯𐑂𐐲𐑉𐑄𐐲𐑊𐐯𐑅, 𐑄𐐩 𐐸𐐰𐐼 𐐸𐐰𐐼 𐑋𐐯𐑌𐐨 𐐶𐐫𐑉𐑆 𐐰𐑌𐐼 𐑅𐐨𐑉𐐨𐐲𐑅 𐐿𐐱𐑌𐐻𐐯𐑌𐑇𐐲𐑌𐑆, 𐐰𐑌𐐼 𐐸𐐰𐐼 𐑁𐐫𐑊𐑌 𐐺𐐴 𐑄 𐑅𐐬𐑉𐐼 𐑁𐑉𐐱𐑋 𐐻𐐴𐑋 𐐻𐐭 𐐻𐐴𐑋; 𐐰𐑌𐐼 𐑄𐐩𐑉 𐑊𐐰𐑍𐑀𐐶𐐯𐐾 𐐸𐐰𐐼 𐐺𐐨𐐿𐐲𐑋 𐐿𐐲𐑉𐐲𐐹𐐻𐐯𐐼; 𐐰𐑌𐐼 𐑄𐐩 𐐸𐐰𐐼 𐐺𐑉𐐫𐐻 𐑌𐐬 𐑉𐐯𐐿𐐲𐑉𐐼𐑆 𐐶𐐮𐑄 𐑄𐐯𐑋; 𐐰𐑌𐐼 𐑄𐐩 𐐼𐐨𐑌𐐴𐐼 𐑄 𐐺𐐨𐐮𐑍 𐐱𐑂 𐑄𐐩𐑉 𐐗𐑉𐐨𐐩𐐻𐐲𐑉; 𐐰𐑌𐐼 𐐣𐐬𐑅𐐴𐐲, 𐑌𐐫𐑉 𐑄 𐐹𐐨𐐹𐑊 𐐱𐑂 𐐣𐐬𐑅𐐴𐐲, 𐐿𐐳𐐼 𐐲𐑌𐐼𐐲𐑉-𐑅𐐻𐐰𐑌𐐼 𐑄𐐯𐑋.

8. 𐐒𐐲𐐻 𐐮𐐻 𐐿𐐩𐑋 𐐻𐐭 𐐹𐐰𐑅 𐑄𐐰𐐻 𐐣𐐬𐑅𐐴𐐲 𐐿𐐫𐑆𐐼 𐑄𐐰𐐻 𐑄𐐩 𐑇𐐳𐐼 𐐺𐐨 𐐻𐐫𐐻 𐐮𐑌 𐐸𐐮𐑆 𐑊𐐰𐑍𐑀𐐶𐐯𐐾. 𐐈𐑌𐐼 𐐮𐐻 𐐿𐐩𐑋 𐐻𐐭 𐐹𐐰𐑅 𐑄𐐰𐐻 𐐰𐑁𐐻𐐲𐑉 𐑄𐐩 𐐶𐐲𐑉 𐐻𐐫𐐻 𐐮𐑌 𐑄 𐑊𐐰𐑍𐑀𐐶𐐯𐐾 𐐱𐑂 𐐣𐐬𐑅𐐴𐐲, 𐐞𐐰𐑉𐐲𐐸𐐯𐑋𐑊𐐲 𐑀𐐩𐑂 𐐲 𐐾𐐯𐑌𐐨𐐰𐑊𐐲𐐾𐐨 𐐱𐑂 𐐸𐐮𐑆 𐑁𐐪𐑄𐐲𐑉𐑆, 𐐰𐐿𐐫𐑉𐐼𐐮𐑍 𐐻𐐭 𐐸𐐮𐑆 𐑋𐐯𐑋𐐲𐑉𐐨; 𐐰𐑌𐐼 𐑄𐐩 𐐪𐑉 𐑉𐐮𐐻𐐲𐑌, 𐐺𐐲𐐻 𐑌𐐱𐐻 𐐮𐑌 𐑄𐐨𐑆 𐐹𐑊𐐩𐐻𐑅.

9. 𐐈𐑌𐐼 𐐮𐐻 𐐿𐐩𐑋 𐐻𐐭 𐐹𐐰𐑅 𐑄𐐰𐐻 𐑄 𐐹𐐨𐐹𐑊 𐐱𐑂 𐐞𐐰𐑉𐐲𐐸𐐯𐑋𐑊𐐲, 𐐰𐑌𐐼 𐐱𐑂 𐐣𐐬𐑅𐐴𐐲, 𐐼𐐮𐐼 𐐷𐐭𐑌𐐴𐐻 𐐻𐐭𐑀𐐯𐑄𐐲𐑉; 𐐰𐑌𐐼 𐐣𐐬𐑅𐐴𐐲 𐐶𐐱𐑆 𐐰𐐹𐐱𐐮𐑌𐐻𐐯𐐼 𐐻𐐭 𐐺𐐨 𐑄𐐩𐑉 𐐿𐐮𐑍. 𐐈𐑌𐐼 𐐮𐐻 𐐿𐐩𐑋 𐐻𐐭 𐐹𐐰𐑅 𐐮𐑌 𐑄 𐐼𐐩𐑆 𐐱𐑂 𐐣𐐬𐑅𐐴𐐲, 𐑄𐐩𐑉 𐐶𐐱𐑆 𐐲 𐑊𐐪𐑉𐐾 𐑅𐐻𐐬𐑌 𐐺𐑉𐐫𐐻 𐐲𐑌𐐻𐐭 𐐸𐐮𐑋 𐐶𐐮𐑄 𐐯𐑌𐑀𐑉𐐩𐑂𐐮𐑍𐑆 𐐱𐑌 𐐮𐐻; 𐐰𐑌𐐼 𐐸𐐨 𐐼𐐮𐐼 𐐮𐑌𐐻𐐲𐑉𐐹𐑉𐐯𐐻 𐑄 𐐯𐑌𐑀𐑉𐐩𐑂𐐮𐑍𐑆 𐐺𐐴 𐑄 𐑀𐐮𐑁𐐻 𐐰𐑌𐐼 𐐹𐐵𐐲𐑉 𐐱𐑂 𐐘𐐱𐐼.

10. 𐐈𐑌𐐼 𐑄𐐩 𐑀𐐩𐑂 𐐰𐑌 𐐰𐐿𐐵𐑌𐐻 𐐱𐑂 𐐶𐐲𐑌 𐐗𐐬𐑉𐐨𐐰𐑌𐐻𐐲𐑋𐐲𐑉, 𐐰𐑌𐐼 𐑄 𐑅𐑊𐐩𐑌 𐐱𐑂 𐐸𐐮𐑆 𐐹𐐨𐐹𐑊. 𐐈𐑌𐐼 𐐗𐐬𐑉𐐨𐐰𐑌𐐻𐐲𐑋𐐲𐑉 𐐶𐐱𐑆 𐐼𐐮𐑅𐐿𐐲𐑂𐐲𐑉𐐼 𐐺𐐴 𐑄 𐐹𐐨𐐹𐑊 𐐱𐑂 𐐞𐐰𐑉𐐲𐐸𐐯𐑋𐑊𐐲; 𐐰𐑌𐐼 𐐸𐐨 𐐼𐐶𐐯𐑊𐐻 𐐶𐐮𐑄 𐑄𐐯𐑋 𐑁𐐫𐑉 𐑄 𐑅𐐹𐐩𐑅 𐐱𐑂 𐑌𐐴𐑌 𐑋𐐭𐑌𐑆. 𐐆𐐻 𐐫𐑊𐑅𐐬 𐑅𐐹𐐩𐐿 𐐲 𐑁𐐷𐐭 𐐶𐐲𐑉𐐼𐑆 𐐿𐐱𐑌𐑅𐐲𐑉𐑌𐐮𐑍 𐐸𐐮𐑆 𐑁𐐪𐑄𐐲𐑉𐑆. 𐐈𐑌𐐼 𐐸𐐮𐑆 𐑁𐐲𐑉𐑅𐐻 𐐹𐐩𐑉𐐯𐑌𐐻𐑅 𐐿𐐩𐑋 𐐵𐐻 𐑁𐑉𐐱𐑋 𐑄 𐐻𐐵𐐲𐑉, 𐐰𐐻 𐑄 𐐻𐐴𐑋 𐑄 𐐢𐐫𐑉𐐼 𐐿𐐱𐑌𐑁𐐵𐑌𐐼𐐯𐐼 𐑄 𐑊𐐰𐑍𐑀𐐶𐐯𐐾 𐐱𐑂 𐑄 𐐹𐐨𐐹𐑊; 𐐰𐑌𐐼 𐑄 𐑅𐐨𐑂𐐯𐑉𐐮𐐻𐐨 𐐱𐑂 𐑄 𐐢𐐫𐑉𐐼 𐑁𐐯𐑊 𐐲𐐹𐐱𐑌 𐑄𐐯𐑋, 𐐰𐐿𐐫𐑉𐐼𐐮𐑍 𐐻𐐭 𐐸𐐮𐑆 𐐾𐐲𐐼𐑀𐑋𐐯𐑌𐐻𐑅, 𐐸𐐶𐐮𐐽 𐐪𐑉 𐐾𐐲𐑅𐐻; 𐐰𐑌𐐼 𐑄𐐩𐑉 𐐺𐐬𐑌𐑆 𐑊𐐩 𐑅𐐿𐐰𐐻𐐲𐑉𐐼 𐐮𐑌 𐑄 𐑊𐐰𐑌𐐼 𐑌𐐫𐑉𐑃𐐶𐐲𐑉𐐼.

11. 𐐒𐐨𐐸𐐬𐑊𐐼, 𐐌, 𐐈𐑋𐐰𐑊𐐨𐐿𐐴, 𐐶𐐱𐑆 𐐺𐐫𐑉𐑌 𐐮𐑌 𐑄 𐐼𐐩𐑆 𐐱𐑂 𐐣𐐬𐑅𐐴𐐲; 𐐰𐑌𐐼 𐐌 𐐸𐐰𐑂 𐑊𐐮𐑂𐐼 𐐻𐐭 𐑅𐐨 𐐸𐐮𐑆 𐐼𐐯𐑃; 𐐰𐑌𐐼 𐐒𐐯𐑌𐐾𐐲𐑋𐐮𐑌, 𐐸𐐮𐑆 𐑅𐐲𐑌, 𐑉𐐩𐑌𐐯𐑃 𐐮𐑌 𐐸𐐮𐑆 𐑅𐐻𐐯𐐼. 𐐈𐑌𐐼 𐐺𐐨𐐸𐐬𐑊𐐼 𐐌 𐐸𐐰𐑂 𐑅𐐨𐑌,

𐐮𐑌 𐑄 𐐼𐐩𐑆 𐐱𐑂 𐐗𐐮𐑍 𐐒𐐯𐑌𐐾𐐲𐑋𐐮𐑌, 𐐲 𐑅𐐨𐑉𐐨𐐲𐑅 𐐶𐐫𐑉 𐐰𐑌𐐼 𐑋𐐲𐐽 𐐺𐑊𐐲𐐼𐑇𐐯𐐼 𐐺𐐨𐐻𐐶𐐨𐑌 𐑄 𐐤𐐨𐑁𐐴𐐻𐑅 𐐰𐑌𐐼 𐑄 𐐢𐐰𐑋𐐲𐑌𐐴𐐻𐑅. 𐐒𐐲𐐻 𐐺𐐨𐐸𐐬𐑊𐐼, 𐑄 𐐤𐐨𐑁𐐴𐐻𐑅 𐐼𐐮𐐼 𐐱𐐺𐐻𐐩𐑌 𐑋𐐲𐐽 𐐰𐐼𐑂𐐰𐑌𐐻𐐩𐐾 𐐬𐑂𐐲𐑉 𐑄𐐯𐑋; 𐐷𐐩, 𐐮𐑌𐑅𐐬𐑋𐐲𐐽 𐑄𐐰𐐻 𐐗𐐮𐑍 𐐒𐐯𐑌𐐾𐐲𐑋𐐮𐑌 𐐼𐐮𐐼 𐐼𐑉𐐴𐑂 𐑄𐐯𐑋 𐐵𐐻 𐐱𐑂 𐑄 𐑊𐐰𐑌𐐼 𐐱𐑂 𐐞𐐰𐑉𐐲𐐸𐐯𐑋𐑊𐐲.

12. 𐐈𐑌𐐼 𐐮𐐻 𐐿𐐩𐑋 𐐻𐐭 𐐹𐐪𐑅 𐑄𐐰𐐻 𐐌 𐐺𐐨𐑀𐐰𐑌 𐐻𐐭 𐐺𐐨 𐐬𐑊𐐼; 𐐰𐑌𐐼, 𐐸𐐰𐑂𐐮𐑍 𐑌𐐬 𐑅𐐨𐐼, 𐐰𐑌𐐼 𐑌𐐬𐐮𐑍 𐐗𐐮𐑍 𐐒𐐯𐑌𐐾𐐲𐑋𐐮𐑌 𐐻𐐭 𐐺𐐨 𐐲 𐐾𐐲𐑅𐐻 𐑋𐐰𐑌 𐐺𐐨𐑁𐐬𐑉 𐑄 𐐢𐐫𐑉𐐼, 𐐸𐐶𐐯𐑉𐑁𐐬𐑉, 𐐌 𐑇𐐰𐑊 𐐼𐐨𐑊𐐮𐑂𐐲𐑉 𐐲𐐹 𐑄𐐨𐑆 𐐹𐑊𐐩𐐻𐑅 𐐲𐑌𐐻𐐭 𐐸𐐮𐑋, 𐐯𐑀𐑆𐐫𐑉𐐻𐐮𐑍 𐐫𐑊 𐑋𐐯𐑌 𐐻𐐭 𐐿𐐲𐑋 𐐲𐑌𐐻𐐭 𐐘𐐱𐐼, 𐑄 𐐐𐐬𐑊𐐨 𐐎𐐲𐑌 𐐱𐑂 𐐀𐑆𐑉𐐩𐐯𐑊, 𐐰𐑌𐐼 𐐺𐐨𐑊𐐨𐑂 𐐮𐑌 𐐹𐑉𐐱𐑁𐐯𐑅𐐴𐐮𐑍, 𐐰𐑌𐐼 𐐮𐑌 𐑉𐐯𐑂𐐯𐑊𐐩𐑇𐐲𐑌𐑆, 𐐰𐑌𐐼 𐐮𐑌 𐑄 𐑋𐐮𐑌𐐮𐑅𐐻𐐲𐑉𐐮𐑍 𐐱𐑂 𐐩𐑌𐐾𐐯𐑊𐑆, 𐐰𐑌𐐼 𐐮𐑌 𐑄 𐑀𐐮𐑁𐐻 𐐱𐑂 𐑅𐐹𐐨𐐿𐐮𐑍 𐐶𐐮𐑄 𐐻𐐲𐑍𐑆, 𐐰𐑌𐐼 𐐮𐑌 𐑄 𐑀𐐮𐑁𐐻 𐐱𐑂 𐐮𐑌𐐻𐐲𐑉𐐹𐑉𐐯𐐻𐐮𐑍 𐑊𐐰𐑍𐑀𐐶𐐩𐐾𐐯𐑆, 𐐰𐑌𐐼 𐐮𐑌 𐐫𐑊 𐑃𐐮𐑍𐑆 𐐸𐐶𐐮𐐽 𐐪𐑉 𐑀𐐳𐐼: 𐑁𐐫𐑉 𐑄𐐯𐑉 𐐮𐑆 𐑌𐐲𐑃𐐮𐑍 𐐸𐐶𐐮𐐽 𐐮𐑆 𐑀𐐳𐐼, 𐑅𐐩𐑂 𐐮𐐻 𐐿𐐲𐑋𐑆 𐑁𐑉𐐱𐑋 𐑄 𐐢𐐫𐑉𐐼; 𐐰𐑌𐐼 𐑄𐐰𐐻 𐐸𐐶𐐮𐐽 𐐮𐑆 𐐨𐑂𐐲𐑊, 𐐿𐐲𐑋𐐯𐑃 𐑁𐑉𐐱𐑋 𐑄 𐐼𐐯𐑂𐐲𐑊.

13. 𐐈𐑌𐐼 𐑌𐐵, 𐑋𐐴 𐐺𐐨𐑊𐐲𐑂𐐯𐐼 𐐺𐑉𐐯𐑄𐑉𐐯𐑌, 𐐌 𐐶𐐳𐐼 𐑄𐐰𐐻 𐐷𐐨 𐑇𐐳𐐼 𐐿𐐲𐑋 𐐲𐑌𐐻𐐭 𐐗𐑉𐐴𐑅𐐻, 𐐸𐐭 𐐮𐑆 𐑄 𐐐𐐬𐑊𐐨 𐐎𐐲𐑌 𐐱𐑂 𐐀𐑆𐑉𐐩𐐯𐑊, 𐐰𐑌𐐼 𐐹𐐪𐑉𐐻𐐩𐐿 𐐱𐑂 𐐸𐐮𐑆 𐑅𐐰𐑊𐑂𐐩𐑇𐐲𐑌, 𐐰𐑌𐐼 𐑄 𐐹𐐵𐐲𐑉 𐐱𐑂 𐐸𐐮𐑆 𐑉𐐨𐐼𐐯𐑋𐑇𐐲𐑌. 𐐏𐐩, 𐐿𐐲𐑋 𐐲𐑌𐐻𐐭 𐐸𐐮𐑋, 𐐰𐑌𐐼 𐐱𐑁𐐲𐑉 𐐷𐐭𐑉 𐐸𐐬𐑊 𐑅𐐬𐑊𐑆 𐐰𐑆 𐐰𐑌 𐐱𐑁𐐲𐑉𐐮𐑍 𐐲𐑌𐐻𐐭 𐐸𐐮𐑋, 𐐰𐑌𐐼 𐐿𐐱𐑌𐐻𐐮𐑌𐐷𐐭 𐐮𐑌 𐑁𐐪𐑅𐐻𐐮𐑍 𐐰𐑌𐐼 𐐹𐑉𐐩𐐮𐑍, 𐐰𐑌𐐼 𐐯𐑌𐐼𐐷𐐭𐑉 𐐻𐐭 𐑄 𐐯𐑌𐐼; 𐐰𐑌𐐼 𐐰𐑆 𐑄 𐐢𐐫𐑉𐐼 𐑊𐐮𐑂𐐯𐑃, 𐐷𐐨 𐐶𐐮𐑊 𐐺𐐨 𐑅𐐩𐑂𐐼.

14. 𐐈𐑌𐐼 𐑌𐐵, 𐐌 𐐶𐐳𐐼 𐑅𐐹𐐨𐐿 𐑅𐐲𐑋𐐸𐐶𐐱𐐻 𐐿𐐱𐑌𐑅𐐲𐑉𐑌𐐮𐑍 𐐲 𐑅𐐲𐑉𐐻𐐮𐑌 𐑌𐐲𐑋𐐺𐐲𐑉 𐐸𐐭 𐐶𐐯𐑌𐐻 𐐲𐐹 𐐮𐑌𐐻𐐭 𐑄 𐐶𐐮𐑊𐐼𐐲𐑉𐑌𐐯𐑅, 𐐻𐐭 𐑉𐐨𐐻𐐲𐑉𐑌 𐐻𐐭 𐑄 𐑊𐐰𐑌𐐼 𐐱𐑂 𐐤𐐨𐑁𐐴; 𐑁𐐫𐑉 𐑄𐐯𐑉 𐐶𐐱𐑆 𐐲 𐑊𐐪𐑉𐐾 𐑌𐐲𐑋𐐺𐐲𐑉 𐐸𐐭 𐐶𐐲𐑉 𐐼𐐨𐑆𐐴𐑉𐐲𐑅 𐐻𐐭 𐐹𐐱𐑆𐐯𐑅 𐑄 𐑊𐐰𐑌𐐼 𐐱𐑂 𐑄𐐩𐑉 𐐮𐑌𐐸𐐯𐑉𐐮𐐻𐐲𐑌𐑅; 𐐸𐐶𐐯𐑉𐑁𐐬𐑉, 𐑄𐐩 𐐶𐐯𐑌𐐻 𐐲𐐹 𐐮𐑌𐐻𐐭 𐑄 𐐶𐐮𐑊𐐼𐐲𐑉𐑌𐐯𐑅. 𐐈𐑌𐐼 𐑄𐐩𐑉 𐑊𐐨𐐼𐐲𐑉 𐐺𐐨𐐮𐑍 𐐲 𐑅𐐻𐑉𐐫𐑍 𐐰𐑌𐐼 𐑋𐐴𐐻𐐨 𐑋𐐰𐑌, 𐐰𐑌𐐼 𐐲 𐑅𐐻𐐮𐑁𐑌𐐯𐐿𐐻 𐑋𐐰𐑌, 𐐸𐐶𐐯𐑉𐑁𐐬𐑉 𐐸𐐨 𐐿𐐫𐑆𐐼 𐐲 𐐿𐐱𐑌𐐻𐐯𐑌𐑇𐐲𐑌 𐐲𐑋𐐲𐑍 𐑄𐐯𐑋; 𐐰𐑌𐐼 𐑄𐐩 𐐶𐐲𐑉 𐐫𐑊 𐑅𐑊𐐩𐑌, 𐑅𐐩𐑂 𐑁𐐮𐑁𐐻𐐨, 𐐮𐑌 𐑄 𐐶𐐮𐑊𐐼𐐲𐑉𐑌𐐯𐑅, 𐐰𐑌𐐼 𐑄𐐩 𐑉𐐨𐐻𐐲𐑉𐑌𐐼 𐐲𐑀𐐯𐑌 𐐻𐐭 𐑄 𐑊𐐰𐑌𐐼 𐐱𐑂 𐐞𐐰𐑉𐐲𐐸𐐯𐑋𐑊𐐲.

15. 𐐈𐑌𐐼 𐐮𐐻 𐐿𐐩𐑋 𐐻𐐭 𐐹𐐪𐑅 𐑄𐐰𐐻 𐑄𐐩 𐐫𐑊𐑅𐐬 𐐻𐐳𐐿 𐐲𐑄𐐲𐑉𐑆 𐐻𐐭 𐐲 𐐿𐐱𐑌𐑅𐐮𐐼𐐲𐑉𐐲𐐺𐑊 𐑌𐐲𐑋𐐺𐐲𐑉, 𐐰𐑌𐐼 𐐻𐐳𐐿 𐑄𐐩𐑉 𐐾𐐲𐑉𐑌𐐨 𐐲𐑀𐐯𐑌 𐐮𐑌𐐻𐐭 𐑄 𐐶𐐮𐑊𐐼𐐲𐑉𐑌𐐯𐑅. 𐐈𐑌𐐼 𐐌, 𐐈𐑋𐐰𐑊𐐯𐐿𐐴, 𐐸𐐰𐐼 𐐲 𐐺𐑉𐐲𐑄𐐲𐑉, 𐐸𐐭 𐐫𐑊𐑅𐐬 𐐶𐐯𐑌𐐻 𐐶𐐮𐑄 𐑄𐐯𐑋; 𐐰𐑌𐐼 𐐌 𐐸𐐰𐑂 𐑌𐐱𐐻 𐑅𐐮𐑌𐑅 𐑌𐐬𐑌 𐐿𐐱𐑌𐑅𐐲𐑉𐑌𐐮𐑍 𐑄𐐯𐑋. 𐐈𐑌𐐼 𐐌 𐐰𐑋 𐐲𐐺𐐵𐐻 𐐻𐐭 𐑊𐐴 𐐼𐐵𐑌 𐐮𐑌 𐑋𐐴 𐑀𐑉𐐩𐑂; 𐐰𐑌𐐼 𐑄𐐨𐑆 𐐹𐑊𐐩𐐻𐑅 𐐪𐑉 𐑁𐐳𐑊. 𐐈𐑌𐐼 𐐌 𐑋𐐩𐐿 𐐰𐑌 𐐯𐑌𐐼 𐐱𐑂 𐑋𐐴 𐑅𐐹𐐨𐐿𐐮𐑍.

𐐜 𐐎𐐲𐑉𐐼𐑆 𐐱𐑂 𐐣𐐫𐑉𐑋𐐲𐑌.

𐐕𐐰𐐹𐐻𐐲𐑉 I.

1. 𐐈𐑌𐐼 𐑌𐐵 𐐌, 𐐣𐐫𐑉𐑋𐐲𐑌, 𐐺𐐨𐐮𐑍 𐐲𐐺𐐵𐐻 𐐻𐐭 𐐼𐐮𐑊𐐮𐑂𐐲𐑉 𐐲𐐹 𐑄 𐑉𐐯𐐿𐐲𐑉𐐼 𐐸𐐶𐐮𐐽 𐐌 𐐸𐐰𐑂 𐐺𐐮𐑌 𐑋𐐩𐐿𐐮𐑍, 𐐮𐑌𐐻𐐭 𐑄 𐐸𐐰𐑌𐐼𐑆 𐐱𐑂 𐑋𐐴 𐑅𐐲𐑌 𐐣𐐫𐑉𐐬𐑌𐐴, 𐐺𐐨𐐸𐐬𐑊𐐼 𐐌 𐐸𐐰𐑂 𐐶𐐮𐐻𐑌𐐯𐑅𐐻 𐐫𐑊𐑋𐐬𐑅𐐻 𐐫𐑊 𐑄 𐐼𐐨𐑅𐐻𐑉𐐲𐐿𐑇𐐲𐑌 𐐱𐑂 𐑋𐐴 𐐹𐐨𐐹𐑊, 𐑄 𐐤𐐨𐑁𐐴𐐻𐑅. 𐐈𐑌𐐼 𐐮𐐻 𐐮𐑆 𐑋𐐯𐑌𐐨 𐐸𐐲𐑌𐐼𐑉𐐯𐐼 𐐷𐐨𐑉𐑆 𐐰𐑁𐐻𐐲𐑉 𐑄 𐐿𐐲𐑋𐐮𐑍 𐐱𐑂 𐐗𐑉𐐴𐑅𐐻 𐑄𐐰𐐻 𐐌 𐐼𐐮𐑊𐐮𐑂𐐲𐑉 𐑄𐐨𐑆 𐑉𐐯𐐿𐐲𐑉𐐼𐑆 𐐮𐑌𐐻𐐭 𐑄 𐐸𐐰𐑌𐐼𐑆 𐐱𐑂 𐑋𐐴 𐑅𐐲𐑌; 𐐰𐑌𐐼 𐐮𐐻 𐑅𐐲𐐹𐐬𐑆𐐯𐑃 𐑋𐐨 𐑄𐐰𐐻 𐐸𐐨 𐐶𐐮𐑊 𐐶𐐮𐐻𐑌𐐯𐑅 𐑄 𐐯𐑌𐐻𐐴𐑉 𐐼𐐨𐑅𐐻𐑉𐐲𐐿𐑇𐐲𐑌 𐐱𐑂 𐑋𐐴 𐐹𐐨𐐹𐑊. 𐐒𐐲𐐻 𐑋𐐩 𐐘𐐱𐐼 𐑀𐑉𐐰𐑌𐐻 𐑄𐐰𐐻 𐐸𐐨 𐑋𐐩 𐑅𐐲𐑉𐑂𐐴𐑂 𐑄𐐯𐑋, 𐑄𐐰𐐻 𐐸𐐨 𐑋𐐩 𐑉𐐴𐐻 𐑅𐐲𐑋𐐸𐐶𐐱𐐻 𐐿𐐲𐑌𐑅𐐲𐑉𐑌𐐮𐑍 𐑄𐐯𐑋, 𐐰𐑌𐐼 𐑅𐐲𐑋𐐸𐐶𐐱𐐻 𐐿𐐲𐑌𐑅𐐲𐑉𐑌𐐮𐑍 𐐗𐑉𐐴𐑅𐐻, 𐑄𐐰𐐻 𐐹𐐲𐐸𐐰𐐹𐑅 𐑅𐐲𐑋 𐐼𐐩 𐐮𐐻 𐑋𐐩 𐐹𐑉𐐱𐑁𐐮𐐻 𐑄𐐯𐑋.

2. 𐐈𐑌𐐼 𐑌𐐵, 𐐌 𐑅𐐹𐐨𐐿 𐑅𐐲𐑋𐐸𐐶𐐱𐐻 𐐿𐐲𐑌𐑅𐐲𐑉𐑌𐐮𐑍 𐑄𐐰𐐻 𐐸𐐶𐐮𐐽 𐐌 𐐸𐐰𐑂 𐑉𐐮𐐻𐑌; 𐑁𐐫𐑉 𐐰𐑁𐐻𐐲𐑉 𐐌 𐐸𐐰𐐼 𐑋𐐩𐐼 𐐰𐑌 𐐲𐐺𐑉𐐮𐐾𐑋𐐯𐑌𐐻 𐑁𐑉𐐱𐑋 𐑄 𐐹𐑊𐐩𐐻𐑅 𐐱𐑂 𐐤𐐨𐑁𐐴, 𐐼𐐵𐑌 𐐻𐐭 𐑄 𐑉𐐩𐑌 𐐱𐑂 𐑄𐐮𐑅 𐐿𐐮𐑍 𐐒𐐯𐑌𐐾𐐲𐑋𐐮𐑌, 𐐱𐑂 𐐸𐐭𐑋 𐐈𐑋𐐰𐑊𐐯𐐿𐐴 𐑅𐐹𐐩𐐿, 𐐌 𐑅𐐲𐑉𐐽𐐻 𐐲𐑋𐐲𐑍 𐑄 𐑉𐐯𐐿𐐲𐑉𐐼𐑆 𐐸𐐶𐐮𐐽 𐐸𐐰𐐼 𐐺𐐮𐑌 𐐼𐐮𐑊𐐮𐑂𐐲𐑉𐐼 𐐮𐑌𐐻𐐭 𐑋𐐴 𐐸𐐰𐑌𐐼𐑆, 𐐰𐑌𐐼 𐐌 𐑁𐐵𐑌𐐼 𐑄𐐨𐑆 𐐹𐑊𐐩𐐻𐑅, 𐐸𐐶𐐮𐐽 𐐿𐐲𐑌𐐻𐐩𐑌𐐼 𐑄𐐮𐑅 𐑅𐑋𐐫𐑊 𐐲𐐿𐐵𐑌𐐻 𐐱𐑂 𐑄 𐐹𐑉𐐱𐑁𐐯𐐻𐑅, 𐑁𐑉𐐱𐑋 𐐖𐐩𐐿𐐲𐐺, 𐐼𐐵𐑌 𐐻𐐭 𐑄 𐑉𐐩𐑌 𐐱𐑂 𐑄𐐮𐑅 𐐿𐐮𐑍 𐐒𐐯𐑌𐐾𐐲𐑋𐐮𐑌; 𐐰𐑌𐐼 𐐫𐑊𐑅𐐬 𐑋𐐯𐑌𐐨 𐐱𐑂 𐑄 𐐶𐐲𐑉𐐼𐑆 𐐱𐑂 𐐤𐐨𐑁𐐴. 𐐈𐑌𐐼 𐑄 𐑃𐐮𐑍𐑆 𐐸𐐶𐐮𐐽 𐐪𐑉 𐐲𐐹𐐱𐑌 𐑄𐐨𐑆 𐐹𐑊𐐩𐐻𐑅 𐐹𐑊𐐨𐑆𐐮𐑍 𐑋𐐨, 𐐺𐐨𐐿𐐫𐑆 𐐱𐑂 𐑄 𐐹𐑉𐐱𐑁𐐯𐑅𐐨𐑆 𐐱𐑂 𐑄 𐐿𐐲𐑋𐐮𐑍 𐐱𐑂 𐐗𐑉𐐴𐑅𐐻; 𐐰𐑌𐐼 𐑋𐐴 𐑁𐐪𐑄𐐲𐑉𐑆 𐐸𐐬𐐮𐑍 𐑄𐐰𐐻 𐑋𐐯𐑌𐐨 𐐱𐑂 𐑄𐐯𐑋 𐐸𐐰𐑂 𐐺𐐮𐑌 𐑁𐐳𐑊𐑁𐐮𐑊𐐼; 𐐷𐐩, 𐐰𐑌𐐼 𐐌 𐐫𐑊𐑅𐐬 𐑌𐐬 𐑄𐐰𐐻 𐐰𐑆 𐑋𐐯𐑌𐐨 𐑃𐐮𐑍𐑆 𐐰𐑆 𐐸𐐰𐑂 𐐺𐐮𐑌 𐐹𐑉𐐱𐑁𐐯𐑅𐐴𐐼 𐐿𐐲𐑌𐑅𐐲𐑉𐑌𐐮𐑍 𐐲𐑅 𐐼𐐵𐑌 𐐻𐐭 𐑄𐐮𐑅 𐐼𐐩, 𐐸𐐰𐑂 𐐺𐐮𐑌 𐑁𐐳𐑊𐑁𐐮𐑊𐐼, 𐐰𐑌𐐼 𐐰𐑆 𐑋𐐯𐑌𐐨 𐐰𐑆 𐑀𐐬 𐐺𐐨𐐷𐐱𐑌𐐼 𐑄𐐮𐑅 𐐼𐐩, 𐑋𐐲𐑅𐐻 𐑇𐐳𐑉𐑊𐐨 𐐿𐐲𐑋 𐐻𐐭 𐐹𐐰𐑅; 𐐸𐐶𐐯𐑉𐑁𐐫𐑉, 𐐌 𐐽𐐬𐑆 𐑄𐐨𐑆 𐑃𐐮𐑍𐑆, 𐐻𐐭 𐑁𐐮𐑌𐐮𐑇 𐑋𐐴 𐑉𐐯𐐿𐐲𐑉𐐼 𐐲𐐹𐐱𐑌 𐑄𐐯𐑋, 𐐸𐐶𐐮𐐽 𐑉𐐨𐑋𐐩𐑌𐐼𐐲𐑉 𐐱𐑂 𐑋𐐴 𐑉𐐯𐐿𐐲𐑉𐐼 𐐌 𐑇𐐰𐑊 𐐻𐐩𐐿 𐑁𐑉𐐱𐑋 𐑄 𐐹𐑊𐐩𐐻𐑅 𐐱𐑂 𐐤𐐨𐑁𐐴; 𐐰𐑌𐐼 𐐌 𐐿𐐰𐑌𐐱𐐻 𐑉𐐴𐐻 𐑄 𐐸𐐲𐑌𐐼𐑉𐐯𐐼𐑃 𐐹𐐪𐑉𐐻 𐐱𐑂 𐑄 𐑃𐐮𐑍𐑆 𐐱𐑂 𐑋𐐴 𐐹𐐨𐐹𐑊.

3. 𐐒𐐲𐐻 𐐺𐐨𐐸𐐬𐑊𐐼, 𐐌 𐑇𐐰𐑊 𐐻𐐩𐐿 𐑄𐐨𐑆 𐐹𐑊𐐩𐐻𐑅, 𐐸𐐶𐐮𐐽 𐐿𐐲𐑌𐐻𐐩𐑌 𐑄𐐨𐑆 𐐹𐑉𐐱𐑁𐐯𐑅𐐴𐐮𐑍𐑆 𐐰𐑌𐐼 𐑉𐐯𐑂𐐯𐑊𐐩𐑇𐐲𐑌𐑆, 𐐰𐑌𐐼 𐐹𐐳𐐻 𐑄𐐯𐑋 𐐶𐐮𐑄 𐑄 𐑉𐐨𐑋𐐩𐑌𐐼𐐲𐑉 𐐱𐑂 𐑋𐐴 𐑉𐐯𐐿𐐲𐑉𐐼, 𐑁𐐫𐑉 𐑄𐐩 𐐪𐑉 𐐽𐐦𐑅 𐐲𐑌𐐻𐐭 𐑋𐐨; 𐐰𐑌𐐼 𐐌 𐑌𐐬 𐑄𐐩 𐐶𐐮𐑊 𐐺𐐨 𐐽𐐦𐑅 𐐲𐑌𐐻𐐭 𐑋𐐴 𐐺𐑉𐐯𐑄𐑉𐐯𐑌. 𐐈𐑌𐐼 𐐌 𐐼𐐭 𐑄𐐮𐑅 𐑁𐐫𐑉 𐐩 𐐶𐐴𐑆 𐐹𐐲𐑉𐐹𐐲𐑅; 𐑁𐐫𐑉 𐑄𐐲𐑅 𐐮𐐻 𐐸𐐶𐐮𐑅𐐹𐐲𐑉𐐯𐑃 𐑋𐐨, 𐐰𐐿𐐫𐑉𐐼𐐮𐑍 𐐻𐐭 𐑄 𐐶𐐲𐑉𐐿𐐮𐑍𐑆 𐐱𐑂 𐑄 𐐝𐐹𐐮𐑉𐐮𐐻 𐐱𐑂 𐑄 𐐢𐐫𐑉𐐼 𐐸𐐶𐐮𐐽 𐐮𐑆 𐐮𐑌 𐑋𐐨. 𐐈𐑌𐐼 𐑌𐐵, 𐐌 𐐼𐐭 𐑌𐐱𐐻 𐑌𐐬 𐐫𐑊 𐑃𐐮𐑍𐑆; 𐐺𐐲𐐻 𐑄 𐐢𐐫𐑉𐐼 𐑌𐐬𐐯𐑃 𐐫𐑊 𐑃𐐮𐑍𐑆 𐐸𐐶𐐮𐐽 𐐪𐑉 𐐻𐐭 𐐿𐐲𐑋; 𐐸𐐶𐐯𐑉𐑁𐐫𐑉, 𐐸𐐨 𐐶𐐲𐑉𐐿𐐯𐑃 𐐮𐑌 𐑋𐐨 𐐻𐐭 𐐼𐐭 𐐰𐐿𐐫𐑉𐐼𐐮𐑍 𐐻𐐭 𐐸𐐮𐑆 𐐶𐐮𐑊. 𐐈𐑌𐐼 𐑋𐐴 𐐹𐑉𐐩𐐲𐑉 𐐻𐐭 𐐘𐐱𐐼 𐐮𐑆 𐐿𐐲𐑌𐑅𐐲𐑉𐑌𐐮𐑍 𐑋𐐴 𐐺𐑉𐐯𐑄𐑉𐐯𐑌, 𐑄𐐰𐐻 𐑄𐐩 𐑋𐐩 𐐶𐐲𐑌𐑅 𐐲𐑀𐐯𐑌 𐐿𐐲𐑋 𐐻𐐭 𐑄 𐑌𐐱𐑊𐐯𐐾 𐐱𐑂 𐐘𐐱𐐼; 𐐷𐐩, 𐑄 𐑉𐐨𐐼𐐯𐑋𐑇𐐲𐑌 𐐱𐑂 𐐗𐑉𐐴𐑅𐐻; 𐑄𐐰𐐻 𐑄𐐩 𐑋𐐩 𐐶𐐲𐑌𐑅 𐐲𐑀𐐯𐑌 𐐺𐐨 𐐩 𐐼𐐨𐑊𐐴𐐻𐑅𐐲𐑋 𐐹𐐨𐐹𐑊.

4. 𐐈𐑌𐐼 𐑌𐐵 𐐌, 𐐣𐐫𐑉𐑋𐐲𐑌, 𐐹𐑉𐐬𐑅𐐨𐐼 𐐻𐐭 𐑁𐐮𐑌𐐮𐑇 𐐵𐐻 𐑋𐐴 𐑉𐐯𐐿𐐲𐑉𐐼, 𐐸𐐶𐐮𐐽 𐐌 𐐻𐐩𐐿 𐑁𐑉𐐱𐑋 𐑄 𐐹𐑊𐐩𐐻𐑅 𐐱𐑂 𐐤𐐨𐑁𐐴; 𐐰𐑌𐐼 𐐌 𐑋𐐩𐐿 𐐮𐐻 𐐰𐐿𐐫𐑉𐐼𐐮𐑍 𐐻𐐭 𐑄 𐑌𐐱𐑊𐐯𐐾 𐐰𐑌𐐼 𐑄 𐐲𐑌𐐼𐐲𐑉𐑅𐐻𐐰𐑌𐐼𐐮𐑍 𐐸𐐶𐐮𐐽 𐐘𐐱𐐼 𐐸𐐰𐑃 𐑀𐐮𐑂𐑌 𐑋𐐨. 𐐐𐐶𐐯𐑉𐑁𐐫𐑉 𐐮𐐻 𐐿𐐩𐑋 𐐻𐐭 𐐹𐐰𐑅 𐑄𐐰𐐻 𐐰𐑁𐐻𐐲𐑉 𐐈𐑋𐐰𐑊𐐯𐐿𐐴 𐐸𐐰𐐼 𐐼𐐮𐑊𐐮𐑂𐐲𐑉𐐼 𐐲𐐹 𐑄𐐨𐑆 𐐹𐑊𐐩𐐻𐑅 𐐮𐑌𐐻𐐭 𐑄 𐐸𐐰𐑌𐐼𐑆 𐐱𐑂 𐐿𐐮𐑍 𐐒𐐯𐑌𐐾𐐲𐑋𐐮𐑌, 𐐸𐐨 𐐻𐐳𐐿 𐑄𐐯𐑋 𐐰𐑌𐐼 𐐹𐐳𐐻 𐑄𐐯𐑋 𐐶𐐮𐑄 𐑄 𐐲𐑄𐐲𐑉 𐐹𐑊𐐩𐐻𐑅,

𐐸𐐶𐐮𐐽 𐐿𐐲𐑌𐐻𐐩𐑌𐐼 𐑉𐐯𐐿𐐲𐑉𐐼𐑆 𐐸𐐶𐐮𐐽 𐐸𐐰𐐼 𐐺𐐮𐑌 𐐸𐐰𐑌𐐼𐐯𐐼 𐐼𐐵𐑌 𐐺𐐴 𐑄 𐐿𐐮𐑍𐑆, 𐑁𐑉𐐱𐑋 𐐾𐐯𐑌𐐯𐑉𐐩𐑇𐐲𐑌 𐐻𐐭 𐐾𐐯𐑌𐐯𐑉𐐩𐑇𐐲𐑌, 𐐲𐑌𐐻𐐮𐑊 𐑄 𐐼𐐩𐑆 𐐱𐑂 𐐿𐐮𐑍 𐐒𐐯𐑌𐐾𐐲𐑋𐐮𐑌; 𐐰𐑌𐐼 𐑄𐐩 𐐶𐐲𐑉 𐐸𐐰𐑌𐐼𐐯𐐼 𐐼𐐵𐑌 𐑁𐑉𐐱𐑋 𐐿𐐮𐑍 𐐒𐐯𐑌𐐾𐐲𐑋𐐮𐑌, 𐑁𐑉𐐱𐑋 𐐾𐐯𐑌𐐯𐑉𐐩𐑇𐐲𐑌 𐐻𐐭 𐐾𐐯𐑌𐐯𐑉𐐩𐑇𐐲𐑌, 𐐲𐑌𐐻𐐮𐑊 𐑄𐐩 𐐸𐐰𐑂 𐑁𐐫𐑊𐐲𐑌 𐐮𐑌𐐻𐐭 𐑋𐐴 𐐸𐐰𐑌𐐼𐑆. 𐐰𐑌𐐼 𐐌, 𐐣𐐫𐑉𐑋𐐲𐑌, 𐐹𐑉𐐩 𐐻𐐭 𐐘𐐱𐐼 𐑄𐐰𐐻 𐑄𐐩 𐑋𐐩 𐐺 𐐹𐑉𐐨𐑆𐐲𐑉𐑂𐐼 𐑁𐑉𐐱𐑋 𐑄𐐮𐑅 𐐻𐐴𐑋 𐐸𐐯𐑌𐑅𐑁𐐫𐑉𐑃. 𐐰𐑌𐐼 𐐌 𐑌𐐬 𐑄𐐰𐐻 𐑄𐐩 𐐶𐐮𐑊 𐐺 𐐹𐑉𐐨𐑆𐐲𐑉𐑂𐐼; 𐑁𐐫𐑉 𐑄𐐩𐑉 𐐪𐑉 𐑀𐑉𐐩𐐻 𐑃𐐮𐑍𐑆 𐑉𐐮𐐻𐑌 𐐲𐐹𐐱𐑌 𐑄𐐯𐑋, 𐐵𐐻 𐐱𐑂 𐐸𐐶𐐮𐐽 𐑋𐐴 𐐹𐐨𐐹𐑊 𐐰𐑌𐐼 𐑄𐐩𐑉 𐐺𐑉𐐯𐑄𐑉𐐯𐑌, 𐑇𐐰𐑊 𐐺 𐐾𐐲𐐾𐐼 𐐰𐐻 𐑄 𐑀𐑉𐐩𐐻 𐐰𐑌𐐼 𐑊𐐰𐑅𐐻 𐐼𐐩, 𐐰𐐿𐐫𐑉𐐼𐐮𐑍 𐐻𐐭 𐑄 𐐶𐐲𐑉𐐼 𐐱𐑂 𐐘𐐱𐐼 𐐸𐐶𐐮𐐽 𐐮𐑆 𐑉𐐮𐐻𐑌.

5. 𐐰𐑌𐐼 𐑌𐐵, 𐐿𐐲𐑌𐑅𐐲𐑉𐑌𐐮𐑍 𐑄𐐮𐑅 𐐿𐐮𐑍 𐐒𐐯𐑌𐐾𐐲𐑋𐐮𐑌: 𐐸𐐨 𐐸𐐰𐐼 𐑅𐐲𐑋𐐸𐐶𐐱𐐻 𐐱𐑂 𐐿𐐲𐑌𐐻𐐯𐑌𐑇𐐲𐑌𐑆 𐐲𐑋𐐲𐑍 𐐸𐐮𐑆 𐐬𐑌 𐐹𐐨𐐹𐑊. 𐐰𐑌𐐼 𐐮𐐻 𐐿𐐩𐑋 𐐻𐐭 𐐹𐐰𐑅 𐐫𐑊𐑅𐐬, 𐑄𐐰𐐻 𐑄 𐐪𐑉𐑋𐐨𐑆 𐐱𐑂 𐑄 𐐢𐐰𐑋𐐲𐑌𐐴𐐻𐑅 𐐿𐐩𐑋 𐐼𐐵𐑌 𐐵𐐻 𐐱𐑂 𐑄 𐑊𐐰𐑌𐐼 𐐱𐑂 𐐤𐐨𐑁𐐴, 𐐻𐐭 𐐺𐐰𐐻𐑊 𐐰𐑀𐐯𐑌𐑅𐐻 𐐸𐐮𐑆 𐐹𐐨𐐹𐑊. 𐐒𐐲𐐻 𐐺𐐨𐐸𐐬𐑊𐐼, 𐐿𐐮𐑍 𐐒𐐯𐑌𐐾𐐲𐑋𐐮𐑌 𐑀𐐰𐑄𐐲𐑉𐐼 𐐻𐐭𐑀𐐯𐑄𐐲𐑉 𐐸𐐮𐑆 𐐪𐑉𐑋𐐨𐑆, 𐐰𐑌𐐼 𐐸𐐨 𐐼𐐮𐐼 𐑅𐐻𐐰𐑌𐐼 𐐰𐑀𐐯𐑌𐑅𐐻 𐑄𐐯𐑋; 𐐰𐑌𐐼 𐐸𐐨 𐐼𐐮𐐼 𐑁𐐴𐐻 𐐶𐐮𐑄 𐑄 𐑅𐐻𐑉𐐯𐑍𐑃 𐐱𐑂 𐐸𐐮𐑆 𐐬𐑌 𐐪𐑉𐑋, 𐐶𐐮𐑄 𐑄 𐑅𐐬𐑉𐐼 𐐱𐑂 𐐢𐐩𐐺𐐲𐑌; 𐐰𐑌𐐼 𐐮𐑌 𐑄 𐑅𐐻𐑉𐐯𐑍𐑃 𐐱𐑂 𐑄 𐐢𐐫𐑉𐐼 𐑄𐐩 𐐼𐐮𐐼 𐐿𐐲𐑌𐐻𐐯𐑌𐐼 𐐰𐑀𐐯𐑌𐑅𐐻 𐑄𐐩𐑉 𐐯𐑌𐐯𐑋𐐨𐑆, 𐐲𐑌𐐻𐐮𐑊 𐑄𐐩 𐐸𐐰𐐼 𐑅𐑊𐐩𐑌 𐑋𐐯𐑌𐐨 𐑃𐐵𐑆𐐲𐑌𐐼𐑆 𐐱𐑂 𐑄 𐐢𐐰𐑋𐐲𐑌𐐴𐐻𐑅. 𐐰𐑌𐐼 𐐮𐐻 𐐿𐐩𐑋 𐐻𐐭 𐐹𐐰𐑅 𐑄𐐰𐐻 𐑄𐐩 𐐼𐐮𐐼 𐐿𐐲𐑌𐐻𐐯𐑌𐐼 𐐰𐑀𐐯𐑌𐑅𐐻 𐑄 𐐢𐐰𐑋𐐲𐑌𐐴𐐻𐑅, 𐐲𐑌𐐻𐐮𐑊 𐑄𐐩 𐐸𐐰𐐼 𐐼𐑉𐐮𐑂𐑌 𐑄𐐯𐑋 𐐵𐐻 𐐱𐑂 𐐫𐑊 𐑄 𐑊𐐰𐑌𐐼𐑆 𐐱𐑂 𐑄𐐩𐑉 𐐮𐑌𐐸𐐯𐑉𐐮𐐻𐐲𐑌𐑅.

6. 𐐰𐑌𐐼 𐐮𐐻 𐐿𐐩𐑋 𐐻𐐭 𐐹𐐰𐑅 𐑄𐐰𐐻 𐐪𐑁𐐻𐐲𐑉 𐑄𐐩𐑉 𐐸𐐰𐐼 𐐺𐐮𐑌 𐑁𐐫𐑊𐑅 𐐗𐑉𐐴𐑅𐐻𐑅, 𐐰𐑌𐐼 𐑄𐐩𐑉 𐑋𐐵𐑄𐑆 𐐸𐐰𐐼 𐐺𐐮𐑌 𐑇𐐲𐐻, 𐐰𐑌𐐼 𐑄𐐩 𐐹𐐲𐑌𐐮𐑇𐐻 𐐰𐐿𐐫𐑉𐐼𐐮𐑍 𐐻𐐭 𐑄𐐩𐑉 𐐿𐑉𐐴𐑋𐑆; 𐐰𐑌𐐼 𐐪𐑁𐐻𐐲𐑉 𐑄𐐩𐑉 𐐸𐐰𐐼 𐐺𐐮𐑌 𐑁𐐫𐑊𐑅 𐐹𐑉𐐱𐑁𐐯𐐻𐑅, 𐐰𐑌𐐼 𐑁𐐫𐑊𐑅 𐐹𐑉𐐨𐐽𐐲𐑉𐑆 𐐰𐑌𐐼 𐐻𐐨𐐽𐐲𐑉𐑆 𐐲𐑋𐐲𐑍 𐑄 𐐹𐐨𐐹𐑊, 𐐰𐑌𐐼 𐐫𐑊 𐑄𐐨𐑆 𐐸𐐰𐑂𐐮𐑍 𐐺𐐮𐑌 𐐹𐐲𐑌𐐮𐑇𐐻 𐐰𐐿𐐫𐑉𐐼𐐮𐑍 𐐻𐐭 𐑄𐐩𐑉 𐐿𐑉𐐴𐑋𐑆; 𐐰𐑌𐐼 𐐪𐑁𐐻𐐲𐑉 𐑄𐐩𐑉 𐐸𐐰𐑂𐐮𐑍 𐐺𐐮𐑌 𐑋𐐲𐐽 𐐿𐐲𐑌𐐻𐐯𐑌𐑇𐐲𐑌 𐐰𐑌𐐼 𐑋𐐯𐑌𐐨 𐐼𐐮𐑅𐐯𐑌𐑇𐐲𐑌𐑆, 𐐲𐐶𐐩 𐐲𐑌𐐻𐐭 𐑄 𐐢𐐰𐑋𐐲𐑌𐐴𐐻𐑅, 𐐺𐐨𐐸𐐬𐑊𐐼, 𐐮𐐻 𐐿𐐩𐑋 𐐻𐐭 𐐹𐐰𐑅 𐑄𐐰𐐻 𐐿𐐮𐑍 𐐒𐐯𐑌𐐾𐐲𐑋𐐮𐑌, 𐐶𐐮𐑄 𐑄 𐐲𐑅𐐮𐑅𐐻𐐲𐑌𐑅 𐐱𐑂 𐑄 𐐸𐐬𐑊𐐨 𐐹𐑉𐐱𐑁𐐯𐐻𐑅 𐐸𐐭 𐐶𐐲𐑉 𐐲𐑋𐐲𐑍 𐐸𐐮𐑆 𐐹𐐨𐐹𐑊; 𐑁𐐫𐑉 𐐺𐐨𐐸𐐬𐑊𐐼, 𐐿𐐮𐑍 𐐒𐐯𐑌𐐾𐐲𐑋𐐮𐑌 𐐶𐐱𐑆 𐐲 𐐸𐐬𐑊𐐨 𐑋𐐰𐑌, 𐐰𐑌𐐼 𐐸𐐨 𐐼𐐮𐐼 𐑉𐐩𐑌 𐐬𐑂𐐲𐑉 𐐸𐐮𐑆 𐐹𐐨𐐹𐑊 𐐮𐑌 𐑉𐐴𐐽𐐲𐑅𐑌𐐯𐑅; 𐐰𐑌𐐼 𐑄𐐩𐑉 𐐶𐐲𐑉 𐑋𐐯𐑌𐐨 𐐸𐐬𐑊𐐨 𐑋𐐯𐑌 𐐮𐑌 𐑄 𐑊𐐰𐑌𐐼; 𐐰𐑌𐐼 𐑄𐐩 𐐼𐐮𐐼 𐑅𐐹𐐨𐐿 𐑄 𐐶𐐲𐑉𐐼 𐐱𐑂 𐐘𐐱𐐼 𐐶𐐮𐑄 𐐹𐐵𐐲𐑉 𐐰𐑌𐐼 𐐶𐐮𐑄 𐐫𐑃𐐲𐑉𐐮𐐻𐐨; 𐐰𐑌𐐼 𐑄𐐩 𐐼𐐮𐐼 𐐷𐐭𐑆 𐑋𐐲𐐽 𐑇𐐪𐑉𐐹𐑌𐐯𐑅 𐐺𐐨𐐿𐐫𐑆 𐐱𐑂 𐑄 𐑅𐐻𐐮𐑁𐑌𐐯𐐿𐐯𐐼𐑌𐐯𐑅 𐐱𐑂 𐑄 𐐹𐐨𐐹𐑊; 𐐸𐐶𐐯𐑉𐑁𐐫𐑉, 𐐶𐐮𐑄 𐑄 𐐸𐐯𐑊𐐹 𐐱𐑂 𐑄𐐨𐑆, 𐐿𐐮𐑍 𐐒𐐯𐑌𐐾𐐲𐑋𐐮𐑌, 𐐺𐐴 𐑊𐐩𐐺𐐲𐑉𐐮𐑍 𐐶𐐮𐑄 𐐫𐑊 𐑄 𐑋𐐴𐐻 𐐱𐑂 𐐸𐐮𐑆 𐐺𐐱𐐼𐐨 𐐰𐑌𐐼 𐑄 𐑁𐐰𐐿𐐲𐑊𐐻𐐨 𐐱𐑂 𐐸𐐮𐑆 𐐸𐐬𐑊 𐑅𐐬𐑊, 𐐰𐑌𐐼 𐐫𐑊𐑅𐐬 𐑄 𐐹𐑉𐐱𐑁𐐯𐐻𐑅, 𐐼𐐮𐐼 𐐶𐐲𐑌𐑅 𐑋𐐬𐑉 𐐯𐑅𐐻𐐰𐐺𐑊𐐮𐑇 𐐹𐐨𐑅 𐐮𐑌 𐑄 𐑊𐐰𐑌𐐼.

𐐜 𐐒𐐳𐐿 𐐱𐑂 𐐣𐐬𐑆𐐴𐐲.

𐐗𐐰𐐹𐐻𐐲𐑉 I.

1. 𐐰𐑌𐐼 𐑌𐐵 𐑄𐐩𐑉 𐐶𐐱𐑆 𐑌𐐬 𐑋𐐬𐑉 𐐿𐐱𐑌𐐻𐐯𐑌𐑇𐐲𐑌 𐐮𐑌 𐐫𐑊 𐑄 𐑊𐐰𐑌𐐼 𐐱𐑂 𐐞𐐩𐑉𐐲𐐸𐐯𐑋𐑊𐐲, 𐐲𐑋𐐲𐑍 𐐫𐑊 𐑄 𐐹𐐨𐐹𐑊 𐐸𐐭 𐐺𐐨𐑊𐐱𐑍𐐼 𐐻𐐭 𐐿𐐮𐑍 𐐒𐐯𐑌𐐾𐐲𐑋𐐮𐑌, 𐑅𐐬 𐑄𐐰𐐻 𐐿𐐮𐑍 𐐒𐐯𐑌𐐾𐐲𐑋𐐮𐑌 𐐸𐐰𐐼 𐐿𐐱𐑌𐐻𐐮𐑌𐐷𐐭𐐲𐑊 𐐹𐐨𐑅 𐐫𐑊 𐑄 𐑉𐐨𐑋𐐩𐑌𐐼𐐲𐑉 𐐱𐑂 𐐸𐐮𐑆 𐐼𐐩𐑆. 𐐰𐑌𐐼 𐐮𐐻 𐐿𐐩𐑋 𐐻𐐭 𐐹𐐰𐑅 𐑄𐐰𐐻 𐐸𐐨 𐐸𐐰𐐼 𐑃𐑉𐐨 𐑅𐐲𐑌𐑆; 𐐰𐑌𐐼 𐐸𐐨 𐐿𐐫𐑊𐐼 𐑄𐐩𐑉 𐑌𐐩𐑋𐑆 𐐣𐐬𐑆𐐴𐐲, 𐐰𐑌𐐼 𐐐𐐯𐑊𐐬𐑉𐐲𐑋, 𐐰𐑌𐐼 𐐐𐐨𐑊𐐲𐑋𐐲𐑌. 𐐰𐑌𐐼 𐐸𐐨 𐐿𐐫𐑆𐐼 𐑄𐐰𐐻 𐑄𐐩 𐑇𐐳𐐼 𐐺𐐨 𐐻𐐫𐐻 𐐮𐑌 𐐫𐑊 𐑄 𐑊𐐰𐑍𐑀𐐶𐐩𐐾 𐐱𐑂 𐐸𐐮𐑆 𐑁𐐪𐑄𐐲𐑉𐑆, 𐑄𐐰𐐻 𐑄𐐩𐑉𐐺𐐴 𐑄𐐩 𐑋𐐴𐐻 𐐺𐐨𐐿𐐲𐑋 𐑋𐐯𐑌 𐐱𐑂 𐐲𐑌𐐼𐐲𐑉𐑅𐐻𐐰𐑌𐐼𐐮𐑍; 𐐰𐑌𐐼 𐑄𐐰𐐻 𐑄𐐩 𐑋𐐴𐐻 𐑌𐐬 𐐿𐐱𐑌𐑅𐐲𐑉𐑌𐐮𐑍 𐑄 𐐹𐑉𐐱𐑁𐐯𐑅𐐨𐑆 𐐸𐐶𐐮𐐽 𐐸𐐰𐐼 𐐺𐐮𐑌 𐑅𐐹𐐬𐐿𐐲𐑌 𐐺𐐴 𐑄 𐑋𐐵𐑃𐑅 𐐱𐑂 𐑄𐐩𐑉 𐑁𐐪𐑄𐐲𐑉𐑆, 𐐸𐐶𐐮𐐽 𐐶𐐲𐑉 𐐼𐐨𐑊𐐮𐑂𐐲𐑉𐐼 𐑄𐐯𐑋 𐐺𐐴 𐑄 𐐸𐐰𐑌𐐼 𐐱𐑂 𐑄 𐐢𐐫𐑉𐐼. 𐐰𐑌𐐼 𐐸𐐨 𐐫𐑊𐑅𐐬 𐐻𐐫𐐻 𐑄𐐯𐑋 𐐿𐐱𐑌𐑅𐐲𐑉𐑌𐐮𐑍 𐑄 𐑉𐐯𐐿𐐲𐑉𐐼𐑆 𐐸𐐶𐐮𐐽 𐐶𐐲𐑉 𐐯𐑌𐑀𐑉𐐩𐑂𐐲𐑌 𐐱𐑌 𐑄 𐐹𐑊𐐩𐐻𐑅 𐐱𐑂 𐐺𐑉𐐰𐑅, 𐑅𐐩𐐮𐑍, 𐑋𐐴 𐑅𐐲𐑌𐑆, 𐐌 𐐶𐐳𐐼 𐑄𐐰𐐻 𐐷𐐨 𐑇𐐳𐐼 𐑉𐐨𐑋𐐯𐑋𐐺𐐲𐑉 𐑄𐐰𐐻 𐐶𐐲𐑉 𐐮𐐻 𐑌𐐱𐐻 𐑁𐐫𐑉 𐑄𐐨𐑆 𐐹𐑊𐐩𐐻𐑅, 𐐸𐐶𐐮𐐽 𐐿𐐱𐑌𐐻𐐩𐑌 𐑄𐐨𐑆 𐑉𐐯𐐿𐐲𐑉𐐼𐑆 𐐰𐑌𐐼 𐑄𐐨𐑆 𐐿𐐱𐑋𐐰𐑌𐐼𐑋𐐯𐑌𐐻𐑅, 𐐶𐐨 𐑋𐐲𐑅𐐻 𐐸𐐰𐑂 𐑅𐐲𐑁𐐲𐑉𐐼 𐐮𐑌 𐐮𐑀𐑌𐐬𐑉𐐰𐑌𐑅, 𐐨𐑂𐐲𐑌 𐐰𐐻 𐑄𐐮𐑅 𐐹𐑉𐐯𐑆𐐯𐑌𐐻 𐐻𐐴𐑋, 𐑌𐐱𐐻 𐑌𐐬𐐮𐑍 𐑄 𐑋𐐮𐑅𐐻𐐲𐑉𐐨𐑆 𐐱𐑂 𐐘𐐱𐐼; 𐑁𐐫𐑉 𐐮𐐻 𐐶𐐲𐑉 𐑌𐐱𐐻 𐐹𐐱𐑅𐐮𐐺𐐲𐑊 𐑄𐐰𐐻 𐐵𐑉 𐑁𐐪𐑄𐐲𐑉, 𐐢𐐨𐐸𐐴, 𐐿𐐳𐐼 𐐸𐐰𐑂 𐑉𐐨𐑋𐐯𐑋𐐺𐐲𐑉𐐼 𐐫𐑊 𐑄𐐨𐑆 𐑃𐐮𐑍𐑆, 𐐻𐐭 𐐸𐐰𐑂 𐐻𐐫𐐻 𐑄𐐯𐑋 𐐻𐐭 𐐸𐐮𐑆 𐐽𐐮𐑊𐐼𐑉𐐯𐑌, 𐐯𐐿𐑅𐐯𐐹𐐻 𐐮𐐻 𐐶𐐲𐑉 𐑁𐐫𐑉 𐑄 𐐸𐐯𐑊𐐹 𐐱𐑂 𐑄𐐨𐑆 𐐹𐑊𐐩𐐻𐑅: 𐑁𐐫𐑉 𐐸𐐨 𐐸𐐰𐑂𐐮𐑍 𐐺𐐮𐑌 𐐻𐐫𐐻 𐐮𐑌 𐑄 𐑊𐐰𐑍𐑀𐐶𐐩𐐾 𐐱𐑂 𐑄 𐐀𐐾𐐮𐐹𐑇𐐲𐑌𐑆, 𐑄𐐩𐑉𐑁𐐬𐑉 𐐸𐐨 𐐿𐐳𐐼 𐑉𐐨𐐼 𐑄𐐨𐑆 𐐯𐑌𐑀𐑉𐐩𐑂𐐮𐑍𐑆, 𐐰𐑌𐐼 𐐻𐐨𐐽 𐑄𐐯𐑋 𐐻𐐭 𐐸𐐮𐑆 𐐽𐐮𐑊𐐼𐑉𐐯𐑌, 𐑄𐐰𐐻 𐑄𐐩𐑉𐐺𐐴 𐑄𐐩 𐐿𐐳𐐼 𐐻𐐨𐐽 𐑄𐐯𐑋 𐐻𐐭 𐑄𐐩𐑉 𐐽𐐮𐑊𐐼𐑉𐐯𐑌, 𐐰𐑌𐐼 𐑅𐐬 𐑁𐐳𐑊𐑁𐐮𐑊𐐮𐑍 𐑄 𐐿𐐱𐑋𐐰𐑌𐐼𐑋𐐯𐑌𐐻𐑅 𐐱𐑂 𐐘𐐱𐐼, 𐐨𐑂𐐲𐑌 𐐼𐐵𐑌 𐐻𐐭 𐑄𐐮𐑅 𐐹𐑉𐐯𐑆𐐯𐑌𐐻 𐐻𐐴𐑋. 𐐌 𐑅𐐩 𐐲𐑌𐐻𐐭 𐐷𐐭, 𐑋𐐴 𐑅𐐲𐑌𐑆, 𐐶𐐲𐑉 𐐮𐐻 𐑌𐐱𐐻 𐑁𐐫𐑉 𐑄𐐨𐑆 𐑃𐐮𐑍𐑆, 𐐸𐐶𐐮𐐽 𐐸𐐰𐑂 𐐺𐐮𐑌 𐐿𐐯𐐹𐐻 𐐰𐑌𐐼 𐐹𐑉𐐨𐑆𐐲𐑉𐑂𐐼 𐐺𐐴 𐑄 𐐸𐐰𐑌𐐼 𐐱𐑂 𐐘𐐱𐐼, 𐑄𐐰𐐻 𐐶𐐨 𐑋𐐴𐐻 𐑉𐐨𐐼 𐐰𐑌𐐼 𐐲𐑌𐐼𐐲𐑉𐑅𐐻𐐰𐑌𐐼 𐐱𐑂 𐐸𐐮𐑆 𐑋𐐮𐑅𐐻𐐲𐑉𐐨𐑆, 𐐰𐑌𐐼 𐐸𐐰𐑂 𐐸𐐮𐑆 𐐿𐐱𐑋𐐰𐑌𐐼𐑋𐐯𐑌𐐻𐑅 𐐫𐑊𐐶𐐩𐑆 𐐺𐐨𐑁𐐬𐑉 𐐵𐑉 𐐴𐑆, 𐑄𐐰𐐻 𐐨𐑂𐐲𐑌 𐐵𐑉 𐑁𐐪𐑄𐐲𐑉𐑆 𐐶𐐳𐐼 𐐸𐐰𐑂 𐐼𐐶𐐮𐑌𐐼𐑊𐐼 𐐮𐑌 𐐲𐑌𐐺𐐨𐑊𐐨𐑁, 𐐰𐑌𐐼 𐐶𐐨 𐑇𐐳𐐼 𐐸𐐰𐑂 𐐺𐐮𐑌 𐑊𐐴𐐿 𐐲𐑌𐐻𐐭 𐐵𐑉 𐐺𐑉𐐯𐑄𐑉𐐯𐑌, 𐑄 𐐢𐐩𐑋𐐲𐑌𐐴𐐻𐑅, 𐐸𐐭 𐑌𐐬 𐑌𐐲𐑃𐐮𐑍 𐐿𐐱𐑌𐑅𐐲𐑉𐑌𐐮𐑍 𐑄𐐨𐑆 𐑃𐐮𐑍𐑆, 𐐫𐑉 𐐨𐑂𐐲𐑌 𐐼𐐭 𐑌𐐱𐐻 𐐺𐐨𐑊𐐨𐑂 𐑄𐐯𐑋 𐐸𐐶𐐯𐑌 𐑄𐐩 𐐪𐑉 𐐻𐐫𐐻 𐑄𐐯𐑋, 𐐺𐐨𐐿𐐫𐑆 𐐱𐑂 𐑄 𐐻𐑉𐐲𐐼𐐮𐑇𐐲𐑌𐑆 𐐱𐑂 𐑄𐐩𐑉 𐑁𐐪𐑄𐐲𐑉𐑆, 𐐸𐐶𐐮𐐽 𐐪𐑉 𐑌𐐱𐐻 𐐿𐐱𐑉𐐯𐐿𐐻. 𐐄 𐑋𐐴 𐑅𐐲𐑌𐑆, 𐐌 𐐶𐐳𐐼 𐑄𐐰𐐻 𐐷𐐨 𐑇𐐳𐐼 𐑉𐐨𐑋𐐯𐑋𐐺𐐲𐑉 𐑄𐐰𐐻 𐑄𐐨𐑆 𐑅𐐩𐐮𐑍𐑆 𐐪𐑉 𐐻𐑉𐐭; 𐐰𐑌𐐼 𐐫𐑊𐑅𐐬, 𐑄𐐰𐐻 𐑄𐐨𐑆 𐑉𐐯𐐿𐐲𐑉𐐼𐑆 𐐪𐑉 𐐻𐑉𐐭. 𐐰𐑌𐐼 𐐺𐐨𐐸𐐬𐑊𐐼, 𐐫𐑊𐑅𐐬 𐑄 𐐹𐑊𐐩𐐻𐑅 𐐱𐑂 𐐤𐐨𐑁𐐴, 𐐸𐐶𐐮𐐽 𐐿𐐱𐑌𐐻𐐩𐑌 𐑄 𐑉𐐯𐐿𐐲𐑉𐐼𐑆 𐐰𐑌𐐼 𐑄 𐑅𐐩𐐮𐑍𐑆 𐐱𐑂 𐐵𐑉 𐑁𐐪𐑄𐐲𐑉𐑆 𐑁𐑉𐐱𐑋 𐑄 𐐻𐐴𐑋 𐑄𐐩 𐑊𐐯𐑁𐐻 𐐖𐐨𐑉𐐭𐑅𐐲𐑊𐐯𐑋 𐐲𐑌𐐻𐐮𐑊 𐑌𐐵; 𐐰𐑌𐐼 𐑄𐐩 𐐪𐑉 𐐻𐑉𐐭; 𐐰𐑌𐐼 𐐶𐐨 𐐿𐐰𐑌 𐑌𐐬 𐐱𐑂 𐑄𐐩𐑉 𐑇𐐭𐑉𐐮𐐻𐐨, 𐐺𐐨𐐿𐐫𐑆 𐐶𐐨 𐐸𐐰𐑂 𐑄𐐯𐑋 𐐺𐐨𐑁𐐬𐑉 𐐵𐑉 𐐴𐑆. 𐐰𐑌𐐼 𐑌𐐵, 𐑋𐐴 𐑅𐐲𐑌𐑆, 𐐌 𐐶𐐳𐐼 𐑄𐐰𐐻 𐐷𐐨 𐑇𐐳𐐼 𐑉𐐨𐑋𐐯𐑋𐐺𐐲𐑉 𐐻𐐭 𐑅𐐲𐑉𐐽 𐑄𐐯𐑋 𐐼𐐮𐑊𐐮𐐾𐐯𐑌𐐻𐑊𐐨, 𐑄𐐰𐐻 𐐷𐐨 𐑋𐐩 𐐹𐑉𐐱𐑁𐐮𐐻 𐑄𐐩𐑉𐐺𐐴; 𐐰𐑌𐐼 𐐌 𐐶𐐳𐐼 𐑄𐐰𐐻 𐐷𐐨 𐑇𐐳𐐼 𐐿𐐨𐐹 𐑄 𐐿𐐱𐑋𐐰𐑌𐐼𐑋𐐯𐑌𐐻𐑅 𐐱𐑂 𐐘𐐱𐐼, 𐑄𐐰𐐻 𐐷𐐨 𐑋𐐩 𐐹𐑉𐐱𐑅𐐹𐐲𐑉 𐐮𐑌 𐑄 𐑊𐐰𐑌𐐼, 𐐰𐐿𐐫𐑉𐐼𐐮𐑍 𐐻𐐭 𐑄 𐐹𐑉𐐱𐑋𐐮𐑅𐐯𐑆 𐐸𐐶𐐮𐐽 𐑄 𐐢𐐫𐑉𐐼 𐑋𐐩𐐼 𐐲𐑌𐐻𐐭 𐐵𐑉 𐑁𐐪𐑄𐐲𐑉𐑆. 𐐰𐑌𐐼 𐑋𐐯𐑌𐐨 𐑋𐐬𐑉 𐑃𐐮𐑍𐑆 𐐼𐐮𐐼 𐐿𐐮𐑍 𐐒𐐯𐑌𐐾𐐲𐑋𐐮𐑌 𐐻𐐨𐐽 𐐸𐐮𐑆 𐑅𐐲𐑌𐑆, 𐐸𐐶𐐮𐐽 𐐪𐑉 𐑌𐐱𐐻 𐑉𐐮𐐻𐐲𐑌 𐐮𐑌 𐑄𐐮𐑅 𐐺𐐳𐐿.

2. 𐐰𐑌𐐼 𐐮𐐻 𐐿𐐩𐑋 𐐻𐐭 𐐹𐐰𐑅 𐑄𐐰𐐻 𐐰𐑁𐐻𐐲𐑉 𐐿𐐮𐑍 𐐒𐐯𐑌𐐾𐐲𐑋𐐮𐑌 𐐸𐐰𐐼 𐑋𐐩𐐼 𐐰𐑌 𐐯𐑌𐐼 𐐱𐑂 𐐻𐐨𐐽𐐮𐑍 𐐸𐐮𐑆

𐑅𐐲𐑌𐑆, 𐑄𐐰𐐻 𐐸𐐨 𐐶𐐰𐐿𐑅𐐻 𐐬𐑊𐐼, 𐐰𐑌𐐼 𐐸𐐨 𐑅𐐫 𐑄𐐰𐐻 𐐸𐐨 𐑋𐐲𐑅𐐻 𐑂𐐯𐑉𐐨 𐑅𐐭𐑌 𐑀𐐬 𐑄 𐐶𐐩 𐐱𐑂 𐐫𐑊 𐑄 𐐲𐑉𐑃; 𐑄𐐯𐑉𐑁𐐬𐑉, 𐐸𐐨 𐑃𐐫𐐻 𐐮𐐻 𐐯𐐿𐑅𐐹𐐨𐐼𐐨𐐯𐑌𐐻 𐑄𐐰𐐻 𐐸𐐨 𐑇𐐳𐐼 𐐿𐐱𐑌𐑁𐐲𐑉 𐑄 𐐿𐐮𐑍𐐼𐐲𐑋 𐐲𐐹𐐱𐑌 𐐶𐐲𐑌 𐐱𐑂 𐐸𐐮𐑆 𐑅𐐲𐑌𐑆. 𐐜𐐯𐑉𐑁𐐬𐑉, 𐐸𐐨 𐐸𐐰𐐼 𐐣𐐬𐑅𐐴𐐲 𐐺𐑉𐐫𐐻 𐐺𐐨𐑁𐐬𐑉 𐐸𐐮𐑋; 𐐰𐑌𐐼 𐑄𐐨𐑆 𐐪𐑉 𐑄 𐐶𐐲𐑉𐐼𐑆 𐐸𐐶𐐮𐐽 𐐸𐐨 𐑅𐐹𐐩𐐿 𐐲𐑌𐐻𐐭 𐐸𐐮𐑋, 𐑅𐐩𐐮𐑍; 𐐣𐐴 𐑅𐐲𐑌, 𐐌 𐐶𐐳𐐼 𐑄𐐰𐐻 𐐷𐐨 𐑇𐐳𐐼 𐑋𐐩𐐿 𐐲 𐐹𐑉𐐱𐐿𐑊𐐲𐑋𐐩𐑇𐐲𐑌 𐑃𐑉𐐭𐐵𐐻 𐐫𐑊 𐑄𐐮𐑅 𐑊𐐰𐑌𐐼, 𐐲𐑋𐐲𐑍 𐐫𐑊 𐑄𐐮𐑅 𐐹𐐨𐐹𐑊, 𐐫𐑉 𐑄 𐐹𐐨𐐹𐑊 𐐱𐑂 𐐞𐐰𐑉𐐲𐐸𐐯𐑋𐑊𐐲, 𐐰𐑌𐐼 𐑄 𐐹𐐨𐐹𐑊 𐐱𐑂 𐐣𐐬𐑅𐐴𐐲 𐐸𐐭 𐐼𐐶𐐯𐑊 𐐮𐑌 𐑄 𐑊𐐰𐑌𐐼, 𐑄𐐰𐐻 𐑄𐐯𐑉𐐺𐐴 𐑄𐐩 𐑋𐐩 𐐺𐐨 𐑀𐐰𐑄𐐲𐑉𐐼 𐐻𐐳𐑀𐐯𐑄𐐲𐑉; 𐑁𐐫𐑉 𐐱𐑌 𐑄 𐑋𐐱𐑉𐐬 𐐌 𐑇𐐰𐑊 𐐹𐑉𐐬𐐿𐑊𐐩𐑋 𐐲𐑌𐐻𐐭 𐑄𐐮𐑅 𐑋𐐴 𐐹𐐨𐐹𐑊 𐐵𐐻 𐐱𐑂 𐑋𐐴𐑌 𐐬𐑌 𐑋𐐵𐑃, 𐑄𐐰𐐻 𐑄𐐵 𐐪𐑉𐐻 𐐲 𐐿𐐮𐑍 𐐰𐑌𐐼 𐐲 𐑉𐐭𐑊𐐲𐑉 𐐬𐑂𐐲𐑉 𐑄𐐮𐑅 𐐹𐐨𐐹𐑊, 𐐸𐐭𐑋 𐑄 𐐢𐐫𐑉𐐼 𐐵𐑉 𐐘𐐱𐐼 𐐸𐐰𐑃 𐑀𐐮𐑂𐑌 𐐲𐑅. 𐐈𐑌𐐼 𐑋𐐬𐑉𐐬𐑂𐐲𐑉, 𐐌 𐑇𐐰𐑊 𐑀𐐮𐑂 𐑄𐐮𐑅 𐐹𐐨𐐹𐑊 𐐲 𐑌𐐩𐑋, 𐑄𐐰𐐻 𐑄𐐯𐑉𐐺𐐴 𐑄𐐩 𐑋𐐩 𐐺𐐨 𐐼𐐮𐑅𐐻𐐮𐑍𐑀𐐶𐐮𐑇𐐻 𐐲𐐺𐐲𐑂 𐐫𐑊 𐑄 𐐹𐐨𐐹𐑊 𐐸𐐶𐐮𐐽 𐑄 𐐢𐐫𐑉𐐼 𐐘𐐱𐐼 𐐸𐐰𐑃 𐐺𐑉𐐫𐐻 𐐵𐐻 𐐱𐑂 𐑄 𐑊𐐰𐑌𐐼 𐐱𐑂 𐐖𐐨𐑉𐐭𐑅𐐲𐑊𐐯𐑋; 𐐰𐑌𐐼 𐑄𐐮𐑅 𐐌 𐐼𐐭, 𐐺𐐨𐐿𐐫𐑆 𐑄𐐩 𐐸𐐰𐑂 𐐺𐐮𐑌 𐐲 𐐼𐐮𐑊𐐮𐐾𐐯𐑌𐐻 𐐹𐐨𐐹𐑊 𐐮𐑌 𐐿𐐨𐐹𐐮𐑍 𐑄 𐐿𐐱𐑋𐐰𐑌𐐼𐑋𐐯𐑌𐐻𐑅 𐐱𐑂 𐑄 𐐢𐐫𐑉𐐼. 𐐈𐑌𐐼 𐐌 𐑀𐐮𐑂 𐐲𐑌𐐻𐐭 𐑄𐐯𐑋 𐐲 𐑌𐐩𐑋 𐑄𐐰𐐻 𐑌𐐯𐑂𐐲𐑉 𐑇𐐰𐑊 𐐺𐐨 𐐺𐑊𐐱𐐻𐐯𐐼 𐐵𐐻, 𐐯𐐿𐑅𐐯𐐹𐐻 𐐮𐐻 𐐺𐐨 𐑃𐑉𐐭 𐐻𐑉𐐰𐑌𐑆𐑀𐑉𐐯𐑇𐐲𐑌. 𐐏𐐩, 𐐰𐑌𐐼 𐑋𐐬𐑉𐐬𐑂𐐲𐑉 𐐌 𐑅𐐩 𐐲𐑌𐐻𐐭 𐐷𐐭, 𐑄𐐰𐐻 𐐮𐑁 𐑄𐐮𐑅 𐐸𐐴𐑊𐐨 𐑁𐐩𐑂𐐲𐑉𐐼 𐐹𐐨𐐹𐑊 𐐱𐑂 𐑄 𐐢𐐫𐑉𐐼 𐑇𐐳𐐼 𐑁𐐫𐑊 𐐮𐑌𐐻𐐭 𐐻𐑉𐐰𐑌𐑆𐑀𐑉𐐯𐑇𐐲𐑌, 𐐰𐑌𐐼 𐐺𐐨𐐿𐐲𐑋 𐐲 𐐶𐐮𐐿𐐯𐐼 𐐰𐑌𐐼 𐐰𐑌 𐐰𐐼𐐲𐑊𐐻𐐲𐑉𐐲𐑅 𐐹𐐨𐐹𐑊, 𐑄𐐰𐐻 𐑄 𐐢𐐫𐑉𐐼 𐐶𐐮𐑊 𐐼𐐨𐑊𐐮𐑂𐐲𐑉 𐑄𐐯𐑋 𐐲𐐹, 𐑄𐐰𐐻 𐑄𐐯𐑉𐐺𐐴 𐑄𐐩 𐐺𐐨𐐿𐐲𐑋 𐐶𐐨𐐿 𐑊𐐴𐐿 𐐲𐑌𐐻𐐭 𐑄𐐩𐑉 𐐺𐑉𐐯𐑄𐑉𐐯𐑌; 𐐰𐑌𐐼 𐐸𐐨 𐐶𐐮𐑊 𐑌𐐬 𐑋𐐬𐑉 𐐹𐑉𐐨𐑆𐐲𐑉𐑂 𐑄𐐯𐑋 𐐺𐐴 𐐸𐐮𐑆 𐑋𐐰𐐽𐑊𐐯𐑅 𐐰𐑌𐐼 𐑋𐐪𐑉𐑂𐐯𐑊𐐲𐑅 𐐹𐐵𐐲𐑉, 𐐰𐑆 𐐸𐐨 𐐸𐐰𐑆 𐐸𐐮𐑄𐐲𐑉𐐻𐐭 𐐹𐑉𐐨𐑆𐐲𐑉𐑂𐐼 𐐵𐑉 𐑁𐐪𐑄𐐲𐑉𐑆. 𐐙𐐫𐑉 𐐌 𐑅𐐩 𐐲𐑌𐐻𐐭 𐐷𐐭, 𐑄𐐰𐐻 𐐮𐑁 𐐸𐐨 𐐸𐐰𐐼 𐑌𐐱𐐻 𐐯𐐿𐑅𐐻𐐯𐑌𐐼𐐯𐐼 𐐸𐐮𐑆 𐐪𐑉𐑋 𐐮𐑌 𐑄 𐐹𐑉𐐯𐑆𐐲𐑉𐑂𐐩𐑇𐐲𐑌 𐐱𐑂 𐐵𐑉 𐑁𐐪𐑄𐐲𐑉𐑆, 𐑄𐐩 𐑋𐐲𐑅𐐻 𐐸𐐰𐑂 𐑁𐐫𐑊𐑌 𐐮𐑌𐐻𐐭 𐑄 𐐸𐐰𐑌𐐼𐑆 𐐱𐑂 𐑄 𐐢𐐩𐑋𐐲𐑌𐐴𐐻𐑅, 𐐰𐑌𐐼 𐐺𐐨𐐿𐐲𐑋 𐑂𐐮𐐿𐐻𐐮𐑋𐑆 𐐻𐐭 𐑄𐐩𐑉 𐐸𐐩𐐻𐑉𐐯𐐼.

3. 𐐈𐑌𐐼 𐐮𐐻 𐐿𐐩𐑋 𐐻𐐭 𐐹𐐰𐑅 𐑄𐐰𐐻 𐐰𐑁𐐻𐐲𐑉 𐐿𐐮𐑍 𐐒𐐯𐑌𐐾𐐲𐑋𐐮𐑌 𐐸𐐰𐐼 𐑋𐐩𐐼 𐐰𐑌 𐐯𐑌𐐼 𐐱𐑂 𐑄𐐨𐑆 𐑅𐐩𐐮𐑍𐑆 𐐻𐐭 𐐸𐐮𐑆 𐑅𐐲𐑌, 𐑄𐐰𐐻 𐐸𐐨 𐑀𐐩𐑂 𐐸𐐮𐑋 𐐽𐐪𐑉𐐾 𐐿𐐱𐑌𐑅𐐲𐑉𐑌𐐮𐑍 𐐫𐑊 𐑄 𐐰𐑁𐐩𐑉𐑆 𐐱𐑂 𐑄 𐐿𐐮𐑍𐐼𐐲𐑋. 𐐈𐑌𐐼 𐑋𐐬𐑉𐐬𐑂𐐲𐑉, 𐐸𐐨 𐐫𐑊𐑅𐐬 𐑀𐐩𐑂 𐐸𐐮𐑋 𐐽𐐪𐑉𐐾 𐐿𐐱𐑌𐑅𐐲𐑉𐑌𐐮𐑍 𐑄 𐑉𐐯𐐿𐐲𐑉𐐼𐑆 𐐸𐐶𐐮𐐽 𐐶𐐲𐑉 𐐯𐑌𐑀𐑉𐐩𐑂𐑌 𐐱𐑌 𐑄 𐐹𐑊𐐩𐐻𐑅 𐐱𐑂 𐐺𐑉𐐰𐑅; 𐐰𐑌𐐼 𐐫𐑊𐑅𐐬, 𐑄 𐐹𐑊𐐩𐐻𐑅 𐐱𐑂 𐐤𐐨𐑁𐐴; 𐐰𐑌𐐼 𐐫𐑊𐑅𐐬, 𐑄 𐑅𐐬𐑉𐐼 𐐱𐑂 𐐢𐐩𐐺𐐲𐑌, 𐐰𐑌𐐼 𐑄 𐐺𐐫𐑊 𐐫𐑉 𐐼𐐴𐑉𐐯𐐿𐐻𐐲𐑉, 𐐸𐐶𐐮𐐽 𐑊𐐯𐐼 𐐵𐑉 𐑁𐐪𐑄𐐲𐑉𐑆 𐑃𐑉𐐭 𐑄 𐐶𐐮𐑊𐐼𐐲𐑉𐑌𐐯𐑅, 𐐸𐐶𐐮𐐽 𐐶𐐱𐑆 𐐹𐑉𐐨𐐹𐐩𐑉𐐼 𐐺𐐴 𐑄 𐐸𐐰𐑌𐐼 𐐱𐑂 𐑄 𐐢𐐫𐑉𐐼, 𐑄𐐰𐐻 𐑄𐐯𐑉𐐺𐐴 𐑄𐐩 𐑋𐐴𐐻 𐐺𐐨 𐑊𐐯𐐼, 𐐯𐑂𐐲𐑉𐐨 𐐶𐐲𐑌 𐐰𐐿𐐫𐑉𐐼𐐮𐑍 𐐻𐐭 𐑄 𐐸𐐨𐐼 𐐰𐑌𐐼 𐐼𐐮𐑊𐐮𐐾𐐯𐑌𐑅 𐐸𐐶𐐮𐐽 𐑄𐐩 𐑀𐐩𐑂 𐐲𐑌𐐻𐐭 𐐸𐐮𐑋. 𐐜𐐯𐑉𐑁𐐬𐑉, 𐐰𐑆 𐑄𐐩 𐐶𐐲𐑉 𐐲𐑌𐑁𐐩𐑃𐑁𐐳𐑊, 𐑄𐐩 𐐼𐐮𐐼 𐑌𐐱𐐻 𐐹𐑉𐐱𐑅𐐹𐐲𐑉 𐑌𐐫𐑉 𐐹𐑉𐐱𐑀𐑉𐐯𐑅 𐐮𐑌 𐑄𐐩𐑉 𐐾𐐲𐑉𐑌𐐨, 𐐺𐐲𐐻 𐐶𐐲𐑉 𐐼𐑉𐐮𐑂𐑌 𐐺𐐰𐐿, 𐐰𐑌𐐼 𐐮𐑌𐐿𐐲𐑉𐐼 𐑄 𐐼𐐮𐑅𐐹𐑊𐐯𐑈𐐲𐑉 𐐱𐑂 𐐘𐐱𐐼 𐐲𐐹𐐱𐑌 𐑄𐐯𐑋; 𐐰𐑌𐐼 𐑄𐐯𐑉𐑁𐐬𐑉, 𐑄𐐩 𐐶𐐲𐑉 𐑅𐑋𐐮𐐻𐑌 𐐶𐐮𐑃 𐑁𐐰𐑋𐐮𐑌 𐐰𐑌𐐼 𐑅𐐬𐑉 𐐰𐑁𐑊𐐮𐐿𐑇𐐲𐑌𐑆, 𐐻𐐭 𐑅𐐻𐐲𐑉 𐑄𐐯𐑋 𐐲𐐹 𐐮𐑌 𐑉𐐨𐑋𐐯𐑋𐐺𐑉𐐲𐑌𐑅 𐐱𐑂 𐑄𐐩𐑉 𐐼𐐧𐐻𐐨.

4. 𐐈𐑌𐐼 𐑌𐐵, 𐐮𐐻 𐐿𐐩𐑋 𐐻𐐭 𐐹𐐰𐑅 𐑄𐐰𐐻 𐐣𐐬𐑅𐐴𐐲 𐐶𐐯𐑌𐐻 𐐰𐑌𐐼 𐐼𐐮𐐼 𐐰𐑆 𐐸𐐮𐑆 𐑁𐐪𐑄𐐲𐑉 𐐸𐐰𐐼 𐐿𐐱𐑋𐐰𐑌𐐼𐐯𐐼 𐐸𐐮𐑋, 𐐰𐑌𐐼 𐐹𐑉𐐬𐐿𐑊𐐩𐑋𐐼 𐐲𐑌𐐻𐐭 𐐫𐑊 𐑄 𐐹𐐨𐐹𐑊 𐐸𐐭 𐐶𐐲𐑉 𐐮𐑌 𐑄 𐑊𐐰𐑌𐐼 𐐱𐑂 𐐞𐐰𐑉𐐲𐐸𐐯𐑋𐑊𐐲, 𐑄𐐰𐐻 𐑄𐐯𐑉𐐺𐐴 𐑄𐐩 𐑋𐐴𐐻 𐑀𐐰𐑄𐐲𐑉 𐑄𐐯𐑋𐑅𐐯𐑊𐑂𐑆 𐐻𐐳𐑀𐐯𐑄𐐲𐑉, 𐐻𐐭 𐑀𐐬 𐐲𐐹 𐐻𐐭 𐑄 𐐻𐐯𐑋𐐹𐑊 𐐻𐐭 𐐸𐐨𐑉 𐑄 𐐶𐐲𐑉𐐼𐑆 𐐸𐐶𐐮𐐽 𐐸𐐮𐑆 𐑁𐐪𐑄𐐲𐑉 𐑇𐐳𐐼 𐑅𐐹𐐨𐐿 𐐲𐑌𐐻𐐭 𐑄𐐯𐑋.

5. 𐐈𐑌𐐼 𐐮𐐻 𐐿𐐩𐑋 𐐻𐐭 𐐹𐐰𐑅 𐑄𐐰𐐻 𐐰𐑁𐐻𐐲𐑉 𐐣𐐬𐑅𐐴𐐲 𐐸𐐰𐐼 𐐼𐐲𐑌 𐐰𐑆 𐐸𐐮𐑆 𐑁𐐪𐑄𐐲𐑉 𐐸𐐰𐐼 𐐿𐐱𐑋𐐰𐑌𐐼𐐯𐐼 𐐸𐐮𐑋, 𐐰𐑌𐐼 𐐸𐐰𐐼 𐑋𐐩𐐼 𐐲 𐐹𐑉𐐱𐐿𐑊𐐲𐑋𐐩𐑇𐐲𐑌 𐑃𐑉𐐭𐐵𐐻 𐐫𐑊 𐑄 𐑊𐐰𐑌𐐼, 𐑄𐐰𐐻 𐑄 𐐹𐐨𐐹𐑊 𐑀𐐰𐑄𐐲𐑉𐐼 𐑄𐐯𐑋𐑅𐐯𐑊𐑂𐑆 𐐻𐐳𐑀𐐯𐑄𐐲𐑉 𐑃𐑉𐐭𐐵𐐻 𐐫𐑊 𐑄 𐑊𐐰𐑌𐐼, 𐑄𐐰𐐻 𐑄𐐩 𐑋𐐴𐐻 𐑀𐐬 𐐲𐐹 𐐻𐐭 𐑄 𐐻𐐯𐑋𐐹𐑊 𐐻𐐭 𐐸𐐨𐑉 𐑄 𐐶𐐲𐑉𐐼𐑆 𐐸𐐶𐐮𐐽 𐐿𐐮𐑍 𐐒𐐯𐑌𐐾𐐲𐑋𐐮𐑌 𐑇𐐳𐐼 𐑅𐐹𐐨𐐿 𐐲𐑌𐐻𐐭 𐑄𐐯𐑋. 𐐈𐑌𐐼 𐑄𐐩𐑉 𐐶𐐲𐑉 𐐲 𐑀𐑉𐐩𐐻 𐑌𐐲𐑋𐐺𐐲𐑉, 𐐨𐑂𐑌 𐑅𐐬 𐑋𐐯𐑌𐐨 𐑄𐐰𐐻 𐑄𐐩 𐐼𐐮𐐼 𐑌𐐱𐐻 𐑌𐐲𐑋𐐺𐐲𐑉 𐑄𐐯𐑋; 𐑁𐐫𐑉 𐑄𐐩 𐐸𐐰𐐼 𐑋𐐲𐑊𐐻𐐮𐐹𐑊𐐴𐐼 𐐯𐐿𐑅𐐨𐐼𐐮𐑍𐑊𐐨, 𐐰𐑌𐐼 𐐶𐐰𐐿𐑅𐐻 𐑀𐑉𐐩𐐻 𐐮𐑌 𐑄 𐑊𐐰𐑌𐐼. 𐐈𐑌𐐼 𐑄𐐩 𐐫𐑊𐑅𐐬 𐐻𐐳𐐿 𐐱𐑂 𐑄 𐑁𐐲𐑉𐑅𐐻𐑊𐐮𐑍𐑆 𐐱𐑂 𐑄𐐩𐑉 𐑁𐑊𐐱𐐿𐑅, 𐑄𐐰𐐻 𐑄𐐩 𐑋𐐴𐐻 𐐱𐑁𐐲𐑉 𐑅𐐰𐐿𐑉𐐮𐑁𐐴𐑅 𐐰𐑌𐐼 𐐺𐐲𐑉𐑌𐐻 𐐱𐑁𐐲𐑉𐐮𐑍𐑆, 𐐰𐐿𐐫𐑉𐐼𐐮𐑍 𐐻𐐭 𐑄 𐑊𐐫 𐐱𐑂 𐐣𐐬𐑆𐐯𐑆; 𐐰𐑌𐐼 𐐫𐑊𐑅𐐬, 𐑄𐐰𐐻 𐑄𐐩 𐑋𐐴𐐻 𐑀𐐮𐑂 𐑃𐐰𐑍𐐿𐑅 𐐻𐐭 𐑄 𐐢𐐫𐑉𐐼 𐑄𐐩𐑉 𐐘𐐱𐐼, 𐐸𐐭 𐐸𐐰𐐼 𐐺𐑉𐐫𐐻 𐑄𐐯𐑋 𐐵𐐻 𐐱𐑂 𐑄 𐑊𐐰𐑌𐐼 𐐱𐑂 𐐖𐐨𐑉𐐭𐑅𐐲𐑊𐐯𐑋, 𐐰𐑌𐐼 𐐸𐐭 𐐸𐐰𐐼 𐐼𐐨𐑊𐐮𐑂𐐲𐑉𐐼 𐑄𐐯𐑋 𐐵𐐻 𐐱𐑂 𐑄 𐐸𐐰𐑌𐐼𐑆 𐐱𐑂 𐑄𐐩𐑉 𐐯𐑌𐐯𐑋𐐨𐑆, 𐐰𐑌𐐼 𐐸𐐰𐐼 𐐰𐐹𐑎𐑌𐐻𐐯𐐼 𐐾𐐲𐑅𐐻 𐑋𐐯𐑌 𐐻𐐭 𐐺𐐨 𐑄𐐩𐑉

𐐻𐐨𐐽𐐲𐑉𐑆; 𐐰𐑌𐐼 𐐫𐑊𐑅𐐬 𐐲 𐐾𐐲𐑅𐐻 𐑋𐐰𐑌 𐐻𐐭 𐐺𐐨 𐑄𐐯𐑉 𐐿𐐮𐑍, 𐐸𐐭 𐐸𐐰𐐼 𐐯𐑅𐐻𐐰𐐺𐑊𐐮𐑇𐐻 𐐹𐐨𐑅 𐐮𐑌 𐑄 𐑊𐐰𐑌𐐼 𐐱𐑂 𐐞𐐯𐑉𐐲𐐸𐐯𐑋𐑊𐐲, 𐐰𐑌𐐼 𐐸𐐭 𐐸𐐰𐐼 𐐻𐐫𐐻 𐑄𐐯𐑋 𐐻𐐭 𐐿𐐨𐐹 𐑄 𐐿𐐱𐑋𐐰𐑌𐐼𐑋𐐯𐑌𐐻𐑅 𐐱𐑂 𐐘𐐱𐐼, 𐑄𐐰𐐻 𐑄𐐩 𐑋𐐴𐐻 𐑉𐐨𐐾𐐱𐐮𐑅, 𐐰𐑌𐐼 𐐺𐐨 𐑁𐐮𐑊𐐼 𐐶𐐮𐑄 𐑊𐐲𐑂 𐐻𐐬𐐲𐑉𐐼𐑆 𐐘𐐱𐐼 𐐰𐑌𐐼 𐐫𐑊 𐑋𐐯𐑌.

6. 𐐈𐑌𐐼 𐐮𐐻 𐐿𐐩𐑋 𐐻𐐭 𐐹𐐪𐑅 𐑄𐐰𐐻 𐐸𐐶𐐯𐑌 𐑄𐐩 𐐿𐐩𐑋 𐐲𐐹 𐐻𐐭 𐑄 𐐻𐐯𐑋𐐹𐑊, 𐑄𐐩 𐐹𐐮𐐽𐐻 𐑄𐐯𐑉 𐐻𐐯𐑌𐐻𐑅 𐑉𐐵𐑌𐐼 𐐲𐐺𐐵𐐻, 𐐯𐑂𐐲𐑉𐐨 𐑋𐐰𐑌 𐐰𐐿𐐫𐑉𐐼𐐮𐑍 𐐻𐐭 𐐸𐐮𐑆 𐑁𐐰𐑋𐐮𐑊𐐨, 𐐿𐐱𐑌𐑅𐐮𐑅𐐻𐐮𐑍 𐐱𐑂 𐐸𐐮𐑆 𐐶𐐴𐑁, 𐐰𐑌𐐼 𐐸𐐮𐑆 𐑅𐐲𐑌𐑆, 𐐰𐑌𐐼 𐐸𐐮𐑆 𐐼𐐫𐐻𐐲𐑉𐑆, 𐐰𐑌𐐼 𐑄𐐯𐑉 𐑅𐐲𐑌𐑆, 𐐰𐑌𐐼 𐑄𐐯𐑉 𐐼𐐫𐐻𐐲𐑉𐑆, 𐑁𐑉𐐱𐑋 𐑄 𐐯𐑊𐐼𐐯𐑅𐐻 𐐼𐐵𐑌 𐐻𐐭 𐑄 𐐷𐐲𐑍𐑀𐐯𐑅𐐻, 𐐯𐑂𐐲𐑉𐐨 𐑁𐐰𐑋𐐮𐑊𐐨 𐐺𐐨𐐮𐑍 𐑅𐐯𐐹𐐲𐑉𐐩𐐻 𐐶𐐲𐑌 𐑁𐑉𐐱𐑋 𐐰𐑌𐐲𐑄𐐲𐑉; 𐐰𐑌𐐼 𐑄𐐩 𐐹𐐮𐐽𐐻 𐑄𐐯𐑉 𐐻𐐯𐑌𐐻𐑅 𐑉𐐵𐑌𐐼 𐐲𐐺𐐵𐐻 𐑄 𐐻𐐯𐑋𐐹𐑊, 𐐯𐑂𐐲𐑉𐐨 𐑋𐐰𐑌 𐐸𐐰𐑂𐐮𐑍 𐐸𐐮𐑆 𐐻𐐯𐑌𐐻 𐐶𐐮𐑄 𐑄 𐐼𐐬𐑉 𐑄𐐯𐑉𐐱𐑂 𐐻𐐬𐐲𐑉𐐼𐑆 𐑄 𐐻𐐯𐑋𐐹𐑊, 𐑄𐐰𐐻 𐑄𐐯𐑉𐐺𐐴 𐑄𐐩 𐑋𐐴𐐻 𐑉𐐨𐑋𐐩𐑌 𐐮𐑌 𐑄𐐯𐑉 𐐻𐐯𐑌𐐻𐑅 𐐰𐑌𐐼 𐐸𐐨𐑉 𐑄 𐐶𐐲𐑉𐐼𐑆 𐐸𐐶𐐮𐐽 𐐿𐐮𐑍 𐐒𐐯𐑌𐐾𐐲𐑋𐐮𐑌 𐑇𐐳𐐼 𐑅𐐹𐐨𐐿 𐐲𐑌𐐻𐐭 𐑄𐐯𐑋; 𐑁𐐫𐑉 𐑄 𐑋𐐲𐑊𐐻𐐮𐐻𐐷𐐭𐐼 𐐺𐐨𐐮𐑍 𐑅𐐬 𐑀𐑉𐐩𐐻 𐑄𐐰𐐻 𐐿𐐮𐑍 𐐒𐐯𐑌𐐾𐐲𐑋𐐮𐑌 𐐿𐐳𐐼 𐑌𐐱𐐻 𐐻𐐨𐐽 𐑄𐐯𐑋 𐐫𐑊 𐐶𐐮𐑄𐐮𐑌 𐑄 𐐶𐐫𐑊𐑆 𐐱𐑂 𐑄 𐐻𐐯𐑋𐐹𐑊, 𐑄𐐯𐑉𐑁𐐬𐑉 𐐸𐐨 𐐿𐐫𐑆𐐼 𐐲 𐐻𐐵𐐲𐑉 𐐻𐐭 𐐺𐐨 𐐨𐑉𐐯𐐿𐐻𐐯𐐼, 𐑄𐐰𐐻 𐑄𐐯𐑉𐐺𐐴 𐐸𐐮𐑆 𐐹𐐨𐐹𐑊 𐑋𐐴𐐻 𐐸𐐨𐑉 𐑄 𐐶𐐲𐑉𐐼𐑆 𐐸𐐶𐐮𐐽 𐐸𐐨 𐑇𐐳𐐼 𐑅𐐹𐐨𐐿 𐐲𐑌𐐻𐐭 𐑄𐐯𐑋.

7. 𐐈𐑌𐐼 𐐮𐐻 𐐿𐐩𐑋 𐐻𐐭 𐐹𐐪𐑅 𐑄𐐰𐐻 𐐸𐐨 𐐺𐐨𐑀𐐰𐑌 𐐻𐐭 𐑅𐐹𐐨𐐿 𐐻𐐭 𐐸𐐮𐑆 𐐹𐐨𐐹𐑊 𐑁𐑉𐐱𐑋 𐑄 𐐻𐐵𐐲𐑉; 𐐰𐑌𐐼 𐑄𐐩 𐐿𐐳𐐼 𐑌𐐱𐐻 𐐫𐑊 𐐸𐐨𐑉 𐐸𐐮𐑆 𐐶𐐲𐑉𐐼𐑆, 𐐺𐐨𐐿𐐫𐑆 𐐱𐑂 𐑄 𐑀𐑉𐐩𐐻𐑌𐐯𐑅 𐐱𐑂 𐑄 𐑋𐐲𐑊𐐻𐐮𐐻𐐷𐐭𐐼; 𐑄𐐯𐑉𐑁𐐬𐑉 𐐸𐐨 𐐿𐐫𐑆𐐼 𐑄𐐰𐐻 𐑄 𐐶𐐲𐑉𐐼𐑆 𐐸𐐶𐐮𐐽 𐐸𐐨 𐑅𐐹𐐩𐐿 𐑇𐐳𐐼 𐐺𐐨 𐑉𐐮𐐻𐑌 𐐰𐑌𐐼 𐑅𐐯𐑌𐐻 𐑁𐐬𐑉𐑃 𐐲𐑋𐐲𐑍 𐑄𐐬𐑆 𐑄𐐰𐐻 𐐶𐐲𐑉 𐑌𐐱𐐻 𐐲𐑌𐐼𐐲𐑉 𐑄 𐑅𐐵𐑌𐐼 𐐱𐑂 𐐸𐐮𐑆 𐑂𐐱𐐮𐑅, 𐑄𐐰𐐻 𐑄𐐩 𐑋𐐴𐐻 𐐫𐑊𐑅𐐬 𐑉𐐨𐑅𐐨𐑂 𐐸𐐮𐑆 𐐶𐐲𐑉𐐼𐑆. 𐐈𐑌𐐼 𐑄𐐨𐑆 𐐪𐑉 𐑄 𐐶𐐲𐑉𐐼𐑆 𐐸𐐶𐐮𐐽 𐐸𐐨 𐑅𐐹𐐩𐐿 𐐰𐑌𐐼 𐐿𐐫𐑆𐐼 𐐻𐐭 𐐺𐐨 𐑉𐐮𐐻𐑌, 𐑅𐐩𐐮𐑍: 𐐣𐐴 𐐺𐑉𐐯𐑄𐑉𐐯𐑌, 𐐫𐑊 𐐷𐐨 𐑄𐐰𐐻 𐐸𐐰𐑂 𐐰𐑅𐐯𐑋𐐺𐑊𐐼 𐐷𐐭𐑉𐑅𐐯𐑊𐑂𐑆 𐐻𐐭𐑀𐐯𐑄𐐲𐑉, 𐐷𐐭 𐑄𐐰𐐻 𐐿𐐰𐑌 𐐸𐐨𐑉 𐑋𐐴 𐐶𐐲𐑉𐐼𐑆 𐐸𐐶𐐮𐐽 𐐌 𐑇𐐰𐑊 𐑅𐐹𐐨𐐿 𐐲𐑌𐐻𐐭 𐐷𐐭 𐑄𐐮𐑅 𐐼𐐩; 𐑁𐐫𐑉 𐐌 𐐸𐐰𐑂 𐑌𐐱𐐻 𐐿𐐱𐑋𐐰𐑌𐐼𐐯𐐼 𐐷𐐭 𐐻𐐭 𐐿𐐲𐑋 𐐲𐐹 𐐸𐐮𐑄𐐲𐑉 𐐻𐐭 𐐻𐑉𐐴𐑁𐑊 𐐶𐐮𐑄 𐑄 𐐶𐐲𐑉𐐼𐑆 𐐸𐐶𐐮𐐽 𐐌 𐑇𐐰𐑊 𐑅𐐹𐐨𐐿, 𐐺𐐲𐐻 𐑄𐐰𐐻 𐐷𐐭 𐑇𐐳𐐼 𐐸𐐪𐑉𐐿𐐲𐑌 𐐲𐑌𐐻𐐭 𐑋𐐨, 𐐰𐑌𐐼 𐐬𐐹𐐲𐑌 𐐷𐐭𐑉 𐐨𐑉𐑆 𐑄𐐰𐐻 𐐷𐐨 𐑋𐐩 𐐸𐐨𐑉, 𐐰𐑌𐐼 𐐷𐐭𐑉 𐐸𐐪𐑉𐐻𐑅 𐑄𐐰𐐻 𐐷𐐨 𐑋𐐩 𐐲𐑌𐐼𐐲𐑉𐑅𐐻𐐰𐑌𐐼, 𐐰𐑌𐐼 𐐷𐐭𐑉 𐑋𐐴𐑌𐐼𐑆 𐑄𐐰𐐻 𐑄 𐑋𐐮𐑅𐐻𐐲𐑉𐐨𐑆 𐐱𐑂 𐐘𐐱𐐼 𐑋𐐩 𐐺𐐨 𐐲𐑌𐑁𐐬𐑊𐐼𐐯𐐼 𐐻𐐭 𐐷𐐭𐑉 𐑂𐐷𐐭. 𐐌 𐐸𐐰𐑂 𐑌𐐱𐐻 𐐿𐐱𐑋𐐰𐑌𐐼𐐯𐐼 𐐷𐐭 𐐻𐐭 𐐿𐐲𐑋 𐐲𐐹 𐐸𐐮𐑄𐐲𐑉 𐑄𐐰𐐻 𐐷𐐨 𐑇𐐳𐐼 𐑁𐐨𐑉 𐑋𐐨, 𐐫𐑉 𐑄𐐰𐐻 𐐷𐐨 𐑇𐐳𐐼 𐑃𐐮𐑍𐐿 𐑄𐐰𐐻 𐐌 𐐱𐑂 𐑋𐐴𐑅𐐯𐑊𐑁 𐐰𐑋 𐑋𐐬𐑉 𐑄𐐰𐑌 𐐲 𐑋𐐫𐑉𐐻𐐲𐑊 𐑋𐐰𐑌. 𐐒𐐲𐐻 𐐌 𐐰𐑋 𐑊𐐴𐐿 𐐰𐑆 𐐷𐐭𐑉𐑅𐐯𐑊𐑂𐑆, 𐑅𐐲𐐺𐐾𐐯𐐿𐐻 𐐻𐐭 𐐫𐑊 𐑋𐐰𐑌𐐲𐑉 𐐱𐑂 𐐮𐑌𐑁𐐲𐑉𐑋𐐮𐐻𐐨𐑆 𐐮𐑌 𐐺𐐱𐐼𐐨 𐐰𐑌𐐼 𐑋𐐴𐑌𐐼; 𐐷𐐯𐐻 𐐌 𐐸𐐰𐑂 𐐺𐐨𐑌 𐐽𐐬𐑆𐐲𐑌 𐐺𐐴 𐑄𐐮𐑅 𐐹𐐨𐐹𐑊, 𐐰𐑌𐐼 𐐿𐐱𐑌𐑅𐐯𐐿𐑉𐐩𐐻𐐯𐐼 𐐺𐐴 𐑋𐐴 𐑁𐐪𐑄𐐲𐑉, 𐐰𐑌𐐼 𐐶𐐱𐑆 𐑅𐐲𐑁𐐲𐑉𐐼 𐐺𐐴 𐑄 𐐸𐐰𐑌𐐼 𐐱𐑂 𐑄 𐐢𐐫𐑉𐐼 𐑄𐐰𐐻 𐐌 𐑇𐐳𐐼 𐐺𐐨 𐐲 𐑉𐐭𐑊𐐲𐑉 𐐰𐑌𐐼 𐐲 𐐿𐐮𐑍 𐐬𐑂𐐲𐑉 𐑄𐐮𐑅 𐐹𐐨𐐹𐑊; 𐐰𐑌𐐼 𐐸𐐰𐑂 𐐺𐐨𐑌 𐐿𐐯𐐹𐐻 𐐰𐑌𐐼 𐐹𐑉𐐨𐑆𐐲𐑉𐑂𐐼 𐐺𐐴 𐐸𐐮𐑆 𐑋𐐰𐐽𐑊𐐯𐑅 𐐹𐐵𐐲𐑉, 𐐻𐐭 𐑅𐐲𐑉𐑂 𐐷𐐭 𐐶𐐮𐑄 𐐫𐑊 𐑄 𐑋𐐴𐐻, 𐑋𐐴𐑌𐐼 𐐰𐑌𐐼 𐑅𐐻𐑉𐐯𐑍𐑃 𐐸𐐶𐐮𐐽 𐑄 𐐢𐐫𐑉𐐼 𐐸𐐰𐑃 𐑀𐑉𐐪𐑌𐐻𐐯𐐼 𐐲𐑌𐐻𐐭 𐑋𐐨. 𐐌 𐑅𐐩 𐐲𐑌𐐻𐐭 𐐷𐐭, 𐑄𐐰𐐻 𐐰𐑆 𐐌 𐐸𐐰𐑂 𐐺𐐨𐑌 𐑅𐐲𐑁𐐲𐑉𐐼 𐐻𐐭 𐑅𐐹𐐯𐑌𐐼 𐑋𐐴 𐐼𐐩𐑆 𐐮𐑌 𐐷𐐭𐑉 𐑅𐐲𐑉𐑂𐐮𐑅, 𐐨𐑂𐐲𐑌 𐐲𐐹 𐐻𐐭 𐑄𐐮𐑅 𐐻𐐴𐑋, 𐐰𐑌𐐼 𐐸𐐰𐑂 𐑌𐐱𐐻 𐑅𐐫𐐻 𐑀𐐬𐑊𐐼 𐑌𐐫𐑉 𐑅𐐮𐑊𐑂𐐲𐑉 𐑌𐐫𐑉 𐐯𐑌𐐨 𐑋𐐰𐑌𐐲𐑉 𐐱𐑂 𐑉𐐮𐐽𐐯𐑆 𐐱𐑂 𐐷𐐭; 𐑌𐐨𐑄𐐲𐑉 𐐸𐐰𐑂 𐐌 𐑅𐐲𐑁𐐲𐑉𐐼 𐑄𐐰𐐻 𐐷𐐨 𐑇𐐳𐐼 𐐺𐐨 𐐿𐐱𐑌𐑁𐐴𐑌𐐼 𐐮𐑌 𐐼𐐲𐑌𐐾𐐲𐑌𐑆, 𐑌𐐫𐑉 𐑄𐐰𐐻 𐐷𐐨 𐑇𐐳𐐼 𐑋𐐩𐐿 𐑅𐑊𐐩𐑂𐑆 𐐶𐐲𐑌 𐐱𐑂 𐐰𐑌𐐲𐑄𐐲𐑉, 𐑌𐐫𐑉 𐑄𐐰𐐻 𐐷𐐨 𐑇𐐳𐐼 𐑋𐐲𐑉𐐼𐐲𐑉, 𐐫𐑉 𐐹𐑊𐐲𐑌𐐼𐐲𐑉, 𐐫𐑉 𐑅𐐻𐐨𐑊, 𐐫𐑉 𐐿𐐱𐑋𐐮𐐻 𐐲𐐼𐐲𐑊𐐻𐐲𐑉𐐨; 𐑌𐐫𐑉 𐐨𐑂𐐲𐑌 𐐸𐐰𐑂 𐐌 𐑅𐐲𐑁𐐲𐑉𐐼 𐑄𐐰𐐻 𐐷𐐨 𐑇𐐳𐐼 𐐿𐐱𐑋𐐮𐐻 𐐯𐑌𐐨 𐑋𐐰𐑌𐐲𐑉 𐐱𐑂 𐐶𐐮𐐿𐐯𐐼𐑌𐐯𐑅, 𐐰𐑌𐐼 𐐸𐐰𐑂 𐐻𐐫𐐻 𐐷𐐭 𐑄𐐰𐐻 𐐷𐐨 𐑇𐐳𐐼 𐐿𐐨𐐹 𐑄 𐐿𐐱𐑋𐐰𐑌𐐼𐑋𐐯𐑌𐐻𐑅 𐐱𐑂 𐑄 𐐢𐐫𐑉𐐼, 𐐮𐑌 𐐫𐑊 𐑃𐐮𐑍𐑆 𐐸𐐶𐐮𐐽 𐐸𐐨 𐐸𐐰𐑃 𐐿𐐱𐑋𐐰𐑌𐐼𐐯𐐼 𐐷𐐭; 𐐰𐑌𐐼 𐐨𐑂𐐲𐑌 𐐌 𐑋𐐴𐑅𐐯𐑊𐑁 𐐸𐐰𐑂 𐑊𐐩𐐺𐐲𐑉𐐼 𐐶𐐮𐑄 𐑋𐐴𐑌 𐐬𐑌 𐐸𐐰𐑌𐐼𐑆, 𐑄𐐰𐐻 𐐌 𐑋𐐴𐐻 𐑅𐐲𐑉𐑂 𐐷𐐭, 𐐰𐑌𐐼 𐑄𐐰𐐻 𐐷𐐨 𐑇𐐳𐐼 𐑌𐐱𐐻 𐐺𐐨 𐑊𐐩𐐼𐑌 𐐶𐐮𐑄 𐐻𐐰𐐿𐑅𐐯𐑆, 𐐰𐑌𐐼 𐑄𐐰𐐻 𐑄𐐯𐑉 𐑇𐐳𐐼 𐑌𐐲𐑃𐐮𐑍 𐐿𐐲𐑋 𐐲𐐹𐐱𐑌 𐐷𐐭 𐐸𐐶𐐮𐐽 𐐶𐐱𐑆 𐑀𐑉𐐨𐑂𐐲𐑅 𐐻𐐭 𐐺𐐨 𐐺𐐬𐑉𐑌; 𐐰𐑌𐐼 𐐱𐑂 𐐫𐑊 𐑄𐐨𐑆 𐑃𐐮𐑍𐑆 𐐸𐐶𐐮𐐽 𐐌 𐐸𐐰𐑂 𐑅𐐹𐐬𐐿𐐲𐑌, 𐐷𐐨 𐐷𐐭𐑉𐑅𐐯𐑊𐑂𐑆 𐐪𐑉 𐐶𐐮𐐻𐑌𐐯𐑅𐐯𐑆 𐑄𐐮𐑅 𐐼𐐩. 𐐏𐐯𐐻, 𐑋𐐴 𐐺𐑉𐐯𐑄𐑉𐐯𐑌, 𐐌 𐐸𐐰𐑂 𐑌𐐱𐐻 𐐼𐐲𐑌 𐑄𐐨𐑆 𐑃𐐮𐑍𐑆 𐑄𐐰𐐻 𐐌 𐑋𐐴𐐻 𐐺𐐬𐑅𐐻, 𐑌𐐨𐑄𐐲𐑉 𐐼𐐭 𐐌 𐐻𐐯𐑊 𐑄𐐨𐑆 𐑃𐐮𐑍𐑆 𐑄𐐰𐐻 𐑄𐐯𐑉𐐺𐐴 𐐌 𐑋𐐴𐐻 𐐰𐐿𐐷𐐭𐑆 𐐷𐐭; 𐐺𐐲𐐻 𐐌 𐐻𐐯𐑊 𐐷𐐭 𐑄𐐨𐑆 𐑃𐐮𐑍𐑆 𐑄𐐰𐐻 𐐷𐐨 𐑋𐐩 𐑌𐐬 𐑄𐐰𐐻 𐐌 𐐿𐐰𐑌 𐐰𐑌𐑅𐐲𐑉 𐐲 𐐿𐑊𐐨𐑉 𐐿𐐱𐑌𐑇𐐯𐑌𐑅 𐐺𐐨𐑁𐐬𐑉 𐐘𐐱𐐼 𐑄𐐮𐑅 𐐼𐐩. 𐐒𐐨𐐸𐐬𐑊𐐼, 𐐌 𐑅𐐩 𐐲𐑌𐐻𐐭 𐐷𐐭, 𐑄𐐰𐐻 𐐺𐐨𐐿𐐫𐑆 𐐌 𐑅𐐯𐐼 𐐲𐑌𐐻𐐭 𐐷𐐭 𐑄𐐰𐐻 𐐌 𐐸𐐰𐐼 𐑅𐐹𐐯𐑌𐐻 𐑋𐐴 𐐼𐐩𐑆 𐐮𐑌 𐐷𐐭𐑉 𐑅𐐲𐑉𐑂𐐮𐑅, 𐐌 𐐼𐐭 𐑌𐐱𐐻 𐐼𐐨𐑆𐐴𐑉 𐐻𐐭 𐐺𐐬𐑅𐐻, 𐑁𐐫𐑉 𐐌 𐐸𐐰𐑂 𐐬𐑌𐑊𐐨 𐐺𐐨𐑌 𐐮𐑌 𐑄 𐑅𐐲𐑉𐑂𐐮𐑅 𐐱𐑂 𐐘𐐱𐐼.

8. 𐐈𐑌𐐼 𐐺𐐨𐐸𐐬𐑊𐐼, 𐐌 𐐻𐐯𐑊 𐐷𐐭 𐑄𐐨𐑆 𐑃𐐮𐑍𐑆 𐑄𐐰𐐻 𐐷 𐑋𐐩 𐑊𐐲𐑉𐑌 𐐶𐐮𐑆𐐼𐐲𐑋; 𐑄𐐰𐐻 𐐷 𐑋𐐩 𐑊𐐲𐑉𐑌 𐑄𐐰𐐻 𐐸𐐶𐐯𐑌 𐐷 𐐪𐑉 𐐮𐑌 𐑄 𐑅𐐲𐑉𐑂𐐮𐑅 𐐱𐑂 𐐷𐐬𐑉 𐑁𐐯𐑊𐐬 𐐺𐐨𐐮𐑍𐑆, 𐐷 𐐪𐑉 𐐬𐑌𐑊𐐮 𐐮𐑌 𐑄 𐑅𐐲𐑉𐑂𐐮𐑅 𐐱𐑂 𐐷𐐬𐑉 𐐘𐐱𐐼. 𐐒𐐨𐐸𐐬𐑊𐐼, 𐐷 𐐸𐐰𐑂 𐐿𐐫𐑊𐐼 𐑋𐐨 𐐷𐐬𐑉 𐐿𐐮𐑍; 𐐰𐑌𐐼 𐐮𐑁 𐐌, 𐐸𐐭𐑋 𐐷 𐐿𐐫𐑊 𐐷𐐬𐑉 𐐿𐐮𐑍, 𐐼𐐭 𐑊𐐩𐐺𐐲𐑉 𐐻𐐭 𐑅𐐲𐑉𐑂 𐐷𐐭, 𐑄𐐯𐑌 𐐸𐐰𐐼 𐑌𐐱𐐻 𐐷 𐐫𐐻 𐐻𐐭 𐑊𐐩𐐺𐐲𐑉 𐐻𐐭 𐑅𐐲𐑉𐑂 𐐶𐐲𐑌 𐐰𐑌𐐲𐑄𐐲𐑉? 𐐈𐑌𐐼 𐐺𐐨𐐸𐐬𐑊𐐼 𐐫𐑊𐑅𐐬, 𐐮𐑁 𐐌, 𐐸𐐭𐑋 𐐷 𐐿𐐫𐑊 𐐷𐐬𐑉 𐐿𐐮𐑍, 𐐸𐐭 𐐸𐐰𐑆 𐑅𐐹𐐯𐑌𐐻 𐐸𐐮𐑆 𐐼𐐩𐑆 𐐮𐑌 𐐷𐐬𐑉 𐑅𐐲𐑉𐑂𐐮𐑅, 𐐰𐑌𐐼 𐐷𐐯𐐻 𐐸𐐰𐑆 𐐺𐐮𐑌 𐐮𐑌 𐑄 𐑅𐐲𐑉𐑂𐐮𐑅 𐐱𐑂 𐐘𐐱𐐼, 𐐼𐐭 𐑋𐐯𐑉𐐮𐐻 𐐯𐑌𐐮 𐑃𐐰𐑍𐐿𐑅 𐑁𐑉𐐱𐑋 𐐷𐐭, 𐐄 𐐸𐐵 𐐸𐐰𐐼 𐐷𐐭 𐐫𐐻 𐐻𐐭 𐑃𐐰𐑍𐐿 𐐷𐐬𐑉 𐐸𐐯𐑂𐐲𐑌𐑊𐐮 𐐗𐐮𐑍! 𐐌 𐑅𐐩 𐐲𐑌𐐻𐐭 𐐷𐐭, 𐑋𐐴 𐐺𐑉𐐯𐑄𐑉𐐯𐑌, 𐑄𐐰𐐻 𐐮𐑁 𐐷𐐭 𐑇𐐳𐐼 𐑉𐐯𐑌𐐼𐐲𐑉 𐐫𐑊 𐑄 𐑃𐐰𐑍𐐿𐑅 𐐰𐑌𐐼 𐐹𐑉𐐩𐑆 𐐸𐐶𐐮𐐽 𐐷𐐬𐑉 𐐸𐐬𐑊 𐑅𐐬𐑊 𐐸𐐰𐑆 𐐹𐐵𐑉 𐐻𐐭 𐐹𐐲𐑆𐐯𐑅, 𐐻𐐭 𐑄𐐰𐐻 𐐘𐐱𐐼 𐐸𐐭 𐐸𐐰𐑆 𐐿𐑉𐐨𐐩𐐻𐐯𐐼 𐐷𐐭, 𐐰𐑌𐐼 𐐸𐐰𐑆 𐐿𐐯𐐹𐐻 𐐰𐑌𐐼 𐐹𐑉𐐨𐑆𐐲𐑉𐑂𐐼 𐐷𐐭, 𐐰𐑌𐐼 𐐸𐐰𐑆 𐐿𐐫𐑆𐐼 𐑄𐐰𐐻 𐐷 𐑇𐐳𐐼 𐑉𐐨𐐾𐐦𐑅, 𐐰𐑌𐐼 𐐸𐐰𐑆 𐑀𐑉𐐰𐑌𐐻𐐯𐐼 𐑄𐐰𐐻 𐐷 𐑇𐐳𐐼 𐑊𐐮𐑂 𐐮𐑌 𐐹𐐨𐑅 𐐶𐐲𐑌 𐐶𐐮𐑄 𐐰𐑌𐐲𐑄𐐲𐑉; 𐐌 𐑅𐐩 𐐲𐑌𐐻𐐭 𐐷𐐭, 𐑄𐐰𐐻 𐐮𐑁 𐐷 𐑇𐐳𐐼 𐑅𐐲𐑉𐑂 𐐸𐐮𐑋 𐐸𐐭 𐐸𐐰𐑆 𐐿𐑉𐐨𐐩𐐻𐐯𐐼 𐐷𐐭 𐑁𐑉𐐱𐑋 𐑄 𐐺𐐨𐑀𐐮𐑌𐐮𐑍, 𐐰𐑌𐐼 𐐪𐑉𐐻 𐐹𐑉𐐨𐑆𐐲𐑉𐑂𐐮𐑍 𐐷𐐭 𐑁𐑉𐐱𐑋 𐐼𐐩 𐐻𐐭 𐐼𐐩, 𐐺𐐴 𐑊𐐯𐑌𐐼𐐮𐑍 𐐷𐐭 𐐺𐑉𐐯𐑃, 𐑄𐐰𐐻 𐐷 𐑋𐐩 𐑊𐐮𐑂 𐐰𐑌𐐼 𐑋𐐭𐑂, 𐐰𐑌𐐼 𐐼𐐭 𐐰𐐿𐐫𐑉𐐼𐐮𐑍 𐐻𐐭 𐐷𐐬𐑉 𐐬𐑌 𐐶𐐮𐑊, 𐐰𐑌𐐼 𐐨𐑂𐑌 𐑅𐐲𐐹𐐬𐑉𐐻𐐮𐑍 𐐷𐐭 𐑁𐑉𐐱𐑋 𐐶𐐲𐑌 𐑋𐐬𐑋𐐯𐑌𐐻 𐐻𐐭 𐐰𐑌𐐲𐑄𐐲𐑉; 𐐌 𐑅𐐩, 𐐮𐑁 𐐷 𐑇𐐳𐐼 𐑅𐐲𐑉𐑂 𐐸𐐮𐑋 𐐶𐐮𐑄 𐐫𐑊 𐐷𐐬𐑉 𐐸𐐬𐑊 𐑅𐐬𐑊𐑆, 𐑄𐐰𐐻 𐐷 𐐶𐐳𐐼 𐐺 𐐲𐑌𐐹𐑉𐐱𐑁𐐮𐐻𐐲𐐺𐑊 𐑅𐐲𐑉𐑂𐐲𐑌𐐻𐑅. 𐐈𐑌𐐼 𐐺𐐨𐐸𐐬𐑊𐐼, 𐐫𐑊 𐑄𐐰𐐻 𐐸𐐨 𐑉𐐨𐐿𐐶𐐴𐑉𐑆 𐐱𐑂 𐐷𐐭 𐐮𐑆 𐐻𐐭 𐐿𐐨𐐹 𐐸𐐮𐑆 𐐿𐐱𐑋𐐰𐑌𐐼𐑋𐐯𐑌𐐻𐑅; 𐐰𐑌𐐼 𐐸𐐨 𐐸𐐰𐑆 𐐹𐑉𐐱𐑋𐐮𐑅𐐻 𐐷𐐭 𐑄𐐰𐐻 𐐮𐑁 𐐷 𐐶𐐳𐐼 𐐿𐐨𐐹 𐐸𐐮𐑆 𐐿𐐱𐑋𐐰𐑌𐐼𐑋𐐯𐑌𐐻𐑅, 𐐷 𐑇𐐳𐐼 𐐹𐑉𐐱𐑅𐐹𐐲𐑉 𐐮𐑌 𐑄 𐑊𐐰𐑌𐐼; 𐐰𐑌𐐼 𐐸𐐨 𐑌𐐯𐑂𐐲𐑉 𐐼𐐲𐑃 𐑂𐐩𐑉𐐨 𐑁𐑉𐐱𐑋 𐑄𐐰𐐻 𐐸𐐶𐐮𐐽 𐐸𐐨 𐐸𐐰𐑃 𐑅𐐯𐐼; 𐑄𐐯𐑉𐑁𐐬𐑉, 𐐮𐑁 𐐷 𐐼𐐭 𐐿𐐨𐐹 𐐸𐐮𐑆 𐐿𐐱𐑋𐐰𐑌𐐼𐑋𐐯𐑌𐐻𐑅, 𐐸𐐨 𐐼𐐲𐑃 𐐺𐑊𐐯𐑅 𐐷𐐭 𐐰𐑌𐐼 𐐹𐑉𐐱𐑅𐐹𐐲𐑉 𐐷𐐭.

9. 𐐈𐑌𐐼 𐑌𐐵, 𐐮𐑌 𐑄 𐑁𐐲𐑉𐑅𐐻 𐐹𐑊𐐩𐑅, 𐐸𐐨 𐐸𐐰𐑃 𐐿𐑉𐐨𐐩𐐻𐐯𐐼 𐐷𐐭, 𐐰𐑌𐐼 𐑀𐑉𐐰𐑌𐐻𐐯𐐼 𐐲𐑌𐐻𐐭 𐐷𐐭 𐐷𐐬𐑉 𐑊𐐴𐑂𐑆, 𐑁𐐬𐑉 𐐸𐐶𐐮𐐽 𐐷 𐐪𐑉 𐐮𐑌𐐼𐐯𐐻𐐯𐐼 𐐲𐑌𐐻𐐭 𐐸𐐮𐑋. 𐐈𐑌𐐼 𐑅𐐯𐐿𐐲𐑌𐐼𐑊𐐨: 𐐸𐐨 𐐼𐐲𐑃 𐑉𐐨𐐿𐐶𐐴𐑉 𐑄𐐰𐐻 𐐷 𐑇𐐳𐐼 𐐼𐐭 𐐰𐑆 𐐸𐐨 𐐸𐐰𐑃 𐐿𐐱𐑋𐐰𐑌𐐼𐐯𐐼 𐐷𐐭; 𐑁𐐬𐑉 𐐸𐐶𐐮𐐽 𐐮𐑁 𐐷 𐐼𐐭, 𐐸𐐨 𐐼𐐲𐑃 𐐮𐑋𐐨𐐼𐐨𐐩𐐻𐑊𐐨 𐐺𐑊𐐯𐑅 𐐷𐐭; 𐐰𐑌𐐼 𐑄𐐯𐑉𐑁𐐬𐑉 𐐸𐐨 𐐸𐐰𐑃 𐐹𐐩𐐼 𐐷𐐭. 𐐈𐑌𐐼 𐐷 𐐪𐑉 𐑅𐐻𐐮𐑊 𐐮𐑌𐐼𐐯𐐻𐐯𐐼 𐐲𐑌𐐻𐐭 𐐸𐐮𐑋; 𐐰𐑌𐐼 𐐪𐑉, 𐐰𐑌𐐼 𐐶𐐮𐑊 𐐺, 𐑁𐐬𐑉 𐐯𐑂𐐲𐑉 𐐰𐑌𐐼 𐐯𐑂𐐲𐑉; 𐑄𐐯𐑉𐑁𐐬𐑉, 𐐱𐑂 𐐸𐐶𐐱𐐻 𐐸𐐰𐑂 𐐷 𐐻𐐭 𐐺𐐬𐑅𐐻? 𐐈𐑌𐐼 𐑌𐐵 𐐌 𐐰𐑅𐐿, 𐐿𐐰𐑌 𐐷 𐑅𐐩 𐐫𐐻 𐐱𐑂 𐐷𐐬𐑉𐑅𐐯𐑊𐑂𐑆? 𐐌 𐐰𐑌𐑅𐐲𐑉 𐐷𐐭, 𐑌𐐩. 𐐏 𐐿𐐰𐑌𐐱𐐻 𐑅𐐩 𐑄𐐰𐐻 𐐷 𐐪𐑉 𐐨𐑂𐑌 𐐰𐑆 𐑋𐐲𐐽 𐐰𐑆 𐑄 𐐼𐐲𐑅𐐻 𐐱𐑂 𐑄 𐐲𐑉𐑃: 𐐷𐐯𐐻 𐐷 𐐶𐐲𐑉 𐐿𐑉𐐨𐐩𐐻𐐯𐐼 𐐱𐑂 𐑄 𐐼𐐲𐑅𐐻 𐐱𐑂 𐑄 𐐲𐑉𐑃: 𐐺𐐲𐐻 𐐺𐐨𐐸𐐬𐑊𐐼, 𐐮𐐻 𐐺𐐨𐑊𐐱𐑍𐐯𐑃 𐐻𐐭 𐐸𐐮𐑋 𐐸𐐭 𐐿𐑉𐐨𐐩𐐻𐐯𐐼 𐐷𐐭. 𐐈𐑌𐐼 𐐌, 𐐨𐑂𐑌 𐐌, 𐐸𐐭𐑋 𐐷 𐐿𐐫𐑊 𐐷𐐬𐑉 𐐿𐐮𐑍, 𐐰𐑋 𐑌𐐬 𐐺𐐯𐐻𐐲𐑉 𐑄𐐰𐑌 𐐷 𐐷𐐬𐑉𐑅𐐯𐑊𐑂𐑆 𐐪𐑉; 𐑁𐐬𐑉 𐐌 𐐰𐑋 𐐫𐑊𐑅𐐬 𐐱𐑂 𐑄 𐐼𐐲𐑅𐐻. 𐐈𐑌𐐼 𐐷 𐐺𐐨𐐸𐐬𐑊𐐼 𐑄𐐰𐐻 𐐌 𐐰𐑋 𐐬𐑊𐐼, 𐐰𐑌𐐼 𐐰𐑋 𐐰𐐺𐐵𐐻 𐐻𐐭 𐐷𐐨𐑊𐐼 𐐲𐐹 𐑄𐐮𐑅 𐑋𐐫𐑉𐐻𐐲𐑊 𐑁𐑉𐐩𐑋 𐐻𐐭 𐐮𐐻𐑅 𐑋𐐲𐑄𐐲𐑉 𐐲𐑉𐑃; 𐑄𐐯𐑉𐑁𐐬𐑉, 𐐰𐑆 𐐌 𐑅𐐯𐐼 𐐲𐑌𐐻𐐭 𐐷𐐭 𐑄𐐰𐐻 𐐌 𐐸𐐰𐐼 𐑅𐐲𐑉𐑂𐐼 𐐷𐐭, 𐐶𐐫𐐿𐐮𐑍 𐐶𐐮𐑄 𐐲 𐐿𐑊𐐨𐑉 𐐿𐐱𐑌𐑇𐐯𐑌𐑅 𐐺𐐨𐑁𐐬𐑉 𐐘𐐱𐐼, 𐐨𐑂𐑌 𐑅𐐬 𐐌 𐐰𐐻 𐑄𐐮𐑅 𐐻𐐴𐑋 𐐸𐐰𐑂 𐐿𐐫𐑆𐐼 𐑄𐐰𐐻 𐐷 𐑇𐐳𐐼 𐐰𐑅𐐯𐑋𐐺𐑊 𐐷𐐬𐑉𐑅𐐯𐑊𐑂𐑆 𐐻𐐳𐑀𐐯𐑄𐐲𐑉, 𐑄𐐰𐐻 𐐌 𐑋𐐴𐐻 𐐺 𐑁𐐵𐑌𐐼 𐐺𐑊𐐩𐑋𐑊𐐯𐑅, 𐐰𐑌𐐼 𐑄𐐰𐐻 𐐷𐐬𐑉 𐐺𐑊𐐲𐐼 𐑇𐐳𐐼 𐑌𐐱𐐻 𐐿𐐲𐑋 𐐲𐐹𐐱𐑌 𐑋𐐨, 𐐸𐐶𐐯𐑌 𐐌 𐑇𐐰𐑊 𐑅𐐻𐐰𐑌𐐼 𐐻𐐭 𐐺 𐐾𐐲𐐾𐐼 𐐱𐑂 𐐘𐐱𐐼 𐐱𐑂 𐑄 𐑃𐐮𐑍𐑆 𐐸𐐶𐐯𐑉𐐱𐑂 𐐸𐐨 𐐸𐐰𐑃 𐐿𐐱𐑋𐐰𐑌𐐼𐐯𐐼 𐑋𐐨 𐐿𐐱𐑌𐑅𐐲𐑉𐑌𐐮𐑍 𐐷𐐭. 𐐌 𐑅𐐩 𐐲𐑌𐐻𐐭 𐐷𐐭, 𐑄𐐰𐐻 𐐌 𐐸𐐰𐑂 𐐿𐐫𐑆𐐼 𐑄𐐰𐐻 𐐷 𐑇𐐳𐐼 𐐰𐑅𐐯𐑋𐐺𐑊 𐐷𐐬𐑉𐑅𐐯𐑊𐑂𐑆 𐐻𐐳𐑀𐐯𐑄𐐲𐑉, 𐑄𐐰𐐻 𐐌 𐑋𐐴𐐻 𐑉𐐮𐐼 𐑋𐐴 𐑀𐐪𐑉𐑋𐐯𐑌𐐻𐑅 𐐱𐑂 𐐷𐐬𐑉 𐐺𐑊𐐲𐐼, 𐐰𐐻 𐑄𐐮𐑅 𐐹𐐨𐑉𐐨𐐲𐐼 𐐱𐑂 𐐻𐐴𐑋 𐐸𐐶𐐯𐑌 𐐌 𐐰𐑋 𐐰𐐺𐐵𐐻 𐐻𐐭 𐑀𐐬 𐐼𐐵𐑌 𐐻𐐭 𐑋𐐴 𐑀𐑉𐐩𐑂, 𐑄𐐰𐐻 𐐌 𐑋𐐴𐐻 𐑀𐐬 𐐼𐐵𐑌 𐐮𐑌 𐐹𐐨𐑅, 𐐰𐑌𐐼 𐑋𐐴 𐐮𐑋𐐫𐑉𐐻𐐲𐑊 𐑅𐐹𐐮𐑉𐐮𐐻 𐑋𐐩 𐐾𐐦𐑌 𐑄 𐐿𐐶𐐴𐑉𐑆 𐐰𐐺𐐲𐑂 𐐮𐑌 𐑅𐐮𐑍𐐮𐑍 𐑄 𐐹𐑉𐐩𐑆𐐯𐑆 𐐱𐑂 𐐲 𐐾𐐲𐑅𐐻 𐐘𐐱𐐼. 𐐈𐑌𐐼 𐑋𐐬𐑉𐐬𐑂𐐲𐑉, 𐐌 𐑅𐐩 𐐲𐑌𐐻𐐭 𐐷𐐭, 𐑄𐐰𐐻 𐐌 𐐸𐐰𐑂 𐐿𐐫𐑆𐐼 𐑄𐐰𐐻 𐐷 𐑇𐐳𐐼 𐐰𐑅𐐯𐑋𐐺𐑊 𐐷𐐬𐑉𐑅𐐯𐑊𐑂𐑆 𐐻𐐳𐑀𐐯𐑄𐐲𐑉, 𐑄𐐰𐐻 𐐌 𐑋𐐴𐐻 𐐼𐐨𐐿𐑊𐐯𐑉 𐐲𐑌𐐻𐐭 𐐷𐐭 𐑄𐐰𐐻 𐐌 𐐿𐐰𐑌 𐑌𐐬 𐑊𐐱𐑍𐑀𐐲𐑉 𐐺 𐐷𐐬𐑉 𐐻𐐨𐐽𐐲𐑉, 𐑌𐐫𐑉 𐐷𐐬𐑉 𐐿𐐮𐑍; 𐑁𐐬𐑉 𐐨𐑂𐑌 𐐰𐐻 𐑄𐐮𐑅 𐐻𐐴𐑋, 𐑋𐐴 𐐸𐐬𐑊 𐑁𐑉𐐩𐑋 𐐼𐐲𐑃 𐐻𐑉𐐯𐑋𐐺𐑊 𐐯𐐿𐑅𐐨𐐼𐐮𐑍𐑊𐐨, 𐐸𐐶𐐴𐑊 𐐰𐐻𐐯𐑋𐐹𐐻𐐮𐑍 𐐻𐐭 𐑅𐐹𐐨𐐿 𐐲𐑌𐐻𐐭 𐐷𐐭; 𐐺𐐲𐐻 𐑄 𐐢𐐫𐑉𐐼 𐐘𐐱𐐼 𐐼𐐲𐑃 𐑅𐐲𐐹𐐬𐑉𐐻 𐑋𐐨, 𐐰𐑌𐐼 𐐸𐐰𐑃 𐑅𐐲𐑁𐐲𐑉𐐼 𐑋𐐨 𐑄𐐰𐐻 𐐌 𐑇𐐳𐐼 𐑅𐐹𐐨𐐿 𐐲𐑌𐐻𐐭 𐐷𐐭, 𐐰𐑌𐐼 𐐸𐐰𐑃 𐐿𐐱𐑋𐐰𐑌𐐼𐐯𐐼 𐑋𐐨 𐑄𐐰𐐻 𐐌 𐑇𐐳𐐼 𐐼𐐨𐐿𐑊𐐯𐑉 𐐲𐑌𐐻𐐭 𐐷𐐭 𐑄𐐮𐑅 𐐼𐐩, 𐑄𐐰𐐻 𐑋𐐴 𐑅𐐲𐑌 𐐣𐐬𐑆𐐴𐐲 𐐮𐑆 𐐲 𐐿𐐮𐑍 𐐰𐑌𐐼 𐐲 𐑉𐐭𐑊𐐲𐑉 𐐬𐑂𐐲𐑉 𐐷𐐭.

10. 𐐈𐑌𐐼 𐑌𐐵, 𐑋𐐴 𐐺𐑉𐐯𐑄𐑉𐐯𐑌, 𐐴 𐐶𐐳𐐼 𐑄𐐰𐐻 𐐷 𐑇𐐳𐐼 𐐼𐐭 𐐰𐑆 𐐷 𐐸𐐰𐑂 𐐸𐐮𐑄𐐲𐑉𐐻𐐭 𐐼𐐲𐑌. 𐐈𐑆 𐐷 𐐸𐐰𐑂 𐐿𐐯𐐹𐐻 𐑋𐐴 𐐿𐐱𐑋𐐰𐑌𐐼𐑋𐐯𐑌𐐻𐑅, 𐐰𐑌𐐼 𐐫𐑊𐑅𐐬 𐑄 𐐿𐐱𐑋𐐰𐑌𐐼𐑋𐐯𐑌𐐻𐑅 𐐱𐑂 𐑋𐐴 𐑁𐐪𐑄𐐲𐑉, 𐐰𐑌𐐼 𐐸𐐰𐑂 𐐹𐑉𐐱𐑅𐐹𐐲𐑉𐐼, 𐐰𐑌𐐼 𐐸𐐰𐑂 𐐺𐐨𐑌 𐐿𐐯𐐹𐐻 𐑁𐑉𐐱𐑋 𐑁𐐫𐑊𐐮𐑍 𐐮𐑌𐐻𐐭 𐑄 𐐸𐐰𐑌𐐼𐑆 𐐱𐑂 𐐷𐐬𐑉 𐐯𐑌𐐯𐑋𐐨𐑆, 𐐨𐑂𐐲𐑌 𐑅𐐬 𐐮𐑁 𐐷 𐑇𐐰𐑊 𐐿𐐨𐐹 𐑄 𐐿𐐱𐑋𐐰𐑌𐐼𐑋𐐯𐑌𐐻𐑅 𐐱𐑂 𐑋𐐴 𐑅𐐲𐑌, 𐐫𐑉 𐑄 𐐿𐐱𐑋𐐰𐑌𐐼𐑋𐐯𐑌𐐻𐑅 𐐱𐑂 𐐘𐐱𐐼, 𐐸𐐶𐐮𐐽 𐑇𐐰𐑊 𐐺𐐨 𐐼𐐯𐑊𐐮𐑂𐐲𐑉𐐼 𐐲𐑌𐐻𐐭 𐐷𐐭 𐐺𐐴 𐐸𐐮𐑋, 𐐷 𐑇𐐰𐑊 𐐹𐑉𐐱𐑅𐐹𐐲𐑉 𐐮𐑌 𐑄 𐑊𐐰𐑌𐐼, 𐐰𐑌𐐼 𐐷𐐬𐑉 𐐯𐑌𐐯𐑋𐐨𐑆 𐑇𐐰𐑊 𐐸𐐰𐑂 𐑌𐐬 𐐹𐐵𐐲𐑉 𐐬𐑂𐐲𐑉 𐐷𐐭. 𐐒𐐲𐐻, 𐐄 𐑋𐐴 𐐹𐐨𐐹𐑊, 𐐺𐐨𐐶𐐩𐑉 𐑊𐐯𐑅𐐻 𐑄𐐯𐑉 𐑇𐐰𐑊 𐐲𐑉𐐴𐑆 𐐿𐐱𐑌𐐻𐐯𐑌𐑇𐐲𐑌𐑆 𐐲𐑋𐐲𐑍 𐐷𐐭, 𐐰𐑌𐐼 𐐷 𐑊𐐮𐑅𐐻 𐐻𐐭 𐐬𐐺𐐩 𐑄 𐐨𐑂𐐮𐑊 𐑅𐐹𐐮𐑉𐐮𐐻, 𐐸𐐶𐐮𐐽 𐐶𐐱𐑆 𐑅𐐹𐐬𐐿𐐲𐑌 𐐱𐑂 𐐺𐐴 𐑋𐐴 𐑁𐐪𐑄𐐲𐑉 𐐣𐐬𐑅𐐴𐐲. 𐐙𐐫𐑉 𐐺𐐨𐐸𐐬𐑊𐐼, 𐑄𐐯𐑉 𐐮𐑆 𐐰 𐐶𐐬 𐐹𐑉𐐬𐑌𐐵𐑌𐑅𐐻 𐐲𐐹𐐱𐑌 𐐸𐐮𐑋 𐐸𐐭 𐑊𐐮𐑅𐐻𐐯𐑃 𐐻𐐭 𐐬𐐺𐐩 𐑄𐐰𐐻 𐑅𐐹𐐮𐑉𐐮𐐻; 𐑁𐐫𐑉 𐐮𐑁 𐐸𐐨 𐑊𐐮𐑅𐐻𐐯𐑃 𐐻𐐭 𐐬𐐺𐐩 𐐸𐐮𐑋, 𐐰𐑌𐐼 𐑉𐐨𐑋𐐩𐑌𐐯𐑃 𐐰𐑌𐐼 𐐼𐐴𐐯𐑃 𐐮𐑌 𐐸𐐮𐑆 𐑅𐐮𐑌𐑆, 𐑄 𐑅𐐩𐑋 𐐼𐑉𐐮𐑍𐐿𐐯𐑃 𐐼𐐰𐑋𐑌𐐩𐑇𐐲𐑌 𐐻𐐭 𐐸𐐮𐑆 𐐬𐑌 𐑅𐐬𐑊; 𐑁𐐫𐑉 𐐸𐐨 𐑉𐐨𐑅𐐨𐑂𐐯𐑃 𐑁𐐫𐑉 𐐸𐐮𐑆 𐐶𐐩𐐾𐐯𐑆 𐐰𐑌 𐐯𐑂𐐲𐑉𐑊𐐰𐑅𐐻𐐮𐑍 𐐹𐐲𐑌𐐮𐑇𐑋𐐯𐑌𐐻, 𐐸𐐰𐑂𐐮𐑍 𐐻𐑉𐐰𐑌𐑆𐑀𐑉𐐯𐑅𐐻 𐑄 𐑊𐐫 𐐱𐑂 𐐘𐐱𐐼, 𐐿𐐱𐑌𐐻𐑉𐐯𐑉𐐨 𐐻𐐭 𐐸𐐮𐑆 𐐬𐑌 𐑌𐐱𐑊𐐯𐐾. 𐐌 𐑅𐐩 𐐲𐑌𐐻𐐭 𐐷𐐭, 𐑄𐐰𐐻 𐑄𐐯𐑉 𐐪𐑉 𐑌𐐱𐐻 𐐯𐑌𐐨 𐐲𐑋𐐲𐑍 𐐷𐐭, 𐐯𐐿𐑅𐐯𐐹𐐻 𐐮𐐻 𐐺𐐨 𐐷𐐬𐑉 𐑊𐐮𐐻𐑊 𐐽𐐮𐑊𐐼𐑉𐐯𐑌 𐑄𐐰𐐻 𐐸𐐰𐑂 𐑌𐐱𐐻 𐐺𐐨𐑌 𐐻𐐫𐐻 𐐿𐐱𐑌𐑅𐐲𐑉𐑌𐐮𐑍 𐑄𐐨𐑆 𐑃𐐮𐑍𐑆, 𐐺𐐲𐐻 𐐸𐐶𐐱𐐻 𐑌𐐬𐐯𐑃 𐑄𐐰𐐻 𐐷 𐐪𐑉 𐐯𐐻𐐲𐑉𐑌𐐲𐑊𐐨 𐐮𐑌𐐼𐐯𐐻𐐯𐐼 𐐻𐐭 𐐷𐐬𐑉 𐐸𐐯𐑂𐐲𐑌𐑊𐐨 𐐙𐐪𐑄𐐲𐑉, 𐐻𐐭 𐑉𐐯𐑌𐐼𐐲𐑉 𐐻𐐭 𐐸𐐮𐑋 𐐫𐑊 𐑄𐐰𐐻 𐐷𐐭 𐐸𐐰𐑂 𐐰𐑌𐐼 𐐪𐑉, 𐐰𐑌𐐼 𐐫𐑊𐑅𐐬 𐐸𐐰𐑂 𐐺𐐨𐑌 𐐻𐐫𐐻 𐐿𐐱𐑌𐑅𐐲𐑉𐑌𐐮𐑍 𐑄 𐑉𐐯𐐿𐐲𐑉𐐼𐑆 𐐸𐐶𐐮𐐽 𐐿𐐱𐑌𐐻𐐩𐑌 𐑄 𐐹𐑉𐐱𐑁𐐯𐑅𐐨𐑆 𐐸𐐶𐐮𐐽 𐐸𐐰𐑂 𐐺𐐨𐑌 𐑅𐐹𐐬𐐿𐐲𐑌 𐐺𐐴 𐑄 𐐸𐐬𐑊𐐨 𐐹𐑉𐐱𐑁𐐯𐐻𐑅, 𐐨𐑂𐐲𐑌 𐐼𐐵𐑌 𐐻𐐭 𐑄 𐐻𐐴𐑋 𐐵𐐲𐑉 𐑁𐐪𐑄𐐲𐑉 𐐢𐐨𐐸𐐴 𐑊𐐯𐑁𐐻 𐐖𐐯𐑉𐐭𐑅𐐲𐑊𐐯𐑋; 𐐰𐑌𐐼 𐐫𐑊𐑅𐐬, 𐐫𐑊 𐑄𐐰𐐻 𐐸𐐰𐑆 𐐺𐐨𐑌 𐑅𐐹𐐬𐐿𐐲𐑌 𐐺𐐴 𐐵𐐲𐑉 𐑁𐐪𐑄𐐲𐑉𐑆 𐐲𐑌𐐻𐐮𐑊 𐑌𐐵. 𐐈𐑌𐐼 𐐺𐐨𐐸𐐬𐑊𐐼, 𐐫𐑊𐑅𐐬, 𐑄𐐩 𐑅𐐹𐐪𐐿 𐑄𐐰𐐻 𐐸𐐶𐐮𐐽 𐐶𐐱𐑆 𐐿𐐱𐑋𐐰𐑌𐐼𐐯𐐼 𐑄𐐯𐑋 𐐱𐑂 𐑄 𐐢𐐫𐑉𐐼; 𐑄𐐯𐑉𐑁𐐫𐑉, 𐑄𐐩 𐐪𐑉 𐐾𐐲𐑅𐐻 𐐰𐑌𐐼 𐐻𐑉𐐭.

11. 𐐈𐑌𐐼 𐑌𐐵, 𐐴 𐑅𐐩 𐐲𐑌𐐻𐐭 𐐷𐐭, 𐑋𐐴 𐐺𐑉𐐯𐑄𐑉𐐯𐑌, 𐑄𐐰𐐻 𐐰𐑁𐐻𐐲𐑉 𐐷 𐐸𐐰𐑂 𐑌𐐬𐑌 𐐰𐑌𐐼 𐐸𐐰𐑂 𐐺𐐨𐑌 𐐻𐐫𐐻 𐐫𐑊 𐑄𐐨𐑆 𐑃𐐮𐑍𐑆, 𐐮𐑁 𐐷 𐑇𐐳𐐼 𐐻𐑉𐐰𐑌𐑆𐑀𐑉𐐯𐑅, 𐐰𐑌𐐼 𐑀𐐬 𐐿𐐱𐑌𐐻𐑉𐐯𐑉𐐨 𐐻𐐭 𐑄𐐰𐐻 𐐸𐐶𐐮𐐽 𐐸𐐰𐑆 𐐺𐐨𐑌 𐑅𐐹𐐬𐐿𐐲𐑌, 𐑄𐐰𐐻 𐐷 𐐼𐐭 𐐶𐐮𐑃𐐼𐑉𐐫 𐐷𐐬𐑉𐑅𐐯𐑊𐑂𐑆 𐑁𐑉𐐱𐑋 𐑄 𐐝𐐹𐐮𐑉𐐮𐐻 𐐱𐑂 𐑄 𐐢𐐫𐑉𐐼, 𐑄𐐰𐐻 𐐮𐐻 𐑋𐐩 𐐸𐐰𐑂 𐑌𐐬 𐐹𐑊𐐩𐑅 𐐮𐑌 𐐷𐐭 𐐻𐐭 𐑀𐐴𐐼 𐐷𐐭 𐐮𐑌 𐐶𐐮𐑆𐐼𐐲𐑋'𐑆 𐐹𐐪𐑃𐑅, 𐑄𐐰𐐻 𐐷 𐑋𐐩 𐐺𐐨 𐐺𐑊𐐯𐑅𐐻, 𐐹𐑉𐐱𐑅𐐹𐐲𐑉𐐼, 𐐰𐑌𐐼 𐐹𐑉𐐨𐑆𐐲𐑉𐑂𐐼. 𐐌 𐑅𐐩 𐐲𐑌𐐻𐐭 𐐷𐐭, 𐑄𐐰𐐻 𐑄 𐑋𐐰𐑌 𐑄𐐰𐐻 𐐼𐐭𐐯𐑃 𐑄𐐮𐑅, 𐑄 𐑅𐐩𐑋 𐐿𐐲𐑋𐐯𐑃 𐐵𐐻 𐐮𐑌 𐐬𐐹𐐯𐑌 𐑉𐐨𐐺𐐯𐑊𐐷𐐲𐑌 𐐲𐑀𐐯𐑌𐑅𐐻 𐐘𐐱𐐼; 𐑄𐐯𐑉𐑁𐐫𐑉 𐐸𐐨 𐑊𐐮𐑅𐐻𐐯𐑃 𐐻𐐭 𐐬𐐺𐐩 𐑄 𐐨𐑂𐐮𐑊 𐑅𐐹𐐮𐑉𐐮𐐻, 𐐰𐑌𐐼 𐐺𐐨𐐿𐐲𐑋𐐯𐑃 𐐰𐑌 𐐯𐑌𐐯𐑋𐐨 𐐻𐐭 𐐫𐑊 𐑉𐐴𐐽𐐲𐑅𐑌𐐯𐑅; 𐑄𐐯𐑉𐑁𐐫𐑉, 𐑄 𐐢𐐫𐑉𐐼 𐐸𐐰𐑆 𐑌𐐬 𐐹𐑊𐐩𐑅 𐐮𐑌 𐐸𐐮𐑋, 𐑁𐐫𐑉 𐐸𐐨 𐐼𐐶𐐯𐑊𐐯𐑃 𐑌𐐱𐐻 𐐮𐑌 𐐲𐑌𐐸𐐬𐑊𐐨 𐐻𐐯𐑋𐐹𐑊𐑆. 𐐜𐐯𐑉𐑁𐐫𐑉 𐐮𐑁 𐑄𐐰𐐻 𐑋𐐰𐑌 𐑉𐐨𐐹𐐯𐑌𐐻𐐯𐑃 𐑌𐐱𐐻, 𐐰𐑌𐐼 𐑉𐐨𐑋𐐩𐑌𐐯𐑃 𐐰𐑌𐐼 𐐼𐐴𐐯𐑃 𐐰𐑌 𐐯𐑌𐐯𐑋𐐨 𐐻𐐭 𐐘𐐱𐐼, 𐑄 𐐼𐐨𐑋𐐰𐑌𐐼𐑆 𐐱𐑂 𐐼𐐮𐑂𐐴𐑌 𐐾𐐲𐑅𐐻𐐮𐑅 𐐼𐐭 𐐲𐐶𐐩𐐿𐐲𐑌 𐐸𐐮𐑆 𐐮𐑋𐐫𐑉𐐻𐐲𐑊 𐑅𐐬𐑊 𐐻𐐭 𐐰 𐑊𐐴𐑂𐑊𐐨 𐑅𐐯𐑌𐑅 𐐱𐑂 𐐸𐐮𐑆 𐐬𐑌 𐑀𐐮𐑊𐐻, 𐐸𐐶𐐮𐐽 𐐼𐐲𐑃 𐐿𐐫𐑆 𐐸𐐮𐑋 𐐻𐐭 𐑇𐑉𐐮𐑍𐐿 𐑁𐑉𐐱𐑋 𐑄 𐐹𐑉𐐯𐑆𐐯𐑌𐑅 𐐱𐑂 𐑄 𐐢𐐫𐑉𐐼, 𐐰𐑌𐐼 𐐼𐐲𐑃 𐑁𐐮𐑊 𐐸𐐮𐑆 𐐺𐑉𐐯𐑅𐐻 𐐶𐐮𐑄 𐑀𐐮𐑊𐐻, 𐐰𐑌𐐼 𐐹𐐩𐑌, 𐐰𐑌𐐼 𐐰𐑍𐑀𐐶𐐮𐑇, 𐐸𐐶𐐮𐐽 𐐮𐑆 𐑊𐐴𐐿 𐐰𐑌 𐐲𐑌𐐿𐐶𐐯𐑌𐐽𐐲𐐺𐑊 𐑁𐐴𐑉, 𐐸𐐭𐑆 𐑁𐑊𐐩𐑋 𐐰𐑅𐐯𐑌𐐼𐐯𐑃 𐐲𐐹 𐑁𐐫𐑉𐐯𐑂𐐲𐑉 𐐰𐑌𐐼 𐐯𐑂𐐲𐑉. 𐐈𐑌𐐼 𐑌𐐵 𐐴 𐑅𐐩 𐐲𐑌𐐻𐐭 𐐷𐐭, 𐑄𐐰𐐻 𐑋𐐲𐑉𐑅𐐨 𐐸𐐰𐑃 𐑌𐐬 𐐿𐑊𐐩𐑋 𐐱𐑌 𐑄𐐰𐐻 𐑋𐐰𐑌; 𐑄𐐯𐑉𐑁𐐫𐑉, 𐐸𐐮𐑆 𐑁𐐴𐑌𐐲𐑊 𐐼𐐭𐑋 𐐮𐑆 𐐻𐐭 𐐯𐑌𐐼𐐭𐑉 𐐰 𐑌𐐯𐑂𐐲𐑉-𐐯𐑌𐐼𐐮𐑍 𐐻𐐫𐑉𐑋𐐯𐑌𐐻.

12. 𐐄, 𐐫𐑊 𐐷 𐐬𐑊𐐼 𐑋𐐯𐑌, 𐐰𐑌𐐼 𐐫𐑊𐑅𐐬 𐐷 𐐷𐐲𐑍 𐑋𐐯𐑌, 𐐰𐑌𐐼 𐐷𐐭 𐑊𐐮𐐻𐑊 𐐽𐐮𐑊𐐼𐑉𐐯𐑌, 𐐸𐐭 𐐿𐐰𐑌 𐐲𐑌𐐼𐐲𐑉𐑅𐐻𐐰𐑌𐐼 𐑋𐐴 𐐶𐐲𐑉𐐼𐑆, (𐑁𐐫𐑉 𐐴 𐐸𐐰𐑂 𐑅𐐹𐐬𐐿𐐲𐑌 𐐹𐑊𐐩𐑌𐑊𐐨 𐐲𐑌𐐻𐐭 𐐷𐐭, 𐑄𐐰𐐻 𐐷 𐑋𐐴𐐻 𐐲𐑌𐐼𐐲𐑉𐑅𐐻𐐰𐑌𐐼,) 𐐴 𐐹𐑉𐐩 𐑄𐐰𐐻 𐐷 𐑇𐐳𐐼 𐐲𐐶𐐩𐐿 𐐻𐐭 𐐰 𐑉𐐨𐑋𐐯𐑋𐐺𐑉𐐲𐑌𐑅 𐐱𐑂 𐑄 𐐫𐑁𐐳𐑊 𐑅𐐮𐐻𐐷𐐭𐐩𐑇𐐲𐑌 𐐱𐑂 𐑄𐐬𐑆 𐑄𐐰𐐻 𐐸𐐰𐑂 𐑁𐐫𐑊𐐲𐑌 𐐮𐑌𐐻𐐭 𐐻𐑉𐐰𐑌𐑆𐑀𐑉𐐯𐑇𐐲𐑌; 𐐰𐑌𐐼 𐑋𐐬𐑉𐐬𐑂𐐲𐑉, 𐐴 𐐶𐐳𐐼 𐐼𐐨𐑆𐐴𐑉 𐑄𐐰𐐻 𐐷 𐑇𐐳𐐼 𐐿𐐱𐑌𐑅𐐮𐐼𐐲𐑉 𐐱𐑌 𐑄 𐐺𐑊𐐯𐑅𐐯𐐼 𐐰𐑌𐐼 𐐸𐐰𐐹𐐨 𐑅𐐻𐐩𐐻 𐐱𐑂 𐑄𐐬𐑆 𐑄𐐰𐐻 𐐿𐐨𐐹 𐑄 𐐿𐐱𐑋𐐰𐑌𐐼𐑋𐐯𐑌𐐻𐑅 𐐱𐑂 𐐘𐐱𐐼. 𐐙𐐫𐑉 𐐺𐐨𐐸𐐬𐑊𐐼, 𐑄𐐩 𐐪𐑉 𐐺𐑊𐐯𐑅𐐯𐐼 𐐮𐑌 𐐫𐑊 𐑃𐐮𐑍𐑆, 𐐺𐐬𐑃 𐐻𐐯𐑋𐐹𐐬𐑉𐐲𐑊 𐐰𐑌𐐼 𐑅𐐹𐐮𐑉𐐮𐐻𐐷𐐭𐐲𐑊; 𐐰𐑌𐐼 𐐮𐑁 𐑄𐐩 𐐸𐐬𐑊𐐼 𐐵𐐻 𐑁𐐩𐑃𐑁𐐳𐑊 𐐻𐐭 𐑄 𐐯𐑌𐐼, 𐑄𐐩 𐐪𐑉 𐑉𐐨𐑅𐐨𐑂𐐼 𐐮𐑌𐐻𐐭 𐐸𐐯𐑂𐐲𐑌, 𐑄𐐰𐐻 𐑄𐐯𐑉𐐺𐐴 𐑄𐐩 𐑋𐐩 𐐼𐐶𐐯𐑊 𐐶𐐮𐑄 𐐘𐐱𐐼 𐐮𐑌 𐐰 𐑅𐐻𐐩𐐻 𐐱𐑂 𐑌𐐯𐑂𐐲𐑉-𐐯𐑌𐐼𐐮𐑍 𐐸𐐰𐐹𐐨𐑌𐐯𐑅. 𐐄 𐑉𐐨𐑋𐐯𐑋𐐺𐐲𐑉, 𐑉𐐨𐑋𐐯𐑋𐐺𐐲𐑉 𐑄𐐰𐐻 𐑄𐐨𐑆 𐑃𐐮𐑍𐑆 𐐪𐑉 𐐻𐑉𐐭; 𐑁𐐫𐑉 𐑄 𐐢𐐫𐑉𐐼 𐐘𐐱𐐼 𐐸𐐰𐑃 𐑅𐐹𐐬𐐿𐐲𐑌 𐐮𐐻.

13. 𐐈𐑌𐐼 𐐰𐑀𐐯𐑌 𐑋𐐴 𐐺𐑉𐐯𐑃𐑉𐐯𐑌, 𐐌 𐐶𐐳𐐼 𐐿𐐫𐑊 𐐷𐐫𐑉 𐐰𐐻𐐯𐑌𐑇𐐲𐑌, 𐑁𐐫𐑉 𐐌 𐐸𐐰𐑂 𐑅𐐲𐑋𐐶𐐱𐐻 𐑋𐐫𐑉 𐐻𐐭 𐑅𐐹𐐨𐐿 𐐲𐑌𐐻𐐭 𐐷𐐭; 𐑁𐐫𐑉 𐐺𐐨𐐸𐐬𐑊𐐼, 𐐌 𐐸𐐰𐑂 𐑃𐐮𐑍𐑆 𐐻𐐭 𐐻𐐯𐑊 𐐷𐐭 𐐿𐐲𐑌𐑅𐐲𐑉𐑌𐐮𐑍 𐑄𐐰𐐻 𐐸𐐶𐐮𐐽 𐐮𐑆 𐐻𐐭 𐐿𐐲𐑋; 𐐰𐑌𐐼 𐑄 𐑃𐐮𐑍𐑆 𐐸𐐶𐐮𐐽 𐐌 𐑇𐐰𐑊 𐐻𐐯𐑊 𐐷𐐭 𐐪𐑉 𐑋𐐩𐐼 𐑌𐐬𐑌 𐐲𐑌𐐻𐐭 𐑋𐐨, 𐐺𐐴 𐐰𐑌 𐐩𐑌𐐾𐐯𐑊 𐑁𐑉𐐱𐑋 𐐘𐐱𐐼. 𐐈𐑌𐐼 𐐸𐐨 𐑅𐐯𐐼 𐐲𐑌𐐻𐐭 𐑋𐐨, 𐐈𐐶𐐩𐐿; 𐐰𐑌𐐼 𐐌 𐐰𐐶𐐬𐐿, 𐐰𐑌𐐼 𐐺𐐨𐐸𐐬𐑊𐐼 𐐸𐐨 𐑅𐐻𐐳𐐼 𐐺𐐨𐑁𐐫𐑉 𐑋𐐨. 𐐈𐑌𐐼 𐐸𐐨 𐑅𐐯𐐼 𐐲𐑌𐐻𐐭 𐑋𐐨, 𐐈𐐶𐐩𐐿, 𐐰𐑌𐐼 𐐸𐐨𐑉 𐑄 𐐶𐐲𐑉𐐼𐑆 𐐸𐐶𐐮𐐽 𐐌 𐑇𐐰𐑊 𐐻𐐯𐑊 𐑄; 𐑁𐐫𐑉 𐐺𐐨𐐸𐐬𐑊𐐼, 𐐌 𐐰𐑋 𐐿𐐲𐑋 𐐻𐐭 𐐼𐐨𐐿𐑊𐐩𐑉 𐐲𐑌𐐻𐐭 𐐷𐐭 𐑄 𐑀𐑊𐐰𐐼 𐐻𐐴𐐼𐐮𐑍𐑆 𐐱𐑂 𐑀𐑉𐐩𐐻 𐐾𐐱𐐮. 𐐙𐐫𐑉 𐑄 𐐢𐐫𐑉𐐼 𐐸𐐰𐑃 𐐸𐐲𐑉𐐼 𐑄𐐴 𐐹𐑉𐐩𐑉𐑆, 𐐰𐑌𐐼 𐐸𐐰𐑃 𐐾𐐲𐐾𐐼 𐐱𐑂 𐑄𐐴 𐑉𐐴𐐽𐐲𐑅𐑌𐐯𐑅, 𐐰𐑌𐐼 𐐸𐐰𐑃 𐑅𐐯𐑌𐐻 𐑋𐐨 𐐻𐐭 𐐼𐐨𐐿𐑊𐐩𐑉 𐐲𐑌𐐻𐐭 𐑄 𐑄𐐰𐐻 𐑄𐐵 𐑋𐐩𐐯𐑅𐐻 𐑉𐐨𐐾𐐱𐐮𐑅; 𐐰𐑌𐐼 𐑄𐐰𐐻 𐑄𐐵 𐑋𐐩𐐯𐑅𐐻 𐐼𐐨𐐿𐑊𐐩𐑉 𐐲𐑌𐐻𐐭 𐑄𐐴 𐐹𐐨𐐹𐑊, 𐑄𐐰𐐻 𐑄𐐩 𐑋𐐩 𐐫𐑊𐑅𐐬 𐐺 𐑁𐐮𐑊𐐼 𐐶𐐮𐑄 𐐾𐐱𐐮. 𐐙𐐫𐑉 𐐺𐐨𐐸𐐬𐑊𐐼, 𐑄 𐐻𐐴𐑋 𐐿𐐲𐑋𐐯𐑃, 𐐰𐑌𐐼 𐐮𐑆 𐑌𐐱𐐻 𐑁𐐪𐑉 𐐼𐐮𐑅𐐻𐐲𐑌𐐻, 𐑄𐐰𐐻 𐐶𐐮𐑄 𐐹𐐵𐑉, 𐑄 𐐢𐐫𐑉𐐼 𐐉𐑋𐑌𐐮𐐹𐐬𐐻𐐯𐑌𐐻 𐐸𐐭 𐑉𐐩𐑌𐐯𐑃, 𐐸𐐭 𐐶𐐱𐑆, 𐐰𐑌𐐼 𐐮𐑆 𐑁𐑉𐐱𐑋 𐐫𐑊 𐐨𐐻𐐲𐑉𐑌𐐮𐐻𐐨 𐐻𐐭 𐐫𐑊 𐐨𐐻𐐲𐑉𐑌𐐮𐐻𐐨, 𐑇𐐰𐑊 𐐿𐐲𐑋 𐐼𐐵𐑌 𐑁𐑉𐐱𐑋 𐐸𐐯𐑂𐐲𐑌 𐐲𐑋𐐲𐑍 𐑄 𐐽𐐮𐑊𐐼𐑉𐐯𐑌 𐐱𐑂 𐑋𐐯𐑌, 𐐰𐑌𐐼 𐑇𐐰𐑊 𐐼𐐶𐐯𐑊 𐐮𐑌 𐐩 𐐻𐐰𐐺𐐲𐑉𐑌𐐰𐐿𐑊 𐐱𐑂 𐐿𐑊𐐩, 𐐰𐑌𐐼 𐑇𐐰𐑊 𐑀𐐬 𐑁𐐫𐑉𐑃 𐐲𐑋𐐲𐑍𐑅𐐻 𐑋𐐯𐑌, 𐐶𐐲𐑉𐐿𐐮𐑍 𐑋𐐴𐐻𐐨 𐑋𐐮𐑉𐐲𐐿𐑊𐑆, 𐑅𐐲𐐽 𐐰𐑆 𐐸𐐨𐑊𐐮𐑍 𐑄 𐑅𐐮𐐿, 𐑉𐐩𐑆𐐮𐑍 𐑄 𐐼𐐯𐐼, 𐐿𐐫𐑆𐐮𐑍 𐑄 𐑊𐐩𐑋 𐐻𐐭 𐐶𐐫𐐿, 𐑄 𐐺𐑊𐐴𐑌𐐼 𐐻𐐭 𐑉𐐨𐑅𐐨𐑂 𐑄𐐩𐑉 𐑅𐐴𐐻, 𐐰𐑌𐐼 𐑄 𐐼𐐯𐑁 𐐻𐐭 𐐸𐐨𐑉, 𐐰𐑌𐐼 𐐿𐐷𐐭𐑉𐐮𐑍 𐐫𐑊 𐑋𐐰𐑌𐐲𐑉 𐐱𐑂 𐐼𐐮𐑆𐐨𐑆𐐯𐑆; 𐐰𐑌𐐼 𐐸𐐨 𐑇𐐰𐑊 𐐿𐐰𐑅𐐻 𐐵𐐻 𐐼𐐯𐑂𐐲𐑊𐑆, 𐐫𐑉 𐑄 𐐨𐑂𐐲𐑊 𐑅𐐹𐐮𐑉𐐮𐐻𐑅 𐐸𐐶𐐮𐐽 𐐼𐐶𐐯𐑊 𐐮𐑌 𐑄 𐐸𐐪𐑉𐐻𐑅 𐐱𐑂 𐑄 𐐽𐐮𐑊𐐼𐑉𐐯𐑌 𐐱𐑂 𐑋𐐯𐑌. 𐐈𐑌𐐼 𐑊𐐬, 𐐸𐐨 𐑇𐐰𐑊 𐑅𐐲𐑁𐐲𐑉 𐐻𐐯𐑋𐐻𐐩𐑇𐐲𐑌𐑆, 𐐰𐑌𐐼 𐐹𐐩𐑌 𐐱𐑂 𐐺𐐱𐐼𐐨, 𐐸𐐲𐑍𐑀𐐲𐑉, 𐑃𐐲𐑉𐑅𐐻, 𐐰𐑌𐐼 𐑁𐐰𐐻𐐨𐑀, 𐐨𐑂𐐯𐑌 𐑋𐐫𐑉 𐑄𐐰𐑌 𐑋𐐰𐑌 𐐿𐐰𐑌 𐑅𐐲𐑁𐐲𐑉, 𐐯𐐿𐑅𐐯𐐹𐐻 𐐮𐐻 𐐺 𐐲𐑌𐐻𐐭 𐐼𐐯𐑃; 𐑁𐐫𐑉 𐐺𐐨𐐸𐐬𐑊𐐼, 𐐺𐑊𐐲𐐼 𐐿𐐲𐑋𐐯𐑃 𐑁𐑉𐐱𐑋 𐐯𐑂𐑉𐐨 𐐹𐐫𐑉, 𐑅𐐬 𐑀𐑉𐐩𐐻 𐑇𐐰𐑊 𐐺 𐐸𐐮𐑆 𐐰𐑍𐑀𐐶𐐮𐑇 𐑁𐐫𐑉 𐑄 𐐶𐐮𐐿𐐯𐐼𐑌𐐯𐑅 𐐰𐑌𐐼 𐑄 𐐰𐐺𐐱𐑋𐐮𐑌𐐩𐑇𐐲𐑌𐑆 𐐱𐑂 𐐸𐐮𐑆 𐐹𐐨𐐹𐑊.

14. 𐐈𐑌𐐼 𐐸𐐨 𐑇𐐰𐑊 𐐺 𐐿𐐫𐑊𐐼 𐐖𐐨𐑆𐐲𐑅 𐐗𐑉𐐴𐑅𐐻, 𐑄 𐐝𐐲𐑌 𐐱𐑂 𐐘𐐱𐐼, 𐑄 𐐙𐐪𐑄𐐲𐑉 𐐱𐑂 𐐸𐐯𐑂𐐲𐑌 𐐰𐑌𐐼 𐐲𐑉𐑃, 𐑄 𐐗𐑉𐐨𐐩𐐻𐐲𐑉 𐐱𐑂 𐐫𐑊 𐑃𐐮𐑍𐑆 𐑁𐑉𐐱𐑋 𐑄 𐐺𐐨𐑀𐐮𐑌𐐮𐑍; 𐐰𐑌𐐼 𐐸𐐮𐑆 𐑋𐐲𐑄𐐲𐑉 𐑇𐐰𐑊 𐐺 𐐿𐐫𐑊𐐼 𐐣𐐩𐑉𐐨. 𐐈𐑌𐐼 𐑊𐐬, 𐐸𐐨 𐐿𐐲𐑋𐐯𐑃 𐐲𐑌𐐻𐐭 𐐸𐐮𐑆 𐐬𐑌, 𐑄𐐰𐐻 𐑅𐐰𐑊𐑂𐐩𐑇𐐲𐑌 𐑋𐐴𐐻 𐐿𐐲𐑋 𐐲𐑌𐐻𐐭 𐑄 𐐽𐐮𐑊𐐼𐑉𐐯𐑌 𐐱𐑂 𐑋𐐯𐑌, 𐐨𐑂𐐯𐑌 𐑃𐑉𐐭 𐑁𐐩𐑃 𐐱𐑌 𐐸𐐮𐑆 𐑌𐐩𐑋; 𐐰𐑌𐐼 𐐨𐑂𐐯𐑌 𐐰𐑁𐐻𐐲𐑉 𐐫𐑊 𐑄𐐮𐑅, 𐑄𐐩 𐑇𐐰𐑊 𐐿𐐲𐑌𐑅𐐮𐐼𐐲𐑉 𐐸𐐮𐑋 𐐩 𐑋𐐰𐑌, 𐐰𐑌𐐼 𐑅𐐩 𐑄𐐰𐐻 𐐸𐐨 𐐸𐐰𐑃 𐐩 𐐼𐐯𐑂𐐲𐑊, 𐐰𐑌𐐼 𐑇𐐰𐑊 𐑅𐐿𐐲𐑉𐐾 𐐸𐐮𐑋, 𐐰𐑌𐐼 𐑇𐐰𐑊 𐐿𐑉𐐭𐑅𐐮𐑁𐐴 𐐸𐐮𐑋. 𐐈𐑌𐐼 𐐸𐐨 𐑇𐐰𐑊 𐑉𐐴𐑆 𐑄 𐑃𐐲𐑉𐐼 𐐼𐐩 𐑁𐑉𐐱𐑋 𐑄 𐐼𐐯𐐼; 𐐰𐑌𐐼 𐐺𐐨𐐸𐐬𐑊𐐼, 𐐸𐐨 𐑅𐐻𐐰𐑌𐐼𐐯𐑃 𐐻𐐭 𐐾𐐲𐐾 𐑄 𐐶𐐲𐑉𐑊𐐼; 𐐰𐑌𐐼 𐐺𐐨𐐸𐐬𐑊𐐼, 𐐫𐑊 𐑄𐐨𐑆 𐑃𐐮𐑍𐑆 𐐪𐑉 𐐼𐐲𐑌 𐑄𐐰𐐻 𐐩 𐑉𐐴𐐽𐐲𐑅 𐐾𐐲𐐾𐑋𐐯𐑌𐐻 𐑋𐐴𐐻 𐐿𐐲𐑋 𐐲𐐹𐐱𐑌 𐑄 𐐽𐐮𐑊𐐼𐑉𐐯𐑌 𐐱𐑂 𐑋𐐯𐑌. 𐐙𐐫𐑉 𐐺𐐨𐐸𐐬𐑊𐐼, 𐐰𐑌𐐼 𐐫𐑊𐑅𐐬 𐐸𐐮𐑆 𐐺𐑊𐐲𐐼 𐐰𐐻𐐬𐑌𐐯𐑃 𐑁𐐫𐑉 𐑄 𐑅𐐮𐑌𐑆 𐐱𐑂 𐑄𐐬𐑆 𐐸𐐭 𐐸𐐰𐑂 𐑁𐐫𐑊𐐲𐑌 𐐺𐐴 𐑄 𐐻𐑉𐐰𐑌𐑆-𐑀𐑉𐐯𐑇𐐲𐑌 𐐱𐑂 𐐈𐐼𐐲𐑋, 𐐸𐐭 𐐸𐐰𐑂 𐐼𐐴𐐼, 𐑌𐐱𐐻 𐑌𐐬𐐮𐑍 𐑄 𐐶𐐮𐑊 𐐱𐑂 𐐘𐐱𐐼 𐐿𐐲𐑌𐑅𐐲𐑉𐑌𐐮𐑍 𐑄𐐯𐑋, 𐐫𐑉 𐐸𐐭 𐐸𐐰𐑂 𐐮𐑀𐑌𐐬𐑉𐐲𐑌𐐻𐑊𐐨 𐑅𐐮𐑌𐐼. 𐐒𐐲𐐻 𐐶𐐬, 𐐶𐐬 𐐲𐑌𐐻𐐭 𐐸𐐮𐑋 𐐸𐐭 𐑌𐐬𐐯𐑃 𐑄𐐰𐐻 𐐸𐐨 𐑉𐐨𐐺𐐯𐑊𐐯𐑃 𐐲𐑀𐐯𐑌𐑅𐐻 𐐘𐐱𐐼; 𐑁𐐫𐑉 𐑅𐐰𐑊𐑂𐐩𐑇𐐲𐑌 𐐿𐐲𐑋𐐯𐑃 𐐻𐐭 𐑌𐐲𐑌 𐑅𐐲𐐽, 𐐯𐐿𐑅𐐯𐐹𐐻 𐐮𐐻 𐐺 𐑃𐑉𐐭 𐑉𐐨𐐹𐐯𐑌𐐻𐐲𐑌𐑅 𐐰𐑌𐐼 𐑁𐐩𐑃 𐐱𐑌 𐑄 𐐢𐐫𐑉𐐼 𐐖𐐨𐑆𐐲𐑅 𐐗𐑉𐐴𐑅𐐻. 𐐈𐑌𐐼 𐑄 𐐢𐐫𐑉𐐼 𐐘𐐱𐐼 𐐸𐐰𐑃 𐑅𐐯𐑌𐐻 𐐸𐐮𐑆 𐐸𐐬𐑊𐐨 𐐹𐑉𐐱𐑁𐐯𐐻𐑅 𐐲𐑋𐐲𐑍 𐐫𐑊 𐑄 𐐽𐐮𐑊𐐼𐑉𐐯𐑌 𐐱𐑂 𐑋𐐯𐑌, 𐐻𐐭 𐐼𐐨𐐿𐑊𐐩𐑉 𐑄𐐨𐑆 𐑃𐐮𐑍𐑆 𐐻𐐭 𐐯𐑂𐑉𐐨 𐐿𐐮𐑌𐐼𐑉𐐯𐐼, 𐑌𐐩𐑇𐐲𐑌, 𐐰𐑌𐐼 𐐻𐐲𐑍, 𐑄𐐰𐐻 𐑄𐐩𐑉𐐺𐐴 𐐸𐐭𐑅𐐬-𐐯𐑂𐐲𐑉 𐑇𐐳𐐼 𐐺𐐨𐑊𐐨𐑂 𐑄𐐰𐐻 𐐗𐑉𐐴𐑅𐐻 𐑇𐐳𐐼 𐐿𐐲𐑋, 𐑄 𐑅𐐩𐑋 𐑋𐐴𐐻 𐑉𐐨𐑅𐐨𐑂 𐑉𐐨𐑋𐐮𐑇𐐲𐑌 𐐱𐑂 𐑄𐐩𐑉 𐑅𐐮𐑌𐑆, 𐐰𐑌𐐼 𐑉𐐨𐐾𐐱𐐮𐑅 𐐶𐐮𐑄 𐐯𐐿𐑅𐐨𐐼𐐮𐑍𐑊𐐨 𐑀𐑉𐐩𐐻 𐐾𐐱𐐮, 𐐨𐑂𐐯𐑌 𐐰𐑆 𐑄𐐬 𐐸𐐨 𐐸𐐰𐐼 𐐫𐑊𐑉𐐯𐐼𐐨 𐐿𐐲𐑋 𐐲𐑋𐐲𐑍 𐑄𐐯𐑋. 𐐏𐐯𐐻 𐑄 𐐢𐐫𐑉𐐼 𐐘𐐱𐐼 𐑅𐐫 𐑄𐐰𐐻 𐐸𐐮𐑆 𐐹𐐨𐐹𐑊 𐐶𐐲𐑉 𐐩 𐑅𐐻𐐮𐑁𐑌𐐯𐐿𐐻 𐐹𐐨𐐹𐑊, 𐐰𐑌𐐼 𐐸𐐨 𐐰𐐹𐐱𐐮𐑌𐐻𐐯𐐼 𐐲𐑌𐐻𐐭 𐑄𐐯𐑋 𐐩 𐑊𐐫, 𐐨𐑂𐐯𐑌 𐑄 𐑊𐐫 𐐱𐑂 𐐣𐐬𐑆𐐯𐑆. 𐐈𐑌𐐼 𐑋𐐯𐑌𐐨 𐑅𐐴𐑌𐑆, 𐐰𐑌𐐼 𐐶𐐲𐑌𐐼𐐲𐑉𐑆, 𐐰𐑌𐐼 𐐻𐐴𐐹𐑅, 𐐰𐑌𐐼 𐑇𐐰𐐼𐐬𐑆 𐑇𐐬𐐼 𐐸𐐨 𐐲𐑌𐐻𐐭 𐑄𐐯𐑋, 𐐿𐐲𐑌𐑅𐐲𐑉𐑌𐐮𐑍 𐐸𐐮𐑆 𐐿𐐲𐑋𐐮𐑍; 𐐰𐑌𐐼 𐐫𐑊𐑅𐐬 𐐸𐐬𐑊𐐨 𐐹𐑉𐐱𐑁𐐯𐐻𐑅 𐑅𐐹𐐩𐐿 𐐲𐑌𐐻𐐭 𐑄𐐯𐑋 𐐿𐐲𐑌𐑅𐐲𐑉𐑌𐐮𐑍 𐐸𐐮𐑆 𐐿𐐲𐑋𐐮𐑍; 𐐰𐑌𐐼 𐐷𐐯𐐻 𐑄𐐩 𐐸𐐪𐑉𐐼𐐯𐑌𐐼 𐑄𐐩𐑉 𐐸𐐪𐑉𐐻𐑅, 𐐰𐑌𐐼 𐐲𐑌𐐼𐐲𐑉𐑅𐐻𐐳𐐼 𐑌𐐱𐐻 𐑄𐐰𐐻 𐑄 𐑊𐐫 𐐱𐑂 𐐣𐐬𐑆𐐯𐑆 𐐰𐑂𐐩𐑊𐐯𐑃 𐑌𐐲𐑃𐐮𐑍, 𐐯𐐿𐑅𐐯𐐹𐐻 𐐮𐐻 𐐶𐐲𐑉 𐑃𐑉𐐭 𐑄 𐐰𐐻𐐬𐑌𐑋𐐯𐑌𐐻 𐐱𐑂 𐐸𐐮𐑆 𐐺𐑊𐐲𐐼; 𐐰𐑌𐐼 𐐨𐑂𐐯𐑌 𐐮𐑁 𐐮𐐻 𐐶𐐲𐑉 𐐹𐐱𐑅𐐮𐐺𐑊 𐑄𐐰𐐻 𐑊𐐮𐐻𐑊 𐐽𐐮𐑊𐐼𐑉𐐯𐑌 𐐿𐐳𐐼 𐑅𐐮𐑌, 𐑄𐐩 𐐿𐐳𐐼 𐑌𐐱𐐻 𐐺 𐑅𐐩𐑂𐐼; 𐐺𐐲𐐻 𐐌 𐑅𐐩 𐐲𐑌𐐻𐐭 𐐷𐐭 𐑄𐐩 𐐪𐑉 𐐺𐑊𐐯𐑅𐐻; 𐑁𐐫𐑉 𐐺𐐨𐐸𐐬𐑊𐐼, 𐐰𐑆 𐐮𐑌 𐐈𐐼𐐲𐑋, 𐐫𐑉 𐐺𐐴 𐑌𐐩𐐽𐐲𐑉, 𐑄𐐩 𐑁𐐫𐑊, 𐐨𐑂𐐯𐑌 𐑅𐐬 𐑄 𐐺𐑊𐐲𐐼 𐐱𐑂 𐐗𐑉𐐴𐑅𐐻 𐐰𐐻𐐬𐑌𐐯𐑃 𐑁𐐫𐑉 𐑄𐐩𐑉 𐑅𐐮𐑌𐑆.

15. 𐐈𐑌𐐼 𐑋𐐬𐑉𐐬𐑂𐐲𐑉, 𐐌 𐑅𐐩 𐐲𐑌𐐻𐐭 𐐷𐐭, 𐑄𐐰𐐻 𐑄𐐯𐑉 𐑇𐐰𐑊 𐐺 𐑌𐐬 𐐲𐑄𐐲𐑉 𐑌𐐩𐑋 𐑀𐐮𐑂𐑌, 𐑌𐐫𐑉 𐐯𐑌𐐨 𐐲𐑄𐐲𐑉 𐐶𐐩 𐑌𐐫𐑉 𐑋𐐨𐑌𐑆 𐐸𐐶𐐯𐑉𐐺𐐴 𐑅𐐰𐑊𐑂𐐩𐑇𐐲𐑌 𐐿𐐰𐑌 𐐿𐐲𐑋 𐐲𐑌𐐻𐐭 𐑄 𐐽𐐮𐑊𐐼𐑉𐐲𐑌 𐐱𐑂 𐑋𐐯𐑌, 𐐬𐑌𐑊𐐨 𐐮𐑌 𐐰𐑌𐐼 𐑃𐑉𐐭 𐑄 𐑌𐐩𐑋 𐐱𐑂 𐐗𐑉𐐴𐑅𐐻, 𐑄 𐐢𐐫𐑉𐐼 𐐉𐑋𐑌𐐮𐐹𐐬𐐻𐐲𐑌𐐻. 𐐙𐐫𐑉 𐐺𐐨𐐸𐐬𐑊𐐼, 𐐸𐐨 𐐾𐐲𐐾𐐯𐑃, 𐐰𐑌𐐼 𐐸𐐮𐑆 𐐾𐐲𐐾𐑋𐐯𐑌𐐻 𐐮𐑆 𐐾𐐲𐑅𐐻, 𐐰𐑌𐐼 𐑄 𐐮𐑌𐑁𐐲𐑌𐐻 𐐹𐐯𐑉𐐮𐑇𐐯𐑃 𐑌𐐱𐐻 𐑄𐐰𐐻 𐐼𐐴𐐯𐑃 𐐮𐑌 𐐸𐐮𐑆 𐐮𐑌𐑁𐐲𐑌𐑅𐐨; 𐐺𐐲𐐻 𐑋𐐯𐑌 𐐼𐑉𐐮𐑍𐐿 𐐼𐐰𐑋𐑌𐐩𐑇𐐲𐑌 𐐻𐐭 𐑄𐐯𐑉 𐐬𐑌 𐑅𐐬𐑊𐑆, 𐐯𐐿𐑅𐐯𐐹𐐻 𐑄𐐩 𐐸𐐲𐑋𐐺𐑊 𐑄𐐯𐑋𐑅𐐯𐑊𐑂𐑆 𐐰𐑌𐐼 𐐺𐐨𐐿𐐲𐑋 𐐰𐑆 𐑊𐐮𐐻𐑊 𐐽𐐮𐑊𐐼𐑉𐐲𐑌, 𐐰𐑌𐐼 𐐺𐐨𐑊𐐨𐑂 𐑄𐐰𐐻 𐑅𐐰𐑊𐑂𐐩𐑇𐐲𐑌 𐐶𐐱𐑆, 𐐰𐑌𐐼 𐐮𐑆, 𐐰𐑌𐐼 𐐮𐑆 𐐻𐐭 𐐿𐐲𐑋, 𐐮𐑌 𐐰𐑌𐐼 𐑃𐑉𐐭 𐑄 𐐲𐐻𐐬𐑌𐐮𐑍 𐐺𐑊𐐲𐐼 𐐱𐑂 𐐗𐑉𐐴𐑅𐐻, 𐑄 𐐢𐐫𐑉𐐼 𐐉𐑋𐑌𐐮𐐹𐐬𐐻𐐲𐑌𐐻; 𐑁𐐫𐑉 𐑄 𐑌𐐰𐐽𐐲𐑉𐐲𐑊 𐑋𐐰𐑌 𐐮𐑆 𐐰𐑌 𐐯𐑌𐐲𐑋𐐨 𐐻𐐭 𐐘𐐱𐐼, 𐐰𐑌𐐼 𐐸𐐰𐑆 𐐺𐐨𐑌 𐑁𐑉𐐱𐑋 𐑄 𐑁𐐫𐑊 𐐱𐑂 𐐈𐐼𐐲𐑋, 𐐰𐑌𐐼 𐐶𐐮𐑊 𐐺, 𐑁𐐫𐑉𐐯𐑂𐐲𐑉 𐐰𐑌𐐼 𐐯𐑂𐐲𐑉; 𐐺𐐲𐐻 𐐮𐑁 𐐸𐐨 𐐷𐐨𐑊𐐼𐑆 𐐻𐐭 𐑄 𐐯𐑌𐐻𐐴𐑅𐐮𐑍𐑆 𐐱𐑂 𐑄 𐐐𐐬𐑊𐐨 𐐝𐐹𐐮𐑉𐐮𐐻, 𐐰𐑌𐐼 𐐹𐐳𐐻𐐯𐑃 𐐫𐑁 𐑄 𐑌𐐰𐐽𐐲𐑉𐐲𐑊 𐑋𐐰𐑌, 𐐰𐑌𐐼 𐐺𐐨𐐿𐐲𐑋𐐯𐑃 𐐲 𐑅𐐩𐑌𐐻, 𐑃𐑉𐐭 𐑄 𐐲𐐻𐐬𐑌𐑋𐐲𐑌𐐻 𐐱𐑂 𐐗𐑉𐐴𐑅𐐻 𐑄 𐐢𐐫𐑉𐐼, 𐐰𐑌𐐼 𐐺𐐨𐐿𐐲𐑋𐐯𐑃 𐐰𐑆 𐐲 𐐽𐐴𐑊𐐼, 𐑅𐐲𐐺𐑋𐐮𐑅𐐮𐑂, 𐑋𐐨𐐿, 𐐸𐐲𐑋𐐺𐑊, 𐐹𐐩𐑇𐐲𐑌𐐻, 𐑁𐐳𐑊 𐐱𐑂 𐑊𐐲𐑂, 𐐶𐐮𐑊𐐮𐑍 𐐻𐐭 𐑅𐐲𐐺𐑋𐐮𐐻 𐐻𐐭 𐐫𐑊 𐑃𐐮𐑍𐑆 𐐸𐐶𐐮𐐽 𐑄 𐐢𐐫𐑉𐐼 𐑅𐐨𐐯𐑃 𐑁𐐮𐐻 𐐻𐐭 𐐮𐑌𐑁𐑊𐐮𐐿𐐻 𐐲𐐹𐐱𐑌 𐐸𐐮𐑋, 𐐨𐑂𐑌 𐐰𐑆 𐐲 𐐽𐐴𐑊𐐼 𐐼𐐲𐑃 𐑅𐐲𐐺𐑋𐐮𐐻 𐐻𐐭 𐐸𐐮𐑆 𐑁𐐱𐑄𐐲𐑉. 𐐈𐑌𐐼 𐑋𐐬𐑉𐐬𐑂𐐲𐑉, 𐐌 𐑅𐐩 𐐲𐑌𐐻𐐭 𐐷𐐭, 𐑄𐐰𐐻 𐑄 𐐻𐐴𐑋 𐑇𐐰𐑊 𐐿𐐲𐑋 𐐸𐐶𐐯𐑌 𐑄 𐑌𐐱𐑊𐐯𐐾 𐐱𐑂 𐐲 𐐝𐐩𐑂𐐷𐐲𐑉 𐑇𐐰𐑊 𐑅𐐹𐑉𐐯𐐼 𐑃𐑉𐐭𐐵𐐻 𐐯𐑂𐑉𐐨 𐑌𐐩𐑇𐐲𐑌, 𐐿𐐮𐑌𐐼𐑉𐐯𐐼, 𐐻𐐲𐑍, 𐐰𐑌𐐼 𐐹𐐨𐐹𐑊. 𐐈𐑌𐐼 𐐺𐐨𐐸𐐬𐑊𐐼, 𐐸𐐶𐐯𐑌 𐑄𐐰𐐻 𐐻𐐴𐑋 𐐿𐐲𐑋𐐯𐑃, 𐑌𐐲𐑌 𐑇𐐰𐑊 𐐺 𐑁𐐵𐑌𐐼 𐐺𐑊𐐩𐑋𐑊𐐯𐑅 𐐺𐐨𐑁𐐫𐑉 𐐘𐐱𐐼, 𐐯𐐿𐑅𐐯𐐹𐐻 𐐮𐐻 𐐺 𐑊𐐮𐐻𐑊 𐐽𐐮𐑊𐐼𐑉𐐲𐑌, 𐐬𐑌𐑊𐐨 𐑃𐑉𐐭 𐑉𐐯𐐹𐐯𐑌𐐻𐐲𐑌𐑅 𐐰𐑌𐐼 𐑁𐐩𐑃 𐐱𐑌 𐑄 𐑌𐐩𐑋 𐐱𐑂 𐑄 𐐢𐐫𐑉𐐼 𐐘𐐱𐐼 𐐉𐑋𐑌𐐮𐐹𐐬𐐻𐐲𐑌𐐻; 𐐰𐑌𐐼 𐐨𐑂𐑌 𐐰𐐻 𐑄𐐮𐑅 𐐻𐐴𐑋, 𐐸𐐶𐐯𐑌 𐑄𐐵 𐑇𐐰𐑊𐐻 𐐸𐐰𐑂 𐐻𐐫𐐻 𐑄𐐴 𐐹𐐨𐐹𐑊 𐑄 𐑃𐐮𐑍𐑆 𐐸𐐶𐐮𐐽 𐑄 𐐢𐐫𐑉𐐼 𐑄𐐴 𐐘𐐱𐐼 𐐸𐐰𐑃 𐐿𐐱𐑋𐐰𐑌𐐼𐐯𐐼 𐑄𐐨, 𐐨𐑂𐑌 𐑄𐐯𐑌 𐐪𐑉 𐑄𐐩 𐑁𐐵𐑌𐐼 𐑌𐐬 𐑋𐐬𐑉 𐐺𐑊𐐩𐑋𐑊𐐯𐑅 𐐮𐑌 𐑄 𐑅𐐴𐐻 𐐱𐑂 𐐘𐐱𐐼, 𐐬𐑌𐑊𐐨 𐐰𐐿𐐫𐑉𐐼𐐮𐑍 𐐻𐐭 𐑄 𐐶𐐲𐑉𐐼𐑆 𐐸𐐶𐐮𐐽 𐐌 𐐸𐐰𐑂 𐑅𐐹𐐬𐐿𐑌 𐐲𐑌𐐻𐐭 𐑄𐐨.

16. 𐐈𐑌𐐼 𐑌𐐵 𐐌 𐐸𐐰𐑂 𐑅𐐹𐐬𐐿𐑌 𐑄 𐐶𐐲𐑉𐐼𐑆 𐐸𐐶𐐮𐐽 𐑄 𐐢𐐫𐑉𐐼 𐐘𐐱𐐼 𐐸𐐰𐑃 𐐿𐐱𐑋𐐰𐑌𐐼𐐯𐐼 𐑋𐐨. 𐐈𐑌𐐼 𐑄𐐲𐑅 𐑅𐐯𐑃 𐑄 𐐢𐐫𐑉𐐼: 𐐜𐐩 𐑇𐐰𐑊 𐑅𐐻𐐰𐑌𐐼 𐐰𐑆 𐐲 𐐺𐑉𐐴𐐻 𐐻𐐯𐑅𐐻𐐮𐑋𐐬𐑌𐐨 𐐲𐑀𐐯𐑌𐑅𐐻 𐑄𐐮𐑅 𐐹𐐨𐐹𐑊, 𐐰𐐻 𐑄 𐐾𐐲𐐾𐑋𐐯𐑌𐐻 𐐼𐐩; 𐐸𐐶𐐯𐑉𐐱𐑂 𐑄𐐩 𐑇𐐰𐑊 𐐺 𐐾𐐲𐐾𐐼, 𐐯𐑂𐑉𐐨 𐑋𐐰𐑌 𐐰𐐿𐐫𐑉𐐼𐐮𐑍 𐐻𐐭 𐐸𐐮𐑆 𐐶𐐲𐑉𐐿𐑅, 𐐸𐐶𐐯𐑄𐐲𐑉 𐑄𐐩 𐐺 𐑀𐐳𐐼 𐐫𐑉 𐐸𐐶𐐯𐑄𐐲𐑉 𐑄𐐩 𐐺 𐐨𐑂𐑊; 𐐰𐑌𐐼 𐐮𐑁 𐑄𐐩 𐐺 𐐨𐑂𐑊, 𐑄𐐩 𐐪𐑉 𐐿𐐱𐑌𐑅𐐴𐑌𐐼 𐐻𐐭 𐐰𐑌 𐐫𐑁𐐳𐑊 𐑂𐐷𐐭 𐐱𐑂 𐑄𐐯𐑉 𐐬𐑌 𐑀𐐮𐑊𐐻 𐐰𐑌𐐼 𐐲𐐺𐐱𐑋𐐮𐑌𐐩𐑇𐐲𐑌𐑆, 𐐸𐐶𐐮𐐽 𐐼𐐲𐑃 𐐿𐐫𐑆 𐑄𐐯𐑋 𐐻𐐭 𐑇𐑉𐐮𐑍𐐿 𐑁𐑉𐐱𐑋 𐑄 𐐹𐑉𐐯𐑆𐐯𐑌𐑅 𐐱𐑂 𐑄 𐐢𐐫𐑉𐐼, 𐐮𐑌𐐻𐐭 𐐲 𐑅𐐻𐐩𐐻 𐐱𐑂 𐑋𐐮𐑆𐐲𐑉𐐨 𐐰𐑌𐐼 𐐯𐑌𐐼𐑊𐐯𐑅 𐐻𐐫𐑉𐑋𐐯𐑌𐐻, 𐑁𐑉𐐱𐑋 𐐸𐐶𐐯𐑌𐑅 𐑄𐐩 𐐿𐐰𐑌 𐑌𐐬 𐑋𐐬𐑉 𐑉𐐨𐐻𐐲𐑉𐑌; 𐑄𐐯𐑉𐑁𐐫𐑉, 𐑄𐐩 𐐸𐐰𐑂 𐐼𐑉𐐲𐑍𐐿 𐐼𐐰𐑋𐑌𐐩𐑇𐐲𐑌 𐐻𐐭 𐑄𐐯𐑉 𐐬𐑌 𐑅𐐬𐑊𐑆. 𐐜𐐯𐑉𐑁𐐫𐑉 𐑄𐐩 𐐸𐐰𐑂 𐐼𐑉𐐲𐑍𐐿 𐐵𐐻 𐐱𐑂 𐑄 𐐿𐐲𐐹 𐐱𐑂 𐑄 𐑉𐐱𐑃 𐐱𐑂 𐐘𐐱𐐼, 𐐸𐐶𐐮𐐽 𐐾𐐲𐑅𐐻𐐮𐑅 𐐿𐐳𐐼 𐑌𐐬 𐑋𐐬𐑉 𐐼𐐨𐑌𐐴 𐐲𐑌𐐻𐐭 𐑄𐐯𐑋 𐑄𐐰𐑌 𐐮𐐻 𐐿𐐳𐐼 𐐼𐐨𐑌𐐴 𐑄𐐰𐐻 𐐈𐐼𐐲𐑋 𐑇𐐳𐐼 𐑁𐐫𐑊 𐐺𐐨𐐿𐐫𐑆 𐐱𐑂 𐐸𐐮𐑆 𐐹𐐪𐑉𐐻𐐩𐐿𐐮𐑍 𐐱𐑂 𐑄 𐑁𐐫𐑉𐐺𐐮𐐼𐑌 𐑁𐑉𐐭𐐻; 𐑄𐐯𐑉𐑁𐐫𐑉, 𐑋𐐲𐑉𐑅𐐨 𐐿𐐳𐐼 𐐸𐐰𐑂 𐐿𐑊𐐩𐑋 𐐱𐑌 𐑄𐐯𐑋 𐑌𐐬 𐑋𐐬𐑉 𐑁𐐫𐑉𐐯𐑂𐐲𐑉. 𐐈𐑌𐐼 𐑄𐐯𐑉 𐐻𐐫𐑉𐑋𐐯𐑌𐐻 𐐮𐑆 𐐰𐑆 𐐲 𐑊𐐩𐐿 𐐱𐑂 𐑁𐐴𐑉 𐐰𐑌𐐼 𐐺𐑉𐐮𐑋𐑅𐐻𐐬𐑌, 𐐸𐐭𐑆 𐑁𐑊𐐩𐑋𐑆 𐐪𐑉 𐐲𐑌𐐿𐐶𐐯𐑌𐐽𐐲𐐺𐑊, 𐐰𐑌𐐼 𐐸𐐭𐑆 𐑅𐑋𐐬𐐿 𐐲𐑅𐐯𐑌𐐼𐐯𐑃 𐐲𐐹 𐑁𐐫𐑉𐐯𐑂𐐲𐑉 𐐰𐑌𐐼 𐐯𐑂𐐲𐑉. 𐐜𐐲𐑅 𐐸𐐰𐑃 𐑄 𐐢𐐫𐑉𐐼 𐐿𐐱𐑋𐐰𐑌𐐼𐐯𐐼 𐑋𐐨. 𐐁𐑋𐐯𐑌.

𐐕𐐰𐐹𐐻𐐲𐑉 II.

1. 𐐈𐑌𐐼 𐑌𐐵, 𐐮𐐻 𐐿𐐩𐑋 𐐻𐐭 𐐹𐐪𐑅 𐑄𐐰𐐻 𐐸𐐶𐐯𐑌 𐐗𐐮𐑍 𐐒𐐯𐑌𐐾𐐲𐑋𐐲𐑌 𐐸𐐰𐐼 𐑋𐐩𐐼 𐐰𐑌 𐐯𐑌𐐼 𐐱𐑂 𐑅𐐹𐐨𐐿𐐮𐑍 𐑄 𐐶𐐲𐑉𐐼𐑆 𐐸𐐶𐐮𐐽 𐐸𐐰𐐼 𐐺𐐨𐑌 𐐼𐐯𐑊𐐮𐑂𐐲𐑉𐐼 𐐲𐑌𐐻𐐭 𐐸𐐮𐑋 𐐺𐐴 𐑄 𐐩𐑌𐐾𐐯𐑊 𐐱𐑂 𐑄 𐐢𐐫𐑉𐐼, 𐑄𐐰𐐻 𐐸𐐨 𐐿𐐰𐑅𐐻 𐐸𐐮𐑆 𐐴𐑆 𐑉𐐵𐑌𐐼 𐐲𐐺𐐵𐐻 𐐱𐑌 𐑄 𐑋𐐲𐑊𐐻𐐮𐐻𐐷𐐭𐐼, 𐐰𐑌𐐼 𐐺𐐨𐐸𐐬𐑊𐐼 𐑄𐐩 𐐸𐐰𐐼 𐑁𐐫𐑊𐑌 𐐻𐐭 𐑄 𐐲𐑉𐑃, 𐑁𐐫𐑉 𐑄 𐑁𐐨𐑉 𐐱𐑂 𐑄 𐐢𐐫𐑉𐐼 𐐸𐐰𐐼 𐐿𐐲𐑋 𐐲𐐹𐐱𐑌 𐑄𐐯𐑋; 𐐰𐑌𐐼 𐑄𐐩 𐐸𐐰𐐼 𐑂𐐷𐐭𐐼 𐑄𐐯𐑋𐑅𐐯𐑊𐑂𐑆 𐐮𐑌 𐑄𐐯𐑉 𐐬𐑌 𐐿𐐪𐑉𐑌𐐲𐑊 𐑅𐐻𐐩𐐻, 𐐨𐑂𐑌 𐑊𐐯𐑅 𐑄𐐰𐑌 𐑄 𐐼𐐲𐑅𐐻 𐐱𐑂 𐑄 𐐲𐑉𐑃. 𐐈𐑌𐐼 𐑄𐐩 𐐫𐑊 𐐿𐑉𐐴𐐼 𐐲𐑊𐐵𐐼 𐐶𐐮𐑄 𐐶𐐲𐑌 𐑂𐑎𐑅, 𐑅𐐩𐐮𐑍, 𐐄 𐐸𐐰𐑂 𐑋𐐲𐑉𐑅𐐨, 𐐰𐑌𐐼 𐐰𐐹𐑊𐐴 𐑄 𐐲𐐻𐐬𐑌𐐮𐑍 𐐺𐑊𐐲𐐼 𐐱𐑂 𐐗𐑉𐐴𐑅𐐻, 𐑄𐐰𐐻 𐐶𐐨 𐑋𐐩 𐑉𐐨𐑅𐐨𐑂 𐑁𐐫𐑉𐑀𐐮𐑂-

𐑀𐐮𐑂𐑌𐐯𐑅 𐐱𐑂 𐐵𐑉 𐑅𐐮𐑌𐑆, 𐐰𐑌𐐼 𐐵𐑉 𐐸𐐪𐑉𐐻𐑅 𐑋𐐩 𐐺 𐐹𐐷𐐭𐑉𐐮𐑁𐐴𐐼; 𐑁𐐫𐑉 𐐶𐐨 𐐺𐐨𐑊𐐨𐑂 𐐮𐑌 𐐖𐐨𐑆𐐲𐑅 𐐗𐑉𐐴𐑅𐐻, 𐑄 𐐝𐐲𐑌 𐐱𐑂 𐐘𐐱𐐼, 𐐸𐐭 𐐿𐑉𐐨𐐩𐐻𐐯𐐼 𐐸𐐯𐑂𐑌 𐐰𐑌𐐼 𐐲𐑉𐑃, 𐐰𐑌𐐼 𐐫𐑊 𐑃𐐮𐑍𐑆, 𐐸𐐭 𐑇𐐰𐑊 𐐿𐐲𐑋 𐐼𐐵𐑌 𐐰𐑋𐐲𐑍 𐑄 𐐽𐐮𐑊𐐼𐑉𐐯𐑌 𐐱𐑂 𐑋𐐯𐑌.

2. 𐐈𐑌𐐼 𐐮𐐻 𐐿𐐩𐑋 𐐻𐐭 𐐹𐐪𐑅 𐑄𐐰𐐻 𐐪𐑁𐐻𐐲𐑉 𐑄𐐩 𐐸𐐰𐐼 𐑅𐐹𐐬𐐿𐐲𐑌 𐑄𐐨𐑆 𐐶𐐲𐑉𐐼𐑆, 𐑄 𐐝𐐹𐐮𐑉𐐮𐐻 𐐱𐑂 𐑄 𐐢𐐫𐑉𐐼 𐐿𐐩𐑋 𐐲𐐹𐐱𐑌 𐑄𐐯𐑋, 𐐰𐑌𐐼 𐑄𐐩 𐐶𐐲𐑉 𐑁𐐮𐑊𐐼 𐐶𐐮𐑄 𐐾𐑎, 𐐸𐐰𐑂𐐮𐑍 𐑉𐐨𐑅𐐨𐑂𐐼 𐐪 𐑉𐐨𐑋𐐮𐑇𐐲𐑌 𐐱𐑂 𐑄𐐩𐑉 𐑅𐐮𐑌𐑆, 𐐰𐑌𐐼 𐐸𐐰𐑂𐐮𐑍 𐐹𐐨𐑅 𐐱𐑂 𐐿𐐱𐑌𐑇𐐯𐑌𐑅, 𐐺𐐨𐐿𐐫𐑆 𐐱𐑂 𐑄 𐐯𐐿𐑅𐐨𐐼𐐮𐑍 𐑁𐐩𐑃 𐐸𐐶𐐮𐐽 𐑄𐐩 𐐸𐐰𐐼 𐐮𐑌 𐐖𐐨𐑆𐐲𐑅 𐐗𐑉𐐴𐑅𐐻 𐐸𐐭 𐑇𐐳𐐼 𐐿𐐲𐑋, 𐐰𐐿𐐫𐑉𐐼𐐮𐑍 𐐻𐐭 𐑄 𐐶𐐲𐑉𐐼𐑆 𐐸𐐶𐐮𐐽 𐐗𐐮𐑍 𐐒𐐯𐑌𐐾𐐰𐑋𐐮𐑌 𐐸𐐰𐐼 𐑅𐐹𐐬𐐿𐐲𐑌 𐐲𐑌𐐻𐐭 𐑄𐐯𐑋. 𐐈𐑌𐐼 𐐗𐐮𐑍 𐐒𐐯𐑌𐐾𐐰𐑋𐐮𐑌 𐐰𐑀𐐯𐑌 𐐬𐐹𐑌𐐼 𐐸𐐮𐑆 𐑋𐐵𐑃, 𐐰𐑌𐐼 𐐺𐐯𐑀𐐰𐑌 𐐻𐐭 𐑅𐐹𐐨𐐿 𐐲𐑌𐐻𐐭 𐑄𐐯𐑋, 𐑅𐐩𐐮𐑍, 𐑋𐐴 𐑁𐑉𐐯𐑌𐐼𐑆 𐐰𐑌𐐼 𐑋𐐴 𐐺𐑉𐐯𐑄𐑉𐐯𐑌, 𐑋𐐴 𐐿𐐮𐑌𐐼𐑉𐐯𐐼 𐐰𐑌𐐼 𐑋𐐴 𐐹𐐨𐐹𐑊, 𐐌 𐐶𐐳𐐼 𐐰𐑀𐐯𐑌 𐐿𐐫𐑊 𐐷𐐫𐑉 𐐰𐐻𐐯𐑌𐑇𐐲𐑌, 𐑄𐐰𐐻 𐐷 𐑋𐐩 𐐸𐐨𐑉 𐐰𐑌𐐼 𐐲𐑌𐐼𐐲𐑉𐑅𐐻𐐰𐑌𐐼 𐑄 𐑉𐐨𐑋𐐩𐑌𐐼𐐲𐑉 𐐱𐑂 𐑋𐐴 𐐶𐐲𐑉𐐼𐑆 𐐸𐐶𐐮𐐽 𐐌 𐑇𐐰𐑊 𐑅𐐹𐐨𐐿 𐐲𐑌𐐻𐐭 𐐷𐐭; 𐑁𐐫𐑉 𐐺𐐨𐐸𐐬𐑊𐐼, 𐐮𐑁 𐑄 𐑌𐐱𐑊𐐯𐐾 𐐱𐑂 𐑄 𐑀𐐳𐐼𐑌𐐯𐑅 𐐱𐑂 𐐘𐐱𐐼 𐐰𐐻 𐑄𐐮𐑅 𐐻𐐴𐑋 𐐸𐐰𐑆 𐐰𐐶𐐩𐐿𐐲𐑌𐐼 𐐷𐐭 𐐻𐐭 𐐪 𐑅𐐯𐑌𐑅 𐐱𐑂 𐐷𐐫𐑉 𐑌𐐲𐑃𐐮𐑍𐑌𐐯𐑅, 𐐰𐑌𐐼 𐐷𐐫𐑉 𐐶𐐲𐑉𐑃𐑊𐐯𐑅 𐐰𐑌𐐼 𐑁𐐫𐑊𐑌 𐑅𐐻𐐩𐐻; 𐐌 𐑅𐐩 𐐲𐑌𐐻𐐭 𐐷𐐭, 𐐮𐑁 𐐷 𐐸𐐰𐑂 𐐿𐐲𐑋 𐐻𐐭 𐐪 𐑌𐐱𐑊𐐯𐐾 𐐱𐑂 𐑄 𐑀𐐳𐐼𐑌𐐯𐑅 𐐱𐑂 𐐘𐐱𐐼, 𐐰𐑌𐐼 𐐸𐐮𐑆 𐑋𐐰𐐽𐑊𐐯𐑅 𐐹𐐵𐑉, 𐐰𐑌𐐼 𐐸𐐮𐑆 𐐶𐐮𐑆𐐼𐐲𐑋, 𐐰𐑌𐐼 𐐸𐐮𐑆 𐐹𐐩𐑇𐐯𐑌𐑅, 𐐰𐑌𐐼 𐐸𐐮𐑆 𐑊𐐱𐑍𐑅𐐲𐑁𐐲𐑉𐐮𐑍 𐐻𐐬𐐲𐑉𐐼𐑆 𐑄 𐐽𐐮𐑊𐐼𐑉𐐯𐑌 𐐱𐑂 𐑋𐐯𐑌, 𐐰𐑌𐐼 𐐫𐑊𐑅𐐬, 𐑄 𐐰𐐻𐐬𐑌𐑋𐐯𐑌𐐻 𐐸𐐶𐐮𐐽 𐐸𐐰𐑆 𐐺𐐨𐑌 𐐹𐑉𐐨𐐹𐐩𐑉𐐼 𐑁𐑉𐐱𐑋 𐑄 𐑁𐐵𐑌𐐼𐐩𐑇𐐲𐑌 𐐱𐑂 𐑄 𐐶𐐲𐑉𐑊𐐼, 𐑄𐐰𐐻 𐑄𐐯𐑉𐐺𐐴 𐑅𐐰𐑊𐑂𐐩𐑇𐐲𐑌 𐑋𐐴𐐻 𐐿𐐲𐑋 𐐻𐐭 𐐸𐐮𐑋 𐑄𐐰𐐻 𐑇𐐳𐐼 𐐹𐐳𐐻 𐐸𐐮𐑆 𐐻𐑉𐐲𐑅𐐻 𐐮𐑌 𐑄 𐐢𐐫𐑉𐐼, 𐐰𐑌𐐼 𐑇𐐳𐐼 𐐺 𐐼𐐮𐑊𐐮𐐾𐐯𐑌𐐻 𐐮𐑌 𐐿𐐨𐐹𐐮𐑍 𐐸𐐮𐑆 𐐿𐐱𐑋𐐰𐑌𐐼𐑋𐐯𐑌𐐻𐑅, 𐐰𐑌𐐼 𐐿𐐱𐑌𐐻𐐮𐑌𐐷𐐭 𐐮𐑌 𐑄 𐑁𐐩𐑃 𐐨𐑂𐑌 𐐲𐑌𐐻𐐭 𐑄 𐐯𐑌𐐼 𐐱𐑂 𐐸𐐮𐑆 𐑊𐐴𐑁; 𐐌 𐑋𐐨𐑌 𐑄 𐑊𐐴𐑁 𐐱𐑂 𐑄 𐑋𐐫𐑉𐐻𐐲𐑊 𐐺𐐱𐐼𐐨; 𐐌 𐑅𐐩, 𐑄𐐰𐐻 𐑄𐐮𐑅 𐐮𐑆 𐑄 𐑋𐐰𐑌 𐐸𐐭 𐑉𐐨𐑅𐐨𐑂𐐯𐑃 𐑅𐐰𐑊𐑂𐐩𐑇𐐲𐑌, 𐑃𐑉𐐭 𐑄 𐐰𐐻𐐬𐑌𐑋𐐯𐑌𐐻 𐐸𐐶𐐮𐐽 𐐶𐐱𐑆 𐐹𐑉𐐨𐐹𐐩𐑉𐐼 𐑁𐑉𐐱𐑋 𐑄 𐑁𐐵𐑌𐐼𐐩𐑇𐐲𐑌 𐐱𐑂 𐑄 𐐶𐐲𐑉𐑊𐐼 𐑁𐐫𐑉 𐐫𐑊 𐑋𐐰𐑌𐐿𐐴𐑌𐐼, 𐐸𐐶𐐮𐐽 𐐯𐑂𐐲𐑉 𐐶𐐲𐑉 𐑅𐐮𐑌𐑅 𐑄 𐑁𐐫𐑊 𐐱𐑂 𐐈𐐼𐐲𐑋, 𐐫𐑉 𐐸𐐭 𐐪𐑉, 𐐫𐑉 𐐸𐐭 𐐯𐑂𐐲𐑉 𐑇𐐰𐑊 𐐺, 𐐨𐑂𐑌 𐐲𐑌𐐻𐐭 𐑄 𐐯𐑌𐐼 𐐱𐑂 𐑄 𐐶𐐲𐑉𐑊𐐼; 𐐰𐑌𐐼 𐑄𐐮𐑅 𐐮𐑆 𐑄 𐑋𐐨𐑌𐑆 𐐸𐐶𐐯𐑉𐐺𐐴 𐑅𐐰𐑊𐑂𐐩𐑇𐐲𐑌 𐐿𐐲𐑋𐐯𐑃. 𐐈𐑌𐐼 𐑄𐐩𐑉 𐐮𐑆 𐑌𐐲𐑌 𐐲𐑄𐐲𐑉 𐑅𐐰𐑊𐑂𐐩𐑇𐐲𐑌, 𐑅𐐩𐑂 𐑄𐐮𐑅 𐐸𐐶𐐮𐐽 𐐸𐐰𐑃 𐐺𐐨𐑌 𐑅𐐹𐐬𐐿𐐲𐑌 𐐱𐑂; 𐑌𐐨𐑄𐐲𐑉 𐐪𐑉 𐑄𐐩𐑉 𐐯𐑌𐐨 𐐿𐐱𐑌𐐼𐐮𐑇𐐲𐑌𐑆 𐐸𐐶𐐯𐑉𐐺𐐴 𐑋𐐰𐑌 𐐿𐐰𐑌 𐐺 𐑅𐐩𐑂𐐼, 𐐯𐐿𐑅𐐯𐐹𐐻 𐑄 𐐿𐐱𐑌𐐼𐐮𐑇𐐲𐑌𐑆 𐐸𐐶𐐮𐐽 𐐌 𐐸𐐰𐑂 𐐻𐐬𐑊𐐼 𐐷𐐭. 𐐒𐐨𐑊𐐨𐑂 𐐮𐑌 𐐘𐐱𐐼; 𐐺𐐨𐑊𐐨𐑂 𐑄𐐰𐐻 𐐸𐐨 𐐮𐑆, 𐐰𐑌𐐼 𐑄𐐰𐐻 𐐸𐐨 𐐿𐑉𐐨𐐩𐐻𐐯𐐼 𐐫𐑊 𐑃𐐮𐑍𐑆, 𐐺𐐬𐑃 𐐮𐑌 𐐸𐐯𐑂𐑌 𐐰𐑌𐐼 𐐮𐑌 𐐲𐑉𐑃; 𐐺𐐨𐑊𐐨𐑂 𐑄𐐰𐐻 𐐸𐐨 𐐸𐐰𐑆 𐐫𐑊 𐐶𐐮𐑆𐐼𐐲𐑋, 𐐰𐑌𐐼 𐐫𐑊 𐐹𐐵𐑉, 𐐺𐐬𐑃 𐐮𐑌 𐐸𐐯𐑂𐑌 𐐰𐑌𐐼 𐐮𐑌 𐐲𐑉𐑃; 𐐺𐐨𐑊𐐨𐑂 𐑄𐐰𐐻 𐑋𐐰𐑌 𐐼𐐲𐑃 𐑌𐐱𐐻 𐐿𐐱𐑋𐐹𐑉𐐨𐐸𐐯𐑌𐐼 𐐫𐑊 𐑄 𐑃𐐮𐑍𐑆 𐐸𐐶𐐮𐐽 𐑄 𐐢𐐫𐑉𐐼 𐐿𐐰𐑌 𐐿𐐱𐑋𐐹𐑉𐐨𐐸𐐯𐑌𐐼.

3. 𐐈𐑌𐐼 𐐰𐑀𐐯𐑌: 𐐒𐐨𐑊𐐨𐑂 𐑄𐐰𐐻 𐐷 𐑋𐐲𐑅𐐻 𐑉𐐨𐐹𐐯𐑌𐐻 𐐱𐑂 𐐷𐐫𐑉 𐑅𐐮𐑌𐑆 𐐰𐑌𐐼 𐑁𐐫𐑉𐑅𐐩𐐿 𐑄𐐯𐑋, 𐐰𐑌𐐼 𐐸𐐲𐑋𐐺𐑊 𐐷𐐫𐑉𐑅𐐯𐑊𐑂𐑆 𐐺𐐨𐑁𐐫𐑉 𐐘𐐱𐐼; 𐐰𐑌𐐼 𐐪𐑅𐐿 𐐮𐑌 𐑅𐐮𐑌𐑅𐐯𐑉𐐮𐐻𐐨 𐐱𐑂 𐐸𐐪𐑉𐐻 𐑄𐐰𐐻 𐐸𐐨 𐐶𐐳𐐼 𐑁𐐫𐑉𐑀𐐮𐑂 𐐷𐐭; 𐐰𐑌𐐼 𐑌𐐵, 𐐮𐑁 𐐷𐐭 𐐺𐐨𐑊𐐨𐑂 𐐫𐑊 𐑄𐐨𐑆 𐑃𐐮𐑍𐑆 𐑅𐐨 𐑄𐐰𐐻 𐐷 𐐼𐐭 𐑄𐐯𐑋. 𐐈𐑌𐐼 𐐰𐑀𐐯𐑌 𐐌 𐑅𐐩 𐐲𐑌𐐻𐐭 𐐷𐐭 𐐰𐑆 𐐌 𐐸𐐰𐑂 𐑅𐐯𐐼 𐐺𐐨𐑁𐐫𐑉, 𐑄𐐰𐐻 𐐰𐑆 𐐷 𐐸𐐰𐑂 𐐿𐐲𐑋 𐐻𐐭 𐑄 𐑌𐐱𐑊𐐯𐐾 𐐱𐑂 𐑄 𐑀𐑊𐐫𐑉𐐨 𐐱𐑂 𐐘𐐱𐐼, 𐐫𐑉 𐐮𐑁 𐐷 𐐸𐐰𐑂 𐑌𐐬𐑌 𐐱𐑂 𐐸𐐮𐑆 𐑀𐐳𐐼𐑌𐐯𐑅, 𐐰𐑌𐐼 𐐸𐐰𐑂 𐐻𐐩𐑅𐐻𐐯𐐼 𐐱𐑂 𐐸𐐮𐑆 𐑊𐐲𐑂, 𐐰𐑌𐐼 𐐸𐐰𐑂 𐑉𐐨𐑅𐐨𐑂𐐼 𐐪 𐑉𐐨𐑋𐐮𐑇𐐲𐑌 𐐱𐑂 𐐷𐐫𐑉 𐑅𐐮𐑌𐑆, 𐐸𐐶𐐮𐐽 𐐿𐐫𐑆𐐯𐑃 𐑅𐐲𐐽 𐐯𐐿𐑅𐐨𐐼𐐮𐑍𐑊𐐨 𐑀𐑉𐐩𐐻 𐐾𐑎 𐐮𐑌 𐐷𐐫𐑉 𐑅𐐬𐑊𐑆, 𐐨𐑂𐑌 𐑅𐐬 𐐌 𐐶𐐳𐐼 𐑄𐐰𐐻 𐐷 𐑇𐐳𐐼 𐑉𐐨𐑋𐐯𐑋𐐺𐐲𐑉, 𐐰𐑌𐐼 𐐫𐑊𐐶𐐩𐑆 𐑉𐐨𐐻𐐩𐑌 𐐮𐑌 𐑉𐐨𐑋𐐯𐑋𐐺𐐲𐑉𐐲𐑌𐑅, 𐑄 𐑀𐑉𐐩𐐻𐑌𐐯𐑅 𐐱𐑂 𐐘𐐱𐐼, 𐐰𐑌𐐼 𐐷𐐫𐑉 𐐬𐑌 𐑌𐐲𐑃𐐮𐑍𐑌𐐯𐑅, 𐐰𐑌𐐼 𐐸𐐮𐑆 𐑀𐐳𐐼𐑌𐐯𐑅 𐐰𐑌𐐼 𐑊𐐱𐑍𐑅𐐲𐑁𐐲𐑉𐐮𐑍 𐐻𐐬𐐲𐑉𐐼𐑆 𐐷𐐭, 𐐲𐑌𐐶𐐲𐑉𐑄𐐨 𐐿𐑉𐐨𐐽𐐲𐑉𐑆, 𐐰𐑌𐐼 𐐸𐐲𐑋𐐺𐑊 𐐷𐐫𐑉𐑅𐐯𐑊𐑂𐑆 𐐨𐑂𐑌 𐐮𐑌 𐑄 𐐼𐐯𐐹𐑃𐑅 𐐱𐑂 𐐸𐐷𐐭𐑋𐐮𐑊𐐮𐐻𐐨, 𐐿𐐫𐑊𐐮𐑍 𐐱𐑌 𐑄 𐑌𐐩𐑋 𐐱𐑂 𐑄 𐐢𐐫𐑉𐐼 𐐼𐐩𐑊𐐨, 𐐰𐑌𐐼 𐑅𐐻𐐰𐑌𐐼𐐮𐑍 𐑅𐐻𐐯𐐼𐑁𐐰𐑅𐐻𐑊𐐨 𐐮𐑌 𐑄 𐑁𐐩𐑃 𐐱𐑂 𐑄𐐰𐐻 𐐸𐐶𐐮𐐽 𐐮𐑆 𐐻𐐭 𐐿𐐲𐑋, 𐐸𐐶𐐮𐐽 𐐶𐐱𐑆 𐑅𐐹𐐬𐐿𐐲𐑌 𐐺𐐴 𐑄 𐑋𐐵𐑃 𐐱𐑂 𐑄 𐐩𐑌𐐾𐐯𐑊; 𐐰𐑌𐐼 𐐺𐐨𐐸𐐬𐑊𐐼, 𐐌 𐑅𐐩 𐐲𐑌𐐻𐐭 𐐷𐐭, 𐑄𐐰𐐻 𐐮𐑁 𐐷 𐐼𐐭 𐑄𐐮𐑅, 𐐷 𐑇𐐰𐑊 𐐫𐑊𐐶𐐩𐑆 𐑉𐐨𐐾𐐱𐐮𐑅, 𐐰𐑌𐐼 𐐺 𐑁𐐮𐑊𐐼 𐐶𐐮𐑄 𐑄 𐑊𐐲𐑂 𐐱𐑂 𐐘𐐱𐐼, 𐐰𐑌𐐼 𐐫𐑊𐐶𐐩𐑆 𐑉𐐨𐐻𐐩𐑌 𐐪 𐑉𐐨𐑋𐐮𐑇𐐲𐑌 𐐱𐑂 𐐷𐐫𐑉 𐑅𐐮𐑌𐑆; 𐐰𐑌𐐼 𐐷 𐑇𐐰𐑊 𐑀𐑉𐐬 𐐮𐑌 𐑄 𐑌𐐱𐑊𐐯𐐾 𐐱𐑂 𐑄 𐑀𐑊𐐫𐑉𐐨 𐐱𐑂 𐐸𐐮𐑋 𐑄𐐰𐐻 𐐿𐑉𐐨𐐩𐐻𐐯𐐼 𐐷𐐭, 𐐫𐑉 𐐮𐑌 𐑄 𐑌𐐱𐑊𐐯𐐾 𐐱𐑂 𐑄𐐰𐐻 𐐸𐐶𐐮𐐽 𐐮𐑆 𐐾𐐲𐑅𐐻 𐐰𐑌𐐼 𐐻𐑉𐐭. 𐐈𐑌𐐼 𐐷 𐐶𐐮𐑊 𐑌𐐱𐐻 𐐸𐐰𐑂 𐐪 𐑋𐐴𐑌𐐼 𐐻𐐭

𐐮𐑌𐐾𐐲𐑉 𐐶𐐲𐑌 𐐰𐑌𐐲𐑄𐐲𐑉, 𐐺𐐲𐐻 𐐻𐐭 𐑊𐐮𐑂 𐐹𐐨𐑅𐐲𐐺𐑊𐐨, 𐐰𐑌𐐼 𐐻𐐭 𐑉𐐯𐑌𐐼𐐲𐑉 𐐻𐐭 𐐯𐑂𐐲𐑉𐐨 𐑋𐐰𐑌 𐐰𐐿𐐫𐑉𐐼𐐮𐑍 𐐻𐐭 𐑄𐐰𐐻 𐐸𐐶𐐮𐐽 𐐮𐑆 𐐸𐐮𐑆 𐐼𐐭. 𐐈𐑌𐐼 𐐷 𐐶𐐮𐑊 𐑌𐐱𐐻 𐑅𐐲𐑁𐐲𐑉 𐐷𐐫𐑉 𐐽𐐮𐑊𐐼𐑉𐐯𐑌, 𐑄𐐰𐐻 𐑄𐐩 𐑀𐐬 𐐸𐐲𐑍𐑀𐑉𐐨, 𐐫𐑉 𐑌𐐩𐐿𐐯𐐼; 𐑌𐐨𐑄𐐲𐑉 𐐶𐐮𐑊 𐐷 𐑅𐐲𐑁𐐲𐑉 𐑄𐐰𐐻 𐑄𐐩 𐐻𐑉𐐰𐑌𐑅𐑀𐑉𐐯𐑅 𐑄 𐑊𐐫𐑆 𐐱𐑂 𐐘𐐱𐐼, 𐐰𐑌𐐼 𐑁𐐴𐐻 𐐰𐑌𐐼 𐐿𐐶𐐫𐑉𐐲𐑊 𐐶𐐲𐑌 𐐶𐐮𐑄 𐐰𐑌𐐲𐑄𐐲𐑉, 𐐰𐑌𐐼 𐑅𐐲𐑉𐑂 𐑄 𐐼𐐯𐑂𐐮𐑊, 𐐸𐐭 𐐮𐑆 𐑄 𐑋𐐰𐑅𐐻𐐲𐑉 𐐱𐑂 𐑅𐐮𐑌, 𐐫𐑉 𐐸𐐭 𐐮𐑆 𐑄 𐐨𐑂𐐮𐑊 𐑅𐐹𐐮𐑉𐐮𐐻 𐐸𐐶𐐮𐐽 𐐸𐐰𐑃 𐐺𐐮𐑌 𐑅𐐹𐐬𐐿𐐲𐑌 𐐱𐑂 𐐺𐐴 𐐵𐑉 𐑁𐐪𐑄𐐲𐑉𐑆, 𐐸𐐨 𐐺𐐨𐐮𐑍 𐐰𐑌 𐐯𐑌𐐲𐑋𐐨 𐐻𐐭 𐐫𐑊 𐑉𐐴𐐽𐐲𐑅𐑌𐐯𐑅; 𐐺𐐲𐐻 𐐷 𐐶𐐮𐑊 𐐻𐐨𐐽 𐑄𐐯𐑋 𐐻𐐭 𐐶𐐫𐐿 𐐮𐑌 𐑄 𐐶𐐩𐑆 𐐱𐑂 𐐻𐑉𐐭𐑃 𐐰𐑌𐐼 𐑅𐐬𐐺𐐲𐑉𐑌𐐯𐑅; 𐐷 𐐶𐐮𐑊 𐐻𐐨𐐽 𐑄𐐯𐑋 𐐻𐐭 𐑊𐐲𐑂 𐐶𐐲𐑌 𐐰𐑌𐐲𐑄𐐲𐑉, 𐐰𐑌𐐼 𐐻𐐭 𐑅𐐲𐑉𐑂 𐐶𐐲𐑌 𐐰𐑌𐐲𐑄𐐲𐑉; 𐐰𐑌𐐼 𐐫𐑊𐑅𐐬, 𐐷 𐐷𐐫𐑉𐑅𐐯𐑊𐑂𐑆 𐐶𐐮𐑊 𐑅𐐲𐐿𐐲𐑉 𐑄𐐬𐑆 𐑄𐐰𐐻 𐑅𐐻𐐰𐑌𐐼 𐐮𐑌 𐑌𐐨𐐼 𐐱𐑂 𐐷𐐫𐑉 𐑅𐐲𐐿𐐲𐑉; 𐐷 𐐶𐐮𐑊 𐐰𐐼𐑋𐐮𐑌𐐮𐑅𐐻𐐲𐑉 𐐱𐑂 𐐷𐐫𐑉 𐑅𐐲𐐺𐑅𐐻𐐲𐑌𐑅 𐐲𐑌𐐻𐐭 𐐸𐐮𐑋 𐑄𐐰𐐻 𐑅𐐻𐐰𐑌𐐼𐐯𐑃 𐐮𐑌 𐑌𐐨𐐼; 𐐰𐑌𐐼 𐐷 𐐶𐐮𐑊 𐑌𐐱𐐻 𐑅𐐲𐑁𐐲𐑉 𐑄𐐰𐐻 𐑄 𐐺𐐯𐑀𐐲𐑉 𐐹𐐳𐐻𐐯𐑃 𐐲𐐹 𐐸𐐮𐑆 𐐹𐐯𐐻𐐮𐑇𐐲𐑌 𐐻𐐭 𐐷𐐭 𐐮𐑌 𐑂𐐩𐑌, 𐐰𐑌𐐼 𐐻𐐲𐑉𐑌 𐐸𐐮𐑋 𐐵𐐻 𐐻𐐭 𐐹𐐯𐑉𐐮𐑇. 𐐑𐐲𐑉𐐸𐐰𐐹𐑅 𐑄𐐵 𐑇𐐰𐑊𐐻 𐑅𐐩, 𐑄 𐑋𐐰𐑌 𐐸𐐰𐑆 𐐺𐑉𐐫𐐻 𐐲𐐹𐐱𐑌 𐐸𐐮𐑋𐑅𐐯𐑊𐑁 𐐸𐐮𐑆 𐑋𐐮𐑆𐐲𐑉𐐨, 𐑄𐐯𐑉𐑁𐐫𐑉 𐐌 𐐶𐐮𐑊 𐑅𐐻𐐩 𐑋𐐴 𐐸𐐰𐑌𐐼, 𐐰𐑌𐐼 𐐶𐐮𐑊 𐑌𐐱𐐻 𐑀𐐮𐑂 𐐲𐑌𐐻𐐭 𐐸𐐮𐑋 𐐱𐑂 𐑋𐐴 𐑁𐐭𐐼, 𐑌𐐫𐑉 𐐮𐑋𐐹𐐪𐑉𐐻 𐐲𐑌𐐻𐐭 𐐸𐐮𐑋 𐐱𐑂 𐑋𐐴 𐑅𐐲𐐺𐑅𐐻𐐲𐑌𐑅 𐑄𐐰𐐻 𐐸𐐨 𐑋𐐩 𐑌𐐱𐐻 𐑅𐐲𐑁𐐲𐑉, 𐑁𐐫𐑉 𐐸𐐮𐑆 𐐹𐐲𐑌𐐮𐑇𐑋𐐯𐑌𐐻𐑅 𐐪𐑉 𐐾𐐲𐑅𐐻. 𐐒𐐲𐐻 𐐌 𐑅𐐩 𐐲𐑌𐐻𐐭 𐐷𐐭, 𐐄 𐑋𐐰𐑌, 𐐸𐐭𐑅𐐬𐐯𐑂𐐲𐑉 𐐼𐐭𐐯𐑃 𐑄𐐮𐑅 𐑄 𐑅𐐩𐑋 𐐸𐐰𐑃 𐑀𐑉𐐩𐐻 𐐿𐐫𐑆 𐐻𐐭 𐑉𐐨𐐹𐐯𐑌𐐻; 𐐰𐑌𐐼 𐐯𐐿𐑅𐐯𐐹𐐻 𐐸𐐨 𐑉𐐨𐐹𐐯𐑌𐐻𐐯𐑃 𐐱𐑂 𐑄𐐰𐐻 𐐸𐐶𐐮𐐽 𐐸𐐨 𐐸𐐰𐑃 𐐼𐐲𐑌, 𐐸𐐨 𐐹𐐯𐑉𐐮𐑇𐐯𐑃 𐑁𐐫𐑉𐐯𐑂𐐲𐑉, 𐐰𐑌𐐼 𐐸𐐰𐑃 𐑌𐐬 𐐮𐑌𐐻𐐲𐑉𐐯𐑅𐐻 𐐮𐑌 𐑄 𐐿𐐮𐑍𐐼𐐲𐑋 𐐱𐑂 𐐘𐐱𐐼.

4. 𐐙𐐫𐑉 𐐺𐐨𐐸𐐬𐑊𐐼, 𐐪𐑉 𐐶𐐨 𐑌𐐱𐐻 𐐫𐑊 𐐺𐐯𐑀𐐲𐑉𐑆? 𐐔𐐭 𐐶𐐨 𐑌𐐱𐐻 𐐫𐑊 𐐼𐐨𐐹𐐯𐑌𐐼 𐐲𐐹𐐱𐑌 𐑄 𐑅𐐩𐑋 𐐺𐐨𐐮𐑍, 𐐨𐑂𐐯𐑌 𐐘𐐱𐐼, 𐑁𐐫𐑉 𐐫𐑊 𐑄 𐑅𐐲𐐺𐑅𐐻𐐲𐑌𐑅 𐐸𐐶𐐮𐐽 𐐶𐐨 𐐸𐐰𐑂; 𐑁𐐫𐑉 𐐺𐐬𐑃 𐑁𐐭𐐼 𐐰𐑌𐐼 𐑉𐐩𐑋𐐯𐑌𐐻, 𐐰𐑌𐐼 𐑁𐐫𐑉 𐑀𐐬𐑊𐐼, 𐐰𐑌𐐼 𐑁𐐫𐑉 𐑅𐐮𐑊𐑂𐐲𐑉, 𐐰𐑌𐐼 𐑁𐐫𐑉 𐐫𐑊 𐑄 𐑉𐐮𐐽𐐯𐑆 𐐸𐐶𐐮𐐽 𐐶𐐨 𐐸𐐰𐑂 𐐱𐑂 𐐯𐑂𐐲𐑉𐐨 𐐿𐐴𐑌𐐼? 𐐈𐑌𐐼 𐐺𐐨𐐸𐐬𐑊𐐼, 𐐨𐑂𐐯𐑌 𐐰𐐻 𐑄𐐮𐑅 𐐻𐐴𐑋, 𐐷 𐐸𐐰𐑂 𐐺𐐮𐑌 𐐿𐐫𐑊𐐮𐑍 𐐱𐑌 𐐸𐐮𐑆 𐑌𐐩𐑋, 𐐰𐑌𐐼 𐐺𐐯𐑀𐐮𐑍 𐑁𐐫𐑉 𐐩 𐑉𐐨𐑋𐐮𐑇𐐲𐑌 𐐱𐑂 𐐷𐐫𐑉 𐑅𐐮𐑌𐑆. 𐐈𐑌𐐼 𐐸𐐰𐑆 𐐸𐐨 𐑅𐐲𐑁𐐲𐑉𐐯𐐼 𐑄𐐰𐐻 𐐷 𐐸𐐰𐑂 𐐺𐐯𐑀𐐼 𐐮𐑌 𐑂𐐩𐑌? 𐐤𐐩; 𐐸𐐨 𐐸𐐰𐑆 𐐹𐐫𐑉𐐼 𐐵𐐻 𐐸𐐮𐑆 𐐝𐐹𐐮𐑉𐐮𐐻 𐐲𐐹𐐱𐑌 𐐷𐐭, 𐐰𐑌𐐼 𐐸𐐰𐑆 𐐿𐐫𐑆𐐼 𐑄𐐰𐐻 𐐷𐐫𐑉 𐐸𐐪𐑉𐐻𐑅 𐑇𐐳𐐼 𐐺𐐨 𐑁𐐮𐑊𐐼 𐐶𐐮𐑄 𐐾𐐱𐐮, 𐐰𐑌𐐼 𐐸𐐰𐑆 𐐿𐐫𐑆𐐼 𐑄𐐰𐐻 𐐷𐐫𐑉 𐑋𐐵𐑄𐑅 𐑇𐐳𐐼 𐐺𐐨 𐑅𐐻𐐱𐐹𐐻, 𐑄𐐰𐐻 𐐷 𐐿𐐳𐐼 𐑌𐐱𐐻 𐑁𐐴𐑌𐐼 𐐲𐐻𐐲𐑉𐐰𐑌𐑅, 𐑅𐐬 𐐯𐐿𐑅𐐨𐐼𐐮𐑍𐑊𐐨 𐑀𐑉𐐩𐐻 𐐶𐐱𐑆 𐐷𐐫𐑉 𐐾𐐱𐐮. 𐐈𐑌𐐼 𐑌𐐵, 𐐮𐑁 𐐘𐐱𐐼, 𐐸𐐭 𐐸𐐰𐑆 𐐿𐑉𐐨𐐩𐐻𐐯𐐼 𐐷𐐭, 𐐱𐑌 𐐸𐐭𐑋 𐐷 𐐪𐑉 𐐼𐐨𐐹𐐯𐑌𐐼𐐯𐑌𐐻 𐑁𐐫𐑉 𐐷𐐫𐑉 𐑊𐐴𐑂𐑆, 𐐰𐑌𐐼 𐑁𐐫𐑉 𐐫𐑊 𐑄𐐰𐐻 𐐷 𐐸𐐰𐑂 𐐰𐑌𐐼 𐐪𐑉, 𐐼𐐲𐑃 𐑀𐑉𐐰𐑌𐐻 𐐲𐑌𐐻𐐭 𐐷𐐭 𐐸𐐶𐐱𐐻𐑅𐐬𐐯𐑂𐐲𐑉 𐐷 𐐰𐑅𐐿 𐑄𐐰𐐻 𐐮𐑆 𐑉𐐴𐐻, 𐐮𐑌 𐑁𐐩𐑃, 𐐺𐐨𐑊𐐨𐑂𐐮𐑍 𐑄𐐰𐐻 𐐷 𐑇𐐰𐑊 𐑉𐐨𐑅𐐨𐑂, 𐐄 𐑄𐐯𐑌, 𐐸𐐵 𐐷 𐐫𐐻 𐐻𐐭 𐐮𐑋𐐹𐐪𐑉𐐻 𐐱𐑂 𐑄 𐑅𐐲𐐺𐑅𐐻𐐲𐑌𐑅 𐑄𐐰𐐻 𐐷 𐐸𐐰𐑂 𐐶𐐲𐑌 𐐻𐐭 𐐰𐑌𐐲𐑄𐐲𐑉? 𐐈𐑌𐐼 𐐮𐑁 𐐷 𐐾𐐲𐐾 𐑄 𐑋𐐰𐑌 𐐸𐐭 𐐹𐐳𐐻𐐯𐑃 𐐲𐐹 𐐸𐐮𐑆 𐐹𐐯𐐻𐐮𐑇𐐲𐑌 𐐻𐐭 𐐷𐐭 𐑁𐐫𐑉 𐐷𐐫𐑉 𐑅𐐲𐐺𐑅𐐻𐐲𐑌𐑅 𐑄𐐰𐐻 𐐸𐐨 𐐹𐐯𐑉𐐮𐑇 𐑌𐐱𐐻, 𐐰𐑌𐐼 𐐿𐐱𐑌𐐼𐐯𐑋 𐐸𐐮𐑋, 𐐸𐐵 𐑋𐐲𐐽 𐑋𐐬𐑉 𐐾𐐲𐑅𐐻 𐐶𐐮𐑊 𐐺𐐨 𐐷𐐫𐑉 𐐿𐐱𐑌𐐼𐐯𐑋𐑌𐐩𐑇𐐲𐑌 𐑁𐐫𐑉 𐐶𐐮𐑄𐐸𐐬𐑊𐐼𐐮𐑍 𐐷𐐫𐑉 𐑅𐐲𐐺𐑅𐐻𐐲𐑌𐑅, 𐐸𐐶𐐮𐐽 𐐼𐐲𐑃 𐑌𐐱𐐻 𐐺𐐨𐑊𐐱𐑍 𐐻𐐭 𐐷𐐭 𐐺𐐲𐐻 𐐻𐐭 𐐘𐐱𐐼, 𐐻𐐭 𐐸𐐭𐑋 𐐫𐑊𐑅𐐬 𐐷𐐫𐑉 𐑊𐐴𐑁 𐐺𐐨𐑊𐐱𐑍𐐯𐑃; 𐐰𐑌𐐼 𐐷𐐯𐐻 𐐷 𐐹𐐳𐐻 𐐲𐐹 𐑌𐐬 𐐹𐐯𐐻𐐮𐑇𐐲𐑌, 𐑌𐐫𐑉 𐑉𐐨𐐹𐐯𐑌𐐻 𐐱𐑂 𐑄 𐑃𐐮𐑍 𐐸𐐶𐐮𐐽 𐑄𐐵 𐐸𐐰𐑅𐐻 𐐼𐐲𐑌. 𐐌 𐑅𐐩 𐐲𐑌𐐻𐐭 𐐷𐐭, 𐐶𐐬 𐐺𐐨 𐐲𐑌𐐻𐐭 𐑄𐐰𐐻 𐑋𐐰𐑌, 𐑁𐐫𐑉 𐐸𐐮𐑆 𐑅𐐲𐐺𐑅𐐻𐐲𐑌𐑅 𐑇𐐰𐑊 𐐹𐐯𐑉𐐮𐑇 𐐶𐐮𐑄 𐐸𐐮𐑋; 𐐰𐑌𐐼 𐑌𐐵, 𐐌 𐑅𐐩 𐑄𐐨𐑆 𐑃𐐮𐑍𐑆 𐐲𐑌𐐻𐐭 𐑄𐐬𐑆 𐐸𐐭 𐐪𐑉 𐑉𐐮𐐽 𐐰𐑆 𐐹𐐲𐑉𐐻𐐩𐑌𐐮𐑍 𐐻𐐭 𐑄 𐑃𐐮𐑍𐑆 𐐱𐑂 𐑄𐐮𐑅 𐐶𐐲𐑉𐑊𐐼. 𐐈𐑌𐐼 𐐰𐑀𐐯𐑌, 𐐌 𐑅𐐩 𐐲𐑌𐐻𐐭 𐑄 𐐹𐐭𐑉, 𐐷 𐐸𐐭 𐐸𐐰𐑂 𐑌𐐱𐐻 𐐰𐑌𐐼 𐐷𐐯𐐻 𐐸𐐰𐑂 𐑅𐐲𐑁𐐮𐑇𐐯𐑌𐐻, 𐑄𐐰𐐻 𐐷 𐑉𐐨𐑋𐐩𐑌 𐑁𐑉𐐱𐑋 𐐼𐐩 𐐻𐐭 𐐼𐐩; 𐐌 𐑋𐐨𐑌 𐐫𐑊 𐐷𐐭 𐐸𐐭 𐐼𐐨𐑌𐐴 𐑄 𐐺𐐯𐑀𐐲𐑉, 𐐺𐐨𐐿𐐫𐑆 𐐷 𐐸𐐰𐑂 𐑌𐐱𐐻; 𐐌 𐐶𐐳𐐼 𐑄𐐰𐐻 𐐷 𐑅𐐩 𐐮𐑌 𐐷𐐫𐑉 𐐸𐐪𐑉𐐻𐑅 𐑄𐐰𐐻, 𐐌 𐑀𐐮𐑂 𐑌𐐱𐐻 𐐺𐐨𐐿𐐫𐑆 𐐌 𐐸𐐰𐑂 𐑌𐐱𐐻; 𐐺𐐲𐐻 𐐮𐑁 𐐌 𐐸𐐰𐐼, 𐐌 𐐶𐐳𐐼 𐑀𐐮𐑂. 𐐈𐑌𐐼 𐑌𐐵, 𐐮𐑁 𐐷 𐑅𐐩 𐑄𐐮𐑅 𐐮𐑌 𐐷𐐫𐑉 𐐸𐐪𐑉𐐻𐑅, 𐐷 𐑉𐐨𐑋𐐩𐑌 𐑀𐐮𐑊𐐻𐑊𐐯𐑅, 𐐲𐑄𐐲𐑉𐐶𐐴𐑆 𐐷 𐐪𐑉 𐐿𐐱𐑌𐐼𐐯𐑋𐐼, 𐐰𐑌𐐼 𐐷𐐫𐑉 𐐿𐐱𐑌𐐼𐐯𐑋𐑌𐐩𐑇𐐲𐑌 𐐮𐑆 𐐾𐐲𐑅𐐻; 𐑁𐐫𐑉 𐐷 𐐿𐐲𐑂𐐯𐐻 𐑄𐐰𐐻 𐐸𐐶𐐮𐐽 𐐷 𐐸𐐰𐑂 𐑌𐐱𐐻 𐑉𐐨𐑅𐐨𐑂𐐼.

5. 𐐈𐑌𐐼 𐑌𐐵, 𐑁𐐫𐑉 𐑄 𐑅𐐩𐐿 𐐱𐑂 𐑄𐐨𐑆 𐑃𐐮𐑍𐑆 𐐸𐐶𐐮𐐽 𐐌 𐐸𐐰𐑂 𐑅𐐹𐐬𐐿𐐲𐑌 𐐲𐑌𐐻𐐭 𐐷𐐭; 𐑄𐐰𐐻 𐐮𐑆, 𐑁𐐫𐑉 𐑄 𐑅𐐩𐐿 𐐱𐑂 𐑉𐐨𐐻𐐩𐑌𐐮𐑍 𐐩 𐑉𐐨𐑋𐐮𐑇𐐲𐑌 𐐱𐑂 𐐷𐐫𐑉 𐑅𐐮𐑌𐑆 𐑁𐑉𐐱𐑋 𐐼𐐩 𐐻𐐭 𐐼𐐩, 𐑄𐐰𐐻 𐐷 𐑋𐐩 𐐶𐐫𐐿 𐑀𐐮𐑊𐐻𐑊𐐯𐑅 𐐺𐐨𐑁𐐫𐑉 𐐘𐐱𐐼, 𐐌 𐐶𐐳𐐼 𐑄𐐰𐐻 𐐷 𐑇𐐳𐐼 𐐮𐑋𐐹𐐪𐑉𐐻 𐐱𐑂 𐐷𐐫𐑉 𐑅𐐲𐐺𐑅𐐻𐐲𐑌𐑅 𐐻𐐭 𐑄 𐐹𐐭𐑉, 𐐯𐑂𐐲𐑉𐐨 𐑋𐐰𐑌 𐐰𐐿𐐫𐑉𐐼𐐮𐑍 𐐻𐐭 𐑄𐐰𐐻 𐐸𐐶𐐮𐐽 𐐸𐐨 𐐸𐐰𐑃, 𐑅𐐲𐐽 𐐰𐑆 𐑁𐐨𐐼𐐮𐑍 𐑄 𐐸𐐲𐑍𐑀𐑉𐐨, 𐐿𐑊𐐬𐑄𐐮𐑍 𐑄 𐑌𐐩𐐿𐐯𐐼, 𐑂𐐮𐑆𐐮𐐻𐐮𐑍 𐑄

𐑅𐐮𐐿, 𐐰𐑌𐐼 𐐰𐐼𐑋𐐮𐑌𐐮𐑅𐐻𐐲𐑉𐐮𐑍 𐐻𐐭 𐑄𐐯𐑉 𐑉𐐨𐑊𐐨𐑁, 𐐺𐐬𐑃 𐑅𐐹𐐮𐑉𐐮𐐻𐐷𐐭𐐲𐑊𐐨 𐐰𐑌𐐼 𐐻𐐯𐑋𐐹𐐬𐑉𐐲𐑊𐐨, 𐐰𐐿𐐫𐑉𐐼𐐮𐑍 𐐻𐐭 𐑄𐐯𐑉 𐐶𐐪𐑌𐐻𐑅, 𐐰𐑌𐐼 𐑅𐐨 𐑄𐐰𐐻 𐐫𐑊 𐑄𐐨𐑆 𐑃𐐮𐑍𐑆 𐐪𐑉 𐐼𐐲𐑌 𐐮𐑌 𐐶𐐮𐑆𐐼𐐲𐑋 𐐰𐑌𐐼 𐐫𐑉𐐼𐐲𐑉; 𐑁𐐫𐑉 𐐮𐐻 𐐮𐑆 𐑌𐐪𐐻 𐑉𐐯𐐿𐐶𐐮𐑆𐐮𐐻 𐑄𐐰𐐻 𐐲 𐑋𐐰𐑌 𐑇𐐳𐐼 𐑉𐐲𐑌 𐑁𐐰𐑅𐐻𐐲𐑉 𐑄𐐰𐑌 𐐸𐐨 𐐸𐐰𐑆 𐑅𐐻𐑉𐐯𐑍𐑃. 𐐰𐑌𐐼 𐐲𐑀𐐯𐑌: 𐐮𐐻 𐐮𐑆 𐐯𐐿𐑅𐐹𐐨𐐼𐐨𐐲𐑌𐐻 𐑄𐐰𐐻 𐐸𐐨 𐑇𐐳𐐼 𐐺𐐨 𐐼𐐮𐑊𐐮𐐾𐐲𐑌𐐻, 𐑄𐐰𐐻 𐑄𐐯𐑉𐐺𐐴 𐐸𐐨 𐑋𐐴𐐻 𐐶𐐮𐑌 𐑄 𐐹𐑉𐐴𐑆; 𐑄𐐯𐑉𐑁𐐬𐑉, 𐐫𐑊 𐑃𐐮𐑍𐑆 𐑋𐐲𐑅𐐻 𐐺𐐨 𐐼𐐲𐑌 𐐮𐑌 𐐫𐑉𐐼𐐲𐑉. 𐐰𐑌𐐼 𐐴 𐐶𐐳𐐼 𐑄𐐰𐐻 𐐷𐐨 𐑇𐐳𐐼 𐑉𐐨𐑋𐐯𐑋𐐺𐐲𐑉, 𐑄𐐰𐐻 𐐸𐐭𐑅𐐬𐐯𐑂𐐲𐑉 𐐲𐑋𐐲𐑍 𐐷𐐭 𐑄𐐰𐐻 𐐺𐐫𐑉𐐬𐐯𐑃 𐐱𐑂 𐐸𐐮𐑆 𐑌𐐩𐐺𐐲𐑉, 𐑇𐐳𐐼 𐑉𐐨𐐻𐐲𐑉𐑌 𐑄 𐑃𐐮𐑍 𐑄𐐰𐐻 𐐸𐐨 𐐺𐐫𐑉𐐬𐐯𐑃, 𐐰𐐿𐐫𐑉𐐼𐐮𐑍 𐐰𐑆 𐐸𐐨 𐐼𐐲𐑃 𐐲𐑀𐑉𐐨, 𐐫𐑉 𐐯𐑊𐑅 𐑄𐐵 𐑇𐐰𐑊𐐻 𐐿𐐲𐑋𐐮𐐻 𐑅𐐮𐑌, 𐐰𐑌𐐼 𐐹𐐲𐑉𐐸𐐰𐐹𐑅 𐑄𐐵 𐑇𐐰𐑊𐐻 𐐿𐐫𐑆 𐑄𐐴 𐑌𐐩𐐺𐐲𐑉 𐐻𐐭 𐐿𐐲𐑋𐐮𐐻 𐑅𐐮𐑌 𐐫𐑊𐑅𐐬. 𐐰𐑌𐐼 𐑁𐐴𐑌𐐲𐑊𐐨, 𐐴 𐐿𐐰𐑌𐐪𐐻 𐐻𐐯𐑊 𐐷𐐭 𐐫𐑊 𐑄 𐑃𐐮𐑍𐑆 𐐸𐐶𐐯𐑉𐐺𐐴 𐐷𐐨 𐑋𐐩 𐐿𐐲𐑋𐐮𐐻 𐑅𐐮𐑌; 𐑁𐐫𐑉 𐑄𐐯𐑉 𐐪𐑉 𐐼𐐴𐑂𐐲𐑉𐑆 𐐶𐐩𐑆 𐐰𐑌𐐼 𐑋𐐨𐑌𐑆, 𐐨𐑂𐐲𐑌 𐑅𐐬 𐑋𐐯𐑌𐐨, 𐑄𐐰𐐻 𐐴 𐐿𐐰𐑌𐐪𐐻 𐑌𐐲𐑋𐐺𐐲𐑉 𐑄𐐯𐑋. 𐐒𐐲𐐻 𐑄𐐮𐑅 𐑋𐐲𐐽 𐐴 𐐿𐐰𐑌 𐐻𐐯𐑊 𐐷𐐭, 𐑄𐐰𐐻 𐐮𐑁 𐐷𐐨 𐐼𐐭 𐑌𐐪𐐻 𐐶𐐪𐐽 𐐷𐐭𐑉𐑅𐐯𐑊𐑂𐑆, 𐐰𐑌𐐼 𐐷𐐭𐑉 𐑃𐐫𐐻𐑅, 𐐰𐑌𐐼 𐐷𐐭𐑉 𐐶𐐲𐑉𐐼𐑆, 𐐰𐑌𐐼 𐐷𐐭𐑉 𐐼𐐨𐐼𐑆, 𐐰𐑌𐐼 𐐫𐐺𐑆𐐲𐑉𐑂 𐑄 𐐿𐐲𐑋𐐰𐑌𐐼𐑋𐐯𐑌𐐻𐑅 𐐱𐑂 𐐘𐐱𐐼, 𐐰𐑌𐐼 𐐿𐐲𐑌𐐻𐐮𐑌𐐷𐐭 𐐮𐑌 𐑄 𐑁𐐩𐑃 𐐱𐑂 𐐸𐐶𐐱𐐻 𐐷𐐨 𐐸𐐰𐑂 𐐸𐐲𐑉𐐼 𐐿𐐲𐑌𐑅𐐲𐑉𐑌𐐮𐑍 𐑄 𐐿𐐲𐑋𐐮𐑍 𐐱𐑂 𐐵𐑉 𐐢𐐫𐑉𐐼, 𐐨𐑂𐐲𐑌 𐐲𐑌𐐻𐐭 𐑄 𐐯𐑌𐐼 𐐱𐑂 𐐷𐐭𐑉 𐑊𐐴𐑂𐑆, 𐐷𐐨 𐑋𐐲𐑅𐐻 𐐹𐐯𐑉𐐮𐑇. 𐐰𐑌𐐼 𐑌𐐵, 𐐄 𐑋𐐰𐑌, 𐑉𐐨𐑋𐐯𐑋𐐺𐐲𐑉, 𐐰𐑌𐐼 𐐹𐐯𐑉𐐮𐑇 𐑌𐐪𐐻.

𐐕𐐰𐐹𐐻𐐲𐑉 III.

1. 𐐰𐑌𐐼 𐑌𐐵, 𐐮𐐻 𐐿𐐩𐑋 𐐻𐐭 𐐹𐐰𐑅 𐑄𐐰𐐻 𐐸𐐶𐐯𐑌 𐐿𐐨𐑍 𐐒𐐯𐑌𐐾𐐲𐑋𐐮𐑌 𐐸𐐰𐐼 𐑄𐐲𐑅 𐑅𐐹𐐬𐐿𐐲𐑌 𐐻𐐭 𐐸𐐮𐑆 𐐹𐐨𐐹𐐲𐑊, 𐐸𐐨 𐑅𐐯𐑌𐐻 𐐲𐑋𐐲𐑍 𐑄𐐯𐑋, 𐐼𐐨𐑆𐐴𐑉𐐮𐑍 𐐻𐐭 𐑌𐐬 𐐱𐑂 𐐸𐐮𐑆 𐐹𐐨𐐹𐐲𐑊, 𐐮𐑁 𐑄𐐩 𐐺𐐨𐑊𐐨𐑂𐐼 𐑄 𐐶𐐲𐑉𐐼𐑆 𐐸𐐶𐐮𐐽 𐐸𐐨 𐐸𐐰𐐼 𐑅𐐹𐐬𐐿𐐲𐑌 𐐲𐑌𐐻𐐭 𐑄𐐯𐑋. 𐐰𐑌𐐼 𐑄𐐩 𐐫𐑊 𐐿𐑉𐐴𐐼 𐐶𐐮𐑄 𐐶𐐲𐑌 𐑂𐐱𐐮𐑅, 𐑅𐐩𐐮𐑍, 𐐷𐐩, 𐐶𐐨 𐐺𐐨𐑊𐐨𐑂 𐐫𐑊 𐑄 𐐶𐐲𐑉𐐼𐑆 𐐸𐐶𐐮𐐽 𐑄𐐵 𐐸𐐰𐑅𐐻 𐑅𐐹𐐬𐐿𐐲𐑌 𐐲𐑌𐐻𐐭 𐐲𐑅; 𐐰𐑌𐐼 𐐫𐑊𐑅𐐬, 𐐶𐐨 𐑌𐐬 𐐱𐑂 𐑄𐐯𐑉 𐑇𐐭𐑉𐐻𐐨 𐐰𐑌𐐼 𐑃𐑉𐐭𐑃, 𐐺𐐨𐐿𐐫𐑆 𐐱𐑂 𐑄 𐐝𐐹𐐮𐑉𐐮𐐻 𐐱𐑂 𐑄 𐐢𐐫𐑉𐐼 𐐱𐑋𐑌𐐮𐐹𐐬𐐻𐐯𐑌𐐻, 𐐸𐐶𐐮𐐽 𐐸𐐰𐑆 𐑉𐐫𐐻 𐐲 𐑋𐐴𐐻𐐨 𐐽𐐩𐑌𐐾 𐐮𐑌 𐐲𐑅, 𐐫𐑉 𐐮𐑌 𐐵𐑉 𐐸𐐪𐑉𐐻𐑅, 𐑄𐐰𐐻 𐐶𐐨 𐐸𐐰𐑂 𐑌𐐬 𐑋𐐬𐑉 𐐼𐐮𐑅𐐹𐐬𐑆𐐮𐑇𐐲𐑌 𐐻𐐭 𐐼𐐭 𐐨𐑂𐐲𐑊, 𐐺𐐲𐐻 𐐻𐐭 𐐼𐐭 𐑀𐐳𐐼 𐐿𐐲𐑌𐐻𐐮𐑌𐐷𐐭𐐲𐑊𐐨. 𐐰𐑌𐐼 𐐶𐐨 𐐵𐑉𐑅𐐯𐑊𐑂𐑆, 𐐫𐑊𐑅𐐬, 𐑃𐑉𐐭 𐑄 𐐮𐑌𐑁𐐮𐑌𐐮𐐻 𐑀𐐳𐐼𐑌𐐯𐑅 𐐱𐑂 𐐘𐐱𐐼, 𐐰𐑌𐐼 𐑄 𐑋𐐰𐑌𐐮𐑁𐐯𐑅𐐻𐐩𐑇𐐲𐑌𐑆 𐐱𐑂 𐐸𐐮𐑆 𐐝𐐹𐐮𐑉𐐮𐐻, 𐐸𐐰𐑂 𐑀𐑉𐐩𐐻 𐑂𐐷𐐭𐑆 𐐱𐑂 𐑄𐐰𐐻 𐐸𐐶𐐮𐐽 𐐮𐑆 𐐻𐐭 𐐿𐐲𐑋; 𐐰𐑌𐐼 𐐶𐐲𐑉 𐐮𐐻 𐐯𐐿𐑅𐐹𐐨𐐼𐐨𐐲𐑌𐐻, 𐐶𐐨 𐐿𐐳𐐼 𐐹𐑉𐐱𐑁𐐯𐑅𐐴 𐐱𐑂 𐐫𐑊 𐑃𐐮𐑍𐑆. 𐐰𐑌𐐼 𐐮𐐻 𐐮𐑆 𐑄 𐑁𐐩𐑃 𐐸𐐶𐐮𐐽 𐐶𐐨 𐐸𐐰𐑂 𐐸𐐰𐐼 𐐱𐑌 𐑄 𐑃𐐮𐑍𐑆 𐐸𐐶𐐮𐐽 𐐵𐑉 𐐿𐐨𐑍 𐐸𐐰𐑆 𐑅𐐹𐐬𐐿𐐲𐑌 𐐲𐑌𐐻𐐭 𐐲𐑅, 𐑄𐐰𐐻 𐐸𐐰𐑆 𐐺𐑉𐐫𐐻 𐐲𐑅 𐐻𐐭 𐑄𐐮𐑅 𐑀𐑉𐐩𐐻 𐑌𐐱𐑊𐐯𐐾, 𐐸𐐶𐐯𐑉𐐺𐐴 𐐶𐐨 𐐼𐐭 𐑉𐐨𐐾𐐱𐐮𐑅 𐐶𐐮𐑄 𐑅𐐲𐐽 𐐯𐐿𐑅𐐨𐐼𐐮𐑍𐑊𐐨 𐑀𐑉𐐩𐐻 𐐾𐐱𐐮; 𐐰𐑌𐐼 𐐶𐐨 𐐪𐑉 𐐶𐐮𐑊𐐮𐑍 𐐻𐐭 𐐯𐑌𐐻𐐲𐑉 𐐮𐑌𐐻𐐭 𐐲 𐐿𐐲𐑂𐐯𐑌𐐰𐑌𐐻 𐐶𐐮𐑄 𐐵𐑉 𐐘𐐱𐐼 𐐻𐐭 𐐼𐐭 𐐸𐐮𐑆 𐐶𐐮𐑊, 𐐰𐑌𐐼 𐐻𐐭 𐐺𐐨 𐐬𐐺𐐨𐐼𐐨𐐲𐑌𐐻 𐐻𐐭 𐐸𐐮𐑆 𐐿𐐲𐑋𐐰𐑌𐐼𐑋𐐯𐑌𐐻𐑅 𐐮𐑌 𐐫𐑊 𐑃𐐮𐑍𐑆 𐑄𐐰𐐻 𐐸𐐨 𐑇𐐰𐑊 𐐿𐐲𐑋𐐰𐑌𐐼 𐐲𐑅, 𐐫𐑊 𐑄 𐑉𐐨𐑋𐐩𐑌𐐼𐐲𐑉 𐐱𐑂 𐐵𐑉 𐐼𐐩𐑆, 𐑄𐐰𐐻 𐐶𐐨 𐑋𐐩 𐑌𐐪𐐻 𐐺𐑉𐐮𐑍 𐐲𐐹𐐱𐑌 𐐵𐑉𐑅𐐯𐑊𐑂𐑆 𐐲 𐑌𐐯𐑂𐐲𐑉 𐐯𐑌𐐼𐐮𐑍 𐐻𐐫𐑉𐑋𐐯𐑌𐐻, 𐐰𐑆 𐐸𐐰𐑆 𐐺𐐮𐑌 𐑅𐐹𐐬𐐿𐐲𐑌 𐐺𐐴 𐑄 𐐩𐑌𐐾𐐯𐑊, 𐑄𐐰𐐻 𐐶𐐨 𐑋𐐩 𐑌𐐪𐐻 𐐼𐑉𐐮𐑍𐐿 𐐵𐐻 𐐱𐑂 𐑄 𐐿𐐲𐐹 𐐱𐑂 𐑄 𐑉𐐪𐑃 𐐱𐑂 𐐘𐐱𐐼.

2. 𐐰𐑌𐐼 𐑌𐐵, 𐑄𐐨𐑆 𐐪𐑉 𐑄 𐐶𐐲𐑉𐐼𐑆 𐐸𐐶𐐮𐐽 𐐿𐐨𐑍 𐐒𐐯𐑌𐐾𐐲𐑋𐐮𐑌 𐐼𐐨𐑆𐐴𐑉𐐼 𐐱𐑂 𐑄𐐯𐑋; 𐐰𐑌𐐼 𐑄𐐯𐑉𐑁𐐬𐑉 𐐸𐐨 𐑅𐐯𐐼 𐐲𐑌𐐻𐐭 𐑄𐐯𐑋, 𐐷𐐨 𐐸𐐰𐑂 𐑅𐐹𐐬𐐿𐐲𐑌 𐑄 𐐶𐐲𐑉𐐼𐑆 𐑄𐐰𐐻 𐐴 𐐼𐐨𐑆𐐴𐑉𐐼; 𐐰𐑌𐐼 𐑄 𐐿𐐲𐑂𐐯𐑌𐐰𐑌𐐻 𐐸𐐶𐐮𐐽 𐐷𐐨 𐐸𐐰𐑂 𐑋𐐩𐐼 𐐮𐑆 𐐲 𐑉𐐴𐐽𐐲𐑅 𐐿𐐲𐑂𐐯𐑌𐐰𐑌𐐻. 𐐰𐑌𐐼 𐑌𐐵, 𐐺𐐨𐐿𐐫𐑆 𐐱𐑂 𐑄 𐐿𐐲𐑂𐐯𐑌𐐰𐑌𐐻 𐐸𐐶𐐮𐐽 𐐷𐐨 𐐸𐐰𐑂 𐑋𐐩𐐼 𐐷𐐨 𐑇𐐰𐑊 𐐺𐐨 𐐿𐐫𐑊𐐼 𐑄 𐐽𐐮𐑊𐐼𐑉𐐯𐑌 𐐱𐑂 𐐗𐑉𐐴𐑅𐐻, 𐐸𐐮𐑆 𐑅𐐲𐑌𐑆, 𐐰𐑌𐐼 𐐸𐐮𐑆 𐐼𐐫𐐻𐐲𐑉𐑆; 𐑁𐐫𐑉 𐐺𐐨𐐸𐐬𐑊𐐼, 𐑄𐐮𐑅 𐐼𐐩 𐐸𐐨 𐐸𐐰𐑃 𐑅𐐹𐐮𐑉𐐮𐐻𐐷𐐭𐐲𐑊𐐨 𐐺𐐨𐑀𐐱𐐻𐐲𐑌 𐐷𐐭; 𐑁𐐫𐑉 𐐷𐐨 𐑅𐐩 𐑄𐐰𐐻 𐐷𐐭𐑉 𐐸𐐪𐑉𐐻𐑅 𐐪𐑉 𐐽𐐩𐑌𐐾𐐼 𐑃𐑉𐐭 𐑁𐐩𐑃 𐐱𐑌 𐐸𐐮𐑆 𐑌𐐩𐑋; 𐑄𐐯𐑉𐑁𐐬𐑉, 𐐷𐐨 𐐪𐑉 𐐺𐐫𐑉𐑌 𐐱𐑂 𐐸𐐮𐑋, 𐐰𐑌𐐼 𐐸𐐰𐑂 𐐺𐐨𐐿𐐲𐑋 𐐸𐐮𐑆 𐑅𐐲𐑌𐑆 𐐰𐑌𐐼 𐐸𐐮𐑆 𐐼𐐫𐐻𐐲𐑉𐑆. 𐐰𐑌𐐼 𐐲𐑌𐐼𐐲𐑉 𐑄𐐮𐑅 𐐸𐐯𐐼 𐐷𐐨 𐐪𐑉 𐑋𐐩𐐼 𐑁𐑉𐐨, 𐐰𐑌𐐼 𐑄𐐯𐑉 𐐮𐑆 𐑌𐐬 𐐲𐑄𐐲𐑉 𐐸𐐯𐐼 𐐸𐐶𐐯𐑉𐐺𐐴 𐐷𐐨 𐐿𐐰𐑌 𐐺𐐨 𐑋𐐩𐐼 𐑁𐑉𐐨. 𐑄𐐯𐑉 𐐮𐑆 𐑌𐐬 𐐲𐑄𐐲𐑉 𐑌𐐩𐑋 𐑀𐐮𐑂𐐲𐑌 𐐸𐐶𐐯𐑉𐐺𐐴 𐑅𐐰𐑊𐑂𐐩𐑇𐐲𐑌 𐐿𐐲𐑋𐐯𐑃; 𐑄𐐯𐑉𐑁𐐬𐑉, 𐐴 𐐶𐐳𐐼 𐑄𐐰𐐻 𐐷𐐨 𐑇𐐳𐐼 𐐻𐐩𐐿 𐐲𐐹𐐱𐑌 𐐷𐐭 𐑄 𐑌𐐩𐑋 𐐱𐑂 𐐗𐑉𐐴𐑅𐐻, 𐐫𐑊 𐐷𐐭 𐑄𐐰𐐻 𐐸𐐰𐑂 𐐯𐑌𐐻𐐲𐑉𐐼 𐐮𐑌𐐻𐐭 𐑄 𐐿𐐲𐑂𐐯𐑌𐐰𐑌𐐻 𐐶𐐮𐑄 𐐘𐐱𐐼, 𐑄𐐰𐐻 𐐷𐐨 𐑇𐐳𐐼 𐐺𐐨 𐐬𐐺𐐨𐐼𐐨𐐲𐑌𐐻 𐐲𐑌𐐻𐐭 𐑄 𐐯𐑌𐐼 𐐱𐑂 𐐷𐐭𐑉 𐑊𐐴𐑂𐑆. 𐐰𐑌𐐼 𐐮𐐻

𐑇𐐰𐑊 𐐿𐐲𐑋 𐐻𐐭 𐐹𐐰𐑅 𐑄𐐰𐐻 𐐸𐐭𐑅𐐬𐐯𐑂𐐲𐑉 𐐼𐐲𐑃 𐑄𐐮𐑅, 𐑇𐐰𐑊 𐐺𐐨 𐑁𐐵𐑌𐐼 𐐰𐐻 𐑄 𐑉𐐴𐐻 𐐸𐐰𐑌𐐼 𐐱𐑂 𐐘𐐱𐐼, 𐑁𐐫𐑉 𐐸𐐨 𐑇𐐰𐑊 𐑌𐐬 𐑄 𐑌𐐩𐑋 𐐺𐐴 𐐸𐐶𐐮𐐽 𐐸𐐨 𐐮𐑆 𐐿𐐫𐑊𐐼; 𐑁𐐫𐑉 𐐸𐐨 𐑇𐐰𐑊 𐐺𐐨 𐐿𐐫𐑊𐐼 𐐺𐐴 𐑄 𐑌𐐩𐑋 𐐱𐑂 𐐗𐑉𐐴𐑅𐐻.

3. 𐐈𐑌𐐼 𐑌𐐵 𐐮𐐻 𐑇𐐰𐑊 𐐿𐐲𐑋 𐐻𐐭 𐐹𐐰𐑅, 𐑄𐐰𐐻 𐐸𐐭𐑅𐐬𐐯𐑂𐐲𐑉 𐑇𐐰𐑊 𐑌𐐱𐐻 𐐻𐐩𐐿 𐐲𐐹𐐱𐑌 𐐸𐐮𐑋 𐑄 𐑌𐐩𐑋 𐐱𐑂 𐐗𐑉𐐴𐑅𐐻, 𐑋𐐲𐑅𐐻 𐐺𐐨 𐐿𐐫𐑊𐐼 𐐺𐐴 𐑅𐐲𐑋 𐐲𐑄𐐲𐑉 𐑌𐐩𐑋; 𐑄𐐯𐑉𐑁𐐫𐑉, 𐐸𐐨 𐑁𐐴𐑌𐐼𐐯𐑃 𐐸𐐮𐑋𐑅𐐯𐑊𐑁 𐐱𐑌 𐑄 𐑊𐐯𐑁𐐻 𐐸𐐰𐑌𐐼 𐐱𐑂 𐐘𐐱𐐼. 𐐈𐑌𐐼 𐐌 𐐶𐐳𐐼 𐑄𐐰𐐻 𐐷𐐨 𐑇𐐳𐐼 𐑉𐐨𐑋𐐯𐑋𐐺𐐲𐑉 𐐫𐑊𐑅𐐬, 𐑄𐐰𐐻 𐑄𐐮𐑅 𐐮𐑆 𐑄 𐑌𐐩𐑋 𐑄𐐰𐐻 𐐌 𐑅𐐯𐐼 𐐌 𐑇𐐳𐐼 𐑀𐐮𐑂 𐐲𐑌𐐻𐐭 𐐷𐐭 𐑄𐐰𐐻 𐑌𐐯𐑂𐐲𐑉 𐑇𐐳𐐼 𐐺𐐨 𐐺𐑊𐐱𐐻𐐲𐐼 𐐵𐐻, 𐐯𐐿𐑅𐐯𐐹𐐻 𐐮𐐻 𐐺𐐨 𐑃𐑉𐐭 𐐻𐑉𐐰𐑌𐑆𐑀𐑉𐐯𐑇𐐲𐑌; 𐑄𐐯𐑉𐑁𐐫𐑉, 𐐻𐐩𐐿 𐐸𐐨𐐼 𐑄𐐰𐐻 𐐷𐐨 𐐼𐐭 𐑌𐐱𐐻 𐐻𐑉𐐰𐑌𐑆𐑀𐑉𐐯𐑅, 𐑄𐐰𐐻 𐑄 𐑌𐐩𐑋 𐐺𐐨 𐑌𐐱𐐻 𐐺𐑊𐐱𐐻𐐲𐐼 𐐵𐐻 𐐱𐑂 𐐷𐐫𐑉 𐐸𐐪𐑉𐐻𐑅. 𐐌 𐑅𐐩 𐐲𐑌𐐻𐐭 𐐷𐐭, 𐐌 𐐶𐐳𐐼 𐑄𐐰𐐻 𐐷𐐨 𐑇𐐳𐐼 𐑉𐐨𐑋𐐯𐑋𐐺𐐲𐑉 𐐻𐐭 𐑉𐐨𐐻𐐩𐑌 𐑄 𐑌𐐩𐑋 𐑉𐐮𐐻𐑌 𐐫𐑊𐐶𐐩𐑆 𐐮𐑌 𐐷𐐫𐑉 𐐸𐐪𐑉𐐻𐑅, 𐑄𐐰𐐻 𐐷𐐨 𐐪𐑉 𐑌𐐱𐐻 𐑁𐐵𐑌𐐼 𐐱𐑌 𐑄 𐑊𐐯𐑁𐐻 𐐸𐐰𐑌𐐼 𐐱𐑂 𐐘𐐱𐐼, 𐐺𐐲𐐻 𐑄𐐰𐐻 𐐷𐐨 𐐸𐐨𐑉 𐐰𐑌𐐼 𐑌𐐬 𐑄 𐑂𐐱𐐮𐑅 𐐺𐐴 𐐸𐐶𐐮𐐽 𐐷𐐨 𐑇𐐰𐑊 𐐺𐐨 𐐿𐐫𐑊𐐼, 𐐰𐑌𐐼 𐐫𐑊𐑅𐐬, 𐑄 𐑌𐐩𐑋 𐐺𐐴 𐐸𐐶𐐮𐐽 𐐸𐐨 𐑇𐐰𐑊 𐐿𐐫𐑊 𐐷𐐭. 𐐙𐐫𐑉 𐐸𐐵 𐑌𐐬𐐯𐑃 𐐩 𐑋𐐰𐑌 𐑄 𐑋𐐰𐑅𐐻𐐲𐑉 𐐸𐐭𐑋 𐐸𐐨 𐐸𐐰𐑆 𐑌𐐱𐐻 𐑅𐐲𐑉𐑂𐐼, 𐐰𐑌𐐼 𐐸𐐭 𐐮𐑆 𐐩 𐑅𐐻𐑉𐐩𐑌𐐾𐐲𐑉 𐐲𐑌𐐻𐐭 𐐸𐐮𐑋, 𐐰𐑌𐐼 𐐮𐑆 𐑁𐐪𐑉 𐑁𐑉𐐱𐑋 𐑄 𐑃𐐫𐐻𐑅 𐐰𐑌𐐼 𐐮𐑌𐐻𐐯𐑌𐐻𐑅 𐐱𐑂 𐐸𐐮𐑆 𐐸𐐪𐑉𐐻? 𐐈𐑌𐐼 𐐲𐑀𐐯𐑌, 𐐼𐐲𐑃 𐐩 𐑋𐐰𐑌 𐐻𐐩𐐿 𐐰𐑌 𐐰𐑅 𐐸𐐶𐐮𐐽 𐐺𐐨𐑊𐐱𐑍𐐯𐑃 𐐻𐐭 𐐸𐐮𐑆 𐑌𐐩𐐺𐐲𐑉, 𐐰𐑌𐐼 𐐿𐐨𐐹 𐐸𐐮𐑋? 𐐌 𐑅𐐩 𐐲𐑌𐐻𐐭 𐐷𐐭, 𐑌𐐩; 𐐸𐐨 𐐶𐐮𐑊 𐑌𐐱𐐻 𐐨𐑂𐐲𐑌 𐑅𐐲𐑁𐐲𐑉 𐑄𐐰𐐻 𐐸𐐨 𐑇𐐰𐑊 𐑁𐐨𐐼 𐐲𐑋𐐲𐑍 𐐸𐐮𐑆 𐑁𐑊𐐱𐐿𐑅, 𐐺𐐲𐐻 𐐶𐐮𐑊 𐐼𐑉𐐴𐑂 𐐸𐐮𐑋 𐐲𐐶𐐩, 𐐰𐑌𐐼 𐐿𐐰𐑅𐐻 𐐸𐐮𐑋 𐐵𐐻. 𐐌 𐑅𐐩 𐐲𐑌𐐻𐐭 𐐷𐐭, 𐑄𐐰𐐻 𐐨𐑂𐐲𐑌 𐑅𐐬 𐑇𐐰𐑊 𐐮𐐻 𐐺𐐨 𐐲𐑋𐐲𐑍 𐐷𐐭, 𐐮𐑁 𐐷𐐨 𐑌𐐬 𐑌𐐱𐐻 𐑄 𐑌𐐩𐑋 𐐺𐐴 𐐸𐐶𐐮𐐽 𐐷𐐨 𐐪𐑉 𐐿𐐫𐑊𐐼. 𐐜𐐯𐑉𐑁𐐫𐑉, 𐐌 𐐶𐐳𐐼 𐑄𐐰𐐻 𐐷𐐨 𐑇𐐳𐐼 𐐺𐐨 𐑅𐐻𐐯𐐼𐑁𐐰𐑅𐐻 𐐰𐑌𐐼 𐐮𐑋𐐭𐑂𐐲𐐺𐑊, 𐐫𐑊𐐶𐐩𐑆 𐐲𐐺𐐵𐑌𐐼𐐮𐑍 𐐮𐑌 𐑀𐐳𐐼 𐐶𐐲𐑉𐐿𐑅, 𐑄𐐰𐐻 𐐗𐑉𐐴𐑅𐐻, 𐑄 𐐢𐐫𐑉𐐼 𐐘𐐱𐐼 𐐉𐑋𐑌𐐮𐐹𐐬𐐻𐐯𐑌𐐻, 𐑋𐐩 𐑅𐐨𐑊 𐐷𐐭 𐐸𐐮𐑆, 𐑄𐐰𐐻 𐐷𐐭 𐑋𐐩 𐐺𐐨 𐐺𐑉𐐫𐐻 𐐻𐐭 𐐸𐐯𐑂𐐲𐑌, 𐑄𐐰𐐻 𐐷𐐨 𐑋𐐩 𐐸𐐰𐑂 𐐯𐑂𐐲𐑉𐑊𐐰𐑅𐐻𐐮𐑍 𐑅𐐰𐑊𐑂𐐩𐑇𐐲𐑌 𐐰𐑌𐐼 𐐨𐐻𐐲𐑉𐑌𐐲𐑊 𐑊𐐴𐑁, 𐑃𐑉𐐭 𐑄 𐐶𐐮𐑆𐐼𐐲𐑋, 𐐰𐑌𐐼 𐐹𐐵𐐲𐑉, 𐐰𐑌𐐼 𐐾𐐲𐑅𐐻𐐮𐑅, 𐐰𐑌𐐼 𐑋𐐲𐑉𐑅𐐨 𐐱𐑂 𐐸𐐮𐑋 𐐸𐐭 𐐿𐑉𐐨𐐩𐐻𐐯𐐼 𐐫𐑊 𐑃𐐮𐑍𐑆, 𐐮𐑌 𐐸𐐯𐑂𐐲𐑌 𐐰𐑌𐐼 𐐮𐑌 𐐲𐑉𐑃, 𐐸𐐭 𐐮𐑆 𐐘𐐱𐐼 𐐲𐐺𐐲𐑂 𐐫𐑊. 𐐁𐑋𐐯𐑌.

𐐕𐐈𐐑𐐓𐐇𐐡 IV.

1. 𐐈𐑌𐐼 𐑌𐐵 𐐗𐐮𐑍 𐐒𐐯𐑌𐐾𐐲𐑋𐐮𐑌 𐑃𐐫𐐻 𐐮𐐻 𐐯𐐿𐑅𐐹𐐨𐐼𐐨𐐲𐑌𐐻, 𐐰𐑁𐐻𐐲𐑉 𐐸𐐰𐑂𐐮𐑍 𐑁𐐮𐑌𐐮𐑇𐐻 𐑅𐐹𐐨𐐿𐐮𐑍 𐐻𐐭 𐑄 𐐹𐐨𐐹𐑊, 𐑄𐐰𐐻 𐐸𐐨 𐑇𐐳𐐼 𐐻𐐩𐐿 𐑄 𐑌𐐩𐑋𐑆 𐐱𐑂 𐐫𐑊 𐑄𐐬𐑆 𐐸𐐭 𐐸𐐰𐐼 𐐯𐑌𐐻𐐲𐑉𐐼 𐐮𐑌𐐻𐐭 𐐩 𐐿𐐲𐑂𐐯𐑌𐐰𐑌𐐻 𐐶𐐮𐑃 𐐘𐐱𐐼 𐐻𐐭 𐐿𐐨𐐹 𐐸𐐮𐑆 𐐿𐐲𐑋𐐰𐑌𐐼𐑋𐐯𐑌𐐻𐑅. 𐐈𐑌𐐼 𐐮𐐻 𐐿𐐩𐑋 𐐻𐐭 𐐹𐐰𐑅 𐑄𐐰𐐻 𐑄𐐯𐑉 𐐶𐐱𐑆 𐑌𐐱𐐻 𐐶𐐲𐑌 𐑅𐐬𐑊, 𐐯𐐿𐑅𐐯𐐹𐐻 𐐮𐐻 𐐶𐐲𐑉 𐑊𐐮𐐻𐑊 𐐽𐐮𐑊𐐼𐑉𐐲𐑌, 𐐺𐐲𐐻 𐐸𐐭 𐐸𐐰𐐼 𐐯𐑌𐐻𐐲𐑉𐐼 𐐮𐑌𐐻𐐭 𐑄 𐐿𐐲𐑂𐐯𐑌𐐰𐑌𐐻, 𐐰𐑌𐐼 𐐸𐐰𐐼 𐐻𐐩𐐿𐑌 𐐲𐐹𐐱𐑌 𐑄𐐯𐑋 𐑄 𐑌𐐩𐑋 𐐱𐑂 𐐗𐑉𐐴𐑅𐐻. 𐐈𐑌𐐼 𐐲𐑀𐐯𐑌: 𐐮𐐻 𐐿𐐩𐑋 𐐻𐐭 𐐹𐐰𐑅 𐑄𐐰𐐻 𐐸𐐶𐐯𐑌 𐐗𐐮𐑍 𐐒𐐯𐑌𐐾𐐲𐑋𐐮𐑌 𐐸𐐰𐐼 𐑋𐐩𐐼 𐐰𐑌 𐐯𐑌𐐼 𐐱𐑂 𐐫𐑊 𐑄𐐨𐑆 𐑃𐐮𐑍𐑆, 𐐰𐑌𐐼 𐐸𐐰𐐼 𐐿𐐱𐑌𐑅𐐨𐐿𐑉𐐩𐐻𐐲𐐼 𐐸𐐮𐑆 𐑅𐐲𐑌 𐐣𐐬𐑆𐐴𐐲 𐐻𐐭 𐐺𐐨 𐐩 𐑉𐐭𐑊𐐲𐑉 𐐰𐑌𐐼 𐐩 𐐿𐐮𐑍 𐐬𐑂𐐲𐑉 𐐸𐐮𐑆 𐐹𐐨𐐹𐑊, 𐐰𐑌𐐼 𐐸𐐰𐐼 𐑀𐐮𐑂𐑌 𐐸𐐮𐑋 𐐫𐑊 𐑄 𐐽𐐪𐑉𐐾𐐲𐑆 𐐿𐐲𐑌𐑅𐐲𐑉𐑌𐐮𐑍 𐑄 𐐿𐐮𐑍𐐼𐐲𐑋, 𐐰𐑌𐐼 𐐫𐑊𐑅𐐬 𐐸𐐰𐐼 𐐲𐐹𐐱𐐮𐑌𐐻𐐲𐐼 𐐹𐑉𐐨𐑅𐐻𐑅 𐐻𐐭 𐐻𐐨𐐽 𐑄 𐐹𐐨𐐹𐑊, 𐑄𐐰𐐻 𐑄𐐯𐑉𐐺𐐴 𐑄𐐩 𐑋𐐴𐐻 𐐸𐐨𐑉 𐐰𐑌𐐼 𐑌𐐬 𐑄 𐐿𐐲𐑋𐐰𐑌𐐼𐑋𐐯𐑌𐐻𐑅 𐐱𐑂 𐐘𐐱𐐼, 𐐰𐑌𐐼 𐐻𐐭 𐑅𐐻𐐲𐑉 𐑄𐐯𐑋 𐐲𐐹 𐐮𐑌 𐑉𐐨𐑋𐐯𐑋𐐺𐑉𐐲𐑌𐑅 𐐱𐑂 𐑄 𐐬𐑃 𐐸𐐶𐐮𐐽 𐑄𐐩 𐐸𐐰𐐼 𐑋𐐩𐐼, 𐐸𐐨 𐐼𐐮𐑅𐑋𐐮𐑅𐐻 𐑄 𐑋𐐲𐑊𐐻𐐮𐐻𐐭𐐼, 𐐰𐑌𐐼 𐑄𐐩 𐑉𐐨𐐻𐐲𐑉𐑌𐐼, 𐐯𐑂𐐲𐑉𐐨 𐐶𐐲𐑌, 𐐲𐐿𐐫𐑉𐐼𐐮𐑍 𐐻𐐭 𐑄𐐯𐑉 𐑁𐐰𐑋𐐮𐑊𐐨𐑆, 𐐻𐐭 𐑄𐐯𐑉 𐐬𐑌 𐐸𐐵𐑆𐐲𐑆.

2. 𐐈𐑌𐐼 𐐣𐐬𐑆𐐴𐐲 𐐺𐐨𐑀𐐰𐑌 𐐻𐐭 𐑉𐐩𐑌 𐐮𐑌 𐐸𐐮𐑆 𐑁𐐪𐑄𐐲𐑉'𐑆 𐑅𐐻𐐯𐐼. 𐐈𐑌𐐼 𐐸𐐨 𐐺𐐨𐑀𐐰𐑌 𐐻𐐭 𐑉𐐩𐑌 𐐮𐑌 𐑄 𐑃𐐲𐑉𐐻𐐨𐐯𐑃 𐐷𐐨𐑉 𐐱𐑂 𐐸𐐮𐑆 𐐩𐐾, 𐑋𐐩𐐿𐐮𐑍, 𐐮𐑌 𐑄 𐐸𐐬𐑊, 𐐲𐐺𐐵𐐻 𐑁𐐫𐑉 𐐸𐐲𐑌𐐼𐑉𐐲𐐼 𐐰𐑌𐐼 𐑅𐐯𐑂𐑌𐐻𐐨-𐑅𐐮𐐿𐑅 𐐷𐐨𐑉𐑆 𐑁𐑉𐐱𐑋 𐑄 𐐻𐐴𐑋 𐑄𐐰𐐻 𐐢𐐨𐐸𐐴 𐑊𐐯𐑁𐐻 𐐖𐐲𐑉𐐭𐑅𐐲𐑊𐐲𐑋. 𐐈𐑌𐐼 𐐗𐐮𐑍 𐐒𐐯𐑌𐐾𐐲𐑋𐐮𐑌 𐑊𐐮𐑂𐐼 𐑃𐑉𐐨 𐐷𐐨𐑉𐑆 𐐰𐑌𐐼 𐐸𐐨 𐐼𐐴𐐼. 𐐈𐑌𐐼 𐐮𐐻 𐐿𐐩𐑋 𐐻𐐭 𐐹𐐰𐑅 𐑄𐐰𐐻 𐐗𐐮𐑍 𐐣𐐬𐑆𐐴𐐲 𐐼𐐮𐐼 𐐶𐐫𐐿 𐐮𐑌 𐑄 𐐶𐐩𐑆 𐐱𐑂 𐑄 𐐢𐐫𐑉𐐼,

𐐰𐑌𐐼 𐐼𐐮𐐼 𐐱𐐺𐑆𐐲𐑉𐑂 𐐸𐐮𐑆 𐐾𐐲𐐾𐑋𐐯𐑌𐐻𐑅, 𐐰𐑌𐐼 𐐸𐐮𐑆 𐑅𐐻𐐰𐐻𐐷𐐭𐐻𐑅, 𐐰𐑌𐐼 𐐼𐐮𐐼 𐐿𐐨𐐹 𐐸𐐮𐑆 𐐿𐐱𐑋𐐰𐑌𐐼𐑋𐐯𐑌𐐻𐑅 𐐮𐑌 𐐫𐑊 𐑃𐐮𐑍𐑆 𐐸𐐶𐐱𐐻𐑅𐐬𐐯𐑂𐐲𐑉 𐐸𐐨 𐐿𐐱𐑋𐐰𐑌𐐼𐐯𐐼 𐐸𐐮𐑋.

3. 𐐈𐑌𐐼 𐐿𐐮𐑍 𐐣𐐬𐑅𐐴𐐲 𐐼𐐮𐐼 𐐿𐐫𐑆 𐐸𐐮𐑆 𐐹𐐨𐐹𐑊 𐑄𐐰𐐻 𐑄𐐩 𐑇𐐳𐐼 𐐻𐐮𐑊 𐑄 𐐲𐑉𐑃. 𐐈𐑌𐐼 𐐸𐐨 𐐫𐑊𐑅𐐬 𐐸𐐮𐑋𐑅𐐯𐑊𐑁 𐐼𐐮𐐼 𐐻𐐮𐑊 𐑄 𐐲𐑉𐑃, 𐑄𐐰𐐻 𐑄𐐯𐑉𐐺𐐴 𐐸𐐨 𐑋𐐴𐐻 𐑌𐐱𐐻 𐐺𐐨𐐿𐐲𐑋 𐐺𐐲𐑉𐐼𐐲𐑌𐑅𐐲𐑋 𐐻𐐭 𐐸𐐮𐑆 𐐹𐐨𐐹𐑊, 𐑄𐐰𐐻 𐐸𐐨 𐑋𐐴𐐻 𐐼𐐭 𐐰𐐿𐐫𐑉𐐼𐐮𐑍 𐐻𐐭 𐑄𐐰𐐻 𐐸𐐶𐐮𐐽 𐐸𐐮𐑆 𐑁𐐪𐑄𐐲𐑉 𐐸𐐰𐐼 𐐼𐐲𐑌 𐐮𐑌 𐐫𐑊 𐑃𐐮𐑍𐑆. 𐐈𐑌𐐼 𐑄𐐯𐑉 𐐶𐐱𐑆 𐑌𐐬 𐐿𐐱𐑌𐐻𐐯𐑌𐑇𐐲𐑌 𐐲𐑋𐐲𐑍 𐐫𐑊 𐐸𐐮𐑆 𐐹𐐨𐐹𐑊 𐑁𐐫𐑉 𐑄 𐑅𐐹𐐩𐑅 𐐱𐑂 𐑃𐑉𐐨 𐐷𐐨𐑉𐑆.

𐐕𐐰𐐹𐐻𐐲𐑉 V.

1. 𐐈𐑌𐐼 𐑌𐐵, 𐐮𐐻 𐐿𐐩𐑋 𐐻𐐭 𐐹𐐰𐑅 𐑄𐐰𐐻 𐐰𐑁𐐻𐐲𐑉 𐐿𐐮𐑍 𐐣𐐬𐑅𐐴𐐲 𐐸𐐰𐐼 𐐸𐐰𐐼 𐐿𐐱𐑌𐐻𐐮𐑌𐐷𐐲𐑊 𐐹𐐨𐑅 𐑁𐐫𐑉 𐑄 𐑅𐐹𐐩𐑅 𐐱𐑂 𐑃𐑉𐐨 𐐷𐐨𐑉𐑆, 𐐸𐐨 𐐶𐐱𐑆 𐐼𐐯𐑆𐐴𐑉𐐲𐑅 𐐻𐐭 𐑌𐐬 𐐿𐐱𐑌𐑅𐐲𐑉𐑌𐐮𐑍 𐑄 𐐹𐐨𐐹𐑊 𐐸𐐭 𐐶𐐯𐑌𐐻 𐐲𐐹 𐐻𐐭 𐐼𐐶𐐯𐑊 𐐮𐑌 𐑄 𐑊𐐰𐑌𐐼 𐐱𐑂 𐐢𐐨𐐸𐐴-𐐤𐐨𐑁𐐴, 𐐫𐑉 𐐮𐑌 𐑄 𐑅𐐮𐐻𐐨 𐐱𐑂 𐐢𐐨𐐸𐐴-𐐤𐐨𐑁𐐴; 𐑁𐐫𐑉 𐐸𐐮𐑆 𐐹𐐨𐐹𐑊 𐐸𐐰𐐼 𐐸𐐲𐑉𐐼 𐑌𐐲𐑃𐐮𐑍 𐑁𐑉𐐱𐑋 𐑄𐐯𐑋 𐑁𐑉𐐱𐑋 𐑄 𐐻𐐴𐑋 𐑄𐐩 𐑊𐐯𐑁𐐻 𐑄 𐑊𐐰𐑌𐐼 𐐱𐑂 𐐞𐐯𐑉𐐲𐐸𐐯𐑋𐑊𐐲; 𐑄𐐯𐑉𐑁𐐬𐑉, 𐑄𐐩 𐐶𐐨𐑉𐐨𐐼 𐐸𐐮𐑋 𐐶𐐮𐑄 𐑄𐐯𐑉 𐐻𐐨𐑆𐐮𐑍𐑆.

2. 𐐈𐑌𐐼 𐐮𐐻 𐐿𐐩𐑋 𐐻𐐭 𐐹𐐰𐑅 𐑄𐐰𐐻 𐐿𐐮𐑍 𐐣𐐬𐑅𐐴𐐲 𐑀𐑉𐐪𐑌𐐻𐐯𐐼 𐑄𐐰𐐻 𐑅𐐮𐐿𐑅𐐻𐐨𐑌 𐐱𐑂 𐑄𐐯𐑉 𐑅𐐻𐑉𐐱𐑍 𐑋𐐯𐑌 𐑋𐐴𐐻 𐑀𐐬 𐐲𐐹 𐐻𐐭 𐑄 𐑊𐐰𐑌𐐼 𐐱𐑂 𐐢𐐨𐐸𐐴-𐐤𐐨𐑁𐐴, 𐐻𐐭 𐐮𐑌𐐿𐐶𐐴𐑉 𐐿𐐱𐑌𐑅𐐲𐑉𐑌𐐮𐑍 𐑄𐐯𐑉 𐐺𐑉𐐯𐑄𐑉𐐯𐑌. 𐐈𐑌𐐼 𐐮𐐻 𐐿𐐩𐑋 𐐻𐐭 𐐹𐐰𐑅 𐑄𐐰𐐻 𐐱𐑌 𐑄 𐑋𐐱𐑉𐐬 𐑄𐐩 𐑅𐐻𐐪𐑉𐐻𐐯𐐼 𐐻𐐭 𐑀𐐬 𐐲𐐹, 𐐸𐐰𐑂𐐮𐑍 𐐶𐐮𐑄 𐑄𐐯𐑋 𐐶𐐲𐑌 𐐈𐑋𐐲𐑌, 𐐸𐐨 𐐺𐐨𐐮𐑍 𐐲 𐑅𐐻𐑉𐐱𐑍 𐐰𐑌𐐼 𐑋𐐴𐐻𐐨 𐑋𐐰𐑌, 𐐰𐑌𐐼 𐐲 𐐼𐐯𐑅𐐯𐑌𐐼𐐲𐑌𐐻 𐐱𐑂 𐐞𐐯𐑉𐐲𐐸𐐯𐑋𐑊𐐲; 𐐰𐑌𐐼 𐐸𐐨 𐐶𐐱𐑆 𐐫𐑊𐑅𐐬 𐑄𐐯𐑉 𐑊𐐨𐐼𐐲𐑉. 𐐈𐑌𐐼 𐑌𐐵, 𐑄𐐩 𐑌𐐭 𐑌𐐱𐐻 𐑄 𐐿𐐬𐑉𐑅 𐑄𐐩 𐑇𐐳𐐼 𐐻𐑉𐐰𐑂𐐯𐑊 𐐮𐑌 𐑄 𐐶𐐮𐑊𐐼𐐲𐑉𐑌𐐯𐑅 𐐻𐐭 𐑀𐐬 𐐲𐐹 𐐻𐐭 𐑄 𐑊𐐰𐑌𐐼 𐐱𐑂 𐐢𐐨𐐸𐐴-𐐤𐐨𐑁𐐴; 𐑄𐐯𐑉𐑁𐐬𐑉 𐑄𐐩 𐐶𐐱𐑌𐐼𐐲𐑉𐐼 𐑋𐐯𐑌𐐨 𐐼𐐩𐑆 𐐮𐑌 𐑄 𐐶𐐮𐑊𐐼𐐲𐑉𐑌𐐯𐑅, 𐐨𐑂𐐲𐑌 𐑁𐐫𐑉𐐻𐐨 𐐼𐐩𐑆 𐐼𐐮𐐼 𐑄𐐩 𐐶𐐱𐑌𐐼𐐲𐑉. 𐐈𐑌𐐼 𐐸𐐶𐐯𐑌 𐑄𐐩 𐐸𐐰𐐼 𐐶𐐱𐑌𐐼𐐲𐑉𐐼 𐑁𐐫𐑉𐐻𐐨 𐐼𐐩𐑆 𐑄𐐩 𐐿𐐩𐑋 𐐻𐐭 𐐲 𐐸𐐮𐑊, 𐐸𐐶𐐮𐐽 𐐮𐑆 𐑌𐐫𐑉𐑃 𐐱𐑂 𐑄 𐑊𐐰𐑌𐐼 𐐱𐑂 𐐟𐐴𐑊𐐲𐑋, 𐐰𐑌𐐼 𐑄𐐯𐑉 𐑄𐐩 𐐹𐐮𐐽𐐻 𐑄𐐯𐑉 𐐻𐐯𐑌𐐻𐑅. 𐐈𐑌𐐼 𐐈𐑋𐐲𐑌 𐐻𐐳𐐿 𐑃𐑉𐐨 𐐱𐑂 𐐸𐐮𐑆 𐐺𐑉𐐯𐑄𐑉𐐯𐑌, 𐐰𐑌𐐼 𐑄𐐯𐑉 𐑌𐐩𐑋𐑆 𐐶𐐲𐑉 𐐈𐑋𐐰𐑊𐐯𐐿𐐴, 𐐐𐐨𐑊𐐯𐑋, 𐐰𐑌𐐼 𐐐𐐯𐑋, 𐐰𐑌𐐼 𐑄𐐩 𐐶𐐯𐑌𐐻 𐐼𐐵𐑌 𐐮𐑌𐐻𐐭 𐑄 𐑊𐐰𐑌𐐼 𐐱𐑂 𐐤𐐨𐑁𐐴. 𐐈𐑌𐐼 𐐺𐐨𐐸𐐬𐑊𐐼, 𐑄𐐩 𐑋𐐯𐐻 𐑄 𐐿𐐮𐑍 𐐱𐑂 𐑄 𐐹𐐨𐐹𐑊 𐐸𐐭 𐐶𐐲𐑉 𐐮𐑌 𐑄 𐑊𐐰𐑌𐐼 𐐱𐑂 𐐤𐐨𐑁𐐴, 𐐰𐑌𐐼 𐐮𐑌 𐑄 𐑊𐐰𐑌𐐼 𐐱𐑂 𐐟𐐴𐑊𐐲𐑋; 𐐰𐑌𐐼 𐑄𐐩 𐐶𐐲𐑉 𐑅𐐲𐑉𐐵𐑌𐐼𐐯𐐼 𐐺𐐴 𐑄 𐐿𐐮𐑍'𐑆 𐑀𐐪𐑉𐐼, 𐐰𐑌𐐼 𐐶𐐲𐑉 𐐻𐐩𐐿𐑌, 𐐰𐑌𐐼 𐐶𐐲𐑉 𐐺𐐵𐑌𐐼, 𐐰𐑌𐐼 𐐶𐐲𐑉 𐐿𐐱𐑋𐐮𐐻𐐯𐐼 𐐻𐐭 𐐹𐑉𐐮𐑆𐐲𐑌. 𐐈𐑌𐐼 𐐮𐐻 𐐿𐐩𐑋 𐐻𐐭 𐐹𐐰𐑅 𐐸𐐶𐐯𐑌 𐑄𐐩 𐐸𐐰𐐼 𐐺𐐮𐑌 𐐮𐑌 𐐹𐑉𐐮𐑆𐐲𐑌 𐐻𐐭 𐐼𐐩𐑆 𐑄𐐩 𐐶𐐲𐑉 𐐲𐑀𐐯𐑌 𐐺𐑉𐐫𐐻 𐐺𐐨𐑁𐐬𐑉 𐑄 𐐿𐐮𐑍, 𐐰𐑌𐐼 𐑄𐐯𐑉 𐐺𐐰𐑌𐐼𐑆 𐐶𐐲𐑉 𐑊𐐭𐑅𐐯𐐼; 𐐰𐑌𐐼 𐑄𐐩 𐑅𐐻𐐳𐐼 𐐺𐐨𐑁𐐬𐑉 𐑄 𐐿𐐮𐑍, 𐐰𐑌𐐼 𐐶𐐲𐑉 𐐹𐐲𐑉𐑋𐐮𐐻𐐯𐐼, 𐐫𐑉 𐑉𐐪𐑄𐐲𐑉 𐐿𐐱𐑋𐐰𐑌𐐼𐐯𐐼, 𐑄𐐰𐐻 𐑄𐐩 𐑇𐐳𐐼 𐐰𐑌𐑅𐐲𐑉 𐑄 𐐿𐐶𐐯𐑅𐐽𐐲𐑌𐑆 𐐸𐐶𐐮𐐽 𐐸𐐨 𐑇𐐳𐐼 𐐰𐑅𐐿 𐑄𐐯𐑋. 𐐈𐑌𐐼 𐐸𐐨 𐑅𐐯𐐼 𐐲𐑌𐐻𐐭 𐑄𐐯𐑋, 𐐒𐐨𐐸𐐬𐑊𐐼, 𐐌 𐐰𐑋 𐐢𐐮𐑋𐐸𐐴, 𐑄 𐑅𐐲𐑌 𐐱𐑂 𐐤𐐬𐐲, 𐐸𐐭 𐐶𐐱𐑆 𐑄 𐑅𐐲𐑌 𐐱𐑂 𐐞𐐨𐑌𐐮𐑁, 𐐸𐐭 𐐿𐐩𐑋 𐐲𐐹 𐐵𐐻 𐐱𐑂 𐑄 𐑊𐐰𐑌𐐼 𐐱𐑂 𐐞𐐯𐑉𐐲𐐸𐐯𐑋𐑊𐐲, 𐐻𐐭 𐐮𐑌𐐸𐐯𐑉𐐮𐐻 𐑄𐐮𐑅 𐑊𐐰𐑌𐐼, 𐐸𐐶𐐮𐐽 𐐶𐐱𐑆 𐑄 𐑊𐐰𐑌𐐼 𐐱𐑂 𐑄𐐯𐑉 𐑁𐐪𐑄𐐲𐑉𐑆, 𐐸𐐭 𐐶𐐱𐑆 𐑋𐐩𐐼 𐐲 𐐿𐐮𐑍 𐐺𐐴 𐑄 𐑂𐐱𐐮𐑅 𐐱𐑂 𐑄 𐐹𐐨𐐹𐑊. 𐐈𐑌𐐼 𐑌𐐵, 𐐌 𐐼𐐯𐑆𐐴𐑉 𐐻𐐭 𐑌𐐬 𐑄 𐐿𐐫𐑆 𐐸𐐶𐐯𐑉𐐺𐐴 𐐷 𐐶𐐲𐑉 𐑅𐐬 𐐺𐐬𐑊𐐼 𐐰𐑆 𐐻𐐭 𐐿𐐲𐑋 𐑌𐐨𐑉 𐑄 𐐶𐐫𐑊𐑆 𐐱𐑂 𐑄 𐑅𐐮𐐻𐐨, 𐐸𐐶𐐯𐑌 𐐌, 𐑋𐐴𐑅𐐯𐑊𐑁, 𐐶𐐱𐑆 𐐶𐐮𐑄 𐑋𐐴 𐑀𐐪𐑉𐐼𐑆 𐐶𐐮𐑄𐐵𐐻 𐑄 𐑀𐐩𐐻? 𐐈𐑌𐐼 𐑌𐐵, 𐑁𐐫𐑉 𐑄𐐮𐑅 𐐿𐐫𐑆 𐐸𐐰𐑂 𐐌 𐑅𐐲𐑁𐐲𐑉𐐼 𐑄𐐰𐐻 𐐷 𐑇𐐳𐐼 𐐺𐐨 𐐹𐑉𐐨𐑆𐐲𐑉𐑂𐐼, 𐑄𐐰𐐻 𐐌 𐑋𐐴𐐻 𐐮𐑌𐐿𐐶𐐴𐑉 𐐱𐑂 𐐷𐐭, 𐐫𐑉 𐐯𐑊𐑅 𐐌 𐑇𐐳𐐼 𐐸𐐰𐑂 𐐿𐐫𐑆𐐼 𐑄𐐰𐐻 𐑋𐐴 𐑀𐐪𐑉𐐼𐑆 𐑇𐐳𐐼 𐐸𐐰𐑂 𐐹𐐳𐐻 𐐷𐐭 𐐻𐐭 𐐼𐐯𐑃. 𐐏 𐐪𐑉 𐐹𐐲𐑉𐑋𐐮𐐻𐐯𐐼 𐐻𐐭 𐑅𐐹𐐨𐐿.

3. 𐐈𐑌𐐼 𐑌𐐵, 𐐸𐐶𐐯𐑌 𐐈𐑋𐐲𐑌 𐑅𐐫 𐑄𐐰𐐻 𐐸𐐨 𐐶𐐱𐑆 𐐹𐐲𐑉𐑋𐐮𐐻𐐯𐐼 𐐻𐐭 𐑅𐐹𐐨𐐿, 𐐸𐐨 𐐶𐐯𐑌𐐻 𐑁𐐬𐑉𐑃 𐐰𐑌𐐼 𐐺𐐵𐐼 𐐸𐐮𐑋𐑅𐐯𐑊𐑁 𐐺𐐨𐑁𐐬𐑉 𐑄 𐐿𐐮𐑍; 𐐰𐑌𐐼 𐑉𐐴𐑆𐐮𐑍 𐐲𐑀𐐯𐑌 𐐸𐐨 𐑅𐐯𐐼, 𐐄 𐐿𐐮𐑍, 𐐌 𐐰𐑋 𐑂𐐯𐑉𐐨 𐑃𐐰𐑍𐐿𐑁𐐳𐑊 𐐺𐐨𐑁𐐬𐑉 𐐘𐐱𐐼 𐑄𐐮𐑅 𐐼𐐩, 𐑄𐐰𐐻 𐐌 𐐰𐑋 𐐷𐐯𐐻 𐐲𐑊𐐴𐑂, 𐐰𐑌𐐼 𐐰𐑋 𐐹𐐲𐑉𐑋𐐮𐐻𐐯𐐼 𐐻𐐭 𐑅𐐹𐐨𐐿; 𐐰𐑌𐐼 𐐌 𐐶𐐮𐑊 𐐯𐑌𐐼𐐯𐑂𐐲𐑉 𐐻𐐭 𐑅𐐹𐐨𐐿 𐐶𐐮𐑄 𐐺𐐬𐑊𐐼𐑌𐐯𐑅; 𐑁𐐫𐑉 𐐌 𐐰𐑋 𐐰𐑇𐐳𐑉𐐼 𐑄𐐰𐐻 𐐮𐑁 𐐷 𐐸𐐰𐐼 𐑌𐐬𐑌 𐑋𐐨, 𐐷 𐐶𐐳𐐼 𐑌𐐱𐐻

𐐸𐐰𐑂 𐑅𐐲𐑁𐐲𐑉𐐼 𐑄𐐰𐐻 𐐌 𐑇𐐳𐐼 𐐸𐐰𐑂 𐐶𐐬𐑉 𐑄𐐨𐑆 𐐺𐐰𐑌𐐼𐑆. 𐐙𐐫𐑉 𐐌 𐐰𐑋 𐐈𐑋𐐲𐑌, 𐐰𐑌𐐼 𐐰𐑋 𐐲 𐐼𐐨𐑅𐐯𐑌𐐼𐐲𐑌𐐻 𐐱𐑂 𐐞𐐯𐑉𐐰𐐸𐐯𐑋𐑊𐐰, 𐐰𐑌𐐼 𐐸𐐰𐑂 𐐿𐐲𐑋 𐐲𐐹 𐐵𐐻 𐐱𐑂 𐑄 𐑊𐐰𐑌𐐼 𐐱𐑂 𐐞𐐯𐑉𐐰𐐸𐐯𐑋𐑊𐐰, 𐐻𐐭 𐐮𐑌𐐿𐐶𐐴𐑉 𐐿𐐲𐑌𐑅𐐲𐑉𐑌𐐮𐑍 𐐵𐑉 𐐺𐑉𐐯𐑃𐑉𐐯𐑌, 𐐸𐐭𐑋 𐐞𐐨𐑌𐐮𐑁 𐐺𐑉𐐫𐐻 𐐲𐐹 𐐵𐐻 𐐱𐑂 𐑄𐐰𐐻 𐑊𐐰𐑌𐐼.

4. 𐐈𐑌𐐼 𐑌𐐵, 𐐮𐐻 𐐿𐐩𐑋 𐐻𐐭 𐐹𐐰𐑅 𐑄𐐰𐐻 𐐰𐑁𐐻𐐲𐑉 𐐢𐐮𐑋𐐸𐐴 𐐸𐐰𐐼 𐐸𐐲𐑉𐐼 𐑄 𐐶𐐲𐑉𐐼𐑆 𐐱𐑂 𐐈𐑋𐐲𐑌, 𐐸𐐨 𐐶𐐱𐑆 𐐯𐐿𐑅𐐨𐐼𐐮𐑍𐑊𐐨 𐑀𐑊𐐰𐐼, 𐐰𐑌𐐼 𐑅𐐯𐐼, 𐐤𐐵, 𐐌 𐑌𐐬 𐐱𐑂 𐐲 𐑇𐐭𐑉𐐮𐐻𐐨 𐑄𐐰𐐻 𐑋𐐴 𐐺𐑉𐐯𐑃𐑉𐐯𐑌 𐐸𐐭 𐐶𐐲𐑉 𐐮𐑌 𐑄 𐑊𐐰𐑌𐐼 𐐱𐑂 𐐞𐐯𐑉𐐰𐐸𐐯𐑋𐑊𐐰 𐐪𐑉 𐐷𐐯𐐻 𐐲𐑊𐐴𐑂. 𐐈𐑌𐐼 𐑌𐐵, 𐐌 𐐶𐐮𐑊 𐑉𐐨𐐾𐑎𐑅; 𐐰𐑌𐐼 𐐱𐑌 𐑄 𐑋𐐱𐑉𐐬, 𐐌 𐐶𐐮𐑊 𐐿𐐫𐑆 𐑄𐐰𐐻 𐑋𐐴 𐐹𐐨𐐹𐑊 𐑇𐐰𐑊 𐑉𐐨𐐾𐑎𐑅 𐐫𐑊𐑅𐐬. 𐐙𐐫𐑉 𐐺𐐨𐐸𐐬𐑊𐐼, 𐐶𐐨 𐐪𐑉 𐐮𐑌 𐐺𐐱𐑌𐐼𐐩𐐾 𐐻𐐭 𐑄 𐐢𐐩𐑋𐐲𐑌𐐴𐐻𐑅, 𐐰𐑌𐐼 𐐪𐑉 𐐻𐐰𐐿𐑅𐐻 𐐶𐐮𐑄 𐐲 𐐻𐐰𐐿𐑅 𐐸𐐶𐐮𐐽 𐐮𐑆 𐑀𐑉𐐨𐑂𐐲𐑅 𐐻𐐭 𐐺𐐨 𐐺𐐬𐑉𐑌. 𐐈𐑌𐐼 𐑌𐐵, 𐐺𐐨𐐸𐐬𐑊𐐼, 𐐵𐑉 𐐺𐑉𐐯𐑃𐑉𐐯𐑌 𐐶𐐮𐑊 𐐼𐐨𐑊𐐮𐑂𐐲𐑉 𐐲𐑅 𐐵𐐻 𐐱𐑂 𐐵𐑉 𐐺𐐱𐑌𐐼𐐩𐐾, 𐐫𐑉 𐐵𐐻 𐐱𐑂 𐑄 𐐸𐐰𐑌𐐼𐑆 𐐱𐑂 𐑄 𐐢𐐩𐑋𐐲𐑌𐐴𐐻𐑅, 𐐰𐑌𐐼 𐐶𐐨 𐐶𐐮𐑊 𐐺𐐨 𐑄𐐩𐑉 𐑅𐑊𐐩𐑂𐑆; 𐑁𐐫𐑉 𐐮𐐻 𐐮𐑆 𐐺𐐯𐐻𐐲𐑉 𐑄𐐰𐐻 𐐶𐐨 𐐺𐐨 𐑅𐑊𐐩𐑂𐑆 𐐻𐐭 𐑄 𐐤𐐨𐑁𐐴𐐻𐑅, 𐑄𐐰𐑌 𐐻𐐭 𐐹𐐩 𐐻𐑉𐐮𐐺𐐷𐐭𐐻 𐐻𐐭 𐑄 𐐿𐐮𐑍 𐐱𐑂 𐑄 𐐢𐐩𐑋𐐲𐑌𐐴𐐻𐑅.

5. 𐐈𐑌𐐼 𐑌𐐵, 𐐿𐐮𐑍 𐐢𐐮𐑋𐐸𐐴 𐐿𐐲𐑋𐐰𐑌𐐼𐐯𐐼 𐐸𐐮𐑆 𐑀𐐪𐑉𐐼𐑆 𐑄𐐰𐐻 𐑄𐐩 𐑇𐐳𐐼 𐑌𐐬 𐑋𐐬𐑉 𐐺𐐴𐑌𐐼 𐐈𐑋𐐲𐑌, 𐑌𐐫𐑉 𐐸𐐮𐑆 𐐺𐑉𐐯𐑃𐑉𐐯𐑌, 𐐺𐐲𐐻 𐐿𐐫𐑆𐐼 𐑄𐐰𐐻 𐑄𐐩 𐑇𐐳𐐼 𐑀𐐬 𐐻𐐭 𐑄 𐐸𐐮𐑊 𐐸𐐶𐐮𐐽 𐐶𐐱𐑆 𐑌𐐫𐑉𐑃 𐐱𐑂 𐐟𐐴𐑊𐐲𐑋, 𐐰𐑌𐐼 𐐺𐑉𐐮𐑍 𐑄𐐩𐑉 𐐺𐑉𐐯𐑃𐑉𐐯𐑌 𐐮𐑌𐐻𐐭 𐑄 𐑅𐐮𐐻𐐨, 𐑄𐐰𐐻 𐑄𐐩𐑉𐐺𐐴 𐑄𐐩 𐑋𐐴𐐻 𐐨𐐻, 𐐰𐑌𐐼 𐐼𐑉𐐮𐑍𐐿, 𐐰𐑌𐐼 𐑉𐐯𐑅𐐻 𐑄𐐯𐑋𐑅𐐯𐑊𐑂𐑆 𐑁𐑉𐐱𐑋 𐑄 𐑊𐐩𐐺𐐲𐑉𐑆 𐐱𐑂 𐑄𐐩𐑉 𐐾𐐲𐑉𐑌𐐨; 𐑁𐐫𐑉 𐑄𐐩 𐐸𐐰𐐼 𐑅𐐲𐑁𐐲𐑉𐐼 𐑋𐐯𐑌𐐨 𐑃𐐮𐑍𐑆; 𐑄𐐩 𐐸𐐰𐐼 𐑅𐐲𐑁𐐲𐑉𐐼 𐐸𐐲𐑍𐑀𐐲𐑉, 𐑃𐐲𐑉𐑅𐐻, 𐐰𐑌𐐼 𐑁𐐲𐐻𐐨𐑀.

6. 𐐈𐑌𐐼 𐑌𐐵, 𐐮𐐻 𐐿𐐩𐑋 𐐻𐐭 𐐹𐐰𐑅 𐐱𐑌 𐑄 𐑋𐐱𐑉𐐬, 𐑄𐐰𐐻 𐐿𐐮𐑍 𐐢𐐮𐑋𐐸𐐴 𐑅𐐯𐑌𐐻 𐐲 𐐹𐑉𐐱𐐿𐑊𐐲𐑋𐐩𐑇𐐲𐑌 𐐲𐑋𐐲𐑍 𐐫𐑊 𐐸𐐮𐑆 𐐹𐐨𐐹𐑊, 𐑄𐐰𐐻 𐑄𐐩𐑉𐐺𐐴 𐑄𐐩 𐑋𐐴𐐻 𐑀𐐰𐑄𐐲𐑉 𐑄𐐯𐑋𐑅𐐯𐑊𐑂𐑆 𐐻𐐭𐑀𐐯𐑄𐐲𐑉 𐐻𐐭 𐑄 𐐻𐐯𐑋𐐹𐑊, 𐐻𐐭 𐐸𐐨𐑉 𐑄 𐐶𐐲𐑉𐐼𐑆 𐐸𐐶𐐮𐐽 𐐸𐐨 𐑇𐐳𐐼 𐑅𐐹𐐨𐐿 𐐲𐑌𐐻𐐭 𐑄𐐯𐑋. 𐐈𐑌𐐼 𐐮𐐻 𐐿𐐩𐑋 𐐻𐐭 𐐹𐐰𐑅 𐑄𐐰𐐻 𐐸𐐶𐐯𐑌 𐑄𐐩 𐐸𐐰𐐼 𐑀𐐰𐑄𐐲𐑉𐐼 𐑄𐐯𐑋𐑅𐐯𐑊𐑂𐑆 𐐻𐐭𐑀𐐯𐑄𐐲𐑉, 𐑄𐐰𐐻 𐐸𐐨 𐑅𐐹𐐩𐐿 𐐲𐑌𐐻𐐭 𐑄𐐯𐑋 𐐮𐑌 𐑄𐐮𐑅 𐐶𐐴𐑆, 𐑅𐐩𐐮𐑍, 𐐄 𐐷𐐨, 𐑋𐐴 𐐹𐐨𐐹𐑊, 𐑊𐐮𐑁𐐻 𐐲𐐹 𐐷𐐭𐑉 𐐸𐐯𐐼𐑆 𐐰𐑌𐐼 𐐺𐐨 𐐿𐐲𐑋𐑁𐐲𐑉𐐻𐐯𐐼; 𐑁𐐫𐑉 𐐺𐐨𐐸𐐬𐑊𐐼, 𐑄 𐐻𐐴𐑋 𐐮𐑆 𐐰𐐻 𐐸𐐰𐑌𐐼, 𐐫𐑉 𐐮𐑆 𐑌𐐱𐐻 𐑁𐐪𐑉 𐐼𐐮𐑅𐐻𐐲𐑌𐐻, 𐐸𐐶𐐯𐑌 𐐶𐐨 𐑇𐐰𐑊 𐑌𐐬 𐑊𐐱𐑍𐑀𐐲𐑉 𐐺𐐨 𐐮𐑌 𐑅𐐲𐐺𐐾𐐯𐐿𐑇𐐲𐑌 𐐻𐐭 𐐵𐑉 𐐯𐑌𐐯𐑋𐐨𐑆, 𐑌𐐱𐐻𐐶𐐮𐑄𐑅𐐻𐐰𐑌𐐼𐐮𐑍 𐐵𐑉 𐑋𐐯𐑌𐐨 𐑅𐐻𐑉𐐴𐑂𐐮𐑍𐑆, 𐐸𐐶𐐮𐐽 𐐸𐐰𐑂 𐐺𐐮𐑌 𐐮𐑌 𐑂𐐩𐑌; 𐐷𐐯𐐻 𐐌 𐐻𐑉𐐲𐑅𐐻 𐑄𐐩𐑉 𐑉𐐨𐑋𐐩𐑌𐐯𐑃 𐐰𐑌 𐐯𐑁𐐯𐐿𐐽𐐭𐐲𐑊 𐑅𐐻𐑉𐐲𐑀𐑊 𐐻𐐭 𐐺𐐨 𐑋𐐩𐐼. 𐐜𐐩𐑉𐑁𐐬𐑉, 𐑊𐐮𐑁𐐻 𐐲𐐹 𐐷𐐭𐑉 𐐸𐐯𐐼𐑆, 𐐰𐑌𐐼 𐑉𐐨𐐾𐑎𐑅, 𐐰𐑌𐐼 𐐹𐐳𐐻 𐐷𐐭𐑉 𐐻𐑉𐐲𐑅𐐻 𐐮𐑌 𐐘𐐱𐐼, 𐐮𐑌 𐑄𐐰𐐻 𐐘𐐱𐐼 𐐸𐐭 𐐶𐐱𐑆 𐑄 𐐘𐐱𐐼 𐐱𐑂 𐐁𐐺𐑉𐐲𐐸𐐰𐑋, 𐐰𐑌𐐼 𐐌𐑆𐐲𐐿, 𐐰𐑌𐐼 𐐖𐐩𐐿𐐲𐐺; 𐐰𐑌𐐼 𐐫𐑊𐑅𐐬, 𐑄𐐰𐐻 𐐘𐐱𐐼 𐐸𐐭 𐐺𐑉𐐫𐐻 𐑄 𐐽𐐮𐑊𐐼𐑉𐐯𐑌 𐐱𐑂 𐐆𐑆𐑉𐐩𐐯𐑊 𐐵𐐻 𐐱𐑂 𐑄 𐑊𐐰𐑌𐐼 𐐱𐑂 𐐀𐐾𐐮𐐹𐐻, 𐐰𐑌𐐼 𐐿𐐫𐑆𐐼 𐑄𐐰𐐻 𐑄𐐩 𐑇𐐳𐐼 𐐶𐐫𐐿 𐑃𐑉𐐭 𐑄 𐐡𐐯𐐼 𐐝𐐨 𐐱𐑌 𐐼𐑉𐐴 𐑀𐑉𐐵𐑌𐐼, 𐐰𐑌𐐼 𐑁𐐯𐐼 𐑄𐐯𐑋 𐐶𐐮𐑄 𐑋𐐰𐑌𐐲, 𐑄𐐰𐐻 𐑄𐐩 𐑋𐐴𐐻 𐑌𐐱𐐻 𐐹𐐯𐑉𐐮𐑇 𐐮𐑌 𐑄 𐐶𐐮𐑊𐐼𐐲𐑉𐑌𐐯𐑅; 𐐰𐑌𐐼 𐑋𐐯𐑌𐐨 𐑋𐐬𐑉 𐑃𐐮𐑍𐑆 𐐼𐐮𐐼 𐐸𐐨 𐐼𐐭 𐑁𐐫𐑉 𐑄𐐯𐑋. 𐐈𐑌𐐼 𐐲𐑀𐐯𐑌: 𐐜𐐰𐐻 𐑅𐐩𐑋 𐐘𐐱𐐼 𐐸𐐰𐑆 𐐺𐑉𐐫𐐻 𐐵𐑉 𐑁𐐪𐑄𐐲𐑉𐑆 𐐵𐐻 𐐱𐑂 𐑄 𐑊𐐰𐑌𐐼 𐐱𐑂 𐐖𐐲𐑉𐐭𐑅𐐲𐑊𐐯𐑋, 𐐰𐑌𐐼 𐐸𐐰𐑆 𐐿𐐯𐐹𐐻 𐐰𐑌𐐼 𐐹𐑉𐐨𐑆𐐲𐑉𐑂𐐼 𐐸𐐮𐑆 𐐹𐐨𐐹𐑊, 𐐨𐑂𐐲𐑌 𐐲𐑌𐐻𐐮𐑊 𐑌𐐵. 𐐈𐑌𐐼 𐐺𐐨𐐸𐐬𐑊𐐼, 𐐮𐐻 𐐮𐑆 𐐺𐐨𐐿𐐫𐑆 𐐱𐑂 𐐵𐑉 𐐮𐑌𐐮𐐿𐐶𐐮𐐻𐐨𐑆 𐐰𐑌𐐼 𐐲𐐺𐐱𐑋𐐮𐑌𐐩𐑇𐐲𐑌𐑆 𐑄𐐰𐐻 𐐸𐐨 𐐸𐐰𐑆 𐐺𐑉𐐫𐐻 𐐲𐑅 𐐮𐑌𐐻𐐭 𐐺𐐱𐑌𐐼𐐩𐐾. 𐐈𐑌𐐼 𐐷𐐨 𐐫𐑊 𐐪𐑉 𐐶𐐮𐐻𐑌𐐯𐑅𐐯𐑆 𐑄𐐮𐑅 𐐼𐐩, 𐑄𐐰𐐻 𐐞𐐨𐑌𐐮𐑁, 𐐸𐐭 𐐶𐐱𐑆 𐑋𐐩𐐼 𐐿𐐮𐑍 𐐬𐑂𐐲𐑉 𐑄𐐮𐑅 𐐹𐐨𐐹𐑊, 𐐸𐐨 𐐺𐐨𐐮𐑍 𐐬𐑂𐐲𐑉-𐑆𐐯𐑊𐐲𐑅 𐐻𐐭 𐐮𐑌𐐸𐐯𐑉𐐮𐐻 𐑄 𐑊𐐰𐑌𐐼 𐐱𐑂 𐐸𐐮𐑆 𐑁𐐪𐑄𐐲𐑉𐑆, 𐑄𐐩𐑉𐑁𐐬𐑉 𐐺𐐨𐐮𐑍 𐐼𐐨𐑅𐐨𐑂𐐼 𐐺𐐴 𐑄 𐐿𐐲𐑌𐐮𐑍 𐐰𐑌𐐼 𐐿𐑉𐐰𐑁𐐻𐐨𐑌𐐯𐑅 𐐱𐑂 𐐿𐐮𐑍 𐐢𐐩𐑋𐐲𐑌, 𐐸𐐭 𐐸𐐰𐑂𐐮𐑍 𐐯𐑌𐐻𐐲𐑉𐐼 𐐮𐑌𐐻𐐭 𐐲 𐐻𐑉𐐨𐐻𐐨 𐐶𐐮𐑄 𐐿𐐮𐑍 𐐞𐐨𐑌𐐮𐑁, 𐐰𐑌𐐼 𐐸𐐰𐑂𐐮𐑍 𐐷𐐨𐑊𐐼𐐯𐐼 𐐲𐐹 𐐮𐑌𐐻𐐭 𐐸𐐮𐑆 𐐸𐐰𐑌𐐼𐑆 𐑄 𐐹𐐱𐑆𐐯𐑇𐐲𐑌𐑆 𐐱𐑂 𐐲 𐐹𐐪𐑉𐐻 𐐱𐑂 𐑄 𐑊𐐰𐑌𐐼, 𐐫𐑉 𐐨𐑂𐐲𐑌 𐑄 𐑅𐐮𐐻𐐨 𐐱𐑂 𐐢𐐨𐐸𐐴-𐐤𐐨𐑁𐐴, 𐐰𐑌𐐼 𐑄 𐑅𐐮𐐻𐐨 𐐱𐑂 𐐟𐐴𐑊𐐲𐑋; 𐐰𐑌𐐼 𐑄 𐑊𐐰𐑌𐐼 𐑉𐐵𐑌𐐼 𐐲𐐺𐐵𐐻; 𐐰𐑌𐐼 𐐫𐑊 𐑄𐐮𐑅 𐐸𐐨 𐐼𐐮𐐼, 𐑁𐐫𐑉 𐑄 𐑅𐐬𐑊 𐐹𐐲𐑉𐐹𐐲𐑅 𐐱𐑂 𐐺𐑉𐐮𐑍𐐮𐑍 𐑄𐐮𐑅 𐐹𐐨𐐹𐑊 𐐮𐑌𐐻𐐭 𐑅𐐲𐐺𐐾𐐯𐐿𐑇𐐲𐑌 𐐫𐑉 𐐮𐑌𐐻𐐭 𐐺𐐱𐑌𐐼𐐩𐐾. 𐐈𐑌𐐼 𐐺𐐨𐐸𐐬𐑊𐐼, 𐐶𐐨 𐐰𐐻 𐑄𐐮𐑅 𐐻𐐴𐑋 𐐼𐐭 𐐹𐐩 𐐻𐑉𐐮𐐺𐐷𐐭𐐻 𐐻𐐭 𐑄 𐐿𐐮𐑍 𐐱𐑂 𐑄 𐐢𐐩𐑋𐐲𐑌𐐴𐐻𐑅, 𐐻𐐭 𐑄 𐐲𐑋𐐵𐑌𐐻 𐐱𐑂 𐐶𐐲𐑌 𐐸𐐪𐑁 𐐱𐑂 𐐵𐑉 𐐿𐐫𐑉𐑌, 𐐰𐑌𐐼 𐐵𐑉 𐐺𐐪𐑉𐑊𐐨, 𐐰𐑌𐐼 𐐨𐑂𐐲𐑌 𐐫𐑊 𐐵𐑉 𐑀𐑉𐐩𐑌 𐐱𐑂 𐐯𐑂𐐲𐑉𐐨 𐐿𐐴𐑌𐐼, 𐐰𐑌𐐼 𐐶𐐲𐑌 𐐸𐐪𐑁 𐐱𐑂 𐑄 𐐮𐑌𐐿𐑉𐐨𐑅 𐐱𐑂 𐐵𐑉 𐑁𐑊𐐱𐐿𐑅 𐐰𐑌𐐼 𐐵𐑉 𐐸𐐲𐑉𐐼𐑆; 𐐰𐑌𐐼 𐐨𐑂𐐲𐑌 𐐶𐐲𐑌 𐐸𐐪𐑁 𐐱𐑂 𐐫𐑊 𐐶𐐨 𐐸𐐰𐑂 𐐫𐑉 𐐹𐐱𐑆𐐯𐑅, 𐑄 𐐿𐐮𐑍 𐐱𐑂 𐑄 𐐢𐐩𐑋𐐲𐑌𐐴𐐻𐑅 𐐼𐐲𐑃 𐐯𐑆𐐰𐐿𐐻 𐐱𐑂 𐐲𐑅, 𐐫𐑉 𐐵𐑉 𐑊𐐴𐑂𐑆.

𐐈𐑌𐐼 𐑌𐐵, 𐐮𐑆 𐑌𐐱𐐻 𐑄𐐮𐑅 𐑀𐑉𐐨𐑂𐐲𐑅 𐐻𐐭 𐐺 𐐺𐐫𐑉𐑌? 𐐈𐑌𐐼 𐐮𐑆 𐑌𐐱𐐻 𐑄𐐮𐑅, 𐐵𐑉 𐐰𐑁𐑊𐐮𐐿𐑇𐐲𐑌, 𐑀𐑉𐐩𐐻? 𐐤𐐵 𐐺𐐨𐐸𐐬𐑊𐐼, 𐐸𐐵 𐑀𐑉𐐩𐐻 𐑉𐐨𐑆𐑌 𐐶𐐨 𐐸𐐰𐑂 𐐻𐐭 𐑋𐐬𐑉𐑌.

7. 𐐏𐐩, 𐐌 𐑅𐐩 𐐲𐑌𐐻𐐭 𐐷𐐭, 𐑀𐑉𐐩𐐻 𐐪𐑉 𐑄 𐑉𐐨𐑆𐑌𐑆 𐐸𐐶𐐮𐐽 𐐶𐐨 𐐸𐐰𐑂 𐐻𐐭 𐑋𐐬𐑉𐑌; 𐑁𐐫𐑉 𐐺𐐨𐐸𐐬𐑊𐐼, 𐐸𐐵 𐑋𐐯𐑌𐐨 𐐱𐑂 𐐵𐑉 𐐺𐑉𐐯𐑄𐑉𐐯𐑌 𐐸𐐰𐑂 𐐺𐐮𐑌 𐑅𐑊𐐩𐑌, 𐐰𐑌𐐼 𐑄𐐩𐑉 𐐺𐑊𐐲𐐼 𐐸𐐰𐑆 𐐺𐐮𐑌 𐑅𐐹𐐮𐑊𐐻 𐐮𐑌 𐑂𐐩𐑌, 𐐰𐑌𐐼 𐐫𐑊 𐐺𐐨𐐿𐐫𐑆 𐐱𐑂 𐐮𐑌𐐮𐐿𐐶𐐮𐐻𐐨. 𐐙𐐫𐑉 𐐮𐑁 𐑄𐐮𐑅 𐐹𐐨𐐹𐑊 𐐸𐐰𐐼 𐑌𐐱𐐻 𐑁𐐫𐑊𐑌 𐐮𐑌𐐻𐐭 𐐻𐑉𐐰𐑌𐑅𐑀𐑉𐐯𐑇𐐲𐑌, 𐑄 𐐢𐐫𐑉𐐼 𐐶𐐳𐐼 𐑌𐐱𐐻 𐐸𐐰𐑂 𐑅𐐲𐑁𐐲𐑉𐐼 𐑄𐐰𐐻 𐑄𐐮𐑅 𐑀𐑉𐐩𐐻 𐐨𐑂𐑊 𐑇𐐳𐐼 𐐿𐐲𐑋 𐐲𐐹𐐱𐑌 𐑄𐐯𐑋. 𐐒𐐲𐐻 𐐺𐐨𐐸𐐬𐑊𐐼, 𐑄𐐩 𐐶𐐳𐐼 𐑌𐐱𐐻 𐐸𐐪𐑉𐐿𐑌 𐐲𐑌𐐻𐐭 𐐸𐐮𐑆 𐐶𐐲𐑉𐐼𐑆; 𐐺𐐲𐐻 𐑄𐐩𐑉 𐐲𐑉𐐬𐑆 𐐿𐐲𐑌𐐻𐐯𐑌𐑇𐐲𐑌𐑆 𐐲𐑋𐐲𐑍 𐑄𐐯𐑋, 𐐨𐑂𐑌 𐑅𐐬 𐑋𐐲𐐽 𐑄𐐰𐐻 𐑄𐐩 𐐼𐐮𐐼 𐑇𐐯𐐼 𐐺𐑊𐐲𐐼 𐐲𐑋𐐲𐑍 𐑄𐐯𐑋𐑅𐐯𐑊𐑂𐑆. 𐐈𐑌𐐼 𐐩 𐐹𐑉𐐱𐑁𐐯𐐻 𐐱𐑂 𐑄 𐐢𐐫𐑉𐐼 𐐸𐐰𐑂 𐑄𐐩 𐑅𐑊𐐩𐑌; 𐐷𐐩, 𐐩 𐐽𐐬𐑆𐑌 𐑋𐐰𐑌 𐐱𐑂 𐐘𐐱𐐼, 𐐸𐐭 𐐻𐐬𐑊𐐼 𐑄𐐯𐑋 𐐱𐑂 𐑄𐐩𐑉 𐐶𐐮𐐿𐐯𐐼𐑌𐐯𐑅 𐐰𐑌𐐼 𐐲𐐺𐐱𐑋𐐮𐑌𐐩𐑇𐐲𐑌𐑆, 𐐰𐑌𐐼 𐐹𐑉𐐱𐑁𐐯𐑅𐐴𐐼 𐐱𐑂 𐑋𐐯𐑌𐐨 𐑃𐐮𐑍𐑆 𐐸𐐶𐐮𐐽 𐐪𐑉 𐐻𐐭 𐐿𐐲𐑋, 𐐷𐐩, 𐐨𐑂𐑌 𐑄 𐐿𐐲𐑋𐐮𐑍 𐐱𐑂 𐐗𐑉𐐴𐑅𐐻. 𐐈𐑌𐐼 𐐺𐐨𐐿𐐫𐑆 𐐸𐐨 𐑅𐐯𐐼 𐐲𐑌𐐻𐐭 𐑄𐐯𐑋 𐑄𐐰𐐻 𐐗𐑉𐐴𐑅𐐻 𐐶𐐱𐑆 𐑄 𐐘𐐱𐐼, 𐑄 𐐙𐐪𐑄𐐲𐑉 𐐱𐑂 𐐫𐑊 𐑃𐐮𐑍𐑆, 𐐰𐑌𐐼 𐑅𐐯𐐼 𐑄𐐰𐐻 𐐸𐐨 𐑇𐐳𐐼 𐐻𐐩𐐿 𐐲𐐹𐐱𐑌 𐐸𐐮𐑋 𐑄 𐐮𐑋𐐯𐐾 𐐱𐑂 𐑋𐐰𐑌, 𐐰𐑌𐐼 𐐮𐐻 𐑇𐐳𐐼 𐐺 𐑄 𐐮𐑋𐐯𐐾 𐐪𐑁𐐻𐐲𐑉 𐐸𐐶𐐮𐐽 𐑋𐐰𐑌 𐐶𐐱𐑆 𐐿𐑉𐐨𐐩𐐻𐐯𐐼 𐐮𐑌 𐑄 𐐺𐐨𐑀𐐮𐑌𐐮𐑍; 𐐫𐑉 𐐮𐑌 𐐲𐑄𐐲𐑉 𐐶𐐲𐑉𐐼𐑆, 𐐸𐐨 𐑅𐐯𐐼 𐑄𐐰𐐻 𐑋𐐰𐑌 𐐶𐐱𐑆 𐐿𐑉𐐨𐐩𐐻𐐯𐐼 𐐪𐑁𐐻𐐲𐑉 𐑄 𐐮𐑋𐐯𐐾 𐐱𐑂 𐐘𐐱𐐼, 𐐰𐑌𐐼 𐑄𐐰𐐻 𐐘𐐱𐐼 𐑇𐐳𐐼 𐐿𐐲𐑋 𐐼𐐵𐑌 𐐲𐑋𐐲𐑍 𐑄 𐐽𐐮𐑊𐐼𐑉𐐯𐑌 𐐱𐑂 𐑋𐐯𐑌, 𐐰𐑌𐐼 𐐻𐐩𐐿 𐐲𐐹𐐱𐑌 𐐸𐐮𐑋 𐑁𐑊𐐯𐑇 𐐰𐑌𐐼 𐐺𐑊𐐲𐐼, 𐐰𐑌𐐼 𐑀𐐬 𐑁𐐬𐑉𐑃 𐐲𐐹𐐱𐑌 𐑄 𐑁𐐩𐑅 𐐱𐑂 𐑄 𐐲𐑉𐑃; 𐐰𐑌𐐼 𐑌𐐵, 𐐺𐐨𐐿𐐫𐑆 𐐸𐐨 𐑅𐐯𐐼 𐑄𐐮𐑅, 𐑄𐐩 𐐼𐐮𐐼 𐐹𐐳𐐻 𐐸𐐮𐑋 𐐻𐐭 𐐼𐐯𐑃; 𐐰𐑌𐐼 𐑋𐐯𐑌𐐨 𐑋𐐬𐑉 𐑃𐐮𐑍𐑆 𐐼𐐮𐐼 𐑄𐐩 𐐼𐐭 𐐸𐐶𐐮𐐽 𐐺𐑉𐐫𐐻 𐐼𐐵𐑌 𐑄 𐑉𐐰𐑃 𐐱𐑂 𐐘𐐱𐐼 𐐲𐐹𐐱𐑌 𐑄𐐯𐑋. 𐐜𐐩𐑉𐑁𐐬𐑉, 𐐸𐐭 𐐶𐐲𐑌𐐼𐐲𐑉𐐯𐑃 𐑄𐐰𐐻 𐑄𐐩 𐐪𐑉 𐐮𐑌 𐐺𐐱𐑌𐐼𐐯𐐾, 𐐰𐑌𐐼 𐑄𐐰𐐻 𐑄𐐩 𐐪𐑉 𐑅𐑋𐐮𐐻𐑌 𐐶𐐮𐑄 𐑅𐐬𐑉 𐐰𐑁𐑊𐐮𐐿𐑇𐐲𐑌𐑆. 𐐙𐐫𐑉 𐐺𐐨𐐸𐐬𐑊𐐼, 𐑄 𐐢𐐫𐑉𐐼 𐐸𐐰𐑃 𐑅𐐯𐐼, 𐐌 𐐶𐐮𐑊 𐑌𐐱𐐻 𐑅𐐲𐐿𐐲𐑉 𐑋𐐴 𐐹𐐨𐐹𐑊 𐐮𐑌 𐑄 𐐼𐐩 𐐱𐑂 𐑄𐐩𐑉 𐐻𐑉𐐰𐑌𐑅𐑀𐑉𐐯𐑇𐐲𐑌; 𐐺𐐲𐐻 𐐌 𐐶𐐮𐑊 𐐸𐐯𐐾 𐐲𐐹 𐑄𐐩𐑉 𐐶𐐩𐑆 𐑄𐐰𐐻 𐑄𐐩 𐐹𐑉𐐱𐑅𐐹𐐲𐑉 𐑌𐐱𐐻; 𐐰𐑌𐐼 𐑄𐐩𐑉 𐐼𐐭𐐮𐑍𐑆 𐑇𐐰𐑊 𐐺 𐐰𐑆 𐐩 𐑅𐐻𐐲𐑋𐐺𐑊𐐮𐑍 𐐺𐑊𐐱𐐿 𐐺𐐨𐑁𐐬𐑉 𐑄𐐯𐑋. 𐐈𐑌𐐼 𐐲𐑀𐐯𐑌, 𐐸𐐨 𐑅𐐯𐑃, 𐐆𐑁 𐑋𐐴 𐐹𐐨𐐹𐑊 𐑇𐐰𐑊 𐑅𐐬 𐑁𐐮𐑊𐑃𐐮𐑌𐐯𐑅, 𐑄𐐩 𐑇𐐰𐑊 𐑉𐐨𐐹 𐑄 𐐽𐐰𐑁 𐑄𐐩𐑉𐐱𐑂 𐐮𐑌 𐑄 𐐸𐐶𐐲𐑉𐑊𐐶𐐮𐑌𐐼; 𐐰𐑌𐐼 𐑄 𐐯𐑁𐐯𐐿𐐻 𐑄𐐩𐑉𐐱𐑂 𐐮𐑆 𐐹𐐫𐐮𐑆𐑌. 𐐈𐑌𐐼 𐐲𐑀𐐯𐑌, 𐐸𐐨 𐑅𐐯𐑃, 𐐆𐑁 𐑋𐐴 𐐹𐐨𐐹𐑊 𐑇𐐰𐑊 𐑅𐐬 𐑁𐐮𐑊𐑃𐐮𐑌𐐯𐑅, 𐑄𐐩 𐑇𐐰𐑊 𐑉𐐨𐐹 𐑄 𐐨𐑅𐐻 𐐶𐐮𐑌𐐼, 𐐸𐐶𐐮𐐽 𐐺𐑉𐐮𐑍𐐯𐑃 𐐮𐑋𐐨𐐼𐐨𐐯𐐻 𐐼𐐯𐑅𐐻𐑉𐐲𐐿𐑇𐐲𐑌. 𐐈𐑌𐐼 𐑌𐐵, 𐐺𐐨𐐸𐐬𐑊𐐼, 𐑄 𐐹𐑉𐐱𐑋𐐮𐑅 𐐱𐑂 𐑄 𐐢𐐫𐑉𐐼 𐐮𐑆 𐑁𐐳𐑊𐑁𐐮𐑊𐐼; 𐐰𐑌𐐼 𐐷 𐐪𐑉 𐑅𐑋𐐮𐐻𐑌 𐐰𐑌𐐼 𐐰𐑁𐑊𐐮𐐿𐐻𐐯𐐼. 𐐒𐐲𐐻 𐐮𐑁 𐐷 𐐶𐐮𐑊 𐐻𐐲𐑉𐑌 𐐻𐐭 𐑄 𐐢𐐫𐑉𐐼 𐐶𐐮𐑄 𐑁𐐳𐑊 𐐹𐐲𐑉𐐹𐐲𐑅 𐐱𐑂 𐐸𐐪𐑉𐐻, 𐐰𐑌𐐼 𐐹𐐳𐐻 𐐷𐐬𐑉 𐐻𐑉𐐲𐑅𐐻 𐐮𐑌 𐐸𐐮𐑋, 𐐰𐑌𐐼 𐑅𐐲𐑉𐑂 𐐸𐐮𐑋 𐐶𐐮𐑄 𐐫𐑊 𐐼𐐮𐑊𐐮𐐾𐐯𐑌𐑅 𐐱𐑂 𐑋𐐴𐑌𐐼; 𐐮𐑁 𐐷 𐐼𐐭 𐑄𐐮𐑅, 𐐸𐐨 𐐶𐐮𐑊, 𐐰𐐿𐐫𐑉𐐼𐐮𐑍 𐐻𐐭 𐐸𐐮𐑆 𐐬𐑌 𐐶𐐮𐑊 𐐰𐑌𐐼 𐐹𐑊𐐯𐑈𐐲𐑉, 𐐼𐐨𐑊𐐮𐑂𐐲𐑉 𐐷𐐭 𐐵𐐻 𐐱𐑂 𐐺𐐱𐑌𐐼𐐯𐐾.

8. 𐐈𐑌𐐼 𐐮𐐻 𐐿𐐩𐑋 𐐻𐐭 𐐹𐐪𐑅 𐑄𐐰𐐻 𐐪𐑁𐐻𐐲𐑉 𐐿𐐮𐑍 𐐢𐐮𐑋𐐸𐐴 𐐸𐐰𐐼 𐑋𐐩𐐼 𐐰𐑌 𐐯𐑌𐐼 𐐱𐑂 𐑅𐐹𐐨𐐿𐐮𐑍 𐐻𐐭 𐐸𐐮𐑆 𐐹𐐨𐐹𐑊, 𐑁𐐫𐑉 𐐸𐐨 𐑅𐐹𐐩𐐿 𐑋𐐯𐑌𐐨 𐑃𐐮𐑍𐑆 𐐲𐑌𐐻𐐭 𐑄𐐯𐑋, 𐐰𐑌𐐼 𐐬𐑌𐑊𐐨 𐐩 𐑁𐐷𐐭 𐐱𐑂 𐑄𐐯𐑋 𐐸𐐰𐑂 𐐌 𐑉𐐮𐐻𐑌 𐐮𐑌 𐑄𐐮𐑅 𐐺𐐳𐐿, 𐐸𐐨 𐐻𐐬𐑊𐐼 𐐸𐐮𐑆 𐐹𐐨𐐹𐑊 𐐫𐑊 𐑄 𐑃𐐮𐑍𐑆 𐐿𐐱𐑌𐑅𐐲𐑉𐑌𐐮𐑍 𐑄𐐩𐑉 𐐺𐑉𐐯𐑄𐑉𐐯𐑌 𐐸𐐭 𐐶𐐲𐑉 𐐮𐑌 𐑄 𐑊𐐰𐑌𐐼 𐐱𐑂 𐐞𐐰𐑉𐐲𐐸𐐯𐑋𐑊𐐲; 𐐰𐑌𐐼 𐐸𐐨 𐐿𐐫𐑆𐐼 𐑄𐐰𐐻 𐐈𐑋𐐲𐑌 𐑇𐐳𐐼 𐑅𐐻𐐰𐑌𐐼 𐐲𐐹 𐐺𐐨𐑁𐐬𐑉 𐑄 𐑋𐐲𐑊𐐻𐐮𐐻𐐷𐐭𐐼, 𐐰𐑌𐐼 𐑉𐐨𐐸𐐲𐑉𐑅 𐐲𐑌𐐻𐐭 𐑄𐐯𐑋 𐐫𐑊 𐑄𐐰𐐻 𐐸𐐰𐐼 𐐸𐐰𐐹𐑌𐐼 𐐲𐑌𐐻𐐭 𐑄𐐩𐑉 𐐺𐑉𐐯𐑄𐑉𐐯𐑌 𐑁𐑉𐐱𐑋 𐑄 𐐻𐐴𐑋 𐑄𐐰𐐻 𐐞𐐨𐑌𐐮𐑁 𐐶𐐯𐑌𐐻 𐐲𐐹 𐐵𐐻 𐐱𐑂 𐑄 𐑊𐐰𐑌𐐼, 𐐨𐑂𐑌 𐐲𐑌𐐻𐐮𐑊 𐑄 𐐻𐐴𐑋 𐑄𐐰𐐻 𐐸𐐨 𐐸𐐮𐑋𐑅𐐯𐑊𐑁 𐐿𐐩𐑋 𐐲𐐹 𐐵𐐻 𐐱𐑂 𐑄 𐑊𐐰𐑌𐐼. 𐐈𐑌𐐼 𐐸𐐨 𐐫𐑊𐑅𐐬 𐑉𐐨𐐸𐐲𐑉𐑅𐐻 𐐲𐑌𐐻𐐭 𐑄𐐯𐑋 𐑄 𐑊𐐪𐑅𐐻 𐐶𐐲𐑉𐐼𐑆 𐐸𐐶𐐮𐐽 𐐿𐐮𐑍 𐐒𐐯𐑌𐐾𐐲𐑋𐐮𐑌 𐐸𐐰𐐼 𐐻𐐫𐐻 𐑄𐐯𐑋, 𐐰𐑌𐐼 𐐯𐐿𐑅-𐐹𐑊𐐩𐑌𐐼 𐑄𐐯𐑋 𐐻𐐭 𐑄 𐐹𐐨𐐹𐑊 𐐱𐑂 𐐿𐐮𐑍 𐐢𐐮𐑋𐐸𐐴, 𐑅𐐬 𐑄𐐰𐐻 𐑄𐐩 𐑋𐐴𐐻 𐐲𐑌𐐼𐐲𐑉𐑅𐐻𐐰𐑌𐐼 𐐫𐑊 𐑄 𐐶𐐲𐑉𐐼𐑆 𐐸𐐶𐐮𐐽 𐐸𐐨 𐑅𐐹𐐩𐐿. 𐐈𐑌𐐼 𐐮𐐻 𐐿𐐩𐑋 𐐻𐐭 𐐹𐐪𐑅 𐑄𐐰𐐻 𐐪𐑁𐐻𐐲𐑉 𐐸𐐨 𐐸𐐰𐐼 𐐼𐐲𐑌 𐐫𐑊 𐑄𐐮𐑅, 𐑄𐐰𐐻 𐐿𐐮𐑍 𐐢𐐮𐑋𐐸𐐴 𐐼𐐮𐑅-𐑋𐐮𐑅𐐻 𐑄 𐑋𐐲𐑊𐐻𐐮𐐻𐐷𐐭𐐼, 𐐰𐑌𐐼 𐐿𐐫𐑆𐐼 𐑄𐐰𐐻 𐑄𐐩 𐑇𐐳𐐼 𐑉𐐨𐐻𐐲𐑉𐑌 𐐯𐑂𐑉𐐨 𐐶𐐲𐑌 𐐲𐑌𐐻𐐭 𐐸𐐮𐑆 𐐬𐑌 𐐸𐐵𐑅.

9. 𐐈𐑌𐐼 𐐮𐐻 𐐿𐐩𐑋 𐐻𐐭 𐐹𐐪𐑅 𐑄𐐰𐐻 𐐸𐐨 𐐿𐐫𐑆𐐼 𐑄𐐰𐐻 𐑄 𐐹𐑊𐐩𐐻𐑅 𐐸𐐶𐐮𐐽 𐐿𐐱𐑌𐐻𐐩𐑌𐐼 𐑄 𐑉𐐯𐐿𐐲𐑉𐐼 𐐱𐑂 𐐸𐐮𐑆 𐐹𐐨𐐹𐑊, 𐑁𐑉𐐱𐑋 𐑄 𐐻𐐴𐑋 𐑄𐐰𐐻 𐑄𐐩 𐑊𐐯𐑁𐐻 𐑄 𐑊𐐰𐑌𐐼 𐐱𐑂 𐐞𐐰𐑉𐐲𐐸𐐯𐑋𐑊𐐲, 𐑇𐐳𐐼 𐐺 𐐺𐑉𐐫𐐻 𐐺𐐨𐑁𐐬𐑉 𐐈𐑋𐐲𐑌, 𐑄𐐰𐐻 𐐸𐐨 𐑋𐐴𐐻 𐑉𐐨𐐼 𐑄𐐯𐑋. 𐐤𐐵, 𐐰𐑆 𐑅𐐭𐑌 𐐰𐑆 𐐈𐑋𐐲𐑌 𐐸𐐰𐐼 𐑉𐐯𐐼 𐑄 𐑉𐐯𐐿𐐲𐑉𐐼, 𐑄 𐐿𐐮𐑍 𐐮𐑌-𐐿𐐶𐐴𐑉𐐼 𐐱𐑂 𐐸𐐮𐑋 𐐻𐐭 𐑌𐐬 𐐮𐑁 𐐸𐐨 𐐿𐐳𐐼 𐐮𐑌𐐻𐐲𐑉𐐹𐑉𐐯𐐻 𐑊𐐰𐑍𐑀𐐶𐐯𐐾𐐯𐑆, 𐐰𐑌𐐼 𐐈𐑋𐐲𐑌 𐐻𐐬𐑊𐐼 𐐸𐐮𐑋 𐑄𐐰𐐻 𐐸𐐨

𐐿𐐳𐐼 𐑌𐐱𐐻. 𐐈𐑌𐐼 𐑄 𐐿𐐮𐑍 𐑅𐐯𐐼 𐐲𐑌𐐻𐐭 𐐸𐐮𐑋, 𐐺𐐨𐐮𐑍 𐑀𐑉𐐨𐑂𐐼 𐑁𐐫𐑉 𐑄 𐐰𐑁𐑊𐐮𐐿𐑇𐐲𐑌𐑆 𐐱𐑂 𐑋𐐴 𐐹𐐨𐐹𐑊, 𐐌 𐐿𐐫𐑆𐐼 𐑄𐐰𐐻 𐑁𐐫𐑉𐐻𐐨 𐐰𐑌𐐼 𐑃𐑉𐐨 𐐱𐑂 𐑋𐐴 𐐹𐐨𐐹𐑊 𐑇𐐳𐐼 𐐻𐐩𐐿 𐐲 𐐾𐐲𐑉𐑌𐐨 𐐮𐑌𐐻𐐭 𐑄 𐐶𐐮𐑊𐐼𐐲𐑉𐑌𐐯𐑅, 𐑄𐐰𐐻 𐑄𐐯𐑉𐐺𐐴 𐑄𐐩 𐑋𐐴𐐻 𐑁𐐴𐑌𐐼 𐑄 𐑊𐐰𐑌𐐼 𐐱𐑂 𐐞𐐰𐑉𐐲𐐸𐐯𐑋𐑊𐐲, 𐑄𐐰𐐻 𐐶𐐨 𐑋𐐴𐐻 𐐲𐐹𐐨𐑊 𐐲𐑌𐐻𐐭 𐐵𐑉 𐐺𐑉𐐯𐑄𐑉𐐯𐑌 𐐻𐐭 𐐼𐐯𐑊𐐮𐑂𐐲𐑉 𐐲𐑅 𐐵𐐻 𐐱𐑂 𐐺𐐱𐑌𐐼𐐩𐐾; 𐐰𐑌𐐼 𐑄𐐩 𐐶𐐲𐑉 𐑊𐐫𐑅𐐻 𐐮𐑌 𐑄 𐐶𐐮𐑊𐐼𐐲𐑉𐑌𐐯𐑅 𐑁𐐫𐑉 𐑄 𐑅𐐹𐐩𐑅 𐐱𐑂 𐑋𐐯𐑌𐐨 𐐼𐐩𐑆, 𐐷𐐯𐐻 𐑄𐐩 𐐶𐐲𐑉 𐐼𐐮𐑊𐐮𐐾𐐯𐑌𐐻, 𐐰𐑌𐐼 𐑁𐐵𐑌𐐼 𐑌𐐱𐐻 𐑄 𐑊𐐰𐑌𐐼 𐐱𐑂 𐐞𐐰𐑉𐐲𐐸𐐯𐑋𐑊𐐲, 𐐺𐐲𐐻 𐑉𐐨𐐻𐐲𐑉𐑌𐐼 𐐻𐐭 𐑄𐐮𐑅 𐑊𐐰𐑌𐐼, 𐐸𐐰𐑂𐐮𐑍 𐐻𐑉𐐰𐑂𐐯𐑊𐐼 𐐮𐑌 𐐲 𐑊𐐰𐑌𐐼 𐐲𐑋𐐲𐑍 𐑋𐐯𐑌𐐨 𐐶𐐫𐐻𐐲𐑉𐑆; 𐐸𐐰𐑂𐐮𐑍 𐐼𐐮𐑅𐐿𐐲𐑂𐐲𐑉𐐼 𐐲 𐑊𐐰𐑌𐐼 𐐸𐐶𐐮𐐽 𐐶𐐱𐑆 𐐿𐐲𐑂𐐲𐑉𐐼 𐐶𐐮𐑄 𐐺𐐬𐑌𐑆 𐐱𐑂 𐑋𐐯𐑌, 𐐰𐑌𐐼 𐐱𐑂 𐐺𐐨𐑅𐐻𐑅, 𐐯𐐻𐑅., 𐐰𐑌𐐼 𐐶𐐱𐑆 𐐫𐑊𐑅𐐬 𐐿𐐲𐑂𐐲𐑉𐐼 𐐶𐐮𐑄 𐑉𐐭𐐮𐑌𐑆 𐐱𐑂 𐐺𐐮𐑊𐐼𐐮𐑍𐑆 𐐱𐑂 𐐯𐑂𐐲𐑉𐐨 𐐿𐐴𐑌𐐼; 𐐸𐐰𐑂𐐮𐑍 𐐼𐐮𐑅𐐿𐐲𐑂𐐲𐑉𐐼 𐐲 𐑊𐐰𐑌𐐼 𐐸𐐶𐐮𐐽 𐐸𐐰𐐼 𐐺𐐮𐑌 𐐹𐐨𐐹𐑊𐐼 𐐶𐐮𐑄 𐐲 𐐹𐐨𐐹𐑊 𐐸𐐭 𐐶𐐲𐑉 𐐰𐑆 𐑌𐐭𐑋𐐲𐑉𐐲𐑅 𐐰𐑆 𐑄 𐐸𐐬𐑅𐐻𐑅 𐐱𐑂 𐐆𐑆𐑉𐐩𐐯𐑊. 𐐈𐑌𐐼 𐑁𐐫𐑉 𐐲 𐐻𐐯𐑅𐐻𐐮𐑋𐐬𐑌𐐨 𐑄𐐰𐐻 𐑄 𐑃𐐮𐑍𐑆 𐑄𐐰𐐻 𐑄𐐩 𐐸𐐰𐐼 𐑅𐐯𐐼 𐐪𐑉 𐐻𐑉𐐭, 𐑄𐐩 𐐸𐐰𐑂 𐐺𐑉𐐫𐐻 𐐻𐐶𐐯𐑌𐐻𐐨-𐑁𐐬𐑉 𐐹𐑊𐐩𐐻𐑅 𐐸𐐶𐐮𐐽 𐐪𐑉 𐑁𐐮𐑊𐐼 𐐶𐐮𐑄 𐐯𐑌𐑀𐑉𐐩𐑂𐐮𐑍𐑆, 𐐰𐑌𐐼 𐑄𐐩 𐐪𐑉 𐐱𐑂 𐐹𐐷𐐭𐑉 𐑀𐐬𐑊𐐼. 𐐈𐑌𐐼 𐐺𐐨𐐸𐐬𐑊𐐼, 𐐫𐑊𐑅𐐬, 𐑄𐐩 𐐸𐐰𐑂 𐐺𐑉𐐫𐐻 𐐺𐑉𐐯𐑅𐐻-𐐹𐑊𐐩𐐻𐑅, 𐐸𐐶𐐮𐐽 𐐪𐑉 𐑊𐐪𐑉𐐾, 𐐰𐑌𐐼 𐑄𐐩 𐐪𐑉 𐐱𐑂 𐐺𐑉𐐰𐑅 𐐰𐑌𐐼 𐐱𐑂 𐐿𐐱𐐹𐐲𐑉, 𐐰𐑌𐐼 𐐪𐑉 𐐹𐐲𐑉𐑁𐐯𐐿𐐻𐑊𐐨 𐑅𐐵𐑌𐐼. 𐐈𐑌𐐼 𐐲𐑀𐐯𐑌, 𐑄𐐩 𐐸𐐰𐑂 𐐺𐑉𐐫𐐻 𐑅𐐬𐑉𐐼𐑆, 𐑄 𐐸𐐮𐑊𐐻𐑅 𐑄𐐯𐑉𐐱𐑂 𐐸𐐰𐑂 𐐹𐐯𐑉𐐮𐑇𐐻, 𐐰𐑌𐐼 𐑄 𐐺𐑊𐐩𐐼𐑆 𐑄𐐯𐑉𐐱𐑂 𐐶𐐲𐑉 𐐿𐐰𐑍𐐿𐐲𐑉𐐼 𐐶𐐮𐑄 𐑉𐐲𐑅𐐻; 𐐰𐑌𐐼 𐑄𐐯𐑉 𐐮𐑆 𐑌𐐬 𐐶𐐲𐑌 𐐮𐑌 𐑄 𐑊𐐰𐑌𐐼 𐑄𐐰𐐻 𐐮𐑆 𐐩𐐺𐑊 𐐻𐐭 𐐮𐑌𐐻𐐲𐑉𐐹𐑉𐐯𐐻 𐑄 𐑊𐐰𐑍𐑀𐐶𐐩𐐾 𐐫𐑉 𐑄 𐐯𐑌𐑀𐑉𐐩𐑂𐐮𐑍𐑆 𐑄𐐰𐐻 𐐪𐑉 𐐱𐑌 𐑄 𐐹𐑊𐐩𐐻𐑅. 𐐜𐐯𐑉𐑁𐐬𐑉, 𐐌 𐑅𐐯𐐼 𐐲𐑌𐐻𐐭 𐑄𐐨, 𐐗𐐰𐑌𐑅𐐻 𐑄𐐵 𐐻𐑉𐐰𐑌𐑅𐑊𐐩𐐻? 𐐈𐑌𐐼 𐐌 𐑅𐐩 𐐲𐑌𐐻𐐭 𐑄𐐨 𐐲𐑀𐐯𐑌, 𐐤𐐬𐐯𐑅𐐻 𐑄𐐵 𐐱𐑂 𐐯𐑌𐐨 𐐶𐐲𐑌 𐑄𐐰𐐻 𐐿𐐰𐑌 𐐻𐑉𐐰𐑌𐑅𐑊𐐩𐐻? 𐐙𐐫𐑉 𐐌 𐐰𐑋 𐐼𐐨𐑆𐐴𐑉𐐲𐑅 𐑄𐐰𐐻 𐑄𐐨𐑆 𐑉𐐯𐐿𐐲𐑉𐐼𐑆 𐑇𐐳𐐼 𐐺𐐨 𐐻𐑉𐐰𐑌𐑅𐑊𐐩𐐻𐐯𐐼 𐐮𐑌𐐻𐐭 𐐵𐑉 𐑊𐐰𐑍𐑀𐐶𐐩𐐾; 𐑁𐐫𐑉, 𐐹𐐲𐑉𐐸𐐰𐐹𐑅, 𐑄𐐩 𐐶𐐮𐑊 𐑀𐐮𐑂 𐐲𐑅 𐐲 𐑌𐐱𐑊𐐯𐐾 𐐱𐑂 𐐲 𐑉𐐯𐑋𐑌𐐰𐑌𐐻 𐐱𐑂 𐑄 𐐹𐐨𐐹𐑊 𐐸𐐭 𐐸𐐰𐑂 𐐺𐐮𐑌 𐐼𐐯𐑅𐐻𐑉𐐱𐐮𐐼, 𐑁𐑉𐐱𐑋 𐐸𐐶𐐯𐑌𐑅 𐑄𐐨𐑆 𐑉𐐯𐐿𐐲𐑉𐐼𐑆 𐐿𐐩𐑋; 𐐫𐑉, 𐐹𐐲𐑉𐐸𐐰𐐹𐑅, 𐑄𐐩 𐐶𐐮𐑊 𐑀𐐮𐑂 𐐲𐑅 𐐲 𐑌𐐱𐑊𐐯𐐾 𐐱𐑂 𐑄𐐮𐑅 𐑂𐐯𐑉𐐨 𐐹𐐨𐐹𐑊 𐐸𐐭 𐐸𐐰𐑂 𐐺𐐮𐑌 𐐼𐐯𐑅𐐻𐑉𐐱𐐮𐐼; 𐐰𐑌𐐼 𐐌 𐐰𐑋 𐐼𐐨𐑆𐐴𐑉𐐲𐑅 𐐻𐐭 𐑌𐐬 𐑄 𐐿𐐫𐑆 𐐱𐑂 𐑄𐐩𐑉 𐐼𐐯𐑅𐐻𐑉𐐲𐐿𐑇𐐲𐑌.

10. 𐐤𐐵 𐐈𐑋𐐲𐑌 𐑅𐐯𐐼 𐐲𐑌𐐻𐐭 𐐸𐐮𐑋, 𐐌 𐐿𐐰𐑌 𐐰𐑇𐐭𐑉𐐯𐐼𐑊𐐨 𐐻𐐯𐑊 𐑄𐐨, 𐐄 𐐿𐐮𐑍, 𐐱𐑂 𐐲 𐑋𐐰𐑌 𐑄𐐰𐐻 𐐿𐐰𐑌 𐐻𐑉𐐰𐑌𐑅𐑊𐐩𐐻 𐑄 𐑉𐐯𐐿𐐲𐑉𐐼𐑆; 𐑁𐐫𐑉 𐐸𐐨 𐐸𐐰𐑆 𐐸𐐶𐐯𐑉𐐶𐐮𐑄 𐑄𐐰𐐻 𐐸𐐨 𐐿𐐰𐑌 𐑊𐐳𐐿, 𐐰𐑌𐐼 𐐻𐑉𐐰𐑌𐑅𐑊𐐩𐐻 𐐫𐑊 𐑉𐐯𐐿𐐲𐑉𐐼𐑆 𐑄𐐰𐐻 𐐪𐑉 𐐱𐑂 𐐩𐑌𐑇𐐯𐑌𐐻 𐐼𐐩𐐻; 𐐰𐑌𐐼 𐐮𐐻 𐐮𐑆 𐐲 𐑀𐐮𐑁𐐻 𐑁𐑉𐐱𐑋 𐐘𐐱𐐼. 𐐈𐑌𐐼 𐑄 𐑃𐐮𐑍𐑆 𐐪𐑉 𐐿𐐫𐑊𐐼 𐐮𐑌𐐻𐐲𐑉𐐹𐑉𐐯𐐻𐐲𐑉𐑆, 𐐰𐑌𐐼 𐑌𐐬 𐑋𐐰𐑌 𐐿𐐰𐑌 𐑊𐐳𐐿 𐐮𐑌 𐑄𐐯𐑋, 𐐯𐐿𐑅𐐯𐐹𐐻 𐐸𐐨 𐐺𐐨 𐐿𐐱𐑋𐐰𐑌𐐼𐐯𐐼, 𐑊𐐯𐑅𐐻 𐐸𐐨 𐑇𐐳𐐼 𐑊𐐳𐐿 𐑁𐐫𐑉 𐑄𐐰𐐻 𐐸𐐨 𐐫𐐻 𐑌𐐱𐐻, 𐐰𐑌𐐼 𐐸𐐨 𐑇𐐳𐐼 𐐹𐐯𐑉𐐮𐑇. 𐐈𐑌𐐼 𐐸𐐭𐑅𐐬𐐯𐑂𐐲𐑉 𐐮𐑆 𐐿𐐱𐑋𐐰𐑌𐐼𐐯𐐼 𐐻𐐭 𐑊𐐳𐐿 𐐮𐑌 𐑄𐐯𐑋, 𐑄 𐑅𐐩𐑋 𐐮𐑆 𐐿𐐫𐑊𐐼 𐑅𐐨𐐲𐑉. 𐐈𐑌𐐼 𐐺𐐨𐐸𐐬𐑊𐐼, 𐑄 𐐿𐐮𐑍 𐐱𐑂 𐑄 𐐹𐐨𐐹𐑊 𐐸𐐭 𐐪𐑉 𐐮𐑌 𐑄 𐑊𐐰𐑌𐐼 𐐱𐑂 𐐞𐐰𐑉𐐲𐐸𐐯𐑋𐑊𐐲, 𐐮𐑆 𐑄 𐑋𐐰𐑌 𐑄𐐰𐐻 𐐮𐑆 𐐿𐐱𐑋𐐰𐑌𐐼𐐯𐐼 𐐻𐐭 𐐼𐐭 𐑄𐐨𐑆 𐑃𐐮𐑍𐑆, 𐐰𐑌𐐼 𐐸𐐭 𐐸𐐰𐑆 𐑄𐐮𐑅 𐐸𐐴 𐑀𐐮𐑁𐐻 𐑁𐑉𐐱𐑋 𐐘𐐱𐐼. 𐐈𐑌𐐼 𐑄 𐐿𐐮𐑍 𐑅𐐯𐐼 𐑄𐐰𐐻 𐐲 𐑅𐐨𐐲𐑉 𐐮𐑆 𐑀𐑉𐐩𐐻𐐲𐑉 𐑄𐐰𐑌 𐐲 𐐹𐑉𐐱𐑁𐐯𐐻. 𐐈𐑌𐐼 𐐈𐑋𐐲𐑌 𐑅𐐯𐐼 𐑄𐐰𐐻 𐐲 𐑅𐐨𐐲𐑉 𐐮𐑆 𐐲 𐑉𐐯𐑂𐐯𐑊𐐩𐐻𐐲𐑉 𐐰𐑌𐐼 𐐲 𐐹𐑉𐐱𐑁𐐯𐐻 𐐫𐑊𐑅𐐬; 𐐰𐑌𐐼 𐐲 𐑀𐐮𐑁𐐻 𐐸𐐶𐐮𐐽 𐐮𐑆 𐑀𐑉𐐩𐐻𐐲𐑉 𐐿𐐰𐑌 𐑌𐐬 𐑋𐐰𐑌 𐐸𐐰𐑂, 𐐯𐐿𐑅𐐯𐐹𐐻 𐐸𐐨 𐑇𐐳𐐼 𐐹𐐲𐑆𐐯𐑅 𐑄 𐐹𐐵𐐲𐑉 𐐱𐑂 𐐘𐐱𐐼, 𐐸𐐶𐐮𐐽 𐑌𐐬 𐑋𐐰𐑌 𐐿𐐰𐑌; 𐐷𐐯𐐻 𐐲 𐑋𐐰𐑌 𐑋𐐩 𐐸𐐰𐑂 𐑀𐑉𐐩𐐻 𐐹𐐵𐐲𐑉 𐑀𐐮𐑂𐐲𐑌 𐐸𐐮𐑋 𐑁𐑉𐐱𐑋 𐐘𐐱𐐼. 𐐒𐐲𐐻 𐐲 𐑅𐐨𐐲𐑉 𐐿𐐰𐑌 𐑌𐐬 𐐱𐑂 𐑃𐐮𐑍𐑆 𐐸𐐶𐐮𐐽 𐐪𐑉 𐐹𐐰𐑅𐐻, 𐐰𐑌𐐼 𐐫𐑊𐑅𐐬 𐐱𐑂 𐑃𐐮𐑍𐑆 𐐸𐐶𐐮𐐽 𐐪𐑉 𐐻𐐭 𐐿𐐲𐑋, 𐐰𐑌𐐼 𐐺𐐴 𐑄𐐯𐑋 𐑇𐐰𐑊 𐐫𐑊 𐑃𐐮𐑍𐑆 𐐺𐐨 𐑉𐐯𐑂𐐨𐑊𐐼, 𐐫𐑉, 𐑉𐐪𐑄𐐲𐑉, 𐑇𐐰𐑊 𐑅𐐨𐐿𐑉𐐯𐐻 𐑃𐐮𐑍𐑆 𐐺𐐨 𐑋𐐩𐐼 𐑋𐐰𐑌𐐮𐑁𐐯𐑅𐐻, 𐐰𐑌𐐼 𐐸𐐮𐐼𐐲𐑌 𐑃𐐮𐑍𐑆 𐑇𐐰𐑊 𐐿𐐲𐑋 𐐻𐐭 𐑊𐐴𐐻, 𐐰𐑌𐐼 𐑃𐐮𐑍𐑆 𐐸𐐶𐐮𐐽 𐐪𐑉 𐑌𐐱𐐻 𐑌𐐬𐑌 𐑇𐐰𐑊 𐐺𐐨 𐑋𐐩𐐼 𐑌𐐬𐑌 𐐺𐐴 𐑄𐐯𐑋, 𐐰𐑌𐐼 𐐫𐑊𐑅𐐬 𐑃𐐮𐑍𐑆 𐑇𐐰𐑊 𐐺𐐨 𐑋𐐩𐐼 𐑌𐐬𐑌 𐐺𐐴 𐑄𐐯𐑋 𐐸𐐶𐐮𐐽 𐐲𐑄𐐲𐑉𐐶𐐴𐑆 𐐿𐐳𐐼 𐑌𐐱𐐻 𐐺𐐨 𐑌𐐬𐑌. 𐐜𐐲𐑅 𐐘𐐱𐐼 𐐸𐐰𐑆 𐐹𐑉𐐬𐑂𐐴𐐼𐐯𐐼 𐐲 𐑋𐐨𐑌𐑆 𐑄𐐰𐐻 𐑋𐐰𐑌, 𐑃𐑉𐐭 𐑁𐐩𐑃, 𐑋𐐴𐐻 𐐶𐐲𐑉𐐿 𐑋𐐴𐐻𐐨 𐑋𐐮𐑉𐐲𐐿𐑊𐑆; 𐑄𐐯𐑉𐑁𐐬𐑉 𐐸𐐨 𐐺𐐨𐐿𐐲𐑋𐐯𐑃 𐐲 𐑀𐑉𐐩𐐻 𐐺𐐯𐑌𐐯𐑁𐐮𐐻 𐐻𐐭 𐐸𐐮𐑆 𐑁𐐯𐑊𐐬-𐐺𐐨𐐮𐑍𐑆.

11. 𐐈𐑌𐐼 𐑌𐐵 𐐸𐐶𐐯𐑌 𐐈𐑋𐐲𐑌 𐐸𐐰𐐼 𐑋𐐩𐐼 𐐰𐑌 𐐯𐑌𐐼 𐐱𐑂 𐑅𐐹𐐨𐐿𐐮𐑍 𐑄𐐨𐑆 𐐶𐐲𐑉𐐼𐑆, 𐑄 𐐿𐐮𐑍 𐑉𐐨𐐾𐐱𐐮𐑅𐐻 𐐯𐐿𐑅𐐨𐐼𐐮𐑍𐑊𐐨, 𐐰𐑌𐐼 𐑀𐐩𐑂 𐑃𐐰𐑍𐐿𐑅 𐐻𐐭 𐐘𐐱𐐼, 𐑅𐐩𐐮𐑍, 𐐔𐐵𐐻𐑊𐐯𐑅 𐐲 𐑀𐑉𐐩𐐻 𐑋𐐮𐑅𐐻𐐲𐑉𐐨 𐐮𐑆 𐐿𐐱𐑌𐐻𐐩𐑌𐐼 𐐶𐐮𐑄𐐮𐑌 𐑄𐐨𐑆 𐐹𐑊𐐩𐐻𐑅, 𐐰𐑌𐐼 𐑄𐐨𐑆 𐐮𐑌𐐻𐐲𐑉𐐹𐑉𐐯𐐻𐐲𐑉𐑆 𐐶𐐲𐑉 𐐼𐐵𐐻𐑊𐐯𐑅 𐐹𐑉𐐨𐐹𐐩𐑉𐐼 𐑁𐐫𐑉 𐑄 𐐹𐐲𐑉𐐹𐐲𐑅 𐐱𐑂

𐐲𐑌𐑁𐐬𐑊𐐼𐐮𐑍 𐐫𐑊 𐑅𐐲𐐽 𐑋𐐮𐑅𐐻𐐲𐑉𐐨𐑆 𐐻𐐭 𐑄 𐐽𐐮𐑊𐐼𐑉𐐯𐑌 𐐱𐑂 𐑋𐐯𐑌. 𐐄 𐐸𐐵 𐑋𐐪𐑉𐑂𐐯𐑊𐐲𐑅 𐐪𐑉 𐑄 𐐶𐐲𐑉𐐿𐑅 𐐱𐑂 𐑄 𐐢𐐫𐑉𐐼, 𐐰𐑌𐐼 𐐸𐐵 𐑊𐐱𐑍 𐐼𐐲𐑃 𐐸𐐨 𐑅𐐲𐑁𐐲𐑉 𐐶𐐮𐑄 𐐸𐐮𐑆 𐐹𐐨𐐹𐐲𐑊; 𐐷𐐩, 𐐰𐑌𐐼 𐐸𐐵 𐐺𐑊𐐴𐑌𐐼 𐐰𐑌𐐼 𐐮𐑋𐐹𐐯𐑌𐐯𐐻𐑉𐐲𐐺𐑊 𐐪𐑉 𐑄 𐐲𐑌𐐼𐐲𐑉𐑅𐐻𐐰𐑌𐐼𐐮𐑍𐑆 𐐱𐑂 𐑄 𐐽𐐮𐑊𐐼𐑉𐐯𐑌 𐐱𐑂 𐑋𐐯𐑌, 𐑁𐐫𐑉 𐑄𐐩 𐐶𐐮𐑊 𐑌𐐱𐐻 𐑅𐐨𐐿 𐐶𐐮𐑆𐐼𐐲𐑋, 𐑌𐐨𐑄𐐲𐑉 𐐼𐐭 𐑄𐐩 𐐼𐐮𐑆𐐴𐐲𐑉 𐑄𐐰𐐻 𐑇𐐨 𐑇𐐳𐐼 𐑉𐐭𐑊 𐐬𐑂𐐲𐑉 𐑄𐐯𐑋. 𐐏𐐩, 𐑄𐐩 𐐪𐑉 𐐰𐑆 𐐲 𐐶𐐴𐑊𐐼 𐑁𐑊𐐱𐐿 𐐸𐐶𐐮𐐽 𐑁𐑊𐐨𐑃 𐑁𐑉𐐱𐑋 𐑄 𐑇𐐯𐐹𐐲𐑉𐐼, 𐐰𐑌𐐼 𐑅𐐿𐐰𐐻𐐲𐑉𐐯𐑃, 𐐰𐑌𐐼 𐐪𐑉 𐐼𐑉𐐴𐑂𐐯𐑌, 𐐰𐑌𐐼 𐐪𐑉 𐐼𐐨𐑂𐐵𐑉𐐼 𐐺𐐴 𐑄 𐐺𐐨𐑅𐐻𐑅 𐐱𐑂 𐑄 𐑁𐐱𐑉𐐯𐑅𐐻.

𐐕𐐰𐐹𐐻𐐲𐑉 VI.

𐑄 𐐡𐐯𐐿𐐲𐑉𐐼 𐐱𐑂 𐐞𐐨𐑌𐐮𐑁.—𐐈𐑌 𐐲𐐿𐐵𐑌𐐻 𐐱𐑂 𐐸𐐮𐑆 𐐹𐐨𐐹𐐲𐑊, 𐑁𐑉𐐱𐑋 𐑄 𐐻𐐴𐑋 𐑄𐐩 𐑊𐐯𐑁𐐻 𐑄 𐑊𐐰𐑌𐐼 𐐱𐑂 𐐞𐐯𐑉𐐲𐐸𐐯𐑋𐑊𐐲, 𐐲𐑌𐐻𐐮𐑊 𐑄 𐐻𐐴𐑋 𐑄𐐰𐐻 𐑄𐐩 𐐶𐐲𐑉 𐐼𐐯𐑊𐐮𐑂𐐲𐑉𐐼 𐐵𐐻 𐐱𐑂 𐑄 𐐸𐐰𐑌𐐼𐑆 𐐱𐑂 𐑄 𐐢𐐩𐑋𐐲𐑌𐐴𐐻𐑅.

1. 𐐌, 𐐞𐐨𐑌𐐮𐑁, 𐐸𐐰𐑂𐐮𐑍 𐐺𐐮𐑌 𐐻𐐫𐐻 𐐮𐑌 𐐫𐑊 𐑄 𐑊𐐰𐑍𐑀𐐶𐐯𐐾 𐐱𐑂 𐑄 𐐤𐐨𐑁𐐴𐐻𐑅, 𐐰𐑌𐐼 𐐸𐐰𐑂𐐮𐑍 𐐸𐐰𐐼 𐐲 𐑌𐐱𐑊𐐯𐐾 𐐱𐑂 𐑄 𐑊𐐰𐑌𐐼 𐐱𐑂 𐐤𐐨𐑁𐐴, 𐐫𐑉 𐐱𐑂 𐑄 𐑊𐐰𐑌𐐼 𐐱𐑂 𐐵𐑉 𐑁𐐪𐑄𐐲𐑉𐑆' 𐑁𐐲𐑉𐑅𐐻 𐐮𐑌𐐸𐐯𐑉𐐮𐐻𐐲𐑌𐑅, 𐐰𐑌𐐼 𐐸𐐰𐑂𐐮𐑍 𐐺𐐮𐑌 𐑅𐐯𐑌𐐻 𐐰𐑆 𐐲 𐑅𐐹𐐴 𐐲𐑋𐐲𐑍 𐑄 𐐢𐐩𐑋𐐲𐑌𐐴𐐻𐑅, 𐑄𐐰𐐻 𐐌 𐑋𐐴𐐻 𐑅𐐹𐐴 𐐵𐐻 𐑄𐐯𐑉 𐑁𐐫𐑉𐑅𐐯𐑆, 𐑄𐐰𐐻 𐐵𐑉 𐐪𐑉𐑋𐐨 𐑋𐐴𐐻 𐐿𐐲𐑋 𐐲𐐹𐐱𐑌 𐑄𐐯𐑋 𐐰𐑌𐐼 𐐼𐐨𐑅𐐻𐑉𐐱𐐴 𐑄𐐯𐑋; 𐐺𐐲𐐻 𐐸𐐶𐐯𐑌 𐐌 𐑅𐐫 𐑄𐐰𐐻 𐐸𐐶𐐮𐐽 𐐶𐐱𐑆 𐑀𐐳𐐼 𐐲𐑋𐐲𐑍 𐑄𐐯𐑋, 𐐌 𐐶𐐱𐑆 𐐼𐐨𐑆𐐴𐑉𐐲𐑅 𐑄𐐰𐐻 𐑄𐐩 𐑇𐐳𐐼 𐑌𐐱𐐻 𐐺𐐨 𐐼𐐨𐑅𐐻𐑉𐐱𐐴𐐼; 𐑄𐐯𐑉𐑁𐐫𐑉 𐐌 𐐿𐐱𐑌𐐻𐐯𐑌𐐼𐐯𐐼 𐐶𐐮𐑄 𐑋𐐴 𐐺𐑉𐐯𐑃𐑉𐐯𐑌 𐐮𐑌 𐑄 𐐶𐐮𐑊𐐼𐐲𐑉𐑌𐐯𐑅, 𐑁𐐫𐑉 𐐌 𐐶𐐳𐐼 𐑄𐐰𐐻 𐐵𐑉 𐑉𐐭𐑊𐐲𐑉 𐑇𐐳𐐼 𐑋𐐩𐐿 𐐲 𐐻𐑉𐐨𐐻𐐨 𐐶𐐮𐑄 𐑄𐐯𐑋; 𐐺𐐲𐐻 𐐸𐐨 𐐺𐐨𐐮𐑍 𐐰𐑌 𐐫𐑅𐐻𐐨𐑉 𐐰𐑌𐐼 𐐲 𐐺𐑊𐐲𐐼-𐑃𐐲𐑉𐑅𐐻𐐨 𐑋𐐰𐑌, 𐐿𐐱𐑋𐐰𐑌𐐼𐐯𐐼 𐑄𐐰𐐻 𐐌 𐑇𐐳𐐼 𐐺𐐨 𐑅𐑊𐐩𐑌, 𐐺𐐲𐐻 𐐌 𐐶𐐱𐑆 𐑉𐐯𐑅𐐿𐐷𐐭𐐼 𐐺𐐴 𐑄 𐑇𐐯𐐼𐐮𐑍 𐐱𐑂 𐑋𐐲𐐽 𐐺𐑊𐐲𐐼; 𐑁𐐫𐑉 𐑁𐐪𐑄𐐲𐑉 𐑁𐐫𐐻 𐐲𐑀𐐯𐑌𐑅𐐻 𐑁𐐪𐑄𐐲𐑉, 𐐰𐑌𐐼 𐐺𐑉𐐲𐑄𐐲𐑉 𐐲𐑀𐐯𐑌𐑅𐐻 𐐺𐑉𐐲𐑄𐐲𐑉, 𐐲𐑌𐐻𐐮𐑊 𐑄 𐑀𐑉𐐩𐐻𐐲𐑉 𐑌𐐲𐑋𐐺𐐲𐑉 𐐱𐑂 𐐵𐑉 𐐪𐑉𐑋𐐨 𐐶𐐱𐑆 𐐼𐐨𐑅𐐻𐑉𐐱𐐴𐐼 𐐮𐑌 𐑄 𐐶𐐮𐑊𐐼𐐲𐑉𐑌𐐯𐑅; 𐐰𐑌𐐼 𐐶𐐨 𐑉𐐨𐐻𐐲𐑉𐑌𐐼, 𐑄𐐬𐑆 𐐱𐑂 𐐲𐑅 𐑄𐐰𐐻 𐐶𐐲𐑉 𐑅𐐹𐐩𐑉𐐼, 𐐻𐐭 𐑄 𐑊𐐰𐑌𐐼 𐐱𐑂 𐐞𐐯𐑉𐐲𐐸𐐯𐑋𐑊𐐲, 𐐻𐐭 𐑉𐐨𐑊𐐩𐐻 𐑄𐐰𐐻 𐐻𐐩𐑊 𐐻𐐭 𐑄𐐯𐑉 𐐶𐐴𐑂𐑆 𐐰𐑌𐐼 𐑄𐐯𐑉 𐐽𐐮𐑊𐐼𐑉𐐯𐑌. 𐐈𐑌𐐼 𐐷𐐯𐐻, 𐐌 𐐺𐐨𐐮𐑍 𐐬𐑂𐐲𐑉-𐑆𐐯𐑊𐐲𐑅 𐐻𐐭 𐐮𐑌𐐸𐐯𐑉𐐮𐐻 𐑄 𐑊𐐰𐑌𐐼 𐐱𐑂 𐐵𐑉 𐑁𐐪𐑄𐐲𐑉𐑆, 𐐿𐐲𐑊𐐯𐐿𐐻𐐯𐐼 𐐰𐑆 𐑋𐐯𐑌𐐨 𐐰𐑆 𐐶𐐲𐑉 𐐼𐐨𐑆𐐴𐑉𐐲𐑅 𐐻𐐭 𐑀𐐬 𐐲𐐹 𐐻𐐭 𐐹𐐲𐑆𐐯𐑅 𐑄 𐑊𐐰𐑌𐐼, 𐐰𐑌𐐼 𐑅𐐻𐐪𐑉𐐻𐐯𐐼 𐐲𐑀𐐯𐑌 𐐱𐑌 𐐵𐑉 𐐾𐐲𐑉𐑌𐐨 𐐮𐑌𐐻𐐭 𐑄 𐐶𐐮𐑊𐐼𐐲𐑉𐑌𐐯𐑅 𐐻𐐭 𐑀𐐬 𐐲𐐹 𐐻𐐭 𐑄 𐑊𐐰𐑌𐐼; 𐐺𐐲𐐻 𐐶𐐨 𐐶𐐲𐑉 𐑅𐑋𐐮𐐻𐐯𐑌 𐐶𐐮𐑄 𐑁𐐰𐑋𐐮𐑌 𐐰𐑌𐐼 𐑅𐐬𐑉 𐐲𐑁𐑊𐐮𐐿𐑇𐐲𐑌𐑆, 𐑁𐐫𐑉 𐐶𐐨 𐐶𐐲𐑉 𐑅𐑊𐐬 𐐻𐐭 𐑉𐐨𐑋𐐯𐑋𐐺𐐲𐑉 𐑄 𐐢𐐫𐑉𐐼 𐐵𐑉 𐐘𐐱𐐼. 𐐤𐐯𐑂𐐲𐑉𐑄𐐯𐑊𐐯𐑅, 𐐰𐑁𐐻𐐲𐑉 𐑋𐐯𐑌𐐨 𐐼𐐩𐑆' 𐐶𐐪𐑌𐐼𐐲𐑉𐐮𐑍 𐐮𐑌 𐑄 𐐶𐐮𐑊𐐼𐐲𐑉𐑌𐐯𐑅, 𐐶𐐨 𐐹𐐮𐐽𐐻 𐐵𐑉 𐐻𐐯𐑌𐐻𐑅 𐐮𐑌 𐑄 𐐹𐑊𐐩𐑅 𐐸𐐶𐐯𐑉 𐐵𐑉 𐐺𐑉𐐯𐑃𐑉𐐯𐑌 𐐶𐐲𐑉 𐑅𐑊𐐩𐑌, 𐐸𐐶𐐮𐐽 𐐶𐐱𐑆 𐑌𐐨𐑉 𐐻𐐭 𐑄 𐑊𐐰𐑌𐐼 𐐱𐑂 𐐵𐑉 𐑁𐐪𐑄𐐲𐑉𐑆.

2. 𐐈𐑌𐐼 𐐮𐐻 𐐿𐐩𐑋 𐐻𐐭 𐐹𐐰𐑅 𐑄𐐰𐐻 𐐌 𐐶𐐯𐑌𐐻 𐐲𐑀𐐯𐑌 𐐶𐐮𐑄 𐑁𐐬𐑉 𐐱𐑂 𐑋𐐴 𐑋𐐯𐑌 𐐮𐑌𐐻𐐭 𐑄 𐑅𐐮𐐻𐐨, 𐐮𐑌 𐐲𐑌𐐻𐐭 𐑄 𐐿𐐮𐑍, 𐑄𐐰𐐻 𐐌 𐑋𐐴𐐻 𐑌𐐬 𐐱𐑂 𐑄 𐐼𐐮𐑅𐐹𐐬𐑆𐐮𐑇𐐲𐑌 𐐱𐑂 𐑄 𐐿𐐮𐑍, 𐐰𐑌𐐼 𐑄𐐰𐐻 𐐌 𐑋𐐴𐐻 𐑌𐐬 𐐮𐑁 𐐌 𐑋𐐴𐐻 𐑀𐐬 𐐮𐑌 𐐶𐐮𐑄 𐑋𐐴 𐐹𐐨𐐹𐐲𐑊 𐐰𐑌𐐼 𐐹𐐲𐑆𐐯𐑅 𐑄 𐑊𐐰𐑌𐐼 𐐮𐑌 𐐹𐐨𐑅. 𐐈𐑌𐐼 𐐌 𐐶𐐯𐑌𐐻 𐐮𐑌 𐐲𐑌𐐻𐐭 𐑄 𐐿𐐮𐑍, 𐐰𐑌𐐼 𐐸𐐨 𐐿𐐲𐑂𐐯𐑌𐐰𐑌𐐻𐐯𐐼 𐐶𐐮𐑄 𐑋𐐨 𐑄𐐰𐐻 𐐌 𐑋𐐴𐐻 𐐹𐐲𐑆𐐯𐑅 𐑄 𐑊𐐰𐑌𐐼 𐐱𐑂 𐐢𐐨𐐸𐐴-𐐤𐐨𐑁𐐴, 𐐰𐑌𐐼 𐑄 𐑊𐐰𐑌𐐼 𐐱𐑂 𐐟𐐴𐑊𐐲𐑋. 𐐈𐑌𐐼 𐐸𐐨 𐐫𐑊𐑅𐐬 𐐿𐐱𐑋𐐰𐑌𐐼𐐯𐐼 𐑄𐐰𐐻 𐐸𐐮𐑆 𐐹𐐨𐐹𐐲𐑊 𐑇𐐳𐐼 𐐼𐐨𐐹𐐪𐑉𐐻 𐐵𐐻 𐐱𐑂 𐑄 𐑊𐐰𐑌𐐼, 𐐰𐑌𐐼 𐐌 𐐰𐑌𐐼 𐑋𐐴 𐐹𐐨𐐹𐐲𐑊 𐐶𐐯𐑌𐐻 𐐮𐑌𐐻𐐭 𐑄 𐑊𐐰𐑌𐐼 𐑄𐐰𐐻 𐐶𐐨 𐑋𐐴𐐻 𐐹𐐲𐑆𐐯𐑅 𐐮𐐻. 𐐈𐑌𐐼 𐐶𐐨 𐐺𐐨𐑀𐐰𐑌 𐐻𐐭 𐐺𐐮𐑊𐐼 𐐺𐐮𐑊𐐼𐐮𐑍𐑆, 𐐰𐑌𐐼 𐐻𐐭 𐑉𐐨𐐹𐐩𐑉 𐑄 𐐶𐐫𐑊𐑆 𐐱𐑂 𐑄 𐑅𐐮𐐻𐐨, 𐐷𐐩, 𐐨𐑂𐐯𐑌 𐑄 𐐶𐐫𐑊𐑆 𐐱𐑂 𐑄 𐑅𐐮𐐻𐐨 𐐱𐑂 𐐢𐐨𐐸𐐴-𐐤𐐨𐑁𐐴, 𐐰𐑌𐐼 𐑄 𐑅𐐮𐐻𐐨 𐐱𐑂 𐐟𐐴𐑊𐐲𐑋. 𐐈𐑌𐐼 𐐶𐐨 𐐺𐐨𐑀𐐰𐑌 𐐻𐐭 𐐻𐐮𐑊 𐑄 𐑀𐑉𐐵𐑌𐐼, 𐐷𐐩, 𐐨𐑂𐐯𐑌 𐐶𐐮𐑄 𐐫𐑊 𐑋𐐰𐑌𐐲𐑉 𐐱𐑂 𐑅𐐨𐐼𐑆, 𐐶𐐮𐑄 𐑅𐐨𐐼𐑆 𐐱𐑂 𐐿𐐫𐑉𐑌, 𐐰𐑌𐐼 𐐱𐑂 𐐸𐐶𐐨𐐻, 𐐰𐑌𐐼 𐐱𐑂 𐐺𐐪𐑉𐑊𐐨, 𐐰𐑌𐐼 𐐶𐐮𐑄 𐑌𐐨𐐰𐑅, 𐐰𐑌𐐼 𐐶𐐮𐑄 𐑇𐐨𐐲𐑋, 𐐰𐑌𐐼 𐐶𐐮𐑄 𐑅𐐨𐐼𐑆 𐐱𐑂 𐐫𐑊 𐑋𐐰𐑌𐐲𐑉 𐐱𐑂 𐑁𐑉𐐭𐐻𐑅; 𐐰𐑌𐐼 𐐶𐐨 𐐼𐐮𐐼 𐐺𐐨𐑀𐐮𐑌 𐐻𐐭 𐑋𐐲𐑊𐐻𐐨𐐹𐑊𐐴 𐐰𐑌𐐼 𐐹𐑉𐐱𐑅𐐹𐐲𐑉 𐐮𐑌 𐑄 𐑊𐐰𐑌𐐼. 𐐤𐐵 𐐮𐐻 𐐶𐐱𐑆 𐑄 𐐿𐐲𐑌𐐮𐑍 𐐰𐑌𐐼 𐑄 𐐿𐑉𐐰𐑁𐐻𐐨𐑌𐐯𐑅 𐐱𐑂 𐐿𐐮𐑍 𐐢𐐩𐑋𐐲𐑌, 𐐻𐐭 𐐺𐑉𐐮𐑍 𐑋𐐴 𐐹𐐨𐐹𐐲𐑊 𐐮𐑌𐐻𐐭 𐐺𐐱𐑌𐐼𐐩𐐾, 𐑄𐐰𐐻 𐐸𐐨 𐐷𐐨𐑊𐐼𐐯𐐼 𐐲𐐹 𐑄 𐑊𐐰𐑌𐐼 𐑄𐐰𐐻 𐐶𐐨 𐑋𐐴𐐻 𐐹𐐲𐑆𐐯𐑅 𐐮𐐻.

3. 𐐜𐐩𐑉𐑁𐐬𐑉, 𐐮𐐻 𐐿𐐩𐑋 𐐻𐐭 𐐹𐐰𐑅, 𐑄𐐰𐐻 𐐰𐑁𐐻𐐲𐑉 𐐶𐐨 𐐸𐐰𐐼 𐐼𐐶𐐯𐑊𐐻 𐐮𐑌 𐑄 𐑊𐐰𐑌𐐼 𐑁𐐬𐑉 𐑄 𐑅𐐹𐐩𐑅 𐐱𐑂 𐐻𐐶𐐯𐑊𐑂 𐐷𐐨𐑉𐑆, 𐑄𐐰𐐻 𐐗𐐮𐑍 𐐢𐐩𐑋𐐲𐑌 𐐺𐐨𐑀𐐰𐑌 𐐻𐐭 𐑀𐑉𐐬 𐐲𐑌𐐨𐑆𐐨, 𐑊𐐯𐑅𐐻 𐐺𐐴 𐐯𐑌𐐨 𐑋𐐨𐑌𐑆 𐑋𐐴 𐐹𐐨𐐹𐑊 𐑇𐐳𐐼 𐐶𐐰𐐿𐑅 𐑅𐐻𐑉𐐫𐑍 𐐮𐑌 𐑄 𐑊𐐰𐑌𐐼, 𐐰𐑌𐐼 𐑄𐐰𐐻 𐑄𐐩 𐐿𐐳𐐼 𐑌𐐱𐐻 𐐬𐑂𐐲𐑉𐐹𐐵𐐲𐑉 𐑄𐐯𐑋 𐐰𐑌𐐼 𐐺𐑉𐐮𐑍 𐑄𐐯𐑋 𐐮𐑌𐐻𐐭 𐐺𐐱𐑌𐐼𐐲𐐾. 𐐤𐐵 𐑄𐐩 𐐶𐐲𐑉 𐐩 𐑊𐐩𐑆𐐨 𐐰𐑌𐐼 𐐰𐑌 𐐴𐐼𐐱𐑊𐐲𐐻𐑉𐐲𐑅 𐐹𐐨𐐹𐑊: 𐑄𐐩𐑉𐑁𐐬𐑉 𐑄𐐩 𐐶𐐲𐑉 𐐼𐐯𐑆𐐴𐑉𐐲𐑅 𐐻𐐭 𐐺𐑉𐐮𐑍 𐐲𐑅 𐐮𐑌𐐻𐐭 𐐺𐐱𐑌𐐼𐐲𐐾, 𐑄𐐰𐐻 𐑄𐐩 𐑋𐐴𐐻 𐑀𐑊𐐲𐐻 𐑄𐐯𐑋𐑅𐐯𐑊𐑂𐑆 𐐶𐐮𐑄 𐑄 𐑊𐐩𐐺𐐲𐑉𐑆 𐐱𐑂 𐐵𐑉 𐐸𐐰𐑌𐐼𐑆; 𐐷𐐩, 𐑄𐐰𐐻 𐑄𐐩 𐑋𐐴𐐻 𐑁𐐨𐑅𐐻 𐑄𐐯𐑋𐑅𐐯𐑊𐑂𐑆 𐐲𐐹𐐱𐑌 𐑄 𐑁𐑊𐐱𐐿𐑅 𐐱𐑂 𐐵𐑉 𐑁𐐨𐑊𐐼𐑆.

4. 𐐜𐐩𐑉𐑁𐐬𐑉 𐐮𐐻 𐐿𐐩𐑋 𐐻𐐭 𐐹𐐰𐑅 𐑄𐐰𐐻 𐐗𐐮𐑍 𐐢𐐩𐑋𐐲𐑌 𐐺𐐨𐑀𐐰𐑌 𐐻𐐭 𐑅𐐻𐐲𐑉 𐐲𐐹 𐐸𐐮𐑆 𐐹𐐨𐐹𐑊, 𐑄𐐰𐐻 𐑄𐐩 𐑇𐐳𐐼 𐐿𐐱𐑌𐐻𐐯𐑌𐐼 𐐶𐐮𐑄 𐑋𐐴 𐐹𐐨𐐹𐑊; 𐑄𐐩𐑉𐑁𐐬𐑉 𐑄𐐩𐑉 𐐺𐐨𐑀𐐰𐑌 𐐻𐐭 𐐺𐐨 𐐶𐐫𐑉𐑆 𐐰𐑌𐐼 𐐿𐐱𐑌𐐻𐐯𐑌𐑇𐐲𐑌𐑆 𐐮𐑌 𐑄 𐑊𐐰𐑌𐐼; 𐑁𐐬𐑉, 𐐮𐑌 𐑄 𐑃𐐲𐑉𐐻𐐨𐑌𐑃 𐐷𐐨𐑉 𐐱𐑂 𐑋𐐴 𐑉𐐩𐑌 𐐮𐑌 𐑄 𐑊𐐰𐑌𐐼 𐐱𐑂 𐐤𐐨𐑁𐐴, 𐐲𐐶𐐩 𐐱𐑌 𐑄 𐑅𐐵𐑃 𐐱𐑂 𐑄 𐑊𐐰𐑌𐐼 𐐱𐑂 𐐟𐐴𐑊𐐲𐑋, 𐐸𐐶𐐯𐑌 𐑋𐐴 𐐹𐐨𐐹𐑊 𐐶𐐲𐑉 𐐶𐐫𐐻𐐲𐑉𐐮𐑍 𐐰𐑌𐐼 𐑁𐐨𐐼𐐮𐑍 𐑄𐐯𐑉 𐑁𐑊𐐱𐐿𐑅, 𐐰𐑌𐐼 𐐻𐐮𐑊𐐮𐑍 𐑄𐐯𐑉 𐑊𐐰𐑌𐐼𐑆, 𐐩 𐑌𐐭𐑋𐐲𐑉𐐲𐑅 𐐸𐐬𐑅𐐻 𐐱𐑂 𐐢𐐩𐑋𐐲𐑌𐐴𐐻𐑅 𐐿𐐩𐑋 𐐲𐐹𐐱𐑌 𐑄𐐯𐑋, 𐐰𐑌𐐼 𐐺𐐨𐑀𐐰𐑌 𐐻𐐭 𐑅𐑊𐐩 𐑄𐐯𐑋, 𐐰𐑌𐐼 𐐻𐐭 𐐻𐐩𐐿 𐐱𐑁 𐑄𐐯𐑉 𐑁𐑊𐐱𐐿𐑅, 𐐰𐑌𐐼 𐑄 𐐿𐐫𐑉𐑌 𐐱𐑂 𐑄𐐯𐑉 𐑁𐐨𐑊𐐼𐑆. 𐐏𐐩, 𐐰𐑌𐐼 𐐮𐐻 𐐿𐐩𐑋 𐐻𐐭 𐐹𐐰𐑅 𐑄𐐰𐐻 𐑄𐐩 𐑁𐑊𐐯𐐼, 𐐫𐑊 𐑄𐐰𐐻 𐐶𐐲𐑉 𐑌𐐱𐐻 𐐬𐑂𐐲𐑉𐐻𐐩𐐿𐐲𐑌, 𐐨𐑂𐐲𐑌 𐐮𐑌𐐻𐐭 𐑄 𐑅𐐮𐐻𐐨 𐐱𐑂 𐐤𐐨𐑁𐐴, 𐐰𐑌𐐼 𐐼𐐮𐐼 𐐿𐐫𐑊 𐐲𐐹𐐱𐑌 𐑋𐐨 𐑁𐐬𐑉 𐐹𐑉𐐬𐐻𐐯𐐿𐑇𐐲𐑌.

5. 𐐈𐑌𐐼 𐐮𐐻 𐐿𐐩𐑋 𐐻𐐭 𐐹𐐰𐑅 𐑄𐐰𐐻 𐐌 𐐼𐐮𐐼 𐐪𐑉𐑋 𐑄𐐯𐑋 𐐶𐐮𐑄 𐐺𐐬𐑆, 𐐰𐑌𐐼 𐐶𐐮𐑄 𐐰𐑉𐐬𐑆, 𐐶𐐮𐑄 𐑅𐐬𐑉𐐼𐑆, 𐐰𐑌𐐼 𐐶𐐮𐑄 𐑅𐐮𐑋𐐮𐐻𐐲𐑉𐑆, 𐐰𐑌𐐼 𐐶𐐮𐑄 𐐿𐑊𐐲𐐺𐑆, 𐐰𐑌𐐼 𐐶𐐮𐑄 𐑅𐑊𐐮𐑍𐑆, 𐐰𐑌𐐼 𐐶𐐮𐑄 𐐫𐑊 𐑋𐐰𐑌𐐲𐑉 𐐱𐑂 𐐶𐐯𐐹𐐲𐑌𐑆 𐐸𐐶𐐮𐐽 𐐶𐐨 𐐿𐐳𐐼 𐐮𐑌𐑂𐐯𐑌𐐻, 𐐰𐑌𐐼 𐐌 𐐰𐑌𐐼 𐑋𐐴 𐐹𐐨𐐹𐑊 𐐼𐐮𐐼 𐑀𐐬 𐑁𐐬𐑉𐑃 𐐲𐑀𐐯𐑌𐑅𐐻 𐑄 𐐢𐐩𐑋𐐲𐑌𐐴𐐻𐑅 𐐻𐐭 𐐺𐐰𐐻𐑊; 𐐷𐐩, 𐐮𐑌 𐑄 𐑅𐐻𐑉𐐯𐑍𐑃 𐐱𐑂 𐑄 𐐢𐐫𐑉𐐼 𐐼𐐮𐐼 𐐶𐐨 𐑀𐐬 𐑁𐐬𐑉𐑃 𐐻𐐭 𐐺𐐰𐐻𐑊 𐐲𐑀𐐯𐑌𐑅𐐻 𐑄 𐐢𐐩𐑋𐐲𐑌𐐴𐐻𐑅; 𐑁𐐬𐑉 𐐌 𐐰𐑌𐐼 𐑋𐐴 𐐹𐐨𐐹𐑊 𐐼𐐮𐐼 𐐿𐑉𐐴 𐑋𐐴𐐻𐐮𐑊𐐨 𐐻𐐭 𐑄 𐐢𐐫𐑉𐐼 𐑄𐐰𐐻 𐐸𐐨 𐐶𐐳𐐼 𐐼𐐮𐑊𐐮𐑂𐐲𐑉 𐐲𐑅 𐐵𐐻 𐐱𐑂 𐑄 𐐸𐐰𐑌𐐼𐑆 𐐱𐑂 𐐵𐑉 𐐯𐑌𐐲𐑋𐐨𐑆, 𐑁𐐬𐑉 𐐶𐐨 𐐶𐐲𐑉 𐐲𐐶𐐩𐐿𐐲𐑌𐐼 𐐻𐐭 𐐩 𐑉𐐨𐑋𐐯𐑋𐐺𐑉𐐲𐑌𐑅 𐐱𐑂 𐑄 𐐼𐐮𐑊𐐮𐑂𐐲𐑉𐐲𐑌𐑅 𐐱𐑂 𐐵𐑉 𐑁𐐪𐑄𐐲𐑉𐑆. 𐐈𐑌𐐼 𐐘𐐱𐐼 𐐼𐐮𐐼 𐐸𐐨𐑉 𐐵𐑉 𐐿𐑉𐐴𐑆 𐐰𐑌𐐼 𐐼𐐮𐐼 𐐰𐑌𐑅𐐲𐑉 𐐵𐑉 𐐹𐑉𐐩𐐲𐑉𐑆; 𐐰𐑌𐐼 𐐶𐐨 𐐼𐐮𐐼 𐑀𐐬 𐑁𐐬𐑉𐑃 𐐮𐑌 𐐸𐐮𐑆 𐑋𐐴𐐻; 𐐷𐐩, 𐐶𐐨 𐐼𐐮𐐼 𐑀𐐬 𐑁𐐬𐑉𐑃 𐐲𐑀𐐯𐑌𐑅𐐻 𐑄 𐐢𐐩𐑋𐐲𐑌𐐴𐐻𐑅, 𐐰𐑌𐐼 𐐮𐑌 𐐶𐐲𐑌 𐐼𐐩 𐐰𐑌𐐼 𐐩 𐑌𐐴𐐻, 𐐶𐐨 𐐼𐐮𐐼 𐑅𐑊𐐩 𐑃𐑉𐐨 𐑃𐐵𐑆𐐲𐑌𐐼 𐐰𐑌𐐼 𐑁𐐫𐑉𐐻𐐨-𐑃𐑉𐐨: 𐐶𐐨 𐐼𐐮𐐼 𐑅𐑊𐐩 𐑄𐐯𐑋, 𐐨𐑂𐐲𐑌 𐐲𐑌𐐻𐐮𐑊 𐐶𐐨 𐐸𐐰𐐼 𐐼𐑉𐐮𐑂𐐲𐑌 𐑄𐐯𐑋 𐐵𐐻 𐐱𐑂 𐐵𐑉 𐑊𐐰𐑌𐐼. 𐐈𐑌𐐼 𐐌, 𐑋𐐴𐑅𐐯𐑊𐑁, 𐐶𐐮𐑄 𐑋𐐴𐑌 𐐬𐑌 𐐸𐐰𐑌𐐼𐑆, 𐐼𐐮𐐼 𐐸𐐯𐑊𐐹 𐐻𐐭 𐐺𐐯𐑉𐐨 𐑄𐐯𐑉 𐐼𐐯𐐼. 𐐈𐑌𐐼 𐐺𐐨𐐸𐐬𐑊𐐼, 𐐻𐐭 𐐵𐑉 𐑀𐑉𐐩𐐻 𐑅𐐱𐑉𐐬 𐐰𐑌𐐼 𐑊𐐰𐑋𐐲𐑌𐐻𐐩𐑇𐐲𐑌, 𐐻𐐭 𐐸𐐲𐑌𐐼𐑉𐐲𐐼 𐐰𐑌𐐼 𐑅𐐯𐑂𐐲𐑌𐐻𐐨-𐑌𐐴𐑌 𐐱𐑂 𐐵𐑉 𐐺𐑉𐐯𐑄𐑉𐐲𐑌 𐐶𐐲𐑉 𐑅𐑊𐐩𐑌.

6. 𐐈𐑌𐐼 𐐮𐐻 𐐿𐐩𐑋 𐐻𐐭 𐐹𐐰𐑅 𐑄𐐰𐐻 𐐶𐐨 𐐲𐑀𐐯𐑌 𐐺𐐨𐑀𐐰𐑌 𐐻𐐭 𐐯𐑅𐐻𐐰𐐺𐑊𐐮𐑇 𐑄 𐐿𐐮𐑍𐐼𐐲𐑋, 𐐰𐑌𐐼 𐐶𐐨 𐐲𐑀𐐯𐑌 𐐺𐐨𐑀𐐰𐑌 𐐻𐐭 𐐹𐐲𐑆𐐯𐑅 𐑄 𐑊𐐰𐑌𐐼 𐐮𐑌 𐐹𐐨𐑅. 𐐈𐑌𐐼 𐐌 𐐿𐐫𐑆𐐼 𐑄𐐰𐐻 𐑄𐐩𐑉 𐑇𐐳𐐼 𐐺𐐨 𐐶𐐯𐐹𐐲𐑌𐑆 𐐱𐑂 𐐶𐐫𐑉 𐑋𐐩𐐼 𐐱𐑂 𐐯𐑂𐐲𐑉𐐨 𐐿𐐴𐑌𐐼, 𐑄𐐰𐐻 𐑄𐐩𐑉𐐺𐐴 𐐌 𐑋𐐴𐐻 𐐸𐐰𐑂 𐐶𐐯𐐹𐐲𐑌𐑆 𐑁𐐬𐑉 𐑋𐐴 𐐹𐐨𐐹𐑊 𐐲𐑀𐐯𐑌𐑅𐐻 𐑄 𐐻𐐴𐑋 𐑄 𐐢𐐩𐑋𐐲𐑌𐐴𐐻𐑅 𐑇𐐳𐐼 𐐿𐐲𐑋 𐐲𐐹 𐐲𐑀𐐯𐑌 𐐻𐐭 𐐶𐐫𐑉 𐐲𐑀𐐯𐑌𐑅𐐻 𐑋𐐴 𐐹𐐨𐐹𐑊. 𐐈𐑌𐐼 𐐌 𐑅𐐯𐐻 𐑀𐐪𐑉𐐼𐑆 𐑉𐐵𐑌𐐼 𐐲𐐺𐐵𐐻 𐑄 𐑊𐐰𐑌𐐼, 𐑄𐐰𐐻 𐑄 𐐢𐐩𐑋𐐲𐑌𐐴𐐻𐑅 𐑋𐐴𐐻 𐑌𐐱𐐻 𐐿𐐲𐑋 𐐲𐐹𐐱𐑌 𐐲𐑅 𐐲𐑀𐐯𐑌 𐐲𐑌𐐶𐐩𐑉𐑆 𐐰𐑌𐐼 𐐼𐐨𐑅𐐻𐑉𐐱𐐴 𐐲𐑅; 𐐰𐑌𐐼 𐑄𐐲𐑅 𐐌 𐐼𐐮𐐼 𐑀𐐪𐑉𐐼 𐑋𐐴 𐐹𐐨𐐹𐑊 𐐰𐑌𐐼 𐑋𐐴 𐑁𐑊𐐱𐐿𐑅, 𐐰𐑌𐐼 𐐿𐐨𐐹 𐑄𐐯𐑋 𐑁𐑉𐐱𐑋 𐑁𐐫𐑊𐐮𐑍 𐐮𐑌𐐻𐐭 𐑄 𐐸𐐰𐑌𐐼𐑆 𐐱𐑂 𐐵𐑉 𐐯𐑌𐐲𐑋𐐨𐑆.

7. 𐐈𐑌𐐼 𐐮𐐻 𐐿𐐩𐑋 𐐻𐐭 𐐹𐐰𐑅 𐑄𐐰𐐻 𐐶𐐨 𐐼𐐮𐐼 𐐮𐑌𐐸𐐯𐑉𐐮𐐻 𐑄 𐑊𐐰𐑌𐐼 𐐱𐑂 𐐵𐑉 𐑁𐐪𐑄𐐲𐑉𐑆 𐑁𐐬𐑉 𐑋𐐯𐑌𐐨 𐐷𐐨𐑉𐑆, 𐐷𐐩, 𐑁𐐬𐑉 𐑄 𐑅𐐹𐐩𐑅 𐐱𐑂 𐐻𐐶𐐯𐑌𐐻𐐨 𐐰𐑌𐐼 𐐻𐐭 𐐷𐐨𐑉𐑆. 𐐈𐑌𐐼 𐐌 𐐼𐐮𐐼 𐐿𐐫𐑆 𐑄𐐰𐐻 𐑄 𐑋𐐯𐑌 𐑇𐐳𐐼 𐐻𐐮𐑊 𐑄 𐑀𐑉𐐵𐑌𐐼, 𐐰𐑌𐐼 𐑉𐐩𐑆 𐐫𐑊 𐑋𐐰𐑌𐐲𐑉 𐐱𐑂 𐑀𐑉𐐩𐑌 𐐰𐑌𐐼 𐐫𐑊 𐑋𐐰𐑌𐐲𐑉 𐐱𐑂 𐑁𐑉𐐭𐐻 𐐱𐑂 𐐯𐑂𐐲𐑉𐐨 𐐿𐐴𐑌𐐼. 𐐈𐑌𐐼 𐐌 𐐼𐐮𐐼 𐐿𐐫𐑆 𐑄𐐰𐐻 𐑄 𐐶𐐮𐑋𐐲𐑌 𐑇𐐳𐐼 𐑅𐐹𐐮𐑌, 𐐰𐑌𐐼 𐐻𐐶𐐮𐑊, 𐐰𐑌𐐼 𐐶𐐲𐑉𐐿, 𐐰𐑌𐐼 𐐶𐐲𐑉𐐿 𐐫𐑊 𐑋𐐰𐑌𐐲𐑉 𐐱𐑂 𐑁𐐴𐑌 𐑊𐐮𐑌𐐲𐑌; 𐐷𐐩, 𐐰𐑌𐐼 𐐿𐑊𐐱𐑃 𐐱𐑂 𐐯𐑂𐐲𐑉𐐨 𐐿𐐴𐑌𐐼, 𐑄𐐰𐐻 𐐶𐐨 𐑋𐐴𐐻 𐐿𐑊𐐬𐑄 𐐵𐑉 𐑌𐐩𐐿𐐯𐐼𐑌𐐯𐑅; 𐐰𐑌𐐼 𐑄𐐲𐑅 𐐶𐐨 𐐼𐐮𐐼 𐐹𐑉𐐱𐑅𐐹𐐲𐑉 𐐮𐑌 𐑄 𐑊𐐰𐑌𐐼—𐑄𐐲𐑅 𐐶𐐨 𐐼𐐮𐐼 𐐸𐐰𐑂 𐐿𐐱𐑌𐐻𐐮𐑌𐐷𐐭𐐲𐑊 𐐹𐐨𐑅 𐐮𐑌 𐑄 𐑊𐐰𐑌𐐼 𐑁𐐬𐑉 𐑄 𐑅𐐹𐐩𐑅 𐐱𐑂 𐐻𐐶𐐯𐑌𐐻𐐨 𐐰𐑌𐐼 𐐻𐐭 𐐷𐐨𐑉𐑆.

8. 𐐈𐑌𐐼 𐐮𐐻 𐐿𐐩𐑋 𐐻𐐭 𐐹𐐰𐑅 𐑄𐐰𐐻 𐐗𐐮𐑍 𐐢𐐩𐑋𐐲𐑌 𐐼𐐴𐐼, 𐐰𐑌𐐼 𐐸𐐮𐑆 𐑅𐐲𐑌 𐐺𐐨𐑀𐐰𐑌 𐐻𐐭 𐑉𐐩𐑌 𐐮𐑌 𐐸𐐮𐑆

𐑅𐐻𐐯𐐼. 𐐈𐑌𐐼 𐐸𐐨 𐐺𐐨𐑀𐐰𐑌 𐐻𐐭 𐑅𐐻𐐲𐑉 𐐸𐐮𐑆 𐐹𐐨𐐹𐐲𐑊 𐐲𐐹 𐐮𐑌 𐑉𐐨𐐺𐐯𐑊𐐷𐐲𐑌 𐐲𐑀𐐯𐑌𐑅𐐻 𐑋𐐴 𐐹𐐨𐐹𐐲𐑊; 𐑄𐐯𐑉𐑁𐐬𐑉 𐑄𐐩 𐐺𐐨𐑀𐐰𐑌 𐐻𐐭 𐐹𐑉𐐨𐐹𐐯𐑉 𐑁𐐫𐑉 𐐶𐐫𐑉, 𐐰𐑌𐐼 𐐻𐐭 𐐿𐐲𐑋 𐐲𐐹 𐐻𐐭 𐐺𐐰𐐻𐐲𐑊 𐐲𐑀𐐯𐑌𐑅𐐻 𐑋𐐴 𐐹𐐨𐐹𐐲𐑊. 𐐒𐐲𐐻 𐐴 𐐸𐐰𐐼 𐑅𐐯𐑌𐐻 𐑋𐐴 𐑅𐐹𐐴𐑆 𐐵𐐻 𐑉𐐵𐑌𐐼 𐐲𐐺𐐵𐐻 𐑄 𐑊𐐰𐑌𐐼 𐐱𐑂 𐐟𐐯𐑋𐑊𐐱𐑌, 𐑄𐐰𐐻 𐐴 𐑋𐐴𐐻 𐐼𐐮𐑅𐐿𐐲𐑂𐐲𐑉 𐑄𐐩𐑉 𐐹𐑉𐐯𐐹𐐲𐑉𐐩𐑇𐐲𐑌𐑆, 𐑄𐐰𐐻 𐐴 𐑋𐐴𐐻 𐑀𐐪𐑉𐐼 𐐲𐑀𐐯𐑌𐑅𐐻 𐑄𐐯𐑋, 𐑄𐐰𐐻 𐑄𐐩 𐑋𐐴𐐻 𐑌𐐱𐐻 𐐿𐐲𐑋 𐐲𐐹𐐱𐑌 𐑋𐐴 𐐹𐐨𐐹𐐲𐑊 𐐰𐑌𐐼 𐐼𐐨𐑅𐐻𐑉𐐱𐐮 𐑄𐐯𐑋.

9. 𐐈𐑌𐐼 𐐮𐐻 𐐿𐐩𐑋 𐐻𐐭 𐐹𐐰𐑅 𐑄𐐰𐐻 𐑄𐐩 𐐿𐐩𐑋 𐐲𐐹 𐐲𐐹𐐱𐑌 𐑄 𐑌𐐫𐑉𐑃 𐐱𐑂 𐑄 𐑊𐐰𐑌𐐼 𐐱𐑂 𐐟𐐴𐑊𐐱𐑋, 𐐶𐐮𐑄 𐑄𐐩𐑉 𐑌𐐭𐑋𐐲𐑉𐐲𐑅 𐐸𐐬𐑅𐐻𐑅, 𐑋𐐯𐑌 𐐪𐑉𐑋𐐼 𐐶𐐮𐑄 𐐺𐐬𐑆, 𐐰𐑌𐐼 𐐶𐐮𐑄 𐐰𐑉𐐬𐑆, 𐐰𐑌𐐼 𐐶𐐮𐑄 𐑅𐐫𐑉𐐼𐑆, 𐐰𐑌𐐼 𐐶𐐮𐑄 𐑅𐐮𐑋𐐨𐐻𐐲𐑉𐑆, 𐐰𐑌𐐼 𐐶𐐮𐑄 𐑅𐐻𐐬𐑌𐑆, 𐐰𐑌𐐼 𐐶𐐮𐑄 𐑅𐑊𐐮𐑍𐑆; 𐐰𐑌𐐼 𐑄𐐩 𐐸𐐰𐐼 𐑄𐐩𐑉 𐐸𐐯𐐼𐑆 𐑇𐐩𐑂𐐼, 𐑄𐐰𐐻 𐑄𐐩 𐐶𐐲𐑉 𐑌𐐩𐐿𐐯𐐼: 𐐰𐑌𐐼 𐑄𐐩 𐐶𐐲𐑉 𐑀𐐲𐑉𐐼𐐯𐐼 𐐶𐐮𐑄 𐐰 𐑊𐐯𐑄𐐲𐑉𐑌 𐑀𐐲𐑉𐐼𐐲𐑊 𐐲𐐺𐐵𐐻 𐑄𐐩𐑉 𐑊𐐱𐐮𐑌𐑆.

10. 𐐈𐑌𐐼 𐐮𐐻 𐐿𐐩𐑋 𐐻𐐭 𐐹𐐰𐑅 𐑄𐐰𐐻 𐐴 𐐿𐐫𐑆𐐼 𐑄𐐰𐐻 𐑄 𐐶𐐮𐑋𐐯𐑌 𐐰𐑌𐐼 𐐽𐐮𐑊𐐼𐑉𐐯𐑌 𐐱𐑂 𐑋𐐴 𐐹𐐨𐐹𐐲𐑊 𐑇𐐳𐐼 𐐺𐐨 𐐸𐐮𐐼 𐐮𐑌 𐑄 𐐶𐐮𐑊𐐼𐐲𐑉𐑌𐐯𐑅: 𐐰𐑌𐐼 𐐴 𐐫𐑊𐑅𐐬 𐐿𐐫𐑆𐐼 𐑄𐐰𐐻 𐐫𐑊 𐑋𐐴 𐐬𐑊𐐼 𐑋𐐯𐑌 𐑄𐐰𐐻 𐐿𐐳𐐼 𐐺𐐩𐑉 𐐪𐑉𐑋𐑆, 𐐰𐑌𐐼 𐐫𐑊𐑅𐐬 𐐫𐑊 𐑋𐐴 𐐷𐐲𐑍 𐑋𐐯𐑌 𐑄𐐰𐐻 𐐶𐐲𐑉 𐐩𐐺𐐲𐑊 𐐻𐐭 𐐺𐐩𐑉 𐐪𐑉𐑋𐑆, 𐑇𐐳𐐼 𐑀𐐰𐑄𐐲𐑉 𐑄𐐯𐑋𐑅𐐯𐑊𐑂𐑆 𐐻𐐭𐑀𐐯𐑄𐐲𐑉 𐐻𐐭 𐑀𐐬 𐐻𐐭 𐐺𐐰𐐻𐐲𐑊 𐐲𐑀𐐯𐑌𐑅𐐻 𐑄 𐐢𐐩𐑋𐐲𐑌𐐴𐐻𐑅; 𐐰𐑌𐐼 𐐴 𐐼𐐮𐐼 𐐹𐑊𐐩𐑅 𐑄𐐯𐑋 𐐮𐑌 𐑄𐐩𐑉 𐑉𐐰𐑍𐐿𐑅, 𐐯𐑂𐑉𐐨 𐑋𐐰𐑌 𐐰𐐿𐐫𐑉𐐼𐐮𐑍 𐐻𐐭 𐐸𐐮𐑆 𐐩𐐾.

11. 𐐈𐑌𐐼 𐐮𐐻 𐐿𐐩𐑋 𐐻𐐭 𐐹𐐰𐑅 𐑄𐐰𐐻 𐐶𐐨 𐐼𐐮𐐼 𐑀𐐬 𐐲𐐹 𐐻𐐭 𐐺𐐰𐐻𐐲𐑊 𐐲𐑀𐐯𐑌𐑅𐐻 𐑄 𐐢𐐩𐑋𐐲𐑌𐐴𐐻𐑅; 𐐰𐑌𐐼 𐐴, 𐐨𐑂𐐲𐑌 𐐴, 𐐮𐑌 𐑋𐐴 𐐬𐑊𐐼 𐐩𐐾, 𐐼𐐮𐐼 𐑀𐐬 𐐲𐐹 𐐻𐐭 𐐺𐐰𐐻𐐲𐑊 𐐲𐑀𐐯𐑌𐑅𐐻 𐑄 𐐢𐐩𐑋𐐲𐑌𐐴𐐻𐑅. 𐐈𐑌𐐼 𐐮𐐻 𐐿𐐩𐑋 𐐻𐐭 𐐹𐐰𐑅 𐑄𐐰𐐻 𐐶𐐨 𐐼𐐮𐐼 𐑀𐐬 𐐲𐐹 𐐮𐑌 𐑄 𐑅𐐻𐑉𐐯𐑍𐑃 𐐱𐑂 𐑄 𐐢𐐫𐑉𐐼 𐐻𐐭 𐐺𐐰𐐻𐐲𐑊.

12. 𐐤𐐵, 𐑄 𐐢𐐩𐑋𐐲𐑌𐐴𐐻𐑅 𐑌𐐭 𐑌𐐲𐑃𐐮𐑍 𐐿𐐱𐑌𐑅𐐲𐑉𐑌𐐮𐑍 𐑄 𐐢𐐫𐑉𐐼, 𐑌𐐫𐑉 𐑄 𐑅𐐻𐑉𐐯𐑍𐑃 𐐱𐑂 𐑄 𐐢𐐫𐑉𐐼, 𐑄𐐯𐑉𐑁𐐬𐑉 𐑄𐐩 𐐼𐐯𐐹𐐯𐑌𐐼𐐯𐐼 𐐲𐐹𐐱𐑌 𐑄𐐩𐑉 𐐬𐑌 𐑅𐐻𐑉𐐯𐑍𐑃. 𐐏𐐯𐐻 𐑄𐐩 𐐶𐐲𐑉 𐐰 𐑅𐐻𐑉𐐫𐑍 𐐹𐐨𐐹𐐲𐑊, 𐐰𐑆 𐐻𐐭 𐑄 𐑅𐐻𐑉𐐯𐑍𐑃 𐐱𐑂 𐑋𐐯𐑌—𐑄𐐩 𐐶𐐲𐑉 𐐰 𐐶𐐴𐑊𐐼, 𐐰𐑌𐐼 𐑁𐐯𐑉𐐬𐑇𐐲𐑅, 𐐰𐑌𐐼 𐐰 𐐺𐑊𐐲𐐼-𐑃𐐲𐑉𐑅𐐻𐐨 𐐹𐐨𐐹𐐲𐑊, 𐐺𐐨𐑊𐐨𐑂𐐮𐑍 𐐮𐑌 𐑄 𐐻𐑉𐐲𐐼𐐮𐑇𐐲𐑌 𐐱𐑂 𐑄𐐩𐑉 𐑁𐐪𐑄𐐲𐑉𐑆, 𐐸𐐶𐐮𐐽 𐐮𐑆 𐑄𐐮𐑅:—𐐒𐐨𐑊𐐨𐑂𐐮𐑍 𐑄𐐰𐐻 𐑄𐐩 𐐶𐐲𐑉 𐐼𐑉𐐮𐑂𐐲𐑌 𐐵𐐻 𐐱𐑂 𐑄 𐑊𐐰𐑌𐐼 𐐱𐑂 𐐖𐐨𐑉𐐭𐑅𐐲𐑊𐐯𐑋, 𐐺𐐨𐐿𐐫𐑆 𐐱𐑂 𐑄 𐐮𐑌𐐮𐐿𐐶𐐮𐐻𐐨𐑆 𐐱𐑂 𐑄𐐩𐑉 𐑁𐐪𐑄𐐲𐑉𐑆, 𐐰𐑌𐐼 𐑄𐐰𐐻 𐑄𐐩 𐐶𐐲𐑉 𐑉𐐫𐑍𐐼 𐐮𐑌 𐑄 𐐶𐐮𐑊𐐼𐐲𐑉𐑌𐐯𐑅 𐐺𐐴 𐑄𐐩𐑉 𐐺𐑉𐐯𐑄𐑉𐐯𐑌, 𐐰𐑌𐐼 𐑄𐐩 𐐶𐐲𐑉 𐐫𐑊𐑅𐐬 𐑉𐐫𐑍𐐼 𐐸𐐶𐐴𐑊 𐐿𐑉𐐫𐑅𐐮𐑍 𐑄 𐑅𐐨. 𐐈𐑌𐐼 𐐲𐑀𐐯𐑌: 𐑄𐐰𐐻 𐑄𐐩 𐐶𐐲𐑉 𐑉𐐫𐑍𐐼 𐐸𐐶𐐴𐑊 𐐮𐑌 𐑄 𐑊𐐰𐑌𐐼 𐐱𐑂 𐑄𐐩𐑉 𐑁𐐲𐑉𐑅𐐻 𐐮𐑌𐐸𐐯𐑉𐐮𐐻𐐲𐑌𐑅, 𐐰𐑁𐐻𐐲𐑉 𐑄𐐩 𐐸𐐰𐐼 𐐿𐑉𐐫𐑅𐐻 𐑄 𐑅𐐨, 𐐰𐑌𐐼 𐐫𐑊 𐑄𐐮𐑅 𐐺𐐨𐐿𐐫𐑆 𐑄𐐰𐐻 𐐤𐐨𐑁𐐴 𐐶𐐱𐑆 𐑋𐐬𐑉 𐑁𐐩𐑃𐑁𐐳𐑊 𐐮𐑌 𐐿𐐨𐐹𐐮𐑍 𐑄 𐐿𐐱𐑋𐐰𐑌𐐼𐑋𐐯𐑌𐐻𐑅 𐐱𐑂 𐑄 𐐢𐐫𐑉𐐼; 𐑄𐐯𐑉𐑁𐐬𐑉 𐐸𐐨 𐐶𐐱𐑆 𐑁𐐩𐑂𐐲𐑉𐐼 𐐱𐑂 𐑄 𐐢𐐫𐑉𐐼, 𐑁𐐫𐑉 𐑄 𐐢𐐫𐑉𐐼 𐐸𐐲𐑉𐐼 𐐸𐐮𐑆 𐐹𐑉𐐩𐑉𐑆 𐐰𐑌𐐼 𐐰𐑌𐑅𐐲𐑉𐐼 𐑄𐐯𐑋, 𐐰𐑌𐐼 𐐸𐐨 𐐻𐐳𐐿 𐑄 𐑊𐐨𐐼 𐐱𐑂 𐑄𐐩𐑉 𐐾𐐲𐑉𐑌𐐨 𐐮𐑌 𐑄 𐐶𐐮𐑊𐐼𐐲𐑉𐑌𐐯𐑅. 𐐈𐑌𐐼 𐐸𐐮𐑆 𐐺𐑉𐐯𐑄𐑉𐐯𐑌 𐐶𐐲𐑉 𐑉𐐫𐑃 𐐶𐐮𐑄 𐐸𐐮𐑋 𐐺𐐨𐐿𐐫𐑆 𐑄𐐩 𐐲𐑌𐐼𐐲𐑉𐑅𐐻𐐳𐐼 𐑌𐐱𐐻 𐑄 𐐼𐐨𐑊𐐮𐑍𐑆 𐐱𐑂 𐑄 𐐢𐐫𐑉𐐼; 𐑄𐐩 𐐶𐐲𐑉 𐐫𐑊𐑅𐐬 𐑉𐐫𐑃 𐐶𐐮𐑄 𐐸𐐮𐑋 𐐲𐐹𐐱𐑌 𐑄 𐐶𐐫𐐻𐐲𐑉𐑆, 𐐺𐐨𐐿𐐫𐑆 𐑄𐐩 𐐸𐐪𐑉𐐼𐐲𐑌𐐼 𐑄𐐩𐑉 𐐸𐐪𐑉𐐻𐑅 𐐲𐑀𐐯𐑌𐑅𐐻 𐑄 𐐢𐐫𐑉𐐼. 𐐈𐑌𐐼 𐐲𐑀𐐯𐑌: 𐑄𐐩 𐐶𐐲𐑉 𐑉𐐫𐑃 𐐶𐐮𐑄 𐐸𐐮𐑋 𐐸𐐶𐐯𐑌 𐑄𐐩 𐐸𐐰𐐼 𐐲𐑉𐐴𐑂𐐼 𐐮𐑌 𐑄 𐐹𐑉𐐱𐑋𐐮𐑅𐐼 𐑊𐐰𐑌𐐼, 𐐺𐐨𐐿𐐫𐑆 𐑄𐐩 𐑅𐐯𐐼 𐑄𐐰𐐻 𐐸𐐨 𐐸𐐰𐐼 𐐻𐐩𐐿𐐲𐑌 𐑄 𐑉𐐭𐑊𐐮𐑍 𐐱𐑂 𐑄 𐐹𐐨𐐹𐐲𐑊 𐐵𐐻 𐐱𐑂 𐑄𐐩𐑉 𐐸𐐰𐑌𐐼𐑆; 𐐰𐑌𐐼 𐑄𐐩 𐑅𐐫𐐻 𐐻𐐭 𐐿𐐮𐑊 𐐸𐐮𐑋. 𐐈𐑌𐐼 𐐲𐑀𐐯𐑌: 𐑄𐐩 𐐶𐐲𐑉 𐑉𐐫𐑃 𐐶𐐮𐑄 𐐸𐐮𐑋, 𐐺𐐨𐐿𐐫𐑆 𐐸𐐨 𐐼𐐨𐐹𐐪𐑉𐐻𐐲𐐼 𐐮𐑌𐐻𐐭 𐑄 𐐶𐐮𐑊𐐼𐐲𐑉𐑌𐐯𐑅 𐐰𐑆 𐑄 𐐢𐐫𐑉𐐼 𐐸𐐰𐐼 𐐿𐐱𐑋𐐰𐑌𐐼𐐲𐐼 𐐸𐐮𐑋, 𐐰𐑌𐐼 𐐻𐐳𐐿 𐑄 𐑉𐐯𐐿𐐲𐑉𐐼𐑆 𐐸𐐶𐐮𐐽 𐐶𐐲𐑉 𐐯𐑌𐑀𐑉𐐩𐑂𐐲𐑌 𐐱𐑌 𐑄 𐐹𐑊𐐩𐐻𐑅 𐐱𐑂 𐐺𐑉𐐰𐑅; 𐑁𐐫𐑉 𐑄𐐩 𐑅𐐯𐐼 𐑄𐐰𐐻 𐐸𐐨 𐑉𐐱𐐺𐐼 𐑄𐐯𐑋. 𐐈𐑌𐐼 𐑄𐐲𐑅 𐑄𐐩 𐐸𐐰𐑂 𐐻𐐫𐐻 𐑄𐐩𐑉 𐐽𐐮𐑊𐐼𐑉𐐯𐑌, 𐑄𐐰𐐻 𐑄𐐩 𐑇𐐳𐐼 𐐸𐐩𐐻 𐑄𐐯𐑋, 𐐰𐑌𐐼 𐑄𐐰𐐻 𐑄𐐩 𐑇𐐳𐐼 𐑋𐐲𐑉𐐼𐐲𐑉 𐑄𐐯𐑋, 𐐰𐑌𐐼 𐑄𐐰𐐻 𐑄𐐩 𐑇𐐳𐐼 𐑉𐐱𐐺 𐐰𐑌𐐼 𐐹𐑊𐐲𐑌𐐼𐐲𐑉 𐑄𐐯𐑋, 𐐰𐑌𐐼 𐐼𐐭 𐐫𐑊 𐑄𐐩 𐐿𐐳𐐼 𐐻𐐭 𐐼𐐨𐑅𐐻𐑉𐐱𐐮 𐑄𐐯𐑋: 𐑄𐐯𐑉𐑁𐐬𐑉 𐑄𐐩 𐐸𐐰𐑂 𐐰𐑌 𐐨𐐻𐐲𐑉𐑌𐐲𐑊 𐐸𐐩𐐻𐑉𐐯𐐼 𐐻𐐫𐑉𐐼𐑆 𐑄 𐐽𐐮𐑊𐐼𐑉𐐯𐑌 𐐱𐑂 𐐤𐐨𐑁𐐴. 𐐙𐐫𐑉 𐑄𐐮𐑅 𐑂𐐯𐑉𐐨 𐐿𐐫𐑆 𐐸𐐰𐑆 𐐿𐐮𐑍 𐐢𐐩𐑋𐐲𐑌, 𐐺𐐴 𐐸𐐮𐑆 𐐿𐐲𐑌𐐮𐑍, 𐐰𐑌𐐼 𐑊𐐴𐐮𐑍 𐐿𐑉𐐰𐑁𐐻𐐨𐑌𐐯𐑅, 𐐰𐑌𐐼 𐐸𐐮𐑆 𐑁𐐩𐑉 𐐹𐑉𐐱𐑋𐐮𐑅𐐯𐑆, 𐐼𐐨𐑅𐐨𐑂𐐼 𐑋𐐨, 𐑄𐐰𐐻 𐐴 𐐸𐐰𐑂 𐐺𐑉𐐫𐐻 𐑄𐐮𐑅 𐑋𐐴 𐐹𐐨𐐹𐐲𐑊 𐐲𐐹 𐐮𐑌𐐻𐐭 𐑄𐐮𐑅 𐑊𐐰𐑌𐐼, 𐑄𐐰𐐻 𐑄𐐩 𐑋𐐩 𐐼𐐨𐑅𐐻𐑉𐐱𐐮 𐑄𐐯𐑋; 𐐷𐐩, 𐐰𐑌𐐼 𐐶𐐨 𐐸𐐰𐑂 𐑅𐐲𐑁𐐲𐑉𐐼 𐑄𐐨𐑆 𐑋𐐯𐑌𐐨 𐐷𐐨𐑉𐑆 𐐮𐑌 𐑄 𐑊𐐰𐑌𐐼.

13. 𐐈𐑌𐐼 𐑌𐐵 𐐴, 𐐞𐐨𐑌𐐮𐑁, 𐐰𐑁𐐻𐐲𐑉 𐐸𐐰𐑂𐐮𐑍 𐐻𐐬𐑊𐐼 𐐫𐑊 𐑄𐐨𐑆 𐑃𐐮𐑍𐑆 𐐲𐑌𐐻𐐭 𐑋𐐴 𐐹𐐨𐐹𐐲𐑊 𐐿𐐱𐑌𐑅𐐲𐑉𐑌𐐮𐑍 𐑄 𐐢𐐩𐑋𐐲𐑌𐐴𐐻𐑅, 𐐴 𐐼𐐮𐐼 𐑅𐐻𐐲𐑉 𐑄𐐯𐑋 𐐲𐐹 𐐻𐐭 𐑀𐐬 𐐻𐐭 𐐺𐐰𐐻𐐲𐑊 𐐶𐐮𐑄 𐑄𐐩𐑉 𐑋𐐴𐐻, 𐐹𐐳𐐻𐐮𐑍 𐑄𐐩𐑉 𐐻𐑉𐐲𐑅𐐻

𐐮𐑌 𐑄 𐐢𐐫𐑉𐐼; 𐑄𐐯𐑉𐑁𐐫𐑉, 𐐶𐐨 𐐼𐐮𐐼 𐐿𐐱𐑌𐐻𐐯𐑌𐐼 𐐶𐐮𐑄 𐑄𐐯𐑋, 𐑁𐐩𐑅 𐐻𐐭 𐑁𐐩𐑅. 𐐈𐑌𐐼 𐐮𐐻 𐐿𐐩𐑋 𐐻𐐭 𐐹𐐪𐑅 𐑄𐐰𐐻 𐐶𐐨 𐐼𐐮𐐼 𐐼𐑉𐐴𐑂 𐑄𐐯𐑋 𐐰𐑀𐐯𐑌 𐐵𐐻 𐐱𐑂 𐐵𐑉 𐑊𐐰𐑌𐐼; 𐐰𐑌𐐼 𐐶𐐨 𐑅𐑊𐐭 𐑄𐐯𐑋 𐐶𐐮𐑄 𐐲 𐑀𐑉𐐩𐐻 𐑅𐑊𐐫𐐻𐐲𐑉, 𐐨𐑂𐑌 𐑅𐐬 𐑋𐐯𐑌𐐨 𐑄𐐰𐐻 𐐶𐐨 𐐼𐐮𐐼 𐑌𐐱𐐻 𐑌𐐲𐑋𐐺𐐲𐑉 𐑄𐐯𐑋.

14. 𐐈𐑌𐐼 𐐮𐐻 𐐿𐐩𐑋 𐐻𐐭 𐐹𐐪𐑅 𐑄𐐰𐐻 𐐶𐐨 𐑉𐐨𐐻𐐲𐑉𐑌𐐼 𐐰𐑀𐐯𐑌 𐐻𐐭 𐐵𐑉 𐐬𐑌 𐑊𐐰𐑌𐐼, 𐐰𐑌𐐼 𐑋𐐴 𐐹𐐨𐐹𐑊 𐐰𐑀𐐯𐑌 𐐺𐐨𐑀𐐰𐑌 𐐻𐐭 𐐻𐐯𐑌𐐼 𐑄𐐩𐑉 𐑁𐑊𐐱𐐿𐑅, 𐐰𐑌𐐼 𐐻𐐭 𐐻𐐮𐑊 𐑄𐐩𐑉 𐑀𐑉𐐵𐑌𐐼. 𐐈𐑌𐐼 𐑌𐐵 𐐌, 𐐺𐐨𐐮𐑍 𐐬𐑊𐐼, 𐐼𐐮𐐼 𐐿𐐱𐑌𐑁𐐲𐑉 𐑄 𐐿𐐮𐑍𐐼𐐲𐑋 𐐲𐐹𐐱𐑌 𐐶𐐲𐑌 𐐱𐑂 𐑋𐐴 𐑅𐐲𐑌𐑆; 𐑄𐐯𐑉𐑁𐐫𐑉, 𐐌 𐑅𐐩 𐑌𐐬 𐑋𐐫𐑉. 𐐈𐑌𐐼 𐑋𐐩 𐑄 𐐢𐐫𐑉𐐼 𐐺𐑊𐐯𐑅 𐑋𐐴 𐐹𐐨𐐹𐑊. 𐐁𐑋𐐯𐑌.

𐐕𐐈𐐑𐐓𐐊𐐡 VII.

1. 𐐈𐑌𐐼 𐑌𐐵 𐐮𐐻 𐐿𐐩𐑋 𐐻𐐭 𐐹𐐪𐑅 𐑄𐐰𐐻 𐐞𐐯𐑌𐐮𐑁 𐐿𐐱𐑌𐑁𐐲𐑉𐐼 𐑄 𐐿𐐮𐑍𐐼𐐲𐑋 𐐲𐐹𐐱𐑌 𐐤𐐬𐐲, 𐐶𐐲𐑌 𐐱𐑂 𐐸𐐮𐑆 𐑅𐐲𐑌𐑆; 𐑄𐐯𐑉𐑁𐐫𐑉 𐐤𐐬𐐲 𐐺𐐨𐑀𐐰𐑌 𐐻𐐭 𐑉𐐩𐑌 𐐮𐑌 𐐸𐐮𐑆 𐑅𐐻𐐯𐐼; 𐐰𐑌𐐼 𐐸𐐨 𐐼𐐮𐐼 𐑌𐐱𐐻 𐐶𐐫𐐿 𐐮𐑌 𐑄 𐐶𐐩𐑆 𐐱𐑂 𐐸𐐮𐑆 𐑁𐐪𐑄𐐲𐑉. 𐐙𐐫𐑉 𐐺𐐨𐐸𐐬𐑊𐐼, 𐐸𐐨 𐐼𐐮𐐼 𐑌𐐱𐐻 𐐿𐐨𐐹 𐑄 𐐿𐐲𐑋𐐰𐑌𐐼𐑋𐐯𐑌𐐻𐑅 𐐱𐑂 𐐘𐐱𐐼, 𐐺𐐲𐐻 𐐸𐐨 𐐼𐐮𐐼 𐐶𐐫𐐿 𐐰𐑁𐐻𐐲𐑉 𐑄 𐐼𐐨𐑆𐐴𐑉𐑆 𐐱𐑂 𐐸𐐮𐑆 𐐬𐑌 𐐸𐐪𐑉𐐻. 𐐈𐑌𐐼 𐐸𐐨 𐐸𐐰𐐼 𐑋𐐯𐑌𐐨 𐐶𐐴𐑂𐑆 𐐰𐑌𐐼 𐐿𐐱𐑍𐐿𐐷𐐭𐐺𐐴𐑌𐑆. 𐐈𐑌𐐼 𐐸𐐨 𐐼𐐮𐐼 𐐿𐐫𐑆 𐐸𐐮𐑆 𐐹𐐨𐐹𐑊 𐐻𐐭 𐐿𐐲𐑋𐐮𐐻 𐑅𐐮𐑌, 𐐰𐑌𐐼 𐐼𐐭 𐑄𐐰𐐻 𐐸𐐶𐐮𐐽 𐐶𐐱𐑆 𐐰𐐺𐐱𐑋𐐮𐑌𐐲𐐺𐑊 𐐮𐑌 𐑄 𐑅𐐴𐐻 𐐱𐑂 𐑄 𐐢𐐫𐑉𐐼. 𐐏𐐩, 𐐰𐑌𐐼 𐑄𐐩 𐐼𐐮𐐼 𐐿𐐲𐑋𐐮𐐻 𐐸𐐬𐑉𐐼𐐲𐑋𐑆 𐐰𐑌𐐼 𐐫𐑊 𐑋𐐰𐑌𐐲𐑉 𐐱𐑂 𐐶𐐮𐐿𐐯𐐼𐑌𐐯𐑅. 𐐈𐑌𐐼 𐐸𐐨 𐑊𐐩𐐼 𐐲 𐐻𐐰𐐿𐑅 𐐱𐑂 𐐶𐐲𐑌 𐑁𐐮𐑁𐑃 𐐹𐐪𐑉𐐻 𐐱𐑂 𐐫𐑊 𐑄𐐩 𐐹𐐲𐑆𐐯𐑅𐐻: 𐐲 𐑁𐐮𐑁𐑃 𐐹𐐪𐑉𐐻 𐐱𐑂 𐑄𐐩𐑉 𐑀𐐬𐑊𐐼 𐐰𐑌𐐼 𐐱𐑂 𐑄𐐩𐑉 𐑅𐐮𐑊𐑂𐐲𐑉, 𐐰𐑌𐐼 𐐲 𐑁𐐮𐑁𐑃 𐐹𐐪𐑉𐐻 𐐱𐑂 𐑄𐐩𐑉 𐑆𐐮𐑁, 𐐰𐑌𐐼 𐐱𐑂 𐑄𐐩𐑉 𐐿𐐱𐐹𐐲𐑉, 𐐰𐑌𐐼 𐐱𐑂 𐑄𐐩𐑉 𐐺𐑉𐐰𐑅 𐐰𐑌𐐼 𐑄𐐩𐑉 𐐴𐐲𐑉𐑌; 𐐰𐑌𐐼 𐐲 𐑁𐐮𐑁𐑃 𐐹𐐪𐑉𐐻 𐐱𐑂 𐑄𐐩𐑉 𐑁𐐰𐐻𐑊𐐮𐑍𐑆; 𐐰𐑌𐐼 𐐫𐑊𐑅𐐬 𐐲 𐑁𐐮𐑁𐑃 𐐹𐐪𐑉𐐻 𐐱𐑂 𐐫𐑊 𐑄𐐩𐑉 𐑀𐑉𐐩𐑌. 𐐈𐑌𐐼 𐐫𐑊 𐑄𐐮𐑅 𐐼𐐮𐐼 𐐸𐐨 𐐻𐐩𐐿 𐐻𐐭 𐑅𐐲𐐹𐐬𐑉𐐻 𐐸𐐮𐑋𐑅𐐯𐑊𐑁, 𐐰𐑌𐐼 𐐸𐐮𐑆 𐐶𐐴𐑂𐑆, 𐐰𐑌𐐼 𐐸𐐮𐑆 𐐿𐐱𐑍𐐿𐐷𐐭𐐺𐐴𐑌𐑆; 𐐰𐑌𐐼 𐐫𐑊𐑅𐐬 𐐸𐐮𐑆 𐐹𐑉𐐨𐑅𐐻𐑅, 𐐰𐑌𐐼 𐑄𐐩𐑉 𐐶𐐴𐑂𐑆, 𐐰𐑌𐐼 𐑄𐐩𐑉 𐐿𐐱𐑍𐐿𐐷𐐭𐐺𐐴𐑌𐑆; 𐑄𐐲𐑅 𐐸𐐨 𐐸𐐰𐐼 𐐽𐐩𐑌𐐾𐐼 𐑄 𐐰𐑁𐐩𐑉𐑆 𐐱𐑂 𐑄 𐐿𐐮𐑍𐐼𐐲𐑋. 𐐙𐐫𐑉 𐐸𐐨 𐐹𐐳𐐻 𐐼𐐵𐑌 𐐫𐑊 𐑄 𐐹𐑉𐐨𐑅𐐻𐑅 𐑄𐐰𐐻 𐐸𐐰𐐼 𐐺𐐮𐑌 𐐿𐐱𐑌𐑅𐐲𐐿𐑉𐐩𐐻𐐯𐐼 𐐺𐐴 𐐸𐐮𐑆 𐑁𐐪𐑄𐐲𐑉; 𐐰𐑌𐐼 𐐿𐐱𐑌𐑅𐐲𐐿𐑉𐐩𐐻𐐯𐐼 𐑌𐐭 𐐶𐐲𐑌𐑆 𐐮𐑌 𐑄𐐩𐑉 𐑅𐐻𐐯𐐼, 𐑅𐐲𐐽 𐐰𐑆 𐐶𐐲𐑉 𐑊𐐮𐑁𐐻𐐯𐐼 𐐲𐐹 𐐮𐑌 𐑄 𐐹𐑉𐐴𐐼 𐐱𐑂 𐑄𐐩𐑉 𐐸𐐪𐑉𐐻𐑅. 𐐏𐐩, 𐐰𐑌𐐼 𐑄𐐲𐑅 𐑄𐐩 𐐶𐐲𐑉 𐑅𐐲𐐹𐐬𐑉𐐻𐐯𐐼 𐐮𐑌 𐑄𐐩𐑉 𐑊𐐩𐑆𐐮𐑌𐐯𐑅, 𐐰𐑌𐐼 𐐮𐑌 𐑄𐐩𐑉 𐐴𐐼𐐱𐑊𐐰𐐻𐑉𐐨, 𐐰𐑌𐐼 𐐮𐑌 𐑄𐐩𐑉 𐐸𐐬𐑉𐐼𐐲𐑋𐑆, 𐐺𐐴 𐑄 𐐻𐐰𐐿𐑅𐐯𐑆 𐐸𐐶𐐮𐐽 𐐿𐐮𐑍 𐐤𐐬𐐲 𐐸𐐰𐐼 𐐹𐐳𐐻 𐐲𐐹𐐱𐑌 𐐸𐐮𐑆 𐐹𐐨𐐹𐑊; 𐑄𐐲𐑅 𐐼𐐮𐐼 𐑄 𐐹𐐨𐐹𐑊 𐑊𐐩𐐺𐐲𐑉 𐐯𐐿𐑅𐐨𐐼𐐮𐑍𐑊𐐨 𐐻𐐭 𐑅𐐲𐐹𐐬𐑉𐐻 𐐮𐑌𐐮𐐿𐐶𐐮𐐻𐐨. 𐐏𐐩, 𐐰𐑌𐐼 𐑄𐐩 𐐫𐑊𐑅𐐬 𐐺𐐨𐐿𐐩𐑋 𐐴𐐼𐐱𐑊𐐰𐐻𐑉𐐲𐑅, 𐐺𐐨𐐿𐐫𐑆 𐑄𐐩 𐐶𐐲𐑉 𐐼𐐨𐑅𐐨𐑂𐐼 𐐺𐐴 𐑄 𐑂𐐩𐑌 𐐰𐑌𐐼 𐑁𐑊𐐰𐐻𐐲𐑉𐐮𐑍 𐐶𐐲𐑉𐐼𐑆 𐐱𐑂 𐑄 𐐿𐐮𐑍 𐐰𐑌𐐼 𐐹𐑉𐐨𐑅𐐻𐑅; 𐑁𐐫𐑉 𐑄𐐩 𐐼𐐮𐐼 𐑅𐐹𐐨𐐿 𐑁𐑊𐐰𐐻𐐲𐑉𐐮𐑍 𐑃𐐮𐑍𐑆 𐐲𐑌𐐻𐐭 𐑄𐐯𐑋.

2. 𐐈𐑌𐐼 𐐮𐐻 𐐿𐐩𐑋 𐐻𐐭 𐐹𐐪𐑅 𐑄𐐰𐐻 𐐿𐐮𐑍 𐐤𐐬𐐲 𐐺𐐮𐑊𐐻 𐑋𐐯𐑌𐐨 𐐯𐑊𐐯𐑀𐐲𐑌𐐻 𐐰𐑌𐐼 𐑅𐐹𐐩𐑇𐐲𐑅 𐐺𐐮𐑊𐐼𐐮𐑍𐑆; 𐐰𐑌𐐼 𐐸𐐨 𐐫𐑉𐑌𐐲𐑋𐐯𐑌𐐻𐐯𐐼 𐑄𐐯𐑋 𐐶𐐮𐑄 𐑁𐐴𐑌 𐐶𐐲𐑉𐐿 𐐱𐑂 𐐶𐐳𐐼, 𐐰𐑌𐐼 𐐱𐑂 𐐫𐑊 𐑋𐐰𐑌𐐲𐑉 𐐱𐑂 𐐹𐑉𐐯𐑇𐐲𐑅 𐑃𐐮𐑍𐑆, 𐐱𐑂 𐑀𐐬𐑊𐐼, 𐐰𐑌𐐼 𐐱𐑂 𐑅𐐮𐑊𐑂𐐲𐑉, 𐐰𐑌𐐼 𐐱𐑂 𐐴𐐲𐑉𐑌, 𐐰𐑌𐐼 𐐱𐑂 𐐺𐑉𐐰𐑅, 𐐰𐑌𐐼 𐐱𐑂 𐑆𐐮𐑁, 𐐰𐑌𐐼 𐐱𐑂 𐐿𐐱𐐹𐐲𐑉; 𐐰𐑌𐐼 𐐸𐐨 𐐫𐑊𐑅𐐬 𐐺𐐮𐑊𐐻 𐐸𐐮𐑋 𐐲 𐑅𐐹𐐩𐑇𐐲𐑅 𐐹𐐰𐑊𐐲𐑅, 𐐰𐑌𐐼 𐐲 𐑃𐑉𐐬𐑌 𐐮𐑌 𐑄 𐑋𐐮𐐼𐑅𐐻 𐑄𐐩𐑉𐐱𐑂, 𐐫𐑊 𐐱𐑂 𐐸𐐶𐐮𐐽 𐐶𐐱𐑆 𐐱𐑂 𐑁𐐴𐑌 𐐶𐐳𐐼, 𐐰𐑌𐐼 𐐶𐐱𐑆 𐐫𐑉𐑌𐐲𐑋𐐯𐑌𐐻𐐯𐐼 𐐶𐐮𐑄 𐑀𐐬𐑊𐐼 𐐰𐑌𐐼 𐑅𐐮𐑊𐑂𐐲𐑉, 𐐰𐑌𐐼 𐐶𐐮𐑄 𐐹𐑉𐐯𐑇𐐲𐑅 𐑃𐐮𐑍𐑆. 𐐈𐑌𐐼 𐐸𐐨 𐐫𐑊𐑅𐐬 𐐿𐐫𐑆𐐼 𐑄𐐰𐐻 𐐸𐐮𐑆 𐐶𐐲𐑉𐐿𐑋𐐯𐑌 𐑇𐐳𐐼 𐐶𐐲𐑉𐐿 𐐫𐑊 𐑋𐐰𐑌𐐲𐑉 𐐱𐑂 𐑁𐐴𐑌 𐐶𐐲𐑉𐐿 𐐶𐐮𐑄𐐮𐑌 𐑄 𐐶𐐫𐑊𐑆 𐐱𐑂 𐑄 𐐻𐐯𐑋𐐹𐐲𐑊, 𐐱𐑂 𐑁𐐴𐑌 𐐶𐐳𐐼, 𐐰𐑌𐐼 𐐱𐑂 𐐿𐐱𐐹𐐲𐑉, 𐐰𐑌𐐼 𐐱𐑂 𐐺𐑉𐐰𐑅; 𐐰𐑌𐐼 𐑄 𐑅𐐨𐐻𐑅 𐐸𐐶𐐮𐐽 𐐶𐐲𐑉 𐑅𐐯𐐻 𐐰𐐹𐐪𐑉𐐻 𐑁𐐫𐑉 𐑄 𐐸𐐴 𐐹𐑉𐐨𐑅𐐻𐑅, 𐐸𐐶𐐮𐐽 𐐶𐐲𐑉 𐐰𐐺𐐲𐑂 𐐫𐑊 𐑄 𐐲𐑄𐐲𐑉 𐑅𐐨𐐻𐑅, 𐐸𐐨 𐐼𐐮𐐼 𐐫𐑉𐑌𐐲𐑋𐐯𐑌𐐻 𐐶𐐮𐑄 𐐹𐐷𐐭𐑉 𐑀𐐬𐑊𐐼: 𐐰𐑌𐐼 𐐸𐐨 𐐿𐐫𐑆𐐼 𐐲 𐐺𐑉𐐯𐑅𐐻𐐶𐐲𐑉𐐿 𐐻𐐭 𐐺 𐐺𐐮𐑊𐐻 𐐺𐐨𐑁𐐫𐑉 𐑄𐐯𐑋, 𐑄𐐰𐐻 𐑄𐐩 𐑋𐐴𐐻 𐑉𐐯𐑅𐐻 𐑄𐐩𐑉 𐐺𐐱𐐼𐐨𐑆 𐐰𐑌𐐼 𐑄𐐩𐑉 𐐪𐑉𐑋𐑆 𐐲𐐹𐐱𐑌, 𐐸𐐶𐐴𐑊 𐑄𐐩 𐑇𐐳𐐼 𐑅𐐹𐐨𐐿 𐑊𐐴𐐮𐑍 𐐰𐑌𐐼 𐑂𐐩𐑌 𐐶𐐲𐑉𐐼𐑆 𐐻𐐭 𐐸𐐮𐑆 𐐹𐐨𐐹𐑊.

3. 𐐈𐑌𐐼 𐐮𐐻 𐐿𐐩𐑋 𐐻𐐭 𐐹𐐪𐑅 𐑄𐐰𐐻 𐐸𐐨 𐐺𐐮𐑊𐐻 𐐲 𐐻𐐵𐐲𐑉 𐑌𐐨𐑉 𐑄 𐐻𐐯𐑋𐐹𐐲𐑊; 𐐷𐐩, 𐐲 𐑂𐐯𐑉𐐨 𐐸𐐴 𐐻𐐵𐐲𐑉,

𐐨𐑂𐐲𐑌 𐑅𐐬 𐐸𐐴 𐑄𐐰𐐻 𐐸𐐨 𐐿𐐳𐐼 𐑅𐐻𐐰𐑌𐐼 𐐲𐐹𐐱𐑌 𐑄 𐐻𐐱𐐹 𐑄𐐯𐑉𐐱𐑂 𐐰𐑌𐐼 𐐬𐑂𐐲𐑉𐑊𐐳𐐿 𐑄 𐑊𐐰𐑌𐐼 𐐱𐑂 𐐖𐐴𐑊𐐲𐑋, 𐐰𐑌𐐼 𐐫𐑊𐑅𐐬 𐑄 𐑊𐐰𐑌𐐼 𐐱𐑂 𐐖𐐯𐑋𐑊𐐲𐑌, 𐐸𐐶𐐮𐐽 𐐶𐐱𐑆 𐐹𐐲𐑆𐐯𐑅𐐻 𐐺𐐴 𐑄 𐐢𐐰𐑋𐐲𐑌𐐴𐐻𐑅; 𐐰𐑌𐐼 𐐸𐐨 𐐿𐐳𐐼 𐐨𐑂𐐲𐑌 𐑊𐐳𐐿 𐐬𐑂𐐲𐑉 𐐫𐑊 𐑄 𐑊𐐰𐑌𐐼 𐑉𐐵𐑌𐐼 𐐲𐐺𐐵𐐻.

4. 𐐰𐑌𐐼 𐐮𐐻 𐐿𐐩𐑋 𐐻𐐭 𐐹𐐰𐑅 𐑄𐐰𐐻 𐐸𐐨 𐐿𐐫𐑆𐐼 𐑋𐐯𐑌𐐨 𐐺𐐮𐑊𐐼𐐮𐑍𐑆 𐐻𐐭 𐐺𐐨 𐐺𐐮𐑊𐐻 𐐮𐑌 𐑄 𐑊𐐰𐑌𐐼 𐐱𐑂 𐐖𐐴𐑊𐐲𐑋; 𐐰𐑌𐐼 𐐸𐐨 𐐿𐐫𐑆𐐼 𐐲 𐑀𐑉𐐩𐐻 𐐻𐐵𐐲𐑉 𐐻𐐭 𐐺𐐨 𐐺𐐮𐑊𐐻 𐐱𐑌 𐑄 𐐸𐐮𐑊 𐑌𐐫𐑉𐑃 𐐱𐑂 𐑄 𐑊𐐰𐑌𐐼 𐐖𐐴𐑊𐐲𐑋, 𐐸𐐶𐐮𐐽 𐐸𐐰𐐼 𐐺𐐮𐑌 𐐲 𐑉𐐨𐑆𐐫𐑉𐐻 𐑁𐐫𐑉 𐑄 𐐽𐐮𐑊𐐼𐑉𐐯𐑌 𐐱𐑂 𐐤𐐨𐑁𐐴 𐐰𐐻 𐑄 𐐻𐐴𐑋 𐑄𐐩 𐑁𐑊𐐯𐐼 𐐵𐐻 𐐱𐑂 𐑄 𐑊𐐰𐑌𐐼; 𐐰𐑌𐐼 𐑄𐐲𐑅 𐐸𐐨 𐐼𐐮𐐼 𐐼𐐭 𐐶𐐮𐑃 𐑄 𐑉𐐮𐐽𐐯𐑆 𐐸𐐶𐐮𐐽 𐐸𐐨 𐐱𐐺𐐻𐐩𐑌𐐼 𐐺𐐴 𐑄 𐐻𐐰𐐿𐑅𐐩𐑇𐐲𐑌 𐐱𐑂 𐐸𐐮𐑆 𐐹𐐨𐐹𐑊.

4. 𐐰𐑌𐐼 𐐮𐐻 𐐿𐐩𐑋 𐐻𐐭 𐐹𐐰𐑅 𐑄𐐰𐐻 𐐸𐐨 𐐹𐑊𐐩𐑅𐐻 𐐸𐐮𐑆 𐐸𐐪𐑉𐐻 𐐲𐐹𐐱𐑌 𐐸𐐮𐑆 𐑉𐐮𐐽𐐯𐑆, 𐐰𐑌𐐼 𐐸𐐨 𐑅𐐹𐐯𐑌𐐻 𐐸𐐮𐑆 𐐻𐐴𐑋 𐐮𐑌 𐑉𐐴𐐲𐐻𐐲𐑅 𐑊𐐮𐑂𐐮𐑍 𐐶𐐮𐑃 𐐸𐐮𐑆 𐐶𐐴𐑂𐑆 𐐰𐑌𐐼 𐐸𐐮𐑆 𐐿𐐱𐑍𐐿𐐷𐐭𐐺𐐴𐑌𐑆; 𐐰𐑌𐐼 𐑅𐐬 𐐼𐐮𐐼 𐐫𐑊𐑅𐐬 𐐸𐐮𐑆 𐐹𐑉𐐨𐑅𐐻𐑅 𐑅𐐹𐐯𐑌𐐼 𐑄𐐩𐑉 𐐻𐐴𐑋 𐐶𐐮𐑃 𐐸𐐪𐑉𐑊𐐲𐐻𐑅. 𐐰𐑌𐐼 𐐮𐐻 𐐿𐐩𐑋 𐐻𐐭 𐐹𐐰𐑅 𐑄𐐰𐐻 𐐸𐐨 𐐹𐑊𐐰𐑌𐐻𐐯𐐼 𐑂𐐮𐑌𐐷𐐲𐑉𐐼𐑆 𐑉𐐵𐑌𐐼 𐐲𐐺𐐵𐐻 𐐮𐑌 𐑄 𐑊𐐰𐑌𐐼; 𐐰𐑌𐐼 𐐸𐐨 𐐺𐐮𐑊𐐻 𐐶𐐴𐑌-𐐹𐑉𐐯𐑅𐐯𐑆, 𐐰𐑌𐐼 𐑋𐐩𐐼 𐐶𐐴𐑌 𐐮𐑌 𐐲𐐺𐐲𐑌𐐼𐐲𐑌𐑅; 𐐰𐑌𐐼 𐑄𐐯𐑉𐑁𐐬𐑉 𐐸𐐨 𐐺𐐨𐐿𐐩𐑋 𐐲 𐐶𐐴𐑌-𐐺𐐮𐐺𐐲𐑉, 𐐰𐑌𐐼 𐐫𐑊𐑅𐐬 𐐸𐐮𐑆 𐐹𐐨𐐹𐑊.

6. 𐐰𐑌𐐼 𐐮𐐻 𐐿𐐩𐑋 𐐻𐐭 𐐹𐐰𐑅 𐑄𐐰𐐻 𐑄 𐐢𐐰𐑋𐐲𐑌𐐴𐐻𐑅 𐐺𐐨𐑀𐐰𐑌 𐐻𐐭 𐐿𐐲𐑋 𐐮𐑌 𐐲𐐹𐐱𐑌 𐐸𐐮𐑆 𐐹𐐨𐐹𐑊, 𐐲𐐹𐐱𐑌 𐑅𐑋𐐫𐑊 𐑌𐐲𐑋𐐺𐐲𐑉𐑆, 𐐰𐑌𐐼 𐐻𐐭 𐑅𐑊𐐩 𐑄𐐯𐑋 𐐮𐑌 𐑄𐐩𐑉 𐑁𐐨𐑊𐐼𐑆, 𐐰𐑌𐐼 𐐸𐐶𐐴𐑊 𐑄𐐩 𐐶𐐲𐑉 𐐻𐐯𐑌𐐼𐐮𐑍 𐑄𐐩𐑉 𐑁𐑊𐐱𐐿𐑅. 𐐰𐑌𐐼 𐐿𐐮𐑍 𐐤𐐬𐐲 𐑅𐐯𐑌𐐻 𐑀𐐪𐑉𐐼𐑆 𐑉𐐵𐑌𐐼 𐐲𐐺𐐵𐐻 𐑄 𐑊𐐰𐑌𐐼 𐐻𐐭 𐐿𐐨𐐹 𐑄𐐯𐑋 𐐫𐑁; 𐐺𐐲𐐻 𐐸𐐨 𐐼𐐮𐐼 𐑌𐐱𐐻 𐑅𐐯𐑌𐐼 𐐲 𐑅𐐲𐑁𐐮𐑇𐐯𐑌𐐻 𐑌𐐲𐑋𐐺𐐲𐑉, 𐐰𐑌𐐼 𐑄 𐐢𐐰𐑋𐐲𐑌𐐴𐐻𐑅 𐐿𐐩𐑋 𐐲𐐹𐐱𐑌 𐑄𐐯𐑋 𐐰𐑌𐐼 𐐿𐐮𐑊𐐼 𐑄𐐯𐑋, 𐐰𐑌𐐼 𐐼𐑉𐐬𐑂 𐑋𐐯𐑌𐐨 𐐱𐑂 𐑄𐐩𐑉 𐑁𐑊𐐱𐐿𐑅 𐐵𐐻 𐐱𐑂 𐑄 𐑊𐐰𐑌𐐼: 𐑄𐐲𐑅 𐑄 𐐢𐐰𐑋𐐲𐑌𐐴𐐻𐑅 𐐺𐐨𐑀𐐰𐑌 𐐻𐐭 𐐼𐐯𐑅𐐻𐑉𐑎 𐑄𐐯𐑋, 𐐰𐑌𐐼 𐐻𐐭 𐐯𐐿𐑅𐐲𐑉𐑅𐐴𐑆 𐑄𐐩𐑉 𐐸𐐩𐐻𐑉𐐯𐐼 𐐲𐐹𐐱𐑌 𐑄𐐯𐑋.

7. 𐐰𐑌𐐼 𐐮𐐻 𐐿𐐩𐑋 𐐻𐐭 𐐹𐐰𐑅 𐑄𐐰𐐻 𐐿𐐮𐑍 𐐤𐐬𐐲 𐑅𐐯𐑌𐐻 𐐸𐐮𐑆 𐐪𐑉𐑋𐐨𐑆 𐐲𐑀𐐯𐑌𐑅𐐻 𐑄𐐯𐑋, 𐐰𐑌𐐼 𐑄𐐩 𐐶𐐲𐑉 𐐼𐑉𐐮𐑂𐐲𐑌 𐐺𐐰𐐿, 𐐫𐑉 𐑄𐐩 𐐼𐑉𐐬𐑂 𐑄𐐯𐑋 𐐺𐐰𐐿 𐑁𐐫𐑉 𐐲 𐐻𐐴𐑋; 𐑄𐐯𐑉𐑁𐐬𐑉, 𐑄𐐩 𐑉𐐨𐐻𐐲𐑉𐑌𐐼 𐑉𐐨𐐾𐑎𐑅𐐮𐑍 𐐮𐑌 𐑄𐐩𐑉 𐑅𐐹𐑎𐑊. 𐐰𐑌𐐼 𐑌𐐵, 𐐺𐐨𐐿𐐫𐑆 𐐱𐑂 𐑄𐐮𐑅 𐑀𐑉𐐩𐐻 𐑂𐐮𐐿𐐻𐐬𐑉𐐨, 𐑄𐐩 𐐶𐐲𐑉 𐑊𐐮𐑁𐐻𐐯𐐼 𐐲𐐹 𐐮𐑌 𐑄 𐐹𐑉𐐴𐐼 𐐱𐑂 𐑄𐐩𐑉 𐐸𐐪𐑉𐐻𐑅: 𐑄𐐩 𐐼𐐮𐐼 𐐺𐐬𐑅𐐻 𐐮𐑌 𐑄𐐩𐑉 𐐬𐑌 𐑅𐐻𐑉𐐯𐑍𐑃, 𐑅𐐩𐐮𐑍, 𐑄𐐰𐐻 𐑄𐐩𐑉 𐑁𐐮𐑁𐐻𐐨 𐐿𐐳𐐼 𐑅𐐻𐐰𐑌𐐼 𐐲𐑀𐐯𐑌𐑅𐐻 𐑃𐐵𐑆𐐲𐑌𐐼𐑆 𐐱𐑂 𐑄 𐐢𐐰𐑋𐐲𐑌𐐴𐐻𐑅; 𐐰𐑌𐐼 𐑄𐐲𐑅 𐑄𐐩 𐐼𐐮𐐼 𐐺𐐬𐑅𐐻, 𐐰𐑌𐐼 𐐼𐐮𐐼 𐐼𐐨𐑊𐐴𐐻 𐐮𐑌 𐐺𐑊𐐲𐐼, 𐐰𐑌𐐼 𐑄 𐑇𐐯𐐼𐐮𐑍 𐐱𐑂 𐑄 𐐺𐑊𐐲𐐼 𐐱𐑂 𐑄𐐩𐑉 𐐺𐑉𐐯𐑄𐑉𐐯𐑌, 𐐰𐑌𐐼 𐑄𐐮𐑅 𐐺𐐨𐐿𐐫𐑆 𐐱𐑂 𐑄 𐐶𐐮𐐿𐐯𐐼𐑌𐐯𐑅 𐐱𐑂 𐑄𐐩𐑉 𐐿𐐮𐑍 𐐰𐑌𐐼 𐐹𐑉𐐨𐑅𐐻𐑅.

8. 𐐰𐑌𐐼 𐐮𐐻 𐐿𐐩𐑋 𐐻𐐭 𐐹𐐰𐑅 𐑄𐐰𐐻 𐑄𐐩𐑉 𐐶𐐱𐑆 𐐲 𐑋𐐰𐑌 𐐲𐑋𐐲𐑍 𐑄𐐯𐑋 𐐸𐐭𐑆 𐑌𐐩𐑋 𐐶𐐱𐑆 𐐈𐐺𐐮𐑌𐐲𐐼𐐴; 𐐰𐑌𐐼 𐐸𐐨 𐐶𐐯𐑌𐐻 𐑁𐐬𐑉𐑃 𐐲𐑋𐐲𐑍 𐑄𐐯𐑋, 𐐰𐑌𐐼 𐐺𐐨𐑀𐐰𐑌 𐐻𐐭 𐐹𐑉𐐱𐑁𐐯𐑅𐐴, 𐑅𐐩𐐮𐑍, 𐐒𐐨𐐸𐐬𐑊𐐼, 𐑄𐐲𐑅 𐑅𐐯𐑃 𐑄 𐐢𐐫𐑉𐐼, 𐐰𐑌𐐼 𐑄𐐲𐑅 𐐸𐐰𐑃 𐐸𐐨 𐐿𐐱𐑋𐐰𐑌𐐼𐐯𐐼 𐑋𐐨, 𐑅𐐩𐐮𐑍, 𐐘𐐬 𐑁𐐬𐑉𐑃, 𐐰𐑌𐐼 𐑅𐐩 𐐲𐑌𐐻𐐭 𐑄𐐮𐑅 𐐹𐐨𐐹𐑊, 𐑄𐐲𐑅 𐑅𐐯𐑃 𐑄 𐐢𐐫𐑉𐐼: 𐐎𐐬 𐐺𐐨 𐐲𐑌𐐻𐐭 𐑄𐐮𐑅 𐐹𐐨𐐹𐑊, 𐑁𐐫𐑉 𐐌 𐐸𐐰𐑂 𐑅𐐨𐑌 𐑄𐐩𐑉 𐐲𐐺𐐱𐑋𐐮𐑌𐐩𐑇𐐲𐑌𐑆, 𐐰𐑌𐐼 𐑄𐐩𐑉 𐐶𐐮𐐿𐐯𐐼𐑌𐐯𐑅, 𐐰𐑌𐐼 𐑄𐐩𐑉 𐐸𐐬𐑉𐐼𐐲𐑋𐑆; 𐐰𐑌𐐼 𐐯𐐿𐑅𐐯𐐹𐐻 𐑄𐐩 𐑉𐐨𐐹𐐯𐑌𐐻, 𐐌 𐐶𐐮𐑊 𐑂𐐮𐑆𐐮𐐻 𐑄𐐯𐑋 𐐮𐑌 𐑋𐐴𐑌 𐐰𐑍𐑀𐐲𐑉. 𐐰𐑌𐐼 𐐯𐐿𐑅𐐯𐐹𐐻 𐑄𐐩 𐑉𐐨𐐹𐐯𐑌𐐻 𐐰𐑌𐐼 𐐻𐐲𐑉𐑌 𐐻𐐭 𐑄 𐐢𐐫𐑉𐐼 𐑄𐐩𐑉 𐐘𐐱𐐼, 𐐺𐐨𐐸𐐬𐑊𐐼, 𐐌 𐐶𐐮𐑊 𐐼𐐨𐑊𐐮𐑂𐐲𐑉 𐑄𐐯𐑋 𐐮𐑌𐐻𐐭 𐑄 𐐸𐐰𐑌𐐼𐑆 𐐱𐑂 𐑄𐐩𐑉 𐐯𐑌𐐯𐑋𐐨𐑆: 𐐷𐐩, 𐐰𐑌𐐼 𐑄𐐩 𐑇𐐰𐑊 𐐺𐐨 𐐺𐑉𐐫𐐻 𐐮𐑌𐐻𐐭 𐐺𐐱𐑌𐐼𐐩𐐾; 𐐰𐑌𐐼 𐑄𐐩 𐑇𐐰𐑊 𐐺𐐨 𐐲𐑁𐑊𐐮𐐿𐐻𐐯𐐼 𐐺𐐴 𐑄 𐐸𐐰𐑌𐐼 𐐱𐑂 𐑄𐐩𐑉 𐐯𐑌𐐯𐑋𐐨𐑆. 𐐰𐑌𐐼 𐐮𐐻 𐑇𐐰𐑊 𐐿𐐲𐑋 𐐻𐐭 𐐹𐐰𐑅 𐑄𐐰𐐻 𐑄𐐩 𐑇𐐰𐑊 𐑌𐐬 𐑄𐐰𐐻 𐐌 𐐰𐑋 𐑄 𐐢𐐫𐑉𐐼 𐑄𐐩𐑉 𐐘𐐱𐐼, 𐐰𐑌𐐼 𐐰𐑋 𐐲 𐐾𐐯𐑊𐐲𐑅 𐐘𐐱𐐼, 𐑂𐐮𐑆𐐮𐐻𐐮𐑍 𐑄 𐐮𐑌𐐮𐐿𐐶𐐮𐐻𐐨𐑆 𐐱𐑂 𐑋𐐴 𐐹𐐨𐐹𐑊. 𐐰𐑌𐐼 𐐮𐐻 𐑇𐐰𐑊 𐐿𐐲𐑋 𐐻𐐭 𐐹𐐰𐑅 𐑄𐐰𐐻 𐐯𐐿𐑅𐐯𐐹𐐻 𐑄𐐮𐑅 𐐹𐐨𐐹𐑊 𐑉𐐨𐐹𐐯𐑌𐐻 𐐰𐑌𐐼 𐐻𐐲𐑉𐑌 𐐲𐑌𐐻𐐭 𐑄 𐐢𐐫𐑉𐐼 𐑄𐐩𐑉 𐐘𐐱𐐼, 𐑄𐐩 𐑇𐐰𐑊 𐐺𐐨 𐐺𐑉𐐫𐐻 𐐮𐑌𐐻𐐭 𐐺𐐱𐑌𐐼𐐩𐐾; 𐐰𐑌𐐼 𐑌𐐲𐑌 𐑇𐐰𐑊 𐐼𐐨𐑊𐐮𐑂𐐲𐑉 𐑄𐐯𐑋, 𐐯𐐿𐑅𐐯𐐹𐐻 𐐮𐐻 𐐺𐐨 𐑄 𐐢𐐫𐑉𐐼 𐑄 𐐉𐑊𐑋𐐴𐐻𐐨 𐐘𐐱𐐼. 𐐏𐐩, 𐐰𐑌𐐼 𐐮𐐻 𐑇𐐰𐑊 𐐿𐐲𐑋 𐐻𐐭 𐐹𐐰𐑅 𐑄𐐰𐐻 𐐸𐐶𐐯𐑌 𐑄𐐩 𐑇𐐰𐑊 𐐿𐑉𐐴 𐐲𐑌𐐻𐐭 𐑋𐐨, 𐐌 𐐶𐐮𐑊 𐐺𐐨 𐑅𐑊𐐬 𐐻𐐭 𐐸𐐨𐑉 𐑄𐐩𐑉 𐐿𐑉𐐴𐑆; 𐐷𐐩, 𐐰𐑌𐐼 𐐌 𐐶𐐮𐑊 𐑅𐐲𐑁𐐲𐑉 𐑄𐐯𐑋 𐑄𐐰𐐻 𐑄𐐩 𐐺𐐨 𐑅𐑋𐐮𐐻𐐲𐑌 𐐺𐐴 𐑄𐐩𐑉 𐐯𐑌𐐯𐑋𐐨𐑆. 𐐰𐑌𐐼 𐐯𐐿𐑅𐐯𐐹𐐻 𐑄𐐩 𐑉𐐨𐐹𐐯𐑌𐐻 𐐮𐑌 𐑅𐐰𐐿-𐐿𐑊𐐫𐑃 𐐰𐑌𐐼 𐐰𐑇𐐯𐑆, 𐐰𐑌𐐼 𐐿𐑉𐐴 𐑋𐐴𐐻𐐮𐑊𐐨 𐐻𐐭 𐑄 𐐢𐐫𐑉𐐼 𐑄𐐩𐑉 𐐘𐐱𐐼, 𐐌 𐐶𐐮𐑊 𐑌𐐱𐐻 𐐸𐐨𐑉 𐑄𐐩𐑉 𐐹𐑉𐐩𐐲𐑉𐑆, 𐑌𐐨𐑄𐐲𐑉 𐐶𐐮𐑊 𐐌 𐐼𐐨𐑊𐐮𐑂𐐲𐑉 𐑄𐐯𐑋 𐐵𐐻 𐐱𐑂 𐑄𐐩𐑉 𐐲𐑁𐑊𐐮𐐿𐑇𐐲𐑌𐑆; 𐐰𐑌𐐼 𐑄𐐲𐑅 𐑅𐐯𐑃 𐑄 𐐢𐐫𐑉𐐼, 𐐰𐑌𐐼 𐑄𐐲𐑅 𐐸𐐰𐑃 𐐸𐐨 𐐿𐐱𐑋𐐰𐑌𐐼𐐯𐐼 𐑋𐐨.

9. 𐐤𐐵 𐐮𐐻 𐐿𐐩𐑋 𐐻𐐭 𐐹𐐰𐑅 𐑄𐐰𐐻 𐐸𐐶𐐯𐑌 𐐈𐐺𐐮𐑌𐐰𐐼𐐴 𐐸𐐰𐐼 𐑅𐐹𐐬𐐿𐐲𐑌 𐑄𐐨𐑆 𐐶𐐲𐑉𐐼𐑆 𐐲𐑌𐐻𐐭 𐑄𐐯𐑋, 𐑄𐐩 𐐶𐐲𐑉 𐑉𐐫𐑃 𐐶𐐮𐑄 𐐸𐐮𐑋, 𐐰𐑌𐐼 𐑅𐐫𐐻 𐐻𐐭 𐐻𐐩𐐿 𐐰𐐶𐐩 𐐸𐐮𐑆 𐑊𐐴𐑁; 𐐺𐐲𐐻 𐑄 𐐢𐐫𐑉𐐼 𐐼𐐯𐑊𐐮𐑂𐐲𐑉𐐼 𐐸𐐮𐑋 𐐵𐐻 𐐲𐑂 𐑄𐐯𐑉 𐐸𐐰𐑌𐐼𐑆. 𐐤𐐵 𐐸𐐶𐐯𐑌 𐐿𐐮𐑍 𐐤𐐬𐐰 𐐸𐐰𐐼 𐐸𐐲𐑉𐐼 𐐲𐑂 𐑄 𐐶𐐲𐑉𐐼𐑆 𐐸𐐶𐐮𐐽 𐐈𐐺𐐮𐑌𐐰𐐼𐐴 𐐸𐐰𐐼 𐑅𐐹𐐬𐐿𐐲𐑌 𐐲𐑌𐐻𐐭 𐑄 𐐹𐐨𐐹𐑊, 𐐸𐐨 𐐶𐐲𐑆 𐐫𐑊𐑅𐐬 𐑉𐐫𐑃; 𐐰𐑌𐐼 𐐸𐐨 𐑅𐐯𐐼, 𐐐𐐭 𐐮𐑆 𐐈𐐺𐐮𐑌𐐰𐐼𐐴, 𐑄𐐰𐐻 𐐌 𐐰𐑌𐐼 𐑋𐐴 𐐹𐐨𐐹𐑊 𐑇𐐳𐐼 𐐺𐐨 𐐾𐐲𐐾𐐼 𐐲𐑂 𐐸𐐮𐑋? 𐐱𐑉 𐐸𐐭 𐐮𐑆 𐑄 𐐢𐐫𐑉𐐼, 𐑄𐐰𐐻 𐑇𐐰𐑊 𐐺𐑉𐐮𐑍 𐐲𐐹𐐱𐑌 𐑋𐐴 𐐹𐐨𐐹𐑊 𐑅𐐲𐐽 𐑀𐑉𐐩𐐻 𐐰𐑁𐑊𐐮𐐿𐑇𐐲𐑌? 𐐌 𐐿𐐲𐑋𐐰𐑌𐐼 𐐷𐐭 𐐻𐐭 𐐺𐑉𐐮𐑍 𐐈𐐺𐐮𐑌𐐰𐐼𐐴 𐐸𐐮𐑄𐐲𐑉, 𐑄𐐰𐐻 𐐌 𐑋𐐩 𐑅𐑊𐐩 𐐸𐐮𐑋: 𐑁𐐫𐑉 𐐸𐐨 𐐸𐐰𐑆 𐑅𐐯𐐼 𐑄𐐨𐑆 𐑃𐐮𐑍𐑆 𐑄𐐰𐐻 𐐸𐐨 𐑋𐐴𐐻 𐑅𐐻𐐲𐑉 𐐲𐐹 𐑋𐐴 𐐹𐐨𐐹𐑊 𐐻𐐭 𐐰𐑍𐑀𐐲𐑉 𐐶𐐲𐑌 𐐶𐐮𐑄 𐐰𐑌𐐲𐑄𐐲𐑉, 𐐰𐑌𐐼 𐐻𐐭 𐑉𐐩𐑆 𐐿𐐱𐑌𐐻𐐯𐑌𐑇𐐲𐑌𐑆 𐐲𐑋𐐲𐑍 𐑋𐐴 𐐹𐐨𐐹𐑊; 𐑄𐐯𐑉𐑁𐐫𐑉 𐐌 𐐶𐐮𐑊 𐑅𐑊𐐩 𐐸𐐮𐑋. 𐐤𐐵 𐑄 𐐴𐑆 𐐲𐑂 𐑄 𐐹𐐨𐐹𐑊 𐐶𐐲𐑉 𐐺𐑊𐐴𐑌𐐼𐐲𐐼: 𐑄𐐯𐑉𐑁𐐫𐑉 𐑄𐐩 𐐸𐐪𐑉𐐼𐐲𐑌𐐼 𐑄𐐯𐑉 𐐸𐐪𐑉𐐻𐑅 𐐲𐑀𐐯𐑌𐑅𐐻 𐑄 𐐶𐐲𐑉𐐼𐑆 𐐲𐑂 𐐈𐐺𐐮𐑌𐐰𐐼𐐴, 𐐰𐑌𐐼 𐑄𐐩 𐑅𐐫𐐻 𐑁𐑉𐐱𐑋 𐑄𐐰𐐻 𐐻𐐴𐑋 𐑁𐐫𐑉𐐶𐐲𐑉𐐼 𐐻𐐭 𐐻𐐩𐐿 𐐸𐐮𐑋. 𐐈𐑌𐐼 𐐿𐐮𐑍 𐐤𐐬𐐰 𐐸𐐪𐑉𐐼𐐲𐑌𐐼 𐐸𐐮𐑆 𐐸𐐪𐑉𐐻 𐐲𐑀𐐯𐑌𐑅𐐻 𐑄 𐐶𐐲𐑉𐐼 𐐲𐑂 𐑄 𐐢𐐫𐑉𐐼, 𐐰𐑌𐐼 𐐸𐐨 𐐼𐐮𐐼 𐑌𐐱𐐻 𐑉𐐯𐐹𐐯𐑌𐐻 𐐲𐑂 𐐸𐐮𐑆 𐐨𐑂𐐲𐑊 𐐼𐐭𐐮𐑍𐑆.

10. 𐐈𐑌𐐼 𐐮𐐻 𐐿𐐩𐑋 𐐻𐐭 𐐹𐐰𐑅 𐑄𐐰𐐻 𐐰𐑁𐐻𐐲𐑉 𐑄 𐑅𐐹𐐩𐑅 𐐲𐑂 𐐻𐐭 𐐷𐐨𐑉𐑆, 𐑄𐐰𐐻 𐐈𐐺𐐮𐑌𐐰𐐼𐐴 𐐿𐐩𐑋 𐐲𐑋𐐲𐑍 𐑄𐐯𐑋 𐐮𐑌 𐐼𐐮𐑅𐑀𐐴𐑆, 𐑄𐐰𐐻 𐑄𐐩 𐑌𐐭 𐐸𐐮𐑋 𐑌𐐱𐐻, 𐐰𐑌𐐼 𐐺𐐨𐑀𐐰𐑌 𐐻𐐭 𐐹𐑉𐐱𐑁𐐯𐑅𐐴 𐐲𐑋𐐲𐑍 𐑄𐐯𐑋, 𐑅𐐩𐐮𐑍, 𐐜𐐲𐑅 𐐸𐐰𐑆 𐑄 𐐢𐐫𐑉𐐼 𐐿𐐲𐑋𐐰𐑌𐐼𐐲𐐼 𐑋𐐨, 𐑅𐐩𐐮𐑍: 𐐈𐐺𐐮𐑌𐐰𐐼𐐴, 𐑀𐐬 𐐰𐑌𐐼 𐐹𐑉𐐱𐑁𐐯𐑅𐐴 𐐲𐑌𐐻𐐭 𐑄𐐮𐑅 𐑋𐐴 𐐹𐐨𐐹𐑊, 𐑁𐐫𐑉 𐑄𐐩 𐐸𐐰𐑂 𐐸𐐪𐑉𐐼𐐲𐑌𐐼 𐑄𐐯𐑉 𐐸𐐪𐑉𐐻𐑅 𐐲𐑀𐐯𐑌𐑅𐐻 𐑋𐐴 𐐶𐐲𐑉𐐼𐑆: 𐑄𐐩 𐐸𐐰𐑂 𐑉𐐯𐐹𐐯𐑌𐐻𐐲𐐼 𐑌𐐱𐐻 𐐲𐑂 𐑄𐐯𐑉 𐐨𐑂𐐲𐑊 𐐼𐐭𐐮𐑍𐑆; 𐑄𐐯𐑉𐑁𐐫𐑉, 𐐌 𐐶𐐮𐑊 𐑂𐐮𐑆𐐮𐐻 𐑄𐐯𐑋 𐐮𐑌 𐑋𐐴 𐐰𐑍𐑀𐐲𐑉, 𐐷𐐩, 𐐮𐑌 𐑋𐐴 𐑁𐐨𐑉𐑅 𐐰𐑍𐑀𐐲𐑉 𐐶𐐮𐑊 𐐌 𐑂𐐮𐑆𐐮𐐻 𐑄𐐯𐑋 𐐮𐑌 𐑄𐐯𐑉 𐐮𐑌𐐮𐐿𐐶𐐮𐐻𐐨𐑆 𐐰𐑌𐐼 𐐰𐐺𐐱𐑋𐐮𐑌𐐩𐑇𐐲𐑌𐑆; 𐐏𐐩, 𐐶𐐬 𐐺𐐨 𐐲𐑌𐐻𐐭 𐑄𐐮𐑅 𐐾𐐯𐑌𐐲𐑉𐐩𐑇𐐲𐑌. 𐐈𐑌𐐼 𐑄 𐐢𐐫𐑉𐐼 𐑅𐐯𐐼 𐐲𐑌𐐻𐐭 𐑋𐐨, 𐐝𐐻𐑉𐐯𐐽 𐑁𐐬𐑉𐑃 𐑄𐐴 𐐸𐐰𐑌𐐼 𐐰𐑌𐐼 𐐹𐑉𐐱𐑁𐐯𐑅𐐴, 𐑅𐐩𐐮𐑍, 𐐜𐐲𐑅 𐑅𐐯𐑃 𐑄 𐐢𐐫𐑉𐐼: 𐐮𐐻 𐑇𐐰𐑊 𐐿𐐲𐑋 𐐻𐐭 𐐹𐐰𐑅 𐑄𐐰𐐻 𐑄𐐮𐑅 𐐾𐐯𐑌𐐲𐑉𐐩𐑇𐐲𐑌, 𐐺𐐨𐐿𐐫𐑆 𐐲𐑂 𐑄𐐯𐑉 𐐮𐑌𐐮𐐿𐐶𐐮𐐻𐐨𐑆, 𐑇𐐰𐑊 𐐺𐐨 𐐺𐑉𐐫𐐻 𐐮𐑌𐐻𐐭 𐐺𐐱𐑌𐐼𐐮𐐾, 𐐰𐑌𐐼 𐑇𐐰𐑊 𐐺𐐨 𐑅𐑋𐐮𐐻𐐲𐑌 𐐱𐑌 𐑄 𐐽𐐨𐐿; 𐐷𐐩, 𐐰𐑌𐐼 𐑇𐐰𐑊 𐐺𐐨 𐐼𐑉𐐮𐑂𐐲𐑌 𐐺𐐴 𐑋𐐯𐑌, 𐐰𐑌𐐼 𐑇𐐰𐑊 𐐺𐐨 𐑅𐑊𐐩𐑌; 𐐰𐑌𐐼 𐑄 𐑂𐐲𐑊𐐽𐐲𐑉𐑆 𐐲𐑂 𐑄 𐐩𐑉, 𐐰𐑌𐐼 𐑄 𐐼𐐫𐑀𐑆, 𐐷𐐩, 𐐰𐑌𐐼 𐑄 𐐶𐐴𐑊𐐼 𐐺𐐨𐑅𐐻𐑅, 𐑇𐐰𐑊 𐐼𐐯𐑂𐐵𐑉 𐑄𐐯𐑉 𐑁𐑊𐐯𐑇.

11. 𐐈𐑌𐐼 𐐮𐐻 𐑇𐐰𐑊 𐐿𐐲𐑋 𐐻𐐭 𐐹𐐰𐑅 𐑄𐐰𐐻 𐑄 𐑊𐐴𐑁 𐐲𐑂 𐐿𐐮𐑍 𐐤𐐬𐐰 𐑇𐐰𐑊 𐐺𐐨 𐑂𐐰𐑊𐐷𐐭𐐼 𐐨𐑂𐐲𐑌 𐐰𐑆 𐐰 𐑀𐐪𐑉𐑋𐐲𐑌𐐻 𐐮𐑌 𐐰 𐐸𐐱𐐻 𐑁𐐲𐑉𐑌𐐲𐑅; 𐑁𐐫𐑉 𐐸𐐨 𐑇𐐰𐑊 𐑌𐐬 𐑄𐐰𐐻 𐐌 𐐰𐑋 𐑄 𐐢𐐫𐑉𐐼. 𐐈𐑌𐐼 𐐮𐐻 𐑇𐐰𐑊 𐐿𐐲𐑋 𐐻𐐭 𐐹𐐰𐑅 𐑄𐐰𐐻 𐐌 𐐶𐐮𐑊 𐑅𐑋𐐴𐐻 𐑄𐐮𐑅 𐑋𐐴 𐐹𐐨𐐹𐑊 𐐶𐐮𐑄 𐑅𐐬𐑉 𐐰𐑁𐑊𐐮𐐿𐑇𐐲𐑌𐑆; 𐐷𐐩, 𐐶𐐮𐑄 𐑁𐐰𐑋𐐮𐑌 𐐰𐑌𐐼 𐐶𐐮𐑄 𐐹𐐯𐑅𐐻𐐮𐑊𐐯𐑌𐑅; 𐐰𐑌𐐼 𐐌 𐐶𐐮𐑊 𐐿𐐫𐑆 𐑄𐐰𐐻 𐑄𐐩 𐑇𐐰𐑊 𐐸𐐵𐑊 𐐫𐑊 𐑄 𐐼𐐩 𐑊𐐱𐑍. 𐐏𐐩, 𐐰𐑌𐐼 𐐌 𐐶𐐮𐑊 𐐿𐐫𐑆 𐑄𐐰𐐻 𐑄𐐩 𐑇𐐰𐑊 𐐸𐐰𐑂 𐐺𐐲𐑉𐐼𐐲𐑌𐑆 𐑊𐐰𐑇𐐻 𐐲𐐹𐐱𐑌 𐑄𐐯𐑉 𐐺𐐰𐐿𐑅; 𐐰𐑌𐐼 𐑄𐐩 𐑇𐐰𐑊 𐐺𐐨 𐐼𐑉𐐮𐑂𐐲𐑌 𐐺𐐨𐑁𐐬𐑉 𐑊𐐴𐐿 𐐰 𐐼𐐲𐑋 𐐰𐑅.

12. 𐐈𐑌𐐼 𐐮𐐻 𐑇𐐰𐑊 𐐿𐐲𐑋 𐐻𐐭 𐐹𐐰𐑅 𐑄𐐰𐐻 𐐌 𐐶𐐮𐑊 𐑅𐐯𐑌𐐼 𐑁𐐬𐑉𐑃 𐐸𐐩𐑊 𐐲𐑋𐐲𐑍 𐑄𐐯𐑋, 𐐰𐑌𐐼 𐐮𐐻 𐑇𐐰𐑊 𐑅𐑋𐐴𐐻 𐑄𐐯𐑋; 𐐰𐑌𐐼 𐑄𐐩 𐑇𐐰𐑊 𐐫𐑊𐑅𐐬 𐐺𐐨 𐑅𐑋𐐮𐐻𐐲𐑌 𐐶𐐮𐑄 𐑄 𐐨𐑅𐐻 𐐶𐐮𐑌𐐼; 𐐰𐑌𐐼 𐐮𐑌𐑅𐐯𐐿𐐻𐑅 𐑇𐐰𐑊 𐐹𐐯𐑅𐐻𐐲𐑉 𐑄𐐯𐑉 𐑊𐐰𐑌𐐼 𐐫𐑊𐑅𐐬, 𐐰𐑌𐐼 𐐼𐐯𐑂𐐵𐑉 𐑄𐐯𐑉 𐑀𐑉𐐩𐑌. 𐐈𐑌𐐼 𐑄𐐩 𐑇𐐰𐑊 𐐺𐐨 𐑅𐑋𐐮𐐻𐐲𐑌 𐐶𐐮𐑄 𐐰 𐑀𐑉𐐩𐐻 𐐹𐐯𐑅𐐻𐐮𐑊𐐯𐑌𐑅: 𐐰𐑌𐐼 𐐫𐑊 𐑄𐐮𐑅 𐐶𐐮𐑊 𐐌 𐐼𐐭 𐐺𐐨𐐿𐐫𐑆 𐐲𐑂 𐑄𐐯𐑉 𐐮𐑌𐐮𐐿𐐶𐐮𐐻𐐨𐑆 𐐰𐑌𐐼 𐐰𐐺𐐱𐑋𐐮𐑌𐐩𐑇𐐲𐑌𐑆.

13. 𐐈𐑌𐐼 𐐮𐐻 𐑇𐐰𐑊 𐐿𐐲𐑋 𐐻𐐭 𐐹𐐰𐑅 𐑄𐐰𐐻 𐐯𐐿𐑅𐐯𐐹𐐻 𐑄𐐩 𐑉𐐯𐐹𐐯𐑌𐐻, 𐐌 𐐶𐐮𐑊 𐐲𐐻𐐲𐑉𐑊𐐨 𐐼𐐯𐑅𐐻𐑉𐐱𐐴 𐑄𐐯𐑋 𐑁𐑉𐐱𐑋 𐐫𐑁 𐑄 𐑁𐐩𐑅 𐐲𐑂 𐑄 𐐲𐑉𐑃; 𐐷𐐯𐐻 𐑄𐐩 𐑇𐐰𐑊 𐑊𐐨𐑂 𐐰 𐑉𐐯𐐿𐐲𐑉𐐼 𐐺𐐨𐐸𐐴𐑌𐐼 𐑄𐐯𐑋, 𐐰𐑌𐐼 𐐌 𐐶𐐮𐑊 𐐹𐑉𐐨𐑆𐐲𐑉𐑂 𐑄𐐯𐑋 𐑁𐐫𐑉 𐐲𐑄𐐲𐑉 𐑌𐐩𐑇𐐲𐑌𐑆 𐐸𐐶𐐮𐐽 𐑇𐐰𐑊 𐐹𐐲𐑆𐐯𐑅 𐑄 𐑊𐐰𐑌𐐼; 𐐷𐐩, 𐐨𐑂𐐲𐑌 𐑄𐐮𐑅 𐐶𐐮𐑊 𐐌 𐐼𐐭 𐑄𐐰𐐻 𐐌 𐑋𐐩 𐐼𐐮𐑅𐐿𐐲𐑂𐐲𐑉 𐑄 𐐰𐐺𐐱𐑋𐐮𐑌𐐩𐑇𐐲𐑌𐑆 𐐲𐑂 𐑄𐐮𐑅 𐐹𐐨𐐹𐑊 𐐻𐐭 𐐲𐑄𐐲𐑉 𐑌𐐩𐑇𐐲𐑌𐑆. 𐐈𐑌𐐼 𐑋𐐯𐑌𐐨 𐑃𐐮𐑍𐑆 𐐼𐐮𐐼 𐐈𐐺𐐮𐑌𐐰𐐼𐐴 𐐹𐑉𐐱𐑁𐐯𐑅𐐴 𐐲𐑀𐐯𐑌𐑅𐐻 𐑄𐐮𐑅 𐐹𐐨𐐹𐑊.

14. 𐐈𐑌𐐼 𐐮𐐻 𐐿𐐩𐑋 𐐻𐐭 𐐹𐐰𐑅 𐑄𐐰𐐻 𐑄𐐩 𐐶𐐲𐑉 𐐰𐑍𐑀𐑉𐐨 𐐶𐐮𐑄 𐐸𐐮𐑋; 𐐰𐑌𐐼 𐑄𐐩 𐐻𐐳𐐿 𐐸𐐮𐑋 𐐰𐑌𐐼 𐐿𐐰𐑉𐐨𐐼 𐐸𐐮𐑋 𐐺𐐵𐑌𐐼 𐐺𐐨𐑁𐐬𐑉 𐑄 𐐿𐐮𐑍, 𐐰𐑌𐐼 𐑅𐐯𐐼 𐐲𐑌𐐻𐐭 𐑄 𐐿𐐮𐑍, 𐐒𐐨𐐸𐐬𐑊𐐼, 𐐶𐐨 𐐸𐐰𐑂 𐐺𐑉𐐫𐐻 𐐰 𐑋𐐰𐑌 𐐺𐐨𐑁𐐬𐑉 𐑄𐐨 𐐸𐐭 𐐸𐐰𐑆 𐐹𐑉𐐱𐑁𐐯𐑅𐐴𐐼 𐐨𐑂𐐲𐑊 𐐿𐐱𐑌𐑅𐐲𐑉𐑌𐐮𐑍 𐑄𐐴 𐐹𐐨𐐹𐑊, 𐐰𐑌𐐼 𐑅𐐯𐑃 𐑄𐐰𐐻 𐐘𐐱𐐼 𐐶𐐮𐑊 𐐼𐐯𐑅𐐻𐑉𐐱𐐴 𐑄𐐯𐑋. 𐐈𐑌𐐼 𐐸𐐨 𐐫𐑊𐑅𐐬 𐐹𐑉𐐱𐑁𐐯𐑅𐐴𐐯𐑃 𐐨𐑂𐐲𐑊 𐐿𐐱𐑌𐑅𐐲𐑉𐑌𐐮𐑍 𐑄𐐴 𐑊𐐴𐑁, 𐐰𐑌𐐼 𐑅𐐯𐑃 𐑄𐐰𐐻 𐑄𐐴

𐑊𐐴𐑁 𐑇𐐰𐑊 𐐺𐐨 𐐰𐑆 𐐩 𐑀𐐪𐑉𐑋𐐲𐑌𐐻 𐐮𐑌 𐐩 𐑁𐐲𐑉𐑌𐐲𐑅 𐐱𐑂 𐑁𐐴𐑉. 𐐈𐑌𐐼 𐐲𐑀𐐯𐑌, 𐐸𐐨 𐑅𐐯𐑃 𐑄𐐰𐐻 𐑄𐐵 𐑇𐐰𐑊𐐻 𐐺𐐨 𐐰𐑆 𐐩 𐑅𐐻𐐫𐐿, 𐐨𐑂𐐲𐑌 𐐰𐑆 𐐩 𐐼𐑉𐐴 𐑅𐐻𐐫𐐿 𐐱𐑂 𐑄 𐑁𐐨𐑊𐐼, 𐐸𐐶𐐮𐐽 𐐮𐑆 𐑉𐐲𐑌 𐐬𐑂𐐲𐑉 𐐺𐐴 𐑄 𐐺𐐨𐑅𐐻𐑅, 𐐰𐑌𐐼 𐐻𐑉𐐱𐐼𐑌 𐐲𐑌𐐼𐐲𐑉 𐑁𐐳𐐻. 𐐈𐑌𐐼 𐐲𐑀𐐯𐑌, 𐐸𐐨 𐑅𐐯𐑃 𐑄𐐵 𐑇𐐰𐑊𐐻 𐐺𐐨 𐐰𐑆 𐑄 𐐺𐑊𐐱𐑅𐐲𐑋𐑆 𐐱𐑂 𐐩 𐑃𐐮𐑅𐑊, 𐐸𐐶𐐮𐐽, 𐐸𐐶𐐯𐑌 𐐮𐐻 𐐮𐑆 𐑁𐐳𐑊𐐨 𐑉𐐴𐐹, 𐐮𐑁 𐑄 𐐶𐐮𐑌𐐼 𐐺𐑊𐐬𐐲𐑃 𐐮𐐻 𐐮𐑆 𐐼𐑉𐐮𐑂𐑌 𐑁𐐫𐑉𐑃 𐐲𐐹𐐱𐑌 𐑄 𐑁𐐩𐑅 𐐱𐑂 𐑄 𐑊𐐰𐑌𐐼; 𐐰𐑌𐐼 𐐸𐐨 𐐹𐑉𐐨𐐻𐐯𐑌𐐼𐐲𐑃 𐑄 𐐢𐐫𐑉𐐼 𐐸𐐰𐑃 𐑅𐐹𐐬𐐿𐑌 𐐮𐐻. 𐐈𐑌𐐼 𐐸𐐨 𐑅𐐯𐑃 𐐫𐑊 𐑄𐐮𐑅 𐑇𐐰𐑊 𐐿𐐲𐑋 𐐲𐐹𐐱𐑌 𐑄𐐨 𐐯𐐿𐑅𐐯𐐹𐐻 𐑄𐐵 𐑉𐐨𐐹𐐯𐑌𐐻, 𐐰𐑌𐐼 𐑄𐐮𐑅 𐐺𐐨𐐿𐐫𐑆 𐐱𐑂 𐑄𐐴𐑌 𐐮𐑌𐐮𐐿𐐶𐐮𐐻𐐮𐑆.

15. 𐐈𐑌𐐼 𐑌𐐵, 𐐄 𐐿𐐮𐑍, 𐐸𐐶𐐱𐐻 𐑀𐑉𐐩𐐻 𐐨𐑂𐐮𐑊 𐐸𐐰𐑅𐐻 𐑄𐐵 𐐼𐐲𐑌, 𐐫𐑉 𐐸𐐶𐐱𐐻 𐑀𐑉𐐩𐐻 𐑅𐐮𐑌𐑆 𐐸𐐰𐑂 𐑄𐐴 𐐹𐐨𐐹𐑊 𐐿𐐲𐑋𐐮𐐻𐐲𐐼, 𐑄𐐰𐐻 𐐶𐐨 𐑇𐐳𐐼 𐐺𐐨 𐐿𐐲𐑌𐐼𐐯𐑋𐐼 𐐱𐑂 𐐘𐐱𐐼 𐐫𐑉 𐐾𐐲𐐾𐐼 𐐱𐑂 𐑄𐐮𐑅 𐑋𐐰𐑌? 𐐈𐑌𐐼 𐑌𐐵, 𐐄 𐐿𐐮𐑍, 𐐺𐐨𐐸𐐬𐑊𐐼, 𐐶𐐨 𐐪𐑉 𐑀𐐮𐑊𐐻𐑊𐐯𐑅, 𐐰𐑌𐐼 𐑄𐐵, 𐐄 𐐿𐐮𐑍, 𐐸𐐰𐑅𐐻 𐑌𐐱𐐻 𐑅𐐮𐑌𐐼; 𐑄𐐯𐑉𐑁𐐫𐑉 𐑄𐐮𐑅 𐑋𐐰𐑌 𐐸𐐰𐑆 𐑊𐐴𐐼 𐐿𐐲𐑌𐑅𐐲𐑉𐑌𐐮𐑍 𐐷𐐭, 𐐰𐑌𐐼 𐐸𐐨 𐐸𐐰𐑆 𐐹𐑉𐐱𐑁𐐯𐑅𐐴𐐼 𐐮𐑌 𐑂𐐩𐑌. 𐐈𐑌𐐼 𐐺𐐨𐐸𐐬𐑊𐐼, 𐐶𐐨 𐐪𐑉 𐑅𐐻𐑉𐐱𐑍, 𐐶𐐨 𐑇𐐰𐑊 𐑌𐐱𐐻 𐐿𐐲𐑋 𐐮𐑌𐐻𐐭 𐐺𐐱𐑌𐐼𐐩𐐾, 𐐫𐑉 𐐺𐐨 𐐻𐐩𐐿𐑌 𐐿𐐰𐐹𐐻𐐮𐑂 𐐺𐐴 𐐵𐑉 𐐯𐑌𐐯𐑋𐐮𐑆; 𐐷𐐩, 𐐰𐑌𐐼 𐑄𐐵 𐐸𐐰𐑅𐐻 𐐹𐑉𐐱𐑅𐐹𐐲𐑉𐐼 𐐮𐑌 𐑄 𐑊𐐰𐑌𐐼, 𐐰𐑌𐐼 𐑄𐐵 𐑇𐐰𐑊𐐻 𐐫𐑊𐑅𐐬 𐐹𐑉𐐱𐑅𐐹𐐲𐑉. 𐐒𐐨𐐸𐐬𐑊𐐼, 𐐸𐐨𐑉 𐐮𐑆 𐑄 𐑋𐐰𐑌, 𐐶𐐨 𐐼𐐯𐑊𐐮𐑂𐐲𐑉 𐐸𐐮𐑋 𐐮𐑌𐐻𐐭 𐑄𐐴 𐐸𐐰𐑌𐐼𐑆; 𐑄𐐵 𐑋𐐩𐐯𐑅𐐻 𐐼𐐭 𐐶𐐮𐑃 𐐸𐐮𐑋 𐐰𐑆 𐑅𐐨𐑋𐐯𐑃 𐑄𐐨 𐑀𐐳𐐼.

16. 𐐈𐑌𐐼 𐐮𐐻 𐐿𐐩𐑋 𐐻𐐭 𐐹𐐰𐑅 𐑄𐐰𐐻 𐐿𐐮𐑍 𐐤𐐬𐐲 𐐿𐐫𐑆𐐼 𐑄𐐰𐐻 𐐈𐐺𐐮𐑌𐐲𐐼𐐴 𐑇𐐳𐐼 𐐺𐐨 𐐿𐐰𐑅𐐻 𐐮𐑌𐐻𐐭 𐐹𐑉𐐮𐑆𐑌; 𐐰𐑌𐐼 𐐸𐐨 𐐿𐐲𐑋𐐰𐑌𐐼𐐲𐐼 𐑄𐐰𐐻 𐑄 𐐹𐑉𐐨𐑅𐐻𐑅 𐑇𐐳𐐼 𐑀𐐰𐑄𐐲𐑉 𐑄𐐯𐑋𐑅𐐯𐑊𐑂𐑆 𐐻𐐭𐑀𐐯𐑄𐐲𐑉, 𐑄𐐰𐐻 𐐸𐐨 𐑋𐐴𐐻 𐐸𐐬𐑊𐐼 𐐩 𐐿𐐵𐑌𐑅𐐮𐑊 𐐶𐐮𐑃 𐑄𐐯𐑋 𐐸𐐶𐐱𐐻 𐐸𐐨 𐑇𐐳𐐼 𐐼𐐭 𐐶𐐮𐑃 𐐸𐐮𐑋. 𐐈𐑌𐐼 𐐮𐐻 𐐿𐐩𐑋 𐐻𐐭 𐐹𐐰𐑅 𐑄𐐰𐐻 𐑄𐐩 𐑅𐐯𐐼 𐐲𐑌𐐻𐐭 𐑄 𐐿𐐮𐑍, 𐐒𐑉𐐮𐑍 𐐸𐐮𐑋 𐐸𐐮𐑄𐐲𐑉 𐑄𐐰𐐻 𐐶𐐨 𐑋𐐩 𐐿𐐶𐐯𐑅𐐽𐐲𐑌 𐐸𐐮𐑋; 𐐰𐑌𐐼 𐑄 𐐿𐐮𐑍 𐐿𐐲𐑋𐐰𐑌𐐼𐐲𐐼 𐑄𐐰𐐻 𐐸𐐨 𐑇𐐳𐐼 𐐺𐐨 𐐺𐑉𐐫𐐻 𐐺𐐨𐑁𐐫𐑉 𐑄𐐯𐑋. 𐐈𐑌𐐼 𐑄𐐩 𐐺𐐨𐑀𐐰𐑌 𐐻𐐭 𐐿𐐶𐐯𐑅𐐽𐐲𐑌 𐐸𐐮𐑋, 𐑄𐐰𐐻 𐑄𐐩 𐑋𐐴𐐻 𐐿𐑉𐐱𐑅 𐐸𐐮𐑋, 𐑄𐐰𐐻 𐑄𐐯𐑉𐐺𐐴 𐑄𐐩 𐑋𐐴𐐻 𐐸𐐰𐑂 𐐸𐐶𐐯𐑉𐐶𐐮𐑃 𐐻𐐭 𐐰𐐿𐐷𐐭𐑆 𐐸𐐮𐑋; 𐐺𐐲𐐻 𐐸𐐨 𐐰𐑌𐑅𐐲𐑉𐐼 𐑄𐐯𐑋 𐐺𐐬𐑊𐐼𐑊𐐨, 𐐰𐑌𐐼 𐐶𐐮𐑄𐑅𐐻𐐳𐐼 𐐫𐑊 𐑄𐐯𐑉 𐐿𐐶𐐯𐑅𐐽𐐲𐑌𐑆, 𐐷𐐩, 𐐻𐐭 𐑄𐐯𐑉 𐐰𐑅𐐻𐐱𐑌𐐮𐑇𐑋𐐲𐑌𐐻: 𐑁𐐫𐑉 𐐸𐐨 𐐼𐐮𐐼 𐐶𐐮𐑄𐑅𐐻𐐰𐑌𐐼 𐑄𐐯𐑋 𐐮𐑌 𐐫𐑊 𐑄𐐯𐑉 𐐿𐐶𐐯𐑅𐐽𐐲𐑌𐑆, 𐐰𐑌𐐼 𐐼𐐮𐐼 𐐿𐐲𐑌𐑁𐐵𐑌𐐼 𐑄𐐯𐑋 𐐮𐑌 𐐫𐑊 𐑄𐐯𐑉 𐐶𐐲𐑉𐐼𐑆.

17. 𐐈𐑌𐐼 𐐮𐐻 𐐿𐐩𐑋 𐐻𐐭 𐐹𐐰𐑅 𐑄𐐰𐐻 𐐶𐐲𐑌 𐐱𐑂 𐑄𐐯𐑋 𐑅𐐯𐐼 𐐲𐑌𐐻𐐭 𐐸𐐮𐑋, 𐐐𐐶𐐱𐐻 𐑋𐐨𐑌𐐲𐑃 𐑄 𐐶𐐲𐑉𐐼𐑆 𐐸𐐶𐐮𐐽 𐐪𐑉 𐑉𐐮𐐻𐑌, 𐐰𐑌𐐼 𐐸𐐶𐐮𐐽 𐐸𐐰𐑂 𐐺𐐨𐑌 𐐻𐐫𐐻 𐐺𐐴 𐐵𐑉 𐑁𐐪𐑄𐐲𐑉𐑆, 𐑅𐐩𐐮𐑍: 𐐐𐐵 𐐺𐐷𐐭𐐻𐐮𐑁𐐳𐑊 𐐲𐐹𐐱𐑌 𐑄 𐑋𐐵𐑌𐐻𐐲𐑌𐑆 𐐪𐑉 𐑄 𐑁𐐨𐐻 𐐱𐑂 𐐸𐐮𐑋 𐑄𐐰𐐻 𐐺𐑉𐐮𐑍𐐲𐑃 𐑀𐐳𐐼 𐐻𐐴𐐼𐐮𐑍𐑆; 𐑄𐐰𐐻 𐐹𐐲𐐺𐑊𐐮𐑇𐐲𐑃 𐐹𐐨𐑅; 𐑄𐐰𐐻 𐐺𐑉𐐮𐑍𐐲𐑃 𐑀𐐳𐐼 𐐻𐐴𐐼𐐮𐑍𐑆 𐐱𐑂 𐑀𐐳𐐼; 𐑄𐐰𐐻 𐐹𐐲𐐺𐑊𐐮𐑇𐐲𐑃 𐑅𐐰𐑊𐑂𐐩𐑇𐐲𐑌; 𐑄𐐰𐐻 𐑅𐐯𐑃 𐐲𐑌𐐻𐐭 𐐞𐐴𐐲𐑌, 𐐜𐐴 𐐘𐐱𐐼 𐑉𐐩𐑌𐐲𐑃; 𐐜𐐴 𐐶𐐱𐐽𐑋𐐯𐑌 𐑇𐐰𐑊 𐑊𐐮𐑁𐐻 𐐲𐐹 𐑄 𐑂𐐱𐐮𐑅; 𐐶𐐮𐑃 𐑄 𐑂𐐱𐐮𐑅 𐐻𐐭𐑀𐐯𐑄𐐲𐑉 𐑇𐐰𐑊 𐑄𐐩 𐑅𐐮𐑍, 𐑁𐐫𐑉 𐑄𐐩 𐑇𐐰𐑊 𐑅𐐨 𐐴 𐐻𐐭 𐐴 𐐸𐐶𐐯𐑌 𐑄 𐐢𐐫𐑉𐐼 𐑇𐐰𐑊 𐐺𐑉𐐮𐑍 𐐲𐑀𐐯𐑌 𐐞𐐴𐐲𐑌. 𐐒𐑉𐐩𐐿 𐑁𐐫𐑉𐑃 𐐮𐑌𐐻𐐭 𐐾𐐱𐐮; 𐑅𐐮𐑍 𐐻𐐭𐑀𐐯𐑄𐐲𐑉 𐐷𐐨 𐐶𐐩𐑅𐐻 𐐹𐑊𐐩𐑅𐐲𐑆 𐐱𐑂 𐐖𐐲𐑉𐐭𐑅𐐲𐑊𐐲𐑋: 𐑁𐐫𐑉 𐑄 𐐢𐐫𐑉𐐼 𐐸𐐰𐑃 𐐿𐐲𐑋𐑁𐐲𐑉𐐻𐐲𐐼 𐐸𐐮𐑆 𐐹𐐨𐐹𐑊, 𐐸𐐨 𐐸𐐰𐑃 𐑉𐐨𐐼𐐨𐑋𐐼 𐐖𐐲𐑉𐐭𐑅𐐲𐑊𐐲𐑋. 𐐜 𐐢𐐫𐑉𐐼 𐐸𐐰𐑃 𐑋𐐩𐐼 𐐺𐐯𐑉 𐐸𐐮𐑆 𐐸𐐬𐑊𐐨 𐐪𐑉𐑋 𐐮𐑌 𐑄 𐐴𐑆 𐐱𐑂 𐐫𐑊 𐑄 𐑌𐐩𐑇𐐲𐑌𐑆, 𐐰𐑌𐐼 𐐫𐑊 𐑄 𐐯𐑌𐐼𐑆 𐐱𐑂 𐑄 𐐲𐑉𐑃 𐑇𐐰𐑊 𐑅𐐨 𐑄 𐑅𐐰𐑊𐑂𐐩𐑇𐐲𐑌 𐐱𐑂 𐐵𐑉 𐐘𐐱𐐼. 𐐈𐑌𐐼 𐑌𐐵 𐐈𐐺𐐮𐑌𐐲𐐼𐐴 𐑅𐐯𐐼 𐐲𐑌𐐻𐐭 𐑄𐐯𐑋, 𐐂𐑉 𐐷𐐭 𐐹𐑉𐐨𐑅𐐻𐑅, 𐐰𐑌𐐼 𐐹𐑉𐐨𐐻𐐯𐑌𐐼 𐐻𐐭 𐐻𐐨𐐽 𐑄𐐮𐑅 𐐹𐐨𐐹𐑊, 𐐰𐑌𐐼 𐐻𐐭 𐐲𐑌𐐼𐐲𐑉𐑅𐐻𐐰𐑌𐐼 𐑄 𐑅𐐹𐐮𐑉𐐮𐐻 𐐱𐑂 𐐹𐑉𐐱𐑁𐐯𐑅𐐴𐐮𐑍, 𐐰𐑌𐐼 𐐷𐐯𐐻 𐐼𐐯𐑆𐐴𐑉 𐐻𐐭 𐑌𐐬 𐐱𐑂 𐑋𐐨 𐐸𐐶𐐱𐐻 𐑄𐐨𐑆 𐑃𐐮𐑍𐑆 𐑋𐐨𐑌? 𐐌 𐑅𐐩 𐐲𐑌𐐻𐐭 𐐷𐐭, 𐐎𐐬 𐐺𐐨 𐐲𐑌𐐻𐐭 𐐷𐐭 𐑁𐐫𐑉 𐐹𐐲𐑉𐑂𐐲𐑉𐐻𐐮𐑍 𐑄 𐐶𐐩𐑆 𐐱𐑂 𐑄 𐐢𐐫𐑉𐐼. 𐐙𐐫𐑉 𐐮𐑁 𐐷𐐨 𐐲𐑌𐐼𐐲𐑉𐑅𐐻𐐰𐑌𐐼 𐑄𐐨𐑆 𐑃𐐮𐑍𐑆 𐐷𐐨 𐐸𐐰𐑂 𐑌𐐱𐐻 𐐻𐐫𐐻 𐑄𐐯𐑋: 𐑄𐐯𐑉𐑁𐐫𐑉, 𐐷𐐨 𐐸𐐰𐑂 𐐹𐐲𐑉𐑂𐐲𐑉𐐻𐐲𐐼 𐑄 𐐶𐐩𐑆 𐐱𐑂 𐑄 𐐢𐐫𐑉𐐼. 𐐏𐐨 𐐸𐐰𐑂 𐑌𐐱𐐻 𐐰𐐹𐑊𐐴𐐼 𐐷𐐫𐑉 𐐸𐐪𐑉𐐻𐑅 𐐻𐐭 𐐲𐑌𐐼𐐲𐑉𐑅𐐻𐐰𐑌𐐼𐐮𐑍; 𐑄𐐯𐑉𐑁𐐫𐑉, 𐐷𐐨 𐐸𐐰𐑂 𐑌𐐱𐐻 𐐺𐐨𐑌 𐐶𐐴𐑆. 𐐜𐐯𐑉𐑁𐐫𐑉, 𐐸𐐶𐐱𐐻 𐐻𐐨𐐽 𐐷𐐨 𐑄𐐮𐑅 𐐹𐐨𐐹𐑊? 𐐈𐑌𐐼 𐑄𐐩 𐑅𐐯𐐼, 𐐎𐐨 𐐻𐐨𐐽 𐑄 𐑊𐐫 𐐱𐑂 𐐣𐐬𐑆𐐯𐑆. 𐐈𐑌𐐼 𐐲𐑀𐐯𐑌 𐐸𐐨 𐑅𐐯𐐼 𐐲𐑌𐐻𐐭 𐑄𐐯𐑋, 𐐆𐑁 𐐷𐐨 𐐻𐐨𐐽 𐑄 𐑊𐐫 𐐱𐑂 𐐣𐐬𐑆𐐯𐑆 𐐸𐐶𐐴 𐐼𐐭 𐐷𐐨 𐑌𐐱𐐻 𐐿𐐨𐐹 𐐮𐐻? 𐐐𐐶𐐴 𐐼𐐭 𐐷𐐨 𐑅𐐯𐐻 𐐷𐐫𐑉 𐐸𐐪𐑉𐐻𐑅 𐐲𐐹𐐱𐑌 𐑉𐐮𐐽𐐯𐑆? 𐐐𐐶𐐴 𐐼𐐭 𐐷𐐨 𐐿𐐲𐑋𐐮𐐻 𐐸𐐬𐑉𐐼𐐲𐑋𐑆 𐐰𐑌𐐼 𐑅𐐹𐐯𐑌𐐼 𐐷𐐫𐑉 𐑅𐐻𐑉𐐯𐑍𐑃 𐐶𐐮𐑃 𐐸𐐪𐑉𐑊𐐱𐐻𐑅, 𐐷𐐩, 𐐰𐑌𐐼 𐐿𐐫𐑆 𐑄𐐮𐑅 𐐹𐐨𐐹𐑊 𐐻𐐭 𐐿𐐲𐑋𐐮𐐻 𐑅𐐮𐑌, 𐑄𐐰𐐻 𐑄 𐐢𐐫𐑉𐐼 𐐸𐐰𐑆 𐐿𐐫𐑆 𐐻𐐭 𐑅𐐯𐑌𐐼 𐑋𐐨 𐐻𐐭 𐐹𐑉𐐱𐑁𐐯𐑅𐐴 𐐲𐑀𐐯𐑌𐑅𐐻 𐑄𐐮𐑅 𐐹𐐨𐐹𐑊, 𐐷𐐩, 𐐨𐑂𐐲𐑌 𐐩 𐑀𐑉𐐩𐐻 𐐨𐑂𐐮𐑊 𐐲𐑀𐐯𐑌𐑅𐐻 𐑄𐐮𐑅 𐐹𐐨𐐹𐑊? 𐐤𐐬 𐐷𐐨 𐑌𐐱𐐻 𐑄𐐰𐐻 𐐌 𐑅𐐹𐐨𐐿 𐑄 𐐻𐑉𐐭𐑃? 𐐏𐐩, 𐐷𐐨 𐑌𐐬 𐑄𐐰𐐻 𐐌 𐑅𐐹𐐨𐐿 𐑄 𐐻𐑉𐐭𐑃; 𐐰𐑌𐐼 𐐷𐐭 𐐫𐐻 𐐻𐐭 𐐻𐑉𐐯𐑋𐐺𐑊 𐐺𐐨𐑁𐐫𐑉 𐐘𐐱𐐼.

18. 𐐈𐑌𐐼 𐐮𐐻 𐑇𐐰𐑊 𐐿𐐲𐑋 𐐻𐐭 𐐹𐐰𐑅 𐑄𐐰𐐻 𐐷 𐑇𐐰𐑊 𐐺 𐑅𐑋𐐮𐐻𐑌 𐑁𐐫𐑉 𐐷𐐫𐑉 𐐮𐑌𐐮𐐿𐐶𐐮𐐻𐐮𐑆: 𐑁𐐫𐑉 𐐷 𐐸𐐰𐑂 𐑅𐐯𐐼 𐑄𐐰𐐻 𐐷 𐐻𐐨𐐽 𐑄 𐑊𐐫 𐐲𐑂 𐐣𐐬𐑆𐐯𐑆. 𐐈𐑌𐐼 𐐸𐐶𐐱𐐻 𐑌𐐬 𐐷 𐐿𐐱𐑌𐑅𐐲𐑉𐑌𐐮𐑍 𐑄 𐑊𐐫 𐐲𐑂 𐐣𐐬𐑆𐐯𐑆? 𐐔𐐲𐑃 𐑅𐐰𐑊𐑂𐐩𐑇𐐲𐑌 𐐿𐐲𐑋 𐐺𐐴 𐑄 𐑊𐐫 𐐲𐑂 𐐣𐐬𐑆𐐯𐑆? 𐐐𐐶𐐱𐐻 𐑅𐐩 𐐷? 𐐈𐑌𐐼 𐑄𐐩 𐐰𐑌𐑅𐐲𐑉𐐼 𐐰𐑌𐐼 𐑅𐐯𐐼, 𐐜𐐰𐐻 𐑅𐐰𐑊𐑂𐐩𐑇𐐲𐑌 𐐼𐐮𐐼 𐐿𐐲𐑋 𐐺𐐴 𐑄 𐑊𐐫 𐐲𐑂 𐐣𐐬𐑆𐐯𐑆. 𐐒𐐲𐐻 𐑌𐐵 𐐈𐐺𐐮𐑌𐐩𐐼𐐴 𐑅𐐯𐐼 𐐲𐑌𐐻𐐭 𐑄𐐯𐑋, 𐐌 𐑌𐐬 𐐮𐑁 𐐷 𐐿𐐨𐐹 𐑄 𐐿𐐲𐑋𐐰𐑌𐐼𐑋𐐯𐑌𐐻𐑅 𐐲𐑂 𐐘𐐱𐐼 𐐷 𐑇𐐰𐑊 𐐺 𐑅𐐩𐑂𐐼; 𐐷𐐩, 𐐮𐑁 𐐷 𐐿𐐨𐐹 𐑄 𐐿𐐲𐑋𐐰𐑌𐐼𐑋𐐯𐑌𐐻𐑅 𐐸𐐶𐐮𐐽 𐑄 𐐢𐐫𐑉𐐼 𐐼𐐮𐑊𐐮𐑂𐐲𐑉𐐼 𐐲𐑌𐐻𐐭 𐐣𐐬𐑆𐐯𐑆 𐐮𐑌 𐑄 𐑋𐐵𐑌𐐻 𐐲𐑂 𐐝𐐴𐑌𐐴, 𐑅𐐩𐐮𐑍, 𐐌 𐐰𐑋 𐑄 𐐢𐐫𐑉𐐼 𐑄𐐴 𐐘𐐱𐐼, 𐐸𐐭 𐐸𐐰𐑃 𐐺𐑉𐐫𐐻 𐑄𐐨 𐐵𐐻 𐐲𐑂 𐑄 𐑊𐐰𐑌𐐼 𐐲𐑂 𐐀𐐾𐐮𐐹𐐻, 𐐵𐐻 𐐲𐑂 𐑄 𐐸𐐵𐑅 𐐲𐑂 𐐺𐐱𐑌𐐼𐐩𐐾. 𐐜𐐵 𐑇𐐰𐑊𐐻 𐐸𐐰𐑂 𐑌𐐬 𐐲𐑄𐐲𐑉 𐐘𐐱𐐼 𐐺𐐨𐑁𐐬𐑉 𐑋𐐨. 𐐜𐐵 𐑇𐐰𐑊𐐻 𐑌𐐱𐐻 𐑋𐐩𐐿 𐐲𐑌𐐻𐐭 𐑄𐐨 𐐯𐑌𐐨 𐑀𐑉𐐩𐑂𐐲𐑌 𐐮𐑋𐐲𐐾, 𐐫𐑉 𐐯𐑌𐐨 𐑊𐐴𐐿𐑌𐐯𐑅 𐐲𐑂 𐐯𐑌𐐨 𐑃𐐮𐑍 𐐮𐑌 𐐸𐐯𐑂𐐲𐑌 𐐲𐐺𐐲𐑂, 𐐫𐑉 𐑃𐐮𐑍𐑆 𐐸𐐶𐐮𐐽 𐐪𐑉 𐐮𐑌 𐑄 𐐲𐑉𐑃 𐐺𐐨𐑌𐐨𐑃. 𐐤𐐵 𐐈𐐺𐐮𐑌𐐩𐐼𐐴 𐑅𐐯𐐼 𐐲𐑌𐐻𐐭 𐑄𐐯𐑋, 𐐐𐐰𐑂 𐐷 𐐼𐐲𐑌 𐐫𐑊 𐑄𐐮𐑅? 𐐌 𐑅𐐩 𐐲𐑌𐐻𐐭 𐐷𐐭, 𐐤𐐩, 𐐷 𐐸𐐰𐑂 𐑌𐐱𐐻. 𐐈𐑌𐐼 𐐸𐐰𐑂 𐐷 𐐻𐐫𐐻 𐑄𐐮𐑅 𐐹𐐨𐐹𐐲𐑊 𐑄𐐰𐐻 𐑄𐐩 𐑇𐐳𐐼 𐐼𐐭 𐐫𐑊 𐑄𐐨𐑆 𐑃𐐮𐑍𐑆? 𐐌 𐑅𐐩 𐐲𐑌𐐻𐐭 𐐷𐐭, 𐐤𐐩, 𐐷 𐐸𐐰𐑂 𐑌𐐱𐐻.

19. 𐐈𐑌𐐼 𐑌𐐵 𐐸𐐶𐐯𐑌 𐑄 𐐿𐐮𐑍 𐐸𐐰𐐼 𐐸𐐲𐑉𐐼 𐑄𐐨𐑆 𐐶𐐲𐑉𐐼𐑆, 𐐸𐐨 𐑅𐐯𐐼 𐐲𐑌𐐻𐐭 𐐸𐐮𐑆 𐐹𐑉𐐨𐑅𐐻𐑅, 𐐊𐐶𐐩 𐐶𐐮𐑄 𐑄𐐮𐑅 𐑁𐐯𐑊𐐬, 𐐰𐑌𐐼 𐑅𐑊𐐩 𐐸𐐮𐑋: 𐑁𐐫𐑉 𐐸𐐶𐐱𐐻 𐐸𐐰𐑂 𐐶𐐨 𐐻𐐭 𐐼𐐭 𐐶𐐮𐑄 𐐸𐐮𐑋, 𐑁𐐫𐑉 𐐸𐐨 𐐮𐑆 𐑋𐐰𐐼. 𐐈𐑌𐐼 𐑄𐐩 𐑅𐐻𐐳𐐼 𐑁𐐬𐑉𐑃 𐐰𐑌𐐼 𐐲𐐻𐐯𐑋𐐹𐐻𐐲𐐼 𐐻𐐭 𐑊𐐩 𐑄𐐯𐑉 𐐸𐐰𐑌𐐼𐑆 𐐱𐑌 𐐸𐐮𐑋; 𐐺𐐲𐐻 𐐸𐐨 𐐶𐐮𐑄𐑅𐐻𐐳𐐼 𐑄𐐯𐑋, 𐐰𐑌𐐼 𐑅𐐯𐐼 𐐲𐑌𐐻𐐭 𐑄𐐯𐑋, 𐐓𐐲𐐽 𐑋𐐨 𐑌𐐱𐐻, 𐑁𐐫𐑉 𐐘𐐱𐐼 𐑇𐐰𐑊 𐑅𐑋𐐴𐐻 𐐷𐐭 𐐮𐑁 𐐷 𐑊𐐩 𐐷𐐫𐑉 𐐸𐐰𐑌𐐼𐑆 𐐲𐐹𐐱𐑌 𐑋𐐨, 𐑁𐐫𐑉 𐐌 𐐸𐐰𐑂 𐑌𐐱𐐻 𐐼𐐮𐑊𐐮𐑂𐐲𐑉𐐼 𐑄 𐑋𐐯𐑅𐐯𐐾 𐐸𐐶𐐮𐐽 𐑄 𐐢𐐫𐑉𐐼 𐑅𐐯𐑌𐐻 𐑋𐐨 𐐻𐐭 𐐼𐐮𐑊𐐮𐑂𐐲𐑉; 𐑌𐐨𐑄𐐲𐑉 𐐸𐐰𐑂 𐐌 𐐻𐐬𐑊𐐼 𐐷𐐭 𐑄𐐰𐐻 𐐸𐐶𐐮𐐽 𐐷 𐑉𐐨𐐿𐐶𐐯𐑅𐐻𐐲𐐼 𐑄𐐰𐐻 𐐌 𐑇𐐳𐐼 𐐻𐐯𐑊; 𐑄𐐯𐑉𐑁𐐫𐑉, 𐐘𐐱𐐼 𐐶𐐮𐑊 𐑌𐐱𐐻 𐑅𐐲𐑁𐐲𐑉 𐑄𐐰𐐻 𐐌 𐑇𐐰𐑊 𐐺 𐐼𐐨𐑅𐐻𐑉𐐱𐐮𐐼 𐐰𐐻 𐑄𐐮𐑅 𐐻𐐴𐑋. 𐐒𐐲𐐻 𐐌 𐑋𐐲𐑅𐐻 𐑁𐐳𐑊𐑁𐐮𐑊 𐑄 𐐿𐐲𐑋𐐰𐑌𐐼𐑋𐐯𐑌𐐻𐑅 𐐸𐐶𐐯𐑉𐐶𐐮𐑄 𐐘𐐱𐐼 𐐸𐐰𐑆 𐐿𐐲𐑋𐐰𐑌𐐼𐐲𐐼 𐑋𐐨; 𐐰𐑌𐐼 𐐺𐐨𐐿𐐫𐑆 𐐌 𐐸𐐰𐑂 𐐻𐐬𐑊𐐼 𐐷𐐭 𐑄 𐐻𐑉𐐭𐑃 𐐷 𐐪𐑉 𐐰𐑍𐑀𐑉𐐨 𐐶𐐮𐑄 𐑋𐐨. 𐐈𐑌𐐼 𐐲𐑀𐐯𐑌, 𐐺𐐨𐐿𐐫𐑆 𐐌 𐐸𐐰𐑂 𐑅𐐹𐐬𐐿𐑌 𐑄 𐐶𐐲𐑉𐐼 𐐲𐑂 𐐘𐐱𐐼, 𐐷 𐐸𐐰𐑂 𐐾𐐲𐐾𐐼 𐑋𐐨 𐑄𐐰𐐻 𐐌 𐐰𐑋 𐑋𐐰𐐼.

20. 𐐤𐐵 𐐮𐐻 𐐿𐐩𐑋 𐐻𐐭 𐐹𐐰𐑅 𐐰𐑁𐐻𐐲𐑉 𐐈𐐺𐐮𐑌𐐩𐐼𐐴 𐐸𐐰𐐼 𐑅𐐹𐐬𐐿𐑌 𐑄𐐨𐑆 𐐶𐐲𐑉𐐼𐑆 𐑄𐐰𐐻 𐑄 𐐹𐐨𐐹𐐲𐑊 𐐲𐑂 𐐗𐐮𐑍 𐐤𐐬𐐲 𐐼𐐲𐑉𐑅𐐻 𐑌𐐱𐐻 𐑊𐐩 𐑄𐐯𐑉 𐐸𐐰𐑌𐐼𐑆 𐐱𐑌 𐐸𐐮𐑋, 𐑁𐐫𐑉 𐑄 𐐝𐐹𐐮𐑉𐐮𐐻 𐐲𐑂 𐑄 𐐢𐐫𐑉𐐼 𐐶𐐱𐑆 𐐲𐐹𐐱𐑌 𐐸𐐮𐑋; 𐐰𐑌𐐼 𐐸𐐮𐑆 𐑁𐐩𐑅 𐑇𐐬𐑌 𐐶𐐮𐑄 𐐯𐐿𐑅𐐨𐐼𐐮𐑍 𐑊𐐲𐑅𐐻𐐲𐑉, 𐐨𐑂𐑌 𐐰𐑆 𐐣𐐬𐑆𐐯𐑆' 𐐼𐐮𐐼 𐐸𐐶𐐴𐑊 𐐮𐑌 𐑄 𐑋𐐵𐑌𐐻 𐐲𐑂 𐐝𐐴𐑌𐐴, 𐐸𐐶𐐴𐑊 𐑅𐐹𐐨𐐿𐐮𐑍 𐐶𐐮𐑄 𐑄 𐐢𐐫𐑉𐐼. 𐐈𐑌𐐼 𐐸𐐨 𐑅𐐹𐐩𐐿 𐐶𐐮𐑄 𐐹𐐵𐐲𐑉 𐐰𐑌𐐼 𐐫𐑃𐐱𐑉𐐮𐐻𐐨 𐑁𐑉𐐱𐑋 𐐘𐐱𐐼; 𐐰𐑌𐐼 𐐸𐐨 𐐿𐐱𐑌𐐻𐐮𐑌𐐷𐐭𐐼 𐐸𐐮𐑆 𐐶𐐲𐑉𐐼𐑆, 𐑅𐐩𐐮𐑍, 𐐏 𐑅𐐨 𐑄𐐰𐐻 𐐷 𐐸𐐰𐑂 𐑌𐐱𐐻 𐐹𐐵𐐲𐑉 𐐻𐐭 𐑅𐑊𐐩 𐑋𐐨, 𐑄𐐯𐑉𐑁𐐫𐑉 𐐌 𐑁𐐮𐑌𐐮𐑇 𐑋𐐴 𐑋𐐯𐑅𐐯𐐾. 𐐏𐐩, 𐐰𐑌𐐼 𐐌 𐐹𐐲𐑉𐑅𐐨𐑂 𐑄𐐰𐐻 𐐮𐐻 𐐿𐐲𐐻𐑅 𐐷𐐭 𐐻𐐭 𐐷𐐫𐑉 𐐸𐐪𐑉𐐻𐑅, 𐐺𐐨𐐿𐐫𐑆 𐐌 𐐻𐐯𐑊 𐐷𐐭 𐑄 𐐻𐑉𐐭𐑃 𐐿𐐱𐑌𐑅𐐲𐑉𐑌𐐮𐑍 𐐷𐐫𐑉 𐐮𐑌𐐮𐐿𐐶𐐮𐐻𐐮𐑆; 𐐷𐐩, 𐐰𐑌𐐼 𐑋𐐴 𐐶𐐲𐑉𐐼𐑆 𐑁𐐮𐑊 𐐷𐐭 𐐶𐐮𐑄 𐐶𐐲𐑌𐐼𐐲𐑉 𐐰𐑌𐐼 𐐰𐑋𐐩𐑆𐑋𐐯𐑌𐐻, 𐐰𐑌𐐼 𐐶𐐮𐑄 𐐰𐑍𐑀𐐲𐑉. 𐐒𐐲𐐻 𐐌 𐑁𐐮𐑌𐐮𐑇 𐑋𐐴 𐑋𐐯𐑅𐐯𐐾; 𐐰𐑌𐐼 𐑄𐐯𐑌 𐐮𐐻 𐑋𐐰𐐻𐐲𐑉𐑆 𐑌𐐱𐐻 𐐸𐐶𐐮𐑄𐐲𐑉 𐐌 𐑀𐐬, 𐐮𐑁 𐐮𐐻 𐑅𐐬 𐐺 𐑄𐐰𐐻 𐐌 𐐰𐑋 𐑅𐐩𐑂𐐼. 𐐒𐐲𐐻 𐑄𐐮𐑅 𐑋𐐲𐐽 𐐌 𐐻𐐯𐑊 𐐷𐐭; 𐐸𐐶𐐱𐐻 𐐷𐐭 𐐼𐐭 𐐶𐐮𐑄 𐑋𐐨, 𐐰𐑁𐐻𐐲𐑉 𐑄𐐮𐑅, 𐑇𐐰𐑊 𐐺 𐐰𐑆 𐐩 𐐻𐐴𐐹 𐐰𐑌𐐼 𐐩 𐑇𐐰𐐼𐐬 𐐲𐑂 𐑃𐐮𐑍𐑆 𐐸𐐶𐐮𐐽 𐐪𐑉 𐐻𐐭 𐐿𐐲𐑋. 𐐈𐑌𐐼 𐑌𐐵 𐐌 𐑉𐐨𐐼 𐐲𐑌𐐻𐐭 𐐷𐐭 𐑄 𐑉𐐨𐑋𐐩𐑌𐐼𐐲𐑉 𐐲𐑂 𐑄 𐐿𐐲𐑋𐐰𐑌𐐼𐑋𐐯𐑌𐐻𐑅 𐐲𐑂 𐐘𐐱𐐼, 𐑁𐐫𐑉 𐐌 𐐹𐐲𐑉𐑅𐐨𐑂 𐑄𐐰𐐻 𐑄𐐩 𐐪𐑉 𐑌𐐱𐐻 𐑉𐐮𐐻𐑌 𐐮𐑌 𐐷𐐫𐑉 𐐸𐐪𐑉𐐻𐑅; 𐐌 𐐹𐐲𐑉𐑅𐐨𐑂 𐑄𐐰𐐻 𐐷 𐐸𐐰𐑂 𐑅𐐻𐐲𐐼𐐨𐐼 𐐰𐑌𐐼 𐐻𐐫𐐻 𐐮𐑌𐐮𐐿𐐶𐐮𐐻𐐨 𐑄 𐑋𐐬𐑅𐐻 𐐹𐐪𐑉𐐻 𐐲𐑂 𐐷𐐫𐑉 𐑊𐐴𐑂𐑆.

21. 𐐈𐑌𐐼 𐑌𐐵, 𐐷 𐑉𐐨𐑋𐐯𐑋𐐺𐐲𐑉 𐑄𐐰𐐻 𐐌 𐑅𐐯𐐼 𐐲𐑌𐐻𐐭 𐐷𐐭, 𐐜𐐵 𐑇𐐰𐑊𐐻 𐑌𐐱𐐻 𐑋𐐩𐐿 𐐲𐑌𐐻𐐭 𐑄𐐨 𐐯𐑌𐐨 𐑀𐑉𐐩𐑂𐐲𐑌 𐐮𐑋𐐲𐐾, 𐐫𐑉 𐐯𐑌𐐨 𐑊𐐴𐐿𐑌𐐯𐑅 𐐲𐑂 𐑃𐐮𐑍𐑆 𐐸𐐶𐐮𐐽 𐐪𐑉 𐐮𐑌 𐐸𐐯𐑂𐐲𐑌 𐐲𐐺𐐲𐑂, 𐐫𐑉 𐐸𐐶𐐮𐐽 𐐪𐑉 𐐮𐑌 𐑄 𐐲𐑉𐑃 𐐺𐐨𐑌𐐨𐑃, 𐐫𐑉 𐐸𐐶𐐮𐐽 𐐪𐑉 𐐮𐑌 𐑄 𐐶𐐫𐐻𐐲𐑉 𐐲𐑌𐐼𐐲𐑉 𐑄 𐐲𐑉𐑃. 𐐈𐑌𐐼 𐐲𐑀𐐯𐑌; 𐑄𐐵 𐑇𐐰𐑊𐐻 𐑌𐐱𐐻 𐐺𐐵 𐐼𐐵𐑌 𐑄𐐴𐑅𐐯𐑊𐑁 𐐲𐑌𐐻𐐭 𐑄𐐯𐑋, 𐑌𐐫𐑉 𐑅𐐲𐑉𐑂 𐑄𐐯𐑋; 𐑁𐐫𐑉 𐐌 𐑄 𐐢𐐫𐑉𐐼 𐑄𐐴 𐐘𐐱𐐼 𐐰𐑋 𐐩 𐐾𐐯𐑊𐐲𐑅 𐐘𐐱𐐼, 𐑂𐐮𐑆𐐮𐐻-𐐮𐑍 𐑄 𐐮𐑌𐐮𐐿𐐶𐐮𐐻𐐮𐑆 𐐲𐑂 𐑄 𐑁𐐪𐑄𐐲𐑉𐑆 𐐲𐐹𐐱𐑌 𐑄 𐐽𐐮𐑊𐐼𐑉𐐯𐑌 𐐲𐑌𐐻𐐭 𐑄 𐑃𐐲𐑉𐐼 𐐰𐑌𐐼 𐑁𐐬𐑉𐑃 𐑈𐐯𐑌𐐲𐑉𐐩𐑇𐐲𐑌𐑆 𐐲𐑂 𐑄𐐯𐑋 𐑄𐐰𐐻 𐐸𐐩𐐻 𐑋𐐨; 𐐰𐑌𐐼 𐑇𐐬𐐮𐑍 𐑋𐐲𐑉𐑅𐐨 𐐲𐑌𐐻𐐭 𐑃𐐵𐑆𐐲𐑌𐐼𐑆 𐐲𐑂 𐑄𐐯𐑋 𐑄𐐰𐐻 𐑊𐐲𐑂 𐑋𐐨 𐐰𐑌𐐼 𐐿𐐨𐐹

𐑋𐐴 𐐿𐐱𐑋𐐰𐑌𐐼𐑋𐐲𐑌𐐻𐑅. 𐐜𐐵 𐑇𐐰𐑊𐐻 𐑌𐐱𐐻 𐐻𐐩𐐿 𐑄 𐑌𐐩𐑋 𐐱𐑂 𐑄 𐐢𐐫𐑉𐐼 𐑄𐐴 𐐘𐐱𐐼 𐐮𐑌 𐑂𐐩𐑌; 𐑁𐐫𐑉 𐑄 𐐢𐐫𐑉𐐼 𐑇𐐰𐑊 𐑌𐐱𐐻 𐐸𐐬𐑊𐐼 𐐸𐐮𐑋 𐑀𐐮𐑊𐐻𐑊𐐯𐑅 𐑄𐐰𐐻 𐐻𐐩𐐿𐐯𐑃 𐐸𐐮𐑆 𐑌𐐩𐑋 𐐮𐑌 𐑂𐐩𐑌. 𐐡𐐨𐑋𐐯𐑋𐐺𐐲𐑉 𐑄 𐑅𐐰𐐺𐐲𐑃 𐐼𐐩, 𐐻𐐭 𐐿𐐨𐐹 𐐮𐐻 𐐸𐐬𐑊𐐨. 𐐝𐐮𐐿𐑅 𐐼𐐩𐑆 𐑇𐐰𐑊𐐻 𐑄𐐵 𐑊𐐩𐐺𐐲𐑉, 𐐰𐑌𐐼 𐐼𐐭 𐐫𐑊 𐑄𐐴 𐐶𐐲𐑉𐐿; 𐐺𐐲𐐻 𐑄 𐑅𐐯𐑂𐐲𐑌𐑃 𐐼𐐩, 𐑄 𐑅𐐰𐐺𐐲𐑃 𐐱𐑂 𐑄 𐐢𐐫𐑉𐐼 𐑄𐐴 𐐘𐐱𐐼, 𐑄𐐵 𐑇𐐰𐑊𐐻 𐑌𐐱𐐻 𐐼𐐭 𐐯𐑌𐐨 𐐶𐐲𐑉𐐿, 𐑄𐐵, 𐑌𐐫𐑉 𐑄𐐴 𐑅𐐲𐑌, 𐑌𐐫𐑉 𐑄𐐴 𐐼𐐫𐐻𐐲𐑉, 𐑄𐐴 𐑋𐐰𐑌-𐑅𐐲𐑉𐑂𐐲𐑌𐐻, 𐑌𐐫𐑉 𐑄𐐴 𐑋𐐩𐐼-𐑅𐐲𐑉𐑂𐐲𐑌𐐻, 𐑌𐐫𐑉 𐑄𐐴 𐐿𐐰𐐻𐐲𐑊, 𐑌𐐫𐑉 𐑄𐐴 𐑅𐐻𐑉𐐩𐑌𐐾𐐲𐑉 𐑄𐐰𐐻 𐐮𐑆 𐐶𐐮𐑄𐐮𐑌 𐑄𐐴 𐑀𐐩𐐻𐑅: 𐑁𐐫𐑉 𐐮𐑌 𐑅𐐮𐐿𐑅 𐐼𐐩𐑆 𐑄 𐐢𐐫𐑉𐐼 𐑋𐐩𐐼 𐐸𐐯𐑂𐐲𐑌 𐐰𐑌𐐼 𐐲𐑉𐑃, 𐐰𐑌𐐼 𐑄 𐑅𐐨, 𐐰𐑌𐐼 𐐫𐑊 𐑄𐐰𐐻 𐐮𐑌 𐑄𐐯𐑋 𐐮𐑆; 𐐸𐐶𐐯𐑉𐑁𐐫𐑉 𐑄 𐐢𐐫𐑉𐐼 𐐺𐑊𐐯𐑅𐐻 𐑄 𐑅𐐰𐐺𐐲𐑃 𐐼𐐩, 𐐰𐑌𐐼 𐐸𐐰𐑊𐐬𐐼 𐐮𐐻. 𐐉𐑌𐐲𐑉 𐑄𐐴 𐑁𐐪𐑄𐐲𐑉 𐐰𐑌𐐼 𐑄𐐴 𐑋𐐲𐑄𐐲𐑉, 𐑄𐐰𐐻 𐑄𐐴 𐐼𐐩𐑆 𐑋𐐩 𐐺 𐑊𐐱𐑍 𐐲𐐹𐐱𐑌 𐑄 𐑊𐐰𐑌𐐼 𐐸𐐶𐐮𐐽 𐑄 𐐢𐐫𐑉𐐼 𐑄𐐴 𐐘𐐱𐐼 𐑀𐐮𐑂𐐯𐑃 𐑄𐐨. 𐐜𐐵 𐑇𐐰𐑊𐐻 𐑌𐐱𐐻 𐐿𐐮𐑊. 𐐜𐐵 𐑇𐐰𐑊𐐻 𐑌𐐱𐐻 𐐿𐐲𐑋𐐮𐐻 𐐰𐐼𐐲𐑊𐐻𐐲𐑉𐐨. 𐐜𐐵 𐑇𐐰𐑊𐐻 𐑌𐐱𐐻 𐑅𐐻𐐨𐑊. 𐐜𐐵 𐑇𐐰𐑊𐐻 𐑌𐐱𐐻 𐐺𐐯𐑉 𐑁𐐫𐑊𐑅 𐐶𐐮𐐻𐑌𐐯𐑅 𐐰𐑀𐐯𐑌𐑅𐐻 𐑄𐐴 𐑌𐐩𐐺𐐲𐑉. 𐐜𐐵 𐑇𐐰𐑊𐐻 𐑌𐐱𐐻 𐐿𐐲𐑂𐐯𐐻 𐑄𐐴 𐑌𐐩𐐺𐐲𐑉'𐑆 𐐸𐐵𐑅, 𐑄𐐵 𐑇𐐰𐑊𐐻 𐑌𐐱𐐻 𐐿𐐲𐑂𐐯𐐻 𐑄𐐴 𐑌𐐩𐐺𐐲𐑉'𐑆 𐐶𐐴𐑁, 𐑌𐐫𐑉 𐐸𐐮𐑆 𐑋𐐰𐑌-𐑅𐐲𐑉𐑂𐐲𐑌𐐻, 𐑌𐐫𐑉 𐐸𐐮𐑆 𐑋𐐩𐐼-𐑅𐐲𐑉𐑂𐐲𐑌𐐻, 𐑌𐐫𐑉 𐐸𐐮𐑆 𐐱𐐿𐑅, 𐑌𐐫𐑉 𐐸𐐮𐑆 𐐰𐑅, 𐑌𐐫𐑉 𐐯𐑌𐐨 𐑃𐐮𐑍 𐑄𐐰𐐻 𐐮𐑆 𐑄𐐴 𐑌𐐩𐐺𐐲𐑉'𐑆.

𐐕𐐈𐐑𐐓𐐊𐐡 VIII.

1. 𐐈𐑌𐐼 𐐮𐐻 𐐿𐐩𐑋 𐐻𐐭 𐐹𐐰𐑅 𐑄𐐰𐐻 𐐰𐑁𐐻𐐲𐑉 𐐈𐐺𐐮𐑌𐐪𐐼𐐴 𐐸𐐰𐐼 𐑋𐐩𐐼 𐐰𐑌 𐐯𐑌𐐼 𐐱𐑂 𐑄𐐨𐑆 𐑅𐐩𐐮𐑍𐑆, 𐑄𐐰𐐻 𐐸𐐨 𐑅𐐯𐐼 𐐲𐑌𐐻𐐭 𐑄𐐯𐑋, 𐐐𐐰𐑂 𐐷𐐨 𐐻𐐫𐐻 𐑄𐐮𐑅 𐐹𐐨𐐹𐐲𐑊 𐑄𐐰𐐻 𐑄𐐩 𐑇𐐳𐐼 𐐱𐐺𐑆𐐲𐑉𐑂 𐐻𐐭 𐐼𐐭 𐐫𐑊 𐑄𐐨𐑆 𐑃𐐮𐑍𐑆, 𐑁𐐫𐑉 𐐻𐐭 𐐿𐐨𐐹 𐑄𐐨𐑆 𐐿𐐱𐑋𐐰𐑌𐐼𐑋𐐲𐑌𐐻𐑅? 𐐌 𐑅𐐩 𐐲𐑌𐐻𐐭 𐐷𐐭, 𐐤𐐩; 𐑁𐐫𐑉 𐐮𐑁 𐐷𐐨 𐐸𐐰𐐼, 𐑄 𐐢𐐫𐑉𐐼 𐐶𐐳𐐼 𐑌𐐱𐐻 𐐸𐐰𐑂 𐐿𐐫𐑆𐐼 𐑋𐐨 𐐻𐐭 𐐿𐐲𐑋 𐑁𐐬𐑉𐑃 𐐰𐑌𐐼 𐐻𐐭 𐐹𐑉𐐱𐑁𐐲𐑅𐐴 𐐨𐑂𐐲𐑊 𐐿𐐱𐑌𐑅𐐲𐑉𐑌𐐮𐑍 𐑄𐐮𐑅 𐐹𐐨𐐹𐐲𐑊. 𐐈𐑌𐐼 𐑌𐐵 𐐷𐐨 𐐸𐐰𐑂 𐑅𐐯𐐼 𐑄𐐰𐐻 𐑅𐐰𐑊𐑂𐐩𐑇𐐲𐑌 𐐿𐐲𐑋𐐯𐑃 𐐺𐐴 𐑄 𐑊𐐫 𐐱𐑂 𐐣𐐬𐑆𐐯𐑆. 𐐌 𐑅𐐩 𐐲𐑌𐐻𐐭 𐐷𐐭 𐑄𐐰𐐻 𐐮𐐻 𐐮𐑆 𐐯𐐿𐑅𐐹𐐨𐐼𐐨𐐲𐑌𐐻 𐑄𐐰𐐻 𐐷𐐨 𐑇𐐳𐐼 𐐿𐐨𐐹 𐑄 𐑊𐐫 𐐱𐑂 𐐣𐐬𐑆𐐯𐑆 𐐰𐑆 𐐷𐐯𐐻; 𐐺𐐲𐐻 𐐌 𐑅𐐩 𐐲𐑌𐐻𐐭 𐐷𐐭, 𐑄𐐰𐐻 𐑄 𐐻𐐴𐑋 𐑇𐐰𐑊 𐐿𐐲𐑋 𐐸𐐶𐐯𐑌 𐐮𐐻 𐑇𐐰𐑊 𐑌𐐬 𐑋𐐬𐑉 𐐺 𐐯𐐿𐑅𐐹𐐨𐐼𐐨𐐲𐑌𐐻 𐐻𐐭 𐐿𐐨𐐹 𐑄 𐑊𐐫 𐐱𐑂 𐐣𐐬𐑆𐐯𐑆. 𐐈𐑌𐐼 𐑋𐐬𐑉𐐬𐑂𐐲𐑉, 𐐌 𐑅𐐩 𐐲𐑌𐐻𐐭 𐐷𐐭, 𐑄𐐰𐐻 𐑅𐐰𐑊𐑂𐐩𐑇𐐲𐑌 𐐼𐐲𐑆 𐑌𐐱𐐻 𐐿𐐲𐑋 𐐺𐐴 𐑄 𐑊𐐫 𐐰𐑊𐐬𐑌; 𐐰𐑌𐐼 𐐶𐐲𐑉 𐐮𐐻 𐑌𐐱𐐻 𐑁𐐫𐑉 𐑄 𐐰𐐻𐐬𐑌𐑋𐐯𐑌𐐻, 𐐸𐐶𐐮𐐽 𐐘𐐱𐐼 𐐸𐐮𐑋𐑅𐐯𐑊𐑁 𐑇𐐰𐑊 𐑋𐐩𐐿 𐑁𐐫𐑉 𐑄 𐑅𐐮𐑌𐑆 𐐰𐑌𐐼 𐐮𐑌𐐮𐐿𐐶𐐮𐐻𐐨𐑆 𐐱𐑂 𐐸𐐮𐑆 𐐹𐐨𐐹𐐲𐑊, 𐑄𐐰𐐻 𐑄𐐩 𐑋𐐲𐑅𐐻 𐐲𐑌𐐲𐑂𐐬𐐮𐐼𐐲𐐺𐑊𐐨 𐐹𐐯𐑉𐐮𐑇, 𐑌𐐱𐐻𐐶𐐮𐑄𐑅𐐻𐐰𐑌𐐼𐐮𐑍 𐑄 𐑊𐐫 𐐱𐑂 𐐣𐐬𐑆𐐯𐑆. 𐐈𐑌𐐼 𐑌𐐵 𐐌 𐑅𐐩 𐐲𐑌𐐻𐐭 𐐷𐐭, 𐑄𐐰𐐻 𐐮𐐻 𐐶𐐱𐑆 𐐯𐐿𐑅𐐹𐐨𐐼𐐨𐐲𐑌𐐻 𐑄𐐰𐐻 𐑄𐐯𐑉 𐑇𐐳𐐼 𐐺 𐐰 𐑊𐐫 𐑀𐐮𐑂𐐲𐑌 𐐻𐐭 𐑄 𐐽𐐮𐑊𐐼𐑉𐐯𐑌 𐐱𐑂 𐐆𐑆𐑉𐐩𐐯𐑊, 𐐷𐐩, 𐐨𐑂𐐲𐑌 𐐰 𐑂𐐯𐑉𐐨 𐑅𐐻𐑉𐐮𐐿𐐻 𐑊𐐫; 𐑁𐐫𐑉 𐑄𐐩 𐐶𐐲𐑉 𐐰 𐑅𐐻𐐮𐑁-𐑌𐐯𐐿𐐻 𐐹𐐨𐐹𐐲𐑊, 𐐿𐐶𐐮𐐿 𐐻𐐭 𐐼𐐭 𐐮𐑌𐐮𐐿𐐶𐐮𐐻𐐨, 𐐰𐑌𐐼 𐑅𐑊𐐬 𐐻𐐭 𐑉𐐨𐑋𐐯𐑋𐐺𐐲𐑉 𐑄 𐐢𐐫𐑉𐐼 𐑄𐐩𐑉 𐐘𐐱𐐼; 𐐸𐐶𐐯𐑉𐑁𐐫𐑉 𐑄𐐯𐑉 𐐶𐐱𐑆 𐐰 𐑊𐐫 𐑀𐐮𐑂𐐲𐑌 𐑄𐐯𐑋, 𐐷𐐩, 𐐰 𐑊𐐫 𐐱𐑂 𐐹𐐲𐑉𐑁𐐫𐑉𐑋𐐲𐑌𐑅𐐯𐑆 𐐰𐑌𐐼 𐐱𐑂 𐐫𐑉𐐼𐐮𐑌𐐲𐑌𐑅𐐯𐑆, 𐐰 𐑊𐐫 𐐸𐐶𐐮𐐽 𐑄𐐩 𐐶𐐲𐑉 𐐻𐐭 𐐱𐐺𐑆𐐲𐑉𐑂 𐑅𐐻𐑉𐐮𐐿𐐻𐑊𐐨 𐑁𐑉𐐱𐑋 𐐼𐐩 𐐻𐐭 𐐼𐐩, 𐐻𐐭 𐐿𐐨𐐹 𐑄𐐯𐑋 𐐮𐑌 𐑉𐐨𐑋𐐯𐑋𐐺𐐲𐑉𐐲𐑌𐑅 𐐱𐑂 𐐘𐐱𐐼 𐐰𐑌𐐼 𐑄𐐩𐑉 𐐼𐐭𐐻𐐨 𐐻𐐬-𐐶𐐫𐑉𐐼𐑆 𐐸𐐮𐑋.

2. 𐐒𐐲𐐻 𐐺𐐨𐐸𐐬𐑊𐐼, 𐐌 𐑅𐐩 𐐲𐑌𐐻𐐭 𐐷𐐭, 𐑄𐐰𐐻 𐐫𐑊 𐑄𐐨𐑆 𐑃𐐮𐑍𐑆 𐐶𐐲𐑉 𐐻𐐴𐐹𐑅 𐐱𐑂 𐑃𐐮𐑍𐑆 𐐻𐐭 𐐿𐐲𐑋. 𐐈𐑌𐐼 𐑌𐐵, 𐐼𐐮𐐼 𐑄𐐩 𐐲𐑌𐐼𐐲𐑉𐑅𐐻𐐰𐑌𐐼 𐑄 𐑊𐐫? 𐐌 𐑅𐐩 𐐲𐑌𐐻𐐭 𐐷𐐭, 𐐤𐐩, 𐑄𐐩 𐐼𐐮𐐼 𐑌𐐱𐐻 𐐫𐑊 𐐲𐑌𐐼𐐲𐑉𐑅𐐻𐐰𐑌𐐼 𐑄 𐑊𐐫; 𐐰𐑌𐐼 𐑄𐐮𐑅 𐐺𐐨𐐿𐐫𐑆 𐐱𐑂 𐑄 𐐸𐐪𐑉𐐼𐑌𐐯𐑅 𐐱𐑂 𐑄𐐩𐑉 𐐸𐐪𐑉𐐻𐑅; 𐑁𐐫𐑉 𐑄𐐩 𐐲𐑌𐐼𐐲𐑉𐑅𐐻𐐳𐐼 𐑌𐐱𐐻 𐑄𐐰𐐻 𐑄𐐯𐑉 𐐿𐐳𐐼 𐑌𐐱𐐻 𐐯𐑌𐐨 𐑋𐐰𐑌 𐐺 𐑅𐐩𐑂𐐼, 𐐯𐐿𐑅𐐯𐐹𐐻 𐐮𐐻 𐐶𐐲𐑉 𐑃𐑉𐐭 𐑄 𐑉𐐨𐐼𐐯𐑋𐑇𐐲𐑌 𐐱𐑂 𐐘𐐱𐐼. 𐐙𐐫𐑉 𐐺𐐨𐐸𐐬𐑊𐐼, 𐐼𐐮𐐼 𐑌𐐱𐐻 𐐣𐐬𐑆𐐯𐑆 𐐹𐑉𐐱𐑁𐐲𐑅𐐴 𐐲𐑌𐐻𐐭 𐑄𐐯𐑋 𐐿𐐱𐑌𐑅𐐲𐑉𐑌𐐮𐑍 𐑄 𐐿𐐲𐑋𐐮𐑍 𐐱𐑂 𐑄 𐐣𐐯𐑅𐐴𐐲, 𐐰𐑌𐐼 𐑄𐐰𐐻 𐐘𐐱𐐼 𐑇𐐳𐐼 𐑉𐐨𐐼𐐨𐑋 𐐸𐐮𐑆 𐐹𐐨𐐹𐐲𐑊? 𐐏𐐩, 𐐰𐑌𐐼 𐐨𐑂𐐲𐑌 𐐫𐑊 𐑄 𐐹𐑉𐐱𐑁𐐯𐐻𐑅 𐐸𐐭 𐐸𐐰𐑂 𐐹𐑉𐐱𐑁𐐲𐑅𐐴𐐼 𐐯𐑂𐐲𐑉 𐑅𐐮𐑌𐑅 𐑄 𐐶𐐲𐑉𐑊𐐼 𐐺𐐨𐑀𐐰𐑌, 𐐸𐐰𐑂 𐑄𐐩 𐑌𐐱𐐻 𐑅𐐹𐐬𐐿𐐲𐑌 𐑋𐐬𐑉 𐐫𐑉 𐑊𐐯𐑅 𐐿𐐱𐑌𐑅𐐲𐑉𐑌𐐮𐑍 𐑄𐐨𐑆 𐑃𐐮𐑍𐑆? 𐐐𐐰𐑂 𐑄𐐩 𐑌𐐱𐐻 𐑅𐐯𐐼 𐑄𐐰𐐻 𐐘𐐱𐐼 𐐸𐐮𐑋𐑅𐐯𐑊𐑁 𐑇𐐳𐐼 𐐿𐐲𐑋 𐐼𐐵𐑌 𐐲𐑋𐐱𐑍 𐑄 𐐽𐐮𐑊𐐼𐑉𐐯𐑌 𐐱𐑂 𐑋𐐯𐑌, 𐐰𐑌𐐼 𐐻𐐩𐐿 𐐲𐐹𐐱𐑌 𐐸𐐮𐑋 𐑄 𐑁𐐫𐑉𐑋 𐐱𐑂 𐑋𐐰𐑌, 𐐰𐑌𐐼 𐑀𐐬 𐑁𐐬𐑉𐑃 𐐮𐑌 𐑋𐐴𐐻𐐨 𐐹𐐵𐐲𐑉 𐐲𐐹𐐱𐑌 𐑄 𐑁𐐩𐑅 𐐱𐑂 𐑄 𐐲𐑉𐑃? 𐐏𐐩,

𐐰𐑌𐐼 𐐸𐐰𐑂 𐑄𐐩 𐑌𐐱𐐻 𐑅𐐯𐐼 𐐫𐑊𐑅𐐬, 𐑄𐐰𐐻 𐐸𐐨 𐑇𐐳𐐼 𐐺𐑉𐐮𐑍 𐐻𐐭 𐐹𐐰𐑅 𐑄 𐑉𐐯𐑆𐐲𐑉𐐯𐐿𐑇𐐲𐑌 𐐲𐑂 𐑄 𐐼𐐯𐐼, 𐐰𐑌𐐼 𐑄𐐰𐐻 𐐸𐐨, 𐐸𐐮𐑋𐑅𐐯𐑊𐑁, 𐑇𐐳𐐼 𐐺𐐨 𐐱𐐹𐑉𐐯𐑅𐐻 𐐰𐑌𐐼 𐐰𐑁𐑊𐐮𐐿𐐻𐐯𐐼? 𐐏𐐩, 𐐨𐑂𐐲𐑌 𐐼𐐲𐑃 𐑌𐐱𐐻 𐐌𐑆𐐩𐐲 𐑅𐐩, 𐐐𐐭 𐐸𐐰𐑃 𐐺𐐨𐑊𐐨𐑂𐐼 𐐵𐑉 𐑉𐐨𐐹𐐫𐑉𐐻, 𐐰𐑌𐐼 𐐻𐐭 𐐸𐐭𐑋 𐐮𐑆 𐑄 𐐪𐑉𐑋 𐐲𐑂 𐑄 𐐢𐐫𐑉𐐼 𐑉𐐨𐑂𐐨𐑊𐐼? 𐐙𐐫𐑉 𐐸𐐨 𐑇𐐰𐑊 𐑀𐑉𐐬 𐐲𐐹 𐐺𐐨𐑁𐐬𐑉 𐐸𐐮𐑋 𐐰𐑆 𐐩 𐐻𐐯𐑌𐐼𐐲𐑉 𐐹𐑊𐐰𐑌𐐻, 𐐰𐑌𐐼 𐐰𐑆 𐐩 𐑉𐐭𐐻 𐐵𐐻 𐐲𐑂 𐐼𐑉𐐴 𐑀𐑉𐐵𐑌𐐼; 𐐸𐐨 𐐸𐐰𐑃 𐑌𐐬 𐑁𐐫𐑉𐑋 𐑌𐐫𐑉 𐐿𐐲𐑋𐑊𐐨𐑌𐐯𐑅; 𐐰𐑌𐐼 𐐸𐐶𐐯𐑌 𐐶𐐨 𐑇𐐰𐑊 𐑅𐐨 𐐸𐐮𐑋, 𐑄𐐯𐑉 𐐮𐑆 𐑌𐐬 𐐺𐐷𐐭𐐻𐐨 𐑄𐐰𐐻 𐐶𐐨 𐑇𐐳𐐼 𐐼𐐨𐑆𐐴𐑉 𐐸𐐮𐑋. 𐐐𐐨 𐐮𐑆 𐐼𐐯𐑅𐐹𐐴𐑆𐐼 𐐰𐑌𐐼 𐑉𐐨𐐾𐐯𐐿𐐻𐐯𐐼 𐐲𐑂 𐑋𐐯𐑌; 𐐩 𐑋𐐰𐑌 𐐲𐑂 𐑅𐐱𐑉𐐬𐑆, 𐐰𐑌𐐼 𐐰𐐿𐐶𐐩𐑌𐐻𐐯𐐼 𐐶𐐮𐑄 𐑀𐑉𐐨𐑁; 𐐰𐑌𐐼 𐐶𐐨 𐐸𐐮𐐼 𐐰𐑆 𐐮𐐻 𐐶𐐲𐑉 𐐵𐑉 𐑁𐐩𐑅𐐯𐑆 𐑁𐑉𐐱𐑋 𐐸𐐮𐑋; 𐐸𐐨 𐐶𐐱𐑆 𐐼𐐯𐑅𐐹𐐴𐑆𐐼, 𐐰𐑌𐐼 𐐶𐐨 𐐯𐑅𐐻𐐨𐑋𐐼 𐐸𐐮𐑋 𐑌𐐱𐐻.

3. 𐐟𐐭𐑉𐑊𐐨 𐐸𐐨 𐐸𐐰𐑆 𐐺𐐫𐑉𐑌 𐐵𐑉 𐑀𐑉𐐨𐑁𐑅, 𐐰𐑌𐐼 𐐿𐐰𐑉𐐨𐐼 𐐵𐑉 𐑅𐐱𐑉𐐬𐑆; 𐐷𐐯𐐻 𐐶𐐨 𐐼𐐮𐐼 𐐯𐑅𐐻𐐨𐑋 𐐸𐐮𐑋 𐑅𐐻𐑉𐐮𐐿𐐲𐑌, 𐑅𐑋𐐮𐐻𐐲𐑌 𐐲𐑂 𐐘𐐱𐐼, 𐐰𐑌𐐼 𐐰𐑁𐑊𐐮𐐿𐐻𐐯𐐼. 𐐒𐐲𐐻 𐐸𐐨 𐐶𐐱𐑆 𐐶𐐭𐑌𐐼𐐯𐐼 𐑁𐐫𐑉 𐐵𐑉 𐐻𐑉𐐰𐑌𐑅𐑀𐑉𐐯𐑇𐐲𐑌𐑆, 𐐸𐐨 𐐶𐐱𐑆 𐐺𐑉𐐭𐑆𐐼 𐑁𐐫𐑉 𐐵𐑉 𐐮𐑌𐐮𐐿𐐶𐐮𐐻𐐨𐑆; 𐑄 𐐽𐐰𐑅𐐻𐐴𐑆𐑋𐐯𐑌𐐻 𐐲𐑂 𐐵𐑉 𐐹𐐨𐑅 𐐶𐐱𐑆 𐐲𐐹𐐱𐑌 𐐸𐐮𐑋; 𐐰𐑌𐐼 𐐶𐐮𐑄 𐐸𐐮𐑆 𐑅𐐻𐑉𐐴𐐹𐑅 𐐶𐐨 𐐪𐑉 𐐸𐐨𐑊𐐼. 𐐄𐑊 𐐶𐐨, 𐑊𐐴𐐿 𐑇𐐨𐐹, 𐐸𐐰𐑂 𐑀𐐱𐑌 𐐲𐑅𐐻𐑉𐐩; 𐐶𐐨 𐐸𐐰𐑂 𐐻𐐲𐑉𐑌𐐼 𐐯𐑂𐑉𐐨 𐐶𐐲𐑌 𐐻𐐭 𐐸𐐮𐑆 𐐬𐑌 𐐶𐐩; 𐐰𐑌𐐼 𐑄 𐐢𐐫𐑉𐐼 𐐸𐐰𐑃 𐑊𐐩𐐼 𐐱𐑌 𐐸𐐮𐑋 𐑄 𐐮𐑌𐐮𐐿𐐶𐐮𐐻𐐨𐑆 𐐲𐑂 𐐲𐑅 𐐫𐑊. 𐐐𐐨 𐐶𐐱𐑆 𐐱𐐹𐑉𐐯𐑅𐐻, 𐐰𐑌𐐼 𐐸𐐨 𐐶𐐱𐑆 𐐰𐑁𐑊𐐮𐐿𐐻𐐯𐐼, 𐐷𐐯𐐻 𐐸𐐨 𐐬𐐹𐐲𐑌𐐼 𐑌𐐱𐐻 𐐸𐐮𐑆 𐑋𐐵𐑃; 𐐸𐐨 𐐮𐑆 𐐺𐑉𐐫𐐻 𐐰𐑆 𐐩 𐑊𐐰𐑋 𐐻𐐭 𐑄 𐑅𐑊𐐫𐐻𐐲𐑉, 𐐰𐑌𐐼 𐐰𐑆 𐐩 𐑇𐐨𐐹 𐐺𐐨𐑁𐐬𐑉 𐐸𐐲𐑉 𐑇𐐨𐑉𐐲𐑉𐑆 𐐮𐑆 𐐼𐐲𐑋, 𐑅𐐬 𐐸𐐨 𐐬𐐹𐐲𐑌𐐼 𐑌𐐱𐐻 𐐸𐐮𐑆 𐑋𐐵𐑃. 𐐐𐐨 𐐶𐐱𐑆 𐐻𐐩𐐿𐐲𐑌 𐑁𐑉𐐱𐑋 𐐹𐑉𐐮𐑆𐐲𐑌 𐐰𐑌𐐼 𐑁𐑉𐐱𐑋 𐐾𐐲𐐾𐑋𐐯𐑌𐐻; 𐐰𐑌𐐼 𐐸𐐭 𐑇𐐰𐑊 𐐼𐐯𐐿𐑊𐐯𐑉 𐐸𐐮𐑆 𐐾𐐯𐑌𐐲𐑉𐐩𐑇𐐲𐑌? 𐐙𐐫𐑉 𐐸𐐨 𐐶𐐱𐑆 𐐿𐐲𐐻 𐐱𐑁 𐐵𐐻 𐐲𐑂 𐑄 𐑊𐐰𐑌𐐼 𐐲𐑂 𐑄 𐑊𐐮𐑂𐐮𐑍; 𐑁𐐫𐑉 𐑄 𐐻𐑉𐐰𐑌𐑅𐑀𐑉𐐯𐑇𐐲𐑌𐑆 𐐲𐑂 𐑋𐐴 𐐹𐐨𐐹𐑊 𐐶𐐱𐑆 𐐸𐐨 𐑅𐐻𐑉𐐮𐐿𐐲𐑌. 𐐈𐑌𐐼 𐐸𐐨 𐑋𐐩𐐼 𐐸𐐮𐑆 𐑀𐑉𐐩𐑂 𐐶𐐮𐑄 𐑄 𐐶𐐮𐐿𐐯𐐼, 𐐰𐑌𐐼 𐐶𐐮𐑄 𐑄 𐑉𐐮𐐽 𐐮𐑌 𐐸𐐮𐑆 𐐼𐐯𐑃; 𐐺𐐨𐐿𐐫𐑆 𐐸𐐨 𐐸𐐰𐐼 𐐼𐐲𐑌 𐑌𐐬 𐐨𐑂𐐮𐑊, 𐑌𐐨𐑄𐐲𐑉 𐐶𐐱𐑆 𐐯𐑌𐐨 𐐼𐐨𐑅𐐨𐐻 𐐮𐑌 𐐸𐐮𐑆 𐑋𐐵𐑃.

4. 𐐏𐐯𐐻 𐐮𐐻 𐐹𐑊𐐨𐑆𐐼 𐑄 𐐢𐐫𐑉𐐼 𐐻𐐭 𐐺𐑉𐐭𐑆 𐐸𐐮𐑋; 𐐸𐐨 𐐸𐐰𐑃 𐐹𐐳𐐻 𐐸𐐮𐑋 𐐻𐐭 𐑀𐑉𐐨𐑁; 𐐸𐐶𐐯𐑌 𐑄𐐵 𐑇𐐰𐑊𐐻 𐑋𐐩𐐿 𐐸𐐮𐑆 𐑅𐐬𐑊 𐐰𐑌 𐐱𐑁𐐲𐑉𐐮𐑍 𐑁𐐫𐑉 𐑅𐐮𐑌, 𐐸𐐨 𐑇𐐰𐑊 𐑅𐐨 𐐸𐐮𐑆 𐑅𐐨𐐼, 𐐸𐐨 𐑇𐐰𐑊 𐐹𐑉𐐬𐑊𐐱𐑍 𐐸𐐮𐑆 𐐼𐐩𐑆, 𐐰𐑌𐐼 𐑄 𐐹𐑊𐐯𐑈𐐲𐑉 𐐲𐑂 𐑄 𐐢𐐫𐑉𐐼 𐑇𐐰𐑊 𐐹𐑉𐐱𐑅𐐹𐐲𐑉 𐐮𐑌 𐐸𐐮𐑆 𐐸𐐰𐑌𐐼. 𐐐𐐨 𐑇𐐰𐑊 𐑅𐐨 𐐲𐑂 𐑄 𐐻𐑉𐐰𐑂𐐩𐑊 𐐲𐑂 𐐸𐐮𐑆 𐑅𐐬𐑊, 𐐰𐑌𐐼 𐑇𐐰𐑊 𐐺𐐨 𐑅𐐰𐐻𐐮𐑅𐑁𐐴𐐼; 𐐺𐐴 𐐸𐐮𐑆 𐑌𐐱𐑊𐐯𐐾 𐑇𐐰𐑊 𐑋𐐴 𐑉𐐴𐐽𐐲𐑅 𐑅𐐲𐑉𐑂𐐲𐑌𐐻 𐐾𐐲𐑅𐐻𐐮𐑁𐐴 𐑋𐐯𐑌𐐨; 𐑁𐐫𐑉 𐐸𐐨 𐑇𐐰𐑊 𐐺𐐯𐑉 𐑄𐐯𐑉 𐐮𐑌𐐮𐐿𐐶𐐮𐐻𐐨𐑆. 𐐜𐐯𐑉𐑁𐐬𐑉 𐐶𐐮𐑊 𐐌 𐐼𐐮𐑂𐐴𐐼 𐐸𐐮𐑋 𐐩 𐐹𐐬𐑉𐑇𐐲𐑌 𐐶𐐮𐑄 𐑄 𐑀𐑉𐐩𐐻, 𐐰𐑌𐐼 𐐸𐐨 𐑇𐐰𐑊 𐐼𐐮𐑂𐐴𐐼 𐑄 𐑅𐐹𐑎𐑊 𐐶𐐮𐑄 𐑄 𐑅𐐻𐑉𐐱𐑍; 𐐺𐐨𐐿𐐫𐑆 𐐸𐐨 𐐸𐐰𐑃 𐐹𐐬𐑉𐐼 𐐵𐐻 𐐸𐐮𐑆 𐑅𐐬𐑊 𐐲𐑌𐐻𐐭 𐐼𐐯𐑃; 𐐰𐑌𐐼 𐐸𐐨 𐐶𐐱𐑆 𐑌𐐲𐑋𐐺𐐲𐑉𐐼 𐐶𐐮𐑄 𐑄 𐐻𐑉𐐰𐑌𐑅𐑀𐑉𐐯𐑅𐐲𐑉𐑆; 𐐰𐑌𐐼 𐐸𐐨 𐐺𐐯𐑉 𐑄 𐑅𐐮𐑌𐑆 𐐲𐑂 𐑋𐐯𐑌𐐨, 𐐰𐑌𐐼 𐑋𐐩𐐼 𐐮𐑌𐐻𐐲𐑉𐑅𐐯𐑇𐐲𐑌 𐑁𐐫𐑉 𐑄 𐐻𐑉𐐰𐑌𐑅𐑀𐑉𐐯𐑅𐐲𐑉𐑆.

5. 𐐈𐑌𐐼 𐑌𐐵 𐐈𐐺𐐮𐑌𐐲𐐼𐐴 𐑅𐐯𐐼 𐐲𐑌𐐻𐐭 𐑄𐐯𐑋, 𐐌 𐐶𐐳𐐼 𐑄𐐰𐐻 𐐷𐐨 𐑇𐐳𐐼 𐐲𐑌𐐼𐐲𐑉𐑅𐐻𐐰𐑌𐐼 𐑄𐐰𐐻 𐐘𐐱𐐼 𐐸𐐮𐑋𐑅𐐯𐑊𐑁 𐑇𐐰𐑊 𐐿𐐲𐑋 𐐼𐐵𐑌 𐐲𐑋𐐲𐑍 𐑄 𐐽𐐮𐑊𐐼𐑉𐐯𐑌 𐐲𐑂 𐑋𐐯𐑌, 𐐰𐑌𐐼 𐑇𐐰𐑊 𐑉𐐨𐐼𐐨𐑋 𐐸𐐮𐑆 𐐹𐐨𐐹𐑊; 𐐰𐑌𐐼 𐐺𐐨𐐿𐐫𐑆 𐐸𐐨 𐐼𐐶𐐯𐑊𐐯𐑃 𐐮𐑌 𐑁𐑊𐐯𐑇, 𐐸𐐨 𐑇𐐰𐑊 𐐺𐐨 𐐿𐐫𐑊𐐼 𐑄 𐐝𐐲𐑌 𐐲𐑂 𐐘𐐱𐐼: 𐐰𐑌𐐼 𐐸𐐰𐑂𐐮𐑍 𐑅𐐲𐐺𐐾𐐯𐐿𐐻𐐯𐐼 𐑄 𐑁𐑊𐐯𐑇 𐐻𐐭 𐑄 𐐶𐐮𐑊 𐐲𐑂 𐑄 𐐙𐐪𐑄𐐲𐑉, 𐐺𐐨𐐮𐑍 𐑄 𐐙𐐪𐑄𐐲𐑉 𐐰𐑌𐐼 𐑄 𐐝𐐲𐑌; 𐑄 𐐙𐐪𐑄𐐲𐑉, 𐐺𐐨𐐿𐐫𐑆 𐐸𐐨 𐐶𐐱𐑆 𐐿𐐲𐑌𐑅𐐨𐑂𐐼 𐐺𐐴 𐑄 𐐹𐐵𐐲𐑉 𐐲𐑂 𐐘𐐱𐐼; 𐐰𐑌𐐼 𐑄 𐐝𐐲𐑌, 𐐺𐐨𐐿𐐫𐑆 𐐲𐑂 𐑄 𐑁𐑊𐐯𐑇; 𐑄𐐲𐑅 𐐺𐐨𐐿𐐲𐑋𐐮𐑍 𐑄 𐐙𐐪𐑄𐐲𐑉 𐐰𐑌𐐼 𐐝𐐲𐑌: 𐐰𐑌𐐼 𐑄𐐩 𐐪𐑉 𐐶𐐲𐑌 𐐘𐐱𐐼, 𐐷𐐩, 𐑄 𐑂𐐯𐑉𐐨 𐐩𐐻𐐲𐑉𐑌𐐲𐑊 𐐙𐐪𐑄𐐲𐑉 𐐲𐑂 𐐸𐐯𐑂𐐲𐑌 𐐰𐑌𐐼 𐐲𐑂 𐐲𐑉𐑃; 𐐰𐑌𐐼 𐑄𐐲𐑅 𐑄 𐑁𐑊𐐯𐑇 𐐺𐐨𐐿𐐲𐑋𐐮𐑍 𐑅𐐲𐐺𐐾𐐯𐐿𐐻 𐐻𐐭 𐑄 𐐝𐐹𐐮𐑉𐐮𐐻, 𐐫𐑉 𐑄 𐐝𐐲𐑌 𐐻𐐭 𐑄 𐐙𐐪𐑄𐐲𐑉, 𐐺𐐨𐐮𐑍 𐐶𐐲𐑌 𐐘𐐱𐐼, 𐑅𐐲𐑁𐐲𐑉𐐯𐑃 𐐻𐐯𐑋𐐻𐐩𐑇𐐲𐑌, 𐐰𐑌𐐼 𐐷𐐨𐑊𐐼𐐯𐑃 𐑌𐐱𐐻 𐐻𐐭 𐑄 𐐻𐐯𐑋𐐻𐐩𐑇𐐲𐑌, 𐐺𐐲𐐻 𐑅𐐲𐑁𐐲𐑉𐐯𐑃 𐐸𐐮𐑋𐑅𐐯𐑊𐑁 𐐻𐐭 𐐺𐐨 𐑋𐐱𐐿𐐻, 𐐰𐑌𐐼 𐑅𐐿𐐫𐑉𐐾𐐼, 𐐰𐑌𐐼 𐐿𐐰𐑅𐐻 𐐵𐐻, 𐐰𐑌𐐼 𐐼𐐮𐑅𐐬𐑌𐐼 𐐺𐐴 𐐸𐐮𐑆 𐐹𐐨𐐹𐑊. 𐐈𐑌𐐼 𐐰𐑁𐐻𐐲𐑉 𐐫𐑊 𐑄𐐮𐑅, 𐐰𐑁𐐻𐐲𐑉 𐐶𐐲𐑉𐐿𐐮𐑍 𐑋𐐯𐑌𐐨 𐑋𐐴𐐻𐐨 𐑋𐐮𐑉𐐲𐐿𐐲𐑊𐑆 𐐲𐑋𐐲𐑍 𐑄 𐐽𐐮𐑊𐐼𐑉𐐯𐑌 𐐲𐑂 𐑋𐐯𐑌, 𐐸𐐨 𐑇𐐰𐑊 𐐺𐐨 𐑊𐐯𐐼, 𐐷𐐩, 𐐨𐑂𐐲𐑌 𐐰𐑆 𐐌𐑆𐐩𐐲 𐑅𐐯𐐼, 𐐰𐑆 𐐩 𐑇𐐨𐐹 𐐺𐐨𐑁𐐬𐑉 𐑄 𐑇𐐨𐑉𐐲𐑉 𐐮𐑆 𐐼𐐲𐑋, 𐑅𐐬 𐐸𐐨 𐐬𐐹𐐲𐑌𐐼 𐑌𐐱𐐻 𐐸𐐮𐑆 𐑋𐐵𐑃; 𐐷𐐩, 𐐨𐑂𐐲𐑌 𐑅𐐬 𐐸𐐨 𐑇𐐰𐑊 𐐺𐐨 𐑊𐐯𐐼, 𐐿𐑉𐐭𐑅𐐮𐑁𐐴𐐼, 𐐰𐑌𐐼 𐑅𐑊𐐩𐑌, 𐑄 𐑁𐑊𐐯𐑇 𐐺𐐨𐐿𐐲𐑋𐐮𐑍 𐑅𐐲𐐺𐐾𐐯𐐿𐐻 𐐨𐑂𐐲𐑌 𐐲𐑌𐐻𐐭 𐐼𐐯𐑃, 𐑄 𐐶𐐮𐑊 𐐲𐑂 𐑄 𐐝𐐲𐑌 𐐺𐐨𐐮𐑍 𐑅𐐶𐐱𐑊𐐬𐐼 𐐲𐐹 𐐮𐑌 𐑄 𐐶𐐮𐑊 𐐲𐑂 𐑄 𐐙𐐪𐑄𐐲𐑉; 𐐰𐑌𐐼 𐑄𐐲𐑅 𐐘𐐱𐐼 𐐺𐑉𐐩𐐿𐐯𐑃 𐑄 𐐺𐐰𐑌𐐼𐑆 𐐲𐑂 𐐼𐐯𐑃, 𐐸𐐰𐑂𐐮𐑍 𐑀𐐩𐑌𐐼 𐑄 𐑂𐐮𐐿𐐻𐐲𐑉𐐨 𐐬𐑂𐐲𐑉 𐐼𐐯𐑃; 𐑀𐐮𐑂𐐮𐑍 𐑄 𐐝𐐲𐑌 𐐹𐐵𐐲𐑉 𐐻𐐭 𐑋𐐩𐐿 𐐮𐑌𐐻𐐲𐑉𐑅𐐯𐑇𐐲𐑌 𐑁𐐫𐑉 𐑄 𐐽𐐮𐑊𐐼𐑉𐐯𐑌 𐐲𐑂 𐑋𐐯𐑌: 𐐸𐐰𐑂𐐮𐑍 𐐰𐑅𐐯𐑌𐐼𐐯𐐼 𐐮𐑌𐐻𐐭 𐐸𐐯𐑂𐐲𐑌; 𐐸𐐰𐑂𐐮𐑍 𐑄 𐐺𐐵𐐯𐑊𐑆 𐐲𐑂 𐑋𐐲𐑉𐑅𐐨;

𐐺𐐨𐐮𐑍 𐑁𐐮𐑊𐐼 𐐶𐐮𐑃 𐐿𐐲𐑋𐐹𐐰𐑇𐐲𐑌 𐐻𐐬𐑉𐐼𐑆 𐑄 𐐽𐐮𐑊𐐼𐑉𐐯𐑌 𐐱𐑂 𐑋𐐯𐑌; 𐑅𐐻𐐰𐑌𐐼𐐮𐑍 𐐺𐐨𐐻𐐶𐐮𐐿𐑅𐐻 𐑄𐐯𐑋 𐐰𐑌𐐼 𐐾𐐲𐑅𐐻𐐮𐑅; 𐐸𐐰𐑂𐐮𐑍 𐐺𐑉𐐬𐐿𐐲𐑌 𐑄 𐐺𐐰𐑌𐐼𐑆 𐐱𐑂 𐐼𐐯𐑃, 𐐻𐐩𐐿𐐲𐑌 𐐲𐐹𐐱𐑌 𐐸𐐮𐑋𐑅𐐯𐑊𐑁 𐑄𐐩𐑉 𐐮𐑌𐐮𐐿𐐶𐐮𐐻𐐨 𐐰𐑌𐐼 𐑄𐐩𐑉 𐐻𐑉𐐰𐑌𐑆𐑀𐑉𐐯𐑇𐐲𐑌𐑆; 𐐸𐐰𐑂𐐮𐑍 𐑉𐐨𐐼𐐨𐑋𐐼 𐑄𐐯𐑋, 𐐰𐑌𐐼 𐑅𐐰𐐻𐐮𐑅𐑁𐐴𐐼 𐑄 𐐼𐐨𐑋𐐰𐑌𐐼𐑆 𐐱𐑂 𐐾𐐲𐑅𐐻𐐮𐑅. 𐐈𐑌𐐼 𐑌𐐵 𐐌 𐑅𐐩 𐐲𐑌𐐻𐐭 𐐷𐐭, 𐐐𐐭 𐑇𐐰𐑊 𐐼𐐨𐐿𐑊𐐩𐑉 𐐸𐐮𐑆 𐐾𐐯𐑌𐐲𐑉𐐩𐑇𐐲𐑌? 𐐒𐐨𐐸𐐬𐑊𐐼, 𐐌 𐑅𐐩 𐐲𐑌𐐻𐐭 𐐷𐐭, 𐐜𐐰𐐻 𐐸𐐶𐐯𐑌 𐐸𐐮𐑆 𐑅𐐬𐑊 𐐸𐐰𐑆 𐐺𐐮𐑌 𐑋𐐩𐐼 𐐰𐑌 𐐱𐑁𐐲𐑉𐐮𐑍 𐑁𐐫𐑉 𐑅𐐮𐑌, 𐐸𐐨 𐑇𐐰𐑊 𐑅𐐨 𐐸𐐮𐑆 𐑅𐐨𐐼. 𐐈𐑌𐐼 𐑌𐐵 𐐸𐐶𐐱𐐻 𐑅𐐩 𐐷𐐨? 𐐈𐑌𐐼 𐐸𐐭 𐑇𐐰𐑊 𐐺𐐨 𐐸𐐮𐑆 𐑅𐐨𐐼? 𐐒𐐨𐐸𐐬𐑊𐐼 𐐌 𐑅𐐩 𐐲𐑌𐐻𐐭 𐐷𐐭, 𐐜𐐰𐐻 𐐸𐐭𐑅𐐬𐐯𐑂𐐲𐑉 𐐸𐐰𐑆 𐐸𐐲𐑉𐐼 𐑄 𐐶𐐲𐑉𐐼𐑆 𐐱𐑂 𐑄 𐐹𐑉𐐱𐑁𐐯𐐻𐑅, 𐐷𐐩, 𐐫𐑊 𐑄 𐐸𐐬𐑊𐐨 𐐹𐑉𐐱𐑁𐐯𐐻𐑅 𐐸𐐭 𐐸𐐰𐑂 𐐹𐑉𐐱𐑁𐐯𐑅𐐴𐐼 𐐿𐐱𐑌𐑅𐐲𐑉𐑌𐐮𐑍 𐑄 𐐿𐐲𐑋𐐮𐑍 𐐱𐑂 𐑄 𐐢𐐫𐑉𐐼; 𐐌 𐑅𐐩 𐐲𐑌𐐻𐐭 𐐷𐐭, 𐐜𐐰𐐻 𐐫𐑊 𐑄𐐬𐑆 𐐸𐐭 𐐸𐐰𐑂 𐐸𐐪𐑉𐐿𐐲𐑌𐐼 𐐲𐑌𐐻𐐭 𐑄𐐩𐑉 𐐶𐐲𐑉𐐼𐑆, 𐐰𐑌𐐼 𐐺𐐨𐑊𐐨𐑂𐐼 𐑄𐐰𐐻 𐑄 𐐢𐐫𐑉𐐼 𐐶𐐳𐐼 𐑉𐐨𐐼𐐨𐑋 𐐸𐐮𐑆 𐐹𐐨𐐹𐐲𐑊, 𐐰𐑌𐐼 𐐸𐐰𐑂 𐑊𐐳𐐿𐐻 𐑁𐐫𐑉𐐶𐐲𐑉𐐼 𐐻𐐭 𐑄𐐰𐐻 𐐼𐐩 𐑁𐐫𐑉 𐐲 𐑉𐐨𐑋𐐮𐑇𐐲𐑌 𐐱𐑂 𐑄𐐩𐑉 𐑅𐐮𐑌𐑆; 𐐌 𐑅𐐩 𐐲𐑌𐐻𐐭 𐐷𐐭, 𐑄𐐰𐐻 𐑄𐐨𐑆 𐐪𐑉 𐐸𐐮𐑆 𐑅𐐨𐐼, 𐐫𐑉 𐑄𐐩 𐐪𐑉 𐑄 𐐩𐑉𐑆 𐐱𐑂 𐑄 𐐿𐐮𐑍𐐼𐐲𐑋 𐐱𐑂 𐐘𐐱𐐼: 𐑁𐐫𐑉 𐑄𐐨𐑆 𐐪𐑉 𐑄𐐩 𐐸𐐭𐑆 𐑅𐐮𐑌𐑆 𐐸𐐨 𐐸𐐰𐑆 𐐺𐐬𐑉𐑌; 𐑄𐐨𐑆 𐐪𐑉 𐑄𐐩 𐑁𐐫𐑉 𐐸𐐭𐑋 𐐸𐐨 𐐸𐐰𐑆 𐐼𐐴𐐼, 𐐻𐐭 𐑉𐐨𐐼𐐨𐑋 𐑄𐐯𐑋 𐑁𐑉𐐱𐑋 𐑄𐐩𐑉 𐐻𐑉𐐰𐑌𐑆𐑀𐑉𐐯𐑇𐐲𐑌𐑆. 𐐈𐑌𐐼 𐑌𐐵, 𐐪𐑉 𐑄𐐩 𐑌𐐱𐐻 𐐸𐐮𐑆 𐑅𐐨𐐼? 𐐏𐐩, 𐐰𐑌𐐼 𐐪𐑉 𐑌𐐱𐐻 𐑄 𐐹𐑉𐐱𐑁𐐯𐐻𐑅, 𐐯𐑂𐐲𐑉𐐨 𐐶𐐲𐑌 𐑄𐐰𐐻 𐐸𐐰𐑆 𐐬𐐹𐐲𐑌𐐼 𐐸𐐮𐑆 𐑋𐐵𐑃 𐐻𐐭 𐐹𐑉𐐱𐑁𐐯𐑅𐐴, 𐑄𐐰𐐻 𐐸𐐰𐑆 𐑌𐐱𐐻 𐑁𐐫𐑊𐐲𐑌 𐐮𐑌𐐻𐐭 𐐻𐑉𐐰𐑌𐑆𐑀𐑉𐐯𐑇𐐲𐑌; 𐐌 𐑋𐐨𐑌 𐐫𐑊 𐑄 𐐸𐐬𐑊𐐨 𐐹𐑉𐐱𐑁𐐯𐐻𐑅 𐐯𐑂𐐲𐑉 𐑅𐐮𐑌𐑅 𐑄 𐐶𐐲𐑉𐑊𐐼 𐐺𐐨𐑀𐐰𐑌? 𐐌 𐑅𐐩 𐐲𐑌𐐻𐐭 𐐷𐐭 𐑄𐐰𐐻 𐑄𐐩 𐐪𐑉 𐐸𐐮𐑆 𐑅𐐨𐐼; 𐐰𐑌𐐼 𐑄𐐨𐑆 𐐪𐑉 𐑄𐐩 𐐸𐐭 𐐸𐐰𐑂 𐐹𐐲𐐺𐑊𐐮𐑇𐐻 𐐹𐐨𐑅, 𐐸𐐭 𐐸𐐰𐑂 𐐺𐑉𐐫𐐻 𐑀𐐳𐐼 𐐻𐐴𐐼𐐮𐑍𐑆 𐐱𐑂 𐑀𐐳𐐼, 𐐸𐐭 𐐸𐐰𐑂 𐐹𐐲𐐺𐑊𐐮𐑇𐐻 𐑅𐐰𐑊𐑂𐐩𐑇𐐲𐑌; 𐐰𐑌𐐼 𐑅𐐯𐐼 𐐲𐑌𐐻𐐭 𐐞𐐴𐐲𐑌, 𐐜𐐴 𐐘𐐱𐐼 𐑉𐐩𐑌𐐯𐑃! 𐐈𐑌𐐼 𐐄 𐐸𐐵 𐐺𐐧𐐻𐐮𐑁𐐳𐑊 𐐲𐐹𐐱𐑌 𐑄 𐑋𐐵𐑌𐐻𐐩𐑌𐑆 𐐶𐐲𐑉 𐑄𐐩𐑉 𐑁𐐨𐐻! 𐐈𐑌𐐼 𐐰𐑀𐐯𐑌, 𐐸𐐵 𐐺𐐧𐐻𐐮𐑁𐐳𐑊 𐐲𐐹𐐱𐑌 𐑄 𐑋𐐵𐑌𐐻𐐩𐑌𐑆 𐐪𐑉 𐑄 𐑁𐐨𐐻 𐐱𐑂 𐑄𐐬𐑆 𐑄𐐰𐐻 𐐪𐑉 𐑅𐐻𐐮𐑊 𐐹𐐲𐐺𐑊𐐮𐑇𐐮𐑍 𐐹𐐨𐑅! 𐐈𐑌𐐼 𐐰𐑀𐐯𐑌, 𐐸𐐵 𐐺𐐧𐐻𐐮𐑁𐐳𐑊 𐐲𐐹𐐱𐑌 𐑄 𐑋𐐵𐑌𐐻𐐩𐑌𐑆 𐐪𐑉 𐑄 𐑁𐐨𐐻 𐐱𐑂 𐑄𐐬𐑆 𐐸𐐭 𐑇𐐰𐑊 𐐸𐐨𐑉𐐰𐑁𐐻𐐲𐑉 𐐹𐐲𐐺𐑊𐐮𐑇 𐐹𐐨𐑅, 𐐷𐐩, 𐑁𐑉𐐱𐑋 𐑄𐐮𐑅 𐐻𐐴𐑋 𐐸𐐯𐑌𐑅𐑁𐐬𐑉𐑃 𐐰𐑌𐐼 𐑁𐐫𐑉 𐐯𐑂𐐲𐑉!

6. 𐐈𐑌𐐼 𐐺𐐨𐐸𐐬𐑊𐐼, 𐐌 𐑅𐐩 𐐲𐑌𐐻𐐭 𐐷𐐭, 𐐜𐐮𐑅 𐐮𐑆 𐑌𐐱𐐻 𐐫𐑊: 𐑁𐐫𐑉 𐐄 𐐸𐐵 𐐺𐐧𐐻𐐮𐑁𐐳𐑊 𐐲𐐹𐐱𐑌 𐑄 𐑋𐐵𐑌𐐻𐐩𐑌𐑆 𐐪𐑉 𐑄 𐑁𐐨𐐻 𐐱𐑂 𐐸𐐮𐑋 𐑄𐐰𐐻 𐐺𐑉𐐮𐑍𐐯𐑃 𐑀𐐳𐐼 𐐻𐐴𐐼𐐮𐑍𐑆, 𐑄𐐰𐐻 𐐮𐑆 𐑄 𐑁𐐵𐑌𐐼𐐲𐑉 𐐱𐑂 𐐹𐐨𐑅: 𐐷𐐩, 𐐨𐑂𐐲𐑌 𐑄 𐐢𐐫𐑉𐐼, 𐐸𐐭 𐐸𐐰𐑆 𐑉𐐨𐐼𐐨𐑋𐐼 𐐸𐐮𐑆 𐐹𐐨𐐹𐐲𐑊: 𐐷𐐩, 𐐸𐐮𐑋 𐐸𐐭 𐐸𐐰𐑆 𐑀𐑉𐐰𐑌𐐻𐐯𐐼 𐑅𐐰𐑊𐑂𐐩𐑇𐐲𐑌 𐐲𐑌𐐻𐐭 𐐸𐐮𐑆 𐐹𐐨𐐹𐐲𐑊: 𐑁𐐫𐑉 𐐶𐐲𐑉 𐐮𐐻 𐑌𐐱𐐻 𐑁𐐫𐑉 𐑄 𐑉𐐨𐐼𐐯𐑋𐑇𐐲𐑌 𐐸𐐶𐐮𐐽 𐐸𐐨 𐐸𐐰𐑃 𐑋𐐩𐐼 𐑁𐐫𐑉 𐐸𐐮𐑆 𐐹𐐨𐐹𐐲𐑊, 𐐸𐐶𐐮𐐽 𐐶𐐱𐑆 𐐹𐑉𐐨𐐹𐐩𐑉𐐼 𐑁𐑉𐐱𐑋 𐑄 𐑁𐐵𐑌𐐼𐐩𐑇𐐲𐑌 𐐱𐑂 𐑄 𐐶𐐲𐑉𐑊𐐼; 𐐌 𐑅𐐩 𐐲𐑌𐐻𐐭 𐐷𐐭, 𐐶𐐲𐑉 𐐮𐐻 𐑌𐐱𐐻 𐑁𐐫𐑉 𐑄𐐮𐑅, 𐐫𐑊 𐑋𐐰𐑌𐐿𐐴𐑌𐐼 𐑋𐐲𐑅𐐻 𐐸𐐰𐑂 𐐹𐐯𐑉𐐮𐑇𐐻. 𐐒𐐲𐐻 𐐺𐐨𐐸𐐬𐑊𐐼, 𐑄 𐐺𐐰𐑌𐐼𐑆 𐐱𐑂 𐐼𐐯𐑃 𐑇𐐰𐑊 𐐺𐐨 𐐺𐑉𐐬𐐿𐐲𐑌, 𐐰𐑌𐐼 𐑄 𐐝𐐲𐑌 𐑉𐐩𐑌𐐯𐑃, 𐐰𐑌𐐼 𐐸𐐰𐑃 𐐹𐐵𐐲𐑉 𐐬𐑂𐐲𐑉 𐑄 𐐼𐐯𐐼; 𐑄𐐩𐑉𐑁𐐬𐑉, 𐐸𐐨 𐐺𐑉𐐮𐑍𐐯𐑃 𐐻𐐭 𐐹𐐰𐑅 𐑄 𐑉𐐯𐑆𐐲𐑉𐐯𐐿𐑇𐐲𐑌 𐐱𐑂 𐑄 𐐼𐐯𐐼. 𐐈𐑌𐐼 𐑄𐐩𐑉 𐐿𐐲𐑋𐐯𐑃 𐐲 𐑉𐐯𐑆𐐲𐑉𐐯𐐿𐑇𐐲𐑌, 𐐨𐑂𐐲𐑌 𐐲 𐑁𐐲𐑉𐑅𐐻 𐑉𐐯𐑆𐐲𐑉𐐯𐐿𐑇𐐲𐑌; 𐐷𐐩, 𐐨𐑂𐐲𐑌 𐐲 𐑉𐐯𐑆𐐲𐑉𐐯𐐿𐑇𐐲𐑌 𐐱𐑂 𐑄𐐬𐑆 𐑄𐐰𐐻 𐐸𐐰𐑂 𐐺𐐮𐑌, 𐐰𐑌𐐼 𐐸𐐭 𐐪𐑉, 𐐰𐑌𐐼 𐐸𐐭 𐑇𐐰𐑊 𐐺𐐨, 𐐨𐑂𐐲𐑌 𐐲𐑌𐐻𐐮𐑊 𐑄 𐑉𐐯𐑆𐐲𐑉𐐯𐐿𐑇𐐲𐑌 𐐱𐑂 𐐗𐑉𐐴𐑅𐐻: 𐑁𐐫𐑉 𐑅𐐬 𐑇𐐰𐑊 𐐸𐐨 𐐺𐐨 𐐿𐐫𐑊𐐼. 𐐈𐑌𐐼 𐑌𐐵 𐑄 𐑉𐐯𐑆𐐲𐑉𐐯𐐿𐑇𐐲𐑌 𐐱𐑂 𐐫𐑊 𐑄 𐐹𐑉𐐱𐑁𐐯𐐻𐑅, 𐐰𐑌𐐼 𐐫𐑊 𐑄𐐬𐑆 𐑄𐐰𐐻 𐐸𐐰𐑂 𐐺𐐨𐑊𐐨𐑂𐐼 𐐮𐑌 𐑄𐐩𐑉 𐐶𐐲𐑉𐐼𐑆, 𐐫𐑉 𐐫𐑊 𐑄𐐬𐑆 𐑄𐐰𐐻 𐐸𐐰𐑂 𐐿𐐯𐐹𐐻 𐑄 𐐿𐐱𐑋𐐰𐑌𐐼𐑋𐐯𐑌𐐻𐑅 𐐱𐑂 𐐘𐐱𐐼, 𐑇𐐰𐑊 𐐿𐐲𐑋 𐑁𐐬𐑉𐑃 𐐮𐑌 𐑄 𐑁𐐲𐑉𐑅𐐻 𐑉𐐯𐑆𐐲𐑉𐐯𐐿𐑇𐐲𐑌; 𐑄𐐩𐑉𐑁𐐬𐑉, 𐑄𐐩 𐐪𐑉 𐑄 𐑁𐐲𐑉𐑅𐐻 𐑉𐐯𐑆𐐲𐑉𐐯𐐿𐑇𐐲𐑌. 𐐜𐐩 𐐪𐑉 𐑉𐐩𐑆𐐼 𐐻𐐭 𐐼𐐶𐐯𐑊 𐐶𐐮𐑃 𐐘𐐱𐐼 𐐸𐐭 𐐸𐐰𐑆 𐑉𐐨𐐼𐐨𐑋𐐼 𐑄𐐯𐑋: 𐑄𐐲𐑅 𐑄𐐩 𐐸𐐰𐑂 𐐨𐐻𐐲𐑉𐑌𐐲𐑊 𐑊𐐴𐑁 𐑃𐑉𐐭 𐐗𐑉𐐴𐑅𐐻, 𐐸𐐭 𐐸𐐰𐑆 𐐺𐑉𐐬𐐿𐐲𐑌 𐑄 𐐺𐐰𐑌𐐼𐑆 𐐱𐑂 𐐼𐐯𐑃. 𐐈𐑌𐐼 𐑄𐐨𐑆 𐐪𐑉 𐑄𐐬𐑆 𐐸𐐭 𐐸𐐰𐑂 𐐹𐐪𐑉𐐻 𐐮𐑌 𐑄 𐑁𐐲𐑉𐑅𐐻 𐑉𐐯𐑆𐐲𐑉𐐯𐐿𐑇𐐲𐑌; 𐐰𐑌𐐼 𐑄𐐨𐑆 𐐪𐑉 𐑄𐐩 𐑄𐐰𐐻 𐐸𐐰𐑂 𐐼𐐴𐐼 𐐺𐐨𐑁𐐬𐑉 𐐗𐑉𐐴𐑅𐐻 𐐿𐐩𐑋, 𐐮𐑌 𐑄𐐩𐑉 𐐮𐑀𐑌𐐬𐑉𐐰𐑌𐑅, 𐑌𐐱𐐻 𐐸𐐰𐑂𐐮𐑍 𐑅𐐰𐑊𐑂𐐩𐑇𐐲𐑌 𐐼𐐨𐐿𐑊𐐩𐑉𐐼 𐐲𐑌𐐻𐐭 𐑄𐐯𐑋. 𐐈𐑌𐐼 𐑄𐐲𐑅 𐑄 𐐢𐐫𐑉𐐼 𐐺𐑉𐐮𐑍𐐯𐑃 𐐲𐐺𐐵𐐻 𐑄 𐑉𐐯𐑅𐐻𐐬𐑉𐐩𐑇𐐲𐑌 𐐱𐑂 𐑄𐐨𐑆; 𐐰𐑌𐐼 𐑄𐐩 𐐸𐐰𐑂 𐐲 𐐹𐐪𐑉𐐻 𐐮𐑌 𐑄 𐑁𐐲𐑉𐑅𐐻 𐑉𐐯𐑆𐐲𐑉𐐯𐐿𐑇𐐲𐑌, 𐐫𐑉 𐐸𐐰𐑂 𐐨𐐻𐐲𐑉𐑌𐐲𐑊 𐑊𐐴𐑁, 𐐺𐐨𐐮𐑍 𐑉𐐨𐐼𐐨𐑋𐐼 𐐺𐐴 𐑄 𐐢𐐫𐑉𐐼. 𐐈𐑌𐐼 𐑊𐐮𐐻𐐲𐑊 𐐽𐐮𐑊𐐼𐑉𐐯𐑌 𐐫𐑊𐑅𐐬 𐐸𐐰𐑂 𐐨𐐻𐐲𐑉𐑌𐐲𐑊 𐑊𐐴𐑁. 𐐒𐐲𐐻 𐐺𐐨𐐸𐐬𐑊𐐼, 𐐰𐑌𐐼 𐑁𐐨𐑉, 𐐰𐑌𐐼 𐐻𐑉𐐯𐑋𐐺𐐲𐑊 𐐺𐐨𐑁𐐬𐑉 𐐘𐐱𐐼; 𐑁𐐫𐑉 𐐷𐐨 𐐫𐐻 𐐻𐐭 𐐻𐑉𐐯𐑋𐐺𐐲𐑊: 𐑁𐐫𐑉 𐑄 𐐢𐐫𐑉𐐼 𐑉𐐨𐐼𐐨𐑋𐐯𐑃 𐑌𐐲𐑌 𐑅𐐲𐐽 𐑄𐐰𐐻 𐑉𐐨𐐺𐐯𐑊 𐐰𐑀𐐯𐑌𐑅𐐻 𐐸𐐮𐑋, 𐐰𐑌𐐼 𐐼𐐴 𐐮𐑌 𐑄𐐩𐑉 𐑅𐐮𐑌𐑆; 𐐷𐐩, 𐐨𐑂𐐲𐑌 𐐫𐑊 𐑄𐐬𐑆 𐑄𐐰𐐻 𐐸𐐰𐑂 𐐹𐐯𐑉𐐮𐑇𐐻 𐐮𐑌 𐑄𐐩𐑉 𐑅𐐮𐑌𐑆 𐐯𐑂𐐲𐑉 𐑅𐐮𐑌𐑅 𐑄 𐐶𐐲𐑉𐑊𐐼 𐐺𐐨𐑀𐐰𐑌, 𐑄𐐰𐐻 𐐸𐐰𐑂 𐐶𐐮𐑊-

𐑁𐐳𐑊𐐨 𐑉𐐨𐐺𐐯𐑊𐐼 𐐲𐑀𐐯𐑌𐑅𐐻 𐐘𐐱𐐼, 𐑄𐐰𐐻 𐐸𐐰𐑂 𐑌𐐬𐑌 𐑄 𐐿𐐱𐑋𐐰𐑌𐐼𐑋𐐯𐑌𐐻𐑅 𐐱𐑂 𐐘𐐱𐐼, 𐐰𐑌𐐼 𐐶𐐳𐐼 𐑌𐐱𐐻 𐐿𐐨𐐹 𐑄𐐯𐑋; 𐑄𐐨𐑆 𐐪𐑉 𐑄𐐩 𐑄𐐰𐐻 𐐸𐐰𐑂 𐑌𐐬 𐐹𐐪𐑉𐐻 𐐮𐑌 𐑄 𐑁𐐲𐑉𐑅𐐻 𐑉𐐯𐑆𐐲𐑉𐐯𐐿𐑇𐐲𐑌. 𐐜𐐩𐑉𐑁𐐬𐑉 𐐫𐐻 𐐷𐐨 𐑌𐐱𐐻 𐐻𐐭 𐐻𐑉𐐯𐑋𐐺𐑊? 𐐙𐐫𐑉 𐑅𐐰𐑊𐑂𐐩𐑇𐐲𐑌 𐐿𐐲𐑋𐐯𐑃 𐐻𐐭 𐑌𐐲𐑌 𐑅𐐲𐐽; 𐑁𐐫𐑉 𐑄 𐐢𐐫𐑉𐐼 𐐸𐐰𐑃 𐑉𐐨𐐼𐐨𐑋𐐼 𐑌𐐲𐑌 𐑅𐐲𐐽; 𐐷𐐩, 𐑌𐐨𐑄𐐲𐑉 𐐿𐐰𐑌 𐑄 𐐢𐐫𐑉𐐼 𐑉𐐨𐐼𐐨𐑋 𐑅𐐲𐐽; 𐑁𐐫𐑉 𐐸𐐨 𐐿𐐰𐑌𐐱𐐻 𐐼𐐨𐑌𐐴 𐐸𐐮𐑋𐑅𐐯𐑊𐑁; 𐑁𐐫𐑉 𐐸𐐨 𐐿𐐰𐑌𐐱𐐻 𐐼𐐨𐑌𐐴 𐐾𐐲𐑅𐐻𐐮𐑅 𐐸𐐶𐐯𐑌 𐐮𐐻 𐐸𐐰𐑆 𐐮𐐻𐑅 𐐿𐑊𐐩𐑋.

7. 𐐈𐑌𐐼 𐑌𐐵 𐐴 𐑅𐐩 𐐲𐑌𐐻𐐭 𐐷𐐭, 𐑄𐐰𐐻 𐑄 𐐻𐐴𐑋 𐑇𐐰𐑊 𐐿𐐲𐑋 𐑄𐐰𐐻 𐑄 𐑅𐐰𐑊𐑂𐐩𐑇𐐲𐑌 𐐱𐑂 𐑄 𐐢𐐫𐑉𐐼 𐑇𐐰𐑊 𐐺𐐨 𐐼𐐯𐐿𐑊𐐩𐑉𐐼 𐐻𐐭 𐐯𐑂𐑉𐐨 𐑌𐐩𐑇𐐲𐑌, 𐐿𐐮𐑌𐐼𐑉𐐯𐐼, 𐐻𐐲𐑍, 𐐰𐑌𐐼 𐐹𐐨𐐹𐑊. 𐐧𐐩, 𐐢𐐫𐑉𐐼, 𐑄𐐴 𐐶𐐱𐐽𐑋𐐯𐑌 𐑇𐐰𐑊 𐑊𐐮𐑁𐐻 𐐲𐐹 𐑄𐐩𐑉 𐑂𐑎𐑅; 𐐶𐐮𐑄 𐑄 𐑂𐑎𐑅 𐐻𐐭𐑀𐐯𐑄𐐲𐑉 𐑇𐐰𐑊 𐑄𐐩 𐑅𐐮𐑍: 𐑁𐐫𐑉 𐑄𐐩 𐑇𐐰𐑊 𐑅𐐨 𐐴 𐐻𐐭 𐐴, 𐐸𐐶𐐯𐑌 𐑄 𐐢𐐫𐑉𐐼 𐑇𐐰𐑊 𐐺𐑉𐐮𐑍 𐐲𐑀𐐯𐑌 𐐞𐐴𐐲𐑌. 𐐒𐑉𐐩𐐿 𐑁𐐬𐑉𐑃 𐐮𐑌𐐻𐐭 𐐾𐑎, 𐑅𐐮𐑍 𐐻𐐭𐑀𐐯𐑄𐐲𐑉 𐐷𐐨 𐐶𐐩𐑅𐐻 𐐹𐑊𐐩𐑅𐐯𐑆 𐐱𐑂 𐐖𐐯𐑉𐐭𐑅𐐲𐑊𐐯𐑋: 𐑁𐐫𐑉 𐑄 𐐢𐐫𐑉𐐼 𐐸𐐰𐑃 𐐿𐐲𐑋𐑁𐐲𐑉𐐻𐐯𐐼 𐐸𐐮𐑆 𐐹𐐨𐐹𐑊, 𐐸𐐨 𐐸𐐰𐑃 𐑉𐐨𐐼𐐨𐑋𐐼 𐐖𐐯𐑉𐐭𐑅𐐲𐑊𐐯𐑋. 𐐜 𐐢𐐫𐑉𐐼 𐐸𐐰𐑃 𐑋𐐩𐐼 𐐺𐐩𐑉 𐐸𐐮𐑆 𐐸𐐬𐑊𐐨 𐐪𐑉𐑋 𐐮𐑌 𐑄 𐐴𐑆 𐐱𐑂 𐐫𐑊 𐑄 𐑌𐐩𐑇𐐲𐑌𐑆: 𐐰𐑌𐐼 𐐫𐑊 𐑄 𐐯𐑌𐐼𐑆 𐐱𐑂 𐑄 𐐲𐑉𐑃 𐑇𐐰𐑊 𐑅𐐨 𐑄 𐑅𐐰𐑊𐑂𐐩𐑇𐐲𐑌 𐐱𐑂 𐐵𐑉 𐐘𐐱𐐼.

8. 𐐈𐑌𐐼 𐑌𐐵 𐐮𐐻 𐐿𐐩𐑋 𐐻𐐭 𐐹𐐰𐑅 𐑄𐐰𐐻 𐐰𐑁𐐻𐐲𐑉 𐐂𐐺𐐮𐑌𐐪𐐼𐐴 𐐸𐐰𐐼 𐑅𐐹𐐬𐐿𐐲𐑌 𐑄𐐨𐑆 𐐶𐐲𐑉𐐼𐑆, 𐐸𐐨 𐑅𐐻𐑉𐐯𐐽𐐻 𐑁𐐬𐑉𐑃 𐐸𐐮𐑆 𐐸𐐰𐑌𐐼 𐐰𐑌𐐼 𐑅𐐯𐐼, 𐐜 𐐻𐐴𐑋 𐑇𐐰𐑊 𐐿𐐲𐑋 𐐸𐐶𐐯𐑌 𐐫𐑊 𐑇𐐰𐑊 𐑅𐐨 𐑄 𐑅𐐰𐑊𐑂𐐩𐑇𐐲𐑌 𐐱𐑂 𐑄 𐐢𐐫𐑉𐐼: 𐐸𐐶𐐯𐑌 𐐯𐑂𐑉𐐨 𐑌𐐩𐑇𐐲𐑌, 𐐿𐐮𐑌𐐼𐑉𐐯𐐼, 𐐻𐐲𐑍, 𐐰𐑌𐐼 𐐹𐐨𐐹𐑊, 𐑇𐐰𐑊 𐑅𐐨 𐐴 𐐻𐐭 𐐴, 𐐰𐑌𐐼 𐑇𐐰𐑊 𐐿𐐱𐑌𐑁𐐯𐑅 𐐺𐐨𐑁𐐬𐑉 𐐘𐐱𐐼 𐑄𐐰𐐻 𐐸𐐮𐑆 𐐾𐐲𐐾𐑋𐐯𐑌𐐻𐑅 𐐪𐑉 𐐾𐐲𐑅𐐻; 𐐰𐑌𐐼 𐑄𐐯𐑌 𐑇𐐰𐑊 𐑄 𐐶𐐮𐐿𐐯𐐼 𐐺𐐨 𐐿𐐪𐑅𐐻 𐐵𐐻, 𐐰𐑌𐐼 𐑄𐐩 𐑇𐐰𐑊 𐐸𐐰𐑂 𐐿𐐫𐑆 𐐻𐐭 𐐸𐐵𐑊, 𐐰𐑌𐐼 𐐶𐐨𐐹, 𐐰𐑌𐐼 𐐶𐐩𐑊, 𐐰𐑌𐐼 𐑌𐐰𐑇 𐑄𐐩𐑉 𐐻𐐨𐑃; 𐐰𐑌𐐼 𐑄𐐮𐑅 𐐺𐐨𐐿𐐫𐑆 𐑄𐐩 𐐶𐐳𐐼 𐑌𐐱𐐻 𐐸𐐪𐑉𐐿𐐲𐑌 𐐲𐑌𐐻𐐭 𐑄 𐑂𐑎𐑅 𐐱𐑂 𐑄 𐐢𐐫𐑉𐐼; 𐑄𐐩𐑉𐑁𐐬𐑉 𐑄 𐐢𐐫𐑉𐐼 𐑉𐐨𐐼𐐨𐑋𐐯𐑃 𐑄𐐯𐑋 𐑌𐐱𐐻, 𐑁𐐫𐑉 𐑄𐐩 𐐪𐑉 𐐿𐐪𐑉𐑌𐐲𐑊 𐐰𐑌𐐼 𐐼𐐯𐑂𐐮𐑊𐐮𐑇, 𐐰𐑌𐐼 𐑄 𐐼𐐯𐑂𐐮𐑊 𐐸𐐰𐑃 𐐹𐐵𐐲𐑉 𐐬𐑂𐐲𐑉 𐑄𐐯𐑋; 𐐷𐐩, 𐐨𐑂𐐯𐑌 𐑄𐐰𐐻 𐐬𐑊𐐼 𐑅𐐲𐑉𐐹𐐯𐑌𐐻 𐑄𐐰𐐻 𐐼𐐮𐐼 𐐺𐐨𐑀𐐴𐑊 𐐵𐑉 𐑁𐐲𐑉𐑅𐐻 𐐹𐐩𐑉𐐯𐑌𐐻𐑅, 𐐸𐐶𐐮𐐽 𐐶𐐱𐑆 𐑄 𐐿𐐫𐑆 𐐱𐑂 𐑄𐐩𐑉 𐑁𐐫𐑊; 𐐸𐐶𐐮𐐽 𐐶𐐱𐑆 𐑄 𐐿𐐫𐑆 𐐱𐑂 𐐫𐑊 𐑋𐐰𐑌𐐿𐐴𐑌𐐼 𐐺𐐨𐐿𐐲𐑋𐐮𐑍 𐐿𐐪𐑉𐑌𐐲𐑊, 𐑅𐐯𐑌𐑇𐐭𐐲𐑊, 𐐼𐐯𐑂𐐮𐑊𐐮𐑇, 𐑌𐐬𐐮𐑍 𐐨𐑂𐐮𐑊 𐑁𐑉𐐱𐑋 𐑀𐐳𐐼, 𐑅𐐲𐐺𐐾𐐯𐐿𐐻𐐮𐑍 𐑄𐐯𐑋𐑅𐐯𐑊𐑂𐑆 𐐻𐐭 𐑄 𐐼𐐯𐑂𐐮𐑊. 𐐜𐐲𐑅 𐐫𐑊 𐑋𐐰𐑌𐐿𐐴𐑌𐐼 𐐶𐐲𐑉 𐑊𐐱𐑅𐐻; 𐐰𐑌𐐼 𐐺𐐨𐐸𐐬𐑊𐐼, 𐑄𐐩 𐐶𐐳𐐼 𐐸𐐰𐑂 𐐺𐐮𐑌 𐐯𐑌𐐼𐑊𐐯𐑅𐑊𐐨 𐑊𐐱𐑅𐐻, 𐐶𐐲𐑉 𐐮𐐻 𐑌𐐱𐐻 𐑄𐐰𐐻 𐐘𐐱𐐼 𐑉𐐨𐐼𐐨𐑋𐐼 𐐸𐐮𐑆 𐐹𐐨𐐹𐑊 𐑁𐑉𐐱𐑋 𐑄𐐩𐑉 𐑊𐐱𐑅𐐻 𐐰𐑌𐐼 𐑁𐐫𐑊𐐲𐑌 𐑅𐐻𐐩𐐻. 𐐒𐐲𐐻 𐑉𐐨𐑋𐐯𐑋𐐺𐐲𐑉, 𐑄𐐰𐐻 𐐸𐐨 𐑄𐐰𐐻 𐐹𐐲𐑉𐑅𐐮𐑅𐐻𐑅 𐐮𐑌 𐐸𐐮𐑆 𐐬𐑌 𐐿𐐪𐑉𐑌𐐲𐑊 𐑌𐐩𐐽𐐲𐑉, 𐐰𐑌𐐼 𐑀𐐬𐑆 𐐱𐑌 𐐮𐑌 𐑄 𐐶𐐩𐑆 𐐱𐑂 𐑅𐐮𐑌 𐐰𐑌𐐼 𐑉𐐨𐐺𐐯𐑊𐐷𐐲𐑌 𐐲𐑀𐐯𐑌𐑅𐐻 𐐘𐐱𐐼, 𐑉𐐨𐑋𐐩𐑌𐐯𐑃 𐐮𐑌 𐐸𐐮𐑆 𐑁𐐫𐑊𐐲𐑌 𐑅𐐻𐐩𐐻, 𐐰𐑌𐐼 𐑄 𐐼𐐯𐑂𐐮𐑊 𐐸𐐰𐑃 𐐫𐑊 𐐹𐐵𐐲𐑉 𐐬𐑂𐐲𐑉 𐐸𐐮𐑋. 𐐜𐐩𐑉𐑁𐐬𐑉 𐐸𐐨 𐐮𐑆 𐐰𐑆 𐑄𐐬 𐑄𐐩𐑉 𐐶𐐱𐑆 𐑌𐐬 𐑉𐐨𐐼𐐯𐑋𐑇𐐲𐑌 𐑋𐐩𐐼; 𐐺𐐨𐐮𐑍 𐐰𐑌 𐐯𐑌𐐯𐑋𐐨 𐐻𐐭 𐐘𐐱𐐼; 𐐰𐑌𐐼 𐐫𐑊𐑅𐐬 𐐮𐑆 𐑄 𐐼𐐯𐑂𐐮𐑊 𐐰𐑌 𐐯𐑌𐐯𐑋𐐨 𐐻𐐭 𐐘𐐱𐐼. 𐐈𐑌𐐼 𐑌𐐵 𐐮𐑁 𐐗𐑉𐐴𐑅𐐻 𐐸𐐰𐐼 𐑌𐐱𐐻 𐐿𐐲𐑋 𐐮𐑌𐐻𐐭 𐑄 𐐶𐐲𐑉𐑊𐐼, 𐑅𐐹𐐨𐐿𐐮𐑍 𐐱𐑂 𐑃𐐮𐑍𐑆 𐐻𐐭 𐐿𐐲𐑋, 𐐰𐑆 𐑄𐐬 𐑄𐐩 𐐸𐐰𐐼 𐐫𐑊𐑉𐐯𐐼𐐨 𐐿𐐲𐑋, 𐑄𐐩𐑉 𐐿𐐳𐐼 𐐸𐐰𐑂 𐐺𐐮𐑌 𐑌𐐬 𐑉𐐨𐐼𐐯𐑋𐑇𐐲𐑌.

9. 𐐈𐑌𐐼 𐐮𐑁 𐐗𐑉𐐴𐑅𐐻 𐐸𐐰𐐼 𐑌𐐱𐐻 𐑉𐐮𐑆𐐲𐑌 𐑁𐑉𐐱𐑋 𐑄 𐐼𐐯𐐼, 𐐫𐑉 𐐸𐐰𐑂 𐐺𐑉𐐬𐐿𐐲𐑌 𐑄 𐐺𐐰𐑌𐐼𐑆 𐐱𐑂 𐐼𐐯𐑃, 𐑄𐐰𐐻 𐑄 𐑀𐑉𐐩𐑂 𐑇𐐳𐐼 𐐸𐐰𐑂 𐑌𐐬 𐑂𐐮𐐿𐐻𐐬𐑉𐐨, 𐐰𐑌𐐼 𐑄𐐰𐐻 𐐼𐐯𐑃 𐑇𐐳𐐼 𐐸𐐰𐑂 𐑌𐐬 𐑅𐐻𐐮𐑍, 𐑄𐐩𐑉 𐐿𐐳𐐼 𐐸𐐰𐑂 𐐺𐐮𐑌 𐑌𐐬 𐑉𐐯𐑆𐐲𐑉𐐯𐐿𐑇𐐲𐑌. 𐐒𐐲𐐻 𐑄𐐩𐑉 𐐮𐑆 𐐰 𐑉𐐯𐑆𐐲𐑉𐐯𐐿𐑇𐐲𐑌, 𐑄𐐩𐑉𐑁𐐬𐑉 𐑄 𐑀𐑉𐐩𐑂 𐐸𐐰𐑃 𐑌𐐬 𐑂𐐮𐐿𐐻𐐬𐑉𐐨, 𐐰𐑌𐐼 𐑄 𐑅𐐻𐐮𐑍 𐐱𐑂 𐐼𐐯𐑃 𐐮𐑆 𐑅𐐶𐐱𐑊𐐬𐐼 𐐲𐐹 𐐮𐑌 𐐗𐑉𐐴𐑅𐐻: 𐐐𐐨 𐐮𐑆 𐑄 𐑊𐐴𐐻 𐐰𐑌𐐼 𐑄 𐑊𐐴𐑁 𐐱𐑂 𐑄 𐐶𐐲𐑉𐑊𐐼; 𐐷𐐩, 𐐰 𐑊𐐴𐐻 𐑄𐐰𐐻 𐐮𐑆 𐐯𐑌𐐼𐑊𐐯𐑅, 𐑄𐐰𐐻 𐐿𐐰𐑌 𐑌𐐯𐑂𐐲𐑉 𐐺𐐨 𐐼𐐪𐑉𐐿𐐲𐑌𐐼; 𐐷𐐩, 𐐰𐑌𐐼 𐐫𐑊𐑅𐐬 𐐰 𐑊𐐴𐑁 𐐸𐐶𐐮𐐽 𐐮𐑆 𐐯𐑌𐐼𐑊𐐯𐑅, 𐑄𐐰𐐻 𐑄𐐩𐑉 𐐿𐐰𐑌 𐐺𐐨 𐑌𐐬 𐑋𐐬𐑉 𐐼𐐯𐑃. 𐐀𐑂𐐯𐑌 𐑄𐐮𐑅 𐑋𐐫𐑉𐐻𐐲𐑊 𐑇𐐰𐑊 𐐹𐐳𐐻 𐐱𐑌 𐐮𐑋𐐫𐑉𐐻𐐰𐑊𐐮𐐻𐐨, 𐐰𐑌𐐼 𐑄𐐮𐑅 𐐿𐐫𐑉𐐲𐐹𐑇𐐲𐑌 𐑇𐐰𐑊 𐐹𐐳𐐻 𐐱𐑌 𐐮𐑌𐐿𐐫𐑉𐐲𐐹𐑇𐐲𐑌, 𐐰𐑌𐐼 𐑇𐐰𐑊 𐐺𐐨 𐐺𐑉𐐫𐐻 𐐻𐐭 𐑅𐐻𐐰𐑌𐐼 𐐺𐐨𐑁𐐬𐑉 𐑄 𐐺𐐪𐑉 𐐱𐑂 𐐘𐐱𐐼, 𐐻𐐭 𐐺𐐨 𐐾𐐲𐐾𐐼 𐐱𐑂 𐐸𐐮𐑋 𐐰𐐿𐐫𐑉𐐼𐐮𐑍 𐐻𐐭 𐑄𐐩𐑉 𐐶𐐲𐑉𐐿𐑅, 𐐸𐐶𐐯𐑄𐐲𐑉 𐑄𐐩 𐐺𐐨 𐑀𐐳𐐼, 𐐫𐑉 𐐸𐐶𐐯𐑄𐐲𐑉 𐑄𐐩 𐐺𐐨 𐐨𐑂𐐮𐑊. 𐐆𐑁 𐑄𐐩 𐐺𐐨 𐑀𐐳𐐼, 𐐻𐐭 𐑄 𐑉𐐯𐑆𐐲𐑉𐐯𐐿𐑇𐐲𐑌 𐐱𐑂 𐐯𐑌𐐼𐑊𐐯𐑅 𐑊𐐴𐑁 𐐰𐑌𐐼 𐐸𐐰𐐹𐐨𐑌𐐯𐑅, 𐐰𐑌𐐼 𐐮𐑁 𐑄𐐩 𐐺𐐨 𐐨𐑂𐐮𐑊, 𐐻𐐭 𐑄 𐑉𐐯𐑆𐐲𐑉𐐯𐐿𐑇𐐲𐑌 𐐱𐑂 𐐯𐑌𐐼𐑊𐐯𐑅 𐐼𐐰𐑋𐑌𐐩𐑇𐐲𐑌; 𐐺𐐨𐐮𐑍 𐐼𐐨𐑊𐐮𐑂𐐲𐑉𐐼 𐐲𐐹 𐐻𐐭 𐑄 𐐼𐐯𐑂𐐮𐑊, 𐐸𐐭 𐐸𐐰𐑃 𐑅𐐲𐐺𐐾𐐯𐐿𐐻𐐯𐐼 𐑄𐐯𐑋, 𐐸𐐶𐐮𐐽 𐐮𐑆 𐐼𐐰𐑋𐑌𐐩𐑇𐐲𐑌: 𐐸𐐰𐑂𐐮𐑍 𐑀𐐱𐑌 𐐰𐐿𐐫𐑉𐐼𐐮𐑍 𐐻𐐭 𐑄𐐩𐑉 𐐬𐑌 𐐿𐐪𐑉𐑌𐐲𐑊 𐐶𐐮𐑊𐑆 𐐰𐑌𐐼 𐐼𐐨𐑆𐐴𐑉𐑆; 𐐸𐐰𐑂𐐮𐑍 𐑌𐐯𐑂𐐲𐑉 𐐿𐐫𐑊𐐼 𐐲𐐹𐐱𐑌 𐑄 𐐢𐐫𐑉𐐼 𐐸𐐶𐐴𐑊 𐑄 𐐪𐑉𐑋𐑆 𐐱𐑂 𐑋𐐲𐑉𐑅𐐨 𐐶𐐲𐑉

𐐯𐐿𐑅𐐻𐐯𐑌𐐼𐐯𐐼 𐐻𐐬𐑉𐐼𐑆 𐑄𐐯𐑋, 𐐰𐑌𐐼 𐑄𐐩 𐐶𐐳𐐼 𐑌𐐱𐐻; 𐑄𐐩 𐐺𐐨𐐮𐑍 𐐶𐐫𐑉𐑌𐐼 𐐱𐑂 𐑄𐐯𐑉 𐐮𐑌𐐮𐐿𐐶𐐮𐐻𐐨𐑆, 𐐰𐑌𐐼 𐐷𐐯𐐻 𐑄𐐩 𐐶𐐳𐐼 𐑌𐐱𐐻 𐐼𐐨𐐹𐐪𐑉𐐻 𐑁𐑉𐐱𐑋 𐑄𐐯𐑋; 𐐰𐑌𐐼 𐑄𐐩 𐐶𐐲𐑉 𐐿𐐱𐑋𐐰𐑌𐐼𐐯𐐼 𐐻𐐭 𐑉𐐨𐐹𐐯𐑌𐐻, 𐐰𐑌𐐼 𐐷𐐯𐐻 𐑄𐐩 𐐶𐐳𐐼 𐑌𐐱𐐻 𐑉𐐨𐐹𐐯𐑌𐐻. 𐐈𐑌𐐼 𐑌𐐵 𐐫𐐻 𐐷𐐨 𐑌𐐱𐐻 𐐻𐐭 𐐻𐑉𐐯𐑋𐐺𐐲𐑊 𐐰𐑌𐐼 𐑉𐐨𐐹𐐯𐑌𐐻 𐐱𐑂 𐐷𐐬𐑉 𐑅𐐮𐑌𐑆, 𐐰𐑌𐐼 𐑉𐐨𐑋𐐯𐑋𐐺𐐲𐑉 𐑄𐐰𐐻 𐐬𐑌𐑊𐐨 𐐮𐑌 𐐰𐑌𐐼 𐑃𐑉𐐭 𐐗𐑉𐐴𐑅𐐻 𐐷𐐨 𐐿𐐰𐑌 𐐺𐐨 𐑅𐐩𐑂𐐼? 𐐜𐐯𐑉𐑁𐐬𐑉, 𐐮𐑁 𐐷𐐨 𐐻𐐨𐐽 𐑄 𐑊𐐫 𐐱𐑂 𐐣𐐬𐑆𐐯𐑆, 𐐫𐑊𐑅𐐬 𐐻𐐨𐐽 𐑄𐐰𐐻 𐐮𐐻 𐐮𐑆 𐐰 𐑇𐐰𐐼𐐬 𐐱𐑂 𐑄𐐬𐑆 𐑃𐐮𐑍𐑆 𐐸𐐶𐐮𐐽 𐐪𐑉 𐐻𐐭 𐐿𐐲𐑋; 𐐻𐐨𐐽 𐑄𐐯𐑋 𐑄𐐰𐐻 𐑉𐐨𐐼𐐯𐑋𐑇𐐲𐑌 𐐿𐐲𐑋𐐯𐑃 𐑃𐑉𐐭 𐐗𐑉𐐴𐑅𐐻 𐑄 𐐢𐐫𐑉𐐼, 𐐸𐐭 𐐮𐑆 𐑄 𐑂𐐯𐑉𐐨 𐐀𐐻𐐲𐑉𐑌𐐲𐑊 𐐙𐐪𐑄𐐲𐑉. 𐐁𐑋𐐯𐑌.

𐐗𐐰𐐹𐐻𐐲𐑉 IX.

1. 𐐈𐑌𐐼 𐑌𐐵 𐐮𐐻 𐐿𐐩𐑋 𐐻𐐭 𐐹𐐰𐑅 𐑄𐐰𐐻 𐐸𐐶𐐯𐑌 𐐈𐐺𐐮𐑌𐐲𐐼𐐴 𐐸𐐰𐐼 𐑁𐐮𐑌𐐮𐑇𐐻 𐑄𐐨𐑆 𐑅𐐩𐐮𐑍𐑆, 𐑄𐐰𐐻 𐑄 𐐿𐐮𐑍 𐐿𐐱𐑋𐐰𐑌𐐼𐐯𐐼 𐑄𐐰𐐻 𐑄 𐐹𐑉𐐨𐑅𐐻𐑅 𐑇𐐳𐐼 𐐻𐐩𐐿 𐐸𐐮𐑋 𐐰𐑌𐐼 𐐿𐐫𐑆 𐑄𐐰𐐻 𐐸𐐨 𐑇𐐳𐐼 𐐺𐐨 𐐹𐐳𐐻 𐐻𐐭 𐐼𐐯𐑃. 𐐒𐐲𐐻 𐑄𐐯𐑉 𐐶𐐱𐑆 𐐶𐐲𐑌 𐐲𐑋𐐲𐑍 𐑄𐐯𐑋 𐐸𐐭𐑆 𐑌𐐩𐑋 𐐶𐐱𐑆 𐐈𐑊𐑋𐐲, 𐐸𐐨 𐐫𐑊𐑅𐐬 𐐺𐐨𐐮𐑍 𐐰 𐐼𐐨𐑅𐐯𐑌𐐼𐐲𐑌𐐻 𐐱𐑂 𐐤𐐨𐑁𐐴. 𐐈𐑌𐐼 𐐸𐐨 𐐶𐐱𐑆 𐐰 𐐷𐐲𐑍 𐑋𐐰𐑌, 𐐰𐑌𐐼 𐐸𐐨 𐐺𐐨𐑊𐐨𐑂𐐼 𐑄 𐐶𐐲𐑉𐐼𐑆 𐐸𐐶𐐮𐐽 𐐈𐐺𐐮𐑌𐐲𐐼𐐴 𐐸𐐰𐐼 𐑅𐐹𐐬𐐿𐐲𐑌, 𐑁𐐫𐑉 𐐸𐐨 𐑌𐐭 𐐿𐐱𐑌𐑅𐐲𐑉𐑌𐐮𐑍 𐑄 𐐮𐑌𐐮𐐿𐐶𐐮𐐻𐐨 𐐸𐐶𐐮𐐽 𐐈𐐺𐐮𐑌𐐲𐐼𐐴 𐐸𐐰𐐼 𐐻𐐯𐑅𐐻𐐮𐑁𐐴𐐼 𐐲𐑀𐐯𐑌𐑅𐐻 𐑄𐐯𐑋; 𐑄𐐯𐑉𐑁𐐬𐑉 𐐸𐐨 𐐺𐐨𐑀𐐰𐑌 𐐻𐐭 𐐹𐑊𐐨𐐼 𐐶𐐮𐑄 𐑄 𐐿𐐮𐑍 𐑄𐐰𐐻 𐐸𐐨 𐐶𐐳𐐼 𐑌𐐱𐐻 𐐺𐐨 𐐰𐑍𐑀𐑉𐐨 𐐶𐐮𐑄 𐐈𐐺𐐮𐑌𐐲𐐼𐐴, 𐐺𐐲𐐻 𐑅𐐲𐑁𐐲𐑉 𐑄𐐰𐐻 𐐸𐐨 𐑋𐐴𐐻 𐐼𐐨𐐹𐐪𐑉𐐻 𐐮𐑌 𐐹𐐨𐑅. 𐐒𐐲𐐻 𐑄 𐐿𐐮𐑍 𐐶𐐱𐑆 𐑋𐐬𐑉 𐑉𐐫𐑃, 𐐰𐑌𐐼 𐐿𐐫𐑆𐐼 𐑄𐐰𐐻 𐐈𐑊𐑋𐐲 𐑇𐐳𐐼 𐐺𐐨 𐐿𐐰𐑅𐐻 𐐵𐐻 𐑁𐑉𐐱𐑋 𐐲𐑋𐐲𐑍 𐑄𐐯𐑋, 𐐰𐑌𐐼 𐑅𐐯𐑌𐐻 𐐸𐐮𐑆 𐑅𐐲𐑉𐑂𐐲𐑌𐐻𐑅 𐐰𐑁𐐻𐐲𐑉 𐐸𐐮𐑋 𐑄𐐰𐐻 𐑄𐐩 𐑋𐐴𐐻 𐑅𐑊𐐩 𐐸𐐮𐑋. 𐐒𐐲𐐻 𐐸𐐨 𐑁𐑊𐐯𐐼 𐑁𐑉𐐱𐑋 𐐺𐐨𐑁𐐬𐑉 𐑄𐐯𐑋 𐐰𐑌𐐼 𐐸𐐮𐐼 𐐸𐐮𐑋𐑅𐐯𐑊𐑁 𐑄𐐰𐐻 𐑄𐐩 𐑁𐐵𐑌𐐼 𐐸𐐮𐑋 𐑌𐐱𐐻. 𐐈𐑌𐐼 𐐸𐐨 𐐺𐐨𐐮𐑍 𐐿𐐱𐑌𐑅𐐨𐑊𐐼 𐑁𐐫𐑉 𐑋𐐯𐑌𐐨 𐐼𐐩𐑆 𐐼𐐮𐐼 𐑉𐐴𐐻 𐐫𐑊 𐑄 𐐶𐐲𐑉𐐼𐑆 𐐸𐐶𐐮𐐽 𐐈𐐺𐐮𐑌𐐲𐐼𐐴 𐐸𐐰𐐼 𐑅𐐹𐐬𐐿𐐲𐑌.

2. 𐐈𐑌𐐼 𐐮𐐻 𐐿𐐩𐑋 𐐻𐐭 𐐹𐐰𐑅 𐑄𐐰𐐻 𐑄 𐐿𐐮𐑍 𐐿𐐫𐑆𐐼 𐑄𐐰𐐻 𐐸𐐮𐑆 𐑀𐐪𐑉𐐼𐑆 𐑇𐐳𐐼 𐑅𐐲𐑉𐐵𐑌𐐼 𐐈𐐺𐐮𐑌𐐲𐐼𐐴, 𐐰𐑌𐐼 𐐻𐐩𐐿 𐐸𐐮𐑋; 𐐰𐑌𐐼 𐑄𐐩 𐐺𐐵𐑌𐐼 𐐸𐐮𐑋 𐐰𐑌𐐼 𐐿𐐰𐑅𐐻 𐐸𐐮𐑋 𐐮𐑌𐐻𐐭 𐐹𐑉𐐮𐑆𐐲𐑌. 𐐈𐑌𐐼 𐐰𐑁𐐻𐐲𐑉 𐑃𐑉𐐨 𐐼𐐩𐑆, 𐐸𐐰𐑂𐐮𐑍 𐐿𐐵𐑌𐑅𐐯𐑊𐐼 𐐶𐐮𐑄 𐐸𐐮𐑆 𐐹𐑉𐐨𐑅𐐻𐑅, 𐐸𐐨 𐐿𐐫𐑆𐐼 𐑄𐐰𐐻 𐐸𐐨 𐑇𐐳𐐼 𐐲𐑀𐐯𐑌 𐐺𐐨 𐐺𐑉𐐫𐐻 𐐺𐐨𐑁𐐬𐑉 𐐸𐐮𐑋. 𐐈𐑌𐐼 𐐸𐐨 𐑅𐐯𐐼 𐐲𐑌𐐻𐐭 𐐸𐐮𐑋: 𐐈𐐺𐐮𐑌𐐲𐐼𐐴, 𐐶𐐨 𐐸𐐰𐑂 𐑁𐐵𐑌𐐼 𐐰𐑌 𐐰𐐿𐐷𐐭𐑆𐐩𐑇𐐲𐑌 𐐲𐑀𐐯𐑌𐑅𐐻 𐑄𐐨, 𐐰𐑌𐐼 𐑄𐐵 𐐪𐑉𐐻 𐐶𐐲𐑉𐑄𐐨 𐐱𐑂 𐐼𐐯𐑃. 𐐙𐐫𐑉 𐑄𐐵 𐐸𐐰𐑅𐐻 𐑅𐐯𐐼 𐑄𐐰𐐻 𐐘𐐱𐐼 𐐸𐐮𐑋𐑅𐐯𐑊𐑁 𐑇𐐳𐐼 𐐿𐐲𐑋 𐐼𐐵𐑌 𐐲𐑋𐐲𐑍 𐑄 𐐽𐐮𐑊𐐼𐑉𐐯𐑌 𐐱𐑂 𐑋𐐯𐑌; 𐐰𐑌𐐼 𐑌𐐵, 𐑁𐐫𐑉 𐑄𐐮𐑅 𐐿𐐫𐑆 𐑄𐐵 𐑇𐐰𐑊𐐻 𐐺𐐨 𐐹𐐳𐐻 𐐻𐐭 𐐼𐐯𐑃, 𐐲𐑌𐑊𐐯𐑅 𐑄𐐵 𐐶𐐮𐑊𐐻 𐑉𐐨𐐿𐐫𐑊 𐐫𐑊 𐑄 𐐶𐐲𐑉𐐼𐑆 𐐸𐐶𐐮𐐽 𐑄𐐵 𐐸𐐰𐑅𐐻 𐑅𐐹𐐬𐐿𐐲𐑌 𐐨𐑂𐐲𐑊 𐐿𐐱𐑌𐑅𐐲𐑉𐑌𐐮𐑍 𐑋𐐨 𐐰𐑌𐐼 𐑋𐐴 𐐹𐐨𐐹𐐲𐑊.

3. 𐐤𐐵 𐐈𐐺𐐮𐑌𐐲𐐼𐐴 𐑅𐐯𐐼 𐐲𐑌𐐻𐐭 𐐸𐐮𐑋: 𐐌 𐑅𐐩 𐐲𐑌𐐻𐐭 𐐷𐐭, 𐐌 𐐶𐐮𐑊 𐑌𐐱𐐻 𐑉𐐨𐐿𐐫𐑊 𐑄 𐐶𐐲𐑉𐐼𐑆 𐐸𐐶𐐮𐐽 𐐌 𐐸𐐰𐑂 𐑅𐐹𐐬𐐿𐐲𐑌 𐐲𐑌𐐻𐐭 𐐷𐐭 𐐿𐐱𐑌𐑅𐐲𐑉𐑌𐐮𐑍 𐑄𐐮𐑅 𐐹𐐨𐐹𐐲𐑊, 𐑁𐐫𐑉 𐑄𐐩 𐐪𐑉 𐐻𐑉𐐭; 𐐰𐑌𐐼 𐑄𐐰𐐻 𐐷𐐨 𐑋𐐩 𐑌𐐬 𐐱𐑂 𐑄𐐯𐑉 𐑇𐐭𐑉𐐻𐐨, 𐐌 𐐸𐐰𐑂 𐑅𐐲𐑁𐐲𐑉𐐼 𐑋𐐴𐑅𐐯𐑊𐑁 𐑄𐐰𐐻 𐐌 𐐸𐐰𐑂 𐑁𐐫𐑊𐐲𐑌 𐐮𐑌𐐻𐐭 𐐷𐐬𐑉 𐐸𐐰𐑌𐐼𐑆. 𐐏𐐩, 𐐰𐑌𐐼 𐐌 𐐶𐐮𐑊 𐑅𐐲𐑁𐐲𐑉 𐐨𐑂𐐲𐑌 𐐲𐑌𐐻𐐮𐑊 𐐼𐐯𐑃, 𐐰𐑌𐐼 𐐌 𐐶𐐮𐑊 𐑌𐐱𐐻 𐑉𐐨𐐿𐐫𐑊 𐑋𐐴 𐐶𐐲𐑉𐐼𐑆, 𐐰𐑌𐐼 𐑄𐐩 𐑇𐐰𐑊 𐑅𐐻𐐰𐑌𐐼 𐐰𐑆 𐐰 𐐻𐐯𐑅𐐻𐐮𐑋𐐬𐑌𐐨 𐐲𐑀𐐯𐑌𐑅𐐻 𐐷𐐭. 𐐈𐑌𐐼 𐐮𐑁 𐐷𐐨 𐑅𐑊𐐩 𐑋𐐨, 𐐷𐐨 𐐶𐐮𐑊 𐑇𐐯𐐼 𐐮𐑌𐐬𐑅𐐯𐑌𐐻 𐐺𐑊𐐲𐐼, 𐐰𐑌𐐼 𐑄𐐮𐑅 𐑇𐐰𐑊 𐐫𐑊𐑅𐐬 𐑅𐐻𐐰𐑌𐐼 𐐰𐑆 𐐰 𐐻𐐯𐑅𐐻𐐮𐑋𐐬𐑌𐐨 𐐲𐑀𐐯𐑌𐑅𐐻 𐐷𐐭 𐐰𐐻 𐑄 𐑊𐐰𐑅𐐻 𐐼𐐩.

4. 𐐈𐑌𐐼 𐑌𐐵 𐐗𐐮𐑍 𐐤𐐬𐐲 𐐶𐐱𐑆 𐐲𐐺𐐵𐐻 𐐻𐐭 𐑉𐐨𐑊𐐨𐑅 𐐸𐐮𐑋, 𐑁𐐫𐑉 𐐸𐐨 𐑁𐐨𐑉𐐼 𐐸𐐮𐑆 𐐶𐐲𐑉𐐼; 𐑁𐐫𐑉 𐐸𐐨 𐑁𐐨𐑉𐐼 𐑄𐐰𐐻 𐑄 𐐾𐐲𐐾𐑋𐐯𐑌𐐻𐑅 𐐱𐑂 𐐘𐐱𐐼 𐐶𐐳𐐼 𐐿𐐲𐑋 𐐲𐐹𐐱𐑌 𐐸𐐮𐑋. 𐐒𐐲𐐻 𐑄 𐐹𐑉𐐨𐑅𐐻𐑅 𐑊𐐮𐑁𐐻𐐯𐐼 𐐲𐐹 𐑄𐐯𐑉 𐑂𐐱𐐮𐑅𐐯𐑆 𐐲𐑀𐐯𐑌𐑅𐐻 𐐸𐐮𐑋, 𐐰𐑌𐐼 𐐺𐐨𐑀𐐰𐑌 𐐻𐐭 𐐰𐐿𐐷𐐭𐑆 𐐸𐐮𐑋, 𐑅𐐩𐐮𐑍: 𐐐𐐨 𐐸𐐰𐑆 𐑉𐐨𐑂𐐴𐑊𐐼 𐑄 𐐿𐐮𐑍. 𐐜𐐯𐑉𐑁𐐬𐑉 𐑄 𐐿𐐮𐑍 𐐶𐐱𐑆 𐑅𐐻𐐲𐑉𐐼 𐐲𐐹 𐐮𐑌 𐐰𐑍𐑀𐐲𐑉 𐐲𐑀𐐯𐑌𐑅𐐻 𐐸𐐮𐑋, 𐐰𐑌𐐼 𐐸𐐨 𐐼𐐨𐑊𐐮𐑂𐐲𐑉𐐼 𐐸𐐮𐑋 𐐲𐐹 𐑄𐐰𐐻 𐐸𐐨 𐑋𐐴𐐻 𐐺𐐨 𐑅𐑊𐐩𐑌.

5. 𐐈𐑌𐐼 𐐮𐐻 𐐿𐐩𐑋 𐐻𐐭 𐐹𐐰𐑅 𐑄𐐰𐐻 𐑄𐐩 𐐻𐐳𐐿 𐐸𐐮𐑋 𐐰𐑌𐐼 𐐺𐐵𐑌𐐼 𐐸𐐮𐑋, 𐐰𐑌𐐼 𐑅𐐿𐐲𐑉𐐾𐐼 𐐸𐐮𐑆 𐑅𐐿𐐮𐑌 𐐶𐐮𐑄 𐑁𐐰𐑀𐐲𐐻𐑅, 𐐷𐐩, 𐐨𐑂𐐲𐑌 𐐲𐑌𐐻𐐭 𐐼𐐯𐑃. 𐐈𐑌𐐼 𐑌𐐵 𐐸𐐶𐐯𐑌 𐑄 𐑁𐑊𐐩𐑋𐑆 𐐺𐐨𐑀𐐰𐑌 𐐻𐐭 𐑅𐐿𐐫𐑉𐐽 𐐸𐐮𐑋, 𐐸𐐨 𐐿𐑉𐐴𐐼 𐐲𐑌𐐻𐐭 𐑄𐐯𐑋, 𐑅𐐩𐐮𐑍: 𐐒𐐨𐐸𐐬𐑊𐐼, 𐐨𐑂𐐲𐑌 𐐰𐑆 𐐷𐐨 𐐸𐐰𐑂 𐐼𐐲𐑌 𐐲𐑌𐐻𐐭 𐑋𐐨, 𐑅𐐬 𐑇𐐰𐑊 𐐮𐐻 𐐿𐐲𐑋 𐐻𐐭 𐐹𐐰𐑅 𐑄𐐰𐐻 𐑄𐐴 𐑅𐐨𐐼

𐑇𐐰𐑊 𐐿𐐫𐑆 𐑄𐐰𐐻 𐑋𐐯𐑌𐐨 𐑇𐐰𐑊 𐑅𐐲𐑁𐐲𐑉 𐑄 𐐹𐐩𐑌𐑆 𐑄𐐰𐐻 𐐌 𐐼𐐭 𐑅𐐲𐑁𐐲𐑉, 𐐨𐑂𐑌 𐑄 𐐹𐐩𐑌𐑆 𐐱𐑂 𐐼𐐯𐑃 𐐺𐐴 𐑁𐐴𐑉; 𐐰𐑌𐐼 𐑄𐐮𐑅 𐐺𐐨𐐿𐐫𐑆 𐑄𐐩 𐐺𐐨𐑊𐐨𐑂 𐐮𐑌 𐑄 𐑅𐐰𐑊𐑂𐐩𐑇𐐲𐑌 𐐱𐑂 𐑄 𐐢𐐫𐑉𐐼 𐑄𐐩𐑉 𐐘𐐪𐐼. 𐐈𐑌𐐼 𐐮𐐻 𐐶𐐮𐑊 𐐿𐐲𐑋 𐐻𐐭 𐐹𐐰𐑅 𐑄𐐰𐐻 𐐷𐐨 𐑇𐐰𐑊 𐐺 𐐰𐑁𐑊𐐮𐐿𐐻𐐯𐐼 𐐶𐐮𐑄 𐐫𐑊 𐑋𐐰𐑌𐐲𐑉 𐐱𐑂 𐐼𐐮𐑆𐐨𐑆𐐯𐑆 𐐺𐐨𐐿𐐫𐑆 𐐱𐑂 𐐷𐐬𐑉 𐐮𐑌𐐮𐐿𐐶𐐮𐐻𐐮𐑆. 𐐏𐐩, 𐐰𐑌𐐼 𐐷𐐨 𐑇𐐰𐑊 𐐺 𐑅𐑋𐐮𐐻𐑌 𐐱𐑌 𐐯𐑂𐐲𐑉𐐨 𐐸𐐰𐑌𐐼, 𐐰𐑌𐐼 𐑇𐐰𐑊 𐐺 𐐼𐑉𐐮𐑂𐑌 𐐰𐑌𐐼 𐑅𐐿𐐰𐐻𐐲𐑉𐐼 𐐻𐐭 𐐰𐑌𐐼 𐑁𐑉𐐬, 𐐨𐑂𐑌 𐐰𐑆 𐐲 𐐶𐐴𐑊𐐼 𐑁𐑊𐐱𐐿 𐐮𐑆 𐐼𐑉𐐮𐑂𐑌 𐐺𐐴 𐐶𐐴𐑊𐐼 𐐰𐑌𐐼 𐑁𐐯𐑉𐐬𐑇𐐲𐑅 𐐺𐐨𐑅𐐻𐑅. 𐐈𐑌𐐼 𐐮𐑌 𐑄𐐰𐐻 𐐼𐐩 𐐷𐐨 𐑇𐐰𐑊 𐐺 𐐸𐐲𐑌𐐻𐐯𐐼, 𐐰𐑌𐐼 𐐷𐐨 𐑇𐐰𐑊 𐐺 𐐻𐐩𐐿𐑌 𐐺𐐴 𐑄 𐐸𐐰𐑌𐐼 𐐱𐑂 𐐷𐐬𐑉 𐐯𐑌𐐯𐑋𐐨𐑆, 𐐰𐑌𐐼 𐑄𐐯𐑌 𐐷𐐨 𐑇𐐰𐑊 𐑅𐐲𐑁𐐲𐑉, 𐐰𐑆 𐐌 𐑅𐐲𐑁𐐲𐑉, 𐑄 𐐹𐐩𐑌𐑆 𐐱𐑂 𐐼𐐯𐑃 𐐺𐐴 𐑁𐐴𐑉. 𐐜𐐲𐑅 𐐘𐐪𐐼 𐐯𐐿𐑅𐐯𐐿𐐷𐐭𐐻𐐯𐑃 𐑂𐐯𐑌𐐾𐐲𐑌𐑅 𐐲𐐹𐐱𐑌 𐑄𐐬𐑆 𐑄𐐰𐐻 𐐼𐐨𐑅𐐻𐑉𐐱𐐮 𐐸𐐮𐑆 𐐹𐐨𐐹𐑊. 𐐄 𐐘𐐪𐐼, 𐑉𐐨𐑅𐐨𐑂 𐑋𐐴 𐑅𐐬𐑊. 𐐈𐑌𐐼 𐑌𐐵 𐐸𐐶𐐯𐑌 𐐈𐐺𐐨𐑌𐐪𐐼𐐴 𐐸𐐰𐐼 𐑅𐐯𐐼 𐑄𐐨𐑆 𐐶𐐲𐑉𐐼𐑆, 𐐸𐐨 𐑁𐐯𐑊, 𐐸𐐰𐑂𐐮𐑍 𐑅𐐲𐑁𐐲𐑉𐐼 𐐼𐐯𐑃 𐐺𐐴 𐑁𐐴𐑉; 𐐏𐐩, 𐐸𐐰𐑂𐐮𐑍 𐐺𐐨𐑌 𐐹𐐳𐐻 𐐻𐐭 𐐼𐐯𐑃 𐐺𐐨𐐿𐐫𐑆 𐐸𐐨 𐐶𐐳𐐼 𐑌𐐱𐐻 𐐼𐐨𐑌𐐴 𐑄 𐐿𐐲𐑋𐐰𐑌𐐼𐑋𐐯𐑌𐐻𐑅 𐐱𐑂 𐐘𐐪𐐼: 𐐸𐐰𐑂𐐮𐑍 𐑅𐐨𐑊𐐼 𐑄 𐐻𐑉𐐭𐑃 𐐱𐑂 𐐸𐐮𐑆 𐐶𐐲𐑉𐐼𐑆 𐐺𐐴 𐐸𐐮𐑆 𐐼𐐯𐑃.

6. 𐐈𐑌𐐼 𐑌𐐵 𐐮𐐻 𐐿𐐩𐑋 𐐻𐐭 𐐹𐐰𐑅 𐑄𐐰𐐻 𐐈𐑊𐑋𐐲, 𐐸𐐭 𐑁𐑊𐐯𐐼 𐑁𐑉𐐱𐑋 𐑄 𐑅𐐲𐑉𐑂𐐰𐑌𐐻𐑅 𐐱𐑂 𐐿𐐮𐑍 𐐤𐐬𐐲, 𐑉𐐯𐐹𐐯𐑌𐐻𐐯𐐼 𐐱𐑂 𐐸𐐮𐑆 𐑅𐐮𐑌𐑆 𐐰𐑌𐐼 𐐮𐑌𐐮𐐿𐐶𐐮𐐻𐐮𐑆, 𐐰𐑌𐐼 𐐶𐐯𐑌𐐻 𐐲𐐺𐐵𐐻 𐐹𐑉𐐴𐑂𐐲𐐻𐑊𐐨 𐐲𐑋𐐲𐑍 𐑄 𐐹𐐨𐐹𐑊, 𐐰𐑌𐐼 𐐺𐐨𐑀𐐰𐑌 𐐻𐐭 𐐻𐐨𐐽 𐑄 𐐶𐐲𐑉𐐼𐑆 𐐱𐑂 𐐈𐐺𐐨𐑌𐐪𐐼𐐴: 𐐏𐐩, 𐐿𐐱𐑌𐑅𐐲𐑉𐑌𐐮𐑍 𐑄𐐰𐐻 𐐸𐐶𐐮𐐽 𐐶𐐱𐑆 𐐻𐐭 𐐿𐐲𐑋, 𐐰𐑌𐐼 𐐫𐑊𐑅𐐬 𐐿𐐱𐑌𐑅𐐲𐑉𐑌𐐮𐑍 𐑄 𐑉𐐯𐑆𐐲𐑉𐐯𐐿𐑇𐐲𐑌 𐐱𐑂 𐑄 𐐼𐐯𐐼, 𐐰𐑌𐐼 𐑄 𐑉𐐨𐐼𐐯𐑋𐑇𐐲𐑌 𐐱𐑂 𐑄 𐐹𐐨𐐹𐑊, 𐐸𐐶𐐮𐐽 𐐶𐐱𐑆 𐐻𐐭 𐐺 𐐺𐑉𐐫𐐻 𐐻𐐭 𐐹𐐰𐑅 𐑃𐑉𐐭 𐑄 𐐹𐐵𐐲𐑉, 𐐰𐑌𐐼 𐑅𐐲𐑁𐐲𐑉𐐮𐑍𐑆, 𐐰𐑌𐐼 𐐼𐐯𐑃 𐐱𐑂 𐐗𐑉𐐴𐑅𐐻, 𐐰𐑌𐐼 𐐸𐐮𐑆 𐑉𐐯𐑆𐐲𐑉𐐯𐐿𐑇𐐲𐑌 𐐰𐑌𐐼 𐐰𐑅𐐯𐑌𐑇𐐲𐑌 𐐮𐑌𐐻𐐭 𐐸𐐯𐑂𐑌. 𐐈𐑌𐐼 𐐰𐑆 𐑋𐐯𐑌𐐨 𐐰𐑆 𐐶𐐳𐐼 𐐸𐐨𐑉 𐐸𐐮𐑆 𐐶𐐲𐑉𐐼 𐐸𐐨 𐐼𐐮𐐼 𐐻𐐨𐐽. 𐐈𐑌𐐼 𐐸𐐨 𐐻𐐫𐐻 𐑄𐐯𐑋 𐐹𐑉𐐴𐑂𐐲𐐻𐑊𐐨, 𐑄𐐰𐐻 𐐮𐐻 𐑋𐐴𐐻 𐑌𐐱𐐻 𐐿𐐲𐑋 𐐻𐐭 𐑄 𐑌𐐱𐑊𐐯𐐾 𐐱𐑂 𐑄 𐐿𐐮𐑍. 𐐈𐑌𐐼 𐑋𐐯𐑌𐐨 𐐼𐐮𐐼 𐐺𐐨𐑊𐐨𐑂 𐐸𐐮𐑆 𐐶𐐲𐑉𐐼𐑆. 𐐈𐑌𐐼 𐐮𐐻 𐐿𐐩𐑋 𐐻𐐭 𐐹𐐰𐑅 𐑄𐐰𐐻 𐐰𐑆 𐑋𐐯𐑌𐐨 𐐰𐑆 𐐼𐐮𐐼 𐐺𐐨𐑊𐐨𐑂 𐐸𐐮𐑋, 𐐼𐐮𐐼 𐑀𐐬 𐑁𐐬𐑉𐑃 𐐻𐐭 𐐲 𐐹𐑊𐐩𐑅 𐐸𐐶𐐮𐐽 𐐶𐐱𐑆 𐐿𐐫𐑊𐐼 𐐣𐐫𐑉𐑋𐐲𐑌, 𐐸𐐰𐑂𐐮𐑍 𐑉𐐨𐑅𐐨𐑂𐐼 𐐮𐐻𐑅 𐑌𐐩𐑋 𐑁𐑉𐐱𐑋 𐑄 𐐿𐐮𐑍, 𐐺𐐨𐐮𐑍 𐐮𐑌 𐑄 𐐺𐐫𐑉𐐼𐐲𐑉𐑆 𐐱𐑂 𐑄 𐑊𐐰𐑌𐐼 𐐸𐐰𐑂𐐮𐑍 𐐺𐐨𐑌 𐐮𐑌𐑁𐐯𐑅𐐻𐐯𐐼, 𐐺𐐴 𐐻𐐴𐑋𐑆 𐐫𐑉 𐐰𐐻 𐑅𐐨𐑆𐑌𐑆, 𐐺𐐴 𐐶𐐴𐑊𐐼 𐐺𐐨𐑅𐐻𐑅. 𐐤𐐵 𐑄𐐯𐑉 𐐶𐐱𐑆 𐐮𐑌 𐐣𐐫𐑉𐑋𐐲𐑌 𐐲 𐑁𐐵𐑌𐐻𐐯𐑌 𐐱𐑂 𐐹𐐷𐐭𐑉 𐐶𐐫𐐻𐐲𐑉, 𐐰𐑌𐐼 𐐈𐑊𐑋𐐲 𐑉𐐨𐑆𐐫𐑉𐐻𐐯𐐼 𐑃𐐮𐑄𐐲𐑉, 𐑄𐐯𐑉 𐐺𐐨𐐮𐑍 𐑌𐐨𐑉 𐑄 𐐶𐐫𐐻𐐲𐑉 𐐲 𐑃𐐮𐐿𐐯𐐻 𐐱𐑂 𐑅𐑋𐐫𐑊 𐐻𐑉𐐨𐑆, 𐐸𐐶𐐯𐑉 𐐸𐐨 𐐼𐐮𐐼 𐐸𐐴𐐼 𐐸𐐮𐑋𐑅𐐯𐑊𐑁 𐐮𐑌 𐑄 𐐼𐐩-𐐻𐐴𐑋, 𐑁𐑉𐐱𐑋 𐑄 𐑅𐐲𐑉𐐽𐐯𐑆 𐐱𐑂 𐑄 𐐿𐐮𐑍. 𐐈𐑌𐐼 𐐮𐐻 𐐿𐐩𐑋 𐐻𐐭 𐐹𐐰𐑅 𐑄𐐰𐐻 𐐰𐑆 𐑋𐐯𐑌𐐨 𐐰𐑆 𐐺𐐨𐑊𐐨𐑂𐐼 𐐸𐐮𐑋, 𐐶𐐯𐑌𐐻 𐑄𐐮𐑄𐐲𐑉 𐐻𐐭 𐐸𐐨𐑉 𐐸𐐮𐑆 𐐶𐐲𐑉𐐼𐑆. 𐐈𐑌𐐼 𐐮𐐻 𐐿𐐩𐑋 𐐻𐐭 𐐹𐐰𐑅 𐐰𐑁𐐻𐐲𐑉 𐑋𐐯𐑌𐐨 𐐼𐐩𐑆, 𐑄𐐯𐑉 𐐶𐐲𐑉 𐐲 𐑀𐐳𐐼𐑊𐐨 𐑌𐐲𐑋𐐺𐐲𐑉 𐑀𐐰𐑄𐐲𐑉𐐼 𐐻𐐭𐑀𐐯𐑄𐐲𐑉 𐐰𐐻 𐑄 𐐹𐑊𐐩𐑅 𐐱𐑂 𐐣𐐫𐑉𐑋𐐲𐑌, 𐐻𐐭 𐐸𐐨𐑉 𐑄 𐐶𐐲𐑉𐐼𐑆 𐐱𐑂 𐐈𐑊𐑋𐐲. 𐐏𐐩, 𐐫𐑊 𐐶𐐲𐑉 𐑀𐐰𐑄𐐲𐑉𐐼 𐐻𐐭𐑀𐐯𐑄𐐲𐑉 𐑄𐐰𐐻 𐐺𐐨𐑊𐐨𐑂𐐼 𐐱𐑌 𐐸𐐮𐑆 𐐶𐐲𐑉𐐼, 𐐻𐐭 𐐸𐐨𐑉 𐐸𐐮𐑋. 𐐈𐑌𐐼 𐐸𐐨 𐐼𐐮𐐼 𐐻𐐨𐐽 𐑄𐐯𐑋, 𐐰𐑌𐐼 𐐼𐐮𐐼 𐐹𐑉𐐨𐐽 𐐲𐑌𐐻𐐭 𐑄𐐯𐑋 𐑉𐐨𐐹𐐯𐑌𐐻𐐲𐑌𐑅, 𐐰𐑌𐐼 𐑉𐐨𐐼𐐯𐑋𐑇𐐲𐑌, 𐐰𐑌𐐼 𐑁𐐩𐑃 𐐱𐑌 𐑄 𐐢𐐫𐑉𐐼.

7. 𐐈𐑌𐐼 𐐮𐐻 𐐿𐐩𐑋 𐐻𐐭 𐐹𐐰𐑅 𐑄𐐰𐐻 𐐸𐐨 𐑅𐐯𐐼 𐐲𐑌𐐻𐐭 𐑄𐐯𐑋, 𐐒𐐨𐐸𐐬𐑊𐐼, 𐐸𐐨𐑉 𐐪𐑉 𐑄 𐐶𐐫𐐻𐐲𐑉𐑆 𐐱𐑂 𐐣𐐫𐑉𐑋𐐲𐑌; 𐑁𐐫𐑉 𐑄𐐲𐑅 𐐶𐐲𐑉 𐑄𐐩 𐐿𐐫𐑊𐐼. 𐐈𐑌𐐼 𐑌𐐵, 𐐰𐑆 𐐷𐐨 𐐪𐑉 𐐼𐐨𐑆𐐴𐑉𐐲𐑅 𐐻𐐭 𐐿𐐲𐑋 𐐮𐑌𐐻𐐭 𐑄 𐑁𐐬𐑊𐐼 𐐱𐑂 𐐘𐐪𐐼, 𐐰𐑌𐐼 𐐻𐐭 𐐺 𐐿𐐫𐑊𐐼 𐐸𐐮𐑆 𐐹𐐨𐐹𐑊, 𐐰𐑌𐐼 𐐪𐑉 𐐶𐐮𐑊𐐮𐑍 𐐻𐐭 𐐺𐐯𐑉 𐐶𐐲𐑌 𐐲𐑌𐐲𐑄𐐲𐑉'𐑆 𐐺𐐲𐑉𐐼𐑌𐑆, 𐑄𐐰𐐻 𐑄𐐩 𐑋𐐩 𐐺 𐑊𐐴𐐻; 𐐏𐐩, 𐐰𐑌𐐼 𐐪𐑉 𐐶𐐮𐑊𐐮𐑍 𐐻𐐭 𐑋𐐬𐑉𐑌 𐐶𐐮𐑄 𐑄𐐬𐑆 𐑄𐐰𐐻 𐑋𐐬𐑉𐑌; 𐐏𐐩, 𐐰𐑌𐐼 𐐿𐐲𐑋𐑁𐐲𐑉𐐻 𐑄𐐬𐑆 𐑄𐐰𐐻 𐑅𐐻𐐰𐑌𐐼 𐐮𐑌 𐑌𐐨𐐼 𐐱𐑂 𐐿𐐲𐑋𐑁𐐲𐑉𐐻, 𐐰𐑌𐐼 𐐻𐐭 𐑅𐐻𐐰𐑌𐐼 𐐰𐑆 𐐶𐐮𐐻𐑌𐐯𐑅𐐯𐑆 𐐱𐑂 𐐘𐐪𐐼 𐐰𐐻 𐐫𐑊 𐐻𐐴𐑋𐑆, 𐐰𐑌𐐼 𐐮𐑌 𐐫𐑊 𐑃𐐮𐑍𐑆, 𐐰𐑌𐐼 𐐮𐑌 𐐫𐑊 𐐹𐑊𐐩𐑅𐐯𐑆 𐑄𐐰𐐻 𐐷𐐨 𐑋𐐩 𐐺 𐐮𐑌, 𐐨𐑂𐑌 𐐲𐑌𐐻𐐮𐑊 𐐼𐐯𐑃, 𐑄𐐰𐐻 𐐷𐐨 𐑋𐐩 𐐺 𐑉𐐨𐐼𐐨𐑋𐐼 𐐱𐑂 𐐘𐐪𐐼, 𐐰𐑌𐐼 𐐺 𐑌𐐲𐑋𐐺𐐲𐑉𐐼 𐐶𐐮𐑄 𐑄𐐬𐑆 𐐱𐑂 𐑄 𐑁𐐲𐑉𐑅𐐻 𐑉𐐯𐑆𐐲𐑉𐐯𐐿𐑇𐐲𐑌, 𐑄𐐰𐐻 𐐷𐐨 𐑋𐐩 𐐸𐐰𐑂 𐐨𐐻𐐲𐑉𐑌𐐲𐑊 𐑊𐐴𐑁: 𐐤𐐵 𐐌 𐑅𐐩 𐐲𐑌𐐻𐐭 𐐷𐐭, 𐐮𐑁 𐑄𐐮𐑅 𐐺 𐑄 𐐼𐐨𐑆𐐴𐑉 𐐱𐑂 𐐷𐐬𐑉 𐐸𐐪𐑉𐐻𐑅, 𐐸𐐶𐐱𐐻 𐐸𐐰𐑂 𐐷𐐭 𐐲𐑀𐐯𐑌𐑅𐐻 𐐺𐐨𐐮𐑍 𐐺𐐰𐐹𐐻𐐴𐑆𐐼 𐐮𐑌 𐑄 𐑌𐐩𐑋 𐐱𐑂 𐑄 𐐢𐐫𐑉𐐼, 𐐰𐑆 𐐲 𐐶𐐮𐐻𐑌𐐯𐑅 𐐺𐐨𐑁𐐬𐑉 𐐸𐐮𐑋 𐑄𐐰𐐻 𐐷𐐨 𐐸𐐰𐑂 𐐯𐑌𐐻𐐲𐑉𐐼 𐐮𐑌𐐻𐐭 𐐲 𐐿𐐲𐑂𐐯𐑌𐐲𐑌𐐻 𐐶𐐮𐑄 𐐸𐐮𐑋, 𐑄𐐰𐐻 𐐷𐐨 𐐶𐐮𐑊 𐑅𐐲𐑉𐑂 𐐸𐐮𐑋, 𐐰𐑌𐐼 𐐿𐐨𐐹 𐐸𐐮𐑆 𐐿𐐲𐑋𐐰𐑌𐐼𐑋𐐯𐑌𐐻𐑅, 𐑄𐐰𐐻 𐐸𐐨 𐑋𐐩 𐐹𐐫𐑉 𐐵𐐻 𐐸𐐮𐑆 𐐝𐐹𐐮𐑉𐐮𐐻 𐑋𐐬𐑉 𐐲𐐺𐐲𐑌𐐼𐐲𐑌𐐻𐑊𐐨 𐐲𐐹𐐱𐑌 𐐷𐐭? 𐐈𐑌𐐼 𐑌𐐵 𐐸𐐶𐐯𐑌 𐑄 𐐹𐐨𐐹𐑊 𐐸𐐰𐐼 𐐸𐐲𐑉𐐼 𐑄𐐨𐑆 𐐶𐐲𐑉𐐼𐑆, 𐑄𐐩 𐐿𐑊𐐰𐐹𐐻 𐑄𐐩𐑉 𐐸𐐰𐑌𐐼𐑆 𐑁𐐫𐑉 𐐾𐐱𐐮, 𐐰𐑌𐐼 𐐯𐐿𐑅𐐿𐑊𐐩𐑋𐐼, 𐐜𐐮𐑅 𐐮𐑆 𐑄 𐐼𐐨𐑆𐐴𐑉 𐐱𐑂 𐐵𐑉 𐐸𐐪𐑉𐐻𐑅.

8. 𐐈𐑌𐐔 𐑌𐐵 𐐮𐐻 𐐿𐐩𐑋 𐐻𐐭 𐐹𐐰𐑅 𐑄𐐰𐐻 𐐈𐑊𐑋𐐲 𐐻𐐳𐐿 𐐐𐐨𐑊𐐲𐑋, 𐐸𐐨 𐐺𐐨𐐮𐑍 𐐶𐐲𐑌 𐐱𐑂 𐑄 𐑁𐐲𐑉𐑅𐐻, 𐐰𐑌𐐼 𐐶𐐯𐑌𐐻 𐐰𐑌𐐼 𐑅𐐻𐐳𐐼 𐑁𐐫𐑉𐑃 𐐮𐑌 𐑄 𐐶𐐫𐐻𐐲𐑉, 𐐰𐑌𐐼 𐐿𐑉𐐴𐐼, 𐑅𐐩𐐮𐑍, 𐐄 𐐢𐐫𐑉𐐼, 𐐹𐐬𐑉 𐐵𐐻 𐑄𐐴 𐐝𐐹𐐮𐑉𐐮𐐻 𐐲𐐹𐐱𐑌 𐑄𐐴 𐑅𐐲𐑉𐑂𐐲𐑌𐐻, 𐑄𐐰𐐻 𐐸𐐨 𐑋𐐩 𐐼𐐭 𐑄𐐮𐑅 𐐶𐐲𐑉𐐿 𐐶𐐮𐑄 𐐸𐐬𐑊𐐨𐑌𐐯𐑅 𐐱𐑂 𐐸𐐪𐑉𐐻. 𐐈𐑌𐐼 𐐸𐐶𐐯𐑌 𐐸𐐨 𐐸𐐰𐐼 𐑅𐐯𐐼 𐑄𐐨𐑆 𐐶𐐲𐑉𐐼𐑆, 𐑄 𐐝𐐹𐐮𐑉𐐮𐐻 𐐱𐑂 𐑄 𐐢𐐫𐑉𐐼 𐐶𐐱𐑆 𐐲𐐹𐐱𐑌 𐐸𐐮𐑋, 𐐰𐑌𐐼 𐐸𐐨 𐑅𐐯𐐼, 𐐐𐐨𐑊𐐲𐑋, 𐐌 𐐺𐐰𐐹𐐻𐐴𐑆 𐑄𐐨, 𐐸𐐰𐑂𐐮𐑍 𐐫𐑃𐐱𐑉𐐮𐐻𐐨 𐑁𐑉𐐱𐑋 𐑄 𐐃𐑊𐑋𐐴𐐻𐐨 𐐘𐐱𐐼, 𐐰𐑆 𐐲 𐐻𐐯𐑅𐐻𐐮𐑋𐐬𐑌𐐨 𐑄𐐰𐐻 𐐷𐐨 𐐸𐐰𐑂 𐐯𐑌𐐻𐐲𐑉𐐼 𐐮𐑌𐐻𐐭 𐐲 𐐿𐐲𐑂𐐲𐑌𐐰𐑌𐐻 𐐻𐐭 𐑅𐐲𐑉𐑂 𐐸𐐮𐑋 𐐲𐑌𐐻𐐮𐑊 𐐷𐐭 𐐪𐑉 𐐼𐐯𐐼 𐐰𐑆 𐐻𐐭 𐑄 𐑋𐐫𐑉𐐻𐐲𐑊 𐐺𐐱𐐼𐐨; 𐐰𐑌𐐼 𐑋𐐩 𐑄 𐐝𐐹𐐮𐑉𐐮𐐻 𐐱𐑂 𐑄 𐐢𐐫𐑉𐐼 𐐺𐐨 𐐹𐐬𐑉𐐼 𐐵𐐻 𐐲𐐹𐐱𐑌 𐐷𐐭; 𐐰𐑌𐐼 𐑋𐐩 𐐸𐐨 𐑀𐑉𐐰𐑌𐐻 𐐲𐑌𐐻𐐭 𐐷𐐭 𐐨𐐻𐐲𐑉𐑌𐐲𐑊 𐑊𐐴𐑁, 𐑃𐑉𐐭 𐑄 𐑉𐐨𐐼𐐯𐑋𐑇𐐲𐑌 𐐱𐑂 𐐗𐑉𐐴𐑅𐐻, 𐐸𐐭𐑋 𐐸𐐨 𐐸𐐰𐑆 𐐹𐑉𐐨𐐹𐐩𐑉𐐼 𐑁𐑉𐐱𐑋 𐑄 𐑁𐐵𐑌𐐼𐐩𐑇𐐲𐑌 𐐱𐑂 𐑄 𐐶𐐲𐑉𐑊𐐼. 𐐈𐑌𐐼 𐐰𐑁𐐻𐐲𐑉 𐐈𐑊𐑋𐐲 𐐸𐐰𐐼 𐑅𐐯𐐼 𐑄𐐨𐑆 𐐶𐐲𐑉𐐼𐑆, 𐐺𐐬𐑃 𐐈𐑊𐑋𐐲 𐐰𐑌𐐼 𐐐𐐨𐑊𐐲𐑋 𐐶𐐲𐑉 𐐺𐐯𐑉𐐨𐐼 𐐮𐑌 𐑄 𐐶𐐫𐐻𐐲𐑉; 𐐰𐑌𐐼 𐑄𐐩 𐐲𐑉𐐬𐑆, 𐐰𐑌𐐼 𐐿𐐩𐑋 𐑁𐐫𐑉𐑃 𐐵𐐻 𐐱𐑂 𐑄 𐐶𐐫𐐻𐐲𐑉 𐑉𐐨𐐾𐐦𐑅𐐮𐑍, 𐐺𐐨𐐮𐑍 𐑁𐐮𐑊𐐼 𐐶𐐮𐑄 𐑄 𐐝𐐹𐐮𐑉𐐮𐐻. 𐐈𐑌𐐼 𐐲𐑀𐐯𐑌, 𐐈𐑊𐑋𐐲 𐐻𐐳𐐿 𐐲𐑌𐐲𐑄𐐲𐑉, 𐐰𐑌𐐼 𐐶𐐯𐑌𐐻 𐑁𐐫𐑉𐑃 𐐲 𐑅𐐯𐐿𐐲𐑌𐐼 𐐻𐐴𐑋 𐐮𐑌𐐻𐐭 𐑄 𐐶𐐫𐐻𐐲𐑉, 𐐰𐑌𐐼 𐐺𐐰𐐹𐐻𐐴𐑆𐐼 𐐸𐐮𐑋 𐐰𐐿𐐫𐑉𐐼𐐮𐑍 𐐻𐐭 𐑄 𐑁𐐲𐑉𐑅𐐻, 𐐬𐑌𐑊𐐨 𐐸𐐨 𐐼𐐮𐐼 𐑌𐐱𐐻 𐐺𐐯𐑉𐐨 𐐸𐐮𐑋𐑅𐐯𐑊𐑁 𐐲𐑀𐐯𐑌 𐐮𐑌 𐑄 𐐶𐐫𐐻𐐲𐑉. 𐐈𐑌𐐼 𐐰𐑁𐐻𐐲𐑉 𐑄𐐮𐑅 𐑋𐐰𐑌𐐲𐑉 𐐸𐐨 𐐼𐐮𐐼 𐐺𐐰𐐹𐐻𐐴𐑆 𐐯𐑂𐑉𐐨 𐐶𐐲𐑌 𐑄𐐰𐐻 𐐶𐐯𐑌𐐻 𐑁𐐫𐑉𐑃 𐐻𐐭 𐑄 𐐹𐑊𐐩𐑅 𐐱𐑂 𐐣𐐫𐑉𐑋𐐲𐑌: 𐐰𐑌𐐼 𐑄𐐩 𐐶𐐲𐑉 𐐮𐑌 𐑌𐐲𐑋𐐺𐐲𐑉 𐐲𐐺𐐵𐐻 𐐻𐐭 𐐸𐐲𐑌𐐼𐑉𐐯𐐼 𐐰𐑌𐐼 𐑁𐐬𐑉 𐑅𐐬𐑊𐑆; 𐐷𐐩, 𐐰𐑌𐐼 𐑄𐐩 𐐶𐐲𐑉 𐐺𐐰𐐹𐐻𐐴𐑆𐐼 𐐮𐑌 𐑄 𐐶𐐫𐐻𐐲𐑉𐑆 𐐱𐑂 𐐣𐐫𐑉𐑋𐐲𐑌, 𐐰𐑌𐐼 𐐶𐐲𐑉 𐑁𐐮𐑊𐐼 𐐶𐐮𐑄 𐑄 𐑀𐑉𐐩𐑅 𐐱𐑂 𐐘𐐱𐐼; 𐐰𐑌𐐼 𐑄𐐩 𐐶𐐲𐑉 𐐿𐐫𐑊𐐼 𐑄 𐐕𐐲𐑉𐐽 𐐱𐑂 𐐘𐐱𐐼, 𐐫𐑉 𐑄 𐐕𐐲𐑉𐐽 𐐱𐑂 𐐗𐑉𐐴𐑅𐐻, 𐑁𐑉𐐱𐑋 𐑄𐐰𐐻 𐐻𐐴𐑋 𐑁𐐫𐑉𐐶𐐲𐑉𐐼. 𐐈𐑌𐐼 𐐮𐐻 𐐿𐐩𐑋 𐐻𐐭 𐐹𐐰𐑅 𐑄𐐰𐐻 𐐸𐐭𐑅𐐬𐐯𐑂𐐲𐑉 𐐶𐐱𐑆 𐐺𐐰𐐹𐐻𐐴𐑆𐐼 𐐺𐐴 𐑄 𐐹𐐵𐐲𐑉 𐐰𐑌𐐼 𐐫𐑃𐐱𐑉𐐮𐐻𐐨 𐐱𐑂 𐐘𐐱𐐼, 𐐶𐐱𐑆 𐐰𐐼𐐯𐐼 𐐻𐐭 𐐸𐐮𐑆 𐐕𐐲𐑉𐐽.

9. 𐐈𐑌𐐼 𐐮𐐻 𐐿𐐩𐑋 𐐻𐐭 𐐹𐐰𐑅 𐑄𐐰𐐻 𐐈𐑊𐑋𐐲, 𐐸𐐰𐑂𐐮𐑍 𐐫𐑃𐐱𐑉𐐮𐐻𐐨 𐑁𐑉𐐱𐑋 𐐘𐐱𐐼, 𐐫𐑉𐐼𐐩𐑌𐐼 𐐹𐑉𐐨𐑅𐐻𐑅; 𐐨𐑂𐐲𐑌 𐐶𐐲𐑌 𐐹𐑉𐐨𐑅𐐻 𐐻𐐭 𐐯𐑂𐑉𐐨 𐑁𐐮𐑁𐐻𐐨 𐐱𐑂 𐑄𐐯𐑉 𐑌𐐲𐑋𐐺𐐲𐑉 𐐼𐐮𐐼 𐐸𐐨 𐐫𐑉𐐼𐐩𐑌 𐐻𐐭 𐐹𐑉𐐨𐐽 𐐲𐑌𐐻𐐭 𐑄𐐯𐑋, 𐐰𐑌𐐼 𐐻𐐭 𐐻𐐨𐐽 𐑄𐐯𐑋 𐐿𐐱𐑌𐑅𐐲𐑉𐑌𐐮𐑍 𐑄 𐑃𐐮𐑍𐑆 𐐹𐐲𐑉𐐻𐐩𐑌𐐮𐑍 𐐻𐐭 𐑄 𐐿𐐮𐑍𐐼𐐲𐑋 𐐱𐑂 𐐘𐐱𐐼. 𐐈𐑌𐐼 𐐸𐐨 𐐿𐐱𐑋𐐰𐑌𐐼𐐯𐐼 𐑄𐐯𐑋 𐑄𐐰𐐻 𐑄𐐩 𐑇𐐳𐐼 𐐻𐐨𐐽 𐑌𐐲𐑃𐐮𐑍 𐑅𐐩𐑂 𐐮𐐻 𐐶𐐲𐑉 𐑄 𐑃𐐮𐑍𐑆 𐐸𐐶𐐮𐐽 𐐸𐐨 𐐸𐐰𐐼 𐐻𐐫𐐻, 𐐰𐑌𐐼 𐐸𐐶𐐮𐐽 𐐸𐐰𐐼 𐐺𐐮𐑌 𐑅𐐹𐐬𐐿𐐲𐑌 𐐺𐐴 𐑄 𐑋𐐵𐑃 𐐱𐑂 𐑄 𐐸𐐬𐑊𐐨 𐐹𐑉𐐱𐑁𐐯𐐻𐑅. 𐐏𐐩, 𐐨𐑂𐐲𐑌 𐐸𐐨 𐐿𐐱𐑋𐐰𐑌𐐼𐐯𐐼 𐑄𐐯𐑋 𐑄𐐰𐐻 𐑄𐐩 𐑇𐐳𐐼 𐐹𐑉𐐨𐐽 𐑌𐐲𐑃𐐮𐑍 𐑅𐐩𐑂 𐐮𐐻 𐐶𐐲𐑉 𐑉𐐨𐐹𐐯𐑌𐐻𐐲𐑌𐑅 𐐰𐑌𐐼 𐑁𐐩𐑃 𐐱𐑌 𐑄 𐐢𐐫𐑉𐐼, 𐐸𐐭 𐐸𐐰𐐼 𐑉𐐨𐐼𐐨𐑋𐐼 𐐸𐐮𐑆 𐐹𐐨𐐹𐐲𐑊. 𐐈𐑌𐐼 𐐸𐐨 𐐿𐐱𐑋𐐰𐑌𐐼𐐯𐐼 𐑄𐐯𐑋 𐑄𐐰𐐻 𐑄𐐯𐑉 𐑇𐐳𐐼 𐐺𐐨 𐑌𐐬 𐐿𐐱𐑌𐐻𐐯𐑌𐑇𐐲𐑌 𐐶𐐲𐑌 𐐶𐐮𐑄 𐐲𐑌𐐲𐑄𐐲𐑉, 𐐺𐐲𐐻 𐑄𐐰𐐻 𐑄𐐩 𐑇𐐳𐐼 𐑊𐐳𐐿 𐑁𐐫𐑉𐐶𐐲𐑉𐐼 𐐶𐐮𐑄 𐐶𐐲𐑌 𐐴, 𐐸𐐰𐑂𐐮𐑍 𐐶𐐲𐑌 𐑁𐐩𐑃 𐐰𐑌𐐼 𐐶𐐲𐑌 𐐺𐐰𐐹𐐻𐐮𐑆𐑋, 𐐸𐐰𐑂𐐮𐑍 𐑄𐐯𐑉 𐐸𐐪𐑉𐐻𐑅 𐑌𐐮𐐻 𐐻𐐭𐑀𐐯𐑄𐐲𐑉 𐐮𐑌 𐐷𐐭𐑌𐐮𐐻𐐨 𐐰𐑌𐐼 𐐮𐑌 𐑊𐐲𐑂 𐐶𐐲𐑌 𐐻𐐬𐐲𐑉𐐼𐑆 𐐲𐑌𐐲𐑄𐐲𐑉. 𐐈𐑌𐐼 𐑄𐐲𐑅 𐐸𐐨 𐐿𐐱𐑋𐐰𐑌𐐼𐐯𐐼 𐑄𐐯𐑋 𐐻𐐭 𐐹𐑉𐐨𐐽. 𐐈𐑌𐐼 𐑄𐐲𐑅 𐑄𐐩 𐐺𐐨𐐿𐐩𐑋 𐑄 𐐽𐐮𐑊𐐼𐑉𐐯𐑌 𐐱𐑂 𐐘𐐱𐐼. 𐐈𐑌𐐼 𐐸𐐨 𐐿𐐱𐑋𐐰𐑌𐐼𐐯𐐼 𐑄𐐯𐑋 𐑄𐐰𐐻 𐑄𐐩 𐑇𐐳𐐼 𐐱𐐺𐑆𐐲𐑉𐑂 𐑄 𐑅𐐰𐐺𐐲𐑃 𐐼𐐩, 𐐰𐑌𐐼 𐐿𐐨𐐹 𐐮𐐻 𐐸𐐬𐑊𐐨, 𐐰𐑌𐐼 𐐫𐑊𐑅𐐬 𐐯𐑂𐑉𐐨 𐐼𐐩 𐑄𐐩 𐑇𐐳𐐼 𐑀𐐮𐑂 𐑃𐐰𐑍𐐿𐑅 𐐻𐐭 𐑄 𐐢𐐫𐑉𐐼 𐑄𐐯𐑉 𐐘𐐱𐐼. 𐐈𐑌𐐼 𐐸𐐨 𐐫𐑊𐑅𐐬 𐐿𐐱𐑋𐐰𐑌𐐼𐐯𐐼 𐑄𐐯𐑋 𐑄𐐰𐐻 𐑄 𐐹𐑉𐐨𐑅𐐻𐑅 𐐸𐐭𐑋 𐐸𐐨 𐐸𐐰𐐼 𐐫𐑉𐐼𐐩𐑌𐐼 𐑇𐐳𐐼 𐑊𐐩𐐺𐐲𐑉 𐐶𐐮𐑄 𐑄𐐯𐑉 𐐬𐑌 𐐸𐐰𐑌𐐼𐑆 𐑁𐐫𐑉 𐑄𐐯𐑉 𐑅𐐲𐐹𐐬𐑉𐐻; 𐐰𐑌𐐼 𐑄𐐯𐑉 𐐶𐐱𐑆 𐐶𐐲𐑌 𐐼𐐩 𐐮𐑌 𐐯𐑂𐑉𐐨 𐐶𐐨𐐿 𐑄𐐰𐐻 𐐶𐐱𐑆 𐑅𐐯𐐻 𐐲𐐹𐐪𐑉𐐻 𐑄𐐰𐐻 𐑄𐐩 𐑇𐐳𐐼 𐑀𐐰𐑄𐐲𐑉 𐑄𐐯𐑋𐑅𐐯𐑊𐑂𐑆 𐐻𐐭𐑀𐐯𐑄𐐲𐑉 𐐻𐐭 𐐻𐐨𐐽 𐑄 𐐹𐐨𐐹𐐲𐑊, 𐐰𐑌𐐼 𐐻𐐭 𐐶𐐲𐑉𐑇𐐮𐐹 𐑄 𐐢𐐫𐑉𐐼 𐑄𐐯𐑉 𐐘𐐱𐐼, 𐐰𐑌𐐼 𐐫𐑊𐑅𐐬, 𐐰𐑆 𐐱𐑁𐐲𐑌 𐐰𐑆 𐐮𐐻 𐐶𐐱𐑆 𐐮𐑌 𐑄𐐯𐑉 𐐹𐐵𐐲𐑉, 𐐻𐐭 𐐲𐑅𐐯𐑋𐐺𐐲𐑊 𐑄𐐯𐑋𐑅𐐯𐑊𐑂𐑆 𐐻𐐭𐑀𐐯𐑄𐐲𐑉. 𐐈𐑌𐐼 𐑄 𐐹𐑉𐐨𐑅𐐻𐑅 𐐶𐐲𐑉 𐑌𐐱𐐻 𐐻𐐭 𐐼𐐨𐐹𐐯𐑌𐐼 𐐲𐐹𐐱𐑌 𐑄 𐐹𐐨𐐹𐐲𐑊 𐑁𐐫𐑉 𐑄𐐯𐑉 𐑅𐐲𐐹𐐬𐑉𐐻; 𐐺𐐲𐐻 𐑁𐐫𐑉 𐑄𐐯𐑉 𐑊𐐩𐐺𐐲𐑉 𐑄𐐩 𐐶𐐲𐑉 𐐻𐐭 𐑉𐐨𐑅𐐨𐑂 𐑄 𐑀𐑉𐐩𐑅 𐐱𐑂 𐐘𐐱𐐼, 𐑄𐐰𐐻 𐑄𐐩 𐑋𐐴𐐻 𐐶𐐰𐐿𐑅 𐑅𐐻𐑉𐐱𐑍 𐐮𐑌 𐑄 𐐝𐐹𐐮𐑉𐐮𐐻, 𐐸𐐰𐑂𐐮𐑍 𐑄 𐑌𐐱𐑊𐐯𐐾 𐐱𐑂 𐐘𐐱𐐼, 𐑄𐐰𐐻 𐑄𐐩 𐑋𐐴𐐻 𐐻𐐨𐐽 𐐶𐐮𐑄 𐐹𐐵𐐲𐑉 𐐰𐑌𐐼 𐐫𐑃𐐱𐑉𐐮𐐻𐐨 𐑁𐑉𐐱𐑋 𐐘𐐱𐐼. 𐐈𐑌𐐼 𐐲𐑀𐐯𐑌 𐐈𐑊𐑋𐐲 𐐿𐐱𐑋𐐰𐑌𐐼𐐯𐐼 𐑄𐐰𐐻 𐑄 𐐹𐐨𐐹𐐲𐑊 𐐱𐑂 𐑄 𐐕𐐲𐑉𐐽 𐑇𐐳𐐼 𐐮𐑋𐐹𐐪𐑉𐐻 𐐱𐑂 𐑄𐐯𐑉 𐑅𐐲𐐺𐑅𐐻𐐲𐑌𐑅, 𐐯𐑂𐑉𐐨 𐐶𐐲𐑌 𐐰𐐿𐐫𐑉𐐼𐐮𐑍 𐐻𐐭 𐑄𐐰𐐻 𐐸𐐶𐐮𐐽 𐐸𐐨 𐐸𐐰𐐼; 𐐮𐑁 𐐸𐐨 𐐸𐐰𐑂 𐑋𐐬𐑉 𐐲𐐺𐐲𐑌𐐼𐐲𐑌𐐻𐑊𐐨, 𐐸𐐨 𐑇𐐳𐐼 𐐮𐑋𐐹𐐪𐑉𐐻 𐑋𐐬𐑉 𐐲𐐺𐐲𐑌𐐼𐐲𐑌𐐻𐑊𐐨; 𐐰𐑌𐐼 𐐱𐑂 𐐸𐐮𐑋 𐑄𐐰𐐻 𐐸𐐰𐐼 𐐺𐐲𐐻 𐑊𐐮𐐻𐑊, 𐐺𐐲𐐻 𐑊𐐮𐐻𐑊 𐑇𐐳𐐼 𐐺𐐨 𐑉𐐨𐐿𐐶𐐴𐑉𐐼; 𐐰𐑌𐐼 𐐻𐐭 𐐸𐐮𐑋 𐑄𐐰𐐻 𐐸𐐰𐐼 𐑌𐐱𐐻 𐑇𐐳𐐼 𐐺𐐨 𐑀𐐮𐑂𐐲𐑌. 𐐈𐑌𐐼 𐑄𐐲𐑅 𐑄𐐩 𐑇𐐳𐐼 𐐮𐑋𐐹𐐪𐑉𐐻 𐐱𐑂 𐑄𐐯𐑉 𐑅𐐲𐐺𐑅𐐻𐐲𐑌𐑅, 𐐱𐑂 𐑄𐐯𐑉 𐐬𐑌 𐑁𐑉𐐨 𐐶𐐮𐑊 𐐰𐑌𐐼 𐑀𐐳𐐼 𐐼𐐨𐑆𐐴𐑉𐑆 𐐻𐐬𐐲𐑉𐐼𐑆 𐐘𐐱𐐼, 𐐰𐑌𐐼 𐐻𐐭 𐑄𐐬𐑆

𐐹𐑉𐐨𐑅𐐻𐑅 𐑄𐐰𐐻 𐑅𐐻𐐳𐐼 𐐮𐑌 𐑌𐐨𐐼, 𐐷𐐩, 𐐰𐑌𐐼 𐐻𐐭 𐐯𐑂𐐲𐑉𐐨 𐑌𐐨𐐼𐐨, 𐑌𐐩𐐿𐐯𐐼 𐑅𐐬𐑊. 𐐈𐑌𐐼 𐑄𐐮𐑅 𐐸𐐨 𐑅𐐯𐐼 𐐲𐑌𐐻𐐭 𐑄𐐯𐑋, 𐐸𐐰𐑂𐐮𐑍 𐐺𐐮𐑌 𐐿𐐲𐑋𐐰𐑌𐐼𐐯𐐼 𐐱𐑂 𐐘𐐱𐐼; 𐐰𐑌𐐼 𐑄𐐩 𐐼𐐮𐐼 𐐶𐐫𐐿 𐐲𐐹𐑉𐐴𐐻𐑊𐐨 𐐺𐐨𐑁𐐬𐑉 𐐘𐐱𐐼, 𐐮𐑋𐐹𐐪𐑉𐐻𐐮𐑍 𐐻𐐭 𐐶𐐲𐑌 𐐲𐑌𐐲𐑄𐐲𐑉 𐐺𐐬𐑃 𐐻𐐯𐑋𐐹𐐲𐑉𐐲𐑊𐐨 𐐰𐑌𐐼 𐑅𐐹𐐮𐑉𐐮𐐻𐐷𐐭𐐰𐑊𐐨, 𐐰𐐿𐐫𐑉𐐼𐐮𐑍 𐐻𐐭 𐑄𐐩𐑉 𐑌𐐨𐐼𐑆 𐐰𐑌𐐼 𐑄𐐩𐑉 𐐶𐐱𐑌𐐻𐑅.

10. 𐐈𐑌𐐼 𐑌𐐵 𐐮𐐻 𐐿𐐩𐑋 𐐻𐐭 𐐹𐐰𐑅 𐑄𐐰𐐻 𐐫𐑊 𐑄𐐮𐑅 𐐶𐐱𐑆 𐐼𐐲𐑌 𐐮𐑌 𐐣𐐫𐑉𐑋𐐲𐑌; 𐐷𐐩, 𐐺𐐴 𐑄 𐐶𐐫𐐻𐐲𐑉𐑆 𐐱𐑂 𐐣𐐫𐑉𐑋𐐲𐑌, 𐐮𐑌 𐑄 𐑁𐐱𐑉𐐯𐑅𐐻 𐑄𐐰𐐻 𐐶𐐱𐑆 𐑌𐐨𐑉 𐑄 𐐶𐐫𐐻𐐲𐑉𐑆 𐐱𐑂 𐐣𐐫𐑉𐑋𐐲𐑌; 𐐷𐐩, 𐑄 𐐹𐑊𐐩𐑅 𐐱𐑂 𐐣𐐫𐑉𐑋𐐲𐑌, 𐑄 𐐶𐐫𐐻𐐲𐑉𐑆 𐐱𐑂 𐐣𐐫𐑉𐑋𐐲𐑌, 𐑄 𐑁𐐱𐑉𐐯𐑅𐐻 𐐱𐑂 𐐣𐐫𐑉𐑋𐐲𐑌, 𐐸𐐵 𐐺𐐷𐐭𐐻𐐮𐑁𐐳𐑊 𐐪𐑉 𐑄𐐩 𐐻𐐭 𐑄 𐐴𐑆 𐐱𐑂 𐑄𐐯𐑋 𐐸𐐭 𐑄𐐩𐑉 𐐿𐐩𐑋 𐐻𐐭 𐑄 𐑌𐐱𐑊𐐯𐐾 𐐱𐑂 𐑄𐐩𐑉 𐑉𐐨𐐼𐐨𐑋𐐲𐑉; 𐐷𐐩, 𐐰𐑌𐐼 𐐸𐐵 𐐺𐑊𐐯𐑅𐐯𐐼 𐐪𐑉 𐑄𐐩, 𐑁𐐫𐑉 𐑄𐐩 𐑇𐐰𐑊 𐑅𐐮𐑍 𐐻𐐭 𐐸𐐮𐑆 𐐹𐑉𐐩𐑆 𐑁𐐫𐑉𐐯𐑂𐐲𐑉. 𐐈𐑌𐐼 𐑄𐐨𐑆 𐑃𐐮𐑍𐑆 𐐶𐐲𐑉 𐐼𐐲𐑌 𐐮𐑌 𐑄 𐐺𐐫𐑉𐐼𐐲𐑉𐑆 𐐱𐑂 𐑄 𐑊𐐰𐑌𐐼, 𐑄𐐰𐐻 𐑄𐐩 𐑋𐐴𐐻 𐑌𐐱𐐻 𐐿𐐲𐑋 𐐻𐐭 𐑄 𐑌𐐱𐑊𐐯𐐾 𐐱𐑂 𐑄 𐐿𐐮𐑍. 𐐒𐐲𐐻 𐐺𐐨𐐸𐐬𐑊𐐼, 𐐮𐐻 𐐿𐐩𐑋 𐐻𐐭 𐐹𐐰𐑅 𐑄𐐰𐐻 𐑄 𐐿𐐮𐑍, 𐐸𐐰𐑂𐐮𐑍 𐐼𐐮𐑅𐐿𐐲𐑂𐐲𐑉𐐼 𐐲 𐑋𐐭𐑂𐑋𐐯𐑌𐐻 𐐲𐑋𐐲𐑍 𐑄 𐐹𐐨𐐹𐑊, 𐑅𐐯𐑌𐐻 𐐸𐐮𐑆 𐑅𐐲𐑉𐑂𐐰𐑌𐐻𐑅 𐐻𐐭 𐐶𐐱𐐽 𐑄𐐯𐑋. 𐐜𐐩𐑉𐑁𐐬𐑉 𐐱𐑌 𐑄 𐐼𐐩 𐑄𐐰𐐻 𐑄𐐩 𐐶𐐲𐑉 𐐰𐑅𐐯𐑋𐐺𐑊𐐮𐑍 𐑄𐐯𐑋𐑅𐐯𐑊𐑂𐑆 𐐻𐐭𐑀𐐯𐑄𐐲𐑉 𐐻𐐭 𐐸𐐨𐑉 𐑄 𐐶𐐲𐑉𐐼 𐐱𐑂 𐑄 𐐢𐐫𐑉𐐼, 𐑄𐐩 𐐶𐐲𐑉 𐐼𐐮𐑅𐐿𐐲𐑂𐐲𐑉𐐼 𐐲𐑌𐐻𐐭 𐑄 𐐿𐐮𐑍. 𐐈𐑌𐐼 𐑌𐐵 𐑄 𐐿𐐮𐑍 𐑅𐐯𐐼 𐑄𐐰𐐻 𐐈𐑊𐑋𐐲 𐐶𐐱𐑆 𐑅𐐻𐐲𐑉𐐮𐑍 𐐲𐐹 𐑄 𐐹𐐨𐐹𐑊 𐐻𐐭 𐑉𐐨𐐺𐐯𐑊𐐷𐐲𐑌 𐐰𐑀𐐯𐑌𐑅𐐻 𐐸𐐮𐑋; 𐑄𐐩𐑉𐑁𐐬𐑉 𐐸𐐨 𐑅𐐯𐑌𐐻 𐐸𐐮𐑆 𐐪𐑉𐑋𐐨 𐐻𐐭 𐐼𐐨𐑅𐐻𐑉𐑎 𐑄𐐯𐑋. 𐐈𐑌𐐼 𐐮𐐻 𐐿𐐩𐑋 𐐻𐐭 𐐹𐐰𐑅 𐑄𐐰𐐻 𐐈𐑊𐑋𐐲 𐐰𐑌𐐼 𐑄 𐐹𐐨𐐹𐑊 𐐱𐑂 𐑄 𐐢𐐫𐑉𐐼 𐐶𐐲𐑉 𐐰𐐹𐑉𐐴𐑆𐐼 𐐱𐑂 𐑄 𐐿𐐲𐑋𐐮𐑍 𐐱𐑂 𐑄 𐐿𐐮𐑍𐑆 𐐪𐑉𐑋𐐨; 𐑄𐐩𐑉𐑁𐐬𐑉 𐑄𐐩 𐐻𐐳𐐿 𐑄𐐩𐑉 𐐻𐐯𐑌𐐻𐑅 𐐰𐑌𐐼 𐑄𐐩𐑉 𐑁𐐰𐑋𐐮𐑊𐐨𐑆, 𐐰𐑌𐐼 𐐼𐐨𐐹𐐪𐑉𐐻𐐯𐐼 𐐮𐑌𐐻𐐭 𐑄 𐐶𐐮𐑊𐐼𐐲𐑉𐑌𐐯𐑅. 𐐈𐑌𐐼 𐑄𐐩 𐐶𐐲𐑉 𐐮𐑌 𐑌𐐲𐑋𐐺𐐲𐑉 𐐲𐐺𐐵𐐻 𐑁𐐬𐑉 𐐸𐐲𐑌𐐼𐑉𐐯𐐼 𐐰𐑌𐐼 𐑁𐐮𐑁𐐻𐐨 𐑅𐐬𐑊𐑆.

11. 𐐈𐑌𐐼 𐐮𐐻 𐐿𐐩𐑋 𐐻𐐭 𐐹𐐰𐑅 𐑄𐐰𐐻 𐑄 𐐪𐑉𐑋𐐨 𐐱𐑂 𐑄 𐐿𐐮𐑍 𐑉𐐨𐐻𐐲𐑉𐑌𐐼, 𐐸𐐰𐑂𐐮𐑍 𐑅𐐲𐑉𐐽𐐻 𐐮𐑌 𐑂𐐩𐑌 𐑁𐐫𐑉 𐑄 𐐹𐐨𐐹𐑊 𐐱𐑂 𐑄 𐐢𐐫𐑉𐐼. 𐐈𐑌𐐼 𐐺𐐨𐐸𐐬𐑊𐐼, 𐑄 𐑁𐐬𐑉𐑅𐐯𐑆 𐐱𐑂 𐑄 𐐿𐐮𐑍 𐐶𐐲𐑉 𐑅𐑋𐐫𐑊, 𐐸𐐰𐑂𐐮𐑍 𐐺𐐮𐑌 𐑉𐐨𐐼𐐷𐐭𐑅𐐻, 𐐰𐑌𐐼 𐑄𐐩𐑉 𐐺𐐨𐑀𐐰𐑌 𐐻𐐭 𐐺𐐨 𐐲 𐐼𐐮𐑂𐐮𐑈𐐲𐑌 𐐲𐑋𐐲𐑍 𐑄 𐑉𐐨𐑋𐐩𐑌𐐼𐐲𐑉 𐐱𐑂 𐑄 𐐹𐐨𐐹𐑊. 𐐈𐑌𐐼 𐑄 𐑊𐐯𐑅𐐲𐑉 𐐹𐐪𐑉𐐻 𐐺𐐨𐑀𐐰𐑌 𐐻𐐭 𐐺𐑉𐐨𐑄 𐐵𐐻 𐑃𐑉𐐯𐐻𐑌𐐮𐑍𐑆 𐐰𐑀𐐯𐑌𐑅𐐻 𐑄 𐐿𐐮𐑍, 𐐰𐑌𐐼 𐑄𐐩𐑉 𐐺𐐨𐑀𐐰𐑌 𐐻𐐭 𐐺𐐨 𐐲 𐑀𐑉𐐩𐐻 𐐿𐐱𐑌𐐻𐐯𐑌𐑇𐐲𐑌 𐐲𐑋𐐲𐑍 𐑄𐐯𐑋. 𐐈𐑌𐐼 𐑌𐐵 𐑄𐐩𐑉 𐐶𐐱𐑆 𐐲 𐑋𐐰𐑌 𐐲𐑋𐐲𐑍 𐑄𐐯𐑋 𐐸𐐭𐑆 𐑌𐐩𐑋 𐐶𐐱𐑆 𐐘𐐮𐐼𐐨𐐲𐑌, 𐐰𐑌𐐼 𐐸𐐨 𐐺𐐨𐐮𐑍 𐐲 𐑅𐐻𐑉𐐱𐑍 𐑋𐐰𐑌 𐐰𐑌𐐼 𐐰𐑌 𐐯𐑌𐐯𐑋𐐨 𐐻𐐭 𐑄 𐐿𐐮𐑍, 𐑄𐐩𐑉𐑁𐐬𐑉 𐐸𐐨 𐐼𐑉𐐭 𐐸𐐮𐑆 𐑅𐐬𐑉𐐼, 𐐰𐑌𐐼 𐑅𐐶𐐬𐑉 𐐮𐑌 𐐸𐐮𐑆 𐑉𐐫𐑃 𐑄𐐰𐐻 𐐸𐐨 𐐶𐐳𐐼 𐑅𐑊𐐩 𐑄 𐐿𐐮𐑍. 𐐈𐑌𐐼 𐐮𐐻 𐐿𐐩𐑋 𐐻𐐭 𐐹𐐰𐑅 𐑄𐐰𐐻 𐐸𐐨 𐑁𐐫𐐻 𐐶𐐮𐑄 𐑄 𐐿𐐮𐑍; 𐐰𐑌𐐼 𐐸𐐶𐐯𐑌 𐑄 𐐿𐐮𐑍 𐑅𐐫 𐑄𐐰𐐻 𐐸𐐨 𐐶𐐱𐑆 𐐲𐐺𐐵𐐻 𐐻𐐭 𐐬𐑂𐐲𐑉𐐹𐐵𐐲𐑉 𐐸𐐮𐑋, 𐐸𐐨 𐑁𐑊𐐯𐐼 𐐰𐑌𐐼 𐑉𐐰𐑌 𐐰𐑌𐐼 𐑀𐐱𐐻 𐐲𐐹𐐱𐑌 𐑄 𐐻𐐵𐐲𐑉 𐐸𐐶𐐮𐐽 𐐶𐐱𐑆 𐑌𐐨𐑉 𐑄 𐐻𐐯𐑋𐐹𐑊. 𐐈𐑌𐐼 𐐘𐐮𐐼𐐨𐐲𐑌 𐐹𐐲𐑉𐑅𐐭𐐼 𐐰𐑁𐐻𐐲𐑉 𐐸𐐮𐑋 𐐰𐑌𐐼 𐐶𐐱𐑆 𐐲𐐺𐐵𐐻 𐐻𐐭 𐑀𐐯𐐻 𐐲𐐹𐐱𐑌 𐑄 𐐻𐐵𐐲𐑉 𐐻𐐭 𐑅𐑊𐐩 𐑄 𐐿𐐮𐑍, 𐐰𐑌𐐼 𐑄 𐐿𐐮𐑍 𐐿𐐰𐑅𐐻 𐐸𐐮𐑆 𐐴𐑆 𐑉𐐵𐑌𐐼 𐐲𐐺𐐵𐐻 𐐻𐐬𐑉𐐼𐑆 𐑄 𐑊𐐰𐑌𐐼 𐐱𐑂 𐐟𐐯𐑋𐑊𐐲𐑌, 𐐰𐑌𐐼 𐐺𐐨𐐸𐐬𐑊𐐼, 𐑄 𐐪𐑉𐑋𐐨 𐐱𐑂 𐑄 𐐢𐐰𐑋𐐲𐑌𐐴𐐻𐑅 𐐶𐐲𐑉 𐐶𐐮𐑄𐐮𐑌 𐑄 𐐺𐐫𐑉𐐼𐐲𐑉𐑆 𐐱𐑂 𐑄 𐑊𐐰𐑌𐐼. 𐐈𐑌𐐼 𐑌𐐵 𐑄 𐐿𐐮𐑍 𐐿𐑉𐐴𐐼 𐐵𐐻 𐐮𐑌 𐑄 𐐰𐑍𐑀𐐶𐐮𐑇 𐐱𐑂 𐐸𐐮𐑆 𐑅𐐬𐑊, 𐑅𐐩𐐮𐑍, 𐐘𐐮𐐼𐐨𐐲𐑌, 𐑅𐐹𐐩𐑉 𐑋𐐨, 𐑁𐐫𐑉 𐑄 𐐢𐐰𐑋𐐲𐑌𐐴𐐻𐑅 𐐪𐑉 𐐲𐐹𐐱𐑌 𐐲𐑅, 𐐰𐑌𐐼 𐑄𐐩 𐐶𐐮𐑊 𐐼𐐨𐑅𐐻𐑉𐑎 𐐲𐑅; 𐐷𐐩, 𐑄𐐩 𐐶𐐮𐑊 𐐼𐐨𐑅𐐻𐑉𐑎 𐑋𐐴 𐐹𐐨𐐹𐑊. 𐐈𐑌𐐼 𐑌𐐵 𐑄 𐐿𐐮𐑍 𐐶𐐱𐑆 𐑌𐐱𐐻 𐑅𐐬 𐑋𐐲𐐽 𐐿𐐲𐑌𐑅𐐲𐑉𐑌𐐼 𐐲𐐺𐐵𐐻 𐐸𐐮𐑆 𐐹𐐨𐐹𐑊 𐐰𐑆 𐐸𐐨 𐐶𐐱𐑆 𐐲𐐺𐐵𐐻 𐐸𐐮𐑆 𐐬𐑌 𐑊𐐴𐑁; 𐑌𐐯𐑂𐐲𐑉𐑄𐐯𐑊𐐯𐑅, 𐐘𐐮𐐼𐐨𐐲𐑌 𐐼𐐮𐐼 𐑅𐐹𐐩𐑉 𐐸𐐮𐑆 𐑊𐐴𐑁. 𐐈𐑌𐐼 𐑄 𐐿𐐮𐑍 𐐿𐐲𐑋𐐰𐑌𐐼𐐯𐐼 𐑄 𐐹𐐨𐐹𐑊 𐑄𐐰𐐻 𐑄𐐩 𐑇𐐳𐐼 𐑁𐑊𐐨 𐐺𐐨𐑁𐐬𐑉 𐑄 𐐢𐐰𐑋𐐲𐑌𐐴𐐻𐑅, 𐐰𐑌𐐼 𐐸𐐨 𐐸𐐮𐑋𐑅𐐯𐑊𐑁 𐐼𐐮𐐼 𐑀𐐬 𐐺𐐨𐑁𐐬𐑉 𐑄𐐯𐑋, 𐐰𐑌𐐼 𐑄𐐩 𐐼𐐮𐐼 𐑁𐑊𐐨 𐐮𐑌𐐻𐐭 𐑄 𐐶𐐮𐑊𐐼𐐲𐑉𐑌𐐯𐑅, 𐐶𐐮𐑄 𐑄𐐩𐑉 𐐶𐐮𐑋𐐯𐑌 𐐰𐑌𐐼 𐑄𐐩𐑉 𐐽𐐮𐑊𐐼𐑉𐐯𐑌. 𐐈𐑌𐐼 𐐮𐐻 𐐿𐐩𐑋 𐐻𐐭 𐐹𐐰𐑅 𐑄𐐰𐐻 𐑄 𐐢𐐰𐑋𐐲𐑌𐐴𐐻𐑅 𐐼𐐮𐐼 𐐹𐐲𐑉𐑅𐐭 𐑄𐐯𐑋, 𐐰𐑌𐐼 𐐼𐐮𐐼 𐐬𐑂𐐲𐑉𐐻𐐩𐐿 𐑄𐐯𐑋, 𐐰𐑌𐐼 𐐺𐐨𐑀𐐰𐑌 𐐻𐐭 𐑅𐑊𐐩 𐑄𐐯𐑋.

12. 𐐤𐐵 𐐮𐐻 𐐿𐐩𐑋 𐐻𐐭 𐐹𐐰𐑅 𐑄𐐰𐐻 𐑄 𐐿𐐮𐑍 𐐿𐐲𐑋𐐰𐑌𐐼𐐯𐐼 𐑄𐐯𐑋 𐑄𐐰𐐻 𐐫𐑊 𐑄 𐑋𐐯𐑌 𐑇𐐳𐐼 𐑊𐐨𐑂 𐑄𐐩𐑉 𐐶𐐴𐑂𐑆 𐐰𐑌𐐼 𐑄𐐩𐑉 𐐽𐐮𐑊𐐼𐑉𐐯𐑌, 𐐰𐑌𐐼 𐑁𐑊𐐨 𐐺𐐨𐑁𐐬𐑉 𐑄 𐐢𐐰𐑋𐐲𐑌𐐴𐐻𐑅. 𐐤𐐵 𐑄𐐩𐑉 𐐶𐐲𐑉 𐑋𐐯𐑌𐐨 𐑄𐐰𐐻 𐐶𐐳𐐼 𐑌𐐱𐐻 𐑊𐐨𐑂 𐑄𐐯𐑋, 𐐺𐐲𐐻 𐐸𐐰𐐼 𐑉𐐰𐑄𐐲𐑉 𐑅𐐻𐐩 𐐰𐑌𐐼 𐐹𐐯𐑉𐐮𐑇 𐐶𐐮𐑄 𐑄𐐯𐑋. 𐐈𐑌𐐼 𐑄 𐑉𐐯𐑅𐐻 𐑊𐐯𐑁𐐻 𐑄𐐩𐑉 𐐶𐐴𐑂𐑆 𐐰𐑌𐐼 𐑄𐐩𐑉 𐐽𐐮𐑊𐐼𐑉𐐯𐑌 𐐰𐑌𐐼 𐑁𐑊𐐯𐐼. 𐐈𐑌𐐼 𐐮𐐻 𐐿𐐩𐑋 𐐻𐐭 𐐹𐐰𐑅 𐑄𐐰𐐻 𐑄𐐬𐑆 𐐸𐐭 𐐻𐐰𐑉𐐨𐐼 𐐶𐐮𐑄 𐑄𐐩𐑉 𐐶𐐴𐑂𐑆 𐐰𐑌𐐼 𐑄𐐩𐑉 𐐽𐐮𐑊𐐼𐑉𐐯𐑌, 𐐿𐐫𐑆𐐼 𐑄𐐰𐐻 𐑄𐐩𐑉 𐑁𐐩𐑉 𐐼𐐫𐐻𐐲𐑉𐑆 𐑇𐐳𐐼 𐑅𐐻𐐰𐑌𐐼 𐑁𐐬𐑉𐑃 𐐰𐑌𐐼 𐐹𐑊𐐨𐐼 𐐶𐐮𐑄

𐑄 𐐢𐐰𐑋𐐲𐑌𐐴𐐻𐑅, 𐑄𐐰𐐻 𐑄𐐩 𐐶𐐳𐐼 𐑌𐐱𐐻 𐑅𐑊𐐩 𐑄𐐯𐑋. 𐐈𐑌𐐼 𐐮𐐻 𐐿𐐩𐑋 𐐻𐐭 𐐹𐐰𐑅 𐑄𐐰𐐻 𐑄 𐐢𐐰𐑋𐐲𐑌𐐴𐐻𐑅 𐐸𐐰𐐼 𐐿𐐱𐑋𐐹𐐰𐑇𐐲𐑌 𐐱𐑌 𐑄𐐯𐑋, 𐑁𐐫𐑉 𐑄𐐩 𐐶𐐲𐑉 𐐽𐐪𐑉𐑋𐐼 𐐶𐐮𐑄 𐑄 𐐺𐐧𐐻𐐨 𐐱𐑂 𐑄𐐯𐑉 𐐶𐐮𐑋𐐯𐑌; 𐑄𐐯𐑉𐑁𐐬𐑉, 𐑄 𐐢𐐰𐑋𐐲𐑌𐐴𐐻𐑅 𐐼𐐮𐐼 𐑅𐐹𐐯𐑉 𐑄𐐯𐑉 𐑊𐐴𐑂𐑆, 𐐰𐑌𐐼 𐐻𐐳𐐿 𐑄𐐯𐑋 𐐿𐐰𐐹𐐻𐐮𐑂𐑆, 𐐰𐑌𐐼 𐐿𐐰𐑉𐐨𐐼 𐑄𐐯𐑋 𐐺𐐰𐐿 𐐻𐐭 𐑄 𐑊𐐰𐑌𐐼 𐐱𐑂 𐐤𐐨𐑁𐐴, 𐐰𐑌𐐼 𐑀𐑉𐐪𐑌𐐻𐐯𐐼 𐐲𐑌𐐻𐐭 𐑄𐐯𐑋 𐑄𐐰𐐻 𐑄𐐩 𐑋𐐴𐐻 𐐹𐐲𐑆𐐯𐑅 𐑄 𐑊𐐰𐑌𐐼, 𐐲𐑌𐐼𐐲𐑉 𐑄 𐐿𐐱𐑌𐐼𐐮𐑇𐐲𐑌𐑆 𐑄𐐰𐐻 𐑄𐐩 𐐶𐐳𐐼 𐐼𐐯𐑊𐐮𐑂𐐲𐑉 𐐲𐐹 𐐿𐐮𐑍 𐐤𐐬𐐲 𐐮𐑌𐐻𐐭 𐑄 𐐸𐐰𐑌𐐼𐑆 𐐱𐑂 𐑄 𐐢𐐰𐑋𐐲𐑌𐐴𐐻𐑅, 𐐰𐑌𐐼 𐐼𐐯𐑊𐐮𐑂𐐲𐑉 𐐲𐐹 𐑄𐐯𐑉 𐐹𐑉𐐱𐐹𐐲𐑉𐐻𐐨, 𐐨𐑂𐐯𐑌 𐐶𐐲𐑌 𐐸𐐪𐑁 𐐱𐑂 𐐫𐑊 𐑄𐐩 𐐹𐐲𐑆𐐯𐑅𐐻, 𐐶𐐲𐑌 𐐸𐐪𐑁 𐐱𐑂 𐑄𐐯𐑉 𐑀𐐬𐑊𐐼, 𐐰𐑌𐐼 𐑄𐐯𐑉 𐑅𐐮𐑊𐑂𐐲𐑉, 𐐰𐑌𐐼 𐐫𐑊 𐑄𐐯𐑉 𐐹𐑉𐐯𐑇𐐲𐑅 𐑃𐐮𐑍𐑆, 𐐰𐑌𐐼 𐑄𐐲𐑅 𐑄𐐩 𐑇𐐳𐐼 𐐹𐐩 𐐻𐑉𐐮𐐺𐐧𐐻 𐐻𐐭 𐑄 𐐿𐐮𐑍 𐐱𐑂 𐑄 𐐢𐐰𐑋𐐲𐑌𐐴𐐻𐑅, 𐑁𐑉𐐱𐑋 𐐷𐐨𐑉 𐐻𐐭 𐐷𐐨𐑉. 𐐈𐑌𐐼 𐑌𐐵 𐑄𐐯𐑉 𐐶𐐱𐑆 𐐶𐐲𐑌 𐐱𐑂 𐑄 𐑅𐐲𐑌𐑆 𐐱𐑂 𐑄 𐐿𐐮𐑍 𐐲𐑋𐐲𐑍 𐑄𐐬𐑆 𐑄𐐰𐐻 𐐶𐐲𐑉 𐐻𐐩𐐿𐐯𐑌 𐐿𐐰𐐹𐐻𐐮𐑂, 𐐸𐐭𐑆 𐑌𐐩𐑋 𐐶𐐱𐑆 𐐢𐐮𐑋𐐸𐐴. 𐐈𐑌𐐼 𐑌𐐵 𐐢𐐮𐑋𐐸𐐴 𐐶𐐱𐑆 𐐼𐐯𐑆𐐴𐑉𐐲𐑅 𐑄𐐰𐐻 𐐸𐐮𐑆 𐑁𐐪𐑄𐐲𐑉 𐑇𐐳𐐼 𐑌𐐱𐐻 𐐺𐐨 𐐼𐐯𐑅𐐻𐑉𐑎𐐼; 𐑌𐐯𐑂𐐲𐑉𐑄𐐯𐑊𐐯𐑅, 𐐢𐐮𐑋𐐸𐐴 𐐶𐐱𐑆 𐑌𐐱𐐻 𐐮𐑀𐑌𐐬𐑉𐐰𐑌𐐻 𐐱𐑂 𐑄 𐐮𐑌𐐮𐐿𐐶𐐮𐐻𐐨𐑆 𐐱𐑂 𐐸𐐮𐑆 𐑁𐐪𐑄𐐲𐑉, 𐐸𐐨 𐐸𐐮𐑋𐑅𐐯𐑊𐑁 𐐺𐐨𐐮𐑍 𐐲 𐐾𐐲𐑅𐐻 𐑋𐐰𐑌.

13. 𐐈𐑌𐐼 𐐮𐐻 𐐿𐐩𐑋 𐐻𐐭 𐐹𐐰𐑅 𐑄𐐰𐐻 𐐘𐐮𐐼𐐨𐐲𐑌 𐑅𐐯𐑌𐐻 𐑋𐐯𐑌 𐐮𐑌𐐻𐐭 𐑄 𐐶𐐮𐑊𐐼𐐲𐑉𐑌𐐯𐑅 𐑅𐐨𐐿𐑉𐐯𐐻𐑊𐐨, 𐐻𐐭 𐑅𐐲𐑉𐐽 𐑁𐐫𐑉 𐑄 𐐿𐐮𐑍, 𐐰𐑌𐐼 𐑄𐐬𐑆 𐑄𐐰𐐻 𐐶𐐲𐑉 𐐶𐐮𐑄 𐐸𐐮𐑋. 𐐈𐑌𐐼 𐐮𐐻 𐐿𐐩𐑋 𐐻𐐭 𐐹𐐰𐑅 𐑄𐐰𐐻 𐑄𐐩 𐑋𐐯𐐻 𐑄 𐐹𐐨𐐹𐑊 𐐮𐑌 𐑄 𐐶𐐮𐑊𐐼𐐲𐑉𐑌𐐯𐑅, 𐐫𐑊 𐑅𐐩𐑂 𐑄 𐐿𐐮𐑍 𐐰𐑌𐐼 𐐸𐐮𐑆 𐐹𐑉𐐨𐑅𐐻𐑅. 𐐤𐐵 𐑄𐐩 𐐸𐐰𐐼 𐑅𐐶𐐬𐑉𐑌 𐐮𐑌 𐑄𐐯𐑉 𐐸𐐪𐑉𐐻𐑅 𐑄𐐰𐐻 𐑄𐐩 𐐶𐐳𐐼 𐑉𐐨𐐻𐐲𐑉𐑌 𐐻𐐭 𐑄 𐑊𐐰𐑌𐐼 𐐱𐑂 𐐤𐐨𐑁𐐴, 𐐰𐑌𐐼 𐐮𐑁 𐑄𐐯𐑉 𐐶𐐴𐑂𐑆 𐐰𐑌𐐼 𐑄𐐯𐑉 𐐽𐐮𐑊𐐼𐑉𐐯𐑌 𐐶𐐲𐑉 𐑅𐑊𐐩𐑌, 𐐰𐑌𐐼 𐐫𐑊𐑅𐐬 𐑄𐐬𐑆 𐑄𐐰𐐻 𐐸𐐰𐐼 𐐻𐐰𐑉𐐨𐐼 𐐶𐐮𐑄 𐑄𐐯𐑋, 𐑄𐐰𐐻 𐑄𐐩 𐐶𐐳𐐼 𐑅𐐨𐐿 𐑉𐐨𐑂𐐯𐑌𐐾, 𐐰𐑌𐐼 𐐫𐑊𐑅𐐬 𐐹𐐯𐑉𐐮𐑇 𐐶𐐮𐑄 𐑄𐐯𐑋. 𐐈𐑌𐐼 𐑄 𐐿𐐮𐑍 𐐿𐐱𐑋𐐪𐑌𐐼𐐯𐐼 𐑄𐐯𐑋 𐑄𐐰𐐻 𐑄𐐩 𐑇𐐳𐐼 𐑌𐐱𐐻 𐑉𐐨𐐻𐐲𐑉𐑌; 𐐰𐑌𐐼 𐑄𐐩 𐐶𐐲𐑉 𐐰𐑍𐑀𐑉𐐨 𐐶𐐮𐑄 𐑄 𐐿𐐮𐑍, 𐐰𐑌𐐼 𐐿𐐫𐑆𐐼 𐑄𐐰𐐻 𐐸𐐨 𐑇𐐳𐐼 𐑅𐐲𐑁𐐲𐑉, 𐐨𐑂𐐯𐑌 𐐲𐑌𐐻𐐭 𐐼𐐯𐑃 𐐺𐐴 𐑁𐐴𐑉. 𐐈𐑌𐐼 𐑄𐐩 𐐶𐐲𐑉 𐐲𐐺𐐵𐐻 𐐻𐐭 𐐻𐐩𐐿 𐑄 𐐹𐑉𐐨𐑅𐐻𐑅 𐐫𐑊𐑅𐐬 𐐰𐑌𐐼 𐐹𐐳𐐻 𐑄𐐯𐑋 𐐻𐐭 𐐼𐐯𐑃, 𐐰𐑌𐐼 𐑄𐐩 𐑁𐑊𐐯𐐼 𐐺𐐨𐑁𐐬𐑉 𐑄𐐯𐑋.

14. 𐐈𐑌𐐼 𐐮𐐻 𐐿𐐩𐑋 𐐻𐐭 𐐹𐐰𐑅 𐑄𐐰𐐻 𐑄𐐩 𐐶𐐲𐑉 𐐲𐐺𐐵𐐻 𐐻𐐭 𐑉𐐨𐐻𐐲𐑉𐑌 𐐻𐐭 𐑄 𐑊𐐰𐑌𐐼 𐐱𐑂 𐐤𐐨𐑁𐐴, 𐐰𐑌𐐼 𐑄𐐩 𐑋𐐯𐐻 𐑄 𐑋𐐯𐑌 𐐱𐑂 𐐘𐐮𐐼𐐨𐐲𐑌. 𐐈𐑌𐐼 𐑄 𐑋𐐯𐑌 𐐱𐑂 𐐘𐐮𐐼𐐨𐐲𐑌 𐐻𐐬𐑊𐐼 𐑄𐐯𐑋 𐐱𐑂 𐐫𐑊 𐑄𐐰𐐻 𐐸𐐰𐐼 𐐸𐐰𐐹𐐲𐑌𐐼 𐐻𐐭 𐑄𐐯𐑉 𐐶𐐴𐑂𐑆 𐐰𐑌𐐼 𐑄𐐯𐑉 𐐽𐐮𐑊𐐼𐑉𐐯𐑌; 𐐰𐑌𐐼 𐑄𐐰𐐻 𐑄 𐐢𐐰𐑋𐐲𐑌𐐴𐐻𐑅 𐐸𐐰𐐼 𐑀𐑉𐐪𐑌𐐻𐐯𐐼 𐐲𐑌𐐻𐐭 𐑄𐐯𐑋 𐑄𐐰𐐻 𐑄𐐩 𐑋𐐴𐐻 𐐹𐐲𐑆𐐯𐑅 𐑄 𐑊𐐰𐑌𐐼, 𐐺𐐴 𐐹𐐩𐐮𐑍 𐐲 𐐻𐑉𐐮𐐺𐐧𐐻 𐐻𐐭 𐑄 𐐢𐐰𐑋𐐲𐑌𐐴𐐻𐑅 𐐱𐑂 𐐶𐐲𐑌 𐐸𐐪𐑁 𐐱𐑂 𐐫𐑊 𐑄𐐩 𐐹𐐲𐑆𐐯𐑅𐐻. 𐐈𐑌𐐼 𐑄 𐐹𐐨𐐹𐑊 𐐻𐐬𐑊𐐼 𐑄 𐑋𐐯𐑌 𐐱𐑂 𐐘𐐮𐐼𐐨𐐲𐑌 𐑄𐐰𐐻 𐑄𐐩 𐐸𐐰𐐼 𐑅𐑊𐐩𐑌 𐑄 𐐿𐐮𐑍, 𐐰𐑌𐐼 𐐸𐐮𐑆 𐐹𐑉𐐨𐑅𐐻𐑅 𐐸𐐰𐐼 𐑁𐑊𐐯𐐼 𐑁𐑉𐐱𐑋 𐑄𐐯𐑋 𐑁𐐪𐑉𐑄𐐲𐑉 𐐮𐑌𐐻𐐭 𐑄 𐐶𐐮𐑊𐐼𐐲𐑉𐑌𐐯𐑅. 𐐈𐑌𐐼 𐐮𐐻 𐐿𐐩𐑋 𐐻𐐭 𐐹𐐰𐑅 𐑄𐐰𐐻 𐐪𐑁𐐻𐐲𐑉 𐑄𐐩 𐐸𐐰𐐼 𐐯𐑌𐐼𐐯𐐼 𐑄 𐑅𐐯𐑉𐐨𐑋𐐬𐑌𐐨, 𐑄𐐰𐐻 𐑄𐐩 𐑉𐐨𐐻𐐲𐑉𐑌𐐼 𐐻𐐭 𐑄 𐑊𐐰𐑌𐐼 𐐱𐑂 𐐤𐐨𐑁𐐴, 𐑉𐐨𐐾𐑎𐑅𐐮𐑍, 𐐺𐐨𐐿𐐫𐑆 𐑄𐐯𐑉 𐐶𐐴𐑂𐑆 𐐰𐑌𐐼 𐑄𐐯𐑉 𐐽𐐮𐑊𐐼𐑉𐐯𐑌 𐐶𐐲𐑉 𐑌𐐱𐐻 𐑅𐑊𐐩𐑌; 𐐰𐑌𐐼 𐑄𐐩 𐐻𐐬𐑊𐐼 𐐘𐐮𐐼𐐨𐐲𐑌 𐐸𐐶𐐱𐐻 𐑄𐐩 𐐸𐐰𐐼 𐐼𐐲𐑌 𐐻𐐭 𐑄 𐐿𐐮𐑍.

15. 𐐈𐑌𐐼 𐐮𐐻 𐐿𐐩𐑋 𐐻𐐭 𐐹𐐰𐑅 𐑄𐐰𐐻 𐑄 𐐿𐐮𐑍 𐐱𐑂 𐑄 𐐢𐐰𐑋𐐲𐑌𐐴𐐻𐑅 𐑋𐐩𐐼 𐐰𐑌 𐐬𐑃 𐐲𐑌𐐻𐐭 𐑄𐐯𐑋, 𐑄𐐰𐐻 𐐸𐐮𐑆 𐐹𐐨𐐹𐑊 𐑇𐐳𐐼 𐑌𐐱𐐻 𐑅𐑊𐐩 𐑄𐐯𐑋. 𐐈𐑌𐐼 𐐫𐑊𐑅𐐬 𐐢𐐮𐑋𐐸𐐴, 𐐺𐐨𐐮𐑍 𐑄 𐑅𐐲𐑌 𐐱𐑂 𐑄 𐐿𐐮𐑍, 𐐸𐐰𐑂𐐮𐑍 𐑄 𐐿𐐮𐑍𐐼𐐲𐑋 𐐿𐐱𐑌𐑁𐐲𐑉𐐼 𐐲𐐹𐐱𐑌 𐐸𐐮𐑋 𐐺𐐴 𐑄 𐐹𐐨𐐹𐑊, 𐑋𐐩𐐼 𐐬𐑃 𐐲𐑌𐐻𐐭 𐑄 𐐿𐐮𐑍 𐐱𐑂 𐑄 𐐢𐐰𐑋𐐲𐑌𐐴𐐻𐑅, 𐑄𐐰𐐻 𐐸𐐮𐑆 𐐹𐐨𐐹𐑊 𐑇𐐳𐐼 𐐹𐐩 𐐻𐑉𐐮𐐺𐐧𐐻 𐐲𐑌𐐻𐐭 𐐸𐐮𐑋, 𐐨𐑂𐐯𐑌 𐐶𐐲𐑌 𐐸𐐪𐑁 𐐱𐑂 𐐫𐑊 𐑄𐐩 𐐹𐐲𐑆𐐯𐑅𐐻.

16. 𐐈𐑌𐐼 𐐮𐐻 𐐿𐐩𐑋 𐐻𐐭 𐐹𐐰𐑅 𐑄𐐰𐐻 𐐢𐐮𐑋𐐸𐐴 𐐺𐐨𐑀𐐰𐑌 𐐻𐐭 𐐯𐑅𐐻𐐰𐐺𐑊𐐮𐑇 𐑄 𐐿𐐮𐑍𐐼𐐲𐑋, 𐐰𐑌𐐼 𐐻𐐭 𐐯𐑅𐐻𐐰𐐺𐑊𐐮𐑇 𐐹𐐨𐑅 𐐲𐑋𐐲𐑍 𐐸𐐮𐑆 𐐹𐐨𐐹𐑊. 𐐈𐑌𐐼 𐑄 𐐿𐐮𐑍 𐐱𐑂 𐑄 𐐢𐐰𐑋𐐲𐑌𐐴𐐻𐑅 𐑅𐐯𐐻 𐑀𐐪𐑉𐐼𐑆 𐑉𐐵𐑌𐐼 𐐲𐐺𐐵𐐻 𐑄 𐑊𐐰𐑌𐐼, 𐑄𐐰𐐻 𐐸𐐨 𐑋𐐴𐐻 𐐿𐐨𐐹 𐑄 𐐹𐐨𐐹𐑊 𐐱𐑂 𐐢𐐮𐑋𐐸𐐴 𐐮𐑌 𐑄 𐑊𐐰𐑌𐐼, 𐑄𐐰𐐻 𐑄𐐩 𐑋𐐴𐐻 𐑌𐐱𐐻 𐐼𐐨𐐹𐐪𐑉𐐻 𐐮𐑌𐐻𐐭 𐑄 𐐶𐐮𐑊𐐼𐐲𐑉𐑌𐐯𐑅; 𐐰𐑌𐐼 𐐸𐐨 𐐼𐐮𐐼 𐑅𐐲𐐹𐐬𐑉𐐻 𐐸𐐮𐑆 𐑀𐐪𐑉𐐼𐑆 𐐵𐐻 𐐱𐑂 𐑄 𐐻𐑉𐐮𐐺𐐧𐐻 𐐸𐐶𐐮𐐽 𐐸𐐨 𐐼𐐮𐐼 𐑉𐐨𐑅𐐨𐑂 𐑁𐑉𐐱𐑋 𐑄 𐐤𐐨𐑁𐐴𐐻𐑅. 𐐈𐑌𐐼 𐑌𐐵 𐐿𐐮𐑍 𐐢𐐮𐑋𐐸𐐴 𐐼𐐮𐐼 𐐸𐐰𐑂 𐐿𐐱𐑌𐐻𐐮𐑌𐐧𐐲𐑊 𐐹𐐨𐑅 𐐮𐑌 𐐸𐐮𐑆 𐐿𐐮𐑍𐐼𐐲𐑋, 𐑁𐐫𐑉 𐑄 𐑅𐐹𐐩𐑅 𐐱𐑂 𐐻𐐭 𐐷𐐨𐑉𐑆, 𐑄𐐰𐐻 𐑄 𐐢𐐰𐑋𐐲𐑌𐐴𐐻𐑅 𐐼𐐮𐐼 𐑌𐐱𐐻 𐑋𐐬𐑊𐐯𐑅𐐻 𐑄𐐯𐑋 𐑌𐐫𐑉 𐑅𐐨𐐿 𐐻𐐭 𐐼𐐯𐑅𐐻𐑉𐑎 𐑄𐐯𐑋.

17. 𐐤𐐵 𐑄𐐯𐑉 𐐶𐐱𐑆 𐐲 𐐹𐑊𐐩𐑅 𐐮𐑌 𐐟𐐯𐑋𐑊𐐱𐑌, 𐐸𐐶𐐯𐑉 𐑄 𐐼𐐫𐐻𐐲𐑉𐑆 𐐱𐑂 𐑄 𐐢𐐰𐑋𐐲𐑌𐐴𐐻𐑅 𐐼𐐮𐐼 𐑀𐐰𐑄𐐲𐑉

𐑄𐐯𐑋𐑅𐐯𐑊𐑂𐑆 𐐻𐐭𐑀𐐯𐑄𐐲𐑉 𐐻𐐭 𐑅𐐮𐑍, 𐐰𐑌𐐼 𐐻𐐭 𐐼𐐰𐑌𐑅, 𐐰𐑌𐐼 𐐻𐐭 𐑋𐐩𐐿 𐑄𐐯𐑋𐑅𐐯𐑊𐑂𐑆 𐑋𐐯𐑉𐐨. 𐐈𐑌𐐼 𐐮𐐻 𐐿𐐩𐑋 𐐻𐐭 𐐹𐐰𐑅 𐑄𐐰𐐻 𐑄𐐯𐑉 𐐶𐐱𐑆 𐐶𐐲𐑌 𐐼𐐩 𐐫 𐑅𐑋𐐫𐑊 𐑌𐐲𐑋𐐺𐐲𐑉 𐐱𐑂 𐑄𐐯𐑋 𐑀𐐰𐑄𐐲𐑉𐐼 𐐻𐐭𐑀𐐯𐑄𐐲𐑉 𐐻𐐭 𐑅𐐮𐑍 𐐰𐑌𐐼 𐐻𐐭 𐐼𐐰𐑌𐑅. 𐐈𐑌𐐼 𐑌𐐵 𐑄 𐐹𐑉𐐨𐑅𐐻𐑅 𐐱𐑂 𐐿𐐮𐑍 𐐤𐐬𐐲, 𐐺𐐨𐐮𐑍 𐐲𐑇𐐩𐑋𐐼 𐐻𐐭 𐑉𐐨𐐻𐐲𐑉𐑌 𐐻𐐭 𐑄 𐑅𐐮𐐻𐐨 𐐱𐑂 𐐤𐐨𐑁𐐴, 𐐷𐐩, 𐐰𐑌𐐼 𐐫𐑊𐑅𐐬 𐑁𐐨𐑉𐐮𐑍 𐑄𐐰𐐻 𐑄 𐐹𐐨𐐹𐑊 𐑇𐐳𐐼 𐑅𐑊𐐩 𐑄𐐯𐑋, 𐑄𐐯𐑉𐑁𐐬𐑉 𐑄𐐩 𐐼𐐲𐑉𐑅𐐻 𐑌𐐱𐐻 𐑉𐐨𐐻𐐲𐑉𐑌 𐐻𐐭 𐑄𐐯𐑉 𐐶𐐴𐑂𐑆 𐐰𐑌𐐼 𐑄𐐯𐑉 𐐽𐐮𐑊𐐼𐑉𐐲𐑌. 𐐈𐑌𐐼 𐐸𐐰𐑂𐐮𐑍 𐐻𐐰𐑉𐐨𐐼 𐐮𐑌 𐑄 𐐶𐐮𐑊𐐼𐐲𐑉𐑌𐐯𐑅, 𐐰𐑌𐐼 𐐸𐐰𐑂𐐮𐑍 𐐼𐐮𐑅𐐿𐐲𐑂𐐲𐑉𐐼 𐑄 𐐼𐐫𐐻𐐲𐑉𐑆 𐐱𐑂 𐑄 𐐢𐐩𐑋𐐲𐑌𐐴𐐻𐑅, 𐑄𐐩 𐑊𐐩𐐼 𐐰𐑌𐐼 𐐶𐐱𐐽𐐻 𐑄𐐯𐑋; 𐐰𐑌𐐼 𐐶𐐯𐑌 𐑄𐐯𐑉 𐐶𐐲𐑉 𐐺𐐲𐐻 𐑁𐐷𐐭 𐐱𐑂 𐑄𐐯𐑋 𐑀𐐰𐑄𐐲𐑉𐐼 𐐻𐐭𐑀𐐯𐑄𐐲𐑉 𐐻𐐭 𐐼𐐰𐑌𐑅, 𐑄𐐩 𐐿𐐩𐑋 𐑁𐐬𐑉𐑃 𐐵𐐻 𐐱𐑂 𐑄𐐯𐑉 𐑅𐐨𐐿𐑉𐐯𐐻 𐐹𐑊𐐩𐑅𐐯𐑆, 𐐰𐑌𐐼 𐐻𐐳𐐿 𐑄𐐯𐑋 𐐰𐑌𐐼 𐐿𐐰𐑉𐐨𐐼 𐑄𐐯𐑋 𐐮𐑌𐐻𐐭 𐑄 𐐶𐐮𐑊𐐼𐐲𐑉𐑌𐐯𐑅; 𐐷𐐩, 𐐻𐐶𐐯𐑌𐐻𐐨 𐐰𐑌𐐼 𐑁𐐬𐑉 𐐱𐑂 𐑄 𐐼𐐫𐐻𐐲𐑉𐑆 𐐱𐑂 𐑄 𐐢𐐩𐑋𐐲𐑌𐐴𐐻𐑅 𐑄𐐩 𐐿𐐰𐑉𐐨𐐼 𐐮𐑌𐐻𐐭 𐑄 𐐶𐐮𐑊𐐼𐐲𐑉𐑌𐐯𐑅.

18. 𐐈𐑌𐐼 𐐮𐐻 𐐿𐐩𐑋 𐐻𐐭 𐐹𐐰𐑅 𐑄𐐰𐐻 𐐶𐐯𐑌 𐑄 𐐢𐐩𐑋𐐲𐑌𐐴𐐻𐑅 𐑁𐐵𐑌𐐼 𐑄𐐰𐐻 𐑄𐐯𐑉 𐐼𐐫𐐻𐐲𐑉𐑆 𐐸𐐰𐐼 𐐺𐐨𐑌 𐑋𐐮𐑅𐐮𐑍, 𐑄𐐩 𐐶𐐲𐑉 𐐰𐑍𐑀𐑉𐐨 𐐶𐐮𐑄 𐑄 𐐹𐐨𐐹𐑊 𐐱𐑂 𐐢𐐮𐑋𐐸𐐴; 𐑁𐐫𐑉 𐑄𐐩 𐑃𐐫𐐻 𐐮𐐻 𐐶𐐱𐑆 𐑄 𐐹𐐨𐐹𐑊 𐐱𐑂 𐐢𐐮𐑋𐐸𐐴. 𐐜𐐯𐑉𐑁𐐬𐑉 𐑄𐐩 𐑅𐐯𐑌𐐻 𐑄𐐯𐑉 𐐪𐑉𐑋𐐨𐑆 𐑁𐐬𐑉𐑃; 𐐷𐐩, 𐐨𐑂𐐲𐑌 𐑄 𐐿𐐮𐑍 𐐸𐐮𐑋𐑅𐐯𐑊𐑁 𐐶𐐯𐑌𐐻 𐐺𐐨𐑁𐐬𐑉 𐐸𐐮𐑆 𐐹𐐨𐐹𐑊; 𐐰𐑌𐐼 𐑄𐐩 𐐶𐐯𐑌𐐻 𐐲𐐹 𐐻𐐭 𐑄 𐑊𐐰𐑌𐐼 𐐱𐑂 𐐤𐐨𐑁𐐴, 𐐻𐐭 𐐼𐐨𐑅𐐻𐑉𐐱𐐫 𐑄 𐐹𐐨𐐹𐑊 𐐱𐑂 𐐢𐐮𐑋𐐸𐐴. 𐐈𐑌𐐼 𐑌𐐵 𐐢𐐮𐑋𐐸𐐴 𐐸𐐰𐐼 𐐼𐐮𐑅𐐿𐐲𐑂𐐲𐑉𐐼 𐑄𐐯𐑋 𐑁𐑉𐐱𐑋 𐑄 𐐻𐐵𐐲𐑉, 𐐨𐑂𐐲𐑌 𐐫𐑊 𐑄𐐯𐑉 𐐹𐑉𐐯𐐹𐐲𐑉𐐩𐑇𐐲𐑌𐑆 𐑁𐐬𐑉 𐐶𐐫𐑉 𐐼𐐮𐐼 𐐸𐐨 𐐼𐐮𐑅𐐿𐐲𐑂𐐲𐑉; 𐑄𐐯𐑉𐑁𐐬𐑉 𐐸𐐨 𐑀𐐰𐑄𐐲𐑉𐐼 𐐸𐐮𐑆 𐐹𐐨𐐹𐑊 𐐻𐐭𐑀𐐯𐑄𐐲𐑉, 𐐰𐑌𐐼 𐑊𐐩𐐼 𐐶𐐩𐐻 𐑁𐐬𐑉 𐑄𐐯𐑋 𐐮𐑌 𐑄 𐑁𐐨𐑊𐐼𐑆, 𐐰𐑌𐐼 𐐮𐑌 𐑄 𐑁𐐱𐑉𐐯𐑅𐐻𐑅. 𐐈𐑌𐐼 𐐮𐐻 𐐿𐐩𐑋 𐐻𐐭 𐐹𐐰𐑅 𐑄𐐰𐐻 𐐶𐐯𐑌 𐑄 𐐢𐐩𐑋𐐲𐑌𐐴𐐻𐑅 𐐸𐐰𐐼 𐐿𐐲𐑋 𐐲𐐹, 𐑄𐐰𐐻 𐑄 𐐹𐐨𐐹𐑊 𐐱𐑂 𐐢𐐮𐑋𐐸𐐴 𐐺𐐨𐑀𐐰𐑌 𐐻𐐭 𐑁𐐫𐑊 𐐲𐐹𐐱𐑌 𐑄𐐯𐑋 𐑁𐑉𐐱𐑋 𐑄𐐯𐑉 𐐶𐐩𐐻𐐮𐑍 𐐹𐑊𐐩𐑅𐐯𐑆, 𐐰𐑌𐐼 𐐺𐐨𐑀𐐰𐑌 𐐻𐐭 𐑅𐑊𐐩 𐑄𐐯𐑋.

19. 𐐈𐑌𐐼 𐐮𐐻 𐐿𐐩𐑋 𐐻𐐭 𐐹𐐰𐑅 𐑄𐐰𐐻 𐑄 𐐺𐐰𐐻𐑊 𐐺𐐨𐐿𐐩𐑋 𐐯𐐿𐑅𐐨𐐼𐐮𐑍𐑊𐐨 𐑅𐐬𐑉, 𐑁𐐬𐑉 𐑄𐐩 𐑁𐐫𐐻 𐑊𐐴𐐿 𐑊𐐴𐐲𐑌𐑆 𐑁𐐬𐑉 𐑄𐐯𐑉 𐐹𐑉𐐩. 𐐈𐑌𐐼 𐐮𐐻 𐐿𐐩𐑋 𐐻𐐭 𐐹𐐰𐑅 𐑄𐐰𐐻 𐑄 𐐹𐐨𐐹𐑊 𐐱𐑂 𐐢𐐮𐑋𐐸𐐴 𐐺𐐨𐑀𐐰𐑌 𐐻𐐭 𐐼𐑉𐐴𐑂 𐑄 𐐢𐐩𐑋𐐲𐑌𐐴𐐻𐑅 𐐺𐐨𐑁𐐬𐑉 𐑄𐐯𐑋; 𐐷𐐯𐐻 𐑄𐐩 𐐶𐐲𐑉 𐑌𐐱𐐻 𐐸𐐪𐑁 𐑅𐐬 𐑌𐐷𐐭𐑋𐐲𐑉𐐲𐑅 𐐰𐑆 𐑄 𐐢𐐩𐑋𐐲𐑌𐐴𐐻𐑅. 𐐒𐐲𐐻 𐑄𐐩 𐑁𐐫𐐻 𐑁𐐬𐑉 𐑄𐐯𐑉 𐑊𐐴𐑂𐑆, 𐐰𐑌𐐼 𐑁𐐬𐑉 𐑄𐐯𐑉 𐐶𐐴𐑂𐑆, 𐐰𐑌𐐼 𐑁𐐬𐑉 𐑄𐐯𐑉 𐐽𐐮𐑊𐐼𐑉𐐲𐑌; 𐑄𐐯𐑉𐑁𐐬𐑉 𐑄𐐩 𐐯𐑀𐑆𐐲𐑉𐐻𐐲𐐼 𐑄𐐯𐑋𐑅𐐯𐑊𐑂𐑆, 𐐰𐑌𐐼 𐑊𐐴𐐿 𐐼𐑉𐐰𐑀𐐲𐑌𐑆 𐐼𐐮𐐼 𐑄𐐩 𐑁𐐴𐐻.

20. 𐐈𐑌𐐼 𐐮𐐻 𐐿𐐩𐑋 𐐻𐐭 𐐹𐐰𐑅 𐑄𐐰𐐻 𐑄𐐩 𐑁𐐵𐑌𐐼 𐑄 𐐿𐐮𐑍 𐐱𐑂 𐑄 𐐢𐐩𐑋𐐲𐑌𐐴𐐻𐑅 𐐲𐑋𐐲𐑍 𐑄 𐑌𐐲𐑋𐐺𐐲𐑉 𐐱𐑂 𐑄𐐯𐑉 𐐼𐐯𐐼; 𐐷𐐯𐐻 𐐸𐐨 𐐶𐐱𐑆 𐑌𐐱𐐻 𐐼𐐯𐐼, 𐐸𐐰𐑂𐐮𐑍 𐐺𐐨𐑌 𐐶𐐭𐑌𐐼𐐲𐐼 𐐰𐑌𐐼 𐑊𐐯𐑁𐐻 𐐲𐐹𐐱𐑌 𐑄 𐑀𐑉𐐵𐑌𐐼, 𐑅𐐬 𐑅𐐹𐐨𐐼𐐨 𐐶𐐱𐑆 𐑄 𐑁𐑊𐐴𐐻 𐐱𐑂 𐐸𐐮𐑆 𐐹𐐨𐐹𐑊. 𐐈𐑌𐐼 𐑄𐐩 𐐻𐐳𐐿 𐐸𐐮𐑋 𐐰𐑌𐐼 𐐺𐐵𐑌𐐼 𐐲𐐹 𐐸𐐮𐑆 𐐶𐐭𐑌𐐼𐑆, 𐐰𐑌𐐼 𐐺𐑉𐐫𐐻 𐐸𐐮𐑋 𐐺𐐨𐑁𐐬𐑉 𐐢𐐮𐑋𐐸𐐴, 𐐰𐑌𐐼 𐑅𐐯𐐼, 𐐒𐐨𐐸𐐬𐑊𐐼, 𐐸𐐨𐑉 𐐮𐑆 𐑄 𐐿𐐮𐑍 𐐱𐑂 𐑄 𐐢𐐩𐑋𐐲𐑌𐐴𐐻𐑅; 𐐸𐐨 𐐸𐐰𐑂𐐮𐑍 𐑉𐐨𐑅𐐨𐑂𐐼 𐐫 𐐶𐐭𐑌𐐼, 𐐸𐐰𐑆 𐑁𐐫𐑊𐐲𐑌 𐐲𐑋𐐲𐑍 𐑄𐐯𐑉 𐐼𐐯𐐼, 𐐰𐑌𐐼 𐑄𐐩 𐐸𐐰𐑂 𐑊𐐯𐑁𐐻 𐐸𐐮𐑋; 𐐰𐑌𐐼 𐐺𐐨𐐸𐐬𐑊𐐼, 𐐶𐐨 𐐸𐐰𐑂 𐐺𐑉𐐫𐐻 𐐸𐐮𐑋 𐐺𐐨𐑁𐐬𐑉 𐐷𐐭; 𐐰𐑌𐐼 𐑌𐐵 𐑊𐐯𐐻 𐐲𐑅 𐑅𐑊𐐩 𐐸𐐮𐑋. 𐐒𐐲𐐻 𐐢𐐮𐑋𐐸𐐴 𐑅𐐯𐐼 𐐲𐑌𐐻𐐭 𐑄𐐯𐑋, 𐐐𐐨 𐑇𐐰𐑊 𐑌𐐱𐐻 𐑅𐑊𐐩 𐐸𐐮𐑋, 𐐺𐐲𐐻 𐐺𐑉𐐮𐑍 𐐸𐐮𐑋 𐐸𐐮𐑄𐐲𐑉 𐑄𐐰𐐻 𐐌 𐑋𐐩 𐑅𐐨 𐐸𐐮𐑋. 𐐈𐑌𐐼 𐑄𐐩 𐐺𐑉𐐫𐐻 𐐸𐐮𐑋. 𐐈𐑌𐐼 𐐢𐐮𐑋𐐸𐐴 𐑅𐐯𐐼 𐐲𐑌𐐻𐐭 𐐸𐐮𐑋, 𐐐𐐶𐐱𐐻 𐐿𐐫𐑆 𐐸𐐰𐑂 𐐷𐐨 𐐻𐐭 𐐿𐐲𐑋 𐐲𐐹 𐐻𐐭 𐐶𐐫𐑉 𐐰𐑀𐐯𐑌𐑅𐐻 𐑋𐐴 𐐹𐐨𐐹𐑊? 𐐒𐐨𐐸𐐬𐑊𐐼, 𐑋𐐴 𐐹𐐨𐐹𐑊 𐐸𐐰𐑂 𐑌𐐱𐐻 𐐺𐑉𐐬𐐿𐑌 𐑄 𐐬𐑃 𐑄𐐰𐐻 𐐌 𐑋𐐩𐐼 𐐲𐑌𐐻𐐭 𐐷𐐭; 𐑄𐐯𐑉𐑁𐐬𐑉 𐐸𐐶𐐴 𐑇𐐳𐐼 𐐷𐐨 𐐺𐑉𐐩𐐿 𐑄 𐐬𐑃 𐐸𐐶𐐮𐐽 𐐷𐐨 𐑋𐐩𐐼 𐐲𐑌𐐻𐐭 𐑋𐐴 𐐹𐐨𐐹𐑊?

21. 𐐈𐑌𐐼 𐑌𐐵 𐑄 𐐿𐐮𐑍 𐑅𐐯𐐼, 𐐌 𐐸𐐰𐑂 𐐺𐑉𐐬𐐿𐑌 𐑄 𐐬𐑃, 𐐺𐐨𐐿𐐫𐑆 𐑄𐐴 𐐹𐐨𐐹𐑊 𐐼𐐮𐐼 𐐿𐐰𐑉𐐨 𐐲𐐶𐐩 𐑄 𐐼𐐫𐐻𐐲𐑉𐑆 𐐱𐑂 𐑋𐐴 𐐹𐐨𐐹𐑊; 𐑄𐐯𐑉𐑁𐐬𐑉, 𐐮𐑌 𐑋𐐴 𐐰𐑍𐑀𐐲𐑉 𐐌 𐐼𐐮𐐼 𐐿𐐫𐑆 𐑋𐐴 𐐹𐐨𐐹𐑊 𐐻𐐭 𐐿𐐲𐑋 𐐲𐐹 𐐻𐐭 𐐶𐐫𐑉 𐐰𐑀𐐯𐑌𐑅𐐻 𐑄𐐴 𐐹𐐨𐐹𐑊. 𐐈𐑌𐐼 𐑌𐐵 𐐢𐐮𐑋𐐸𐐴 𐐸𐐰𐐼 𐐸𐐲𐑉𐐼 𐑌𐐲𐑃𐐮𐑍 𐐿𐐲𐑌𐑅𐐲𐑉𐑌𐐮𐑍 𐑄𐐮𐑅 𐑋𐐰𐐻𐐲𐑉; 𐑄𐐯𐑉𐑁𐐬𐑉 𐐸𐐨 𐑅𐐯𐐼, 𐐌 𐐶𐐮𐑊 𐑅𐐲𐑉𐐽 𐐲𐑋𐐲𐑍 𐑋𐐴 𐐹𐐨𐐹𐑊, 𐐰𐑌𐐼 𐐸𐐭𐑅𐐬𐐯𐑂𐐲𐑉 𐐸𐐰𐑆 𐐼𐐲𐑌 𐑄𐐮𐑅 𐑃𐐮𐑍 𐑇𐐰𐑊 𐐹𐐯𐑉𐐮𐑇. 𐐜𐐯𐑉𐑁𐐬𐑉 𐐸𐐨 𐐿𐐫𐑆𐐼 𐐫 𐑅𐐲𐑉𐐽 𐐻𐐭 𐐺𐐨 𐑋𐐩𐐼 𐐲𐑋𐐲𐑍 𐐸𐐮𐑆 𐐹𐐨𐐹𐑊. 𐐤𐐵 𐐸𐐶𐐯𐑌 𐐘𐐮𐐼𐐨𐐲𐑌 𐐸𐐰𐐼 𐐸𐐲𐑉𐐼 𐑄𐐨𐑆 𐑃𐐮𐑍𐑆, 𐐸𐐨 𐐺𐐨𐐮𐑍 𐑄 𐐿𐐮𐑍'𐑆 𐐿𐐰𐐹𐐻𐐲𐑌, 𐐸𐐨 𐐶𐐯𐑌𐐻 𐑁𐐬𐑉𐑃 𐐰𐑌𐐼 𐑅𐐯𐐼 𐐲𐑌𐐻𐐭 𐑄 𐐿𐐮𐑍, 𐐌 𐐹𐑉𐐩 𐑄𐐨 𐑁𐐬𐑉𐐺𐐯𐑉, 𐐰𐑌𐐼 𐐼𐐭 𐑌𐐱𐐻 𐑅𐐲𐑉𐐽 𐑄𐐮𐑅 𐐹𐐨𐐹𐑊, 𐐰𐑌𐐼 𐑊𐐩 𐑌𐐱𐐻 𐑄𐐮𐑅 𐑃𐐮𐑍 𐐻𐐭 𐑄𐐯𐑉 𐐽𐐪𐑉𐑈. 𐐙𐐬𐑉 𐐼𐐭 𐐷𐐨 𐑌𐐱𐐻 𐑉𐐨𐑋𐐯𐑋𐐺𐐲𐑉 𐑄 𐐹𐑉𐐨𐑅𐐻𐑅 𐐱𐑂 𐑄𐐴 𐑁𐐪𐑄𐐲𐑉, 𐐸𐐭𐑋 𐑄𐐮𐑅 𐐹𐐨𐐹𐑊 𐑅𐐫𐐻 𐐻𐐭 𐐼𐐨𐑅𐐻𐑉𐐱𐐫? 𐐈𐑌𐐼 𐐪𐑉 𐑄𐐩 𐑌𐐱𐐻 𐐮𐑌 𐑄 𐐶𐐮𐑊𐐼𐐲𐑉𐑌𐐯𐑅? 𐐈𐑌𐐼 𐐪𐑉 𐑌𐐱𐐻 𐑄𐐩 𐑄 𐐶𐐲𐑌𐑆 𐐸𐐭 𐐸𐐰𐑂 𐑅𐐻𐐬𐑊𐑌 𐑄 𐐼𐐫𐐻𐐲𐑉𐑆 𐐱𐑂 𐑄

𐐢𐐰𐑋𐐲𐑌𐐴𐐻𐑅? 𐐈𐑌𐐼 𐑌𐐵 𐐺𐐨𐐸𐐬𐑊𐐼, 𐐰𐑌𐐼 𐐻𐐯𐑊 𐑄 𐐿𐐮𐑍 𐐱𐑂 𐑄𐐨𐑆 𐑃𐐮𐑍𐑆, 𐑄𐐰𐐻 𐐸𐐨 𐑋𐐩 𐐻𐐯𐑊 𐐸𐐮𐑆 𐐹𐐨𐐹𐑊 𐑄𐐰𐐻 𐑄𐐩 𐑋𐐩 𐐺𐐨 𐐹𐐰𐑅𐐮𐑁𐐴𐐼 𐐻𐐬𐐲𐑉𐐼𐑆 𐐲𐑅: 𐑁𐐫𐑉 𐐺𐐨𐐸𐐬𐑊𐐼 𐑄𐐩 𐐪𐑉 𐐫𐑊𐑉𐐯𐐼𐐨 𐐹𐑉𐐨𐐹𐐩𐑉𐐮𐑍 𐐻𐐭 𐐿𐐲𐑋 𐐰𐑀𐐯𐑌𐑅𐐻 𐐲𐑅; 𐐰𐑌𐐼 𐐺𐐨𐐸𐐬𐑊𐐼 𐐫𐑊𐑅𐐬, 𐑄𐐩𐑉 𐐪𐑉 𐐺𐐲𐐻 𐑁𐐷𐐭 𐐱𐑂 𐐲𐑅. 𐐈𐑌𐐼 𐐺𐐨𐐸𐐬𐑊𐐼, 𐑄𐐩 𐐿𐐲𐑋 𐐶𐐮𐑄 𐑄𐐩𐑉 𐑌𐐷𐐭𐑋𐐲𐑉𐐲𐑅 𐐸𐐬𐑅𐐻𐑅; 𐐰𐑌𐐼 𐐯𐐿𐑅𐐯𐐹𐐻 𐑄 𐐿𐐮𐑍 𐐼𐐲𐑃 𐐹𐐰𐑅𐐮𐑁𐐴 𐑄𐐯𐑋 𐐻𐐬𐐲𐑉𐐼𐑆 𐐲𐑅, 𐐶𐐨 𐑋𐐲𐑅𐐻 𐐹𐐯𐑉𐐮𐑇. 𐐙𐐫𐑉 𐐪𐑉 𐑌𐐱𐐻 𐑄 𐐶𐐲𐑉𐐼𐑆 𐐱𐑂 𐐈𐐺𐐮𐑌𐐪𐐼𐐴 𐑁𐐳𐑊𐑁𐐮𐑊𐐼, 𐐸𐐶𐐮𐐽 𐐸𐐨 𐐹𐑉𐐱𐑁𐐯𐑅𐐴𐐼 𐐰𐑀𐐯𐑌𐑅𐐻 𐐲𐑅? 𐐈𐑌𐐼 𐐫𐑊 𐑄𐐮𐑅 𐐺𐐨𐐿𐐫𐑆 𐐶𐐨 𐐶𐐳𐐼 𐑌𐐱𐐻 𐐸𐐪𐑉𐐿𐑌 𐐲𐑌𐐻𐐭 𐑄 𐐶𐐲𐑉𐐼𐑆 𐐱𐑂 𐑄 𐐢𐐫𐑉𐐼, 𐐰𐑌𐐼 𐐻𐐲𐑉𐑌 𐑁𐑉𐐱𐑋 𐐵𐑉 𐐮𐑌𐐮𐐿𐐶𐐮𐐻𐐮𐑆? 𐐈𐑌𐐼 𐑌𐐵 𐑊𐐯𐐻 𐐲𐑅 𐐹𐐰𐑅𐐮𐑁𐐴 𐑄 𐐿𐐮𐑍, 𐐰𐑌𐐼 𐐶𐐨 𐑁𐐳𐑊𐑁𐐮𐑊 𐑄 𐐬𐑃 𐐸𐐶𐐮𐐽 𐐶𐐨 𐐸𐐰𐑂 𐑋𐐩𐐼 𐐲𐑌𐐻𐐭 𐐸𐐮𐑋: 𐑁𐐫𐑉 𐐮𐐻 𐐮𐑆 𐐺𐐯𐐻𐐲𐑉 𐑄𐐰𐐻 𐐶𐐨 𐑇𐐳𐐼 𐐺𐐨 𐐮𐑌 𐐺𐐱𐑌𐐼𐐩𐐾, 𐑄𐐰𐑌 𐑄𐐰𐐻 𐐶𐐨 𐑇𐐳𐐼 𐑊𐐭𐑆 𐐵𐑉 𐑊𐐴𐑂𐑆; 𐑄𐐩𐑉𐑁𐐫𐑉, 𐑊𐐯𐐻 𐐲𐑅 𐐹𐐳𐐻 𐐲 𐑅𐐻𐐱𐐹 𐐻𐐭 𐑄 𐑇𐐯𐐼𐐮𐑍 𐐱𐑂 𐑅𐐬 𐑋𐐲𐐽 𐐺𐑊𐐲𐐼. 𐐈𐑌𐐼 𐑌𐐵 𐐢𐐮𐑋𐐸𐐴 𐐻𐐬𐑊𐐼 𐑄 𐐿𐐮𐑍 𐐫𐑊 𐑄 𐑃𐐮𐑍𐑆 𐐿𐐲𐑌𐑅𐐲𐑉𐑌𐐮𐑍 𐐸𐐮𐑆 𐑁𐐪𐑄𐐲𐑉, 𐐰𐑌𐐼 𐑄 𐐹𐑉𐐨𐑅𐐻𐑅 𐑄𐐰𐐻 𐐸𐐰𐐼 𐑁𐑊𐐯𐐼 𐐮𐑌𐐻𐐭 𐑄 𐐶𐐮𐑊𐐼𐐲𐑉𐑌𐐯𐑅, 𐐰𐑌𐐼 𐐰𐐻𐐻𐑉𐐮𐐺𐐷𐐭𐐻𐐯𐐼 𐑄 𐐿𐐰𐑉𐐨𐐮𐑍 𐐰𐐶𐐩 𐐱𐑂 𐑄𐐩𐑉 𐐼𐐫𐐻𐐲𐑉𐑆 𐐻𐐭 𐑄𐐯𐑋.

22. 𐐈𐑌𐐼 𐐮𐐻 𐐿𐐩𐑋 𐐻𐐭 𐐹𐐪𐑅 𐑄𐐰𐐻 𐑄 𐐿𐐮𐑍 𐐶𐐱𐑆 𐐹𐐰𐑅𐐮𐑁𐐴𐐼 𐐻𐐬𐐲𐑉𐐼𐑆 𐐸𐐮𐑆 𐐹𐐨𐐹𐑊: 𐐰𐑌𐐼 𐐸𐐨 𐑅𐐯𐐼 𐐲𐑌𐐻𐐭 𐑄𐐯𐑋, 𐐢𐐯𐐻 𐐲𐑅 𐑀𐐬 𐑁𐐫𐑉𐑃 𐐻𐐭 𐑋𐐨𐐻 𐑋𐐴 𐐹𐐨𐐹𐑊, 𐐶𐐮𐑄𐐵𐐻 𐐪𐑉𐑋𐑆; 𐐰𐑌𐐼 𐐌 𐑅𐐶𐐩𐑉 𐐲𐑌𐐻𐐭 𐐷𐐭 𐐶𐐮𐑄 𐐰𐑌 𐐬𐑃, 𐑄𐐰𐐻 𐑋𐐴 𐐹𐐨𐐹𐑊 𐑇𐐰𐑊 𐑌𐐱𐐻 𐑅𐑊𐐩 𐑄𐐴 𐐹𐐨𐐹𐑊. 𐐈𐑌𐐼 𐐮𐐻 𐐿𐐩𐑋 𐐻𐐭 𐐹𐐪𐑅 𐑄𐐰𐐻 𐑄𐐩 𐑁𐐱𐑊𐐬𐐼 𐑄 𐐿𐐮𐑍, 𐐰𐑌𐐼 𐐶𐐯𐑌𐐻 𐑁𐐫𐑉𐑃 𐐶𐐮𐑄𐐵𐐻 𐐪𐑉𐑋𐑆 𐐻𐐭 𐑋𐐨𐐻 𐑄 𐐢𐐰𐑋𐐲𐑌𐐴𐐻𐑅. 𐐈𐑌𐐼 𐐮𐐻 𐐿𐐩𐑋 𐐻𐐭 𐐹𐐪𐑅 𐑄𐐰𐐻 𐑄𐐩 𐐼𐐮𐐼 𐑋𐐨𐐻 𐑄 𐐢𐐰𐑋𐐲𐑌𐐴𐐻𐑅; 𐐰𐑌𐐼 𐑄 𐐿𐐮𐑍 𐐱𐑂 𐑄 𐐢𐐰𐑋𐐲𐑌𐐴𐐻𐑅 𐐼𐐮𐐼 𐐺𐐵 𐐸𐐮𐑋𐑅𐐯𐑊𐑁 𐐼𐐵𐑌 𐐺𐐨𐑁𐐬𐑉 𐑄𐐯𐑋, 𐐰𐑌𐐼 𐐼𐐮𐐼 𐐹𐑊𐐨𐐼 𐐮𐑌 𐐺𐐨𐐸𐐪𐑁 𐐱𐑂 𐑄 𐐹𐐨𐐹𐑊 𐐱𐑂 𐐢𐐮𐑋𐐸𐐴. 𐐈𐑌𐐼 𐐸𐐶𐐯𐑌 𐑄 𐐢𐐰𐑋𐐲𐑌𐐴𐐻𐑅 𐑅𐐫 𐑄 𐐹𐐨𐐹𐑊 𐐱𐑂 𐐢𐐮𐑋𐐸𐐴, 𐑄𐐰𐐻 𐑄𐐩 𐐶𐐲𐑉 𐐶𐐮𐑄𐐵𐐻 𐐪𐑉𐑋𐑆, 𐑄𐐩 𐐸𐐰𐐼 𐐿𐐱𐑋𐐹𐐰𐑇𐐲𐑌 𐐱𐑌 𐑄𐐯𐑋, 𐐰𐑌𐐼 𐐶𐐲𐑉 𐐹𐐰𐑅𐐮𐑁𐐴𐐼 𐐻𐐬𐐲𐑉𐐼𐑆 𐑄𐐯𐑋, 𐐰𐑌𐐼 𐑉𐐨𐐻𐐲𐑉𐑌𐐼 𐐶𐐮𐑄 𐑄𐐩𐑉 𐐿𐐮𐑍 𐐮𐑌 𐐹𐐨𐑅 𐐻𐐭 𐑄𐐩𐑉 𐐬𐑌 𐑊𐐰𐑌𐐼.

23. 𐐈𐑌𐐼 𐐮𐐻 𐐿𐐩𐑋 𐐻𐐭 𐐹𐐪𐑅 𐑄𐐰𐐻 𐐢𐐮𐑋𐐸𐐴 𐐰𐑌𐐼 𐐸𐐮𐑆 𐐹𐐨𐐹𐑊 𐑉𐐨𐐻𐐲𐑉𐑌𐐼 𐐻𐐭 𐑄 𐑅𐐮𐐻𐐨 𐐱𐑂 𐐤𐐨𐑁𐐴, 𐐰𐑌𐐼 𐐺𐐨𐑀𐐰𐑌 𐐻𐐭 𐐼𐐶𐐯𐑊 𐐮𐑌 𐑄 𐑊𐐰𐑌𐐼 𐐰𐑀𐐯𐑌 𐐮𐑌 𐐹𐐨𐑅. 𐐈𐑌𐐼 𐐮𐐻 𐐿𐐩𐑋 𐐻𐐭 𐐹𐐪𐑅 𐑄𐐰𐐻 𐐪𐑁𐐻𐐲𐑉 𐑋𐐯𐑌𐐨 𐐼𐐩𐑆, 𐑄 𐐢𐐰𐑋𐐲𐑌𐐴𐐻𐑅 𐐺𐐨𐑀𐐰𐑌 𐐰𐑀𐐯𐑌 𐐻𐐭 𐐺𐐨 𐑅𐐻𐐲𐑉𐐼 𐐲𐐹 𐐮𐑌 𐐰𐑍𐑀𐐲𐑉 𐐰𐑀𐐯𐑌𐑅𐐻 𐑄 𐐤𐐨𐑁𐐴𐐻𐑅, 𐐰𐑌𐐼 𐑄𐐩 𐐺𐐨𐑀𐐰𐑌 𐐻𐐭 𐐿𐐲𐑋 𐐮𐑌𐐻𐐭 𐑄 𐐺𐐫𐑉𐐼𐐲𐑉𐑆 𐐱𐑂 𐑄 𐑊𐐰𐑌𐐼 𐑉𐐵𐑌𐐼 𐐰𐐺𐐵𐐻. 𐐤𐐵 𐑄𐐩 𐐼𐐲𐑉𐑅𐐻 𐑌𐐱𐐻 𐑅𐑊𐐩 𐑄𐐯𐑋, 𐐺𐐨𐐿𐐫𐑆 𐐱𐑂 𐑄 𐐬𐑃 𐐸𐐶𐐮𐐽 𐑄𐐩𐑉 𐐿𐐮𐑍 𐐸𐐰𐐼 𐑋𐐩𐐼 𐐲𐑌𐐻𐐭 𐐢𐐮𐑋𐐸𐐴; 𐐺𐐲𐐻 𐑄𐐩 𐐶𐐳𐐼 𐑅𐑋𐐴𐐻 𐑄𐐯𐑋 𐐱𐑌 𐑄𐐩𐑉 𐐽𐐨𐐿𐑅, 𐐰𐑌𐐼 𐐯𐐿𐑅𐐲𐑉𐑅𐐴𐑆 𐐫𐑃𐐱𐑉𐐮𐐻𐐨 𐐬𐑂𐐲𐑉 𐑄𐐯𐑋; 𐐰𐑌𐐼 𐐺𐐨𐑀𐐰𐑌 𐐻𐐭 𐐹𐐳𐐻 𐐸𐐯𐑂𐐨 𐐺𐐲𐑉𐐼𐑌𐑆 𐐲𐐹𐐱𐑌 𐑄𐐩𐑉 𐐺𐐰𐐿𐑅, 𐐰𐑌𐐼 𐐼𐑉𐐴𐑂 𐑄𐐯𐑋 𐐰𐑆 𐑄𐐩 𐐶𐐳𐐼 𐐲 𐐼𐐲𐑋 𐐰𐑅; 𐐏𐐩, 𐐫𐑊 𐑄𐐮𐑅 𐐶𐐱𐑆 𐐼𐐲𐑌 𐑄𐐰𐐻 𐑄 𐐶𐐲𐑉𐐼 𐐱𐑂 𐑄 𐐢𐐫𐑉𐐼 𐑋𐐴𐐻 𐐺𐐨 𐑁𐐳𐑊𐑁𐐮𐑊𐐼. 𐐈𐑌𐐼 𐑌𐐵 𐑄 𐐰𐑁𐑊𐐮𐐿𐑇𐐲𐑌𐑆 𐐱𐑂 𐑄 𐐤𐐨𐑁𐐴𐐻𐑅 𐐶𐐲𐑉 𐑀𐑉𐐩𐐻, 𐐰𐑌𐐼 𐑄𐐩𐑉 𐐶𐐱𐑆 𐑌𐐬 𐐶𐐩 𐑄𐐰𐐻 𐑄𐐩 𐐿𐐳𐐼 𐐼𐐨𐑊𐐮𐑂𐐲𐑉 𐑄𐐯𐑋𐑅𐐯𐑊𐑂𐑆 𐐵𐐻 𐐱𐑂 𐑄𐐩𐑉 𐐸𐐰𐑌𐐼𐑆, 𐑁𐐫𐑉 𐑄 𐐢𐐰𐑋𐐲𐑌𐐴𐐻𐑅 𐐸𐐰𐐼 𐑅𐐲𐑉𐐵𐑌𐐼𐐯𐐼 𐑄𐐯𐑋 𐐱𐑌 𐐯𐑂𐐲𐑉𐐨 𐑅𐐴𐐼.

24. 𐐈𐑌𐐼 𐐮𐐻 𐐿𐐩𐑋 𐐻𐐭 𐐹𐐪𐑅 𐑄𐐰𐐻 𐑄 𐐹𐐨𐐹𐑊 𐐺𐐨𐑀𐐰𐑌 𐐻𐐭 𐑋𐐲𐑉𐑋𐐲𐑉 𐐶𐐮𐑄 𐑄 𐐿𐐮𐑍, 𐐺𐐨𐐿𐐫𐑆 𐐱𐑂 𐑄𐐩𐑉 𐐰𐑁𐑊𐐮𐐿𐑇𐐲𐑌𐑆; 𐐰𐑌𐐼 𐑄𐐩 𐐺𐐨𐑀𐐰𐑌 𐐻𐐭 𐐺𐐨 𐐼𐐨𐑆𐐴𐑉𐐲𐑅 𐐻𐐭 𐑀𐐬 𐐰𐑀𐐯𐑌𐑅𐐻 𐑄𐐯𐑋 𐐻𐐭 𐐺𐐰𐐻𐑊. 𐐈𐑌𐐼 𐑄𐐩 𐐼𐐮𐐼 𐐰𐑁𐑊𐐮𐐿𐐻 𐑄 𐐿𐐮𐑍 𐑅𐐬𐑉𐑊𐐨 𐐶𐐮𐑄 𐑄𐐩𐑉 𐐿𐐱𐑋𐐹𐑊𐐩𐑌𐐻𐑅; 𐑄𐐩𐑉𐑁𐐫𐑉 𐐸𐐨 𐑀𐑉𐐰𐑌𐐻𐐯𐐼 𐐲𐑌𐐻𐐭 𐑄𐐯𐑋 𐑄𐐰𐐻 𐑄𐐩 𐑇𐐳𐐼 𐐼𐐭 𐐰𐐿𐐫𐑉𐐼𐐮𐑍 𐐻𐐭 𐑄𐐩𐑉 𐐼𐐨𐑆𐐴𐑉𐑆. 𐐈𐑌𐐼 𐑄𐐩 𐑀𐐰𐑄𐐲𐑉𐐼 𐑄𐐯𐑋𐑅𐐯𐑊𐑂𐑆 𐐻𐐭𐑀𐐯𐑄𐐲𐑉 𐐰𐑀𐐯𐑌, 𐐰𐑌𐐼 𐐹𐐳𐐻 𐐱𐑌 𐑄𐐩𐑉 𐐪𐑉𐑋𐐲𐑉, 𐐰𐑌𐐼 𐐶𐐯𐑌𐐻 𐑁𐐫𐑉𐑃 𐐰𐑀𐐯𐑌𐑅𐐻 𐑄 𐐢𐐰𐑋𐐲𐑌𐐴𐐻𐑅 𐐻𐐭 𐐼𐑉𐐴𐑂 𐑄𐐯𐑋 𐐵𐐻 𐐱𐑂 𐑄𐐩𐑉 𐑊𐐰𐑌𐐼. 𐐈𐑌𐐼 𐐮𐐻 𐐿𐐩𐑋 𐐻𐐭 𐐹𐐪𐑅 𐑄𐐰𐐻 𐑄 𐐢𐐰𐑋𐐲𐑌𐐴𐐻𐑅 𐐼𐐮𐐼 𐐺𐐨𐐻 𐑄𐐯𐑋, 𐐰𐑌𐐼 𐐼𐑉𐐬𐑂 𐑄𐐯𐑋 𐐺𐐰𐐿, 𐐰𐑌𐐼 𐑅𐑊𐐭 𐑋𐐯𐑌𐐨 𐐱𐑂 𐑄𐐯𐑋. 𐐈𐑌𐐼 𐑌𐐵 𐑄𐐩𐑉 𐐶𐐱𐑆 𐐲 𐑀𐑉𐐩𐐻 𐑋𐐬𐑉𐑌𐐮𐑍 𐐰𐑌𐐼 𐑊𐐰𐑋𐐯𐑌𐐻𐐩𐑇𐐲𐑌 𐐰𐑋𐐲𐑍 𐑄 𐐹𐐨𐐹𐑊 𐐱𐑂 𐐢𐐮𐑋𐐸𐐴; 𐑄 𐐶𐐮𐐼𐐬 𐑋𐐬𐑉𐑌𐐮𐑍 𐑁𐐫𐑉 𐐸𐐲𐑉 𐐸𐐲𐑆𐐺𐐲𐑌𐐼; 𐑄 𐑅𐐲𐑌 𐐰𐑌𐐼 𐑄 𐐼𐐫𐐻𐐲𐑉 𐑋𐐬𐑉𐑌𐐮𐑍 𐑁𐐫𐑉 𐑄𐐩𐑉 𐑁𐐪𐑄𐐲𐑉; 𐐰𐑌𐐼 𐑄 𐐺𐑉𐐲𐑄𐐲𐑉𐑆 𐑁𐐫𐑉 𐑄𐐩𐑉 𐐺𐑉𐐯𐑄𐑉𐐯𐑌. 𐐤𐐵 𐑄𐐩𐑉 𐐶𐐲𐑉 𐐲 𐑀𐑉𐐩𐐻 𐑋𐐯𐑌𐐨 𐐶𐐮𐐼𐐬𐑆 𐐮𐑌 𐑄 𐑊𐐰𐑌𐐼, 𐐰𐑌𐐼 𐑄𐐩 𐐼𐐮𐐼 𐐿𐑉𐐴 𐑋𐐴𐐻𐐮𐑊𐐨 𐑁𐑉𐐱𐑋 𐐼𐐩 𐐻𐐭 𐐼𐐩, 𐑁𐐫𐑉 𐐲 𐑀𐑉𐐩𐐻 𐑁𐐨𐑉 𐐱𐑂 𐑄 𐐢𐐰𐑋𐐲𐑌𐐴𐐻𐑅 𐐸𐐰𐐼 𐐿𐐲𐑋 𐐲𐐹𐐱𐑌 𐑄𐐯𐑋. 𐐈𐑌𐐼 𐐮𐐻 𐐿𐐩𐑋 𐐻𐐭 𐐹𐐪𐑅 𐑄𐐰𐐻 𐑄𐐩𐑉 𐐿𐐱𐑌𐐻𐐮𐑌𐐷𐐭𐐲𐑊 𐐿𐑉𐐴𐑆 𐐼𐐮𐐼 𐑅𐐻𐐲𐑉 𐐲𐐹 𐑄 𐑉𐐯𐑋𐑌𐐰𐑌𐐻 𐐱𐑂 𐑄 𐐹𐐨𐐹𐑊 𐐱𐑂 𐐢𐐮𐑋𐐸𐐴 𐐻𐐭 𐐰𐑍𐑀𐐲𐑉 𐐰𐑀𐐯𐑌𐑅𐐻 𐑄 𐐢𐐰𐑋𐐲𐑌𐐴𐐻𐑅; 𐐰𐑌𐐼

𐑄𐐩 𐐶𐐯𐑌𐐻 𐐲𐑀𐐯𐑌 𐐻𐐭 𐐺𐐰𐐻𐑊, 𐐺𐐲𐐻 𐑄𐐩 𐐶𐐲𐑉 𐐼𐑉𐐮𐑂𐑌 𐐺𐐰𐐿 𐐲𐑀𐐯𐑌, 𐑅𐐲𐑁𐐲𐑉𐐮𐑍 𐑋𐐲𐐽 𐑊𐐱𐑅. 𐐏𐐩, 𐑄𐐩 𐐶𐐯𐑌𐐻 𐐲𐑀𐐯𐑌 𐐨𐑂𐑌 𐑄 𐑃𐐲𐑉𐐼 𐐻𐐴𐑋, 𐐰𐑌𐐼 𐑅𐐲𐑁𐐲𐑉𐐼 𐐮𐑌 𐑄 𐑊𐐴𐐿 𐑋𐐰𐑌𐐲𐑉; 𐐰𐑌𐐼 𐑄𐐬𐑆 𐑄𐐰𐐻 𐐶𐐲𐑉 𐑌𐐱𐐻 𐑅𐑊𐐩𐑌 𐑉𐐨𐐻𐐲𐑉𐑌𐐼 𐐲𐑀𐐯𐑌 𐐻𐐭 𐑄 𐑅𐐮𐐻𐐮 𐐱𐑂 𐐤𐐨𐑁𐐴. 𐐰𐑌𐐼 𐑄𐐩 𐐼𐐮𐐼 𐐸𐐲𐑋𐐺𐑊 𐑄𐐯𐑋𐑅𐐯𐑊𐑂𐑆 𐐨𐑂𐑌 𐐻𐐭 𐑄 𐐼𐐲𐑅𐐻, 𐑅𐐲𐐺𐐾𐐯𐐿𐐻𐐮𐑍 𐑄𐐯𐑋𐑅𐐯𐑊𐑂𐑆 𐐻𐐭 𐑄 𐐷𐐬𐐿 𐐱𐑂 𐐺𐐱𐑌𐐼𐐩𐐾, 𐑅𐐲𐐺𐑋𐐮𐐻𐐮𐑍 𐑄𐐯𐑋𐑅𐐯𐑊𐑂𐑆 𐐻𐐭 𐐺𐐨 𐑅𐑋𐐮𐐻𐑌, 𐐰𐑌𐐼 𐐻𐐭 𐐺𐐨 𐐼𐑉𐐮𐑂𐑌 𐐻𐐭 𐐰𐑌𐐼 𐑁𐑉𐐬, 𐐰𐑌𐐼 𐐺𐐲𐑉𐐼𐑌𐐼, 𐐰𐐿𐐫𐑉𐐼𐐮𐑍 𐐻𐐭 𐑄 𐐼𐐨𐑆𐐴𐑉𐑆 𐐱𐑂 𐑄𐐩𐑉 𐐯𐑌𐐯𐑋𐐮𐑆. 𐐰𐑌𐐼 𐑄𐐩 𐐼𐐮𐐼 𐐸𐐲𐑋𐐺𐑊 𐑄𐐯𐑋𐑅𐐯𐑊𐑂𐑆 𐐨𐑂𐑌 𐐮𐑌 𐑄 𐐼𐐯𐐹𐑃𐑅 𐐱𐑂 𐐸𐐷𐐭𐑋𐐮𐑊𐐮𐐻𐐮; 𐐰𐑌𐐼 𐑄𐐩 𐐼𐐮𐐼 𐐿𐑉𐐴 𐑋𐐴𐐻𐐮𐑊𐐮 𐐻𐐭 𐐘𐐱𐐼; 𐐏𐐩, 𐐨𐑂𐑌 𐐫𐑊 𐑄 𐐼𐐩 𐑊𐐱𐑍 𐐼𐐮𐐼 𐑄𐐩 𐐿𐑉𐐴 𐐲𐑌𐐻𐐭 𐑄𐐩𐑉 𐐘𐐱𐐼 𐑄𐐰𐐻 𐐸𐐨 𐐶𐐳𐐼 𐐼𐐨𐑊𐐮𐑂𐐲𐑉 𐑄𐐯𐑋 𐐵𐐻 𐐱𐑂 𐑄𐐩𐑉 𐐰𐑁𐑊𐐮𐐿𐑇𐐲𐑌𐑆. 𐐰𐑌𐐼 𐑌𐐵 𐑄 𐐢𐐫𐑉𐐼 𐐶𐐱𐑆 𐑅𐑊𐐬 𐐻𐐭 𐐸𐐨𐑉 𐑄𐐩𐑉 𐐿𐑉𐐴, 𐐺𐐨𐐿𐐫𐑆 𐐱𐑂 𐑄𐐩𐑉 𐐮𐑌𐐮𐐿𐐶𐐮𐐻𐐮𐑆; 𐑌𐐯𐑂𐐲𐑉𐑄𐐲𐑊𐐯𐑅 𐑄 𐐢𐐫𐑉𐐼 𐐼𐐮𐐼 𐐸𐐨𐑉 𐑄𐐩𐑉 𐐿𐑉𐐴𐑆, 𐐰𐑌𐐼 𐐺𐐨𐑀𐐰𐑌 𐐻𐐭 𐑅𐐫𐑁𐑌 𐑄 𐐸𐐪𐑉𐐻𐑅 𐐱𐑂 𐑄 𐐢𐐩𐑋𐐲𐑌𐐴𐐻𐑅, 𐑄𐐰𐐻 𐑄𐐩 𐐺𐐨𐑀𐐰𐑌 𐐻𐐭 𐐨𐑆 𐑄𐐩𐑉 𐐺𐐲𐑉𐐼𐑌𐑆: 𐐏𐐯𐐻 𐑄 𐐢𐐫𐑉𐐼 𐐼𐐮𐐼 𐑌𐐱𐐻 𐑅𐐨 𐑁𐐮𐐻 𐐻𐐭 𐐼𐐨𐑊𐐮𐑂𐐲𐑉 𐑄𐐯𐑋 𐐵𐐻 𐐱𐑂 𐐺𐐱𐑌𐐼𐐩𐐾.

25. 𐐰𐑌𐐼 𐐮𐐻 𐐿𐐩𐑋 𐐻𐐭 𐐹𐐰𐑅 𐑄𐐰𐐻 𐑄𐐩 𐐺𐐨𐑀𐐰𐑌 𐐻𐐭 𐐹𐑉𐐱𐑅𐐹𐐲𐑉 𐐺𐐴 𐐼𐐨𐑀𐑉𐐨𐑆 𐐮𐑌 𐑄 𐑊𐐰𐑌𐐼, 𐐰𐑌𐐼 𐐺𐐨𐑀𐐰𐑌 𐐻𐐭 𐑉𐐩𐑆 𐑀𐑉𐐩𐑌 𐑋𐐬𐑉 𐐲𐐺𐐲𐑌𐐼𐐲𐑌𐐻𐑊𐐮, 𐐰𐑌𐐼 𐑁𐑊𐐱𐐿𐑅, 𐐰𐑌𐐼 𐐸𐐲𐑉𐐼𐑆, 𐑄𐐰𐐻 𐑄𐐩 𐐼𐐮𐐼 𐑌𐐱𐐻 𐑅𐐲𐑁𐐲𐑉 𐐶𐐮𐑄 𐐸𐐲𐑍𐑀𐐲𐑉. 𐐤𐐵 𐑄𐐯𐑉 𐐶𐐱𐑆 𐐲 𐑀𐑉𐐩𐐻 𐑌𐐲𐑋𐐺𐐲𐑉 𐐱𐑂 𐐶𐐮𐑋𐐯𐑌, 𐑋𐐬𐑉 𐑄𐐰𐑌 𐑄𐐯𐑉 𐐶𐐱𐑆 𐐱𐑂 𐑋𐐯𐑌; 𐑄𐐯𐑉𐑁𐐬𐑉 𐐿𐐮𐑍 𐐢𐐮𐑋𐐸𐐴 𐐿𐐱𐑋𐐰𐑌𐐼𐐯𐐼 𐑄𐐰𐐻 𐐯𐑂𐐲𐑉𐐮 𐑋𐐰𐑌 𐑇𐐳𐐼 𐐮𐑋𐐹𐐪𐑉𐐻 𐐻𐐭 𐑄 𐑅𐐲𐐹𐐬𐑉𐐻 𐐱𐑂 𐑄 𐐶𐐮𐐼𐐬𐑆 𐐰𐑌𐐼 𐑄𐐩𐑉 𐐽𐐮𐑊𐐼𐑉𐐯𐑌, 𐑄𐐰𐐻 𐑄𐐩 𐑋𐐴𐐻 𐑌𐐱𐐻 𐐹𐐯𐑉𐐮𐑇 𐐶𐐮𐑄 𐐸𐐲𐑍𐑀𐐲𐑉; 𐐰𐑌𐐼 𐑄𐐮𐑅 𐑄𐐩 𐐼𐐮𐐼 𐐺𐐨𐐿𐐫𐑆 𐐱𐑂 𐑄 𐑀𐑉𐐩𐐻𐑌𐐯𐑅 𐐱𐑂 𐑄𐐩𐑉 𐑌𐐲𐑋𐐺𐐲𐑉 𐑄𐐰𐐻 𐐸𐐰𐐼 𐐺𐐮𐑌 𐑅𐑊𐐩𐑌. 𐐤𐐵 𐑄 𐐹𐐨𐐹𐑊 𐐱𐑂 𐐢𐐮𐑋𐐸𐐴 𐐿𐐯𐐹𐐻 𐐻𐐭𐑀𐐯𐑄𐐲𐑉 𐐮𐑌 𐐲 𐐺𐐱𐐼𐐮 𐐰𐑆 𐑋𐐲𐐽 𐐰𐑆 𐐮𐐻 𐐶𐐱𐑆 𐐹𐐱𐑅𐐮𐐺𐑊, 𐐰𐑌𐐼 𐑅𐐨𐐿𐐷𐐭𐑉𐐼 𐑄𐐩𐑉 𐑀𐑉𐐩𐑌 𐐰𐑌𐐼 𐑄𐐩𐑉 𐑁𐑊𐐱𐐿𐑅; 𐐰𐑌𐐼 𐑄 𐐿𐐮𐑍 𐐸𐐮𐑋𐑅𐐯𐑊𐑁 𐐼𐐮𐐼 𐑌𐐱𐐻 𐐻𐑉𐐲𐑅𐐻 𐐸𐐮𐑆 𐐹𐐲𐑉𐑅𐑌 𐐶𐐮𐑄𐐵𐐻 𐑄 𐐶𐐫𐑊𐑆 𐐱𐑂 𐑄 𐑅𐐮𐐻𐐮, 𐐲𐑌𐑊𐐯𐑅 𐐸𐐨 𐐻𐐳𐐿 𐐸𐐮𐑆 𐑀𐐪𐑉𐐼𐑆 𐐶𐐮𐑄 𐐸𐐮𐑋, 𐑁𐐨𐑉𐐮𐑍 𐑄𐐰𐐻 𐐸𐐨 𐑋𐐴𐐻 𐐺𐐴 𐑅𐐲𐑋 𐑋𐐨𐑌𐑆 𐑁𐐫𐑊 𐐮𐑌𐐻𐐭 𐑄 𐐸𐐰𐑌𐐼𐑆 𐐱𐑂 𐑄 𐐢𐐩𐑋𐐲𐑌-𐐴𐐻𐑅. 𐐰𐑌𐐼 𐐸𐐨 𐐿𐐫𐑆𐐼 𐑄𐐰𐐻 𐐸𐐮𐑆 𐐹𐐨𐐹𐑊 𐑇𐐳𐐼 𐐶𐐱𐐽 𐑄 𐑊𐐰𐑌𐐼 𐑉𐐵𐑌𐐼 𐐲𐐺𐐵𐐻, 𐑄𐐰𐐻 𐐺𐐴 𐑅𐐲𐑋 𐑋𐐨𐑌𐑆 𐑄𐐩 𐑋𐐴𐐻 𐐻𐐩𐐿 𐑄𐐬𐑆 𐐹𐑉𐐨𐑅𐐻𐑅 𐑄𐐰𐐻 𐑁𐑊𐐯𐐼 𐐮𐑌𐐻𐐭 𐑄 𐐶𐐮𐑊𐐼𐐲𐑉𐑌𐐯𐑅, 𐐸𐐭 𐐸𐐰𐐼 𐑅𐐻𐐬𐑊𐑌 𐑄 𐐼𐐫𐐻𐐲𐑉𐑆 𐐱𐑂 𐑄 𐐢𐐩𐑋𐐲𐑌𐐴𐐻𐑅, 𐐰𐑌𐐼 𐑄𐐰𐐻 𐐸𐐰𐐼 𐐿𐐫𐑆𐐼 𐑅𐐲𐐽 𐐲 𐑀𐑉𐐩𐐻 𐐼𐐯𐑅𐐻𐑉𐐲𐐿𐑇𐐲𐑌 𐐻𐐭 𐐿𐐲𐑋 𐐲𐐹𐐱𐑌 𐑄𐐯𐑋; 𐑁𐐫𐑉 𐑄𐐩 𐐶𐐲𐑉 𐐼𐐨𐑆𐐴𐑉𐐲𐑅 𐐻𐐭 𐐻𐐩𐐿 𐑄𐐯𐑋, 𐑄𐐰𐐻 𐑄𐐩 𐑋𐐴𐐻 𐐹𐐲𐑌𐐮𐑇 𐑄𐐯𐑋; 𐑁𐐫𐑉 𐑄𐐩 𐐸𐐰𐐼 𐐿𐐲𐑋 𐐮𐑌𐐻𐐭 𐑄 𐑊𐐰𐑌𐐼 𐐱𐑂 𐐤𐐨𐑁𐐴 𐐺𐐴 𐑌𐐴𐐻, 𐐰𐑌𐐼 𐐿𐐰𐑉𐐮𐐼 𐐫𐑁 𐑄𐐩𐑉 𐑀𐑉𐐩𐑌, 𐐰𐑌𐐼 𐑋𐐯𐑌𐐮 𐐱𐑂 𐑄𐐩𐑉 𐐹𐑉𐐯𐑇𐐲𐑅 𐑃𐐮𐑍𐑆; 𐑄𐐯𐑉𐑁𐐬𐑉 𐑄𐐩 𐑊𐐩𐐼 𐐶𐐩𐐻 𐑁𐐫𐑉 𐑄𐐯𐑋.

26. 𐐰𐑌𐐼 𐐮𐐻 𐐿𐐩𐑋 𐐻𐐭 𐐹𐐰𐑅 𐑄𐐰𐐻 𐑄𐐯𐑉 𐐶𐐱𐑆 𐑌𐐬 𐑋𐐬𐑉 𐐼𐐮𐑅𐐻𐐲𐑉𐐺𐐰𐑌𐑅 𐐺𐐨𐐻𐐶𐐨𐑌 𐑄 𐐢𐐩𐑋𐐲𐑌𐐴𐐻𐑅 𐐰𐑌𐐼 𐑄 𐐹𐐨𐐹𐑊 𐐱𐑂 𐐢𐐮𐑋𐐸𐐴, 𐐨𐑂𐑌 𐐲𐑌𐐻𐐮𐑊 𐑄 𐐻𐐴𐑋 𐑄𐐰𐐻 𐐈𐑋𐐲𐑌 𐐰𐑌𐐼 𐐸𐐮𐑆 𐐺𐑉𐐯𐑄𐑉𐐯𐑌 𐐿𐐩𐑋 𐐮𐑌𐐻𐐭 𐑄 𐑊𐐰𐑌𐐼. 𐐰𐑌𐐼 𐑄 𐐿𐐮𐑍 𐐸𐐰𐑂𐐮𐑍 𐐺𐐮𐑌 𐐶𐐮𐑄𐐵𐐻 𐑄 𐑀𐐩𐐻𐑅 𐐱𐑂 𐑄 𐑅𐐮𐐻𐐮 𐐶𐐮𐑄 𐐸𐐮𐑆 𐑀𐐪𐑉𐐼, 𐐼𐐮𐑅𐐿𐐲𐑂𐐲𐑉𐐼 𐐈𐑋𐐲𐑌 𐐰𐑌𐐼 𐐸𐐮𐑆 𐐺𐑉𐐯𐑄𐑉𐐯𐑌; 𐐰𐑌𐐼 𐑅𐐲𐐹𐐬𐑆𐐮𐑍 𐑄𐐯𐑋 𐐻𐐭 𐐺𐐨 𐐹𐑉𐐨𐑅𐐻𐑅 𐐱𐑂 𐐤𐐬𐐲, 𐑄𐐯𐑉𐑁𐐬𐑉 𐐸𐐨 𐐿𐐫𐑆𐐼 𐑄𐐰𐐻 𐑄𐐩 𐑇𐐳𐐼 𐐺𐐨 𐐻𐐩𐐿𐑌, 𐐰𐑌𐐼 𐐺𐐵𐑌𐐼, 𐐰𐑌𐐼 𐐿𐐰𐑅𐐻 𐐮𐑌𐐻𐐭 𐐹𐑉𐐮𐑆𐑌. 𐐰𐑌𐐼 𐐸𐐰𐐼 𐑄𐐩 𐐺𐐮𐑌 𐑄 𐐹𐑉𐐨𐑅𐐻𐑅 𐐱𐑂 𐐤𐐬𐐲, 𐐸𐐨 𐐶𐐳𐐼 𐐸𐐰𐑂 𐐿𐐫𐑆𐐼 𐑄𐐰𐐻 𐑄𐐩 𐑇𐐳𐐼 𐐺𐐨 𐐹𐐳𐐻 𐐻𐐭 𐐼𐐯𐑃; 𐐺𐐲𐐻 𐐸𐐶𐐯𐑌 𐐸𐐨 𐑁𐐵𐑌𐐼 𐑄𐐰𐐻 𐑄𐐩 𐐶𐐲𐑉 𐑌𐐱𐐻, 𐐺𐐲𐐻 𐑄𐐰𐐻 𐑄𐐩 𐐶𐐲𐑉 𐐸𐐮𐑆 𐐺𐑉𐐯𐑄𐑉𐐯𐑌, 𐐰𐑌𐐼 𐐸𐐰𐐼 𐐿𐐲𐑋 𐑁𐑉𐐱𐑋 𐑄 𐑊𐐰𐑌𐐼 𐐱𐑂 𐐞𐐰𐑉𐐲𐐸𐐯𐑋𐑊𐐲, 𐐸𐐨 𐐶𐐱𐑆 𐑁𐐮𐑊𐐼 𐐶𐐮𐑄 𐐯𐐿𐑅𐐨𐐼𐐮𐑍𐑊𐐮 𐑀𐑉𐐩𐐻 𐐾𐐦. 𐐤𐐵 𐐿𐐮𐑍 𐐢𐐮𐑋𐐸𐐴 𐐸𐐰𐐼 𐑅𐐯𐑌𐐻, 𐐹𐑉𐐨𐑂𐐨𐐲𐑅 𐐻𐐭 𐑄 𐐿𐐲𐑋-𐐮𐑍 𐐱𐑂 𐐈𐑋𐐲𐑌, 𐐲 𐑅𐑋𐐫𐑊 𐑌𐐲𐑋𐐺𐐲𐑉 𐐱𐑂 𐑋𐐯𐑌 𐐻𐐭 𐑅𐐲𐑉𐐽 𐑁𐐫𐑉 𐑄 𐑊𐐰𐑌𐐼 𐐱𐑂 𐐞𐐰𐑉𐐲𐐸𐐯𐑋𐑊𐐲; 𐐺𐐲𐐻 𐑄𐐩 𐐿𐐳𐐼 𐑌𐐱𐐻 𐑁𐐴𐑌𐐼 𐐮𐐻, 𐐰𐑌𐐼 𐑄𐐩 𐐶𐐲𐑉 𐑊𐐱𐑅𐐻 𐐮𐑌 𐑄 𐐶𐐮𐑊𐐼𐐲𐑉𐑌𐐯𐑅. 𐑌𐐯𐑂𐐲𐑉𐑄𐐲𐑊𐐯𐑅 𐑄𐐩 𐐼𐐮𐐼 𐑁𐐴𐑌𐐼 𐐲 𐑊𐐰𐑌𐐼 𐐸𐐶𐐮𐐽 𐐸𐐰𐐼 𐐺𐐮𐑌 𐐹𐐨𐐹𐑊𐐼; 𐐏𐐩, 𐐲 𐑊𐐰𐑌𐐼 𐐸𐐶𐐮𐐽 𐐶𐐱𐑆 𐐿𐐲𐑂𐐲𐑉𐐼 𐐶𐐮𐑄 𐐼𐑉𐐴 𐐺𐐬𐑌𐑆; 𐐏𐐩, 𐐲 𐑊𐐰𐑌𐐼 𐐸𐐶𐐮𐐽 𐐸𐐰𐐼 𐐺𐐮𐑌 𐐹𐐨𐐹𐑊𐐼 𐐰𐑌𐐼 𐐸𐐶𐐮𐐽 𐐸𐐰𐐼 𐐺𐐮𐑌 𐐼𐐯𐑅𐐻𐑉𐐦𐐼; 𐐰𐑌𐐼 𐑄𐐩, 𐐸𐐰𐑂𐐮𐑍 𐑅𐐲𐐹𐐬𐑆𐐼 𐐮𐐻 𐐻𐐭 𐐺𐐨 𐑄 𐑊𐐰𐑌𐐼 𐐱𐑂 𐐞𐐰𐑉𐐲𐐸𐐯𐑋𐑊𐐲, 𐑉𐐨𐐻𐐲𐑉𐑌𐐼 𐐻𐐭 𐑄 𐑊𐐰𐑌𐐼 𐐱𐑂 𐐤𐐨𐑁𐐴, 𐐸𐐰𐑂𐐮𐑍 𐐲𐑉𐐴𐑂𐐼 𐐮𐑌 𐑄 𐐺𐐫𐑉-𐐼𐐲𐑉𐑆 𐐱𐑂 𐑄 𐑊𐐰𐑌𐐼 𐑌𐐱𐐻 𐑋𐐯𐑌𐐮 𐐼𐐩𐑆 𐐺𐐨𐑁𐐬𐑉 𐑄 𐐿𐐲𐑋𐐮𐑍 𐐱𐑂 𐐈𐑋𐐲𐑌. 𐐰𐑌𐐼 𐑄𐐩 𐐺𐑉𐐫𐐻 𐐲 𐑉𐐯𐐿𐐲𐑉𐐼 𐐶𐐮𐑄 𐑄𐐯𐑋, 𐐨𐑂𐑌 𐐲 𐑉𐐯𐐿𐐲𐑉𐐼 𐐱𐑂 𐑄 𐐹𐐨𐐹𐑊 𐐸𐐭𐑆 𐐺𐐬𐑌𐑆 𐑄𐐩 𐐸𐐰𐐼 𐑁𐐵𐑌𐐼: 𐐰𐑌𐐼 𐐮𐐻 𐐶𐐱𐑆 𐐯𐑌𐑀𐑉𐐩𐑂𐑌

𐐲𐑌 𐐹𐑊𐐩𐐻𐑅 𐐲𐑂 𐐬𐑉. 𐐈𐑌𐐼 𐑌𐐵 𐐢𐐮𐑋𐐸𐐴 𐐶𐐱𐑆 𐐲𐑀𐐯𐑌 𐑁𐐮𐑊𐐼 𐐶𐐮𐑄 𐐾𐑎 𐐲𐑌 𐑊𐐲𐑉𐑌𐐮𐑍 𐑁𐑉𐐲𐑋 𐑄 𐑋𐐵𐑃 𐐲𐑂 𐐈𐑋𐐲𐑌 𐑄𐐰𐐻 𐐿𐐮𐑍 𐐣𐐬𐑅𐐴𐐲 𐐸𐐰𐐼 𐐲 𐑀𐐮𐑁𐐻 𐑁𐑉𐐲𐑋 𐐘𐐱𐐼, 𐐸𐐶𐐯𐑉𐐺𐐴 𐐸𐐨 𐐿𐐳𐐼 𐐮𐑌𐐻𐐲𐑉𐐹𐑉𐐯𐐻 𐑅𐐲𐐽 𐐯𐑌𐑀𐑉𐐩𐑂𐐮𐑍𐑆; 𐐷𐐩, 𐐰𐑌𐐼 𐐈𐑋𐐲𐑌 𐐫𐑊𐑅𐐬 𐐼𐐮𐐼 𐑉𐐨𐐾𐑎𐑅. 𐐏𐐯𐐻 𐐈𐑋𐐲𐑌 𐐰𐑌𐐼 𐐸𐐮𐑆 𐐺𐑉𐐯𐑄𐑉𐐯𐑌 𐐶𐐲𐑉 𐑁𐐮𐑊𐐼 𐐶𐐮𐑄 𐑅𐐱𐑉𐐬 𐐺𐐨𐐿𐐫𐑆 𐑅𐐬 𐑋𐐯𐑌𐐨 𐐲𐑂 𐑄𐐩𐑉 𐐺𐑉𐐯𐑄𐑉𐐯𐑌 𐐸𐐰𐐼 𐐺𐐮𐑌 𐑅𐑊𐐩𐑌; 𐐰𐑌𐐼 𐐫𐑊𐑅𐐬 𐑄𐐰𐐻 𐐿𐐮𐑍 𐐤𐐬𐐲 𐐰𐑌𐐼 𐐸𐐮𐑆 𐐹𐑉𐐨𐑅𐐻𐑅 𐐸𐐰𐐼 𐐿𐐫𐑆𐐼 𐑄 𐐹𐐨𐐹𐑊 𐐻𐐭 𐐿𐐱𐑋𐐮𐐻 𐑅𐐬 𐑋𐐯𐑌𐐨 𐑅𐐮𐑌𐑆 𐐰𐑌𐐼 𐐮𐑌𐐮𐐿𐐶𐐮𐐻𐐨𐑆 𐐲𐑀𐐯𐑌𐑅𐐻 𐐘𐐱𐐼; 𐐰𐑌𐐼 𐑄𐐩 𐐫𐑊𐑅𐐬 𐐼𐐮𐐼 𐑋𐐬𐑉𐑌 𐑁𐐫𐑉 𐑄 𐐼𐐯𐑃 𐐲𐑂 𐐈𐐺𐐮𐑌𐐲𐐼𐐴; 𐐰𐑌𐐼 𐐫𐑊𐑅𐐬 𐑁𐐫𐑉 𐑄 𐐼𐐨𐐹𐐪𐑉𐐽𐐲𐑉 𐐲𐑂 𐐈𐑊𐑋𐐲 𐐰𐑌𐐼 𐑄 𐐹𐐨𐐹𐑊 𐑄𐐰𐐻 𐐶𐐯𐑌𐐻 𐐶𐐮𐑄 𐐸𐐮𐑋, 𐐸𐐭 𐐸𐐰𐐼 𐑁𐐫𐑉𐑋𐐼 𐐲 𐐽𐐲𐑉𐐽 𐐲𐑂 𐐘𐐱𐐼 𐑃𐑉𐐭 𐑄 𐑅𐐻𐑉𐐯𐑍𐑃 𐐰𐑌𐐼 𐐹𐐵𐐲𐑉 𐐲𐑂 𐐘𐐱𐐼, 𐐰𐑌𐐼 𐑁𐐩𐑃 𐐲𐑌 𐑄 𐐶𐐲𐑉𐐼𐑆 𐐸𐐶𐐮𐐽 𐐸𐐰𐐼 𐐺𐐮𐑌 𐑅𐐹𐐬𐐿𐑌 𐐺𐐴 𐐈𐐺𐐮𐑌𐐲𐐼𐐴; 𐐷𐐩, 𐑄𐐩 𐐼𐐮𐐼 𐑋𐐬𐑉𐑌 𐑁𐐫𐑉 𐑄𐐩𐑉 𐐼𐐨𐐹𐐪𐑉𐐽𐐲𐑉, 𐑁𐐫𐑉 𐑄𐐩 𐑌𐐭 𐑌𐐱𐐻 𐐸𐐶𐐮𐑄𐐲𐑉 𐑄𐐩 𐐸𐐰𐐼 𐑁𐑊𐐯𐐼. 𐐤𐐵 𐑄𐐩 𐐶𐐳𐐼 𐐸𐐰𐑂 𐑀𐑊𐐰𐐼𐑊𐐨 𐐾𐑎𐑌𐐼 𐐶𐐮𐑄 𐑄𐐯𐑋, 𐑁𐐫𐑉 𐑄𐐩 𐑄𐐯𐑋𐑅𐐯𐑊𐑂𐑆 𐐸𐐰𐐼 𐐯𐑌𐐻𐐲𐑉𐐼 𐐮𐑌𐐻𐐭 𐐲 𐐿𐐲𐑂𐐯𐑌𐐲𐑌𐐻 𐐶𐐮𐑄 𐐘𐐱𐐼 𐐻𐐭 𐑅𐐲𐑉𐑂 𐐸𐐮𐑋 𐐰𐑌𐐼 𐐿𐐨𐐹 𐐸𐐮𐑆 𐐿𐐱𐑋𐐰𐑌𐐼𐑋𐐯𐑌𐐻𐑅. 𐐈𐑌𐐼 𐑌𐐵 𐑅𐐮𐑌𐑅 𐑄 𐐿𐐲𐑋𐐮𐑍 𐐲𐑂 𐐈𐑋𐐲𐑌, 𐐿𐐮𐑍 𐐢𐐮𐑋𐐸𐐴 𐐸𐐰𐐼 𐐫𐑊𐑅𐐬 𐐯𐑌𐐻𐐲𐑉𐐼 𐐮𐑌𐐻𐐭 𐐲 𐐿𐐲𐑂𐐯𐑌𐐲𐑌𐐻 𐐶𐐮𐑄 𐐘𐐱𐐼, 𐐰𐑌𐐼 𐐫𐑊𐑅𐐬 𐑋𐐯𐑌𐐨 𐐲𐑂 𐐸𐐮𐑆 𐐹𐐨𐐹𐑊, 𐐻𐐭 𐑅𐐲𐑉𐑂 𐐸𐐮𐑋 𐐰𐑌𐐼 𐐿𐐨𐐹 𐐸𐐮𐑆 𐐿𐐱𐑋𐐰𐑌𐐼𐑋𐐯𐑌𐐻𐑅.

27. 𐐈𐑌𐐼 𐐮𐐻 𐐿𐐩𐑋 𐐻𐐭 𐐹𐐰𐑅 𐑄𐐰𐐻 𐐿𐐮𐑍 𐐢𐐮𐑋𐐸𐐴 𐐰𐑌𐐼 𐑋𐐯𐑌𐐨 𐐲𐑂 𐐸𐐮𐑆 𐐹𐐨𐐹𐑊 𐐶𐐲𐑉 𐐼𐐨𐑆𐐴𐑉𐐲𐑅 𐐻𐐭 𐐺𐐨 𐐺𐐰𐐹𐐻𐐴𐑆𐐼; 𐐺𐐲𐐻 𐑄𐐩𐑉 𐐶𐐱𐑆 𐑌𐐲𐑌 𐐮𐑌 𐑄 𐑊𐐰𐑌𐐼 𐑄𐐰𐐻 𐐸𐐰𐐼 𐐫𐑃𐐱𐑉𐐮𐐻𐐨 𐑁𐑉𐐲𐑋 𐐘𐐱𐐼. 𐐈𐑌𐐼 𐐈𐑋𐐲𐑌 𐐼𐐨𐐿𐑊𐐴𐑌𐐼 𐐼𐐭𐐮𐑍 𐑄𐐮𐑅 𐑃𐐮𐑍, 𐐿𐐱𐑌𐑅𐐮𐐼𐐲𐑉𐐮𐑍 𐐸𐐮𐑋𐑅𐐯𐑊𐑁 𐐰𐑌 𐐲𐑌𐐶𐐲𐑉𐑄𐐨 𐑅𐐲𐑉𐑂𐐲𐑌𐐻. 𐐜𐐩𐑉𐑁𐐫𐑉 𐑄𐐩 𐐼𐐮𐐼 𐑌𐐱𐐻 𐐰𐐻 𐑄𐐰𐐻 𐐻𐐴𐑋 𐑁𐐫𐑉𐑋 𐑄𐐯𐑋𐑅𐐯𐑊𐑂𐑆 𐐮𐑌𐐻𐐭 𐐲 𐐽𐐲𐑉𐐽, 𐐶𐐩𐐻𐐮𐑍 𐐲𐐹𐐱𐑌 𐑄 𐐝𐐹𐐮𐑉𐐮𐐻 𐐲𐑂 𐑄 𐐢𐐫𐑉𐐼. 𐐤𐐵 𐑄𐐩 𐐶𐐲𐑉 𐐼𐐨𐑆𐐴𐑉𐐲𐑅 𐐻𐐭 𐐺𐐨𐐿𐐲𐑋 𐐨𐑂𐐯𐑌 𐐰𐑆 𐐈𐑊𐑋𐐲 𐐰𐑌𐐼 𐐸𐐮𐑆 𐐺𐑉𐐯𐑄𐑉𐐯𐑌, 𐐸𐐭 𐐸𐐰𐐼 𐑁𐑊𐐯𐐼 𐐮𐑌𐐻𐐭 𐑄 𐐶𐐮𐑊𐐼𐐲𐑉𐑌𐐯𐑅. 𐐜𐐩 𐐶𐐲𐑉 𐐼𐐨𐑆𐐴𐑉𐐲𐑅 𐐻𐐭 𐐺𐐨 𐐺𐐰𐐹𐐻𐐴𐑆𐐼 𐐰𐑆 𐐲 𐐶𐐮𐐻𐑌𐐯𐑅 𐐰𐑌𐐼 𐐲 𐐻𐐯𐑅𐐻𐐮𐑋𐐬𐑌𐐨 𐑄𐐰𐐻 𐑄𐐩 𐐶𐐲𐑉 𐐶𐐮𐑊𐐮𐑍 𐐻𐐭 𐑅𐐲𐑉𐑂 𐐘𐐱𐐼 𐐶𐐮𐑄 𐐫𐑊 𐑄𐐩𐑉 𐐸𐐪𐑉𐐻𐑅; 𐑌𐐯𐑂𐐲𐑉𐑄𐐲𐑊𐐯𐑅 𐑄𐐩 𐐼𐐮𐐼 𐐹𐑉𐐬𐑊𐐱𐑍 𐑄 𐐻𐐴𐑋; 𐐰𐑌𐐼 𐐰𐑌 𐐲𐐿𐐵𐑌𐐻 𐐲𐑂 𐑄𐐩𐑉 𐐺𐐰𐐹𐐻𐐮𐑆𐑋 𐑇𐐰𐑊 𐐺𐐨 𐑀𐐮𐑂𐑌 𐐸𐐨𐑉𐐰𐑁𐐻𐐲𐑉: 𐐰𐑌𐐼 𐑌𐐵 𐐫𐑊 𐑄 𐑅𐐻𐐲𐐼𐐨 𐐲𐑂 𐐈𐑋𐐲𐑌 𐐰𐑌𐐼 𐐸𐐮𐑆 𐐹𐐨𐐹𐑊, 𐐰𐑌𐐼 𐐿𐐮𐑍 𐐢𐐮𐑋𐐸𐐴 𐐰𐑌𐐼 𐐸𐐮𐑆 𐐹𐐨𐐹𐑊, 𐐶𐐱𐑆 𐐻𐐭 𐐼𐐮𐑊𐐮𐑂𐐲𐑉 𐑄𐐯𐑋𐑅𐐯𐑊𐑂𐑆 𐐵𐐻 𐐲𐑂 𐑄 𐐸𐐰𐑌𐐼𐑆 𐐲𐑂 𐑄 𐐢𐐰𐑋𐐲𐑌𐐴𐐻𐑅, 𐐰𐑌𐐼 𐑁𐑉𐐲𐑋 𐐺𐐱𐑌𐐼𐐮𐐾.

𐐕𐐰𐐹𐐻𐐲𐑉 X.

1. 𐐈𐑌𐐼 𐑌𐐵 𐐮𐐻 𐐿𐐩𐑋 𐐻𐐭 𐐹𐐰𐑅 𐑄𐐰𐐻 𐐈𐑋𐐲𐑌 𐐰𐑌𐐼 𐐿𐐮𐑍 𐐢𐐮𐑋𐐸𐐴 𐐺𐐨𐑀𐐰𐑌 𐐻𐐭 𐐿𐐱𐑌𐑅𐐲𐑊𐐻 𐐶𐐮𐑄 𐑄 𐐹𐐨𐐹𐑊 𐐸𐐵 𐑄𐐩 𐑇𐐳𐐼 𐐼𐐮𐑊𐐮𐑂𐐲𐑉 𐑄𐐯𐑋𐑅𐐯𐑊𐑂𐑆 𐐵𐐻 𐐲𐑂 𐐺𐐱𐑌𐐼𐐮𐐾; 𐐰𐑌𐐼 𐐨𐑂𐐯𐑌 𐑄𐐩 𐐼𐐮𐐼 𐐿𐐫𐑆 𐑄𐐰𐐻 𐐫𐑊 𐑄 𐐹𐐨𐐹𐑊 𐑇𐐳𐐼 𐑀𐐰𐑄𐐲𐑉 𐑄𐐯𐑋𐑅𐐯𐑊𐑂𐑆 𐐻𐐲𐑀𐐯𐑄𐐲𐑉: 𐐰𐑌𐐼 𐑄𐐮𐑅 𐑄𐐩 𐐼𐐮𐐼 𐑄𐐰𐐻 𐑄𐐩 𐑋𐐴𐐻 𐐸𐐰𐑂 𐑄 𐑂𐑎𐑅 𐐲𐑂 𐑄 𐐹𐐨𐐹𐑊 𐐿𐐱𐑌𐑅𐐲𐑉𐑌𐐮𐑍 𐑄 𐑋𐐰𐐻𐐲𐑉. 𐐈𐑌𐐼 𐐮𐐻 𐐿𐐩𐑋 𐐻𐐭 𐐹𐐰𐑅 𐑄𐐰𐐻 𐑄𐐩 𐐿𐐳𐐼 𐑁𐐴𐑌𐐼 𐑌𐐬 𐐶𐐩 𐐻𐐭 𐐼𐐮𐑊𐐮𐑂𐐲𐑉 𐑄𐐯𐑋𐑅𐐯𐑊𐑂𐑆 𐐵𐐻 𐐲𐑂 𐐺𐐱𐑌𐐼𐐮𐐾, 𐐯𐐿𐑅𐐯𐐹𐐻 𐐮𐐻 𐐶𐐲𐑉 𐐻𐐭 𐐻𐐩𐐿 𐑄𐐩𐑉 𐐶𐐳𐑋𐐲𐑌 𐐰𐑌𐐼 𐐽𐐮𐑊𐐼𐑉𐐯𐑌, 𐐰𐑌𐐼 𐑄𐐩𐑉 𐑁𐑊𐐱𐐿𐑅, 𐐰𐑌𐐼 𐑄𐐩𐑉 𐐸𐐲𐑉𐐼𐑆, 𐐰𐑌𐐼 𐑄𐐩𐑉 𐐻𐐯𐑌𐐻𐑅, 𐐰𐑌𐐼 𐐼𐐨𐐹𐐪𐑉𐐻 𐐮𐑌𐐻𐐭 𐑄 𐐶𐐮𐑊𐐼𐐲𐑉𐑌𐐯𐑅; 𐑁𐐫𐑉 𐑄 𐐢𐐰𐑋𐐲𐑌𐐴𐐻𐑅 𐐺𐐨𐐮𐑍 𐑅𐐬 𐑌𐐭𐑋𐐲𐑉𐐲𐑅, 𐐮𐐻 𐐶𐐱𐑆 𐐮𐑋𐐹𐐱𐑅𐐮𐐺𐑊 𐑁𐐫𐑉 𐑄 𐐹𐐨𐐹𐑊 𐐲𐑂 𐐢𐐮𐑋𐐸𐐴 𐐻𐐭 𐐿𐐱𐑌𐐻𐐯𐑌𐐼 𐐶𐐮𐑄 𐑄𐐯𐑋, 𐑃𐐮𐑍𐐿𐐮𐑍 𐐻𐐭 𐐼𐐮𐑊𐐮𐑂𐐲𐑉 𐑄𐐯𐑋𐑅𐐯𐑊𐑂𐑆 𐐵𐐻 𐐲𐑂 𐐺𐐱𐑌𐐼𐐮𐐾 𐐺𐐴 𐑄 𐑅𐐫𐑉𐐼.

2. 𐐤𐐵 𐐮𐐻 𐐿𐐩𐑋 𐐻𐐭 𐐹𐐰𐑅 𐑄𐐰𐐻 𐐘𐐮𐐼𐐨𐐲𐑌 𐐶𐐯𐑌𐐻 𐑁𐐫𐑉𐑃 𐐰𐑌𐐼 𐑅𐐻𐐳𐐼 𐐺𐐨𐑁𐐫𐑉 𐑄 𐐿𐐮𐑍, 𐐰𐑌𐐼 𐑅𐐯𐐼 𐐲𐑌𐐻𐐭 𐐸𐐮𐑋, 𐐤𐐵, 𐐄 𐐿𐐮𐑍, 𐑄𐐵 𐐸𐐰𐑅𐐻 𐐸𐐮𐑄𐐲𐑉𐐻𐐭 𐐸𐐪𐑉𐐿𐑌𐐼 𐐲𐑌𐐻𐐭 𐑋𐐴 𐐶𐐲𐑉𐐼𐑆 𐑋𐐯𐑌𐐨 𐐻𐐴𐑋𐑆 𐐸𐐶𐐯𐑌 𐐶𐐨 𐐸𐐰𐑂 𐐺𐐮𐑌 𐐿𐐱𐑌𐐻𐐯𐑌𐐼𐐮𐑍 𐐶𐐮𐑄 𐐵𐑉 𐐺𐑉𐐯𐑄𐑉𐐯𐑌, 𐑄 𐐢𐐰𐑋𐐲𐑌𐐴𐐻𐑅. 𐐈𐑌𐐼 𐑌𐐵, 𐐄 𐐿𐐮𐑍, 𐐮𐑁 𐑄𐐵 𐐸𐐰𐑅𐐻 𐑌𐐱𐐻 𐑁𐐵𐑌𐐼 𐑋𐐨 𐐻𐐭 𐐺𐐨 𐐰𐑌 𐐲𐑌𐐹𐑉𐐱𐑁𐐮𐐻𐐲𐐺𐑊 𐑅𐐲𐑉𐑂𐐲𐑌𐐻, 𐐱𐑉 𐐮𐑁 𐑄𐐵 𐐸𐐰𐑅𐐻 𐐸𐐮𐑄𐐲𐑉𐐻𐐭 𐑊𐐮𐑅𐑌𐐼 𐐻𐐭 𐑋𐐴 𐐶𐐲𐑉𐐼𐑆 𐐮𐑌 𐐯𐑌𐐨 𐐼𐐨𐑀𐑉𐐨, 𐐰𐑌𐐼 𐑄𐐩 𐐸𐐰𐑂 𐐺𐐮𐑌 𐐲𐑂 𐑅𐐲𐑉𐑂𐐮𐑅 𐐻𐐭 𐑄𐐨, 𐐨𐑂𐐯𐑌 𐑅𐐬 𐐌 𐐼𐐨𐑆𐐴𐑉 𐑄𐐰𐐻 𐑄𐐵 𐐶𐐳𐐼𐑅𐐻 𐑊𐐮𐑅𐑌 𐐻𐐭 𐑋𐐴 𐐶𐐲𐑉𐐼𐑆 𐐰𐐻 𐑄𐐮𐑅 𐐻𐐴𐑋, 𐐰𐑌𐐼 𐐌 𐐶𐐮𐑊 𐐺𐐨 𐑄𐐴 𐑅𐐲𐑉𐑂𐐲𐑌𐐻, 𐐰𐑌𐐼 𐐼𐐮𐑊𐐮𐑂𐐲𐑉 𐑄𐐮𐑅

𐐹𐐨𐐹𐐲𐑊 𐐵𐐻 𐐱𐑂 𐐺𐐱𐑌𐐼𐐩𐐾. 𐐈𐑌𐐼 𐑄 𐐿𐐮𐑍 𐑀𐑉𐐰𐑌𐐻𐐯𐐼 𐐲𐑌𐐻𐐭 𐐸𐐮𐑋 𐑄𐐰𐐻 𐐸𐐨 𐑋𐐴𐐻 𐑅𐐹𐐨𐐿. 𐐈𐑌𐐼 𐐘𐐮𐐼-𐐨𐐲𐑌 𐑅𐐯𐐼 𐐲𐑌𐐻𐐭 𐐸𐐮𐑋, 𐐒𐐨𐐸𐐬𐑊𐐼 𐑄 𐐺𐐰𐐿 𐐹𐐪𐑅, 𐑃𐑉𐐭 𐑄 𐐺𐐰𐐿 𐐶𐐫𐑊, 𐐱𐑌 𐑄 𐐺𐐰𐐿 𐑅𐐴𐐼 𐐱𐑂 𐑄 𐑅𐐮𐐻𐐨. 𐐜 𐐢𐐰𐑋𐐲𐑌𐐴𐐻𐑅, 𐐫𐑉 𐑄 𐑀𐐪𐑉𐐼𐑆 𐐱𐑂 𐑄 𐐢𐐰𐑋𐐲𐑌𐐴𐐻𐑅, 𐐺𐐴 𐑌𐐴𐐻, 𐐪𐑉 𐐼𐑉𐐲𐑍𐐿𐐲𐑌; 𐑄𐐯𐑉𐑁𐐬𐑉 𐑊𐐯𐐻 𐐲𐑅 𐑅𐐯𐑌𐐼 𐐰 𐐹𐑉𐐬𐐿𐑊𐐰𐑋𐐩𐑇𐐲𐑌 𐐰𐑋𐐲𐑍 𐐫𐑊 𐑄𐐮𐑅 𐐹𐐨𐐹𐐲𐑊, 𐑄𐐰𐐻 𐑄𐐩 𐑀𐐰𐑄𐐲𐑉 𐐻𐐭𐑀𐐯𐑄𐐲𐑉 𐑄𐐯𐑉 𐑁𐑊𐐱𐐿𐑅 𐐰𐑌𐐼 𐐸𐐲𐑉𐐼𐑆, 𐑄𐐰𐐻 𐑄𐐩 𐑋𐐩 𐐼𐑉𐐴𐑂 𐑄𐐯𐑋 𐐮𐑌𐐻𐐭 𐑄 𐐶𐐮𐑊𐐼𐐲𐑉𐑌𐐯𐑅 𐐺𐐴 𐑌𐐴𐐻. 𐐈𐑌𐐼 𐐌 𐐶𐐮𐑊 𐑀𐐬 𐐰𐐿𐐫𐑉𐐼𐐮𐑍 𐐻𐐭 𐑄𐐴 𐐿𐐲𐑋𐐰𐑌𐐼, 𐐰𐑌𐐼 𐐹𐐩 𐑄 𐑊𐐪𐑅𐐻 𐐻𐑉𐐮𐐺𐐷𐐭𐐻 𐐱𐑂 𐐶𐐴𐑌 𐐻𐐭 𐑄 𐐢𐐰𐑋𐐲𐑌𐐴𐐻𐑅, 𐐰𐑌𐐼 𐑄𐐩 𐐶𐐮𐑊 𐐺𐐨 𐐼𐑉𐐲𐑍𐐿𐐲𐑌; 𐐰𐑌𐐼 𐐶𐐨 𐐶𐐮𐑊 𐐹𐐪𐑅 𐑃𐑉𐐭 𐑄 𐑅𐐨𐐿𐑉𐐯𐐻 𐐹𐐪𐑅 𐐱𐑌 𐑄 𐑊𐐯𐑁𐐻 𐐱𐑂 𐑄 𐐿𐐰𐑋𐐹, 𐐸𐐶𐐯𐑌 𐑄𐐩 𐐪𐑉 𐐼𐑉𐐲𐑍𐐿𐐲𐑌 𐐰𐑌𐐼 𐐰𐑅𐑊𐐨𐐹: 𐑄𐐲𐑅 𐐶𐐨 𐐶𐐮𐑊 𐐼𐐨𐐹𐐪𐑉𐐻 𐐶𐐮𐑄 𐐵𐑉 𐐶𐐮𐑋𐐯𐑌 𐐰𐑌𐐼 𐐵𐑉 𐐽𐐮𐑊𐐼𐑉𐐯𐑌, 𐐵𐑉 𐑁𐑊𐐱𐐿𐑅 𐐰𐑌𐐼 𐐵𐑉 𐐸𐐲𐑉𐐼𐑆, 𐐮𐑌𐐻𐐭 𐑄 𐐶𐐮𐑊𐐼𐐲𐑉𐑌𐐯𐑅; 𐐰𐑌𐐼 𐐶𐐨 𐐶𐐮𐑊 𐐻𐑉𐐰𐑂𐐯𐑊 𐐰𐑉𐐵𐑌𐐼 𐑄 𐑊𐐰𐑌𐐼 𐐱𐑂 𐐟𐐴𐑊𐐲𐑋. 𐐈𐑌𐐼 𐐮𐐻 𐐿𐐩𐑋 𐐻𐐭 𐐹𐐪𐑅 𐑄𐐰𐐻 𐑄 𐐿𐐮𐑍 𐐸𐐪𐑉𐐿𐐲𐑌𐐼 𐐲𐑌𐐻𐐭 𐑄 𐐶𐐲𐑉𐐼𐑆 𐐱𐑂 𐐘𐐮𐐼𐐨𐐲𐑌. 𐐈𐑌𐐼 𐐿𐐮𐑍 𐐢𐐮𐑋𐐸𐐴 𐐿𐐫𐑆𐐼 𐑄𐐰𐐻 𐐸𐐮𐑆 𐐹𐐨𐐹𐐲𐑊 𐑇𐐳𐐼 𐑀𐐰𐑄𐐲𐑉 𐑄𐐯𐑉 𐑁𐑊𐐱𐐿𐑅 𐐻𐐭𐑀𐐯𐑄𐐲𐑉; 𐐰𐑌𐐼 𐐸𐐨 𐑅𐐯𐑌𐐻 𐑄 𐐻𐑉𐐮𐐺𐐷𐐭𐐻 𐐱𐑂 𐐶𐐴𐑌 𐐻𐐭 𐑄 𐐢𐐰𐑋𐐲𐑌𐐴𐐻𐑅; 𐐰𐑌𐐼 𐐸𐐨 𐐫𐑊𐑅𐐬 𐑅𐐯𐑌𐐻 𐑋𐐬𐑉 𐐶𐐴𐑌, 𐐰𐑆 𐐰 𐐹𐑉𐐯𐑆𐐯𐑌𐐻 𐐲𐑌𐐻𐐭 𐑄𐐯𐑋: 𐐰𐑌𐐼 𐑄𐐩 𐐼𐐮𐐼 𐐼𐑉𐐮𐑍𐐿 𐑁𐑉𐐨𐑊𐐨 𐐱𐑂 𐑄 𐐶𐐴𐑌 𐐸𐐶𐐮𐐽 𐐿𐐮𐑍 𐐢𐐮𐑋𐐸𐐴 𐐼𐐮𐐼 𐑅𐐯𐑌𐐼 𐐲𐑌𐐻𐐭 𐑄𐐯𐑋.

3. 𐐈𐑌𐐼 𐐮𐐻 𐐿𐐩𐑋 𐐻𐐭 𐐹𐐪𐑅 𐑄𐐰𐐻 𐑄 𐐹𐐨𐐹𐐲𐑊 𐐱𐑂 𐐿𐐮𐑍 𐐢𐐮𐑋𐐸𐐴 𐐼𐐮𐐼 𐐼𐐨𐐹𐐪𐑉𐐻 𐐺𐐴 𐑌𐐴𐐻 𐐮𐑌𐐻𐐭 𐑄 𐐶𐐮𐑊𐐼𐐲𐑉𐑌𐐯𐑅 𐐶𐐮𐑄 𐑄𐐯𐑉 𐑁𐑊𐐱𐐿𐑅 𐐰𐑌𐐼 𐑄𐐯𐑉 𐐸𐐲𐑉𐐼𐑆, 𐐰𐑌𐐼 𐑄𐐩 𐐶𐐯𐑌𐐻 𐑉𐐵𐑌𐐼 𐐰𐐺𐐵𐐻 𐑄 𐑊𐐰𐑌𐐼 𐐱𐑂 𐐟𐐴𐑊𐐲𐑋 𐐮𐑌 𐑄 𐐶𐐮𐑊𐐼𐐲𐑉𐑌𐐯𐑅, 𐐰𐑌𐐼 𐐺𐐯𐑌𐐻 𐑄𐐯𐑉 𐐿𐐬𐑉𐑅 𐐻𐐬𐑉𐐼𐑆 𐑄 𐑊𐐰𐑌𐐼 𐐱𐑂 𐐞𐐰𐑉𐐲𐐸𐐯𐑋𐑊𐐲, 𐐺𐐨𐐮𐑍 𐑊𐐯𐐼 𐐺𐐴 𐐈𐑋𐐲𐑌 𐐰𐑌𐐼 𐐸𐐮𐑆 𐐺𐑉𐐯𐑄𐑉𐐯𐑌. 𐐈𐑌𐐼 𐑄𐐩 𐐸𐐰𐐼 𐐻𐐩𐐿𐐲𐑌 𐐫𐑊 𐑄𐐯𐑉 𐑀𐐬𐑊𐐼, 𐐰𐑌𐐼 𐑅𐐮𐑊𐑂𐐲𐑉, 𐐰𐑌𐐼 𐑄𐐯𐑉 𐐹𐑉𐐯𐑇𐐲𐑅 𐑃𐐮𐑍𐑆, 𐐸𐐶𐐮𐐽 𐑄𐐩 𐐿𐐳𐐼 𐐿𐐰𐑉𐐨; 𐐰𐑌𐐼 𐐫𐑊𐑅𐐬 𐑄𐐯𐑉 𐐹𐑉𐐬𐑂𐐮𐑈𐐲𐑌𐑆 𐐶𐐮𐑄 𐑄𐐯𐑋, 𐐮𐑌𐐻𐐭 𐑄 𐐶𐐮𐑊𐐼𐐲𐑉𐑌𐐯𐑅; 𐐰𐑌𐐼 𐑄𐐩 𐐹𐐲𐑉𐑅𐐭𐐼 𐑄𐐯𐑉 𐐾𐐲𐑉𐑌𐐨. 𐐈𐑌𐐼 𐐰𐑁𐐻𐐲𐑉 𐐺𐐨𐐮𐑍 𐑋𐐯𐑌𐐨 𐐼𐐩𐑆 𐐮𐑌 𐑄 𐐶𐐮𐑊𐐼𐐲𐑉𐑌𐐯𐑅, 𐑄𐐩 𐐰𐑉𐐴𐑂𐐼 𐐮𐑌 𐑄 𐑊𐐰𐑌𐐼 𐐱𐑂 𐐞𐐰𐑉𐐲𐐸𐐯𐑋𐑊𐐲, 𐐰𐑌𐐼 𐐾𐑎𐑌𐐼 𐐸𐐮𐑆 𐐹𐐨𐐹𐐲𐑊, 𐐰𐑌𐐼 𐐺𐐨𐐿𐐩𐑋 𐐸𐐮𐑆 𐑅𐐲𐐺𐐾𐐯𐐿𐐻𐑅. 𐐈𐑌𐐼 𐐮𐐻 𐐿𐐩𐑋 𐐻𐐭 𐐹𐐪𐑅 𐑄𐐰𐐻 𐐣𐐬𐑅𐐴𐐪 𐑉𐐨𐑅𐐨𐑂𐐼 𐑄𐐯𐑋 𐐶𐐮𐑄 𐐾𐑎; 𐐰𐑌𐐼 𐐸𐐨 𐐫𐑊𐑅𐐬 𐑉𐐨𐑅𐐨𐑂𐐼 𐑄𐐯𐑉 𐑉𐐯𐐿𐐲𐑉𐐼𐑆, 𐐰𐑌𐐼 𐐫𐑊𐑅𐐬 𐑄 𐑉𐐯𐐿𐐲𐑉𐐼𐑆 𐐸𐐶𐐮𐐽 𐐸𐐰𐐼 𐐺𐐮𐑌 𐑁𐐵𐑌𐐼 𐐺𐐴 𐑄 𐐹𐐨𐐹𐐲𐑊 𐐱𐑂 𐐢𐐮𐑋𐐸𐐴. 𐐈𐑌𐐼 𐑌𐐵 𐐮𐐻 𐐿𐐩𐑋 𐐻𐐭 𐐹𐐪𐑅 𐐸𐐶𐐯𐑌 𐑄 𐐢𐐰𐑋𐐲𐑌𐐴𐐻𐑅 𐐸𐐰𐐼 𐑁𐐵𐑌𐐼 𐑄𐐰𐐻 𐑄 𐐹𐐨𐐹𐐲𐑊 𐐱𐑂 𐐢𐐮𐑋𐐸𐐴 𐐸𐐰𐐼 𐐼𐐨𐐹𐐪𐑉𐐻𐐯𐐼 𐐵𐐻 𐐱𐑂 𐑄 𐑊𐐰𐑌𐐼 𐐺𐐴 𐑌𐐴𐐻, 𐑄𐐰𐐻 𐑄𐐩 𐑅𐐯𐑌𐐻 𐐰𐑌 𐐪𐑉𐑋𐐨 𐐮𐑌𐐻𐐭 𐑄 𐐶𐐮𐑊𐐼𐐲𐑉𐑌𐐯𐑅 𐐻𐐭 𐐹𐐲𐑉𐑅𐐭 𐑄𐐯𐑋; 𐐰𐑌𐐼 𐐰𐑁𐐻𐐲𐑉 𐑄𐐩 𐐸𐐰𐐼 𐐹𐐲𐑉𐑅𐐭𐐼 𐑄𐐯𐑋 𐐻𐐭 𐐼𐐩𐑆, 𐑄𐐩 𐐿𐐳𐐼 𐑌𐐬 𐑊𐐱𐑍𐑀𐐲𐑉 𐑁𐐱𐑊𐐬 𐑄𐐯𐑉 𐐻𐑉𐐰𐐿𐑅; 𐑄𐐯𐑉𐑁𐐬𐑉 𐑄𐐩 𐐶𐐲𐑉 𐑊𐐱𐑅𐐻 𐐮𐑌 𐑄 𐐶𐐮𐑊𐐼𐐲𐑉𐑌𐐯𐑅.

𐐕𐐈𐐑𐐓𐐊𐐡 XI.

𐐈𐑌 𐐰𐐿𐐵𐑌𐐻 𐐱𐑂 𐐈𐑊𐑋𐐲 𐐰𐑌𐐼 𐑄 𐐹𐐨𐐹𐐲𐑊 𐐱𐑂 𐑄 𐐢𐐫𐑉𐐼, 𐐸𐐭 𐐶𐐲𐑉 𐐼𐑉𐐮𐑂𐐲𐑌 𐐮𐑌𐐻𐐭 𐑄 𐐶𐐮𐑊𐐼𐐲𐑉𐑌𐐯𐑅 𐐺𐐴 𐑄 𐐹𐐨𐐹𐐲𐑊 𐐱𐑂 𐐿𐐮𐑍 𐐤𐐬𐐲.

1. 𐐤𐐵 𐐈𐑊𐑋𐐲, 𐐸𐐰𐑂𐐮𐑍 𐐺𐐮𐑌 𐐶𐐫𐑉𐑌𐐼 𐐱𐑂 𐑄 𐐢𐐫𐑉𐐼 𐑄𐐰𐐻 𐑄 𐐪𐑉𐑋𐐨𐑆 𐐱𐑂 𐐿𐐮𐑍 𐐤𐐬𐐲 𐐶𐐳𐐼 𐐿𐐲𐑋 𐐲𐐹𐐱𐑌 𐑄𐐯𐑋, 𐐰𐑌𐐼 𐐸𐐰𐐼 𐑋𐐩𐐼 𐐮𐐻 𐑌𐐬𐑌 𐐻𐐭 𐐸𐐮𐑆 𐐹𐐨𐐹𐐲𐑊, 𐑄𐐯𐑉𐑁𐐬𐑉 𐑄𐐩 𐑀𐐰𐑄𐐲𐑉𐐼 𐐻𐐭𐑀𐐯𐑄𐐲𐑉 𐑄𐐯𐑉 𐑁𐑊𐐱𐐿𐑅, 𐐰𐑌𐐼 𐐻𐐳𐐿 𐐱𐑂 𐑄𐐯𐑉 𐑀𐑉𐐩𐑌, 𐐰𐑌𐐼 𐐼𐐨𐐹𐐪𐑉𐐻𐐯𐐼 𐐮𐑌𐐻𐐭 𐑄 𐐶𐐮𐑊𐐼𐐲𐑉𐑌𐐯𐑅 𐐺𐐨𐑁𐐬𐑉 𐑄 𐐪𐑉𐑋𐐨𐑆 𐐱𐑂 𐐿𐐮𐑍 𐐤𐐬𐐲. 𐐈𐑌𐐼 𐑄 𐐢𐐫𐑉𐐼 𐐼𐐮𐐼 𐑅𐐻𐑉𐐯𐑍𐑃𐐲𐑌 𐑄𐐯𐑋, 𐑄𐐰𐐻 𐑄 𐐹𐐨𐐹𐐲𐑊 𐐱𐑂 𐐿𐐮𐑍 𐐤𐐬𐐲 𐐿𐐳𐐼 𐑌𐐱𐐻 𐐬𐑂𐐲𐑉𐐻𐐩𐐿 𐑄𐐯𐑋, 𐐻𐐭 𐐼𐐨𐑅𐐻𐑉𐑎 𐑄𐐯𐑋. 𐐈𐑌𐐼 𐑄𐐩 𐑁𐑊𐐯𐐼 𐐩𐐻 𐐼𐐩𐑆' 𐐾𐐲𐑉𐑌𐐨 𐐮𐑌𐐻𐐭 𐑄 𐐶𐐮𐑊𐐼𐐲𐑉𐑌𐐯𐑅. 𐐈𐑌𐐼 𐑄𐐩 𐐿𐐩𐑋 𐐻𐐭 𐐰 𐑊𐐰𐑌𐐼, 𐐷𐐩, 𐐨𐑂𐐲𐑌 𐐰 𐑂𐐯𐑉𐐨 𐐺𐐷𐐭𐐻𐐮𐑁𐐳𐑊 𐐰𐑌𐐼 𐐹𐑊𐐯𐑆𐐲𐑌𐐻 𐑊𐐰𐑌𐐼; 𐐰 𐑊𐐰𐑌𐐼 𐐱𐑂 𐐹𐐷𐐭𐑉 𐐶𐐫𐐻𐐲𐑉. 𐐈𐑌𐐼 𐑄𐐩 𐐹𐐮𐐽𐐻 𐑄𐐯𐑉 𐐻𐐯𐑌𐐻𐑅, 𐐰𐑌𐐼 𐐺𐐨𐑀𐐰𐑌 𐐻𐐭 𐐻𐐮𐑊 𐑄 𐑀𐑉𐐵𐑌𐐼, 𐐰𐑌𐐼 𐐺𐐨𐑀𐐰𐑌 𐐻𐐭 𐐺𐐮𐑊𐐼 𐐺𐐮𐑊𐐼𐐮𐑍𐑆, 𐐯𐐻𐑅.; 𐐷𐐩, 𐑄𐐩 𐐶𐐲𐑉 𐐮𐑌𐐼𐐲𐑅𐐻𐑉𐐨𐐲𐑅, 𐐰𐑌𐐼 𐐼𐐮𐐼 𐑊𐐩𐐺𐐲𐑉 𐐯𐐿𐑅𐐨𐐼𐐮𐑍𐑊𐐨. 𐐈𐑌𐐼 𐑄 𐐹𐐨𐐹𐐲𐑊 𐐶𐐲𐑉 𐐼𐐨𐑆𐐴𐑉𐐲𐑅 𐑄𐐰𐐻 𐐈𐑊𐑋𐐲 𐑇𐐳𐐼 𐐺𐐨 𐑄𐐯𐑉 𐐿𐐮𐑍, 𐑁𐐫𐑉 𐐸𐐨 𐐶𐐱𐑆 𐐺𐐨𐑊𐐲𐑂𐐯𐐼 𐐺𐐴 𐐸𐐮𐑆 𐐹𐐨𐐹𐐲𐑊. 𐐒𐐲𐐻 𐐸𐐨

𐑅𐐯𐐼 𐐲𐑌𐐻𐐭 𐑄𐐯𐑋, 𐐒𐐨𐐸𐐬𐑊𐐼, 𐐮𐐻 𐐮𐑆 𐑌𐐱𐐻 𐐯𐐿𐑅𐐹𐐨𐐼𐐨𐐲𐑌𐐻 𐑄𐐰𐐻 𐐶𐐨 𐑇𐐳𐐼 𐐸𐐰𐑂 𐐲 𐐿𐐮𐑍: 𐑁𐐫𐑉 𐑄𐐲𐑅 𐑅𐐯𐑃 𐑄 𐐢𐐫𐑉𐐼: 𐐏 𐑇𐐰𐑊 𐑌𐐱𐐻 𐐯𐑅𐐻𐐨𐑋 𐐶𐐲𐑌 𐑁𐑊𐐯𐑇 𐐲𐐺𐐲𐑂 𐐰𐑌𐐲𐑄𐐲𐑉, 𐐫𐑉 𐐶𐐲𐑌 𐑋𐐰𐑌 𐑇𐐰𐑊 𐑌𐐱𐐻 𐑃𐐮𐑍𐐿 𐐸𐐮𐑋𐑅𐐯𐑊𐑁 𐐲𐐺𐐲𐑂 𐐰𐑌𐐲𐑄𐐲𐑉; 𐑄𐐯𐑉𐑁𐐫𐑉 𐐌 𐑅𐐩 𐐲𐑌𐐻𐐭 𐐷𐐭, 𐐮𐐻 𐐮𐑆 𐑌𐐱𐐻 𐐯𐐿𐑅𐐹𐐨𐐼𐐨𐐲𐑌𐐻 𐑄𐐰𐐻 𐐷𐐨 𐑇𐐳𐐼 𐐸𐐰𐑂 𐐲 𐐿𐐮𐑍. 𐐤𐐯𐑂𐐲𐑉𐑄𐐲𐑊𐐯𐑅 𐐮𐑁 𐐮𐐻 𐐶𐐲𐑉 𐐹𐐱𐑅𐐮𐐺𐑊 𐑄𐐰𐐻 𐐷𐐨 𐐿𐐳𐐼 𐐫𐑊𐐶𐐩𐑆 𐐸𐐰𐑂 𐐾𐐲𐑅𐐻 𐑋𐐯𐑌 𐐻𐐭 𐐺𐐨 𐐷𐐭𐑉 𐐿𐐮𐑍𐑆, 𐐮𐐻 𐐶𐐳𐐼 𐐺𐐨 𐐶𐐯𐑊 𐑁𐐫𐑉 𐐷𐐭 𐐻𐐭 𐐸𐐰𐑂 𐐲 𐐿𐐮𐑍. 𐐒𐐲𐐻 𐑉𐐨𐑋𐐯𐑋𐐺𐐲𐑉 𐑄 𐐮𐑌𐐮𐐿𐐶𐐮𐐻𐐨 𐐱𐑂 𐐿𐐮𐑍 𐐤𐐬𐐲 𐐰𐑌𐐼 𐐸𐐮𐑆 𐐹𐑉𐐨𐑅𐐻𐑅: 𐐰𐑌𐐼 𐐌 𐑋𐐴𐑅𐐯𐑊𐑁 𐐶𐐱𐑆 𐐿𐐫𐐻 𐐮𐑌 𐐲 𐑅𐑌𐐩𐑉, 𐐰𐑌𐐼 𐐼𐐮𐐼 𐑋𐐯𐑌𐐨 𐑃𐐮𐑍𐑆 𐐸𐐶𐐮𐐽 𐐶𐐲𐑉 𐐲𐐺𐐱𐑋𐐮𐑌𐐲𐐺𐑊 𐐮𐑌 𐑄 𐑅𐐴𐐻 𐐱𐑂 𐑄 𐐢𐐫𐑉𐐼, 𐐸𐐶𐐮𐐽 𐐿𐐫𐑆𐐼 𐑋𐐨 𐑅𐐬𐑉 𐑉𐐨𐐹𐐯𐑌𐐻𐐲𐑌𐑅; 𐑌𐐯𐑂𐐲𐑉𐑄𐐲𐑊𐐯𐑅, 𐐰𐑁𐐻𐐲𐑉 𐑋𐐲𐐽 𐐻𐑉𐐮𐐺𐐷𐐭𐑊𐐩𐑇𐐲𐑌, 𐑄 𐐢𐐫𐑉𐐼 𐐼𐐮𐐼 𐐸𐐨𐑉 𐑋𐐴 𐐿𐑉𐐴𐑆, 𐐰𐑌𐐼 𐐼𐐮𐐼 𐐰𐑌𐑅𐐲𐑉 𐑋𐐴 𐐹𐑉𐐩𐑉𐑆, 𐐰𐑌𐐼 𐐸𐐰𐑆 𐑋𐐩𐐼 𐑋𐐨 𐐰𐑌 𐐮𐑌𐑅𐐻𐑉𐐭𐑋𐐯𐑌𐐻 𐐮𐑌 𐐸𐐮𐑆 𐐸𐐰𐑌𐐼𐑆, 𐐮𐑌 𐐺𐑉𐐮𐑍𐐮𐑍 𐑅𐐬 𐑋𐐯𐑌𐐨 𐐱𐑂 𐐷𐐭 𐐻𐐭 𐐲 𐑌𐐱𐑊𐐯𐐾 𐐱𐑂 𐐸𐐮𐑆 𐐻𐑉𐐭𐑃. 𐐤𐐯𐑂𐐲𐑉𐑄𐐲𐑊𐐯𐑅, 𐐮𐑌 𐑄𐐮𐑅 𐐌 𐐼𐐭 𐑌𐐱𐐻 𐑀𐑊𐐬𐑉𐐨, 𐑁𐐫𐑉 𐐌 𐐰𐑋 𐐲𐑌𐐶𐐲𐑉𐑄𐐨 𐐻𐐭 𐑀𐑊𐐬𐑉𐐨 𐐱𐑂 𐑋𐐴𐑅𐐯𐑊𐑁. 𐐈𐑌𐐼 𐑌𐐵 𐐌 𐑅𐐩 𐐲𐑌𐐻𐐭 𐐷𐐭, 𐐏 𐐸𐐰𐑂 𐐺𐐮𐑌 𐐱𐐹𐑉𐐯𐑅𐐻 𐐺𐐴 𐐿𐐮𐑍 𐐤𐐬𐐲, 𐐰𐑌𐐼 𐐸𐐰𐑂 𐐺𐐮𐑌 𐐮𐑌 𐐺𐐱𐑌𐐼𐐩𐐾 𐐻𐐭 𐐸𐐮𐑋 𐐰𐑌𐐼 𐐸𐐮𐑆 𐐹𐑉𐐨𐑅𐐻𐑅, 𐐰𐑌𐐼 𐐸𐐰𐑂 𐐺𐐮𐑌 𐐺𐑉𐐫𐐻 𐐮𐑌𐐻𐐭 𐐮𐑌𐐮𐐿𐐶𐐮𐐻𐐨 𐐺𐐴 𐑄𐐯𐑋; 𐑄𐐯𐑉𐑁𐐫𐑉 𐐷𐐨 𐐶𐐲𐑉 𐐺𐐵𐑌𐐼 𐐶𐐮𐑄 𐑄 𐐺𐐰𐑌𐐼𐑆 𐐱𐑂 𐐮𐑌𐐮𐐿𐐶𐐮𐐻𐐨.

2. 𐐈𐑌𐐼 𐑌𐐵 𐐰𐑆 𐐷𐐨 𐐸𐐰𐑂 𐐺𐐮𐑌 𐐼𐐮𐑊𐐮𐑂𐐲𐑉𐐼 𐐺𐐴 𐑄 𐐹𐐵𐐲𐑉 𐐱𐑂 𐐘𐐱𐐼 𐐵𐐻 𐐱𐑂 𐑄𐐨𐑆 𐐺𐐱𐑌𐐼𐑆; 𐐷𐐩, 𐐨𐑂𐐲𐑌 𐐵𐐻 𐐱𐑂 𐑄 𐐸𐐰𐑌𐐼𐑆 𐐱𐑂 𐐿𐐮𐑍 𐐤𐐬𐐲 𐐰𐑌𐐼 𐐸𐐮𐑆 𐐹𐐨𐐹𐑊, 𐐰𐑌𐐼 𐐫𐑊𐑅𐐬 𐑁𐑉𐐱𐑋 𐑄 𐐺𐐱𐑌𐐼𐑆 𐐱𐑂 𐐮𐑌𐐮𐐿𐐶𐐮𐐻𐐨, 𐐨𐑂𐐲𐑌 𐑅𐐬 𐐌 𐐼𐐨𐑆𐐴𐑉 𐑄𐐰𐐻 𐐷𐐨 𐑇𐐳𐐼 𐑅𐐻𐐰𐑌𐐼 𐑁𐐰𐑅𐐻 𐐮𐑌 𐑄𐐮𐑅 𐑊𐐮𐐺𐐲𐑉𐐻𐐨 𐐸𐐶𐐯𐑉𐐶𐐮𐑄 𐐷𐐨 𐐸𐐰𐑂 𐐺𐐮𐑌 𐑋𐐩𐐼 𐑁𐑉𐐨, 𐐰𐑌𐐼 𐑄𐐰𐐻 𐐷𐐨 𐐻𐑉𐐲𐑅𐐻 𐑌𐐬 𐑋𐐰𐑌 𐐻𐐭 𐐺𐐨 𐐲 𐐿𐐮𐑍 𐐬𐑂𐐲𐑉 𐐷𐐭; 𐐰𐑌𐐼 𐐫𐑊𐑅𐐬 𐐻𐑉𐐲𐑅𐐻 𐑌𐐬 𐐶𐐲𐑌 𐐻𐐭 𐐺𐐨 𐐷𐐭𐑉 𐐻𐐨𐐽𐐲𐑉 𐑌𐐫𐑉 𐐷𐐭𐑉 𐑋𐐮𐑌𐐮𐑅𐐻𐐲𐑉, 𐐯𐐿𐑅𐐯𐐹𐐻 𐐸𐐨 𐐺𐐨 𐐲 𐑋𐐰𐑌 𐐱𐑂 𐐘𐐱𐐼, 𐐶𐐫𐐿𐐮𐑍 𐐮𐑌 𐐸𐐮𐑆 𐐶𐐩𐑆 𐐰𐑌𐐼 𐐿𐐨𐐹𐐮𐑍 𐐸𐐮𐑆 𐐿𐐱𐑋𐐰𐑌𐐼𐑋𐐯𐑌𐐻𐑅. 𐐜𐐲𐑅 𐐼𐐮𐐼 𐐈𐑊𐑋𐐲 𐐻𐐨𐐽 𐐸𐐮𐑆 𐐹𐐨𐐹𐑊, 𐑄𐐰𐐻 𐐯𐑂𐐲𐑉𐐨 𐑋𐐰𐑌 𐑇𐐳𐐼 𐑊𐐲𐑂 𐐸𐐮𐑆 𐑌𐐩𐐺𐐲𐑉 𐐰𐑆 𐐸𐐮𐑋𐑅𐐯𐑊𐑁, 𐑄𐐰𐐻 𐑄𐐯𐑉 𐑇𐐳𐐼 𐐺𐐨 𐑌𐐬 𐐿𐐱𐑌𐐻𐐯𐑌𐑇𐐲𐑌 𐐲𐑋𐐲𐑍 𐑄𐐯𐑋. 𐐈𐑌𐐼 𐑌𐐵 𐐈𐑊𐑋𐐲 𐐶𐐱𐑆 𐑄𐐯𐑉 𐐸𐐴 𐐹𐑉𐐨𐑅𐐻, 𐐸𐐨 𐐺𐐨𐐮𐑍 𐑄 𐑁𐐵𐑌𐐼𐐲𐑉 𐐱𐑂 𐑄𐐯𐑉 𐐽𐐲𐑉𐐽. 𐐈𐑌𐐼 𐐮𐐻 𐐿𐐩𐑋 𐐻𐐭 𐐹𐐰𐑅 𐑄𐐰𐐻 𐑌𐐲𐑌 𐑉𐐨𐑅𐐨𐑂𐐼 𐐫𐑃𐐱𐑉𐐮𐐻𐐨 𐐻𐐭 𐐹𐑉𐐨𐐽 𐐫𐑉 𐐻𐐭 𐐻𐐨𐐽, 𐐯𐐿𐑅𐐯𐐹𐐻 𐐮𐐻 𐐶𐐲𐑉 𐐺𐐴 𐐸𐐮𐑋 𐑁𐑉𐐱𐑋 𐐘𐐱𐐼. 𐐜𐐯𐑉𐑁𐐫𐑉 𐐸𐐨 𐐿𐐱𐑌𐑅𐐨𐐿𐑉𐐩𐐻𐐯𐐼 𐐫𐑊 𐑄𐐯𐑉 𐐹𐑉𐐨𐑅𐐻𐑅 𐐰𐑌𐐼 𐐫𐑊 𐑄𐐯𐑉 𐐻𐐨𐐽𐐲𐑉𐑆; 𐐰𐑌𐐼 𐑌𐐲𐑌 𐐶𐐲𐑉 𐐿𐐱𐑌𐑅𐐨𐐿𐑉𐐩𐐻𐐯𐐼 𐐯𐐿𐑅𐐯𐐹𐐻 𐑄𐐩 𐐶𐐲𐑉 𐐾𐐲𐑅𐐻 𐑋𐐯𐑌. 𐐜𐐯𐑉𐑁𐐫𐑉 𐑄𐐩 𐐼𐐮𐐼 𐐶𐐱𐐽 𐐬𐑂𐐲𐑉 𐑄𐐯𐑉 𐐹𐐨𐐹𐑊, 𐐰𐑌𐐼 𐐼𐐮𐐼 𐑌𐐲𐑉𐐮𐑇 𐑄𐐯𐑋 𐐶𐐮𐑄 𐑃𐐮𐑍𐑆 𐐹𐐲𐑉𐐻𐐩𐑌𐐮𐑍 𐐻𐐭 𐑉𐐴𐐽𐐲𐑅𐑌𐐯𐑅. 𐐈𐑌𐐼 𐐮𐐻 𐐿𐐩𐑋 𐐻𐐭 𐐹𐐰𐑅 𐑄𐐰𐐻 𐑄𐐩 𐐺𐐨𐑀𐐰𐑌 𐐻𐐭 𐐹𐑉𐐱𐑅𐐹𐐲𐑉 𐐯𐐿𐑅𐐨𐐼𐐮𐑍𐑊𐐨 𐐮𐑌 𐑄 𐑊𐐰𐑌𐐼; 𐐰𐑌𐐼 𐑄𐐩 𐐿𐐫𐑊𐐼 𐑄 𐑊𐐰𐑌𐐼 𐐐𐐨𐑊𐐲𐑋. 𐐈𐑌𐐼 𐐮𐐻 𐐿𐐩𐑋 𐐻𐐭 𐐹𐐰𐑅 𐑄𐐰𐐻 𐑄𐐩 𐐼𐐮𐐼 𐑋𐐲𐑊𐐻𐐮𐐹𐑊𐐴 𐐰𐑌𐐼 𐐹𐑉𐐱𐑅𐐹𐐲𐑉 𐐯𐐿𐑅𐐨𐐼𐐮𐑍𐑊𐐨 𐐮𐑌 𐑄 𐑊𐐰𐑌𐐼 𐐱𐑂 𐐐𐐨𐑊𐐲𐑋; 𐐰𐑌𐐼 𐑄𐐩 𐐺𐐮𐑊𐐻 𐐲 𐑅𐐮𐐻𐐨, 𐐸𐐶𐐮𐐽 𐑄𐐩 𐐿𐐫𐑊𐐼 𐑄 𐑅𐐮𐐻𐐨 𐐱𐑂 𐐐𐐨𐑊𐐲𐑋. 𐐤𐐯𐑂𐐲𐑉𐑄𐐲𐑊𐐯𐑅 𐑄 𐐢𐐫𐑉𐐼 𐑅𐐨𐐯𐑃 𐑁𐐮𐐻 𐐻𐐭 𐐽𐐩𐑅𐐲𐑌 𐐸𐐮𐑆 𐐹𐐨𐐹𐑊; 𐐷𐐩, 𐐸𐐨 𐐻𐑉𐐴𐐯𐑃 𐑄𐐯𐑉 𐐹𐐩𐑇𐐯𐑌𐑅 𐐰𐑌𐐼 𐑄𐐯𐑉 𐑁𐐩𐑃. 𐐤𐐯𐑂𐐲𐑉𐑄𐐲𐑊𐐯𐑅, 𐐸𐐭𐑅𐐬𐐯𐑂𐐲𐑉 𐐹𐐳𐐻𐐯𐑃 𐐸𐐮𐑆 𐐻𐑉𐐲𐑅𐐻 𐐮𐑌 𐐸𐐮𐑋, 𐑄 𐑅𐐩𐑋 𐑇𐐰𐑊 𐐺𐐨 𐑊𐐮𐑁𐐻𐐯𐐼 𐐲𐐹 𐐰𐐻 𐑄 𐑊𐐰𐑅𐐻 𐐼𐐩. 𐐏𐐩, 𐐰𐑌𐐼 𐑄𐐲𐑅 𐐮𐐻 𐐶𐐱𐑆 𐐶𐐮𐑄 𐑄𐐮𐑅 𐐹𐐨𐐹𐑊. 𐐙𐐫𐑉 𐐺𐐨𐐸𐐬𐑊𐐼, 𐐌 𐐶𐐮𐑊 𐑇𐐬 𐐲𐑌𐐻𐐭 𐐷𐐭 𐑄𐐰𐐻 𐑄𐐩 𐐶𐐲𐑉 𐐺𐑉𐐫𐐻 𐐮𐑌𐐻𐐭 𐐺𐐱𐑌𐐼𐐩𐐾, 𐐰𐑌𐐼 𐑌𐐲𐑌 𐐿𐐳𐐼 𐐼𐐮𐑊𐐮𐑂𐐲𐑉 𐑄𐐯𐑋 𐐺𐐲𐐻 𐑄 𐐢𐐫𐑉𐐼 𐑄𐐯𐑉 𐐘𐐱𐐼; 𐐷𐐩, 𐐨𐑂𐐲𐑌 𐑄 𐐘𐐱𐐼 𐐱𐑂 𐐁𐐺𐑉𐐲𐐸𐐰𐑋 𐐰𐑌𐐼 𐐌𐑆𐐲𐐿, 𐐰𐑌𐐼 𐐱𐑂 𐐖𐐩𐐿𐐲𐐺. 𐐈𐑌𐐼 𐐮𐐻 𐐿𐐩𐑋 𐐻𐐭 𐐹𐐰𐑅 𐑄𐐰𐐻 𐐸𐐨 𐐼𐐮𐐼 𐐼𐐮𐑊𐐮𐑂𐐲𐑉 𐑄𐐯𐑋, 𐐰𐑌𐐼 𐐼𐐮𐐼 𐑇𐐬 𐑁𐐬𐑉𐑃 𐐸𐐮𐑆 𐑋𐐴𐐻𐐨 𐐹𐐵𐐲𐑉 𐐲𐑌𐐻𐐭 𐑄𐐯𐑋, 𐐰𐑌𐐼 𐑀𐑉𐐩𐐻 𐐶𐐲𐑉 𐑄𐐯𐑉 𐑉𐐨𐐾𐐱𐐮𐑅𐐮𐑍𐑆.

3. 𐐙𐐫𐑉 𐐺𐐨𐐸𐐬𐑊𐐼, 𐐮𐐻 𐐿𐐩𐑋 𐐻𐐭 𐐹𐐰𐑅 𐑄𐐰𐐻 𐐸𐐶𐐴𐑊 𐑄𐐩 𐐶𐐲𐑉 𐐮𐑌 𐑄 𐑊𐐰𐑌𐐼 𐐱𐑂 𐐐𐐨𐑊𐐲𐑋, 𐐷𐐩, 𐐮𐑌 𐑄 𐑅𐐮𐐻𐐨 𐐱𐑂 𐐐𐐨𐑊𐐲𐑋, 𐐸𐐶𐐴𐑊 𐐻𐐮𐑊𐐮𐑍 𐑄 𐑊𐐰𐑌𐐼 𐑉𐐵𐑌𐐼 𐐲𐐺𐐵𐐻, 𐐺𐐨𐐸𐐬𐑊𐐼 𐐰𐑌 𐐪𐑉𐑋𐐨 𐐱𐑂 𐑄 𐐢𐐩𐑋𐐲𐑌𐐴𐐻𐑅 𐐶𐐱𐑆 𐐮𐑌 𐑄 𐐺𐐫𐑉𐐼𐐲𐑉𐑆 𐐱𐑂 𐑄 𐑊𐐰𐑌𐐼. 𐐤𐐵 𐐮𐐻 𐐿𐐩𐑋 𐐻𐐭 𐐹𐐰𐑅 𐑄𐐰𐐻 𐑄 𐐺𐑉𐐯𐑄𐑉𐐯𐑌 𐐱𐑂 𐐈𐑊𐑋𐐲 𐑁𐑊𐐯𐐼 𐑁𐑉𐐱𐑋 𐑄𐐯𐑉 𐑁𐐨𐑊𐐼𐑆, 𐐰𐑌𐐼 𐑀𐐰𐑄𐐲𐑉𐐼 𐑄𐐯𐑋𐑅𐐯𐑊𐑂𐑆 𐐻𐐭𐑀𐐯𐑄𐐲𐑉 𐐮𐑌 𐑄 𐑅𐐮𐐻𐐨 𐐱𐑂 𐐐𐐨𐑊𐐲𐑋; 𐐰𐑌𐐼 𐑄𐐩 𐐶𐐲𐑉 𐑋𐐲𐐽 𐑁𐑉𐐴𐐻𐐲𐑌𐐼 𐐺𐐨𐐿𐐫𐑆 𐐱𐑂 𐑄 𐐲𐐹𐐨𐑉𐐲𐑌𐑅 𐐱𐑂 𐑄 𐐢𐐩𐑋𐐲𐑌𐐴𐐻𐑅. 𐐒𐐲𐐻 𐐈𐑊𐑋𐐲 𐐶𐐯𐑌𐐻 𐑁𐐬𐑉𐑃 𐐰𐑌𐐼 𐑅𐐻𐐳𐐼 𐐲𐑋𐐲𐑍 𐑄𐐯𐑋, 𐐰𐑌𐐼 𐐯𐑀𐑆𐐫𐑉𐐻𐐯𐐼 𐑄𐐯𐑋 𐑄𐐰𐐻 𐑄𐐩 𐑇𐐳𐐼 𐑌𐐱𐐻 𐐺𐐨 𐑁𐑉𐐴𐐻𐐲𐑌𐐼, 𐐺𐐲𐐻 𐑄𐐰𐐻 𐑄𐐩 𐑇𐐳𐐼 𐑉𐐨𐑋𐐯𐑋𐐺𐐲𐑉 𐑄 𐐢𐐫𐑉𐐼 𐑄𐐯𐑉 𐐘𐐱𐐼, 𐐰𐑌𐐼 𐐸𐐨 𐐶𐐳𐐼 𐐼𐐮𐑊𐐮𐑂𐐲𐑉 𐑄𐐯𐑋; 𐑄𐐯𐑉𐑁𐐫𐑉 𐑄𐐩 𐐸𐐲𐑇𐐻 𐑄𐐯𐑉 𐑁𐐨𐑉𐑆, 𐐰𐑌𐐼

𐐺𐐨𐑀𐐰𐑌 𐐻𐐭 𐐿𐑉𐐴 𐐲𐑌𐐻𐐭 𐑄 𐐢𐐫𐑉𐐼, 𐑄𐐰𐐻 𐐸𐐨 𐐶𐐳𐐼 𐑅𐐫𐑁𐑌 𐑄 𐐸𐐪𐑉𐐻𐑅 𐐲𐑂 𐑄 𐐢𐐩𐑋𐐲𐑌𐐴𐐻𐑅, 𐑄𐐰𐐻 𐑄𐐩 𐐶𐐳𐐼 𐑅𐐹𐐩𐑉 𐑄𐐯𐑋, 𐐰𐑌𐐼 𐑄𐐩𐑉 𐐶𐐴𐑂𐑆, 𐐰𐑌𐐼 𐑄𐐩𐑉 𐐽𐐮𐑊𐐼𐑉𐐯𐑌. 𐐈𐑌𐐼 𐐮𐐻 𐐿𐐩𐑋 𐐻𐐭 𐐹𐐰𐑅 𐑄𐐰𐐻 𐑄 𐐢𐐫𐑉𐐼 𐐼𐐮𐐼 𐑅𐐫𐑁𐑌 𐑄 𐐸𐐪𐑉𐐻𐑅 𐐲𐑂 𐑄 𐐢𐐩𐑋𐐲𐑌𐐴𐐻𐑅. 𐐈𐑌𐐼 𐐈𐑊𐑋𐐲 𐐰𐑌𐐼 𐐸𐐮𐑆 𐐺𐑉𐐯𐑄𐑉𐐯𐑌 𐐶𐐯𐑌𐐻 𐑁𐐬𐑉𐑃 𐐰𐑌𐐼 𐐼𐐨𐑊𐐮𐑂𐐲𐑉𐐼 𐑄𐐯𐑋𐑅𐐯𐑊𐑂𐑆 𐐲𐐹 𐐮𐑌𐐻𐐭 𐑄𐐩𐑉 𐐸𐐰𐑌𐐼𐑆; 𐐰𐑌𐐼 𐑄 𐐢𐐩𐑋𐐲𐑌𐐴𐐻𐑅 𐐻𐐳𐐿 𐐹𐐲𐑆𐐯𐑇𐐲𐑌 𐐲𐑂 𐑄 𐑊𐐰𐑌𐐼 𐐲𐑂 𐐐𐐨𐑊𐐲𐑋. 𐐤𐐵 𐑄 𐐪𐑉𐑋𐐨𐑆 𐐲𐑂 𐑄 𐐢𐐩𐑋𐐲𐑌𐐴𐐻𐑅 𐐸𐐶𐐮𐐽 𐐸𐐰𐐼 𐑁𐐱𐑊𐐬𐐼 𐐰𐑁𐐻𐐲𐑉 𐑄 𐐹𐐨𐐹𐑊 𐐲𐑂 𐐿𐐮𐑍 𐐢𐐮𐑋𐐸𐐴, 𐐸𐐰𐐼 𐐺𐐮𐑌 𐑊𐐱𐑅𐐻 𐐮𐑌 𐑄 𐐶𐐮𐑊𐐼𐐲𐑉𐑌𐐯𐑅 𐑁𐐫𐑉 𐑋𐐯𐑌𐐨 𐐼𐐩𐑆. 𐐈𐑌𐐼 𐐺𐐨𐐸𐐬𐑊𐐼, 𐑄𐐩 𐐸𐐰𐐼 𐑁𐐵𐑌𐐼 𐑄𐐬𐑆 𐐹𐑉𐐨𐑅𐐻𐑅 𐐲𐑂 𐐿𐐮𐑍 𐐤𐐬𐐲, 𐐮𐑌 𐐲 𐐹𐑊𐐩𐑅 𐐸𐐶𐐮𐐽 𐑄𐐩 𐐿𐐫𐑊𐐼 𐐈𐑋𐐷𐐭𐑊𐐲𐑌; 𐐰𐑌𐐼 𐑄𐐩 𐐸𐐰𐐼 𐐺𐐨𐑀𐐲𐑌 𐐻𐐭 𐐹𐐲𐑆𐐯𐑅 𐑄 𐑊𐐰𐑌𐐼 𐐲𐑂 𐐈𐑋𐐷𐐭𐑊𐐲𐑌, 𐐰𐑌𐐼 𐐸𐐰𐐼 𐐺𐐨𐑀𐐲𐑌 𐐻𐐭 𐐻𐐮𐑊 𐑄 𐑀𐑉𐐵𐑌𐐼. 𐐤𐐵 𐑄 𐑌𐐩𐑋 𐐲𐑂 𐑄 𐑊𐐨𐐼𐐲𐑉 𐐲𐑂 𐑄𐐬𐑆 𐐹𐑉𐐨𐑅𐐻𐑅 𐐶𐐱𐑆 𐐈𐑋𐐷𐐭𐑊𐐲𐑌. 𐐈𐑌𐐼 𐐮𐐻 𐐿𐐩𐑋 𐐻𐐭 𐐹𐐰𐑅 𐑄𐐰𐐻 𐐈𐑋𐐷𐐭𐑊𐐲𐑌 𐐼𐐮𐐼 𐐹𐑊𐐨𐐼 𐐶𐐮𐑄 𐑄 𐐢𐐩𐑋𐐲𐑌𐐴𐐻𐑅; 𐐰𐑌𐐼 𐐸𐐨 𐐫𐑊𐑅𐐬 𐑅𐐯𐑌𐐻 𐑁𐐬𐑉𐑃 𐑄𐐩𐑉 𐐶𐐴𐑂𐑆, 𐐸𐐭 𐐶𐐲𐑉 𐑄 𐐼𐐫𐐻𐐲𐑉𐑆 𐐲𐑂 𐑄 𐐢𐐩𐑋𐐲𐑌𐐴𐐻𐑅, 𐐻𐐭 𐐹𐑊𐐨𐐼 𐐶𐐮𐑄 𐑄𐐩𐑉 𐐺𐑉𐐯𐑄𐑉𐐯𐑌, 𐑄𐐰𐐻 𐑄𐐩 𐑇𐐳𐐼 𐑌𐐱𐐻 𐐼𐐨𐑅𐐻𐑉𐐦 𐑄𐐩𐑉 𐐸𐐲𐑆𐐺𐐲𐑌𐐼𐑆. 𐐈𐑌𐐼 𐑄 𐐢𐐩𐑋𐐲𐑌𐐴𐐻𐑅 𐐸𐐰𐐼 𐐿𐐲𐑋𐐹𐐰𐑇𐐲𐑌 𐐱𐑌 𐐈𐑋𐐷𐐭𐑊𐐲𐑌 𐐰𐑌𐐼 𐐸𐐮𐑆 𐐺𐑉𐐯𐑄𐑉𐐯𐑌, 𐐰𐑌𐐼 𐐼𐐮𐐼 𐑌𐐱𐐻 𐐼𐐨𐑅𐐻𐑉𐐦 𐑄𐐯𐑋, 𐐺𐐨𐐿𐐫𐑆 𐐲𐑂 𐑄𐐩𐑉 𐐶𐐴𐑂𐑆. 𐐈𐑌𐐼 𐐈𐑋𐐷𐐭𐑊𐐲𐑌 𐐰𐑌𐐼 𐐸𐐮𐑆 𐐺𐑉𐐯𐑄𐑉𐐯𐑌 𐐼𐐮𐐼 𐐾𐐦𐑌 𐑄 𐐢𐐩𐑋𐐲𐑌𐐴𐐻𐑅, 𐐰𐑌𐐼 𐑄𐐩 𐐶𐐲𐑉 𐐻𐑉𐐰𐑂𐐯𐑊𐐮𐑍 𐐮𐑌 𐑄 𐐶𐐮𐑊𐐼𐐲𐑉𐑌𐐯𐑅 𐐮𐑌 𐑅𐐲𐑉𐐽 𐐲𐑂 𐑄 𐑊𐐰𐑌𐐼 𐐲𐑂 𐐤𐐨𐑁𐐴, 𐐸𐐶𐐯𐑌 𐑄𐐩 𐐼𐐮𐑅𐐿𐐲𐑂𐐲𐑉𐐼 𐑄 𐑊𐐰𐑌𐐼 𐐲𐑂 𐐐𐐨𐑊𐐲𐑋, 𐐸𐐶𐐮𐐽 𐐶𐐱𐑆 𐐹𐐲𐑆𐐯𐑅𐐻 𐐺𐐴 𐐈𐑊𐑋𐐲 𐐰𐑌𐐼 𐐸𐐮𐑆 𐐺𐑉𐐯𐑄𐑉𐐯𐑌. 𐐈𐑌𐐼 𐐮𐐻 𐐿𐐩𐑋 𐐻𐐭 𐐹𐐰𐑅 𐑄𐐰𐐻 𐑄 𐐢𐐩𐑋𐐲𐑌𐐴𐐻𐑅 𐐹𐑉𐐱𐑋𐐮𐑅𐐻 𐐲𐑌𐐻𐐭 𐐈𐑊𐑋𐐲 𐐰𐑌𐐼 𐐸𐐮𐑆 𐐺𐑉𐐯𐑄𐑉𐐯𐑌, 𐑄𐐰𐐻 𐐮𐑁 𐑄𐐩 𐐶𐐳𐐼 𐑇𐐬 𐑄𐐯𐑋 𐑄 𐐶𐐩 𐐸𐐶𐐮𐐽 𐑊𐐯𐐼 𐐻𐐭 𐑄 𐑊𐐰𐑌𐐼 𐐲𐑂 𐐤𐐨𐑁𐐴, 𐑄𐐰𐐻 𐑄𐐩 𐐶𐐳𐐼 𐑀𐑉𐐰𐑌𐐻 𐐲𐑌𐐻𐐭 𐑄𐐯𐑋 𐑄𐐩𐑉 𐑊𐐴𐑂𐑆 𐐰𐑌𐐼 𐑄𐐩𐑉 𐑊𐐮𐐺𐐲𐑉𐐻𐐨. 𐐒𐐲𐐻 𐐰𐑁𐐻𐐲𐑉 𐐈𐑊𐑋𐐲 𐐸𐐰𐐼 𐑇𐐬𐑌 𐑄𐐯𐑋 𐑄 𐐶𐐩 𐑄𐐰𐐻 𐑊𐐯𐐼 𐐻𐐭 𐑄 𐑊𐐰𐑌𐐼 𐐲𐑂 𐐤𐐨𐑁𐐴, 𐑄 𐐢𐐩𐑋𐐲𐑌𐐴𐐻𐑅 𐐶𐐳𐐼 𐑌𐐱𐐻 𐐿𐐨𐐹 𐑄𐐩𐑉 𐐹𐑉𐐱𐑋𐐮𐑅; 𐐺𐐲𐐻 𐑄𐐩 𐑅𐐯𐐻 𐑀𐐪𐑉𐐼𐑆 𐑉𐐵𐑌𐐼 𐐲𐐺𐐵𐐻 𐑄 𐑊𐐰𐑌𐐼 𐐲𐑂 𐐐𐐨𐑊𐐲𐑋, 𐐬𐑂𐐲𐑉 𐐈𐑊𐑋𐐲 𐐰𐑌𐐼 𐐸𐐮𐑆 𐐺𐑉𐐯𐑄𐑉𐐯𐑌. 𐐈𐑌𐐼 𐑄 𐑉𐐨𐑋𐐩𐑌𐐼𐐲𐑉 𐐲𐑂 𐑄𐐯𐑋 𐐶𐐯𐑌𐐻 𐐻𐐭 𐑄 𐑊𐐰𐑌𐐼 𐐲𐑂 𐐤𐐨𐑁𐐴: 𐐰𐑌𐐼 𐐲 𐐹𐐪𐑉𐐻 𐐲𐑂 𐑄𐐯𐑋 𐑉𐐨𐐻𐐲𐑉𐑌𐐼 𐐻𐐭 𐑄 𐑊𐐰𐑌𐐼 𐐲𐑂 𐐐𐐨𐑊𐐲𐑋, 𐐰𐑌𐐼 𐐫𐑊𐑅𐐬 𐐺𐑉𐐫𐐻 𐐶𐐮𐑄 𐑄𐐯𐑋 𐑄 𐐶𐐴𐑂𐑆 𐐰𐑌𐐼 𐑄 𐐽𐐮𐑊𐐼𐑉𐐯𐑌 𐐲𐑂 𐑄 𐑀𐐪𐑉𐐼𐑆 𐐸𐐭 𐐸𐐰𐐼 𐐺𐐮𐑌 𐑊𐐯𐑁𐐻 𐐮𐑌 𐑄 𐑊𐐰𐑌𐐼. 𐐈𐑌𐐼 𐑄 𐐿𐐮𐑍 𐐲𐑂 𐑄 𐐢𐐩𐑋𐐲𐑌𐐴𐐻𐑅 𐐸𐐰𐐼 𐑀𐑉𐐰𐑌𐐻𐐯𐐼 𐐲𐑌𐐻𐐭 𐐈𐑋𐐷𐐭𐑊𐐲𐑌 𐑄𐐰𐐻 𐐸𐐨 𐑇𐐳𐐼 𐐺𐐨 𐐲 𐐿𐐮𐑍 𐐰𐑌𐐼 𐐲 𐑉𐐭𐑊𐐲𐑉 𐐬𐑂𐐲𐑉 𐐸𐐮𐑆 𐐹𐐨𐐹𐑊, 𐐸𐐭 𐐶𐐲𐑉 𐐮𐑌 𐑄 𐑊𐐰𐑌𐐼 𐐲𐑂 𐐐𐐨𐑊𐐲𐑋; 𐑌𐐯𐑂𐐲𐑉𐑄𐐯𐑊𐐯𐑅 𐐸𐐨 𐑇𐐳𐐼 𐐸𐐰𐑂 𐑌𐐬 𐐹𐐵𐐲𐑉 𐐻𐐭 𐐼𐐭 𐐯𐑌𐐮𐑃𐐮𐑍 𐐿𐐱𐑌𐐻𐑉𐐯𐑉𐐮 𐐻𐐭 𐑄 𐐶𐐮𐑊 𐐲𐑂 𐑄 𐐿𐐮𐑍 𐐲𐑂 𐑄 𐐢𐐩𐑋𐐲𐑌𐐴𐐻𐑅.

4. 𐐈𐑌𐐼 𐐮𐐻 𐐿𐐩𐑋 𐐻𐐭 𐐹𐐰𐑅 𐑄𐐰𐐻 𐐈𐑋𐐷𐐭𐑊𐐲𐑌 𐐼𐐮𐐼 𐑀𐐩𐑌 𐑁𐐩𐑂𐐲𐑉 𐐮𐑌 𐑄 𐐴𐑆 𐐲𐑂 𐑄 𐐿𐐮𐑍 𐐲𐑂 𐑄 𐐢𐐩𐑋𐐲𐑌𐐴𐐻𐑅; 𐑄𐐯𐑉𐑁𐐬𐑉, 𐑄 𐐿𐐮𐑍 𐐲𐑂 𐑄 𐐢𐐩𐑋𐐲𐑌𐐴𐐻𐑅 𐑀𐑉𐐰𐑌𐐻𐐯𐐼 𐐲𐑌𐐻𐐭 𐐸𐐮𐑋 𐐰𐑌𐐼 𐐸𐐮𐑆 𐐺𐑉𐐯𐑄𐑉𐐯𐑌, 𐑄𐐰𐐻 𐑄𐐩 𐑇𐐳𐐼 𐐺𐐨 𐐲𐐹𐐦𐑌𐐻𐐯𐐼 𐐻𐐨𐐽𐐲𐑉𐑆 𐐬𐑂𐐲𐑉 𐐸𐐮𐑆 𐐹𐐨𐐹𐑊; 𐐷𐐩, 𐐨𐑂𐐲𐑌 𐐬𐑂𐐲𐑉 𐑄 𐐹𐐨𐐹𐑊 𐐸𐐭 𐐶𐐲𐑉 𐐮𐑌 𐑄 𐑊𐐰𐑌𐐼 𐐲𐑂 𐐟𐐯𐑋𐑊𐐲𐑌, 𐐰𐑌𐐼 𐐮𐑌 𐑄 𐑊𐐰𐑌𐐼 𐐲𐑂 𐐟𐐴𐑊𐐲𐑋, 𐐰𐑌𐐼 𐐮𐑌 𐑄 𐑊𐐰𐑌𐐼 𐐲𐑂 𐐈𐑋𐐷𐐭𐑊𐐲𐑌: 𐑁𐐫𐑉 𐑄 𐐢𐐩𐑋𐐲𐑌𐐴𐐻𐑅 𐐸𐐰𐐼 𐐻𐐩𐐿𐑌 𐐹𐐲𐑆𐐯𐑇𐐲𐑌 𐐲𐑂 𐐫𐑊 𐑄𐐨𐑆 𐑊𐐰𐑌𐐼𐑆; 𐑄𐐯𐑉𐑁𐐬𐑉, 𐑄 𐐿𐐮𐑍 𐐲𐑂 𐑄 𐐢𐐩𐑋𐐲𐑌𐐴𐐻𐑅 𐐸𐐰𐐼 𐐲𐐹𐐦𐑌𐐻𐐯𐐼 𐐿𐐮𐑍𐑆 𐐬𐑂𐐲𐑉 𐐫𐑊 𐑄𐐨𐑆 𐑊𐐰𐑌𐐼𐑆. 𐐈𐑌𐐼 𐑌𐐵 𐑄 𐑌𐐩𐑋 𐐲𐑂 𐑄 𐐿𐐮𐑍 𐐲𐑂 𐑄 𐐢𐐩𐑋𐐲𐑌𐐴𐐻𐑅 𐐶𐐱𐑆 𐐢𐐩𐑋𐐲𐑌, 𐐺𐐨𐐮𐑍 𐐿𐐫𐑊𐐼 𐐰𐑁𐐻𐐲𐑉 𐑄 𐑌𐐩𐑋 𐐲𐑂 𐐸𐐮𐑆 𐑁𐐪𐑄𐐲𐑉; 𐐰𐑌𐐼 𐑄𐐯𐑉𐑁𐐬𐑉 𐐸𐐨 𐐶𐐱𐑆 𐐿𐐫𐑊𐐼 𐐿𐐮𐑍 𐐢𐐩𐑋𐐲𐑌. 𐐈𐑌𐐼 𐐸𐐨 𐐶𐐱𐑆 𐐿𐐮𐑍 𐐬𐑂𐐲𐑉 𐐲 𐑌𐐷𐐭𐑋𐐲𐑉𐐲𐑅 𐐹𐐨𐐹𐑊; 𐐰𐑌𐐼 𐐸𐐨 𐐲𐐹𐐦𐑌𐐻𐐯𐐼 𐐻𐐨𐐽𐐲𐑉𐑆 𐐲𐑂 𐑄 𐐺𐑉𐐯𐑄𐑉𐐯𐑌 𐐲𐑂 𐐈𐑋𐐷𐐭𐑊𐐲𐑌, 𐐮𐑌 𐐯𐑂𐐲𐑉𐐨 𐑊𐐰𐑌𐐼 𐐸𐐶𐐮𐐽 𐐶𐐱𐑆 𐐹𐐲𐑆𐐯𐑅𐐻 𐐺𐐴 𐐸𐐮𐑆 𐐹𐐨𐐹𐑊: 𐐰𐑌𐐼 𐑄𐐲𐑅 𐑄 𐑊𐐰𐑍𐑀𐐶𐐩𐐾 𐐲𐑂 𐐤𐐨𐑁𐐴 𐐺𐐨𐑀𐐰𐑌 𐐻𐐭 𐐺𐐨 𐐻𐐫𐐻 𐐲𐑋𐐲𐑍 𐐫𐑊 𐑄 𐐹𐐨𐐹𐑊 𐐲𐑂 𐑄 𐐢𐐩𐑋𐐲𐑌𐐴𐐻𐑅. 𐐈𐑌𐐼 𐑄𐐩 𐐶𐐲𐑉 𐐲 𐐹𐐨𐐹𐑊 𐑁𐑉𐐯𐑌𐐼𐑊𐐨 𐐶𐐲𐑌 𐐶𐐮𐑄 𐐲𐑌𐐲𐑄𐐲𐑉; 𐑌𐐯𐑂𐐲𐑉𐑄𐐯𐑊𐐯𐑅 𐑄𐐩 𐑌𐐭 𐑌𐐱𐐻 𐐘𐐱𐐼; 𐑌𐐨𐑄𐐲𐑉 𐐼𐐮𐐼 𐑄 𐐺𐑉𐐯𐑄𐑉𐐯𐑌 𐐲𐑂 𐐈𐑋𐐷𐐭𐑊𐐲𐑌 𐐻𐐨𐐽 𐑄𐐯𐑋 𐐯𐑌𐐮𐑃𐐮𐑍 𐐿𐐱𐑌𐑅𐐲𐑉𐑌𐐮𐑍 𐑄 𐐢𐐫𐑉𐐼 𐑄𐐩𐑉 𐐘𐐱𐐼, 𐑌𐐨𐑄𐐲𐑉 𐑄 𐑊𐐫 𐐲𐑂 𐐣𐐬𐑆𐐯𐑆; 𐑌𐐫𐑉 𐐼𐐮𐐼 𐑄𐐩 𐐻𐐨𐐽 𐑄𐐯𐑋 𐑄 𐐶𐐲𐑉𐐼𐑆 𐐲𐑂 𐐈𐐺𐐮𐑌𐐪𐐼𐐴; 𐐺𐐲𐐻 𐑄𐐩 𐐻𐐫𐐻 𐑄𐐯𐑋 𐑄𐐰𐐻 𐑄𐐩 𐑇𐐳𐐼 𐐿𐐨𐐹 𐑄𐐩𐑉 𐑉𐐯𐐿𐐲𐑉𐐼, 𐐰𐑌𐐼 𐑄𐐰𐐻 𐑄𐐩 𐑋𐐴𐐻 𐑉𐐴𐐻 𐐶𐐲𐑌 𐐻𐐭 𐐲𐑌𐐲𐑄𐐲𐑉. 𐐈𐑌𐐼 𐑄𐐲𐑅 𐑄 𐐢𐐩𐑋𐐲𐑌𐐴𐐻𐑅 𐐺𐐨𐑀𐐰𐑌 𐐻𐐭 𐐮𐑌𐐿𐑉𐐨𐑅 𐐮𐑌 𐑉𐐮𐐽𐐯𐑆, 𐐰𐑌𐐼 𐐺𐐨𐑀𐐰𐑌 𐐻𐐭 𐐻𐑉𐐩𐐼 𐐶𐐲𐑌 𐐶𐐮𐑄 𐐲𐑌𐐲𐑄𐐲𐑉, 𐐰𐑌𐐼 𐐶𐐰𐐿𐑅 𐑀𐑉𐐩𐐻, 𐐰𐑌𐐼 𐐺𐐨𐑀𐐰𐑌 𐐻𐐭 𐐺𐐨 𐐲 𐐿𐐲𐑌𐐮𐑍 𐐰𐑌𐐼 𐐲 𐐶𐐴𐑆 𐐹𐐨𐐹𐑊, 𐐰𐑆 𐐻𐐭 𐑄 𐐶𐐮𐑆𐐼𐐲𐑋 𐐲𐑂 𐑄 𐐶𐐲𐑉𐑊𐐼; 𐐷𐐩, 𐐲

𐑂𐐯𐑉𐐨 𐐿𐐲𐑌𐐮𐑍 𐐹𐐨𐐹𐑊; 𐐼𐐨𐑊𐐴𐐻𐐮𐑍 𐐮𐑌 𐐫𐑊 𐑋𐐰𐑌𐐲𐑉 𐐲𐑂 𐐶𐐮𐐿𐐯𐐼𐑌𐐯𐑅 𐐰𐑌𐐼 𐐹𐑊𐐲𐑌𐐼𐐲𐑉, 𐐯𐐿𐑅𐐯𐐹𐐻 𐐮𐐻 𐐶𐐲𐑉 𐐲𐑋𐐲𐑍 𐑄𐐩𐑉 𐐬𐑌 𐐺𐑉𐐯𐑄𐑉𐐯𐑌.

5. 𐐈𐑌𐐼 𐑌𐐵 𐐮𐐻 𐐿𐐩𐑋 𐐻𐐭 𐐹𐐪𐑅 𐑄𐐰𐐻 𐐈𐑋𐐷𐐭𐑊𐐪𐑌 𐐺𐐨𐑀𐐰𐑌 𐐻𐐭 𐐯𐐿𐑅𐐲𐑉𐑅𐐴𐑆 𐐫𐑃𐐱𐑉𐐮𐐻𐐨 𐐬𐑂𐐲𐑉 𐐈𐑊𐑋𐐲 𐐰𐑌𐐼 𐐸𐐮𐑆 𐐺𐑉𐐯𐑄𐑉𐐯𐑌, 𐐰𐑌𐐼 𐐺𐐨𐑀𐐰𐑌 𐐻𐐭 𐐹𐐲𐑉𐑅𐐨𐐿𐐷𐐭𐐻 𐐸𐐮𐑋, 𐐰𐑌𐐼 𐐿𐐫𐑆 𐑄𐐰𐐻 𐐸𐐮𐑆 𐐽𐐮𐑊𐐼𐑉𐐯𐑌 𐑇𐐳𐐼 𐐹𐐲𐑉𐑅𐐨𐐿𐐷𐐭𐐻 𐑄𐐩𐑉 𐐽𐐮𐑊𐐼𐑉𐐯𐑌: 𐑁𐐫𐑉 𐐈𐑋𐐷𐐭𐑊𐐪𐑌 𐑌𐐭 𐐈𐑊𐑋𐐲, 𐑄𐐰𐐻 𐐸𐐨 𐐸𐐰𐐼 𐐺𐐮𐑌 𐐶𐐲𐑌 𐐲𐑂 𐑄 𐐿𐐮𐑍'𐑆 𐐹𐑉𐐨𐑅𐐻𐑅, 𐐰𐑌𐐼 𐑄𐐰𐐻 𐐮𐐻 𐐶𐐱𐑆 𐐸𐐨 𐑄𐐰𐐻 𐐺𐐨𐑊𐐨𐑂𐐼 𐑄 𐐶𐐲𐑉𐐼𐑆 𐐲𐑂 𐐈𐐺𐐮𐑌𐐲𐐼𐐴, 𐐰𐑌𐐼 𐐶𐐱𐑆 𐐼𐑉𐐮𐑂𐐲𐑌 𐐵𐐻 𐐺𐐨𐑁𐐬𐑉 𐑄 𐐿𐐮𐑍; 𐐰𐑌𐐼 𐑄𐐯𐑉𐑁𐐬𐑉 𐐸𐐨 𐐶𐐱𐑆 𐑉𐐫𐑃 𐐶𐐮𐑄 𐐸𐐮𐑋, 𐑁𐐫𐑉 𐐸𐐨 𐐶𐐱𐑆 𐑅𐐲𐐺𐐾𐐯𐐿𐐻 𐐻𐐭 𐐿𐐮𐑍 𐐢𐐩𐑋𐐲𐑌; 𐐷𐐯𐐻 𐐸𐐨 𐐯𐐿𐑅𐐲𐑉𐑅𐐴𐑆𐐼 𐐫𐑃𐐱𐑉𐐮𐐻𐐨 𐐬𐑂𐐲𐑉 𐑄𐐯𐑋, 𐐰𐑌𐐼 𐐹𐐳𐐻 𐐻𐐪𐑅𐐿𐑅 𐐲𐐹𐐱𐑌 𐑄𐐯𐑋, 𐐰𐑌𐐼 𐐹𐐳𐐻 𐐻𐐪𐑅𐐿-𐑋𐐪𐑅𐐻𐐲𐑉𐑆 𐐬𐑂𐐲𐑉 𐑄𐐯𐑋. 𐐈𐑌𐐼 𐐮𐐻 𐐿𐐩𐑋 𐐻𐐭 𐐹𐐪𐑅 𐑄𐐰𐐻 𐑅𐐬 𐑀𐑉𐐩𐐻 𐐶𐐲𐑉 𐑄𐐩𐑉 𐐰𐑁𐑊𐐮𐐿𐑇𐐲𐑌𐑆, 𐑄𐐰𐐻 𐑄𐐩 𐐺𐐨𐑀𐐰𐑌 𐐻𐐭 𐐿𐑉𐐴 𐑋𐐴𐐻𐐮𐑊𐐨 𐐻𐐭 𐐘𐐪𐐼. 𐐈𐑌𐐼 𐐈𐑋𐐷𐐭𐑊𐐪𐑌 𐐿𐐱𐑋𐐪𐑌𐐼𐐯𐐼 𐑄𐐯𐑋 𐑄𐐰𐐻 𐑄𐐩 𐑇𐐳𐐼 𐑅𐐻𐐱𐐹 𐑄𐐩𐑉 𐐿𐑉𐐴𐑆; 𐐰𐑌𐐼 𐐸𐐨 𐐹𐐳𐐻 𐑀𐐪𐑉𐐼𐑆 𐐬𐑂𐐲𐑉 𐑄𐐯𐑋 𐐻𐐭 𐐶𐐱𐐽 𐑄𐐯𐑋, 𐑄𐐰𐐻 𐐸𐐭𐑅𐐬𐐯𐑂𐐲𐑉 𐑇𐐳𐐼 𐐺𐐨 𐑁𐐵𐑌𐐼 𐐿𐐫𐑊𐐮𐑍 𐐲𐐹𐐱𐑌 𐐘𐐪𐐼 𐑇𐐳𐐼 𐐺𐐨 𐐹𐐳𐐻 𐐻𐐭 𐐼𐐯𐑃. 𐐈𐑌𐐼 𐐈𐑊𐑋𐐲 𐐰𐑌𐐼 𐐸𐐮𐑆 𐐹𐐨𐐹𐑊 𐐼𐐮𐐼 𐑌𐐱𐐻 𐑉𐐩𐑆 𐑄𐐩𐑉 𐑂𐑎𐑅𐐯𐑆 𐐻𐐭 𐑄 𐐢𐐫𐑉𐐼 𐑄𐐩𐑉 𐐘𐐪𐐼, 𐐺𐐲𐐻 𐐼𐐮𐐼 𐐹𐐬𐑉 𐐵𐐻 𐑄𐐩𐑉 𐐸𐐪𐑉𐐻𐑅 𐐻𐐭 𐐸𐐮𐑋; 𐐰𐑌𐐼 𐐸𐐨 𐐼𐐮𐐼 𐑌𐐬 𐑄 𐑃𐐫𐐻𐑅 𐐲𐑂 𐑄𐐩𐑉 𐐸𐐪𐑉𐐻𐑅.

6. 𐐈𐑌𐐼 𐐮𐐻 𐐿𐐩𐑋 𐐻𐐭 𐐹𐐪𐑅 𐑄𐐰𐐻 𐑄 𐑂𐑎𐑅 𐐲𐑂 𐑄 𐐢𐐫𐑉𐐼 𐐿𐐩𐑋 𐐻𐐭 𐑄𐐯𐑋 𐐮𐑌 𐑄𐐩𐑉 𐐰𐑁𐑊𐐮𐐿𐑇𐐲𐑌𐑆, 𐑅𐐩𐐮𐑍, 𐐢𐐮𐑁𐐻 𐐲𐐹 𐐷𐐭𐑉 𐐸𐐯𐐼𐑆 𐐰𐑌𐐼 𐐺𐐨 𐐲𐑂 𐑀𐐳𐐼 𐐿𐐲𐑋𐑁𐐲𐑉𐐻, 𐑁𐐫𐑉 𐐌 𐑌𐐬 𐐲𐑂 𐑄 𐐿𐐲𐑂𐐯𐑌𐐰𐑌𐐻 𐐸𐐶𐐮𐐽 𐐷𐐨 𐐸𐐰𐑂 𐑋𐐩𐐼 𐐲𐑌𐐻𐐭 𐑋𐐨; 𐐰𐑌𐐼 𐐌 𐐶𐐮𐑊 𐐿𐐲𐑂𐐯𐑌𐐰𐑌𐐻 𐐶𐐮𐑄 𐑋𐐴 𐐹𐐨𐐹𐑊, 𐐰𐑌𐐼 𐐼𐐨𐑊𐐮𐑂𐐲𐑉 𐑄𐐯𐑋 𐐵𐐻 𐐲𐑂 𐐺𐐱𐑌𐐼𐐯𐐾. 𐐈𐑌𐐼 𐐌 𐐶𐐮𐑊 𐐫𐑊𐑅𐐬 𐐨𐑆 𐑄 𐐺𐐲𐑉𐐼𐐲𐑌𐑆 𐐸𐐶𐐮𐐽 𐐪𐑉 𐐹𐐳𐐻 𐐲𐐹𐐱𐑌 𐐷𐐭𐑉 𐑇𐐬𐑊𐐼𐐲𐑉𐑆, 𐑄𐐰𐐻 𐐨𐑂𐐲𐑌 𐐷𐐭 𐐿𐐰𐑌𐐱𐐻 𐑁𐐨𐑊 𐑄𐐯𐑋 𐐲𐐹𐐱𐑌 𐐷𐐭𐑉 𐐺𐐰𐐿𐑅, 𐐨𐑂𐐲𐑌 𐐸𐐶𐐴𐑊 𐐷𐐭 𐐪𐑉 𐐮𐑌 𐐺𐐱𐑌𐐼𐐯𐐾; 𐐰𐑌𐐼 𐑄𐐮𐑅 𐐶𐐮𐑊 𐐌 𐐼𐐭, 𐑄𐐰𐐻 𐐷𐐨 𐑋𐐩 𐑅𐐻𐐰𐑌𐐼 𐐰𐑆 𐐶𐐮𐐻𐑌𐐯𐑅𐐯𐑆 𐑁𐐫𐑉 𐑋𐐨 𐐸𐐨𐑉𐐰𐑁𐐻𐐲𐑉, 𐐰𐑌𐐼 𐑄𐐰𐐻 𐐷𐐨 𐑋𐐩 𐑌𐐬 𐐲𐑂 𐐲 𐑇𐐳𐑉𐐯𐐻𐐨 𐑄𐐰𐐻 𐐌, 𐑄 𐐢𐐫𐑉𐐼 𐐘𐐪𐐼, 𐐼𐐭 𐑂𐐮𐑆𐐮𐐻 𐑋𐐴 𐐹𐐨𐐹𐑊 𐐮𐑌 𐑄𐐩𐑉 𐐰𐑁𐑊𐐮𐐿𐑇𐐲𐑌𐑆. 𐐈𐑌𐐼 𐑌𐐵 𐐮𐐻 𐐿𐐩𐑋 𐐻𐐭 𐐹𐐪𐑅 𐑄𐐰𐐻 𐑄 𐐺𐐲𐑉𐐼𐐲𐑌𐑆 𐐸𐐶𐐮𐐽 𐐶𐐲𐑉 𐑊𐐩𐐼 𐐲𐐹𐐱𐑌 𐐈𐑊𐑋𐐲 𐐰𐑌𐐼 𐐸𐐮𐑆 𐐺𐑉𐐯𐑄𐑉𐐯𐑌 𐐶𐐲𐑉 𐑋𐐩𐐼 𐑊𐐴𐐻; 𐐷𐐩, 𐑄 𐐢𐐫𐑉𐐼 𐐼𐐮𐐼 𐑅𐐻𐑉𐐯𐑍𐑃𐐲𐑌 𐑄𐐯𐑋 𐑄𐐰𐐻 𐑄𐐩 𐐿𐐳𐐼 𐐺𐐩𐑉 𐐲𐐹 𐑄𐐩𐑉 𐐺𐐲𐑉𐐼𐐲𐑌𐑆 𐐶𐐮𐑄 𐐨𐑆, 𐐰𐑌𐐼 𐑄𐐩 𐐼𐐮𐐼 𐑅𐐲𐐺𐑋𐐮𐐻 𐐽𐐨𐑉𐑁𐐳𐑊𐐨 𐐰𐑌𐐼 𐐶𐐮𐑄 𐐹𐐩𐑇𐐯𐑌𐑅 𐐻𐐭 𐐫𐑊 𐑄 𐐶𐐮𐑊 𐐲𐑂 𐑄 𐐢𐐫𐑉𐐼. 𐐈𐑌𐐼 𐐮𐐻 𐐿𐐩𐑋 𐐻𐐭 𐐹𐐪𐑅 𐑄𐐰𐐻 𐑅𐐬 𐑀𐑉𐐩𐐻 𐐶𐐱𐑆 𐑄𐐩𐑉 𐑁𐐩𐑃 𐐰𐑌𐐼 𐑄𐐩𐑉 𐐹𐐩𐑇𐐯𐑌𐑅, 𐑄𐐰𐐻 𐑄 𐑂𐑎𐑅 𐐲𐑂 𐑄 𐐢𐐫𐑉𐐼 𐐿𐐩𐑋 𐐲𐑌𐐻𐐭 𐑄𐐯𐑋 𐐲𐑀𐐯𐑌, 𐑅𐐩𐐮𐑍, 𐐒𐐨 𐐲𐑂 𐑀𐐳𐐼 𐐿𐐲𐑋𐑁𐐲𐑉𐐻, 𐑁𐐫𐑉 𐐱𐑌 𐑄 𐑋𐐱𐑉𐐬 𐐌 𐐶𐐮𐑊 𐐼𐐨𐑊𐐮𐑂𐐲𐑉 𐐷𐐭 𐐵𐐻 𐐲𐑂 𐐺𐐱𐑌𐐼𐐯𐐾. 𐐈𐑌𐐼 𐐸𐐨 𐑅𐐯𐐼 𐐲𐑌𐐻𐐭 𐐈𐑊𐑋𐐲, 𐐜𐐵 𐑇𐐰𐑊𐐻 𐑀𐐬 𐐺𐐨𐑁𐐬𐑉 𐑄𐐮𐑅 𐐹𐐨𐐹𐑊, 𐐰𐑌𐐼 𐐌 𐐶𐐮𐑊 𐑀𐐬 𐐶𐐮𐑄 𐑄𐐨, 𐐰𐑌𐐼 𐐼𐐨𐑊𐐮𐑂𐐲𐑉 𐑄𐐮𐑅 𐐹𐐨𐐹𐑊 𐐵𐐻 𐐲𐑂 𐐺𐐱𐑌𐐼𐐯𐐾.

7. 𐐤𐐵 𐐮𐐻 𐐿𐐩𐑋 𐐻𐐭 𐐹𐐪𐑅 𐑄𐐰𐐻 𐐈𐑊𐑋𐐲 𐐰𐑌𐐼 𐐸𐐮𐑆 𐐹𐐨𐐹𐑊, 𐐮𐑌 𐑄 𐑌𐐴𐐻-𐐻𐐴𐑋, 𐑀𐐰𐑄𐐲𐑉𐐼 𐑄𐐩𐑉 𐑁𐑊𐐱𐐿𐑅 𐐻𐐳𐑀𐐯𐑄𐐲𐑉, 𐐰𐑌𐐼 𐐫𐑊𐑅𐐬 𐐲𐑂 𐑄𐐩𐑉 𐑀𐑉𐐩𐑌; 𐐷𐐩, 𐐨𐑂𐐲𐑌 𐐫𐑊 𐑄 𐑌𐐴𐐻-𐐻𐐴𐑋 𐐶𐐲𐑉 𐑄𐐩 𐑀𐐰𐑄𐐲𐑉𐐮𐑍 𐑄𐐩𐑉 𐑁𐑊𐐱𐐿𐑅 𐐻𐐳𐑀𐐯𐑄𐐲𐑉. 𐐈𐑌𐐼 𐐮𐑌 𐑄 𐑋𐐫𐑉𐑌𐐮𐑍 𐑄 𐐢𐐫𐑉𐐼 𐐿𐐫𐑆𐐼 𐐲 𐐼𐐨𐐹 𐑅𐑊𐐨𐐹 𐐻𐐭 𐐿𐐲𐑋 𐐲𐐹𐐱𐑌 𐑄 𐐢𐐩𐑋𐐲𐑌𐐴𐐻𐑅, 𐐷𐐩, 𐐰𐑌𐐼 𐐫𐑊 𐑄𐐩𐑉 𐐻𐐪𐑅𐐿-𐑋𐐪𐑅𐐻𐐲𐑉𐑆 𐐶𐐲𐑉 𐐮𐑌 𐐲 𐐹𐑉𐐬𐑁𐐵𐑌𐐼 𐑅𐑊𐐨𐐹. 𐐈𐑌𐐼 𐐈𐑊𐑋𐐲 𐐰𐑌𐐼 𐐸𐐮𐑆 𐐹𐐨𐐹𐑊 𐐼𐐨𐐹𐐪𐑉𐐻𐐯𐐼 𐐮𐑌𐐻𐐭 𐑄 𐐶𐐮𐑊𐐼𐐲𐑉𐑌𐐯𐑅; 𐐰𐑌𐐼 𐐸𐐶𐐯𐑌 𐑄𐐩 𐐸𐐰𐐼 𐐻𐑉𐐰𐑂𐐯𐑊𐐼 𐐫𐑊 𐐼𐐩, 𐑄𐐩 𐐹𐐮𐐽𐐻 𐑄𐐩𐑉 𐐻𐐯𐑌𐐻𐑅 𐐮𐑌 𐐲 𐑂𐐰𐑊𐐨, 𐐰𐑌𐐼 𐑄𐐩 𐐿𐐫𐑊𐐼 𐑄 𐑂𐐰𐑊𐐨 𐐈𐑊𐑋𐐲, 𐐺𐐨𐐿𐐫𐑆 𐐸𐐨 𐑊𐐯𐐼 𐑄𐐩𐑉 𐐶𐐩 𐐮𐑌 𐑄 𐐶𐐮𐑊𐐼𐐲𐑉𐑌𐐯𐑅; 𐐷𐐩, 𐐰𐑌𐐼 𐐮𐑌 𐑄 𐑂𐐰𐑊𐐨 𐐲𐑂 𐐈𐑊𐑋𐐲 𐑄𐐩 𐐹𐐬𐑉𐐼 𐐵𐐻 𐑄𐐩𐑉 𐑃𐐰𐑍𐐿𐑅 𐐻𐐭 𐐘𐐪𐐼, 𐐺𐐨𐐿𐐫𐑆 𐐸𐐨 𐐸𐐰𐐼 𐐺𐐮𐑌 𐑋𐐲𐑉𐑅𐐮𐑁𐐳𐑊 𐐲𐑌𐐻𐐭 𐑄𐐯𐑋, 𐐰𐑌𐐼 𐐨𐑆𐐼 𐑄𐐩𐑉 𐐺𐐲𐑉𐐼𐐲𐑌𐑆, 𐐰𐑌𐐼 𐐸𐐰𐐼 𐐼𐐨𐑊𐐮𐑂𐐲𐑉𐐼 𐑄𐐯𐑋 𐐵𐐻 𐐲𐑂 𐐺𐐱𐑌𐐼𐐯𐐾; 𐑁𐐫𐑉 𐑄𐐩 𐐶𐐲𐑉 𐐮𐑌 𐐺𐐱𐑌𐐼𐐯𐐾, 𐐰𐑌𐐼 𐑌𐐲𐑌 𐐿𐐳𐐼 𐐼𐐨𐑊𐐮𐑂𐐲𐑉 𐑄𐐯𐑋, 𐐯𐐿𐑅𐐯𐐹𐐻 𐐮𐐻 𐐶𐐲𐑉 𐑄 𐐢𐐫𐑉𐐼 𐑄𐐩𐑉 𐐘𐐪𐐼. 𐐈𐑌𐐼 𐑄𐐩 𐑀𐐩𐑂 𐑃𐐰𐑍𐐿𐑅 𐐻𐐭 𐐘𐐪𐐼, 𐐷𐐩, 𐐫𐑊 𐑄𐐩𐑉 𐑋𐐯𐑌, 𐐰𐑌𐐼 𐐫𐑊 𐑄𐐩𐑉 𐐶𐐮𐑋𐐯𐑌, 𐐰𐑌𐐼 𐐫𐑊 𐑄𐐩𐑉 𐐽𐐮𐑊𐐼𐑉𐐯𐑌 𐑄𐐰𐐻 𐐿𐐳𐐼 𐑅𐐹𐐨𐐿, 𐑊𐐮𐑁𐐻𐐯𐐼 𐑄𐐩𐑉 𐑂𐑎𐑅𐐯𐑆 𐐮𐑌 𐑄 𐐹𐑉𐐩𐑆𐐯𐑆 𐐲𐑂 𐑄𐐩𐑉 𐐘𐐪𐐼.

8. 𐐈𐑌𐐼 𐑌𐐵 𐑄 𐐢𐐫𐑉𐐼 𐑅𐐯𐐼 𐐲𐑌𐐻𐐭 𐐈𐑊𐑋𐐲, 𐐐𐐩𐑅𐐻 𐑄𐐨 𐐰𐑌𐐼 𐑀𐐯𐐻 𐑄𐐵 𐐰𐑌𐐼 𐑄𐐮𐑅 𐐹𐐨𐐹𐑊 𐐵𐐻 𐐲𐑂

𐑄𐐮𐑅 𐐹𐐨𐐹𐑊, 𐑁𐐫𐑉 𐑄 𐐢𐐰𐑋𐐲𐑌𐐴𐐻𐑅 𐐸𐐰𐑂 𐐲𐐶𐐬𐐿 𐐰𐑌𐐼 𐐼𐐭 𐐹𐐲𐑉𐑅𐐷𐐭 𐑄; 𐑄𐐩𐑉𐑁𐐫𐑉 𐑀𐐯𐐻 𐑄 𐐵𐐻 𐐱𐑂 𐑄𐐮𐑅 𐑊𐐰𐑌𐐼, 𐐰𐑌𐐼 𐐌 𐐶𐐮𐑊 𐑅𐐻𐐱𐐹 𐑄 𐐢𐐰𐑋𐐲𐑌𐐴𐐻𐑅 𐐮𐑌 𐑄𐐮𐑅 𐑂𐐰𐑊𐐨, 𐑄𐐰𐐻 𐑄𐐩 𐐿𐐲𐑋 𐑌𐐬 𐑁𐐲𐑉𐑄𐐲𐑉 𐐮𐑌 𐐹𐐲𐑉𐑅𐐷𐐭𐐻 𐐱𐑂 𐑄𐐮𐑅 𐐹𐐨𐐹𐑊. 𐐈𐑌𐐼 𐐮𐐻 𐐿𐐩𐑋 𐐻𐐭 𐐹𐐰𐑅 𐑄𐐰𐐻 𐑄𐐩 𐐼𐐨𐐹𐐪𐑉𐐻𐐯𐐼 𐐵𐐻 𐐱𐑂 𐑄 𐑂𐐰𐑊𐐨, 𐐰𐑌𐐼 𐐻𐐳𐐿 𐑄𐐩𐑉 𐐾𐐲𐑉𐑌𐐨 𐐮𐑌𐐻𐐭 𐑄 𐐶𐐮𐑊𐐼𐐲𐑉𐑌𐐯𐑅. 𐐈𐑌𐐼 𐐪𐑁𐐻𐐲𐑉 𐑄𐐩 𐐸𐐰𐐼 𐐺𐐮𐑌 𐐮𐑌 𐑄 𐐶𐐮𐑊𐐼𐐲𐑉𐑌𐐯𐑅 𐐻𐐶𐐯𐑊𐑂 𐐼𐐩𐑆, 𐑄𐐩 𐐲𐑉𐐴𐑂𐐼 𐐮𐑌 𐑄 𐑊𐐰𐑌𐐼 𐐱𐑂 𐐞𐐩𐑉𐐲𐐸𐐯𐑋𐑊𐐲; 𐐰𐑌𐐼 𐐿𐐮𐑍 𐐣𐐬𐑆𐐴𐐲 𐐼𐐮𐐼 𐐫𐑊𐑅𐐬 𐑉𐐨𐑅𐐨𐑂 𐑄𐐯𐑋 𐐶𐐮𐑄 𐐾𐐫𐐮. 𐐈𐑌𐐼 𐑌𐐵 𐐿𐐮𐑍 𐐣𐐬𐑆𐐴𐐲 𐐿𐐫𐑆𐐼 𐑄𐐰𐐻 𐐫𐑊 𐑄 𐐹𐐨𐐹𐑊 𐑇𐐳𐐼 𐐺𐐨 𐑀𐐰𐑄𐐲𐑉𐐼 𐐻𐐭𐑀𐐯𐑄𐐲𐑉. 𐐤𐐵 𐑄𐐩𐑉 𐐶𐐲𐑉 𐑌𐐱𐐻 𐑅𐐬 𐑋𐐯𐑌𐐨 𐐱𐑂 𐑄 𐐽𐐮𐑊𐐼𐑉𐐯𐑌 𐐱𐑂 𐐤𐐨𐑁𐐴, 𐐫𐑉 𐑅𐐬 𐑋𐐯𐑌𐐨 𐐱𐑂 𐑄𐐬𐑆 𐐸𐐭 𐐶𐐲𐑉 𐐼𐐨𐑅𐐯𐑌𐐼𐐲𐑌𐐻𐑅 𐐱𐑂 𐐤𐐨𐑁𐐴, 𐐰𐑆 𐑄𐐩𐑉 𐐶𐐲𐑉 𐐱𐑂 𐑄 𐐹𐐨𐐹𐑊 𐐱𐑂 𐐞𐐩𐑉𐐲𐐸𐐯𐑋𐑊𐐲, 𐐸𐐭 𐐶𐐱𐑆 𐐰 𐐼𐐨𐑅𐐯𐑌𐐼𐐲𐑌𐐻 𐐱𐑂 𐐣𐐷𐐭𐑊𐐯𐐿, 𐐰𐑌𐐼 𐑄𐐬𐑆 𐐸𐐭 𐐿𐐩𐑋 𐐶𐐮𐑄 𐐸𐐮𐑋 𐐮𐑌𐐻𐐭 𐑄 𐐶𐐮𐑊𐐼𐐲𐑉𐑌𐐯𐑅. 𐐈𐑌𐐼 𐑄𐐩𐑉 𐐶𐐲𐑉 𐑌𐐱𐐻 𐑅𐐬 𐑋𐐯𐑌𐐨 𐐱𐑂 𐑄 𐐹𐐨𐐹𐑊 𐐱𐑂 𐐤𐐨𐑁𐐴 𐐰𐑌𐐼 𐐱𐑂 𐑄 𐐹𐐨𐐹𐑊 𐐱𐑂 𐐞𐐩𐑉𐐲𐐸𐐯𐑋𐑊𐐲 𐐰𐑆 𐑄𐐩𐑉 𐐶𐐲𐑉 𐐱𐑂 𐑄 𐐢𐐰𐑋𐐲𐑌𐐴𐐻𐑅: 𐐷𐐩, 𐑄𐐩 𐐶𐐲𐑉 𐑌𐐱𐐻 𐐸𐐪𐑁 𐑅𐐬 𐑌𐐷𐐭𐑋𐐲𐑉𐐲𐑅. 𐐈𐑌𐐼 𐑌𐐵 𐐫𐑊 𐑄 𐐹𐐨𐐹𐑊 𐐱𐑂 𐐤𐐨𐑁𐐴 𐐶𐐲𐑉 𐐲𐑅𐐯𐑋𐐺𐑊𐐼 𐐻𐐭𐑀𐐯𐑄𐐲𐑉, 𐐰𐑌𐐼 𐐫𐑊𐑅𐐬 𐐫𐑊 𐑄 𐐹𐐨𐐹𐑊 𐐱𐑂 𐐞𐐩𐑉𐐲𐐸𐐯𐑋𐑊𐐲, 𐐰𐑌𐐼 𐑄𐐩 𐐶𐐲𐑉 𐑀𐐰𐑄𐐲𐑉𐐼 𐐻𐐭𐑀𐐯𐑄𐐲𐑉 𐐮𐑌 𐐻𐐭 𐐺𐐱𐐼𐐨𐑆.

9. 𐐈𐑌𐐼 𐐮𐐻 𐐿𐐩𐑋 𐐻𐐭 𐐹𐐰𐑅 𐑄𐐰𐐻 𐐣𐐬𐑆𐐴𐐲 𐐼𐐮𐐼 𐑉𐐨𐐼, 𐐰𐑌𐐼 𐐿𐐫𐑆𐐼 𐐻𐐭 𐐺𐐨 𐑉𐐯𐐼, 𐑄 𐑉𐐯𐐿𐐲𐑉𐐼𐑆 𐐱𐑂 𐐞𐐨𐑌𐐮𐑁 𐐻𐐭 𐐸𐐮𐑆 𐐹𐐨𐐹𐑊; 𐐷𐐩, 𐐸𐐨 𐑉𐐯𐐼 𐑄 𐑉𐐯𐐿𐐲𐑉𐐼𐑆 𐐱𐑂 𐑄 𐐹𐐨𐐹𐑊 𐐱𐑂 𐐞𐐨𐑌𐐮𐑁, 𐑁𐑉𐐱𐑋 𐑄 𐐻𐐴𐑋 𐑄𐐩 𐑊𐐯𐑁𐐻 𐑄 𐑊𐐰𐑌𐐼 𐐱𐑂 𐐞𐐩𐑉𐐲𐐸𐐯𐑋𐑊𐐲 𐐲𐑌𐐻𐐮𐑊 𐑄𐐩 𐑉𐐨𐐻𐐲𐑉𐑌𐐼 𐐲𐑀𐐯𐑌. 𐐈𐑌𐐼 𐐸𐐨 𐐫𐑊𐑅𐐬 𐑉𐐯𐐼 𐑄 𐐲𐐿𐐵𐑌𐐻 𐐱𐑂 𐐈𐑊𐑋𐐲 𐐰𐑌𐐼 𐐸𐐮𐑆 𐐺𐑉𐐯𐑄𐑉𐐯𐑌, 𐐰𐑌𐐼 𐐫𐑊 𐑄𐐩𐑉 𐐲𐑁𐑊𐐮𐐿𐑇𐐲𐑌𐑆, 𐑁𐑉𐐱𐑋 𐑄 𐐻𐐴𐑋 𐑄𐐩 𐑊𐐯𐑁𐐻 𐑄 𐑊𐐰𐑌𐐼 𐐱𐑂 𐐞𐐩𐑉𐐲𐐸𐐯𐑋𐑊𐐲 𐐲𐑌𐐻𐐮𐑊 𐑄 𐐻𐐴𐑋 𐑄𐐩 𐑉𐐨𐐻𐐲𐑉𐑌𐐼 𐐲𐑀𐐯𐑌. 𐐈𐑌𐐼 𐑌𐐵, 𐐸𐐶𐐯𐑌 𐐣𐐬𐑆𐐴𐐲 𐐸𐐰𐐼 𐑋𐐩𐐼 𐐰𐑌 𐐯𐑌𐐼 𐐱𐑂 𐑉𐐨𐐼𐐮𐑍 𐑄 𐑉𐐯𐐿𐐲𐑉𐐼𐑆, 𐐸𐐮𐑆 𐐹𐐨𐐹𐑊 𐐸𐐭 𐐻𐐰𐑉𐐨𐐼 𐐮𐑌 𐑄 𐑊𐐰𐑌𐐼 𐐶𐐲𐑉 𐑅𐐻𐑉𐐲𐐿 𐐶𐐮𐑄 𐐶𐐲𐑌𐐼𐐲𐑉 𐐰𐑌𐐼 𐐲𐑋𐐩𐑆𐑋𐐯𐑌𐐻, 𐑁𐐫𐑉 𐑄𐐩 𐑌𐐷𐐭 𐑌𐐱𐐻 𐐸𐐶𐐱𐐻 𐐻𐐭 𐑃𐐮𐑍𐐿; 𐑁𐐫𐑉 𐐸𐐶𐐯𐑌 𐑄𐐩 𐐺𐐨𐐸𐐯𐑊𐐼 𐑄𐐬𐑆 𐑄𐐰𐐻 𐐸𐐰𐐼 𐐺𐐮𐑌 𐐼𐐨𐑊𐐮𐑂𐐲𐑉𐐼 𐐵𐐻 𐐱𐑂 𐐺𐐱𐑌𐐼𐐩𐐾, 𐑄𐐩 𐐶𐐲𐑉 𐑁𐐮𐑊𐐼 𐐶𐐮𐑄 𐐯𐐿𐑅𐐨𐐼𐐮𐑍𐑊𐐨 𐑀𐑉𐐩𐐻 𐐾𐐫𐐮. 𐐈𐑌𐐼 𐐲𐑀𐐯𐑌, 𐐸𐐶𐐯𐑌 𐑄𐐩 𐑃𐐫𐐻 𐐱𐑂 𐑄𐐩𐑉 𐐺𐑉𐐯𐑄𐑉𐐯𐑌 𐐸𐐭 𐐸𐐰𐐼 𐐺𐐮𐑌 𐑅𐑊𐐩𐑌 𐐺𐐴 𐑄 𐐢𐐰𐑋𐐲𐑌𐐴𐐻𐑅, 𐑄𐐩 𐐶𐐲𐑉 𐑁𐐮𐑊𐐼 𐐶𐐮𐑄 𐑅𐐱𐑉𐐬, 𐐰𐑌𐐼 𐐨𐑂𐐲𐑌 𐑇𐐯𐐼 𐑋𐐯𐑌𐐨 𐐻𐐨𐑉𐑆 𐐱𐑂 𐑅𐐱𐑉𐐬; 𐐰𐑌𐐼 𐐲𐑀𐐯𐑌, 𐐸𐐶𐐯𐑌 𐑄𐐩 𐑃𐐫𐐻 𐐱𐑂 𐑄 𐐮𐑋𐐨𐐼𐐷𐐲𐐻 𐑀𐐳𐐼𐑌𐐯𐑅 𐐱𐑂 𐐘𐐱𐐼, 𐐰𐑌𐐼 𐐸𐐮𐑆 𐐹𐐵𐐲𐑉 𐐮𐑌 𐐼𐐨𐑊𐐮𐑂𐐲𐑉𐐮𐑍 𐐈𐑊𐑋𐐲 𐐰𐑌𐐼 𐐸𐐮𐑆 𐐺𐑉𐐯𐑄𐑉𐐯𐑌 𐐵𐐻 𐐱𐑂 𐑄 𐐸𐐰𐑌𐐼𐑆 𐐱𐑂 𐑄 𐐢𐐰𐑋𐐲𐑌𐐴𐐻𐑅, 𐐰𐑌𐐼 𐐱𐑂 𐐺𐐱𐑌𐐼𐐩𐐾, 𐑄𐐩 𐐼𐐮𐐼 𐑉𐐩𐑆 𐑄𐐩𐑉 𐑂𐐫𐐮𐑅𐐯𐑆, 𐐰𐑌𐐼 𐑀𐐮𐑂 𐑃𐐰𐑍𐐿𐑅 𐐻𐐭 𐐘𐐱𐐼. 𐐈𐑌𐐼 𐐲𐑀𐐯𐑌, 𐐸𐐶𐐯𐑌 𐑄𐐩 𐑃𐐫𐐻 𐐲𐐹𐐱𐑌 𐑄 𐐢𐐰𐑋𐐲𐑌𐐴𐐻𐑅, 𐐸𐐭 𐐶𐐲𐑉 𐑄𐐩𐑉 𐐺𐑉𐐯𐑄𐑉𐐯𐑌, 𐐱𐑂 𐑄𐐩𐑉 𐑅𐐮𐑌𐑁𐐳𐑊 𐐰𐑌𐐼 𐐹𐐱𐑊𐐷𐐭𐐻𐐯𐐼 𐑅𐐻𐐩𐐻, 𐑄𐐩 𐐶𐐲𐑉 𐑁𐐮𐑊𐐼 𐐶𐐮𐑄 𐐹𐐩𐑌 𐐰𐑌𐐼 𐐰𐑍𐑀𐐶𐐮𐑇 𐑁𐐫𐑉 𐑄 𐐶𐐯𐑊𐑁𐐩𐑉 𐐱𐑂 𐑄𐐩𐑉 𐑅𐐬𐑊𐑆.

10. 𐐈𐑌𐐼 𐐮𐐻 𐐿𐐩𐑋 𐐻𐐭 𐐹𐐰𐑅 𐑄𐐰𐐻 𐑄𐐬𐑆 𐐸𐐭 𐐶𐐲𐑉 𐑄 𐐽𐐮𐑊𐐼𐑉𐐯𐑌 𐐱𐑂 𐐈𐑋𐐷𐐭𐑊𐐲𐑌 𐐰𐑌𐐼 𐐸𐐮𐑆 𐐺𐑉𐐯𐑄𐑉𐐯𐑌, 𐐸𐐭 𐐸𐐰𐐼 𐐻𐐩𐐿𐐲𐑌 𐐻𐐭 𐐶𐐴𐑁 𐑄 𐐼𐐫𐐻𐐲𐑉𐑆 𐐱𐑂 𐑄 𐐢𐐰𐑋𐐲𐑌𐐴𐐻𐑅, 𐐶𐐲𐑉 𐐼𐐮𐑅𐐹𐑊𐐨𐑆𐐼 𐐶𐐮𐑄 𐑄 𐐿𐐱𐑌𐐼𐐲𐐿𐐻 𐐱𐑂 𐑄𐐩𐑉 𐑁𐐪𐑄𐐲𐑉𐑆, 𐐰𐑌𐐼 𐑄𐐩 𐐶𐐳𐐼 𐑌𐐬 𐑊𐐱𐑍𐑀𐐲𐑉 𐐺𐐨 𐐿𐐫𐑊𐐼 𐐺𐐴 𐑄 𐑌𐐩𐑋𐑆 𐐱𐑂 𐑄𐐩𐑉 𐑁𐐪𐑄𐐲𐑉𐑆, 𐑄𐐩𐑉𐑁𐐫𐑉 𐑄𐐩 𐐻𐐳𐐿 𐐲𐐹𐐱𐑌 𐑄𐐯𐑋𐑅𐐯𐑊𐑂𐑆 𐑄 𐑌𐐩𐑋 𐐱𐑂 𐐤𐐨𐑁𐐴, 𐑄𐐰𐐻 𐑄𐐩 𐑋𐐴𐐻 𐐺𐐨 𐐿𐐫𐑊𐐼 𐑄 𐐽𐐮𐑊𐐼𐑉𐐯𐑌 𐐱𐑂 𐐤𐐨𐑁𐐴, 𐐰𐑌𐐼 𐐺𐐨 𐑌𐐲𐑋𐐺𐐲𐑉𐐼 𐐲𐑋𐐲𐑍 𐑄𐐬𐑆 𐐸𐐭 𐐶𐐲𐑉 𐐿𐐫𐑊𐐼 𐐤𐐨𐑁𐐴𐐻𐑅. 𐐈𐑌𐐼 𐑌𐐵 𐐫𐑊 𐑄 𐐹𐐨𐐹𐑊 𐐱𐑂 𐐞𐐩𐑉𐐲𐐸𐐯𐑋𐑊𐐲 𐐶𐐲𐑉 𐑌𐐲𐑋𐐺𐐲𐑉𐐼 𐐶𐐮𐑄 𐑄 𐐤𐐨𐑁𐐴𐐻𐑅, 𐐰𐑌𐐼 𐑄𐐮𐑅 𐐺𐐨𐐿𐐫𐑆 𐑄 𐐿𐐮𐑍𐐼𐐲𐑋 𐐸𐐰𐐼 𐐺𐐮𐑌 𐐿𐐲𐑌𐑁𐐲𐑉𐐼 𐐲𐐹𐐱𐑌 𐑌𐐲𐑌 𐐺𐐲𐐻 𐑄𐐬𐑆 𐐸𐐭 𐐶𐐲𐑉 𐐼𐐨𐑅𐐯𐑌𐐼𐐲𐑌𐐻𐑅 𐐱𐑂 𐐤𐐨𐑁𐐴.

11. 𐐈𐑌𐐼 𐑌𐐵 𐐮𐐻 𐐿𐐩𐑋 𐐻𐐭 𐐹𐐰𐑅 𐑄𐐰𐐻 𐐸𐐶𐐯𐑌 𐐣𐐬𐑆𐐴𐐲 𐐸𐐰𐐼 𐑋𐐩𐐼 𐐰𐑌 𐐯𐑌𐐼 𐐱𐑂 𐑅𐐹𐐨𐐿𐐮𐑍 𐐰𐑌𐐼 𐑉𐐨𐐼𐐮𐑍 𐐻𐐭 𐑄 𐐹𐐨𐐹𐑊, 𐐸𐐨 𐐼𐐨𐑆𐐴𐑉𐐼 𐑄𐐰𐐻 𐐈𐑊𐑋𐐲 𐑇𐐳𐐼 𐐫𐑊𐑅𐐬 𐑅𐐹𐐨𐐿 𐐻𐐭 𐑄 𐐹𐐨𐐹𐑊. 𐐈𐑌𐐼 𐐈𐑊𐑋𐐲 𐐼𐐮𐐼 𐑅𐐹𐐨𐐿 𐐲𐑌𐐻𐐭 𐑄𐐯𐑋, 𐐸𐐶𐐯𐑌 𐑄𐐩 𐐶𐐲𐑉 𐐲𐑅𐐯𐑋𐐺𐑊𐐼 𐐻𐐭𐑀𐐯𐑄𐐲𐑉 𐐮𐑌 𐑊𐐪𐑉𐐾 𐐺𐐱𐐼𐐨𐑆, 𐐰𐑌𐐼 𐐸𐐨 𐐶𐐯𐑌𐐻 𐑁𐑉𐐱𐑋 𐐶𐐲𐑌 𐐺𐐱𐐼𐐨 𐐻𐐭 𐐲𐑌𐐲𐑄𐐲𐑉, 𐐹𐑉𐐨𐐽𐐮𐑍 𐐲𐑌𐐻𐐭 𐑄 𐐹𐐨𐐹𐑊 𐑉𐐨𐐹𐐯𐑌𐐻𐐲𐑌𐑅 𐐰𐑌𐐼 𐑁𐐩𐑃 𐐱𐑌 𐑄 𐐢𐐫𐑉𐐼. 𐐈𐑌𐐼 𐐸𐐨 𐐼𐐮𐐼 𐐯𐑀𐑆𐐫𐑉𐐻 𐑄 𐐹𐐨𐐹𐑊 𐐱𐑂 𐐢𐐮𐑋𐐸𐐴 𐐰𐑌𐐼 𐐸𐐮𐑆 𐐺𐑉𐐯𐑄𐑉𐐯𐑌, 𐐫𐑊 𐑄𐐬𐑆 𐑄𐐰𐐻 𐐸𐐰𐐼 𐐺𐐮𐑌 𐐼𐐨𐑊𐐮𐑂𐐲𐑉𐐼 𐐵𐐻 𐐱𐑂 𐐺𐐱𐑌𐐼𐐩𐐾, 𐑄𐐰𐐻 𐑄𐐩 𐑇𐐳𐐼 𐑉𐐨𐑋𐐯𐑋𐐺𐐲𐑉 𐑄𐐰𐐻 𐐮𐐻 𐐶𐐱𐑆 𐑄 𐐢𐐫𐑉𐐼 𐑄𐐰𐐻 𐐼𐐮𐐼 𐐼𐐨𐑊𐐮𐑂𐐲𐑉 𐑄𐐯𐑋. 𐐈𐑌𐐼 𐐮𐐻 𐐿𐐩𐑋 𐐻𐐭 𐐹𐐰𐑅 𐑄𐐰𐐻 𐐪𐑁𐐻𐐲𐑉 𐐈𐑊𐑋𐐲 𐐸𐐰𐐼 𐐻𐐫𐐻 𐑄 𐐹𐐨𐐹𐑊 𐑋𐐯𐑌𐐨 𐑃𐐮𐑍𐑆, 𐐰𐑌𐐼 𐐸𐐰𐐼 𐑋𐐩𐐼 𐐰𐑌 𐐯𐑌𐐼 𐐱𐑂 𐑅𐐹𐐨𐐿𐐮𐑍 𐐻𐐭 𐑄𐐯𐑋, 𐑄𐐰𐐻 𐐿𐐮𐑍 𐐢𐐮𐑋𐐸𐐴 𐐶𐐱𐑆 𐐼𐐨𐑆𐐴𐑉𐐲𐑅 𐑄𐐰𐐻 𐐸𐐨 𐑋𐐴𐐻 𐐺𐐨 𐐺𐐰𐐹-

𐐻𐐴𐑆𐐼; 𐐰𐑌𐐼 𐐫𐑊 𐐸𐐮𐑆 𐐹𐐨𐐹𐑊 𐐶𐐲𐑉 𐐼𐐨𐑆𐐴𐑉𐐲𐑅 𐑄𐐰𐐻 𐑄𐐩 𐑋𐐴𐐻 𐐺 𐐺𐐰𐐹𐐻𐐴𐑆𐐼 𐐫𐑊𐑅𐐬. 𐐜𐐯𐑉𐑁𐐬𐑉 𐐈𐑊𐑋𐐰 𐐼𐐮𐐼 𐑀𐐬 𐑁𐐬𐑉𐑃 𐐮𐑌𐐻𐐭 𐑄 𐐶𐐫𐐻𐐲𐑉, 𐐰𐑌𐐼 𐐼𐐮𐐼 𐐺𐐰𐐹𐐻𐐴𐑆 𐑄𐐯𐑋; 𐐷𐐩, 𐐸𐐨 𐐼𐐮𐐼 𐐺𐐰𐐹𐐻𐐴𐑆 𐑄𐐯𐑋 𐐰𐑁𐐻𐐲𐑉 𐑄 𐑋𐐰𐑌𐐲𐑉 𐐸𐐨 𐐼𐐮𐐼 𐐸𐐮𐑆 𐐺𐑉𐐯𐑃𐑉𐐯𐑌 𐐮𐑌 𐑄 𐐶𐐫𐐻𐐲𐑉𐑆 𐐱𐑂 𐐣𐐫𐑉𐑋𐐲𐑌; 𐐷𐐩, 𐐰𐑌𐐼 𐐰𐑆 𐑋𐐯𐑌𐐨 𐐰𐑆 𐐸𐐨 𐐼𐐮𐐼 𐐺𐐰𐐹𐐻𐐴𐑆 𐐼𐐮𐐼 𐐺𐐨𐑊𐐱𐑍 𐐻𐐭 𐑄 𐐽𐐲𐑉𐐽 𐐱𐑂 𐐘𐐱𐐼; 𐐰𐑌𐐼 𐑄𐐮𐑅 𐐺𐐨𐐿𐐫𐑆 𐐱𐑂 𐑄𐐩𐑉 𐐺𐐨𐑊𐐨𐑁 𐐱𐑌 𐑄 𐐶𐐲𐑉𐐼𐑆 𐐱𐑂 𐐈𐑊𐑋𐐰.

12. 𐐈𐑌𐐼 𐐮𐐻 𐐿𐐩𐑋 𐐻𐐭 𐐹𐐰𐑅 𐑄𐐰𐐻 𐐿𐐮𐑍 𐐣𐐬𐑆𐐴𐐰 𐑀𐑉𐐰𐑌𐐻𐐯𐐼 𐐲𐑌𐐻𐐭 𐐈𐑊𐑋𐐰, 𐑄𐐰𐐻 𐐸𐐨 𐑋𐐴𐐻 𐐯𐑅𐐻𐐰𐐺𐑊𐐮𐑇 𐐽𐐲𐑉𐐽𐐯𐑆 𐑃𐑉𐐭𐐵𐐻 𐐫𐑊 𐑄 𐑊𐐰𐑌𐐼 𐐱𐑂 𐐞𐐯𐑉𐐰𐐸𐐯𐑋𐑊𐐰; 𐐰𐑌𐐼 𐑀𐐩𐑂 𐐸𐐮𐑋 𐐹𐐵𐐲𐑉 𐐻𐐭 𐐫𐑉𐐼𐐩𐑌 𐐹𐑉𐐨𐑅𐐻𐑅 𐐰𐑌𐐼 𐐻𐐨𐐽𐐲𐑉𐑆 𐐬𐑂𐐲𐑉 𐐯𐑂𐐲𐑉𐐨 𐐽𐐲𐑉𐐽. 𐐤𐐵 𐑄𐐮𐑅 𐐶𐐱𐑆 𐐼𐐲𐑌 𐐺𐐨𐐿𐐫𐑆 𐑄𐐯𐑉 𐐶𐐲𐑉 𐑅𐐬 𐑋𐐯𐑌𐐨 𐐹𐐨𐐹𐑊 𐑄𐐰𐐻 𐑄𐐩 𐐿𐐳𐐼 𐑌𐐱𐐻 𐐫𐑊 𐐺 𐑀𐐲𐑂𐐲𐑉𐑌𐐼 𐐺𐐴 𐐶𐐲𐑌 𐐻𐐨𐐽𐐲𐑉; 𐑌𐐨𐑄𐐲𐑉 𐐿𐐳𐐼 𐑄𐐩 𐐫𐑊 𐐸𐐨𐑉 𐑄 𐐶𐐲𐑉𐐼 𐐱𐑂 𐐘𐐱𐐼 𐐮𐑌 𐐶𐐲𐑌 𐐰𐑅𐐯𐑋𐐺𐑊𐐨; 𐑄𐐯𐑉𐑁𐐬𐑉 𐑄𐐩 𐐼𐐮𐐼 𐐰𐑅𐐯𐑋𐐺𐑊 𐑄𐐯𐑋𐑅𐐯𐑊𐑂𐑆 𐐻𐐭𐑀𐐯𐑄𐐲𐑉 𐐮𐑌 𐐼𐐮𐑁𐐲𐑉𐐯𐑌𐐻 𐐺𐐱𐐼𐐨𐑆, 𐐺𐐨𐐮𐑍 𐐿𐐫𐑊𐐼 𐐽𐐲𐑉𐐽𐐯𐑆; 𐐯𐑂𐐲𐑉𐐨 𐐽𐐲𐑉𐐽 𐐸𐐰𐑂𐐮𐑍 𐑄𐐯𐑉 𐐹𐑉𐐨𐑅𐐻𐑅 𐐰𐑌𐐼 𐑄𐐯𐑉 𐐻𐐨𐐽𐐲𐑉𐑆, 𐐰𐑌𐐼 𐐯𐑂𐐲𐑉𐐨 𐐹𐑉𐐨𐑅𐐻 𐐹𐑉𐐨𐐽𐐮𐑍 𐑄 𐐶𐐲𐑉𐐼 𐐰𐐿𐐫𐑉𐐼𐐮𐑍 𐐰𐑆 𐐮𐐻 𐐶𐐱𐑆 𐐼𐐯𐑊𐐮𐑂𐐲𐑉𐐼 𐐻𐐭 𐐸𐐮𐑋 𐐺𐐴 𐑄 𐑋𐐵𐑃 𐐱𐑂 𐐈𐑊𐑋𐐰; 𐐰𐑌𐐼 𐑄𐐲𐑅, 𐑌𐐱𐐻𐐶𐐮𐑃𐑅𐐻𐐰𐑌𐐼𐐮𐑍 𐑄𐐯𐑉 𐐺𐐨𐐮𐑍 𐑋𐐯𐑌𐐨 𐐽𐐲𐑉𐐽𐐯𐑆, 𐑄𐐩 𐐶𐐲𐑉 𐐫𐑊 𐐶𐐲𐑌 𐐽𐐲𐑉𐐽; 𐐷𐐩, 𐐨𐑂𐐯𐑌 𐑄 𐐽𐐲𐑉𐐽 𐐱𐑂 𐐘𐐱𐐼; 𐑁𐐫𐑉 𐑄𐐯𐑉 𐐶𐐱𐑆 𐑌𐐲𐑃𐐮𐑍 𐐹𐑉𐐨𐐽𐐻 𐐮𐑌 𐐫𐑊 𐑄 𐐽𐐲𐑉𐐽𐐯𐑆 𐐯𐐿𐑅𐐯𐐹𐐻 𐐮𐐻 𐐶𐐲𐑉 𐑉𐐨𐐹𐐯𐑌𐐻𐐰𐑌𐑅 𐐰𐑌𐐼 𐑁𐐩𐑃 𐐮𐑌 𐐘𐐱𐐼. 𐐈𐑌𐐼 𐑌𐐵 𐑄𐐯𐑉 𐐶𐐲𐑉 𐑅𐐯𐑂𐐯𐑌 𐐽𐐲𐑉𐐽𐐯𐑆 𐐮𐑌 𐑄 𐑊𐐰𐑌𐐼 𐐱𐑂 𐐞𐐯𐑉𐐰𐐸𐐯𐑋𐑊𐐰. 𐐈𐑌𐐼 𐐮𐐻 𐐿𐐩𐑋 𐐻𐐭 𐐹𐐰𐑅 𐑄𐐰𐐻 𐐸𐐭𐑅𐐬𐐯𐑂𐐲𐑉 𐐶𐐲𐑉 𐐼𐐨𐑆𐐴𐑉𐐲𐑅 𐐻𐐭 𐐻𐐩𐐿 𐐲𐐹𐐱𐑌 𐑄𐐯𐑋 𐑄 𐑌𐐩𐑋 𐐱𐑂 𐐗𐑉𐐴𐑅𐐻, 𐐫𐑉 𐐱𐑂 𐐘𐐱𐐼, 𐑄𐐩 𐐼𐐮𐐼 𐐾𐑎𐑌 𐑄 𐐽𐐲𐑉𐐽𐐯𐑆 𐐱𐑂 𐐘𐐱𐐼; 𐐰𐑌𐐼 𐑄𐐩 𐐶𐐲𐑉 𐐿𐐫𐑊𐐼 𐑄 𐐹𐐨𐐹𐑊 𐐱𐑂 𐐘𐐱𐐼. 𐐈𐑌𐐼 𐑄 𐐢𐐫𐑉𐐼 𐐼𐐮𐐼 𐐹𐐬𐑉 𐐵𐐻 𐐸𐐮𐑆 𐐝𐐹𐐮𐑉𐐮𐐻 𐐲𐐹𐐱𐑌 𐑄𐐯𐑋, 𐐰𐑌𐐼 𐑄𐐩 𐐶𐐲𐑉 𐐺𐑊𐐯𐑅𐐼, 𐐰𐑌𐐼 𐐹𐑉𐐱𐑅𐐹𐐲𐑉𐐼 𐐮𐑌 𐑄 𐑊𐐰𐑌𐐼.

13. 𐐤𐐵 𐐮𐐻 𐐿𐐩𐑋 𐐻𐐭 𐐹𐐰𐑅 𐑄𐐰𐐻 𐑄𐐯𐑉 𐐶𐐲𐑉 𐑋𐐯𐑌𐐨 𐐱𐑂 𐑄 𐑉𐐴𐑆𐐮𐑍 𐑀𐐯𐑌𐐲𐑉𐐩𐑇𐐲𐑌 𐑄𐐰𐐻 𐐿𐐳𐐼 𐑌𐐱𐐻 𐐲𐑌𐐼𐐲𐑉𐑅𐐻𐐰𐑌𐐼 𐑄 𐐶𐐲𐑉𐐼𐑆 𐐱𐑂 𐐿𐐮𐑍 𐐒𐐯𐑌𐐾𐐲𐑋𐐮𐑌, 𐐺𐐨𐐮𐑍 𐑊𐐮𐐻𐑊 𐐽𐐮𐑊𐐼𐑉𐐯𐑌 𐐰𐐻 𐑄 𐐻𐐴𐑋 𐐸𐐨 𐑅𐐹𐐩𐐿 𐐲𐑌𐐻𐐭 𐐸𐐮𐑆 𐐹𐐨𐐹𐑊; 𐐰𐑌𐐼 𐑄𐐩 𐐼𐐮𐐼 𐑌𐐱𐐻 𐐺𐐨𐑊𐐨𐑂 𐑄 𐐻𐑉𐐰𐐼𐐮𐑇𐐲𐑌 𐐱𐑂 𐑄𐐯𐑉 𐑁𐐪𐑄𐐲𐑉𐑆. 𐐜𐐩 𐐼𐐮𐐼 𐑌𐐱𐐻 𐐺𐐨𐑊𐐨𐑂 𐐸𐐶𐐱𐐻 𐐸𐐰𐐼 𐐺𐐨𐑌 𐑅𐐯𐐼 𐐿𐐱𐑌𐑅𐐲𐑉𐑌𐐮𐑍 𐑄 𐑉𐐯𐑆𐐲𐑉𐐯𐐿𐑇𐐲𐑌 𐐱𐑂 𐑄 𐐼𐐯𐐼, 𐑌𐐨𐑄𐐲𐑉 𐐼𐐮𐐼 𐑄𐐩 𐐺𐐨𐑊𐐨𐑂 𐐿𐐱𐑌𐑅𐐲𐑉𐑌𐐮𐑍 𐑄 𐐿𐐲𐑋𐐮𐑍 𐐱𐑂 𐐗𐑉𐐴𐑅𐐻. 𐐈𐑌𐐼 𐑌𐐵 𐐺𐐨𐐿𐐫𐑆 𐐱𐑂 𐑄𐐯𐑉 𐐲𐑌𐐺𐐨𐑊𐐨𐑁 𐑄𐐩 𐐿𐐳𐐼 𐑌𐐱𐐻 𐐲𐑌𐐼𐐲𐑉𐑅𐐻𐐰𐑌𐐼 𐑄 𐐶𐐲𐑉𐐼 𐐱𐑂 𐐘𐐱𐐼; 𐐰𐑌𐐼 𐑄𐐯𐑉 𐐸𐐪𐑉𐐻𐑅 𐐶𐐲𐑉 𐐸𐐪𐑉𐐼𐐲𐑌𐐼. 𐐈𐑌𐐼 𐑄𐐩 𐐶𐐳𐐼 𐑌𐐱𐐻 𐐺 𐐺𐐰𐐹𐐻𐐴𐑆𐐼; 𐑌𐐨𐑄𐐲𐑉 𐐶𐐳𐐼 𐑄𐐩 𐐾𐑎𐑌 𐑄 𐐽𐐲𐑉𐐽. 𐐈𐑌𐐼 𐑄𐐩 𐐶𐐲𐑉 𐐰 𐑅𐐯𐐹𐐲𐑉𐐩𐐻 𐐹𐐨𐐹𐑊 𐐰𐑆 𐐻𐐭 𐑄𐐯𐑉 𐑁𐐩𐑃, 𐐰𐑌𐐼 𐑉𐐨𐑋𐐩𐑌𐐼 𐑅𐐬 𐐯𐑂𐐲𐑉 𐐰𐑁𐐻𐐲𐑉, 𐐨𐑂𐐯𐑌 𐐮𐑌 𐑄𐐯𐑉 𐐿𐐪𐑉𐑌𐐲𐑊 𐐰𐑌𐐼 𐑅𐐮𐑌𐑁𐐳𐑊 𐑅𐐻𐐩𐐻; 𐑁𐐫𐑉 𐑄𐐩 𐐶𐐳𐐼 𐑌𐐱𐐻 𐐿𐐫𐑊 𐐲𐐹𐐱𐑌 𐑄 𐐢𐐫𐑉𐐼 𐑄𐐯𐑉 𐐘𐐱𐐼. 𐐈𐑌𐐼 𐑌𐐵 𐐮𐑌 𐑄 𐑉𐐩𐑌 𐐱𐑂 𐐣𐐬𐑆𐐴𐐰 𐑄𐐩 𐐶𐐲𐑉 𐑌𐐱𐐻 𐐸𐐪𐑁 𐑅𐐬 𐑌𐐭𐑋𐐲𐑉𐐲𐑅 𐐰𐑆 𐑄 𐐹𐐨𐐹𐑊 𐐱𐑂 𐐘𐐱𐐼; 𐐺𐐲𐐻 𐐺𐐨𐐿𐐫𐑆 𐐱𐑂 𐑄 𐐼𐐮𐑅𐐯𐑌𐑇𐐲𐑌𐑆 𐐲𐑋𐐲𐑍 𐑄 𐐺𐑉𐐯𐑄𐑉𐐯𐑌 𐑄𐐩 𐐺𐐨𐐿𐐩𐑋 𐑋𐐬𐑉 𐑌𐐭𐑋𐐲𐑉𐐲𐑅. 𐐙𐐫𐑉 𐐮𐐻 𐐿𐐩𐑋 𐐻𐐭 𐐹𐐰𐑅 𐑄𐐰𐐻 𐑄𐐩 𐐼𐐮𐐼 𐐼𐐨𐑅𐐨𐑂 𐑋𐐯𐑌𐐨 𐐶𐐮𐑄 𐑄𐐯𐑉 𐑁𐑊𐐰𐐻𐐲𐑉𐐮𐑍 𐐶𐐲𐑉𐐼𐑆, 𐐸𐐭 𐐶𐐲𐑉 𐐮𐑌 𐑄 𐐽𐐲𐑉𐐽, 𐐰𐑌𐐼 𐐼𐐮𐐼 𐐿𐐫𐑆 𐑄𐐯𐑋 𐐻𐐭 𐐿𐐲𐑋𐐮𐐻 𐑋𐐯𐑌𐐨 𐑅𐐮𐑌𐑆; 𐑄𐐯𐑉𐑁𐐬𐑉 𐐮𐐻 𐐺𐐨𐐿𐐩𐑋 𐐯𐐿𐑅𐐹𐐨𐐼𐐨𐐲𐑌𐐻 𐑄𐐰𐐻 𐑄𐐬𐑆 𐐸𐐭 𐐿𐐲𐑋𐐮𐐻𐐯𐐼 𐑅𐐮𐑌, 𐑄𐐰𐐻 𐐶𐐲𐑉 𐐮𐑌 𐑄 𐐽𐐲𐑉𐐽, 𐑇𐐳𐐼 𐐺 𐐰𐐼𐑋𐐱𐑌𐐮𐑇𐐻 𐐺𐐴 𐑄 𐐽𐐲𐑉𐐽.

14. 𐐈𐑌𐐼 𐐮𐐻 𐐿𐐩𐑋 𐐻𐐭 𐐹𐐰𐑅 𐑄𐐰𐐻 𐑄𐐩 𐐶𐐲𐑉 𐐺𐑉𐐱𐐻 𐐺𐐨𐑁𐐬𐑉 𐑄 𐐹𐑉𐐨𐑅𐐻𐑅, 𐐰𐑌𐐼 𐐼𐐨𐑊𐐮𐑂𐐲𐑉𐐼 𐐲𐐹 𐐲𐑌𐐻𐐭 𐑄 𐐹𐑉𐐨𐑅𐐻𐑅 𐐺𐐴 𐑄 𐐻𐐨𐐽𐐲𐑉𐑆; 𐐰𐑌𐐼 𐑄 𐐹𐑉𐐨𐑅𐐻𐑅 𐐺𐑉𐐱𐐻 𐑄𐐯𐑋 𐐺𐐨𐑁𐐬𐑉 𐐈𐑊𐑋𐐰, 𐐸𐐭 𐐶𐐱𐑆 𐑄 𐐸𐐴 𐐹𐑉𐐨𐑅𐐻. 𐐤𐐵 𐐿𐐮𐑍 𐐣𐐬𐑆𐐴𐐰 𐐸𐐰𐐼 𐑀𐐮𐑂𐑌 𐐈𐑊𐑋𐐰 𐑄 𐐫𐑃𐐱𐑉𐐮𐐻𐐨 𐐬𐑂𐐲𐑉 𐑄 𐐽𐐲𐑉𐐽. 𐐈𐑌𐐼 𐐮𐐻 𐐿𐐩𐑋 𐐻𐐭 𐐹𐐰𐑅 𐑄𐐰𐐻 𐐈𐑊𐑋𐐰 𐐼𐐮𐐼 𐑌𐐱𐐻 𐑌𐐬 𐐿𐐱𐑌𐑅𐐲𐑉𐑌𐐮𐑍 𐑄𐐯𐑋, 𐑁𐐫𐑉 𐑄𐐯𐑉 𐐶𐐲𐑉 𐑋𐐯𐑌𐐨 𐐶𐐮𐐻𐑌𐐯𐑅𐐯𐑆 𐐲𐑀𐐯𐑌𐑅𐐻 𐑄𐐯𐑋; 𐐷𐐩, 𐑄 𐐹𐐨𐐹𐑊 𐑅𐐻𐐳𐐼 𐐰𐑌𐐼 𐐻𐐯𐑅𐐻𐐮𐑁𐐴𐐼 𐐱𐑂 𐑄𐐯𐑉 𐐮𐑌𐐮𐐿𐐶𐐮𐐻𐐨 𐐮𐑌 𐐰𐐺𐐲𐑌𐐼𐐲𐑌𐑅. 𐐤𐐵 𐑄𐐯𐑉 𐐸𐐰𐐼 𐑌𐐱𐐻 𐐯𐑌𐐨 𐑅𐐲𐐽 𐑃𐐮𐑍 𐐸𐐰𐐹𐑌𐐼 𐐺𐐨𐑁𐐬𐑉 𐐮𐑌 𐑄 𐐽𐐲𐑉𐐽; 𐑄𐐯𐑉𐑁𐐬𐑉 𐐈𐑊𐑋𐐰 𐐶𐐱𐑆 𐐻𐑉𐐲𐐺𐑊𐐼 𐐮𐑌 𐐸𐐮𐑆 𐑅𐐹𐐮𐑉𐐮𐐻, 𐐰𐑌𐐼 𐐸𐐨 𐐿𐐫𐑆𐐼 𐑄𐐰𐐻 𐑄𐐩 𐑇𐐳𐐼 𐐺 𐐺𐑉𐐱𐐻 𐐺𐐨𐑁𐐬𐑉 𐑄 𐐿𐐮𐑍. 𐐈𐑌𐐼 𐐸𐐨 𐑅𐐯𐐼 𐐲𐑌𐐻𐐭 𐑄 𐐿𐐮𐑍, 𐐒𐐨𐐸𐐬𐑊𐐼, 𐐸𐐨𐑉 𐐪𐑉 𐑋𐐯𐑌𐐨 𐐸𐐭𐑋 𐐶𐐨 𐐸𐐰𐑂 𐐺𐑉𐐱𐐻 𐐺𐐨𐑁𐐬𐑉 𐑄𐐨, 𐐸𐐭 𐐪𐑉 𐐰𐐿𐐷𐐭𐑆𐐼 𐐱𐑂 𐑄𐐯𐑉 𐐺𐑉𐐯𐑄𐑉𐐯𐑌; 𐐷𐐩, 𐐰𐑌𐐼 𐑄𐐩 𐐸𐐰𐑂 𐐺𐐨𐑌 𐐻𐐩𐐿𐑌 𐐮𐑌 𐐼𐐴𐑂𐐲𐑉𐑆 𐐮𐑌𐐮𐐿𐐶𐐮𐐻𐐨𐑆. 𐐈𐑌𐐼 𐑄𐐩 𐐼𐐭 𐑌𐐱𐐻 𐑉𐐨𐐹𐐯𐑌𐐻 𐐱𐑂 𐑄𐐯𐑉 𐐮𐑌𐐮𐐿𐐶𐐮𐐻𐐨𐑆;

𐑄𐐩𐑉𐑁𐐬𐑉 𐐶𐐨 𐐸𐐰𐑂 𐐺𐑉𐐫𐐻 𐑄𐐯𐑋 𐐺𐐨𐑁𐐬𐑉 𐑄, 𐑄𐐰𐐻 𐑄𐐵 𐑋𐐩𐐯𐑅𐐻 𐐾𐐲𐐾 𐑄𐐯𐑋 𐐰𐐿𐐫𐑉𐐼𐐮𐑍 𐐻𐐭 𐑄𐐩𐑉 𐐿𐑉𐐴𐑋𐑆. 𐐒𐐲𐐻 𐐿𐐮𐑍 𐐣𐐬𐑅𐐴𐐲 𐑅𐐯𐐼 𐐲𐑌𐐻𐐭 𐐈𐑊𐑋𐐲, 𐐒𐐨𐐸𐐬𐑊𐐼, 𐐌 𐐾𐐲𐐾 𐑄𐐯𐑋 𐑌𐐱𐐻; 𐑄𐐩𐑉𐑁𐐬𐑉 𐐌 𐐼𐐨𐑊𐐮𐑂𐐲𐑉 𐑄𐐯𐑋 𐐮𐑌𐐻𐐭 𐑄𐐴 𐐸𐐰𐑌𐐼𐑆 𐐻𐐭 𐐺𐐨 𐐾𐐲𐐾𐐼. 𐐈𐑌𐐼 𐑌𐐵 𐑄 𐑅𐐹𐐮𐑉𐐮𐐻 𐐱𐑂 𐐈𐑊𐑋𐐲 𐐶𐐱𐑆 𐐲𐑀𐐯𐑌 𐐻𐑉𐐲𐐺𐑊𐐼; 𐐰𐑌𐐼 𐐸𐐨 𐐶𐐯𐑌𐐻 𐐰𐑌𐐼 𐐮𐑌𐐿𐐶𐐴𐑉𐐼 𐐱𐑂 𐑄 𐐢𐐫𐑉𐐼 𐐸𐐶𐐱𐐻 𐐸𐐨 𐑇𐐳𐐼 𐐼𐐭 𐐿𐐱𐑌𐑅𐐲𐑉𐑌𐐮𐑍 𐑄𐐮𐑅 𐑋𐐰𐐻𐐲𐑉, 𐑁𐐬𐑉 𐐸𐐨 𐑁𐐨𐑉𐐼 𐑄𐐰𐐻 𐐸𐐨 𐑇𐐳𐐼 𐐼𐐭 𐑉𐐱𐑍 𐐮𐑌 𐑄 𐑅𐐴𐐻 𐐱𐑂 𐐘𐐱𐐼.

15. 𐐈𐑌𐐼 𐐮𐐻 𐐿𐐩𐑋 𐐻𐐭 𐐹𐐰𐑅 𐑄𐐰𐐻 𐐰𐑁𐐻𐐲𐑉 𐐸𐐨 𐐸𐐰𐐼 𐐹𐐬𐑉𐐼 𐐵𐐻 𐐸𐐮𐑆 𐐸𐐬𐑊 𐑅𐐬𐑊 𐐻𐐭 𐐘𐐱𐐼, 𐑄 𐑂𐐦𐑅 𐐱𐑂 𐑄 𐐢𐐫𐑉𐐼 𐐿𐐩𐑋 𐐻𐐭 𐐸𐐮𐑋, 𐑅𐐩𐐮𐑍, 𐐒𐑊𐐯𐑅𐐯𐐼 𐐪𐑉𐐻 𐑄𐐵, 𐐈𐑊𐑋𐐲, 𐐰𐑌𐐼 𐐺𐑊𐐯𐑅𐐯𐐼 𐐪𐑉 𐑄𐐩 𐐸𐐭 𐐶𐐲𐑉 𐐺𐐰𐐹𐐻𐐴𐑆𐐼 𐐮𐑌 𐑄 𐐶𐐫𐐻𐐲𐑉𐑆 𐐱𐑂 𐐣𐐫𐑉𐑋𐐲𐑌. 𐐜𐐵 𐐪𐑉𐐻 𐐺𐑊𐐯𐑅𐐯𐐼 𐐺𐐨𐐿𐐫𐑆 𐐱𐑂 𐑄𐐴 𐐯𐐿𐑅𐐨𐐼𐐮𐑍 𐑁𐐩𐑃 𐐮𐑌 𐑄 𐐶𐐲𐑉𐐼𐑆 𐐰𐑊𐐬𐑌 𐐱𐑂 𐑋𐐴 𐑅𐐲𐑉𐑂𐐰𐑌𐐻 𐐈𐐺𐐮𐑌𐐲𐐼𐐴. 𐐈𐑌𐐼 𐐺𐑊𐐯𐑅𐐯𐐼 𐐪𐑉 𐑄𐐩 𐐺𐐨𐐿𐐫𐑆 𐐱𐑂 𐑄𐐩𐑉 𐐯𐐿𐑅𐐨𐐼𐐮𐑍 𐑁𐐩𐑃 𐐮𐑌 𐑄 𐐶𐐲𐑉𐐼𐑆 𐐰𐑊𐐬𐑌 𐐸𐐶𐐮𐐽 𐑄𐐵 𐐸𐐰𐑅𐐻 𐑅𐐹𐐬𐐿𐐲𐑌 𐐲𐑌𐐻𐐭 𐑄𐐯𐑋. 𐐈𐑌𐐼 𐐺𐑊𐐯𐑅𐐯𐐼 𐐪𐑉𐐻 𐑄𐐵 𐐺𐐨𐐿𐐫𐑆 𐑄𐐵 𐐸𐐰𐑅𐐻 𐐯𐑅𐐻𐐰𐐺𐑊𐐮𐑇𐐻 𐐲 𐐽𐐲𐑉𐐽 𐐲𐑋𐐲𐑍 𐑄𐐮𐑅 𐐹𐐨𐐹𐑊; 𐐰𐑌𐐼 𐑄𐐩 𐑇𐐰𐑊 𐐺𐐨 𐐯𐑅𐐻𐐰𐐺𐑊𐐮𐑇𐐻, 𐐰𐑌𐐼 𐑄𐐩 𐑇𐐰𐑊 𐐺𐐨 𐑋𐐴 𐐹𐐨𐐹𐑊. 𐐏𐐩, 𐐺𐑊𐐯𐑅𐐯𐐼 𐐮𐑆 𐑄𐐮𐑅 𐐹𐐨𐐹𐑊 𐐸𐐭 𐐪𐑉 𐐶𐐮𐑊𐐮𐑍 𐐻𐐭 𐐺𐐩𐑉 𐑋𐐴 𐑌𐐩𐑋; 𐑁𐐬𐑉 𐐮𐑌 𐑋𐐴 𐑌𐐩𐑋 𐑇𐐰𐑊 𐑄𐐩 𐐺𐐨 𐐿𐐫𐑊𐐼; 𐐰𐑌𐐼 𐑄𐐩 𐐪𐑉 𐑋𐐴𐑌. 𐐈𐑌𐐼 𐐺𐐨𐐿𐐫𐑆 𐑄𐐵 𐐸𐐰𐑅𐐻 𐐮𐑌𐐿𐐶𐐴𐑉𐐼 𐐱𐑂 𐑋𐐨 𐐿𐐱𐑌𐑅𐐲𐑉𐑌𐐮𐑍 𐑄 𐐻𐑉𐐰𐑌𐑅𐑀𐑉𐐯𐑅𐐲𐑉, 𐑄𐐵 𐐪𐑉𐐻 𐐺𐑊𐐯𐑅𐐯𐐼. 𐐜𐐵 𐐪𐑉𐐻 𐑋𐐴 𐑅𐐲𐑉𐑂𐐰𐑌𐐻; 𐐰𐑌𐐼 𐐌 𐐿𐐲𐑂𐐯𐑌𐐰𐑌𐐻 𐐶𐐮𐑄 𐑄, 𐑄𐐰𐐻 𐑄𐐵 𐑇𐐰𐑊𐐻 𐐸𐐰𐑂 𐐨𐐻𐐲𐑉𐑌𐐲𐑊 𐑊𐐴𐑁; 𐐰𐑌𐐼 𐑄𐐵 𐑇𐐰𐑊𐐻 𐑅𐐲𐑉𐑂 𐑋𐐨, 𐐰𐑌𐐼 𐑀𐐬 𐑁𐐬𐑉𐑃 𐐮𐑌 𐑋𐐴 𐑌𐐩𐑋, 𐐰𐑌𐐼 𐑇𐐰𐑊𐐻 𐑀𐐰𐑄𐐲𐑉 𐐻𐐭𐑀𐐯𐑄𐐲𐑉 𐑋𐐴 𐑇𐐨𐐹. 𐐈𐑌𐐼 𐐸𐐨 𐑄𐐰𐐻 𐐶𐐮𐑊 𐐸𐐨𐑉 𐑋𐐴 𐑂𐐦𐑅 𐑇𐐰𐑊 𐐺𐐨 𐑋𐐴 𐑇𐐨𐐹; 𐐰𐑌𐐼 𐐸𐐮𐑋 𐑇𐐰𐑊 𐐷𐐨 𐑉𐐨𐑅𐐨𐑂 𐐮𐑌𐐻𐐭 𐑄 𐐽𐐲𐑉𐐽, 𐐰𐑌𐐼 𐐸𐐮𐑋 𐐶𐐮𐑊 𐐌 𐐫𐑊𐑅𐐬 𐑉𐐨𐑅𐐨𐑂. 𐐙𐐬𐑉 𐐺𐐨𐐸𐐬𐑊𐐼, 𐑄𐐮𐑅 𐐮𐑆 𐑋𐐴 𐐽𐐲𐑉𐐽: 𐐸𐐭𐑅𐐬𐐯𐑂𐐲𐑉 𐐮𐑆 𐐺𐐰𐐹𐐻𐐴𐑆𐐼 𐑇𐐰𐑊 𐐺𐐨 𐐺𐐰𐐹𐐻𐐴𐑆𐐼 𐐲𐑌𐐻𐐭 𐑉𐐨𐐹𐐯𐑌𐐻𐐰𐑌𐑅. 𐐈𐑌𐐼 𐐸𐐭𐑋𐑅𐐬𐐯𐑂𐐲𐑉 𐐷𐐨 𐑉𐐨𐑅𐐨𐑂 𐑇𐐰𐑊 𐐺𐐨𐑊𐐨𐑂 𐐮𐑌 𐑋𐐴 𐑌𐐩𐑋; 𐐰𐑌𐐼 𐐸𐐮𐑋 𐐶𐐮𐑊 𐐌 𐑁𐑉𐐨𐑊𐐨 𐑁𐐫𐑉𐑀𐐮𐑂: 𐑁𐐬𐑉 𐐮𐐻 𐐮𐑆 𐐌 𐑄𐐰𐐻 𐐻𐐩𐐿𐐯𐑃 𐐲𐐹𐐱𐑌 𐑋𐐨 𐑄 𐑅𐐮𐑌𐑆 𐐱𐑂 𐑄 𐐶𐐲𐑉𐑊𐐼; 𐑁𐐬𐑉 𐐮𐐻 𐐮𐑆 𐐌 𐑄𐐰𐐻 𐐸𐐰𐑃 𐐿𐑉𐐨𐐩𐐻𐐯𐐼 𐑄𐐯𐑋; 𐐰𐑌𐐼 𐐮𐐻 𐐮𐑆 𐐌 𐑄𐐰𐐻 𐑀𐑉𐐰𐑌𐐻𐐯𐑃 𐐲𐑌𐐻𐐭 𐐸𐐮𐑋 𐑄𐐰𐐻 𐐺𐐨𐑊𐐨𐑂𐐯𐑃 𐐲𐑌𐐻𐐭 𐑄 𐐯𐑌𐐼, 𐐲 𐐹𐑊𐐩𐑅 𐐰𐐻 𐑋𐐴 𐑉𐐴𐐻 𐐸𐐰𐑌𐐼. 𐐙𐐬𐑉 𐐺𐐨𐐸𐐬𐑊𐐼, 𐐮𐑌 𐑋𐐴 𐑌𐐩𐑋 𐐪𐑉 𐑄𐐩 𐐿𐐫𐑊𐐼; 𐐰𐑌𐐼 𐐮𐑁 𐑄𐐩 𐑌𐐬 𐑋𐐨 𐑄𐐩 𐑇𐐰𐑊 𐐿𐐲𐑋 𐑁𐐬𐑉𐑃, 𐐰𐑌𐐼 𐑇𐐰𐑊 𐐸𐐰𐑂 𐐲 𐐹𐑊𐐩𐑅 𐐨𐐻𐐲𐑉𐑌𐐲𐑊𐐨 𐐰𐐻 𐑋𐐴 𐑉𐐴𐐻 𐐸𐐰𐑌𐐼.

16. 𐐈𐑌𐐼 𐐮𐐻 𐑇𐐰𐑊 𐐿𐐲𐑋 𐐻𐐭 𐐹𐐰𐑅 𐑄𐐰𐐻 𐐸𐐶𐐯𐑌 𐑄 𐑅𐐯𐐿𐐲𐑌𐐼 𐐻𐑉𐐲𐑋𐐹 𐑇𐐰𐑊 𐑅𐐵𐑌𐐼, 𐑄𐐯𐑌 𐑇𐐰𐑊 𐑄𐐩 𐑄𐐰𐐻 𐑌𐐯𐑂𐐲𐑉 𐑌𐐭 𐑋𐐨 𐐿𐐲𐑋 𐑁𐐬𐑉𐑃 𐐰𐑌𐐼 𐑇𐐰𐑊 𐑅𐐻𐐰𐑌𐐼 𐐺𐐨𐑁𐐬𐑉 𐑋𐐨; 𐐰𐑌𐐼 𐑄𐐯𐑌 𐑇𐐰𐑊 𐑄𐐩 𐑌𐐬 𐑄𐐰𐐻 𐐌 𐐰𐑋 𐑄 𐐢𐐫𐑉𐐼 𐑄𐐩𐑉 𐐘𐐱𐐼, 𐑄𐐰𐐻 𐐌 𐐰𐑋 𐑄𐐩𐑉 𐐡𐐨𐐼𐐨𐑋𐐲𐑉; 𐐺𐐲𐐻 𐑄𐐩 𐐶𐐳𐐼 𐑌𐐱𐐻 𐐺𐐨 𐑉𐐨𐐼𐐨𐑋𐐼. 𐐈𐑌𐐼 𐑄𐐯𐑌 𐐶𐐮𐑊 𐐌 𐐿𐐱𐑌𐑁𐐯𐑅 𐐲𐑌𐐻𐐭 𐑄𐐯𐑋 𐑄𐐰𐐻 𐐌 𐑌𐐯𐑂𐐲𐑉 𐑌𐐭 𐑄𐐯𐑋; 𐐰𐑌𐐼 𐑄𐐩 𐑇𐐰𐑊 𐐼𐐨𐐹𐐪𐑉𐐻 𐐮𐑌𐐻𐐭 𐐯𐑂𐐲𐑉𐑊𐐰𐑅𐐻𐐮𐑍 𐑁𐐴𐑉, 𐐹𐑉𐐨𐐹𐐩𐑉𐐼 𐑁𐐬𐑉 𐑄 𐐼𐐯𐑂𐐲𐑊 𐐰𐑌𐐼 𐐸𐐮𐑆 𐐩𐑌𐐾𐐯𐑊𐑆. 𐐜𐐩𐑉𐑁𐐬𐑉 𐐌 𐑅𐐩 𐐲𐑌𐐻𐐭 𐐷𐐭, 𐑄𐐰𐐻 𐐸𐐨 𐑄𐐰𐐻 𐐶𐐮𐑊 𐑌𐐱𐐻 𐐸𐐨𐑉 𐑋𐐴 𐑂𐐦𐑅, 𐑄 𐑅𐐩𐑋 𐑇𐐰𐑊 𐐷𐐨 𐑌𐐱𐐻 𐑉𐐨𐑅𐐨𐑂 𐐮𐑌𐐻𐐭 𐑋𐐴 𐐽𐐲𐑉𐐽, 𐑁𐐬𐑉 𐐸𐐮𐑋 𐐌 𐐶𐐮𐑊 𐑌𐐱𐐻 𐑉𐐨𐑅𐐨𐑂 𐐰𐐻 𐑄 𐑊𐐰𐑅𐐻 𐐼𐐩; 𐑄𐐩𐑉𐑁𐐬𐑉 𐐌 𐑅𐐩 𐐲𐑌𐐻𐐭 𐐷𐐭, 𐐘𐐬; 𐐰𐑌𐐼 𐐸𐐭𐑅𐐬𐐯𐑂𐐲𐑉 𐐻𐑉𐐰𐑌𐑅𐑀𐑉𐐯𐑅𐐯𐑃 𐐲𐑀𐐯𐑌𐑅𐐻 𐑋𐐨, 𐐸𐐮𐑋 𐑇𐐰𐑊 𐐷𐐨 𐐾𐐲𐐾 𐐰𐐿𐐫𐑉𐐼𐐮𐑍 𐐻𐐭 𐑄 𐑅𐐮𐑌𐑆 𐐸𐐶𐐮𐐽 𐐸𐐨 𐐸𐐰𐑆 𐐿𐐱𐑋𐐮𐐻𐐯𐐼; 𐐰𐑌𐐼 𐐮𐑁 𐐸𐐨 𐐿𐐱𐑌𐑁𐐯𐑅 𐐸𐐮𐑆 𐑅𐐮𐑌𐑆 𐐺𐐨𐑁𐐬𐑉 𐑄 𐐰𐑌𐐼 𐑋𐐨, 𐐰𐑌𐐼 𐑉𐐨𐐹𐐯𐑌𐐻𐐯𐑃 𐐮𐑌 𐑄 𐑅𐐮𐑌𐑅𐐯𐑉𐐮𐐻𐐨 𐐱𐑂 𐐸𐐮𐑆 𐐸𐐪𐑉𐐻, 𐐸𐐮𐑋 𐑇𐐰𐑊 𐐷𐐨 𐑁𐐫𐑉𐑀𐐮𐑂, 𐐰𐑌𐐼 𐐌 𐐶𐐮𐑊 𐑁𐐫𐑉𐑀𐐮𐑂 𐐸𐐮𐑋 𐐫𐑊𐑅𐐬; 𐐷𐐩, 𐐰𐑌𐐼 𐐰𐑆 𐐫𐑁𐐲𐑌 𐐰𐑆 𐑋𐐴 𐐹𐐨𐐹𐑊 𐑉𐐨𐐹𐐯𐑌𐐻, 𐐶𐐮𐑊 𐐌 𐑁𐐫𐑉𐑀𐐮𐑂 𐑄𐐯𐑋 𐑄𐐩𐑉 𐐻𐑉𐐯𐑅𐐹𐐲𐑅𐐯𐑆 𐐲𐑀𐐯𐑌𐑅𐐻 𐑋𐐨. 𐐈𐑌𐐼 𐐷𐐨 𐑇𐐰𐑊 𐐫𐑊𐑅𐐬 𐑁𐐫𐑉𐑀𐐮𐑂 𐐶𐐲𐑌 𐐲𐑌𐐲𐑄𐐲𐑉 𐐷𐐭𐑉 𐐻𐑉𐐯𐑅𐐹𐐲𐑅𐐯𐑆; 𐑁𐐬𐑉 𐑂𐐯𐑉𐐮𐑊𐐨 𐐌 𐑅𐐩 𐐲𐑌𐐻𐐭 𐐷𐐭, 𐐐𐐨 𐑄𐐰𐐻 𐑁𐐫𐑉𐑀𐐮𐑂𐐯𐑃 𐑌𐐱𐐻 𐐸𐐮𐑆 𐑌𐐩𐐺𐐲𐑉'𐑆 𐐻𐑉𐐯𐑅𐐹𐐲𐑅𐐯𐑆, 𐐸𐐶𐐯𐑌 𐐸𐐨 𐑅𐐯𐑆 𐑄𐐰𐐻 𐐸𐐨 𐑉𐐨𐐹𐐯𐑌𐐻𐑅, 𐑄 𐑅𐐩𐑋 𐐸𐐰𐑃 𐐺𐑉𐐫𐐻 𐐸𐐮𐑋𐑅𐐯𐑊𐑁 𐐲𐑌𐐼𐐲𐑉 𐐿𐐱𐑌𐐼𐐯𐑋𐑌𐐩𐑇𐐲𐑌. 𐐤𐐵 𐐌 𐑅𐐩 𐐲𐑌𐐻𐐭 𐐷𐐭, 𐐘𐐬; 𐐰𐑌𐐼 𐐸𐐭𐑅𐐬𐐯𐑂𐐲𐑉 𐐶𐐮𐑊 𐑌𐐱𐐻 𐑉𐐨𐐹𐐯𐑌𐐻 𐐱𐑂 𐐸𐐮𐑆 𐑅𐐮𐑌𐑆, 𐑄 𐑅𐐩𐑋 𐑇𐐰𐑊 𐑌𐐱𐐻 𐐺𐐨 𐑌𐐲𐑋𐐺𐐲𐑉𐐼 𐐲𐑋𐐲𐑍 𐑋𐐴 𐐹𐐨𐐹𐑊; 𐐰𐑌𐐼 𐑄𐐮𐑅 𐑇𐐰𐑊 𐐺𐐨 𐐱𐐺𐑆𐐲𐑉𐑂𐐼 𐑁𐑉𐐱𐑋 𐑄𐐮𐑅 𐐻𐐴𐑋 𐑁𐐫𐑉𐐶𐐲𐑉𐐼.

17. 𐐈𐑌𐐼 𐐮𐐻 𐐿𐐩𐑋 𐐻𐐭 𐐹𐐰𐑅 𐐸𐐶𐐯𐑌 𐐈𐑊𐑋𐐲 𐐸𐐰𐐼 𐐸𐐲𐑉𐐼 𐑄𐐨𐑆 𐐶𐐲𐑉𐐼𐑆, 𐐸𐐨 𐑉𐐬𐐻 𐑄𐐯𐑋 𐐼𐐵𐑌 𐑄𐐰𐐻 𐐸𐐨 𐑋𐐴𐐻 𐐸𐐰𐑂 𐑄𐐯𐑋, 𐐰𐑌𐐼 𐑄𐐰𐐻 𐐸𐐨 𐑋𐐴𐐻 𐐾𐐲𐐾 𐑄 𐐹𐐨𐐹𐑊 𐐱𐑂 𐑄𐐰𐐻 𐐽𐐲𐑉𐐽, 𐐰𐐿𐐫𐑉𐐼𐐮𐑍 𐐻𐐭 𐑄 𐐿𐐱𐑋𐐰𐑌𐐼-

𐑋𐐲𐑌𐐻𐑅 𐐱𐑂 𐐘𐐱𐐼. 𐐈𐑌𐐼 𐐮𐐻 𐐿𐐩𐑋 𐐻𐐭 𐐹𐐰𐑅 𐑄𐐰𐐻 𐐈𐑊𐑋𐐲 𐐶𐐯𐑌𐐻 𐐰𐑌𐐼 𐐾𐐲𐐾𐐼 𐑄𐐬𐑆 𐑄𐐰𐐻 𐐸𐐰𐐼 𐐺𐐨𐑌 𐐻𐐩𐐿𐑌 𐐮𐑌 𐐮𐑌𐐮𐐿𐐶𐐮𐐻𐐨, 𐐰𐐿𐐫𐑉𐐼𐐮𐑍 𐐻𐐭 𐑄 𐐶𐐲𐑉𐐼 𐐱𐑂 𐑄 𐐢𐐫𐑉𐐼. 𐐈𐑌𐐼 𐐸𐐭𐑅𐐬𐐯𐑂𐐲𐑉 𐑉𐐨𐐹𐐯𐑌𐐻𐐯𐐼 𐐱𐑂 𐑄𐐩𐑉 𐑅𐐮𐑌𐑆 𐐰𐑌𐐼 𐐼𐐮𐐼 𐐿𐐱𐑌𐑁𐐯𐑅 𐑄𐐯𐑋, 𐑄𐐯𐑋 𐐸𐐨 𐐼𐐮𐐼 𐑌𐐲𐑋𐐺𐐲𐑉 𐐰𐑋𐐲𐑍 𐑄 𐐹𐐨𐐹𐑊 𐐱𐑂 𐑄 𐐕𐐲𐑉𐐽; 𐐰𐑌𐐼 𐑄𐐬𐑆 𐑄𐐰𐐻 𐐶𐐳𐐼 𐑌𐐱𐐻 𐐿𐐱𐑌𐑁𐐯𐑅 𐑄𐐩𐑉 𐑅𐐮𐑌𐑆 𐐰𐑌𐐼 𐑉𐐨𐐹𐐯𐑌𐐻 𐐱𐑂 𐑄𐐩𐑉 𐐮𐑌𐐮𐐿𐐶𐐮𐐻𐐨, 𐑄 𐑅𐐩𐑋 𐐶𐐲𐑉 𐑌𐐱𐐻 𐑌𐐲𐑋𐐺𐐲𐑉𐐼 𐐰𐑋𐐲𐑍 𐑄 𐐹𐐨𐐹𐑊 𐐱𐑂 𐑄 𐐕𐐲𐑉𐐽, 𐐰𐑌𐐼 𐑄𐐩𐑉 𐑌𐐩𐑋𐑆 𐐶𐐲𐑉 𐐺𐑊𐐱𐐻𐐯𐐼 𐐵𐐻. 𐐈𐑌𐐼 𐐮𐐻 𐐿𐐩𐑋 𐐻𐐭 𐐹𐐰𐑅 𐑄𐐰𐐻 𐐈𐑊𐑋𐐲 𐐼𐐮𐐼 𐑉𐐯𐑀𐐷𐐳𐑊𐐩𐐻 𐐫𐑊 𐑄 𐐰𐑁𐐩𐑉𐑆 𐐱𐑂 𐑄 𐐕𐐲𐑉𐐽; 𐐰𐑌𐐼 𐑄𐐩 𐐺𐐨𐑀𐐰𐑌 𐐰𐑀𐐯𐑌 𐐻𐐭 𐐸𐐰𐑂 𐐹𐐨𐑅 𐐰𐑌𐐼 𐐻𐐭 𐐹𐑉𐐱𐑅𐐹𐐲𐑉 𐐯𐐿𐑅𐐨𐐼𐐮𐑍𐑊𐐨 𐐮𐑌 𐑄 𐐰𐑁𐐩𐑉𐑆 𐐱𐑂 𐑄 𐐕𐐲𐑉𐐽; 𐐶𐐫𐐿𐐮𐑍 𐑅𐐲𐑉𐐿𐐲𐑋𐑅𐐹𐐯𐐿𐐻𐑊𐐨 𐐺𐐨𐑁𐐬𐑉 𐐘𐐱𐐼; 𐑉𐐨𐑅𐐨𐑂𐐮𐑍 𐑋𐐯𐑌𐐨, 𐐰𐑌𐐼 𐐺𐐰𐐹𐐻𐐴𐑆𐐮𐑍 𐑋𐐯𐑌𐐨. 𐐈𐑌𐐼 𐑌𐐵 𐐫𐑊 𐑄𐐮𐑅 𐐼𐐮𐐼 𐐈𐑊𐑋𐐲 𐐰𐑌𐐼 𐐸𐐮𐑆 𐑁𐐯𐑊𐐬 𐑊𐐩𐐺𐐲𐑉𐐲𐑉𐑆 𐐼𐐭 𐐸𐐭 𐐶𐐲𐑉 𐐬𐑂𐐲𐑉 𐑄 𐐕𐐲𐑉𐐽; 𐐶𐐫𐐿𐐮𐑍 𐐮𐑌 𐐫𐑊 𐐼𐐮𐑊𐐮𐐾𐐯𐑌𐑅; 𐐻𐐨𐐽𐐮𐑍 𐑄 𐐶𐐲𐑉𐐼 𐐱𐑂 𐐘𐐱𐐼 𐐮𐑌 𐐫𐑊 𐑃𐐮𐑍𐑆; 𐑅𐐲𐑁𐐲𐑉𐐮𐑍 𐐫𐑊 𐑋𐐰𐑌𐐲𐑉 𐐱𐑂 𐐰𐑁𐑊𐐮𐐿𐑇𐐲𐑌𐑆; 𐐺𐐨𐐮𐑍 𐐹𐐲𐑉𐑅𐐯𐐿𐐷𐐭𐐻𐐯𐐼 𐐺𐐴 𐐫𐑊 𐑄𐐬𐑆 𐐸𐐭 𐐼𐐮𐐼 𐑌𐐱𐐻 𐐺𐐨𐑊𐐫𐑍 𐐻𐐭 𐑄 𐐕𐐲𐑉𐐽 𐐱𐑂 𐐘𐐱𐐼. 𐐈𐑌𐐼 𐑄𐐩 𐐼𐐮𐐼 𐐰𐐼𐑋𐐱𐑌𐐮𐑇 𐑄𐐩𐑉 𐐺𐑉𐐯𐑄𐑉𐐯𐑌; 𐐰𐑌𐐼 𐑄𐐩 𐐶𐐲𐑉 𐐫𐑊𐑅𐐬 𐐰𐐼𐑋𐐱𐑌𐐮𐑇𐐻, 𐐯𐑂𐐲𐑉𐐨 𐐶𐐲𐑌 𐐺𐐴 𐑄 𐐶𐐲𐑉𐐼 𐐱𐑂 𐐘𐐱𐐼, 𐐰𐐿𐐫𐑉𐐼𐐮𐑍 𐐻𐐭 𐐸𐐮𐑆 𐑅𐐮𐑌𐑆, 𐐫𐑉 𐐻𐐭 𐑄 𐑅𐐮𐑌𐑆 𐐸𐐶𐐮𐐽 𐐸𐐨 𐐸𐐰𐐼 𐐿𐐱𐑋𐐮𐐻𐐯𐐼, 𐐺𐐨𐐮𐑍 𐐿𐐱𐑋𐐰𐑌𐐼𐐯𐐼 𐐱𐑂 𐐘𐐱𐐼 𐐻𐐭 𐐹𐑉𐐩 𐐶𐐮𐑄𐐵𐐻 𐑅𐐨𐑅𐐮𐑍, 𐐰𐑌𐐼 𐐻𐐭 𐑀𐐮𐑂 𐑃𐐰𐑍𐐿𐑅 𐐮𐑌 𐐫𐑊 𐑃𐐮𐑍𐑆. 𐐈𐑌𐐼 𐑌𐐵 𐐮𐐻 𐐿𐐩𐑋 𐐻𐐭 𐐹𐐰𐑅 𐑄𐐰𐐻 𐑄 𐐹𐐲𐑉𐑅𐐯𐐿𐐷𐐭𐑇𐐲𐑌𐑆 𐐸𐐶𐐮𐐽 𐐶𐐲𐑉 𐐮𐑌𐑁𐑊𐐮𐐿𐐻𐐯𐐼 𐐱𐑌 𐑄 𐐕𐐲𐑉𐐽 𐐺𐐴 𐑄 𐐲𐑌𐐺𐐨𐑊𐐨𐑂𐐲𐑉𐑆 𐐺𐐨𐐿𐐩𐑋 𐑅𐐬 𐑀𐑉𐐩𐐻, 𐑄𐐰𐐻 𐑄 𐐕𐐲𐑉𐐽 𐐺𐐨𐑀𐐰𐑌 𐐻𐐭 𐑋𐐲𐑉𐑋𐐲𐑉, 𐐰𐑌𐐼 𐐿𐐱𐑋𐐹𐑊𐐩𐑌 𐐻𐐭 𐑄𐐩𐑉 𐑊𐐨𐐼𐐲𐑉𐑆 𐐿𐐱𐑌𐑅𐐲𐑉𐑌𐐮𐑍 𐑄 𐑋𐐰𐐻𐐲𐑉; 𐐰𐑌𐐼 𐑄𐐩 𐐼𐐮𐐼 𐐿𐐱𐑋𐐹𐑊𐐩𐑌 𐐻𐐭 𐐈𐑊𐑋𐐲. 𐐈𐑌𐐼 𐐈𐑊𐑋𐐲 𐑊𐐩𐐼 𐑄 𐐿𐐩𐑅 𐐺𐐨𐑁𐐬𐑉 𐑄𐐩𐑉 𐐿𐐮𐑍, 𐐣𐐬𐑆𐐴𐐲. 𐐈𐑌𐐼 𐐣𐐬𐑆𐐴𐐲 𐐿𐐱𐑌𐑅𐐲𐑊𐐻𐐯𐐼 𐐶𐐮𐑄 𐐸𐐮𐑆 𐐹𐑉𐐨𐑅𐐻𐑅.

18. 𐐈𐑌𐐼 𐐮𐐻 𐐿𐐩𐑋 𐐻𐐭 𐐹𐐰𐑅 𐑄𐐰𐐻 𐐿𐐮𐑍 𐐣𐐬𐑆𐐴𐐲 𐑅𐐯𐑌𐐻 𐐩 𐐹𐑉𐐱𐐿𐑊𐐲𐑋𐐩𐑇𐐲𐑌 𐑃𐑉𐐭𐐵𐐻 𐑄 𐑊𐐰𐑌𐐼 𐑉𐐵𐑌𐐼 𐐲𐐺𐐵𐐻, 𐑄𐐰𐐻 𐑄𐐩𐑉 𐑇𐐳𐐼 𐑌𐐱𐐻 𐐯𐑌𐐨 𐐲𐑌𐐺𐐨𐑊𐐨𐑂𐐲𐑉 𐐹𐐲𐑉𐑅𐐯𐐿𐐷𐐭𐐻 𐐯𐑌𐐨 𐐱𐑂 𐑄𐐬𐑆 𐐸𐐭 𐐺𐐨𐑊𐐫𐑍𐐼 𐐻𐐭 𐑄 𐐕𐐲𐑉𐐽 𐐱𐑂 𐐘𐐱𐐼; 𐐰𐑌𐐼 𐑄𐐩𐑉 𐐶𐐱𐑆 𐐩 𐑅𐐻𐑉𐐮𐐿𐐻 𐐿𐐱𐑋𐐰𐑌𐐼 𐑃𐑉𐐭𐐵𐐻 𐐫𐑊 𐑄 𐐽𐐲𐑉𐐽𐐯𐑆, 𐑄𐐰𐐻 𐑄𐐩𐑉 𐑇𐐳𐐼 𐐺𐐨 𐑌𐐬 𐐹𐐲𐑉𐑅𐐯𐐿𐐷𐐭𐑇𐐲𐑌𐑆 𐐰𐑋𐐲𐑍 𐑄𐐯𐑋, 𐑄𐐰𐐻 𐑄𐐩𐑉 𐑇𐐳𐐼 𐐺𐐨 𐐰𐑌 𐐨𐐿𐐶𐐱𐑊𐐮𐐻𐐨 𐐰𐑋𐐲𐑍 𐐫𐑊 𐑋𐐯𐑌; 𐑄𐐰𐐻 𐑄𐐩 𐑇𐐳𐐼 𐑊𐐯𐐻 𐑌𐐬 𐐹𐑉𐐴𐐼 𐑌𐐫𐑉 𐐸𐐫𐐻𐐨𐑌𐐯𐑅 𐐼𐐮𐑅𐐻𐐲𐑉𐐺 𐑄𐐩𐑉 𐐹𐐨𐑅; 𐑄𐐰𐐻 𐐯𐑂𐐲𐑉𐐨 𐑋𐐰𐑌 𐑇𐐳𐐼 𐐯𐑅𐐻𐐨𐑋 𐐸𐐮𐑆 𐑌𐐩𐐺𐐲𐑉 𐐰𐑆 𐐸𐐮𐑋𐑅𐐯𐑊𐑁, 𐑊𐐩𐐺𐐲𐑉𐐮𐑍 𐐶𐐮𐑄 𐑄𐐩𐑉 𐐬𐑌 𐐸𐐰𐑌𐐼𐑆 𐑁𐐫𐑉 𐑄𐐩𐑉 𐑅𐐲𐐹𐐬𐑉𐐻; 𐐷𐐩, 𐐰𐑌𐐼 𐐫𐑊 𐑄𐐩𐑉 𐐹𐑉𐐨𐑅𐐻𐑅 𐐰𐑌𐐼 𐐻𐐨𐐽𐐲𐑉𐑆 𐑇𐐳𐐼 𐑊𐐩𐐺𐐲𐑉 𐐶𐐮𐑄 𐑄𐐩𐑉 𐐬𐑌 𐐸𐐰𐑌𐐼𐑆 𐑁𐐫𐑉 𐑄𐐩𐑉 𐑅𐐲𐐹𐐬𐑉𐐻, 𐐮𐑌 𐐫𐑊 𐐿𐐩𐑅𐐯𐑆 𐑅𐐩𐑂 𐐮𐐻 𐐶𐐲𐑉 𐐮𐑌 𐑅𐐮𐐿𐑌𐐯𐑅, 𐐫𐑉 𐐮𐑌 𐑋𐐲𐐽 𐐶𐐱𐑌𐐻; 𐐰𐑌𐐼 𐐼𐐭𐐮𐑍 𐑄𐐨𐑆 𐑃𐐮𐑍𐑆, 𐑄𐐩 𐐼𐐮𐐼 𐐲𐐺𐐵𐑌𐐼 𐐮𐑌 𐑄 𐑀𐑉𐐩𐑅 𐐱𐑂 𐐘𐐱𐐼. 𐐈𐑌𐐼 𐑄𐐩𐑉 𐐺𐐨𐑀𐐰𐑌 𐐻𐐭 𐐺𐐨 𐑋𐐲𐐽 𐐹𐐨𐑅 𐐰𐑀𐐯𐑌 𐐮𐑌 𐑄 𐑊𐐰𐑌𐐼; 𐐰𐑌𐐼 𐑄 𐐹𐐨𐐹𐑊 𐐺𐐨𐑀𐐰𐑌 𐐻𐐭 𐐺𐐨 𐑂𐐯𐑉𐐨 𐑌𐐷𐐭𐑋𐐲𐑉𐐲𐑅, 𐐰𐑌𐐼 𐐺𐐨𐑀𐐰𐑌 𐐻𐐭 𐑅𐐿𐐰𐐻𐐲𐑉 𐐲𐐺𐑉𐐫𐐼 𐐲𐐹𐐱𐑌 𐑄 𐑁𐐩𐑅 𐐱𐑂 𐑄 𐐲𐑉𐑃, 𐐷𐐩, 𐐱𐑌 𐑄 𐑌𐐫𐑉𐑃 𐐰𐑌𐐼 𐐱𐑌 𐑄 𐑅𐐵𐑃, 𐐱𐑌 𐑄 𐐨𐑅𐐻 𐐰𐑌𐐼 𐐱𐑌 𐑄 𐐶𐐯𐑅𐐻, 𐐺𐐮𐑊𐐼𐐮𐑍 𐑊𐐪𐑉𐐾 𐑅𐐮𐐻𐐨𐑆 𐐰𐑌𐐼 𐑂𐐮𐑊𐐯𐐾𐐯𐑆 𐐮𐑌 𐐫𐑊 𐐿𐐶𐐫𐑉𐐻𐐲𐑉𐑆 𐐱𐑂 𐑄 𐑊𐐰𐑌𐐼. 𐐈𐑌𐐼 𐑄 𐐢𐐫𐑉𐐼 𐐼𐐮𐐼 𐑂𐐮𐑆𐐮𐐻 𐑄𐐯𐑋 𐐰𐑌𐐼 𐐹𐑉𐐱𐑅𐐹𐐲𐑉 𐑄𐐯𐑋, 𐐰𐑌𐐼 𐑄𐐩 𐐺𐐨𐐿𐐩𐑋 𐐩 𐑊𐐪𐑉𐐾 𐐰𐑌𐐼 𐐶𐐯𐑊𐑃𐐨 𐐹𐐨𐐹𐑊.

19. 𐐤𐐵 𐑄 𐑅𐐲𐑌𐑆 𐐱𐑂 𐐣𐐬𐑆𐐴𐐲 𐐶𐐲𐑉 𐑌𐐲𐑋𐐺𐐲𐑉𐐼 𐐰𐑋𐐲𐑍 𐑄 𐐲𐑌𐐺𐐨𐑊𐐨𐑂𐐲𐑉𐑆; 𐐰𐑌𐐼 𐐫𐑊𐑅𐐬 𐐶𐐲𐑌 𐐱𐑂 𐑄 𐑅𐐲𐑌𐑆 𐐱𐑂 𐐈𐑊𐑋𐐲 𐐶𐐱𐑆 𐑌𐐲𐑋𐐺𐐲𐑉𐐼 𐐰𐑋𐐲𐑍 𐑄𐐯𐑋, 𐐸𐐨 𐐺𐐨𐐮𐑍 𐐿𐐫𐑊𐐼 𐐈𐑊𐑋𐐲, 𐐰𐑁𐐻𐐲𐑉 𐐸𐐮𐑆 𐑁𐐪𐑄𐐲𐑉; 𐑌𐐯𐑂𐐲𐑉𐑄𐐯𐑊𐐯𐑅, 𐐸𐐨 𐐺𐐨𐐿𐐩𐑋 𐐩 𐑂𐐯𐑉𐐨 𐐶𐐮𐐿𐐯𐐼 𐐰𐑌𐐼 𐐰𐑌 𐐴𐐼𐐱𐑊𐐲𐐻𐑉𐐲𐑅 𐑋𐐰𐑌. 𐐈𐑌𐐼 𐐸𐐨 𐐶𐐱𐑆 𐐩 𐑋𐐰𐑌 𐐱𐑂 𐑋𐐯𐑌𐐨 𐐶𐐲𐑉𐐼𐑆, 𐐰𐑌𐐼 𐐼𐐮𐐼 𐑅𐐹𐐨𐐿 𐑋𐐲𐐽 𐑁𐑊𐐰𐐻𐐲𐑉𐐨 𐐻𐐭 𐑄 𐐹𐐨𐐹𐑊; 𐑄𐐩𐑉𐑁𐐬𐑉 𐐸𐐨 𐑊𐐯𐐼 𐑋𐐯𐑌𐐨 𐐱𐑂 𐑄 𐐹𐐨𐐹𐑊 𐐻𐐭 𐐼𐐭 𐐰𐑁𐐻𐐲𐑉 𐑄 𐑋𐐰𐑌𐐲𐑉 𐐱𐑂 𐐸𐐮𐑆 𐐮𐑌𐐮𐐿𐐶𐐮𐐻𐐨𐑆. 𐐈𐑌𐐼 𐐸𐐨 𐐺𐐨𐐿𐐩𐑋 𐐩 𐑀𐑉𐐩𐐻 𐐸𐐮𐑌𐐼𐐲𐑉𐑋𐐯𐑌𐐻 𐐻𐐭 𐑄 𐐹𐑉𐐱𐑅𐐹𐐯𐑉𐐮𐐻𐐨 𐐱𐑂 𐑄 𐐕𐐲𐑉𐐽 𐐱𐑂 𐐘𐐱𐐼; 𐑅𐐻𐐨𐑊𐐮𐑍 𐐲𐐶𐐩 𐑄 𐐸𐐪𐑉𐐻𐑅 𐐱𐑂 𐑄 𐐹𐐨𐐹𐑊; 𐐿𐐫𐑆𐐮𐑍 𐑋𐐲𐐽 𐐼𐐮𐑅𐑅𐐯𐑌𐑇𐐲𐑌 𐐰𐑋𐐲𐑍 𐑄 𐐹𐐨𐐹𐑊; 𐑀𐐮𐑂𐐮𐑍 𐐩 𐐽𐐰𐑌𐑅 𐑁𐐫𐑉 𐑄 𐐯𐑌𐐯𐑋𐐨 𐐱𐑂 𐐘𐐱𐐼 𐐻𐐭 𐐯𐐿𐑅𐐲𐑉𐑅𐐴𐑆 𐐸𐐮𐑆 𐐹𐐵𐐲𐑉 𐐬𐑂𐐲𐑉 𐑄𐐯𐑋.

20. 𐐈𐑌𐐼 𐑌𐐵 𐐮𐐻 𐐿𐐩𐑋 𐐻𐐭 𐐹𐐰𐑅, 𐑄𐐰𐐻 𐐸𐐶𐐴𐑊 𐐸𐐨 𐐶𐐱𐑆 𐑀𐐬𐐮𐑍 𐐲𐐺𐐵𐐻 𐐻𐐭 𐐼𐐯𐑅𐐻𐑉𐐦 𐑄 𐐕𐐲𐑉𐐽 𐐱𐑂 𐐘𐐱𐐼; 𐑁𐐫𐑉 𐐸𐐨 𐐼𐐮𐐼 𐑀𐐬 𐐲𐐺𐐵𐐻 𐑅𐐨𐐿𐑉𐐯𐐻𐑊𐐨 𐐶𐐮𐑄 𐑄 𐑅𐐲𐑌𐑆 𐐱𐑂 𐐣𐐬𐑆𐐴𐐲, 𐑅𐐨𐐿𐐮𐑍 𐐻𐐭 𐐼𐐯𐑅𐐻𐑉𐐦

𐑄 𐐕𐐲𐑉𐐕, 𐐰𐑌𐐼 𐐻𐐭 𐑊𐐨𐐼 𐐰𐑅𐐻𐑉𐐩 𐑄 𐐹𐐨𐐹𐑊 𐐱𐑂 𐑄 𐐢𐐫𐑉𐐼, 𐐗𐐱𐑌𐐻𐑉𐐯𐑉𐐮 𐐻𐐭 𐑄 𐐗𐐲𐑋𐐰𐑌𐐼𐑋𐐯𐑌𐐻𐑅 𐐱𐑂 𐐘𐐱𐐼, 𐐫𐑉 𐐨𐑂𐑌 𐑄 𐐗𐐮𐑍; 𐐰𐑌𐐼 𐐰𐑆 𐐌 𐑅𐐯𐐼 𐐲𐑌𐐻𐐭 𐐷𐐭, 𐐰𐑆 𐑄𐐩 𐐶𐐲𐑉 𐑀𐐬𐐮𐑍 𐐰𐐺𐐵𐐻 𐑉𐐨𐐺𐐯𐑊𐐮𐑍 𐐰𐑀𐐯𐑌𐑅𐐻 𐐘𐐱𐐼, 𐐺𐐨𐐸𐐬𐑊𐐼, 𐑄 𐐩𐑌𐐾𐐯𐑊 𐐱𐑂 𐑄 𐐢𐐫𐑉𐐼 𐐰𐐹𐐨𐑉𐐼 𐐲𐑌𐐻𐐭 𐑄𐐯𐑋; 𐐰𐑌𐐼 𐐸𐐨 𐐼𐐨𐑅𐐯𐑌𐐼𐐯𐐼 𐐰𐑆 𐐮𐐻 𐐶𐐲𐑉 𐐮𐑌 𐐩 𐐿𐑊𐐵𐐼; 𐐰𐑌𐐼 𐐸𐐨 𐑅𐐹𐐩𐐿 𐐰𐑆 𐐮𐐻 𐐶𐐲𐑉 𐐶𐐮𐑃 𐐩 𐑂𐐦𐑅 𐐱𐑂 𐑃𐐲𐑌𐐼𐐯𐑉, 𐐸𐐶𐐮𐐽 𐐿𐐫𐑆𐐼 𐑄 𐐲𐑉𐑃 𐐻𐐭 𐑇𐐩𐐿 𐐲𐐹𐐱𐑌 𐐸𐐶𐐮𐐽 𐑄𐐩 𐑅𐐻𐐳𐐼; 𐐰𐑌𐐼 𐑅𐐬 𐑀𐑉𐐩𐐻 𐐶𐐱𐑆 𐑄𐐩𐑉 𐐰𐑅𐐻𐐱𐑌𐐮𐑇𐑋𐐯𐑌𐐻, 𐑄𐐰𐐻 𐑄𐐩 𐑁𐐯𐑊 𐐻𐐭 𐑄 𐐲𐑉𐑃, 𐐰𐑌𐐼 𐐲𐑌𐐼𐐯𐑉𐑅𐐻𐐳𐐼 𐑌𐐱𐐻 𐑄 𐐶𐐲𐑉𐐼𐑆 𐐸𐐶𐐮𐐽 𐐸𐐨 𐑅𐐹𐐩𐐿 𐐲𐑌𐐻𐐭 𐑄𐐯𐑋. 𐑌𐐯𐑂𐐯𐑉𐑄𐐯𐑊𐐯𐑅 𐐸𐐨 𐐗𐑉𐐴𐐼 𐐰𐑀𐐯𐑌, 𐑅𐐩𐐮𐑍, 𐐰𐑊𐑋𐐲, 𐐲𐑉𐐴𐑆 𐐰𐑌𐐼 𐑅𐐻𐐰𐑌𐐼 𐑁𐐫𐑉𐑃, 𐑁𐐫𐑉 𐐸𐐶𐐴 𐐹𐐲𐑉𐑅𐐨𐐿𐐷𐐭𐐻𐐯𐑅𐐻 𐑄𐐵 𐑄 𐐕𐐲𐑉𐐕 𐐱𐑂 𐐘𐐱𐐼? 𐑁𐐫𐑉 𐑄 𐐢𐐫𐑉𐐼 𐐸𐐰𐑃 𐑅𐐯𐐼, 𐐜𐐮𐑅 𐐮𐑆 𐑋𐐴 𐐕𐐲𐑉𐐕, 𐐰𐑌𐐼 𐐌 𐐶𐐮𐑊 𐐯𐑅𐐻𐐰𐐺𐑊𐐮𐑇 𐐮𐐻; 𐐰𐑌𐐼 𐑌𐐲𐑃𐐮𐑍 𐑇𐐰𐑊 𐐬𐑂𐐲𐑉𐑃𐑉𐐬 𐐮𐐻, 𐑅𐐩𐑂 𐐮𐐻 𐐮𐑆 𐑄 𐐻𐑉𐐰𐑌𐑅𐑀𐑉𐐯𐑇𐐲𐑌 𐐱𐑂 𐑋𐐴 𐐹𐐨𐐹𐑊. 𐐰𐑌𐐼 𐐰𐑀𐐯𐑌, 𐑄 𐐩𐑌𐐾𐐯𐑊 𐑅𐐯𐐼, 𐐒𐐨𐐸𐐬𐑊𐐼, 𐑄 𐐢𐐫𐑉𐐼 𐐸𐐰𐑃 𐐸𐐲𐑉𐐼 𐑄 𐐹𐑉𐐩𐑉𐑆 𐐱𐑂 𐐸𐐮𐑆 𐐹𐐨𐐹𐑊, 𐐰𐑌𐐼 𐐫𐑊𐑅𐐬 𐑄 𐐹𐑉𐐩𐑉𐑆 𐐱𐑂 𐐸𐐮𐑆 𐑅𐐲𐑉𐑂𐐯𐑌𐐻 𐐰𐑊𐑋𐐲, 𐐸𐐭 𐐮𐑆 𐑄𐐴 𐑁𐐪𐑄𐐲𐑉: 𐑁𐐫𐑉 𐐸𐐨 𐐸𐐰𐑆 𐐹𐑉𐐩𐐼 𐐶𐐮𐑃 𐑋𐐲𐐽 𐑁𐐩𐑃 𐐿𐐱𐑌𐑅𐐲𐑉𐑌𐐮𐑍 𐑄, 𐑄𐐰𐐻 𐑄𐐵 𐑋𐐴𐐻𐐯𐑅𐐻 𐐺 𐐺𐑉𐐱𐐻 𐐻𐐭 𐑄 𐑌𐐱𐑊𐐯𐐾 𐐱𐑂 𐑄 𐐻𐑉𐐭𐑃: 𐑄𐐯𐑉𐑁𐐫𐑉, 𐑁𐐫𐑉 𐑄𐐮𐑅 𐐹𐐲𐑉𐐹𐐲𐑅 𐐸𐐰𐑂 𐐌 𐐿𐐲𐑋 𐐻𐐭 𐐿𐐱𐑌𐑂𐐮𐑌𐑅 𐑄 𐐱𐑂 𐑄 𐐹𐐵𐐲𐑉 𐐰𐑌𐐼 𐐫𐑃𐐱𐑉𐐮𐐻𐐮 𐐱𐑂 𐐘𐐱𐐼, 𐑄𐐰𐐻 𐑄 𐐹𐑉𐐩𐑉𐑆 𐐱𐑂 𐐸𐐮𐑆 𐑅𐐲𐑉𐑂𐐯𐑌𐐻𐑅 𐑋𐐴𐐻 𐐺 𐐰𐑌𐑅𐐲𐑉𐐼 𐐰𐐿𐐫𐑉𐐼𐐮𐑍 𐐻𐐭 𐑄𐐩𐑉 𐑁𐐩𐑃. 𐐰𐑌𐐼 𐑌𐐵 𐐺𐐨𐐸𐐬𐑊𐐼, 𐐿𐐰𐑌 𐐷 𐐼𐐮𐑅𐐹𐐷𐐭𐐻 𐑄 𐐹𐐵𐐲𐑉 𐐱𐑂 𐐘𐐱𐐼? 𐑁𐐫𐑉 𐐺𐐨𐐸𐐬𐑊𐐼, 𐐼𐐲𐑃 𐑌𐐱𐐻 𐑋𐐴 𐑂𐐦𐑅 𐑇𐐩𐐿 𐑄 𐐲𐑉𐑃? 𐐰𐑌𐐼 𐐿𐐰𐑌 𐐷 𐑌𐐱𐐻 𐐫𐑊𐑅𐐬 𐐺𐐨𐐸𐐬𐑊𐐼 𐑋𐐨 𐐺𐐨𐑁𐐫𐑉 𐐷𐐭? 𐐰𐑌𐐼 𐐌 𐐰𐑋 𐑅𐐯𐑌𐐻 𐑁𐑉𐐱𐑋 𐐘𐐱𐐼. 𐐤𐐵 𐐌 𐑅𐐩 𐐲𐑌𐐻𐐭 𐑄, 𐐘𐐬, 𐐰𐑌𐐼 𐑉𐐨𐑋𐐯𐑋𐐺𐐲𐑉 𐑄 𐐿𐐰𐐹𐐻𐐮𐑂𐐮𐐻𐐮 𐐱𐑂 𐑄𐐴 𐑁𐐪𐑄𐐲𐑉𐑆 𐐮𐑌 𐑄 𐑊𐐰𐑌𐐼 𐐱𐑂 𐐸𐐨𐑊𐐲𐑋, 𐐰𐑌𐐼 𐐮𐑌 𐑄 𐑊𐐰𐑌𐐼 𐐱𐑂 𐑌𐐨𐑁𐐴; 𐐰𐑌𐐼 𐑉𐐨𐑋𐐯𐑋𐐺𐐲𐑉 𐐸𐐵 𐑀𐑉𐐩𐐻 𐑃𐐮𐑍𐑆 𐐸𐐨 𐐸𐐰𐑆 𐐼𐐲𐑌 𐑁𐐫𐑉 𐑄𐐯𐑋: 𐑁𐐫𐑉 𐑄𐐩 𐐶𐐲𐑉 𐐮𐑌 𐐺𐐱𐑌𐐼𐐯𐐾, 𐐰𐑌𐐼 𐐸𐐨 𐐸𐐰𐑆 𐐼𐐨𐑊𐐮𐑂𐐲𐑉𐐼 𐑄𐐯𐑋. 𐐰𐑌𐐼 𐑌𐐵 𐐌 𐑅𐐩 𐐲𐑌𐐻𐐭 𐑄, 𐐰𐑊𐑋𐐲, 𐐘𐐬 𐑄𐐴 𐐶𐐩, 𐐰𐑌𐐼 𐑅𐐨𐐿 𐐻𐐭 𐐼𐐨𐑅𐐻𐑉𐐶𐐦 𐑄 𐐕𐐲𐑉𐐕 𐑌𐐬 𐑋𐐫𐑉, 𐑄𐐰𐐻 𐑄𐐩𐑉 𐐹𐑉𐐩𐑉𐑆 𐑋𐐩 𐐺 𐐰𐑌𐑅𐐲𐑉𐐼; 𐐰𐑌𐐼 𐑄𐐮𐑅 𐐨𐑂𐑌 𐐮𐑁 𐑄𐐵 𐐶𐐮𐑊𐐻 𐐱𐑂 𐑄𐐴𐑅𐐯𐑊𐑁 𐐺 𐐿𐐰𐑅𐐻 𐐫𐑁.

21. 𐐰𐑌𐐼 𐑌𐐵 𐐮𐐻 𐐿𐐩𐑋 𐐻𐐭 𐐹𐐰𐑅 𐑄𐐰𐐻 𐑄𐐨𐑆 𐐶𐐲𐑉 𐑄 𐑊𐐰𐑅𐐻 𐐶𐐲𐑉𐐼𐑆 𐐸𐐶𐐮𐐽 𐑄 𐐩𐑌𐐾𐐯𐑊 𐑅𐐹𐐩𐐿 𐐲𐑌𐐻𐐭 𐐰𐑊𐑋𐐲, 𐐰𐑌𐐼 𐐸𐐨 𐐼𐐨𐐹𐐪𐑉𐐻𐐯𐐼. 𐐰𐑌𐐼 𐑌𐐵 𐐰𐑊𐑋𐐲, 𐐰𐑌𐐼 𐑄𐐬𐑆 𐑄𐐰𐐻 𐐶𐐲𐑉 𐐶𐐮𐑃 𐐸𐐮𐑋, 𐑁𐐯𐑊 𐐰𐑀𐐯𐑌 𐐻𐐭 𐑄 𐐲𐑉𐑃, 𐑁𐐫𐑉 𐑀𐑉𐐩𐐻 𐐶𐐱𐑆 𐑄𐐩𐑉 𐐰𐑅𐐻𐐱𐑌𐐮𐑇𐑋𐐯𐑌𐐻: 𐑁𐐫𐑉 𐐶𐐮𐑃 𐑄𐐩𐑉 𐐬𐑌 𐐌𐑆 𐑄𐐩 𐐸𐐰𐐼 𐐺𐐨𐐸𐐯𐑊𐐼 𐐰𐑌 𐐩𐑌𐐾𐐯𐑊 𐐱𐑂 𐑄 𐐢𐐫𐑉𐐼; 𐐰𐑌𐐼 𐐸𐐮𐑆 𐑂𐐦𐑅 𐐶𐐱𐑆 𐐰𐑆 𐑃𐐲𐑌𐐼𐐯𐑉, 𐐸𐐶𐐮𐐽 𐑇𐐳𐐿 𐑄 𐐲𐑉𐑃; 𐐰𐑌𐐼 𐑄𐐩 𐑌𐐭 𐑄𐐰𐐻 𐑄𐐩𐑉 𐐶𐐱𐑆 𐑌𐐲𐑃𐐮𐑍 𐑅𐐩𐑂 𐑄 𐐹𐐵𐐲𐑉 𐐱𐑂 𐐘𐐱𐐼 𐑄𐐰𐐻 𐐿𐐳𐐼 𐑇𐐩𐐿 𐑄 𐐲𐑉𐑃 𐐰𐑌𐐼 𐐿𐐫𐑆 𐐮𐐻 𐐻𐐭 𐐻𐑉𐐯𐑋𐐺𐑊, 𐐰𐑆 𐑄𐐬 𐐮𐐻 𐐶𐐳𐐼 𐐹𐐪𐑉𐐻 𐐰𐑅𐐲𐑌𐐼𐐯𐑉. 𐐰𐑌𐐼 𐑌𐐵 𐑄 𐐰𐑅𐐻𐐱𐑌𐐮𐑇𐑋𐐯𐑌𐐻 𐐱𐑂 𐐰𐑊𐑋𐐲 𐐶𐐱𐑆 𐑅𐐬 𐑀𐑉𐐩𐐻, 𐑄𐐰𐐻 𐐸𐐨 𐐺𐐨𐐿𐐩𐑋 𐐼𐐲𐑋, 𐑄𐐰𐐻 𐐸𐐨 𐐿𐐳𐐼 𐑌𐐱𐐻 𐐬𐐹𐐯𐑌 𐐸𐐮𐑆 𐑋𐐵𐑃; 𐐷𐐩, 𐐰𐑌𐐼 𐐸𐐨 𐐺𐐨𐐿𐐩𐑋 𐐶𐐨𐐿, 𐐨𐑂𐑌 𐑄𐐰𐐻 𐐸𐐨 𐐿𐐳𐐼 𐑌𐐱𐐻 𐑋𐐭𐑂 𐐸𐐮𐑆 𐐸𐐰𐑌𐐼𐑆; 𐑄𐐯𐑉𐑁𐐫𐑉 𐐸𐐨 𐐶𐐱𐑆 𐐻𐐩𐐿𐐲𐑌 𐐺𐐴 𐑄𐐬𐑆 𐑄𐐰𐐻 𐐶𐐲𐑉 𐐶𐐮𐑃 𐐸𐐮𐑋, 𐐰𐑌𐐼 𐐿𐐰𐑉𐐮𐐼 𐐸𐐯𐑊𐐹𐑊𐐯𐑅, 𐐨𐑂𐑌 𐐲𐑌𐐻𐐮𐑊 𐐸𐐨 𐐶𐐱𐑆 𐑊𐐩𐐼 𐐺𐐨𐑁𐐫𐑉 𐐸𐐮𐑆 𐑁𐐪𐑄𐐲𐑉. 𐐰𐑌𐐼 𐑄𐐩 𐑉𐐨𐐸𐐲𐑉𐑅𐐻 𐐲𐑌𐐻𐐭 𐐸𐐮𐑆 𐑁𐐪𐑄𐐲𐑉 𐐫𐑊 𐑄𐐰𐐻 𐐸𐐰𐐼 𐐸𐐰𐐹𐐯𐑌𐐼 𐐲𐑌𐐻𐐭 𐑄𐐯𐑋; 𐐰𐑌𐐼 𐐸𐐮𐑆 𐑁𐐪𐑄𐐲𐑉 𐑉𐐨𐐾𐐦𐑅𐐻, 𐑁𐐫𐑉 𐐸𐐨 𐑌𐐭 𐑄𐐰𐐻 𐐮𐐻 𐐶𐐱𐑆 𐑄 𐐹𐐵𐐲𐑉 𐐱𐑂 𐐘𐐱𐐼. 𐐰𐑌𐐼 𐐸𐐨 𐐿𐐫𐑆𐐼 𐑄𐐰𐐻 𐐩 𐑋𐐲𐑊𐐻𐐮𐐻𐐷𐐭𐐼 𐑇𐐳𐐼 𐐺 𐑀𐐰𐑄𐐲𐑉𐐼 𐐻𐐲𐑀𐐯𐑄𐐲𐑉, 𐑄𐐰𐐻 𐑄𐐩 𐑋𐐴𐐻 𐐶𐐮𐐻𐑌𐐯𐑅 𐐸𐐶𐐲𐐻 𐑄 𐐢𐐫𐑉𐐼 𐐸𐐰𐐼 𐐼𐐲𐑌 𐑁𐐫𐑉 𐐸𐐮𐑆 𐑅𐐲𐑌, 𐐰𐑌𐐼 𐐫𐑊𐑅𐐬 𐑁𐐫𐑉 𐑄𐐬𐑆 𐑄𐐰𐐻 𐐶𐐲𐑉 𐐶𐐮𐑃 𐐸𐐮𐑋. 𐐰𐑌𐐼 𐐸𐐨 𐐿𐐫𐑆𐐼 𐑄𐐰𐐻 𐑄 𐐹𐑉𐐨𐑅𐐻𐑅 𐑇𐐳𐐼 𐐰𐑅𐐯𐑋𐐺𐑊 𐑄𐐯𐑋𐑅𐐯𐑊𐑂𐑆 𐐻𐐲𐑀𐐯𐑄𐐲𐑉; 𐐰𐑌𐐼 𐑄𐐩 𐐺𐐨𐑀𐐰𐑌 𐐻𐐭 𐑁𐐰𐑅𐐻, 𐐰𐑌𐐼 𐐻𐐭 𐐹𐑉𐐩 𐐻𐐭 𐑄 𐐢𐐫𐑉𐐼 𐑄𐐩𐑉 𐐘𐐱𐐼, 𐑄𐐰𐐻 𐐸𐐨 𐐶𐐳𐐼 𐐬𐐹𐐯𐑌 𐑄 𐑋𐐵𐑃 𐐱𐑂 𐐰𐑊𐑋𐐲, 𐑄𐐰𐐻 𐐸𐐨 𐑋𐐴𐐻 𐑅𐐹𐐨𐐿; 𐐰𐑌𐐼 𐐫𐑊𐑅𐐬 𐑄𐐰𐐻 𐐸𐐮𐑆 𐑊𐐮𐑋𐑆 𐑋𐐴𐐻 𐑉𐐨𐑅𐐨𐑂 𐑄𐐩𐑉 𐑅𐐻𐑉𐐯𐑍𐑃, 𐑄𐐰𐐻 𐑄 𐐌𐑆 𐐱𐑂 𐑄 𐐹𐐨𐐹𐑊 𐑋𐐴𐐻 𐐺 𐐬𐐹𐐯𐑌𐐼 𐐻𐐭 𐑅𐐨 𐐰𐑌𐐼 𐑌𐐬 𐐱𐑂 𐑄 𐑀𐐳𐐼𐑌𐐯𐑅 𐐰𐑌𐐼 𐑀𐑊𐐫𐑉𐐨 𐐱𐑂 𐐘𐐱𐐼.

22. 𐐰𐑌𐐼 𐐮𐐻 𐐿𐐩𐑋 𐐻𐐭 𐐹𐐰𐑅 𐐰𐑁𐐻𐐲𐑉 𐑄𐐩 𐐸𐐰𐐼 𐑁𐐰𐑅𐐻𐐯𐐼 𐐰𐑌𐐼 𐐹𐑉𐐩𐐼 𐑁𐐫𐑉 𐑄 𐑅𐐹𐐩𐑅 𐐱𐑂 𐐻𐐭 𐐼𐐩𐑆 𐐰𐑌𐐼 𐐻𐐭 𐑌𐐴𐐻𐑅, 𐑄 𐑊𐐮𐑋𐑆 𐐱𐑂 𐐰𐑊𐑋𐐲 𐑉𐐨𐑅𐐨𐑂𐐼 𐑄𐐩𐑉 𐑅𐐻𐑉𐐯𐑍𐑃, 𐐰𐑌𐐼 𐐸𐐨 𐑅𐐻𐐳𐐼 𐐲𐐹 𐐰𐑌𐐼 𐐺𐐨𐑀𐐰𐑌 𐐻𐐭 𐑅𐐹𐐨𐐿 𐐲𐑌𐐻𐐭 𐑄𐐯𐑋, 𐐺𐐮𐐼𐐮𐑍 𐑄𐐯𐑋 𐐻𐐭 𐐺 𐐱𐑂 𐑀𐐳𐐼 𐐿𐐲𐑋𐑁𐐲𐑉𐐻: 𐑁𐐫𐑉, 𐑅𐐯𐐼 𐐸𐐨, 𐐌 𐐸𐐰𐑂 𐑉𐐨𐐹𐐯𐑌𐐻𐐯𐐼 𐐱𐑂 𐑋𐐴 𐑅𐐮𐑌𐑆, 𐐰𐑌𐐼 𐐸𐐰𐑂 𐐺𐐮𐑌 𐑉𐐨𐐼𐐨𐑋𐐼 𐐱𐑂 𐑄 𐐢𐐫𐑉𐐼; 𐐺𐐨𐐸𐐬𐑊𐐼, 𐐌 𐐰𐑋 𐐺𐐫𐑉𐑌 𐐱𐑂 𐑄

𐑅𐐹𐐮𐑉𐐮𐐻. 𐐈𐑌𐐼 𐑄 𐐢𐐫𐑉𐐼 𐑅𐐯𐐼 𐐲𐑌𐐻𐐭 𐑋𐐨, 𐐣𐐪𐑉𐑂𐐯𐑊 𐑌𐐱𐐻 𐑄𐐰𐐻 𐐫𐑊 𐑋𐐰𐑌𐐿𐐴𐑌𐐼, 𐐷𐐩, 𐑋𐐯𐑌 𐐰𐑌𐐼 𐐶𐐮𐑋𐐯𐑌, 𐐫𐑊 𐑌𐐩𐑇𐐲𐑌𐑆, 𐐿𐐮𐑌𐐼𐑉𐐯𐐼𐑆, 𐐻𐐲𐑍𐑆, 𐐰𐑌𐐼 𐐹𐐨𐐹𐑊, 𐑋𐐲𐑅𐐻 𐐺𐐨 𐐺𐐫𐑉𐑌 𐐰𐑀𐐯𐑌; 𐐷𐐩, 𐐺𐐫𐑉𐑌 𐐱𐑂 𐐘𐐱𐐼, 𐐽𐐩𐑌𐐾𐐼 𐑁𐑉𐐱𐑋 𐑄𐐩𐑉 𐐿𐐪𐑉𐑌𐐲𐑊 𐐰𐑌𐐼 𐑁𐐫𐑊𐐲𐑌 𐑅𐐻𐐩𐐻 𐐻𐐭 𐐩 𐑅𐐻𐐩𐐻 𐐱𐑂 𐑉𐐴𐐽𐐲𐑅𐑌𐐯𐑅, 𐐺𐐨𐐮𐑍 𐑉𐐨𐐼𐐨𐑋𐐼 𐐱𐑂 𐐘𐐱𐐼, 𐐺𐐨𐐿𐐲𐑋𐐮𐑍 𐐸𐐮𐑆 𐑅𐐲𐑌𐑆 𐐰𐑌𐐼 𐐼𐐫𐐻𐐲𐑉𐑆; 𐐰𐑌𐐼 𐑄𐐲𐑅 𐑄𐐩 𐐺𐐨𐐿𐐲𐑋 𐑌𐐭 𐐿𐑉𐐨𐐽𐐲𐑉𐑆; 𐐰𐑌𐐼 𐐲𐑌𐑊𐐯𐑅 𐑄𐐩 𐐼𐐭 𐑄𐐮𐑅, 𐑄𐐩 𐐿𐐰𐑌 𐐮𐑌 𐑌𐐬 𐐶𐐴𐑆 𐐮𐑌𐐸𐐯𐑉𐐮𐐻 𐑄 𐐿𐐮𐑍𐐼𐐲𐑋 𐐱𐑂 𐐘𐐱𐐼. 𐐌 𐑅𐐩 𐐲𐑌𐐻𐐭 𐐷𐐭, 𐐲𐑌𐑊𐐯𐑅 𐑄𐐮𐑅 𐐺𐐨 𐑄 𐐿𐐩𐑅, 𐑄𐐩 𐑋𐐲𐑅𐐻 𐐺𐐨 𐐿𐐰𐑅𐐻 𐐫𐑁; 𐐰𐑌𐐼 𐑄𐐮𐑅 𐐌 𐑌𐐬, 𐐺𐐨𐐿𐐫𐑆 𐐌 𐐶𐐲𐑆 𐑊𐐴𐐿 𐐻𐐭 𐐺𐐨 𐐿𐐰𐑅𐐻 𐐫𐑁. 𐐤𐐯𐑂𐐲𐑉𐑄𐐯𐑊𐐯𐑅, 𐐰𐑁𐐻𐐲𐑉 𐐶𐐩𐐼𐐮𐑍 𐑃𐑉𐐭 𐑋𐐲𐐽 𐐻𐑉𐐮𐐺𐐷𐐭𐑊𐐩𐑇𐐲𐑌, 𐑉𐐨𐐹𐐯𐑌𐐻𐐮𐑍 𐑌𐐴 𐐲𐑌𐐻𐐭 𐐼𐐯𐑃, 𐑄 𐐢𐐫𐑉𐐼 𐐮𐑌 𐑋𐐲𐑉𐑅𐐨 𐐸𐐰𐑃 𐑅𐐨𐑌 𐑁𐐮𐐻 𐐻𐐭 𐑅𐑌𐐰𐐽 𐑋𐐨 𐐵𐐻 𐐱𐑂 𐐰𐑌 𐐯𐑂𐐲𐑉𐑊𐐰𐑅𐐻𐐮𐑍 𐐺𐐲𐑉𐑌𐐮𐑍, 𐐰𐑌𐐼 𐐌 𐐰𐑋 𐐺𐐫𐑉𐑌 𐐱𐑂 𐐘𐐱𐐼. 𐐣𐐴 𐑅𐐬𐑊 𐐸𐐰𐑆 𐐺𐐨𐑌 𐑉𐐨𐐼𐐨𐑋𐐼 𐑁𐑉𐐱𐑋 𐑄 𐑀𐐫𐑊 𐐱𐑂 𐐺𐐮𐐻𐐲𐑉𐑌𐐯𐑅 𐐰𐑌𐐼 𐐺𐐱𐑌𐐼𐑆 𐐱𐑂 𐐮𐑌𐐮𐐿𐐶𐐮𐐻𐐨. 𐐌 𐐶𐐲𐑆 𐐮𐑌 𐑄 𐐼𐐪𐑉𐐿𐐯𐑅𐐻 𐐰𐐺𐐮𐑅; 𐐺𐐲𐐻 𐑌𐐵 𐐌 𐐺𐐨𐐸𐐬𐑊𐐼 𐑄 𐑋𐐪𐑉𐑂𐐯𐑊𐐲𐑅 𐑊𐐴𐐻 𐐱𐑂 𐐘𐐱𐐼. 𐐣𐐴 𐑅𐐬𐑊 𐐶𐐲𐑆 𐑉𐐰𐐿𐐻 𐐶𐐮𐑄 𐐨𐐻𐐲𐑉𐑌𐐲𐑊 𐐻𐐫𐑉𐑋𐐯𐑌𐐻; 𐐺𐐲𐐻 𐐌 𐐰𐑋 𐑅𐑌𐐰𐐽𐐻, 𐐰𐑌𐐼 𐑋𐐴 𐑅𐐬𐑊 𐐮𐑆 𐐹𐐩𐑌𐐼 𐑌𐐬 𐑋𐐬𐑉. 𐐌 𐑉𐐨𐐾𐐯𐐿𐐻𐐯𐐼 𐑋𐐴 𐐡𐐨𐐼𐐨𐑋𐐲𐑉, 𐐰𐑌𐐼 𐐼𐐨𐑌𐐴𐐼 𐑄𐐰𐐻 𐐸𐐶𐐮𐐽 𐐸𐐰𐐼 𐐺𐐨𐑌 𐑅𐐹𐐬𐐿𐐲𐑌 𐐱𐑂 𐐺𐐴 𐐵𐑉 𐑁𐐪𐑄𐐲𐑉𐑆; 𐐺𐐲𐐻 𐑌𐐵 𐑄𐐰𐐻 𐑄𐐩 𐑋𐐩 𐑁𐐬𐑉𐑅𐐨 𐑄𐐰𐐻 𐐸𐐨 𐐶𐐮𐑊 𐐿𐐲𐑋, 𐐰𐑌𐐼 𐑄𐐰𐐻 𐐸𐐨 𐑉𐐨𐑋𐐯𐑋𐐺𐐲𐑉𐐯𐑃 𐐯𐑂𐐲𐑉𐐨 𐐿𐑉𐐨𐐽𐐲𐑉 𐐱𐑂 𐐸𐐮𐑆 𐐿𐑉𐐨𐐩𐐻𐐮𐑍, 𐐸𐐨 𐐶𐐮𐑊 𐑋𐐩𐐿 𐐸𐐮𐑋𐑅𐐯𐑊𐑁 𐑋𐐰𐑌𐐮𐑁𐐯𐑅𐐻 𐐲𐑌𐐻𐐭 𐐫𐑊. 𐐏𐐩, 𐐯𐑂𐐲𐑉𐐨 𐑌𐐨 𐑇𐐰𐑊 𐐺𐐵, 𐐰𐑌𐐼 𐐯𐑂𐐲𐑉𐐨 𐐻𐐲𐑍 𐐿𐐱𐑌𐑁𐐯𐑅 𐐺𐐨𐑁𐐬𐑉 𐐸𐐮𐑋. 𐐏𐐩, 𐐨𐑂𐐯𐑌 𐐰𐐻 𐑄 𐑊𐐰𐑅𐐻 𐐼𐐩, 𐐸𐐶𐐯𐑌 𐐫𐑊 𐑋𐐯𐑌 𐑇𐐰𐑊 𐑅𐐻𐐰𐑌𐐼 𐐻𐐭 𐐺𐐨 𐐾𐐲𐐾𐐼 𐐱𐑂 𐐸𐐮𐑋, 𐑄𐐯𐑌 𐑇𐐰𐑊 𐑄𐐩 𐐿𐐱𐑌𐑁𐐯𐑅 𐑄𐐰𐐻 𐐸𐐨 𐐮𐑆 𐐘𐐱𐐼; 𐑄𐐯𐑌 𐑇𐐰𐑊 𐑄𐐩 𐐿𐐱𐑌𐑁𐐯𐑅, 𐐸𐐭 𐑊𐐮𐑂 𐐶𐐮𐑄𐐵𐐻 𐐘𐐱𐐼 𐐮𐑌 𐑄 𐐶𐐲𐑉𐑊𐐼, 𐑄𐐰𐐻 𐑄 𐐾𐐲𐐾𐑋𐐯𐑌𐐻 𐐱𐑂 𐐰𐑌 𐐯𐑂𐐲𐑉𐑊𐐰𐑅𐐻𐐮𐑍 𐐹𐐲𐑌𐐮𐑇𐑋𐐯𐑌𐐻 𐐮𐑆 𐐾𐐲𐑅𐐻 𐐲𐐹𐐱𐑌 𐑄𐐯𐑋; 𐐰𐑌𐐼 𐑄𐐩 𐑇𐐰𐑊 𐐿𐐶𐐩𐐿, 𐐰𐑌𐐼 𐐻𐑉𐐯𐑋𐐺𐑊, 𐐰𐑌𐐼 𐑇𐑉𐐮𐑍𐐿 𐐺𐐨𐑌𐐨𐑃 𐑄 𐑀𐑊𐐰𐑌𐑅 𐐱𐑂 𐐸𐐮𐑆 𐐫𐑊-𐑅𐐲𐑉𐐽𐐮𐑍 𐐴.

23. 𐐈𐑌𐐼 𐑌𐐵 𐐮𐐻 𐐿𐐩𐑋 𐐻𐐭 𐐹𐐰𐑅 𐑄𐐰𐐻 𐐈𐑊𐑋𐐲 𐐺𐐨𐑀𐐰𐑌 𐑁𐑉𐐱𐑋 𐑄𐐮𐑅 𐐻𐐴𐑋 𐑁𐐬𐑉𐐶𐐲𐑉𐐼, 𐐻𐐭 𐐻𐐨𐐽 𐑄 𐐹𐐨𐐹𐑊, 𐐰𐑌𐐼 𐑄𐐬𐑆 𐐸𐐭 𐐶𐐲𐑉 𐐶𐐮𐑄 𐐈𐑊𐑋𐐲 𐐰𐐻 𐑄 𐐻𐐴𐑋 𐑄 𐐩𐑌𐐾𐐯𐑊 𐐰𐐹𐐨𐑉𐐼 𐐲𐑌𐐻𐐭 𐑄𐐯𐑋: 𐐻𐑉𐐰𐑂𐐯𐑊𐐮𐑍 𐑉𐐵𐑌𐐼 𐐰𐐺𐐵𐐻 𐑃𐑉𐐭 𐐫𐑊 𐑄 𐑊𐐰𐑌𐐼, 𐐹𐐲𐐺𐑊𐐮𐑇𐐮𐑍 𐐻𐐭 𐐫𐑊 𐑄 𐐹𐐨𐐹𐑊 𐑄 𐑃𐐮𐑍𐑆 𐐸𐐶𐐮𐐽 𐑄𐐩 𐐸𐐰𐐼 𐐸𐐲𐑉𐐼 𐐰𐑌𐐼 𐑅𐐨𐑌, 𐐰𐑌𐐼 𐐹𐑉𐐨𐐽𐐮𐑍 𐑄 𐐶𐐲𐑉𐐼 𐐱𐑂 𐐘𐐱𐐼 𐐮𐑌 𐑋𐐲𐐽 𐐻𐑉𐐮𐐺𐐷𐐭𐑊𐐩𐑇𐐲𐑌, 𐐺𐐨𐐮𐑍 𐑀𐑉𐐩𐐻𐑊𐐨 𐐹𐐲𐑉𐑅𐐨𐐿𐐷𐐭𐐻𐐯𐐼 𐐺𐐴 𐑄𐐬𐑆 𐐸𐐭 𐐶𐐲𐑉 𐐲𐑌𐐺𐐨𐑊𐐨𐑂𐐲𐑉𐑆, 𐐺𐐨𐐮𐑍 𐑅𐑋𐐮𐐻𐑌 𐐺𐐴 𐑋𐐯𐑌𐐨 𐐱𐑂 𐑄𐐯𐑋. 𐐒𐐲𐐻 𐑌𐐱𐐻𐐶𐐮𐑄𐑅𐐻𐐰𐑌𐐼𐐮𐑍 𐐫𐑊 𐑄𐐮𐑅, 𐑄𐐩 𐐼𐐮𐐼 𐐮𐑋𐐹𐐪𐑉𐐻 𐑋𐐲𐐽 𐐿𐐱𐑌𐑅𐐬𐑊𐐩𐑇𐐲𐑌 𐐻𐐭 𐑄 𐐕𐐲𐑉𐐽, 𐐿𐐱𐑌𐑁𐐲𐑉𐑋𐐮𐑍 𐑄𐐩𐑉 𐑁𐐩𐑃, 𐐰𐑌𐐼 𐐯𐑀𐑆𐐫𐑉𐐻𐐮𐑍 𐑄𐐯𐑋 𐐶𐐮𐑄 𐑊𐐱𐑍 𐑅𐐲𐑁𐐲𐑉𐐮𐑍 𐐰𐑌𐐼 𐑋𐐲𐐽 𐐻𐑉𐐰𐑂𐐯𐑊 𐐻𐐭 𐐿𐐨𐐹 𐑄 𐐿𐐱𐑋𐐰𐑌𐐼𐑋𐐯𐑌𐐻𐑅 𐐱𐑂 𐐘𐐱𐐼. 𐐈𐑌𐐼 𐑁𐐬𐑉 𐐱𐑂 𐑄𐐯𐑋 𐐶𐐲𐑉 𐑄 𐑅𐐲𐑌𐑆 𐐱𐑂 𐐣𐐬𐑅𐐴𐐲; 𐐰𐑌𐐼 𐑄𐐩𐑉 𐑌𐐩𐑋𐑆 𐐶𐐲𐑉 𐐈𐑋𐐲𐑌, 𐐰𐑌𐐼 𐐁𐑉𐐲𐑌, 𐐰𐑌𐐼 𐐉𐑋𐑌𐐲𐑉, 𐐰𐑌𐐼 𐐐𐐮𐑋𐑌𐐴: 𐑄𐐨𐑆 𐐶𐐲𐑉 𐑄 𐑌𐐩𐑋𐑆 𐐱𐑂 𐑄 𐑅𐐲𐑌𐑆 𐐱𐑂 𐐣𐐬𐑅𐐴𐐲. 𐐈𐑌𐐼 𐑄𐐩 𐐻𐑉𐐰𐑂𐐯𐑊𐐼 𐑃𐑉𐐭𐐵𐐻 𐐫𐑊 𐑄 𐑊𐐰𐑌𐐼 𐐱𐑂 𐐞𐐰𐑉𐐲𐐸𐐯𐑋𐑊𐐲, 𐐰𐑌𐐼 𐐲𐑋𐐲𐑍 𐐫𐑊 𐑄 𐐹𐐨𐐹𐑊 𐐸𐐭 𐐶𐐲𐑉 𐐲𐑌𐐼𐐲𐑉 𐑄 𐑉𐐩𐑌 𐐱𐑂 𐐿𐐮𐑍 𐐣𐐬𐑅𐐴𐐲, 𐑆𐐯𐑊𐐲𐑅𐑊𐐨 𐑅𐐻𐑉𐐴𐑂𐐮𐑍 𐐻𐐭 𐑉𐐨𐐹𐐩𐑉 𐐫𐑊 𐑄 𐐮𐑌𐐾𐐲𐑉𐐨𐑆 𐐸𐐶𐐮𐐽 𐑄𐐩 𐐸𐐰𐐼 𐐼𐐲𐑌 𐐻𐐭 𐑄 𐐕𐐲𐑉𐐽, 𐐿𐐱𐑌𐑁𐐯𐑅𐐮𐑍 𐐫𐑊 𐑄𐐩𐑉 𐑅𐐮𐑌𐑆, 𐐰𐑌𐐼 𐐹𐐲𐐺𐑊𐐮𐑇𐐮𐑍 𐐫𐑊 𐑄 𐑃𐐮𐑍𐑆 𐐸𐐶𐐮𐐽 𐑄𐐩 𐐸𐐰𐐼 𐑅𐐨𐑌, 𐐰𐑌𐐼 𐐯𐐿𐑅𐐹𐑊𐐩𐑌𐐮𐑍 𐑄 𐐹𐑉𐐱𐑁𐐯𐑅𐐨𐑆 𐐰𐑌𐐼 𐑄 𐑅𐐿𐑉𐐮𐐹𐐽𐐲𐑉𐑆 𐐻𐐭 𐐫𐑊 𐐸𐐭 𐐼𐐨𐑆𐐴𐑉𐐼 𐐻𐐭 𐐸𐐨𐑉 𐑄𐐯𐑋. 𐐈𐑌𐐼 𐑄𐐲𐑅 𐑄𐐩 𐐶𐐲𐑉 𐐮𐑌𐑅𐐻𐑉𐐭𐑋𐐯𐑌𐐻𐑅 𐐮𐑌 𐑄 𐐸𐐰𐑌𐐼𐑆 𐐱𐑂 𐐘𐐱𐐼, 𐐮𐑌 𐐺𐑉𐐮𐑍𐐮𐑍 𐑋𐐯𐑌𐐨 𐐻𐐭 𐑄 𐑌𐐱𐑊𐐯𐐾 𐐱𐑂 𐑄 𐐻𐑉𐐭𐑃, 𐐷𐐩, 𐐻𐐭 𐑄 𐑌𐐱𐑊𐐯𐐾 𐐱𐑂 𐑄𐐩𐑉 𐐡𐐨𐐼𐐨𐑋𐐲𐑉. 𐐈𐑌𐐼 𐐸𐐵 𐐺𐑊𐐯𐑅𐐯𐐼 𐐪𐑉 𐑄𐐩! 𐐙𐐬𐑉 𐑄𐐩 𐐼𐐮𐐼 𐐹𐐲𐐺𐑊𐐮𐑇 𐐹𐐨𐑅: 𐑄𐐩 𐐼𐐮𐐼 𐐹𐐲𐐺𐑊𐐮𐑇 𐑀𐐳𐐼 𐐻𐐴𐐼𐐮𐑍𐑆 𐐱𐑂 𐑀𐐳𐐼; 𐐰𐑌𐐼 𐑄𐐩 𐐼𐐮𐐼 𐐼𐐨𐐿𐑊𐐩𐑉 𐐲𐑌𐐻𐐭 𐑄 𐐹𐐨𐐹𐑊 𐑄𐐰𐐻 𐑄 𐐢𐐫𐑉𐐼 𐑉𐐩𐑌𐐯𐑃.

𐐕𐐈𐐑𐐓𐐊𐐡 XII.

1. 𐐤𐐵 𐐮𐐻 𐐿𐐩𐑋 𐐻𐐭 𐐹𐐰𐑅 𐑄𐐰𐐻 𐐰𐑁𐐻𐐲𐑉 𐑄 𐑅𐐲𐑌𐑆 𐐱𐑂 𐐣𐐬𐑅𐐴𐐲 𐐸𐐰𐐼 𐐼𐐲𐑌 𐐫𐑊 𐑄𐐨𐑆 𐑃𐐮𐑍𐑆, 𐑄𐐩 𐐻𐐳𐐿 𐐰 𐑅𐑋𐐫𐑊 𐑌𐐲𐑋𐐺𐐲𐑉 𐐶𐐮𐑄 𐑄𐐯𐑋 𐐰𐑌𐐼 𐑉𐐨𐐻𐐲𐑉𐑌𐐼 𐐻𐐭 𐑄𐐩𐑉 𐑁𐐪𐑄𐐲𐑉, 𐑄 𐐿𐐮𐑍, 𐐰𐑌𐐼 𐐼𐐨𐑆𐐴𐑉𐐼 𐐱𐑂 𐐸𐐮𐑋 𐑄𐐰𐐻 𐐸𐐨 𐐶𐐳𐐼 𐑀𐑉𐐪𐑌𐐻 𐐲𐑌𐐻𐐭 𐑄𐐯𐑋 𐑄𐐰𐐻 𐑄𐐩 𐑋𐐴𐐻, 𐐶𐐮𐑄 𐑄𐐨𐑆 𐐸𐐭𐑋 𐑄𐐩 𐐸𐐰𐐼 𐑅𐐯𐑊𐐯𐐿𐐻𐐯𐐼, 𐑀𐐬 𐐲𐐹 𐐻𐐭 𐑄 𐑊𐐰𐑌𐐼 𐐱𐑂 𐐤𐐨𐑁𐐴, 𐑄𐐰𐐻 𐑄𐐩 𐑋𐐴𐐻 𐐹𐑉𐐨𐐽 𐑄 𐑃𐐮𐑍𐑆 𐐸𐐶𐐮𐐽 𐑄𐐩 𐐸𐐰𐐼 𐐸𐐲𐑉𐐼, 𐐰𐑌𐐼 𐑄𐐰𐐻 𐑄𐐩 𐑋𐐴𐐻 𐐮𐑋𐐹𐐫𐑉𐐻 𐑄 𐐶𐐲𐑉𐐼 𐐱𐑂 𐐘𐐱𐐼 𐐻𐐭 𐑄𐐩𐑉 𐐺𐑉𐐯𐑄𐑉𐐯𐑌, 𐑄 𐐢𐐩𐑋𐐲𐑌𐐴𐐻𐑅, 𐑄𐐰𐐻 𐐹𐐲𐑉𐐸𐐰𐐹𐑅 𐑄𐐩 𐑋𐐴𐐻 𐐺𐑉𐐮𐑍 𐑄𐐯𐑋 𐐻𐐭 𐑄 𐑌𐐱𐑊𐐯𐐾 𐐱𐑂 𐑄 𐐢𐐫𐑉𐐼 𐑄𐐩𐑉 𐐘𐐱𐐼, 𐐰𐑌𐐼 𐐿𐐲𐑌𐑂𐐮𐑌𐑅 𐑄𐐯𐑋 𐐱𐑂 𐑄 𐐮𐑌𐐮𐐿𐐶𐐮𐐻𐐨 𐐱𐑂 𐑄𐐩𐑉 𐑁𐐪𐑄𐐲𐑉𐑆; 𐐰𐑌𐐼 𐑄𐐰𐐻 𐐹𐐲𐑉𐐸𐐰𐐹𐑅 𐑄𐐩 𐑋𐐴𐐻 𐐿𐐷𐐭𐑉 𐑄𐐯𐑋 𐐱𐑂 𐑄𐐩𐑉 𐐸𐐩𐐻𐑉𐐯𐐼 𐐻𐐬𐐲𐑉𐐼𐑆 𐑄 𐐤𐐨𐑁𐐴𐐻𐑅, 𐑄𐐰𐐻 𐑄𐐩 𐑋𐐴𐐻 𐐫𐑊𐑅𐐬 𐐺𐐨 𐐺𐑉𐐫𐐻 𐐻𐐭 𐑉𐐨𐐾𐐱𐐮𐑅 𐐮𐑌 𐑄 𐐢𐐫𐑉𐐼 𐑄𐐩𐑉 𐐘𐐱𐐼, 𐑄𐐰𐐻 𐑄𐐩 𐑋𐐴𐐻 𐐺𐐨𐐿𐐲𐑋 𐑁𐑉𐐯𐑌𐐼𐑊𐐨 𐐻𐐭 𐐶𐐲𐑌 𐐰𐑌𐐲𐑄𐐲𐑉, 𐐰𐑌𐐼 𐑄𐐰𐐻 𐑄𐐯𐑉 𐑇𐐳𐐼 𐐺𐐨 𐑌𐐬 𐑋𐐬𐑉 𐐿𐐲𐑌𐐻𐐯𐑌𐑇𐐲𐑌𐑆 𐐮𐑌 𐐫𐑊 𐑄 𐑊𐐰𐑌𐐼 𐐸𐐶𐐮𐐽 𐑄 𐐢𐐫𐑉𐐼 𐑄𐐩𐑉 𐐘𐐱𐐼 𐐸𐐰𐐼 𐑀𐐮𐑂𐐲𐑌 𐑄𐐯𐑋. 𐐤𐐵 𐑄𐐩 𐐶𐐲𐑉 𐐼𐐯𐑆𐐴𐑉𐐲𐑅 𐑄𐐰𐐻 𐑅𐐰𐑊𐑂𐐩𐑇𐐲𐑌 𐑇𐐳𐐼 𐐺𐐨 𐐼𐐯𐐿𐑊𐐩𐑉𐐼 𐐻𐐭 𐐯𐑂𐐲𐑉𐐨 𐐿𐑉𐐨𐐽𐐲𐑉, 𐑁𐐫𐑉 𐑄𐐩 𐐿𐐳𐐼 𐑌𐐱𐐻 𐐺𐐯𐑉 𐑄𐐰𐐻 𐐯𐑌𐐨 𐐸𐐷𐐭𐑋𐐲𐑌 𐑅𐐬𐑊 𐑇𐐳𐐼 𐐹𐐯𐑉𐐮𐑇; 𐐷𐐩, 𐐨𐑂𐐲𐑌 𐑄 𐑂𐐯𐑉𐐨 𐑃𐐫𐐻𐑅 𐑄𐐰𐐻 𐐯𐑌𐐨 𐑅𐐬𐑊 𐑇𐐳𐐼 𐐯𐑌𐐼𐐷𐐭𐑉 𐐯𐑌𐐼𐑊𐐯𐑅 𐐻𐐫𐑉𐑋𐐯𐑌𐐻 𐐼𐐮𐐼 𐐿𐐫𐑆 𐑄𐐯𐑋 𐐻𐐭 𐐿𐐶𐐩𐐿 𐐰𐑌𐐼 𐐻𐑉𐐯𐑋𐐺𐑊. 𐐈𐑌𐐼 𐑄𐐲𐑅 𐐼𐐮𐐼 𐑄 𐐝𐐹𐐮𐑉𐐮𐐻 𐐱𐑂 𐑄 𐐢𐐫𐑉𐐼 𐐶𐐲𐑉𐐿 𐐲𐐹𐐱𐑌 𐑄𐐯𐑋, 𐑁𐐫𐑉 𐑄𐐩 𐐶𐐲𐑉 𐑄 𐑂𐐯𐑉𐐨 𐑂𐐴𐑊𐐯𐑅𐐻 𐐱𐑂 𐑅𐐮𐑌𐐲𐑉𐑆. 𐐈𐑌𐐼 𐑄 𐐢𐐫𐑉𐐼 𐑅𐐫 𐑁𐐮𐐻 𐐮𐑌 𐐸𐐮𐑆 𐐮𐑌𐑁𐐮𐑌𐐮𐐻 𐑋𐐲𐑉𐑅𐐨 𐐻𐐭 𐑅𐐹𐐩𐑉 𐑄𐐯𐑋; 𐑌𐐯𐑂𐐲𐑉𐑄𐐲𐑊𐐯𐑅 𐑄𐐩 𐑅𐐲𐑁𐐲𐑉𐐼 𐑋𐐲𐐽 𐐰𐑍𐑀𐐶𐐮𐑇 𐐱𐑂 𐑅𐐬𐑊, 𐐺𐐨𐐿𐐫𐑆 𐐱𐑂 𐑄𐐩𐑉 𐐮𐑌𐐮𐐿𐐶𐐮𐐻𐐨𐑆; 𐑅𐐲𐑁𐐲𐑉𐐮𐑍 𐑋𐐲𐐽 𐐰𐑌𐐼 𐑁𐐨𐑉𐐮𐑍 𐑄𐐰𐐻 𐑄𐐩 𐑇𐐳𐐼 𐐺𐐨 𐐿𐐰𐑅𐐻 𐐱𐑁 𐑁𐐫𐑉 𐐯𐑂𐐲𐑉.

2. 𐐈𐑌𐐼 𐐮𐐻 𐐿𐐩𐑋 𐐻𐐭 𐐹𐐰𐑅 𐑄𐐰𐐻 𐑄𐐩 𐐼𐐮𐐼 𐐹𐑊𐐨𐐼 𐐶𐐮𐑄 𐑄𐐩𐑉 𐑁𐐪𐑄𐐲𐑉 𐑋𐐯𐑌𐐨 𐐼𐐩𐑆 𐑄𐐰𐐻 𐑄𐐩 𐑋𐐴𐐻 𐑀𐐬 𐐲𐐹 𐐻𐐭 𐑄 𐑊𐐰𐑌𐐼 𐐱𐑂 𐐤𐐨𐑁𐐴. 𐐈𐑌𐐼 𐐿𐐮𐑍 𐐣𐐬𐑅𐐴𐐲 𐐶𐐯𐑌𐐻 𐐰𐑌𐐼 𐐮𐑌𐐿𐐶𐐴𐑉𐐼 𐐱𐑂 𐑄 𐐢𐐫𐑉𐐼, 𐐮𐑁 𐐸𐐨 𐑇𐐳𐐼 𐑊𐐯𐐻 𐐸𐐮𐑆 𐑅𐐲𐑌𐑆 𐑀𐐬 𐐲𐐹 𐐰𐑋𐐲𐑍 𐑄 𐐢𐐩𐑋𐐲𐑌𐐴𐐻𐑅 𐐻𐐭 𐐹𐑉𐐨𐐽 𐑄 𐐶𐐲𐑉𐐼. 𐐈𐑌𐐼 𐑄 𐐢𐐫𐑉𐐼 𐑅𐐯𐐼 𐐲𐑌𐐻𐐭 𐐣𐐬𐑅𐐴𐐲, 𐐢𐐯𐐻 𐑄𐐯𐑋 𐑀𐐬 𐐲𐐹, 𐑁𐐫𐑉 𐑋𐐯𐑌𐐨 𐑇𐐰𐑊 𐐺𐐨𐑊𐐨𐑂 𐐱𐑌 𐑄𐐩𐑉 𐐶𐐲𐑉𐐼𐑆, 𐐰𐑌𐐼 𐑄𐐩 𐑇𐐰𐑊 𐐸𐐰𐑂 𐐨𐐻𐐲𐑉𐑌𐐲𐑊 𐑊𐐴𐑁; 𐐰𐑌𐐼 𐐌 𐐶𐐮𐑊 𐐼𐐯𐑊𐐮𐑂𐐲𐑉 𐑄𐐴 𐑅𐐲𐑌𐑆 𐐵𐐻 𐐱𐑂 𐑄 𐐸𐐰𐑌𐐼𐑆 𐐱𐑂 𐑄 𐐢𐐩𐑋𐐲𐑌𐐴𐐻𐑅.

3. 𐐈𐑌𐐼 𐐮𐐻 𐐿𐐩𐑋 𐐻𐐭 𐐹𐐰𐑅 𐑄𐐰𐐻 𐐣𐐬𐑅𐐴𐐲 𐑀𐑉𐐪𐑌𐐻𐐯𐐼 𐑄𐐰𐐻 𐑄𐐩 𐑋𐐴𐐻 𐑀𐐬, 𐐰𐑌𐐼 𐐼𐐭 𐐰𐐿𐐫𐑉𐐼𐐮𐑍 𐐻𐐭 𐑄𐐩𐑉 𐑉𐐨𐐿𐐶𐐯𐑅𐐻; 𐐰𐑌𐐼 𐑄𐐩 𐐻𐐳𐐿 𐑄𐐩𐑉 𐐾𐐲𐑉𐑌𐐨 𐐮𐑌𐐻𐐭 𐑄 𐐶𐐮𐑊𐐼𐐲𐑉𐑌𐐯𐑅, 𐐻𐐭 𐑀𐐬 𐐲𐐹 𐐻𐐭 𐐹𐑉𐐨𐐽 𐑄 𐐶𐐲𐑉𐐼 𐐰𐑋𐐲𐑍 𐑄 𐐢𐐩𐑋𐐲𐑌𐐴𐐻𐑅: 𐐰𐑌𐐼 𐐌 𐑇𐐰𐑊 𐑀𐐮𐑂 𐐰𐑌 𐐰𐐿𐐵𐑌𐐻 𐐱𐑂 𐑄𐐩𐑉 𐐹𐑉𐐬𐑅𐐨𐐼𐐮𐑍𐑆 𐐸𐐨𐑉𐐰𐑁𐐻𐐲𐑉. 𐐤𐐵 𐐿𐐮𐑍 𐐣𐐬𐑅𐐴𐐲 𐐸𐐰𐐼 𐑌𐐬 𐐶𐐲𐑌 𐐻𐐭 𐐿𐐲𐑌𐑁𐐲𐑉 𐑄 𐐿𐐮𐑍𐐼𐐲𐑋 𐐲𐐹𐐱𐑌, 𐑁𐐫𐑉 𐑄𐐯𐑉 𐐶𐐱𐑆 𐑌𐐱𐐻 𐐯𐑌𐐨 𐐱𐑂 𐐸𐐮𐑆 𐑅𐐲𐑌𐑆 𐐸𐐭 𐐶𐐳𐐼 𐐰𐐿𐑅𐐯𐐹𐐻 𐐱𐑂 𐑄 𐐿𐐮𐑍𐐼𐐲𐑋; 𐑄𐐯𐑉𐑁𐐫𐑉 𐐸𐐨 𐐻𐐳𐐿 𐑄 𐑉𐐯𐐿𐐲𐑉𐐼𐑆 𐐸𐐶𐐮𐐽 𐐶𐐲𐑉 𐐯𐑌𐑀𐑉𐐩𐑂𐐲𐑌 𐐱𐑌 𐑄 𐐹𐑊𐐩𐐻𐑅 𐐱𐑂 𐐺𐑉𐐰𐑅, 𐐰𐑌𐐼 𐐫𐑊𐑅𐐬 𐑄 𐐹𐑊𐐩𐐻𐑅 𐐱𐑂 𐐤𐐨𐑁𐐴, 𐐰𐑌𐐼 𐐫𐑊 𐑄 𐑃𐐮𐑍𐑆 𐐸𐐶𐐮𐐽 𐐸𐐨 𐐸𐐰𐐼 𐐿𐐯𐐹𐐻 𐐰𐑌𐐼 𐐹𐑉𐐨𐑆𐐲𐑉𐑂𐐼 𐐰𐐿𐐫𐑉𐐼𐐮𐑍 𐐻𐐭 𐑄 𐐿𐐲𐑋𐐰𐑌𐐼𐑋𐐯𐑌𐐻𐑅 𐐱𐑂 𐐘𐐱𐐼, 𐐰𐑁𐐻𐐲𐑉 𐐸𐐰𐑂𐐮𐑍 𐐻𐑉𐐰𐑌𐑅𐑊𐐩𐐻𐐯𐐼 𐐰𐑌𐐼 𐐿𐐫𐑆𐐼 𐐻𐐭 𐐺𐐨 𐑉𐐮𐐻𐑌 𐑄 𐑉𐐯𐐿𐐲𐑉𐐼𐑆 𐐸𐐶𐐮𐐽 𐐶𐐲𐑉 𐐱𐑌 𐑄 𐐹𐑊𐐩𐐻𐑅 𐐱𐑂 𐑀𐐬𐑊𐐼, 𐐸𐐶𐐮𐐽 𐐸𐐰𐐼 𐐺𐐨𐑌 𐑁𐐵𐑌𐐼 𐐺𐐴 𐑄 𐐹𐐨𐐹𐑊 𐐱𐑂 𐐢𐐮𐑋𐐸𐐴, 𐐸𐐶𐐮𐐽 𐐶𐐲𐑉 𐐼𐐯𐑊𐐮𐑂𐐲𐑉𐐼 𐐻𐐭 𐐸𐐮𐑋 𐐺𐐴 𐑄 𐐸𐐰𐑌𐐼 𐐱𐑂 𐐢𐐮𐑋𐐸𐐴; 𐐰𐑌𐐼 𐑄𐐮𐑅 𐐸𐐨 𐐼𐐮𐐼 𐐺𐐨𐐿𐐫𐑆 𐐱𐑂 𐑄 𐑀𐑉𐐩𐐻 𐐰𐑍𐑆𐐴𐐲𐐻𐐨 𐐱𐑂 𐐸𐐮𐑆 𐐹𐐨𐐹𐑊, 𐑁𐐫𐑉 𐑄𐐩 𐐶𐐲𐑉 𐐼𐐯𐑆𐐴𐑉𐐲𐑅 𐐺𐐨𐐷𐐱𐑌𐐼 𐑋𐐯𐑈𐐲𐑉 𐐻𐐭 𐑌𐐬 𐐿𐐲𐑌𐑅𐐲𐑉𐑌𐐮𐑍 𐑄𐐬𐑆 𐐹𐐨𐐹𐑊 𐐸𐐭 𐐸𐐰𐐼 𐐺𐐨𐑌 𐐼𐐯𐑅𐐻𐑉𐐱𐐮𐐼. 𐐈𐑌𐐼 𐑌𐐵 𐐸𐐨 𐐻𐑉𐐰𐑌𐑅𐑊𐐩𐐻𐐯𐐼 𐑄𐐯𐑋 𐐺𐐴 𐑄 𐑋𐐨𐑌𐑆 𐐱𐑂 𐑄𐐬𐑆 𐐻𐐭 𐑅𐐻𐐬𐑌𐑆 𐐸𐐶𐐮𐐽 𐐶𐐲𐑉 𐑁𐐪𐑅𐑌𐐯𐐼 𐐮𐑌𐐻𐐭 𐑄 𐐻𐐭 𐑉𐐮𐑋𐑆 𐐱𐑂 𐐰 𐐺𐐬. 𐐤𐐵 𐑄𐐨𐑆 𐑃𐐮𐑍𐑆 𐐶𐐲𐑉 𐐹𐑉𐐨𐐹𐐩𐑉𐐼 𐑁𐑉𐐱𐑋 𐑄 𐐺𐐨𐑀𐐮𐑌𐐮𐑍, 𐐰𐑌𐐼 𐐶𐐲𐑉 𐐸𐐰𐑌𐐼𐐯𐐼 𐐼𐐵𐑌 𐑁𐑉𐐱𐑋 𐐾𐐯𐑌𐐲𐑉𐐩𐑇𐐲𐑌 𐐻𐐭 𐐾𐐯𐑌𐐲𐑉𐐩𐑇𐐲𐑌, 𐑁𐐫𐑉 𐑄 𐐹𐐲𐑉𐐹𐐲𐑅 𐐱𐑂 𐐮𐑌𐐻𐐲𐑉𐐹𐑉𐐯𐐻𐐮𐑍 𐑊𐐰𐑍𐑀𐐶𐐯𐐾𐐯𐑆; 𐐰𐑌𐐼 𐑄𐐩 𐐸𐐰𐑂 𐐺𐐨𐑌 𐐿𐐯𐐹𐐻 𐐰𐑌𐐼 𐐹𐑉𐐨𐑆𐐲𐑉𐑂𐐼 𐐺𐐴 𐑄 𐐸𐐰𐑌𐐼 𐐱𐑂 𐑄 𐐢𐐫𐑉𐐼, 𐑄𐐰𐐻 𐐸𐐨 𐑇𐐳𐐼 𐐼𐐮𐑅𐐿𐐲𐑂𐐲𐑉 𐐻𐐭 𐐯𐑂𐐲𐑉𐐨 𐐿𐑉𐐨𐐽𐐲𐑉 𐐸𐐭 𐑇𐐳𐐼 𐐹𐐲𐑆𐐯𐑅 𐑄 𐑊𐐰𐑌𐐼 𐑄 𐐮𐑌𐐮𐐿𐐶𐐮𐐻𐐨𐑆 𐐰𐑌𐐼 𐐰𐐺𐐱𐑋𐐮𐑌𐐩𐑇𐐲𐑌𐑆 𐐱𐑂 𐐸𐐮𐑆 𐐹𐐨𐐹𐑊: 𐐰𐑌𐐼 𐐸𐐭𐑅𐐬𐐯𐑂𐐲𐑉 𐐸𐐰𐑆 𐑄𐐨𐑆 𐑃𐐮𐑍𐑆 𐐮𐑆 𐐿𐐫𐑊𐐼 𐑅𐐨𐐲𐑉, 𐐰𐑁𐐻𐐲𐑉 𐑄 𐑋𐐰𐑌𐐲𐑉 𐐱𐑂 𐐬𐑊𐐼 𐐻𐐴𐑋𐑆.

4. 𐐤𐐵, 𐐰𐑁𐐻𐐲𐑉 𐐣𐐬𐑅𐐴𐐲 𐐸𐐰𐐼 𐑁𐐮𐑌𐐮𐑇𐐻 𐐻𐑉𐐰𐑌𐑅𐑊𐐩𐐻𐐮𐑍 𐑄𐐨𐑆 𐑉𐐯𐐿𐐲𐑉𐐼𐑆, 𐐺𐐨𐐸𐐬𐑊𐐼 𐐮𐐻 𐑀𐐩𐑂 𐐰𐑌 𐐰𐐿𐐵𐑌𐐻 𐐱𐑂 𐑄 𐐹𐐨𐐹𐑊 𐐸𐐶𐐮𐐽 𐐶𐐲𐑉 𐐼𐐯𐑅𐐻𐑉𐑎𐐼, 𐑁𐑉𐐱𐑋 𐑄 𐐻𐐴𐑋 𐑄𐐰𐐻 𐑄𐐩 𐐶𐐲𐑉 𐐼𐐯𐑅𐐻𐑉𐑎𐐼, 𐐺𐐰𐐿 𐐻𐐭 𐑄 𐐺𐐮𐑊𐐼𐐮𐑍 𐐱𐑂 𐑄 𐑀𐑉𐐩𐐻 𐐻𐐵𐐲𐑉, 𐐰𐐻 𐑄 𐐻𐐴𐑋 𐑄 𐐢𐐫𐑉𐐼 𐐿𐐱𐑌𐑁𐐵𐑌𐐼𐐯𐐼 𐑄 𐑊𐐰𐑍𐑀𐐶𐐯𐐾 𐐱𐑂 𐑄 𐐹𐐨𐐹𐑊, 𐐰𐑌𐐼 𐑄𐐩 𐐶𐐲𐑉 𐑅𐐿𐐰𐐻𐐲𐑉𐐼 𐐲𐐺𐑉𐐫𐐼 𐐲𐐹𐐱𐑌 𐑄 𐑁𐐩𐑅 𐐱𐑂 𐐫𐑊 𐑄 𐐲𐑉𐑃; 𐐷𐐩, 𐐰𐑌𐐼 𐐨𐑂𐐲𐑌 𐑁𐑉𐐱𐑋 𐑄𐐰𐐻 𐐻𐐴𐑋, 𐐺𐐰𐐿 𐐲𐑌𐐻𐐮𐑊 𐑄 𐐿𐑉𐐨𐐩𐑇𐐲𐑌 𐐱𐑂 𐐁𐐼𐐲𐑋. 𐐤𐐵 𐑄𐐮𐑅 𐐰𐐿𐐵𐑌𐐻 𐐼𐐮𐐼 𐐿𐐫𐑆 𐑄 𐐹𐐨𐐹𐑊 𐐱𐑂 𐐣𐐬𐑅𐐴𐐲 𐐻𐐭 𐑋𐐬𐑉𐑌 𐐯𐐿𐑅𐐨𐐼𐐮𐑍𐑊𐐨, 𐐷𐐩, 𐑄𐐩 𐐶𐐲𐑉 𐑁𐐮𐑊𐐼 𐐶𐐮𐑄 𐑅𐐱𐑉𐐬; 𐑌𐐯𐑂𐐲𐑉𐑄𐐲𐑊𐐯𐑅 𐐮𐐻 𐑀𐐩𐑂 𐑄𐐯𐑋 𐑋𐐲𐐽 𐑌𐐱𐑊𐐯𐐾, 𐐮𐑌 𐑄 𐐸𐐶𐐮𐐽 𐑄𐐩 𐐼𐐮𐐼 𐑉𐐨𐐾𐑎𐑅. 𐐈𐑌𐐼 𐑄𐐮𐑅 𐐰𐐿𐐵𐑌𐐻 𐑇𐐰𐑊 𐐺𐐨 𐑉𐐮𐐻𐐲𐑌 𐐸𐐨𐑉𐐰𐑁𐐻𐐲𐑉: 𐑁𐐫𐑉 𐐺𐐨𐐸𐐬𐑊𐐼, 𐐮𐐻 𐐮𐑆 𐐯𐐿𐑅𐐹𐐨𐐼𐐨𐐯𐑌𐐻 𐑄𐐰𐐻 𐐫𐑊 𐐹𐐨𐐹𐑊 𐑇𐐳𐐼 𐑌𐐬 𐑄 𐑃𐐮𐑍𐑆 𐐸𐐶𐐮𐐽 𐐪𐑉 𐑉𐐮𐐻𐐲𐑌 𐐮𐑌 𐑄𐐮𐑅 𐐰𐐿𐐵𐑌𐐻.

𐐕𐐰𐐹𐐻𐐲𐑉 XIII.

1. 𐐈𐑌𐐼 𐑌𐐵, 𐐰𐑆 𐐌 𐑅𐐯𐐼 𐐲𐑌𐐻𐐭 𐐷𐐭, 𐑄𐐰𐐻 𐐰𐑁𐐻𐐲𐑉 𐐿𐐮𐑍 𐐣𐐬𐑅𐐴𐐲 𐐸𐐰𐐼 𐐼𐐲𐑌 𐑄𐐨𐑆 𐑃𐐮𐑍𐑆, 𐐸𐐨 𐐻𐐳𐐿 𐑄 𐐹𐑊𐐩𐐻𐑅 𐐱𐑂 𐐺𐑉𐐰𐑅, 𐐰𐑌𐐼 𐐫𐑊 𐑄 𐑃𐐮𐑍𐑆 𐐸𐐶𐐮𐐽 𐐸𐐨 𐐸𐐰𐐼 𐐿𐐯𐐹𐐻, 𐐰𐑌𐐼 𐐿𐐱𐑌𐑁𐐲𐑉𐐼 𐑄𐐯𐑋 𐐲𐐹𐐱𐑌 𐐈𐑊𐑋𐐲, 𐐸𐐭 𐐶𐐱𐑆 𐑄 𐑅𐐲𐑌 𐐱𐑂 𐐈𐑊𐑋𐐲; 𐐷𐐩, 𐐫𐑊 𐑄 𐑉𐐯𐐿𐐲𐑉𐐼𐑆, 𐐰𐑌𐐼 𐐫𐑊𐑅𐐬 𐑄 𐐮𐑌𐐻𐐲𐑉𐐹𐑉𐐯𐐻𐐲𐑉𐑆, 𐐰𐑌𐐼 𐐿𐐱𐑌𐑁𐐲𐑉𐐼 𐑄𐐯𐑋 𐐲𐐹𐐱𐑌 𐐸𐐮𐑋, 𐐰𐑌𐐼 𐐿𐐱𐑋𐐰𐑌𐐼𐐯𐐼 𐐸𐐮𐑋 𐑄𐐰𐐻 𐐸𐐨 𐑇𐐳𐐼 𐐿𐐨𐐹 𐐰𐑌𐐼 𐐹𐑉𐐨𐑆𐐲𐑉𐑂 𐑄𐐯𐑋, 𐐰𐑌𐐼 𐐫𐑊𐑅𐐬 𐐿𐐨𐐹 𐐩 𐑉𐐯𐐿𐐲𐑉𐐼 𐐱𐑂 𐑄 𐐹𐐨𐐹𐑊, 𐐸𐐰𐑌𐐼𐐮𐑍 𐑄𐐯𐑋 𐐼𐐵𐑌 𐑁𐑉𐐱𐑋 𐐶𐐲𐑌 𐐾𐐯𐑌𐐲𐑉𐐩𐑇𐐲𐑌 𐐻𐐭 𐐲𐑌𐐲𐑄𐐲𐑉, 𐐨𐑂𐐲𐑌 𐐰𐑆 𐑄𐐩 𐐸𐐰𐐼 𐐺𐐮𐑌 𐐸𐐰𐑌𐐼𐐯𐐼 𐐼𐐵𐑌 𐑁𐑉𐐱𐑋 𐑄 𐐻𐐴𐑋 𐑄𐐰𐐻 𐐢𐐨𐐸𐐴 𐑊𐐯𐑁𐐻 𐐖𐐯𐑉𐐭𐑅𐐲𐑊𐐯𐑋. 𐐤𐐵 𐐸𐐶𐐯𐑌 𐐣𐐬𐑅𐐴𐐲 𐐸𐐰𐐼 𐐼𐐲𐑌 𐑄𐐮𐑅, 𐐸𐐨 𐑅𐐯𐑌𐐻 𐐵𐐻 𐑃𐑉𐐭𐐵𐐻 𐐫𐑊 𐑄 𐑊𐐰𐑌𐐼, 𐐲𐑋𐐲𐑍 𐐫𐑊 𐑄 𐐹𐐨𐐹𐑊, 𐐼𐐯𐑆𐐴𐑉𐐮𐑍 𐐻𐐭 𐑌𐐬 𐑄𐐩𐑉 𐐶𐐮𐑊 𐐿𐐱𐑌𐑅𐐲𐑉𐑌𐐮𐑍 𐐸𐐭 𐑇𐐳𐐼 𐐺𐐨 𐑄𐐩𐑉 𐐿𐐮𐑍. 𐐈𐑌𐐼 𐐮𐐻 𐐿𐐩𐑋 𐐻𐐭 𐐹𐐪𐑅 𐑄𐐰𐐻 𐑄 𐑂𐑎𐑅 𐐱𐑂 𐑄 𐐹𐐨𐐹𐑊 𐐿𐐩𐑋, 𐑅𐐩𐐮𐑍, 𐐎𐐨 𐐪𐑉 𐐼𐐯𐑆𐐴𐑉𐐲𐑅 𐑄𐐰𐐻 𐐇𐑉𐐲𐑌, 𐑄𐐴 𐑅𐐲𐑌, 𐑇𐐳𐐼 𐐺𐐨 𐐵𐑉 𐐿𐐮𐑍, 𐐰𐑌𐐼 𐐵𐑉 𐑉𐐭𐑊𐐲𐑉. 𐐤𐐵 𐐇𐑉𐐲𐑌 𐐸𐐰𐐼 𐑀𐐱𐑌 𐐲𐐹 𐐻𐐭 𐑄 𐑊𐐰𐑌𐐼 𐐱𐑂 𐐤𐐨𐑁𐐴, 𐑄𐐯𐑉𐑁𐐬𐑉 𐑄 𐐿𐐮𐑍 𐐿𐐳𐐼 𐑌𐐱𐐻 𐐿𐐱𐑌𐑁𐐲𐑉 𐑄 𐐿𐐮𐑍𐐼𐐲𐑋 𐐲𐐹𐐱𐑌 𐐸𐐮𐑋; 𐑌𐐨𐑄𐐲𐑉 𐐶𐐳𐐼 𐐇𐑉𐐲𐑌 𐐻𐐩𐐿 𐐲𐐹𐐱𐑌 𐐸𐐮𐑋 𐑄 𐐿𐐮𐑍𐐼𐐲𐑋; 𐑌𐐨𐑄𐐲𐑉 𐐶𐐲𐑉 𐐯𐑌𐐨 𐐱𐑂 𐑄 𐑅𐐲𐑌𐑆 𐐱𐑂 𐐣𐐬𐑅𐐴𐐲 𐐶𐐮𐑊𐐮𐑍 𐐻𐐭 𐐻𐐩𐐿 𐐲𐐹𐐱𐑌 𐑄𐐯𐑋 𐑄 𐐿𐐮𐑍𐐼𐐲𐑋; 𐑄𐐯𐑉𐑁𐐬𐑉 𐐿𐐮𐑍 𐐣𐐬𐑅𐐴𐐲 𐑅𐐯𐑌𐐻 𐐲𐑀𐐯𐑌 𐐲𐑋𐐲𐑍 𐑄 𐐹𐐨𐐹𐑊; 𐐷𐐩, 𐐨𐑂𐐲𐑌 𐐩 𐑉𐐮𐐻𐐲𐑌 𐐶𐐲𐑉𐐼 𐑅𐐯𐑌𐐻 𐐸𐐨 𐐲𐑋𐐲𐑍 𐑄 𐐹𐐨𐐹𐑊. 𐐈𐑌𐐼 𐑄𐐨𐑆 𐐶𐐲𐑉 𐑄 𐐶𐐲𐑉𐐼𐑆 𐑄𐐰𐐻 𐐶𐐲𐑉 𐑉𐐮𐐻𐐲𐑌, 𐑅𐐩𐐮𐑍:—𐐒𐐨𐐸𐐬𐑊𐐼, 𐐄 𐐷𐐨 𐑋𐐴 𐐹𐐨𐐹𐑊, 𐐫𐑉 𐑋𐐴 𐐺𐑉𐐯𐑄𐑉𐐯𐑌, 𐑁𐐫𐑉 𐐌 𐐯𐑅𐐻𐐨𐑋 𐐷𐐭 𐐰𐑆 𐑅𐐲𐐽; 𐑁𐐫𐑉 𐐌 𐐼𐐯𐑆𐐴𐑉 𐑄𐐰𐐻 𐐷𐐨 𐑇𐐳𐐼 𐐿𐐱𐑌𐑅𐐮𐐼𐐲𐑉 𐑄 𐐿𐐫𐑆 𐐸𐐶𐐮𐐽 𐐷𐐨 𐐪𐑉 𐐿𐐫𐑊𐐼 𐐻𐐭 𐐿𐐱𐑌𐑅𐐮𐐼𐐲𐑉; 𐑁𐐫𐑉 𐐷𐐨 𐐪𐑉 𐐼𐐯𐑆𐐴𐑉𐐲𐑅 𐐻𐐭 𐐸𐐰𐑂 𐐩 𐐿𐐮𐑍. 𐐤𐐵 𐐌 𐐼𐐯𐐿𐑊𐐩𐑉 𐐲𐑌𐐻𐐭 𐐷𐐭 𐑄𐐰𐐻 𐐸𐐨 𐐻𐐭 𐐸𐐭𐑋 𐑄 𐐿𐐮𐑍𐐼𐐲𐑋 𐐼𐐲𐑃 𐑉𐐴𐐻𐑊𐐨 𐐺𐐨𐑊𐐱𐑍, 𐐸𐐰𐑆 𐐼𐐯𐐿𐑊𐐴𐑌𐐼, 𐐰𐑌𐐼 𐐶𐐮𐑊 𐑌𐐱𐐻 𐐻𐐩𐐿 𐐲𐐹𐐱𐑌 𐐸𐐮𐑋 𐑄 𐐿𐐮𐑍𐐼𐐲𐑋.

2. 𐐈𐑌𐐼 𐑌𐐵 𐐮𐑁 𐑄𐐩𐑉 𐑇𐐳𐐼 𐐺𐐨 𐐲𐑌𐐲𐑄𐐲𐑉 𐐲𐐹𐑎𐑌𐐻𐐯𐐼 𐐮𐑌 𐐸𐐮𐑆 𐑅𐐻𐐯𐐼, 𐐺𐐨𐐸𐐬𐑊𐐼 𐐌 𐑁𐐨𐑉 𐑄𐐩𐑉 𐐶𐐳𐐼 𐑉𐐴𐑆 𐐿𐐱𐑌𐐻𐐯𐑌𐑇𐐲𐑌𐑆 𐐲𐑋𐐲𐑍 𐐷𐐭; 𐐰𐑌𐐼 𐐸𐐭 𐑌𐐬𐐯𐑃 𐐺𐐲𐐻 𐐸𐐶𐐱𐐻 𐑋𐐴 𐑅𐐲𐑌, 𐐻𐐭 𐐸𐐭𐑋 𐑄 𐐿𐐮𐑍𐐼𐐲𐑋 𐐼𐐲𐑃 𐐺𐐨𐑊𐐱𐑍, 𐑇𐐳𐐼 𐐻𐐲𐑉𐑌 𐐻𐐭 𐐺𐐨 𐐰𐑍𐑀𐑉𐐨, 𐐰𐑌𐐼 𐐼𐑉𐐫 𐐲𐐶𐐩 𐐩 𐐹𐐪𐑉𐐻 𐐱𐑂 𐑄𐐮𐑅 𐐹𐐨𐐹𐑊 𐐰𐑁𐐻𐐲𐑉 𐐸𐐮𐑋, 𐐸𐐶𐐮𐐽 𐐶𐐳𐐼 𐐿𐐫𐑆 𐐶𐐫𐑉𐑆 𐐰𐑌𐐼 𐐿𐐱𐑌𐐻𐐯𐑌𐑇𐐲𐑌𐑆 𐐲𐑋𐐲𐑍 𐐷𐐭, 𐐸𐐶𐐮𐐽 𐐶𐐳𐐼 𐐺𐐨 𐑄 𐐿𐐫𐑆 𐐱𐑂 𐑇𐐯𐐼𐐮𐑍 𐑋𐐲𐐽 𐐺𐑊𐐲𐐼, 𐐰𐑌𐐼 𐐹𐐲𐑉𐑂𐐲𐑉𐐻𐐮𐑍 𐑄 𐐶𐐩 𐐱𐑂 𐑄 𐐢𐐫𐑉𐐼; 𐐷𐐩, 𐐰𐑌𐐼 𐐼𐐯𐑅𐐻𐑉𐑎 𐑄 𐑅𐐬𐑊𐑆 𐐱𐑂 𐑋𐐯𐑌𐐨 𐐹𐐨𐐹𐑊. 𐐤𐐵 𐐌 𐑅𐐩 𐐲𐑌𐐻𐐭 𐐷𐐭, 𐑊𐐯𐐻 𐐲𐑅 𐐺𐐨 𐐶𐐴𐑆 𐐰𐑌𐐼 𐐿𐐱𐑌𐑅𐐮𐐼𐐲𐑉 𐑄𐐨𐑆 𐑃𐐮𐑍𐑆, 𐑁𐐫𐑉 𐐶𐐨 𐐸𐐰𐑂 𐑌𐐬 𐑉𐐴𐐻 𐐻𐐭 𐐼𐐯𐑅𐐻𐑉𐑎 𐑋𐐴 𐑅𐐲𐑌, 𐑌𐐨𐑄𐐲𐑉 𐑇𐐳𐐼 𐐶𐐨 𐐸𐐰𐑂 𐐯𐑌𐐨 𐑉𐐴𐐻 𐐻𐐭 𐐼𐐯𐑅𐐻𐑉𐑎 𐐲𐑌𐐲𐑄𐐲𐑉 𐐮𐑁 𐐸𐐨 𐑇𐐳𐐼 𐐺𐐨 𐐲𐐹𐑎𐑌𐐻𐐯𐐼 𐐮𐑌 𐐸𐐮𐑆 𐑅𐐻𐐯𐐼. 𐐈𐑌𐐼 𐐮𐑁 𐑋𐐴 𐑅𐐲𐑌 𐑇𐐳𐐼 𐐻𐐲𐑉𐑌 𐐲𐑀𐐯𐑌 𐐻𐐭 𐐸𐐮𐑆 𐐹𐑉𐐴𐐼 𐐰𐑌𐐼 𐑂𐐩𐑌 𐑃𐐮𐑍𐑆, 𐐸𐐨 𐐶𐐳𐐼 𐑉𐐨𐐿𐐫𐑊 𐑄 𐑃𐐮𐑍𐑆 𐐸𐐶𐐮𐐽 𐐸𐐨 𐐸𐐰𐐼 𐑅𐐯𐐼, 𐐰𐑌𐐼 𐐿𐑊𐐩𐑋 𐐸𐐮𐑆 𐑉𐐴𐐻 𐐻𐐭 𐑄 𐐿𐐮𐑍𐐼𐐲𐑋, 𐐸𐐶𐐮𐐽 𐐶𐐳𐐼 𐐿𐐫𐑆 𐐸𐐮𐑋 𐐰𐑌𐐼 𐐫𐑊𐑅𐐬 𐑄𐐮𐑅 𐐹𐐨𐐹𐑊 𐐻𐐭 𐐿𐐱𐑋𐐮𐐻 𐑋𐐲𐐽 𐑅𐐮𐑌. 𐐈𐑌𐐼 𐑌𐐵 𐑊𐐯𐐻 𐐲𐑅 𐐺𐐨 𐐶𐐴𐑆 𐐰𐑌𐐼 𐑊𐐳𐐿 𐑁𐐫𐑉𐐶𐐲𐑉𐐼 𐐻𐐭 𐑄𐐨𐑆 𐑃𐐮𐑍𐑆, 𐐰𐑌𐐼 𐐼𐐭 𐑄𐐰𐐻 𐐸𐐶𐐮𐐽 𐐶𐐮𐑊 𐑋𐐩𐐿 𐑁𐐫𐑉 𐑄 𐐹𐐨𐑅 𐐱𐑂 𐑄𐐮𐑅 𐐹𐐨𐐹𐑊. 𐐜𐐯𐑉𐑁𐐬𐑉 𐐌 𐐶𐐮𐑊 𐐺𐐨 𐐷𐐭𐑉 𐐿𐐮𐑍 𐑄 𐑉𐐨𐑋𐐩𐑌𐐼𐐲𐑉 𐐱𐑂 𐑋𐐴 𐐼𐐩𐑆; 𐑌𐐯𐑂𐐲𐑉𐑄𐐲𐑊𐐯𐑅, 𐑊𐐯𐐻 𐐲𐑅 𐐲𐐹𐑎𐑌𐐻 𐐾𐐲𐐾𐐯𐑆, 𐐻𐐭 𐐾𐐲𐐾 𐑄𐐮𐑅

𐐹𐐨𐐹𐐲𐑊 𐐰𐐿𐐫𐑉𐐼𐐮𐑍 𐐻𐐭 𐐵𐑉 𐑊𐐫, 𐐰𐑌𐐼 𐐶𐐨 𐐶𐐮𐑊 𐑌𐐭𐑊𐐨 𐐲𐑉𐐩𐑌𐐾 𐑄 𐐰𐑁𐐯𐑉𐑆 𐐱𐑂 𐑄𐐮𐑅 𐐹𐐨𐐹𐐲𐑊, 𐑁𐐫𐑉 𐐶𐐨 𐐶𐐮𐑊 𐐲𐐹𐑎𐑌𐐻 𐐶𐐴𐑆 𐑋𐐯𐑌 𐐻𐐭 𐐺𐐨 𐐾𐐲𐐾𐐯𐑆, 𐑄𐐰𐐻 𐐶𐐮𐑊 𐐾𐐲𐐾 𐑄𐐮𐑅 𐐹𐐨𐐹𐐲𐑊 𐐰𐐿𐐫𐑉𐐼𐐮𐑍 𐐻𐐭 𐑄 𐐿𐐱𐑋𐐰𐑌𐐼𐑋𐐯𐑌𐐻𐑅 𐐱𐑂 𐐘𐐱𐐼. 𐐤𐐵 𐐮𐐻 𐐮𐑆 𐐺𐐯𐐻𐐲𐑉 𐑄𐐰𐐻 𐐲 𐑋𐐰𐑌 𐑇𐐳𐐼 𐐺𐐨 𐐾𐐲𐐾𐐼 𐐱𐑂 𐐘𐐱𐐼 𐑄𐐰𐑌 𐐱𐑂 𐑋𐐰𐑌, 𐑁𐐫𐑉 𐑄 𐐾𐐲𐐾-𐑋𐐯𐑌𐐻𐑅 𐐱𐑂 𐐘𐐱𐐼 𐐪𐑉 𐐫𐑊𐐶𐐩𐑆 𐐾𐐲𐑅𐐻, 𐐺𐐲𐐻 𐑄 𐐾𐐲𐐾𐑋𐐯𐑌𐐻𐑅 𐐱𐑂 𐑋𐐰𐑌 𐐪𐑉 𐑌𐐱𐐻 𐐫𐑊𐐶𐐩𐑆 𐐾𐐲𐑅𐐻; 𐐜𐐯𐑉-𐑁𐐬𐑉 𐐮𐑁 𐐮𐐻 𐐶𐐲𐑉 𐐹𐐱𐑅𐐮𐐺𐐲𐑊 𐑄𐐰𐐻 𐐷𐐭 𐐿𐐳𐐼 𐐸𐐰𐑂 𐐾𐐲𐑅𐐻 𐑋𐐯𐑌 𐐻𐐭 𐐺𐐨 𐐷𐐭𐑉 𐐿𐐮𐑍𐑆, 𐐸𐐭 𐐶𐐳𐐼 𐐯𐑅𐐻𐐰𐐺-𐑊𐐮𐑇 𐑄 𐑊𐐫𐑆 𐐱𐑂 𐐘𐐱𐐼, 𐐰𐑌𐐼 𐐾𐐲𐐾 𐑄𐐮𐑅 𐐹𐐨𐐹𐐲𐑊 𐐰𐐿𐐫𐑉𐐼𐐮𐑍 𐐻𐐭 𐐸𐐮𐑆 𐐿𐐱𐑋𐐰𐑌𐐼𐑋𐐯𐑌𐐻𐑅; 𐐷𐐩, 𐐮𐑁 𐐷𐐨 𐐿𐐳𐐼 𐐸𐐰𐑂 𐑋𐐯𐑌 𐑁𐐫𐑉 𐐷𐐭𐑉 𐐿𐐮𐑍𐑆 𐐸𐐭 𐐶𐐳𐐼 𐐼𐐭 𐐨𐑂𐐲𐑌 𐐰𐑆 𐑋𐐴 𐑁𐐪𐑄𐐲𐑉 𐐒𐐯𐑌𐐾𐐲𐑋𐐮𐑌 𐐼𐐮𐐼 𐑁𐐫𐑉 𐑄𐐮𐑅 𐐹𐐨𐐹𐐲𐑊: 𐐌 𐑅𐐩 𐐲𐑌𐐻𐐭 𐐷𐐭, 𐐮𐑁 𐑄𐐮𐑅 𐐿𐐳𐐼 𐐫𐑊𐐶𐐩𐑆 𐐺𐐨 𐑄 𐐿𐐩𐑅, 𐑄𐐯𐑌 𐐮𐐻 𐐶𐐳𐐼 𐐺𐐨 𐐯𐐿𐑅𐐹𐐨𐐼𐐨𐐲𐑌𐐻 𐑄𐐰𐐻 𐐷𐐨 𐑇𐐳𐐼 𐐫𐑊𐐶𐐩𐑆 𐐸𐐰𐑂 𐐿𐐮𐑍𐑆 𐐻𐐭 𐑉𐐭𐑊 𐐬𐑂𐐲𐑉 𐐷𐐭. 𐐈𐑌𐐼 𐐨𐑂𐐲𐑌 𐐌 𐑋𐐴𐑅𐐯𐑊𐑁 𐐸𐐰𐑂 𐑊𐐩𐐺𐐲𐑉𐐼 𐐶𐐮𐑄 𐐫𐑊 𐑄 𐐹𐐵𐐲𐑉 𐐰𐑌𐐼 𐑁𐐰𐐿𐐲𐑊𐐻𐐮𐑆 𐐸𐐶𐐮𐐽 𐐌 𐐸𐐰𐑂 𐐹𐐲𐑆𐐯𐑅𐐻, 𐐻𐐭 𐐻𐐨𐐽 𐐷𐐭 𐑄 𐐿𐐱𐑋𐐰𐑌𐐼𐑋𐐯𐑌𐐻𐑅 𐐱𐑂 𐐘𐐱𐐼, 𐐰𐑌𐐼 𐐻𐐭 𐐯𐑅𐐻𐐰𐐺𐑊𐐮𐑇 𐐹𐐨𐑅 𐑃𐑉𐐭𐐵𐐻 𐑄 𐑊𐐰𐑌𐐼, 𐑄𐐰𐐻 𐑄𐐯𐑉 𐑇𐐳𐐼 𐐺𐐨 𐑌𐐬 𐐶𐐫𐑉𐑆 𐑌𐐫𐑉 𐐿𐐱𐑌𐐻𐐯𐑌𐑇𐐲𐑌𐑆, 𐑌𐐬 𐑅𐐻𐐨𐑊𐐮𐑍, 𐑌𐐫𐑉 𐐹𐑊𐐲𐑌𐐼𐐲𐑉𐐮𐑍, 𐑌𐐫𐑉 𐑋𐐲𐑉𐐼𐐲𐑉𐐮𐑍, 𐑌𐐫𐑉 𐐯𐑌𐐨 𐑋𐐰𐑌𐐲𐑉 𐐱𐑂 𐐮𐑌𐐮𐐿𐐶𐐮𐐻𐐨: 𐐰𐑌𐐼 𐐸𐐭𐑅𐐬-𐐯𐑂𐐲𐑉 𐐸𐐰𐑆 𐐿𐐱𐑋𐐮𐐻𐐯𐐼 𐐮𐑌𐐮𐐿𐐶𐐮𐐻𐐨, 𐐸𐐮𐑋 𐐸𐐰𐑂 𐐌 𐐹𐐲𐑌𐐮𐑇𐐻 𐐰𐐿𐐫𐑉𐐼𐐮𐑍 𐐻𐐭 𐑄 𐑊𐐫 𐐸𐐶𐐮𐐽 𐐸𐐰𐑆 𐐺𐐮𐑌 𐑀𐐮𐑂𐐲𐑌 𐐻𐐭 𐐲𐑅 𐐺𐐴 𐐵𐑉 𐑁𐐪𐑄𐐲𐑉𐑆.

3. 𐐤𐐵 𐐌 𐑅𐐩 𐐲𐑌𐐻𐐭 𐐷𐐭, 𐑄𐐰𐐻 𐐺𐐨𐐿𐐫𐑆 𐐫𐑊 𐑋𐐯𐑌 𐐪𐑉 𐑌𐐱𐐻 𐐾𐐲𐑅𐐻, 𐐮𐐻 𐐮𐑆 𐑌𐐱𐐻 𐐯𐐿𐑅𐐹𐐨𐐼𐐨𐐲𐑌𐐻 𐑄𐐰𐐻 𐐷𐐨 𐑇𐐳𐐼 𐐸𐐰𐑂 𐐲 𐐿𐐮𐑍 𐐫𐑉 𐐿𐐮𐑍𐑆 𐐻𐐭 𐑉𐐭𐑊 𐐬𐑂𐐲𐑉 𐐷𐐭. 𐐙𐐫𐑉 𐐺𐐨𐐸𐐬𐑊𐐼, 𐐸𐐵 𐑋𐐲𐐽 𐐮𐑌𐐮𐐿𐐶𐐮𐐻𐐨 𐐼𐐲𐑃 𐐶𐐲𐑌 𐐶𐐮𐐿𐐯𐐼 𐐿𐐮𐑍 𐐿𐐫𐑆 𐐻𐐭 𐐺𐐨 𐐿𐐱𐑋𐐮𐐻𐐯𐐼! 𐐷𐐩, 𐐰𐑌𐐼 𐐸𐐶𐐱𐐻 𐑀𐑉𐐩𐐻 𐐼𐐯𐑅𐐻𐑉𐐲𐐿𐑇𐐲𐑌! 𐐏𐐩, 𐑉𐐨𐑋𐐯𐑋𐐺𐐲𐑉 𐐿𐐮𐑍 𐐤𐐬𐐲, 𐐸𐐮𐑆 𐐶𐐮𐐿𐐯𐐼𐑌𐐯𐑅 𐐰𐑌𐐼 𐐸𐐮𐑆 𐐲𐐺𐐱𐑋𐐮𐑌𐐩𐑇𐐲𐑌𐑆; 𐐰𐑌𐐼 𐐫𐑊𐑅𐐬 𐑄 𐐶𐐮𐐿𐐯𐐼𐑌𐐯𐑅 𐐰𐑌𐐼 𐐲𐐺𐐱𐑋𐐮𐑌𐐩𐑇𐐲𐑌𐑆 𐐱𐑂 𐐸𐐮𐑆 𐐹𐐨𐐹𐐲𐑊. 𐐒𐐨𐐸𐐬𐑊𐐼 𐐸𐐶𐐱𐐻 𐑀𐑉𐐩𐐻 𐐼𐐯𐑅𐐻𐑉𐐲𐐿𐑇𐐲𐑌 𐐼𐐮𐐼 𐐿𐐲𐑋 𐐲𐐹𐐱𐑌 𐑄𐐯𐑋; 𐐰𐑌𐐼 𐐫𐑊𐑅𐐬 𐐺𐐨𐐿𐐫𐑆 𐐱𐑂 𐑄𐐩𐑉 𐐮𐑌𐐮𐐿𐐶𐐮𐐻𐐨𐑆, 𐑄𐐩 𐐶𐐲𐑉 𐐺𐑉𐐫𐐻 𐐮𐑌𐐻𐐭 𐐺𐐱𐑌𐐼𐐩𐐾. 𐐈𐑌𐐼 𐐶𐐲𐑉 𐐮𐐻 𐑌𐐱𐐻 𐑁𐐫𐑉 𐑄 𐐮𐑌𐐻𐐲𐑉𐐹𐐬𐑆𐐮𐑇𐐲𐑌 𐐱𐑂 𐑄𐐩𐑉 𐐫𐑊-𐐶𐐴𐑆 𐐗𐑉𐐨𐐩𐐻𐐲𐑉, 𐐰𐑌𐐼 𐑄𐐮𐑅 𐐺𐐨𐐿𐐫𐑆 𐐱𐑂 𐑄𐐩𐑉 𐑅𐐮𐑌𐑅𐐨𐑉 𐑉𐐨𐐹𐐯𐑌𐐻𐐰𐑌𐑅, 𐑄𐐩 𐑋𐐲𐑅𐐻 𐐲𐑌𐐲𐑂𐑎𐐼𐐲𐐺𐑊𐐨 𐑉𐐨𐑋𐐩𐑌 𐐮𐑌 𐐺𐐱𐑌𐐼𐐩𐐾 𐐲𐑌𐐻𐐮𐑊 𐑌𐐵. 𐐒𐐲𐐻 𐐺𐐨𐐸𐐬𐑊𐐼, 𐐸𐐨 𐐼𐐮𐐼 𐐼𐐨𐑊𐐮𐑂𐐲𐑉 𐑄𐐯𐑋 𐐺𐐨𐐿𐐫𐑆 𐑄𐐩 𐐼𐐮𐐼 𐐸𐐲𐑋𐐺𐐲𐑊 𐑄𐐯𐑋𐑅𐐯𐑊𐑂𐑆 𐐺𐐨𐑁𐐬𐑉 𐐸𐐮𐑋; 𐐰𐑌𐐼 𐐺𐐨𐐿𐐫𐑆 𐑄𐐩 𐐿𐑉𐐴𐐼 𐑋𐐴𐐻𐐮𐑊𐐨 𐐲𐑌𐐻𐐭 𐐸𐐮𐑋 𐐸𐐨 𐐼𐐮𐐼 𐐼𐐨𐑊𐐮𐑂𐐲𐑉 𐑄𐐯𐑋 𐐵𐐻 𐐱𐑂 𐐺𐐱𐑌𐐼𐐩𐐾: 𐐰𐑌𐐼 𐑄𐐲𐑅 𐐼𐐲𐑃 𐑄 𐐢𐐫𐑉𐐼 𐐶𐐲𐑉𐐿 𐐶𐐮𐑄 𐐸𐐮𐑆 𐐹𐐵𐐲𐑉 𐐮𐑌 𐐫𐑊 𐐿𐐩𐑅𐐯𐑆 𐐲𐑋𐐲𐑍 𐑄 𐐽𐐮𐑊𐐼𐑉𐐯𐑌 𐐱𐑂 𐑋𐐯𐑌, 𐐯𐐿𐑅𐐻𐐯𐑌𐐼𐐮𐑍 𐑄 𐐪𐑉𐑋 𐐱𐑂 𐑋𐐲𐑉𐑅𐐨 𐐻𐐬𐑉𐐼𐑆 𐑄𐐯𐑋 𐑄𐐰𐐻 𐐹𐐳𐐻 𐑄𐐩𐑉 𐐻𐑉𐐲𐑅𐐻 𐐮𐑌 𐐸𐐮𐑋. 𐐈𐑌𐐼 𐐺𐐨𐐸𐐬𐑊𐐼, 𐑌𐐵 𐐌 𐑅𐐩 𐐲𐑌𐐻𐐭 𐐷𐐭, 𐐷𐐨 𐐿𐐰𐑌𐐱𐐻 𐐼𐐨-𐑃𐑉𐐬𐑌 𐐰𐑌 𐐮𐑌𐐮𐐿𐐶𐐮𐐻𐐲𐑅 𐐿𐐮𐑍, 𐑅𐐩𐑂 𐐮𐐻 𐐺𐐨 𐑃𐑉𐐭 𐑋𐐲𐐽 𐐿𐐱𐑌𐐻𐐯𐑌𐑇𐐲𐑌, 𐐰𐑌𐐼 𐑄 𐑇𐐯𐐼𐐮𐑍 𐐱𐑂 𐑋𐐲𐐽 𐐺𐑊𐐲𐐼. 𐐙𐐫𐑉 𐐺𐐨𐐸𐐬𐑊𐐼, 𐐸𐐨 𐐸𐐰𐑆 𐐸𐐮𐑆 𐑁𐑉𐐯𐑌𐐼𐑆 𐐮𐑌 𐐮𐑌𐐮𐐿𐐶𐐮𐐻𐐨, 𐐰𐑌𐐼 𐐸𐐨 𐐿𐐨𐐹𐐯𐑃 𐐸𐐮𐑆 𐑀𐐪𐑉𐐼𐑆 𐐲𐐺𐐵𐐻 𐐸𐐮𐑋: 𐐰𐑌𐐼 𐐸𐐨 𐐻𐐩𐑉𐐯𐑃 𐐲𐐹 𐑄 𐑊𐐫𐑆 𐐱𐑂 𐑄𐐬𐑆 𐐸𐐭 𐐸𐐰𐑂 𐑉𐐩𐑌𐐼 𐐮𐑌 𐑉𐐴𐐽𐐲𐑅𐑌𐐯𐑅 𐐺𐐨𐑁𐐬𐑉 𐐸𐐮𐑋: 𐐰𐑌𐐼 𐐸𐐨 𐐻𐑉𐐰𐑋𐐹𐑊𐐯𐑃 𐐲𐑌𐐼𐐲𐑉 𐐸𐐮𐑆 𐑁𐐨𐐻 𐑄 𐐿𐐱𐑋𐐰𐑌𐐼𐑋𐐯𐑌𐐻𐑅 𐐱𐑂 𐐘𐐱𐐼; 𐐰𐑌𐐼 𐐸𐐨 𐐯𐑌𐐰𐐿𐐻𐐯𐑃 𐑊𐐫𐑆, 𐐰𐑌𐐼 𐑅𐐯𐑌𐐼𐐯𐑃 𐑄𐐯𐑋 𐑁𐐬𐑉𐑃 𐐲𐑋𐐲𐑍 𐐸𐐮𐑆 𐐹𐐨𐐹𐐲𐑊; 𐐷𐐩, 𐑊𐐫𐑆 𐐰𐑁𐐻𐐲𐑉 𐑄 𐑋𐐰𐑌𐐲𐑉 𐐱𐑂 𐐸𐐮𐑆 𐐬𐑌 𐐶𐐮𐐿𐐯𐐼𐑌𐐯𐑅; 𐐰𐑌𐐼 𐐸𐐭𐑅𐐬-𐐯𐑂𐐲𐑉 𐐼𐐲𐑃 𐑌𐐱𐐻 𐐬𐐺𐐩 𐐸𐐮𐑆 𐑊𐐫𐑆, 𐐸𐐨 𐐿𐐫𐑆𐐯𐑃 𐐻𐐭 𐐺𐐨 𐐼𐐯𐑅𐐻𐑉𐑎𐐼; 𐐰𐑌𐐼 𐐸𐐭𐑅𐐬𐐯𐑂𐐲𐑉 𐐼𐐲𐑃 𐑉𐐨𐐺𐐯𐑊 𐐲𐑀𐐯𐑌𐑅𐐻 𐐸𐐮𐑋, 𐐸𐐨 𐐶𐐮𐑊 𐑅𐐯𐑌𐐼 𐐸𐐮𐑆 𐐪𐑉𐑋𐐮𐑆 𐐲𐑀𐐯𐑌𐑅𐐻 𐑄𐐯𐑋 𐐻𐐭 𐐶𐐫𐑉, 𐐰𐑌𐐼 𐐮𐑁 𐐸𐐨 𐐿𐐰𐑌 𐐸𐐨 𐐶𐐮𐑊 𐐼𐐯-𐑅𐐻𐑉𐑎 𐑄𐐯𐑋: 𐐰𐑌𐐼 𐑄𐐲𐑅 𐐰𐑌 𐐲𐑌𐑉𐐴𐐽𐐲𐑅 𐐿𐐮𐑍 𐐼𐐲𐑃 𐐹𐐲𐑉𐑂𐐲𐑉𐐻 𐑄 𐐶𐐩𐑆 𐐱𐑂 𐐫𐑊 𐑉𐐴𐐽𐐲𐑅𐑌𐐯𐑅. 𐐈𐑌𐐼 𐑌𐐵 𐐺𐐨𐐸𐐬𐑊𐐼, 𐐌 𐑅𐐩 𐐲𐑌𐐻𐐭 𐐷𐐭, 𐐮𐐻 𐐮𐑆 𐑌𐐱𐐻 𐐯𐐿𐑅𐐹𐐨𐐼𐐨𐐲𐑌𐐻 𐑄𐐰𐐻 𐑅𐐲𐐽 𐐲𐐺𐐱𐑋𐐮𐑌𐐩𐑇𐐲𐑌𐑆 𐑇𐐳𐐼 𐐿𐐲𐑋 𐐲𐐹𐐱𐑌 𐐷𐐭; 𐑄𐐯𐑉𐑁𐐬𐑉 𐐽𐐭𐑆 𐐷𐐭 𐐺𐐴 𐑄 𐑂𐑎𐑅 𐐱𐑂 𐑄𐐮𐑅 𐐹𐐨𐐹𐐲𐑊, 𐐾𐐲𐐾𐐯𐑆, 𐑄𐐰𐐻 𐐷𐐨 𐑋𐐩 𐐺𐐨 𐐾𐐲𐐾𐐼 𐐰𐐿𐐫𐑉𐐼𐐮𐑍 𐐻𐐭 𐑄 𐑊𐐫𐑆 𐐸𐐶𐐮𐐽 𐐸𐐰𐑂 𐐺𐐮𐑌 𐑀𐐮𐑂𐐲𐑌 𐐷𐐭 𐐺𐐴 𐐵𐑉 𐑁𐐪𐑄𐐲𐑉𐑆, 𐐸𐐶𐐮𐐽 𐐪𐑉 𐐿𐐱𐑉𐐯𐐿𐐻, 𐐰𐑌𐐼 𐐸𐐶𐐮𐐽 𐐶𐐲𐑉 𐑀𐐮𐑂𐐲𐑌 𐑄𐐯𐑋 𐐺𐐴 𐑄 𐐸𐐰𐑌𐐼 𐐱𐑂 𐑄 𐐢𐐫𐑉𐐼.

4. 𐐤𐐵 𐐮𐐻 𐐮𐑆 𐑌𐐱𐐻 𐐿𐐱𐑋𐐲𐑌 𐑄𐐰𐐻 𐑄 𐑂𐑎𐑅 𐐱𐑂 𐑄 𐐹𐐨𐐹𐐲𐑊 𐐼𐐨𐑆𐐴𐑉𐐯𐑃 𐐯𐑌𐐨𐑃𐐮𐑍 𐐿𐐱𐑌𐐻𐑉𐐯𐑉𐐨 𐐻𐐭 𐑄𐐰𐐻 𐐸𐐶𐐮𐐽 𐐮𐑆 𐑉𐐴𐐻; 𐐺𐐲𐐻 𐐮𐐻 𐐮𐑆 𐐿𐐱𐑋𐐲𐑌 𐑁𐐫𐑉 𐑄 𐑊𐐯𐑅𐐲𐑉 𐐹𐐪𐑉𐐻 𐐱𐑂 𐑄 𐐹𐐨𐐹𐐲𐑊 𐐻𐐭 𐐼𐐨𐑆𐐴𐑉 𐑄𐐰𐐻 𐐸𐐶𐐮𐐽 𐐮𐑆 𐑌𐐱𐐻 𐑉𐐴𐐻; 𐑄𐐯𐑉𐑁𐐬𐑉 𐑄𐐮𐑅 𐑇𐐰𐑊 𐐷𐐨 𐐱𐐺𐑆𐐲𐑉𐑂, 𐐰𐑌𐐼 𐑋𐐩𐐿 𐐮𐐻 𐐷𐐭𐑉 𐑊𐐫 𐐻𐐭 𐐼𐐭 𐐷𐐭𐑉 𐐺𐐮𐑆-

𐑌𐐯𐑅 𐐺𐐴 𐑄 𐑂𐐱𐐮𐑅 𐐱𐑂 𐑄 𐐹𐐨𐐹𐑊. 𐐈𐑌𐐼 𐐮𐑁 𐑄 𐐻𐐴𐑋 𐐿𐐲𐑋𐑆 𐑄𐐰𐐻 𐑄 𐑂𐐱𐐮𐑅 𐐱𐑂 𐑄 𐐹𐐨𐐹𐑊 𐐼𐐲𐑃 𐐽𐐭𐑆 𐐮𐑌𐐮𐐿𐐶𐐮𐐻𐐨, 𐑄𐐯𐑌 𐐮𐑆 𐑄 𐐻𐐴𐑋 𐑄𐐰𐐻 𐑄 𐐾𐐲𐐾𐑋𐐯𐑌𐐻𐑅 𐐱𐑂 𐐘𐐱𐐼 𐐶𐐮𐑊 𐐿𐐲𐑋 𐐲𐐹𐐱𐑌 𐐷𐐭, 𐐷𐐩, 𐑄𐐯𐑌 𐐮𐑆 𐑄 𐐻𐐴𐑋 𐐸𐐨 𐐶𐐮𐑊 𐑂𐐮𐑆𐐮𐐻 𐐷𐐭 𐐶𐐮𐑃 𐑀𐑉𐐩𐐻 𐐼𐐯𐑅𐐻𐑉𐐲𐐿𐑇𐐲𐑌 𐐨𐑂𐐲𐑌 𐐰𐑆 𐐸𐐨 𐐸𐐰𐑆 𐐸𐐮𐑄𐐲𐑉𐐻𐐭 𐑂𐐮𐑆𐐮𐐻𐐯𐐼 𐑄𐐮𐑅 𐑊𐐰𐑌𐐼. 𐐈𐑌𐐼 𐑌𐐵 𐐮𐑁 𐐷𐐨 𐐸𐐰𐑂 𐐾𐐲𐐾𐐯𐑆, 𐐰𐑌𐐼 𐑄𐐩 𐐼𐐭 𐑌𐐱𐐻 𐐾𐐲𐐾 𐐷𐐭 𐐰𐐿𐐫𐑉𐐼𐐮𐑍 𐐻𐐭 𐑄 𐑊𐐫 𐐸𐐶𐐮𐐽 𐐸𐐰𐑆 𐐺𐐮𐑌 𐑀𐐮𐑂𐐲𐑌, 𐐷𐐨 𐐿𐐰𐑌 𐐿𐐫𐑆 𐑄𐐰𐐻 𐑄𐐩 𐑋𐐩 𐐺𐐨 𐐾𐐲𐐾𐐼 𐐱𐑂 𐐲 𐐸𐐴𐐲𐑉 𐐾𐐲𐐾. 𐐆𐑁 𐐷𐐳𐑉 𐐸𐐴𐐲𐑉 𐐾𐐲𐐾𐐯𐑆 𐐼𐐭 𐑌𐐱𐐻 𐐾𐐲𐐾 𐑉𐐴𐐽𐐲𐑅 𐐾𐐲𐐾𐑋𐐯𐑌𐐻𐑅, 𐐷𐐨 𐑇𐐰𐑊 𐐿𐐫𐑆 𐑄𐐰𐐻 𐐲 𐑅𐑋𐐫𐑊 𐑌𐐲𐑋𐐺𐐲𐑉 𐐱𐑂 𐐷𐐳𐑉 𐑊𐐬𐐲𐑉 𐐾𐐲𐐾𐐯𐑆 𐑇𐐳𐐼 𐐺𐐨 𐑀𐐰𐑄𐐲𐑉𐐼 𐐻𐐭𐑀𐐯𐑄𐐲𐑉, 𐐰𐑌𐐼 𐑄𐐩 𐑇𐐰𐑊 𐐾𐐲𐐾 𐐷𐐳𐑉 𐐸𐐴𐐲𐑉 𐐾𐐲𐐾𐐯𐑆, 𐐰𐐿𐐫𐑉𐐼𐐮𐑍 𐐻𐐭 𐑄 𐑂𐐱𐐮𐑅 𐐱𐑂 𐑄 𐐹𐐨𐐹𐑊. 𐐈𐑌𐐼 𐐌 𐐿𐐲𐑋𐐰𐑌𐐼 𐐷𐐭 𐐻𐐭 𐐼𐐭 𐑄𐐨𐑆 𐑃𐐮𐑍𐑆 𐐮𐑌 𐑄 𐑁𐐨𐑉 𐐱𐑂 𐑄 𐐢𐐫𐑉𐐼; 𐐰𐑌𐐼 𐐌 𐐿𐐲𐑋𐐰𐑌𐐼 𐐷𐐭 𐐻𐐭 𐐼𐐭 𐑄𐐨𐑆 𐑃𐐮𐑍𐑆, 𐐰𐑌𐐼 𐑄𐐰𐐻 𐐷𐐨 𐐸𐐰𐑂 𐑌𐐬 𐐿𐐮𐑍; 𐑄𐐰𐐻 𐐮𐑁 𐑄𐐨𐑆 𐐹𐐨𐐹𐑊 𐐿𐐲𐑋𐐮𐐻 𐑅𐐮𐑌𐑆 𐐰𐑌𐐼 𐐮𐑌𐐮𐐿𐐶𐐮𐐻𐐨𐑆, 𐑄𐐩 𐑇𐐰𐑊 𐐺𐐨 𐐰𐑌𐑅𐐲𐑉𐐼 𐐲𐐹𐐱𐑌 𐑄𐐩𐑉 𐐬𐑌 𐐸𐐯𐐼𐑆. 𐐙𐐫𐑉 𐐺𐐨𐐸𐐬𐑊𐐼 𐐌 𐑅𐐩 𐐲𐑌𐐻𐐭 𐐷𐐭, 𐑄 𐑅𐐮𐑌𐑆 𐐱𐑂 𐑋𐐯𐑌𐐨 𐐹𐐨𐐹𐑊 𐐸𐐰𐑂 𐐺𐐮𐑌 𐐿𐐫𐑆𐐼 𐐺𐐴 𐑄 𐐮𐑌𐐮𐐿𐐶𐐮𐐻𐐨𐑆 𐐱𐑂 𐑄𐐩𐑉 𐐿𐐮𐑍𐑆; 𐑄𐐩𐑉𐑁𐐫𐑉 𐑄𐐩𐑉 𐐮𐑌𐐮𐐿𐐶𐐮𐐻𐐨𐑆 𐐪𐑉 𐐰𐑌𐑅𐐲𐑉𐐼 𐐲𐐹𐐱𐑌 𐑄 𐐸𐐯𐐼𐑆 𐐱𐑂 𐑄𐐩𐑉 𐐿𐐮𐑍𐑆. 𐐈𐑌𐐼 𐑌𐐵 𐐌 𐐼𐐨𐑆𐐴𐑉 𐑄𐐰𐐻 𐑄𐐮𐑅 𐐮𐑌𐐨𐐿𐐶𐐱𐑊𐐮𐐻𐐨 𐑇𐐳𐐼 𐐺𐐨 𐑌𐐬 𐑋𐐫𐑉 𐐮𐑌 𐑄𐐮𐑅 𐑊𐐰𐑌𐐼, 𐐯𐑅𐐹𐐯𐑇𐐲𐑊𐐨 𐐲𐑋𐐲𐑍 𐑄𐐮𐑅 𐑋𐐴 𐐹𐐨𐐹𐑊; 𐐺𐐲𐐻 𐐌 𐐼𐐨𐑆𐐴𐑉 𐑄𐐰𐐻 𐑄𐐮𐑅 𐑊𐐰𐑌𐐼 𐐺𐐨 𐐲 𐑊𐐰𐑌𐐼 𐐱𐑂 𐑊𐐮𐐺𐐲𐑉𐐻𐐨, 𐐰𐑌𐐼 𐐯𐑂𐐲𐑉𐐨 𐑋𐐰𐑌 𐑋𐐩 𐐯𐑌𐐾𐐱𐐮 𐐸𐐮𐑆 𐑉𐐴𐐻𐑅 𐐰𐑌𐐼 𐐹𐑉𐐮𐑂𐐮𐑊𐐯𐐾𐐯𐑆 𐐲𐑊𐐴𐐿, 𐑅𐐬 𐑊𐐱𐑍 𐐰𐑆 𐑄 𐐢𐐫𐑉𐐼 𐑅𐐨𐑆 𐑁𐐮𐐻, 𐑄𐐰𐐻 𐐶𐐨 𐑋𐐩 𐑊𐐮𐑂 𐐰𐑌𐐼 𐐮𐑌𐐸𐐯𐑉𐐮𐐻 𐑄 𐑊𐐰𐑌𐐼, 𐐷𐐩, 𐐨𐑂𐐲𐑌 𐐰𐑆 𐑊𐐱𐑍 𐐰𐑆 𐐯𐑌𐐨 𐐱𐑂 𐐵𐑉 𐐹𐐱𐑅𐐻𐐯𐑉𐐮𐐻𐐨 𐑉𐐨𐑋𐐩𐑌𐑆 𐐲𐐹𐐱𐑌 𐑄 𐑁𐐩𐑅 𐐱𐑂 𐑄 𐑊𐐰𐑌𐐼. 𐐈𐑌𐐼 𐑋𐐯𐑌𐐨 𐑋𐐫𐑉 𐑃𐐮𐑍𐑆 𐐼𐐮𐐼 𐐿𐐮𐑍 𐐣𐐬𐑆𐐴𐐲 𐑉𐐴𐐻 𐐲𐑌𐐻𐐭 𐑄𐐯𐑋, 𐐲𐑌𐑁𐐬𐑊𐐼𐐮𐑍 𐐲𐑌𐐻𐐭 𐑄𐐯𐑋 𐐫𐑊 𐑄 𐐻𐑉𐐴𐐲𐑊𐑆 𐐰𐑌𐐼 𐐻𐑉𐐲𐐺𐑊𐑆 𐐱𐑂 𐐲 𐑉𐐴𐐽𐐲𐑅 𐐿𐐮𐑍; 𐐷𐐩, 𐐫𐑊 𐑄 𐐻𐑉𐐰𐑂𐐩𐑊𐑆 𐐱𐑂 𐑅𐐬𐑊 𐑁𐐫𐑉 𐑄𐐩𐑉 𐐹𐐨𐐹𐑊, 𐐰𐑌𐐼 𐐫𐑊𐑅𐐬 𐐫𐑊 𐑄 𐑋𐐲𐑉𐑋𐐲𐑉𐐮𐑍𐑆 𐐱𐑂 𐑄 𐐹𐐨𐐹𐑊 𐐻𐐭 𐑄𐐩𐑉 𐐿𐐮𐑍; 𐐰𐑌𐐼 𐐸𐐨 𐐯𐐿𐑅𐐹𐑊𐐩𐑌𐐼 𐐮𐐻 𐐫𐑊 𐐲𐑌𐐻𐐭 𐑄𐐯𐑋. 𐐈𐑌𐐼 𐐸𐐨 𐐻𐐬𐑊𐐼 𐑄𐐯𐑋 𐑄𐐰𐐻 𐑄𐐨𐑆 𐑃𐐮𐑍𐑆 𐐫𐐻 𐑌𐐱𐐻 𐐻𐐭 𐐺𐐨; 𐐺𐐲𐐻 𐑄𐐰𐐻 𐑄 𐐺𐐲𐑉𐐼𐐲𐑌 𐑇𐐳𐐼 𐐿𐐲𐑋 𐐲𐐹𐐱𐑌 𐐫𐑊 𐑄 𐐹𐐨𐐹𐑊, 𐑄𐐰𐐻 𐐯𐑂𐐲𐑉𐐨 𐑋𐐰𐑌 𐑋𐐴𐐻 𐐺𐐩𐑉 𐐸𐐮𐑆 𐐹𐐪𐑉𐐻. 𐐈𐑌𐐼 𐐸𐐨 𐐫𐑊𐑅𐐬 𐐲𐑌𐑁𐐬𐑊𐐼𐐯𐐼 𐐲𐑌𐐻𐐭 𐑄𐐯𐑋 𐐫𐑊 𐑄 𐐼𐐮𐑅𐐰𐐼𐑂𐐰𐑌𐐻𐐯𐐾𐐯𐑆 𐑄𐐩 𐑊𐐩𐐺𐐲𐑉𐐼 𐐲𐑌𐐼𐐲𐑉, 𐐺𐐴 𐐸𐐰𐑂𐐮𐑍 𐐰𐑌 𐐲𐑌𐑉𐐴𐐽𐐲𐑅 𐐿𐐮𐑍 𐐻𐐭 𐑉𐐭𐑊 𐐬𐑂𐐲𐑉 𐑄𐐯𐑋; 𐐷𐐩, 𐐫𐑊 𐐸𐐮𐑆 𐐮𐑌𐐮𐐿𐐶𐐮𐐻𐐨𐑆 𐐰𐑌𐐼 𐐲𐐺𐐱𐑋𐐮𐑌𐐩𐑇𐐲𐑌𐑆, 𐐰𐑌𐐼 𐐫𐑊 𐑄 𐐶𐐫𐑉𐑆, 𐐰𐑌𐐼 𐐿𐐱𐑌𐐻𐐯𐑌𐑇𐐲𐑌𐑆, 𐐰𐑌𐐼 𐐺𐑊𐐲𐐼𐑇𐐯𐐼, 𐐰𐑌𐐼 𐑄 𐑅𐐻𐐨𐑊𐐮𐑍, 𐐰𐑌𐐼 𐑄 𐐹𐑊𐐲𐑌𐐼𐐲𐑉𐐮𐑍, 𐐰𐑌𐐼 𐑄 𐐿𐐲𐑋𐐮𐐻𐐮𐑍 𐐱𐑂 𐐸𐐬𐑉𐐼𐐲𐑋𐑆, 𐐰𐑌𐐼 𐐫𐑊 𐑋𐐰𐑌𐐲𐑉 𐐱𐑂 𐐮𐑌𐐮𐐿𐐶𐐮𐐻𐐨𐑆 𐐸𐐶𐐮𐐽 𐐿𐐰𐑌𐐱𐐻 𐐺𐐨 𐐨𐑌𐐷𐐭𐑋𐐲𐑉𐐩𐐻𐐯𐐼; 𐐻𐐯𐑊𐐮𐑍 𐑄𐐯𐑋 𐑄𐐰𐐻 𐑄𐐨𐑆 𐑃𐐮𐑍𐑆 𐐫𐐻 𐑌𐐱𐐻 𐐻𐐭 𐐺𐐨; 𐑄𐐰𐐻 𐑄𐐩 𐐶𐐲𐑉 𐐯𐐿𐑅𐐹𐑉𐐯𐑅𐑊𐐨 𐑉𐐨𐐹𐐲𐑀𐑌𐐰𐑌𐐻 𐐻𐐭 𐑄 𐐿𐐲𐑋𐐰𐑌𐐼𐑋𐐯𐑌𐐻𐑅 𐐱𐑂 𐐘𐐱𐐼.

5. 𐐈𐑌𐐼 𐑌𐐵 𐐮𐐻 𐐿𐐩𐑋 𐐻𐐭 𐐹𐐰𐑅, 𐐰𐑁𐐻𐐲𐑉 𐐿𐐮𐑍 𐐣𐐬𐑆𐐴𐐲 𐐸𐐰𐐼 𐑅𐐯𐑌𐐻 𐑄𐐨𐑆 𐑃𐐮𐑍𐑆 𐑁𐐬𐑉𐑃 𐐲𐑋𐐲𐑍 𐑄 𐐹𐐨𐐹𐑊, 𐑄𐐩 𐐶𐐲𐑉 𐐿𐐱𐑌𐑂𐐮𐑌𐑅𐐻 𐐱𐑂 𐑄 𐐻𐑉𐐭𐑃 𐐱𐑂 𐐸𐐮𐑆 𐐶𐐲𐑉𐐼𐑆; 𐑄𐐩𐑉𐑁𐐫𐑉 𐑄𐐩 𐑉𐐨𐑊𐐮𐑍𐐿𐐶𐐮𐑇𐐻 𐑄𐐩𐑉 𐐼𐐨𐑆𐐴𐑉𐑆 𐑁𐐫𐑉 𐐲 𐐿𐐮𐑍, 𐐰𐑌𐐼 𐐺𐐨𐐿𐐩𐑋 𐐯𐐿𐑅𐐨𐐼𐐮𐑍𐑊𐐨 𐐰𐑍𐐿𐑇𐐲𐑅 𐑄𐐰𐐻 𐐯𐑂𐐲𐑉𐐨 𐑋𐐰𐑌 𐑇𐐳𐐼 𐐸𐐰𐑂 𐐰𐑌 𐐨𐐿𐐶𐐲𐑊 𐐽𐐰𐑌𐑅 𐑃𐑉𐐭𐐵𐐻 𐐫𐑊 𐑄 𐑊𐐰𐑌𐐼; 𐐷𐐩, 𐐰𐑌𐐼 𐐯𐑂𐐲𐑉𐐨 𐑋𐐰𐑌 𐐯𐐿𐑅𐐹𐑉𐐯𐑅𐐻 𐐲 𐐶𐐮𐑊𐐮𐑍𐑌𐐯𐑅 𐐻𐐭 𐐰𐑌𐑅𐐲𐑉 𐑁𐐫𐑉 𐐸𐐮𐑆 𐐬𐑌 𐑅𐐮𐑌𐑆. 𐐜𐐩𐑉𐑁𐐫𐑉, 𐐮𐐻 𐐿𐐩𐑋 𐐻𐐭 𐐹𐐰𐑅 𐑄𐐰𐐻 𐑄𐐩 𐐲𐑅𐐯𐑋𐐺𐑊𐐼 𐑄𐐯𐑋𐑅𐐯𐑊𐑂𐑆 𐐻𐐭𐑀𐐯𐑄𐐲𐑉 𐐮𐑌 𐐺𐐱𐐼𐐨𐑆 𐑃𐑉𐐭𐐵𐐻 𐑄 𐑊𐐰𐑌𐐼, 𐐻𐐭 𐐿𐐰𐑅𐐻 𐐮𐑌 𐑄𐐩𐑉 𐑂𐐱𐐮𐑅𐐯𐑆 𐐿𐐱𐑌𐑅𐐲𐑉𐑌𐐮𐑍 𐐸𐐭 𐑇𐐳𐐼 𐐺𐐨 𐑄𐐩𐑉 𐐾𐐲𐐾𐐯𐑆, 𐐻𐐭 𐐾𐐲𐐾 𐑄𐐯𐑋 𐐰𐐿𐐫𐑉𐐼𐐮𐑍 𐐻𐐭 𐑄 𐑊𐐫 𐐸𐐶𐐮𐐽 𐐸𐐰𐐼 𐐺𐐮𐑌 𐑀𐐮𐑂𐐲𐑌 𐑄𐐯𐑋; 𐐰𐑌𐐼 𐑄𐐩 𐐶𐐲𐑉 𐐯𐐿𐑅𐐨𐐼𐐮𐑍𐑊𐐨 𐑉𐐨𐐾𐐱𐐮𐑅𐐻 𐐺𐐨𐐿𐐫𐑆 𐐱𐑂 𐑄 𐑊𐐮𐐺𐐲𐑉𐐻𐐨 𐐸𐐶𐐮𐐽 𐐸𐐰𐐼 𐐺𐐮𐑌 𐑀𐑉𐐰𐑌𐐻𐐯𐐼 𐐲𐑌𐐻𐐭 𐑄𐐯𐑋. 𐐈𐑌𐐼 𐑄𐐩 𐐼𐐮𐐼 𐐶𐐰𐐿𐑅 𐑅𐐻𐑉𐐱𐑍 𐐮𐑌 𐑊𐐲𐑂 𐐻𐐬𐐲𐑉𐐼𐑆 𐐣𐐬𐑆𐐴𐐲; 𐐷𐐩, 𐑄𐐩 𐐼𐐮𐐼 𐐯𐑅𐐻𐐨𐑋 𐐸𐐮𐑋 𐑋𐐫𐑉 𐑄𐐰𐑌 𐐯𐑌𐐨 𐐲𐑄𐐲𐑉 𐑋𐐰𐑌; 𐑁𐐫𐑉 𐑄𐐩 𐐼𐐮𐐼 𐑌𐐱𐐻 𐑊𐐳𐐿 𐐲𐐹𐐱𐑌 𐐸𐐮𐑋 𐐰𐑆 𐐲 𐐻𐐴𐑉𐐲𐑌𐐻 𐐸𐐭 𐐶𐐱𐑆 𐑅𐐨𐐿𐐮𐑍 𐑁𐐫𐑉 𐑀𐐩𐑌, 𐐷𐐩, 𐑁𐐫𐑉 𐑄𐐰𐐻 𐑊𐐭𐐿𐐲𐑉 𐐸𐐶𐐮𐐽 𐐼𐐲𐑃 𐐿𐐲𐑉𐐲𐐹𐐻 𐑄 𐑅𐐬𐑊; 𐑁𐐫𐑉 𐐸𐐨 𐐸𐐰𐐼 𐑌𐐱𐐻 𐐯𐑀𐑆𐐰𐐿𐐻𐐯𐐼 𐑉𐐮𐐽𐐯𐑆 𐐱𐑂 𐑄𐐯𐑋, 𐑌𐐨𐑄𐐲𐑉 𐐸𐐰𐐼 𐐸𐐨 𐐼𐐨𐑊𐐴𐐻𐐯𐐼 𐐮𐑌 𐑄 𐑇𐐯𐐼𐐮𐑍 𐐱𐑂 𐐺𐑊𐐲𐐼; 𐐺𐐲𐐻 𐐸𐐨 𐐸𐐰𐐼 𐐯𐑅𐐻𐐰𐐺𐑊𐐮𐑇𐐻 𐐹𐐨𐑅 𐐮𐑌 𐑄 𐑊𐐰𐑌𐐼, 𐐰𐑌𐐼 𐐸𐐨 𐐸𐐰𐐼 𐑀𐑉𐐰𐑌𐐻𐐯𐐼 𐐲𐑌𐐻𐐭 𐐸𐐮𐑆 𐐹𐐨𐐹𐑊 𐑄𐐰𐐻 𐑄𐐩 𐑇𐐳𐐼 𐐺𐐨 𐐼𐐨𐑊𐐮𐑂𐐲𐑉𐐼 𐑁𐑉𐐱𐑋 𐐫𐑊 𐑋𐐰𐑌𐐲𐑉 𐐱𐑂 𐐺𐐱𐑌𐐼𐐯𐐾; 𐑄𐐩𐑉𐑁𐐫𐑉 𐑄𐐩 𐐼𐐮𐐼 𐐯𐑅𐐻𐐨𐑋 𐐸𐐮𐑋, 𐐷𐐩, 𐐯𐐿𐑅𐐨𐐼𐐮𐑍𐑊𐐨, 𐐺𐐨𐐷𐐱𐑌𐐼 𐑋𐐯𐑈𐐲𐑉. 𐐈𐑌𐐼 𐐮𐐻 𐐿𐐩𐑋 𐐻𐐭 𐐹𐐰𐑅 𐑄𐐰𐐻 𐑄𐐩 𐐼𐐮𐐼 𐐲𐐹𐐱𐐮𐑌𐐻 𐐾𐐲𐐾𐐯𐑆 𐐻𐐭 𐑉𐐭𐑊 𐐬𐑂𐐲𐑉 𐑄𐐯𐑋, 𐐫𐑉 𐐻𐐭 𐐾𐐲𐐾 𐑄𐐯𐑋 𐐰𐐿𐐫𐑉𐐼𐐮𐑍 𐐻𐐭 𐑄 𐑊𐐫; 𐐰𐑌𐐼 𐑄𐐮𐑅 𐑄𐐩 𐐼𐐮𐐼 𐑃𐑉𐐭𐐵𐐻 𐐫𐑊 𐑄 𐑊𐐰𐑌𐐼.

6. 𐐈𐑌𐐼 𐐮𐐻 𐐿𐐩𐑋 𐐻𐐭 𐐹𐐰𐑅 𐑄𐐰𐐻 𐐈𐑊𐑋𐐲 𐐶𐐲𐑆 𐐲𐐹𐐱𐐮𐑌𐐻𐐲𐐼 𐐻𐐭 𐐺 𐑄 𐑁𐐲𐑉𐑅𐐻 𐐕𐐨𐑁 𐐖𐐲𐐾; 𐐸𐐨 𐐺𐐨𐐮𐑍 𐐫𐑊𐑅𐐬 𐑄 𐐸𐐴 𐐹𐑉𐐨𐑅𐐻; 𐐸𐐮𐑆 𐑁𐐪𐑄𐐲𐑉 𐐸𐐰𐑂𐐮𐑍 𐐿𐐲𐑌𐑁𐐲𐑉𐐼 𐑄 𐐱𐑁𐐮𐑅 𐐲𐐹𐐱𐑌 𐐸𐐮𐑋, 𐐰𐑌𐐼 𐐸𐐰𐑂𐐮𐑍 𐑀𐐮𐑂𐐲𐑌 𐐸𐐮𐑋 𐑄 𐐽𐐪𐑉𐐾 𐐿𐐱𐑌𐑅𐐲𐑉𐑌𐐮𐑍 𐐫𐑊 𐑄 𐐰𐑁𐐩𐑉𐑆 𐐱𐑂 𐑄 𐐕𐐲𐑉𐐽. 𐐈𐑌𐐼 𐑌𐐵 𐐮𐐻 𐐿𐐩𐑋 𐐻𐐭 𐐹𐐰𐑅 𐑄𐐰𐐻 𐐈𐑊𐑋𐐲 𐐼𐐮𐐼 𐐶𐐫𐐿 𐐮𐑌 𐑄 𐐶𐐩𐑆 𐐱𐑂 𐑄 𐐢𐐫𐑉𐐼, 𐐰𐑌𐐼 𐐸𐐨 𐐼𐐮𐐼 𐐿𐐨𐐹 𐐸𐐮𐑆 𐐿𐐲𐑋𐐰𐑌𐐼𐑋𐐲𐑌𐐻𐑅, 𐐰𐑌𐐼 𐐸𐐨 𐐼𐐮𐐼 𐐾𐐲𐐾 𐑉𐐴𐐽𐐲𐑅 𐐾𐐲𐐾𐑋𐐲𐑌𐐻; 𐐰𐑌𐐼 𐑄𐐯𐑉 𐐶𐐲𐑆 𐐿𐐲𐑌𐐻𐐮𐑌𐐷𐐭𐐲𐑊 𐐹𐐨𐑅 𐑃𐑉𐐭 𐑄 𐑊𐐰𐑌𐐼; 𐐰𐑌𐐼 𐑄𐐲𐑅 𐐿𐐲𐑋𐐯𐑌𐑅𐐻 𐑄 𐑉𐐩𐑌 𐐱𐑂 𐑄 𐐾𐐲𐐾𐐯𐑆 𐑃𐑉𐐭𐐵𐐻 𐐫𐑊 𐑄 𐑊𐐰𐑌𐐼 𐐱𐑂 𐐞𐐰𐑉𐐲𐐸𐐯𐑋𐑊𐐲, 𐐲𐑋𐐲𐑍 𐐫𐑊 𐑄 𐐹𐐨𐐹𐑊 𐐸𐐭 𐐶𐐲𐑉 𐐿𐐫𐑊𐐼 𐑄 𐐤𐐨𐑁𐐴𐐻𐑅: 𐐰𐑌𐐼 𐐈𐑊𐑋𐐲 𐐶𐐲𐑆 𐑄 𐑁𐐲𐑉𐑅𐐻 𐐰𐑌𐐼 𐐕𐐨𐑁 𐐖𐐲𐐾. 𐐈𐑌𐐼 𐑌𐐵 𐐸𐐮𐑆 𐑁𐐪𐑄𐐲𐑉 𐐼𐐴𐐼, 𐐺𐐨𐐮𐑍 𐐩𐐻𐐨 𐐰𐑌𐐼 𐐻𐐭 𐐷𐐨𐑉𐑆 𐐬𐑊𐐼, 𐐸𐐰𐑂𐐮𐑍 𐑊𐐮𐑂𐐼 𐐻𐐭 𐑁𐐳𐑊𐑁𐐮𐑊 𐑄 𐐿𐐲𐑋𐐰𐑌𐐼𐑋𐐲𐑌𐐻𐑅 𐐱𐑂 𐐘𐐱𐐼.

7. 𐐈𐑌𐐼 𐐮𐐻 𐐿𐐩𐑋 𐐻𐐭 𐐹𐐰𐑅 𐑄𐐰𐐻 𐐣𐐬𐑅𐐴𐐲 𐐼𐐴𐐼 𐐫𐑊𐑅𐐬, 𐐮𐑌 𐑄 𐑃𐐲𐑉𐐻𐐨 𐐰𐑌𐐼 𐑃𐐲𐑉𐐼 𐐷𐐨𐑉 𐐱𐑂 𐐸𐐮𐑆 𐑉𐐩𐑌, 𐐺𐐨𐐮𐑍 𐑅𐐮𐐿𐑅𐐻𐐨 𐐰𐑌𐐼 𐑃𐑉𐐨 𐐷𐐨𐑉𐑆 𐐬𐑊𐐼; 𐑋𐐩𐐿𐐮𐑍 𐐮𐑌 𐑄 𐐸𐐬𐑊, 𐑁𐐴𐑂 𐐸𐐲𐑌𐐼𐑉𐐯𐐼 𐐰𐑌𐐼 𐑌𐐴𐑌 𐐷𐐨𐑉𐑆 𐑁𐑉𐐱𐑋 𐑄 𐐻𐐴𐑋 𐐢𐐨𐐸𐐴 𐑊𐐯𐑁𐐻 𐐖𐐨𐑉𐐭𐑅𐐲𐑊𐐯𐑋; 𐐰𐑌𐐼 𐑄𐐲𐑅 𐐯𐑌𐐼𐐯𐐼 𐑄 𐑉𐐩𐑌 𐐱𐑂 𐑄 𐐿𐐮𐑍𐑆 𐐬𐑂𐐲𐑉 𐑄 𐐹𐐨𐐹𐑊 𐐱𐑂 𐐤𐐨𐑁𐐴: 𐐰𐑌𐐼 𐑄𐐲𐑅 𐐯𐑌𐐼𐐯𐐼 𐑄 𐐼𐐩𐑆 𐐱𐑂 𐐈𐑊𐑋𐐲, 𐐸𐐭 𐐶𐐲𐑆 𐑄 𐑁𐐵𐑌𐐼𐐲𐑉 𐐱𐑂 𐑄𐐩𐑉 𐐕𐐲𐑉𐐽.

𐐜 𐐒𐐳𐐿 𐐱𐑂 𐐈𐑊𐑋𐐲,

𐐜 𐐝𐐲𐑌 𐐱𐑂 𐐈𐑊𐑋𐐲.

𐐕𐐰𐐹𐐻𐐲𐑉 I.

𐐜 𐐰𐐿𐐵𐑌𐐻 𐐱𐑂 𐐈𐑊𐑋𐐲, 𐐸𐐭 𐐶𐐱𐑆 𐑄 𐑅𐐲𐑌 𐐱𐑂 𐐈𐑊𐑋𐐲 𐑄 𐑁𐐲𐑉𐑅𐐻, 𐐰𐑌𐐼 𐐕𐐨𐑁 𐐖𐐲𐐾 𐐬𐑂𐐲𐑉 𐑄 𐐹𐐨𐐹𐑊 𐐱𐑂 𐐤𐐨𐑁𐐴, 𐐰𐑌𐐼 𐐫𐑊𐑅𐐬 𐑄 𐐐𐐴 𐐑𐑉𐐨𐑅𐐻 𐐬𐑂𐐲𐑉 𐑄 𐐕𐐲𐑉𐐽. 𐐈𐑌 𐐰𐐿𐐵𐑌𐐻 𐐱𐑂 𐑄 𐑉𐐩𐑌 𐐱𐑂 𐑄 𐐖𐐲𐐾𐐯𐑆, 𐐰𐑌𐐼 𐑄 𐐶𐐫𐑉𐑆 𐐰𐑌𐐼 𐐿𐐪𐑌𐐻𐐯𐑌𐑇𐐲𐑌𐑆 𐐲𐑋𐐲𐑍 𐑄 𐐹𐐨𐐹𐑊. 𐐈𐑌𐐼 𐐫𐑊𐑅𐐬 𐐰𐑌 𐐰𐐿𐐵𐑌𐐻 𐐱𐑂 𐐲 𐐶𐐫𐑉 𐐺𐐨𐐻𐐶𐐨𐑌 𐑄 𐐤𐐨𐑁𐐴𐐻𐑅 𐐰𐑌𐐼 𐑄 𐐢𐐩𐑋𐐲𐑌𐐴𐐻𐑅, 𐐰𐐿𐐫𐑉𐐼𐐮𐑍 𐐻𐐭 𐑄 𐑉𐐯𐐿𐐫𐑉𐐼 𐐱𐑂 𐐈𐑊𐑋𐐲 𐑄 𐑁𐐲𐑉𐑅𐐻 𐐰𐑌𐐼 𐐕𐐨𐑁 𐐖𐐲𐐾.

1. 𐐤𐐵 𐐮𐐻 𐐿𐐩𐑋 𐐻𐐭 𐐹𐐰𐑅 𐑄𐐰𐐻 𐐮𐑌 𐑄 𐑁𐐲𐑉𐑅𐐻 𐐷𐐨𐑉 𐐱𐑂 𐑄 𐑉𐐩𐑌 𐐱𐑂 𐑄 𐐖𐐲𐐾𐐯𐑆 𐐬𐑂𐐲𐑉 𐑄 𐐹𐐨𐐹𐑊 𐐱𐑂 𐐤𐐨𐑁𐐴, 𐑁𐑉𐐱𐑋 𐑄𐐮𐑅 𐐻𐐴𐑋 𐑁𐐫𐑉𐐶𐐲𐑉𐐼, 𐐿𐐮𐑍 𐐣𐐬𐑅𐐴𐐲 𐐸𐐰𐑂𐐮𐑍 𐑀𐐱𐑌 𐑄 𐐶𐐩 𐐱𐑂 𐐫𐑊 𐑄 𐐲𐑉𐑃, 𐐸𐐰𐑂𐐮𐑍 𐐶𐐫𐑉𐐼 𐐲 𐑀𐐳𐐼 𐐶𐐫𐑉𐑁𐐩𐑉, 𐐶𐐫𐐿𐐮𐑍 𐐲𐐹𐑉𐐴𐐻𐑊𐐨 𐐺𐐨𐑁𐐬𐑉 𐐘𐐱𐐼, 𐑊𐐨𐑂𐐮𐑍 𐑌𐐲𐑌 𐐻𐐭 𐑉𐐩𐑌 𐐮𐑌 𐐸𐐮𐑆 𐑅𐐻𐐯𐐼; 𐑌𐐯𐑂𐐲𐑉𐑄𐐯𐑊𐐯𐑅 𐐸𐐨 𐐸𐐰𐐼 𐐯𐑅𐐻𐐰𐐺𐑊𐐮𐑇𐐻 𐑊𐐫𐑆, 𐐰𐑌𐐼 𐑄𐐩 𐐶𐐲𐑉 𐐰𐐿𐑌𐐱𐑊𐐯𐐾𐐼 𐐺𐐴 𐑄 𐐹𐐨𐐹𐑊; 𐑄𐐯𐑉𐑁𐐬𐑉 𐑄𐐩 𐐶𐐲𐑉 𐐬𐐺𐑊𐐴𐐾𐐼 𐐻𐐭 𐐲𐐺𐐴𐐼 𐐺𐐴 𐑄 𐑊𐐫𐑆 𐐸𐐶𐐮𐐽 𐐸𐐨 𐐸𐐰𐐼 𐑋𐐩𐐼.

2. 𐐈𐑌𐐼 𐐮𐐻 𐐿𐐩𐑋 𐐻𐐭 𐐹𐐰𐑅 𐑄𐐰𐐻 𐐮𐑌 𐑄 𐑁𐐲𐑉𐑅𐐻 𐐷𐐨𐑉 𐐱𐑂 𐑄 𐑉𐐩𐑌 𐐱𐑂 𐐈𐑊𐑋𐐲 𐐮𐑌 𐑄 𐐾𐐲𐐾𐑋𐐯𐑌𐐻-𐑅𐐨𐐻, 𐑄𐐯𐑉 𐐶𐐱𐑆 𐐲 𐑋𐐰𐑌 𐐺𐑉𐐫𐐻 𐐺𐐨𐑁𐐬𐑉 𐐸𐐮𐑋 𐐻𐐭 𐐺𐐨 𐐾𐐲𐐾𐐼; 𐐲 𐑋𐐰𐑌 𐐸𐐭 𐐶𐐱𐑆 𐑊𐐪𐑉𐐾, 𐐰𐑌𐐼 𐐶𐐱𐑆 𐑌𐐬𐐻𐐯𐐼 𐑁𐐫𐑉 𐐸𐐮𐑆 𐑋𐐲𐐽 𐑅𐐻𐑉𐐯𐑍𐑃; 𐐰𐑌𐐼 𐐸𐐨 𐐸𐐰𐐼 𐑀𐐱𐑌 𐐲𐐺𐐵𐐻 𐐲𐑋𐐲𐑍 𐑄 𐐹𐐨𐐹𐑊, 𐐹𐑉𐐨𐐽𐐮𐑍 𐐻𐐭 𐑄𐐯𐑋 𐑄𐐰𐐻 𐐸𐐶𐐮𐐽 𐐸𐐨 𐐻𐐲𐑉𐑋𐐼 𐐻𐐭 𐐺𐐨 𐑄 𐐶𐐲𐑉𐐼 𐐱𐑂 𐐘𐐱𐐼, 𐐺𐐯𐑉𐐮𐑍 𐐼𐐵𐑌 𐐲𐑀𐐯𐑌𐑅𐐻 𐑄 𐐽𐐲𐑉𐐽; 𐐼𐐯𐐿𐑊𐐯𐑉𐐮𐑍 𐐲𐑌𐐻𐐭 𐑄 𐐹𐐨𐐹𐑊 𐑄𐐰𐐻 𐐯𐑂𐐲𐑉𐐨 𐐹𐑉𐐨𐑅𐐻 𐐰𐑌𐐼 𐐻𐐨𐐽𐐲𐑉 𐐫𐐻 𐐻𐐭 𐐺𐐨𐐿𐐲𐑋 𐐹𐐱𐐹𐐷𐐭𐑊𐐲𐑉; 𐐰𐑌𐐼 𐑄𐐩 𐐫𐐻 𐑌𐐱𐐻 𐐻𐐭 𐑊𐐩𐐺𐐲𐑉 𐐶𐐮𐑄 𐑄𐐯𐑉 𐐸𐐰𐑌𐐼𐑆, 𐐺𐐲𐐻 𐑄𐐰𐐻 𐑄𐐩 𐐫𐐻 𐐻𐐭 𐐺𐐨 𐑅𐐲𐐹𐐬𐑉𐐻𐐯𐐼 𐐺𐐴 𐑄 𐐹𐐨𐐹𐑊; 𐐰𐑌𐐼 𐐸𐐨 𐐫𐑊𐑅𐐬 𐐻𐐯𐑅𐐻𐐮𐑁𐐴𐐼 𐐲𐑌𐐻𐐭 𐑄 𐐹𐐨𐐹𐑊 𐑄𐐰𐐻 𐐫𐑊 𐑋𐐰𐑌𐐿𐐴𐑌𐐼 𐑇𐐳𐐼 𐐺𐐨 𐑅𐐩𐑂𐐼 𐐰𐐻 𐑄 𐑊𐐰𐑅𐐻 𐐼𐐩, 𐐰𐑌𐐼 𐑄𐐰𐐻 𐑄𐐩 𐑌𐐨𐐼 𐑌𐐱𐐻 𐑁𐐨𐑉 𐑌𐐫𐑉 𐐻𐑉𐐯𐑋𐐺𐑊, 𐐺𐐲𐐻 𐑄𐐰𐐻 𐑄𐐩 𐑋𐐴𐐻 𐑊𐐮𐑁𐐻 𐐲𐐹 𐑄𐐯𐑉 𐐸𐐯𐐼𐑆 𐐰𐑌𐐼 𐑉𐐨𐐾𐐱𐐮𐑅: 𐑁𐐫𐑉 𐑄 𐐢𐐫𐑉𐐼 𐐸𐐰𐐼 𐐿𐑉𐐨𐐩𐐻𐐯𐐼 𐐫𐑊 𐑋𐐯𐑌, 𐐰𐑌𐐼 𐐸𐐰𐐼 𐐫𐑊𐑅𐐬 𐑉𐐨𐐼𐐨𐑋𐐼 𐐫𐑊 𐑋𐐯𐑌; 𐐰𐑌𐐼 𐐮𐑌 𐑄 𐐯𐑌𐐼, 𐐫𐑊 𐑋𐐯𐑌 𐑇𐐳𐐼 𐐸𐐰𐑂 𐐨𐐻𐐲𐑉𐑌𐐲𐑊 𐑊𐐴𐑁. 𐐈𐑌𐐼 𐐮𐐻 𐐿𐐩𐑋 𐐻𐐭 𐐹𐐰𐑅 𐑄𐐰𐐻 𐐸𐐨 𐐼𐐮𐐼 𐐻𐐨𐐽 𐑄𐐨𐑆 𐑃𐐮𐑍𐑆 𐑅𐐬 𐑋𐐲𐐽, 𐑄𐐰𐐻 𐑋𐐯𐑌𐐨 𐐼𐐮𐐼 𐐺𐐨𐑊𐐨𐑂 𐐱𐑌 𐐸𐐮𐑆 𐐶𐐲𐑉𐐼𐑆, 𐐨𐑂𐐯𐑌 𐑅𐐬 𐑋𐐯𐑌𐐨 𐑄𐐰𐐻 𐑄𐐩 𐐺𐐨𐑀𐐰𐑌 𐐻𐐭 𐑅𐐲𐐹𐐬𐑉𐐻 𐐸𐐮𐑋 𐐰𐑌𐐼 𐑀𐐮𐑂 𐐸𐐮𐑋 𐑋𐐲𐑌𐐨; 𐐰𐑌𐐼 𐐸𐐨 𐐺𐐨𐑀𐐰𐑌 𐐻𐐭 𐐺𐐨 𐑊𐐮𐑁𐐻𐐯𐐼 𐐲𐐹 𐐮𐑌 𐑄 𐐹𐑉𐐴𐐼 𐐱𐑂 𐐸𐐮𐑆 𐐸𐐪𐑉𐐻, 𐐰𐑌𐐼 𐐻𐐭 𐐶𐐯𐑉 𐑂𐐯𐑉𐐨 𐐿𐐱𐑅𐐻𐑊𐐨 𐐲𐐹𐐯𐑉𐐯𐑊; 𐐷𐐩, 𐐰𐑌𐐼 𐐨𐑂𐐯𐑌 𐐺𐐨𐑀𐐰𐑌 𐐻𐐭 𐐯𐑅𐐻𐐰𐐺𐑊𐐮𐑇 𐐲 𐐽𐐲𐑉𐐽, 𐐰𐑁𐐻𐐲𐑉 𐑄 𐑋𐐰𐑌𐐲𐑉 𐐱𐑂 𐐸𐐮𐑆 𐐹𐑉𐐨𐐽𐐮𐑍.

3. 𐐈𐑌𐐼 𐐮𐐻 𐐿𐐩𐑋 𐐻𐐭 𐐹𐐰𐑅 𐐰𐑆 𐐸𐐨 𐐶𐐱𐑆 𐑀𐐬𐐮𐑍 𐐻𐐭 𐐹𐑉𐐨𐐽 𐐻𐐭 𐑄𐐬𐑆 𐐸𐐭 𐐺𐐨𐑊𐐨𐑂𐐼 𐐱𐑌 𐐸𐐮𐑆 𐐶𐐲𐑉𐐼, 𐐸𐐨 𐑋𐐯𐐻 𐐲 𐑋𐐰𐑌 𐐸𐐭 𐐺𐐨𐑊𐐱𐑍𐐼 𐐻𐐭 𐑄 𐐽𐐲𐑉𐐽 𐐱𐑂 𐐘𐐱𐐼, 𐐷𐐩, 𐐨𐑂𐐯𐑌 𐐶𐐲𐑌 𐐱𐑂 𐑄𐐯𐑉 𐐻𐐨𐐽𐐲𐑉𐑆; 𐐰𐑌𐐼 𐐸𐐨 𐐺𐐨𐑀𐐰𐑌 𐐻𐐭 𐐿𐐱𐑌𐐻𐐯𐑌𐐼 𐐶𐐮𐑄 𐐸𐐮𐑋 𐑇𐐪𐑉𐐹𐑊𐐨, 𐑄𐐰𐐻 𐐸𐐨 𐑋𐐴𐐻 𐑊𐐨𐐼 𐐲𐐶𐐩 𐑄 𐐹𐐨𐐹𐑊 𐐱𐑂 𐑄 𐐽𐐲𐑉𐐽; 𐐺𐐲𐐻 𐑄 𐑋𐐰𐑌 𐐶𐐮𐑄𐑅𐐻𐐳𐐼 𐐸𐐮𐑋, 𐐰𐐼𐑋𐐱𐑌𐐮𐑇𐐮𐑍 𐐸𐐮𐑋 𐐶𐐮𐑄 𐑄 𐐶𐐲𐑉𐐼𐑆 𐐱𐑂 𐐘𐐱𐐼. 𐐤𐐵 𐑄 𐑌𐐩𐑋 𐐱𐑂 𐑄 𐑋𐐰𐑌 𐐶𐐱𐑆 𐐘𐐮𐐼𐐨𐐲𐑌; 𐐰𐑌𐐼 𐐮𐐻 𐐶𐐱𐑆 𐐸𐐨 𐐸𐐭 𐐶𐐱𐑆 𐐰𐑌 𐐮𐑌𐑅𐐻𐑉𐐭𐑋𐐯𐑌𐐻 𐐮𐑌 𐑄 𐐸𐐰𐑌𐐼𐑆 𐐱𐑂 𐐘𐐱𐐼, 𐐮𐑌 𐐼𐐯𐑊𐐮𐑂𐐲𐑉𐐮𐑍 𐑄 𐐹𐐨𐐹𐑊 𐐱𐑂 𐐢𐐮𐑋𐐸𐐴 𐐵𐐻 𐐱𐑂 𐐺𐐱𐑌𐐼𐐲𐐾. 𐐤𐐵, 𐐺𐐨𐐿𐐫𐑆 𐐘𐐮𐐼𐐨𐐲𐑌 𐐶𐐮𐑄𐑅𐐻𐐳𐐼 𐐸𐐮𐑋

𐐶𐐮𐑄 𐑄 𐐶𐐲𐑉𐐼𐑆 𐐱𐑂 𐐘𐐱𐐼, 𐐸𐐨 𐐶𐐱𐑆 𐑉𐐫𐑃 𐐶𐐮𐑄 𐐘𐐮𐐼𐐨𐐲𐑌, 𐐰𐑌𐐼 𐐼𐑉𐐭 𐐸𐐮𐑆 𐑅𐐬𐑉𐐼 𐐰𐑌𐐼 𐐺𐐨𐑀𐐰𐑌 𐐻𐐭 𐑅𐑋𐐴𐐻 𐐸𐐮𐑋. 𐐤𐐵 𐐘𐐮𐐼𐐨𐐲𐑌 𐐺𐐨𐐮𐑍 𐑅𐐻𐑉𐐮𐐿𐐲𐑌 𐐶𐐮𐑄 𐑋𐐯𐑌𐐨 𐐷𐐨𐑉𐑆, 𐑄𐐯𐑉𐑁𐐬𐑉 𐐸𐐨 𐐶𐐱𐑆 𐑌𐐱𐐻 𐐩𐐺𐑊 𐐻𐐭 𐐶𐐮𐑄𐑅𐐻𐐰𐑌𐐼 𐐸𐐮𐑆 𐐺𐑊𐐬𐑆, 𐑄𐐯𐑉𐑁𐐬𐑉 𐐸𐐨 𐐶𐐱𐑆 𐑅𐑊𐐩𐑌 𐐺𐐴 𐑄 𐑅𐐬𐑉𐐼; 𐐰𐑌𐐼 𐑄 𐑋𐐰𐑌 𐐸𐐭 𐑅𐑊𐐭 𐐸𐐮𐑋 𐐶𐐱𐑆 𐐻𐐩𐐿𐐲𐑌 𐐺𐐴 𐑄 𐐹𐐨𐐹𐑊 𐐱𐑂 𐑄 𐐕𐐲𐑉𐐽, 𐐰𐑌𐐼 𐐶𐐱𐑆 𐐺𐑉𐐫𐐻 𐐺𐐨𐑁𐐬𐑉 𐐈𐑊𐑋𐐲, 𐐻𐐭 𐐺𐐨 𐐾𐐲𐐾𐐼 𐐲𐐿𐐫𐑉𐐼𐐮𐑍 𐐻𐐭 𐑄 𐐿𐑉𐐴𐑋𐑆 𐐸𐐶𐐮𐐽 𐐸𐐨 𐐸𐐰𐐼 𐐿𐐱𐑋𐐮𐐻𐐲𐐼. 𐐈𐑌𐐼 𐐮𐐻 𐐿𐐩𐑋 𐐻𐐭 𐐹𐐪𐑅 𐑄𐐰𐐻 𐐸𐐨 𐑅𐐻𐐳𐐼 𐐺𐐨𐑁𐐬𐑉 𐐈𐑊𐑋𐐲, 𐐰𐑌𐐼 𐐹𐑊𐐯𐐼 𐑁𐐫𐑉 𐐸𐐮𐑋𐑅𐐯𐑊𐑁 𐐶𐐮𐑄 𐑋𐐲𐐽 𐐺𐐬𐑊𐐼𐑌𐐯𐑅. 𐐒𐐲𐐻 𐐈𐑊𐑋𐐲 𐑅𐐯𐐼 𐐲𐑌𐐻𐐭 𐐸𐐮𐑋, 𐐒𐐨𐐸𐐬𐑊𐐼, 𐑄𐐮𐑅 𐐮𐑆 𐑄 𐑁𐐲𐑉𐑅𐐻 𐐻𐐴𐑋 𐑄𐐰𐐻 𐐹𐑉𐐨𐑅𐐻𐐿𐑉𐐰𐑁𐐻 𐐸𐐰𐑆 𐐺𐐨𐑌 𐐮𐑌𐐻𐑉𐐬𐐼𐐷𐐭𐑅𐐻 𐐲𐑋𐐲𐑍 𐑄𐐮𐑅 𐐹𐐨𐐹𐑊. 𐐈𐑌𐐼 𐐺𐐨𐐸𐐬𐑊𐐼 𐑄𐐵 𐐪𐑉𐐻 𐑌𐐱𐐻 𐐬𐑌𐑊𐐨 𐑀𐐮𐑊𐐻𐐨 𐐱𐑂 𐐹𐑉𐐨𐑅𐐻𐐿𐑉𐐰𐑁𐐻, 𐐺𐐲𐐻 𐐸𐐰𐑅𐐻 𐐯𐑌𐐼𐐯𐑂𐐲𐑉𐐼 𐐻𐐭 𐐯𐑌𐑁𐐬𐑉𐑅 𐐮𐐻 𐐺𐐴 𐑄 𐑅𐐬𐑉𐐼; 𐐰𐑌𐐼 𐐶𐐲𐑉 𐐹𐑉𐐨𐑅𐐻𐐿𐑉𐐰𐑁𐐻 𐐻𐐭 𐐺𐐨 𐐯𐑌𐑁𐐬𐑉𐑅𐐻 𐐲𐑋𐐲𐑍 𐑄𐐮𐑅 𐐹𐐨𐐹𐑊, 𐐮𐐻 𐐶𐐳𐐼 𐐹𐑉𐐭𐑂 𐑄𐐩𐑉 𐐯𐑌𐐻𐐴𐑉 𐐼𐐨𐑅𐐻𐑉𐐲𐐿𐑇𐐲𐑌. 𐐈𐑌𐐼 𐑄𐐵 𐐸𐐰𐑅𐐻 𐑇𐐯𐐼 𐑄 𐐺𐑊𐐲𐐼 𐐱𐑂 𐐩 𐑉𐐴𐐽𐐲𐑅 𐑋𐐰𐑌, 𐐷𐐩, 𐐩 𐑋𐐰𐑌 𐐸𐐭 𐐸𐐰𐑆 𐐼𐐲𐑌 𐑋𐐲𐐽 𐑀𐐳𐐼 𐐲𐑋𐐲𐑍 𐑄𐐮𐑅 𐐹𐐨𐐹𐑊; 𐐰𐑌𐐼 𐐶𐐲𐑉 𐐶𐐨 𐐻𐐭 𐑅𐐹𐐩𐑉 𐑄𐐨, 𐐸𐐮𐑆 𐐺𐑊𐐲𐐼 𐐶𐐳𐐼 𐐿𐐲𐑋 𐐲𐐹𐐱𐑌 𐐲𐑅 𐑁𐐫𐑉 𐑂𐐯𐑌𐐾𐐲𐑌𐑅; 𐑄𐐯𐑉𐑁𐐬𐑉 𐑄𐐵 𐐪𐑉𐐻 𐐿𐐱𐑌𐐼𐐯𐑋𐐼 𐐻𐐭 𐐼𐐴, 𐐲𐐿𐐫𐑉𐐼𐐮𐑍 𐐻𐐭 𐑄 𐑊𐐫 𐐸𐐶𐐮𐐽 𐐸𐐰𐑆 𐐺𐐨𐑌 𐑀𐐮𐑂𐐲𐑌 𐐲𐑅 𐐺𐐴 𐐣𐐬𐑆𐐴𐐲, 𐐵𐐲𐑉 𐑊𐐪𐑅𐐻 𐐿𐐮𐑍; 𐐰𐑌𐐼 𐐮𐐻 𐐸𐐰𐑆 𐐺𐐨𐑌 𐐰𐐿𐑌𐐱𐑊𐐯𐐾𐐼 𐐺𐐴 𐑄𐐮𐑅 𐐹𐐨𐐹𐑊; 𐑄𐐯𐑉𐑁𐐬𐑉, 𐑄𐐮𐑅 𐐹𐐨𐐹𐑊 𐑋𐐲𐑅𐐻 𐐲𐐺𐐴𐐼 𐐺𐐴 𐑄 𐑊𐐫.

4. 𐐈𐑌𐐼 𐐮𐐻 𐐿𐐩𐑋 𐐻𐐭 𐐹𐐪𐑅 𐑄𐐰𐐻 𐐸𐐨 𐐶𐐱𐑆 𐐿𐐰𐑉𐐨𐐼 𐐲𐐹𐐱𐑌 𐑄 𐐻𐐱𐐹 𐐱𐑂 𐑄 𐐸𐐮𐑊 𐐣𐐰𐑌𐐻𐐴, 𐐰𐑌𐐼 𐑄𐐯𐑉 𐐸𐐨 𐐶𐐱𐑆 𐐿𐐫𐑆𐐼, 𐐫𐑉 𐑉𐐪𐑄𐐲𐑉 𐐼𐐮𐐼 𐐰𐐿𐑌𐐱𐑊𐐯𐐾, 𐐺𐐨𐐻𐐶𐐨𐑌 𐑄 𐐸𐐯𐑂𐐲𐑌𐑆 𐐰𐑌𐐼 𐑄 𐐲𐑉𐑃, 𐑄𐐰𐐻 𐐸𐐶𐐱𐐻 𐐸𐐨 𐐸𐐰𐐼 𐐻𐐫𐐻 𐐻𐐭 𐑄 𐐹𐐨𐐹𐑊 𐐶𐐱𐑆 𐐿𐐱𐑌𐐻𐑉𐐯𐑉𐐨 𐐻𐐭 𐑄 𐐶𐐲𐑉𐐼 𐐱𐑂 𐐘𐐱𐐼; 𐐰𐑌𐐼 𐑄𐐯𐑉 𐐸𐐨 𐑅𐐲𐑁𐐲𐑉𐐼 𐐰𐑌 𐐮𐑀𐑌𐐬𐑋𐐮𐑌𐐨𐐲𐑅 𐐼𐐯𐑃. 𐐤𐐯𐑂𐐲𐑉𐑄𐐲𐑊𐐯𐑅, 𐑄𐐮𐑅 𐐼𐐮𐐼 𐑌𐐱𐐻 𐐹𐐳𐐻 𐐰𐑌 𐐯𐑌𐐼 𐐻𐐭 𐑄 𐑅𐐹𐑉𐐯𐐼𐐮𐑍 𐐱𐑂 𐐹𐑉𐐨𐑅𐐻𐐿𐑉𐐰𐑁𐐻 𐑃𐑉𐐭 𐑄 𐑊𐐰𐑌𐐼; 𐑁𐐫𐑉 𐑄𐐯𐑉 𐐶𐐲𐑉 𐑋𐐯𐑌𐐨 𐐸𐐭 𐑊𐐲𐑂𐐼 𐑄 𐑂𐐩𐑌 𐑃𐐮𐑍𐑆 𐐱𐑂 𐑄 𐐶𐐲𐑉𐑊𐐼, 𐐰𐑌𐐼 𐑄𐐩 𐐶𐐯𐑌𐐻 𐑁𐐬𐑉𐑃 𐐹𐑉𐐨𐐽𐐮𐑍 𐑁𐐫𐑊𐑅 𐐼𐐱𐐿𐐻𐑉𐐮𐑌𐑆; 𐐰𐑌𐐼 𐑄𐐮𐑅 𐑄𐐩 𐐼𐐮𐐼 𐑁𐐫𐑉 𐑄 𐑅𐐩𐐿 𐐱𐑂 𐑉𐐮𐐽𐐯𐑆 𐐰𐑌𐐼 𐐱𐑌𐐲𐑉. 𐐤𐐯𐑂𐐲𐑉𐑄𐐲𐑊𐐯𐑅, 𐑄𐐩 𐐼𐐲𐑉𐑅𐐻 𐑌𐐱𐐻 𐑊𐐴, 𐐮𐑁 𐐮𐐻 𐐶𐐲𐑉 𐑌𐐬𐑌, 𐑁𐐫𐑉 𐑁𐐨𐑉 𐐱𐑂 𐑄 𐑊𐐫, 𐑁𐐫𐑉 𐑊𐐴𐐲𐑉𐑆 𐐶𐐲𐑉 𐐹𐐲𐑌𐐮𐑇𐐻; 𐑄𐐯𐑉𐑁𐐬𐑉 𐑄𐐩 𐐹𐑉𐐨𐐻𐐯𐑌𐐼𐐲𐐼 𐐻𐐭 𐐹𐑉𐐨𐐽 𐐲𐐿𐐫𐑉𐐼𐐮𐑍 𐐻𐐭 𐑄𐐩𐑉 𐐺𐐨𐑊𐐨𐑁: 𐐰𐑌𐐼 𐑌𐐵 𐑄 𐑊𐐫 𐐿𐐳𐐼 𐐸𐐰𐑂 𐑌𐐬 𐐹𐐵𐐲𐑉 𐐱𐑌 𐐯𐑌𐐨 𐑋𐐰𐑌 𐑁𐐫𐑉 𐐸𐐮𐑆 𐐺𐐨𐑊𐐨𐑁. 𐐈𐑌𐐼 𐑄𐐩 𐐼𐐲𐑉𐑅𐐻 𐑌𐐱𐐻 𐑅𐐻𐐨𐑊, 𐑁𐐫𐑉 𐑁𐐨𐑉 𐐱𐑂 𐑄 𐑊𐐫; 𐑁𐐫𐑉 𐑅𐐲𐐽 𐐶𐐲𐑉 𐐹𐐲𐑌𐐮𐑇𐐻; 𐑌𐐨𐑄𐐲𐑉 𐐼𐐲𐑉𐑅𐐻 𐑄𐐩 𐑉𐐱𐐺, 𐑌𐐫𐑉 𐑋𐐲𐑉𐐼𐐲𐑉: 𐑁𐐫𐑉 𐐸𐐨 𐑄𐐰𐐻 𐑋𐐲𐑉𐐼𐐲𐑉𐐼 𐐶𐐱𐑆 𐐹𐐲𐑌𐐮𐑇𐐻 𐐲𐑌𐐻𐐭 𐐼𐐯𐑃.

5. 𐐤𐐵 𐐮𐐻 𐐿𐐩𐑋 𐐻𐐭 𐐹𐐪𐑅 𐑄𐐰𐐻 𐐸𐐭𐑅𐐬𐐯𐑂𐐲𐑉 𐐼𐐮𐐼 𐑌𐐱𐐻 𐐺𐐨𐑊𐐱𐑍 𐐻𐐭 𐑄 𐐕𐐲𐑉𐐽 𐐱𐑂 𐐘𐐱𐐼, 𐐺𐐨𐑀𐐰𐑌 𐐻𐐭 𐐹𐐲𐑉𐑅𐐨𐐿𐐷𐐭𐐻 𐑄𐐬𐑆 𐑄𐐰𐐻 𐐼𐐮𐐼 𐐺𐐨𐑊𐐱𐑍 𐐻𐐭 𐑄 𐐕𐐲𐑉𐐽 𐐱𐑂 𐐘𐐱𐐼, 𐐰𐑌𐐼 𐐸𐐰𐐼 𐐻𐐩𐐿𐐲𐑌 𐐲𐐹𐐱𐑌 𐑄𐐯𐑋 𐑄 𐑌𐐩𐑋 𐐱𐑂 𐐗𐑉𐐴𐑅𐐻; 𐐷𐐩, 𐑄𐐩 𐐼𐐮𐐼 𐐹𐐲𐑉𐑅𐐨𐐿𐐷𐐭𐐻 𐑄𐐯𐑋, 𐐰𐑌𐐼 𐐰𐑁𐑊𐐮𐐿𐐻 𐑄𐐯𐑋 𐐶𐐮𐑄 𐐫𐑊 𐑋𐐰𐑌𐐲𐑉 𐐱𐑂 𐐶𐐲𐑉𐐼𐑆, 𐐰𐑌𐐼 𐑄𐐮𐑅 𐐺𐐨𐐿𐐫𐑆 𐐱𐑂 𐑄𐐩𐑉 𐐸𐐷𐐭𐑋𐐮𐑊𐐮𐐻𐐨; 𐐺𐐨𐐿𐐫𐑆 𐑄𐐩 𐐶𐐲𐑉 𐑌𐐱𐐻 𐐹𐑉𐐵𐐼 𐐮𐑌 𐑄𐐩𐑉 𐐬𐑌 𐐴𐑆, 𐐰𐑌𐐼 𐐺𐐨𐐿𐐫𐑆 𐑄𐐩 𐐼𐐮𐐼 𐐮𐑋𐐹𐐪𐑉𐐻 𐑄 𐐶𐐲𐑉𐐼 𐐱𐑂 𐐘𐐱𐐼, 𐐶𐐲𐑌 𐐶𐐮𐑄 𐐲𐑌𐐲𐑄𐐲𐑉, 𐐶𐐮𐑄𐐵𐐻 𐑋𐐲𐑌𐐨, 𐐰𐑌𐐼 𐐶𐐮𐑄𐐵𐐻 𐐹𐑉𐐴𐑅. 𐐤𐐵 𐑄𐐯𐑉 𐐶𐐱𐑆 𐐩 𐑅𐐻𐑉𐐮𐐿𐐻 𐑊𐐫 𐐲𐑋𐐲𐑍 𐑄 𐐹𐐨𐐹𐑊 𐐱𐑂 𐑄 𐐕𐐲𐑉𐐽, 𐑄𐐰𐐻 𐑄𐐯𐑉 𐑇𐐳𐐼 𐑌𐐱𐐻 𐐯𐑌𐐨 𐑋𐐰𐑌, 𐐺𐐨𐑊𐐱𐑍𐐮𐑍 𐐻𐐭 𐑄 𐐕𐐲𐑉𐐽, 𐐲𐑉𐐴𐑆 𐐰𐑌𐐼 𐐹𐐲𐑉𐑅𐐨𐐿𐐷𐐭𐐻 𐑄𐐬𐑆 𐑄𐐰𐐻 𐐼𐐮𐐼 𐑌𐐱𐐻 𐐺𐐨𐑊𐐱𐑍 𐐻𐐭 𐑄 𐐕𐐲𐑉𐐽, 𐐰𐑌𐐼 𐑄𐐰𐐻 𐑄𐐯𐑉 𐑇𐐳𐐼 𐐺𐐨 𐑌𐐬 𐐹𐐲𐑉𐑅𐐨𐐿𐐷𐐭𐑇𐐲𐑌 𐐲𐑋𐐲𐑍 𐑄𐐯𐑋𐑅𐐯𐑊𐑂𐑆. 𐐤𐐯𐑂𐐲𐑉𐑄𐐲𐑊𐐯𐑅, 𐑄𐐯𐑉 𐐶𐐲𐑉 𐑋𐐯𐑌𐐨 𐐲𐑋𐐲𐑍 𐑄𐐯𐑋 𐐸𐐭 𐐺𐐨𐑀𐐰𐑌 𐐻𐐭 𐐺𐐨 𐐹𐑉𐐵𐐼, 𐐰𐑌𐐼 𐐺𐐨𐑀𐐰𐑌 𐐻𐐭 𐐿𐐱𐑌𐐻𐐯𐑌𐐼 𐐶𐐫𐑉𐑋𐑊𐐨 𐐶𐐮𐑄 𐑄𐐩𐑉 𐐰𐐼𐑂𐐲𐑉𐑅𐐯𐑉𐐨𐑆, 𐐨𐑂𐐲𐑌 𐐲𐑌𐐻𐐭 𐐺𐑊𐐬𐑆; 𐐷𐐩, 𐑄𐐩 𐐶𐐳𐐼 𐑅𐑋𐐴𐐻 𐐶𐐲𐑌 𐐲𐑌𐐲𐑄𐐲𐑉 𐐶𐐮𐑄 𐑄𐐩𐑉 𐑁𐐮𐑅𐐻𐑅. 𐐤𐐵, 𐑄𐐮𐑅 𐐶𐐱𐑆 𐐮𐑌 𐑄 𐑅𐐯𐐿𐐲𐑌𐐼 𐐷𐐨𐑉 𐐱𐑂 𐑄 𐑉𐐩𐑌 𐐱𐑂 𐐈𐑊𐑋𐐲, 𐐰𐑌𐐼 𐐮𐐻 𐐶𐐱𐑆 𐐩 𐐿𐐫𐑆 𐐱𐑂 𐑋𐐲𐐽 𐐰𐑁𐑊𐐮𐐿𐑇𐐲𐑌 𐐻𐐭 𐑄 𐐕𐐲𐑉𐐽; 𐐷𐐩, 𐐮𐐻 𐐶𐐱𐑆 𐑄 𐐿𐐫𐑆 𐐱𐑂 𐑋𐐲𐐽 𐐻𐑉𐐴𐐲𐑊 𐐶𐐮𐑄 𐑄 𐐕𐐲𐑉𐐽; 𐑁𐐫𐑉 𐑄 𐐸𐐪𐑉𐐻𐑅 𐐱𐑂 𐑋𐐯𐑌𐐨 𐐶𐐲𐑉 𐐸𐐪𐑉𐐼𐐲𐑌𐐼, 𐐰𐑌𐐼 𐑄𐐩𐑉 𐑌𐐩𐑋𐑆 𐐶𐐲𐑉 𐐺𐑊𐐱𐐻𐐲𐐼 𐐵𐐻, 𐑄𐐰𐐻 𐑄𐐩 𐐶𐐲𐑉 𐑉𐐨𐑋𐐯𐑋𐐺𐐲𐑉𐐼 𐑌𐐬 𐑋𐐬𐑉 𐐲𐑋𐐲𐑍 𐑄 𐐹𐐨𐐹𐑊 𐐱𐑂 𐐘𐐱𐐼. 𐐈𐑌𐐼 𐐫𐑊𐑅𐐬 𐑋𐐯𐑌𐐨 𐐶𐐮𐑄𐐼𐑉𐐭 𐑄𐐯𐑋𐑅𐐯𐑊𐑂𐑆 𐑁𐑉𐐱𐑋 𐐲𐑋𐐲𐑍 𐑄𐐯𐑋. 𐐤𐐵 𐑄𐐮𐑅 𐐶𐐱𐑆 𐐩 𐑀𐑉𐐩𐐻 𐐻𐑉𐐴𐐲𐑊 𐐻𐐭 𐑄𐐬𐑆 𐑄𐐰𐐻 𐐼𐐮𐐼 𐑅𐐻𐐰𐑌𐐼 𐑁𐐪𐑅𐐻 𐐮𐑌 𐑄 𐑁𐐩𐑃; 𐑌𐐯𐑂𐐲𐑉𐑄𐐲𐑊𐐯𐑅, 𐑄𐐩 𐐶𐐲𐑉 𐑅𐐻𐐯𐐼𐑁𐐪𐑅𐐻 𐐰𐑌𐐼 𐐮𐑋𐐭𐑂𐐲𐐺𐑊 𐐮𐑌 𐐿𐐨𐐹𐐮𐑍 𐑄 𐐿𐐱𐑋𐐰𐑌𐐼𐑋𐐲𐑌𐐻𐑅 𐐱𐑂 𐐘𐐱𐐼, 𐐰𐑌𐐼 𐑄𐐩 𐐺𐐬𐑉 𐐶𐐮𐑄 𐐹𐐩𐑇𐐯𐑌𐑅 𐑄 𐐹𐐲𐑉𐑅𐐨𐐿𐐷𐐭𐑇𐐲𐑌 𐐸𐐶𐐮𐐽 𐐶𐐱𐑆 𐐸𐐨𐐹𐐻 𐐲𐐹𐐱𐑌 𐑄𐐯𐑋.

6. 𐐰𐑌𐐼 𐐶𐐯𐑌 𐑄 𐐹𐑉𐐨𐑅𐐻𐑅 𐑊𐐯𐑁𐐻 𐑄𐐩𐑉 𐑊𐐩𐐺𐐲𐑉 𐐻𐐭 𐐮𐑋𐐹𐐪𐑉𐐻 𐑄 𐐶𐐲𐑉𐐼 𐐱𐑂 𐐘𐐱𐐼 𐐲𐑌𐐻𐐭 𐑄 𐐹𐐨𐐹𐑊, 𐑄 𐐹𐐨𐐹𐑊 𐐫𐑊𐑅𐐬 𐑊𐐯𐑁𐐻 𐑄𐐩𐑉 𐑊𐐩𐐺𐐲𐑉𐑆 𐐻𐐭 𐐸𐐨𐑉 𐑄 𐐶𐐲𐑉𐐼 𐐱𐑂 𐐘𐐱𐐼. 𐐰𐑌𐐼 𐐶𐐯𐑌 𐑄 𐐹𐑉𐐨𐑅𐐻 𐐸𐐰𐐼 𐐮𐑋𐐹𐐪𐑉𐐻𐐯𐐼 𐐲𐑌𐐻𐐭 𐑄𐐯𐑋 𐑄 𐐶𐐲𐑉𐐼 𐐱𐑂 𐐘𐐱𐐼, 𐑄𐐩 𐐫𐑊 𐑉𐐨𐐻𐐲𐑉𐑌𐐼 𐐲𐑀𐐯𐑌 𐐼𐐮𐑊𐐮𐐾𐐯𐑌𐐻𐑊𐐨 𐐲𐑌𐐻𐐭 𐑄𐐩𐑉 𐑊𐐩𐐺𐐲𐑉𐑆; 𐐰𐑌𐐼 𐑄 𐐹𐑉𐐨𐑅𐐻, 𐑌𐐱𐐻 𐐯𐑅𐐻𐐨𐑋𐐮𐑍 𐐸𐐮𐑋𐑅𐐯𐑊𐑁 𐐲𐐺𐐲𐑂 𐐸𐐮𐑆 𐐸𐐨𐑉𐐲𐑉𐑆; 𐑁𐐫𐑉 𐑄 𐐹𐑉𐐨𐐽𐐲𐑉 𐐶𐐱𐑆 𐑌𐐬 𐐺𐐯𐐻𐐲𐑉 𐑄𐐰𐑌 𐑄 𐐸𐐨𐑉𐐲𐑉, 𐑌𐐨𐑄𐐲𐑉 𐐶𐐱𐑆 𐑄 𐐻𐐨𐐽𐐲𐑉 𐐯𐑌𐐨 𐐺𐐯𐐻𐐲𐑉 𐑄𐐰𐑌 𐑄 𐑊𐐲𐑉𐑌𐐲𐑉; 𐐰𐑌𐐼 𐑄𐐲𐑅 𐑄𐐩 𐐶𐐲𐑉 𐐫𐑊 𐐨𐐿𐐶𐐲𐑊, 𐐰𐑌𐐼 𐑄𐐩 𐐼𐐮𐐼 𐐫𐑊 𐑊𐐩𐐺𐐲𐑉, 𐐯𐑂𐐲𐑉𐐨 𐑋𐐰𐑌 𐐰𐐿𐐫𐑉𐐼𐐮𐑍 𐐻𐐭 𐐸𐐮𐑆 𐑅𐐻𐑉𐐯𐑍𐑃: 𐐰𐑌𐐼 𐑄𐐩 𐐼𐐮𐐼 𐐮𐑋𐐹𐐪𐑉𐐻 𐐱𐑂 𐑄𐐩𐑉 𐑅𐐲𐐺𐑅𐐻𐐰𐑌𐑅, 𐐯𐑂𐐲𐑉𐐨 𐑋𐐰𐑌 𐐰𐐿𐐫𐑉𐐼𐐮𐑍 𐐻𐐭 𐑄𐐰𐐻 𐐸𐐶𐐮𐐽 𐐸𐐨 𐐸𐐰𐐼, 𐐻𐐭 𐑄 𐐹𐐭𐑉, 𐐰𐑌𐐼 𐑄 𐑌𐐨𐐼𐐨, 𐐰𐑌𐐼 𐑄 𐑅𐐮𐐿, 𐐰𐑌𐐼 𐑄 𐐰𐑁𐑊𐐮𐐿𐐻𐐯𐐼; 𐐰𐑌𐐼 𐑄𐐩 𐐼𐐮𐐼 𐑌𐐱𐐻 𐐶𐐩𐑉 𐐿𐐱𐑅𐐻𐑊𐐨 𐐰𐐹𐐰𐑉𐐯𐑊, 𐐷𐐯𐐻 𐑄𐐩 𐐶𐐲𐑉 𐑌𐐨𐐻 𐐰𐑌𐐼 𐐿𐐲𐑋𐑊𐐨; 𐐰𐑌𐐼 𐑄𐐲𐑅 𐑄𐐩 𐐼𐐮𐐼 𐐯𐑅𐐻𐐰𐐺𐑊𐐮𐑇 𐑄 𐐰𐑁𐐩𐑉𐑆 𐐱𐑂 𐑄 𐐕𐐲𐑉𐐽; 𐐰𐑌𐐼 𐑄𐐲𐑅 𐑄𐐩 𐐺𐐨𐑀𐐰𐑌 𐐻𐐭 𐐸𐐰𐑂 𐐿𐐱𐑌𐐻𐐮𐑌𐐷𐐭𐐲𐑊 𐐹𐐨𐑅 𐐲𐑀𐐯𐑌, 𐑌𐐱𐐻𐐶𐐮𐑄𐑅𐐻𐐰𐑌𐐼𐐮𐑍 𐐫𐑊 𐑄𐐩𐑉 𐐹𐐲𐑉𐑅𐐨𐐿𐐷𐐭𐑇𐐲𐑌𐑆. 𐐰𐑌𐐼 𐑌𐐵, 𐐺𐐨𐐿𐐫𐑆 𐐱𐑂 𐑄 𐑅𐐻𐐯𐐼𐐨𐑌𐐯𐑅 𐐱𐑂 𐑄 𐐕𐐲𐑉𐐽, 𐑄𐐩 𐐺𐐨𐑀𐐰𐑌 𐐻𐐭 𐐺𐐨 𐐯𐐿𐑅𐐨𐐼𐐮𐑍𐑊𐐨 𐑉𐐮𐐽, 𐐸𐐰𐑂𐐮𐑍 𐐰𐐺𐐲𐑌𐐼𐐰𐑌𐑅 𐐱𐑂 𐐫𐑊 𐑃𐐮𐑍𐑆 𐐸𐐶𐐱𐐻𐑅𐐬𐐯𐑂𐐲𐑉 𐑄𐐩 𐑅𐐻𐐳𐐼 𐐮𐑌 𐑌𐐨𐐼; 𐐰𐑌 𐐰𐐺𐐲𐑌𐐼𐐰𐑌𐑅 𐐱𐑂 𐑁𐑊𐐱𐐿𐑅 𐐰𐑌𐐼 𐐸𐐲𐑉𐐼𐑆, 𐐰𐑌𐐼 𐑁𐐰𐐻𐑊𐐮𐑍𐑆 𐐱𐑂 𐐯𐑂𐐲𐑉𐐨 𐐿𐐴𐑌𐐼, 𐐰𐑌𐐼 𐐫𐑊𐑅𐐬 𐐰𐐺𐐲𐑌𐐼𐐰𐑌𐑅 𐐱𐑂 𐑀𐑉𐐩𐑌, 𐐰𐑌𐐼 𐐱𐑂 𐑀𐐬𐑊𐐼, 𐐰𐑌𐐼 𐐱𐑂 𐑅𐐮𐑊𐑂𐐲𐑉, 𐐰𐑌𐐼 𐐱𐑂 𐐹𐑉𐐯𐑇𐐲𐑅 𐑃𐐮𐑍𐑆; 𐐰𐑌𐐼 𐐰𐐺𐐲𐑌𐐼𐐰𐑌𐑅 𐐱𐑂 𐑅𐐮𐑊𐐿 𐐰𐑌𐐼 𐑁𐐴𐑌 𐐻𐐶𐐴𐑌𐐼 𐑊𐐮𐑌𐐯𐑌, 𐐰𐑌𐐼 𐐫𐑊 𐑋𐐰𐑌𐐲𐑉 𐐱𐑂 𐑀𐐳𐐼 𐐸𐐬𐑋𐑊𐐨 𐐿𐑊𐐱𐑃. 𐐰𐑌𐐼 𐑄𐐲𐑅, 𐐮𐑌 𐑄𐐩𐑉 𐐹𐑉𐐱𐑅𐐹𐐲𐑉𐐲𐑅 𐑅𐐲𐑉𐐿𐐲𐑋𐑅𐐻𐐰𐑌𐑅𐐯𐑆, 𐑄𐐩 𐐼𐐮𐐼 𐑌𐐱𐐻 𐑅𐐯𐑌𐐼 𐐲𐐶𐐩 𐐯𐑌𐐨 𐐸𐐭 𐐶𐐲𐑉 𐑌𐐩𐐿𐐯𐐼, 𐐫𐑉 𐑄𐐰𐐻 𐐶𐐲𐑉 𐐸𐐲𐑍𐑀𐑉𐐨, 𐐫𐑉 𐑄𐐰𐐻 𐐶𐐲𐑉 𐐲𐑃𐐲𐑉𐑅𐐻, 𐐫𐑉 𐑄𐐰𐐻 𐐶𐐲𐑉 𐑅𐐮𐐿, 𐐫𐑉 𐑄𐐰𐐻 𐐸𐐰𐐼 𐑌𐐱𐐻 𐐺𐐮𐑌 𐑌𐐲𐑉𐐮𐑇𐐻; 𐐰𐑌𐐼 𐑄𐐩 𐐼𐐮𐐼 𐑌𐐱𐐻 𐑅𐐯𐐻 𐑄𐐩𐑉 𐐸𐐪𐑉𐐻𐑅 𐐲𐐹𐐱𐑌 𐑉𐐮𐐽𐐯𐑆; 𐑄𐐩𐑉𐑁𐐬𐑉 𐑄𐐩 𐐶𐐲𐑉 𐑊𐐮𐐺𐐲𐑉𐐲𐑊 𐐻𐐭 𐐫𐑊, 𐐺𐐬𐑃 𐐬𐑊𐐼 𐐰𐑌𐐼 𐐷𐐲𐑍, 𐐺𐐬𐑃 𐐺𐐱𐑌𐐼 𐐰𐑌𐐼 𐑁𐑉𐐨, 𐐺𐐬𐑃 𐑋𐐩𐑊 𐐰𐑌𐐼 𐑁𐐨𐑋𐐩𐑊, 𐐸𐐶𐐯𐑄𐐲𐑉 𐐵𐐻 𐐱𐑂 𐑄 𐐕𐐲𐑉𐐽 𐐫𐑉 𐐮𐑌 𐑄 𐐕𐐲𐑉𐐽, 𐐸𐐰𐑂𐐮𐑍 𐑌𐐬 𐑉𐐨𐑅𐐹𐐯𐐿𐐻 𐐻𐐭 𐐹𐐲𐑉𐑅𐐲𐑌𐑆 𐐰𐑆 𐐻𐐭 𐑄𐐬𐑆 𐐸𐐭 𐑅𐐻𐐳𐐼 𐐮𐑌 𐑌𐐨𐐼; 𐐰𐑌𐐼 𐑄𐐲𐑅 𐑄𐐩 𐐼𐐮𐐼 𐐹𐑉𐐱𐑅𐐹𐐲𐑉 𐐰𐑌𐐼 𐐺𐐨𐐿𐐲𐑋 𐑁𐐪𐑉 𐑋𐐬𐑉 𐐶𐐯𐑊𐑃𐐨 𐑄𐐰𐑌 𐑄𐐬𐑆 𐐸𐐭 𐐼𐐮𐐼 𐑌𐐱𐐻 𐐺𐐨𐑊𐐱𐑍 𐐻𐐭 𐑄𐐩𐑉 𐐕𐐲𐑉𐐽. 𐑁𐐫𐑉 𐑄𐐬𐑆 𐐸𐐭 𐐼𐐮𐐼 𐑌𐐱𐐻 𐐺𐐨𐑊𐐱𐑍 𐐻𐐭 𐑄𐐩𐑉 𐐕𐐲𐑉𐐽, 𐐼𐐮𐐼 𐐮𐑌𐐼𐐲𐑊𐐾 𐑄𐐯𐑋𐑅𐐯𐑊𐑂𐑆 𐐮𐑌 𐑅𐐫𐑉𐑅𐐲𐑉𐐨𐑆, 𐐰𐑌𐐼 𐐮𐑌 𐐴𐐼𐐱𐑊𐐲𐐻𐑉𐐨 𐐫𐑉 𐐴𐐼𐑊𐑌𐐯𐑅, 𐐰𐑌𐐼 𐐮𐑌 𐐺𐐰𐐺𐑊𐐮𐑍𐑆, 𐐰𐑌𐐼 𐐮𐑌 𐐯𐑌𐑂𐐨𐐮𐑍𐑆 𐐰𐑌𐐼 𐑅𐐻𐑉𐐴𐑁; 𐐶𐐩𐑉𐐮𐑍 𐐿𐐱𐑅𐐻𐑊𐐨 𐐰𐐹𐐰𐑉𐐯𐑊; 𐐺𐐨𐐮𐑍 𐑊𐐮𐑁𐐻𐐯𐐼 𐐲𐐹 𐐮𐑌 𐑄 𐐹𐑉𐐴𐐼 𐐱𐑂 𐑄𐐩𐑉 𐐬𐑌 𐐴𐑆; 𐐹𐐲𐑉𐑅𐐨𐐿𐐷𐐭𐐻𐐮𐑍, 𐑊𐐴𐐮𐑍, 𐑃𐐨𐑂𐐮𐑍, 𐑉𐐱𐐺𐐮𐑍, 𐐿𐐱𐑋𐐮𐐻𐐮𐑍 𐐸𐐬𐑉𐐼𐐲𐑋𐑆, 𐐰𐑌𐐼 𐑋𐐲𐑉𐐼𐐲𐑉𐐮𐑍, 𐐰𐑌𐐼 𐐫𐑊 𐑋𐐰𐑌𐐲𐑉 𐐱𐑂 𐐶𐐮𐐿𐐯𐐼𐑌𐐯𐑅; 𐑌𐐯𐑂𐐲𐑉𐑄𐐲𐑊𐐯𐑅, 𐑄 𐑊𐐫 𐐶𐐱𐑆 𐐹𐐳𐐻 𐐮𐑌 𐑁𐐬𐑉𐑅 𐐲𐐹𐐱𐑌 𐐫𐑊 𐑄𐐬𐑆 𐐸𐐭 𐐼𐐮𐐼 𐐻𐑉𐐰𐑌𐑅𐑀𐑉𐐯𐑅 𐐮𐐻, 𐐮𐑌𐐰𐑆𐑋𐐲𐐽 𐐰𐑆 𐐮𐐻 𐐶𐐲𐑉 𐐹𐐱𐑅𐐮𐐺𐑊.

7. 𐐰𐑌𐐼 𐐮𐐻 𐐿𐐩𐑋 𐐻𐐭 𐐹𐐰𐑅 𐑄𐐰𐐻 𐐺𐐴 𐑄𐐲𐑅 𐐯𐐿𐑅𐐲𐑉𐑅𐐴𐑆𐐮𐑍 𐑄 𐑊𐐫 𐐲𐐹𐐱𐑌 𐑄𐐯𐑋, 𐐯𐑂𐐲𐑉𐐨 𐑋𐐰𐑌 𐑅𐐲𐑁𐐲𐑉𐐮𐑍 𐐰𐐿𐐫𐑉𐐼𐐮𐑍 𐐻𐐭 𐑄𐐰𐐻 𐐸𐐶𐐮𐐽 𐐸𐐨 𐐸𐐰𐐼 𐐼𐐲𐑌, 𐑄𐐩 𐐺𐐨𐐿𐐩𐑋 𐑋𐐬𐑉 𐑅𐐻𐐮𐑊, 𐐰𐑌𐐼 𐐼𐐲𐑉𐑅𐐻 𐑌𐐱𐐻 𐐿𐐱𐑋𐐮𐐻 𐐯𐑌𐐨 𐐶𐐮𐐿𐐯𐐼𐑌𐐯𐑅 𐐮𐑁 𐐮𐐻 𐐶𐐲𐑉 𐑌𐐬𐑌; 𐑄𐐩𐑉𐑁𐐬𐑉, 𐑄𐐩𐑉 𐐶𐐱𐑆 𐑋𐐲𐐽 𐐹𐐨𐑅 𐐲𐑋𐐲𐑍 𐑄 𐐹𐐨𐐹𐑊 𐐱𐑂 𐐤𐐨𐑁𐐴 𐐲𐑌𐐻𐐮𐑊 𐑄 𐑁𐐮𐑁𐑃 𐐷𐐨𐑉 𐐱𐑂 𐑄 𐑉𐐩𐑌 𐐱𐑂 𐑄 𐐾𐐲𐐾𐐯𐑆. 𐐰𐑌𐐼 𐐮𐐻 𐐿𐐩𐑋 𐐻𐐭 𐐹𐐰𐑅 𐐮𐑌 𐑄 𐐿𐐱𐑋𐐯𐑌𐑅𐑋𐐯𐑌𐐻 𐐱𐑂 𐑄 𐑁𐐮𐑁𐑃 𐐷𐐨𐑉 𐐱𐑂 𐑄𐐩𐑉 𐑉𐐩𐑌, 𐑄𐐩𐑉 𐐺𐐨𐑀𐐰𐑌 𐐻𐐭 𐐺𐐨 𐐲 𐐿𐐱𐑌𐐻𐐯𐑌𐑇𐐲𐑌 𐐲𐑋𐐲𐑍 𐑄 𐐹𐐨𐐹𐑊; 𐑁𐐫𐑉 𐐲 𐑅𐐲𐑉𐐻𐐯𐑌 𐑋𐐰𐑌, 𐐺𐐨𐐮𐑍 𐐿𐐫𐑊𐐼 𐐈𐑋𐑊𐐮𐑅𐐴, 𐐸𐐨, 𐐺𐐨𐐮𐑍 𐐲 𐑂𐐯𐑉𐐨 𐐿𐐲𐑌𐐮𐑍 𐑋𐐰𐑌, 𐐷𐐩, 𐐲 𐐶𐐴𐑆 𐑋𐐰𐑌 𐐰𐑆 𐐻𐐭 𐑄 𐐶𐐮𐑆𐐼𐐲𐑋 𐐱𐑂 𐑄 𐐶𐐲𐑉𐑊𐐼; 𐐸𐐨 𐐺𐐨𐐮𐑍 𐐰𐑁𐐻𐐲𐑉 𐑄 𐐫𐑉𐐼𐐲𐑉 𐐱𐑂 𐑄 𐑋𐐰𐑌 𐑄𐐰𐐻 𐑅𐑊𐐭 𐐘𐐮𐐼𐐨𐐲𐑌 𐐺𐐴 𐑄 𐑅𐐬𐑉𐐼, 𐐸𐐭 𐐶𐐱𐑆 𐐯𐐿𐑅𐐨𐐿𐐷𐐭𐐻𐐯𐐼 𐐰𐐿𐐫𐑉𐐼𐐮𐑍 𐐻𐐭 𐑄 𐑊𐐫. 𐐤𐐵 𐑄𐐮𐑅 𐐈𐑋𐑊𐐮𐑅𐐴 𐐸𐐰𐐼, 𐐺𐐴 𐐸𐐮𐑆 𐐿𐐲𐑌𐐮𐑍, 𐐼𐑉𐐫𐑌 𐐲𐐶𐐩 𐑋𐐲𐐽 𐐹𐐨𐐹𐑊 𐐰𐑁𐐻𐐲𐑉 𐐸𐐮𐑋; 𐐨𐑂𐐯𐑌 𐑅𐐬 𐑋𐐲𐐽 𐑄𐐰𐐻 𐑄𐐩 𐐺𐐨𐑀𐐰𐑌 𐐻𐐭 𐐺𐐨 𐑂𐐯𐑉𐐨 𐐹𐐵𐐲𐑉𐑁𐐳𐑊; 𐐰𐑌𐐼 𐑄𐐩 𐐺𐐨𐑀𐐰𐑌 𐐻𐐭 𐐯𐑌𐐼𐐯𐑂𐐲𐑉 𐐻𐐭 𐐯𐑅𐐻𐐰𐐺𐑊𐐮𐑇 𐐈𐑋𐑊𐐮𐑅𐐴 𐐻𐐭 𐐺𐐨 𐐲 𐐿𐐮𐑍 𐐬𐑂𐐲𐑉 𐑄 𐐹𐐨𐐹𐑊. 𐐤𐐵 𐑄𐐮𐑅 𐐶𐐱𐑆 𐐰𐑊𐐪𐑉𐑋𐐮𐑍 𐐻𐐭 𐑄 𐐹𐐨𐐹𐑊 𐐱𐑂 𐑄 𐐕𐐲𐑉𐐽, 𐐰𐑌𐐼 𐐫𐑊𐑅𐐬 𐐻𐐭 𐐫𐑊 𐑄𐐬𐑆 𐐸𐐭 𐐸𐐰𐐼 𐑌𐐱𐐻 𐐺𐐮𐑌 𐐼𐑉𐐫𐑌 𐐲𐐶𐐩 𐐰𐑁𐐻𐐲𐑉 𐑄 𐐹𐐲𐑉𐑅𐐶𐐩𐑈𐐲𐑌𐑆 𐐱𐑂 𐐈𐑋𐑊𐐮𐑅𐐴; 𐑁𐐫𐑉 𐑄𐐩 𐑌𐐭 𐑄𐐰𐐻 𐐰𐐿𐐫𐑉𐐼𐐮𐑍 𐐻𐐭 𐑄𐐩𐑉 𐑊𐐫 𐑄𐐰𐐻 𐑅𐐲𐐽 𐑃𐐮𐑍𐑆 𐑋𐐲𐑅𐐻 𐐺𐐨 𐐯𐑅𐐻𐐰𐐺𐑊𐐮𐑇𐐻 𐐺𐐴 𐑄 𐑂𐐱𐐮𐑅 𐐱𐑂 𐑄 𐐹𐐨𐐹𐑊; 𐑄𐐩𐑉𐑁𐐬𐑉, 𐐮𐑁 𐐮𐐻 𐐶𐐲𐑉 𐐹𐐱𐑅𐐮𐐺𐑊 𐑄𐐰𐐻 𐐈𐑋𐑊𐐮𐑅𐐴 𐑇𐐳𐐼 𐑀𐐩𐑌 𐑄 𐑂𐐱𐐮𐑅 𐐱𐑂 𐑄 𐐹𐐨𐐹𐑊, 𐐸𐐨, 𐐺𐐨𐐮𐑍 𐐲 𐐶𐐮𐐿𐐯𐐼 𐑋𐐰𐑌, 𐐶𐐳𐐼 𐐼𐐨𐐹𐑉𐐴𐑂 𐑄𐐯𐑋

𐐱𐑂 𐑄𐐩𐑉 𐑉𐐴𐐻𐑅 𐐰𐑌𐐼 𐐹𐑉𐐮𐑂𐐮𐑊𐐯𐐾𐐯𐑆 𐐱𐑂 𐑄 𐐕𐐲𐑉𐐽, 𐐯𐐻𐑅.; 𐑁𐐫𐑉 𐐮𐐻 𐐶𐐱𐑆 𐐸𐐮𐑆 𐐮𐑌𐐻𐐯𐑌𐐻 𐐻𐐭 𐐼𐐨𐑅𐐻𐑉𐑎 𐑄 𐐕𐐲𐑉𐐽 𐐱𐑂 𐐘𐐱𐐼.

8. 𐐰𐑌𐐼 𐐮𐐻 𐐿𐐩𐑋 𐐻𐐭 𐐹𐐪𐑅 𐑄𐐰𐐻 𐑄 𐐹𐐨𐐹𐑊 𐐰𐑅𐐯𐑋𐐺𐑊𐐼 𐑄𐐯𐑋𐑅𐐯𐑊𐑂𐑆 𐐻𐐭𐑀𐐯𐑄𐐯𐑉 𐑃𐑉𐐭𐐵𐐻 𐐫𐑊 𐑄 𐑊𐐰𐑌𐐼, 𐐯𐑂𐐲𐑉𐐨 𐑋𐐰𐑌 𐐰𐐿𐐫𐑉𐐼𐐮𐑍 𐐻𐐭 𐐸𐐮𐑆 𐑋𐐴𐑌𐐼, 𐐸𐐶𐐯𐑄𐐯𐑉 𐐮𐐻 𐐶𐐲𐑉 𐑁𐐫𐑉 𐐫𐑉 𐐰𐑀𐐯𐑌𐑅𐐻 𐐰𐑋𐑊𐐮𐑅𐐴, 𐐮𐑌 𐑅𐐯𐐹𐐲𐑉𐐩𐐻 𐐺𐐱𐐼𐐨𐑆, 𐐸𐐰𐑂𐐮𐑍 𐑋𐐲𐐽 𐐼𐐮𐑅𐐹𐐷𐐭𐐻 𐐰𐑌𐐼 𐐶𐐲𐑌𐐼𐐲𐑉𐑁𐐳𐑊 𐐿𐐱𐑌𐐻𐐯𐑌𐑇𐐲𐑌𐑆 𐐶𐐲𐑌 𐐶𐐮𐑄 𐐰𐑌𐐲𐑄𐐲𐑉; 𐐰𐑌𐐼 𐑄𐐲𐑅 𐑄𐐩 𐐼𐐮𐐼 𐐰𐑅𐐯𐑋𐐺𐑊 𐑄𐐯𐑋𐑅𐐯𐑊𐑂𐑆 𐐻𐐭𐑀𐐯𐑄𐐯𐑉 𐐻𐐭 𐐿𐐪𐑅𐐻 𐐮𐑌 𐑄𐐩𐑉 𐑂𐑎𐑅𐐯𐑆 𐐿𐐱𐑌𐑅𐐲𐑉𐑌𐐮𐑍 𐑄 𐑋𐐰𐐻𐐲𐑉; 𐐰𐑌𐐼 𐑄𐐩 𐐶𐐲𐑉 𐑊𐐩𐐼 𐐺𐐨𐑁𐐫𐑉 𐑄 𐐾𐐲𐐾𐐯𐑆. 𐐰𐑌𐐼 𐐮𐐻 𐐿𐐩𐑋 𐐻𐐭 𐐹𐐪𐑅 𐑄𐐰𐐻 𐑄 𐑂𐑎𐑅 𐐱𐑂 𐑄 𐐹𐐨𐐹𐑊 𐐿𐐩𐑋 𐐰𐑀𐐯𐑌𐑅𐐻 𐐰𐑋𐑊𐐮𐑅𐐴, 𐑄𐐰𐐻 𐐸𐐨 𐐶𐐱𐑆 𐑌𐐱𐐻 𐑋𐐩𐐼 𐐿𐐮𐑍 𐐬𐑂𐐲𐑉 𐑄 𐐹𐐨𐐹𐑊. 𐑌𐐵 𐑄𐐮𐑅 𐐼𐐮𐐼 𐐿𐐫𐑆 𐑋𐐲𐐽 𐐾𐑎 𐐮𐑌 𐑄 𐐸𐐪𐑉𐐻𐑅 𐐱𐑂 𐑄𐐬𐑆 𐐸𐐭 𐐶𐐲𐑉 𐐰𐑀𐐯𐑌𐑅𐐻 𐐸𐐮𐑋; 𐐺𐐲𐐻 𐐰𐑋𐑊𐐮𐑅𐐴 𐐼𐐮𐐼 𐑅𐐻𐐲𐑉 𐐲𐐹 𐑄𐐬𐑆 𐐸𐐭 𐐶𐐲𐑉 𐐮𐑌 𐐸𐐮𐑆 𐑁𐐩𐑂𐐲𐑉, 𐐻𐐭 𐐰𐑍𐑀𐐲𐑉 𐐰𐑀𐐯𐑌𐑅𐐻 𐑄𐐬𐑆 𐐸𐐭 𐐶𐐲𐑉 𐑌𐐱𐐻 𐐮𐑌 𐐸𐐮𐑆 𐑁𐐩𐑂𐐲𐑉.

9. 𐐰𐑌𐐼 𐐮𐐻 𐐿𐐩𐑋 𐐻𐐭 𐐹𐐪𐑅 𐑄𐐰𐐻 𐑄𐐩 𐑀𐐰𐑄𐐲𐑉𐐼 𐑄𐐯𐑋𐑅𐐯𐑊𐑂𐑆 𐐻𐐭𐑀𐐯𐑄𐐯𐑉, 𐐰𐑌𐐼 𐐼𐐮𐐼 𐐿𐐱𐑌𐑅𐐨𐐿𐑉𐐩𐐻 𐐰𐑋𐑊𐐮𐑅𐐴 𐐻𐐭 𐐺𐐨 𐑄𐐩𐑉 𐐿𐐮𐑍. 𐑌𐐵 𐐸𐐶𐐯𐑌 𐐰𐑋𐑊𐐮𐑅𐐴 𐐶𐐱𐑆 𐑋𐐩𐐼 𐐿𐐮𐑍 𐐬𐑂𐐲𐑉 𐑄𐐯𐑋, 𐐸𐐨 𐐿𐐱𐑋𐐪𐑌𐐼𐐯𐐼 𐑄𐐯𐑋 𐑄𐐰𐐻 𐑄𐐩 𐑇𐐳𐐼 𐐻𐐩𐐿 𐐲𐐹 𐐪𐑉𐑋𐑆 𐐰𐑀𐐯𐑌𐑅𐐻 𐑄𐐩𐑉 𐐺𐑉𐐯𐑄𐑉𐐯𐑌; 𐐰𐑌𐐼 𐑄𐐮𐑅 𐐸𐐨 𐐼𐐮𐐼 𐑄𐐰𐐻 𐐸𐐨 𐑋𐐴𐐻 𐑅𐐲𐐺𐐾𐐯𐐿𐐻 𐑄𐐯𐑋 𐐻𐐭 𐐸𐐮𐑋. 𐑌𐐵 𐑄 𐐹𐐨𐐹𐑊 𐐱𐑂 𐐰𐑋𐑊𐐮𐑅𐐴 𐐶𐐲𐑉 𐐼𐐮𐑅𐐻𐐮𐑍𐑀𐐶𐐮𐑇𐐻 𐐺𐐴 𐑄 𐑌𐐩𐑋 𐐱𐑂 𐐰𐑋-𐑊𐐮𐑅𐐴, 𐐺𐐨𐐮𐑍 𐐿𐐫𐑊𐐼 𐐰𐑋𐑊𐐮𐑅𐐴𐐻𐑅; 𐐰𐑌𐐼 𐑄 𐑉𐐨𐑋𐐩𐑌𐐼𐐲𐑉 𐐶𐐲𐑉 𐐿𐐫𐑊𐐼 𐐤𐐨𐑁𐐴𐐻𐑅, 𐐫𐑉 𐑄 𐐹𐐨𐐹𐑊 𐐱𐑂 𐐘𐐱𐐼; 𐑄𐐯𐑉𐑁𐐫𐑉 𐑄 𐐹𐐨𐐹𐑊 𐐱𐑂 𐑄 𐐤𐐨𐑁𐐴𐐻𐑅 𐐶𐐲𐑉 𐐰𐐶𐐯𐑉 𐐱𐑂 𐑄 𐐮𐑌𐐻𐐯𐑌𐐻 𐐱𐑂 𐑄 𐐰𐑋𐑊𐐮𐑅𐐴𐐻𐑅, 𐐰𐑌𐐼 𐑄𐐯𐑉𐑁𐐫𐑉 𐑄𐐩 𐐼𐐮𐐼 𐐹𐑉𐐨𐐹𐐯𐑉 𐐻𐐭 𐑋𐐨𐐻 𐑄𐐯𐑋; 𐐷𐐩, 𐑄𐐩 𐐼𐐮𐐼 𐐪𐑉𐑋 𐑄𐐯𐑋𐑅𐐯𐑊𐑂𐑆 𐐶𐐮𐑄 𐑅𐐫𐑉𐐼𐑆, 𐐰𐑌𐐼 𐐶𐐮𐑄 𐑅𐐮𐑋𐐨𐐻𐐲𐑉𐑆, 𐐰𐑌𐐼 𐐶𐐮𐑄 𐐺𐐬𐑆, 𐐰𐑌𐐼 𐐶𐐮𐑄 𐐰𐑉𐐬𐑆, 𐐰𐑌𐐼 𐐶𐐮𐑄 𐑅𐐻𐐬𐑌𐑆, 𐐰𐑌𐐼 𐐶𐐮𐑄 𐑅𐑊𐐮𐑍𐑆, 𐐰𐑌𐐼 𐐶𐐮𐑄 𐐫𐑊 𐑋𐐰𐑌𐐲𐑉 𐐱𐑂 𐐶𐐯𐐹𐐲𐑌𐑆 𐐱𐑂 𐐶𐐫𐑉, 𐐱𐑂 𐐯𐑂𐐲𐑉𐐨 𐐿𐐴𐑌𐐼; 𐐰𐑌𐐼 𐑄𐐲𐑅 𐑄𐐩 𐐶𐐲𐑉 𐐹𐑉𐐨𐐹𐐯𐑉𐐼 𐐻𐐭 𐑋𐐨𐐻 𐑄 𐐰𐑋𐑊𐐮𐑅𐐴𐐻𐑅 𐐰𐐻 𐑄 𐐻𐐴𐑋 𐐱𐑂 𐑄𐐩𐑉 𐐿𐐲𐑋𐐮𐑍. 𐐰𐑌𐐼 𐑄𐐩𐑉 𐐶𐐲𐑉 𐐰𐐹𐐱𐐮𐑌𐐻𐐯𐐼 𐐿𐐰𐐹𐐻𐐮𐑌𐑆, 𐐰𐑌𐐼 𐐸𐐴𐐲𐑉 𐐿𐐰𐐹-𐐻𐐮𐑌𐑆, 𐐰𐑌𐐼 𐐽𐐨𐑁 𐐿𐐰𐐹𐐻𐐮𐑌𐑆, 𐐰𐐿𐐫𐑉𐐼𐐮𐑍 𐐻𐐭 𐑄𐐩𐑉 𐑌𐐲𐑋𐐺𐐲𐑉𐑆.

10. 𐐰𐑌𐐼 𐐮𐐻 𐐿𐐩𐑋 𐐻𐐭 𐐹𐐪𐑅 𐑄𐐰𐐻 𐐰𐑋𐑊𐐮𐑅𐐴 𐐼𐐮𐐼 𐐪𐑉𐑋 𐐸𐐮𐑆 𐑋𐐯𐑌 𐐶𐐮𐑄 𐐫𐑊 𐑋𐐰𐑌𐐲𐑉 𐐱𐑂 𐐶𐐯𐐹𐐲𐑌𐑆 𐐱𐑂 𐐶𐐫𐑉, 𐐱𐑂 𐐯𐑂𐐲𐑉𐐨 𐐿𐐴𐑌𐐼; 𐐰𐑌𐐼 𐐸𐐨 𐐫𐑊𐑅𐐬 𐐰𐐹𐐱𐐮𐑌𐐻𐐯𐐼 𐑉𐐭𐑊𐐲𐑉𐑆 𐐰𐑌𐐼 𐑊𐐨𐐼𐐲𐑉𐑆 𐐬𐑂𐐲𐑉 𐐸𐐮𐑆 𐐹𐐨𐐹𐑊, 𐐻𐐭 𐑊𐐨𐐼 𐑄𐐯𐑋 𐐻𐐭 𐐶𐐫𐑉 𐐰𐑀𐐯𐑌𐑅𐐻 𐑄𐐩𐑉 𐐺𐑉𐐯𐑄𐑉𐐯𐑌. 𐐰𐑌𐐼 𐐮𐐻 𐐿𐐩𐑋 𐐻𐐭 𐐹𐐪𐑅 𐑄𐐰𐐻 𐑄 𐐰𐑋𐑊𐐮𐑅𐐴𐐻𐑅 𐐿𐐩𐑋 𐐲𐐹𐐱𐑌 𐑄 𐐸𐐮𐑊 𐐰𐑋𐑌𐐴𐐸𐐭, 𐐸𐐶𐐮𐐽 𐐶𐐱𐑆 𐑄 𐐨𐑅𐐻 𐐱𐑂 𐑄 𐑉𐐮𐑂𐐲𐑉 𐐝𐐴𐐼𐐲𐑌, 𐐸𐐶𐐮𐐽 𐑉𐐰𐑌 𐐺𐐴 𐑄 𐑊𐐰𐑌𐐼 𐐞𐐩𐑉𐐰𐐸𐐯𐑋𐑊𐐰,, 𐐰𐑌𐐼 𐑄𐐯𐑉 𐑄𐐩 𐐺𐐨𐑀𐐰𐑌 𐐻𐐭 𐑋𐐩𐐿 𐐶𐐫𐑉 𐐶𐐮𐑄 𐑄 𐐤𐐨𐑁𐐴𐐻𐑅. 𐑌𐐵 𐐰𐑊𐑋𐐰, 𐐺𐐨𐐮𐑍 𐑄 𐐕𐐨𐑁 𐐖𐐲𐐾, 𐐰𐑌𐐼 𐑄 𐑀𐐲𐑂𐐲𐑉𐑌𐐲𐑉 𐐱𐑂 𐑄 𐐹𐐨𐐹𐑊 𐐱𐑂 𐐤𐐨𐑁𐐴, 𐑄𐐯𐑉𐑁𐐫𐑉 𐐸𐐨 𐐶𐐯𐑌𐐻 𐐲𐐹 𐐶𐐮𐑄 𐐸𐐮𐑆 𐐹𐐨𐐹𐑊, 𐐷𐐩, 𐐶𐐮𐑄 𐐸𐐮𐑆 𐐿𐐰𐐹𐐻𐐮𐑌𐑆, 𐐰𐑌𐐼 𐐽𐐨𐑁 𐐿𐐰𐐹𐐻𐐮𐑌𐑆, 𐐷𐐩, 𐐰𐐻 𐑄 𐐸𐐯𐐼 𐐱𐑂 𐐸𐐮𐑆 𐐪𐑉𐑋𐐨𐑆, 𐐰𐑀𐐯𐑌𐑅𐐻 𐑄 𐐰𐑋-𐑊𐐮𐑅𐐴𐐻𐑅 𐐻𐐭 𐐺𐐰𐐻𐑊; 𐐰𐑌𐐼 𐑄𐐩 𐐺𐐨𐑀𐐰𐑌 𐐻𐐭 𐑅𐑊𐐩 𐑄 𐐰𐑋𐑊𐐮𐑅𐐴𐐻𐑅 𐐲𐐹𐐱𐑌 𐑄 𐐸𐐮𐑊 𐐨𐑅𐐻 𐐱𐑂 𐐝𐐴𐐼𐐲𐑌. 𐐰𐑌𐐼 𐑄 𐐰𐑋𐑊𐐮𐑅𐐴𐐻𐑅 𐐼𐐮𐐼 𐐿𐐲𐑌𐐻𐐯𐑌𐐼 𐐶𐐮𐑄 𐑄 𐐤𐐨𐑁𐐴𐐻𐑅 𐐶𐐮𐑄 𐑀𐑉𐐩𐐻 𐑅𐐻𐑉𐐯𐑍𐑃, 𐐮𐑌𐑅𐐬𐑋𐐲𐐽 𐑄𐐰𐐻 𐑋𐐯𐑌𐐨 𐐱𐑂 𐑄 𐐤𐐨𐑁𐐴𐐻𐑅 𐐼𐐮𐐼 𐑁𐐫𐑊 𐐺𐐨𐑁𐐫𐑉 𐑄 𐐰𐑋𐑊𐐮𐑅𐐴𐐻𐑅; 𐑌𐐯𐑂𐐲𐑉𐑄𐐯𐑊𐐯𐑅 𐑄 𐐢𐐫𐑉𐐼 𐐼𐐮𐐼 𐑅𐐻𐑉𐐯𐑍𐑃𐐯𐑌 𐑄 𐐸𐐰𐑌𐐼 𐐱𐑂 𐑄 𐐤𐐨𐑁𐐴𐐻𐑅, 𐑄𐐰𐐻 𐑄𐐩 𐑅𐑊𐐭 𐑄 𐐰𐑋𐑊𐐮𐑅𐐴𐐻𐑅 𐐶𐐮𐑄 𐐩 𐑀𐑉𐐩𐐻 𐑅𐑊𐐫𐐻𐐲𐑉, 𐑄𐐰𐐻 𐑄𐐩 𐐺𐐨𐑀𐐰𐑌 𐐻𐐭 𐑁𐑊𐐨 𐐺𐐨𐑁𐐫𐑉 𐑄𐐯𐑋. 𐐰𐑌𐐼 𐐮𐐻 𐐿𐐩𐑋 𐐻𐐭 𐐹𐐪𐑅 𐑄𐐰𐐻 𐑄 𐐤𐐨𐑁𐐴𐐻𐑅 𐐼𐐮𐐼 𐐹𐐲𐑉𐑅𐐭 𐑄 𐐰𐑋𐑊𐐮𐑅𐐴𐐻𐑅 𐐫𐑊 𐑄𐐰𐐻 𐐼𐐩, 𐐰𐑌𐐼 𐐼𐐮𐐼 𐑅𐑊𐐩 𐑄𐐯𐑋 𐐶𐐮𐑄 𐑋𐐲𐐽 𐑅𐑊𐐫𐐻𐐲𐑉, 𐐮𐑌𐑅𐐬𐑋𐐲𐐽 𐑄𐐰𐐻 𐑄𐐯𐑉 𐐶𐐱𐑆 𐑅𐑊𐐩𐑌 𐐱𐑂 𐑄 𐐰𐑋𐑊𐐮𐑅𐐴𐐻𐑅 𐐻𐐶𐐯𐑊𐑂 𐑃𐐵𐑆𐐲𐑌𐐼 𐑁𐐴𐑂 𐐸𐐲𐑌𐐼𐑉𐐯𐐼 𐑃𐐲𐑉𐐻𐐨 𐐰𐑌𐐼 𐐻𐐭 𐑅𐐬𐑊𐑆; 𐐰𐑌𐐼 𐑄𐐯𐑉 𐐶𐐱𐑆 𐑅𐑊𐐩𐑌 𐐱𐑂 𐑄 𐐤𐐨𐑁𐐴𐐻𐑅 𐑅𐐮𐐿𐑅 𐑃𐐵𐑆𐐲𐑌𐐼 𐑁𐐴𐑂 𐐸𐐲𐑌𐐼𐑉𐐯𐐼 𐑅𐐮𐐿𐑅𐐻𐐨 𐐰𐑌𐐼 𐐻𐐭 𐑅𐐬𐑊𐑆.

11. 𐐰𐑌𐐼 𐐮𐐻 𐐿𐐩𐑋 𐐻𐐭 𐐹𐐪𐑅 𐑄𐐰𐐻 𐐸𐐶𐐯𐑌 𐐰𐑊𐑋𐐰 𐐿𐐳𐐼 𐐹𐐲𐑉𐑅𐐭 𐑄 𐐰𐑋𐑊𐐮𐑅𐐴𐐻𐑅 𐑌𐐬 𐑊𐐱𐑍𐑀𐐲𐑉, 𐐸𐐨 𐐿𐐫𐑆𐐼 𐑄𐐰𐐻 𐐸𐐮𐑆 𐐹𐐨𐐹𐑊 𐑇𐐳𐐼 𐐹𐐮𐐽 𐑄𐐩𐑉 𐐻𐐯𐑌𐐻𐑅 𐐮𐑌 𐑄 𐑂𐐰𐑊𐐨 𐐱𐑂 𐐘𐐮𐐼𐐨𐐲𐑌, 𐑄 𐑂𐐰𐑊𐐨 𐐺𐐨𐐮𐑍 𐐿𐐫𐑊𐐼 𐐰𐑁𐐻𐐲𐑉 𐑄𐐰𐐻 𐐘𐐮𐐼𐐨𐐲𐑌 𐐸𐐶𐐮𐐽 𐐶𐐱𐑆 𐑅𐑊𐐩𐑌 𐐺𐐴 𐑄 𐐸𐐰𐑌𐐼 𐐱𐑂 𐐤𐐨𐐸𐐫𐑉 𐐶𐐮𐑄 𐑄 𐑅𐐫𐑉𐐼; 𐐰𐑌𐐼 𐐮𐑌 𐑄𐐮𐑅 𐑂𐐰𐑊𐐨 𐑄 𐐤𐐨𐑁𐐴𐐻𐑅 𐐼𐐮𐐼 𐐹𐐮𐐽 𐑄𐐩𐑉 𐐻𐐯𐑌𐐻𐑅 𐑁𐐫𐑉 𐑄 𐑌𐐴𐐻. 𐐰𐑌𐐼 𐐰𐑊𐑋𐐰 𐑅𐐯𐑌𐐻 𐑅𐐹𐐴𐑆 𐐻𐐭 𐑁𐐱𐑊𐐬 𐑄 𐑉𐐯𐑋𐑌𐐰𐑌𐐻 𐐱𐑂 𐑄 𐐰𐑋𐑊𐐮𐑅𐐴𐐻𐑅, 𐑄𐐰𐐻 𐐸𐐨 𐑋𐐴𐐻 𐑌𐐬 𐐱𐑂 𐑄𐐩𐑉 𐐹𐑊𐐰𐑌𐑆 𐐰𐑌𐐼 𐑄𐐩𐑉 𐐹𐑊𐐱𐐻𐑅, 𐐸𐐶𐐯𐑉𐐺𐐴

𐐸𐐨 𐑋𐐴𐐻 𐑀𐐪𐑉𐐼 𐐸𐐮𐑋𐑅𐐯𐑊𐑁 𐐰𐑀𐐯𐑌𐑅𐐻 𐑄𐐯𐑋, 𐑄𐐰𐐻 𐐸𐐨 𐑋𐐴𐐻 𐐹𐑉𐐨𐑆𐐲𐑉𐑂 𐐸𐐮𐑆 𐐹𐐨𐐹𐑊 𐑁𐑉𐐱𐑋 𐐺𐐨𐐮𐑍 𐐼𐐨𐑅𐐻𐑉𐐱𐐮𐐼. 𐐤𐐵 𐑄𐐬𐑆 𐐸𐐭𐑋 𐐸𐐨 𐐸𐐰𐐼 𐑅𐐯𐑌𐐻 𐐵𐐻 𐐻𐐭 𐐶𐐱𐐽 𐑄 𐐿𐐰𐑋𐐹 𐐱𐑂 𐑄 𐐈𐑋𐑊𐐲𐑅𐐴𐐻𐑅 𐐶𐐲𐑉 𐐿𐐫𐑊𐐼 𐐞𐐨𐑉𐐰𐑋, 𐐰𐑌𐐼 𐐈𐑋𐑌𐐱𐑉, 𐐰𐑌𐐼 𐐣𐐰𐑌𐐻𐐴, 𐐰𐑌𐐼 𐐢𐐮𐑋𐐸𐐲𐑉; 𐑄𐐨𐑆 𐐶𐐲𐑉 𐑄𐐩 𐐸𐐭 𐐶𐐯𐑌𐐻 𐐵𐐻 𐐶𐐮𐑄 𐑄𐐯𐑉 𐑋𐐯𐑌 𐐻𐐭 𐐶𐐱𐐽 𐑄 𐐿𐐰𐑋𐐹 𐐱𐑂 𐑄 𐐈𐑋𐑊𐐲𐑅𐐴𐐻𐑅.

12. 𐐈𐑌𐐼 𐐮𐐻 𐐿𐐩𐑋 𐐻𐐭 𐐹𐐰𐑅 𐑄𐐰𐐻 𐐱𐑌 𐑄 𐑋𐐱𐑉𐐬 𐑄𐐩 𐑉𐐨𐐻𐐲𐑉𐑌𐐼 𐐮𐑌𐐻𐐭 𐑄 𐐿𐐰𐑋𐐹 𐐱𐑂 𐑄 𐐤𐐨𐑁𐐴𐐻𐑅 𐐮𐑌 𐑀𐑉𐐩𐐻 𐐸𐐩𐑅𐐻, 𐐺𐐨𐐮𐑍 𐑀𐑉𐐩𐐻𐑊𐐨 𐐰𐑅𐐻𐐱𐑌𐐮𐑇𐐻, 𐐰𐑌𐐼 𐑅𐐻𐑉𐐲𐐿 𐐶𐐮𐑄 𐑋𐐲𐐽 𐑁𐐨𐑉, 𐑅𐐩𐐮𐑍, 𐐒𐐨𐐸𐐬𐑊𐐼, 𐐶𐐨 𐑁𐐱𐑊𐐬𐐼 𐑄 𐐿𐐰𐑋𐐹 𐐱𐑂 𐑄 𐐈𐑋𐑊𐐲𐑅𐐴𐐻𐑅, 𐐰𐑌𐐼 𐐻𐐭 𐐵𐑉 𐑀𐑉𐐩𐐻 𐐰𐑅𐐻𐐱𐑌𐐮𐑇𐑋𐐯𐑌𐐻, 𐐮𐑌 𐑄 𐑊𐐰𐑌𐐼 𐐱𐑂 𐐣𐐴𐑌𐐱𐑌, 𐐰𐐺𐐲𐑂 𐑄 𐑊𐐰𐑌𐐼 𐐱𐑂 𐐞𐐩𐑉𐐲𐐸𐐯𐑋𐑊𐐲, 𐐮𐑌 𐑄 𐐿𐐬𐑉𐑅 𐐱𐑂 𐑄 𐑊𐐰𐑌𐐼 𐐱𐑂 𐐤𐐨𐑁𐐴, 𐐶𐐨 𐑅𐐫 𐐲 𐑌𐐭𐑋𐐲𐑉𐐲𐑅 𐐸𐐬𐑅𐐻 𐐱𐑂 𐑄 𐐢𐐩𐑋𐐲𐑌𐐴𐐻𐑅; 𐐰𐑌𐐼 𐐺𐐨𐐸𐐬𐑊𐐼, 𐑄 𐐈𐑋𐑊𐐲𐑅𐐴𐐻𐑅 𐐸𐐰𐑂 𐐾𐐱𐐮𐑌𐐼 𐑄𐐯𐑋; 𐐰𐑌𐐼 𐑄𐐩 𐐪𐑉 𐐲𐐹𐐱𐑌 𐐵𐑉 𐐺𐑉𐐯𐑄𐑉𐐯𐑌 𐐮𐑌 𐑄𐐰𐐻 𐑊𐐰𐑌𐐼; 𐐰𐑌𐐼 𐑄𐐩 𐐪𐑉 𐑁𐑊𐐨𐐮𐑍 𐐺𐐨𐑁𐐬𐑉 𐑄𐐯𐑋 𐐶𐐮𐑄 𐑄𐐯𐑉 𐑁𐑊𐐱𐐿𐑅, 𐐰𐑌𐐼 𐑄𐐯𐑉 𐐶𐐴𐑂𐑆, 𐐰𐑌𐐼 𐑄𐐯𐑉 𐐽𐐮𐑊𐐼𐑉𐐯𐑌, 𐐻𐐬𐐲𐑉𐐼𐑆 𐐵𐑉 𐑅𐐮𐐻𐐨; 𐐰𐑌𐐼 𐐯𐐿𐑅𐐯𐐹𐐻 𐐶𐐨 𐑋𐐩𐐿 𐐸𐐩𐑅𐐻 𐑄𐐩 𐐱𐐺𐐻𐐩𐑌 𐐹𐐱𐑆𐐯𐑇𐐲𐑌 𐐱𐑂 𐐵𐑉 𐑅𐐮𐐻𐐨; 𐐰𐑌𐐼 𐐵𐑉 𐑁𐐪𐑄𐐲𐑉𐑆, 𐐰𐑌𐐼 𐐵𐑉 𐐶𐐴𐑂𐑆, 𐐰𐑌𐐼 𐐵𐑉 𐐽𐐮𐑊𐐼𐑉𐐯𐑌 𐐺𐐨 𐑅𐑊𐐩𐑌.

13. 𐐈𐑌𐐼 𐐮𐐻 𐐿𐐩𐑋 𐐻𐐭 𐐹𐐰𐑅 𐑄𐐰𐐻 𐑄 𐐹𐐨𐐹𐑊 𐐱𐑂 𐐤𐐨𐑁𐐴 𐐻𐐳𐐿 𐑄𐐯𐑉 𐐻𐐯𐑌𐐻𐑅, 𐐰𐑌𐐼 𐐼𐐨𐐹𐐪𐑉𐐻𐐯𐐼 𐐵𐐻 𐐱𐑂 𐑄 𐑂𐐰𐑊𐐨 𐐱𐑂 𐐘𐐮𐐼𐐨𐐱𐑌 𐐻𐐬𐐲𐑉𐐼𐑆 𐑄𐐯𐑉 𐑅𐐮𐐻𐐨, 𐐸𐐶𐐮𐐽 𐐶𐐱𐑆 𐑄 𐑅𐐮𐐻𐐨 𐐱𐑂 𐐞𐐩𐑉𐐲𐐸𐐯𐑋𐑊𐐲. 𐐈𐑌𐐼 𐐺𐐨𐐸𐐬𐑊𐐼, 𐐰𐑆 𐑄𐐩 𐐶𐐲𐑉 𐐿𐑉𐐱𐑅𐐮𐑍 𐑄 𐑉𐐮𐑂𐐲𐑉 𐐝𐐴𐐼𐐱𐑌, 𐑄 𐐢𐐩𐑋𐐲𐑌𐐴𐐻𐑅 𐐰𐑌𐐼 𐑄 𐐈𐑋𐑊𐐲𐑅𐐴𐐻𐑅, 𐐺𐐨𐐮𐑍 𐐰𐑆 𐑌𐐭𐑋𐐲𐑉𐐲𐑅 𐐫𐑊𐑋𐐬𐑅𐐻, 𐐰𐑆 𐐮𐐻 𐐶𐐲𐑉, 𐐰𐑆 𐑄 𐑅𐐰𐑌𐐼𐑆 𐐱𐑂 𐑄 𐑅𐐨, 𐐿𐐩𐑋 𐐲𐐹𐐱𐑌 𐑄𐐯𐑋 𐐻𐐭 𐐼𐐨𐑅𐐻𐑉𐐱𐐮 𐑄𐐯𐑋; 𐑌𐐯𐑂𐐲𐑉𐑄𐐲𐑊𐐯𐑅, 𐑄 𐐤𐐨𐑁𐐴𐐻𐑅 𐐺𐐨𐐮𐑍 𐑅𐐻𐑉𐐯𐑍𐑃𐐲𐑌𐐼 𐐺𐐴 𐑄 𐐸𐐰𐑌𐐼 𐐱𐑂 𐑄 𐐢𐐫𐑉𐐼, 𐐸𐐰𐑂𐐮𐑍 𐐹𐑉𐐩𐐼 𐑋𐐴𐐻𐐮𐑊𐐨 𐐻𐐭 𐐸𐐮𐑋 𐑄𐐰𐐻 𐐸𐐨 𐐶𐐳𐐼 𐐼𐐨𐑊𐐮𐑂𐐲𐑉 𐑄𐐯𐑋 𐐵𐐻 𐐱𐑂 𐑄 𐐸𐐰𐑌𐐼𐑆 𐐱𐑂 𐑄𐐯𐑉 𐐯𐑌𐐯𐑋𐐨𐑆; 𐑄𐐯𐑉𐑁𐐬𐑉 𐑄 𐐢𐐫𐑉𐐼 𐐼𐐮𐐼 𐐸𐐨𐑉 𐑄𐐯𐑉 𐐿𐑉𐐴𐑆, 𐐰𐑌𐐼 𐐼𐐮𐐼 𐑅𐐻𐑉𐐯𐑍𐑃𐐲𐑌 𐑄𐐯𐑋, 𐐰𐑌𐐼 𐑄 𐐢𐐩𐑋𐐲𐑌𐐴𐐻𐑅 𐐰𐑌𐐼 𐑄 𐐈𐑋𐑊𐐲𐑅𐐴𐐻𐑅 𐐼𐐮𐐼 𐑁𐐫𐑊 𐐺𐐨𐑁𐐬𐑉 𐑄𐐯𐑋. 𐐈𐑌𐐼 𐐮𐐻 𐐿𐐩𐑋 𐐻𐐭 𐐹𐐰𐑅 𐑄𐐰𐐻 𐐈𐑊𐑋𐐲 𐑁𐐫𐐻 𐐶𐐮𐑄 𐐈𐑋𐑊𐐲𐑅𐐴 𐐶𐐮𐑄 𐑄 𐑅𐐬𐑉𐐼, 𐑁𐐩𐑅 𐐻𐐭 𐑁𐐩𐑅; 𐐰𐑌𐐼 𐑄𐐩 𐐼𐐮𐐼 𐐿𐐱𐑌𐐻𐐯𐑌𐐼 𐑋𐐴𐐻𐐮𐑊𐐨 𐐶𐐲𐑌 𐐶𐐮𐑄 𐐲𐑌𐐲𐑄𐐲𐑉.

14. 𐐈𐑌𐐼 𐐮𐐻 𐐿𐐩𐑋 𐐻𐐭 𐐹𐐰𐑅 𐑄𐐰𐐻 𐐈𐑊𐑋𐐲, 𐐺𐐨𐐮𐑍 𐐲 𐑋𐐰𐑌 𐐱𐑂 𐐘𐐱𐐼, 𐐺𐐨𐐮𐑍 𐐯𐐿𐑅𐐲𐑉𐑅𐐴𐑆𐐼 𐐶𐐮𐑄 𐑋𐐲𐐽 𐑁𐐩𐑃, 𐐿𐑉𐐴𐐼, 𐑅𐐩𐐮𐑍, 𐐄 𐐢𐐫𐑉𐐼, 𐐸𐐰𐑂 𐑋𐐲𐑉𐑅𐐨 𐐰𐑌𐐼 𐑅𐐹𐐩𐑉 𐑋𐐴 𐑊𐐴𐑁, 𐑄𐐰𐐻 𐐌 𐑋𐐩 𐐺𐐨 𐐰𐑌 𐐮𐑌𐑅𐐻𐑉𐐭𐑋𐐯𐑌𐐻 𐐮𐑌 𐑄𐐴 𐐸𐐰𐑌𐐼𐑆 𐐻𐐭 𐑅𐐩𐑂 𐐰𐑌𐐼 𐐹𐑉𐐨𐑆𐐲𐑉𐑂 𐑄𐐮𐑅 𐐹𐐨𐐹𐑊. 𐐤𐐵 𐐸𐐶𐐯𐑌 𐐈𐑊𐑋𐐲 𐐸𐐰𐐼 𐑅𐐯𐐼 𐑄𐐨𐑆 𐐶𐐲𐑉𐐼𐑆, 𐐸𐐨 𐐿𐐱𐑌𐐻𐐯𐑌𐐼𐐯𐐼 𐐰𐑀𐐯𐑌 𐐶𐐮𐑄 𐐈𐑋𐑊𐐲𐑅𐐴; 𐐰𐑌𐐼 𐐸𐐨 𐐶𐐱𐑆 𐑅𐐻𐑉𐐯𐑍𐑃𐐲𐑌𐐼, 𐐮𐑌𐑅𐐬𐑋𐐲𐐽 𐑄𐐰𐐻 𐐸𐐨 𐑅𐑊𐐭 𐐈𐑋𐑊𐐲𐑅𐐴 𐐶𐐮𐑄 𐑄 𐑅𐐬𐑉𐐼. 𐐈𐑌𐐼 𐐸𐐨 𐐫𐑊𐑅𐐬 𐐿𐐱𐑌𐐻𐐯𐑌𐐼𐐯𐐼 𐐶𐐮𐑄 𐑄 𐐿𐐮𐑍 𐐱𐑂 𐑄 𐐢𐐩𐑋𐐲𐑌𐐴𐐻𐑅; 𐐺𐐲𐐻 𐑄 𐐿𐐮𐑍 𐐱𐑂 𐑄 𐐢𐐩𐑋𐐲𐑌𐐴𐐻𐑅 𐑁𐑊𐐯𐐼 𐐺𐐰𐐿 𐑁𐑉𐐱𐑋 𐐺𐐨𐑁𐐬𐑉 𐐈𐑊𐑋𐐲, 𐐰𐑌𐐼 𐑅𐐯𐑌𐐻 𐐸𐐮𐑆 𐑀𐐪𐑉𐐼𐑆 𐐻𐐭 𐐿𐐱𐑌𐐻𐐯𐑌𐐼 𐐶𐐮𐑄 𐐈𐑊𐑋𐐲. 𐐒𐐲𐐻 𐐈𐑊𐑋𐐲, 𐐶𐐮𐑄 𐐸𐐮𐑆 𐑀𐐪𐑉𐐼𐑆, 𐐿𐐱𐑌𐐻𐐯𐑌𐐼𐐯𐐼 𐐶𐐮𐑄 𐑄 𐑀𐐪𐑉𐐼𐑆 𐐱𐑂 𐑄 𐐿𐐮𐑍 𐐱𐑂 𐑄 𐐢𐐩𐑋𐐲𐑌𐐴𐐻𐑅, 𐐲𐑌𐐻𐐮𐑊 𐐸𐐨 𐑅𐑊𐐭 𐐰𐑌𐐼 𐐼𐑉𐐬𐑂 𐑄𐐯𐑋 𐐺𐐰𐐿; 𐐰𐑌𐐼 𐑄𐐲𐑅 𐐸𐐨 𐐿𐑊𐐨𐑉𐐼 𐑄 𐑀𐑉𐐵𐑌𐐼, 𐐫𐑉 𐑉𐐪𐑄𐐲𐑉 𐑄 𐐺𐐰𐑍𐐿, 𐐸𐐶𐐮𐐽 𐐶𐐱𐑆 𐐱𐑌 𐑄 𐐶𐐯𐑅𐐻 𐐱𐑂 𐑄 𐑉𐐮𐑂𐐲𐑉 𐐝𐐴𐐼𐐱𐑌, 𐑃𐑉𐐬𐐮𐑍 𐑄 𐐺𐐱𐐼𐐨𐑆 𐐱𐑂 𐑄 𐐢𐐩𐑋𐐲𐑌𐐴𐐻𐑅 𐐸𐐭 𐐸𐐰𐐼 𐐺𐐮𐑌 𐑅𐑊𐐩𐑌 𐐮𐑌𐐻𐐭 𐑄 𐐶𐐫𐐻𐐲𐑉𐑆 𐐱𐑂 𐐝𐐴𐐼𐐱𐑌, 𐑄𐐰𐐻 𐑄𐐯𐑉𐐺𐐴 𐐸𐐮𐑆 𐐹𐐨𐐹𐑊 𐑋𐐴𐐻 𐐸𐐰𐑂 𐑉𐐭𐑋 𐐻𐐭 𐐿𐑉𐐱𐑅 𐐰𐑌𐐼 𐐿𐐱𐑌𐐻𐐯𐑌𐐼 𐐶𐐮𐑄 𐑄 𐐢𐐩𐑋𐐲𐑌𐐴𐐻𐑅 𐐰𐑌𐐼 𐑄 𐐈𐑋𐑊𐐲𐑅𐐴𐐻𐑅, 𐐱𐑌 𐑄 𐐶𐐯𐑅𐐻 𐑅𐐴𐐼 𐐱𐑂 𐑄 𐑉𐐮𐑂𐐲𐑉 𐐝𐐴𐐼𐐱𐑌.

15. 𐐈𐑌𐐼 𐐮𐐻 𐐿𐐩𐑋 𐐻𐐭 𐐹𐐰𐑅 𐑄𐐰𐐻 𐐸𐐶𐐯𐑌 𐑄𐐩 𐐸𐐰𐐼 𐐫𐑊 𐐿𐑉𐐱𐑅𐐻 𐑄 𐑉𐐮𐑂𐐲𐑉 𐐝𐐴𐐼𐐱𐑌, 𐑄𐐰𐐻 𐑄 𐐢𐐩𐑋𐐲𐑌𐐴𐐻𐑅 𐐰𐑌𐐼 𐑄 𐐈𐑋𐑊𐐲𐑅𐐴𐐻𐑅 𐐺𐐨𐑀𐐰𐑌 𐐻𐐭 𐑁𐑊𐐨 𐐺𐐨𐑁𐐬𐑉 𐑄𐐯𐑋, 𐑌𐐱𐐻𐐶𐐮𐑄𐑅𐐻𐐰𐑌𐐼𐐮𐑍 𐑄𐐩 𐐶𐐲𐑉 𐑅𐐬 𐑌𐐭𐑋𐐲𐑉𐐲𐑅 𐑄𐐰𐐻 𐑄𐐩 𐐿𐐳𐐼 𐑌𐐱𐐻 𐐺𐐨 𐑌𐐲𐑋𐐺𐐲𐑉𐐼; 𐐰𐑌𐐼 𐑄𐐩 𐑁𐑊𐐯𐐼 𐐺𐐨𐑁𐐬𐑉 𐑄 𐐤𐐨𐑁𐐴𐐻𐑅 𐐻𐐬𐐲𐑉𐐼𐑆 𐑄 𐐶𐐮𐑊𐐼𐐲𐑉𐑌𐐯𐑅 𐐸𐐶𐐮𐐽 𐐶𐐱𐑆 𐐶𐐯𐑅𐐻 𐐰𐑌𐐼 𐑌𐐫𐑉𐑃, 𐐰𐐶𐐩 𐐺𐐨𐐷𐐱𐑌𐐼 𐑄 𐐺𐐫𐑉𐐼𐐲𐑉𐑆 𐐱𐑂 𐑄 𐑊𐐰𐑌𐐼; 𐐰𐑌𐐼 𐑄 𐐤𐐨𐑁𐐴𐐻𐑅 𐐼𐐮𐐼 𐐹𐐲𐑉𐑅𐐭 𐑄𐐯𐑋 𐐶𐐮𐑄 𐑄𐐯𐑉 𐑋𐐴𐐻, 𐐰𐑌𐐼 𐐼𐐮𐐼 𐑅𐑊𐐩 𐑄𐐯𐑋; 𐐷𐐩, 𐑄𐐩 𐐶𐐲𐑉 𐑋𐐯𐐻 𐐱𐑌 𐐯𐑂𐐲𐑉𐐨 𐐸𐐰𐑌𐐼, 𐐰𐑌𐐼 𐑅𐑊𐐩𐑌, 𐐰𐑌𐐼 𐐼𐑉𐐮𐑂𐐲𐑌, 𐐲𐑌𐐻𐐮𐑊 𐑄𐐩 𐐶𐐲𐑉 𐑅𐐿𐐰𐐻𐐲𐑉𐐼 𐐱𐑌 𐑄 𐐶𐐯𐑅𐐻, 𐐰𐑌𐐼 𐐱𐑌 𐑄 𐑌𐐫𐑉𐑃, 𐐲𐑌𐐻𐐮𐑊 𐑄𐐩 𐐸𐐰𐐼 𐑉𐐨𐐽𐐻 𐑄 𐐶𐐮𐑊𐐼𐐲𐑉𐑌𐐯𐑅, 𐐸𐐶𐐮𐐽 𐐶𐐱𐑆 𐐿𐐫𐑊𐐼 𐐐𐐲𐑉𐑋𐐵𐑌𐐻𐑅; 𐐰𐑌𐐼 𐐮𐐻 𐐶𐐱𐑆 𐑄𐐰𐐻 𐐹𐐪𐑉𐐻

𐐱𐑂 𐑄 𐐶𐐮𐑊𐐼𐐲𐑉𐑌𐐯𐑅 𐐸𐐶𐐮𐐽 𐐶𐐱𐑆 𐐮𐑌𐑁𐐯𐑅𐐻𐐲𐐼 𐐺𐐴 𐐶𐐴𐑊𐐼 𐐰𐑌𐐼 𐑉𐐰𐑂𐐲𐑌𐐲𐑅 𐐺𐐨𐑅𐐻𐑅. 𐐈𐑌𐐼 𐐮𐐻 𐐿𐐩𐑋 𐐻𐐭 𐐹𐐪𐑅 𐑄𐐰𐐻 𐑋𐐯𐑌𐐨 𐐼𐐴𐐼 𐐮𐑌 𐑄 𐐶𐐮𐑊𐐼𐐲𐑉𐑌𐐯𐑅 𐐱𐑂 𐑄𐐯𐑉 𐐶𐐭𐑌𐐼𐑆, 𐐰𐑌𐐼 𐐶𐐲𐑉 𐐼𐐨𐑂𐐵𐑉𐐼 𐐺𐐴 𐑄𐐬𐑆 𐐺𐐨𐑅𐐻𐑅, 𐐰𐑌𐐼 𐐫𐑊𐑅𐐬 𐑄 𐑂𐐲𐑊𐐽𐐲𐑉𐑆 𐐱𐑂 𐑄 𐐩𐑉; 𐐰𐑌𐐼 𐑄𐐯𐑉 𐐺𐐬𐑌𐑆 𐐸𐐰𐑂 𐐺𐐮𐑌 𐑁𐐵𐑌𐐼, 𐐰𐑌𐐼 𐐸𐐰𐑂 𐐺𐐮𐑌 𐐸𐐨𐐹𐐼 𐐲𐐹 𐐱𐑌 𐑄 𐐲𐑉𐑃.

16. 𐐈𐑌𐐼 𐐮𐐻 𐐿𐐩𐑋 𐐻𐐭 𐐹𐐪𐑅 𐑄𐐰𐐻 𐑄 𐐤𐐨𐑁𐐴𐐻𐑅 𐐸𐐭 𐐶𐐲𐑉 𐑌𐐱𐐻 𐑅𐑊𐐩𐑌 𐐺𐐴 𐑄 𐐶𐐯𐐹𐐲𐑌𐑆 𐐱𐑂 𐐶𐐫𐑉, 𐐰𐑁𐐻𐐲𐑉 𐐸𐐰𐑂𐐮𐑍 𐐺𐐯𐑉𐐨𐐼 𐑄𐐬𐑆 𐐸𐐭 𐐸𐐰𐐼 𐐺𐐮𐑌 𐑅𐑊𐐩𐑌,—𐑌𐐵 𐑄 𐑌𐐲𐑋𐐺𐐲𐑉 𐐱𐑂 𐑄 𐑅𐑊𐐩𐑌 𐐶𐐲𐑉 𐑌𐐱𐐻 𐑌𐐲𐑋𐐺𐐲𐑉𐐼, 𐐺𐐨𐐿𐐫𐑆 𐐱𐑂 𐑄 𐑀𐑉𐐩𐐻𐑌𐐯𐑅 𐐱𐑂 𐑄𐐯𐑉 𐑌𐐲𐑋𐐺𐐲𐑉;—𐐰𐑁𐐻𐐲𐑉 𐑄𐐩 𐐸𐐰𐐼 𐑁𐐮𐑌𐐮𐑇𐐻 𐐺𐐯𐑉𐐨𐐮𐑍 𐑄𐐯𐑉 𐐼𐐯𐐼, 𐑄𐐩 𐐫𐑊 𐑉𐐨𐐻𐐲𐑉𐑌𐐼 𐐻𐐭 𐑄𐐯𐑉 𐑊𐐰𐑌𐐼𐑆, 𐐰𐑌𐐼 𐐻𐐭 𐑄𐐯𐑉 𐐸𐐵𐑆𐐲𐑆, 𐐰𐑌𐐼 𐑄𐐯𐑉 𐐶𐐴𐑂𐑆, 𐐰𐑌𐐼 𐑄𐐯𐑉 𐐽𐐮𐑊𐐼𐑉𐐯𐑌. 𐐤𐐵 𐑋𐐯𐑌𐐨 𐐶𐐮𐑋𐐯𐑌 𐐰𐑌𐐼 𐐽𐐮𐑊𐐼𐑉𐐯𐑌 𐐸𐐰𐐼 𐐺𐐮𐑌 𐑅𐑊𐐩𐑌 𐐶𐐮𐑄 𐑄 𐑅𐐬𐑉𐐼, 𐐰𐑌𐐼 𐐫𐑊𐑅𐐬 𐑋𐐯𐑌𐐨 𐐱𐑂 𐑄𐐯𐑉 𐑁𐑊𐐱𐐿𐑅 𐐰𐑌𐐼 𐑄𐐯𐑉 𐐸𐐲𐑉𐐼𐑆; 𐐰𐑌𐐼 𐐫𐑊𐑅𐐬 𐑋𐐯𐑌𐐨 𐐱𐑂 𐑄𐐯𐑉 𐑁𐐨𐑊𐐼𐑆 𐐱𐑂 𐑀𐑉𐐩𐑌 𐐶𐐲𐑉 𐐼𐐮𐑅𐐻𐑉𐐱𐐮𐐼, 𐑁𐐫𐑉 𐑄𐐩 𐐶𐐲𐑉 𐐻𐑉𐐱𐐼𐐲𐑌 𐐼𐐵𐑌 𐐺𐐴 𐑄 𐐸𐐬𐑅𐐻𐑅 𐐱𐑂 𐑋𐐯𐑌. 𐐈𐑌𐐼 𐑌𐐵 𐐰𐑆 𐑋𐐯𐑌𐐨 𐐱𐑂 𐑄 𐐢𐐰𐑋𐐲𐑌𐐴𐐻𐑅 𐐰𐑌𐐼 𐑄 𐐈𐑋𐑊𐐮𐑅𐐴𐐻𐑅 𐐸𐐭 𐐸𐐰𐐼 𐐺𐐮𐑌 𐑅𐑊𐐩𐑌 𐐲𐐹𐐱𐑌 𐑄 𐐺𐐰𐑍𐐿 𐐱𐑂 𐑄 𐑉𐐮𐑂𐐲𐑉 𐐝𐐴𐐼𐐲𐑌, 𐐶𐐲𐑉 𐐿𐐰𐑅𐐻 𐐮𐑌𐐻𐐭 𐑄 𐐶𐐫𐐻𐐲𐑉𐑆 𐐱𐑂 𐐝𐐴𐐼𐐲𐑌; 𐐰𐑌𐐼 𐐺𐐨𐐸𐐬𐑊𐐼 𐑄𐐯𐑉 𐐺𐐬𐑌𐑆 𐐪𐑉 𐐮𐑌 𐑄 𐐼𐐯𐐹𐑃𐑅 𐐱𐑂 𐑄 𐑅𐐨, 𐐰𐑌𐐼 𐑄𐐩 𐐪𐑉 𐑋𐐯𐑌𐐨. 𐐈𐑌𐐼 𐑄 𐐈𐑋𐑊𐐮𐑅𐐴𐐻𐑅 𐐶𐐲𐑉 𐐼𐐮𐑅𐐻𐐮𐑍𐑀𐐶𐐮𐑇𐐻 𐑁𐑉𐐱𐑋 𐑄 𐐤𐐨𐑁𐐴𐐻𐑅, 𐑁𐐫𐑉 𐑄𐐩 𐐸𐐰𐐼 𐑋𐐪𐑉𐐿𐐻 𐑄𐐯𐑋𐑅𐐯𐑊𐑂𐑆 𐐶𐐮𐑄 𐑉𐐯𐐼 𐐮𐑌 𐑄𐐯𐑉 𐑁𐐫𐑉𐐸𐐯𐐼𐑆 𐐰𐑁𐐻𐐲𐑉 𐑄 𐑋𐐰𐑌𐐲𐑉 𐐱𐑂 𐑄 𐐢𐐰𐑋𐐲𐑌𐐴𐐻𐑅; 𐑌𐐯𐑂𐐲𐑉𐑄𐐲𐑊𐐯𐑅 𐑄𐐩 𐐸𐐰𐐼 𐑌𐐱𐐻 𐑇𐐫𐑉𐑌 𐑄𐐯𐑉 𐐸𐐯𐐼𐑆 𐑊𐐴𐐿 𐐲𐑌𐐻𐐭 𐑄 𐐢𐐰𐑋𐐲𐑌𐐴𐐻𐑅. 𐐤𐐵 𐑄 𐐸𐐯𐐼𐑆 𐐱𐑂 𐑄 𐐢𐐰𐑋𐐲𐑌𐐴𐐻𐑅 𐐶𐐲𐑉 𐑇𐐫𐑉𐑌; 𐐰𐑌𐐼 𐑄𐐩 𐐶𐐲𐑉 𐑌𐐩𐐿𐐯𐐼, 𐑅𐐩𐑂 𐐮𐐻 𐐶𐐲𐑉 𐑅𐐿𐐮𐑌 𐐸𐐶𐐮𐐽 𐐶𐐱𐑆 𐑀𐐲𐑉𐐼𐐯𐐼 𐐲𐐺𐐵𐐻 𐑄𐐯𐑉 𐑊𐐱𐐮𐑌𐑆, 𐐰𐑌𐐼 𐐫𐑊𐑅𐐬 𐑄𐐯𐑉 𐐪𐑉𐑋𐐲𐑉, 𐐸𐐶𐐮𐐽 𐐶𐐱𐑆 𐑀𐐲𐑉𐐼𐐯𐐼 𐐲𐐺𐐵𐐻 𐑄𐐯𐑋, 𐐰𐑌𐐼 𐑄𐐯𐑉 𐐺𐐬𐑆, 𐐰𐑌𐐼 𐑄𐐯𐑉 𐐰𐑉𐐬𐑆, 𐐰𐑌𐐼 𐑄𐐯𐑉 𐑅𐐻𐐬𐑌𐑆, 𐐰𐑌𐐼 𐑄𐐯𐑉 𐑅𐑊𐐮𐑍𐑆, 𐐯𐐻𐑅. 𐐈𐑌𐐼 𐑄 𐑅𐐿𐐮𐑌𐑆 𐐱𐑂 𐑄 𐐢𐐰𐑋𐐲𐑌𐐴𐐻𐑅 𐐶𐐲𐑉 𐐼𐐪𐑉𐐿, 𐐰𐐿𐐫𐑉𐐼𐐮𐑍 𐐻𐐭 𐑄 𐑋𐐪𐑉𐐿 𐐸𐐶𐐮𐐽 𐐶𐐱𐑆 𐑅𐐯𐐻 𐐱𐑌 𐑄𐐯𐑉 𐑁𐐪𐑄𐐲𐑉𐑆, 𐐸𐐶𐐮𐐽 𐐶𐐱𐑆 𐐩 𐐿𐐲𐑉𐑅 𐐲𐐹𐐱𐑌 𐑄𐐯𐑋 𐐺𐐨𐐿𐐫𐑆 𐐱𐑂 𐑄𐐯𐑉 𐐻𐑉𐐰𐑌𐑆𐑀𐑉𐐯𐑇𐐲𐑌 𐐰𐑌𐐼 𐑄𐐯𐑉 𐑉𐐨𐐺𐐯𐑊𐐷𐐲𐑌 𐐲𐑀𐐯𐑌𐑅𐐻 𐑄𐐯𐑉 𐐺𐑉𐐯𐑄𐑉𐐯𐑌, 𐐸𐐭 𐐿𐐱𐑌𐑅𐐮𐑅𐐻𐐲𐐼 𐐱𐑂 𐐤𐐨𐑁𐐴, 𐐖𐐩𐐿𐐲𐐺, 𐐰𐑌𐐼 𐐖𐐬𐑆𐐯𐑁, 𐐰𐑌𐐼 𐐝𐐰𐑋, 𐐸𐐭 𐐶𐐲𐑉 𐐾𐐲𐑅𐐻 𐐰𐑌𐐼 𐐸𐐬𐑊𐐨 𐑋𐐯𐑌. 𐐈𐑌𐐼 𐑄𐐯𐑉 𐐺𐑉𐐯𐑄𐑉𐐯𐑌 𐑅𐐫𐐻 𐐻𐐭 𐐼𐐮𐑅𐐻𐑉𐐱𐐮 𐑄𐐯𐑋, 𐑄𐐯𐑉𐑁𐐫𐑉 𐑄𐐩 𐐶𐐲𐑉 𐐿𐐲𐑉𐑅𐐻; 𐐰𐑌𐐼 𐑄 𐐢𐐫𐑉𐐼 𐐘𐐱𐐼 𐑅𐐯𐐻 𐐩 𐑋𐐪𐑉𐐿 𐐲𐐹𐐱𐑌 𐑄𐐯𐑋, 𐐷𐐩, 𐐲𐐹𐐱𐑌 𐐢𐐩𐑋𐐲𐑌 𐐰𐑌𐐼 𐐢𐐯𐑋𐐷𐐭𐐯𐑊, 𐐰𐑌𐐼 𐐫𐑊𐑅𐐬 𐑄 𐑅𐐲𐑌𐑆 𐐱𐑂 𐐆𐑇𐑋𐐩𐐯𐑊, 𐐰𐑌𐐼 𐐆𐑇𐑋𐐩𐐯𐑊𐐴𐐻𐐮𐑇 𐐶𐐮𐑋𐐯𐑌. 𐐈𐑌𐐼 𐑄𐐮𐑅 𐐶𐐱𐑆 𐐼𐐲𐑌 𐑄𐐰𐐻 𐑄𐐯𐑉 𐑅𐐨𐐼 𐑋𐐴𐐻 𐐺𐐨 𐐼𐐮𐑅𐐻𐐮𐑍𐑀𐐶𐐮𐑇𐐻 𐑁𐑉𐐱𐑋 𐑄 𐑅𐐨𐐼 𐐱𐑂 𐑄𐐯𐑉 𐐺𐑉𐐯𐑄𐑉𐐯𐑌, 𐑄𐐰𐐻 𐑄𐐯𐑉𐐺𐐴 𐑄 𐐢𐐫𐑉𐐼 𐐘𐐱𐐼 𐑋𐐴𐐻 𐐹𐑉𐐨𐑆𐐲𐑉𐑂 𐐸𐐮𐑆 𐐹𐐨𐐹𐑊, 𐑄𐐰𐐻 𐑄𐐩 𐑋𐐴𐐻 𐑌𐐱𐐻 𐑋𐐮𐐿𐑅 𐐰𐑌𐐼 𐐺𐐨𐑊𐐨𐑂 𐐮𐑌 𐐮𐑌𐐿𐐱𐑉𐐯𐐿𐐻 𐐻𐑉𐐲𐐼𐐮𐑇𐐲𐑌𐑆 𐐸𐐶𐐮𐐽 𐐶𐐳𐐼 𐐹𐑉𐐭𐑂 𐑄𐐯𐑉 𐐼𐐮𐑅𐐻𐑉𐐲𐐿𐑇𐐲𐑌.

17. 𐐈𐑌𐐼 𐐮𐐻 𐐿𐐩𐑋 𐐻𐐭 𐐹𐐪𐑅 𐑄𐐰𐐻 𐐸𐐭𐑅𐐬𐐯𐑂𐐲𐑉 𐐼𐐮𐐼 𐑋𐐮𐑍𐑀𐑊 𐐸𐐮𐑆 𐑅𐐨𐐼 𐐶𐐮𐑄 𐑄𐐰𐐻 𐐱𐑂 𐑄 𐐢𐐰𐑋𐐲𐑌𐐴𐐻𐑅 𐐼𐐮𐐼 𐐺𐑉𐐮𐑍 𐑄 𐑅𐐩𐑋 𐐿𐐲𐑉𐑅 𐐲𐐹𐐱𐑌 𐐸𐐮𐑆 𐑅𐐨𐐼; 𐑄𐐯𐑉𐑁𐐫𐑉 𐐸𐐭𐑅𐐬𐐯𐑂𐐲𐑉 𐑅𐐲𐑁𐐲𐑉𐐼 𐐸𐐮𐑋𐑅𐐯𐑊𐑁 𐐻𐐭 𐐺𐐨 𐑊𐐯𐐼 𐐲𐐶𐐩 𐐺𐐴 𐑄 𐐢𐐰𐑋𐐲𐑌𐐴𐐻𐑅 𐐶𐐱𐑆 𐐿𐐫𐑊𐐼 𐐲𐑌𐐼𐐲𐑉 𐑄𐐰𐐻 𐐸𐐯𐐼, 𐐰𐑌𐐼 𐑄𐐯𐑉 𐐶𐐱𐑆 𐐩 𐑋𐐪𐑉𐐿 𐑅𐐯𐐻 𐐲𐐹𐐱𐑌 𐐸𐐮𐑋. 𐐈𐑌𐐼 𐐮𐐻 𐐿𐐩𐑋 𐐻𐐭 𐐹𐐪𐑅 𐑄𐐰𐐻 𐐸𐐭𐑅𐐬𐐯𐑂𐐲𐑉 𐐶𐐳𐐼 𐑌𐐱𐐻 𐐺𐐨𐑊𐐨𐑂 𐐮𐑌 𐑄 𐐻𐑉𐐲𐐼𐐮𐑇𐐲𐑌 𐐱𐑂 𐑄 𐐢𐐰𐑋𐐲𐑌𐐴𐐻𐑅, 𐐺𐐲𐐻 𐐺𐐨𐑊𐐨𐑂𐐼 𐑄𐐬𐑆 𐑉𐐯𐐿𐐲𐑉𐐼𐑆 𐐸𐐶𐐮𐐽 𐐶𐐲𐑉 𐐺𐑉𐐱𐐻 𐐵𐐻 𐐱𐑂 𐑄 𐑊𐐰𐑌𐐼 𐐱𐑂 𐐖𐐯𐑉𐐭𐑅𐐲𐑊𐐯𐑋, 𐐰𐑌𐐼 𐐫𐑊𐑅𐐬 𐐮𐑌 𐑄 𐐻𐑉𐐲𐐼𐐮𐑇𐐲𐑌 𐐱𐑂 𐑄𐐯𐑉 𐑁𐐪𐑄𐐲𐑉𐑆, 𐐸𐐶𐐮𐐽 𐐶𐐲𐑉 𐐿𐐱𐑉𐐯𐐿𐐻, 𐐸𐐭 𐐺𐐨𐑊𐐨𐑂𐐼 𐐮𐑌 𐑄 𐐿𐐱𐑋𐐰𐑌𐐼𐑋𐐯𐑌𐐻𐑅 𐐱𐑂 𐐘𐐱𐐼, 𐐰𐑌𐐼 𐐿𐐯𐐹𐐻 𐑄𐐯𐑋, 𐐶𐐲𐑉 𐐿𐐫𐑊𐐼 𐑄 𐐤𐐨𐑁𐐴𐐻𐑅, 𐐫𐑉 𐑄 𐐹𐐨𐐹𐑊 𐐱𐑂 𐐤𐐨𐑁𐐴, 𐑁𐑉𐐱𐑋 𐑄𐐰𐐻 𐐻𐐴𐑋 𐑁𐐫𐑉𐑃; 𐐰𐑌𐐼 𐐮𐐻 𐐮𐑆 𐑄𐐩 𐐸𐐭 𐐸𐐰𐑂 𐐿𐐯𐐹𐐻 𐑄 𐑉𐐯𐐿𐐲𐑉𐐼𐑆 𐐸𐐶𐐮𐐽 𐐪𐑉 𐐻𐑉𐐭 𐐱𐑂 𐑄𐐯𐑉 𐐹𐐨𐐹𐑊, 𐐰𐑌𐐼 𐐫𐑊𐑅𐐬 𐐱𐑂 𐑄 𐐹𐐨𐐹𐑊 𐐱𐑂 𐑄 𐐢𐐰𐑋𐐲𐑌𐐴𐐻𐑅. 𐐤𐐵 𐐶𐐨 𐐶𐐮𐑊 𐑉𐐨𐐻𐐲𐑉𐑌 𐐲𐑀𐐯𐑌 𐐻𐐭 𐑄 𐐈𐑋𐑊𐐮𐑅𐐴𐐻𐑅, 𐑁𐐫𐑉 𐑄𐐩 𐐫𐑊𐑅𐐬 𐐸𐐰𐐼 𐐩 𐑋𐐪𐑉𐐿 𐑅𐐯𐐻 𐐲𐐹𐐱𐑌 𐑄𐐯𐑋; 𐐷𐐩, 𐑄𐐩 𐑅𐐯𐐻 𐑄 𐑋𐐪𐑉𐐿 𐐲𐐹𐐱𐑌 𐑄𐐯𐑋𐑅𐐯𐑊𐑂𐑆, 𐐷𐐩, 𐐨𐑂𐐲𐑌 𐐩 𐑋𐐪𐑉𐐿 𐐱𐑂 𐑉𐐯𐐼 𐐲𐐹𐐱𐑌 𐑄𐐯𐑉 𐑁𐐫𐑉𐐸𐐯𐐼𐑆. 𐐜𐐲𐑅 𐑄 𐐶𐐲𐑉𐐼 𐐱𐑂 𐐘𐐱𐐼 𐐮𐑆 𐑁𐐳𐑊𐑁𐐮𐑊𐐼, 𐑁𐐫𐑉 𐑄𐐨𐑆 𐐪𐑉 𐑄 𐐶𐐲𐑉𐐼𐑆 𐐸𐐶𐐮𐐽 𐐸𐐨 𐑅𐐯𐐼 𐐻𐐭 𐐤𐐨𐑁𐐴—𐐒𐐨𐐸𐐬𐑊𐐼, 𐑄 𐐢𐐰𐑋𐐲𐑌𐐴𐐻𐑅 𐐸𐐰𐑂 𐐌 𐐿𐐲𐑉𐑅𐐻, 𐐰𐑌𐐼 𐐌 𐐶𐐮𐑊 𐑅𐐯𐐻 𐐩 𐑋𐐪𐑉𐐿 𐐱𐑌 𐑄𐐯𐑋, 𐑄𐐰𐐻 𐑄𐐩 𐐰𐑌𐐼 𐑄𐐯𐑉 𐑅𐐨𐐼 𐑋𐐩 𐐺𐐨 𐑅𐐯𐐹𐐲𐑉𐐩𐐻𐐯𐐼 𐑁𐑉𐐱𐑋 𐑄𐐨 𐐰𐑌𐐼 𐑄𐐴 𐑅𐐨𐐼, 𐑁𐑉𐐱𐑋 𐑄𐐮𐑅 𐐻𐐴𐑋 𐐸𐐯𐑌𐑅𐑁𐐫𐑉𐑃 𐐰𐑌𐐼 𐑁𐐫𐑉𐐯𐑂𐐲𐑉, 𐐯𐐿𐑅𐐯𐐹𐐻 𐑄𐐩 𐑉𐐨𐐹𐐯𐑌𐐻 𐐱𐑂 𐑄𐐯𐑉 𐐶𐐮𐐿𐐯𐐼𐑌𐐯𐑅 𐐰𐑌𐐼 𐐻𐐲𐑉𐑌 𐐻𐐭

𐑋𐐨, 𐑄𐐰𐐻 𐐴 𐑋𐐩 𐐸𐐰𐑂 𐑋𐐲𐑉𐑅𐐨 𐐲𐐹𐐱𐑌 𐑄𐐯𐑋. 𐐈𐑌𐐼 𐐲𐑀𐐯𐑌: 𐐴 𐐶𐐮𐑊 𐑅𐐯𐐻 𐐲 𐑋𐐪𐑉𐐿 𐐱𐑌 𐐸𐐮𐑋 𐑄𐐰𐐻 𐑋𐐮𐑍𐑀𐑊𐐯𐑃 𐐸𐐮𐑆 𐑅𐐨𐐼 𐐶𐐮𐑄 𐑄𐐴 𐐺𐑉𐐯𐑄𐑉𐐯𐑌, 𐑄𐐰𐐻 𐑄𐐩 𐑋𐐩 𐐺𐐨 𐐿𐐲𐑉𐑅𐐻 𐐫𐑊𐑅𐐬. 𐐈𐑌𐐼 𐐲𐑀𐐯𐑌, 𐐴 𐐶𐐮𐑊 𐑅𐐯𐐻 𐐲 𐑋𐐪𐑉𐐿 𐐲𐐹𐐱𐑌 𐐸𐐮𐑋 𐑄𐐰𐐻 𐑁𐐴𐐻𐐯𐑃 𐐲𐑀𐐯𐑌𐑅𐐻 𐑄𐐨 𐐰𐑌𐐼 𐑄𐐴 𐑅𐐨𐐼. 𐐈𐑌𐐼 𐐲𐑀𐐯𐑌 𐐴 𐑅𐐩, 𐐸𐐨 𐑄𐐰𐐻 𐐼𐐨𐐹𐐪𐑉𐐻𐐯𐑃 𐑁𐑉𐐱𐑋 𐑄𐐨 𐑇𐐰𐑊 𐑌𐐬 𐑋𐐬𐑉 𐐺𐐨 𐐿𐐫𐑊𐐼 𐑄𐐴 𐑅𐐨𐐼; 𐐰𐑌𐐼 𐐴 𐐶𐐮𐑊 𐐺𐑊𐐯𐑅 𐑄𐐨, 𐐰𐑌𐐼 𐐸𐐭𐑋𐑅𐐬𐐯𐑂𐐲𐑉 𐑇𐐰𐑊 𐐺𐐨 𐐿𐐫𐑊𐐼 𐑄𐐴 𐑅𐐨𐐼 𐐸𐐯𐑌𐑅𐑁𐐬𐑉𐑃 𐐰𐑌𐐼 𐑁𐐱𐑉𐐯𐑂𐐲𐑉; 𐐰𐑌𐐼 𐑄𐐨𐑆 𐐶𐐲𐑉 𐑄𐐲 𐐹𐑉𐐱𐑋𐐮𐑅𐐯𐑆 𐐱𐑂 𐑄𐐲 𐐢𐐫𐑉𐐼 𐐲𐑌𐐻𐐭 𐐤𐐨𐑁𐐴 𐐰𐑌𐐼 𐐻𐐭 𐐸𐐮𐑆 𐑅𐐨𐐼. 𐐤𐐵 𐑄𐐲 𐐈𐑋𐑊𐐮𐑅𐐴𐐻𐑅 𐑌𐐭 𐑌𐐱𐐻 𐑄𐐰𐐻 𐑄𐐩 𐐶𐐲𐑉 𐑁𐐳𐑊𐑁𐐮𐑊𐐮𐑍 𐑄𐐲 𐐶𐐲𐑉𐐼𐑆 𐐱𐑂 𐐘𐐱𐐼, 𐐸𐐶𐐯𐑌 𐑄𐐩 𐐺𐐨𐑀𐐰𐑌 𐐻𐐭 𐑋𐐪𐑉𐐿 𐑄𐐯𐑋𐑅𐐯𐑊𐑂𐑆 𐐮𐑌 𐑄𐐩𐑉 𐑁𐐱𐑉𐐸𐐯𐐼𐑆; 𐑌𐐯𐑂𐐲𐑉𐑄𐐯𐑊𐐯𐑅 𐑄𐐩 𐐸𐐰𐐼 𐐿𐐲𐑋 𐐵𐐻 𐐮𐑌 𐐬𐐹𐑌 𐑉𐐨𐐺𐐯𐑊𐐷𐐲𐑌 𐐲𐑀𐐯𐑌𐑅𐐻 𐐘𐐱𐐼; 𐑄𐐯𐑉𐑁𐐬𐑉 𐐮𐐻 𐐶𐐱𐑆 𐐯𐐿𐑅𐐹𐐨𐐼𐐨𐐯𐑌𐐻 𐑄𐐰𐐻 𐑄𐐲 𐐿𐐲𐑉𐑅 𐑇𐐳𐐼 𐑁𐐫𐑊 𐐲𐐹𐐱𐑌 𐑄𐐯𐑋. 𐐤𐐵 𐐴 𐐶𐐳𐐼 𐑄𐐰𐐻 𐐷𐐨 𐑇𐐳𐐼 𐑅𐐨 𐑄𐐰𐐻 𐑄𐐩 𐐺𐑉𐐫𐐻 𐐲𐐹𐐱𐑌 𐑄𐐯𐑋𐑅𐐯𐑊𐑂𐑆 𐑄𐐲 𐐿𐐲𐑉𐑅; 𐐰𐑌𐐼 𐐨𐑂𐐲𐑌 𐑅𐐬 𐐼𐐲𐑃 𐐯𐑂𐑉𐐨 𐑋𐐰𐑌 𐑄𐐰𐐻 𐐮𐑆 𐐿𐐲𐑉𐑅𐐻 𐐺𐑉𐐮𐑍 𐐲𐐹𐐱𐑌 𐐸𐐮𐑋𐑅𐐯𐑊𐑁 𐐸𐐮𐑆 𐐬𐑌 𐐿𐐱𐑌𐐼𐐯𐑋𐑌𐐩𐑇𐐲𐑌.

18. 𐐈𐑌𐐼 𐐮𐐻 𐐿𐐩𐑋 𐐻𐐭 𐐹𐐰𐑅 𐑄𐐰𐐻 𐑌𐐱𐐻 𐑋𐐯𐑌𐐨 𐐼𐐩𐑆 𐐰𐑁𐐻𐐲𐑉 𐑄𐐲 𐐺𐐰𐐻𐐲𐑊 𐐸𐐶𐐮𐐽 𐐶𐐱𐑆 𐑁𐐫𐐻 𐐮𐑌 𐑄𐐲 𐑊𐐰𐑌𐐼 𐐱𐑂 𐐞𐐰𐑉𐐲𐐸𐐯𐑋𐑊𐐲, 𐐺𐐴 𐑄𐐲 𐐢𐐰𐑋𐐲𐑌𐐴𐐻𐑅 𐐰𐑌𐐼 𐑄𐐲 𐐈𐑋𐑊𐐮𐑅𐐴𐐻𐑅, 𐑄𐐰𐐻 𐑄𐐯𐑉 𐐶𐐱𐑆 𐐰𐑌𐐲𐑄𐐲𐑉 𐐪𐑉𐑋𐐨 𐐱𐑂 𐑄𐐲 𐐢𐐰𐑋𐐲𐑌𐐴𐐻𐑅 𐐿𐐩𐑋 𐐮𐑌 𐐲𐐹𐐱𐑌 𐑄𐐲 𐐹𐐨𐐹𐐲𐑊 𐐱𐑂 𐐤𐐨𐑁𐐴, 𐐮𐑌 𐑄𐐲 𐑅𐐩𐑋 𐐹𐑊𐐩𐑅 𐐸𐐶𐐯𐑉 𐑄𐐲 𐑁𐐲𐑉𐑅𐐻 𐐪𐑉𐑋𐐨 𐑋𐐯𐐻 𐑄𐐲 𐐈𐑋𐑊𐐮𐑅𐐴𐐻𐑅. 𐐈𐑌𐐼 𐐮𐐻 𐐿𐐩𐑋 𐐻𐐭 𐐹𐐰𐑅 𐑄𐐰𐐻 𐑄𐐯𐑉 𐐶𐐱𐑆 𐐰𐑌 𐐪𐑉𐑋𐐨 𐑅𐐯𐑌𐐻 𐐻𐐭 𐐼𐑉𐐴𐑂 𐑄𐐯𐑋 𐐵𐐻 𐐱𐑂 𐑄𐐩𐑉 𐑊𐐰𐑌𐐼. 𐐤𐐵 𐐈𐑊𐑋𐐲 𐐸𐐮𐑋𐑅𐐯𐑊𐑁 𐐺𐐨𐐮𐑍 𐐰𐑁𐑊𐐮𐐿𐐻𐐯𐐼 𐐶𐐮𐑄 𐐲 𐐶𐐭𐑌𐐼, 𐐼𐐮𐐼 𐑌𐐱𐐻 𐑀𐐬 𐐲𐐹 𐐻𐐭 𐐺𐐰𐐻𐐲𐑊 𐐰𐐻 𐑄𐐮𐑅 𐐻𐐴𐑋 𐐲𐑀𐐯𐑌𐑅𐐻 𐑄𐐲 𐐢𐐰𐑋𐐲𐑌𐐴𐐻𐑅; 𐐒𐐲𐐻 𐐸𐐨 𐑅𐐯𐑌𐐻 𐐲𐐹 𐐲 𐑌𐐭𐑋𐐲𐑉𐐲𐑅 𐐪𐑉𐑋𐐨 𐐲𐑀𐐯𐑌𐑅𐐻 𐑄𐐯𐑋; 𐐰𐑌𐐼 𐑄𐐩 𐐶𐐯𐑌𐐻 𐐲𐐹 𐐰𐑌𐐼 𐑅𐑊𐐭 𐑋𐐯𐑌𐐨 𐐱𐑂 𐑄𐐲 𐐢𐐰𐑋𐐲𐑌𐐴𐐻𐑅, 𐐰𐑌𐐼 𐐼𐑉𐐬𐑂 𐑄𐐲 𐑉𐐨𐑋𐐩𐑌𐐼𐐲𐑉 𐐱𐑂 𐑄𐐯𐑋 𐐵𐐻 𐐱𐑂 𐑄𐐲 𐐺𐐫𐑉𐐼𐐲𐑉𐑆 𐐱𐑂 𐑄𐐩𐑉 𐑊𐐰𐑌𐐼; 𐐰𐑌𐐼 𐑄𐐯𐑌 𐑄𐐩 𐑉𐐨𐐻𐐲𐑉𐑌𐐼 𐐲𐑀𐐯𐑌, 𐐰𐑌𐐼 𐐺𐐨𐑀𐐰𐑌 𐐻𐐭 𐐯𐑅𐐻𐐰𐐺𐑊𐐮𐑇 𐐹𐐨𐑅 𐐮𐑌 𐑄𐐲 𐑊𐐰𐑌𐐼, 𐐺𐐨𐐮𐑍 𐐻𐑉𐐲𐐺𐐲𐑊𐐼 𐑌𐐬 𐑋𐐬𐑉 𐑁𐐫𐑉 𐐲 𐐻𐐴𐑋 𐐶𐐮𐑄 𐑄𐐩𐑉 𐐯𐑌𐐯𐑋𐐨𐑆. 𐐤𐐵 𐐫𐑊 𐑄𐐨𐑆 𐑃𐐮𐑍𐑆 𐐶𐐲𐑉 𐐼𐐲𐑌, 𐐷𐐩, 𐐫𐑊 𐑄𐐨𐑆 𐐶𐐫𐑉𐑆 𐐰𐑌𐐼 𐐿𐐱𐑌𐐻𐐯𐑌𐑇𐐲𐑌𐑆 𐐶𐐲𐑉 𐐿𐐱𐑋𐐯𐑌𐑅𐐻 𐐰𐑌𐐼 𐐯𐑌𐐼𐐯𐐼 𐐮𐑌 𐑄𐐲 𐑁𐐮𐑁𐑃 𐐷𐐨𐑉 𐐱𐑂 𐑄𐐲 𐑉𐐩𐑌 𐐱𐑂 𐑄𐐲 𐐾𐐲𐐾𐐯𐑆; 𐐰𐑌𐐼 𐐮𐑌 𐐶𐐲𐑌 𐐷𐐨𐑉 𐐶𐐲𐑉 𐑃𐐵𐑆𐐲𐑌𐐼𐑆 𐐰𐑌𐐼 𐐻𐐯𐑌𐑆 𐐱𐑂 𐑃𐐵𐑆𐐲𐑌𐐼𐑆 𐐱𐑂 𐑅𐐬𐑊𐑆 𐑅𐐯𐑌𐐻 𐐻𐐭 𐑄𐐲 𐐨𐐻𐐲𐑉𐑌𐐲𐑊 𐐶𐐲𐑉𐑊𐐼, 𐑄𐐰𐐻 𐑄𐐩 𐑋𐐴𐐻 𐑉𐐨𐐹 𐑄𐐩𐑉 𐑉𐐨𐐶𐐫𐑉𐐼𐑆 𐐰𐐿𐐫𐑉𐐼𐐮𐑍 𐐻𐐭 𐑄𐐩𐑉 𐐶𐐲𐑉𐐿𐑅, 𐐸𐐶𐐯𐑄𐐲𐑉 𐑄𐐩 𐐶𐐲𐑉 𐑀𐐳𐐼 𐐫𐑉 𐐸𐐶𐐯𐑄𐐲𐑉 𐑄𐐩 𐐶𐐲𐑉 𐐺𐐰𐐼, 𐐻𐐭 𐑉𐐨𐐹 𐐨𐐻𐐲𐑉𐑌𐐲𐑊 𐐸𐐰𐐹𐐨𐑌𐐯𐑅 𐐫𐑉 𐐨𐐻𐐲𐑉𐑌𐐲𐑊 𐑋𐐮𐑆𐐲𐑉𐐨, 𐐰𐐿𐐫𐑉𐐼𐐮𐑍 𐐻𐐭 𐑄𐐲 𐑅𐐹𐐮𐑉𐐮𐐻 𐐸𐐶𐐮𐐽 𐑄𐐩 𐑊𐐮𐑅𐐻𐐯𐐼 𐐻𐐭 𐐬𐐺𐐩, 𐐸𐐶𐐯𐑄𐐲𐑉 𐐮𐐻 𐐺𐐨 𐐲 𐑀𐐳𐐼 𐑅𐐹𐐮𐑉𐐮𐐻 𐐫𐑉 𐐲 𐐺𐐰𐐼 𐐶𐐲𐑌; 𐑁𐐫𐑉 𐐯𐑂𐑉𐐨 𐑋𐐰𐑌 𐑉𐐨𐑅𐐨𐑂𐐯𐑃 𐐶𐐩𐐾𐐯𐑆 𐐱𐑂 𐐸𐐮𐑋 𐐸𐐭𐑋 𐐸𐐨 𐑊𐐮𐑅𐐻𐐯𐑃 𐐻𐐭 𐐬𐐺𐐩, 𐐰𐑌𐐼 𐑄𐐮𐑅 𐐰𐐿𐐫𐑉𐐼𐐮𐑍 𐐻𐐭 𐑄𐐲 𐐶𐐲𐑉𐐼𐑆 𐐱𐑂 𐑄𐐲 𐑅𐐹𐐮𐑉𐐮𐐻 𐐱𐑂 𐐹𐑉𐐱𐑁𐐯𐑅𐐨; 𐑄𐐯𐑉𐑁𐐬𐑉 𐑊𐐯𐐻 𐐮𐐻 𐐺𐐨 𐐰𐐿𐐫𐑉𐐼𐐮𐑍 𐐻𐐭 𐑄𐐲 𐐻𐑉𐐭𐑃. 𐐈𐑌𐐼 𐑄𐐲𐑅 𐐯𐑌𐐼𐐯𐑃 𐑄𐐲 𐑁𐐮𐑁𐑃 𐐷𐐨𐑉 𐐱𐑂 𐑄𐐲 𐑉𐐩𐑌 𐐱𐑂 𐑄𐐲 𐐾𐐲𐐾𐐯𐑆.

𐐕𐐰𐐹𐐻𐐲𐑉 II.

1. 𐐤𐐵 𐐮𐐻 𐐿𐐩𐑋 𐐻𐐭 𐐹𐐰𐑅 𐐮𐑌 𐑄𐐲 𐑅𐐮𐐿𐑅𐑃 𐐷𐐨𐑉 𐐱𐑂 𐑄𐐲 𐑉𐐩𐑌 𐐱𐑂 𐑄𐐲 𐐾𐐲𐐾𐐯𐑆 𐐬𐑂𐐲𐑉 𐑄𐐲 𐐹𐐨𐐹𐐲𐑊 𐐱𐑂 𐐤𐐨𐑁𐐴, 𐑄𐐯𐑉 𐐶𐐲𐑉 𐑌𐐬 𐐿𐐱𐑌𐐻𐐯𐑌𐑇𐐲𐑌𐑆 𐑌𐐫𐑉 𐐶𐐫𐑉𐑆 𐐮𐑌 𐑄𐐲 𐑊𐐰𐑌𐐼 𐐱𐑂 𐐞𐐰𐑉𐐲𐐸𐐯𐑋𐑊𐐲; 𐐒𐐲𐐻 𐑄𐐲 𐐹𐐨𐐹𐐲𐑊 𐐶𐐲𐑉 𐐰𐑁𐑊𐐮𐐿𐐻𐐯𐐼, 𐐷𐐩, 𐑀𐑉𐐩𐐻𐑊𐐨 𐐰𐑁𐑊𐐮𐐿𐐻𐐯𐐼 𐑁𐐫𐑉 𐑄𐐲 𐑊𐐱𐑅 𐐱𐑂 𐑄𐐩𐑉 𐐺𐑉𐐯𐑄𐑉𐐯𐑌, 𐐰𐑌𐐼 𐐫𐑊𐑅𐐬 𐑁𐐫𐑉 𐑄𐐲 𐑊𐐱𐑅 𐐱𐑂 𐑄𐐩𐑉 𐑁𐑊𐐱𐐿𐑅 𐐰𐑌𐐼 𐐸𐐲𐑉𐐼𐑆, 𐐰𐑌𐐼 𐐫𐑊𐑅𐐬 𐑁𐐫𐑉 𐑄𐐲 𐑊𐐱𐑅 𐐱𐑂 𐑄𐐩𐑉 𐑁𐐨𐑊𐐼𐑆 𐐱𐑂 𐑀𐑉𐐩𐑌, 𐐸𐐶𐐮𐐽 𐐶𐐲𐑉 𐐻𐑉𐐱𐐼𐐲𐑌 𐐲𐑌𐐼𐐲𐑉 𐑁𐐳𐐻 𐐰𐑌𐐼 𐐼𐐨𐑅𐐻𐑉𐐱𐐮𐐼 𐐺𐐴 𐑄𐐲 𐐢𐐰𐑋𐐲𐑌𐐴𐐻𐑅. 𐐈𐑌𐐼 𐑅𐐬 𐑀𐑉𐐩𐐻 𐐶𐐲𐑉 𐑄𐐩𐑉 𐐰𐑁𐑊𐐮𐐿𐑇𐐲𐑌𐑆 𐑄𐐰𐐻 𐐯𐑂𐑉𐐨 𐑅𐐬𐑊 𐐸𐐰𐐼 𐐿𐐫𐑆 𐐻𐐭 𐑋𐐬𐑉𐑌; 𐐰𐑌𐐼 𐑄𐐩 𐐺𐐨𐑊𐐨𐑂𐐼 𐑄𐐰𐐻 𐐮𐐻 𐐶𐐱𐑆 𐑄𐐲 𐐾𐐲𐐾𐑋𐐯𐑌𐐻𐑅 𐐱𐑂 𐐘𐐱𐐼 𐑅𐐯𐑌𐐻 𐐲𐐹𐐱𐑌 𐑄𐐯𐑋 𐐺𐐨𐐿𐐫𐑆 𐐱𐑂 𐑄𐐩𐑉 𐐶𐐮𐐿𐐯𐐼𐑌𐐯𐑅 𐐰𐑌𐐼 𐑄𐐩𐑉 𐐲𐐺𐐱𐑋𐐮𐑌𐐩𐑇𐐲𐑌𐑆; 𐑄𐐯𐑉𐑁𐐬𐑉 𐑄𐐩 𐐶𐐲𐑉 𐐰𐐶𐐩𐐿𐐲𐑌𐐼 𐐻𐐭 𐐲 𐑉𐐨𐑋𐐯𐑋𐐺𐑉𐐲𐑌𐑅 𐐱𐑂 𐑄𐐩𐑉 𐐼𐐭𐐻𐐨. 𐐈𐑌𐐼 𐑄𐐩 𐐺𐐨𐑀𐐰𐑌 𐐻𐐭 𐐯𐑅𐐻𐐰𐐺𐑊𐐮𐑇 𐑄𐐲 𐐽𐐲𐑉𐐽 𐑋𐐬𐑉 𐑁𐐳𐑊𐐨; 𐐷𐐩, 𐐰𐑌𐐼 𐑋𐐯𐑌𐐨 𐐶𐐲𐑉 𐐺𐐰𐐹𐐻𐐴𐑆𐐼 𐐮𐑌 𐑄𐐲 𐐶𐐫𐐻𐐲𐑉𐑆 𐐱𐑂 𐐝𐐴𐐼𐐲𐑌, 𐐰𐑌𐐼 𐐶𐐲𐑉 𐐾𐐱𐐮𐑌𐐼 𐐻𐐭 𐑄𐐲 𐐽𐐲𐑉𐐽

𐐱𐑂 𐐘𐐱𐐼; 𐐷𐐩, 𐑄𐐩 𐐶𐐲𐑉 𐐺𐐰𐐹𐐻𐐴𐑆𐐼 𐐺𐐴 𐑄 𐐸𐐰𐑌𐐼 𐐱𐑂 𐐈𐑊𐑋𐐲, 𐐸𐐭 𐐸𐐰𐐼 𐐺𐐨𐑌 𐐿𐐱𐑌𐑅𐐨𐐿𐑉𐐩𐐻𐐯𐐼 𐑄 𐐸𐐴 𐐹𐑉𐐨𐑅𐐻 𐐬𐑂𐐲𐑉 𐑄 𐐹𐐨𐐹𐑊 𐐱𐑂 𐑄 𐐕𐐲𐑉𐐽, 𐐺𐐴 𐑄 𐐸𐐰𐑌𐐼 𐐱𐑂 𐐸𐐮𐑆 𐑁𐐪𐑄𐐲𐑉 𐐈𐑊𐑋𐐲.

2. 𐐈𐑌𐐼 𐐮𐐻 𐐿𐐩𐑋 𐐻𐐭 𐐹𐐰𐑅 𐐮𐑌 𐑄 𐑅𐐯𐑂𐐯𐑌𐑃 𐐷𐐨𐑉 𐐱𐑂 𐑄 𐑉𐐩𐑌 𐐱𐑂 𐑄 𐐖𐐲𐐾𐐯𐑆 𐑄𐐩𐑉 𐐶𐐲𐑉 𐐰𐐺𐐵𐐻 𐑃𐑉𐐨 𐑃𐐵𐑆𐐰𐑌𐐼 𐑁𐐴𐑂 𐐸𐐲𐑌𐐼𐑉𐐯𐐼 𐑅𐐬𐑊𐑆 𐑄𐐰𐐻 𐐷𐐭𐑌𐐴𐐻𐐯𐐼 𐑄𐐯𐑋𐑅𐐯𐑊𐑂𐑆 𐐻𐐭 𐑄 𐐕𐐲𐑉𐐽 𐐱𐑂 𐐘𐐱𐐼, 𐐰𐑌𐐼 𐐶𐐲𐑉 𐐺𐐰𐐹𐐻𐐴𐑆𐐼. 𐐈𐑌𐐼 𐑄𐐲𐑅 𐐯𐑌𐐼𐐯𐐼 𐑄 𐑅𐐯𐑂𐐯𐑌𐑃 𐐷𐐨𐑉 𐐱𐑂 𐑄 𐑉𐐩𐑌 𐐱𐑂 𐑄 𐐖𐐲𐐾𐐯𐑆 𐐬𐑂𐐲𐑉 𐑄 𐐹𐐨𐐹𐑊 𐐱𐑂 𐐤𐐨𐑁𐐴; 𐐰𐑌𐐼 𐑄𐐩𐑉 𐐶𐐱𐑆 𐐿𐐱𐑌𐐻𐐮𐑌𐐷𐐭𐐲𐑊 𐐹𐐨𐑅 𐐮𐑌 𐐫𐑊 𐑄𐐰𐐻 𐐻𐐴𐑋.

3. 𐐈𐑌𐐼 𐐮𐐻 𐐿𐐩𐑋 𐐻𐐭 𐐹𐐰𐑅 𐐮𐑌 𐑄 𐐩𐐻𐑃 𐐷𐐨𐑉 𐐱𐑂 𐑄 𐑉𐐩𐑌 𐐱𐑂 𐑄 𐐖𐐲𐐾𐐯𐑆 𐑄𐐰𐐻 𐑄 𐐹𐐨𐐹𐑊 𐐱𐑂 𐑄 𐐕𐐲𐑉𐐽 𐐺𐐨𐑀𐐰𐑌 𐐻𐐭 𐐶𐐰𐐿𐑅 𐐹𐑉𐐵𐐼, 𐐺𐐨𐐿𐐫𐑆 𐐱𐑂 𐑄𐐩𐑉 𐐯𐐿𐑅𐐨𐐼𐐮𐑍 𐑉𐐮𐐽𐐯𐑆, 𐐰𐑌𐐼 𐑄𐐩𐑉 𐑁𐐴𐑌 𐑅𐐮𐑊𐐿𐑅, 𐐰𐑌𐐼 𐑄𐐩𐑉 𐑁𐐴𐑌 𐐻𐐶𐐴𐑌𐐼 𐑊𐐮𐑌𐐯𐑌, 𐐰𐑌𐐼 𐐺𐐨𐐿𐐫𐑆 𐐱𐑂 𐑄𐐩𐑉 𐑋𐐯𐑌𐐨 𐑁𐑊𐐱𐐿𐑅 𐐰𐑌𐐼 𐐸𐐲𐑉𐐼𐑆, 𐐰𐑌𐐼 𐑄𐐩𐑉 𐑀𐐬𐑊𐐼 𐐰𐑌𐐼 𐑄𐐩𐑉 𐑅𐐮𐑊𐑂𐐲𐑉, 𐐰𐑌𐐼 𐐫𐑊 𐑋𐐰𐑌𐐲𐑉 𐐱𐑂 𐐹𐑉𐐯𐑇𐐲𐑅 𐑃𐐮𐑍𐑆, 𐐸𐐶𐐮𐐽 𐑄𐐩 𐐸𐐰𐐼 𐐱𐐺𐐻𐐩𐑌𐐼 𐐺𐐴 𐑄𐐩𐑉 𐐮𐑌𐐼𐐲𐑅𐐻𐑉𐐨; 𐐰𐑌𐐼 𐐮𐑌 𐐫𐑊 𐑄𐐨𐑆 𐑃𐐮𐑍𐑆 𐐶𐐲𐑉 𐑄𐐩 𐑊𐐮𐑁𐐻𐐯𐐼 𐐲𐐹 𐐮𐑌 𐑄 𐐹𐑉𐐴𐐼 𐐱𐑂 𐑄𐐩𐑉 𐐴𐑆, 𐑁𐐫𐑉 𐑄𐐩 𐐺𐐨𐑀𐐰𐑌 𐐻𐐭 𐐶𐐩𐑉 𐑂𐐯𐑉𐐨 𐐿𐐱𐑅𐐻𐑊𐐨 𐐰𐐹𐐰𐑉𐐯𐑊. 𐐤𐐵 𐑄𐐮𐑅 𐐶𐐱𐑆 𐑄 𐐿𐐫𐑆 𐐱𐑂 𐑋𐐲𐐽 𐐰𐑁𐑊𐐮𐐿𐑇𐐲𐑌 𐐻𐐭 𐐈𐑊𐑋𐐲, 𐐷𐐩, 𐐰𐑌𐐼 𐐻𐐭 𐑋𐐯𐑌𐐨 𐐱𐑂 𐑄 𐐹𐐨𐐹𐑊 𐐸𐐭𐑋 𐐈𐑊𐑋𐐲 𐐸𐐰𐐼 𐐿𐐱𐑌𐑅𐐨𐐿𐑉𐐩𐐻𐐯𐐼 𐐻𐐭 𐐺𐐨 𐐻𐐨𐐽𐐲𐑉𐑆, 𐐰𐑌𐐼 𐐹𐑉𐐨𐑅𐐻𐑅, 𐐰𐑌𐐼 𐐯𐑊𐐼𐐲𐑉𐑆 𐐬𐑂𐐲𐑉 𐑄 𐐕𐐲𐑉𐐽; 𐐷𐐩, 𐑋𐐯𐑌𐐨 𐐱𐑂 𐑄𐐯𐑋 𐐶𐐲𐑉 𐑅𐐬𐑉𐑊𐐨 𐑀𐑉𐐨𐑂𐐼 𐑁𐐫𐑉 𐑄 𐐶𐐮𐐿𐐯𐐼𐑌𐐯𐑅 𐐸𐐶𐐮𐐽 𐑄𐐩 𐑅𐐫 𐐸𐐰𐐼 𐐺𐐨𐑀𐐲𐑌 𐐻𐐭 𐐺𐐨 𐐰𐑋𐐲𐑍 𐑄𐐩𐑉 𐐹𐐨𐐹𐑊. 𐐙𐐫𐑉 𐑄𐐩 𐑅𐐫 𐐰𐑌𐐼 𐐺𐐨𐐸𐐯𐑊𐐼 𐐶𐐮𐑄 𐑀𐑉𐐩𐐻 𐑅𐐱𐑉𐐬, 𐑄𐐰𐐻 𐑄 𐐹𐐨𐐹𐑊 𐐱𐑂 𐑄 𐐕𐐲𐑉𐐽 𐐺𐐨𐑀𐐰𐑌 𐐻𐐭 𐐺𐐨 𐑊𐐮𐑁𐐻𐐯𐐼 𐐲𐐹 𐐮𐑌 𐑄 𐐹𐑉𐐴𐐼 𐐱𐑂 𐑄𐐩𐑉 𐐴𐑆, 𐐰𐑌𐐼 𐐻𐐭 𐑅𐐯𐐻 𐑄𐐩𐑉 𐐸𐐪𐑉𐐻𐑅 𐐲𐐹𐐱𐑌 𐑉𐐮𐐽𐐯𐑆, 𐐰𐑌𐐼 𐐲𐐹𐐱𐑌 𐑄 𐑂𐐩𐑌 𐑃𐐮𐑍𐑆 𐐱𐑂 𐑄 𐐶𐐲𐑉𐑊𐐼; 𐑄𐐰𐐻 𐑄𐐩 𐐺𐐨𐑀𐐰𐑌 𐐻𐐭 𐐺𐐨 𐑅𐐿𐐫𐑉𐑌𐑁𐐳𐑊, 𐐶𐐲𐑌 𐐻𐐬𐐲𐑉𐐼𐑆 𐐰𐑌𐐲𐑄𐐲𐑉, 𐐰𐑌𐐼 𐑄𐐩 𐐺𐐨𐑀𐐰𐑌 𐐻𐐭 𐐹𐐲𐑉𐑅𐐨𐐿𐐷𐐭𐐻 𐑄𐐬𐑆 𐑄𐐰𐐻 𐐼𐐮𐐼 𐑌𐐱𐐻 𐐺𐐨𐑊𐐨𐑂 𐐰𐐿𐐫𐑉𐐼𐐮𐑍 𐐻𐐭 𐑄𐐩𐑉 𐐬𐑌 𐐶𐐮𐑊 𐐰𐑌𐐼 𐐹𐑊𐐯𐑈𐐲𐑉. 𐐈𐑌𐐼 𐑄𐐲𐑅, 𐐮𐑌 𐑄𐐮𐑅 𐐩𐐻𐑃 𐐷𐐨𐑉 𐐱𐑂 𐑄 𐑉𐐩𐑌 𐐱𐑂 𐑄 𐐖𐐲𐐾𐐯𐑆, 𐑄𐐩𐑉 𐐺𐐨𐑀𐐰𐑌 𐐻𐐭 𐐺𐐨 𐑀𐑉𐐩𐐻 𐐿𐐱𐑌𐐻𐐯𐑌𐑇𐐲𐑌𐑆 𐐰𐑋𐐲𐑍 𐑄 𐐹𐐨𐐹𐑊 𐐱𐑂 𐑄 𐐕𐐲𐑉𐐽; 𐐷𐐩, 𐑄𐐩𐑉 𐐶𐐲𐑉 𐐯𐑌𐑂𐐨𐐮𐑍𐑆, 𐐰𐑌𐐼 𐑅𐐻𐑉𐐴𐑁𐑅, 𐐰𐑌𐐼 𐑋𐐰𐑊𐐮𐑅, 𐐰𐑌𐐼 𐐹𐐲𐑉𐑅𐐨𐐿𐐷𐐭𐑇𐐲𐑌𐑆, 𐐰𐑌𐐼 𐐹𐑉𐐴𐐼, 𐐨𐑂𐐯𐑌 𐐻𐐭 𐐯𐐿𐑅𐐨𐐼 𐑄 𐐹𐑉𐐴𐐼 𐐱𐑂 𐑄𐐬𐑆 𐐸𐐭 𐐼𐐮𐐼 𐑌𐐱𐐻 𐐺𐐨𐑊𐐫𐑍 𐐻𐐭 𐑄 𐐕𐐲𐑉𐐽 𐐱𐑂 𐐘𐐱𐐼. 𐐈𐑌𐐼 𐑄𐐲𐑅 𐐯𐑌𐐼𐐯𐐼 𐑄 𐐩𐐻𐑃 𐐷𐐨𐑉 𐐱𐑂 𐑄 𐑉𐐩𐑌 𐐱𐑂 𐑄 𐐖𐐲𐐾𐐯𐑆; 𐐰𐑌𐐼 𐑄 𐐶𐐮𐐿𐐯𐐼𐑌𐐯𐑅 𐐱𐑂 𐑄 𐐕𐐲𐑉𐐽 𐐶𐐱𐑆 𐐰 𐑀𐑉𐐩𐐻 𐑅𐐻𐐲𐑋𐐺𐑊𐐮𐑍-𐐺𐑊𐐱𐐿 𐐻𐐭 𐑄𐐬𐑆 𐐸𐐭 𐐼𐐮𐐼 𐑌𐐱𐐻 𐐺𐐨𐑊𐐫𐑍 𐐻𐐭 𐑄 𐐕𐐲𐑉𐐽; 𐐰𐑌𐐼 𐑄𐐲𐑅 𐑄 𐐕𐐲𐑉𐐽 𐐺𐐨𐑀𐐰𐑌 𐐻𐐭 𐑁𐐩𐑊 𐐮𐑌 𐐮𐐻𐑅 𐐹𐑉𐐱𐑀𐑉𐐯𐑅.

4. 𐐈𐑌𐐼 𐐮𐐻 𐐿𐐩𐑋 𐐻𐐭 𐐹𐐰𐑅 𐐮𐑌 𐑄 𐐿𐐱𐑋𐐯𐑌𐑅𐑋𐐯𐑌𐐻 𐐱𐑂 𐑄 𐑌𐐴𐑌𐑃 𐐷𐐨𐑉, 𐐈𐑊𐑋𐐲 𐑅𐐫 𐑄 𐐶𐐮𐐿𐐯𐐼𐑌𐐯𐑅 𐐱𐑂 𐑄 𐐕𐐲𐑉𐐽, 𐐰𐑌𐐼 𐐸𐐨 𐑅𐐫 𐐫𐑊𐑅𐐬 𐑄𐐰𐐻 𐑄 𐐯𐑀𐑆𐐰𐑋𐐹𐑊 𐐱𐑂 𐑄 𐐕𐐲𐑉𐐽 𐐺𐐨𐑀𐐰𐑌 𐐻𐐭 𐑊𐐨𐐼 𐑄𐐬𐑆 𐐸𐐭 𐐶𐐲𐑉 𐐲𐑌𐐺𐐨𐑊𐐨𐑂𐐲𐑉𐑆 𐐱𐑌 𐑁𐑉𐐱𐑋 𐐶𐐲𐑌 𐐹𐐨𐑅 𐐱𐑂 𐐮𐑌𐐮𐐿𐐶𐐮𐐻𐐨 𐐻𐐭 𐐰𐑌𐐲𐑄𐐲𐑉, 𐑄𐐲𐑅 𐐺𐑉𐐮𐑍𐐮𐑍 𐐱𐑌 𐑄 𐐼𐐯𐑅𐐻𐑉𐐲𐐿𐑇𐐲𐑌 𐐱𐑂 𐑄 𐐹𐐨𐐹𐑊; 𐐷𐐩, 𐐸𐐨 𐑅𐐫 𐑀𐑉𐐩𐐻 𐐮𐑌𐐨𐐿𐐶𐐱𐑊𐐮𐐻𐐨 𐐰𐑋𐐲𐑍 𐑄 𐐹𐐨𐐹𐑊, 𐑅𐐲𐑋 𐑊𐐮𐑁𐐻𐐮𐑍 𐑄𐐯𐑋𐑅𐐯𐑊𐑂𐑆 𐐲𐐹 𐐶𐐮𐑄 𐑄𐐩𐑉 𐐹𐑉𐐴𐐼, 𐐼𐐯𐑅𐐹𐐴𐑆𐐮𐑍 𐐲𐑄𐐲𐑉𐑆, 𐐻𐐲𐑉𐑌𐐮𐑍 𐑄𐐩𐑉 𐐺𐐰𐐿𐑅 𐐲𐐹𐐱𐑌 𐑄 𐑌𐐨𐐼𐐨 𐐰𐑌𐐼 𐑄 𐑌𐐩𐐿𐐯𐐼, 𐐰𐑌𐐼 𐑄𐐬𐑆 𐐸𐐭 𐐶𐐲𐑉 𐐸𐐲𐑍𐑀𐑉𐐨, 𐐰𐑌𐐼 𐑄𐐬𐑆 𐐸𐐭 𐐶𐐲𐑉 𐐰𐑃𐐲𐑉𐑅𐐻, 𐐰𐑌𐐼 𐑄𐐬𐑆 𐐸𐐭 𐐶𐐲𐑉 𐑅𐐮𐐿 𐐰𐑌𐐼 𐐰𐑁𐑊𐐮𐐿𐐻𐐯𐐼. 𐐤𐐵 𐑄𐐮𐑅 𐐶𐐱𐑆 𐐰 𐑀𐑉𐐩𐐻 𐐿𐐫𐑆 𐑁𐐫𐑉 𐑊𐐰𐑋𐐯𐑌𐐻𐐩𐑇𐐲𐑌𐑆 𐐰𐑋𐐲𐑍 𐑄 𐐹𐐨𐐹𐑊, 𐐸𐐶𐐴𐑊 𐐲𐑄𐐲𐑉𐑆 𐐶𐐲𐑉 𐐰𐐺𐐩𐑅𐐮𐑍 𐑄𐐯𐑋𐑅𐐯𐑊𐑂𐑆, 𐑅𐐲𐐿𐐲𐑉𐐮𐑍 𐑄𐐬𐑆 𐐸𐐭 𐑅𐐻𐐳𐐼 𐐮𐑌 𐑌𐐨𐐼 𐐱𐑂 𐑄𐐩𐑉 𐑅𐐲𐐿𐐲𐑉, 𐑅𐐲𐐽 𐐰𐑆 𐐮𐑋𐐹𐐪𐑉𐐻𐐮𐑍 𐑄𐐩𐑉 𐑅𐐲𐐺𐑅𐐻𐐰𐑌𐑅 𐐻𐐭 𐑄 𐐹𐐭𐑉 𐐰𐑌𐐼 𐑄 𐑌𐐨𐐼𐐨; 𐑁𐐨𐐼𐐮𐑍 𐑄 𐐸𐐲𐑍𐑀𐑉𐐨, 𐐰𐑌𐐼 𐑅𐐲𐑁𐐲𐑉𐐮𐑍 𐐫𐑊 𐑋𐐰𐑌𐐲𐑉 𐐱𐑂 𐐰𐑁𐑊𐐮𐐿𐑇𐐲𐑌𐑆, 𐑁𐐫𐑉 𐐗𐑉𐐴𐑅𐐻'𐑅 𐑅𐐩𐐿, 𐐸𐐭 𐑇𐐳𐐼 𐐿𐐲𐑋 𐐰𐐿𐐫𐑉𐐼𐐮𐑍 𐐻𐐭 𐑄 𐑅𐐹𐐮𐑉𐐮𐐻 𐐱𐑂 𐐹𐑉𐐱𐑁𐐯𐑅𐐨, 𐑊𐐳𐐿𐐮𐑍 𐑁𐐫𐑉𐐶𐐲𐑉𐐼 𐐻𐐭 𐑄𐐰𐐻 𐐼𐐩, 𐑄𐐲𐑅 𐑉𐐨𐐻𐐩𐑌𐐮𐑍 𐐰 𐑉𐐨𐑋𐐮𐑇𐐲𐑌 𐐱𐑂 𐑄𐐩𐑉 𐑅𐐮𐑌𐑆; 𐐺𐐨𐐮𐑍 𐑁𐐮𐑊𐐼 𐐶𐐮𐑄 𐑀𐑉𐐩𐐻 𐐾𐐦, 𐐺𐐨𐐿𐐫𐑆 𐐱𐑂 𐑄 𐑉𐐯𐑆𐐲𐑉𐐯𐐿𐑇𐐲𐑌 𐐱𐑂 𐑄 𐐼𐐯𐐼, 𐐰𐐿𐐫𐑉𐐼𐐮𐑍 𐐻𐐭 𐑄 𐐶𐐮𐑊, 𐐰𐑌𐐼 𐐹𐐵𐐲𐑉, 𐐰𐑌𐐼 𐐼𐐨𐑊𐐮𐑂𐐲𐑉𐐰𐑌𐑅 𐐱𐑂 𐐖𐐨𐑆𐐲𐑅 𐐗𐑉𐐴𐑅𐐻 𐑁𐑉𐐱𐑋 𐑄 𐐺𐐰𐑌𐐼𐑆 𐐱𐑂 𐐼𐐯𐑃.

5. 𐐈𐑌𐐼 𐑌𐐵 𐐮𐐻 𐐿𐐩𐑋 𐐻𐐭 𐐹𐐰𐑅 𐑄𐐰𐐻 𐐈𐑊𐑋𐐲, 𐐸𐐰𐑂𐐮𐑍 𐑅𐐨𐑌 𐑄 𐐰𐑁𐑊𐐮𐐿𐑇𐐲𐑌𐑆 𐐱𐑂 𐑄 𐐸𐐲𐑋𐐺𐑊 𐑁𐐱𐑊𐐬𐐲𐑉𐑆 𐐱𐑂 𐐘𐐱𐐼, 𐐰𐑌𐐼 𐑄 𐐹𐐲𐑉𐑅𐐨𐐿𐐷𐐭𐑇𐐲𐑌𐑆 𐐸𐐶𐐮𐐽 𐐶𐐲𐑉 𐐸𐐨𐐹𐐻 𐐲𐐹𐐱𐑌 𐑄𐐯𐑋 𐐺𐐴 𐑄 𐑉𐐨𐑋𐐩𐑌𐐼𐐲𐑉 𐐱𐑂 𐐸𐐮𐑆 𐐹𐐨𐐹𐑊, 𐐰𐑌𐐼 𐑅𐐨𐐮𐑍 𐐫𐑊 𐑄𐐩𐑉 𐐮𐑌𐐨𐐿𐐶𐐱𐑊𐐮𐐻𐐨, 𐐺𐐨𐑀𐐰𐑌 𐐻𐐭 𐐺𐐨 𐑂𐐯𐑉𐐨 𐑅𐐱𐑉𐐬𐑁𐐳𐑊; 𐑌𐐯𐑂𐐲𐑉𐑄𐐯𐑊𐐯𐑅

𐑄 𐐝𐐹𐐮𐑉𐐮𐐻 𐐱𐑂 𐑄 𐐢𐐫𐑉𐐼 𐐼𐐮𐐼 𐑌𐐱𐐻 𐑁𐐩𐑊 𐐸𐐮𐑋. 𐐈𐑌𐐼 𐐸𐐨 𐑅𐐯𐑊𐐯𐐿𐐻𐐯𐐼 𐐲 𐐶𐐴𐑆 𐑋𐐰𐑌 𐐸𐐭 𐐶𐐱𐑆 𐐲𐑋𐐲𐑍 𐑄 𐐯𐑊𐐼𐐲𐑉𐑆 𐐱𐑂 𐑄 𐐽𐐲𐑉𐐽, 𐐰𐑌𐐼 𐑀𐐩𐑂 𐐸𐐮𐑋 𐐹𐐵𐐲𐑉 𐐰𐐿𐐫𐑉𐐼𐐮𐑍 𐐻𐐭 𐑄 𐑂𐐦𐑅 𐐱𐑂 𐑄 𐐹𐐨𐐹𐑊, 𐑄𐐰𐐻 𐐸𐐨 𐑋𐐴𐐻 𐐸𐐰𐑂 𐐹𐐵𐐲𐑉 𐐻𐐭 𐐯𐑌𐐰𐐿𐐻 𐑊𐐫𐑆 𐐰𐐿𐐫𐑉𐐼𐐮𐑍 𐐻𐐭 𐑄 𐑊𐐫𐑆 𐐸𐐶𐐮𐐽 𐐸𐐰𐐼 𐐺𐐮𐑌 𐑀𐐮𐑂𐐲𐑌, 𐐰𐑌𐐼 𐐻𐐭 𐐹𐐳𐐻 𐑄𐐯𐑋 𐐮𐑌 𐑁𐐬𐑉𐑅, 𐐰𐐿𐐫𐑉𐐼𐐮𐑍 𐐻𐐭 𐑄 𐐶𐐮𐐿𐐯𐐼𐑌𐐯𐑅 𐐰𐑌𐐼 𐑄 𐐿𐑉𐐴𐑋𐑆 𐐱𐑂 𐑄 𐐹𐐨𐐹𐑊. 𐐤𐐵 𐑄𐐮𐑅 𐑋𐐰𐑌'𐑆 𐑌𐐩𐑋 𐐶𐐱𐑆 𐐤𐐨𐑁𐐴𐐸𐐪, 𐐰𐑌𐐼 𐐸𐐨 𐐶𐐱𐑆 𐐰𐐹𐐶𐐮𐑌𐐻𐐯𐐼 𐐽𐐨𐑁 𐐖𐐲𐐾; 𐐰𐑌𐐼 𐐸𐐨 𐑅𐐰𐐻 𐐮𐑌 𐑄 𐐾𐐲𐐾𐑋𐐯𐑌𐐻-𐑅𐐨𐐻 𐐻𐐭 𐐾𐐲𐐾 𐐰𐑌𐐼 𐐻𐐭 𐑀𐐲𐑂𐐲𐑉𐑌 𐑄 𐐹𐐨𐐹𐑊. 𐐤𐐵 𐐈𐑊𐑋𐐲 𐐼𐐮𐐼 𐑌𐐱𐐻 𐑀𐑉𐐪𐑌𐐻 𐐲𐑌𐐻𐐭 𐐸𐐮𐑋 𐑄 𐐱𐑁𐐮𐑅 𐐱𐑂 𐐺𐐨𐐮𐑍 𐐸𐐴 𐐹𐑉𐐨𐑅𐐻 𐐬𐑂𐐲𐑉 𐑄 𐐽𐐲𐑉𐐽, 𐐺𐐲𐐻 𐐸𐐨 𐑉𐐨𐐻𐐩𐑌𐐼 𐑄 𐐱𐑁𐐮𐑅 𐐱𐑂 𐐸𐐴 𐐹𐑉𐐨𐑅𐐻 𐐲𐑌𐐻𐐭 𐐸𐐮𐑋𐑅𐐯𐑊𐑁; 𐐺𐐲𐐻 𐐸𐐨 𐐼𐐯𐑊𐐮𐑂𐐲𐑉𐐼 𐑄 𐐾𐐲𐐾𐑋𐐯𐑌𐐻-𐑅𐐨𐐻 𐐲𐑌𐐻𐐭 𐐤𐐨𐑁𐐴𐐸𐐪. 𐐈𐑌𐐼 𐑄𐐮𐑅 𐐸𐐨 𐐼𐐮𐐼 𐑄𐐰𐐻 𐐸𐐨 𐐸𐐮𐑋𐑅𐐯𐑊𐑁 𐑋𐐴𐐻 𐑀𐐬 𐑁𐐬𐑉𐑃 𐐲𐑋𐐲𐑍 𐐸𐐮𐑆 𐐹𐐨𐐹𐑊, 𐐫𐑉 𐐲𐑋𐐲𐑍 𐑄 𐐹𐐨𐐹𐑊 𐐱𐑂 𐐤𐐨𐑁𐐴, 𐑄𐐰𐐻 𐐸𐐨 𐑋𐐴𐐻 𐐹𐑉𐐨𐐽 𐑄 𐐶𐐲𐑉𐐼 𐐱𐑂 𐐘𐐱𐐼 𐐲𐑌𐐻𐐭 𐑄𐐯𐑋, 𐐻𐐭 𐑅𐐻𐐲𐑉 𐑄𐐯𐑋 𐐲𐐹 𐐮𐑌 𐑉𐐮𐑋𐐯𐑋𐐺𐑉𐐲𐑌𐑅 𐐱𐑂 𐑄𐐩𐑉 𐐼𐑏𐐻𐐨, 𐐰𐑌𐐼 𐑄𐐰𐐻 𐐸𐐨 𐑋𐐴𐐻 𐐹𐐳𐑊 𐐼𐐵𐑌, 𐐺𐐴 𐑄 𐐶𐐲𐑉𐐼 𐐱𐑂 𐐘𐐱𐐼, 𐐫𐑊 𐑄 𐐹𐑉𐐴𐐼 𐐰𐑌𐐼 𐐿𐑉𐐰𐑁𐐻𐐨𐑌𐐯𐑅 𐐰𐑌𐐼 𐐫𐑊 𐑄 𐐿𐐱𐑌𐐻𐐯𐑌𐑇𐐲𐑌𐑆 𐐸𐐶𐐮𐐽 𐐶𐐲𐑉 𐐲𐑋𐐲𐑍 𐐸𐐮𐑆 𐐹𐐨𐐹𐑊, 𐑅𐐨𐐮𐑍 𐑌𐐬 𐐶𐐩 𐑄𐐰𐐻 𐐸𐐨 𐑋𐐴𐐻 𐑉𐐨𐐿𐑊𐐩𐑋 𐑄𐐯𐑋 𐑅𐐩𐑂 𐐮𐐻 𐐶𐐲𐑉 𐐮𐑌 𐐺𐐩𐑉𐐮𐑍 𐐼𐐵𐑌 𐐮𐑌 𐐹𐑏𐑉 𐐻𐐯𐑅𐐻𐐮𐑋𐐬𐑌𐐨 𐐲𐑀𐐯𐑌𐑅𐐻 𐑄𐐯𐑋. 𐐈𐑌𐐼 𐑄𐐲𐑅 𐐮𐑌 𐑄 𐐿𐐱𐑋𐐯𐑌𐑅𐑋𐐯𐑌𐐻 𐐱𐑂 𐑄 𐑌𐐴𐑌𐑃 𐐷𐐨𐑉 𐐱𐑂 𐑄 𐑉𐐩𐑌 𐐱𐑂 𐑄 𐐾𐐲𐐾𐐯𐑆 𐐬𐑂𐐲𐑉 𐑄 𐐹𐐨𐐹𐑊 𐐱𐑂 𐐤𐐨𐑁𐐴, 𐐈𐑊𐑋𐐲 𐐼𐐯𐑊𐐮𐑂𐐲𐑉𐐼 𐐲𐐹 𐑄 𐐾𐐲𐐾𐑋𐐯𐑌𐐻-𐑅𐐨𐐻 𐐻𐐭 𐐤𐐨𐑁𐐴𐐸𐐪, 𐐰𐑌𐐼 𐐿𐐱𐑌𐑁𐐴𐑌𐐼 𐐸𐐮𐑋𐑅𐐯𐑊𐑁 𐐸𐐬𐑊𐐨 𐐻𐐭 𐑄 𐐸𐐴 𐐹𐑉𐐨𐑅𐐻𐐸𐐳𐐼 𐐱𐑂 𐑄 𐐸𐐬𐑊𐐨 𐐫𐑉𐐼𐐲𐑉 𐐱𐑂 𐐘𐐱𐐼, 𐐻𐐭 𐑄 𐐻𐐯𐑅𐐻𐐮𐑋𐐬𐑌𐐨 𐐱𐑂 𐑄 𐐶𐐲𐑉𐐼, 𐐰𐐿𐐫𐑉𐐼𐐮𐑍 𐐻𐐭 𐑄 𐑅𐐹𐐮𐑉𐐮𐐻 𐐱𐑂 𐑉𐐯𐑂𐐯𐑊𐐩𐑇𐐲𐑌 𐐰𐑌𐐼 𐐹𐑉𐐱𐑁𐐯𐑅𐐨.

𐐕𐐈𐐑𐐓𐐊𐐡 III.

𐐜 𐐶𐐲𐑉𐐼𐑆 𐐸𐐶𐐮𐐽 𐐈𐑊𐑋𐐲, 𐑄 𐐐𐐴 𐐑𐑉𐐨𐑅𐐻, 𐐰𐐿𐐫𐑉𐐼𐐮𐑍 𐐻𐐭 𐑄 𐐸𐐬𐑊𐐨 𐐫𐑉𐐼𐐲𐑉 𐐱𐑂 𐐘𐐱𐐼, 𐐼𐐯𐑊𐐮𐑂𐐲𐑉𐐼 𐐻𐐭 𐑄 𐐹𐐨𐐹𐑊 𐐮𐑌 𐑄𐐩𐑉 𐑅𐐮𐐻𐐨𐑆 𐐰𐑌𐐼 𐑂𐐮𐑊𐐯𐐾𐐯𐑆 𐑃𐑉𐐭𐐵𐐻 𐑄 𐑊𐐰𐑌𐐼.

1. 𐐤𐐵 𐐮𐐻 𐐿𐐩𐑋 𐐻𐐭 𐐹𐐪𐑅 𐑄𐐰𐐻 𐐈𐑊𐑋𐐲 𐐺𐐨𐑀𐐰𐑌 𐐻𐐭 𐐼𐐯𐑊𐐮𐑂𐐲𐑉 𐑄 𐐶𐐲𐑉𐐼 𐐱𐑂 𐐘𐐱𐐼 𐐲𐑌𐐻𐐭 𐑄 𐐹𐐨𐐹𐑊, 𐑁𐐲𐑉𐑅𐐻 𐐮𐑌 𐑄 𐑊𐐰𐑌𐐼 𐐱𐑂 𐐞𐐰𐑉𐐲𐐸𐐯𐑋𐑊𐐲, 𐐰𐑌𐐼 𐑁𐑉𐐱𐑋 𐑄𐐯𐑌𐑅 𐑃𐑉𐐭𐐵𐐻 𐐫𐑊 𐑄 𐑊𐐰𐑌𐐼. 𐐈𐑌𐐼 𐑄𐐨𐑆 𐐪𐑉 𐑄 𐐶𐐲𐑉𐐼𐑆 𐐸𐐶𐐮𐐽 𐐸𐐨 𐑅𐐹𐐩𐐿 𐐻𐐭 𐑄 𐐹𐐨𐐹𐑊 𐐮𐑌 𐑄 𐐽𐐲𐑉𐐽 𐐸𐐶𐐮𐐽 𐐶𐐱𐑆 𐐯𐑅𐐻𐐰𐐺𐑊𐐮𐑇𐐻 𐐮𐑌 𐑄 𐑅𐐮𐐻𐐨 𐐱𐑂 𐐞𐐰𐑉𐐲𐐸𐐯𐑋𐑊𐐲, 𐐰𐐿𐐫𐑉𐐼𐐮𐑍 𐐻𐐭 𐐸𐐮𐑆 𐐬𐑌 𐑉𐐯𐐿𐐲𐑉𐐼, 𐑅𐐩𐐮𐑍: 𐐌, 𐐈𐑊𐑋𐐲, 𐐸𐐰𐑂𐐮𐑍 𐐺𐐮𐑌 𐐿𐐱𐑌𐑅𐐯𐐿𐑉𐐩𐐻𐐯𐐼 𐐺𐐴 𐑋𐐴 𐑁𐐪𐑄𐐲𐑉, 𐐈𐑊𐑋𐐲, 𐐻𐐭 𐐺𐐨 𐐲 𐐸𐐴 𐐹𐑉𐐨𐑅𐐻 𐐬𐑂𐐲𐑉 𐑄 𐐽𐐲𐑉𐐽 𐐱𐑂 𐐘𐐱𐐼, 𐐸𐐨 𐐸𐐰𐑂𐐮𐑍 𐐹𐐵𐐲𐑉 𐐰𐑌𐐼 𐐫𐑃𐐱𐑉𐐮𐐻𐐨 𐑁𐑉𐐱𐑋 𐐘𐐱𐐼 𐐻𐐭 𐐼𐐭 𐑄𐐨𐑆 𐑃𐐮𐑍𐑆, 𐐺𐐨𐐸𐐬𐑊𐐼, 𐐌 𐑅𐐩 𐐲𐑌𐐻𐐭 𐐷𐐭, 𐑄𐐰𐐻 𐐸𐐨 𐐺𐐨𐑀𐐰𐑌 𐐻𐐭 𐐯𐑅𐐻𐐰𐐺𐑊𐐮𐑇 𐐲 𐐽𐐲𐑉𐐽 𐐮𐑌 𐑄 𐑊𐐰𐑌𐐼 𐐸𐐶𐐮𐐽 𐐶𐐱𐑆 𐐮𐑌 𐑄 𐐺𐐫𐑉𐐼𐐲𐑉𐑆 𐐱𐑂 𐐤𐐨𐑁𐐴; 𐐷𐐩, 𐑄 𐑊𐐰𐑌𐐼 𐐸𐐶𐐮𐐽 𐐶𐐱𐑆 𐐿𐐫𐑊𐐼 𐑄 𐑊𐐰𐑌𐐼 𐐱𐑂 𐐣𐐫𐑉𐑋𐐲𐑌; 𐐷𐐩, 𐐰𐑌𐐼 𐐸𐐨 𐐼𐐮𐐼 𐐺𐐰𐐹𐐻𐐴𐑆 𐐸𐐮𐑆 𐐺𐑉𐐯𐑄𐑉𐐯𐑌 𐐮𐑌 𐑄 𐐶𐐫𐐻𐐲𐑉𐑆 𐐱𐑂 𐐣𐐫𐑉𐑋𐐲𐑌. 𐐈𐑌𐐼 𐐺𐐨𐐸𐐬𐑊𐐼, 𐐌 𐑅𐐩 𐐲𐑌𐐻𐐭 𐐷𐐭, 𐑄𐐩 𐐶𐐲𐑉 𐐼𐐯𐑊𐐮𐑂𐐲𐑉𐐼 𐐵𐐻 𐐱𐑂 𐑄 𐐸𐐰𐑌𐐼𐑆 𐐱𐑂 𐑄 𐐹𐐨𐐹𐑊 𐐱𐑂 𐐿𐐮𐑍 𐐤𐐬𐐪, 𐐺𐐴 𐑄 𐑋𐐲𐑉𐑅𐐨 𐐰𐑌𐐼 𐐹𐐵𐐲𐑉 𐐱𐑂 𐐘𐐱𐐼. 𐐈𐑌𐐼 𐐺𐐨𐐸𐐬𐑊𐐼, 𐐪𐑁𐐻𐐲𐑉 𐑄𐐰𐐻, 𐑄𐐩 𐐶𐐲𐑉 𐐺𐑉𐐫𐐻 𐐮𐑌𐐻𐐭 𐐺𐐱𐑌𐐼𐐩𐐾 𐐺𐐴 𐑄 𐐸𐐰𐑌𐐼𐑆 𐐱𐑂 𐑄 𐐢𐐩𐑋𐐲𐑌𐐴𐐻𐑅 𐐮𐑌 𐑄 𐐶𐐮𐑊𐐼𐐲𐑉𐑌𐐯𐑅; 𐐷𐐩, 𐐌 𐑅𐐩 𐐲𐑌𐐻𐐭 𐐷𐐭, 𐑄𐐩 𐐶𐐲𐑉 𐐮𐑌 𐐿𐐰𐐹𐐻𐐮𐑂𐐮𐐻𐐨, 𐐰𐑌𐐼 𐐲𐑀𐐯𐑌 𐑄 𐐢𐐫𐑉𐐼 𐐼𐐮𐐼 𐐼𐐯𐑊𐐮𐑂𐐲𐑉 𐑄𐐯𐑋 𐐵𐐻 𐐱𐑂 𐐺𐐱𐑌𐐼𐐩𐐾 𐐺𐐴 𐑄 𐐹𐐵𐐲𐑉 𐐱𐑂 𐐸𐐮𐑆 𐐶𐐲𐑉𐐼; 𐐰𐑌𐐼 𐐶𐐨 𐐶𐐲𐑉 𐐺𐑉𐐫𐐻 𐐮𐑌𐐻𐐭 𐑄𐐮𐑅 𐑊𐐰𐑌𐐼, 𐐰𐑌𐐼 𐐸𐐨𐑉 𐐶𐐨 𐐺𐐨𐑀𐐰𐑌 𐐻𐐭 𐐯𐑅𐐻𐐰𐐺𐑊𐐮𐑇 𐑄 𐐽𐐲𐑉𐐽 𐐱𐑂 𐐘𐐱𐐼 𐑃𐑉𐐭𐐵𐐻 𐑄𐐮𐑅 𐑊𐐰𐑌𐐼 𐐫𐑊𐑅𐐬.

2. 𐐈𐑌𐐼 𐑌𐐵 𐐺𐐨𐐸𐐬𐑊𐐼, 𐐌 𐑅𐐩 𐐲𐑌𐐻𐐭 𐐷𐐭, 𐑋𐐴 𐐺𐑉𐐯𐑄𐑉𐐯𐑌, 𐐷𐐭 𐑄𐐰𐐻 𐐺𐐨𐑊𐐱𐑍 𐐻𐐭 𐑄𐐮𐑅 𐐽𐐲𐑉𐐽, 𐐸𐐰𐑂 𐐷𐐭 𐑅𐐲𐑁𐐮𐑇𐐯𐑌𐐻𐑊𐐨 𐑉𐐨𐐻𐐩𐑌𐐼 𐐮𐑌 𐑉𐐮𐑋𐐯𐑋𐐺𐑉𐐲𐑌𐑅 𐑄 𐐿𐐰𐐹𐐻𐐮𐑂𐐮𐐻𐐨 𐐱𐑂 𐐷𐐭𐑉 𐑁𐐪𐑄𐐲𐑉𐑆? 𐐏𐐩, 𐐰𐑌𐐼 𐐸𐐰𐑂 𐐷𐐭 𐑅𐐲𐑁𐐮𐑇𐐯𐑌𐐻𐑊𐐨 𐑉𐐨𐐻𐐩𐑌𐐼 𐐮𐑌 𐑉𐐮𐑋𐐯𐑋𐐺𐑉𐐲𐑌𐑅 𐐸𐐮𐑆 𐑋𐐲𐑉𐑅𐐨 𐐰𐑌𐐼 𐑊𐐱𐑍-𐑅𐐲𐑁𐐲𐑉𐐮𐑍 𐐻𐐬𐐲𐑉𐐼𐑆 𐑄𐐯𐑋?

𐐰𐑌𐐼 𐑋𐐬𐑉𐐬𐑂𐐲𐑉, 𐐸𐐰𐑂 𐐷 𐑅𐐲𐑁𐐮𐑇𐐲𐑌𐐻𐑊𐐨 𐑉𐐨𐐻𐐩𐑌𐐼 𐐮𐑌 𐑉𐐨𐑋𐐯𐑋𐐺𐑉𐐲𐑌𐑅 𐑄𐐰𐐻 𐐸𐐨 𐐸𐐰𐑆 𐐼𐐨𐑊𐐮𐑂𐐲𐑉𐐼 𐑄𐐯𐑉
𐑅𐐬𐑊𐑆 𐑁𐑉𐐱𐑋 𐐸𐐯𐑊? 𐐒𐐨𐐸𐐬𐑊𐐼, 𐐸𐐨 𐐽𐐩𐑌𐐾𐐼 𐑄𐐯𐑉 𐐸𐐪𐑉𐐻𐑅; 𐐷𐐩, 𐐸𐐨 𐐰𐐶𐐩𐐿𐐲𐑌𐐼 𐑄𐐯𐑋 𐐵𐐻 𐐱𐑂 𐐩 𐐼𐐨𐐹
𐑅𐑊𐐨𐐹, 𐐰𐑌𐐼 𐑄𐐩 𐐰𐐶𐐬𐐿 𐐲𐑌𐐻𐐭 𐐘𐐪𐐼. 𐐒𐐨𐐸𐐬𐑊𐐼, 𐑄𐐩 𐐶𐐲𐑉 𐐮𐑌 𐑄 𐑋𐐮𐐼𐑅𐐻 𐐱𐑂 𐐼𐐪𐑉𐐿𐑌𐐯𐑅: 𐑌𐐯𐑂𐐲𐑉𐑄𐐲𐑊𐐯𐑅, 𐑄𐐯𐑉 𐑅𐐬𐑊𐑆 𐐶𐐲𐑉 𐐮𐑊𐐭𐑋𐐮𐑌𐐩𐐻𐐯𐐼 𐐺𐐴 𐑄 𐑊𐐴𐐻 𐐱𐑂 𐑄 𐐯𐑂𐐲𐑉𐑊𐐰𐑅𐐻𐐮𐑍 𐐶𐐲𐑉𐐼; 𐐷𐐩, 𐑄𐐩 𐐶𐐲𐑉
𐐯𐑌𐑅𐐲𐑉𐐿𐑊𐐼 𐐰𐐺𐐵𐐻 𐐺𐐴 𐑄 𐐺𐐰𐑌𐐼𐑆 𐐱𐑂 𐐼𐐯𐑃, 𐐰𐑌𐐼 𐑄 𐐽𐐩𐑌𐑆 𐐱𐑂 𐐸𐐯𐑊, 𐐰𐑌𐐼 𐐰𐑌 𐐯𐑂𐐲𐑉𐑊𐐰𐑅𐐻𐐮𐑍 𐐼𐐨𐑅𐐻𐑉𐐲𐐿𐑇𐐲𐑌 𐐼𐐮𐐼 𐐰𐐶𐐩𐐻 𐑄𐐯𐑋. 𐐈𐑌𐐼 𐑌𐐵 𐐴 𐐰𐑅𐐿 𐐱𐑂 𐐷𐐭, 𐑋𐐴 𐐺𐑉𐐯𐑄𐑉𐐯𐑌, 𐐶𐐲𐑉 𐑄𐐩 𐐼𐐨𐑅𐐻𐑉𐐱𐐮𐐼?
𐐒𐐨𐐸𐐬𐑊𐐼, 𐐌 𐑅𐐩 𐐲𐑌𐐻𐐭 𐐷𐐭, 𐐤𐐩, 𐑄𐐩 𐐶𐐲𐑉 𐑌𐐱𐐻. 𐐈𐑌𐐼 𐐰𐑀𐐯𐑌 𐐴 𐐰𐑅𐐿, 𐐶𐐲𐑉 𐑄 𐐺𐐰𐑌𐐼𐑆 𐐱𐑂
𐐼𐐯𐑃 𐐺𐑉𐐬𐐿𐐲𐑌, 𐐰𐑌𐐼 𐑄 𐐽𐐩𐑌𐑆 𐐱𐑂 𐐸𐐯𐑊 𐐸𐐶𐐮𐐽 𐐯𐑌𐑅𐐲𐑉𐐿𐑊𐐼 𐑄𐐯𐑋 𐐰𐐺𐐵𐐻, 𐐶𐐲𐑉 𐑄𐐩 𐑊𐐭𐑅𐐻? 𐐌 𐑅𐐩
𐐲𐑌𐐻𐐭 𐐷𐐭, 𐐏𐐩, 𐑄𐐩 𐐶𐐲𐑉 𐑊𐐭𐑅𐐻, 𐐰𐑌𐐼 𐑄𐐯𐑉 𐑅𐐬𐑊𐑆 𐐼𐐮𐐼 𐐯𐐿𐑅𐐹𐐰𐑌𐐼, 𐐰𐑌𐐼 𐑄𐐩 𐐼𐐮𐐼 𐑅𐐮𐑍 𐑉𐐨𐐼𐐨𐑋𐐮𐑍
𐑊𐐲𐑂. 𐐈𐑌𐐼 𐐌 𐑅𐐩 𐐲𐑌𐐻𐐭 𐐷𐐭 𐑄𐐰𐐻 𐑄𐐩 𐐪𐑉 𐑅𐐩𐑂𐐼. 𐐈𐑌𐐼 𐑌𐐵 𐐴 𐐰𐑅𐐿 𐐱𐑂 𐐷𐐭 𐐱𐑌 𐐸𐐶𐐱𐐻 𐐿𐐱𐑌𐐼𐐮𐑇𐐲𐑌𐑆 𐐪𐑉 𐑄𐐩 𐑅𐐩𐑂𐐼? 𐐏𐐩, 𐐸𐐶𐐱𐐻 𐑀𐑉𐐵𐑌𐐼𐑆 𐐸𐐰𐐼 𐑄𐐩 𐐻𐐭 𐐸𐐬𐐹 𐑁𐐫𐑉 𐑅𐐰𐑊𐑂𐐩𐑇𐐲𐑌? 𐐐𐐶𐐱𐐻
𐐮𐑆 𐑄 𐐿𐐫𐑆 𐐱𐑂 𐑄𐐯𐑉 𐐺𐐨𐐮𐑍 𐑊𐐭𐑅𐐻 𐑁𐑉𐐱𐑋 𐑄 𐐺𐐰𐑌𐐼𐑆 𐐱𐑂 𐐼𐐯𐑃? 𐐏𐐩, 𐐰𐑌𐐼 𐐫𐑊𐑅𐐬 𐑄 𐐽𐐩𐑌𐑆 𐐱𐑂
𐐸𐐯𐑊? 𐐒𐐨𐐸𐐬𐑊𐐼, 𐐌 𐐿𐐰𐑌 𐐻𐐯𐑊 𐐷𐐭: 𐐔𐐮𐐼 𐑌𐐱𐐻 𐑋𐐴 𐑁𐐪𐑄𐐲𐑉 𐐈𐑊𐑋𐐲 𐐺𐐨𐑊𐐨𐑂 𐐮𐑌 𐑄 𐐶𐐲𐑉𐐼𐑆 𐐸𐐶𐐮𐐽
𐐶𐐲𐑉 𐐼𐐨𐑊𐐮𐑂𐐲𐑉𐐼 𐐺𐐴 𐑄 𐑋𐐵𐑃 𐐱𐑂 𐐈𐐺𐐮𐑌𐐰𐐼𐐴? 𐐈𐑌𐐼 𐐶𐐱𐑆 𐐸𐐨 𐑌𐐱𐐻 𐐩 𐐸𐐬𐑊𐐨 𐐹𐑉𐐱𐑁𐐯𐐻? 𐐔𐐮𐐼 𐐸𐐨
𐑌𐐱𐐻 𐑅𐐹𐐨𐐿 𐑄 𐐶𐐲𐑉𐐼𐑆 𐐱𐑂 𐐘𐐪𐐼, 𐐰𐑌𐐼 𐑋𐐴 𐑁𐐪𐑄𐐲𐑉 𐐈𐑊𐑋𐐲 𐐺𐐨𐑊𐐨𐑂 𐑄𐐯𐑋? 𐐈𐑌𐐼 𐐰𐐿𐐫𐑉𐐼𐐮𐑍 𐐻𐐭
𐐸𐐮𐑆 𐑁𐐩𐑃 𐑄𐐯𐑉 𐐶𐐱𐑆 𐐩 𐑋𐐴𐐻𐐨 𐐽𐐩𐑌𐐾 𐑉𐐫𐐻 𐐮𐑌 𐐸𐐮𐑆 𐐸𐐪𐑉𐐻. 𐐒𐐨𐐸𐐬𐑊𐐼 𐐌 𐑅𐐩 𐐲𐑌𐐻𐐭 𐐷𐐭, 𐑄𐐰𐐻 𐑄𐐮𐑅
𐐮𐑆 𐐫𐑊 𐐻𐑉𐐭. 𐐈𐑌𐐼 𐐺𐐨𐐸𐐬𐑊𐐼 𐐸𐐨 𐐹𐑉𐐨𐐽𐐻 𐑄 𐐶𐐲𐑉𐐼 𐐲𐑌𐐻𐐭 𐐷𐐭𐑉 𐑁𐐪𐑄𐐲𐑉𐑆, 𐐰𐑌𐐼 𐐩 𐑋𐐴𐐻𐐨 𐐽𐐩𐑌𐐾
𐐶𐐱𐑆 𐐫𐑊𐑅𐐬 𐑉𐐫𐐻 𐐮𐑌 𐑄𐐯𐑉 𐐸𐐪𐑉𐐻𐑅, 𐐰𐑌𐐼 𐑄𐐩 𐐸𐐲𐑋𐐺𐑊𐐼 𐑄𐐯𐑋𐑅𐐯𐑊𐑂𐑆, 𐐰𐑌𐐼 𐐹𐐳𐐻 𐑄𐐯𐑉 𐐻𐑉𐐲𐑅𐐻 𐐮𐑌 𐑄
𐐻𐑉𐐭 𐐰𐑌𐐼 𐑊𐐮𐑂𐐮𐑍 𐐘𐐪𐐼. 𐐈𐑌𐐼 𐐺𐐨𐐸𐐬𐑊𐐼 𐑄𐐩 𐐶𐐲𐑉 𐑁𐐩𐑃𐑁𐐳𐑊 𐐲𐑌𐐻𐐮𐑊 𐑄 𐐯𐑌𐐼; 𐑄𐐯𐑉𐑁𐐬𐑉 𐑄𐐩 𐐶𐐲𐑉 𐑅𐐩𐑂𐐼.

3. 𐐈𐑌𐐼 𐑌𐐵 𐐺𐐨𐐸𐐬𐑊𐐼, 𐐌 𐐰𐑅𐐿 𐐱𐑂 𐐷𐐭, 𐑋𐐴 𐐺𐑉𐐯𐑄𐑉𐐯𐑌 𐐱𐑂 𐑄 𐐕𐐲𐑉𐐽, 𐐸𐐰𐑂 𐐷 𐑅𐐹𐐮𐑉𐐮𐐽𐐭𐐲𐑊𐐨
𐐺𐐨𐑌 𐐺𐐫𐑉𐑌 𐐱𐑂 𐐘𐐪𐐼? 𐐐𐐰𐑂 𐐷 𐑉𐐨𐑅𐐨𐑂𐐼 𐐸𐐮𐑆 𐐮𐑋𐐩𐐾 𐐮𐑌 𐐷𐐭𐑉 𐐿𐐵𐑌𐐻𐐲𐑌𐐲𐑌𐑅𐐯𐑆? 𐐐𐐰𐑂 𐐷
𐐯𐐿𐑅𐐹𐐨𐑉𐐨𐐲𐑌𐑅𐐻 𐑄𐐮𐑅 𐑋𐐴𐐻𐐨 𐐽𐐩𐑌𐐾 𐐮𐑌 𐐷𐐭𐑉 𐐸𐐪𐑉𐐻𐑅? 𐐔𐐭 𐐷 𐐯𐐿𐑅𐐲𐑉𐑅𐐴𐑆 𐑁𐐩𐑃 𐐮𐑌 𐑄 𐑉𐐨𐐼𐐯𐑋𐑇𐐲𐑌 𐐱𐑂 𐐸𐐮𐑋 𐐸𐐭 𐐿𐑉𐐨𐐩𐐻𐐯𐐼 𐐷𐐭? 𐐔𐐭 𐐷𐐭 𐑊𐐳𐐿 𐑁𐐫𐑉𐐶𐐲𐑉𐐼 𐐶𐐮𐑄 𐐰𐑌 𐐴 𐐱𐑂 𐑁𐐩𐑃, 𐐰𐑌𐐼 𐑂𐐭
𐑄𐐮𐑅 𐑋𐐫𐑉𐐻𐐲𐑊 𐐺𐐱𐐼𐐨 𐑉𐐩𐑆𐐼 𐐮𐑌 𐐮𐑋𐐫𐑉𐐻𐐰𐑊𐐮𐐻𐐨, 𐐰𐑌𐐼 𐑄𐐮𐑅 𐐿𐐱𐑉𐐲𐐹𐑇𐐲𐑌 𐑉𐐩𐑆𐐼 𐐮𐑌 𐐮𐑌𐐿𐐱𐑉𐐲𐐹𐑇𐐲𐑌, 𐐻𐐭
𐑅𐐻𐐰𐑌𐐼 𐐺𐐨𐑁𐐬𐑉 𐐘𐐪𐐼, 𐐻𐐭 𐐺𐐨 𐐾𐐲𐐾𐐼 𐐰𐐿𐐫𐑉𐐼𐐮𐑍 𐐻𐐭 𐑄 𐐼𐐨𐐼𐑆 𐐸𐐶𐐮𐐽 𐐸𐐰𐑂 𐐺𐐨𐑌 𐐼𐐲𐑌 𐐮𐑌 𐑄 𐑋𐐫𐑉𐐻𐐲𐑊
𐐺𐐱𐐼𐐨? 𐐌 𐑅𐐩 𐐲𐑌𐐻𐐭 𐐷𐐭, 𐐿𐐰𐑌 𐐷𐐭 𐐮𐑋𐐰𐐾𐐮𐑌 𐐻𐐭 𐐷𐐭𐑉𐑅𐐯𐑊𐑂𐑆 𐑄𐐰𐐻 𐐷 𐐸𐐨𐑉 𐑄 𐑂𐐱𐐮𐑅 𐐱𐑂 𐑄 𐐢𐐫𐑉𐐼,
𐑅𐐩𐐮𐑍 𐐲𐑌𐐻𐐭 𐐷𐐭, 𐐮𐑌 𐑄𐐰𐐻 𐐼𐐩: 𐐗𐐲𐑋 𐐲𐑌𐐻𐐭 𐑋𐐨 𐐷 𐐺𐑊𐐯𐑅𐐯𐐼, 𐑁𐐫𐑉 𐐺𐐨𐐸𐐬𐑊𐐼, 𐐷𐐭𐑉 𐐶𐐲𐑉𐐿𐑅 𐐸𐐰𐑂
𐐺𐐨𐑌 𐑄 𐐶𐐲𐑉𐐿𐑅 𐐱𐑂 𐑉𐐴𐐽𐐲𐑅𐑌𐐯𐑅 𐐲𐐹𐐱𐑌 𐑄 𐑁𐐩𐑅 𐐱𐑂 𐑄 𐐲𐑉𐑃? 𐐃𐑉 𐐼𐐭 𐐷 𐐮𐑋𐐰𐐾𐐮𐑌 𐐻𐐭 𐐷𐐭𐑉𐑅𐐯𐑊𐑂𐑆
𐑄𐐰𐐻 𐐷 𐐿𐐰𐑌 𐑊𐐴 𐐲𐑌𐐻𐐭 𐑄 𐐢𐐫𐑉𐐼 𐐮𐑌 𐑄𐐰𐐻 𐐼𐐩, 𐐰𐑌𐐼 𐑅𐐩, 𐐢𐐫𐑉𐐼, 𐐵𐑉 𐐶𐐲𐑉𐐿𐑅 𐐸𐐰𐑂 𐐺𐐨𐑌 𐑉𐐴𐐽𐐲𐑅
𐐶𐐲𐑉𐐿𐑅 𐐲𐐹𐐱𐑌 𐑄 𐑁𐐩𐑅 𐐱𐑂 𐑄 𐐲𐑉𐑃, 𐐰𐑌𐐼 𐑄𐐰𐐻 𐐸𐐨 𐐶𐐮𐑊 𐑅𐐩𐑂 𐐷𐐭? 𐐃𐑉 𐐲𐑄𐐲𐑉𐐶𐐴𐑆, 𐐿𐐰𐑌 𐐷 𐐮𐑋𐐰𐐾𐐮𐑌 𐐷𐐭𐑉𐑅𐐯𐑊𐑂𐑆 𐐺𐑉𐐫𐐻 𐐺𐐨𐑁𐐬𐑉 𐑄 𐐻𐑉𐐴𐐺𐐷𐐭𐑌𐐲𐑊 𐐱𐑂 𐐘𐐪𐐼, 𐐶𐐮𐑄 𐐷𐐭𐑉 𐑅𐐬𐑊𐑆 𐑁𐐮𐑊𐐼 𐐶𐐮𐑄 𐑀𐐮𐑊𐐻
𐐰𐑌𐐼 𐑉𐐨𐑋𐐫𐑉𐑅: 𐐸𐐰𐑂𐐮𐑍 𐐩 𐑉𐐨𐑋𐐯𐑋𐐺𐑉𐐲𐑌𐑅 𐐱𐑂 𐐫𐑊 𐐷𐐭𐑉 𐑀𐐮𐑊𐐻; 𐐷𐐩, 𐐩 𐐹𐐲𐑉𐑁𐐯𐐿𐐻 𐑉𐐨𐑋𐐯𐑋𐐺𐑉𐐲𐑌𐑅 𐐱𐑂
𐐫𐑊 𐐷𐐭𐑉 𐐶𐐮𐐿𐐯𐐼𐑌𐐯𐑅; 𐐷𐐩, 𐐩 𐑉𐐨𐑋𐐯𐑋𐐺𐑉𐐲𐑌𐑅 𐑄𐐰𐐻 𐐷 𐐸𐐰𐑂 𐑅𐐯𐐻 𐐰𐐻 𐐼𐐨𐑁𐐴𐐲𐑌𐑅 𐑄 𐐿𐐱𐑋𐐰𐑌𐐼𐑋𐐯𐑌𐐻𐑅
𐐱𐑂 𐐘𐐪𐐼? 𐐌 𐑅𐐩 𐐲𐑌𐐻𐐭 𐐷𐐭, 𐐿𐐰𐑌 𐐷 𐑊𐐳𐐿 𐐲𐐹 𐐻𐐭 𐐘𐐪𐐼 𐐰𐐻 𐑄𐐰𐐻 𐐼𐐩 𐐶𐐮𐑄 𐐩 𐐹𐐷𐐭𐑉 𐐸𐐪𐑉𐐻
𐐰𐑌𐐼 𐐿𐑊𐐨𐑌 𐐸𐐰𐑌𐐼𐑆? 𐐌 𐑅𐐩 𐐲𐑌𐐻𐐭 𐐷𐐭, 𐐿𐐰𐑌 𐐷𐐭 𐑊𐐳𐐿 𐐲𐐹, 𐐸𐐰𐑂𐐮𐑍 𐑄 𐐮𐑋𐐰𐐾 𐐱𐑂 𐐘𐐪𐐼 𐐯𐑌𐑀𐑉𐐩𐑂𐐲𐑌 𐐲𐐹𐐱𐑌 𐐷𐐭𐑉 𐐿𐐵𐑌𐐻𐐲𐑌𐐲𐑌𐑅𐐯𐑆? 𐐌 𐑅𐐩 𐐲𐑌𐐻𐐭 𐐷𐐭, 𐐿𐐰𐑌 𐐷 𐑃𐐮𐑍𐐿 𐐱𐑂 𐐺𐐨𐐮𐑍 𐑅𐐩𐑂𐐼 𐐸𐐶𐐯𐑌
𐐷𐐭 𐐸𐐰𐑂 𐐷𐐨𐑊𐐼𐐯𐐼 𐐷𐐭𐑉𐑅𐐯𐑊𐑂𐑆 𐐻𐐭 𐐺𐐨𐐿𐐲𐑋 𐑅𐐲𐐺𐐾𐐯𐐿𐐻𐑅 𐐻𐐭 𐑄 𐐼𐐯𐑂𐐮𐑊? 𐐌 𐑅𐐩 𐐲𐑌𐐻𐐭 𐐷𐐭, 𐐷
𐐶𐐮𐑊 𐑌𐐬 𐐰𐐻 𐑄𐐰𐐻 𐐼𐐩, 𐑄𐐰𐐻 𐐷 𐐿𐐰𐑌𐐱𐐻 𐐺𐐨 𐑅𐐩𐑂𐐼; 𐑁𐐫𐑉 𐑄𐐯𐑉 𐐿𐐰𐑌 𐑌𐐬 𐑋𐐰𐑌 𐐺𐐨 𐑅𐐩𐑂𐐼 𐐯𐐿𐑅𐐯𐐹𐐻
𐐸𐐮𐑆 𐑀𐐪𐑉𐑋𐐯𐑌𐐻𐑅 𐐪𐑉 𐐶𐐱𐑇𐐻 𐐸𐐶𐐴𐐻; 𐐷𐐩, 𐐸𐐮𐑆 𐑀𐐪𐑉𐑋𐐯𐑌𐐻𐑅 𐑋𐐲𐑅𐐻 𐐺𐐨 𐐹𐐷𐐭𐑉𐐮𐑁𐐴𐐼 𐐲𐑌𐐻𐐮𐑊 𐑄𐐩 𐐪𐑉
𐐿𐑊𐐯𐑌𐑆𐐼 𐑁𐑉𐐱𐑋 𐐫𐑊 𐑅𐐻𐐩𐑌, 𐑃𐑉𐐭 𐑄 𐐺𐑊𐐲𐐼 𐐱𐑂 𐐸𐐮𐑋 𐐱𐑂 𐐸𐐭𐑋 𐐮𐐻 𐐸𐐰𐑆 𐐺𐐨𐑌 𐑅𐐹𐐬𐐿𐐲𐑌 𐐺𐐴 𐐵𐑉 𐑁𐐪𐑄𐐲𐑉𐑆
𐐸𐐭 𐑇𐐳𐐼 𐐿𐐲𐑋 𐐻𐐭 𐑉𐐨𐐼𐐨𐑋 𐐸𐐮𐑆 𐐹𐐨𐐹𐑊 𐑁𐑉𐐱𐑋 𐑄𐐯𐑉 𐑅𐐮𐑌𐑆.

4. 𐐈𐑌𐐼 𐑌𐐵 𐐌 𐐰𐑅𐐿 𐐱𐑂 𐐷𐐭, 𐑋𐐴 𐐺𐑉𐐯𐑄𐑉𐐯𐑌, 𐐸𐐵 𐐶𐐮𐑊 𐐯𐑌𐐨 𐐱𐑂 𐐷𐐭 𐑁𐐨𐑊, 𐐮𐑁 𐐷 𐑇𐐰𐑊 𐑅𐐻𐐰𐑌𐐼 𐐺𐐨𐑁𐐬𐑉 𐑄 𐐺𐐪𐑉 𐐱𐑂 𐐘𐐱𐐼, 𐐸𐐰𐑂𐐮𐑍 𐐷𐐬𐑉 𐑀𐐪𐑉𐑋𐐯𐑌𐐻𐑅 𐑅𐐻𐐩𐑌𐐼 𐐶𐐮𐑄 𐐺𐑊𐐲𐐼 𐐰𐑌𐐼 𐐫𐑊 𐑋𐐰𐑌𐐲𐑉 𐐱𐑂 𐑁𐐮𐑊𐑃𐐨𐑌𐐯𐑅? 𐐒𐐨𐐸𐐬𐑊𐐼, 𐐸𐐶𐐱𐐻 𐐶𐐮𐑊 𐑄𐐨𐑆 𐑃𐐮𐑍𐑆 𐐻𐐯𐑅𐐻𐐮𐑁𐐴 𐐰𐑀𐐯𐑌𐑅𐐻 𐐷𐐭? 𐐒𐐨𐐸𐐬𐑊𐐼, 𐐶𐐮𐑊 𐑄𐐩 𐑌𐐱𐐻 𐐻𐐯𐑅𐐻𐐮𐑁𐐴 𐑄𐐰𐐻 𐐷 𐐪𐑉 𐑋𐐲𐑉𐐼𐐲𐑉𐐲𐑉𐑆, 𐐷𐐩, 𐐰𐑌𐐼 𐐫𐑊𐑅𐐬 𐑄𐐰𐐻 𐐷 𐐪𐑉 𐑀𐐮𐑊𐐻𐐨 𐐱𐑂 𐐫𐑊 𐑋𐐰𐑌𐐲𐑉 𐐱𐑂 𐐶𐐮𐐿𐐯𐐼𐑌𐐯𐑅? 𐐒𐐨𐐸𐐬𐑊𐐼, 𐑋𐐴 𐐺𐑉𐐯𐑄𐑉𐐯𐑌, 𐐔𐐭 𐐷 𐑅𐐲𐐹𐐬𐑆 𐑄𐐰𐐻 𐑅𐐲𐐽 𐐰𐑌 𐐶𐐲𐑌 𐐿𐐰𐑌 𐐸𐐰𐑂 𐐰 𐐹𐑊𐐩𐑅 𐐻𐐭 𐑅𐐮𐐻 𐐼𐐵𐑌 𐐮𐑌 𐑄 𐐿𐐮𐑍𐐼𐐲𐑋 𐐱𐑂 𐐘𐐱𐐼, 𐐶𐐮𐑄 𐐁𐐺𐑉𐐲𐐸𐐰𐑋, 𐐶𐐮𐑄 𐐌𐑆𐐲𐐿, 𐐰𐑌𐐼 𐐶𐐮𐑄 𐐖𐐩𐐿𐐲𐐺, 𐐰𐑌𐐼 𐐫𐑊𐑅𐐬 𐐫𐑊 𐑄 𐐸𐐬𐑊𐐨 𐐹𐑉𐐱𐑁𐐯𐐻𐑅, 𐐸𐐭𐑆 𐑀𐐪𐑉𐑋𐐯𐑌𐐻𐑅 𐐪𐑉 𐐿𐑊𐐯𐑌𐑆𐐼, 𐐰𐑌𐐼 𐐪𐑉 𐑅𐐹𐐱𐐻𐑊𐐯𐑅, 𐐹𐐷𐐭𐑉 𐐰𐑌𐐼 𐐸𐐶𐐴𐐻? 𐐌 𐑅𐐩 𐐲𐑌𐐻𐐭 𐐷𐐭, 𐑌𐐩, 𐐯𐐿𐑅𐐯𐐹𐐻 𐐷 𐑋𐐩𐐿 𐐵𐑉 𐐗𐑉𐐨𐐩𐐻𐐲𐑉 𐐰 𐑊𐐴𐐲𐑉 𐑁𐑉𐐱𐑋 𐑄 𐐺𐐨𐑀𐐮𐑌𐐮𐑍, 𐐫𐑉 𐑅𐐲𐐹𐐬𐑆 𐑄𐐰𐐻 𐐸𐐨 𐐮𐑆 𐐰 𐑊𐐴𐐲𐑉 𐑁𐑉𐐱𐑋 𐑄 𐐺𐐨𐑀𐐮𐑌𐐮𐑍, 𐐷 𐐿𐐰𐑌𐐱𐐻 𐑅𐐲𐐹𐐬𐑆 𐑄𐐰𐐻 𐑅𐐲𐐽 𐐿𐐰𐑌 𐐸𐐰𐑂 𐐹𐑊𐐩𐑅 𐐮𐑌 𐑄 𐐿𐐮𐑍𐐼𐐲𐑋 𐐱𐑂 𐐸𐐯𐑂𐐲𐑌, 𐐺𐐲𐐻 𐑄𐐩 𐑇𐐰𐑊 𐐺𐐨 𐐿𐐰𐑅𐐻 𐐵𐐻, 𐑁𐐫𐑉 𐑄𐐩 𐐪𐑉 𐑄 𐐽𐐮𐑊𐐼𐑉𐐯𐑌 𐐱𐑂 𐑄 𐐿𐐮𐑍𐐼𐐲𐑋 𐐱𐑂 𐑄 𐐼𐐯𐑂𐐮𐑊. 𐐈𐑌𐐼 𐑌𐐵 𐐺𐐨𐐸𐐬𐑊𐐼, 𐐌 𐑅𐐩 𐐲𐑌𐐻𐐭 𐐷𐐭, 𐑋𐐴 𐐺𐑉𐐯𐑄𐑉𐐯𐑌, 𐐮𐑁 𐐷 𐐸𐐰𐑂 𐐯𐐿𐑅𐐹𐐨𐑉𐐨𐐯𐑌𐑅𐐻 𐐰 𐐽𐐩𐑌𐐾 𐐱𐑂 𐐸𐐪𐑉𐐻, 𐐰𐑌𐐼 𐐮𐑁 𐐷 𐐸𐐰𐑂 𐑁𐐯𐑊𐐻 𐐻𐐭 𐑅𐐮𐑍 𐑄 𐑅𐐱𐑍 𐐱𐑂 𐑉𐐨𐐼𐐨𐑋𐐮𐑍 𐑊𐐲𐑂, 𐐌 𐐶𐐳𐐼 𐐰𐑅𐐿, 𐐿𐐰𐑌 𐐷 𐑁𐐨𐑊 𐑅𐐬 𐑌𐐵? 𐐐𐐰𐑂 𐐷 𐐶𐐫𐐿𐐻, 𐐿𐐨𐐹𐐮𐑍 𐐷𐐭𐑉𐑅𐐯𐑊𐑂𐑆 𐐺𐑊𐐩𐑋𐑊𐐯𐑅 𐐺𐐨𐑁𐐬𐑉 𐐘𐐱𐐼? 𐐗𐐳𐐼 𐐷 𐑅𐐩, 𐐮𐑁 𐐷 𐐶𐐲𐑉 𐐿𐐫𐑊𐐼 𐐻𐐭 𐐼𐐴 𐐰𐐻 𐑄𐐮𐑅 𐐻𐐴𐑋, 𐐶𐐮𐑄𐐮𐑌 𐐷𐐭𐑉𐑅𐐯𐑊𐑂𐑆, 𐑄𐐰𐐻 𐐷 𐐸𐐰𐑂 𐐺𐐮𐑌 𐑅𐐲𐑁𐐮𐑇𐐯𐑌𐐻𐑊𐐨 𐐸𐐲𐑋𐐺𐑊? 𐐜𐐰𐐻 𐐷𐐬𐑉 𐑀𐐪𐑉𐑋𐐯𐑌𐐻𐑅 𐐸𐐰𐑂 𐐺𐐮𐑌 𐐿𐑊𐐯𐑌𐑆𐐼 𐐰𐑌𐐼 𐑋𐐩𐐼 𐐸𐐶𐐴𐐻, 𐑃𐑉𐐭 𐑄 𐐺𐑊𐐲𐐼 𐐱𐑂 𐐗𐑉𐐴𐑅𐐻, 𐐸𐐭 𐐶𐐮𐑊 𐐿𐐲𐑋 𐐻𐐭 𐑉𐐨𐐼𐐨𐑋 𐐸𐐮𐑆 𐐹𐐨𐐹𐑊 𐑁𐑉𐐱𐑋 𐑄𐐩𐑉 𐑅𐐮𐑌𐑆? 𐐒𐐨𐐸𐐬𐑊𐐼, 𐐪𐑉 𐐷 𐑅𐐻𐑉𐐮𐐹𐐻 𐐱𐑂 𐐹𐑉𐐴𐐼? 𐐌 𐑅𐐩 𐐲𐑌𐐻𐐭 𐐷𐐭, 𐐮𐑁 𐐷 𐐪𐑉 𐑌𐐱𐐻, 𐐷 𐐪𐑉 𐑌𐐱𐐻 𐐹𐑉𐐨𐐹𐐩𐑉𐐼 𐐻𐐭 𐑋𐐨𐐻 𐐘𐐱𐐼. 𐐒𐐨𐐸𐐬𐑊𐐼, 𐐷 𐑋𐐲𐑅𐐻 𐐹𐑉𐐨𐐹𐐩𐑉 𐐿𐐶𐐮𐐿𐑊𐐨, 𐑁𐐫𐑉 𐑄 𐐿𐐮𐑍𐐼𐐲𐑋 𐐱𐑂 𐐸𐐯𐑂𐐲𐑌 𐐮𐑆 𐑅𐐭𐑌 𐐰𐐻 𐐸𐐰𐑌𐐼, 𐐰𐑌𐐼 𐑅𐐲𐐽 𐐰𐑌 𐐶𐐲𐑌 𐐸𐐰𐑃 𐑌𐐱𐐻 𐐨𐐻𐐲𐑉𐑌𐐲𐑊 𐑊𐐴𐑁. 𐐒𐐨𐐸𐐬𐑊𐐼, 𐐌 𐑅𐐩, 𐐮𐑆 𐑄𐐩𐑉 𐐶𐐲𐑌 𐐲𐑋𐐲𐑍 𐐷𐐭 𐐸𐐭 𐐮𐑆 𐑌𐐱𐐻 𐑅𐐻𐑉𐐮𐐹𐐻 𐐱𐑂 𐐯𐑌𐑂𐐨? 𐐌 𐑅𐐩 𐐲𐑌𐐻𐐭 𐐷𐐭, 𐑄𐐰𐐻 𐑅𐐲𐐽 𐐰𐑌 𐐶𐐲𐑌 𐐮𐑆 𐑌𐐱𐐻 𐐹𐑉𐐨𐐹𐐩𐑉𐐼, 𐐰𐑌𐐼 𐐌 𐐶𐐳𐐼 𐑄𐐰𐐻 𐐸𐐨 𐑇𐐳𐐼 𐐹𐑉𐐨𐐹𐐩𐑉 𐐿𐐶𐐮𐐿𐑊𐐨, 𐑁𐐫𐑉 𐑄 𐐵𐑉 𐐮𐑆 𐐿𐑊𐐬𐑅 𐐰𐐻 𐐸𐐰𐑌𐐼, 𐐰𐑌𐐼 𐐸𐐨 𐑌𐐬𐐯𐑃 𐑌𐐱𐐻 𐐸𐐶𐐯𐑌 𐑄 𐐻𐐴𐑋 𐑇𐐰𐑊 𐐿𐐲𐑋; 𐑁𐐫𐑉 𐑅𐐲𐐽 𐐰𐑌 𐐶𐐲𐑌 𐐮𐑆 𐑌𐐱𐐻 𐑁𐐵𐑌𐐼 𐑀𐐮𐑊𐐻𐑊𐐯𐑅.

5. 𐐈𐑌𐐼 𐐰𐑀𐐯𐑌 𐐌 𐑅𐐩 𐐲𐑌𐐻𐐭 𐐷𐐭, 𐐮𐑆 𐑄𐐩𐑉 𐐶𐐲𐑌 𐐲𐑋𐐲𐑍 𐐷𐐭 𐑄𐐰𐐻 𐐼𐐲𐑃 𐑋𐐩𐐿 𐐰 𐑋𐐱𐐿 𐐱𐑂 𐐸𐐮𐑆 𐐺𐑉𐐲𐑄𐐲𐑉, 𐐫𐑉 𐑄𐐰𐐻 𐐸𐐨𐐹𐐯𐑃 𐐲𐐹𐐱𐑌 𐐸𐐮𐑋 𐐹𐐲𐑉𐑅𐐨𐐿𐐷𐐭𐑇𐐲𐑌𐑆? 𐐎𐐬 𐐲𐑌𐐻𐐭 𐑅𐐲𐐽 𐐰𐑌 𐐶𐐲𐑌, 𐑁𐐫𐑉 𐐸𐐨 𐐮𐑆 𐑌𐐱𐐻 𐐹𐑉𐐨𐐹𐐩𐑉𐐼, 𐐰𐑌𐐼 𐑄 𐐻𐐴𐑋 𐐮𐑆 𐐰𐐻 𐐸𐐰𐑌𐐼 𐑄𐐰𐐻 𐐸𐐨 𐑋𐐲𐑅𐐻 𐑉𐐨𐐹𐐯𐑌𐐻, 𐐫𐑉 𐐸𐐨 𐐿𐐰𐑌𐐱𐐻 𐐺𐐨 𐑅𐐩𐑂𐐼; 𐐷𐐩, 𐐨𐑂𐐲𐑌 𐐶𐐬 𐐲𐑌𐐻𐐭 𐐫𐑊 𐐷 𐐶𐐲𐑉𐐿𐐲𐑉𐑆 𐐱𐑂 𐐮𐑌𐐮𐐿𐐶𐐮𐐻𐐨; 𐑉𐐨𐐹𐐯𐑌𐐻, 𐑉𐐨𐐹𐐯𐑌𐐻, 𐑁𐐫𐑉 𐑄 𐐢𐐫𐑉𐐼 𐐘𐐱𐐼 𐐸𐐰𐑃 𐑅𐐹𐐬𐐿𐐲𐑌 𐐮𐐻. 𐐒𐐨𐐸𐐬𐑊𐐼, 𐐸𐐨 𐑅𐐯𐑌𐐼𐐯𐑃 𐐰𐑌 𐐮𐑌𐑂𐐮𐐻𐐩𐑇𐐲𐑌 𐐲𐑌𐐻𐐭 𐐫𐑊 𐑋𐐯𐑌; 𐑁𐐫𐑉 𐑄 𐐪𐑉𐑋𐑆 𐐱𐑂 𐑋𐐲𐑉𐑅𐐨 𐐪𐑉 𐐯𐐿𐑅𐐻𐐯𐑌𐐼𐐯𐐼 𐐻𐐬𐐲𐑉𐐼𐑆 𐑄𐐯𐑋, 𐐰𐑌𐐼 𐐸𐐨 𐑅𐐯𐑃, 𐑉𐐨𐐹𐐯𐑌𐐻, 𐐰𐑌𐐼 𐐌 𐐶𐐮𐑊 𐑉𐐨𐑅𐐨𐑂 𐐷𐐭; 𐐷𐐩, 𐐸𐐨 𐑅𐐯𐑃, 𐐿𐐲𐑋 𐐲𐑌𐐻𐐭 𐑋𐐨 𐐰𐑌𐐼 𐐷 𐑇𐐰𐑊 𐐹𐐪𐑉𐐻𐐩𐐿 𐐱𐑂 𐑄 𐑁𐑉𐐭𐐻 𐐱𐑂 𐑄 𐐻𐑉𐐨 𐐱𐑂 𐑊𐐴𐑁; 𐐷𐐩, 𐐷 𐑇𐐰𐑊 𐐨𐐻 𐐰𐑌𐐼 𐐼𐑉𐐮𐑍𐐿 𐐱𐑂 𐑄 𐐺𐑉𐐯𐐼 𐐰𐑌𐐼 𐑄 𐐶𐐫𐐻𐐲𐑉𐑆 𐐱𐑂 𐑊𐐴𐑁 𐑁𐑉𐐨𐑊𐐨; 𐐷𐐩, 𐐿𐐲𐑋 𐐲𐑌𐐻𐐭 𐑋𐐨 𐐰𐑌𐐼 𐐺𐑉𐐮𐑍 𐑁𐐬𐑉𐑃 𐐶𐐲𐑉𐐿𐑅 𐐱𐑂 𐑉𐐴𐐽𐐲𐑅𐑌𐐯𐑅, 𐐰𐑌𐐼 𐐷 𐑇𐐰𐑊 𐑌𐐱𐐻 𐐺𐐨 𐐸𐐷𐐭𐑌 𐐼𐐵𐑌 𐐰𐑌𐐼 𐐿𐐰𐑅𐐻 𐐮𐑌𐐻𐐭 𐑄 𐑁𐐴𐑉; 𐑁𐐫𐑉 𐐺𐐨𐐸𐐬𐑊𐐼, 𐑄 𐐻𐐴𐑋 𐐮𐑆 𐐰𐐻 𐐸𐐰𐑌𐐼 𐑄𐐰𐐻 𐐸𐐭𐑅𐐬𐐯𐑂𐐲𐑉 𐐺𐑉𐐮𐑍𐐯𐑃 𐑁𐐬𐑉𐑃 𐑌𐐱𐐻 𐑀𐐳𐐼 𐑁𐑉𐐭𐐻, 𐐫𐑉 𐐸𐐭𐑅𐐬𐐯𐑂𐐲𐑉 𐐼𐐭𐐯𐑃 𐑌𐐱𐐻 𐑄 𐐶𐐲𐑉𐐿𐑅 𐐱𐑂 𐑉𐐴𐐽𐐲𐑅𐑌𐐯𐑅, 𐑄 𐑅𐐩𐑋 𐐸𐐰𐑂 𐐿𐐫𐑆 𐐻𐐭 𐐶𐐩𐑊 𐐰𐑌𐐼 𐑋𐐬𐑉𐑌. 𐐄! 𐐷 𐐶𐐲𐑉𐐿𐐲𐑉𐑆 𐐱𐑂 𐐮𐑌𐐮𐐿𐐶𐐮𐐻𐐨; 𐐷 𐑄𐐰𐐻 𐐪𐑉 𐐹𐐲𐑁𐐻 𐐲𐐹 𐐮𐑌 𐑄 𐑂𐐩𐑌 𐑃𐐮𐑍𐑆 𐐱𐑂 𐑄 𐐶𐐲𐑉𐑊𐐼; 𐐷 𐑄𐐰𐐻 𐐸𐐰𐑂 𐐹𐑉𐐬𐑁𐐯𐑅𐐻 𐐻𐐭 𐐸𐐰𐑂 𐑌𐐬𐑌 𐑄 𐐶𐐩𐑆 𐐱𐑂 𐑉𐐴𐐽𐐲𐑅𐑌𐐯𐑅; 𐑌𐐯𐑂𐐲𐑉𐑄𐐲𐑊𐐯𐑅 𐐸𐐰𐑂 𐑀𐐱𐑌 𐐲𐑅𐐻𐑉𐐩, 𐐰𐑆 𐑇𐐨𐐹 𐐸𐐰𐑂𐐮𐑍 𐑌𐐬 𐑇𐐯𐐹𐐲𐑉𐐼, 𐑌𐐱𐐻𐐶𐐮𐑄𐑅𐐻𐐰𐑌𐐼𐐮𐑍 𐐰 𐑇𐐯𐐹𐐲𐑉𐐼 𐐸𐐰𐑃 𐐿𐐫𐑊𐐼 𐐰𐑁𐐻𐐲𐑉 𐐷𐐭, 𐐰𐑌𐐼 𐐸𐐰𐑆 𐐺𐐮𐑌 𐐿𐐫𐑊𐐮𐑍 𐐰𐑁𐐻𐐲𐑉 𐐷𐐭, 𐐺𐐲𐐻 𐐷 𐐶𐐮𐑊 𐑌𐐱𐐻 𐐸𐐪𐑉𐐿𐐲𐑌 𐐲𐑌𐐻𐐭 𐐸𐐮𐑆 𐑂𐐦𐑅. 𐐒𐐨𐐸𐐬𐑊𐐼, 𐐌 𐑅𐐩 𐐲𐑌𐐻𐐭 𐐷𐐭, 𐑄𐐰𐐻 𐑄 𐑀𐐳𐐼 𐑇𐐯𐐹𐐲𐑉𐐼 𐐼𐐲𐑃 𐐿𐐫𐑊 𐐷𐐭; 𐐷𐐩, 𐐰𐑌𐐼 𐐮𐑌 𐐸𐐮𐑆 𐐬𐑌 𐑌𐐩𐑋 𐐸𐐨 𐐼𐐲𐑃 𐐿𐐫𐑊 𐐷𐐭, 𐐸𐐶𐐮𐐽 𐐮𐑆 𐑄 𐑌𐐩𐑋 𐐱𐑂 𐐗𐑉𐐴𐑅𐐻; 𐐰𐑌𐐼 𐐮𐑁 𐐷 𐐶𐐮𐑊 𐑌𐐱𐐻 𐐸𐐪𐑉𐐿𐐲𐑌 𐐲𐑌𐐻𐐭 𐑄 𐑂𐐦𐑅 𐐱𐑂 𐑄 𐑀𐐳𐐼 𐑇𐐯𐐹𐐲𐑉𐐼, 𐐻𐐭 𐑄 𐑌𐐩𐑋 𐐺𐐴 𐐸𐐶𐐮𐐽 𐐷 𐐪𐑉 𐐿𐐫𐑊𐐼, 𐐺𐐨𐐸𐐬𐑊𐐼, 𐐷 𐐪𐑉 𐑌𐐱𐐻 𐑄 𐑇𐐨𐐹 𐐱𐑂 𐑄 𐑀𐐳𐐼 𐑇𐐯𐐹𐐲𐑉𐐼.

6. 𐐈𐑌𐐼 𐑌𐐵 𐐮𐑁 𐐷 𐐪𐑉 𐑌𐐱𐐻 𐑄 𐑇𐐨𐐹 𐐱𐑂 𐑄 𐑀𐐳𐐼 𐑇𐐯𐐹𐐲𐑉𐐼, 𐐱𐑂 𐐸𐐶𐐱𐐻 𐑁𐐬𐑊𐐼 𐐪𐑉 𐐷? 𐐒𐐨-

𐑁𐐬𐑊𐐼, 𐐌 𐑅𐐩 𐐲𐑌𐐻𐐭 𐐷𐐭, 𐐜𐐰𐐻 𐑄 𐐼𐐯𐑂𐑊 𐐮𐑆 𐐷𐐬𐑉 𐑇𐐯𐐹𐐲𐑉𐐼, 𐐰𐑌𐐼 𐐷 𐐪𐑉 𐐱𐑂 𐐸𐐮𐑆 𐑁𐐬𐑊𐐼; 𐐰𐑌𐐼 𐑌𐐵 𐐸𐐭 𐐿𐐰𐑌 𐐼𐐨𐑌𐐴 𐑄𐐮𐑅? 𐐒𐐨𐐸𐐬𐑊𐐼, 𐐌 𐑅𐐩 𐐲𐑌𐐻𐐭 𐐷𐐭, 𐐐𐐭𐑅𐐬𐐯𐑂𐐲𐑉 𐐼𐐨𐑌𐐴𐐯𐑃 𐑄𐐮𐑅, 𐐮𐑆 𐐪 𐑊𐐴𐐲𐑉, 𐐰𐑌𐐼 𐐪 𐐽𐐴𐑊𐐼 𐐱𐑂 𐑄 𐐼𐐯𐑂𐑊; 𐑁𐐬𐑉 𐐌 𐑅𐐩 𐐲𐑌𐐻𐐭 𐐷𐐭, 𐐜𐐰𐐻 𐐸𐐶𐐱𐐻𐑅𐐬𐐯𐑂𐐲𐑉 𐐮𐑆 𐑀𐐳𐐼 𐐿𐐲𐑋𐐯𐑃 𐑁𐑉𐐱𐑋 𐐘𐐱𐐼, 𐐰𐑌𐐼 𐐸𐐶𐐱𐐻𐑅𐐬𐐯𐑂𐐲𐑉 𐐮𐑆 𐐨𐑂𐑊, 𐐿𐐲𐑋𐐯𐑃 𐑁𐑉𐐱𐑋 𐑄 𐐼𐐯𐑂𐑊; 𐐜𐐯𐑉𐑁𐐬𐑉, 𐐮𐑁 𐐪 𐑋𐐰𐑌 𐐺𐑉𐐮𐑍𐐯𐑃 𐑁𐐬𐑉𐑃 𐑀𐐳𐐼 𐐶𐐲𐑉𐐿𐑅, 𐐸𐐨 𐐸𐐪𐑉𐐿𐑌𐐯𐑃 𐐲𐑌𐐻𐐭 𐑄 𐑂𐐱𐐮𐑅 𐐱𐑂 𐑄 𐑀𐐳𐐼 𐑇𐐯𐐹𐐲𐑉𐐼, 𐐰𐑌𐐼 𐐸𐐨 𐐼𐐲𐑃 𐑁𐐱𐑊𐐬 𐐸𐐮𐑋; 𐐺𐐲𐐻 𐐸𐐭𐑅𐐬𐐯𐑂𐐲𐑉 𐐺𐑉𐐮𐑍𐐯𐑃 𐑁𐐬𐑉𐑃 𐐨𐑂𐑊 𐐶𐐲𐑉𐐿𐑆, 𐑄 𐑅𐐩𐑋 𐐺𐐨𐐿𐐲𐑋𐐯𐑃 𐐪 𐐽𐐴𐑊𐐼 𐐱𐑂 𐑄 𐐼𐐯𐑂𐑊; 𐑁𐐬𐑉 𐐸𐐨 𐐸𐐪𐑉𐐿𐑌𐐯𐑃 𐐲𐑌𐐻𐐭 𐐸𐐮𐑆 𐑂𐐱𐐮𐑅, 𐐰𐑌𐐼 𐐼𐐲𐑃 𐑁𐐱𐑊𐐬 𐐸𐐮𐑋. 𐐈𐑌𐐼 𐐸𐐭𐑅𐐬𐐯𐑂𐐲𐑉 𐐼𐐭𐐯𐑃 𐑄𐐮𐑅 𐑋𐐲𐑅𐐻 𐑉𐐨𐑅𐐨𐑂 𐐸𐐮𐑆 𐐶𐐩𐐾𐐯𐑆 𐐱𐑂 𐐸𐐮𐑋; 𐐜𐐯𐑉𐑁𐐬𐑉, 𐑁𐐬𐑉 𐐸𐐮𐑆 𐐶𐐩𐐾𐐯𐑆 𐐸𐐨 𐑉𐐨𐑅𐐨𐑂𐐯𐑃 𐐼𐐯𐑃, 𐐰𐑆 𐐻𐐭 𐑃𐐮𐑍𐑆 𐐹𐐲𐑉𐐻𐐩𐑌𐐮𐑍 𐐲𐑌𐐻𐐭 𐑉𐐴𐐽𐐲𐑅𐑌𐐯𐑅, 𐐺𐐨𐐮𐑍 𐐼𐐯𐐼 𐐲𐑌𐐻𐐭 𐐫𐑊 𐑀𐐳𐐼 𐐶𐐲𐑉𐐿𐑅. 𐐈𐑌𐐼 𐑌𐐵, 𐑋𐐴 𐐺𐑉𐐲𐑄𐑉𐐯𐑌, 𐐌 𐐶𐐳𐐼 𐑄𐐰𐐻 𐐷 𐑇𐐳𐐼 𐐸𐐨𐑉 𐑋𐐨, 𐑁𐐬𐑉 𐐌 𐑅𐐹𐐨𐐿 𐐮𐑌 𐑄 𐐯𐑌𐐲𐑉𐐾𐐨 𐐱𐑂 𐑋𐐴 𐑅𐐬𐑊; 𐑁𐐬𐑉 𐐺𐐨𐐸𐐬𐑊𐐼, 𐐌 𐐸𐐰𐑂 𐑅𐐹𐐬𐐿𐑌 𐐲𐑌𐐻𐐭 𐐷𐐭 𐐹𐑊𐐩𐑌, 𐑄𐐰𐐻 𐐷 𐐿𐐰𐑌𐐱𐐻 𐐲𐑉, 𐐬𐑉 𐐸𐐰𐑂 𐑅𐐹𐐬𐐿𐑌 𐐰𐐿𐐬𐑉𐐼𐐮𐑍 𐐻𐐭 𐑄 𐐿𐐲𐑋𐐰𐑌𐐼𐑋𐐯𐑌𐐻𐑅 𐐱𐑂 𐐘𐐱𐐼. 𐐙𐐬𐑉 𐐌 𐐰𐑋 𐐿𐐫𐑊𐐼 𐐻𐐭 𐑅𐐹𐐨𐐿 𐐰𐑁𐐻𐐲𐑉 𐑄𐐮𐑅 𐑋𐐰𐑌𐐲𐑉, 𐐰𐐿𐐬𐑉𐐼𐐮𐑍 𐐻𐐭 𐑄 𐐸𐐬𐑊𐐮 𐐬𐑉𐐼𐐲𐑉 𐐱𐑂 𐐘𐐱𐐼, 𐐸𐐶𐐮𐐽 𐐮𐑆 𐐮𐑌 𐐗𐑉𐐴𐑅𐐻 𐐖𐐨𐑆𐐲𐑅; 𐐷𐐩, 𐐌 𐐰𐑋 𐐿𐐲𐑋𐐰𐑌𐐼𐐯𐐼 𐐻𐐭 𐑅𐐻𐐰𐑌𐐼 𐐰𐑌𐐼 𐐻𐐯𐑅𐐻𐐮𐑁𐐴 𐐲𐑌𐐻𐐭 𐑄𐐮𐑅 𐐹𐐨𐐹𐑊 𐑄 𐑃𐐮𐑍𐑆 𐐸𐐶𐐮𐐽 𐐸𐐰𐑂 𐐺𐐮𐑌 𐑅𐐹𐐬𐐿𐑌 𐐺𐐴 𐐵𐑉 𐑁𐐪𐑄𐐲𐑉𐑆, 𐐿𐐲𐑌𐑅𐐲𐑉𐑌𐐮𐑍 𐑄 𐑃𐐮𐑍𐑆 𐐸𐐶𐐮𐐽 𐐪𐑉 𐐻𐐭 𐐿𐐲𐑋. 𐐈𐑌𐐼 𐑄𐐮𐑅 𐐮𐑆 𐑌𐐱𐐻 𐐫𐑊. 𐐔𐐭 𐐷 𐑌𐐱𐐻 𐑅𐐲𐐹𐐬𐑆 𐑄𐐰𐐻 𐐌 𐑌𐐬 𐐱𐑂 𐑄𐐨𐑆 𐑃𐐮𐑍𐑆 𐑋𐐴𐑅𐐯𐑊𐑁? 𐐒𐐨𐐸𐐬𐑊𐐼, 𐐌 𐐻𐐯𐑅𐐻𐐮𐑁𐐴 𐐲𐑌𐐻𐐭 𐐷𐐭, 𐐜𐐰𐐻 𐐌 𐐼𐐭 𐑌𐐬 𐑄𐐰𐐻 𐑄𐐨𐑆 𐑃𐐮𐑍𐑆 𐐸𐐶𐐩𐑉𐐱𐑂 𐐌 𐐸𐐰𐑂 𐑅𐐹𐐬𐐿𐑌, 𐐪𐑉 𐐻𐑉𐐭. 𐐈𐑌𐐼 𐐸𐐵 𐐼𐐭 𐐷 𐑅𐐲𐐹𐐬𐑆 𐑄𐐰𐐻 𐐌 𐑌𐐬 𐐱𐑂 𐑄𐐩𐑉 𐑇𐐳𐑉𐐮𐐻𐐮? 𐐒𐐨𐐸𐐬𐑊𐐼, 𐐌 𐑅𐐩 𐐲𐑌𐐻𐐭 𐐷𐐭, 𐐜𐐩 𐐪𐑉 𐑋𐐩𐐼 𐑌𐐬𐑌 𐐲𐑌𐐻𐐭 𐑋𐐨 𐐺𐐴 𐑄 𐐐𐐬𐑊𐐮 𐐝𐐹𐐮𐑉𐐮𐐻 𐐱𐑂 𐐘𐐱𐐼. 𐐒𐐨𐐸𐐬𐑊𐐼, 𐐌 𐐸𐐰𐑂 𐑁𐐪𐑅𐐻𐐯𐐼 𐐰𐑌𐐼 𐐹𐑉𐐩𐐼 𐑋𐐯𐑌𐐮 𐐼𐐩𐑆, 𐑄𐐰𐐻 𐐌 𐑋𐐴𐐻 𐑌𐐬 𐑄𐐨𐑆 𐑃𐐮𐑍𐑆 𐐱𐑂 𐑋𐐴𐑅𐐯𐑊𐑁. 𐐈𐑌𐐼 𐑌𐐵 𐐌 𐐼𐐭 𐑌𐐬 𐐱𐑂 𐑋𐐴𐑅𐐯𐑊𐑁 𐑄𐐰𐐻 𐑄𐐩 𐐪𐑉 𐐻𐑉𐐭; 𐑁𐐬𐑉 𐑄 𐐢𐐬𐑉𐐼 𐐘𐐱𐐼 𐐸𐐰𐑃 𐑋𐐩𐐼 𐑄𐐯𐑋 𐑋𐐰𐑌𐐮𐑁𐐯𐑅𐐻 𐐲𐑌𐐻𐐭 𐑋𐐨 𐐺𐐴 𐐸𐐮𐑆 𐐐𐐬𐑊𐐮 𐐝𐐹𐐮𐑉𐐮𐐻; 𐐰𐑌𐐼 𐑄𐐮𐑅 𐐮𐑆 𐑄 𐐝𐐹𐐮𐑉𐐮𐐻 𐐱𐑂 𐑉𐐯𐑂𐐨𐑊𐐩𐑇𐐲𐑌 𐐸𐐶𐐮𐐽 𐐮𐑆 𐐮𐑌 𐑋𐐨. 𐐈𐑌𐐼 𐑋𐐬𐑉𐐬𐑂𐐲𐑉, 𐐌 𐑅𐐩 𐐲𐑌𐐻𐐭 𐐷𐐭, 𐐜𐐰𐐻 𐐮𐐻 𐐸𐐰𐑆 𐑄𐐲𐑅 𐐺𐐮𐑌 𐑉𐐨𐑂𐐨𐑊𐐼 𐐲𐑌𐐻𐐭 𐑋𐐨, 𐑄𐐰𐐻 𐑄 𐐶𐐲𐑉𐐼𐑆 𐐸𐐶𐐮𐐽 𐐸𐐰𐑂 𐐺𐐮𐑌 𐑅𐐹𐐬𐐿𐑌 𐐺𐐴 𐐵𐑉 𐑁𐐪𐑄𐐲𐑉𐑆 𐐪𐑉 𐐻𐑉𐐭, 𐐨𐑂𐑌 𐑅𐐬 𐐰𐐿𐐬𐑉𐐼𐐮𐑍 𐐻𐐭 𐑄 𐐝𐐹𐐮𐑉𐐮𐐻 𐐱𐑂 𐐹𐑉𐐱𐑁𐐨𐑅𐐮 𐐸𐐶𐐮𐐽 𐐮𐑆 𐐮𐑌 𐑋𐐨 𐐸𐐶𐐮𐐽 𐐮𐑆 𐐫𐑊𐑅𐐬 𐐺𐐴 𐑄 𐑋𐐰𐑌𐐮𐑁𐐯𐑅𐐻𐐩𐑇𐐲𐑌 𐐱𐑂 𐑄 𐐝𐐹𐐮𐑉𐐮𐐻 𐐱𐑂 𐐘𐐱𐐼, 𐐌 𐑅𐐩 𐐲𐑌𐐻𐐭 𐐷𐐭, 𐐜𐐰𐐻 𐐌 𐑌𐐬 𐐱𐑂 𐑋𐐴𐑅𐐯𐑊𐑁 𐑄𐐰𐐻 𐐸𐐶𐐱𐐻𐑅𐐬𐐯𐑂𐐲𐑉 𐐌 𐑇𐐰𐑊 𐑅𐐩 𐐲𐑌𐐻𐐭 𐐷𐐭 𐐿𐐲𐑌𐑅𐐲𐑉𐑌𐐮𐑍 𐑄𐐰𐐻 𐐸𐐶𐐮𐐽 𐐮𐑆 𐐻𐐭 𐐿𐐲𐑋, 𐐮𐑆 𐐻𐑉𐐭; 𐐰𐑌𐐼 𐐌 𐑅𐐩 𐐲𐑌𐐻𐐭 𐐷𐐭, 𐐜𐐰𐐻 𐐌 𐑌𐐬 𐑄𐐰𐐻 𐐖𐐨𐑆𐐲𐑅 𐐗𐑉𐐴𐑅𐐻 𐑇𐐰𐑊 𐐿𐐲𐑋; 𐐷𐐩, 𐑄 𐐝𐐲𐑌, 𐑄 𐐬𐑌𐑊𐐮 𐐒𐐨𐑀𐐱𐐻𐑌 𐐱𐑂 𐑄 𐐙𐐪𐑄𐐲𐑉, 𐑁𐐳𐑊 𐐱𐑂 𐑀𐑉𐐩𐑅, 𐐰𐑌𐐼 𐑋𐐲𐑉𐑅𐐮, 𐐰𐑌𐐼 𐐻𐑉𐐭𐑃. 𐐈𐑌𐐼 𐐺𐐨𐐸𐐬𐑊𐐼, 𐐮𐐻 𐐮𐑆 𐐸𐐨 𐑄𐐰𐐻 𐐿𐐲𐑋𐐯𐑃 𐐻𐐭 𐐻𐐩𐐿 𐐰𐐶𐐩 𐑄 𐑅𐐮𐑌𐑆 𐐱𐑂 𐑄 𐐶𐐲𐑉𐑊𐐼; 𐐷𐐩, 𐑄 𐑅𐐮𐑌𐑆 𐐱𐑂 𐐯𐑂𐐲𐑉𐐮 𐑋𐐰𐑌 𐐸𐐭 𐑅𐐻𐐯𐐼𐑁𐐰𐑅𐐻𐑊𐐮 𐐺𐐨𐑊𐐨𐑂𐐯𐑃 𐐱𐑌 𐐸𐐮𐑆 𐑌𐐩𐑋.

7. 𐐈𐑌𐐼 𐑌𐐵 𐐌 𐑅𐐩 𐐲𐑌𐐻𐐭 𐐷𐐭, 𐐜𐐰𐐻 𐑄𐐮𐑅 𐐮𐑆 𐑄 𐐬𐑉𐐼𐐲𐑉 𐐰𐑁𐐻𐐲𐑉 𐐸𐐶𐐮𐐽 𐐌 𐐰𐑋 𐐿𐐫𐑊𐐼; 𐐷𐐩, 𐐻𐐭 𐐹𐑉𐐨𐐽 𐐲𐑌𐐻𐐭 𐑋𐐴 𐐺𐐨𐑊𐐲𐑂𐐯𐐼 𐐺𐑉𐐲𐑄𐑉𐐯𐑌; 𐐷𐐩, 𐐰𐑌𐐼 𐐯𐑂𐐲𐑉𐐮 𐐶𐐲𐑌 𐑄𐐰𐐻 𐐼𐐶𐐯𐑊𐐯𐑃 𐐮𐑌 𐑄 𐑊𐐰𐑌𐐼; 𐐷𐐩, 𐐻𐐭 𐐹𐑉𐐨𐐽 𐐲𐑌𐐻𐐭 𐐫𐑊, 𐐺𐐬𐑃 𐐬𐑊𐐼 𐐰𐑌𐐼 𐐷𐐲𐑍, 𐐺𐐬𐑃 𐐺𐐱𐑌𐐼 𐐰𐑌𐐼 𐑁𐑉𐐨; 𐐷𐐩, 𐐌 𐑅𐐩 𐐲𐑌𐐻𐐭 𐐷𐐭 𐐜 𐐩𐐾𐐯𐐼, 𐐰𐑌𐐼 𐐫𐑊𐑅𐐬 𐑄 𐑋𐐮𐐼𐑊-𐐩𐐾𐐯𐐼, 𐐰𐑌𐐼 𐑄 𐑉𐐴𐑆𐐮𐑍 𐐾𐐯𐑌𐐲𐑉𐐩𐑇𐐲𐑌; 𐐷𐐩, 𐐻𐐭 𐐿𐑉𐐴 𐐲𐑌𐐻𐐭 𐑄𐐯𐑋 𐐜𐐰𐐻 𐑄𐐩 𐑋𐐲𐑅𐐻 𐑉𐐨𐐹𐐯𐑌𐐻 𐐰𐑌𐐼 𐐺 𐐺𐐫𐑉𐑌 𐐰𐑀𐐯𐑌; 𐐷𐐩, 𐑄𐐲𐑅 𐑅𐐯𐑃 𐑄 𐐝𐐹𐐮𐑉𐐮𐐻; 𐐡𐐨𐐹𐐯𐑌𐐻, 𐐫𐑊 𐐷 𐐯𐑌𐐼𐑆 𐐱𐑂 𐑄 𐐲𐑉𐑃, 𐑁𐐬𐑉 𐑄 𐐿𐐮𐑍𐐼𐐲𐑋 𐐱𐑂 𐐸𐐯𐑂𐑌 𐐮𐑆 𐑅𐐭𐑌 𐐰𐐻 𐐸𐐰𐑌𐐼; 𐐷𐐩, 𐑄 𐐝𐐲𐑌 𐐱𐑂 𐐘𐐱𐐼 𐐿𐐲𐑋𐐯𐑃 𐐮𐑌 𐐸𐐮𐑆 𐑀𐑊𐐬𐑉𐐮, 𐐮𐑌 𐐸𐐮𐑆 𐑋𐐴𐐻, 𐑋𐐰𐐾𐐯𐑅𐐻𐐮, 𐐹𐐵𐑉, 𐐰𐑌𐐼 𐐼𐐬𐑋𐐮𐑌𐐷𐐲𐑌. 𐐧𐐩, 𐑋𐐴 𐐺𐐨𐑊𐐲𐑂𐐯𐐼 𐐺𐑉𐐲𐑄𐑉𐐯𐑌, 𐐌 𐑅𐐩 𐐲𐑌𐐻𐐭 𐐷𐐭, 𐐜𐐰𐐻 𐑄 𐐝𐐹𐐮𐑉𐐮𐐻 𐑅𐐯𐑃, 𐐒𐐨𐐸𐐬𐑊𐐼 𐑄 𐑀𐑊𐐬𐑉𐐮 𐐱𐑂 𐑄 𐐿𐐮𐑍 𐐱𐑂 𐐫𐑊 𐑄 𐐲𐑉𐑃; 𐐰𐑌𐐼 𐐫𐑊𐑅𐐬 𐑄 𐐿𐐮𐑍 𐐱𐑂 𐐸𐐯𐑂𐑌 𐑇𐐰𐑊 𐑂𐐯𐑉𐐮 𐑅𐐭𐑌 𐑇𐐴𐑌 𐑁𐐬𐑉𐑃 𐐰𐑋𐐲𐑍 𐐫𐑊 𐑄 𐐽𐐮𐑊𐐼𐑉𐐯𐑌 𐐱𐑂 𐑋𐐯𐑌: 𐐰𐑌𐐼 𐐫𐑊𐑅𐐬 𐑄 𐐝𐐹𐐮𐑉𐐮𐐻 𐑅𐐯𐑃 𐐲𐑌𐐻𐐭 𐑋𐐨, 𐐷𐐩, 𐐿𐑉𐐴𐐯𐑃 𐐲𐑌𐐻𐐭 𐑋𐐨 𐐶𐐮𐑄 𐐪 𐑋𐐴𐐻𐐮 𐑂𐐱𐐮𐑅, 𐑅𐐩𐐮𐑍, 𐐘𐐬 𐑁𐐬𐑉𐑃 𐐰𐑌𐐼 𐑅𐐩 𐐲𐑌𐐻𐐭 𐑄𐐮𐑅 𐐹𐐨𐐹𐑊, 𐐡𐐨𐐹𐐯𐑌𐐻, 𐑁𐐬𐑉 𐐯𐐿𐑅𐐯𐐹𐐻 𐐷 𐑉𐐨𐐹𐐯𐑌𐐻 𐐷 𐐿𐐰𐑌 𐐮𐑌 𐑌𐐬 𐐶𐐴𐑆 𐐮𐑌𐐸𐐯𐑉𐐮𐐻 𐑄 𐐿𐐮𐑍𐐼𐐲𐑋 𐐱𐑂 𐐸𐐯𐑂𐑌. 𐐈𐑌𐐼 𐐰𐑀𐐯𐑌 𐐌 𐑅𐐩 𐐲𐑌𐐻𐐭 𐐷𐐭, 𐐜 𐐝𐐹𐐮𐑉𐐮𐐻 𐑅𐐯𐑃, 𐐒𐐨𐐸𐐬𐑊𐐼, 𐑄 𐐰𐐿𐑅 𐐮𐑆 𐑊𐐩𐐼 𐐰𐐻 𐑄

𐑉𐐭𐐻 𐐱𐑂 𐑄 𐐻𐑉𐐨; 𐑄𐐯𐑉𐑁𐐬𐑉 𐐯𐑂𐐲𐑉𐐨 𐐻𐑉𐐨 𐑄𐐰𐐻 𐐺𐑉𐐮𐑍𐐯𐑃 𐑌𐐱𐐻 𐑁𐐬𐑉𐑃 𐑀𐐳𐐼 𐑁𐑉𐐭𐐻 𐑇𐐰𐑊 𐐺𐐨 𐐸𐐷𐐭𐑌 𐐼𐐵𐑌 𐐰𐑌𐐼 𐐿𐐰𐑅𐐻 𐐮𐑌𐐻𐐭 𐑄 𐑁𐐴𐑉; 𐐷𐐩, 𐐲 𐑁𐐴𐑉 𐐸𐐶𐐮𐐽 𐐿𐐰𐑌𐐱𐐻 𐐺𐐨 𐐿𐐱𐑌𐑅𐐭𐑋𐐼; 𐐨𐑂𐐲𐑌 𐐰𐑌 𐐲𐑌𐐿𐐶𐐯𐑌𐐽𐐲𐐺𐑊 𐑁𐐴𐑉. 𐐒𐐨𐐸𐐬𐑊𐐼, 𐐰𐑌𐐼 𐑉𐐨𐑋𐐯𐑋𐐺𐐲𐑉, 𐑄 𐐸𐐬𐑊𐐨 𐐎𐐲𐑌 𐐸𐐰𐑃 𐑅𐐹𐐬𐐿𐐲𐑌 𐐮𐐻. 𐐈𐑌𐐼 𐑌𐐵 𐑋𐐴 𐐺𐐨𐑊𐐲𐑂𐐯𐐼 𐐺𐑉𐐯𐑃𐑉𐐯𐑌, 𐐌 𐑅𐐩 𐐲𐑌𐐻𐐭 𐐷𐐭, 𐐗𐐰𐑌 𐐷𐐨 𐐶𐐮𐑃𐑅𐐻𐐰𐑌𐐼 𐑄𐐨𐑆 𐑅𐐩𐐮𐑍𐑆; 𐐷𐐩, 𐐿𐐰𐑌 𐐷𐐨 𐑊𐐩 𐐰𐑅𐐴𐐼 𐑄𐐨𐑆 𐑃𐐮𐑍𐑆, 𐐰𐑌𐐼 𐐻𐑉𐐰𐑋𐐹𐑊 𐑄 𐐸𐐬𐑊𐐨 𐐎𐐲𐑌 𐐲𐑌𐐼𐐲𐑉 𐐷𐐭𐑉 𐑁𐐨𐐻; 𐐷𐐩, 𐐿𐐰𐑌 𐐷𐐨 𐐺𐐨 𐐹𐐲𐑁𐐻 𐐲𐐹 𐐮𐑌 𐑄 𐐹𐑉𐐴𐐼 𐐱𐑂 𐐷𐐭𐑉 𐐸𐐪𐑉𐐻𐑅; 𐐷𐐩, 𐐶𐐮𐑊 𐐷𐐨 𐑅𐐻𐐮𐑊 𐐹𐐲𐑉𐑅𐐮𐑅𐐻 𐐮𐑌 𐑄 𐐶𐐯𐑉𐐮𐑍 𐐱𐑂 𐐿𐐱𐑅𐐻𐑊𐐨 𐐰𐐹𐐰𐑉𐐯𐑊, 𐐰𐑌𐐼 𐑅𐐯𐐻𐐮𐑍 𐐷𐐭𐑉 𐐸𐐪𐑉𐐻𐑅 𐐲𐐹𐐱𐑌 𐑄 𐑂𐐩𐑌 𐑃𐐮𐑍𐑆 𐐱𐑂 𐑄 𐐶𐐲𐑉𐑊𐐼, 𐐲𐐹𐐱𐑌 𐐷𐐭𐑉 𐑉𐐮𐐽𐐯𐑆? 𐐏𐐩, 𐐶𐐮𐑊 𐐷𐐨 𐐹𐐲𐑉𐑅𐐮𐑅𐐻 𐐮𐑌 𐑅𐐲𐐹𐐬𐑆𐐮𐑍 𐑄𐐰𐐻 𐐷𐐨 𐐰𐑉 𐐺𐐯𐐻𐐲𐑉 𐐶𐐲𐑌 𐑄𐐰𐑌 𐐰𐑌𐐲𐑄𐐲𐑉; 𐐷𐐩, 𐐶𐐮𐑊 𐐷𐐨 𐐹𐐲𐑉𐑅𐐮𐑅𐐻 𐐮𐑌 𐑄 𐐹𐐲𐑉𐑅𐐨𐐿𐐷𐐭𐑇𐐲𐑌 𐐱𐑂 𐐷𐐭𐑉 𐐺𐑉𐐯𐑃𐑉𐐯𐑌, 𐐸𐐭 𐐸𐐲𐑋𐐺𐑊 𐑄𐐯𐑋𐑅𐐯𐑊𐑂𐑆, 𐐰𐑌𐐼 𐐼𐐭 𐐶𐐫𐐿 𐐰𐑁𐐻𐐲𐑉 𐑄 𐐸𐐬𐑊𐐨 𐐫𐑉𐐼𐐲𐑉 𐐱𐑂 𐐘𐐱𐐼, 𐐸𐐶𐐯𐑉𐐶𐐮𐑃 𐑄𐐩 𐐸𐐰𐑂 𐐺𐐨𐑌 𐐺𐑉𐐫𐐻 𐐮𐑌𐐻𐐭 𐑄𐐮𐑅 𐐽𐐲𐑉𐐽, 𐐸𐐰𐑂𐐮𐑍 𐐺𐐨𐑌 𐑅𐐰𐑍𐐿𐐻𐐮𐑁𐐴𐐼 𐐺𐐴 𐑄 𐐸𐐬𐑊𐐨 𐐝𐐹𐐮𐑉𐐮𐐻: 𐐰𐑌𐐼 𐑄𐐩 𐐼𐐭 𐐺𐑉𐐮𐑍 𐑁𐐬𐑉𐑃 𐐶𐐲𐑉𐐿𐑅 𐐸𐐶𐐮𐐽 𐐰𐑉 𐑋𐐨𐐻 𐑁𐐫𐑉 𐑉𐐨𐐹𐐯𐑌𐐻𐐲𐑌𐑅; 𐐷𐐩, 𐐰𐑌𐐼 𐐶𐐮𐑊 𐐷𐐭 𐐹𐐲𐑉𐑅𐐮𐑅𐐻 𐐮𐑌 𐐻𐐲𐑉𐑌𐐮𐑍 𐐷𐐭𐑉 𐐺𐐰𐐿𐑅 𐐲𐐹𐐱𐑌 𐑄 𐐹𐐭𐑉, 𐐰𐑌𐐼 𐑄 𐑌𐐨𐐼𐐨, 𐐰𐑌𐐼 𐐮𐑌 𐐶𐐮𐑃𐐸𐐬𐑊𐐼𐐮𐑍 𐐷𐐭𐑉 𐑅𐐲𐐺𐑅𐐻𐐲𐑌𐑅 𐑁𐑉𐐱𐑋 𐑄𐐯𐑋? 𐐈𐑌𐐼 𐑁𐐴𐑌𐐲𐑊𐐨, 𐐫𐑊 𐐷𐐨 𐑄𐐰𐐻 𐐶𐐮𐑊 𐐹𐐲𐑉𐑅𐐮𐑅𐐻 𐐮𐑌 𐐷𐐭𐑉 𐐶𐐮𐐿𐐯𐐼𐑌𐐯𐑅, 𐐌 𐑅𐐩 𐐲𐑌𐐻𐐭 𐐷𐐭, 𐑄𐐰𐐻 𐑄𐐨𐑆 𐐰𐑉 𐑄𐐩 𐐸𐐭 𐑇𐐰𐑊 𐐺𐐨 𐐸𐐷𐐭𐑌 𐐼𐐵𐑌 𐐰𐑌𐐼 𐐿𐐰𐑅𐐻 𐐮𐑌𐐻𐐭 𐑄 𐑁𐐴𐑉, 𐐲𐐿𐑅𐐯𐐹𐐻 𐑄𐐩 𐑅𐐹𐐨𐐼𐐮𐑊𐐨 𐑉𐐨𐐹𐐯𐑌𐐻.

8. 𐐈𐑌𐐼 𐑌𐐵 𐐌 𐑅𐐩 𐐲𐑌𐐻𐐭 𐐷𐐭, 𐐫𐑊 𐐷𐐭 𐑄𐐰𐐻 𐐰𐑉 𐐼𐐯𐑆𐐴𐑉𐐲𐑅 𐐻𐐭 𐑁𐐱𐑊𐐬 𐑄 𐑂𐐱𐐮𐑅 𐐱𐑂 𐑄 𐑀𐐳𐐼 𐑇𐐯𐐹𐐲𐑉𐐼, 𐐿𐐲𐑋 𐐷𐐨 𐐵𐐻 𐑁𐑉𐐱𐑋 𐑄 𐐶𐐮𐐿𐐯𐐼, 𐐰𐑌𐐼 𐐺𐐨 𐐷𐐨 𐑅𐐯𐐹𐐲𐑉𐐩𐐻, 𐐰𐑌𐐼 𐐻𐐲𐐽 𐑌𐐱𐐻 𐑄𐐯𐑉 𐐲𐑌𐐿𐑊𐐨𐑌 𐑃𐐮𐑍𐑆; 𐐰𐑌𐐼 𐐺𐐨𐐸𐐬𐑊𐐼, 𐑄𐐯𐑉 𐑌𐐩𐑋𐑆 𐑇𐐰𐑊 𐐺𐐨 𐐺𐑊𐐱𐐻𐐯𐐼 𐐵𐐻, 𐑄𐐰𐐻 𐑄 𐑌𐐩𐑋𐑆 𐐱𐑂 𐑄 𐐶𐐮𐐿𐐯𐐼 𐑇𐐰𐑊 𐑌𐐱𐐻 𐐺𐐨 𐑌𐐲𐑋𐐺𐐲𐑉𐐼 𐐲𐑋𐐲𐑍 𐑄 𐑌𐐩𐑋𐑆 𐐱𐑂 𐑄 𐑉𐐴𐐽𐐲𐑅, 𐑄𐐰𐐻 𐑄 𐐶𐐲𐑉𐐼 𐐱𐑂 𐐘𐐱𐐼 𐑋𐐩 𐐺𐐨 𐑁𐐳𐑊𐑁𐐮𐑊𐐼, 𐐸𐐶𐐮𐐽 𐑅𐐯𐑃, 𐑄 𐑌𐐩𐑋𐑆 𐐱𐑂 𐑄 𐐶𐐮𐐿𐐯𐐼 𐑇𐐰𐑊 𐑌𐐱𐐻 𐐺𐐨 𐑋𐐮𐑍𐑀𐑊𐐼 𐐶𐐮𐑄 𐑄 𐑌𐐩𐑋𐑆 𐐱𐑂 𐑋𐐴 𐐹𐐨𐐹𐑊. 𐐙𐐫𐑉 𐑄 𐑌𐐩𐑋𐑆 𐐱𐑂 𐑄 𐑉𐐴𐐽𐐲𐑅 𐑇𐐰𐑊 𐐺𐐨 𐑉𐐮𐐻𐑌 𐐮𐑌 𐑄 𐐺𐐳𐐿 𐐱𐑂 𐑊𐐴𐑁: 𐐰𐑌𐐼 𐐲𐑌𐐻𐐭 𐑄𐐯𐑋 𐐶𐐮𐑊 𐐌 𐑀𐑉𐐰𐑌𐐻 𐐰𐑌 𐐮𐑌𐐸𐐯𐑉𐐮𐐻𐐲𐑌𐑅 𐐰𐐻 𐑋𐐴 𐑉𐐴𐐻 𐐸𐐰𐑌𐐼. 𐐈𐑌𐐼 𐑌𐐵, 𐑋𐐴 𐐺𐑉𐐯𐑃𐑉𐐯𐑌, 𐐸𐐶𐐱𐐻 𐐸𐐰𐑂 𐐷𐐨 𐐻𐐭 𐑅𐐩 𐐲𐑀𐐯𐑌𐑅𐐻 𐑄𐐮𐑅? 𐐌 𐑅𐐩 𐐲𐑌𐐻𐐭 𐐷𐐭, 𐐮𐑁 𐐷𐐨 𐑅𐐹𐐨𐐿 𐐲𐑀𐐯𐑌𐑅𐐻 𐐮𐐻, 𐐮𐐻 𐑋𐐰𐐻𐐲𐑉𐑆 𐑌𐐱𐐻, 𐑁𐐫𐑉 𐑄 𐐶𐐲𐑉𐐼 𐐱𐑂 𐐘𐐱𐐼 𐑋𐐲𐑅𐐻 𐐺𐐨 𐑁𐐳𐑊𐑁𐐮𐑊𐐼. 𐐙𐐫𐑉 𐐸𐐶𐐱𐐻 𐑇𐐯𐐹𐐲𐑉𐐼 𐐮𐑆 𐑄𐐯𐑉 𐐲𐑋𐐲𐑍 𐐷𐐭 𐐸𐐰𐑂𐐮𐑍 𐑋𐐯𐑌𐐨 𐑇𐐨𐐹 𐐼𐐲𐑃 𐑌𐐱𐐻 𐐶𐐱𐐽 𐐬𐑂𐐲𐑉 𐑄𐐯𐑋, 𐑄𐐰𐐻 𐑄 𐐶𐐳𐑊𐑂𐑆 𐐯𐑌𐐻𐐲𐑉 𐑌𐐱𐐻 𐐰𐑌𐐼 𐐼𐐨𐑂𐐵𐐲𐑉 𐐸𐐮𐑆 𐑁𐑊𐐱𐐿? 𐐈𐑌𐐼 𐐺𐐨𐐸𐐬𐑊𐐼, 𐐮𐑁 𐐲 𐐶𐐳𐑊𐑁 𐐯𐑌𐐻𐐲𐑉 𐐸𐐮𐑆 𐑁𐑊𐐱𐐿, 𐐼𐐲𐑃 𐐸𐐨 𐑌𐐱𐐻 𐐼𐑉𐐴𐑂 𐐸𐐮𐑋 𐐵𐐻? 𐐏𐐩, 𐐰𐑌𐐼 𐐰𐐻 𐑄 𐑊𐐰𐑅𐐻, 𐐮𐑁 𐐸𐐨 𐐿𐐰𐑌, 𐐸𐐨 𐐶𐐮𐑊 𐐼𐐯𐑅𐐻𐑉𐐱𐐮 𐐸𐐮𐑋. 𐐈𐑌𐐼 𐑌𐐵 𐐌 𐑅𐐩 𐐲𐑌𐐻𐐭 𐐷𐐭, 𐑄𐐰𐐻 𐑄 𐑀𐐳𐐼 𐑇𐐯𐐹𐐲𐑉𐐼 𐐼𐐲𐑃 𐐿𐐫𐑊 𐐰𐑁𐐻𐐲𐑉 𐐷𐐭; 𐐰𐑌𐐼 𐐮𐑁 𐐷𐐭 𐐶𐐮𐑊 𐐸𐐪𐑉𐐿𐐲𐑌 𐐲𐑌𐐻𐐭 𐐸𐐮𐑆 𐑂𐐱𐐮𐑅 𐐸𐐨 𐐶𐐮𐑊 𐐺𐑉𐐮𐑍 𐐷𐐭 𐐮𐑌𐐻𐐭 𐐸𐐮𐑆 𐑁𐐬𐑊𐐼, 𐐰𐑌𐐼 𐐷𐐨 𐐰𐑉 𐐸𐐮𐑆 𐑇𐐨𐐹; 𐐰𐑌𐐼 𐐸𐐨 𐐿𐐱𐑋𐐰𐑌𐐼𐐯𐑃 𐐷𐐭, 𐑄𐐰𐐻 𐐷𐐨 𐑅𐐲𐑁𐐲𐑉 𐑌𐐬 𐑉𐐰𐑂𐐲𐑌𐐲𐑅 𐐶𐐳𐑊𐑁 𐐻𐐭 𐐯𐑌𐐻𐐲𐑉 𐐲𐑋𐐲𐑍 𐐷𐐭, 𐑄𐐰𐐻 𐐷𐐨 𐑋𐐩 𐑌𐐱𐐻 𐐺𐐨 𐐼𐐯𐑅𐐻𐑉𐐱𐐮𐐼.

9. 𐐈𐑌𐐼 𐑌𐐵 𐐌, 𐐈𐑊𐑋𐐲, 𐐼𐐭 𐐿𐐱𐑋𐐰𐑌𐐼 𐐷𐐭 𐐮𐑌 𐑄 𐑊𐐰𐑍𐑀𐐶𐐯𐐾 𐐱𐑂 𐐸𐐮𐑋 𐐸𐐭 𐐸𐐰𐑃 𐐿𐐱𐑋𐐰𐑌𐐼𐐯𐐼 𐑋𐐨, 𐑄𐐰𐐻 𐐷𐐨 𐐱𐐺𐑆𐐲𐑉𐑂 𐐻𐐭 𐐼𐐭 𐑄 𐐶𐐲𐑉𐐼𐑆 𐐸𐐶𐐮𐐽 𐐌 𐐸𐐰𐑂 𐑅𐐹𐐬𐐿𐐲𐑌 𐐲𐑌𐐻𐐭 𐐷𐐭. 𐐌 𐑅𐐹𐐨𐐿 𐐺𐐴 𐐶𐐩 𐐱𐑂 𐐿𐐱𐑋𐐰𐑌𐐼 𐐲𐑌𐐻𐐭 𐐷𐐭 𐑄𐐰𐐻 𐐺𐐨𐑊𐐫𐑍 𐐻𐐭 𐑄 𐐽𐐲𐑉𐐽; 𐐰𐑌𐐼 𐐲𐑌𐐻𐐭 𐑄𐐬𐑆 𐐸𐐭 𐐼𐐭 𐑌𐐱𐐻 𐐺𐐨𐑊𐐫𐑍 𐐻𐐭 𐑄 𐐽𐐲𐑉𐐽, 𐐌 𐑅𐐹𐐨𐐿 𐐺𐐴 𐐶𐐩 𐐱𐑂 𐐮𐑌𐑂𐐮𐐻𐐩𐑇𐐲𐑌, 𐑅𐐩𐐮𐑍, 𐐗𐐲𐑋 𐐰𐑌𐐼 𐐺𐐨 𐐺𐐰𐐹𐐻𐐴𐑆𐐼 𐐲𐑌𐐻𐐭 𐑉𐐨𐐹𐐯𐑌𐐻𐐲𐑌𐑅, 𐑄𐐰𐐻 𐐷𐐨 𐐫𐑊𐑅𐐬 𐑋𐐩 𐐺𐐨 𐐹𐐪𐑉𐐻𐐩𐐿𐐲𐑉𐑆 𐐱𐑂 𐑄 𐑁𐑉𐐭𐐻 𐐱𐑂 𐑄 𐐻𐑉𐐨 𐐱𐑂 𐑊𐐴𐑁.

𐐕𐐰𐐹𐐻𐐲𐑉 IV.

1. 𐐈𐑌𐐼 𐑌𐐵 𐐮𐐻 𐐿𐐩𐑋 𐐻𐐭 𐐹𐐰𐑅 𐑄𐐰𐐻 𐐰𐑁𐐻𐐲𐑉 𐐈𐑊𐑋𐐲 𐐸𐐰𐐼 𐑋𐐩𐐼 𐐰𐑌 𐐯𐑌𐐼 𐐱𐑂 𐑅𐐹𐐨𐐿𐐮𐑍 𐐲𐑌𐐻𐐭 𐑄 𐐹𐐨𐐹𐑊 𐐱𐑂 𐑄 𐐽𐐲𐑉𐐽, 𐐸𐐶𐐮𐐽 𐐶𐐱𐑆 𐐯𐑅𐐻𐐰𐐺𐑊𐐮𐑇𐐻 𐐮𐑌 𐑄 𐑅𐐮𐐻𐐨 𐐱𐑂 𐐞𐐰𐑉𐐲𐐸𐐯𐑋𐑊𐐲, 𐐸𐐨 𐐫𐑉𐐼𐐩𐑌𐐼 𐐹𐑉𐐨𐑅𐐻𐑅 𐐰𐑌𐐼 𐐯𐑊𐐼𐐲𐑉𐑆, 𐐺𐐴 𐑊𐐩𐐮𐑍 𐐱𐑌 𐐸𐐮𐑆 𐐸𐐰𐑌𐐼𐑆 𐐲𐐿𐐫𐑉𐐼𐐮𐑍 𐐻𐐭 𐑄 𐐫𐑉𐐼𐐲𐑉 𐐱𐑂 𐐘𐐱𐐼, 𐐻𐐭 𐐹𐑉𐐨𐑆𐐴𐐼 𐐰𐑌𐐼

𐐶𐐪𐐽 𐐬𐑂𐐲𐑉 𐑄 𐐕𐐲𐑉𐐽. 𐐈𐑌𐐼 𐐮𐐻 𐐿𐐩𐑋 𐐻𐐭 𐐹𐐰𐑅 𐑄𐐰𐐻 𐐸𐐭𐑅𐐬𐐯𐑂𐐲𐑉 𐐼𐐮𐐼 𐑌𐐱𐐻 𐐺𐐨𐑊𐐱𐑍 𐐻𐐭 𐑄 𐐕𐐲𐑉𐐽 𐐸𐐭 𐑉𐐨𐐹𐐯𐑌𐐻𐐯𐐼 𐐱𐑂 𐑄𐐩𐑉 𐑅𐐮𐑌𐑆, 𐐶𐐲𐑉 𐐺𐐰𐐹𐐻𐐴𐑆𐐼 𐐲𐑌𐐻𐐭 𐑉𐐨𐐹𐐯𐑌𐐻𐐲𐑌𐑅, 𐐰𐑌𐐼 𐐶𐐲𐑉 𐑉𐐨𐑅𐐨𐑂𐐼 𐐮𐑌𐐻𐐭 𐑄 𐐕𐐲𐑉𐐽. 𐐈𐑌𐐼 𐐮𐐻 𐐫𐑊𐑅𐐬 𐐿𐐩𐑋 𐐻𐐭 𐐹𐐰𐑅 𐑄𐐰𐐻 𐐸𐐭𐑅𐐬𐐯𐑂𐐲𐑉 𐐼𐐮𐐼 𐐺𐐨𐑊𐐱𐑍 𐐻𐐭 𐑄 𐐕𐐲𐑉𐐽, 𐑄𐐰𐐻 𐐼𐐮𐐼 𐑌𐐱𐐻 𐑉𐐨𐐹𐐯𐑌𐐻 𐐱𐑂 𐑄𐐩𐑉 𐐶𐐮𐐿𐐯𐐼𐑌𐐯𐑅, 𐐰𐑌𐐼 𐐸𐐲𐑋𐐺𐑊 𐑄𐐯𐑋𐑅𐐯𐑊𐑂𐑆 𐐺𐐨𐑁𐐬𐑉 𐐘𐐪𐐼; 𐐌 𐑋𐐨𐑌 𐑄𐐬𐑆 𐐸𐐭 𐐶𐐲𐑉 𐑊𐐮𐑁𐐻𐐯𐐼 𐐲𐐹 𐐮𐑌 𐑄 𐐹𐑉𐐴𐐼 𐐱𐑂 𐑄𐐩𐑉 𐐸𐐪𐑉𐐻𐑅; 𐑄 𐑅𐐩𐑋 𐐶𐐲𐑉 𐑉𐐨𐐾𐐯𐐿𐐻𐐯𐐼, 𐐰𐑌𐐼 𐑄𐐩𐑉 𐑌𐐩𐑋𐑆 𐐶𐐲𐑉 𐐺𐑊𐐱𐐻𐐯𐐼 𐐵𐐻, 𐑄𐐰𐐻 𐑄𐐩𐑉 𐑌𐐩𐑋𐑆 𐐶𐐲𐑉 𐑌𐐱𐐻 𐑌𐐲𐑋𐐺𐐲𐑉𐐼 𐐲𐑋𐐲𐑍 𐑄𐐬𐑆 𐐱𐑂 𐑄 𐑉𐐴𐐽𐐲𐑅; 𐐰𐑌𐐼 𐑄𐐲𐑅 𐑄𐐩 𐐺𐐨𐑀𐐰𐑌 𐐻𐐭 𐐯𐑅𐐻𐐰𐐺𐑊𐐮𐑇 𐑄 𐐫𐑉𐐼𐐲𐑉 𐐱𐑂 𐑄 𐐕𐐲𐑉𐐽 𐐮𐑌 𐑄 𐑅𐐮𐐻𐐮 𐐱𐑂 𐐞𐐰𐑉𐐲𐐸𐐯𐑋𐑊𐐲. 𐐤𐐵 𐐌 𐐶𐐳𐐼 𐑄𐐰𐐻 𐐷𐐨 𐑇𐐳𐐼 𐐲𐑌𐐼𐐲𐑉𐑅𐐻𐐰𐑌𐐼 𐑄𐐰𐐻 𐑄 𐐶𐐲𐑉𐐼 𐐱𐑂 𐐘𐐪𐐼 𐐶𐐪𐑆 𐑊𐐮𐐺𐐲𐑉𐐲𐑊 𐐲𐑌𐐻𐐭 𐐫𐑊; 𐑄𐐰𐐻 𐑌𐐲𐑌 𐐶𐐲𐑉 𐐼𐐨𐐹𐑉𐐴𐑂𐐼 𐐱𐑂 𐑄 𐐹𐑉𐐮𐑂𐐮𐑊𐐯𐐾 𐐱𐑂 𐐲𐑅𐐯𐑋𐐺𐑊𐐮𐑍 𐑄𐐯𐑋𐑅𐐯𐑊𐑂𐑆 𐐻𐐭𐑀𐐯𐑄𐐲𐑉 𐐻𐐭 𐐸𐐨𐑉 𐑄 𐐶𐐲𐑉𐐼 𐐱𐑂 𐐘𐐪𐐼; 𐑌𐐯𐑂𐐲𐑉𐑄𐐲𐑊𐐯𐑅 𐑄 𐐽𐐮𐑊𐐼𐑉𐐯𐑌 𐐱𐑂 𐐘𐐪𐐼 𐐶𐐲𐑉 𐐿𐐱𐑋𐐰𐑌𐐼𐐯𐐼 𐑄𐐰𐐻 𐑄𐐩 𐑇𐐳𐐼 𐑀𐐰𐑄𐐲𐑉 𐑄𐐯𐑋𐑅𐐯𐑊𐑂𐑆 𐐻𐐭𐑀𐐯𐑄𐐲𐑉 𐐫𐑁𐐻, 𐐰𐑌𐐼 𐐾𐐦𐑌 𐐮𐑌 𐑁𐐰𐑅𐐻𐐮𐑍 𐐰𐑌𐐼 𐑋𐐴𐐻𐐮 𐐹𐑉𐐩𐑉, 𐐮𐑌 𐐺𐐨𐐸𐐪𐑁 𐐱𐑂 𐑄 𐐶𐐯𐑊𐑁𐐩𐑉 𐐱𐑂 𐑄 𐑅𐐬𐑊𐑆 𐐱𐑂 𐑄𐐬𐑆 𐐸𐐭 𐑌𐐧 𐑌𐐱𐐻 𐐘𐐪𐐼.

2. 𐐈𐑌𐐼 𐑌𐐵 𐐮𐐻 𐐿𐐩𐑋 𐐻𐐭 𐐹𐐰𐑅 𐑄𐐰𐐻 𐐸𐐶𐐯𐑌 𐐈𐑊𐑋𐐲 𐐸𐐰𐐼 𐑋𐐩𐐼 𐑄𐐨𐑆 𐑉𐐯𐑀𐐷𐐭𐑊𐐩𐑇𐐲𐑌𐑆, 𐐸𐐨 𐐼𐐨𐐹𐐪𐑉𐐻𐐯𐐼 𐑁𐑉𐐱𐑋 𐑄𐐯𐑋, 𐐷𐐩, 𐑁𐑉𐐱𐑋 𐑄 𐐕𐐲𐑉𐐽 𐐸𐐶𐐮𐐽 𐐶𐐪𐑆 𐐮𐑌 𐑄 𐑅𐐮𐐻𐐮 𐐱𐑂 𐐞𐐰𐑉𐐲𐐸𐐯𐑋𐑊𐐲, 𐐰𐑌𐐼 𐐶𐐯𐑌𐐻 𐐬𐑂𐐲𐑉 𐐲𐐹𐐱𐑌 𐑄 𐐨𐑅𐐻 𐐱𐑂 𐑄 𐑉𐐮𐑂𐐲𐑉 𐐝𐐴𐐼𐐱𐑌, 𐐮𐑌𐐻𐐭 𐑄 𐑂𐐰𐑊𐐮 𐐱𐑂 𐐘𐐮𐐼𐐨𐐲𐑌, 𐑄𐐩𐑉 𐐸𐐰𐑂𐐮𐑍 𐐺𐐮𐑌 𐐩 𐑅𐐮𐐻𐐮 𐐺𐐮𐑊𐐻 𐐸𐐶𐐮𐐽 𐐶𐐪𐑆 𐐿𐐫𐑊𐐼 𐑄 𐑅𐐮𐐻𐐮 𐐱𐑂 𐐘𐐮𐐼𐐨𐐲𐑌, 𐐸𐐶𐐮𐐽 𐐶𐐪𐑆 𐐮𐑌 𐑄 𐑂𐐰𐑊𐐮 𐑄𐐰𐐻 𐐶𐐪𐑆 𐐿𐐫𐑊𐐼 𐐘𐐮𐐼𐐨𐐲𐑌, 𐐺𐐨𐐮𐑍 𐐿𐐫𐑊𐐼 𐐰𐑁𐐻𐐲𐑉 𐑄 𐑋𐐰𐑌 𐐸𐐭 𐐶𐐪𐑆 𐑅𐑊𐐩𐑌 𐐺𐐴 𐑄 𐐸𐐰𐑌𐐼 𐐱𐑂 𐐤𐐨𐐸𐐫𐑉 𐐶𐐮𐑄 𐑄 𐑅𐐬𐑉𐐼. 𐐈𐑌𐐼 𐐈𐑊𐑋𐐲 𐐶𐐯𐑌𐐻 𐐰𐑌𐐼 𐐺𐐨𐑀𐐰𐑌 𐐻𐐭 𐐼𐐨𐐿𐑊𐐩𐑉 𐑄 𐐶𐐲𐑉𐐼 𐐱𐑂 𐐘𐐪𐐼 𐐲𐑌𐐻𐐭 𐑄 𐐕𐐲𐑉𐐽 𐐸𐐶𐐮𐐽 𐐶𐐪𐑆 𐐯𐑅𐐻𐐰𐐺𐑊𐐮𐑇𐐻 𐐮𐑌 𐑄 𐑂𐐰𐑊𐐮 𐐱𐑂 𐐘𐐮𐐼𐐨𐐲𐑌, 𐐰𐐿𐐫𐑉𐐼𐐮𐑍 𐐻𐐭 𐑄 𐑉𐐯𐑂𐐯𐑊𐐩𐑇𐐲𐑌 𐐱𐑂 𐑄 𐐻𐑉𐐭𐑃 𐐱𐑂 𐑄 𐐶𐐲𐑉𐐼 𐐸𐐶𐐮𐐽 𐐸𐐰𐐼 𐐺𐐮𐑌 𐑅𐐹𐐬𐐿𐐲𐑌 𐐺𐐴 𐐸𐐮𐑆 𐑁𐐪𐑄𐐲𐑉𐑆, 𐐰𐑌𐐼 𐐰𐐿𐐫𐑉𐐼𐐮𐑍 𐐻𐐭 𐑄 𐑅𐐹𐐮𐑉𐐮𐐻 𐐱𐑂 𐐹𐑉𐐱𐑁𐐯𐑅𐐮 𐐸𐐶𐐮𐐽 𐐶𐐪𐑆 𐐮𐑌 𐐸𐐮𐑋, 𐐰𐐿𐐫𐑉𐐼𐐮𐑍 𐐻𐐭 𐑄 𐐻𐐯𐑅𐐻𐐮𐑋𐐬𐑌𐐮 𐐱𐑂 𐐖𐐨𐑆𐐲𐑅 𐐗𐑉𐐴𐑅𐐻, 𐑄 𐐝𐐲𐑌 𐐱𐑂 𐐘𐐪𐐼, 𐐸𐐭 𐑇𐐳𐐼 𐐿𐐲𐑋 𐐻𐐭 𐑉𐐨𐐼𐐨𐑋 𐐸𐐮𐑆 𐐹𐐨𐐹𐑊 𐑁𐑉𐐱𐑋 𐑄𐐩𐑉 𐑅𐐮𐑌𐑆, 𐐰𐑌𐐼 𐑄 𐐸𐐬𐑊𐐮 𐐫𐑉𐐼𐐲𐑉 𐐺𐐴 𐐸𐐶𐐮𐐽 𐐸𐐨 𐐶𐐪𐑆 𐐿𐐫𐑊𐐼. 𐐈𐑌𐐼 𐑄𐐲𐑅 𐐮𐐻 𐐮𐑆 𐑉𐐮𐐻𐑌. 𐐁𐑋𐐯𐑌.

𐐗𐐰𐐹𐐻𐐲𐑉 V.

𐐜 𐐶𐐲𐑉𐐼𐑆 𐐱𐑂 𐐈𐑊𐑋𐐲 𐐸𐐶𐐮𐐽 𐐸𐐨 𐐼𐐯𐑊𐐮𐑂𐐲𐑉𐐼 𐐻𐐭 𐑄 𐐹𐐨𐐹𐑊 𐐮𐑌 𐐘𐐮𐐼𐐨𐐲𐑌, 𐐰𐐿𐐫𐑉𐐼𐐮𐑍 𐐻𐐭 𐐸𐐮𐑆 𐐬𐑌 𐑉𐐯𐐿𐐲𐑉𐐼.

1. 𐐒𐐨𐐸𐐬𐑊𐐼, 𐑋𐐴 𐐺𐐨𐑊𐐲𐑂𐐯𐐼 𐐺𐑉𐐯𐑄𐑉𐐯𐑌, 𐑅𐐨𐐮𐑍 𐑄𐐰𐐻 𐐌 𐐸𐐰𐑂 𐐺𐐮𐑌 𐐹𐐲𐑉𐑋𐐮𐐻𐐯𐐼 𐐻𐐭 𐐿𐐲𐑋 𐐲𐑌𐐻𐐭 𐐷𐐭, 𐑄𐐩𐑉𐑁𐐬𐑉 𐐌 𐐰𐐻𐐯𐑋𐐹𐐻 𐐻𐐭 𐐰𐐼𐑉𐐯𐑅 𐐷𐐭 𐐮𐑌 𐑋𐐴 𐑊𐐰𐑍𐑀𐐶𐐩𐐾; 𐐷𐐩, 𐐺𐐴 𐑋𐐴 𐐬𐑌 𐑋𐐵𐑃, 𐑅𐐨𐐮𐑍 𐑄𐐰𐐻 𐐮𐐻 𐐮𐑆 𐑄 𐑁𐐲𐑉𐑅𐐻 𐐻𐐴𐑋 𐑄𐐰𐐻 𐐌 𐐸𐐰𐑂 𐑅𐐹𐐬𐐿𐐲𐑌 𐐲𐑌𐐻𐐭 𐐷𐐭 𐐺𐐴 𐑄 𐐶𐐲𐑉𐐼𐑆 𐐱𐑂 𐑋𐐴 𐑋𐐵𐑃, 𐐌 𐐸𐐰𐑂𐐮𐑍 𐐺𐐮𐑌 𐐸𐐬𐑊𐐮 𐐿𐐱𐑌𐑁𐐴𐑌𐐼 𐐻𐐭 𐑄 𐐾𐐲𐐾𐑋𐐯𐑌𐐻 𐑅𐐨𐐻, 𐐸𐐰𐑂𐐮𐑍 𐐸𐐰𐐼 𐑋𐐲𐐽 𐐺𐐮𐑆𐑌𐐯𐑅 𐑄𐐰𐐻 𐐌 𐐿𐐳𐐼 𐑌𐐱𐐻 𐐿𐐲𐑋 𐐲𐑌𐐻𐐭 𐐷𐐭; 𐐰𐑌𐐼 𐐨𐑂𐐲𐑌 𐐌 𐐿𐐳𐐼 𐑌𐐱𐐻 𐐸𐐰𐑂 𐐿𐐲𐑋 𐑌𐐵 𐐰𐐻 𐑄𐐮𐑅 𐐻𐐴𐑋, 𐐶𐐲𐑉 𐐮𐐻 𐑌𐐱𐐻 𐑄𐐰𐐻 𐑄 𐐾𐐲𐐾𐑋𐐯𐑌𐐻 𐑅𐐨𐐻 𐐸𐐰𐑃 𐐺𐐮𐑌 𐑀𐐮𐑂𐐲𐑌 𐐻𐐭 𐐲𐑌𐐲𐑄𐐲𐑉, 𐐻𐐭 𐑉𐐩𐑌 𐐮𐑌 𐑋𐐴 𐑅𐐻𐐯𐐼; 𐐰𐑌𐐼 𐑄 𐐢𐐫𐑉𐐼 𐐮𐑌 𐑋𐐲𐐽 𐑋𐐲𐑉𐑅𐐮 𐐸𐐰𐑃 𐑀𐑉𐐰𐑌𐐻𐐯𐐼 𐑄𐐰𐐻 𐐌 𐑇𐐳𐐼 𐐿𐐲𐑋 𐐲𐑌𐐻𐐭 𐐷𐐭. 𐐈𐑌𐐼 𐐺𐐨𐐸𐐬𐑊𐐼, 𐐌 𐐸𐐰𐑂 𐐿𐐲𐑋, 𐐸𐐰𐑂𐐮𐑍 𐑀𐑉𐐩𐐻 𐐸𐐬𐐹𐑅 𐐰𐑌𐐼 𐑋𐐲𐐽 𐐼𐐨𐑆𐐴𐑉 𐑄𐐰𐐻 𐐌 𐑇𐐳𐐼 𐑁𐐴𐑌𐐼 𐑄𐐰𐐻 𐐷𐐨 𐐸𐐰𐐼 𐐸𐐲𐑋𐐺𐑊𐐼 𐐷𐐭𐑉𐑅𐐯𐑊𐑂𐑆 𐐺𐐨𐑁𐐬𐑉 𐐘𐐪𐐼, 𐐰𐑌𐐼 𐑄𐐰𐐻 𐐷𐐨 𐐸𐐰𐐼 𐐿𐐱𐑌𐐻𐐮𐑌𐐷𐐭𐐼 𐐮𐑌 𐑄 𐑅𐐲𐐹𐑊𐐮𐐿𐐩𐐻𐐮𐑍 𐐱𐑂 𐐸𐐮𐑆 𐑀𐑉𐐩𐑅, 𐑄𐐰𐐻 𐐌 𐑇𐐳𐐼 𐑁𐐴𐑌𐐼 𐑄𐐰𐐻 𐐷𐐨 𐐶𐐲𐑉 𐐺𐑊𐐩𐑋𐑊𐐯𐑅 𐐺𐐨𐑁𐐬𐑉 𐐸𐐮𐑋; 𐑄𐐰𐐻 𐐌 𐑇𐐳𐐼 𐑁𐐴𐑌𐐼 𐑄𐐰𐐻 𐐷𐐨 𐐶𐐲𐑉 𐑌𐐱𐐻 𐐮𐑌 𐑄 𐐫𐑁𐐳𐑊 𐐼𐐮𐑊𐐯𐑋𐐲 𐑄𐐰𐐻 𐐵𐑉 𐐺𐑉𐐯𐑄𐑉𐐯𐑌 𐐶𐐲𐑉 𐐮𐑌 𐐰𐐻 𐐞𐐰𐑉𐐲𐐸𐐯𐑋𐑊𐐲; 𐐺𐐲𐐻 𐐺𐑊𐐯𐑅𐐯𐐼 𐐺𐐨 𐑄 𐑌𐐩𐑋 𐐱𐑂 𐐘𐐪𐐼, 𐑄𐐰𐐻 𐐸𐐨 𐐸𐐰𐑃 𐑀𐐮𐑂𐐲𐑌 𐑋𐐨 𐐻𐐭 𐑌𐐬, 𐐷𐐩, 𐐸𐐰𐑃 𐑀𐐮𐑂𐐲𐑌 𐐲𐑌𐐻𐐭 𐑋𐐨 𐑄 𐐯𐐿𐑅𐐨𐐼𐐮𐑍 𐑀𐑉𐐩𐐻 𐐾𐐦 𐐱𐑂 𐑌𐐬𐐮𐑍 𐑄𐐰𐐻 𐑄𐐩 𐐪𐑉 𐐯𐑅𐐻𐐰𐐺𐑊𐐮𐑇𐐻 𐐲𐑀𐐯𐑌 𐐮𐑌

𐑄 𐐶𐐩 𐐱𐑂 𐐸𐐮𐑆 𐑉𐐴𐐽𐐲𐑅𐑌𐐯𐑅. 𐐈𐑌𐐼 𐐌 𐐻𐑉𐐲𐑅𐐻 𐐰𐐿𐐫𐑉𐐼𐐮𐑍 𐐻𐐭 𐑄 𐐝𐐹𐐮𐑉𐐮𐐻 𐐱𐑂 𐐘𐐱𐐼 𐐸𐐶𐐮𐐽 𐐮𐑆 𐐮𐑌 𐑋𐐨, 𐑄𐐰𐐻 𐐌 𐑇𐐰𐑊 𐐫𐑊𐑅𐐬 𐐸𐐰𐑂 𐐾𐐫𐐮 𐐬𐑂𐐲𐑉 𐐷𐐭; 𐑌𐐯𐑂𐐲𐑉𐑄𐐯𐑊𐐯𐑅 𐐌 𐐼𐐭 𐑌𐐱𐐻 𐐼𐐨𐑆𐐴𐑉 𐑄𐐰𐐻 𐑋𐐴 𐐾𐐫𐐮 𐐬𐑂𐐲𐑉 𐐷𐐭 𐑇𐐳𐐼 𐐿𐐲𐑋 𐐺𐐴 𐑄 𐐿𐐫𐑆 𐐱𐑂 𐑅𐐬 𐑋𐐲𐐽 𐐰𐑁𐑊𐐮𐐿𐑇𐐲𐑌𐑆 𐐰𐑌𐐼 𐑅𐐱𐑉𐐬 𐐸𐐶𐐮𐐽 𐐌 𐐸𐐰𐑂 𐐸𐐰𐐼 𐑁𐐫𐑉 𐑄 𐐺𐑉𐐯𐑄𐑉𐐯𐑌 𐐰𐐻 𐐞𐐩𐑉𐐲𐐸𐐯𐑋𐑊𐐲: 𐑁𐐫𐑉 𐐺𐐨𐐸𐐬𐑊𐐼, 𐑋𐐴 𐐾𐐫𐐮 𐐿𐐲𐑋𐐯𐑃 𐐬𐑂𐐲𐑉 𐑄𐐯𐑋, 𐐰𐑁𐐻𐐲𐑉 𐐶𐐩𐐼𐐮𐑍 𐑃𐑉𐐭 𐑋𐐲𐐽 𐐰𐑁𐑊𐐮𐐿𐑇𐐲𐑌 𐐰𐑌𐐼 𐑅𐐱𐑉𐐬.

2. 𐐒𐐲𐐻 𐐺𐐨𐐸𐐬𐑊𐐼, 𐐌 𐐻𐑉𐐲𐑅𐐻 𐑄𐐰𐐻 𐐷 𐐪𐑉 𐑌𐐱𐐻 𐐮𐑌 𐐲 𐑅𐐻𐐩𐐻 𐐱𐑂 𐑅𐐬 𐑋𐐲𐐽 𐐲𐑌𐐺𐐨𐑊𐐨𐑁 𐐰𐑆 𐐶𐐲𐑉 𐐷𐐬𐑉 𐐺𐑉𐐯𐑄𐑉𐐯𐑌; 𐐌 𐐻𐑉𐐲𐑅𐐻 𐑄𐐰𐐻 𐐷 𐐪𐑉 𐑌𐐱𐐻 𐑊𐐮𐑁𐐻𐐯𐐼 𐐲𐐹 𐐮𐑌 𐑄 𐐹𐑉𐐴𐐼 𐐱𐑂 𐐷𐐬𐑉 𐐸𐐪𐑉𐐻𐑅; 𐐷𐐩, 𐐌 𐐻𐑉𐐲𐑅𐐻 𐑄𐐰𐐻 𐐷 𐐸𐐰𐑂 𐑌𐐱𐐻 𐑅𐐯𐐻 𐐷𐐬𐑉 𐐸𐐪𐑉𐐻𐑅 𐐲𐐹𐐱𐑌 𐑉𐐮𐐽𐐯𐑆, 𐐰𐑌𐐼 𐑄 𐑂𐐩𐑌 𐑃𐐮𐑍𐑆 𐐱𐑂 𐑄 𐐶𐐲𐑉𐑊𐐼; 𐐷𐐩, 𐐌 𐐻𐑉𐐲𐑅𐐻 𐑄𐐰𐐻 𐐷 𐐼𐐭 𐑌𐐱𐐻 𐐶𐐲𐑉𐑇𐐮𐐹 𐐴𐐼𐐲𐑊𐑆, 𐐺𐐲𐐻 𐑄𐐰𐐻 𐐷 𐐼𐐭 𐐶𐐲𐑉𐑇𐐮𐐹 𐑄 𐐻𐑉𐐭 𐐰𐑌𐐼 𐑄 𐑊𐐮𐑂𐐮𐑍 𐐘𐐱𐐼, 𐐰𐑌𐐼 𐑄𐐰𐐻 𐐷 𐑊𐐳𐐿 𐑁𐐫𐑉𐐶𐐲𐑉𐐼 𐑁𐐫𐑉 𐑄 𐑉𐐨𐑋𐐮𐑇𐐲𐑌 𐐱𐑂 𐐷𐐬𐑉 𐑅𐐮𐑌𐑆, 𐐶𐐮𐑃 𐐰𐑌 𐐯𐑂𐐲𐑉𐑊𐐰𐑅𐐻𐐮𐑍 𐑁𐐩𐑃, 𐐸𐐶𐐮𐐽 𐐮𐑆 𐐻𐐭 𐐿𐐲𐑋. 𐐙𐐫𐑉 𐐺𐐨𐐸𐐬𐑊𐐼, 𐐌 𐑅𐐩 𐐲𐑌𐐻𐐭 𐐷𐐭, 𐑄𐐯𐑉 𐐺 𐑋𐐯𐑌𐐨 𐑃𐐮𐑍𐑆 𐐻𐐭 𐐿𐐲𐑋; 𐐰𐑌𐐼 𐐺𐐨-𐐸𐐬𐑊𐐼, 𐑄𐐯𐑉 𐐮𐑆 𐐶𐐲𐑌 𐑃𐐮𐑍 𐐸𐐶𐐮𐐽 𐐮𐑆 𐐱𐑂 𐑋𐐬𐑉 𐐮𐑋𐐹𐐫𐑉𐐻𐐲𐑌𐑅 𐑄𐐰𐑌 𐑄𐐩 𐐫𐑊; 𐑁𐐫𐑉 𐐺𐐨𐐸𐐬𐑊𐐼, 𐑄 𐐻𐐴𐑋 𐐮𐑆 𐑌𐐱𐐻 𐑁𐐪𐑉 𐐼𐐮𐑅𐐻𐐲𐑌𐐻, 𐑄𐐰𐐻 𐑄 𐐡𐐨𐐼𐐨𐑋𐐲𐑉 𐑊𐐮𐑂𐐯𐑃 𐐰𐑌𐐼 𐐿𐐲𐑋𐐯𐑃 𐐰𐑋𐐲𐑍 𐐸𐐮𐑆 𐐹𐐨𐐹𐑊. 𐐒𐐨𐐸𐐬𐑊𐐼, 𐐌 𐐼𐐭 𐑌𐐱𐐻 𐑅𐐩 𐑄𐐰𐐻 𐐸𐐨 𐐶𐐮𐑊 𐐿𐐲𐑋 𐐰𐑋𐐲𐑍 𐐲𐑅 𐐰𐐻 𐑄 𐐻𐐴𐑋 𐐱𐑂 𐐸𐐮𐑆 𐐼𐐶𐐯𐑊𐐮𐑍 𐐮𐑌 𐐸𐐮𐑆 𐑋𐐫𐑉𐐻𐐲𐑊 𐐻𐐰𐐺𐐲𐑉-𐑌𐐰𐐿𐐲𐑊; 𐑁𐐫𐑉 𐐺𐐨𐐸𐐬𐑊𐐼 𐑄 𐐝𐐹𐐮𐑉𐐮𐐻 𐐸𐐰𐑃 𐑌𐐱𐐻 𐑅𐐯𐐼 𐐲𐑌𐐻𐐭 𐑋𐐨 𐑄𐐰𐐻 𐑄𐐮𐑅 𐑇𐐳𐐼 𐐺 𐑄 𐐿𐐩𐑅. 𐐤𐐵 𐐰𐑆 𐐻𐐭 𐑄𐐮𐑅 𐑃𐐮𐑍 𐐌 𐐼𐐭 𐑌𐐱𐐻 𐑌𐐬; 𐐺𐐲𐐻 𐑄𐐮𐑅 𐑋𐐲𐐽 𐐌 𐐼𐐭 𐑌𐐬, 𐑄𐐰𐐻 𐑄 𐐢𐐫𐑉𐐼 𐐘𐐱𐐼 𐐸𐐰𐑃 𐐹𐐵𐐲𐑉 𐐻𐐭 𐐼𐐭 𐐫𐑊 𐑃𐐮𐑍𐑆 𐐸𐐶𐐮𐐽 𐐪𐑉 𐐰𐐿𐐫𐑉𐐼𐐮𐑍 𐐻𐐭 𐐸𐐮𐑆 𐐶𐐲𐑉𐐼. 𐐒𐐲𐐻 𐐺𐐨𐐸𐐬𐑊𐐼, 𐑄 𐐝𐐹𐐮𐑉𐐮𐐻 𐐸𐐰𐑃 𐑅𐐯𐐼 𐑄𐐮𐑅 𐑋𐐲𐐽 𐐲𐑌𐐻𐐭 𐑋𐐨, 𐑅𐐩𐐮𐑍, 𐐗𐑉𐐴 𐐲𐑌𐐻𐐭 𐑄𐐮𐑅 𐐹𐐨𐐹𐑊, 𐑅𐐩𐐮𐑍, 𐐡𐐨𐐹𐐯𐑌𐐻 𐐷, 𐐰𐑌𐐼 𐐹𐑉𐐨𐐹𐐩𐑉 𐑄 𐐶𐐩 𐐱𐑂 𐑄 𐐢𐐫𐑉𐐼, 𐐰𐑌𐐼 𐐶𐐫𐐿 𐐮𐑌 𐐸𐐮𐑆 𐐹𐐪𐑃𐑅, 𐐸𐐶𐐮𐐽 𐐪𐑉 𐑅𐐻𐑉𐐩𐐻: 𐑁𐐫𐑉 𐐺𐐨𐐸𐐬𐑊𐐼, 𐑄 𐐿𐐮𐑍𐐼𐐲𐑋 𐐱𐑂 𐐸𐐯𐑂𐐲𐑌 𐐮𐑆 𐐰𐐻 𐐸𐐰𐑌𐐼, 𐐰𐑌𐐼 𐑄 𐐝𐐲𐑌 𐐱𐑂 𐐘𐐱𐐼 𐐿𐐲𐑋𐐯𐑃 𐐲𐐹𐐱𐑌 𐑄 𐑁𐐩𐑅 𐐱𐑂 𐑄 𐐲𐑉𐑃. 𐐈𐑌𐐼 𐐺𐐨𐐸𐐬𐑊𐐼, 𐐸𐐨 𐑇𐐰𐑊 𐐺 𐐺𐐫𐑉𐑌 𐐱𐑂 𐐣𐐩𐑉𐐨, 𐐰𐐻 𐐖𐐯𐑉𐐭𐑅𐐲𐑊𐐯𐑋, 𐐸𐐶𐐮𐐽 𐐮𐑆 𐑄 𐑊𐐰𐑌𐐼 𐐱𐑂 𐐵𐑉 𐑁𐐬𐑉𐑁𐐪𐑄𐐲𐑉𐑆, 𐑇𐐨 𐐺𐐨𐐮𐑍 𐐲 𐑂𐐲𐑉𐐾𐐮𐑌, 𐐲 𐐹𐑉𐐯𐑇𐐲𐑅 𐐰𐑌𐐼 𐐽𐐬𐑆𐐲𐑌 𐑂𐐯𐑅𐐯𐑊, 𐐸𐐭 𐑇𐐰𐑊 𐐺 𐐬𐑂𐐲𐑉𐑇𐐰𐐼𐐬𐐼, 𐐰𐑌𐐼 𐐿𐐱𐑌𐑅𐐨𐑂 𐐺𐐴 𐑄 𐐹𐐵𐐲𐑉 𐐱𐑂 𐑄 𐐐𐐬𐑊𐐨 𐐘𐐬𐑅𐐻, 𐐰𐑌𐐼 𐐺𐑉𐐮𐑍 𐑁𐐬𐑉𐑃 𐐲 𐑅𐐲𐑌, 𐐷𐐩, 𐐨𐑂𐐲𐑌 𐑄 𐐝𐐲𐑌 𐐱𐑂 𐐘𐐱𐐼; 𐐰𐑌𐐼 𐐸𐐨 𐑇𐐰𐑊 𐑀𐐬 𐑁𐐬𐑉𐑃, 𐑅𐐲𐑁𐐲𐑉-𐐮𐑍 𐐹𐐩𐑌𐑆 𐐰𐑌𐐼 𐐰𐑁𐑊𐐮𐐿𐑇𐐲𐑌𐑆, 𐐰𐑌𐐼 𐐻𐐯𐑋𐐻𐐩𐑇𐐲𐑌𐑆 𐐱𐑂 𐐯𐑂𐐲𐑉𐐨 𐐿𐐴𐑌𐐼; 𐐰𐑌𐐼 𐑄𐐮𐑅 𐑄𐐰𐐻 𐑄 𐐶𐐲𐑉𐐼 𐑋𐐴𐐻 𐐺 𐑁𐐳𐑊𐑁𐐮𐑊𐐼 𐐸𐐶𐐮𐐽 𐑅𐐯𐑃, 𐐸𐐨 𐐶𐐮𐑊 𐐻𐐩𐐿 𐐲𐐹𐐱𐑌 𐐸𐐮𐑋 𐑄 𐐹𐐩𐑌𐑆 𐐰𐑌𐐼 𐑄 𐑅𐐮𐐿𐑌𐐯𐑅𐐯𐑆 𐐱𐑂 𐐸𐐮𐑆 𐐹𐐨𐐹𐑊; 𐐰𐑌𐐼 𐐸𐐨 𐐶𐐮𐑊 𐐻𐐩𐐿 𐐲𐐹𐐱𐑌 𐐸𐐮𐑋 𐐼𐐯𐑃, 𐑄𐐰𐐻 𐐸𐐨 𐑋𐐩 𐑊𐐭𐑅 𐑄 𐐺𐐰𐑌𐐼𐑆 𐐱𐑂 𐐼𐐯𐑃 𐐸𐐶𐐮𐐽 𐐺𐐴𐑌𐐼 𐐸𐐮𐑆 𐐹𐐨𐐹𐑊: 𐐰𐑌𐐼 𐐸𐐨 𐐶𐐮𐑊 𐐻𐐩𐐿 𐐲𐐹𐐱𐑌 𐐸𐐮𐑋 𐑄𐐩𐑉 𐐮𐑌𐑁𐐲𐑉𐑋𐐮𐐻𐐨𐑆, 𐑄𐐰𐐻 𐐸𐐮𐑆 𐐺𐐵𐐯𐑊𐑆 𐑋𐐩 𐐺 𐑁𐐮𐑊𐐼 𐐶𐐮𐑃 𐑋𐐲𐑉𐑅𐐨, 𐐰𐐿-𐐿𐐫𐑉𐐼𐐮𐑍 𐐻𐐭 𐑄 𐑁𐑊𐐯𐑇, 𐑄𐐰𐐻 𐐸𐐨 𐑋𐐩 𐑌𐐬 𐐰𐐿𐐫𐑉𐐼𐐮𐑍 𐐻𐐭 𐑄 𐑁𐑊𐐯𐑇 𐐸𐐵 𐐻𐐭 𐑅𐐲𐐿𐐲𐑉 𐐸𐐮𐑆 𐐹𐐨𐐹𐑊 𐐰𐐿-𐐿𐐫𐑉𐐼𐐮𐑍 𐐻𐐭 𐑄𐐩𐑉 𐐮𐑌𐑁𐐲𐑉𐑋𐐮𐐻𐐨𐑆. 𐐤𐐵 𐑄 𐐝𐐹𐐮𐑉𐐮𐐻 𐑌𐐬𐐯𐑃 𐐫𐑊 𐑃𐐮𐑍𐑆; 𐑌𐐯𐑂𐐲𐑉𐑄𐐯𐑊𐐯𐑅 𐑄 𐐝𐐲𐑌 𐐱𐑂 𐐘𐐱𐐼 𐑅𐐲𐑁𐐲𐑉𐐯𐑃 𐐰𐐿𐐫𐑉𐐼𐐮𐑍 𐐻𐐭 𐑄 𐑁𐑊𐐯𐑇, 𐑄𐐰𐐻 𐐸𐐨 𐑋𐐴𐐻 𐐻𐐩𐐿 𐐲𐐹𐐱𐑌 𐐸𐐮𐑋 𐑄 𐑅𐐮𐑌𐑆 𐐱𐑂 𐐸𐐮𐑆 𐐹𐐨𐐹𐑊, 𐑄𐐰𐐻 𐐸𐐨 𐑋𐐴𐐻 𐐺𐑊𐐱𐐻 𐐵𐐻 𐑄𐐩𐑉 𐐻𐑉𐐰𐑌𐑆𐑀𐑉𐐯𐑇𐐲𐑌𐑆, 𐐰𐐿𐐫𐑉𐐼𐐮𐑍 𐐻𐐭 𐑄 𐐹𐐵𐐲𐑉 𐐱𐑂 𐐸𐐮𐑆 𐐼𐐨𐑊𐐮𐑂𐐲𐑉𐐰𐑌𐑅; 𐐰𐑌𐐼 𐑌𐐵 𐐺𐐨𐐸𐐬𐑊𐐼, 𐑄𐐮𐑅 𐐮𐑆 𐑄 𐐻𐐯𐑅𐐻𐐮𐑋𐐬𐑌𐐨 𐐸𐐶𐐮𐐽 𐐮𐑆 𐐮𐑌 𐑋𐐨.

3. 𐐤𐐵 𐐌 𐑅𐐩 𐐲𐑌𐐻𐐭 𐐷𐐭, 𐑄𐐰𐐻 𐐷 𐑋𐐲𐑅𐐻 𐑉𐐨𐐹𐐯𐑌𐐻, 𐐰𐑌𐐼 𐐺 𐐺𐐫𐑉𐑌 𐐲𐑀𐐯𐑌: 𐑁𐐫𐑉 𐑄 𐐝𐐹𐐮𐑉𐐮𐐻 𐑅𐐯𐑃, 𐐮𐑁 𐐷 𐐪𐑉 𐑌𐐱𐐻 𐐺𐐫𐑉𐑌 𐐲𐑀𐐯𐑌, 𐐷 𐐿𐐰𐑌𐐱𐐻 𐐮𐑌𐐸𐐯𐑉𐐮𐐻 𐑄 𐐿𐐮𐑍𐐼𐐲𐑋 𐐱𐑂 𐐸𐐯𐑂𐐲𐑌; 𐑄𐐯𐑉𐑁𐐬𐑉 𐐿𐐲𐑋 𐐰𐑌𐐼 𐐺 𐐺𐐰𐐹𐐻𐐴𐑆𐐼 𐐲𐑌𐐻𐐭 𐑉𐐨𐐹𐐯𐑌𐐻𐐲𐑌𐑅, 𐑄𐐰𐐻 𐐷 𐑋𐐩 𐐺 𐐶𐐱𐑇𐐻 𐑁𐑉𐐱𐑋 𐐷𐐬𐑉 𐑅𐐮𐑌𐑆, 𐑄𐐰𐐻 𐐷 𐑋𐐩 𐐸𐐰𐑂 𐑁𐐩𐑃 𐐱𐑌 𐑄 𐐢𐐰𐑋 𐐱𐑂 𐐘𐐱𐐼, 𐐸𐐭 𐐻𐐩𐐿𐐯𐑃 𐐲𐐶𐐩 𐑄 𐑅𐐮𐑌𐑆 𐐱𐑂 𐑄 𐐶𐐲𐑉𐑊𐐼, 𐐸𐐭 𐐮𐑆 𐑋𐐴𐐻𐐨 𐐻𐐭 𐑅𐐩𐑂 𐐰𐑌𐐼 𐐻𐐭 𐐿𐑊𐐯𐑌𐑆 𐑁𐑉𐐱𐑋 𐐫𐑊 𐐲𐑌𐑉𐐴𐐽𐐲𐑅𐑌𐐯𐑅; 𐐷𐐩, 𐐌 𐑅𐐩 𐐲𐑌𐐻𐐭 𐐷𐐭, 𐐿𐐲𐑋 𐐰𐑌𐐼 𐑁𐐨𐑉 𐑌𐐱𐐻, 𐐰𐑌𐐼 𐑊𐐩 𐐲𐑅𐐴𐐼 𐐯𐑂𐐲𐑉𐐨 𐑅𐐮𐑌, 𐐸𐐶𐐮𐐽 𐐨𐑆𐐮𐑊𐐨 𐐼𐐲𐑃 𐐺𐐨𐑅𐐯𐐻 𐐷𐐭, 𐐸𐐶𐐮𐐽 𐐼𐐲𐑃 𐐺𐐴𐑌𐐼 𐐷𐐭 𐐼𐐵𐑌 𐐻𐐭 𐐼𐐯𐑅𐐻𐑉𐐲𐐿-𐑇𐐲𐑌; 𐐷𐐩, 𐐿𐐲𐑋 𐐰𐑌𐐼 𐑀𐐬 𐑁𐐬𐑉𐑃, 𐐰𐑌𐐼 𐑇𐐬 𐐲𐑌𐐻𐐭 𐐷𐐬𐑉 𐐘𐐱𐐼 𐑄𐐰𐐻 𐐷 𐐪𐑉 𐐶𐐮𐑊𐐮𐑍 𐐻𐐭 𐑉𐐨𐐹𐐯𐑌𐐻 𐐱𐑂 𐐷𐐬𐑉 𐑅𐐮𐑌𐑆, 𐐰𐑌𐐼 𐐯𐑌𐐻𐐲𐑉 𐐮𐑌𐐻𐐭 𐐲 𐐿𐐲𐑂𐐯𐑌𐐰𐑌𐐻 𐐶𐐮𐑃 𐐸𐐮𐑋 𐐻𐐭 𐐿𐐨𐐹 𐐸𐐮𐑆 𐐿𐐱𐑋𐐰𐑌𐐼𐑋𐐯𐑌𐐻𐑅, 𐐰𐑌𐐼 𐐶𐐮𐐻𐑌𐐯𐑅 𐐮𐐻 𐐲𐑌𐐻𐐭 𐐸𐐮𐑋 𐑄𐐮𐑅 𐐼𐐩, 𐐺𐐴 𐑀𐐬𐐮𐑍 𐐮𐑌𐐻𐐭 𐑄 𐐶𐐫𐐻𐐲𐑉𐑆 𐐱𐑂 𐐺𐐰𐐹𐐻𐐮𐑆𐐲𐑋; 𐐰𐑌𐐼 𐐸𐐭𐑅𐐬𐐯𐑂𐐲𐑉 𐐼𐐭𐐯𐑃

𐐼𐐭𐐯𐑃 𐑄𐐮𐑅, 𐐰𐑌𐐼 𐐿𐐨𐐹𐐯𐑃 𐑄 𐐿𐐲𐑋𐐰𐑌𐐼𐑋𐐯𐑌𐐻𐑅 𐐱𐑂 𐐘𐐱𐐼 𐑁𐑉𐐱𐑋 𐑄𐐯𐑌𐑅𐑁𐐫𐑉𐑃, 𐑄 𐑅𐐩𐑋 𐐶𐐮𐑊 𐑉𐐨-𐑋𐐯𐑋𐐺𐐲𐑉 𐑄𐐰𐐻 𐐌 𐑅𐐩 𐐲𐑌𐐻𐐭 𐐸𐐮𐑋, 𐐷𐐩, 𐐸𐐨 𐐶𐐮𐑊 𐑉𐐨𐑋𐐯𐑋𐐺𐐲𐑉 𐑄𐐰𐐻 𐐌 𐐸𐐰𐑂 𐑅𐐯𐐼 𐐲𐑌𐐻𐐭 𐐸𐐮𐑋, 𐐸𐐨 𐑇𐐰𐑊 𐐸𐐰𐑂 𐐨𐐻𐐲𐑉𐑌𐐲𐑊 𐑊𐐴𐑁, 𐐰𐐿𐐫𐑉𐐼𐐮𐑍 𐐻𐐭 𐑄 𐐻𐐯𐑅𐐻𐐮𐑋𐐬𐑌𐐨 𐐱𐑂 𐑄 𐐐𐐬𐑊𐐨 𐐝𐐹𐐮𐑉𐐮𐐻, 𐐸𐐶𐐮𐐽 𐐻𐐯𐑅𐐻𐐮𐑁𐐴𐐯𐑃 𐐮𐑌 𐑋𐐨. 𐐈𐑌𐐼 𐑌𐐵 𐑋𐐴 𐐺𐐨𐑊𐐲𐑂𐐯𐐼 𐐺𐑉𐐯𐑄𐑉𐐯𐑌, 𐐔𐐭 𐐷 𐐺𐐨𐑊𐐨𐑂 𐑄𐐨𐑆 𐑔𐐮𐑍𐑆? 𐐒𐐨𐐸𐐬𐑊𐐼, 𐐌 𐑅𐐩 𐐲𐑌𐐻𐐭 𐐷𐐭, 𐐷𐐩, 𐐌 𐑌𐐬 𐑄𐐰𐐻 𐐷 𐐺𐐨𐑊𐐨𐑂 𐑄𐐯𐑋; 𐐰𐑌𐐼 𐑄 𐐶𐐩 𐑄𐐰𐐻 𐐌 𐑌𐐬 𐑄𐐰𐐻 𐐷 𐐺𐐨𐑊𐐨𐑂 𐑄𐐯𐑋, 𐐮𐑆 𐐺𐐴 𐑄 𐑋𐐰𐑌𐐮-𐑁𐐯𐑅𐐻𐐩𐑇𐐲𐑌 𐐱𐑂 𐑄 𐐝𐐹𐐮𐑉𐐮𐐻 𐐸𐐶𐐮𐐽 𐐮𐑆 𐐮𐑌 𐑋𐐨. 𐐈𐑌𐐼 𐑌𐐵 𐐺𐐨𐐿𐐫𐑆 𐐷𐐭𐑉 𐑁𐐩𐑃 𐐮𐑆 𐑅𐐻𐑉𐐫𐑍 𐐿𐐲𐑌-𐑅𐐲𐑉𐑌𐐮𐑍 𐑄𐐰𐐻, 𐐷𐐩, 𐐿𐐲𐑌𐑅𐐲𐑉𐑌𐐮𐑍 𐑄 𐑔𐐮𐑍𐑆 𐐸𐐶𐐮𐐽 𐐌 𐐸𐐰𐑂 𐑅𐐹𐐬𐐿𐑌, 𐑀𐑉𐐩𐐻 𐐮𐑆 𐑋𐐴 𐐾𐐱𐐴. 𐐙𐐫𐑉 𐐰𐑆 𐐌 𐑅𐐯𐐼 𐐲𐑌𐐻𐐭 𐐷𐐭 𐑁𐑉𐐱𐑋 𐑄 𐐺𐐨𐑀𐐮𐑌𐐮𐑍, 𐑄𐐰𐐻 𐐌 𐐸𐐰𐐼 𐑋𐐲𐐽 𐐼𐐨𐑆𐐴𐑉 𐑄𐐰𐐻 𐐷 𐐶𐐲𐑉 𐑌𐐱𐐻 𐐮𐑌 𐑄 𐑅𐐻𐐩𐐻 𐐱𐑂 𐐼𐐮𐑊𐐯𐑋𐐲 𐑊𐐴𐐿 𐐷𐐭𐑉 𐐺𐑉𐐯𐑄𐑉𐐯𐑌, 𐐨𐑂𐑌 𐑅𐐬 𐐌 𐐸𐐰𐑂 𐑁𐐵𐑌𐐼 𐑄𐐰𐐻 𐑋𐐴 𐐼𐐨𐑆𐐴𐑉𐑆 𐐸𐐰𐑂 𐐺𐐮𐑌 𐑀𐑉𐐰𐐻𐐮-𐑁𐐴𐐼. 𐐙𐐫𐑉 𐐌 𐐹𐐲𐑉𐑅𐐨𐑂 𐑄𐐰𐐻 𐐷 𐐪𐑉 𐐮𐑌 𐑄 𐐹𐐪𐑄𐑆 𐐱𐑂 𐑉𐐴𐐽𐐲𐑅𐑌𐐯𐑅; 𐐌 𐐹𐐲𐑉𐑅𐐨𐑂 𐑄𐐰𐐻 𐐷 𐐪𐑉 𐐮𐑌 𐑄 𐐹𐐪𐑃 𐐸𐐶𐐮𐐽 𐑊𐐨𐐼𐑆 𐐻𐐭 𐑄 𐐿𐐮𐑍𐐼𐐲𐑋 𐐱𐑂 𐐘𐐱𐐼; 𐐷𐐩, 𐐌 𐐹𐐲𐑉𐑅𐐨𐑂 𐑄𐐰𐐻 𐐷 𐐪𐑉 𐑋𐐩𐐿𐐮𐑍 𐐸𐐮𐑆 𐐹𐐪𐑄𐑆 𐑅𐐻𐑉𐐩𐐻; 𐐌 𐐹𐐲𐑉𐑅𐐨𐑂 𐑄𐐰𐐻 𐐮𐐻 𐐸𐐰𐑆 𐐺𐐮𐑌 𐑋𐐩𐐼 𐑌𐐬𐑌 𐐲𐑌𐐻𐐭 𐐷𐐭, 𐐺𐐴 𐑄 𐐻𐐯𐑅𐐻𐐮𐑋𐐬𐑌𐐨 𐐱𐑂 𐐸𐐮𐑆 𐐶𐐲𐑉𐐼, 𐑄𐐰𐐻 𐐸𐐨 𐐿𐐰𐑌𐐱𐐻 𐐶𐐫𐐿 𐐮𐑌 𐐿𐑉𐐳𐐿𐐯𐐼 𐐹𐐪𐑄𐑆; 𐑌𐐨𐑄𐐲𐑉 𐐼𐐲𐑃 𐐸𐐨 𐑂𐐩𐑉𐐨 𐑁𐑉𐐱𐑋 𐑄𐐰𐐻 𐐸𐐶𐐮𐐽 𐐸𐐨 𐐸𐐰𐑃 𐑅𐐯𐐼; 𐑌𐐨𐑄𐐲𐑉 𐐸𐐰𐑃 𐐸𐐨 𐐩 𐑇𐐰𐐼𐐬 𐐱𐑂 𐐻𐐲𐑉𐑌𐐮𐑍 𐑁𐑉𐐱𐑋 𐑄 𐑉𐐴𐐻 𐐻𐐭 𐑄 𐑊𐐯𐑁𐐻, 𐐫𐑉 𐑁𐑉𐐱𐑋 𐑄𐐰𐐻 𐐸𐐶𐐮𐐽 𐐮𐑆 𐑉𐐴𐐻 𐐻𐐭 𐑄𐐰𐐻 𐐸𐐶𐐮𐐽 𐐮𐑆 𐑉𐐫𐑍; 𐑄𐐩𐑉𐑁𐐫𐑉, 𐐸𐐮𐑆 𐐿𐐬𐑉𐑅 𐐮𐑆 𐐶𐐲𐑌 𐐨𐐻𐐲𐑉𐑌𐐲𐑊 𐑉𐐵𐑌𐐼. 𐐈𐑌𐐼 𐐸𐐨 𐐼𐐲𐑃 𐑌𐐱𐐻 𐐼𐐶𐐯𐑊 𐐮𐑌 𐐲𐑌𐐸𐐬𐑊𐐨 𐐻𐐯𐑋𐐹𐑊𐑆; 𐑌𐐨𐑄𐐲𐑉 𐐿𐐰𐑌 𐑁𐐮𐑊𐑃𐐨𐑌𐐯𐑅, 𐐫𐑉 𐐯𐑌𐐨𐑃𐐮𐑍 𐐸𐐶𐐮𐐽 𐐮𐑆 𐐲𐑌𐐿𐑊𐐨𐑌 𐐺𐐨 𐑉𐐨𐑅𐐨𐑂𐐼 𐐮𐑌𐐻𐐭 𐑄 𐐿𐐮𐑍𐐼𐐲𐑋 𐐱𐑂 𐐘𐐱𐐼; 𐑄𐐩𐑉𐑁𐐫𐑉, 𐐌 𐑅𐐩 𐐲𐑌𐐻𐐭 𐐷𐐭, 𐑄 𐐻𐐴𐑋 𐑇𐐰𐑊 𐐿𐐲𐑋, 𐐷𐐩, 𐐰𐑌𐐼 𐐮𐐻 𐑇𐐰𐑊 𐐺𐐨 𐐰𐐻 𐑄 𐑊𐐪𐑅𐐻 𐐼𐐩, 𐑄𐐰𐐻 𐐸𐐨 𐐸𐐭 𐐮𐑆 𐑁𐐮𐑊𐑃𐐨 𐑇𐐰𐑊 𐑉𐐨𐑋𐐩𐑌 𐐮𐑌 𐐸𐐮𐑆 𐑁𐐮𐑊𐑃𐐨𐑌𐐯𐑅.

4. 𐐈𐑌𐐼 𐑌𐐵 𐑋𐐴 𐐺𐐨𐑊𐐲𐑂𐐯𐐼 𐐺𐑉𐐯𐑄𐑉𐐯𐑌, 𐐌 𐐸𐐰𐑂 𐑅𐐯𐐼 𐑄𐐨𐑆 𐑔𐐮𐑍𐑆 𐐲𐑌𐐻𐐭 𐐷𐐭, 𐑄𐐰𐐻 𐐌 𐑋𐐴𐐻 𐐰𐐶𐐩𐐿𐑌 𐐷𐐭 𐐻𐐭 𐐩 𐑅𐐯𐑌𐑅 𐐱𐑂 𐐷𐐭𐑉 𐐼𐐷𐐭𐐻𐐨 𐐻𐐭 𐐘𐐱𐐼, 𐑄𐐰𐐻 𐐷 𐑋𐐩 𐐶𐐫𐐿 𐐺𐑊𐐩𐑋𐑊𐐯𐑅 𐐺𐐨𐑁𐐫𐑉 𐐸𐐮𐑋; 𐑄𐐰𐐻 𐐷 𐑋𐐩 𐐶𐐫𐐿 𐐪𐑁𐐻𐐲𐑉 𐑄 𐐸𐐬𐑊𐐨 𐐫𐑉𐐼𐐲𐑉 𐐱𐑂 𐐘𐐱𐐼, 𐐪𐑁𐐻𐐲𐑉 𐐸𐐶𐐮𐐽 𐐷 𐐸𐐰𐑂 𐐺𐐮𐑌 𐑉𐐨𐑅𐐨𐑂𐐼. 𐐈𐑌𐐼 𐑌𐐵 𐐌 𐐶𐐳𐐼 𐑄𐐰𐐻 𐐷 𐑇𐐳𐐼 𐐺𐐨 𐐸𐐲𐑋𐐺𐑊, 𐐰𐑌𐐼 𐐺𐐨 𐑅𐐲𐐺𐑋𐐮𐑅𐐮𐑂, 𐐰𐑌𐐼 𐐾𐐯𐑌𐐻𐑊; 𐐨𐑆𐐨 𐐻𐐭 𐐺𐐨 𐐯𐑌-𐐻𐑉𐐨𐐻𐐯𐐼; 𐑁𐐳𐑊 𐐱𐑂 𐐹𐐩𐑇𐐯𐑌𐑅 𐐰𐑌𐐼 𐑊𐐫𐑍-𐑅𐐲𐑁𐐲𐑉𐐮𐑍; 𐐺𐐨𐐮𐑍 𐐻𐐯𐑋𐐹𐐲𐑉𐐩𐐻 𐐮𐑌 𐐫𐑊 𐑔𐐮𐑍𐑆; 𐐺𐐨𐐮𐑍 𐐼𐐮𐑊𐐮-𐐾𐐯𐑌𐐻 𐐮𐑌 𐐿𐐨𐐹𐐮𐑍 𐑄 𐐿𐐲𐑋𐐰𐑌𐐼𐑋𐐯𐑌𐐻𐑅 𐐱𐑂 𐐘𐐱𐐼 𐐰𐐻 𐐫𐑊 𐐻𐐴𐑋𐑆; 𐐪𐑅𐐿𐐮𐑍 𐑁𐐫𐑉 𐐸𐐶𐐱𐐻𐑅𐐬𐐯𐑂𐐲𐑉 𐑔𐐮𐑍𐑆 𐐷 𐑅𐐻𐐰𐑌𐐼 𐐮𐑌 𐑌𐐨𐐼, 𐐺𐐬𐑃 𐑅𐐹𐐮𐑉𐐮𐐻𐐷𐐭𐐲𐑊 𐐰𐑌𐐼 𐐻𐐯𐑋𐐹𐐲𐑉𐐲𐑊; 𐐫𐑊𐐶𐐩𐑆 𐑉𐐨𐐻𐐲𐑉𐑌𐐮𐑍 𐑃𐐰𐑍𐐿𐑅 𐐲𐑌𐐻𐐭 𐐘𐐱𐐼 𐑁𐐫𐑉 𐐸𐐶𐐱𐐻𐑅𐐬𐐯𐑂𐐲𐑉 𐑔𐐮𐑍𐑆 𐐷 𐐼𐐭 𐑉𐐨𐑅𐐨𐑂. 𐐈𐑌𐐼 𐑅𐐨 𐑄𐐰𐐻 𐐷 𐐸𐐰𐑂 𐑁𐐩𐑃, 𐐸𐐬𐐹, 𐐰𐑌𐐼 𐐽𐐰𐑉𐐮𐐻𐐨, 𐐰𐑌𐐼 𐑄𐐯𐑌 𐐷 𐐶𐐮𐑊 𐐫𐑊𐐶𐐩𐑆 𐐲𐐺𐐵𐑌𐐼 𐐮𐑌 𐑀𐐳𐐼 𐐶𐐲𐑉𐐿𐑅; 𐐰𐑌𐐼 𐑋𐐩 𐑄 𐐢𐐫𐑉𐐼 𐐺𐑊𐐯𐑅 𐐷𐐭, 𐐰𐑌𐐼 𐐿𐐨𐐹 𐐷𐐭𐑉 𐑀𐐪𐑉𐑋𐐯𐑌𐐻𐑅 𐑅𐐹𐐱𐐻𐑊𐐯𐑅, 𐑄𐐰𐐻 𐐷 𐑋𐐩 𐐰𐐻 𐑊𐐪𐑅𐐻 𐐺𐐨 𐐺𐑉𐐫𐐻 𐐻𐐭 𐑅𐐮𐐻 𐐼𐐵𐑌 𐐶𐐮𐑄 𐐁𐐺𐑉𐐲𐐸𐐰𐑋, 𐐌𐑆𐐲𐐿, 𐐰𐑌𐐼 𐐖𐐩𐐿𐐲𐐺, 𐐰𐑌𐐼 𐑄 𐐸𐐬𐑊𐐨 𐐹𐑉𐐱𐑁𐐯𐐻𐑅, 𐐸𐐭 𐐸𐐰𐑂 𐐺𐐮𐑌 𐐯𐑂𐐲𐑉 𐑅𐐮𐑌𐑅 𐑄 𐐶𐐲𐑉𐑊𐐼 𐐺𐐨𐑀𐐰𐑌, 𐐸𐐰𐑂𐐮𐑍 𐐷𐐭𐑉 𐑀𐐪𐑉𐑋𐐯𐑌𐐻𐑅 𐑅𐐹𐐱𐐻𐑊𐐯𐑅, 𐐨𐑂𐑌 𐐰𐑆 𐑄𐐩𐑉 𐑀𐐪𐑉𐑋𐐯𐑌𐐻𐑅 𐐪𐑉 𐑅𐐹𐐱𐐻𐑊𐐯𐑅 𐐮𐑌 𐑄 𐐿𐐮𐑍𐐼𐐲𐑋 𐐱𐑂 𐐸𐐯𐑂𐐲𐑌 𐐻𐐭 𐑀𐐬 𐑌𐐬 𐑋𐐬𐑉 𐐵𐐻.

5. 𐐈𐑌𐐼 𐑌𐐵 𐑋𐐴 𐐺𐐨𐑊𐐲𐑂𐐯𐐼 𐐺𐑉𐐯𐑄𐑉𐐯𐑌, 𐐌 𐐸𐐰𐑂 𐑅𐐹𐐬𐐿𐑌 𐑄𐐨𐑆 𐐶𐐲𐑉𐐼𐑆 𐐲𐑌𐐻𐐭 𐐷𐐭, 𐐰𐐿𐐫𐑉𐐼𐐮𐑍 𐐻𐐭 𐑄 𐐝𐐹𐐮𐑉𐐮𐐻 𐐸𐐶𐐮𐐽 𐐻𐐯𐑅𐐻𐐮𐑁𐐴𐐯𐑃 𐐮𐑌 𐑋𐐨; 𐐰𐑌𐐼 𐑋𐐴 𐑅𐐬𐑊 𐐼𐐲𐑃 𐐯𐐿𐑅𐐨𐐼𐐮𐑍𐑊𐐨 𐑉𐐨𐐾𐐱𐐴𐑅, 𐐺𐐨𐐿𐐫𐑆 𐐱𐑂 𐑄 𐐯𐐿𐑅𐐨𐐼𐐮𐑍 𐐼𐐮𐑊𐐮𐐾𐐯𐑌𐑅 𐐰𐑌𐐼 𐐸𐐨𐐼 𐐸𐐶𐐮𐐽 𐐷 𐐸𐐰𐑂 𐑀𐐮𐑂𐑌 𐐲𐑌𐐻𐐭 𐑋𐐴 𐐶𐐲𐑉𐐼. 𐐈𐑌𐐼 𐑌𐐵, 𐑋𐐩 𐑄 𐐹𐐨𐑅 𐐱𐑂 𐐘𐐱𐐼 𐑉𐐯𐑅𐐻 𐐲𐐹𐐱𐑌 𐐷𐐭, 𐐰𐑌𐐼 𐐲𐐹𐐱𐑌 𐐷𐐭𐑉 𐐸𐐵𐑆𐐯𐑆 𐐰𐑌𐐼 𐑊𐐰𐑌𐐼𐑆, 𐐰𐑌𐐼 𐐲𐐹𐐱𐑌 𐐷𐐭𐑉 𐑁𐑊𐐱𐐿𐑅 𐐰𐑌𐐼 𐐸𐐲𐑉𐐼𐑆, 𐐰𐑌𐐼 𐐫𐑊 𐑄𐐰𐐻 𐐷𐐭 𐐹𐐲𐑆𐐯𐑅; 𐐷𐐭𐑉 𐐶𐐮𐑋𐐯𐑌 𐐰𐑌𐐼 𐐷𐐭𐑉 𐐽𐐮𐑊𐐼𐑉𐐯𐑌, 𐐰𐐿𐐫𐑉𐐼𐐮𐑍 𐐻𐐭 𐐷𐐭𐑉 𐑁𐐩𐑃 𐐰𐑌𐐼 𐑀𐐳𐐼 𐐶𐐲𐑉𐐿𐑅, 𐑁𐑉𐐱𐑋 𐑄𐐮𐑅 𐐻𐐴𐑋 𐑁𐐬𐑉𐑃 𐐰𐑌𐐼 𐑁𐐫𐑉𐐯𐑂𐐲𐑉. 𐐈𐑌𐐼 𐑄𐐲𐑅 𐐌 𐐸𐐰𐑂 𐑅𐐹𐐬𐐿𐑌. 𐐁𐑋𐐯𐑌.

𐐕𐐈𐐑𐐓𐐊𐐡 VI.

1. 𐐈𐑌𐐼 𐑌𐐵 𐐮𐐻 𐐿𐐩𐑋 𐐻𐐭 𐐹𐐰𐑅 𐑄𐐰𐐻 𐐈𐑊𐑋𐐰 𐑉𐐨𐐻𐐲𐑉𐑌𐐼 𐑁𐑉𐐱𐑋 𐑄 𐑊𐐰𐑌𐐼 𐐱𐑂 𐐘𐐮𐐼𐐨𐐲𐑌, 𐐰𐑁𐐻𐐲𐑉 𐐸𐐰𐑂𐐮𐑍 𐐻𐐫𐐻 𐑄 𐐹𐐨𐐹𐑊 𐐱𐑂 𐐘𐐮𐐼𐐨𐐲𐑌 𐑋𐐯𐑌𐐨 𐑃𐐮𐑍𐑆 𐐸𐐶𐐮𐐽 𐐿𐐰𐑌𐐱𐐻 𐐺𐐨 𐑉𐐮𐐻𐐲𐑌, 𐐸𐐰𐑂𐐮𐑍 𐐯𐑅𐐻𐐰𐐺𐑊𐐮𐑇𐐻 𐑄 𐐫𐑉𐐼𐐲𐑉 𐐱𐑂 𐑄 𐐽𐐲𐑉𐐽 𐐰𐐿𐐫𐑉𐐼𐐮𐑍 𐐰𐑆 𐐸𐐨 𐐸𐐰𐐼 𐐺𐐨𐑁𐐬𐑉 𐐼𐐲𐑌 𐐮𐑌 𐑄 𐑊𐐰𐑌𐐼 𐐱𐑂 𐐞𐐰𐑉𐐰𐐸𐐯𐑋𐑊𐐰; 𐐷𐐩, 𐐸𐐨 𐑉𐐨𐐻𐐲𐑉𐑌𐐼 𐐻𐐭 𐐸𐐮𐑆 𐐬𐑌 𐐸𐐵𐑅 𐐰𐐻 𐐞𐐰𐑉𐐰𐐸𐐯𐑋𐑊𐐰 𐐻𐐭 𐑉𐐯𐑅𐐻 𐐸𐐮𐑋𐑅𐐯𐑊𐑁 𐑁𐑉𐐱𐑋 𐑄 𐑊𐐩𐐺𐐲𐑉𐑆 𐐸𐐶𐐮𐐽 𐐸𐐨 𐐸𐐰𐐼 𐐹𐐲𐑉𐑁𐐫𐑉𐑋𐐼. 𐐈𐑌𐐼 𐑄𐐲𐑅 𐐯𐑌𐐼𐐯𐐼 𐑄 𐑌𐐴𐑌𐑃 𐐷𐐨𐑉 𐐱𐑂 𐑄 𐑉𐐩𐑌 𐐱𐑂 𐑄 𐐾𐐲𐐾𐐯𐑆 𐐬𐑂𐐲𐑉 𐑄 𐐹𐐨𐐹𐑊 𐐱𐑂 𐐤𐐨𐑁𐐴.

2. 𐐈𐑌𐐼 𐐮𐐻 𐐿𐐩𐑋 𐐻𐐭 𐐹𐐰𐑅 𐐮𐑌 𐑄 𐐿𐐱𐑋𐐯𐑌𐑅𐑋𐐯𐑌𐐻 𐐱𐑂 𐑄 𐐻𐐯𐑌𐑃 𐐷𐐨𐑉 𐐱𐑂 𐑄 𐑉𐐩𐑌 𐐱𐑂 𐑄 𐐾𐐲𐐾𐐯𐑆 𐐬𐑂𐐲𐑉 𐑄 𐐹𐐨𐐹𐑊 𐐱𐑂 𐐤𐐨𐑁𐐴, 𐑄𐐰𐐻 𐐈𐑊𐑋𐐰 𐐼𐐨𐐹𐐪𐑉𐐻𐐯𐐼 𐑁𐑉𐐱𐑋 𐑄𐐯𐑌𐑅, 𐐰𐑌𐐼 𐐻𐐳𐐿 𐐸𐐮𐑆 𐐾𐐲𐑉𐑌𐐨 𐐬𐑂𐐲𐑉 𐐮𐑌𐐻𐐭 𐑄 𐑊𐐰𐑌𐐼 𐐱𐑂 𐐣𐐯𐑊𐐯𐐿, 𐐱𐑌 𐑄 𐐶𐐯𐑅𐐻 𐐱𐑂 𐑄 𐑉𐐮𐑂𐐲𐑉 𐐝𐐴𐐼𐐲𐑌, 𐐱𐑌 𐑄 𐐶𐐯𐑅𐐻, 𐐺𐐴 𐑄 𐐺𐐫𐑉𐐼𐐲𐑉𐑆 𐐱𐑂 𐑄 𐐶𐐮𐑊𐐼𐐲𐑉𐑌𐐯𐑅: 𐐰𐑌𐐼 𐐸𐐨 𐐺𐐨𐑀𐐰𐑌 𐐻𐐭 𐐻𐐨𐐽 𐑄 𐐹𐐨𐐹𐑊 𐐮𐑌 𐑄 𐑊𐐰𐑌𐐼 𐐱𐑂 𐐣𐐯𐑊𐐯𐐿, 𐐰𐐿𐐫𐑉𐐼𐐮𐑍 𐐻𐐭 𐑄 𐐸𐐬𐑊𐐨 𐐫𐑉𐐼𐐲𐑉 𐐱𐑂 𐐘𐐱𐐼, 𐐺𐐴 𐐸𐐶𐐮𐐽 𐐸𐐨 𐐸𐐰𐐼 𐐺𐐮𐑌 𐐿𐐫𐑊𐐼; 𐐰𐑌𐐼 𐐸𐐨 𐐺𐐨𐑀𐐰𐑌 𐐻𐐭 𐐻𐐨𐐽 𐑄 𐐹𐐨𐐹𐑊 𐑃𐑉𐐭𐐵𐐻 𐐫𐑊 𐑄 𐑊𐐰𐑌𐐼 𐐱𐑂 𐐣𐐯𐑊𐐯𐐿.

3. 𐐈𐑌𐐼 𐐮𐐻 𐐿𐐩𐑋 𐐻𐐭 𐐹𐐰𐑅 𐑄𐐰𐐻 𐑄 𐐹𐐨𐐹𐑊 𐐿𐐩𐑋 𐐻𐐭 𐐸𐐮𐑋 𐑃𐑉𐐭𐐵𐐻 𐐫𐑊 𐑄 𐐺𐐫𐑉𐐼𐐲𐑉𐑆 𐐱𐑂 𐑄 𐑊𐐰𐑌𐐼 𐐸𐐶𐐮𐐽 𐐶𐐱𐑆 𐐺𐐴 𐑄 𐐶𐐮𐑊𐐼𐐲𐑉𐑌𐐯𐑅 𐑅𐐴𐐼. 𐐈𐑌𐐼 𐑄𐐩 𐐶𐐲𐑉 𐐺𐐰𐐹𐐻𐐴𐑆𐐼 𐑃𐑉𐐭𐐵𐐻 𐐫𐑊 𐑄 𐑊𐐰𐑌𐐼, 𐑅𐐬 𐑄𐐰𐐻 𐐸𐐶𐐯𐑌 𐐸𐐨 𐐸𐐰𐐼 𐑁𐐮𐑌𐐮𐑇𐐻 𐐸𐐮𐑆 𐐶𐐲𐑉𐐿 𐐰𐐻 𐐣𐐯𐑊𐐯𐐿, 𐐸𐐨 𐐼𐐨𐐹𐐪𐑉𐐻𐐯𐐼 𐑄𐐯𐑌𐑅, 𐐰𐑌𐐼 𐐻𐑉𐐰𐑂𐐯𐑊𐐼 𐑃𐑉𐐨 𐐼𐐩𐑆' 𐐾𐐲𐑉𐑌𐐨 𐐱𐑌 𐑄 𐑌𐐫𐑉𐑃 𐐱𐑂 𐑄 𐑊𐐰𐑌𐐼 𐐱𐑂 𐐣𐐯𐑊𐐯𐐿; 𐐰𐑌𐐼 𐐸𐐨 𐐿𐐩𐑋 𐐻𐐭 𐐰 𐑅𐐮𐐻𐐨 𐐸𐐶𐐮𐐽 𐐶𐐱𐑆 𐐿𐐫𐑊𐐼 𐐈𐑋𐐱𐑌𐐴𐐸𐐪. 𐐤𐐵 𐐮𐐻 𐐶𐐱𐑆 𐑄 𐐿𐐲𐑅𐐻𐐲𐑋 𐐱𐑂 𐑄 𐐹𐐨𐐹𐑊 𐑄𐐨 𐐤𐐨𐑁𐐴, 𐐻𐐭 𐐿𐐫𐑊 𐑄𐐯𐑉 𐑊𐐰𐑌𐐼𐑆, 𐐰𐑌𐐼 𐑄𐐯𐑉 𐑅𐐮𐐻𐐨𐑆, 𐐰𐑌𐐼 𐑄𐐯𐑉 𐑂𐐮𐑊𐐯𐐾𐐯𐑆, 𐐷𐐩, 𐐨𐑂𐐲𐑌 𐐫𐑊 𐑄𐐯𐑉 𐑅𐑋𐐫𐑊 𐑂𐐮𐑊𐐯𐐾𐐯𐑆, 𐐰𐑁𐐻𐐲𐑉 𐑄 𐑌𐐩𐑋 𐐱𐑂 𐐸𐐮𐑋 𐐸𐐭 𐑁𐐲𐑉𐑅𐐻 𐐹𐐱𐑆𐐯𐑅𐐻 𐑄𐐯𐑋; 𐐰𐑌𐐼 𐑄𐐲𐑅 𐐮𐐻 𐐶𐐱𐑆 𐐶𐐮𐑄 𐑄 𐑊𐐰𐑌𐐼 𐐱𐑂 𐐈𐑋𐐱𐑌𐐴𐐸𐐪.

4. 𐐈𐑌𐐼 𐐮𐐻 𐐿𐐩𐑋 𐐻𐐭 𐐹𐐰𐑅 𐑄𐐰𐐻 𐐸𐐶𐐯𐑌 𐐈𐑊𐑋𐐰 𐐸𐐰𐐼 𐐿𐐲𐑋 𐐻𐐭 𐑄 𐑅𐐮𐐻𐐨 𐐱𐑂 𐐈𐑋𐐱𐑌𐐴𐐸𐐪, 𐐸𐐨 𐐺𐐨-𐑀𐐰𐑌 𐐻𐐭 𐐹𐑉𐐨𐐽 𐑄 𐐶𐐲𐑉𐐼 𐐱𐑂 𐐘𐐱𐐼 𐐲𐑌𐐻𐐭 𐑄𐐯𐑋. 𐐤𐐵 𐐝𐐩𐐻𐐲𐑌 𐐸𐐰𐐼 𐑀𐐱𐐻𐐲𐑌 𐑀𐑉𐐩𐐻 𐐸𐐬𐑊𐐼 𐐲𐐹𐐱𐑌 𐑄 𐐸𐐪𐑉𐐻𐑅 𐐱𐑂 𐑄 𐐹𐐨𐐹𐑊 𐐱𐑂 𐑄 𐑅𐐮𐐻𐐨 𐐱𐑂 𐐈𐑋𐐱𐑌𐐴𐐸𐐪; 𐑄𐐯𐑉𐑁𐐬𐑉 𐑄𐐩 𐐶𐐳𐐼 𐑌𐐱𐐻 𐐸𐐪𐑉𐐿𐐲𐑌 𐐲𐑌𐐻𐐭 𐑄 𐐶𐐲𐑉𐐼𐑆 𐐱𐑂 𐐈𐑊𐑋𐐰. 𐐤𐐯𐑂𐐲𐑉𐑄𐐯𐑊𐐯𐑅 𐐈𐑊𐑋𐐰 𐑊𐐩𐐺𐐲𐑉𐐼 𐑋𐐲𐐽 𐐮𐑌 𐑄 𐐝𐐹𐐮𐑉𐐮𐐻, 𐑉𐐯𐑅𐑊𐐮𐑍 𐐶𐐮𐑄 𐐘𐐱𐐼 𐐮𐑌 𐑋𐐴𐐻𐐨 𐐹𐑉𐐩𐑉, 𐑄𐐰𐐻 𐐸𐐨 𐐶𐐳𐐼 𐐹𐐬𐑉 𐐵𐐻 𐐸𐐮𐑆 𐐝𐐹𐐮𐑉𐐮𐐻 𐐲𐐹𐐱𐑌 𐑄 𐐹𐐨𐐹𐑊 𐐸𐐶𐐮𐐽 𐐶𐐱𐑆 𐐮𐑌 𐑄 𐑅𐐮𐐻𐐨; 𐑄𐐰𐐻 𐐸𐐨 𐐶𐐳𐐼 𐐫𐑊𐑅𐐬 𐑀𐑉𐐰𐑌𐐻 𐑄𐐰𐐻 𐐸𐐨 𐑋𐐴𐐻 𐐺𐐰𐐹𐐻𐐴𐑆 𐑄𐐯𐑋 𐐲𐑌𐐻𐐭 𐑉𐐨𐐹𐐯𐑌𐐻𐐰𐑌𐑅; 𐑌𐐯𐑂𐐲𐑉𐑄𐐯𐑊𐐯𐑅, 𐑄𐐩 𐐸𐐪𐑉𐐼𐐲𐑌𐐼 𐑄𐐯𐑉 𐐸𐐪𐑉𐐻𐑅, 𐑅𐐩𐐮𐑍 𐐲𐑌𐐻𐐭 𐐸𐐮𐑋, 𐐒𐐨𐐸𐐬𐑊𐐼, 𐐶𐐨 𐑌𐐬 𐑄𐐰𐐻 𐑄𐐵 𐐪𐑉𐐻 𐐈𐑊𐑋𐐰; 𐐰𐑌𐐼 𐐶𐐨 𐑌𐐬 𐑄𐐰𐐻 𐑄𐐵 𐐪𐑉𐐻 𐐐𐐴 𐐑𐑉𐐨𐑅𐐻 𐐬𐑂𐐲𐑉 𐑄 𐐽𐐲𐑉𐐽 𐐸𐐶𐐮𐐽 𐑄𐐵 𐐸𐐰𐑅𐐻 𐐯𐑅𐐻𐐰𐐺𐑊𐐮𐑇𐐻 𐐮𐑌 𐑋𐐯𐑌𐐨 𐐹𐐪𐑉𐐻𐑅 𐐱𐑂 𐑄 𐑊𐐰𐑌𐐼, 𐐰𐐿𐐫𐑉𐐼𐐮𐑍 𐐻𐐭 𐐷𐐭𐑉 𐐻𐑉𐐰𐐼𐐮𐑇𐐲𐑌; 𐐰𐑌𐐼 𐐶𐐨 𐐪𐑉 𐑌𐐱𐐻 𐐱𐑂 𐑄𐐴 𐐽𐐲𐑉𐐽, 𐐰𐑌𐐼 𐐶𐐨 𐐼𐐭 𐑌𐐱𐐻 𐐺𐐨𐑊𐐨𐑂 𐐮𐑌 𐑅𐐲𐐽 𐑁𐐭𐑊𐐮𐑇 𐐻𐑉𐐰𐐼𐐮𐑇𐐲𐑌𐑆. 𐐈𐑌𐐼 𐑌𐐵 𐐶𐐨 𐑌𐐬 𐑄𐐰𐐻 𐐺𐐨𐐿𐐫𐑆 𐐶𐐨 𐐪𐑉 𐑌𐐱𐐻 𐐱𐑂 𐑄𐐴 𐐽𐐲𐑉𐐽, 𐐶𐐨 𐑌𐐬 𐑄𐐰𐐻 𐑄𐐵 𐐸𐐰𐑅𐐻 𐑌𐐬 𐐹𐐵𐐲𐑉 𐐬𐑂𐐲𐑉 𐐲𐑅; 𐐰𐑌𐐼 𐑄𐐵 𐐸𐐰𐑅𐐻 𐐼𐐨𐑊𐐮𐑂𐐲𐑉𐐼 𐐲𐐹 𐑄 𐐾𐐲𐐾𐑋𐐯𐑌𐐻 𐑅𐐨𐐻 𐐲𐑌𐐻𐐭 𐐤𐐨𐑁𐐴𐐸𐐪; 𐑄𐐯𐑉𐑁𐐬𐑉 𐑄𐐵 𐐪𐑉𐐻 𐑌𐐱𐐻 𐑄 𐐕𐐨𐑁 𐐖𐐲𐐾 𐐬𐑂𐐲𐑉 𐐲𐑅. 𐐤𐐵 𐐸𐐶𐐯𐑌 𐑄 𐐹𐐨𐐹𐑊 𐐸𐐰𐐼 𐑅𐐯𐐼 𐑄𐐮𐑅, 𐐰𐑌𐐼 𐐶𐐮𐑄𐑅𐐻𐐳𐐼 𐐫𐑊 𐐸𐐮𐑆 𐐶𐐲𐑉𐐼𐑆, 𐐰𐑌𐐼 𐑉𐐨𐑂𐐴𐑊𐐼 𐐸𐐮𐑋, 𐐰𐑌𐐼 𐑅𐐹𐐮𐐻 𐐲𐐹𐐱𐑌 𐐸𐐮𐑋, 𐐰𐑌𐐼 𐐿𐐫𐑆𐐼 𐑄𐐰𐐻 𐐸𐐨 𐑇𐐳𐐼 𐐺𐐨 𐐿𐐰𐑅𐐻 𐐵𐐻 𐐱𐑂 𐑄𐐯𐑉 𐑅𐐮𐐻𐐨, 𐐸𐐨 𐐼𐐨𐐹𐐪𐑉𐐻𐐯𐐼 𐑄𐐯𐑌𐑅 𐐰𐑌𐐼 𐐻𐐳𐐿 𐐸𐐮𐑆 𐐾𐐲𐑉𐑌𐐨 𐐻𐐬𐐲𐑉𐐼𐑆 𐑄 𐑅𐐮𐐻𐐨 𐐸𐐶𐐮𐐽 𐐶𐐱𐑆 𐐿𐐫𐑊𐐼 𐐁𐑉𐐲𐑌.

5. 𐐈𐑌𐐼 𐐮𐐻 𐐿𐐩𐑋 𐐻𐐭 𐐹𐐰𐑅 𐑄𐐰𐐻 𐐸𐐶𐐴𐑊 𐐸𐐨 𐐶𐐱𐑆 𐐾𐐲𐑉𐑌𐐨𐐮𐑍 𐑄𐐮𐑄𐐲𐑉, 𐐺𐐨𐐮𐑍 𐐶𐐩𐐼 𐐼𐐵𐑌 𐐶𐐮𐑄 𐑅𐐱𐑉𐐬, 𐐶𐐩𐐼𐐮𐑍 𐑃𐑉𐐭 𐑋𐐲𐐽 𐐻𐑉𐐮𐐺𐐷𐐭𐑊𐐩𐑇𐐲𐑌 𐐰𐑌𐐼 𐐰𐑍𐑀𐐶𐐮𐑇 𐐱𐑂 𐑅𐐬𐑊, 𐐺𐐨𐐿𐐫𐑆 𐐱𐑂 𐑄 𐐶𐐮𐐿𐐯𐐼𐑌𐐯𐑅 𐐱𐑂 𐑄 𐐹𐐨𐐹𐑊 𐐸𐐶𐐮𐐽 𐐶𐐱𐑆 𐐮𐑌 𐑄 𐑅𐐮𐐻𐐨 𐐱𐑂 𐐈𐑋𐐱𐑌𐐴𐐸𐐪, 𐐮𐐻 𐐿𐐩𐑋 𐐻𐐭 𐐹𐐰𐑅 𐐸𐐶𐐴𐑊 𐐈𐑊𐑋𐐰 𐐶𐐱𐑆 𐑄𐐲𐑅 𐐶𐐩𐐼

𐐼𐐵𐑌 𐐶𐐮𐑄 𐑅𐐪𐑉𐐬, 𐐺𐐨𐐸𐐬𐑊𐐼 𐐰𐑌 𐐩𐑌𐐾𐐯𐑊 𐐱𐑂 𐑄 𐐢𐐫𐑉𐐼 𐐰𐐹𐐨𐑉𐐼 𐐲𐑌𐐻𐐭 𐐸𐐮𐑋, 𐑅𐐩𐐮𐑍, 𐐒𐑊𐐯𐑅𐐯𐐼 𐐪𐑉𐐻 𐑄𐐵 𐐈𐑊𐑋𐐲; 𐑄𐐯𐑉𐑁𐐬𐑉 𐑊𐐮𐑁𐐻 𐐲𐐹 𐑄𐐴 𐐸𐐯𐐼 𐐰𐑌𐐼 𐑉𐐨𐐾𐐱𐐮𐑅, 𐑁𐐫𐑉 𐑄𐐵 𐐸𐐰𐑅𐐻 𐑀𐑉𐐩𐐻 𐐿𐐫𐑆 𐐻𐐭 𐑉𐐨𐐾𐐱𐐮𐑅: 𐑁𐐫𐑉 𐑄𐐵 𐐸𐐰𐑅𐐻 𐐺𐐮𐑌 𐑁𐐩𐑃𐑁𐐳𐑊 𐐮𐑌 𐐿𐐨𐐹𐐮𐑍 𐑄 𐐿𐐱𐑋𐐰𐑌𐐼𐑋𐐯𐑌𐐻𐑅 𐐱𐑂 𐐘𐐱𐐼 𐑁𐑉𐐱𐑋 𐑄 𐐻𐐴𐑋 𐐸𐐶𐐮𐐽 𐑄𐐵 𐑉𐐨𐑅𐐨𐑂𐐼𐑅𐐻 𐑄𐐴 𐑁𐐲𐑉𐑅𐐻 𐑋𐐯𐑅𐐯𐐾 𐑁𐑉𐐱𐑋 𐐸𐐮𐑋. 𐐒𐐨𐐸𐐬𐑊𐐼, 𐐌 𐐰𐑋 𐐸𐐨 𐑄𐐰𐐻 𐐼𐐯𐑊𐐮𐑂𐐲𐑉𐐼 𐐮𐐻 𐐲𐑌𐐻𐐭 𐐷𐐭; 𐐰𐑌𐐼 𐐺𐐨𐐸𐐬𐑊𐐼, 𐐌 𐐰𐑋 𐑅𐐯𐑌𐐻 𐐻𐐭 𐐿𐐱𐑋𐐰𐑌𐐼 𐑄 𐑄𐐰𐐻 𐑄𐐵 𐑉𐐨𐐻𐐲𐑉𐑌 𐐻𐐭 𐑄 𐑅𐐮𐐻𐐮 𐐱𐑂 𐐈𐑋𐐱𐑌𐐴𐐸𐐪, 𐐰𐑌𐐼 𐐹𐑉𐐨𐐽 𐐰𐑀𐐯𐑌 𐐲𐑌𐐻𐐭 𐑄 𐐹𐐨𐐹𐑊 𐐱𐑂 𐑄 𐑅𐐮𐐻𐐮; 𐐷𐐩, 𐐹𐑉𐐨𐐽 𐐲𐑌𐐻𐐭 𐑄𐐯𐑋. 𐐏𐐩, 𐑅𐐩 𐐲𐑌𐐻𐐭 𐑄𐐯𐑋, 𐐯𐐿𐑅𐐯𐐹𐐻 𐑄𐐩 𐑉𐐨𐐹𐐯𐑌𐐻, 𐑄 𐐢𐐫𐑉𐐼 𐐘𐐱𐐼 𐐶𐐮𐑊 𐐼𐐨𐑅𐐻𐑉𐐱𐐮 𐑄𐐯𐑋. 𐐙𐐫𐑉 𐐺𐐨𐐸𐐬𐑊𐐼, 𐑄𐐩 𐐼𐐭 𐑅𐐻𐐲𐐼𐐮 𐐰𐐻 𐑄𐐮𐑅 𐐻𐐴𐑋 𐑄𐐰𐐻 𐑄𐐩 𐑋𐐩 𐐼𐐨𐑅𐐻𐑉𐐱𐐮 𐑄 𐑊𐐮𐐺𐐲𐑉𐐻𐐮 𐐱𐑂 𐑄𐐴 𐐹𐐨𐐹𐑊, (𐑁𐐫𐑉 𐑄𐐲𐑅 𐑅𐐯𐑃 𐑄 𐐢𐐫𐑉𐐼,) 𐐸𐐶𐐮𐐽 𐐮𐑆 𐐿𐐱𐑌𐐻𐑉𐐯𐑉𐐮 𐐻𐐭 𐑄 𐑅𐐻𐐰𐐻𐐷𐐭𐐻𐑅, 𐐰𐑌𐐼 𐐾𐐲𐐾𐑋𐐯𐑌𐐻𐑅, 𐐰𐑌𐐼 𐐿𐐱𐑋𐐰𐑌𐐼𐑋𐐯𐑌𐐻𐑅 𐐸𐐶𐐮𐐽 𐐸𐐨 𐐸𐐰𐑆 𐑀𐐮𐑂𐐯𐑌 𐐲𐑌𐐻𐐭 𐐸𐐮𐑆 𐐹𐐨𐐹𐑊.

6. 𐐤𐐵 𐐮𐐻 𐐿𐐩𐑋 𐐻𐐭 𐐹𐐰𐑅 𐑄𐐰𐐻 𐐰𐑁𐐻𐐲𐑉 𐐈𐑊𐑋𐐲 𐐸𐐰𐐼 𐑉𐐨𐑅𐐨𐑂𐐼 𐐸𐐮𐑆 𐑋𐐯𐑅𐐯𐐾 𐑁𐑉𐐱𐑋 𐑄 𐐩𐑌𐐾𐐯𐑊 𐐱𐑂 𐑄 𐐢𐐫𐑉𐐼, 𐐸𐐨 𐑉𐐨𐐻𐐲𐑉𐑌𐐼 𐑅𐐹𐐨𐐼𐐮𐑊𐐮 𐐻𐐭 𐑄 𐑊𐐰𐑌𐐼 𐐱𐑂 𐐈𐑋𐐱𐑌𐐴𐐸𐐪. 𐐈𐑌𐐼 𐐸𐐨 𐐯𐑌𐐻𐐲𐑉𐐼 𐑄 𐑅𐐮𐐻𐐮 𐐺𐐴 𐐰𐑌𐐲𐑄𐐲𐑉 𐐶𐐩, 𐐷𐐩, 𐐺𐐴 𐑄 𐐶𐐩 𐐸𐐶𐐮𐐽 𐐮𐑆 𐐱𐑌 𐑄 𐑅𐐵𐑃 𐐱𐑂 𐑄 𐑅𐐮𐐻𐐮 𐐱𐑂 𐐈𐑋𐐱𐑌𐐴𐐸𐐪. 𐐈𐑌𐐼 𐐰𐑆 𐐸𐐨 𐐯𐑌𐐻𐐲𐑉𐐼 𐑄 𐑅𐐮𐐻𐐮 𐐸𐐨 𐐶𐐱𐑆 𐐰𐑌 𐐸𐐲𐑍𐑀𐐲𐑉𐐼, 𐐰𐑌𐐼 𐐸𐐨 𐑅𐐯𐐼 𐐻𐐭 𐐲 𐑋𐐰𐑌, 𐐎𐐮𐑊 𐐷𐐨 𐑀𐐮𐑂 𐐻𐐭 𐐰𐑌 𐐸𐐲𐑋𐐺𐑊 𐑅𐐲𐑉𐑂𐐰𐑌𐐻 𐐱𐑂 𐐘𐐱𐐼 𐑅𐐲𐑋𐑃𐐮𐑍 𐐻𐐭 𐐨𐐻? 𐐈𐑌𐐼 𐑄 𐑋𐐰𐑌 𐑅𐐯𐐼 𐐲𐑌𐐻𐐭 𐐸𐐮𐑋, 𐐌 𐐰𐑋 𐐲 𐐤𐐨𐑁𐐴𐐻, 𐐰𐑌𐐼 𐐌 𐑌𐐬 𐑄𐐰𐐻 𐑄𐐵 𐐪𐑉𐐻 𐐰𐑌 𐐸𐐬𐑊𐐮 𐐹𐑉𐐱𐑁𐐯𐐻 𐐱𐑂 𐐘𐐱𐐼, 𐑁𐐫𐑉 𐑄𐐵 𐐪𐑉𐐻 𐑄 𐑋𐐰𐑌 𐐸𐐭𐑋 𐐰𐑌 𐐩𐑌𐐾𐐯𐑊 𐑅𐐯𐐼 𐐮𐑌 𐐲 𐑂𐐮𐑈𐐲𐑌, 𐐜𐐵 𐑇𐐰𐑊𐐻 𐑉𐐨𐑅𐐨𐑂; 𐑄𐐯𐑉𐑁𐐬𐑉, 𐑀𐐬 𐐶𐐮𐑄 𐑋𐐨 𐐮𐑌𐐻𐐭 𐑋𐐴 𐐸𐐵𐑅, 𐐰𐑌𐐼 𐐌 𐐶𐐮𐑊 𐐮𐑋𐐹𐐪𐑉𐐻 𐐲𐑌𐐻𐐭 𐑄 𐐱𐑂 𐑋𐐴 𐑁𐐭𐐼; 𐐰𐑌𐐼 𐐌 𐑌𐐬 𐑄𐐰𐐻 𐑄𐐵 𐐶𐐮𐑊𐐻 𐐺𐐨 𐐲 𐐺𐑊𐐯𐑅𐐮𐑍 𐐲𐑌𐐻𐐭 𐑋𐐨 𐐰𐑌𐐼 𐑋𐐴 𐐸𐐵𐑅. 𐐈𐑌𐐼 𐐮𐐻 𐐿𐐩𐑋 𐐻𐐭 𐐹𐐰𐑅 𐑄𐐰𐐻 𐑄 𐑋𐐰𐑌 𐑉𐐨𐑅𐐨𐑂𐐼 𐐸𐐮𐑋 𐐮𐑌𐐻𐐭 𐐸𐐮𐑆 𐐸𐐵𐑅; 𐐰𐑌𐐼 𐑄 𐑋𐐰𐑌 𐐶𐐱𐑆 𐐿𐐫𐑊𐐼 𐐈𐑋𐐷𐐭𐑊𐐯𐐿; 𐐰𐑌𐐼 𐐸𐐨 𐐺𐑉𐐫𐐻 𐑁𐐬𐑉𐑃 𐐺𐑉𐐯𐐼 𐐰𐑌𐐼 𐑋𐐨𐐻, 𐐰𐑌𐐼 𐑅𐐯𐐻 𐐺𐐨𐑁𐐬𐑉 𐐈𐑊𐑋𐐲.

7. 𐐈𐑌𐐼 𐐮𐐻 𐐿𐐩𐑋 𐐻𐐭 𐐹𐐰𐑅 𐑄𐐰𐐻 𐐈𐑊𐑋𐐲 𐐩𐐻 𐐺𐑉𐐯𐐼 𐐰𐑌𐐼 𐐶𐐱𐑆 𐑁𐐮𐑊𐐼; 𐐰𐑌𐐼 𐐸𐐨 𐐺𐑊𐐯𐑅𐐻 𐐈𐑋𐐷𐐭𐑊𐐯𐐿 𐐰𐑌𐐼 𐐸𐐮𐑆 𐐸𐐵𐑅, 𐐰𐑌𐐼 𐐸𐐨 𐑀𐐩𐑂 𐑃𐐰𐑍𐐿𐑅 𐐲𐑌𐐻𐐭 𐐘𐐱𐐼. 𐐈𐑌𐐼 𐐰𐑁𐐻𐐲𐑉 𐐸𐐨 𐐸𐐰𐐼 𐐨𐐻𐐯𐑌 𐐰𐑌𐐼 𐐶𐐱𐑆 𐑁𐐮𐑊𐐼, 𐐸𐐨 𐑅𐐯𐐼 𐐲𐑌𐐻𐐭 𐐈𐑋𐐷𐐭𐑊𐐯𐐿, 𐐌 𐐰𐑋 𐐈𐑊𐑋𐐲, 𐐰𐑌𐐼 𐐰𐑋 𐑄 𐐸𐐴 𐐹𐑉𐐨𐑅𐐻 𐐬𐑂𐐲𐑉 𐑄 𐐽𐐲𐑉𐐽 𐐱𐑂 𐐘𐐱𐐼 𐑃𐑉𐐭𐐵𐐻 𐑄 𐑊𐐰𐑌𐐼. 𐐈𐑌𐐼 𐐺𐐨𐐸𐐬𐑊𐐼, 𐐌 𐐸𐐰𐑂 𐐺𐐮𐑌 𐐿𐐫𐑊𐐼 𐐻𐐭 𐐹𐑉𐐨𐐽 𐑄 𐐶𐐲𐑉𐐼 𐐱𐑂 𐐘𐐱𐐼 𐐰𐑋𐐲𐑍 𐐫𐑊 𐑄𐐮𐑅 𐐹𐐨𐐹𐑊, 𐐰𐐿𐐫𐑉𐐼𐐮𐑍 𐐻𐐭 𐑄 𐑅𐐹𐐮𐑉𐐮𐐻 𐐱𐑂 𐑉𐐯𐑂𐐯𐑊𐐩𐑇𐐲𐑌 𐐰𐑌𐐼 𐐹𐑉𐐱𐑁𐐯𐑅𐐮; 𐐰𐑌𐐼 𐐌 𐐶𐐱𐑆 𐐮𐑌 𐑄𐐮𐑅 𐑊𐐰𐑌𐐼, 𐐰𐑌𐐼 𐑄𐐩 𐐶𐐳𐐼 𐑌𐐱𐐻 𐑉𐐨𐑅𐐨𐑂 𐑋𐐨, 𐐺𐐲𐐻 𐑄𐐩 𐐿𐐰𐑅𐐻 𐑋𐐨 𐐵𐐻, 𐐰𐑌𐐼 𐐌 𐐶𐐱𐑆 𐐰𐐺𐐵𐐻 𐐻𐐭 𐑅𐐯𐐻 𐑋𐐴 𐐺𐐰𐐿 𐐻𐐭𐐶𐐫𐑉𐐼𐑆 𐑄𐐮𐑅 𐑊𐐰𐑌𐐼 𐑁𐐫𐑉𐐯𐑂𐐲𐑉. 𐐒𐐲𐐻 𐐺𐐨𐐸𐐬𐑊𐐼, 𐐌 𐐸𐐰𐑂 𐐺𐐮𐑌 𐐿𐐱𐑋𐐰𐑌𐐼𐐯𐐼 𐑄𐐰𐐻 𐐌 𐑇𐐳𐐼 𐐻𐐲𐑉𐑌 𐐰𐑀𐐯𐑌 𐐰𐑌𐐼 𐐹𐑉𐐱𐑁𐐯𐑅𐐴 𐐲𐑌𐐻𐐭 𐑄𐐮𐑅 𐐹𐐨𐐹𐑊, 𐐷𐐩, 𐐰𐑌𐐼 𐐻𐐭 𐐻𐐯𐑅𐐻𐐮𐑁𐐴 𐐰𐑀𐐯𐑌𐑅𐐻 𐑄𐐯𐑋 𐐿𐐱𐑌𐑅𐐲𐑉𐑌𐐮𐑍 𐑄𐐩𐑉 𐐮𐑌𐐮𐐿𐐶𐐮𐐻𐐮𐑆. 𐐈𐑌𐐼 𐑌𐐵 𐐈𐑋𐐷𐐭𐑊𐐯𐐿, 𐐺𐐨𐐿𐐫𐑆 𐑄𐐵 𐐸𐐰𐑅𐐻 𐑁𐐯𐐼 𐑋𐐨 𐐰𐑌𐐼 𐐻𐐩𐐿𐐯𐑌 𐑋𐐨 𐐮𐑌, 𐑄𐐵 𐐪𐑉𐐻 𐐺𐑊𐐯𐑅𐐻; 𐑁𐐫𐑉 𐐌 𐐶𐐱𐑆 𐐰𐑌 𐐸𐐲𐑍𐑀𐐲𐑉𐐼, 𐑁𐐫𐑉 𐐌 𐐸𐐰𐐼 𐑁𐐰𐑅𐐻𐐯𐐼 𐑋𐐯𐑌𐐮 𐐼𐐩𐑆. 𐐈𐑌𐐼 𐐈𐑊𐑋𐐲 𐐻𐐰𐑉𐐮𐐼 𐑋𐐯𐑌𐐮 𐐼𐐩𐑆 𐐶𐐮𐑄 𐐈𐑋𐐷𐐭𐑊𐐯𐐿 𐐺𐐨𐑁𐐬𐑉 𐐸𐐨 𐐺𐐨𐑀𐐰𐑌 𐐻𐐭 𐐹𐑉𐐨𐐽 𐐲𐑌𐐻𐐭 𐑄 𐐹𐐨𐐹𐑊.

8. 𐐈𐑌𐐼 𐐮𐐻 𐐿𐐩𐑋 𐐻𐐭 𐐹𐐰𐑅 𐑄𐐰𐐻 𐑄 𐐹𐐨𐐹𐑊 𐐼𐐮𐐼 𐐶𐐰𐐿𐑅 𐑋𐐬𐑉 𐑀𐑉𐐬𐑅 𐐮𐑌 𐑄𐐩𐑉 𐐮𐑌𐐮𐐿𐐶𐐮𐐻𐐮𐑆. 𐐈𐑌𐐼 𐑄 𐐶𐐲𐑉𐐼 𐐿𐐩𐑋 𐐻𐐭 𐐈𐑊𐑋𐐲, 𐑅𐐩𐐮𐑍, 𐐘𐐬; 𐐰𐑌𐐼 𐐫𐑊𐑅𐐬 𐑅𐐩 𐐲𐑌𐐻𐐭 𐑋𐐴 𐑅𐐲𐑉𐑂𐐰𐑌𐐻 𐐈𐑋𐐷𐐭𐑊𐐯𐐿, 𐐘𐐬 𐑁𐐬𐑉𐑃 𐐰𐑌𐐼 𐐹𐑉𐐱𐑁𐐯𐑅𐐴 𐐲𐑌𐐻𐐭 𐑄𐐮𐑅 𐐹𐐨𐐹𐑊, 𐑅𐐩𐐮𐑍, 𐐡𐐨𐐹𐐯𐑌𐐻 𐐷𐐨, 𐑁𐐫𐑉 𐑄𐐲𐑅 𐑅𐐯𐑃 𐑄 𐐢𐐫𐑉𐐼, 𐐯𐐿𐑅𐐯𐐹𐐻 𐐷𐐨 𐑉𐐨𐐹𐐯𐑌𐐻, 𐐌 𐐶𐐮𐑊 𐑂𐐮𐑆𐐮𐐻 𐑄𐐮𐑅 𐐹𐐨𐐹𐑊 𐐮𐑌 𐑋𐐴𐑌 𐐰𐑍𐑀𐐲𐑉; 𐐷𐐩, 𐐰𐑌𐐼 𐐌 𐐶𐐮𐑊 𐑌𐐱𐐻 𐐻𐐲𐑉𐑌 𐑋𐐴 𐑁𐐨𐑉𐑅 𐐰𐑍𐑀𐐲𐑉 𐐰𐐶𐐩. 𐐈𐑌𐐼 𐐈𐑊𐑋𐐲 𐐶𐐯𐑌𐐻 𐑁𐐬𐑉𐑃, 𐐰𐑌𐐼 𐐫𐑊𐑅𐐬 𐐈𐑋𐐷𐐭𐑊𐐯𐐿, 𐐰𐑋𐐲𐑍 𐑄 𐐹𐐨𐐹𐑊, 𐐻𐐭 𐐼𐐨𐐿𐑊𐐩𐑉 𐑄 𐐶𐐲𐑉𐐼𐑆 𐐱𐑂 𐐘𐐱𐐼 𐐲𐑌𐐻𐐭 𐑄𐐯𐑋; 𐐰𐑌𐐼 𐑄𐐩 𐐶𐐲𐑉 𐑁𐐮𐑊𐐼 𐐶𐐮𐑄 𐑄 𐐐𐐬𐑊𐐮 𐐘𐐬𐑅𐐻; 𐐰𐑌𐐼 𐑄𐐩 𐐸𐐰𐐼 𐐹𐐵𐐲𐑉 𐑀𐐮𐑂𐐯𐑌 𐐲𐑌𐐻𐐭 𐑄𐐯𐑋, 𐐮𐑌𐑅𐐬𐑋𐐲𐐽 𐑄𐐰𐐻 𐑄𐐩 𐐿𐐳𐐼 𐑌𐐱𐐻 𐐺𐐨 𐐿𐐱𐑌𐑁𐐴𐑌𐐼 𐐮𐑌 𐐼𐐲𐑌𐐾𐐲𐑌𐑆; 𐑌𐐨𐑄𐐲𐑉 𐐶𐐱𐑆 𐐮𐐻 𐐹𐐱𐑅𐐮𐐺𐑊 𐑄𐐰𐐻 𐐯𐑌𐐮 𐑋𐐰𐑌 𐐿𐐳𐐼 𐑅𐑊𐐩 𐑄𐐯𐑋; 𐑌𐐯𐑂𐐲𐑉𐑄𐐯𐑊𐐯𐑅 𐑄𐐩 𐐼𐐮𐐼 𐑌𐐱𐐻 𐐯𐐿𐑅𐐲𐑉𐑅𐐴𐑆 𐑄𐐩𐑉 𐐹𐐵𐐲𐑉 𐐲𐑌𐐻𐐮𐑊 𐑄𐐩 𐐶𐐲𐑉 𐐺𐐵𐑌𐐼 𐐮𐑌 𐐺𐐰𐑌𐐼𐑆 𐐰𐑌𐐼 𐐿𐐰𐑅𐐻 𐐮𐑌𐐻𐐭 𐐹𐑉𐐮𐑆𐐲𐑌. 𐐤𐐵, 𐑄𐐮𐑅 𐐶𐐱𐑆 𐐼𐐲𐑌 𐑄𐐰𐐻 𐑄 𐐢𐐫𐑉𐐼 𐑋𐐴𐐻 𐑇𐐬 𐑁𐐬𐑉𐑃 𐐸𐐮𐑆 𐐹𐐵𐐲𐑉 𐐮𐑌 𐑄𐐯𐑋.

9. 𐐰𐑌𐐼 𐐮𐐻 𐐿𐐩𐑋 𐐻𐐭 𐐹𐐰𐑅 𐑄𐐰𐐻 𐑄𐐩 𐐶𐐯𐑌𐐻 𐑁𐐬𐑉𐑃 𐐰𐑌𐐼 𐐺𐐨𐑀𐐰𐑌 𐐻𐐭 𐐹𐑉𐐨𐐽 𐐰𐑌𐐼 𐐻𐐭 𐐹𐑉𐐱𐑁𐐯𐑅𐐴 𐐲𐑌𐐻𐐭 𐑄 𐐹𐐨𐐹𐑊, 𐐰𐐿𐐫𐑉𐐼𐐮𐑍 𐐻𐐭 𐑄 𐑅𐐹𐐮𐑉𐐮𐐻 𐐰𐑌𐐼 𐐹𐐵𐐲𐑉 𐐸𐐶𐐮𐐽 𐑄 𐐢𐐫𐑉𐐼 𐐸𐐰𐐼 𐑀𐐮𐑂𐑌 𐑄𐐯𐑋.

𐐕𐐈𐐑𐐓𐐊𐐡 VII.

𐐜 𐐶𐐲𐑉𐐼𐑆 𐐱𐑂 𐐈𐑊𐑋𐐲, 𐐰𐑌𐐼 𐐫𐑊𐑅𐐬 𐑄 𐐶𐐲𐑉𐐼𐑆 𐐱𐑂 𐐈𐑋𐐷𐐭𐑊𐐯𐐿, 𐐸𐐶𐐮𐐽 𐐪𐑉 𐐼𐐨𐐿𐑊𐐩𐑉𐐼 𐐲𐑌𐐻𐐭 𐑄 𐐹𐐨𐐹𐑊 𐐸𐐭 𐐪𐑉 𐐮𐑌 𐑄 𐑊𐐰𐑌𐐼 𐐱𐑂 𐐈𐑋𐐱𐑌𐐴𐐸𐐪. 𐐈𐑌𐐼 𐐫𐑊𐑅𐐬 𐑄𐐩 𐐪𐑉 𐐿𐐰𐑅𐐻 𐐮𐑌𐐻𐐭 𐐹𐑉𐐮𐑆𐑌, 𐐰𐑌𐐼 𐐼𐐨𐑊𐐮𐑂𐐲𐑉𐐼 𐐺𐐴 𐑄 𐑋𐐮𐑉𐐰𐐿𐐷𐐭𐑊𐐲𐑅 𐐹𐐵𐐲𐑉 𐐱𐑂 𐐘𐐱𐐼 𐐸𐐶𐐮𐐽 𐐶𐐱𐑆 𐐮𐑌 𐑄𐐯𐑋, 𐐰𐐿𐐫𐑉𐐼𐐮𐑍 𐐻𐐭 𐑄 𐑉𐐯𐐿𐐫𐑉𐐼 𐐱𐑂 𐐈𐑊𐑋𐐲.

1. 𐐈𐑌𐐼 𐐰𐑀𐐯𐑌, 𐐌 𐐈𐑊𐑋𐐲, 𐐸𐐰𐑂𐐮𐑍 𐐺𐐮𐑌 𐐿𐐱𐑋𐐰𐑌𐐼𐐯𐐼 𐐱𐑂 𐐘𐐱𐐼 𐑄𐐰𐐻 𐐌 𐑇𐐳𐐼 𐐻𐐩𐐿 𐐈𐑋𐐷𐐭𐑊𐐯𐐿 𐐰𐑌𐐼 𐑀𐐬 𐑁𐐬𐑉𐑃 𐐰𐑌𐐼 𐐹𐑉𐐨𐐽 𐐰𐑀𐐯𐑌 𐐲𐑌𐐻𐐭 𐑄𐐮𐑅 𐐹𐐨𐐹𐑊, 𐐫𐑉 𐑄 𐐹𐐨𐐹𐑊 𐐸𐐭 𐐶𐐲𐑉 𐐮𐑌 𐑄 𐑅𐐮𐐻𐐨 𐐱𐑂 𐐈𐑋𐐱𐑌𐐴𐐸𐐪, 𐐮𐐻 𐐿𐐩𐑋 𐐻𐐭 𐐹𐐰𐑅 𐐰𐑆 𐐌 𐐺𐐨𐑀𐐰𐑌 𐐻𐐭 𐐹𐑉𐐨𐐽 𐐲𐑌𐐻𐐭 𐑄𐐯𐑋, 𐑄𐐩 𐐺𐐨𐑀𐐰𐑌 𐐻𐐭 𐐿𐐱𐑌𐐻𐐯𐑌𐐼 𐐶𐐮𐑄 𐑋𐐨, 𐑅𐐩𐐮𐑍, 𐐐𐐭 𐐪𐑉𐐻 𐑄𐐵? 𐐝𐐲𐐹𐐬𐑆 𐐷𐐨 𐑄𐐰𐐻 𐐶𐐨 𐑇𐐰𐑊 𐐺𐐨𐑊𐐨𐑂 𐑄 𐐻𐐯𐑅𐐻𐐮𐑋𐐬𐑌𐐨 𐐱𐑂 𐐶𐐲𐑌 𐑋𐐰𐑌, 𐐫𐑊𐑄𐐬 𐐸𐐨 𐑇𐐳𐐼 𐐹𐑉𐐨𐐽 𐐲𐑌𐐻𐐭 𐐲𐑅 𐑄𐐰𐐻 𐑄 𐐲𐑉𐑃 𐑇𐐳𐐼 𐐹𐐰𐑅 𐐰𐐶𐐩? 𐐤𐐵 𐑄𐐩 𐐲𐑌𐐼𐐲𐑉𐑅𐐻𐐳𐐼 𐑌𐐱𐐻 𐑄 𐐶𐐲𐑉𐐼𐑆 𐐸𐐶𐐮𐐽 𐑄𐐩 𐑅𐐹𐐩𐐿; 𐑁𐐫𐑉 𐑄𐐩 𐑌𐐭 𐑌𐐱𐐻 𐑄𐐰𐐻 𐑄 𐐲𐑉𐑃 𐑇𐐳𐐼 𐐹𐐰𐑅 𐐰𐐶𐐩. 𐐈𐑌𐐼 𐑄𐐩 𐑅𐐯𐐼 𐐫𐑊𐑅𐐬, 𐐎𐐨 𐐶𐐮𐑊 𐑌𐐱𐐻 𐐺𐐨𐑊𐐨𐑂 𐑄𐐴 𐐶𐐲𐑉𐐼𐑆, 𐐮𐑁 𐑄𐐵 𐑇𐐳𐐼𐑅𐐻 𐐹𐑉𐐱𐑁𐐯𐑅𐐴 𐑄𐐰𐐻 𐑄𐐮𐑅 𐑀𐑉𐐩𐐻 𐑅𐐮𐐻𐐨 𐑇𐐳𐐼 𐐺𐐨 𐐼𐐨𐑅𐐻𐑉𐑎𐐼 𐐮𐑌 𐐶𐐲𐑌 𐐼𐐩. 𐐤𐐵 𐑄𐐩 𐑌𐐭 𐑌𐐱𐐻 𐑄𐐰𐐻 𐐘𐐱𐐼 𐐿𐐳𐐼 𐐼𐐭 𐑅𐐲𐐽 𐑋𐐪𐑉𐑂𐐯𐑊𐐲𐑅 𐐶𐐲𐑉𐐿𐑅, 𐑁𐐫𐑉 𐑄𐐩 𐐶𐐲𐑉 𐐲 𐐸𐐪𐑉𐐼-𐐸𐐪𐑉𐐻𐐯𐐼 𐐰𐑌𐐼 𐐲 𐑅𐐻𐐮𐑁𐑌𐐯𐐿𐐻 𐐹𐐨𐐹𐑊. 𐐈𐑌𐐼 𐑄𐐩 𐑅𐐯𐐼, 𐐐𐐭 𐐮𐑆 𐐘𐐱𐐼, 𐑄𐐰𐐻 𐑅𐐯𐑌𐐼𐐯𐑃 𐑌𐐬 𐑋𐐬𐑉 𐐫𐑃𐐱𐑉𐐮𐐻𐐨 𐑄𐐰𐑌 𐐶𐐲𐑌 𐑋𐐰𐑌 𐐰𐑋𐐲𐑍 𐑄𐐮𐑅 𐐹𐐨𐐹𐑊, 𐐻𐐭 𐐼𐐨𐐿𐑊𐐩𐑉 𐐲𐑌𐐻𐐭 𐑄𐐯𐑋 𐑄 𐐻𐑉𐐭𐑃 𐐱𐑂 𐑅𐐲𐐽 𐑀𐑉𐐩𐐻 𐐰𐑌𐐼 𐑋𐐪𐑉𐑂𐐯𐑊𐐲𐑅 𐑃𐐮𐑍𐑆? 𐐈𐑌𐐼 𐑄𐐩 𐑅𐐻𐐳𐐼 𐑁𐐬𐑉𐑃 𐐻𐐭 𐑊𐐩 𐑄𐐩𐑉 𐐸𐐰𐑌𐐼𐑆 𐐱𐑌 𐑋𐐨; 𐐺𐐲𐐻 𐐺𐐨𐐸𐐬𐑊𐐼 𐑄𐐩 𐐼𐐮𐐼 𐑌𐐱𐐻. 𐐈𐑌𐐼 𐐌 𐑅𐐻𐐳𐐼 𐐶𐐮𐑄 𐐺𐐬𐑊𐐼𐑌𐐯𐑅 𐐻𐐭 𐐼𐐨𐐿𐑊𐐩𐑉 𐐲𐑌𐐻𐐭 𐑄𐐯𐑋, 𐐷𐐩, 𐐌 𐐼𐐮𐐼 𐐺𐐬𐑊𐐼𐑊𐐨 𐐻𐐯𐑅𐐻𐐮𐑁𐐴 𐐲𐑌𐐻𐐭 𐑄𐐯𐑋, 𐑅𐐩𐐮𐑍: 𐐒𐐨𐐸𐐬𐑊𐐼, 𐐄 𐐷𐐨 𐐶𐐮𐐿𐐯𐐼 𐐰𐑌𐐼 𐐹𐐲𐑉𐑂𐐲𐑉𐑅 𐐾𐐯𐑌𐐲𐑉𐐩𐑇𐐲𐑌, 𐐸𐐵 𐐸𐐰𐑂 𐐷𐐨 𐑁𐐫𐑉𐑀𐐱𐐻𐑌 𐑄 𐐻𐑉𐐰𐐼𐐮𐑇𐐲𐑌 𐐱𐑂 𐐷𐐭𐑉 𐑁𐐪𐑄𐐲𐑉𐑆; 𐐷𐐩, 𐐸𐐵 𐑅𐐭𐑌 𐐷𐐨 𐐸𐐰𐑂 𐑁𐐫𐑉𐑀𐐱𐐻𐑌 𐑄 𐐿𐐱𐑋𐐰𐑌𐐼𐑋𐐯𐑌𐐻𐑅 𐐱𐑂 𐐘𐐱𐐼. 𐐔𐐭 𐐷𐐨 𐑌𐐱𐐻 𐑉𐐨𐑋𐐯𐑋𐐺𐐲𐑉 𐑄𐐰𐐻 𐐵𐑉 𐑁𐐪𐑄𐐲𐑉 𐐢𐐨𐐸𐐴 𐐶𐐱𐑆 𐐺𐑉𐐫𐐻 𐐵𐐻 𐐱𐑂 𐐖𐐯𐑉𐐭𐑅𐐰𐑊𐐯𐑋 𐐺𐐴 𐑄 𐐸𐐰𐑌𐐼 𐐱𐑂 𐐘𐐱𐐼? 𐐔𐐭 𐐷𐐨 𐑌𐐱𐐻 𐑉𐐨𐑋𐐯𐑋𐐺𐐲𐑉 𐑄𐐰𐐻 𐑄𐐩 𐐶𐐲𐑉 𐐫𐑊 𐑊𐐯𐐼 𐐺𐐴 𐐸𐐮𐑋 𐑃𐑉𐐭 𐑄 𐐶𐐮𐑊𐐼𐐲𐑉𐑌𐐯𐑅? 𐐈𐑌𐐼 𐐸𐐰𐑂 𐐷𐐨 𐑁𐐫𐑉𐑀𐐱𐐻𐑌 𐑅𐐬 𐑅𐐭𐑌 𐐸𐐵 𐑋𐐯𐑌𐐨 𐐻𐐴𐑋𐑆 𐐸𐐨 𐐼𐐨𐑊𐐮𐑂𐐲𐑉𐐼 𐐵𐑉 𐑁𐐪𐑄𐐲𐑉𐑆 𐐵𐐻 𐐱𐑂 𐑄 𐐸𐐰𐑌𐐼𐑆 𐐱𐑂 𐑄𐐩𐑉 𐐯𐑌𐐯𐑋𐐨𐑆, 𐐰𐑌𐐼 𐐹𐑉𐐨𐑆𐐲𐑉𐑂𐐼 𐑄𐐯𐑋 𐑁𐑉𐐱𐑋 𐐺𐐨𐐮𐑍 𐐼𐐨𐑅𐐻𐑉𐑎𐐼, 𐐨𐑂𐑌 𐐺𐐴 𐑄 𐐸𐐰𐑌𐐼𐑆 𐐱𐑂 𐑄𐐩𐑉 𐐬𐑌 𐐺𐑉𐐯𐑄𐑉𐐯𐑌? 𐐏𐐩, 𐐰𐑌𐐼 𐐮𐑁 𐐮𐐻 𐐸𐐰𐐼 𐑌𐐱𐐻 𐐺𐐮𐑌 𐑁𐐫𐑉 𐐸𐐮𐑆 𐑋𐐰𐐽𐑊𐐯𐑅 𐐹𐐵𐐲𐑉, 𐐰𐑌𐐼 𐐸𐐮𐑆 𐑋𐐲𐑉𐑅𐐨, 𐐰𐑌𐐼 𐐸𐐮𐑆 𐑊𐐱𐑍-𐑅𐐲𐑁𐐲𐑉𐐮𐑍 𐐻𐐬𐐲𐑉𐐼𐑆 𐐲𐑅, 𐐶𐐨 𐑇𐐳𐐼 𐐲𐑌𐐰𐑂𐑎𐐼𐐲𐐺𐑊𐐨 𐐸𐐰𐑂 𐐺𐐮𐑌 𐐿𐐲𐐻 𐐫𐑁 𐑁𐑉𐐱𐑋 𐑄 𐑁𐐩𐑅 𐐱𐑂 𐑄 𐐲𐑉𐑃 𐑊𐐱𐑍 𐐺𐐨𐑁𐐬𐑉 𐑄𐐮𐑅 𐐹𐐨𐑉𐐨𐐲𐐼 𐐱𐑂 𐐻𐐴𐑋, 𐐰𐑌𐐼 𐐹𐐲𐑉𐐸𐐰𐐹𐑅 𐐺𐐮𐑌 𐐿𐐱𐑌𐑅𐐴𐑌𐐼 𐐻𐐭 𐐲 𐑅𐐻𐐩𐐻 𐐱𐑂 𐐯𐑌𐐼𐑊𐐯𐑅 𐑋𐐮𐑆𐐲𐑉𐐨 𐐰𐑌𐐼 𐐶𐐬. 𐐒𐐨𐐸𐐬𐑊𐐼, 𐑌𐐵 𐐌 𐑅𐐩 𐐲𐑌𐐻𐐭 𐐷𐐭, 𐑄𐐰𐐻 𐐸𐐨 𐐿𐐱𐑋𐐰𐑌𐐼𐐯𐑃 𐐷𐐭 𐐻𐐭 𐑉𐐨𐐹𐐯𐑌𐐻; 𐐰𐑌𐐼 𐐯𐐿𐑅𐐯𐐹𐐻 𐐷𐐨 𐑉𐐨𐐹𐐯𐑌𐐻, 𐐷𐐨 𐐿𐐰𐑌 𐐮𐑌 𐑌𐐬 𐐶𐐴𐑆 𐐮𐑌𐐸𐐯𐑉𐐮𐐻 𐑄 𐐿𐐮𐑍𐐼𐐲𐑋 𐐱𐑂 𐐘𐐱𐐼. 𐐒𐐲𐐻 𐐺𐐨𐐸𐐬𐑊𐐼, 𐑄𐐰𐐻 𐐮𐑆 𐑌𐐱𐐻 𐐫𐑊: 𐐸𐐨 𐐸𐐰𐑆 𐐿𐐱𐑋𐐰𐑌𐐼𐐯𐐼 𐐷𐐭 𐐻𐐭 𐑉𐐨𐐹𐐯𐑌𐐻, 𐐫𐑉 𐐸𐐨 𐐶𐐮𐑊 𐐲𐐻𐐲𐑉𐑊𐐨 𐐼𐐨𐑅𐐻𐑉𐑎 𐐷𐐭 𐑁𐑉𐐱𐑋 𐐫𐑁 𐑄 𐑁𐐩𐑅 𐐱𐑂 𐑄 𐐲𐑉𐑃; 𐐷𐐩, 𐐸𐐨 𐐶𐐮𐑊 𐑂𐐮𐑆𐐮𐐻 𐐷𐐭 𐐮𐑌 𐐸𐐮𐑆 𐐰𐑍𐑀𐐲𐑉, 𐐰𐑌𐐼 𐐮𐑌 𐐸𐐮𐑆 𐑁𐐨𐑉𐑅 𐐰𐑍𐑀𐐲𐑉 𐐸𐐨 𐐶𐐮𐑊 𐑌𐐱𐐻 𐐻𐐲𐑉𐑌 𐐰𐐶𐐩. 𐐒𐐨𐐸𐐬𐑊𐐼, 𐐼𐐭 𐐷𐐨 𐑌𐐱𐐻 𐑉𐐨𐑋𐐯𐑋𐐺𐐲𐑉 𐑄 𐐶𐐲𐑉𐐼𐑆 𐐸𐐶𐐮𐐽 𐐸𐐨 𐑅𐐹𐐩𐐿 𐐲𐑌𐐻𐐭 𐐢𐐨𐐸𐐴, 𐑅𐐩𐐮𐑍, 𐐜𐐰𐐻 𐐮𐑌𐐰𐑆𐑋𐐲𐐽 𐐰𐑆 𐐷𐐨 𐑇𐐰𐑊 𐐿𐐨𐐹 𐑋𐐴 𐐿𐐱𐑋𐐰𐑌𐐼𐑋𐐯𐑌𐐻𐑅, 𐐷𐐨 𐑇𐐰𐑊 𐐹𐑉𐐱𐑅𐐹𐐲𐑉 𐐮𐑌 𐑄 𐑊𐐰𐑌𐐼? 𐐈𐑌𐐼 𐐰𐑀𐐯𐑌 𐐮𐐻 𐐮𐑆 𐑅𐐯𐐼, 𐐜𐐰𐐻 𐐮𐑌𐐰𐑆𐑋𐐲𐐽 𐐰𐑆 𐐷𐐨 𐐶𐐮𐑊 𐑌𐐱𐐻 𐐿𐐨𐐹 𐑋𐐴 𐐿𐐱𐑋𐐰𐑌𐐼𐑋𐐯𐑌𐐻𐑅, 𐐷𐐨 𐑇𐐰𐑊 𐐺𐐨 𐐿𐐲𐐻 𐐫𐑁 𐑁𐑉𐐱𐑋 𐑄 𐐹𐑉𐐯𐑆𐐯𐑌𐑅 𐐱𐑂 𐑄 𐐢𐐫𐑉𐐼.

2. 𐐤𐐵 𐐌 𐐶𐐳𐐼 𐑄𐐰𐐻 𐐷𐐨 𐑇𐐳𐐼 𐑉𐐨𐑋𐐯𐑋𐐺𐐲𐑉, 𐑄𐐰𐐻 𐐮𐑌𐐰𐑆𐑋𐐲𐐽 𐐰𐑆 𐑄 𐐢𐐩𐑋𐐲𐑌𐐴𐐻𐑅 𐐸𐐰𐑂 𐑌𐐱𐐻 𐐿𐐯𐐹𐐻 𐑄 𐐿𐐱𐑋𐐰𐑌𐐼𐑋𐐯𐑌𐐻𐑅 𐐱𐑂 𐐘𐐱𐐼, 𐑄𐐩 𐐸𐐰𐑂 𐐺𐐮𐑌 𐐿𐐲𐐻 𐐫𐑁 𐑁𐑉𐐱𐑋 𐑄 𐐹𐑉𐐯𐑆𐐯𐑌𐑅 𐐱𐑂 𐑄 𐐢𐐫𐑉𐐼. 𐐤𐐵 𐐶𐐨

𐑅𐐬 𐑄𐐰𐐻 𐑄 𐐶𐐲𐑉𐐼 𐐱𐑂 𐑄 𐐢𐐫𐑉𐐼 𐐸𐐰𐑆 𐐺𐐮𐑌 𐑂𐐯𐑉𐐮𐑁𐐴𐐼 𐐮𐑌 𐑄𐐮𐑅 𐑃𐐮𐑍, 𐐰𐑌𐐼 𐑄 𐐢𐐩𐑋𐐲𐑌𐐴𐐻𐑅 𐐸𐐰𐑆 𐐺𐐮𐑌 𐐿𐐲𐐻 𐐱𐑁 𐑁𐑉𐐱𐑋 𐐸𐐮𐑆 𐐹𐑉𐐯𐑆𐐯𐑌𐑅, 𐑁𐑉𐐱𐑋 𐑄 𐐺𐐨𐑀𐐮𐑌𐐮𐑍 𐐱𐑂 𐑄𐐩𐑉 𐐻𐑉𐐰𐑌𐑆𐑀𐑉𐐯𐑇𐐲𐑌𐑆 𐐮𐑌 𐑄 𐑊𐐰𐑌𐐼. 𐐤𐐯𐑂𐐲𐑉𐑄𐐲𐑊𐐯𐑅 𐐌 𐑅𐐩 𐐲𐑌𐐻𐐭 𐐷𐐭, 𐑄𐐰𐐻 𐐮𐐻 𐑇𐐰𐑊 𐐺𐐨 𐑋𐐬𐑉 𐐻𐐱𐑊𐐲𐑉𐐲𐐺𐑊 𐑁𐐫𐑉 𐑄𐐯𐑋 𐐮𐑌 𐑄 𐐼𐐩 𐐱𐑂 𐐾𐐲𐐾𐑋𐐯𐑌𐐻 𐑄𐐰𐑌 𐑁𐐫𐑉 𐐷𐐭, 𐐮𐑁 𐐷𐐨 𐑉𐐨𐑋𐐩𐑌 𐐮𐑌 𐐷𐐲𐑉 𐑅𐐮𐑌𐑆: 𐐷𐐩, 𐐰𐑌𐐼 𐐨𐑂𐐲𐑌 𐑋𐐬𐑉 𐐻𐐱𐑊𐐲𐑉𐐲𐐺𐑊 𐑁𐐫𐑉 𐑄𐐯𐑋 𐐮𐑌 𐑄𐐮𐑅 𐑊𐐴𐑁, 𐑄𐐰𐑌 𐑁𐐫𐑉 𐐷𐐭, 𐐯𐐿𐑅𐐯𐐹𐐻 𐐷𐐨 𐑉𐐨𐐹𐐯𐑌𐐻, 𐑁𐐫𐑉 𐑄𐐩𐑉 𐐪𐑉 𐑋𐐯𐑌𐐨 𐐹𐑉𐐱𐑋𐐮𐑅𐐯𐑆 𐐸𐐶𐐮𐐽 𐐪𐑉 𐐯𐐿𐑅𐐻𐐯𐑌𐐼𐐯𐐼 𐐻𐐭 𐑄 𐐢𐐩𐑋𐐲𐑌𐐴𐐻𐑅: 𐑁𐐫𐑉 𐐮𐐻 𐐮𐑆 𐐺𐐨𐐿𐐫𐑆 𐐱𐑂 𐑄 𐐻𐑉𐐲𐐼𐐮𐑇𐐲𐑌𐑆 𐐱𐑂 𐑄𐐩𐑉 𐑁𐐪𐑄𐐲𐑉𐑆, 𐑄𐐰𐐻 𐐿𐐫𐑆𐐼 𐑄𐐯𐑋 𐐻𐐭 𐑉𐐨𐑋𐐩𐑌 𐐮𐑌 𐑄𐐩𐑉 𐑅𐐻𐐩𐐻 𐐱𐑂 𐐮𐑀𐑌𐐬𐑉𐐲𐑌𐑅; 𐑄𐐯𐑉𐑁𐐫𐑉 𐑄 𐐢𐐫𐑉𐐼 𐐶𐐮𐑊 𐐺𐐨 𐑋𐐲𐑉𐑅𐐮𐑁𐐳𐑊 𐐲𐑌𐐻𐐭 𐑄𐐯𐑋, 𐐰𐑌𐐼 𐐹𐑉𐐬𐑊𐐱𐑍 𐑄𐐩𐑉 𐐯𐑀𐑆𐐮𐑅𐐻𐐲𐑌𐑅 𐐮𐑌 𐑄 𐑊𐐰𐑌𐐼. 𐐈𐑌𐐼 𐐰𐐻 𐑅𐐲𐑋 𐐹𐐨𐑉𐐨𐐲𐐼 𐐱𐑂 𐐻𐐴𐑋 𐑄𐐩 𐐶𐐮𐑊 𐐺𐐨 𐐺𐑉𐐫𐐻 𐐻𐐭 𐐺𐐨𐑊𐐨𐑂 𐐮𐑌 𐐸𐐮𐑆 𐐶𐐲𐑉𐐼, 𐐰𐑌𐐼 𐐻𐐭 𐑌𐐬 𐐱𐑂 𐑄 𐐮𐑌𐐿𐐫𐑉𐐯𐐿𐐻𐑌𐐯𐑅 𐐱𐑂 𐑄 𐐻𐑉𐐲𐐼𐐮𐑇𐐲𐑌𐑆 𐐱𐑂 𐑄𐐩𐑉 𐑁𐐪𐑄𐐲𐑉𐑆; 𐐰𐑌𐐼 𐑋𐐯𐑌𐐨 𐐱𐑂 𐑄𐐯𐑋 𐐶𐐮𐑊 𐐺𐐨 𐑅𐐩𐑂𐐼, 𐑁𐐫𐑉 𐑄 𐐢𐐫𐑉𐐼 𐐶𐐮𐑊 𐐺𐐨 𐑋𐐲𐑉𐑅𐐮𐑁𐐳𐑊 𐐲𐑌𐐻𐐭 𐐫𐑊 𐐸𐐭 𐐿𐐫𐑊 𐐱𐑌 𐐸𐐮𐑆 𐑌𐐩𐑋. 𐐒𐐲𐐻 𐐺𐐨𐐸𐐬𐑊𐐼, 𐐌 𐑅𐐩 𐐲𐑌𐐻𐐭 𐐷𐐭, 𐑄𐐰𐐻 𐐮𐑁 𐐷𐐨 𐐹𐐲𐑉𐑅𐐮𐑅𐐻 𐐮𐑌 𐐷𐐲𐑉 𐐶𐐮𐐿𐐯𐐼𐑌𐐯𐑅, 𐑄𐐰𐐻 𐐷𐐲𐑉 𐐼𐐩𐑆 𐑇𐐰𐑊 𐑌𐐱𐐻 𐐺𐐨 𐐹𐑉𐐬𐑊𐐱𐑍𐐼 𐐮𐑌 𐑄 𐑊𐐰𐑌𐐼, 𐑁𐐫𐑉 𐑄 𐐢𐐩𐑋𐐲𐑌𐐴𐐻𐑅 𐑇𐐰𐑊 𐐺𐐨 𐑅𐐯𐑌𐐻 𐐲𐐹𐐱𐑌 𐐷𐐭; 𐐰𐑌𐐼 𐐮𐑁 𐐷𐐨 𐑉𐐨𐐹𐐯𐑌𐐻 𐑌𐐱𐐻, 𐑄𐐩 𐑇𐐰𐑊 𐐿𐐲𐑋 𐐮𐑌 𐐩 𐐻𐐴𐑋 𐐸𐐶𐐯𐑌 𐐷𐐭 𐑌𐐬 𐑌𐐱𐐻, 𐐰𐑌𐐼 𐐷𐐨 𐑇𐐰𐑊 𐐺𐐨 𐑂𐐮𐑆𐐮𐐻𐐯𐐼 𐐶𐐮𐑄 𐐲𐐻𐐲𐑉 𐐼𐐯𐑅𐐻𐑉𐐲𐐿𐑇𐐲𐑌; 𐐰𐑌𐐼 𐐮𐐻 𐑇𐐰𐑊 𐐺𐐨 𐐰𐐿𐐫𐑉𐐼𐐮𐑍 𐐻𐐭 𐑄 𐑁𐐨𐑉𐑅 𐐰𐑍𐑀𐐲𐑉 𐐱𐑂 𐑄 𐐢𐐫𐑉𐐼; 𐑁𐐫𐑉 𐐸𐐨 𐐶𐐮𐑊 𐑌𐐱𐐻 𐑅𐐲𐑁𐐲𐑉 𐐷𐐭 𐑄𐐰𐐻 𐐷𐐨 𐑇𐐰𐑊 𐑊𐐮𐑂 𐐮𐑌 𐐷𐐲𐑉 𐐮𐑌𐐮𐐿𐐶𐐮𐐻𐐨𐑆, 𐐻𐐭 𐐼𐐯𐑅𐐻𐑉𐐱𐐴 𐐸𐐮𐑆 𐐹𐐨𐐹𐑊. 𐐌 𐑅𐐩 𐐲𐑌𐐻𐐭 𐐷𐐭, 𐐤𐐩: 𐐸𐐨 𐐶𐐳𐐼 𐑉𐐰𐑄𐐲𐑉 𐑅𐐲𐑁𐐲𐑉 𐑄𐐰𐐻 𐑄 𐐢𐐩𐑋𐐲𐑌𐐴𐐻𐑅 𐑋𐐴𐐻 𐐼𐐯𐑅𐐻𐑉𐐱𐐴 𐐫𐑊 𐐸𐐮𐑆 𐐹𐐨𐐹𐑊 𐐸𐐶𐐮𐐽 𐐪𐑉 𐐿𐐫𐑊𐐼 𐑄 𐐹𐐨𐐹𐑊 𐐱𐑂 𐐤𐐨𐑁𐐴, 𐐮𐑁 𐐮𐐻 𐐶𐐲𐑉 𐐹𐐱𐑅𐐮𐐺𐑊 𐑄𐐰𐐻 𐑄𐐩 𐐿𐐳𐐼 𐑁𐐫𐑊 𐐮𐑌𐐻𐐭 𐑅𐐮𐑌𐑆 𐐰𐑌𐐼 𐐻𐑉𐐰𐑌𐑆𐑀𐑉𐐯𐑇𐐲𐑌𐑆, 𐐰𐑁𐐻𐐲𐑉 𐐸𐐰𐑂𐐮𐑍 𐐸𐐰𐐼 𐑅𐐬 𐑋𐐲𐐽 𐑊𐐴𐐻 𐐰𐑌𐐼 𐑅𐐬 𐑋𐐲𐐽 𐑌𐐱𐑊𐐯𐐾 𐑀𐐮𐑂𐐲𐑌 𐐲𐑌𐐻𐐭 𐑄𐐯𐑋 𐐱𐑂 𐑄 𐐢𐐫𐑉𐐼 𐑄𐐩𐑉 𐐘𐐱𐐼; 𐐷𐐩, 𐐰𐑁𐐻𐐲𐑉 𐐸𐐰𐑂𐐮𐑍 𐐺𐐮𐑌 𐑅𐐲𐐽 𐐩 𐐸𐐴𐑊𐐨 𐑁𐐩𐑂𐐲𐑉𐐼 𐐹𐐨𐐹𐑊 𐐱𐑂 𐑄 𐐢𐐫𐑉𐐼; 𐐷𐐩, 𐐰𐑁𐐻𐐲𐑉 𐐸𐐰𐑂𐐮𐑍 𐐺𐐮𐑌 𐑁𐐩𐑂𐐲𐑉𐐼 𐐲𐐺𐐲𐑂 𐐯𐑂𐐲𐑉𐐨 𐐲𐑄𐐲𐑉 𐑌𐐩𐑇𐐲𐑌, 𐐿𐐮𐑌𐐼𐑉𐐯𐐼, 𐐻𐐲𐑍, 𐐫𐑉 𐐹𐐨𐐹𐑊; 𐐰𐑁𐐻𐐲𐑉 𐐸𐐰𐑂𐐮𐑍 𐐸𐐰𐐼 𐐫𐑊 𐑃𐐮𐑍𐑆 𐑋𐐩𐐼 𐑌𐐬𐑌 𐐲𐑌𐐻𐐭 𐑄𐐯𐑋, 𐐰𐐿𐐫𐑉𐐼𐐮𐑍 𐐻𐐭 𐑄𐐩𐑉 𐐼𐐨𐑆𐐴𐑉𐑆, 𐐰𐑌𐐼 𐑄𐐩𐑉 𐑁𐐩𐑃, 𐐰𐑌𐐼 𐐹𐑉𐐩𐑉𐑆, 𐐱𐑂 𐑄𐐰𐐻 𐐸𐐶𐐮𐐽 𐐸𐐰𐑆 𐐺𐐮𐑌, 𐐰𐑌𐐼 𐐸𐐶𐐮𐐽 𐐮𐑆, 𐐰𐑌𐐼 𐐸𐐶𐐮𐐽 𐐮𐑆 𐐻𐐭 𐐿𐐲𐑋; 𐐸𐐰𐑂𐐮𐑍 𐐺𐐮𐑌 𐑂𐐮𐑆𐐮𐐻𐐯𐐼 𐐺𐐴 𐑄 𐐝𐐹𐐮𐑉𐐮𐐻 𐐱𐑂 𐐘𐐱𐐼; 𐐸𐐰𐑂𐐮𐑍 𐐿𐐱𐑌𐑂𐐲𐑉𐑅𐐻 𐐶𐐮𐑄 𐐩𐑌𐐾𐐯𐑊𐑆, 𐐰𐑌𐐼 𐐸𐐰𐑂𐐮𐑍 𐐺𐐮𐑌 𐑅𐐹𐐬𐐿𐐲𐑌 𐐲𐑌𐐻𐐭 𐐺𐐴 𐑄 𐑂𐐱𐐮𐑅 𐐱𐑂 𐑄 𐐢𐐫𐑉𐐼; 𐐰𐑌𐐼 𐐸𐐰𐑂𐐮𐑍 𐑄 𐐝𐐹𐐮𐑉𐐮𐐻 𐐱𐑂 𐐑𐑉𐐱𐑁𐐯𐑅𐐨 𐐰𐑌𐐼 𐑄 𐐝𐐹𐐮𐑉𐐮𐐻 𐐱𐑂 𐐡𐐯𐑂𐐯𐑊𐐩𐑇𐐲𐑌, 𐐰𐑌𐐼 𐐫𐑊𐑅𐐬 𐑋𐐯𐑌𐐨 𐑀𐐮𐑁𐐻𐑅: 𐑄 𐑀𐐮𐑁𐐻 𐐱𐑂 𐑅𐐹𐐨𐐿𐐮𐑍 𐐶𐐮𐑄 𐐻𐐲𐑍𐑆, 𐐰𐑌𐐼 𐑄 𐑀𐐮𐑁𐐻 𐐱𐑂 𐐹𐑉𐐨𐐽𐐮𐑍, 𐐰𐑌𐐼 𐑄 𐑀𐐮𐑁𐐻 𐐱𐑂 𐑄 𐐐𐐬𐑊𐐨 𐐘𐐬𐑅𐐻, 𐐰𐑌𐐼 𐑄 𐑀𐐮𐑁𐐻 𐐱𐑂 𐐻𐑉𐐰𐑌𐑆𐑊𐐩𐑇𐐲𐑌; 𐐷𐐩, 𐐰𐑌𐐼 𐐰𐑁𐐻𐐲𐑉 𐐸𐐰𐑂𐐮𐑍 𐐺𐐮𐑌 𐐼𐐯𐑊𐐮𐑂𐐲𐑉𐐼 𐐱𐑂 𐐘𐐱𐐼 𐐵𐐻 𐐱𐑂 𐑄 𐑊𐐰𐑌𐐼 𐐱𐑂 𐐖𐐯𐑉𐐭𐑅𐐲𐑊𐐲𐑋, 𐐺𐐴 𐑄 𐐸𐐰𐑌𐐼 𐐱𐑂 𐑄 𐐢𐐫𐑉𐐼; 𐐸𐐰𐑂𐐮𐑍 𐐺𐐮𐑌 𐑅𐐩𐑂𐐼 𐑁𐑉𐐱𐑋 𐑁𐐰𐑋𐐮𐑌, 𐐰𐑌𐐼 𐑁𐑉𐐱𐑋 𐑅𐐮𐐿𐑌𐐯𐑅, 𐐰𐑌𐐼 𐐫𐑊 𐑋𐐰𐑌𐐲𐑉 𐐱𐑂 𐐼𐐮𐑆𐐨𐑆𐐯𐑆 𐐱𐑂 𐐯𐑂𐐲𐑉𐐨 𐐿𐐴𐑌𐐼; 𐐰𐑌𐐼 𐑄𐐩 𐐸𐐰𐑂𐐮𐑍 𐐶𐐰𐐿𐑅𐐻 𐑅𐐻𐑉𐐱𐑍 𐐮𐑌 𐐺𐐰𐐻𐑊, 𐑄𐐰𐐻 𐑄𐐩 𐑋𐐴𐐻 𐑌𐐱𐐻 𐐺𐐨 𐐼𐐯𐑅𐐻𐑉𐐱𐐮𐐼; 𐐸𐐰𐑂𐐮𐑍 𐐺𐐮𐑌 𐐺𐑉𐐫𐐻 𐐵𐐻 𐐱𐑂 𐐺𐐱𐑌𐐼𐐮𐐾 𐐻𐐴𐑋 𐐰𐑁𐐻𐐲𐑉 𐐻𐐴𐑋, 𐐰𐑌𐐼 𐐸𐐰𐑂𐐮𐑍 𐐺𐐮𐑌 𐐿𐐯𐐹𐐻 𐐰𐑌𐐼 𐐹𐑉𐐨𐑆𐐲𐑉𐑂𐐼 𐐲𐑌𐐻𐐮𐑊 𐑌𐐵; 𐐰𐑌𐐼 𐑄𐐩 𐐸𐐰𐑂 𐐺𐐮𐑌 𐐹𐑉𐐱𐑅𐐹𐐲𐑉𐐼 𐐲𐑌𐐻𐐮𐑊 𐑄𐐩 𐐪𐑉 𐑉𐐮𐐽 𐐮𐑌 𐐫𐑊 𐑋𐐰𐑌𐐲𐑉 𐐱𐑂 𐑃𐐮𐑍𐑆.

3. 𐐈𐑌𐐼 𐑌𐐵 𐐺𐐨𐐸𐐬𐑊𐐼 𐐌 𐑅𐐩 𐐲𐑌𐐻𐐭 𐐷𐐭, 𐑄𐐰𐐻 𐐮𐑁 𐑄𐐮𐑅 𐐹𐐨𐐹𐑊, 𐐸𐐭 𐐸𐐰𐑂 𐑉𐐨𐑅𐐨𐑂𐐼 𐑅𐐬 𐑋𐐯𐑌𐐨 𐐺𐑊𐐯𐑅𐐮𐑍𐑆 𐑁𐑉𐐱𐑋 𐑄 𐐸𐐰𐑌𐐼 𐐱𐑂 𐑄 𐐢𐐫𐑉𐐼, 𐑇𐐳𐐼 𐐻𐑉𐐰𐑌𐑆𐑀𐑉𐐯𐑅 𐐿𐐱𐑌𐐻𐑉𐐯𐑉𐐨 𐐻𐐭 𐑄 𐑊𐐴𐐻 𐐰𐑌𐐼 𐑌𐐱𐑊𐐯𐐾 𐐸𐐶𐐮𐐽 𐑄𐐩 𐐼𐐭 𐐸𐐰𐑂: 𐐌 𐑅𐐩 𐐲𐑌𐐻𐐭 𐐷𐐭 𐑄𐐰𐐻 𐐮𐑁 𐑄𐐮𐑅 𐐺𐐨 𐑄 𐐿𐐩𐑅, 𐑄𐐰𐐻 𐐮𐑁 𐑄𐐩 𐑇𐐳𐐼 𐑁𐐫𐑊 𐐮𐑌𐐻𐐭 𐐻𐑉𐐰𐑌𐑆𐑀𐑉𐐯𐑇𐐲𐑌, 𐐮𐐻 𐐶𐐳𐐼 𐐺𐐨 𐑁𐐪𐑉 𐑋𐐬𐑉 𐐻𐐱𐑊𐐲𐑉𐐲𐐺𐑊 𐑁𐐫𐑉 𐑄 𐐢𐐩𐑋𐐲𐑌𐐴𐐻𐑅 𐑄𐐰𐑌 𐑁𐐫𐑉 𐑄𐐯𐑋. 𐐙𐐫𐑉 𐐺𐐨𐐸𐐬𐑊𐐼, 𐑄 𐐹𐑉𐐱𐑋𐐮𐑅𐐯𐑆 𐐱𐑂 𐑄 𐐢𐐫𐑉𐐼 𐐪𐑉 𐐯𐐿𐑅𐐻𐐯𐑌𐐼𐐯𐐼 𐐻𐐭 𐑄 𐐢𐐩𐑋𐐲𐑌𐐴𐐻𐑅, 𐐺𐐲𐐻 𐑄𐐩 𐐪𐑉 𐑌𐐱𐐻 𐐲𐑌𐐻𐐭 𐐷𐐭, 𐐮𐑁 𐐷𐐨 𐐻𐑉𐐰𐑌𐑆𐑀𐑉𐐯𐑅: 𐑁𐐫𐑉 𐐸𐐰𐑆 𐑌𐐱𐐻 𐑄 𐐢𐐫𐑉𐐼 𐐯𐐿𐑅𐐹𐑉𐐯𐑅𐑊𐐨 𐐹𐑉𐐱𐑋𐐮𐑅𐐻 𐐰𐑌𐐼 𐑁𐐲𐑉𐑋𐑊𐐨 𐐼𐐨𐐿𐑉𐐨𐐻, 𐑄𐐰𐐻 𐐮𐑁 𐐷𐐨 𐐶𐐮𐑊 𐑉𐐨𐐺𐐯𐑊 𐐰𐑀𐐯𐑌𐑅𐐻 𐐸𐐮𐑋, 𐑄𐐰𐐻 𐐷𐐨 𐑇𐐰𐑊 𐐲𐐻𐐲𐑉𐑊𐐨 𐐺𐐨 𐐼𐐯𐑅𐐻𐑉𐐱𐐮𐐼 𐑁𐑉𐐱𐑋 𐐱𐑁 𐑄 𐑁𐐩𐑅 𐐱𐑂 𐑄 𐐲𐑉𐑃? 𐐈𐑌𐐼 𐑌𐐵 𐑁𐐫𐑉 𐑄𐐮𐑅 𐐿𐐫𐑆, 𐑄𐐰𐐻 𐐷𐐨 𐑋𐐩 𐑌𐐱𐐻 𐐺𐐨 𐐼𐐯𐑅𐐻𐑉𐐱𐐮𐐼, 𐑄 𐐢𐐫𐑉𐐼 𐐸𐐰𐑆 𐑅𐐯𐑌𐐻 𐐸𐐮𐑆 𐐩𐑌𐐾𐐯𐑊 𐐻𐐭 𐑂𐐮𐑆𐐮𐐻 𐑋𐐯𐑌𐐨 𐐱𐑂 𐐸𐐮𐑆 𐐹𐐨𐐹𐑊, 𐐼𐐯𐐿𐑊𐐯𐑉𐐮𐑍 𐐲𐑌𐐻𐐭 𐑄𐐯𐑋 𐑄𐐰𐐻 𐑄𐐩 𐑋𐐲𐑅𐐻 𐑀𐐬 𐑁𐐫𐑉𐑃 𐐰𐑌𐐼 𐐿𐑉𐐴 𐑋𐐴𐐻𐐮𐑊𐐨 𐐲𐑌𐐻𐐭 𐑄𐐮𐑅 𐐹𐐨𐐹𐑊, 𐑅𐐩𐐮𐑍, 𐐡𐐨𐐹𐐯𐑌𐐻 𐐷𐐨, 𐑁𐐫𐑉 𐑄 𐐿𐐮𐑍𐐼𐐲𐑋 𐐱𐑂 𐐸𐐯𐑂𐐲𐑌 𐐮𐑆

𐐮𐑆 𐐰𐐻 𐐸𐐰𐑌𐐼; 𐐰𐑌𐐼 𐑌𐐱𐐻 𐑋𐐯𐑌𐐨 𐐼𐐩𐑆 𐐸𐐯𐑌𐑅 𐑄 𐐝𐐲𐑌 𐐱𐑂 𐐘𐐱𐐼 𐑇𐐰𐑊 𐐿𐐲𐑋 𐐮𐑌 𐐸𐐮𐑆 𐑀𐑊𐐬𐑉𐐨; 𐐰𐑌𐐼 𐐸𐐮𐑆 𐑀𐑊𐐬𐑉𐐨 𐑇𐐰𐑊 𐐺𐐨 𐑄 𐑀𐑊𐐬𐑉𐐨 𐐱𐑂 𐑄 𐐄𐑌𐑊𐐨 𐐒𐐨𐑀𐐱𐐻𐐲𐑌 𐐱𐑂 𐑄 𐐙𐐪𐑄𐐲𐑉, 𐑁𐐳𐑊 𐐱𐑂 𐑀𐑉𐐩𐑅, 𐐯𐐿𐐶𐐮𐐻𐐨, 𐐰𐑌𐐼 𐐻𐑉𐐭𐑃, 𐑁𐐳𐑊 𐐱𐑂 𐐹𐐩𐑇𐐯𐑌𐑅, 𐑋𐐲𐑉𐑅𐐨, 𐐰𐑌𐐼 𐑊𐐱𐑍 𐑅𐐲𐑁𐐲𐑉𐐮𐑍, 𐐿𐐶𐐮𐐿 𐐻𐐭 𐐸𐐨𐑉 𐑄 𐐿𐑉𐐴𐑆 𐐱𐑂 𐐸𐐮𐑆 𐐹𐐨𐐹𐑊 𐐰𐑌𐐼 𐐻𐐭 𐐰𐑌𐑅𐐲𐑉 𐑄𐐯𐑉 𐐹𐑉𐐯𐑉𐑆. 𐐈𐑌𐐼 𐐺𐐨𐐸𐐬𐑊𐐼 𐐸𐐨 𐐿𐐲𐑋𐐯𐑃 𐐻𐐭 𐑉𐐨𐐼𐐨𐑋 𐑄𐐬𐑆 𐐸𐐭 𐐶𐐮𐑊 𐐺𐐨 𐐺𐐰𐐹𐐻𐐴𐑆𐐼 𐐲𐑌𐐻𐐭 𐑉𐐨𐐹𐐯𐑌𐐻𐐰𐑌𐑅, 𐑃𐑉𐐭 𐑁𐐩𐑃 𐐱𐑌 𐐸𐐮𐑆 𐑌𐐩𐑋; 𐑄𐐯𐑉𐑁𐐬𐑉 𐐹𐑉𐐨𐐹𐐯𐑉 𐐷𐐨 𐑄 𐐶𐐩 𐐱𐑂 𐑄 𐐢𐐫𐑉𐐼, 𐑁𐐫𐑉 𐑄 𐐻𐐴𐑋 𐐮𐑆 𐐰𐐻 𐐸𐐰𐑌𐐼 𐑄𐐰𐐻 𐐫𐑊 𐑋𐐯𐑌 𐑇𐐰𐑊 𐑉𐐨𐐹 𐐲 𐑉𐐨𐐶𐐫𐑉𐐼 𐐱𐑂 𐑄𐐯𐑉 𐐶𐐲𐑉𐐿𐑅, 𐐰𐐿𐐫𐑉𐐼𐐮𐑍 𐐻𐐭 𐑄𐐰𐐻 𐐸𐐶𐐮𐐽 𐑄𐐩 𐐸𐐰𐑂 𐐺𐐮𐑌: 𐐮𐑁 𐑄𐐩 𐐸𐐰𐑂 𐐺𐐮𐑌 𐑉𐐴𐐽𐐲𐑅, 𐑄𐐩 𐑇𐐰𐑊 𐑉𐐨𐐹 𐑄 𐑅𐐰𐑊𐑂𐐩𐑇𐐲𐑌 𐐱𐑂 𐑄𐐯𐑉 𐑅𐐬𐑊𐑆, 𐐰𐐿𐐫𐑉𐐼𐐮𐑍 𐐻𐐭 𐑄 𐐹𐐵𐐲𐑉 𐐰𐑌𐐼 𐐼𐐮𐑊𐐮𐑂𐐲𐑉𐐰𐑌𐑅 𐐱𐑂 𐐖𐐨𐑆𐐲𐑅 𐐗𐑉𐐴𐑅𐐻: 𐐰𐑌𐐼 𐐮𐑁 𐑄𐐩 𐐸𐐰𐑂 𐐺𐐮𐑌 𐐨𐑂𐐮𐑊, 𐑄𐐩 𐑇𐐰𐑊 𐑉𐐨𐐹 𐑄 𐐼𐐰𐑋𐑌𐐩𐑇𐐲𐑌 𐐱𐑂 𐑄𐐯𐑉 𐑅𐐬𐑊𐑆, 𐐰𐐿𐐫𐑉𐐼𐐮𐑍 𐐻𐐭 𐑄 𐐹𐐵𐐲𐑉 𐐰𐑌𐐼 𐐿𐐰𐐹𐐻𐐮𐑂𐐩𐑇𐐲𐑌 𐐱𐑂 𐑄 𐐼𐐯𐑂𐐮𐑊. 𐐤𐐵 𐐺𐐨𐐸𐐬𐑊𐐼, 𐑄𐐮𐑅 𐐮𐑆 𐑄 𐑂𐐦𐑅 𐐱𐑂 𐑄 𐐩𐑌𐐾𐐯𐑊, 𐐿𐑉𐐴𐐮𐑍 𐐲𐑌𐐻𐐭 𐑄 𐐹𐐨𐐹𐑊. 𐐈𐑌𐐼 𐑌𐐵 𐑋𐐴 𐐺𐐨𐑊𐐲𐑂𐐯𐐼 𐐺𐑉𐐯𐑄𐑉𐐯𐑌, 𐑁𐐫𐑉 𐐷𐐨 𐐪𐑉 𐑋𐐴 𐐺𐑉𐐯𐑄𐑉𐐯𐑌, 𐐰𐑌𐐼 𐐷𐐨 𐐫𐐻 𐐻𐐭 𐐺𐐨 𐐺𐐨𐑊𐐲𐑂𐐯𐐼, 𐐰𐑌𐐼 𐐷𐐨 𐐫𐐻 𐐻𐐭 𐐺𐑉𐐮𐑍 𐑁𐐫𐑉𐑃 𐐶𐐲𐑉𐐿𐑅 𐐸𐐶𐐮𐐽 𐐪𐑉 𐑋𐐨𐐻 𐑁𐐫𐑉 𐑉𐐨𐐹𐐯𐑌𐐻𐐰𐑌𐑅, 𐑅𐐨𐐮𐑍 𐑄𐐰𐐻 𐐷𐐭𐑉 𐐸𐐪𐑉𐐻𐑅 𐐸𐐰𐑂 𐐺𐐮𐑌 𐑀𐑉𐐬𐑅𐑊𐐨 𐐸𐐪𐑉𐐼𐐲𐑌𐐼 𐐰𐑀𐐯𐑌𐑅𐐻 𐑄 𐐶𐐲𐑉𐐼 𐐱𐑂 𐐘𐐱𐐼, 𐐰𐑌𐐼 𐑅𐐨𐐮𐑍 𐑄𐐰𐐻 𐐷𐐨 𐐪𐑉 𐐲 𐑊𐐱𐑅𐐻 𐐰𐑌𐐼 𐐲 𐑁𐐫𐑊𐐲𐑌 𐐹𐐨𐐹𐑊.

4. 𐐈𐑌𐐼 𐐮𐐻 𐐿𐐩𐑋 𐐻𐐭 𐐹𐐪𐑅 𐑄𐐰𐐻 𐐸𐐶𐐯𐑌 𐐌, 𐐈𐑊𐑋𐐲, 𐐸𐐰𐐼 𐑅𐐹𐐬𐐿𐐲𐑌 𐑄𐐨𐑆 𐐶𐐲𐑉𐐼𐑆, 𐐺𐐨𐐸𐐬𐑊𐐼, 𐑄 𐐹𐐨𐐹𐑊 𐐶𐐲𐑉 𐑉𐐫𐑃 𐐶𐐮𐑄 𐑋𐐨, 𐐺𐐨𐐿𐐫𐑆 𐐌 𐑅𐐯𐐼 𐐲𐑌𐐻𐐭 𐑄𐐯𐑋 𐑄𐐰𐐻 𐑄𐐩 𐐶𐐲𐑉 𐐲 𐐸𐐪𐑉𐐼 𐐸𐐪𐑉𐐻𐐯𐐼 𐐰𐑌𐐼 𐐲 𐑅𐐻𐐮𐑁𐑌𐐯𐐿𐐻 𐐹𐐨𐐹𐑊; 𐐰𐑌𐐼 𐐫𐑊𐑅𐐬 𐐺𐐨𐐿𐐫𐑆 𐐌 𐑅𐐯𐐼 𐐲𐑌𐐻𐐭 𐑄𐐯𐑋 𐑄𐐰𐐻 𐑄𐐩 𐐶𐐲𐑉 𐐲 𐑊𐐱𐑅𐐻 𐐰𐑌𐐼 𐐲 𐑁𐐫𐑊𐐲𐑌 𐐹𐐨𐐹𐑊, 𐑄𐐩 𐐶𐐲𐑉 𐐰𐑍𐑀𐑉𐐨 𐐶𐐮𐑄 𐑋𐐨, 𐐰𐑌𐐼 𐑅𐐫𐐻 𐐻𐐭 𐑊𐐩 𐑄𐐯𐑉 𐐸𐐰𐑌𐐼𐑆 𐐲𐐹𐐱𐑌 𐑋𐐨, 𐑄𐐰𐐻 𐑄𐐩 𐑋𐐴𐐻 𐐿𐐰𐑅𐐻 𐑋𐐨 𐐮𐑌𐐻𐐭 𐐹𐑉𐐮𐑆𐐲𐑌; 𐐺𐐲𐐻 𐐮𐐻 𐐿𐐩𐑋 𐐻𐐭 𐐹𐐪𐑅 𐑄𐐰𐐻 𐑄 𐐢𐐫𐑉𐐼 𐐼𐐮𐐼 𐑌𐐱𐐻 𐑅𐐲𐑁𐐲𐑉 𐑄𐐯𐑋 𐑄𐐰𐐻 𐑄𐐩 𐑇𐐳𐐼 𐐻𐐩𐐿 𐑋𐐨 𐐰𐐻 𐑄𐐰𐐻 𐐻𐐴𐑋 𐐰𐑌𐐼 𐐿𐐰𐑅𐐻 𐑋𐐨 𐐮𐑌𐐻𐐭 𐐹𐑉𐐮𐑆𐐲𐑌.

5. 𐐈𐑌𐐼 𐐮𐐻 𐐿𐐩𐑋 𐐻𐐭 𐐹𐐪𐑅 𐑄𐐰𐐻 𐐈𐑋𐐷𐐭𐑊𐐯𐐿 𐐶𐐯𐑌𐐻 𐐰𐑌𐐼 𐑅𐐻𐐳𐐼 𐑁𐐫𐑉𐑃, 𐐰𐑌𐐼 𐐺𐐨𐑀𐐰𐑌 𐐻𐐭 𐐹𐑉𐐨𐐽 𐐲𐑌𐐻𐐭 𐑄𐐯𐑋 𐐫𐑊𐑅𐐬. 𐐈𐑌𐐼 𐑌𐐵 𐑄 𐐶𐐲𐑉𐐼𐑆 𐐱𐑂 𐐈𐑋𐐷𐐭𐑊𐐯𐐿 𐐪𐑉 𐑌𐐱𐐻 𐐫𐑊 𐑉𐐮𐐻𐐲𐑌, 𐑌𐐯𐑂𐐲𐑉𐑄𐐯𐑊𐐯𐑅 𐐲 𐐹𐐪𐑉𐐻 𐐱𐑂 𐐸𐐮𐑆 𐐶𐐲𐑉𐐼𐑆 𐐪𐑉 𐑉𐐮𐐻𐐲𐑌 𐐮𐑌 𐑄𐐮𐑅 𐐺𐐳𐐿.

𐐗𐐰𐐹𐐻𐐲𐑉 VIII.

1. 𐐤𐐵 𐑄𐐨𐑆 𐐪𐑉 𐑄 𐐶𐐲𐑉𐐼𐑆 𐐸𐐶𐐮𐐽 𐐈𐑋𐐷𐐭𐑊𐐯𐐿 𐐹𐑉𐐨𐐽𐐻 𐐲𐑌𐐻𐐭 𐑄 𐐹𐐨𐐹𐑊 𐐸𐐭 𐐶𐐲𐑉 𐐮𐑌 𐑄 𐑊𐐰𐑌𐐼 𐐱𐑂 𐐈𐑋𐐱𐑌𐐴𐐸𐐪, 𐑅𐐩𐐮𐑍: 𐐌 𐐰𐑋 𐐈𐑋𐐷𐐭𐑊𐐯𐐿; 𐐌 𐐰𐑋 𐑄 𐑅𐐲𐑌 𐐱𐑂 𐐘𐐮𐐼𐐬𐑌𐐪, 𐐸𐐭 𐐶𐐱𐑆 𐑄 𐑅𐐲𐑌 𐐱𐑂 𐐌𐑇𐑋𐐩𐐯𐑊, 𐐸𐐭 𐐶𐐱𐑆 𐐲 𐐼𐐨𐑅𐐯𐑌𐐼𐐰𐑌𐐻 𐐱𐑂 𐐈𐑋𐐮𐑌𐐰𐐼𐐴; 𐐰𐑌𐐼 𐐮𐐻 𐐶𐐱𐑆 𐑄𐐰𐐻 𐑅𐐩𐑋 𐐈𐑋𐐮𐑌𐐰𐐼𐐴 𐐸𐐭 𐐮𐑌𐐻𐐲𐑉𐐹𐑉𐐯𐐻𐐯𐐼 𐑄 𐑉𐐴𐐻𐐮𐑍 𐐸𐐶𐐮𐐽 𐐶𐐱𐑆 𐐲𐐹𐐱𐑌 𐑄 𐐶𐐫𐑊 𐐱𐑂 𐑄 𐐻𐐯𐑋𐐹𐐲𐑊, 𐐸𐐶𐐮𐐽 𐐶𐐱𐑆 𐑉𐐮𐐻𐐲𐑌 𐐺𐐴 𐑄 𐑁𐐮𐑍𐑀𐐲𐑉 𐐱𐑂 𐐘𐐱𐐼. 𐐈𐑌𐐼 𐐈𐑋𐐮𐑌𐐰𐐼𐐴 𐐶𐐱𐑆 𐐲 𐐼𐐨𐑅𐐯𐑌𐐼𐐰𐑌𐐻 𐐱𐑂 𐐤𐐨𐑁𐐴, 𐐸𐐭 𐐶𐐱𐑆 𐑄 𐑅𐐲𐑌 𐐱𐑂 𐐢𐐨𐐸𐐴, 𐐸𐐭 𐐿𐐩𐑋 𐐵𐐻 𐐱𐑂 𐑄 𐑊𐐰𐑌𐐼 𐐱𐑂 𐐖𐐨𐑉𐐭𐑅𐐲𐑊𐐯𐑋, 𐐸𐐭 𐐶𐐱𐑆 𐐲 𐐼𐐨𐑅𐐯𐑌𐐼𐐰𐑌𐐻 𐐱𐑂 𐐣𐐰𐑌𐐰𐑅𐐲, 𐐸𐐭 𐐶𐐱𐑆 𐑄 𐑅𐐲𐑌 𐐱𐑂 𐐖𐐬𐑆𐐯𐑁, 𐐸𐐭 𐐶𐐱𐑆 𐑅𐐬𐑊𐐼 𐐮𐑌𐐻𐐭 𐐇𐐾𐐮𐐹𐐻 𐐺𐐴 𐑄 𐐸𐐰𐑌𐐼𐑆 𐐱𐑂 𐐸𐐮𐑆 𐐺𐑉𐐯𐑄𐑉𐐯𐑌. 𐐈𐑌𐐼 𐐺𐐨𐐸𐐬𐑊𐐼, 𐐌 𐐰𐑋 𐐫𐑊𐑅𐐬 𐐲 𐑋𐐰𐑌 𐐱𐑂 𐑌𐐬 𐑅𐑋𐐫𐑊 𐑉𐐯𐐹𐐷𐐭𐐻𐐩𐑇𐐲𐑌 𐐲𐑋𐐲𐑍 𐐫𐑊 𐑄𐐬𐑆 𐐸𐐭 𐑌𐐬 𐑋𐐨; 𐐷𐐩, 𐐰𐑌𐐼 𐐺𐐨𐐸𐐬𐑊𐐼, 𐐌 𐐸𐐰𐑂 𐑋𐐯𐑌𐐨 𐐿𐐮𐑌𐐼𐑉𐐯𐐼𐑆 𐐰𐑌𐐼 𐑁𐑉𐐯𐑌𐐼𐑆, 𐐰𐑌𐐼 𐐌 𐐸𐐰𐑂 𐐫𐑊𐑅𐐬 𐐰𐐿𐐶𐐴𐑉𐐼 𐑋𐐲𐐽 𐑉𐐮𐐽𐐯𐑆 𐐺𐐴 𐑄 𐐸𐐰𐑌𐐼 𐐱𐑂 𐑋𐐴 𐐮𐑌𐐼𐐲𐑅𐐻𐑉𐐨; 𐑌𐐯𐑂𐐲𐑉𐑄𐐯𐑊𐐯𐑅, 𐐰𐑁𐐻𐐲𐑉 𐐫𐑊 𐑄𐐮𐑅, 𐐌 𐑌𐐯𐑂𐐲𐑉 𐐸𐐰𐑂 𐑌𐐬𐑌 𐑋𐐲𐐽 𐐱𐑂 𐑄 𐐶𐐩𐑆 𐐱𐑂 𐑄 𐐢𐐫𐑉𐐼, 𐐰𐑌𐐼 𐐸𐐮𐑆 𐑋𐐮𐑅𐐻𐐲𐑉𐐨𐑆 𐐰𐑌𐐼 𐑋𐐪𐑉𐑂𐐯𐑊𐐲𐑅 𐐹𐐵𐐲𐑉. 𐐌 𐑅𐐯𐐼 𐐌 𐑌𐐯𐑂𐐲𐑉 𐐸𐐰𐐼 𐑌𐐬𐑌 𐑋𐐲𐐽 𐐱𐑂 𐑄𐐨𐑆 𐑃𐐮𐑍𐑆; 𐐺𐐲𐐻 𐐺𐐨𐐸𐐬𐑊𐐼, 𐐌 𐑋𐐮𐑅𐐻𐐩𐐿, 𐑁𐐫𐑉 𐐌 𐐸𐐰𐑂 𐑅𐐨𐑌 𐑋𐐲𐐽 𐐱𐑂 𐐸𐐮𐑆 𐑋𐐮𐑅𐐻𐐲𐑉𐐨𐑆 𐐰𐑌𐐼 𐐸𐐮𐑆 𐑋𐐪𐑉𐑂𐐯𐑊𐐲𐑅 𐐹𐐵𐐲𐑉; 𐐷𐐩, 𐐨𐑂𐐯𐑌 𐐮𐑌 𐑄 𐐹𐑉𐐯𐑆𐐲𐑉𐑂𐐩𐑇𐐲𐑌 𐐱𐑂 𐑄 𐑊𐐴𐑂𐑆 𐐱𐑂 𐑄𐐮𐑅 𐐹𐐨𐐹𐑊; 𐑌𐐯𐑂𐐲𐑉𐑄𐐯𐑊𐐯𐑅 𐐌 𐐼𐐮𐐼 𐐸𐐪𐑉𐐼𐐲𐑌 𐑋𐐴 𐐸𐐪𐑉𐐻, 𐑁𐐫𐑉 𐐌 𐐶𐐱𐑆 𐐿𐐫𐑊𐐼 𐑋𐐯𐑌𐐨 𐐻𐐴𐑋𐑆, 𐐰𐑌𐐼 𐐌 𐐶𐐳𐐼 𐑌𐐱𐐻 𐐸𐐨𐑉; 𐑄𐐯𐑉𐑁𐐬𐑉 𐐌 𐑌𐐭

𐑌𐐯𐑂𐐲𐑉𐑄𐐯𐑊𐐯𐑅 𐐌 𐐼𐐮𐐼 𐐸𐐪𐑉𐐼𐑌 𐑋𐐴 𐐸𐐪𐑉𐐻, 𐑁𐐫𐑉 𐐌 𐐶𐐱𐑆 𐐿𐐫𐑊𐐼 𐑋𐐯𐑌𐐨 𐐻𐐴𐑋𐑆, 𐐰𐑌𐐼 𐐌 𐐶𐐳𐐼 𐑌𐐱𐐻 𐐸𐐨𐑉; 𐑄𐐯𐑉𐑁𐐫𐑉 𐐌 𐑌𐐭 𐐿𐐲𐑌𐑅𐐲𐑉𐑌𐐮𐑍 𐑄𐐨𐑆 𐑃𐐮𐑍𐑆, 𐐷𐐯𐐻 𐐌 𐐶𐐳𐐼 𐑌𐐱𐐻 𐑌𐐬; 𐑄𐐯𐑉𐑁𐐫𐑉 𐐌 𐐶𐐯𐑌𐐻 𐐱𐑌 𐑉𐐯𐐺𐐯𐑊𐐮𐑍 𐐲𐑀𐐯𐑌𐑅𐐻 𐐘𐐱𐐼, 𐐮𐑌 𐑄 𐐶𐐮𐐿𐐯𐐼𐑌𐐯𐑅 𐐱𐑂 𐑋𐐴 𐐸𐐪𐑉𐐻, 𐐨𐑂𐑌 𐐲𐑌𐐻𐐮𐑊 𐑄 𐑁𐐬𐑉𐑃 𐐼𐐩 𐐱𐑂 𐑄𐐮𐑅 𐑅𐐯𐑂𐑌𐑃 𐑋𐐲𐑌𐑃, 𐐸𐐶𐐮𐐽 𐐮𐑆 𐐮𐑌 𐑄 𐐻𐐯𐑌𐑃 𐐷𐐨𐑉 𐐱𐑂 𐑄 𐑉𐐩𐑌 𐐱𐑂 𐑄 𐐾𐐲𐐾𐐯𐑆. 𐐈𐑆 𐐌 𐐶𐐱𐑆 𐐾𐐲𐑉𐑌𐐨𐐮𐑍 𐐻𐐭 𐑅𐐨 𐐲 𐑂𐐯𐑉𐐨 𐑌𐐨𐑉 𐐿𐐮𐑌𐐼𐑉𐐯𐐼, 𐐺𐐨𐐸𐐬𐑊𐐼 𐐰𐑌 𐐩𐑌𐐾𐐯𐑊 𐐱𐑂 𐑄 𐐢𐐫𐑉𐐼 𐐰𐐹𐐨𐑉𐐼 𐐲𐑌𐐻𐐭 𐑋𐐨 𐐰𐑌𐐼 𐑅𐐯𐐼, 𐐈𐑋𐐷𐑊𐐯𐐿, 𐑉𐐨𐐻𐐲𐑉𐑌 𐐻𐐭 𐑄𐐴𐑌 𐐬𐑌 𐐸𐐵𐑅, 𐑁𐐫𐑉 𐑄𐐵 𐑇𐐰𐑊𐐻 𐑁𐐨𐐼 𐐲 𐐹𐑉𐐱𐑁𐐯𐐻 𐐱𐑂 𐑄 𐐢𐐫𐑉𐐼; 𐐷𐐩, 𐐲 𐐸𐐬𐑊𐐨 𐑋𐐰𐑌, 𐐸𐐭 𐐮𐑆 𐐲 𐐽𐐬𐑆𐑌 𐑋𐐰𐑌 𐐱𐑂 𐐘𐐱𐐼; 𐑁𐐫𐑉 𐐸𐐨 𐐸𐐰𐑆 𐑁𐐪𐑅𐐻𐐯𐐼 𐑋𐐯𐑌𐐨 𐐼𐐩𐑆 𐐺𐐨𐐿𐐫𐑆 𐐱𐑂 𐑄 𐑅𐐮𐑌𐑆 𐐱𐑂 𐑄𐐮𐑅 𐐹𐐨𐐹𐑊, 𐐰𐑌𐐼 𐐸𐐨 𐐮𐑆 𐐰𐑌 𐐸𐐲𐑍𐑀𐐲𐑉𐐼, 𐐰𐑌𐐼 𐑄𐐵 𐑇𐐰𐑊𐐻 𐑉𐐨𐑅𐐨𐑂 𐐸𐐮𐑋 𐐮𐑌𐐻𐐭 𐑄𐐴 𐐸𐐵𐑅 𐐰𐑌𐐼 𐑁𐐨𐐼 𐐸𐐮𐑋, 𐐰𐑌𐐼 𐐸𐐨 𐑇𐐰𐑊 𐐺𐑊𐐯𐑅 𐑄𐐨 𐐰𐑌𐐼 𐑄𐐴 𐐸𐐵𐑅; 𐐰𐑌𐐼 𐑄 𐐺𐑊𐐯𐑅𐐮𐑍 𐐱𐑂 𐑄 𐐢𐐫𐑉𐐼 𐑇𐐰𐑊 𐑉𐐯𐑅𐐻 𐐲𐐹𐐱𐑌 𐑄𐐨 𐐰𐑌𐐼 𐑄𐐴 𐐸𐐵𐑅.

2. 𐐈𐑌𐐼 𐐮𐐻 𐐿𐐩𐑋 𐐻𐐭 𐐹𐐪𐑅 𐑄𐐰𐐻 𐐌 𐐬𐐺𐐩𐐼 𐑄 𐑂𐐱𐐮𐑅 𐐱𐑂 𐑄 𐐩𐑌𐐾𐐯𐑊, 𐐰𐑌𐐼 𐑉𐐨𐐻𐐲𐑉𐑌𐐼 𐐻𐐬𐐲𐑉𐐼𐑆 𐑋𐐴 𐐸𐐵𐑅. 𐐈𐑌𐐼 𐐰𐑆 𐐌 𐐶𐐱𐑆 𐑀𐐬𐐮𐑍 𐑄𐐮𐑄𐐲𐑉 𐐌 𐑁𐐵𐑌𐐼 𐑄 𐑋𐐰𐑌 𐐸𐐭𐑋 𐑄 𐐩𐑌𐐾𐐯𐑊 𐑅𐐯𐐼 𐐲𐑌𐐻𐐭 𐑋𐐨, 𐐜𐐵 𐑇𐐰𐑊𐐻 𐑉𐐨𐑅𐐨𐑂 𐐮𐑌𐐻𐐭 𐑄𐐴 𐐸𐐵𐑅; 𐐰𐑌𐐼 𐐺𐐨𐐸𐐬𐑊𐐼 𐐮𐐻 𐐶𐐱𐑆 𐑄𐐮𐑅 𐑅𐐩𐑋 𐑋𐐰𐑌 𐐸𐐭 𐐸𐐰𐑆 𐐺𐐨𐑌 𐑅𐐹𐐨𐐿𐐮𐑍 𐐲𐑌𐐻𐐭 𐐷𐐭 𐐿𐐲𐑌𐑅𐐲𐑉𐑌𐐮𐑍 𐑄 𐑃𐐮𐑍𐑆 𐐱𐑂 𐐘𐐱𐐼. 𐐈𐑌𐐼 𐑄 𐐩𐑌𐐾𐐯𐑊 𐑅𐐯𐐼 𐐲𐑌𐐻𐐭 𐑋𐐨 𐐸𐐨 𐐮𐑆 𐐲 𐐸𐐬𐑊𐐨 𐑋𐐰𐑌; 𐐸𐐶𐐯𐑉𐑁𐐫𐑉 𐐌 𐑌𐐬 𐐸𐐨 𐐮𐑆 𐐲 𐐸𐐬𐑊𐐨 𐑋𐐰𐑌 𐐺𐐨𐐿𐐫𐑆 𐐮𐐻 𐐶𐐱𐑆 𐑅𐐯𐐼 𐐺𐐴 𐐰𐑌 𐐩𐑌𐐾𐐯𐑊 𐐱𐑂 𐐘𐐱𐐼. 𐐈𐑌𐐼 𐐲𐑀𐐯𐑌, 𐐌 𐑌𐐬 𐑄𐐰𐐻 𐑄 𐑃𐐮𐑍𐑆 𐐸𐐶𐐯𐑉𐐱𐑂 𐐸𐐨 𐐸𐐰𐑃 𐐻𐐯𐑅𐐻𐐮𐑁𐐴𐐼 𐐪𐑉 𐐻𐑉𐐭; 𐑁𐐫𐑉 𐐺𐐨𐐸𐐬𐑊𐐼 𐐌 𐑅𐐩 𐐲𐑌𐐻𐐭 𐐷𐐭, 𐑄𐐰𐐻 𐐰𐑆 𐑄 𐐢𐐫𐑉𐐼 𐑊𐐮𐑂𐐯𐑃, 𐐨𐑂𐑌 𐑅𐐬 𐐸𐐰𐑆 𐐸𐐨 𐑅𐐯𐑌𐐻 𐐸𐐮𐑆 𐐩𐑌𐐾𐐯𐑊 𐐻𐐭 𐑋𐐩𐐿 𐑄𐐨𐑆 𐑃𐐮𐑍𐑆 𐑋𐐰𐑌𐐮𐑁𐐯𐑅𐐻 𐐲𐑌𐐻𐐭 𐑋𐐨; 𐐰𐑌𐐼 𐑄𐐮𐑅 𐐸𐐨 𐐸𐐰𐑆 𐐼𐐲𐑌 𐐸𐐶𐐴𐑊 𐑄𐐮𐑅 𐐈𐑊𐑋𐐲 𐐸𐐰𐑃 𐐼𐐶𐐯𐑊𐐻 𐐰𐐻 𐑋𐐴 𐐸𐐵𐑅: 𐑁𐐫𐑉 𐐺𐐨𐐸𐐬𐑊𐐼, 𐐸𐐨 𐐸𐐰𐑃 𐐺𐑊𐐯𐑅𐐻 𐑋𐐴𐑌 𐐸𐐵𐑅, 𐐸𐐨 𐐸𐐰𐑃 𐐺𐑊𐐯𐑅𐐻 𐑋𐐨, 𐐰𐑌𐐼 𐑋𐐴 𐐶𐐮𐑋𐐯𐑌, 𐐰𐑌𐐼 𐑋𐐴 𐐽𐐮𐑊𐐼𐑉𐐯𐑌, 𐐰𐑌𐐼 𐑋𐐴 𐑁𐐪𐑄𐐲𐑉, 𐐰𐑌𐐼 𐑋𐐴 𐐿𐐮𐑌𐑆𐑁𐐬𐐿; 𐐷𐐩, 𐐨𐑂𐑌 𐐫𐑊 𐑋𐐴 𐐿𐐮𐑌𐐼𐑉𐐯𐐼 𐐸𐐰𐑃 𐐸𐐨 𐐺𐑊𐐯𐑅𐐻, 𐐰𐑌𐐼 𐑄 𐐺𐑊𐐯𐑅𐐮𐑍 𐐱𐑂 𐑄 𐐢𐐫𐑉𐐼 𐐸𐐰𐑃 𐑉𐐯𐑅𐐻𐐯𐐼 𐐲𐐹𐐱𐑌 𐐲𐑅 𐐰𐐿𐐫𐑉𐐼𐐮𐑍 𐐻𐐭 𐑄 𐐶𐐲𐑉𐐼𐑆 𐐸𐐶𐐮𐐽 𐐸𐐨 𐑅𐐹𐐩𐐿.

3. 𐐈𐑌𐐼 𐑌𐐵, 𐐸𐐶𐐯𐑌 𐐈𐑋𐐷𐑊𐐯𐐿 𐐸𐐰𐐼 𐑅𐐹𐐬𐐿𐑌 𐑄𐐨𐑆 𐐶𐐲𐑉𐐼𐑆, 𐑄 𐐹𐐨𐐹𐑊 𐐺𐐨𐑀𐐰𐑌 𐐻𐐭 𐐺𐐨 𐐰𐑅𐐻𐐱𐑌𐐮𐑇𐐻, 𐑅𐐨𐐮𐑍 𐑄𐐯𐑉 𐐶𐐱𐑆 𐑋𐐬𐑉 𐑄𐐰𐑌 𐐶𐐲𐑌 𐐶𐐮𐐻𐑌𐐯𐑅 𐐸𐐭 𐐻𐐯𐑅𐐻𐐮𐑁𐐴𐐼 𐐱𐑂 𐑄 𐑃𐐮𐑍𐑆 𐐸𐐶𐐯𐑉𐐱𐑂 𐑄𐐩 𐐶𐐲𐑉 𐐰𐐿𐐷𐐭𐑆𐐼, 𐐰𐑌𐐼 𐐫𐑊𐑅𐐬 𐐱𐑂 𐑄 𐑃𐐮𐑍𐑆 𐐸𐐶𐐮𐐽 𐐶𐐲𐑉 𐐻𐐭 𐐿𐐲𐑋, 𐐰𐐿𐐫𐑉𐐼𐐮𐑍 𐐻𐐭 𐑄 𐑅𐐹𐐮𐑉𐐮𐐻 𐐱𐑂 𐐹𐑉𐐱𐑁𐐯𐑅𐐨 𐐸𐐶𐐮𐐽 𐐶𐐱𐑆 𐐮𐑌 𐑄𐐯𐑋. 𐐤𐐯𐑂𐐲𐑉𐑄𐐯𐑊𐐯𐑅, 𐑄𐐯𐑉 𐐶𐐲𐑉 𐑅𐐲𐑋 𐐲𐑋𐐲𐑍 𐑄𐐯𐑋 𐐸𐐭 𐑃𐐫𐐻 𐐻𐐭 𐐿𐐶𐐯𐑅𐐽𐐲𐑌 𐑄𐐯𐑋, 𐑄𐐰𐐻 𐐺𐐴 𐑄𐐯𐑉 𐐿𐐲𐑌𐐮𐑍 𐐼𐐯𐑂𐐴𐑅𐐯𐑆 𐑄𐐩 𐑋𐐴𐐻 𐐿𐐰𐐽 𐑄𐐯𐑋 𐐮𐑌 𐑄𐐯𐑉 𐐶𐐲𐑉𐐼𐑆, 𐑄𐐰𐐻 𐑄𐐩 𐑋𐐴𐐻 𐑁𐐴𐑌𐐼 𐐶𐐮𐐻𐑌𐐯𐑅 𐐲𐑀𐐯𐑌𐑅𐐻 𐑄𐐯𐑋, 𐑄𐐰𐐻 𐑄𐐩 𐑋𐐴𐐻 𐐼𐐯𐑊𐐮𐑂𐐲𐑉 𐑄𐐯𐑋 𐐻𐐭 𐑄𐐯𐑉 𐐾𐐲𐐾𐐯𐑆 𐑄𐐰𐐻 𐑄𐐩 𐑋𐐴𐐻 𐐺𐐨 𐐾𐐲𐐾𐐼 𐐰𐐿𐐫𐑉𐐼𐐮𐑍 𐐻𐐭 𐑄 𐑊𐐫, 𐐰𐑌𐐼 𐑄𐐰𐐻 𐑄𐐩 𐑋𐐴𐐻 𐐺𐐨 𐑅𐑊𐐩𐑌 𐐫𐑉 𐐿𐐰𐑅𐐻 𐐮𐑌𐐻𐐭 𐐹𐑉𐐮𐑆𐑌, 𐐰𐐿𐐫𐑉𐐼𐐮𐑍 𐐻𐐭 𐑄 𐐿𐑉𐐴𐑋 𐐸𐐶𐐮𐐽 𐑄𐐩 𐐿𐐳𐐼 𐑋𐐩𐐿 𐐰𐐹𐐨𐑉 𐐫𐑉 𐐶𐐮𐐻𐑌𐐯𐑅 𐐲𐑀𐐯𐑌𐑅𐐻 𐑄𐐯𐑋. 𐐤𐐵 𐐮𐐻 𐐶𐐱𐑆 𐑄𐐬𐑆 𐑋𐐯𐑌 𐐸𐐭 𐑅𐐫𐐻 𐐻𐐭 𐐼𐐯𐑅𐐻𐑉𐐱𐐮 𐑄𐐯𐑋, 𐐸𐐭 𐐶𐐲𐑉 𐑊𐐫𐐷𐐲𐑉𐑆, 𐐸𐐭 𐐶𐐲𐑉 𐐸𐐴𐑉𐐼 𐐫𐑉 𐐰𐐹𐐱𐐮𐑌𐐻𐐯𐐼 𐐺𐐴 𐑄 𐐹𐐨𐐹𐑊 𐐻𐐭 𐐰𐐼𐑋𐐮𐑌𐐮𐑅𐐻𐐲𐑉 𐑄 𐑊𐐫 𐐰𐐻 𐑄𐐯𐑉 𐐻𐐴𐑋𐑆 𐐱𐑂 𐐻𐑉𐐴𐐲𐑊𐑆, 𐐫𐑉 𐐰𐐻 𐑄 𐐻𐑉𐐴𐐲𐑊𐑆 𐐱𐑂 𐑄 𐐿𐑉𐐴𐑋𐑆 𐐱𐑂 𐑄 𐐹𐐨𐐹𐑊 𐐺𐐨𐑁𐐬𐑉 𐑄 𐐾𐐲𐐾𐐯𐑆. 𐐤𐐵 𐑄𐐨𐑆 𐑊𐐫𐐷𐐲𐑉𐑆 𐐶𐐲𐑉 𐑊𐐲𐑉𐑌𐐯𐐼 𐐮𐑌 𐐫𐑊 𐑄 𐐪𐑉𐐻𐑅 𐐰𐑌𐐼 𐐿𐐲𐑌𐐮𐑍 𐐱𐑂 𐑄 𐐹𐐨𐐹𐑊; 𐐰𐑌𐐼 𐑄𐐮𐑅 𐐶𐐱𐑆 𐐻𐐭 𐐯𐑌𐐩𐐺𐑊 𐑄𐐯𐑋 𐑄𐐰𐐻 𐑄𐐩 𐑋𐐴𐐻 𐐺𐐨 𐑅𐐿𐐮𐑊𐑁𐐳𐑊 𐐮𐑌 𐑄𐐯𐑉 𐐹𐑉𐐬𐑁𐐯𐑇𐐲𐑌. 𐐈𐑌𐐼 𐐮𐐻 𐐿𐐩𐑋 𐐻𐐭 𐐹𐐪𐑅 𐑄𐐰𐐻 𐑄𐐩 𐐺𐐨𐑀𐐰𐑌 𐐻𐐭 𐐿𐐶𐐯𐑅𐐽𐐲𐑌 𐐈𐑋𐐷𐑊𐐯𐐿, 𐑄𐐰𐐻 𐑄𐐯𐑉𐐺𐐴 𐑄𐐩 𐑋𐐴𐐻 𐑋𐐩𐐿 𐐸𐐮𐑋 𐐿𐑉𐐱𐑅 𐐸𐐮𐑆 𐐶𐐲𐑉𐐼𐑆, 𐐫𐑉 𐐿𐐱𐑌𐐻𐑉𐐲𐐼𐐮𐐿𐐻 𐑄 𐐶𐐲𐑉𐐼𐑆 𐐸𐐶𐐮𐐽 𐐸𐐨 𐑇𐐳𐐼 𐑅𐐹𐐨𐐿.

4. 𐐤𐐵 𐑄𐐩 𐑌𐐭 𐑌𐐱𐐻 𐑄𐐰𐐻 𐐈𐑋𐐷𐑊𐐯𐐿 𐐿𐐳𐐼 𐑌𐐬 𐐱𐑂 𐑄𐐯𐑉 𐐼𐐯𐑆𐐴𐑌𐑆. 𐐒𐐲𐐻 𐐮𐐻 𐐿𐐩𐑋 𐐻𐐭 𐐹𐐪𐑅 𐐰𐑆 𐑄𐐩 𐐺𐐨𐑀𐐰𐑌 𐐻𐐭 𐐿𐐶𐐯𐑅𐐽𐐲𐑌 𐐸𐐮𐑋, 𐐸𐐨 𐐹𐐲𐑉𐑅𐐨𐑂𐐼 𐑄𐐯𐑉 𐑃𐐫𐐻𐑅, 𐐰𐑌𐐼 𐐸𐐨 𐑅𐐯𐐼 𐐲𐑌𐐻𐐭 𐑄𐐯𐑋, 𐐄 𐐷𐐨 𐐶𐐮𐐿𐐯𐐼 𐐰𐑌𐐼 𐐹𐐲𐑉𐑂𐐲𐑉𐑅 𐐾𐐯𐑌𐐲𐑉𐐩𐑇𐐲𐑌; 𐐷𐐨 𐑊𐐫𐐷𐐲𐑉𐑆 𐐰𐑌𐐼 𐐸𐐮𐐹𐐬𐐿𐑉𐐮𐐻𐑅; 𐑁𐐫𐑉 𐐷𐐨 𐐪𐑉 𐑊𐐩𐐮𐑍 𐑄 𐑁𐐵𐑌𐐼𐐩𐑇𐐲𐑌𐑆 𐐱𐑂 𐑄 𐐼𐐯𐑂𐐮𐑊; 𐑁𐐫𐑉 𐐷𐐨 𐐪𐑉 𐑊𐐩𐐮𐑍 𐐻𐑉𐐰𐐹𐑅 𐐰𐑌𐐼 𐑅𐑌𐐯𐑉𐑆 𐐻𐐭 𐐿𐐰𐐽 𐑄 𐐸𐐬𐑊𐐨 𐐶𐐲𐑌𐑆 𐐱𐑂 𐐘𐐱𐐼; 𐐷𐐨 𐐪𐑉 𐑊𐐩𐐮𐑍 𐐹𐑊𐐰𐑌𐑆 𐐻𐐭 𐐹𐐲𐑉𐑂𐐲𐑉𐐻 𐑄 𐐶𐐩𐑆 𐐱𐑂 𐑄 𐑉𐐴𐐽𐐲𐑅, 𐐰𐑌𐐼 𐐻𐐭 𐐺𐑉𐐮𐑍 𐐼𐐵𐑌 𐑄 𐑉𐐪𐑃 𐐱𐑂 𐐘𐐱𐐼 𐐲𐐹𐐱𐑌 𐐷𐐭𐑉 𐐸𐐯𐐼𐑆, 𐐨𐑂𐑌 𐐻𐐭 𐑄 𐐲𐐻𐐲𐑉 𐐼𐐯𐑅𐐻𐑉𐐲𐐿𐑇𐐲𐑌 𐐱𐑂 𐑄𐐮𐑅 𐐹𐐨𐐹𐑊; 𐐷𐐩,

𐐶𐐯𐑊 𐐼𐐮𐐼 𐐣𐐬𐑆𐐴𐐲 𐑅𐐩, 𐐸𐐭 𐐶𐐱𐑆 𐐵𐑉 𐑊𐐪𐑅𐐻 𐐿𐐮𐑍, 𐐸𐐶𐐯𐑌 𐐸𐐨 𐐶𐐱𐑆 𐐲𐐺𐐵𐐻 𐐻𐐭 𐐼𐐨𐑊𐐮𐑂𐐲𐑉 𐐲𐐹 𐑄 𐐿𐐮𐑍𐐼𐐲𐑋, 𐐸𐐰𐑂𐐮𐑍 𐑌𐐬 𐐶𐐲𐑌 𐐻𐐭 𐐿𐐱𐑌𐑁𐐲𐑉 𐐮𐐻 𐐲𐐹𐐱𐑌, 𐐿𐐫𐑆𐐮𐑍 𐑄𐐰𐐻 𐑄𐐮𐑅 𐐹𐐨𐐹𐑊 𐑇𐐳𐐼 𐐺 𐑀𐐲𐑂𐐲𐑉𐑌𐐼 𐐺𐐴 𐑄𐐩𐑉 𐐬𐑌 𐑂𐐫𐐮𐑅𐐯𐑆; 𐐏𐐩, 𐐶𐐯𐑊 𐐼𐐮𐐼 𐐸𐐨 𐑅𐐩, 𐑄𐐰𐐻 𐐮𐑁 𐑄 𐐻𐐴𐑋 𐑇𐐳𐐼 𐐿𐐲𐑋 𐑄𐐰𐐻 𐑄 𐑂𐐫𐐮𐑅 𐐱𐑂 𐑄𐐮𐑅 𐐹𐐨𐐹𐑊 𐑇𐐳𐐼 𐐽𐐭𐑆 𐐮𐑌𐐮𐐿𐐶𐐮𐐻𐐨; 𐑄𐐰𐐻 𐐮𐑆, 𐐮𐑁 𐑄 𐐻𐐴𐑋 𐑇𐐳𐐼 𐐿𐐲𐑋 𐑄𐐰𐐻 𐑄𐐮𐑅 𐐹𐐨𐐹𐑊 𐑇𐐳𐐼 𐑁𐐫𐑊 𐐮𐑌𐐻𐐭 𐐻𐑉𐐰𐑌𐑆𐑀𐑉𐐯𐑇𐐲𐑌, 𐑄𐐩 𐐶𐐳𐐼 𐐺 𐑉𐐴𐐹 𐑁𐐫𐑉 𐐼𐐯𐑅𐐻𐑉𐐲𐐿𐑇𐐲𐑌. 𐐈𐑌𐐼 𐑌𐐵 𐐌 𐑅𐐩 𐐲𐑌𐐻𐐭 𐐷𐐭, 𐑄𐐰𐐻 𐐶𐐯𐑊 𐐼𐐲𐑃 𐑄 𐐢𐐫𐑉𐐼 𐐾𐐲𐐾 𐐱𐑂 𐐷𐐬𐑉 𐐮𐑌𐐮𐐿𐐶𐐮𐐻𐐨𐑆; 𐐶𐐯𐑊 𐐼𐐲𐑃 𐐸𐐨 𐐿𐑉𐐴 𐐲𐑌𐐻𐐭 𐑄𐐮𐑅 𐐹𐐨𐐹𐑊, 𐐺𐐴 𐑄 𐑂𐐫𐐮𐑅 𐐱𐑂 𐐸𐐮𐑆 𐐩𐑌𐐾𐐯𐑊𐑆, 𐐡𐐯𐐹𐐯𐑌𐐻 𐐷, 𐑉𐐯𐐹𐐯𐑌𐐻, 𐑁𐐫𐑉 𐑄 𐐿𐐮𐑍𐐼𐐲𐑋 𐐱𐑂 𐐸𐐯𐑂𐐲𐑌 𐐮𐑆 𐐰𐐻 𐐸𐐰𐑌𐐼. 𐐏𐐩, 𐐶𐐯𐑊 𐐼𐐲𐑃 𐐸𐐨 𐐿𐑉𐐴 𐐺𐐴 𐑄 𐑂𐐫𐐮𐑅 𐐱𐑂 𐐸𐐮𐑆 𐐩𐑌𐐾𐐯𐑊𐑆, 𐑄𐐰𐐻 𐐌 𐐶𐐮𐑊 𐐿𐐲𐑋 𐐼𐐵𐑌 𐐲𐑋𐐲𐑍 𐑋𐐴 𐐹𐐨𐐹𐑊, 𐐶𐐮𐑄 𐐯𐐿𐐶𐐮𐐻𐐨 𐐰𐑌𐐼 𐐾𐐲𐑅𐐻𐐮𐑅 𐐮𐑌 𐑋𐐴 𐐸𐐰𐑌𐐼𐑆. 𐐏𐐩, 𐐰𐑌𐐼 𐐌 𐑅𐐩 𐐲𐑌𐐻𐐭 𐐷𐐭, 𐑄𐐰𐐻 𐐮𐑁 𐐮𐐻 𐐶𐐲𐑉 𐑌𐐱𐐻 𐑁𐐫𐑉 𐑄 𐐹𐑉𐐩𐐲𐑉𐑆 𐐱𐑂 𐑄 𐑉𐐴𐐽𐐲𐑅, 𐐸𐐭 𐐪𐑉 𐑌𐐵 𐐮𐑌 𐑄 𐑊𐐰𐑌𐐼, 𐑄𐐰𐐻 𐐷 𐐶𐐳𐐼 𐐨𐑂𐑌 𐑌𐐵 𐐺 𐑂𐐮𐑆𐐮𐐻𐐯𐐼 𐐶𐐮𐑄 𐐲𐐻𐐲𐑉 𐐼𐐯𐑅𐐻𐑉𐐲𐐿𐑇𐐲𐑌; 𐐷𐐯𐐻 𐐮𐐻 𐐶𐐳𐐼 𐑌𐐱𐐻 𐐺 𐐺𐐴 𐑁𐑊𐐲𐐼, 𐐰𐑆 𐐶𐐲𐑉 𐑄 𐐹𐐨𐐹𐑊 𐐮𐑌 𐑄 𐐼𐐩𐑆 𐐱𐑂 𐐤𐐬𐐲, 𐐺𐐲𐐻 𐐮𐐻 𐐶𐐳𐐼 𐐺 𐐺𐐴 𐑁𐐰𐑋𐐮𐑌, 𐐰𐑌𐐼 𐐺𐐴 𐐹𐐯𐑅𐐻𐐮𐑊𐐯𐑌𐑅, 𐐰𐑌𐐼 𐑄 𐑅𐐫𐑉𐐼. 𐐒𐐲𐐻 𐐮𐐻 𐐮𐑆 𐐺𐐴 𐑄 𐐹𐑉𐐩𐐲𐑉𐑆 𐐱𐑂 𐑄 𐑉𐐴𐐽𐐲𐑅 𐑄𐐰𐐻 𐐷 𐐪𐑉 𐑅𐐹𐐩𐑉𐐼; 𐑌𐐵 𐑄𐐯𐑉𐑁𐐫𐑉 𐐮𐑁 𐐷 𐐶𐐮𐑊 𐐿𐐪𐑅𐐻 𐐵𐐻 𐑄 𐑉𐐴𐐽𐐲𐑅 𐑁𐑉𐐲𐑋 𐐲𐑋𐐲𐑍 𐐷𐐭, 𐑄𐐯𐑌 𐐶𐐮𐑊 𐑌𐐱𐐻 𐑄 𐐢𐐫𐑉𐐼 𐑅𐐻𐐩 𐐸𐐮𐑆 𐐸𐐰𐑌𐐼; 𐐺𐐲𐐻 𐐮𐑌 𐐸𐐮𐑆 𐑁𐐨𐑉𐑅 𐐰𐑍𐑀𐐲𐑉 𐐸𐐨 𐐶𐐮𐑊 𐐿𐐲𐑋 𐐵𐐻 𐐲𐑀𐐯𐑌𐑅𐐻 𐐷𐐭; 𐑄𐐯𐑌 𐐷 𐑇𐐰𐑊 𐐺 𐑅𐑋𐐮𐐻𐑌 𐐺𐐴 𐑁𐐰𐑋𐐮𐑌, 𐐰𐑌𐐼 𐐺𐐴 𐐹𐐯𐑅𐐻𐐮𐑊𐐯𐑌𐑅, 𐐰𐑌𐐼 𐐺𐐴 𐑄 𐑅𐐫𐑉𐐼; 𐐰𐑌𐐼 𐑄 𐐻𐐴𐑋 𐐮𐑆 𐑅𐐭𐑌 𐐰𐐻 𐐸𐐰𐑌𐐼, 𐐯𐐿𐑅𐐯𐐹𐐻 𐐷 𐑉𐐯𐐹𐐯𐑌𐐻.

5. 𐐈𐑌𐐼 𐑌𐐵 𐐮𐐻 𐐿𐐩𐑋 𐐻𐐭 𐐹𐐪𐑅 𐑄𐐰𐐻 𐑄 𐐹𐐨𐐹𐑊 𐐶𐐲𐑉 𐑋𐐬𐑉 𐐰𐑍𐑀𐑉𐐨 𐐶𐐮𐑄 𐐈𐑋𐐷𐐭𐑊𐐯𐐿, 𐐰𐑌𐐼 𐑄𐐩 𐐿𐑉𐐴𐐼 𐐵𐐻, 𐑅𐐩𐐮𐑍: 𐐜𐐮𐑅 𐑋𐐰𐑌 𐐼𐐲𐑃 𐑉𐐨𐑂𐐴𐑊 𐐲𐑀𐐯𐑌𐑅𐐻 𐐵𐑉 𐑊𐐫𐑆 𐐸𐐶𐐮𐐽 𐐪𐑉 𐐾𐐲𐑅𐐻, 𐐰𐑌𐐼 𐐵𐑉 𐐶𐐴𐑆 𐑊𐐫𐐷𐐲𐑉𐑆 𐐸𐐭𐑋 𐐶𐐨 𐐸𐐰𐑂 𐑅𐐯𐑊𐐯𐐿𐐻𐐯𐐼. 𐐒𐐲𐐻 𐐈𐑋𐐷𐐭𐑊𐐯𐐿 𐑅𐐻𐑉𐐯𐐽𐐻 𐑁𐐫𐑉𐑃 𐐸𐐮𐑆 𐐸𐐰𐑌𐐼, 𐐰𐑌𐐼 𐐿𐑉𐐴𐐼 𐑄 𐑋𐐴𐐻𐐨𐐲𐑉 𐐲𐑌𐐻𐐭 𐑄𐐯𐑋, 𐑅𐐩𐐮𐑍: 𐐄 𐐷 𐐶𐐮𐐿𐐯𐐼 𐐰𐑌𐐼 𐐹𐐲𐑉𐑂𐐲𐑉𐑅 𐐾𐐯𐑌𐐲𐑉𐐩𐑇𐐲𐑌; 𐐸𐐶𐐴 𐐸𐐰𐑃 𐐝𐐩𐐻𐐲𐑌 𐑀𐐱𐐻 𐑅𐐲𐐽 𐑀𐑉𐐩𐐻 𐐸𐐬𐑊𐐼 𐐲𐐹𐐱𐑌 𐐷𐐬𐑉 𐐸𐐪𐑉𐐻𐑅? 𐐐𐐶𐐴 𐐶𐐮𐑊 𐐷 𐐷𐐨𐑊𐐼 𐐷𐐬𐑉𐑅𐐯𐑊𐑂𐑆 𐐲𐑌𐐻𐐭 𐐸𐐮𐑋 𐑄𐐰𐐻 𐐸𐐨 𐑋𐐩 𐐸𐐰𐑂 𐐹𐐵𐐲𐑉 𐐬𐑂𐐲𐑉 𐐷𐐭, 𐐻𐐭 𐐺𐑊𐐴𐑌𐐼 𐐷𐐬𐑉 𐐴𐑆, 𐑄𐐰𐐻 𐐷 𐐶𐐮𐑊 𐑌𐐱𐐻 𐐲𐑌𐐼𐐲𐑉𐑅𐐻𐐰𐑌𐐼 𐑄 𐐶𐐲𐑉𐐼𐑆 𐐸𐐶𐐮𐐽 𐐪𐑉 𐑅𐐹𐐬𐐿𐑌, 𐐰𐐿𐐫𐑉𐐼𐐮𐑍 𐐻𐐭 𐑄𐐩𐑉 𐐻𐑉𐐭𐑃? 𐐙𐐫𐑉 𐐺𐐨𐐸𐐬𐑊𐐼, 𐐸𐐰𐑂 𐐌 𐐻𐐯𐑅𐐻𐐮𐑁𐐴𐐼 𐐲𐑀𐐯𐑌𐑅𐐻 𐐷𐐬𐑉 𐑊𐐫? 𐐏 𐐼𐐭 𐑌𐐱𐐻 𐐲𐑌𐐼𐐲𐑉𐑅𐐻𐐰𐑌𐐼; 𐐷 𐑅𐐩 𐑄𐐰𐐻 𐐌 𐐸𐐰𐑂 𐑅𐐹𐐬𐐿𐑌 𐐲𐑀𐐯𐑌𐑅𐐻 𐐷𐐬𐑉 𐑊𐐫; 𐐺𐐲𐐻 𐐌 𐐸𐐰𐑂 𐑌𐐱𐐻, 𐐺𐐲𐐻 𐐌 𐐸𐐰𐑂 𐑅𐐹𐐬𐐿𐑌 𐐮𐑌 𐑁𐐩𐑂𐐲𐑉 𐐱𐑂 𐐷𐐬𐑉 𐑊𐐫, 𐐻𐐭 𐐷𐐬𐑉 𐐿𐐱𐑌𐐼𐐯𐑋𐑌𐐩𐑇𐐲𐑌. 𐐈𐑌𐐼 𐑌𐐵 𐐺𐐨𐐸𐐬𐑊𐐼, 𐐌 𐑅𐐩 𐐲𐑌𐐻𐐭 𐐷𐐭, 𐑄𐐰𐐻 𐑄 𐑁𐐵𐑌𐐼𐐩𐑇𐐲𐑌 𐐱𐑂 𐑄 𐐼𐐯𐑅𐐻𐑉𐐲𐐿𐑇𐐲𐑌 𐐱𐑂 𐑄𐐮𐑅 𐐹𐐨𐐹𐑊 𐐮𐑆 𐐺𐐨𐑀𐐮𐑌𐐮𐑍 𐐻𐐭 𐐺 𐑊𐐩𐐼 𐐺𐐴 𐑄 𐐲𐑌𐑉𐐴𐐽𐐲𐑅𐑌𐐯𐑅 𐐱𐑂 𐐷𐐬𐑉 𐑊𐐫𐐷𐐲𐑉𐑆 𐐰𐑌𐐼 𐐷𐐬𐑉 𐐾𐐲𐐾𐐯𐑆.

6. 𐐈𐑌𐐼 𐑌𐐵 𐐮𐐻 𐐿𐐩𐑋 𐐻𐐭 𐐹𐐪𐑅, 𐑄𐐰𐐻 𐐸𐐶𐐯𐑌 𐐈𐑋𐐷𐐭𐑊𐐯𐐿 𐐸𐐰𐐼 𐑅𐐹𐐬𐐿𐑌 𐑄𐐨𐑆 𐐶𐐲𐑉𐐼𐑆, 𐑄 𐐹𐐨𐐹𐑊 𐐿𐑉𐐴𐐼 𐐵𐐻 𐐲𐑀𐐯𐑌𐑅𐐻 𐐸𐐮𐑋, 𐑅𐐩𐐮𐑍, 𐐤𐐵 𐐶𐐨 𐑌𐐬 𐑄𐐰𐐻 𐑄𐐮𐑅 𐑋𐐰𐑌 𐐮𐑆 𐐩 𐐽𐐴𐑊𐐼 𐐱𐑂 𐑄 𐐼𐐯𐑂𐑊, 𐑁𐐫𐑉 𐐸𐐨 𐐸𐐰𐑃 𐑊𐐴𐐼 𐐲𐑌𐐻𐐭 𐐲𐑅; 𐑁𐐫𐑉 𐐸𐐨 𐐸𐐰𐑃 𐑅𐐹𐐬𐐿𐑌 𐐲𐑀𐐯𐑌𐑅𐐻 𐐵𐑉 𐑊𐐫. 𐐈𐑌𐐼 𐑌𐐵 𐐸𐐨 𐑅𐐯𐑆 𐑄𐐰𐐻 𐐸𐐨 𐐸𐐰𐑆 𐑌𐐱𐐻 𐑅𐐹𐐬𐐿𐑌 𐐲𐑀𐐯𐑌𐑅𐐻 𐐮𐐻. 𐐈𐑌𐐼 𐐲𐑀𐐯𐑌: 𐐸𐐨 𐐸𐐰𐑆 𐑉𐐨𐑂𐐴𐑊𐐼 𐐲𐑀𐐯𐑌𐑅𐐻 𐐵𐑉 𐑊𐐫𐐷𐐲𐑉𐑆, 𐐰𐑌𐐼 𐐵𐑉 𐐾𐐲𐐾𐐯𐑆, 𐐫𐑊𐑅𐐬. 𐐈𐑌𐐼 𐐮𐐻 𐐿𐐩𐑋 𐐻𐐭 𐐹𐐪𐑅 𐑄𐐰𐐻 𐑄 𐑊𐐫𐐷𐐲𐑉𐑆 𐐹𐐳𐐻 𐐮𐐻 𐐮𐑌𐐻𐐭 𐑄𐐩𐑉 𐐸𐐪𐑉𐐻𐑅, 𐑄𐐰𐐻 𐑄𐐩 𐑇𐐳𐐼 𐑉𐐨𐑋𐐯𐑋𐐺𐐲𐑉 𐑄𐐨𐑆 𐑃𐐮𐑍𐑆 𐐲𐑀𐐯𐑌𐑅𐐻 𐐸𐐮𐑋. 𐐈𐑌𐐼 𐑄𐐩𐑉 𐐶𐐱𐑆 𐐶𐐲𐑌 𐐲𐑋𐐲𐑍 𐑄𐐯𐑋 𐐸𐐭𐑆 𐑌𐐩𐑋 𐐶𐐱𐑆 𐐞𐐨𐑆𐑉𐐱𐑋. 𐐤𐐵 𐐸𐐨 𐐺𐐨𐐮𐑍 𐑄 𐑁𐐲𐑉𐑅𐐻 𐐻𐐭 𐐰𐐿𐐷𐐭𐑆 𐐈𐑋𐐷𐐭𐑊𐐯𐐿 𐐰𐑌𐐼 𐐈𐑊𐑋𐐲, 𐐸𐐨 𐐺𐐨𐐮𐑍 𐐶𐐲𐑌 𐐱𐑂 𐑄 𐑋𐐬𐑅𐐻 𐐯𐐿𐑅𐐹𐐲𐑉𐐻 𐐲𐑋𐐲𐑍 𐑄𐐯𐑋, 𐐸𐐰𐑂𐐮𐑍 𐑋𐐲𐐽 𐐺𐐮𐑆𐑌𐐯𐑅 𐐻𐐭 𐐼𐐭 𐐲𐑋𐐲𐑍 𐑄 𐐹𐐨𐐹𐑊. 𐐤𐐵 𐑄 𐐱𐐺𐐾𐐯𐐿𐐻 𐐱𐑂 𐑄𐐨𐑆 𐑊𐐫𐐷𐐲𐑉𐑆 𐐶𐐱𐑆 𐐻𐐭 𐑀𐐯𐐻 𐑀𐐩𐑌: 𐐰𐑌𐐼 𐑄𐐩 𐑀𐐱𐐻 𐑀𐐩𐑌 𐐰𐐿𐐫𐑉𐐼𐐮𐑍 𐐻𐐭 𐑄𐐩𐑉 𐐯𐑋𐐹𐑊𐐫𐐮.

7. 𐐤𐐵 𐐮𐐻 𐐶𐐱𐑆 𐐮𐑌 𐑄 𐑊𐐫 𐐱𐑂 𐐣𐐬𐑆𐐴𐐲 𐑄𐐰𐐻 𐐯𐑂𐐲𐑉𐐨 𐑋𐐰𐑌 𐐸𐐭 𐐶𐐱𐑆 𐐩 𐐾𐐲𐐾 𐐱𐑂 𐑄 𐑊𐐫, 𐐫𐑉 𐑄𐐬𐑆 𐐸𐐭 𐐶𐐲𐑉 𐐰𐐹𐐱𐐮𐑌𐐻𐐯𐐼 𐐻𐐭 𐐺 𐐾𐐲𐐾𐐯𐑆, 𐑇𐐳𐐼 𐑉𐐨𐑅𐐨𐑂 𐐶𐐩𐐾𐐯𐑆 𐐰𐐿𐐫𐑉𐐼𐐮𐑍 𐐻𐐭 𐑄 𐐻𐐴𐑋 𐐸𐐶𐐮𐐽 𐑄𐐩 𐑊𐐩𐐺𐐲𐑉𐐼 𐐻𐐭 𐐾𐐲𐐾 𐑄𐐬𐑆 𐐸𐐭 𐐶𐐲𐑉 𐐺𐑉𐐫𐐻 𐐺𐐨𐑁𐐫𐑉 𐑄𐐯𐑋 𐐻𐐭 𐐺 𐐾𐐲𐐾𐐼.

8. 𐐤𐐵 𐐮𐑁 𐐩 𐑋𐐰𐑌 𐐬𐐼 𐐲𐑌𐐲𐑄𐐲𐑉, 𐐰𐑌𐐼 𐐸𐐨 𐐶𐐳𐐼 𐑌𐐱𐐻 𐐹𐐩 𐑄𐐰𐐻 𐐸𐐶𐐮𐐽 𐐸𐐨 𐐼𐐮𐐼 𐐬, 𐐸𐐨 𐐶𐐱𐑆

𐐿𐐲𐑋𐐹𐑊𐐩𐑌𐐼 𐐱𐑂 𐐻𐐭 𐑄 𐐾𐐲𐐾; 𐐰𐑌𐐼 𐑄 𐐾𐐲𐐾 𐐯𐐿𐑅𐐯𐐿𐐷𐐭𐐻𐐯𐐼 𐐫𐑃𐐱𐑉𐐮𐐻𐐨, 𐐰𐑌𐐼 𐑅𐐯𐑌𐐻 𐑁𐐬𐑉𐑃 𐐱𐑁𐐮𐑅𐐲𐑉𐑆 𐑄𐐰𐐻 𐑄 𐑋𐐰𐑌 𐑇𐐳𐐼 𐐺𐐨 𐐺𐑉𐐫𐐻 𐐺𐐨𐑁𐐬𐑉 𐐸𐐮𐑋; 𐐰𐑌𐐼 𐐸𐐨 𐐾𐐲𐐾𐐼 𐑄 𐑋𐐰𐑌 𐐰𐐿𐐫𐑉𐐼𐐮𐑍 𐐻𐐭 𐑄 𐑊𐐫 𐐰𐑌𐐼 𐑄 𐐯𐑂𐐮𐐼𐐯𐑌𐑅𐐯𐑆 𐐸𐐶𐐮𐐽 𐐶𐐲𐑉 𐐺𐑉𐐫𐐻 𐐰𐑀𐐯𐑌𐑅𐐻 𐐸𐐮𐑋, 𐐰𐑌𐐼 𐑄𐐲𐑅 𐑄 𐑋𐐰𐑌 𐐶𐐱𐑆 𐐿𐐲𐑋𐐹𐐯𐑊𐐼 𐐻𐐭 𐐹𐐩 𐑄𐐰𐐻 𐐸𐐶𐐮𐐽 𐐸𐐨 𐐬𐐼, 𐐫𐑉 𐐺𐐨 𐑅𐐻𐑉𐐮𐐹𐐻, 𐐫𐑉 𐐺𐐨 𐐿𐐰𐑅𐐻 𐐵𐐻 𐑁𐑉𐐱𐑋 𐐲𐑋𐐲𐑍 𐑄 𐐹𐐨𐐹𐑊 𐐰𐑆 𐐲 𐑃𐐨𐑁 𐐰𐑌𐐼 𐐲 𐑉𐐱𐐺𐐲𐑉. 𐐈𐑌𐐼 𐑄 𐐾𐐲𐐾 𐑉𐐨𐑅𐐨𐑂𐐼 𐑁𐐫𐑉 𐐸𐐮𐑆 𐐶𐐩𐐾𐐯𐑆 𐐰𐐿𐐫𐑉𐐼𐐮𐑍 𐐻𐐭 𐐸𐐮𐑆 𐐻𐐴𐑋: 𐐲 𐑅𐐯𐑌𐐴𐑌 𐐱𐑂 𐑀𐐬𐑊𐐼 𐑁𐐫𐑉 𐐲 𐐼𐐩, 𐐫𐑉 𐐲 𐑅𐐯𐑌𐐲𐑋 𐐱𐑂 𐑅𐐮𐑊𐑂𐐲𐑉, 𐐸𐐶𐐮𐐽 𐐮𐑆 𐐨𐐿𐐶𐐲𐑊 𐐻𐐭 𐐲 𐑅𐐯𐑌𐐴𐑌 𐐱𐑂 𐑀𐐬𐑊𐐼; 𐐰𐑌𐐼 𐑄𐐮𐑅 𐐮𐑆 𐐰𐐿𐐫𐑉𐐼𐐮𐑍 𐐻𐐭 𐑄 𐑊𐐫 𐐸𐐶𐐮𐐽 𐐶𐐱𐑆 𐑀𐐮𐑂𐐲𐑌. 𐐤𐐵 𐑄𐐨𐑆 𐐪𐑉 𐑄 𐑌𐐩𐑋𐑆 𐐱𐑂 𐑄 𐐼𐐮𐑁𐐲𐑉𐐯𐑌𐐻 𐐹𐐨𐑅𐐯𐑆 𐐱𐑂 𐑄𐐩𐑉 𐑀𐐬𐑊𐐼, 𐐰𐑌𐐼 𐐱𐑂 𐑄𐐩𐑉 𐑅𐐮𐑊𐑂𐐲𐑉, 𐐰𐐿𐐫𐑉𐐼𐐮𐑍 𐐻𐐭 𐑄𐐩𐑉 𐑂𐐰𐑊𐐷𐐭. 𐐈𐑌𐐼 𐑄 𐑌𐐩𐑋𐑆 𐐪𐑉 𐑀𐐮𐑂𐐲𐑌 𐐺𐐴 𐑄 𐐤𐐨𐑁𐐴𐐻𐑅: 𐑁𐐫𐑉 𐑄𐐩 𐐼𐐮𐐼 𐑌𐐱𐐻 𐑉𐐯𐐿𐐲𐑌 𐐰𐑁𐐻𐐲𐑉 𐑄 𐑋𐐰𐑌𐐲𐑉 𐐱𐑂 𐑄 𐐖𐐭𐑆 𐐸𐐭 𐐶𐐲𐑉 𐐰𐐻 𐐖𐐯𐑉𐐭𐑅𐐲𐑊𐐯𐑋; 𐑌𐐨𐑄𐐲𐑉 𐐼𐐮𐐼 𐑄𐐩 𐑋𐐯𐑈𐐲𐑉 𐐰𐑁𐐻𐐲𐑉 𐑄 𐑋𐐰𐑌𐐲𐑉 𐐱𐑂 𐑄 𐐖𐐭𐑆, 𐐺𐐲𐐻 𐑄𐐩 𐐫𐑊𐐻𐐲𐑉𐐼 𐑄𐐩𐑉 𐑉𐐯𐐿𐐲𐑌𐐮𐑍 𐐰𐑌𐐼 𐑄𐐩𐑉 𐑋𐐯𐑈𐐲𐑉, 𐐰𐐿𐐫𐑉𐐼𐐮𐑍 𐐻𐐭 𐑄 𐑋𐐴𐑌𐐼𐑆 𐐰𐑌𐐼 𐑄 𐑅𐐲𐑉𐐿𐐲𐑋𐑅𐐻𐐰𐑌𐑅𐐯𐑆 𐐱𐑂 𐑄 𐐹𐐨𐐹𐑊, 𐐮𐑌 𐐯𐑂𐐲𐑉𐐨 𐐾𐐯𐑌𐐲𐑉𐐩𐑇𐐲𐑌, 𐐲𐑌𐐻𐐮𐑊 𐑄 𐑉𐐩𐑌 𐐱𐑂 𐑄 𐐾𐐲𐐾𐐯𐑆; 𐑄𐐩 𐐸𐐰𐑂𐐮𐑍 𐐺𐐮𐑌 𐐯𐑅𐐻𐐰𐐺𐑊𐐮𐑇𐐻 𐐺𐐴 𐐿𐐮𐑍 𐐣𐐬𐑆𐐴𐐲. 𐐤𐐵 𐑄 𐑉𐐯𐐿𐐲𐑌𐐮𐑍 𐐮𐑆 𐑄𐐲𐑅: 𐐲 𐑅𐐯𐑌𐐴𐑌 𐐱𐑂 𐑀𐐬𐑊𐐼, 𐐲 𐑅𐐨𐐱𐑌 𐐱𐑂 𐑀𐐬𐑊𐐼, 𐐲 𐑇𐐲𐑋 𐐱𐑂 𐑀𐐬𐑊𐐼, 𐐰𐑌𐐼 𐐲 𐑊𐐮𐑋𐑌𐐪 𐐱𐑂 𐑀𐐬𐑊𐐼. 𐐊 𐑅𐐯𐑌𐐲𐑋 𐐱𐑂 𐑅𐐮𐑊𐑂𐐲𐑉, 𐐰𐑌 𐐰𐑋𐑌𐐫𐑉 𐐱𐑂 𐑅𐐮𐑊𐑂𐐲𐑉, 𐐰𐑌 𐐯𐑆𐑉𐐱𐑋 𐐱𐑂 𐑅𐐮𐑊𐑂𐐲𐑉, 𐐰𐑌𐐼 𐐰𐑌 𐐱𐑌𐐻𐐴 𐐱𐑂 𐑅𐐮𐑊𐑂𐐲𐑉. 𐐊 𐑅𐐯𐑌𐐲𐑋 𐐱𐑂 𐑅𐐮𐑊𐑂𐐲𐑉 𐐶𐐱𐑆 𐐨𐐿𐐶𐐲𐑊 𐐻𐐭 𐐲 𐑅𐐯𐑌𐐴𐑌 𐐱𐑂 𐑀𐐬𐑊𐐼: 𐐰𐑌𐐼 𐐨𐑄𐐲𐑉 𐑁𐐫𐑉 𐐲 𐑋𐐯𐑈𐐲𐑉 𐐱𐑂 𐐺𐐪𐑉𐑊𐐨, 𐐰𐑌𐐼 𐐫𐑊𐑅𐐬 𐑁𐐫𐑉 𐐲 𐑋𐐯𐑈𐐲𐑉 𐐱𐑂 𐐯𐑂𐐲𐑉𐐨 𐐿𐐴𐑌𐐼 𐐱𐑂 𐑀𐑉𐐩𐑌. 𐐤𐐵 𐑄 𐐲𐑋𐐵𐑌𐐻 𐐱𐑂 𐐲 𐑅𐐨𐐱𐑌 𐐱𐑂 𐑀𐐬𐑊𐐼, 𐐶𐐱𐑆 𐐻𐐶𐐴𐑅 𐑄 𐑂𐐰𐑊𐐷𐐭 𐐱𐑂 𐐲 𐑅𐐯𐑌𐐴𐑌; 𐐰𐑌𐐼 𐐲 𐑇𐐲𐑋 𐐱𐑂 𐑀𐐬𐑊𐐼 𐐶𐐱𐑆 𐐻𐐶𐐴𐑅 𐑄 𐑂𐐰𐑊𐐷𐐭 𐐱𐑂 𐐲 𐑅𐐨𐐱𐑌; 𐐰𐑌𐐼 𐐲 𐑊𐐮𐑋𐑌𐐪 𐐱𐑂 𐑀𐐬𐑊𐐼 𐐶𐐱𐑆 𐑄 𐑂𐐰𐑊𐐷𐐭 𐐱𐑂 𐑄𐐯𐑋 𐐫𐑊; 𐐰𐑌𐐼 𐐰𐑌 𐐰𐑋𐑌𐐫𐑉 𐐱𐑂 𐑅𐐮𐑊𐑂𐐲𐑉 𐐶𐐱𐑆 𐐰𐑆 𐑀𐑉𐐩𐐻 𐐰𐑆 𐐻𐐭 𐑅𐐯𐑌𐐲𐑋𐑆; 𐐰𐑌𐐼 𐐰𐑌 𐐯𐑆𐑉𐐱𐑋 𐐱𐑂 𐑅𐐮𐑊𐑂𐐲𐑉 𐐶𐐱𐑆 𐐰𐑆 𐑀𐑉𐐩𐐻 𐐰𐑆 𐑁𐐬𐑉 𐑅𐐯𐑌𐐲𐑋𐑆; 𐐰𐑌𐐼 𐐰𐑌 𐐱𐑌𐐻𐐴 𐐶𐐱𐑆 𐐰𐑆 𐑀𐑉𐐩𐐻 𐐰𐑆 𐑄𐐯𐑋 𐐫𐑊. 𐐤𐐵 𐑄𐐮𐑅 𐐮𐑆 𐑄 𐑂𐐰𐑊𐐷𐐭 𐐱𐑂 𐑄 𐑊𐐯𐑅𐐲𐑉 𐑌𐐲𐑋𐐺𐐲𐑉𐑆 𐐱𐑂 𐑄𐐩𐑉 𐑉𐐯𐐿𐐲𐑌𐐮𐑍: 𐐲 𐑇𐐮𐐺𐑊𐐱𐑌 𐐮𐑆 𐐸𐐪𐑁 𐐱𐑂 𐐲 𐑅𐐯𐑌𐐲𐑋: 𐑄𐐯𐑉𐑁𐐬𐑉, 𐐲 𐑇𐐮𐐺𐑊𐐱𐑌 𐑁𐐫𐑉 𐐸𐐪𐑁 𐐲 𐑋𐐯𐑈𐐲𐑉 𐐱𐑂 𐐺𐐪𐑉𐑊𐐨; 𐐰𐑌𐐼 𐐲 𐑇𐐮𐐺𐑊𐐲𐑋 𐐮𐑆 𐐲 𐐸𐐪𐑁 𐐱𐑂 𐐲 𐑇𐐮𐐺𐑊𐐱𐑌: 𐐰𐑌𐐼 𐐲 𐑊𐐨𐐪 𐐮𐑆 𐑄 𐐸𐐪𐑁 𐐱𐑂 𐐲 𐑇𐐮𐐺𐑊𐐲𐑋. 𐐤𐐵 𐑄𐐮𐑅 𐐮𐑆 𐑄𐐩𐑉 𐑌𐐲𐑋𐐺𐐲𐑉, 𐐰𐐿𐐫𐑉𐐼𐐮𐑍 𐐻𐐭 𐑄𐐩𐑉 𐑉𐐯𐐿𐐲𐑌𐐮𐑍. 𐐤𐐵 𐐰𐑌 𐐰𐑌𐐻𐐨𐐱𐑌 𐐱𐑂 𐑀𐐬𐑊𐐼 𐐮𐑆 𐐨𐐿𐐶𐐲𐑊 𐐻𐐭 𐑃𐑉𐐨 𐑇𐐮𐐺𐑊𐐱𐑌𐑆.

9. 𐐤𐐵, 𐐮𐐻 𐐶𐐱𐑆 𐑁𐐫𐑉 𐑄 𐑅𐐬𐑊 𐐹𐐲𐑉𐐹𐐲𐑅 𐐻𐐭 𐑀𐐯𐐻 𐑀𐐩𐑌, 𐐺𐐨𐐿𐐫𐑆 𐑄𐐩 𐑉𐐨𐑅𐐨𐑂𐐼 𐑄𐐩𐑉 𐐶𐐩𐐾𐐯𐑆 𐐰𐐿𐐫𐑉𐐼𐐮𐑍 𐐻𐐭 𐑄𐐩𐑉 𐐯𐑋𐐹𐑊𐐱𐐶, 𐑄𐐯𐑉𐑁𐐬𐑉 𐑄𐐩 𐐼𐐮𐐼 𐑅𐐻𐐲𐑉 𐐲𐐹 𐑄 𐐹𐐨𐐹𐑊 𐐻𐐭 𐑉𐐴𐐲𐐻𐐮𐑍𐑆, 𐐰𐑌𐐼 𐐫𐑊 𐑋𐐰𐑌𐐲𐑉 𐐱𐑂 𐐼𐐮𐑅𐐻𐐲𐑉𐐺𐐲𐑌𐑅𐐯𐑆 𐐰𐑌𐐼 𐐶𐐮𐐿𐐯𐐼𐑌𐐯𐑅, 𐑄𐐰𐐻 𐑄𐐩 𐑋𐐴𐐻 𐐸𐐰𐑂 𐑋𐐬𐑉 𐐯𐑋𐐹𐑊𐐱𐐶; 𐑄𐐰𐐻 𐑄𐐩 𐑋𐐴𐐻 𐑀𐐯𐐻 𐑋𐐲𐑌𐐨 𐐰𐐿𐐫𐑉𐐼𐐮𐑍 𐐻𐐭 𐑄 𐑅𐐭𐐻𐑅 𐐸𐐶𐐮𐐽 𐐶𐐲𐑉 𐐺𐑉𐐫𐐻 𐐺𐐨𐑁𐐬𐑉 𐑄𐐯𐑋: 𐑄𐐯𐑉𐑁𐐬𐑉 𐑄𐐩 𐐼𐐮𐐼 𐑅𐐻𐐲𐑉 𐐲𐐹 𐑄 𐐹𐐨𐐹𐑊 𐐰𐑀𐐯𐑌𐑅𐐻 𐐈𐑊𐑋𐐰 𐐰𐑌𐐼 𐐈𐑋𐐷𐐭𐑊𐐯𐐿. 𐐈𐑌𐐼 𐑄𐐮𐑅 𐐞𐐨𐐯𐑆𐑉𐐱𐑋 𐐺𐐨𐑀𐐰𐑌 𐐻𐐭 𐐿𐐶𐐯𐑅𐐽𐐲𐑌 𐐈𐑋𐐷𐐭𐑊𐐯𐐿, 𐑅𐐩𐐮𐑍: 𐐎𐐮𐑊 𐐷𐐨 𐐰𐑌𐑅𐐲𐑉 𐑋𐐨 𐐲 𐑁𐐷𐐭 𐐿𐐶𐐯𐑅𐐽𐐲𐑌𐑆 𐐸𐐶𐐮𐐽 𐐌 𐑇𐐰𐑊 𐐰𐑅𐐿 𐐷𐐭? 𐐤𐐵 𐐞𐐨𐐯𐑆𐑉𐐱𐑋 𐐶𐐱𐑆 𐐲 𐑋𐐰𐑌 𐐸𐐭 𐐶𐐱𐑆 𐐯𐐿𐑅𐐹𐐲𐑉𐐻 𐐮𐑌 𐑄 𐐼𐐨𐑂𐐴𐑅𐐯𐑆 𐐱𐑂 𐑄 𐐼𐐯𐑂𐐮𐑊, 𐑄𐐰𐐻 𐐸𐐨 𐑋𐐴𐐻 𐐼𐐯𐑅𐐻𐑉𐐱𐐮 𐑄𐐰𐐻 𐐸𐐶𐐮𐐽 𐐶𐐱𐑆 𐑀𐐳𐐼; 𐑄𐐯𐑉𐑁𐐬𐑉 𐐸𐐨 𐑅𐐯𐐼 𐐲𐑌𐐻𐐭 𐐈𐑋𐐷𐐭𐑊𐐯𐐿, 𐐎𐐮𐑊 𐐷𐐨 𐐰𐑌𐑅𐐲𐑉 𐑄 𐐿𐐶𐐯𐑅𐐽𐐲𐑌𐑆 𐐸𐐶𐐮𐐽 𐐌 𐑇𐐰𐑊 𐐹𐐳𐐻 𐐲𐑌𐐻𐐭 𐐷𐐭? 𐐈𐑌𐐼 𐐈𐑋𐐷𐐭𐑊𐐯𐐿 𐑅𐐯𐐼 𐐲𐑌𐐻𐐭 𐐸𐐮𐑋, 𐐏𐐩, 𐐮𐑁 𐐮𐐻 𐐺𐐨 𐐰𐐿𐐫𐑉𐐼𐐮𐑍 𐐻𐐭 𐑄 𐐝𐐹𐐮𐑉𐐮𐐻 𐐱𐑂 𐑄 𐐢𐐫𐑉𐐼, 𐐸𐐶𐐮𐐽 𐐮𐑆 𐐮𐑌 𐑋𐐨; 𐑁𐐫𐑉 𐐌 𐑇𐐰𐑊 𐑅𐐩 𐑌𐐲𐑃𐐮𐑍 𐐸𐐶𐐮𐐽 𐐮𐑆 𐐿𐐱𐑌𐐻𐑉𐐯𐑉𐐨 𐐻𐐭 𐑄 𐐝𐐹𐐮𐑉𐐮𐐻 𐐱𐑂 𐑄 𐐢𐐫𐑉𐐼. 𐐈𐑌𐐼 𐐞𐐨𐐯𐑆𐑉𐐱𐑋 𐑅𐐯𐐼 𐐲𐑌𐐻𐐭 𐐸𐐮𐑋, 𐐒𐐨𐐸𐐬𐑊𐐼, 𐐸𐐨𐑉 𐐮𐑆 𐑅𐐮𐐿𐑅 𐐱𐑌𐐻𐐴𐑆 𐐱𐑂 𐑅𐐮𐑊𐑂𐐲𐑉, 𐐰𐑌𐐼 𐐫𐑊 𐑄𐐨𐑆 𐐶𐐮𐑊 𐐌 𐑀𐐮𐑂 𐑄𐐨 𐐮𐑁 𐑄𐐵 𐐶𐐮𐑊𐐻 𐐼𐐨𐑌𐐴 𐑄 𐐯𐑀𐑆𐐮𐑅𐐻𐐯𐑌𐑅 𐐱𐑂 𐐲 𐐝𐐭𐐹𐑉𐐨𐑋 𐐒𐐨𐐮𐑍. 𐐤𐐵 𐐈𐑋𐐷𐐭𐑊𐐯𐐿 𐑅𐐯𐐼, 𐐄 𐑄𐐵 𐐽𐐴𐑊𐐼 𐐱𐑂 𐐸𐐯𐑊, 𐐸𐐶𐐴 𐐻𐐯𐑋𐐹𐐻 𐐷𐐨 𐑋𐐨? 𐐤𐐬𐐯𐑅𐐻 𐑄𐐵 𐑄𐐰𐐻 𐑄 𐑉𐐴𐐽𐐲𐑅 𐐷𐐨𐑊𐐼𐐯𐑃 𐐻𐐭 𐑌𐐬 𐑅𐐲𐐽 𐐻𐐯𐑋𐐹𐐻𐐩𐑇𐐲𐑌𐑆? 𐐒𐐨𐑊𐐨𐑂𐐯𐑅𐐻 𐑄𐐵 𐑄𐐰𐐻 𐑄𐐩𐑉 𐐮𐑆 𐑌𐐬 𐐘𐐱𐐼? 𐐌 𐑅𐐩 𐐲𐑌𐐻𐐭 𐐷𐐭, 𐐤𐐩: 𐑄𐐵 𐑌𐐬𐐯𐑅𐐻 𐑄𐐰𐐻 𐑄𐐩𐑉 𐐮𐑆 𐐲 𐐘𐐱𐐼, 𐐺𐐲𐐻 𐑄𐐵 𐑊𐐲𐑂𐐯𐑅𐐻 𐑄𐐰𐐻 𐑊𐐭𐐿𐐲𐑉 𐑋𐐬𐑉 𐑄𐐰𐑌 𐐸𐐮𐑋. 𐐈𐑌𐐼 𐑌𐐵 𐑄𐐵 𐐸𐐰𐑅𐐻 𐑊𐐴𐐼 𐐺𐐨𐑁𐐬𐑉 𐐘𐐱𐐼 𐐲𐑌𐐻𐐭 𐑋𐐨. 𐐜𐐵 𐑅𐐯𐐼𐐯𐑅𐐻 𐐲𐑌𐐻𐐭 𐑋𐐨, 𐐒𐐨𐐸𐐬𐑊𐐼 𐑄𐐨𐑆 𐑅𐐮𐐿𐑅 𐐱𐑌𐐻𐐴𐑆, 𐐸𐐶𐐮𐐽 𐐪𐑉 𐐱𐑂 𐑀𐑉𐐩𐐻 𐐶𐐲𐑉𐑃, 𐐌 𐐶𐐮𐑊 𐑀𐐮𐑂 𐐲𐑌𐐻𐐭 𐑄𐐨, 𐐸𐐶𐐯𐑌 𐑄𐐵 𐐸𐐰𐐼𐐮𐐻

𐐮𐑌 𐑄𐐴 𐐸𐐪𐑉𐐻 𐐻𐐭 𐑉𐐨𐐻𐐩𐑌 𐑄𐐯𐑋 𐑁𐑉𐐱𐑋 𐑋𐐨; 𐐰𐑌𐐼 𐐮𐐻 𐐶𐐱𐑆 𐐬𐑌𐑊𐐨 𐑄𐐴 𐐼𐐨𐑆𐐴𐑉 𐑄𐐰𐐻 𐐴 𐑇𐐳𐐼 𐐼𐐨𐑌𐐴 𐑄 𐐻𐑉𐐭 𐐰𐑌𐐼 𐑊𐐮𐑂𐐮𐑍 𐐘𐐱𐐼, 𐑄𐐰𐐻 𐑄𐐵 𐑋𐐴𐐻𐐯𐑅𐐻 𐐸𐐰𐑂 𐐿𐐫𐑆 𐐻𐐭 𐐼𐐯𐑅𐐻𐑉𐑎 𐑋𐐨. 𐐈𐑌𐐼 𐑌𐐵 𐐺𐐨𐐸𐐬𐑊𐐼, 𐑁𐐫𐑉 𐑄𐐮𐑅 𐑀𐑉𐐩𐐻 𐐨𐑂𐐮𐑊 𐑄𐐵 𐑇𐐰𐑊𐐻 𐐸𐐰𐑂 𐑄𐐴 𐑉𐐨𐐶𐐫𐑉𐐼. 𐐈𐑌𐐼 𐐞𐐨𐑆𐑉𐐱𐑋 𐑅𐐯𐐼 𐐲𐑌𐐻𐐭 𐐸𐐮𐑋, 𐐜𐐵 𐑅𐐩-𐐯𐑅𐐻 𐑄𐐰𐐻 𐑄𐐩𐑉 𐐮𐑆 𐐲 𐐻𐑉𐐭 𐐰𐑌𐐼 𐑊𐐮𐑂𐐮𐑍 𐐘𐐱𐐼? 𐐈𐑌𐐼 𐐈𐑋𐐭𐑊𐐯𐐿 𐑅𐐯𐐼, 𐐏𐐩, 𐑄𐐩𐑉 𐐮𐑆 𐐲 𐐻𐑉𐐭 𐐰𐑌𐐼 𐑊𐐮𐑂𐐮𐑍 𐐘𐐱𐐼. 𐐤𐐵 𐐞𐐨𐑆𐑉𐐱𐑋 𐑅𐐯𐐼, 𐐆𐑆 𐑄𐐩𐑉 𐑋𐐬𐑉 𐑄𐐰𐑌 𐐶𐐲𐑌 𐐘𐐱𐐼? 𐐈𐑌𐐼 𐐸𐐨 𐐰𐑌𐑅𐐲𐑉𐐼, 𐐤𐐬. 𐐤𐐵 𐐞𐐨𐑆𐑉𐐱𐑋 𐑅𐐯𐐼 𐐲𐑌𐐻𐐭 𐐸𐐮𐑋 𐐲𐑀𐐯𐑌, 𐐐𐐵 𐑌𐐬𐐯𐑅𐐻 𐑄𐐵 𐑄𐐨𐑆 𐑃𐐮𐑍𐑆? 𐐈𐑌𐐼 𐐸𐐨 𐑅𐐯𐐼, 𐐈𐑌 𐐩𐑌𐐾𐐯𐑊 𐐸𐐰𐑃 𐑋𐐩𐐼 𐑄𐐯𐑋 𐑌𐐬𐑌 𐐲𐑌𐐻𐐭 𐑋𐐨. 𐐈𐑌𐐼 𐐞𐐨𐑆𐑉𐐱𐑋 𐑅𐐯𐐼 𐐲𐑀𐐯𐑌, 𐐐𐐭 𐐮𐑆 𐐸𐐨 𐑄𐐰𐐻 𐑇𐐰𐑊 𐐿𐐲𐑋? 𐐆𐑆 𐐮𐐻 𐑄 𐐝𐐲𐑌 𐐱𐑂 𐐘𐐱𐐼? 𐐈𐑌𐐼 𐐸𐐨 𐑅𐐯𐐼 𐐲𐑌𐐻𐐭 𐐸𐐮𐑋, 𐐏𐐩. 𐐈𐑌𐐼 𐐞𐐨𐑆𐑉𐐱𐑋 𐑅𐐯𐐼 𐐲𐑀𐐯𐑌, 𐐟𐐰𐑊 𐐸𐐨 𐑅𐐩𐑂 𐐸𐐮𐑆 𐐹𐐨𐐹𐑊 𐐮𐑌 𐑄𐐩𐑉 𐑅𐐮𐑌𐑆? 𐐈𐑌𐐼 𐐈𐑋𐐭𐑊𐐯𐐿 𐐰𐑌𐑅𐐲𐑉𐐼 𐐰𐑌𐐼 𐑅𐐯𐐼 𐐲𐑌𐐻𐐭 𐐸𐐮𐑋, 𐐴 𐑅𐐩 𐐲𐑌𐐻𐐭 𐐷𐐭 𐐸𐐨 𐑇𐐰𐑊 𐑌𐐱𐐻, 𐑁𐐫𐑉 𐐮𐐻 𐐮𐑆 𐐮𐑋𐐹𐐱𐑅𐐮𐐺𐑊 𐑁𐐫𐑉 𐐸𐐮𐑋 𐐻𐐭 𐐼𐐨𐑌𐐴 𐐸𐐮𐑆 𐐶𐐲𐑉𐐼.

10. 𐐤𐐵 𐐞𐐨𐑆𐑉𐐱𐑋 𐑅𐐯𐐼 𐐲𐑌𐐻𐐭 𐑄 𐐹𐐨𐐹𐑊, 𐐝𐐨 𐑄𐐰𐐻 𐐷𐐨 𐑉𐐨𐑋𐐯𐑋𐐺𐐲𐑉 𐑄𐐨𐑆 𐑃𐐮𐑍𐑆; 𐑁𐐫𐑉 𐐸𐐨 𐑅𐐯𐐼 𐑄𐐩𐑉 𐐮𐑆 𐐺𐐲𐐻 𐐶𐐲𐑌 𐐘𐐱𐐼; 𐐷𐐯𐐻 𐐸𐐨 𐑅𐐯𐑃 𐑄𐐰𐐻 𐑄 𐐝𐐲𐑌 𐐱𐑂 𐐘𐐱𐐼 𐑇𐐰𐑊 𐐿𐐲𐑋, 𐐺𐐲𐐻 𐐸𐐨 𐑇𐐰𐑊 𐑌𐐱𐐻 𐑅𐐩𐑂 𐐸𐐮𐑆 𐐹𐐨𐐹𐑊, 𐐰𐑆 𐑄𐐬 𐐸𐐨 𐐸𐐰𐐼 𐐫𐑃𐐱𐑉𐐮𐐻𐐨 𐐻𐐭 𐐿𐐱𐑋𐐰𐑌𐐼 𐐘𐐱𐐼. 𐐤𐐵 𐐈𐑋𐐭𐑊𐐯𐐿 𐑅𐐯𐑃 𐐲𐑀𐐯𐑌 𐐲𐑌𐐻𐐭 𐐸𐐮𐑋, 𐐒𐐨𐐸𐐬𐑊𐐼 𐑄𐐵 𐐸𐐰𐑅𐐻 𐑊𐐴𐐼, 𐑁𐐫𐑉 𐑄𐐵 𐑅𐐩𐐯𐑅𐐻 𐑄𐐰𐐻 𐐴 𐑅𐐹𐐩𐐿 𐐰𐑆 𐑄𐐬 𐐴 𐐸𐐰𐐼 𐐫𐑃𐐱𐑉𐐮𐐻𐐨 𐐻𐐭 𐐿𐐱𐑋𐐰𐑌𐐼 𐐘𐐱𐐼, 𐐺𐐨𐐿𐐫𐑆 𐐴 𐑅𐐯𐐼 𐐸𐐨 𐑇𐐰𐑊 𐑌𐐱𐐻 𐑅𐐩𐑂 𐐸𐐮𐑆 𐐹𐐨𐐹𐑊 𐐮𐑌 𐑄𐐩𐑉 𐑅𐐮𐑌𐑆. 𐐈𐑌𐐼 𐐴 𐑅𐐩 𐐲𐑌𐐻𐐭 𐐷𐐭 𐐲𐑀𐐯𐑌, 𐑄𐐰𐐻 𐐸𐐨 𐐿𐐰𐑌𐐱𐐻 𐑅𐐩𐑂 𐑄𐐯𐑋 𐐮𐑌 𐑄𐐩𐑉 𐑅𐐮𐑌𐑆; 𐑁𐐫𐑉 𐐴 𐐿𐐰𐑌𐐱𐐻 𐐼𐐨𐑌𐐴 𐐸𐐮𐑆 𐐶𐐲𐑉𐐼, 𐐰𐑌𐐼 𐐸𐐨 𐐸𐐰𐑃 𐑅𐐯𐐼 𐑄𐐰𐐻 𐑌𐐬 𐐲𐑌𐐿𐑊𐐨𐑌 𐑃𐐮𐑍 𐐿𐐰𐑌 𐐮𐑌𐐸𐐯𐑉𐐮𐐻 𐑄 𐐿𐐮𐑍𐐼𐐲𐑋 𐐱𐑂 𐐸𐐯𐑂𐐲𐑌; 𐑄𐐩𐑉𐑁𐐬𐑉, 𐐸𐐵 𐐿𐐰𐑌 𐐷𐐨 𐐺𐐨 𐑅𐐩𐑂𐐼, 𐐯𐐿𐑅𐐯𐐹𐐻 𐐷𐐨 𐐮𐑌𐐸𐐯𐑉𐐮𐐻 𐑄 𐐿𐐮𐑍𐐼𐐲𐑋 𐐱𐑂 𐐸𐐯𐑂𐐲𐑌? 𐐜𐐩𐑉𐑁𐐬𐑉, 𐐷𐐨 𐐿𐐰𐑌𐐱𐐻 𐐺𐐨 𐑅𐐩𐑂𐐼 𐐮𐑌 𐐷𐐳𐑉 𐑅𐐮𐑌𐑆. 𐐤𐐵 𐐞𐐨𐑆𐑉𐐱𐑋 𐑅𐐯𐑃 𐐲𐑀𐐯𐑌 𐐲𐑌𐐻𐐭 𐐸𐐮𐑋, 𐐆𐑆 𐑄 𐐝𐐲𐑌 𐐱𐑂 𐐘𐐱𐐼 𐑄 𐑂𐐯𐑉𐐨 𐐀𐐻𐐲𐑉𐑌𐐲𐑊 𐐙𐐪𐑄𐐲𐑉? 𐐈𐑌𐐼 𐐈𐑋𐐭𐑊𐐯𐐿 𐑅𐐯𐐼 𐐲𐑌𐐻𐐭 𐐸𐐮𐑋, 𐐏𐐩, 𐐸𐐨 𐐮𐑆 𐑄 𐑂𐐯𐑉𐐨 𐐀𐐻𐐲𐑉𐑌𐐲𐑊 𐐙𐐪𐑄𐐲𐑉 𐐱𐑂 𐐸𐐯𐑂𐐲𐑌 𐐰𐑌𐐼 𐐱𐑂 𐐲𐑉𐑃, 𐐰𐑌𐐼 𐐫𐑊 𐑃𐐮𐑍𐑆 𐐸𐐶𐐮𐐽 𐐮𐑌 𐑄𐐯𐑋 𐐪𐑉; 𐐸𐐨 𐐮𐑆 𐑄 𐐺𐐨𐑀𐐮𐑌𐐮𐑍 𐐰𐑌𐐼 𐑄 𐐯𐑌𐐼, 𐑄 𐑁𐐲𐑉𐑅𐐻 𐐰𐑌𐐼 𐑄 𐑊𐐰𐑅𐐻; 𐐰𐑌𐐼 𐐸𐐨 𐑇𐐰𐑊 𐐿𐐲𐑋 𐐮𐑌𐐻𐐭 𐑄 𐐶𐐲𐑉𐑊𐐼 𐐻𐐭 𐑉𐐨𐐼𐐨𐑋 𐐸𐐮𐑆 𐐹𐐨𐐹𐑊; 𐐰𐑌𐐼 𐐸𐐨 𐑇𐐰𐑊 𐐻𐐩𐐿 𐐲𐐹𐐱𐑌 𐐸𐐮𐑋 𐑄 𐐻𐑉𐐰𐑌𐑆𐑀𐑉𐐯𐑇𐐲𐑌𐑆 𐐱𐑂 𐑄𐐬𐑆 𐐸𐐭 𐐺𐐨𐑊𐐨𐑂 𐐱𐑌 𐐸𐐮𐑆 𐑌𐐩𐑋; 𐐰𐑌𐐼 𐑄𐐨𐑆 𐐪𐑉 𐑄𐐩 𐑄𐐰𐐻 𐑇𐐰𐑊 𐐸𐐰𐑂 𐐀𐐻𐐲𐑉𐑌𐐲𐑊 𐑊𐐴𐑁, 𐐰𐑌𐐼 𐑅𐐰𐑊𐑂𐐩𐑇𐐲𐑌 𐐿𐐲𐑋𐐯𐑃 𐐻𐐭 𐑌𐐲𐑌 𐐯𐑊𐑅; 𐑄𐐩𐑉𐑁𐐬𐑉 𐑄 𐐶𐐮𐐿𐐯𐐼 𐑉𐐨𐑋𐐩𐑌 𐐰𐑆 𐑄𐐬 𐑄𐐩𐑉 𐐸𐐰𐐼 𐐺𐐮𐑌 𐑌𐐬 𐑉𐐨𐐼𐐯𐑋𐑇𐐲𐑌 𐑋𐐩𐐼, 𐐯𐐿𐑅𐐯𐐹𐐻 𐐮𐐻 𐐺𐐨 𐑄 𐑊𐐭𐑆𐐮𐑍 𐐱𐑂 𐑄 𐐺𐐰𐑌𐐼𐑆 𐐱𐑂 𐐼𐐯𐑃; 𐑁𐐫𐑉 𐐺𐐨𐐸𐐬𐑊𐐼 𐑄 𐐼𐐩 𐐿𐐲𐑋𐐯𐑃 𐑄𐐰𐐻 𐐫𐑊 𐑇𐐰𐑊 𐑉𐐴𐑆 𐑁𐑉𐐱𐑋 𐑄 𐐼𐐯𐐼 𐐰𐑌𐐼 𐑅𐐻𐐰𐑌𐐼 𐐺𐐨𐑁𐐬𐑉 𐐘𐐱𐐼, 𐐰𐑌𐐼 𐐺𐐨 𐐾𐐲𐐾𐐼 𐐰𐐿𐐫𐑉𐐼𐐮𐑍 𐐻𐐭 𐑄𐐩𐑉 𐐶𐐲𐑉𐐿𐑅. 𐐤𐐵, 𐑄𐐩𐑉 𐐮𐑆 𐐲 𐐼𐐯𐑃 𐐸𐐶𐐮𐐽 𐐮𐑆 𐐿𐐫𐑊𐐼 𐐲 𐐻𐐯𐑋𐐹𐐬𐑉𐐲𐑊 𐐼𐐯𐑃: 𐐰𐑌𐐼 𐑄 𐐼𐐯𐑃 𐐱𐑂 𐐗𐑉𐐴𐑅𐐻 𐑇𐐰𐑊 𐑊𐐭𐑆 𐑄 𐐺𐐰𐑌𐐼𐑆 𐐱𐑂 𐑄𐐮𐑅 𐐻𐐯𐑋𐐹𐐬𐑉𐐲𐑊 𐐼𐐯𐑃, 𐑄𐐰𐐻 𐐫𐑊 𐑇𐐰𐑊 𐐺𐐨 𐑉𐐩𐑆𐐼 𐑁𐑉𐐱𐑋 𐑄𐐮𐑅 𐐻𐐯𐑋𐐹𐐬𐑉𐐲𐑊 𐐼𐐯𐑃; 𐑄 𐑅𐐹𐐮𐑉𐐮𐐻 𐐰𐑌𐐼 𐑄 𐐺𐐱𐐼𐐨 𐑇𐐰𐑊 𐐺𐐨 𐑉𐐨-𐐷𐐭𐑌𐐴𐐻𐐯𐐼 𐐲𐑀𐐯𐑌 𐐮𐑌 𐐮𐐻𐑅 𐐹𐐲𐑉𐑁𐐯𐐿𐐻 𐑁𐐫𐑉𐑋; 𐐺𐐬𐑃 𐑊𐐮𐑋 𐐰𐑌𐐼 𐐾𐑎𐑌𐐻 𐑇𐐰𐑊 𐐺𐐨 𐑉𐐨𐑅𐐻𐐬𐑉𐐼 𐐻𐐭 𐐮𐐻𐑅 𐐹𐑉𐐱𐐹𐐲𐑉 𐑁𐑉𐐩𐑋, 𐐨𐑂𐐲𐑌 𐐰𐑆 𐐶𐐨 𐑌𐐵 𐐪𐑉 𐐰𐐻 𐑄𐐮𐑅 𐐻𐐴𐑋; 𐐰𐑌𐐼 𐐶𐐨 𐑇𐐰𐑊 𐐺𐐨 𐐺𐑉𐐫𐐻 𐐻𐐭 𐑅𐐻𐐰𐑌𐐼 𐐺𐐨𐑁𐐬𐑉 𐐘𐐱𐐼, 𐑌𐐬𐐮𐑍 𐐨𐑂𐐲𐑌 𐐰𐑆 𐐶𐐨 𐑌𐐬 𐑌𐐵, 𐐰𐑌𐐼 𐐸𐐰𐑂 𐐲 𐐺𐑉𐐴𐐻 𐑉𐐯𐐿𐐱𐑊𐐯𐐿𐑇𐐲𐑌 𐐱𐑂 𐐫𐑊 𐐵𐑉 𐑀𐐮𐑊𐐻. 𐐤𐐵 𐑄𐐮𐑅 𐑉𐐯𐑅𐐻𐐬𐑉𐐩𐑇𐐲𐑌 𐑇𐐰𐑊 𐐿𐐲𐑋 𐐻𐐭 𐐫𐑊, 𐐺𐐬𐑃 𐐬𐑊𐐼 𐐰𐑌𐐼 𐐷𐐲𐑍, 𐐺𐐬𐑃 𐐺𐐱𐑌𐐼 𐐰𐑌𐐼 𐑁𐑉𐐨, 𐐺𐐬𐑃 𐑋𐐩𐑊 𐐰𐑌𐐼 𐑁𐐨𐑋𐐩𐑊, 𐐺𐐬𐑃 𐑄 𐐶𐐮𐐿𐐯𐐼 𐐰𐑌𐐼 𐑄 𐑉𐐴𐐽𐐲𐑅; 𐐰𐑌𐐼 𐐨𐑂𐐲𐑌 𐑄𐐩𐑉 𐑇𐐰𐑊 𐑌𐐱𐐻 𐑅𐐬 𐑋𐐲𐐽 𐐰𐑆 𐐲 𐐸𐐩𐑉 𐐱𐑂 𐑄𐐩𐑉 𐐸𐐯𐐼𐑆 𐐺𐐨 𐑊𐐱𐑅𐐻; 𐐺𐐲𐐻 𐐫𐑊 𐑃𐐮𐑍𐑆 𐑇𐐰𐑊 𐐺𐐨 𐑉𐐨𐑅𐐻𐐬𐑉𐐼 𐐻𐐭 𐐮𐐻𐑅 𐐹𐐲𐑉𐑁𐐯𐐿𐐻 𐑁𐑉𐐩𐑋, 𐐰𐑆 𐐮𐐻 𐐮𐑆 𐑌𐐵, 𐐫𐑉 𐐮𐑌 𐑄 𐐺𐐱𐐼𐐨, 𐐰𐑌𐐼 𐑇𐐰𐑊 𐐺𐐨 𐐺𐑉𐐫𐐻 𐐰𐑌𐐼 𐐺𐐨 𐐲𐑉𐐩𐑌𐐼 𐐺𐐨𐑁𐐬𐑉 𐑄 𐐺𐐪𐑉 𐐱𐑂 𐐗𐑉𐐴𐑅𐐻 𐑄 𐐝𐐲𐑌, 𐐰𐑌𐐼 𐐘𐐱𐐼 𐑄 𐐙𐐪𐑄𐐲𐑉, 𐐰𐑌𐐼 𐑄 𐐐𐐬𐑊𐐨 𐐝𐐹𐐮𐑉𐐮𐐻, 𐐸𐐶𐐮𐐽 𐐮𐑆 𐐶𐐲𐑌 𐐀𐐻𐐲𐑉𐑌𐐲𐑊 𐐘𐐱𐐼, 𐐻𐐭 𐐺𐐨 𐐾𐐲𐐾𐐼 𐐰𐐿𐐫𐑉𐐼𐐮𐑍 𐐻𐐭 𐑄𐐩𐑉 𐐶𐐲𐑉𐐿𐑅, 𐐸𐐶𐐯𐑄𐐲𐑉 𐑄𐐩 𐐺𐐨 𐑀𐐳𐐼 𐐫𐑉 𐐸𐐶𐐯𐑄𐐲𐑉 𐑄𐐩 𐐺𐐨 𐐨𐑂𐐮𐑊.

11. 𐐤𐐵 𐐺𐐨𐐸𐐬𐑊𐐼, 𐐴 𐐸𐐰𐑂 𐑅𐐹𐐬𐐿𐐲𐑌 𐐲𐑌𐐻𐐭 𐐷𐐭 𐐿𐐱𐑌𐑅𐐲𐑉𐑌𐐮𐑍 𐑄 𐐼𐐯𐑃 𐐱𐑂 𐑄 𐑋𐐫𐑉𐐻𐐲𐑊 𐐺𐐱𐐼𐐨, 𐐰𐑌𐐼 𐐫𐑊𐑅𐐬 𐐿𐐱𐑌𐑅𐐲𐑉𐑌𐐮𐑍 𐑄 𐑉𐐯𐑆𐐲𐑉𐐯𐐿𐑇𐐲𐑌 𐐱𐑂 𐑄 𐑋𐐫𐑉𐐻𐐲𐑊 𐐺𐐱𐐼𐐨. 𐐌 𐑅𐐩 𐐲𐑌𐐻𐐭 𐐷𐐭, 𐑄𐐰𐐻 𐑄𐐮𐑅 𐑋𐐫𐑉𐐻𐐲𐑊 𐐺𐐱𐐼𐐨 𐐮𐑆 𐑉𐐩𐑆𐐼 𐐻𐐭 𐐰𐑌 𐐮𐑋𐐫𐑉𐐻𐐲𐑊 𐐺𐐱𐐼𐐨; 𐑄𐐰𐐻 𐐮𐑆 𐑁𐑉𐐱𐑋 𐐼𐐯𐑃, 𐐨𐑂𐐲𐑌 𐑁𐑉𐐱𐑋 𐑄 𐑁𐐲𐑉𐑅𐐻

𐐼𐐯𐑃 𐐲𐑌𐐻𐐭 𐑊𐐴𐑁, 𐑄𐐰𐐻 𐑄𐐩 𐐿𐐰𐑌 𐐼𐐴 𐑌𐐬 𐑋𐐬𐑉; 𐑄𐐩𐑉 𐑅𐐹𐐮𐑉𐐮𐐻𐑅 𐐷𐐭𐑌𐐴𐐻𐐮𐑍 𐐶𐐮𐑄 𐑄𐐩𐑉 𐐺𐐱𐐼𐐨𐑆, 𐑌𐐯𐑂𐐲𐑉 𐐻𐐭 𐐺𐐨 𐐼𐐨𐑂𐐴𐐼𐐯𐐼; 𐑄𐐲𐑅 𐑄 𐐸𐐬𐑊 𐐺𐐨𐐿𐐲𐑋𐐮𐑍 𐑅𐐹𐐮𐑉𐐮𐐻𐐷𐐭𐐲𐑊 𐐰𐑌𐐼 𐐮𐑋𐐫𐑉𐐻𐐲𐑊, 𐑄𐐰𐐻 𐑄𐐩 𐐿𐐰𐑌 𐑌𐐬 𐑋𐐬𐑉 𐑅𐐨 𐐿𐐲𐑉𐐲𐐹𐑇𐐲𐑌.

12. 𐑌𐐵, 𐐸𐐶𐐯𐑌 𐐰𐑋𐐷𐐭𐑊𐐯𐐿 𐐸𐐰𐐼 𐑁𐐮𐑌𐐮𐑇𐐻 𐑄𐐨𐑆 𐐶𐐲𐑉𐐼𐑆, 𐑄 𐐹𐐨𐐹𐑊 𐐺𐐨𐑀𐐰𐑌 𐐰𐑀𐐯𐑌 𐐻𐐭 𐐺𐐨 𐐰𐑅𐐻𐐱𐑌𐐮𐑇𐐻, 𐐰𐑌𐐼 𐐫𐑊𐑅𐐬 𐑆𐐨𐐯𐑆𐑉𐐲𐑋 𐐺𐐨𐑀𐐰𐑌 𐐻𐐭 𐐻𐑉𐐯𐑋𐐺𐑊. 𐐰𐑌𐐼 𐑄𐐲𐑅 𐐯𐑌𐐼𐐯𐐼 𐑄 𐐶𐐲𐑉𐐼𐑆 𐐱𐑂 𐐰𐑋𐐷𐐭𐑊𐐯𐐿, 𐐫𐑉 𐑄𐐮𐑅 𐐮𐑆 𐐫𐑊 𐑄𐐰𐐻 𐐌 𐐸𐐰𐑂 𐑉𐐮𐐻𐐲𐑌.

𐐕𐐰𐐹𐐻𐐲𐑉 IX.

1. 𐑌𐐵 𐐰𐑊𐑋𐐲, 𐑅𐐨𐐮𐑍 𐑄𐐰𐐻 𐑄 𐐶𐐲𐑉𐐼𐑆 𐐱𐑂 𐐰𐑋𐐷𐐭𐑊𐐯𐐿 𐐸𐐰𐐼 𐑅𐐴𐑊𐐯𐑌𐑅𐐻 𐑆𐐨𐐯𐑆𐑉𐐲𐑋, 𐑁𐐫𐑉 𐐸𐐨 𐐺𐐨𐐸𐐯𐑊𐐼 𐑄𐐰𐐻 𐐰𐑋𐐷𐐭𐑊𐐯𐐿 𐐸𐐰𐐼 𐐿𐐫𐐻 𐐸𐐮𐑋 𐐮𐑌 𐐸𐐮𐑆 𐑊𐐴𐐮𐑍 𐐰𐑌𐐼 𐐼𐐨𐑅𐐨𐑂𐐮𐑍 𐐻𐐭 𐐼𐐯𐑅𐐻𐑉𐐱𐐮 𐐸𐐮𐑋, 𐐰𐑌𐐼 𐑅𐐨𐐮𐑍 𐑄𐐰𐐻 𐐸𐐨 𐐺𐐨𐑀𐐰𐑌 𐐻𐐭 𐐻𐑉𐐯𐑋𐐺𐑊 𐐲𐑌𐐼𐐲𐑉 𐐰 𐐿𐐱𐑌𐑇𐐲𐑅𐑌𐐯𐑅 𐐱𐑂 𐐸𐐮𐑆 𐑀𐐮𐑊𐐻, 𐐸𐐨 𐐬𐐹𐐲𐑌𐐼 𐐸𐐮𐑆 𐑋𐐵𐑃 𐐰𐑌𐐼 𐐺𐐨𐑀𐐰𐑌 𐐻𐐭 𐑅𐐹𐐨𐐿 𐐲𐑌𐐻𐐭 𐐸𐐮𐑋, 𐐰𐑌𐐼 𐐻𐐭 𐐯𐑅𐐻𐐰𐐺𐑊𐐮𐑇 𐑄 𐐶𐐲𐑉𐐼𐑆 𐐱𐑂 𐐰𐑋𐐷𐐭𐑊𐐯𐐿, 𐐰𐑌𐐼 𐐻𐐭 𐐯𐐿𐑅𐐹𐑊𐐩𐑌 𐑃𐐮𐑍𐑆 𐐺𐐨𐐷𐐱𐑌𐐼, 𐐫𐑉 𐐻𐐭 𐐲𐑌𐑁𐐬𐑊𐐼 𐑄 𐐝𐐿𐑉𐐮𐐹𐐽𐐲𐑉𐑆 𐐺𐐨𐐷𐐱𐑌𐐼 𐑄𐐰𐐻 𐐸𐐶𐐮𐐽 𐐰𐑋𐐷𐐭𐑊𐐯𐐿 𐐸𐐰𐐼 𐐼𐐲𐑌. 𐑌𐐵 𐑄 𐐶𐐲𐑉𐐼𐑆 𐑄𐐰𐐻 𐐰𐑊𐑋𐐲 𐑅𐐹𐐩𐐿 𐐲𐑌𐐻𐐭 𐑆𐐨𐐯𐑆𐑉𐐲𐑋, 𐐶𐐲𐑉 𐐸𐐲𐑉𐐼 𐐺𐐴 𐑄 𐐹𐐨𐐹𐑊 𐑉𐐵𐑌𐐼 𐐰𐐺𐐵𐐻; 𐑁𐐫𐑉 𐑄 𐑋𐐲𐑊𐐻𐐮𐐻𐐷𐐭𐐼 𐐶𐐱𐑆 𐑀𐑉𐐩𐐻, 𐐰𐑌𐐼 𐐸𐐨 𐑅𐐹𐐩𐐿 𐐱𐑌 𐑄𐐮𐑅 𐐶𐐴𐑆: 𐑌𐐵 𐐞𐐨𐐯𐑆𐑉𐐲𐑋, 𐑅𐐨𐐮𐑍 𐑄𐐰𐐻 𐑄𐐵 𐐸𐐰𐑅𐐻 𐐺𐐮𐑌 𐐻𐐩𐐿𐐲𐑌 𐐮𐑌 𐑄𐐴 𐑊𐐴𐐮𐑍 𐐰𐑌𐐼 𐐿𐑉𐐰𐑁𐐻𐐮𐑌𐐯𐑅, 𐑁𐐫𐑉 𐑄𐐵 𐐸𐐰𐑅𐐻 𐑌𐐱𐐻 𐑊𐐴𐐼 𐐲𐑌𐐻𐐭 𐑋𐐯𐑌 𐐬𐑌𐑊𐐨, 𐐺𐐲𐐻 𐑄𐐵 𐐸𐐰𐑅𐐻 𐑊𐐴𐐼 𐐲𐑌𐐻𐐭 𐐘𐐱𐐼; 𐑁𐐫𐑉 𐐺𐐨𐐸𐐬𐑊𐐼, 𐐸𐐨 𐑌𐐬𐑆 𐐫𐑊 𐑄𐐴 𐑃𐐫𐐻𐑅, 𐐰𐑌𐐼 𐑄𐐵 𐑅𐐨𐐯𐑅𐐻 𐑄𐐰𐐻 𐑄𐐴 𐑃𐐫𐐻𐑅 𐐪𐑉 𐑋𐐩𐐼 𐑌𐐬𐑌 𐐲𐑌𐐻𐐭 𐐲𐑅 𐐺𐐴 𐐸𐐮𐑆 𐐝𐐹𐐮𐑉𐐮𐐻; 𐐰𐑌𐐼 𐑄𐐵 𐑅𐐨𐐯𐑅𐐻 𐑄𐐰𐐻 𐐶𐐨 𐑌𐐬 𐑄𐐰𐐻 𐑄𐐴 𐐹𐑊𐐰𐑌 𐐶𐐱𐑆 𐐰 𐑂𐐯𐑉𐐨 𐑅𐐲𐐻𐑊 𐐹𐑊𐐰𐑌, 𐐰𐑆 𐐻𐐭 𐑄 𐑅𐐲𐐻𐑊𐐻𐐨 𐐱𐑂 𐑄 𐐼𐐯𐑂𐐮𐑊, 𐑁𐐫𐑉 𐐻𐐭 𐑊𐐴 𐐰𐑌𐐼 𐐻𐐭 𐐼𐐨𐑅𐐨𐑂 𐑄𐐮𐑅 𐐹𐐨𐐹𐑊, 𐑄𐐰𐐻 𐑄𐐵 𐑋𐐴𐐻𐐯𐑅𐐻 𐑅𐐯𐐻 𐑄𐐯𐑋 𐐰𐑀𐐯𐑌𐑅𐐻 𐐲𐑅, 𐐻𐐭 𐑉𐐨𐑂𐐴𐑊 𐐲𐑅 𐐰𐑌𐐼 𐐻𐐭 𐐿𐐰𐑅𐐻 𐐲𐑅 𐐵𐐻. 𐑌𐐵 𐑄𐐮𐑅 𐐶𐐱𐑆 𐐰 𐐹𐑊𐐰𐑌 𐐱𐑂 𐑄𐐴𐑌 𐐰𐐼𐑂𐐲𐑉𐑅𐐯𐑉𐐨, 𐐰𐑌𐐼 𐐸𐐨 𐐸𐐰𐑃 𐐯𐐿𐑅𐐲𐑉𐑅𐐴𐑆𐐼 𐐸𐐮𐑆 𐐹𐐵𐐲𐑉 𐐮𐑌 𐑄𐐨. 𐑌𐐵 𐐌 𐐶𐐳𐐼 𐑄𐐰𐐻 𐐷𐐨 𐑇𐐳𐐼 𐑉𐐨𐑋𐐯𐑋𐐺𐐲𐑉 𐑄𐐰𐐻 𐐸𐐶𐐱𐐻 𐐌 𐑅𐐩 𐐲𐑌𐐻𐐭 𐑄𐐨 𐐌 𐑅𐐩 𐐲𐑌𐐻𐐭 𐐫𐑊. 𐐰𐑌𐐼 𐐺𐐨𐐸𐐬𐑊𐐼 𐐌 𐑅𐐩 𐐲𐑌𐐻𐐭 𐐷𐐭 𐐫𐑊 𐑄𐐰𐐻 𐑄𐐮𐑅 𐐶𐐱𐑆 𐐰 𐑅𐑌𐐩𐑉 𐐱𐑂 𐑄 𐐰𐐼𐑂𐐲𐑉𐑅𐐯𐑉𐐨, 𐐸𐐶𐐮𐐽 𐐸𐐨 𐐸𐐰𐑆 𐑊𐐩𐐼 𐐻𐐭 𐐿𐐰𐐽 𐑄𐐮𐑅 𐐹𐐨𐐹𐑊, 𐑄𐐰𐐻 𐐸𐐨 𐑋𐐴𐐻 𐐺𐑉𐐮𐑍 𐐷𐐭 𐐮𐑌𐐻𐐭 𐑅𐐲𐐺𐐾𐐯𐐿𐑇𐐲𐑌 𐐲𐑌𐐻𐐭 𐐸𐐮𐑋, 𐑄𐐰𐐻 𐐸𐐨 𐑋𐐴𐐻 𐐯𐑌𐑅𐐲𐑉𐐿𐑊 𐐷𐐭 𐐰𐐺𐐵𐐻 𐐶𐐮𐑄 𐐸𐐮𐑆 𐐽𐐩𐑌𐑆, 𐑄𐐰𐐻 𐐸𐐨 𐑋𐐴𐐻 𐐽𐐩𐑌 𐐷𐐭 𐐼𐐵𐑌 𐐻𐐭 𐐯𐑂𐐲𐑉𐑊𐐰𐑅𐐻𐐮𐑍 𐐼𐐯𐑅𐐻𐑉𐐲𐐿𐑇𐐲𐑌, 𐐰𐐿𐐫𐑉𐐼𐐮𐑍 𐐻𐐭 𐑄 𐐹𐐵𐐲𐑉 𐐱𐑂 𐐸𐐮𐑆 𐐿𐐰𐐹𐐻𐐮𐑂𐐮𐐻𐐨.

2. 𐑌𐐵 𐐸𐐶𐐯𐑌 𐐰𐑊𐑋𐐲 𐐸𐐰𐐼 𐑅𐐹𐐬𐐿𐐲𐑌 𐑄𐐨𐑆 𐐶𐐲𐑉𐐼𐑆, 𐐞𐐨𐐯𐑆𐑉𐐲𐑋 𐐺𐐨𐑀𐐰𐑌 𐐻𐐭 𐐻𐑉𐐯𐑋𐐺𐑊 𐑋𐐬𐑉 𐐯𐐿𐑅𐐨𐐼𐐮𐑍𐑊𐐨, 𐑁𐐫𐑉 𐐸𐐨 𐐶𐐱𐑆 𐐿𐐱𐑌𐑂𐐮𐑌𐑅𐐻 𐑋𐐬𐑉 𐐰𐑌𐐼 𐑋𐐬𐑉 𐐱𐑂 𐑄 𐐹𐐵𐐲𐑉 𐐱𐑂 𐐘𐐱𐐼; 𐐰𐑌𐐼 𐐸𐐨 𐐶𐐱𐑆 𐐫𐑊𐑅𐐬 𐐿𐐱𐑌𐑂𐐮𐑌𐑅𐐻 𐑄𐐰𐐻 𐐰𐑊𐑋𐐲 𐐰𐑌𐐼 𐐰𐑋𐐷𐐭𐑊𐐯𐐿 𐐸𐐰𐐼 𐐰 𐑌𐐱𐑊𐐯𐐾 𐐱𐑂 𐐸𐐮𐑋, 𐑁𐐫𐑉 𐐸𐐨 𐐶𐐱𐑆 𐐿𐐱𐑌𐑂𐐮𐑌𐑅𐐻 𐑄𐐰𐐻 𐑄𐐩 𐑌𐐷𐐭 𐑄 𐑃𐐫𐐻𐑅 𐐰𐑌𐐼 𐐮𐑌𐐻𐐯𐑌𐐻𐑅 𐐱𐑂 𐐸𐐮𐑆 𐐸𐐪𐑉𐐻; 𐑁𐐫𐑉 𐐹𐐵𐐲𐑉 𐐶𐐱𐑆 𐑀𐐮𐑂𐐲𐑌 𐐲𐑌𐐻𐐭 𐑄𐐯𐑋 𐑄𐐰𐐻 𐑄𐐩 𐑋𐐴𐐻 𐑌𐐬 𐐱𐑂 𐑄𐐨𐑆 𐑃𐐮𐑍𐑆 𐐰𐐿𐐫𐑉𐐼𐐮𐑍 𐐻𐐭 𐑄 𐑅𐐹𐐮𐑉𐐮𐐻 𐐱𐑂 𐐹𐑉𐐱𐑁𐐯𐑅𐐨. 𐐰𐑌𐐼 𐐞𐐨𐐯𐑆𐑉𐐲𐑋 𐐺𐐨𐑀𐐰𐑌 𐐻𐐭 𐐮𐑌𐐿𐐶𐐴𐑉 𐐱𐑂 𐑄𐐯𐑋 𐐼𐐮𐑊𐐮𐐾𐐯𐑌𐐻𐑊𐐨, 𐑄𐐰𐐻 𐐸𐐨 𐑋𐐴𐐻 𐑌𐐬 𐑋𐐬𐑉 𐐿𐐱𐑌𐑅𐐲𐑉𐑌𐐮𐑍 𐑄 𐐿𐐮𐑍𐐼𐐲𐑋 𐐱𐑂 𐐘𐐱𐐼. 𐐰𐑌𐐼 𐐸𐐨 𐑅𐐯𐐼 𐐲𐑌𐐻𐐭 𐐰𐑊𐑋𐐲, 𐐸𐐶𐐱𐐻 𐐼𐐲𐑆 𐑄𐐮𐑅 𐑋𐐨𐑌 𐐸𐐶𐐮𐐽 𐐰𐑋𐐷𐐭𐑊𐐯𐐿 𐐸𐐰𐑃 𐑅𐐹𐐬𐐿𐐲𐑌 𐐿𐐱𐑌𐑅𐐲𐑉𐑌𐐮𐑍 𐑄 𐑉𐐯𐑆𐐲𐑉𐐯𐐿𐑇𐐲𐑌 𐐱𐑂 𐑄 𐐼𐐯𐐼, 𐑄𐐰𐐻 𐐫𐑊 𐑇𐐰𐑊 𐑉𐐴𐑆 𐑁𐑉𐐱𐑋 𐑄 𐐼𐐯𐐼, 𐐺𐐬𐑃 𐑄 𐐾𐐲𐑅𐐻 𐐰𐑌𐐼 𐑄 𐐲𐑌𐐾𐐲𐑅𐐻, 𐐰𐑌𐐼 𐐪𐑉 𐐺𐑉𐐫𐐻 𐐻𐐭 𐑅𐐻𐐰𐑌𐐼 𐐺𐐨𐑁𐐬𐑉 𐐘𐐱𐐼 𐐻𐐭 𐐺𐐨 𐐾𐐲𐐾𐐼 𐐰𐐿𐐫𐑉𐐼𐐮𐑍 𐐻𐐭 𐑄𐐩𐑉 𐐶𐐲𐑉𐐿𐑅? 𐐰𐑌𐐼 𐑌𐐵 𐐰𐑊𐑋𐐲 𐐺𐐨𐑀𐐰𐑌 𐐻𐐭 𐐯𐐿𐑅𐐹𐐵𐑌𐐼 𐑄𐐨𐑆 𐑃𐐮𐑍𐑆 𐐲𐑌𐐻𐐭 𐐸𐐮𐑋, 𐑅𐐩𐐮𐑍, 𐐮𐐻 𐐮𐑆 𐑀𐐮𐑂𐐲𐑌 𐐲𐑌𐐻𐐭 𐑋𐐯𐑌𐐨 𐐻𐐭 𐑌𐐬 𐑄 𐑋𐐮𐑅𐐻𐐲𐑉𐐨𐑆 𐐱𐑂 𐐘𐐱𐐼; 𐑌𐐯𐑂𐐲𐑉𐑄𐐲𐑊𐐯𐑅 𐑄𐐩 𐐪𐑉 𐑊𐐩𐐼 𐐲𐑌𐐼𐐲𐑉 𐐰 𐑅𐐻𐑉𐐮𐐿𐐻 𐐿𐐱𐑋𐐰𐑌𐐼 𐑄𐐰𐐻 𐑄𐐩 𐑇𐐰𐑊 𐑌𐐱𐐻 𐐮𐑋𐐹𐐪𐑉𐐻 𐐬𐑌𐑊𐐨 𐐰𐐿𐐫𐑉𐐼𐐮𐑍 𐐻𐐭 𐑄 𐐹𐐬𐑉𐑇𐐲𐑌 𐐱𐑂 𐐸𐐮𐑆 𐐶𐐲𐑉𐐼 𐐸𐐶𐐮𐐽 𐐸𐐨 𐐼𐐲𐑃 𐑀𐑉𐐰𐑌𐐻 𐐲𐑌𐐻𐐭 𐑄 𐐽𐐮𐑊𐐼𐑉𐐯𐑌 𐐱𐑂 𐑋𐐯𐑌, 𐐰𐐿𐐫𐑉𐐼𐐮𐑍 𐐻𐐭 𐑄 𐐸𐐨𐐼 𐐰𐑌𐐼 𐐼𐐮𐑊𐐮𐐾𐐯𐑌𐑅 𐐸𐐶𐐮𐐽 𐑄𐐩 𐑀𐐮𐑂 𐐲𐑌𐐻𐐭 𐐸𐐮𐑋;

𐐰𐑌𐐼 𐑄𐐩𐑉𐑁𐐬𐑉 𐐸𐐨 𐑄𐐰𐐻 𐐶𐐮𐑊 𐐸𐐪𐑉𐐼𐑌 𐐸𐐮𐑆 𐐸𐐪𐑉𐐻, 𐑄 𐑅𐐩𐑋 𐑉𐐨𐑅𐐨𐑂𐐯𐑃 𐑄 𐑊𐐯𐑅𐐲𐑉 𐐹𐐬𐑉𐑇𐐲𐑌 𐐱𐑂 𐑄 𐐶𐐲𐑉𐐼; 𐐰𐑌𐐼 𐐸𐐨 𐑄𐐰𐐻 𐐶𐐮𐑊 𐑌𐐱𐐻 𐐸𐐪𐑉𐐼𐑌 𐐸𐐮𐑆 𐐸𐐪𐑉𐐻, 𐐻𐐭 𐐸𐐮𐑋 𐐮𐑆 𐑀𐐮𐑂𐑌 𐑄 𐑀𐑉𐐩𐐻𐐲𐑉 𐐹𐐬𐑉𐑇𐐲𐑌 𐐱𐑂 𐑄 𐐶𐐲𐑉𐐼, 𐐲𐑌𐐻𐐮𐑊 𐐮𐐻 𐐮𐑆 𐑀𐐮𐑂𐑌 𐐲𐑌𐐻𐐭 𐐸𐐮𐑋 𐐻𐐭 𐑌𐐬 𐑄 𐑋𐐮𐑅𐐻𐐲𐑉𐐨𐑆 𐐱𐑂 𐐘𐐱𐐼, 𐐲𐑌𐐻𐐮𐑊 𐑄𐐩 𐑌𐐬 𐑄𐐯𐑋 𐐮𐑌 𐑁𐐳𐑊; 𐐰𐑌𐐼 𐑄𐐩 𐑄𐐰𐐻 𐐶𐐮𐑊 𐐸𐐪𐑉𐐼𐑌 𐑄𐐩𐑉 𐐸𐐪𐑉𐐻𐑅, 𐐻𐐭 𐑄𐐯𐑋 𐐮𐑆 𐑀𐐮𐑂𐑌 𐑄 𐑊𐐯𐑅𐐲𐑉 𐐹𐐬𐑉𐑇𐐲𐑌 𐐱𐑂 𐑄 𐐶𐐲𐑉𐐼, 𐐲𐑌𐐻𐐮𐑊 𐑄𐐩 𐑌𐐬 𐑌𐐲𐑃𐐮𐑍 𐐿𐐲𐑌𐑅𐐲𐑉𐑌𐐮𐑍 𐐸𐐮𐑆 𐑋𐐮𐑅𐐻𐐲𐑉𐐨𐑆; 𐐰𐑌𐐼 𐑄𐐯𐑌 𐑄𐐩 𐐪𐑉 𐐻𐐩𐐿𐑌 𐐿𐐰𐐹𐐻𐐮𐑂 𐐺𐐴 𐑄 𐐼𐐯𐑂𐑊, 𐐰𐑌𐐼 𐑊𐐯𐐼 𐐺𐐴 𐐸𐐮𐑆 𐐶𐐮𐑊 𐐼𐐵𐑌 𐐻𐐭 𐐼𐐨𐑅𐐻𐑉𐐲𐐿𐑇𐐲𐑌. 𐐤𐐵 𐑄𐐮𐑅 𐐮𐑆 𐐸𐐶𐐱𐐻 𐐮𐑆 𐑋𐐯𐑌𐐻 𐐺𐐴 𐑄 𐐽𐐩𐑌𐑆 𐐱𐑂 𐐸𐐯𐑊; 𐐰𐑌𐐼 𐐈𐑋𐐷𐐭𐑊𐐯𐐿 𐐸𐐰𐑃 𐑅𐐹𐐬𐐿𐑌 𐐹𐑊𐐩𐑌𐑊𐐨 𐐿𐐲𐑌𐑅𐐲𐑉𐑌𐐮𐑍 𐐼𐐯𐑃, 𐐰𐑌𐐼 𐐺𐐨𐐮𐑍 𐑉𐐩𐑆𐐼 𐑁𐑉𐐱𐑋 𐑄𐐮𐑅 𐑋𐐫𐑉𐐻𐐰𐑊𐐮𐐻𐐨 𐐻𐐭 𐐲 𐑅𐐻𐐩𐐻 𐐱𐑂 𐐮𐑋𐐫𐑉𐐻𐐰𐑊𐐮𐐻𐐨, 𐐰𐑌𐐼 𐐺𐐨𐐮𐑍 𐐺𐑉𐐫𐐻 𐐺𐐨𐑁𐐬𐑉 𐑄 𐐺𐐪𐑉 𐐱𐑂 𐐘𐐱𐐼, 𐐻𐐭 𐐺 𐐾𐐲𐐾𐐼 𐐰𐐿𐐫𐑉𐐼𐐮𐑍 𐐻𐐭 𐐵𐑉 𐐶𐐲𐑉𐐿𐑅. 𐐜𐐯𐑌 𐐮𐑁 𐐵𐑉 𐐸𐐪𐑉𐐻𐑅 𐐸𐐰𐑂 𐐺𐐮𐑌 𐐸𐐪𐑉𐐼𐑌𐐼, 𐐷𐐩, 𐐮𐑁 𐐶𐐨 𐐸𐐰𐑂 𐐸𐐪𐑉𐐼𐑌𐐼 𐐵𐑉 𐐸𐐪𐑉𐐻𐑅 𐐲𐑀𐐯𐑌𐑅𐐻 𐑄 𐐶𐐲𐑉𐐼, 𐐮𐑌𐑅𐐬𐑋𐐲𐐽 𐑄𐐰𐐻 𐐮𐐻 𐐸𐐰𐑆 𐑌𐐱𐐻 𐐺𐐮𐑌 𐑁𐐵𐑌𐐼 𐐮𐑌 𐐲𐑅, 𐑄𐐯𐑌 𐐶𐐮𐑊 𐐵𐑉 𐑅𐐻𐐩𐐻 𐐺 𐐫𐑁𐐳𐑊, 𐑁𐐫𐑉 𐑄𐐯𐑌 𐐶𐐨 𐑇𐐰𐑊 𐐺 𐐿𐐲𐑌𐐼𐐯𐑋𐐼; 𐑁𐐫𐑉 𐐵𐑉 𐐶𐐲𐑉𐐼𐑆 𐐶𐐮𐑊 𐐿𐐲𐑌𐐼𐐯𐑋 𐐲𐑅, 𐐷𐐩, 𐐫𐑊 𐐵𐑉 𐐶𐐲𐑉𐐿𐑅 𐐶𐐮𐑊 𐐿𐐲𐑌𐐼𐐯𐑋 𐐲𐑅; 𐐶𐐨 𐑇𐐰𐑊 𐑌𐐱𐐻 𐐺 𐑁𐐵𐑌𐐼 𐑅𐐹𐐱𐐻𐑊𐐯𐑅; 𐐰𐑌𐐼 𐐵𐑉 𐑃𐐫𐐻𐑅 𐐶𐐮𐑊 𐐫𐑊𐑅𐐬 𐐿𐐲𐑌𐐼𐐯𐑋 𐐲𐑅; 𐐰𐑌𐐼 𐐮𐑌 𐑄𐐮𐑅 𐐫𐑁𐐳𐑊 𐑅𐐻𐐩𐐻 𐐶𐐨 𐑇𐐰𐑊 𐑌𐐱𐐻 𐐼𐐩𐑉 𐐻𐐭 𐑊𐐳𐐿 𐐲𐐹 𐐻𐐭 𐐵𐑉 𐐘𐐱𐐼; 𐐰𐑌𐐼 𐐶𐐨 𐐶𐐳𐐼 𐑁𐐩𐑌 𐐺 𐑀𐑊𐐰𐐼 𐐮𐑁 𐐶𐐨 𐐿𐐳𐐼 𐐿𐐲𐑋𐐰𐑌𐐼 𐑄 𐑉𐐱𐐿𐑅 𐐰𐑌𐐼 𐑄 𐑋𐐵𐑌𐐻𐐮𐑌𐑆 𐐻𐐭 𐑁𐐫𐑊 𐐲𐐹𐐱𐑌 𐐲𐑅, 𐐻𐐭 𐐸𐐴𐐼 𐐲𐑅 𐑁𐑉𐐱𐑋 𐐸𐐮𐑆 𐐹𐑉𐐯𐑆𐐯𐑌𐑅. 𐐒𐐲𐐻 𐑄𐐮𐑅 𐐿𐐰𐑌𐐱𐐻 𐐺; 𐐶𐐨 𐑋𐐲𐑅𐐻 𐐿𐐲𐑋 𐑁𐐬𐑉𐑃 𐐰𐑌𐐼 𐑅𐐻𐐰𐑌𐐼 𐐺𐐨𐑁𐐬𐑉 𐐸𐐮𐑋 𐐮𐑌 𐐸𐐮𐑆 𐑀𐑊𐐬𐑉𐐨, 𐐰𐑌𐐼 𐐮𐑌 𐐸𐐮𐑆 𐐹𐐵𐐲𐑉, 𐐰𐑌𐐼 𐐮𐑌 𐐸𐐮𐑆 𐑋𐐴𐐻, 𐑋𐐰𐐾𐐯𐑅𐐻𐐨, 𐐰𐑌𐐼 𐐼𐐱𐑋𐐮𐑌𐐷𐐲𐑌, 𐐰𐑌𐐼 𐐰𐐿𐑌𐐱𐑊𐐯𐐾 𐐻𐐭 𐐵𐑉 𐐯𐑂𐐲𐑉𐑊𐐰𐑅𐐻𐐮𐑍 𐑇𐐩𐑋, 𐑄𐐰𐐻 𐐫𐑊 𐐸𐐮𐑆 𐐾𐐲𐐾𐑋𐐯𐑌𐐻𐑅 𐐪𐑉 𐐾𐐲𐑅𐐻; 𐑄𐐰𐐻 𐐸𐐨 𐐮𐑆 𐐾𐐲𐑅𐐻 𐐮𐑌 𐐫𐑊 𐐸𐐮𐑆 𐐶𐐲𐑉𐐿𐑅, 𐐰𐑌𐐼 𐑄𐐰𐐻 𐐸𐐨 𐐮𐑆 𐑋𐐲𐑉𐑅𐐮𐑁𐐳𐑊 𐐲𐑌𐐻𐐭 𐑄 𐐽𐐮𐑊𐐼𐑉𐐯𐑌 𐐱𐑂 𐑋𐐯𐑌, 𐐰𐑌𐐼 𐑄𐐰𐐻 𐐸𐐨 𐐸𐐰𐑆 𐐫𐑊 𐐹𐐵𐐲𐑉 𐐻𐐭 𐑅𐐩𐑂 𐐯𐑂𐑉𐐨 𐑋𐐰𐑌 𐑄𐐰𐐻 𐐺𐐨𐑊𐐨𐑂𐐯𐑃 𐐱𐑌 𐐸𐐮𐑆 𐑌𐐩𐑋, 𐐰𐑌𐐼 𐐺𐑉𐐮𐑍𐐯𐑃 𐑁𐐬𐑉𐑃 𐑁𐑉𐐭𐐻 𐑋𐐨𐐻 𐑁𐐫𐑉 𐑉𐐨𐐹𐐯𐑌𐐻𐐲𐑌𐑅.

3. 𐐰𐑌𐐼 𐑌𐐵 𐐺𐐨𐐸𐐬𐑊𐐼 𐐌 𐑅𐐩 𐐲𐑌𐐻𐐭 𐐷𐐭, 𐑄𐐯𐑌 𐐿𐐲𐑋𐐯𐑃 𐐲 𐐼𐐯𐑃, 𐐨𐑂𐐯𐑌 𐐲 𐑅𐐯𐐿𐐲𐑌𐐼 𐐼𐐯𐑃, 𐐸𐐶𐐮𐐽 𐐮𐑆 𐐲 𐑅𐐹𐐮𐑉𐐮𐐻𐐷𐐭𐐲𐑊 𐐼𐐯𐑃; 𐑄𐐯𐑌 𐐮𐑆 𐐲 𐐻𐐴𐑋 𐑄𐐰𐐻 𐐸𐐭𐑅𐐬𐐯𐑂𐐲𐑉 𐐼𐐴𐐯𐑃 𐐮𐑌 𐐸𐐮𐑆 𐑅𐐮𐑌𐑆, 𐐰𐑆 𐐻𐐭 𐐲 𐐻𐐯𐑋𐐹𐐬𐑉𐐲𐑊 𐐼𐐯𐑃, 𐑇𐐰𐑊 𐐫𐑊𐑅𐐬 𐐼𐐴 𐐲 𐑅𐐹𐐮𐑉𐐮𐐻𐐷𐐭𐐲𐑊 𐐼𐐯𐑃; 𐐷𐐩, 𐐸𐐨 𐑇𐐰𐑊 𐐼𐐴 𐐰𐑆 𐐻𐐭 𐑃𐐮𐑍𐑆 𐐹𐐲𐑉𐐻𐐩𐑌𐐮𐑍 𐐲𐑌𐐻𐐭 𐑉𐐴𐐽𐐲𐑅𐑌𐐯𐑅; 𐑄𐐯𐑌 𐐮𐑆 𐑄 𐐻𐐴𐑋 𐐸𐐶𐐯𐑌 𐑄𐐩𐑉 𐐻𐐫𐑉𐑋𐐯𐑌𐐻𐑅 𐑇𐐰𐑊 𐐺 𐐰𐑆 𐐲 𐑊𐐩𐐿 𐐱𐑂 𐑁𐐴𐑉 𐐰𐑌𐐼 𐐺𐑉𐐮𐑋𐑅𐐻𐐬𐑌, 𐐸𐐭𐑆 𐑁𐑊𐐩𐑋 𐐰𐑅𐐯𐑌𐐼𐐯𐑃 𐐲𐐹 𐑁𐐫𐑉 𐐯𐑂𐐲𐑉 𐐰𐑌𐐼 𐐯𐑂𐐲𐑉; 𐐰𐑌𐐼 𐑄𐐯𐑌 𐐮𐑆 𐑄 𐐻𐐴𐑋 𐑄𐐰𐐻 𐑄𐐩 𐑇𐐰𐑊 𐐺 𐐽𐐩𐑌𐐼 𐐼𐐵𐑌 𐐻𐐭 𐐰𐑌 𐐯𐑂𐐲𐑉𐑊𐐰𐑅𐐻𐐮𐑍 𐐼𐐨𐑅𐐻𐑉𐐲𐐿𐑇𐐲𐑌, 𐐰𐐿𐐫𐑉𐐼𐐮𐑍 𐐻𐐭 𐑄 𐐹𐐵𐐲𐑉 𐐰𐑌𐐼 𐐿𐐰𐐹𐐻𐐮𐑂𐐮𐐻𐐨 𐐱𐑂 𐐝𐐩𐐻𐐲𐑌; 𐐸𐐨 𐐸𐐰𐑂𐐮𐑍 𐑅𐐲𐐺𐐾𐐯𐐿𐐻𐐯𐐼 𐑄𐐯𐑋 𐐰𐐿𐐫𐑉𐐼𐐮𐑍 𐐻𐐭 𐐸𐐮𐑆 𐐶𐐮𐑊. 𐐜𐐯𐑌 𐐌 𐑅𐐩 𐐲𐑌𐐻𐐭 𐐷𐐭, 𐑄𐐩 𐑇𐐰𐑊 𐐺 𐐰𐑆 𐑄𐐬 𐑄𐐩𐑉 𐐸𐐰𐐼 𐐺𐐮𐑌 𐑌𐐬 𐑉𐐨𐐼𐐯𐑋𐑇𐐲𐑌 𐑋𐐩𐐼; 𐑁𐐫𐑉 𐑄𐐩 𐐿𐐰𐑌𐐱𐐻 𐐺 𐑉𐐨𐐼𐐨𐑋𐐼 𐐰𐐿𐐫𐑉𐐼𐐮𐑍 𐐻𐐭 𐐘𐐱𐐼'𐑆 𐐾𐐲𐑅𐐻𐐮𐑅; 𐐰𐑌𐐼 𐑄𐐩 𐐿𐐰𐑌𐐱𐐻 𐐼𐐴, 𐑅𐐨𐐮𐑍 𐑄𐐩𐑉 𐐮𐑆 𐑌𐐬 𐑋𐐬𐑉 𐐿𐐫𐑉𐐲𐐹𐑇𐐲𐑌.

4. 𐐤𐐵 𐐮𐐻 𐐿𐐩𐑋 𐐻𐐭 𐐹𐐰𐑅 𐑄𐐰𐐻 𐐸𐐶𐐯𐑌 𐐈𐑊𐑋𐐲 𐐸𐐰𐐼 𐑋𐐩𐐼 𐐰𐑌 𐐯𐑌𐐼 𐐱𐑂 𐑅𐐹𐐨𐐿𐐮𐑍 𐑄𐐨𐑆 𐐶𐐲𐑉𐐼𐑆, 𐑄 𐐹𐐨𐐹𐑊 𐐺𐐨𐑀𐐰𐑌 𐐻𐐭 𐐺 𐑋𐐬𐑉 𐐰𐑅𐐻𐐱𐑌𐐮𐑇𐐻; 𐐒𐐲𐐻 𐑄𐐩𐑉 𐐶𐐱𐑆 𐐶𐐲𐑌 𐐈𐑌𐐻𐐨𐐬𐑌𐐲, 𐐸𐐭 𐐶𐐱𐑆 𐐲 𐐽𐐨𐑁 𐑉𐐭𐑊𐐲𐑉 𐐲𐑋𐐲𐑍 𐑄𐐯𐑋, 𐐿𐐩𐑋 𐑁𐐬𐑉𐑃 𐐰𐑌𐐼 𐑅𐐯𐐼 𐐲𐑌𐐻𐐭 𐐸𐐮𐑋, 𐐐𐐶𐐱𐐻 𐐮𐑆 𐑄𐐮𐑅 𐑄𐐰𐐻 𐑄𐐵 𐐸𐐰𐑅𐐻 𐑅𐐯𐐼, 𐑄𐐰𐐻 𐑋𐐰𐑌 𐑇𐐳𐐼 𐑉𐐴𐑆 𐑁𐑉𐐱𐑋 𐑄 𐐼𐐯𐐼 𐐰𐑌𐐼 𐐺 𐐽𐐩𐑌𐐾𐐼 𐑁𐑉𐐱𐑋 𐑄𐐮𐑅 𐑋𐐫𐑉𐐻𐐰𐑊 𐐻𐐭 𐐰𐑌 𐐮𐑋𐐫𐑉𐐻𐐰𐑊 𐑅𐐻𐐩𐐻, 𐑄𐐰𐐻 𐑄 𐑅𐐬𐑊 𐐿𐐰𐑌 𐑌𐐯𐑂𐐲𐑉 𐐼𐐴? 𐐐𐐶𐐱𐐻 𐐼𐐲𐑆 𐑄 𐐝𐐿𐑉𐐮𐐹𐐽𐐲𐑉 𐑋𐐨𐑌, 𐐸𐐶𐐮𐐽 𐑅𐐯𐑃 𐑄𐐰𐐻 𐐘𐐱𐐼 𐐹𐑊𐐩𐑅𐐻 𐐽𐐯𐑉𐐲𐐺𐐮𐑋𐑆 𐐰𐑌𐐼 𐐲 𐑁𐑊𐐩𐑋𐐮𐑍 𐑅𐐬𐑉𐐼 𐐱𐑌 𐑄 𐐨𐑅𐐻 𐐱𐑂 𐑄 𐑀𐐪𐑉𐐼𐑌 𐐱𐑂 𐐀𐐼𐐯𐑌, 𐑊𐐯𐑅𐐻 𐐵𐑉 𐑁𐐲𐑉𐑅𐐻 𐐹𐐩𐑉𐐯𐑌𐐻𐑅 𐑇𐐳𐐼 𐐯𐑌𐐻𐐲𐑉 𐐰𐑌𐐼 𐐹𐐪𐑉𐐻𐐩𐐿 𐐱𐑂 𐑄 𐑁𐑉𐐭𐐻 𐐱𐑂 𐑄 𐐻𐑉𐐨 𐐱𐑂 𐑊𐐴𐑁, 𐐰𐑌𐐼 𐑊𐐮𐑂 𐑁𐐫𐑉 𐐯𐑂𐐲𐑉? 𐐰𐑌𐐼 𐑄𐐲𐑅 𐐶𐐨 𐑅𐐨 𐑄𐐰𐐻 𐑄𐐩𐑉 𐐶𐐱𐑆 𐑌𐐬 𐐹𐐱𐑅𐐮𐐺𐑊 𐐽𐐰𐑌𐑅 𐑄𐐰𐐻 𐑄𐐩 𐑇𐐳𐐼 𐑊𐐮𐑂 𐑁𐐫𐑉 𐐯𐑂𐐲𐑉. 𐐤𐐵 𐐈𐑊𐑋𐐲 𐑅𐐯𐐼 𐐲𐑌𐐻𐐭 𐐸𐐮𐑋, 𐐜𐐮𐑅 𐐮𐑆 𐑄 𐑃𐐮𐑍 𐐸𐐶𐐮𐐽 𐐌 𐐶𐐱𐑆 𐐲𐐺𐐵𐐻 𐐻𐐭 𐐯𐐿𐑅𐐹𐑊𐐩𐑌. 𐐤𐐵 𐐶𐐨 𐑅𐐨 𐑄𐐰𐐻 𐐈𐐼𐐲𐑋 𐐼𐐮𐐼 𐑁𐐫𐑊 𐐺𐐴 𐑄 𐐹𐐪𐑉𐐻𐐩𐐿𐐮𐑍 𐐱𐑂 𐑄 𐑁𐐫𐑉𐐺𐐮𐐼𐑌 𐑁𐑉𐐭𐐻, 𐐰𐐿𐐫𐑉𐐼𐐮𐑍 𐐻𐐭 𐑄 𐐶𐐲𐑉𐐼 𐐱𐑂 𐐘𐐱𐐼; 𐐰𐑌𐐼 𐑄𐐲𐑅 𐐶𐐨 𐑅𐐨, 𐑄𐐰𐐻 𐐺𐐴 𐐸𐐮𐑆 𐑁𐐫𐑊, 𐐫𐑊 𐑋𐐰𐑌𐐿𐐴𐑌𐐼 𐐺𐐨𐐿𐐩𐑋 𐐲 𐑊𐐱𐑅𐐻 𐐰𐑌𐐼 𐑁𐐫𐑊𐑌 𐐹𐐨𐐹𐑊. 𐐈𐑌𐐼 𐑌𐐵 𐐺𐐨𐐸𐐬𐑊𐐼, 𐐌 𐑅𐐩 𐐲𐑌𐐻𐐭 𐐷𐐭, 𐑄𐐰𐐻 𐐮𐑁 𐐮𐐻 𐐸𐐰𐐼 𐐺𐐮𐑌 𐐹𐐱𐑅𐐮𐐺𐑊 𐑁𐐫𐑉 𐐈𐐼𐐲𐑋 𐐻𐐭 𐐸𐐰𐑂 𐐹𐐪𐑉-

𐐻𐐩𐐿𐐲𐑌 𐐱𐑂 𐑄 𐑁𐑉𐐭𐐻 𐐱𐑂 𐑄 𐐻𐑉𐐨 𐐱𐑂 𐑊𐐴𐑁 𐐰𐐻 𐑄𐐰𐐻 𐐻𐐴𐑋, 𐑄𐐯𐑉 𐐶𐐳𐐼 𐐸𐐰𐑂 𐐺𐐮𐑌 𐑌𐐬 𐐼𐐯𐑃, 𐐰𐑌𐐼 𐑄 𐐶𐐲𐑉𐐼 𐐶𐐳𐐼 𐐸𐐰𐑂 𐐺𐐮𐑌 𐑂𐐦𐐼, 𐑋𐐩𐐿𐐮𐑍 𐐘𐐱𐐼 𐐲 𐑊𐐴𐐲𐑉: 𐑁𐐫𐑉 𐐸𐐨 𐑅𐐯𐐼, 𐐆𐑁 𐑄𐐵 𐐨𐐻, 𐑄𐐵 𐑇𐐰𐑊𐐻 𐑇𐐳𐑉𐑊𐐨 𐐼𐐴. 𐐈𐑌𐐼 𐐶𐐨 𐑅𐐨 𐑄𐐰𐐻 𐐼𐐯𐑃 𐐿𐐲𐑋𐑆 𐐲𐐹𐐱𐑌 𐑋𐐰𐑌𐐿𐐴𐑌𐐼, 𐐷𐐩, 𐑄 𐐼𐐯𐑃 𐐸𐐶𐐮𐐽 𐐸𐐰𐑆 𐐺𐐮𐑌 𐑅𐐹𐐬𐐿𐐲𐑌 𐐱𐑂 𐐺𐐴 𐐈𐑋𐐷𐐭𐑊𐐯𐐿, 𐐸𐐶𐐮𐐽 𐐮𐑆 𐑄 𐐻𐐯𐑋𐐹𐐬𐑉𐐲𐑊 𐐼𐐯𐑃; 𐑌𐐯𐑂𐐲𐑉𐑄𐐲𐑊𐐯𐑅 𐑄𐐯𐑉 𐐶𐐱𐑆 𐐲 𐑅𐐹𐐩𐑅 𐑀𐑉𐐰𐑌𐐻𐐯𐐼 𐐲𐑌𐐻𐐭 𐑋𐐰𐑌 𐐮𐑌 𐐸𐐶𐐮𐐽 𐐸𐐨 𐑋𐐴𐐻 𐑉𐐯𐐹𐐯𐑌𐐻; 𐑄𐐯𐑉𐑁𐐬𐑉 𐑄𐐮𐑅 𐑊𐐴𐑁 𐐺𐐨𐐿𐐩𐑋 𐐲 𐐹𐑉𐐬𐐺𐐩𐑇𐐲𐑌𐐯𐑉𐐨 𐑅𐐻𐐩𐐻; 𐐲 𐐻𐐴𐑋 𐐻𐐭 𐐹𐑉𐐨𐐹𐐯𐑉 𐐻𐐭 𐑋𐐨𐐻 𐐘𐐱𐐼; 𐐲 𐐻𐐴𐑋 𐐻𐐭 𐐹𐑉𐐨𐐹𐐯𐑉 𐑁𐐫𐑉 𐑄𐐰𐐻 𐐯𐑌𐐼𐑊𐐯𐑅 𐑅𐐻𐐩𐐻, 𐐸𐐶𐐮𐐽 𐐸𐐰𐑆 𐐺𐐮𐑌 𐑅𐐹𐐬𐐿𐐲𐑌 𐐱𐑂 𐐺𐐴 𐐲𐑅, 𐐸𐐶𐐮𐐽 𐐮𐑆 𐐰𐑁𐐻𐐲𐑉 𐑄 𐑉𐐯𐑆𐐲𐑉𐐯𐐿𐑇𐐲𐑌 𐐱𐑂 𐑄 𐐼𐐯𐐼.

5. 𐐤𐐵 𐐮𐑁 𐐮𐐻 𐐸𐐰𐐼 𐑌𐐱𐐻 𐐺𐐮𐑌 𐑁𐐫𐑉 𐑄 𐐹𐑊𐐰𐑌 𐐱𐑂 𐑉𐐨𐐼𐐯𐑋𐐹𐑇𐐲𐑌, 𐐸𐐶𐐮𐐽 𐐶𐐱𐑆 𐑊𐐩𐐼 𐑁𐑉𐐱𐑋 𐑄 𐑁𐐵𐑌𐐼𐐩𐑇𐐲𐑌 𐐱𐑂 𐑄 𐐶𐐲𐑉𐑊𐐼, 𐑄𐐯𐑉 𐐿𐐳𐐼 𐐸𐐰𐑂 𐐺𐐮𐑌 𐑌𐐬 𐑉𐐯𐑆𐐲𐑉𐐯𐐿𐑇𐐲𐑌 𐐱𐑂 𐑄 𐐼𐐯𐐼; 𐐺𐐲𐐻 𐑄𐐯𐑉 𐐶𐐱𐑆 𐐲 𐐹𐑊𐐰𐑌 𐐱𐑂 𐑉𐐨𐐼𐐯𐑋𐐹𐑇𐐲𐑌 𐑊𐐩𐐼, 𐐸𐐶𐐮𐐽 𐑇𐐰𐑊 𐐺𐑉𐐮𐑍 𐐻𐐭 𐐹𐐰𐑅 𐑄 𐑉𐐯𐑆𐐲𐑉𐐯𐐿𐑇𐐲𐑌 𐐱𐑂 𐑄 𐐼𐐯𐐼, 𐐱𐑂 𐐸𐐶𐐮𐐽 𐐸𐐰𐑆 𐐺𐐮𐑌 𐑅𐐹𐐬𐐿𐐲𐑌. 𐐈𐑌𐐼 𐑌𐐵 𐐺𐐨𐐸𐐬𐑊𐐼, 𐐮𐑁 𐐮𐐻 𐐶𐐲𐑉 𐐹𐐱𐑅𐐮𐐺𐑊 𐑄𐐰𐐻 𐐵𐑉 𐑁𐐲𐑉𐑅𐐻 𐐹𐐯𐑉𐐯𐑌𐐻𐑅 𐐿𐐳𐐼 𐐸𐐰𐑂 𐑀𐐱𐑌 𐑁𐐬𐑉𐑃 𐐰𐑌𐐼 𐐹𐐪𐑉𐐻𐐩𐐿𐐲𐑌 𐐱𐑂 𐑄 𐐻𐑉𐐨 𐐱𐑂 𐑊𐐴𐑁, 𐑄𐐩 𐐶𐐳𐐼 𐐸𐐰𐑂 𐐺𐐮𐑌 𐑁𐐫𐑉𐐯𐑂𐐲𐑉 𐑋𐐮𐑆𐐲𐑉𐐲𐐺𐑊, 𐐸𐐰𐑂𐐮𐑍 𐑌𐐬 𐐹𐑉𐐨𐐹𐐰𐑉𐐲𐐻𐐬𐑉𐐨 𐑅𐐻𐐩𐐻; 𐐰𐑌𐐼 𐑄𐐲𐑅 𐑄 𐐹𐑊𐐰𐑌 𐐱𐑂 𐑉𐐨𐐼𐐯𐑋𐐹𐑇𐐲𐑌 𐐶𐐳𐐼 𐐸𐐰𐑂 𐐺𐐮𐑌 𐑁𐑉𐐲𐑅𐐻𐑉𐐩𐐻𐐯𐐼, 𐐰𐑌𐐼 𐑄 𐐶𐐲𐑉𐐼 𐐱𐑂 𐐘𐐱𐐼 𐐶𐐳𐐼 𐐸𐐰𐑂 𐐺𐐮𐑌 𐑂𐐦𐐼, 𐐻𐐩𐐿𐐮𐑍 𐑌𐐲𐑌 𐐯𐑁𐐯𐐿𐐻. 𐐒𐐲𐐻 𐐺𐐨𐐸𐐬𐑊𐐼, 𐐮𐐻 𐐶𐐱𐑆 𐑌𐐱𐐻 𐑅𐐬; 𐐺𐐲𐐻 𐐮𐐻 𐐶𐐱𐑆 𐐲𐐹𐐦𐑌𐐻𐐯𐐼 𐐲𐑌𐐻𐐭 𐑋𐐯𐑌 𐑄𐐰𐐻 𐑄𐐩 𐑋𐐲𐑅𐐻 𐐼𐐴; 𐐰𐑌𐐼 𐐰𐑁𐐻𐐲𐑉 𐐼𐐯𐑃, 𐑄𐐩 𐑋𐐲𐑅𐐻 𐐿𐐲𐑋 𐐻𐐭 𐐾𐐲𐐾𐑋𐐯𐑌𐐻, 𐐨𐑂𐐯𐑌 𐑄𐐰𐐻 𐑅𐐩𐑋 𐐾𐐲𐐾𐑋𐐯𐑌𐐻 𐐱𐑂 𐐸𐐶𐐮𐐽 𐐶𐐨 𐐸𐐰𐑂 𐑅𐐹𐐬𐐿𐐲𐑌, 𐐸𐐶𐐮𐐽 𐐮𐑆 𐑄 𐐯𐑌𐐼. 𐐈𐑌𐐼 𐐰𐑁𐐻𐐲𐑉 𐐘𐐱𐐼 𐐸𐐰𐐼 𐐲𐐹𐐦𐑌𐐻𐐯𐐼 𐑄𐐰𐐻 𐑄𐐨𐑆 𐑃𐐮𐑍𐑆 𐑇𐐳𐐼 𐐿𐐲𐑋 𐐲𐑌𐐻𐐭 𐑋𐐰𐑌, 𐐺𐐨𐐸𐐬𐑊𐐼, 𐑄𐐯𐑌 𐐸𐐨 𐑅𐐫 𐑄𐐰𐐻 𐐮𐐻 𐐶𐐱𐑆 𐐯𐐿𐑅𐐹𐐨𐐼𐐨𐐯𐑌𐐻 𐑄𐐰𐐻 𐑋𐐰𐑌 𐑇𐐳𐐼 𐑌𐐬 𐐿𐐱𐑌𐑅𐐲𐑉𐑌𐐮𐑍 𐑄 𐑃𐐮𐑍𐑆 𐐸𐐶𐐯𐑉𐐱𐑂 𐐸𐐨 𐐸𐐰𐐼 𐐲𐐹𐐦𐑌𐐻𐐯𐐼 𐐲𐑌𐐻𐐭 𐑄𐐯𐑋; 𐑄𐐯𐑉𐑁𐐬𐑉 𐐸𐐨 𐑅𐐯𐑌𐐻 𐐩𐑌𐐾𐐯𐑊𐑆 𐐻𐐭 𐐿𐐱𐑌𐑂𐐲𐑉𐑅 𐐶𐐮𐑄 𐑄𐐯𐑋, 𐐸𐐭 𐐿𐐫𐑆𐐼 𐑋𐐯𐑌 𐐻𐐭 𐐺𐐨𐐸𐐬𐑊𐐼 𐐱𐑂 𐐸𐐮𐑆 𐑀𐑊𐐬𐑉𐐨. 𐐈𐑌𐐼 𐑄𐐩 𐐺𐐨𐑀𐐰𐑌 𐑁𐑉𐐱𐑋 𐑄𐐰𐐻 𐐻𐐴𐑋 𐑁𐐬𐑉𐑃 𐐻𐐭 𐐿𐐫𐑊 𐐱𐑌 𐐸𐐮𐑆 𐑌𐐩𐑋; 𐑄𐐯𐑉𐑁𐐬𐑉 𐐘𐐱𐐼 𐐿𐐱𐑌𐑂𐐲𐑉𐑅𐐻 𐐶𐐮𐑄 𐑋𐐯𐑌, 𐐰𐑌𐐼 𐑋𐐩𐐼 𐑌𐐬𐑌 𐐲𐑌𐐻𐐭 𐑄𐐯𐑋 𐑄 𐐹𐑊𐐰𐑌 𐐱𐑂 𐑉𐐨𐐼𐐯𐑋𐐹𐑇𐐲𐑌, 𐐸𐐶𐐮𐐽 𐐸𐐰𐐼 𐐺𐐮𐑌 𐐹𐑉𐐨𐐹𐐯𐑉𐐼 𐑁𐑉𐐱𐑋 𐑄 𐑁𐐵𐑌𐐼𐐩𐑇𐐲𐑌 𐐱𐑂 𐑄 𐐶𐐲𐑉𐑊𐐼; 𐐰𐑌𐐼 𐑄𐐮𐑅 𐐸𐐨 𐑋𐐩𐐼 𐑌𐐬𐑌 𐐲𐑌𐐻𐐭 𐑄𐐯𐑋 𐐰𐐿𐐫𐑉𐐼𐐮𐑍 𐐻𐐭 𐑄𐐯𐑉 𐑁𐐩𐑃 𐐰𐑌𐐼 𐑉𐐯𐐹𐐯𐑌𐐻𐐲𐑌𐑅 𐐰𐑌𐐼 𐑄𐐯𐑉 𐐸𐐬𐑊𐐨 𐐶𐐲𐑉𐐿𐑅; 𐐸𐐶𐐯𐑉𐑁𐐬𐑉 𐐸𐐨 𐑀𐐩𐑂 𐐿𐐱𐑋𐐰𐑌𐐼𐑋𐐯𐑌𐐻𐑅 𐐲𐑌𐐻𐐭 𐑋𐐯𐑌, 𐑄𐐩 𐐸𐐰𐑂𐐮𐑍 𐑁𐐲𐑉𐑅𐐻 𐐻𐑉𐐰𐑌𐑅𐑀𐑉𐐯𐑅𐐻 𐑄 𐑁𐐲𐑉𐑅𐐻 𐐿𐐱𐑋𐐰𐑌𐐼𐑋𐐯𐑌𐐻𐑅 𐐰𐑆 𐐻𐐭 𐑃𐐮𐑍𐑆 𐐸𐐶𐐮𐐽 𐐶𐐲𐑉 𐐻𐐯𐑋𐐹𐐬𐑉𐐲𐑊, 𐐰𐑌𐐼 𐐺𐐨𐐿𐐲𐑋𐐮𐑍 𐐰𐑆 𐐘𐐱𐐼𐑆, 𐑌𐐬𐐮𐑍 𐑀𐐳𐐼 𐑁𐑉𐐱𐑋 𐐨𐑂𐐮𐑊, 𐐹𐑊𐐩𐑅𐐮𐑍 𐑄𐐯𐑋𐑅𐐯𐑊𐑂𐑆 𐐮𐑌 𐐲 𐑅𐐻𐐩𐐻 𐐻𐐭 𐐰𐐿𐐻, 𐐫𐑉 𐐺𐐨𐐮𐑍 𐐹𐑊𐐩𐑅𐐻 𐐮𐑌 𐐲 𐑅𐐻𐐩𐐻 𐐻𐐭 𐐰𐐿𐐻 𐐰𐐿𐐫𐑉𐐼𐐮𐑍 𐐻𐐭 𐑄𐐯𐑉 𐐶𐐮𐑊𐑆 𐐰𐑌𐐼 𐐹𐑊𐐯𐑈𐐲𐑉𐑆, 𐐸𐐶𐐯𐑄𐐲𐑉 𐐻𐐭 𐐼𐐭 𐐨𐑂𐐮𐑊 𐐫𐑉 𐐻𐐭 𐐼𐐭 𐑀𐐳𐐼; 𐑄𐐯𐑉𐑁𐐬𐑉 𐐘𐐱𐐼 𐑀𐐩𐑂 𐐲𐑌𐐻𐐭 𐑄𐐯𐑋 𐐿𐐱𐑋𐐰𐑌𐐼𐑋𐐯𐑌𐐻𐑅, 𐐰𐑁𐐻𐐲𐑉 𐐸𐐰𐑂𐐮𐑍 𐑋𐐩𐐼 𐑌𐐬𐑌 𐐲𐑌𐐻𐐭 𐑄𐐯𐑋 𐑄 𐐹𐑊𐐰𐑌 𐐱𐑂 𐑉𐐨𐐼𐐯𐑋𐐹𐑇𐐲𐑌, 𐑄𐐰𐐻 𐑄𐐩 𐑇𐐳𐐼 𐑌𐐱𐐻 𐐼𐐭 𐐨𐑂𐐮𐑊, 𐑄 𐐹𐐯𐑌𐐲𐑊𐐻𐐨 𐑄𐐯𐑉𐐱𐑂 𐐺𐐨𐐮𐑍 𐐲 𐑅𐐯𐐿𐐲𐑌𐐼 𐐼𐐯𐑃, 𐐸𐐶𐐮𐐽 𐐶𐐱𐑆 𐐰𐑌 𐐯𐑂𐐲𐑉𐑊𐐰𐑅𐐻𐐮𐑍 𐐼𐐯𐑃 𐐰𐑆 𐐻𐐭 𐑃𐐮𐑍𐑆 𐐹𐐲𐑉𐐻𐐩𐑌𐐮𐑍 𐐲𐑌𐐻𐐭 𐑉𐐴𐐽𐐲𐑅𐑌𐐯𐑅; 𐑁𐐫𐑉 𐐱𐑌 𐑅𐐲𐐽 𐑄 𐐹𐑊𐐰𐑌 𐐱𐑂 𐑉𐐨𐐼𐐯𐑋𐐹𐑇𐐲𐑌 𐐿𐐳𐐼 𐐸𐐰𐑂 𐑌𐐬 𐐹𐐵𐐲𐑉, 𐑁𐐫𐑉 𐑄 𐐶𐐲𐑉𐐿𐑅 𐐱𐑂 𐐾𐐲𐑅𐐻𐐮𐑅 𐐿𐐳𐐼 𐑌𐐱𐐻 𐐺𐐨 𐐼𐐯𐑅𐐻𐑉𐐦𐐼, 𐐰𐐿𐐫𐑉𐐼𐐮𐑍 𐐻𐐭 𐑄 𐑅𐐭𐐹𐑉𐐨𐑋 𐑀𐐳𐐼𐑌𐐯𐑅 𐐱𐑂 𐐘𐐱𐐼. 𐐒𐐲𐐻 𐐘𐐱𐐼 𐐼𐐮𐐼 𐐿𐐫𐑊 𐐱𐑌 𐑋𐐯𐑌, 𐐮𐑌 𐑄 𐑌𐐩𐑋 𐐱𐑂 𐐸𐐮𐑆 𐐝𐐲𐑌, (𐑄𐐮𐑅 𐐺𐐨𐐮𐑍 𐑄 𐐹𐑊𐐰𐑌 𐐱𐑂 𐑉𐐨𐐼𐐯𐑋𐐹𐑇𐐲𐑌 𐐸𐐶𐐮𐐽 𐐶𐐱𐑆 𐑊𐐩𐐼,) 𐑅𐐩𐐮𐑍, 𐐆𐑁 𐐷𐐨 𐐶𐐮𐑊 𐑉𐐯𐐹𐐯𐑌𐐻, 𐐰𐑌𐐼 𐐸𐐪𐑉𐐼𐐲𐑌 𐑌𐐱𐐻 𐐷𐐬𐑉 𐐸𐐪𐑉𐐻𐑅, 𐑄𐐯𐑌 𐐶𐐮𐑊 𐐌 𐐸𐐰𐑂 𐑋𐐲𐑉𐑅𐐨 𐐲𐐹𐐱𐑌 𐐷𐐭, 𐑃𐑉𐐭 𐑋𐐴𐑌 𐐄𐑌𐑊𐐨 𐐒𐐨𐑀𐐱𐐻𐐲𐑌 𐐝𐐲𐑌; 𐑄𐐯𐑉𐑁𐐬𐑉, 𐐸𐐭𐑅𐐬𐐯𐑂𐐲𐑉 𐑉𐐯𐐹𐐯𐑌𐐻𐐯𐑃, 𐐰𐑌𐐼 𐐸𐐪𐑉𐐼𐐲𐑌𐐯𐑃 𐑌𐐱𐐻 𐐸𐐮𐑆 𐐸𐐪𐑉𐐻, 𐐸𐐨 𐑇𐐰𐑊 𐐸𐐰𐑂 𐐿𐑊𐐩𐑋 𐐱𐑌 𐑋𐐲𐑉𐑅𐐨 𐑃𐑉𐐭 𐑋𐐴𐑌 𐐄𐑌𐑊𐐨 𐐒𐐨𐑀𐐱𐐻𐐲𐑌 𐐝𐐲𐑌, 𐐲𐑌𐐻𐐭 𐐲 𐑉𐐨𐑋𐐮𐑇𐐲𐑌 𐐱𐑂 𐐸𐐮𐑆 𐑅𐐮𐑌𐑆; 𐐰𐑌𐐼 𐑄𐐨𐑆 𐑇𐐰𐑊 𐐯𐑌𐐻𐐲𐑉 𐐮𐑌𐐻𐐭 𐑋𐐴 𐑉𐐯𐑅𐐻. 𐐈𐑌𐐼 𐐸𐐭𐑅𐐬𐐯𐑂𐐲𐑉 𐐶𐐮𐑊 𐐸𐐪𐑉𐐼𐐲𐑌 𐐸𐐮𐑆 𐐸𐐪𐑉𐐻 𐐰𐑌𐐼 𐐶𐐮𐑊 𐐼𐐭 𐐮𐑌𐐮𐐿𐐶𐐮𐐻𐐨, 𐐺𐐨𐐸𐐬𐑊𐐼, 𐐌 𐑅𐐶𐐯𐑉 𐐮𐑌 𐑋𐐴 𐑉𐐪𐑃 𐑄𐐰𐐻 𐐸𐐨 𐑇𐐰𐑊 𐑌𐐱𐐻 𐐯𐑌𐐻𐐲𐑉 𐐮𐑌𐐻𐐭 𐑋𐐴 𐑉𐐯𐑅𐐻. 𐐈𐑌𐐼 𐑌𐐵, 𐑋𐐴 𐐺𐑉𐐯𐑄𐑉𐐯𐑌, 𐐺𐐨𐐸𐐬𐑊𐐼, 𐐌 𐑅𐐩 𐐲𐑌𐐻𐐭 𐐷𐐭, 𐑄𐐰𐐻 𐐮𐑁 𐐷𐐨 𐐶𐐮𐑊 𐐸𐐪𐑉𐐼𐐲𐑌 𐐷𐐬𐑉 𐐸𐐪𐑉𐐻𐑅, 𐐷𐐨 𐑇𐐰𐑊 𐑌𐐱𐐻 𐐯𐑌𐐻𐐲𐑉 𐐮𐑌𐐻𐐭 𐑄 𐑉𐐯𐑅𐐻 𐐱𐑂 𐑄 𐐢𐐫𐑉𐐼; 𐑄𐐯𐑉𐑁𐐬𐑉 𐐷𐐬𐑉 𐐮𐑌𐐮𐐿𐐶𐐮𐐻𐐨 𐐹𐑉𐐬𐑂𐐬𐐿𐐯𐑃 𐐸𐐮𐑋 𐑄𐐰𐐻 𐐸𐐨 𐑅𐐯𐑌𐐼𐐯𐑃 𐐼𐐵𐑌 𐐸𐐮𐑆 𐑉𐐪𐑃 𐐲𐐹𐐱𐑌 𐐷𐐭 𐐰𐑆 𐐮𐑌 𐑄 𐑁𐐲𐑉𐑅𐐻 𐐹𐑉𐐱𐑂𐐬𐐿𐐩𐑇𐐲𐑌, 𐐷𐐩, 𐐰𐐿𐐫𐑉𐐼𐐮𐑍 𐐻𐐭 𐐸𐐮𐑆 𐐶𐐲𐑉𐐼 𐐮𐑌 𐑄 𐑊𐐰𐑅𐐻 𐐹𐑉𐐱𐑂𐐬𐐿𐐩𐑇𐐲𐑌 𐐰𐑆 𐐶𐐯𐑊 𐐰𐑆 𐑄 𐑁𐐲𐑉𐑅𐐻, 𐐻𐐭

𐑄 𐐯𐑂𐐲𐑉𐑊𐐰𐑅𐐻𐐮𐑍 𐐼𐐯𐑅𐐻𐑉𐐲𐐿𐑇𐐲𐑌 𐐱𐑂 𐐷𐐬𐑉 𐑅𐐬𐑊𐑆; 𐑄𐐯𐑉𐑁𐐬𐑉, 𐐰𐐿𐐫𐑉𐐼𐐮𐑍 𐐻𐐭 𐐸𐐮𐑆 𐐶𐐲𐑉𐐼, 𐐲𐑌𐐻𐐭 𐑄 𐑊𐐪𐑅𐐻 𐐼𐐯𐑃, 𐐰𐑆 𐐶𐐯𐑊 𐐰𐑆 𐑄 𐑁𐐲𐑉𐑅𐐻.

6. 𐐈𐑌𐐼 𐑌𐐵, 𐑋𐐴 𐐺𐑉𐐯𐑄𐑉𐐯𐑌, 𐑅𐐨𐐮𐑍 𐐶𐐨 𐑌𐐬 𐑄𐐨𐑆 𐑃𐐮𐑍𐑆, 𐐰𐑌𐐼 𐑄𐐩 𐐪𐑉 𐐻𐑉𐐭, 𐑊𐐯𐐻 𐐲𐑅 𐑉𐐨𐐹𐐯𐑌𐐻, 𐐰𐑌𐐼 𐐸𐐪𐑉𐐼𐐲𐑌 𐑌𐐱𐐻 𐐵𐑉 𐐸𐐪𐑉𐐻𐑅, 𐑄𐐰𐐻 𐐶𐐨 𐐹𐑉𐐬𐑂𐐬𐐿 𐑌𐐱𐐻 𐑄 𐐢𐐫𐑉𐐼 𐐵𐑉 𐐘𐐱𐐼 𐐻𐐭 𐐹𐐳𐑊 𐐼𐐵𐑌 𐐸𐐮𐑆 𐑉𐐰𐑃 𐐲𐐹𐐱𐑌 𐐲𐑅 𐐮𐑌 𐑄𐐨𐑆 𐐸𐐮𐑆 𐑅𐐯𐐿𐐲𐑌𐐼 𐐿𐐱𐑋𐐰𐑌𐐼𐑋𐐯𐑌𐐻𐑅 𐐸𐐶𐐮𐐽 𐐸𐐨 𐐸𐐰𐑆 𐑀𐐮𐑂𐐲𐑌 𐐲𐑌𐐻𐐭 𐐲𐑅; 𐐺𐐲𐐻 𐑊𐐯𐐻 𐐲𐑅 𐐯𐑌𐐻𐐲𐑉 𐐮𐑌𐐻𐐭 𐑄 𐑉𐐯𐑅𐐻 𐐱𐑂 𐐘𐐱𐐼, 𐐸𐐶𐐮𐐽 𐐮𐑆 𐐹𐑉𐐨𐐹𐐩𐑉𐐼 𐐰𐐿𐐫𐑉𐐼𐐮𐑍 𐐻𐐭 𐐸𐐮𐑆 𐐶𐐲𐑉𐐼. 𐐈𐑌𐐼 𐐰𐑀𐐯𐑌: 𐐣𐐴 𐐺𐑉𐐯𐑄𐑉𐐯𐑌, 𐐌 𐐶𐐳𐐼 𐑅𐐴𐐻 𐐷𐐬𐑉 𐑋𐐴𐑌𐐼𐑆 𐑁𐐫𐑉𐐶𐐲𐑉𐐼 𐐻𐐭 𐑄 𐐻𐐴𐑋 𐑄 𐐢𐐫𐑉𐐼 𐐘𐐱𐐼 𐑀𐐩𐑂 𐑄𐐨𐑆 𐐿𐐱𐑋𐐰𐑌𐐼𐑋𐐯𐑌𐐻𐑅 𐐲𐑌𐐻𐐭 𐐸𐐮𐑆 𐐽𐐮𐑊𐐼𐑉𐐯𐑌; 𐐰𐑌𐐼 𐐌 𐐶𐐳𐐼 𐑄𐐰𐐻 𐐷𐐨 𐑇𐐳𐐼 𐑉𐐨𐑋𐐯𐑋𐐺𐐲𐑉 𐑄𐐰𐐻 𐑄 𐐢𐐫𐑉𐐼 𐐘𐐱𐐼 𐐫𐑉𐐼𐐩𐑌𐐼 𐐹𐑉𐐨𐑅𐐻𐑅, 𐐪𐑁𐐻𐐲𐑉 𐐸𐐮𐑆 𐐸𐐬𐑊𐐨 𐐫𐑉𐐼𐐲𐑉, 𐐸𐐶𐐮𐐽 𐐶𐐱𐑆 𐐪𐑁𐐻𐐲𐑉 𐑄 𐐫𐑉𐐼𐐲𐑉 𐐱𐑂 𐐸𐐮𐑆 𐐝𐐲𐑌, 𐐻𐐭 𐐻𐐨𐐽 𐑄𐐨𐑆 𐑃𐐮𐑍𐑆 𐐲𐑌𐐻𐐭 𐑄 𐐹𐐨𐐹𐑊; 𐐰𐑌𐐼 𐑄𐐬𐑆 𐐹𐑉𐐨𐑅𐐻𐑅 𐐶𐐲𐑉 𐐫𐑉𐐼𐐩𐑌𐐼 𐐪𐑁𐐻𐐲𐑉 𐑄 𐐫𐑉𐐼𐐲𐑉 𐐱𐑂 𐐸𐐮𐑆 𐐝𐐲𐑌, 𐐮𐑌 𐐰 𐑋𐐰𐑌𐐲𐑉 𐑄𐐰𐐻 𐑄𐐯𐑉𐐺𐐴 𐑄 𐐹𐐨𐐹𐑊 𐑋𐐴𐐻 𐑌𐐬 𐐮𐑌 𐐸𐐶𐐱𐐻 𐑋𐐰𐑌𐐲𐑉 𐐻𐐭 𐑊𐐳𐐿 𐑁𐐫𐑉𐐶𐐲𐑉𐐼 𐐻𐐭 𐐸𐐮𐑆 𐐝𐐲𐑌 𐑁𐐫𐑉 𐑉𐐨𐐼𐐯𐑋𐑇𐐲𐑌. 𐐈𐑌𐐼 𐑄𐐮𐑅 𐐮𐑆 𐑄 𐑋𐐰𐑌𐐲𐑉 𐐪𐑁𐐻𐐲𐑉 𐐸𐐶𐐮𐐽 𐑄𐐩 𐐶𐐲𐑉 𐐫𐑉𐐼𐐩𐑌𐐼: 𐐺𐐨𐐮𐑍 𐐿𐐫𐑊𐐼 𐐰𐑌𐐼 𐐹𐑉𐐨𐐹𐐩𐑉𐐼 𐑁𐑉𐐱𐑋 𐑄 𐑁𐐵𐑌𐐼𐐩𐑇𐐲𐑌 𐐱𐑂 𐑄 𐐶𐐲𐑉𐑊𐐼, 𐐰𐐿𐐫𐑉𐐼𐐮𐑍 𐐻𐐭 𐑄 𐑁𐐬𐑉𐑌𐐱𐑊𐐯𐐾 𐐱𐑂 𐐘𐐱𐐼, 𐐱𐑌 𐐰𐐿𐐵𐑌𐐻 𐐱𐑂 𐑄𐐯𐑉 𐐯𐐿𐑅𐐨𐐼𐐮𐑍 𐑁𐐩𐑃 𐐰𐑌𐐼 𐑀𐐳𐐼 𐐶𐐲𐑉𐐿𐑅; 𐐮𐑌 𐑄 𐑁𐐲𐑉𐑅𐐻 𐐹𐑊𐐩𐑅 𐐺𐐨𐐮𐑍 𐑊𐐯𐑁𐐻 𐐻𐐭 𐐽𐐭𐑆 𐑀𐐳𐐼 𐐫𐑉 𐐨𐑂𐑊; 𐑄𐐯𐑉𐑁𐐬𐑉 𐑄𐐩 𐐸𐐰𐑂𐐮𐑍 𐐽𐐬𐑆𐐲𐑌 𐑀𐐳𐐼, 𐐰𐑌𐐼 𐐯𐐿𐑅𐐲𐑉𐑅𐐴𐑆𐐮𐑍 𐐯𐐿𐑅𐐨𐐼𐐮𐑍 𐑀𐑉𐐩𐐻 𐑁𐐩𐑃, 𐐪𐑉 𐐿𐐫𐑊𐐼 𐐶𐐮𐑄 𐐰 𐐸𐐬𐑊𐐨 𐐿𐐫𐑊𐐮𐑍, 𐐷𐐩, 𐐶𐐮𐑄 𐑄𐐰𐐻 𐐸𐐬𐑊𐐨 𐐿𐐫𐑊𐐮𐑍 𐐸𐐶𐐮𐐽 𐐶𐐱𐑆 𐐹𐑉𐐨𐐹𐐩𐑉𐐼 𐐶𐐮𐑄, 𐐰𐑌𐐼 𐐰𐐿𐐫𐑉𐐼𐐮𐑍 𐐻𐐭, 𐐰 𐐹𐑉𐐨𐐹𐐰𐑉𐐲𐐻𐐲𐑉𐐨 𐑉𐐨𐐼𐐯𐑋𐑇𐐲𐑌 𐑁𐐫𐑉 𐑅𐐲𐐽; 𐐰𐑌𐐼 𐑄𐐲𐑅 𐑄𐐩 𐐸𐐰𐑂 𐐺𐐮𐑌 𐐿𐐫𐑊𐐼 𐐻𐐭 𐑄𐐮𐑅 𐐸𐐬𐑊𐐨 𐐿𐐫𐑊𐐮𐑍 𐐱𐑌 𐐰𐐿𐐵𐑌𐐻 𐐱𐑂 𐑄𐐯𐑉 𐑁𐐩𐑃, 𐐸𐐶𐐴𐑊 𐐲𐑄𐐲𐑉𐑆 𐐶𐐳𐐼 𐑉𐐨𐐾𐐯𐐿𐐻 𐑄 𐐝𐐹𐐮𐑉𐐮𐐻 𐐱𐑂 𐐘𐐱𐐼 𐐱𐑌 𐐰𐐿𐐵𐑌𐐻 𐐱𐑂 𐑄 𐐸𐐪𐑉𐐼𐑌𐐯𐑅 𐐱𐑂 𐑄𐐯𐑉 𐐸𐐪𐑉𐐻𐑅 𐐰𐑌𐐼 𐐺𐑊𐐴𐑌𐐼𐑌𐐯𐑅 𐐱𐑂 𐑄𐐯𐑉 𐑋𐐴𐑌𐐼𐑆, 𐐸𐐶𐐴𐑊, 𐐮𐑁 𐐮𐐻 𐐸𐐰𐐼 𐑌𐐱𐐻 𐐺𐐮𐑌 𐑁𐐫𐑉 𐑄𐐮𐑅 𐑄𐐩 𐑋𐐴𐐻 𐐸𐐰𐑂 𐐸𐐰𐐼 𐐰𐑆 𐑀𐑉𐐩𐐻 𐐹𐑉𐐮𐑂𐐮𐑊𐐯𐐾 𐐰𐑆 𐑄𐐯𐑉 𐐺𐑉𐐯𐑄𐑉𐐯𐑌. 𐐉𐑉 𐐮𐑌 𐑁𐐴𐑌; 𐐮𐑌 𐑄 𐑁𐐲𐑉𐑅𐐻 𐐹𐑊𐐩𐑅 𐑄𐐩 𐐶𐐲𐑉 𐐱𐑌 𐑄 𐑅𐐩𐑋 𐑅𐐻𐐰𐑌𐐼𐐮𐑍 𐐶𐐮𐑄 𐑄𐐯𐑉 𐐺𐑉𐐯𐑄𐑉𐐯𐑌; 𐑄𐐲𐑅 𐑄𐐮𐑅 𐐸𐐬𐑊𐐨 𐐿𐐫𐑊𐐮𐑍 𐐺𐐨𐐮𐑍 𐐹𐑉𐐨𐐹𐐩𐑉𐐼 𐑁𐑉𐐱𐑋 𐑄 𐑁𐐵𐑌𐐼𐐩𐑇𐐲𐑌 𐐱𐑂 𐑄 𐐶𐐲𐑉𐑊𐐼 𐑁𐐫𐑉 𐑅𐐲𐐽 𐐰𐑆 𐐶𐐳𐐼 𐑌𐐱𐐻 𐐸𐐪𐑉𐐼𐐲𐑌 𐑄𐐯𐑉 𐐸𐐪𐑉𐐻𐑅, 𐐺𐐨𐐮𐑍 𐐮𐑌 𐐰𐑌𐐼 𐑃𐑉𐐭 𐑄 𐐲𐐻𐐬𐑌𐑋𐐯𐑌𐐻 𐐱𐑂 𐑄 𐐄𐑌𐑊𐐨 𐐒𐐨𐑀𐐱𐐻𐑌 𐐝𐐲𐑌, 𐐸𐐭 𐐶𐐱𐑆 𐐹𐑉𐐨𐐹𐐩𐑉𐐼; 𐐰𐑌𐐼 𐑄𐐲𐑅 𐐺𐐨𐐮𐑍 𐐿𐐫𐑊𐐼 𐐺𐐴 𐑄𐐮𐑅 𐐸𐐬𐑊𐐨 𐐿𐐫𐑊𐐮𐑍, 𐐰𐑌𐐼 𐐫𐑉𐐼𐐩𐑌𐐼 𐐲𐑌𐐻𐐭 𐑄 𐐸𐐴 𐐹𐑉𐐨𐑅𐐻𐐸𐐳𐐼 𐐱𐑂 𐑄 𐐸𐐬𐑊𐐨 𐐫𐑉𐐼𐐲𐑉 𐐱𐑂 𐐘𐐱𐐼, 𐐻𐐭 𐐻𐐨𐐽 𐐸𐐮𐑆 𐐿𐐱𐑋𐐰𐑌𐐼𐑋𐐯𐑌𐐻𐑅 𐐲𐑌𐐻𐐭 𐑄 𐐽𐐮𐑊𐐼𐑉𐐯𐑌 𐐱𐑂 𐑋𐐯𐑌, 𐑄𐐰𐐻 𐑄𐐩 𐐫𐑊𐑅𐐬 𐑋𐐴𐐻 𐐯𐑌𐐻𐐲𐑉 𐐮𐑌𐐻𐐭 𐐸𐐮𐑆 𐑉𐐯𐑅𐐻, 𐑄𐐮𐑅 𐐸𐐴 𐐹𐑉𐐨𐑅𐐻𐐸𐐳𐐼 𐐺𐐨𐐮𐑍 𐐪𐑁𐐻𐐲𐑉 𐑄 𐐫𐑉𐐼𐐲𐑉 𐐱𐑂 𐐸𐐮𐑆 𐐝𐐲𐑌, 𐐸𐐶𐐮𐐽 𐐫𐑉𐐼𐐲𐑉 𐐶𐐱𐑆 𐑁𐑉𐐱𐑋 𐑄 𐑁𐐵𐑌𐐼𐐩𐑇𐐲𐑌 𐐱𐑂 𐑄 𐐶𐐲𐑉𐑊𐐼; 𐐫𐑉 𐐮𐑌 𐐲𐑄𐐲𐑉 𐐶𐐲𐑉𐐼𐑆, 𐐺𐐨𐐮𐑍 𐐶𐐮𐑄𐐵𐐻 𐐺𐐨𐑀𐐮𐑌𐐮𐑍 𐐱𐑂 𐐼𐐩𐑆 𐐫𐑉 𐐯𐑌𐐼 𐐱𐑂 𐐷𐐨𐑉𐑆, 𐐺𐐨𐐮𐑍 𐐹𐑉𐐨𐐹𐐩𐑉𐐼 𐑁𐑉𐐱𐑋 𐐨𐐻𐐲𐑉𐑌𐐮𐐻𐐨 𐐻𐐭 𐐫𐑊 𐐨𐐻𐐲𐑉𐑌𐐮𐐻𐐨, 𐐰𐐿𐐫𐑉𐐼𐐮𐑍 𐐻𐐭 𐐸𐐮𐑆 𐑁𐐬𐑉𐑌𐐱𐑊𐐯𐐾 𐐱𐑂 𐐫𐑊 𐑃𐐮𐑍𐑆. 𐐤𐐵 𐑄𐐩 𐐶𐐲𐑉 𐐫𐑉𐐼𐐩𐑌𐐼 𐐪𐑁𐐻𐐲𐑉 𐑄𐐮𐑅 𐑋𐐰𐑌𐐲𐑉: 𐐒𐐨𐐮𐑍 𐐿𐐫𐑊𐐼 𐐶𐐮𐑄 𐐰 𐐸𐐬𐑊𐐨 𐐿𐐫𐑊𐐮𐑍, 𐐰𐑌𐐼 𐐫𐑉𐐼𐐩𐑌𐐼 𐐶𐐮𐑄 𐐰 𐐸𐐬𐑊𐐨 𐐫𐑉𐐼𐐮𐑌𐐰𐑌𐑅, 𐐰𐑌𐐼 𐐻𐐩𐐿𐐮𐑍 𐐲𐐹𐐱𐑌 𐑄𐐯𐑋 𐑄 𐐸𐐴 𐐹𐑉𐐨𐑅𐐻𐐸𐐳𐐼 𐐱𐑂 𐑄 𐐸𐐬𐑊𐐨 𐐫𐑉𐐼𐐲𐑉, 𐐸𐐶𐐮𐐽 𐐿𐐫𐑊𐐮𐑍, 𐐰𐑌𐐼 𐐫𐑉𐐼𐐮𐑌𐐰𐑌𐑅, 𐐰𐑌𐐼 𐐸𐐴 𐐹𐑉𐐨𐑅𐐻𐐸𐐳𐐼, 𐐮𐑆 𐐶𐐮𐑄𐐵𐐻 𐐺𐐨𐑀𐐮𐑌𐐮𐑍 𐐫𐑉 𐐯𐑌𐐼; 𐑄𐐲𐑅 𐑄𐐩 𐐺𐐨𐐿𐐲𐑋 𐐸𐐴 𐐹𐑉𐐨𐑅𐐻𐑅 𐑁𐐫𐑉𐐯𐑂𐐲𐑉, 𐐪𐑁𐐻𐐲𐑉 𐑄 𐐫𐑉𐐼𐐲𐑉 𐐱𐑂 𐑄 𐐝𐐲𐑌, 𐑄 𐐄𐑌𐑊𐐨 𐐒𐐨𐑀𐐱𐐻𐑌 𐐱𐑂 𐑄 𐐙𐐪𐑄𐐲𐑉, 𐐸𐐭 𐐮𐑆 𐐶𐐮𐑄𐐵𐐻 𐐺𐐨𐑀𐐮𐑌𐐮𐑍 𐐱𐑂 𐐼𐐩𐑆 𐐫𐑉 𐐯𐑌𐐼 𐐱𐑂 𐐷𐐨𐑉𐑆, 𐐸𐐭 𐐮𐑆 𐑁𐐳𐑊 𐐱𐑂 𐑀𐑉𐐩𐑅, 𐐯𐐿𐐶𐐮𐐻𐐨, 𐐰𐑌𐐼 𐐻𐑉𐐭𐑃. 𐐈𐑌𐐼 𐑄𐐲𐑅 𐐮𐐻 𐐮𐑆. 𐐁𐑋𐐯𐑌.

𐐕𐐰𐐹𐐻𐐲𐑉 X.

1. 𐐤𐐵 𐐰𐑆 𐐌 𐑅𐐯𐐼 𐐿𐐱𐑌𐑅𐐲𐑉𐑌𐐮𐑍 𐑄 𐐸𐐬𐑊𐐨 𐐫𐑉𐐼𐐲𐑉 𐐱𐑂 𐑄𐐮𐑅 𐐸𐐴 𐐹𐑉𐐨𐑅𐐻𐐸𐐳𐐼: 𐑄𐐯𐑉 𐐶𐐲𐑉 𐑋𐐯𐑌𐐨 𐐸𐐭 𐐶𐐲𐑉 𐐫𐑉𐐼𐐩𐑌𐐼 𐐰𐑌𐐼 𐐺𐐨𐐿𐐩𐑋 𐐸𐐴 𐐹𐑉𐐨𐑅𐐻𐑅 𐐱𐑂 𐐘𐐱𐐼; 𐐰𐑌𐐼 𐐮𐐻 𐐶𐐱𐑆 𐐱𐑌 𐐰𐐿𐐵𐑌𐐻 𐐱𐑂 𐑄𐐯𐑉 𐐯𐐿𐑅𐐨𐐼𐐮𐑍 𐑁𐐩𐑃 𐐰𐑌𐐼 𐑉𐐨𐐹𐐯𐑌𐐻𐐰𐑌𐑅, 𐐰𐑌𐐼 𐑄𐐯𐑉 𐑉𐐴𐐽𐐲𐑅𐑌𐐯𐑅 𐐺𐐨𐑁𐐬𐑉 𐐘𐐱𐐼, 𐑄𐐩 𐐽𐐭𐑆𐐮𐑍 𐐻𐐭 𐑉𐐨𐐹𐐯𐑌𐐻

𐐰𐑌𐐼 𐐶𐐲𐑉𐐿 𐑉𐐴𐐽𐐲𐑅𐑌𐐯𐑅, 𐑉𐐪𐑄𐐲𐑉 𐑄𐐰𐑌 𐐻𐐭 𐐹𐐯𐑉𐐮𐑇; 𐑄𐐯𐑉𐑁𐐬𐑉 𐑄𐐩 𐐶𐐲𐑉 𐐿𐐫𐑊𐐼 𐐪𐑁𐐻𐐲𐑉 𐑄𐐮𐑅 𐐸𐐬𐑊𐐨 𐐫𐑉𐐼𐐲𐑉, 𐐰𐑌𐐼 𐐶𐐲𐑉 𐑅𐐰𐑍𐐿𐐻𐐮𐑁𐐴𐐼, 𐐰𐑌𐐼 𐑄𐐩𐑉 𐑀𐐪𐑉𐑋𐐯𐑌𐐻𐑅 𐐶𐐲𐑉 𐐶𐐱𐑇𐐻 𐐸𐐶𐐴𐐻, 𐑃𐑉𐐭 𐑄 𐐺𐑊𐐲𐐼 𐐱𐑂 𐑄 𐐢𐐰𐑋. 𐐤𐐵 𐑄𐐩, 𐐪𐑁𐐻𐐲𐑉 𐐺𐐨𐐮𐑍 𐑅𐐰𐑍𐐿𐐻𐐮𐑁𐐴𐐼 𐐺𐐴 𐑄 𐐐𐐬𐑊𐐨 𐐘𐐬𐑅𐐻, 𐐸𐐰𐑂𐐮𐑍 𐑄𐐩𐑉 𐑀𐐪𐑉𐑋𐐯𐑌𐐻𐑅 𐑋𐐩𐐼 𐐸𐐶𐐴𐐻, 𐐺𐐨𐐮𐑍 𐐹𐐷𐐭𐑉 𐐰𐑌𐐼 𐑅𐐹𐐱𐐻𐑊𐐯𐑅 𐐺𐐨𐑁𐐬𐑉 𐐘𐐱𐐼, 𐐿𐐳𐐼 𐑌𐐱𐐻 𐑊𐐳𐐿 𐐲𐐹𐐱𐑌 𐑅𐐮𐑌, 𐑅𐐩𐑂 𐐮𐐻 𐐶𐐲𐑉 𐐶𐐮𐑄 𐐰𐐺𐐸𐐱𐑉𐐯𐑌𐑅; 𐐰𐑌𐐼 𐑄𐐩𐑉 𐐶𐐲𐑉 𐑋𐐯𐑌𐐨, 𐐯𐐿𐑅𐐨𐐼𐐮𐑍𐑊𐐨 𐑀𐑉𐐩𐐻 𐑋𐐯𐑌𐐨, 𐐸𐐭 𐐶𐐲𐑉 𐑋𐐩𐐼 𐐹𐐷𐐭𐑉, 𐐰𐑌𐐼 𐐯𐑌𐐻𐐲𐑉𐐼 𐐮𐑌𐐻𐐭 𐑄 𐑉𐐯𐑅𐐻 𐐱𐑂 𐑄 𐐢𐐫𐑉𐐼 𐑄𐐩𐑉 𐐘𐐱𐐼. 𐐈𐑌𐐼 𐑌𐐵, 𐑋𐐴 𐐺𐑉𐐯𐑄𐑉𐐯𐑌, 𐐌 𐐶𐐳𐐼 𐑄𐐰𐐻 𐐷𐐨 𐑇𐐳𐐼 𐐸𐐲𐑋𐐺𐑊 𐐷𐐭𐑉𐑅𐐯𐑊𐑂𐑆 𐐺𐐨𐑁𐐬𐑉 𐐘𐐱𐐼, 𐐰𐑌𐐼 𐐺𐑉𐐮𐑍 𐑁𐐬𐑉𐑃 𐑁𐑉𐐭𐐻 𐑋𐐨𐐻 𐑁𐐫𐑉 𐑉𐐨𐐹𐐯𐑌𐐻𐐰𐑌𐑅, 𐑄𐐰𐐻 𐐷𐐨 𐑋𐐩 𐐫𐑊𐑅𐐬 𐐯𐑌𐐻𐐲𐑉 𐐮𐑌𐐻𐐭 𐑄𐐰𐐻 𐑉𐐯𐑅𐐻; 𐐷𐐩, 𐐸𐐲𐑋𐐺𐑊 𐐷𐐭𐑉𐑅𐐯𐑊𐑂𐑆 𐐨𐑂𐐲𐑌 𐐰𐑆 𐑄 𐐹𐐨𐐹𐑊 𐐮𐑌 𐑄 𐐼𐐩𐑆 𐐱𐑂 𐐣𐐯𐑊𐐿𐐮𐑆𐐯𐐼𐐯𐐿, 𐐸𐐭 𐐶𐐱𐑆 𐐫𐑊𐑅𐐬 𐐰 𐐸𐐴 𐐹𐑉𐐨𐑅𐐻 𐐪𐑁𐐻𐐲𐑉 𐑄𐐮𐑅 𐑅𐐩𐑋 𐐫𐑉𐐼𐐲𐑉 𐐸𐐶𐐮𐐽 𐐌 𐐸𐐰𐑂 𐑅𐐹𐐬𐐿𐐲𐑌, 𐐸𐐭 𐐫𐑊𐑅𐐬 𐐻𐐳𐐿 𐐲𐐹𐐱𐑌 𐐸𐐮𐑋 𐑄 𐐸𐐴 𐐹𐑉𐐨𐑅𐐻𐐸𐐳𐐼 𐑁𐐫𐑉 𐐯𐑂𐐲𐑉. 𐐈𐑌𐐼 𐐮𐐻 𐐶𐐱𐑆 𐑄𐐮𐑅 𐑅𐐩𐑋 𐐣𐐯𐑊𐐿𐐮𐑆𐐯𐐼𐐯𐐿 𐐻𐐭 𐐸𐐭𐑋 𐐁𐐺𐑉𐐰𐐸𐐰𐑋 𐐹𐐩𐐼 𐐻𐐴𐑄𐑆; 𐐷𐐩, 𐐨𐑂𐐲𐑌 𐐵𐑉 𐑁𐐪𐑄𐐲𐑉 𐐁𐐺𐑉𐐰𐐸𐐰𐑋 𐐹𐐩𐐼 𐐻𐐴𐑄𐑆 𐐱𐑂 𐐶𐐲𐑌 𐐻𐐯𐑌𐑃 𐐹𐐪𐑉𐐻 𐐱𐑂 𐐫𐑊 𐐸𐐨 𐐹𐐲𐑆𐐯𐑅𐐻. 𐐤𐐵 𐑄𐐨𐑆 𐐫𐑉𐐼𐐮𐑌𐐰𐑌𐑅𐐯𐑆 𐐶𐐲𐑉 𐑀𐐮𐑂𐐲𐑌 𐐪𐑁𐐻𐐲𐑉 𐑄𐐮𐑅 𐑋𐐰𐑌𐐲𐑉, 𐑄𐐰𐐻 𐑄𐐩𐑉𐐺𐐴 𐑄 𐐹𐐨𐐹𐑊 𐑋𐐴𐐻 𐑊𐐳𐐿 𐑁𐐫𐑉𐐶𐐲𐑉𐐼 𐐱𐑌 𐑄 𐐝𐐲𐑌 𐐱𐑂 𐐘𐐱𐐼, 𐐮𐐻 𐐺𐐨𐐮𐑍 𐐰 𐐻𐐴𐐹 𐐱𐑂 𐐸𐐮𐑆 𐐫𐑉𐐼𐐲𐑉, 𐐫𐑉 𐐮𐐻 𐐺𐐨𐐮𐑍 𐐸𐐮𐑆 𐐫𐑉𐐼𐐲𐑉; 𐐰𐑌𐐼 𐑄𐐮𐑅 𐑄𐐰𐐻 𐑄𐐩 𐑋𐐴𐐻 𐑊𐐳𐐿 𐑁𐐫𐑉𐐶𐐲𐑉𐐼 𐐻𐐭 𐐸𐐮𐑋 𐑁𐐫𐑉 𐐰 𐑉𐐨𐑋𐐮𐑇𐐲𐑌 𐐱𐑂 𐑄𐐩𐑉 𐑅𐐮𐑌𐑆, 𐑄𐐰𐐻 𐑄𐐩 𐑋𐐴𐐻 𐐯𐑌𐐻𐐲𐑉 𐐮𐑌𐐻𐐭 𐑄 𐑉𐐯𐑅𐐻 𐐱𐑂 𐑄 𐐢𐐫𐑉𐐼.

2. 𐐤𐐵 𐑄𐐮𐑅 𐐣𐐯𐑊𐐿𐐮𐑆𐐯𐐼𐐯𐐿 𐐶𐐱𐑆 𐐰 𐐿𐐮𐑍 𐐬𐑂𐐲𐑉 𐑄 𐑊𐐰𐑌𐐼 𐐱𐑂 𐐝𐐩𐑊𐐯𐑋; 𐐰𐑌𐐼 𐐸𐐮𐑆 𐐹𐐨𐐹𐑊 𐐸𐐰𐐼 𐐶𐐰𐐿𐑅𐐻 𐑅𐐻𐑉𐐱𐑍 𐐮𐑌 𐐮𐑌𐐮𐐿𐐶𐐮𐐻𐐨 𐐰𐑌𐐼 𐐲𐐺𐐱𐑋𐐮𐑌𐐩𐑇𐐲𐑌; 𐐷𐐩, 𐑄𐐩 𐐸𐐰𐐼 𐐫𐑊 𐑀𐐱𐑌 𐐲𐑅𐐻𐑉𐐩: 𐑄𐐩 𐐶𐐲𐑉 𐑁𐐳𐑊 𐐱𐑂 𐐫𐑊 𐑋𐐰𐑌𐐲𐑉 𐐱𐑂 𐐶𐐮𐐿𐐯𐐼𐑌𐐯𐑅: 𐐺𐐲𐐻 𐐣𐐯𐑊𐐿𐐮𐑆𐐯𐐼𐐯𐐿 𐐸𐐰𐑂𐐮𐑍 𐐯𐐿𐑅𐐲𐑉𐑅𐐴𐑆𐐼 𐑋𐐴𐐻𐐨 𐑁𐐩𐑃, 𐐰𐑌𐐼 𐑉𐐨𐑅𐐨𐑂𐐼 𐑄 𐐱𐑁𐐮𐑅 𐐱𐑂 𐑄 𐐸𐐴 𐐹𐑉𐐨𐑅𐐻𐐸𐐳𐐼, 𐐰𐐿𐐫𐑉𐐼𐐮𐑍 𐐻𐐭 𐑄 𐐸𐐬𐑊𐐨 𐐫𐑉𐐼𐐲𐑉 𐐱𐑂 𐐘𐐱𐐼, 𐐼𐐮𐐼 𐐹𐑉𐐨𐐽 𐑉𐐨𐐹𐐯𐑌𐐻𐐰𐑌𐑅 𐐲𐑌𐐻𐐭 𐐸𐐮𐑆 𐐹𐐨𐐹𐑊. 𐐈𐑌𐐼 𐐺𐐨𐐸𐐬𐑊𐐼, 𐑄𐐩 𐐼𐐮𐐼 𐑉𐐨𐐹𐐯𐑌𐐻; 𐐰𐑌𐐼 𐐣𐐯𐑊𐐿𐐮𐑆𐐯𐐼𐐯𐐿 𐐼𐐮𐐼 𐐯𐑅𐐻𐐰𐐺𐑊𐐮𐑇 𐐹𐐨𐑅 𐐮𐑌 𐑄 𐑊𐐰𐑌𐐼 𐐮𐑌 𐐸𐐮𐑆 𐐼𐐩𐑆; 𐑄𐐯𐑉𐑁𐐬𐑉 𐐸𐐨 𐐶𐐱𐑆 𐐿𐐫𐑊𐐼 𐑄 𐐹𐑉𐐮𐑌𐑅 𐐱𐑂 𐐹𐐨𐑅, 𐑁𐐫𐑉 𐐸𐐨 𐐶𐐱𐑆 𐑄 𐐿𐐮𐑍 𐐱𐑂 𐐝𐐩𐑊𐐯𐑋; 𐐰𐑌𐐼 𐐸𐐨 𐐼𐐮𐐼 𐑉𐐩𐑌 𐐲𐑌𐐼𐐲𐑉 𐐸𐐮𐑆 𐑁𐐪𐑄𐐲𐑉. 𐐤𐐵, 𐑄𐐩𐑉 𐐶𐐲𐑉 𐑋𐐯𐑌𐐨 𐐺𐐨𐑁𐐬𐑉 𐐸𐐮𐑋, 𐐰𐑌𐐼 𐐫𐑊𐑅𐐬 𐑄𐐩𐑉 𐐶𐐲𐑉 𐑋𐐯𐑌𐐨 𐐪𐑁𐐻𐐲𐑉𐐶𐐲𐑉𐐼𐑆, 𐐺𐐲𐐻 𐑌𐐲𐑌 𐐶𐐲𐑉 𐑀𐑉𐐩𐐻𐐲𐑉; 𐑄𐐯𐑉𐑁𐐬𐑉, 𐐱𐑂 𐐸𐐮𐑋 𐑄𐐩 𐐸𐐰𐑂 𐑋𐐬𐑉 𐐹𐐪𐑉𐐻𐐮𐐿𐐷𐐭𐑊𐐲𐑉𐑊𐐨 𐑋𐐩𐐼 𐑋𐐯𐑌𐑇𐐲𐑌. 𐐤𐐵 𐐌 𐑌𐐨𐐼 𐑌𐐱𐐻 𐑉𐐨𐐸𐐲𐑉𐑅 𐑄 𐑋𐐰𐐻𐐲𐑉; 𐐸𐐶𐐱𐐻 𐐌 𐐸𐐰𐑂 𐑅𐐯𐐼 𐑋𐐩 𐑅𐐲𐑁𐐴𐑅. 𐐒𐐨𐐸𐐬𐑊𐐼, 𐑄 𐑅𐐿𐑉𐐮𐐹𐐽𐐲𐑉𐑆 𐐪𐑉 𐐺𐐨𐑁𐐬𐑉 𐐷𐐭; 𐐮𐑁 𐐷𐐨 𐐶𐐮𐑊 𐑉𐐯𐑅𐐻 𐑄𐐯𐑋 𐐮𐐻 𐑇𐐰𐑊 𐐺𐐨 𐐻𐐭 𐐷𐐭𐑉 𐐬𐑌 𐐼𐐯𐑅𐐻𐑉𐐲𐐿𐑇𐐲𐑌.

3. 𐐈𐑌𐐼 𐑌𐐵 𐐮𐐻 𐐿𐐩𐑋 𐐻𐐭 𐐹𐐪𐑅 𐑄𐐰𐐻 𐐸𐐶𐐯𐑌 𐐈𐑊𐑋𐐲 𐐸𐐰𐐼 𐑅𐐯𐐼 𐑄𐐨𐑆 𐐶𐐲𐑉𐐼𐑆 𐐲𐑌𐐻𐐭 𐑄𐐯𐑋, 𐐸𐐨 𐑅𐐻𐑉𐐯𐐽𐐻 𐑁𐐬𐑉𐑃 𐐸𐐮𐑆 𐐸𐐰𐑌𐐼 𐐲𐑌𐐻𐐭 𐑄𐐯𐑋 𐐰𐑌𐐼 𐐿𐑉𐐴𐐼 𐐶𐐮𐑄 𐐰 𐑋𐐴𐐻𐐨 𐑂𐐦𐑅, 𐑅𐐩𐐮𐑍, 𐐤𐐵 𐐮𐑆 𐑄 𐐻𐐴𐑋 𐐻𐐭 𐑉𐐨𐐹𐐯𐑌𐐻, 𐑁𐐫𐑉 𐑄 𐐼𐐩 𐐱𐑂 𐑅𐐰𐑊𐑂𐐩𐑇𐐲𐑌 𐐼𐑉𐐫𐐯𐑃 𐑌𐐴; 𐐷𐐩, 𐐰𐑌𐐼 𐑄 𐑂𐐦𐑅 𐐱𐑂 𐑄 𐐢𐐫𐑉𐐼, 𐐺𐐴 𐑄 𐑋𐐵𐑃 𐐱𐑂 𐐩𐑌𐐾𐐯𐑊𐑆, 𐐼𐐲𐑃 𐐼𐐨𐐿𐑊𐐩𐑉 𐐮𐐻 𐐲𐑌𐐻𐐭 𐐫𐑊 𐑌𐐩𐑇𐐲𐑌𐑆: 𐐷𐐩, 𐐼𐐲𐑃 𐐼𐐨𐐿𐑊𐐩𐑉 𐐮𐐻, 𐑄𐐰𐐻 𐑄𐐩 𐑋𐐩 𐐸𐐰𐑂 𐑀𐑊𐐰𐐼 𐐻𐐴𐐼𐐮𐑍𐑆 𐐱𐑂 𐑀𐑉𐐩𐐻 𐐾𐐦; 𐐷𐐩, 𐐰𐑌𐐼 𐐸𐐨 𐐼𐐲𐑃 𐑅𐐵𐑌𐐼 𐑄𐐨𐑆 𐑀𐑊𐐰𐐼 𐐻𐐴𐐼𐐮𐑍𐑆 𐐲𐑋𐐲𐑍 𐐫𐑊 𐐸𐐮𐑆 𐐹𐐨𐐹𐑊, 𐐷𐐩, 𐐨𐑂𐐲𐑌 𐐻𐐭 𐑄𐐯𐑋 𐑄𐐰𐐻 𐐪𐑉 𐑅𐐿𐐰𐐻𐐲𐑉𐐼 𐐲𐐺𐑉𐐫𐐼 𐐲𐐹𐐱𐑌 𐑄 𐑁𐐩𐑅 𐐱𐑂 𐑄 𐐲𐑉𐑃; 𐐸𐐶𐐩𐑉𐑁𐐬𐑉 𐑄𐐩 𐐸𐐰𐑂 𐐿𐐲𐑋 𐐲𐑌𐐻𐐭 𐐲𐑅. 𐐈𐑌𐐼 𐑄𐐩 𐐪𐑉 𐑋𐐩𐐼 𐑌𐐬𐑌 𐐲𐑌𐐻𐐭 𐐲𐑅 𐐮𐑌 𐐹𐑊𐐩𐑌 𐐻𐐲𐑉𐑋𐑆, 𐑄𐐰𐐻 𐐶𐐨 𐑋𐐩 𐐲𐑌𐐼𐐲𐑉𐑅𐐻𐐰𐑌𐐼, 𐑄𐐰𐐻 𐐶𐐨 𐐿𐐰𐑌𐑌𐐱𐐻 𐐲𐑉; 𐐰𐑌𐐼 𐑄𐐮𐑅 𐐺𐐨𐐿𐐫𐑆 𐐱𐑂 𐐵𐑉 𐐺𐐨𐐮𐑍 𐐶𐐱𐑌𐐼𐐲𐑉𐐲𐑉𐑆 𐐮𐑌 𐐰 𐑅𐐻𐑉𐐩𐑌𐐾 𐑊𐐰𐑌𐐼; 𐑄𐐯𐑉𐑁𐐬𐑉, 𐐶𐐨 𐐪𐑉 𐑄𐐲𐑅 𐐸𐐴𐑊𐐨 𐑁𐐩𐑂𐐲𐑉𐐼, 𐑁𐐫𐑉 𐐶𐐨 𐐸𐐰𐑂 𐑄𐐨𐑆 𐑀𐑊𐐰𐐼 𐐻𐐴𐐼𐐮𐑍𐑆 𐐼𐐨𐐿𐑊𐐩𐑉𐐼 𐐲𐑌𐐻𐐭 𐐲𐑅 𐐮𐑌 𐐫𐑊 𐐹𐐪𐑉𐐻𐑅 𐐱𐑂 𐐵𐑉 𐑂𐐮𐑌𐐷𐐲𐑉𐐼. 𐐙𐐫𐑉 𐐺𐐨𐐸𐐬𐑊𐐼, 𐐩𐑌𐐾𐐯𐑊𐑆 𐐪𐑉 𐐼𐐨𐐿𐑊𐐩𐑉𐐮𐑍 𐐮𐐻 𐐲𐑌𐐻𐐭 𐑋𐐯𐑌𐐨 𐐰𐐻 𐑄𐐮𐑅 𐐻𐐴𐑋 𐐮𐑌 𐐵𐑉 𐑊𐐰𐑌𐐼; 𐐰𐑌𐐼 𐑄𐐮𐑅 𐐮𐑆 𐑁𐐫𐑉 𐑄 𐐹𐐲𐑉𐐹𐐲𐑅 𐐱𐑂 𐐹𐑉𐐨𐐹𐐩𐑉𐐮𐑍 𐑄 𐐸𐐪𐑉𐐻𐑅 𐐱𐑂 𐑄 𐐽𐐮𐑊𐐼𐑉𐐯𐑌 𐐱𐑂 𐑋𐐯𐑌 𐐻𐐭 𐑉𐐨𐑅𐐨𐑂 𐐸𐐮𐑆 𐐶𐐲𐑉𐐼 𐐰𐐻 𐑄 𐐻𐐴𐑋 𐐱𐑂 𐐸𐐮𐑆 𐐿𐐲𐑋𐐮𐑍 𐐮𐑌 𐐸𐐮𐑆 𐑀𐑊𐐬𐑉𐐨. 𐐈𐑌𐐼 𐑌𐐵 𐐶𐐨 𐐬𐑌𐑊𐐨 𐐶𐐩𐐻 𐐻𐐭 𐐸𐐨𐑉 𐑄 𐐾𐐦𐑁𐐳𐑊 𐑌𐐧𐑆 𐐼𐐨𐐿𐑊𐐩𐑉𐐼 𐐲𐑌𐐻𐐭 𐐲𐑅 𐐺𐐴 𐑄 𐑋𐐵𐑃 𐐱𐑂 𐐩𐑌𐐾𐐯𐑊𐑆, 𐐱𐑂 𐐸𐐮𐑆 𐐿𐐲𐑋𐐮𐑍: 𐑁𐐫𐑉 𐑄 𐐻𐐴𐑋 𐐿𐐲𐑋𐐯𐑃, 𐐶𐐨 𐑌𐐬 𐑌𐐱𐐻 𐐸𐐵 𐑅𐐭𐑌. 𐐎𐐳𐐼 𐐻𐐭 𐐘𐐱𐐼 𐑄𐐰𐐻 𐐮𐐻 𐑋𐐴𐐻 𐐺𐐨 𐐮𐑌 𐑋𐐴 𐐼𐐩; 𐐺𐐲𐐻 𐑊𐐯𐐻 𐐮𐐻 𐐺𐐨 𐑅𐐭𐑌𐐲𐑉 𐐫𐑉 𐑊𐐩𐐻𐐲𐑉, 𐐮𐑌 𐐮𐐻 𐐌 𐐶𐐮𐑊 𐑉𐐨𐐾𐐦𐑅. 𐐈𐑌𐐼 𐐮𐐻 𐑇𐐰𐑊 𐐺𐐨 𐑋𐐩𐐼 𐑌𐐬𐑌

𐐲𐑌𐐻𐐭 𐐾𐐲𐑅𐐻 𐐰𐑌𐐼 𐐸𐐬𐑊𐐨 𐑋𐐯𐑌, 𐐺𐐴 𐑄 𐑋𐐵𐑃 𐐱𐑂 𐐩𐑌𐐾𐐯𐑊𐑆, 𐐰𐐻 𐑄 𐐻𐐴𐑋 𐐱𐑂 𐐸𐐮𐑆 𐐿𐐲𐑋𐐮𐑍, 𐑄𐐰𐐻 𐑄 𐐶𐐲𐑉𐐼𐑆 𐐱𐑂 𐐵𐑉 𐑁𐐪𐑄𐐲𐑉𐑆 𐑋𐐩 𐐺𐐨 𐑁𐐳𐑊𐑁𐐮𐑊𐐼, 𐐰𐐿𐐫𐑉𐐼𐐮𐑍 𐐻𐐭 𐑄𐐰𐐻 𐐸𐐶𐐮𐐽 𐑄𐐩 𐐸𐐰𐑂 𐑅𐐹𐐬𐐿𐐲𐑌 𐐿𐐱𐑌𐑅𐐲𐑉𐑌𐐮𐑍 𐐸𐐮𐑋, 𐐸𐐶𐐮𐐽 𐐶𐐱𐑆 𐐰𐐿𐐫𐑉𐐼𐐮𐑍 𐐻𐐭 𐑄 𐑅𐐹𐐮𐑉𐐮𐐻 𐐱𐑂 𐐹𐑉𐐱𐑁𐐯𐑅𐐨 𐐸𐐶𐐮𐐽 𐐶𐐱𐑆 𐐮𐑌 𐑄𐐯𐑋.

4. 𐐈𐑌𐐼 𐑌𐐵 𐑋𐐴 𐐺𐑉𐐯𐑄𐑉𐐯𐑌, 𐐌 𐐶𐐮𐑇 𐑁𐑉𐐱𐑋 𐑄 𐐮𐑌𐑋𐐬𐑅𐐻 𐐹𐐪𐑉𐐻 𐐱𐑂 𐑋𐐴 𐐸𐐪𐑉𐐻, 𐐷𐐩, 𐐶𐐮𐑄 𐑀𐑉𐐩𐐻 𐐰𐑍𐑆𐐴𐐲𐐻𐐨 𐐨𐑂𐑌 𐐲𐑌𐐻𐐭 𐐹𐐩𐑌, 𐑄𐐰𐐻 𐐷𐐨 𐐶𐐳𐐼 𐐸𐐪𐑉𐐿𐐲𐑌 𐐲𐑌𐐻𐐭 𐑋𐐴 𐐶𐐲𐑉𐐼𐑆, 𐐰𐑌𐐼 𐐿𐐰𐑅𐐻 𐐫𐑁 𐐷𐐭𐑉 𐑅𐐮𐑌𐑆, 𐐰𐑌𐐼 𐑌𐐱𐐻 𐐹𐑉𐐬𐐿𐑉𐐰𐑅𐐻𐐮𐑌𐐩𐐻 𐑄 𐐼𐐩 𐐱𐑂 𐐷𐐭𐑉 𐑉𐐨𐐹𐐯𐑌𐐻𐐲𐑌𐑅; 𐐺𐐲𐐻 𐑄𐐰𐐻 𐐷𐐨 𐐶𐐳𐐼 𐐸𐐲𐑋𐐺𐑊 𐐷𐐭𐑉𐑅𐐯𐑊𐑂𐑆 𐐺𐐨𐑁𐐬𐑉 𐑄 𐐢𐐫𐑉𐐼, 𐐰𐑌𐐼 𐐿𐐫𐑊 𐐱𐑌 𐐸𐐮𐑆 𐐸𐐬𐑊𐐨 𐑌𐐩𐑋, 𐐰𐑌𐐼 𐐶𐐱𐐽 𐐰𐑌𐐼 𐐹𐑉𐐩 𐐿𐐱𐑌𐐻𐐮𐑌𐐷𐐭𐐲𐑊𐐨, 𐑄𐐰𐐻 𐐷𐐨 𐑋𐐩 𐑌𐐱𐐻 𐐺𐐨 𐐻𐐯𐑋𐐻𐐯𐐼 𐐲𐐺𐐲𐑂 𐑄𐐰𐐻 𐐸𐐶𐐮𐐽 𐐷𐐨 𐐿𐐰𐑌 𐐺𐐩𐑉, 𐐰𐑌𐐼 𐑄𐐲𐑅 𐐺𐐨 𐑊𐐯𐐼 𐐺𐐴 𐑄 𐐐𐐬𐑊𐐨 𐐝𐐹𐐮𐑉𐐮𐐻, 𐐺𐐨𐐿𐐲𐑋𐐮𐑍 𐐸𐐲𐑋𐐺𐑊, 𐑋𐐨𐐿, 𐑅𐐲𐐺𐑋𐐮𐑅𐐮𐑂, 𐐹𐐩𐑇𐐯𐑌𐐻, 𐑁𐐳𐑊 𐐱𐑂 𐑊𐐲𐑂 𐐰𐑌𐐼 𐐫𐑊 𐑊𐐫𐑍-𐑅𐐲𐑁𐐲𐑉𐐮𐑍; 𐐸𐐰𐑂𐐮𐑍 𐑁𐐩𐑃 𐐱𐑌 𐑄 𐐢𐐫𐑉𐐼; 𐐸𐐰𐑂𐐮𐑍 𐐩 𐐸𐐬𐐹 𐑄𐐰𐐻 𐐷𐐨 𐑇𐐰𐑊 𐑉𐐨𐑅𐐨𐑂 𐐨𐐻𐐲𐑉𐑌𐐲𐑊 𐑊𐐴𐑁; 𐐸𐐰𐑂𐐮𐑍 𐑄 𐑊𐐲𐑂 𐐱𐑂 𐐘𐐱𐐼 𐐫𐑊𐐶𐐩𐑆 𐐮𐑌 𐐷𐐭𐑉 𐐸𐐪𐑉𐐻𐑅, 𐑄𐐰𐐻 𐐷𐐨 𐑋𐐩 𐐺𐐨 𐑊𐐮𐑁𐐻𐐯𐐼 𐐲𐐹 𐐰𐐻 𐑄 𐑊𐐰𐑅𐐻 𐐼𐐩 𐐰𐑌𐐼 𐐯𐑌𐐻𐐲𐑉 𐐮𐑌𐐻𐐭 𐐸𐐮𐑆 𐑉𐐯𐑅𐐻: 𐐰𐑌𐐼 𐑋𐐩 𐑄 𐐢𐐫𐑉𐐼 𐑀𐑉𐐰𐑌𐐻 𐐲𐑌𐐻𐐭 𐐷𐐭 𐑉𐐨𐐹𐐯𐑌𐐻𐐲𐑌𐑅, 𐑄𐐰𐐻 𐐷𐐨 𐑋𐐩 𐑌𐐱𐐻 𐐺𐑉𐐮𐑍 𐐼𐐵𐑌 𐐸𐐮𐑆 𐑉𐐪𐑃 𐐲𐐹𐐱𐑌 𐐷𐐭, 𐑄𐐰𐐻 𐐷𐐨 𐑋𐐩 𐑌𐐱𐐻 𐐺𐐨 𐐺𐐵𐑌𐐼 𐐼𐐵𐑌 𐐺𐐴 𐑄 𐐽𐐩𐑌𐑆 𐐱𐑂 𐐸𐐯𐑊, 𐑄𐐰𐐻 𐐷𐐨 𐑋𐐩 𐑌𐐱𐐻 𐑅𐐲𐑁𐐲𐑉 𐑄 𐑅𐐯𐐿𐐲𐑌𐐼 𐐼𐐯𐑃. 𐐈𐑌𐐼 𐐈𐑊𐑋𐐲 𐑅𐐹𐐩𐐿 𐑋𐐯𐑌𐐨 𐑋𐐬𐑉 𐐶𐐲𐑉𐐼𐑆 𐐲𐑌𐐻𐐭 𐑄 𐐹𐐨𐐹𐑊, 𐐸𐐶𐐮𐐽 𐐪𐑉 𐑌𐐱𐐻 𐑉𐐮𐐻𐑌 𐐮𐑌 𐑄𐐮𐑅 𐐺𐐳𐐿.

5. 𐐈𐑌𐐼 𐐮𐐻 𐐿𐐩𐑋 𐐻𐐭 𐐹𐐰𐑅 𐐰𐑁𐐻𐐲𐑉 𐐸𐐨 𐐸𐐰𐐼 𐑋𐐩𐐼 𐐰𐑌 𐐯𐑌𐐼 𐐱𐑂 𐑅𐐹𐐨𐐿𐐮𐑍 𐐲𐑌𐐻𐐭 𐑄 𐐹𐐨𐐹𐑊, 𐑋𐐯𐑌𐐨 𐐱𐑂 𐑄𐐯𐑋 𐐼𐐮𐐼 𐐺𐐨𐑊𐐨𐑂 𐐱𐑌 𐐸𐐮𐑆 𐐶𐐲𐑉𐐼𐑆, 𐐰𐑌𐐼 𐐺𐐨𐑀𐐰𐑌 𐐻𐐭 𐑉𐐨𐐹𐐯𐑌𐐻, 𐐰𐑌𐐼 𐐻𐐭 𐑅𐐲𐑉𐐽 𐑄 𐑅𐐿𐑉𐐮𐐹𐐽𐐲𐑉𐑆; 𐐺𐐲𐐻 𐑄 𐑋𐐬𐑉 𐐹𐐪𐑉𐐻 𐐱𐑂 𐑄𐐯𐑋 𐐶𐐲𐑉 𐐼𐐨𐑆𐐴𐑉𐐲𐑅 𐑄𐐰𐐻 𐑄𐐩 𐑋𐐴𐐻 𐐼𐐯𐑅𐐻𐑉𐐦 𐐈𐑊𐑋𐐲 𐐰𐑌𐐼 𐐈𐑋𐐷𐐭𐑊𐐯𐐿; 𐑁𐐫𐑉 𐑄𐐩 𐐶𐐲𐑉 𐐰𐑍𐑀𐑉𐐨 𐐶𐐮𐑄 𐐈𐑊𐑋𐐲, 𐐺𐐨𐐿𐐫𐑆 𐐱𐑂 𐑄 𐐹𐑊𐐩𐑌𐑌𐐯𐑅 𐐱𐑂 𐐸𐐮𐑆 𐐶𐐲𐑉𐐼𐑆 𐐲𐑌𐐻𐐭 𐐞𐐨𐑆𐑉𐐱𐑋; 𐐰𐑌𐐼 𐑄𐐩 𐐫𐑊𐑅𐐬 𐑅𐐯𐐼 𐑄𐐰𐐻 𐐈𐑋𐐷𐐭𐑊𐐯𐐿 𐐸𐐰𐐼 𐑊𐐴𐐼 𐐲𐑌𐐻𐐭 𐑄𐐯𐑋, 𐐰𐑌𐐼 𐐸𐐰𐐼 𐑉𐐨𐑂𐐴𐑊𐐼 𐐲𐑀𐐯𐑌𐑅𐐻 𐑄𐐯𐑉 𐑊𐐫, 𐐰𐑌𐐼 𐐫𐑊𐑅𐐬 𐐲𐑀𐐯𐑌𐑅𐐻 𐑄𐐯𐑉 𐑊𐐫𐐷𐐲𐑉𐑆 𐐰𐑌𐐼 𐐾𐐲𐐾𐐯𐑆. 𐐈𐑌𐐼 𐑄𐐩 𐐶𐐲𐑉 𐐫𐑊𐑅𐐬 𐐰𐑍𐑀𐑉𐐨 𐐶𐐮𐑄 𐐈𐑊𐑋𐐲 𐐰𐑌𐐼 𐐈𐑋𐐷𐐭𐑊𐐯𐐿; 𐐰𐑌𐐼 𐐺𐐨𐐿𐐫𐑆 𐑄𐐩 𐐸𐐰𐐼 𐐻𐐯𐑅𐐻𐐮𐑁𐐴𐐼 𐑅𐐬 𐐹𐑊𐐩𐑌𐑊𐐨 𐐲𐑀𐐯𐑌𐑅𐐻 𐑄𐐯𐑉 𐐶𐐮𐐿𐐯𐐼𐑌𐐯𐑅, 𐑄𐐩 𐑅𐐫𐐻 𐐻𐐭 𐐹𐐳𐐻 𐑄𐐯𐑋 𐐲𐐶𐐩 𐐹𐑉𐐮𐑂𐐮𐑊𐐨. 𐐒𐐲𐐻 𐐮𐐻 𐐿𐐩𐑋 𐐻𐐭 𐐹𐐰𐑅 𐑄𐐰𐐻 𐑄𐐩 𐐼𐐮𐐼 𐑌𐐱𐐻; 𐐺𐐲𐐻 𐑄𐐩 𐐻𐐳𐐿 𐑄𐐯𐑋 𐐰𐑌𐐼 𐐺𐐵𐑌𐐼 𐑄𐐯𐑋 𐐶𐐮𐑄 𐑅𐐻𐑉𐐫𐑍 𐐿𐐫𐑉𐐼𐑆, 𐐰𐑌𐐼 𐐻𐐳𐐿 𐑄𐐯𐑋 𐐺𐐨𐑁𐐬𐑉 𐑄 𐐽𐐨𐑁 𐐾𐐲𐐾 𐐱𐑂 𐑄 𐑊𐐰𐑌𐐼. 𐐈𐑌𐐼 𐑄 𐐹𐐨𐐹𐑊 𐐶𐐯𐑌𐐻 𐑁𐐬𐑉𐑃 𐐰𐑌𐐼 𐐶𐐮𐐻𐑌𐐯𐑅𐐻 𐐲𐑀𐐯𐑌𐑅𐐻 𐑄𐐯𐑋, 𐐻𐐯𐑅𐐻𐐮𐑁𐐴𐐮𐑍 𐑄𐐰𐐻 𐑄𐐩 𐐸𐐰𐐼 𐑉𐐨𐑂𐐴𐑊𐐼 𐐲𐑀𐐯𐑌𐑅𐐻 𐑄 𐑊𐐫, 𐐰𐑌𐐼 𐑄𐐯𐑉 𐑊𐐫𐐷𐐲𐑉𐑆 𐐰𐑌𐐼 𐐾𐐲𐐾𐐯𐑆 𐐱𐑂 𐑄 𐑊𐐰𐑌𐐼, 𐐰𐑌𐐼 𐐫𐑊𐑅𐐬 𐐱𐑂 𐐫𐑊 𐑄 𐐹𐐨𐐹𐑊 𐑄𐐰𐐻 𐐶𐐲𐑉 𐐮𐑌 𐑄 𐑊𐐰𐑌𐐼; 𐐰𐑌𐐼 𐐫𐑊𐑅𐐬 𐐻𐐯𐑅𐐻𐐮𐑁𐐴𐐼 𐑄𐐰𐐻 𐑄𐐯𐑉 𐐶𐐱𐑆 𐐺𐐲𐐻 𐐶𐐲𐑌 𐐘𐐱𐐼, 𐐰𐑌𐐼 𐑄𐐰𐐻 𐐸𐐨 𐑇𐐳𐐼 𐑅𐐯𐑌𐐼 𐐸𐐮𐑆 𐐝𐐲𐑌 𐐲𐑋𐐲𐑍 𐑄 𐐹𐐨𐐹𐑊, 𐐺𐐲𐐻 𐐸𐐨 𐑇𐐳𐐼 𐑌𐐱𐐻 𐑅𐐩𐑂 𐑄𐐯𐑋; 𐐰𐑌𐐼 𐑋𐐯𐑌𐐨 𐑅𐐲𐐽 𐑃𐐮𐑍𐑆 𐐼𐐮𐐼 𐑄 𐐹𐐨𐐹𐑊 𐐻𐐯𐑅𐐻𐐮𐑁𐐴 𐐲𐑀𐐯𐑌𐑅𐐻 𐐈𐑊𐑋𐐲 𐐰𐑌𐐼 𐐈𐑋𐐷𐐭𐑊𐐯𐐿. 𐐤𐐵 𐑄𐐮𐑅 𐐶𐐱𐑆 𐐼𐐲𐑌 𐐺𐐨𐑁𐐬𐑉 𐑄 𐐽𐐨𐑁 𐐾𐐲𐐾 𐐱𐑂 𐑄 𐑊𐐰𐑌𐐼. 𐐈𐑌𐐼 𐐮𐐻 𐐿𐐩𐑋 𐐻𐐭 𐐹𐐰𐑅 𐑄𐐰𐐻 𐐞𐐨𐑆𐑉𐐱𐑋 𐐶𐐱𐑆 𐐰𐑅𐐻𐐱𐑌𐐮𐑇𐐻 𐐰𐐻 𐑄 𐐶𐐲𐑉𐐼𐑆 𐐸𐐶𐐮𐐽 𐐸𐐰𐐼 𐐺𐐮𐑌 𐑅𐐹𐐬𐐿𐐲𐑌; 𐐰𐑌𐐼 𐐸𐐨 𐐫𐑊𐑅𐐬 𐑌𐐭 𐐿𐐱𐑌𐑅𐐲𐑉𐑌𐐮𐑍 𐑄 𐐺𐑊𐐴𐑌𐐼𐑌𐐯𐑅 𐐱𐑂 𐑄 𐑋𐐴𐑌𐐼𐑆, 𐐸𐐶𐐮𐐽 𐐸𐐨 𐐸𐐰𐐼 𐐿𐐫𐑆𐐼 𐐲𐑋𐐲𐑍 𐑄 𐐹𐐨𐐹𐑊 𐐺𐐴 𐐸𐐮𐑆 𐑊𐐴𐐮𐑍 𐐶𐐲𐑉𐐼𐑆; 𐐰𐑌𐐼 𐐸𐐮𐑆 𐑅𐐬𐑊 𐐺𐐨𐑀𐐰𐑌 𐐻𐐭 𐐺𐐨 𐐸𐐰𐑉𐐬𐐼 𐐲𐐹 𐐲𐑌𐐼𐐲𐑉 𐐩 𐐿𐐱𐑌𐑇𐐲𐑅𐑌𐐯𐑅 𐐱𐑂 𐐸𐐮𐑆 𐐬𐑌 𐑀𐐮𐑊𐐻; 𐐷𐐩, 𐐸𐐨 𐐺𐐨𐑀𐐰𐑌 𐐻𐐭 𐐺𐐨 𐐯𐑌𐑅𐐲𐑉𐐿𐑊𐐼 𐐲𐐺𐐵𐐻 𐐺𐐴 𐑄 𐐹𐐩𐑌𐑆 𐐱𐑂 𐐸𐐯𐑊.

6. 𐐈𐑌𐐼 𐐮𐐻 𐐿𐐩𐑋 𐐻𐐭 𐐹𐐰𐑅 𐑄𐐰𐐻 𐐸𐐨 𐐺𐐨𐑀𐐰𐑌 𐐻𐐭 𐐿𐑉𐐴 𐐲𐑌𐐻𐐭 𐑄 𐐹𐐨𐐹𐑊, 𐑅𐐩𐐮𐑍: 𐐒𐐨𐐸𐐬𐑊𐐼, 𐐌 𐐰𐑋 𐑀𐐮𐑊𐐻𐐨, 𐐰𐑌𐐼 𐑄𐐨𐑆 𐑋𐐯𐑌 𐐪𐑉 𐑅𐐹𐐱𐐻𐑊𐐯𐑅 𐐺𐐨𐑁𐐬𐑉 𐐘𐐱𐐼. 𐐈𐑌𐐼 𐐸𐐨 𐐺𐐨𐑀𐐰𐑌 𐐻𐐭 𐐹𐑊𐐨𐐼 𐑁𐐫𐑉 𐑄𐐯𐑋 𐑁𐑉𐐱𐑋 𐑄𐐰𐐻 𐐻𐐴𐑋 𐑁𐐬𐑉𐑃; 𐐺𐐲𐐻 𐑄𐐩 𐑉𐐨𐑂𐐴𐑊𐐼 𐐸𐐮𐑋, 𐑅𐐩𐐮𐑍: 𐐂𐑉𐐻 𐑄𐐵 𐐫𐑊𐑅𐐬 𐐹𐐲𐑆𐐯𐑅𐐻 𐐶𐐮𐑄 𐑄 𐐼𐐯𐑂𐐮𐑊? 𐐈𐑌𐐼 𐑄𐐩 𐑅𐐹𐐮𐐻 𐐲𐐹𐐱𐑌 𐐸𐐮𐑋, 𐐰𐑌𐐼 𐐿𐐰𐑅𐐻 𐐸𐐮𐑋 𐐵𐐻 𐑁𐑉𐐱𐑋 𐐲𐑋𐐲𐑍 𐑄𐐯𐑋, 𐐰𐑌𐐼 𐐫𐑊𐑅𐐬 𐐫𐑊 𐑄𐐬𐑆 𐐸𐐭 𐐺𐐨𐑊𐐨𐑂𐐼 𐐫𐑉 𐐸𐐰𐐼 𐐺𐐮𐑌 𐐻𐐫𐐻 𐐻𐐭 𐐺𐐨𐑊𐐨𐑂 𐐮𐑌 𐑄 𐐶𐐲𐑉𐐼𐑆 𐐸𐐶𐐮𐐽 𐐸𐐰𐐼 𐐺𐐮𐑌 𐑅𐐹𐐬𐐿𐐲𐑌 𐐺𐐴 𐐈𐑊𐑋𐐲 𐐰𐑌𐐼 𐐈𐑋𐐷𐐭𐑊𐐯𐐿; 𐐰𐑌𐐼 𐑄𐐩 𐐿𐐰𐑅𐐻 𐑄𐐯𐑋 𐐵𐐻, 𐐰𐑌𐐼 𐑅𐐯𐑌𐐻 𐑋𐐯𐑌 𐐻𐐭 𐐿𐐰𐑅𐐻 𐑅𐐻𐐬𐑌𐑆 𐐰𐐻 𐑄𐐯𐑋. 𐐈𐑌𐐼 𐑄𐐩 𐐺𐑉𐐫𐐻 𐑄𐐯𐑉 𐐶𐐴𐑂𐑆 𐐰𐑌𐐼 𐐽𐐮𐑊𐐼𐑉𐐯𐑌 𐐻𐐭𐑀𐐯𐑄𐐲𐑉, 𐐰𐑌𐐼 𐐸𐐭𐑅𐐬𐐯𐑂𐐲𐑉 𐐺𐐨𐑊𐐨𐑂𐐼, 𐐫𐑉 𐐸𐐰𐐼 𐐺𐐮𐑌 𐐻𐐫𐐻 𐐻𐐭 𐐺𐐨𐑊𐐨𐑂 𐐮𐑌 𐑄 𐐶𐐲𐑉𐐼

𐐱𐑂 𐐘𐐱𐐼, 𐑄𐐩 𐐿𐐫𐑆𐐼 𐑄𐐰𐐻 𐑄𐐩 𐑇𐐳𐐼 𐐺𐐨 𐐿𐐰𐑅𐐻 𐐮𐑌𐐻𐐭 𐑄 𐑁𐐴𐑉; 𐐰𐑌𐐼 𐑄𐐩 𐐫𐑊𐑅𐐬 𐐺𐑉𐐫𐐻 𐑁𐐫𐑉𐑃 𐑄𐐩𐑉 𐑉𐐯𐐿𐐫𐑉𐐼𐑆 𐐸𐐶𐐮𐐽 𐐿𐐱𐑌𐐻𐐩𐑌𐐼 𐑄 𐐸𐐬𐑊𐐨 𐐝𐐿𐑉𐐮𐐹𐐽𐐲𐑉𐑆, 𐐰𐑌𐐼 𐐿𐐰𐑅𐐻 𐑄𐐯𐑋 𐐮𐑌𐐻𐐭 𐑄 𐑁𐐴𐑉 𐐫𐑊𐑅𐐬, 𐑄𐐰𐐻 𐑄𐐩 𐑋𐐴𐐻 𐐺𐐨 𐐺𐐲𐑉𐑌𐐼 𐐰𐑌𐐼 𐐼𐐯𐑅𐐻𐑉𐐦𐐼 𐐺𐐴 𐑁𐐴𐑉.

7. 𐐈𐑌𐐼 𐐮𐐻 𐐿𐐩𐑋 𐐻𐐭 𐐹𐐪𐑅 𐑄𐐰𐐻 𐑄𐐩 𐐻𐐳𐐿 𐐈𐑊𐑋𐐲 𐐰𐑌𐐼 𐐈𐑋𐐷𐐭𐑊𐐯𐐿, 𐐰𐑌𐐼 𐐿𐐰𐑉𐐨𐐼 𐑄𐐯𐑋 𐑁𐐫𐑉𐑃 𐐻𐐭 𐑄 𐐹𐑊𐐩𐑅 𐐱𐑂 𐑋𐐪𐑉𐐻𐐲𐑉𐐼𐐲𐑋, 𐑄𐐰𐐻 𐑄𐐩 𐑋𐐴𐐻 𐐶𐐮𐐻𐑌𐐯𐑅 𐑄 𐐼𐐯𐑅𐐻𐑉𐐲𐐿𐑇𐐲𐑌 𐐱𐑂 𐑄𐐬𐑆 𐐸𐐭 𐐶𐐲𐑉 𐐿𐐱𐑌𐑅𐐭𐑋𐐼 𐐺𐐴 𐑁𐐴𐑉. 𐐈𐑌𐐼 𐐸𐐶𐐯𐑌 𐐈𐑋𐐷𐐭𐑊𐐯𐐿 𐑅𐐫 𐑄 𐐹𐐩𐑌𐑆 𐐱𐑂 𐑄 𐐶𐐮𐑋𐐯𐑌 𐐰𐑌𐐼 𐐽𐐮𐑊𐐼𐑉𐐯𐑌 𐐸𐐭 𐐶𐐲𐑉 𐐿𐐱𐑌𐑅𐐭𐑋𐐮𐑍 𐐮𐑌 𐑄 𐑁𐐴𐑉, 𐐸𐐨 𐐫𐑊𐑅𐐬 𐐶𐐱𐑆 𐐹𐐩𐑌𐐼; 𐐰𐑌𐐼 𐐸𐐨 𐑅𐐯𐐼 𐐲𐑌𐐻𐐭 𐐈𐑊𐑋𐐲, 𐐐𐐵 𐐿𐐰𐑌 𐐶𐐨 𐐶𐐮𐐻𐑌𐐯𐑅 𐑄𐐮𐑅 𐐫𐑁𐐳𐑊 𐑅𐐨𐑌? 𐐜𐐯𐑉𐑁𐐬𐑉 𐑊𐐯𐐻 𐐲𐑅 𐑅𐐻𐑉𐐯𐐽 𐑁𐐫𐑉𐑃 𐐵𐑉 𐐸𐐰𐑌𐐼𐑆, 𐐰𐑌𐐼 𐐯𐐿𐑅𐐲𐑉𐑅𐐴𐑆 𐑄 𐐹𐐵𐐲𐑉 𐐱𐑂 𐐘𐐱𐐼 𐐸𐐶𐐮𐐽 𐐮𐑆 𐐮𐑌 𐐲𐑅, 𐐰𐑌𐐼 𐑅𐐩𐑂 𐑄𐐯𐑋 𐑁𐑉𐐱𐑋 𐑄 𐑁𐑊𐐩𐑋𐑆. 𐐒𐐲𐐻 𐐈𐑊𐑋𐐲 𐑅𐐯𐐼 𐐲𐑌𐐻𐐭 𐐸𐐮𐑋, 𐐜 𐐝𐐹𐐮𐑉𐐮𐐻 𐐿𐐱𐑌𐑅𐐻𐑉𐐩𐑌𐐯𐑃 𐑋𐐨 𐑄𐐰𐐻 𐐌 𐑋𐐲𐑅𐐻 𐑌𐐱𐐻 𐑅𐐻𐑉𐐯𐐽 𐑁𐐫𐑉𐑃 𐑋𐐴𐑌 𐐸𐐰𐑌𐐼; 𐑁𐐫𐑉 𐐺𐐨𐐸𐐬𐑊𐐼 𐑄 𐐢𐐫𐑉𐐼 𐑉𐐨𐑅𐐨𐑂𐐯𐑃 𐑄𐐯𐑋 𐐲𐐹 𐐲𐑌𐐻𐐭 𐐸𐐮𐑋𐑅𐐯𐑊𐑁, 𐐮𐑌 𐑀𐑊𐐬𐑉𐐨; 𐐰𐑌𐐼 𐐸𐐨 𐐼𐐲𐑃 𐑅𐐲𐑁𐐲𐑉 𐑄𐐰𐐻 𐑄𐐩 𐑋𐐩 𐐼𐐭 𐑄𐐮𐑅 𐑃𐐮𐑍, 𐐫𐑉 𐑄𐐰𐐻 𐑄 𐐹𐐨𐐹𐐲𐑊 𐑋𐐩 𐐼𐐭 𐑄𐐮𐑅 𐑃𐐮𐑍 𐐲𐑌𐐻𐐭 𐑄𐐯𐑋, 𐐰𐐿𐐫𐑉𐐼𐐮𐑍 𐐻𐐭 𐑄 𐐸𐐪𐑉𐐼𐑌𐐯𐑅 𐐱𐑂 𐑄𐐩𐑉 𐐸𐐪𐑉𐐻𐑅, 𐑄𐐰𐐻 𐑄 𐐾𐐲𐐾𐑋𐐯𐑌𐐻𐑅 𐐸𐐶𐐮𐐽 𐐸𐐨 𐑇𐐰𐑊 𐐯𐐿𐑅𐐲𐑉𐑅𐐴𐑆 𐐲𐐹𐐱𐑌 𐑄𐐯𐑋 𐐮𐑌 𐐸𐐮𐑆 𐑉𐐪𐑃 𐑋𐐩 𐐺𐐨 𐐾𐐲𐑅𐐻; 𐐰𐑌𐐼 𐑄 𐐺𐑊𐐲𐐼 𐐱𐑂 𐑄 𐐮𐑌𐐬𐑅𐐯𐑌𐐻 𐑇𐐰𐑊 𐑅𐐻𐐰𐑌𐐼 𐐰𐑆 𐐲 𐐶𐐮𐐻𐑌𐐯𐑅 𐐲𐑀𐐯𐑌𐑅𐐻 𐑄𐐯𐑋, 𐐷𐐩, 𐐰𐑌𐐼 𐐿𐑉𐐴 𐑋𐐴𐐻𐐮𐑊𐐨 𐐲𐑀𐐯𐑌𐑅𐐻 𐑄𐐯𐑋 𐐰𐐻 𐑄 𐑊𐐪𐑅𐐻 𐐼𐐩. 𐐤𐐵 𐐈𐑋𐐷𐐭𐑊𐐯𐐿 𐑅𐐯𐐼 𐐲𐑌𐐻𐐭 𐐈𐑊𐑋𐐲, 𐐒𐐨𐐸𐐬𐑊𐐼, 𐐹𐐲𐑉𐐸𐐰𐐹𐑅 𐑄𐐩 𐐶𐐮𐑊 𐐺𐐲𐑉𐑌 𐐲𐑅 𐐫𐑊𐑅𐐬? 𐐈𐑌𐐼 𐐈𐑊𐑋𐐲 𐑅𐐯𐐼, 𐐒𐐨 𐐮𐐻 𐐰𐐿𐐫𐑉𐐼𐐮𐑍 𐐻𐐭 𐑄 𐐶𐐮𐑊 𐐱𐑂 𐑄 𐐢𐐫𐑉𐐼. 𐐒𐐲𐐻 𐐺𐐨𐐸𐐬𐑊𐐼, 𐐵𐑉 𐐶𐐲𐑉𐐿 𐐮𐑆 𐑌𐐱𐐻 𐑁𐐮𐑌𐐮𐑇𐐻; 𐑄𐐯𐑉𐑁𐐬𐑉 𐑄𐐩 𐐺𐐲𐑉𐑌 𐐲𐑅 𐑌𐐱𐐻.

8. 𐐤𐐵 𐐮𐐻 𐐿𐐩𐑋 𐐻𐐭 𐐹𐐪𐑅 𐑄𐐰𐐻 𐐸𐐶𐐯𐑌 𐑄 𐐺𐐱𐐼𐐨𐑆 𐐱𐑂 𐑄𐐬𐑆 𐐸𐐭 𐐸𐐰𐐼 𐐺𐐨𐐯𐑌 𐐿𐐰𐑅𐐻 𐐮𐑌𐐻𐐭 𐑄 𐑁𐐴𐑉 𐐶𐐲𐑉 𐐿𐐱𐑌𐑅𐐭𐑋𐐼, 𐐰𐑌𐐼 𐐫𐑊𐑅𐐬 𐑄 𐑉𐐯𐐿𐐫𐑉𐐼𐑆 𐐸𐐶𐐮𐐽 𐐶𐐲𐑉 𐐿𐐰𐑅𐐻 𐐮𐑌 𐐶𐐮𐑄 𐑄𐐯𐑋, 𐑄 𐐕𐐨𐑁 𐐖𐐲𐐾 𐐱𐑂 𐑄 𐑊𐐰𐑌𐐼 𐐿𐐩𐑋 𐐰𐑌𐐼 𐑅𐐻𐐳𐐼 𐐺𐐨𐑁𐐬𐑉 𐐈𐑊𐑋𐐲 𐐰𐑌𐐼 𐐈𐑋𐐷𐐭𐑊𐐯𐐿, 𐐰𐑆 𐑄𐐩 𐐶𐐲𐑉 𐐺𐐵𐑌𐐼; 𐐰𐑌𐐼 𐐸𐐨 𐑅𐑋𐐬𐐻 𐑄𐐯𐑋 𐐶𐐮𐑄 𐐸𐐮𐑆 𐐸𐐰𐑌𐐼 𐐲𐐹𐐱𐑌 𐑄𐐩𐑉 𐐽𐐨𐐿𐑅, 𐐰𐑌𐐼 𐑅𐐯𐐼 𐐲𐑌𐐻𐐭 𐑄𐐯𐑋, 𐐀𐑁𐐻𐐲𐑉 𐐸𐐶𐐱𐐻 𐐷𐐨 𐐸𐐰𐑂 𐑅𐐨𐑌, 𐐶𐐮𐑊 𐐷𐐨 𐐹𐑉𐐨𐐽 𐐲𐑀𐐯𐑌 𐐲𐑌𐐻𐐭 𐑄𐐮𐑅 𐐹𐐨𐐹𐐲𐑊, 𐑄𐐰𐐻 𐑄𐐩 𐑇𐐰𐑊 𐐺𐐨 𐐿𐐰𐑅𐐻 𐐮𐑌𐐻𐐭 𐐲 𐑊𐐩𐐿 𐐱𐑂 𐑁𐐴𐑉 𐐰𐑌𐐼 𐐺𐑉𐐮𐑋𐑅𐐻𐐬𐑌? 𐐒𐐨𐐸𐐬𐑊𐐼, 𐐷𐐨 𐑅𐐨 𐑄𐐰𐐻 𐐷𐐨 𐐸𐐰𐐼 𐑌𐐱𐐻 𐐹𐐵𐐲𐑉 𐐻𐐭 𐑅𐐩𐑂 𐑄𐐬𐑆 𐐸𐐭 𐐸𐐰𐐼 𐐺𐐨𐐯𐑌 𐐿𐐰𐑅𐐻 𐐮𐑌𐐻𐐭 𐑄 𐑁𐐴𐑉; 𐑌𐐨𐑄𐐲𐑉 𐐸𐐰𐑆 𐐘𐐱𐐼 𐑅𐐩𐑂𐐼 𐑄𐐯𐑋 𐐺𐐨𐐿𐐫𐑆 𐑄𐐩 𐐶𐐲𐑉 𐐱𐑂 𐑄𐐴 𐑁𐐩𐑃. 𐐈𐑌𐐼 𐑄 𐐖𐐲𐐾 𐑅𐑋𐐬𐐻 𐑄𐐯𐑋 𐐲𐑀𐐯𐑌 𐐲𐐹𐐱𐑌 𐑄𐐩𐑉 𐐽𐐨𐐿𐑅, 𐐰𐑌𐐼 𐐰𐑅𐐿𐐻, 𐐐𐐶𐐱𐐻 𐑅𐐩 𐐷𐐨 𐑁𐐫𐑉 𐐷𐐫𐑉𐑅𐐯𐑊𐑂𐑆? 𐐤𐐵 𐑄𐐮𐑅 𐐖𐐲𐐾 𐐶𐐱𐑆 𐐪𐑁𐐻𐐲𐑉 𐑄 𐐫𐑉𐐼𐐲𐑉 𐐰𐑌𐐼 𐑁𐐩𐑃 𐐱𐑂 𐐤𐐨𐐸𐐫𐑉, 𐐸𐐭 𐑅𐑊𐐭 𐐘𐐮𐐼𐐨𐐲𐑌. 𐐈𐑌𐐼 𐐮𐐻 𐐿𐐩𐑋 𐐻𐐭 𐐹𐐪𐑅 𐑄𐐰𐐻 𐐈𐑊𐑋𐐲 𐐰𐑌𐐼 𐐈𐑋𐐷𐐭𐑊𐐯𐐿 𐐰𐑌𐑅𐐲𐑉𐐼 𐐸𐐮𐑋 𐑌𐐲𐑃𐐮𐑍; 𐐰𐑌𐐼 𐐸𐐨 𐑅𐑋𐐬𐐻 𐑄𐐯𐑋 𐐲𐑀𐐯𐑌, 𐐰𐑌𐐼 𐐼𐐯𐑊𐐮𐑂𐐲𐑉𐐼 𐑄𐐯𐑋 𐐻𐐭 𐑄 𐐱𐑁𐐮𐑅𐐲𐑉𐑆 𐐻𐐭 𐐺𐐨 𐐿𐐰𐑅𐐻 𐐮𐑌𐐻𐐭 𐐹𐑉𐐮𐑆𐐲𐑌. 𐐈𐑌𐐼 𐐸𐐶𐐯𐑌 𐑄𐐩 𐐸𐐰𐐼 𐐺𐐨𐐯𐑌 𐐿𐐰𐑅𐐻 𐐮𐑌𐐻𐐭 𐐹𐑉𐐮𐑆𐐲𐑌 𐑃𐑉𐐨 𐐼𐐩𐑆, 𐑄𐐯𐑉 𐐿𐐩𐑋 𐑋𐐯𐑌𐐨 𐑊𐐫𐐷𐐲𐑉𐑆, 𐐰𐑌𐐼 𐐾𐐲𐐾𐐯𐑆, 𐐰𐑌𐐼 𐐹𐑉𐐨𐑅𐐻𐑅, 𐐰𐑌𐐼 𐐻𐐨𐐽𐐲𐑉𐑆, 𐐸𐐭 𐐶𐐲𐑉 𐐱𐑂 𐑄 𐐹𐑉𐐬𐑁𐐯𐑇𐐲𐑌 𐐱𐑂 𐐤𐐨𐐸𐐫𐑉; 𐐰𐑌𐐼 𐑄𐐩 𐐿𐐩𐑋 𐐮𐑌 𐐲𐑌𐐻𐐭 𐑄 𐐹𐑉𐐮𐑆𐐲𐑌 𐐻𐐭 𐑅𐐨 𐑄𐐯𐑋, 𐐰𐑌𐐼 𐑄𐐩 𐐿𐐶𐐯𐑅𐐽𐐲𐑌𐐼 𐑄𐐯𐑋 𐐲𐐺𐐵𐐻 𐑋𐐯𐑌𐐨 𐐶𐐲𐑉𐐼𐑆; 𐐺𐐲𐐻 𐑄𐐩 𐐰𐑌𐑅𐐲𐑉𐐼 𐑄𐐯𐑋 𐑌𐐲𐑃𐐮𐑍. 𐐈𐑌𐐼 𐐮𐐻 𐐿𐐩𐑋 𐐻𐐭 𐐹𐐪𐑅 𐑄𐐰𐐻 𐑄 𐐖𐐲𐐾 𐑅𐐻𐐳𐐼 𐐺𐐨𐑁𐐬𐑉 𐑄𐐯𐑋, 𐐰𐑌𐐼 𐑅𐐯𐐼, 𐐐𐐶𐐴 𐐼𐐭 𐐷𐐨 𐑌𐐱𐐻 𐐰𐑌𐑅𐐲𐑉 𐑄 𐐶𐐲𐑉𐐼𐑆 𐐱𐑂 𐑄𐐮𐑅 𐐹𐐨𐐹𐐲𐑊? 𐐤𐐬 𐐷𐐨 𐑌𐐱𐐻 𐑄𐐰𐐻 𐐌 𐐸𐐰𐑂 𐐹𐐵𐐲𐑉 𐐻𐐭 𐐼𐐯𐑊𐐮𐑂𐐲𐑉 𐐷𐐭 𐐲𐐹 𐐲𐑌𐐻𐐭 𐑄 𐑁𐑊𐐩𐑋𐑆? 𐐈𐑌𐐼 𐐸𐐨 𐐿𐐱𐑋𐐰𐑌𐐼𐐯𐐼 𐑄𐐯𐑋 𐐻𐐭 𐑅𐐹𐐨𐐿; 𐐺𐐲𐐻 𐑄𐐩 𐐰𐑌𐑅𐐲𐑉𐐼 𐑌𐐲𐑃𐐮𐑍.

9. 𐐈𐑌𐐼 𐐮𐐻 𐐿𐐩𐑋 𐐻𐐭 𐐹𐐪𐑅 𐑄𐐰𐐻 𐑄𐐩 𐐼𐐯𐐹𐐪𐑉𐐻𐐯𐐼 𐐰𐑌𐐼 𐐶𐐯𐑌𐐻 𐑄𐐩𐑉 𐐶𐐩𐑆, 𐐺𐐲𐐻 𐐿𐐩𐑋 𐐲𐑀𐐯𐑌 𐐱𐑌 𐑄 𐑋𐐱𐑉𐐬; 𐐰𐑌𐐼 𐑄 𐐖𐐲𐐾 𐐫𐑊𐑅𐐬 𐑅𐑋𐐬𐐻 𐑄𐐯𐑋 𐐲𐑀𐐯𐑌 𐐱𐑌 𐑄𐐩𐑉 𐐽𐐨𐐿𐑅. 𐐈𐑌𐐼 𐑋𐐯𐑌𐐨 𐐿𐐩𐑋 𐑁𐐫𐑉𐑃 𐐫𐑊𐑅𐐬, 𐐰𐑌𐐼 𐑅𐑋𐐬𐐻 𐑄𐐯𐑋, 𐑅𐐩𐐮𐑍, 𐐎𐐮𐑊 𐐷𐐨 𐑅𐐻𐐰𐑌𐐼 𐐲𐑀𐐯𐑌 𐐰𐑌𐐼 𐐾𐐲𐐾 𐑄𐐮𐑅 𐐹𐐨𐐹𐐲𐑊, 𐐰𐑌𐐼 𐐿𐐱𐑌𐐼𐐯𐑋 𐐵𐑉 𐑊𐐫? 𐐆𐑁 𐐷𐐨 𐐸𐐰𐑂 𐑅𐐲𐐽 𐑀𐑉𐐩𐐻 𐐹𐐵𐐲𐑉, 𐐸𐐶𐐴 𐐼𐐭 𐐷𐐨 𐑌𐐱𐐻 𐐼𐐯𐑊𐐮𐑂𐐲𐑉 𐐷𐐫𐑉𐑅𐐯𐑊𐑂𐑆? 𐐈𐑌𐐼 𐑋𐐯𐑌𐐨 𐑅𐐲𐐽 𐑃𐐮𐑍𐑆 𐑅𐐯𐐼 𐑄𐐩 𐐲𐑌𐐻𐐭 𐑄𐐯𐑋, 𐑌𐐰𐑇𐐮𐑍 𐑄𐐩𐑉 𐐻𐐨𐑃 𐐲𐐹𐐱𐑌 𐑄𐐯𐑋, 𐐰𐑌𐐼 𐑅𐐹𐐮𐐻𐐮𐑍 𐐲𐐹𐐱𐑌 𐑄𐐯𐑋, 𐐰𐑌𐐼 𐑅𐐩𐐮𐑍, 𐐐𐐵 𐑇𐐰𐑊 𐐶𐐨 𐑊𐐳𐐿 𐐸𐐶𐐯𐑌 𐐶𐐨 𐐪𐑉 𐐼𐐰𐑋𐐼? 𐐈𐑌𐐼 𐑋𐐯𐑌𐐨 𐑅𐐲𐐽 𐑃𐐮𐑍𐑆, 𐐷𐐩, 𐐫𐑊 𐑋𐐰𐑌𐐲𐑉 𐐱𐑂 𐑅𐐲𐐽 𐑃𐐮𐑍𐑆 𐐼𐐮𐐼 𐑄𐐩 𐑅𐐩 𐐲𐑌𐐻𐐭 𐑄𐐯𐑋; 𐐰𐑌𐐼 𐑄𐐲𐑅 𐑄𐐩 𐐼𐐮𐐼 𐑋𐐱𐐿 𐑄𐐯𐑋 𐑁𐐫𐑉 𐑋𐐯𐑌𐐨 𐐼𐐩𐑆. 𐐈𐑌𐐼 𐑄𐐩 𐐼𐐮𐐼

𐐶𐐮𐑄𐐸𐐬𐑊𐐼 𐑁𐐭𐐼 𐑁𐑉𐐱𐑋 𐑄𐐯𐑋 𐑄𐐰𐐻 𐑄𐐩 𐑋𐐴𐐻 𐐸𐐲𐑍𐑀𐐲𐑉, 𐐰𐑌𐐼 𐐶𐐫𐐻𐐲𐑉 𐑁𐑉𐐱𐑋 𐑄𐐯𐑋, 𐑄𐐰𐐻 𐑄𐐩 𐑋𐐴𐐻 𐑃𐐲𐑉𐑅𐐻; 𐐰𐑌𐐼 𐑄𐐩 𐐫𐑊𐑅𐐬 𐐼𐐮𐐼 𐐻𐐩𐐿 𐑁𐑉𐐱𐑋 𐑄𐐯𐑋 𐑄𐐩𐑉 𐐿𐑊𐐬𐑄𐑆, 𐑄𐐰𐐻 𐑄𐐩 𐐶𐐲𐑉 𐑌𐐩𐐿𐐯𐐼; 𐐰𐑌𐐼 𐑄𐐲𐑅 𐑄𐐩 𐐶𐐲𐑉 𐐺𐐵𐑌𐐼 𐐶𐐮𐑄 𐑅𐐻𐑉𐐱𐑍 𐐿𐐫𐑉𐐼𐑆, 𐐰𐑌𐐼 𐐿𐐱𐑌𐑁𐐴𐑌𐐼 𐐮𐑌 𐐹𐑉𐐮𐑆𐐲𐑌.

10. 𐐈𐑌𐐼 𐐮𐐻 𐐿𐐩𐑋 𐐻𐐭 𐐹𐐰𐑅 𐐰𐑁𐐻𐐲𐑉 𐑄𐐩 𐐸𐐰𐐼 𐑅𐐲𐑁𐐲𐑉𐐼 𐑁𐐫𐑉 𐑋𐐯𐑌𐐨 𐐼𐐩𐑆, (𐐰𐑌𐐼 𐐮𐐻 𐐶𐐱𐑆 𐐱𐑌 𐑄 𐐻𐐶𐐯𐑊𐑁𐑃 𐐼𐐩, 𐐮𐑌 𐑄 𐐻𐐯𐑌𐑃 𐑋𐐲𐑌𐑃, 𐐮𐑌 𐑄 𐐻𐐯𐑌𐑃 𐐷𐐨𐑉 𐐱𐑂 𐑄 𐑉𐐩𐑌 𐐱𐑂 𐑄 𐐖𐐲𐐾𐐯𐑆 𐐬𐑂𐐲𐑉 𐑄 𐐹𐐨𐐹𐐲𐑊 𐐱𐑂 𐐤𐐨𐑁𐐴,) 𐑄𐐰𐐻 𐑄 𐐕𐐨𐑁 𐐖𐐲𐐾 𐐬𐑂𐐲𐑉 𐑄 𐑊𐐰𐑌𐐼 𐐱𐑂 𐐈𐑋𐐱𐑌𐐴𐐸𐐪, 𐐰𐑌𐐼 𐑋𐐯𐑌𐐨 𐐱𐑂 𐑄𐐩𐑉 𐐻𐐨𐐽𐐲𐑉𐑆 𐐰𐑌𐐼 𐑄𐐩𐑉 𐑊𐐫𐐷𐐲𐑉𐑆, 𐐶𐐯𐑌𐐻 𐐮𐑌 𐐲𐑌𐐻𐐭 𐑄 𐐹𐑉𐐮𐑆𐐲𐑌 𐐸𐐶𐐩𐑉 𐐈𐑊𐑋𐐲 𐐰𐑌𐐼 𐐈𐑋𐐷𐐭𐑊𐐯𐐿 𐐶𐐲𐑉 𐐺𐐵𐑌𐐼 𐐶𐐮𐑄 𐐿𐐫𐑉𐐼𐑆, 𐐰𐑌𐐼 𐑄 𐐕𐐨𐑁 𐐖𐐲𐐾 𐑅𐐻𐐳𐐼 𐐺𐐨𐑁𐐬𐑉 𐑄𐐯𐑋, 𐐰𐑌𐐼 𐑅𐑋𐐬𐐻 𐑄𐐯𐑋 𐐲𐑀𐐯𐑌, 𐐰𐑌𐐼 𐑅𐐯𐐼 𐐲𐑌𐐻𐐭 𐑄𐐯𐑋, 𐐆𐑁 𐐷𐐨 𐐸𐐰𐑂 𐑄 𐐹𐐵𐐲𐑉 𐐱𐑂 𐐘𐐱𐐼, 𐐼𐐯𐑊𐐮𐑂𐐲𐑉 𐐷𐐫𐑉𐑅𐐯𐑊𐑂𐑆 𐑁𐑉𐐱𐑋 𐑄𐐨𐑆 𐐺𐐰𐑌𐐼𐑆, 𐐰𐑌𐐼 𐑄𐐯𐑌 𐐶𐐨 𐐶𐐮𐑊 𐐺𐐨𐑊𐐨𐑂 𐑄𐐰𐐻 𐑄 𐐢𐐫𐑉𐐼 𐐶𐐮𐑊 𐐼𐐯𐑅𐐻𐑉𐐱𐐴 𐑄𐐮𐑅 𐐹𐐨𐐹𐐲𐑊 𐐲𐐿𐐫𐑉𐐼𐐮𐑍 𐐻𐐭 𐐷𐐫𐑉 𐐶𐐲𐑉𐐼𐑆. 𐐈𐑌𐐼 𐐮𐐻 𐐿𐐩𐑋 𐐻𐐭 𐐹𐐰𐑅 𐑄𐐰𐐻 𐑄𐐩 𐐫𐑊 𐐶𐐯𐑌𐐻 𐑁𐐬𐑉𐑃 𐐰𐑌𐐼 𐑅𐑋𐐬𐐻 𐑄𐐯𐑋, 𐑅𐐩𐐮𐑍 𐑄 𐑅𐐩𐑋 𐐶𐐲𐑉𐐼𐑆, 𐐨𐑂𐐲𐑌 𐐲𐑌𐐻𐐮𐑊 𐑄 𐑊𐐰𐑅𐐻; 𐐰𐑌𐐼 𐐸𐐶𐐯𐑌 𐑄 𐑊𐐰𐑅𐐻 𐐸𐐰𐐼 𐑅𐐹𐐬𐐿𐐲𐑌 𐐲𐑌𐐻𐐭 𐑄𐐯𐑋, 𐑄 𐐹𐐵𐐲𐑉 𐐱𐑂 𐐘𐐱𐐼 𐐶𐐱𐑆 𐐲𐐹𐐱𐑌 𐐈𐑊𐑋𐐲 𐐰𐑌𐐼 𐐈𐑋𐐷𐐭𐑊𐐯𐐿, 𐐰𐑌𐐼 𐑄𐐩 𐑉𐐬𐑆 𐐰𐑌𐐼 𐑅𐐻𐐳𐐼 𐐲𐐹𐐱𐑌 𐑄𐐩𐑉 𐑁𐐨𐐻; 𐐰𐑌𐐼 𐐈𐑊𐑋𐐲 𐐿𐑉𐐴𐐼, 𐑅𐐩𐐮𐑍, 𐐐𐐵 𐑊𐐱𐑍 𐑇𐐰𐑊 𐐶𐐨 𐑅𐐲𐑁𐐲𐑉 𐑄𐐨𐑆 𐑀𐑉𐐩𐐻 𐐰𐑁𐑊𐐮𐐿𐑇𐐲𐑌𐑆, 𐐄 𐐢𐐫𐑉𐐼? 𐐄 𐐢𐐫𐑉𐐼, 𐑀𐐮𐑂 𐐲𐑅 𐑅𐐻𐑉𐐯𐑍𐑃 𐐲𐐿𐐫𐑉𐐼𐐮𐑍 𐐻𐐭 𐐵𐑉 𐑁𐐩𐑃 𐐸𐐶𐐮𐐽 𐐮𐑆 𐐮𐑌 𐐗𐑉𐐴𐑅𐐻, 𐐨𐑂𐐲𐑌 𐐲𐑌𐐻𐐭 𐐼𐐯𐑊𐐮𐑂𐐲𐑉𐐲𐑌𐑅: 𐐰𐑌𐐼 𐑄𐐩 𐐺𐑉𐐬𐐿 𐑄 𐐿𐐫𐑉𐐼𐑆 𐐶𐐮𐑄 𐐸𐐶𐐮𐐽 𐑄𐐩 𐐶𐐲𐑉 𐐺𐐵𐑌𐐼; 𐐰𐑌𐐼 𐐸𐐶𐐯𐑌 𐑄 𐐹𐐨𐐹𐐲𐑊 𐑅𐐫 𐑄𐐮𐑅, 𐑄𐐩 𐐺𐐨𐑀𐐰𐑌 𐐻𐐭 𐑁𐑊𐐨, 𐑁𐐫𐑉 𐑄 𐑁𐐨𐑉 𐐱𐑂 𐐼𐐯𐑅𐐻𐑉𐐲𐐿𐑇𐐲𐑌 𐐸𐐰𐐼 𐐿𐐲𐑋 𐐲𐐹𐐱𐑌 𐑄𐐯𐑋.

11. 𐐈𐑌𐐼 𐐮𐐻 𐐿𐐩𐑋 𐐻𐐭 𐐹𐐰𐑅 𐑄𐐰𐐻 𐑅𐐬 𐑀𐑉𐐩𐐻 𐐶𐐱𐑆 𐑄𐐩𐑉 𐑁𐐨𐑉, 𐑄𐐰𐐻 𐑄𐐩 𐑁𐐯𐑊 𐐻𐐭 𐑄 𐐲𐑉𐑃, 𐐰𐑌𐐼 𐐼𐐮𐐼 𐑌𐐱𐐻 𐐱𐐺𐐻𐐩𐑌 𐑄 𐐵𐐻𐐲𐑉 𐐼𐐬𐑉 𐐱𐑂 𐑄 𐐹𐑉𐐮𐑆𐐲𐑌; 𐐰𐑌𐐼 𐑄 𐐲𐑉𐑃 𐑇𐐳𐐿 𐑋𐐴𐐻𐐮𐑊𐐨, 𐐰𐑌𐐼 𐑄 𐐶𐐫𐑊𐑆 𐐱𐑂 𐑄 𐐹𐑉𐐮𐑆𐐲𐑌 𐐶𐐲𐑉 𐑉𐐯𐑌𐐻 𐐮𐑌 𐐻𐐶𐐩𐑌, 𐑅𐐬 𐑄𐐰𐐻 𐑄𐐩 𐑁𐐯𐑊 𐐻𐐭 𐑄 𐐲𐑉𐑃; 𐐰𐑌𐐼 𐑄 𐐕𐐨𐑁 𐐖𐐲𐐾, 𐐰𐑌𐐼 𐑄 𐑊𐐫𐐷𐐲𐑉𐑆, 𐐰𐑌𐐼 𐐹𐑉𐐨𐑅𐐻𐑅, 𐐰𐑌𐐼 𐐻𐐨𐐽𐐲𐑉𐑆, 𐐸𐐭 𐑅𐑋𐐬𐐻 𐐲𐐹𐐱𐑌 𐐈𐑊𐑋𐐲 𐐰𐑌𐐼 𐐈𐑋𐐷𐐭𐑊𐐯𐐿, 𐐶𐐲𐑉 𐑅𐑊𐐩𐑌 𐐺𐐴 𐑄 𐑁𐐫𐑊 𐑄𐐩𐑉𐐱𐑂. 𐐈𐑌𐐼 𐐈𐑊𐑋𐐲 𐐰𐑌𐐼 𐐈𐑋𐐷𐐭𐑊𐐯𐐿 𐐿𐐩𐑋 𐑁𐐬𐑉𐑃 𐐵𐐻 𐐱𐑂 𐑄 𐐹𐑉𐐮𐑆𐐲𐑌, 𐐰𐑌𐐼 𐑄𐐩 𐐶𐐲𐑉 𐑌𐐱𐐻 𐐸𐐲𐑉𐐻; 𐑁𐐫𐑉 𐑄 𐐢𐐫𐑉𐐼 𐐸𐐰𐐼 𐑀𐑉𐐰𐑌𐐻𐐯𐐼 𐐲𐑌𐐻𐐭 𐑄𐐯𐑋 𐐹𐐵𐐲𐑉, 𐐲𐐿𐐫𐑉𐐼𐐮𐑍 𐐻𐐭 𐑄𐐩𐑉 𐑁𐐩𐑃 𐐸𐐶𐐮𐐽 𐐶𐐱𐑆 𐐮𐑌 𐐗𐑉𐐴𐑅𐐻. 𐐈𐑌𐐼 𐑄𐐩 𐑅𐐻𐑉𐐩𐐻𐐶𐐩 𐐿𐐩𐑋 𐑁𐐬𐑉𐑃 𐐵𐐻 𐐱𐑂 𐑄 𐐹𐑉𐐮𐑆𐐲𐑌; 𐐰𐑌𐐼 𐑄𐐩 𐐶𐐲𐑉 𐑊𐐭𐑅𐐻 𐑁𐑉𐐱𐑋 𐑄𐐩𐑉 𐐺𐐰𐑌𐐼𐑆; 𐐰𐑌𐐼 𐑄 𐐹𐑉𐐮𐑆𐐲𐑌 𐐸𐐰𐐼 𐑁𐐫𐑊𐐲𐑌 𐐻𐐭 𐑄 𐐲𐑉𐑃, 𐐰𐑌𐐼 𐐯𐑂𐑉𐐨 𐑅𐐬𐑊 𐐶𐐮𐑄𐐮𐑌 𐑄 𐐶𐐫𐑊𐑆 𐑄𐐩𐑉𐐱𐑂, 𐑅𐐩𐑂 𐐮𐐻 𐐶𐐲𐑉 𐐈𐑊𐑋𐐲 𐐰𐑌𐐼 𐐈𐑋𐐷𐐭𐑊𐐯𐐿, 𐐶𐐱𐑆 𐑅𐑊𐐩𐑌: 𐐰𐑌𐐼 𐑄𐐩 𐑅𐐻𐑉𐐩𐐻𐐶𐐩 𐐿𐐩𐑋 𐑁𐐬𐑉𐑃 𐐮𐑌𐐻𐐭 𐑄 𐑅𐐮𐐻𐐨. 𐐤𐐵 𐑄 𐐹𐐨𐐹𐐲𐑊 𐐸𐐰𐑂𐐮𐑍 𐐸𐐲𐑉𐐼 𐐩 𐑀𐑉𐐩𐐻 𐑌𐑎𐑆, 𐐿𐐩𐑋 𐑉𐐲𐑌𐐮𐑍 𐐻𐐭𐑀𐐯𐑄𐐲𐑉 𐐺𐐴 𐑋𐐲𐑊𐐻𐐮𐐻𐐷𐐭𐐼𐑆, 𐐻𐐭 𐑌𐐬 𐑄 𐐿𐐫𐑆 𐐱𐑂 𐐮𐐻; 𐐰𐑌𐐼 𐐸𐐶𐐯𐑌 𐑄𐐩 𐑅𐐫 𐐈𐑊𐑋𐐲 𐐰𐑌𐐼 𐐈𐑋𐐷𐐭𐑊𐐯𐐿 𐐿𐐲𐑋𐐮𐑍 𐑁𐐬𐑉𐑃 𐐵𐐻 𐐱𐑂 𐑄 𐐹𐑉𐐮𐑆𐐲𐑌, 𐐰𐑌𐐼 𐑄 𐐶𐐫𐑊𐑆 𐑄𐐩𐑉𐐱𐑂 𐐸𐐰𐐼 𐑁𐐫𐑊𐐲𐑌 𐐻𐐭 𐑄 𐐲𐑉𐑃, 𐑄𐐩 𐐶𐐲𐑉 𐑅𐐻𐑉𐐲𐐿 𐐶𐐮𐑄 𐑀𐑉𐐩𐐻 𐑁𐐨𐑉, 𐐰𐑌𐐼 𐑁𐑊𐐯𐐼 𐑁𐑉𐐱𐑋 𐑄 𐐹𐑉𐐯𐑆𐐲𐑌𐑅 𐐱𐑂 𐐈𐑊𐑋𐐲 𐐰𐑌𐐼 𐐈𐑋𐐷𐐭𐑊𐐯𐐿, 𐐨𐑂𐐲𐑌 𐐰𐑆 𐐩 𐑀𐐬𐐻 𐑁𐑊𐐨𐐲𐑃 𐐶𐐮𐑄 𐐸𐐲𐑉 𐐷𐐲𐑍 𐑁𐑉𐐱𐑋 𐐻𐐭 𐑊𐐴𐐲𐑌𐑆; 𐐰𐑌𐐼 𐑄𐐲𐑅 𐑄𐐩 𐐼𐐮𐐼 𐑁𐑊𐐨 𐑁𐑉𐐱𐑋 𐑄 𐐹𐑉𐐯𐑆𐐲𐑌𐑅 𐐱𐑂 𐐈𐑊𐑋𐐲 𐐰𐑌𐐼 𐐈𐑋𐐷𐐭𐑊𐐯𐐿.

12. 𐐈𐑌𐐼 𐐮𐐻 𐐿𐐩𐑋 𐐻𐐭 𐐹𐐰𐑅 𐑄𐐰𐐻 𐐈𐑊𐑋𐐲 𐐰𐑌𐐼 𐐈𐑋𐐷𐐭𐑊𐐯𐐿 𐐶𐐲𐑉 𐐿𐐱𐑋𐐰𐑌𐐼𐐯𐐼 𐐻𐐭 𐐼𐐯𐐹𐐪𐑉𐐻 𐐵𐐻 𐐱𐑂 𐑄𐐰𐐻 𐑅𐐮𐐻𐐨; 𐐰𐑌𐐼 𐑄𐐩 𐐼𐐯𐐹𐐪𐑉𐐻𐐯𐐼, 𐐰𐑌𐐼 𐐿𐐩𐑋 𐐵𐐻 𐐨𐑂𐐲𐑌 𐐮𐑌𐐻𐐭 𐑄 𐑊𐐰𐑌𐐼 𐐱𐑂 𐐝𐐴𐐼𐐱𐑋: 𐐰𐑌𐐼 𐐺𐐨𐐸𐐬𐑊𐐼, 𐑄𐐩𐑉 𐑄𐐩 𐑁𐐵𐑌𐐼 𐐫𐑊 𐑄 𐐹𐐨𐐹𐐲𐑊 𐐸𐐶𐐮𐐽 𐐸𐐰𐐼 𐐼𐐯𐐹𐐪𐑉𐐻𐐯𐐼 𐐵𐐻 𐐱𐑂 𐑄 𐑊𐐰𐑌𐐼 𐐱𐑂 𐐈𐑋𐐱𐑌𐐴𐐸𐐪, 𐐸𐐭 𐐸𐐰𐐼 𐐺𐐨𐑌 𐐿𐐰𐑅𐐻 𐐵𐐻 𐐰𐑌𐐼 𐑅𐐻𐐬𐑌𐐼, 𐐺𐐨𐐿𐐫𐑆 𐑄𐐩 𐐺𐐨𐑊𐐨𐑂𐐼 𐐮𐑌 𐑄 𐐶𐐲𐑉𐐼𐑆 𐐱𐑂 𐐈𐑊𐑋𐐲. 𐐈𐑌𐐼 𐑄𐐩 𐑉𐐨𐑊𐐩𐐻𐐯𐐼 𐐲𐑌𐐻𐐭 𐑄𐐯𐑋 𐐫𐑊 𐑄𐐰𐐻 𐐸𐐰𐐼 𐐸𐐰𐐹𐐲𐑌𐐼 𐐲𐑌𐐻𐐭 𐑄𐐩𐑉 𐐶𐐴𐑂𐑆 𐐰𐑌𐐼 𐐽𐐮𐑊𐐼𐑉𐐯𐑌, 𐐰𐑌𐐼 𐐫𐑊𐑅𐐬 𐐿𐐱𐑌𐑅𐐲𐑉𐑌𐐮𐑍 𐑄𐐯𐑋𐑅𐐯𐑊𐑂𐑆, 𐐰𐑌𐐼 𐐱𐑂 𐑄𐐩𐑉 𐐹𐐵𐐲𐑉 𐐱𐑂 𐐼𐐯𐑊𐐮𐑂𐐲𐑉𐐲𐑌𐑅. 𐐈𐑌𐐼 𐐫𐑊𐑅𐐬 𐐞𐐨𐑆𐑉𐐱𐑋 𐑊𐐩 𐑅𐐮𐐿 𐐰𐐻 𐐝𐐴𐐼𐐱𐑋, 𐐶𐐮𐑄 𐐩 𐐺𐐲𐑉𐑌𐐮𐑍 𐑁𐐨𐑂𐐲𐑉, 𐐸𐐶𐐮𐐽 𐐶𐐱𐑆 𐐿𐐫𐑆𐐼 𐐺𐐴 𐑄 𐑀𐑉𐐩𐐻 𐐻𐑉𐐮𐐺𐐷𐐭𐑊𐐩𐑇𐐲𐑌𐑆 𐐱𐑂 𐐸𐐮𐑆 𐑋𐐴𐑌𐐼, 𐐱𐑌 𐐲𐐿𐐵𐑌𐐻 𐐱𐑂 𐐸𐐮𐑆 𐐶𐐮𐐿𐐯𐐼𐑌𐐯𐑅, 𐑁𐐫𐑉 𐐸𐐨 𐑅𐐲𐐹𐐬𐑆𐐼 𐑄𐐰𐐻 𐐈𐑊𐑋𐐲 𐐰𐑌𐐼 𐐈𐑋𐐷𐐭𐑊𐐯𐐿 𐐶𐐲𐑉 𐑌𐐬 𐑋𐐬𐑉; 𐐰𐑌𐐼 𐐸𐐨 𐑅𐐲𐐹𐐬𐑆𐐼 𐑄𐐰𐐻 𐑄𐐩 𐐸𐐰𐐼 𐐺𐐨𐑌 𐑅𐑊𐐩𐑌 𐐺𐐨𐐿𐐫𐑆 𐐱𐑂 𐐸𐐮𐑆 𐐮𐑌𐐮𐐿𐐶𐐮𐐻𐐨. 𐐈𐑌𐐼 𐑄𐐮𐑅 𐑀𐑉𐐩𐐻 𐑅𐐮𐑌, 𐐰𐑌𐐼 𐐸𐐮𐑆 𐑋𐐯𐑌𐐨 𐐲𐑄𐐲𐑉 𐑅𐐮𐑌𐑆, 𐐼𐐮𐐼 𐐸𐐰𐑉𐐬 𐐲𐐹 𐐸𐐮𐑆 𐑋𐐴𐑌𐐼 𐐲𐑌𐐻𐐮𐑊 𐐮𐐻 𐐼𐐮𐐼 𐐺𐐨𐐿𐐲𐑋

𐐯𐐿𐑅𐐨𐐼𐐮𐑍 𐑅𐐬𐑉, 𐐸𐐰𐑂𐐮𐑍 𐑌𐐬 𐐼𐐯𐑊𐐮𐑂𐐲𐑉𐐰𐑌𐑅; 𐑄𐐯𐑉𐑁𐐬𐑉 𐐸𐐨 𐐺𐐨𐑀𐐰𐑌 𐐻𐐭 𐐺 𐑅𐐿𐐬𐑉𐐽𐐻 𐐶𐐮𐑄 𐐲 𐐺𐐲𐑉𐑌𐐮𐑍 𐐸𐐨𐐻. 𐐤𐐵 𐐸𐐶𐐯𐑌 𐐸𐐨 𐐸𐐲𐑉𐐼 𐑄𐐰𐐻 𐐈𐑊𐑋𐐲 𐐰𐑌𐐼 𐐈𐑋𐐷𐐭𐑊𐐯𐐿 𐐶𐐲𐑉 𐐮𐑌 𐑄 𐑊𐐰𐑌𐐼 𐐱𐑂 𐐝𐐴𐐼𐐲𐑋, 𐐸𐐮𐑆 𐐸𐐪𐑉𐐻 𐐺𐐨𐑀𐐰𐑌 𐐻𐐭 𐐻𐐩𐐿 𐐿𐐲𐑉𐐯𐐾; 𐐰𐑌𐐼 𐐸𐐨 𐑅𐐯𐑌𐐻 𐐲 𐑋𐐯𐑅𐐯𐐾 𐐮𐑋𐐨𐐼𐐮𐐰𐐻𐑊𐐮 𐐲𐑌𐐻𐐭 𐑄𐐯𐑋, 𐐼𐐯𐑆𐐴𐑉𐐮𐑍 𐑄𐐯𐑋 𐐻𐐭 𐐿𐐲𐑋 𐐲𐑌𐐻𐐭 𐐸𐐮𐑋.

13. 𐐈𐑌𐐼 𐐮𐐻 𐐿𐐩𐑋 𐐻𐐭 𐐹𐐰𐑅 𐑄𐐰𐐻 𐑄𐐩 𐐶𐐯𐑌𐐻 𐐮𐑋𐐨𐐼𐐮𐐰𐐻𐑊𐐮, 𐐬𐐺𐐩𐐮𐑍 𐑄 𐑋𐐯𐑅𐐯𐐾 𐐸𐐶𐐮𐐽 𐐸𐐨 𐐸𐐰𐐼 𐑅𐐯𐑌𐐻 𐐲𐑌𐐻𐐭 𐑄𐐯𐑋; 𐐰𐑌𐐼 𐑄𐐩 𐐶𐐯𐑌𐐻 𐐮𐑌 𐐲𐑌𐐻𐐭 𐑄 𐐸𐐵𐑅 𐐲𐑌𐐻𐐭 𐐞𐐨𐑆𐑉𐐲𐑋; 𐐰𐑌𐐼 𐑄𐐩 𐑁𐐵𐑌𐐼 𐐸𐐮𐑋 𐐲𐐹𐐱𐑌 𐐸𐐮𐑆 𐐺𐐯𐐼, 𐑅𐐮𐐿, 𐐺𐐨𐐮𐑍 𐑂𐐯𐑉𐐮 𐑊𐐬 𐐶𐐮𐑄 𐐲 𐐺𐐲𐑉𐑌𐐮𐑍 𐑁𐐨𐑂𐐲𐑉; 𐐰𐑌𐐼 𐐸𐐮𐑆 𐑋𐐴𐑌𐐼 𐐫𐑊𐑅𐐬 𐐶𐐱𐑆 𐐯𐐿𐑅𐐨𐐼𐐮𐑍 𐑅𐐬𐑉 𐐺𐐨𐐿𐐫𐑆 𐐱𐑂 𐐸𐐮𐑆 𐐮𐑌𐐮𐐿𐐶𐐮𐐻𐐮𐑆; 𐐰𐑌𐐼 𐐸𐐶𐐯𐑌 𐐸𐐨 𐑅𐐫 𐑄𐐯𐑋 𐐸𐐨 𐑅𐐻𐑉𐐯𐐽𐐻 𐑁𐐬𐑉𐑃 𐐸𐐮𐑆 𐐸𐐰𐑌𐐼, 𐐰𐑌𐐼 𐐺𐐨𐑅𐐫𐐻 𐑄𐐯𐑋 𐑄𐐰𐐻 𐑄𐐩 𐐶𐐳𐐼 𐐸𐐨𐑊 𐐸𐐮𐑋.

14. 𐐈𐑌𐐼 𐐮𐐻 𐐿𐐩𐑋 𐐻𐐭 𐐹𐐰𐑅 𐑄𐐰𐐻 𐐈𐑊𐑋𐐲 𐑅𐐯𐐼 𐐲𐑌𐐻𐐭 𐐸𐐮𐑋, 𐐻𐐩𐐿𐐮𐑍 𐐸𐐮𐑋 𐐺𐐴 𐑄 𐐸𐐰𐑌𐐼, 𐐒𐐨𐑊𐐨𐑂𐐯𐑅𐐻 𐑄𐐵 𐐮𐑌 𐑄 𐐹𐐵𐐲𐑉 𐐱𐑂 𐐗𐑉𐐴𐑅𐐻 𐐲𐑌𐐻𐐭 𐑅𐐰𐑊𐑂𐐩𐑇𐐲𐑌? 𐐈𐑌𐐼 𐐸𐐨 𐐰𐑌𐑅𐐲𐑉𐐼 𐐰𐑌𐐼 𐑅𐐯𐐼, 𐐏𐐩, 𐐌 𐐺𐐨𐑊𐐨𐑂 𐐫𐑊 𐑄 𐐶𐐲𐑉𐐼𐑆 𐑄𐐰𐐻 𐑄𐐵 𐐸𐐰𐑅𐐻 𐐻𐐫𐐻. 𐐈𐑌𐐼 𐐈𐑊𐑋𐐲 𐑅𐐯𐐼, 𐐆𐑁 𐑄𐐵 𐐺𐐨𐑊𐐨𐑂𐐯𐑅𐐻 𐐮𐑌 𐑄 𐑉𐐨𐐼𐐯𐑋𐑇𐐲𐑌 𐐱𐑂 𐐗𐑉𐐴𐑅𐐻, 𐑄𐐵 𐐿𐐰𐑌𐑅𐐻 𐐺 𐐸𐐨𐑊𐐼. 𐐈𐑌𐐼 𐐸𐐨 𐑅𐐯𐐼, 𐐏𐐩, 𐐌 𐐺𐐨𐑊𐐨𐑂 𐐰𐐿𐐫𐑉𐐼𐐮𐑍 𐐻𐐭 𐑄𐐴 𐐶𐐲𐑉𐐼𐑆. 𐐈𐑌𐐼 𐑄𐐯𐑌 𐐈𐑊𐑋𐐲 𐐿𐑉𐐴𐐼 𐐲𐑌𐐻𐐭 𐑄 𐐢𐐫𐑉𐐼, 𐑅𐐩𐐮𐑍, 𐐄 𐐢𐐫𐑉𐐼 𐐵𐑉 𐐘𐐱𐐼, 𐐸𐐰𐑂 𐑋𐐲𐑉𐑅𐐮 𐐱𐑌 𐑄𐐮𐑅 𐑋𐐰𐑌, 𐐰𐑌𐐼 𐐸𐐨𐑊 𐐸𐐮𐑋 𐐰𐐿𐐫𐑉𐐼𐐮𐑍 𐐻𐐭 𐐸𐐮𐑆 𐑁𐐩𐑃 𐐸𐐶𐐮𐐽 𐐮𐑆 𐐮𐑌 𐐗𐑉𐐴𐑅𐐻. 𐐈𐑌𐐼 𐐸𐐶𐐯𐑌 𐐈𐑊𐑋𐐲 𐐸𐐰𐐼 𐑅𐐯𐐼 𐑄𐐨𐑆 𐐶𐐲𐑉𐐼𐑆, 𐐞𐐨𐑆𐑉𐐲𐑋 𐑊𐐨𐐹𐐻 𐐲𐐹𐐱𐑌 𐐸𐐮𐑆 𐑁𐐨𐐻, 𐐰𐑌𐐼 𐐺𐐨𐑀𐐰𐑌 𐐻𐐭 𐐶𐐫𐐿; 𐐰𐑌𐐼 𐑄𐐮𐑅 𐐶𐐱𐑆 𐐼𐐲𐑌 𐐻𐐭 𐑄 𐑀𐑉𐐩𐐻 𐐰𐑅𐐻𐐱𐑌𐐮𐑇𐑋𐐯𐑌𐐻 𐐱𐑂 𐐫𐑊 𐑄 𐐹𐐨𐐹𐑊; 𐐰𐑌𐐼 𐑄 𐑌𐐱𐑊𐐯𐐾 𐐱𐑂 𐑄𐐮𐑅 𐐶𐐯𐑌𐐻 𐑁𐐬𐑉𐑃 𐑃𐑉𐐭𐐵𐐻 𐐫𐑊 𐑄 𐑊𐐰𐑌𐐼 𐐱𐑂 𐐝𐐴𐐼𐐲𐑋. 𐐈𐑌𐐼 𐐈𐑊𐑋𐐲 𐐺𐐰𐐹𐐻𐐴𐑆𐐼 𐐞𐐨𐑆𐑉𐐲𐑋 𐐲𐑌𐐻𐐭 𐑄 𐐢𐐫𐑉𐐼; 𐐰𐑌𐐼 𐐸𐐨 𐐺𐐨𐑀𐐰𐑌 𐑁𐑉𐐱𐑋 𐑄𐐰𐐻 𐐻𐐴𐑋 𐑁𐐬𐑉𐑃 𐐻𐐭 𐐹𐑉𐐨𐐽 𐐲𐑌𐐻𐐭 𐑄 𐐹𐐨𐐹𐑊. 𐐈𐑌𐐼 𐐈𐑊𐑋𐐲 𐐯𐑅𐐻𐐰𐐺𐑊𐐮𐑇𐐻 𐐲 𐐽𐐲𐑉𐐽 𐐮𐑌 𐑄 𐑊𐐰𐑌𐐼 𐐱𐑂 𐐝𐐴𐐼𐐲𐑋, 𐐰𐑌𐐼 𐐿𐐱𐑌𐑅𐐨𐐿𐑉𐐩𐐻𐐯𐐼 𐐹𐑉𐐨𐑅𐐻𐑅 𐐰𐑌𐐼 𐐻𐐨𐐽𐐲𐑉𐑆 𐐮𐑌 𐑄 𐑊𐐰𐑌𐐼, 𐐻𐐭 𐐺𐐰𐐹𐐻𐐴𐑆 𐐲𐑌𐐻𐐭 𐑄 𐐢𐐫𐑉𐐼 𐐸𐐭𐑅𐐬𐐯𐑂𐐲𐑉 𐐶𐐲𐑉 𐐼𐐯𐑆𐐴𐑉𐐲𐑅 𐐻𐐭 𐐺 𐐺𐐰𐐹𐐻𐐴𐑆𐐼.

15. 𐐈𐑌𐐼 𐐮𐐻 𐐿𐐩𐑋 𐐻𐐭 𐐹𐐰𐑅 𐑄𐐰𐐻 𐑄𐐩 𐐶𐐲𐑉 𐑋𐐯𐑌𐐮; 𐑁𐐫𐑉 𐑄𐐩 𐐼𐐮𐐼 𐑁𐑊𐐱𐐿 𐐮𐑌 𐑁𐑉𐐱𐑋 𐐫𐑊 𐑄 𐑉𐐨𐐾𐐲𐑌 𐑉𐐵𐑌𐐼 𐐲𐐺𐐵𐐻 𐐝𐐴𐐼𐐲𐑋, 𐐰𐑌𐐼 𐐶𐐲𐑉 𐐺𐐰𐐹𐐻𐐴𐑆𐐼; 𐐺𐐲𐐻 𐐰𐑆 𐐻𐐭 𐑄 𐐹𐐨𐐹𐑊 𐑄𐐰𐐻 𐐶𐐲𐑉 𐐮𐑌 𐑄 𐑊𐐰𐑌𐐼 𐐱𐑂 𐐈𐑋𐐬𐑌𐐴𐐸𐐪, 𐑄𐐩 𐐷𐐯𐐻 𐑉𐐨𐑋𐐩𐑌𐐼 𐐲 𐐸𐐪𐑉𐐼-𐐸𐐪𐑉𐐻𐐯𐐼 𐐰𐑌𐐼 𐐲 𐑅𐐻𐐮𐑁𐑌𐐯𐐿𐐻 𐐹𐐨𐐹𐑊; 𐐰𐑌𐐼 𐑄𐐩 𐑉𐐨𐐹𐐯𐑌𐐻𐐯𐐼 𐑌𐐱𐐻 𐐱𐑂 𐑄𐐩𐑉 𐑅𐐮𐑌𐑆, 𐐰𐑅𐐿𐑉𐐴𐐺𐐮𐑍 𐐫𐑊 𐑄 𐐹𐐵𐐲𐑉 𐐱𐑂 𐐈𐑊𐑋𐐲 𐐰𐑌𐐼 𐐈𐑋𐐷𐐭𐑊𐐯𐐿 𐐻𐐭 𐑄 𐐼𐐯𐑂𐐮𐑊; 𐑁𐐫𐑉 𐑄𐐩 𐐶𐐲𐑉 𐐱𐑂 𐑄 𐐹𐑉𐐬𐑁𐐯𐑇𐐲𐑌 𐐱𐑂 𐐤𐐨𐐸𐐫𐑉, 𐐰𐑌𐐼 𐐼𐐮𐐼 𐑌𐐱𐐻 𐐺𐐨𐑊𐐨𐑂 𐐮𐑌 𐑄 𐑉𐐨𐐹𐐯𐑌𐐻𐐰𐑌𐑅 𐐱𐑂 𐑄𐐩𐑉 𐑅𐐮𐑌𐑆.

16. 𐐈𐑌𐐼 𐐮𐐻 𐐿𐐩𐑋 𐐻𐐭 𐐹𐐰𐑅 𐑄𐐰𐐻 𐐈𐑊𐑋𐐲 𐐰𐑌𐐼 𐐈𐑋𐐷𐐭𐑊𐐯𐐿, 𐐈𐑋𐐷𐐭𐑊𐐯𐐿 𐐸𐐰𐑂𐐮𐑍 𐑁𐐫𐑉𐑅𐐩𐐿𐐲𐑌 𐐫𐑊 𐐸𐐮𐑆 𐑀𐐬𐑊𐐼, 𐐰𐑌𐐼 𐑅𐐮𐑊𐑂𐐲𐑉, 𐐰𐑌𐐼 𐐸𐐮𐑆 𐐹𐑉𐐯𐑇𐐲𐑅 𐑃𐐮𐑍𐑆, 𐐸𐐶𐐮𐐽 𐐶𐐲𐑉 𐐮𐑌 𐑄 𐑊𐐰𐑌𐐼 𐐱𐑂 𐐈𐑋𐐬𐑌𐐴𐐸𐐪, 𐑁𐐫𐑉 𐑄 𐐶𐐲𐑉𐐼 𐐱𐑂 𐐘𐐱𐐼, 𐐸𐐨 𐐺𐐨𐐮𐑍 𐑉𐐨𐐾𐐯𐐿𐐻𐐯𐐼 𐐺𐐴 𐑄𐐬𐑆 𐐸𐐭 𐐶𐐲𐑉 𐐶𐐲𐑌𐑅 𐐸𐐮𐑆 𐑁𐑉𐐯𐑌𐐼𐑆, 𐐰𐑌𐐼 𐐫𐑊𐑅𐐬 𐐺𐐴 𐐸𐐮𐑆 𐑁𐐪𐑄𐐲𐑉 𐐰𐑌𐐼 𐐸𐐮𐑆 𐐿𐐮𐑌𐐼𐑉𐐯𐐼; 𐑄𐐯𐑉𐑁𐐬𐑉, 𐐰𐑁𐐻𐐲𐑉 𐐈𐑊𐑋𐐲 𐐸𐐰𐑂𐐮𐑍 𐐯𐑅𐐻𐐰𐐺𐑊𐐮𐑇𐐻 𐑄 𐐽𐐲𐑉𐐽 𐐰𐐻 𐐝𐐴𐐼𐐲𐑋, 𐑅𐐨𐐮𐑍 𐐲 𐑀𐑉𐐩𐐻 𐐽𐐯𐐿, 𐐷𐐩, 𐑅𐐨𐐮𐑍 𐑄𐐰𐐻 𐑄 𐐹𐐨𐐹𐑊 𐐶𐐲𐑉 𐐽𐐯𐐿𐐻 𐐰𐑆 𐐻𐐭 𐑄 𐐹𐑉𐐴𐐼 𐐱𐑂 𐑄𐐩𐑉 𐐸𐐪𐑉𐐻𐑅, 𐐰𐑌𐐼 𐐺𐐨𐑀𐐰𐑌 𐐻𐐭 𐐸𐐲𐑋𐐺𐑊 𐑄𐐯𐑋𐑅𐐯𐑊𐑂𐑆 𐐺𐐨𐑁𐐬𐑉 𐐘𐐱𐐼, 𐐰𐑌𐐼 𐐺𐐨𐑀𐐰𐑌 𐐻𐐭 𐐰𐑅𐐯𐑋𐐺𐑊 𐑄𐐯𐑋𐑅𐐯𐑊𐑂𐑆 𐐻𐐭𐑀𐐯𐑄𐐲𐑉 𐐰𐐻 𐑄𐐩𐑉 𐑅𐐰𐑍𐐿𐐻𐐷𐐭𐐯𐑉𐐮𐑆 𐐻𐐭 𐐶𐐲𐑉𐑇𐐮𐐹 𐐘𐐱𐐼 𐐺𐐨𐑁𐐬𐑉 𐑄 𐐫𐑊𐐻𐐲𐑉, 𐐶𐐱𐐽𐐮𐑍 𐐰𐑌𐐼 𐐹𐑉𐐩𐐮𐑍 𐐿𐐱𐑌𐐻𐐮𐑌𐐷𐐭𐐰𐑊𐐮, 𐑄𐐰𐐻 𐑄𐐩 𐑋𐐴𐐻 𐐺 𐐼𐐯𐑊𐐮𐑂𐐲𐑉𐐼 𐑁𐑉𐐱𐑋 𐐝𐐩𐐻𐐲𐑌, 𐐰𐑌𐐼 𐑁𐑉𐐱𐑋 𐐼𐐯𐑃, 𐐰𐑌𐐼 𐑁𐑉𐐱𐑋 𐐼𐐯𐑅𐐻𐑉𐐲𐐿𐑇𐐲𐑌; 𐑌𐐵 𐐰𐑆 𐐌 𐑅𐐯𐐼, 𐐈𐑊𐑋𐐲 𐐸𐐰𐑂𐐮𐑍 𐑅𐐨𐑌 𐐫𐑊 𐑄𐐨𐑆 𐑃𐐮𐑍𐑆, 𐑄𐐯𐑉𐑁𐐬𐑉 𐐸𐐨 𐐻𐐳𐐿 𐐈𐑋𐐷𐐭𐑊𐐯𐐿 𐐰𐑌𐐼 𐐿𐐩𐑋 𐐬𐑂𐐲𐑉 𐐻𐐭 𐑄 𐑊𐐰𐑌𐐼 𐐱𐑂 𐐞𐐰𐑉𐐲𐐸𐐯𐑋𐑊𐐲, 𐐰𐑌𐐼 𐐻𐐳𐐿 𐐸𐐮𐑋 𐐻𐐭 𐐸𐐮𐑆 𐐬𐑌 𐐸𐐵𐑅, 𐐰𐑌𐐼 𐐼𐐮𐐼 𐐰𐐼𐑋𐐮𐑌𐐮𐑅𐐻𐐲𐑉 𐐲𐑌𐐻𐐭 𐐸𐐮𐑋 𐐮𐑌 𐐸𐐮𐑆 𐐻𐑉𐐮𐐺𐐷𐐭𐑊𐐩𐑇𐐲𐑌𐑆, 𐐰𐑌𐐼 𐑅𐐻𐑉𐐯𐑍𐑃𐐲𐑌𐐼 𐐸𐐮𐑋 𐐮𐑌 𐑄 𐐢𐐫𐑉𐐼. 𐐈𐑌𐐼 𐑄𐐲𐑅 𐐯𐑌𐐼𐐯𐐼 𐑄 𐐻𐐯𐑌𐑃 𐐷𐐨𐑉 𐐱𐑂 𐑄 𐑉𐐩𐑌 𐐱𐑂 𐑄 𐐖𐐲𐐾𐐯𐑆 𐐬𐑂𐐲𐑉 𐑄 𐐹𐐨𐐹𐑊 𐐱𐑂 𐐤𐐨𐑁𐐴.

𐐕𐐰𐐹𐐻𐐲𐑉 XI.

1. 𐐰𐑌𐐼 𐐮𐐻 𐐿𐐩𐑋 𐐻𐐭 𐐹𐐰𐑅 𐐮𐑌 𐑄 𐐨𐑊𐐯𐑂𐑌𐑃 𐐷𐐨𐑉 𐐲𐑂 𐑄 𐑉𐐩𐑌 𐐲𐑂 𐑄 𐐾𐐲𐐾𐐯𐑆 𐐬𐑂𐐲𐑉 𐑄 𐐹𐐨𐐹𐐲𐑊 𐐲𐑂 𐐤𐐨𐑁𐐴, 𐐱𐑌 𐑄 𐑁𐐮𐑁𐑃 𐐼𐐩 𐐲𐑂 𐑄 𐑅𐐯𐐿𐐲𐑌𐐼 𐑋𐐲𐑌𐑃, 𐑄𐐯𐑉 𐐸𐐰𐑂𐐮𐑍 𐐺𐐮𐑌 𐑋𐐲𐐽 𐐹𐐨𐑅 𐐮𐑌 𐑄 𐑊𐐰𐑌𐐼 𐐲𐑂 𐐞𐐩𐑉𐐲𐐸𐐯𐑋𐑊𐐲; 𐑄𐐯𐑉 𐐸𐐰𐑂𐐮𐑍 𐐺𐐮𐑌 𐑌𐐬 𐐶𐐫𐑉𐑆 𐑌𐐫𐑉 𐐿𐐱𐑌𐐻𐐯𐑌𐑇𐐲𐑌𐑆 𐑁𐐫𐑉 𐐲 𐑅𐐲𐑉𐐻𐐮𐑌 𐑌𐐲𐑋𐐺𐐲𐑉 𐐲𐑂 𐐷𐐨𐑉𐑆; 𐐨𐑂𐐲𐑌 𐐲𐑌𐐻𐐮𐑊 𐑄 𐑁𐐮𐑁𐑃 𐐼𐐩 𐐲𐑂 𐑄 𐑅𐐯𐐿𐐲𐑌𐐼 𐑋𐐲𐑌𐑃, 𐐮𐑌 𐑄 𐐨𐑊𐐯𐑂𐑌𐑃 𐐷𐐨𐑉, 𐑄𐐯𐑉 𐐶𐐱𐑆 𐐲 𐐿𐑉𐐴 𐐲𐑂 𐐶𐐫𐑉 𐐸𐐲𐑉𐐼 𐑃𐑉𐐭𐐵𐐻 𐑄 𐑊𐐰𐑌𐐼; 𐑁𐐫𐑉 𐐺𐐨𐐸𐐬𐑊𐐼, 𐑄 𐐪𐑉𐑋𐐨𐑆 𐐲𐑂 𐑄 𐐢𐐩𐑋𐐲𐑌𐐴𐐻𐑅 𐐸𐐰𐐼 𐐿𐐲𐑋 𐐮𐑌 𐐲𐐹𐐱𐑌 𐑄 𐐶𐐮𐑊𐐼𐐲𐑉𐑌𐐯𐑅 𐑅𐐴𐐼, 𐐮𐑌𐐻𐐭 𐑄 𐐺𐐫𐑉𐐼𐐲𐑉𐑆 𐐲𐑂 𐑄 𐑊𐐰𐑌𐐼, 𐐨𐑂𐐲𐑌 𐐮𐑌𐐻𐐭 𐑄 𐑅𐐮𐐻𐐮 𐐲𐑂 𐐈𐑋𐐲𐑌𐐴𐐸𐐲, 𐐰𐑌𐐼 𐐺𐐨𐑀𐐰𐑌 𐐻𐐭 𐑅𐑊𐐩 𐑄 𐐹𐐨𐐹𐐲𐑊, 𐐰𐑌𐐼 𐐼𐐨𐑅𐐻𐑉𐑎 𐑄 𐑅𐐮𐐻𐐮.

2. 𐐰𐑌𐐼 𐑌𐐵 𐐮𐐻 𐐿𐐩𐑋 𐐻𐐭 𐐹𐐰𐑅 𐐺𐐨𐑁𐐬𐑉 𐑄 𐐤𐐨𐑁𐐴𐐻𐑅 𐐿𐐳𐐼 𐑉𐐩𐑆 𐐲 𐑅𐐲𐑁𐐮𐑇𐐲𐑌𐐻 𐐪𐑉𐑋𐐨 𐐻𐐭 𐐼𐑉𐐴𐑂 𐑄𐐯𐑋 𐐵𐐻 𐐲𐑂 𐑄 𐑊𐐰𐑌𐐼, 𐑄𐐩 𐐸𐐰𐐼 𐐼𐐨𐑅𐐻𐑉𐑎𐐼 𐑄 𐐹𐐨𐐹𐐲𐑊 𐐸𐐭 𐐶𐐲𐑉 𐐮𐑌 𐑄 𐑅𐐮𐐻𐐮 𐐲𐑂 𐐈𐑋𐐲𐑌𐐴𐐸𐐲, 𐐰𐑌𐐼 𐐫𐑊𐑅𐐬 𐑅𐐲𐑋 𐐲𐑉𐐵𐑌𐐼 𐑄 𐐺𐐫𐑉𐐼𐐲𐑉𐑆 𐐲𐑂 𐐤𐐬𐐲, 𐐰𐑌𐐼 𐐻𐐩𐐿𐑌 𐐲𐑄𐐲𐑉𐑆 𐐿𐐰𐐹𐐻𐐮𐑂 𐐮𐑌𐐻𐐭 𐑄 𐐶𐐮𐑊𐐼𐐲𐑉𐑌𐐯𐑅.

3. 𐑌𐐵 𐐮𐐻 𐐿𐐩𐑋 𐐻𐐭 𐐹𐐰𐑅 𐑄𐐰𐐻 𐑄 𐐤𐐨𐑁𐐴𐐻𐑅 𐐶𐐲𐑉 𐐼𐐨𐑆𐐴𐑉𐐲𐑅 𐐻𐐭 𐐱𐐺𐐻𐐩𐑌 𐑄𐐬𐑆 𐐸𐐭 𐐸𐐰𐐼 𐐺𐐮𐑌 𐐿𐐰𐑉𐐨𐐼 𐐲𐐶𐐩 𐐿𐐰𐐹𐐻𐐮𐑂 𐐮𐑌𐐻𐐭 𐑄 𐐶𐐮𐑊𐐼𐐲𐑉𐑌𐐯𐑅; 𐑄𐐯𐑉𐑁𐐬𐑉 𐐸𐐨 𐑄𐐰𐐻 𐐸𐐰𐐼 𐐺𐐮𐑌 𐐲𐐹𐑎𐑌𐐻𐐯𐐼 𐐽𐐨𐑁 𐐿𐐰𐐹𐐻𐐲𐑌 𐐬𐑂𐐲𐑉 𐑄 𐐪𐑉𐑋𐐨𐑆 𐐲𐑂 𐑄 𐐤𐐨𐑁𐐴𐐻𐑅, (𐐰𐑌𐐼 𐐸𐐮𐑆 𐑌𐐩𐑋 𐐶𐐱𐑆 𐐞𐐬𐑉𐐲𐑋, 𐐰𐑌𐐼 𐐸𐐨 𐐸𐐰𐐼 𐐻𐐭 𐑅𐐲𐑌𐑆, 𐐢𐐨𐐸𐐴 𐐰𐑌𐐼 𐐁𐐸𐐲.) 𐑌𐐵 𐐞𐐬𐑉𐐲𐑋 𐐰𐑌𐐼 𐐸𐐮𐑆 𐐻𐐭 𐑅𐐲𐑌𐑆, 𐑌𐐬𐐮𐑍 𐑄𐐰𐐻 𐐈𐑊𐑋𐐲 𐐶𐐱𐑆 𐐸𐐴 𐐹𐑉𐐨𐑅𐐻 𐐬𐑂𐐲𐑉 𐑄 𐐽𐐲𐑉𐐽, 𐐰𐑌𐐼 𐐸𐐰𐑂𐐮𐑍 𐐸𐐲𐑉𐐼 𐑄𐐰𐐻 𐐸𐐨 𐐸𐐰𐐼 𐑄 𐑅𐐹𐐮𐑉𐐮𐐻 𐐲𐑂 𐐹𐑉𐐱𐑁𐐯𐑅𐐨, 𐑄𐐯𐑉𐑁𐐬𐑉 𐑄𐐩 𐐶𐐯𐑌𐐻 𐐲𐑌𐐻𐐭 𐐸𐐮𐑋 𐐰𐑌𐐼 𐐼𐐨𐑆𐐴𐑉𐐼 𐐲𐑂 𐐸𐐮𐑋 𐐻𐐭 𐑌𐐬 𐐸𐐶𐐮𐑄𐐲𐑉 𐑄 𐐢𐐫𐑉𐐼 𐐶𐐳𐐼 𐑄𐐰𐐻 𐑄𐐩 𐑇𐐳𐐼 𐑀𐐬 𐐮𐑌𐐻𐐭 𐑄 𐐶𐐮𐑊𐐼𐐲𐑉𐑌𐐯𐑅 𐐮𐑌 𐑅𐐲𐑉𐐽 𐐲𐑂 𐑄𐐯𐑉 𐐺𐑉𐐯𐑄𐑉𐐯𐑌, 𐐸𐐭 𐐸𐐰𐐼 𐐺𐐮𐑌 𐐻𐐩𐐿𐑌 𐐿𐐰𐐹𐐻𐐮𐑂 𐐺𐐴 𐑄 𐐢𐐩𐑋𐐲𐑌𐐴𐐻𐑅.

4. 𐐰𐑌𐐼 𐐮𐐻 𐐿𐐩𐑋 𐐻𐐭 𐐹𐐰𐑅 𐑄𐐰𐐻 𐐈𐑊𐑋𐐲 𐐮𐑌𐐿𐐶𐐴𐑉𐐼 𐐲𐑂 𐑄 𐐢𐐫𐑉𐐼 𐐿𐐱𐑌𐑅𐐲𐑉𐑌𐐮𐑍 𐑄 𐑋𐐰𐐻𐐲𐑉. 𐐰𐑌𐐼 𐐈𐑊𐑋𐐲 𐑉𐐨𐐻𐐲𐑉𐑌𐐼 𐐰𐑌𐐼 𐑅𐐯𐐼 𐐲𐑌𐐻𐐭 𐑄𐐯𐑋, 𐐺𐐨𐐸𐐬𐑊𐐼, 𐑄 𐐢𐐩𐑋𐐲𐑌𐐴𐐻𐑅 𐐶𐐮𐑊 𐐿𐑉𐐫𐑅 𐑄 𐑉𐐮𐑂𐐲𐑉 𐐝𐐴𐐼𐐲𐑌 𐐮𐑌 𐑄 𐑅𐐵𐑃 𐐶𐐮𐑊𐐼𐐲𐑉𐑌𐐯𐑅, 𐐲𐐶𐐩 𐐲𐐹 𐐺𐐨𐐷𐐱𐑌𐐼 𐑄 𐐺𐐫𐑉𐐼𐐲𐑉𐑆 𐐲𐑂 𐑄 𐑊𐐰𐑌𐐼 𐐲𐑂 𐐣𐐰𐑌𐐻𐐴. 𐐰𐑌𐐼 𐐺𐐨𐐸𐐬𐑊𐐼 𐑄𐐯𐑉 𐑇𐐰𐑊 𐐷𐐨 𐑋𐐨𐐻 𐑄𐐯𐑋, 𐐱𐑌 𐑄 𐐨𐑅𐐻 𐐲𐑂 𐑄 𐑉𐐮𐑂𐐲𐑉 𐐝𐐴𐐼𐐲𐑌, 𐐰𐑌𐐼 𐑄𐐯𐑉 𐑄 𐐢𐐫𐑉𐐼 𐐶𐐮𐑊 𐐼𐐨𐑊𐐮𐑂𐐲𐑉 𐐲𐑌𐐻𐐭 𐑄𐐨 𐑄𐐴 𐐺𐑉𐐯𐑄𐑉𐐯𐑌 𐐸𐐭 𐐸𐐰𐑂 𐐺𐐮𐑌 𐐻𐐩𐐿𐑌 𐐿𐐰𐐹𐐻𐐮𐑂 𐐺𐐴 𐑄 𐐢𐐩𐑋𐐲𐑌𐐴𐐻𐑅.

5. 𐐰𐑌𐐼 𐐮𐐻 𐐿𐐩𐑋 𐐻𐐭 𐐹𐐰𐑅 𐑄𐐰𐐻 𐐞𐐬𐑉𐐲𐑋 𐐰𐑌𐐼 𐐸𐐮𐑆 𐑅𐐲𐑌𐑆 𐐿𐑉𐐫𐑅𐐻 𐐬𐑂𐐲𐑉 𐑄 𐑉𐐮𐑂𐐲𐑉 𐐝𐐴𐐼𐐲𐑌, 𐐶𐐮𐑄 𐑄𐐯𐑉 𐐪𐑉𐑋𐐨𐑆, 𐐰𐑌𐐼 𐑋𐐪𐑉𐐽𐐻 𐐲𐐶𐐩 𐐺𐐨𐐷𐐱𐑌𐐼 𐑄 𐐺𐐫𐑉𐐼𐐲𐑉𐑆 𐐲𐑂 𐐣𐐰𐑌𐐻𐐴, 𐐮𐑌𐐻𐐭 𐑄 𐑅𐐵𐑃 𐐶𐐮𐑊𐐼𐐲𐑉𐑌𐐯𐑅, 𐐸𐐶𐐮𐐽 𐐶𐐱𐑆 𐐱𐑌 𐑄 𐐨𐑅𐐻 𐑅𐐴𐐼 𐐲𐑂 𐑄 𐑉𐐮𐑂𐐲𐑉 𐐝𐐴𐐼𐐲𐑌. 𐐰𐑌𐐼 𐑄𐐩 𐐿𐐩𐑋 𐐲𐐹𐐱𐑌 𐑄 𐐪𐑉𐑋𐐨𐑆 𐐲𐑂 𐑄 𐐢𐐩𐑋𐐲𐑌𐐴𐐻𐑅, 𐐰𐑌𐐼 𐑄 𐐢𐐩𐑋𐐲𐑌𐐴𐐻𐑅 𐐶𐐲𐑉 𐑅𐐿𐐰𐐻𐐲𐑉𐐼 𐐰𐑌𐐼 𐐼𐑉𐐮𐑂𐑌 𐐮𐑌𐐻𐐭 𐑄 𐐶𐐮𐑊𐐼𐐲𐑉𐑌𐐯𐑅; 𐐰𐑌𐐼 𐑄𐐩 𐐻𐐳𐐿 𐑄𐐯𐑉 𐐺𐑉𐐯𐑄𐑉𐐯𐑌 𐐸𐐭 𐐸𐐰𐐼 𐐺𐐮𐑌 𐐻𐐩𐐿𐑌 𐐿𐐰𐐹𐐻𐐮𐑂 𐐺𐐴 𐑄 𐐢𐐩𐑋𐐲𐑌𐐴𐐻𐑅, 𐐰𐑌𐐼 𐑄𐐯𐑉 𐐶𐐱𐑆 𐑌𐐱𐐻 𐐶𐐲𐑌 𐑅𐐬𐑊 𐐲𐑂 𐑄𐐯𐑋 𐐸𐐰𐐼 𐐺𐐮𐑌 𐑊𐐫𐑅𐐻, 𐑄𐐰𐐻 𐐶𐐲𐑉 𐐻𐐩𐐿𐑌 𐐿𐐰𐐹𐐻𐐮𐑂. 𐐰𐑌𐐼 𐑄𐐩 𐐶𐐲𐑉 𐐺𐑉𐐫𐐻 𐐺𐐴 𐑄𐐯𐑉 𐐺𐑉𐐯𐑄𐑉𐐯𐑌 𐐻𐐭 𐐹𐐲𐑆𐐯𐑅 𐑄𐐯𐑉 𐐬𐑌 𐑊𐐰𐑌𐐼𐑆. 𐐰𐑌𐐼 𐑄𐐲𐑅 𐐯𐑌𐐼𐐯𐐼 𐑄 𐐨𐑊𐐯𐑂𐑌𐑃 𐐷𐐨𐑉 𐐲𐑂 𐑄 𐐾𐐲𐐾𐐯𐑆, 𐑄 𐐢𐐩𐑋𐐲𐑌𐐴𐐻𐑅 𐐸𐐰𐑂𐐮𐑍 𐐺𐐮𐑌 𐐼𐑉𐐮𐑂𐑌 𐐵𐐻 𐐲𐑂 𐑄 𐑊𐐰𐑌𐐼, 𐐰𐑌𐐼 𐑄 𐐹𐐨𐐹𐐲𐑊 𐐲𐑂 𐐈𐑋𐐲𐑌𐐴𐐸𐐲 𐐶𐐲𐑉 𐐼𐐨𐑅𐐻𐑉𐑎𐐼; 𐐷𐐩, 𐐯𐑂𐐲𐑉𐐨 𐑊𐐮𐑂𐐮𐑍 𐑅𐐬𐑊 𐐲𐑂 𐑄 𐐈𐑋𐐲𐑌𐐴𐐸𐐲𐐴𐐻𐑅 𐐶𐐱𐑆 𐐼𐐨𐑅𐐻𐑉𐑎𐐼, 𐐰𐑌𐐼 𐐫𐑊𐑅𐐬 𐑄𐐯𐑉 𐑀𐑉𐐩𐐻 𐑅𐐮𐐻𐐮, 𐐸𐐶𐐮𐐽 𐑄𐐩 𐑅𐐯𐐼 𐐘𐐱𐐼 𐐿𐐳𐐼 𐑌𐐱𐐻 𐐼𐐨𐑅𐐻𐑉𐑎, 𐐺𐐨𐐿𐐫𐑆 𐐲𐑂 𐐮𐐻𐑅 𐑀𐑉𐐩𐐻𐑌𐐯𐑅. 𐐺𐐲𐐻 𐐺𐐨𐐸𐐬𐑊𐐼, 𐐮𐑌 𐐶𐐲𐑌 𐐼𐐩 𐐮𐐻 𐐶𐐱𐑆 𐑊𐐯𐑁𐐻 𐐼𐐯𐑅𐐬𐑊𐐩𐐻; 𐐰𐑌𐐼 𐑄 𐐿𐐪𐑉𐐿𐐲𐑅𐐯𐑆 𐐶𐐲𐑉 𐑋𐐰𐑍𐑀𐑊𐐼 𐐺𐐴 𐐼𐐫𐑀𐑆 𐐰𐑌𐐼 𐐶𐐴𐑊𐐼 𐐺𐐨𐑅𐐻𐑅 𐐲𐑂 𐑄 𐐶𐐮𐑊𐐼𐐲𐑉𐑌𐐯𐑅: 𐑌𐐯𐑂𐐲𐑉𐑄𐐲𐑊𐐯𐑅, 𐐰𐑁𐐻𐐲𐑉 𐑋𐐯𐑌𐐨 𐐼𐐩𐑆, 𐑄𐐯𐑉 𐐼𐐯𐐼 𐐺𐐱𐐼𐐨𐑆 𐐶𐐲𐑉 𐐸𐐨𐐹𐐻 𐐲𐐹 𐐲𐐹𐐱𐑌 𐑄 𐑁𐐩𐑅 𐐲𐑂 𐑄 𐐲𐑉𐑃, 𐐰𐑌𐐼 𐑄𐐩 𐐶𐐲𐑉 𐐿𐐲𐑂𐐲𐑉𐐼 𐐶𐐮𐑄 𐐲 𐑇𐐰𐑊𐐬 𐐿𐐲𐑂𐐲𐑉𐐮𐑍. 𐐰𐑌𐐼 𐑌𐐵 𐑅𐐬 𐑀𐑉𐐩𐐻 𐐶𐐱𐑆 𐑄 𐑅𐐯𐑌𐐻 𐑄𐐯𐑉𐐱𐑂, 𐑄𐐰𐐻 𐑄 𐐹𐐨𐐹𐐲𐑊 𐐼𐐮𐐼 𐑌𐐱𐐻 𐑀𐐬 𐐮𐑌 𐐻𐐭 𐐹𐐲𐑆𐐯𐑅 𐑄 𐑊𐐰𐑌𐐼 𐐲𐑂 𐐈𐑋𐐲𐑌𐐴𐐸𐐲 𐑁𐐫𐑉 𐑋𐐯𐑌𐐨

𐐷𐐨𐑉𐑆. 𐐈𐑌𐐼 𐐮𐐻 𐐶𐐱𐑆 𐐿𐐫𐑊𐐼 𐐔𐐯𐑅𐐬𐑊𐐩𐑇𐐲𐑌 𐐱𐑂 𐐤𐐨𐐸𐐫𐑉𐑆; 𐑁𐐫𐑉 𐑄𐐩 𐐶𐐲𐑉 𐐱𐑂 𐑄 𐐹𐑉𐐬𐑁𐐯𐑇𐐲𐑌 𐐱𐑂 𐐤𐐨𐐸𐐫𐑉, 𐐸𐐭 𐐶𐐲𐑉 𐑅𐑊𐐩𐑌; 𐐰𐑌𐐼 𐑄𐐩𐑉 𐑊𐐰𐑌𐐼𐑆 𐑉𐐨𐑋𐐩𐑌𐐼 𐐼𐐯𐑅𐐬𐑊𐐩𐐻. 𐐈𐑌𐐼 𐑄 𐐢𐐰𐑋𐐲𐑌𐐴𐐻𐑅 𐐼𐐮𐐼 𐑌𐐱𐐻 𐐿𐐲𐑋 𐐲𐑀𐐯𐑌 𐐻𐐭 𐐶𐐫𐑉 𐐲𐑀𐐯𐑌𐑅𐐻 𐑄 𐐤𐐨𐑁𐐴𐐻𐑅 𐐲𐑌𐐻𐐮𐑊 𐑄 𐑁𐐬𐑉𐐻𐐨𐑌𐑃 𐐷𐐨𐑉 𐐱𐑂 𐑄 𐑉𐐩𐑌 𐐱𐑂 𐑄 𐐾𐐲𐐾𐐯𐑆 𐐬𐑂𐐲𐑉 𐑄 𐐹𐐨𐐹𐑊 𐐱𐑂 𐐤𐐨𐑁𐐴. 𐐈𐑌𐐼 𐑄𐐲𐑅 𐑁𐐫𐑉 𐑃𐑉𐐨 𐐷𐐨𐑉𐑆 𐐼𐐮𐐼 𐑄 𐐹𐐨𐐹𐑊 𐐱𐑂 𐐤𐐨𐑁𐐴 𐐸𐐰𐑂 𐐿𐐱𐑌𐐻𐐮𐑌𐐷𐐭𐐲𐑊 𐐹𐐨𐑅 𐐮𐑌 𐐫𐑊 𐑄 𐑊𐐰𐑌𐐼.

6. 𐐈𐑌𐐼 𐐈𐑊𐑋𐐲 𐐰𐑌𐐼 𐐈𐑋𐐷𐐭𐑊𐐯𐐿 𐐶𐐯𐑌𐐻 𐑁𐐫𐑉𐑃 𐐹𐑉𐐨𐐽𐐮𐑍 𐑉𐐨𐐹𐐯𐑌𐐻𐐲𐑌𐑅 𐐻𐐭 𐑄 𐐹𐐨𐐹𐑊 𐐮𐑌 𐑄𐐩𐑉 𐐻𐐯𐑋𐐹𐑊𐑆, 𐐰𐑌𐐼 𐐮𐑌 𐑄𐐩𐑉 𐑅𐐰𐑍𐐿𐐽𐐷𐐭𐐯𐑉𐐮𐑆, 𐐰𐑌𐐼 𐐫𐑊𐑅𐐬 𐐮𐑌 𐑄𐐩𐑉 𐑅𐐮𐑌𐐲𐑀𐐱𐑀𐑆, 𐐸𐐶𐐮𐐽 𐐶𐐲𐑉 𐐺𐐮𐑊𐐻 𐐰𐑁𐐻𐐲𐑉 𐑄 𐑋𐐰𐑌𐐲𐑉 𐐱𐑂 𐑄 𐐖𐐭𐑆. 𐐈𐑌𐐼 𐐰𐑆 𐑋𐐯𐑌𐐨 𐐰𐑆 𐐶𐐳𐐼 𐐸𐐨𐑉 𐑄𐐩𐑉 𐐶𐐲𐑉𐐼𐑆, 𐐲𐑌𐐻𐐭 𐑄𐐯𐑋 𐑄𐐩 𐐼𐐮𐐼 𐐮𐑋𐐹𐐪𐑉𐐻 𐑄 𐐶𐐲𐑉𐐼 𐐱𐑂 𐐘𐐱𐐼, 𐐶𐐮𐑄𐐵𐐻 𐐯𐑌𐐨 𐑉𐐨𐑅𐐹𐐯𐐿𐐻 𐐱𐑂 𐐹𐐲𐑉𐑅𐐲𐑌𐑆, 𐐿𐐱𐑌𐐻𐐮𐑌𐐷𐐭𐐲𐑊𐐨. 𐐈𐑌𐐼 𐑄𐐲𐑅 𐐼𐐮𐐼 𐐈𐑊𐑋𐐲 𐐰𐑌𐐼 𐐈𐑋𐐷𐐭𐑊𐐯𐐿 𐑀𐐬 𐑁𐐫𐑉𐑃, 𐐰𐑌𐐼 𐐫𐑊𐑅𐐬 𐑋𐐯𐑌𐐨 𐑋𐐬𐑉 𐐸𐐭 𐐸𐐰𐐼 𐐺𐐨𐑌 𐐽𐐬𐑆𐐲𐑌 𐑁𐐫𐑉 𐑄 𐐶𐐲𐑉𐐿, 𐐻𐐭 𐐹𐑉𐐨𐐽 𐑄 𐐶𐐲𐑉𐐼 𐑃𐑉𐐭𐐵𐐻 𐐫𐑊 𐑄 𐑊𐐰𐑌𐐼. 𐐈𐑌𐐼 𐑄 𐐯𐑅𐐻𐐰𐐺𐑊𐐮𐑇𐑋𐐯𐑌𐐻 𐐱𐑂 𐑄 𐐽𐐲𐑉𐐽 𐐺𐐨𐐿𐐩𐑋 𐐾𐐯𐑌𐐲𐑉𐐲𐑊 𐑃𐑉𐐭𐐵𐐻 𐑄 𐑊𐐰𐑌𐐼, 𐐮𐑌 𐐫𐑊 𐑄 𐑉𐐨𐐾𐐲𐑌 𐑉𐐵𐑌𐐼 𐐲𐐺𐐵𐐻, 𐐲𐑋𐐲𐑍 𐐫𐑊 𐑄 𐐹𐐨𐐹𐑊 𐐱𐑂 𐑄 𐐤𐐨𐑁𐐴𐐻𐑅.

7. 𐐈𐑌𐐼 𐑄𐐩𐑉 𐐶𐐱𐑆 𐑌𐐬 𐐮𐑌𐐨𐐿𐐶𐐱𐑊𐐮𐐻𐐨 𐐲𐑋𐐲𐑍 𐑄𐐯𐑋; 𐑄 𐐢𐐫𐑉𐐼 𐐼𐐮𐐼 𐐹𐐬𐑉 𐐵𐐻 𐐸𐐮𐑆 𐐝𐐹𐐮𐑉𐐮𐐻 𐐱𐑌 𐐫𐑊 𐑄 𐑁𐐩𐑅 𐐱𐑂 𐑄 𐑊𐐰𐑌𐐼, 𐐻𐐭 𐐹𐑉𐐨𐐹𐐩𐑉 𐑄 𐑋𐐴𐑌𐐼𐑆 𐐱𐑂 𐑄 𐐽𐐮𐑊𐐼𐑉𐐯𐑌 𐐱𐑂 𐑋𐐯𐑌, 𐐫𐑉 𐐻𐐭 𐐹𐑉𐐨𐐹𐐩𐑉 𐑄𐐩𐑉 𐐸𐐪𐑉𐐻𐑅 𐐻𐐭 𐑉𐐨𐑅𐐨𐑂 𐑄 𐐶𐐲𐑉𐐼 𐐸𐐶𐐮𐐽 𐑇𐐳𐐼 𐐺𐐨 𐐻𐐫𐐻 𐐲𐑋𐐲𐑍 𐑄𐐯𐑋 𐐰𐐻 𐑄 𐐻𐐴𐑋 𐐱𐑂 𐐸𐐮𐑆 𐐿𐐲𐑋𐐮𐑍, 𐑄𐐰𐐻 𐑄𐐩 𐑋𐐴𐐻 𐑌𐐱𐐻 𐐺𐐨 𐐸𐐪𐑉𐐼𐐲𐑌𐐼 𐐲𐑀𐐯𐑌𐑅𐐻 𐑄 𐐶𐐲𐑉𐐼, 𐑄𐐰𐐻 𐑄𐐩 𐑋𐐴𐐻 𐑌𐐱𐐻 𐐺𐐨 𐐲𐑌𐐺𐐨𐑊𐐨𐑂𐐮𐑍, 𐐰𐑌𐐼 𐑀𐐬 𐐱𐑌 𐐻𐐭 𐐼𐐯𐑅𐐻𐑉𐐲𐐿𐑇𐐲𐑌, 𐐺𐐲𐐻 𐑄𐐰𐐻 𐑄𐐩 𐑋𐐴𐐻 𐑉𐐨𐑅𐐨𐑂 𐑄 𐐶𐐲𐑉𐐼 𐐶𐐮𐑄 𐐾𐐱𐐮, 𐐰𐑌𐐼 𐐰𐑆 𐐲 𐐺𐑉𐐰𐑌𐐽 𐐺𐐨 𐑀𐑉𐐰𐑁𐐻𐐲𐐼 𐐮𐑌𐐻𐐭 𐑄 𐐻𐑉𐐭 𐑂𐐴𐑌, 𐑄𐐰𐐻 𐑄𐐩 𐑋𐐴𐐻 𐐯𐑌𐐻𐐲𐑉 𐐮𐑌𐐻𐐭 𐑄 𐑉𐐯𐑅𐐻 𐐱𐑂 𐑄 𐐢𐐫𐑉𐐼 𐑄𐐩𐑉 𐐘𐐱𐐼.

8. 𐐤𐐵 𐑄𐐬𐑆 𐐹𐑉𐐨𐑅𐐻𐑅 𐐸𐐭 𐐼𐐮𐐼 𐑀𐐬 𐑁𐐫𐑉𐑃 𐐲𐑋𐐲𐑍 𐑄 𐐹𐐨𐐹𐑊, 𐐼𐐮𐐼 𐐹𐑉𐐨𐐽 𐐲𐑀𐐯𐑌𐑅𐐻 𐐫𐑊 𐑊𐐴𐐮𐑍𐑆, 𐐰𐑌𐐼 𐐼𐐨𐑅𐐨𐑂𐐮𐑍𐑆, 𐐰𐑌𐐼 𐐯𐑌𐑂𐐨𐐮𐑍𐑆, 𐐰𐑌𐐼 𐑅𐐻𐑉𐐴𐑁𐑅, 𐐰𐑌𐐼 𐑋𐐰𐑊𐐮𐑅, 𐐰𐑌𐐼 𐑉𐐨𐑂𐐴𐑊𐐮𐑍𐑆, 𐐰𐑌𐐼 𐑅𐐻𐐨𐑊𐐮𐑍, 𐑉𐐱𐐺𐐮𐑍, 𐐹𐑊𐐲𐑌𐐼𐐲𐑉𐐮𐑍, 𐑋𐐲𐑉𐐼𐐲𐑉𐐮𐑍, 𐐿𐐱𐑋𐐮𐐻𐐮𐑍 𐐰𐐼𐐲𐑊𐐻𐐲𐑉𐐨, 𐐰𐑌𐐼 𐐫𐑊 𐑋𐐰𐑌𐐲𐑉 𐐱𐑂 𐑊𐐰𐑅𐐮𐑂𐐨𐐲𐑅𐑌𐐯𐑅, 𐐿𐑉𐐴𐐮𐑍 𐑄𐐰𐐻 𐑄𐐨𐑆 𐑃𐐮𐑍𐑆 𐐫𐐻 𐑌𐐱𐐻 𐑅𐐬 𐐻𐐭 𐐺𐐨; 𐐸𐐬𐑊𐐼𐐮𐑍 𐑁𐐫𐑉𐑃 𐑃𐐮𐑍𐑆 𐐸𐐶𐐮𐐽 𐑋𐐲𐑅𐐻 𐑇𐐫𐑉𐐻𐑊𐐨 𐐿𐐲𐑋; 𐐷𐐩, 𐐸𐐬𐑊𐐼𐐮𐑍 𐑁𐐫𐑉𐑃 𐑄 𐐿𐐲𐑋𐐮𐑍 𐐱𐑂 𐑄 𐐝𐐲𐑌 𐐱𐑂 𐐘𐐱𐐼, 𐐸𐐮𐑆 𐑅𐐲𐑁𐐲𐑉𐐮𐑍𐑆 𐐰𐑌𐐼 𐐼𐐯𐑃, 𐐰𐑌𐐼 𐐫𐑊𐑅𐐬 𐑄 𐑉𐐯𐑆𐐲𐑉𐐯𐐿𐑇𐐲𐑌 𐐱𐑂 𐑄 𐐼𐐯𐐼. 𐐈𐑌𐐼 𐑋𐐯𐑌𐐨 𐐱𐑂 𐑄 𐐹𐐨𐐹𐑊 𐐼𐐮𐐼 𐐮𐑌𐐿𐐶𐐴𐑉 𐐿𐐱𐑌𐑅𐐲𐑉𐑌𐐮𐑍 𐑄 𐐹𐑊𐐩𐑅 𐐸𐐶𐐩𐑉 𐑄 𐐝𐐲𐑌 𐐱𐑂 𐐘𐐱𐐼 𐑇𐐳𐐼 𐐿𐐲𐑋; 𐐰𐑌𐐼 𐑄𐐩 𐐶𐐲𐑉 𐐻𐐫𐐻 𐑄𐐰𐐻 𐐸𐐨 𐐶𐐳𐐼 𐐲𐐹𐐨𐑉 𐐲𐑌𐐻𐐭 𐑄𐐯𐑋 𐐰𐑁𐐻𐐲𐑉 𐐸𐐮𐑆 𐑉𐐯𐑆𐐲𐑉𐐯𐐿𐑇𐐲𐑌; 𐐰𐑌𐐼 𐑄𐐮𐑅 𐑄 𐐹𐐨𐐹𐑊 𐐼𐐮𐐼 𐐸𐐨𐑉 𐐶𐐮𐑄 𐑀𐑉𐐩𐐻 𐐾𐐱𐐮 𐐰𐑌𐐼 𐑀𐑊𐐰𐐼𐑌𐐯𐑅. 𐐈𐑌𐐼 𐑌𐐵 𐐰𐑁𐐻𐐲𐑉 𐑄 𐐽𐐲𐑉𐐽 𐐸𐐰𐑂𐐮𐑍 𐐺𐐨𐑌 𐐯𐑅𐐻𐐰𐐺𐑊𐐮𐑇𐐻 𐑃𐑉𐐭𐐵𐐻 𐐫𐑊 𐑄 𐑊𐐰𐑌𐐼, 𐐸𐐰𐑂𐐮𐑍 𐑀𐐱𐐻 𐑄 𐑂𐐮𐐿𐐻𐐲𐑉𐐨 𐐬𐑂𐐲𐑉 𐑄 𐐼𐐯𐑂𐐲𐑊, 𐐰𐑌𐐼 𐑄 𐐶𐐲𐑉𐐼 𐐱𐑂 𐐘𐐱𐐼 𐐺𐐨𐐮𐑍 𐐹𐑉𐐨𐐽𐐻 𐐮𐑌 𐐮𐐻𐑅 𐐹𐐷𐐭𐑉𐐮𐐻𐐨 𐐮𐑌 𐐫𐑊 𐑄 𐑊𐐰𐑌𐐼, 𐐰𐑌𐐼 𐑄 𐐢𐐫𐑉𐐼 𐐹𐐬𐑉𐐮𐑍 𐐵𐐻 𐐸𐐮𐑆 𐐺𐑊𐐯𐑅𐐮𐑍𐑆 𐐲𐐹𐐱𐑌 𐑄 𐐹𐐨𐐹𐑊; 𐑄𐐲𐑅 𐐯𐑌𐐼𐐲𐐼 𐑄 𐑁𐐬𐑉𐐻𐐨𐑌𐑃 𐐷𐐨𐑉 𐐱𐑂 𐑄 𐑉𐐩𐑌 𐐱𐑂 𐑄 𐐾𐐲𐐾𐐯𐑆 𐐬𐑂𐐲𐑉 𐑄 𐐹𐐨𐐹𐑊 𐐱𐑂 𐐤𐐨𐑁𐐴.

𐐕𐐰𐐹𐐻𐐲𐑉 XII.

𐐈𐑌 𐐲𐐿𐐵𐑌𐐻 𐐱𐑂 𐑄 𐑅𐐲𐑌𐑆 𐐱𐑂 𐐣𐐬𐑅𐐴𐐲, 𐐸𐐭 𐑉𐐨𐐾𐐯𐐿𐐻𐐲𐐼 𐑄𐐩𐑉 𐑉𐐴𐐻𐑅 𐐻𐐭 𐑄 𐐿𐐮𐑍𐐼𐐲𐑋 𐑁𐐫𐑉 𐑄 𐐶𐐲𐑉𐐼 𐐱𐑂 𐐘𐐱𐐼, 𐐰𐑌𐐼 𐐶𐐯𐑌𐐻 𐐲𐐹 𐐻𐐭 𐑄 𐑊𐐰𐑌𐐼 𐐱𐑂 𐐤𐐨𐑁𐐴, 𐐻𐐭 𐐹𐑉𐐨𐐽 𐐻𐐭 𐑄 𐐢𐐰𐑋𐐲𐑌𐐴𐐻𐑅. 𐐜𐐩𐑉 𐑅𐐲𐑁𐐲𐑉𐐮𐑍𐑆 𐐰𐑌𐐼 𐐼𐐮𐑊𐐮𐑂𐐲𐑉𐐲𐑌𐑅𐑅, 𐐲𐐿𐐫𐑉𐐼𐐮𐑍 𐐻𐐭 𐑄 𐑉𐐯𐐿𐐲𐑉𐐼 𐐱𐑂 𐐈𐑊𐑋𐐲.

1. 𐐈𐑌𐐼 𐑌𐐵 𐐮𐐻 𐐿𐐩𐑋 𐐻𐐭 𐐹𐐰𐑅 𐑄𐐰𐐻 𐐰𐑆 𐐈𐑊𐑋𐐲 𐐶𐐱𐑆 𐐾𐐲𐑉𐑌𐐨𐐮𐑍 𐑁𐑉𐐱𐑋 𐑄 𐑊𐐰𐑌𐐼 𐐱𐑂 𐐘𐐮𐐼𐐨𐐲𐑌, 𐑅𐐵𐑃𐐶𐐲𐑉𐐼, 𐐲𐐶𐐩 𐐻𐐭 𐑄 𐑊𐐰𐑌𐐼 𐐱𐑂 𐐣𐐰𐑌𐐻𐐴, 𐐺𐐨𐐸𐐬𐑊𐐼, 𐐻𐐭 𐐸𐐮𐑆 𐐲𐑅𐐻𐐱𐑌𐐮𐑇𐑋𐐯𐑌𐐻, 𐐸𐐨 𐑋𐐯𐐻 𐐶𐐮𐑄 𐑄 𐑅𐐲𐑌𐑆 𐐱𐑂 𐐣𐐬𐑅𐐴𐐲, 𐐾𐐲𐑉𐑌𐐨𐐮𐑍 𐐻𐐬𐑉𐐩𐑉𐐼𐑆 𐑄 𐑊𐐰𐑌𐐼 𐐱𐑂 𐐞𐐰𐑉𐐲𐐸𐐯𐑋𐑊𐐲. 𐐤𐐵 𐑄𐐨𐑆 𐑅𐐲𐑌𐑆 𐐱𐑂 𐐣𐐬𐑅𐐴𐐲 𐐶𐐲𐑉 𐐶𐐮𐑄 𐐈𐑊𐑋𐐲 𐐰𐐻 𐑄 𐐻𐐴𐑋 𐑄 𐐩𐑌𐐾𐐯𐑊 𐑁𐐲𐑉𐑅𐐻 𐐲𐐹𐐨𐑉𐐼 𐐲𐑌𐐻𐐭 𐐸𐐮𐑋; 𐑄𐐩𐑉𐑁𐐫𐑉 𐐈𐑊𐑋𐐲 𐐼𐐮𐐼 𐑉𐐨𐐾𐐱𐐮𐑅

𐐯𐐿𐑅𐐨𐐼𐐮𐑍𐑊𐐨 𐐻𐐭 𐑅𐐨 𐐸𐐮𐑆 𐐺𐑉𐐯𐑄𐑉𐐯𐑌; 𐐰𐑌𐐼 𐐸𐐶𐐱𐐻 𐐰𐐼𐐯𐐼 𐑋𐐬𐑉 𐐻𐐭 𐐸𐐮𐑆 𐐾𐑎, 𐑄𐐩 𐐶𐐲𐑉 𐑅𐐻𐐮𐑊 𐐸𐐮𐑆 𐐺𐑉𐐯𐑄𐑉𐐯𐑌 𐐮𐑌 𐑄 𐐢𐐫𐑉𐐼; 𐐷𐐩, 𐐰𐑌𐐼 𐑄𐐩 𐐸𐐰𐐼 𐐶𐐰𐐿𐑅𐐻 𐑅𐐻𐑉𐐱𐑍 𐐮𐑌 𐑄 𐑌𐐱𐑊𐐯𐐾 𐐱𐑂 𐑄 𐐻𐑉𐐭𐑃; 𐑁𐐫𐑉 𐑄𐐩 𐐶𐐲𐑉 𐑋𐐯𐑌 𐐱𐑂 𐐩 𐑅𐐵𐑌𐐼 𐐲𐑌𐐼𐐲𐑉𐑅𐐻𐐰𐑌𐐼𐐮𐑍, 𐐰𐑌𐐼 𐑄𐐩 𐐸𐐰𐐼 𐑅𐐲𐑉𐐽𐐻 𐑄 𐐝𐐿𐑉𐐮𐐹𐐽𐐲𐑉𐑆 𐐼𐐮𐑊𐐮𐐾𐐯𐑌𐐻𐑊𐐨, 𐑄𐐰𐐻 𐑄𐐩 𐑋𐐴𐐻 𐑌𐐬 𐑄 𐐶𐐲𐑉𐐼 𐐱𐑂 𐐘𐐱𐐼. 𐐒𐐲𐐻 𐑄𐐮𐑅 𐐮𐑆 𐑌𐐱𐐻 𐐫𐑊; 𐑄𐐩 𐐸𐐰𐐼 𐑀𐐮𐑂𐐯𐑌 𐑄𐐯𐑋𐑅𐐯𐑊𐑂𐑆 𐐻𐐭 𐑋𐐲𐐽 𐐹𐑉𐐩𐑉, 𐐰𐑌𐐼 𐑁𐐰𐑅𐐻𐐮𐑍, 𐑄𐐩𐑉𐑁𐐫𐑉 𐑄𐐩 𐐸𐐰𐐼 𐑄 𐐝𐐹𐐮𐑉𐐮𐐻 𐐱𐑂 𐐹𐑉𐐱𐑁𐐯𐑅𐐨, 𐐰𐑌𐐼 𐑄 𐐝𐐹𐐮𐑉𐐮𐐻 𐐱𐑂 𐑉𐐯𐑂𐐯𐑊𐐩𐑇𐐲𐑌, 𐐰𐑌𐐼 𐐸𐐶𐐯𐑌 𐑄𐐩 𐐻𐐫𐐻, 𐑄𐐩 𐐻𐐫𐐻 𐐶𐐮𐑄 𐐹𐐵𐑉 𐐰𐑌𐐼 𐐫𐑃𐐱𐑉𐐮𐐻𐐨 𐐱𐑂 𐐘𐐱𐐼. 𐐈𐑌𐐼 𐑄𐐩 𐐸𐐰𐐼 𐐺𐐮𐑌 𐐻𐐨𐐽𐐮𐑍 𐑄 𐐶𐐲𐑉𐐼 𐐱𐑂 𐐘𐐱𐐼 𐑁𐐫𐑉 𐑄 𐑅𐐹𐐩𐑅 𐐱𐑂 𐑁𐐬𐑉𐐻𐐨𐑌 𐐷𐐨𐑉𐑆 𐐰𐑋𐐲𐑍 𐑄 𐐢𐐩𐑋𐐲𐑌𐐴𐐻𐑅, 𐐸𐐰𐑂𐐮𐑍 𐐸𐐰𐐼 𐑋𐐲𐐽 𐑅𐐲𐐿𐑅𐐯𐑅 𐐮𐑌 𐐺𐑉𐐮𐑍𐐮𐑍 𐑋𐐯𐑌𐐨 𐐻𐐭 𐑄 𐑌𐐱𐑊𐐯𐐾 𐐱𐑂 𐑄 𐐻𐑉𐐭𐑃; 𐐷𐐩, 𐐺𐐴 𐑄 𐐹𐐵𐑉 𐐱𐑂 𐑄𐐩𐑉 𐐶𐐲𐑉𐐼𐑆, 𐑋𐐯𐑌𐐨 𐐶𐐲𐑉 𐐺𐑉𐐫𐐻 𐐺𐐨𐑁𐐬𐑉 𐑄 𐐫𐑊𐐻𐐲𐑉 𐐱𐑂 𐐘𐐱𐐼, 𐐻𐐭 𐐿𐐫𐑊 𐐱𐑌 𐐸𐐮𐑆 𐑌𐐩𐑋, 𐐰𐑌𐐼 𐐿𐐱𐑌𐑁𐐯𐑅 𐑄𐐩𐑉 𐑅𐐮𐑌𐑆 𐐺𐐨𐑁𐐬𐑉 𐐸𐐮𐑋. 𐐤𐐵 𐑄𐐨𐑆 𐐪𐑉 𐑄 𐑅𐐲𐑉𐐿𐐲𐑋𐑅𐐻𐐰𐑌𐑅𐐯𐑆 𐐸𐐶𐐮𐐽 𐐰𐐻𐐯𐑌𐐼𐐯𐐼 𐑄𐐯𐑋 𐐮𐑌 𐑄𐐩𐑉 𐐾𐐲𐑉𐑌𐐨𐐮𐑍𐑆, 𐑁𐐫𐑉 𐑄𐐩 𐐸𐐰𐐼 𐑋𐐯𐑌𐐨 𐐰𐑁𐑊𐐮𐐿𐑇𐐲𐑌𐑆; 𐑄𐐩 𐐼𐐮𐐼 𐑅𐐲𐑁𐐲𐑉 𐑋𐐲𐐽, 𐐺𐐬𐑃 𐐮𐑌 𐐺𐐱𐐼𐐨 𐐰𐑌𐐼 𐐮𐑌 𐑋𐐴𐑌𐐼; 𐑅𐐲𐐽 𐐰𐑆 𐐸𐐲𐑍𐑀𐐲𐑉, 𐑃𐐲𐑉𐑅𐐻, 𐐰𐑌𐐼 𐑁𐐰𐐻𐐨𐑀, 𐐰𐑌𐐼 𐐫𐑊𐑅𐐬 𐑋𐐲𐐽 𐑊𐐩𐐺𐐲𐑉 𐐮𐑌 𐑄 𐑅𐐹𐐮𐑉𐐮𐐻. 𐐤𐐵 𐑄𐐨𐑆 𐐶𐐲𐑉 𐑄𐐩𐑉 𐐾𐐲𐑉𐑌𐐨𐐮𐑍𐑆: 𐐐𐐰𐑂𐐮𐑍 𐐻𐐩𐐿𐑌 𐑊𐐨𐑂 𐐱𐑂 𐑄𐐩𐑉 𐑁𐐪𐑄𐐲𐑉 𐐣𐐬𐑅𐐴𐐲, 𐐮𐑌 𐑄 𐑁𐐲𐑉𐑅𐐻 𐐷𐐨𐑉 𐐱𐑂 𐑄 𐐖𐐲𐐾𐐯𐑆; 𐐸𐐰𐑂𐐮𐑍 𐑉𐐯𐑁𐐷𐐭𐑆𐐼 𐑄 𐐿𐐮𐑍𐐼𐐲𐑋 𐐸𐐶𐐮𐐽 𐑄𐐩𐑉 𐑁𐐪𐑄𐐲𐑉 𐐶𐐱𐑆 𐐼𐐨𐑆𐐴𐑉𐐲𐑅 𐐻𐐭 𐐿𐐲𐑌𐑁𐐲𐑉 𐐲𐐹𐐱𐑌 𐑄𐐯𐑋; 𐐰𐑌𐐼 𐐫𐑊𐑅𐐬 𐑄𐐮𐑅 𐐶𐐱𐑆 𐑄 𐑋𐐴𐑌𐐼𐑆 𐐱𐑂 𐑄 𐐹𐐨𐐹𐑊; 𐑌𐐯𐑂𐐲𐑉𐑄𐐯𐑊𐐯𐑅 𐑄𐐩 𐐼𐐨𐐹𐐪𐑉𐐻𐐯𐐼 𐐵𐐻 𐐱𐑂 𐑄 𐑊𐐰𐑌𐐼 𐐱𐑂 𐐞𐐰𐑉𐐲𐐸𐐯𐑋𐑊𐐲, 𐐰𐑌𐐼 𐐻𐐳𐐿 𐑄𐐩𐑉 𐑅𐐬𐑉𐐼𐑆, 𐐰𐑌𐐼 𐑄𐐩𐑉 𐑅𐐹𐐨𐑉𐑆, 𐐰𐑌𐐼 𐑄𐐩𐑉 𐐺𐐬𐑆, 𐐰𐑌𐐼 𐑄𐐩𐑉 𐐰𐑉𐐬𐑆, 𐐰𐑌𐐼 𐑄𐐩𐑉 𐑅𐑊𐐮𐑍𐑆; 𐐰𐑌𐐼 𐑄𐐮𐑅 𐑄𐐩 𐐼𐐮𐐼 𐑄𐐰𐐻 𐑄𐐩 𐑋𐐴𐐻 𐐹𐑉𐐬𐑂𐐴𐐼 𐑁𐐭𐐼 𐑁𐐫𐑉 𐑄𐐯𐑋𐑅𐐯𐑊𐑂𐑆 𐐸𐐶𐐴𐑊 𐐮𐑌 𐑄 𐐶𐐮𐑊𐐼𐐲𐑉𐑌𐐯𐑅, 𐐰𐑌𐐼 𐑄𐐲𐑅 𐑄𐐩 𐐼𐐨𐐹𐐪𐑉𐐻𐐯𐐼 𐐮𐑌𐐻𐐭 𐑄 𐐶𐐮𐑊𐐼𐐲𐑉𐑌𐐯𐑅 𐐶𐐮𐑄 𐑄𐐩𐑉 𐑌𐐲𐑋𐐺𐐲𐑉𐑆 𐐸𐐶𐐮𐐽 𐑄𐐩 𐐸𐐰𐐼 𐑅𐐯𐑊𐐯𐐿𐐻𐐯𐐼, 𐐻𐐭 𐑀𐐬 𐐲𐐹 𐐻𐐭 𐑄 𐑊𐐰𐑌𐐼 𐐱𐑂 𐐤𐐨𐑁𐐴, 𐐻𐐭 𐐹𐑉𐐨𐐽 𐑄 𐐶𐐲𐑉𐐼 𐐱𐑂 𐐘𐐱𐐼 𐐲𐑌𐐻𐐭 𐑄 𐐢𐐩𐑋𐐲𐑌𐐴𐐻𐑅.

2. 𐐈𐑌𐐼 𐐮𐐻 𐐿𐐩𐑋 𐐻𐐭 𐐹𐐰𐑅 𐑄𐐰𐐻 𐑄𐐩 𐐾𐐲𐑉𐑌𐐨𐐯𐐼 𐑋𐐯𐑌𐐨 𐐼𐐩𐑆 𐐮𐑌 𐑄 𐐶𐐮𐑊𐐼𐐲𐑉𐑌𐐯𐑅, 𐐰𐑌𐐼 𐑄𐐩 𐑁𐐰𐑅𐐻𐐯𐐼 𐑋𐐲𐐽, 𐑄𐐰𐐻 𐑄 𐐢𐐫𐑉𐐼 𐐶𐐳𐐼 𐑀𐑉𐐰𐑌𐐻 𐐲𐑌𐐻𐐭 𐑄𐐯𐑋 𐐩 𐐹𐐫𐑉𐑇𐐲𐑌 𐐱𐑂 𐐸𐐮𐑆 𐐝𐐹𐐮𐑉𐐮𐐻 𐐻𐐭 𐑀𐐬 𐐶𐐮𐑄 𐑄𐐯𐑋, 𐐰𐑌𐐼 𐐰𐐺𐐴𐐼 𐐶𐐮𐑄 𐑄𐐯𐑋, 𐑄𐐰𐐻 𐑄𐐩 𐑋𐐴𐐻 𐐺 𐐰𐑌 𐐮𐑌𐑅𐐻𐑉𐐭𐑋𐐯𐑌𐐻 𐐮𐑌 𐑄 𐐸𐐰𐑌𐐼𐑆 𐐱𐑂 𐐘𐐱𐐼 𐐻𐐭 𐐺𐑉𐐮𐑍, 𐐮𐑁 𐐮𐐻 𐐶𐐲𐑉 𐐹𐐱𐑅𐐮𐐺𐑊, 𐑄𐐩𐑉 𐐺𐑉𐐯𐑄𐑉𐐯𐑌, 𐑄 𐐢𐐩𐑋𐐲𐑌𐐴𐐻𐑅, 𐐻𐐭 𐑄 𐑌𐐱𐑊𐐯𐐾 𐐱𐑂 𐑄 𐐻𐑉𐐭𐑃; 𐐻𐐭 𐑄 𐑌𐐱𐑊𐐯𐐾 𐐱𐑂 𐑄 𐐺𐐩𐑅𐑌𐐯𐑅 𐐱𐑂 𐑄 𐐻𐑉𐐰𐐼𐐮𐑇𐐲𐑌𐑆 𐐱𐑂 𐑄𐐩𐑉 𐑁𐐪𐑄𐐲𐑉𐑆, 𐐸𐐶𐐮𐐽 𐐶𐐲𐑉 𐑌𐐱𐐻 𐐿𐐲𐑉𐐯𐐿𐐻.

3. 𐐈𐑌𐐼 𐐮𐐻 𐐿𐐩𐑋 𐐻𐐭 𐐹𐐰𐑅 𐑄𐐰𐐻 𐑄 𐐢𐐫𐑉𐐼 𐐼𐐮𐐼 𐑂𐐮𐑆𐐮𐐻 𐑄𐐯𐑋 𐐶𐐮𐑄 𐐸𐐮𐑆 𐐝𐐹𐐮𐑉𐐮𐐻, 𐐰𐑌𐐼 𐑅𐐯𐐼 𐐲𐑌𐐻𐐭 𐑄𐐯𐑋, 𐐒 𐐿𐐲𐑋𐑁𐐲𐑉𐐻𐐯𐐼; 𐐰𐑌𐐼 𐑄𐐩 𐐶𐐲𐑉 𐐿𐐲𐑋𐑁𐐲𐑉𐐻𐐯𐐼. 𐐈𐑌𐐼 𐑄 𐐢𐐫𐑉𐐼 𐑅𐐯𐐼 𐐲𐑌𐐻𐐭 𐑄𐐯𐑋 𐐫𐑊𐑅𐐬, 𐐘𐐬 𐑁𐐫𐑉𐑃 𐐰𐑋𐐲𐑍 𐑄 𐐢𐐩𐑋𐐲𐑌𐐴𐐻𐑅, 𐑄𐐴 𐐺𐑉𐐯𐑄𐑉𐐯𐑌, 𐐰𐑌𐐼 𐐯𐑅𐐻𐐰𐐺𐑊𐐮𐑇 𐑋𐐴 𐐶𐐲𐑉𐐼; 𐐷𐐯𐐻 𐐷 𐑇𐐰𐑊 𐐺 𐐹𐐩𐑇𐐯𐑌𐐻 𐐮𐑌 𐑊𐐫𐑍 𐑅𐐲𐑁𐐲𐑉𐐮𐑍 𐐰𐑌𐐼 𐐰𐑁𐑊𐐮𐐿𐑇𐐲𐑌𐑆, 𐑄𐐰𐐻 𐐷 𐑋𐐩 𐑇𐐬 𐑁𐐫𐑉𐑃 𐑀𐐳𐐼 𐐯𐑀𐑆𐐰𐑋𐐹𐑊𐑆 𐐲𐑌𐐻𐐭 𐑄𐐯𐑋 𐐮𐑌 𐑋𐐨, 𐐰𐑌𐐼 𐐌 𐐶𐐮𐑊 𐑋𐐩𐐿 𐐰𐑌 𐐮𐑌𐑅𐐻𐑉𐐭𐑋𐐯𐑌𐐻 𐐱𐑂 𐑄 𐐮𐑌 𐑋𐐴 𐐸𐐰𐑌𐐼𐑆 𐐲𐑌𐐻𐐭 𐑄 𐑅𐐰𐑊𐑂𐐩𐑇𐐲𐑌 𐐱𐑂 𐑋𐐯𐑌𐐨 𐑅𐐬𐑊𐑆.

4. 𐐈𐑌𐐼 𐐮𐐻 𐐿𐐩𐑋 𐐻𐐭 𐐹𐐰𐑅 𐑄𐐰𐐻 𐑄 𐐸𐐪𐑉𐐻𐑅 𐐱𐑂 𐑄 𐑅𐐲𐑌𐑆 𐐱𐑂 𐐣𐐬𐑅𐐴𐐲, 𐐰𐑌𐐼 𐐫𐑊𐑅𐐬 𐑄𐐬𐑆 𐐸𐐭 𐐶𐐲𐑉 𐐶𐐮𐑄 𐑄𐐯𐑋, 𐐻𐐳𐐿 𐐿𐐲𐑉𐐯𐐾 𐐻𐐭 𐑀𐐬 𐑁𐐫𐑉𐑃 𐐲𐑌𐐻𐐭 𐑄 𐐢𐐩𐑋𐐲𐑌𐐴𐐻𐑅, 𐐻𐐭 𐐼𐐨𐐿𐑊𐐩𐑉 𐐲𐑌𐐻𐐭 𐑄𐐯𐑋 𐑄 𐐶𐐲𐑉𐐼 𐐱𐑂 𐐘𐐱𐐼. 𐐈𐑌𐐼 𐐮𐐻 𐐿𐐩𐑋 𐐻𐐭 𐐹𐐰𐑅 𐐸𐐶𐐯𐑌 𐑄𐐩 𐐸𐐰𐐼 𐐰𐑉𐐴𐑂𐐼 𐐮𐑌 𐑄 𐐺𐐫𐑉𐐼𐐲𐑉𐑆 𐐱𐑂 𐑄 𐑊𐐰𐑌𐐼 𐐱𐑂 𐑄 𐐢𐐩𐑋𐐲𐑌𐐴𐐻𐑅, 𐑄𐐰𐐻 𐑄𐐩 𐑅𐐯𐐹𐐲𐑉𐐩𐐻𐐯𐐼 𐑄𐐯𐑋𐑅𐐯𐑊𐑂𐑆, 𐐰𐑌𐐼 𐐼𐐨𐐹𐐪𐑉𐐻𐐯𐐼 𐐶𐐲𐑌 𐑁𐑉𐐱𐑋 𐐰𐑌𐐲𐑄𐐲𐑉, 𐐻𐑉𐐲𐑅𐐻𐐮𐑍 𐐮𐑌 𐑄 𐐢𐐫𐑉𐐼 𐑄𐐰𐐻 𐑄𐐩 𐑇𐐳𐐼 𐑋𐐨𐐻 𐐰𐑀𐐯𐑌 𐐰𐐻 𐑄 𐐿𐑊𐐬𐑆 𐐱𐑂 𐑄𐐩𐑉 𐐸𐐪𐑉𐑂𐐯𐑅𐐻, 𐑁𐐫𐑉 𐑄𐐩 𐑅𐐲𐐹𐐬𐑆𐐼 𐑄𐐰𐐻 𐑀𐑉𐐩𐐻 𐐶𐐱𐑆 𐑄 𐐶𐐲𐑉𐐿 𐐸𐐶𐐮𐐽 𐑄𐐩 𐐸𐐰𐐼 𐐲𐑌𐐼𐐲𐑉𐐻𐐩𐐿𐑌. 𐐈𐑌𐐼 𐐰𐑇𐐳𐑉𐐯𐐼𐑊𐐨 𐐮𐐻 𐐶𐐱𐑆 𐑀𐑉𐐩𐐻, 𐑁𐐫𐑉 𐑄𐐩 𐐸𐐰𐐼 𐐲𐑌𐐼𐐲𐑉𐐻𐐩𐐿𐑌 𐐻𐐭 𐐹𐑉𐐨𐐽 𐑄 𐐶𐐲𐑉𐐼 𐐱𐑂 𐐘𐐱𐐼 𐐻𐐭 𐐩 𐐶𐐴𐑊𐐼, 𐐰𐑌𐐼 𐐩 𐐸𐐪𐑉𐐼𐑌𐐼, 𐐰𐑌𐐼 𐐩 𐑁𐐨𐑉𐐬𐑇𐐲𐑅 𐐹𐐨𐐹𐑊; 𐐩 𐐹𐐨𐐹𐑊 𐐸𐐭 𐐼𐐨𐑊𐐴𐐻𐐯𐐼 𐐮𐑌 𐑋𐐲𐑉𐐼𐐲𐑉𐐮𐑍 𐑄 𐐤𐐨𐑁𐐴𐐻𐑅, 𐐰𐑌𐐼 𐑉𐐱𐐺𐐮𐑍 𐐰𐑌𐐼 𐐹𐑊𐐲𐑌𐐼𐐲𐑉𐐮𐑍 𐑄𐐯𐑋; 𐐰𐑌𐐼 𐑄𐐩𐑉 𐐸𐐪𐑉𐐻𐑅 𐐶𐐲𐑉 𐑅𐐯𐐻 𐐲𐐹𐐱𐑌 𐑉𐐮𐐽𐐯𐑆, 𐐫𐑉 𐐲𐐹𐐱𐑌 𐑀𐐬𐑊𐐼, 𐐰𐑌𐐼 𐑅𐐮𐑊𐑂𐐲𐑉, 𐐰𐑌𐐼 𐐹𐑉𐐯𐑇𐐲𐑅 𐑅𐐻𐐬𐑌𐑆; 𐐷𐐯𐐻 𐑄𐐩 𐑅𐐫𐐻 𐐻𐐭 𐐱𐐺𐐻𐐩𐑌 𐑄𐐨𐑆 𐑃𐐮𐑍𐑆 𐐺𐐴 𐑋𐐲𐑉𐐼𐐲𐑉𐐮𐑍 𐐰𐑌𐐼 𐐹𐑊𐐲𐑌𐐼𐐲𐑉𐐮𐑍, 𐑄𐐰𐐻 𐑄𐐩 𐑋𐐴𐐻

𐑌𐐱𐐻 𐑊𐐩𐐺𐐲𐑉 𐑁𐐫𐑉 𐑄𐐯𐑋 𐐶𐐮𐑄 𐑄𐐩𐑉 𐐬𐑌 𐐸𐐰𐑌𐐼𐑆; 𐑄𐐲𐑅 𐑄𐐩 𐐶𐐲𐑉 𐐩 𐑂𐐯𐑉𐐨 𐐮𐑌𐐼𐐬𐑊𐐯𐑌𐐻 𐐹𐐨𐐹𐐲𐑊, 𐑋𐐯𐑌𐐨 𐐱𐑂 𐐸𐐭𐑋 𐐼𐐮𐐼 𐐶𐐲𐑉𐑇𐐮𐐹 𐐴𐐼𐐲𐑊𐑆, 𐐰𐑌𐐼 𐑄 𐐿𐐲𐑉𐑅 𐐱𐑂 𐐘𐐱𐐼 𐐸𐐰𐐼 𐑁𐐫𐑊𐐯𐑌 𐐲𐐹𐐱𐑌 𐑄𐐯𐑋 𐐺𐐨𐐿𐐫𐑆 𐐱𐑂 𐑄 𐐻𐑉𐐰𐐼𐐮𐑇𐐲𐑌𐑆 𐐱𐑂 𐑄𐐩𐑉 𐑁𐐪𐑄𐐲𐑉𐑆; 𐑌𐐱𐐻𐐶𐐮𐑄𐑅𐐻𐐰𐑌𐐼𐐮𐑍 𐑄 𐐹𐑉𐐱𐑋𐐮𐑅𐐯𐑆 𐐱𐑂 𐑄 𐐢𐐫𐑉𐐼 𐐶𐐲𐑉 𐐯𐐿𐑅𐐻𐐯𐑌𐐼𐐯𐐼 𐐲𐑌𐐻𐐭 𐑄𐐯𐑋 𐐱𐑌 𐑄 𐐿𐐱𐑌𐐼𐐮𐑇𐐲𐑌𐑆 𐐱𐑂 𐑉𐐨𐐹𐐯𐑌𐐻𐐰𐑌𐑅; 𐑄𐐩𐑉𐑁𐐫𐑉 𐑄𐐮𐑅 𐐶𐐱𐑆 𐑄 𐐿𐐫𐑆 𐑁𐐫𐑉 𐐸𐐶𐐮𐐽 𐑄 𐑅𐐲𐑌𐑆 𐐱𐑂 𐐣𐐬𐑅𐐴𐐲 𐐸𐐰𐐼 𐐲𐑌𐐼𐐲𐑉𐐻𐐩𐐿𐐯𐑌 𐑄 𐐶𐐲𐑉𐐿, 𐑄𐐰𐐻 𐐹𐐲𐑉𐐸𐐰𐐹𐑅 𐑄𐐩 𐑋𐐴𐐻 𐐺𐑉𐐮𐑍 𐑄𐐯𐑋 𐐲𐑌𐐻𐐭 𐑉𐐨𐐹𐐯𐑌𐐻𐐰𐑌𐑅; 𐑄𐐰𐐻 𐐹𐐲𐑉𐐸𐐰𐐹𐑅 𐑄𐐩 𐑋𐐴𐐻 𐐺𐑉𐐮𐑍 𐑄𐐯𐑋 𐐻𐐭 𐑌𐐬 𐐱𐑂 𐑄 𐐹𐑊𐐰𐑌 𐐱𐑂 𐑉𐐨𐐼𐐯𐑋𐑇𐐲𐑌; 𐑄𐐩𐑉𐑁𐐫𐑉 𐑄𐐩 𐑅𐐯𐐹𐐲𐑉𐐩𐐻𐐯𐐼 𐑄𐐯𐑋𐑅𐐯𐑊𐑂𐑆 𐐶𐐲𐑌 𐑁𐑉𐐱𐑋 𐐰𐑌𐐲𐑄𐐲𐑉, 𐐰𐑌𐐼 𐐶𐐯𐑌𐐻 𐑁𐐬𐑉𐑃 𐐲𐑋𐐲𐑍 𐑄𐐯𐑋, 𐐯𐑂𐐲𐑉𐐨 𐑋𐐰𐑌 𐐲𐑊𐐬𐑌, 𐐰𐐿𐐫𐑉𐐼𐐮𐑍 𐐻𐐭 𐑄 𐐶𐐲𐑉𐐼 𐐰𐑌𐐼 𐐹𐐵𐐲𐑉 𐐱𐑂 𐐘𐐱𐐼 𐐸𐐶𐐮𐐽 𐐶𐐱𐑆 𐑀𐐮𐑂𐐯𐑌 𐐲𐑌𐐻𐐭 𐐸𐐮𐑋.

5. 𐐤𐐵 𐐈𐑋𐐲𐑌 𐐺𐐨𐐮𐑍 𐑄 𐐽𐐨𐑁 𐐲𐑋𐐲𐑍 𐑄𐐯𐑋, 𐐫𐑉 𐑉𐐰𐑄𐐲𐑉 𐐸𐐨 𐐼𐐮𐐼 𐐰𐐼𐑋𐐮𐑌𐐮𐑅𐐻𐐲𐑉 𐐲𐑌𐐻𐐭 𐑄𐐯𐑋: 𐐰𐑌𐐼 𐐸𐐨 𐐼𐐨𐐹𐐪𐑉𐐻𐐯𐐼 𐑁𐑉𐐱𐑋 𐑄𐐯𐑋, 𐐰𐑁𐐻𐐲𐑉 𐐸𐐰𐑂𐐮𐑍 𐐺𐑊𐐯𐑅𐐻 𐑄𐐯𐑋 𐐰𐐿𐐫𐑉𐐼𐐮𐑍 𐐻𐐭 𐑄𐐩𐑉 𐑅𐐯𐑂𐐲𐑉𐐲𐑊 𐑅𐐻𐐩𐑇𐐲𐑌𐑆, 𐐸𐐰𐑂𐐮𐑍 𐐮𐑋𐐹𐐪𐑉𐐻𐐯𐐼 𐑄 𐐶𐐲𐑉𐐼 𐐱𐑂 𐐘𐐱𐐼 𐐲𐑌𐐻𐐭 𐑄𐐯𐑋, 𐐫𐑉 𐐰𐐼𐑋𐐮𐑌𐐮𐑅𐐻𐐲𐑉𐐼 𐐲𐑌𐐻𐐭 𐑄𐐯𐑋 𐐺𐐨𐑁𐐬𐑉 𐐸𐐮𐑆 𐐼𐐨𐐹𐐪𐑉𐐽𐐲𐑉; 𐐰𐑌𐐼 𐑄𐐲𐑅 𐑄𐐩 𐐻𐐳𐐿 𐑄𐐩𐑉 𐑅𐐯𐑂𐐲𐑉𐐲𐑊 𐐾𐐲𐑉𐑌𐐨𐑆 𐑃𐑉𐐭𐐵𐐻 𐑄 𐑊𐐰𐑌𐐼. 𐐈𐑌𐐼 𐐈𐑋𐐲𐑌 𐐶𐐯𐑌𐐻 𐐻𐐭 𐑄 𐑊𐐰𐑌𐐼 𐐱𐑂 𐐆𐑇𐑋𐐩𐐯𐑊, 𐑄 𐑊𐐰𐑌𐐼 𐐺𐐨𐐮𐑍 𐐿𐐫𐑊𐐼 𐐰𐑁𐐻𐐲𐑉 𐑄 𐑅𐐲𐑌𐑆 𐐱𐑂 𐐆𐑇𐑋𐐩𐐯𐑊, 𐐸𐐭 𐐫𐑊𐑅𐐬 𐐺𐐨𐐿𐐩𐑋 𐐢𐐰𐑋𐐲𐑌𐐴𐐻𐑅. 𐐈𐑌𐐼 𐐰𐑆 𐐈𐑋𐐲𐑌 𐐯𐑌𐐻𐐲𐑉𐐼 𐑄 𐑊𐐰𐑌𐐼 𐐱𐑂 𐐆𐑇𐑋𐐩𐐯𐑊, 𐑄 𐐢𐐰𐑋𐐲𐑌𐐴𐐻𐑅 𐐻𐐳𐐿 𐐸𐐮𐑋 𐐰𐑌𐐼 𐐺𐐵𐑌𐐼 𐐸𐐮𐑋, 𐐰𐑆 𐐶𐐱𐑆 𐑄𐐩𐑉 𐐿𐐲𐑅𐐻𐐲𐑋 𐐻𐐭 𐐺𐐴𐑌𐐼 𐐫𐑊 𐑄 𐐤𐐨𐑁𐐴𐐻𐑅 𐐸𐐭 𐑁𐐯𐑊 𐐮𐑌𐐻𐐭 𐑄𐐩𐑉 𐐸𐐰𐑌𐐼𐑆, 𐐰𐑌𐐼 𐐿𐐰𐑉𐐨 𐑄𐐯𐑋 𐐺𐐨𐑁𐐬𐑉 𐑄 𐐿𐐮𐑍; 𐐰𐑌𐐼 𐑄𐐲𐑅 𐐮𐐻 𐐶𐐱𐑆 𐑊𐐯𐑁𐐻 𐐻𐐭 𐑄 𐐹𐑊𐐯𐑈𐐲𐑉 𐐱𐑂 𐑄 𐐿𐐮𐑍 𐐻𐐭 𐑅𐑊𐐩 𐑄𐐯𐑋, 𐐫𐑉 𐐻𐐭 𐑉𐐨𐐻𐐩𐑌 𐑄𐐯𐑋 𐐮𐑌 𐐿𐐰𐐹𐐻𐐮𐑂𐐮𐐻𐐨, 𐐫𐑉 𐐻𐐭 𐐿𐐰𐑅𐐻 𐑄𐐯𐑋 𐐮𐑌𐐻𐐭 𐐹𐑉𐐮𐑆𐐲𐑌, 𐐫𐑉 𐐻𐐭 𐐿𐐰𐑅𐐻 𐑄𐐯𐑋 𐐵𐐻 𐐱𐑂 𐐸𐐮𐑆 𐑊𐐰𐑌𐐼, 𐐰𐐿𐐫𐑉𐐼𐐮𐑍 𐐻𐐭 𐐸𐐮𐑆 𐐶𐐮𐑊 𐐰𐑌𐐼 𐐹𐑊𐐯𐑈𐐲𐑉; 𐐰𐑌𐐼 𐑄𐐲𐑅 𐐈𐑋𐐲𐑌 𐐶𐐱𐑆 𐐿𐐰𐑉𐐨𐐼 𐐺𐐨𐑁𐐬𐑉 𐑄 𐐿𐐮𐑍 𐐸𐐭 𐐶𐐱𐑆 𐐬𐑂𐐲𐑉 𐑄 𐑊𐐰𐑌𐐼 𐐱𐑂 𐐆𐑇𐑋𐐩𐐯𐑊; 𐐰𐑌𐐼 𐐸𐐮𐑆 𐑌𐐩𐑋 𐐶𐐱𐑆 𐐢𐐰𐑋𐐬𐑌𐐴; 𐐰𐑌𐐼 𐐸𐐨 𐐶𐐱𐑆 𐐩 𐐼𐐨𐑅𐐯𐑌𐐼𐐰𐑌𐐻 𐐱𐑂 𐐆𐑇𐑋𐐩𐐯𐑊. 𐐈𐑌𐐼 𐑄 𐐿𐐮𐑍 𐐮𐑌𐐿𐐶𐐴𐑉𐐼 𐐱𐑂 𐐈𐑋𐐲𐑌 𐐮𐑁 𐐮𐐻 𐐶𐐲𐑉 𐐸𐐮𐑆 𐐼𐐨𐑆𐐴𐑉 𐐻𐐭 𐐼𐐶𐐯𐑊 𐐮𐑌 𐑄 𐑊𐐰𐑌𐐼 𐐲𐑋𐐲𐑍 𐑄 𐐢𐐰𐑋𐐲𐑌𐐴𐐻𐑅, 𐐫𐑉 𐐲𐑋𐐲𐑍 𐐸𐐮𐑆 𐐹𐐨𐐹𐐲𐑊? 𐐈𐑌𐐼 𐐈𐑋𐐲𐑌 𐑅𐐯𐐼 𐐲𐑌𐐻𐐭 𐐸𐐮𐑋, 𐐏𐐩, 𐐌 𐐼𐐨𐑆𐐴𐑉 𐐻𐐭 𐐼𐐶𐐯𐑊 𐐲𐑋𐐲𐑍 𐑄𐐮𐑅 𐐹𐐨𐐹𐐲𐑊 𐑁𐐫𐑉 𐐩 𐐻𐐴𐑋; 𐐷𐐩, 𐐰𐑌𐐼 𐐹𐐲𐑉𐐸𐐰𐐹𐑅 𐐲𐑌𐐻𐐮𐑊 𐑄 𐐼𐐩 𐐌 𐐼𐐴.

6. 𐐈𐑌𐐼 𐐮𐐻 𐐿𐐩𐑋 𐐻𐐭 𐐹𐐰𐑅 𐑄𐐰𐐻 𐐿𐐮𐑍 𐐢𐐰𐑋𐐬𐑌𐐴 𐐶𐐱𐑆 𐑋𐐲𐐽 𐐹𐑊𐐨𐑆𐐼 𐐶𐐮𐑄 𐐈𐑋𐐲𐑌, 𐐰𐑌𐐼 𐐿𐐫𐑆𐐼 𐑄𐐰𐐻 𐐸𐐮𐑆 𐐺𐐰𐑌𐐼𐑆 𐑇𐐳𐐼 𐐺𐐨 𐑊𐐭𐑅𐐻; 𐐰𐑌𐐼 𐐸𐐨 𐐶𐐳𐐼 𐑄𐐰𐐻 𐐈𐑋𐐲𐑌 𐑇𐐳𐐼 𐐻𐐩𐐿 𐐶𐐲𐑌 𐐱𐑂 𐐸𐐮𐑆 𐐼𐐫𐐻𐐲𐑉𐑆 𐐻𐐭 𐐶𐐴𐑁. 𐐒𐐲𐐻 𐐈𐑋𐐲𐑌 𐑅𐐯𐐼 𐐲𐑌𐐻𐐭 𐐸𐐮𐑋, 𐐤𐐩, 𐐺𐐲𐐻 𐐌 𐐶𐐮𐑊 𐐺𐐨 𐑄𐐴 𐑅𐐲𐑉𐑂𐐲𐑌𐐻; 𐑄𐐩𐑉𐑁𐐫𐑉 𐐈𐑋𐐲𐑌 𐐺𐐨𐐿𐐩𐑋 𐐩 𐑅𐐲𐑉𐑂𐐲𐑌𐐻 𐐻𐐭 𐐿𐐮𐑍 𐐢𐐰𐑋𐐬𐑌𐐴. 𐐈𐑌𐐼 𐐮𐐻 𐐿𐐩𐑋 𐐻𐐭 𐐹𐐰𐑅 𐑄𐐰𐐻 𐐸𐐨 𐐶𐐱𐑆 𐑅𐐯𐐻 𐐲𐑋𐐲𐑍 𐐲𐑄𐐲𐑉 𐑅𐐲𐑉𐑂𐐲𐑌𐐻𐑅, 𐐻𐐭 𐐶𐐱𐐽 𐑄 𐑁𐑊𐐱𐐿𐑅 𐐱𐑂 𐐢𐐰𐑋𐐬𐑌𐐴, 𐐰𐐿𐐫𐑉𐐼𐐮𐑍 𐐻𐐭 𐑄 𐐿𐐲𐑅𐐻𐐲𐑋 𐐱𐑂 𐑄 𐐢𐐰𐑋𐐲𐑌𐐴𐐻𐑅. 𐐈𐑌𐐼 𐐰𐑁𐐻𐐲𐑉 𐐸𐐨 𐐸𐐰𐐼 𐐺𐐮𐑌 𐐮𐑌 𐑄 𐑅𐐲𐑉𐑂𐐮𐑅 𐐱𐑂 𐑄 𐐿𐐮𐑍 𐑃𐑉𐐨 𐐼𐐩𐑆, 𐐰𐑆 𐐸𐐨 𐐶𐐱𐑆 𐐶𐐮𐑄 𐑄 𐐢𐐰𐑋𐐲𐑌𐐴𐐻𐐮𐑇 𐑅𐐲𐑉𐑂𐐲𐑌𐐻𐑅 𐑀𐐬𐐮𐑍 𐑁𐐬𐑉𐑃 𐐶𐐮𐑄 𐑄𐐩𐑉 𐑁𐑊𐐱𐐿𐑅 𐐻𐐭 𐑄 𐐹𐑊𐐩𐑅 𐐱𐑂 𐐶𐐫𐐻𐐲𐑉, 𐐸𐐶𐐮𐐽 𐐶𐐱𐑆 𐐿𐐫𐑊𐐼 𐑄 𐐶𐐫𐐻𐐲𐑉 𐐱𐑂 𐐝𐐨𐐺𐐲𐑅 (𐐰𐑌𐐼 𐐫𐑊 𐑄 𐐢𐐰𐑋𐐲𐑌𐐴𐐻𐑅 𐐼𐑉𐐴𐑂 𐑄𐐩𐑉 𐑁𐑊𐐱𐐿𐑅 𐐸𐐮𐑄𐐲𐑉, 𐑄𐐰𐐻 𐑄𐐩 𐑋𐐩 𐐸𐐰𐑂 𐐶𐐫𐐻𐐲𐑉); 𐑄𐐩𐑉𐑁𐐫𐑉 𐐰𐑆 𐐈𐑋𐐲𐑌 𐐰𐑌𐐼 𐑄 𐑅𐐲𐑉𐑂𐐲𐑌𐐻𐑅 𐐱𐑂 𐑄 𐐿𐐮𐑍 𐐶𐐲𐑉 𐐼𐑉𐐴𐑂𐐮𐑍 𐑁𐐬𐑉𐑃 𐑄𐐩𐑉 𐑁𐑊𐐱𐐿𐑅 𐐻𐐭 𐑄𐐮𐑅 𐐹𐑊𐐩𐑅 𐐱𐑂 𐐶𐐫𐐻𐐲𐑉, 𐐺𐐨𐐸𐐬𐑊𐐼, 𐐩 𐑅𐐲𐑉𐐻𐐯𐑌 𐑌𐐲𐑋𐐺𐐲𐑉 𐐱𐑂 𐑄 𐐢𐐰𐑋𐐲𐑌𐐴𐐻𐑅, 𐐸𐐭 𐐸𐐰𐐼 𐐺𐐮𐑌 𐐶𐐮𐑄 𐑄𐐩𐑉 𐑁𐑊𐐱𐐿𐑅 𐐻𐐭 𐐶𐐫𐐻𐐲𐑉, 𐑅𐐻𐐳𐐼 𐐰𐑌𐐼 𐑅𐐿𐐰𐐻𐐲𐑉𐐼 𐑄 𐑁𐑊𐐱𐐿𐑅 𐐱𐑂 𐐈𐑋𐐲𐑌, 𐐰𐑌𐐼 𐑄 𐑅𐐲𐑉𐑂𐐲𐑌𐐻𐑅 𐐱𐑂 𐑄 𐐿𐐮𐑍, 𐐰𐑌𐐼 𐑄𐐩 𐑅𐐿𐐰𐐻𐐲𐑉𐐼 𐑄𐐯𐑋 𐐮𐑌𐑅𐐬𐑋𐐲𐐽 𐑄𐐰𐐻 𐑄𐐩 𐑁𐑊𐐯𐐼 𐑋𐐯𐑌𐐨 𐐶𐐩𐑆.

7. 𐐤𐐵 𐑄 𐑅𐐲𐑉𐑂𐐲𐑌𐐻𐑅 𐐱𐑂 𐑄 𐐿𐐮𐑍 𐐺𐐨𐑀𐐰𐑌 𐐻𐐭 𐑋𐐲𐑉𐑋𐐲𐑉, 𐑅𐐩𐐮𐑍, 𐐤𐐵 𐑄 𐐿𐐮𐑍 𐐶𐐮𐑊 𐑅𐑊𐐩 𐐲𐑅, 𐐰𐑆 𐐸𐐨 𐐸𐐰𐑆 𐐵𐑉 𐐺𐑉𐐯𐑄𐑉𐐯𐑌, 𐐺𐐨𐐿𐐫𐑆 𐑄𐐩𐑉 𐑁𐑊𐐱𐐿𐑅 𐐶𐐲𐑉 𐑅𐐿𐐰𐐻𐐲𐑉𐐼 𐐺𐐴 𐑄 𐐶𐐮𐐿𐐯𐐼𐑌𐐯𐑅 𐐱𐑂 𐑄𐐨𐑆 𐑋𐐯𐑌. 𐐈𐑌𐐼 𐑄𐐩 𐐺𐐨𐑀𐐰𐑌 𐐻𐐭 𐐶𐐨𐐹 𐐯𐐿𐑅𐐨𐐼𐐮𐑍𐑊𐐨, 𐑅𐐩𐐮𐑍, 𐐒𐐨𐐸𐐬𐑊𐐼, 𐐵𐑉 𐑁𐑊𐐱𐐿𐑅 𐐪𐑉 𐑅𐐿𐐰𐐻𐐲𐑉𐐼 𐐫𐑊𐑉𐐯𐐼𐐨. 𐐤𐐵 𐑄𐐩 𐐶𐐯𐐹𐐻 𐐺𐐨𐐿𐐫𐑆 𐐱𐑂 𐑄 𐑁𐐨𐑉 𐐱𐑂 𐐺𐐨𐐮𐑍 𐑅𐑊𐐩𐑌. 𐐤𐐵 𐐸𐐶𐐯𐑌 𐐈𐑋𐐲𐑌 𐑅𐐫 𐑄𐐮𐑅, 𐐸𐐮𐑆 𐐸𐐪𐑉𐐻 𐐶𐐱𐑆 𐑅𐐶𐐬𐑊𐐯𐑌 𐐶𐐮𐑄𐐮𐑌 𐐸𐐮𐑋 𐐶𐐮𐑄 𐐾𐑎; 𐑁𐐫𐑉, 𐑅𐐯𐐼 𐐸𐐨, 𐐌 𐐶𐐮𐑊 𐑇𐐬 𐑁𐐬𐑉𐑃 𐑋𐐴 𐐹𐐵𐐲𐑉 𐐲𐑌𐐻𐐭 𐑄𐐨𐑆 𐑋𐐴 𐑁𐐯𐑊𐐬-𐑅𐐲𐑉𐑂𐐲𐑌𐐻𐑅, 𐐫𐑉 𐑄 𐐹𐐵𐐲𐑉 𐐸𐐶𐐮𐐽 𐐮𐑆 𐐮𐑌 𐑋𐐨, 𐐮𐑌 𐑉𐐨𐑅𐐻𐐬𐑉𐐮𐑍 𐑄𐐨𐑆 𐑁𐑊𐐱𐐿𐑅 𐐲𐑌𐐻𐐭 𐑄 𐐿𐐮𐑍, 𐑄𐐰𐐻 𐐌 𐑋𐐩

𐐶𐐮𐑌 𐑄 𐐸𐐪𐑉𐐻𐑅 𐐱𐑂 𐑄𐐨𐑆 𐐸𐐮𐑆 𐑁𐐯𐑊𐐬-𐑅𐐲𐑉𐑂𐐲𐑌𐐻𐑅, 𐑄𐐰𐐻 𐐸𐐨 𐑋𐐴𐐻 𐑊𐐨𐐼 𐑄𐐯𐑋 𐐻𐐭 𐐺𐐮𐑊𐐨𐑂 𐐮𐑌 𐐸𐐮𐑆 𐐶𐐲𐑉𐐼𐑆. 𐐈𐑌𐐼 𐑄𐐨𐑆 𐐶𐐲𐑉 𐑄 𐑃𐐫𐐻𐑅 𐐱𐑂 𐐈𐑋𐐲𐑌, 𐐸𐐶𐐯𐑌 𐐸𐐨 𐑅𐐫 𐑄 𐐰𐑁𐑊𐐮𐐿𐑇𐐲𐑌𐑆 𐐱𐑂 𐑄𐐬𐑆 𐐸𐐭𐑋 𐐸𐐨 𐐻𐐲𐑉𐑋𐐼 𐐻𐐭 𐐺 𐐸𐐮𐑆 𐐺𐑉𐐯𐑄𐑉𐐯𐑌.

8. 𐐈𐑌𐐼 𐐮𐐻 𐐿𐐩𐑋 𐐻𐐭 𐐹𐐰𐑅 𐑄𐐰𐐻 𐐸𐐨 𐑁𐑊𐐰𐐻𐐲𐑉𐐼 𐑄𐐯𐑋 𐐺𐐴 𐐸𐐮𐑆 𐐶𐐲𐑉𐐼𐑆, 𐑅𐐩𐐮𐑍, 𐐣𐐴 𐐺𐑉𐐯𐑄𐑉𐐯𐑌, 𐐺 𐐱𐑂 𐑀𐐳𐐼 𐐽𐐨𐑉, 𐐰𐑌𐐼 𐑊𐐯𐐻 𐐲𐑅 𐑀𐐬 𐐮𐑌 𐑅𐐲𐑉𐐽 𐐱𐑂 𐑄 𐑁𐑊𐐱𐐿𐑅, 𐐰𐑌𐐼 𐐶𐐨 𐐶𐐮𐑊 𐑀𐐰𐑄𐐲𐑉 𐑄𐐯𐑋 𐐻𐐭𐑀𐐯𐑄𐐲𐑉 𐐰𐑌𐐼 𐐺𐑉𐐮𐑍 𐑄𐐯𐑋 𐐺𐐰𐐿 𐐲𐑌𐐻𐐭 𐑄 𐐹𐑊𐐩𐑅 𐐱𐑂 𐐶𐐫𐐻𐐲𐑉; 𐐰𐑌𐐼 𐑄𐐲𐑅 𐐶𐐨 𐐶𐐮𐑊 𐐹𐑉𐐨𐑆𐐲𐑉𐑂 𐑄 𐑁𐑊𐐱𐐿𐑅 𐐲𐑌𐐻𐐭 𐑄 𐐿𐐮𐑍, 𐐰𐑌𐐼 𐐸𐐨 𐐶𐐮𐑊 𐑌𐐱𐐻 𐑅𐑊𐐩 𐐲𐑅. 𐐈𐑌𐐼 𐐮𐐻 𐐿𐐩𐑋 𐐻𐐭 𐐹𐐰𐑅 𐑄𐐰𐐻 𐑄𐐩 𐐶𐐯𐑌𐐻 𐐮𐑌 𐑅𐐲𐑉𐐽 𐐱𐑂 𐑄 𐑁𐑊𐐱𐐿𐑅, 𐐰𐑌𐐼 𐑄𐐩 𐐼𐐮𐐼 𐑁𐐱𐑊𐐬 𐐈𐑋𐐲𐑌, 𐐰𐑌𐐼 𐑄𐐩 𐑉𐐲𐑇𐐻 𐑁𐐫𐑉𐑃 𐐶𐐮𐑄 𐑋𐐲𐐽 𐑅𐐶𐐮𐑁𐐻𐑌𐐯𐑅 𐐰𐑌𐐼 𐐼𐐮𐐼 𐐸𐐯𐐼 𐑄 𐑁𐑊𐐱𐐿𐑅 𐐱𐑂 𐑄 𐐿𐐮𐑍, 𐐰𐑌𐐼 𐐼𐐮𐐼 𐑀𐐰𐑄𐐲𐑉 𐑄𐐯𐑋 𐐻𐐭𐑀𐐯𐑄𐐲𐑉 𐐲𐑀𐐯𐑌 𐐻𐐭 𐑄 𐐹𐑊𐐩𐑅 𐐱𐑂 𐐶𐐫𐐻𐐲𐑉. 𐐈𐑌𐐼 𐑄𐐬𐑆 𐑋𐐯𐑌 𐐲𐑀𐐯𐑌 𐑅𐐻𐐭𐐼 𐐻𐐭 𐑅𐐿𐐰𐐻𐐲𐑉 𐑄𐐩𐑉 𐑁𐑊𐐱𐐿𐑅; 𐐺𐐲𐐻 𐐈𐑋𐐲𐑌 𐑅𐐯𐐼 𐐲𐑌𐐻𐐭 𐐸𐐮𐑆 𐐺𐑉𐐯𐑄𐑉𐐯𐑌, 𐐇𐑌𐑅𐐲𐑉𐐿𐑊 𐑄 𐑁𐑊𐐱𐐿𐑅 𐑉𐐵𐑌𐐼 𐐲𐐺𐐵𐐻, 𐑄𐐰𐐻 𐑄𐐩 𐑁𐑊𐐨 𐑌𐐱𐐻; 𐐰𐑌𐐼 𐐌 𐑀𐐬 𐐰𐑌𐐼 𐐿𐐱𐑌𐐻𐐯𐑌𐐼 𐐶𐐮𐑄 𐑄𐐨𐑆 𐑋𐐯𐑌 𐐸𐐭 𐐼𐐭 𐑅𐐿𐐰𐐻𐐲𐑉 𐐵𐑉 𐑁𐑊𐐱𐐿𐑅. 𐐜𐐯𐑉𐑁𐐫𐑉, 𐑄𐐩 𐐼𐐮𐐼 𐐰𐑆 𐐈𐑋𐐲𐑌 𐐿𐐲𐑋𐐰𐑌𐐼𐐯𐐼 𐑄𐐯𐑋, 𐐰𐑌𐐼 𐐸𐐨 𐐶𐐯𐑌𐐻 𐑁𐐫𐑉𐑃 𐐰𐑌𐐼 𐑅𐐻𐐭𐐼 𐐻𐐭 𐐿𐐱𐑌𐐻𐐯𐑌𐐼 𐐶𐐮𐑄 𐑄𐐬𐑆 𐐸𐐭 𐑅𐐻𐐭𐐼 𐐺𐐴 𐑄 𐐶𐐫𐐻𐐲𐑉𐑆 𐐱𐑂 𐐝𐐨𐐺𐐲𐑅; 𐐰𐑌𐐼 𐑄𐐩 𐐶𐐲𐑉 𐐮𐑌 𐑌𐐲𐑋𐐺𐐲𐑉 𐑌𐐱𐐻 𐐩 𐑁𐐷𐐭. 𐐜𐐯𐑉𐑁𐐫𐑉 𐑄𐐩 𐐼𐐮𐐼 𐑌𐐱𐐻 𐑁𐐨𐑉 𐐈𐑋𐐲𐑌, 𐑁𐐫𐑉 𐑄𐐩 𐑅𐐲𐐹𐐬𐑆𐐼 𐑄𐐰𐐻 𐐶𐐲𐑌 𐐱𐑂 𐑄𐐩𐑉 𐑋𐐯𐑌 𐐿𐐳𐐼 𐑅𐑊𐐩 𐐸𐐮𐑋 𐐲𐐿𐐫𐑉𐐼𐐮𐑍 𐐻𐐭 𐑄𐐩𐑉 𐐹𐑊𐐯𐑠𐐲𐑉, 𐑁𐐫𐑉 𐑄𐐩 𐑌𐐷𐐭 𐑌𐐱𐐻 𐑄𐐰𐐻 𐑄 𐐢𐐫𐑉𐐼 𐐸𐐰𐐼 𐐹𐑉𐐱𐑋𐐮𐑅𐐻 𐐣𐐬𐑆𐐴𐐲 𐑄𐐰𐐻 𐐸𐐨 𐐶𐐳𐐼 𐐼𐐯𐑊𐐮𐑂𐐲𐑉 𐐸𐐮𐑆 𐑅𐐲𐑌𐑆 𐐵𐐻 𐐱𐑂 𐑄𐐩𐑉 𐐸𐐰𐑌𐐼𐑆; 𐑌𐐨𐑄𐐲𐑉 𐐼𐐮𐐼 𐑄𐐩 𐑌𐐬 𐐯𐑌𐐨𐑃𐐮𐑍 𐐿𐐱𐑌𐑅𐐲𐑉𐑌𐐮𐑍 𐑄 𐐢𐐫𐑉𐐼; 𐑄𐐯𐑉𐑁𐐫𐑉 𐑄𐐩 𐐼𐐮𐑊𐐴𐐻𐐯𐐼 𐐮𐑌 𐑄 𐐼𐐮𐑅𐐻𐑉𐐲𐐿𐑇𐐲𐑌 𐐱𐑂 𐑄𐐩𐑉 𐐺𐑉𐐯𐑄𐑉𐐯𐑌; 𐐰𐑌𐐼 𐑁𐐫𐑉 𐑄𐐮𐑅 𐐿𐐫𐑆 𐑄𐐩 𐑅𐐻𐐭𐐼 𐐻𐐭 𐑅𐐿𐐰𐐻𐐲𐑉 𐑄 𐑁𐑊𐐱𐐿𐑅 𐐱𐑂 𐑄 𐐿𐐮𐑍.

9. 𐐒𐐲𐐻 𐐈𐑋𐐲𐑌 𐑅𐐻𐐭𐐼 𐑁𐐫𐑉𐑃 𐐰𐑌𐐼 𐐺𐐯𐑀𐐰𐑌 𐐻𐐭 𐐿𐐰𐑅𐐻 𐑅𐐻𐐬𐑌𐑆 𐐰𐐻 𐑄𐐯𐑋 𐐶𐐮𐑄 𐐸𐐮𐑆 𐑅𐑊𐐮𐑍; 𐐷𐐩, 𐐶𐐮𐑄 𐑋𐐴𐐻𐐨 𐐹𐐵𐐲𐑉 𐐸𐐨 𐐼𐐮𐐼 𐑅𐑊𐐮𐑍 𐑅𐐻𐐬𐑌𐑆 𐐲𐑋𐐲𐑍𐑅𐐻 𐑄𐐯𐑋; 𐐰𐑌𐐼 𐑄𐐲𐑅 𐐸𐐨 𐑅𐑊𐐭 𐐩 𐑅𐐲𐑉𐐻𐐲𐑌 𐑌𐐲𐑋𐐺𐐲𐑉 𐐱𐑂 𐑄𐐯𐑋, 𐐮𐑌𐑅𐐬𐑋𐐲𐐽 𐑄𐐰𐐻 𐑄𐐩 𐐺𐐯𐑀𐐰𐑌 𐐻𐐭 𐐺 𐐰𐑅𐐻𐐱𐑌𐐮𐑇𐐻 𐐰𐐻 𐐸𐐮𐑆 𐐹𐐵𐐲𐑉; 𐑌𐐯𐑂𐐲𐑉𐑄𐐯𐑊𐐯𐑅 𐑄𐐩 𐐶𐐲𐑉 𐐰𐑍𐑀𐑉𐐨 𐐺𐐨𐐿𐐫𐑆 𐐱𐑂 𐑄 𐑅𐑊𐐩𐑌 𐐱𐑂 𐑄𐐩𐑉 𐐺𐑉𐐯𐑄𐑉𐐯𐑌, 𐐰𐑌𐐼 𐑄𐐩 𐐶𐐲𐑉 𐐼𐐨𐐻𐐲𐑉𐑋𐐮𐑌𐐼 𐑄𐐰𐐻 𐐸𐐨 𐑇𐐳𐐼 𐑁𐐫𐑊; 𐑄𐐯𐑉𐑁𐐫𐑉, 𐑅𐐨𐐮𐑍 𐑄𐐰𐐻 𐑄𐐩 𐐿𐐳𐐼 𐑌𐐱𐐻 𐐸𐐮𐐻 𐐸𐐮𐑋 𐐶𐐮𐑄 𐑄𐐩𐑉 𐑅𐐻𐐬𐑌𐑆, 𐑄𐐩 𐐿𐐩𐑋 𐑁𐐫𐑉𐑃 𐐶𐐮𐑄 𐐿𐑊𐐲𐐺𐑆 𐐻𐐭 𐑅𐑊𐐩 𐐸𐐮𐑋. 𐐒𐐲𐐻 𐐺𐐨𐐸𐐬𐑊𐐼, 𐐯𐑂𐐲𐑉𐐨 𐑋𐐰𐑌 𐑄𐐰𐐻 𐑊𐐮𐑁𐐻𐐯𐐼 𐐸𐐮𐑆 𐐿𐑊𐐲𐐺 𐐻𐐭 𐑅𐑋𐐴𐐻 𐐈𐑋𐐲𐑌, 𐐸𐐨 𐑅𐑋𐐬𐐻 𐐱𐑁 𐑄𐐩𐑉 𐐪𐑉𐑋𐑆 𐐶𐐮𐑄 𐐸𐐮𐑆 𐑅𐐫𐑉𐐼; 𐑁𐐫𐑉 𐐸𐐨 𐐼𐐮𐐼 𐐶𐐮𐑄𐑅𐐻𐐰𐑌𐐼 𐑄𐐩𐑉 𐐺𐑊𐐬𐑆 𐐺𐐴 𐑅𐑋𐐴𐐻𐐮𐑍 𐑄𐐩𐑉 𐐪𐑉𐑋𐑆 𐐶𐐮𐑄 𐑄 𐐯𐐾 𐐱𐑂 𐐸𐐮𐑆 𐑅𐐫𐑉𐐼, 𐐮𐑌𐑅𐐬𐑋𐐲𐐽 𐑄𐐰𐐻 𐑄𐐩 𐐺𐐯𐑀𐐰𐑌 𐐻𐐭 𐐺 𐐰𐑅𐐻𐐱𐑌𐐮𐑇𐐻, 𐐰𐑌𐐼 𐐺𐐯𐑀𐐰𐑌 𐐻𐐭 𐑁𐑊𐐨 𐐺𐐨𐑁𐐬𐑉 𐐸𐐮𐑋; 𐐷𐐩, 𐐰𐑌𐐼 𐑄𐐩 𐐶𐐲𐑉 𐑌𐐱𐐻 𐑁𐐷𐐭 𐐮𐑌 𐑌𐐲𐑋𐐺𐐲𐑉; 𐐰𐑌𐐼 𐐸𐐨 𐐿𐐫𐑆𐐼 𐑄𐐯𐑋 𐐻𐐭 𐑁𐑊𐐨 𐐺𐐴 𐑄 𐑅𐐻𐑉𐐯𐑍𐑃 𐐱𐑂 𐐸𐐮𐑆 𐐪𐑉𐑋. 𐐤𐐵 𐑅𐐮𐐿𐑅 𐐱𐑂 𐑄𐐯𐑋 𐐸𐐰𐐼 𐑁𐐫𐑊𐑌 𐐺𐐴 𐑄 𐑅𐑊𐐮𐑍, 𐐺𐐲𐐻 𐐸𐐨 𐑅𐑊𐐭 𐑌𐐲𐑌 𐑅𐐩𐑂 𐐮𐐻 𐐶𐐲𐑉 𐑄𐐩𐑉 𐑊𐐨𐐼𐐲𐑉 𐐶𐐮𐑄 𐐸𐐮𐑆 𐑅𐐫𐑉𐐼; 𐐰𐑌𐐼 𐐸𐐨 𐑅𐑋𐐬𐐻 𐐱𐑁 𐐰𐑆 𐑋𐐯𐑌𐐨 𐐱𐑂 𐑄𐐩𐑉 𐐪𐑉𐑋𐑆 𐐰𐑆 𐐶𐐲𐑉 𐑊𐐮𐑁𐐻𐐯𐐼 𐐲𐑀𐐯𐑌𐑅𐐻 𐐸𐐮𐑋, 𐐰𐑌𐐼 𐑄𐐩 𐐶𐐲𐑉 𐑌𐐱𐐻 𐐩 𐑁𐐷𐐭. 𐐈𐑌𐐼 𐐸𐐶𐐯𐑌 𐐸𐐨 𐐸𐐰𐐼 𐐼𐑉𐐮𐑂𐐲𐑌 𐑄𐐯𐑋 𐐲𐑁𐐪𐑉 𐐱𐑁, 𐐸𐐨 𐑉𐐨𐐻𐐲𐑉𐑌𐐼 𐐰𐑌𐐼 𐑄𐐩 𐐶𐐫𐐻𐐲𐑉𐐼 𐑄𐐩𐑉 𐑁𐑊𐐱𐐿𐑅 𐐰𐑌𐐼 𐑉𐐨𐐻𐐲𐑉𐑌𐐼 𐑄𐐯𐑋 𐐻𐐭 𐑄 𐐹𐐰𐑅𐐽𐐲𐑉 𐐱𐑂 𐑄 𐐿𐐮𐑍, 𐐰𐑌𐐼 𐑄𐐯𐑌 𐐶𐐯𐑌𐐻 𐐮𐑌 𐐲𐑌𐐻𐐭 𐑄 𐐿𐐮𐑍, 𐐺𐐯𐑉𐐮𐑍 𐑄 𐐪𐑉𐑋𐑆 𐐸𐐶𐐮𐐽 𐐸𐐰𐐼 𐐺𐐨𐑌 𐑅𐑋𐐮𐐻𐑌 𐐱𐑁 𐐺𐐴 𐑄 𐑅𐐫𐑉𐐼 𐐱𐑂 𐐈𐑋𐐲𐑌, 𐐱𐑂 𐑄𐐬𐑆 𐐸𐐭 𐑅𐐫𐐻 𐐻𐐭 𐑅𐑊𐐩 𐐸𐐮𐑋; 𐐰𐑌𐐼 𐑄𐐩 𐐶𐐲𐑉 𐐿𐐰𐑉𐐨𐐼 𐐮𐑌 𐐲𐑌𐐻𐐭 𐑄 𐐿𐐮𐑍 𐑁𐐫𐑉 𐐩 𐐻𐐯𐑅𐐻𐐮𐑋𐐬𐑌𐐨 𐐱𐑂 𐑄 𐑃𐐮𐑍𐑆 𐐸𐐶𐐮𐐽 𐑄𐐩 𐐸𐐰𐐼 𐐼𐐲𐑌.

10. 𐐈𐑌𐐼 𐐮𐐻 𐐿𐐩𐑋 𐐻𐐭 𐐹𐐰𐑅 𐑄𐐰𐐻 𐐿𐐮𐑍 𐐢𐐲𐑋𐐬𐑌𐐴 𐐿𐐫𐑆𐐼 𐑄𐐰𐐻 𐐸𐐮𐑆 𐑅𐐲𐑉𐑂𐐲𐑌𐐻𐑅 𐑇𐐳𐐼 𐑅𐐻𐐰𐑌𐐼 𐑁𐐫𐑉𐑃 𐐰𐑌𐐼 𐐻𐐯𐑅𐐻𐐮𐑁𐐴 𐐻𐐭 𐐫𐑊 𐑄 𐑃𐐮𐑍𐑆 𐐸𐐶𐐮𐐽 𐑄𐐩 𐐸𐐰𐐼 𐑅𐐨𐑌 𐐿𐐱𐑌𐑅𐐲𐑉𐑌𐐮𐑍 𐑄 𐑋𐐰𐐻𐐲𐑉. 𐐈𐑌𐐼 𐐸𐐶𐐯𐑌 𐑄𐐩 𐐸𐐰𐐼 𐐫𐑊 𐐻𐐯𐑅𐐻𐐮𐑁𐐴𐐼 𐐻𐐭 𐑄 𐑃𐐮𐑍𐑆 𐐸𐐶𐐮𐐽 𐑄𐐩 𐐸𐐰𐐼 𐑅𐐨𐑌, 𐐰𐑌𐐼 𐐸𐐨 𐐸𐐰𐐼 𐑊𐐲𐑉𐑌𐐼 𐐱𐑂 𐑄 𐑁𐐩𐑃𐑁𐐳𐑊𐑌𐐯𐑅 𐐱𐑂 𐐈𐑋𐐲𐑌 𐐮𐑌 𐐹𐑉𐐨𐑆𐐲𐑉𐑂𐐮𐑍 𐐸𐐮𐑆 𐑁𐑊𐐱𐐿𐑅, 𐐰𐑌𐐼 𐐫𐑊𐑅𐐬 𐐱𐑂 𐐸𐐮𐑆 𐑀𐑉𐐩𐐻 𐐹𐐵𐐲𐑉 𐐮𐑌 𐐿𐐱𐑌𐐻𐐯𐑌𐐼𐐮𐑍 𐐲𐑀𐐯𐑌𐑅𐐻 𐑄𐐬𐑆 𐐸𐐭 𐑅𐐫𐐻 𐐻𐐭 𐑅𐑊𐐩 𐐸𐐮𐑋, 𐐸𐐨 𐐶𐐱𐑆 𐐰𐑅𐐻𐐱𐑌𐐮𐑇𐐻 𐐯𐐿𐑅𐐨𐐼𐐮𐑍𐑊𐐨, 𐐰𐑌𐐼 𐑅𐐯𐐼, 𐐟𐐳𐑉𐑊𐐨, 𐑄𐐮𐑅 𐐮𐑆 𐑋𐐬𐑉 𐑄𐐰𐑌 𐐩 𐑋𐐰𐑌. 𐐒𐐨𐐸𐐬𐑊𐐼, 𐐮𐑆 𐑌𐐱𐐻 𐑄𐐮𐑅 𐑄 𐐘𐑉𐐩𐐻 𐐝𐐹𐐮𐑉𐐮𐐻 𐐸𐐭 𐐼𐐲𐑃 𐑅𐐯𐑌𐐼 𐑅𐐲𐐽 𐑀𐑉𐐩𐐻 𐐹𐐲𐑌𐐮𐑇𐑋𐐲𐑌𐐻𐑅 𐐲𐐹𐐱𐑌 𐑄𐐮𐑅 𐐹𐐨𐐹𐑊, 𐐺𐐨𐐿𐐫𐑆 𐐱𐑂 𐑄𐐩𐑉 𐑋𐐲𐑉𐐼𐐲𐑉𐑆? 𐐈𐑌𐐼 𐑄𐐩 𐐰𐑌𐑅𐐲𐑉𐐼 𐑄 𐐿𐐮𐑍, 𐐰𐑌𐐼

𐑅𐐯𐐼, 𐐸𐐶𐐯𐑄𐐲𐑉 𐐸𐐨 𐐺 𐑄 𐐘𐑉𐐩𐐻 𐐝𐐹𐐮𐑉𐐮𐐻 𐐫𐑉 𐐲 𐑋𐐰𐑌, 𐐶𐐨 𐑌𐐬 𐑌𐐱𐐻; 𐐺𐐲𐐻 𐑄𐐮𐑅 𐑋𐐲𐐽 𐐶𐐨 𐐼𐐭 𐑌𐐬, 𐑄𐐰𐐻 𐐸𐐨 𐐿𐐰𐑌𐐱𐐻 𐐺 𐑅𐑊𐐩𐑌 𐐺𐐴 𐑄 𐐯𐑌𐐯𐑋𐐮𐑆 𐐱𐑂 𐑄 𐐿𐐮𐑍; 𐑌𐐨𐑄𐐲𐑉 𐐿𐐰𐑌 𐑄𐐩 𐑅𐐿𐐰𐐻𐐲𐑉 𐑄 𐐿𐐮𐑍𐑆 𐑁𐑊𐐱𐐿𐑅 𐐸𐐶𐐯𐑌 𐐸𐐨 𐐮𐑆 𐐶𐐮𐑄 𐐲𐑅, 𐐺𐐨𐐿𐐫𐑆 𐐱𐑂 𐐸𐐮𐑆 𐐯𐐿𐑅𐐹𐐲𐑉𐐻𐑌𐐯𐑅 𐐰𐑌𐐼 𐑀𐑉𐐩𐐻 𐑅𐐻𐑉𐐯𐑍𐑃; 𐑄𐐩𐑉𐑁𐐬𐑉, 𐐶𐐨 𐑌𐐬 𐑄𐐰𐐻 𐐸𐐨 𐐮𐑆 𐐲 𐑁𐑉𐐯𐑌𐐼 𐐻𐐭 𐑄 𐐿𐐮𐑍. 𐐈𐑌𐐼 𐑌𐐵, 𐐄 𐐿𐐮𐑍, 𐐶𐐨 𐐼𐐭 𐑌𐐱𐐻 𐐺𐐨𐑊𐐨𐑂 𐑄𐐰𐐻 𐐲 𐑋𐐰𐑌 𐐸𐐰𐑆 𐑅𐐲𐐽 𐑀𐑉𐐩𐐻 𐐹𐐵𐑉, 𐑁𐐫𐑉 𐐶𐐨 𐑌𐐬 𐐸𐐨 𐐿𐐰𐑌𐐱𐐻 𐐺 𐑅𐑊𐐩𐑌. 𐐈𐑌𐐼 𐐸𐐶𐐯𐑌 𐑄 𐐿𐐮𐑍 𐐸𐐲𐑉𐐼 𐑄𐐨𐑆 𐐶𐐲𐑉𐐼𐑆, 𐐸𐐨 𐑅𐐯𐐼 𐐲𐑌𐐻𐐭 𐑄𐐯𐑋, 𐐤𐐵 𐐌 𐑌𐐬 𐑄𐐰𐐻 𐐮𐐻 𐐮𐑆 𐑄 𐐘𐑉𐐩𐐻 𐐝𐐹𐐮𐑉𐐮𐐻; 𐐰𐑌𐐼 𐐸𐐨 𐐸𐐰𐑆 𐐿𐐲𐑋 𐐼𐐵𐑌 𐐰𐐻 𐑄𐐮𐑅 𐐻𐐴𐑋 𐐻𐐭 𐐹𐑉𐐨𐑆𐐲𐑉𐑂 𐐷𐐬𐑉 𐑊𐐴𐑂𐑆, 𐑄𐐰𐐻 𐐌 𐑋𐐴𐐻 𐑌𐐱𐐻 𐑅𐑊𐐩 𐐷𐐭 𐐰𐑆 𐐌 𐐼𐐮𐐼 𐐷𐐬𐑉 𐐺𐑉𐐯𐑄𐑉𐐯𐑌. 𐐤𐐵 𐑄𐐮𐑅 𐐮𐑆 𐑄 𐐘𐑉𐐩𐐻 𐐝𐐹𐐮𐑉𐐮𐐻 𐐱𐑂 𐐸𐐭𐑋 𐐵𐑉 𐑁𐐪𐑄𐐲𐑉𐑆 𐐸𐐰𐑂 𐑅𐐹𐐬𐐿𐑌. 𐐤𐐵 𐑄𐐮𐑅 𐐶𐐱𐑆 𐑄 𐐻𐑉𐐲𐐼𐐮𐑇𐐲𐑌 𐐱𐑂 𐐢𐐩𐑋𐐬𐑌𐐴, 𐐸𐐶𐐮𐐽 𐐸𐐨 𐐸𐐰𐐼 𐑉𐐨𐑅𐐨𐑂𐐼 𐑁𐑉𐐱𐑋 𐐸𐐮𐑆 𐑁𐐪𐑄𐐲𐑉, 𐑄𐐰𐐻 𐑄𐐩𐑉 𐐶𐐱𐑆 𐐲 𐐘𐑉𐐩𐐻 𐐝𐐹𐐮𐑉𐐮𐐻. 𐐤𐐱𐐻𐐶𐐮𐑄𐑅𐐻𐐰𐑌𐐼𐐮𐑍 𐑄𐐩 𐐺𐐨𐑊𐐨𐑂𐐼 𐐮𐑌 𐐲 𐐘𐑉𐐩𐐻 𐐝𐐹𐐮𐑉𐐮𐐻, 𐑄𐐩 𐑅𐐲𐐹𐐬𐑆𐐼 𐑄𐐰𐐻 𐐸𐐶𐐱𐐻𐑅𐐬𐐯𐑂𐐲𐑉 𐑄𐐩 𐐼𐐮𐐼 𐐶𐐱𐑆 𐑉𐐴𐐻; 𐑌𐐯𐑂𐐲𐑉𐑄𐐲𐑊𐐯𐑅, 𐐢𐐩𐑋𐐬𐑌𐐴 𐐺𐐨𐑀𐐰𐑌 𐐻𐐭 𐑁𐐨𐑉 𐐯𐐿𐑅𐐨𐐼𐐮𐑍𐑊𐐨, 𐐶𐐮𐑄 𐑁𐐨𐑉 𐑊𐐯𐑅𐐻 𐐸𐐨 𐐸𐐰𐐼 𐐼𐐲𐑌 𐑉𐐱𐑍 𐐮𐑌 𐑅𐑊𐐩𐐮𐑍 𐐸𐐮𐑆 𐑅𐐲𐑉𐑂𐐲𐑌𐐻𐑅: 𐑁𐐫𐑉 𐐸𐐨 𐐸𐐰𐐼 𐑅𐑊𐐩𐑌 𐑋𐐯𐑌𐐨 𐐱𐑂 𐑄𐐯𐑋, 𐐺𐐨𐐿𐐫𐑆 𐑄𐐩𐑉 𐐺𐑉𐐯𐑄𐑉𐐯𐑌 𐐸𐐰𐐼 𐑅𐐿𐐰𐐻𐐲𐑉𐐼 𐑄𐐩𐑉 𐑁𐑊𐐱𐐿𐑅 𐐰𐐻 𐑄 𐐹𐑊𐐩𐑅 𐐱𐑂 𐐶𐐫𐐻𐐲𐑉; 𐐰𐑌𐐼 𐑄𐐲𐑅 𐐺𐐨𐐿𐐫𐑆 𐑄𐐩 𐐸𐐰𐐼 𐐸𐐰𐐼 𐑄𐐩𐑉 𐑁𐑊𐐱𐐿𐑅 𐑅𐐿𐐰𐐻𐐲𐑉𐐼, 𐑄𐐩 𐐶𐐲𐑉 𐑅𐑊𐐩𐑌. 𐐤𐐵 𐐮𐐻 𐐶𐐱𐑆 𐑄 𐐹𐑉𐐰𐐿𐐻𐐮𐑅 𐐱𐑂 𐑄 𐐢𐐩𐑋𐐲𐑌𐐴𐐻𐑅 𐐻𐐭 𐑅𐐻𐐰𐑌𐐼 𐐺𐐴 𐑄 𐐶𐐫𐐻𐐲𐑉𐑆 𐐱𐑂 𐐝𐐨𐐺𐐲𐑅, 𐐻𐐭 𐑅𐐿𐐰𐐻𐐲𐑉 𐑄 𐑁𐑊𐐱𐐿𐑅 𐐱𐑂 𐑄 𐐹𐐨𐐹𐑊, 𐑄𐐰𐐻 𐑄𐐩𐑉𐐺𐐴 𐑄𐐩 𐑋𐐴𐐻 𐐼𐑉𐐴𐑂 𐐲𐐶𐐩 𐑋𐐯𐑌𐐨 𐑄𐐰𐐻 𐐶𐐲𐑉 𐑅𐐿𐐰𐐻𐐲𐑉𐐼 𐐲𐑌𐐻𐐭 𐑄𐐩𐑉 𐐬𐑌 𐑊𐐰𐑌𐐼, 𐐮𐐻 𐐺𐐨𐐮𐑍 𐐲 𐐹𐑉𐐰𐐿𐐻𐐮𐑅 𐐱𐑂 𐐹𐑊𐐲𐑌𐐼𐐲𐑉 𐐲𐑋𐐲𐑍 𐑄𐐯𐑋.

11. 𐐈𐑌𐐼 𐐮𐐻 𐐿𐐩𐑋 𐐻𐐭 𐐹𐐰𐑅 𐑄𐐰𐐻 𐐿𐐮𐑍 𐐢𐐩𐑋𐐬𐑌𐐴 𐐮𐑌𐐿𐐶𐐴𐑉𐐼 𐐱𐑂 𐐸𐐮𐑆 𐑅𐐲𐑉𐑂𐐲𐑌𐐻𐑅, 𐑅𐐩𐐮𐑍, 𐐐𐐶𐐩𐑉 𐐮𐑆 𐑄𐐮𐑅 𐑋𐐰𐑌 𐑄𐐰𐐻 𐐸𐐰𐑆 𐑅𐐲𐐽 𐑀𐑉𐐩𐐻 𐐹𐐵𐑉? 𐐈𐑌𐐼 𐑄𐐩 𐑅𐐯𐐼 𐐲𐑌𐐻𐐭 𐐸𐐮𐑋, 𐐒𐐨𐐸𐐬𐑊𐐼, 𐐸𐐨 𐐮𐑆 𐑁𐐨𐐼𐐮𐑍 𐑄𐐴 𐐸𐐫𐑉𐑅𐐯𐑆. 𐐤𐐵 𐑄 𐐿𐐮𐑍 𐐸𐐰𐐼 𐐿𐐲𐑋𐐰𐑌𐐼𐐯𐐼 𐐸𐐮𐑆 𐑅𐐲𐑉𐑂𐐲𐑌𐐻𐑅, 𐐹𐑉𐐨𐑂𐐮𐐲𐑅 𐐻𐐭 𐑄 𐐻𐐴𐑋 𐐱𐑂 𐑄 𐐶𐐫𐐻𐐲𐑉𐐮𐑍 𐐱𐑂 𐑄𐐩𐑉 𐑁𐑊𐐱𐐿𐑅, 𐑄𐐰𐐻 𐑄𐐩 𐑇𐐳𐐼 𐐹𐑉𐐨𐐹𐐩𐑉 𐐸𐐮𐑆 𐐸𐐫𐑉𐑅𐐯𐑆 𐐰𐑌𐐼 𐐽𐐰𐑉𐐮𐐲𐐻𐑅, 𐐰𐑌𐐼 𐐿𐐲𐑌𐐼𐐲𐐿𐐻 𐐸𐐮𐑋 𐑁𐐬𐑉𐑃 𐐻𐐭 𐑄 𐑊𐐰𐑌𐐼 𐐱𐑂 𐐤𐐨𐑁𐐴; 𐑁𐐫𐑉 𐑄𐐩𐑉 𐐸𐐰𐐼 𐐺𐐮𐑌 𐐲 𐑀𐑉𐐩𐐻 𐑁𐐨𐑅𐐻 𐐲𐐹𐐫𐐮𐑌𐐻𐐯𐐼 𐐰𐐻 𐑄 𐑊𐐰𐑌𐐼 𐐱𐑂 𐐤𐐨𐑁𐐴, 𐐺𐐴 𐑄 𐑁𐐪𐑄𐐲𐑉 𐐱𐑂 𐐢𐐩𐑋𐐬𐑌𐐴, 𐐸𐐭 𐐶𐐱𐑆 𐐿𐐮𐑍 𐐬𐑂𐐲𐑉 𐐫𐑊 𐑄 𐑊𐐰𐑌𐐼. 𐐤𐐵 𐐸𐐶𐐯𐑌 𐐿𐐮𐑍 𐐢𐐩𐑋𐐬𐑌𐐴 𐐸𐐲𐑉𐐼 𐑄𐐰𐐻 𐐈𐑋𐐲𐑌 𐐶𐐱𐑆 𐐹𐑉𐐨𐐹𐐩𐑉𐐮𐑍 𐐸𐐮𐑆 𐐸𐐫𐑉𐑅𐐯𐑆 𐐰𐑌𐐼 𐐸𐐮𐑆 𐐽𐐰𐑉𐐮𐐲𐐻𐑅, 𐐸𐐨 𐐶𐐱𐑆 𐑋𐐬𐑉 𐐲𐑅𐐻𐐱𐑌𐐮𐑇𐐻, 𐐺𐐨𐐿𐐫𐑆 𐐱𐑂 𐑄 𐑁𐐩𐑃𐑁𐐳𐑊𐑌𐐯𐑅 𐐱𐑂 𐐈𐑋𐐲𐑌, 𐑅𐐩𐐮𐑍, 𐐟𐐳𐑉𐑊𐐨 𐑄𐐩𐑉 𐐸𐐰𐑆 𐑌𐐱𐐻 𐐺𐐮𐑌 𐐯𐑌𐐨 𐑅𐐲𐑉𐑂𐐲𐑌𐐻 𐐲𐑋𐐲𐑍 𐐫𐑊 𐑋𐐴 𐑅𐐲𐑉𐑂𐐲𐑌𐐻𐑅, 𐑄𐐰𐐻 𐐸𐐰𐑆 𐐺𐐮𐑌 𐑅𐐬 𐑁𐐩𐑃𐑁𐐳𐑊 𐐰𐑆 𐑄𐐮𐑅 𐑋𐐰𐑌; 𐑁𐐫𐑉 𐐨𐑂𐐯𐑌 𐐸𐐨 𐐼𐐲𐑃 𐑉𐐨𐑋𐐯𐑋𐐺𐐲𐑉 𐐫𐑊 𐑋𐐴 𐐿𐐲𐑋𐐰𐑌𐐼𐑋𐐯𐑌𐐻𐑅 𐐻𐐭 𐐯𐐿𐑅𐐨𐐿𐐷𐐭𐐻 𐑄𐐯𐑋. 𐐤𐐵 𐐌 𐑇𐐳𐑉𐑊𐐨 𐑌𐐬 𐑄𐐰𐐻 𐑄𐐮𐑅 𐐮𐑆 𐑄 𐐘𐑉𐐩𐐻 𐐝𐐹𐐮𐑉𐐮𐐻, 𐐰𐑌𐐼 𐐌 𐐶𐐳𐐼 𐐼𐐯𐑆𐐴𐑉 𐐸𐐮𐑋 𐑄𐐰𐐻 𐐸𐐨 𐐿𐐲𐑋 𐐮𐑌 𐐲𐑌𐐻𐐭 𐑋𐐨, 𐐺𐐲𐐻 𐐌 𐐼𐐲𐑉𐑅𐐻 𐑌𐐱𐐻.

12. 𐐈𐑌𐐼 𐐮𐐻 𐐿𐐩𐑋 𐐻𐐭 𐐹𐐰𐑅 𐑄𐐰𐐻 𐐸𐐶𐐯𐑌 𐐈𐑋𐐲𐑌 𐐸𐐰𐐼 𐑋𐐩𐐼 𐑉𐐯𐐼𐐨 𐑄 𐐸𐐫𐑉𐑅𐐯𐑆 𐐰𐑌𐐼 𐑄 𐐽𐐰𐑉𐐮𐐲𐐻𐑅 𐑁𐐫𐑉 𐑄 𐐿𐐮𐑍 𐐰𐑌𐐼 𐐸𐐮𐑆 𐑅𐐲𐑉𐑂𐐲𐑌𐐻𐑅, 𐐸𐐨 𐐶𐐯𐑌𐐻 𐐮𐑌 𐐲𐑌𐐻𐐭 𐑄 𐐿𐐮𐑍, 𐐰𐑌𐐼 𐐸𐐨 𐑅𐐫 𐑄𐐰𐐻 𐑄 𐐿𐐵𐑌𐐻𐐯𐑌𐐲𐑌𐑅 𐐱𐑂 𐑄 𐐿𐐮𐑍 𐐶𐐱𐑆 𐐽𐐩𐑌𐐾𐐼; 𐑄𐐩𐑉𐑁𐐬𐑉 𐐸𐐨 𐐶𐐱𐑆 𐐲𐐺𐐵𐐻 𐐻𐐭 𐑉𐐨𐐻𐐲𐑉𐑌 𐐵𐐻 𐐱𐑂 𐐸𐐮𐑆 𐐹𐑉𐐯𐑆𐐯𐑌𐑅; 𐐰𐑌𐐼 𐐶𐐲𐑌 𐐱𐑂 𐑄 𐐿𐐮𐑍𐑆 𐑅𐐲𐑉𐑂𐐲𐑌𐐻𐑅 𐑅𐐯𐐼 𐐲𐑌𐐻𐐭 𐐸𐐮𐑋, 𐐡𐐰𐐺𐐩𐑌𐐪, 𐐸𐐶𐐮𐐽 𐐮𐑆, 𐐺𐐨𐐮𐑍 𐐮𐑌𐐻𐐲𐑉𐐹𐑉𐐯𐐻𐐯𐐼, 𐐹𐐵𐑉𐑁𐐳𐑊 𐐫𐑉 𐑀𐑉𐐩𐐻 𐐿𐐮𐑍, 𐐿𐐲𐑌𐑅𐐮𐐼𐐲𐑉𐐮𐑍 𐑄𐐩𐑉 𐐿𐐮𐑍𐑆 𐐻𐐭 𐐺 𐐹𐐵𐑉𐑁𐐳𐑊; 𐐰𐑌𐐼 𐑄𐐲𐑅 𐐸𐐨 𐑅𐐯𐐼 𐐲𐑌𐐻𐐭 𐐸𐐮𐑋, 𐐡𐐰𐐺𐐩𐑌𐐪, 𐑄 𐐿𐐮𐑍 𐐼𐐯𐑆𐐴𐑉𐐯𐑃 𐑄 𐐻𐐭 𐑅𐐻𐐩; 𐑄𐐩𐑉𐑁𐐬𐑉 𐐈𐑋𐐲𐑌 𐐻𐐲𐑉𐑌𐐼 𐐸𐐮𐑋𐑅𐐯𐑊𐑁 𐐲𐑌𐐻𐐭 𐑄 𐐿𐐮𐑍, 𐐰𐑌𐐼 𐑅𐐯𐐼 𐐲𐑌𐐻𐐭 𐐸𐐮𐑋, 𐐐𐐶𐐱𐐻 𐐶𐐮𐑊𐐻 𐑄𐐵 𐑄𐐰𐐻 𐐌 𐑇𐐳𐐼 𐐼𐐭 𐑁𐐫𐑉 𐑄, 𐐄 𐐿𐐮𐑍? 𐐈𐑌𐐼 𐑄 𐐿𐐮𐑍 𐐰𐑌𐑅𐐲𐑉𐐼 𐐸𐐮𐑋 𐑌𐐱𐐻 𐑁𐐫𐑉 𐑄 𐑅𐐹𐐩𐑅 𐐱𐑂 𐐰𐑌 𐐵𐑉, 𐐰𐐿𐐫𐑉𐐼𐐮𐑍 𐐻𐐭 𐑄𐐩𐑉 𐐻𐐴𐑋, 𐑁𐐫𐑉 𐐸𐐨 𐑌𐐷𐐭 𐑌𐐱𐐻 𐐸𐐶𐐱𐐻 𐐸𐐨 𐑇𐐳𐐼 𐑅𐐩 𐐲𐑌𐐻𐐭 𐐸𐐮𐑋. 𐐈𐑌𐐼 𐐮𐐻 𐐿𐐩𐑋 𐐻𐐭 𐐹𐐰𐑅 𐑄𐐰𐐻 𐐈𐑋𐐲𐑌 𐑅𐐯𐐼 𐐲𐑌𐐻𐐭 𐐸𐐮𐑋 𐐲𐑀𐐯𐑌, 𐐐𐐶𐐱𐐻 𐐼𐐯𐑆𐐴𐑉𐐯𐑅𐐻 𐑄𐐵 𐐱𐑂 𐑋𐐨? 𐐒𐐲𐐻 𐑄 𐐿𐐮𐑍 𐐰𐑌𐑅𐐲𐑉𐐼 𐐸𐐮𐑋 𐑌𐐱𐐻.

13. 𐐈𐑌𐐼 𐐮𐐻 𐐿𐐩𐑋 𐐻𐐭 𐐹𐐰𐑅 𐑄𐐰𐐻 𐐈𐑋𐐲𐑌, 𐐺𐐨𐐮𐑍 𐑁𐐮𐑊𐐼 𐐶𐐮𐑄 𐑄 𐐝𐐹𐐮𐑉𐐮𐐻 𐐱𐑂 𐐘𐐱𐐼, 𐑄𐐩𐑉𐑁𐐬𐑉 𐐸𐐨 𐐹𐐲𐑉𐑅𐐨𐑂𐐼 𐑄 𐑃𐐫𐐻𐑅 𐐱𐑂 𐑄 𐐿𐐮𐑍. 𐐈𐑌𐐼 𐐸𐐨 𐑅𐐯𐐼 𐐲𐑌𐐻𐐭 𐐸𐐮𐑋, 𐐆𐑆 𐐮𐐻 𐐺𐐨𐐿𐐫𐑆 𐑄𐐵 𐐸𐐰𐑅𐐻 𐐸𐐲𐑉𐐼 𐑄𐐰𐐻 𐐌 𐐼𐐨𐑁𐐯𐑌𐐼𐐯𐐼 𐑄𐐴 𐑅𐐲𐑉𐑂𐐲𐑌𐐻𐑅 𐐰𐑌𐐼 𐑄𐐴 𐑁𐑊𐐱𐐿𐑅, 𐐰𐑌𐐼 𐑅𐑊𐐭 𐑅𐐯𐑂𐐯𐑌 𐐱𐑂 𐑄𐐩𐑉 𐐺𐑉𐐯𐑄-

𐑉𐐲𐑌 𐐶𐐮𐑄 𐑄 𐑅𐑊𐐮𐑍, 𐐰𐑌𐐼 𐐶𐐮𐑄 𐑄 𐑅𐐬𐑉𐐼, 𐐰𐑌𐐼 𐑅𐑋𐐬𐐻 𐐫𐑁 𐑄 𐐪𐑉𐑋𐑆 𐐱𐑂 𐐲𐑄𐐲𐑉𐑆, 𐐮𐑌 𐐫𐑉𐐼𐐲𐑉 𐐻𐐭 𐐼𐐨𐑁𐐯𐑌𐐼 𐑄𐐴 𐑁𐑊𐐱𐐿𐑅 𐐰𐑌𐐼 𐑄𐐴 𐑅𐐲𐑉𐑂𐐰𐑌𐐻𐑅; 𐐺𐐨𐐸𐐬𐑊𐐼, 𐐮𐑆 𐐮𐐻 𐑄𐐮𐑅 𐑄𐐰𐐻 𐐿𐐫𐑆𐐯𐑃 𐑄𐐴 𐑋𐐪𐑉𐑂𐐯𐑊𐐮𐑍? 𐐌 𐑅𐐩 𐐲𐑌𐐻𐐭 𐐷𐐭, 𐐸𐐶𐐱𐐻 𐐮𐑆 𐐮𐐻, 𐑄𐐰𐐻 𐑄𐐴 𐑋𐐪𐑉𐑂𐐯𐑊𐐮𐑍 𐐮𐑆 𐑅𐐬 𐑀𐑉𐐩𐐻? 𐐒𐐨𐐸𐐬𐑊𐐼, 𐐌 𐐰𐑋 𐐲 𐑋𐐰𐑌, 𐐰𐑌𐐼 𐐰𐑋 𐑄𐐴 𐑅𐐲𐑉𐑂𐐰𐑌𐐻; 𐑄𐐯𐑉𐑁𐐬𐑉, 𐐸𐐶𐐱𐐻𐑅𐐬𐐯𐑂𐐲𐑉 𐑄𐐵 𐐼𐐨𐑆𐐴𐑉𐐯𐑅𐐻 𐐸𐐶𐐮𐐽 𐐮𐑆 𐑉𐐴𐐻, 𐑄𐐰𐐻 𐐶𐐮𐑊 𐐌 𐐼𐐭. 𐐤𐐵 𐐸𐐶𐐯𐑌 𐑄 𐐿𐐮𐑍 𐐸𐐰𐐼 𐐸𐐲𐑉𐐼 𐑄𐐨𐑆 𐐶𐐲𐑉𐐼𐑆, 𐐸𐐨 𐑋𐐪𐑉𐑂𐐯𐑊𐐼 𐐲𐑀𐐯𐑌, 𐑁𐐫𐑉 𐐸𐐨 𐐺𐐨𐐸𐐯𐑊𐐼 𐑄𐐰𐐻 𐐈𐑋𐐲𐑌 𐐿𐐳𐐼 𐐼𐐮𐑆𐐲𐑉𐑌 𐐸𐐮𐑆 𐑃𐐫𐐻𐑅; 𐐺𐐲𐐻 𐑌𐐱𐐻𐐶𐐮𐑄𐑅𐐻𐐰𐑌𐐼𐐮𐑍 𐑄𐐮𐑅, 𐐿𐐮𐑍 𐐢𐐰𐑋𐐬𐑌𐐴 𐐼𐐮𐐼 𐐬𐐹𐐲𐑌 𐐸𐐮𐑆 𐑋𐐵𐑃, 𐐰𐑌𐐼 𐑅𐐯𐐼 𐐲𐑌𐐻𐐭 𐐸𐐮𐑋, 𐐐𐐭 𐐪𐑉𐐻 𐑄𐐵? 𐐂𐑉𐐻 𐑄𐐵 𐑄𐐰𐐻 𐐘𐑉𐐩𐐻 𐐝𐐹𐐮𐑉𐐮𐐻, 𐐸𐐭 𐑌𐐬𐑆 𐐫𐑊 𐑃𐐮𐑍𐑆? 𐐈𐑋𐐲𐑌 𐐰𐑌𐑅𐐲𐑉𐐼 𐐰𐑌𐐼 𐑅𐐯𐐼 𐐲𐑌𐐻𐐭 𐐸𐐮𐑋, 𐐌 𐐰𐑋 𐑌𐐱𐐻. 𐐈𐑌𐐼 𐑄 𐐿𐐮𐑍 𐑅𐐯𐐼, 𐐐𐐵 𐑌𐐬𐐯𐑅𐐻 𐑄𐐵 𐑄 𐑃𐐫𐐻𐑅 𐐱𐑂 𐑋𐐴 𐐸𐐪𐑉𐐻? 𐐜𐐵 𐑋𐐩𐐯𐑅𐐻 𐑅𐐹𐐨𐐿 𐐺𐐬𐑊𐐼𐑊𐐨, 𐐰𐑌𐐼 𐐻𐐯𐑊 𐑋𐐨 𐐿𐐱𐑌𐑅𐐲𐑉𐑌𐐮𐑍 𐑄𐐨𐑆 𐑃𐐮𐑍𐑆; 𐐰𐑌𐐼 𐐫𐑊𐑅𐐬 𐐻𐐯𐑊 𐑋𐐨 𐐺𐐴 𐐸𐐶𐐱𐐻 𐐹𐐵𐐲𐑉 𐐷𐐨 𐑅𐑊𐐭 𐐰𐑌𐐼 𐑅𐑋𐐬𐐻 𐐫𐑁 𐑄 𐐪𐑉𐑋𐑆 𐐱𐑂 𐑋𐐴 𐐺𐑉𐐯𐑄𐑉𐐲𐑌 𐑄𐐰𐐻 𐑅𐐿𐐰𐐻𐐲𐑉𐐼 𐑋𐐴 𐑁𐑊𐐱𐐿𐑅. 𐐈𐑌𐐼 𐑌𐐵, 𐐮𐑁 𐑄𐐵 𐐶𐐮𐑊𐐻 𐐻𐐯𐑊 𐑋𐐨 𐐿𐐱𐑌𐑅𐐲𐑉𐑌𐐮𐑍 𐑄𐐨𐑆 𐑃𐐮𐑍𐑆, 𐐸𐐶𐐱𐐻𐑅𐐬𐐯𐑂𐐲𐑉 𐑄𐐵 𐐼𐐨𐑆𐐴𐑉𐐯𐑅𐐻 𐐌 𐐶𐐮𐑊 𐑀𐐮𐑂 𐐲𐑌𐐻𐐭 𐑄𐐨; 𐐰𐑌𐐼 𐐮𐑁 𐐮𐐻 𐐶𐐲𐑉 𐑌𐐨𐐼𐐯𐐼, 𐐌 𐐶𐐳𐐼 𐑀𐐪𐑉𐐼 𐑄𐐨 𐐶𐐮𐑄 𐑋𐐴 𐐪𐑉𐑋𐐮𐑆; 𐐺𐐲𐐻 𐐌 𐑌𐐬 𐑄𐐰𐐻 𐑄𐐵 𐐪𐑉𐐻 𐑋𐐬𐑉 𐐹𐐵𐐲𐑉𐑁𐐳𐑊 𐑄𐐰𐑌 𐐫𐑊 𐑄𐐩: 𐑌𐐯𐑂𐐲𐑉𐑄𐐯𐑊𐐯𐑅, 𐐸𐐶𐐱𐐻𐑅𐐬𐐯𐑂𐐲𐑉 𐑄𐐵 𐐼𐐨𐑆𐐴𐑉𐐯𐑅𐐻 𐐱𐑂 𐑋𐐨, 𐐌 𐐶𐐮𐑊 𐑀𐑉𐐰𐑌𐐻 𐐮𐐻 𐐲𐑌𐐻𐐭 𐑄𐐨. 𐐤𐐵 𐐈𐑋𐐲𐑌 𐐺𐐨𐐮𐑍 𐐶𐐴𐑆, 𐐷𐐯𐐻 𐐸𐐪𐑉𐑋𐑊𐐯𐑅, 𐐸𐐨 𐑅𐐯𐐼 𐐲𐑌𐐻𐐭 𐐢𐐰𐑋𐐬𐑌𐐴, 𐐎𐐮𐑊𐐻 𐑄𐐵 𐐸𐐪𐑉𐐿𐐲𐑌 𐐲𐑌𐐻𐐭 𐑋𐐴 𐐶𐐲𐑉𐐼𐑆, 𐐮𐑁 𐐌 𐐻𐐯𐑊 𐑄𐐨 𐐺𐐴 𐐸𐐶𐐱𐐻 𐐹𐐵𐐲𐑉 𐐌 𐐼𐐭 𐑄𐐨𐑆 𐑃𐐮𐑍𐑆? 𐐈𐑌𐐼 𐑄𐐮𐑅 𐐮𐑆 𐑄 𐑃𐐮𐑍 𐑄𐐰𐐻 𐐌 𐐼𐐨𐑆𐐴𐑉 𐐱𐑂 𐑄𐐨. 𐐈𐑌𐐼 𐑄 𐐿𐐮𐑍 𐐰𐑌𐑅𐐲𐑉𐐼 𐐸𐐮𐑋, 𐐰𐑌𐐼 𐑅𐐯𐐼, 𐐏𐐩, 𐐌 𐐶𐐮𐑊 𐐺𐐨𐑊𐐨𐑂 𐐫𐑊 𐑄𐐴 𐐶𐐲𐑉𐐼𐑆; 𐐰𐑌𐐼 𐑄𐐲𐑅 𐐸𐐨 𐐶𐐱𐑆 𐐿𐐫𐐻 𐐶𐐮𐑄 𐑀𐐴𐑊. 𐐈𐑌𐐼 𐐈𐑋𐐲𐑌 𐐺𐐨𐑀𐐰𐑌 𐐻𐐭 𐑅𐐹𐐨𐐿 𐐲𐑌𐐻𐐭 𐐸𐐮𐑋 𐐶𐐮𐑄 𐐺𐐬𐑊𐐼𐑌𐐯𐑅, 𐐰𐑌𐐼 𐑅𐐯𐐼 𐐲𐑌𐐻𐐭 𐐸𐐮𐑋, 𐐒𐐨𐑊𐐨𐑂𐐯𐑅𐐻 𐑄𐐵 𐑄𐐰𐐻 𐑄𐐯𐑉 𐐮𐑆 𐐲 𐐘𐐱𐐼? 𐐈𐑌𐐼 𐐸𐐨 𐐰𐑌𐑅𐐲𐑉𐐼, 𐐰𐑌𐐼 𐑅𐐯𐐼 𐐲𐑌𐐻𐐭 𐐸𐐮𐑋, 𐐌 𐐼𐐭 𐑌𐐱𐐻 𐑌𐐬 𐐸𐐶𐐱𐐻 𐑄𐐰𐐻 𐑋𐐨𐑌𐐯𐑃.

14. 𐐈𐑌𐐼 𐑄𐐯𐑌 𐐈𐑋𐐲𐑌 𐑅𐐯𐐼, 𐐒𐐨𐑊𐐨𐑂𐐯𐑅𐐻 𐑄𐐵 𐑄𐐰𐐻 𐑄𐐯𐑉 𐐮𐑆 𐐲 𐐘𐑉𐐩𐐻 𐐝𐐹𐐮𐑉𐐮𐐻? 𐐈𐑌𐐼 𐐸𐐨 𐑅𐐯𐐼, 𐐏𐐩. 𐐈𐑌𐐼 𐐈𐑋𐐲𐑌 𐑅𐐯𐐼, 𐐜𐐮𐑅 𐐮𐑆 𐐘𐐱𐐼. 𐐈𐑌𐐼 𐐈𐑋𐐲𐑌 𐑅𐐯𐐼 𐐲𐑌𐐻𐐭 𐐸𐐮𐑋 𐐲𐑀𐐯𐑌, 𐐒𐐨𐑊𐐨𐑂𐐯𐑅𐐻 𐑄𐐵 𐑄𐐰𐐻 𐑄𐐮𐑅 𐐘𐑉𐐩𐐻 𐐝𐐹𐐮𐑉𐐮𐐻, 𐐸𐐭 𐐮𐑆 𐐘𐐱𐐼, 𐐿𐑉𐐨𐐩𐐻𐐯𐐼 𐐫𐑊 𐑃𐐮𐑍𐑆 𐐸𐐶𐐮𐐽 𐐪𐑉 𐐮𐑌 𐐸𐐯𐑂𐐲𐑌 𐐰𐑌𐐼 𐐮𐑌 𐑄 𐐲𐑉𐑃? 𐐈𐑌𐐼 𐐸𐐨 𐑅𐐯𐐼, 𐐏𐐩, 𐐌 𐐺𐐨𐑊𐐨𐑂 𐑄𐐰𐐻 𐐸𐐨 𐐿𐑉𐐨𐐩𐐻𐐯𐐼 𐐫𐑊 𐑃𐐮𐑍𐑆 𐐸𐐶𐐮𐐽 𐐪𐑉 𐐮𐑌 𐑄 𐐲𐑉𐑃; 𐐺𐐲𐐻 𐐌 𐐼𐐭 𐑌𐐱𐐻 𐑌𐐬 𐑄 𐐸𐐯𐑂𐐲𐑌𐑆. 𐐈𐑌𐐼 𐐈𐑋𐐲𐑌 𐑅𐐯𐐼 𐐲𐑌𐐻𐐭 𐐸𐐮𐑋, 𐐜 𐐸𐐯𐑂𐐲𐑌𐑆 𐐮𐑆 𐐲 𐐹𐑊𐐩𐑅 𐐸𐐶𐐯𐑉 𐐘𐐱𐐼 𐐼𐐶𐐯𐑊𐑆 𐐰𐑌𐐼 𐐫𐑊 𐐸𐐮𐑆 𐐸𐐬𐑊𐐨 𐐩𐑌𐐾𐐯𐑊𐑆. 𐐈𐑌𐐼 𐐿𐐮𐑍 𐐢𐐰𐑋𐐬𐑌𐐴 𐑅𐐯𐐼, 𐐆𐑆 𐐮𐐻 𐐲𐐺𐐲𐑂 𐑄 𐐲𐑉𐑃? 𐐈𐑌𐐼 𐐈𐑋𐐲𐑌 𐑅𐐯𐐼, 𐐏𐐩, 𐐰𐑌𐐼 𐐸𐐨 𐑊𐐳𐐿𐐯𐑃 𐐼𐐵𐑌 𐐲𐐹𐐱𐑌 𐐫𐑊 𐑄 𐐽𐐮𐑊𐐼𐑉𐐯𐑌 𐐱𐑂 𐑋𐐯𐑌; 𐐰𐑌𐐼 𐐸𐐨 𐑌𐐬𐑆 𐐫𐑊 𐑄 𐑃𐐫𐐻𐑅 𐐰𐑌𐐼 𐐮𐑌𐐻𐐯𐑌𐐻𐑅 𐐱𐑂 𐑄 𐐸𐐪𐑉𐐻: 𐑁𐐫𐑉 𐐺𐐴 𐐸𐐮𐑆 𐐸𐐰𐑌𐐼 𐐶𐐲𐑉 𐑄𐐩 𐐫𐑊 𐐿𐑉𐐨𐐩𐐻𐐯𐐼 𐑁𐑉𐐱𐑋 𐑄 𐐺𐐨𐑀𐐮𐑌𐐮𐑍. 𐐈𐑌𐐼 𐐿𐐮𐑍 𐐢𐐰𐑋𐐬𐑌𐐴 𐑅𐐯𐐼, 𐐌 𐐺𐐨𐑊𐐨𐑂 𐐫𐑊 𐑄𐐨𐑆 𐑃𐐮𐑍𐑆 𐐸𐐶𐐮𐐽 𐑄𐐵 𐐸𐐰𐑅𐐻 𐑅𐐹𐐬𐐿𐐲𐑌. 𐐂𐑉𐐻 𐑄𐐵 𐑅𐐯𐑌𐐻 𐑁𐑉𐐱𐑋 𐐘𐐱𐐼? 𐐈𐑋𐐲𐑌 𐑅𐐯𐐼 𐐲𐑌𐐻𐐭 𐐸𐐮𐑋, 𐐌 𐐰𐑋 𐐲 𐑋𐐰𐑌; 𐐰𐑌𐐼 𐑋𐐰𐑌 𐐮𐑌 𐑄 𐐺𐐨𐑀𐐮𐑌𐐮𐑍 𐐶𐐱𐑆 𐐿𐑉𐐨𐐩𐐻𐐯𐐼 𐐰𐑁𐐻𐐲𐑉 𐑄 𐐮𐑋𐐯𐐾 𐐱𐑂 𐐘𐐱𐐼, 𐐰𐑌𐐼 𐐌 𐐰𐑋 𐐿𐐫𐑊𐐼 𐐺𐐴 𐐸𐐮𐑆 𐐐𐐬𐑊𐐨 𐐝𐐹𐐮𐑉𐐮𐐻 𐐻𐐭 𐐻𐐨𐐽 𐑄𐐨𐑆 𐑃𐐮𐑍𐑆 𐐲𐑌𐐻𐐭 𐑄𐐮𐑅 𐐹𐐨𐐹𐑊, 𐑄𐐰𐐻 𐑄𐐩 𐑋𐐩 𐐺𐐨 𐐺𐑉𐐫𐐻 𐐻𐐭 𐐲 𐑌𐐱𐑊𐐯𐐾 𐐱𐑂 𐑄𐐰𐐻 𐐸𐐶𐐮𐐽 𐐮𐑆 𐐾𐐲𐑅𐐻 𐐰𐑌𐐼 𐐻𐑉𐐭; 𐐰𐑌𐐼 𐐲 𐐹𐐬𐑉𐑇𐐲𐑌 𐐱𐑂 𐑄𐐰𐐻 𐐝𐐹𐐮𐑉𐐮𐐻 𐐼𐐶𐐯𐑊𐐯𐑃 𐐮𐑌 𐑋𐐨, 𐐸𐐶𐐮𐐽 𐑀𐐮𐑂𐐯𐑃 𐑋𐐨 𐑌𐐱𐑊𐐯𐐾, 𐐰𐑌𐐼 𐐫𐑊𐑅𐐬 𐐹𐐵𐐲𐑉, 𐐰𐐿𐐫𐑉𐐼𐐮𐑍 𐐻𐐭 𐑋𐐴 𐑁𐐩𐑃 𐐰𐑌𐐼 𐐼𐐨𐑆𐐴𐑉𐑆 𐐸𐐶𐐮𐐽 𐐪𐑉 𐐮𐑌 𐐘𐐱𐐼. 𐐤𐐵 𐐸𐐶𐐯𐑌 𐐈𐑋𐐲𐑌 𐐸𐐰𐐼 𐑅𐐯𐐼 𐑄𐐨𐑆 𐐶𐐲𐑉𐐼𐑆, 𐐸𐐨 𐐺𐐨𐑀𐐰𐑌 𐐰𐐻 𐑄 𐐿𐑉𐐨𐐩𐑇𐐲𐑌 𐐱𐑂 𐑄 𐐶𐐲𐑉𐑊𐐼, 𐐰𐑌𐐼 𐐫𐑊𐑅𐐬 𐑄 𐐿𐑉𐐨𐐩𐑇𐐲𐑌 𐐱𐑂 𐐁𐐼𐐲𐑋, 𐐰𐑌𐐼 𐐻𐐬𐑊𐐼 𐐸𐐮𐑋 𐐫𐑊 𐑄 𐑃𐐮𐑍𐑆 𐐿𐐱𐑌𐑅𐐲𐑉𐑌𐐮𐑍 𐑄 𐑁𐐫𐑊 𐐱𐑂 𐑋𐐰𐑌, 𐐰𐑌𐐼 𐑉𐐨𐐸𐐲𐑉𐑅𐐻 𐐰𐑌𐐼 𐑊𐐩𐐼 𐐺𐐨𐑁𐐬𐑉 𐐸𐐮𐑋 𐑄 𐑉𐐯𐐿𐐲𐑉𐐼𐑆 𐐰𐑌𐐼 𐑄 𐐸𐐬𐑊𐐨 𐑅𐐿𐑉𐐮𐐹𐐽𐐲𐑉𐑆 𐐱𐑂 𐑄 𐐹𐐨𐐹𐑊, 𐐸𐐶𐐮𐐽 𐐸𐐰𐐼 𐐺𐐮𐑌 𐑅𐐹𐐬𐐿𐐲𐑌 𐐺𐐴 𐑄 𐐹𐑉𐐱𐑁𐐯𐐻𐑅, 𐐨𐑂𐐲𐑌 𐐼𐐵𐑌 𐐻𐐭 𐑄 𐐻𐐴𐑋 𐑄𐐰𐐻 𐑄𐐯𐑉 𐑁𐐪𐑄𐐲𐑉, 𐐢𐐨𐐸𐐴, 𐑊𐐯𐑁𐐻 𐐖𐐯𐑉𐐭𐑅𐐲𐑊𐐯𐑋; 𐐰𐑌𐐼 𐐸𐐨 𐐫𐑊𐑅𐐬 𐑉𐐨𐐸𐐲𐑉𐑅𐐻 𐐲𐑌𐐻𐐭 𐑄𐐯𐑋, (𐑁𐐫𐑉 𐐮𐐻 𐐶𐐱𐑆 𐐲𐑌𐐻𐐭 𐑄 𐐿𐐮𐑍 𐐰𐑌𐐼 𐐻𐐭 𐐸𐐮𐑆 𐑅𐐲𐑉𐑂𐐰𐑌𐐻𐑅,) 𐐫𐑊 𐑄 𐐾𐐲𐑉𐑌𐐨𐐮𐑍𐑆 𐐱𐑂 𐑄𐐯𐑉 𐑁𐐪𐑄𐐲𐑉𐑆 𐐮𐑌 𐑄 𐐶𐐮𐑊𐐼𐐲𐑉𐑌𐐯𐑅, 𐐰𐑌𐐼 𐐫𐑊 𐑄𐐯𐑉 𐑅𐐲𐑁𐐲𐑉𐐮𐑍𐑆 𐐶𐐮𐑄 𐐸𐐲𐑍𐑀𐐲𐑉 𐐰𐑌𐐼 𐑃𐐲𐑉𐑅𐐻, 𐐰𐑌𐐼 𐑄𐐯𐑉 𐐻𐑉𐐰𐑂𐐩𐑊, 𐐯𐐻𐑅.: 𐐰𐑌𐐼 𐐸𐐨 𐐫𐑊𐑅𐐬 𐑉𐐨𐐸𐐲𐑉𐑅𐐻 𐐲𐑌𐐻𐐭

𐑄𐐯𐑋 𐐿𐐱𐑌𐑅𐐲𐑉𐑌𐐮𐑍 𐑄 𐑉𐐯𐐺𐐯𐑊𐐷𐐲𐑌𐑆 𐐱𐑂 𐐢𐐩𐑋𐐲𐑌 𐐰𐑌𐐼 𐐢𐐯𐑋𐐷𐐭𐐯𐑊, 𐐰𐑌𐐼 𐑄 𐑅𐐲𐑌𐑆 𐐱𐑂 𐐆𐑇𐑋𐐩𐐯𐑊, 𐐷𐐩, 𐐫𐑊 𐑄𐐩𐑉 𐑉𐐯𐐺𐐯𐑊𐐷𐐲𐑌𐑆 𐐼𐐮𐐼 𐐸𐐨 𐑉𐐨𐑊𐐩𐐻 𐐲𐑌𐐻𐐭 𐑄𐐯𐑋; 𐐰𐑌𐐼 𐐸𐐨 𐐯𐐿𐑅𐐹𐐵𐑌𐐼𐐯𐐼 𐐲𐑌𐐻𐐭 𐑄𐐯𐑋 𐐫𐑊 𐑄 𐑉𐐯𐐿𐐲𐑉𐐼𐑆 𐐰𐑌𐐼 𐑅𐐿𐑉𐐮𐐹𐐽𐐲𐑉𐑆, 𐑁𐑉𐐱𐑋 𐑄 𐐻𐐴𐑋 𐑄𐐰𐐻 𐐢𐐨𐐸𐐴 𐑊𐐯𐑁𐐻 𐐖𐐯𐑉𐐭𐑅𐐲𐑊𐐯𐑋, 𐐼𐐵𐑌 𐐻𐐭 𐑄 𐐹𐑉𐐯𐑆𐐯𐑌𐐻 𐐻𐐴𐑋; 𐐒𐐲𐐻 𐑄𐐮𐑅 𐐮𐑆 𐑌𐐱𐐻 𐐫𐑊; 𐑁𐐫𐑉 𐐸𐐨 𐐯𐐿𐑅𐐹𐐵𐑌𐐼𐐯𐐼 𐐲𐑌𐐻𐐭 𐑄𐐯𐑋 𐑄 𐐹𐑊𐐰𐑌 𐐱𐑂 𐑉𐐨𐐼𐐯𐑋𐐹𐑇𐐲𐑌, 𐐸𐐶𐐮𐐽 𐐶𐐱𐑆 𐐹𐑉𐐨𐐹𐐩𐑉𐐼 𐑁𐑉𐐱𐑋 𐑄 𐑁𐐵𐑌𐐼𐐩𐑇𐐲𐑌 𐐱𐑂 𐑄 𐐶𐐲𐑉𐑊𐐼; 𐐰𐑌𐐼 𐐸𐐨 𐐫𐑊𐑅𐐬 𐑋𐐩𐐼 𐑌𐐬𐑌 𐐲𐑌𐐻𐐭 𐑄𐐯𐑋 𐐿𐐱𐑌𐑅𐐲𐑉𐑌𐐮𐑍 𐑄 𐐿𐐲𐑋𐐮𐑍 𐐱𐑂 𐐗𐑉𐐴𐑅𐐻, 𐐰𐑌𐐼 𐐫𐑊 𐑄 𐐶𐐲𐑉𐐿𐑅 𐐱𐑂 𐑄 𐐢𐐫𐑉𐐼 𐐼𐐮𐐼 𐐸𐐨 𐑋𐐩𐐿 𐑌𐐬𐑌 𐐲𐑌𐐻𐐭 𐑄𐐯𐑋.

15. 𐐈𐑌𐐼 𐐮𐐻 𐐿𐐩𐑋 𐐻𐐭 𐐹𐐰𐑅 𐑄𐐰𐐻 𐐰𐑁𐐻𐐲𐑉 𐐸𐐨 𐐸𐐰𐐼 𐑅𐐯𐐼 𐐫𐑊 𐑄𐐨𐑆 𐑃𐐮𐑍𐑆, 𐐰𐑌𐐼 𐐯𐐿𐑅𐐹𐐵𐑌𐐼𐐯𐐼 𐑄𐐯𐑋 𐐲𐑌𐐻𐐭 𐑄 𐐿𐐮𐑍, 𐑄𐐰𐐻 𐑄 𐐿𐐮𐑍 𐐺𐐨𐑊𐐨𐑂𐐼 𐐫𐑊 𐐸𐐮𐑆 𐐶𐐲𐑉𐐼𐑆. 𐐈𐑌𐐼 𐐸𐐨 𐐺𐐨𐑀𐐰𐑌 𐐻𐐭 𐐿𐑉𐐴 𐐲𐑌𐐻𐐭 𐑄 𐐢𐐫𐑉𐐼, 𐑅𐐩𐐮𐑍: 𐐄 𐐢𐐫𐑉𐐼, 𐐸𐐰𐑂 𐑋𐐲𐑉𐑅𐐨; 𐐰𐐿𐐫𐑉𐐼𐐮𐑍 𐐻𐐭 𐑄𐐴 𐐲𐐺𐐲𐑌𐐼𐐲𐑌𐐻 𐑋𐐲𐑉𐑅𐐨 𐐸𐐶𐐮𐐽 𐑄𐐵 𐐸𐐰𐑅𐐻 𐐸𐐰𐐼 𐐲𐐹𐐱𐑌 𐑄 𐐹𐐨𐐹𐑊 𐐱𐑂 𐐤𐐨𐑁𐐴, 𐐸𐐰𐑂 𐐲𐐹𐐱𐑌 𐑋𐐨, 𐐰𐑌𐐼 𐑋𐐴 𐐹𐐨𐐹𐑊. 𐐈𐑌𐐼 𐑌𐐵, 𐐸𐐶𐐯𐑌 𐐸𐐨 𐐸𐐰𐐼 𐑅𐐯𐐼 𐑄𐐮𐑅, 𐐸𐐨 𐑁𐐯𐑊 𐐲𐑌𐐻𐐭 𐑄 𐐲𐑉𐑃, 𐐰𐑆 𐐮𐑁 𐐸𐐨 𐐶𐐲𐑉 𐐼𐐯𐐼. 𐐈𐑌𐐼 𐐮𐐻 𐐿𐐩𐑋 𐐻𐐭 𐐹𐐰𐑅 𐑄𐐰𐐻 𐐸𐐮𐑆 𐑅𐐲𐑉𐑂𐐲𐑌𐐻𐑅 𐐻𐐳𐐿 𐐸𐐮𐑋 𐐰𐑌𐐼 𐐿𐐰𐑉𐐨𐐼 𐐸𐐮𐑋 𐐮𐑌 𐐲𐑌𐐻𐐭 𐐸𐐮𐑆 𐐶𐐴𐑁, 𐐰𐑌𐐼 𐑊𐐩𐐼 𐐸𐐮𐑋 𐐲𐐹𐐱𐑌 𐐰 𐐺𐐯𐐼; 𐐰𐑌𐐼 𐐸𐐨 𐑊𐐩 𐐰𐑆 𐐮𐑁 𐐸𐐨 𐐶𐐲𐑉 𐐼𐐯𐐼 𐑁𐐫𐑉 𐑄 𐑅𐐹𐐩𐑅 𐐱𐑂 𐐻𐐭 𐐼𐐩𐑆 𐐰𐑌𐐼 𐐻𐐭 𐑌𐐴𐐻𐑅; 𐐰𐑌𐐼 𐐸𐐮𐑆 𐐶𐐴𐑁, 𐐰𐑌𐐼 𐐸𐐮𐑆 𐑅𐐲𐑌𐑆, 𐐰𐑌𐐼 𐐸𐐮𐑆 𐐼𐐫𐐻𐐲𐑉𐑆, 𐑋𐐬𐑉𐑌𐐼 𐐬𐑂𐐲𐑉 𐐸𐐮𐑋, 𐐰𐑁𐐻𐐲𐑉 𐑄 𐑋𐐰𐑌𐐲𐑉 𐐱𐑂 𐑄 𐐢𐐩𐑋𐐲𐑌𐐴𐐻𐑅, 𐑀𐑉𐐩𐐻𐑊𐐨 𐑊𐐰𐑋𐐯𐑌𐐻𐐮𐑍 𐐸𐐮𐑆 𐑊𐐱𐑅.

16. 𐐈𐑌𐐼 𐐮𐐻 𐐿𐐩𐑋 𐐻𐐭 𐐹𐐰𐑅 𐑄𐐰𐐻 𐐰𐑁𐐻𐐲𐑉 𐐻𐐭 𐐼𐐩𐑆 𐐰𐑌𐐼 𐐻𐐭 𐑌𐐴𐐻𐑅, 𐑄𐐩 𐐶𐐲𐑉 𐐲𐐺𐐵𐐻 𐐻𐐭 𐐻𐐩𐐿 𐐸𐐮𐑆 𐐺𐐱𐐼𐐨 𐐰𐑌𐐼 𐑊𐐩 𐐮𐐻 𐐮𐑌 𐐰 𐑅𐐯𐐹𐐲𐑊𐐿𐐲𐑉, 𐐸𐐶𐐮𐐽 𐑄𐐩 𐐸𐐰𐐼 𐑋𐐩𐐼 𐑁𐐫𐑉 𐑄 𐐹𐐲𐑉𐐹𐐲𐑅 𐐱𐑂 𐐺𐐯𐑉𐐨𐐮𐑍 𐑄𐐩𐑉 𐐼𐐯𐐼. 𐐤𐐵 𐑄 𐐿𐐶𐐨𐑌 𐐸𐐰𐑂𐐮𐑍 𐐸𐐲𐑉𐐼 𐐱𐑂 𐑄 𐑁𐐩𐑋 𐐱𐑂 𐐈𐑋𐐲𐑌, 𐑄𐐯𐑉𐑁𐐬𐑉 𐑇𐐨 𐑅𐐯𐑌𐐻 𐐰𐑌𐐼 𐐼𐐨𐑆𐐴𐑉𐐼 𐑄𐐰𐐻 𐐸𐐨 𐑇𐐳𐐼 𐐿𐐲𐑋 𐐮𐑌 𐐲𐑌𐐻𐐭 𐐸𐐲𐑉. 𐐈𐑌𐐼 𐐮𐐻 𐐿𐐩𐑋 𐐻𐐭 𐐹𐐰𐑅 𐑄𐐰𐐻 𐐈𐑋𐐲𐑌 𐐼𐐮𐐼 𐐰𐑆 𐐸𐐨 𐐶𐐱𐑆 𐐿𐐱𐑋𐐰𐑌𐐼𐐯𐐼, 𐐰𐑌𐐼 𐐶𐐯𐑌𐐻 𐐮𐑌 𐐲𐑌𐐻𐐭 𐑄 𐐿𐐶𐐨𐑌, 𐐰𐑌𐐼 𐐼𐐨𐑆𐐴𐑉𐐼 𐐻𐐭 𐑌𐐬 𐐸𐐶𐐱𐐻 𐑇𐐨 𐐶𐐳𐐼 𐑄𐐰𐐻 𐐸𐐨 𐑇𐐳𐐼 𐐼𐐭. 𐐈𐑌𐐼 𐑇𐐨 𐑅𐐯𐐼 𐐲𐑌𐐻𐐭 𐐸𐐮𐑋, 𐐜 𐑅𐐲𐑉𐑂𐐲𐑌𐐻𐑅 𐐱𐑂 𐑋𐐴 𐐸𐐲𐑆𐐺𐐲𐑌𐐼 𐐸𐐰𐑂 𐑋𐐩𐐼 𐐮𐐻 𐑌𐐬𐑌 𐐲𐑌𐐻𐐭 𐑋𐐨 𐑄𐐰𐐻 𐑄𐐵 𐐪𐑉𐐻 𐐰 𐐹𐑉𐐱𐑁𐐯𐐻 𐐱𐑂 𐐰 𐐸𐐬𐑊𐐨 𐐘𐐱𐐼, 𐐰𐑌𐐼 𐑄𐐰𐐻 𐑄𐐵 𐐸𐐰𐑅𐐻 𐐹𐐵𐐲𐑉 𐐻𐐭 𐐼𐐭 𐑋𐐯𐑌𐐨 𐑋𐐴𐐻𐐨 𐐶𐐲𐑉𐐿𐑅 𐐮𐑌 𐐸𐐮𐑆 𐑌𐐩𐑋; 𐑄𐐯𐑉𐑁𐐬𐑉, 𐐮𐑁 𐑄𐐮𐑅 𐐮𐑆 𐑄 𐐿𐐩𐑅, 𐐌 𐐶𐐳𐐼 𐑄𐐰𐐻 𐐷𐐨 𐑇𐐳𐐼 𐑀𐐬 𐐮𐑌 𐐰𐑌𐐼 𐑅𐐨 𐑋𐐴 𐐸𐐲𐑆𐐺𐐲𐑌𐐼, 𐑁𐐫𐑉 𐐸𐐨 𐐸𐐰𐑆 𐐺𐐮𐑌 𐑊𐐩𐐼 𐐲𐐹𐐱𐑌 𐐸𐐮𐑆 𐐺𐐯𐐼 𐑁𐐫𐑉 𐑄 𐑅𐐹𐐩𐑅 𐐱𐑂 𐐻𐐭 𐐼𐐩𐑆 𐐰𐑌𐐼 𐐻𐐭 𐑌𐐴𐐻𐑅; 𐐰𐑌𐐼 𐑅𐐲𐑋 𐑅𐐩 𐑄𐐰𐐻 𐐸𐐨 𐐮𐑆 𐑌𐐱𐐻 𐐼𐐯𐐼, 𐐺𐐲𐐻 𐐲𐑄𐐲𐑉𐑆 𐑅𐐩 𐑄𐐰𐐻 𐐸𐐨 𐐮𐑆 𐐼𐐯𐐼, 𐐰𐑌𐐼 𐑄𐐰𐐻 𐐸𐐨 𐑅𐐻𐐮𐑍𐐿𐐯𐑃, 𐐰𐑌𐐼 𐑄𐐰𐐻 𐐸𐐨 𐐫𐐻 𐐻𐐭 𐐺𐐨 𐐹𐑊𐐩𐑅𐐻 𐐮𐑌 𐑄 𐑅𐐯𐐹𐐲𐑊𐐿𐐲𐑉; 𐐺𐐲𐐻 𐐰𐑆 𐑁𐐫𐑉 𐑋𐐴𐑅𐐯𐑊𐑁, 𐐻𐐭 𐑋𐐨 𐐸𐐨 𐐼𐐲𐑃 𐑌𐐱𐐻 𐑅𐐻𐐮𐑍𐐿. 𐐤𐐵, 𐑄𐐮𐑅 𐐶𐐱𐑆 𐐸𐐶𐐱𐐻 𐐈𐑋𐐲𐑌 𐐼𐐨𐑆𐐴𐑉𐐼, 𐑁𐐫𐑉 𐐸𐐨 𐑌𐐭 𐑄𐐰𐐻 𐐿𐐮𐑍 𐐢𐐰𐑋𐐬𐑌𐐴 𐐶𐐱𐑆 𐐲𐑌𐐼𐐲𐑉 𐑄 𐐹𐐵𐐲𐑉 𐐱𐑂 𐐘𐐱𐐼; 𐐸𐐨 𐑌𐐭 𐑄𐐰𐐻 𐑄 𐐼𐐪𐑉𐐿 𐑂𐐩𐑊 𐐱𐑂 𐐲𐑌𐐺𐐨𐑊𐐨𐑁 𐐶𐐱𐑆 𐐺𐐨𐐮𐑍 𐐿𐐰𐑅𐐻 𐐰𐐶𐐩 𐑁𐑉𐐱𐑋 𐐸𐐮𐑆 𐑋𐐴𐑌𐐼, 𐐰𐑌𐐼 𐑄 𐑊𐐴𐐻 𐐸𐐶𐐮𐐽 𐐼𐐮𐐼 𐑊𐐴𐐻 𐐲𐐹 𐐸𐐮𐑆 𐑋𐐴𐑌𐐼, 𐐸𐐶𐐮𐐽 𐐶𐐱𐑆 𐑄 𐑊𐐴𐐻 𐐱𐑂 𐑄 𐑀𐑊𐐬𐑉𐐨 𐐱𐑂 𐐘𐐱𐐼, 𐐸𐐶𐐮𐐽 𐐶𐐱𐑆 𐐰 𐑋𐐪𐑉𐑂𐐯𐑊𐐲𐑅 𐑊𐐴𐐻 𐐱𐑂 𐐸𐐮𐑆 𐑀𐐳𐐼𐑌𐐯𐑅; 𐐷𐐩, 𐑄𐐮𐑅 𐑊𐐴𐐻 𐐸𐐰𐐼 𐐮𐑌𐑁𐐷𐐭𐑆𐐼 𐑅𐐲𐐽 𐐾𐐱𐐨 𐐮𐑌𐐻𐐭 𐐸𐐮𐑆 𐑅𐐬𐑊, 𐑄 𐐿𐑊𐐵𐐼 𐐱𐑂 𐐼𐐪𐑉𐐿𐑌𐐯𐑅 𐐸𐐰𐑂𐐮𐑍 𐐺𐐮𐑌 𐐼𐐮𐑅𐐹𐐯𐑊𐐼, 𐐰𐑌𐐼 𐑄𐐰𐐻 𐑄 𐑊𐐴𐐻 𐐱𐑂 𐐯𐑂𐐲𐑉𐑊𐐰𐑅𐐻𐐮𐑍 𐑊𐐴𐑁 𐐶𐐱𐑆 𐑊𐐮𐐻 𐐲𐐹 𐐮𐑌 𐐸𐐮𐑆 𐑅𐐬𐑊; 𐐷𐐩, 𐐸𐐨 𐑌𐐭 𐑄𐐰𐐻 𐑄𐐮𐑅 𐐸𐐰𐐼 𐐬𐑂𐐲𐑉𐐿𐐲𐑋 𐐸𐐮𐑆 𐑌𐐰𐐽𐐲𐑉𐐲𐑊 𐑁𐑉𐐩𐑋, 𐐰𐑌𐐼 𐐸𐐨 𐐶𐐱𐑆 𐐿𐐰𐑉𐐨𐐼 𐐰𐐶𐐩 𐐮𐑌 𐐘𐐱𐐼; 𐑄𐐯𐑉𐑁𐐬𐑉, 𐐸𐐶𐐱𐐻 𐑄 𐐿𐐶𐐨𐑌 𐐼𐐨𐑆𐐴𐑉𐐼 𐐱𐑂 𐐸𐐮𐑋, 𐐶𐐱𐑆 𐐸𐐮𐑆 𐐬𐑌𐑊𐐨 𐐼𐐨𐑆𐐴𐑉. 𐐜𐐯𐑉𐑁𐐬𐑉, 𐐸𐐨 𐐶𐐯𐑌𐐻 𐐮𐑌 𐐻𐐭 𐑅𐐨 𐑄 𐐿𐐮𐑍 𐐰𐐿𐐫𐑉𐐼𐐮𐑍 𐐰𐑆 𐑄 𐐿𐐶𐐨𐑌 𐐸𐐰𐐼 𐐼𐐨𐑆𐐴𐑉𐐼 𐐸𐐮𐑋; 𐐰𐑌𐐼 𐐸𐐨 𐑅𐐫 𐑄 𐐿𐐮𐑍, 𐐰𐑌𐐼 𐐸𐐨 𐑌𐐭 𐑄𐐰𐐻 𐐸𐐨 𐐶𐐱𐑆 𐑌𐐱𐐻 𐐼𐐯𐐼. 𐐈𐑌𐐼 𐐸𐐨 𐑅𐐯𐐼 𐐲𐑌𐐻𐐭 𐑄 𐐿𐐶𐐨𐑌, 𐐐𐐨 𐐮𐑆 𐑌𐐱𐐻 𐐼𐐯𐐼, 𐐺𐐲𐐻 𐐸𐐨 𐑅𐑊𐐨𐐹𐐯𐑃 𐐮𐑌 𐐘𐐱𐐼, 𐐰𐑌𐐼 𐐱𐑌 𐑄 𐑋𐐱𐑉𐐬 𐐸𐐨 𐑇𐐰𐑊 𐑉𐐴𐑆 𐐰𐑀𐐯𐑌; 𐑄𐐯𐑉𐑁𐐬𐑉 𐐺𐐯𐑉𐐨 𐐸𐐮𐑋 𐑌𐐱𐐻. 𐐈𐑌𐐼 𐐈𐑋𐐲𐑌 𐑅𐐯𐐼 𐐲𐑌𐐻𐐭 𐐸𐐲𐑉, 𐐒𐐨𐑊𐐨𐑂𐐯𐑅𐐻 𐑄𐐵 𐑄𐐮𐑅? 𐐈𐑌𐐼 𐑇𐐨 𐑅𐐯𐐼 𐐲𐑌𐐻𐐭 𐐸𐐮𐑋, 𐐌 𐐸𐐰𐑂 𐐸𐐰𐐼 𐑌𐐬 𐐶𐐮𐐻𐑌𐐯𐑅, 𐑅𐐩𐑂 𐑄𐐴 𐐶𐐲𐑉𐐼, 𐐰𐑌𐐼 𐑄 𐐶𐐲𐑉𐐼 𐐱𐑂 𐐵𐑉 𐑅𐐲𐑉𐑂𐐲𐑌𐐻𐑅; 𐑌𐐯𐑂𐐲𐑉𐑄𐐯𐑊𐐯𐑅, 𐐌 𐐺𐐨𐑊𐐨𐑂 𐑄𐐰𐐻 𐐮𐐻 𐑇𐐰𐑊 𐐺𐐨 𐐰𐐿𐐫𐑉𐐼𐐮𐑍 𐐰𐑆 𐑄𐐵 𐐸𐐰𐑅𐐻 𐑅𐐯𐐼. 𐐈𐑌𐐼 𐐈𐑋𐐲𐑌 𐑅𐐯𐐼 𐐲𐑌𐐻𐐭 𐐸𐐲𐑉, 𐐒𐑊𐐯𐑅𐐯𐐼 𐐪𐑉𐐻 𐑄𐐵 𐐺𐐨𐐿𐐫𐑆 𐐱𐑂 𐑄𐐴 𐐯𐐿𐑅𐐨𐐼𐐮𐑍

𐑁𐐩𐑃; 𐐴 𐑅𐐩 𐐲𐑌𐐻𐐭 𐑄, 𐐶𐐳𐑋𐐲𐑌, 𐑄𐐯𐑉 𐐸𐐰𐑆 𐑌𐐪𐐻 𐐺𐐮𐑌 𐑅𐐲𐐽 𐑀𐑉𐐩𐐻 𐑁𐐩𐑃 𐐰𐑋𐐲𐑍 𐐫𐑊 𐑄 𐐹𐐨𐐹𐑊 𐐱𐑂 𐑄 𐐤𐐨𐑁𐐴𐐻𐑅.

17. 𐐰𐑌𐐼 𐐮𐐻 𐐿𐐩𐑋 𐐻𐐭 𐐹𐐩𐑅 𐑄𐐰𐐻 𐑇𐐨 𐐶𐐪𐐽𐐻 𐐬𐑂𐐲𐑉 𐑄 𐐺𐐯𐐼 𐐱𐑂 𐐸𐐲𐑉 𐐸𐐲𐑆𐐺𐐲𐑌𐐼, 𐑁𐑉𐐲𐑋 𐑄𐐰𐐻 𐐻𐐴𐑋, 𐐨𐑂𐐲𐑌 𐐲𐑌𐐻𐐮𐑊 𐑄𐐰𐐻 𐐻𐐴𐑋 𐐪𐑌 𐑄 𐑋𐐪𐑉𐐬 𐐸𐐶𐐮𐐽 𐐈𐑋𐐲𐑌 𐐸𐐰𐐼 𐐰𐐹𐐱𐐮𐑌𐐻𐐯𐐼 𐑄𐐰𐐻 𐐸𐐨 𐑇𐐳𐐼 𐑉𐐴𐑆. 𐐰𐑌𐐼 𐐮𐐻 𐐿𐐩𐑋 𐐻𐐭 𐐹𐐩𐑅 𐑄𐐰𐐻 𐐸𐐨 𐐰𐑉𐐬𐑆, 𐐰𐐿𐐫𐑉𐐼𐐮𐑍 𐐻𐐭 𐑄 𐐶𐐲𐑉𐐼𐑆 𐐱𐑂 𐐈𐑋𐐲𐑌; 𐐰𐑌𐐼 𐐰𐑆 𐐸𐐨 𐐰𐑉𐐬𐑆, 𐐸𐐨 𐑅𐐻𐑉𐐯𐐽𐐻 𐑁𐐬𐑉𐑃 𐐸𐐮𐑆 𐐸𐐰𐑌𐐼 𐐲𐑌𐐻𐐭 𐑄 𐐶𐐳𐑋𐐲𐑌, 𐐰𐑌𐐼 𐑅𐐯𐐼 𐐒𐑊𐐯𐑅𐐯𐐼 𐐺 𐑄 𐑌𐐩𐑋 𐐱𐑂 𐐘𐐪𐐼, 𐐰𐑌𐐼 𐐺𐑊𐐯𐑅𐐯𐐼 𐐪𐑉𐐻 𐑄𐐵; 𐑁𐐫𐑉 𐐰𐑆 𐑇𐐳𐑉 𐐰𐑆 𐑄𐐵 𐑊𐐮𐑂𐐯𐑅𐐻, 𐐺𐐨𐐸𐐬𐑊𐐼, 𐐴 𐐸𐐰𐑂 𐑅𐐨𐑌 𐑋𐐴 𐐡𐐨𐐼𐐨𐑋𐐲𐑉; 𐐰𐑌𐐼 𐐸𐐨 𐑇𐐰𐑊 𐐿𐐲𐑋 𐑁𐐬𐑉𐑃, 𐐰𐑌𐐼 𐐺 𐐺𐐫𐑉𐑌 𐐱𐑂 𐐩 𐐶𐐳𐑋𐐲𐑌, 𐐰𐑌𐐼 𐐸𐐨 𐑇𐐰𐑊 𐑉𐐨𐐼𐐨𐑋 𐐫𐑊 𐑋𐐰𐑌𐐿𐐴𐑌𐐼 𐐸𐐭 𐐺𐐨𐑊𐐨𐑂 𐐪𐑌 𐐸𐐮𐑆 𐑌𐐩𐑋. 𐐤𐐵, 𐐸𐐶𐐯𐑌 𐐸𐐨 𐐸𐐰𐐼 𐑅𐐯𐐼 𐑄𐐨𐑆 𐐶𐐲𐑉𐐼𐑆, 𐐸𐐮𐑆 𐐸𐐪𐑉𐐻 𐐶𐐪𐑆 𐑅𐐶𐐬𐑊𐐲𐑌 𐐶𐐮𐑄𐐮𐑌 𐐸𐐮𐑋, 𐐰𐑌𐐼 𐐸𐐨 𐑅𐐲𐑍𐐿 𐐰𐑀𐐯𐑌 𐐶𐐮𐑄 𐐾𐐦; 𐐰𐑌𐐼 𐑄 𐐿𐐶𐐨𐑌 𐐫𐑊𐑅𐐬 𐑅𐐲𐑍𐐿 𐐼𐐵𐑌, 𐐺𐐨𐐮𐑍 𐐬𐑂𐐲𐑉𐐹𐐵𐐲𐑉𐐼 𐐺𐐴 𐑄 𐐝𐐹𐐮𐑉𐐮𐐻. 𐐤𐐵 𐐈𐑋𐐲𐑌 𐑅𐐨𐐮𐑍 𐑄 𐐝𐐹𐐮𐑉𐐮𐐻 𐐱𐑂 𐑄 𐐢𐐫𐑉𐐼 𐐹𐐬𐑉𐐼 𐐵𐐻 𐐰𐐿𐐫𐑉𐐼𐐮𐑍 𐐻𐐭 𐐸𐐮𐑆 𐐹𐑉𐐯𐑉𐑆 𐐲𐐹𐐪𐑌 𐑄 𐐢𐐩𐑋𐐲𐑌𐐴𐐻𐑅, 𐐸𐐮𐑆 𐐺𐑉𐐯𐑄𐑉𐐯𐑌, 𐐸𐐭 𐐸𐐰𐐼 𐐺𐐮𐑌 𐑄 𐐿𐐫𐑆 𐐱𐑂 𐑅𐐬 𐑋𐐲𐐽 𐑋𐐬𐑉𐑌𐐮𐑍 𐐰𐑋𐐲𐑍 𐑄 𐐤𐐨𐑁𐐴𐐻𐑅, 𐐫𐑉 𐐰𐑋𐐲𐑍 𐐫𐑊 𐑄 𐐹𐐨𐐹𐑊 𐐱𐑂 𐐘𐐪𐐼 𐐺𐐨𐐿𐐫𐑆 𐐱𐑂 𐑄𐐯𐑉 𐐮𐑌𐐮𐐿𐐶𐐮𐐻𐐮𐑆 𐐰𐑌𐐼 𐑄𐐯𐑉 𐐻𐑉𐐰𐐼𐐮𐑇𐐲𐑌𐑆, 𐐸𐐨 𐑁𐐯𐑊 𐐲𐐹𐐪𐑌 𐐸𐐮𐑆 𐑌𐐨𐑆, 𐐰𐑌𐐼 𐐺𐐨𐑀𐐰𐑌 𐐻𐐭 𐐹𐐬𐑉 𐐵𐐻 𐐸𐐮𐑆 𐑅𐐬𐑊 𐐮𐑌 𐐹𐑉𐐯𐑉 𐐰𐑌𐐼 𐑃𐐰𐑍𐐿𐑅𐑀𐐮𐑂𐐮𐑍 𐐻𐐭 𐐘𐐪𐐼, 𐑁𐐫𐑉 𐐸𐐶𐐪𐐻 𐐸𐐨 𐐸𐐰𐐼 𐐼𐐲𐑌 𐑁𐐫𐑉 𐐸𐐮𐑆 𐐺𐑉𐐯𐑄𐑉𐐯𐑌; 𐐰𐑌𐐼 𐐸𐐨 𐐶𐐪𐑆 𐐫𐑊𐑅𐐬 𐐬𐑂𐐲𐑉𐐹𐐵𐐲𐑉𐐼 𐐶𐐮𐑄 𐐾𐐦; 𐐰𐑌𐐼 𐑄𐐲𐑅 𐑄𐐩 𐐫𐑊 𐑃𐑉𐐨 𐐸𐐰𐐼 𐑅𐐲𐑍𐐿 𐐻𐐭 𐑄 𐐲𐑉𐑃. 𐐤𐐵, 𐐸𐐶𐐯𐑌 𐑄 𐑅𐐲𐑉𐑂𐐲𐑌𐐻𐑅 𐐱𐑂 𐑄 𐐿𐐮𐑍 𐐸𐐰𐐼 𐑅𐐨𐑌 𐑄𐐰𐐻 𐑄𐐩 𐐸𐐰𐐼 𐑁𐐫𐑊𐐲𐑌, 𐑄𐐩 𐐫𐑊𐑅𐐬 𐐺𐐨𐑀𐐰𐑌 𐐻𐐭 𐐿𐑉𐐴 𐐲𐑌𐐻𐐭 𐐘𐐪𐐼, 𐑁𐐫𐑉 𐑄 𐑁𐐨𐑉 𐐱𐑂 𐑄 𐐢𐐫𐑉𐐼 𐐸𐐰𐐼 𐐿𐐲𐑋 𐐲𐐹𐐪𐑌 𐑄𐐯𐑋 𐐫𐑊𐑅𐐬, 𐑁𐐫𐑉 𐐮𐐻 𐐶𐐪𐑆 𐑄𐐩 𐐸𐐭 𐐸𐐰𐐼 𐑅𐐻𐐳𐐼 𐐺𐐨𐑁𐐬𐑉 𐑄 𐐿𐐮𐑍, 𐐰𐑌𐐼 𐐻𐐯𐑅𐐻𐐮𐑁𐐴𐐼 𐐲𐑌𐐻𐐭 𐐸𐐮𐑋 𐐿𐐪𐑌𐑅𐐲𐑉𐑌𐐮𐑍 𐑄 𐑀𐑉𐐩𐐻 𐐹𐐵𐐲𐑉 𐐱𐑂 𐐈𐑋𐐲𐑌.

18. 𐐰𐑌𐐼 𐐮𐐻 𐐿𐐩𐑋 𐐻𐐭 𐐹𐐩𐑅 𐑄𐐰𐐻 𐑄𐐩 𐐼𐐮𐐼 𐐿𐐫𐑊 𐐪𐑌 𐑄 𐑌𐐩𐑋 𐐱𐑂 𐑄 𐐢𐐫𐑉𐐼, 𐐮𐑌 𐑄𐐯𐑉 𐑋𐐴𐐻, 𐐨𐑂𐐲𐑌 𐐲𐑌𐐻𐐮𐑊 𐑄𐐩 𐐸𐐰𐐼 𐐫𐑊 𐑁𐐫𐑊𐐲𐑌 𐐻𐐭 𐑄 𐐲𐑉𐑃, 𐑅𐐩𐑂 𐐮𐐻 𐐶𐐲𐑉 𐐶𐐲𐑌 𐐱𐑂 𐑄 𐐢𐐩𐑋𐐲𐑌𐐴𐐻𐐮𐑇 𐐶𐐮𐑋𐐯𐑌, 𐐸𐐭𐑆 𐑌𐐩𐑋 𐐶𐐪𐑆 𐐁𐐺𐐮𐑇, 𐑇𐐨 𐐸𐐰𐑂𐐮𐑍 𐐺𐐮𐑌 𐐿𐐪𐑌𐑂𐐲𐑉𐐻𐐯𐐼 𐐲𐑌𐐻𐐭 𐑄 𐐢𐐫𐑉𐐼 𐑁𐐫𐑉 𐑋𐐯𐑌𐐨 𐐷𐐨𐑉𐑆, 𐐪𐑌 𐐰𐐿𐐵𐑌𐐻 𐐱𐑂 𐐩 𐑉𐐨𐑋𐐪𐑉𐐿𐐲𐐺𐑊 𐑂𐐮𐑈𐐲𐑌 𐐱𐑂 𐐸𐐲𐑉 𐑁𐐪𐑄𐐲𐑉; 𐑄𐐲𐑅 𐐸𐐰𐑂𐐮𐑍 𐐺𐐮𐑌 𐐿𐐪𐑌𐑂𐐲𐑉𐐻𐐯𐐼 𐐻𐐭 𐑄 𐐢𐐫𐑉𐐼, 𐐰𐑌𐐼 𐑌𐐯𐑂𐐲𐑉 𐐸𐐰𐑂𐐮𐑍 𐑋𐐩𐐼 𐐮𐐻 𐑌𐐬𐑌; 𐑄𐐯𐑉𐑁𐐬𐑉, 𐐸𐐶𐐯𐑌 𐑇𐐨 𐑅𐐫 𐑄𐐰𐐻 𐐫𐑊 𐑄 𐑅𐐲𐑉𐑂𐐲𐑌𐐻𐑅 𐐱𐑂 𐐢𐐩𐑋𐐬𐑌𐐴 𐐸𐐰𐐼 𐑁𐐫𐑊𐐲𐑌 𐐻𐐭 𐑄 𐐲𐑉𐑃, 𐐰𐑌𐐼 𐐫𐑊𐑅𐐬 𐐸𐐲𐑉 𐑋𐐮𐑅𐐻𐑉𐐯𐑅, 𐑄 𐐿𐐶𐐨𐑌, 𐐰𐑌𐐼 𐑄 𐐿𐐮𐑍, 𐐰𐑌𐐼 𐐈𐑋𐐲𐑌 𐑊𐐩 𐐹𐑉𐐪𐑅-𐐻𐑉𐐩𐐻 𐐲𐐹𐐪𐑌 𐑄 𐐲𐑉𐑃, 𐑇𐐨 𐑌𐐭 𐑄𐐰𐐻 𐐮𐐻 𐐶𐐪𐑆 𐑄 𐐹𐐵𐐲𐑉 𐐱𐑂 𐐘𐐪𐐼; 𐐰𐑌𐐼 𐑅𐐲𐐹𐐬𐑆𐐮𐑍 𐑄𐐰𐐻 𐑄𐐮𐑅 𐐪𐐹𐐲𐑉-𐐻𐐷𐐭𐑌𐐮𐐻𐐨, 𐐺𐐴 𐑋𐐩𐐿𐐮𐑍 𐑌𐐬𐑌 𐐲𐑌𐐻𐐭 𐑄 𐐹𐐨𐐹𐑊 𐐸𐐶𐐪𐐻 𐐸𐐰𐐼 𐐸𐐰𐐹𐐲𐑌𐐼 𐐰𐑋𐐲𐑍 𐑄𐐯𐑋, 𐑄𐐰𐐻 𐐺𐐴 𐐺𐐨𐐸𐐬𐑊𐐼𐐮𐑍 𐑄𐐮𐑅 𐑅𐐨𐑌, 𐐮𐐻 𐐶𐐳𐐼 𐐿𐐫𐑆 𐑄𐐯𐑋 𐐻𐐭 𐐺𐐨𐑊𐐨𐑂 𐐮𐑌 𐑄 𐐹𐐵𐐲𐑉 𐐱𐑂 𐐘𐐪𐐼, 𐑄𐐯𐑉𐑁𐐬𐑉 𐑇𐐨 𐑉𐐰𐑌 𐑁𐐬𐑉𐑃 𐑁𐑉𐐲𐑋 𐐸𐐵𐑅 𐐻𐐭 𐐸𐐵𐑅, 𐑋𐐩𐐿𐐮𐑍 𐐮𐐻 𐑌𐐬𐑌 𐐲𐑌𐐻𐐭 𐑄 𐐹𐐨𐐹𐑊; 𐐰𐑌𐐼 𐑄𐐩 𐐺𐐨𐑀𐐰𐑌 𐐻𐐭 𐐰𐑅𐐯𐑋𐐺𐑊 𐑄𐐯𐑋-𐑅𐐯𐑊𐑂𐑆 𐐻𐐭𐑀𐐯𐑄𐐲𐑉 𐐲𐑌𐐻𐐭 𐑄 𐐸𐐵𐑅 𐐱𐑂 𐑄 𐐿𐐮𐑍. 𐐰𐑌𐐼 𐑄𐐯𐑉 𐐿𐐩𐑋 𐐩 𐑋𐐲𐑊𐐻𐐮𐐻𐐷𐐭𐐼, 𐐰𐑌𐐼 𐐻𐐭 𐑄𐐯𐑉 𐐰𐑅𐐻𐐪𐑌𐐮𐑇𐑋𐐯𐑌𐐻, 𐑄𐐩 𐐺𐐨𐐸𐐯𐑊𐐼 𐑄 𐐿𐐮𐑍, 𐐰𐑌𐐼 𐑄 𐐿𐐶𐐨𐑌, 𐐰𐑌𐐼 𐑄𐐯𐑉 𐑅𐐲𐑉𐑂𐐲𐑌𐐻𐑅 𐐹𐑉𐐪𐑅𐐻𐑉𐐩𐐻 𐐲𐐹𐐪𐑌 𐑄 𐐲𐑉𐑃, 𐐰𐑌𐐼 𐑄𐐩 𐐫𐑊 𐑊𐐩 𐑄𐐯𐑉 𐐰𐑆 𐑄𐐬 𐑄𐐩 𐐶𐐲𐑉 𐐼𐐯𐐼; 𐐰𐑌𐐼 𐑄𐐩 𐐫𐑊𐑅𐐬 𐑅𐐫 𐐈𐑋𐐲𐑌, 𐐰𐑌𐐼 𐐺𐐨𐐸𐐬𐑊𐐼, 𐐸𐐨 𐐶𐐪𐑆 𐐩 𐐤𐐨𐑁𐐴𐐻. 𐐰𐑌𐐼 𐑌𐐵 𐑄 𐐹𐐨𐐹𐑊 𐐺𐐨𐑀𐐰𐑌 𐐻𐐭 𐑋𐐲𐑉𐑋𐐲𐑉 𐐰𐑋𐐲𐑍 𐑄𐐯𐑋𐑅𐐯𐑊𐑂𐑆; 𐑅𐐲𐑋 𐑅𐐩𐐮𐑍 𐑄𐐰𐐻 𐐮𐐻 𐐶𐐪𐑆 𐐩 𐑀𐑉𐐩𐐻 𐐨𐑂𐐮𐑊 𐑄𐐰𐐻 𐐸𐐰𐐼 𐐿𐐲𐑋 𐐲𐐹𐐪𐑌 𐑄𐐯𐑋, 𐐫𐑉 𐐲𐐹𐐪𐑌 𐑄 𐐿𐐮𐑍 𐐰𐑌𐐼 𐐸𐐮𐑆 𐐸𐐵𐑅, 𐐺𐐨-𐐿𐐫𐑆 𐐸𐐨 𐐸𐐰𐐼 𐑅𐐲𐑁𐐲𐑉𐐼 𐑄𐐰𐐻 𐑄 𐐤𐐨𐑁𐐴𐐻 𐑇𐐳𐐼 𐑉𐐨𐑋𐐩𐑌 𐐮𐑌 𐑄 𐑊𐐰𐑌𐐼. 𐐒𐐲𐐻 𐐲𐑄𐐲𐑉𐑆 𐑉𐐨𐐺𐐷𐐭𐐿𐐻 𐑄𐐯𐑋, 𐑅𐐩𐐮𐑍, 𐐜 𐐿𐐮𐑍 𐐸𐐰𐑃 𐐺𐑉𐐫𐐻 𐑄𐐮𐑅 𐐨𐑂𐐮𐑊 𐐲𐐹𐐪𐑌 𐐸𐐮𐑆 𐐸𐐵𐑅, 𐐺𐐨𐐿𐐫𐑆 𐐸𐐨 𐑅𐑊𐐭 𐐸𐐮𐑆 𐑅𐐲𐑉𐑂𐐲𐑌𐐻𐑅 𐐸𐐭 𐐸𐐰𐐼 𐐸𐐰𐐼 𐑄𐐯𐑉 𐑁𐑊𐐪𐐿𐑅 𐑅𐐿𐐰𐐻𐐲𐑉𐐼 𐐰𐐻 𐑄 𐐶𐐫𐐻𐐲𐑉𐑆 𐐱𐑂 𐐝𐐨𐐺𐐲𐑅; 𐐰𐑌𐐼 𐑄𐐩 𐐶𐐲𐑉 𐐫𐑊𐑅𐐬 𐑉𐐨𐐺𐐷𐐭𐐿𐐻 𐐺𐐴 𐑄𐐬𐑆 𐑋𐐯𐑌 𐐸𐐭 𐐸𐐰𐐼 𐑅𐐻𐐳𐐼 𐐰𐐻 𐑄 𐐶𐐫𐐻𐐲𐑉𐑆 𐐱𐑂 𐐝𐐨𐐺𐐲𐑅, 𐐰𐑌𐐼 𐑅𐐿𐐰𐐻𐐲𐑉𐐼 𐑄 𐑁𐑊𐐪𐐿𐑅 𐐸𐐶𐐮𐐽 𐐺𐐨𐑊𐐫𐑍𐐼 𐐻𐐭 𐑄 𐐿𐐮𐑍, 𐑁𐐫𐑉 𐑄𐐩 𐐶𐐲𐑉 𐐰𐑍𐑀𐑉𐐨 𐐶𐐮𐑄 𐐈𐑋𐐲𐑌 𐐺𐐨𐐿𐐫𐑆 𐐱𐑂 𐑄 𐑌𐐲𐑋𐐺𐐲𐑉 𐐸𐐶𐐮𐐽 𐐸𐐨 𐐸𐐰𐐼 𐑅𐑊𐐩𐑌 𐐱𐑂 𐑄𐐯𐑉 𐐺𐑉𐐯𐑄𐑉𐐯𐑌 𐐰𐐻 𐑄 𐐶𐐫𐐻𐐲𐑉𐑆 𐐱𐑂 𐐝𐐨𐐺𐐲𐑅, 𐐸𐐶𐐴𐑊 𐐼𐐨𐑁𐐯𐑌𐐼𐐮𐑍 𐑄 𐑁𐑊𐐪𐐿𐑅 𐐱𐑂 𐑄 𐐿𐐮𐑍. 𐐤𐐵, 𐐶𐐲𐑌 𐐱𐑂 𐑄𐐯𐑋, 𐐸𐐭𐑆 𐐺𐑉𐐲𐑄𐐲𐑉 𐐸𐐰𐐼 𐐺𐐮𐑌 𐑅𐑊𐐩𐑌 𐐶𐐮𐑄 𐑄 𐑅𐐬𐑉𐐼 𐐱𐑂 𐐈𐑋𐐲𐑌, 𐐺𐐨𐐮𐑍 𐐯𐐿𐑅𐐨𐐼𐐮𐑍𐑊𐐨

𐐰𐑍𐑀𐑉𐐨 𐐶𐐮𐑄 𐐈𐑋𐐲𐑌, 𐐼𐑉𐐭 𐐸𐐮𐑆 𐑅𐐬𐑉𐐼 𐐰𐑌𐐼 𐐶𐐯𐑌𐐻 𐑁𐐫𐑉𐑃 𐑄𐐰𐐻 𐐸𐐨 𐑋𐐴𐐻 𐑊𐐯𐐻 𐐮𐐻 𐑁𐐫𐑊 𐐲𐐹𐐱𐑌 𐐈𐑋𐐲𐑌, 𐐻𐐭 𐑅𐑊𐐩 𐐸𐐮𐑋; 𐐰𐑌𐐼 𐐰𐑆 𐐸𐐨 𐑊𐐮𐑁𐐻𐐯𐐼 𐑄 𐑅𐐬𐑉𐐼 𐐻𐐭 𐑅𐑋𐐴𐐻 𐐸𐐮𐑋, 𐐺𐐨𐐸𐐬𐑊𐐼, 𐐸𐐨 𐑁𐐯𐑊 𐐼𐐯𐐼. 𐐤𐐵 𐐶𐐨 𐑅𐐨 𐑄𐐰𐐻 𐐈𐑋𐐲𐑌 𐐿𐐳𐐼 𐑌𐐱𐐻 𐐺𐐨 𐑅𐑊𐐩𐑌, 𐑁𐐫𐑉 𐑄 𐐢𐐫𐑉𐐼 𐐸𐐰𐐼 𐑅𐐯𐐼 𐐲𐑌𐐻𐐭 𐐣𐐬𐑅𐐴𐐲, 𐐸𐐮𐑆 𐑁𐐪𐑄𐐲𐑉, 𐐌 𐐶𐐮𐑊 𐑅𐐹𐐩𐑉 𐐸𐐮𐑋, 𐐰𐑌𐐼 𐐮𐐻 𐑇𐐰𐑊 𐐺𐐨 𐐲𐑌𐐻𐐭 𐐸𐐮𐑋 𐐰𐐿𐐫𐑉𐐼𐐮𐑍 𐐻𐐭 𐑄𐐴 𐑁𐐩𐑃; 𐑄𐐩𐑉𐑁𐐫𐑉, 𐐣𐐬𐑅𐐴𐐲 𐐻𐑉𐐲𐑅𐐻𐐯𐐼 𐐸𐐮𐑋 𐐲𐑌𐐻𐐭 𐑄 𐐢𐐫𐑉𐐼.

19. 𐐈𐑌𐐼 𐐮𐐻 𐐿𐐩𐑋 𐐻𐐭 𐐹𐐰𐑅 𐑄𐐰𐐻 𐐸𐐶𐐯𐑌 𐑄 𐑋𐐲𐑊𐐻𐐮𐐻𐐭𐐼 𐐺𐐨𐐸𐐯𐑊𐐼 𐑄𐐰𐐻 𐑄 𐑋𐐰𐑌 𐐸𐐰𐐼 𐑁𐐫𐑊𐐯𐑌 𐐼𐐯𐐼, 𐐸𐐭 𐑊𐐮𐑁𐐻𐐯𐐼 𐑄 𐑅𐐬𐑉𐐼 𐐻𐐭 𐑅𐑊𐐩 𐐈𐑋𐐲𐑌, 𐑁𐐨𐑉 𐐿𐐩𐑋 𐐲𐐹𐐱𐑌 𐑄𐐯𐑋 𐐫𐑊, 𐐰𐑌𐐼 𐑄𐐩 𐐼𐐲𐑉𐑅𐐻 𐑌𐐱𐐻 𐐹𐐳𐐻 𐑁𐐫𐑉𐑃 𐑄𐐩𐑉 𐐸𐐰𐑌𐐼𐑆 𐐻𐐭 𐐻𐐲𐐽 𐐸𐐮𐑋, 𐐫𐑉 𐐯𐑌𐐨 𐐱𐑂 𐑄𐐬𐑆 𐐸𐐭 𐐸𐐰𐐼 𐑁𐐫𐑊𐐯𐑌; 𐐰𐑌𐐼 𐑄𐐩 𐐺𐐨𐑀𐐰𐑌 𐐻𐐭 𐑋𐐪𐑉𐑂𐐯𐑊 𐐰𐑀𐐯𐑌 𐐰𐑋𐐲𐑍 𐑄𐐯𐑋𐑅𐐯𐑊𐑂𐑆 𐐸𐐶𐐱𐐻 𐐿𐐳𐐼 𐐺𐐨 𐑄 𐐿𐐫𐑆 𐐱𐑂 𐑄𐐮𐑅 𐑀𐑉𐐩𐐻 𐐹𐐵𐐲𐑉, 𐐫𐑉 𐐸𐐶𐐱𐐻 𐐫𐑊 𐑄𐐨𐑆 𐑃𐐮𐑍𐑆 𐐿𐐳𐐼 𐑋𐐨𐑌.

20. 𐐈𐑌𐐼 𐐮𐐻 𐐿𐐩𐑋 𐐻𐐭 𐐹𐐰𐑅 𐑄𐐰𐐻 𐑄𐐩𐑉 𐐶𐐲𐑉 𐑋𐐯𐑌𐐨 𐐰𐑋𐐲𐑍 𐑄𐐯𐑋 𐐸𐐭 𐑅𐐯𐐼 𐑄𐐰𐐻 𐐈𐑋𐐲𐑌 𐐶𐐱𐑆 𐑄 𐐘𐑉𐐩𐐻 𐐝𐐹𐐮𐑉𐐮𐐻, 𐐰𐑌𐐼 𐐲𐑄𐐲𐑉𐑆 𐑅𐐯𐐼 𐐸𐐨 𐐶𐐱𐑆 𐑅𐐯𐑌𐐻 𐐺𐐴 𐑄 𐐘𐑉𐐩𐐻 𐐝𐐹𐐮𐑉𐐮𐐻; 𐐺𐐲𐐻 𐐲𐑄𐐲𐑉𐑆 𐑉𐐨𐐺𐐭𐐿𐐻 𐑄𐐯𐑋 𐐫𐑊, 𐑅𐐩𐐮𐑍, 𐐜𐐰𐐻 𐐸𐐨 𐐶𐐱𐑆 𐐲 𐑋𐐱𐑌𐑅𐐻𐐲𐑉, 𐐸𐐭 𐐸𐐰𐐼 𐐺𐐮𐑌 𐑅𐐯𐑌𐐻 𐑁𐑉𐐱𐑋 𐑄 𐐤𐐨𐑁𐐴𐐻𐑅 𐐻𐐭 𐐻𐐫𐑉𐑋𐐯𐑌𐐻 𐑄𐐯𐑋. 𐐈𐑌𐐼 𐑄𐐩𐑉 𐐶𐐲𐑉 𐑅𐐲𐑋 𐐸𐐭 𐑅𐐯𐐼 𐑄𐐰𐐻 𐐈𐑋𐐲𐑌 𐐶𐐱𐑆 𐑅𐐯𐑌𐐻 𐐺𐐴 𐑄 𐐘𐑉𐐩𐐻 𐐝𐐹𐐮𐑉𐐮𐐻 𐐻𐐭 𐐰𐑁𐑊𐐮𐐿𐐻 𐑄𐐯𐑋 𐐺𐐨𐐿𐐫𐑆 𐐱𐑂 𐑄𐐩𐑉 𐐮𐑌𐐮𐐿𐐶𐐮𐐻𐐨𐑆; 𐐰𐑌𐐼 𐑄𐐰𐐻 𐐮𐐻 𐐶𐐱𐑆 𐑄 𐐘𐑉𐐩𐐻 𐐝𐐹𐐮𐑉𐐮𐐻 𐑄𐐰𐐻 𐐸𐐰𐐼 𐐫𐑊𐐶𐐩𐑆 𐐰𐐻𐐯𐑌𐐼𐐯𐐼 𐑄 𐐤𐐨𐑁𐐴𐐻𐑅, 𐐸𐐭 𐐸𐐰𐐼 𐐯𐑂𐐲𐑉 𐐼𐐨𐑊𐐮𐑂𐐲𐑉𐐼 𐑄𐐯𐑋 𐐵𐐻 𐐱𐑂 𐑄𐐩𐑉 𐐸𐐰𐑌𐐼𐑆; 𐐰𐑌𐐼 𐑄𐐩 𐑅𐐯𐐼 𐑄𐐰𐐻 𐐮𐐻 𐐶𐐱𐑆 𐑄𐐮𐑅 𐐘𐑉𐐩𐐻 𐐝𐐹𐐮𐑉𐐮𐐻 𐐸𐐭 𐐸𐐰𐐼 𐐼𐐨𐑅𐐻𐑉𐐦𐐼 𐑅𐐬 𐑋𐐯𐑌𐐨 𐐱𐑂 𐑄𐐩𐑉 𐐺𐑉𐐯𐑄𐑉𐐯𐑌, 𐑄 𐐢𐐰𐑋𐐲𐑌𐐴𐐻𐑅. 𐐈𐑌𐐼 𐑄𐐲𐑅 𐑄 𐐿𐐱𐑌𐐻𐐯𐑌𐑇𐐲𐑌 𐐺𐐨𐑀𐐰𐑌 𐐻𐐭 𐐺𐐨 𐐯𐐿𐑅𐐨𐐼𐐮𐑍𐑊𐐨 𐑇𐐪𐑉𐐹 𐐰𐑋𐐲𐑍 𐑄𐐯𐑋. 𐐈𐑌𐐼 𐐸𐐶𐐴𐑊 𐑄𐐩 𐐶𐐲𐑉 𐑄𐐲𐑅 𐐿𐐱𐑌𐐻𐐯𐑌𐐼𐐮𐑍, 𐑄 𐐶𐐳𐑋𐐲𐑌 𐑅𐐲𐑉𐑂𐐲𐑌𐐻 𐐸𐐭 𐐸𐐰𐐼 𐐿𐐫𐑆𐐼 𐑄 𐑋𐐲𐑊𐐻𐐮𐐻𐐭𐐼 𐐻𐐭 𐐺𐐨 𐑀𐐰𐑄𐐲𐑉𐐼 𐐻𐐭𐑀𐐯𐑄𐐲𐑉 𐐿𐐩𐑋, 𐐰𐑌𐐼 𐐸𐐶𐐯𐑌 𐑇𐐨 𐑅𐐫 𐑄 𐐿𐐱𐑌𐐻𐐯𐑌𐑇𐐲𐑌 𐐸𐐶𐐮𐐽 𐐶𐐱𐑆 𐐰𐑋𐐲𐑍 𐑄 𐑋𐐲𐑊𐐻𐐮𐐻𐐭𐐼 𐑇𐐨 𐐶𐐱𐑆 𐐯𐐿𐑅𐐨𐐼𐐮𐑍𐑊𐐨 𐑅𐐱𐑉𐐬𐑁𐐳𐑊, 𐐨𐑂𐐯𐑌 𐐲𐑌𐐻𐐭 𐐻𐐨𐑉𐑆.

21. 𐐈𐑌𐐼 𐐮𐐻 𐐿𐐩𐑋 𐐻𐐭 𐐹𐐰𐑅 𐑄𐐰𐐻 𐑇𐐨 𐐶𐐯𐑌𐐻 𐐰𐑌𐐼 𐐻𐐳𐐿 𐑄 𐐿𐐶𐐨𐑌 𐐺𐐴 𐑄 𐐸𐐰𐑌𐐼, 𐑄𐐰𐐻 𐐹𐐲𐑉𐐸𐐰𐐹𐑅 𐑇𐐨 𐑋𐐴𐐻 𐑉𐐩𐑆 𐐸𐐲𐑉 𐑁𐑉𐐱𐑋 𐑄 𐑀𐑉𐐵𐑌𐐼; 𐐰𐑌𐐼 𐐰𐑆 𐑅𐐭𐑌 𐐰𐑆 𐑇𐐨 𐐻𐐲𐐽𐐻 𐐸𐐲𐑉 𐐸𐐰𐑌𐐼 𐑇𐐨 𐐲𐑉𐐬𐑆 𐐰𐑌𐐼 𐑅𐐻𐐳𐐼 𐐲𐐹𐐱𐑌 𐐸𐐲𐑉 𐑁𐐨𐐻, 𐐰𐑌𐐼 𐐿𐑉𐐴𐐼 𐐶𐐮𐑄 𐐲 𐑊𐐵𐐼 𐑂𐐦𐑅, 𐑅𐐩𐐮𐑍, 𐐄 𐐺𐑊𐐯𐑅𐐯𐐼 𐐖𐐨𐑆𐐲𐑅, 𐐸𐐭 𐐸𐐰𐑆 𐑅𐐩𐑂𐐼 𐑋𐐨 𐑁𐑉𐐱𐑋 𐐰𐑌 𐐫𐑁𐐳𐑊 𐐸𐐯𐑊! 𐐄 𐐺𐑊𐐯𐑅𐐯𐐼 𐐘𐐱𐐼, 𐐸𐐰𐑂 𐑋𐐲𐑉𐑅𐐨 𐐱𐑌 𐑄𐐮𐑅 𐐹𐐨𐐹𐑊! 𐐈𐑌𐐼 𐐸𐐶𐐯𐑌 𐑇𐐨 𐐸𐐰𐐼 𐑅𐐯𐐼 𐑄𐐮𐑅, 𐑇𐐨 𐐿𐑊𐐰𐑅𐐹𐐻 𐐸𐐲𐑉 𐐸𐐰𐑌𐐼𐑆, 𐐺𐐨𐐮𐑍 𐑁𐐮𐑊𐐼 𐐶𐐮𐑄 𐐾𐐦, 𐑅𐐹𐐨𐐿𐐮𐑍 𐑋𐐯𐑌𐐨 𐐶𐐲𐑉𐐼𐑆 𐐸𐐶𐐮𐐽 𐐶𐐲𐑉 𐑌𐐱𐐻 𐐲𐑌𐐼𐐲𐑉𐑅𐐻𐐳𐐼; 𐐰𐑌𐐼 𐐸𐐶𐐯𐑌 𐑇𐐨 𐐸𐐰𐐼 𐐼𐐲𐑌 𐑄𐐮𐑅, 𐑇𐐨 𐐻𐐳𐐿 𐑄 𐐿𐐮𐑍, 𐐢𐐰𐑋𐐬𐑌𐐴, 𐐺𐐴 𐑄 𐐸𐐰𐑌𐐼, 𐐰𐑌𐐼 𐐺𐐨𐐸𐐬𐑊𐐼 𐐸𐐨 𐐲𐑉𐐬𐑆 𐐰𐑌𐐼 𐑅𐐻𐐳𐐼 𐐲𐐹𐐱𐑌 𐐸𐐮𐑆 𐑁𐐨𐐻; 𐐰𐑌𐐼 𐐸𐐨 𐐮𐑋𐐨𐐼𐐨𐐲𐐻𐑊𐐨, 𐑅𐐨𐐮𐑍 𐑄 𐐿𐐱𐑌𐐻𐐯𐑌𐑇𐐲𐑌 𐐰𐑋𐐲𐑍 𐐸𐐮𐑆 𐐹𐐨𐐹𐑊, 𐐶𐐯𐑌𐐻 𐑁𐐫𐑉𐑃 𐐰𐑌𐐼 𐐺𐐨𐑀𐐰𐑌 𐐻𐐭 𐑉𐐨𐐺𐐭𐐿 𐑄𐐯𐑋, 𐐰𐑌𐐼 𐐻𐐭 𐐻𐐨𐐽 𐑄𐐯𐑋 𐑄 𐐶𐐲𐑉𐐼𐑆 𐐸𐐶𐐮𐐽 𐐸𐐨 𐐸𐐰𐐼 𐐸𐐲𐑉𐐼 𐑁𐑉𐐱𐑋 𐑄 𐑋𐐵𐑃 𐐱𐑂 𐐈𐑋𐐲𐑌; 𐐰𐑌𐐼 𐐰𐑆 𐑋𐐯𐑌𐐨 𐐰𐑆 𐐸𐐲𐑉𐐼 𐐸𐐮𐑆 𐐶𐐲𐑉𐐼𐑆 𐐺𐐨𐑊𐐨𐑂𐐼, 𐐰𐑌𐐼 𐐶𐐲𐑉 𐐿𐐱𐑌𐑂𐐲𐑉𐐻𐐯𐐼 𐐲𐑌𐐻𐐭 𐑄 𐐢𐐫𐑉𐐼. 𐐒𐐲𐐻 𐑄𐐩𐑉 𐐶𐐲𐑉 𐑋𐐯𐑌𐐨 𐐰𐑋𐐲𐑍 𐑄𐐯𐑋 𐐸𐐭 𐐶𐐳𐐼 𐑌𐐱𐐻 𐐸𐐨𐑉 𐐸𐐮𐑆 𐐶𐐲𐑉𐐼𐑆; 𐑄𐐩𐑉𐑁𐐫𐑉 𐑄𐐩 𐐶𐐯𐑌𐐻 𐑄𐐩𐑉 𐐶𐐩.

22. 𐐈𐑌𐐼 𐐮𐐻 𐐿𐐩𐑋 𐐻𐐭 𐐹𐐰𐑅 𐑄𐐰𐐻 𐐸𐐶𐐯𐑌 𐐈𐑋𐐲𐑌 𐐲𐑉𐐬𐑆, 𐐸𐐨 𐐫𐑊𐑅𐐬 𐐰𐐼𐑋𐐮𐑌𐐮𐑅𐐻𐐲𐑉𐐼 𐐲𐑌𐐻𐐭 𐑄𐐯𐑋, 𐐰𐑌𐐼 𐐫𐑊𐑅𐐬 𐐼𐐮𐐼 𐐫𐑊 𐑄 𐑅𐐲𐑉𐑂𐐲𐑌𐐻𐑅 𐐱𐑂 𐐢𐐰𐑋𐐬𐑌𐐴; 𐐰𐑌𐐼 𐑄𐐩 𐐼𐐮𐐼 𐐫𐑊 𐐼𐐨𐐿𐑊𐐩𐑉 𐐲𐑌𐐻𐐭 𐑄 𐐹𐐨𐐹𐑊 𐑄 𐑅𐐯𐑊𐑁-𐑅𐐩𐑋 𐑃𐐮𐑍: 𐑄𐐰𐐻 𐑄𐐩𐑉 𐐸𐐪𐑉𐐻𐑅 𐐸𐐰𐐼 𐐺𐐮𐑌 𐐽𐐩𐑌𐐾𐐼; 𐑄𐐰𐐻 𐑄𐐩 𐐸𐐰𐐼 𐑌𐐬 𐑋𐐬𐑉 𐐼𐐨𐑆𐐴𐑉 𐐻𐐭 𐐼𐐭 𐐨𐑂𐐮𐑊. 𐐈𐑌𐐼 𐐺𐐨𐐸𐐬𐑊𐐼, 𐑋𐐯𐑌𐐨 𐐼𐐮𐐼 𐐼𐐨𐐿𐑊𐐩𐑉 𐐲𐑌𐐻𐐭 𐑄 𐐹𐐨𐐹𐑊 𐑄𐐰𐐻 𐑄𐐩 𐐸𐐰𐐼 𐑅𐐨𐑌 𐐩𐑌𐐾𐐯𐑊𐑆 𐐰𐑌𐐼 𐐸𐐰𐐼 𐐿𐐱𐑌𐑂𐐲𐑉𐑅𐐼 𐐶𐐮𐑄 𐑄𐐯𐑋: 𐐰𐑌𐐼 𐑄𐐲𐑅 𐑄𐐩 𐐸𐐰𐐼 𐐻𐐬𐑊𐐼 𐑄𐐯𐑋 𐑃𐐮𐑍𐑆 𐐱𐑂 𐐘𐐱𐐼, 𐐰𐑌𐐼 𐐱𐑂 𐐸𐐮𐑆 𐑉𐐴𐐽𐐲𐑅𐑌𐐯𐑅. 𐐈𐑌𐐼 𐐮𐐻 𐐿𐐩𐑋 𐐻𐐭 𐐹𐐰𐑅 𐑄𐐰𐐻 𐑄𐐩𐑉 𐐶𐐲𐑉 𐑋𐐯𐑌𐐨 𐑄𐐰𐐻 𐐼𐐮𐐼 𐐺𐐨𐑊𐐨𐑂 𐐮𐑌 𐑄𐐩𐑉 𐐶𐐲𐑉𐐼𐑆; 𐐰𐑌𐐼 𐐰𐑆 𐑋𐐯𐑌𐐨 𐐰𐑆 𐐼𐐮𐐼 𐐺𐐨𐑊𐐨𐑂 𐐶𐐲𐑉 𐐺𐐰𐐹𐐻𐐴𐑆𐐼; 𐐰𐑌𐐼 𐑄𐐩 𐐺𐐨𐐿𐐩𐑋 𐐲 𐑉𐐴𐐽𐐲𐑅 𐐹𐐨𐐹𐑊, 𐐰𐑌𐐼 𐑄𐐩 𐐼𐐮𐐼 𐐯𐑅𐐻𐐰𐐺𐑊𐐮𐑇 𐐲 𐐽𐐲𐑉𐐽 𐐰𐑋𐐲𐑍 𐑄𐐯𐑋: 𐐰𐑌𐐼 𐑄𐐲𐑅 𐑄 𐐶𐐲𐑉𐐿 𐐱𐑂 𐑄 𐐢𐐫𐑉𐐼 𐐼𐐮𐐼 𐐿𐐱𐑋𐐯𐑌𐑅 𐐰𐑋𐐲𐑍 𐑄 𐐢𐐰𐑋𐐲𐑌𐐴𐐻𐑅; 𐑄𐐲𐑅 𐑄 𐐢𐐫𐑉𐐼 𐐼𐐮𐐼 𐐺𐐨𐑀𐐮𐑌 𐐻𐐭 𐐹𐐬𐑉 𐐵𐐻 𐐸𐐮𐑆 𐐝𐐹𐐮𐑉𐐮𐐻 𐐲𐐹𐐱𐑌 𐑄𐐯𐑋; 𐐰𐑌𐐼 𐐶𐐨 𐑅𐐨 𐑄𐐰𐐻 𐐸𐐮𐑆 𐐪𐑉𐑋 𐐮𐑆 𐐯𐐿𐑅𐐻𐐯𐑌𐐼𐐯𐐼 𐐻𐐭 𐐫𐑊 𐐹𐐨𐐹𐑊 𐐸𐐭 𐐶𐐮𐑊 𐑉𐐨𐐹𐐯𐑌𐐻 𐐰𐑌𐐼 𐐺𐐨𐑊𐐨𐑂 𐐱𐑌 𐐸𐐮𐑆 𐑌𐐩𐑋.

23. 𐐈𐑌𐐼 𐐮𐐻 𐐿𐐩𐑋 𐐻𐐭 𐐹𐐰𐑅 𐑄𐐰𐐻 𐐸𐐶𐐯𐑌 𐑄𐐩 𐐸𐐰𐐼 𐐯𐑅𐐻𐐰𐐺𐑊𐐮𐑇𐐻 𐐲 𐐽𐐲𐑉𐐽 𐐮𐑌 𐑄𐐰𐐻 𐑊𐐰𐑌𐐼, 𐑄𐐰𐐻 𐐿𐐮𐑍 𐐢𐐪𐑋𐐬𐑌𐐴 𐐼𐐨𐑆𐐴𐑉𐐼 𐑄𐐰𐐻 𐐈𐑋𐐲𐑌 𐑇𐐳𐐼 𐑀𐐬 𐐶𐐮𐑄 𐐸𐐮𐑋 𐐻𐐭 𐑄 𐑊𐐰𐑌𐐼 𐐱𐑂 𐐤𐐨𐑁𐐴, 𐑄𐐰𐐻 𐐸𐐨 𐑋𐐴𐐻 𐑇𐐬 𐐸𐐮𐑋 𐐲𐑌𐐻𐐭 𐐸𐐮𐑆 𐑁𐐪𐑄𐐲𐑉. 𐐈𐑌𐐼 𐑄 𐑂𐑎𐑅 𐐱𐑂 𐑄 𐐢𐐫𐑉𐐼 𐐿𐐩𐑋 𐐻𐐭 𐐈𐑋𐐲𐑌, 𐑅𐐩𐐮𐑍, 𐐜𐐵 𐑇𐐰𐑊𐐻 𐑌𐐱𐐻 𐑀𐐬 𐐲𐐹 𐐻𐐭 𐑄 𐑊𐐰𐑌𐐼 𐐱𐑂 𐐤𐐨𐑁𐐴, 𐑁𐐫𐑉 𐐺𐐨𐐸𐐬𐑊𐐼, 𐑄 𐐿𐐮𐑍 𐐶𐐮𐑊 𐑅𐐨𐐿 𐑄𐐴 𐑊𐐴𐑁; 𐐺𐐲𐐻 𐑄𐐵 𐑇𐐰𐑊𐐻 𐑀𐐬 𐐻𐐭 𐑄 𐑊𐐰𐑌𐐼 𐐱𐑂 𐐣𐐮𐐼𐐬𐑌𐐴; 𐑁𐐫𐑉 𐐺𐐨𐐸𐐬𐑊𐐼, 𐑄𐐴 𐐺𐑉𐐲𐑄𐐲𐑉 𐐁𐑉𐐲𐑌, 𐐰𐑌𐐼 𐐫𐑊𐑅𐐬 𐐣𐐭𐑊𐐬𐐿𐐴 𐐰𐑌𐐼 𐐈𐑋𐐪 𐐪𐑉 𐐮𐑌 𐐹𐑉𐐮𐑆𐐲𐑌.

24. 𐐤𐐵 𐐮𐐻 𐐿𐐩𐑋 𐐻𐐭 𐐹𐐰𐑅 𐑄𐐰𐐻 𐐸𐐶𐐯𐑌 𐐈𐑋𐐲𐑌 𐐸𐐰𐐼 𐐸𐐲𐑉𐐼 𐑄𐐮𐑅, 𐐸𐐨 𐑅𐐯𐐼 𐐲𐑌𐐻𐐭 𐐢𐐪𐑋𐐬𐑌𐐴, 𐐒𐐨𐐸𐐬𐑊𐐼, 𐑋𐐴 𐐺𐑉𐐲𐑄𐐲𐑉 𐐰𐑌𐐼 𐐺𐑉𐐯𐑄𐑉𐐯𐑌 𐐪𐑉 𐐮𐑌 𐐹𐑉𐐮𐑆𐐲𐑌 𐐰𐐻 𐐣𐐮𐐼𐐬𐑌𐐴, 𐐰𐑌𐐼 𐐌 𐑀𐐬 𐑄𐐰𐐻 𐐌 𐑋𐐩 𐐼𐐨𐑊𐐮𐑂𐐲𐑉 𐑄𐐯𐑋. 𐐤𐐵 𐐢𐐪𐑋𐐬𐑌𐐴 𐑅𐐯𐐼 𐐲𐑌𐐻𐐭 𐐈𐑋𐐲𐑌, 𐐌 𐑌𐐬 𐐮𐑌 𐑄 𐑅𐐻𐑉𐐯𐑍𐑃 𐐱𐑂 𐑄 𐐢𐐫𐑉𐐼 𐑄𐐵 𐐿𐐰𐑌𐑅𐐻 𐐼𐐭 𐐫𐑊 𐑃𐐮𐑍𐑆. 𐐒𐐲𐐻 𐐺𐐨𐐸𐐬𐑊𐐼 𐐌 𐐶𐐮𐑊 𐑀𐐬 𐐶𐐮𐑄 𐑄 𐐻𐐭 𐑄 𐑊𐐰𐑌𐐼 𐐱𐑂 𐐣𐐮𐐼𐐬𐑌𐐴; 𐑁𐐫𐑉 𐑄 𐐿𐐮𐑍 𐐱𐑂 𐑄 𐑊𐐰𐑌𐐼 𐐱𐑂 𐐣𐐮𐐼𐐬𐑌𐐴, 𐐸𐐭𐑆 𐑌𐐩𐑋 𐐮𐑆 𐐈𐑌𐐻𐐨𐐱𐑋𐑌𐐬, 𐐮𐑆 𐐲 𐑁𐑉𐐯𐑌𐐼 𐐲𐑌𐐻𐐭 𐑋𐐨; 𐑄𐐯𐑉𐑁𐐬𐑉 𐐌 𐑀𐐬 𐐻𐐭 𐑄 𐑊𐐰𐑌𐐼 𐐱𐑂 𐐣𐐮𐐼𐐬𐑌𐐴, 𐑄𐐰𐐻 𐐌 𐑋𐐩 𐑁𐑊𐐰𐐻𐐲𐑉 𐑄 𐐿𐐮𐑍; 𐐰𐑌𐐼 𐐸𐐨 𐐶𐐮𐑊 𐐿𐐰𐑅𐐻 𐑄𐐴 𐐺𐑉𐐯𐑄𐑉𐐯𐑌 𐐵𐐻 𐐱𐑂 𐐹𐑉𐐮𐑆𐐲𐑌. 𐐤𐐵 𐐢𐐪𐑋𐐬𐑌𐐴 𐑅𐐯𐐼 𐐲𐑌𐐻𐐭 𐐸𐐮𐑋, 𐐐𐐭 𐐻𐐬𐑊𐐼 𐑄 𐑄𐐰𐐻 𐑄𐐴 𐐺𐑉𐐯𐑄𐑉𐐯𐑌 𐐶𐐲𐑉 𐐮𐑌 𐐹𐑉𐐮𐑆𐐲𐑌? 𐐈𐑌𐐼 𐐈𐑋𐐲𐑌 𐑅𐐯𐐼 𐐲𐑌𐐻𐐭 𐐸𐐮𐑋, 𐐤𐐬 𐐶𐐲𐑌 𐐸𐐰𐑃 𐐻𐐬𐑊𐐼 𐑋𐐨, 𐑅𐐩𐑂 𐐮𐐻 𐐺 𐐘𐐱𐐼: 𐐰𐑌𐐼 𐐸𐐨 𐑅𐐯𐐼 𐐲𐑌𐐻𐐭 𐑋𐐨, 𐐘𐐬 𐐰𐑌𐐼 𐐼𐐨𐑊𐐮𐑂𐐲𐑉 𐑄𐐴 𐐺𐑉𐐯𐑄𐑉𐐯𐑌, 𐑁𐐫𐑉 𐑄𐐩 𐐪𐑉 𐐮𐑌 𐐹𐑉𐐮𐑆𐐲𐑌 𐐮𐑌 𐑄 𐑊𐐰𐑌𐐼 𐐱𐑂 𐐣𐐮𐐼𐐬𐑌𐐴. 𐐤𐐵 𐐸𐐶𐐯𐑌 𐐢𐐪𐑋𐐬𐑌𐐴 𐐸𐐰𐐼 𐐸𐐲𐑉𐐼 𐑄𐐮𐑅, 𐐸𐐨 𐐿𐐫𐑆𐐼 𐑄𐐰𐐻 𐐸𐐮𐑆 𐑅𐐲𐑉𐑂𐐰𐑌𐐻𐑅 𐑇𐐳𐐼 𐑋𐐩𐐿 𐑉𐐯𐐼𐐨 𐐸𐐮𐑆 𐐸𐐫𐑉𐑅𐐯𐑆 𐐰𐑌𐐼 𐐸𐐮𐑆 𐐽𐐰𐑉𐐨𐐲𐐻𐑅. 𐐈𐑌𐐼 𐐸𐐨 𐑅𐐯𐐼 𐐲𐑌𐐻𐐭 𐐈𐑋𐐲𐑌, 𐐗𐐲𐑋, 𐐌 𐐶𐐮𐑊 𐑀𐐬 𐐶𐐮𐑄 𐑄 𐐼𐐵𐑌 𐐻𐐭 𐑄 𐑊𐐰𐑌𐐼 𐐱𐑂 𐐣𐐮𐐼𐐬𐑌𐐴, 𐐰𐑌𐐼 𐑄𐐯𐑉 𐐌 𐐶𐐮𐑊 𐐹𐑊𐐨𐐼 𐐶𐐮𐑄 𐑄 𐐿𐐮𐑍, 𐑄𐐰𐐻 𐐸𐐨 𐐶𐐮𐑊 𐐿𐐰𐑅𐐻 𐑄𐐴 𐐺𐑉𐐯𐑄𐑉𐐯𐑌 𐐵𐐻 𐐱𐑂 𐐹𐑉𐐮𐑆𐐲𐑌.

25. 𐐈𐑌𐐼 𐐮𐐻 𐐿𐐩𐑋 𐐻𐐭 𐐹𐐰𐑅 𐑄𐐰𐐻 𐐰𐑆 𐐈𐑋𐐲𐑌 𐐰𐑌𐐼 𐐢𐐪𐑋𐐬𐑌𐐴 𐐶𐐲𐑉 𐐾𐐲𐑉𐑌𐐨𐐮𐑍 𐑄𐐮𐑄𐐲𐑉, 𐑄𐐰𐐻 𐑄𐐩 𐑋𐐯𐐻 𐑄 𐑁𐐪𐑄𐐲𐑉 𐐱𐑂 𐐢𐐪𐑋𐐬𐑌𐐴, 𐐸𐐭 𐐶𐐱𐑆 𐐿𐐮𐑍 𐐬𐑂𐐲𐑉 𐐫𐑊 𐑄 𐑊𐐰𐑌𐐼. 𐐈𐑌𐐼 𐐺𐐨𐐸𐐬𐑊𐐼, 𐑄 𐑁𐐪𐑄𐐲𐑉 𐐱𐑂 𐐢𐐪𐑋𐐬𐑌𐐴 𐑅𐐯𐐼 𐐲𐑌𐐻𐐭 𐐸𐐮𐑋, 𐐐𐐶𐐴 𐐼𐐮𐐼 𐐷 𐑌𐐱𐐻 𐐿𐐲𐑋 𐐻𐐭 𐑄 𐑁𐐨𐑅𐐻 𐐱𐑌 𐑄𐐰𐐻 𐑀𐑉𐐩𐐻 𐐼𐐩 𐐸𐐶𐐯𐑌 𐐌 𐑋𐐩𐐼 𐐲 𐑁𐐨𐑅𐐻 𐐲𐑌𐐻𐐭 𐑋𐐴 𐑅𐐲𐑌𐑆, 𐐰𐑌𐐼 𐐲𐑌𐐻𐐭 𐑋𐐴 𐐹𐐨𐐹𐑊? 𐐈𐑌𐐼 𐐸𐐨 𐐫𐑊𐑅𐐬 𐑅𐐯𐐼, 𐐐𐐶𐐮𐑄𐐲𐑉 𐐪𐑉𐐻 𐑄𐐵 𐑀𐐬𐐮𐑍 𐐶𐐮𐑄 𐑄𐐮𐑅 𐐤𐐨𐑁𐐴𐐻, 𐐸𐐭 𐐮𐑆 𐐶𐐲𐑌 𐐱𐑂 𐑄 𐐽𐐮𐑊𐐼𐑉𐐯𐑌 𐐱𐑂 𐐲 𐑊𐐴𐐲𐑉? 𐐈𐑌𐐼 𐐮𐐻 𐐿𐐩𐑋 𐐻𐐭 𐐹𐐰𐑅 𐑄𐐰𐐻 𐐢𐐪𐑋𐐬𐑌𐐴 𐑉𐐨𐐸𐐲𐑉𐑅𐐻 𐐲𐑌𐐻𐐭 𐐸𐐮𐑋 𐐸𐐶𐐮𐑄𐐲𐑉 𐐸𐐨 𐐶𐐱𐑆 𐑀𐐬𐐮𐑍, 𐑁𐐫𐑉 𐐸𐐨 𐑁𐐨𐑉𐐼 𐐻𐐭 𐐫𐑁𐐯𐑌𐐼 𐐸𐐮𐑋. 𐐈𐑌𐐼 𐐸𐐨 𐐫𐑊𐑅𐐬 𐐻𐐬𐑊𐐼 𐐸𐐮𐑋 𐐫𐑊 𐑄 𐐿𐐫𐑆 𐐱𐑂 𐐸𐐮𐑆 𐐻𐐰𐑉𐐨𐐮𐑍 𐐮𐑌 𐐸𐐮𐑆 𐐬𐑌 𐐿𐐮𐑍𐐼𐐲𐑋, 𐑄𐐰𐐻 𐐸𐐨 𐐼𐐮𐐼 𐑌𐐱𐐻 𐑀𐐬 𐐲𐑌𐐻𐐭 𐐸𐐮𐑆 𐑁𐐪𐑄𐐲𐑉 𐐻𐐭 𐑄 𐑁𐐨𐑅𐐻 𐐸𐐶𐐮𐐽 𐐸𐐨 𐐸𐐰𐐼 𐐹𐑉𐐨𐐹𐐩𐑉𐐼. 𐐈𐑌𐐼 𐑌𐐵 𐐸𐐶𐐯𐑌 𐐢𐐪𐑋𐐬𐑌𐐴 𐐸𐐰𐐼 𐑉𐐨𐐸𐐲𐑉𐑅𐐻 𐐲𐑌𐐻𐐭 𐐸𐐮𐑋 𐐫𐑊 𐑄𐐨𐑆 𐑃𐐮𐑍𐑆, 𐐺𐐨𐐸𐐬𐑊𐐼, 𐐻𐐭 𐐸𐐮𐑆 𐐲𐑅𐐻𐐱𐑌𐐮𐑇𐑋𐐯𐑌𐐻, 𐐸𐐮𐑆 𐑁𐐪𐑄𐐲𐑉 𐐶𐐱𐑆 𐐰𐑍𐑀𐑉𐐨 𐐶𐐮𐑄 𐐸𐐮𐑋, 𐐰𐑌𐐼 𐑅𐐯𐐼, 𐐢𐐪𐑋𐐬𐑌𐐴, 𐑄𐐵 𐐪𐑉𐐻 𐑀𐐬𐐮𐑍 𐐻𐐭 𐐼𐐨𐑊𐐮𐑂𐐲𐑉 𐑄𐐨𐑆 𐐤𐐨𐑁𐐴𐐻𐑅, 𐐸𐐭 𐐪𐑉 𐑅𐐲𐑌𐑆 𐐱𐑂 𐐲 𐑊𐐴𐐲𐑉. 𐐒𐐨𐐸𐐬𐑊𐐼, 𐐸𐐨 𐑉𐐱𐐺𐐼 𐐵𐑉 𐑁𐐪𐑄𐐲𐑉𐑆; 𐐰𐑌𐐼 𐑌𐐵 𐐸𐐮𐑆 𐐽𐐮𐑊𐐼𐑉𐐯𐑌 𐐪𐑉 𐐫𐑊𐑅𐐬 𐐿𐐲𐑋 𐐲𐑋𐐲𐑍𐑅𐐻 𐐲𐑅, 𐑄𐐰𐐻 𐑄𐐩 𐑋𐐩, 𐐺𐐴 𐑄𐐯𐑉 𐐿𐐲𐑌𐐮𐑍 𐐰𐑌𐐼 𐑄𐐯𐑉 𐑊𐐴𐐮𐑍𐑆, 𐐼𐐨𐑅𐐨𐑂 𐐲𐑅, 𐑄𐐰𐐻 𐑄𐐩 𐐲𐑀𐐯𐑌 𐑋𐐩 𐑉𐐱𐐺 𐐲𐑅 𐐱𐑂 𐐵𐑉 𐐹𐑉𐐱𐐹𐐲𐑉𐐻𐐨. 𐐤𐐵 𐑄 𐑁𐐪𐑄𐐲𐑉 𐐱𐑂 𐐢𐐪𐑋𐐬𐑌𐐴 𐐿𐐱𐑋𐐰𐑌𐐼𐐯𐐼 𐐸𐐮𐑋 𐑄𐐰𐐻 𐐸𐐨 𐑇𐐳𐐼 𐑅𐑊𐐩 𐐈𐑋𐐲𐑌 𐐶𐐮𐑄 𐑄 𐑅𐐫𐑉𐐼. 𐐈𐑌𐐼 𐐸𐐨 𐐫𐑊𐑅𐐬 𐐿𐐱𐑋𐐰𐑌𐐼𐐯𐐼 𐐸𐐮𐑋 𐑄𐐰𐐻 𐐸𐐨 𐑇𐐳𐐼 𐑌𐐱𐐻 𐑀𐐬 𐐻𐐭 𐑄 𐑊𐐰𐑌𐐼 𐐱𐑂 𐐣𐐮𐐼𐐬𐑌𐐴, 𐐺𐐲𐐻 𐑄𐐰𐐻 𐐸𐐨 𐑇𐐳𐐼 𐑉𐐨𐐻𐐲𐑉𐑌 𐐶𐐮𐑄 𐐸𐐮𐑋 𐐻𐐭 𐑄 𐑊𐐰𐑌𐐼 𐐱𐑂 𐐆𐑇𐑋𐐩𐐯𐑊. 𐐒𐐲𐐻 𐐢𐐪𐑋𐐬𐑌𐐴 𐑅𐐯𐐼 𐐲𐑌𐐻𐐭 𐐸𐐮𐑆 𐑁𐐪𐑄𐐲𐑉, 𐐌 𐐶𐐮𐑊 𐑌𐐱𐐻 𐑅𐑊𐐩 𐐈𐑋𐐲𐑌, 𐑌𐐨𐑄𐐲𐑉 𐐶𐐮𐑊 𐐌 𐑉𐐨𐐻𐐲𐑉𐑌 𐐻𐐭 𐑄 𐑊𐐰𐑌𐐼 𐐱𐑂 𐐆𐑇𐑋𐐩𐐯𐑊, 𐐺𐐲𐐻 𐐌 𐑀𐐬 𐐻𐐭 𐑄 𐑊𐐰𐑌𐐼 𐐱𐑂 𐐣𐐮𐐼𐐬𐑌𐐴, 𐑄𐐰𐐻 𐐌 𐑋𐐩 𐑉𐐨𐑊𐐨𐑅 𐑄 𐐺𐑉𐐯𐑄𐑉𐐯𐑌 𐐱𐑂 𐐈𐑋𐐲𐑌, 𐑁𐐫𐑉 𐐌 𐑌𐐬 𐑄𐐰𐐻 𐑄𐐩 𐐪𐑉 𐐾𐐲𐑅𐐻 𐑋𐐯𐑌, 𐐰𐑌𐐼 𐐸𐐬𐑊𐐨 𐐹𐑉𐐱𐑁𐐯𐐻𐑅 𐐱𐑂 𐑄 𐐻𐑉𐐭 𐐘𐐱𐐼. 𐐤𐐵 𐐸𐐶𐐯𐑌 𐐸𐐮𐑆 𐑁𐐪𐑄𐐲𐑉 𐐸𐐰𐐼 𐐸𐐲𐑉𐐼 𐑄𐐨𐑆 𐐶𐐲𐑉𐐼𐑆, 𐐸𐐨 𐐶𐐱𐑆 𐐰𐑍𐑀𐑉𐐨 𐐶𐐮𐑄 𐐸𐐮𐑋, 𐐰𐑌𐐼 𐐸𐐨 𐐼𐑉𐐭 𐐸𐐮𐑆 𐑅𐐫𐑉𐐼 𐑄𐐰𐐻 𐐸𐐨 𐑋𐐴𐐻 𐑅𐑋𐐴𐐻 𐐸𐐮𐑋 𐐻𐐭 𐑄 𐐲𐑉𐑃. 𐐒𐐲𐐻 𐐈𐑋𐐲𐑌 𐑅𐐻𐐳𐐼 𐑁𐐫𐑉𐑃 𐐰𐑌𐐼 𐑅𐐯𐐼 𐐲𐑌𐐻𐐭 𐐸𐐮𐑋, 𐐒𐐨𐐸𐐬𐑊𐐼, 𐑄𐐵 𐑇𐐰𐑊𐐻 𐑌𐐱𐐻 𐑅𐑊𐐩 𐑄𐐴 𐑅𐐲𐑌; 𐑌𐐯𐑂𐐲𐑉𐑄𐐲𐑊𐐯𐑅, 𐐮𐐻 𐐶𐐲𐑉 𐐺𐐯𐐻𐐲𐑉 𐑄𐐰𐐻 𐐸𐐨 𐑇𐐳𐐼 𐑁𐐫𐑊 𐑄𐐰𐑌 𐑄: 𐑁𐐫𐑉 𐐺𐐨𐐸𐐬𐑊𐐼, 𐐸𐐨 𐐸𐐰𐑆 𐑉𐐨𐐹𐐯𐑌𐐻𐐯𐐼 𐐱𐑂 𐐸𐐮𐑆 𐑅𐐮𐑌𐑆; 𐐺𐐲𐐻 𐐮𐑁 𐑄𐐵 𐑇𐐳𐐼𐑅𐐻 𐑁𐐫𐑊 𐐰𐐻 𐑄𐐮𐑅 𐐻𐐴𐑋, 𐐮𐑌 𐑄𐐴𐑌 𐐰𐑍𐑀𐐲𐑉, 𐑄𐐴 𐑅𐐬𐑊 𐐿𐐳𐐼 𐑌𐐱𐐻 𐐺 𐑅𐐩𐑂𐐼. 𐐈𐑌𐐼

𐐰𐑀𐐯𐑌, 𐐮𐐻 𐐮𐑆 𐐯𐐿𐑅𐐹𐐨𐐼𐐨𐐲𐑌𐐻 𐑄𐐰𐐻 𐑄𐐵 𐑇𐐳𐐼𐑅𐐻 𐑁𐐫𐑉𐐺𐐯𐑉; 𐑁𐐫𐑉 𐐮𐑁 𐑄𐐵 𐑇𐐳𐐼𐑅𐐻 𐑅𐑊𐐩 𐑄𐐴 𐑅𐐲𐑌, (𐐸𐐨 𐐺𐐨𐐮𐑍 𐐰𐑌 𐐮𐑌𐐬𐑅𐐲𐑌𐐻 𐑋𐐰𐑌,) 𐐸𐐮𐑆 𐐺𐑊𐐲𐐼 𐐶𐐳𐐼 𐐿𐑉𐐴 𐑁𐑉𐐲𐑋 𐑄 𐑀𐑉𐐵𐑌𐐼, 𐐻𐐭 𐑄 𐐢𐐫𐑉𐐼 𐐸𐐮𐑆 𐐘𐐱𐐼, 𐑁𐐫𐑉 𐑂𐐯𐑌𐐾𐐲𐑌𐑅 𐐻𐐭 𐐿𐐲𐑋 𐐲𐐹𐐱𐑌 𐑄; 𐐰𐑌𐐼 𐐹𐐲𐑉𐐸𐐰𐐹𐑅 𐑄𐐵 𐐶𐐳𐐼𐑅𐐻 𐑊𐐭𐑆 𐑄𐐴 𐑅𐐬𐑊. 𐐤𐐵 𐐸𐐶𐐯𐑌 𐐈𐑋𐐲𐑌 𐐸𐐰𐐼 𐑅𐐯𐐼 𐑄𐐨𐑆 𐐶𐐲𐑉𐐼𐑆 𐐲𐑌𐐻𐐭 𐐸𐐮𐑋, 𐐸𐐨 𐐰𐑌𐑅𐐲𐑉𐐼 𐐸𐐮𐑋, 𐑅𐐩𐐮𐑍, 𐐌 𐑌𐐬 𐑄𐐰𐐻 𐐮𐑁 𐐌 𐑇𐐳𐐼 𐑅𐑊𐐩 𐑋𐐴 𐑅𐐲𐑌, 𐑄𐐰𐐻 𐐌 𐑇𐐳𐐼 𐑇𐐯𐐼 𐐮𐑌𐐬𐑅𐐲𐑌𐐻 𐐺𐑊𐐲𐐼; 𐑁𐐫𐑉 𐐮𐐻 𐐮𐑆 𐑄𐐵 𐑄𐐰𐐻 𐐸𐐰𐑅𐐻 𐑅𐐫𐐻 𐐻𐐭 𐐼𐐯𐑅𐐻𐑉𐐱𐐴 𐐸𐐮𐑋: 𐐰𐑌𐐼 𐐸𐐨 𐑅𐐻𐑉𐐯𐐽𐐻 𐑁𐐫𐑉𐑃 𐐸𐐮𐑆 𐐸𐐰𐑌𐐼 𐐻𐐭 𐑅𐑊𐐩 𐐈𐑋𐐲𐑌. 𐐒𐐲𐐻 𐐈𐑋𐐲𐑌 𐐶𐐮𐑄𐑅𐐻𐐳𐐼 𐐸𐐮𐑆 𐐺𐑊𐐬𐑆, 𐐰𐑌𐐼 𐐫𐑊𐑅𐐬 𐑅𐑋𐐬𐐻 𐐸𐐮𐑆 𐐪𐑉𐑋 𐑄𐐰𐐻 𐐸𐐨 𐐿𐐳𐐼 𐑌𐐱𐐻 𐐷𐐭𐑆 𐐮𐐻. 𐐤𐐵 𐐸𐐶𐐯𐑌 𐑄 𐐿𐐮𐑍 𐑅𐐫 𐑄𐐰𐐻 𐐈𐑋𐐲𐑌 𐐿𐐳𐐼 𐑅𐑊𐐩 𐐸𐐮𐑋, 𐐸𐐨 𐐺𐐨𐑀𐐰𐑌 𐐻𐐭 𐐹𐑊𐐨𐐼 𐐶𐐮𐑄 𐐈𐑋𐐲𐑌, 𐑄𐐰𐐻 𐐸𐐨 𐐶𐐳𐐼 𐑅𐐹𐐩𐑉 𐐸𐐮𐑆 𐑊𐐴𐑁. 𐐒𐐲𐐻 𐐈𐑋𐐲𐑌 𐑉𐐩𐑆𐐼 𐐸𐐮𐑆 𐑅𐐫𐑉𐐼, 𐐰𐑌𐐼 𐑅𐐯𐐼 𐐲𐑌𐐻𐐭 𐐸𐐮𐑋, 𐐒𐐨𐐸𐐬𐑊𐐼, 𐐌 𐐶𐐮𐑊 𐑅𐑋𐐴𐐻 𐑄, 𐐯𐐿𐑅𐐯𐐹𐐻 𐑄𐐵 𐐶𐐮𐑊𐐻 𐑀𐑉𐐪𐑌𐐻 𐐲𐑌𐐻𐐭 𐑋𐐨 𐑄𐐰𐐻 𐑋𐐴 𐐺𐑉𐐯𐑃𐑉𐐯𐑌 𐑋𐐩 𐐺𐐨 𐐿𐐪𐑅𐐻 𐐵𐐻 𐐱𐑂 𐐹𐑉𐐮𐑆𐐲𐑌. 𐐤𐐵 𐑄 𐐿𐐮𐑍, 𐑁𐐨𐑉𐐮𐑍 𐐸𐐨 𐑇𐐳𐐼 𐑊𐐭𐑆 𐐸𐐮𐑆 𐑊𐐴𐑁, 𐑅𐐯𐐼, 𐐆𐑁 𐑄𐐵 𐐶𐐮𐑊𐐻 𐑅𐐹𐐩𐑉 𐑋𐐨 𐐌 𐐶𐐮𐑊 𐑀𐑉𐐪𐑌𐐻 𐐲𐑌𐐻𐐭 𐑄 𐐸𐐶𐐱𐐻𐑅𐐬𐐯𐑂𐐲𐑉 𐑄𐐵 𐐶𐐮𐑊𐐻 𐐪𐑅𐐿, 𐐨𐑂𐐲𐑌 𐐻𐐭 𐐸𐐪𐑁 𐐱𐑂 𐑄 𐐿𐐮𐑍𐐼𐐲𐑋.

26. 𐐤𐐵 𐐸𐐶𐐯𐑌 𐐈𐑋𐐲𐑌 𐑅𐐫 𐑄𐐰𐐻 𐐸𐐨 𐐸𐐰𐐼 𐑉𐐫𐐻 𐐲𐐹𐐱𐑌 𐑄 𐐬𐑊𐐼 𐐿𐐮𐑍 𐐰𐐿𐐫𐑉𐐼𐐮𐑍 𐐻𐐭 𐐸𐐮𐑆 𐐼𐐨𐑆𐐴𐑉, 𐐸𐐨 𐑅𐐯𐐼 𐐲𐑌𐐻𐐭 𐐸𐐮𐑋, 𐐆𐑁 𐑄𐐵 𐐶𐐮𐑊𐐻 𐑀𐑉𐐪𐑌𐐻 𐑄𐐰𐐻 𐑋𐐴 𐐺𐑉𐐯𐑃𐑉𐐯𐑌 𐑋𐐩 𐐺𐐨 𐐿𐐪𐑅𐐻 𐐵𐐻 𐐱𐑂 𐐹𐑉𐐮𐑆𐐲𐑌, 𐐰𐑌𐐼 𐐫𐑊𐑅𐐬 𐑄𐐰𐐻 𐐢𐐰𐑋𐐬𐑌𐐴 𐑋𐐩 𐑉𐐨𐐻𐐩𐑌 𐐸𐐮𐑆 𐐿𐐮𐑍𐐼𐐲𐑋, 𐐰𐑌𐐼 𐑄𐐰𐐻 𐐷𐐨 𐐺𐐨 𐑌𐐱𐐻 𐐼𐐮𐑅𐐹𐑊𐐨𐑆𐐼 𐐶𐐮𐑄 𐐸𐐮𐑋, 𐐺𐐲𐐻 𐑀𐑉𐐪𐑌𐐻 𐑄𐐰𐐻 𐐸𐐨 𐑋𐐩 𐐼𐐭 𐐰𐐿𐐫𐑉𐐼𐐮𐑍 𐐻𐐭 𐐸𐐮𐑆 𐐬𐑌 𐐼𐐨𐑆𐐴𐑉𐑆 𐐮𐑌 𐐸𐐶𐐱𐐻𐑅𐐬𐐯𐑂𐐲𐑉 𐑃𐐮𐑍 𐐸𐐨 𐑃𐐮𐑍𐐿𐐯𐑃, 𐑄𐐯𐑌 𐐶𐐮𐑊 𐐌 𐑅𐐹𐐩𐑉 𐑄; 𐐱𐑄𐐲𐑉𐐶𐐴𐑆 𐐌 𐐶𐐮𐑊 𐑅𐑋𐐴𐐻 𐑄 𐐻𐐭 𐑄 𐐲𐑉𐑃. 𐐈𐑌𐐼 𐐸𐐶𐐯𐑌 𐐈𐑋𐐲𐑌 𐐸𐐰𐐼 𐑅𐐯𐐼 𐑄𐐨𐑆 𐐶𐐲𐑉𐐼𐑆, 𐑄 𐐿𐐮𐑍 𐐺𐐨𐑀𐐰𐑌 𐐻𐐭 𐑉𐐨𐐾𐐱𐐮𐑅 𐐺𐐨𐐿𐐫𐑆 𐐱𐑂 𐐸𐐮𐑆 𐑊𐐴𐑁. 𐐈𐑌𐐼 𐐸𐐶𐐯𐑌 𐐸𐐨 𐑅𐐫 𐑄𐐰𐐻 𐐈𐑋𐐲𐑌 𐐸𐐰𐐼 𐑌𐐬 𐐼𐐨𐑆𐐴𐑉 𐐻𐐭 𐐼𐐯𐑅𐐻𐑉𐐱𐐴 𐐸𐐮𐑋, 𐐰𐑌𐐼 𐐸𐐶𐐯𐑌 𐐸𐐨 𐐫𐑊𐑅𐐬 𐑅𐐫 𐑄 𐑀𐑉𐐩𐐻 𐑊𐐲𐑂 𐐸𐐨 𐐸𐐰𐐼 𐑁𐐫𐑉 𐐸𐐮𐑆 𐑅𐐲𐑌 𐐢𐐰𐑋𐐬𐑌𐐴, 𐐸𐐨 𐐶𐐱𐑆 𐐰𐑅𐐻𐐱𐑌𐐮𐑇𐐻 𐐯𐐿𐑅𐐨𐐼𐐮𐑍𐑊𐐨, 𐐰𐑌𐐼 𐑅𐐯𐐼, 𐐒𐐨𐐿𐐫𐑆 𐑄𐐮𐑅 𐐮𐑆 𐐫𐑊 𐑄𐐰𐐻 𐑄𐐵 𐐸𐐰𐑅𐐻 𐐼𐐨𐑆𐐴𐑉𐐼, 𐑄𐐰𐐻 𐐌 𐐶𐐳𐐼 𐑉𐐨𐑊𐐨𐑅 𐑄𐐴 𐐺𐑉𐐯𐑃𐑉𐐯𐑌, 𐐰𐑌𐐼 𐑅𐐲𐑁𐐲𐑉 𐑄𐐰𐐻 𐑋𐐴 𐑅𐐲𐑌 𐐢𐐰𐑋𐐬𐑌𐐴 𐑇𐐳𐐼 𐑉𐐨𐐻𐐩𐑌 𐐸𐐮𐑆 𐐿𐐮𐑍𐐼𐐲𐑋, 𐐺𐐨𐐸𐐬𐑊𐐼, 𐐌 𐐶𐐮𐑊 𐑀𐑉𐐪𐑌𐐻 𐐲𐑌𐐻𐐭 𐐷𐐭 𐑄𐐰𐐻 𐑋𐐴 𐑅𐐲𐑌 𐑋𐐩 𐑉𐐨𐐻𐐩𐑌 𐐸𐐮𐑆 𐐿𐐮𐑍𐐼𐐲𐑋 𐑁𐑉𐐲𐑋 𐑄𐐮𐑅 𐐻𐐴𐑋 𐐰𐑌𐐼 𐑁𐐫𐑉 𐐯𐑂𐐲𐑉; 𐐰𐑌𐐼 𐐌 𐐶𐐮𐑊 𐑀𐐲𐑂𐐲𐑉𐑌 𐐸𐐮𐑋 𐑌𐐬 𐑋𐐬𐑉; 𐐰𐑌𐐼 𐐌 𐐶𐐮𐑊 𐐫𐑊𐑅𐐬 𐑀𐑉𐐪𐑌𐐻 𐐲𐑌𐐻𐐭 𐑄 𐑄𐐰𐐻 𐑄𐐴 𐐺𐑉𐐯𐑃𐑉𐐯𐑌 𐑋𐐩 𐐺𐐨 𐐿𐐪𐑅𐐻 𐐵𐐻 𐐱𐑂 𐐹𐑉𐐮𐑆𐐲𐑌, 𐐰𐑌𐐼 𐑄𐐵 𐐰𐑌𐐼 𐑄𐐴 𐐺𐑉𐐯𐑃𐑉𐐯𐑌 𐑋𐐩 𐐿𐐲𐑋 𐐲𐑌𐐻𐐭 𐑋𐐨, 𐐮𐑌 𐑋𐐴 𐐿𐐮𐑍𐐼𐐲𐑋; 𐑁𐐫𐑉 𐐌 𐑇𐐰𐑊 𐑀𐑉𐐩𐐻𐑊𐐨 𐐼𐐨𐑆𐐴𐑉 𐐻𐐭 𐑅𐐨 𐑄. 𐐙𐐫𐑉 𐑄 𐐿𐐮𐑍 𐐶𐐱𐑆 𐑀𐑉𐐩𐐻𐑊𐐨 𐐰𐑅𐐻𐐱𐑌𐐮𐑇𐐻 𐐰𐐻 𐑄 𐐶𐐲𐑉𐐼𐑆 𐐸𐐶𐐮𐐽 𐐸𐐨 𐐸𐐰𐐼 𐑅𐐹𐐬𐐿𐐲𐑌, 𐐰𐑌𐐼 𐐫𐑊𐑅𐐬 𐐰𐐻 𐑄 𐐶𐐲𐑉𐐼𐑆 𐐸𐐶𐐮𐐽 𐐸𐐰𐐼 𐐺𐐨𐑌 𐑅𐐹𐐬𐐿𐐲𐑌 𐐺𐐴 𐐸𐐮𐑆 𐑅𐐲𐑌 𐐢𐐰𐑋𐐬𐑌𐐴, 𐑄𐐯𐑉𐑁𐐬𐑉 𐐸𐐨 𐐶𐐱𐑆 𐐼𐐨𐑆𐐴𐑉𐐲𐑅 𐐻𐐭 𐑊𐐲𐑉𐑌 𐑄𐐯𐑋.

27. 𐐈𐑌𐐼 𐐮𐐻 𐐿𐐩𐑋 𐐻𐐭 𐐹𐐰𐑅 𐑄𐐰𐐻 𐐈𐑋𐐲𐑌 𐐰𐑌𐐼 𐐢𐐰𐑋𐐬𐑌𐐴 𐐹𐑉𐐬𐑅𐐨𐐼𐐯𐐼 𐐱𐑌 𐑄𐐯𐑉 𐐾𐐲𐑉𐑌𐐨 𐐻𐐬𐑉𐐼𐑆 𐑄 𐑊𐐰𐑌𐐼 𐐱𐑂 𐐣𐐮𐐼𐐬𐑌𐐴. 𐐈𐑌𐐼 𐐢𐐰𐑋𐐬𐑌𐐴 𐑁𐐵𐑌𐐼 𐑁𐐩𐑂𐐲𐑉 𐐮𐑌 𐑄 𐐴𐑆 𐐱𐑂 𐑄 𐐿𐐮𐑍 𐐱𐑂 𐑄 𐑊𐐰𐑌𐐼; 𐑄𐐯𐑉𐑁𐐬𐑉 𐑄 𐐺𐑉𐐯𐑃𐑉𐐯𐑌 𐐱𐑂 𐐈𐑋𐐲𐑌 𐐶𐐲𐑉 𐐺𐑉𐐫𐐻 𐑁𐐬𐑉𐑃 𐐵𐐻 𐐱𐑂 𐐹𐑉𐐮𐑆𐐲𐑌. 𐐈𐑌𐐼 𐐸𐐶𐐯𐑌 𐐈𐑋𐐲𐑌 𐐼𐐮𐐼 𐑋𐐨𐐻 𐑄𐐯𐑋 𐐸𐐨 𐐶𐐱𐑆 𐐯𐐿𐑅𐐨𐐼𐐮𐑍 𐑅𐐱𐑉𐐬𐑁𐐳𐑊, 𐑁𐐫𐑉 𐐺𐐨𐐸𐐬𐑊𐐼 𐑄𐐩 𐐶𐐲𐑉 𐑌𐐩𐐿𐐯𐐼, 𐐰𐑌𐐼 𐑄𐐯𐑉 𐑅𐐿𐐮𐑌𐑆 𐐶𐐲𐑉 𐐶𐐬𐑉𐑌 𐐯𐐿𐑅𐐨𐐼𐐮𐑍𐑊𐐨, 𐐺𐐨𐐿𐐫𐑆 𐐱𐑂 𐐺𐐨𐐮𐑍 𐐺𐐵𐑌𐐼 𐐶𐐮𐑄 𐑅𐐻𐑉𐐱𐑍 𐐿𐐬𐑉𐐼𐑆. 𐐈𐑌𐐼 𐑄𐐩 𐐫𐑊𐑅𐐬 𐐸𐐰𐐼 𐑅𐐲𐑁𐐲𐑉𐐼 𐐸𐐲𐑍𐑀𐐲𐑉, 𐑃𐐲𐑉𐑅𐐻, 𐐰𐑌𐐼 𐐫𐑊 𐐿𐐴𐑌𐐼𐑆 𐐱𐑂 𐐰𐑁𐑊𐐮𐐿𐑇𐐲𐑌𐑆; 𐑌𐐯𐑂𐐲𐑉𐑄𐐯𐑊𐐯𐑅 𐑄𐐩 𐐶𐐲𐑉 𐐹𐐩𐑇𐐲𐑌𐐻 𐐮𐑌 𐐫𐑊 𐑄𐐯𐑉 𐑅𐐲𐑁𐐲𐑉𐐮𐑍𐑆. 𐐈𐑌𐐼 𐐰𐑆 𐐮𐐻 𐐸𐐰𐐹𐐲𐑌𐐼, 𐐮𐐻 𐐶𐐱𐑆 𐑄𐐯𐑉 𐑊𐐱𐐻 𐐻𐐭 𐐸𐐰𐑂 𐑁𐐫𐑊𐐲𐑌 𐐮𐑌𐐻𐐭 𐑄 𐐸𐐰𐑌𐐼𐑆 𐐱𐑂 𐐲 𐑋𐐬𐑉 𐐸𐐪𐑉𐐼𐐲𐑌𐐼 𐐰𐑌𐐼 𐐲 𐑋𐐬𐑉 𐑅𐐻𐐮𐑁𐑌𐐯𐐿𐐻 𐐹𐐨𐐹𐑊; 𐑄𐐯𐑉𐑁𐐬𐑉 𐑄𐐩 𐐶𐐳𐐼 𐑌𐐱𐐻 𐐸𐐪𐑉𐐿𐐲𐑌 𐐲𐑌𐐻𐐭 𐑄𐐯𐑉 𐐶𐐲𐑉𐐼𐑆, 𐐰𐑌𐐼 𐑄𐐩 𐐸𐐰𐐼 𐐿𐐪𐑅𐐻 𐑄𐐯𐑋 𐐵𐐻, 𐐰𐑌𐐼 𐐸𐐰𐐼 𐑅𐑋𐐮𐐻𐐲𐑌 𐑄𐐯𐑋, 𐐰𐑌𐐼 𐐸𐐰𐐼 𐐼𐑉𐐮𐑂𐐲𐑌 𐑄𐐯𐑋 𐑁𐑉𐐲𐑋 𐐸𐐵𐑅 𐐻𐐭 𐐸𐐵𐑅, 𐐰𐑌𐐼 𐑁𐑉𐐲𐑋 𐐹𐑊𐐩𐑅 𐐻𐐭 𐐹𐑊𐐩𐑅, 𐐨𐑂𐐲𐑌 𐐲𐑌𐐻𐐮𐑊 𐑄𐐩 𐐸𐐰𐐼 𐐲𐑉𐐴𐑂𐐼 𐐮𐑌 𐑄 𐑊𐐰𐑌𐐼 𐐱𐑂 𐐣𐐮𐐼𐐬𐑌𐐴; 𐐰𐑌𐐼 𐑄𐐯𐑉 𐑄𐐩 𐐶𐐲𐑉 𐐻𐐩𐐿𐐲𐑌 𐐰𐑌𐐼 𐐿𐐪𐑅𐐻 𐐮𐑌𐐻𐐭 𐐹𐑉𐐮𐑆𐐲𐑌, 𐐰𐑌𐐼 𐐺𐐵𐑌𐐼 𐐶𐐮𐑄 𐑅𐐻𐑉𐐱𐑍 𐐿𐐬𐑉𐐼𐑆, 𐐰𐑌𐐼 𐐿𐐯𐐹𐐻 𐐮𐑌 𐐹𐑉𐐮𐑆𐐲𐑌 𐑁𐐫𐑉 𐑋𐐯𐑌𐐨 𐐼𐐩𐑆, 𐐰𐑌𐐼 𐐶𐐲𐑉 𐐼𐐨𐑊𐐮𐑂𐐲𐑉𐐼 𐐺𐐴 𐐢𐐰𐑋𐐬𐑌𐐴 𐐰𐑌𐐼 𐐈𐑋𐐲𐑌.

𐐕𐐈𐐑𐐓𐐊𐐡 XIII.

𐐈𐑌 𐐰𐐿𐐵𐑌𐐻 𐐱𐑂 𐑄 𐐹𐑉𐐨𐐽𐐮𐑍 𐐱𐑂 𐐁𐑉𐐲𐑌, 𐐰𐑌𐐼 𐐣𐐷𐐭𐑊𐐬𐐿𐐴, 𐐰𐑌𐐼 𐑄𐐯𐑉 𐐺𐑉𐐯𐑄𐑉𐐯𐑌, 𐐻𐐭 𐑄 𐐢𐐩𐑋𐐲𐑌𐐴𐐻𐑅.

1. 𐐤𐐵 𐐸𐐶𐐯𐑌 𐐈𐑋𐐲𐑌 𐐰𐑌𐐼 𐐸𐐮𐑆 𐐺𐑉𐐯𐑄𐑉𐐯𐑌 𐑅𐐯𐐹𐐲𐑉𐐩𐐻𐐯𐐼 𐑄𐐯𐑋𐑅𐐯𐑊𐑂𐑆 𐐮𐑌 𐑄 𐐺𐐫𐑉𐐼𐐲𐑉𐑆 𐐱𐑂 𐑄 𐑊𐐰𐑌𐐼 𐐱𐑂 𐑄 𐐢𐐩𐑋𐐲𐑌𐐴𐐻𐑅, 𐐺𐐨𐐸𐐬𐑊𐐼 𐐁𐑉𐐲𐑌 𐐻𐐳𐐿 𐐸𐐮𐑆 𐐾𐐲𐑉𐑌𐐨 𐐻𐐬𐑉𐐼𐑆 𐑄 𐑊𐐰𐑌𐐼 𐐸𐐶𐐮𐐽 𐐶𐐱𐑆 𐐿𐐫𐑊𐐼 𐐺𐐴 𐑄 𐐢𐐩𐑋𐐲𐑌𐐴𐐻𐑅, 𐐖𐐲𐑉𐐭𐑅𐐲𐑊𐐯𐑋; 𐐿𐐫𐑊𐐮𐑍 𐐮𐐻 𐐰𐑁𐐻𐐲𐑉 𐑄 𐑊𐐰𐑌𐐼 𐐱𐑂 𐑄𐐯𐑉 𐑁𐐪𐑄𐐲𐑉𐑆' 𐑌𐐩𐐻𐐮𐑂𐐮𐐻𐐨; 𐐰𐑌𐐼 𐐮𐐻 𐐶𐐱𐑆 𐐰𐐶𐐩 𐐾𐐱𐐮𐑌𐐮𐑍 𐑄 𐐺𐐫𐑉𐐼𐐲𐑉𐑆 𐐱𐑂 𐐣𐐫𐑉𐑋𐐲𐑌. 𐐤𐐵 𐑄 𐐢𐐩𐑋𐐲𐑌𐐴𐐻𐑅, 𐐰𐑌𐐼 𐑄 𐐈𐑋𐐰𐑊𐐯𐐿𐐴𐐻𐑅, 𐐰𐑌𐐼 𐑄 𐐹𐐨𐐹𐑊 𐐱𐑂 𐐈𐑋𐐷𐐭𐑊𐐱𐑌, 𐐸𐐰𐐼 𐐺𐐮𐑊𐐻 𐐩 𐑀𐑉𐐩𐐻 𐑅𐐮𐐻𐐨, 𐐸𐐶𐐮𐐽 𐐶𐐱𐑆 𐐿𐐫𐑊𐐼 𐐖𐐲𐑉𐐭𐑅𐐲𐑊𐐯𐑋. 𐐤𐐵 𐑄 𐐢𐐩𐑋𐐲𐑌𐐴𐐻𐑅 𐐱𐑂 𐑄𐐯𐑋𐑅𐐯𐑊𐑂𐑆 𐐶𐐲𐑉 𐑅𐐲𐑁𐐮𐑇𐐲𐑌𐐻𐑊𐐨 𐐸𐐪𐑉𐐼𐐲𐑌𐐼, 𐐺𐐲𐐻 𐑄 𐐈𐑋𐐰𐑊𐐯𐐿𐐴𐐻𐑅 𐐰𐑌𐐼 𐑄 𐐈𐑋𐐷𐐭𐑊𐐱𐑌𐐴𐐻𐑅 𐐶𐐲𐑉 𐑅𐐻𐐮𐑊 𐐸𐐪𐑉𐐼𐐲𐑉; 𐑄𐐯𐑉𐑁𐐬𐑉 𐑄𐐩 𐐼𐐮𐐼 𐐿𐐫𐑆 𐑄 𐐢𐐩𐑋𐐲𐑌𐐴𐐻𐑅 𐑄𐐰𐐻 𐑄𐐩 𐑇𐐳𐐼 𐐸𐐪𐑉𐐼𐐲𐑌 𐑄𐐯𐑉 𐐸𐐪𐑉𐐻𐑅, 𐑄𐐰𐐻 𐑄𐐩 𐑇𐐳𐐼 𐐶𐐰𐐿𐑅 𐑅𐐻𐑉𐐫𐑍 𐐮𐑌 𐐶𐐮𐐿𐐯𐐼𐑌𐐯𐑅 𐐰𐑌𐐼 𐑄𐐯𐑉 𐐰𐐺𐐱𐑋𐐮𐑌𐐩𐑇𐐲𐑌𐑆.

2. 𐐈𐑌𐐼 𐐮𐐻 𐐿𐐩𐑋 𐐻𐐭 𐐹𐐰𐑅 𐑄𐐰𐐻 𐐁𐑉𐐲𐑌 𐐿𐐩𐑋 𐐻𐐭 𐑄 𐑅𐐮𐐻𐐨 𐐱𐑂 𐐖𐐲𐑉𐐭𐑅𐐲𐑊𐐯𐑋, 𐐰𐑌𐐼 𐑁𐐲𐑉𐑅𐐻 𐐺𐐨𐑀𐐰𐑌 𐐻𐐭 𐐹𐑉𐐨𐐽 𐐻𐐭 𐑄 𐐈𐑋𐐰𐑊𐐯𐐿𐐴𐐻𐑅. 𐐈𐑌𐐼 𐐸𐐨 𐐺𐐨𐑀𐐰𐑌 𐐻𐐭 𐐹𐑉𐐨𐐽 𐐻𐐭 𐑄𐐯𐑋 𐐮𐑌 𐑄𐐯𐑉 𐑅𐐮𐑌𐐲𐑀𐐱𐑀𐑆, 𐑁𐐫𐑉 𐑄𐐩 𐐸𐐰𐐼 𐐺𐐮𐑊𐐻 𐑅𐐮𐑌𐐲𐑀𐐱𐑀𐑆 𐐰𐑁𐐻𐐲𐑉 𐑄 𐐫𐑉𐐼𐐲𐑉 𐐱𐑂 𐑄 𐐤𐐨𐐸𐐫𐑉𐑆; 𐑁𐐫𐑉 𐑋𐐯𐑌𐐨 𐐱𐑂 𐑄 𐐈𐑋𐐰𐑊𐐯𐐿𐐴𐐻𐑅 𐐰𐑌𐐼 𐑄 𐐈𐑋𐐷𐐭𐑊𐐱𐑌𐐴𐐻𐑅 𐐶𐐲𐑉 𐐰𐑁𐐻𐐲𐑉 𐑄 𐐫𐑉𐐼𐐲𐑉 𐐱𐑂 𐑄 𐐤𐐨𐐸𐐫𐑉𐑆. 𐐜𐐯𐑉𐑁𐐬𐑉, 𐐰𐑆 𐐁𐑉𐐲𐑌 𐐯𐑌𐐻𐐲𐑉𐐼 𐐮𐑌𐐻𐐭 𐐶𐐲𐑌 𐐱𐑂 𐑄𐐯𐑉 𐑅𐐮𐑌𐐲𐑀𐐱𐑀𐑆 𐐻𐐭 𐐹𐑉𐐨𐐽 𐐲𐑌𐐻𐐭 𐑄 𐐹𐐨𐐹𐑊, 𐐰𐑌𐐼 𐐰𐑆 𐐸𐐨 𐐶𐐱𐑆 𐑅𐐹𐐨𐐿𐐮𐑍 𐐲𐑌𐐻𐐭 𐑄𐐯𐑋, 𐐺𐐨𐐸𐐬𐑊𐐼, 𐑄𐐯𐑉 𐐲𐑉𐐬𐑆 𐐰𐑌 𐐈𐑋𐐰𐑊𐐯𐐿𐐴𐐻 𐐰𐑌𐐼 𐐺𐐨𐑀𐐰𐑌 𐐻𐐭 𐐿𐐱𐑌𐐻𐐯𐑌𐐼 𐐶𐐮𐑄 𐐸𐐮𐑋, 𐑅𐐩𐐮𐑍, 𐐐𐐶𐐱𐐻 𐐮𐑆 𐑄𐐰𐐻 𐑄𐐵 𐐸𐐰𐑅𐐻 𐐻𐐯𐑅𐐻𐐮𐑁𐐴𐐼? 𐐐𐐰𐑅𐐻 𐑄𐐵 𐑅𐐨𐑌 𐐰𐑌 𐐩𐑌𐐾𐐯𐑊? 𐐐𐐶𐐴 𐐼𐐭 𐑌𐐱𐐻 𐐩𐑌𐐾𐐯𐑊𐑆 𐐰𐐹𐐨𐑉 𐐲𐑌𐐻𐐭 𐐲𐑅? 𐐒𐐨𐐸𐐬𐑊𐐼, 𐐪𐑉 𐑌𐐱𐐻 𐑄𐐮𐑅 𐐹𐐨𐐹𐑊 𐐰𐑆 𐑀𐐳𐐼 𐐰𐑆 𐑄𐐴 𐐹𐐨𐐹𐑊? 𐐜𐐵 𐐫𐑊𐑅𐐬 𐑅𐐩𐐯𐑅𐐻, 𐐯𐐿𐑅𐐯𐐹𐐻 𐐶𐐨 𐑉𐐨𐐹𐐯𐑌𐐻 𐐶𐐨 𐑇𐐰𐑊 𐐹𐐯𐑉𐐮𐑇. 𐐐𐐵 𐑌𐐬𐐯𐑅𐐻 𐑄𐐵 𐑄 𐑃𐐫𐐻 𐐰𐑌𐐼 𐐮𐑌𐐻𐐯𐑌𐐻 𐐱𐑂 𐐵𐑉 𐐸𐐪𐑉𐐻𐑅? 𐐐𐐵 𐑌𐐬𐐯𐑅𐐻 𐑄𐐵 𐑄𐐰𐐻 𐐶𐐨 𐐸𐐰𐑂 𐐿𐐫𐑆 𐐻𐐭 𐑉𐐨𐐹𐐯𐑌𐐻? 𐐐𐐵 𐑌𐐬𐐯𐑅𐐻 𐑄𐐵 𐑄𐐰𐐻 𐐶𐐨 𐐪𐑉 𐑌𐐱𐐻 𐐩 𐑉𐐴𐐽𐐲𐑅 𐐹𐐨𐐹𐑊? 𐐒𐐨𐐸𐐬𐑊𐐼, 𐐶𐐨 𐐸𐐰𐑂 𐐺𐐮𐑊𐐻 𐑅𐐰𐑍𐐿𐐻𐐷𐐭𐐯𐑉𐐨𐑆, 𐐰𐑌𐐼 𐐶𐐨 𐐼𐐭 𐐰𐑅𐐯𐑋𐐺𐑊 𐐵𐑉𐑅𐐯𐑊𐑂𐑆 𐐻𐐭𐑀𐐯𐑄𐐲𐑉 𐐻𐐭 𐐶𐐲𐑉𐑇𐐮𐐹 𐐘𐐱𐐼. 𐐎𐐨 𐐼𐐭 𐐺𐐨𐑊𐐨𐑂 𐑄𐐰𐐻 𐐘𐐱𐐼 𐐶𐐮𐑊 𐑅𐐩𐑂 𐐫𐑊 𐑋𐐯𐑌. 𐐤𐐵 𐐁𐑉𐐲𐑌 𐑅𐐯𐐼 𐐲𐑌𐐻𐐭 𐐸𐐮𐑋, 𐐒𐐨𐑊𐐨𐑂𐐯𐑅𐐻 𐑄𐐵 𐑄𐐰𐐻 𐑄 𐐝𐐲𐑌 𐐱𐑂 𐐘𐐱𐐼 𐑇𐐰𐑊 𐐿𐐲𐑋 𐐻𐐭 𐑉𐐨𐐼𐐨𐑋 𐑋𐐰𐑌𐐿𐐴𐑌𐐼 𐑁𐑉𐐱𐑋 𐑄𐐯𐑉 𐑅𐐮𐑌𐑆? 𐐈𐑌𐐼 𐑄 𐑋𐐰𐑌 𐑅𐐯𐐼 𐐲𐑌𐐻𐐭 𐐸𐐮𐑋, 𐐎𐐨 𐐼𐐭 𐑌𐐱𐐻 𐐺𐐨𐑊𐐨𐑂 𐑄𐐰𐐻 𐑄𐐵 𐑌𐐬𐐯𐑅𐐻 𐐯𐑌𐐨 𐑅𐐲𐐽 𐑃𐐮𐑍. 𐐎𐐨 𐐼𐐭 𐑌𐐱𐐻 𐐺𐐨𐑊𐐨𐑂 𐐮𐑌 𐑄𐐨𐑆 𐑁𐐭𐑊𐐮𐑇 𐐻𐑉𐐲𐐼𐐮𐑇𐐲𐑌𐑆. 𐐎𐐨 𐐼𐐭 𐑌𐐱𐐻 𐐺𐐨𐑊𐐨𐑂 𐑄𐐰𐐻 𐑄𐐵 𐑌𐐬𐐯𐑅𐐻 𐐱𐑂 𐑃𐐮𐑍𐑆 𐐻𐐭 𐐿𐐲𐑋, 𐑌𐐨𐑄𐐲𐑉 𐐼𐐭 𐐶𐐨 𐐺𐐨𐑊𐐨𐑂 𐑄𐐰𐐻 𐑄𐐴 𐑁𐐪𐑄𐐲𐑉𐑆, 𐐰𐑌𐐼 𐐫𐑊𐑅𐐬 𐑄𐐰𐐻 𐐵𐑉 𐑁𐐪𐑄𐐲𐑉𐑆, 𐐼𐐮𐐼 𐑌𐐬 𐐿𐐱𐑌𐑅𐐲𐑉𐑌𐐮𐑍 𐑄 𐑃𐐮𐑍𐑆 𐐸𐐶𐐮𐐽 𐑄𐐩 𐑅𐐹𐐩𐐿, 𐐱𐑂 𐑄𐐰𐐻 𐐸𐐶𐐮𐐽 𐐮𐑆 𐐻𐐭 𐐿𐐲𐑋.

3. 𐐤𐐵 𐐁𐑉𐐲𐑌 𐐺𐐨𐑀𐐰𐑌 𐐻𐐭 𐐬𐐹𐐲𐑌 𐑄 𐑅𐐿𐑉𐐮𐐹𐐽𐐲𐑉𐑆 𐐲𐑌𐐻𐐭 𐑄𐐯𐑋 𐐿𐐱𐑌𐑅𐐲𐑉𐑌𐐮𐑍 𐑄 𐐿𐐲𐑋𐐮𐑍 𐐱𐑂 𐐗𐑉𐐴𐑅𐐻, 𐐰𐑌𐐼 𐐫𐑊𐑅𐐬 𐐿𐐱𐑌𐑅𐐲𐑉𐑌𐐮𐑍 𐑄 𐑉𐐯𐑆𐐲𐑉𐐯𐐿𐑇𐐲𐑌 𐐱𐑂 𐑄 𐐼𐐯𐐼, 𐐰𐑌𐐼 𐑄𐐰𐐻 𐑄𐐯𐑉 𐐿𐐳𐐼 𐐺𐐨 𐑌𐐬 𐑉𐐨𐐼𐐯𐑋𐑇𐐲𐑌 𐑁𐐫𐑉 𐑋𐐰𐑌𐐿𐐴𐑌𐐼, 𐑅𐐩𐑂 𐐮𐐻 𐐶𐐲𐑉 𐑃𐑉𐐭 𐑄 𐐼𐐯𐑃 𐐰𐑌𐐼 𐑅𐐲𐑁𐐲𐑉𐐮𐑍𐑆 𐐱𐑂 𐐗𐑉𐐴𐑅𐐻, 𐐰𐑌𐐼 𐑄 𐐰𐐻𐐬𐑌𐑋𐐯𐑌𐐻 𐐱𐑂 𐐸𐐮𐑆 𐐺𐑊𐐲𐐼. 𐐈𐑌𐐼 𐐮𐐻 𐐿𐐩𐑋 𐐻𐐭 𐐹𐐰𐑅 𐐰𐑆 𐐸𐐨 𐐺𐐨𐑀𐐰𐑌 𐐻𐐭 𐐯𐐿𐑅𐐹𐐵𐑌𐐼 𐑄𐐨𐑆 𐑃𐐮𐑍𐑆 𐐲𐑌𐐻𐐭 𐑄𐐯𐑋, 𐑄𐐩 𐐶𐐲𐑉 𐐰𐑍𐑀𐑉𐐨 𐐶𐐮𐑄 𐐸𐐮𐑋, 𐐰𐑌𐐼 𐐺𐐨𐑀𐐰𐑌 𐐻𐐭 𐑋𐐱𐐿 𐐸𐐮𐑋; 𐐰𐑌𐐼 𐑄𐐩 𐐶𐐳𐐼 𐑌𐐱𐐻 𐐸𐐨𐑉 𐑄 𐐶𐐲𐑉𐐼𐑆 𐐸𐐶𐐮𐐽 𐐸𐐨 𐑅𐐹𐐩𐐿: 𐑄𐐯𐑉𐑁𐐬𐑉, 𐐸𐐶𐐯𐑌 𐐸𐐨 𐑅𐐫 𐑄𐐰𐐻 𐑄𐐩 𐐶𐐳𐐼 𐑌𐐱𐐻 𐐸𐐨𐑉 𐐸𐐮𐑆 𐐶𐐲𐑉𐐼𐑆, 𐐸𐐨 𐐼𐐨𐐹𐐪𐑉𐐻𐐯𐐼 𐐵𐐻 𐐱𐑂 𐑄𐐯𐑉 𐑅𐐮𐑌𐐲𐑀𐐱𐑀, 𐐰𐑌𐐼 𐐿𐐩𐑋 𐐬𐑂𐐲𐑉 𐐻𐐭 𐐩 𐑂𐐮𐑊𐐯𐐾 𐐸𐐶𐐮𐐽 𐐶𐐱𐑆 𐐿𐐫𐑊𐐼 𐐁𐑌𐐴-𐐈𐑌𐐻𐐴, 𐐰𐑌𐐼 𐑄𐐯𐑉 𐐸𐐨 𐑁𐐵𐑌𐐼 𐐣𐐷𐐭𐑊𐐬𐐿𐐴 𐐹𐑉𐐨𐐽𐐮𐑍 𐑄 𐐶𐐲𐑉𐐼 𐐲𐑌𐐻𐐭 𐑄𐐯𐑋; 𐐰𐑌𐐼 𐐫𐑊𐑅𐐬 𐐈𐑋𐐲 𐐰𐑌𐐼 𐐸𐐮𐑆 𐐺𐑉𐐯𐑄𐑉𐐯𐑌. 𐐈𐑌𐐼 𐑄𐐩 𐐿𐐱𐑌𐐻𐐯𐑌𐐼𐐯𐐼 𐐶𐐮𐑄 𐑋𐐯𐑌𐐨 𐐲𐐺𐐵𐐻 𐑄 𐐶𐐲𐑉𐐼. 𐐈𐑌𐐼 𐐮𐐻 𐐿𐐩𐑋 𐐻𐐭 𐐹𐐰𐑅 𐑄𐐰𐐻 𐑄𐐩 𐑅𐐫 𐑄𐐰𐐻 𐑄 𐐹𐐨𐐹𐑊 𐐶𐐳𐐼 𐐸𐐪𐑉𐐼𐐲𐑌 𐑄𐐯𐑉 𐐸𐐪𐑉𐐻𐑅, 𐑄𐐯𐑉𐑁𐐬𐑉 𐑄𐐩 𐐼𐐨𐐹𐐪𐑉𐐻𐐯𐐼 𐐰𐑌𐐼 𐐿𐐩𐑋 𐐬𐑂𐐲𐑉 𐐮𐑌𐐻𐐭 𐑄 𐑊𐐰𐑌𐐼 𐐱𐑂 𐐣𐐮𐐼𐐬𐑌𐐴. 𐐈𐑌𐐼 𐑄𐐩 𐐼𐐮𐐼 𐐹𐑉𐐨𐐽 𐑄 𐐶𐐲𐑉𐐼 𐐲𐑌𐐻𐐭 𐑋𐐯𐑌𐐨, 𐐰𐑌𐐼 𐑁𐐷𐐭 𐐺𐐨𐑊𐐨𐑂𐐼

𐐱𐑌 𐑄 𐐶𐐲𐑉𐐼𐑆 𐐸𐐶𐐮𐐽 𐑄𐐩 𐐻𐐫𐐻. 𐐤𐐯𐑂𐐲𐑉𐑄𐐯𐑊𐐯𐑅, 𐐁𐑉𐐲𐑌 𐐰𐑌𐐼 𐐲 𐑅𐐲𐑉𐐻𐐮𐑌 𐑌𐐲𐑋𐐺𐐲𐑉 𐐱𐑂 𐐸𐐮𐑆 𐐺𐑉𐐯𐑄𐑉𐐯𐑌 𐐶𐐲𐑉 𐐻𐐩𐐿𐐲𐑌 𐐰𐑌𐐼 𐐿𐐰𐑅𐐻 𐐮𐑌𐐻𐐭 𐐹𐑉𐐮𐑆𐐲𐑌, 𐐰𐑌𐐼 𐑄 𐑉𐐨𐑋𐐩𐑌𐐼𐐲𐑉 𐐱𐑂 𐑄𐐯𐑋 𐑁𐑊𐐯𐐼 𐐵𐐻 𐐱𐑂 𐑄 𐑊𐐰𐑌𐐼 𐐱𐑂 𐐣𐐮𐐼𐐬𐑌𐐴, 𐐲𐑌𐐻𐐭 𐑄 𐑉𐐨𐐾𐐲𐑌𐑆 𐑉𐐵𐑌𐐼 𐐲𐐺𐐵𐐻. 𐐈𐑌𐐼 𐑄𐐬𐑆 𐐸𐐭 𐐶𐐲𐑉 𐐿𐐰𐑅𐐻 𐐮𐑌𐐻𐐭 𐐹𐑉𐐮𐑆𐐲𐑌 𐑅𐐲𐑁𐐲𐑉𐐼 𐑋𐐯𐑌𐐨 𐑃𐐮𐑍𐑆, 𐐰𐑌𐐼 𐑄𐐩 𐐶𐐲𐑉 𐐼𐐯𐑊𐐮𐑂𐐲𐑉𐐼 𐐺𐐴 𐑄 𐐸𐐰𐑌𐐼 𐐱𐑂 𐐢𐐰𐑋𐐬𐑌𐐴 𐐰𐑌𐐼 𐐈𐑋𐐲𐑌, 𐐰𐑌𐐼 𐑄𐐩 𐐶𐐲𐑉 𐑁𐐯𐐼 𐐰𐑌𐐼 𐐿𐑊𐐬𐑄𐐼. 𐐈𐑌𐐼 𐑄𐐩 𐐶𐐯𐑌𐐻 𐑁𐐫𐑉𐑃 𐐲𐑀𐐯𐑌 𐐻𐐭 𐐼𐐨𐐿𐑊𐐩𐑉 𐑄 𐐶𐐲𐑉𐐼, 𐐰𐑌𐐼 𐑄𐐲𐑅 𐑄𐐩 𐐶𐐲𐑉 𐐼𐐯𐑊𐐮𐑂𐐲𐑉𐐼 𐑁𐐫𐑉 𐑄 𐑁𐐲𐑉𐑅𐐻 𐐻𐐴𐑋 𐐵𐐻 𐐱𐑂 𐐹𐑉𐐮𐑆𐐲𐑌; 𐐰𐑌𐐼 𐑄𐐲𐑅 𐑄𐐩 𐐸𐐰𐐼 𐑅𐐲𐑁𐐲𐑉𐐼. 𐐈𐑌𐐼 𐑄𐐩 𐐶𐐯𐑌𐐻 𐑁𐐫𐑉𐑃 𐐸𐐶𐐮𐑄𐐲𐑉𐑅𐐬𐐯𐑂𐐲𐑉 𐑄𐐩 𐐶𐐲𐑉 𐑊𐐯𐐼 𐐺𐐴 𐑄 𐐝𐐹𐐮𐑉𐐮𐐻 𐐱𐑂 𐑄 𐐢𐐫𐑉𐐼, 𐐹𐑉𐐨𐐽𐐮𐑍 𐑄 𐐶𐐲𐑉𐐼 𐐱𐑂 𐐘𐐱𐐼 𐐮𐑌 𐐯𐑂𐑉𐐨 𐑅𐐮𐑌𐐲𐑀𐐱𐑀 𐐱𐑂 𐑄 𐐈𐑋𐐰𐑊𐐯𐐿𐐴𐐻𐑅, 𐐫𐑉 𐐮𐑌 𐐯𐑂𐑉𐐨 𐐲𐑅𐐯𐑋𐐺𐑊𐐨 𐐱𐑂 𐑄 𐐢𐐰𐑋𐐲𐑌𐐴𐐻𐑅 𐐸𐐶𐐩𐑉 𐑄𐐩 𐐿𐐳𐐼 𐐺𐐨 𐐰𐐼𐑋𐐮𐐻𐐯𐐼.

4. 𐐈𐑌𐐼 𐐮𐐻 𐐿𐐩𐑋 𐐻𐐭 𐐹𐐰𐑅 𐑄𐐰𐐻 𐑄 𐐢𐐫𐑉𐐼 𐐺𐐨𐑀𐐰𐑌 𐐻𐐭 𐐺𐑊𐐯𐑅 𐑄𐐯𐑋, 𐐮𐑌𐑅𐐬𐑋𐐲𐐽 𐑄𐐰𐐻 𐑄𐐩 𐐺𐑉𐐫𐐻 𐑋𐐯𐑌𐐨 𐐻𐐭 𐑄 𐑌𐐱𐑊𐐯𐐾 𐐱𐑂 𐑄 𐐻𐑉𐐭𐑃; 𐐷𐐩, 𐑄𐐩 𐐼𐐮𐐼 𐐿𐐱𐑌𐑂𐐮𐑌𐑅 𐑋𐐯𐑌𐐨 𐐱𐑂 𐑄𐐩𐑉 𐑅𐐮𐑌𐑆, 𐐰𐑌𐐼 𐐱𐑂 𐑄 𐐻𐑉𐐲𐐼𐐮𐑇𐐲𐑌𐑆 𐐱𐑂 𐑄𐐩𐑉 𐑁𐐪𐑄𐐲𐑉𐑆, 𐐸𐐶𐐮𐐽 𐐶𐐲𐑉 𐑌𐐱𐐻 𐐿𐐱𐑉𐐯𐐿𐐻.

5. 𐐈𐑌𐐼 𐐮𐐻 𐐿𐐩𐑋 𐐻𐐭 𐐹𐐰𐑅 𐑄𐐰𐐻 𐐈𐑋𐐲𐑌 𐐰𐑌𐐼 𐐢𐐰𐑋𐐬𐑌𐐴 𐑉𐐨𐐻𐐲𐑉𐑌𐐼 𐑁𐑉𐐱𐑋 𐑄 𐑊𐐰𐑌𐐼 𐐱𐑂 𐐣𐐮𐐼𐐬𐑌𐐴, 𐐻𐐭 𐑄 𐑊𐐰𐑌𐐼 𐐱𐑂 𐐆𐑇𐑋𐐩𐐯𐑊, 𐐸𐐶𐐮𐐽 𐐶𐐱𐑆 𐑄 𐑊𐐰𐑌𐐼 𐐱𐑂 𐑄𐐩𐑉 𐐮𐑌𐐸𐐯𐑉𐐮𐐻𐐲𐑌𐑅. 𐐈𐑌𐐼 𐐿𐐮𐑍 𐐢𐐰𐑋𐐬𐑌𐐴 𐐶𐐳𐐼 𐑌𐐱𐐻 𐑅𐐲𐑁𐐲𐑉 𐑄𐐰𐐻 𐐈𐑋𐐲𐑌 𐑇𐐳𐐼 𐑅𐐲𐑉𐑂 𐐸𐐮𐑋, 𐐫𐑉 𐐺𐐨 𐐸𐐮𐑆 𐑅𐐲𐑉𐑂𐐲𐑌𐐻; 𐐺𐐲𐐻 𐐸𐐨 𐐿𐐫𐑆𐐼 𐑄𐐰𐐻 𐑄𐐩𐑉 𐑇𐐳𐐼 𐐺𐐨 𐑅𐐮𐑌𐐲𐑀𐐱𐑀𐑆 𐐺𐐮𐑊𐐻 𐐮𐑌 𐑄 𐑊𐐰𐑌𐐼 𐐱𐑂 𐐆𐑇𐑋𐐩𐐯𐑊; 𐐰𐑌𐐼 𐐸𐐨 𐐿𐐫𐑆𐐼 𐑄𐐰𐐻 𐐸𐐮𐑆 𐐹𐐨𐐹𐑊, 𐐫𐑉 𐑄 𐐹𐐨𐐹𐑊 𐐸𐐭 𐐶𐐲𐑉 𐐲𐑌𐐼𐐲𐑉 𐐸𐐮𐑆 𐑉𐐩𐑌, 𐑇𐐳𐐼 𐐲𐑅𐐯𐑋𐐺𐑊 𐑄𐐯𐑋𐑅𐐯𐑊𐑂𐑆 𐐻𐐭𐑀𐐯𐑄𐐲𐑉. 𐐈𐑌𐐼 𐐸𐐨 𐐼𐐮𐐼 𐑉𐐨𐐾𐑎𐑅 𐐬𐑂𐐲𐑉 𐑄𐐯𐑋, 𐐰𐑌𐐼 𐐸𐐨 𐐼𐐮𐐼 𐐻𐐨𐐽 𐑄𐐯𐑋 𐑋𐐯𐑌𐐨 𐑃𐐮𐑍𐑆. 𐐈𐑌𐐼 𐐸𐐨 𐐼𐐮𐐼 𐐫𐑊𐑅𐐬 𐐼𐐨𐐿𐑊𐐩𐑉 𐐲𐑌𐐻𐐭 𐑄𐐯𐑋, 𐑄𐐰𐐻 𐑄𐐩 𐐶𐐲𐑉 𐐲 𐐹𐐨𐐹𐑊 𐐸𐐭 𐐶𐐲𐑉 𐐲𐑌𐐼𐐲𐑉 𐐸𐐮𐑋, 𐐰𐑌𐐼 𐑄𐐰𐐻 𐑄𐐩 𐐶𐐲𐑉 𐐲 𐑁𐑉𐐨 𐐹𐐨𐐹𐑊; 𐑄𐐰𐐻 𐑄𐐩 𐐶𐐲𐑉 𐑁𐑉𐐨 𐑁𐑉𐐱𐑋 𐑄 𐐱𐐹𐑉𐐯𐑇𐐲𐑌𐑆 𐐱𐑂 𐑄 𐐿𐐮𐑍, 𐐸𐐮𐑆 𐑁𐐪𐑄𐐲𐑉; 𐑁𐐫𐑉 𐑄𐐰𐐻 𐐸𐐮𐑆 𐑁𐐪𐑄𐐲𐑉 𐐸𐐰𐐼 𐑀𐑉𐐰𐑌𐐻𐐯𐐼 𐐲𐑌𐐻𐐭 𐐸𐐮𐑋 𐑄𐐰𐐻 𐐸𐐨 𐑋𐐴𐐻 𐑉𐐩𐑌 𐐬𐑂𐐲𐑉 𐑄 𐐹𐐨𐐹𐑊 𐐸𐐭 𐐶𐐲𐑉 𐐮𐑌 𐑄 𐑊𐐰𐑌𐐼 𐐱𐑂 𐐆𐑇𐑋𐐩𐐯𐑊, 𐐰𐑌𐐼 𐐮𐑌 𐐫𐑊 𐑄 𐑊𐐰𐑌𐐼 𐑉𐐵𐑌𐐼 𐐲𐐺𐐵𐐻. 𐐈𐑌𐐼 𐐸𐐨 𐐫𐑊𐑅𐐬 𐐼𐐨𐐿𐑊𐐩𐑉𐐼 𐐲𐑌𐐻𐐭 𐑄𐐯𐑋 𐑄𐐰𐐻 𐑄𐐩 𐑋𐐴𐐻 𐐸𐐰𐑂 𐑄 𐑊𐐮𐐺𐐲𐑉𐐻𐐨 𐐱𐑂 𐐶𐐲𐑉𐑇𐐮𐐹𐐮𐑍 𐑄 𐐢𐐫𐑉𐐼 𐑄𐐩𐑉 𐐘𐐱𐐼, 𐐰𐐿𐐫𐑉𐐼𐐮𐑍 𐐻𐐭 𐑄𐐩𐑉 𐐼𐐨𐑆𐐴𐑉𐑆, 𐐮𐑌 𐐸𐐶𐐱𐐻𐑅𐐬𐐯𐑂𐐲𐑉 𐐹𐑊𐐩𐑅 𐑄𐐩 𐐶𐐲𐑉 𐐮𐑌, 𐐮𐑁 𐐮𐐻 𐐶𐐲𐑉 𐐮𐑌 𐑄 𐑊𐐰𐑌𐐼 𐐸𐐶𐐮𐐽 𐐶𐐱𐑆 𐐲𐑌𐐼𐐲𐑉 𐑄 𐑉𐐩𐑌 𐐱𐑂 𐐿𐐮𐑍 𐐢𐐰𐑋𐐬𐑌𐐴. 𐐈𐑌𐐼 𐐈𐑋𐐲𐑌 𐐼𐐮𐐼 𐐹𐑉𐐨𐐽 𐐲𐑌𐐻𐐭 𐑄 𐐹𐐨𐐹𐑊 𐐱𐑂 𐐿𐐮𐑍 𐐢𐐰𐑋𐐬𐑌𐐴; 𐐰𐑌𐐼 𐐮𐐻 𐐿𐐩𐑋 𐐻𐐭 𐐹𐐰𐑅 𐑄𐐰𐐻 𐐸𐐨 𐐼𐐮𐐼 𐐻𐐨𐐽 𐑄𐐯𐑋 𐐫𐑊 𐑃𐐮𐑍𐑆 𐐿𐐱𐑌𐑅𐐲𐑉𐑌𐐮𐑍 𐑃𐐮𐑍𐑆 𐐹𐐲𐑉𐐻𐐩𐑌𐐮𐑍 𐐻𐐭 𐑉𐐴𐐽𐐲𐑅𐑌𐐯𐑅. 𐐈𐑌𐐼 𐐸𐐨 𐐼𐐮𐐼 𐐯𐑀𐑆𐐫𐑉𐐻 𐑄𐐯𐑋 𐐼𐐩𐑊𐐨, 𐐶𐐮𐑄 𐐫𐑊 𐐼𐐮𐑊𐐮𐐾𐐯𐑌𐑅; 𐐰𐑌𐐼 𐑄𐐩 𐑀𐐩𐑂 𐐸𐐨𐐼 𐐲𐑌𐐻𐐭 𐐸𐐮𐑆 𐐶𐐲𐑉𐐼, 𐐰𐑌𐐼 𐑄𐐩 𐐶𐐲𐑉 𐑆𐐯𐑊𐐲𐑅 𐑁𐐫𐑉 𐐿𐐨𐐹𐐮𐑍 𐑄 𐐿𐐱𐑋𐐰𐑌𐐼𐑋𐐯𐑌𐐻𐑅 𐐱𐑂 𐐘𐐱𐐼. 𐐤𐐵 𐐰𐑆 𐐈𐑋𐐲𐑌 𐐶𐐱𐑆 𐑄𐐲𐑅 𐐻𐐨𐐽𐐮𐑍 𐑄 𐐹𐐨𐐹𐑊 𐐱𐑂 𐐢𐐰𐑋𐐬𐑌𐐴 𐐿𐐱𐑌𐐻𐐮𐑌𐐷𐐭𐐰𐑊𐐨, 𐐶𐐨 𐐶𐐮𐑊 𐑉𐐨𐐻𐐲𐑉𐑌 𐐻𐐭 𐑄 𐐰𐐿𐐵𐑌𐐻 𐐱𐑂 𐐁𐑉𐐲𐑌 𐐰𐑌𐐼 𐐸𐐮𐑆 𐐺𐑉𐐯𐑄𐑉𐐯𐑌; 𐑁𐐫𐑉 𐐰𐑁𐐻𐐲𐑉 𐐸𐐨 𐐼𐐨𐐹𐐪𐑉𐐻𐐯𐐼 𐑁𐑉𐐱𐑋 𐑄 𐑊𐐰𐑌𐐼 𐐱𐑂 𐐣𐐮𐐼𐐬𐑌𐐴, 𐐸𐐨 𐐶𐐱𐑆 𐑊𐐯𐐼 𐐺𐐴 𐑄 𐐝𐐹𐐮𐑉𐐮𐐻 𐐻𐐭 𐑄 𐑊𐐰𐑌𐐼 𐐱𐑂 𐐤𐐨𐑁𐐴, 𐐨𐑂𐐯𐑌 𐐻𐐭 𐑄 𐐸𐐵𐑅 𐐱𐑂 𐑄 𐐿𐐮𐑍 𐐸𐐶𐐮𐐽 𐐶𐐱𐑆 𐐬𐑂𐐲𐑉 𐐫𐑊 𐑄 𐑊𐐰𐑌𐐼, 𐑅𐐩𐑂 𐐮𐐻 𐐶𐐲𐑉 𐑄 𐑊𐐰𐑌𐐼 𐐱𐑂 𐐆𐑇𐑋𐐩𐐯𐑊: 𐐰𐑌𐐼 𐐸𐐨 𐐶𐐱𐑆 𐑄 𐑁𐐪𐑄𐐲𐑉 𐐱𐑂 𐐢𐐰𐑋𐐬𐑌𐐴.

6. 𐐈𐑌𐐼 𐐮𐐻 𐐿𐐩𐑋 𐐻𐐭 𐐹𐐰𐑅 𐑄𐐰𐐻 𐐸𐐨 𐐶𐐯𐑌𐐻 𐐮𐑌 𐐲𐑌𐐻𐐭 𐐸𐐮𐑋 𐐮𐑌𐐻𐐭 𐑄 𐐿𐐮𐑍'𐑆 𐐹𐐰𐑊𐐲𐑅, 𐐶𐐮𐑄 𐐸𐐮𐑆 𐐺𐑉𐐯𐑄𐑉𐐯𐑌, 𐐰𐑌𐐼 𐐺𐐵𐐼 𐐸𐐮𐑋𐑅𐐯𐑊𐑁 𐐺𐐨𐑁𐐬𐑉 𐑄 𐐿𐐮𐑍, 𐐰𐑌𐐼 𐑅𐐯𐐼 𐐲𐑌𐐻𐐭 𐐸𐐮𐑋, 𐐒𐐨𐐸𐐬𐑊𐐼, 𐐄 𐐿𐐮𐑍, 𐐶𐐨 𐐪𐑉 𐑄 𐐺𐑉𐐯𐑄𐑉𐐯𐑌 𐐱𐑂 𐐈𐑋𐐲𐑌, 𐐸𐐭𐑋 𐑄𐐵 𐐸𐐰𐑅𐐻 𐐼𐐯𐑊𐐮𐑂𐐲𐑉𐐼 𐐵𐐻 𐐱𐑂 𐐹𐑉𐐮𐑆𐐲𐑌. 𐐈𐑌𐐼 𐑌𐐵, 𐐄 𐐿𐐮𐑍, 𐐮𐑁 𐑄𐐵 𐐶𐐮𐑊𐐻 𐑅𐐹𐐩𐑉 𐐵𐑉 𐑊𐐴𐑂𐑆, 𐐶𐐨 𐐶𐐮𐑊 𐐺𐐨 𐑄𐐴 𐑅𐐲𐑉𐑂𐐲𐑌𐐻𐑅. 𐐈𐑌𐐼 𐑄 𐐿𐐮𐑍 𐑅𐐯𐐼 𐐲𐑌𐐻𐐭 𐑄𐐯𐑋, 𐐊𐑉𐐴𐑆, 𐑁𐐫𐑉 𐐌 𐐶𐐮𐑊 𐑀𐑉𐐰𐑌𐐻 𐐲𐑌𐐻𐐭 𐐷𐐭 𐐷𐐭𐑉 𐑊𐐴𐑂𐑆, 𐐰𐑌𐐼 𐐌 𐐶𐐮𐑊 𐑌𐐱𐐻 𐑅𐐲𐑁𐐲𐑉 𐑄𐐰𐐻 𐐷𐐨 𐑇𐐰𐑊 𐐺𐐨 𐑋𐐴 𐑅𐐲𐑉𐑂𐐲𐑌𐐻𐑅; 𐐺𐐲𐐻 𐐌 𐐶𐐮𐑊 𐐮𐑌𐑅𐐮𐑅𐐻 𐑄𐐰𐐻 𐐷𐐨 𐑇𐐰𐑊 𐐰𐐼𐑋𐐮𐑌𐐮𐑅𐐻𐐲𐑉 𐐲𐑌𐐻𐐭 𐑋𐐨; 𐑁𐐫𐑉 𐐌 𐐸𐐰𐑂 𐐺𐐮𐑌 𐑅𐐲𐑋𐐸𐐶𐐱𐐻 𐐻𐑉𐐲𐐺𐐲𐑊𐐼 𐐮𐑌 𐑋𐐴𐑌𐐼, 𐐺𐐨𐐿𐐫𐑆 𐐱𐑂 𐑄 𐐾𐐯𐑌𐐲𐑉𐐱𐑅𐐮𐐻𐐨 𐐰𐑌𐐼 𐑄 𐑀𐑉𐐩𐐻𐑌𐐯𐑅 𐐱𐑂 𐑄 𐐶𐐲𐑉𐐼𐑆 𐐱𐑂 𐑄𐐴 𐐺𐑉𐐲𐑄𐐲𐑉 𐐈𐑋𐐲𐑌; 𐐰𐑌𐐼 𐐌 𐐼𐐨𐑆𐐴𐑉 𐐻𐐭 𐑌𐐬 𐑄 𐐿𐐫𐑆 𐐸𐐶𐐴 𐐸𐐨 𐐸𐐰𐑆 𐑌𐐱𐐻 𐐿𐐲𐑋 𐐲𐐹 𐐵𐐻 𐐱𐑂 𐐣𐐮𐐼𐐬𐑌𐐴 𐐶𐐮𐑄 𐑄𐐨. 𐐈𐑌𐐼 𐐁𐑉𐐲𐑌 𐑅𐐯𐐼 𐐲𐑌𐐻𐐭 𐑄 𐐿𐐮𐑍, 𐐒𐐨𐐸𐐬𐑊𐐼, 𐑄 𐐝𐐹𐐮𐑉𐐮𐐻 𐐱𐑂 𐑄 𐐢𐐫𐑉𐐼 𐐸𐐰𐑆 𐐿𐐫𐑊𐐼 𐐸𐐮𐑋

𐐲𐑌𐐲𐑄𐐲𐑉 𐐶𐐩: 𐐸𐐨 𐐸𐐰𐑆 𐑀𐐱𐑌 𐐻𐐭 𐑄 𐑊𐐰𐑌𐐼 𐐱𐑂 𐐆𐑇𐑋𐐩𐐯𐑊, 𐐻𐐭 𐐻𐐨𐐽 𐑄 𐐹𐐨𐐹𐑊 𐐱𐑂 𐐢𐐩𐑋𐐬𐑌𐐴. 𐐤𐐵 𐑄 𐐿𐐮𐑍 𐑅𐐯𐐼 𐐲𐑌𐐻𐐭 𐑄𐐯𐑋, 𐐐𐐶𐐱𐐻 𐐮𐑆 𐑄𐐮𐑅 𐑄𐐰𐐻 𐐷𐐨 𐐸𐐰𐑂 𐑅𐐯𐐼 𐐿𐐲𐑌𐑅𐐲𐑉𐑌𐐮𐑍 𐑄 𐐝𐐹𐐮𐑉𐐮𐐻 𐐱𐑂 𐑄 𐐢𐐫𐑉𐐼? 𐐒𐐨𐐸𐐬𐑊𐐼, 𐑄𐐮𐑅 𐐮𐑆 𐑄 𐑃𐐮𐑍 𐐸𐐶𐐮𐐽 𐐼𐐲𐑃 𐐻𐑉𐐲𐐺𐑊 𐑋𐐨. 𐐈𐑌𐐼 𐐫𐑊𐑅𐐬, 𐐸𐐶𐐱𐐻 𐐮𐑆 𐑄𐐮𐑅 𐑄𐐰𐐻 𐐈𐑋𐐲𐑌 𐑅𐐯𐐼—𐐆𐑁 𐐷𐐨 𐐶𐐮𐑊 𐑉𐐨𐐹𐐯𐑌𐐻 𐐷𐐨 𐑇𐐰𐑊 𐐺 𐑅𐐩𐑂𐐼, 𐐰𐑌𐐼 𐐮𐑁 𐐷𐐨 𐐶𐐮𐑊 𐑌𐐱𐐻 𐑉𐐨𐐹𐐯𐑌𐐻, 𐐷𐐨 𐑇𐐰𐑊 𐐺 𐐿𐐰𐑅𐐻 𐐫𐑁 𐐰𐐻 𐑄 𐑊𐐰𐑅𐐻 𐐼𐐩? 𐐈𐑌𐐼 𐐁𐑉𐐲𐑌 𐐰𐑌𐑅𐐲𐑉𐐼 𐐸𐐮𐑋 𐐰𐑌𐐼 𐑅𐐯𐐼 𐐲𐑌𐐻𐐭 𐐸𐐮𐑋, 𐐒𐐮𐑊𐐨𐑂𐐯𐑅𐐻 𐑄𐐵 𐑄𐐰𐐻 𐑄𐐯𐑉 𐐮𐑆 𐐲 𐐘𐐱𐐼? 𐐈𐑌𐐼 𐑄 𐐿𐐮𐑍 𐑅𐐯𐐼 𐐌 𐑌𐐬 𐑄𐐰𐐻 𐑄 𐐈𐑋𐐰𐑊𐐯𐐿𐐴𐐻𐑅 𐑅𐐩 𐑄𐐰𐐻 𐑄𐐯𐑉 𐐮𐑆 𐐲 𐐘𐐱𐐼, 𐐰𐑌𐐼 𐐌 𐐸𐐰𐑂 𐑀𐑉𐐰𐑌𐐻𐐯𐐼 𐐲𐑌𐐻𐐭 𐑄𐐯𐑋 𐑄𐐰𐐻 𐑄𐐩 𐑇𐐳𐐼 𐐺𐐮𐑊𐐼 𐑅𐐰𐑍𐐿𐐽𐐭𐐯𐑉𐐮𐑆, 𐑄𐐰𐐻 𐑄𐐩 𐑋𐐩 𐐲𐑅𐐯𐑋𐐺𐑊 𐑄𐐯𐑋𐑅𐐯𐑊𐑂𐑆 𐐻𐐭𐑀𐐯𐑄𐐲𐑉 𐐻𐐭 𐐶𐐲𐑉𐑇𐐮𐐹 𐐸𐐮𐑋. 𐐈𐑌𐐼 𐐮𐑁 𐑌𐐵 𐑄𐐵 𐑅𐐩𐐯𐑅𐐻 𐑄𐐯𐑉 𐐮𐑆 𐐲 𐐘𐐱𐐼, 𐐺𐐨𐐸𐐬𐑊𐐼 𐐌 𐐶𐐮𐑊 𐐺𐐮𐑊𐐨𐑂.

7. 𐐈𐑌𐐼 𐑌𐐵 𐐸𐐶𐐯𐑌 𐐁𐑉𐐲𐑌 𐐸𐐲𐑉𐐼 𐑄𐐮𐑅, 𐐸𐐮𐑆 𐐸𐐪𐑉𐐻 𐐺𐐨𐑀𐐰𐑌 𐐻𐐭 𐑉𐐨𐐾𐐦𐑅, 𐐰𐑌𐐼 𐐸𐐨 𐑅𐐯𐐼, 𐐒𐐨𐐸𐐬𐑊𐐼, 𐐰𐑇𐐳𐑉𐐯𐐼𐑊𐐨 𐐰𐑆 𐑄𐐵 𐑊𐐮𐑂𐐯𐑅𐐻, 𐐄 𐐿𐐮𐑍, 𐑄𐐯𐑉 𐐮𐑆 𐐲 𐐘𐐱𐐼. 𐐈𐑌𐐼 𐑄 𐐿𐐮𐑍 𐑅𐐯𐐼, 𐐆𐑆 𐐘𐐱𐐼 𐑄𐐰𐐻 𐐘𐑉𐐩𐐻 𐐝𐐹𐐮𐑉𐐮𐐻 𐑄𐐰𐐻 𐐺𐑉𐐫𐐻 𐐵𐑉 𐑁𐐪𐑄𐐲𐑉𐑆 𐐵𐐻 𐐱𐑂 𐑄 𐑊𐐰𐑌𐐼 𐐱𐑂 𐐖𐐯𐑉𐐭𐑅𐐲𐑊𐐯𐑋? 𐐈𐑌𐐼 𐐁𐑉𐐲𐑌 𐑅𐐯𐐼 𐐲𐑌𐐻𐐭 𐐸𐐮𐑋, 𐐏𐐩, 𐐸𐐨 𐐮𐑆 𐑄𐐰𐐻 𐐘𐑉𐐩𐐻 𐐝𐐹𐐮𐑉𐐮𐐻, 𐐰𐑌𐐼 𐐸𐐨 𐐿𐑉𐐨𐐩𐐻𐐯𐐼 𐐫𐑊 𐑃𐐮𐑍𐑆 𐐺𐐬𐑃 𐐮𐑌 𐐸𐐯𐑂𐐲𐑌 𐐰𐑌𐐼 𐐮𐑌 𐐲𐑉𐑃: 𐐒𐐮𐑊𐐨𐑂𐐯𐑅𐐻 𐑄𐐵 𐑄𐐮𐑅? 𐐈𐑌𐐼 𐐸𐐨 𐑅𐐯𐐼, 𐐏𐐩, 𐐌 𐐺𐐮𐑊𐐨𐑂 𐑄𐐰𐐻 𐑄 𐐘𐑉𐐩𐐻 𐐝𐐹𐐮𐑉𐐮𐐻 𐐿𐑉𐐨𐐩𐐻𐐯𐐼 𐐫𐑊 𐑃𐐮𐑍𐑆, 𐐰𐑌𐐼 𐐌 𐐼𐐯𐑆𐐴𐑉 𐑄𐐰𐐻 𐐷𐐨 𐑇𐐳𐐼 𐐻𐐯𐑊 𐑋𐐨 𐐿𐐲𐑌𐑅𐐲𐑉𐑌𐐮𐑍 𐐫𐑊 𐑄𐐨𐑆 𐑃𐐮𐑍𐑆, 𐐰𐑌𐐼 𐐌 𐐶𐐮𐑊 𐐺𐐮𐑊𐐨𐑂 𐑄𐐴 𐐶𐐲𐑉𐐼𐑆.

8. 𐐈𐑌𐐼 𐐮𐐻 𐐿𐐩𐑋 𐐻𐐭 𐐹𐐰𐑅 𐑄𐐰𐐻 𐐸𐐶𐐯𐑌 𐐁𐑉𐐲𐑌 𐑅𐐫 𐑄𐐰𐐻 𐑄 𐐿𐐮𐑍 𐐶𐐳𐐼 𐐺𐐮𐑊𐐨𐑂 𐐸𐐮𐑆 𐐶𐐲𐑉𐐼𐑆, 𐐸𐐨 𐐺𐐨𐑀𐐰𐑌 𐑁𐑉𐐱𐑋 𐑄 𐐿𐑉𐐨𐐩𐑇𐐲𐑌 𐐱𐑂 𐐈𐐼𐐲𐑋, 𐑉𐐨𐐼𐐮𐑍 𐑄 𐑅𐐿𐑉𐐮𐐹𐐽𐐲𐑉𐑆 𐐲𐑌𐐻𐐭 𐑄 𐐿𐐮𐑍: 𐐸𐐵 𐐘𐐱𐐼 𐐿𐑉𐐨𐐩𐐻𐐯𐐼 𐑋𐐰𐑌 𐐰𐑁𐐻𐐲𐑉 𐐸𐐮𐑆 𐐬𐑌 𐐮𐑋𐐮𐐾, 𐐰𐑌𐐼 𐑄𐐰𐐻 𐐘𐐱𐐼 𐑀𐐩𐑂 𐐸𐐮𐑋 𐐿𐐲𐑋𐐰𐑌𐐼𐑋𐐯𐑌𐐻𐑅, 𐐰𐑌𐐼 𐑄𐐰𐐻 𐐺𐐨𐐿𐐫𐑆 𐐱𐑂 𐐻𐑉𐐰𐑌𐑅𐑀𐑉𐐯𐑇𐐲𐑌, 𐑋𐐰𐑌 𐐸𐐰𐐼 𐑁𐐫𐑊𐐲𐑌. 𐐈𐑌𐐼 𐐁𐑉𐐲𐑌 𐐼𐐮𐐼 𐐯𐐿𐑅𐐹𐐵𐑌𐐼 𐐲𐑌𐐻𐐭 𐐸𐐮𐑋 𐑄 𐑅𐐿𐑉𐐮𐐹𐐽𐐲𐑉𐑆, 𐑁𐑉𐐱𐑋 𐑄 𐐿𐑉𐐨𐐩𐑇𐐲𐑌 𐐱𐑂 𐐈𐐼𐐲𐑋, 𐑊𐐩𐐮𐑍 𐑄 𐑁𐐫𐑊 𐐱𐑂 𐑋𐐰𐑌 𐐺𐐨𐑁𐐬𐑉 𐐸𐐮𐑋, 𐐰𐑌𐐼 𐑄𐐯𐑉 𐐿𐐪𐑉𐑌𐐲𐑊 𐑅𐐻𐐩𐐻, 𐐰𐑌𐐼 𐐫𐑊𐑅𐐬 𐑄 𐐹𐑊𐐰𐑌 𐐱𐑂 𐑉𐐨𐐼𐐯𐑋𐐹𐑇𐐲𐑌, 𐐸𐐶𐐮𐐽 𐐶𐐱𐑆 𐐹𐑉𐐨𐐹𐐯𐑉𐐼 𐑁𐑉𐐱𐑋 𐑄 𐑁𐐵𐑌𐐼𐐩𐑇𐐲𐑌 𐐱𐑂 𐑄 𐐶𐐲𐑉𐑊𐐼, 𐑃𐑉𐐭 𐐗𐑉𐐴𐑅𐐻, 𐑁𐐫𐑉 𐐫𐑊 𐐸𐐭𐑅𐐬𐐯𐑂𐐲𐑉 𐐶𐐳𐐼 𐐺𐐮𐑊𐐨𐑂 𐐱𐑌 𐐸𐐮𐑆 𐑌𐐩𐑋. 𐐈𐑌𐐼 𐑅𐐮𐑌𐑅 𐑋𐐰𐑌 𐐸𐐰𐐼 𐑁𐐫𐑊𐐲𐑌, 𐐸𐐨 𐐿𐐳𐐼 𐑌𐐱𐐻 𐑋𐐯𐑉𐐮𐐻 𐐯𐑌𐐮𐑃𐐮𐑍 𐐱𐑂 𐐸𐐮𐑋𐑅𐐯𐑊𐑁; 𐐺𐐲𐐻 𐑄 𐑅𐐲𐑁𐐲𐑉𐐮𐑍𐑆 𐐰𐑌𐐼 𐐼𐐯𐑃 𐐱𐑂 𐐗𐑉𐐴𐑅𐐻, 𐐰𐐻𐐬𐑌𐐯𐑃 𐑁𐐫𐑉 𐑄𐐯𐑉 𐑅𐐮𐑌𐑆, 𐑃𐑉𐐭 𐑁𐐩𐑃 𐐰𐑌𐐼 𐑉𐐨𐐹𐐯𐑌𐐻𐐰𐑌𐑅, 𐐯𐐻𐑅.; 𐐰𐑌𐐼 𐑄𐐰𐐻 𐐸𐐨 𐐺𐑉𐐩𐐿𐐯𐑃 𐑄 𐐺𐐰𐑌𐐼𐑆 𐐱𐑂 𐐼𐐯𐑃, 𐑄𐐰𐐻 𐑄 𐑀𐑉𐐩𐑂 𐑇𐐰𐑊 𐐸𐐰𐑂 𐑌𐐬 𐑂𐐮𐐿𐐻𐐲𐑉𐐨, 𐐰𐑌𐐼 𐑄𐐰𐐻 𐑄 𐑅𐐻𐐮𐑍 𐐱𐑂 𐐼𐐯𐑃 𐑇𐐳𐐼 𐐺 𐑅𐐶𐐱𐑊𐐬𐐼 𐐲𐐹 𐐮𐑌 𐑄 𐐸𐐬𐐹𐑅 𐐱𐑂 𐑀𐑊𐐬𐑉𐐨: 𐐰𐑌𐐼 𐐁𐑉𐐲𐑌 𐐼𐐮𐐼 𐐯𐐿𐑅𐐹𐐵𐑌𐐼 𐐫𐑊 𐑄𐐨𐑆 𐑃𐐮𐑍𐑆 𐐲𐑌𐐻𐐭 𐑄 𐐿𐐮𐑍. 𐐈𐑌𐐼 𐐮𐐻 𐐿𐐩𐑋 𐐻𐐭 𐐹𐐰𐑅 𐑄𐐰𐐻 𐐰𐑁𐐻𐐲𐑉 𐐁𐑉𐐲𐑌 𐐸𐐰𐐼 𐐯𐐿𐑅𐐹𐐵𐑌𐐼𐐯𐐼 𐑄𐐨𐑆 𐑃𐐮𐑍𐑆 𐐲𐑌𐐻𐐭 𐐸𐐮𐑋, 𐑄 𐐿𐐮𐑍 𐑅𐐯𐐼, 𐐐𐐶𐐱𐐻 𐑇𐐰𐑊 𐐌 𐐼𐐭 𐑄𐐰𐐻 𐐌 𐑋𐐩 𐐸𐐰𐑂 𐑄𐐮𐑅 𐐨𐐻𐐲𐑉𐑌𐐲𐑊 𐑊𐐴𐑁 𐐱𐑂 𐐸𐐶𐐮𐐽 𐑄𐐵 𐐸𐐰𐑅𐐻 𐑅𐐹𐐬𐐿𐐲𐑌? 𐐏𐐩, 𐐸𐐶𐐱𐐻 𐑇𐐰𐑊 𐐌 𐐼𐐭 𐑄𐐰𐐻 𐐌 𐑋𐐩 𐐺 𐐺𐐫𐑉𐑌 𐐱𐑂 𐐘𐐱𐐼, 𐐸𐐰𐑂𐐮𐑍 𐑄𐐮𐑅 𐐶𐐮𐐿𐐯𐐼 𐑅𐐹𐐮𐑉𐐮𐐻 𐑉𐐭𐐻𐐯𐐼 𐐵𐐻 𐐱𐑂 𐑋𐐴 𐐺𐑉𐐯𐑅𐐻, 𐐰𐑌𐐼 𐑉𐐨𐑅𐐨𐑂 𐐸𐐮𐑆 𐐝𐐹𐐮𐑉𐐮𐐻, 𐑄𐐰𐐻 𐐌 𐑋𐐩 𐐺 𐑁𐐮𐑊𐐼 𐐶𐐮𐑄 𐐾𐐦, 𐑄𐐰𐐻 𐐌 𐑋𐐩 𐑌𐐱𐐻 𐐺 𐐿𐐰𐑅𐐻 𐐫𐑁 𐐰𐐻 𐑄 𐑊𐐰𐑅𐐻 𐐼𐐩? 𐐒𐐨𐐸𐐬𐑊𐐼, 𐑅𐐯𐐼 𐐸𐐨, 𐐌 𐐶𐐮𐑊 𐑀𐐮𐑂 𐐲𐐹 𐐫𐑊 𐑄𐐰𐐻 𐐌 𐐹𐐲𐑆𐐯𐑅; 𐐷𐐩, 𐐌 𐐶𐐮𐑊 𐑁𐐫𐑉𐑅𐐩𐐿 𐑋𐐴 𐐿𐐮𐑍𐐼𐐲𐑋, 𐑄𐐰𐐻 𐐌 𐑋𐐩 𐑉𐐨𐑅𐐨𐑂 𐑄𐐮𐑅 𐑀𐑉𐐩𐐻 𐐾𐐦. 𐐒𐐲𐐻 𐐁𐑉𐐲𐑌 𐑅𐐯𐐼 𐐲𐑌𐐻𐐭 𐐸𐐮𐑋, 𐐆𐑁 𐑄𐐵 𐐼𐐯𐑆𐐴𐑉𐐯𐑅𐐻 𐑄𐐮𐑅 𐑃𐐮𐑍, 𐐮𐑁 𐑄𐐵 𐐶𐐮𐑊𐐻 𐐺𐐵 𐐼𐐵𐑌 𐐺𐐨𐑁𐐬𐑉 𐐘𐐱𐐼, 𐐷𐐩, 𐐮𐑁 𐑄𐐵 𐐶𐐮𐑊𐐻 𐑉𐐨𐐹𐐯𐑌𐐻 𐐱𐑂 𐐫𐑊 𐑄𐐴 𐑅𐐮𐑌𐑆, 𐐰𐑌𐐼 𐐶𐐮𐑊 𐐺𐐵 𐐼𐐵𐑌 𐐺𐐨𐑁𐐬𐑉 𐐘𐐱𐐼, 𐐰𐑌𐐼 𐐿𐐫𐑊 𐐱𐑌 𐐸𐐮𐑆 𐑌𐐩𐑋 𐐮𐑌 𐑁𐐩𐑃, 𐐺𐐮𐑊𐐨𐑂𐐮𐑍 𐑄𐐰𐐻 𐐷𐐨 𐑇𐐰𐑊 𐑉𐐨𐑅𐐨𐑂, 𐑄𐐯𐑌 𐑇𐐰𐑊𐐻 𐑄𐐵 𐑉𐐨𐑅𐐨𐑂 𐑄 𐐸𐐬𐐹 𐐸𐐶𐐮𐐽 𐑄𐐵 𐐼𐐯𐑆𐐴𐑉𐐯𐑅𐐻.

9. 𐐈𐑌𐐼 𐐮𐐻 𐐿𐐩𐑋 𐐻𐐭 𐐹𐐰𐑅 𐑄𐐰𐐻 𐐸𐐶𐐯𐑌 𐐁𐑉𐐲𐑌 𐐸𐐰𐐼 𐑅𐐯𐐼 𐑄𐐨𐑆 𐐶𐐲𐑉𐐼𐑆, 𐑄 𐐿𐐮𐑍 𐐼𐐮𐐼 𐐺𐐵 𐐼𐐵𐑌 𐐺𐐨𐑁𐐬𐑉 𐑄 𐐢𐐫𐑉𐐼, 𐐲𐐹𐐱𐑌 𐐸𐐮𐑆 𐑌𐐨𐑆; 𐐷𐐩, 𐐨𐑂𐐲𐑌 𐐸𐐨 𐐼𐐮𐐼 𐐹𐑉𐐱𐑅𐐻𐑉𐐩𐐻 𐐸𐐮𐑋𐑅𐐯𐑊𐑁 𐐲𐐹𐐱𐑌 𐑄 𐐲𐑉𐑃, 𐐰𐑌𐐼 𐐿𐑉𐐴𐐼 𐑋𐐴𐐻𐐮𐑊𐐨, 𐑅𐐩𐐮𐑍, 𐐄 𐐘𐐱𐐼, 𐐁𐑉𐐲𐑌 𐐸𐐰𐑃 𐐻𐐬𐑊𐐼 𐑋𐐨 𐑄𐐰𐐻 𐑄𐐯𐑉 𐐮𐑆 𐐲 𐐘𐐱𐐼; 𐐰𐑌𐐼 𐐮𐑁 𐑄𐐯𐑉 𐐮𐑆 𐐲 𐐘𐐱𐐼, 𐐰𐑌𐐼 𐐮𐑁 𐑄𐐵 𐐪𐑉𐐻 𐐘𐐱𐐼, 𐐶𐐮𐑊𐐻 𐑄𐐵 𐑋𐐩𐐿 𐑄𐐴𐑅𐐯𐑊𐑁 𐑌𐐬𐑌 𐐲𐑌𐐻𐐭 𐑋𐐨, 𐐰𐑌𐐼 𐐌 𐐶𐐮𐑊 𐑀𐐮𐑂 𐐲𐐶𐐩 𐐫𐑊 𐑋𐐴 𐑅𐐮𐑌𐑆 𐐻𐐭 𐑌𐐬 𐑄𐐨, 𐐰𐑌𐐼 𐑄𐐰𐐻 𐐌 𐑋𐐩 𐐺 𐑉𐐩𐑆𐐼 𐑁𐑉𐐱𐑋 𐑄 𐐼𐐯𐐼, 𐐰𐑌𐐼 𐐺 𐑅𐐩𐑂𐐼 𐐰𐐻

𐑄 𐑊𐐪𐑅𐐻 𐐼𐐩. 𐐈𐑌𐐼 𐑌𐐵 𐐸𐐶𐐯𐑌 𐑄 𐐿𐐮𐑍 𐐸𐐰𐐼 𐑅𐐯𐐼 𐑄𐐨𐑆 𐐶𐐲𐑉𐐼𐑆, 𐐸𐐨 𐐶𐐱𐑆 𐑅𐐻𐑉𐐲𐐿 𐐰𐑆 𐐮𐑁 𐐸𐐨 𐐶𐐲𐑉 𐐼𐐯𐐼.

10. 𐐈𐑌𐐼 𐐮𐐻 𐐿𐐩𐑋 𐐻𐐭 𐐹𐐪𐑅 𐑄𐐰𐐻 𐐸𐐮𐑆 𐑅𐐲𐑉𐑂𐐰𐑌𐐻𐑅 𐑉𐐰𐑌 𐐰𐑌𐐼 𐐻𐐬𐑊𐐼 𐑄 𐐿𐐶𐐨𐑌 𐐫𐑊 𐑄𐐰𐐻 𐐸𐐰𐐼 𐐸𐐰𐐹𐐲𐑌𐐼 𐐲𐑌𐐻𐐭 𐑄 𐐿𐐮𐑍. 𐐈𐑌𐐼 𐑇𐐨 𐐿𐐩𐑋 𐐮𐑌 𐐲𐑌𐐻𐐭 𐑄 𐐿𐐮𐑍; 𐐰𐑌𐐼 𐐸𐐶𐐯𐑌 𐑇𐐨 𐑅𐐫 𐐸𐐮𐑋 𐑊𐐩 𐐰𐑆 𐐮𐑁 𐐸𐐨 𐐶𐐲𐑉 𐐼𐐯𐐼, 𐐰𐑌𐐼 𐐫𐑊𐑅𐐬 𐐁𐑉𐐲𐑌 𐐰𐑌𐐼 𐐸𐐮𐑆 𐐺𐑉𐐯𐑄𐑉𐐯𐑌 𐑅𐐻𐐰𐑌𐐼𐐮𐑍 𐐰𐑆 𐑄𐐬 𐑄𐐩 𐐸𐐰𐐼 𐐺𐐮𐑌 𐑄 𐐿𐐫𐑆 𐐱𐑂 𐐸𐐮𐑆 𐑁𐐫𐑊, 𐑇𐐨 𐐶𐐱𐑆 𐐰𐑍𐑀𐑉𐐨 𐐶𐐮𐑄 𐑄𐐯𐑋, 𐐰𐑌𐐼 𐐿𐐲𐑋𐐰𐑌𐐼𐐯𐐼 𐑄𐐰𐐻 𐐸𐐲𐑉 𐑅𐐲𐑉𐑂𐐰𐑌𐐻𐑅, 𐐫𐑉 𐑄 𐑅𐐲𐑉𐑂𐐰𐑌𐐻𐑅 𐐱𐑂 𐑄 𐐿𐐮𐑍, 𐑇𐐳𐐼 𐐻𐐩𐐿 𐑄𐐯𐑋 𐐰𐑌𐐼 𐑅𐑊𐐩 𐑄𐐯𐑋. 𐐤𐐵 𐑄 𐑅𐐲𐑉𐑂𐐰𐑌𐐻𐑅 𐐸𐐰𐐼 𐑅𐐨𐑌 𐑄 𐐿𐐫𐑆 𐐱𐑂 𐑄 𐐿𐐮𐑍𐑆 𐑁𐐫𐑊, 𐑄𐐯𐑉𐑁𐐬𐑉 𐑄𐐩 𐐼𐐲𐑉𐑅𐐻 𐑌𐐱𐐻 𐑊𐐩 𐑄𐐩𐑉 𐐸𐐰𐑌𐐼𐑆 𐐱𐑌 𐐁𐑉𐐲𐑌 𐐰𐑌𐐼 𐐸𐐮𐑆 𐐺𐑉𐐯𐑄𐑉𐐯𐑌; 𐐰𐑌𐐼 𐑄𐐩 𐐹𐑊𐐯𐐼 𐐶𐐮𐑄 𐑄 𐐿𐐶𐐨𐑌, 𐑅𐐩𐐮𐑍, 𐐐𐐶𐐴 𐐿𐐲𐑋𐐰𐑌𐐼𐐯𐑅𐐻 𐑄𐐵 𐑄𐐰𐐻 𐐶𐐨 𐑇𐐳𐐼 𐑅𐑊𐐩 𐑄𐐨𐑆 𐑋𐐯𐑌, 𐐸𐐶𐐯𐑌 𐐺𐐨𐐸𐐬𐑊𐐼 𐐶𐐲𐑌 𐐱𐑂 𐑄𐐯𐑋 𐐮𐑆 𐑋𐐴𐐻𐐨𐐲𐑉 𐑄𐐰𐑌 𐐲𐑅 𐐫𐑊? 𐐜𐐯𐑉𐑁𐐬𐑉 𐐶𐐨 𐑇𐐰𐑊 𐑁𐐫𐑊 𐐺𐐨𐑁𐐬𐑉 𐑄𐐯𐑋. 𐐤𐐵 𐐸𐐶𐐯𐑌 𐑄 𐐿𐐶𐐨𐑌 𐑅𐐫 𐑄 𐑁𐐨𐑉 𐐱𐑂 𐑄 𐑅𐐲𐑉𐑂𐐰𐑌𐐻𐑅, 𐑇𐐨 𐐫𐑊𐑅𐐬 𐐺𐐨𐑀𐐰𐑌 𐐻𐐭 𐑁𐐨𐑉 𐐯𐐿𐑅𐐨𐐼𐐮𐑍𐑊𐐨, 𐑊𐐯𐑅𐐻 𐑄𐐯𐑉 𐑇𐐳𐐼 𐑅𐐲𐑋 𐐨𐑂𐐲𐑊 𐐿𐐲𐑋 𐐲𐐹𐐱𐑌 𐐸𐐲𐑉. 𐐈𐑌𐐼 𐑇𐐨 𐐿𐐲𐑋𐐰𐑌𐐼𐐯𐐼 𐐸𐐲𐑉 𐑅𐐲𐑉𐑂𐐰𐑌𐐻𐑅 𐑄𐐰𐐻 𐑄𐐩 𐑇𐐳𐐼 𐑀𐐬 𐐰𐑌𐐼 𐐿𐐫𐑊 𐑄 𐐹𐐨𐐹𐑊, 𐑄𐐰𐐻 𐑄𐐩 𐑋𐐴𐐻 𐑅𐑊𐐩 𐐁𐑉𐐲𐑌 𐐰𐑌𐐼 𐐸𐐮𐑆 𐐺𐑉𐐯𐑄𐑉𐐯𐑌. 𐐤𐐵 𐐸𐐶𐐯𐑌 𐐁𐑉𐐲𐑌 𐑅𐐫 𐑄 𐐼𐐨𐐻𐐲𐑉𐑋𐐮𐑌𐐩𐑇𐐲𐑌 𐐱𐑂 𐑄 𐐿𐐶𐐨𐑌, 𐐰𐑌𐐼 𐐸𐐨 𐐫𐑊𐑅𐐬 𐑌𐐬𐐮𐑍 𐑄 𐐸𐐪𐑉𐐼𐑌𐐯𐑅 𐐱𐑂 𐑄 𐐸𐐪𐑉𐐻𐑅 𐐱𐑂 𐑄 𐐹𐐨𐐹𐑊, 𐑁𐐨𐑉𐐼 𐑊𐐯𐑅𐐻 𐑄𐐰𐐻 𐐰 𐑋𐐲𐑊𐐻𐐮𐐻𐐭𐐼 𐑇𐐳𐐼 𐐰𐑅𐐯𐑋𐐺𐐲𐑊 𐑄𐐯𐑋𐑅𐐯𐑊𐑂𐑆 𐐻𐐭𐑀𐐯𐑄𐐲𐑉, 𐐰𐑌𐐼 𐑄𐐯𐑉 𐑇𐐳𐐼 𐐺𐐨 𐐰 𐑀𐑉𐐩𐐻 𐐿𐐱𐑌𐐻𐐯𐑌𐑇𐐲𐑌, 𐐰𐑌𐐼 𐐰 𐐼𐐮𐑅𐐻𐐲𐑉𐐺𐐰𐑌𐑅 𐐰𐑋𐐲𐑍 𐑄𐐯𐑋; 𐑄𐐯𐑉𐑁𐐬𐑉 𐐸𐐨 𐐹𐐳𐐻 𐑁𐐬𐑉𐑃 𐐸𐐮𐑆 𐐸𐐰𐑌𐐼 𐐰𐑌𐐼 𐑉𐐩𐑆𐐼 𐑄 𐐿𐐮𐑍 𐑁𐑉𐐱𐑋 𐑄 𐐲𐑉𐑃, 𐐰𐑌𐐼 𐑅𐐯𐐼 𐐲𐑌𐐻𐐭 𐐸𐐮𐑋, 𐐝𐐻𐐰𐑌𐐼: 𐐰𐑌𐐼 𐐸𐐨 𐑅𐐻𐐳𐐼 𐐲𐐹𐐱𐑌 𐐸𐐮𐑆 𐑁𐐨𐐻, 𐑉𐐨𐑅𐐨𐑂𐐮𐑍 𐐸𐐮𐑆 𐑅𐐻𐑉𐐯𐑍𐑃. 𐐤𐐵 𐑄𐐮𐑅 𐐶𐐱𐑆 𐐼𐐲𐑌 𐐮𐑌 𐑄 𐐹𐑉𐐯𐑆𐐯𐑌𐑅 𐐱𐑂 𐑄 𐐿𐐶𐐨𐑌 𐐰𐑌𐐼 𐑋𐐯𐑌𐐨 𐐱𐑂 𐑄 𐑅𐐲𐑉𐑂𐐰𐑌𐐻𐑅. 𐐈𐑌𐐼 𐐸𐐶𐐯𐑌 𐑄𐐩 𐑅𐐫 𐐮𐐻, 𐑄𐐩 𐑀𐑉𐐩𐐻𐑊𐐨 𐑋𐐪𐑉𐑂𐐯𐑊𐐼, 𐐰𐑌𐐼 𐐺𐐨𐑀𐐰𐑌 𐐻𐐭 𐑁𐐨𐑉. 𐐈𐑌𐐼 𐑄 𐐿𐐮𐑍 𐑅𐐻𐐳𐐼 𐑁𐐬𐑉𐑃, 𐐰𐑌𐐼 𐐺𐐨𐑀𐐰𐑌 𐐻𐐭 𐑋𐐮𐑌𐐮𐑅𐐻𐐲𐑉 𐐲𐑌𐐻𐐭 𐑄𐐯𐑋. 𐐈𐑌𐐼 𐐸𐐨 𐐼𐐮𐐼 𐑋𐐮𐑌𐐮𐑅𐐻𐐲𐑉 𐐲𐑌𐐻𐐭 𐑄𐐯𐑋, 𐐮𐑌𐑅𐐬𐑋𐐲𐐽 𐑄𐐰𐐻 𐐸𐐮𐑆 𐐸𐐬𐑊 𐐸𐐵𐑅𐐸𐐬𐑊𐐼 𐐶𐐲𐑉 𐐿𐐱𐑌𐑂𐐲𐑉𐐻𐐯𐐼 𐐲𐑌𐐻𐐭 𐑄 𐐢𐐫𐑉𐐼. 𐐤𐐵 𐑄𐐯𐑉 𐐶𐐱𐑆 𐐰 𐑋𐐲𐑊𐐻𐐮𐐻𐐭𐐼 𐑀𐐰𐑄𐐲𐑉𐐼 𐐻𐐭𐑀𐐯𐑄𐐲𐑉 𐐺𐐨𐐿𐐫𐑆 𐐱𐑂 𐑄 𐐿𐐲𐑋𐐰𐑌𐐼𐑋𐐯𐑌𐐻 𐐱𐑂 𐑄 𐐿𐐶𐐨𐑌, 𐐰𐑌𐐼 𐑄𐐯𐑉 𐐺𐐨𐑀𐐰𐑌 𐐻𐐭 𐐺𐐨 𐑀𐑉𐐩𐐻 𐑋𐐲𐑉𐑋𐐲𐑉𐐮𐑍𐑆 𐐰𐑋𐐲𐑍 𐑄𐐯𐑋 𐐺𐐨𐐿𐐫𐑆 𐐱𐑂 𐐁𐑉𐐲𐑌 𐐰𐑌𐐼 𐐸𐐮𐑆 𐐺𐑉𐐯𐑄𐑉𐐯𐑌. 𐐒𐐲𐐻 𐑄 𐐿𐐮𐑍 𐑅𐐻𐐳𐐼 𐑁𐐬𐑉𐑃 𐐰𐑋𐐲𐑍 𐑄𐐯𐑋, 𐐰𐑌𐐼 𐐰𐐼𐑋𐐮𐑌𐐮𐑅𐐻𐐲𐑉𐐼 𐐲𐑌𐐻𐐭 𐑄𐐯𐑋. 𐐈𐑌𐐼 𐑄𐐩 𐐶𐐲𐑉 𐐹𐐰𐑅𐐮𐑁𐐴𐐼 𐐻𐐬𐐲𐑉𐐼𐑆 𐐁𐑉𐐲𐑌, 𐐰𐑌𐐼 𐑄𐐬𐑆 𐐸𐐭 𐐶𐐲𐑉 𐐶𐐮𐑄 𐐸𐐮𐑋.

11. 𐐈𐑌𐐼 𐐮𐐻 𐐿𐐩𐑋 𐐻𐐭 𐐹𐐪𐑅 𐑄𐐰𐐻 𐐸𐐶𐐯𐑌 𐑄 𐐿𐐮𐑍 𐑅𐐫 𐑄𐐰𐐻 𐑄 𐐹𐐨𐐹𐑊 𐐶𐐲𐑉 𐐹𐐰𐑅𐐮𐑁𐐴𐐼, 𐐸𐐨 𐐿𐐫𐑆𐐼 𐑄𐐰𐐻 𐐁𐑉𐐲𐑌 𐐰𐑌𐐼 𐐸𐐮𐑆 𐐺𐑉𐐯𐑄𐑉𐐯𐑌 𐑇𐐳𐐼 𐑅𐐻𐐰𐑌𐐼 𐑁𐐬𐑉𐑃 𐐮𐑌 𐑄 𐑋𐐮𐐼𐑅𐐻 𐐱𐑂 𐑄 𐑋𐐲𐑊𐐻𐐮𐐻𐐭𐐼, 𐐰𐑌𐐼 𐑄𐐰𐐻 𐑄𐐩 𐑇𐐳𐐼 𐐹𐑉𐐨𐐽 𐑄 𐐶𐐲𐑉𐐼 𐐲𐑌𐐻𐐭 𐑄𐐯𐑋. 𐐈𐑌𐐼 𐐮𐐻 𐐿𐐩𐑋 𐐻𐐭 𐐹𐐪𐑅 𐑄𐐰𐐻 𐑄 𐐿𐐮𐑍 𐑅𐐯𐑌𐐻 𐐰 𐐹𐑉𐐱𐐿𐑊𐐰𐑋𐐩𐑇𐐲𐑌 𐑃𐑉𐐭𐐵𐐻 𐐫𐑊 𐑄 𐑊𐐰𐑌𐐼, 𐐰𐑋𐐲𐑍𐑅𐐻 𐐫𐑊 𐐸𐐮𐑆 𐐹𐐨𐐹𐑊 𐐸𐐭 𐐶𐐲𐑉 𐐮𐑌 𐐫𐑊 𐐸𐐮𐑆 𐑊𐐰𐑌𐐼, 𐐸𐐭 𐐶𐐲𐑉 𐐮𐑌 𐐫𐑊 𐑄 𐑉𐐨𐐾𐐲𐑌𐑆 𐑉𐐵𐑌𐐼 𐐰𐐺𐐵𐐻, 𐐸𐐶𐐮𐐽 𐐶𐐱𐑆 𐐺𐐫𐑉𐐼𐐲𐑉𐐮𐑍 𐐨𐑂𐐲𐑌 𐐻𐐭 𐑄 𐑅𐐨, 𐐱𐑌 𐑄 𐐨𐑅𐐻 𐐰𐑌𐐼 𐐱𐑌 𐑄 𐐶𐐯𐑅𐐻, 𐐰𐑌𐐼 𐐸𐐶𐐮𐐽 𐐶𐐱𐑆 𐐼𐐮𐑂𐐴𐐼𐐯𐐼 𐑁𐑉𐐱𐑋 𐑄 𐑊𐐰𐑌𐐼 𐐱𐑂 𐐞𐐯𐑉𐐲𐐸𐐯𐑋𐑊𐐲 𐐺𐐴 𐐰 𐑌𐐰𐑉𐐬 𐑅𐐻𐑉𐐮𐐹 𐐱𐑂 𐐶𐐮𐑊𐐼𐐲𐑉𐑌𐐯𐑅, 𐐸𐐶𐐮𐐽 𐑉𐐰𐑌 𐑁𐑉𐐱𐑋 𐑄 𐑅𐐨 𐐨𐑅𐐻 𐐨𐑂𐐲𐑌 𐐻𐐭 𐑄 𐑅𐐨 𐐶𐐯𐑅𐐻, 𐐰𐑌𐐼 𐑉𐐵𐑌𐐼 𐐰𐐺𐐵𐐻 𐐱𐑌 𐑄 𐐺𐐫𐑉𐐼𐐲𐑉𐑆 𐐱𐑂 𐑄 𐑅𐐨𐑇𐐬𐑉, 𐐰𐑌𐐼 𐑄 𐐺𐐫𐑉𐐼𐐲𐑉𐑆 𐐱𐑂 𐑄 𐐶𐐮𐑊𐐼𐐲𐑉𐑌𐐯𐑅 𐐸𐐶𐐮𐐽 𐐶𐐱𐑆 𐐱𐑌 𐑄 𐑌𐐫𐑉𐑃 𐐺𐐴 𐑄 𐑊𐐰𐑌𐐼 𐐱𐑂 𐐞𐐯𐑉𐐲𐐸𐐯𐑋𐑊𐐲, 𐑃𐑉𐐭 𐑄 𐐺𐐫𐑉𐐼𐐲𐑉𐑆 𐐱𐑂 𐐣𐐰𐑌𐐻𐐴, 𐐺𐐴 𐑄 𐐸𐐯𐐼 𐐱𐑂 𐑄 𐑉𐐮𐑂𐐲𐑉 𐐝𐐴𐐼𐐲𐑌, 𐑉𐐲𐑌𐐮𐑍 𐑁𐑉𐐱𐑋 𐑄 𐐨𐑅𐐻 𐐻𐐬𐐲𐑉𐐼𐑆 𐑄 𐐶𐐯𐑅𐐻: 𐐰𐑌𐐼 𐑄𐐲𐑅 𐐶𐐲𐑉 𐑄 𐐢𐐩𐑋𐐲𐑌𐐴𐐻𐑅 𐐰𐑌𐐼 𐑄 𐐤𐐨𐑁𐐴𐐻𐑅 𐐼𐐮𐑂𐐴𐐼𐐯𐐼. 𐐤𐐵, 𐑄 𐑋𐐬𐑉 𐐴𐐼𐐲𐑊 𐐹𐐪𐑉𐐻 𐐱𐑂 𐑄 𐐢𐐩𐑋𐐲𐑌𐐴𐐻𐑅 𐑊𐐮𐑂𐐼 𐐮𐑌 𐑄 𐐶𐐮𐑊𐐼𐐲𐑉𐑌𐐯𐑅, 𐐰𐑌𐐼 𐐼𐐶𐐯𐑊𐐻 𐐮𐑌 𐐻𐐯𐑌𐐻𐑅; 𐐰𐑌𐐼 𐑄𐐩 𐐶𐐲𐑉 𐑅𐐹𐑉𐐯𐐼 𐑃𐑉𐐭 𐑄 𐐶𐐮𐑊𐐼𐐲𐑉𐑌𐐯𐑅, 𐐱𐑌 𐑄 𐐶𐐯𐑅𐐻, 𐐮𐑌 𐑄 𐑊𐐰𐑌𐐼 𐐱𐑂 𐐤𐐨𐑁𐐴: 𐐷𐐩, 𐐰𐑌𐐼 𐐫𐑊𐑅𐐬 𐐱𐑌 𐑄 𐐶𐐯𐑅𐐻 𐐱𐑂 𐑄 𐑊𐐰𐑌𐐼 𐐱𐑂 𐐞𐐯𐑉𐐲𐐸𐐯𐑋𐑊𐐲, 𐐮𐑌 𐑄 𐐺𐐫𐑉𐐼𐐲𐑉𐑆 𐐺𐐴 𐑄 𐑅𐐨𐑇𐐬𐑉, 𐐰𐑌𐐼 𐐱𐑌 𐑄 𐐶𐐯𐑅𐐻 𐐮𐑌 𐑄 𐑊𐐰𐑌𐐼 𐐱𐑂 𐐤𐐨𐑁𐐴, 𐐮𐑌 𐑄 𐐹𐑊𐐩𐑅 𐐱𐑂 𐑄𐐩𐑉 𐑁𐐪𐑄𐐲𐑉𐑆' 𐑁𐐲𐑉𐑅𐐻 𐐮𐑌𐐸𐐯𐑉𐐮𐐻𐐰𐑌𐑅, 𐐰𐑌𐐼 𐑄𐐲𐑅 𐐺𐐫𐑉𐐼𐐲𐑉𐐮𐑍 𐐰𐑊𐐱𐑍 𐐺𐐴 𐑄 𐑅𐐨𐑇𐐬𐑉. 𐐈𐑌𐐼 𐐫𐑊𐑅𐐬 𐑄𐐯𐑉 𐐶𐐲𐑉 𐑋𐐯𐑌𐐨 𐐢𐐩𐑋𐐲𐑌𐐴𐐻𐑅 𐐱𐑌 𐑄 𐐨𐑅𐐻 𐐺𐐴 𐑄 𐑅𐐨𐑇𐐬𐑉, 𐐸𐐶𐐮𐑄𐐲𐑉 𐑄 𐐤𐐨𐑁𐐴𐐻𐑅 𐐸𐐰𐐼 𐐼𐑉𐐮𐑂𐐲𐑌 𐑄𐐯𐑋. 𐐈𐑌𐐼 𐑄𐐲𐑅 𐑄 𐐤𐐨𐑁𐐴𐐻𐑅 𐐶𐐲𐑉 𐑌𐐨𐑉𐑊𐐨 𐑅𐐲𐑉𐐵𐑌𐐼𐐯𐐼 𐐺𐐴 𐑄

𐐢𐐩𐑋𐐲𐑌𐐴𐐻𐑅; 𐑌𐐯𐑂𐐲𐑉𐑄𐐲𐑊𐐯𐑅 𐑄 𐐤𐐨𐑁𐐴𐐻𐑅 𐐸𐐰𐐼 𐐻𐐩𐐿𐑌 𐐹𐐲𐑆𐐯𐑇𐐲𐑌 𐐱𐑂 𐐫𐑊 𐑄 𐑌𐐫𐑉𐑄𐐲𐑉𐑌 𐐹𐐪𐑉𐐻𐑅 𐐱𐑂
𐑄 𐑊𐐰𐑌𐐼, 𐐺𐐫𐑉𐐼𐐲𐑉𐐮𐑍 𐐱𐑌 𐑄 𐐶𐐮𐑊𐐼𐐲𐑉𐑌𐐯𐑅, 𐐰𐐻 𐑄 𐐸𐐯𐐼 𐐱𐑂 𐑄 𐑉𐐮𐑂𐐲𐑉 𐐝𐐴𐐼𐐲𐑌, 𐑁𐑉𐐱𐑋 𐑄 𐐨𐑅𐐻 𐐻𐐭
𐑄 𐐶𐐯𐑅𐐻 𐑉𐐵𐑌𐐼 𐐰𐐺𐐵𐐻 𐐱𐑌 𐑄 𐐶𐐮𐑊𐐼𐐲𐑉𐑌𐐯𐑅 𐑅𐐴𐐼; 𐐱𐑌 𐑄 𐑌𐐫𐑉𐑃, 𐐨𐑂𐑌 𐐲𐑌𐐻𐐮𐑊 𐑄𐐩 𐐿𐐩𐑋 𐐻𐐭 𐑄 𐑊𐐰𐑌𐐼
𐐸𐐶𐐮𐐽 𐑄𐐩 𐐿𐐫𐑊𐐼 𐐒𐐵𐑌𐐻𐐮𐑁𐐳𐑊. 𐐈𐑌𐐼 𐐮𐐻 𐐺𐐫𐑉𐐼𐐲𐑉𐐼 𐐲𐐹𐐱𐑌 𐑄 𐑊𐐰𐑌𐐼 𐐸𐐶𐐮𐐽 𐑄𐐩 𐐿𐐫𐑊𐐼 𐐔𐐯𐑅𐐬𐑊𐐩𐑇𐐲𐑌; 𐐮𐐻 𐐺𐐨𐐮𐑍 𐑅𐐬 𐑁𐐪𐑉 𐑌𐐫𐑉𐑃𐐶𐐲𐑉𐐼 𐑄𐐰𐐻 𐐮𐐻 𐐿𐐩𐑋 𐐮𐑌𐐻𐐭 𐑄 𐑊𐐰𐑌𐐼 𐐸𐐶𐐮𐐽 𐐸𐐰𐐼 𐐺𐐮𐑌 𐐹𐐨𐐹𐑊𐐼, 𐐰𐑌𐐼
𐐺𐐮𐑌 𐐼𐐯𐑅𐐻𐑉𐐱𐐮𐐼, 𐐱𐑂 𐐸𐐭𐑆 𐐺𐐬𐑌𐑆 𐐶𐐨 𐐸𐐰𐑂 𐑅𐐹𐐬𐐿𐑌, 𐐸𐐶𐐮𐐽 𐐶𐐱𐑆 𐐼𐐮𐑅𐐿𐐲𐑂𐐲𐑉𐐼 𐐺𐐴 𐑄 𐐹𐐨𐐹𐑊 𐐱𐑂
𐐞𐐯𐑉𐐲𐐸𐐯𐑋𐑊𐐲; 𐐮𐐻 𐐺𐐨𐐮𐑍 𐑄 𐐹𐑊𐐩𐑅 𐐱𐑂 𐑄𐐯𐑉 𐑁𐐲𐑉𐑅𐐻 𐑊𐐰𐑌𐐼𐐮𐑍. 𐐈𐑌𐐼 𐑄𐐩 𐐿𐐩𐑋 𐑁𐑉𐐱𐑋 𐑄𐐯𐑉 𐐲𐐹
𐐮𐑌𐐻𐐭 𐑄 𐑅𐐵𐑃 𐐶𐐮𐑊𐐼𐐲𐑉𐑌𐐯𐑅. 𐐛𐐲𐑅 𐑄 𐑊𐐰𐑌𐐼 𐐱𐑌 𐑄 𐑌𐐫𐑉𐑃𐐶𐐲𐑉𐐼 𐐶𐐱𐑆 𐐿𐐫𐑊𐐼 𐐔𐐯𐑅𐐬𐑊𐐩𐑇𐐲𐑌, 𐐰𐑌𐐼
𐑄 𐑊𐐰𐑌𐐼 𐐱𐑌 𐑄 𐑅𐐲𐑄𐐲𐑉𐑌 𐐶𐐱𐑆 𐐿𐐫𐑊𐐼 𐐒𐐵𐑌𐐻𐐮𐑁𐐳𐑊; 𐐮𐐻 𐐺𐐨𐐮𐑍 𐑄 𐐶𐐮𐑊𐐼𐐲𐑉𐑌𐐯𐑅 𐐸𐐶𐐮𐐽 𐐮𐑆 𐑁𐐮𐑊𐐼
𐐶𐐮𐑄 𐐫𐑊 𐑋𐐰𐑌𐐲𐑉 𐐱𐑂 𐐶𐐴𐑊𐐼 𐐰𐑌𐐮𐑋𐐲𐑊𐑆 𐐱𐑂 𐐯𐑂𐐲𐑉𐐨 𐐿𐐴𐑌𐐼; 𐐲 𐐹𐐪𐑉𐐻 𐐱𐑂 𐐸𐐶𐐮𐐽 𐐸𐐰𐐼 𐐿𐐲𐑋 𐑁𐑉𐐱𐑋 𐑄
𐑊𐐰𐑌𐐼 𐑌𐐫𐑉𐑃𐐶𐐲𐑉𐐼 𐑁𐐫𐑉 𐑁𐐭𐐼. 𐐈𐑌𐐼 𐑌𐐵 𐐮𐐻 𐐶𐐱𐑆 𐐬𐑌𐑊𐐨 𐑄 𐐼𐐮𐑅𐐻𐐲𐑌𐑅 𐐱𐑂 𐐲 𐐼𐐩 𐐰𐑌𐐼 𐐲 𐐸𐐰𐑁'𐑅
𐑈𐐲𐑉𐑌𐐨 𐑁𐐫𐑉 𐐲 𐐤𐐨𐑁𐐴𐐻, 𐐱𐑌 𐑄 𐑊𐐴𐑌 𐐒𐐵𐑌𐐻𐐮𐑁𐐳𐑊, 𐐰𐑌𐐼 𐑄 𐑊𐐰𐑌𐐼 𐐔𐐯𐑅𐐬𐑊𐐩𐑇𐐲𐑌, 𐑁𐑉𐐱𐑋 𐑄 𐐨𐑅𐐻 𐐻𐐭
𐑄 𐐶𐐯𐑅𐐻 𐑅𐐨; 𐐰𐑌𐐼 𐑄𐐲𐑅 𐑄 𐑊𐐰𐑌𐐼 𐐱𐑂 𐐤𐐨𐑁𐐴, 𐐰𐑌𐐼 𐑄 𐑊𐐰𐑌𐐼 𐐱𐑂 𐐞𐐯𐑉𐐲𐐸𐐯𐑋𐑊𐐲, 𐐶𐐲𐑉 𐑌𐐨𐑉𐑊𐐨
𐑅𐐲𐑉𐐵𐑌𐐼𐐲𐐼 𐐺𐐴 𐐶𐐫𐐻𐐲𐑉; 𐑄𐐯𐑉 𐐺𐐨𐐮𐑍 𐐲 𐑅𐑋𐐫𐑊 𐑌𐐯𐐿 𐐱𐑂 𐑊𐐰𐑌𐐼 𐐺𐐮𐐻𐐶𐐨𐑌 𐑄 𐑊𐐰𐑌𐐼 𐑌𐐫𐑉𐑃𐐶𐐲𐑉𐐼
𐐰𐑌𐐼 𐑄 𐑊𐐰𐑌𐐼 𐑅𐐲𐑄𐐲𐑉𐑌.

12. 𐐈𐑌𐐼 𐐮𐐻 𐐿𐐩𐑋 𐐻𐐭 𐐹𐐰𐑅 𐑄𐐰𐐻 𐑄 𐐤𐐨𐑁𐐴𐐻𐑅 𐐸𐐰𐐼 𐐮𐑌𐐸𐐰𐐺𐐮𐐻𐐲𐐼 𐑄 𐑊𐐰𐑌𐐼 𐐒𐐵𐑌𐐻𐐮𐑁𐐳𐑊, 𐐨𐑂𐑌
𐑁𐑉𐐱𐑋 𐑄 𐐨𐑅𐐻 𐐲𐑌𐐻𐐭 𐑄 𐐶𐐯𐑅𐐻 𐑅𐐨, 𐐰𐑌𐐼 𐑄𐐲𐑅 𐑄 𐐤𐐨𐑁𐐴𐐻𐑅 𐐮𐑌 𐑄𐐯𐑉 𐐶𐐮𐑆𐐼𐐲𐑋, 𐐶𐐮𐑄 𐑄𐐯𐑉 𐑀𐐪𐑉𐐼𐑆
𐐰𐑌𐐼 𐑄𐐯𐑉 𐐪𐑉𐑋𐐨𐑆, 𐐸𐐰𐐼 𐐸𐐯𐑋𐐼 𐐮𐑌 𐑄 𐐢𐐩𐑋𐐲𐑌𐐴𐐻𐑅 𐐱𐑌 𐑄 𐑅𐐵𐑃, 𐑄𐐰𐐻 𐑄𐐯𐑉𐐺𐐴 𐑄𐐩 𐑇𐐳𐐼 𐐸𐐰𐑂 𐑌𐐬
𐑋𐐬𐑉 𐐹𐐲𐑆𐐯𐑇𐐲𐑌 𐐱𐑌 𐑄 𐑌𐐫𐑉𐑃, 𐑄𐐰𐐻 𐑄𐐩 𐑋𐐴𐐻 𐑌𐐱𐐻 𐐬𐑂𐐲𐑉𐑉𐐲𐑌 𐑄 𐑊𐐰𐑌𐐼 𐑌𐐫𐑉𐑃𐐶𐐲𐑉𐐼; 𐑄𐐯𐑉𐑁𐐬𐑉 𐑄
𐐢𐐩𐑋𐐲𐑌𐐴𐐻𐑅 𐐿𐐳𐐼 𐐸𐐰𐑂 𐑌𐐬 𐑋𐐬𐑉 𐐹𐐲𐑆𐐯𐑇𐐲𐑌𐑆 𐐬𐑌𐑊𐐨 𐐮𐑌 𐑄 𐑊𐐰𐑌𐐼 𐐱𐑂 𐐤𐐨𐑁𐐴, 𐐰𐑌𐐼 𐑄 𐐶𐐮𐑊𐐼𐐲𐑉𐑌𐐯𐑅
𐑉𐐵𐑌𐐼 𐐰𐐺𐐵𐐻. 𐐤𐐵 𐑄𐐮𐑅 𐐶𐐱𐑆 𐐶𐐮𐑆𐐼𐐲𐑋 𐐮𐑌 𐑄 𐐤𐐨𐑁𐐴𐐻𐑅; 𐐰𐑆 𐑄 𐐢𐐩𐑋𐐲𐑌𐐴𐐻𐑅 𐐶𐐲𐑉 𐐰𐑌 𐐯𐑌𐐲𐑋𐐨 𐐻𐐭
𐑄𐐯𐑋, 𐑄𐐩 𐐶𐐳𐐼 𐑌𐐱𐐻 𐑅𐐲𐑁𐐲𐑉 𐑄𐐯𐑉 𐐰𐑁𐑊𐐮𐐿𐑇𐐲𐑌𐑆 𐐱𐑌 𐐯𐑂𐐲𐑉𐐨 𐐸𐐰𐑌𐐼, 𐐰𐑌𐐼 𐐫𐑊𐑅𐐬 𐑄𐐰𐐻 𐑄𐐩 𐑋𐐴𐐻 𐐸𐐰𐑂
𐐲 𐐿𐐲𐑌𐐻𐑉𐐨 𐐸𐐶𐐮𐑄𐐲𐑉 𐑄𐐩 𐑋𐐴𐐻 𐑁𐑊𐐨, 𐐰𐐿𐐫𐑉𐐼𐐮𐑍 𐐻𐐭 𐑄𐐯𐑉 𐐼𐐨𐑆𐐴𐑉𐑆. 𐐈𐑌𐐼 𐑌𐐵 𐐌, 𐐰𐑁𐐻𐐲𐑉 𐐸𐐰𐑂𐐮𐑍
𐑅𐐯𐐼 𐑄𐐮𐑅, 𐑉𐐨𐐻𐐲𐑉𐑌 𐐲𐑀𐐯𐑌 𐐻𐐭 𐑄 𐐲𐐿𐐵𐑌𐐻 𐐱𐑂 𐐈𐑋𐐲𐑌 𐐰𐑌𐐼 𐐇𐑉𐐲𐑌, 𐐉𐑋𐑌𐐲𐑉 𐐰𐑌𐐼 𐐐𐐮𐑋𐑌𐐴, 𐐰𐑌𐐼 𐑄𐐯𐑉
𐐺𐑉𐐯𐑄𐑉𐐲𐑌.

𐐗𐐰𐐹𐐻𐐲𐑉 XIV.

1. 𐐒𐐨𐐸𐐬𐑊𐐼, 𐑌𐐵 𐐮𐐻 𐐿𐐩𐑋 𐐻𐐭 𐐹𐐰𐑅 𐑄𐐰𐐻 𐑄 𐐿𐐮𐑍 𐐱𐑂 𐑄 𐐢𐐩𐑋𐐲𐑌𐐴𐐻𐑅 𐑅𐐯𐑌𐐻 𐐲 𐐹𐑉𐐱𐐿𐑊𐐲𐑋𐐩𐑇𐐲𐑌
𐐲𐑋𐐲𐑍 𐐫𐑊 𐐸𐐮𐑆 𐐹𐐨𐐹𐑊, 𐑄𐐰𐐻 𐑄𐐩 𐑇𐐳𐐼 𐑌𐐱𐐻 𐑊𐐩 𐑄𐐯𐑉 𐐸𐐰𐑌𐐼𐑆 𐐱𐑌 𐐈𐑋𐐲𐑌, 𐐫𐑉 𐐇𐑉𐐲𐑌, 𐐫𐑉 𐐉𐑋𐑌𐐲𐑉, 𐐫𐑉
𐐐𐐮𐑋𐑌𐐴, 𐑌𐐫𐑉 𐐨𐑄𐐲𐑉 𐐱𐑂 𐑄𐐯𐑉 𐐺𐑉𐐯𐑄𐑉𐐲𐑌 𐐸𐐭 𐑇𐐳𐐼 𐑀𐐬 𐑁𐐬𐑉𐑃 𐐹𐑉𐐨𐐽𐐮𐑍 𐑄 𐐶𐐲𐑉𐐼 𐐱𐑂 𐐘𐐱𐐼, 𐐮𐑌
𐐸𐐶𐐱𐐻𐑅𐐬𐐯𐑂𐐲𐑉 𐐹𐑊𐐩𐑅 𐐮𐐻 𐑇𐐳𐐼 𐐺𐐨, 𐐮𐑌 𐐯𐑌𐐨 𐐹𐐪𐑉𐐻 𐐱𐑂 𐑄𐐯𐑉 𐑊𐐰𐑌𐐼; 𐐷𐐩, 𐐸𐐨 𐑅𐐯𐑌𐐻 𐐲 𐐼𐐨𐐿𐑉𐐨 𐐲𐑋𐐲𐑍
𐑄𐐯𐑋, 𐑄𐐰𐐻 𐑄𐐩 𐑇𐐳𐐼 𐑌𐐱𐐻 𐑊𐐩 𐑄𐐯𐑉 𐐸𐐰𐑌𐐼𐑆 𐐱𐑌 𐑄𐐯𐑋 𐐻𐐭 𐐺𐐴𐑌𐐼 𐑄𐐯𐑋, 𐐫𐑉 𐐻𐐭 𐐿𐐰𐑅𐐻 𐑄𐐯𐑋 𐐮𐑌𐐻𐐭
𐐹𐑉𐐮𐑆𐑌; 𐑌𐐨𐑄𐐲𐑉 𐑇𐐳𐐼 𐑄𐐩 𐑅𐐹𐐮𐐻 𐐲𐐹𐐱𐑌 𐑄𐐯𐑋, 𐑌𐐫𐑉 𐑅𐑋𐐴𐐻 𐑄𐐯𐑋, 𐑌𐐫𐑉 𐐿𐐰𐑅𐐻 𐑄𐐯𐑋 𐐵𐐻 𐐱𐑂 𐑄𐐯𐑉 𐑅𐐮𐑌𐐲𐑀𐐱𐑀𐑆, 𐑌𐐫𐑉 𐑅𐐿𐐲𐑉𐑈 𐑄𐐯𐑋; 𐑌𐐨𐑄𐐲𐑉 𐑇𐐳𐐼 𐑄𐐩 𐐿𐐰𐑅𐐻 𐑅𐐻𐐬𐑌𐑆 𐐰𐐻 𐑄𐐯𐑋, 𐐺𐐲𐐻 𐑄𐐰𐐻 𐑄𐐩 𐑇𐐳𐐼 𐐸𐐰𐑂
𐑁𐑉𐐨 𐐰𐐿𐑅𐐯𐑅 𐐻𐐭 𐑄𐐯𐑉 𐐸𐐵𐑆𐐲𐑆, 𐐰𐑌𐐼 𐐫𐑊𐑅𐐬 𐑄𐐯𐑉 𐐻𐐯𐑋𐐹𐑊𐑆, 𐐰𐑌𐐼 𐑄𐐯𐑉 𐑅𐐰𐑍𐐿𐐻𐐷𐐭𐐲𐑉𐐨𐑆; 𐐰𐑌𐐼 𐑄𐐲𐑅
𐑄𐐩 𐑋𐐴𐐻 𐑀𐐬 𐑁𐐬𐑉𐑃 𐐰𐑌𐐼 𐐹𐑉𐐨𐐽 𐑄 𐐶𐐲𐑉𐐼 𐐰𐐿𐐫𐑉𐐼𐐮𐑍 𐐻𐐭 𐑄𐐯𐑉 𐐼𐐨𐑆𐐴𐑉𐑆, 𐑁𐐫𐑉 𐑄 𐐿𐐮𐑍 𐐸𐐰𐐼 𐐺𐐮𐑌
𐐿𐐲𐑌𐑂𐐲𐑉𐐻𐐲𐐼 𐐲𐑌𐐻𐐭 𐑄 𐐢𐐫𐑉𐐼, 𐐰𐑌𐐼 𐐫𐑊 𐐸𐐮𐑆 𐐸𐐵𐑅𐐸𐐬𐑊𐐼: 𐑄𐐯𐑉𐑁𐐬𐑉 𐐸𐐨 𐑅𐐯𐑌𐐻 𐐸𐐮𐑆 𐐹𐑉𐐱𐐿𐑊𐐲𐑋𐐩𐑇𐐲𐑌
𐑃𐑉𐐭𐐵𐐻 𐑄 𐑊𐐰𐑌𐐼 𐐲𐑌𐐻𐐭 𐐸𐐮𐑆 𐐹𐐨𐐹𐑊, 𐑄𐐰𐐻 𐑄 𐐶𐐲𐑉𐐼 𐐱𐑂 𐐘𐐱𐐼 𐑋𐐴𐐻 𐐸𐐰𐑂 𐑌𐐬 𐐲𐐺𐑅𐐻𐑉𐐲𐐿𐑇𐐲𐑌, 𐐺𐐲𐐻
𐑄𐐰𐐻 𐐮𐐻 𐑋𐐴𐐻 𐑀𐐬 𐑁𐐬𐑉𐑃 𐑃𐑉𐐭𐐵𐐻 𐐫𐑊 𐑄 𐑊𐐰𐑌𐐼, 𐑄𐐰𐐻 𐐸𐐮𐑆 𐐹𐐨𐐹𐑊 𐑋𐐴𐐻 𐐺𐐨 𐐿𐐲𐑌𐑂𐐮𐑌𐑅𐐻 𐐿𐐲𐑌𐑅𐐲𐑉𐑌𐐮𐑍 𐑄
𐐶𐐮𐐿𐐲𐐼 𐐻𐑉𐐲𐐼𐐮𐑇𐐲𐑌𐑆 𐐱𐑂 𐑄𐐯𐑉 𐑁𐐪𐑄𐐲𐑉𐑆, 𐐰𐑌𐐼 𐑄𐐰𐐻 𐑄𐐩 𐑋𐐴𐐻 𐐺𐐨 𐐿𐐲𐑌𐑂𐐮𐑌𐑅𐐻 𐑄𐐰𐐻 𐑄𐐩 𐐶𐐲𐑉 𐐫𐑊 𐐺𐑉𐐯𐑄-

𐑉𐐯𐑌, 𐐰𐑌𐐼 𐑄𐐰𐐻 𐑄𐐩 𐐫𐐻 𐑌𐐱𐐻 𐐻𐐭 𐑋𐐲𐑉𐐼𐐲𐑉, 𐑌𐐫𐑉 𐐻𐐭 𐐹𐑊𐐲𐑌𐐼𐐲𐑉, 𐑌𐐫𐑉 𐐻𐐭 𐑅𐐻𐐨𐑊, 𐑌𐐫𐑉 𐐻𐐭 𐐿𐐱𐑋𐐮𐐻 𐐲𐐼𐐲𐑊𐐻𐐲𐑉𐐨, 𐑌𐐫𐑉 𐐻𐐭 𐐿𐐱𐑋𐐮𐐻 𐐯𐑌𐐨 𐑋𐐰𐑌𐐲𐑉 𐐱𐑂 𐐶𐐮𐐿𐐯𐐼𐑌𐐯𐑅.

2. 𐐈𐑌𐐼 𐑌𐐵 𐐮𐐻 𐐿𐐩𐑋 𐐻𐐭 𐐹𐐰𐑅 𐑄𐐰𐐻 𐐸𐐶𐐯𐑌 𐑄 𐐿𐐮𐑍 𐐸𐐰𐐼 𐑅𐐯𐑌𐐻 𐑁𐐬𐑉𐑃 𐑄𐐮𐑅 𐐹𐑉𐐱𐐿𐑊𐐰𐑋𐐩𐑇𐐲𐑌, 𐑄𐐰𐐻 𐐁𐑉𐐲𐑌 𐐰𐑌𐐼 𐐸𐐮𐑆 𐐺𐑉𐐯𐑄𐑉𐐯𐑌 𐐶𐐯𐑌𐐻 𐑁𐐬𐑉𐑃 𐑁𐑉𐐱𐑋 𐑅𐐮𐐻𐐨 𐐻𐐭 𐑅𐐮𐐻𐐨, 𐐰𐑌𐐼 𐑁𐑉𐐱𐑋 𐐶𐐲𐑌 𐐸𐐵𐑅 𐐱𐑂 𐐶𐐲𐑉𐑇𐐮𐐹 𐐻𐐭 𐐰𐑌𐐲𐑄𐐲𐑉, 𐐯𐑅𐐻𐐰𐐺𐑊𐐮𐑇𐐮𐑍 𐐽𐐲𐑉𐐽𐐯𐑆 𐐰𐑌𐐼 𐐿𐐱𐑌𐑅𐐯𐐿𐑉𐐩𐐻𐐮𐑍 𐐹𐑉𐐨𐑅𐐻𐑅 𐐰𐑌𐐼 𐐻𐐨𐐽𐐲𐑉𐑆 𐑃𐑉𐐭𐐵𐐻 𐑄 𐑊𐐰𐑌𐐼 𐐲𐑋𐐲𐑍 𐑄 𐐢𐐰𐑋𐐲𐑌𐐴𐐻𐑅, 𐐻𐐭 𐐹𐑉𐐨𐐽 𐐰𐑌𐐼 𐐻𐐭 𐐻𐐨𐐽 𐑄 𐐶𐐲𐑉𐐼 𐐱𐑂 𐐘𐐱𐐼 𐐲𐑋𐐲𐑍 𐑄𐐯𐑋; 𐐰𐑌𐐼 𐑄𐐲𐑅 𐑄𐐩 𐐺𐐨𐑀𐐰𐑌 𐐻𐐭 𐐸𐐰𐑂 𐑀𐑉𐐩𐐻 𐑅𐐲𐐿𐑅𐐯𐑅. 𐐈𐑌𐐼 𐑃𐐵𐑆𐐲𐑌𐐼𐑆 𐐶𐐲𐑉 𐐺𐑉𐐫𐐻 𐐻𐐭 𐑄 𐑌𐐱𐑊𐐯𐐾 𐐱𐑂 𐑄 𐐢𐐫𐑉𐐼, 𐐷𐐩, 𐑃𐐵𐑆𐐲𐑌𐐼𐑆 𐐶𐐲𐑉 𐐺𐑉𐐫𐐻 𐐻𐐭 𐐺𐐨𐑊𐐨𐑂 𐐮𐑌 𐑄 𐐻𐑉𐐲𐐼𐐮𐑇𐐲𐑌𐑆 𐐱𐑂 𐑄 𐐤𐐨𐑁𐐴𐐻𐑅, 𐐰𐑌𐐼 𐑄𐐩 𐐶𐐲𐑉 𐐻𐐫𐐻 𐑄 𐑉𐐯𐐿𐐲𐑉𐐼𐑆 𐐰𐑌𐐼 𐐹𐑉𐐱𐑁𐐯𐑅𐐴𐑆 𐐸𐐶𐐮𐐽 𐐶𐐲𐑉 𐐸𐐰𐑌𐐼𐐯𐐼 𐐼𐐵𐑌, 𐐨𐑂𐐲𐑌 𐐻𐐭 𐑄 𐐹𐑉𐐯𐑆𐐯𐑌𐐻 𐐻𐐴𐑋; 𐐰𐑌𐐼 𐐰𐑆 𐑇𐐭𐑉 𐐰𐑆 𐑄 𐐢𐐫𐑉𐐼 𐑊𐐮𐑂𐐯𐑃, 𐑅𐐬 𐑇𐐭𐑉 𐐰𐑆 𐑋𐐯𐑌𐐨 𐐰𐑆 𐐺𐐨𐑊𐐨𐑂𐐼, 𐐫𐑉 𐐰𐑆 𐑋𐐯𐑌𐐨 𐐰𐑆 𐐶𐐲𐑉 𐐺𐑉𐐫𐐻 𐐻𐐭 𐑄 𐑌𐐱𐑊𐐯𐐾 𐐱𐑂 𐑄 𐐻𐑉𐐭𐑃, 𐑃𐑉𐐭 𐑄 𐐹𐑉𐐨𐐽𐐮𐑍 𐐱𐑂 𐐈𐑋𐐲𐑌 𐐰𐑌𐐼 𐐸𐐮𐑆 𐐺𐑉𐐯𐑄𐑉𐐯𐑌, 𐐰𐐿𐐫𐑉𐐼𐐮𐑍 𐐻𐐭 𐑄 𐑅𐐹𐐮𐑉𐐮𐐻 𐐱𐑂 𐑉𐐯𐑂𐐯𐑊𐐩𐑇𐐲𐑌 𐐰𐑌𐐼 𐐱𐑂 𐐹𐑉𐐱𐑁𐐯𐑅𐐨, 𐐰𐑌𐐼 𐑄 𐐹𐐵𐐲𐑉 𐐱𐑂 𐐘𐐱𐐼 𐐶𐐲𐑉𐐿𐐮𐑍 𐑋𐐮𐑉𐐲𐐿𐐲𐑊𐑆 𐐮𐑌 𐑄𐐯𐑋; 𐐷𐐩, 𐐌 𐑅𐐩 𐐲𐑌𐐻𐐭 𐐷𐐭, 𐐰𐑆 𐑄 𐐢𐐫𐑉𐐼 𐑊𐐮𐑂𐐯𐑃, 𐐰𐑆 𐑋𐐯𐑌𐐨 𐐱𐑂 𐑄 𐐢𐐰𐑋𐐲𐑌𐐴𐐻𐑅 𐐰𐑆 𐐺𐐨𐑊𐐨𐑂𐐼 𐐮𐑌 𐑄𐐩𐑉 𐐹𐑉𐐨𐐽𐐮𐑍, 𐐰𐑌𐐼 𐐶𐐲𐑉 𐐿𐐱𐑌𐑂𐐲𐑉𐐻𐐯𐐼 𐐲𐑌𐐻𐐭 𐑄 𐐢𐐫𐑉𐐼, 𐑌𐐯𐑂𐐲𐑉 𐐼𐐮𐐼 𐑁𐐫𐑊 𐐲𐐶𐐩; 𐑁𐐫𐑉 𐑄𐐩 𐐺𐐨𐐿𐐩𐑋 𐐲 𐑉𐐴𐐽𐐲𐑅 𐐹𐐨𐐹𐐲𐑊: 𐑄𐐩 𐐼𐐮𐐼 𐑊𐐩 𐐼𐐵𐑌 𐑄 𐐶𐐯𐐹𐐲𐑌𐑆 𐐱𐑂 𐑄𐐩𐑉 𐑉𐐯𐐺𐐯𐑊𐐷𐐲𐑌, 𐑄𐐰𐐻 𐑄𐐩 𐐼𐐮𐐼 𐑌𐐱𐐻 𐑁𐐴𐐻 𐐲𐑀𐐯𐑌𐑅𐐻 𐐘𐐱𐐼 𐐯𐑌𐐨 𐑋𐐬𐑉, 𐑌𐐨𐑄𐐲𐑉 𐐲𐑀𐐯𐑌𐑅𐐻 𐐯𐑌𐐨 𐐱𐑂 𐑄𐐩𐑉 𐐺𐑉𐐯𐑄𐑉𐐯𐑌. 𐐤𐐵 𐑄𐐨𐑆 𐐪𐑉 𐑄𐐩 𐐸𐐭 𐐶𐐲𐑉 𐐿𐐱𐑌𐑂𐐲𐑉𐐻𐐯𐐼 𐐲𐑌𐐻𐐭 𐑄 𐐢𐐫𐑉𐐼: 𐑄 𐐹𐐨𐐹𐐲𐑊 𐐱𐑂 𐑄 𐐢𐐰𐑋𐐲𐑌𐐴𐐻𐑅 𐐸𐐭 𐐶𐐲𐑉 𐐮𐑌 𐑄 𐑊𐐰𐑌𐐼 𐐱𐑂 𐐆𐑇𐑋𐐩𐐯𐑊, 𐐰𐑌𐐼 𐐫𐑊𐑅𐐬 𐐱𐑂 𐑄 𐐹𐐨𐐹𐐲𐑊 𐐱𐑂 𐑄 𐐢𐐰𐑋𐐲𐑌𐐴𐐻𐑅 𐐸𐐭 𐐶𐐲𐑉 𐐮𐑌 𐑄 𐑊𐐰𐑌𐐼 𐐱𐑂 𐐣𐐮𐐼𐐬𐑌𐐴, 𐐰𐑌𐐼 𐐫𐑊𐑅𐐬 𐐱𐑂 𐑄 𐐹𐐨𐐹𐐲𐑊 𐐱𐑂 𐑄 𐐢𐐰𐑋𐐲𐑌𐐴𐐻𐑅 𐐸𐐭 𐐶𐐲𐑉 𐐮𐑌 𐑄 𐑅𐐮𐐻𐐨 𐐱𐑂 𐐤𐐨𐑁𐐴, 𐐰𐑌𐐼 𐐫𐑊𐑅𐐬 𐐱𐑂 𐑄 𐐹𐐨𐐹𐐲𐑊 𐐱𐑂 𐑄 𐐢𐐰𐑋𐐲𐑌𐐴𐐻𐑅 𐐸𐐭 𐐶𐐲𐑉 𐐮𐑌 𐑄 𐑊𐐰𐑌𐐼 𐐱𐑂 𐐟𐐴𐑊𐐲𐑋, 𐐰𐑌𐐼 𐐸𐐭 𐐶𐐲𐑉 𐐮𐑌 𐑄 𐑊𐐰𐑌𐐼 𐐱𐑂 𐐟𐐯𐑋𐑊𐐱𐑌, 𐐰𐑌𐐼 𐐮𐑌 𐑄 𐑅𐐮𐐻𐐨 𐐱𐑂 𐐢𐐨𐑋𐐷𐐭𐐯𐑊, 𐐰𐑌𐐼 𐐮𐑌 𐑄 𐑅𐐮𐐻𐐨 𐐱𐑂 𐐟𐐮𐑋𐑌𐐴𐑊𐐲𐑋, 𐐰𐑌𐐼 𐑄𐐨𐑆 𐐪𐑉 𐑄 𐑌𐐩𐑋𐑆 𐐱𐑂 𐑄 𐑅𐐮𐐻𐐨𐑆 𐐱𐑂 𐑄 𐐢𐐰𐑋𐐲𐑌𐐴𐐻𐑅 𐐸𐐶𐐮𐐽 𐐶𐐲𐑉 𐐿𐐱𐑌𐑂𐐲𐑉𐐻𐐯𐐼 𐐲𐑌𐐻𐐭 𐑄 𐐢𐐫𐑉𐐼; 𐐰𐑌𐐼 𐑄𐐨𐑆 𐐪𐑉 𐑄𐐩 𐑄𐐰𐐻 𐑊𐐩𐐼 𐐼𐐵𐑌 𐑄 𐐶𐐯𐐹𐐲𐑌𐑆 𐐱𐑂 𐑄𐐩𐑉 𐑉𐐯𐐺𐐯𐑊𐐷𐐲𐑌, 𐐷𐐩, 𐐫𐑊 𐑄𐐩𐑉 𐐶𐐯𐐹𐐲𐑌𐑆 𐐱𐑂 𐐶𐐫𐑉; 𐐰𐑌𐐼 𐑄𐐩 𐐶𐐲𐑉 𐐫𐑊 𐐢𐐰𐑋𐐲𐑌𐐴𐐻𐑅. 𐐈𐑌𐐼 𐑄 𐐈𐑋𐐰𐑊𐐯𐐿𐐴𐐻𐑅 𐐶𐐲𐑉 𐑌𐐱𐐻 𐐿𐐱𐑌𐑂𐐲𐑉𐐻𐐯𐐼, 𐑅𐐩𐑂 𐐬𐑌𐑊𐐨 𐐶𐐲𐑌; 𐑌𐐨𐑄𐐲𐑉 𐐶𐐲𐑉 𐐯𐑌𐐨 𐐱𐑂 𐑄 𐐈𐑋𐐲𐑊𐐱𐑌𐐴𐐻𐑅; 𐐺𐐲𐐻 𐑄𐐩 𐐼𐐮𐐼 𐐸𐐪𐑉𐐼𐐲𐑌 𐑄𐐩𐑉 𐐸𐐪𐑉𐐻𐑅, 𐐰𐑌𐐼 𐐫𐑊𐑅𐐬 𐑄 𐐸𐐪𐑉𐐻𐑅 𐐱𐑂 𐑄 𐐢𐐰𐑋𐐲𐑌𐐴𐐻𐑅 𐐮𐑌 𐑄𐐰𐐻 𐐹𐐪𐑉𐐻 𐐱𐑂 𐑄 𐑊𐐰𐑌𐐼 𐐸𐐶𐐩𐑉𐑅𐐬𐐯𐑂𐐲𐑉 𐑄𐐩 𐐼𐐶𐐯𐑊𐐻; 𐐷𐐩, 𐐰𐑌𐐼 𐐫𐑊 𐑄𐐩𐑉 𐑂𐐮𐑊𐐯𐐾𐐯𐑆, 𐐰𐑌𐐼 𐐫𐑊 𐑄𐐩𐑉 𐑅𐐮𐐻𐐨𐑆; 𐑄𐐩𐑉𐑁𐐬𐑉 𐐶𐐨 𐐸𐐰𐑂 𐑌𐐩𐑋𐐼 𐐫𐑊 𐑄 𐑅𐐮𐐻𐐨𐑆 𐐱𐑂 𐑄 𐐢𐐰𐑋𐐲𐑌𐐴𐐻𐑅 𐐮𐑌 𐐸𐐶𐐮𐐽 𐑄𐐩 𐐼𐐮𐐼 𐑉𐐨𐐹𐐯𐑌𐐻 𐐰𐑌𐐼 𐐿𐐲𐑋 𐐻𐐭 𐑄 𐑌𐐱𐑊𐐯𐐾 𐐱𐑂 𐑄 𐐻𐑉𐐭𐑃, 𐐰𐑌𐐼 𐐶𐐲𐑉 𐐿𐐱𐑌𐑂𐐲𐑉𐐻𐐯𐐼.

3. 𐐈𐑌𐐼 𐑌𐐵 𐐮𐐻 𐐿𐐩𐑋 𐐻𐐭 𐐹𐐰𐑅 𐑄𐐰𐐻 𐑄 𐐿𐐮𐑍, 𐐰𐑌𐐼 𐑄𐐬𐑆 𐐸𐐭 𐐶𐐲𐑉 𐐿𐐱𐑌𐑂𐐲𐑉𐐻𐐯𐐼, 𐐶𐐲𐑉 𐐼𐐯𐑆𐐴𐑉𐐲𐑅 𐑄𐐰𐐻 𐑄𐐩 𐑋𐐴𐐻 𐐸𐐰𐑂 𐐲 𐑌𐐩𐑋, 𐑄𐐰𐐻 𐑄𐐩𐑉𐐺𐐴 𐑄𐐩 𐑋𐐴𐐻 𐐺𐐨 𐐼𐐮𐑅𐐻𐐮𐑍𐑀𐐶𐐮𐑇𐐻 𐑁𐑉𐐱𐑋 𐑄𐐩𐑉 𐐺𐑉𐐯𐑄𐑉𐐯𐑌; 𐑄𐐩𐑉𐑁𐐬𐑉 𐑄 𐐿𐐮𐑍 𐐿𐐱𐑌𐑅𐐲𐑊𐐻𐐯𐐼 𐐶𐐮𐑄 𐐁𐑉𐐲𐑌, 𐐰𐑌𐐼 𐑋𐐯𐑌𐐨 𐐱𐑂 𐑄𐐩𐑉 𐐹𐑉𐐨𐑅𐐻𐑅, 𐐿𐐱𐑌𐑅𐐲𐑉𐑌𐐮𐑍 𐑄 𐑌𐐩𐑋 𐑄𐐰𐐻 𐑄𐐩 𐑇𐐳𐐼 𐐻𐐩𐐿 𐐲𐐹𐐱𐑌 𐑄𐐯𐑋, 𐑄𐐰𐐻 𐑄𐐩 𐑋𐐴𐐻 𐐺𐐨 𐐼𐐮𐑅𐐻𐐮𐑍𐑀𐐶𐐮𐑇𐐻. 𐐈𐑌𐐼 𐐮𐐻 𐐿𐐩𐑋 𐐻𐐭 𐐹𐐰𐑅 𐑄𐐰𐐻 𐑄𐐩 𐐿𐐫𐑊𐐼 𐑄𐐩𐑉 𐑌𐐩𐑋𐑆 𐐈𐑌𐐻𐐴-𐐤𐐨𐑁𐐴-𐐢𐐨𐐸𐐴𐑆; 𐐰𐑌𐐼 𐑄𐐩 𐐶𐐲𐑉 𐐿𐐫𐑊𐐼 𐐺𐐴 𐑄𐐮𐑅 𐑌𐐩𐑋, 𐐰𐑌𐐼 𐐶𐐲𐑉 𐑌𐐬 𐑋𐐬𐑉 𐐿𐐫𐑊𐐼 𐐢𐐰𐑋𐐲𐑌𐐴𐐻𐑅. 𐐈𐑌𐐼 𐑄𐐩 𐐺𐐨𐑀𐐰𐑌 𐐻𐐭 𐐺𐐨 𐐲 𐑂𐐯𐑉𐐨 𐐮𐑌𐐼𐐲𐑅𐐻𐑉𐐨𐐲𐑅 𐐹𐐨𐐹𐐲𐑊: 𐐷𐐩, 𐐰𐑌𐐼 𐑄𐐩 𐐶𐐲𐑉 𐑁𐑉𐐯𐑌𐐼𐑊𐐨 𐐶𐐮𐑄 𐑄 𐐤𐐨𐑁𐐴𐐻𐑅; 𐑄𐐩𐑉𐑁𐐬𐑉, 𐑄𐐩 𐐼𐐮𐐼 𐐬𐐹𐐲𐑌 𐐲 𐐿𐐱𐑉𐐯𐑅𐐹𐐱𐑌𐐼𐐯𐑌𐑅 𐐶𐐮𐑄 𐑄𐐯𐑋, 𐐰𐑌𐐼 𐑄 𐐿𐐲𐑉𐑅 𐐱𐑂 𐐘𐐱𐐼 𐐼𐐮𐐼 𐑌𐐬 𐑋𐐬𐑉 𐑁𐐱𐑊𐐬 𐑄𐐯𐑋.

4. 𐐈𐑌𐐼 𐐮𐐻 𐐿𐐩𐑋 𐐻𐐭 𐐹𐐰𐑅 𐑄𐐰𐐻 𐑄 𐐈𐑋𐐰𐑊𐐯𐐿𐐴𐐻𐑅, 𐐰𐑌𐐼 𐑄 𐐈𐑋𐐲𐑊𐐱𐑌𐐴𐐻𐑅, 𐐰𐑌𐐼 𐑄 𐐢𐐰𐑋𐐲𐑌𐐴𐐻𐑅 𐐸𐐭 𐐶𐐲𐑉 𐐮𐑌 𐑄 𐑊𐐰𐑌𐐼 𐐱𐑂 𐐈𐑋𐐲𐑊𐐱𐑌, 𐐰𐑌𐐼 𐐫𐑊𐑅𐐬 𐐮𐑌 𐑄 𐑊𐐰𐑌𐐼 𐐱𐑂 𐐐𐐨𐑊𐐰𐑋, 𐐰𐑌𐐼 𐐸𐐭 𐐶𐐲𐑉 𐐮𐑌 𐑄 𐑊𐐰𐑌𐐼 𐐱𐑂 𐐖𐐯𐑉𐐭𐑅𐐲𐑊𐐯𐑋, 𐐰𐑌𐐼 𐐮𐑌 𐑁𐐴𐑌, 𐐮𐑌 𐐫𐑊 𐑄 𐑊𐐰𐑌𐐼 𐑉𐐵𐑌𐐼 𐐲𐐺𐐵𐐻, 𐐸𐐭 𐐸𐐰𐐼 𐑌𐐱𐐻 𐐺𐐮𐑌 𐐿𐐱𐑌𐑂𐐲𐑉𐐻𐐯𐐼, 𐐰𐑌𐐼 𐐸𐐰𐐼 𐑌𐐱𐐻 𐐻𐐩𐐿𐐲𐑌 𐐲𐐹𐐱𐑌 𐑄𐐯𐑋 𐑄 𐑌𐐩𐑋 𐐱𐑂 𐐈𐑌𐐻𐐴-𐐤𐐨𐑁𐐴-𐐢𐐨𐐸𐐴, 𐐶𐐲𐑉 𐑅𐐻𐐲𐑉𐐼 𐐲𐐹 𐐺𐐴 𐑄 𐐈𐑋𐐰𐑊𐐯𐐿𐐴𐐻𐑅 𐐰𐑌𐐼 𐐺𐐴 𐑄 𐐈𐑋𐐲𐑊𐐱𐑌𐐴𐐻𐑅 𐐻𐐭 𐐰𐑍𐑀𐐲𐑉 𐐲𐑀𐐯𐑌𐑅𐐻 𐑄𐐩𐑉 𐐺𐑉𐐯𐑄𐑉𐐯𐑌; 𐐰𐑌𐐼 𐑄𐐩𐑉

𐐸𐐩𐐻𐑉𐐯𐐼 𐐺𐐨𐐿𐐩𐑋 𐐯𐐿𐑅𐐨𐐼𐐮𐑍𐑊𐐨 𐑅𐐬𐑉 𐐰𐑀𐐯𐑌𐑅𐐻 𐑄𐐯𐑋, 𐐨𐑂𐐲𐑌 𐐮𐑌𐑅𐐬𐑋𐐲𐐽 𐑄𐐰𐐻 𐑄𐐩 𐐺𐐨𐑀𐐰𐑌 𐐻𐐭 𐑉𐐨𐐺𐐯𐑊 𐐰𐑀𐐯𐑌𐑅𐐻 𐑄𐐩𐑉 𐐿𐐮𐑍, 𐐮𐑌𐑅𐐬𐑋𐐲𐐽 𐑄𐐰𐐻 𐑄𐐩 𐐶𐐳𐐼 𐑌𐐱𐐻 𐑄𐐰𐐻 𐐸𐐨 𐑇𐐳𐐼 𐐺𐐨 𐑄𐐩𐑉 𐐿𐐮𐑍; 𐑄𐐩𐑉𐑁𐐬𐑉, 𐑄𐐩 𐐻𐐳𐐿 𐐲𐐹 𐐪𐑉𐑋𐑆 𐐰𐑀𐐯𐑌𐑅𐐻 𐑄 𐐹𐐨𐐹𐑊 𐐱𐑂 𐐈𐑌𐐻𐐴-𐐤𐐨𐑁𐐴-𐐢𐐨𐐸𐐴.

5. 𐐤𐐵 𐑄 𐐿𐐮𐑍 𐐿𐐱𐑌𐑁𐐲𐑉𐐼 𐑄 𐐿𐐮𐑍𐐼𐐲𐑋 𐐲𐐹𐐱𐑌 𐐸𐐮𐑆 𐑅𐐲𐑌, 𐐰𐑌𐐼 𐐸𐐨 𐐿𐐫𐑊𐐼 𐐸𐐮𐑆 𐑌𐐩𐑋 𐐈𐑌𐐻𐐴-𐐤𐐨𐑁𐐴-𐐢𐐨𐐸𐐴. 𐐈𐑌𐐼 𐑄 𐐿𐐮𐑍 𐐼𐐴𐐼 𐐮𐑌 𐑄𐐰𐐻 𐑅𐐯𐑊𐑁 𐑅𐐩𐑋 𐐷𐐨𐑉 𐑄𐐰𐐻 𐑄 𐐢𐐰𐑋𐐲𐑌𐐴𐐻𐑅 𐐺𐐨𐑀𐐰𐑌 𐐻𐐭 𐑋𐐩𐐿 𐐹𐑉𐐯𐐹𐐲𐑉𐐩𐑇𐐲𐑌𐑆 𐑁𐐫𐑉 𐐶𐐫𐑉 𐐰𐑀𐐯𐑌𐑅𐐻 𐑄 𐐹𐐨𐐹𐑊 𐐱𐑂 𐐘𐐱𐐼. 𐐤𐐵 𐐸𐐶𐐯𐑌 𐐈𐑋𐐲𐑌 𐐰𐑌𐐼 𐐸𐐮𐑆 𐐺𐑉𐐯𐑄𐑉𐐯𐑌 𐐰𐑌𐐼 𐐫𐑊 𐑄𐐬𐑆 𐐸𐐭 𐐸𐐰𐐼 𐐿𐐲𐑋 𐐲𐐹 𐐶𐐮𐑄 𐐸𐐮𐑋 𐑅𐐫 𐑄 𐐹𐑉𐐯𐐹𐐲𐑉𐐩𐑇𐐲𐑌𐑆 𐐱𐑂 𐑄 𐐢𐐰𐑋𐐲𐑌𐐴𐐻𐑅 𐐻𐐭 𐐼𐐯𐑅𐐻𐑉𐑎 𐑄𐐩𐑉 𐐺𐑉𐐯𐑄𐑉𐐯𐑌, 𐑄𐐩 𐐿𐐩𐑋 𐑁𐐬𐑉𐑃 𐐻𐐭 𐑄 𐑊𐐰𐑌𐐼 𐐱𐑂 𐐣𐐮𐐼𐐨𐐲𐑌, 𐐰𐑌𐐼 𐑄𐐩𐑉 𐐈𐑋𐐲𐑌 𐑋𐐯𐐻 𐐫𐑊 𐐸𐐮𐑆 𐐺𐑉𐐯𐑄𐑉𐐯𐑌; 𐐰𐑌𐐼 𐑁𐑉𐐱𐑋 𐑄𐐯𐑌𐑅 𐑄𐐩 𐐿𐐩𐑋 𐐻𐐭 𐑄 𐑊𐐰𐑌𐐼 𐐱𐑂 𐐆𐑇𐑋𐐩𐐯𐑊, 𐑄𐐰𐐻 𐑄𐐩 𐑋𐐴𐐻 𐐸𐐬𐑊𐐼 𐐩 𐐿𐐵𐑌𐑅𐐮𐑊 𐐶𐐮𐑄 𐐢𐐰𐑋𐐬𐑌𐐴, 𐐰𐑌𐐼 𐐫𐑊𐑅𐐬 𐐶𐐮𐑄 𐐸𐐮𐑆 𐐺𐑉𐐲𐑄𐐲𐑉 𐐈𐑌𐐻𐐴-𐐤𐐨𐑁𐐴-𐐢𐐨𐐸𐐴, 𐐸𐐶𐐱𐐻 𐑄𐐩 𐑇𐐳𐐼 𐐼𐐭 𐐻𐐭 𐐼𐐨𐑁𐐯𐑌𐐼 𐑄𐐯𐑋𐑅𐐯𐑊𐑂𐑆 𐐰𐑀𐐯𐑌𐑅𐐻 𐑄 𐐢𐐰𐑋𐐲𐑌𐐴𐐻𐑅. 𐐤𐐵 𐑄𐐩𐑉 𐐶𐐱𐑆 𐑌𐐱𐐻 𐐶𐐲𐑌 𐑅𐐬𐑊 𐐰𐑋𐐲𐑍 𐐫𐑊 𐑄 𐐹𐐨𐐹𐑊 𐐸𐐭 𐐸𐐰𐐼 𐐺𐐮𐑌 𐐿𐐱𐑌𐑂𐐲𐑉𐐻𐐯𐐼 𐐲𐑌𐐻𐐭 𐑄 𐐢𐐫𐑉𐐼, 𐑄𐐰𐐻 𐐶𐐳𐐼 𐐻𐐩𐐿 𐐲𐐹 𐐪𐑉𐑋𐑆 𐐰𐑀𐐯𐑌𐑅𐐻 𐑄𐐩𐑉 𐐺𐑉𐐯𐑄𐑉𐐯𐑌; 𐑌𐐩, 𐑄𐐩 𐐶𐐳𐐼 𐑌𐐱𐐻 𐐨𐑂𐐲𐑌 𐑋𐐩𐐿 𐐯𐑌𐐨 𐐹𐑉𐐯𐐹𐐲𐑉𐐩𐑇𐐲𐑌𐑆 𐑁𐐫𐑉 𐐶𐐫𐑉; 𐐷𐐩, 𐐰𐑌𐐼 𐐫𐑊𐑅𐐬 𐑄𐐩𐑉 𐐿𐐮𐑍 𐐿𐐱𐑋𐐰𐑌𐐼𐐯𐐼 𐑄𐐯𐑋 𐑄𐐰𐐻 𐑄𐐩 𐑇𐐳𐐼 𐑌𐐱𐐻. 𐐤𐐵, 𐑄𐐨𐑆 𐐪𐑉 𐑄 𐐶𐐲𐑉𐐼𐑆 𐐸𐐶𐐮𐐽 𐐸𐐨 𐑅𐐯𐐼 𐐲𐑌𐐻𐐭 𐑄 𐐹𐐨𐐹𐑊 𐐿𐐱𐑌𐑅𐐲𐑉𐑌𐐮𐑍 𐑄 𐑋𐐰𐐻𐐲𐑉: 𐐌 𐑃𐐰𐑍𐐿 𐑋𐐴 𐐘𐐱𐐼, 𐑋𐐴 𐐺𐐨𐑊𐐲𐑂𐐯𐐼 𐐹𐐨𐐹𐑊, 𐑄𐐰𐐻 𐐵𐑉 𐑀𐑉𐐩𐐻 𐐘𐐱𐐼 𐐸𐐰𐑆 𐐮𐑌 𐑀𐐳𐐼𐑌𐐯𐑅 𐑅𐐯𐑌𐐻 𐑄𐐨𐑆 𐐵𐑉 𐐺𐑉𐐯𐑄𐑉𐐯𐑌, 𐑄 𐐤𐐨𐑁𐐴𐐻𐑅, 𐐲𐑌𐐻𐐭 𐐲𐑅 𐐻𐐭 𐐹𐑉𐐨𐐽 𐐲𐑌𐐻𐐭 𐐲𐑅, 𐐰𐑌𐐼 𐐻𐐭 𐐿𐐱𐑌𐑂𐐮𐑌𐑅 𐐲𐑅 𐐱𐑂 𐑄 𐐻𐑉𐐰𐐼𐐮𐑇𐐲𐑌𐑆 𐐱𐑂 𐐵𐑉 𐐶𐐮𐐿𐐯𐐼 𐑁𐐪𐑄𐐲𐑉𐑆. 𐐈𐑌𐐼 𐐺𐐨𐐸𐐬𐑊𐐼, 𐐌 𐑃𐐰𐑍𐐿 𐑋𐐴 𐑀𐑉𐐩𐐻 𐐘𐐱𐐼 𐑄𐐰𐐻 𐐸𐐨 𐐸𐐰𐑆 𐑀𐐮𐑂𐐲𐑌 𐐲𐑅 𐐩 𐐹𐐬𐑉𐑇𐐲𐑌 𐐱𐑂 𐐸𐐮𐑆 𐐝𐐹𐐮𐑉𐐮𐐻 𐐻𐐭 𐑅𐐱𐑁𐐲𐑌 𐐵𐑉 𐐸𐐪𐑉𐐻𐑅, 𐑄𐐰𐐻 𐐶𐐨 𐐸𐐰𐑂 𐐬𐐹𐐲𐑌𐐼 𐐩 𐐿𐐱𐑉𐐯𐑅𐐹𐐱𐑌𐐼𐐯𐑌𐑅 𐐶𐐮𐑄 𐑄𐐨𐑆 𐐺𐑉𐐯𐑄𐑉𐐯𐑌, 𐑄 𐐤𐐨𐑁𐐴𐐻𐑅. 𐐈𐑌𐐼 𐐺𐐨𐐸𐐬𐑊𐐼, 𐐌 𐐫𐑊𐑅𐐬 𐑃𐐰𐑍𐐿 𐑋𐐴 𐐘𐐱𐐼, 𐑄𐐰𐐻 𐐺𐐴 𐐬𐐹𐐲𐑌𐐮𐑍 𐑄𐐮𐑅 𐐿𐐱𐑉𐐯𐑅𐐹𐐱𐑌𐐼𐐯𐑌𐑅 𐐶𐐨 𐐸𐐰𐑂 𐐺𐐮𐑌 𐐿𐐱𐑌𐑂𐐮𐑌𐑅𐐻 𐐱𐑂 𐐵𐑉 𐑅𐐮𐑌𐑆, 𐐰𐑌𐐼 𐐱𐑂 𐑄 𐑋𐐯𐑌𐐨 𐑋𐐲𐑉𐐼𐐲𐑉𐑆 𐐸𐐶𐐮𐐽 𐐶𐐨 𐐸𐐰𐑂 𐐿𐐱𐑋𐐮𐐻𐐯𐐼. 𐐈𐑌𐐼 𐐌 𐐫𐑊𐑅𐐬 𐑃𐐰𐑍𐐿 𐑋𐐴 𐐘𐐱𐐼, 𐐷𐐩, 𐑋𐐴 𐑀𐑉𐐩𐐻 𐐘𐐱𐐼, 𐑄𐐰𐐻 𐐸𐐨 𐐸𐐰𐑃 𐑀𐑉𐐰𐑌𐐻𐐯𐐼 𐐲𐑌𐐻𐐭 𐐲𐑅 𐑄𐐰𐐻 𐐶𐐨 𐑋𐐴𐐻 𐑉𐐨𐐹𐐯𐑌𐐻 𐐱𐑂 𐑄𐐨𐑆 𐑃𐐮𐑍𐑆, 𐐰𐑌𐐼 𐐫𐑊𐑅𐐬, 𐑄𐐰𐐻 𐐸𐐨 𐐸𐐰𐑃 𐑁𐐫𐑉𐑀𐐮𐑂𐐲𐑌 𐐲𐑅 𐐱𐑂 𐑄𐐬𐑆 𐐵𐑉 𐑋𐐯𐑌𐐨 𐑅𐐮𐑌𐑆 𐐰𐑌𐐼 𐑋𐐲𐑉𐐼𐐲𐑉𐑆 𐐸𐐶𐐮𐐽 𐐶𐐨 𐐸𐐰𐑂 𐐿𐐱𐑋𐐮𐐻𐐯𐐼, 𐐰𐑌𐐼 𐐻𐐩𐐿𐐲𐑌 𐐰𐐶𐐩 𐑄 𐑀𐐮𐑊𐐻 𐑁𐑉𐐱𐑋 𐐵𐑉 𐐸𐐪𐑉𐐻𐑅, 𐑃𐑉𐐭 𐑄 𐑋𐐯𐑉𐐮𐐻𐑅 𐐱𐑂 𐐸𐐮𐑆 𐐝𐐲𐑌. 𐐈𐑌𐐼 𐑌𐐵 𐐺𐐨𐐸𐐬𐑊𐐼, 𐑋𐐴 𐐺𐑉𐐯𐑄𐑉𐐯𐑌, 𐑅𐐮𐑌𐑅 𐐮𐐻 𐐸𐐰𐑆 𐐺𐐮𐑌 𐐫𐑊 𐑄𐐰𐐻 𐐶𐐨 𐐿𐐳𐐼 𐐼𐐭, (𐐰𐑆 𐐶𐐨 𐐶𐐲𐑉 𐑄 𐑋𐐬𐑅𐐻 𐑊𐐱𐑅𐐻 𐐱𐑂 𐐫𐑊 𐑋𐐰𐑌𐐿𐐴𐑌𐐼,) 𐐻𐐭 𐑉𐐨𐐹𐐯𐑌𐐻 𐐱𐑂 𐐫𐑊 𐐵𐑉 𐑅𐐮𐑌𐑆 𐐰𐑌𐐼 𐑄 𐑋𐐯𐑌𐐨 𐑋𐐲𐑉𐐼𐐲𐑉𐑆 𐐸𐐶𐐮𐐽 𐐶𐐨 𐐸𐐰𐑂 𐐿𐐱𐑋𐐮𐐻𐐯𐐼, 𐐰𐑌𐐼 𐐻𐐭 𐑀𐐯𐐻 𐐘𐐱𐐼 𐐻𐐭 𐐻𐐩𐐿 𐑄𐐯𐑋 𐐰𐐶𐐩 𐑁𐑉𐐱𐑋 𐐵𐑉 𐐸𐐪𐑉𐐻𐑅, 𐑁𐐫𐑉 𐐮𐐻 𐐶𐐱𐑆 𐐫𐑊 𐐶𐐨 𐐿𐐳𐐼 𐐼𐐭 𐐻𐐭 𐑉𐐨𐐹𐐯𐑌𐐻 𐑅𐐲𐑁𐐮𐑇𐐯𐑌𐐻𐑊𐐨 𐐺𐐨𐑁𐐬𐑉 𐐘𐐱𐐼 𐑄𐐰𐐻 𐐸𐐨 𐐶𐐳𐐼 𐐻𐐩𐐿 𐐰𐐶𐐩 𐐵𐑉 𐑅𐐻𐐩𐑌.

6. 𐐤𐐵, 𐑋𐐴 𐐺𐐯𐑅𐐻 𐐺𐐨𐑊𐐲𐑂𐐯𐐼 𐐺𐑉𐐯𐑄𐑉𐐯𐑌, 𐑅𐐮𐑌𐑅 𐐘𐐱𐐼 𐐸𐐰𐑃 𐐻𐐩𐐿𐐲𐑌 𐐰𐐶𐐩 𐐵𐑉 𐑅𐐻𐐩𐑌𐑆, 𐐰𐑌𐐼 𐐵𐑉 𐑅𐐬𐑉𐐼𐑆 𐐸𐐰𐑂 𐐺𐐨𐐿𐐲𐑋 𐐺𐑉𐐴𐐻, 𐑄𐐯𐑌 𐑊𐐯𐐻 𐐲𐑅 𐑅𐐻𐐩𐑌 𐐵𐑉 𐑅𐐬𐑉𐐼𐑆 𐑌𐐬 𐑋𐐬𐑉 𐐶𐐮𐑄 𐑄 𐐺𐑊𐐲𐐼 𐐱𐑂 𐐵𐑉 𐐺𐑉𐐯𐑄𐑉𐐯𐑌. 𐐒𐐨𐐸𐐬𐑊𐐼, 𐐌 𐑅𐐩 𐐲𐑌𐐻𐐭 𐐷𐐭, 𐐤𐐩, 𐑊𐐯𐐻 𐐲𐑅 𐑉𐐨𐐻𐐩𐑌 𐐵𐑉 𐑅𐐬𐑉𐐼𐑆 𐑄𐐰𐐻 𐑄𐐩 𐐺𐐨 𐑌𐐱𐐻 𐑅𐐻𐐩𐑌𐐼 𐐶𐐮𐑄 𐑄 𐐺𐑊𐐲𐐼 𐐱𐑂 𐐵𐑉 𐐺𐑉𐐯𐑄𐑉𐐯𐑌: 𐑁𐐫𐑉 𐐹𐐲𐑉𐐸𐐰𐐹𐑅, 𐐮𐑁 𐐶𐐨 𐑇𐐳𐐼 𐑅𐐻𐐩𐑌 𐐵𐑉 𐑅𐐬𐑉𐐼𐑆 𐐰𐑀𐐯𐑌, 𐑄𐐩 𐐿𐐰𐑌 𐑌𐐬 𐑋𐐬𐑉 𐐺𐐨 𐐶𐐱𐑇𐐻 𐐺𐑉𐐴𐐻 𐑃𐑉𐐭 𐑄 𐐺𐑊𐐲𐐼 𐐱𐑂 𐑄 𐐝𐐲𐑌 𐐱𐑂 𐐵𐑉 𐑀𐑉𐐩𐐻 𐐘𐐱𐐼, 𐐸𐐶𐐮𐐽 𐑇𐐰𐑊 𐐺𐐨 𐑇𐐯𐐼 𐑁𐐫𐑉 𐑄 𐐰𐐻𐐬𐑌𐑋𐐯𐑌𐐻 𐐱𐑂 𐐵𐑉 𐑅𐐮𐑌𐑆. 𐐈𐑌𐐼 𐑄 𐑀𐑉𐐩𐐻 𐐘𐐱𐐼 𐐸𐐰𐑆 𐐸𐐰𐐼 𐑋𐐲𐑉𐑅𐐨 𐐱𐑌 𐐲𐑅, 𐐰𐑌𐐼 𐑋𐐩𐐼 𐑄𐐨𐑆 𐑃𐐮𐑍𐑆 𐑌𐐬𐑌 𐐲𐑌𐐻𐐭 𐐲𐑅 𐑄𐐰𐐻 𐐶𐐨 𐑋𐐴𐐻 𐑌𐐱𐐻 𐐹𐐯𐑉𐐮𐑇: 𐐷𐐩, 𐐰𐑌𐐼 𐐸𐐨 𐐸𐐰𐑆 𐑋𐐩𐐼 𐑄𐐨𐑆 𐑃𐐮𐑍𐑆 𐑌𐐬𐑌 𐐲𐑌𐐻𐐭 𐐲𐑅 𐐺𐐨𐑁𐐬𐑉𐐸𐐰𐑌𐐼, 𐐺𐐨𐐿𐐫𐑆 𐐸𐐨 𐑊𐐲𐑂𐐯𐑃 𐐵𐑉 𐑅𐐬𐑊𐑆 𐐰𐑆 𐐶𐐯𐑊 𐐰𐑆 𐐸𐐨 𐑊𐐲𐑂𐐯𐑃 𐐵𐑉 𐐽𐐮𐑊𐐼𐑉𐐯𐑌; 𐑄𐐩𐑉𐑁𐐬𐑉, 𐐮𐑌 𐐸𐐮𐑆 𐑋𐐲𐑉𐑅𐐨 𐐸𐐨 𐐼𐐲𐑃 𐑂𐐮𐑆𐐮𐐻 𐐲𐑅 𐐺𐐴 𐐸𐐮𐑆 𐐩𐑌𐐾𐐯𐑊𐑆, 𐑄𐐰𐐻 𐑄 𐐹𐑊𐐰𐑌 𐐱𐑂 𐑅𐐰𐑊𐑂𐐩𐑇𐐲𐑌 𐑋𐐴𐐻 𐐺𐐨 𐑋𐐩𐐼 𐑌𐐬𐑌 𐐲𐑌𐐻𐐭 𐐲𐑅 𐐰𐑆 𐐶𐐯𐑊 𐐰𐑆 𐐲𐑌𐐻𐐭 𐑁𐑏𐐽𐐲𐑉 𐐾𐐯𐑌𐐲𐑉𐐩𐑇𐐲𐑌𐑆. 𐐄, 𐐸𐐵 𐑋𐐲𐑉𐑅𐐮𐑁𐐳𐑊 𐐮𐑆 𐐵𐑉 𐐘𐐱𐐼! 𐐈𐑌𐐼 𐑌𐐵 𐐺𐐨𐐸𐐬𐑊𐐼, 𐑅𐐮𐑌𐑅 𐐮𐐻 𐐸𐐰𐑆 𐐺𐐮𐑌 𐐰𐑆 𐑋𐐲𐐽 𐐰𐑆 𐐶𐐨 𐐿𐐳𐐼 𐐼𐐭 𐐻𐐭 𐑀𐐯𐐻 𐐵𐑉 𐑅𐐻𐐩𐑌𐑆 𐐻𐐩𐐿𐐲𐑌 𐐰𐐶𐐩 𐑁𐑉𐐱𐑋 𐐲𐑅, 𐐰𐑌𐐼 𐐵𐑉 𐑅𐐬𐑉𐐼𐑆 𐐪𐑉 𐑋𐐩𐐼 𐐺𐑉𐐴𐐻, 𐑊𐐯𐐻 𐐲𐑅 𐐸𐐴𐐼 𐑄𐐯𐑋 𐐰𐐶𐐩 𐑄𐐰𐐻 𐑄𐐩 𐑋𐐩 𐐺𐐨 𐐿𐐯𐐹𐐻 𐐺𐑉𐐴𐐻, 𐐰𐑆 𐐩 𐐻𐐯𐑅𐐻𐐮𐑋𐐬𐑌𐐨 𐐻𐐭 𐐵𐑉 𐐘𐐱𐐼 𐐰𐐻 𐑄 𐑊𐐰𐑅𐐻 𐐼𐐩, 𐐫𐑉 𐐰𐐻 𐑄 𐐼𐐩 𐑄𐐰𐐻 𐐶𐐨

𐑇𐐰𐑊 𐐺𐐨 𐐺𐑉𐐫𐐻 𐐻𐐭 𐑅𐐻𐐰𐑌𐐼 𐐺𐐨𐑁𐐬𐑉 𐐸𐐮𐑋 𐐻𐐭 𐐺𐐨 𐐾𐐲𐐾𐐼, 𐑄𐐰𐐻 𐐶𐐨 𐐸𐐰𐑂 𐑌𐐱𐐻 𐑅𐐻𐐩𐑌𐐼 𐐵𐑉 𐑅𐐬𐑉𐐼𐑆 𐐮𐑌 𐑄 𐐺𐑊𐐲𐐼 𐐱𐑂 𐐵𐑉 𐐺𐑉𐐯𐑄𐑉𐐯𐑌 𐑅𐐮𐑌𐑅 𐐸𐐨 𐐮𐑋𐐹𐐪𐑉𐐻𐐲𐐼 𐐸𐐮𐑆 𐐶𐐲𐑉𐐼 𐐲𐑌𐐻𐐭 𐐲𐑅 𐐰𐑌𐐼 𐐸𐐰𐑆 𐑋𐐩𐐼 𐐲𐑅 𐐿𐑊𐐨𐑌 𐑄𐐯𐑉𐐺𐐴. 𐐈𐑌𐐼 𐑌𐐵, 𐑋𐐴 𐐺𐑉𐐯𐑄𐑉𐐯𐑌, 𐐮𐑁 𐐵𐑉 𐐺𐑉𐐯𐑄𐑉𐐯𐑌 𐑅𐐨𐐿 𐐻𐐭 𐐼𐐯𐑅𐐻𐑉𐐱𐐮 𐐲𐑅, 𐐺𐐨𐐸𐐬𐑊𐐼, 𐐶𐐨 𐐶𐐮𐑊 𐐸𐐴𐐼 𐐲𐐶𐐩 𐐵𐑉 𐑅𐐬𐑉𐐼𐑆, 𐐷𐐩, 𐐨𐑂𐐲𐑌 𐐶𐐨 𐐶𐐮𐑊 𐐺𐐯𐑉𐐨 𐑄𐐯𐑋 𐐼𐐨𐐹 𐐮𐑌 𐑄 𐐲𐑉𐑃, 𐑄𐐰𐐻 𐑄𐐩 𐑋𐐩 𐐺𐐨 𐐿𐐯𐐹𐐻 𐐺𐑉𐐴𐐻, 𐐰𐑆 𐐩 𐐻𐐯𐑅𐐻𐐮𐑋𐐬𐑌𐐨 𐑄𐐰𐐻 𐐶𐐨 𐐸𐐰𐑂 𐑌𐐯𐑂𐐲𐑉 𐐷𐐭𐑆𐐼 𐑄𐐯𐑋, 𐐰𐐻 𐑄 𐑊𐐪𐑅𐐻 𐐼𐐩; 𐐰𐑌𐐼 𐐮𐑁 𐐵𐑉 𐐺𐑉𐐯𐑄𐑉𐐯𐑌 𐐼𐐯𐑅𐐻𐑉𐐱𐐮 𐐲𐑅, 𐐺𐐨𐐸𐐬𐑊𐐼, 𐐶𐐨 𐑇𐐰𐑊 𐑀𐐬 𐐻𐐭 𐐵𐑉 𐐘𐐱𐐼 𐐰𐑌𐐼 𐑇𐐰𐑊 𐐺𐐨 𐑅𐐩𐑂𐐼.

7. 𐐈𐑌𐐼 𐑌𐐵 𐐮𐐻 𐐿𐐩𐑋 𐐻𐐭 𐐹𐐪𐑅 𐑄𐐰𐐻 𐐸𐐶𐐯𐑌 𐑄 𐐿𐐮𐑍 𐐸𐐰𐐼 𐑋𐐩𐐼 𐐰𐑌 𐐯𐑌𐐼 𐐱𐑂 𐑄𐐨𐑆 𐑅𐐩𐐮𐑍𐑆, 𐐰𐑌𐐼 𐐫𐑊 𐑄 𐐹𐐨𐐹𐑊 𐐶𐐲𐑉 𐐲𐑅𐐯𐑋𐐺𐑊𐐼 𐐻𐐲𐑀𐐯𐑄𐐲𐑉, 𐑄𐐩 𐐻𐐳𐐿 𐑄𐐯𐑉 𐑅𐐬𐑉𐐼𐑆, 𐐰𐑌𐐼 𐐫𐑊 𐑄 𐐶𐐯𐐹𐐲𐑌𐑆 𐐸𐐶𐐮𐐽 𐐶𐐲𐑉 𐐷𐐭𐑆𐐼 𐑁𐐫𐑉 𐑄 𐑇𐐯𐐼𐐮𐑍 𐐱𐑂 𐑋𐐰𐑌'𐑆 𐐺𐑊𐐲𐐼, 𐐰𐑌𐐼 𐑄𐐩 𐐼𐐮𐐼 𐐺𐐯𐑉𐐨 𐑄𐐯𐑋 𐐲𐐹 𐐼𐐨𐐹 𐐮𐑌 𐑄 𐐲𐑉𐑃; 𐐰𐑌𐐼 𐑄𐐮𐑅 𐑄𐐩 𐐼𐐮𐐼, 𐐮𐐻 𐐺𐐨𐐮𐑍 𐐮𐑌 𐑄𐐯𐑉 𐑂𐐷𐐭 𐐩 𐐻𐐯𐑅𐐻𐐮𐑋𐐬𐑌𐐨 𐐻𐐭 𐐘𐐱𐐼, 𐐰𐑌𐐼 𐐫𐑊𐑅𐐬 𐐻𐐭 𐑋𐐯𐑌, 𐑄𐐰𐐻 𐑄𐐩 𐑌𐐯𐑂𐐲𐑉 𐐶𐐳𐐼 𐐷𐐭𐑆 𐐶𐐯𐐹𐐲𐑌𐑆 𐐲𐑀𐐯𐑌 𐑁𐐫𐑉 𐑄 𐑇𐐯𐐼𐐮𐑍 𐐱𐑂 𐑋𐐰𐑌'𐑆 𐐺𐑊𐐲𐐼; 𐐰𐑌𐐼 𐑄𐐮𐑅 𐑄𐐩 𐐼𐐮𐐼, 𐑂𐐵𐐽𐐮𐑍 𐐰𐑌𐐼 𐐿𐐲𐑂𐐯𐑌𐐰𐑌𐐻𐐮𐑍 𐐶𐐮𐑄 𐐘𐐱𐐼, 𐑄𐐰𐐻 𐑉𐐪𐑄𐐲𐑉 𐑄𐐰𐑌 𐑇𐐯𐐼 𐑄 𐐺𐑊𐐲𐐼 𐐱𐑂 𐑄𐐯𐑉 𐐺𐑉𐐯𐑄𐑉𐐯𐑌, 𐑄𐐩 𐐶𐐳𐐼 𐑀𐐮𐑂 𐐲𐐹 𐑄𐐯𐑉 𐐬𐑌 𐑊𐐴𐑂𐑆; 𐐰𐑌𐐼 𐑉𐐪𐑄𐐲𐑉 𐑄𐐰𐑌 𐐻𐐩𐐿 𐐲𐐶𐐩 𐑁𐑉𐐱𐑋 𐐩 𐐺𐑉𐐲𐑄𐐲𐑉, 𐑄𐐩 𐐶𐐳𐐼 𐑀𐐮𐑂 𐐲𐑌𐐻𐐭 𐐸𐐮𐑋; 𐐰𐑌𐐼 𐑉𐐪𐑄𐐲𐑉 𐑄𐐰𐑌 𐑅𐐹𐐯𐑌𐐼 𐑄𐐯𐑉 𐐼𐐩𐑆 𐐮𐑌 𐐴𐐼𐑊𐑌𐐯𐑅, 𐑄𐐩 𐐶𐐳𐐼 𐑊𐐩𐐺𐐲𐑉 𐐲𐐺𐐲𐑌𐐼𐐲𐑌𐐻𐑊𐐨 𐐶𐐮𐑄 𐑄𐐯𐑉 𐐸𐐰𐑌𐐼𐑆; 𐐰𐑌𐐼 𐑄𐐲𐑅 𐐶𐐨 𐑅𐐨 𐑄𐐰𐐻, 𐐸𐐶𐐯𐑌 𐑄𐐨𐑆 𐐢𐐰𐑋𐐲𐑌𐐴𐐻𐑅 𐐶𐐲𐑉 𐐺𐑉𐐫𐐻 𐐻𐐭 𐐺𐐨𐑊𐐨𐑂 𐐰𐑌𐐼 𐐻𐐭 𐑌𐐬 𐑄 𐐻𐑉𐐭𐑃, 𐑄𐐩 𐐶𐐲𐑉 𐑁𐐲𐑉𐑋, 𐐰𐑌𐐼 𐐶𐐳𐐼 𐑅𐐲𐑁𐐲𐑉 𐐨𐑂𐐲𐑌 𐐲𐑌𐐻𐐭 𐐼𐐯𐑃 𐑉𐐪𐑄𐐲𐑉 𐑄𐐰𐑌 𐐿𐐲𐑋𐐮𐐻 𐑅𐐮𐑌; 𐐰𐑌𐐼 𐑄𐐲𐑅 𐐶𐐨 𐑅𐐨 𐑄𐐰𐐻 𐑄𐐩 𐐺𐐯𐑉𐐨𐐼 𐑄𐐯𐑉 𐐶𐐯𐐹𐐲𐑌𐑆 𐐱𐑂 𐐹𐐨𐑅, 𐐫𐑉 𐑄𐐩 𐐺𐐯𐑉𐐨𐐼 𐑄 𐐶𐐯𐐹𐐲𐑌𐑆 𐐱𐑂 𐐶𐐫𐑉, 𐑁𐐫𐑉 𐐹𐐨𐑅.

8. 𐐈𐑌𐐼 𐐮𐐻 𐐿𐐩𐑋 𐐻𐐭 𐐹𐐪𐑅 𐑄𐐰𐐻 𐑄𐐯𐑉 𐐺𐑉𐐯𐑄𐑉𐐯𐑌, 𐑄 𐐢𐐰𐑋𐐲𐑌𐐴𐐻𐑅, 𐑋𐐩𐐼 𐐹𐑉𐐯𐐹𐐲𐑉𐐩𐑇𐐲𐑌𐑆 𐑁𐐫𐑉 𐐶𐐫𐑉, 𐐰𐑌𐐼 𐐿𐐩𐑋 𐐲𐐹 𐐻𐐭 𐑄 𐑊𐐰𐑌𐐼 𐐱𐑂 𐐤𐐨𐑁𐐴, 𐑁𐐫𐑉 𐑄 𐐹𐐲𐑉𐐹𐐲𐑅 𐐱𐑂 𐐼𐐯𐑅𐐻𐑉𐐱𐐮𐐮𐑍 𐑄 𐐿𐐮𐑍, 𐐰𐑌𐐼 𐐻𐐭 𐐹𐑊𐐩𐑅 𐐲𐑌𐐲𐑄𐐲𐑉 𐐮𐑌 𐐸𐐮𐑆 𐑅𐐻𐐯𐐼, 𐐰𐑌𐐼 𐐫𐑊𐑅𐐬 𐐱𐑂 𐐼𐐯𐑅𐐻𐑉𐐱𐐮𐐮𐑍 𐑄 𐐹𐐨𐐹𐑊 𐐱𐑂 𐐈𐑌𐐻𐐴-𐐤𐐨𐑁𐐴-𐐢𐐨𐐸𐐴 𐐵𐐻 𐐱𐑂 𐑄 𐑊𐐰𐑌𐐼. 𐐤𐐵 𐐸𐐶𐐯𐑌 𐑄 𐐹𐐨𐐹𐑊 𐑅𐐫 𐑄𐐰𐐻 𐑄𐐩 𐐶𐐲𐑉 𐐿𐐬𐐮𐑍 𐐲𐑀𐐯𐑌𐑅𐐻 𐑄𐐯𐑋, 𐑄𐐩 𐐶𐐯𐑌𐐻 𐐵𐐻 𐐻𐐭 𐑋𐐨𐐻 𐑄𐐯𐑋, 𐐰𐑌𐐼 𐐹𐑉𐐱𐑅𐐻𐑉𐐩𐐻𐐲𐐼 𐑄𐐯𐑋𐑅𐐯𐑊𐑂𐑆 𐐺𐐨𐑁𐐬𐑉 𐑄𐐯𐑋 𐐻𐐭 𐑄 𐐲𐑉𐑃, 𐐰𐑌𐐼 𐐺𐐨𐑀𐐰𐑌 𐐻𐐭 𐐿𐐫𐑊 𐐱𐑌 𐑄 𐑌𐐩𐑋 𐐱𐑂 𐑄 𐐢𐐫𐑉𐐼; 𐐰𐑌𐐼 𐑄𐐲𐑅 𐑄𐐩 𐐶𐐲𐑉 𐐮𐑌 𐑄𐐮𐑅 𐐰𐐻𐐮𐐻𐐷𐐭𐐼 𐐸𐐶𐐯𐑌 𐑄 𐐢𐐰𐑋𐐲𐑌𐐴𐐻𐑅 𐐺𐐨𐑀𐐰𐑌 𐐻𐐭 𐑁𐐫𐑊 𐐲𐐹𐐱𐑌 𐑄𐐯𐑋, 𐐰𐑌𐐼 𐐺𐐨𐑀𐐰𐑌 𐐻𐐭 𐑅𐑊𐐩 𐑄𐐯𐑋 𐐶𐐮𐑄 𐑄 𐑅𐐬𐑉𐐼; 𐐰𐑌𐐼 𐑄𐐲𐑅 𐐶𐐮𐑄𐐵𐐻 𐑋𐐨𐐻𐐮𐑍 𐐯𐑌𐐨 𐑉𐐨𐑆𐐮𐑅𐐻𐐰𐑌𐑅, 𐑄𐐩 𐐼𐐮𐐼 𐑅𐑊𐐩 𐐩 𐑃𐐵𐑆𐐰𐑌𐐼 𐐰𐑌𐐼 𐑁𐐴𐑂 𐐱𐑂 𐑄𐐯𐑋; 𐐰𐑌𐐼 𐐶𐐨 𐑌𐐬 𐑄𐐰𐐻 𐑄𐐩 𐐪𐑉 𐐺𐑊𐐯𐑅𐐲𐐼, 𐑁𐐫𐑉 𐑄𐐩 𐐸𐐰𐑂 𐑀𐐱𐑌 𐐻𐐭 𐐼𐐶𐐯𐑊 𐐶𐐮𐑄 𐑄𐐯𐑉 𐐘𐐱𐐼. 𐐤𐐵 𐐸𐐶𐐯𐑌 𐑄 𐐢𐐰𐑋𐐲𐑌𐐴𐐻𐑅 𐑅𐐫 𐑄𐐰𐐻 𐑄𐐯𐑉 𐐺𐑉𐐯𐑄𐑉𐐯𐑌 𐐶𐐳𐐼 𐑌𐐱𐐻 𐑁𐑊𐐨 𐑁𐑉𐐱𐑋 𐑄 𐑅𐐬𐑉𐐼, 𐑌𐐨𐑄𐐲𐑉 𐐶𐐳𐐼 𐑄𐐩 𐐻𐐲𐑉𐑌 𐐲𐑅𐐴𐐼 𐐻𐐭 𐑄 𐑉𐐴𐐻 𐐸𐐰𐑌𐐼 𐐫𐑉 𐐻𐐭 𐑄 𐑊𐐯𐑁𐐻, 𐐺𐐲𐐻 𐑄𐐰𐐻 𐑄𐐩 𐐶𐐳𐐼 𐑊𐐴 𐐼𐐵𐑌 𐐰𐑌𐐼 𐐹𐐯𐑉𐐮𐑇, 𐐰𐑌𐐼 𐐹𐑉𐐩𐑆𐐼 𐐘𐐱𐐼 𐐨𐑂𐐲𐑌 𐐮𐑌 𐑄 𐑂𐐯𐑉𐐨 𐐰𐐿𐐻 𐐱𐑂 𐐹𐐯𐑉𐐮𐑇𐐮𐑍 𐐲𐑌𐐼𐐲𐑉 𐑄 𐑅𐐬𐑉𐐼; 𐐸𐐨 𐐸𐐶𐐯𐑌 𐑄 𐐢𐐰𐑋𐐲𐑌𐐴𐐻𐑅 𐑅𐐫 𐑄𐐮𐑅 𐑄𐐩 𐐼𐐮𐐼 𐑁𐐫𐑉𐐺𐐯𐑉 𐑁𐑉𐐱𐑋 𐑅𐑊𐐩𐐮𐑍 𐑄𐐯𐑋; 𐐰𐑌𐐼 𐑄𐐯𐑉 𐐶𐐲𐑉 𐑋𐐯𐑌𐐨 𐐸𐐭𐑆 𐐸𐐪𐑉𐐻𐑅 𐐸𐐰𐐼 𐑅𐐶𐐬𐑊𐑌 𐐮𐑌 𐑄𐐯𐑋 𐑁𐐫𐑉 𐑄𐐬𐑆 𐐱𐑂 𐑄𐐯𐑉 𐐺𐑉𐐯𐑄𐑉𐐯𐑌 𐐸𐐭 𐐸𐐰𐐼 𐑁𐐫𐑊𐑌 𐐲𐑌𐐼𐐲𐑉 𐑄 𐑅𐐬𐑉𐐼, 𐑁𐐫𐑉 𐑄𐐩 𐑉𐐨𐐹𐐯𐑌𐐻𐐲𐐼 𐐱𐑂 𐑄 𐑃𐐮𐑍𐑆 𐐸𐐶𐐮𐐽 𐑄𐐩 𐐸𐐰𐐼 𐐼𐐲𐑌.

9. 𐐈𐑌𐐼 𐐮𐐻 𐐿𐐩𐑋 𐐻𐐭 𐐹𐐪𐑅 𐑄𐐰𐐻 𐑄𐐩 𐑃𐑉𐐭 𐐼𐐵𐑌 𐑄𐐯𐑉 𐐶𐐯𐐹𐐲𐑌𐑆 𐐱𐑂 𐐶𐐫𐑉, 𐐰𐑌𐐼 𐑄𐐩 𐐶𐐳𐐼 𐑌𐐱𐐻 𐐻𐐩𐐿 𐑄𐐯𐑋 𐐲𐑀𐐯𐑌, 𐑁𐐫𐑉 𐑄𐐩 𐐶𐐲𐑉 𐑅𐐻𐐲𐑍 𐑁𐐫𐑉 𐑄 𐑋𐐲𐑉𐐼𐐲𐑉𐑆 𐐸𐐶𐐮𐐽 𐑄𐐩 𐐸𐐰𐐼 𐐿𐐲𐑋𐐮𐐻𐐲𐐼; 𐐰𐑌𐐼 𐑄𐐩 𐐿𐐩𐑋 𐐼𐐵𐑌 𐐨𐑂𐐲𐑌 𐐰𐑆 𐑄𐐯𐑉 𐐺𐑉𐐯𐑄𐑉𐐯𐑌, 𐑉𐐨𐑊𐐴𐐮𐑍 𐐲𐐹𐐱𐑌 𐑄 𐑋𐐲𐑉𐑅𐐨𐑆 𐐱𐑂 𐑄𐐬𐑆 𐐸𐐭𐑆 𐐪𐑉𐑋𐑆 𐐶𐐲𐑉 𐑊𐐮𐑁𐐻𐐲𐐼 𐐻𐐭 𐑅𐑊𐐩 𐑄𐐯𐑋.

10. 𐐈𐑌𐐼 𐐮𐐻 𐐿𐐩𐑋 𐐻𐐭 𐐹𐐪𐑅 𐑄𐐰𐐻 𐑄 𐐹𐐨𐐹𐑊 𐐱𐑂 𐐘𐐱𐐼 𐐶𐐲𐑉 𐐾𐐱𐐮𐑌𐐼 𐑄𐐰𐐻 𐐼𐐩 𐐺𐐴 𐑋𐐬𐑉 𐑄𐐰𐑌 𐑄 𐑌𐐲𐑋𐐺𐐲𐑉 𐐸𐐭 𐐸𐐰𐐼 𐐺𐐨𐑌 𐑅𐑊𐐩𐑌; 𐐰𐑌𐐼 𐑄𐐬𐑆 𐐸𐐭 𐐸𐐰𐐼 𐐺𐐨𐑌 𐑅𐑊𐐩𐑌 𐐶𐐲𐑉 𐑉𐐴𐐽𐐲𐑅 𐐹𐐨𐐹𐑊; 𐑄𐐯𐑉𐑁𐐬𐑉 𐐶𐐨 𐐸𐐰𐑂 𐑌𐐬 𐑉𐐨𐑆𐐲𐑌 𐐻𐐭 𐐼𐐵𐐻 𐐺𐐲𐐻 𐐸𐐶𐐱𐐻 𐑄𐐩 𐐶𐐲𐑉 𐑅𐐩𐑂𐐼. 𐐈𐑌𐐼 𐑄𐐯𐑉 𐐶𐐱𐑆 𐑌𐐱𐐻 𐐩 𐐶𐐮𐐿𐐲𐐼 𐑋𐐰𐑌 𐑅𐑊𐐩𐑌 𐐲𐑋𐐲𐑍 𐑄𐐯𐑋; 𐐺𐐲𐐻 𐑄𐐯𐑉 𐐶𐐲𐑉 𐑋𐐬𐑉 𐑄𐐰𐑌 𐐩 𐑃𐐵𐑆𐐰𐑌𐐼 𐐺𐑉𐐫𐐻 𐐻𐐭 𐑄 𐑌𐐱𐑊𐐯𐐾 𐐱𐑂 𐑄 𐐻𐑉𐐭𐑃; 𐑄𐐲𐑅 𐐶𐐨 𐑅𐐨 𐑄𐐰𐐻 𐑄 𐐢𐐫𐑉𐐼 𐐶𐐲𐑉𐐿𐐯𐑃 𐐮𐑌 𐑋𐐯𐑌𐐨 𐐶𐐩𐑆 𐐻𐐭 𐑄 𐑅𐐰𐑊𐑂𐐩𐑇𐐲𐑌 𐐱𐑂 𐐸𐐮𐑆 𐐹𐐨𐐹𐑊. 𐐤𐐵 𐑄 𐑀𐑉𐐩𐐻𐐯𐑅𐐻

𐑌𐐲𐑋𐐺𐐲𐑉 𐐲𐑂 𐑄𐐬𐑆 𐐲𐑂 𐑄 𐐢𐐩𐑋𐐲𐑌𐐴𐐻𐑅 𐐸𐐭 𐑅𐑊𐐭 𐑅𐐬 𐑋𐐯𐑌𐐨 𐐲𐑂 𐑄𐐩𐑉 𐐺𐑉𐐯𐑄𐑉𐐯𐑌, 𐐶𐐲𐑉 𐐈𐑋𐐰𐑊𐐯𐐿𐐴𐐻𐑅 𐐰𐑌𐐼 𐐈𐑋𐐷𐐭𐑊𐐲𐑌𐐴𐐻𐑅, 𐑄 𐑀𐑉𐐩𐐻𐐯𐑅𐐻 𐑌𐐲𐑋𐐺𐐲𐑉 𐐲𐑂 𐐸𐐭𐑋 𐐶𐐲𐑉 𐐰𐑁𐐻𐐲𐑉 𐑄 𐐫𐑉𐐼𐐲𐑉 𐐲𐑂 𐑄 𐐤𐐨𐐸𐐬𐑉𐑆. 𐐤𐐵 𐐲𐑋𐐲𐑍 𐑄𐐬𐑆 𐐸𐐭 𐐖𐐱𐐮𐑌𐐼 𐑄 𐐹𐐨𐐹𐐲𐑊 𐐲𐑂 𐑄 𐐢𐐫𐑉𐐼, 𐑄𐐩𐑉 𐐶𐐲𐑉 𐑌𐐲𐑌 𐐸𐐭 𐐶𐐲𐑉 𐐈𐑋𐐰𐑊𐐯𐐿𐐴𐐻𐑅 𐐫𐑉 𐐈𐑋𐐷𐐭𐑊𐐲𐑌𐐴𐐻𐑅, 𐐫𐑉 𐐸𐐭 𐐶𐐲𐑉 𐐲𐑂 𐑄 𐐫𐑉𐐼𐐲𐑉 𐐲𐑂 𐐤𐐨𐐸𐐬𐑉, 𐐺𐐲𐐻 𐑄𐐩 𐐶𐐲𐑉 𐐰𐐿𐐽𐐭𐐲𐑊 𐐼𐐨𐑅𐐯𐑌𐐼𐐲𐑌𐐻𐑅 𐐲𐑂 𐐢𐐩𐑋𐐲𐑌 𐐰𐑌𐐼 𐐢𐐯𐑋𐐷𐐭𐐯𐑊; 𐐰𐑌𐐼 𐑄𐐲𐑅 𐐶𐐨 𐐿𐐰𐑌 𐐹𐑊𐐩𐑌𐑊𐐨 𐐼𐐮𐑆𐐲𐑉𐑌, 𐑄𐐰𐐻 𐐰𐑁𐐻𐐲𐑉 𐐰 𐐹𐐨𐐹𐐲𐑊 𐐸𐐰𐑂 𐐺𐐮𐑌 𐐶𐐲𐑌𐑅 𐐯𐑌𐑊𐐴𐐻𐐲𐑌𐐼 𐐺𐐴 𐑄 𐐝𐐹𐐮𐑉𐐮𐐻 𐐲𐑂 𐐘𐐪𐐼, 𐐰𐑌𐐼 𐐸𐐰𐑂 𐐸𐐰𐐼 𐑀𐑉𐐩𐐻 𐑌𐐪𐑊𐐯𐐾 𐐲𐑂 𐑃𐐮𐑍𐑆 𐐹𐐲𐑉𐐻𐐩𐑌𐐮𐑍 𐐻𐐭 𐑉𐐴𐐽𐐲𐑅𐑌𐐯𐑅, 𐐰𐑌𐐼 𐑄𐐯𐑌 𐐸𐐰𐑂 𐑁𐐫𐑊𐑌 𐐲𐐶𐐩 𐐮𐑌𐐻𐐭 𐑅𐐮𐑌 𐐰𐑌𐐼 𐐻𐑉𐐰𐑌𐑆𐑀𐑉𐐯𐑇𐐲𐑌, 𐑄𐐩 𐐺𐐨𐐿𐐲𐑋 𐑋𐐬𐑉 𐐸𐐪𐑉𐐼𐐲𐑌𐐼, 𐐰𐑌𐐼 𐑄𐐲𐑅 𐑄𐐩𐑉 𐑅𐐻𐐩𐐻 𐐺𐐨𐐿𐐲𐑋𐑆 𐐶𐐲𐑉𐑅 𐑄𐐰𐑌 𐑄𐐬 𐑄𐐩 𐐸𐐰𐐼 𐑌𐐯𐑂𐐲𐑉 𐑌𐐬𐑌 𐑃𐐨𐑆 𐑃𐐮𐑍𐑆.

11. 𐐈𐑌𐐼 𐐺𐐨𐐸𐐬𐑊𐐼, 𐑌𐐵 𐐮𐐻 𐐿𐐩𐑋 𐐻𐐭 𐐹𐐰𐑅 𐑄𐐰𐐻 𐑄𐐬𐑆 𐐢𐐩𐑋𐐲𐑌𐐴𐐻𐑅 𐐶𐐲𐑉 𐑋𐐬𐑉 𐐰𐑍𐑀𐑉𐐨, 𐐺𐐨𐐿𐐫𐑆 𐑄𐐩 𐐸𐐰𐐼 𐑅𐑊𐐩𐑌 𐑄𐐩𐑉 𐐺𐑉𐐯𐑄𐑉𐐯𐑌; 𐑄𐐩𐑉𐑁𐐬𐑉 𐑄𐐩 𐑅𐐶𐐬𐑉 𐑂𐐯𐑌𐐾𐐲𐑌𐑅 𐐲𐐹𐐪𐑌 𐑄 𐐤𐐨𐑁𐐴𐐻𐑅; 𐐰𐑌𐐼 𐑄𐐩 𐐼𐐮𐐼 𐑌𐐬 𐑋𐐬𐑉 𐐲𐐻𐐯𐑋𐐻 𐐻𐐭 𐑅𐑊𐐩 𐑄 𐐹𐐨𐐹𐐲𐑊 𐐲𐑂 𐐈𐑌𐐻𐐴-𐐤𐐨𐑁𐐴-𐐢𐐨𐐸𐐴 𐐰𐐻 𐑄𐐰𐐻 𐐻𐐴𐑋; 𐐺𐐲𐐻 𐑄𐐩 𐐻𐐳𐐿 𐑄𐐩𐑉 𐐪𐑉𐑋𐐨𐑆 𐐰𐑌𐐼 𐐶𐐯𐑌𐐻 𐐬𐑂𐐲𐑉 𐐮𐑌𐐻𐐭 𐑄 𐐺𐐫𐑉𐐼𐐲𐑉𐑆 𐐲𐑂 𐑄 𐑊𐐰𐑌𐐼 𐐲𐑂 𐐞𐐩𐑉𐐲𐐸𐐯𐑋𐑊𐐲, 𐐰𐑌𐐼 𐑁𐐯𐑊 𐐲𐐹𐐪𐑌 𐑄 𐐹𐐨𐐹𐐲𐑊 𐐸𐐭 𐐶𐐲𐑉 𐐮𐑌 𐑄 𐑊𐐰𐑌𐐼 𐐲𐑂 𐐈𐑋𐐲𐑌𐐴𐐸𐐪, 𐐰𐑌𐐼 𐐼𐐨𐑅𐐻𐑉𐐱𐐮𐐼 𐑄𐐯𐑋. 𐐈𐑌𐐼 𐐰𐑁𐐻𐐲𐑉 𐑄𐐰𐐻 𐑄𐐩 𐐸𐐰𐐼 𐑋𐐯𐑌𐐨 𐐺𐐰𐐻𐑊𐑆 𐐶𐐮𐑄 𐑄 𐐤𐐨𐑁𐐴𐐻𐑅, 𐐮𐑌 𐑄 𐐸𐐶𐐮𐐽 𐑄𐐩 𐐶𐐲𐑉 𐐼𐑉𐐮𐑂𐑌 𐐰𐑌𐐼 𐑅𐑊𐐩𐑌; 𐐰𐑌𐐼 𐐲𐑋𐐲𐑍 𐑄 𐐢𐐩𐑋𐐲𐑌𐐴𐐻𐑅 𐐸𐐭 𐐶𐐲𐑉 𐑅𐑊𐐩𐑌, 𐐶𐐲𐑉 𐐫𐑊𐑋𐐬𐑅𐐻 𐐫𐑊 𐑄 𐑅𐐨𐐼 𐐲𐑂 𐐈𐑋𐐷𐐭𐑊𐐲𐑌 𐐰𐑌𐐼 𐐸𐐮𐑆 𐐺𐑉𐐯𐑄𐑉𐐯𐑌, 𐐸𐐭 𐐶𐐲𐑉 𐑄 𐐹𐑉𐐨𐑅𐐻𐑅 𐐲𐑂 𐐤𐐬𐐲, 𐐰𐑌𐐼 𐑄𐐩 𐐶𐐲𐑉 𐑅𐑊𐐩𐑌 𐐺𐐴 𐑄 𐐸𐐰𐑌𐐼𐑆 𐐲𐑂 𐑄 𐐤𐐨𐑁𐐴𐐻𐑅; 𐐰𐑌𐐼 𐑄 𐑉𐐨𐑋𐐩𐑌𐐼𐐲𐑉 𐐸𐐰𐑂𐐮𐑍 𐑁𐑊𐐯𐐼 𐐮𐑌𐐻𐐭 𐑄 𐐨𐑅𐐻 𐐶𐐮𐑊𐐼𐐲𐑉𐑌𐐯𐑅, 𐐰𐑌𐐼 𐐸𐐰𐑂𐐮𐑍 𐐷𐐭𐑆𐐲𐑉𐐹𐐻 𐑄 𐐹𐐵𐐲𐑉 𐐰𐑌𐐼 𐐫𐑃𐐫𐑉𐐮𐐻𐐨 𐐬𐑂𐐲𐑉 𐑄 𐐢𐐩𐑋𐐲𐑌𐐴𐐻𐑅, 𐐿𐐫𐑆𐐼 𐑄𐐰𐐻 𐑋𐐯𐑌𐐨 𐐲𐑂 𐑄 𐐢𐐩𐑋𐐲𐑌𐐴𐐻𐑅 𐑇𐐳𐐼 𐐹𐐯𐑉𐐮𐑇 𐐺𐐴 𐑁𐐴𐑉 𐐺𐐨𐐿𐐫𐑆 𐐲𐑂 𐑄𐐩𐑉 𐐺𐐨𐑊𐐨𐑁; 𐑁𐐫𐑉 𐑋𐐯𐑌𐐨 𐐲𐑂 𐑄𐐯𐑋, 𐐰𐑁𐐻𐐲𐑉 𐐸𐐰𐑂𐐮𐑍 𐑅𐐲𐑁𐐲𐑉𐐼 𐑋𐐲𐐽 𐑊𐐫𐑅 𐐰𐑌𐐼 𐑅𐐬 𐑋𐐯𐑌𐐨 𐐰𐑁𐑊𐐮𐐿𐑇𐐲𐑌𐑆, 𐐺𐐨𐑀𐐰𐑌 𐐻𐐭 𐐺𐐨 𐑅𐐻𐐲𐑉𐐼 𐐲𐐹 𐐮𐑌 𐑉𐐨𐑋𐐯𐑋𐐺𐑉𐐲𐑌𐑅 𐐲𐑂 𐑄 𐐶𐐲𐑉𐐼𐑆 𐐸𐐶𐐮𐐽 𐐁𐑉𐐲𐑌 𐐰𐑌𐐼 𐐸𐐮𐑆 𐐺𐑉𐐯𐑄𐑉𐐯𐑌 𐐸𐐰𐐼 𐐹𐑉𐐨𐐽𐐻 𐐻𐐭 𐑄𐐯𐑋 𐐮𐑌 𐑄𐐩𐑉 𐑊𐐰𐑌𐐼; 𐑄𐐩𐑉𐑁𐐬𐑉 𐑄𐐩 𐐺𐐨𐑀𐐰𐑌 𐐻𐐭 𐐼𐐮𐑅𐐺𐐨𐑊𐐨𐑂 𐑄 𐐻𐑉𐐲𐐼𐐮𐑇𐐲𐑌𐑆 𐐲𐑂 𐑄𐐩𐑉 𐑁𐐪𐑄𐐲𐑉𐑆, 𐐰𐑌𐐼 𐐻𐐭 𐐺𐐨𐑊𐐨𐑂 𐐮𐑌 𐑄 𐐢𐐫𐑉𐐼, 𐐰𐑌𐐼 𐑄𐐰𐐻 𐐸𐐨 𐑀𐐩𐑂 𐑀𐑉𐐩𐐻 𐐹𐐵𐐲𐑉 𐐲𐑌𐐻𐐭 𐑄 𐐤𐐨𐑁𐐴𐐻𐑅; 𐐰𐑌𐐼 𐑄𐐲𐑅 𐑄𐐩𐑉 𐐶𐐲𐑉 𐑋𐐯𐑌𐐨 𐐲𐑂 𐑄𐐯𐑋 𐐿𐐲𐑌𐑂𐐲𐑉𐐻𐐲𐐼 𐐮𐑌 𐑄 𐐶𐐮𐑊𐐼𐐲𐑉𐑌𐐯𐑅.

12. 𐐈𐑌𐐼 𐐮𐐻 𐐿𐐩𐑋 𐐻𐐭 𐐹𐐰𐑅 𐑄𐐰𐐻 𐑄𐐬𐑆 𐑉𐐭𐑊𐐲𐑉𐑆 𐐸𐐭 𐐶𐐲𐑉 𐑄 𐑉𐐯𐑋𐑌𐐲𐑌𐐻 𐐲𐑂 𐑄 𐐽𐐮𐑊𐐼𐑉𐐯𐑌 𐐲𐑂 𐐈𐑋𐐷𐐭𐑊𐐲𐑌, 𐐿𐐫𐑆𐐼 𐑄𐐰𐐻 𐑄𐐩 𐑇𐐳𐐼 𐐺𐐨 𐐹𐐳𐐻 𐐻𐐭 𐐼𐐯𐑃, 𐐷𐐩, 𐐫𐑊 𐑄𐐬𐑆 𐑄𐐰𐐻 𐐺𐐨𐑊𐐨𐑂𐐼 𐐮𐑌 𐑃𐐨𐑆 𐑃𐐮𐑍𐑆. 𐐤𐐵 𐑄𐐮𐑅 𐑋𐐪𐑉𐐻𐐲𐑉𐐼𐐲𐑋 𐐿𐐫𐑆𐐼 𐑄𐐰𐐻 𐑋𐐯𐑌𐐨 𐐲𐑂 𐑄𐐩𐑉 𐐺𐑉𐐯𐑄𐑉𐐯𐑌 𐑇𐐳𐐼 𐐺𐐨 𐑅𐐻𐐲𐑉𐐼 𐐲𐐹 𐐻𐐭 𐐰𐑍𐑀𐐲𐑉; 𐐰𐑌𐐼 𐑄𐐩𐑉 𐐺𐐨𐑀𐐰𐑌 𐐻𐐭 𐐺𐐨 𐐿𐐲𐑌𐐻𐐯𐑌𐑇𐐲𐑌 𐐮𐑌 𐑄 𐐶𐐮𐑊𐐼𐐲𐑉𐑌𐐯𐑅; 𐐰𐑌𐐼 𐑄 𐐢𐐩𐑋𐐲𐑌𐐴𐐻𐑅 𐐺𐐨𐑀𐐰𐑌 𐐻𐐭 𐐸𐐲𐑌𐐻 𐑄 𐑅𐐨𐐼 𐐲𐑂 𐐈𐑋𐐷𐐭𐑊𐐲𐑌 𐐰𐑌𐐼 𐐸𐐮𐑆 𐐺𐑉𐐯𐑄𐑉𐐯𐑌, 𐐰𐑌𐐼 𐐺𐐨𐑀𐐰𐑌 𐐻𐐭 𐑅𐑊𐐩 𐑄𐐯𐑋, 𐐰𐑌𐐼 𐑄𐐩 𐑁𐑊𐐯𐐼 𐐮𐑌𐐻𐐭 𐑄 𐐨𐑅𐐻 𐐶𐐮𐑊𐐼𐐲𐑉𐑌𐐯𐑅. 𐐈𐑌𐐼 𐐺𐐨𐐸𐐬𐑊𐐼, 𐑄𐐩 𐐪𐑉 𐐸𐐲𐑌𐐻𐐯𐐼 𐐰𐐻 𐑄𐐮𐑅 𐐼𐐩 𐐺𐐴 𐑄 𐐢𐐩𐑋𐐲𐑌𐐴𐐻𐑅; 𐑄𐐲𐑅 𐑄 𐐶𐐲𐑉𐐼𐑆 𐐲𐑂 𐐈𐐺𐐮𐑌𐐲𐐼𐐴 𐐶𐐲𐑉 𐐺𐑉𐐫𐐻 𐐻𐐭 𐐹𐐰𐑅, 𐐸𐐶𐐮𐐽 𐐸𐐨 𐑅𐐯𐐼 𐐿𐐲𐑌𐑅𐐲𐑉𐑌𐐮𐑍 𐑄 𐑅𐐨𐐼 𐐲𐑂 𐑄 𐐹𐑉𐐨𐑅𐐻𐑅 𐐸𐐭 𐐿𐐫𐑆𐐼 𐑄𐐰𐐻 𐐸𐐨 𐑇𐐳𐐼 𐑅𐐲𐑁𐐲𐑉 𐐼𐐯𐑃 𐐺𐐴 𐑁𐐴𐑉. 𐐙𐐫𐑉 𐐸𐐨 𐑅𐐯𐐼 𐐲𐑌𐐻𐐭 𐑄𐐯𐑋, 𐐐𐐶𐐪𐐻 𐐷𐐨 𐑇𐐰𐑊 𐐼𐐭 𐐲𐑌𐐻𐐭 𐑋𐐨, 𐑇𐐰𐑊 𐐺𐐨 𐐰 𐐻𐐴𐐹 𐐲𐑂 𐑃𐐮𐑍𐑆 𐐻𐐭 𐐿𐐲𐑋. 𐐈𐑌𐐼 𐑌𐐵 𐐈𐐺𐐮𐑌𐐲𐐼𐐴 𐐶𐐪𐑆 𐑄 𐑁𐐲𐑉𐑅𐐻 𐑄𐐰𐐻 𐑅𐐲𐑁𐐲𐑉𐐼 𐐼𐐯𐑃 𐐺𐐴 𐑁𐐴𐑉, 𐐺𐐨𐐿𐐫𐑆 𐐲𐑂 𐐸𐐮𐑆 𐐺𐐨𐑊𐐨𐑁 𐐮𐑌 𐐘𐐪𐐼; 𐑌𐐵 𐑄𐐮𐑅 𐐮𐑆 𐐸𐐶𐐪𐐻 𐐸𐐨 𐑋𐐯𐑌𐐻, 𐑄𐐰𐐻 𐑋𐐯𐑌𐐨 𐑇𐐳𐐼 𐑅𐐲𐑁𐐲𐑉 𐐼𐐯𐑃 𐐺𐐴 𐑁𐐴𐑉, 𐐰𐐿𐐫𐑉𐐼𐐮𐑍 𐐰𐑆 𐐸𐐨 𐐸𐐰𐐼 𐑅𐐲𐑁𐐲𐑉𐐼. 𐐈𐑌𐐼 𐐸𐐨 𐑅𐐯𐐼 𐐲𐑌𐐻𐐭 𐑄 𐐹𐑉𐐨𐑅𐐻𐑅 𐐲𐑂 𐐤𐐬𐐲, 𐑄𐐰𐐻 𐑄𐐩𐑉 𐑅𐐨𐐼 𐑇𐐳𐐼 𐐿𐐫𐑆 𐑋𐐯𐑌𐐨 𐐻𐐭 𐐺𐐨 𐐹𐐳𐐻 𐐻𐐭 𐐼𐐯𐑃, 𐐮𐑌 𐑄 𐑊𐐴𐐿 𐑋𐐰𐑌𐐲𐑉 𐐰𐑆 𐐸𐐨 𐐶𐐪𐑆, 𐐰𐑌𐐼 𐑄𐐰𐐻 𐑄𐐩 𐑇𐐳𐐼 𐐺𐐨 𐑅𐐿𐐰𐐻𐐲𐑉𐐼 𐐲𐐺𐑉𐐫𐐼 𐐰𐑌𐐼 𐑅𐑊𐐩𐑌, 𐐨𐑂𐑌 𐐰𐑆 𐐰 𐑇𐐨𐐹 𐐸𐐰𐑂𐐮𐑍 𐑌𐐬 𐑇𐐯𐐹𐐲𐑉𐐼 𐐮𐑆 𐐼𐑉𐐮𐑂𐑌 𐐰𐑌𐐼 𐑅𐑊𐐩𐑌 𐐺𐐴 𐐶𐐴𐑊𐐼 𐐺𐐨𐑅𐐻𐑅; 𐐰𐑌𐐼 𐑌𐐵 𐐺𐐨𐐸𐐬𐑊𐐼, 𐑃𐐨𐑆 𐐶𐐲𐑉𐐼𐑆 𐐶𐐲𐑉 𐑂𐐯𐑉𐐮𐑁𐐴𐐼, 𐑁𐐫𐑉 𐑄𐐩 𐐶𐐲𐑉 𐐼𐑉𐐮𐑂𐑌 𐐺𐐴 𐑄 𐐢𐐩𐑋𐐲𐑌𐐴𐐻𐑅, 𐐰𐑌𐐼 𐑄𐐩 𐐶𐐲𐑉 𐐸𐐲𐑌𐐻𐐯𐐼, 𐐰𐑌𐐼 𐑄𐐩 𐐶𐐲𐑉 𐑅𐑋𐐮𐐻𐑌.

13. 𐐈𐑌𐐼 𐐮𐐻 𐐿𐐩𐑋 𐐻𐐭 𐐹𐐰𐑅 𐑄𐐰𐐻 𐐸𐐶𐐯𐑌 𐑄 𐐢𐐩𐑋𐐲𐑌𐐴𐐻𐑅 𐑅𐐫 𐑄𐐰𐐻 𐑄𐐩 𐐿𐐳𐐼 𐑌𐐪𐐻 𐐬𐑂𐐲𐑉𐐹𐐵𐐲𐑉 𐑄 𐐤𐐨𐑁𐐴𐐻𐑅, 𐑄𐐩 𐑉𐐨𐐻𐐲𐑉𐑌𐐼 𐐲𐑀𐐯𐑌 𐐻𐐭 𐑄𐐩𐑉 𐐬𐑌 𐑊𐐰𐑌𐐼; 𐐰𐑌𐐼 𐑋𐐯𐑌𐐨 𐐲𐑂 𐑄𐐯𐑋 𐐿𐐩𐑋 𐐬𐑂𐐲𐑉 𐐻𐐭 𐐼𐐶𐐯𐑊

𐐮𐑌 𐑄 𐑊𐐰𐑌𐐼 𐐱𐑂 𐐃𐑇𐑋𐐩𐐯𐑊 𐐰𐑌𐐼 𐑄 𐑊𐐰𐑌𐐼 𐐱𐑂 𐐤𐐨𐑁𐐴, 𐐰𐑌𐐼 𐐼𐐮𐐼 𐐾𐑎𐑌 𐑄𐐯𐑋𐑅𐐯𐑊𐑂𐑆 𐐻𐐭 𐑄 𐐹𐐨𐐹𐑊 𐐱𐑂 𐐘𐐱𐐼, 𐐸𐐭 𐐶𐐲𐑉 𐑄 𐐹𐐨𐐹𐑊 𐐱𐑂 𐐈𐑌𐐻𐐴-𐐤𐐨𐑁𐐴-𐐢𐐨𐐸𐐴; 𐐰𐑌𐐼 𐑄𐐩 𐐼𐐮𐐼 𐐫𐑊𐑅𐐬 𐐺𐐯𐑉𐐨 𐑄𐐩𐑉 𐐶𐐯𐐹𐐲𐑌𐑆 𐐱𐑂 𐐶𐐫𐑉, 𐐰𐐿𐐫𐑉𐐼𐐮𐑍 𐐰𐑆 𐑄𐐩𐑉 𐐺𐑉𐐯𐑄𐑉𐐯𐑌 𐐸𐐰𐐼, 𐐰𐑌𐐼 𐑄𐐩 𐐺𐐨𐑀𐐰𐑌 𐐻𐐭 𐐺𐐨 𐐲 𐑉𐐴𐐽𐐲𐑅 𐐹𐐨𐐹𐑊; 𐐰𐑌𐐼 𐑄𐐩 𐐼𐐮𐐼 𐐶𐐫𐐿 𐐮𐑌 𐑄 𐐶𐐩𐑆 𐐱𐑂 𐑄 𐐢𐐫𐑉𐐼, 𐐰𐑌𐐼 𐐼𐐮𐐼 𐐱𐐺𐑆𐐲𐑉𐑂 𐐻𐐭 𐐿𐐨𐐹 𐐸𐐮𐑆 𐐿𐐱𐑋𐐰𐑌𐐼𐑋𐐯𐑌𐐻𐑅 𐐰𐑌𐐼 𐐸𐐮𐑆 𐑅𐐻𐐰𐐻𐑏𐐻𐑅, 𐐷𐐩, 𐐰𐑌𐐼 𐑄𐐩 𐐼𐐮𐐼 𐐿𐐨𐐹 𐑄 𐑊𐐫 𐐱𐑂 𐐣𐐬𐑆𐐯𐑆; 𐑁𐐫𐑉 𐐮𐐻 𐐶𐐱𐑆 𐐯𐐿𐑅𐐹𐐨𐐼𐐨𐐯𐑌𐐻 𐑄𐐰𐐻 𐑄𐐩 𐑇𐐳𐐼 𐐿𐐨𐐹 𐑄 𐑊𐐫 𐐱𐑂 𐐣𐐬𐑆𐐯𐑆 𐐰𐑆 𐐷𐐯𐐻, 𐑁𐐫𐑉 𐐮𐐻 𐐶𐐱𐑆 𐑌𐐱𐐻 𐐫𐑊 𐑁𐐳𐑊𐑁𐐮𐑊𐐼. 𐐒𐐲𐐻 𐑌𐐱𐐻𐐶𐐮𐑄𐑅𐐻𐐰𐑌𐐼𐐮𐑍 𐑄 𐑊𐐫 𐐱𐑂 𐐣𐐬𐑆𐐯𐑆, 𐑄𐐩 𐐼𐐮𐐼 𐑊𐐳𐐿 𐑁𐐫𐑉𐐶𐐲𐑉𐐼 𐐻𐐭 𐑄 𐐿𐐲𐑋𐐮𐑍 𐐱𐑂 𐐗𐑉𐐴𐑅𐐻, 𐐿𐐱𐑌𐑅𐐮𐐼𐐲𐑉𐐮𐑍 𐑄𐐰𐐻 𐑄 𐑊𐐫 𐐱𐑂 𐐣𐐬𐑆𐐯𐑆 𐐶𐐱𐑆 𐐲 𐐻𐐴𐐹 𐐱𐑂 𐐸𐐮𐑆 𐐿𐐲𐑋𐐮𐑍, 𐐰𐑌𐐼 𐐺𐐨𐑊𐐨𐑂𐐮𐑍 𐑄𐐰𐐻 𐑄𐐩 𐑋𐐲𐑅𐐻 𐐿𐐨𐐹 𐑄𐐬𐑆 𐐵𐐻𐐶𐐲𐑉𐐼 𐐹𐐲𐑉𐑁𐐫𐑉𐑋𐐰𐑌𐑅𐐯𐑆, 𐐲𐑌𐐻𐐮𐑊 𐑄 𐐻𐐴𐑋 𐑄𐐰𐐻 𐐸𐐨 𐑇𐐳𐐼 𐐺𐐨 𐑉𐐨𐑂𐐨𐑊𐐼 𐐲𐑌𐐻𐐭 𐑄𐐯𐑋. 𐐤𐐵 𐑄𐐩 𐐼𐐮𐐼 𐑌𐐱𐐻 𐑅𐐲𐐹𐐬𐑆 𐑄𐐰𐐻 𐑅𐐰𐑊𐑂𐐩𐑇𐐲𐑌 𐐿𐐩𐑋 𐐺𐐴 𐑄 𐑊𐐫 𐐱𐑂 𐐣𐐬𐑆𐐯𐑆; 𐐺𐐲𐐻 𐑄 𐑊𐐫 𐐱𐑂 𐐣𐐬𐑆𐐯𐑆 𐐼𐐮𐐼 𐑅𐐲𐑉𐑂 𐐻𐐭 𐑅𐐻𐑉𐐯𐑍𐑃𐐯𐑌 𐑄𐐩𐑉 𐑁𐐩𐑃 𐐮𐑌 𐐗𐑉𐐴𐑅𐐻; 𐐰𐑌𐐼 𐑄𐐲𐑅 𐑄𐐩 𐐼𐐮𐐼 𐑉𐐨𐐻𐐩𐑌 𐐲 𐐸𐐬𐐹 𐑃𐑉𐐭 𐑁𐐩𐑃, 𐐲𐑌𐐻𐐭 𐐨𐐻𐐲𐑉𐑌𐐰𐑊 𐑅𐐰𐑊𐑂𐐩𐑇𐐲𐑌, 𐑉𐐨𐑊𐐴𐐮𐑍 𐐲𐐹𐐱𐑌 𐑄 𐐝𐐹𐐮𐑉𐐮𐐻 𐐱𐑂 𐐹𐑉𐐱𐑁𐐯𐑅𐐨, 𐐸𐐶𐐮𐐽 𐑅𐐹𐐩𐐿 𐐱𐑂 𐑄𐐬𐑆 𐑃𐐮𐑍𐑆 𐐻𐐭 𐐿𐐲𐑋. 𐐈𐑌𐐼 𐑌𐐵 𐐺𐐨𐐸𐐬𐑊𐐼, 𐐈𐑋𐐲𐑌, 𐐰𐑌𐐼 𐐁𐑉𐐲𐑌, 𐐰𐑌𐐼 𐐉𐑋𐑌𐐲𐑉, 𐐰𐑌𐐼 𐐐𐐮𐑋𐑌𐐴, 𐐰𐑌𐐼 𐑄𐐩𐑉 𐐺𐑉𐐯𐑄𐑉𐐯𐑌, 𐐼𐐮𐐼 𐑉𐐨𐐾𐑎𐑅 𐐯𐐿𐑅𐐨𐐼𐐮𐑍𐑊𐐨, 𐑁𐐫𐑉 𐑄 𐑅𐐲𐐿𐑅𐐯𐑅 𐐸𐐶𐐮𐐽 𐑄𐐩 𐐸𐐰𐐼 𐐸𐐰𐐼 𐐰𐑋𐐲𐑍 𐑄 𐐢𐐩𐑋𐐲𐑌𐐴𐐻𐑅, 𐑅𐐨𐐮𐑍 𐑄𐐰𐐻 𐑄 𐐢𐐫𐑉𐐼 𐐸𐐰𐐼 𐑀𐑉𐐪𐑌𐐻𐐯𐐼 𐐲𐑌𐐻𐐭 𐑄𐐯𐑋 𐐰𐐿𐐫𐑉𐐼𐐮𐑍 𐐻𐐭 𐑄𐐩𐑉 𐐹𐑉𐐩𐑉𐑆, 𐐰𐑌𐐼 𐑄𐐰𐐻 𐐸𐐨 𐐸𐐰𐐼 𐐫𐑊𐑅𐐬 𐑂𐐯𐑉𐐮𐑁𐐴𐐼 𐐸𐐮𐑆 𐐶𐐲𐑉𐐼 𐐲𐑌𐐻𐐭 𐑄𐐯𐑋 𐐮𐑌 𐐯𐑂𐑉𐐨 𐐹𐐪𐑉𐐻𐐮𐐿𐐷𐐭𐑊𐐲𐑉.

14. 𐐈𐑌𐐼 𐑄𐐨𐑆 𐐪𐑉 𐑄 𐐶𐐲𐑉𐐼𐑆 𐐱𐑂 𐐈𐑋𐐲𐑌 𐐻𐐭 𐐸𐐮𐑆 𐐺𐑉𐐯𐑄𐑉𐐯𐑌, 𐐸𐐶𐐮𐐽 𐑅𐐩 𐑄𐐲𐑅: 𐐣𐐴 𐐺𐑉𐐲𐑄𐐲𐑉𐑆 𐐰𐑌𐐼 𐑋𐐴 𐐺𐑉𐐯𐑄𐑉𐐯𐑌, 𐐺𐐨𐐸𐐬𐑊𐐼 𐐌 𐑅𐐩 𐐲𐑌𐐻𐐭 𐐷𐐭, 𐐸𐐵 𐑀𐑉𐐩𐐻 𐑉𐐨𐑆𐐲𐑌 𐐸𐐰𐑂 𐐶𐐨 𐐻𐐭 𐑉𐐨𐐾𐑎𐑅; 𐑁𐐫𐑉 𐐿𐐳𐐼 𐐶𐐨 𐐸𐐰𐑂 𐑅𐐲𐐹𐐬𐑆𐐼, 𐐸𐐶𐐯𐑌 𐐶𐐨 𐑅𐐻𐐪𐑉𐐻𐐯𐐼 𐑁𐑉𐐱𐑋 𐑄 𐑊𐐰𐑌𐐼 𐐱𐑂 𐐞𐐰𐑉𐐲𐐸𐐯𐑋𐑊𐐲, 𐑄𐐰𐐻 𐐘𐐱𐐼 𐐶𐐳𐐼 𐐸𐐰𐑂 𐑀𐑉𐐪𐑌𐐻𐐯𐐼 𐐲𐑌𐐻𐐭 𐐲𐑅 𐑅𐐲𐐽 𐑀𐑉𐐩𐐻 𐐺𐑊𐐯𐑅𐐮𐑍𐑆? 𐐈𐑌𐐼 𐑌𐐵, 𐐌 𐐰𐑅𐐿, 𐐸𐐶𐐱𐐻 𐑀𐑉𐐩𐐻 𐐺𐑊𐐯𐑅𐐮𐑍𐑆 𐐸𐐰𐑆 𐐸𐐨 𐐺𐐨𐑅𐐻𐐬𐐼 𐐲𐐹𐐱𐑌 𐐲𐑅? 𐐗𐐰𐑌 𐐷𐐨 𐐻𐐯𐑊? 𐐒𐐨𐐸𐐬𐑊𐐼 𐐌 𐐰𐑌𐑅𐐲𐑉 𐑁𐐫𐑉 𐐷𐐭, 𐑁𐐫𐑉 𐐵𐑉 𐐺𐑉𐐯𐑄𐑉𐐯𐑌, 𐑄 𐐢𐐩𐑋𐐲𐑌𐐴𐐻𐑅, 𐐶𐐲𐑉 𐐮𐑌 𐐼𐐪𐑉𐐿𐑌𐐯𐑅, 𐐷𐐩, 𐐨𐑂𐐲𐑌 𐐮𐑌 𐑄 𐐼𐐪𐑉𐐿𐐯𐑅𐐻 𐐰𐐺𐐮𐑅; 𐐺𐐲𐐻 𐐺𐐨𐐸𐐬𐑊𐐼, 𐐸𐐵 𐑋𐐯𐑌𐐨 𐐱𐑂 𐑄𐐯𐑋 𐐪𐑉 𐐺𐑉𐐫𐐻 𐐻𐐭 𐐺𐐨𐐸𐐬𐑊𐐼 𐑄 𐑋𐐪𐑉𐑂𐐯𐑊𐐲𐑅 𐑊𐐴𐐻 𐐱𐑂 𐐘𐐱𐐼? 𐐈𐑌𐐼 𐑄𐐮𐑅 𐐮𐑆 𐑄 𐐺𐑊𐐯𐑅𐐮𐑍 𐐸𐐶𐐮𐐽 𐐸𐐰𐑃 𐐺𐐨𐑌 𐐺𐐨𐑅𐐻𐐬𐐼 𐐲𐐹𐐱𐑌 𐐲𐑅, 𐑄𐐰𐐻 𐐶𐐨 𐐸𐐰𐑂 𐐺𐐨𐑌 𐑋𐐩𐐼 𐐮𐑌𐑅𐐻𐑉𐐭𐑋𐐯𐑌𐐻𐑅 𐐮𐑌 𐑄 𐐸𐐰𐑌𐐼𐑆 𐐱𐑂 𐐘𐐱𐐼 𐐻𐐭 𐐺𐑉𐐮𐑍 𐐲𐐺𐐵𐐻 𐑄𐐮𐑅 𐑀𐑉𐐩𐐻 𐐶𐐲𐑉𐐿. 𐐒𐐨𐐸𐐬𐑊𐐼, 𐑃𐐵𐑆𐐲𐑌𐐼𐑆 𐐱𐑂 𐑄𐐯𐑋 𐐼𐐭 𐑉𐐨𐐾𐑎𐑅, 𐐰𐑌𐐼 𐐸𐐰𐑂 𐐺𐐨𐑌 𐐺𐑉𐐫𐐻 𐐮𐑌𐐻𐐭 𐑄 𐑁𐐬𐑊𐐼 𐐱𐑂 𐐘𐐱𐐼. 𐐒𐐨𐐸𐐬𐑊𐐼, 𐑄 𐑁𐐨𐑊𐐼 𐐶𐐱𐑆 𐑉𐐴𐐹, 𐐰𐑌𐐼 𐐺𐑊𐐯𐑅𐐯𐐼 𐐪𐑉 𐐷𐐨, 𐑁𐐫𐑉 𐐷𐐨 𐐼𐐮𐐼 𐑃𐑉𐐲𐑅𐐻 𐐮𐑌 𐑄 𐑅𐐮𐐿𐑊, 𐐰𐑌𐐼 𐐼𐐮𐐼 𐑉𐐨𐐹 𐐶𐐮𐑄 𐐷𐐭𐑉 𐑋𐐴𐐻, 𐐷𐐩, 𐐫𐑊 𐑄 𐐼𐐩 𐑊𐐫𐑍 𐐼𐐮𐐼 𐐷𐐨 𐑊𐐩𐐺𐐲𐑉; 𐐰𐑌𐐼 𐐺𐐨𐐸𐐬𐑊𐐼 𐑄 𐑌𐐲𐑋𐐺𐐲𐑉 𐐱𐑂 𐐷𐐭𐑉 𐑇𐐨𐑂𐑆! 𐐰𐑌𐐼 𐑄𐐩 𐑇𐐰𐑊 𐐺𐐨 𐑀𐐰𐑄𐐲𐑉𐐼 𐐮𐑌𐐻𐐭 𐑄 𐑀𐐪𐑉𐑌𐐲𐑉𐑆, 𐑄𐐰𐐻 𐑄𐐩 𐐪𐑉 𐑌𐐱𐐻 𐐶𐐩𐑅𐐻𐐯𐐼; 𐐷𐐩, 𐑄𐐩 𐑇𐐰𐑊 𐑌𐐱𐐻 𐐺𐐨 𐐺𐐨𐐻𐐲𐑌 𐐼𐐵𐑌 𐐺𐐴 𐑄 𐑅𐐻𐐫𐑉𐑋 𐐰𐐻 𐑄 𐑊𐐰𐑅𐐻 𐐼𐐩; 𐐷𐐩, 𐑌𐐨𐑄𐐲𐑉 𐑇𐐰𐑊 𐑄𐐩 𐐺𐐨 𐐸𐐰𐑉𐐬𐐼 𐐲𐐹 𐐺𐐴 𐑄 𐐸𐐶𐐲𐑉𐑊𐐶𐐮𐑌𐐼𐑆; 𐐺𐐲𐐻 𐐸𐐶𐐯𐑌 𐑄 𐑅𐐻𐐫𐑉𐑋 𐐿𐐲𐑋𐐯𐑃, 𐑄𐐩 𐑇𐐰𐑊 𐐺𐐨 𐑀𐐰𐑄𐐲𐑉𐐼 𐐻𐐭𐑀𐐯𐑄𐐲𐑉 𐐮𐑌 𐑄𐐩𐑉 𐐹𐑊𐐩𐑅, 𐑄𐐰𐐻 𐑄 𐑅𐐻𐐫𐑉𐑋 𐐿𐐰𐑌𐐱𐐻 𐐹𐐯𐑌𐐯𐐻𐑉𐐩𐐻 𐐻𐐭 𐑄𐐯𐑋; 𐐷𐐩, 𐑌𐐨𐑄𐐲𐑉 𐑇𐐰𐑊 𐑄𐐩 𐐺𐐨 𐐼𐑉𐐮𐑂𐐲𐑌 𐐶𐐮𐑄 𐑁𐐨𐑉𐑅 𐐶𐐮𐑌𐐼𐑆 𐐸𐐶𐐲𐑉𐑅𐐬𐐯𐑂𐐲𐑉 𐑄 𐐯𐑌𐐯𐑋𐐨 𐑊𐐮𐑅𐐻𐐯𐑃 𐐻𐐭 𐐿𐐰𐑉𐐨 𐑄𐐯𐑋. 𐐒𐐲𐐻 𐐺𐐨𐐸𐐬𐑊𐐼, 𐑄𐐩 𐐪𐑉 𐐮𐑌 𐑄 𐐸𐐰𐑌𐐼𐑆 𐐱𐑂 𐑄 𐐢𐐫𐑉𐐼 𐐱𐑂 𐑄 𐐸𐐪𐑉𐑂𐐯𐑅𐐻, 𐐰𐑌𐐼 𐑄𐐩 𐐪𐑉 𐐸𐐮𐑆; 𐐰𐑌𐐼 𐐸𐐨 𐐶𐐮𐑊 𐑉𐐩𐑆 𐑄𐐯𐑋 𐐲𐐹 𐐰𐐻 𐑄 𐑊𐐰𐑅𐐻 𐐼𐐩. 𐐒𐑊𐐯𐑅𐐯𐐼 𐐺𐐨 𐑄 𐑌𐐩𐑋 𐐱𐑂 𐐵𐑉 𐐘𐐱𐐼; 𐑊𐐯𐐻 𐐲𐑅 𐑅𐐮𐑍 𐐻𐐭 𐐸𐐮𐑆 𐐹𐑉𐐩𐑆, 𐐷𐐩, 𐑊𐐯𐐻 𐐲𐑅 𐑀𐐮𐑂 𐑃𐐰𐑍𐐿𐑅 𐐻𐐭 𐐸𐐮𐑆 𐐸𐐬𐑊𐐨 𐑌𐐩𐑋, 𐑁𐐫𐑉 𐐸𐐨 𐐼𐐲𐑃 𐐶𐐲𐑉𐐿 𐑉𐐴𐐽𐐲𐑅𐑌𐐯𐑅 𐑁𐐫𐑉𐐯𐑂𐐲𐑉. 𐐙𐐫𐑉 𐐮𐑁 𐐶𐐨 𐐸𐐰𐐼 𐑌𐐱𐐻 𐐿𐐲𐑋 𐐲𐐹 𐐵𐐻 𐐱𐑂 𐑄 𐑊𐐰𐑌𐐼 𐐱𐑂 𐐞𐐰𐑉𐐲𐐸𐐯𐑋𐑊𐐲, 𐑄𐐨𐑆 𐐵𐑉 𐐼𐐨𐑉𐑊𐐨 𐐺𐐨𐑊𐐲𐑂𐐯𐐼 𐐺𐑉𐐯𐑄𐑉𐐯𐑌, 𐐸𐐭 𐐸𐐰𐑂 𐑅𐐬 𐐼𐐨𐑉𐑊𐐨 𐐺𐐨𐑊𐐲𐑂𐐯𐐼 𐐲𐑅, 𐐶𐐳𐐼 𐑅𐐻𐐮𐑊 𐐸𐐰𐑂 𐐺𐐨𐑌 𐑉𐐰𐐿𐐻 𐐶𐐮𐑄 𐐸𐐩𐐻𐑉𐐯𐐼 𐐰𐑀𐐯𐑌𐑅𐐻 𐐲𐑅, 𐐷𐐩, 𐐰𐑌𐐼 𐑄𐐩 𐐶𐐳𐐼 𐐫𐑊𐑅𐐬 𐐸𐐰𐑂 𐐺𐐨𐑌 𐑅𐐻𐑉𐐩𐑌𐐾𐐲𐑉𐑆 𐐻𐐭 𐐘𐐱𐐼.

15. 𐐈𐑌𐐼 𐐮𐐻 𐐿𐐩𐑋 𐐻𐐭 𐐹𐐰𐑅 𐑄𐐰𐐻 𐐸𐐶𐐯𐑌 𐐈𐑋𐐲𐑌 𐐸𐐰𐐼 𐑅𐐯𐐼 𐑄𐐨𐑆 𐐶𐐲𐑉𐐼𐑆, 𐐸𐐮𐑆 𐐺𐑉𐐲𐑄𐐲𐑉 𐐁𐑉𐐲𐑌 𐑉𐐨𐐺𐐷𐐭𐐿𐐻 𐐸𐐮𐑋, 𐑅𐐩𐐮𐑍, 𐐈𐑋𐐲𐑌, 𐐌 𐑁𐐨𐑉 𐑄𐐰𐐻 𐑄𐐴 𐐾𐑎 𐐼𐐲𐑃 𐐿𐐰𐑉𐐨 𐑄𐐨 𐐰𐐶𐐩 𐐲𐑌𐐻𐐭 𐐺𐐬𐑅𐐻𐐮𐑍; 𐐒𐐲𐐻 𐐈𐑋𐐲𐑌 𐑅𐐯𐐼 𐐲𐑌𐐻𐐭 𐐸𐐮𐑋, 𐐌 𐐼𐐭 𐑌𐐱𐐻 𐐺𐐬𐑅𐐻 𐐮𐑌 𐑋𐐴 𐐬𐑌 𐑅𐐻𐑉𐐯𐑍𐑃, 𐑌𐐫𐑉 𐐮𐑌 𐑋𐐴 𐐬𐑌 𐐶𐐮𐑆𐐼𐐲𐑋; 𐐺𐐲𐐻

𐐒𐐨𐐸𐐬𐑊𐐼, 𐑋𐐴 𐐾𐐫𐐮 𐐮𐑆 𐑁𐐳𐑊, 𐐷𐐩, 𐑋𐐴 𐐸𐐪𐑉𐐻 𐐮𐑆 𐐺𐑉𐐮𐑋 𐐶𐐮𐑄 𐐾𐐫𐐮, 𐐰𐑌𐐼 𐐌 𐐶𐐮𐑊 𐑉𐐨𐐾𐐫𐐮𐑅 𐐮𐑌 𐑋𐐴 𐐘𐐪𐐼; 𐐷𐐩, 𐐌 𐑌𐐬 𐑄𐐰𐐻 𐐌 𐐰𐑋 𐑌𐐲𐑃𐐮𐑍; 𐐰𐑆 𐐻𐐭 𐑋𐐴 𐑅𐐻𐑉𐐯𐑍𐑃 𐐌 𐐰𐑋 𐐶𐐨𐐿; 𐑄𐐯𐑉𐑁𐐬𐑉 𐐌 𐐶𐐮𐑊 𐑌𐐱𐐻 𐐺𐐬𐑅𐐻 𐐱𐑂 𐑋𐐴𐑅𐐯𐑊𐑁, 𐐺𐐲𐐻 𐐌 𐐶𐐮𐑊 𐐺𐐬𐑅𐐻 𐐱𐑂 𐑋𐐴 𐐘𐐪𐐼, 𐑁𐐬𐑉 𐐮𐑌 𐐸𐐮𐑆 𐑅𐐻𐑉𐐯𐑍𐑃 𐐌 𐐿𐐰𐑌 𐐼𐐭 𐐫𐑊 𐑃𐐮𐑍𐑆; 𐐷𐐩, 𐐺𐐨𐐸𐐬𐑊𐐼, 𐑋𐐯𐑌𐐨 𐑋𐐴𐐻𐐨 𐑋𐐮𐑉𐐲𐐿𐑊𐑆 𐐶𐐨 𐐸𐐰𐑂 𐑉𐐫𐐻 𐐮𐑌 𐑄𐐮𐑅 𐑊𐐰𐑌𐐼, 𐑁𐐬𐑉 𐐸𐐶𐐮𐐽 𐐶𐐨 𐐶𐐮𐑊 𐐹𐑉𐐩𐑆 𐐸𐐮𐑆 𐑌𐐩𐑋 𐑁𐐬𐑉𐐯𐑂𐐲𐑉. 𐐒𐐨𐐸𐐬𐑊𐐼, 𐐸𐐵 𐑋𐐯𐑌𐐨 𐑃𐐵𐑆𐐲𐑌𐐼𐑆 𐐱𐑂 𐐵𐑉 𐐺𐑉𐐯𐑄𐑉𐐯𐑌 𐐸𐐰𐑃 𐐸𐐨 𐑊𐐭𐑅𐐻 𐑁𐑉𐐱𐑋 𐑄 𐐹𐐩𐑌𐑆 𐐱𐑂 𐐸𐐯𐑊; 𐐰𐑌𐐼 𐑄𐐩 𐐪𐑉 𐐺𐑉𐐫𐐻 𐐻𐐭 𐑅𐐮𐑍 𐑉𐐨𐐼𐐨𐑋𐐮𐑍 𐑊𐐲𐑂, 𐐰𐑌𐐼 𐑄𐐮𐑅 𐐺𐐨𐐿𐐫𐑆 𐐱𐑂 𐑄 𐐹𐐵𐐲𐑉 𐐱𐑂 𐐸𐐮𐑆 𐐶𐐲𐑉𐐼 𐐸𐐶𐐮𐐽 𐐮𐑆 𐐮𐑌 𐐲𐑅, 𐑄𐐯𐑉𐑁𐐬𐑉 𐐸𐐰𐑂 𐐶𐐨 𐑌𐐱𐐻 𐑀𐑉𐐩𐐻 𐑉𐐨𐑆𐐲𐑌 𐐻𐐭 𐑉𐐨𐐾𐐫𐐮𐑅? 𐐏𐐩, 𐐶𐐨 𐐸𐐰𐑂 𐑉𐐨𐑆𐐲𐑌 𐐻𐐭 𐐹𐑉𐐩𐑆 𐐸𐐮𐑋 𐑁𐐬𐑉𐐯𐑂𐐲𐑉, 𐑁𐐬𐑉 𐐸𐐨 𐐮𐑆 𐑄 𐐣𐐬𐑅𐐻 𐐐𐐴 𐐘𐐪𐐼, 𐐰𐑌𐐼 𐐸𐐰𐑆 𐑊𐐭𐑅𐐻 𐐵𐑉 𐐺𐑉𐐯𐑄𐑉𐐯𐑌 𐑁𐑉𐐱𐑋 𐑄 𐐽𐐩𐑌𐑆 𐐱𐑂 𐐸𐐯𐑊. 𐐏𐐩, 𐑄𐐩 𐐶𐐲𐑉 𐐯𐑌𐑅𐐲𐑉𐐿𐐲𐑊𐐼 𐐲𐐺𐐵𐐻 𐐶𐐮𐑄 𐐯𐑂𐐲𐑉𐑊𐐰𐑅𐐻𐐮𐑍 𐐼𐐪𐑉𐐿𐑌𐐯𐑅 𐐰𐑌𐐼 𐐼𐐯𐑅𐐻𐑉𐐲𐐿𐑇𐐲𐑌; 𐐺𐐲𐐻 𐐺𐐨𐐸𐐬𐑊𐐼, 𐐸𐐨 𐐸𐐰𐑆 𐐺𐑉𐐫𐐻 𐑄𐐯𐑋 𐐮𐑌𐐻𐐭 𐐸𐐮𐑆 𐐯𐑂𐐲𐑉𐑊𐐰𐑅𐐻𐐮𐑍 𐑊𐐴𐐻; 𐐷𐐩, 𐐮𐑌𐐻𐐭 𐐯𐑂𐐲𐑉𐑊𐐰𐑅𐐻𐐮𐑍 𐑅𐐰𐑊𐑂𐐩𐑇𐐲𐑌; 𐐰𐑌𐐼 𐑄𐐩 𐐪𐑉 𐐯𐑌𐑅𐐲𐑉𐐿𐐲𐑊𐐼 𐐲𐐺𐐵𐐻 𐐶𐐮𐑄 𐑄 𐑋𐐰𐐽𐑊𐐯𐑅 𐐺𐐵𐑌𐐻𐐨 𐐱𐑂 𐐸𐐮𐑆 𐑊𐐲𐑂; 𐐷𐐩, 𐐰𐑌𐐼 𐐶𐐨 𐐸𐐰𐑂 𐐺𐐮𐑌 𐐮𐑌𐑅𐐻𐑉𐐭𐑋𐐯𐑌𐐻𐑅 𐐮𐑌 𐐸𐐮𐑆 𐐸𐐰𐑌𐐼𐑆 𐐱𐑂 𐐼𐐭𐐮𐑍 𐑄𐐮𐑅 𐑀𐑉𐐩𐐻 𐐰𐑌𐐼 𐑋𐐪𐑉𐑂𐐯𐑊𐐲𐑅 𐐶𐐲𐑉𐐿; 𐑄𐐯𐑉𐑁𐐬𐑉, 𐑊𐐯𐐻 𐐲𐑅 𐑀𐑊𐐬𐑉𐐨, 𐐷𐐩, 𐐶𐐨 𐐶𐐮𐑊 𐑀𐑊𐐬𐑉𐐨 𐐮𐑌 𐑄 𐐢𐐫𐑉𐐼; 𐐷𐐩, 𐐶𐐨 𐐶𐐮𐑊 𐑉𐐨𐐾𐐫𐐮𐑅, 𐑁𐐬𐑉 𐐵𐑉 𐐾𐐫𐐮 𐐮𐑆 𐑁𐐳𐑊; 𐐷𐐩, 𐐶𐐨 𐐶𐐮𐑊 𐐹𐑉𐐩𐑆 𐐵𐑉 𐐘𐐪𐐼 𐑁𐐬𐑉𐐯𐑂𐐲𐑉. 𐐒𐐨𐐸𐐬𐑊𐐼, 𐐸𐐭 𐐿𐐰𐑌 𐑀𐑊𐐬𐑉𐐨 𐐻𐐭 𐑋𐐲𐐽 𐐮𐑌 𐑄 𐐢𐐫𐑉𐐼? 𐐏𐐩, 𐐸𐐭 𐐿𐐰𐑌 𐑅𐐩 𐐻𐐭 𐑋𐐲𐐽 𐐱𐑂 𐐸𐐮𐑆 𐑀𐑉𐐩𐐻 𐐹𐐵𐐲𐑉, 𐐰𐑌𐐼 𐐱𐑂 𐐸𐐮𐑆 𐑋𐐲𐑉𐑅𐐨, 𐐰𐑌𐐼 𐐱𐑂 𐐸𐐮𐑆 𐑊𐐱𐑍 𐑅𐐲𐑁𐐲𐑉𐐮𐑍 𐐻𐐬𐐲𐑉𐐼𐑆 𐑄 𐐽𐐮𐑊𐐼𐑉𐐯𐑌 𐐱𐑂 𐑋𐐯𐑌? 𐐒𐐨𐐸𐐬𐑊𐐼, 𐐌 𐑅𐐩 𐐲𐑌𐐻𐐭 𐐷𐐭, 𐐌 𐐿𐐰𐑌𐑌𐐱𐐻 𐑅𐐩 𐑄 𐑅𐑋𐐫𐑊𐐯𐑅𐐻 𐐹𐐪𐑉𐐻 𐐸𐐶𐐮𐐽 𐐌 𐑁𐐨𐑊. 𐐐𐐭 𐐿𐐳𐐼 𐐸𐐰𐑂 𐑅𐐲𐐹𐐬𐑆𐐼 𐑄𐐰𐐻 𐐵𐑉 𐐘𐐪𐐼 𐐶𐐳𐐼 𐐸𐐰𐑂 𐐺𐐮𐑌 𐑅𐐬 𐑋𐐲𐑉𐑅𐐮𐑁𐐳𐑊 𐐰𐑆 𐐻𐐭 𐐸𐐰𐑂 𐑅𐑌𐐰𐐽𐐻 𐐲𐑅 𐑁𐑉𐐱𐑋 𐐵𐑉 𐐫𐑁𐐳𐑊, 𐑅𐐮𐑌𐑁𐐳𐑊, 𐐰𐑌𐐼 𐐹𐐲𐑊𐐭𐐻𐐯𐐼 𐑅𐐻𐐩𐐻? 𐐒𐐨𐐸𐐬𐑊𐐼, 𐐶𐐨 𐐶𐐯𐑌𐐻 𐑁𐐬𐑉𐑃 𐐨𐑂𐐲𐑌 𐐮𐑌 𐑉𐐪𐑃, 𐐶𐐮𐑄 𐑋𐐴𐐻𐐨 𐑃𐑉𐐯𐐻𐐲𐑌𐐮𐑍𐑆 𐐻𐐭 𐐼𐐯𐑅𐐻𐑉𐐫𐐮 𐐸𐐮𐑆 𐐕𐐲𐑉𐐽. 𐐄 𐑄𐐯𐑌, 𐐸𐐶𐐴 𐐼𐐮𐐼 𐐸𐐨 𐑌𐐱𐐻 𐐿𐐱𐑌𐑅𐐴𐑌 𐐲𐑅 𐐻𐐭 𐐰𐑌 𐐫𐑁𐐳𐑊 𐐼𐐯𐑅𐐻𐑉𐐲𐐿𐑇𐐲𐑌? 𐐷𐐩, 𐐸𐐶𐐴 𐐼𐐮𐐼 𐐸𐐨 𐑌𐐱𐐻 𐑊𐐯𐐻 𐑄 𐑅𐐬𐑉𐐼 𐐱𐑂 𐐸𐐮𐑆 𐐾𐐲𐑅𐐻𐐮𐑅 𐑁𐐫𐑊 𐐲𐐹𐐱𐑌 𐐲𐑅, 𐐰𐑌𐐼 𐐼𐐭𐑋 𐐲𐑅 𐐻𐐭 𐐨𐐻𐐲𐑉𐑌𐐲𐑊 𐐼𐐯𐑅𐐹𐐩𐑉? 𐐄 𐑋𐐴 𐑅𐐬𐑊, 𐐫𐑊𐑋𐐬𐑅𐐻 𐐰𐑆 𐐮𐐻 𐐶𐐲𐑉, 𐑁𐑊𐐨𐐯𐑃 𐐰𐐻 𐑄 𐑃𐐫𐐻. 𐐒𐐨𐐸𐐬𐑊𐐼, 𐐸𐐨 𐐼𐐮𐐼 𐑌𐐱𐐻 𐐯𐐿𐑅𐐲𐑉𐑅𐐴𐑆 𐐸𐐮𐑆 𐐾𐐲𐑅𐐻𐐮𐑅 𐐲𐐹𐐱𐑌 𐐲𐑅, 𐐺𐐲𐐻 𐐮𐑌 𐐸𐐮𐑆 𐑀𐑉𐐩𐐻 𐑋𐐲𐑉𐑅𐐨 𐐸𐐰𐑃 𐐺𐑉𐐫𐐻 𐐲𐑅 𐐬𐑂𐐲𐑉 𐑄𐐰𐐻 𐐯𐑂𐐲𐑉𐑊𐐰𐑅𐐻𐐮𐑍 𐑀𐐲𐑊𐑁 𐐱𐑂 𐐼𐐯𐑃 𐐰𐑌𐐼 𐑋𐐮𐑆𐐲𐑉𐐨, 𐐨𐑂𐐲𐑌 𐐻𐐭 𐑄 𐑅𐐰𐑊𐑂𐐩𐑇𐐲𐑌 𐐱𐑂 𐐵𐑉 𐑅𐐬𐑊𐑆.

16. 𐐈𐑌𐐼 𐑌𐐵 𐐺𐐨𐐸𐐬𐑊𐐼, 𐑋𐐴 𐐺𐑉𐐯𐑄𐑉𐐯𐑌, 𐐸𐐶𐐱𐐻 𐑌𐐰𐐽𐐲𐑉𐐲𐑊 𐑋𐐰𐑌 𐐮𐑆 𐑄𐐯𐑉 𐑄𐐰𐐻 𐑌𐐬𐐯𐑃 𐑄𐐨𐑆 𐑃𐐮𐑍𐑆? 𐐌 𐑅𐐩 𐐲𐑌𐐻𐐭 𐐷𐐭, 𐐜𐐯𐑉 𐐮𐑆 𐑌𐐲𐑌 𐑄𐐰𐐻 𐑌𐐬𐐯𐑃 𐑄𐐨𐑆 𐑃𐐮𐑍𐑆, 𐑅𐐩𐑂 𐐮𐐻 𐐺𐐨 𐑄 𐐹𐐯𐑌𐐮𐐻𐐯𐑌𐐻: 𐐷𐐩, 𐐸𐐨 𐑄𐐰𐐻 𐑉𐐨𐐹𐐯𐑌𐐻𐐯𐑃 𐐰𐑌𐐼 𐐯𐐿𐑅𐐲𐑉𐑅𐐴𐑆𐐯𐑃 𐑁𐐩𐑃, 𐐰𐑌𐐼 𐐺𐑉𐐮𐑍𐐯𐑃 𐑁𐐬𐑉𐑃 𐑀𐐳𐐼 𐐶𐐲𐑉𐐿𐑅, 𐐰𐑌𐐼 𐐹𐑉𐐩𐐯𐑃 𐐿𐐱𐑌𐐻𐐮𐑌𐐷𐐭𐐲𐑊𐐨 𐐶𐐮𐑄𐐵𐐻 𐑅𐐨𐑅𐐮𐑍: 𐐲𐑌𐐻𐐭 𐑅𐐲𐐽 𐐮𐐻 𐐮𐑆 𐑀𐐮𐑂𐐲𐑌 𐐻𐐭 𐑌𐐬 𐑄 𐑋𐐮𐑅𐐻𐐲𐑉𐐨𐑆 𐐱𐑂 𐐘𐐪𐐼; 𐐷𐐩, 𐐲𐑌𐐻𐐭 𐑅𐐲𐐽 𐐮𐐻 𐑇𐐰𐑊 𐐺𐐨 𐑀𐐮𐑂𐐲𐑌 𐐻𐐭 𐑉𐐨𐑂𐐨𐑊 𐑃𐐮𐑍𐑆 𐐸𐐶𐐮𐐽 𐑌𐐯𐑂𐐲𐑉 𐐸𐐰𐑂 𐐺𐐮𐑌 𐑉𐐨𐑂𐐨𐑊𐐼; 𐐷𐐩, 𐐰𐑌𐐼 𐐮𐐻 𐑇𐐰𐑊 𐐺𐐨 𐑀𐐮𐑂𐐲𐑌 𐐲𐑌𐐻𐐭 𐑅𐐲𐐽 𐐻𐐭 𐐺𐑉𐐮𐑍 𐑃𐐵𐑆𐐲𐑌𐐼𐑆 𐐱𐑂 𐑅𐐬𐑊𐑆 𐐻𐐭 𐑉𐐨𐐹𐐯𐑌𐐻𐐰𐑌𐑅, 𐐨𐑂𐐲𐑌 𐐰𐑆 𐐮𐐻 𐐸𐐰𐑆 𐐺𐐮𐑌 𐑀𐐮𐑂𐐲𐑌 𐐲𐑌𐐻𐐭 𐐲𐑅 𐐻𐐭 𐐺𐑉𐐮𐑍 𐑄𐐨𐑆 𐐵𐑉 𐐺𐑉𐐯𐑄𐑉𐐯𐑌 𐐻𐐭 𐑉𐐨𐐹𐐯𐑌𐐻𐐰𐑌𐑅. 𐐤𐐵 𐐼𐐭 𐐷 𐑉𐐨𐑋𐐯𐑋𐐺𐐲𐑉, 𐑋𐐴 𐐺𐑉𐐯𐑄𐑉𐐯𐑌, 𐑄𐐰𐐻 𐐶𐐨 𐑅𐐯𐐼 𐐲𐑌𐐻𐐭 𐐵𐑉 𐐺𐑉𐐯𐑄𐑉𐐯𐑌 𐐮𐑌 𐑄 𐑊𐐰𐑌𐐼 𐐱𐑂 𐐞𐐰𐑉𐐲𐐸𐐯𐑋𐑊𐐲, 𐐎𐐨 𐑀𐐬 𐐲𐐹 𐐻𐐭 𐑄 𐑊𐐰𐑌𐐼 𐐱𐑂 𐐤𐐨𐑁𐐴, 𐐻𐐭 𐐹𐑉𐐨𐐽 𐐲𐑌𐐻𐐭 𐐵𐑉 𐐺𐑉𐐯𐑄𐑉𐐯𐑌 𐑄 𐐢𐐩𐑋𐐲𐑌𐐴𐐻𐑅, 𐐰𐑌𐐼 𐑄𐐩 𐑊𐐪𐑁𐐻 𐐲𐑅 𐐻𐐭 𐑅𐐿𐐫𐑉𐑌? 𐐙𐐬𐑉 𐑄𐐩 𐑅𐐯𐐼 𐐲𐑌𐐻𐐭 𐐲𐑅, 𐐔𐐭 𐐷 𐑅𐐲𐐹𐐬𐑆 𐑄𐐰𐐻 𐐷 𐐿𐐰𐑌 𐐺𐑉𐐮𐑍 𐑄 𐐢𐐩𐑋𐐲𐑌𐐴𐐻𐑅 𐐻𐐭 𐑄 𐑌𐐱𐑊𐐯𐐾 𐐱𐑂 𐑄 𐐻𐑉𐐭𐑃? 𐐔𐐭 𐐷 𐑅𐐲𐐹𐐬𐑆 𐑄𐐰𐐻 𐐷 𐐿𐐰𐑌 𐐿𐐱𐑌𐑂𐐮𐑌𐑅 𐑄 𐐢𐐩𐑋𐐲𐑌𐐴𐐻𐑅 𐐱𐑂 𐑄 𐐮𐑌𐐿𐐱𐑉𐐯𐐿𐐻𐑌𐐯𐑅 𐐱𐑂 𐑄 𐐻𐑉𐐲𐐼𐐮𐑇𐐲𐑌𐑆 𐐱𐑂 𐑄𐐯𐑉 𐑁𐐪𐑄𐐲𐑉𐑆, 𐐰𐑆 𐑅𐐻𐐮𐑁𐑌𐐯𐐿𐐻 𐐰 𐐹𐐨𐐹𐑊 𐐰𐑆 𐑄𐐩 𐐪𐑉; 𐐸𐐭𐑆 𐐸𐐪𐑉𐐻𐑅 𐐼𐐨𐑊𐐴𐐻 𐐮𐑌 𐑄 𐑇𐐯𐐼𐐮𐑍 𐐱𐑂 𐐺𐑊𐐲𐐼; 𐐸𐐭𐑆 𐐼𐐩𐑆 𐐸𐐰𐑂 𐐺𐐮𐑌 𐑅𐐹𐐯𐑌𐐻 𐐮𐑌 𐑄 𐑀𐑉𐐬𐑅𐐯𐑅𐐻 𐐮𐑌𐐮𐐿𐐶𐐮𐐻𐐨; 𐐸𐐭𐑆 𐐶𐐩𐑆 𐐸𐐰𐑂 𐐺𐐮𐑌 𐑄 𐐶𐐩𐑆 𐐱𐑂 𐑄 𐐻𐑉𐐰𐑌𐑅𐑀𐑉𐐯𐑅𐐲𐑉 𐑁𐑉𐐱𐑋 𐑄 𐐺𐐨𐑀𐐮𐑌𐐮𐑍? 𐐤𐐵 𐑋𐐴 𐐺𐑉𐐯𐑄𐑉𐐯𐑌, 𐐷 𐑉𐐨𐑋𐐯𐑋𐐺𐐲𐑉 𐑄𐐰𐐻 𐑄𐐮𐑅 𐐶𐐱𐑆 𐑄𐐯𐑉 𐑊𐐰𐑍𐑀𐐶𐐯𐐾?

17. 𐐈𐑌𐐼 𐑋𐐬𐑉𐐬𐑂𐐲𐑉 𐑄𐐩 𐐼𐐮𐐼 𐑅𐐩, 𐐢𐐯𐐻 𐐲𐑅 𐐻𐐩𐐿 𐐲𐐹 𐐪𐑉𐑋𐑆 𐐲𐑀𐐯𐑌𐑅𐐻 𐑄𐐯𐑋, 𐑄𐐰𐐻 𐐶𐐨 𐐼𐐯𐑅𐐻𐑉𐐫𐐮 𐑄𐐯𐑋 𐐰𐑌𐐼 𐑄𐐯𐑉 𐐮𐑌𐐮𐐿𐐶𐐮𐐻𐐨 𐐵𐐻 𐐱𐑂 𐑄 𐑊𐐰𐑌𐐼, 𐑊𐐯𐑅𐐻 𐑄𐐩 𐐬𐑂𐐲𐑉𐑉𐐲𐑌 𐐲𐑅 𐐰𐑌𐐼 𐐼𐐯𐑅𐐻𐑉𐐫𐐮 𐐲𐑅.

𐐒𐐲𐐻 𐐺𐐨𐐸𐐬𐑊𐐼, 𐑋𐐴 𐐺𐐨𐑊𐐲𐑂𐐯𐐼 𐐺𐑉𐐯𐑄𐑉𐐯𐑌, 𐐶𐐨 𐐿𐐩𐑋 𐐮𐑌𐐻𐐭 𐑄 𐐶𐐮𐑊𐐼𐐲𐑉𐑌𐐯𐑅 𐑌𐐱𐐻 𐐶𐐮𐑄 𐑄 𐐮𐑌𐐻𐐯𐑌𐐻 𐐻𐐭 𐐼𐐨𐑅𐐻𐑉𐑎 𐐵𐑉 𐐺𐑉𐐯𐑄𐑉𐐯𐑌, 𐐺𐐲𐐻 𐐶𐐮𐑄 𐑄 𐐮𐑌𐐻𐐯𐑌𐐻 𐑄𐐰𐐻 𐐹𐐲𐑉𐐸𐐰𐐹𐑅 𐐶𐐨 𐑋𐐴𐐻 𐑅𐐩𐑂 𐑅𐐲𐑋 𐑁𐑏 𐐲𐑂 𐑄𐐩𐑉 𐑅𐐬𐑊𐑆. 𐐤𐐵 𐐸𐐶𐐯𐑌 𐐵𐑉 𐐸𐐪𐑉𐐻𐑅 𐐶𐐲𐑉 𐐼𐐨𐐹𐑉𐐯𐑅𐐻, 𐐰𐑌𐐼 𐐶𐐨 𐐶𐐲𐑉 𐐲𐐺𐐵𐐻 𐐻𐐭 𐐻𐐲𐑉𐑌 𐐺𐐰𐐿, 𐐺𐐨𐐸𐐬𐑊𐐼, 𐑄 𐐢𐐫𐑉𐐼 𐐿𐐲𐑋𐑁𐐲𐑉𐐻𐐯𐐼 𐐲𐑅, 𐐰𐑌𐐼 𐑅𐐯𐐼, 𐐘𐐬 𐐲𐑋𐐲𐑍𐑅𐐻 𐑄𐐴 𐐺𐑉𐐯𐑄𐑉𐐯𐑌, 𐑄 𐐢𐐩𐑋𐐲𐑌𐐴𐐻𐑅, 𐐰𐑌𐐼 𐐺𐐩𐑉 𐐶𐐮𐑄 𐐹𐐩𐑇𐐯𐑌𐑅 𐑄𐐴𐑌 𐐰𐑁𐑊𐐮𐐿𐑇𐐲𐑌𐑆, 𐐰𐑌𐐼 𐐌 𐐶𐐮𐑊 𐑀𐐮𐑂 𐐲𐑌𐐻𐐭 𐐷𐐭 𐑅𐐲𐐿𐑅𐐯𐑅. 𐐈𐑌𐐼 𐑌𐐵 𐐺𐐨𐐸𐐬𐑊𐐼, 𐐶𐐨 𐐸𐐰𐑂 𐐿𐐲𐑋, 𐐰𐑌𐐼 𐐺𐐨𐑌 𐑁𐐫𐑉𐑃 𐐲𐑋𐐲𐑍𐑅𐐻 𐑄𐐯𐑋; 𐐰𐑌𐐼 𐐶𐐨 𐐸𐐰𐑂 𐐺𐐨𐑌 𐐹𐐩𐑇𐐯𐑌𐐻 𐐮𐑌 𐐵𐑉 𐑅𐐲𐑁𐐲𐑉𐐮𐑍𐑆, 𐐰𐑌𐐼 𐐶𐐨 𐐸𐐰𐑂 𐑅𐐲𐑁𐐲𐑉𐐼 𐐯𐑂𐐲𐑉𐐨 𐐹𐑉𐐴𐑂𐐩𐑇𐐲𐑌; 𐐷𐐩, 𐐶𐐨 𐐸𐐰𐑂 𐐻𐑉𐐰𐑂𐐯𐑊𐐼 𐑁𐑉𐐲𐑋 𐐸𐐵𐑅 𐐻𐐭 𐐸𐐵𐑅, 𐑉𐐨𐑊𐐴𐐮𐑍 𐐲𐐹𐐱𐑌 𐑄 𐑋𐐲𐑉𐑅𐐨𐑆 𐐲𐑂 𐑄 𐐶𐐲𐑉𐑊𐐼; 𐑌𐐱𐐻 𐐲𐐹𐐱𐑌 𐑄 𐑋𐐲𐑉𐑅𐐨𐑆 𐐲𐑂 𐑄 𐐶𐐲𐑉𐑊𐐼 𐐲𐑊𐐬𐑌, 𐐺𐐲𐐻 𐐲𐐹𐐱𐑌 𐑄 𐑋𐐲𐑉𐑅𐐨𐑆 𐐲𐑂 𐐘𐐱𐐼. 𐐈𐑌𐐼 𐐶𐐨 𐐸𐐰𐑂 𐐯𐑌𐐻𐐲𐑉𐐼 𐐮𐑌𐐻𐐭 𐑄𐐩𐑉 𐐸𐐵𐑆𐐯𐑆 𐐰𐑌𐐼 𐐻𐐫𐐻 𐑄𐐯𐑋, 𐐰𐑌𐐼 𐐶𐐨 𐐸𐐰𐑂 𐐻𐐫𐐻 𐑄𐐯𐑋 𐐮𐑌 𐑄𐐩𐑉 𐑅𐐻𐑉𐐨𐐻𐑅; 𐐷𐐩, 𐐰𐑌𐐼 𐐶𐐨 𐐸𐐰𐑂 𐐻𐐫𐐻 𐑄𐐯𐑋 𐐲𐐹𐐱𐑌 𐑄𐐩𐑉 𐐸𐐮𐑊𐑆; 𐐰𐑌𐐼 𐐶𐐨 𐐸𐐰𐑂 𐐫𐑊𐑅𐐬 𐐯𐑌𐐻𐐲𐑉𐐼 𐐮𐑌𐐻𐐭 𐑄𐐩𐑉 𐐻𐐯𐑋𐐹𐑊𐑆 𐐰𐑌𐐼 𐑄𐐩𐑉 𐑅𐐮𐑌𐐲𐑀𐐱𐑀𐑆 𐐰𐑌𐐼 𐐻𐐫𐐻 𐑄𐐯𐑋; 𐐰𐑌𐐼 𐐶𐐨 𐐸𐐰𐑂 𐐺𐐨𐑌 𐐿𐐰𐑅𐐻 𐐵𐐻, 𐐰𐑌𐐼 𐑋𐐱𐐿𐐻, 𐐰𐑌𐐼 𐑅𐐹𐐮𐐻 𐐲𐐹𐐱𐑌, 𐐰𐑌𐐼 𐑅𐑋𐐬𐐻 𐐲𐐹𐐱𐑌 𐐵𐑉 𐐽𐐨𐐿𐑅; 𐐰𐑌𐐼 𐐶𐐨 𐐸𐐰𐑂 𐐺𐐨𐑌 𐑅𐐻𐐬𐑌𐐼, 𐐰𐑌𐐼 𐐻𐐩𐐿𐐲𐑌 𐐰𐑌𐐼 𐐺𐐵𐑌𐐼 𐐶𐐮𐑄 𐑅𐐻𐑉𐐱𐑍 𐐿𐐫𐑉𐐼𐑆, 𐐰𐑌𐐼 𐐿𐐰𐑅𐐻 𐐮𐑌𐐻𐐭 𐐹𐑉𐐮𐑆𐐲𐑌; 𐐰𐑌𐐼 𐑃𐑉𐐭 𐑄 𐐹𐐵𐐲𐑉 𐐰𐑌𐐼 𐐶𐐮𐑆𐐼𐐲𐑋 𐐲𐑂 𐐘𐐱𐐼 𐐶𐐨 𐐸𐐰𐑂 𐐺𐐨𐑌 𐐼𐐨𐑊𐐮𐑂𐐲𐑉𐐼 𐐲𐑀𐐯𐑌. 𐐈𐑌𐐼 𐐶𐐨 𐐸𐐰𐑂 𐑅𐐲𐑁𐐲𐑉𐐼 𐐫𐑊 𐑋𐐰𐑌𐐲𐑉 𐐲𐑂 𐐰𐑁𐑊𐐮𐐿𐑇𐐲𐑌𐑆, 𐐰𐑌𐐼 𐐫𐑊 𐑄𐐮𐑅, 𐑄𐐰𐐻 𐐹𐐲𐑉𐐸𐐰𐐹𐑅 𐐶𐐨 𐑋𐐴𐐻 𐐺𐐨 𐑄 𐑋𐐨𐑌𐑆 𐐲𐑂 𐑅𐐩𐑂𐐮𐑍 𐑅𐐲𐑋 𐑅𐐬𐑊; 𐐰𐑌𐐼 𐐶𐐨 𐑅𐐲𐐹𐐬𐑆𐐼 𐑄𐐰𐐻 𐐵𐑉 𐐾𐑎 𐐶𐐳𐐼 𐐺𐐨 𐑁𐐳𐑊 𐐮𐑁 𐐹𐐲𐑉𐐸𐐰𐐹𐑅 𐐶𐐨 𐐿𐐳𐐼 𐐺𐐨 𐑄 𐑋𐐨𐑌𐑆 𐐲𐑂 𐑅𐐩𐑂𐐮𐑍 𐑅𐐲𐑋.

18. 𐐤𐐵 𐐺𐐨𐐸𐐬𐑊𐐼, 𐐶𐐨 𐐿𐐰𐑌 𐑊𐐳𐐿 𐑁𐐫𐑉𐑃 𐐰𐑌𐐼 𐑅𐐨 𐑄 𐑁𐑉𐐭𐐻𐑅 𐐲𐑂 𐐵𐑉 𐑊𐐩𐐺𐐲𐑉𐑆; 𐐰𐑌𐐼 𐐪𐑉 𐑄𐐩 𐑁𐑏? 𐐌 𐑅𐐩 𐐲𐑌𐐻𐐭 𐐷𐐭, 𐐤𐐩, 𐑄𐐩 𐐪𐑉 𐑋𐐯𐑌𐐨; 𐐷𐐩, 𐐰𐑌𐐼 𐐶𐐨 𐐿𐐰𐑌 𐐶𐐮𐐻𐑌𐐯𐑅 𐐲𐑂 𐑄𐐩𐑉 𐑅𐐮𐑌𐑅𐐯𐑉𐐮𐐻𐐨, 𐐺𐐨𐐿𐐫𐑆 𐐲𐑂 𐑄𐐩𐑉 𐑊𐐲𐑂 𐐻𐐬𐑉𐐼𐑆 𐑄𐐩𐑉 𐐺𐑉𐐯𐑄𐑉𐐯𐑌, 𐐰𐑌𐐼 𐐫𐑊𐑅𐐬 𐐻𐐬𐑉𐐼𐑆 𐐲𐑅. 𐐙𐐫𐑉 𐐺𐐨𐐸𐐬𐑊𐐼, 𐑄𐐩 𐐸𐐰𐐼 𐑉𐐪𐑄𐐲𐑉 𐑅𐐰𐐿𐑉𐐮𐑁𐐴𐑆 𐑄𐐩𐑉 𐑊𐐴𐑂𐑆, 𐑄𐐰𐑌 𐐨𐑂𐐲𐑌 𐐻𐐭 𐐻𐐩𐐿 𐑄 𐑊𐐴𐑁 𐐲𐑂 𐑄𐐩𐑉 𐐯𐑌𐐯𐑋𐐨; 𐐰𐑌𐐼 𐑄𐐩 𐐸𐐰𐑂 𐐺𐐯𐑉𐐨𐐼 𐑄𐐩𐑉 𐐶𐐯𐐹𐐲𐑌𐑆 𐐲𐑂 𐐶𐐫𐑉 𐐼𐐨𐐹 𐐮𐑌 𐑄 𐐲𐑉𐑃, 𐐺𐐨𐐿𐐫𐑆 𐐲𐑂 𐑄𐐩𐑉 𐑊𐐲𐑂 𐐻𐐬𐑉𐐼𐑆 𐑄𐐩𐑉 𐐺𐑉𐐯𐑄𐑉𐐯𐑌. 𐐈𐑌𐐼 𐑌𐐵 𐐺𐐨𐐸𐐬𐑊𐐼 𐐌 𐑅𐐩 𐐲𐑌𐐻𐐭 𐐷𐐭, 𐐸𐐰𐑆 𐑄𐐩𐑉 𐐺𐐨𐑌 𐑅𐐬 𐑀𐑉𐐩𐐻 𐑊𐐲𐑂 𐐮𐑌 𐐫𐑊 𐑄 𐑊𐐰𐑌𐐼? 𐐒𐐨𐐸𐐬𐑊𐐼, 𐐌 𐑅𐐩 𐐲𐑌𐐻𐐭 𐐷𐐭, 𐐤𐐩, 𐑄𐐩𐑉 𐐸𐐰𐑆 𐑌𐐱𐐻, 𐐨𐑂𐐲𐑌 𐐲𐑋𐐲𐑍 𐑄 𐐤𐐨𐑁𐐴𐐻𐑅. 𐐙𐐫𐑉 𐐺𐐨𐐸𐐬𐑊𐐼, 𐑄𐐩 𐐶𐐳𐐼 𐐻𐐩𐐿 𐐲𐐹 𐐪𐑉𐑋𐑆 𐐲𐑀𐐯𐑌𐑅𐐻 𐑄𐐩𐑉 𐐺𐑉𐐯𐑄𐑉𐐯𐑌; 𐑄𐐩 𐐶𐐳𐐼 𐑌𐐱𐐻 𐑅𐐲𐑁𐐲𐑉 𐑄𐐯𐑋𐑅𐐯𐑊𐑂𐑆 𐐻𐐭 𐐺𐐨 𐑅𐑊𐐩𐑌. 𐐒𐐲𐐻 𐐺𐐨𐐸𐐬𐑊𐐼 𐐸𐐵 𐑋𐐯𐑌𐐨 𐐲𐑂 𐑄𐐨𐑆 𐐸𐐰𐑂 𐑊𐐩𐐼 𐐼𐐵𐑌 𐑄𐐩𐑉 𐑊𐐴𐑂𐑆; 𐐰𐑌𐐼 𐐶𐐨 𐑌𐐬 𐑄𐐰𐐻 𐑄𐐩 𐐸𐐰𐑂 𐑀𐐱𐑌 𐐻𐐭 𐑄𐐩𐑉 𐐘𐐱𐐼, 𐐺𐐨𐐿𐐫𐑆 𐐲𐑂 𐑄𐐩𐑉 𐑊𐐲𐑂 𐐰𐑌𐐼 𐐲𐑂 𐑄𐐩𐑉 𐐸𐐩𐐻𐑉𐐯𐐼 𐐻𐐭 𐑅𐐮𐑌. 𐐤𐐵 𐐸𐐰𐑂 𐐶𐐨 𐑌𐐱𐐻 𐑉𐐨𐑆𐐲𐑌 𐐻𐐭 𐑉𐐨𐐾𐑎𐑅? 𐐏𐐩, 𐐌 𐑅𐐩 𐐲𐑌𐐻𐐭 𐐷𐐭, 𐑄𐐩𐑉 𐑌𐐯𐑂𐐲𐑉 𐐶𐐲𐑉 𐑋𐐯𐑌 𐑄𐐰𐐻 𐐸𐐰𐐼 𐑅𐐬 𐑀𐑉𐐩𐐻 𐑉𐐨𐑆𐐲𐑌 𐐻𐐭 𐑉𐐨𐐾𐑎𐑅 𐐰𐑆 𐐶𐐨, 𐑅𐐮𐑌𐑅 𐑄 𐐶𐐲𐑉𐑊𐐼 𐐺𐐨𐑀𐐰𐑌; 𐐷𐐩, 𐐰𐑌𐐼 𐑋𐐴 𐐾𐑎 𐐮𐑆 𐐿𐐰𐑉𐐨𐐼 𐐲𐐶𐐩, 𐐨𐑂𐐲𐑌 𐐲𐑌𐐻𐐭 𐐺𐐬𐑅𐐻𐐮𐑍 𐐮𐑌 𐑋𐐴 𐐘𐐱𐐼; 𐑁𐐫𐑉 𐐸𐐨 𐐸𐐰𐑆 𐐫𐑊 𐐹𐐵𐐲𐑉, 𐐫𐑊 𐐶𐐮𐑆𐐼𐐲𐑋, 𐐰𐑌𐐼 𐐫𐑊 𐐲𐑌𐐼𐐲𐑉𐑅𐐻𐐰𐑌𐐼𐐮𐑍; 𐐸𐐨 𐐿𐐱𐑋𐐹𐑉𐐨𐐸𐐯𐑌𐐼𐐯𐑃 𐐫𐑊 𐑃𐐮𐑍𐑆, 𐐰𐑌𐐼 𐐸𐐨 𐐮𐑆 𐐲 𐑋𐐲𐑉𐑅𐐮𐑁𐐳𐑊 𐐒𐐨𐐮𐑍, 𐐨𐑂𐐲𐑌 𐐲𐑌𐐻𐐭 𐑅𐐰𐑊𐑂𐐩𐑇𐐲𐑌, 𐐻𐐭 𐑄𐐬𐑆 𐐸𐐭 𐐶𐐮𐑊 𐑉𐐨𐐹𐐯𐑌𐐻 𐐰𐑌𐐼 𐐺𐐨𐑊𐐨𐑂 𐐱𐑌 𐐸𐐮𐑆 𐑌𐐩𐑋. 𐐤𐐵 𐐮𐑁 𐑄𐐮𐑅 𐐮𐑆 𐐺𐐬𐑅𐐻𐐮𐑍, 𐐨𐑂𐐲𐑌 𐑅𐐬 𐐶𐐮𐑊 𐐌 𐐺𐐬𐑅𐐻; 𐑁𐐫𐑉 𐑄𐐮𐑅 𐐮𐑆 𐑋𐐴 𐑊𐐴𐑁 𐐰𐑌𐐼 𐑋𐐴 𐑊𐐴𐐻, 𐑋𐐴 𐐾𐑎 𐐰𐑌𐐼 𐑋𐐴 𐑅𐐰𐑊𐑂𐐩𐑇𐐲𐑌, 𐐰𐑌𐐼 𐑋𐐴 𐑉𐐨𐐼𐐯𐑋𐑇𐐲𐑌 𐑁𐑉𐐲𐑋 𐐯𐑂𐐲𐑉𐑊𐐰𐑅𐐻𐐮𐑍 𐐶𐐬. 𐐏𐐩, 𐐺𐑊𐐯𐑅𐐯𐐼 𐐮𐑆 𐑄 𐑌𐐩𐑋 𐐲𐑂 𐑋𐐴 𐐘𐐱𐐼, 𐐸𐐭 𐐸𐐰𐑆 𐐺𐐨𐑌 𐑋𐐴𐑌𐐼𐑁𐐳𐑊 𐐲𐑂 𐑄𐐮𐑅 𐐹𐐨𐐹𐑊, 𐐸𐐭 𐐪𐑉 𐐲 𐐺𐑉𐐰𐑌𐐽 𐐲𐑂 𐑄 𐐻𐑉𐐨 𐐲𐑂 𐐆𐑆𐑉𐐩𐐯𐑊, 𐐰𐑌𐐼 𐐸𐐰𐑆 𐐺𐐨𐑌 𐑊𐐱𐑅𐐻 𐑁𐑉𐐲𐑋 𐐮𐐻𐑅 𐐺𐐱𐐼𐐨 𐐮𐑌 𐐲 𐑅𐐻𐑉𐐩𐑌𐐾 𐑊𐐰𐑌𐐼; 𐐷𐐩, 𐐌 𐑅𐐩, 𐐒𐑊𐐯𐑅𐐯𐐼 𐐺𐐨 𐑄 𐑌𐐩𐑋 𐐲𐑂 𐑋𐐴 𐐘𐐱𐐼, 𐐸𐐭 𐐸𐐰𐑆 𐐺𐐨𐑌 𐑋𐐴𐑌𐐼𐑁𐐳𐑊 𐐲𐑂 𐐲𐑅 𐐶𐐱𐑌𐐼𐐲𐑉𐐲𐑉𐑆 𐐮𐑌 𐐲 𐑅𐐻𐑉𐐩𐑌𐐾 𐑊𐐰𐑌𐐼. 𐐤𐐵 𐑋𐐴 𐐺𐑉𐐯𐑄𐑉𐐯𐑌, 𐐶𐐨 𐑅𐐨 𐑄𐐰𐐻 𐐘𐐱𐐼 𐐮𐑆 𐑋𐐴𐑌𐐼𐑁𐐳𐑊 𐐲𐑂 𐐯𐑂𐐲𐑉𐐨 𐐹𐐨𐐹𐑊, 𐐸𐐶𐐱𐐻𐑅𐐬𐐯𐑂𐐲𐑉 𐑊𐐰𐑌𐐼 𐑄𐐩 𐑋𐐩 𐐺𐐨 𐐮𐑌; 𐐷𐐩, 𐐸𐐨 𐑌𐐲𐑋𐐺𐐲𐑉𐐯𐑃 𐐸𐐮𐑆 𐐹𐐨𐐹𐑊, 𐐰𐑌𐐼 𐐸𐐮𐑆 𐐺𐐵𐐯𐑊𐑆 𐐲𐑂 𐑋𐐲𐑉𐑅𐐨 𐐪𐑉 𐐬𐑂𐐲𐑉 𐐫𐑊 𐑄 𐐲𐑉𐑃. 𐐤𐐵 𐑄𐐮𐑅 𐐮𐑆 𐑋𐐴 𐐾𐑎, 𐐰𐑌𐐼 𐑋𐐴 𐑀𐑉𐐩𐐻 𐑃𐐰𐑍𐐿𐑅𐑀𐐮𐑂𐐮𐑍; 𐐷𐐩, 𐐰𐑌𐐼 𐐌 𐐶𐐮𐑊 𐑀𐐮𐑂 𐑃𐐰𐑍𐐿𐑅 𐐲𐑌𐐻𐐭 𐑋𐐴 𐐘𐐱𐐼 𐑁𐐫𐑉 𐐯𐑂𐐲𐑉. 𐐁𐑋𐐯𐑌.

𐐕𐐰𐐹𐐻𐐲𐑉 XV.

1. 𐐤𐐵 𐐮𐐻 𐐿𐐩𐑋 𐐻𐐭 𐐹𐐰𐑅 𐑄𐐰𐐻 𐐸𐐶𐐯𐑌 𐑄𐐬𐑆 𐐢𐐰𐑋𐐲𐑌𐐴𐐻𐑅 𐐸𐐭 𐐸𐐰𐐼 𐑀𐐫𐑌 𐐻𐐭 𐐶𐐫𐑉 𐐰𐑀𐐯𐑌𐑅𐐻 𐑄 𐐤𐐨𐑁𐐴𐐻𐑅 𐐸𐐰𐐼 𐑁𐐵𐑌𐐼, 𐐪𐑁𐐻𐐲𐑉 𐑄𐐩𐑉 𐑋𐐯𐑌𐐨 𐑅𐐻𐑉𐐲𐑀𐑊𐑆 𐐻𐐭 𐐼𐐯𐑅𐐻𐑉𐑎 𐑄𐐯𐑋, 𐑄𐐰𐐻 𐐮𐐻 𐐶𐐱𐑆 𐐮𐑌 𐑂𐐩𐑌 𐐻𐐭 𐑅𐐨𐐿 𐑄𐐩𐑉 𐐼𐐯𐑅𐐻𐑉𐐲𐐿𐑇𐐲𐑌, 𐑄𐐩 𐑉𐐨𐐻𐐲𐑉𐑌𐐼 𐐰𐑀𐐯𐑌 𐐻𐐭 𐑄 𐑊𐐰𐑌𐐼 𐐱𐑂 𐐤𐐨𐑁𐐴. 𐐈𐑌𐐼 𐐮𐐻 𐐿𐐩𐑋 𐐻𐐭 𐐹𐐰𐑅 𐑄𐐰𐐻 𐑄 𐐈𐑋𐐰𐑊𐐯𐐿𐐴𐐻𐑅, 𐐺𐐨𐐿𐐫𐑆 𐐱𐑂 𐑄𐐩𐑉 𐑊𐐫𐑅, 𐐶𐐲𐑉 𐐯𐐿𐑅𐐨𐐼𐐮𐑍𐑊𐐨 𐐰𐑍𐑀𐑉𐐨. 𐐈𐑌𐐼 𐐸𐐶𐐯𐑌 𐑄𐐩 𐑅𐐫 𐑄𐐰𐐻 𐑄𐐩 𐐿𐐳𐐼 𐑌𐐱𐐻 𐑅𐐨𐐿 𐑉𐐨𐑂𐐯𐑌𐐾 𐑁𐑉𐐱𐑋 𐑄 𐐤𐐨𐑁𐐴𐐻𐑅, 𐑄𐐩 𐐺𐐨𐑀𐐰𐑌 𐐻𐐭 𐑅𐐻𐐲𐑉 𐐲𐐹 𐑄 𐐹𐐨𐐹𐑊 𐐮𐑌 𐐰𐑍𐑀𐐲𐑉 𐐰𐑀𐐯𐑌𐑅𐐻 𐑄𐐩𐑉 𐐺𐑉𐐯𐑄𐑉𐐯𐑌, 𐑄 𐐹𐐨𐐹𐑊 𐐱𐑂 𐐈𐑌𐐻𐐴-𐐤𐐨𐑁𐐴-𐐢𐐨𐐸𐐴; 𐑄𐐩𐑉𐑁𐐬𐑉 𐑄𐐩 𐐺𐐨𐑀𐐰𐑌 𐐰𐑀𐐯𐑌 𐐻𐐭 𐐼𐐯𐑅𐐻𐑉𐑎 𐑄𐐯𐑋. 𐐤𐐵 𐑄𐐮𐑅 𐐹𐐨𐐹𐑊 𐐰𐑀𐐯𐑌 𐑉𐐨𐑁𐐷𐐭𐑆𐐼 𐐻𐐭 𐐻𐐩𐐿 𐑄𐐩𐑉 𐐪𐑉𐑋𐑆, 𐐰𐑌𐐼 𐑄𐐩 𐑅𐐲𐑁𐐲𐑉𐐼 𐑄𐐯𐑋𐑅𐐯𐑊𐑂𐑆 𐐻𐐭 𐐺𐐨 𐑅𐑊𐐩𐑌 𐐰𐐿𐐫𐑉𐐼𐐮𐑍 𐐻𐐭 𐑄 𐐼𐐨𐑆𐐴𐑉𐑆 𐐱𐑂 𐑄𐐩𐑉 𐐯𐑌𐐯𐑋𐐨𐑆. 𐐤𐐵 𐐸𐐶𐐯𐑌 𐐈𐑋𐐲𐑌 𐐰𐑌𐐼 𐐸𐐮𐑆 𐐺𐑉𐐯𐑄𐑉𐐯𐑌 𐑅𐐫 𐑄𐐮𐑅 𐐶𐐲𐑉𐐿 𐐱𐑂 𐐼𐐯𐑅𐐻𐑉𐐲𐐿𐑇𐐲𐑌 𐐰𐑋𐐲𐑍 𐑄𐐬𐑆 𐐸𐐭𐑋 𐑄𐐩 𐑅𐐬 𐐼𐐨𐑉𐑊𐐨 𐐺𐐨𐑊𐐲𐑂𐐼, 𐐰𐑌𐐼 𐐰𐑋𐐲𐑍 𐑄𐐬𐑆 𐐸𐐭 𐐸𐐰𐐼 𐑅𐐬 𐐼𐐨𐑉𐑊𐐨 𐐺𐐨𐑊𐐲𐑂𐐼 𐑄𐐯𐑋; 𐑁𐐫𐑉 𐑄𐐩 𐐶𐐲𐑉 𐐻𐑉𐐨𐐻𐐯𐐼 𐐰𐑆 𐑄𐐬 𐑄𐐩 𐐶𐐲𐑉 𐐩𐑌𐐾𐐯𐑊𐑆 𐑅𐐯𐑌𐐻 𐑁𐑉𐐱𐑋 𐐘𐐱𐐼 𐐻𐐭 𐑅𐐩𐑂 𐑄𐐯𐑋 𐑁𐑉𐐱𐑋 𐐯𐑂𐐲𐑉𐑊𐐪𐑅𐐻𐐮𐑍 𐐼𐐯𐑅𐐻𐑉𐐲𐐿𐑇𐐲𐑌; 𐑄𐐩𐑉𐑁𐐬𐑉, 𐐸𐐶𐐯𐑌 𐐈𐑋𐐲𐑌 𐐰𐑌𐐼 𐐸𐐮𐑆 𐐺𐑉𐐯𐑄𐑉𐐯𐑌 𐑅𐐫 𐑄𐐮𐑅 𐑀𐑉𐐩𐐻 𐐶𐐲𐑉𐐿 𐐱𐑂 𐐼𐐯𐑅𐐻𐑉𐐲𐐿𐑇𐐲𐑌, 𐑄𐐩 𐐶𐐲𐑉 𐑋𐐭𐑂𐐼 𐐶𐐮𐑄 𐐿𐐱𐑋𐐹𐐰𐑇𐐲𐑌, 𐐰𐑌𐐼 𐑄𐐩 𐑅𐐯𐐼 𐐲𐑌𐐻𐐭 𐑄 𐐿𐐮𐑍, 𐐢𐐯𐐻 𐐲𐑅 𐑀𐐰𐑄𐐲𐑉 𐐻𐐭𐑀𐐯𐑄𐐲𐑉 𐑄𐐮𐑅 𐐹𐐨𐐹𐑊 𐐱𐑂 𐑄 𐐢𐐫𐑉𐐼, 𐐰𐑌𐐼 𐑊𐐯𐐻 𐐲𐑅 𐑀𐐬 𐐼𐐵𐑌 𐐻𐐭 𐑄 𐑊𐐰𐑌𐐼 𐐱𐑂 𐐞𐐯𐑉𐐲𐐸𐐯𐑋𐑊𐐲, 𐐻𐐭 𐐵𐑉 𐐺𐑉𐐯𐑄𐑉𐐯𐑌 𐑄 𐐤𐐨𐑁𐐴𐐻𐑅, 𐐰𐑌𐐼 𐑁𐑊𐐨 𐐵𐐻 𐐱𐑂 𐑄 𐐸𐐰𐑌𐐼𐑆 𐐱𐑂 𐐵𐑉 𐐯𐑌𐐯𐑋𐐨𐑆, 𐑄𐐰𐐻 𐐶𐐨 𐐺𐐨 𐑌𐐱𐐻 𐐼𐐯𐑅𐐻𐑉𐑎𐐼. 𐐒𐐲𐐻 𐑄 𐐿𐐮𐑍 𐑅𐐯𐐼 𐐲𐑌𐐻𐐭 𐑄𐐯𐑋, 𐐒𐐨𐐸𐐬𐑊𐐼, 𐑄 𐐤𐐨𐑁𐐴𐐻𐑅 𐐶𐐮𐑊 𐐼𐐯𐑅𐐻𐑉𐑎 𐐲𐑅, 𐐺𐐨𐐿𐐫𐑆 𐐱𐑂 𐑄 𐑋𐐯𐑌𐐨 𐑋𐐲𐑉𐐼𐐲𐑉𐑆 𐐰𐑌𐐼 𐑅𐐮𐑌𐑆 𐐶𐐨 𐐸𐐰𐑂 𐐿𐐱𐑋𐐮𐐻𐐯𐐼 𐐰𐑀𐐯𐑌𐑅𐐻 𐑄𐐯𐑋. 𐐈𐑌𐐼 𐐈𐑋𐐲𐑌 𐑅𐐯𐐼, 𐐌 𐐶𐐮𐑊 𐑀𐐬 𐐰𐑌𐐼 𐐮𐑌𐐿𐐶𐐴𐑉 𐐱𐑂 𐑄 𐐢𐐫𐑉𐐼, 𐐰𐑌𐐼 𐐮𐑁 𐐸𐐨 𐑅𐐩 𐐲𐑌𐐻𐐭 𐐲𐑅, 𐑀𐐬 𐐼𐐵𐑌 𐐲𐑌𐐻𐐭 𐐵𐑉 𐐺𐑉𐐯𐑄𐑉𐐯𐑌, 𐐶𐐮𐑊 𐐷𐐨 𐑀𐐬? 𐐈𐑌𐐼 𐑄 𐐿𐐮𐑍 𐑅𐐯𐐼 𐐲𐑌𐐻𐐭 𐐸𐐮𐑋, 𐐏𐐩: 𐐮𐑁 𐑄 𐐢𐐫𐑉𐐼 𐑅𐐯𐑃 𐐲𐑌𐐻𐐭 𐐲𐑅 𐑀𐐬, 𐐶𐐨 𐐶𐐮𐑊 𐑀𐐬 𐐼𐐵𐑌 𐐲𐑌𐐻𐐭 𐐵𐑉 𐐺𐑉𐐯𐑄𐑉𐐯𐑌, 𐐰𐑌𐐼 𐐶𐐨 𐐶𐐮𐑊 𐐺𐐨 𐑄𐐩𐑉 𐑅𐑊𐐩𐑂𐑆 𐐲𐑌𐐻𐐮𐑊 𐐶𐐨 𐑉𐐨𐐹𐐩𐑉 𐐲𐑌𐐻𐐭 𐑄𐐯𐑋 𐑄 𐑋𐐯𐑌𐐨 𐑋𐐲𐑉𐐼𐐲𐑉𐑆 𐐰𐑌𐐼 𐑅𐐮𐑌𐑆 𐐸𐐶𐐮𐐽 𐐶𐐨 𐐸𐐰𐑂 𐐿𐐱𐑋𐐮𐐻𐐯𐐼 𐐰𐑀𐐯𐑌𐑅𐐻 𐑄𐐯𐑋. 𐐒𐐲𐐻 𐐈𐑋𐐲𐑌 𐑅𐐯𐐼 𐐲𐑌𐐻𐐭 𐐸𐐮𐑋, 𐐆𐐻 𐐮𐑆 𐐰𐑀𐐯𐑌𐑅𐐻 𐑄 𐑊𐐫 𐐱𐑂 𐐵𐑉 𐐺𐑉𐐯𐑄𐑉𐐯𐑌, 𐐸𐐶𐐮𐐽 𐐶𐐱𐑆 𐐯𐑅𐐻𐐰𐐺𐑊𐐮𐑇𐐻 𐐺𐐴 𐑋𐐴 𐑁𐐪𐑄𐐲𐑉, 𐑄𐐰𐐻 𐑄𐐩𐑉 𐑇𐐳𐐼 𐐺𐐨 𐐯𐑌𐐨 𐑅𐑊𐐩𐑂𐑆 𐐰𐑋𐐲𐑍 𐑄𐐯𐑋; 𐑄𐐩𐑉𐑁𐐬𐑉 𐑊𐐯𐐻 𐐲𐑅 𐑀𐐬 𐐼𐐵𐑌 𐐰𐑌𐐼 𐑉𐐨𐑊𐐴 𐐲𐐹𐐱𐑌 𐑄 𐑋𐐲𐑉𐑅𐐨𐑆 𐐱𐑂 𐐵𐑉 𐐺𐑉𐐯𐑄𐑉𐐯𐑌. 𐐒𐐲𐐻 𐑄 𐐿𐐮𐑍 𐑅𐐯𐐼 𐐲𐑌𐐻𐐭 𐐸𐐮𐑋, 𐐆𐑌𐐿𐐶𐐴𐑉 𐐱𐑂 𐑄 𐐢𐐫𐑉𐐼, 𐐰𐑌𐐼 𐐮𐑁 𐐸𐐨 𐑅𐐯𐑃 𐐲𐑌𐐻𐐭 𐐲𐑅 𐑀𐐬, 𐐶𐐨 𐐶𐐮𐑊 𐑀𐐬; 𐐲𐑄𐐲𐑉𐐶𐐴𐑆 𐐶𐐨 𐐶𐐮𐑊 𐐹𐐯𐑉𐐮𐑇 𐐮𐑌 𐑄 𐑊𐐰𐑌𐐼.

2. 𐐈𐑌𐐼 𐐮𐐻 𐐿𐐩𐑋 𐐻𐐭 𐐹𐐰𐑅 𐑄𐐰𐐻 𐐈𐑋𐐲𐑌 𐐶𐐯𐑌𐐻 𐐰𐑌𐐼 𐐮𐑌𐐿𐐶𐐴𐑉𐐼 𐐱𐑂 𐑄 𐐢𐐫𐑉𐐼, 𐐰𐑌𐐼 𐑄 𐐢𐐫𐑉𐐼 𐑅𐐯𐐼 𐐲𐑌𐐻𐐭 𐐸𐐮𐑋, 𐐘𐐯𐐻 𐑄𐐮𐑅 𐐹𐐨𐐹𐑊 𐐵𐐻 𐐱𐑂 𐑄𐐮𐑅 𐑊𐐰𐑌𐐼, 𐑄𐐰𐐻 𐑄𐐩 𐐹𐐯𐑉𐐮𐑇 𐑌𐐱𐐻; 𐑁𐐫𐑉 𐐝𐐩𐐻𐐲𐑌 𐐸𐐰𐑆 𐑀𐑉𐐩𐐻 𐐸𐐬𐑊𐐼 𐐱𐑌 𐑄 𐐸𐐪𐑉𐐻𐑅 𐐱𐑂 𐑄 𐐈𐑋𐐰𐑊𐐯𐐿𐐴𐐻𐑅, 𐐸𐐭 𐐼𐐭 𐑅𐐻𐐲𐑉 𐐲𐐹 𐑄 𐐢𐐰𐑋𐐲𐑌𐐴𐐻𐑅 𐐻𐐭 𐐰𐑍𐑀𐐲𐑉 𐐰𐑀𐐯𐑌𐑅𐐻 𐑄𐐩𐑉 𐐺𐑉𐐯𐑄𐑉𐐯𐑌 𐐻𐐭 𐑅𐑊𐐩 𐑄𐐯𐑋; 𐑄𐐩𐑉𐑁𐐬𐑉 𐑀𐐯𐐻 𐑄𐐵 𐐵𐐻 𐐱𐑂 𐑄𐐮𐑅 𐑊𐐰𐑌𐐼; 𐐰𐑌𐐼 𐐺𐑊𐐯𐑅𐐯𐐼 𐐪𐑉 𐑄𐐮𐑅 𐐹𐐨𐐹𐑊 𐐮𐑌 𐑄𐐮𐑅 𐐾𐐯𐑌𐐲𐑉𐐩𐑇𐐲𐑌, 𐑁𐐫𐑉 𐐌 𐐶𐐮𐑊 𐐹𐑉𐐨𐑆𐐲𐑉𐑂 𐑄𐐯𐑋.

3. 𐐈𐑌𐐼 𐑌𐐵 𐐮𐐻 𐐿𐐩𐑋 𐐻𐐭 𐐹𐐰𐑅 𐑄𐐰𐐻 𐐈𐑋𐐲𐑌 𐐶𐐯𐑌𐐻 𐐰𐑌𐐼 𐐻𐐬𐑊𐐼 𐑄 𐐿𐐮𐑍 𐐫𐑊 𐑄 𐐶𐐲𐑉𐐼𐑆 𐐸𐐶𐐮𐐽 𐑄 𐐢𐐫𐑉𐐼 𐐸𐐰𐐼 𐑅𐐯𐐼 𐐲𐑌𐐻𐐭 𐐸𐐮𐑋. 𐐈𐑌𐐼 𐑄𐐩 𐑀𐐰𐑄𐐲𐑉𐐼 𐐻𐐭𐑀𐐯𐑄𐐲𐑉 𐐫𐑊 𐑄𐐩𐑉 𐐹𐐨𐐹𐑊; 𐐷𐐩, 𐐫𐑊 𐑄 𐐹𐐨𐐹𐑊 𐐱𐑂 𐑄 𐐢𐐫𐑉𐐼, 𐐰𐑌𐐼 𐐼𐐮𐐼 𐑀𐐰𐑄𐐲𐑉 𐐻𐐭𐑀𐐯𐑄𐐲𐑉 𐐫𐑊 𐑄𐐩𐑉 𐑁𐑊𐐱𐐿𐑅 𐐰𐑌𐐼 𐐸𐐲𐑉𐐼𐑆, 𐐰𐑌𐐼 𐐼𐐨𐐹𐐪𐑉𐐻𐐯𐐼 𐐵𐐻 𐐱𐑂 𐑄 𐑊𐐰𐑌𐐼, 𐐰𐑌𐐼 𐐿𐐩𐑋 𐐮𐑌𐐻𐐭 𐑄 𐐶𐐮𐑊𐐼𐐲𐑉𐑌𐐯𐑅 𐐸𐐶𐐮𐐽 𐐼𐐮𐑂𐐴𐐼𐐯𐐼 𐑄 𐑊𐐰𐑌𐐼 𐐱𐑂 𐐤𐐨𐑁𐐴 𐑁𐑉𐐱𐑋 𐑄 𐑊𐐰𐑌𐐼 𐐱𐑂 𐐞𐐯𐑉𐐲𐐸𐐯𐑋𐑊𐐲, 𐐰𐑌𐐼 𐐿𐐩𐑋 𐐬𐑂𐐲𐑉 𐑌𐐨𐑉 𐑄 𐐺𐐫𐑉𐐼𐐲𐑉𐑆 𐐱𐑂 𐑄 𐑊𐐰𐑌𐐼.

4. 𐐈𐑌𐐼 𐐮𐐻 𐐿𐐩𐑋 𐐻𐐭 𐐹𐐰𐑅 𐑄𐐰𐐻 𐐈𐑋𐐲𐑌 𐑅𐐯𐐼 𐐲𐑌𐐻𐐭 𐑄𐐯𐑋, 𐐒𐐨𐐸𐐬𐑊𐐼, 𐐌 𐐰𐑌𐐼 𐑋𐐴 𐐺𐑉𐐯𐑄𐑉𐐯𐑌 𐐶𐐮𐑊 𐑀𐐬 𐑁𐐬𐑉𐑃 𐐮𐑌𐐻𐐭 𐑄 𐑊𐐰𐑌𐐼 𐐱𐑂 𐐞𐐯𐑉𐐲𐐸𐐯𐑋𐑊𐐲, 𐐰𐑌𐐼 𐐷𐐨 𐑇𐐰𐑊 𐑉𐐨𐑋𐐩𐑌 𐐸𐐨𐑉 𐐲𐑌𐐻𐐮𐑊 𐐶𐐨 𐑉𐐨𐐻𐐲𐑉𐑌;

𐐰𐑌𐐼 𐐶𐐨 𐐶𐐮𐑊 𐐻𐑉𐐴 𐑄 𐐸𐐪𐑉𐐻𐑅 𐐱𐑂 𐐵𐑉 𐐺𐑉𐐯𐑄𐑉𐐯𐑌, 𐐸𐐶𐐯𐑄𐐲𐑉 𐑄𐐩 𐐶𐐮𐑊 𐑄𐐰𐐻 𐐷 𐑇𐐰𐑊 𐐿𐐲𐑋 𐐮𐑌𐐻𐐭 𐑄𐐩𐑉 𐑊𐐰𐑌𐐼.

5. 𐐈𐑌𐐼 𐐮𐐻 𐐿𐐩𐑋 𐐻𐐭 𐐹𐐪𐑅 𐑄𐐰𐐻 𐐰𐑆 𐐈𐑋𐐲𐑌 𐐶𐐱𐑆 𐑀𐐬𐐮𐑍 𐑁𐐫𐑉𐑃 𐐮𐑌𐐻𐐭 𐑄 𐑊𐐰𐑌𐐼, 𐑄𐐰𐐻 𐐸𐐨 𐐰𐑌𐐼 𐐸𐐮𐑆 𐐺𐑉𐐯𐑄𐑉𐐯𐑌 𐑋𐐯𐐻 𐐈𐑊𐑋𐐲, 𐐬𐑂𐐲𐑉 𐐮𐑌 𐑄 𐐹𐑊𐐩𐑅 𐐱𐑂 𐐸𐐶𐐮𐐽 𐐸𐐰𐑆 𐐺𐐮𐑌 𐑅𐐹𐐬𐐿𐑌; 𐐰𐑌𐐼 𐐺𐐨𐐸𐐬𐑊𐐼, 𐑄𐐮𐑅 𐐶𐐱𐑆 𐐲 𐐾𐐱𐐮𐑁𐐳𐑊 𐑋𐐨𐐻𐐮𐑍. 𐐤𐐵 𐑄 𐐾𐐱𐐮 𐐱𐑂 𐐈𐑋𐐲𐑌 𐐶𐐱𐑆 𐑅𐐬 𐑀𐑉𐐩𐐻 𐐨𐑂𐑌 𐑄𐐰𐐻 𐐸𐐨 𐐶𐐱𐑆 𐑁𐐳𐑊; 𐐷𐐩, 𐐸𐐨 𐐶𐐱𐑆 𐑅𐐶𐐱𐑊𐐬𐐼 𐐲𐐹 𐐮𐑌 𐑄 𐐾𐐱𐐮 𐐱𐑂 𐐸𐐮𐑆 𐐘𐐱𐐼, 𐐨𐑂𐑌 𐐻𐐭 𐑄 𐐯𐑀𐑆𐐫𐑅𐐻𐐮𐑍 𐐱𐑂 𐐸𐐮𐑆 𐑅𐐻𐑉𐐯𐑍𐑃, 𐐰𐑌𐐼 𐐸𐐨 𐑁𐐯𐑊 𐐲𐑀𐐯𐑌 𐐻𐐭 𐑄 𐐲𐑉𐑃. 𐐤𐐵 𐐶𐐱𐑆 𐑌𐐱𐐻 𐑄𐐮𐑅 𐐯𐐿𐑅𐐨𐐼𐐮𐑍 𐐾𐐱𐐮? 𐐒𐐨𐐸𐐬𐑊𐐼, 𐑄𐐮𐑅 𐐮𐑆 𐐾𐐱𐐮 𐐸𐐶𐐮𐐽 𐑌𐐲𐑌 𐑉𐐨𐑅𐐨𐑂𐐯𐑃 𐑅𐐩𐑂 𐐮𐐻 𐐺 𐑄 𐐻𐑉𐐭𐑊𐐨 𐐹𐐯𐑌𐐮𐐻𐐯𐑌𐐻 𐐰𐑌𐐼 𐐸𐐲𐑋𐐺𐑊 𐑅𐐨𐐿𐐲𐑉 𐐱𐑂 𐐸𐐰𐐹𐐮𐑌𐐯𐑅. 𐐤𐐵 𐑄 𐐾𐐱𐐮 𐐱𐑂 𐐈𐑊𐑋𐐲 𐐮𐑌 𐑋𐐨𐐻𐐮𐑍 𐐸𐐮𐑆 𐐺𐑉𐐯𐑄𐑉𐐯𐑌 𐐶𐐱𐑆 𐐻𐑉𐐭𐑊𐐨 𐑀𐑉𐐩𐐻, 𐐰𐑌𐐼 𐐫𐑊𐑅𐐬 𐑄 𐐾𐐱𐐮 𐐱𐑂 𐐁𐑉𐐲𐑌, 𐐱𐑂 𐐉𐑋𐑌𐐲𐑉, 𐐰𐑌𐐼 𐐐𐐮𐑋𐑌𐐴; 𐐺𐐲𐐻 𐐺𐐨𐐸𐐬𐑊𐐼 𐑄𐐩𐑉 𐐾𐐱𐐮 𐐶𐐱𐑆 𐑌𐐱𐐻 𐑄𐐰𐐻 𐐻𐐭 𐐯𐐿𐑅𐐨𐐼 𐑄𐐩𐑉 𐑅𐐻𐑉𐐯𐑍𐑃.

6. 𐐈𐑌𐐼 𐑌𐐵 𐐮𐐻 𐐿𐐩𐑋 𐐻𐐭 𐐹𐐪𐑅 𐑄𐐰𐐻 𐐈𐑊𐑋𐐲 𐐿𐐲𐑌𐐼𐐲𐐿𐐻𐐯𐐼 𐐸𐐮𐑆 𐐺𐑉𐐯𐑄𐑉𐐯𐑌 𐐺𐐰𐐿 𐐻𐐭 𐑄 𐑊𐐰𐑌𐐼 𐐱𐑂 𐐞𐐩𐑉𐐲𐐸𐐯𐑋𐑊𐐲; 𐐨𐑂𐑌 𐐻𐐭 𐐸𐐮𐑆 𐐬𐑌 𐐸𐐵𐑅. 𐐈𐑌𐐼 𐑄𐐩 𐐶𐐯𐑌𐐻 𐐰𐑌𐐼 𐐻𐐬𐑊𐐼 𐑄 𐐽𐐨𐑁 𐐾𐐲𐐾 𐐫𐑊 𐑄 𐑃𐐮𐑍𐑆 𐑄𐐰𐐻 𐐸𐐰𐐼 𐐸𐐰𐐹𐐯𐑌𐐼 𐐲𐑌𐐻𐐭 𐑄𐐯𐑋 𐐮𐑌 𐑄 𐑊𐐰𐑌𐐼 𐐱𐑂 𐐤𐐨𐑁𐐴, 𐐲𐑋𐐲𐑍 𐑄𐐩𐑉 𐐺𐑉𐐯𐑄𐑉𐐯𐑌, 𐑄 𐐢𐐩𐑋𐐲𐑌𐐴𐐻𐑅.

7. 𐐈𐑌𐐼 𐐮𐐻 𐐿𐐩𐑋 𐐻𐐭 𐐹𐐪𐑅 𐑄𐐰𐐻 𐑄 𐐽𐐨𐑁 𐐾𐐲𐐾 𐑅𐐯𐑌𐐻 𐐲 𐐹𐑉𐐱𐐿𐑊𐐲𐑋𐐩𐑇𐐲𐑌 𐑃𐑉𐐭𐐵𐐻 𐐫𐑊 𐑄 𐑊𐐰𐑌𐐼, 𐐼𐐨𐑆𐐴𐑉𐐮𐑍 𐑄 𐑂𐐱𐐮𐑅 𐐱𐑂 𐑄 𐐹𐐨𐐹𐑊 𐐿𐐲𐑌𐑅𐐲𐑉𐑌𐐮𐑍 𐑄 𐐰𐐼𐑋𐐮𐐻𐐮𐑍 𐑄𐐩𐑉 𐐺𐑉𐐯𐑄𐑉𐐯𐑌, 𐐸𐐭 𐐶𐐲𐑉 𐑄 𐐹𐐨𐐹𐑊 𐐱𐑂 𐐈𐑌𐐻𐐴-𐐤𐐨𐑁𐐴-𐐢𐐨𐐸𐐴. 𐐈𐑌𐐼 𐐮𐐻 𐐿𐐩𐑋 𐐻𐐭 𐐹𐐪𐑅 𐑄𐐰𐐻 𐑄 𐑂𐐱𐐮𐑅 𐐱𐑂 𐑄 𐐹𐐨𐐹𐑊 𐐿𐐩𐑋, 𐑅𐐩𐐮𐑍, 𐐒𐐨𐐸𐐬𐑊𐐼, 𐐶𐐨 𐐶𐐮𐑊 𐑀𐐮𐑂 𐐲𐐹 𐑄 𐑊𐐰𐑌𐐼 𐐱𐑂 𐐖𐐲𐑉𐑇𐐲𐑌, 𐐸𐐶𐐮𐐽 𐐮𐑆 𐐱𐑌 𐑄 𐐨𐑅𐐻 𐐺𐐴 𐑄 𐑅𐐨, 𐐸𐐶𐐮𐐽 𐐾𐐱𐐮𐑌𐑆 𐑄 𐑊𐐰𐑌𐐼 𐐒𐐵𐑌𐐻𐐮𐑁𐐳𐑊; 𐐸𐐶𐐮𐐽 𐐮𐑆 𐐱𐑌 𐑄 𐑅𐐵𐑃 𐐱𐑂 𐑄 𐑊𐐰𐑌𐐼 𐐒𐐵𐑌𐐻𐐮𐑁𐐳𐑊; 𐐰𐑌𐐼 𐑄𐐮𐑅 𐑊𐐰𐑌𐐼 𐐖𐐲𐑉𐑇𐐲𐑌 𐐮𐑆 𐑄 𐑊𐐰𐑌𐐼 𐐸𐐶𐐮𐐽 𐐶𐐨 𐐶𐐮𐑊 𐑀𐐮𐑂 𐐲𐑌𐐻𐐭 𐐵𐑉 𐐺𐑉𐐯𐑄𐑉𐐯𐑌 𐑁𐐫𐑉 𐐰𐑌 𐐮𐑌𐐸𐐯𐑉𐐮𐐻𐐲𐑌𐑅. 𐐈𐑌𐐼 𐐺𐐨𐐸𐐬𐑊𐐼, 𐐶𐐨 𐐶𐐮𐑊 𐑅𐐯𐐻 𐐵𐑉 𐐪𐑉𐑋𐐮𐑆 𐐺𐐨𐐻𐐶𐐨𐑌 𐑄 𐑊𐐰𐑌𐐼 𐐖𐐲𐑉𐑇𐐲𐑌 𐐰𐑌𐐼 𐑄 𐑊𐐰𐑌𐐼 𐐤𐐨𐑁𐐴, 𐑄𐐰𐐻 𐐶𐐨 𐑋𐐩 𐐹𐑉𐐬𐐻𐐯𐐿𐐻 𐐵𐑉 𐐺𐑉𐐯𐑄𐑉𐐯𐑌 𐐮𐑌 𐑄 𐑊𐐰𐑌𐐼 𐐖𐐲𐑉𐑇𐐲𐑌; 𐐰𐑌𐐼 𐑄𐐮𐑅 𐐶𐐨 𐐼𐐭 𐑁𐐫𐑉 𐐵𐑉 𐐺𐑉𐐯𐑄𐑉𐐯𐑌, 𐐱𐑌 𐐰𐐿𐐵𐑌𐐻 𐐱𐑂 𐑄𐐩𐑉 𐑁𐐨𐑉 𐐻𐐭 𐐻𐐩𐐿 𐐲𐐹 𐐪𐑉𐑋𐑆 𐐲𐑀𐐯𐑌𐑅𐐻 𐑄𐐩𐑉 𐐺𐑉𐐯𐑄𐑉𐐯𐑌, 𐑊𐐯𐑅𐐻 𐑄𐐩 𐑇𐐳𐐼 𐐿𐐲𐑋𐐮𐐻 𐑅𐐮𐑌: 𐐰𐑌𐐼 𐑄𐐮𐑅 𐑄𐐩𐑉 𐑀𐑉𐐩𐐻 𐑁𐐨𐑉 𐐿𐐩𐑋, 𐐺𐐨𐐿𐐫𐑆 𐐱𐑂 𐑄𐐩𐑉 𐑅𐐬𐑉 𐑉𐐨𐐹𐐯𐑌𐐻𐐲𐑌𐑅 𐐸𐐶𐐮𐐽 𐑄𐐩 𐐸𐐰𐐼, 𐐱𐑌 𐐰𐐿𐐵𐑌𐐻 𐐱𐑂 𐑄𐐩𐑉 𐑋𐐯𐑌𐐮 𐑋𐐲𐑉𐐼𐐲𐑉𐑆, 𐐰𐑌𐐼 𐑄𐐩𐑉 𐐫𐑁𐐳𐑊 𐐶𐐮𐐿𐐯𐐼𐑌𐐯𐑅. 𐐈𐑌𐐼 𐑌𐐵 𐐺𐐨𐐸𐐬𐑊𐐼, 𐑄𐐮𐑅 𐐶𐐮𐑊 𐐶𐐨 𐐼𐐭 𐐲𐑌𐐻𐐭 𐐵𐑉 𐐺𐑉𐐯𐑄𐑉𐐯𐑌, 𐑄𐐰𐐻 𐑄𐐩 𐑋𐐩 𐐮𐑌𐐸𐐯𐑉𐐮𐐻 𐑄 𐑊𐐰𐑌𐐼 𐐖𐐲𐑉𐑇𐐲𐑌; 𐐰𐑌𐐼 𐐶𐐨 𐐶𐐮𐑊 𐑀𐐪𐑉𐐼 𐑄𐐯𐑋 𐑁𐑉𐐱𐑋 𐑄𐐩𐑉 𐐯𐑌𐐲𐑋𐐮𐑆 𐐶𐐮𐑄 𐐵𐑉 𐐪𐑉𐑋𐐮𐑆, 𐐱𐑌 𐐿𐐲𐑌𐐼𐐮𐑇𐐲𐑌 𐑄𐐰𐐻 𐑄𐐩 𐐶𐐮𐑊 𐑀𐐮𐑂 𐐲𐑅 𐐲 𐐹𐐫𐑉𐑇𐐲𐑌 𐐱𐑂 𐑄𐐩𐑉 𐑅𐐲𐐺𐑅𐐻𐐲𐑌𐑅 𐐻𐐭 𐐰𐑅𐐮𐑅𐐻 𐐲𐑅, 𐑄𐐰𐐻 𐐶𐐨 𐑋𐐩 𐑋𐐩𐑌𐐻𐐩𐑌 𐐵𐑉 𐐪𐑉𐑋𐐮𐑆.

8. 𐐤𐐵, 𐐮𐐻 𐐿𐐩𐑋 𐐻𐐭 𐐹𐐪𐑅 𐑄𐐰𐐻 𐐸𐐶𐐯𐑌 𐐈𐑋𐐲𐑌 𐐸𐐰𐐼 𐐸𐐲𐑉𐐼 𐑄𐐮𐑅, 𐐸𐐨 𐑉𐐨𐐻𐐲𐑉𐑌𐐼 𐐻𐐭 𐑄 𐐹𐐨𐐹𐑊 𐐱𐑂 𐐈𐑌𐐻𐐴-𐐤𐐨𐑁𐐴-𐐢𐐨𐐸𐐴, 𐐰𐑌𐐼 𐐫𐑊𐑅𐐬 𐐈𐑊𐑋𐐲 𐐶𐐮𐑄 𐐸𐐮𐑋, 𐐮𐑌𐐻𐐭 𐑄 𐐶𐐮𐑊𐐼𐐲𐑉𐑌𐐯𐑅, 𐐸𐐶𐐩𐑉 𐑄𐐩 𐐸𐐰𐐼 𐐹𐐮𐐽𐐻 𐑄𐐩𐑉 𐐻𐐯𐑌𐐻𐑅, 𐐰𐑌𐐼 𐑋𐐩𐐼 𐑌𐐬𐑌 𐐲𐑌𐐻𐐭 𐑄𐐯𐑋 𐐫𐑊 𐑄𐐨𐑆 𐑃𐐮𐑍𐑆. 𐐈𐑌𐐼 𐐈𐑊𐑋𐐲 𐐫𐑊𐑅𐐬 𐑉𐐨𐑊𐐩𐐻𐐯𐐼 𐐲𐑌𐐻𐐭 𐑄𐐯𐑋 𐐸𐐮𐑆 𐐿𐐲𐑌𐑂𐐲𐑉𐑇𐐲𐑌 𐐶𐐮𐑄 𐐈𐑋𐐲𐑌, 𐐰𐑌𐐼 𐐁𐑉𐐲𐑌, 𐐰𐑌𐐼 𐐸𐐮𐑆 𐐺𐑉𐐯𐑄𐑉𐐯𐑌. 𐐈𐑌𐐼 𐐮𐐻 𐐿𐐩𐑋 𐐻𐐭 𐐹𐐪𐑅 𐑄𐐰𐐻 𐐮𐐻 𐐼𐐮𐐼 𐐿𐐫𐑆 𐑀𐑉𐐩𐐻 𐐾𐐱𐐮 𐐲𐑋𐐲𐑍 𐑄𐐯𐑋. 𐐈𐑌𐐼 𐑄𐐩 𐐶𐐯𐑌𐐻 𐐼𐐵𐑌 𐐮𐑌𐐻𐐭 𐑄 𐑊𐐰𐑌𐐼 𐐱𐑂 𐐖𐐲𐑉𐑇𐐲𐑌, 𐐰𐑌𐐼 𐐻𐐳𐐿 𐐹𐐲𐑆𐐯𐑇𐐲𐑌 𐐱𐑂 𐑄 𐑊𐐰𐑌𐐼 𐐱𐑂 𐐖𐐲𐑉𐑇𐐲𐑌; 𐐰𐑌𐐼 𐑄𐐩 𐐶𐐲𐑉 𐐿𐐫𐑊𐐼 𐐺𐐴 𐑄 𐐤𐐨𐑁𐐴𐐻𐑅 𐑄 𐐹𐐨𐐹𐑊 𐐱𐑂 𐐈𐑋𐐲𐑌: 𐑄𐐩𐑉𐑁𐐫𐑉, 𐑄𐐩 𐐶𐐲𐑉 𐐼𐐮𐑅𐐻𐐮𐑍𐑀𐐶𐐮𐑇𐐻 𐐺𐐴 𐑄𐐰𐐻 𐑌𐐩𐑋 𐐯𐑂𐐲𐑉 𐐪𐑁𐐻𐐲𐑉; 𐐰𐑌𐐼 𐑄𐐩 𐐶𐐲𐑉 𐐲𐑋𐐲𐑍 𐑄 𐐹𐐨𐐹𐑊 𐐱𐑂 𐐤𐐨𐑁𐐴, 𐐰𐑌𐐼 𐐫𐑊𐑅𐐬 𐑌𐐲𐑋𐐺𐐲𐑉𐐼 𐐲𐑋𐐲𐑍 𐑄 𐐹𐐨𐐹𐑊 𐐸𐐭 𐐶𐐲𐑉 𐐱𐑂 𐑄 𐐽𐐲𐑉𐐽 𐐱𐑂 𐐘𐐱𐐼. 𐐈𐑌𐐼 𐑄𐐩 𐐶𐐲𐑉 𐐫𐑊𐑅𐐬 𐐼𐐮𐑅𐐻𐐮𐑍𐑀𐐶𐐮𐑇𐐻 𐑁𐐫𐑉 𐑄𐐩𐑉 𐑆𐐨𐑊 𐐻𐐬𐐲𐑉𐐼𐑆 𐐘𐐱𐐼, 𐐰𐑌𐐼 𐐫𐑊𐑅𐐬 𐐻𐐬𐐲𐑉𐐼𐑆 𐑋𐐯𐑌; 𐑁𐐫𐑉 𐑄𐐩 𐐶𐐲𐑉 𐐹𐐲𐑉𐑁𐐯𐐿𐐻𐑊𐐨 𐐱𐑌𐐯𐑅𐐻 𐐰𐑌𐐼 𐐲𐐹𐑉𐐴𐐻 𐐮𐑌 𐐫𐑊 𐑃𐐮𐑍𐑆; 𐐰𐑌𐐼 𐑄𐐩 𐐶𐐲𐑉 𐑁𐐲𐑉𐑋 𐐮𐑌 𐑄 𐑁𐐩𐑃 𐐱𐑂 𐐗𐑉𐐴𐑅𐐻, 𐐨𐑂𐑌 𐐲𐑌𐐻𐐭 𐑄 𐐯𐑌𐐼. 𐐈𐑌𐐼 𐑄𐐩 𐐼𐐮𐐼 𐑊𐐳𐐿 𐐲𐐹𐐱𐑌 𐑇𐐯𐐼𐐮𐑍 𐑄 𐐺𐑊𐐲𐐼 𐐱𐑂 𐑄𐐩𐑉 𐐺𐑉𐐯𐑄𐑉𐐯𐑌 𐐶𐐮𐑄 𐑄 𐑀𐑉𐐩𐐻𐐯𐑅𐐻 𐐰𐐺𐐸𐐫𐑉𐐯𐑌𐑅; 𐐰𐑌𐐼 𐑄𐐩 𐑌𐐯𐑂𐐲𐑉 𐐿𐐳𐐼 𐐺 𐐹𐑉𐐨𐑂𐐩𐑊𐐼 𐐲𐐹𐐱𐑌

𐐻𐐭 𐐻𐐩𐐿 𐐲𐐹 𐐪𐑉𐑋𐑆 𐐲𐑀𐐯𐑌𐑅𐐻 𐑄𐐩𐑉 𐐺𐑉𐐯𐑄𐑉𐐯𐑌; 𐐰𐑌𐐼 𐑄𐐩 𐑌𐐯𐑂𐐲𐑉 𐐼𐐮𐐼 𐑊𐐳𐐿 𐐲𐐹𐐱𐑌 𐐼𐐯𐑃 𐐶𐐮𐑄 𐐯𐑌𐐮 𐐼𐐨𐑀𐑉𐐨 𐐱𐑂 𐐻𐐯𐑉𐐲𐑉, 𐑁𐐫𐑉 𐑄𐐩𐑉 𐐸𐐬𐐹 𐐰𐑌𐐼 𐑂𐑏𐑆 𐐱𐑂 𐐗𐑉𐐴𐑅𐐻 𐐰𐑌𐐼 𐑄 𐑉𐐯𐑆𐐲𐑉𐐯𐐿𐑇𐐲𐑌; 𐑄𐐩𐑉𐑁𐐬𐑉, 𐐼𐐯𐑃 𐐶𐐱𐑆 𐑅𐐶𐐱𐑊𐐬𐐼 𐐲𐐹 𐐻𐐭 𐑄𐐯𐑋 𐐺𐐴 𐑄 𐑂𐐮𐐿𐐻𐐲𐑉𐐮 𐐱𐑂 𐐗𐑉𐐴𐑅𐐻 𐐬𐑂𐐲𐑉 𐐮𐐻; 𐑄𐐩𐑉𐑁𐐬𐑉, 𐑄𐐩 𐐶𐐳𐐼 𐑅𐐲𐑁𐐲𐑉 𐐼𐐯𐑃 𐐮𐑌 𐑄 𐑋𐐬𐑅𐐻 𐐰𐑀𐑉𐐲𐑂𐐩𐐻𐐮𐑍 𐐰𐑌𐐼 𐐼𐐮𐑅𐐻𐑉𐐯𐑅𐐮𐑍 𐑋𐐰𐑌𐐲𐑉 𐐸𐐶𐐮𐐽 𐐿𐐳𐐼 𐐺𐐨 𐐮𐑌𐑁𐑊𐐮𐐿𐐻𐐯𐐼 𐐺𐐴 𐑄𐐩𐑉 𐐺𐑉𐐯𐑄𐑉𐐯𐑌, 𐐺𐐨𐑁𐐬𐑉 𐑄𐐩 𐐶𐐳𐐼 𐐻𐐩𐐿 𐑄 𐑅𐐬𐑉𐐼 𐐫𐑉 𐑅𐐮𐑋𐐲𐐻𐐲𐑉 𐐻𐐭 𐑅𐑋𐐴𐐻 𐑄𐐯𐑋. 𐐈𐑌𐐼 𐑄𐐲𐑅 𐑄𐐩 𐐶𐐲𐑉 𐐲 𐑆𐐯𐑊𐐲𐑅 𐐰𐑌𐐼 𐐺𐐨𐑊𐐲𐑂𐐯𐐼 𐐹𐐨𐐹𐑊, 𐐲 𐐸𐐴𐑊𐐨 𐑁𐐩𐑂𐐲𐑉𐐼 𐐹𐐨𐐹𐑊 𐐱𐑂 𐑄 𐐢𐐫𐑉𐐼.

9. 𐐈𐑌𐐼 𐑌𐐵 𐐮𐐻 𐐿𐐩𐑋 𐐻𐐭 𐐹𐐰𐑅, 𐑄𐐰𐐻 𐐰𐑁𐐻𐐲𐑉 𐑄 𐐹𐐨𐐹𐑊 𐐱𐑂 𐐈𐑋𐐲𐑌 𐐶𐐲𐑉 𐐯𐑅𐐻𐐰𐐺𐑊𐐮𐑇𐐻 𐐮𐑌 𐑄 𐑊𐐰𐑌𐐼 𐐱𐑂 𐐖𐐲𐑉𐑇𐐲𐑌, 𐐰𐑌𐐼 𐐲 𐐽𐐲𐑉𐐽 𐐫𐑊𐑅𐐬 𐐯𐑅𐐻𐐰𐐺𐑊𐐮𐑇𐐻 𐐮𐑌 𐑄 𐑊𐐰𐑌𐐼 𐐱𐑂 𐐖𐐲𐑉𐑇𐐲𐑌; 𐐰𐑌𐐼 𐑄 𐐪𐑉𐑋𐐨𐑆 𐐱𐑂 𐑄 𐐤𐐨𐑁𐐴𐐻𐑅 𐐶𐐲𐑉 𐑅𐐯𐐻 𐑉𐐵𐑌𐐼 𐐲𐐺𐐵𐐻 𐑄 𐑊𐐰𐑌𐐼 𐐱𐑂 𐐖𐐲𐑉𐑇𐐲𐑌; 𐐷𐐩, 𐐮𐑌 𐐫𐑊 𐑄 𐐺𐐫𐑉𐐼𐐲𐑉𐑆 𐑉𐐵𐑌𐐼 𐐲𐐺𐐵𐐻 𐑄 𐑊𐐰𐑌𐐼 𐐱𐑂 𐐞𐐰𐑉𐐲𐐸𐐯𐑋𐑊𐐲; 𐐺𐐨𐐸𐐬𐑊𐐼 𐑄 𐐪𐑉𐑋𐐨𐑆 𐐱𐑂 𐑄 𐐢𐐰𐑋𐐲𐑌𐐴𐐻𐑅 𐐸𐐰𐐼 𐑁𐐱𐑊𐐬𐐼 𐑄𐐩𐑉 𐐺𐑉𐐯𐑄𐑉𐐯𐑌 𐐮𐑌𐐻𐐭 𐑄 𐐶𐐮𐑊𐐼𐐲𐑉𐑌𐐯𐑅. 𐐈𐑌𐐼 𐑄𐐲𐑅 𐑄𐐩𐑉 𐐶𐐱𐑆 𐐲 𐐻𐑉𐐨𐑋𐐯𐑌𐐼𐐲𐑅 𐐺𐐰𐐻𐑊; 𐐷𐐩, 𐐨𐑂𐐯𐑌 𐑅𐐲𐐽 𐐰𐑌 𐐶𐐲𐑌 𐐰𐑆 𐑌𐐯𐑂𐐲𐑉 𐐸𐐰𐐼 𐐺𐐮𐑌 𐑌𐐬𐑌 𐐲𐑋𐐲𐑍 𐐫𐑊 𐑄 𐐹𐐨𐐹𐑊 𐐮𐑌 𐑄 𐑊𐐰𐑌𐐼 𐑁𐑉𐐱𐑋 𐑄 𐐻𐐴𐑋 𐐢𐐨𐐸𐐴 𐑊𐐯𐑁𐐻 𐐖𐐯𐑉𐐭𐑅𐐲𐑊𐐯𐑋; 𐐷𐐩, 𐐰𐑌𐐼 𐐻𐐯𐑌𐑆 𐐱𐑂 𐑃𐐵𐑆𐐲𐑌𐐼𐑆 𐐱𐑂 𐑄 𐐢𐐰𐑋𐐲𐑌𐐴𐐻𐑅 𐐶𐐲𐑉 𐑅𐑊𐐩𐑌 𐐰𐑌𐐼 𐑅𐐿𐐰𐐻𐐲𐑉𐐯𐐼 𐐲𐐺𐑉𐐫𐐼. 𐐏𐐩, 𐐰𐑌𐐼 𐐫𐑊𐑅𐐬 𐑄𐐩𐑉 𐐶𐐱𐑆 𐐲 𐐻𐑉𐐨𐑋𐐯𐑌𐐼𐐲𐑅 𐑅𐑊𐐫𐐻𐐲𐑉 𐐲𐑋𐐲𐑍 𐑄 𐐹𐐨𐐹𐑊 𐐱𐑂 𐐤𐐨𐑁𐐴; 𐑌𐐯𐑂𐐲𐑉𐑄𐐯𐑊𐐯𐑅, 𐑄 𐐢𐐰𐑋𐐲𐑌𐐴𐐻𐑅 𐐶𐐲𐑉 𐐼𐑉𐐮𐑂𐐯𐑌 𐐰𐑌𐐼 𐑅𐐿𐐰𐐻𐐲𐑉𐐯𐐼, 𐐰𐑌𐐼 𐑄 𐐹𐐨𐐹𐑊 𐐱𐑂 𐐤𐐨𐑁𐐴 𐑉𐐨𐐻𐐲𐑉𐑌𐐼 𐐲𐑀𐐯𐑌 𐐻𐐭 𐑄𐐩𐑉 𐑊𐐰𐑌𐐼. 𐐈𐑌𐐼 𐑌𐐵 𐑄𐐮𐑅 𐐶𐐱𐑆 𐐲 𐐻𐐴𐑋 𐑄𐐰𐐻 𐑄𐐩𐑉 𐐶𐐱𐑆 𐐲 𐑀𐑉𐐩𐐻 𐑋𐐬𐑉𐑌𐐮𐑍 𐐰𐑌𐐼 𐑊𐐰𐑋𐐯𐑌𐐻𐐩𐑇𐐲𐑌 𐐸𐐲𐑉𐐼 𐑃𐑉𐐭𐐵𐐻 𐐫𐑊 𐑄 𐑊𐐰𐑌𐐼, 𐐲𐑋𐐲𐑍 𐐫𐑊 𐑄 𐐹𐐨𐐹𐑊 𐐱𐑂 𐐤𐐨𐑁𐐴; 𐐷𐐩, 𐑄 𐐿𐑉𐐴 𐐱𐑂 𐐶𐐮𐐼𐐬𐑆 𐑋𐐬𐑉𐑌𐐮𐑍 𐑁𐐫𐑉 𐑄𐐩𐑉 𐐸𐐲𐑆𐐺𐐲𐑌𐐼𐑆, 𐐰𐑌𐐼 𐐫𐑊𐑅𐐬 𐐱𐑂 𐑁𐐪𐑄𐐲𐑉𐑆 𐑋𐐬𐑉𐑌𐐮𐑍 𐑁𐐫𐑉 𐑄𐐩𐑉 𐑅𐐲𐑌𐑆, 𐐰𐑌𐐼 𐑄 𐐼𐐫𐐻𐐲𐑉 𐑁𐐫𐑉 𐑄 𐐺𐑉𐐲𐑄𐐲𐑉; 𐐷𐐩, 𐑄 𐐺𐑉𐐲𐑄𐐲𐑉 𐑁𐐫𐑉 𐑄 𐑁𐐪𐑄𐐲𐑉: 𐐰𐑌𐐼 𐑄𐐲𐑅 𐑄 𐐿𐑉𐐴 𐐱𐑂 𐑋𐐬𐑉𐑌𐐮𐑍 𐐶𐐱𐑆 𐐸𐐲𐑉𐐼 𐐲𐑋𐐲𐑍 𐐫𐑊 𐐱𐑂 𐑄𐐯𐑋: 𐑋𐐬𐑉𐑌𐐮𐑍 𐑁𐐫𐑉 𐑄𐐩𐑉 𐐿𐐮𐑌𐐼𐑉𐐯𐐼 𐐸𐐭 𐐸𐐰𐐼 𐐺𐐮𐑌 𐑅𐑊𐐩𐑌. 𐐈𐑌𐐼 𐑌𐐵 𐑇𐐭𐑉𐑊𐐨 𐑄𐐮𐑅 𐐶𐐱𐑆 𐐲 𐑅𐐱𐑉𐐬𐑁𐐳𐑊 𐐼𐐩; 𐐷𐐩, 𐐲 𐐻𐐴𐑋 𐐱𐑂 𐑅𐐬𐑊𐐯𐑋𐑌𐐮𐐻𐐨, 𐐰𐑌𐐼 𐐲 𐐻𐐴𐑋 𐐱𐑂 𐑋𐐲𐐽 𐑁𐐪𐑅𐐻𐐮𐑍 𐐰𐑌𐐼 𐐹𐑉𐐩𐐲𐑉: 𐐰𐑌𐐼 𐑄𐐲𐑅 𐐯𐑌𐐼𐐯𐑃 𐑄 𐑁𐐮𐑁𐐻𐐨𐑌𐑃 𐐷𐐨𐑉 𐐱𐑂 𐑄 𐑉𐐩𐑌 𐐱𐑂 𐑄 𐐾𐐲𐐾𐐯𐑆 𐐬𐑂𐐲𐑉 𐑄 𐐹𐐨𐐹𐑊 𐐱𐑂 𐐤𐐨𐑁𐐴; 𐐰𐑌𐐼 𐑄𐐮𐑅 𐐮𐑆 𐑄 𐐲𐐿𐐵𐑌𐐻 𐐱𐑂 𐐈𐑋𐐲𐑌 𐐰𐑌𐐼 𐐸𐐮𐑆 𐐺𐑉𐐯𐑄𐑉𐐯𐑌, 𐑄𐐩𐑉 𐐾𐐲𐑉𐑌𐐨𐐮𐑍𐑆 𐐮𐑌 𐑄 𐑊𐐰𐑌𐐼 𐐱𐑂 𐐤𐐨𐑁𐐴, 𐑄𐐩𐑉 𐑅𐐲𐑁𐐲𐑉𐐮𐑍𐑆 𐐮𐑌 𐑄 𐑊𐐰𐑌𐐼, 𐑄𐐩𐑉 𐑅𐐱𐑉𐐬𐑆, 𐐰𐑌𐐼 𐑄𐐩𐑉 𐐰𐑁𐑊𐐮𐐿𐑇𐐲𐑌𐑆, 𐐰𐑌𐐼 𐑄𐐩𐑉 𐐮𐑌𐐿𐐱𐑋𐐹𐑉𐐨𐐸𐐯𐑌𐑅𐐮𐐺𐑊 𐐾𐑎, 𐐰𐑌𐐼 𐑄 𐑉𐐨𐑅𐐯𐐹𐑇𐐲𐑌 𐐰𐑌𐐼 𐑅𐐩𐑁𐐻𐐨 𐐱𐑂 𐑄 𐐺𐑉𐐯𐑄𐑉𐐯𐑌 𐐮𐑌 𐑄 𐑊𐐰𐑌𐐼 𐐱𐑂 𐐖𐐲𐑉𐑇𐐲𐑌. 𐐈𐑌𐐼 𐑌𐐵 𐑋𐐩 𐑄 𐐢𐐫𐑉𐐼, 𐑄 𐐡𐐨𐐼𐐨𐑋𐐲𐑉 𐐱𐑂 𐐫𐑊 𐑋𐐯𐑌, 𐐺𐑊𐐯𐑅 𐑄𐐩𐑉 𐑅𐐬𐑊𐑆 𐑁𐐫𐑉𐐯𐑂𐐲𐑉.

10. 𐐈𐑌𐐼 𐑄𐐮𐑅 𐐮𐑆 𐑄 𐐲𐐿𐐵𐑌𐐻 𐐱𐑂 𐑄 𐐶𐐫𐑉𐑆 𐐰𐑌𐐼 𐐿𐐱𐑌𐐻𐐯𐑌𐑇𐐲𐑌𐑆 𐐲𐑋𐐲𐑍 𐑄 𐐤𐐨𐑁𐐴𐐻𐑅, 𐐰𐑌𐐼 𐐫𐑊𐑅𐐬 𐑄 𐐶𐐫𐑉𐑆 𐐺𐐨𐐻𐐶𐐨𐑌 𐑄 𐐤𐐨𐑁𐐴𐐻𐑅 𐐰𐑌𐐼 𐑄 𐐢𐐰𐑋𐐲𐑌𐐴𐐻𐑅: 𐐰𐑌𐐼 𐑄 𐑁𐐮𐑁𐐻𐐨𐑌𐑃 𐐷𐐨𐑉 𐐱𐑂 𐑄 𐑉𐐩𐑌 𐐱𐑂 𐑄 𐐾𐐲𐐾𐐯𐑆 𐐮𐑆 𐐯𐑌𐐼𐐯𐐼; 𐐰𐑌𐐼 𐑁𐑉𐐱𐑋 𐑄 𐑁𐐲𐑉𐑅𐐻 𐐷𐐨𐑉 𐐻𐐭 𐑄 𐑁𐐮𐑁𐐻𐐨𐑌𐑃, 𐐸𐐰𐑆 𐐺𐑉𐐫𐐻 𐐻𐐭 𐐹𐐰𐑅 𐑄 𐐼𐐯𐑅𐐻𐑉𐐲𐐿𐑇𐐲𐑌 𐐱𐑂 𐑋𐐯𐑌𐐮 𐑃𐐵𐑆𐐲𐑌𐐼 𐑊𐐴𐑂𐑆; 𐐷𐐩, 𐐮𐐻 𐐸𐐰𐑆 𐐺𐑉𐐫𐐻 𐐻𐐭 𐐹𐐰𐑅 𐐰𐑌 𐐫𐑁𐐳𐑊 𐑅𐐨𐑌 𐐱𐑂 𐐺𐑊𐐲𐐼𐑇𐐯𐐼; 𐐰𐑌𐐼 𐑄 𐐺𐐱𐐼𐐨𐑆 𐐱𐑂 𐑋𐐯𐑌𐐮 𐑃𐐵𐑆𐐲𐑌𐐼𐑆 𐐪𐑉 𐑊𐐩𐐼 𐑊𐐬 𐐮𐑌 𐑄 𐐲𐑉𐑃, 𐐸𐐶𐐴𐑊 𐑄 𐐺𐐱𐐼𐐨𐑆 𐐱𐑂 𐑋𐐯𐑌𐐮 𐑃𐐵𐑆𐐲𐑌𐐼𐑆 𐐪𐑉 𐑋𐐬𐑊𐐼𐐲𐑉𐐮𐑍 𐐮𐑌 𐐸𐐨𐐹𐑅 𐐲𐐹𐐱𐑌 𐑄 𐑁𐐩𐑅 𐐱𐑂 𐑄 𐐲𐑉𐑃; 𐐷𐐩, 𐐰𐑌𐐼 𐑋𐐯𐑌𐐮 𐑃𐐵𐑆𐐲𐑌𐐼𐑆 𐐪𐑉 𐑋𐐬𐑉𐑌𐐮𐑍 𐑁𐐫𐑉 𐑄 𐑊𐐱𐑅 𐐱𐑂 𐑄𐐩𐑉 𐐿𐐮𐑌𐐼𐑉𐐯𐐼, 𐐺𐐨𐐿𐐫𐑆 𐑄𐐩 𐐸𐐰𐑂 𐑉𐐨𐑆𐐲𐑌 𐐻𐐭 𐑁𐐨𐑉, 𐐰𐐿𐐫𐑉𐐼𐐮𐑍 𐐻𐐭 𐑄 𐐹𐑉𐐱𐑋𐐮𐑅𐐯𐑆 𐐱𐑂 𐑄 𐐢𐐫𐑉𐐼, 𐑄𐐰𐐻 𐑄𐐩 𐐪𐑉 𐐿𐐱𐑌𐑅𐐴𐑌𐐼 𐐻𐐭 𐐲 𐑅𐐻𐐩𐐻 𐐱𐑂 𐐯𐑌𐐼𐑊𐐯𐑅 𐐶𐐬; 𐐸𐐶𐐴𐑊 𐑋𐐯𐑌𐐮 𐑃𐐵𐑆𐐲𐑌𐐼𐑆 𐐱𐑂 𐐲𐑄𐐲𐑉𐑆 𐐻𐑉𐐭𐑊𐐨 𐑋𐐬𐑉𐑌 𐑁𐐫𐑉 𐑄 𐑊𐐱𐑅 𐐱𐑂 𐑄𐐩𐑉 𐐿𐐮𐑌𐐼𐑉𐐯𐐼, 𐐷𐐯𐐻 𐑄𐐩 𐑉𐐨𐐾𐑎𐑅 𐐰𐑌𐐼 𐐯𐑀𐑆𐐲𐑊𐐻 𐐮𐑌 𐑄 𐐸𐐬𐐹, 𐐰𐑌𐐼 𐐨𐑂𐐯𐑌 𐑌𐐬, 𐐰𐐿𐐫𐑉𐐼𐐮𐑍 𐐻𐐭 𐑄 𐐹𐑉𐐱𐑋𐐮𐑅𐐯𐑆 𐐱𐑂 𐑄 𐐢𐐫𐑉𐐼, 𐑄𐐰𐐻 𐑄𐐩 𐐪𐑉 𐑉𐐩𐑆𐐼 𐐻𐐭 𐐼𐐶𐐯𐑊 𐐰𐐻 𐑄 𐑉𐐴𐐻 𐐸𐐰𐑌𐐼 𐐱𐑂 𐐘𐐱𐐼, 𐐮𐑌 𐐲 𐑅𐐻𐐩𐐻 𐐱𐑂 𐑌𐐯𐑂𐐲𐑉-𐐯𐑌𐐼𐐮𐑍 𐐸𐐰𐐹𐐮𐑌𐐯𐑅: 𐐰𐑌𐐼 𐑄𐐲𐑅 𐐶𐐨 𐑅𐐨 𐐸𐐵 𐑀𐑉𐐩𐐻 𐑄 𐐮𐑌𐐨𐐿𐐶𐐱𐑊𐐮𐐻𐐨 𐐱𐑂 𐑋𐐰𐑌 𐐮𐑆 𐐺𐐨𐐿𐐫𐑆 𐐱𐑂 𐑅𐐮𐑌 𐐰𐑌𐐼 𐐻𐑉𐐰𐑌𐑅𐑀𐑉𐐯𐑇𐐲𐑌, 𐐰𐑌𐐼 𐑄 𐐹𐐵𐐲𐑉 𐐱𐑂 𐑄 𐐼𐐯𐑂𐐮𐑊, 𐐸𐐶𐐮𐐽 𐐿𐐲𐑋𐑆 𐐺𐐴 𐑄 𐐿𐐲𐑌𐐮𐑍 𐐹𐑊𐐰𐑌𐑆 𐐸𐐶𐐮𐐽 𐐸𐐨 𐐸𐐰𐑃 𐐼𐐨𐑂𐐴𐑆𐐼 𐐻𐐭 𐐯𐑌𐑅𐑌𐐩𐑉 𐑄 𐐸𐐪𐑉𐐻𐑅 𐐱𐑂 𐑋𐐯𐑌; 𐐰𐑌𐐼 𐑄𐐲𐑅 𐐶𐐨 𐑅𐐨 𐑄 𐑀𐑉𐐩𐐻 𐐿𐐫𐑊 𐐱𐑂 𐐼𐐮𐑊𐐮𐐾𐐯𐑌𐑅 𐐱𐑂 𐑋𐐯𐑌 𐐻𐐭 𐑊𐐩𐐺𐐲𐑉 𐐮𐑌 𐑄 𐑂𐐮𐑌𐐷𐐲𐑉𐐼𐑆 𐐱𐑂 𐑄 𐐢𐐫𐑉𐐼; 𐐰𐑌𐐼 𐑄𐐲𐑅 𐐶𐐨 𐑅𐐨 𐑄 𐑀𐑉𐐩𐐻 𐑉𐐨𐑆𐐲𐑌 𐐱𐑂 𐑅𐐱𐑉𐐬, 𐐰𐑌𐐼 𐐫𐑊𐑅𐐬 𐐱𐑂 𐑉𐐨-

𐐾𐐱𐐮𐑅𐐮𐑍; 𐑅𐐱𐑉𐐬 𐐺𐐨𐐿𐐫𐑆 𐐱𐑂 𐐼𐐯𐑃 𐐰𐑌𐐼 𐐼𐐨𐑅𐐻𐑉𐐲𐐿𐑇𐐲𐑌 𐐲𐑋𐐲𐑍 𐑋𐐯𐑌, 𐐰𐑌𐐼 𐐾𐐱𐐮 𐐺𐐨𐐿𐐫𐑆 𐐱𐑂 𐑄 𐑊𐐴𐐻 𐐱𐑂 𐐗𐑉𐐴𐑅𐐻 𐐲𐑌𐐻𐐭 𐑊𐐴𐑁.

11. 𐐄 𐑄𐐰𐐻 𐐌 𐐶𐐲𐑉 𐐰𐑌 𐐁𐑌𐐾𐐯𐑊, 𐐰𐑌𐐼 𐐿𐐳𐐼 𐐸𐐰𐑂 𐑄 𐐶𐐮𐑇 𐐱𐑂 𐑋𐐴𐑌 𐐸𐐪𐑉𐐻, 𐑄𐐰𐐻 𐐌 𐑋𐐴𐐻 𐑀𐐬 𐑁𐐫𐑉𐑃 𐐰𐑌𐐼 𐑅𐐹𐐨𐐿 𐐶𐐮𐑄 𐑄 𐐻𐑉𐐲𐑋𐐹 𐐱𐑂 𐐘𐐱𐐼, 𐐶𐐮𐑄 𐐩 𐑂𐐱𐐮𐑅 𐐻𐐭 𐑇𐐩𐐿 𐑄 𐐲𐑉𐑃, 𐐰𐑌𐐼 𐐿𐑉𐐴 𐑉𐐨𐐹𐐯𐑌𐐻𐐲𐑌𐑅 𐐲𐑌𐐻𐐭 𐐯𐑂𐐲𐑉𐐨 𐐹𐐨𐐹𐐲𐑊; 𐐷𐐩, 𐐌 𐐶𐐳𐐼 𐐼𐐨𐐿𐑊𐐩𐑉 𐐲𐑌𐐻𐐭 𐐯𐑂𐐲𐑉𐐨 𐑅𐐬𐑊, 𐐰𐑆 𐐶𐐮𐑄 𐑄 𐑂𐐱𐐮𐑅 𐐱𐑂 𐑃𐐲𐑌𐐼𐐲𐑉, 𐑉𐐨𐐹𐐯𐑌𐐻𐐲𐑌𐑅, 𐐰𐑌𐐼 𐑄 𐐹𐑊𐐰𐑌 𐐱𐑂 𐑉𐐨𐐼𐐯𐑋𐑇𐐲𐑌, 𐑄𐐰𐐻 𐑄𐐩 𐑇𐐳𐐼 𐑉𐐨𐐹𐐯𐑌𐐻 𐐰𐑌𐐼 𐐿𐐲𐑋 𐐲𐑌𐐻𐐭 𐐵𐑉 𐐘𐐱𐐼, 𐑄𐐰𐐻 𐑄𐐯𐑉 𐑋𐐴𐐻 𐑌𐐱𐐻 𐐺 𐑋𐐬𐑉 𐑅𐐱𐑉𐐬 𐐲𐐹𐐱𐑌 𐐫𐑊 𐑄 𐑁𐐩𐑅 𐐱𐑂 𐑄 𐐲𐑉𐑃. 𐐒𐐲𐐻 𐐺𐐨𐐸𐐬𐑊𐐼, 𐐌 𐐰𐑋 𐐩 𐑋𐐰𐑌, 𐐰𐑌𐐼 𐐼𐐭 𐑅𐐮𐑌 𐐮𐑌 𐑋𐐴 𐐶𐐮𐑇; 𐑁𐐫𐑉 𐐌 𐐫𐐻 𐐻𐐭 𐐺 𐐿𐐱𐑌𐐻𐐯𐑌𐐻 𐐶𐐮𐑄 𐑄 𐑃𐐮𐑍𐑆 𐐸𐐶𐐮𐐽 𐑄 𐐢𐐫𐑉𐐼 𐐸𐐰𐑃 𐐰𐑊𐐱𐐻𐐯𐐼 𐐲𐑌𐐻𐐭 𐑋𐐨. 𐐌 𐐫𐐻 𐑌𐐱𐐻 𐐻𐐭 𐐸𐐰𐑉𐐬 𐐲𐐹 𐐮𐑌 𐑋𐐴 𐐼𐐨𐑆𐐴𐑉𐑆, 𐑄 𐑁𐐲𐑉𐑋 𐐼𐐨𐐿𐑉𐐨 𐐱𐑂 𐐩 𐐾𐐲𐑅𐐻 𐐘𐐱𐐼, 𐑁𐐫𐑉 𐐌 𐑌𐐬 𐑄𐐰𐐻 𐐸𐐨 𐑀𐑉𐐰𐑌𐐻𐐯𐑃 𐐲𐑌𐐻𐐭 𐑋𐐯𐑌 𐐰𐐿𐐫𐑉𐐼𐐮𐑍 𐐻𐐭 𐑄𐐯𐑉 𐐼𐐨𐑆𐐴𐑉, 𐐸𐐶𐐯𐑄𐐲𐑉 𐐮𐐻 𐐺 𐐲𐑌𐐻𐐭 𐐼𐐯𐑃 𐐫𐑉 𐐲𐑌𐐻𐐭 𐑊𐐴𐑁; 𐐷𐐩, 𐐌 𐑌𐐬 𐑄𐐰𐐻 𐐸𐐨 𐐰𐑊𐐱𐐻𐐯𐑃 𐐲𐑌𐐻𐐭 𐑋𐐯𐑌, 𐐰𐐿𐐫𐑉𐐼𐐮𐑍 𐐻𐐭 𐑄𐐯𐑉 𐐶𐐮𐑊𐑆; 𐐸𐐶𐐯𐑄𐐲𐑉 𐑄𐐩 𐐺 𐐲𐑌𐐻𐐭 𐑅𐐰𐑊𐑂𐐩𐑇𐐲𐑌 𐐫𐑉 𐐲𐑌𐐻𐐭 𐐼𐐨𐑅𐐻𐑉𐐲𐐿𐑇𐐲𐑌; 𐐷𐐩, 𐐰𐑌𐐼 𐐌 𐑌𐐬 𐑄𐐰𐐻 𐑀𐐳𐐼 𐐰𐑌𐐼 𐐨𐑂𐐲𐑊 𐐸𐐰𐑂 𐐿𐐲𐑋 𐐺𐐨𐑁𐐬𐑉 𐐫𐑊 𐑋𐐯𐑌; 𐐫𐑉 𐐸𐐨 𐑄𐐰𐐻 𐑌𐐬𐐯𐑃 𐑌𐐱𐐻 𐑀𐐳𐐼 𐑁𐑉𐐱𐑋 𐐨𐑂𐐲𐑊 𐐮𐑆 𐐺𐑊𐐩𐑋𐑊𐐯𐑅; 𐐺𐐲𐐻 𐐸𐐨 𐑄𐐰𐐻 𐑌𐐬𐐯𐑃 𐑀𐐳𐐼 𐐰𐑌𐐼 𐐨𐑂𐐲𐑊, 𐐻𐐭 𐐸𐐮𐑋 𐐮𐐻 𐐮𐑆 𐑀𐐮𐑂𐐲𐑌 𐐰𐐿𐐫𐑉𐐼𐐮𐑍 𐐻𐐭 𐐸𐐮𐑆 𐐼𐐨𐑆𐐴𐑉𐑆; 𐐸𐐶𐐯𐑄𐐲𐑉 𐐸𐐨 𐐼𐐨𐑆𐐴𐑉𐐯𐑃 𐑀𐐳𐐼 𐐫𐑉 𐐨𐑂𐐲𐑊, 𐑊𐐴𐑁 𐐫𐑉 𐐼𐐯𐑃, 𐐾𐐱𐐮 𐐫𐑉 𐑉𐐨𐑋𐐫𐑉𐑅 𐐱𐑂 𐐿𐐱𐑌𐑇𐐯𐑌𐑅.

12. 𐐤𐐵 𐑅𐐨𐐮𐑍 𐑄𐐰𐐻 𐐌 𐑌𐐬 𐑄𐐨𐑆 𐑃𐐮𐑍𐑆, 𐐸𐐶𐐴 𐑇𐐳𐐼 𐐌 𐐼𐐨𐑆𐐴𐑉 𐑋𐐬𐑉 𐑄𐐰𐑌 𐐻𐐭 𐐹𐐲𐑉𐑁𐐫𐑉𐑋 𐑄 𐐶𐐲𐑉𐐿 𐐻𐐭 𐐸𐐶𐐮𐐽 𐐌 𐐸𐐰𐑂 𐐺𐐮𐑌 𐐿𐐫𐑊𐐼? 𐐐𐐶𐐴 𐑇𐐳𐐼 𐐌 𐐼𐐨𐑆𐐴𐑉 𐑄𐐰𐐻 𐐌 𐐶𐐱𐑆 𐐰𐑌 𐐁𐑌𐐾𐐯𐑊, 𐑄𐐰𐐻 𐐌 𐐿𐐳𐐼 𐑅𐐹𐐨𐐿 𐐲𐑌𐐻𐐭 𐐫𐑊 𐑄 𐐯𐑌𐐼𐑆 𐐱𐑂 𐑄 𐐲𐑉𐑃? 𐐙𐐫𐑉 𐐺𐐨𐐸𐐬𐑊𐐼, 𐑄 𐐢𐐫𐑉𐐼 𐐼𐐲𐑃 𐑀𐑉𐐰𐑌𐐻 𐐲𐑌𐐻𐐭 𐐫𐑊 𐑌𐐩𐑇𐐲𐑌𐑆, 𐐱𐑂 𐑄𐐯𐑉 𐐬𐑌 𐑌𐐩𐑇𐐲𐑌 𐐰𐑌𐐼 𐐻𐐲𐑍, 𐐻𐐭 𐐻𐐨𐐽 𐐸𐐮𐑆 𐐶𐐲𐑉𐐼, 𐐷𐐩, 𐐮𐑌 𐐶𐐮𐑆𐐼𐐲𐑋, 𐐫𐑊 𐑄𐐰𐐻 𐐸𐐨 𐑅𐐨𐐯𐑃 𐑁𐐮𐐻 𐑄𐐰𐐻 𐑄𐐩 𐑇𐐳𐐼 𐐸𐐰𐑂; 𐑄𐐯𐑉𐑁𐐬𐑉 𐐶𐐨 𐑅𐐨 𐑄𐐰𐐻 𐑄 𐐢𐐫𐑉𐐼 𐐼𐐲𐑃 𐐿𐐵𐑌𐑅𐐯𐑊 𐐮𐑌 𐐶𐐮𐑆𐐼𐐲𐑋, 𐐰𐐿𐐫𐑉𐐼𐐮𐑍 𐐻𐐭 𐑄𐐰𐐻 𐐸𐐶𐐮𐐽 𐐮𐑆 𐐾𐐲𐑅𐐻 𐐰𐑌𐐼 𐐻𐑉𐐭. 𐐌 𐑌𐐬 𐑄𐐰𐐻 𐐸𐐶𐐮𐐽 𐑄 𐐢𐐫𐑉𐐼 𐐸𐐰𐑃 𐐿𐐱𐑋𐐰𐑌𐐼𐐯𐐼 𐑋𐐨, 𐐰𐑌𐐼 𐐌 𐑀𐑊𐐬𐑉𐐨 𐐮𐑌 𐐮𐐻; 𐐌 𐐼𐐭 𐑌𐐱𐐻 𐑀𐑊𐐬𐑉𐐨 𐐱𐑂 𐑋𐐴𐑅𐐯𐑊𐑁, 𐐺𐐲𐐻 𐐌 𐑀𐑊𐐬𐑉𐐨 𐐮𐑌 𐑄𐐰𐐻 𐐸𐐶𐐮𐐽 𐑄 𐐢𐐫𐑉𐐼 𐐸𐐰𐑃 𐐿𐐱𐑋𐐰𐑌𐐼𐐯𐐼 𐑋𐐨; 𐐷𐐩, 𐐰𐑌𐐼 𐑄𐐮𐑅 𐐮𐑆 𐑋𐐴 𐑀𐑊𐐬𐑉𐐨, 𐑄𐐰𐐻 𐐹𐐲𐑉𐐸𐐰𐐹𐑅 𐐌 𐑋𐐩 𐐺 𐐰𐑌 𐐮𐑌𐑅𐐻𐑉𐐭-𐑋𐐯𐑌𐐻 𐐮𐑌 𐑄 𐐸𐐰𐑌𐐼𐑆 𐐱𐑂 𐐘𐐱𐐼, 𐐻𐐭 𐐺𐑉𐐮𐑍 𐑅𐐲𐑋 𐑅𐐬𐑊 𐐻𐐭 𐑉𐐨𐐹𐐯𐑌𐐻𐐲𐑌𐑅; 𐐰𐑌𐐼 𐑄𐐮𐑅 𐐮𐑆 𐑋𐐴 𐐾𐐱𐐮. 𐐈𐑌𐐼 𐐺𐐨𐐸𐐬𐑊𐐼, 𐐸𐐶𐐯𐑌 𐐌 𐑅𐐨 𐑋𐐯𐑌𐐨 𐐱𐑂 𐑋𐐴 𐐺𐑉𐐯𐑄𐑉𐐯𐑌 𐐻𐑉𐐭𐑊𐐨 𐐹𐐯𐑌𐐮𐐻𐐯𐑌𐐻, 𐐰𐑌𐐼 𐐿𐐲𐑋𐐮𐑍 𐐻𐐭 𐑄 𐐢𐐫𐑉𐐼 𐑄𐐯𐑉 𐐘𐐱𐐼, 𐑄𐐯𐑌 𐐮𐑆 𐑋𐐴 𐑅𐐬𐑊 𐑁𐐮𐑊𐐼 𐐶𐐮𐑄 𐐾𐐱𐐮; 𐑄𐐯𐑌 𐐼𐐭 𐐌 𐑉𐐨𐑋𐐯𐑋𐐺𐐲𐑉 𐐸𐐶𐐱𐐻 𐑄 𐐢𐐫𐑉𐐼 𐐸𐐰𐑃 𐐼𐐲𐑌 𐑁𐐫𐑉 𐑋𐐨, 𐐷𐐩, 𐐨𐑂𐐯𐑌 𐑄𐐰𐐻 𐐸𐐨 𐐸𐐰𐑃 𐐸𐐲𐑉𐐼 𐑋𐐴 𐐹𐑉𐐩𐑉; 𐐷𐐩, 𐑄𐐯𐑌 𐐼𐐭 𐐌 𐑉𐐨𐑋𐐯𐑋𐐺𐐲𐑉 𐐸𐐮𐑆 𐑋𐐲𐑉𐑅𐐮𐑁𐐳𐑊 𐐪𐑉𐑋 𐐸𐐶𐐮𐐽 𐐸𐐨 𐐯𐐿𐑅𐐻𐐯𐑌𐐼𐐯𐐼 𐐻𐐬𐐲𐑉𐐼𐑆 𐑋𐐨; 𐐷𐐩, 𐐰𐑌𐐼 𐐌 𐐫𐑊𐑅𐐬 𐑉𐐨𐑋𐐯𐑋𐐺𐐲𐑉 𐑄 𐐿𐐰𐐹𐐻𐐮𐑂𐐮𐐻𐐨 𐐱𐑂 𐑋𐐴 𐑁𐐪𐑄𐐲𐑉𐑆; 𐑁𐐫𐑉 𐐌 𐑇𐐳𐑉𐑊𐐨 𐐼𐐭 𐑌𐐬 𐑄𐐰𐐻 𐑄 𐐢𐐫𐑉𐐼 𐐼𐐮𐐼 𐐼𐐨𐑊𐐮𐑂𐐲𐑉 𐑄𐐯𐑋 𐐵𐐻 𐐱𐑂 𐐺𐐱𐑌𐐼𐐩𐐾, 𐐰𐑌𐐼 𐐺𐐴 𐑄𐐮𐑅 𐐼𐐮𐐼 𐐯𐑅𐐻𐐰𐐺𐑊𐐮𐑇 𐐸𐐮𐑆 𐐽𐐲𐑉𐐽; 𐐷𐐩, 𐑄 𐐢𐐫𐑉𐐼 𐐘𐐱𐐼, 𐑄 𐐘𐐱𐐼 𐐱𐑂 𐐁𐐺𐑉𐐲𐐸𐐰𐑋, 𐑄 𐐘𐐱𐐼 𐐱𐑂 𐐌𐑆𐐲𐐿, 𐐰𐑌𐐼 𐑄 𐐘𐐱𐐼 𐐱𐑂 𐐖𐐩𐐿𐐲𐐺, 𐐼𐐮𐐼 𐐼𐐨𐑊𐐮𐑂𐐲𐑉 𐑄𐐯𐑋 𐐵𐐻 𐐱𐑂 𐐺𐐱𐑌𐐼𐐩𐐾; 𐐷𐐩, 𐐌 𐐸𐐰𐑂 𐐫𐑊𐐶𐐩𐑆 𐑉𐐨𐑋𐐯𐑋𐐺𐐲𐑉𐐼 𐑄 𐐿𐐰𐐹𐐻𐐮𐑂𐐮𐐻𐐨 𐐱𐑂 𐑋𐐴 𐑁𐐪𐑄𐐲𐑉𐑆; 𐐰𐑌𐐼 𐑄𐐰𐐻 𐑅𐐩𐑋 𐐘𐐱𐐼 𐐸𐐭 𐐼𐐨𐑊𐐮𐑂𐐲𐑉𐐼 𐑄𐐯𐑋 𐐵𐐻 𐐱𐑂 𐑄 𐐸𐐰𐑌𐐼𐑆 𐐱𐑂 𐑄 𐐀𐐾𐐮𐐹𐑇𐐲𐑌𐑆, 𐐼𐐮𐐼 𐐼𐐨𐑊𐐮𐑂𐐲𐑉 𐑄𐐯𐑋 𐐵𐐻 𐐱𐑂 𐐺𐐱𐑌𐐼𐐩𐐾; 𐐷𐐩, 𐐰𐑌𐐼 𐑄𐐰𐐻 𐑅𐐩𐑋 𐐘𐐱𐐼 𐐼𐐮𐐼 𐐯𐑅𐐻𐐰𐐺𐑊𐐮𐑇 𐐸𐐮𐑆 𐐽𐐲𐑉𐐽 𐐲𐑋𐐲𐑍 𐑄𐐯𐑋; 𐐷𐐩, 𐐰𐑌𐐼 𐑄𐐰𐐻 𐑅𐐩𐑋 𐐘𐐱𐐼 𐐸𐐰𐑃 𐐿𐐫𐑊𐐼 𐑋𐐨 𐐺𐐴 𐐩 𐐸𐐬𐑊𐐨 𐐿𐐫𐑊𐐮𐑍, 𐐻𐐭 𐐹𐑉𐐨𐐽 𐑄 𐐶𐐲𐑉𐐼 𐐲𐑌𐐻𐐭 𐑄𐐮𐑅 𐐹𐐨𐐹𐐲𐑊, 𐐰𐑌𐐼 𐐸𐐰𐑃 𐑀𐐮𐑂𐐲𐑌 𐑋𐐨 𐑋𐐲𐐽 𐑅𐐲𐐿𐑅𐐯𐑅, 𐐮𐑌 𐑄 𐐸𐐶𐐮𐐽 𐑋𐐴 𐐾𐐱𐐮 𐐮𐑆 𐑁𐐳𐑊; 𐐺𐐲𐐻 𐐌 𐐼𐐭 𐑌𐐱𐐻 𐐾𐐱𐐮 𐐮𐑌 𐑋𐐴 𐐬𐑌 𐑅𐐲𐐿𐑅𐐯𐑅 𐐰𐑊𐐬𐑌, 𐐺𐐲𐐻 𐑋𐐴 𐐾𐐱𐐮 𐐮𐑆 𐑋𐐬𐑉 𐑁𐐳𐑊 𐐺𐐨𐐿𐐫𐑆 𐐱𐑂 𐑄 𐑅𐐲𐐿𐑅𐐯𐑅 𐐱𐑂 𐑋𐐴 𐐺𐑉𐐯𐑄𐑉𐐯𐑌, 𐐸𐐭 𐐸𐐰𐑂 𐐺𐐮𐑌 𐐲𐐹 𐐻𐐭 𐑄 𐑊𐐰𐑌𐐼 𐐱𐑂 𐐤𐐨𐑁𐐴. 𐐒𐐨𐐸𐐬𐑊𐐼, 𐑄𐐩 𐐸𐐰𐑂 𐑊𐐩𐐺𐐲𐑉𐐼 𐐯𐐿𐑅𐐨𐐼𐐮𐑍𐑊𐐨, 𐐰𐑌𐐼 𐐸𐐰𐑂 𐐺𐑉𐐫𐐻 𐑁𐐫𐑉𐑃 𐑋𐐲𐐽 𐑁𐑉𐐭𐐻; 𐐰𐑌𐐼 𐐸𐐵 𐑀𐑉𐐩𐐻 𐑇𐐰𐑊 𐐺 𐑄𐐯𐑉 𐑉𐐨𐐶𐐫𐑉𐐼. 𐐤𐐵 𐐸𐐶𐐯𐑌 𐐌 𐑃𐐮𐑍𐐿 𐐱𐑂 𐑄 𐑅𐐲𐐿𐑅𐐯𐑅 𐐱𐑂 𐑄𐐨𐑆 𐑋𐐴 𐐺𐑉𐐯𐑄𐑉𐐯𐑌, 𐑋𐐴 𐑅𐐬𐑊 𐐮𐑆 𐐿𐐰𐑉𐐨𐐼 𐐰𐐶𐐩, 𐐨𐑂𐐯𐑌 𐐻𐐭 𐑄 𐑅𐐯𐐹𐐲𐑉𐐩𐑇𐐲𐑌 𐐱𐑂 𐐮𐐻 𐑁𐑉𐐱𐑋 𐑄 𐐺𐐱𐐼𐐨, 𐐰𐑆 𐐮𐐻 𐐶𐐲𐑉, 𐑅𐐬 𐑀𐑉𐐩𐐻 𐐮𐑆 𐑋𐐴 𐐾𐐱𐐮.

13. 𐐈𐑌𐐼 𐑌𐐵 𐑋𐐩 𐐘𐐱𐐼 𐑀𐑉𐐰𐑌𐐻 𐐲𐑌𐐻𐐭 𐑄𐐨𐑆 𐑋𐐴 𐐺𐑉𐐯𐑄𐑉𐐯𐑌, 𐑄𐐰𐐻 𐑄𐐩 𐑋𐐩 𐑅𐐮𐐻 𐐼𐐵𐑌 𐐮𐑌 𐑄

𐐿𐐮𐑍𐐼𐐲𐑋 𐐱𐑂 𐐘𐐱𐐼; 𐐷𐐩, 𐐰𐑌𐐼 𐐫𐑊𐑅𐐬 𐐫𐑊 𐑄𐐬𐑆 𐐸𐐭 𐐪𐑉 𐑄 𐑁𐑉𐐭𐐻 𐐱𐑂 𐑄𐐯𐑉 𐑊𐐩𐐺𐐲𐑉𐑆 𐑄𐐰𐐻 𐑄𐐩 𐑋𐐩 𐑀𐐬 𐑌𐐬 𐑋𐐬𐑉 𐐵𐐻, 𐐺𐐲𐐻 𐑄𐐰𐐻 𐑄𐐩 𐑋𐐩 𐐹𐑉𐐩𐑆 𐐸𐐮𐑋 𐑁𐐫𐑉𐐯𐑂𐐲𐑉. 𐐈𐑌𐐼 𐑋𐐩 𐐘𐐱𐐼 𐑀𐑉𐐰𐑌𐐻 𐑄𐐰𐐻 𐐮𐐻 𐑋𐐩 𐐺𐐨 𐐼𐐲𐑌 𐐰𐐿𐐫𐑉𐐼𐐮𐑍 𐐻𐐭 𐑋𐐴 𐐶𐐲𐑉𐐼𐑆, 𐐨𐑂𐐯𐑌 𐐰𐑆 𐐴 𐐸𐐰𐑂 𐑅𐐹𐐬𐐿𐐲𐑌. 𐐁𐑋𐐯𐑌.

𐐕𐐈𐐑𐐓𐐊𐐡 XVI.

1\. 𐐒𐐨𐐸𐐬𐑊𐐼, 𐑌𐐵 𐐮𐐻 𐐿𐐩𐑋 𐐻𐐭 𐐹𐐰𐑅 𐑄𐐰𐐻 𐐰𐑁𐐻𐐲𐑉 𐑄 𐐹𐐨𐐹𐑊 𐐱𐑂 𐐈𐑋𐐲𐑌 𐐶𐐲𐑉 𐐯𐑅𐐻𐐰𐐺𐑊𐐮𐑇𐐻 𐐮𐑌 𐑄 𐑊𐐰𐑌𐐼 𐐱𐑂 𐐖𐐲𐑉𐑇𐐲𐑌, 𐐷𐐩, 𐐰𐑌𐐼 𐐫𐑊𐑅𐐬 𐐰𐑁𐐻𐐲𐑉 𐑄 𐐢𐐩𐑋𐐲𐑌𐐴𐐻𐑅 𐐶𐐲𐑉 𐐼𐑉𐐮𐑂𐐲𐑌 𐐵𐐻 𐐱𐑂 𐑄 𐑊𐐰𐑌𐐼, 𐐰𐑌𐐼 𐑄𐐯𐑉 𐐼𐐯𐐼 𐐶𐐲𐑉 𐐺𐐯𐑉𐐨𐐼 𐐺𐐴 𐑄 𐐹𐐨𐐹𐑊 𐐱𐑂 𐑄 𐑊𐐰𐑌𐐼; 𐑌𐐵 𐑄𐐯𐑉 𐐼𐐯𐐼 𐐶𐐲𐑉 𐑌𐐱𐐻 𐑌𐐲𐑋𐐺𐐲𐑉𐐼 𐐺𐐨𐐿𐐫𐑆 𐐱𐑂 𐑄 𐑀𐑉𐐩𐐻𐑌𐐯𐑅 𐐱𐑂 𐑄𐐯𐑉 𐑌𐐲𐑋𐐺𐐲𐑉𐑆; 𐑌𐐨𐑄𐐲𐑉 𐐶𐐲𐑉 𐑄 𐐼𐐯𐐼 𐐱𐑂 𐑄 𐐤𐐨𐑁𐐴𐐻𐑅 𐑌𐐲𐑋𐐺𐐲𐑉𐐼; 𐐺𐐲𐐻 𐐮𐐻 𐐿𐐩𐑋 𐐻𐐭 𐐹𐐰𐑅 𐐰𐑁𐐻𐐲𐑉 𐑄𐐩 𐐸𐐰𐐼 𐐺𐐯𐑉𐐨𐐼 𐑄𐐯𐑉 𐐼𐐯𐐼, 𐐰𐑌𐐼 𐐫𐑊𐑅𐐬 𐐰𐑁𐐻𐐲𐑉 𐑄 𐐼𐐩𐑆 𐐱𐑂 𐑁𐐰𐑅𐐻𐐮𐑍, 𐐰𐑌𐐼 𐑋𐐬𐑉𐑌𐐮𐑍, 𐐰𐑌𐐼 𐐹𐑉𐐩𐑉, (𐐰𐑌𐐼 𐐮𐐻 𐐶𐐱𐑆 𐐮𐑌 𐑄 𐑅𐐮𐐿𐑅𐐻𐐨𐑌𐑃 𐐷𐐨𐑉 𐐱𐑂 𐑄 𐑉𐐩𐑌 𐐱𐑂 𐑄 𐐾𐐲𐐾𐐯𐑆 𐐬𐑂𐐲𐑉 𐑄 𐐹𐐨𐐹𐑊 𐐱𐑂 𐐤𐐨𐑁𐐴,) 𐑄𐐯𐑉 𐐺𐐨𐑀𐐰𐑌 𐐻𐐭 𐐺𐐨 𐐿𐐱𐑌𐐻𐐮𐑌𐐷𐐭𐐲𐑊 𐐹𐐨𐑅 𐑃𐑉𐐭𐐵𐐻 𐐫𐑊 𐑄 𐑊𐐰𐑌𐐼; 𐐷𐐩, 𐐰𐑌𐐼 𐑄 𐐹𐐨𐐹𐑊 𐐼𐐮𐐼 𐐱𐐺𐑆𐐲𐑉𐑂 𐐻𐐭 𐐿𐐨𐐹 𐑄 𐐿𐐱𐑋𐐰𐑌𐐼𐑋𐐯𐑌𐐻𐑅 𐐱𐑂 𐑄 𐐢𐐫𐑉𐐼; 𐐰𐑌𐐼 𐑄𐐩 𐐶𐐲𐑉 𐑅𐐻𐑉𐐮𐐿𐐻 𐐮𐑌 𐐱𐐺𐑆𐐲𐑉𐑂𐐮𐑍 𐑄 𐐫𐑉𐐼𐐮𐑌𐐰𐑌𐑅𐐯𐑆 𐐱𐑂 𐐘𐐱𐐼, 𐐰𐐿𐐫𐑉𐐼𐐮𐑍 𐐻𐐭 𐑄 𐑊𐐫 𐐱𐑂 𐐣𐐬𐑆𐐯𐑆; 𐑁𐐫𐑉 𐑄𐐩 𐐶𐐲𐑉 𐐻𐐫𐐻 𐐻𐐭 𐐿𐐨𐐹 𐑄 𐑊𐐫 𐐱𐑂 𐐣𐐬𐑆𐐯𐑆, 𐐲𐑌𐐻𐐮𐑊 𐐮𐐻 𐑇𐐳𐐼 𐐺𐐨 𐑁𐐳𐑊𐑁𐐮𐑊𐐼; 𐐰𐑌𐐼 𐑄𐐲𐑅 𐑄 𐐹𐐨𐐹𐑊 𐐼𐐮𐐼 𐐸𐐰𐑂 𐑌𐐬 𐐼𐐮𐑅𐐻𐐲𐑉𐐺𐐰𐑌𐑅 𐐮𐑌 𐐫𐑊 𐑄 𐑅𐐮𐐿𐑅𐐻𐐨𐑌𐑃 𐐷𐐨𐑉 𐐱𐑂 𐑄 𐑉𐐩𐑌 𐐱𐑂 𐑄 𐐾𐐲𐐾𐐯𐑆 𐐬𐑂𐐲𐑉 𐑄 𐐹𐐨𐐹𐑊 𐐱𐑂 𐐤𐐨𐑁𐐴.

2\. 𐐈𐑌𐐼 𐐮𐐻 𐐿𐐩𐑋 𐐻𐐭 𐐹𐐰𐑅 𐐮𐑌 𐑄 𐐿𐐱𐑋𐐯𐑌𐑅𐑋𐐯𐑌𐐻 𐐱𐑂 𐑄 𐑅𐐯𐑂𐐲𐑌𐐻𐐨𐑌𐑃 𐐷𐐨𐑉 𐐱𐑂 𐑄 𐑉𐐩𐑌 𐐱𐑂 𐑄 𐐾𐐲𐐾𐐯𐑆, 𐑄𐐯𐑉 𐐶𐐱𐑆 𐐿𐐱𐑌𐐻𐐮𐑌𐐷𐐭𐐲𐑊 𐐹𐐨𐑅. 𐐒𐐲𐐻 𐐮𐐻 𐐿𐐩𐑋 𐐻𐐭 𐐹𐐰𐑅 𐐮𐑌 𐑄 𐑊𐐰𐐻𐐲𐑉 𐐯𐑌𐐼 𐐱𐑂 𐑄 𐑅𐐯𐑂𐐲𐑌𐐻𐐨𐑌𐑃 𐐷𐐨𐑉, 𐑄𐐯𐑉 𐐿𐐩𐑋 𐐲 𐑋𐐰𐑌 𐐮𐑌𐐻𐐭 𐑄 𐑊𐐰𐑌𐐼 𐐱𐑂 𐐞𐐰𐑉𐐲𐐸𐐯𐑋𐑊𐐲; 𐐰𐑌𐐼 𐐸𐐨 𐐶𐐱𐑆 𐐈𐑌𐐻𐐴-𐐗𐑉𐐴𐑅𐐻, 𐑁𐐫𐑉 𐐸𐐨 𐐺𐐨𐑀𐐰𐑌 𐐻𐐭 𐐹𐑉𐐨𐐽 𐐲𐑌𐐻𐐭 𐑄 𐐹𐐨𐐹𐑊 𐐰𐑀𐐯𐑌𐑅𐐻 𐑄 𐐹𐑉𐐱𐑁𐐯𐑅𐐨𐑆 𐐸𐐶𐐮𐐽 𐐸𐐰𐐼 𐐺𐐮𐑌 𐑅𐐹𐐬𐐿𐐲𐑌 𐐺𐐴 𐑄 𐐹𐑉𐐱𐑁𐐯𐐻𐑅, 𐐿𐐱𐑌𐑅𐐲𐑉𐑌𐐮𐑍 𐑄 𐐿𐐲𐑋𐐮𐑍 𐐱𐑂 𐐗𐑉𐐴𐑅𐐻. 𐐤𐐵 𐑄𐐯𐑉 𐐶𐐱𐑆 𐑌𐐬 𐑊𐐫 𐐰𐑀𐐯𐑌𐑅𐐻 𐐲 𐑋𐐰𐑌'𐑆 𐐺𐐨𐑊𐐨𐑁; 𐑁𐐫𐑉 𐐮𐐻 𐐶𐐱𐑆 𐑅𐐻𐑉𐐮𐐿𐐻𐑊𐐨 𐐿𐐱𐑌𐐻𐑉𐐯𐑉𐐨 𐐻𐐭 𐑄 𐐿𐐱𐑋𐐰𐑌𐐼𐑆 𐐱𐑂 𐐘𐐱𐐼 𐑄𐐰𐐻 𐑄𐐯𐑉 𐑇𐐳𐐼 𐐺𐐨 𐐲 𐑊𐐫 𐐸𐐶𐐮𐐽 𐑇𐐳𐐼 𐐺𐑉𐐮𐑍 𐑋𐐯𐑌 𐐱𐑌 𐐻𐐭 𐐲𐑌𐐨𐐿𐐶𐐲𐑊 𐑀𐑉𐐵𐑌𐐼𐑆. 𐐙𐐫𐑉 𐑄𐐲𐑅 𐑅𐐯𐑃 𐑄 𐑅𐐿𐑉𐐮𐐹𐐽𐐲𐑉, 𐐕𐐭𐑆 𐐷𐐨 𐑄𐐮𐑅 𐐼𐐩 𐐸𐐭𐑋 𐐷𐐨 𐐶𐐮𐑊 𐑅𐐲𐑉𐑂. 𐐤𐐵 𐐮𐑁 𐐲 𐑋𐐰𐑌 𐐼𐐨𐑆𐐴𐑉𐐼 𐐻𐐭 𐑅𐐲𐑉𐑂 𐐘𐐱𐐼 𐐮𐐻 𐐶𐐱𐑆 𐐸𐐮𐑆 𐐹𐑉𐐮𐑂𐐮𐑊𐐯𐐾, 𐐫𐑉 𐑉𐐰𐑄𐐲𐑉 𐐮𐑁 𐐸𐐨 𐐺𐐨𐑊𐐨𐑂𐐼 𐐮𐑌 𐐘𐐱𐐼, 𐐮𐐻 𐐶𐐱𐑆 𐐸𐐮𐑆 𐐹𐑉𐐮𐑂𐐮𐑊𐐯𐐾 𐐻𐐭 𐑅𐐲𐑉𐑂 𐐸𐐮𐑋; 𐐺𐐲𐐻 𐐮𐑁 𐐸𐐨 𐐼𐐮𐐼 𐑌𐐱𐐻 𐐺𐐨𐑊𐐨𐑂 𐐮𐑌 𐐸𐐮𐑋, 𐑄𐐯𐑉 𐐶𐐱𐑆 𐑌𐐬 𐑊𐐫 𐐻𐐭 𐐹𐐲𐑌𐐮𐑇 𐐸𐐮𐑋. 𐐒𐐲𐐻 𐐮𐑁 𐐸𐐨 𐑋𐐲𐑉𐐼𐐲𐑉𐐼, 𐐸𐐨 𐐶𐐱𐑆 𐐹𐐲𐑌𐐮𐑇𐐻 𐐲𐑌𐐻𐐭 𐐼𐐯𐑃; 𐐰𐑌𐐼 𐐮𐑁 𐐸𐐨 𐑉𐐱𐐺𐐼, 𐐸𐐨 𐐶𐐱𐑆 𐐫𐑊𐑅𐐬 𐐹𐐲𐑌𐐮𐑇𐐻; 𐐰𐑌𐐼 𐐮𐑁 𐐸𐐨 𐑅𐐻𐐬𐑊, 𐐸𐐨 𐐶𐐱𐑆 𐐫𐑊𐑅𐐬 𐐹𐐲𐑌𐐮𐑇𐐻; 𐐰𐑌𐐼 𐐮𐑁 𐐸𐐨 𐐿𐐱𐑋𐐮𐐻𐐯𐐼 𐐰𐐼𐐲𐑊𐐻𐐲𐑉𐐨, 𐐸𐐨 𐐶𐐱𐑆 𐐫𐑊𐑅𐐬 𐐹𐐲𐑌𐐮𐑇𐐻; 𐐷𐐩, 𐑁𐐫𐑉 𐐫𐑊 𐑄𐐮𐑅 𐐶𐐮𐐿𐐯𐐼𐑌𐐯𐑅, 𐑄𐐩 𐐶𐐲𐑉 𐐹𐐲𐑌𐐮𐑇𐐻; 𐑁𐐫𐑉 𐑄𐐯𐑉 𐐶𐐱𐑆 𐐲 𐑊𐐫 𐑄𐐰𐐻 𐑋𐐯𐑌 𐑇𐐳𐐼 𐐺𐐨 𐐾𐐲𐐾𐐼 𐐰𐐿𐐫𐑉𐐼𐐮𐑍 𐐻𐐭 𐑄𐐯𐑉 𐐿𐑉𐐴𐑋𐑆. 𐐤𐐯𐑂𐐲𐑉𐑄𐐲𐑊𐐯𐑅, 𐑄𐐯𐑉 𐐶𐐱𐑆 𐑌𐐬 𐑊𐐫 𐐰𐑀𐐯𐑌𐑅𐐻 𐐲 𐑋𐐰𐑌'𐑆 𐐺𐐨𐑊𐐨𐑁; 𐑄𐐯𐑉𐑁𐐬𐑉 𐐲 𐑋𐐰𐑌 𐐶𐐱𐑆 𐐹𐐲𐑌𐐮𐑇𐐻 𐐬𐑌𐑊𐐨 𐑁𐐫𐑉 𐑄 𐐿𐑉𐐴𐑋𐑆 𐐸𐐶𐐮𐐽 𐐸𐐨 𐐸𐐰𐐼 𐐼𐐲𐑌; 𐑄𐐯𐑉𐑁𐐬𐑉 𐐫𐑊 𐑋𐐯𐑌 𐐶𐐲𐑉 𐐱𐑌 𐐨𐐿𐐶𐐲𐑊 𐑀𐑉𐐵𐑌𐐼𐑆. 𐐈𐑌𐐼 𐑄𐐮𐑅 𐐈𐑌𐐻𐐴-𐐗𐑉𐐴𐑅𐐻, 𐐸𐐭𐑆 𐑌𐐩𐑋 𐐶𐐱𐑆 𐐗𐐫𐑉𐐮𐐸𐐫𐑉, (𐐰𐑌𐐼 𐑄 𐑊𐐫 𐐿𐐳𐐼 𐐸𐐰𐑂 𐑌𐐬 𐐸𐐬𐑊𐐼 𐐲𐐹𐐱𐑌 𐐸𐐮𐑋,) 𐐺𐐨𐑀𐐰𐑌 𐐻𐐭 𐐹𐑉𐐨𐐽 𐐲𐑌𐐻𐐭 𐑄 𐐹𐐨𐐹𐑊, 𐑄𐐰𐐻 𐑄𐐯𐑉 𐑇𐐳𐐼 𐐺𐐨 𐑌𐐬 𐐗𐑉𐐴𐑅𐐻. 𐐈𐑌𐐼 𐐰𐑁𐐻𐐲𐑉 𐑄𐐮𐑅 𐑋𐐰𐑌𐐲𐑉 𐐼𐐮𐐼 𐐸𐐨 𐐹𐑉𐐨𐐽, 𐑅𐐩𐐮𐑍, 𐐄 𐐷𐐨 𐑄𐐰𐐻 𐐪𐑉 𐐺𐐵𐑌𐐼 𐐼𐐵𐑌 𐐲𐑌𐐼𐐲𐑉 𐐲 𐑁𐐭𐑊𐐮𐑇 𐐰𐑌𐐼 𐐲 𐑂𐐩𐑌 𐐸𐐬𐐹, 𐐸𐐶𐐴 𐐼𐐭 𐐷𐐨 𐐷𐐬𐐿 𐐷𐐭𐑉𐑅𐐯𐑊𐑂𐑆 𐐶𐐮𐑄 𐑅𐐲𐐽 𐑁𐐭𐑊𐐮𐑇 𐑃𐐮𐑍𐑆? 𐐐𐐶𐐴 𐐼𐐭 𐐷𐐨 𐑊𐐳𐐿 𐑁𐐫𐑉 𐐲 𐐗𐑉𐐴𐑅𐐻? 𐐙𐐫𐑉 𐑌𐐬 𐑋𐐰𐑌 𐐿𐐰𐑌 𐑌𐐬 𐐱𐑂 𐐯𐑌𐐨𐑃𐐮𐑍 𐐸𐐶𐐮𐐽 𐐮𐑆 𐐻𐐭 𐐿𐐲𐑋. 𐐒𐐨𐐸𐐬𐑊𐐼, 𐑄𐐨𐑆 𐑃𐐮𐑍𐑆 𐐸𐐶𐐮𐐽 𐐷𐐨 𐐿𐐫𐑊 𐐹𐑉𐐱𐑁𐐯𐑅𐐨𐑆, 𐐸𐐶𐐮𐐽 𐐷𐐨 𐑅𐐩 𐐪𐑉 𐐸𐐰𐑌𐐼𐐯𐐼 𐐼𐐵𐑌 𐐺𐐴 𐐸𐐬𐑊𐐨 𐐹𐑉𐐱𐑁𐐯𐐻𐑅, 𐐺𐐨𐐸𐐬𐑊𐐼, 𐑄𐐩 𐐪𐑉 𐑁𐐭𐑊𐐮𐑇 𐐻𐑉𐐰𐐼𐐮𐑇𐐲𐑌𐑆 𐐱𐑂 𐐷𐐭𐑉 𐑁𐐪𐑄𐐲𐑉𐑆. 𐐐𐐵 𐐼𐐭 𐐷𐐨 𐑌𐐬 𐐱𐑂 𐑄𐐯𐑉 𐑇𐐭𐑉𐐯𐐻𐐨? 𐐒𐐨𐐸𐐬𐑊𐐼, 𐐷𐐨 𐐿𐐰𐑌𐐱𐐻 𐑌𐐬 𐐱𐑂 𐑃𐐮𐑍𐑆 𐐸𐐶𐐮𐐽 𐐷𐐨 𐐼𐐭 𐑌𐐱𐐻 𐑅𐐨; 𐑄𐐯𐑉𐑁𐐬𐑉 𐐷𐐨 𐐿𐐰𐑌𐐱𐐻 𐑌𐐬 𐑄𐐰𐐻 𐑄𐐯𐑉 𐑇𐐰𐑊 𐐺𐐨 𐐲 𐐗𐑉𐐴𐑅𐐻. 𐐏𐐨 𐑊𐐳𐐿 𐑁𐐬𐑉𐐶𐐲𐑉𐐼 𐐰𐑌𐐼 𐑅𐐩 𐑄𐐰𐐻 𐐷 𐑅𐐨 𐐪 𐑉𐐨𐑋𐐮𐑇𐐲𐑌 𐐱𐑂 𐐷𐐬𐑉 𐑅𐐮𐑌𐑆. 𐐒𐐲𐐻 𐐺𐐨𐐸𐐬𐑊𐐼, 𐐮𐐻 𐐮𐑆 𐑄 𐐯𐑁𐐯𐐿𐐻 𐐱𐑂 𐐪 𐑁𐑉𐐯𐑌𐑆𐐨𐐼 𐑋𐐴𐑌𐐼; 𐐰𐑌𐐼 𐑄𐐮𐑅 𐐼𐐨𐑉𐐩𐑌𐐾𐑋𐐯𐑌𐐻 𐐱𐑂 𐐷𐐬𐑉 𐑋𐐴𐑌𐐼𐑆 𐐿𐐲𐑋𐑆 𐐺𐐨𐐿𐐫𐑆 𐐱𐑂 𐑄 𐐻𐑉𐐰𐐼𐐮𐑇𐐲𐑌𐑆 𐐱𐑂 𐐷𐐬𐑉 𐑁𐐪𐑄𐐲𐑉𐑆, 𐐸𐐶𐐮𐐽 𐑊𐐨𐐼 𐐷𐐭 𐐲𐐶𐐩 𐐮𐑌𐐻𐐭 𐐪 𐐺𐐨𐑊𐐨𐑁 𐐱𐑂 𐑃𐐮𐑍𐑆 𐐸𐐶𐐮𐐽 𐐪𐑉 𐑌𐐱𐐻 𐑅𐐬. 𐐈𐑌𐐼 𐑋𐐯𐑌𐐨 𐑋𐐬𐑉 𐑅𐐲𐐽 𐑃𐐮𐑍𐑆 𐐼𐐮𐐼 𐐸𐐨 𐑅𐐩 𐐲𐑌𐐻𐐭 𐑄𐐯𐑋, 𐐻𐐯𐑊𐐮𐑍 𐑄𐐯𐑋 𐑄𐐰𐐻 𐑄𐐯𐑉 𐐿𐐳𐐼 𐐺 𐑌𐐬 𐐲𐐻𐐬𐑌𐑋𐐯𐑌𐐻 𐑋𐐩𐐼 𐑁𐐬𐑉 𐑄 𐑅𐐮𐑌𐑆 𐐱𐑂 𐑋𐐯𐑌, 𐐺𐐲𐐻 𐐯𐑂𐐲𐑉𐐨 𐑋𐐰𐑌 𐑁𐐯𐑉𐐼 𐐮𐑌 𐑄𐐮𐑅 𐑊𐐴𐑁 𐐰𐐿𐐫𐑉𐐼𐐮𐑍 𐐻𐐭 𐑄 𐑋𐐰𐑌𐐲𐐾𐑋𐐯𐑌𐐻 𐐱𐑂 𐑄 𐐿𐑉𐐨𐐽𐐲𐑉; 𐑄𐐯𐑉𐑁𐐬𐑉 𐐯𐑂𐐲𐑉𐐨 𐑋𐐰𐑌 𐐹𐑉𐐱𐑅𐐹𐐲𐑉𐐼 𐐰𐐿𐐫𐑉𐐼𐐮𐑍 𐐻𐐭 𐐸𐐮𐑆 𐐾𐐨𐑌𐐷𐐲𐑅, 𐐰𐑌𐐼 𐑄𐐰𐐻 𐐯𐑂𐐲𐑉𐐨 𐑋𐐰𐑌 𐐿𐐱𐑍𐐿𐐲𐑉𐐼 𐐰𐐿𐐫𐑉𐐼𐐮𐑍 𐐻𐐭 𐐸𐐮𐑆 𐑅𐐻𐑉𐐯𐑍𐑃; 𐐰𐑌𐐼 𐐸𐐶𐐱𐐻𐑅𐐬𐐯𐑂𐐲𐑉 𐐪 𐑋𐐰𐑌 𐐼𐐮𐐼 𐐶𐐱𐑆 𐑌𐐬 𐐿𐑉𐐴𐑋. 𐐈𐑌𐐼 𐑄𐐲𐑅 𐐸𐐨 𐐼𐐮𐐼 𐐹𐑉𐐨𐐽 𐐲𐑌𐐻𐐭 𐑄𐐯𐑋, 𐑊𐐨𐐼𐐮𐑍 𐐲𐐶𐐩 𐑄 𐐸𐐪𐑉𐐻𐑅 𐐱𐑂 𐑋𐐯𐑌𐐨, 𐐿𐐫𐑆𐐮𐑍 𐑄𐐯𐑋 𐐻𐐭 𐑊𐐮𐑁𐐻 𐐲𐐹 𐑄𐐯𐑉 𐐸𐐯𐐼𐑆 𐐮𐑌 𐑄𐐯𐑉 𐐶𐐮𐐿𐐯𐐼𐑌𐐯𐑅; 𐐷𐐩, 𐑊𐐨𐐼𐐮𐑍 𐐲𐐶𐐩 𐑋𐐯𐑌𐐨 𐐶𐐮𐑋𐐯𐑌, 𐐰𐑌𐐼 𐐫𐑊𐑅𐐬 𐑋𐐯𐑌, 𐐻𐐭 𐐿𐐲𐑋𐐮𐐻 𐐸𐐬𐑉𐐼𐐲𐑋𐑆: 𐐻𐐯𐑊𐐮𐑍 𐑄𐐯𐑋 𐑄𐐰𐐻 𐐸𐐶𐐯𐑌 𐐪 𐑋𐐰𐑌 𐐶𐐱𐑆 𐐼𐐯𐐼, 𐑄𐐰𐐻 𐐶𐐱𐑆 𐑄 𐐯𐑌𐐼 𐑄𐐯𐑉𐐱𐑂.

3. 𐐤𐐵 𐑄𐐮𐑅 𐑋𐐰𐑌 𐐶𐐯𐑌𐐻 𐐬𐑂𐐲𐑉 𐐻𐐭 𐑄 𐑊𐐰𐑌𐐼 𐐱𐑂 𐐖𐐲𐑉𐑇𐐲𐑌 𐐫𐑊𐑅𐐬, 𐐻𐐭 𐐹𐑉𐐨𐐽 𐑄𐐨𐑆 𐑃𐐮𐑍𐑆 𐐲𐑋𐐲𐑍 𐑄 𐐹𐐨𐐹𐑊 𐐱𐑂 𐐈𐑋𐐲𐑌, 𐐸𐐭 𐐶𐐲𐑉 𐐶𐐲𐑌𐑅 𐑄 𐐹𐐨𐐹𐑊 𐐱𐑂 𐑄 𐐢𐐩𐑋𐐲𐑌𐐴𐐻𐑅. 𐐒𐐲𐐻 𐐺𐐨𐐸𐐬𐑊𐐼, 𐑄𐐩 𐐶𐐲𐑉 𐑋𐐬𐑉 𐐶𐐴𐑆 𐑄𐐰𐑌 𐑋𐐯𐑌𐐨 𐐱𐑂 𐑄 𐐤𐐨𐑁𐐴𐐻𐑅; 𐑁𐐬𐑉 𐑄𐐩 𐐻𐐳𐐿 𐐸𐐮𐑋, 𐐰𐑌𐐼 𐐺𐐵𐑌𐐼 𐐸𐐮𐑋, 𐐰𐑌𐐼 𐐿𐐰𐑉𐐨𐐼 𐐸𐐮𐑋 𐐺𐐨𐑁𐐬𐑉 𐐈𐑋𐐲𐑌, 𐐸𐐭 𐐶𐐱𐑆 𐐪 𐐸𐐴 𐐹𐑉𐐨𐑅𐐻 𐐬𐑂𐐲𐑉 𐑄𐐰𐐻 𐐹𐐨𐐹𐑊.

4. 𐐈𐑌𐐼 𐐮𐐻 𐐿𐐩𐑋 𐐻𐐭 𐐹𐐪𐑅 𐑄𐐰𐐻 𐐸𐐨 𐐿𐐫𐑆𐐼 𐑄𐐰𐐻 𐐸𐐨 𐑇𐐳𐐼 𐐺 𐐿𐐰𐑉𐐨𐐼 𐐵𐐻 𐐱𐑂 𐑄 𐑊𐐰𐑌𐐼. 𐐈𐑌𐐼 𐐸𐐨 𐐿𐐩𐑋 𐐬𐑂𐐲𐑉 𐐮𐑌𐐻𐐭 𐑄 𐑊𐐰𐑌𐐼 𐐱𐑂 𐐘𐐮𐐼𐐨𐐲𐑌, 𐐰𐑌𐐼 𐐺𐐨𐑀𐐰𐑌 𐐻𐐭 𐐹𐑉𐐨𐐽 𐐲𐑌𐐻𐐭 𐑄𐐯𐑋 𐐫𐑊𐑅𐐬; 𐐰𐑌𐐼 𐐸𐐨𐑉 𐐸𐐨 𐐼𐐮𐐼 𐑌𐐱𐐻 𐐸𐐰𐑂 𐑋𐐲𐐽 𐑅𐐲𐐿𐑅𐐯𐑅, 𐑁𐐬𐑉 𐐸𐐨 𐐶𐐱𐑆 𐐻𐐩𐐿𐐲𐑌, 𐐰𐑌𐐼 𐐺𐐵𐑌𐐼, 𐐰𐑌𐐼 𐐿𐐰𐑉𐐨𐐼 𐐺𐐨𐑁𐐬𐑉 𐑄 𐐸𐐴 𐐹𐑉𐐨𐑅𐐻, 𐐰𐑌𐐼 𐐫𐑊𐑅𐐬 𐑄 𐐽𐐨𐑁 𐐖𐐲𐐾 𐐬𐑂𐐲𐑉 𐑄 𐑊𐐰𐑌𐐼.

5. 𐐈𐑌𐐼 𐐮𐐻 𐐿𐐩𐑋 𐐻𐐭 𐐹𐐪𐑅 𐑄𐐰𐐻 𐑄 𐐸𐐴 𐐹𐑉𐐨𐑅𐐻 𐑅𐐯𐐼 𐐲𐑌𐐻𐐭 𐐸𐐮𐑋, 𐐐𐐶𐐴 𐐼𐐭 𐐷 𐑀𐐬 𐐲𐐺𐐵𐐻 𐐹𐐲𐑉𐑂𐐲𐑉𐐻𐐮𐑍 𐑄 𐐶𐐩𐑆 𐐱𐑂 𐑄 𐐢𐐫𐑉𐐼? 𐐐𐐶𐐴 𐐼𐐭 𐐷 𐐻𐐨𐐽 𐑄𐐮𐑅 𐐹𐐨𐐹𐑊 𐑄𐐰𐐻 𐑄𐐯𐑉 𐑇𐐰𐑊 𐐺 𐑌𐐬 𐐗𐑉𐐴𐑅𐐻, 𐐻𐐭 𐐮𐑌𐐻𐐲𐑉𐐲𐐹𐐻 𐑄𐐯𐑉 𐑉𐐨𐐾𐐱𐐮𐑅𐐮𐑍𐑆? 𐐐𐐶𐐴 𐐼𐐭 𐐷 𐑅𐐹𐐨𐐿 𐐲𐑀𐐯𐑌𐑅𐐻 𐐫𐑊 𐑄 𐐹𐑉𐐱𐑁𐐯𐑅𐐨𐑆 𐐱𐑂 𐑄 𐐸𐐬𐑊𐐨 𐐹𐑉𐐱𐑁𐐯𐐻𐑅? 𐐤𐐵 𐑄 𐐸𐐴 𐐹𐑉𐐨𐑅𐐻'𐑅 𐑌𐐩𐑋 𐐶𐐱𐑆 𐐘𐐮𐐼𐐬𐑌𐐪. 𐐈𐑌𐐼 𐐗𐐬𐑉𐐴𐐸𐐬𐑉 𐑅𐐯𐐼 𐐲𐑌𐐻𐐭 𐐸𐐮𐑋, 𐐒𐐨𐐿𐐫𐑆 𐐌 𐐼𐐭 𐑌𐐱𐐻 𐐻𐐨𐐽 𐑄 𐑁𐐭𐑊𐐮𐑇 𐐻𐑉𐐰𐐼𐐮𐑇𐐲𐑌𐑆 𐐱𐑂 𐐷𐐬𐑉 𐑁𐐪𐑄𐐲𐑉𐑆, 𐐰𐑌𐐼 𐐺𐐨𐐿𐐫𐑆 𐐌 𐐼𐐭 𐑌𐐱𐐻 𐐻𐐨𐐽 𐑄𐐮𐑅 𐐹𐐨𐐹𐑊 𐐻𐐭 𐐺𐐴𐑌𐐼 𐑄𐐯𐑋𐑅𐐯𐑊𐑂𐑆 𐐲𐑌𐐼𐐲𐑉 𐑄 𐑁𐐭𐑊𐐮𐑇 𐐫𐑉𐐼𐐮𐑌𐐲𐑌𐑅𐐯𐑆 𐐰𐑌𐐼 𐐹𐐲𐑉𐑁𐐫𐑉𐑋𐐲𐑌𐑅𐐯𐑆 𐐸𐐶𐐮𐐽 𐐪𐑉 𐑊𐐩𐐼 𐐼𐐵𐑌 𐐺𐐴 𐐩𐑌𐑇𐐲𐑌𐐻 𐐹𐑉𐐨𐑅𐐻𐑅, 𐐻𐐭 𐐷𐐭𐑆𐐲𐑉𐐹 𐐹𐐵𐐲𐑉 𐐰𐑌𐐼 𐐫𐑃𐐱𐑉𐐮𐐻𐐨 𐐬𐑂𐐲𐑉 𐑄𐐯𐑋, 𐐻𐐭 𐐿𐐨𐐹 𐑄𐐯𐑋 𐐮𐑌 𐐮𐑀𐑌𐐬𐑉𐐲𐑌𐑅, 𐑄𐐰𐐻 𐑄𐐩 𐑋𐐩 𐑌𐐱𐐻 𐑊𐐮𐑁𐐻 𐐲𐐹 𐑄𐐯𐑉 𐐸𐐯𐐼𐑆, 𐐺𐐲𐐻 𐐺 𐐺𐑉𐐫𐐻 𐐼𐐵𐑌 𐐰𐐿𐐫𐑉𐐼𐐮𐑍 𐐻𐐭 𐑄𐐴 𐐶𐐲𐑉𐐼𐑆. 𐐏 𐑅𐐩 𐑄𐐰𐐻 𐑄𐐮𐑅 𐐹𐐨𐐹𐑊 𐐮𐑆 𐐪 𐑁𐑉𐐨 𐐹𐐨𐐹𐑊. 𐐒𐐨𐐸𐐬𐑊𐐼, 𐐌 𐑅𐐩 𐑄𐐩 𐐪𐑉 𐐮𐑌 𐐺𐐱𐑌𐐼𐐲𐐾. 𐐏 𐑅𐐩 𐑄𐐰𐐻 𐑄𐐬𐑆 𐐩𐑌𐑇𐐲𐑌𐐻 𐐹𐑉𐐱𐑁𐐯𐑅𐐨𐑆 𐐪𐑉 𐐻𐑉𐐭. 𐐒𐐨𐐸𐐬𐑊𐐼, 𐐌 𐑅𐐩 𐑄𐐰𐐻 𐐷 𐐼𐐭 𐑌𐐱𐐻 𐑌𐐬 𐑄𐐰𐐻 𐑄𐐩 𐐪𐑉 𐐻𐑉𐐭. 𐐏 𐑅𐐩 𐑄𐐰𐐻 𐑄𐐮𐑅 𐐹𐐨𐐹𐑊 𐐮𐑆 𐐪 𐑀𐐮𐑊𐐻𐐨 𐐰𐑌𐐼 𐐪 𐑁𐐫𐑊𐑌 𐐹𐐨𐐹𐑊, 𐐺𐐨𐐿𐐫𐑆 𐐱𐑂 𐑄 𐐻𐑉𐐰𐑌𐑆𐑀𐑉𐐯𐑇𐐲𐑌 𐐱𐑂 𐐪 𐐹𐐯𐑉𐐯𐑌𐐻. 𐐒𐐨𐐸𐐬𐑊𐐼, 𐐌 𐑅𐐩 𐑄𐐰𐐻 𐐪 𐐽𐐴𐑊𐐼 𐐮𐑆 𐑌𐐱𐐻 𐑀𐐮𐑊𐐻𐐨 𐐺𐐨𐐿𐐫𐑆 𐐱𐑂 𐐮𐐻𐑅 𐐹𐐯𐑉𐐯𐑌𐐻𐑅. 𐐈𐑌𐐼 𐐷 𐐫𐑊𐑅𐐬 𐑅𐐩 𐑄𐐰𐐻 𐐗𐑉𐐴𐑅𐐻 𐑇𐐰𐑊 𐐿𐐲𐑋. 𐐒𐐲𐐻 𐐺𐐨𐐸𐐬𐑊𐐼, 𐐌 𐑅𐐩 𐑄𐐰𐐻 𐐷 𐐼𐐭 𐑌𐐱𐐻 𐑌𐐬 𐑄𐐰𐐻 𐑄𐐯𐑉 𐑇𐐰𐑊 𐐺 𐐪 𐐗𐑉𐐴𐑅𐐻. 𐐈𐑌𐐼 𐐷 𐑅𐐩 𐐫𐑊𐑅𐐬, 𐑄𐐰𐐻 𐐸𐐨 𐑇𐐰𐑊 𐐺 𐑅𐑊𐐩𐑌 𐑁𐐬𐑉 𐑄 𐑅𐐮𐑌𐑆 𐐱𐑂 𐑄 𐐶𐐲𐑉𐑊𐐼; 𐐰𐑌𐐼 𐑄𐐲𐑅 𐐷 𐑊𐐨𐐼 𐐲𐐶𐐩 𐑄𐐮𐑅 𐐹𐐨𐐹𐑊 𐐰𐑁𐐻𐐲𐑉 𐑄 𐑁𐐭𐑊𐐮𐑇 𐐻𐑉𐐰𐐼𐐮𐑇𐐲𐑌𐑆 𐐱𐑂 𐐷𐐬𐑉 𐑁𐐪𐑄𐐲𐑉𐑆, 𐐰𐑌𐐼 𐐰𐐿𐐫𐑉𐐼𐐮𐑍 𐐻𐐭 𐐷𐐬𐑉 𐐬𐑌 𐐼𐐨𐑆𐐴𐑉𐑆; 𐐰𐑌𐐼 𐐷 𐐿𐐨𐐹 𐑄𐐯𐑋 𐐼𐐵𐑌, 𐐨𐑂𐑌 𐐰𐑆 𐐮𐐻 𐐶𐐲𐑉 𐐮𐑌 𐐺𐐱𐑌𐐼𐐲𐐾, 𐑄𐐰𐐻 𐐷 𐑋𐐩 𐑀𐑊𐐲𐐻 𐐷𐐬𐑉𐑅𐐯𐑊𐑂𐑆 𐐶𐐮𐑄 𐑄 𐑊𐐩𐐺𐐲𐑉𐑆 𐐱𐑂 𐑄𐐯𐑉 𐐸𐐰𐑌𐐼𐑆, 𐑄𐐰𐐻 𐑄𐐩 𐐼𐐲𐑉𐑅𐐻 𐑌𐐱𐐻 𐑊𐐳𐐿 𐐲𐐹 𐐶𐐮𐑄 𐐺𐐬𐑊𐐼𐑌𐐯𐑅, 𐐰𐑌𐐼 𐑄𐐰𐐻 𐑄𐐩 𐐼𐐲𐑉𐑅𐐻 𐑌𐐱𐐻 𐐯𐑌𐐾𐐱𐐮 𐑄𐐯𐑉 𐑉𐐴𐐻𐑅 𐐰𐑌𐐼 𐐹𐑉𐐮𐑂𐐮𐑊𐐯𐐾𐐯𐑆; 𐐷𐐩, 𐑄𐐩 𐐼𐐲𐑉𐑅𐐻 𐑌𐐱𐐻 𐑋𐐩𐐿 𐐷𐐭𐑅 𐐱𐑂 𐑄𐐰𐐻 𐐸𐐶𐐮𐐽 𐐮𐑆 𐑄𐐯𐑉 𐐬𐑌, 𐑊𐐯𐑅𐐻 𐑄𐐩 𐑇𐐳𐐼 𐐱𐑁𐐯𐑌𐐼 𐑄𐐯𐑉 𐐹𐑉𐐨𐑅𐐻𐑅, 𐐸𐐭 𐐼𐐭 𐐷𐐬𐐿 𐑄𐐯𐑋 𐐰𐐿𐐫𐑉𐐼𐐮𐑍 𐐻𐐭 𐑄𐐯𐑉 𐐼𐐨𐑆𐐴𐑉𐑆, 𐐰𐑌𐐼 𐐸𐐰𐑂 𐐺𐑉𐐫𐐻 𐑄𐐯𐑋 𐐻𐐭 𐐺𐐨𐑊𐐨𐑂 𐐺𐐴 𐑄𐐯𐑉 𐐻𐑉𐐰𐐼𐐮𐑇𐐲𐑌𐑆, 𐐰𐑌𐐼 𐑄𐐯𐑉 𐐼𐑉𐐨𐑋𐑆, 𐐰𐑌𐐼 𐑄𐐯𐑉 𐐸𐐶𐐮𐑋𐑆, 𐐰𐑌𐐼 𐑄𐐯𐑉 𐑂𐐮𐑈𐐲𐑌𐑆, 𐐰𐑌𐐼 𐑄𐐯𐑉 𐐹𐑉𐐨𐐻𐐯𐑌𐐼𐐯𐐼 𐑋𐐮𐑅𐐻𐐲𐑉𐐨𐑆, 𐑄𐐰𐐻 𐑄𐐩 𐑇𐐳𐐼, 𐐮𐑁 𐑄𐐩 𐐼𐐮𐐼 𐑌𐐱𐐻 𐐼𐐭 𐐰𐐿𐐫𐑉𐐼𐐮𐑍 𐐻𐐭 𐑄𐐯𐑉

𐐶𐐲𐑉𐐼𐑆, 𐐲𐑁𐐯𐑌𐐼 𐑅𐐲𐑋 𐐲𐑌𐑌𐐬𐑌 𐐺𐐨𐐮𐑍, 𐐸𐐭 𐑄𐐩 𐑅𐐩 𐐮𐑆 𐐘𐐱𐐼; 𐐲 𐐺𐐨𐐮𐑍 𐐸𐐭 𐑌𐐯𐑂𐐲𐑉 𐐸𐐰𐑆 𐐺𐐮𐑌 𐑅𐐨𐑌 𐐫𐑉 𐑌𐐬𐑌, 𐐸𐐭 𐑌𐐯𐑂𐐲𐑉 𐐶𐐱𐑆 𐑌𐐫𐑉 𐐯𐑂𐐲𐑉 𐐶𐐮𐑊 𐐺. 𐐤𐐵 𐐸𐐶𐐯𐑌 𐑄 𐐸𐐴 𐐹𐑉𐐨𐑅𐐻 𐐰𐑌𐐼 𐑄 𐐽𐐨𐑁 𐐾𐐲𐐾 𐑅𐐫 𐑄 𐐸𐐪𐑉𐐼𐑌𐐯𐑅 𐐱𐑂 𐐸𐐮𐑆 𐐸𐐪𐑉𐐻; 𐐷𐐩, 𐐸𐐶𐐯𐑌 𐑄𐐩 𐑅𐐫 𐑄𐐰𐐻 𐐸𐐨 𐐶𐐳𐐼 𐑉𐐨𐑂𐐴𐑊 𐐨𐑂𐐲𐑌 𐐰𐑀𐐯𐑌𐑅𐐻 𐐘𐐱𐐼, 𐑄𐐩 𐐶𐐳𐐼 𐑌𐐱𐐻 𐑋𐐩𐐿 𐐯𐑌𐐨 𐑉𐐨𐐹𐑊𐐴 𐐻𐐭 𐐸𐐮𐑆 𐐶𐐲𐑉𐐼𐑆; 𐐺𐐲𐐻 𐑄𐐩 𐐿𐐫𐑆𐐼 𐑄𐐰𐐻 𐐸𐐨 𐑇𐐳𐐼 𐐺 𐐺𐐵𐑌𐐼; 𐐰𐑌𐐼 𐑄𐐩 𐐼𐐮𐑊𐐮𐑂𐐲𐑉𐐼 𐐸𐐮𐑋 𐐲𐐹 𐐮𐑌𐐻𐐭 𐑄 𐐸𐐰𐑌𐐼𐑆 𐐱𐑂 𐑄 𐐱𐑁𐐮𐑅𐐲𐑉𐑆, 𐐰𐑌𐐼 𐑅𐐯𐑌𐐻 𐐸𐐮𐑋 𐐻𐐭 𐑄 𐑊𐐰𐑌𐐼 𐐱𐑂 𐐞𐐯𐑉𐐲𐐸𐐯𐑋𐑊𐐲, 𐑄𐐰𐐻 𐐸𐐨 𐑋𐐴𐐻 𐐺 𐐺𐑉𐐫𐐻 𐐺𐐨𐑁𐐬𐑉 𐐈𐑊𐑋𐐲, 𐐰𐑌𐐼 𐑄 𐐽𐐨𐑁 𐐾𐐲𐐾, 𐐸𐐭 𐐶𐐱𐑆 𐑀𐐲𐑂𐐲𐑉𐑌𐐲𐑉 𐐬𐑂𐐲𐑉 𐐫𐑊 𐑄 𐑊𐐰𐑌𐐼.

6. 𐐈𐑌𐐼 𐐮𐐻 𐐿𐐩𐑋 𐐻𐐭 𐐹𐐪𐑅 𐑄𐐰𐐻 𐐸𐐶𐐯𐑌 𐐸𐐨 𐐶𐐱𐑆 𐐺𐑉𐐫𐐻 𐐺𐐨𐑁𐐬𐑉 𐐈𐑊𐑋𐐲 𐐰𐑌𐐼 𐑄 𐐽𐐨𐑁 𐐾𐐲𐐾, 𐐸𐐨 𐐼𐐮𐐼 𐑀𐐬 𐐱𐑌 𐐮𐑌 𐑄 𐑅𐐩𐑋 𐑋𐐰𐑌𐐲𐑉 𐐰𐑆 𐐸𐐨 𐐼𐐮𐐼 𐐮𐑌 𐑄 𐑊𐐰𐑌𐐼 𐐱𐑂 𐐘𐐮𐐼𐐨𐐲𐑌; 𐐷𐐩, 𐐸𐐨 𐐶𐐯𐑌𐐻 𐐱𐑌 𐐻𐐭 𐐺𐑊𐐰𐑅𐑁𐐨𐑋. 𐐈𐑌𐐼 𐐸𐐨 𐐼𐐮𐐼 𐑉𐐴𐑆 𐐲𐐹 𐐮𐑌 𐑀𐑉𐐩𐐻 𐑅𐐶𐐯𐑊𐐮𐑍 𐐶𐐲𐑉𐐼𐑆 𐐺𐐨𐑁𐐬𐑉 𐐈𐑊𐑋𐐲, 𐐰𐑌𐐼 𐐼𐐮𐐼 𐑉𐐨𐑂𐐴𐑊 𐐰𐑀𐐯𐑌𐑅𐐻 𐑄 𐐹𐑉𐐨𐑅𐐻𐑅 𐐰𐑌𐐼 𐐻𐐨𐐽𐐲𐑉𐑆, 𐐰𐐿𐐷𐐭𐑆𐐮𐑍 𐑄𐐯𐑋 𐐱𐑂 𐑊𐐨𐐼𐐮𐑍 𐐲𐐶𐐩 𐑄 𐐹𐐨𐐹𐑊 𐐰𐑁𐐻𐐲𐑉 𐑄 𐑅𐐮𐑊𐐨 𐐻𐑉𐐲𐐼𐐮𐑇𐐲𐑌𐑆 𐐱𐑂 𐑄𐐯𐑉 𐑁𐐪𐑄𐐲𐑉𐑆, 𐑁𐐫𐑉 𐑄 𐑅𐐩𐐿 𐐱𐑂 𐑀𐑊𐐲𐐻𐐮𐑍 𐐮𐑌 𐑄 𐑊𐐩𐐺𐐲𐑉𐑆 𐐱𐑂 𐑄 𐐹𐐨𐐹𐑊. 𐐤𐐵 𐐈𐑊𐑋𐐲 𐑅𐐯𐐼 𐐲𐑌𐐻𐐭 𐐸𐐮𐑋, 𐐜𐐵 𐑌𐐬𐐯𐑅𐐻 𐑄𐐰𐐻 𐐶𐐨 𐐼𐐭 𐑌𐐱𐐻 𐑀𐑊𐐲𐐻 𐐵𐐲𐑉𐑅𐐯𐑊𐑂𐑆 𐐲𐐹𐐱𐑌 𐑄 𐑊𐐩𐐺𐐲𐑉𐑆 𐐱𐑂 𐑄𐐮𐑅 𐐹𐐨𐐹𐑊; 𐑁𐐫𐑉 𐐺𐐨𐐸𐐬𐑊𐐼 𐐴 𐐸𐐰𐑂 𐑊𐐩𐐺𐐲𐑉𐐼 𐐨𐑂𐐲𐑌 𐑁𐑉𐐱𐑋 𐑄 𐐿𐐱𐑋𐐯𐑌𐑅𐑋𐐯𐑌𐐻 𐐱𐑂 𐑄 𐑉𐐩𐑌 𐐱𐑂 𐑄 𐐾𐐲𐐾𐐯𐑆, 𐐲𐑌𐐻𐐮𐑊 𐑌𐐵, 𐐶𐐮𐑄 𐑋𐐴𐑌 𐐬𐑌 𐐸𐐰𐑌𐐼𐑆, 𐑁𐐫𐑉 𐑋𐐴 𐑅𐐲𐐹𐐬𐑉𐐻, 𐑌𐐱𐐻𐐶𐐮𐑄𐑅𐐻𐐰𐑌𐐼𐐮𐑍 𐑋𐐴 𐑋𐐯𐑌𐐨 𐐻𐑉𐐰𐑂𐐯𐑊𐑆 𐑉𐐵𐑌𐐼 𐐲𐐺𐐵𐐻 𐑄 𐑊𐐰𐑌𐐼 𐐻𐐭 𐐼𐐨𐐿𐑊𐐩𐑉 𐑄 𐐶𐐲𐑉𐐼 𐐱𐑂 𐐘𐐱𐐼 𐐲𐑌𐐻𐐭 𐑋𐐴 𐐹𐐨𐐹𐑊. 𐐈𐑌𐐼 𐑌𐐱𐐻𐐶𐐮𐑄𐑅𐐻𐐰𐑌𐐼𐐮𐑍 𐑄 𐑋𐐯𐑌𐐨 𐑊𐐩𐐺𐐲𐑉𐑆 𐐸𐐶𐐮𐐽 𐐴 𐐸𐐰𐑂 𐐹𐐲𐑉𐑁𐐫𐑉𐑋𐐼 𐐮𐑌 𐑄 𐐽𐐲𐑉𐐽, 𐐴 𐐸𐐰𐑂 𐑌𐐯𐑂𐐲𐑉 𐑉𐐨𐑅𐐨𐑂𐐼 𐑅𐐬 𐑋𐐲𐐽 𐐰𐑆 𐐨𐑂𐐲𐑌 𐐶𐐲𐑌 𐑅𐐯𐑌𐐴𐑌 𐑁𐐫𐑉 𐑋𐐴 𐑊𐐩𐐺𐐲𐑉; 𐑌𐐨𐑄𐐲𐑉 𐐸𐐰𐑆 𐐯𐑌𐐨 𐐱𐑂 𐑋𐐴 𐐺𐑉𐐯𐑄𐑉𐐯𐑌, 𐑅𐐩𐑂 𐐮𐐻 𐐶𐐲𐑉 𐐮𐑌 𐑄 𐐾𐐲𐐾𐑋𐐯𐑌𐐻-𐑅𐐨𐐻; 𐐰𐑌𐐼 𐑄𐐯𐑌 𐐶𐐨 𐐸𐐰𐑂 𐑉𐐨𐑅𐐨𐑂𐐼 𐐬𐑌𐑊𐐨 𐐰𐐿𐐫𐑉𐐼𐐮𐑍 𐐻𐐭 𐑊𐐫 𐑁𐐫𐑉 𐐵𐑉 𐐻𐐴𐑋. 𐐈𐑌𐐼 𐑌𐐵 𐐮𐑁 𐐶𐐨 𐐼𐐭 𐑌𐐱𐐻 𐑉𐐨𐑅𐐨𐑂 𐐯𐑌𐐨𐑃𐐮𐑍 𐑁𐐫𐑉 𐐵𐑉 𐑊𐐩𐐺𐐲𐑉𐑆 𐐮𐑌 𐑄 𐐽𐐲𐑉𐐽, 𐐸𐐶𐐱𐐻 𐐼𐐲𐑃 𐐮𐐻 𐐹𐑉𐐱𐑁𐐮𐐻 𐐲𐑅 𐐻𐐭 𐑊𐐩𐐺𐐲𐑉 𐐮𐑌 𐑄 𐐽𐐲𐑉𐐽, 𐑅𐐩𐑂 𐐮𐐻 𐐶𐐲𐑉 𐐻𐐭 𐐼𐐨𐐿𐑊𐐩𐑉 𐑄 𐐻𐑉𐐭𐑃, 𐑄𐐰𐐻 𐐶𐐨 𐑋𐐩 𐐸𐐰𐑂 𐑉𐐨𐐾𐑎𐑅𐐮𐑍𐑆 𐐮𐑌 𐑄 𐐾𐑎 𐐱𐑂 𐐵𐑉 𐐺𐑉𐐯𐑄𐑉𐐯𐑌? 𐐜𐐯𐑌 𐐸𐐶𐐴 𐑅𐐩𐐯𐑅𐐻 𐑄𐐵 𐑄𐐰𐐻 𐐶𐐨 𐐹𐑉𐐨𐐽 𐐲𐑌𐐻𐐭 𐑄𐐮𐑅 𐐹𐐨𐐹𐑊 𐐻𐐭 𐑀𐐯𐐻 𐑀𐐩𐑌, 𐐸𐐶𐐯𐑌 𐑄𐐵, 𐐱𐑂 𐑄𐐴𐑅𐐯𐑊𐑁, 𐑌𐐬𐐯𐑅𐐻 𐑄𐐰𐐻 𐐶𐐨 𐑉𐐨𐑅𐐨𐑂 𐑌𐐬 𐑀𐐩𐑌? 𐐈𐑌𐐼 𐑌𐐵, 𐐒𐐨𐑊𐐨𐑂𐐯𐑅𐐻 𐑄𐐵 𐑄𐐰𐐻 𐐶𐐨 𐐼𐐨𐑅𐐨𐑂 𐑄𐐮𐑅 𐐹𐐨𐐹𐑊, 𐑄𐐰𐐻 𐐿𐐫𐑆𐐯𐑆 𐑅𐐲𐐽 𐐾𐑎 𐐮𐑌 𐑄𐐯𐑉 𐐸𐐪𐑉𐐻𐑅? 𐐈𐑌𐐼 𐐗𐐫𐑉𐐴𐐸𐐫𐑉 𐐰𐑌-𐑅𐐲𐑉𐐼 𐐸𐐮𐑋, 𐐏𐐩. 𐐈𐑌𐐼 𐑄𐐯𐑌 𐐈𐑊𐑋𐐲 𐑅𐐯𐐼 𐐲𐑌𐐻𐐭 𐐸𐐮𐑋, 𐐒𐐨𐑊𐐨𐑂𐐯𐑅𐐻 𐑄𐐵 𐑄𐐰𐐻 𐑄𐐯𐑉 𐐮𐑆 𐐲 𐐘𐐱𐐼? 𐐈𐑌𐐼 𐐸𐐨 𐐰𐑌𐑅𐐲𐑉𐐼, 𐐤𐐩. 𐐤𐐵 𐐈𐑊𐑋𐐲 𐑅𐐯𐐼 𐐲𐑌𐐻𐐭 𐐸𐐮𐑋, 𐐎𐐮𐑊 𐐷 𐐼𐐨𐑌𐐴 𐐰𐑀𐐯𐑌 𐑄𐐰𐐻 𐑄𐐯𐑉 𐐮𐑆 𐐲 𐐘𐐱𐐼, 𐐰𐑌𐐼 𐐫𐑊𐑅𐐬 𐐼𐐨𐑌𐐴 𐑄 𐐗𐑉𐐴𐑅𐐻? 𐐙𐐫𐑉 𐐺𐐨𐐸𐐬𐑊𐐼, 𐐴 𐑅𐐩 𐐲𐑌𐐻𐐭 𐐷𐐭, 𐐴 𐑌𐐬 𐑄𐐯𐑉 𐐮𐑆 𐐲 𐐘𐐱𐐼, 𐐰𐑌𐐼 𐐫𐑊𐑅𐐬 𐑄𐐰𐐻 𐐗𐑉𐐴𐑅𐐻 𐑇𐐰𐑊 𐐿𐐲𐑋. 𐐈𐑌𐐼 𐑌𐐵 𐐸𐐶𐐱𐐻 𐐯𐑂𐐮𐐼𐐯𐑌𐑅 𐐸𐐰𐑂 𐐷 𐑄𐐰𐐻 𐑄𐐯𐑉 𐐮𐑆 𐑌𐐬 𐐘𐐱𐐼, 𐐫𐑉 𐑄𐐰𐐻 𐐗𐑉𐐴𐑅𐐻 𐐿𐐲𐑋𐐯𐑃 𐑌𐐱𐐻? 𐐌 𐑅𐐩 𐐲𐑌𐐻𐐭 𐐷𐐭 𐑄𐐰𐐻 𐐷 𐐸𐐰𐑂 𐑌𐐲𐑌, 𐑅𐐩𐑂 𐐮𐐻 𐐺 𐐷𐐫𐑉 𐐶𐐲𐑉𐐼 𐐬𐑌𐑊𐐨. 𐐒𐐲𐐻, 𐐺𐐨𐐸𐐬𐑊𐐼, 𐐴 𐐸𐐰𐑂 𐐫𐑊 𐑃𐐮𐑍𐑆 𐐰𐑆 𐐲 𐐻𐐯𐑅𐐻𐐮𐑋𐐬𐑌𐐨 𐑄𐐰𐐻 𐑄𐐨𐑆 𐑃𐐮𐑍𐑆 𐐪𐑉 𐐻𐑉𐐭; 𐐰𐑌𐐼 𐐷 𐐫𐑊𐑅𐐬 𐐸𐐰𐑂 𐐫𐑊 𐑃𐐮𐑍𐑆 𐐰𐑆 𐐲 𐐻𐐯𐑅𐐻𐐮𐑋𐐬𐑌𐐨 𐐲𐑌𐐻𐐭 𐐷𐐭 𐑄𐐰𐐻 𐑄𐐩 𐐪𐑉 𐐻𐑉𐐭; 𐐰𐑌𐐼 𐐶𐐮𐑊 𐐷 𐐼𐐨𐑌𐐴 𐑄𐐯𐑋? 𐐒𐐨𐑊𐐨𐑂𐐯𐑅𐐻 𐑄𐐵 𐑄𐐰𐐻 𐑄𐐨𐑆 𐑃𐐮𐑍𐑆 𐐪𐑉 𐐻𐑉𐐭? 𐐒𐐨𐐸𐐬𐑊𐐼, 𐐴 𐑌𐐬 𐑄𐐰𐐻 𐑄𐐵 𐐺𐐨𐑊𐐨𐑂𐐯𐑅𐐻, 𐐺𐐲𐐻 𐑄𐐵 𐐪𐑉𐐻 𐐹𐐱𐑆𐐯𐑅𐐻 𐐶𐐮𐑄 𐐲 𐑊𐐴𐐮𐑍 𐑅𐐹𐐮𐑉𐐮𐐻, 𐐰𐑌𐐼 𐐷 𐐸𐐰𐑂 𐐹𐐳𐐻 𐐫𐑁 𐑄 𐐝𐐹𐐮𐑉𐐮𐐻 𐐱𐑂 𐐘𐐱𐐼 𐑄𐐰𐐻 𐐮𐐻 𐑋𐐩 𐐸𐐰𐑂 𐑌𐐬 𐐹𐑊𐐩𐑅 𐐮𐑌 𐐷𐐭; 𐐺𐐲𐐻 𐑄 𐐼𐐯𐑂𐐮𐑊 𐐸𐐰𐑆 𐐹𐐵𐐲𐑉 𐐬𐑂𐐲𐑉 𐐷𐐭, 𐐰𐑌𐐼 𐐸𐐨 𐐼𐐲𐑃 𐐿𐐰𐑉𐐨 𐐷𐐭 𐐲𐐺𐐵𐐻, 𐐶𐐲𐑉𐐿𐐮𐑍 𐐼𐐨𐑂𐐴𐑅𐐯𐑆, 𐑄𐐰𐐻 𐐸𐐨 𐑋𐐩 𐐼𐐯𐑅𐐻𐑉𐑎 𐑄 𐐽𐐮𐑊𐐼𐑉𐐯𐑌 𐐱𐑂 𐐘𐐱𐐼.

7. 𐐈𐑌𐐼 𐑌𐐵 𐐗𐐫𐑉𐐴𐐸𐐫𐑉 𐑅𐐯𐐼 𐐲𐑌𐐻𐐭 𐐈𐑊𐑋𐐲, 𐐆𐑁 𐑄𐐵 𐐶𐐮𐑊𐐻 𐑇𐐬 𐑋𐐨 𐐲 𐑅𐐴𐑌, 𐑄𐐰𐐻 𐐴 𐑋𐐩 𐐺 𐐿𐐱𐑌𐑂𐐮𐑌𐑅𐐻 𐑄𐐰𐐻 𐑄𐐯𐑉 𐐮𐑆 𐐲 𐐘𐐱𐐼, 𐐷𐐩, 𐑇𐐬 𐐲𐑌𐐻𐐭 𐑋𐐨 𐑄𐐰𐐻 𐐸𐐨 𐐸𐐰𐑃 𐐹𐐵𐐲𐑉, 𐐰𐑌𐐼 𐑄𐐯𐑌 𐐶𐐮𐑊 𐐴 𐐺 𐐿𐐱𐑌𐑂𐐮𐑌𐑅𐐻 𐐱𐑂 𐑄 𐐻𐑉𐐭𐑃 𐐱𐑂 𐑄𐐴 𐐶𐐲𐑉𐐼𐑆. 𐐒𐐲𐐻 𐐈𐑊𐑋𐐲 𐑅𐐯𐐼 𐐲𐑌𐐻𐐭 𐐸𐐮𐑋, 𐐜𐐵 𐐸𐐰𐑅𐐻 𐐸𐐰𐐼 𐑅𐐴𐑌𐑆 𐐨𐑌𐐲𐑁; 𐐶𐐮𐑊 𐐷 𐐻𐐯𐑋𐐻 𐐷𐐫𐑉 𐐘𐐱𐐼? 𐐎𐐮𐑊 𐐷 𐑅𐐩, 𐐟𐐬 𐐲𐑌𐐻𐐭 𐑋𐐨 𐐲 𐑅𐐴𐑌, 𐐸𐐶𐐯𐑌 𐐷 𐐸𐐰𐑂 𐑄 𐐻𐐯𐑅𐐻𐐮𐑋𐐬𐑌𐐨 𐐱𐑂 𐐫𐑊 𐑄𐐨𐑆 𐑄𐐴 𐐺𐑉𐐯𐑄𐑉𐐯𐑌, 𐐰𐑌𐐼 𐐫𐑊𐑅𐐬 𐐫𐑊 𐑄 𐐸𐐬𐑊𐐨 𐐹𐑉𐐱𐑁𐐯𐐻𐑅? 𐐜 𐑅𐐿𐑉𐐮𐐹-𐐽𐐲𐑉𐑆 𐐪𐑉 𐑊𐐩𐐼 𐐺𐐨𐑁𐐬𐑉 𐑄𐐨, 𐐷𐐩, 𐐰𐑌𐐼 𐐫𐑊 𐑃𐐮𐑍𐑆 𐐼𐐨𐑌𐐬𐐻 𐑄𐐯𐑉 𐐮𐑆 𐐲 𐐘𐐱𐐼; 𐐷𐐩, 𐐨𐑂𐐲𐑌 𐑄 𐐲𐑉𐑃,

𐐰𐑌𐐼 𐐫𐑊 𐑃𐐮𐑍𐑆 𐑄𐐰𐐻 𐐪𐑉 𐐲𐐹𐐱𐑌 𐑄 𐑁𐐩𐑅 𐐱𐑂 𐐮𐐻, 𐐷𐐩, 𐐰𐑌𐐼 𐐮𐐻𐑅 𐑋𐐬𐑇𐐲𐑌; 𐐷𐐩, 𐐰𐑌𐐼 𐐫𐑊𐑅𐐬 𐐫𐑊 𐑄 𐐹𐑊𐐰𐑌𐐯𐐻𐑅, 𐐸𐐶𐐮𐐽 𐑋𐐭𐑂 𐐮𐑌 𐑄𐐩𐑉 𐑉𐐯𐑀𐐷𐐭𐑊𐐲𐑉 𐑁𐐫𐑉𐑋, 𐐼𐐭 𐐶𐐮𐐻𐑌𐐯𐑅 𐑄𐐰𐐻 𐑄𐐩𐑉 𐐮𐑆 𐐲 𐐝𐐭𐐹𐑉𐐨𐑋 𐐗𐑉𐐨𐐩𐐻𐐲𐑉; 𐐰𐑌𐐼 𐐷𐐯𐐻 𐐼𐐭 𐐷𐐨 𐑀𐐬 𐐲𐐺𐐵𐐻, 𐑊𐐨𐐼𐐮𐑍 𐐲𐐶𐐩 𐑄 𐐸𐐪𐑉𐐻𐑅 𐐱𐑂 𐑄𐐮𐑅 𐐹𐐨𐐹𐑊, 𐐻𐐯𐑅𐐻𐐮𐑁𐐴𐐮𐑍 𐐲𐑌𐐻𐐭 𐑄𐐯𐑋 𐑄𐐩𐑉 𐐮𐑆 𐑌𐐬 𐐘𐐱𐐼? 𐐰𐑌𐐼 𐐷𐐯𐐻 𐐶𐐮𐑊 𐐷𐐨 𐐼𐐨𐑌𐐴 𐐲𐑀𐐯𐑌𐑅𐐻 𐐫𐑊 𐑄𐐨𐑆 𐐶𐐮𐐻𐑌𐐯𐑅𐐯𐑆? 𐐰𐑌𐐼 𐐸𐐨 𐑅𐐯𐐼, 𐐏𐐩, 𐐌 𐐶𐐮𐑊 𐐼𐐨𐑌𐐴, 𐐯𐐿𐑅𐐯𐐹𐐻 𐑄𐐵 𐑇𐐰𐑊𐐻 𐑇𐐬 𐑋𐐨 𐐲 𐑅𐐴𐑌.

8. 𐐰𐑌𐐼 𐑌𐐵 𐐮𐐻 𐐿𐐩𐑋 𐐻𐐭 𐐹𐐰𐑅 𐑄𐐰𐐻 𐐈𐑊𐑋𐐲 𐑅𐐯𐐼 𐐲𐑌𐐻𐐭 𐐸𐐮𐑋, 𐐒𐐨𐐸𐐬𐑊𐐼, 𐐌 𐐰𐑋 𐑀𐑉𐐨𐑂𐐼 𐐺𐐨𐐿𐐫𐑆 𐐱𐑂 𐑄 𐐸𐐪𐑉𐐼𐑌𐐯𐑅 𐐱𐑂 𐐷𐐬𐑉 𐐸𐐪𐑉𐐻; 𐐷𐐩, 𐑄𐐰𐐻 𐐷𐐨 𐐶𐐮𐑊 𐑅𐐻𐐮𐑊 𐑉𐐨𐑆𐐮𐑅𐐻 𐑄 𐑅𐐹𐐮𐑉𐐮𐐻 𐐱𐑂 𐑄 𐐻𐑉𐐭𐑃, 𐑄𐐰𐐻 𐑄𐐴 𐑅𐐬𐑊 𐑋𐐩 𐐺𐐨 𐐼𐐯𐑅𐐻𐑉𐐱𐐮𐐼. 𐐒𐐲𐐻 𐐺𐐨𐐸𐐬𐑊𐐼, 𐐮𐐻 𐐮𐑆 𐐺𐐯𐐻𐐲𐑉 𐑄𐐰𐐻 𐑄𐐴 𐑅𐐬𐑊 𐑇𐐳𐐼 𐐺𐐨 𐑊𐐱𐑅𐐻, 𐑄𐐰𐑌 𐑄𐐰𐐻 𐑄𐐵 𐑇𐐳𐐼𐑅𐐻 𐐺𐐨 𐑄 𐑋𐐨𐑌𐑆 𐐱𐑂 𐐺𐑉𐐮𐑍𐐮𐑍 𐑋𐐯𐑌𐐨 𐑅𐐬𐑊𐑆 𐐼𐐵𐑌 𐐻𐐭 𐐼𐐯𐑅𐐻𐑉𐐲𐐿𐑇𐐲𐑌, 𐐺𐐴 𐑄𐐴 𐑊𐐴𐐮𐑍 𐐰𐑌𐐼 𐐺𐐴 𐑄𐐴 𐑁𐑊𐐰𐐻𐐲𐑉𐐮𐑍 𐐶𐐲𐑉𐐼𐑆; 𐑄𐐩𐑉𐑁𐐬𐑉 𐐮𐑁 𐑄𐐵 𐑇𐐰𐑊𐐻 𐐼𐐨𐑌𐐴 𐐲𐑀𐐯𐑌, 𐐺𐐨𐐸𐐬𐑊𐐼, 𐐘𐐱𐐼 𐑇𐐰𐑊 𐑅𐑋𐐴𐐻 𐑄𐐨, 𐑄𐐰𐐻 𐑄𐐵 𐑇𐐰𐑊𐐻 𐐺𐐨𐐿𐐲𐑋 𐐼𐐲𐑋, 𐑄𐐰𐐻 𐑄𐐵 𐑇𐐰𐑊𐐻 𐑌𐐯𐑂𐐲𐑉 𐐬𐐹𐐲𐑌 𐑄𐐴 𐑋𐐵𐑃 𐐯𐑌𐐨 𐑋𐐬𐑉, 𐑄𐐰𐐻 𐑄𐐵 𐑇𐐰𐑊𐐻 𐑌𐐱𐐻 𐐼𐐨𐑅𐐨𐑂 𐑄𐐮𐑅 𐐹𐐨𐐹𐑊 𐐯𐑌𐐨 𐑋𐐬𐑉. 𐐤𐐵 𐐗𐐬𐑉𐐮𐐸𐐬𐑉 𐑅𐐯𐐼 𐐲𐑌𐐻𐐭 𐐸𐐮𐑋, 𐐌 𐐼𐐭 𐑌𐐱𐐻 𐐼𐐨𐑌𐐴 𐑄 𐐯𐑀𐑆𐐮𐑅𐐻𐐯𐑌𐑅 𐐱𐑂 𐐲 𐐘𐐱𐐼, 𐐺𐐲𐐻 𐐌 𐐼𐐭 𐑌𐐱𐐻 𐐺𐐨𐑊𐐨𐑂 𐑄𐐰𐐻 𐑄𐐩𐑉 𐐮𐑆 𐐲 𐐘𐐱𐐼; 𐐰𐑌𐐼 𐐌 𐑅𐐩 𐐫𐑊𐑅𐐬, 𐑄𐐰𐐻 𐐷𐐨 𐐼𐐭 𐑌𐐱𐐻 𐑌𐐬 𐑄𐐰𐐻 𐑄𐐩𐑉 𐐮𐑆 𐐲 𐐘𐐱𐐼; 𐐰𐑌𐐼 𐐯𐐿𐑅𐐯𐐹𐐻 𐐷𐐨 𐑇𐐬 𐑋𐐨 𐐲 𐑅𐐴𐑌, 𐐌 𐐶𐐮𐑊 𐑌𐐱𐐻 𐐺𐐨𐑊𐐨𐑂. 𐐤𐐵 𐐈𐑊𐑋𐐲 𐑅𐐯𐐼 𐐲𐑌𐐻𐐭 𐐸𐐮𐑋, 𐐜𐐮𐑅 𐐶𐐮𐑊 𐐌 𐑀𐐮𐑂 𐐲𐑌𐐻𐐭 𐑄𐐨 𐑁𐐫𐑉 𐐲 𐑅𐐴𐑌, 𐑄𐐰𐐻 𐑄𐐵 𐑇𐐰𐑊𐐻 𐐺𐐨 𐑅𐐻𐑉𐐲𐐿 𐐼𐐲𐑋, 𐐲𐐿𐐫𐑉𐐼𐐮𐑍 𐐻𐐭 𐑋𐐴 𐐶𐐲𐑉𐐼𐑆; 𐐰𐑌𐐼 𐐌 𐑅𐐩, 𐑄𐐰𐐻 𐐮𐑌 𐑄 𐑌𐐩𐑋 𐐱𐑂 𐐘𐐱𐐼, 𐐷𐐨 𐑇𐐰𐑊 𐐺𐐨 𐑅𐐻𐑉𐐲𐐿 𐐼𐐲𐑋, 𐑄𐐰𐐻 𐐷𐐨 𐑇𐐰𐑊 𐑌𐐬 𐑋𐐬𐑉 𐐸𐐰𐑂 𐐲𐐻𐐲𐑉𐐰𐑌𐑅. 𐐤𐐵 𐐸𐐶𐐯𐑌 𐐈𐑊𐑋𐐲 𐐸𐐰𐐼 𐑅𐐯𐐼 𐑄𐐨𐑆 𐐶𐐲𐑉𐐼𐑆, 𐐗𐐬𐑉𐐮𐐸𐐬𐑉 𐐶𐐱𐑆 𐑅𐐻𐑉𐐲𐐿 𐐼𐐲𐑋, 𐑄𐐰𐐻 𐐸𐐨 𐐿𐐳𐐼 𐑌𐐱𐐻 𐐸𐐰𐑂 𐐲𐐻𐐲𐑉𐐰𐑌𐑅, 𐐲𐐿𐐫𐑉𐐼𐐮𐑍 𐐻𐐭 𐑄 𐐶𐐲𐑉𐐼𐑆 𐐱𐑂 𐐈𐑊𐑋𐐲. 𐐰𐑌𐐼 𐑌𐐵 𐐸𐐶𐐯𐑌 𐑄 𐐕𐐨𐑁 𐐖𐐲𐐾 𐑅𐐫 𐑄𐐮𐑅, 𐐸𐐨 𐐹𐐳𐐻 𐑁𐐬𐑉𐑃 𐐸𐐮𐑆 𐐸𐐰𐑌𐐼 𐐰𐑌𐐼 𐑉𐐬𐐻 𐐲𐑌𐐻𐐭 𐐗𐐬𐑉𐐮𐐸𐐬𐑉, 𐑅𐐩𐐮𐑍: 𐐂𐑉𐐻 𐑄𐐵 𐐿𐐲𐑌𐑂𐐮𐑌𐑅𐐻 𐐱𐑂 𐑄 𐐹𐐵𐐲𐑉 𐐱𐑂 𐐘𐐱𐐼? 𐐆𐑌 𐐸𐐭𐑋 𐐼𐐮𐐼 𐐷𐐨 𐐼𐐨𐑆𐐴𐑉 𐑄𐐰𐐻 𐐈𐑊𐑋𐐲 𐑇𐐳𐐼 𐑇𐐬 𐑁𐐬𐑉𐑃 𐐸𐐮𐑆 𐑅𐐴𐑌? 𐐎𐐳𐐼 𐐷𐐨 𐑄𐐰𐐻 𐐸𐐨 𐑇𐐳𐐼 𐐰𐑁𐑊𐐮𐐿𐐻 𐐲𐑄𐐲𐑉𐑆, 𐐻𐐭 𐑇𐐬 𐐲𐑌𐐻𐐭 𐑄𐐨 𐐲 𐑅𐐴𐑌? 𐐒𐐨𐐸𐐬𐑊𐐼, 𐐸𐐨 𐐸𐐰𐑆 𐑇𐐬𐐼 𐐲𐑌𐐻𐐭 𐐷𐐭 𐐲 𐑅𐐴𐑌; 𐐰𐑌𐐼 𐑌𐐵 𐐶𐐮𐑊 𐐷𐐨 𐐼𐐮𐑅𐐹𐐷𐐭𐐻 𐑋𐐬𐑉? 𐐰𐑌𐐼 𐐗𐐬𐑉𐐮𐐸𐐬𐑉 𐐹𐐳𐐻 𐑁𐐬𐑉𐑃 𐐸𐐮𐑆 𐐸𐐰𐑌𐐼 𐐰𐑌𐐼 𐑉𐐬𐐻, 𐑅𐐩𐐮𐑍: 𐐌 𐑌𐐬 𐑄𐐰𐐻 𐐌 𐐰𐑋 𐐼𐐲𐑋, 𐑁𐐫𐑉 𐐌 𐐿𐐰𐑌𐐱𐐻 𐑅𐐹𐐨𐐿; 𐐰𐑌𐐼 𐐌 𐑌𐐬 𐑄𐐰𐐻 𐑌𐐲𐑃𐐮𐑍 𐑅𐐩𐑂 𐐮𐐻 𐐶𐐲𐑉 𐑄 𐐹𐐵𐐲𐑉 𐐱𐑂 𐐘𐐱𐐼 𐐿𐐳𐐼 𐐺𐑉𐐮𐑍 𐑄𐐮𐑅 𐐲𐐹𐐱𐑌 𐑋𐐨; 𐐷𐐩, 𐐰𐑌𐐼 𐐌 𐐫𐑊𐐶𐐩𐑆 𐑌𐐭 𐑄𐐰𐐻 𐑄𐐩𐑉 𐐶𐐱𐑆 𐐲 𐐘𐐱𐐼. 𐐒𐐲𐐻 𐐺𐐨𐐸𐐬𐑊𐐼, 𐑄 𐐼𐐯𐑂𐐮𐑊 𐐸𐐰𐑃 𐐼𐐨𐑅𐐨𐑂𐐼 𐑋𐐨; 𐑁𐐫𐑉 𐐸𐐨 𐐰𐐹𐐨𐑉𐐼 𐐲𐑌𐐻𐐭 𐑋𐐨 𐐮𐑌 𐑄 𐑁𐐫𐑉𐑋 𐐱𐑂 𐐰𐑌 𐐁𐑌𐐾𐐯𐑊, 𐐰𐑌𐐼 𐑅𐐯𐐼 𐐲𐑌𐐻𐐭 𐑋𐐨, 𐐘𐐬 𐐰𐑌𐐼 𐑉𐐨𐐿𐑊𐐩𐑋 𐑄𐐮𐑅 𐐹𐐨𐐹𐑊, 𐑁𐐫𐑉 𐑄𐐩 𐐸𐐰𐑂 𐐫𐑊 𐑀𐐱𐑌 𐐲𐑅𐐻𐑉𐐩 𐐪𐑁𐐻𐐲𐑉 𐐰𐑌 𐐲𐑌𐑌𐐬𐑌 𐐘𐐱𐐼. 𐐰𐑌𐐼 𐐸𐐨 𐑅𐐯𐐼 𐐲𐑌𐐻𐐭 𐑋𐐨, 𐐜𐐩𐑉 𐐮𐑆 𐑌𐐬 𐐘𐐱𐐼; 𐐷𐐩, 𐐰𐑌𐐼 𐐸𐐨 𐐻𐐫𐐻 𐑋𐐨 𐑄𐐰𐐻 𐐸𐐶𐐮𐐽 𐐌 𐑇𐐳𐐼 𐑅𐐩. 𐐰𐑌𐐼 𐐌 𐐸𐐰𐑂 𐐻𐐫𐐻 𐐸𐐮𐑆 𐐶𐐲𐑉𐐼𐑆; 𐐰𐑌𐐼 𐐌 𐐻𐐫𐐻 𐑄𐐯𐑋, 𐐺𐐨𐐿𐐫𐑆 𐑄𐐩 𐐶𐐲𐑉 𐐹𐑊𐐨𐑆𐐮𐑍 𐐲𐑌𐐻𐐭 𐑄 𐐿𐐪𐑉𐑌𐐲𐑊 𐑋𐐴𐑌𐐼; 𐐰𐑌𐐼 𐐌 𐐻𐐫𐐻 𐑄𐐯𐑋 𐐨𐑂𐐯𐑌 𐐲𐑌𐐻𐐮𐑊 𐐌 𐐸𐐰𐐼 𐑋𐐲𐐽 𐑅𐐲𐐿𐑅𐐯𐑅, 𐐮𐑌𐑅𐐬𐑋𐐲𐐽 𐑄𐐰𐐻 𐐌 𐑂𐐯𐑉𐐮𐑊𐐨 𐐺𐐨𐑊𐐨𐑂𐐼 𐑄𐐰𐐻 𐑄𐐩 𐐶𐐲𐑉 𐐻𐑉𐐭; 𐐰𐑌𐐼 𐑁𐐫𐑉 𐑄𐐮𐑅 𐐿𐐫𐑆 𐐌 𐐶𐐮𐑃𐑅𐐻𐐳𐐼 𐑄 𐐻𐑉𐐭𐑃, 𐐨𐑂𐐯𐑌 𐐲𐑌𐐻𐐮𐑊 𐐌 𐐸𐐰𐑂 𐐺𐑉𐐫𐐻 𐑄𐐮𐑅 𐑀𐑉𐐩𐐻 𐐿𐐲𐑉𐑅 𐐲𐐹𐐱𐑌 𐑋𐐨. 𐐤𐐵 𐐸𐐶𐐯𐑌 𐐸𐐨 𐐸𐐰𐐼 𐑅𐐯𐐼 𐑄𐐮𐑅, 𐐸𐐨 𐐺𐐨𐑅𐐫𐐻 𐑄𐐰𐐻 𐐈𐑊𐑋𐐲 𐑇𐐳𐐼 𐐹𐑉𐐩 𐐲𐑌𐐻𐐭 𐐘𐐱𐐼, 𐑄𐐰𐐻 𐑄 𐐿𐐲𐑉𐑅 𐑋𐐴𐐻 𐐺𐐨 𐐻𐐩𐐿𐐲𐑌 𐑁𐑉𐐱𐑋 𐐸𐐮𐑋. 𐐒𐐲𐐻 𐐈𐑊𐑋𐐲 𐑅𐐯𐐼 𐐲𐑌𐐻𐐭 𐐸𐐮𐑋, 𐐆𐑁 𐑄𐐮𐑅 𐐿𐐲𐑉𐑅 𐑇𐐳𐐼 𐐺𐐨 𐐻𐐩𐐿𐐲𐑌 𐑁𐑉𐐱𐑋 𐑄𐐨, 𐑄𐐵 𐐶𐐳𐐼𐑅𐐻 𐐲𐑀𐐯𐑌 𐑊𐐨𐐼 𐐲𐐶𐐩 𐑄 𐐸𐐪𐑉𐐻𐑅 𐐱𐑂 𐑄𐐮𐑅 𐐹𐐨𐐹𐑊; 𐑄𐐩𐑉𐑁𐐬𐑉, 𐐮𐐻 𐑇𐐰𐑊 𐐺𐐨 𐐲𐑌𐐻𐐭 𐑄𐐨, 𐐨𐑂𐐯𐑌 𐐰𐑆 𐑄 𐐢𐐫𐑉𐐼 𐐶𐐮𐑊.

9. 𐐰𐑌𐐼 𐐮𐐻 𐐿𐐩𐑋 𐐻𐐭 𐐹𐐰𐑅 𐑄𐐰𐐻 𐑄 𐐿𐐲𐑉𐑅 𐐶𐐱𐑆 𐑌𐐱𐐻 𐐻𐐩𐐿𐐲𐑌 𐐫𐑁 𐐱𐑂 𐐗𐐬𐑉𐐮𐐸𐐬𐑉; 𐐺𐐲𐐻 𐐸𐐨 𐐶𐐱𐑆 𐐿𐐰𐑅𐐻 𐐵𐐻, 𐐰𐑌𐐼 𐐶𐐯𐑌𐐻 𐐲𐐺𐐵𐐻 𐑁𐑉𐐱𐑋 𐐸𐐵𐑅 𐐻𐐭 𐐸𐐵𐑅, 𐐺𐐯𐑀𐐮𐑍 𐑁𐐫𐑉 𐐸𐐮𐑆 𐑁𐐭𐐼. 𐐤𐐵 𐑄 𐑌𐐱𐑊𐐯𐐾 𐐱𐑂 𐐸𐐶𐐱𐐻 𐐸𐐰𐐼 𐐸𐐰𐐹𐐲𐑌𐐼 𐐲𐑌𐐻𐐭 𐐗𐐬𐑉𐐮𐐸𐐬𐑉 𐐶𐐱𐑆 𐐮𐑋𐐨𐐼𐐨𐐰𐐻𐑊𐐨 𐐹𐐲𐐺𐑊𐐮𐑇𐐻 𐑃𐑉𐐭𐐵𐐻 𐐫𐑊 𐑄 𐑊𐐰𐑌𐐼; 𐐷𐐩, 𐑄 𐐹𐑉𐐱𐐿𐑊𐐲𐑋𐐩𐑇𐐲𐑌 𐐶𐐱𐑆 𐑅𐐯𐑌𐐻 𐑁𐐬𐑉𐑃 𐐺𐐴 𐑄 𐐕𐐨𐑁 𐐖𐐲𐐾 𐐻𐐭 𐐫𐑊 𐑄 𐐹𐐨𐐹𐑊 𐐮𐑌 𐑄 𐑊𐐰𐑌𐐼, 𐐼𐐨𐐿𐑊𐐩𐑉𐐮𐑍 𐐲𐑌𐐻𐐭 𐑄𐐬𐑆 𐐸𐐭 𐐸𐐰𐐼 𐐺𐐨𐑊𐐨𐑂𐐼 𐐮𐑌 𐑄 𐐶𐐲𐑉𐐼𐑆 𐐱𐑂 𐐗𐐬𐑉𐐮𐐸𐐬𐑉, 𐑄𐐰𐐻 𐑄𐐩 𐑋𐐲𐑅𐐻 𐑅𐐹𐐨𐐼𐐮𐑊𐐨 𐑉𐐨𐐹𐐯𐑌𐐻, 𐑊𐐯𐑅𐐻 𐑄 𐑅𐐩𐑋 𐐾𐐲𐐾𐑋𐐯𐑌𐐻𐑅 𐐶𐐳𐐼 𐐿𐐲𐑋 𐐲𐑌𐐻𐐭 𐑄𐐯𐑋.

10. 𐐈𐑌𐐼 𐐮𐐻 𐐿𐐩𐑋 𐐻𐐭 𐐹𐐪𐑅 𐑄𐐰𐐻 𐑄𐐩 𐐶𐐲𐑉 𐐫𐑊 𐐿𐐲𐑌𐑂𐐮𐑌𐑅𐐻 𐐱𐑂 𐑄 𐐶𐐮𐐿𐐯𐐼𐑌𐐯𐑅 𐐱𐑂 𐐗𐐬𐑉𐐴𐐸𐐬𐑉; 𐑄𐐩𐑉𐑁𐐬𐑉 𐑄𐐩 𐐶𐐲𐑉 𐐫𐑊 𐐿𐐲𐑌𐑂𐐲𐑉𐐻𐐯𐐼 𐐲𐑀𐐯𐑌 𐐲𐑌𐐻𐐭 𐑄 𐑊𐐬𐑉𐐼; 𐐰𐑌𐐼 𐑄𐐮𐑅 𐐹𐐳𐐻 𐐰𐑌 𐐯𐑌𐐼 𐐻𐐭 𐑄 𐐮𐑌𐐮𐐿𐐶𐐮𐐻𐐮 𐐪𐑁𐐻𐐲𐑉 𐑄 𐑋𐐰𐑌𐐲𐑉 𐐱𐑂 𐐗𐐬𐑉𐐴𐐸𐐬𐑉. 𐐈𐑌𐐼 𐐗𐐬𐑉𐐴𐐸𐐬𐑉 𐐼𐐮𐐼 𐑀𐐬 𐐲𐐺𐐵𐐻 𐑁𐑉𐐱𐑋 𐐸𐐵𐑅 𐐻𐐭 𐐸𐐵𐑅, 𐐺𐐯𐑀𐐮𐑍 𐑁𐐭𐐼 𐑁𐐬𐑉 𐐸𐐮𐑆 𐑅𐐲𐐹𐐬𐑉𐐻.

11. 𐐈𐑌𐐼 𐐮𐐻 𐐿𐐩𐑋 𐐻𐐭 𐐹𐐪𐑅 𐑄𐐰𐐻 𐐰𐑆 𐐸𐐨 𐐶𐐯𐑌𐐻 𐑁𐐬𐑉𐑃 𐐲𐑋𐐲𐑍 𐑄 𐐹𐐨𐐹𐐲𐑊, 𐐷𐐩, 𐐲𐑋𐐲𐑍 𐐲 𐐹𐐨𐐹𐐲𐑊 𐐸𐐭 𐐸𐐰𐐼 𐑅𐐯𐐹𐐲𐑉𐐩𐐻𐐯𐐼 𐑄𐐯𐑋𐑅𐐯𐑊𐑂𐑆 𐑁𐑉𐐱𐑋 𐑄 𐐤𐐨𐑁𐐴𐐻𐑅, 𐐰𐑌𐐼 𐐿𐐫𐑊𐐼 𐑄𐐯𐑋𐑅𐐯𐑊𐑂𐑆 𐐞𐐬𐑉𐐲𐑋𐐴𐐻𐑅, 𐐺𐐨𐐮𐑍 𐑊𐐯𐐼 𐐺𐐴 𐐲 𐑋𐐰𐑌 𐐸𐐭𐑆 𐑌𐐩𐑋 𐐶𐐱𐑆 𐐞𐐬𐑉𐐲𐑋; 𐐰𐑌𐐼 𐐰𐑆 𐐸𐐨 𐐶𐐯𐑌𐐻 𐑁𐐬𐑉𐑃 𐐲𐑋𐐲𐑍𐑅𐐻 𐑄𐐯𐑋, 𐐺𐐨𐐸𐐬𐑊𐐼, 𐐸𐐨 𐐶𐐱𐑆 𐑉𐐲𐑌 𐐲𐐹𐐱𐑌 𐐰𐑌𐐼 𐐻𐑉𐐱𐐼𐐲𐑌 𐐼𐐵𐑌, 𐐨𐑂𐐲𐑌 𐐲𐑌𐐻𐐮𐑊 𐐸𐐨 𐐶𐐱𐑆 𐐼𐐯𐐼; 𐐰𐑌𐐼 𐑄𐐲𐑅 𐐶𐐨 𐑅𐐨 𐑄 𐐯𐑌𐐼 𐐱𐑂 𐐸𐐮𐑋 𐐸𐐭 𐐹𐐲𐑉𐑂𐐲𐑉𐐻𐐯𐑃 𐑄 𐐶𐐩𐑆 𐐱𐑂 𐑄 𐑊𐐬𐑉𐐼; 𐐰𐑌𐐼 𐑄𐐲𐑅 𐐶𐐨 𐑅𐐨 𐑄𐐰𐐻 𐑄 𐐼𐐯𐑂𐐮𐑊 𐐶𐐮𐑊 𐑌𐐱𐐻 𐑅𐐲𐐹𐐬𐑉𐐻 𐐸𐐮𐑆 𐐽𐐮𐑊𐐼𐑉𐐯𐑌 𐐰𐐻 𐑄 𐑊𐐪𐑅𐐻 𐐼𐐩, 𐐺𐐲𐐻 𐐼𐐲𐑃 𐑅𐐹𐐨𐐼𐐮𐑊𐐮 𐐼𐑉𐐰𐑀 𐑄𐐯𐑋 𐐼𐐵𐑌 𐐻𐐭 𐐸𐐯𐑊.

12. 𐐤𐐵 𐐮𐐻 𐐿𐐩𐑋 𐐻𐐭 𐐹𐐪𐑅 𐑄𐐰𐐻 𐐪𐑁𐐻𐐲𐑉 𐑄 𐐯𐑌𐐼 𐐱𐑂 𐐗𐐬𐑉𐐴𐐸𐐬𐑉, 𐐈𐑊𐑋𐐲 𐐸𐐰𐑂𐐮𐑍 𐑉𐐨𐑅𐐨𐑂𐐼 𐐻𐐴𐐼𐐮𐑍𐑆 𐑄𐐰𐐻 𐑄 𐐞𐐬𐑉𐐲𐑋𐐴𐐻𐑅 𐐶𐐲𐑉 𐐹𐐲𐑉𐑂𐐲𐑉𐐻𐐮𐑍 𐑄 𐐶𐐩𐑆 𐐱𐑂 𐑄 𐑊𐐬𐑉𐐼, 𐐰𐑌𐐼 𐑄𐐰𐐻 𐐞𐐬𐑉𐐲𐑋, 𐐸𐐭 𐐶𐐱𐑆 𐑄𐐩𐑉 𐑊𐐨𐐼𐐲𐑉, 𐐶𐐱𐑆 𐑊𐐨𐐼𐐮𐑍 𐑄 𐐸𐐪𐑉𐐻𐑅 𐐱𐑂 𐑄 𐐹𐐨𐐹𐐲𐑊 𐐻𐐭 𐐺𐐵 𐐼𐐵𐑌 𐐻𐐭 𐐼𐐲𐑋 𐐴𐐼𐐲𐑊𐑆, 𐐯𐐻𐑅., 𐐸𐐮𐑆 𐐸𐐪𐑉𐐻 𐐲𐑀𐐯𐑌 𐐺𐐨𐑀𐐰𐑌 𐐻𐐭 𐑅𐐮𐐿𐐲𐑌, 𐐺𐐨𐐿𐐫𐑆 𐐱𐑂 𐑄 𐐮𐑌𐐮𐐿𐐶𐐮𐐻𐐮 𐐱𐑂 𐑄 𐐹𐐨𐐹𐐲𐑊; 𐑁𐐬𐑉 𐐮𐐻 𐐶𐐱𐑆 𐑄 𐐿𐐫𐑆 𐐱𐑂 𐑀𐑉𐐩𐐻 𐑅𐐱𐑉𐐬 𐐻𐐭 𐐈𐑊𐑋𐐲 𐐻𐐭 𐑌𐐬 𐐱𐑂 𐐮𐑌𐐮𐐿𐐶𐐮𐐻𐐮 𐐲𐑋𐐲𐑍 𐐸𐐮𐑆 𐐹𐐨𐐹𐐲𐑊; 𐑄𐐩𐑉𐑁𐐬𐑉 𐐸𐐮𐑆 𐐸𐐪𐑉𐐻 𐐶𐐱𐑆 𐐯𐐿𐑅𐐨𐐼𐐮𐑍𐑊𐐮 𐑅𐐱𐑉𐐬𐑁𐐳𐑊, 𐐺𐐨𐐿𐐫𐑆 𐐱𐑂 𐑄 𐑅𐐯𐐹𐐲𐑉𐐩𐑇𐐲𐑌 𐐱𐑂 𐑄 𐐞𐐬𐑉𐐲𐑋𐐴𐐻𐑅 𐑁𐑉𐐱𐑋 𐑄 𐐤𐐨𐑁𐐴𐐻𐑅. 𐐤𐐵 𐑄 𐐞𐐬𐑉𐐲𐑋𐐴𐐻𐑅 𐐸𐐰𐐼 𐑀𐐰𐑄𐐲𐑉𐐼 𐑄𐐯𐑋𐑅𐐯𐑊𐑂𐑆 𐐻𐐭𐑀𐐯𐑄𐐲𐑉 𐐮𐑌 𐐲 𐑊𐐰𐑌𐐼 𐐸𐐶𐐮𐐽 𐑄𐐩 𐐿𐐫𐑊𐐼 𐐈𐑌𐐻𐐨𐐬𐑌𐐲𐑋, 𐐸𐐶𐐮𐐽 𐐶𐐱𐑆 𐐨𐑅𐐻 𐐱𐑂 𐑄 𐑊𐐰𐑌𐐼 𐐱𐑂 𐐞𐐰𐑉𐐲𐐸𐐯𐑋𐑊𐐲, 𐐸𐐶𐐮𐐽 𐑊𐐩 𐑌𐐨𐑉𐑊𐐮 𐐺𐐬𐑉𐐼𐐲𐑉𐐮𐑍 𐐲𐐹𐐱𐑌 𐑄 𐑅𐐨 𐑇𐐬𐑉, 𐐸𐐶𐐮𐐽 𐐶𐐱𐑆 𐑅𐐵𐑃 𐐱𐑂 𐑄 𐑊𐐰𐑌𐐼 𐐱𐑂 𐐖𐐲𐑉𐑇𐐲𐑌, 𐐸𐐶𐐮𐐽 𐐫𐑊𐑅𐐬 𐐺𐐬𐑉𐐼𐐲𐑉𐐼 𐐲𐐹𐐱𐑌 𐑄 𐐶𐐮𐑊𐐼𐐲𐑉𐑌𐐯𐑅 𐑅𐐵𐑃, 𐐸𐐶𐐮𐐽 𐐶𐐮𐑊𐐼𐐲𐑉𐑌𐐯𐑅 𐐶𐐱𐑆 𐑁𐐳𐑊 𐐱𐑂 𐑄 𐐢𐐰𐑋𐐲𐑌𐐴𐐻𐑅. 𐐤𐐵 𐑄 𐐤𐐨𐑁𐐴𐐻𐑅 𐑀𐑉𐐩𐐻𐑊𐐮 𐑁𐐨𐑉𐐼 𐑄𐐰𐐻 𐑄 𐐞𐐬𐑉𐐲𐑋-𐐴𐐻𐑅 𐐶𐐳𐐼 𐐯𐑌𐐻𐐲𐑉 𐐮𐑌𐐻𐐭 𐐲 𐐿𐐱𐑉𐐯𐑅𐐹𐐱𐑌𐐼𐐯𐑌𐑅 𐐶𐐮𐑃 𐑄 𐐢𐐰𐑋𐐲𐑌𐐴𐐻𐑅, 𐐰𐑌𐐼 𐑄𐐰𐐻 𐐮𐐻 𐐶𐐳𐐼 𐐺𐐨 𐑄 𐑋𐐨𐑌𐑆 𐐱𐑂 𐑀𐑉𐐩𐐻 𐑊𐐱𐑅 𐐱𐑌 𐑄 𐐹𐐪𐑉𐐻 𐐱𐑂 𐑄 𐐤𐐨𐑁𐐴𐐻𐑅. 𐐈𐑌𐐼 𐑌𐐵 𐐰𐑆 𐑄 𐐹𐑉𐐨𐐽𐐮𐑍 𐐱𐑂 𐑄 𐐶𐐲𐑉𐐼 𐐸𐐰𐐼 𐐲 𐑀𐑉𐐩𐐻 𐐻𐐯𐑌𐐼𐐯𐑌𐑅𐐮 𐐻𐐭 𐑊𐐨𐐼 𐑄 𐐹𐐨𐐹𐐲𐑊 𐐻𐐭 𐐼𐐭 𐑄𐐰𐐻 𐐸𐐶𐐮𐐽 𐐶𐐱𐑆 𐐾𐐲𐑅𐐻; 𐐷𐐩, 𐐮𐐻 𐐸𐐰𐐼 𐐸𐐰𐐼 𐑋𐐬𐑉 𐐹𐐵𐐲𐑉𐑁𐐳𐑊 𐐯𐑁𐐯𐐿𐐻 𐐲𐐹𐐱𐑌 𐑄 𐑋𐐴𐑌𐐼𐑆 𐐱𐑂 𐑄 𐐹𐐨𐐹𐐲𐑊 𐑄𐐰𐑌 𐑄 𐑅𐐬𐑉𐐼, 𐐫𐑉 𐐯𐑌𐐮 𐑃𐐮𐑍 𐐯𐑊𐑅, 𐐸𐐶𐐮𐐽 𐐸𐐰𐐼 𐐸𐐰𐐹𐐲𐑌𐐼 𐐲𐑌𐐻𐐭 𐑄𐐯𐑋; 𐑄𐐩𐑉𐑁𐐬𐑉 𐐈𐑊𐑋𐐲 𐑃𐐫𐐻 𐐮𐐻 𐐶𐐱𐑆 𐐯𐐿𐑅𐐹𐐨𐐼𐐨𐐯𐑌𐐻 𐑄𐐰𐐻 𐑄𐐩 𐑇𐐳𐐼 𐐻𐑉𐐴 𐑄 𐑂𐐲𐑉𐐽𐐭 𐐱𐑂 𐑄 𐐶𐐲𐑉𐐼 𐐱𐑂 𐐘𐐱𐐼. 𐐜𐐩𐑉𐑁𐐬𐑉 𐐸𐐨 𐐻𐐳𐐿 𐐈𐑋𐐲𐑌, 𐐰𐑌𐐼 𐐇𐑉𐐲𐑌, 𐐰𐑌𐐼 𐐉𐑋𐑌𐐲𐑉; 𐐰𐑌𐐼 𐐐𐐮𐑋𐑌𐐴 𐐸𐐨 𐐼𐐮𐐼 𐑊𐐨𐑂 𐐮𐑌 𐑄 𐐽𐐲𐑉𐐽 𐐮𐑌 𐐞𐐰𐑉𐐲𐐸𐐯𐑋𐑊𐐲; 𐐺𐐲𐐻 𐑄 𐑁𐐫𐑉𐑋𐐲𐑉 𐑃𐑉𐐨 𐐸𐐨 𐐻𐐳𐐿 𐐶𐐮𐑃 𐐸𐐮𐑋, 𐐰𐑌𐐼 𐐫𐑊𐑅𐐬 𐐈𐑋𐐷𐐭𐑊𐐯𐐿 𐐰𐑌𐐼 𐐞𐐨𐑆𐑉𐐲𐑋, 𐐸𐐭 𐐶𐐲𐑉 𐐰𐐻 𐐣𐐯𐑊𐐯𐐿; 𐐰𐑌𐐼 𐐸𐐨 𐐫𐑊𐑅𐐬 𐐻𐐳𐐿 𐐻𐐭 𐐱𐑂 𐐸𐐮𐑆 𐑅𐐲𐑌𐑆. 𐐤𐐵 𐑄 𐐯𐑊𐐼𐐯𐑅𐐻 𐐱𐑂 𐐸𐐮𐑆 𐑅𐐲𐑌𐑆 𐐸𐐨 𐐻𐐳𐐿 𐑌𐐱𐐻 𐐶𐐮𐑃 𐐸𐐮𐑋, 𐐰𐑌𐐼 𐐸𐐮𐑆 𐑌𐐩𐑋 𐐶𐐱𐑆 𐐐𐐨𐑊𐐲𐑋𐐲𐑌; 𐐺𐐲𐐻 𐑄 𐑌𐐩𐑋𐑆 𐐱𐑂 𐑄𐐬𐑆 𐐸𐐭𐑋 𐐸𐐨 𐐻𐐳𐐿 𐐶𐐮𐑃 𐐸𐐮𐑋, 𐐶𐐲𐑉 𐐟𐐮𐐺𐑊𐐲𐑌, 𐐰𐑌𐐼 𐐗𐐬𐑉𐐨𐐰𐑌𐐻𐐲𐑌; 𐐰𐑌𐐼 𐑄𐐨𐑆 𐐪𐑉 𐑄 𐑌𐐩𐑋𐑆 𐐱𐑂 𐑄𐐬𐑆 𐐸𐐭 𐐶𐐯𐑌𐐻 𐐶𐐮𐑃 𐐸𐐮𐑋 𐐲𐑋𐐲𐑍 𐑄 𐐞𐐬𐑉𐐲𐑋𐐴𐐻𐑅 𐐻𐐭 𐐹𐑉𐐨𐐽 𐐲𐑌𐐻𐐭 𐑄𐐯𐑋 𐑄 𐐶𐐲𐑉𐐼.

13. 𐐤𐐵 𐑄 𐐞𐐬𐑉𐐲𐑋𐐴𐐻𐑅 𐐶𐐲𐑉 𐐼𐐮𐑅𐐯𐑌𐐻𐐲𐑉𐑆 𐑁𐑉𐐱𐑋 𐑄 𐐤𐐨𐑁𐐴𐐻𐑅; 𐑄𐐩𐑉𐑁𐐬𐑉 𐑄𐐩 𐐸𐐰𐐼 𐐸𐐰𐐼 𐑄 𐐶𐐲𐑉𐐼 𐐱𐑂 𐐘𐐱𐐼 𐐹𐑉𐐨𐐽𐐻 𐐲𐑌𐐻𐐭 𐑄𐐯𐑋. 𐐒𐐲𐐻 𐑄𐐩 𐐸𐐰𐐼 𐑁𐐫𐑊𐐲𐑌 𐐮𐑌𐐻𐐭 𐑀𐑉𐐩𐐻 𐐯𐑉𐐲𐑉𐑆, 𐑁𐐬𐑉 𐑄𐐩 𐐶𐐳𐐼 𐑌𐐱𐐻 𐐱𐐺𐑆𐐲𐑉𐑂 𐐻𐐭 𐐿𐐨𐐹 𐑄 𐐿𐐱𐑋𐐰𐑌𐐼𐑋𐐯𐑌𐐻𐑅 𐐱𐑂 𐐘𐐱𐐼, 𐐰𐑌𐐼 𐐸𐐮𐑆 𐑅𐐻𐐰𐐻𐐭𐐻𐑅, 𐐰𐐿𐐫𐑉𐐼𐐮𐑍 𐐻𐐭 𐑄 𐑊𐐫 𐐱𐑂 𐐣𐐬𐑆𐐯𐑆; 𐑌𐐨𐑄𐐲𐑉 𐐶𐐳𐐼 𐑄𐐩 𐐱𐐺𐑆𐐲𐑉𐑂 𐑄 𐐹𐐲𐑉𐑁𐐫𐑉𐑋𐐲𐑌𐑅𐐯𐑆 𐐱𐑂 𐑄 𐐽𐐲𐑉𐐽, 𐐻𐐭 𐐿𐐱𐑌𐐻𐐮𐑌𐑏 𐐮𐑌 𐐹𐑉𐐩𐐲𐑉 𐐰𐑌𐐼 𐑅𐐲𐐹𐑊𐐮𐐿𐐩𐑇𐐲𐑌 𐐻𐐭 𐐘𐐱𐐼 𐐼𐐩𐑊𐐮, 𐑄𐐰𐐻 𐑄𐐩 𐑋𐐴𐐻 𐑌𐐱𐐻 𐐯𐑌𐐻𐐲𐑉 𐐮𐑌𐐻𐐭 𐐻𐐯𐑋𐐻𐐩𐑇𐐲𐑌; 𐐷𐐩, 𐐮𐑌 𐑁𐐴𐑌, 𐑄𐐩 𐐼𐐮𐐼 𐐹𐐲𐑉𐑂𐐲𐑉𐐻 𐑄 𐐶𐐩𐑆 𐐱𐑂 𐑄 𐑊𐐬𐑉𐐼 𐐮𐑌 𐑂𐐯𐑉𐐮 𐑋𐐯𐑌𐐮 𐐮𐑌𐑅𐐻𐐲𐑌𐑅𐐯𐑆; 𐑄𐐩𐑉𐑁𐐬𐑉, 𐑁𐐬𐑉 𐑄𐐮𐑅 𐐿𐐫𐑆, 𐐈𐑊𐑋𐐲 𐐰𐑌𐐼 𐐸𐐮𐑆 𐐺𐑉𐐯𐑄𐑉𐐯𐑌 𐐶𐐯𐑌𐐻 𐐮𐑌𐐻𐐭 𐑄 𐑊𐐰𐑌𐐼 𐐻𐐭 𐐹𐑉𐐨𐐽 𐑄 𐐶𐐲𐑉𐐼 𐐲𐑌𐐻𐐭 𐑄𐐯𐑋.

14. 𐐤𐐵 𐐸𐐶𐐯𐑌 𐑄𐐩 𐐸𐐰𐐼 𐐿𐐲𐑋 𐐮𐑌𐐻𐐭 𐑄 𐑊𐐰𐑌𐐼, 𐐺𐐨𐐸𐐬𐑊𐐼, 𐐻𐐭 𐑄𐐩𐑉 𐐲𐑅𐐻𐐱𐑌𐐮𐑇𐑋𐐯𐑌𐐻, 𐑄𐐩 𐑁𐐵𐑌𐐼 𐑄𐐰𐐻 𐑄 𐐞𐐬𐑉𐐲𐑋𐐴𐐻𐑅 𐐸𐐰𐐼 𐐺𐐮𐑊𐐻 𐑅𐐮𐑌𐐲𐑀𐐱𐑀𐑆, 𐐰𐑌𐐼 𐑄𐐰𐐻 𐑄𐐩 𐐼𐐮𐐼 𐑀𐐰𐑄𐐲𐑉 𐑄𐐯𐑋𐑅𐐯𐑊𐑂𐑆 𐐻𐐭𐑀𐐯𐑄𐐲𐑉 𐐱𐑌 𐐶𐐲𐑌 𐐼𐐩 𐐱𐑂 𐑄 𐐶𐐨𐐿, 𐐸𐐶𐐮𐐽 𐐼𐐩 𐑄𐐩 𐐼𐐮𐐼 𐐿𐐫𐑊 𐑄 𐐼𐐩 𐐱𐑂 𐑄 𐑊𐐬𐑉𐐼; 𐐰𐑌𐐼 𐑄𐐩 𐐼𐐮𐐼 𐐶𐐲𐑉𐑇𐐮𐐹

𐐰𐑁𐐻𐐲𐑉 𐐲 𐑋𐐰𐑌𐐲𐑉 𐐸𐐶𐐮𐐽 𐐈𐑊𐑋𐐲 𐐰𐑌𐐼 𐐸𐐮𐑆 𐐺𐑉𐐯𐑄𐑉𐐯𐑌 𐐸𐐰𐐼 𐑌𐐯𐑂𐐲𐑉 𐐺𐐨𐐸𐐯𐑊𐐼; 𐑁𐐫𐑉 𐑄𐐩 𐐸𐐰𐐼 𐐲 𐐹𐑊𐐩𐑅 𐐺𐐮𐑊𐐻 𐐲𐐹 𐐮𐑌 𐑄 𐑅𐐯𐑌𐐻𐐲𐑉 𐐱𐑂 𐑄𐐯𐑉 𐑅𐐮𐑌𐐲𐑀𐐱𐑀, 𐐲 𐐹𐑊𐐩𐑅 𐑁𐐫𐑉 𐑅𐐻𐐰𐑌𐐼𐐮𐑍, 𐐸𐐶𐐮𐐽 𐐶𐐱𐑆 𐐸𐐴 𐐲𐐺𐐲𐑂 𐑄 𐐸𐐯𐐼; 𐐰𐑌𐐼 𐑄 𐐻𐐱𐐹 𐑄𐐯𐑉𐐱𐑂 𐐶𐐳𐐼 𐐬𐑌𐑊𐐨 𐐰𐐼𐑋𐐮𐐻 𐐶𐐲𐑌 𐐹𐐲𐑉𐑅𐐲𐑌. 𐐜𐐯𐑉𐑁𐐫𐑉, 𐐸𐐭𐑅𐐬𐐯𐑂𐐲𐑉 𐐼𐐨𐑆𐐴𐑉𐐼 𐐻𐐭 𐐶𐐲𐑉𐑇𐐮𐐹, 𐑋𐐲𐑅𐐻 𐑀𐐬 𐑁𐐫𐑉𐑃 𐐰𐑌𐐼 𐑅𐐻𐐰𐑌𐐼 𐐲𐐹𐐱𐑌 𐑄 𐐻𐐱𐐹 𐑄𐐯𐑉𐐱𐑂, 𐐰𐑌𐐼 𐑅𐐻𐑉𐐯𐐽 𐑁𐐫𐑉𐑃 𐐸𐐮𐑆 𐐸𐐰𐑌𐐼𐑆 𐐻𐐬𐑉𐐼𐑆 𐐸𐐯𐑂𐐲𐑌, 𐐰𐑌𐐼 𐐿𐑉𐐴 𐐶𐐮𐑄 𐐲 𐑊𐐵𐐼 𐑂𐐶𐑅, 𐑅𐐩𐐮𐑍: 𐐐𐐬𐑊𐐨, 𐐸𐐬𐑊𐐨 𐐘𐐱𐐼; 𐐶𐐨 𐐺𐐨𐑊𐐨𐑂 𐑄𐐰𐐻 𐑄𐐵 𐐪𐑉𐐻 𐐘𐐱𐐼, 𐐰𐑌𐐼 𐐶𐐨 𐐺𐐨𐑊𐐨𐑂 𐑄𐐰𐐻 𐑄𐐵 𐐪𐑉𐐻 𐐸𐐬𐑊𐐨, 𐐰𐑌𐐼 𐑄𐐰𐐻 𐑄𐐵 𐐶𐐱𐑅𐐻 𐐲 𐑅𐐹𐐮𐑉𐐮𐐻, 𐐰𐑌𐐼 𐑄𐐰𐐻 𐑄𐐵 𐐪𐑉𐐻 𐐲 𐑅𐐹𐐮𐑉𐐮𐐻, 𐐰𐑌𐐼 𐑄𐐰𐐻 𐑄𐐵 𐐶𐐮𐑊𐐻 𐐺𐐨 𐐲 𐑅𐐹𐐮𐑉𐐮𐐻 𐑁𐐫𐑉 𐐯𐑂𐐲𐑉. 𐐐𐐬𐑊𐐨 𐐘𐐱𐐼, 𐐶𐐨 𐐺𐐨𐑊𐐨𐑂 𐑄𐐰𐐻 𐑄𐐵 𐐸𐐰𐑅𐐻 𐑅𐐯𐐹𐐲𐑉𐐩𐐻𐐯𐐼 𐐲𐑅 𐑁𐑉𐐱𐑋 𐐵𐑉 𐐺𐑉𐐯𐑄𐑉𐐯𐑌; 𐐰𐑌𐐼 𐐶𐐨 𐐼𐐭 𐑌𐐱𐐻 𐐺𐐨𐑊𐐨𐑂 𐐮𐑌 𐑄 𐐻𐑉𐐲𐐼𐐮𐑇𐐲𐑌 𐐱𐑂 𐐵𐑉 𐐺𐑉𐐯𐑄𐑉𐐯𐑌, 𐐸𐐶𐐮𐐽 𐐶𐐱𐑆 𐐸𐐰𐑌𐐼𐐯𐐼 𐐼𐐵𐑌 𐐻𐐭 𐑄𐐯𐑋 𐐺𐐴 𐑄 𐐽𐐴𐑊𐐼𐐮𐑇𐑌𐐯𐑅 𐐱𐑂 𐑄𐐯𐑉 𐑁𐐪𐑄𐐲𐑉𐑆; 𐐺𐐲𐐻 𐐶𐐨 𐐺𐐨𐑊𐐨𐑂 𐑄𐐰𐐻 𐑄𐐵 𐐸𐐰𐑅𐐻 𐐨𐑊𐐯𐐿𐐻𐐯𐐼 𐐲𐑅 𐐻𐐭 𐐺𐐨 𐑄𐐴 𐐸𐐬𐑊𐐨 𐐽𐐮𐑊𐐼𐑉𐐯𐑌; 𐐰𐑌𐐼 𐐫𐑊𐑅𐐬 𐑄𐐵 𐐸𐐰𐑅𐐻 𐑋𐐩𐐼 𐐮𐐻 𐑌𐐬𐑌 𐐲𐑌𐐻𐐭 𐐲𐑅 𐑄𐐰𐐻 𐑄𐐯𐑉 𐑇𐐰𐑊 𐐺𐐨 𐑌𐐬 𐐗𐑉𐐴𐑅𐐻; 𐐺𐐲𐐻 𐑄𐐵 𐐪𐑉𐐻 𐑄 𐑅𐐩𐑋 𐐷𐐯𐑅𐐻𐐲𐑉𐐼𐐩, 𐐻𐐭-𐐼𐐩, 𐐰𐑌𐐼 𐑁𐐫𐑉𐐯𐑂𐐲𐑉; 𐐰𐑌𐐼 𐑄𐐵 𐐸𐐰𐑅𐐻 𐐨𐑊𐐯𐐿𐐻𐐯𐐼 𐐲𐑅, 𐑄𐐰𐐻 𐐶𐐨 𐑇𐐰𐑊 𐐺𐐨 𐑅𐐩𐑂𐐼, 𐐸𐐶𐐴𐑊𐑅𐐻 𐐫𐑊 𐐲𐑉𐐵𐑌𐐼 𐐲𐑅 𐐪𐑉 𐐨𐑊𐐯𐐿𐐻𐐯𐐼 𐐻𐐭 𐐺𐐨 𐐿𐐰𐑅𐐻 𐐺𐐴 𐑄𐐴 𐑉𐐱𐑃 𐐼𐐵𐑌 𐐻𐐭 𐐸𐐯𐑊; 𐑁𐐫𐑉 𐑄 𐐸𐐶𐐮𐐽 𐐸𐐬𐑊𐐨𐑌𐐯𐑅, O 𐐘𐐱𐐼, 𐐶𐐨 𐑃𐐰𐑍𐐿 𐑄𐐨; 𐐰𐑌𐐼 𐐶𐐨 𐐫𐑊𐑅𐐬 𐑃𐐰𐑍𐐿 𐑄𐐨 𐑄𐐰𐐻 𐑄𐐵 𐐸𐐰𐑅𐐻 𐐨𐑊𐐯𐐿𐐻𐐯𐐼 𐐲𐑅, 𐑄𐐰𐐻 𐐶𐐨 𐑋𐐩 𐑌𐐱𐐻 𐐺𐐨 𐑊𐐯𐐼 𐐲𐐶𐐩 𐐰𐑁𐐻𐐲𐑉 𐑄 𐑁𐐭𐑊𐐮𐑇 𐐻𐑉𐐲𐐼𐐮𐑇𐐲𐑌𐑆 𐐱𐑂 𐐵𐑉 𐐺𐑉𐐯𐑄𐑉𐐯𐑌, 𐐸𐐶𐐮𐐽 𐐼𐐲𐑃 𐐺𐐴𐑌𐐼 𐑄𐐯𐑋 𐐼𐐵𐑌 𐐻𐐭 𐐲 𐐺𐐨𐑊𐐨𐑁 𐐱𐑂 𐐗𐑉𐐴𐑅𐐻, 𐐸𐐶𐐮𐐽 𐐼𐐲𐑃 𐑊𐐨𐐼 𐑄𐐯𐑉 𐐸𐐪𐑉𐐻𐑅 𐐻𐐭 𐐶𐐱𐑌𐐼𐐲𐑉 𐑁𐐪𐑉 𐑁𐑉𐐱𐑋 𐑄𐐨, 𐐵𐑉 𐐘𐐱𐐼. 𐐈𐑌𐐼 𐐲𐑀𐐯𐑌: 𐐎𐐨 𐑃𐐰𐑍𐐿 𐑄𐐨, O 𐐘𐐱𐐼, 𐑄𐐰𐐻 𐐶𐐨 𐐪𐑉 𐐲 𐐽𐐬𐑆𐐲𐑌 𐐰𐑌𐐼 𐐲 𐐸𐐬𐑊𐐨 𐐹𐐨𐐹𐑊. 𐐁𐑋𐐯𐑌.

15. 𐐤𐐵 𐐮𐐻 𐐿𐐩𐑋 𐐻𐐭 𐐹𐐰𐑅 𐑄𐐰𐐻 𐐰𐑁𐐻𐐲𐑉 𐐈𐑊𐑋𐐲 𐐰𐑌𐐼 𐐸𐐮𐑆 𐐺𐑉𐐯𐑄𐑉𐐯𐑌, 𐐰𐑌𐐼 𐐸𐐮𐑆 𐑅𐐲𐑌𐑆, 𐐸𐐰𐐼 𐐸𐐲𐑉𐐼 𐑄𐐨𐑆 𐐹𐑉𐐩𐑉𐑆, 𐑄𐐩 𐐶𐐲𐑉 𐐰𐑅𐐻𐐱𐑌𐐮𐑇𐐻 𐐺𐐨𐐷𐐱𐑌𐐼 𐐫𐑊 𐑋𐐯𐑈𐐲𐑉. 𐐙𐐫𐑉 𐐺𐐨𐐸𐐬𐑊𐐼, 𐐯𐑂𐐲𐑉𐐨 𐑋𐐰𐑌 𐐼𐐮𐐼 𐑀𐐬 𐑁𐐫𐑉𐑃 𐐰𐑌𐐼 𐐱𐑁𐐲𐑉 𐐲𐐹 𐑄𐐨𐑆 𐑅𐐩𐑋 𐐹𐑉𐐩𐑉𐑆. 𐐤𐐵 𐑄 𐐹𐑊𐐩𐑅 𐐶𐐱𐑆 𐐿𐐫𐑊𐐼 𐐺𐐴 𐑄𐐯𐑋 𐐡𐐰𐑋𐐨𐐲𐑋𐐹𐐻𐐲𐑋, 𐐸𐐶𐐮𐐽, 𐐺𐐨𐐮𐑍 𐐮𐑌𐐻𐐲𐑉𐐹𐑉𐐯𐐻𐐯𐐼, 𐐮𐑆 𐑄 𐐐𐐬𐑊𐐨 𐐝𐐻𐐰𐑌𐐼. 𐐤𐐵 𐑁𐑉𐐱𐑋 𐑄𐐮𐑅 𐑅𐐻𐐰𐑌𐐼 𐑄𐐩 𐐼𐐮𐐼 𐐱𐑁𐐲𐑉 𐐲𐐹, 𐐯𐑂𐐲𐑉𐐨 𐑋𐐰𐑌, 𐑄 𐑅𐐯𐑊𐑁𐑅𐐩𐑋 𐐹𐑉𐐩𐑉 𐐲𐑌𐐻𐐭 𐐘𐐱𐐼, 𐑃𐐰𐑍𐐿𐐮𐑍 𐑄𐐯𐑉 𐐘𐐱𐐼 𐑄𐐰𐐻 𐑄𐐩 𐐶𐐲𐑉 𐐽𐐬𐑆𐐲𐑌 𐐱𐑂 𐐸𐐮𐑋, 𐐰𐑌𐐼 𐑄𐐰𐐻 𐐸𐐨 𐐼𐐮𐐼 𐑌𐐱𐐻 𐑊𐐨𐐼 𐑄𐐯𐑋 𐐲𐐶𐐩 𐐰𐑁𐐻𐐲𐑉 𐑄 𐐻𐑉𐐲𐐼𐐮𐑇𐐲𐑌 𐐱𐑂 𐑄𐐯𐑉 𐐺𐑉𐐯𐑄𐑉𐐯𐑌; 𐐰𐑌𐐼 𐑄𐐰𐐻 𐑄𐐯𐑉 𐐸𐐪𐑉𐐻𐑅 𐐶𐐲𐑉 𐑌𐐱𐐻 𐑅𐐻𐐬𐑊𐐲𐑌 𐐲𐐶𐐩 𐐻𐐭 𐐺𐐨𐑊𐐨𐑂 𐐮𐑌 𐑃𐐮𐑍𐑆 𐐻𐐭 𐐿𐐲𐑋, 𐐸𐐶𐐮𐐽 𐑄𐐩 𐑌𐐭 𐑌𐐲𐑃𐐮𐑍 𐐲𐐺𐐵𐐻.

16. 𐐤𐐵 𐐰𐑁𐐻𐐲𐑉 𐑄 𐐹𐐨𐐹𐑊 𐐸𐐰𐐼 𐐫𐑊 𐐱𐑁𐐲𐑉𐐼 𐐲𐐹 𐑃𐐰𐑍𐐿𐑅 𐐰𐑁𐐻𐐲𐑉 𐑄𐐮𐑅 𐑋𐐰𐑌𐐲𐑉, 𐑄𐐩 𐑉𐐨𐐻𐐲𐑉𐑌𐐼 𐐻𐐭 𐑄𐐯𐑉 𐐸𐐬𐑋𐑆, 𐑌𐐯𐑂𐐲𐑉 𐑅𐐹𐐨𐐿𐐮𐑍 𐐱𐑂 𐑄𐐯𐑉 𐐘𐐱𐐼 𐐲𐑀𐐯𐑌 𐐲𐑌𐐻𐐮𐑊 𐑄𐐩 𐐸𐐰𐐼 𐐰𐑅𐐯𐑋𐐺𐑊𐐼 𐑄𐐯𐑋𐑅𐐯𐑊𐑂𐑆 𐐻𐐭𐑀𐐯𐑄𐐲𐑉 𐐲𐑀𐐯𐑌 𐐻𐐭 𐑄 𐐐𐐬𐑊𐐨 𐐝𐐻𐐰𐑌𐐼, 𐐻𐐭 𐐱𐑁𐐲𐑉 𐐲𐐹 𐑃𐐰𐑍𐐿𐑅 𐐰𐑁𐐻𐐲𐑉 𐑄𐐯𐑉 𐑋𐐰𐑌𐐲𐑉. 𐐤𐐵 𐐸𐐶𐐯𐑌 𐐈𐑊𐑋𐐲 𐑅𐐫 𐑄𐐮𐑅, 𐐸𐐮𐑆 𐐸𐐪𐑉𐐻 𐐶𐐱𐑆 𐑀𐑉𐐨𐑂𐐼; 𐑁𐐫𐑉 𐐸𐐨 𐑅𐐫 𐑄𐐰𐐻 𐑄𐐩 𐐶𐐲𐑉 𐐲 𐐶𐐮𐐿𐐯𐐼 𐐰𐑌𐐼 𐐲 𐐹𐐲𐑉𐑂𐐲𐑉𐑅 𐐹𐐨𐐹𐑊; 𐐷𐐩, 𐐸𐐨 𐑅𐐫 𐑄𐐰𐐻 𐑄𐐯𐑉 𐐸𐐪𐑉𐐻𐑅 𐐶𐐲𐑉 𐑅𐐯𐐻 𐐲𐐹𐐱𐑌 𐑀𐐬𐑊𐐼, 𐐰𐑌𐐼 𐐲𐐹𐐱𐑌 𐑅𐐮𐑊𐑂𐐲𐑉, 𐐰𐑌𐐼 𐐲𐐹𐐱𐑌 𐐫𐑊 𐑋𐐰𐑌𐐲𐑉 𐐱𐑂 𐑁𐐴𐑌 𐑀𐐳𐐼𐑆. 𐐏𐐩, 𐐰𐑌𐐼 𐐸𐐨 𐐫𐑊𐑅𐐬 𐑅𐐫 𐑄𐐰𐐻 𐑄𐐯𐑉 𐐸𐐪𐑉𐐻𐑅 𐐶𐐲𐑉 𐑊𐐮𐑁𐐻𐐯𐐼 𐐲𐐹 𐐲𐑌𐐻𐐭 𐑀𐑉𐐩𐐻 𐐺𐐬𐑅𐐻𐐮𐑍, 𐐮𐑌 𐑄𐐯𐑉 𐐹𐑉𐐴𐐼. 𐐈𐑌𐐼 𐐸𐐨 𐑊𐐮𐑁𐐻𐐯𐐼 𐐲𐐹 𐐸𐐮𐑆 𐑂𐐶𐑅 𐐻𐐭 𐐸𐐯𐑂𐐲𐑌, 𐐰𐑌𐐼 𐐿𐑉𐐴𐐼, 𐑅𐐩𐐮𐑍: O, 𐐸𐐵 𐑊𐐱𐑍, O 𐐢𐐫𐑉𐐼, 𐐶𐐮𐑊𐐻 𐑄𐐵 𐑅𐐲𐑁𐐲𐑉 𐑄𐐰𐐻 𐑄𐐴 𐑅𐐲𐑉𐑂𐐲𐑌𐐻𐑅 𐑇𐐰𐑊 𐐼𐐶𐐯𐑊 𐐸𐐨𐑉 𐐺𐐨𐑊𐐬 𐐮𐑌 𐑄 𐑁𐑊𐐯𐑇, 𐐻𐐭 𐐺𐐨𐐸𐐬𐑊𐐼 𐑅𐐲𐐽 𐑀𐑉𐐬𐑅 𐐶𐐮𐐿𐐯𐐼𐑌𐐯𐑅 𐐲𐑋𐐲𐑍 𐑄 𐐽𐐮𐑊𐐼𐑉𐐯𐑌 𐐱𐑂 𐑋𐐯𐑌. 𐐒𐐨𐐸𐐬𐑊𐐼, O 𐐘𐐱𐐼, 𐑄𐐩 𐐿𐑉𐐴 𐐲𐑌𐐻𐐭 𐑄𐐨, 𐐰𐑌𐐼 𐐷𐐯𐐻 𐑄𐐯𐑉 𐐸𐐪𐑉𐐻𐑅 𐐪𐑉 𐑅𐐶𐐱𐑊𐐬𐐼 𐐲𐐹 𐐮𐑌 𐑄𐐯𐑉 𐐹𐑉𐐴𐐼. 𐐒𐐨𐐸𐐬𐑊𐐼, O 𐐘𐐱𐐼, 𐑄𐐩 𐐿𐑉𐐴 𐐲𐑌𐐻𐐭 𐑄𐐨 𐐶𐐮𐑄 𐑄𐐯𐑉 𐑋𐐵𐑃𐑅, 𐐸𐐶𐐴𐑊 𐑄𐐩 𐐪𐑉 𐐹𐐲𐑁𐐻 𐐲𐐹, 𐐨𐑂𐐲𐑌 𐐻𐐭 𐑀𐑉𐐩𐐻𐑌𐐯𐑅, 𐐶𐐮𐑄 𐑄 𐑂𐐩𐑌 𐑃𐐮𐑍𐑆 𐐱𐑂 𐑄 𐐶𐐲𐑉𐑊𐐼. 𐐒𐐨𐐸𐐬𐑊𐐼, O 𐑋𐐴 𐐘𐐱𐐼, 𐑄𐐯𐑉 𐐿𐐱𐑅𐐻𐑊𐐨 𐐰𐐹𐐰𐑉𐐯𐑊, 𐐰𐑌𐐼 𐑄𐐯𐑉 𐑉𐐮𐑍𐑊𐐯𐐻𐑅, 𐐰𐑌𐐼 𐑄𐐯𐑉 𐐺𐑉𐐩𐑅𐑊𐐯𐐻𐑅, 𐐰𐑌𐐼 𐑄𐐯𐑉 𐐫𐑉𐑌𐐲𐑋𐐯𐑌𐐻𐑅 𐐱𐑂 𐑀𐐬𐑊𐐼, 𐐰𐑌𐐼 𐐫𐑊 𐑄𐐯𐑉 𐐹𐑉𐐯𐑇𐐲𐑅 𐑃𐐮𐑍𐑆 𐐸𐐶𐐮𐐽 𐑄𐐩 𐐪𐑉 𐐫𐑉𐑌𐐲𐑋𐐯𐑌𐐻𐐯𐐼 𐐶𐐮𐑄; 𐐰𐑌𐐼 𐐺𐐨𐐸𐐬𐑊𐐼, 𐑄𐐯𐑉 𐐸𐐪𐑉𐐻𐑅 𐐪𐑉 𐑅𐐯𐐻 𐐲𐐹𐐱𐑌 𐑄𐐯𐑋, 𐐰𐑌𐐼 𐐷𐐯𐐻 𐑄𐐩 𐐿𐑉𐐴 𐐲𐑌𐐻𐐭 𐑄𐐨 𐐰𐑌𐐼 𐑅𐐩, 𐐎𐐨 𐑃𐐰𐑍𐐿 𐑄𐐨, O 𐐘𐐱𐐼, 𐑁𐐫𐑉 𐐶𐐨 𐐪𐑉 𐐲 𐐽𐐬𐑆𐐲𐑌 𐐹𐐨𐐹𐑊 𐐲𐑌𐐻𐐭 𐑄𐐨, 𐐸𐐶𐐴𐑊 𐐲𐑄𐐲𐑉𐑆 𐑇𐐰𐑊 𐐹𐐯𐑉𐐮𐑇. 𐐏𐐩, 𐐰𐑌𐐼 𐑄𐐩 𐑅𐐩 𐑄𐐰𐐻 𐑄𐐵 𐐸𐐰𐑅𐐻 𐑋𐐩𐐼 𐐮𐐻 𐑌𐐬𐑌

𐐲𐑌𐐻𐐭 𐑄𐐯𐑋, 𐑄𐐰𐐻 𐑄𐐩𐑉 𐑇𐐰𐑊 𐐺 𐑌𐐬 𐐗𐑉𐐴𐑅𐐻. 𐐄 𐐢𐐫𐑉𐐼 𐐘𐐱𐐼, 𐐸𐐵 𐐢𐐱𐑍 𐐶𐐮𐑊𐐻 𐑄𐐵 𐑅𐐲𐑁𐐯𐑉 𐑄𐐰𐐻 𐑅𐐲𐐽 𐐶𐐮𐐿𐐯𐐼𐑌𐐯𐑅 𐐰𐑌𐐼 𐐮𐑌𐐮𐐿𐐶𐐮𐐻𐐨 𐑇𐐰𐑊 𐐺 𐐲𐑋𐐲𐑍 𐑄𐐮𐑅 𐐹𐐨𐐹𐑊? 𐐄 𐐢𐐫𐑉𐐼, 𐐶𐐮𐑊𐐻 𐑄𐐵 𐑀𐐮𐑂 𐑋𐐨 𐑅𐐻𐑉𐐯𐑍𐑃, 𐑄𐐰𐐻 𐐌 𐑋𐐩 𐐺𐐩𐑉 𐐶𐐮𐑄 𐑋𐐴𐑌 𐐮𐑌𐑁𐐲𐑉𐑋𐐮𐐻𐐨𐑆? 𐐙𐐫𐑉 𐐌 𐐰𐑋 𐐮𐑌𐑁𐐲𐑉𐑋, 𐐰𐑌𐐼 𐑅𐐲𐐽 𐐶𐐮𐐿𐐯𐐼𐑌𐐯𐑅 𐐲𐑋𐐲𐑍 𐑄𐐮𐑅 𐐹𐐨𐐹𐑊 𐐼𐐲𐑃 𐐹𐐩𐑌 𐑋𐐴 𐑅𐐬𐑊. 𐐄 𐐢𐐫𐑉𐐼 𐑋𐐴 𐐸𐐪𐑉𐐻 𐐮𐑆 𐐯𐐿𐑅𐐨𐐼𐐮𐑍𐑊𐐨 𐑅𐐱𐑉𐐬𐑁𐐳𐑊; 𐐶𐐮𐑊𐐻 𐑄𐐵 𐐿𐐲𐑋𐑁𐐲𐑉𐐻 𐑋𐐴 𐑅𐐬𐑊 𐐮𐑌 𐐗𐑉𐐴𐑅𐐻? 𐐄 𐐢𐐫𐑉𐐼, 𐐶𐐮𐑊𐐻 𐑄𐐵 𐑀𐑉𐐰𐑌𐐻 𐐲𐑌𐐻𐐭 𐑋𐐨 𐑄𐐰𐐻 𐐌 𐑋𐐩 𐐸𐐰𐑂 𐑅𐐻𐑉𐐯𐑍𐑃, 𐑄𐐰𐐻 𐐌 𐑋𐐩 𐑅𐐲𐑁𐐯𐑉 𐐶𐐮𐑄 𐐹𐐩𐑇𐐯𐑌𐑅 𐑄𐐨𐑆 𐐰𐑁𐑊𐐮𐐿𐑇𐐲𐑌𐑆 𐐸𐐶𐐮𐐽 𐑇𐐰𐑊 𐐿𐐲𐑋 𐐲𐐹𐐱𐑌 𐑋𐐨, 𐐺𐐨𐐿𐐫𐑆 𐐱𐑂 𐑄 𐐮𐑌𐐮𐐿𐐶𐐮𐐻𐐨 𐐱𐑂 𐑄𐐮𐑅 𐐹𐐨𐐹𐑊? 𐐄 𐐢𐐫𐑉𐐼, 𐐶𐐮𐑊𐐻 𐑄𐐵 𐐿𐐲𐑋𐑁𐐲𐑉𐐻 𐑋𐐴 𐑅𐐬𐑊, 𐐰𐑌𐐼 𐑀𐐮𐑂 𐐲𐑌𐐻𐐭 𐑋𐐨 𐑅𐐲𐐿𐑅𐐯𐑅, 𐐰𐑌𐐼 𐐫𐑊𐑅𐐬 𐑋𐐴 𐑁𐐯𐑊𐐬-𐑊𐐩𐐺𐐲𐑉𐐯𐑉𐑆 𐐸𐐭 𐐪𐑉 𐐶𐐮𐑄 𐑋𐐨; 𐐏𐐩, 𐐈𐑋𐐲𐑌, 𐐰𐑌𐐼 𐐁𐑉𐐲𐑌, 𐐰𐑌𐐼 𐐉𐑋𐑌𐐯𐑉, 𐐰𐑌𐐼 𐐫𐑊𐑅𐐬 𐐈𐑋𐐷𐐭𐑊𐐯𐐿 𐐰𐑌𐐼 𐐞𐐨𐐯𐑆𐑉𐐲𐑋, 𐐰𐑌𐐼 𐐫𐑊𐑅𐐬 𐑋𐐴 𐐻𐐭 𐑅𐐲𐑌𐑆; 𐐏𐐩, 𐐨𐑂𐑌 𐐫𐑊 𐑄𐐨𐑆 𐐶𐐮𐑊𐐻 𐑄𐐵 𐐿𐐲𐑋𐑁𐐲𐑉𐐻, 𐐄 𐐢𐐫𐑉𐐼? 𐐏𐐩, 𐐶𐐮𐑊𐐻 𐑄𐐵 𐐿𐐲𐑋𐑁𐐲𐑉𐐻 𐑄𐐩𐑉 𐑅𐐬𐑊𐑆 𐐮𐑌 𐐗𐑉𐐴𐑅𐐻? 𐐎𐐮𐑊𐐻 𐑄𐐵 𐑀𐑉𐐰𐑌𐐻 𐐲𐑌𐐻𐐭 𐑄𐐯𐑋 𐑄𐐰𐐻 𐑄𐐩 𐑋𐐩 𐐸𐐰𐑂 𐑅𐐻𐑉𐐯𐑍𐑃, 𐑄𐐰𐐻 𐑄𐐩 𐑋𐐩 𐐺𐐩𐑉 𐑄𐐩𐑉 𐐰𐑁𐑊𐐮𐐿𐑇𐐲𐑌𐑆 𐐸𐐶𐐮𐐽 𐑇𐐰𐑊 𐐿𐐲𐑋 𐐲𐐹𐐱𐑌 𐑄𐐯𐑋, 𐐺𐐨𐐿𐐫𐑆 𐐱𐑂 𐑄 𐐮𐑌𐐮𐐿𐐶𐐮𐐻𐐨𐑆 𐐱𐑂 𐑄𐐮𐑅 𐐹𐐨𐐹𐑊? 𐐄 𐐢𐐫𐑉𐐼, 𐐶𐐮𐑊𐐻 𐑄𐐵 𐑀𐑉𐐰𐑌𐐻 𐐲𐑌𐐻𐐭 𐐲𐑅 𐑄𐐰𐐻 𐐶𐐨 𐑋𐐩 𐐸𐐰𐑂 𐑅𐐲𐐿𐑅𐐯𐑅 𐐮𐑌 𐐺𐑉𐐮𐑍𐐮𐑍 𐑄𐐯𐑋 𐐲𐑀𐐯𐑌 𐐲𐑌𐐻𐐭 𐑄 𐐮𐑌 𐐗𐑉𐐴𐑅𐐻? 𐐒𐐨𐐸𐐬𐑊𐐼, 𐐄 𐐢𐐫𐑉𐐼, 𐑄𐐩𐑉 𐑅𐐬𐑊𐑆 𐐪𐑉 𐐹𐑉𐐯𐑇𐐲𐑅, 𐐰𐑌𐐼 𐑋𐐯𐑌𐐨 𐐱𐑂 𐑄𐐯𐑋 𐐪𐑉 𐐵𐑉 𐐺𐑉𐐯𐑄𐑉𐐯𐑌, 𐑄𐐩𐑉𐑁𐐬𐑉, 𐑀𐐮𐑂 𐐲𐑌𐐻𐐭 𐐲𐑅, 𐐄 𐐢𐐫𐑉𐐼, 𐐹𐐵𐐯𐑉 𐐰𐑌𐐼 𐐶𐐮𐑆𐐼𐐲𐑋 𐑄𐐰𐐻 𐐶𐐨 𐑋𐐩 𐐺𐑉𐐮𐑍 𐑄𐐨𐑆, 𐐵𐑉 𐐺𐑉𐐯𐑄𐑉𐐯𐑌, 𐐲𐑀𐐯𐑌 𐐲𐑌𐐻𐐭 𐑄.

17. 𐐤𐐵 𐐮𐐻 𐐿𐐩𐑋 𐐻𐐭 𐐹𐐰𐑅 𐑄𐐰𐐻 𐐸𐐶𐐯𐑌 𐐈𐑊𐑋𐐲 𐐸𐐰𐐼 𐑅𐐯𐐼 𐑄𐐨𐑆 𐐶𐐲𐑉𐐼𐑆, 𐑄𐐰𐐻 𐐸𐐨 𐐿𐑊𐐰𐐹𐐻 𐐸𐐮𐑆 𐐸𐐰𐑌𐐼𐑆 𐐲𐐹𐐱𐑌 𐐫𐑊 𐑄𐐯𐑋 𐐸𐐭 𐐶𐐲𐑉 𐐶𐐮𐑄 𐐸𐐮𐑋. 𐐈𐑌𐐼 𐐺𐐨𐐸𐐬𐑊𐐼, 𐐰𐑆 𐐸𐐨 𐐿𐑊𐐰𐐹𐐻 𐐸𐐮𐑆 𐐸𐐰𐑌𐐼𐑆 𐐲𐐹𐐱𐑌 𐑄𐐯𐑋, 𐑄𐐩 𐐶𐐲𐑉 𐑁𐐮𐑊𐐼 𐐶𐐮𐑄 𐑄 𐐐𐐬𐑊𐐨 𐐝𐐹𐐮𐑉𐐮𐐻. 𐐈𐑌𐐼 𐐰𐑁𐐻𐐯𐑉 𐑄𐐰𐐻 𐑄𐐩 𐐼𐐮𐐼 𐑅𐐯𐐹𐐲𐑉𐐩𐐻 𐑄𐐯𐑋𐑅𐐯𐑊𐑂𐑆 𐐶𐐲𐑌 𐑁𐑉𐐲𐑋 𐐲𐑌𐐲𐑄𐐯𐑉; 𐐻𐐩𐐿𐐮𐑍 𐑌𐐬 𐑃𐐫𐐻 𐑁𐐫𐑉 𐑄𐐯𐑋𐑅𐐯𐑊𐑂𐑆 𐐸𐐶𐐱𐐻 𐑄𐐩 𐑇𐐳𐐼 𐐨𐐻, 𐐫𐑉 𐐸𐐶𐐱𐐻 𐑄𐐩 𐑇𐐳𐐼 𐐼𐑉𐐮𐑍𐐿, 𐐫𐑉 𐐸𐐶𐐱𐐻 𐑄𐐩 𐑇𐐳𐐼 𐐹𐐳𐐻 𐐱𐑌. 𐐈𐑌𐐼 𐑄 𐐢𐐫𐑉𐐼 𐐹𐑉𐐬𐑂𐐴𐐼𐐯𐐼 𐑁𐐫𐑉 𐑄𐐯𐑋 𐑄𐐰𐐻 𐑄𐐩 𐑇𐐳𐐼 𐐸𐐲𐑍𐑀𐐯𐑉 𐑌𐐱𐐻, 𐑌𐐨𐑄𐐯𐑉 𐑇𐐳𐐼 𐑄𐐩 𐑃𐐲𐑉𐑅𐐻; 𐐏𐐩, 𐐰𐑌𐐼 𐐸𐐨 𐐫𐑊𐑅𐐬 𐑀𐐩𐑂 𐑄𐐯𐑋 𐑅𐐻𐑉𐐯𐑍𐑃, 𐑄𐐰𐐻 𐑄𐐩 𐑇𐐳𐐼 𐑅𐐲𐑁𐐯𐑉 𐑌𐐬 𐑋𐐰𐑌𐐯𐑉 𐐱𐑂 𐐰𐑁𐑊𐐮𐐿𐑇𐐲𐑌𐑆, 𐑅𐐩𐑂 𐐮𐐻 𐐶𐐲𐑉 𐑅𐐶𐐱𐑊𐐬𐐼 𐐲𐐹 𐐮𐑌 𐑄 𐐾𐐦 𐐱𐑂 𐐗𐑉𐐴𐑅𐐻. 𐐤𐐵 𐑄𐐮𐑅 𐐶𐐱𐑆 𐐰𐐿𐐫𐑉𐐼𐐮𐑍 𐐻𐐭 𐑄 𐐹𐑉𐐩𐐯𐑉 𐐱𐑂 𐐈𐑊𐑋𐐲; 𐐰𐑌𐐼 𐑄𐐮𐑅 𐐺𐐨𐐿𐐫𐑆 𐐸𐐨 𐐹𐑉𐐩𐐼 𐐮𐑌 𐑁𐐩𐑃.

18. 𐐈𐑌𐐼 𐐮𐐻 𐐿𐐩𐑋 𐐻𐐭 𐐹𐐰𐑅 𐑄𐐰𐐻 𐑄𐐩 𐐼𐐮𐐼 𐑀𐐬 𐑁𐐬𐑉𐑃, 𐐰𐑌𐐼 𐐺𐐨𐑀𐐰𐑌 𐐻𐐭 𐐹𐑉𐐨𐐽 𐑄 𐐶𐐲𐑉𐐼 𐐱𐑂 𐐘𐐱𐐼 𐐲𐑌𐐻𐐭 𐑄 𐐹𐐨𐐹𐑊, 𐐯𐑌𐐻𐐯𐑉𐐮𐑍 𐐮𐑌𐐻𐐭 𐑄𐐩𐑉 𐑅𐐮𐑌𐐲𐑀𐐱𐑀𐑆, 𐐰𐑌𐐼 𐐮𐑌𐐻𐐭 𐑄𐐩𐑉 𐐸𐐵𐑆𐐯𐑆; 𐐏𐐩, 𐐰𐑌𐐼 𐐨𐑂𐑌 𐑄𐐩 𐐼𐐮𐐼 𐐹𐑉𐐨𐐽 𐑄 𐐶𐐲𐑉𐐼 𐐮𐑌 𐑄𐐩𐑉 𐑅𐐻𐑉𐐨𐐻𐑅. 𐐈𐑌𐐼 𐐮𐐻 𐐿𐐩𐑋 𐐻𐐭 𐐹𐐰𐑅 𐑄𐐰𐐻 𐐰𐑁𐐻𐐯𐑉 𐑋𐐲𐐽 𐑊𐐩𐐺𐐲𐑉 𐐲𐑋𐐲𐑍 𐑄𐐯𐑋, 𐑄𐐩 𐐺𐐨𐑀𐐰𐑌 𐐻𐐭 𐐸𐐰𐑂 𐑅𐐲𐐿𐑅𐐯𐑅 𐐲𐑋𐐲𐑍 𐑄 𐐹𐐭𐑉 𐐿𐑊𐐰𐑅 𐐱𐑂 𐐹𐐨𐐹𐑊; 𐑁𐐫𐑉 𐐺𐐨𐐸𐐬𐑊𐐼, 𐑄𐐩 𐐶𐐲𐑉 𐐿𐐰𐑅𐐻 𐐵𐐻 𐐱𐑂 𐑄 𐑅𐐮𐑌𐐲𐑀𐐱𐑀𐑆, 𐐺𐐨𐐿𐐫𐑆 𐐱𐑂 𐑄 𐐿𐐬𐑉𐑅𐑌𐐯𐑅 𐐱𐑂 𐑄𐐩𐑉 𐐰𐐹𐐰𐑉𐐯𐑊; 𐑄𐐩𐑉𐑁𐐬𐑉 𐑄𐐩 𐐶𐐲𐑉 𐑌𐐱𐐻 𐐹𐐲𐑉𐑋𐐮𐐻𐐯𐐼 𐐻𐐭 𐐯𐑌𐐻𐐯𐑉 𐐮𐑌𐐻𐐭 𐑄𐐩𐑉 𐑅𐐮𐑌𐐲𐑀𐐱𐑀𐑆 𐐻𐐭 𐐶𐐲𐑉𐑇𐐮𐐹 𐐘𐐱𐐼, 𐐺𐐨𐐮𐑍 𐐯𐑅𐐻𐐨𐑋𐐼 𐐰𐑆 𐑁𐐮𐑊𐑃𐐮𐑌𐐯𐑅; 𐑄𐐩𐑉𐑁𐐬𐑉 𐑄𐐩 𐐶𐐲𐑉 𐐹𐐭𐑉; 𐐏𐐩, 𐑄𐐩 𐐶𐐲𐑉 𐐯𐑅𐐻𐐨𐑋𐐼 𐐺𐐴 𐑄𐐩𐑉 𐐺𐑉𐐯𐑄𐑉𐐯𐑌 𐐰𐑆 𐐼𐑉𐐱𐑅; 𐑄𐐩𐑉𐑁𐐬𐑉 𐑄𐐩 𐐶𐐲𐑉 𐐹𐐭𐑉 𐐰𐑆 𐐻𐐭 𐑃𐐮𐑍𐑆 𐐱𐑂 𐑄 𐐶𐐲𐑉𐑊𐐼; 𐐰𐑌𐐼 𐐫𐑊𐑅𐐬 𐑄𐐩 𐐶𐐲𐑉 𐐹𐐭𐑉 𐐮𐑌 𐐸𐐪𐑉𐐻.

19. 𐐤𐐵 𐐰𐑆 𐐈𐑊𐑋𐐲 𐐶𐐱𐑆 𐐻𐐨𐐽𐐮𐑍 𐐰𐑌𐐼 𐑅𐐹𐐨𐐿𐐮𐑍 𐐲𐑌𐐻𐐭 𐑄 𐐹𐐨𐐹𐑊 𐐲𐐹𐐱𐑌 𐑄 𐐸𐐮𐑊 𐐄𐑌𐐮𐐼𐐲, 𐑄𐐩𐑉 𐐿𐐩𐑋 𐐩 𐑀𐑉𐐩𐐻 𐑋𐐲𐑊𐐻𐐮𐐻𐐭𐐼 𐐲𐑌𐐻𐐭 𐐸𐐮𐑋, 𐐸𐐭 𐐶𐐲𐑉 𐑄𐐬𐑆 𐐱𐑂 𐐸𐐭𐑋 𐐶𐐨 𐐸𐐰𐑂 𐐺𐐮𐑌 𐑅𐐹𐐨𐐿𐐮𐑍, 𐐱𐑂 𐐸𐐭𐑋 𐐶𐐲𐑉 𐐹𐐭𐑉 𐐮𐑌 𐐸𐐪𐑉𐐻, 𐐺𐐨𐐿𐐫𐑆 𐐱𐑂 𐑄𐐩𐑉 𐐹𐐱𐑂𐐲𐑉𐐻𐐨 𐐰𐑆 𐐻𐐭 𐑄 𐑃𐐮𐑍𐑆 𐐱𐑂 𐑄 𐐶𐐲𐑉𐑊𐐼. 𐐈𐑌𐐼 𐑄𐐩 𐐿𐐩𐑋 𐐲𐑌𐐻𐐭 𐐈𐑊𐑋𐐲; 𐐰𐑌𐐼 𐑄 𐐶𐐲𐑌 𐐸𐐭 𐐶𐐱𐑆 𐑄 𐑁𐐬𐑉𐑋𐐬𐑅𐐻 𐐲𐑋𐐲𐑍 𐑄𐐯𐑋 𐑅𐐯𐐼 𐐲𐑌𐐻𐐭 𐐸𐐮𐑋, 𐐒𐐨𐐸𐐬𐑊𐐼, 𐐸𐐶𐐱𐐻 𐑇𐐰𐑊 𐑄𐐨𐑆 𐑋𐐴 𐐺𐑉𐐯𐑄𐑉𐐯𐑌 𐐼𐐭, 𐑁𐐫𐑉 𐑄𐐩 𐐪𐑉 𐐼𐐨𐑅𐐹𐐴𐑆𐐼 𐐱𐑂 𐐫𐑊 𐑋𐐯𐑌 𐐺𐐨𐐿𐐫𐑆 𐐱𐑂 𐑄𐐩𐑉 𐐹𐐱𐑂𐐲𐑉𐐻𐐨; 𐐏𐐩, 𐐰𐑌𐐼 𐑋𐐬𐑉 𐐯𐑅𐐹𐐯𐑇𐐲𐑊𐐨 𐐺𐐴 𐐵𐑉 𐐹𐑉𐐨𐑅𐐻𐑅; 𐑁𐐫𐑉 𐑄𐐩 𐐸𐐰𐑂 𐐿𐐰𐑅𐐻 𐐲𐑅 𐐵𐐻 𐐱𐑂 𐐵𐑉 𐑅𐐮𐑌𐐲𐑀𐐱𐑀𐑆 𐐸𐐶𐐮𐐽 𐐶𐐨 𐐸𐐰𐑂 𐑊𐐩𐐺𐐲𐑉𐐼 𐐲𐐺𐐲𐑌𐐼𐐰𐑌𐐻𐑊𐐨 𐐻𐐭 𐐺𐐮𐑊𐐼 𐐶𐐮𐑄 𐐵𐑉 𐐬𐑌 𐐸𐐰𐑌𐐼𐑆; 𐐰𐑌𐐼 𐐶𐐨 𐐸𐐰𐑂 𐐿𐐰𐑅𐐻 𐐲𐑅 𐐵𐐻 𐐺𐐨𐐿𐐫𐑆 𐐱𐑂 𐐵𐑉 𐐯𐐿𐑅𐐨𐐼𐐮𐑍 𐐹𐐱𐑂𐐲𐑉𐐻𐐨; 𐐰𐑌𐐼 𐐶𐐨 𐐸𐐰𐑂 𐑌𐐬 𐐹𐑊𐐩𐑅 𐐻𐐭 𐐶𐐲𐑉𐑇𐐮𐐹 𐐵𐑉 𐐘𐐱𐐼; 𐐰𐑌𐐼 𐐺𐐨𐐸𐐬𐑊𐐼, 𐐸𐐶𐐱𐐻 𐑇𐐰𐑊 𐐶𐐨 𐐼𐐭? 𐐈𐑌𐐼 𐑌𐐵 𐐸𐐶𐐯𐑌 𐐈𐑊𐑋𐐲 𐐸𐐲𐑉𐐼 𐑄𐐮𐑅, 𐐸𐐨 𐐻𐐲𐑉𐑌𐐼

𐐸𐐮𐑋 𐐲𐐺𐐵𐐻, 𐐸𐐮𐑆 𐑁𐐩𐑅 𐐮𐑋𐐨𐐼𐐮𐐰𐐻𐑊𐐮 𐐻𐐬𐐲𐑉𐐼𐑆 𐐸𐐮𐑋, 𐐰𐑌𐐼 𐐸𐐨 𐐺𐐨𐐸𐐯𐑊𐐼 𐐶𐐮𐑃 𐑀𐑉𐐩𐐻 𐐾𐑎; 𐑁𐐬𐑉 𐐸𐐨 𐐺𐐨𐐸𐐯𐑊𐐼 𐑄𐐰𐐻 𐑄𐐩𐑉 𐐰𐑁𐑊𐐮𐐿𐑇𐐲𐑌𐑆 𐐸𐐰𐐼 𐐻𐑉𐐭𐑊𐐮 𐐸𐐲𐑋𐐺𐑊𐐼 𐑄𐐯𐑋, 𐐰𐑌𐐼 𐑄𐐰𐐻 𐑄𐐩 𐐶𐐲𐑉 𐐮𐑌 𐐲 𐐹𐑉𐐯𐐹𐐲𐑉𐐩𐑇𐐲𐑌 𐐻𐐭 𐐸𐐨𐑉 𐑄 𐐶𐐲𐑉𐐼; 𐑄𐐩𐑉𐑁𐐬𐑉 𐐸𐐨 𐐼𐐮𐐼 𐑅𐐩 𐑌𐐬 𐑋𐐬𐑉 𐐻𐐭 𐑄 𐐲𐑄𐐲𐑉 𐑋𐐲𐑊𐐻𐐮𐐻𐑏𐐼, 𐐺𐐲𐐻 𐐸𐐨 𐑅𐐻𐑉𐐯𐐽𐐻 𐑁𐐬𐑉𐑃 𐐸𐐮𐑆 𐐸𐐰𐑌𐐼, 𐐰𐑌𐐼 𐐿𐑉𐐴𐐼 𐐲𐑌𐐻𐐭 𐑄𐐬𐑆 𐐸𐐭𐑋 𐐸𐐨 𐐺𐐨𐐸𐐯𐑊𐐼, 𐐸𐐭 𐐶𐐲𐑉 𐐻𐑉𐐭𐑊𐐮 𐐹𐐯𐑌𐐮𐐻𐐯𐑌𐐻, 𐐰𐑌𐐼 𐑅𐐯𐐼 𐐲𐑌𐐻𐐭 𐑄𐐯𐑋, 𐐌 𐐺𐐨𐐸𐐬𐑊𐐼 𐑄𐐰𐐻 𐐷 𐐪𐑉 𐑊𐐬𐑊𐐮 𐐮𐑌 𐐸𐐪𐑉𐐻; 𐐰𐑌𐐼 𐐮𐑁 𐑅𐐬, 𐐺𐑊𐐯𐑅𐐯𐐼 𐐪𐑉 𐐷. 𐐒𐐨𐐸𐐬𐑊𐐼, 𐑄𐐴 𐐺𐑉𐐲𐑄𐐲𐑉 𐐸𐐰𐑃 𐑅𐐯𐐼, 𐐐𐐶𐐱𐐻 𐑇𐐰𐑊 𐐶𐐨 𐐼𐐭? 𐑁𐐬𐑉 𐐶𐐨 𐐪𐑉 𐐿𐐰𐑅𐐻 𐐵𐐻 𐐲𐑂 𐐵𐑉 𐑅𐐮𐑌𐐲𐑀𐐱𐑀𐑆, 𐑄𐐰𐐻 𐐶𐐨 𐐿𐐰𐑌𐐱𐐻 𐐶𐐲𐑉𐑇𐐮𐐹 𐐵𐑉 𐐘𐐱𐐼. 𐐒𐐨𐐸𐐬𐑊𐐼, 𐐌 𐑅𐐩 𐐲𐑌𐐻𐐭 𐐷𐐭, 𐐔𐐭 𐐷 𐑅𐐲𐐹𐐬𐑆 𐑄𐐰𐐻 𐐷 𐐿𐐰𐑌𐐱𐐻 𐐶𐐲𐑉𐑇𐐮𐐹 𐐘𐐱𐐼, 𐑅𐐩𐑂 𐐮𐐻 𐐺 𐐮𐑌 𐐷𐐬𐑉 𐑅𐐮𐑌𐐲𐑀𐐱𐑀𐑆 𐐬𐑌𐑊𐐮. 𐐈𐑌𐐼 𐑋𐐬𐑉𐐬𐑂𐐲𐑉, 𐐌 𐐶𐐳𐐼 𐐰𐑅𐐿, 𐐔𐐭 𐐷 𐑅𐐲𐐹𐐬𐑆 𐑄𐐰𐐻 𐐷 𐑋𐐲𐑅𐐻 𐑌𐐱𐐻 𐐶𐐲𐑉𐑇𐐮𐐹 𐐘𐐱𐐼 𐐬𐑌𐑊𐐮 𐐶𐐲𐑌𐑅 𐐮𐑌 𐐲 𐐶𐐨𐐿? 𐐌 𐑅𐐩 𐐲𐑌𐐻𐐭 𐐷𐐭, 𐐮𐐻 𐐮𐑆 𐐶𐐯𐑊 𐑄𐐰𐐻 𐐷 𐐪𐑉 𐐿𐐰𐑅𐐻 𐐵𐐻 𐐲𐑂 𐐷𐐬𐑉 𐑅𐐮𐑌𐐲𐑀𐐱𐑀𐑆, 𐑄𐐰𐐻 𐐷 𐑋𐐩 𐐺 𐐸𐐲𐑋𐐺𐑊, 𐐰𐑌𐐼 𐑄𐐰𐐻 𐐷 𐑋𐐩 𐑊𐐲𐑉𐑌 𐐶𐐮𐑆𐐼𐐲𐑋; 𐑁𐐬𐑉 𐐮𐐻 𐐮𐑆 𐑌𐐯𐑅𐐯𐑅𐐯𐑉𐐮 𐑄𐐰𐐻 𐐷 𐑇𐐳𐐼 𐑊𐐲𐑉𐑌 𐐶𐐮𐑆𐐼𐐲𐑋; 𐑁𐐬𐑉 𐐮𐐻 𐐮𐑆 𐐺𐐨𐐿𐐱𐑆 𐑄𐐰𐐻 𐐷 𐐪𐑉 𐐿𐐰𐑅𐐻 𐐵𐐻, 𐑄𐐰𐐻 𐐷 𐐪𐑉 𐐼𐐨𐑅𐐹𐐴𐑆𐐼 𐐲𐑂 𐐷𐐬𐑉 𐐺𐑉𐐯𐑄𐑉𐐯𐑌, 𐐺𐐨𐐿𐐱𐑆 𐐲𐑂 𐐷𐐬𐑉 𐐯𐐿𐑅𐐨𐐼𐐮𐑍 𐐹𐐱𐑂𐐲𐑉𐐻𐐮, 𐑄𐐰𐐻 𐐷 𐐪𐑉 𐐺𐑉𐐫𐐻 𐐻𐐭 𐐲 𐑊𐐬𐑊𐐮𐑌𐐯𐑅 𐐲𐑂 𐐸𐐪𐑉𐐻; 𐑁𐐬𐑉 𐐷 𐐪𐑉 𐑌𐐯𐑅𐐯𐑅𐐯𐑉𐐮𐑊𐐮 𐐺𐑉𐐫𐐻 𐐻𐐭 𐐺 𐐸𐐲𐑋𐐺𐑊. 𐐈𐑌𐐼 𐑌𐐵, 𐐺𐐨𐐿𐐱𐑆 𐐷 𐐪𐑉 𐐿𐐲𐑋𐐹𐐯𐑊𐐼 𐐻𐐭 𐐺 𐐸𐐲𐑋𐐺𐑊, 𐐺𐑊𐐯𐑅𐐯𐐼 𐐪𐑉 𐐷; 𐑁𐐬𐑉 𐐲 𐑋𐐰𐑌 𐑅𐐲𐑋𐐻𐐴𐑋𐑆, 𐐮𐑁 𐐸𐐨 𐐮𐑆 𐐿𐐲𐑋𐐹𐐯𐑊𐐼 𐐻𐐭 𐐺 𐐸𐐲𐑋𐐺𐑊, 𐑅𐐨𐐿𐐯𐑃 𐑉𐐨𐐹𐐯𐑌𐐻𐐰𐑌𐑅; 𐐰𐑌𐐼 𐑌𐐵 𐑇𐐭𐑉𐑊𐐮, 𐐸𐐭𐑅𐐬𐐯𐑂𐐲𐑉 𐑉𐐨𐐹𐐯𐑌𐐻𐐯𐑃, 𐑇𐐰𐑊 𐑁𐐴𐑌𐐼 𐑋𐐲𐑉𐑅𐐨; 𐐰𐑌𐐼 𐐸𐐨 𐑄𐐰𐐻 𐑁𐐴𐑌𐐼𐐯𐑃 𐑋𐐲𐑉𐑅𐐨, 𐐰𐑌𐐼 𐐯𐑌𐐼𐐷𐐭𐑉𐐯𐑃 𐐻𐐭 𐑄 𐐯𐑌𐐼, 𐑄 𐑅𐐩𐑋 𐑇𐐰𐑊 𐐺 𐑅𐐩𐑂𐐼.

20. 𐐈𐑌𐐼 𐑌𐐵 𐐰𐑆 𐐌 𐑅𐐯𐐼 𐐲𐑌𐐻𐐭 𐐷𐐭, 𐑄𐐰𐐻 𐐺𐐨𐐿𐐱𐑆 𐐷 𐐶𐐲𐑉 𐐿𐐲𐑋𐐹𐐯𐑊𐐼 𐐻𐐭 𐐺 𐐸𐐲𐑋𐐺𐑊, 𐐷 𐐶𐐲𐑉 𐐺𐑊𐐯𐑅𐐻, 𐐼𐐭 𐐷 𐑌𐐱𐐻 𐑅𐐲𐐹𐐬𐑆 𐑄𐐰𐐻 𐑄𐐩 𐐪𐑉 𐑋𐐬𐑉 𐐺𐑊𐐯𐑅𐐻 𐐸𐐭 𐐻𐑉𐐭𐑊𐐮 𐐸𐐲𐑋𐐺𐑊 𐑄𐐯𐑋𐑅𐐯𐑊𐑂𐑆 𐐺𐐨𐐿𐐱𐑆 𐐲𐑂 𐑄 𐐶𐐲𐑉𐐼? 𐐏𐐩, 𐐸𐐨 𐑄𐐰𐐻 𐐻𐑉𐐭𐑊𐐮 𐐸𐐲𐑋𐐺𐑊𐐯𐑃 𐐸𐐮𐑋𐑅𐐯𐑊𐑁 𐐰𐑌𐐼 𐑉𐐨𐐹𐐯𐑌𐐻𐐯𐑃 𐐲𐑂 𐐸𐐮𐑆 𐑅𐐮𐑌𐑆, 𐐰𐑌𐐼 𐐯𐑌𐐼𐐷𐐭𐑉𐐯𐑃 𐐻𐐭 𐑄 𐐯𐑌𐐼, 𐑄 𐑅𐐩𐑋 𐑇𐐰𐑊 𐐺 𐐺𐑊𐐯𐑅𐐻; 𐐷𐐩, 𐑋𐐲𐐽 𐑋𐐬𐑉 𐐺𐑊𐐯𐑅𐐻 𐑄𐐰𐑌 𐑄𐐩 𐐸𐐭 𐐪𐑉 𐐿𐐲𐑋𐐹𐐯𐑊𐐼 𐐻𐐭 𐐺 𐐸𐐲𐑋𐐺𐑊 𐐺𐐨𐐿𐐱𐑆 𐐲𐑂 𐑄𐐩𐑉 𐐯𐐿𐑅𐐨𐐼𐐮𐑍 𐐹𐐱𐑂𐐲𐑉𐐻𐐮; 𐑄𐐩𐑉𐑁𐐬𐑉 𐐺𐑊𐐯𐑅𐐯𐐼 𐐪𐑉 𐑄𐐩 𐐸𐐭 𐐸𐐲𐑋𐐺𐑊 𐑄𐐯𐑋𐑅𐐯𐑊𐑂𐑆 𐐶𐐮𐑄𐐵𐐻 𐐺𐐨𐐮𐑍 𐐿𐐲𐑋𐐹𐐯𐑊𐐼 𐐻𐐭 𐐺 𐐸𐐲𐑋𐐺𐑊; 𐐫𐑉 𐑉𐐪𐑄𐐲𐑉, 𐐮𐑌 𐐲𐑄𐐲𐑉 𐐶𐐲𐑉𐐼𐑆, 𐐺𐑊𐐯𐑅𐐯𐐼 𐐮𐑆 𐐸𐐨 𐑄𐐰𐐻 𐐺𐐨𐑊𐐨𐑂𐐯𐑃 𐐮𐑌 𐑄 𐐶𐐲𐑉𐐼 𐐲𐑂 𐐘𐐱𐐼, 𐐰𐑌𐐼 𐐮𐑆 𐐺𐐰𐐹𐐻𐐴𐑆𐐼 𐐶𐐮𐑄𐐵𐐻 𐑅𐐻𐐲𐐺𐐲𐑉𐑌𐐯𐑅 𐐲𐑂 𐐸𐐪𐑉𐐻; 𐐷𐐩, 𐐶𐐮𐑄𐐵𐐻 𐐺𐐨𐐮𐑍 𐐺𐑉𐐫𐐻 𐐻𐐭 𐑌𐐬 𐑄 𐐶𐐲𐑉𐐼, 𐐫𐑉 𐐨𐑂𐐯𐑌 𐐿𐐲𐑋𐐹𐐯𐑊𐐼 𐐻𐐭 𐑌𐐬, 𐐺𐐨𐑁𐐬𐑉 𐑄𐐩 𐐶𐐮𐑊 𐐺𐐨𐑊𐐨𐑂. 𐐏𐐩, 𐑄𐐩𐑉 𐐪𐑉 𐑋𐐯𐑌𐐮 𐐸𐐭 𐐼𐐭 𐑅𐐩, 𐐆𐑁 𐑄𐐵 𐐶𐐮𐑊𐐻 𐑇𐐬 𐐲𐑌𐐻𐐭 𐐲𐑅 𐐲 𐑅𐐴𐑌 𐑁𐑉𐐱𐑋 𐐸𐐯𐑂𐐲𐑌, 𐑄𐐯𐑌 𐐶𐐨 𐑇𐐰𐑊 𐑌𐐬 𐐲𐑂 𐐲 𐑇𐐭𐑉𐐻𐐮; 𐑄𐐯𐑌 𐐶𐐨 𐑇𐐰𐑊 𐐺𐐨𐑊𐐨𐑂.—𐐤𐐵 𐐌 𐐰𐑅𐐿, 𐐮𐑆 𐑄𐐮𐑅 𐑁𐐩𐑃? 𐐒𐐨𐐸𐐬𐑊𐐼, 𐐌 𐑅𐐩 𐐲𐑌𐐻𐐭 𐐷𐐭, 𐐤𐐩; 𐑁𐐬𐑉 𐐮𐑁 𐐲 𐑋𐐰𐑌 𐑌𐐬𐐯𐑃 𐐲 𐑃𐐮𐑍, 𐐸𐐨 𐐸𐐰𐑃 𐑌𐐬 𐐿𐐫𐑆 𐐻𐐭 𐐺𐐨𐑊𐐨𐑂, 𐑁𐐬𐑉 𐐸𐐨 𐑌𐐬𐐯𐑃 𐐮𐐻. 𐐈𐑌𐐼 𐑌𐐵, 𐐸𐐵 𐑋𐐲𐐽 𐑋𐐬𐑉 𐐿𐐲𐑉𐑅𐐻 𐐮𐑆 𐐸𐐨 𐑄𐐰𐐻 𐑌𐐬𐐯𐑃 𐑄 𐐶𐐮𐑊 𐐲𐑂 𐐘𐐱𐐼 𐐰𐑌𐐼 𐐼𐐭𐐯𐑃 𐐮𐐻 𐑌𐐱𐐻, 𐑄𐐰𐑌 𐐸𐐨 𐑄𐐰𐐻 𐐬𐑌𐑊𐐮 𐐺𐐨𐑊𐐨𐑂𐐯𐑃, 𐐫𐑉 𐐬𐑌𐑊𐐮 𐐸𐐰𐑃 𐐿𐐫𐑆 𐐻𐐭 𐐺𐐨𐑊𐐨𐑂, 𐐰𐑌𐐼 𐑁𐐫𐑊𐐯𐑃 𐐮𐑌𐐻𐐭 𐐻𐑉𐐰𐑌𐑆𐑀𐑉𐐯𐑇𐐲𐑌? 𐐤𐐵 𐐲𐑂 𐑄𐐮𐑅 𐑃𐐮𐑍 𐐷 𐑋𐐲𐑅𐐻 𐐾𐐲𐐾. 𐐒𐐨𐐸𐐬𐑊𐐼, 𐐌 𐑅𐐩 𐐲𐑌𐐻𐐭 𐐷𐐭, 𐐜𐐰𐐻 𐐮𐐻 𐐮𐑆 𐐱𐑌 𐑄 𐐶𐐲𐑌 𐐸𐐰𐑌𐐼 𐐨𐑂𐐯𐑌 𐐰𐑆 𐐮𐐻 𐐮𐑆 𐐱𐑌 𐑄 𐐲𐑄𐐲𐑉; 𐐰𐑌𐐼 𐐮𐐻 𐑇𐐰𐑊 𐐺 𐐲𐑌𐐻𐐭 𐐯𐑂𐐲𐑉𐐮 𐑋𐐰𐑌 𐐰𐐿𐐫𐑉𐐼𐐮𐑍 𐐻𐐭 𐐸𐐮𐑆 𐐶𐐲𐑉𐐿.

21. 𐐈𐑌𐐼 𐑌𐐵 𐐰𐑆 𐐌 𐑅𐐯𐐼 𐐿𐐱𐑌𐑅𐐲𐑉𐑌𐐮𐑍 𐑁𐐩𐑃: 𐐙𐐩𐑃, 𐐮𐑆 𐑌𐐱𐐻 𐐻𐐭 𐐸𐐰𐑂 𐐲 𐐹𐐲𐑉𐑁𐐯𐐿𐐻 𐑌𐐱𐑊𐐯𐐾 𐐲𐑂 𐑃𐐮𐑍𐑆; 𐑄𐐩𐑉𐑁𐐬𐑉 𐐮𐑁 𐐷 𐐸𐐰𐑂 𐑁𐐩𐑃, 𐐷 𐐸𐐬𐐹 𐑁𐐬𐑉 𐑃𐐮𐑍𐑆 𐐸𐐶𐐮𐐽 𐐪𐑉 𐑌𐐱𐐻 𐑅𐐨𐑌, 𐐸𐐶𐐮𐐽 𐐪𐑉 𐐻𐑉𐐭. 𐐈𐑌𐐼 𐑌𐐵, 𐐺𐐨𐐸𐐬𐑊𐐼, 𐐌 𐑅𐐩 𐐲𐑌𐐻𐐭 𐐷𐐭; 𐐰𐑌𐐼 𐐌 𐐶𐐳𐐼 𐑄𐐰𐐻 𐐷 𐑇𐐳𐐼 𐑉𐐨𐑋𐐯𐑋𐐺𐐲𐑉 𐑄𐐰𐐻 𐐘𐐱𐐼 𐐮𐑆 𐑋𐐲𐑉𐑅𐐮𐑁𐐳𐑊 𐐲𐑌𐐻𐐭 𐐫𐑊 𐐸𐐭 𐐺𐐨𐑊𐐨𐑂 𐐱𐑌 𐐸𐐮𐑆 𐑌𐐩𐑋; 𐑄𐐩𐑉𐑁𐐬𐑉 𐐸𐐨 𐐼𐐨𐑆𐐴𐑉𐐯𐑃, 𐐮𐑌 𐑄 𐑁𐐲𐑉𐑅𐐻 𐐹𐑊𐐩𐑅, 𐑄𐐰𐐻 𐐷 𐑇𐐳𐐼 𐐺𐐨𐑊𐐨𐑂, 𐐷𐐩, 𐐨𐑂𐐯𐑌 𐐱𐑌 𐐸𐐮𐑆 𐐶𐐲𐑉𐐼. 𐐈𐑌𐐼 𐑌𐐵, 𐐸𐐨 𐐮𐑋𐐹𐐪𐑉𐐻𐐯𐑃 𐐸𐐮𐑆 𐐶𐐲𐑉𐐼 𐐺𐐴 𐐩𐑌𐐾𐐯𐑊𐑆, 𐐲𐑌𐐻𐐭 𐑋𐐯𐑌; 𐐷𐐩, 𐑌𐐱𐐻 𐐬𐑌𐑊𐐮 𐑋𐐯𐑌, 𐐺𐐲𐐻 𐐶𐐮𐑋𐐯𐑌 𐐫𐑊𐑅𐐬. 𐐤𐐵 𐑄𐐮𐑅 𐐮𐑆 𐑌𐐱𐐻 𐐫𐑊; 𐑊𐐮𐐻𐑊 𐐽𐐮𐑊𐐼𐑉𐐯𐑌 𐐼𐐭 𐐸𐐰𐑂 𐐶𐐲𐑉𐐼𐑆 𐑀𐐮𐑂𐐲𐑌 𐐲𐑌𐐻𐐭 𐑄𐐯𐑋 𐑋𐐯𐑌𐐮 𐐻𐐴𐑋𐑆, 𐐸𐐶𐐮𐐽 𐐿𐐱𐑌𐑁𐐵𐑌𐐼 𐑄 𐐶𐐴𐑆 𐐰𐑌𐐼 𐑄 𐑊𐐲𐑉𐑌𐐯𐐼.

22. 𐐈𐑌𐐼 𐑌𐐵, 𐑋𐐴 𐐺𐐨𐑊𐐲𐑂𐐯𐐼 𐐺𐑉𐐯𐑄𐑉𐐯𐑌, 𐐰𐑆 𐐷 𐐸𐐰𐑂 𐐼𐐨𐑆𐐴𐑉𐐼 𐐻𐐭 𐑌𐐬 𐐲𐑂 𐑋𐐨 𐐸𐐶𐐱𐐻 𐐷 𐑇𐐰𐑊

𐐼𐐭 𐐺𐐨𐐿𐐫𐑆 𐐷 𐐪𐑉 𐐰𐑁𐑊𐐮𐐿𐐻𐐯𐐼 𐐰𐑌𐐼 𐐿𐐰𐑅𐐻 𐐵𐐻; 𐑌𐐵 𐐴 𐐼𐐭 𐑌𐐱𐐻 𐐼𐐨𐑆𐐴𐑉 𐑄𐐰𐐻 𐐷 𐑇𐐳𐐼 𐑅𐐲𐐹𐐬𐑆 𐑄𐐰𐐻 𐐴 𐑋𐐨𐑌 𐐻𐐭 𐐾𐐲𐐾 𐐷𐐭 𐐬𐑌𐑊𐐨 𐐰𐐿𐐫𐑉𐐼𐐮𐑍 𐐻𐐭 𐑄𐐰𐐻 𐐸𐐶𐐮𐐽 𐐮𐑆 𐐻𐑉𐐭; 𐑁𐐫𐑉 𐐴 𐐼𐐭 𐑌𐐱𐐻 𐑋𐐨𐑌 𐑄𐐰𐐻 𐐷 𐐫𐑊 𐐱𐑂 𐐷𐐭 𐐸𐐰𐑂 𐐺𐐮𐑌 𐐿𐐲𐑋𐐹𐐯𐑊𐐼 𐐻𐐭 𐐸𐐲𐑋𐐺𐑊 𐐷𐐭𐑉𐑅𐐯𐑊𐑂𐑆; 𐑁𐐫𐑉 𐐴 𐑂𐐯𐑉𐐮𐑊𐐨 𐐺𐐨𐑊𐐨𐑂 𐑄𐐰𐐻 𐑄𐐩𐑉 𐐪𐑉 𐑅𐐲𐑋 𐐰𐑋𐐲𐑍 𐐷𐐭 𐐸𐐭 𐐶𐐳𐐼 𐐸𐐲𐑋𐐺𐑊 𐑄𐐯𐑋𐑅𐐯𐑊𐑂𐑆, 𐑊𐐯𐐻 𐑄𐐯𐑋 𐐺 𐐮𐑌 𐐸𐐶𐐱𐐻𐑅𐐬𐐯𐑂𐐲𐑉 𐑅𐐲𐑉𐐿𐐲𐑋𐑅𐐻𐐰𐑌𐑅𐐯𐑆 𐑄𐐩 𐑋𐐴𐐻. 𐐤𐐵 𐐰𐑆 𐐴 𐑅𐐯𐐼 𐐿𐐲𐑌𐑅𐐲𐑉𐑌𐐮𐑍 𐑁𐐩𐑃—𐑄𐐰𐐻 𐐮𐐻 𐐶𐐱𐑆 𐑌𐐱𐐻 𐐲 𐐹𐐲𐑉𐑁𐐯𐐿𐐻 𐑌𐐱𐑊𐐯𐐾, 𐐨𐑂𐐯𐑌 𐑅𐐬 𐐮𐐻 𐐮𐑆 𐐶𐐮𐑄 𐑋𐐴 𐐶𐐲𐑉𐐼𐑆. 𐐏 𐐿𐐰𐑌𐑌𐐱𐐻 𐑌𐐬 𐐱𐑂 𐑄𐐩𐑉 𐑇𐐭𐑉𐐮𐐻𐐨 𐐰𐐻 𐑁𐐲𐑉𐑅𐐻, 𐐲𐑌𐐻𐐭 𐐹𐐲𐑉𐑁𐐯𐐿𐑇𐐲𐑌, 𐐯𐑌𐐨 𐑋𐐬𐑉 𐑄𐐰𐑌 𐑁𐐩𐑃 𐐮𐑆 𐐲 𐐹𐐲𐑉𐑁𐐯𐐿𐐻 𐑌𐐱𐑊𐐯𐐾. 𐐒𐐲𐐻 𐐺𐐨𐐸𐐬𐑊𐐼, 𐐮𐑁 𐐷 𐐶𐐮𐑊 𐐰𐐶𐐩𐐿 𐐰𐑌𐐼 𐐰𐑉𐐵𐑆 𐐷𐐭𐑉 𐑁𐐰𐐿𐐲𐑊𐐻𐐮𐑆, 𐐨𐑂𐐯𐑌 𐐻𐐭 𐐰𐑌 𐐯𐐿𐑅𐐹𐐯𐑉𐐮𐑋𐐯𐑌𐐻 𐐲𐐹𐐱𐑌 𐑋𐐴 𐐶𐐲𐑉𐐼𐑆, 𐐰𐑌𐐼 𐐯𐐿𐑅𐐲𐑉𐑅𐐴𐑆 𐐲 𐐹𐐪𐑉𐐻𐐮𐐿𐐲𐑊 𐐱𐑂 𐑁𐐩𐑃; 𐐷𐐩, 𐐨𐑂𐐯𐑌 𐐮𐑁 𐐷 𐐿𐐰𐑌 𐑌𐐬 𐑋𐐬𐑉 𐑄𐐰𐑌 𐐼𐐨𐑆𐐴𐑉 𐐻𐐭 𐐺𐐨𐑊𐐨𐑂, 𐑊𐐯𐐻 𐑄𐐮𐑅 𐐼𐐨𐑆𐐴𐑉 𐐶𐐲𐑉𐐿 𐐮𐑌 𐐷𐐭, 𐐨𐑂𐐯𐑌 𐐲𐑌𐐻𐐮𐑊 𐐷 𐐺𐐨𐑊𐐨𐑂 𐐮𐑌 𐐲 𐑋𐐰𐑌𐐲𐑉 𐑄𐐰𐐻 𐐷 𐐿𐐰𐑌 𐑀𐐮𐑂 𐐹𐑊𐐩𐑅 𐑁𐐫𐑉 𐐲 𐐹𐐬𐑉𐑇𐐲𐑌 𐐱𐑂 𐑋𐐴 𐐶𐐲𐑉𐐼𐑆. 𐐤𐐵 𐐶𐐨 𐐶𐐮𐑊 𐐿𐐲𐑋𐐹𐐩𐑉 𐑄 𐐶𐐲𐑉𐐼 𐐲𐑌𐐻𐐭 𐐲 𐑅𐐨𐐼.

23. 𐐤𐐵 𐐮𐑁 𐐷 𐑀𐐮𐑂 𐐹𐑊𐐩𐑅, 𐑄𐐰𐐻 𐐲 𐑅𐐨𐐼 𐑋𐐩 𐐺 𐐹𐑊𐐰𐑌𐐻𐐯𐐼 𐐮𐑌 𐐷𐐭𐑉 𐐸𐐪𐑉𐐻, 𐐺𐐨𐐸𐐬𐑊𐐼, 𐐮𐑁 𐐮𐐻 𐐺 𐐲 𐐻𐑉𐐭 𐑅𐐨𐐼, 𐐫𐑉 𐐲 𐑀𐐳𐐼 𐑅𐐨𐐼, 𐐮𐑁 𐐷 𐐼𐐭 𐑌𐐱𐐻 𐐿𐐰𐑅𐐻 𐐮𐐻 𐐵𐐻 𐐺𐐴 𐐷𐐭𐑉 𐐲𐑌𐐺𐐨𐑊𐐨𐑁, 𐑄𐐰𐐻 𐐷 𐐶𐐮𐑊 𐑉𐐨𐑆𐐮𐑅𐐻 𐑄 𐐝𐐹𐐮𐑉𐐮𐐻 𐐱𐑂 𐑄 𐐢𐐫𐑉𐐼, 𐐺𐐨𐐸𐐬𐑊𐐼, 𐐮𐐻 𐐶𐐮𐑊 𐐺𐐨𐑀𐐮𐑌 𐐻𐐭 𐑅𐐶𐐯𐑊 𐐶𐐮𐑄𐐮𐑌 𐐷𐐭𐑉 𐐺𐑉𐐯𐑅𐐻𐑅; 𐐰𐑌𐐼 𐐸𐐶𐐯𐑌 𐐷𐐭 𐑁𐐨𐑊 𐑄𐐨𐑆 𐑅𐐶𐐯𐑊𐐮𐑍 𐑋𐐬𐑇𐐲𐑌𐑆, 𐐷 𐐶𐐮𐑊 𐐺𐐨𐑀𐐮𐑌 𐐻𐐭 𐑅𐐩 𐐶𐐮𐑄𐐮𐑌 𐐷𐐭𐑉𐑅𐐯𐑊𐑂𐑆, 𐐆𐐻 𐑋𐐲𐑅𐐻 𐑌𐐨𐐼𐑆 𐐺 𐑄𐐰𐐻 𐑄𐐮𐑅 𐐮𐑆 𐐲 𐑀𐐳𐐼 𐑅𐐨𐐼, 𐐫𐑉 𐑄𐐰𐐻 𐑄 𐐶𐐲𐑉𐐼 𐐮𐑆 𐑀𐐳𐐼, 𐑁𐐫𐑉 𐐮𐐻 𐐺𐐨𐑀𐐮𐑌𐐯𐑃 𐐻𐐭 𐐯𐑌𐑊𐐪𐑉𐐾 𐑋𐐴 𐑅𐐬𐑊: 𐐷𐐩, 𐐮𐐻 𐐺𐐨𐑀𐐮𐑌𐐯𐑃 𐐻𐐭 𐐯𐑌𐑊𐐴𐐻𐐯𐑌 𐑋𐐴 𐐲𐑌𐐼𐐲𐑉𐑅𐐻𐐰𐑌𐐼𐐮𐑍, 𐐷𐐩, 𐐮𐐻 𐐺𐐨𐑀𐐮𐑌𐐯𐑃 𐐻𐐭 𐐺 𐐼𐐨𐑊𐐮𐑇𐐲𐑅 𐐻𐐭 𐑋𐐨.—𐐤𐐵 𐐺𐐨𐐸𐐬𐑊𐐼, 𐐶𐐳𐐼 𐑌𐐱𐐻 𐑄𐐮𐑅 𐐮𐑌𐐿𐑉𐐨𐑅 𐐷𐐭𐑉 𐑁𐐩𐑃? 𐐴 𐑅𐐩 𐐲𐑌𐐻𐐭 𐐷𐐭, 𐐏𐐩; 𐑌𐐯𐑂𐐲𐑉𐑄𐐯𐑊𐐯𐑅 𐐮𐐻 𐐸𐐰𐑃 𐑌𐐱𐐻 𐑀𐑉𐐬𐑌 𐐲𐐹 𐐻𐐭 𐐲 𐐹𐐲𐑉𐑁𐐯𐐿𐐻 𐑌𐐱𐑊𐐯𐐾. 𐐒𐐲𐐻 𐐺𐐨𐐸𐐬𐑊𐐼, 𐐰𐑆 𐑄 𐑅𐐨𐐼 𐑅𐐶𐐯𐑊𐐯𐑃, 𐐰𐑌𐐼 𐑅𐐹𐑉𐐵𐐻𐐯𐑃, 𐐰𐑌𐐼 𐐺𐐨𐑀𐐮𐑌𐐯𐑃 𐐻𐐭 𐑀𐑉𐐬, 𐑄𐐯𐑌 𐐷𐐭 𐑋𐐲𐑅𐐻 𐑌𐐨𐐼𐑆 𐑅𐐩 𐑄𐐰𐐻 𐑄 𐑅𐐨𐐼 𐐮𐑆 𐑀𐐳𐐼; 𐑁𐐫𐑉 𐐺𐐨𐐸𐐬𐑊𐐼 𐐮𐐻 𐑅𐐶𐐯𐑊𐐯𐑃, 𐐰𐑌𐐼 𐑅𐐹𐑉𐐵𐐻𐐯𐑃, 𐐰𐑌𐐼 𐐺𐐨𐑀𐐮𐑌𐐯𐑃 𐐻𐐭 𐑀𐑉𐐬. 𐐈𐑌𐐼 𐑌𐐵, 𐐺𐐨𐐸𐐬𐑊𐐼, 𐐶𐐮𐑊 𐑌𐐱𐐻 𐑄𐐮𐑅 𐑅𐐻𐑉𐐯𐑍𐑃𐐯𐑌 𐐷𐐭𐑉 𐑁𐐩𐑃? 𐐏𐐩, 𐐮𐐻 𐐶𐐮𐑊 𐑅𐐻𐑉𐐯𐑍𐑃𐐯𐑌 𐐷𐐭𐑉 𐑁𐐩𐑃: 𐑁𐐫𐑉 𐐷 𐐶𐐮𐑊 𐑅𐐩 𐐴 𐑌𐐬 𐑄𐐰𐐻 𐑄𐐮𐑅 𐐮𐑆 𐐲 𐑀𐐳𐐼 𐑅𐐨𐐼; 𐑁𐐫𐑉 𐐺𐐨𐐸𐐬𐑊𐐼 𐐮𐐻 𐑅𐐹𐑉𐐵𐐻𐐯𐑃 𐐰𐑌𐐼 𐐺𐐨𐑀𐐮𐑌𐐯𐑃 𐐻𐐭 𐑀𐑉𐐬. 𐐈𐑌𐐼 𐑌𐐵, 𐐺𐐨𐐸𐐬𐑊𐐼, 𐐪𐑉 𐐷 𐑇𐐭𐑉 𐑄𐐰𐐻 𐑄𐐮𐑅 𐐮𐑆 𐐲 𐑀𐐳𐐼 𐑅𐐨𐐼? 𐐴 𐑅𐐩 𐐲𐑌𐐻𐐭 𐐷𐐭, 𐐏𐐩; 𐑁𐐫𐑉 𐐯𐑂𐐲𐑉𐐨 𐑅𐐨𐐼 𐐺𐑉𐐮𐑍𐐯𐑃 𐑁𐐬𐑉𐑃 𐐲𐑌𐐻𐐭 𐐮𐐻𐑅 𐐬𐑌 𐑊𐐴𐐿𐑌𐐯𐑅; 𐑄𐐩𐑉𐑁𐐫𐑉, 𐐮𐑁 𐐲 𐑅𐐨𐐼 𐑀𐑉𐐬𐐯𐑃 𐐮𐐻 𐐮𐑆 𐑀𐐳𐐼, 𐐺𐐲𐐻 𐐮𐑁 𐐮𐐻 𐑀𐑉𐐬𐐯𐑃 𐑌𐐱𐐻, 𐐺𐐨𐐸𐐬𐑊𐐼 𐐮𐐻 𐐮𐑆 𐑌𐐱𐐻 𐑀𐐳𐐼, 𐑄𐐩𐑉𐑁𐐫𐑉 𐐮𐐻 𐐮𐑆 𐐿𐐰𐑅𐐻 𐐰𐐶𐐩. 𐐈𐑌𐐼 𐑌𐐵, 𐐺𐐨𐐸𐐬𐑊𐐼, 𐐺𐐨𐐿𐐫𐑆 𐐷 𐐸𐐰𐑂 𐐻𐑉𐐴𐐼 𐑄 𐐯𐐿𐑅𐐹𐐯𐑉𐐮𐑋𐐯𐑌𐐻, 𐐰𐑌𐐼 𐐹𐑊𐐰𐑌𐐻𐐯𐐼 𐑄 𐑅𐐨𐐼, 𐐰𐑌𐐼 𐐮𐐻 𐑅𐐶𐐯𐑊𐐯𐑃, 𐐰𐑌𐐼 𐑅𐐹𐑉𐐵𐐻𐐯𐑃, 𐐰𐑌𐐼 𐐺𐐨𐑀𐐮𐑌𐐯𐑃 𐐻𐐭 𐑀𐑉𐐬, 𐐷 𐑋𐐲𐑅𐐻 𐑌𐐨𐐼𐑆 𐑌𐐬 𐑄𐐰𐐻 𐑄 𐑅𐐨𐐼 𐐮𐑆 𐑀𐐳𐐼. 𐐈𐑌𐐼 𐑌𐐵, 𐐺𐐨𐐸𐐬𐑊𐐼, 𐐮𐑆 𐐷𐐭𐑉 𐑌𐐱𐑊𐐯𐐾 𐐹𐐲𐑉𐑁𐐯𐐿𐐻? 𐐏𐐩, 𐐷𐐭𐑉 𐑌𐐱𐑊𐐯𐐾 𐐮𐑆 𐐹𐐲𐑉𐑁𐐯𐐿𐐻 𐐮𐑌 𐑄𐐰𐐻 𐑃𐐮𐑍, 𐐰𐑌𐐼 𐐷𐐭𐑉 𐑁𐐩𐑃 𐐮𐑆 𐐼𐐫𐑉𐑋𐐰𐑌𐐻; 𐐰𐑌𐐼 𐑄𐐮𐑅 𐐺𐐨𐐿𐐫𐑆 𐐷𐐭 𐑌𐐬, 𐑁𐐫𐑉 𐐷 𐑌𐐬 𐑄𐐰𐐻 𐑄 𐐶𐐲𐑉𐐼 𐐸𐐰𐑃 𐑅𐐶𐐯𐑊𐐼 𐐷𐐭𐑉 𐑅𐐬𐑊𐑆, 𐐰𐑌𐐼 𐐷 𐐫𐑊𐑅𐐬 𐑌𐐬 𐑄𐐰𐐻 𐐮𐐻 𐐸𐐰𐑃 𐑅𐐹𐑉𐐵𐐻𐐯𐐼 𐐲𐐹, 𐑄𐐰𐐻 𐐷𐐭𐑉 𐐲𐑌𐐼𐐲𐑉𐑅𐐻𐐰𐑌𐐼𐐮𐑍 𐐼𐐲𐑃 𐐺𐐨𐑀𐐮𐑌 𐐻𐐭 𐐺 𐐯𐑌𐑊𐐴𐐻𐐯𐑌𐐼, 𐐰𐑌𐐼 𐐷𐐭𐑉 𐑋𐐴𐑌𐐼 𐐼𐐲𐑃 𐐺𐐨𐑀𐐮𐑌 𐐻𐐭 𐐯𐐿𐑅𐐹𐐰𐑌𐐼. 𐐄 𐑄𐐯𐑌, 𐐮𐑆 𐑌𐐱𐐻 𐑄𐐮𐑅 𐑉𐐨𐐰𐑊? 𐐴 𐑅𐐩 𐐲𐑌𐐻𐐭 𐐷𐐭, 𐐏𐐩, 𐐺𐐨𐐿𐐫𐑆 𐐮𐐻 𐐮𐑆 𐑊𐐴𐐻: 𐐰𐑌𐐼 𐐸𐐶𐐱𐐻𐑅𐐬𐐯𐑂𐐲𐑉 𐐮𐑆 𐑊𐐴𐐻, 𐐮𐑆 𐑀𐐳𐐼, 𐐺𐐨𐐿𐐫𐑆 𐐮𐐻 𐐮𐑆 𐐼𐐮𐑆𐐲𐑉𐑌𐐮𐐺𐑊, 𐑄𐐩𐑉𐑁𐐫𐑉 𐐷 𐑋𐐲𐑅𐐻 𐑌𐐬 𐑄𐐰𐐻 𐐮𐐻 𐐮𐑆 𐑀𐐳𐐼; 𐐰𐑌𐐼 𐑌𐐵 𐐺𐐨𐐸𐐬𐑊𐐼, 𐐰𐑁𐐻𐐲𐑉 𐐷 𐐸𐐰𐑂 𐐻𐐩𐑅𐐻𐐯𐐼 𐑄𐐮𐑅 𐑊𐐴𐐻, 𐐮𐑆 𐐷𐐭𐑉 𐑌𐐱𐑊𐐯𐐾 𐐹𐐲𐑉𐑁𐐯𐐿𐐻? 𐐒𐐨𐐸𐐬𐑊𐐼 𐐴 𐑅𐐩 𐐲𐑌𐐻𐐭 𐐷𐐭, 𐑌𐐩, 𐑌𐐨𐑄𐐲𐑉 𐑋𐐲𐑅𐐻 𐐷 𐑊𐐩 𐐰𐑅𐐴𐐼 𐐷𐐭𐑉 𐑁𐐩𐑃, 𐑁𐐫𐑉 𐐷 𐐸𐐰𐑂 𐐬𐑌𐑊𐐨 𐐯𐐿𐑅𐐲𐑉𐑅𐐴𐑆𐐼 𐐷𐐭𐑉 𐑁𐐩𐑃 𐐻𐐭 𐐹𐑊𐐰𐑌𐐻 𐑄 𐑅𐐨𐐼, 𐑄𐐰𐐻 𐐷 𐑋𐐴𐐻 𐐻𐑉𐐴 𐑄 𐐯𐐿𐑅𐐹𐐯𐑉𐐮𐑋𐐯𐑌𐐻 𐐻𐐭 𐑌𐐬 𐐮𐑁 𐑄 𐑅𐐨𐐼 𐐶𐐱𐑆 𐑀𐐳𐐼. 𐐈𐑌𐐼 𐐺𐐨𐐸𐐬𐑊𐐼, 𐐰𐑆 𐑄 𐐻𐑉𐐨 𐐺𐐨𐑀𐐮𐑌𐐯𐑃 𐐻𐐭 𐑀𐑉𐐬, 𐐷 𐐶𐐮𐑊 𐑅𐐩, 𐑊𐐯𐐻 𐐲𐑅 𐑌𐐲𐑉𐐮𐑇 𐐮𐐻 𐐶𐐮𐑄 𐑀𐑉𐐩𐐻 𐐿𐐩𐑉, 𐑄𐐰𐐻 𐐮𐐻 𐑋𐐩 𐑀𐐯𐐻 𐑉𐐭𐐻, 𐑄𐐰𐐻 𐐮𐐻 𐑋𐐩 𐑀𐑉𐐬 𐐲𐐹, 𐐰𐑌𐐼 𐐺𐑉𐐮𐑍 𐑁𐐬𐑉𐑃 𐑁𐑉𐐭𐐻 𐐲𐑌𐐻𐐭 𐐲𐑅. 𐐈𐑌𐐼 𐑌𐐵 𐐺𐐨𐐸𐐬𐑊𐐼, 𐐮𐑁 𐐷 𐑌𐐲𐑉𐐮𐑇 𐐮𐐻 𐐶𐐮𐑄 𐑋𐐲𐐽 𐐿𐐩𐑉 𐐮𐐻 𐐶𐐮𐑊 𐑀𐐯𐐻 𐑉𐐭𐐻, 𐐰𐑌𐐼 𐑀𐑉𐐬 𐐲𐐹, 𐐰𐑌𐐼 𐐺𐑉𐐮𐑍 𐑁𐐬𐑉𐑃 𐑁𐑉𐐭𐐻.

24. 𐐒𐐲𐐻 𐐮𐑁 𐐷 𐑌𐐯𐑀𐑊𐐯𐐿𐐻 𐑄 𐐻𐑉𐐨, 𐐰𐑌𐐼 𐐻𐐩𐐿 𐑌𐐬 𐑃𐐫𐐻 𐑁𐐫𐑉 𐐮𐐻𐑅 𐑌𐐲𐑉𐐮𐑇𐑋𐐯𐑌𐐻, 𐐺𐐨𐐸𐐬𐑊𐐼 𐐮𐐻 𐐶𐐮𐑊 𐑌𐐱𐐻 𐑀𐐯𐐻 𐐯𐑌𐐨 𐑉𐐭𐐻; 𐐰𐑌𐐼 𐐸𐐶𐐯𐑌 𐑄 𐐸𐐨𐐻 𐐱𐑂 𐑄 𐑅𐐲𐑌 𐐿𐐲𐑋𐐯𐑃 𐐰𐑌𐐼 𐑅𐐿𐐫𐑉𐐽𐐯𐑃 𐐮𐐻, 𐐺𐐨𐐿𐐫𐑆 𐐮𐐻 𐐸𐐰𐑃 𐑌𐐬 𐑉𐐭𐐻 𐐮𐐻 𐐶𐐮𐑄𐐲𐑉𐑆 𐐰𐐶𐐩, 𐐰𐑌𐐼 𐐷 𐐹𐑊𐐲𐐿 𐐮𐐻 𐐲𐐹 𐐰𐑌𐐼 𐐿𐐰𐑅𐐻 𐐮𐐻 𐐵𐐻. 𐐤𐐵 𐑄𐐮𐑅 𐐮𐑆 𐑌𐐱𐐻

𐐺𐐨𐐿𐐫𐑆 𐑄 𐑅𐐨𐐼 𐐶𐐱𐑆 𐑌𐐱𐐻 𐑀𐐳𐐼, 𐑌𐐨𐑄𐐲𐑉 𐐮𐑆 𐐮𐐻 𐐺𐐨𐐿𐐫𐑆 𐑄 𐑁𐑉𐐭𐐻 𐑄𐐩𐑉𐐱𐑂 𐐶𐐳𐐼 𐑌𐐱𐐻 𐐺 𐐼𐐨𐑆𐐴𐑉𐐰𐐺𐑊; 𐐺𐐲𐐻 𐐮𐐻 𐐮𐑆 𐐺𐐨𐐿𐐫𐑆 𐐷𐐫𐑉 𐑀𐑉𐐵𐑌𐐼 𐐮𐑆 𐐺𐐰𐑉𐐲𐑌, 𐐰𐑌𐐼 𐐷 𐐶𐐮𐑊 𐑌𐐱𐐻 𐑌𐐲𐑉𐐮𐑇 𐑄 𐐻𐑉𐐨, 𐑄𐐩𐑉𐑁𐐫𐑉 𐐷 𐐿𐐰𐑌𐐱𐐻 𐐸𐐰𐑂 𐑄 𐑁𐑉𐐭𐐻 𐑄𐐩𐑉𐐱𐑂. 𐐈𐑌𐐼 𐑄𐐲𐑅, 𐐮𐑁 𐐷 𐐶𐐮𐑊 𐑌𐐱𐐻 𐑌𐐲𐑉𐐮𐑇 𐑄 𐐶𐐲𐑉𐐼, 𐑊𐐳𐐿𐐮𐑍 𐑁𐐫𐑉𐐶𐐲𐑉𐐼 𐐶𐐮𐑄 𐐰𐑌 𐐴 𐐱𐑂 𐑁𐐩𐑃 𐐻𐐭 𐑄 𐑁𐑉𐐭𐐻 𐑄𐐩𐑉𐐱𐑂, 𐐷 𐐿𐐰𐑌 𐑌𐐯𐑂𐐲𐑉 𐐹𐑊𐐲𐐿 𐐱𐑂 𐑄 𐑁𐑉𐐭𐐻 𐐱𐑂 𐑄 𐐻𐑉𐐨 𐐱𐑂 𐑊𐐴𐑁. 𐐒𐐲𐐻 𐐮𐑁 𐐷 𐐶𐐮𐑊 𐑌𐐲𐑉𐐮𐑇 𐑄 𐐶𐐲𐑉𐐼, 𐐷𐐩, 𐑌𐐲𐑉𐐮𐑇 𐑄 𐐻𐑉𐐨 𐐰𐑆 𐐮𐐻 𐐺𐐨𐑀𐐮𐑌𐐯𐑃 𐐻𐐭 𐑀𐑉𐐬, 𐐺𐐴 𐐷𐐫𐑉 𐑁𐐩𐑃 𐐶𐐮𐑄 𐑀𐑉𐐩𐐻 𐐼𐐮𐑊𐐮𐐾𐐯𐑌𐑅, 𐐰𐑌𐐼 𐐶𐐮𐑄 𐐹𐐩𐑇𐐯𐑌𐑅, 𐑊𐐳𐐿𐐮𐑍 𐑁𐐫𐑉𐐶𐐲𐑉𐐼 𐐻𐐭 𐑄 𐑁𐑉𐐭𐐻 𐑄𐐩𐑉𐐱𐑂, 𐐮𐐻 𐑇𐐰𐑊 𐐻𐐩𐐿 𐑉𐐭𐐻; 𐐰𐑌𐐼 𐐺𐐨𐐸𐐬𐑊𐐼 𐐮𐐻 𐑇𐐰𐑊 𐐺 𐐰 𐐻𐑉𐐨 𐑅𐐹𐑉𐐮𐑍𐐮𐑍 𐐲𐐹 𐐲𐑌𐐻𐐭 𐐯𐑂𐐲𐑉𐑊𐐰𐑅𐐻𐐮𐑍 𐑊𐐴𐑁; 𐐰𐑌𐐼 𐐺𐐨𐐿𐐫𐑆 𐐱𐑂 𐐷𐐫𐑉 𐐼𐐮𐑊𐐮𐐾𐐯𐑌𐑅, 𐐰𐑌𐐼 𐐷𐐫𐑉 𐑁𐐩𐑃, 𐐰𐑌𐐼 𐐷𐐫𐑉 𐐹𐐩𐑇𐐯𐑌𐑅 𐐶𐐮𐑄 𐑄 𐐶𐐲𐑉𐐼 𐐮𐑌 𐑌𐐲𐑉𐐮𐑇𐐮𐑍 𐐮𐐻, 𐑄𐐰𐐻 𐐮𐐻 𐑋𐐩 𐐻𐐩𐐿 𐑉𐐭𐐻 𐐮𐑌 𐐷𐐭, 𐐺𐐨𐐸𐐬𐑊𐐼, 𐐺𐐴 𐐰𐑌𐐼 𐐺𐐴 𐐷 𐑇𐐰𐑊 𐐹𐑊𐐲𐐿 𐑄 𐑁𐑉𐐭𐐻 𐑄𐐩𐑉𐐱𐑂, 𐐸𐐶𐐮𐐽 𐐮𐑆 𐑋𐐬𐑅𐐻 𐐹𐑉𐐯𐑇𐐲𐑅, 𐐸𐐶𐐮𐐽 𐐮𐑆 𐑅𐐶𐐨𐐻𐐲𐑉 𐐰𐐺𐐲𐑂 𐐫𐑊 𐑄𐐰𐐻 𐐮𐑆 𐑅𐐶𐐨𐐻, 𐐰𐑌𐐼 𐐸𐐶𐐮𐐽 𐐮𐑆 𐐸𐐶𐐴𐐻𐐲𐑉 𐐰𐐺𐐲𐑂 𐐫𐑊 𐑄𐐰𐐻 𐐮𐑆 𐐸𐐶𐐴𐐻; 𐐷𐐩, 𐐰𐑌𐐼 𐐹𐐷𐐭𐑉 𐐰𐐺𐐲𐑂 𐐫𐑊 𐑄𐐰𐐻 𐐮𐑆 𐐹𐐷𐐭𐑉; 𐐰𐑌𐐼 𐐷 𐑇𐐰𐑊 𐑁𐐨𐑅𐐻 𐐲𐐹𐐱𐑌 𐑄𐐮𐑅 𐑁𐑉𐐭𐐻, 𐐨𐑂𐐯𐑌 𐐲𐑌𐐻𐐮𐑊 𐐷 𐐪𐑉 𐑁𐐮𐑊𐐼, 𐑄𐐰𐐻 𐐷 𐐸𐐲𐑍𐑀𐐲𐑉 𐑌𐐱𐐻, 𐑌𐐨𐑄𐐲𐑉 𐑇𐐰𐑊 𐐷 𐑃𐐲𐑉𐑅𐐻. 𐐜𐐯𐑌, 𐑋𐐴 𐐺𐑉𐐯𐑄𐑉𐐯𐑌, 𐐷 𐑇𐐰𐑊 𐑉𐐨𐐹 𐑄 𐑉𐐨𐐶𐐫𐑉𐐼𐑆 𐐱𐑂 𐐷𐐫𐑉 𐑁𐐩𐑃, 𐐰𐑌𐐼 𐐷𐐫𐑉 𐐼𐐮𐑊𐐮𐐾𐐯𐑌𐑅, 𐐰𐑌𐐼 𐐹𐐩𐑇𐐯𐑌𐑅, 𐐰𐑌𐐼 𐑊𐐱𐑍 𐑅𐐲𐑁𐐲𐑉𐐮𐑍, 𐐶𐐩𐐻𐐮𐑍 𐑁𐐫𐑉 𐑄 𐐻𐑉𐐨 𐐻𐐭 𐐺𐑉𐐮𐑍 𐑁𐐫𐑉𐑃 𐑁𐑉𐐭𐐻 𐐲𐑌𐐻𐐭 𐐷𐐭.

25. 𐐤𐐵 𐐪𐑁𐐻𐐲𐑉 𐐈𐑊𐑋𐐲 𐐸𐐰𐐼 𐑅𐐹𐐬𐐿𐐲𐑌 𐑄𐐨𐑆 𐐶𐐲𐑉𐐼𐑆, 𐑄𐐩 𐑅𐐯𐑌𐐻 𐑁𐐫𐑉𐑃 𐐲𐑌𐐻𐐭 𐐸𐐮𐑋 𐐼𐐨𐑆𐐴𐑉𐐮𐑍 𐐻𐐭 𐑌𐐬 𐐸𐐶𐐯𐑄𐐲𐑉 𐑄𐐩 𐑇𐐳𐐼 𐐺𐐨𐑊𐐨𐑂 𐐮𐑌 𐐶𐐲𐑌 𐐘𐐱𐐼, 𐑄𐐰𐐻 𐑄𐐩 𐑋𐐴𐐻 𐐱𐐺𐐻𐐩𐑌 𐑄𐐮𐑅 𐑁𐑉𐐭𐐻 𐐱𐑂 𐐸𐐶𐐮𐐽 𐐸𐐨 𐐸𐐰𐐼 𐑅𐐹𐐬𐐿𐐲𐑌, 𐐫𐑉 𐐸𐐵 𐑄𐐩 𐑇𐐳𐐼 𐐹𐑊𐐰𐑌𐐻 𐑄 𐑅𐐨𐐼, 𐐫𐑉 𐑄 𐐶𐐲𐑉𐐼 𐐱𐑂 𐐸𐐶𐐮𐐽 𐐸𐐨 𐐸𐐰𐐼 𐑅𐐹𐐬𐐿𐐲𐑌, 𐐸𐐶𐐮𐐽 𐐸𐐨 𐑅𐐯𐐼 𐑋𐐲𐑅𐐻 𐐺 𐐹𐑊𐐰𐑌𐐻𐐯𐐼 𐐮𐑌 𐑄𐐩𐑉 𐐸𐐪𐑉𐐻𐑅; 𐐫𐑉 𐐮𐑌 𐐸𐐶𐐱𐐻 𐑋𐐰𐑌𐐲𐑉 𐑄𐐩 𐑇𐐳𐐼 𐐺𐐨𐑀𐐮𐑌 𐐻𐐭 𐐯𐐿𐑅𐐲𐑉𐑅𐐴𐑆 𐑄𐐩𐑉 𐑁𐐩𐑃? 𐐈𐑌𐐼 𐐈𐑊𐑋𐐲 𐑅𐐯𐐼 𐐲𐑌𐐻𐐭 𐑄𐐯𐑋, 𐐒𐐨𐐸𐐬𐑊𐐼 𐐷 𐐸𐐰𐑂 𐑅𐐯𐐼 𐑄𐐰𐐻 𐐷 𐐿𐐳𐐼 𐑌𐐱𐐻 𐐶𐐲𐑉𐑇𐐮𐐹 𐐷𐐫𐑉 𐐘𐐱𐐼, 𐐺𐐨𐐿𐐫𐑆 𐐷 𐐪𐑉 𐐿𐐰𐑅𐐻 𐐵𐐻 𐐱𐑂 𐐷𐐫𐑉 𐑅𐐮𐑌𐐲𐑀𐐱𐑀𐑆. 𐐒𐐲𐐻 𐐺𐐨𐐸𐐬𐑊𐐼 𐐴 𐑅𐐩 𐐲𐑌𐐻𐐭 𐐷𐐭, 𐐮𐑁 𐐷 𐑅𐐲𐐹𐐬𐑆 𐑄𐐰𐐻 𐐷 𐐿𐐰𐑌𐐱𐐻 𐐶𐐲𐑉𐑇𐐮𐐹 𐐘𐐱𐐼, 𐐷 𐐼𐐭 𐑀𐑉𐐩𐐻𐑊𐐨 𐐲𐑉, 𐐰𐑌𐐼 𐐷 𐐫𐐻 𐐻𐐭 𐑅𐐲𐑉𐐽 𐑄 𐑅𐐿𐑉𐐮𐐹𐐻𐐷𐐭𐑉𐑆; 𐐮𐑁 𐐷 𐑅𐐲𐐹𐐬𐑆 𐑄𐐰𐐻 𐑄𐐩 𐐸𐐰𐑂 𐐻𐐫𐐻 𐐷𐐭 𐑄𐐮𐑅, 𐐷 𐐼𐐭 𐑌𐐱𐐻 𐐲𐑌𐐼𐐲𐑉𐑅𐐻𐐰𐑌𐐼 𐑄𐐯𐑋. 𐐔𐐭 𐐷 𐑉𐐨𐑋𐐯𐑋𐐺𐐲𐑉 𐐻𐐭 𐐸𐐰𐑂 𐑉𐐯𐐼 𐐸𐐶𐐱𐐻 𐐞𐐨𐑌𐐲𐑅, 𐑄 𐐹𐑉𐐱𐑁𐐯𐐻 𐐱𐑂 𐐬𐑊𐐼, 𐐸𐐰𐑆 𐑅𐐯𐐼 𐐿𐐱𐑌𐑅𐐲𐑉𐑌𐐮𐑍 𐐹𐑉𐐩𐑉 𐐫𐑉 𐐶𐐲𐑉𐑇𐐮𐐹? 𐐙𐐫𐑉 𐐸𐐨 𐑅𐐯𐐼, 𐐜𐐵 𐐪𐑉𐐻 𐑋𐐲𐑉𐑅𐐮𐑁𐐳𐑊, 𐐄 𐐘𐐱𐐼, 𐑁𐐫𐑉 𐑄𐐵 𐐸𐐰𐑅𐐻 𐐸𐐲𐑉𐐼 𐑋𐐴 𐐹𐑉𐐩𐑉, 𐐨𐑂𐐯𐑌 𐐸𐐶𐐯𐑌 𐐴 𐐶𐐱𐑆 𐐮𐑌 𐑄 𐐶𐐮𐑊𐐼𐐲𐑉𐑌𐐯𐑅; 𐐷𐐩, 𐑄𐐵 𐐶𐐱𐑅𐐻 𐑋𐐲𐑉𐑅𐐮𐑁𐐳𐑊 𐐸𐐶𐐯𐑌 𐐴 𐐹𐑉𐐩𐐼 𐐿𐐱𐑌𐑅𐐲𐑉𐑌𐐮𐑍 𐑄𐐬𐑆 𐐸𐐭 𐐶𐐲𐑉 𐑋𐐴𐑌 𐐯𐑌𐐯𐑋𐐮𐑆, 𐐰𐑌𐐼 𐑄𐐵 𐐼𐐮𐐼𐑅𐐻 𐐻𐐲𐑉𐑌 𐑄𐐯𐑋 𐐻𐐭 𐑋𐐨; 𐐷𐐩, 𐐄 𐐘𐐱𐐼, 𐐰𐑌𐐼 𐑄𐐵 𐐶𐐱𐑅𐐻 𐑋𐐲𐑉𐑅𐐮𐑁𐐳𐑊 𐐲𐑌𐐻𐐭 𐑋𐐨 𐐸𐐶𐐯𐑌 𐐴 𐐼𐐮𐐼 𐐿𐑉𐐴 𐐲𐑌𐐻𐐭 𐑄 𐐮𐑌 𐑋𐐴 𐑁𐐨𐑊𐐼; 𐐸𐐶𐐯𐑌 𐐴 𐐼𐐮𐐼 𐐿𐑉𐐴 𐐲𐑌𐐻𐐭 𐑄 𐐮𐑌 𐑋𐐴 𐐹𐑉𐐩𐑉, 𐐰𐑌𐐼 𐑄𐐵 𐐼𐐮𐐼𐑅𐐻 𐐸𐐨𐑉 𐑋𐐨. 𐐈𐑌𐐼 𐐲𐑀𐐯𐑌, 𐐄 𐐘𐐱𐐼, 𐐸𐐶𐐯𐑌 𐐴 𐐼𐐮𐐼 𐐻𐐲𐑉𐑌 𐐻𐐭 𐑋𐐴 𐐸𐐵𐑅 𐑄𐐵 𐐼𐐮𐐼𐑅𐐻 𐐸𐐨𐑉 𐑋𐐨 𐐮𐑌 𐑋𐐴 𐐹𐑉𐐩𐑉. 𐐈𐑌𐐼 𐐸𐐶𐐯𐑌 𐐴 𐐼𐐮𐐼 𐐻𐐲𐑉𐑌 𐐲𐑌𐐻𐐭 𐑋𐐴 𐐿𐑊𐐱𐑆𐐯𐐻, 𐐄 𐐢𐐫𐑉𐐼, 𐐰𐑌𐐼 𐐹𐑉𐐩𐐼 𐐲𐑌𐐻𐐭 𐑄, 𐑄𐐵 𐐼𐐮𐐼𐑅𐐻 𐐸𐐨𐑉 𐑋𐐨; 𐐷𐐩, 𐑄𐐵 𐐪𐑉𐐻 𐑋𐐲𐑉𐑅𐐮𐑁𐐳𐑊 𐐲𐑌𐐻𐐭 𐑄𐐴 𐐽𐐮𐑊𐐼𐑉𐐲𐑌 𐐸𐐶𐐯𐑌 𐑄𐐩 𐐿𐑉𐐴 𐐲𐑌𐐻𐐭 𐑄 𐐻𐐭 𐐺 𐐸𐐲𐑉𐐼 𐐱𐑂 𐑄, 𐐰𐑌𐐼 𐑌𐐱𐐻 𐐱𐑂 𐑋𐐯𐑌, 𐐰𐑌𐐼 𐑄𐐵 𐐶𐐮𐑊𐐻 𐐸𐐨𐑉 𐑄𐐯𐑋; 𐐷𐐩, 𐐄 𐐘𐐱𐐼, 𐑄𐐵 𐐸𐐰𐑅𐐻 𐐺𐐮𐑌 𐑋𐐲𐑉𐑅𐐮𐑁𐐳𐑊 𐐲𐑌𐐻𐐭 𐑋𐐨, 𐐰𐑌𐐼 𐐸𐐲𐑉𐐼 𐑋𐐴 𐐿𐑉𐐴𐑆 𐐮𐑌 𐑄 𐑋𐐮𐐼𐑅𐐻 𐐱𐑂 𐑄𐐴 𐐿𐐱𐑍𐑀𐑉𐐨𐑀𐐩𐑇𐐲𐑌𐑆; 𐐷𐐩, 𐐰𐑌𐐼 𐑄𐐵 𐐸𐐰𐑅𐐻 𐐫𐑊𐑅𐐬 𐐸𐐲𐑉𐐼 𐑋𐐨 𐐸𐐶𐐯𐑌 𐐴 𐐸𐐰𐑂 𐐺𐐮𐑌 𐐿𐐰𐑅𐐻 𐐵𐐻, 𐐰𐑌𐐼 𐐸𐐰𐑂 𐐺𐐮𐑌 𐐼𐐨𐑅𐐹𐐴𐑆𐐼 𐐺𐐴 𐑋𐐴𐑌 𐐯𐑌𐐯𐑋𐐮𐑆; 𐐷𐐩, 𐑄𐐵 𐐼𐐮𐐼𐑅𐐻 𐐸𐐨𐑉 𐑋𐐴 𐐿𐑉𐐴𐑆, 𐐰𐑌𐐼 𐐶𐐱𐑅𐐻 𐐰𐑍𐑀𐑉𐐨 𐐶𐐮𐑄 𐑋𐐴𐑌 𐐯𐑌𐐯𐑋𐐮𐑆, 𐐰𐑌𐐼 𐑄𐐵 𐐼𐐮𐐼𐑅𐐻 𐑂𐐮𐑆𐐮𐐻 𐑄𐐯𐑋 𐐮𐑌 𐑄𐐴𐑌 𐐰𐑍𐑀𐐲𐑉 𐐶𐐮𐑄 𐑅𐐹𐐨𐐼𐐨 𐐼𐐨𐑅𐐻𐑉𐐲𐐿𐑇𐐲𐑌; 𐐰𐑌𐐼 𐑄𐐵 𐐼𐐮𐐼𐑅𐐻 𐐸𐐨𐑉 𐑋𐐨 𐐺𐐨𐐿𐐫𐑆 𐐱𐑂 𐑋𐐴𐑌 𐐰𐑁𐑊𐐮𐐿𐑇𐐲𐑌𐑆 𐐰𐑌𐐼 𐑋𐐴 𐑅𐐮𐑌𐑅𐐯𐑉𐐮𐐻𐐨; 𐐰𐑌𐐼 𐐮𐐻 𐐮𐑆 𐐺𐐨𐐿𐐫𐑆 𐐱𐑂 𐑄𐐴 𐐝𐐲𐑌 𐑄𐐰𐐻 𐑄𐐵 𐐸𐐰𐑅𐐻 𐐺𐐮𐑌 𐑄𐐲𐑅 𐑋𐐲𐑉𐑅𐐮𐑁𐐳𐑊 𐐲𐑌𐐻𐐭 𐑋𐐨, 𐑄𐐩𐑉𐑁𐐫𐑉 𐐴 𐐶𐐮𐑊 𐐿𐑉𐐴 𐐲𐑌𐐻𐐭 𐑄 𐐮𐑌 𐐫𐑊 𐑋𐐴𐑌 𐐰𐑁𐑊𐐮𐐿𐑇𐐲𐑌𐑆, 𐑁𐐫𐑉 𐐮𐑌 𐑄 𐐮𐑆 𐑋𐐴 𐐾𐑎; 𐑁𐐫𐑉 𐑄𐐵 𐐸𐐰𐑅𐐻 𐐻𐐲𐑉𐑌𐐼 𐑄𐐴 𐐾𐐲𐐾𐑋𐐯𐑌𐐻𐑅 𐐰𐐶𐐩 𐑁𐑉𐐱𐑋 𐑋𐐨, 𐐺𐐨𐐿𐐫𐑆 𐐱𐑂 𐑄𐐴 𐐝𐐲𐑌.

26. 𐐈𐑌𐐼 𐑌𐐵 𐐈𐑊𐑋𐐲 𐑅𐐯𐐼 𐐲𐑌𐐻𐐭 𐑄𐐯𐑋, 𐐔𐐭 𐐷 𐐺𐐨𐑊𐐨𐑂 𐑄𐐬𐑆 𐑅𐐿𐑉𐐮𐐹𐐻𐐷𐐭𐑉𐑆 𐐸𐐶𐐮𐐽 𐐸𐐰𐑂 𐐺𐐮𐑌 𐑉𐐮𐐻𐑌 𐐺𐐴 𐑄𐐯𐑋 𐐱𐑂 𐐬𐑊𐐼? 𐐒𐐨𐐸𐐬𐑊𐐼, 𐐮𐑁 𐐷 𐐼𐐭, 𐐷 𐑋𐐲𐑅𐐻 𐐺𐐨𐑊𐐨𐑂 𐐸𐐶𐐱𐐻 𐐞𐐨𐑌𐐲𐑅 𐑅𐐯𐐼; 𐑁𐐫𐑉,

𐐒𐐨𐐸𐐬𐑊𐐼 𐐸𐐨 𐑅𐐯𐐼, 𐐜𐐵 𐐸𐐰𐑅𐐻 𐐻𐐲𐑉𐑌𐐼 𐐰𐐶𐐩 𐑄𐐴 𐐾𐐲𐐾𐑋𐐯𐑌𐐻𐑅 𐐺𐐨𐐿𐐫𐑆 𐐲𐑂 𐑄𐐴 𐐝𐐲𐑌. 𐐤𐐵, 𐐺𐐨𐐸𐐬𐑊𐐼, 𐑋𐐴 𐐺𐑉𐐯𐑄𐑉𐐯𐑌, 𐐴 𐐶𐐳𐐼 𐐰𐑅𐐿 𐐮𐑁 𐐷 𐐸𐐰𐑂 𐑉𐐯𐐼 𐑄 𐑅𐐿𐑉𐐮𐐹𐐽𐐲𐑉𐑆? 𐐆𐑁 𐐷 𐐸𐐰𐑂, 𐐸𐐵 𐐿𐐰𐑌 𐐷 𐐼𐐮𐑅𐐺𐐨𐑊𐐨𐑂 𐐱𐑌 𐑄 𐐝𐐲𐑌 𐐲𐑂 𐐘𐐱𐐼? 𐐙𐐫𐑉 𐐮𐐻 𐐮𐑆 𐑌𐐱𐐻 𐑉𐐮𐐻𐐲𐑌 𐑄𐐰𐐻 𐐞𐐨𐑌𐐱𐑅 𐐰𐑊𐐬𐑌 𐑅𐐹𐐩𐐿 𐐲𐑂 𐑄𐐨𐑆 𐑃𐐮𐑍𐑆, 𐐺𐐲𐐻 𐐞𐐨𐑌𐐱𐐿 𐐫𐑊𐑅𐐬 𐑅𐐹𐐩𐐿 𐐲𐑂 𐑄𐐨𐑆 𐑃𐐮𐑍𐑆; 𐑁𐐫𐑉 𐐺𐐨𐐸𐐬𐑊𐐼, 𐐸𐐨 𐑅𐐯𐐼, 𐐜𐐵 𐐪𐑉𐐻 𐐰𐑍𐑀𐑉𐐮, 𐐄 𐐢𐐫𐑉𐐼, 𐐶𐐮𐑄 𐑄𐐮𐑅 𐐹𐐨𐐹𐑊, 𐐺𐐨𐐿𐐫𐑆 𐑄𐐩 𐐶𐐮𐑊 𐑌𐐱𐐻 𐐲𐑌𐐼𐐲𐑉𐑅𐐻𐐰𐑌𐐼 𐑄𐐴 𐑋𐐲𐑉𐑅𐐨𐑆 𐐸𐐶𐐮𐐽 𐑄𐐵 𐐸𐐰𐑅𐐻 𐐺𐐨𐑅𐐻𐐬𐐼 𐐲𐐹𐐱𐑌 𐑄𐐯𐑋 𐐺𐐨𐐿𐐫𐑆 𐐲𐑂 𐑄𐐴 𐐝𐐲𐑌. 𐐈𐑌𐐼 𐑌𐐵 𐑋𐐴 𐐺𐑉𐐯𐑄𐑉𐐯𐑌, 𐐷 𐑅𐐨 𐑄𐐰𐐻 𐐰 𐑅𐐯𐐿𐐲𐑌𐐼 𐐹𐑉𐐱𐑁𐐯𐐻 𐐲𐑂 𐐬𐑊𐐼 𐐸𐐰𐑆 𐐻𐐯𐑅𐐻𐐮𐑁𐐴𐐼 𐐲𐑂 𐑄 𐐝𐐲𐑌 𐐲𐑂 𐐘𐐱𐐼, 𐐰𐑌𐐼 𐐺𐐨𐐿𐐫𐑆 𐑄 𐐹𐐨𐐹𐑊 𐐶𐐳𐐼 𐑌𐐱𐐻 𐐲𐑌𐐼𐐲𐑉𐑅𐐻𐐰𐑌𐐼 𐐸𐐮𐑆 𐐶𐐲𐑉𐐼𐑆, 𐑄𐐩 𐑅𐐻𐐬𐑌𐐼 𐐸𐐮𐑋 𐐻𐐭 𐐼𐐯𐑃. 𐐒𐐲𐐻 𐐺𐐨𐐸𐐬𐑊𐐼, 𐑄𐐮𐑅 𐐮𐑆 𐑌𐐱𐐻 𐐫𐑊; 𐑄𐐨𐑆 𐐪𐑉 𐑌𐐱𐐻 𐑄 𐐬𐑌𐑊𐐨 𐐶𐐲𐑌𐑆 𐐸𐐶𐐮𐐽 𐐸𐐰𐑂 𐑅𐐹𐐬𐐿𐐲𐑌 𐐿𐐱𐑌𐑅𐐲𐑉𐑌𐐮𐑍 𐑄 𐐝𐐲𐑌 𐐲𐑂 𐐘𐐱𐐼. 𐐒𐐨𐐸𐐬𐑊𐐼, 𐐸𐐨 𐐶𐐱𐑆 𐑅𐐹𐐬𐐿𐐲𐑌 𐐲𐑂 𐐺𐐴 𐐣𐐬𐑆𐐯𐑆; 𐐷𐐩, 𐐰𐑌𐐼 𐐺𐐨𐐸𐐬𐑊𐐼 𐐰 𐐻𐐴𐐹 𐐶𐐱𐑆 𐑉𐐩𐑆𐐼 𐐲𐐹 𐐮𐑌 𐑄 𐐶𐐮𐑊𐐼𐐲𐑉𐑌𐐯𐑅, 𐑄𐐰𐐻 𐐸𐐭𐑅𐐬𐐯𐑂𐐲𐑉 𐐶𐐳𐐼 𐑊𐐳𐐿 𐐲𐐹𐐱𐑌 𐐮𐐻 𐑋𐐴𐐻 𐑊𐐮𐑂. 𐐈𐑌𐐼 𐑋𐐯𐑌𐐨 𐐼𐐮𐐼 𐑊𐐳𐐿 𐐰𐑌𐐼 𐑊𐐮𐑂. 𐐒𐐲𐐻 𐑁𐑏 𐐲𐑌𐐼𐐲𐑉𐑅𐐻𐐳𐐼 𐑄 𐑋𐐨𐑌𐐮𐑍 𐐲𐑂 𐑄𐐬𐑆 𐑃𐐮𐑍𐑆, 𐐰𐑌𐐼 𐑄𐐮𐑅 𐐺𐐨𐐿𐐫𐑆 𐐲𐑂 𐑄 𐐸𐐪𐑉𐐼𐑌𐐯𐑅 𐐲𐑂 𐑄𐐩𐑉 𐐸𐐪𐑉𐐻𐑅. 𐐒𐐲𐐻 𐑄𐐩𐑉 𐐶𐐲𐑉 𐑋𐐯𐑌𐐨 𐐸𐐭 𐐶𐐲𐑉 𐑅𐐬 𐐸𐐪𐑉𐐼𐐲𐑌𐐼 𐑄𐐰𐐻 𐑄𐐩 𐐶𐐳𐐼 𐑌𐐱𐐻 𐑊𐐳𐐿, 𐑄𐐩𐑉𐑁𐐬𐑉 𐑄𐐩 𐐹𐐯𐑉𐐮𐑇𐐻. 𐐤𐐵 𐑄 𐑉𐐨𐑆𐐲𐑌 𐑄𐐩 𐐶𐐳𐐼 𐑌𐐱𐐻 𐑊𐐳𐐿, 𐐮𐑆 𐐺𐐨𐐿𐐫𐑆 𐑄𐐩 𐐼𐐮𐐼 𐑌𐐱𐐻 𐐺𐐨𐑊𐐨𐑂 𐑄𐐰𐐻 𐐮𐐻 𐐶𐐳𐐼 𐐸𐐨𐑊 𐑄𐐯𐑋. 𐐄 𐑋𐐴 𐐺𐑉𐐯𐑄𐑉𐐯𐑌, 𐐮𐑁 𐐷 𐐿𐐳𐐼 𐐺𐐨 𐐸𐐨𐑊𐐼 𐐺𐐴 𐑋𐐨𐑉𐑊𐐨 𐐿𐐰𐑅𐐻𐐮𐑍 𐐰𐐺𐐵𐐻 𐐷𐐭𐑉 𐐴𐑆 𐑄𐐰𐐻 𐐷 𐑋𐐴𐐻 𐐺𐐨 𐐸𐐨𐑊𐐼, 𐐶𐐳𐐼 𐐷 𐑌𐐱𐐻 𐐺𐐨𐐸𐐬𐑊𐐼 𐐿𐐶𐐮𐐿𐑊𐐨, 𐐫𐑉 𐐶𐐳𐐼 𐐷 𐑉𐐰𐑄𐐲𐑉 𐐸𐐪𐑉𐐼𐐲𐑌 𐐷𐐭𐑉 𐐸𐐪𐑉𐐻𐑅 𐐮𐑌 𐐲𐑌𐐺𐐨𐑊𐐨𐑁, 𐐰𐑌𐐼 𐐺𐐨 𐑅𐑊𐐬𐑃𐑁𐐳𐑊, 𐑄𐐰𐐻 𐐷 𐐶𐐳𐐼 𐑌𐐱𐐻 𐐿𐐰𐑅𐐻 𐐰𐐺𐐵𐐻 𐐷𐐭𐑉 𐐴𐑆, 𐑄𐐰𐐻 𐐷 𐑋𐐴𐐻 𐐹𐐯𐑉𐐮𐑇? 𐐆𐑁 𐑅𐐬, 𐐶𐐬 𐑇𐐰𐑊 𐐿𐐲𐑋 𐐲𐐹𐐱𐑌 𐐷𐐭; 𐐺𐐲𐐻 𐐮𐑁 𐑌𐐱𐐻 𐑅𐐬, 𐑄𐐯𐑌 𐐿𐐰𐑅𐐻 𐐰𐐺𐐵𐐻 𐐷𐐭𐑉 𐐴𐑆 𐐰𐑌𐐼 𐐺𐐨𐑀𐐮𐑌 𐐻𐐭 𐐺𐐨𐑊𐐨𐑂 𐐮𐑌 𐑄 𐐝𐐲𐑌 𐐲𐑂 𐐘𐐱𐐼, 𐑄𐐰𐐻 𐐸𐐨 𐐶𐐮𐑊 𐐿𐐲𐑋 𐐻𐐭 𐑉𐐨𐐼𐐨𐑋 𐐸𐐮𐑆 𐐹𐐨𐐹𐑊, 𐐰𐑌𐐼 𐑄𐐰𐐻 𐐸𐐨 𐑇𐐰𐑊 𐑅𐐲𐑁𐐲𐑉 𐐰𐑌𐐼 𐐼𐐴 𐐻𐐭 𐐰𐐻𐐬𐑌 𐑁𐐫𐑉 𐑄𐐩𐑉 𐑅𐐮𐑌𐑆; 𐐰𐑌𐐼 𐑄𐐰𐐻 𐐸𐐨 𐑇𐐰𐑊 𐑉𐐴𐑆 𐐲𐑀𐐯𐑌 𐑁𐑉𐐱𐑋 𐑄 𐐼𐐯𐐼, 𐐸𐐶𐐮𐐽 𐑇𐐰𐑊 𐐺𐑉𐐮𐑍 𐐻𐐭 𐐹𐐰𐑅 𐑄 𐑉𐐯𐑆𐐲𐑉𐐯𐐿𐑇𐐲𐑌, 𐑄𐐰𐐻 𐐫𐑊 𐑋𐐯𐑌 𐑇𐐰𐑊 𐑅𐐻𐐰𐑌𐐼 𐐺𐐨𐑁𐐬𐑉 𐐸𐐮𐑋, 𐐻𐐭 𐐺𐐨 𐐾𐐲𐐾𐐼 𐐰𐐻 𐑄 𐑊𐐰𐑅𐐻 𐐰𐑌𐐼 𐐾𐐲𐐾𐑋𐐯𐑌𐐻 𐐼𐐩, 𐐰𐐿𐐫𐑉𐐼𐐮𐑍 𐐻𐐭 𐑄𐐩𐑉 𐐶𐐲𐑉𐐿𐑅. 𐐈𐑌𐐼 𐑌𐐵, 𐑋𐐴 𐐺𐑉𐐯𐑄𐑉𐐯𐑌, 𐐴 𐐼𐐨𐑆𐐴𐑉 𐑄𐐰𐐻 𐐷 𐑇𐐰𐑊 𐐹𐑊𐐰𐑌𐐻 𐑄𐐮𐑅 𐐶𐐲𐑉𐐼 𐐮𐑌 𐐷𐐭𐑉 𐐸𐐪𐑉𐐻𐑅, 𐐰𐑌𐐼 𐐰𐑆 𐐮𐐻 𐐺𐐨𐑀𐐮𐑌𐐯𐑃 𐐻𐐭 𐑅𐐶𐐯𐑊, 𐐨𐑂𐐲𐑌 𐑅𐐬 𐑌𐐲𐑉𐐮𐑇 𐐮𐐻 𐐺𐐴 𐐷𐐭𐑉 𐑁𐐩𐑃. 𐐈𐑌𐐼 𐐺𐐨𐐸𐐬𐑊𐐼, 𐐮𐐻 𐐶𐐮𐑊 𐐺𐐨𐐿𐐲𐑋 𐐰 𐐻𐑉𐐨, 𐑅𐐹𐑉𐐮𐑍𐐮𐑍 𐐲𐐹 𐐮𐑌 𐐷𐐭 𐐲𐑌𐐻𐐭 𐐯𐑂𐐲𐑉𐑊𐐰𐑅𐐻𐐮𐑍 𐑊𐐴𐑁. 𐐈𐑌𐐼 𐑄𐐯𐑌 𐑋𐐩 𐐘𐐱𐐼 𐑀𐑉𐐰𐑌𐐻 𐐲𐑌𐐻𐐭 𐐷𐐭 𐑄𐐰𐐻 𐐷𐐭𐑉 𐐺𐐲𐑉𐐼𐐲𐑌𐑆 𐑋𐐩 𐐺𐐨 𐑊𐐴𐐻, 𐑃𐑉𐐭 𐑄 𐐾𐑎 𐐲𐑂 𐐸𐐮𐑆 𐐝𐐲𐑌. 𐐈𐑌𐐼 𐐨𐑂𐐲𐑌 𐐫𐑊 𐑄𐐮𐑅 𐐿𐐰𐑌 𐐷 𐐼𐐭 𐐮𐑁 𐐷 𐐶𐐮𐑊. 𐐁𐑋𐐯𐑌.

27. 𐐈𐑌𐐼 𐑌𐐵 𐐮𐐻 𐐿𐐩𐑋 𐐻𐐭 𐐹𐐰𐑅 𐑄𐐰𐐻 𐐰𐑁𐐻𐐲𐑉 𐐈𐑊𐑋𐐲 𐐸𐐰𐐼 𐑅𐐹𐐬𐐿𐐲𐑌 𐑄𐐨𐑆 𐐶𐐲𐑉𐐼𐑆 𐐲𐑌𐐻𐐭 𐑄𐐯𐑋, 𐐸𐐨 𐑅𐐰𐐻 𐐼𐐵𐑌 𐐲𐐹𐐱𐑌 𐑄 𐑀𐑉𐐵𐑌𐐼, 𐐰𐑌𐐼 𐐈𐑋𐐷𐐭𐑊𐐯𐐿 𐐲𐑉𐐬𐑆 𐐰𐑌𐐼 𐐺𐐨𐑀𐐰𐑌 𐐻𐐭 𐐻𐐨𐐽 𐑄𐐯𐑋, 𐑅𐐩𐐮𐑍, 𐐣𐐴 𐐺𐑉𐐯𐑄𐑉𐐯𐑌, 𐐴 𐑃𐐮𐑍𐐿 𐑄𐐰𐐻 𐐮𐐻 𐐮𐑆 𐐮𐑋𐐹𐐱𐑅𐐮𐐺𐑊 𐑄𐐰𐐻 𐐷 𐑇𐐳𐐼 𐐺𐐨 𐐮𐑀𐑌𐐬𐑉𐐲𐑌𐐻 𐐲𐑂 𐑄 𐑃𐐮𐑍𐑆 𐐸𐐶𐐮𐐽 𐐸𐐰𐑂 𐐺𐐮𐑌 𐑅𐐹𐐬𐐿𐐲𐑌 𐐿𐐱𐑌𐑅𐐲𐑉𐑌𐐮𐑍 𐑄 𐐿𐐲𐑋𐐮𐑍 𐐲𐑂 𐐗𐑉𐐴𐑅𐐻, 𐐸𐐭 𐐮𐑆 𐐻𐐫𐐻 𐐺𐐴 𐐲𐑅 𐐻𐐭 𐐺𐐨 𐑄 𐐝𐐲𐑌 𐐲𐑂 𐐘𐐱𐐼; 𐐷𐐩, 𐐴 𐑌𐐬 𐑄𐐰𐐻 𐑄𐐨𐑆 𐑃𐐮𐑍𐑆 𐐶𐐲𐑉 𐐻𐐫𐐻 𐐲𐑌𐐻𐐭 𐐷𐐭 𐐺𐐵𐑌𐐻𐐮𐑁𐐳𐑊𐐨 𐐺𐐨𐑁𐐬𐑉 𐐷𐐭𐑉 𐐼𐐮𐑅𐐯𐑌𐑇𐐲𐑌 𐑁𐑉𐐱𐑋 𐐰𐑋𐐲𐑍 𐐲𐑅. 𐐈𐑌𐐼 𐐰𐑆 𐐷 𐐸𐐰𐑂 𐐼𐐨𐑆𐐴𐑉𐐼 𐐲𐑂 𐑋𐐴 𐐺𐐨𐑊𐐲𐑂𐐯𐐼 𐐺𐑉𐐲𐑄𐐲𐑉 𐑄𐐰𐐻 𐐸𐐨 𐑇𐐳𐐼 𐑋𐐩𐐿 𐑌𐐬𐑌 𐐲𐑌𐐻𐐭 𐐷𐐭 𐐸𐐶𐐱𐐻 𐐷 𐑇𐐳𐐼 𐐼𐐭, 𐐺𐐨𐐿𐐫𐑆 𐐲𐑂 𐐷𐐭𐑉 𐐰𐑁𐑊𐐮𐐿𐑇𐐲𐑌𐑆; 𐐰𐑌𐐼 𐐸𐐨 𐐸𐐰𐑃 𐑅𐐹𐐬𐐿𐐲𐑌 𐑅𐐲𐑋𐐸𐐶𐐱𐐻 𐐲𐑌𐐻𐐭 𐐷𐐭 𐐻𐐭 𐐹𐑉𐐨𐐹𐐩𐑉 𐐷𐐭𐑉 𐑋𐐴𐑌𐐼𐑆; 𐐷𐐩, 𐐰𐑌𐐼 𐐸𐐨 𐐸𐐰𐑃 𐐯𐑀𐑆𐐫𐑉𐐻𐐯𐐼 𐐷𐐭 𐐲𐑌𐐻𐐭 𐑁𐐩𐑃 𐐰𐑌𐐼 𐐻𐐭 𐐹𐐩𐑇𐐯𐑌𐑅; 𐐷𐐩, 𐐨𐑂𐐲𐑌 𐑄𐐰𐐻 𐐷 𐐶𐐳𐐼 𐐸𐐰𐑂 𐑅𐐬 𐑋𐐲𐐽 𐑁𐐩𐑃 𐐰𐑆 𐐨𐑂𐐲𐑌 𐐻𐐭 𐐹𐑊𐐰𐑌𐐻 𐑄 𐐶𐐲𐑉𐐼 𐐮𐑌 𐐷𐐭𐑉 𐐸𐐪𐑉𐐻𐑅, 𐑄𐐰𐐻 𐐷 𐑋𐐩 𐐻𐑉𐐴 𐑄 𐐯𐐿𐑅𐐹𐐯𐑉𐐮𐑋𐐯𐑌𐐻 𐐲𐑂 𐐮𐐻𐑅 𐑀𐐳𐐼𐑌𐐯𐑅; 𐐰𐑌𐐼 𐐶𐐨 𐐸𐐰𐑂 𐐺𐐨𐐸𐐯𐑊𐐼 𐑄𐐰𐐻 𐑄 𐑀𐑉𐐩𐐻 𐐿𐐶𐐯𐑅𐐽𐐲𐑌 𐐸𐐶𐐮𐐽 𐐮𐑆 𐐮𐑌 𐐷𐐭𐑉 𐑋𐐴𐑌𐐼𐑆, 𐐮𐑆 𐐸𐐶𐐯𐑄𐐲𐑉 𐑄 𐐶𐐲𐑉𐐼 𐐺𐐨 𐐮𐑌 𐑄 𐐝𐐲𐑌 𐐲𐑂 𐐘𐐱𐐼, 𐐫𐑉 𐐸𐐶𐐯𐑄𐐲𐑉 𐑄𐐩𐑉 𐑇𐐰𐑊 𐐺𐐨 𐑌𐐬 𐐗𐑉𐐴𐑅𐐻. 𐐈𐑌𐐼 𐐷 𐐫𐑊𐑅𐐬 𐐺𐐨𐐸𐐯𐑊𐐼 𐑄𐐰𐐻 𐑋𐐴 𐐺𐑉𐐲𐑄𐐲𐑉 𐐸𐐰𐑆 𐐹𐑉𐐭𐑂𐐼 𐐲𐑌𐐻𐐭 𐐷𐐭, 𐐮𐑌 𐑋𐐯𐑌𐐨 𐐮𐑌𐑅𐐻𐐲𐑌𐑅𐐯𐑆, 𐑄𐐰𐐻 𐑄 𐐶𐐲𐑉𐐼 𐐮𐑆 𐐮𐑌 𐐗𐑉𐐴𐑅𐐻 𐐲𐑌𐐻𐐭 𐑅𐐰𐑊𐑂𐐩𐑇𐐲𐑌. 𐐣𐐴 𐐺𐑉𐐲𐑄𐐲𐑉 𐐸𐐰𐑆 𐐿𐐫𐑊𐐼 𐐲𐐹𐐱𐑌 𐑄 𐐶𐐲𐑉𐐼𐑆 𐐲𐑂 𐐞𐐨𐑌𐐱𐑅, 𐑄𐐰𐐻 𐑉𐐨𐐼𐐯𐑋𐑇𐐲𐑌 𐐿𐐲𐑋𐐯𐑃 𐑃𐑉𐐭 𐑄 𐐝𐐲𐑌 𐐲𐑂 𐐘𐐱𐐼, 𐐰𐑌𐐼 𐐫𐑊𐑅𐐬 𐐲𐐹𐐱𐑌 𐑄 𐐶𐐲𐑉𐐼𐑆 𐐲𐑂 𐐞𐐨𐑌𐐱𐐿; 𐐰𐑌𐐼 𐐫𐑊𐑅𐐬 𐐸𐐨 𐐸𐐰𐑆

𐐰𐐹𐐨𐑊𐐼 𐐲𐑌𐐻𐐭 𐐣𐐬𐑆𐐯𐑆, 𐐻𐐭 𐐹𐑉𐐭𐑂 𐑄𐐰𐐻 𐑄𐐨𐑆 𐑃𐐮𐑍𐑆 𐐪𐑉 𐐻𐑉𐐭. 𐐈𐑌𐐼 𐑌𐐵, 𐐺𐐨𐐸𐐬𐑊𐐼, 𐐌 𐐶𐐮𐑊 𐐻𐐯𐑅𐐻𐐮𐑁𐐴 𐐲𐑌𐐻𐐭 𐐷𐐭 𐐱𐑂 𐑋𐐴𐑅𐐯𐑊𐑁 𐑄𐐰𐐻 𐑄𐐨𐑆 𐑃𐐮𐑍𐑆 𐐪𐑉 𐐻𐑉𐐭. 𐐒𐐨𐐸𐐬𐑊𐐼, 𐐌 𐑅𐐩 𐐲𐑌𐐻𐐭 𐐷𐐭, 𐑄𐐰𐐻 𐐌 𐐼𐐭 𐑌𐐬 𐑄𐐰𐐻 𐐗𐑉𐐴𐑅𐐻 𐑇𐐰𐑊 𐐿𐐲𐑋 𐐰𐑋𐐲𐑍 𐑄 𐐽𐐮𐑊𐐼𐑉𐐯𐑌 𐐱𐑂 𐑋𐐯𐑌, 𐐻𐐭 𐐻𐐩𐐿 𐐲𐐹𐐱𐑌 𐐸𐐮𐑋 𐑄 𐐻𐑉𐐰𐑌𐑅𐑀𐑉𐐯𐑇𐐲𐑌𐑆 𐐱𐑂 𐐸𐐮𐑆 𐐹𐐨𐐹𐑊, 𐐰𐑌𐐼 𐑄𐐰𐐻 𐐸𐐨 𐑇𐐰𐑊 𐐰𐐻𐐬𐑌 𐑁𐐫𐑉 𐑄 𐑅𐐮𐑌𐑆 𐐱𐑂 𐑄 𐐶𐐲𐑉𐑊𐐼; 𐑁𐐫𐑉 𐑄 𐐢𐐫𐑉𐐼 𐐘𐐱𐐼 𐐸𐐰𐑃 𐑅𐐹𐐬𐐿𐑌 𐐮𐐻; 𐑁𐐫𐑉 𐐮𐐻 𐐮𐑆 𐐯𐐿𐑅𐐹𐐨𐐼𐐨𐐯𐑌𐐻 𐑄𐐰𐐻 𐐰𐑌 𐐰𐐻𐐬𐑌𐑋𐐯𐑌𐐻 𐑇𐐳𐐼 𐐺 𐑋𐐩𐐼; 𐑁𐐫𐑉 𐐰𐐿𐐫𐑉𐐼𐐮𐑍 𐐻𐐭 𐑄 𐑀𐑉𐐩𐐻 𐐹𐑊𐐰𐑌 𐐱𐑂 𐑄 𐐀𐐻𐐲𐑉𐑌𐐰𐑊 𐐘𐐱𐐼, 𐑄𐐩𐑉 𐑋𐐲𐑅𐐻 𐐺 𐐰𐑌 𐐰𐐻𐐬𐑌𐑋𐐯𐑌𐐻 𐑋𐐩𐐼, 𐐫𐑉 𐐯𐑊𐑅 𐐫𐑊 𐑋𐐰𐑌𐐿𐐴𐑌𐐼 𐑋𐐲𐑅𐐻 𐐲𐑌𐐰𐑂𐐫𐐮𐐼𐐰𐐺𐑊𐐮 𐐹𐐯𐑉𐐮𐑇; 𐐷𐐩, 𐐫𐑊 𐐪𐑉 𐐸𐐪𐑉𐐼𐐯𐑌𐐼; 𐐷𐐩, 𐐫𐑊 𐐪𐑉 𐑁𐐫𐑊𐑌 𐐰𐑌𐐼 𐐪𐑉 𐑊𐐱𐑅𐐻, 𐐰𐑌𐐼 𐑋𐐲𐑅𐐻 𐐹𐐯𐑉𐐮𐑇, 𐐯𐐿𐑅𐐯𐐹𐐻 𐐮𐐻 𐐺 𐑃𐑉𐐭 𐑄 𐐰𐐻𐐬𐑌𐑋𐐯𐑌𐐻 𐐸𐐶𐐮𐐽 𐐮𐐻 𐐮𐑆 𐐯𐐿𐑅𐐹𐐨𐐼𐐨𐐯𐑌𐐻 𐑇𐐳𐐼 𐐺 𐑋𐐩𐐼; 𐑁𐐫𐑉 𐐮𐐻 𐐮𐑆 𐐯𐐿𐑅𐐹𐐨𐐼𐐨𐐯𐑌𐐻 𐑄𐐰𐐻 𐑄𐐩𐑉 𐑇𐐳𐐼 𐐺 𐐩 𐑀𐑉𐐩𐐻 𐐰𐑌𐐼 𐑊𐐰𐑅𐐻 𐑅𐐰𐐿𐑉𐐮𐑁𐐴𐑆; 𐐷𐐩, 𐑌𐐱𐐻 𐐩 𐑅𐐰𐐿𐑉𐐮𐑁𐐴𐑆 𐐱𐑂 𐑋𐐰𐑌, 𐑌𐐨𐑄𐐲𐑉 𐐱𐑂 𐐺𐐨𐑅𐐻, 𐑌𐐨𐑄𐐲𐑉 𐐱𐑂 𐐯𐑌𐐮 𐑋𐐰𐑌𐐲𐑉 𐐱𐑂 𐑁𐐵𐑊; 𐑁𐐫𐑉 𐐮𐐻 𐑇𐐰𐑊 𐑌𐐱𐐻 𐐺 𐐩 𐐸𐐧𐑋𐐲𐑌 𐑅𐐰𐐿𐑉𐐮𐑁𐐴𐑆; 𐐺𐐲𐐻 𐐮𐐻 𐑋𐐲𐑅𐐻 𐐺 𐐰𐑌 𐐮𐑌𐑁𐐮𐑌𐐮𐐻 𐐰𐑌𐐼 𐐨𐐻𐐲𐑉𐑌𐐰𐑊 𐑅𐐰𐐿𐑉𐐮𐑁𐐴𐑆.

28. 𐐤𐐵 𐑄𐐩𐑉 𐐮𐑆 𐑌𐐱𐐻 𐐯𐑌𐐮 𐑋𐐰𐑌 𐑄𐐰𐐻 𐐿𐐰𐑌 𐑅𐐰𐐿𐑉𐐮𐑁𐐴𐑆 𐐸𐐮𐑆 𐐬𐑌 𐐺𐑊𐐲𐐼, 𐐸𐐶𐐮𐐽 𐐶𐐮𐑊 𐐰𐐻𐐬𐑌 𐑁𐐫𐑉 𐑄 𐑅𐐮𐑌𐑆 𐐱𐑂 𐐰𐑌𐐲𐑄𐐲𐑉. 𐐤𐐵 𐐮𐑁 𐐩 𐑋𐐰𐑌 𐑋𐐲𐑉𐐼𐐯𐑉𐐯𐑃, 𐐺𐐨𐐸𐐬𐑊𐐼 𐐶𐐮𐑊 𐐵𐑉 𐑊𐐫, 𐐸𐐶𐐮𐐽 𐐮𐑆 𐐾𐐲𐑅𐐻, 𐐻𐐩𐐿 𐑄 𐑊𐐴𐑁 𐐱𐑂 𐐸𐐮𐑆 𐐺𐑉𐐲𐑄𐐲𐑉? 𐐌 𐑅𐐩 𐐲𐑌𐐻𐐭 𐐷𐐭, 𐐤𐐩. 𐐒𐐲𐐻 𐑄 𐑊𐐫 𐑉𐐨𐐿𐐶𐐴𐑉𐐯𐑃 𐑄 𐑊𐐴𐑁 𐐱𐑂 𐐸𐐮𐑋 𐐸𐐭 𐐸𐐰𐑃 𐑋𐐲𐑉𐐼𐐯𐑉𐐼; 𐑄𐐩𐑉𐑁𐐫𐑉 𐑄𐐩𐑉 𐐿𐐰𐑌 𐐺 𐑌𐐲𐑃𐐮𐑍 𐐸𐐶𐐮𐐽 𐐮𐑆 𐑇𐐫𐑉𐐻 𐐱𐑂 𐐰𐑌 𐐮𐑌𐑁𐐮𐑌𐐮𐐻 𐐰𐐻𐐬𐑌𐑋𐐯𐑌𐐻, 𐐸𐐶𐐮𐐽 𐐶𐐮𐑊 𐑅𐐲𐑁𐐴𐑆 𐑁𐐫𐑉 𐑄 𐑅𐐮𐑌𐑆 𐐱𐑂 𐑄 𐐶𐐲𐑉𐑊𐐼: 𐑄𐐩𐑉𐑁𐐫𐑉 𐐮𐐻 𐐮𐑆 𐐯𐐿𐑅𐐹𐐨𐐼𐐨𐐯𐑌𐐻 𐑄𐐰𐐻 𐑄𐐩𐑉 𐑇𐐳𐐼 𐐺 𐐩 𐑀𐑉𐐩𐐻 𐐰𐑌𐐼 𐑊𐐰𐑅𐐻 𐑅𐐰𐐿𐑉𐐮𐑁𐐴𐑆; 𐐰𐑌𐐼 𐑄𐐯𐑌 𐑇𐐰𐑊 𐑄𐐩𐑉 𐐺, 𐐫𐑉 𐐮𐐻 𐐮𐑆 𐐯𐐿𐑅𐐹𐐨𐐼𐐨𐐯𐑌𐐻 𐑄𐐩𐑉 𐑇𐐳𐐼 𐐺 𐐩 𐑅𐐻𐐱𐐹 𐐻𐐭 𐑄 𐑇𐐯𐐼𐐮𐑍 𐐱𐑂 𐐺𐑊𐐲𐐼; 𐑄𐐯𐑌 𐑇𐐰𐑊 𐑄 𐑊𐐫 𐐱𐑂 𐐣𐐬𐑆𐐯𐑆 𐐺 𐑁𐐳𐑊𐑁𐐮𐑊𐐼; 𐐷𐐩, 𐐮𐐻 𐑇𐐰𐑊 𐐫𐑊 𐐺 𐑁𐐳𐑊𐑁𐐮𐑊𐐼; 𐐯𐑂𐐯𐑉𐐮 𐐾𐐱𐐻 𐐰𐑌𐐼 𐐻𐐮𐐻𐑊, 𐐰𐑌𐐼 𐑌𐐲𐑌 𐑇𐐰𐑊 𐐸𐐰𐑂 𐐹𐐰𐑅𐐻 𐐰𐐶𐐩. 𐐈𐑌𐐼 𐐺𐐨𐐸𐐬𐑊𐐼, 𐑄𐐮𐑅 𐐮𐑆 𐑄 𐐸𐐬𐑊 𐑋𐐨𐑌𐐮𐑍 𐐱𐑂 𐑄 𐑊𐐫; 𐐯𐑂𐐯𐑉𐐮 𐐸𐐶𐐮𐐻 𐐹𐐫𐐮𐑌𐐻𐐮𐑍 𐐻𐐭 𐑄𐐰𐐻 𐑀𐑉𐐩𐐻 𐐰𐑌𐐼 𐑊𐐰𐑅𐐻 𐑅𐐰𐐿𐑉𐐮𐑁𐐴𐑆; 𐐰𐑌𐐼 𐑄𐐰𐐻 𐑀𐑉𐐩𐐻 𐐰𐑌𐐼 𐑊𐐰𐑅𐐻 𐑅𐐰𐐿𐑉𐐮𐑁𐐴𐑆 𐐶𐐮𐑊 𐐺 𐑄 𐐝𐐲𐑌 𐐱𐑂 𐐘𐐱𐐼; 𐐷𐐩, 𐐮𐑌𐑁𐐮𐑌𐐮𐐻 𐐰𐑌𐐼 𐐨𐐻𐐲𐑉𐑌𐐰𐑊; 𐐰𐑌𐐼 𐑄𐐲𐑅 𐐸𐐨 𐑇𐐰𐑊 𐐺𐑉𐐮𐑍 𐑅𐐰𐑊𐑂𐐩𐑇𐐲𐑌 𐐻𐐭 𐐫𐑊 𐑄𐐬𐑆 𐐸𐐭 𐑇𐐰𐑊 𐐺𐐨𐑊𐐨𐑂 𐐱𐑌 𐐸𐐮𐑆 𐑌𐐩𐑋; 𐑄𐐮𐑅 𐐺𐐨𐐮𐑍 𐑄 𐐮𐑌𐐻𐐯𐑌𐐻 𐐱𐑂 𐑄𐐮𐑅 𐑊𐐰𐑅𐐻 𐑅𐐰𐐿𐑉𐐮𐑁𐐴𐑆, 𐐻𐐭 𐐺𐑉𐐮𐑍 𐐰𐐺𐐵𐐻 𐑄 𐐺𐐵𐐯𐑊𐑆 𐐱𐑂 𐑋𐐲𐑉𐑅𐐨, 𐐸𐐶𐐮𐐽 𐐬𐑂𐐲𐑉𐐹𐐵𐐲𐑉𐐯𐑃 𐐾𐐲𐑅𐐻𐐮𐑅 𐐰𐑌𐐼 𐐺𐑉𐐮𐑍𐐯𐑃 𐐰𐐺𐐵𐐻 𐑋𐐨𐑌𐑆 𐐲𐑌𐐻𐐭 𐑋𐐯𐑌 𐑄𐐰𐐻 𐑄𐐩 𐑋𐐩 𐐸𐐰𐑂 𐑁𐐩𐑃 𐐲𐑌𐐻𐐭 𐑉𐐨𐐹𐐯𐑌𐐻𐐰𐑌𐑅. 𐐈𐑌𐐼 𐑄𐐲𐑅 𐑋𐐲𐑉𐑅𐐨 𐐿𐐰𐑌 𐑅𐐰𐐻𐐮𐑅𐑁𐐴 𐑄 𐐼𐐨𐑋𐐰𐑌𐐼𐑆 𐐱𐑂 𐐾𐐲𐑅𐐻𐐮𐑅, 𐐰𐑌𐐼 𐐯𐑌𐑅𐐲𐑉𐐿𐑊𐑆 𐑄𐐯𐑋 𐐮𐑌 𐑄 𐐪𐑉𐑋𐑆 𐐱𐑂 𐑅𐐩𐑁𐐻𐐨, 𐐸𐐶𐐴𐑊 𐐸𐐨 𐑄𐐰𐐻 𐐯𐐿𐑅𐐲𐑉𐑅𐐴𐑆𐐯𐑆 𐑌𐐬 𐑁𐐩𐑃 𐐲𐑌𐐻𐐭 𐑉𐐨𐐹𐐯𐑌𐐻𐐰𐑌𐑅, 𐐮𐑆 𐐯𐐿𐑅𐐹𐐬𐑆𐐼 𐐻𐐭 𐑄 𐐸𐐬𐑊 𐑊𐐫 𐐱𐑂 𐑄 𐐼𐐨𐑋𐐰𐑌𐐼𐑆 𐐱𐑂 𐐾𐐲𐑅𐐻𐐮𐑅; 𐑄𐐩𐑉𐑁𐐫𐑉 𐐬𐑌𐑊𐐨 𐐲𐑌𐐻𐐭 𐐸𐐮𐑋 𐑄𐐰𐐻 𐐸𐐰𐑆 𐑁𐐩𐑃 𐐲𐑌𐐻𐐭 𐑉𐐨𐐹𐐯𐑌𐐻𐐰𐑌𐑅 𐐮𐑆 𐐺𐑉𐐫𐐻 𐐰𐐺𐐵𐐻 𐑄 𐑀𐑉𐐩𐐻 𐐰𐑌𐐼 𐐨𐐻𐐲𐑉𐑌𐐰𐑊 𐐹𐑊𐐰𐑌 𐐱𐑂 𐑉𐐨𐐼𐐯𐑋𐑇𐐲𐑌. 𐐜𐐩𐑉𐑁𐐫𐑉 𐑋𐐩 𐐘𐐱𐐼 𐑀𐑉𐐰𐑌𐐻 𐐲𐑌𐐻𐐭 𐐷𐐭, 𐑋𐐴 𐐺𐑉𐐯𐑃𐑉𐐯𐑌, 𐑄𐐰𐐻 𐐷𐐨 𐑋𐐩 𐐺𐐨𐑀𐐮𐑌 𐐻𐐭 𐐯𐐿𐑅𐐲𐑉𐑅𐐴𐑆 𐐷𐐭𐑉 𐑁𐐩𐑃 𐐲𐑌𐐻𐐭 𐑉𐐨𐐹𐐯𐑌𐐻𐐰𐑌𐑅, 𐑄𐐰𐐻 𐐷𐐨 𐐺𐐨𐑀𐐮𐑌 𐐻𐐭 𐐿𐐫𐑊 𐐲𐐹𐐱𐑌 𐐸𐐮𐑆 𐐸𐐬𐑊𐐨 𐑌𐐩𐑋, 𐑄𐐰𐐻 𐐸𐐨 𐐶𐐳𐐼 𐐸𐐰𐑂 𐑋𐐲𐑉𐑅𐐨 𐐲𐐹𐐱𐑌 𐐷𐐭; 𐐷𐐩, 𐐿𐑉𐐴 𐐲𐑌𐐻𐐭 𐐸𐐮𐑋 𐑁𐐫𐑉 𐑋𐐲𐑉𐑅𐐨; 𐑁𐐫𐑉 𐐸𐐨 𐐮𐑆 𐑋𐐴𐐻𐐨 𐐻𐐭 𐑅𐐩𐑂; 𐐷𐐩, 𐐸𐐲𐑋𐐺𐑊 𐐷𐐭𐑉𐑅𐐯𐑊𐑂𐑆, 𐐰𐑌𐐼 𐐿𐐲𐑌𐐻𐐮𐑌𐐷𐐭 𐐮𐑌 𐐹𐑉𐐩𐑉 𐐲𐑌𐐻𐐭 𐐸𐐮𐑋: 𐐿𐑉𐐴 𐐲𐑌𐐻𐐭 𐐸𐐮𐑋 𐐸𐐶𐐯𐑌 𐐷𐐨 𐐪𐑉 𐐮𐑌 𐐷𐐭𐑉 𐑁𐐨𐑊𐐼𐑆; 𐐷𐐩, 𐐬𐑂𐐲𐑉 𐐫𐑊 𐐷𐐭𐑉 𐑁𐑊𐐱𐐿𐑅: 𐐿𐑉𐐴 𐐲𐑌𐐻𐐭 𐐸𐐮𐑋 𐐮𐑌 𐐷𐐭𐑉 𐐸𐐵𐑆𐐯𐑆; 𐐷𐐩, 𐐬𐑂𐐲𐑉 𐐫𐑊 𐐷𐐭𐑉 𐐸𐐵𐑅𐐸𐐬𐑊𐐼, 𐐺𐐬𐑃 𐑋𐐫𐑉𐑌𐐮𐑍, 𐑋𐐮𐐼-𐐼𐐩, 𐐰𐑌𐐼 𐐨𐑂𐑌𐐮𐑍; 𐐷𐐩, 𐐿𐑉𐐴 𐐲𐑌𐐻𐐭 𐐸𐐮𐑋 𐐰𐑀𐐯𐑌𐑅𐐻 𐑄 𐐹𐐵𐑉 𐐱𐑂 𐐷𐐭𐑉 𐐯𐑌𐐯𐑋𐐮𐑆; 𐐷𐐩, 𐐿𐑉𐐴 𐐲𐑌𐐻𐐭 𐐸𐐮𐑋 𐐰𐑀𐐯𐑌𐑅𐐻 𐑄 𐐼𐐯𐑂𐐮𐑊, 𐐸𐐭 𐐮𐑆 𐐰𐑌 𐐯𐑌𐐯𐑋𐐮 𐐻𐐭 𐐫𐑊 𐑉𐐴𐐽𐐲𐑅𐑌𐐯𐑅. 𐐗𐑉𐐴 𐐲𐑌𐐻𐐭 𐐸𐐮𐑋 𐐬𐑂𐐲𐑉 𐑄 𐐿𐑉𐐱𐐹𐑅 𐐱𐑂 𐐷𐐭𐑉 𐑁𐐨𐑊𐐼𐑆, 𐑄𐐰𐐻 𐐷𐐨 𐑋𐐩 𐐹𐑉𐐱𐑅𐐹𐐲𐑉 𐐮𐑌 𐑄𐐯𐑋: 𐐿𐑉𐐴 𐐬𐑂𐐲𐑉 𐑄 𐑁𐑊𐐱𐐿𐑅 𐐱𐑂 𐐷𐐭𐑉 𐑁𐐨𐑊𐐼𐑆, 𐑄𐐰𐐻 𐑄𐐩 𐑋𐐩 𐐮𐑌𐐿𐑉𐐨𐑅. 𐐒𐐲𐐻 𐑄𐐮𐑅 𐐮𐑆 𐑌𐐱𐐻 𐐫𐑊; 𐐷𐐨 𐑋𐐲𐑅𐐻 𐐹𐐬𐑉 𐐵𐐻 𐐷𐐭𐑉 𐑅𐐬𐑊𐑆 𐐮𐑌 𐐷𐐭𐑉 𐐿𐑊𐐱𐑆𐐯𐐻𐑅, 𐐰𐑌𐐼 𐐷𐐭𐑉 𐑅𐐨𐐿𐑉𐐯𐐻 𐐹𐑊𐐩𐑅𐐯𐑆, 𐐰𐑌𐐼 𐐮𐑌 𐐷𐐭𐑉 𐐶𐐮𐑊𐐼𐐲𐑉𐑌𐐯𐑅; 𐐷𐐩, 𐐰𐑌𐐼 𐐸𐐶𐐯𐑌 𐐷𐐭 𐐼𐐭 𐑌𐐱𐐻 𐐿𐑉𐐴 𐐲𐑌𐐻𐐭 𐑄 𐐢𐐫𐑉𐐼, 𐑊𐐯𐐻 𐐷𐐭𐑉 𐐸𐐪𐑉𐐻𐑅 𐐺 𐑁𐐳𐑊, 𐐼𐑉𐐫𐑌 𐐵𐐻 𐐮𐑌 𐐹𐑉𐐩𐑉 𐐲𐑌𐐻𐐭 𐐸𐐮𐑋 𐐿𐐲𐑌𐐻𐐮𐑌𐐷𐐭𐐰𐑊𐐨 𐑁𐐫𐑉 𐐷𐐭𐑉 𐐶𐐯𐑊𐑁𐐩𐑉, 𐐰𐑌𐐼 𐐫𐑊𐑅𐐬 𐑁𐐫𐑉 𐑄 𐐶𐐯𐑊𐑁𐐩𐑉 𐐱𐑂 𐑄𐐬𐑆 𐐸𐐭 𐐪𐑉 𐐲𐑉𐐵𐑌𐐼 𐐷𐐭.

29. 𐐈𐑌𐐼 𐑌𐐵 𐐺𐐨𐐸𐐬𐑊𐐼, 𐑋𐐴 𐐺𐐨𐑊𐐲𐑝𐐯𐐼 𐐺𐑉𐐯𐑄𐑉𐐯𐑌, 𐐌 𐑅𐐩 𐐲𐑌𐐻𐐭 𐐷𐐭, 𐐔𐐭 𐑌𐐱𐐻 𐑅𐐲𐐹𐐬𐑆 𐑄𐐰𐐻 𐑄𐐮𐑅 𐐮𐑆 𐐫𐑊; 𐑁𐐫𐑉 𐐰𐑁𐐻𐐲𐑉 𐐷𐐨 𐐸𐐰𐑂 𐐼𐐲𐑌 𐐫𐑊 𐑄𐐨𐑆 𐑃𐐮𐑍𐑆, 𐐮𐑁 𐑄 𐐻𐐲𐑉𐑌 𐐲𐐶𐐩 𐑄 𐑌𐐨𐐼𐐨, 𐐰𐑌𐐼 𐑄 𐑌𐐩𐐿𐐯𐐼, 𐐰𐑌𐐼 𐑂𐐮𐑆𐐮𐐻 𐑌𐐱𐐻 𐑄 𐑅𐐮𐐿 𐐰𐑌𐐼 𐐰𐑁𐑊𐐮𐐿𐐻𐐯𐐼, 𐐰𐑌𐐼 𐐮𐑋𐐹𐐪𐑉𐐻 𐐱𐑂 𐐷𐐫𐑉 𐑅𐐲𐐺𐑅𐐻𐐲𐑌𐑅, 𐐮𐑁 𐑄 𐐸𐐰𐑂, 𐐻𐐭 𐑄𐐬𐑆 𐐸𐐭 𐑅𐐻𐐰𐑌𐐼 𐐮𐑌 𐑌𐐨𐐼; 𐐌 𐑅𐐩 𐐲𐑌𐐻𐐭 𐐷𐐭, 𐐮𐑁 𐑄 𐐼𐐭 𐑌𐐱𐐻 𐐯𐑌𐐨 𐐱𐑂 𐑄𐐨𐑆 𐑃𐐮𐑍𐑆, 𐐺𐐨𐐸𐐬𐑊𐐼, 𐐷𐐫𐑉 𐐹𐑉𐐩𐐲𐑉 𐐮𐑆 𐑂𐐩𐑌, 𐐰𐑌𐐼 𐐰𐑂𐐩𐑊𐐯𐑃 𐐷𐐭 𐑌𐐲𐑃𐐮𐑍, 𐐰𐑌𐐼 𐑄 𐐪𐑉 𐐰𐑆 𐐸𐐮𐐹𐐬𐐿𐑉𐐮𐐻𐑅 𐐸𐐭 𐐼𐐭 𐐼𐐨𐑌𐐴 𐑄 𐑁𐐩𐑃. 𐐜𐐯𐑉𐑁𐐬𐑉, 𐐮𐑁 𐑄 𐐼𐐭 𐑌𐐱𐐻 𐑉𐐨𐑋𐐯𐑋𐐺𐐲𐑉 𐐻𐐭 𐐺𐐨 𐐽𐐰𐑉𐐮𐐻𐐲𐐺𐑊, 𐑄 𐐪𐑉 𐐰𐑆 𐐼𐑉𐐱𐑅, 𐐸𐐶𐐮𐐽 𐑄 𐑉𐐨𐑁𐐴𐑌𐐲𐑉𐑆 𐐼𐐭 𐐿𐐰𐑅𐐻 𐐵𐐻, (𐐮𐐻 𐐺𐐨𐐮𐑍 𐐱𐑂 𐑌𐐬 𐐶𐐲𐑉𐑃,) 𐐰𐑌𐐼 𐐮𐑆 𐐻𐑉𐐱𐐼𐑌 𐐲𐑌𐐼𐐲𐑉 𐑁𐐳𐐻 𐐱𐑂 𐑋𐐯𐑌.

30. 𐐈𐑌𐐼 𐑌𐐵, 𐑋𐐴 𐐺𐑉𐐯𐑄𐑉𐐯𐑌, 𐐌 𐐶𐐳𐐼 𐑄𐐰𐐻, 𐐰𐑁𐐻𐐲𐑉 𐑄 𐐸𐐰𐑂 𐑉𐐨𐑅𐐨𐑂𐐼 𐑅𐐬 𐑋𐐯𐑌𐐨 𐐶𐐮𐐻𐑌𐐯𐑅𐐯𐑆, 𐑅𐐨𐐮𐑍 𐑄𐐰𐐻 𐑄 𐐸𐐬𐑊𐐨 𐑅𐐿𐑉𐐮𐐹𐐽𐐲𐑉𐑆 𐐻𐐯𐑅𐐻𐐮𐑁𐐴 𐐱𐑂 𐑄𐐨𐑆 𐑃𐐮𐑍𐑆, 𐑄 𐐿𐐲𐑋 𐑁𐐫𐑉𐑃 𐐰𐑌𐐼 𐐺𐑉𐐮𐑍 𐑁𐑉𐐭𐐻 𐐲𐑌𐐻𐐭 𐑉𐐯𐐹𐐯𐑌𐐻𐐰𐑌𐑅. 𐐏𐐩, 𐐌 𐐶𐐳𐐼 𐑄𐐰𐐻 𐑄 𐐶𐐳𐐼 𐐿𐐲𐑋 𐑁𐐫𐑉𐑃 𐐰𐑌𐐼 𐐸𐐪𐑉𐐼𐑌 𐑌𐐱𐐻 𐐷𐐫𐑉 𐐸𐐪𐑉𐐻𐑅 𐐯𐑌𐐨 𐑊𐐱𐑍𐑀𐐲𐑉; 𐑁𐐫𐑉 𐐺𐐨𐐸𐐬𐑊𐐼, 𐑌𐐵 𐐮𐑆 𐑄 𐐻𐐴𐑋 𐐰𐑌𐐼 𐑄 𐐼𐐩 𐐱𐑂 𐐷𐐫𐑉 𐑅𐐰𐑊𐑂𐐩𐑇𐐲𐑌; 𐐰𐑌𐐼 𐑄𐐯𐑉𐑁𐐬𐑉, 𐐮𐑁 𐑄 𐐶𐐮𐑊 𐑉𐐨𐐹𐐯𐑌𐐻 𐐰𐑌𐐼 𐐸𐐪𐑉𐐼𐑌 𐑌𐐱𐐻 𐐷𐐫𐑉 𐐸𐐪𐑉𐐻𐑅, 𐐮𐑋𐐨𐐼𐐨𐐲𐐻𐑊𐐨 𐑇𐐰𐑊 𐑄 𐑀𐑉𐐩𐐻 𐐹𐑊𐐰𐑌 𐐱𐑂 𐑉𐐨𐐼𐐯𐑋𐑇𐐲𐑌 𐐺𐐨 𐐺𐑉𐐫𐐻 𐐲𐐺𐐵𐐻 𐐲𐑌𐐻𐐭 𐐷𐐭. 𐐙𐐫𐑉 𐐺𐐨𐐸𐐬𐑊𐐼, 𐑄𐐮𐑅 𐑊𐐴𐑁 𐐮𐑆 𐑄 𐐻𐐴𐑋 𐑁𐐫𐑉 𐑋𐐯𐑌 𐐻𐐭 𐐹𐑉𐐨𐐹𐐯𐑉 𐐻𐐭 𐑋𐐨𐐻 𐐘𐐱𐐼; 𐐷𐐩, 𐐺𐐨𐐸𐐬𐑊𐐼 𐑄 𐐼𐐩 𐐱𐑂 𐑄𐐮𐑅 𐑊𐐴𐑁 𐐮𐑆 𐑄 𐐼𐐩 𐑁𐐫𐑉 𐑋𐐯𐑌 𐐻𐐭 𐐹𐐲𐑉𐑁𐐫𐑉𐑋 𐑄𐐯𐑉 𐑊𐐩𐐺𐐲𐑉𐑆. 𐐈𐑌𐐼 𐑌𐐵, 𐐰𐑆 𐐌 𐑅𐐯𐐼 𐐲𐑌𐐻𐐭 𐐷𐐭 𐐺𐐨𐑁𐐬𐑉, 𐐰𐑆 𐑄 𐐸𐐰𐑂 𐐸𐐰𐐼 𐑅𐐬 𐑋𐐯𐑌𐐨 𐐶𐐮𐐻𐑌𐐯𐑅𐐯𐑆, 𐑄𐐯𐑉𐑁𐐬𐑉, 𐐌 𐐺𐐨𐑅𐐨𐐽 𐐱𐑂 𐐷𐐭, 𐑄𐐰𐐻 𐑄 𐐼𐐭 𐑌𐐱𐐻 𐐹𐑉𐐬𐐿𐑉𐐰𐑅𐐻𐐮𐑌𐐩𐐻 𐑄 𐐼𐐩 𐐱𐑂 𐐷𐐫𐑉 𐑉𐐨𐐹𐐯𐑌𐐻𐐰𐑌𐑅 𐐲𐑌𐐻𐐮𐑊 𐑄 𐐯𐑌𐐼; 𐑁𐐫𐑉 𐐰𐑁𐐻𐐲𐑉 𐑄𐐮𐑅 𐐼𐐩 𐐱𐑂 𐑊𐐴𐑁, 𐐸𐐶𐐮𐐽 𐐮𐑆 𐑀𐐮𐑂𐑌 𐐲𐑅 𐐻𐐭 𐐹𐑉𐐨𐐹𐐯𐑉 𐑁𐐫𐑉 𐐨𐐻𐐲𐑉𐑌𐐮𐐻𐐨, 𐐺𐐨𐐸𐐬𐑊𐐼, 𐐮𐑁 𐐶𐐨 𐐼𐐭 𐑌𐐱𐐻 𐐮𐑋𐐹𐑉𐐭𐑂 𐐵𐑉 𐐻𐐴𐑋 𐐸𐐶𐐴𐑊 𐐮𐑌 𐑄𐐮𐑅 𐑊𐐴𐑁, 𐑄𐐯𐑌 𐐿𐐲𐑋𐐯𐑃 𐑄 𐑌𐐴𐐻 𐐱𐑂 𐐼𐐪𐑉𐐿𐑌𐐯𐑅 𐐸𐐶𐐯𐑉𐐮𐑌 𐑄𐐯𐑉 𐐿𐐰𐑌 𐐺𐐨 𐑌𐐬 𐑊𐐩𐐺𐐲𐑉 𐐹𐐲𐑉𐑁𐐫𐑉𐑋𐐼. 𐐏𐐨 𐐿𐐰𐑌𐐱𐐻 𐑅𐐩, 𐐸𐐶𐐯𐑌 𐑄 𐐪𐑉 𐐺𐑉𐐫𐐻 𐐻𐐭 𐑄𐐰𐐻 𐐫𐑁𐐳𐑊 𐐿𐑉𐐴𐑅𐐮𐑅, 𐑄𐐰𐐻 𐐌 𐐶𐐮𐑊 𐑉𐐨𐐹𐐯𐑌𐐻, 𐑄𐐰𐐻 𐐌 𐐶𐐮𐑊 𐑉𐐨𐐻𐐲𐑉𐑌 𐐻𐐭 𐑋𐐴 𐐘𐐱𐐼. 𐐤𐐩, 𐑄 𐐿𐐰𐑌𐐱𐐻 𐑅𐐩 𐑄𐐮𐑅; 𐑁𐐫𐑉 𐑄𐐰𐐻 𐑅𐐩𐑋 𐑅𐐹𐐮𐑉𐐮𐐻 𐐸𐐶𐐮𐐽 𐐼𐐲𐑃 𐐹𐐲𐑆𐐯𐑅 𐐷𐐫𐑉 𐐺𐐱𐐼𐐨𐑆 𐐰𐐻 𐑄 𐐻𐐴𐑋 𐑄𐐰𐐻 𐑄 𐑀𐐬 𐐵𐐻 𐐱𐑂 𐑄𐐮𐑅 𐑊𐐴𐑁, 𐑄𐐰𐐻 𐑅𐐩𐑋 𐑅𐐹𐐮𐑉𐐮𐐻 𐐶𐐮𐑊 𐐸𐐰𐑂 𐐹𐐵𐐲𐑉 𐐻𐐭 𐐹𐐲𐑆𐐯𐑅 𐐷𐐫𐑉 𐐺𐐱𐐼𐐨 𐐮𐑌 𐑄𐐰𐐻 𐐨𐐻𐐲𐑉𐑌𐐲𐑊 𐐶𐐲𐑉𐑊𐐼. 𐐙𐐫𐑉 𐐺𐐨𐐸𐐬𐑊𐐼, 𐐮𐑁 𐑄 𐐸𐐰𐑂 𐐹𐑉𐐬𐐿𐑉𐐰𐑅𐐻𐐮𐑌𐐩𐐻𐐯𐐼 𐑄 𐐼𐐩 𐐱𐑂 𐐷𐐫𐑉 𐑉𐐨𐐹𐐯𐑌𐐻𐐰𐑌𐑅 𐐨𐑂𐑌 𐐲𐑌𐐻𐐮𐑊 𐐼𐐯𐑃, 𐐺𐐨𐐸𐐬𐑊𐐼, 𐑄 𐐸𐐰𐑂 𐐺𐐨𐐿𐐲𐑋 𐑅𐐲𐐺𐐾𐐯𐐿𐐻𐐯𐐼 𐐻𐐭 𐑄 𐑅𐐹𐐮𐑉𐐮𐐻 𐐱𐑂 𐑄 𐐼𐐯𐑂𐐮𐑊, 𐐰𐑌𐐼 𐐸𐐨 𐐼𐐲𐑃 𐑅𐐨𐑊 𐐷𐐭 𐐸𐐮𐑆; 𐑄𐐯𐑉𐑁𐐬𐑉, 𐑄 𐐝𐐹𐐮𐑉𐐮𐐻 𐐱𐑂 𐑄 𐐢𐐫𐑉𐐼 𐐸𐐰𐑃 𐐶𐐮𐑃𐐼𐑉𐐫𐑌 𐑁𐑉𐐱𐑋 𐐷𐐭, 𐐰𐑌𐐼 𐐸𐐰𐑃 𐑌𐐬 𐐹𐑊𐐩𐑅 𐐮𐑌 𐐷𐐭, 𐐰𐑌𐐼 𐑄 𐐼𐐯𐑂𐐮𐑊 𐐸𐐰𐑃 𐐫𐑊 𐐹𐐵𐐲𐑉 𐐬𐑂𐐲𐑉 𐐷𐐭; 𐐰𐑌𐐼 𐑄𐐮𐑅 𐐮𐑆 𐑄 𐑁𐐴𐑌𐐲𐑊 𐑅𐐻𐐩𐐻 𐐱𐑂 𐑄 𐐶𐐮𐐿𐐯𐐼. 𐐈𐑌𐐼 𐑄𐐮𐑅 𐐌 𐑌𐐬, 𐐺𐐨𐐿𐐫𐑆 𐑄 𐐢𐐫𐑉𐐼 𐐸𐐰𐑃 𐑅𐐯𐐼 𐐸𐐨 𐐼𐐶𐐯𐑊𐐯𐑃 𐑌𐐱𐐻 𐐮𐑌 𐐲𐑌𐐸𐐬𐑊𐐨 𐐻𐐯𐑋𐐹𐑊𐑆, 𐐺𐐲𐐻 𐐮𐑌 𐑄 𐐸𐐪𐑉𐐻𐑅 𐐱𐑂 𐑄 𐑉𐐴𐐽𐐲𐑅 𐐼𐐲𐑃 𐐸𐐨 𐐼𐐶𐐯𐑊; 𐐷𐐩, 𐐰𐑌𐐼 𐐸𐐨 𐐸𐐰𐑆 𐐫𐑊𐑅𐐬 𐑅𐐯𐐼 𐑄𐐰𐐻 𐑄 𐑉𐐴𐐽𐐲𐑅 𐑇𐐰𐑊 𐑅𐐮𐐻 𐐼𐐵𐑌 𐐮𐑌 𐐸𐐮𐑆 𐐿𐐮𐑍𐐼𐐲𐑋, 𐐻𐐭 𐑀𐐬 𐑌𐐬 𐑋𐐬𐑉 𐐵𐐻: 𐐺𐐲𐐻 𐑄𐐯𐑉 𐑀𐐪𐑉𐑋𐐯𐑌𐐻𐑅 𐑇𐐳𐐼 𐐺𐐨 𐑋𐐩𐐼 𐐸𐐶𐐴𐐻 𐑃𐑉𐐭 𐑄 𐐺𐑊𐐲𐐼 𐐱𐑂 𐑄 𐐢𐐰𐑋.

31. 𐐈𐑌𐐼 𐑌𐐵 𐑋𐐴 𐐺𐐨𐑊𐐲𐑝𐐯𐐼 𐐺𐑉𐐯𐑄𐑉𐐯𐑌, 𐐌 𐐼𐐨𐑆𐐴𐑉 𐑄𐐰𐐻 𐑄 𐑇𐐳𐐼 𐑉𐐨𐑋𐐯𐑋𐐺𐐲𐑉 𐑄𐐨𐑆 𐑃𐐮𐑍𐑆, 𐐰𐑌𐐼 𐑄𐐰𐐻 𐑄 𐑇𐐳𐐼 𐐶𐐲𐑉𐐿 𐐵𐐻 𐐷𐐫𐑉 𐑅𐐰𐑊𐑂𐐩𐑇𐐲𐑌 𐐶𐐮𐑃 𐑁𐐨𐑉 𐐺𐐨𐑁𐐬𐑉 𐐘𐐱𐐼, 𐐰𐑌𐐼 𐑄𐐰𐐻 𐑄 𐑇𐐳𐐼 𐑌𐐬 𐑋𐐬𐑉 𐐼𐐨𐑌𐐴 𐑄 𐐿𐐲𐑋𐐮𐑍 𐐱𐑂 𐐗𐑉𐐴𐑅𐐻; 𐑄𐐰𐐻 𐑄 𐐿𐐱𐑌𐐻𐐯𐑌𐐼 𐑌𐐬 𐑋𐐬𐑉 𐐲𐑀𐐯𐑌𐑅𐐻 𐑄 𐐐𐐬𐑊𐐨 𐐘𐐬𐑅𐐻, 𐐺𐐲𐐻 𐑄𐐰𐐻 𐑄 𐑉𐐨𐑅𐐨𐑂 𐐮𐐻, 𐐰𐑌𐐼 𐐻𐐩𐐿 𐐲𐐹𐐱𐑌 𐐷𐐭 𐑄 𐑌𐐩𐑋 𐐱𐑂 𐐗𐑉𐐴𐑅𐐻; 𐑄𐐰𐐻 𐑄 𐐸𐐲𐑋𐐺𐑊 𐐷𐐫𐑉𐑅𐐯𐑊𐑂𐑆 𐐨𐑂𐑌 𐐻𐐭 𐑄 𐐼𐐲𐑅𐐻, 𐐰𐑌𐐼 𐐶𐐲𐑉𐑇𐐮𐐹 𐐘𐐱𐐼 𐐮𐑌 𐐸𐐶𐐱𐐻𐑅𐐬𐐯𐑂𐐲𐑉 𐐹𐑊𐐩𐑅 𐑄 𐑋𐐩 𐐺𐐨 𐐮𐑌, 𐐮𐑌 𐑅𐐹𐐮𐑉𐐮𐐻 𐐰𐑌𐐼 𐐮𐑌 𐐻𐑉𐐭𐑃; 𐐰𐑌𐐼 𐑄𐐰𐐻 𐑄 𐑊𐐮𐑂 𐐮𐑌 𐑃𐐰𐑍𐐿𐑅𐑀𐐮𐑂𐐮𐑍 𐐼𐐩𐑊𐐨, 𐑁𐐫𐑉 𐑄 𐑋𐐯𐑌𐐨 𐑋𐐲𐑉𐑅𐐨𐑆 𐐰𐑌𐐼 𐐺𐑊𐐯𐑅𐐮𐑍𐑆 𐐸𐐶𐐮𐐽 𐐸𐐨 𐐼𐐲𐑃 𐐺𐐨𐑅𐐻𐐬 𐐲𐐹𐐱𐑌 𐐷𐐭; 𐐷𐐩, 𐐰𐑌𐐼 𐐌 𐐫𐑊𐑅𐐬 𐐯𐑀𐑆𐐫𐑉𐐻 𐐷𐐭, 𐑋𐐴 𐐺𐑉𐐯𐑄𐑉𐐯𐑌, 𐑄𐐰𐐻 𐑄 𐐺𐐨 𐐶𐐱𐐽𐑁𐐳𐑊 𐐲𐑌𐐻𐐭 𐐹𐑉𐐩𐐲𐑉 𐐿𐐱𐑌𐐻𐐮𐑌𐐷𐐲𐐲𐑊𐐨, 𐑄𐐰𐐻 𐑄 𐑋𐐩 𐑌𐐱𐐻 𐐺𐐨 𐑊𐐯𐐼 𐐲𐐶𐐩 𐐺𐐴 𐑄 𐐻𐐯𐑋𐐻𐐩𐑇𐐲𐑌𐑆 𐐱𐑂 𐑄 𐐼𐐯𐑂𐐮𐑊, 𐑄𐐰𐐻 𐐸𐐨 𐑋𐐩 𐑌𐐱𐐻 𐐬𐑂𐐲𐑉𐐹𐐵𐐲𐑉 𐐷𐐭, 𐑄𐐰𐐻 𐑄 𐑋𐐩 𐑌𐐱𐐻 𐐺𐐨𐐿𐐲𐑋 𐐸𐐮𐑆 𐑅𐐲𐐺𐐾𐐯𐐿𐐻𐑅 𐐰𐐻 𐑄 𐑊𐐰𐑅𐐻 𐐼𐐩: 𐑁𐐫𐑉 𐐺𐐨𐐸𐐬𐑊𐐼, 𐐸𐐨 𐑉𐐨𐐶𐐫𐑉𐐼𐐯𐑃 𐐷𐐭 𐑌𐐬 𐑀𐐳𐐼 𐑃𐐮𐑍. 𐐈𐑌𐐼 𐑌𐐵 𐑋𐐴 𐐺𐐨𐑊𐐲𐑝𐐯𐐼 𐐺𐑉𐐯𐑄𐑉𐐯𐑌, 𐐌 𐐶𐐳𐐼 𐐯𐑀𐑆𐐫𐑉𐐻 𐐷𐐭 𐐻𐐭 𐐸𐐰𐑂 𐐹𐐩𐑇𐐯𐑌𐑅, 𐐰𐑌𐐼 𐑄𐐰𐐻 𐑄 𐐺𐐩𐑉 𐐶𐐮𐑃 𐐫𐑊 𐑋𐐰𐑌𐐲𐑉 𐐱𐑂 𐐰𐑁𐑊𐐮𐐿𐑇𐐲𐑌𐑆;

𐑄𐐰𐐻 𐐷 𐐼𐐭 𐑌𐐱𐐻 𐑉𐐨𐑂𐐴𐑊 𐐰𐑀𐐯𐑌𐑅𐐻 𐑄𐐬𐑆 𐐸𐐭 𐐼𐐭 𐐿𐐪𐑅𐐻 𐐷𐐭 𐐵𐐻 𐐺𐐨𐐿𐐫𐑆 𐐱𐑂 𐐷𐐭𐑉 𐐯𐐿𐑅𐐨𐐼𐐮𐑍 𐐹𐐱𐑂𐐲𐑉𐐻𐐮, 𐑊𐐯𐑅𐐻 𐐷 𐐺𐐨𐐿𐐲𐑋 𐑅𐐮𐑌𐐲𐑉𐑆 𐑊𐐴𐐿 𐐲𐑌𐐻𐐭 𐑄𐐯𐑋; 𐐺𐐲𐐻 𐑄𐐰𐐻 𐐷 𐐸𐐰𐑂 𐐹𐐩𐑇𐐯𐑌𐑅, 𐐰𐑌𐐼 𐐺𐐩𐑉 𐐶𐐮𐑄 𐑄𐐬𐑆 𐐰𐑁𐑊𐐮𐐿𐑇𐐲𐑌𐑆, 𐐶𐐮𐑄 𐐰 𐑁𐐲𐑉𐑋 𐐸𐐬𐐹 𐑄𐐰𐐻 𐐷 𐑇𐐰𐑊 𐐶𐐲𐑌 𐐼𐐩 𐑉𐐯𐑅𐐻 𐑁𐑉𐐱𐑋 𐐫𐑊 𐐷𐐭𐑉 𐐰𐑁𐑊𐐮𐐿𐑇𐐲𐑌𐑆.

32. 𐐤𐐵 𐐮𐐻 𐐿𐐩𐑋 𐐻𐐭 𐐹𐐪𐑅 𐑄𐐰𐐻 𐐪𐑁𐐻𐐯𐑉 𐐈𐑋𐐷𐐭𐑊𐐯𐐿 𐐸𐐰𐐼 𐑋𐐩𐐼 𐐰𐑌 𐐯𐑌𐐼 𐐱𐑂 𐑄𐐨𐑆 𐐶𐐲𐑉𐐼𐑆, 𐑄𐐩 𐐶𐐮𐑄𐐼𐑉𐐭 𐑄𐐯𐑋𐑅𐐯𐑊𐑂𐑆 𐑁𐑉𐐱𐑋 𐑄 𐑋𐐲𐑊𐐻𐐮𐐻𐐷𐐭𐐼, 𐐰𐑌𐐼 𐐿𐐩𐑋 𐐬𐑂𐐯𐑉 𐐮𐑌𐐻𐐭 𐑄 𐑊𐐰𐑌𐐼 𐐱𐑂 𐐖𐐲𐑉𐑇𐐲𐑌; 𐐷𐐩, 𐐰𐑌𐐼 𐑄 𐑉𐐯𐑅𐐻 𐐱𐑂 𐑄 𐐺𐑉𐐯𐑄𐑉𐐯𐑌, 𐐪𐑁𐐻𐐯𐑉 𐑄𐐩 𐐸𐐰𐐼 𐐹𐑉𐐨𐐽𐐻 𐑄 𐐶𐐲𐑉𐐼 𐐲𐑌𐐻𐐭 𐑄 𐐞𐐬𐑉𐐲𐑋𐐴𐐻𐑅, 𐐫𐑊𐑅𐐬 𐐿𐐩𐑋 𐐬𐑂𐐯𐑉 𐐮𐑌𐐻𐐭 𐑄 𐑊𐐰𐑌𐐼 𐐱𐑂 𐐖𐐲𐑉𐑇𐐲𐑌. 𐐈𐑌𐐼 𐐮𐐻 𐐿𐐩𐑋 𐐻𐐭 𐐹𐐪𐑅 𐑄𐐰𐐻 𐐪𐑁𐐻𐐯𐑉 𐑄 𐑋𐐬𐑉 𐐹𐐱𐐹𐐷𐐭𐑊𐐲𐑉 𐐹𐐪𐑉𐐻 𐐱𐑂 𐑄 𐐞𐐬𐑉𐐲𐑋𐐴𐐻𐑅 𐐸𐐰𐐼 𐐿𐐲𐑌𐑅𐐲𐑊𐐻𐐯𐐼 𐐻𐐭𐑀𐐯𐑄𐐯𐑉 𐐿𐐲𐑌𐑅𐐲𐑉𐑌𐐮𐑍 𐑄 𐐶𐐲𐑉𐐼𐑆 𐐸𐐶𐐮𐐽 𐐸𐐰𐐼 𐐺𐐮𐑌 𐐹𐑉𐐨𐐽𐐻 𐐲𐑌𐐻𐐭 𐑄𐐯𐑋, 𐑄𐐩 𐐶𐐲𐑉 𐐰𐑍𐑀𐑉𐐮 𐐺𐐨𐐿𐐫𐑆 𐐱𐑂 𐑄 𐐶𐐲𐑉𐐼, 𐑁𐐬𐑉 𐐮𐐻 𐐼𐐮𐐼 𐐼𐐨𐑅𐐻𐑉𐑎 𐑄𐐩𐑉 𐐿𐑉𐐪𐑁𐐻; 𐑄𐐩𐑉𐑁𐐬𐑉, 𐑄𐐩 𐐶𐐳𐐼 𐑌𐐱𐐻 𐐸𐐪𐑉𐐿𐑌 𐐲𐑌𐐻𐐭 𐑄 𐐶𐐲𐑉𐐼𐑆. 𐐈𐑌𐐼 𐑄𐐩 𐑅𐐯𐑌𐐻 𐐰𐑌𐐼 𐑀𐐰𐑄𐐯𐑉𐐼 𐐻𐐭𐑀𐐯𐑄𐐯𐑉 𐑃𐑉𐐭𐐵𐐻 𐐫𐑊 𐑄 𐑊𐐰𐑌𐐼, 𐐫𐑊 𐑄 𐐹𐐨𐐹𐑊, 𐐰𐑌𐐼 𐐿𐐲𐑌𐑅𐐲𐑊𐐻𐐯𐐼 𐐶𐐮𐑄 𐑄𐐯𐑋, 𐐿𐐲𐑌𐑅𐐲𐑉𐑌𐐮𐑍 𐑄 𐐶𐐲𐑉𐐼𐑆 𐐸𐐶𐐮𐐽 𐐸𐐰𐐼 𐐺𐐮𐑌 𐑅𐐹𐐬𐐿𐑌. 𐐤𐐵 𐑄𐐩𐑉 𐑉𐐭𐑊𐐯𐑉𐑆, 𐐰𐑌𐐼 𐑄𐐩𐑉 𐐹𐑉𐐨𐑅𐐻𐑅, 𐐰𐑌𐐼 𐑄𐐩𐑉 𐐻𐐨𐐽𐐯𐑉𐑆, 𐐼𐐮𐐼 𐑌𐐱𐐻 𐑊𐐯𐐻 𐑄 𐐹𐐨𐐹𐑊 𐑌𐐬 𐐿𐐲𐑌𐑅𐐲𐑉𐑌𐐮𐑍 𐑄𐐩𐑉 𐐼𐐨𐑆𐐴𐑉𐑆; 𐑄𐐩𐑉𐑁𐐬𐑉 𐑄𐐩 𐑁𐐵𐑌𐐼 𐐵𐐻 𐐹𐑉𐐮𐑂𐐮𐑊𐐮 𐑄 𐑋𐐴𐑌𐐼𐑆 𐐱𐑂 𐐫𐑊 𐑄 𐐹𐐨𐐹𐑊. 𐐈𐑌𐐼 𐐮𐐻 𐐿𐐩𐑋 𐐻𐐭 𐐹𐐪𐑅 𐑄𐐰𐐻 𐐪𐑁𐐻𐐯𐑉 𐑄𐐩 𐐸𐐰𐐼 𐑁𐐵𐑌𐐼 𐐵𐐻 𐑄 𐑋𐐴𐑌𐐼𐑆 𐐱𐑂 𐐫𐑊 𐑄 𐐹𐐨𐐹𐑊, 𐑄𐐬𐑆 𐐸𐐭 𐐶𐐲𐑉 𐐮𐑌 𐑁𐐩𐑂𐐲𐑉 𐐱𐑂 𐑄 𐐶𐐲𐑉𐐼𐑆 𐐸𐐶𐐮𐐽 𐐸𐐰𐐼 𐐺𐐮𐑌 𐑅𐐹𐐬𐐿𐑌 𐐺𐐴 𐐈𐐢𐐣𐐊 𐐰𐑌𐐼 𐐸𐐮𐑆 𐐺𐑉𐐯𐑄𐑉𐐯𐑌, 𐐶𐐲𐑉 𐐿𐐪𐑅𐐻 𐐵𐐻 𐐱𐑂 𐑄 𐑊𐐰𐑌𐐼; 𐐰𐑌𐐼 𐑄𐐩 𐐶𐐲𐑉 𐑋𐐯𐑌𐐮; 𐐰𐑌𐐼 𐑄𐐩 𐐿𐐩𐑋 𐐬𐑂𐐯𐑉 𐐫𐑊𐑅𐐬 𐐮𐑌𐐻𐐭 𐑄 𐑊𐐰𐑌𐐼 𐐱𐑂 𐐖𐐲𐑉𐑇𐐲𐑌.

33. 𐐈𐑌𐐼 𐐮𐐻 𐐿𐐩𐑋 𐐻𐐭 𐐹𐐪𐑅 𐑄𐐰𐐻 𐐈𐐢𐐣𐐊 𐐰𐑌𐐼 𐐸𐐮𐑆 𐐺𐑉𐐯𐑄𐑉𐐯𐑌 𐐼𐐮𐐼 𐑋𐐮𐑌𐐮𐑅𐐻𐐲𐑉 𐐲𐑌𐐻𐐭 𐑄𐐯𐑋. 𐐤𐐵 𐑄 𐐹𐐨𐐹𐑊 𐐱𐑂 𐑄 𐐞𐐬𐑉𐐲𐑋𐐴𐐻𐑅 𐐶𐐲𐑉 𐐰𐑍𐑀𐑉𐐮 𐐶𐐮𐑄 𐑄 𐐹𐐨𐐹𐑊 𐐱𐑂 𐐈𐑋𐐲𐑌 𐐸𐐭 𐐶𐐲𐑉 𐐮𐑌 𐐖𐐲𐑉𐑇𐐲𐑌, 𐐰𐑌𐐼 𐑄 𐐽𐐨𐑁 𐑉𐐭𐑊𐐲𐑉 𐐱𐑂 𐑄 𐐞𐐬𐑉𐐲𐑋𐐴𐐻𐑅 𐐺𐐨𐐮𐑍 𐐰 𐑂𐐯𐑉𐐮 𐐶𐐮𐐿𐐯𐐼 𐑋𐐰𐑌, 𐑅𐐯𐑌𐐻 𐐬𐑂𐐯𐑉 𐐲𐑌𐐻𐐭 𐑄 𐐹𐐨𐐹𐑊 𐐱𐑂 𐐈𐑋𐐲𐑌 𐐼𐐨𐑆𐐴𐑉𐐮𐑍 𐑄𐐯𐑋 𐑄𐐰𐐻 𐑄𐐩 𐑇𐐳𐐼 𐐿𐐪𐑅𐐻 𐐵𐐻 𐐱𐑂 𐑄𐐩𐑉 𐑊𐐰𐑌𐐼 𐐫𐑊 𐑄𐐬𐑆 𐐸𐐭 𐐿𐐩𐑋 𐐬𐑂𐐯𐑉 𐑁𐑉𐐱𐑋 𐑄𐐯𐑋 𐐮𐑌𐐻𐐭 𐑄𐐩𐑉 𐑊𐐰𐑌𐐼. 𐐈𐑌𐐼 𐐸𐐨 𐐺𐑉𐐨𐑄𐐼 𐐵𐐻 𐑋𐐯𐑌𐐮 𐑃𐑉𐐯𐐻𐐯𐑌𐐮𐑍𐑆 𐐰𐑀𐐯𐑌𐑅𐐻 𐑄𐐯𐑋. 𐐈𐑌𐐼 𐑌𐐵 𐑄 𐐹𐐨𐐹𐑊 𐐱𐑂 𐐈𐑋𐐲𐑌 𐐼𐐮𐐼 𐑌𐐱𐐻 𐑁𐐨𐑉 𐑄𐐩𐑉 𐐶𐐲𐑉𐐼𐑆, 𐑄𐐩𐑉𐑁𐐬𐑉 𐑄𐐩 𐐼𐐮𐐼 𐑌𐐱𐐻 𐐿𐐪𐑅𐐻 𐑄𐐯𐑋 𐐵𐐻, 𐐺𐐲𐐻 𐑄𐐩 𐐼𐐮𐐼 𐑉𐐨𐑅𐐨𐑂 𐐫𐑊 𐑄 𐐹𐐭𐑉 𐐱𐑂 𐑄 𐐞𐐬𐑉𐐲𐑋𐐴𐐻𐑅 𐑄𐐰𐐻 𐐿𐐩𐑋 𐐬𐑂𐐯𐑉 𐐲𐑌𐐻𐐭 𐑄𐐯𐑋; 𐐰𐑌𐐼 𐑄𐐩 𐐼𐐮𐐼 𐑌𐐲𐑉𐐮𐑇 𐑄𐐯𐑋, 𐐰𐑌𐐼 𐐼𐐮𐐼 𐐿𐑊𐐬𐑄 𐑄𐐯𐑋, 𐐰𐑌𐐼 𐐼𐐮𐐼 𐑀𐐮𐑂 𐐲𐑌𐐻𐐭 𐑄𐐯𐑋 𐑊𐐰𐑌𐐼𐑆 𐑁𐐬𐑉 𐑄𐐩𐑉 𐐮𐑌𐐸𐐯𐑉𐐮𐐻𐐰𐑌𐑅; 𐐰𐑌𐐼 𐑄𐐩 𐐼𐐮𐐼 𐐰𐐼𐑋𐐮𐑌𐐮𐑅𐐻𐐲𐑉 𐐲𐑌𐐻𐐭 𐑄𐐯𐑋 𐐰𐐿𐐬𐑉𐐼𐐮𐑍 𐐻𐐭 𐑄𐐩𐑉 𐐶𐐪𐑌𐐻𐑅. 𐐤𐐵 𐑄𐐮𐑅 𐐼𐐮𐐼 𐑅𐐻𐐲𐑉 𐐲𐐹 𐑄 𐐞𐐬𐑉𐐲𐑋𐐴𐐻𐑅 𐐻𐐭 𐐰𐑍𐑀𐐲𐑉 𐐰𐑀𐐯𐑌𐑅𐐻 𐑄 𐐹𐐨𐐹𐑊 𐐱𐑂 𐐈𐑋𐐲𐑌, 𐐰𐑌𐐼 𐑄𐐩 𐐺𐐨𐑀𐐰𐑌 𐐻𐐭 𐑋𐐮𐐿𐑅 𐐶𐐮𐑄 𐑄 𐐢𐐰𐑋𐐲𐑌𐐴𐐻𐑅, 𐐰𐑌𐐼 𐐻𐐭 𐑅𐐻𐐲𐑉 𐑄𐐯𐑋 𐐲𐐹 𐐫𐑊𐑅𐐬 𐐻𐐭 𐐰𐑍𐑀𐐲𐑉 𐐰𐑀𐐯𐑌𐑅𐐻 𐑄𐐯𐑋: 𐐰𐑌𐐼 𐑄𐐲𐑅 𐑄 𐐞𐐬𐑉𐐲𐑋𐐴𐐻𐑅 𐐰𐑌𐐼 𐑄 𐐢𐐰𐑋𐐲𐑌𐐴𐐻𐑅 𐐺𐐨𐑀𐐰𐑌 𐐻𐐭 𐑋𐐩𐐿 𐐹𐑉𐐯𐐹𐐲𐑉𐐩𐑇𐐲𐑌𐑆 𐑁𐐬𐑉 𐐶𐐫𐑉 𐐰𐑀𐐯𐑌𐑅𐐻 𐑄 𐐹𐐨𐐹𐑊 𐐱𐑂 𐐈𐑋𐐲𐑌, 𐐰𐑌𐐼 𐐫𐑊𐑅𐐬 𐐰𐑀𐐯𐑌𐑅𐐻 𐑄 𐐤𐐨𐑁𐐴𐐻𐑅. 𐐈𐑌𐐼 𐑄𐐲𐑅 𐐯𐑌𐐼𐐯𐐼 𐑄 𐑅𐐯𐑂𐐯𐑌𐐻𐐨𐑌𐑃 𐐷𐐨𐑉 𐐱𐑂 𐑄 𐑉𐐩𐑌 𐐱𐑂 𐑄 𐐾𐐲𐐾𐐯𐑆 𐐬𐑂𐐯𐑉 𐑄 𐐹𐐨𐐹𐑊 𐐱𐑂 𐐤𐐨𐑁𐐴.

34. 𐐈𐑌𐐼 𐑄 𐐹𐐨𐐹𐑊 𐐱𐑂 𐐈𐑋𐐲𐑌 𐐼𐐨𐐹𐐪𐑉𐐻𐐯𐐼 𐐵𐐻 𐐱𐑂 𐑄 𐑊𐐰𐑌𐐼 𐐱𐑂 𐐖𐐲𐑉𐑇𐐲𐑌, 𐐰𐑌𐐼 𐐿𐐩𐑋 𐐬𐑂𐐯𐑉 𐐮𐑌𐐻𐐭 𐑄 𐑊𐐰𐑌𐐼 𐐱𐑂 𐐣𐐯𐑊𐐯𐐿, 𐐰𐑌𐐼 𐑀𐐩𐑂 𐐹𐑊𐐩𐑅 𐐮𐑌 𐑄 𐑊𐐰𐑌𐐼 𐐱𐑂 𐐖𐐲𐑉𐑇𐐲𐑌 𐑁𐐬𐑉 𐑄 𐐪𐑉𐑋𐐮𐑆 𐐱𐑂 𐑄 𐐤𐐨𐑁𐐴𐐻𐑅, 𐑄𐐰𐐻 𐑄𐐩 𐑋𐐴𐐻 𐐿𐐲𐑌𐐻𐐯𐑌𐐼 𐐶𐐮𐑄 𐑄 𐐪𐑉𐑋𐐮𐑆 𐐱𐑂 𐑄 𐐢𐐰𐑋𐐲𐑌𐐴𐐻𐑅 𐐰𐑌𐐼 𐑄 𐐪𐑉𐑋𐐮𐑆 𐐱𐑂 𐑄 𐐞𐐬𐑉𐐲𐑋𐐴𐐻𐑅; 𐐰𐑌𐐼 𐑄𐐲𐑅 𐐿𐐲𐑋𐐯𐑌𐑅𐐻 𐐰 𐐶𐐫𐑉 𐐺𐐨𐐻𐐶𐐮𐐿𐑅𐐻 𐑄 𐐢𐐰𐑋𐐲𐑌𐐴𐐻𐑅 𐐰𐑌𐐼 𐑄 𐐤𐐨𐑁𐐴𐐻𐑅 𐐮𐑌 𐑄 𐐩𐐻𐐨𐑌𐑃 𐐷𐐨𐑉 𐐱𐑂 𐑄 𐑉𐐩𐑌 𐐱𐑂 𐑄 𐐾𐐲𐐾𐐯𐑆; 𐐰𐑌𐐼 𐐰𐑌 𐐰𐐿𐐵𐑌𐐻 𐑇𐐰𐑊 𐐺𐐨 𐑀𐐮𐑂𐐯𐑌 𐐱𐑂 𐑄𐐩𐑉 𐐶𐐫𐑉𐑆 𐐸𐐨𐑉𐐪𐑁𐐻𐐯𐑉. 𐐈𐑌𐐼 𐐈𐐢𐐣𐐊, 𐐰𐑌𐐼 𐐈𐑋𐐲𐑌, 𐐰𐑌𐐼 𐑄𐐩𐑉 𐐺𐑉𐐯𐑄𐑉𐐯𐑌, 𐐰𐑌𐐼 𐐫𐑊𐑅𐐬 𐑄 𐐻𐐭 𐑅𐐲𐑌𐑆 𐐱𐑂 𐐈𐐢𐐣𐐊, 𐑉𐐨𐐻𐐲𐑉𐑌𐐼 𐐻𐐭 𐑄 𐑊𐐰𐑌𐐼 𐐱𐑂 𐐞𐐰𐑉𐐲𐐸𐐯𐑋𐑊𐐲, 𐐪𐑁𐐻𐐯𐑉 𐐸𐐰𐑂𐐮𐑍 𐐺𐐮𐑌 𐐮𐑌𐑅𐐻𐑉𐐭𐑋𐐯𐑌𐐻𐑅 𐐮𐑌 𐑄 𐐸𐐰𐑌𐐼𐑆 𐐱𐑂 𐐘𐐱𐐼 𐐱𐑂 𐐺𐑉𐐮𐑍𐐮𐑍 𐑋𐐯𐑌𐐮 𐐱𐑂 𐑄 𐐞𐐬𐑉𐐲𐑋𐐴𐐻𐑅 𐐻𐐭 𐑉𐐨𐐹𐐯𐑌𐐻𐐰𐑌𐑅; 𐐰𐑌𐐼 𐐰𐑆 𐑋𐐯𐑌𐐮 𐐰𐑆 𐐶𐐲𐑉 𐐺𐑉𐐫𐐻 𐐻𐐭 𐑉𐐨𐐹𐐯𐑌𐐻𐐰𐑌𐑅 𐐶𐐲𐑉 𐐼𐑉𐐮𐑂𐐯𐑌 𐐵𐐻 𐐱𐑂 𐑄𐐩𐑉 𐑊𐐰𐑌𐐼; 𐐺𐐲𐐻 𐑄𐐩 𐐸𐐰𐑂 𐑊𐐰𐑌𐐼𐑆 𐑁𐐬𐑉 𐑄𐐩𐑉 𐐮𐑌𐐸𐐯𐑉𐐮𐐻𐐰𐑌𐑅 𐐮𐑌 𐑄 𐑊𐐰𐑌𐐼 𐐱𐑂 𐐖𐐲𐑉-

𐑇𐐲𐑌, 𐐰𐑌𐐼 𐑄𐐩 𐐸𐐰𐑂 𐐻𐐩𐐿𐑌 𐐲𐐹 𐐪𐑉𐑋𐑆 𐐻𐐭 𐐼𐐨𐑁𐐯𐑌𐐼 𐑄𐐯𐑋𐑅𐐯𐑊𐑂𐑆, 𐐰𐑌𐐼 𐑄𐐩𐑉 𐐶𐐴𐑂𐑆, 𐐰𐑌𐐼 𐐽𐐮𐑊𐐼𐑉𐐯𐑌, 𐐰𐑌𐐼 𐑄𐐩𐑉 𐑊𐐰𐑌𐐼𐑆. 𐐤𐐵 𐐈𐑊𐑋𐐲, 𐐺𐐨𐐮𐑍 𐑀𐑉𐐨𐑂𐐼 𐑁𐐫𐑉 𐑄 𐐮𐑌𐐮𐐿𐐶𐐮𐐻𐐨 𐐱𐑂 𐐸𐐮𐑆 𐐹𐐨𐐹𐑊, 𐐷𐐩, 𐑁𐐫𐑉 𐑄 𐐶𐐫𐑉𐑆, 𐐰𐑌𐐼 𐑄 𐐺𐑊𐐲𐐼𐑇𐐯𐐼𐑆, 𐐰𐑌𐐼 𐑄 𐐿𐐱𐑌𐐻𐐯𐑌𐑇𐐲𐑌𐑆 𐐸𐐶𐐮𐐽 𐐶𐐲𐑉 𐐲𐑋𐐲𐑍 𐑄𐐯𐑋; 𐐰𐑌𐐼 𐐸𐐰𐑂𐐮𐑍 𐐺𐐨𐑌 𐐻𐐭 𐐼𐐨𐐿𐑊𐐩𐑉 𐑄 𐐶𐐲𐑉𐐼, 𐐫𐑉 𐑅𐐯𐑌𐐻 𐐻𐐭 𐐼𐐨𐐿𐑊𐐩𐑉 𐑄 𐐶𐐲𐑉𐐼, 𐐲𐑋𐐲𐑍 𐐫𐑊 𐑄 𐐹𐐨𐐹𐑊 𐐮𐑌 𐐯𐑂𐐲𐑉𐐨 𐑅𐐮𐐻𐐨; 𐐰𐑌𐐼 𐑅𐐨𐐮𐑍 𐑄𐐰𐐻 𐑄 𐐸𐐪𐑉𐐻𐑅 𐐱𐑂 𐑄 𐐹𐐨𐐹𐑊 𐐺𐐯𐑀𐐰𐑌 𐐻𐐭 𐐶𐐰𐐿𐑅 𐐸𐐪𐑉𐐼, 𐐰𐑌𐐼 𐑄𐐰𐐻 𐑄𐐩 𐐺𐐯𐑀𐐰𐑌 𐐻𐐭 𐐺 𐐬𐑁𐐯𐑌𐐼𐐯𐐼 𐐺𐐨𐐿𐐫𐑆 𐐱𐑂 𐑄 𐑅𐐻𐑉𐐮𐐿𐐻𐑌𐐯𐑅 𐐱𐑂 𐑄 𐐶𐐲𐑉𐐼, 𐐸𐐮𐑆 𐐸𐐪𐑉𐐻 𐐶𐐱𐑆 𐐯𐐿𐑅𐐨𐐼𐐮𐑍𐑊𐐨 𐑅𐐱𐑉𐐬𐑁𐐳𐑊; 𐑄𐐩𐑉𐑁𐐫𐑉, 𐐸𐐨 𐐿𐐫𐑆𐐼 𐑄𐐰𐐻 𐐸𐐮𐑆 𐑅𐐲𐑌𐑆 𐑇𐐳𐐼 𐐺 𐑀𐐰𐑄𐐲𐑉𐐼 𐐻𐐳𐑀𐐯𐑄𐐲𐑉, 𐑄𐐰𐐻 𐐸𐐨 𐑋𐐴𐐻 𐑀𐐮𐑂 𐐲𐑌𐐻𐐭 𐑄𐐯𐑋 𐐯𐑂𐐲𐑉𐐨 𐐶𐐲𐑌 𐐸𐐮𐑆 𐐽𐐪𐑉𐐾, 𐑅𐐯𐐹𐐲𐑉𐐩𐐻𐑊𐐨, 𐐿𐐱𐑌𐑅𐐲𐑉𐑌𐐮𐑍 𐑄 𐑃𐐮𐑍𐑆 𐐹𐐲𐑉𐐻𐐩𐑌𐐮𐑍 𐐲𐑌𐐻𐐭 𐑉𐐴𐐽𐐲𐑅𐑌𐐯𐑅. 𐐈𐑌𐐼 𐐶𐐨 𐐸𐐰𐑂 𐐰𐑌 𐐰𐐿𐐵𐑌𐐻 𐐱𐑂 𐐸𐐮𐑆 𐐿𐐲𐑋𐐰𐑌𐐼𐑋𐐯𐑌𐐻𐑅, 𐐸𐐶𐐮𐐽 𐐸𐐨 𐑀𐐩𐑂 𐐲𐑌𐐻𐐭 𐑄𐐯𐑋 𐐰𐐿𐐫𐑉𐐼𐐮𐑍 𐐻𐐭 𐐸𐐮𐑆 𐐬𐑌 𐑉𐐯𐐿𐐫𐑉𐐼.

𐐕𐐈𐐑𐐓𐐊𐐡 XVII.

𐐜 𐐗𐐲𐑋𐐰𐑌𐐼𐑋𐐯𐑌𐐻𐑅 𐐱𐑂 𐐈𐑊𐑋𐐲 𐐻𐐭 𐐸𐐮𐑆 𐑅𐐲𐑌 𐐐𐐨𐑊𐐩𐑋𐐲𐑌.

1. 𐐣𐐴 𐑅𐐲𐑌, 𐑀𐐮𐑂 𐐨𐑉 𐐻𐐭 𐑋𐐴 𐐶𐐲𐑉𐐼𐑆; 𐑁𐐫𐑉 𐐌 𐑅𐐶𐐩𐑉 𐐲𐑌𐐻𐐭 𐐷𐐭, 𐑄𐐰𐐻 𐐮𐑌𐐰𐑆𐑋𐐲𐐽 𐐰𐑆 𐐷 𐑇𐐰𐑊 𐐿𐐨𐐹 𐑄 𐐿𐐲𐑋𐐰𐑌𐐼𐑋𐐯𐑌𐐻𐑅 𐐱𐑂 𐐘𐐱𐐼, 𐐷 𐑇𐐰𐑊 𐐹𐑉𐐱𐑅𐐹𐐲𐑉 𐐮𐑌 𐑄 𐑊𐐰𐑌𐐼. 𐐌 𐐶𐐳𐐼 𐑄𐐰𐐻 𐐷 𐑇𐐳𐐼 𐐼𐐭 𐐰𐑆 𐐌 𐐸𐐰𐑂 𐐼𐐲𐑌, 𐐮𐑌 𐑉𐐨𐑋𐐯𐑋𐐺𐐲𐑉𐐮𐑍 𐑄 𐐿𐐰𐐹𐐻𐐮𐑂𐐮𐐻𐐨 𐐱𐑂 𐐵𐑉 𐑁𐐪𐑄𐐲𐑉𐑆; 𐑁𐐫𐑉 𐑄𐐩 𐐶𐐲𐑉 𐐮𐑌 𐐺𐐱𐑌𐐼𐐩𐐾, 𐐰𐑌𐐼 𐑌𐐲𐑌 𐐿𐐳𐐼 𐐼𐐨𐑊𐐮𐑂𐐲𐑉 𐑄𐐯𐑋 𐐯𐐿𐑅𐐯𐐹𐐻 𐐮𐐻 𐐶𐐱𐑆 𐑄 𐐘𐐱𐐼 𐐱𐑂 𐐁𐐺𐑉𐐲𐐸𐐰𐑋, 𐐰𐑌𐐼 𐑄 𐐘𐐱𐐼 𐐱𐑂 𐐌𐑆𐐲𐐿, 𐐰𐑌𐐼 𐑄 𐐘𐐱𐐼 𐐱𐑂 𐐖𐐩𐐿𐐲𐐺; 𐐰𐑌𐐼 𐐸𐐨 𐑇𐐳𐑉𐑊𐐨 𐐼𐐮𐐼 𐐼𐐨𐑊𐐮𐑂𐐲𐑉 𐑄𐐯𐑋 𐐮𐑌 𐑄𐐩𐑉 𐐰𐑁𐑊𐐮𐐿𐑇𐐲𐑌𐑆. 𐐈𐑌𐐼 𐑌𐐵, 𐐄 𐑋𐐴 𐑅𐐲𐑌 𐐐𐐨𐑊𐐩𐑋𐐲𐑌, 𐐺𐐨𐐸𐐬𐑊𐐼, 𐑄𐐵 𐐪𐑉𐐻 𐐮𐑌 𐑄𐐴 𐐷𐐭𐑃, 𐐰𐑌𐐼 𐑄𐐩𐑉𐑁𐐫𐑉 𐐌 𐐺𐐨𐑅𐐨𐐽 𐐱𐑂 𐑄 𐑄𐐰𐐻 𐑄𐐵 𐐶𐐮𐑊𐐻 𐐸𐐨𐑉 𐑋𐐴 𐐶𐐲𐑉𐐼𐑆, 𐐰𐑌𐐼 𐑊𐐲𐑉𐑌 𐐱𐑂 𐑋𐐨; 𐑁𐐫𐑉 𐐌 𐐼𐐭 𐑌𐐬 𐑄𐐰𐐻 𐐸𐐭𐑅𐐬𐐯𐑂𐐲𐑉 𐑇𐐰𐑊 𐐹𐐳𐐻 𐑄𐐩𐑉 𐐻𐑉𐐲𐑅𐐻 𐐮𐑌 𐐘𐐱𐐼, 𐑇𐐰𐑊 𐐺 𐑅𐐲𐐹𐐬𐑉𐐻𐐯𐐼 𐐮𐑌 𐑄𐐩𐑉 𐐻𐑉𐐴𐐲𐑊𐑆, 𐐰𐑌𐐼 𐑄𐐩𐑉 𐐻𐑉𐐲𐐺𐑊𐑆, 𐐰𐑌𐐼 𐑄𐐩𐑉 𐐰𐑁𐑊𐐮𐐿𐑇𐐲𐑌𐑆, 𐐰𐑌𐐼 𐑇𐐰𐑊 𐐺 𐑊𐐮𐑁𐐻𐐯𐐼 𐐲𐐹 𐐰𐐻 𐑄 𐑊𐐰𐑅𐐻 𐐼𐐩; 𐐰𐑌𐐼 𐐌 𐐶𐐳𐐼 𐑌𐐱𐐻 𐑄𐐰𐐻 𐐷 𐑃𐐮𐑍𐐿 𐑄𐐰𐐻 𐐌 𐑌𐐬 𐐱𐑂 𐑋𐐴𐑅𐐯𐑊𐑁, 𐑌𐐱𐐻 𐐱𐑂 𐑄 𐐻𐐯𐑋𐐹𐐬𐑉𐐲𐑊, 𐐺𐐲𐐻 𐐱𐑂 𐑄 𐑅𐐹𐐮𐑉𐐮𐐻𐐷𐐭𐐲𐑊; 𐑌𐐱𐐻 𐐱𐑂 𐑄 𐐿𐐪𐑉𐑌𐐲𐑊 𐑋𐐴𐑌𐐼, 𐐺𐐲𐐻 𐐱𐑂 𐐘𐐱𐐼. 𐐤𐐵 𐐺𐐨𐐸𐐬𐑊𐐼 𐐌 𐑅𐐩 𐐲𐑌𐐻𐐭 𐐷𐐭, 𐐮𐑁 𐐌 𐐸𐐰𐐼 𐑌𐐱𐐻 𐐺𐐮𐑌 𐐺𐐫𐑉𐑌 𐐱𐑂 𐐘𐐱𐐼, 𐐌 𐑇𐐳𐐼 𐑌𐐱𐐻 𐐸𐐰𐑂 𐑌𐐬𐑌 𐑄𐐨𐑆 𐑃𐐮𐑍𐑆; 𐐺𐐲𐐻 𐐘𐐱𐐼 𐐸𐐰𐑆, 𐐺𐐴 𐑄 𐑋𐐵𐑃 𐐱𐑂 𐐸𐐮𐑆 𐐸𐐬𐑊𐐨 𐐩𐑌𐐾𐐯𐑊, 𐑋𐐩𐐼 𐑄𐐨𐑆 𐑃𐐮𐑍𐑆 𐑌𐐬𐑌 𐐲𐑌𐐻𐐭 𐑋𐐨, 𐑌𐐱𐐻 𐐱𐑂 𐐯𐑌𐐨 𐐶𐐲𐑉𐑄𐐨𐑌𐐯𐑅 𐐱𐑂 𐑋𐐴𐑅𐐯𐑊𐑁, 𐑁𐐫𐑉 𐐌 𐐶𐐯𐑌𐐻 𐐰𐐺𐐵𐐻 𐐶𐐮𐑄 𐑄 𐑅𐐲𐑌𐑆 𐐱𐑂 𐐣𐐬𐑅𐐴𐐲, 𐑅𐐨𐐿𐐮𐑍 𐐻𐐭 𐐼𐐨𐑅𐐻𐑉𐐱𐐴 𐑄 𐐽𐐲𐑉𐐽 𐐱𐑂 𐐘𐐱𐐼; 𐐺𐐲𐐻 𐐺𐐨𐐸𐐬𐑊𐐼, 𐐘𐐱𐐼 𐑅𐐯𐑌𐐻 𐐸𐐮𐑆 𐐸𐐬𐑊𐐨 𐐩𐑌𐐾𐐯𐑊 𐐻𐐭 𐑅𐐻𐐱𐐹 𐐲𐑅 𐐺𐐴 𐑄 𐐶𐐩. 𐐈𐑌𐐼 𐐺𐐨𐐸𐐬𐑊𐐼, 𐐸𐐨 𐑅𐐹𐐩𐐿 𐐲𐑌𐐻𐐭 𐐲𐑅, 𐐰𐑆 𐐮𐐻 𐐶𐐲𐑉 𐑄 𐑂𐐱𐐮𐑅 𐐱𐑂 𐑃𐐲𐑌𐐼𐐲𐑉, 𐐰𐑌𐐼 𐑄 𐐸𐐬𐑊 𐐲𐑉𐑃 𐐼𐐮𐐼 𐐻𐑉𐐯𐑋𐐺𐑊 𐐺𐐨𐑌𐐨𐑃 𐐵𐑉 𐑁𐐨𐐻, 𐐰𐑌𐐼 𐐶𐐨 𐐫𐑊 𐑁𐐯𐑊 𐐻𐐭 𐑄 𐐲𐑉𐑃, 𐑁𐐫𐑉 𐑄 𐑁𐐨𐑉 𐐱𐑂 𐑄 𐐢𐐫𐑉𐐼 𐐿𐐩𐑋 𐐲𐐹𐐱𐑌 𐐲𐑅. 𐐒𐐲𐐻 𐐺𐐨𐐸𐐬𐑊𐐼, 𐑄 𐑂𐐱𐐮𐑅 𐑅𐐯𐐼 𐐲𐑌𐐻𐐭 𐑋𐐨, 𐐈𐑉𐐴𐑆. 𐐈𐑌𐐼 𐐌 𐐰𐑉𐐬𐑆 𐐰𐑌𐐼 𐑅𐐻𐐳𐐼 𐐲𐐹, 𐐰𐑌𐐼 𐐺𐐨𐐸𐐯𐑊𐐼 𐑄 𐐩𐑌𐐾𐐯𐑊. 𐐈𐑌𐐼 𐐸𐐨 𐑅𐐯𐐼 𐐲𐑌𐐻𐐭 𐑋𐐨, 𐐮𐑁 𐑄𐐵 𐐶𐐮𐑊𐐻 𐐱𐑂 𐑄𐐴𐑅𐐯𐑊𐑁 𐐺 𐐼𐐨𐑅𐐻𐑉𐐱𐐴𐐼, 𐑅𐐨𐐿 𐑌𐐬 𐑋𐐬𐑉 𐐻𐐭 𐐼𐐨𐑅𐐻𐑉𐐱𐐴 𐑄 𐐽𐐲𐑉𐐽 𐐱𐑂 𐐘𐐱𐐼.

2. 𐐈𐑌𐐼 𐐮𐐻 𐐿𐐩𐑋 𐐻𐐭 𐐹𐐰𐑅 𐑄𐐰𐐻 𐐌 𐑁𐐯𐑊 𐐻𐐭 𐑄 𐐲𐑉𐑃; 𐐰𐑌𐐼 𐐮𐐻 𐐶𐐱𐑆 𐑁𐐫𐑉 𐑄 𐑅𐐹𐐩𐑅 𐐱𐑂 𐑃𐑉𐐨 𐐼𐐩𐑆 𐐰𐑌𐐼 𐑃𐑉𐐨 𐑌𐐴𐐻𐑅, 𐑄𐐰𐐻 𐐌 𐐿𐐳𐐼 𐑌𐐱𐐻 𐐬𐐹𐑌 𐑋𐐴 𐑋𐐵𐑃: 𐑌𐐨𐑄𐐲𐑉 𐐸𐐰𐐼 𐐌 𐑄 𐐷𐐭𐑆 𐐱𐑂 𐑋𐐴 𐑊𐐮𐑋𐑆. 𐐈𐑌𐐼 𐑄 𐐩𐑌𐐾𐐯𐑊 𐑅𐐹𐐩𐐿 𐑋𐐬𐑉 𐑃𐐮𐑍𐑆 𐐲𐑌𐐻𐐭 𐑋𐐨, 𐐸𐐶𐐮𐐽 𐐶𐐲𐑉 𐐸𐐲𐑉𐐼 𐐺𐐴 𐑋𐐴 𐐺𐑉𐐯𐑄𐑉𐐯𐑌, 𐐺𐐲𐐻 𐐌 𐐼𐐮𐐼 𐑌𐐱𐐻 𐐸𐐨𐑉 𐑄𐐯𐑋; 𐑁𐐫𐑉 𐐸𐐶𐐯𐑌 𐐌 𐐸𐐲𐑉𐐼 𐑄 𐐶𐐲𐑉𐐼𐑆 𐐮𐑁 𐑄𐐵 𐐶𐐮𐑊𐐻 𐐺 𐐼𐐨𐑅𐐻𐑉𐐱𐐴𐐼 𐐱𐑂 𐑄𐐴𐑅𐐯𐑊𐑁, 𐑅𐐨𐐿 𐑌𐐬 𐑋𐐬𐑉 𐐻𐐭 𐐼𐐨𐑅𐐻𐑉𐐱𐐴 𐑄 𐐽𐐲𐑉𐐽 𐐱𐑂 𐐘𐐱𐐼, 𐐌 𐐶𐐱𐑆 𐑅𐐻𐑉𐐲𐐿 𐐶𐐮𐑄 𐑅𐐲𐐽 𐑀𐑉𐐩𐐻 𐑁𐐨𐑉 𐐰𐑌𐐼 𐐰𐑋𐐩𐑆𐑋𐐯𐑌𐐻, 𐑊𐐯𐑅𐐻 𐐹𐐲𐑉𐐸𐐰𐐹𐑅 𐐌 𐑇𐐳𐐼 𐐺 𐐼𐐨𐑅𐐻𐑉𐐱𐐴𐐼, 𐑄𐐰𐐻 𐐌 𐑁𐐯𐑊 𐐻𐐭 𐑄 𐐲𐑉𐑃, 𐐰𐑌𐐼 𐐌 𐐼𐐮𐐼 𐐸𐐨𐑉 𐑌𐐬 𐑋𐐬𐑉; 𐐒𐐲𐐻 𐐌 𐐶𐐱𐑆 𐑉𐐰𐐿𐐻 𐐶𐐮𐑄 𐐨𐐻𐐲𐑉𐑌𐐲𐑊 𐐻𐐫𐑉𐑋𐐯𐑌𐐻, 𐑁𐐫𐑉 𐑋𐐴 𐑅𐐬𐑊 𐐶𐐱𐑆 𐐸𐐰𐑉𐐬𐐼 𐐲𐐹 𐐻𐐭 𐑄 𐑀𐑉𐐩𐐻𐐯𐑅𐐻

𐐼𐐨𐑀𐑉𐐨, 𐐰𐑌𐐼 𐑉𐐰𐐿𐐻 𐐶𐐮𐑄 𐐫𐑊 𐑋𐐴 𐑅𐐮𐑌𐑆. 𐐏𐐩, 𐐌 𐐼𐐮𐐼 𐑉𐐨𐑋𐐯𐑋𐐺𐐲𐑉 𐐫𐑊 𐑋𐐴 𐑅𐐮𐑌𐑆 𐐰𐑌𐐼 𐐮𐑌𐐮𐐿𐐶𐐮𐐻𐐮𐑆, 𐑁𐐫𐑉 𐐸𐐶𐐮𐐽 𐐌 𐐶𐐱𐑆 𐐻𐐫𐑉𐑋𐐯𐑌𐐻𐐯𐐼 𐐶𐐮𐑄 𐑄 𐐹𐐩𐑌𐑆 𐐱𐑂 𐐸𐐯𐑊; 𐐷𐐩, 𐐌 𐑅𐐫 𐑄𐐰𐐻 𐐌 𐐸𐐰𐐼 𐑉𐐨𐐺𐐯𐑊𐐼 𐐰𐑀𐐯𐑌𐑅𐐻 𐑋𐐴 𐐘𐐱𐐼, 𐐰𐑌𐐼 𐑄𐐰𐐻 𐐌 𐐸𐐰𐐼 𐑌𐐱𐐻 𐐿𐐯𐐹𐐻 𐐸𐐮𐑆 𐐸𐐬𐑊𐐨 𐐿𐐱𐑋𐐰𐑌𐐼𐑋𐐯𐑌𐐻𐑅; 𐐷𐐩, 𐐰𐑌𐐼 𐐌 𐐸𐐰𐐼 𐑋𐐲𐑉𐐼𐐲𐑉𐐼 𐑋𐐯𐑌𐐨 𐐱𐑂 𐐸𐐮𐑆 𐐽𐐮𐑊𐐼𐑉𐐯𐑌, 𐐫𐑉 𐑉𐐰𐑄𐐲𐑉 𐑊𐐯𐐼 𐑄𐐯𐑋 𐐲𐐶𐐩 𐐲𐑌𐐻𐐭 𐐼𐐨𐑅𐐻𐑉𐐲𐐿𐑇𐐲𐑌; 𐐷𐐩, 𐐰𐑌𐐼 𐐮𐑌 𐑁𐐴𐑌 𐑅𐐬 𐑀𐑉𐐩𐐻 𐐸𐐰𐐼 𐐺𐐮𐑌 𐑋𐐴 𐐮𐑌𐐮𐐿𐐶𐐮𐐻𐐮𐑆, 𐑄𐐰𐐻 𐑄 𐑂𐐯𐑉𐐨 𐑃𐐫𐐻 𐐱𐑂 𐐿𐐲𐑋𐐮𐑍 𐐮𐑌𐐻𐐭 𐑄 𐐹𐑉𐐯𐑆𐐯𐑌𐑅 𐐱𐑂 𐑋𐐴 𐐘𐐱𐐼 𐐼𐐮𐐼 𐑉𐐰𐐿 𐑋𐐴 𐑅𐐬𐑊 𐐶𐐮𐑄 𐐮𐑌𐐯𐐿𐑅𐐹𐑉𐐯𐑅𐐮𐐺𐑊 𐐸𐐱𐑉𐐲𐑉. 𐐄, 𐑃𐐫𐐻 𐐌, 𐑄𐐰𐐻 𐐌 𐐿𐐳𐐼 𐐺 𐐺𐐰𐑌𐐮𐑇𐐻 𐐰𐑌𐐼 𐐺𐐨𐐿𐐲𐑋 𐐯𐐿𐑅𐐻𐐮𐑍𐐿𐐻 𐐺𐐬𐑃 𐑅𐐬𐑊 𐐰𐑌𐐼 𐐺𐐱𐐼𐐨, 𐑄𐐰𐐻 𐐌 𐑋𐐴𐐻 𐑌𐐱𐐻 𐐺 𐐺𐑉𐐫𐐻 𐐻𐐭 𐑅𐐻𐐰𐑌𐐼 𐐮𐑌 𐑄 𐐹𐑉𐐯𐑆𐐯𐑌𐑅 𐐱𐑂 𐑋𐐴 𐐘𐐱𐐼, 𐐻𐐭 𐐺 𐐾𐐲𐐾𐐼 𐐱𐑂 𐑋𐐴 𐐼𐐨𐐼𐑆. 𐐈𐑌𐐼 𐑌𐐵, 𐑁𐐫𐑉 𐑃𐑉𐐨 𐐼𐐩𐑆 𐐰𐑌𐐼 𐑁𐐫𐑉 𐑃𐑉𐐨 𐑌𐐴𐐻𐑅 𐐶𐐱𐑆 𐐌 𐑉𐐰𐐿𐐻, 𐐨𐑂𐐲𐑌 𐐶𐐮𐑄 𐑄 𐐹𐐩𐑌𐑆 𐐱𐑂 𐐲 𐐼𐐰𐑋𐐼 𐑅𐐬𐑊.

3. 𐐈𐑌𐐼 𐐮𐐻 𐐿𐐩𐑋 𐐻𐐭 𐐹𐐰𐑅 𐑄𐐰𐐻 𐐰𐑆 𐐌 𐐶𐐱𐑆 𐑄𐐲𐑅 𐑉𐐰𐐿𐐻 𐐶𐐮𐑄 𐐻𐐫𐑉𐑋𐐯𐑌𐐻, 𐐸𐐶𐐴𐑊 𐐌 𐐶𐐱𐑆 𐐸𐐰𐑉𐐬𐐼 𐐲𐐹 𐐺𐐴 𐑄 𐑋𐐯𐑋𐐬𐑉𐐨 𐐱𐑂 𐑋𐐴 𐑋𐐯𐑌𐐨 𐑅𐐮𐑌𐑆, 𐐺𐐨𐐸𐐬𐑊𐐼, 𐐌 𐑉𐐨𐑋𐐯𐑋𐐺𐐲𐑉𐐼 𐐫𐑊𐑅𐐬 𐐻𐐭 𐐸𐐰𐑂 𐐸𐐲𐑉𐐼 𐑋𐐴 𐑁𐐪𐑄𐐲𐑉 𐐹𐑉𐐱𐑁𐐯𐑅𐐴 𐐲𐑌𐐻𐐭 𐑄 𐐹𐐨𐐹𐐲𐑊, 𐐿𐐱𐑌𐑅𐐲𐑉𐑌𐐮𐑍 𐑄 𐐿𐐲𐑋𐐮𐑍 𐐱𐑂 𐐶𐐲𐑌 𐐖𐐨𐑆𐐲𐑅 𐐗𐑉𐐴𐑅𐐻, 𐐲 𐐝𐐲𐑌 𐐱𐑂 𐐘𐐱𐐼, 𐐻𐐭 𐐲𐐻𐐬𐑌 𐑁𐐫𐑉 𐑄 𐑅𐐮𐑌𐑆 𐐱𐑂 𐑄 𐐶𐐲𐑉𐑊𐐼. 𐐤𐐵 𐐰𐑆 𐑋𐐴 𐑋𐐴𐑌𐐼 𐐿𐐫𐐻 𐐸𐐬𐑊𐐼 𐐲𐐹𐐱𐑌 𐑄𐐮𐑅 𐑃𐐫𐐻, 𐐌 𐐿𐑉𐐴𐐼 𐐶𐐮𐑄𐐮𐑌 𐑋𐐴 𐐸𐐪𐑉𐐻, 𐐄 𐐖𐐨𐑆𐐲𐑅, 𐑄𐐵 𐐝𐐲𐑌 𐐱𐑂 𐐘𐐱𐐼, 𐐸𐐰𐑂 𐑋𐐲𐑉𐑅𐐨 𐐱𐑌 𐑋𐐨, 𐐸𐐭 𐐰𐑋 𐐮𐑌 𐑄 𐑀𐐫𐑊 𐐱𐑂 𐐺𐐮𐐻𐐲𐑉𐑌𐐯𐑅, 𐐰𐑌𐐼 𐐰𐑋 𐐯𐑌𐑅𐐲𐑉𐐿𐑊𐐼 𐐲𐐺𐐵𐐻 𐐺𐐴 𐑄 𐐯𐑂𐐲𐑉𐑊𐐰𐑅𐐻𐐮𐑍 𐐽𐐩𐑌𐑆 𐐱𐑂 𐐼𐐯𐑃. 𐐈𐑌𐐼 𐑌𐐵, 𐐺𐐨𐐸𐐬𐑊𐐼, 𐐸𐐶𐐯𐑌 𐐌 𐑃𐐫𐐻 𐑄𐐮𐑅, 𐐌 𐐿𐐳𐐼 𐑉𐐨𐑋𐐯𐑋𐐺𐐲𐑉 𐑋𐐴 𐐹𐐩𐑌𐑆 𐑌𐐬 𐑋𐐬𐑉; 𐐷𐐩, 𐐌 𐐶𐐱𐑆 𐐸𐐰𐑉𐐬𐐼 𐐲𐐹 𐐺𐐴 𐑄 𐑋𐐯𐑋𐐬𐑉𐐨 𐐱𐑂 𐑋𐐴 𐑅𐐮𐑌𐑆 𐑌𐐬 𐑋𐐬𐑉. 𐐈𐑌𐐼 𐐄, 𐐸𐐶𐐱𐐻 𐐾𐐦, 𐐰𐑌𐐼 𐐸𐐶𐐱𐐻 𐑋𐐪𐑉𐑂𐐯𐑊𐐲𐑅 𐑊𐐴𐐻 𐐌 𐐼𐐮𐐼 𐐺𐐨𐐸𐐬𐑊𐐼; 𐐷𐐩, 𐑋𐐴 𐑅𐐬𐑊 𐐶𐐱𐑆 𐑁𐐮𐑊𐐼 𐐶𐐮𐑄 𐐾𐐦 𐐰𐑆 𐐯𐐿𐑅𐐨𐐼𐐮𐑍 𐐰𐑆 𐐶𐐱𐑆 𐑋𐐴 𐐹𐐩𐑌; 𐐷𐐩, 𐐌 𐑅𐐩 𐐲𐑌𐐻𐐭 𐐷𐐭, 𐑋𐐴 𐑅𐐲𐑌, 𐑄𐐰𐐻 𐑄𐐩𐑉 𐐿𐐳𐐼 𐐺 𐑌𐐲𐑃𐐮𐑍 𐑅𐐬 𐐯𐐿𐑅𐐿𐐶𐐮𐑆𐐮𐐻 𐐰𐑌𐐼 𐑅𐐬 𐐺𐐮𐐻𐐲𐑉, 𐐰𐑆 𐐶𐐲𐑉 𐑋𐐴 𐐹𐐩𐑌𐑆. 𐐏𐐩, 𐐰𐑌𐐼 𐐲𐑀𐐯𐑌 𐐌 𐑅𐐩 𐐲𐑌𐐻𐐭 𐐷𐐭, 𐑋𐐴 𐑅𐐲𐑌, 𐑄𐐰𐐻 𐐱𐑌 𐑄 𐐲𐑄𐐲𐑉 𐐸𐐰𐑌𐐼 𐑄𐐩𐑉 𐐿𐐰𐑌 𐐺 𐑌𐐲𐑃𐐮𐑍 𐑅𐐬 𐐯𐐿𐑅𐐿𐐶𐐮𐑆𐐮𐐻 𐐰𐑌𐐼 𐑅𐐶𐐨𐐻 𐐰𐑆 𐐶𐐱𐑆 𐑋𐐴 𐐾𐐦; 𐐷𐐩, 𐑋𐐨𐑃𐐫𐐻 𐐌 𐑅𐐫, 𐐨𐑂𐐲𐑌 𐐰𐑆 𐐵𐑉 𐑁𐐪𐑄𐐲𐑉 𐐢𐐨𐐸𐐴 𐑅𐐫, 𐐘𐐱𐐼 𐑅𐐮𐐻𐐮𐑍 𐐲𐐹𐐱𐑌 𐐸𐐮𐑆 𐑃𐑉𐐬𐑌, 𐑅𐐲𐑉𐐵𐑌𐐼𐐯𐐼 𐐶𐐮𐑄 𐑌𐐲𐑋𐐺𐐲𐑉𐑊𐐯𐑅 𐐿𐐱𐑍𐐿𐐬𐑉𐑅𐐯𐑆 𐐱𐑂 𐐩𐑌𐐾𐐯𐑊𐑆, 𐐮𐑌 𐑄 𐐰𐐻𐐮𐐻𐐷𐐭𐐼 𐐱𐑂 𐑅𐐮𐑍𐐮𐑍 𐐰𐑌𐐼 𐐹𐑉𐐩𐑆𐐮𐑍 𐑄𐐩𐑉 𐐘𐐱𐐼; 𐐷𐐩, 𐐰𐑌𐐼 𐑋𐐴 𐑅𐐬𐑊 𐐼𐐮𐐼 𐑊𐐫𐑍 𐐻𐐭 𐐺 𐑄𐐩𐑉. 𐐒𐐲𐐻 𐐺𐐨𐐸𐐬𐑊𐐼, 𐑋𐐴 𐑊𐐮𐑋𐑆 𐐼𐐮𐐼 𐑉𐐨𐑅𐐨𐑂 𐑄𐐩𐑉 𐑅𐐻𐑉𐐯𐑍𐑃 𐐲𐑀𐐯𐑌, 𐐰𐑌𐐼 𐐌 𐑅𐐻𐐳𐐼 𐐲𐐹𐐱𐑌 𐑋𐐴 𐑁𐐨𐐻, 𐐰𐑌𐐼 𐐼𐐮𐐼 𐑋𐐰𐑌𐐮𐑁𐐯𐑅𐐻 𐐲𐑌𐐻𐐭 𐑄 𐐹𐐨𐐹𐐲𐑊 𐑄𐐰𐐻 𐐌 𐐸𐐰𐐼 𐐺𐐮𐑌 𐐺𐐫𐑉𐑌 𐐱𐑂 𐐘𐐱𐐼; 𐐷𐐩, 𐐰𐑌𐐼 𐑁𐑉𐐱𐑋 𐑄𐐰𐐻 𐐻𐐴𐑋 𐐨𐑂𐐲𐑌 𐐲𐑌𐐻𐐮𐑊 𐑌𐐵, 𐐌 𐐸𐐰𐑂 𐑊𐐩𐐺𐐲𐑉𐐼 𐐶𐐮𐑄𐐵𐐻 𐑅𐐨𐑅𐐮𐑍, 𐑄𐐰𐐻 𐐌 𐑋𐐴𐐻 𐐺𐑉𐐮𐑍 𐑅𐐬𐑊𐑆 𐐲𐑌𐐻𐐭 𐑉𐐨𐐹𐐯𐑌𐐻𐐰𐑌𐑅; 𐑄𐐰𐐻 𐐌 𐑋𐐴𐐻 𐐺𐑉𐐮𐑍 𐑄𐐯𐑋 𐐻𐐭 𐐻𐐩𐑅𐐻 𐐱𐑂 𐑄 𐐯𐐿𐑅𐐨𐐼𐐮𐑍 𐐾𐐦 𐐱𐑂 𐐸𐐶𐐮𐐽 𐐌 𐐼𐐮𐐼 𐐻𐐩𐑅𐐻; 𐑄𐐰𐐻 𐑄𐐩 𐑋𐐴𐐻 𐐫𐑊𐑅𐐬 𐐺 𐐺𐐫𐑉𐑌 𐐱𐑂 𐐘𐐱𐐼, 𐐰𐑌𐐼 𐐺 𐑁𐐮𐑊𐐼 𐐶𐐮𐑄 𐑄 𐐐𐐬𐑊𐐨 𐐘𐐬𐑅𐐻. 𐐏𐐩, 𐐰𐑌𐐼 𐑌𐐵 𐐺𐐨𐐸𐐬𐑊𐐼, 𐐄 𐑋𐐴 𐑅𐐲𐑌, 𐑄 𐐢𐐫𐑉𐐼 𐐼𐐲𐑃 𐑀𐐮𐑂 𐑋𐐨 𐐯𐐿𐑅𐐨𐐼𐐮𐑍𐑊𐐨 𐑀𐑉𐐩𐐻 𐐾𐐦 𐐮𐑌 𐑄 𐑁𐑉𐐭𐐻 𐐱𐑂 𐑋𐐴 𐑊𐐩𐐺𐐲𐑉𐑆; 𐑁𐐫𐑉 𐐺𐐨𐐿𐐫𐑆 𐐱𐑂 𐑄 𐐶𐐲𐑉𐐼 𐐸𐐶𐐮𐐽 𐐸𐐨 𐐸𐐰𐑆 𐐮𐑋𐐹𐐪𐑉𐐻𐐯𐐼 𐐲𐑌𐐻𐐭 𐑋𐐨, 𐐺𐐨𐐸𐐬𐑊𐐼, 𐑋𐐯𐑌𐐨 𐐸𐐰𐑂 𐐺𐐮𐑌 𐐺𐐫𐑉𐑌 𐐱𐑂 𐐘𐐱𐐼, 𐐰𐑌𐐼 𐐸𐐰𐑂 𐐻𐐩𐑅𐐻𐐯𐐼 𐐰𐑆 𐐌 𐐸𐐰𐑂 𐐻𐐩𐑅𐐻𐐯𐐼, 𐐰𐑌𐐼 𐐸𐐰𐑂 𐑅𐐨𐑌 𐐴 𐐻𐐭 𐐴, 𐐰𐑆 𐐌 𐐸𐐰𐑂 𐑅𐐨𐑌; 𐑄𐐩𐑉𐑁𐐬𐑉 𐑄𐐩 𐐼𐐭 𐑌𐐬 𐐱𐑂 𐑄𐐨𐑆 𐑃𐐮𐑍𐑆 𐐱𐑂 𐐸𐐶𐐮𐐽 𐐌 𐐸𐐰𐑂 𐑅𐐹𐐬𐐿𐐲𐑌, 𐐰𐑆 𐐌 𐐼𐐭 𐑌𐐬; 𐐰𐑌𐐼 𐑄 𐑌𐐱𐑊𐐯𐐾 𐐸𐐶𐐮𐐽 𐐌 𐐸𐐰𐑂 𐐮𐑆 𐐱𐑂 𐐘𐐱𐐼.

4. 𐐈𐑌𐐼 𐐌 𐐸𐐰𐑂 𐐺𐐮𐑌 𐑅𐐲𐐹𐐬𐑉𐐻𐐯𐐼 𐐲𐑌𐐼𐐲𐑉 𐐻𐑉𐐴𐐲𐑊𐑆 𐐰𐑌𐐼 𐐻𐑉𐐲𐐺𐐲𐑊𐑆 𐐱𐑂 𐐯𐑂𐐲𐑉𐐨 𐐿𐐴𐑌𐐼, 𐐷𐐩, 𐐰𐑌𐐼 𐐮𐑌 𐐫𐑊 𐑋𐐰𐑌𐐲𐑉 𐐱𐑂 𐐰𐑁𐑊𐐮𐐿𐑇𐐲𐑌𐑆; 𐐷𐐩, 𐐘𐐱𐐼 𐐸𐐰𐑆 𐐼𐐨𐑊𐐮𐑂𐐲𐑉𐐼 𐑋𐐨 𐑁𐑉𐐱𐑋 𐐹𐑉𐐮𐑆𐐲𐑌, 𐐰𐑌𐐼 𐑁𐑉𐐱𐑋 𐐺𐐱𐑌𐐼𐑆, 𐐰𐑌𐐼 𐑁𐑉𐐱𐑋 𐐼𐐯𐑃; 𐐷𐐩, 𐐰𐑌𐐼 𐐌 𐐼𐐭 𐐹𐐳𐐻 𐑋𐐴 𐐻𐑉𐐲𐑅𐐻 𐐮𐑌 𐐸𐐮𐑋, 𐐰𐑌𐐼 𐐸𐐨 𐐶𐐮𐑊 𐑅𐐻𐐮𐑊 𐐼𐐨𐑊𐐮𐑂𐐲𐑉 𐑋𐐨; 𐐰𐑌𐐼 𐐌 𐑌𐐬 𐑄𐐰𐐻 𐐸𐐨 𐐶𐐮𐑊 𐑉𐐩𐑆 𐑋𐐨 𐐲𐐹 𐐰𐐻 𐑄 𐑊𐐰𐑅𐐻 𐐼𐐩, 𐐻𐐭 𐐼𐐶𐐯𐑊 𐐶𐐮𐑄 𐐸𐐮𐑋 𐐮𐑌 𐑀𐑊𐐬𐑉𐐨; 𐐷𐐩, 𐐰𐑌𐐼 𐐌 𐐶𐐮𐑊 𐐹𐑉𐐩𐑆 𐐸𐐮𐑋 𐑁𐐫𐑉𐐯𐑂𐐲𐑉, 𐑁𐐫𐑉 𐐸𐐨 𐐸𐐰𐑆 𐐺𐑉𐐫𐐻 𐐵𐑉 𐑁𐐪𐑄𐐲𐑉𐑆 𐐵𐐻 𐐱𐑂 𐐀𐐾𐐮𐐹𐐻, 𐐰𐑌𐐼 𐐸𐐨 𐐸𐐰𐑆 𐑅𐐶𐐱𐑊𐐬𐐼 𐐲𐐹 𐑄 𐐀𐐾𐐮𐐹𐑇𐐲𐑌𐑆 𐐮𐑌 𐑄 𐐡𐐯𐐼 𐐝𐐨; 𐐰𐑌𐐼 𐐸𐐨 𐑊𐐯𐐼 𐑄𐐯𐑋 𐐺𐐴 𐐸𐐮𐑆 𐐹𐐵𐐲𐑉 𐐮𐑌𐐻𐐭 𐑄 𐐹𐑉𐐱𐑋𐐮𐑅𐐻 𐑊𐐰𐑌𐐼; 𐐷𐐩, 𐐰𐑌𐐼 𐐸𐐨 𐐸𐐰𐑆 𐐼𐐨𐑊𐐮𐑂𐐲𐑉𐐼 𐑄𐐯𐑋 𐐵𐐻 𐐱𐑂 𐐺𐐱𐑌𐐼𐐩𐐾 𐐰𐑌𐐼 𐐿𐐰𐐹𐐻𐐮𐑂𐐮𐐻𐐨 𐑁𐑉𐐱𐑋 𐐻𐐴𐑋 𐐻𐐭 𐐻𐐴𐑋; 𐐷𐐩, 𐐰𐑌𐐼 𐐸𐐨 𐐸𐐰𐑆 𐐫𐑊𐑅𐐬 𐐺𐑉𐐫𐐻 𐐵𐑉 𐑁𐐪𐑄𐐲𐑉𐑆 𐐵𐐻 𐐱𐑂 𐑄 𐑊𐐰𐑌𐐼 𐐱𐑂 𐐖𐐯𐑉𐐭𐑅𐐲𐑊𐐯𐑋; 𐐰𐑌𐐼 𐐸𐐨 𐐸𐐰𐑆

𐐱𐑊𐑅𐐬, 𐐺𐐴 𐐸𐐮𐑆 𐐯𐑂𐐲𐑉𐑊𐐰𐑅𐐻𐐮𐑍 𐐹𐐵𐐲𐑉, 𐐼𐐯𐑊𐐮𐑂𐐲𐑉𐐼 𐑄𐐯𐑋 𐐵𐐻 𐐱𐑂 𐐺𐐱𐑌𐐼𐐲𐐾 𐐰𐑌𐐼 𐐿𐐰𐐹𐐻𐐮𐑂𐐮𐐻𐐨, 𐑁𐑉𐐱𐑋 𐐻𐐴𐑋 𐐻𐐭 𐐻𐐴𐑋, 𐐨𐑂𐑌 𐐼𐐵𐑌 𐐻𐐭 𐑄 𐐹𐑉𐐯𐑆𐐲𐑌𐐻 𐐼𐐩; 𐐰𐑌𐐼 𐐌 𐐸𐐰𐑂 𐐱𐑊𐐶𐐩𐑆 𐑉𐐨𐐻𐐩𐑌𐐼 𐐮𐑌 𐑉𐐨𐑋𐐯𐑋𐐺𐑉𐐲𐑌𐑅 𐑄𐐯𐑉 𐐿𐐰𐐹𐐻𐐮𐑂𐐮𐐻𐐨; 𐐷𐐩, 𐐰𐑌𐐼 𐐷𐐨 𐐱𐑊𐑅𐐬 𐐫𐐻 𐐻𐐭 𐑉𐐨𐐻𐐩𐑌 𐐮𐑌 𐑉𐐨𐑋𐐯𐑋𐐺𐑉𐐲𐑌𐑅, 𐐰𐑆 𐐌 𐐸𐐰𐑂 𐐼𐐲𐑌, 𐑄𐐯𐑉 𐐿𐐰𐐹𐐻𐐮𐑂𐐮𐐻𐐨. 𐐒𐐲𐐻 𐐺𐐨𐐸𐐬𐑊𐐼, 𐑋𐐴 𐑅𐐲𐑌, 𐑄𐐮𐑅 𐐮𐑆 𐑌𐐱𐐻 𐐫𐑊: 𐑁𐐬𐑉 𐐷𐐨 𐐫𐐻 𐐻𐐭 𐑌𐐬 𐐰𐑆 𐐌 𐐼𐐭 𐑌𐐬, 𐑄𐐰𐐻 𐐮𐑌𐐰𐑆𐑋𐐲𐐽 𐐰𐑆 𐐷𐐨 𐑇𐐰𐑊 𐐿𐐨𐐹 𐑄 𐐿𐐱𐑋𐐰𐑌𐐼𐑋𐐲𐑌𐐻𐑅 𐐱𐑂 𐐘𐐱𐐼 𐐷𐐨 𐑇𐐰𐑊 𐐹𐑉𐐱𐑅𐐹𐐲𐑉 𐐮𐑌 𐑄 𐑊𐐰𐑌𐐼; 𐐰𐑌𐐼 𐐷𐐨 𐐫𐐻 𐐻𐐭 𐑌𐐬 𐐱𐑊𐑅𐐬, 𐑄𐐰𐐻 𐐮𐑌𐐰𐑆𐑋𐐲𐐽 𐐰𐑆 𐐷𐐨 𐐶𐐮𐑊 𐑌𐐱𐐻 𐐿𐐨𐐹 𐑄 𐐿𐐱𐑋𐐰𐑌𐐼𐑋𐐲𐑌𐐻𐑅 𐐱𐑂 𐐘𐐱𐐼, 𐐷𐐨 𐑇𐐰𐑊 𐐺𐐨 𐐿𐐲𐐻 𐐱𐑁 𐑁𐑉𐐱𐑋 𐐸𐐮𐑆 𐐹𐑉𐐯𐑆𐐲𐑌𐑅. 𐐤𐐵 𐑄𐐮𐑅 𐐮𐑆 𐐰𐐿𐐫𐑉𐐼𐐮𐑍 𐐻𐐭 𐐸𐐮𐑆 𐐶𐐲𐑉𐐼.

5. 𐐈𐑌𐐼 𐑌𐐵 𐑋𐐴 𐑅𐐲𐑌 𐐐𐐯𐑊𐐲𐑋𐐲𐑌, 𐐌 𐐿𐐱𐑋𐐰𐑌𐐼 𐐷𐐭 𐑄𐐰𐐻 𐐷𐐨 𐐻𐐩𐐿 𐑄 𐑉𐐯𐐿𐐫𐑉𐐼𐑆 𐐸𐐶𐐮𐐽 𐐸𐐰𐑂 𐐺𐐨𐑌 𐐯𐑌𐐻𐑉𐐲𐑅𐐻𐐲𐐼 𐐶𐐮𐑄 𐑋𐐨; 𐐰𐑌𐐼 𐐌 𐐱𐑊𐑅𐐬 𐐿𐐱𐑋𐐰𐑌𐐼 𐐷𐐭 𐑄𐐰𐐻 𐐷𐐨 𐐿𐐨𐐹 𐐩 𐑉𐐯𐐿𐐫𐑉𐐼 𐐱𐑂 𐑄𐐮𐑅 𐐹𐐨𐐹𐑊, 𐐰𐐿𐐫𐑉𐐼𐐮𐑍 𐐰𐑆 𐐌 𐐸𐐰𐑂 𐐼𐐲𐑌, 𐐲𐐹𐐱𐑌 𐑄 𐐹𐑊𐐩𐐻𐑅 𐐱𐑂 𐐤𐐨𐑁𐐴, 𐐰𐑌𐐼 𐐿𐐨𐐹 𐐫𐑊 𐑄𐐨𐑆 𐑃𐐮𐑍𐑆 𐑅𐐩𐐿𐑉𐐯𐐼 𐐸𐐶𐐮𐐽 𐐌 𐐸𐐰𐑂 𐐿𐐯𐐹𐐻, 𐐨𐑂𐑌 𐐰𐑆 𐐌 𐐸𐐰𐑂 𐐿𐐯𐐹𐐻 𐑄𐐯𐑋; 𐑁𐐬𐑉 𐐮𐐻 𐐮𐑆 𐑁𐐬𐑉 𐐩 𐐶𐐴𐑆 𐐹𐐲𐑉𐐹𐐲𐑅 𐑄𐐰𐐻 𐑄𐐩 𐐪𐑉 𐐿𐐯𐐹𐐻; 𐐰𐑌𐐼 𐑄𐐨𐑆 𐐹𐑊𐐩𐐻𐑅 𐐱𐑂 𐐺𐑉𐐪𐑅 𐐸𐐶𐐮𐐽 𐐿𐐱𐑌𐐻𐐩𐑌 𐑄𐐨𐑆 𐐯𐑌𐑀𐑉𐐩𐑂𐐮𐑍𐑆, 𐐸𐐶𐐮𐐽 𐐸𐐰𐑂 𐑄 𐑉𐐯𐐿𐐫𐑉𐐼𐑆 𐐱𐑂 𐑄 𐐸𐐬𐑊𐐨 𐑅𐐿𐑉𐐮𐐹𐐽𐐲𐑉𐑆 𐐲𐐹𐐱𐑌 𐑄𐐯𐑋, 𐐸𐐶𐐮𐐽 𐐸𐐰𐑂 𐑄 𐐾𐐨𐑌𐐨𐐰𐑊𐐱𐐾𐐨 𐐱𐑂 𐐵𐐲𐑉 𐑁𐐬𐑉𐑁𐐪𐑄𐐲𐑉𐑆, 𐐨𐑂𐑌 𐑁𐑉𐐱𐑋 𐑄 𐐺𐐨𐑀𐐮𐑌𐐮𐑍. 𐐈𐑌𐐼 𐐺𐐨𐐸𐐬𐑊𐐼, 𐐮𐐻 𐐸𐐰𐑆 𐐺𐐨𐑌 𐐹𐑉𐐱𐑁𐐯𐑅𐐴𐐼 𐐺𐐴 𐐵𐐲𐑉 𐑁𐐪𐑄𐐲𐑉𐑆, 𐑄𐐰𐐻 𐑄𐐩 𐑇𐐳𐐼 𐐺𐐨 𐐿𐐯𐐹𐐻 𐐰𐑌𐐼 𐐸𐐰𐑌𐐼𐐲𐐼 𐐼𐐵𐑌 𐑁𐑉𐐱𐑋 𐐶𐐲𐑌 𐐾𐐯𐑌𐐲𐑉𐐩𐑇𐐲𐑌 𐐻𐐭 𐐰𐑌𐐲𐑄𐐲𐑉, 𐐰𐑌𐐼 𐐺𐐨 𐐿𐐯𐐹𐐻 𐐰𐑌𐐼 𐐹𐑉𐐨𐑆𐐲𐑉𐑂𐐼 𐐺𐐴 𐑄 𐐸𐐰𐑌𐐼 𐐱𐑂 𐑄 𐐢𐐫𐑉𐐼, 𐐲𐑌𐐻𐐮𐑊 𐑄𐐩 𐑇𐐳𐐼 𐑀𐐬 𐑁𐐬𐑉𐑃 𐐲𐑌𐐻𐐭 𐐯𐑂𐐲𐑉𐐨 𐑌𐐩𐑇𐐲𐑌, 𐐿𐐮𐑌𐐼𐑉𐐯𐐼, 𐐻𐐲𐑍, 𐐰𐑌𐐼 𐐹𐐨𐐹𐑊, 𐑄𐐰𐐻 𐑄𐐩 𐑇𐐰𐑊 𐑌𐐬 𐐱𐑂 𐑄 𐑋𐐮𐑅𐐻𐐲𐑉𐐨𐑆 𐐿𐐲𐑌𐐻𐐩𐑌𐐼 𐑄𐐯𐑉𐐱𐑌. 𐐈𐑌𐐼 𐑌𐐵 𐐺𐐨𐐸𐐬𐑊𐐼, 𐐮𐑁 𐑄𐐩 𐐪𐑉 𐐿𐐯𐐹𐐻 𐑄𐐩 𐑋𐐲𐑅𐐻 𐑉𐐨𐐻𐐩𐑌 𐑄𐐯𐑉 𐐺𐑉𐐴𐐻𐑌𐐲𐑅; 𐐷𐐩, 𐐰𐑌𐐼 𐑄𐐩 𐐶𐐮𐑊 𐑉𐐨𐐻𐐩𐑌 𐑄𐐯𐑉 𐐺𐑉𐐴𐐻𐑌𐐲𐑅: 𐐷𐐩, 𐐰𐑌𐐼 𐐱𐑊𐑅𐐬 𐑇𐐰𐑊 𐐫𐑊 𐑄 𐐹𐑊𐐩𐐻𐑅 𐐸𐐶𐐮𐐽 𐐼𐐭 𐐿𐐱𐑌𐐻𐐩𐑌 𐑄𐐰𐐻 𐐸𐐶𐐮𐐽 𐐮𐑆 𐐸𐐬𐑊𐐨 𐑉𐐴𐐻. 𐐤𐐵 𐐷𐐨 𐑋𐐩 𐑅𐐲𐐹𐐬𐑆 𐑄𐐰𐐻 𐑄𐐮𐑅 𐐮𐑆 𐑁𐐭𐑊𐐮𐑇𐑌𐐲𐑅 𐐮𐑌 𐑋𐐨; 𐐺𐐲𐐻 𐐺𐐨𐐸𐐬𐑊𐐼 𐐌 𐑅𐐩 𐐲𐑌𐐻𐐭 𐐷𐐭, 𐑄𐐰𐐻 𐐺𐐴 𐑅𐑋𐐫𐑊 𐐰𐑌𐐼 𐑅𐐮𐑋𐐹𐑊 𐑃𐐮𐑍𐑆, 𐐪𐑉 𐑀𐑉𐐩𐐻 𐑃𐐮𐑍𐑆 𐐺𐑉𐐫𐐻 𐐻𐐭 𐐹𐐪𐑅; 𐐰𐑌𐐼 𐑅𐑋𐐫𐑊 𐑋𐐨𐑌𐑆 𐐮𐑌 𐑋𐐰𐑌𐐨 𐐮𐑌𐑅𐐻𐐲𐑌𐑅𐐲𐑆, 𐐼𐐲𐑃 𐐿𐐱𐑌𐑁𐐵𐑌𐐼 𐑄 𐐶𐐴𐑆. 𐐈𐑌𐐼 𐑄 𐐢𐐫𐑉𐐼 𐐘𐐱𐐼 𐐼𐐲𐑃 𐐶𐐲𐑉𐐿 𐐺𐐴 𐑋𐐨𐑌𐑆 𐐻𐐭 𐐺𐑉𐐮𐑍 𐐲𐐺𐐵𐐻 𐐸𐐮𐑆 𐑀𐑉𐐩𐐻 𐐰𐑌𐐼 𐐨𐐻𐐲𐑉𐑌𐐲𐑊 𐐹𐐲𐑉𐐹𐐲𐑅𐐲𐑆; 𐐰𐑌𐐼 𐐺𐐴 𐑂𐐯𐑉𐐨 𐑅𐑋𐐫𐑊 𐑋𐐨𐑌𐑆 𐑄 𐐢𐐫𐑉𐐼 𐐼𐐲𐑃 𐐿𐐱𐑌𐑁𐐵𐑌𐐼 𐑄 𐐶𐐴𐑆, 𐐰𐑌𐐼 𐐺𐑉𐐮𐑍𐐲𐑃 𐐲𐐺𐐵𐐻 𐑄 𐑅𐐰𐑊𐑂𐐩𐑇𐐲𐑌 𐐱𐑂 𐑋𐐰𐑌𐐨 𐑅𐐬𐑊𐑆.

6. 𐐈𐑌𐐼 𐑌𐐵, 𐐮𐐻 𐐸𐐰𐑆 𐐸𐐮𐑄𐐲𐑉𐐻𐐭 𐐺𐐨𐑌 𐐶𐐮𐑆𐐼𐐲𐑋 𐐮𐑌 𐐘𐐱𐐼, 𐑄𐐰𐐻 𐑄𐐨𐑆 𐑃𐐮𐑍𐑆 𐑇𐐳𐐼 𐐺𐐨 𐐹𐑉𐐨𐑆𐐲𐑉𐑂𐐼; 𐑁𐐬𐑉 𐐺𐐨𐐸𐐬𐑊𐐼, 𐑄𐐩 𐐸𐐰𐑂 𐐯𐑌𐑊𐐪𐑉𐐾𐐼 𐑄 𐑋𐐯𐑋𐐲𐑉𐐨 𐐱𐑂 𐑄𐐮𐑅 𐐹𐐨𐐹𐑊, 𐐷𐐩, 𐐰𐑌𐐼 𐐿𐐲𐑌𐑂𐐮𐑌𐑅𐐻 𐑋𐐰𐑌𐐨 𐐱𐑂 𐑄 𐐯𐑉𐐲𐑉 𐐱𐑂 𐑄𐐯𐑉 𐐶𐐩𐑆, 𐐰𐑌𐐼 𐐺𐑉𐐫𐐻 𐑄𐐯𐑋 𐐻𐐭 𐑄 𐑌𐐱𐑊𐐯𐐾 𐐱𐑂 𐑄𐐯𐑉 𐐘𐐱𐐼, 𐐲𐑌𐐻𐐭 𐑄 𐑅𐐰𐑊𐑂𐐩𐑇𐐲𐑌 𐐱𐑂 𐑄𐐯𐑉 𐑅𐐬𐑊𐑆. 𐐏𐐩, 𐐌 𐑅𐐩 𐐲𐑌𐐻𐐭 𐐷𐐭, 𐐶𐐲𐑉 𐐮𐐻 𐑌𐐱𐐻 𐑁𐐬𐑉 𐑄𐐨𐑆 𐑃𐐮𐑍𐑆 𐑄𐐰𐐻 𐑄𐐨𐑆 𐑉𐐯𐐿𐐫𐑉𐐼𐑆 𐐼𐐭 𐐿𐐱𐑌𐐻𐐩𐑌, 𐐸𐐶𐐮𐐽 𐐪𐑉 𐐱𐑌 𐑄𐐨𐑆 𐐹𐑊𐐩𐐻𐑅, 𐐊𐑋𐐲𐑌 𐐰𐑌𐐼 𐐸𐐮𐑆 𐐺𐑉𐐲𐑄𐑉𐐲𐑌 𐐿𐐳𐐼 𐑌𐐱𐐻 𐐸𐐰𐑂 𐐿𐐱𐑌𐑂𐐮𐑌𐑅𐐻 𐑅𐐬 𐑋𐐰𐑌𐐨 𐑃𐐵𐑆𐐲𐑌𐐼𐑆 𐐱𐑂 𐑄 𐐢𐐩𐑋𐐲𐑌𐐴𐐻𐑅, 𐐱𐑂 𐑄 𐐮𐑌𐐿𐐲𐑉𐐯𐐿𐐻 𐐻𐑉𐐲𐐼𐐮𐑇𐐲𐑌 𐐱𐑂 𐑄𐐯𐑉 𐑁𐐪𐑄𐐲𐑉𐑆; 𐐷𐐩, 𐑄𐐨𐑆 𐑉𐐯𐐿𐐫𐑉𐐼𐑆 𐐰𐑌𐐼 𐑄𐐯𐑉 𐐶𐐲𐑉𐐼𐑆, 𐐺𐑉𐐫𐐻 𐑄𐐯𐑋 𐐲𐑌𐐻𐐭 𐑉𐐯𐐹𐐯𐑌𐐻𐐲𐑌𐑅; 𐑄𐐰𐐻 𐐮𐑆, 𐑄𐐩 𐐺𐑉𐐫𐐻 𐑄𐐯𐑋 𐐻𐐭 𐑄 𐑌𐐱𐑊𐐯𐐾 𐐱𐑂 𐑄 𐐢𐐫𐑉𐐼 𐑄𐐯𐑉 𐐘𐐱𐐼, 𐐰𐑌𐐼 𐐻𐐭 𐑉𐐨𐐾𐐦𐑅 𐐮𐑌 𐐖𐐨𐑆𐐲𐑅 𐐗𐑉𐐴𐑅𐐻 𐑄𐐯𐑉 𐐡𐐨𐐼𐐨𐑋𐐲𐑉. 𐐈𐑌𐐼 𐐸𐐭 𐑌𐐬𐐲𐑃 𐐺𐐲𐐻 𐐸𐐶𐐱𐐻 𐑄𐐩 𐐶𐐮𐑊 𐐺𐐨 𐑄 𐑋𐐨𐑌𐑆 𐐱𐑂 𐐺𐑉𐐮𐑍𐐮𐑍 𐑋𐐰𐑌𐐨 𐑃𐐵𐑆𐐲𐑌𐐼𐑆 𐐱𐑂 𐑄𐐯𐑋, 𐐷𐐩, 𐐰𐑌𐐼 𐐱𐑊𐑅𐐬 𐑃𐐵𐑆𐐲𐑌𐐼𐑆 𐐱𐑂 𐐵𐐲𐑉 𐑅𐐻𐐮𐑁𐑌𐐯𐐿𐐻 𐐺𐑉𐐲𐑄𐑉𐐲𐑌, 𐑄 𐐤𐐨𐑁𐐴𐐻𐑅, 𐐸𐐭 𐐪𐑉 𐑌𐐵 𐐸𐐪𐑉𐐼𐐲𐑌𐐮𐑍 𐑄𐐯𐑉 𐐸𐐪𐑉𐐻𐑅 𐐮𐑌 𐑅𐐮𐑌 𐐰𐑌𐐼 𐐮𐑌𐐮𐐿𐐶𐐮𐐻𐐨𐑆, 𐐻𐐭 𐑄 𐑌𐐱𐑊𐐯𐐾 𐐱𐑂 𐑄𐐯𐑉 𐐡𐐨𐐼𐐨𐑋𐐲𐑉? 𐐤𐐵 𐑄𐐨𐑆 𐑋𐐮𐑅𐐻𐐲𐑉𐐨𐑆 𐐪𐑉 𐑌𐐱𐐻 𐐷𐐯𐐻 𐑁𐐳𐑊𐐨 𐑋𐐩𐐼 𐑌𐐬𐑌 𐐲𐑌𐐻𐐭 𐑋𐐨; 𐑄𐐯𐑉𐑁𐐬𐑉 𐐌 𐑇𐐰𐑊 𐑁𐐬𐑉𐐺𐐯𐑉. 𐐈𐑌𐐼 𐐮𐐻 𐑋𐐩 𐑅𐐲𐑁𐐴𐑅, 𐐮𐑁 𐐌 𐐬𐑌𐑊𐐨 𐑅𐐩, 𐑄𐐩 𐐪𐑉 𐐹𐑉𐐨𐑆𐐲𐑉𐑂𐐼 𐑁𐐬𐑉 𐐩 𐐶𐐴𐑆 𐐹𐐲𐑉𐐹𐐲𐑅, 𐐸𐐶𐐮𐐽 𐐹𐐲𐑉𐐹𐐲𐑅 𐐮𐑆 𐑌𐐬𐑌 𐐲𐑌𐐻𐐭 𐐘𐐱𐐼; 𐑁𐐬𐑉 𐐸𐐨 𐐼𐐲𐑃 𐐿𐐵𐑌𐑅𐐲𐑊 𐐮𐑌 𐐶𐐮𐑆𐐼𐐲𐑋 𐐬𐑂𐐲𐑉 𐐫𐑊 𐐸𐐮𐑆 𐐶𐐲𐑉𐐿𐑅, 𐐰𐑌𐐼 𐐸𐐮𐑆 𐐹𐐪𐑃𐑅 𐐪𐑉 𐑅𐐻𐑉𐐩𐐻, 𐐰𐑌𐐼 𐐸𐐮𐑆 𐐿𐐬𐑉𐑅 𐐮𐑆 𐐶𐐲𐑌 𐐨𐐻𐐲𐑉𐑌𐐲𐑊 𐑉𐐵𐑌𐐼. 𐐄 𐑉𐐨𐑋𐐯𐑋𐐺𐐲𐑉, 𐑉𐐨𐑋𐐯𐑋𐐺𐐲𐑉, 𐑋𐐴 𐑅𐐲𐑌 𐐐𐐯𐑊𐐲𐑋𐐲𐑌, 𐐸𐐵 𐑅𐐻𐑉𐐮𐐿𐐻 𐐪𐑉 𐑄 𐐿𐐱𐑋𐐰𐑌𐐼𐑋𐐲𐑌𐐻𐑅 𐐱𐑂 𐐘𐐱𐐼. 𐐈𐑌𐐼 𐐸𐐨 𐑅𐐯𐐼, 𐐮𐑁 𐐷𐐨 𐐶𐐮𐑊 𐐿𐐨𐐹 𐑋𐐴 𐐿𐐱𐑋𐐰𐑌𐐼𐑋𐐲𐑌𐐻𐑅, 𐐷𐐨 𐑇𐐰𐑊 𐐹𐑉𐐱𐑅𐐹𐐲𐑉 𐐮𐑌 𐑄 𐑊𐐰𐑌𐐼; 𐐺𐐲𐐻 𐐮𐑁 𐐷𐐨 𐐿𐐨𐐹 𐑌𐐱𐐻 𐐸𐐮𐑆 𐐿𐐱𐑋𐐰𐑌𐐼𐑋𐐲𐑌𐐻𐑅, 𐐷𐐨 𐑇𐐰𐑊 𐐺𐐨 𐐿𐐲𐐻 𐐱𐑁 𐑁𐑉𐐱𐑋 𐐸𐐮𐑆

𐐹𐑉𐐯𐑆𐐯𐑌𐑅. 𐐰𐑌𐐼 𐑌𐐵 𐑉𐐨𐑋𐐯𐑋𐐺𐐲𐑉, 𐑋𐐴 𐑅𐐲𐑌, 𐑄𐐰𐐻 𐐘𐐱𐐼 𐐸𐐰𐑆 𐐯𐑌𐐻𐑉𐐲𐑅𐐻𐐯𐐼 𐐷𐐭 𐐶𐐮𐑄 𐑄𐐨𐑆 𐑃𐐮𐑍𐑆, 𐐸𐐶𐐮𐐽 𐐪𐑉 𐑅𐐩𐐿𐑉𐐯𐐼, 𐐸𐐶𐐮𐐽 𐐸𐐨 𐐸𐐰𐑆 𐐿𐐯𐐹𐐻 𐑅𐐩𐐿𐑉𐐯𐐼, 𐐰𐑌𐐼 𐐫𐑊𐑅𐐬 𐐸𐐶𐐮𐐽 𐐸𐐨 𐐶𐐮𐑊 𐐿𐐨𐐹 𐐰𐑌𐐼 𐐹𐑉𐐨𐑆𐐲𐑉𐑂 𐑁𐐫𐑉 𐐲 𐐶𐐴𐑆 𐐹𐐲𐑉𐐹𐐲𐑅 𐐮𐑌 𐐸𐐮𐑋, 𐑄𐐰𐐻 𐐸𐐨 𐑋𐐩 𐑇𐐬 𐑁𐐫𐑉𐑃 𐐸𐐮𐑆 𐐹𐐵𐑉 𐐲𐑌𐐻𐐭 𐑁𐐷𐐭𐐻𐐷𐐭𐑉 𐐖𐐯𐑌𐐲𐑉𐐩𐑇𐐲𐑌𐑆.

7. 𐐰𐑌𐐼 𐑌𐐵 𐐺𐐨𐐸𐐬𐑊𐐼, 𐐌 𐐻𐐯𐑊 𐐷𐐭 𐐺𐐴 𐑄 𐐝𐐹𐐮𐑉𐐮𐐻 𐐱𐑂 𐐹𐑉𐐱𐑁𐐯𐑅𐐨, 𐑄𐐰𐐻 𐐮𐑁 𐐷 𐐻𐑉𐐰𐑌𐑅𐑀𐑉𐐯𐑅 𐑄 𐐿𐐲𐑋𐐰𐑌𐐼𐑋𐐯𐑌𐐻𐑅 𐐱𐑂 𐐘𐐱𐐼, 𐐺𐐨𐐸𐐬𐑊𐐼, 𐑄𐐨𐑆 𐑃𐐮𐑍𐑆 𐐸𐐶𐐮𐐽 𐐪𐑉 𐑅𐐩𐐿𐑉𐐯𐐼 𐑇𐐰𐑊 𐐺 𐐻𐐩𐐿𐑌 𐐲𐐶𐐩 𐑁𐑉𐐱𐑋 𐐷𐐭 𐐺𐐴 𐑄 𐐹𐐵𐑉 𐐱𐑂 𐐘𐐱𐐼, 𐐰𐑌𐐼 𐐷 𐑇𐐰𐑊 𐐺 𐐼𐐨𐑊𐐮𐑂𐐲𐑉𐐼 𐐲𐐹 𐐲𐑌𐐻𐐭 𐐝𐐩𐐻𐐲𐑌, 𐑄𐐰𐐻 𐐸𐐨 𐑋𐐩 𐑅𐐮𐑁𐐻 𐐷𐐭 𐐰𐑆 𐐽𐐰𐑁 𐐺𐐨𐑁𐐫𐑉 𐑄 𐐶𐐮𐑌𐐼; 𐐺𐐲𐐻 𐐮𐑁 𐐷 𐐿𐐨𐐹 𐑄 𐐿𐐲𐑋𐐰𐑌𐐼𐑋𐐯𐑌𐐻𐑅 𐐱𐑂 𐐘𐐱𐐼, 𐐰𐑌𐐼 𐐼𐐭 𐐶𐐮𐑄 𐑄𐐨𐑆 𐑃𐐮𐑍𐑆 𐐸𐐶𐐮𐐽 𐐪𐑉 𐑅𐐩𐐿𐑉𐐯𐐼, 𐐰𐐿𐐫𐑉𐐼𐐮𐑍 𐐻𐐭 𐑄𐐰𐐻 𐐸𐐶𐐮𐐽 𐑄 𐐢𐐫𐑉𐐼 𐐼𐐲𐑃 𐐿𐐲𐑋𐐰𐑌𐐼 𐐷𐐭, (𐑁𐐫𐑉 𐐷𐐭 𐑋𐐲𐑅𐐻 𐐰𐐹𐐨𐑊 𐐲𐑌𐐻𐐭 𐑄 𐐢𐐫𐑉𐐼 𐑁𐐫𐑉 𐐫𐑊 𐑃𐐮𐑍𐑆 𐐸𐐶𐐱𐐻𐑅𐐬𐐯𐑂𐐲𐑉 𐐷 𐑋𐐲𐑅𐐻 𐐼𐐭 𐐶𐐮𐑄 𐑄𐐯𐑋,) 𐐺𐐨𐐸𐐬𐑊𐐼, 𐑌𐐬 𐐹𐐵𐑉 𐐱𐑂 𐐲𐑉𐑃 𐐫𐑉 𐐸𐐯𐑊 𐐿𐐰𐑌 𐐻𐐩𐐿 𐑄𐐯𐑋 𐑁𐑉𐐱𐑋 𐐷𐐭, 𐑁𐐫𐑉 𐐘𐐱𐐼 𐐮𐑆 𐐹𐐵𐑉𐑁𐐳𐑊 𐐻𐐭 𐑄 𐑁𐐳𐑊𐑁𐐮𐑊𐐮𐑍 𐐱𐑂 𐐫𐑊 𐐸𐐮𐑆 𐐶𐐲𐑉𐐼𐑆; 𐑁𐐫𐑉 𐐸𐐨 𐐶𐐮𐑊 𐑁𐐳𐑊𐑁𐐮𐑊 𐐫𐑊 𐐸𐐮𐑆 𐐹𐑉𐐱𐑋𐐮𐑅𐐯𐑆 𐐸𐐶𐐮𐐽 𐐸𐐨 𐑇𐐰𐑊 𐑋𐐩𐐿 𐐲𐑌𐐻𐐭 𐐷𐐭, 𐑁𐐫𐑉 𐐸𐐨 𐐸𐐰𐑆 𐑁𐐳𐑊𐑁𐐮𐑊𐐼 𐐸𐐮𐑆 𐐹𐑉𐐱𐑋𐐮𐑅𐐯𐑆 𐐸𐐶𐐮𐐽 𐐸𐐨 𐐸𐐰𐑆 𐑋𐐩𐐼 𐐲𐑌𐐻𐐭 𐐵𐑉 𐑁𐐪𐑄𐐲𐑉𐑆. 𐑁𐐫𐑉 𐐸𐐨 𐐹𐑉𐐱𐑋𐐮𐑅𐐻 𐐲𐑌𐐻𐐭 𐑄𐐯𐑋 𐑄𐐰𐐻 𐐸𐐨 𐐶𐐳𐐼 𐐹𐑉𐐨𐑆𐐲𐑉𐑂 𐑄𐐨𐑆 𐑃𐐮𐑍𐑆 𐑁𐐫𐑉 𐐲 𐐶𐐴𐑆 𐐹𐐲𐑉𐐹𐐲𐑅 𐐮𐑌 𐐸𐐮𐑋, 𐑄𐐰𐐻 𐐸𐐨 𐑋𐐴𐐻 𐑇𐐬 𐑁𐐫𐑉𐑃 𐐸𐐮𐑆 𐐹𐐵𐑉 𐐲𐑌𐐻𐐭 𐑁𐐷𐐭𐐻𐐷𐐭𐑉 𐐖𐐯𐑌𐐲𐑉𐐩𐑇𐐲𐑌𐑆.

8. 𐐰𐑌𐐼 𐑌𐐵 𐐺𐐨𐐸𐐬𐑊𐐼, 𐐶𐐲𐑌 𐐹𐐲𐑉𐐹𐐲𐑅 𐐸𐐰𐑃 𐐸𐐨 𐑁𐐳𐑊𐑁𐐮𐑊𐐼, 𐐨𐑂𐑌 𐐻𐐭 𐑄 𐑉𐐯𐑅𐐻𐐬𐑉𐐩𐑇𐐲𐑌 𐐱𐑂 𐑋𐐯𐑌𐐮 𐑃𐐵𐑆𐐲𐑌𐐼𐑆 𐐱𐑂 𐑄 𐐢𐐩𐑋𐐲𐑌𐐴𐐻𐑅 𐐻𐐭 𐑄 𐑌𐐱𐑊𐐯𐐾 𐐱𐑂 𐑄 𐐻𐑉𐐭𐑃; 𐐰𐑌𐐼 𐐸𐐨 𐐸𐐰𐑃 𐑇𐐬𐑌 𐑁𐐫𐑉𐑃 𐐸𐐮𐑆 𐐹𐐵𐑉 𐐮𐑌 𐑄𐐯𐑋, 𐐰𐑌𐐼 𐐸𐐨 𐐶𐐮𐑊 𐐫𐑊𐑅𐐬 𐑅𐐻𐐮𐑊 𐑇𐐬 𐑁𐐫𐑉𐑃 𐐸𐐮𐑆 𐐹𐐵𐑉 𐐮𐑌 𐑄𐐯𐑋 𐐲𐑌𐐻𐐭 𐑁𐐷𐐭𐐻𐐷𐐭𐑉 𐐖𐐯𐑌𐐲𐑉𐐩𐑇𐐲𐑌𐑆; 𐑄𐐯𐑉𐑁𐐫𐑉 𐑄𐐩 𐑇𐐰𐑊 𐐺 𐐹𐑉𐐨𐑆𐐲𐑉𐑂𐐼; 𐑄𐐯𐑉𐑁𐐫𐑉 𐐌 𐐿𐐲𐑋𐐰𐑌𐐼 𐐷𐐭, 𐑋𐐴 𐑅𐐲𐑌 𐐐𐐯𐑊𐐲𐑋𐐲𐑌, 𐑄𐐰𐐻 𐐷 𐐺 𐐼𐐮𐑊𐐮𐐾𐐯𐑌𐐻 𐐮𐑌 𐑁𐐳𐑊𐑁𐐮𐑊𐐮𐑍 𐐫𐑊 𐑋𐐴 𐐶𐐲𐑉𐐼𐑆, 𐐰𐑌𐐼 𐑄𐐰𐐻 𐐷 𐐺 𐐼𐐮𐑊𐐮𐐾𐐯𐑌𐐻 𐐮𐑌 𐐿𐐨𐐹𐐮𐑍 𐑄 𐐿𐐲𐑋𐐰𐑌𐐼𐑋𐐯𐑌𐐻𐑅 𐐱𐑂 𐐘𐐱𐐼, 𐐰𐑆 𐑄𐐩 𐐪𐑉 𐑉𐐮𐐻𐑌.

9. 𐐰𐑌𐐼 𐑌𐐵, 𐐌 𐐶𐐮𐑊 𐑅𐐹𐐨𐐿 𐐲𐑌𐐻𐐭 𐐷𐐭 𐐿𐐲𐑌𐑅𐐲𐑉𐑌𐐮𐑍 𐑄𐐬𐑆 𐐻𐐶𐐯𐑌𐐻𐐨-𐑁𐐬𐑉 𐐹𐑊𐐩𐐻𐑅, 𐑄𐐰𐐻 𐐷 𐐿𐐨𐐹 𐑄𐐯𐑋, 𐑄𐐰𐐻 𐑄 𐑋𐐮𐑅𐐻𐐲𐑉𐐨𐑆 𐐰𐑌𐐼 𐑄 𐐶𐐲𐑉𐐿𐑅 𐐱𐑂 𐐼𐐪𐑉𐐿𐑌𐐯𐑅, 𐐰𐑌𐐼 𐑄𐐩𐑉 𐑅𐐨𐐿𐑉𐐯𐐻 𐐶𐐲𐑉𐐿𐑅, 𐐫𐑉 𐑄 𐑅𐐨𐐿𐑉𐐯𐐻 𐐶𐐲𐑉𐐿𐑅 𐐱𐑂 𐑄𐐬𐑆 𐐹𐐨𐐹𐑊, 𐐸𐐭 𐐸𐐰𐑂 𐐺𐐮𐑌 𐐼𐐨𐑅𐐻𐑉𐐦𐐼, 𐑋𐐩 𐐺 𐑋𐐩𐐼 𐑋𐐰𐑌𐐮𐑁𐐯𐑅𐐻 𐐲𐑌𐐻𐐭 𐑄𐐮𐑅 𐐹𐐨𐐹𐑊; 𐐷𐐩, 𐐫𐑊 𐑄𐐩𐑉 𐑋𐐲𐑉𐐼𐐲𐑉𐑆, 𐐰𐑌𐐼 𐑉𐐱𐐺𐐮𐑍𐑆, 𐐰𐑌𐐼 𐑄𐐩𐑉 𐐹𐑊𐐲𐑌𐐼𐐲𐑉𐐮𐑍𐑆, 𐐰𐑌𐐼 𐐫𐑊 𐑄𐐩𐑉 𐐶𐐮𐐿𐐯𐐼𐑌𐐯𐑅, 𐐰𐑌𐐼 𐐲𐐺𐐱𐑋𐐮𐑌𐐩𐑇𐐲𐑌𐑆, 𐑋𐐩 𐐺 𐑋𐐩𐐼 𐑋𐐰𐑌𐐮𐑁𐐯𐑅𐐻 𐐲𐑌𐐻𐐭 𐑄𐐮𐑅 𐐹𐐨𐐹𐑊; 𐐷𐐩, 𐐰𐑌𐐼 𐑄𐐰𐐻 𐐷 𐐹𐑉𐐨𐑆𐐲𐑉𐑂 𐑄𐐨𐑆 𐐼𐐴𐑉𐐯𐐿𐐻𐐲𐑉𐑆. 𐑁𐐫𐑉 𐐺𐐨𐐸𐐬𐑊𐐼, 𐑄 𐐢𐐫𐑉𐐼 𐑅𐐫 𐑄𐐰𐐻 𐐸𐐮𐑆 𐐹𐐨𐐹𐑊 𐐺𐐨𐑀𐐰𐑌 𐐻𐐭 𐐶𐐲𐑉𐐿 𐐮𐑌 𐐼𐐪𐑉𐐿𐑌𐐯𐑅, 𐐷𐐩, 𐐶𐐲𐑉𐐿 𐑅𐐨𐐿𐑉𐐯𐐻 𐑋𐐲𐑉𐐼𐐲𐑉𐑆 𐐰𐑌𐐼 𐐲𐐺𐐱𐑋𐐮𐑌𐐩𐑇𐐲𐑌𐑆; 𐑄𐐯𐑉𐑁𐐫𐑉 𐑄 𐐢𐐫𐑉𐐼 𐑅𐐯𐐼, 𐐮𐑁 𐑄𐐩 𐐼𐐮𐐼 𐑌𐐱𐐻 𐑉𐐨𐐹𐐯𐑌𐐻, 𐑄𐐩 𐑇𐐳𐐼 𐐺 𐐼𐐨𐑅𐐻𐑉𐐦𐐼 𐑁𐑉𐐱𐑋 𐐫𐑁 𐑄 𐑁𐐩𐑅 𐐱𐑂 𐑄 𐐲𐑉𐑃. 𐐰𐑌𐐼 𐑄 𐐢𐐫𐑉𐐼 𐑅𐐯𐐼, 𐐌 𐐶𐐮𐑊 𐐹𐑉𐐨𐐹𐐯𐑉 𐐲𐑌𐐻𐐭 𐑋𐐴 𐑅𐐲𐑉𐑂𐐲𐑌𐐻 𐐘𐐩𐑆𐐯𐑊𐐯𐑋, 𐐲 𐑅𐐻𐐬𐑌, 𐐸𐐶𐐮𐐽 𐑇𐐰𐑊 𐑇𐐴𐑌 𐑁𐐫𐑉𐑃 𐐮𐑌 𐐼𐐪𐑉𐐿𐑌𐐯𐑅 𐐲𐑌𐐻𐐭 𐑊𐐴𐐻, 𐑄𐐰𐐻 𐐌 𐑋𐐩 𐐼𐐮𐑅𐐿𐐲𐑂𐐲𐑉 𐐲𐑌𐐻𐐭 𐑋𐐴 𐐹𐐨𐐹𐑊 𐐸𐐭 𐑅𐐲𐑉𐑂 𐑋𐐨, 𐑄𐐰𐐻 𐐌 𐑋𐐩 𐐼𐐮𐑅𐐿𐐲𐑂𐐲𐑉 𐐲𐑌𐐻𐐭 𐑄𐐯𐑋 𐑄 𐐶𐐲𐑉𐐿𐑅 𐐱𐑂 𐑄𐐩𐑉 𐐺𐑉𐐯𐑄𐑉𐐯𐑌: 𐐷𐐩, 𐑄𐐩𐑉 𐑅𐐨𐐿𐑉𐐯𐐻 𐐶𐐲𐑉𐐿𐑅, 𐑄𐐩𐑉 𐐶𐐲𐑉𐐿𐑅 𐐱𐑂 𐐼𐐪𐑉𐐿𐑌𐐯𐑅, 𐐰𐑌𐐼 𐑄𐐩𐑉 𐐶𐐮𐐿𐐯𐐼𐑌𐐯𐑅 𐐰𐑌𐐼 𐐲𐐺𐐱𐑋𐐮𐑌𐐩𐑇𐐲𐑌𐑆. 𐐰𐑌𐐼 𐑌𐐵, 𐑋𐐴 𐑅𐐲𐑌, 𐑄𐐨𐑆 𐐼𐐴𐑉𐐯𐐿𐐻𐐲𐑉𐑆 𐐶𐐲𐑉 𐐹𐑉𐐨𐐹𐐯𐑉𐐼, 𐑄𐐰𐐻 𐑄 𐐶𐐲𐑉𐐼 𐐱𐑂 𐐘𐐱𐐼 𐑋𐐴𐐻 𐐺 𐑁𐐳𐑊𐑁𐐮𐑊𐐼, 𐐸𐐶𐐮𐐽 𐐸𐐨 𐑅𐐹𐐩𐐿, 𐑅𐐩𐐮𐑍: 𐐌 𐐶𐐮𐑊 𐐺𐑉𐐮𐑍 𐑁𐐫𐑉𐑃 𐐵𐐻 𐐱𐑂 𐐼𐐪𐑉𐐿𐑌𐐯𐑅 𐐲𐑌𐐻𐐭 𐑊𐐴𐐻 𐐫𐑊 𐑄𐐩𐑉 𐑅𐐨𐐿𐑉𐐯𐐻 𐐶𐐲𐑉𐐿𐑅 𐐰𐑌𐐼 𐑄𐐩𐑉 𐐲𐐺𐐱𐑋𐐮𐑌𐐩𐑇𐐲𐑌𐑆; 𐐰𐑌𐐼 𐐯𐐿𐑅𐐯𐐹𐐻 𐑄𐐩 𐑉𐐨𐐹𐐯𐑌𐐻, 𐐌 𐐶𐐮𐑊 𐐼𐐨𐑅𐐻𐑉𐐦 𐑄𐐯𐑋 𐑁𐑉𐐱𐑋 𐐫𐑁 𐑄 𐑁𐐩𐑅 𐐱𐑂 𐑄 𐐲𐑉𐑃; 𐐰𐑌𐐼 𐐌 𐐶𐐮𐑊 𐐺𐑉𐐮𐑍 𐐻𐐭 𐑊𐐴𐐻 𐐫𐑊 𐑄𐐩𐑉 𐑅𐐨𐐿𐑉𐐯𐐻𐑅 𐐰𐑌𐐼 𐐲𐐺𐐱𐑋𐐮𐑌𐐩𐑇𐐲𐑌𐑆, 𐐲𐑌𐐻𐐭 𐐯𐑂𐑉𐐨 𐑌𐐩𐑇𐐲𐑌 𐑄𐐰𐐻 𐑇𐐰𐑊 𐐸𐐨𐑉𐐰𐑁𐐻𐐲𐑉 𐐹𐐲𐑆𐐯𐑅 𐑄 𐑊𐐰𐑌𐐼. 𐐰𐑌𐐼 𐑌𐐵, 𐑋𐐴 𐑅𐐲𐑌, 𐐶𐐨 𐑅𐐨 𐑄𐐰𐐻 𐑄𐐩 𐐼𐐮𐐼 𐑌𐐱𐐻 𐑉𐐨𐐹𐐯𐑌𐐻; 𐑄𐐯𐑉𐑁𐐫𐑉 𐑄𐐩 𐐸𐐰𐑂 𐐺𐐮𐑌 𐐼𐐨𐑅𐐻𐑉𐐦𐐼, 𐐰𐑌𐐼 𐑄𐐲𐑅 𐑁𐐪𐑉 𐑄 𐐶𐐲𐑉𐐼 𐐱𐑂 𐐘𐐱𐐼 𐐸𐐰𐑆 𐐺𐐮𐑌 𐑁𐐳𐑊𐑁𐐮𐑊𐐼; 𐐷𐐩, 𐑄𐐩𐑉 𐑅𐐨𐐿𐑉𐐯𐐻 𐐲𐐺𐐱𐑋𐐮𐑌𐐩𐑇𐐲𐑌𐑆 𐐸𐐰𐑂 𐐺𐐮𐑌 𐐺𐑉𐐫𐐻 𐐵𐐻 𐐱𐑂 𐐼𐐪𐑉𐐿𐑌𐐯𐑅, 𐐰𐑌𐐼 𐑋𐐩𐐼 𐑌𐐬𐑌 𐐲𐑌𐐻𐐭 𐐲𐑅.

10. 𐐰𐑌𐐼 𐑌𐐵 𐑋𐐴 𐑅𐐲𐑌, 𐐌 𐐿𐐲𐑋𐐰𐑌𐐼 𐐷𐐭 𐑄𐐰𐐻 𐐷 𐑉𐐨𐐻𐐩𐑌 𐐫𐑊 𐑄𐐩𐑉 𐐬𐑄𐑆, 𐐰𐑌𐐼 𐑄𐐩𐑉 𐐿𐐲𐑂𐐯-

𐑌𐐲𐑌𐐻𐑅, 𐐰𐑌𐐼 𐑄𐐩𐑉 𐐲𐑀𐑉𐐨𐑋𐐲𐑌𐐻𐑅 𐐮𐑌 𐑄𐐩𐑉 𐑅𐐨𐐿𐑉𐐯𐐻 𐐲𐐺𐐱𐑋𐐮𐑌𐐩𐑇𐐲𐑌𐑆; 𐐷𐐩, 𐐰𐑌𐐼 𐐫𐑊 𐑄𐐩𐑉 𐑅𐐴𐑌𐑆 𐐰𐑌𐐼 𐑄𐐩𐑉 𐐶𐐲𐑌𐐼𐐲𐑉𐑆 𐐷 𐑇𐐰𐑊 𐐿𐐨𐐹 𐑁𐑉𐐱𐑋 𐑄𐐮𐑅 𐐹𐐨𐐹𐑊, 𐑄𐐰𐐻 𐑄𐐩 𐑌𐐬 𐑄𐐯𐑋 𐑌𐐱𐐻, 𐑊𐐯𐑅𐐻 𐐹𐐲𐑉𐐰𐐼𐑂𐐯𐑌𐐽𐐲𐑉 𐑄𐐩 𐑇𐐳𐐼 𐑁𐐫𐑊 𐐮𐑌𐐻𐐭 𐐼𐐪𐑉𐐿𐑌𐐯𐑅 𐐫𐑊𐑅𐐬, 𐐰𐑌𐐼 𐐺 𐐼𐐮𐑅𐐻𐑉𐑎𐐼. 𐐙𐐫𐑉 𐐺𐐨𐐸𐐬𐑊𐐼, 𐑄𐐩𐑉 𐐮𐑆 𐐲 𐐿𐐲𐑉𐑅 𐐲𐐹𐐱𐑌 𐐫𐑊 𐑄𐐮𐑅 𐑊𐐰𐑌𐐼, 𐑄𐐰𐐻 𐐼𐐨𐑅𐐻𐑉𐐲𐐿𐑇𐐲𐑌 𐑇𐐰𐑊 𐐿𐐲𐑋 𐐲𐐹𐐱𐑌 𐐫𐑊 𐑄𐐬𐑆 𐐶𐐲𐑉𐐿𐐲𐑉𐑆 𐐱𐑂 𐐼𐐪𐑉𐐿𐑌𐐯𐑅, 𐐰𐐿𐐫𐑉𐐼𐐮𐑍 𐐻𐐭 𐑄 𐐹𐐵𐐲𐑉 𐐱𐑂 𐐘𐐱𐐼, 𐐸𐐶𐐯𐑌 𐑄𐐩 𐐪𐑉 𐑁𐐳𐑊𐐨 𐑉𐐴𐐹; 𐑄𐐯𐑉𐑁𐐫𐑉 𐐌 𐐼𐐨𐑆𐐴𐑉 𐑄𐐰𐐻 𐑄𐐮𐑅 𐐹𐐨𐐹𐑊 𐑋𐐴𐐻 𐑌𐐱𐐻 𐐺 𐐼𐐮𐑅𐐻𐑉𐑎𐐼. 𐐜𐐯𐑉𐑁𐐫𐑉 𐐷 𐑇𐐰𐑊 𐐿𐐨𐐹 𐑄𐐨𐑆 𐑅𐐨𐐿𐑉𐐯𐐻 𐐹𐑊𐐰𐑌𐑆 𐐱𐑂 𐑄𐐩𐑉 𐐬𐑃𐑅 𐐰𐑌𐐼 𐑄𐐩𐑉 𐐿𐐲𐑂𐐯𐑌𐐲𐑌𐐻𐑅 𐑁𐑉𐐱𐑋 𐑄𐐮𐑅 𐐹𐐨𐐹𐑊, 𐐰𐑌𐐼 𐐬𐑌𐑊𐐨 𐑄𐐩𐑉 𐐶𐐮𐐿𐐯𐐼𐑌𐐯𐑅, 𐐰𐑌𐐼 𐑄𐐩𐑉 𐑋𐐲𐑉𐐼𐐲𐑉𐑆, 𐐰𐑌𐐼 𐑄𐐩𐑉 𐐲𐐺𐐱𐑋𐐮𐑌𐐩𐑇𐐲𐑌𐑆, 𐑇𐐰𐑊 𐐷 𐑋𐐩𐐿 𐑌𐐬𐑌 𐐲𐑌𐐻𐐭 𐑄𐐯𐑋; 𐐰𐑌𐐼 𐐷 𐑇𐐰𐑊 𐐻𐐨𐐽 𐑄𐐯𐑋 𐐻𐐭 𐐰𐐺𐐸𐐫𐑉 𐑅𐐲𐐽 𐐶𐐮𐐿𐐯𐐼𐑌𐐯𐑅, 𐐰𐑌𐐼 𐐲𐐺𐐱𐑋𐐮𐑌𐐩𐑇𐐲𐑌𐑆, 𐐰𐑌𐐼 𐑋𐐲𐑉𐐼𐐲𐑉𐑆; 𐐰𐑌𐐼 𐐷 𐑇𐐰𐑊 𐐫𐑊𐑅𐐬 𐐻𐐨𐐽 𐑄𐐯𐑋, 𐑄𐐰𐐻 𐑄𐐨𐑆 𐐹𐐨𐐹𐑊 𐐶𐐲𐑉 𐐼𐐮𐑅𐐻𐑉𐑎𐐼 𐐱𐑌 𐐰𐐿𐐵𐑌𐐻 𐐱𐑂 𐑄𐐩𐑉 𐐶𐐮𐐿𐐯𐐼𐑌𐐯𐑅, 𐐰𐑌𐐼 𐐲𐐺𐐱𐑋𐐮𐑌𐐩𐑇𐐲𐑌𐑆, 𐐰𐑌𐐼 𐑄𐐩𐑉 𐑋𐐲𐑉𐐼𐐲𐑉𐑆. 𐐙𐐫𐑉 𐐺𐐨𐐸𐐬𐑊𐐼, 𐑄𐐩 𐑋𐐲𐑉𐐼𐐲𐑉𐐼 𐐫𐑊 𐑄 𐐹𐑉𐐱𐑁𐐯𐐻𐑅 𐐱𐑂 𐑄 𐐢𐐫𐑉𐐼 𐐸𐐭 𐐿𐐩𐑋 𐐲𐑋𐐲𐑍 𐑄𐐯𐑋 𐐻𐐭 𐐼𐐨𐐿𐑊𐐩𐑉 𐐲𐑌𐐻𐐭 𐑄𐐯𐑋 𐐿𐐱𐑌𐑅𐐲𐑉𐑌𐐮𐑍 𐑄𐐩𐑉 𐐮𐑌𐐮𐐿𐐶𐐮𐐻𐐨𐑆; 𐐰𐑌𐐼 𐑄 𐐺𐑊𐐲𐐼 𐐱𐑂 𐑄𐐬𐑆 𐐸𐐭𐑋 𐑄𐐩 𐑋𐐲𐑉𐐼𐐲𐑉𐐼 𐐼𐐮𐐼 𐐿𐑉𐐴 𐐲𐑌𐐻𐐭 𐑄 𐐢𐐫𐑉𐐼 𐑄𐐩𐑉 𐐘𐐱𐐼 𐑁𐐫𐑉 𐑂𐐯𐑌𐐾𐐲𐑌𐑅 𐐲𐐹𐐱𐑌 𐑄𐐬𐑆 𐐸𐐭 𐐶𐐲𐑉 𐑄𐐩𐑉 𐑋𐐲𐑉𐐼𐐲𐑉𐐲𐑉𐑆: 𐐰𐑌𐐼 𐑄𐐲𐑅 𐑄 𐐾𐐲𐐾𐑋𐐯𐑌𐐻𐑅 𐐱𐑂 𐐘𐐱𐐼 𐐼𐐮𐐼 𐐿𐐲𐑋 𐐲𐐹𐐱𐑌 𐑄𐐨𐑆 𐐶𐐲𐑉𐐿𐐲𐑉𐑆 𐐱𐑂 𐐼𐐪𐑉𐐿𐑌𐐯𐑅 𐐰𐑌𐐼 𐑅𐐨𐐿𐑉𐐯𐐻 𐐿𐐱𐑋𐐺𐐮𐑌𐐩𐑇𐐲𐑌𐑆; 𐐷𐐩, 𐐰𐑌𐐼 𐐿𐐲𐑉𐑅𐐯𐐼 𐐺 𐑄 𐑊𐐰𐑌𐐼 𐑁𐐫𐑉𐐯𐑂𐐲𐑉 𐐰𐑌𐐼 𐐯𐑂𐐲𐑉 𐐲𐑌𐐻𐐭 𐑄𐐬𐑆 𐐶𐐲𐑉𐐿𐐲𐑉𐑆 𐐱𐑂 𐐼𐐪𐑉𐐿𐑌𐐯𐑅 𐐰𐑌𐐼 𐑅𐐨𐐿𐑉𐐯𐐻 𐐿𐐱𐑋𐐺𐐮𐑌𐐩𐑇𐐲𐑌𐑆; 𐐨𐑂𐐯𐑌 𐐲𐑌𐐻𐐭 𐐼𐐨𐑅𐐻𐑉𐐲𐐿𐑇𐐲𐑌, 𐐯𐐿𐑅𐐯𐐹𐐻 𐑄𐐩 𐑉𐐨𐐹𐐯𐑌𐐻 𐐺𐐨𐑁𐐬𐑉 𐑄𐐩 𐐪𐑉 𐑁𐐳𐑊𐐨 𐑉𐐴𐐹.

11. 𐐈𐑌𐐼 𐑌𐐵 𐑋𐐴 𐑅𐐲𐑌, 𐑉𐐨𐑋𐐯𐑋𐐺𐐲𐑉 𐑄 𐐶𐐲𐑉𐐼𐑆 𐐸𐐶𐐮𐐽 𐐌 𐐸𐐰𐑂 𐑅𐐹𐐬𐐿𐑌 𐐲𐑌𐐻𐐭 𐐷𐐭; 𐐻𐑉𐐲𐑅𐐻 𐑌𐐱𐐻 𐑄𐐬𐑆 𐑅𐐨𐐿𐑉𐐯𐐻 𐐹𐑊𐐰𐑌𐑆 𐐲𐑌𐐻𐐭 𐑄𐐮𐑅 𐐹𐐨𐐹𐑊, 𐐺𐐲𐐻 𐐻𐐨𐐽 𐑄𐐯𐑋 𐐰𐑌 𐐯𐑂𐐲𐑉𐑊𐐰𐑅𐐻𐐮𐑍 𐐸𐐩𐐻𐑉𐐯𐐼 𐐲𐑀𐐯𐑌𐑅𐐻 𐑅𐐮𐑌 𐐰𐑌𐐼 𐐮𐑌𐐮𐐿𐐶𐐮𐐻𐐨; 𐐹𐑉𐐨𐐽 𐐲𐑌𐐻𐐭 𐑄𐐯𐑋 𐑉𐐨𐐹𐐯𐑌𐐻𐐲𐑌𐑅, 𐐰𐑌𐐼 𐑁𐐩𐑃 𐐱𐑌 𐑄 𐐢𐐫𐑉𐐼 𐐖𐐨𐑆𐐲𐑅 𐐗𐑉𐐴𐑅𐐻; 𐐻𐐨𐐽 𐑄𐐯𐑋 𐐻𐐭 𐐸𐐲𐑋𐐺𐑊 𐑄𐐯𐑋𐑅𐐯𐑊𐑂𐑆, 𐐰𐑌𐐼 𐐻𐐭 𐐺 𐑋𐐨𐐿 𐐰𐑌𐐼 𐑊𐐬𐑊𐐨 𐐮𐑌 𐐸𐐪𐑉𐐻; 𐐻𐐨𐐽 𐑄𐐯𐑋 𐐻𐐭 𐐶𐐮𐑄𐑅𐐻𐐰𐑌𐐼 𐐯𐑂𐐲𐑉𐐨 𐐻𐐯𐑋𐐻𐐩𐑇𐐲𐑌 𐐱𐑂 𐑄 𐐼𐐯𐑂𐐮𐑊, 𐐶𐐮𐑄 𐑄𐐩𐑉 𐑁𐐩𐑃 𐐱𐑌 𐑄 𐐢𐐫𐑉𐐼 𐐖𐐨𐑆𐐲𐑅 𐐗𐑉𐐴𐑅𐐻; 𐐻𐐨𐐽 𐑄𐐯𐑋 𐐻𐐭 𐑌𐐯𐑂𐐲𐑉 𐐺 𐐶𐐨𐑉𐐨 𐐱𐑂 𐑀𐐳𐐼 𐐶𐐲𐑉𐐿𐑅, 𐐺𐐲𐐻 𐐻𐐭 𐐺 𐑋𐐨𐐿 𐐰𐑌𐐼 𐑊𐐬𐑊𐐨 𐐮𐑌 𐐸𐐪𐑉𐐻: 𐑁𐐫𐑉 𐑅𐐲𐐽 𐑇𐐰𐑊 𐑁𐐴𐑌𐐼 𐑉𐐯𐑅𐐻 𐐻𐐭 𐑄𐐩𐑉 𐑅𐐬𐑊𐑆. 𐐄 𐑉𐐨𐑋𐐯𐑋𐐺𐐲𐑉, 𐑋𐐴 𐑅𐐲𐑌, 𐐰𐑌𐐼 𐑊𐐲𐑉𐑌 𐐶𐐮𐑆𐐼𐐲𐑋 𐐮𐑌 𐑄𐐴 𐐷𐐭𐑃: 𐐷𐐩, 𐑊𐐲𐑉𐑌 𐐮𐑌 𐑄𐐴 𐐷𐐭𐑃 𐐻𐐭 𐐿𐐨𐐹 𐑄 𐐿𐐲𐑋𐐰𐑌𐐼𐑋𐐯𐑌𐐻𐑅 𐐱𐑂 𐐘𐐱𐐼; 𐐷𐐩, 𐐰𐑌𐐼 𐐿𐑉𐐴 𐐲𐑌𐐻𐐭 𐐘𐐱𐐼 𐑁𐐫𐑉 𐐫𐑊 𐑄𐐴 𐑅𐐲𐐹𐐬𐑉𐐻; 𐐷𐐩, 𐑊𐐯𐐻 𐐫𐑊 𐑄𐐴 𐐼𐐭𐐮𐑍𐑆 𐐺 𐐲𐑌𐐻𐐭 𐑄 𐐢𐐫𐑉𐐼, 𐐰𐑌𐐼 𐐸𐐶𐐮𐑄𐐲𐑉𐑅𐐬𐐯𐑂𐐲𐑉 𐑄𐐵 𐑀𐐬𐐯𐑅𐐻 𐑊𐐯𐐻 𐐮𐐻 𐐺 𐐮𐑌 𐑄 𐐢𐐫𐑉𐐼: 𐐷𐐩, 𐑊𐐯𐐻 𐑄𐐴 𐑃𐐫𐐻𐑅 𐐺 𐐼𐐮𐑉𐐯𐐿𐐻𐐯𐐼 𐐲𐑌𐐻𐐭 𐑄 𐐢𐐫𐑉𐐼; 𐐷𐐩, 𐑊𐐯𐐻 𐑄 𐐰𐑁𐐯𐐿𐑇𐐲𐑌𐑆 𐐱𐑂 𐑄𐐴 𐐸𐐪𐑉𐐻 𐐺 𐐹𐑊𐐩𐑅𐐻 𐐲𐐹𐐱𐑌 𐑄 𐐢𐐫𐑉𐐼 𐑁𐐫𐑉 𐐯𐑂𐐲𐑉; 𐐿𐐵𐑌𐑅𐐯𐑊 𐑄 𐐢𐐫𐑉𐐼 𐐮𐑌 𐐫𐑊 𐑄𐐴 𐐼𐐭𐐮𐑍𐑆, 𐐰𐑌𐐼 𐐸𐐨 𐐶𐐮𐑊 𐐼𐐮𐑉𐐯𐐿𐐻 𐑄 𐑁𐐫𐑉 𐑀𐐳𐐼; 𐐷𐐩, 𐐸𐐶𐐯𐑌 𐑄𐐵 𐑊𐐴𐐯𐑅𐐻 𐐼𐐵𐑌 𐐰𐐻 𐑌𐐴𐐻, 𐑊𐐴 𐐼𐐵𐑌 𐐲𐑌𐐻𐐭 𐑄 𐐢𐐫𐑉𐐼, 𐑄𐐰𐐻 𐐸𐐨 𐑋𐐩 𐐶𐐱𐐽 𐐬𐑂𐐲𐑉 𐐷𐐭 𐐮𐑌 𐐷𐐬𐑉 𐑅𐑊𐐨𐐹; 𐐰𐑌𐐼 𐐸𐐶𐐯𐑌 𐑄𐐵 𐑉𐐴𐑆𐐯𐑅𐐻 𐐮𐑌 𐑄 𐑋𐐫𐑉𐑌𐐮𐑍, 𐑊𐐯𐐻 𐑄𐐴 𐐸𐐪𐑉𐐻 𐐺 𐑁𐐳𐑊 𐐱𐑂 𐑃𐐰𐑍𐐿𐑅 𐐲𐑌𐐻𐐭 𐐘𐐱𐐼: 𐐰𐑌𐐼 𐐮𐑁 𐐷 𐐼𐐭 𐑄𐐨𐑆 𐑃𐐮𐑍𐑆, 𐐷 𐑇𐐰𐑊 𐐺 𐑊𐐮𐑁𐐻𐐯𐐼 𐐲𐐹 𐐰𐐻 𐑄 𐑊𐐰𐑅𐐻 𐐼𐐩.

12. 𐐈𐑌𐐼 𐑌𐐵, 𐑋𐐴 𐑅𐐲𐑌, 𐐌 𐐸𐐰𐑂 𐑅𐐲𐑋𐐸𐐶𐐱𐐻 𐐻𐐭 𐑅𐐩 𐐿𐐱𐑌𐑅𐐲𐑉𐑌𐐮𐑍 𐑄 𐑃𐐮𐑍 𐐸𐐶𐐮𐐽 𐐵𐑉 𐑁𐐪𐑄𐐲𐑉𐑆 𐐿𐐫𐑊 𐐲 𐐺𐐫𐑊, 𐐱𐑉 𐐼𐐮𐑉𐐯𐐿𐐻𐐲𐑉; 𐐱𐑉 𐐵𐑉 𐑁𐐪𐑄𐐲𐑉𐑆 𐐿𐐫𐑊𐐼 𐐮𐐻 𐐢𐐨𐐴𐐪𐐸𐐬𐑌𐐲, 𐐸𐐶𐐮𐐽 𐐮𐑆, 𐐺𐐨𐐮𐑍 𐐮𐑌𐐻𐐲𐑉𐐹𐑉𐐯𐐻𐐯𐐼, 𐐲 𐐿𐐲𐑋𐐹𐐲𐑅; 𐐰𐑌𐐼 𐑄 𐐢𐐫𐑉𐐼 𐐹𐑉𐐨𐐹𐐩𐑉𐐼 𐐮𐐻. 𐐈𐑌𐐼 𐐺𐐨𐐸𐐬𐑊𐐼, 𐑄𐐩𐑉 𐐿𐐰𐑌𐐱𐐻 𐐯𐑌𐐨 𐑋𐐰𐑌 𐐶𐐲𐑉𐐿 𐐪𐑁𐐻𐐲𐑉 𐑄 𐑋𐐰𐑌𐐲𐑉 𐐱𐑂 𐑅𐐬 𐐿𐐷𐐭𐑉𐐨𐐲𐑅 𐐲 𐐶𐐲𐑉𐐿𐑋𐐲𐑌𐑇𐐮𐐹. 𐐈𐑌𐐼 𐐺𐐨𐐸𐐬𐑊𐐼, 𐐮𐐻 𐐶𐐱𐑆 𐐹𐑉𐐨𐐹𐐩𐑉𐐼 𐐻𐐭 𐑇𐐬 𐐲𐑌𐐻𐐭 𐐵𐑉 𐑁𐐪𐑄𐐲𐑉𐑆 𐑄 𐐿𐐬𐑉𐑅 𐐸𐐶𐐮𐐽 𐑄𐐩 𐑇𐐳𐐼 𐐻𐑉𐐰𐑂𐐯𐑊 𐐮𐑌 𐑄 𐐶𐐮𐑊𐐼𐐲𐑉𐑌𐐯𐑅; 𐐰𐑌𐐼 𐐮𐐻 𐐼𐐮𐐼 𐐶𐐲𐑉𐐿 𐑁𐐫𐑉 𐑄𐐯𐑋 𐐰𐐿𐐫𐑉𐐼𐐮𐑍 𐐻𐐭 𐑄𐐩𐑉 𐑁𐐩𐑃 𐐮𐑌 𐐘𐐱𐐼: 𐑄𐐯𐑉𐑁𐐫𐑉, 𐐮𐑁 𐑄𐐩 𐐸𐐰𐐼 𐑁𐐩𐑃 𐐻𐐭 𐐺𐐨𐑊𐐨𐑂 𐑄𐐰𐐻 𐐘𐐱𐐼 𐐿𐐳𐐼 𐐿𐐫𐑆 𐑄𐐰𐐻 𐑄𐐬𐑆 𐑅𐐹𐐮𐑌𐐼𐑊𐑆 𐑇𐐳𐐼 𐐹𐐱𐐮𐑌𐐻 𐑄 𐐶𐐩 𐑄𐐩 𐑇𐐳𐐼 𐑀𐐬, 𐐺𐐨𐐸𐐬𐑊𐐼, 𐐮𐐻 𐐶𐐱𐑆 𐐼𐐲𐑌; 𐑄𐐯𐑉𐑁𐐫𐑉 𐑄𐐩 𐐸𐐰𐐼 𐑄𐐮𐑅 𐑋𐐮𐑉𐐲𐐿𐑊, 𐐰𐑌𐐼 𐐫𐑊𐑅𐐬 𐑋𐐯𐑌𐐨 𐐲𐑄𐐲𐑉 𐑋𐐮𐑉𐐲𐐿𐑊𐑆 𐑉𐐫𐐻 𐐺𐐴 𐑄 𐐹𐐵𐐲𐑉 𐐱𐑂 𐐘𐐱𐐼, 𐐼𐐩 𐐺𐐴 𐐼𐐩; 𐑌𐐯𐑂𐐲𐑉𐑄𐐯𐑊𐐯𐑅 𐐺𐐨𐐿𐐫𐑆 𐑄𐐬𐑆 𐑋𐐮𐑉𐐲𐐿𐑊𐑆 𐐶𐐲𐑉 𐐶𐐲𐑉𐐿𐐻 𐐺𐐴 𐑅𐑋𐐫𐑊 𐑋𐐨𐑌𐑆,

𐐮𐐻 𐐼𐐮𐐼 𐑇𐐬 𐐲𐑌𐐻𐐭 𐑄𐐯𐑋 𐑋𐐪𐑉𐑂𐐯𐑊𐐲𐑅 𐐶𐐲𐑉𐐿𐑅. 𐐜𐐩 𐐶𐐲𐑉 𐑅𐑊𐐱𐑃𐑁𐐳𐑊, 𐐰𐑌𐐼 𐑁𐐲𐑉𐑀𐐱𐐻 𐐻𐐭 𐐯𐐿𐑅𐐲𐑉𐑅𐐴𐑆 𐑄𐐩𐑉 𐑁𐐩𐑃 𐐰𐑌𐐼 𐐼𐐮𐑊𐐮𐐾𐐲𐑌𐑅, 𐐰𐑌𐐼 𐑄𐐯𐑌 𐑄𐐬𐑆 𐑋𐐪𐑉𐑂𐐯𐑊𐐲𐑅 𐐶𐐲𐑉𐐿𐑅 𐑅𐐨𐑅𐐻, 𐐰𐑌𐐼 𐑄𐐩 𐐼𐐮𐐼 𐑌𐐱𐐻 𐐹𐑉𐐬𐑀𐑉𐐯𐑅 𐐮𐑌 𐑄𐐩𐑉 𐐾𐐲𐑉𐑌𐐨; 𐑄𐐩𐑉𐑁𐐬𐑉 𐑄𐐩 𐐻𐐰𐑉𐐨𐐼 𐐮𐑌 𐑄 𐐶𐐮𐑊𐐼𐐲𐑉𐑌𐐯𐑅, 𐐬𐑉 𐐼𐐮𐐼 𐑌𐐱𐐻 𐐻𐑉𐐰𐑂𐐯𐑊 𐐲 𐐼𐐴𐑉𐐯𐐿𐐻 𐐿𐐬𐑉𐑅, 𐐰𐑌𐐼 𐐶𐐲𐑉 𐐰𐑁𐑊𐐮𐐿𐐻𐐯𐐼 𐐶𐐮𐑄 𐐸𐐲𐑍𐑀𐐲𐑉 𐐰𐑌𐐼 𐑃𐐲𐑉𐑅𐐻, 𐐺𐐨𐐿𐐫𐑆 𐐱𐑂 𐑄𐐩𐑉 𐐻𐑉𐐰𐑌𐑅𐑀𐑉𐐯𐑇𐐲𐑌𐑆.

13. 𐐰𐑌𐐼 𐑌𐐵, 𐑋𐐴 𐑅𐐲𐑌, 𐐌 𐐶𐐳𐐼 𐑄𐐰𐐻 𐐷𐐨 𐑇𐐳𐐼 𐐲𐑌𐐼𐐲𐑉𐑅𐐻𐐰𐑌𐐼 𐑄𐐰𐐻 𐑄𐐨𐑆 𐑃𐐮𐑍𐑆 𐐪𐑉 𐑌𐐱𐐻 𐐶𐐮𐑄𐐵𐐻 𐐲 𐑇𐐰𐐼𐐬; 𐑁𐐫𐑉 𐐰𐑆 𐐵𐑉 𐑁𐐪𐑄𐐲𐑉𐑆 𐐶𐐲𐑉 𐑅𐑊𐐱𐑃𐑁𐐳𐑊 𐐻𐐭 𐑀𐐮𐑂 𐐸𐐨𐐼 𐐻𐐭 𐑄𐐮𐑅 𐐿𐐲𐑋𐐹𐐲𐑅, (𐑌𐐵 𐑄𐐨𐑆 𐑃𐐮𐑍𐑆 𐐶𐐲𐑉 𐐻𐐯𐑋𐐹𐐬𐑉𐐲𐑊,) 𐑄𐐩 𐐼𐐮𐐼 𐑌𐐱𐐻 𐐹𐑉𐐱𐑅𐐹𐐲𐑉; 𐐨𐑂𐑌 𐑅𐐬 𐐮𐐻 𐐮𐑆 𐐶𐐮𐑄 𐑃𐐮𐑍𐑆 𐐸𐐶𐐮𐐽 𐐪𐑉 𐑅𐐹𐐮𐑉𐐮𐐻𐐷𐐭𐐲𐑊. 𐐙𐐫𐑉 𐐺𐐨𐐸𐐬𐑊𐐼, 𐐮𐐻 𐐮𐑆 𐐰𐑆 𐐨𐑆𐐨 𐐻𐐭 𐑀𐐮𐑂 𐐸𐐨𐐼 𐐻𐐭 𐑄 𐐶𐐲𐑉𐐼 𐐱𐑂 𐐗𐑉𐐴𐑅𐐻, 𐐸𐐶𐐮𐐽 𐐶𐐮𐑊 𐐹𐐫𐐮𐑌𐐻 𐐻𐐭 𐐷𐐭 𐐲 𐑅𐐻𐑉𐐩𐐻 𐐿𐐬𐑉𐑅 𐐻𐐭 𐐨𐐻𐐲𐑉𐑌𐐲𐑊 𐐺𐑊𐐮𐑅, 𐐰𐑆 𐐮𐐻 𐐶𐐱𐑆 𐑁𐐫𐑉 𐐵𐑉 𐑁𐐪𐑄𐐲𐑉𐑆 𐐻𐐭 𐑀𐐮𐑂 𐐸𐐨𐐼 𐐻𐐭 𐑄𐐮𐑅 𐐿𐐲𐑋𐐹𐐲𐑅, 𐐸𐐶𐐮𐐽 𐐶𐐳𐐼 𐐹𐐫𐐮𐑌𐐻 𐐲𐑌𐐻𐐭 𐑄𐐯𐑋 𐐲 𐑅𐐻𐑉𐐩𐐻 𐐿𐐬𐑉𐑅 𐐻𐐭 𐑄 𐐹𐑉𐐱𐑋𐐮𐑅𐐻 𐑊𐐰𐑌𐐼. 𐐈𐑌𐐼 𐑌𐐵 𐐌 𐑅𐐩, 𐐮𐑆 𐑄𐐩𐑉 𐑌𐐱𐐻 𐐲 𐐻𐐴𐐹 𐐮𐑌 𐑄𐐮𐑅 𐑃𐐮𐑍? 𐐙𐐫𐑉 𐐾𐐲𐑅𐐻 𐐰𐑆 𐑇𐐭𐑉𐑊𐐨 𐐰𐑆 𐑄𐐮𐑅 𐐼𐐴𐑉𐐯𐐿𐐻𐐲𐑉 𐐼𐐮𐐼 𐐺𐑉𐐮𐑍 𐐵𐑉 𐑁𐐪𐑄𐐲𐑉𐑆, 𐐺𐐴 𐑁𐐱𐑊𐐬𐐮𐑍 𐐮𐐻𐑅 𐐿𐐬𐑉𐑅, 𐐻𐐭 𐑄 𐐹𐑉𐐱𐑋𐐮𐑅𐐻 𐑊𐐰𐑌𐐼, 𐑇𐐰𐑊 𐑄 𐐶𐐲𐑉𐐼𐑆 𐐱𐑂 𐐗𐑉𐐴𐑅𐐻, 𐐮𐑁 𐐶𐐨 𐑁𐐱𐑊𐐬 𐑄𐐩𐑉 𐐿𐐬𐑉𐑅, 𐐿𐐰𐑉𐐨 𐐲𐑅 𐐺𐐨𐐷𐐱𐑌𐐼 𐑄𐐮𐑅 𐑂𐐩𐑊 𐐱𐑂 𐑅𐐱𐑉𐐬, 𐐮𐑌𐐻𐐭 𐐲 𐑁𐐪𐑉 𐐺𐐯𐐻𐐲𐑉 𐑊𐐰𐑌𐐼 𐐱𐑂 𐐹𐑉𐐱𐑋𐐮𐑅.

14. 𐐄 𐑋𐐴 𐑅𐐲𐑌, 𐐼𐐭 𐑌𐐱𐐻 𐑊𐐯𐐻 𐐲𐑅 𐐺𐐨 𐑅𐑊𐐱𐑃𐑁𐐳𐑊 𐐺𐐨𐐿𐐫𐑆 𐐱𐑂 𐑄 𐐨𐑆𐐨𐑌𐐯𐑅 𐐱𐑂 𐑄 𐐶𐐩; 𐑁𐐫𐑉 𐑅𐐬 𐐶𐐱𐑆 𐐮𐐻 𐐶𐐮𐑄 𐐵𐑉 𐑁𐐪𐑄𐐲𐑉𐑆; 𐑁𐐫𐑉 𐑅𐐬 𐐶𐐱𐑆 𐐮𐐻 𐐹𐑉𐐨𐐹𐐩𐑉𐐼 𐑁𐐫𐑉 𐑄𐐯𐑋, 𐑄𐐰𐐻 𐐮𐑁 𐑄𐐩 𐐶𐐳𐐼 𐑊𐐳𐐿, 𐑄𐐩 𐑋𐐴𐐻 𐑊𐐮𐑂; 𐐨𐑂𐑌 𐑅𐐬 𐐮𐐻 𐐮𐑆 𐐶𐐮𐑄 𐐲𐑅. 𐐜 𐐶𐐩 𐐮𐑆 𐐹𐑉𐐨𐐹𐐩𐑉𐐼, 𐐰𐑌𐐼 𐐮𐑁 𐐶𐐨 𐐶𐐮𐑊 𐑊𐐳𐐿, 𐐶𐐨 𐑋𐐩 𐑊𐐮𐑂 𐑁𐐫𐑉 𐐯𐑂𐐲𐑉. 𐐈𐑌𐐼 𐑌𐐵, 𐑋𐐴 𐑅𐐲𐑌, 𐑅𐐨 𐑄𐐰𐐻 𐐷𐐨 𐐻𐐩𐐿 𐐿𐐩𐑉 𐐱𐑂 𐑄𐐨𐑆 𐑅𐐩𐐿𐑉𐐯𐐼 𐑃𐐮𐑍𐑆; 𐐷𐐩, 𐑅𐐨 𐑄𐐰𐐻 𐐷𐐨 𐑊𐐳𐐿 𐐻𐐭 𐐘𐐱𐐼 𐐰𐑌𐐼 𐑊𐐮𐑂. 𐐘𐐬 𐐲𐑌𐐻𐐭 𐑄𐐮𐑅 𐐹𐐨𐐹𐑊, 𐐰𐑌𐐼 𐐼𐐨𐐿𐑊𐐩𐑉 𐑄 𐐶𐐲𐑉𐐼, 𐐰𐑌𐐼 𐐺𐐨 𐑅𐐬𐐺𐐲𐑉. 𐐣𐐴 𐑅𐐲𐑌, 𐑁𐐩𐑉𐐶𐐯𐑊.

𐐕𐐈𐐑𐐓𐐊𐐡 XVIII.

𐐜 𐐗𐐲𐑋𐐰𐑌𐐼𐑋𐐲𐑌𐐻𐑅 𐐱𐑂 𐐈𐑊𐑋𐐲 𐐻𐐭 𐐸𐐮𐑆 𐑅𐐲𐑌 𐐟𐐮𐐺𐑊𐐲𐑌.

1. 𐐣𐐴 𐑅𐐲𐑌, 𐑀𐐮𐑂 𐐨𐑉 𐐻𐐭 𐑋𐐴 𐐶𐐲𐑉𐐼𐑆, 𐑁𐐫𐑉 𐐌 𐑅𐐩 𐐲𐑌𐐻𐐭 𐐷𐐭, 𐐨𐑂𐑌 𐐰𐑆 𐐌 𐑅𐐯𐐼 𐐲𐑌𐐻𐐭 𐐐𐐨𐑊𐐩𐑋𐐲𐑌, 𐑄𐐰𐐻 𐐮𐑌𐐰𐑆𐑋𐐲𐐽 𐐰𐑆 𐐷𐐨 𐑇𐐰𐑊 𐐿𐐨𐐹 𐑄 𐐿𐐲𐑋𐐰𐑌𐐼𐑋𐐲𐑌𐐻𐑅 𐐱𐑂 𐐘𐐱𐐼, 𐐷𐐨 𐑇𐐰𐑊 𐐹𐑉𐐱𐑅𐐹𐐲𐑉 𐐮𐑌 𐑄 𐑊𐐰𐑌𐐼; 𐐰𐑌𐐼 𐐮𐑌𐐰𐑆𐑋𐐲𐐽 𐐰𐑆 𐐷𐐨 𐐶𐐮𐑊 𐑌𐐱𐐻 𐐿𐐨𐐹 𐑄 𐐿𐐲𐑋𐐰𐑌𐐼𐑋𐐲𐑌𐐻𐑅 𐐱𐑂 𐐘𐐱𐐼 𐐷𐐨 𐑇𐐰𐑊 𐐺𐐨 𐐿𐐲𐐻 𐐫𐑁 𐑁𐑉𐐱𐑋 𐐸𐐮𐑆 𐐹𐑉𐐯𐑆𐐯𐑌𐑅. 𐐈𐑌𐐼 𐑌𐐵, 𐑋𐐴 𐑅𐐲𐑌, 𐐌 𐐻𐑉𐐲𐑅𐐻 𐑄𐐰𐐻 𐐌 𐑇𐐰𐑊 𐐸𐐰𐑂 𐑀𐑉𐐩𐐻 𐐾𐐫𐐮 𐐮𐑌 𐐷𐐭, 𐐺𐐨𐐿𐐫𐑆 𐐱𐑂 𐐷𐐬𐑉 𐑅𐐻𐐯𐐼𐐨𐑌𐐯𐑅 𐐰𐑌𐐼 𐐷𐐬𐑉 𐑁𐐩𐑃𐑁𐐳𐑊𐑌𐐯𐑅 𐐲𐑌𐐻𐐭 𐐘𐐱𐐼; 𐑁𐐫𐑉 𐐰𐑆 𐐷𐐭 𐐸𐐰𐑂 𐐿𐐲𐑋𐐯𐑌𐑅𐐻 𐐮𐑌 𐐷𐐬𐑉 𐐷𐐭𐑃, 𐐻𐐭 𐑊𐐳𐐿 𐐻𐐭 𐑄 𐐢𐐫𐑉𐐼 𐐷𐐬𐑉 𐐘𐐱𐐼, 𐐨𐑂𐑌 𐑅𐐬 𐐌 𐐸𐐬𐐹 𐑄𐐰𐐻 𐐷𐐭 𐐶𐐮𐑊 𐐿𐐲𐑌𐐻𐐮𐑌𐐷𐐭 𐐮𐑌 𐐿𐐨𐐹𐐮𐑍 𐐸𐐮𐑆 𐐿𐐲𐑋𐐰𐑌𐐼𐑋𐐲𐑌𐐻𐑅; 𐑁𐐫𐑉 𐐺𐑊𐐯𐑅𐐯𐐼 𐐮𐑆 𐐸𐐨 𐑄𐐰𐐻 𐐯𐑌𐐼𐐭𐑉𐐯𐑃 𐐻𐐭 𐑄 𐐯𐑌𐐼. 𐐌 𐑅𐐩 𐐲𐑌𐐻𐐭 𐐷𐐭, 𐑋𐐴 𐑅𐐲𐑌, 𐑄𐐰𐐻 𐐌 𐐸𐐰𐑂 𐐸𐐰𐐼 𐑀𐑉𐐩𐐻 𐐾𐐫𐐮 𐐮𐑌 𐑄𐐨, 𐐫𐑊𐑉𐐯𐐼𐐨, 𐐺𐐨𐐿𐐫𐑆 𐐱𐑂 𐑄𐐴 𐑁𐐩𐑃𐑁𐐳𐑊𐑌𐐯𐑅 𐐰𐑌𐐼 𐑄𐐴 𐐼𐐮𐑊𐐮𐐾𐐲𐑌𐑅, 𐐰𐑌𐐼 𐑄𐐴 𐐹𐐩𐑇𐐯𐑌𐑅, 𐐰𐑌𐐼 𐑄𐐴 𐑊𐐫𐑍 𐑅𐐲𐑁𐐲𐑉𐐮𐑍 𐐲𐑋𐐲𐑍 𐑄 𐐹𐐨𐐹𐑊 𐐱𐑂 𐑄 𐐞𐐬𐑉𐐲𐑋𐐴𐐻𐑅. 𐐙𐐫𐑉 𐐌 𐑌𐐬 𐑄𐐰𐐻 𐑄𐐵 𐐶𐐱𐑅𐐻 𐐮𐑌 𐐺𐐱𐑌𐐼𐑆; 𐐷𐐩, 𐐰𐑌𐐼 𐐌 𐐫𐑊𐑅𐐬 𐑌𐐬 𐑄𐐰𐐻 𐑄𐐵 𐐶𐐱𐑅𐐻 𐑅𐐻𐐬𐑌𐐼 𐑁𐐫𐑉 𐑄 𐐶𐐲𐑉𐐼'𐑆 𐑅𐐩𐐿; 𐐰𐑌𐐼 𐑄𐐵 𐐼𐐮𐐼𐑅𐐻 𐐺𐐩𐑉 𐐫𐑊 𐑄𐐨𐑆 𐑃𐐮𐑍𐑆 𐐶𐐮𐑄 𐐹𐐩𐑇𐐯𐑌𐑅, 𐐺𐐨𐐿𐐫𐑆 𐑄 𐐢𐐫𐑉𐐼 𐐶𐐱𐑆 𐐶𐐮𐑄 𐑄𐐨; 𐐰𐑌𐐼 𐑌𐐵 𐑄𐐵 𐑌𐐬𐐯𐑅𐐻 𐑄𐐰𐐻 𐑄 𐐢𐐫𐑉𐐼 𐐼𐐮𐐼 𐐼𐐨𐑊𐐮𐑂𐐲𐑉 𐑄𐐨.

2. 𐐈𐑌𐐼 𐑌𐐵 𐑋𐐴 𐑅𐐲𐑌, 𐐟𐐮𐐺𐑊𐐲𐑌, 𐐌 𐐶𐐳𐐼 𐑄𐐰𐐻 𐐷𐐨 𐑇𐐳𐐼 𐑉𐐨𐑋𐐯𐑋𐐺𐐲𐑉 𐑄𐐰𐐻 𐐰𐑆 𐑋𐐲𐐽 𐐰𐑆 𐐷𐐨 𐑇𐐰𐑊 𐐹𐐳𐐻 𐐷𐐬𐑉 𐐻𐑉𐐲𐑅𐐻 𐐮𐑌 𐐘𐐱𐐼, 𐐨𐑂𐑌 𐑅𐐬 𐑋𐐲𐐽 𐐷𐐨 𐑇𐐰𐑊 𐐺𐐨 𐐼𐐨𐑊𐐮𐑂𐐲𐑉𐐼 𐐵𐐻 𐐱𐑂 𐐷𐐬𐑉 𐐻𐑉𐐴𐐲𐑊𐑆, 𐐰𐑌𐐼 𐐷𐐬𐑉 𐐻𐑉𐐲𐐺𐑊𐑆, 𐐰𐑌𐐼 𐐷𐐬𐑉 𐐰𐑁𐑊𐐮𐐿𐑇𐐲𐑌𐑆, 𐐰𐑌𐐼 𐐷𐐨 𐑇𐐰𐑊 𐐺𐐨 𐑊𐐮𐑁𐐻𐐯𐐼 𐐲𐐹 𐐰𐐻 𐑄 𐑊𐐰𐑅𐐻 𐐼𐐩. 𐐤𐐵, 𐑋𐐴 𐑅𐐲𐑌,

𐐌 𐐶𐐳𐐼 𐑌𐐱𐐻 𐑄𐐰𐐻 𐐷 𐑇𐐳𐐼 𐑃𐐮𐑍𐐿 𐑄𐐰𐐻 𐐌 𐑌𐐬 𐑄𐐨𐑆 𐑃𐐮𐑍𐑆 𐐱𐑂 𐑋𐐴𐑅𐐯𐑊𐑁, 𐐺𐐲𐐻 𐐮𐐻 𐐮𐑆 𐑄 𐐝𐐹𐐮𐑉𐐮𐐻 𐐱𐑂 𐐘𐐱𐐼 𐐸𐐶𐐮𐐽 𐐮𐑆 𐐮𐑌 𐑋𐐨, 𐐸𐐶𐐮𐐽 𐑋𐐩𐐿𐐯𐑃 𐑄𐐨𐑆 𐑃𐐮𐑍𐑆 𐑌𐐬𐑌 𐐲𐑌𐐻𐐭 𐑋𐐨; 𐑁𐐫𐑉 𐐮𐑁 𐐌 𐐸𐐰𐐼 𐑌𐐱𐐻 𐐺𐐮𐑌 𐐺𐐫𐑉𐑌 𐐱𐑂 𐐘𐐱𐐼, 𐐌 𐑇𐐳𐐼 𐑌𐐱𐐻 𐐸𐐰𐑂 𐑌𐐬𐑌 𐑄𐐨𐑆 𐑃𐐮𐑍𐑆. 𐐒𐐲𐐻 𐐺𐐨𐐸𐐬𐑊𐐼, 𐑄 𐐢𐐫𐑉𐐼 𐐮𐑌 𐐸𐐮𐑆 𐑀𐑉𐐩𐐻 𐑋𐐲𐑉𐑅𐐮 𐑅𐐯𐑌𐐻 𐐸𐐮𐑆 𐐩𐑌𐐾𐐯𐑊 𐐻𐐭 𐐼𐐨𐐿𐑊𐐩𐑉 𐐲𐑌𐐻𐐭 𐑋𐐨, 𐑄𐐰𐐻 𐐌 𐑋𐐲𐑅𐐻 𐑅𐐻𐐱𐐹 𐑄 𐐶𐐲𐑉𐐿 𐐱𐑂 𐐼𐐨𐑅𐐻𐑉𐐲𐐿𐑇𐐲𐑌 𐐰𐑋𐐲𐑍 𐐸𐐮𐑆 𐐹𐐨𐐹𐑊: 𐐷𐐩, 𐐰𐑌𐐼 𐐌 𐐸𐐰𐑂 𐑅𐐨𐑌 𐐰𐑌 𐐩𐑌𐐾𐐯𐑊 𐑁𐐩𐑅 𐐻𐐭 𐑁𐐩𐑅; 𐐰𐑌𐐼 𐐸𐐨 𐑅𐐹𐐩𐐿 𐐶𐐮𐑄 𐑋𐐨, 𐐰𐑌𐐼 𐐸𐐮𐑆 𐑂𐑎𐑅 𐐶𐐱𐑆 𐐰𐑆 𐑃𐐲𐑌𐐼𐐲𐑉, 𐐰𐑌𐐼 𐐮𐐻 𐑇𐐳𐐿 𐑄 𐐸𐐬𐑊 𐐲𐑉𐑃.

3. 𐐈𐑌𐐼 𐐮𐐻 𐐿𐐩𐑋 𐐻𐐭 𐐹𐐰𐑅 𐑄𐐰𐐻 𐐌 𐐶𐐱𐑆 𐑃𐑉𐐨 𐐼𐐩𐑆 𐐰𐑌𐐼 𐑃𐑉𐐨 𐑌𐐴𐐻𐑅 𐐮𐑌 𐑄 𐑋𐐬𐑅𐐻 𐐺𐐮𐐻𐐲𐑉 𐐹𐐩𐑌 𐐰𐑌𐐼 𐐰𐑍𐑀𐐶𐐮𐑇 𐐱𐑂 𐑅𐐬𐑊; 𐐰𐑌𐐼 𐑌𐐯𐑂𐐲𐑉, 𐐲𐑌𐐻𐐮𐑊 𐐌 𐐼𐐮𐐼 𐐿𐑉𐐴 𐐵𐐻 𐐲𐑌𐐻𐐭 𐑄 𐐢𐐫𐑉𐐼 𐐖𐐨𐑆𐐲𐑅 𐐗𐑉𐐴𐑅𐐻 𐑁𐐫𐑉 𐑋𐐲𐑉𐑅𐐮, 𐐼𐐮𐐼 𐐌 𐑉𐐨𐑅𐐨𐑂 𐐩 𐑉𐐨𐑋𐐮𐑇𐐲𐑌 𐐱𐑂 𐑋𐐴 𐑅𐐮𐑌𐑆. 𐐒𐐲𐐻 𐐺𐐨𐐸𐐬𐑊𐐼, 𐐌 𐐼𐐮𐐼 𐐿𐑉𐐴 𐐲𐑌𐐻𐐭 𐐸𐐮𐑋, 𐐰𐑌𐐼 𐐌 𐐼𐐮𐐼 𐑁𐐴𐑌𐐼 𐐹𐐨𐑅 𐐻𐐭 𐑋𐐴 𐑅𐐬𐑊. 𐐈𐑌𐐼 𐑌𐐵, 𐑋𐐴 𐑅𐐲𐑌, 𐐌 𐐸𐐰𐑂 𐐻𐐬𐑊𐐼 𐐷𐐭 𐑄𐐮𐑅, 𐑄𐐰𐐻 𐐷 𐑋𐐩 𐑊𐐲𐑉𐑌 𐐶𐐮𐑆𐐼𐐲𐑋, 𐑄𐐰𐐻 𐐷 𐑋𐐩 𐑊𐐲𐑉𐑌 𐐱𐑂 𐑋𐐨 𐑄𐐰𐐻 𐑄𐐩𐑉 𐐮𐑆 𐑌𐐬 𐐲𐑄𐐲𐑉 𐐶𐐩 𐐫𐑉 𐑋𐐨𐑌𐑆 𐐸𐐶𐐩𐑉𐐺𐐴 𐑋𐐰𐑌 𐐿𐐰𐑌 𐐺 𐑅𐐩𐑂𐐼, 𐐬𐑌𐑊𐐨 𐐮𐑌 𐐰𐑌𐐼 𐑃𐑉𐐭 𐐗𐑉𐐴𐑅𐐻. 𐐒𐐨𐐸𐐬𐑊𐐼, 𐐸𐐨 𐐮𐑆 𐑄 𐑊𐐴𐑁 𐐰𐑌𐐼 𐑄 𐑊𐐴𐐻 𐐱𐑂 𐑄 𐐶𐐲𐑉𐑊𐐼. 𐐒𐐨𐐸𐐬𐑊𐐼, 𐐸𐐨 𐐮𐑆 𐑄 𐐶𐐲𐑉𐐼 𐐱𐑂 𐐻𐑉𐐭𐑃 𐐰𐑌𐐼 𐑉𐐴𐐽𐐲𐑅𐑌𐐯𐑅. 𐐈𐑌𐐼 𐑌𐐵, 𐐰𐑆 𐐷 𐐸𐐰𐑂 𐐺𐐨𐑀𐐲𐑌 𐐻𐐭 𐐻𐐨𐐽 𐑄 𐐶𐐲𐑉𐐼, 𐐨𐑂𐐯𐑌 𐑅𐐬 𐐌 𐐶𐐳𐐼 𐑄𐐰𐐻 𐐷 𐑇𐐳𐐼 𐐿𐐲𐑌𐐻𐐮𐑌𐐷𐐭 𐐻𐐭 𐐻𐐨𐐽; 𐐰𐑌𐐼 𐐌 𐐶𐐳𐐼 𐑄𐐰𐐻 𐐷 𐐶𐐳𐐼 𐐺 𐐼𐐮𐑊𐐮𐐾𐐯𐑌𐐻 𐐰𐑌𐐼 𐐻𐐯𐑋𐐹𐐲𐑉𐐯𐐻 𐐮𐑌 𐐫𐑊 𐑃𐐮𐑍𐑆. 𐐝𐐨 𐑄𐐰𐐻 𐐷 𐐪𐑉 𐑌𐐱𐐻 𐑊𐐮𐑁𐐻𐐯𐐼 𐐲𐐹 𐐲𐑌𐐻𐐭 𐐹𐑉𐐴𐐼: 𐐷𐐩, 𐑅𐐨 𐑄𐐰𐐻 𐐷 𐐼𐐭 𐑌𐐱𐐻 𐐺𐐬𐑅𐐻 𐐮𐑌 𐐷𐐬𐑉 𐐬𐑌 𐐶𐐮𐑆𐐼𐐲𐑋, 𐑌𐐫𐑉 𐐱𐑂 𐐷𐐬𐑉 𐑋𐐲𐐽 𐑅𐐻𐑉𐐯𐑍𐑃; 𐐷𐐭𐑆 𐐺𐐬𐑊𐐼𐑌𐐯𐑅, 𐐺𐐲𐐻 𐑌𐐱𐐻 𐐬𐑂𐐲𐑉𐐺𐐩𐑉𐐲𐑌𐑅; 𐐰𐑌𐐼 𐐫𐑊𐑅𐐬 𐑅𐐨 𐑄𐐰𐐻 𐐷 𐐺𐑉𐐴𐐼𐑊 𐐫𐑊 𐐷𐐬𐑉 𐐹𐐰𐑇𐐲𐑌𐑆, 𐑄𐐰𐐻 𐐷 𐑋𐐩 𐐺 𐑁𐐮𐑊𐐼 𐐶𐐮𐑄 𐑊𐐲𐑂; 𐑅𐐨 𐑄𐐰𐐻 𐐷 𐑉𐐨𐑁𐑉𐐩𐑌 𐑁𐑉𐐱𐑋 𐐴𐐼𐑊𐑌𐐯𐑅; 𐐼𐐭 𐑌𐐱𐐻 𐐹𐑉𐐩 𐐰𐑆 𐑄 𐐞𐐬𐑉𐐲𐑋𐐴𐐻𐑅 𐐼𐐭, 𐑁𐐫𐑉 𐐷 𐐸𐐰𐑂 𐑅𐐨𐑌 𐑄𐐰𐐻 𐑄𐐩 𐐹𐑉𐐩 𐐻𐐭 𐐺 𐐸𐐲𐑉𐐼 𐐱𐑂 𐑋𐐯𐑌, 𐐰𐑌𐐼 𐐻𐐭 𐐺 𐐹𐑉𐐩𐑆𐐼 𐑁𐐫𐑉 𐑄𐐩𐑉 𐐶𐐮𐑆𐐼𐐲𐑋. 𐐔𐐭 𐑌𐐱𐐻 𐑅𐐩, 𐐄 𐐘𐐱𐐼, 𐐌 𐑃𐐰𐑍𐐿 𐑄 𐑄𐐰𐐻 𐐶𐐨 𐐪𐑉 𐐺𐐯𐐻𐐲𐑉 𐑄𐐰𐑌 𐐵𐑉 𐐺𐑉𐐯𐑄𐑉𐐯𐑌; 𐐺𐐲𐐻 𐑉𐐰𐑄𐐲𐑉 𐑅𐐩, 𐐄 𐐢𐐫𐑉𐐼, 𐑁𐐲𐑉𐑀𐐮𐑂 𐑋𐐴 𐐲𐑌𐐶𐐲𐑉𐑄𐐨𐑌𐐯𐑅, 𐐰𐑌𐐼 𐑉𐐨𐑋𐐯𐑋𐐺𐐲𐑉 𐑋𐐴 𐐺𐑉𐐯𐑄𐑉𐐯𐑌 𐐮𐑌 𐑋𐐲𐑉𐑅𐐮; 𐐷𐐩, 𐐰𐐿𐑌𐐱𐑊𐐯𐐾 𐐷𐐬𐑉 𐐲𐑌𐐶𐐲𐑉𐑄𐐨𐑌𐐯𐑅 𐐺𐐨𐑁𐐬𐑉 𐐘𐐱𐐼 𐐰𐐻 𐐫𐑊 𐐻𐐴𐑋𐑆. 𐐈𐑌𐐼 𐑋𐐩 𐑄 𐐢𐐫𐑉𐐼 𐐺𐑊𐐯𐑅 𐐷𐐬𐑉 𐑅𐐬𐑊, 𐐰𐑌𐐼 𐑉𐐨𐑅𐐨𐑂 𐐷𐐭 𐐰𐐻 𐑄 𐑊𐐪𐑅𐐻 𐐼𐐩 𐐮𐑌𐐻𐐭 𐐸𐐮𐑆 𐐿𐐮𐑍𐐼𐐲𐑋, 𐐻𐐭 𐑅𐐮𐐻 𐐼𐐵𐑌 𐐮𐑌 𐐹𐐨𐑅. 𐐤𐐵 𐑀𐐬, 𐑋𐐴 𐑅𐐲𐑌, 𐐰𐑌𐐼 𐐻𐐨𐐽 𐑄 𐐶𐐲𐑉𐐼 𐐲𐑌𐐻𐐭 𐑄𐐮𐑅 𐐹𐐨𐐹𐑊. 𐐒 𐑅𐐬𐐺𐐲𐑉. 𐐣𐐴 𐑅𐐲𐑌, 𐑁𐐩𐑉𐐶𐐯𐑊.

𐐕𐐰𐐹𐐻𐐲𐑉 XIX.

𐑄 𐐿𐐲𐑋𐐰𐑌𐐼𐑋𐐯𐑌𐐻𐑅 𐐱𐑂 𐐈𐑊𐑋𐐲 𐐻𐐭 𐐸𐐮𐑆 𐑅𐐲𐑌 𐐗𐐬𐑉𐐨𐐰𐑌𐐻𐐲𐑌.

1. 𐐈𐑌𐐼 𐑌𐐵, 𐑋𐐴 𐑅𐐲𐑌. 𐐌 𐐸𐐰𐑂 𐑅𐐲𐑋𐐸𐐶𐐱𐐻 𐑋𐐬𐑉 𐐻𐐭 𐑅𐐩 𐐲𐑌𐐻𐐭 𐑄 𐑄𐐰𐑌 𐐸𐐶𐐱𐐻 𐐌 𐑅𐐯𐐼 𐐲𐑌𐐻𐐭 𐑄𐐴 𐐺𐑉𐐲𐑄𐐲𐑉: 𐑁𐐫𐑉 𐐺𐐨𐐸𐐬𐑊𐐼, 𐐸𐐰𐑂 𐐷 𐑌𐐱𐐻 𐐱𐐺𐑆𐐲𐑉𐑂𐐼 𐑄 𐑅𐐻𐐯𐐼𐐨𐑌𐐯𐑅 𐐱𐑂 𐑄𐐴 𐐺𐑉𐐲𐑄𐐲𐑉, 𐐸𐐮𐑆 𐑁𐐩𐑃𐑁𐐳𐑊𐑌𐐯𐑅, 𐐰𐑌𐐼 𐐸𐐮𐑆 𐐼𐐮𐑊𐐮𐐾𐐯𐑌𐑅 𐐮𐑌 𐐿𐐨𐐹𐐮𐑍 𐑄 𐐿𐐲𐑋𐐰𐑌𐐼𐑋𐐯𐑌𐐻𐑅 𐐱𐑂 𐐘𐐱𐐼? 𐐒𐐨𐐸𐐬𐑊𐐼, 𐐸𐐰𐑆 𐐸𐐨 𐑌𐐱𐐻 𐑅𐐯𐐻 𐐩 𐑀𐐳𐐼 𐐯𐑀𐑆𐐰𐑋𐐹𐑊 𐑁𐐫𐑉 𐑄? 𐐙𐐫𐑉 𐑄𐐵 𐐼𐐮𐐼𐑅𐐻 𐑌𐐱𐐻 𐑀𐐮𐑂 𐑅𐐬 𐑋𐐲𐐽 𐐸𐐨𐐼 𐐲𐑌𐐻𐐭 𐑋𐐴 𐐶𐐲𐑉𐐼𐑆 𐐰𐑆 𐐼𐐮𐐼 𐑄𐐴 𐐺𐑉𐐲𐑄𐐲𐑉, 𐐰𐑋𐐲𐑍 𐑄 𐐹𐐨𐐹𐑊 𐐱𐑂 𐑄 𐐞𐐬𐑉𐐲𐑋𐐴𐐻𐑅. 𐐤𐐵 𐑄𐐮𐑅 𐐮𐑆 𐐸𐐶𐐱𐐻 𐐌 𐐸𐐰𐑂 𐐰𐑀𐐯𐑌𐑅𐐻 𐑄; 𐑄𐐵 𐐼𐐮𐐼𐑅𐐻 𐑀𐐬 𐐱𐑌 𐐲𐑌𐐻𐐭 𐐺𐐬𐑅𐐻𐐮𐑍 𐐮𐑌 𐑄𐐴 𐑅𐐻𐑉𐐯𐑍𐑃 𐐰𐑌𐐼 𐑄𐐴 𐐶𐐮𐑆𐐼𐐲𐑋. 𐐈𐑌𐐼 𐑄𐐮𐑅 𐐮𐑆 𐑌𐐱𐐻 𐐫𐑊, 𐑋𐐴 𐑅𐐲𐑌. 𐐜𐐵 𐐼𐐮𐐼𐑅𐐻 𐐼𐐭 𐑄𐐰𐐻 𐐸𐐶𐐮𐐽 𐐶𐐱𐑆 𐑀𐑉𐐨𐑂𐐲𐑅 𐐲𐑌𐐻𐐭 𐑋𐐨; 𐑁𐐫𐑉 𐑄𐐵 𐐼𐐮𐐼𐑅𐐻 𐑁𐐲𐑉𐑅𐐩𐐿 𐑄 𐑋𐐮𐑌𐐮𐑅𐐻𐑉𐐨, 𐐰𐑌𐐼 𐐼𐐮𐐼 𐑀𐐬 𐐬𐑂𐐲𐑉 𐐮𐑌𐐻𐐭 𐑄 𐑊𐐰𐑌𐐼 𐐱𐑂 𐐝𐐴𐑉𐐲𐑌, 𐐰𐑋𐐲𐑍 𐑄 𐐺𐐫𐑉𐐼𐐲𐑉𐑆 𐐱𐑂 𐑄 𐐢𐐰𐑋𐐲𐑌𐐴𐐻𐑅, 𐐰𐑁𐐻𐐲𐑉 𐑄 𐐸𐐪𐑉𐑊𐐱𐐻 𐐆𐑆𐐰𐐺𐐯𐑊; 𐐷𐐩, 𐑇𐐨 𐐼𐐮𐐼 𐑅𐐻𐐨𐑊 𐐰𐐶𐐩 𐑄 𐐸𐐪𐑉𐐻𐑅 𐐱𐑂 𐑋𐐯𐑌𐐨; 𐐺𐐲𐐻 𐑄𐐮𐑅 𐐶𐐱𐑆 𐑌𐐬 𐐯𐐿𐑅𐐿𐐷𐐭𐑆 𐑁𐐫𐑉 𐑄, 𐑋𐐴 𐑅𐐲𐑌. 𐐜𐐵 𐑇𐐳𐐼𐑅𐐻 𐐸𐐰𐑂 𐐻𐐯𐑌𐐼𐐯𐐼 𐐻𐐭 𐑄 𐑋𐐮𐑌𐐮𐑅𐐻𐑉𐐨 𐐸𐐶𐐩𐑉𐐶𐐮𐑃 𐑄𐐵 𐐶𐐱𐑅𐐻 𐐯𐑌𐐻𐑉𐐲𐑅𐐻𐐯𐐼. 𐐤𐐬 𐐷 𐑌𐐱𐐻, 𐑋𐐴 𐑅𐐲𐑌, 𐑄𐐰𐐻 𐑄𐐨𐑆 𐑃𐐮𐑍𐑆 𐐪𐑉 𐐰𐑌 𐐰𐐺𐐱𐑋𐐮𐑌𐐩𐑇𐐲𐑌

𐐮𐑌 𐑄 𐑅𐐴𐐻 𐐱𐑂 𐑄 𐐢𐐫𐑉𐐼; 𐐷𐐩, 𐑋𐐬𐑅𐐻 𐐲𐐺𐐱𐑋𐐮𐑌𐐲𐐺𐑊 𐐲𐐺𐐲𐑂 𐐫𐑊 𐑅𐐮𐑌𐑆 𐑅𐐩𐑂 𐐮𐐻 𐐺 𐑄 𐑇𐐯𐐼𐐮𐑍 𐐱𐑂 𐐮𐑌𐐬𐑅𐐯𐑌𐐻 𐐺𐑊𐐲𐐼, 𐐫𐑉 𐐼𐐨𐑌𐐴𐐮𐑍 𐑄 𐐐𐐬𐑊𐐨 𐐘𐐬𐑅𐐻? 𐐙𐐫𐑉 𐐺𐐨𐐸𐐬𐑊𐐼, 𐐮𐑁 𐐷 𐐼𐐨𐑌𐐴 𐑄 𐐐𐐬𐑊𐐨 𐐘𐐬𐑅𐐻 𐐸𐐶𐐯𐑌 𐐮𐐻 𐐶𐐲𐑌𐑅 𐐸𐐰𐑆 𐐸𐐰𐐼 𐐹𐑊𐐩𐑅 𐐮𐑌 𐐷𐐭, 𐐰𐑌𐐼 𐐷 𐑌𐐬 𐑄𐐰𐐻 𐐷 𐐼𐐨𐑌𐐴 𐐮𐐻, 𐐺𐐨𐐸𐐬𐑊𐐼, 𐑄𐐮𐑅 𐐮𐑆 𐐩 𐑅𐐮𐑌 𐐸𐐶𐐮𐐽 𐐮𐑆 𐐲𐑌𐐹𐐪𐑉𐐼𐐲𐑌𐐲𐐺𐑊; 𐐷𐐩, 𐐰𐑌𐐼 𐐸𐐭𐑅𐐬𐐯𐑂𐐲𐑉 𐑋𐐲𐑉𐐼𐐲𐑉𐐯𐑃 𐐲𐑀𐐯𐑌𐑅𐐻 𐑄 𐑊𐐴𐐻 𐐰𐑌𐐼 𐑌𐐱𐑊𐐯𐐾 𐐱𐑂 𐐘𐐱𐐼, 𐐮𐐻 𐐮𐑆 𐑌𐐱𐐻 𐐨𐑆𐐨 𐑁𐐫𐑉 𐐸𐐮𐑋 𐐻𐐭 𐐱𐐺𐐻𐐩𐑌 𐑁𐐫𐑉𐑀𐐮𐑂𐑌𐐯𐑅; 𐐷𐐩, 𐐴 𐑅𐐩 𐐲𐑌𐐻𐐭 𐐷𐐭, 𐑋𐐴 𐑅𐐲𐑌, 𐑄𐐰𐐻 𐐮𐐻 𐐮𐑆 𐑌𐐱𐐻 𐐨𐑆𐐨 𐑁𐐫𐑉 𐐸𐐮𐑋 𐐻𐐭 𐐱𐐺𐐻𐐩𐑌 𐐩 𐑁𐐫𐑉𐑀𐐮𐑂𐑌𐐯𐑅. 𐐈𐑌𐐼 𐑌𐐵, 𐑋𐐴 𐑅𐐲𐑌, 𐐴 𐐶𐐳𐐼 𐐻𐐭 𐐘𐐱𐐼 𐑄𐐰𐐻 𐐷 𐐸𐐰𐐼 𐑌𐐱𐐻 𐐺𐐮𐑌 𐑀𐐮𐑊𐐻𐐨 𐐱𐑂 𐑅𐐬 𐑀𐑉𐐩𐐻 𐐩 𐐿𐑉𐐴𐑋. 𐐌 𐐶𐐳𐐼 𐑌𐐱𐐻 𐐼𐐶𐐯𐑊 𐐲𐐹𐐱𐑌 𐐷𐐭𐑉 𐐿𐑉𐐴𐑋𐑆, 𐐻𐐭 𐐸𐐰𐑉𐐬 𐐲𐐹 𐐷𐐭𐑉 𐑅𐐬𐑊, 𐐮𐑁 𐐮𐐻 𐐶𐐲𐑉 𐑌𐐱𐐻 𐑁𐐫𐑉 𐐷𐐭𐑉 𐑀𐐳𐐼. 𐐒𐐲𐐻 𐐺𐐨𐐸𐐬𐑊𐐼, 𐐷 𐐿𐐰𐑌𐐱𐐻 𐐸𐐴𐐼 𐐷𐐭𐑉 𐐿𐑉𐐴𐑋𐑆 𐑁𐑉𐐱𐑋 𐐘𐐱𐐼; 𐐰𐑌𐐼 𐐯𐐿𐑅𐐯𐐹𐐻 𐐷 𐑉𐐨𐐹𐐯𐑌𐐻 𐑄𐐩 𐐶𐐮𐑊 𐑅𐐻𐐰𐑌𐐼 𐐰𐑆 𐐩 𐐻𐐯𐑅𐐻𐐮𐑋𐐬𐑌𐐨 𐐲𐑀𐐯𐑌𐑅𐐻 𐐷𐐭 𐐰𐐻 𐑄 𐑊𐐰𐑅𐐻 𐐼𐐩.

2. 𐐤𐐵 𐑋𐐴 𐑅𐐲𐑌, 𐐴 𐐶𐐳𐐼 𐑄𐐰𐐻 𐐷 𐑇𐐳𐐼 𐑉𐐨𐐹𐐯𐑌𐐻 𐐰𐑌𐐼 𐑁𐐫𐑉𐑅𐐩𐐿 𐐷𐐭𐑉 𐑅𐐮𐑌𐑆, 𐐰𐑌𐐼 𐑀𐐬 𐑌𐐬 𐑋𐐬𐑉 𐐪𐑁𐐻𐐲𐑉 𐑄 𐑊𐐲𐑅𐐻𐑅 𐐱𐑂 𐐷𐐭𐑉 𐐴𐑆, 𐐺𐐲𐐻 𐐿𐑉𐐱𐑅 𐐷𐐭𐑉𐑅𐐯𐑊𐑁 𐐮𐑌 𐐫𐑊 𐑄𐐨𐑆 𐑃𐐮𐑍𐑆; 𐑁𐐫𐑉 𐐯𐐿𐑅𐐯𐐹𐐻 𐐷 𐐼𐐭 𐑄𐐮𐑅, 𐐷 𐐿𐐰𐑌 𐐮𐑌 𐑌𐐬 𐐶𐐴𐑆 𐐮𐑌𐐸𐐯𐑉𐐮𐐻 𐑄 𐐿𐐮𐑍𐐼𐐲𐑋 𐐱𐑂 𐐘𐐱𐐼. 𐐄 𐑉𐐨𐑋𐐯𐑋𐐺𐐲𐑉, 𐐰𐑌𐐼 𐐻𐐩𐐿 𐐮𐐻 𐐲𐐹𐐱𐑌 𐐷𐐭, 𐐰𐑌𐐼 𐐿𐑉𐐱𐑅 𐐷𐐭𐑉𐑅𐐯𐑊𐑁 𐐮𐑌 𐑄𐐨𐑆 𐑃𐐮𐑍𐑆. 𐐈𐑌𐐼 𐐴 𐐿𐐱𐑋𐐰𐑌𐐼 𐐷𐐭 𐐻𐐭 𐐻𐐩𐐿 𐐮𐐻 𐐲𐐹𐐱𐑌 𐐷𐐭 𐐻𐐭 𐐿𐐵𐑌𐑅𐐯𐑊 𐐶𐐮𐑃 𐐷𐐭𐑉 𐐯𐑊𐐼𐐲𐑉 𐐺𐑉𐐲𐑄𐐲𐑉𐑆 𐐮𐑌 𐐷𐐭𐑉 𐐲𐑌𐐼𐐲𐑉𐐻𐐩𐐿𐐮𐑍𐑆; 𐑁𐐫𐑉 𐐺𐐨𐐸𐐬𐑊𐐼, 𐑄𐐵 𐐪𐑉𐐻 𐐮𐑌 𐑄𐐴 𐐷𐐭𐑃, 𐐰𐑌𐐼 𐐷 𐑅𐐻𐐰𐑌𐐼 𐐮𐑌 𐑌𐐨𐐼 𐐻𐐭 𐐺 𐑌𐐲𐑉𐐮𐑇𐐻 𐐺𐐴 𐐷𐐭𐑉 𐐺𐑉𐐲𐑄𐐲𐑉𐑆. 𐐈𐑌𐐼 𐑀𐐮𐑂 𐐸𐐨𐐼 𐐻𐐭 𐑄𐐩𐑉 𐐿𐐵𐑌𐑅𐐯𐑊; 𐑅𐐲𐑁𐐲𐑉 𐑌𐐱𐐻 𐐷𐐭𐑉𐑅𐐯𐑊𐑁 𐐻𐐭 𐐺 𐑊𐐯𐐼 𐐲𐐶𐐩 𐐺𐐴 𐐯𐑌𐐨 𐑂𐐩𐑌 𐐫𐑉 𐑁𐐭𐑊𐐮𐑇 𐑃𐐮𐑍; 𐑅𐐲𐑁𐐲𐑉 𐑌𐐱𐐻 𐑄 𐐼𐐯𐑂𐐮𐑊 𐐻𐐭 𐑊𐐨𐐼 𐐲𐐶𐐩 𐐷𐐭𐑉 𐐸𐐪𐑉𐐻 𐐲𐑀𐐯𐑌 𐐪𐑁𐐻𐐲𐑉 𐑄𐐬𐑆 𐐶𐐮𐐿𐐯𐐼 𐐸𐐪𐑉𐑊𐐲𐐻𐑅. 𐐒𐐨𐐸𐐬𐑊𐐼, 𐐄 𐑋𐐴 𐑅𐐲𐑌, 𐐸𐐵 𐑀𐑉𐐩𐐻 𐐮𐑌𐐮𐐿𐐶𐐮𐐻𐐨 𐐷 𐐺𐑉𐐫𐐻 𐐲𐐹𐐱𐑌 𐑄 𐐞𐐬𐑉𐐲𐑋𐐴𐐻𐑅: 𐑁𐐫𐑉 𐐸𐐶𐐯𐑌 𐑄𐐩 𐑅𐐫 𐐷𐐭𐑉 𐐿𐐱𐑌𐐼𐐲𐐿𐐻, 𐑄𐐩 𐐶𐐳𐐼 𐑌𐐱𐐻 𐐺𐐨𐑊𐐨𐑂 𐐮𐑌 𐑋𐐴 𐐶𐐲𐑉𐐼𐑆. 𐐈𐑌𐐼 𐑌𐐵 𐑄 𐐝𐐹𐐮𐑉𐐮𐐻 𐐱𐑂 𐑄 𐐢𐐫𐑉𐐼 𐐼𐐲𐑃 𐑅𐐩 𐐲𐑌𐐻𐐭 𐑋𐐨, 𐐗𐐱𐑋𐐰𐑌𐐼 𐑄𐐴 𐐽𐐮𐑊𐐼𐑉𐐯𐑌 𐐻𐐭 𐐼𐐭 𐑀𐐳𐐼, 𐑊𐐯𐑅𐐻 𐑄𐐩 𐑊𐐨𐐼 𐐲𐐶𐐩 𐑄 𐐸𐐪𐑉𐐻𐑅 𐐱𐑂 𐑋𐐯𐑌𐐨 𐐹𐐨𐐹𐑊 𐐻𐐭 𐐼𐐯𐑅𐐻𐑉𐐲𐐿𐑇𐐲𐑌; 𐑄𐐯𐑉𐑁𐐬𐑉 𐐴 𐐿𐐱𐑋𐐰𐑌𐐼 𐐷𐐭, 𐑋𐐴 𐑅𐐲𐑌, 𐐮𐑌 𐑄 𐑁𐐨𐑉 𐐱𐑂 𐐘𐐱𐐼, 𐑄𐐰𐐻 𐐷 𐑉𐐯𐑁𐑉𐐩𐑌 𐑁𐑉𐐱𐑋 𐐷𐐭𐑉 𐐮𐑌𐐮𐐿𐐶𐐮𐐻𐐨𐑆; 𐑄𐐰𐐻 𐐷 𐐻𐐲𐑉𐑌 𐐻𐐭 𐑄 𐐢𐐫𐑉𐐼 𐐶𐐮𐑃 𐐫𐑊 𐐷𐐭𐑉 𐑋𐐴𐑌𐐼, 𐑋𐐴𐐻, 𐐰𐑌𐐼 𐑅𐐻𐑉𐐯𐑍𐑃; 𐑄𐐰𐐻 𐐷 𐑊𐐨𐐼 𐐲𐐶𐐩 𐑄 𐐸𐐪𐑉𐐻𐑅 𐐱𐑂 𐑌𐐬 𐑋𐐬𐑉 𐐻𐐭 𐐼𐐭 𐐶𐐮𐐿𐐯𐐼𐑊𐐨; 𐐺𐐲𐐻 𐑉𐐪𐑄𐐲𐑉 𐑉𐐨𐐻𐐲𐑉𐑌 𐐲𐑌𐐻𐐭 𐑄𐐯𐑋, 𐐰𐑌𐐼 𐐰𐐿𐑌𐐱𐑊𐐯𐐾 𐐷𐐭𐑉 𐑁𐐫𐑊𐐻𐑅, 𐐰𐑌𐐼 𐑄𐐰𐐻 𐑉𐐫𐑍 𐐸𐐶𐐮𐐽 𐐷 𐐸𐐰𐑂 𐐼𐐲𐑌; 𐑅𐐨𐐿 𐑌𐐱𐐻 𐐪𐑁𐐻𐐲𐑉 𐑉𐐮𐐽𐐯𐑆 𐑌𐐫𐑉 𐑄 𐑂𐐩𐑌 𐑃𐐮𐑍𐑆 𐐱𐑂 𐑄𐐮𐑅 𐐶𐐲𐑉𐑊𐐼, 𐑁𐐫𐑉 𐐺𐐨𐐸𐐬𐑊𐐼, 𐐷𐐭 𐐿𐐰𐑌𐐱𐐻 𐐿𐐰𐑉𐐨 𐑄𐐯𐑋 𐐶𐐮𐑃 𐐷𐐭.

3. 𐐈𐑌𐐼 𐑌𐐵, 𐑋𐐴 𐑅𐐲𐑌, 𐐴 𐐶𐐳𐐼 𐑅𐐩 𐑅𐐲𐑋𐐶𐐱𐐻 𐐲𐑌𐐻𐐭 𐐷𐐭 𐐿𐐱𐑌𐑅𐐲𐑉𐑌𐐮𐑍 𐑄 𐐿𐐲𐑋𐐮𐑍 𐐱𐑂 𐐗𐑉𐐴𐑅𐐻. 𐐒𐐨𐐸𐐬𐑊𐐼, 𐐴 𐑅𐐩 𐐲𐑌𐐻𐐭 𐐷𐐭, 𐑄𐐰𐐻 𐐮𐐻 𐐮𐑆 𐐸𐐨 𐑄𐐰𐐻 𐑇𐐳𐑉𐑊𐐨 𐑇𐐰𐑊 𐐿𐐲𐑋 𐐻𐐭 𐐻𐐩𐐿 𐐲𐐶𐐩 𐑄 𐑅𐐮𐑌𐑆 𐐱𐑂 𐑄 𐐶𐐲𐑉𐑊𐐼; 𐐷𐐩, 𐐸𐐨 𐐿𐐲𐑋𐐯𐑃 𐐻𐐭 𐐼𐐨𐐿𐑊𐐩𐑉 𐑀𐑊𐐰𐐼 𐐻𐐴𐐼𐐮𐑍𐑆 𐐱𐑂 𐑅𐐰𐑊𐑂𐐩𐑇𐐲𐑌 𐐲𐑌𐐻𐐭 𐐸𐐮𐑆 𐐹𐐨𐐹𐑊. 𐐈𐑌𐐼 𐑌𐐵, 𐑋𐐴 𐑅𐐲𐑌, 𐑄𐐮𐑅 𐐶𐐱𐑆 𐑄 𐑋𐐮𐑌𐐮𐑅𐐻𐑉𐐨 𐐲𐑌𐐻𐐭 𐐸𐐶𐐮𐐽 𐐷 𐐶𐐲𐑉 𐐿𐐫𐑊𐐼, 𐐻𐐭 𐐼𐐨𐐿𐑊𐐩𐑉 𐑄𐐨𐑆 𐑀𐑊𐐰𐐼 𐐻𐐴𐐼𐐮𐑍𐑆 𐐲𐑌𐐻𐐭 𐑄𐐮𐑅 𐐹𐐨𐐹𐑊, 𐐻𐐭 𐐹𐑉𐐨𐐹𐐩𐑉 𐑄𐐩𐑉 𐑋𐐴𐑌𐐼𐑆; 𐐫𐑉 𐑉𐐪𐑄𐐲𐑉 𐑄𐐰𐐻 𐑅𐐰𐑊𐑂𐐩𐑇𐐲𐑌 𐑋𐐴𐐻 𐐿𐐲𐑋 𐐲𐑌𐐻𐐭 𐑄𐐯𐑋, 𐑄𐐰𐐻 𐑄𐐩 𐑋𐐩 𐐹𐑉𐐨𐐹𐐩𐑉 𐑄 𐑋𐐴𐑌𐐼𐑆 𐐱𐑂 𐑄𐐩𐑉 𐐽𐐮𐑊𐐼𐑉𐐯𐑌 𐐻𐐭 𐐸𐐨𐑉 𐑄 𐐶𐐲𐑉𐐼 𐐰𐐻 𐑄 𐐻𐐴𐑋 𐐱𐑂 𐐸𐐮𐑆 𐐿𐐲𐑋𐐮𐑍.

4. 𐐈𐑌𐐼 𐑌𐐵 𐐴 𐐶𐐮𐑊 𐐨𐑆 𐐷𐐭𐑉 𐑋𐐴𐑌𐐼 𐑅𐐲𐑋𐐶𐐱𐐻 𐐱𐑌 𐑄𐐮𐑅 𐑅𐐲𐐺𐐾𐐯𐐿𐐻. 𐐒𐐨𐐸𐐬𐑊𐐼, 𐐷𐐭 𐑋𐐪𐑉𐑂𐐯𐑊 𐐸𐐶𐐴 𐑄𐐨𐑆 𐑃𐐮𐑍𐑆 𐑇𐐳𐐼 𐐺 𐑌𐐬𐑌 𐑅𐐬 𐑊𐐫𐑍 𐐺𐐨𐑁𐐬𐑉𐐸𐐰𐑌𐐼. 𐐒𐐨𐐸𐐬𐑊𐐼, 𐐴 𐑅𐐩 𐐲𐑌𐐻𐐭 𐐷𐐭, 𐐮𐑆 𐑌𐐱𐐻 𐐩 𐑅𐐬𐑊 𐐰𐐻 𐑄𐐮𐑅 𐐻𐐴𐑋 𐐰𐑆 𐐹𐑉𐐯𐑇𐐲𐑅 𐐲𐑌𐐻𐐭 𐐘𐐱𐐼, 𐐰𐑆 𐐩 𐑅𐐬𐑊 𐐶𐐮𐑊 𐐺 𐐰𐐻 𐑄 𐐻𐐴𐑋 𐐱𐑂 𐐸𐐮𐑆 𐐿𐐲𐑋𐐮𐑍? 𐐆𐑆 𐐮𐐻 𐑌𐐱𐐻 𐐰𐑆 𐑌𐐯𐑅𐐯𐑅𐐯𐑉𐐨 𐑄𐐰𐐻 𐑄 𐐹𐑊𐐰𐑌 𐐱𐑂 𐑉𐐨𐐼𐐯𐑋𐑇𐐲𐑌 𐑇𐐳𐐼 𐐺 𐑋𐐩𐐼 𐑌𐐬𐑌 𐐲𐑌𐐻𐐭 𐑄𐐮𐑅 𐐹𐐨𐐹𐑊, 𐐰𐑆 𐐶𐐯𐑊 𐐰𐑆 𐐲𐑌𐐻𐐭 𐑄𐐩𐑉 𐐽𐐮𐑊𐐼𐑉𐐯𐑌? 𐐆𐑆 𐐮𐐻 𐑌𐐱𐐻 𐐰𐑆 𐐨𐑆𐐨 𐐰𐐻 𐑄𐐮𐑅 𐐻𐐴𐑋, 𐑁𐐫𐑉 𐑄 𐐢𐐫𐑉𐐼 𐐻𐐭 𐑅𐐯𐑌𐐼 𐐸𐐮𐑆 𐐩𐑌𐐾𐐯𐑊 𐐻𐐭 𐐼𐐨𐐿𐑊𐐩𐑉 𐑄𐐨𐑆 𐑀𐑊𐐰𐐼 𐐻𐐴𐐼𐐮𐑍𐑆 𐐲𐑌𐐻𐐭 𐐲𐑅, 𐐰𐑆 𐐲𐑌𐐻𐐭 𐐵𐑉 𐐽𐐮𐑊𐐼𐑉𐐯𐑌; 𐐫𐑉 𐐰𐑆 𐐪𐑁𐐻𐐲𐑉 𐑄 𐐻𐐴𐑋 𐐱𐑂 𐐸𐐮𐑆 𐐿𐐲𐑋𐐮𐑍? 𐐤𐐵 𐑋𐐴 𐑅𐐲𐑌, 𐐸𐐨𐑉 𐐮𐑆 𐑅𐐲𐑋𐐶𐐱𐐻 𐑋𐐬𐑉 𐐴 𐐶𐐳𐐼 𐑅𐐩 𐐲𐑌𐐻𐐭 𐑄; 𐑁𐐫𐑉 𐐴 𐐹𐐲𐑉𐑅𐐨𐑂 𐑄𐐰𐐻 𐑄𐐴 𐑋𐐴𐑌𐐼 𐐮𐑆 𐐶𐐲𐑉𐐨𐐼 𐐿𐐱𐑌𐑅𐐲𐑉𐑌𐐮𐑍 𐑄 𐑉𐐯𐑆𐐲𐑉𐐯𐐿𐑇𐐲𐑌 𐐱𐑂 𐑄 𐐼𐐯𐐼. 𐐒𐐨𐐸𐐬𐑊𐐼, 𐐴 𐑅𐐩 𐐲𐑌𐐻𐐭 𐐷𐐭, 𐑄𐐰𐐻 𐑄𐐯𐑉 𐐮𐑆 𐑌𐐬 𐑉𐐯𐑆𐐲𐑉𐐯𐐿𐑇𐐲𐑌; 𐐫𐑉, 𐐴 𐐶𐐳𐐼 𐑅𐐩,

𐐮𐑌 𐐲𐑄𐐲𐑉 𐐶𐐲𐑉𐐼𐑆, 𐑄𐐰𐐻 𐑄𐐮𐑅 𐑋𐐫𐑉𐐻𐐲𐑊 𐐼𐐲𐑆 𐑌𐐱𐐻 𐐹𐐳𐐻 𐐱𐑌 𐐮𐑋𐐫𐑉𐐻𐐰𐑊𐐮𐐻𐐨; 𐑄𐐮𐑅 𐐿𐐲𐑉𐐲𐐹𐑇𐐲𐑌 𐐼𐐲𐑆 𐑌𐐱𐐻 𐐹𐐳𐐻 𐐱𐑌 𐐮𐑌𐐿𐐲𐑉𐐲𐐹𐑇𐐲𐑌, 𐐲𐑌𐐻𐐮𐑊 𐐰𐑁𐐻𐐲𐑉 𐑄 𐐿𐐲𐑋𐐮𐑍 𐐲𐑂 𐐗𐑉𐐴𐑅𐐻. 𐐒𐐨𐐸𐐬𐑊𐐼, 𐐸𐐨 𐐺𐑉𐐮𐑍𐐯𐑃 𐐻𐐭 𐐹𐐰𐑅 𐑄 𐑉𐐯𐑆𐐲𐑉𐐯𐐿𐑇𐐲𐑌 𐐲𐑂 𐑄 𐐼𐐯𐐼. 𐐒𐐲𐐻 𐐺𐐨𐐸𐐬𐑊𐐼, 𐑋𐐴 𐑅𐐲𐑌, 𐑄 𐑉𐐯𐑆𐐲𐑉𐐯𐐿𐑇𐐲𐑌 𐐮𐑆 𐑌𐐱𐐻 𐐷𐐯𐐻. 𐐤𐐵 𐐌 𐐲𐑌𐑁𐐬𐑊𐐼 𐐲𐑌𐐻𐐭 𐐷𐐭 𐐰 𐑋𐐮𐑅𐐻𐐲𐑉𐐨; 𐑌𐐯𐑂𐐲𐑉𐑄𐐲𐑊𐐯𐑅, 𐑄𐐯𐑉 𐐪𐑉 𐑋𐐯𐑌𐐨 𐑋𐐮𐑅𐐻𐐲𐑉𐐨𐑆 𐐸𐐶𐐮𐐽 𐐪𐑉 𐐿𐐯𐐹𐐻, 𐑄𐐰𐐻 𐑌𐐬 𐐶𐐲𐑌 𐑌𐐬𐐯𐑃 𐑄𐐯𐑋 𐑅𐐩𐑂 𐐘𐐱𐐼 𐐸𐐮𐑋𐑅𐐯𐑊𐑁. 𐐒𐐲𐐻 𐐌 𐑇𐐬 𐐲𐑌𐐻𐐭 𐐷𐐭 𐐶𐐲𐑌 𐑃𐐮𐑍 𐐸𐐶𐐮𐐽 𐐌 𐐸𐐰𐑂 𐐮𐑌𐐿𐐶𐐴𐑉𐐼 𐐼𐐮𐑊𐐮𐐾𐐯𐑌𐐻𐑊𐐨 𐐲𐑂 𐐘𐐱𐐼, 𐑄𐐰𐐻 𐐌 𐑋𐐴𐐻 𐑌𐐬; 𐑄𐐰𐐻 𐐮𐑆 𐐿𐐱𐑌𐑅𐐲𐑉𐑌𐐮𐑍 𐑄 𐑉𐐯𐑆𐐲𐑉𐐯𐐿𐑇𐐲𐑌. 𐐒𐐨𐐸𐐬𐑊𐐼, 𐑄𐐯𐑉 𐐮𐑆 𐐰 𐐻𐐴𐑋 𐐲𐐹𐑎𐑌𐐻𐐯𐐼 𐑄𐐰𐐻 𐐫𐑊 𐑇𐐰𐑊 𐐿𐐲𐑋 𐑁𐐫𐑉𐑃 𐑁𐑉𐐱𐑋 𐑄 𐐼𐐯𐐼. 𐐤𐐵 𐐸𐐶𐐯𐑌 𐑄𐐮𐑅 𐐻𐐴𐑋 𐐿𐐲𐑋𐐯𐑃 𐑌𐐬 𐐶𐐲𐑌 𐑌𐐬𐑆; 𐐺𐐲𐐻 𐐘𐐱𐐼 𐑌𐐬𐐯𐑃 𐑄 𐐻𐐴𐑋 𐐸𐐶𐐮𐐽 𐐮𐑆 𐐲𐐹𐑎𐑌𐐻𐐯𐐼. 𐐤𐐵 𐐸𐐶𐐯𐑄𐐲𐑉 𐑄𐐯𐑉 𐑇𐐰𐑊 𐐺𐐨 𐐶𐐲𐑌 𐐻𐐴𐑋, 𐐫𐑉 𐐰 𐑅𐐯𐐿𐐲𐑌𐐼 𐐻𐐴𐑋, 𐐫𐑉 𐐰 𐑃𐐲𐑉𐐼 𐐻𐐴𐑋, 𐑄𐐰𐐻 𐑋𐐯𐑌 𐑇𐐰𐑊 𐐿𐐲𐑋 𐑁𐐫𐑉𐑃 𐑁𐑉𐐱𐑋 𐑄 𐐼𐐯𐐼, 𐐮𐐻 𐑋𐐰𐐻𐐲𐑉𐐯𐑃 𐑌𐐱𐐻; 𐑁𐐫𐑉 𐐘𐐱𐐼 𐑌𐐬𐐯𐑃 𐐫𐑊 𐑄𐐨𐑆 𐑃𐐮𐑍𐑆; 𐐰𐑌𐐼 𐐮𐐻 𐑅𐐲𐑁𐐴𐑅𐐯𐑃 𐑋𐐨 𐐻𐐭 𐑌𐐬 𐑄𐐰𐐻 𐑄𐐮𐑅 𐐮𐑆 𐑄 𐐿𐐩𐑅; 𐑄𐐰𐐻 𐑄𐐯𐑉 𐐮𐑆 𐐰 𐐻𐐴𐑋 𐐲𐐹𐑎𐑌𐐻𐐯𐐼 𐑄𐐰𐐻 𐑋𐐯𐑌 𐑇𐐰𐑊 𐑉𐐴𐑆 𐑁𐑉𐐱𐑋 𐑄 𐐼𐐯𐐼. 𐐤𐐵 𐑄𐐯𐑉 𐑋𐐲𐑅𐐻 𐑌𐐨𐐼𐑆 𐐺𐐨 𐐰 𐑅𐐹𐐩𐑅 𐐺𐐨𐐻𐐶𐐮𐐿𐑅𐐻 𐑄 𐐻𐐴𐑋 𐐲𐑂 𐐼𐐯𐑃 𐐰𐑌𐐼 𐑄 𐐻𐐴𐑋 𐐲𐑂 𐑄 𐑉𐐯𐑆𐐲𐑉𐐯𐐿𐑇𐐲𐑌.

5. 𐐈𐑌𐐼 𐑌𐐵 𐐌 𐐶𐐳𐐼 𐐮𐑌𐐿𐐶𐐴𐑉 𐐸𐐶𐐱𐐻 𐐺𐐨𐐿𐐲𐑋𐐯𐑃 𐐲𐑂 𐑄 𐑅𐐬𐑊𐑆 𐐲𐑂 𐑋𐐯𐑌 𐑁𐑉𐐱𐑋 𐑄𐐮𐑅 𐐻𐐴𐑋 𐐲𐑂 𐐼𐐯𐑃 𐐻𐐭 𐑄 𐐻𐐴𐑋 𐐲𐐹𐑎𐑌𐐻𐐯𐐼 𐑁𐐫𐑉 𐑄 𐑉𐐯𐑆𐐲𐑉𐐯𐐿𐑇𐐲𐑌? 𐐤𐐵 𐐸𐐶𐐯𐑄𐐲𐑉 𐑄𐐯𐑉 𐐮𐑆 𐑋𐐬𐑉 𐑄𐐰𐑌 𐐶𐐲𐑌 𐐻𐐴𐑋 𐐲𐐹𐑎𐑌𐐻𐐯𐐼 𐑁𐐫𐑉 𐑋𐐯𐑌 𐐻𐐭 𐑉𐐴𐑆, 𐐮𐐻 𐑋𐐰𐐻𐐲𐑉𐐯𐑃 𐑌𐐱𐐻; 𐑁𐐫𐑉 𐐫𐑊 𐐼𐐭 𐑌𐐱𐐻 𐐼𐐴 𐐰𐐻 𐐶𐐲𐑌𐑅: 𐐰𐑌𐐼 𐑄𐐮𐑅 𐑋𐐰𐐻𐐲𐑉𐐯𐑃 𐑌𐐱𐐻; 𐐫𐑊 𐐮𐑆 𐐰𐑆 𐐶𐐲𐑌 𐐼𐐩, 𐐶𐐮𐑄 𐐘𐐱𐐼; 𐐰𐑌𐐼 𐐻𐐴𐑋 𐐬𐑌𐑊𐐨 𐐮𐑆 𐑋𐐯𐑈𐐲𐑉𐐼 𐐲𐑌𐐻𐐭 𐑋𐐯𐑌; 𐑄𐐯𐑉𐑁𐐬𐑉 𐑄𐐯𐑉 𐐮𐑆 𐐰 𐐻𐐴𐑋 𐐲𐐹𐑎𐑌𐐻𐐯𐐼 𐐲𐑌𐐻𐐭 𐑋𐐯𐑌, 𐑄𐐰𐐻 𐑄𐐩 𐑇𐐰𐑊 𐑉𐐴𐑆 𐑁𐑉𐐱𐑋 𐑄 𐐼𐐯𐐼; 𐐰𐑌𐐼 𐑄𐐯𐑉 𐐮𐑆 𐐰 𐑅𐐹𐐩𐑅 𐐺𐐨𐐻𐐶𐐨𐑌 𐑄 𐐻𐐴𐑋 𐐲𐑂 𐐼𐐯𐑃 𐐰𐑌𐐼 𐑄 𐑉𐐯𐑆𐐲𐑉𐐯𐐿𐑇𐐲𐑌. 𐐈𐑌𐐼 𐑌𐐵 𐐿𐐱𐑌𐑅𐐲𐑉𐑌𐐮𐑍 𐑄𐐮𐑅 𐑅𐐹𐐩𐑅 𐐲𐑂 𐐻𐐴𐑋. 𐐐𐐶𐐱𐐻 𐐺𐐨𐐿𐐲𐑋𐐯𐑃 𐐲𐑂 𐑄 𐑅𐐬𐑊𐑆 𐐲𐑂 𐑋𐐯𐑌, 𐐮𐑆 𐑄 𐑃𐐮𐑍 𐐸𐐶𐐮𐐽 𐐌 𐐸𐐰𐑂 𐐮𐑌𐐿𐐶𐐴𐑉𐐼 𐐼𐐮𐑊𐐮𐐾𐐯𐑌𐐻𐑊𐐨 𐐲𐑂 𐑄 𐐢𐐫𐑉𐐼 𐐻𐐭 𐑌𐐬; 𐐰𐑌𐐼 𐑄𐐮𐑅 𐐮𐑆 𐑄 𐑃𐐮𐑍 𐐲𐑂 𐐸𐐶𐐮𐐽 𐐌 𐐼𐐭 𐑌𐐬. 𐐈𐑌𐐼 𐐸𐐶𐐯𐑌 𐑄 𐐻𐐴𐑋 𐐿𐐲𐑋𐐯𐑃 𐐸𐐶𐐯𐑌 𐐫𐑊 𐑇𐐰𐑊 𐑉𐐴𐑆, 𐑄𐐯𐑌 𐑇𐐰𐑊 𐑄𐐩 𐑌𐐬 𐑄𐐰𐐻 𐐘𐐱𐐼 𐑌𐐬𐐯𐑃 𐐫𐑊 𐑄 𐐻𐐴𐑋𐑆 𐐸𐐶𐐮𐐽 𐐪𐑉 𐐲𐐹𐑎𐑌𐐻𐐯𐐼 𐐲𐑌𐐻𐐭 𐑋𐐰𐑌. 𐐤𐐵 𐐿𐐱𐑌𐑅𐐲𐑉𐑌𐐮𐑍 𐑄 𐑅𐐻𐐩𐐻 𐐲𐑂 𐑄 𐑅𐐬𐑊 𐐺𐐨𐐻𐐶𐐨𐑌 𐐼𐐯𐑃 𐐰𐑌𐐼 𐑄 𐑉𐐯𐑆𐐲𐑉𐐯𐐿𐑇𐐲𐑌. 𐐒𐐨𐐸𐐬𐑊𐐼, 𐐮𐐻 𐐸𐐰𐑆 𐐺𐐮𐑌 𐑋𐐩𐐼 𐑌𐐬𐑌 𐐲𐑌𐐻𐐭 𐑋𐐨 𐐺𐐴 𐐰𐑌 𐐩𐑌𐐾𐐯𐑊, 𐑄𐐰𐐻 𐑄 𐑅𐐹𐐮𐑉𐐮𐐻𐑅 𐐲𐑂 𐐫𐑊 𐑋𐐯𐑌, 𐐰𐑆 𐑅𐐭𐑌 𐐰𐑆 𐑄𐐩 𐐪𐑉 𐐼𐐨𐐹𐐪𐑉𐐻𐐯𐐼 𐑁𐑉𐐱𐑋 𐑄𐐮𐑅 𐑋𐐫𐑉𐐻𐐲𐑊 𐐺𐐱𐐼𐐨; 𐐷𐐩, 𐑄 𐑅𐐹𐐮𐑉𐐮𐐻𐑅 𐐲𐑂 𐐫𐑊 𐑋𐐯𐑌, 𐐸𐐶𐐯𐑄𐐲𐑉 𐑄𐐩 𐐺𐐨 𐑀𐐳𐐼 𐐫𐑉 𐐨𐑂𐐲𐑊, 𐐪𐑉 𐐻𐐩𐐿𐐯𐑌 𐐸𐐬𐑋 𐐻𐐭 𐑄𐐰𐐻 𐐘𐐱𐐼 𐐸𐐭 𐑀𐐩𐑂 𐑄𐐯𐑋 𐑊𐐴𐑁. 𐐈𐑌𐐼 𐑄𐐯𐑌 𐑇𐐰𐑊 𐐮𐐻 𐐿𐐲𐑋 𐐻𐐭 𐐹𐐰𐑅, 𐑄𐐰𐐻 𐑄 𐑅𐐹𐐮𐑉𐐮𐐻𐑅 𐐲𐑂 𐑄𐐬𐑆 𐐸𐐭 𐐪𐑉 𐑉𐐴𐐽𐐲𐑅, 𐐪𐑉 𐑉𐐨𐑅𐐨𐑂𐐼 𐐮𐑌𐐻𐐭 𐐰 𐑅𐐻𐐩𐐻 𐐲𐑂 𐐸𐐰𐐹𐐨𐑌𐐯𐑅, 𐐸𐐶𐐮𐐽 𐐮𐑆 𐐿𐐫𐑊𐐼 𐐹𐐰𐑉𐐲𐐼𐐴𐑅; 𐐰 𐑅𐐻𐐩𐐻 𐐲𐑂 𐑉𐐯𐑅𐐻; 𐐰 𐑅𐐻𐐩𐐻 𐐲𐑂 𐐹𐐨𐑅, 𐐸𐐶𐐯𐑉 𐑄𐐩 𐑇𐐰𐑊 𐑉𐐯𐑅𐐻 𐑁𐑉𐐱𐑋 𐐫𐑊 𐑄𐐯𐑉 𐐻𐑉𐐲𐐺𐑊𐑆, 𐐰𐑌𐐼 𐑁𐑉𐐱𐑋 𐐫𐑊 𐐿𐐯𐑉, 𐐰𐑌𐐼 𐑅𐐱𐑉𐐬, 𐐯𐐻𐑅.

6. 𐐈𐑌𐐼 𐑄𐐯𐑌 𐑇𐐰𐑊 𐐮𐐻 𐐿𐐲𐑋 𐐻𐐭 𐐹𐐰𐑅, 𐑄𐐰𐐻 𐑄 𐑅𐐹𐐮𐑉𐐮𐐻𐑅 𐐲𐑂 𐑄 𐐶𐐮𐐿𐐯𐐼, 𐐷𐐩, 𐐸𐐭 𐐪𐑉 𐐨𐑂𐐲𐑊; 𐑁𐐫𐑉 𐐺𐐨𐐸𐐬𐑊𐐼, 𐑄𐐩 𐐸𐐰𐑂 𐑌𐐬 𐐹𐐪𐑉𐐻 𐑌𐐫𐑉 𐐹𐐬𐑉𐑇𐐲𐑌 𐐲𐑂 𐑄 𐐝𐐹𐐮𐑉𐐮𐐻 𐐲𐑂 𐑄 𐐢𐐫𐑉𐐼; 𐑁𐐫𐑉 𐐺𐐨𐐸𐐬𐑊𐐼, 𐑄𐐩 𐐽𐐬𐑆 𐐨𐑂𐐲𐑊 𐐶𐐲𐑉𐐿𐑅 𐑉𐐰𐑄𐐲𐑉 𐑄𐐰𐑌 𐑀𐐳𐐼; 𐑄𐐯𐑉𐑁𐐬𐑉 𐑄 𐑅𐐹𐐮𐑉𐐮𐐻 𐐲𐑂 𐑄 𐐼𐐯𐑂𐐮𐑊 𐐼𐐮𐐼 𐐯𐑌𐐻𐐲𐑉 𐐮𐑌𐐻𐐭 𐑄𐐯𐑋, 𐐰𐑌𐐼 𐐻𐐩𐐿 𐐹𐐲𐑆𐐯𐑇𐐲𐑌 𐐲𐑂 𐑄𐐯𐑉 𐐸𐐵𐑅; 𐐰𐑌𐐼 𐑄𐐨𐑆 𐑇𐐰𐑊 𐐺𐐨 𐐿𐐰𐑅𐐻 𐐵𐐻 𐐮𐑌𐐻𐐭 𐐵𐐻𐐲𐑉 𐐼𐐪𐑉𐐿𐑌𐐯𐑅; 𐑄𐐯𐑉 𐑇𐐰𐑊 𐐺𐐨 𐐶𐐨𐐹𐐮𐑍, 𐐰𐑌𐐼 𐐶𐐩𐑊𐐮𐑍, 𐐰𐑌𐐼 𐑌𐐰𐑇𐐮𐑍 𐐲𐑂 𐐻𐐨𐑃; 𐐰𐑌𐐼 𐑄𐐮𐑅 𐐺𐐨𐐿𐐫𐑆 𐐲𐑂 𐑄𐐯𐑉 𐐬𐑌 𐐮𐑌𐐮𐐿𐐶𐐮𐐻𐐨; 𐐺𐐨𐐮𐑍 𐑊𐐯𐐼 𐐿𐐰𐐹𐐻𐐮𐑂 𐐺𐐴 𐑄 𐐶𐐮𐑊 𐐲𐑂 𐑄 𐐼𐐯𐑂𐐮𐑊. 𐐤𐐵 𐑄𐐮𐑅 𐐮𐑆 𐑄 𐑅𐐻𐐩𐐻 𐐲𐑂 𐑄 𐑅𐐬𐑊𐑆 𐐲𐑂 𐑄 𐐶𐐮𐐿𐐯𐐼; 𐐷𐐩, 𐐮𐑌 𐐼𐐪𐑉𐐿𐑌𐐯𐑅, 𐐰𐑌𐐼 𐐰 𐑅𐐻𐐩𐐻 𐐲𐑂 𐐫𐑁𐐳𐑊, 𐑁𐐨𐑉𐑁𐐳𐑊 𐑊𐐳𐐿𐐮𐑍 𐑁𐐫𐑉 𐐲𐑂 𐑄 𐑁𐐴𐑉𐐨 𐐮𐑌𐐼𐐮𐑀𐑌𐐩𐑇𐐲𐑌 𐐲𐑂 𐑄 𐑉𐐰𐑃 𐐲𐑂 𐐘𐐱𐐼 𐐲𐐹𐐱𐑌 𐑄𐐯𐑋; 𐑄𐐲𐑅 𐑄𐐩 𐑉𐐨𐑋𐐩𐑌 𐐮𐑌 𐑄𐐮𐑅 𐑅𐐻𐐩𐐻, 𐐰𐑆 𐐶𐐯𐑊 𐐰𐑆 𐑄 𐑉𐐴𐐽𐐲𐑅 𐐮𐑌 𐐹𐐰𐑉𐐲𐐼𐐴𐑅, 𐐲𐑌𐐻𐐮𐑊 𐑄 𐐻𐐴𐑋 𐐲𐑂 𐑄𐐯𐑉 𐑉𐐯𐑆𐐲𐑉𐐯𐐿𐑇𐐲𐑌. 𐐤𐐵 𐑄𐐯𐑉 𐐪𐑉 𐑅𐐲𐑋 𐑄𐐰𐐻 𐐸𐐰𐑂 𐐲𐑌𐐼𐐲𐑉𐑅𐐻𐐳𐐼 𐑄𐐰𐐻 𐑄𐐮𐑅 𐑅𐐻𐐩𐐻 𐐲𐑂 𐐸𐐰𐐹𐐨𐑌𐐯𐑅, 𐐰𐑌𐐼 𐑄𐐮𐑅 𐑅𐐻𐐩𐐻 𐐲𐑂 𐑋𐐮𐑆𐐲𐑉𐐨 𐐲𐑂 𐑄 𐑅𐐬𐑊, 𐐺𐐨𐑁𐐬𐑉 𐑄 𐑉𐐯𐑆𐐲𐑉𐐯𐐿𐑇𐐲𐑌, 𐐶𐐱𐑆 𐐰 𐑁𐐲𐑉𐑅𐐻 𐑉𐐯𐑆𐐲𐑉𐐯𐐿𐑇𐐲𐑌. 𐐏𐐩, 𐐌 𐐰𐐼𐑋𐐮𐐻 𐐮𐐻 𐑋𐐩 𐐺𐐨 𐐻𐐲𐑉𐑋𐐼 𐐰 𐑉𐐯𐑆𐐲𐑉𐐯𐐿𐑇𐐲𐑌; 𐑄 𐑉𐐩𐑆𐐮𐑍 𐐲𐑂 𐑄 𐑅𐐹𐐮𐑉𐐮𐐻 𐐫𐑉 𐑄 𐑅𐐬𐑊, 𐐰𐑌𐐼 𐑄𐐯𐑉 𐐿𐐱𐑌𐑅𐐮𐑀𐑌𐐩𐑇𐐲𐑌 𐐻𐐭 𐐸𐐰𐐹𐐨𐑌𐐯𐑅

𐐫𐑉 𐑋𐐮𐑆𐐲𐑉𐐨, 𐐲𐐿𐐫𐑉𐐼𐐮𐑍 𐐻𐐭 𐑄 𐐶𐐲𐑉𐐼𐑆 𐐸𐐶𐐮𐐽 𐐸𐐰𐑂 𐐺𐐮𐑌 𐑅𐐹𐐬𐐿𐐲𐑌. 𐐈𐑌𐐼 𐐺𐐨𐐸𐐬𐑊𐐼, 𐐲𐑀𐐯𐑌 𐐮𐐻 𐐸𐐰𐑃 𐐺𐐮𐑌 𐑅𐐹𐐬𐐿𐐲𐑌, 𐑄𐐰𐐻 𐑄𐐯𐑉 𐐮𐑆 𐐲 𐑁𐐲𐑉𐑅𐐻 𐑉𐐯𐑆𐐲𐑉𐐯𐐿𐑇𐐲𐑌; 𐐲 𐑉𐐯𐑆𐐲𐑉𐐯𐐿𐑇𐐲𐑌 𐐱𐑂 𐐫𐑊 𐑄𐐬𐑆 𐐸𐐭 𐐸𐐰𐑂 𐐺𐐮𐑌, 𐐫𐑉 𐐸𐐭 𐐪𐑉, 𐐫𐑉 𐐸𐐭 𐑇𐐰𐑊 𐐺𐐨, 𐐼𐐵𐑌 𐐻𐐭 𐑄 𐑉𐐯𐑆𐐲𐑉𐐯𐐿𐑇𐐲𐑌 𐐱𐑂 𐐗𐑉𐐴𐑅𐐻 𐑁𐑉𐐱𐑋 𐑄 𐐼𐐯𐐼.

7. 𐐤𐐵 𐐶𐐨 𐐼𐐭 𐑌𐐱𐐻 𐑅𐐲𐐹𐐬𐑆 𐑄𐐰𐐻 𐑄𐐮𐑅 𐑁𐐲𐑉𐑅𐐻 𐑉𐐯𐑆𐐲𐑉𐐯𐐿𐑇𐐲𐑌 𐐸𐐶𐐮𐐽 𐐮𐑆 𐑅𐐹𐐬𐐿𐐲𐑌 𐐱𐑂 𐐮𐑌 𐑄𐐮𐑅 𐑋𐐰𐑌𐐲𐑉, 𐐿𐐰𐑌 𐐺𐐨 𐑄 𐑉𐐯𐑆𐐲𐑉𐐯𐐿𐑇𐐲𐑌 𐐱𐑂 𐑄 𐑅𐐬𐑊𐑆 𐐰𐑌𐐼 𐑄𐐯𐑉 𐐿𐐱𐑌𐑅𐐮𐑀𐑌𐐩𐑇𐐲𐑌 𐐻𐐭 𐐸𐐰𐐹𐐨𐑌𐐯𐑅 𐐫𐑉 𐑋𐐮𐑆𐐲𐑉𐐨. 𐐏𐐨 𐐿𐐰𐑌𐐱𐐻 𐑅𐐲𐐹𐐬𐑆 𐑄𐐰𐐻 𐑄𐐮𐑅 𐐮𐑆 𐐸𐐶𐐱𐐻 𐐮𐐻 𐑋𐐨𐑌𐐯𐑃. 𐐒𐐨𐐸𐐬𐑊𐐼, 𐐌 𐑅𐐩 𐐲𐑌𐐻𐐭 𐐷𐐭, 𐐤𐐩; 𐐺𐐲𐐻 𐐮𐐻 𐑋𐐨𐑌𐐯𐑃 𐑄 𐑉𐐨-𐐷𐐭𐑌𐐴𐐻𐐮𐑍 𐐱𐑂 𐑄 𐑅𐐬𐑊 𐐶𐐮𐑄 𐑄 𐐺𐐱𐐼𐐨 𐐱𐑂 𐑄𐐬𐑆 𐑁𐑉𐐱𐑋 𐑄 𐐼𐐩𐑆 𐐱𐑂 𐐈𐐼𐐲𐑋, 𐐼𐐵𐑌 𐐻𐐭 𐑄 𐑉𐐯𐑆𐐲𐑉𐐯𐐿𐑇𐐲𐑌 𐐱𐑂 𐐗𐑉𐐴𐑅𐐻. 𐐤𐐵 𐐸𐐶𐐯𐑄𐐲𐑉 𐑄 𐑅𐐬𐑊𐑆 𐐰𐑌𐐼 𐑄 𐐺𐐱𐐼𐐨𐑆 𐐱𐑂 𐑄𐐬𐑆 𐐱𐑂 𐐸𐐭𐑋 𐐸𐐰𐑆 𐐺𐐮𐑌 𐑅𐐹𐐬𐐿𐐲𐑌, 𐑇𐐰𐑊 𐐫𐑊 𐐺𐐨 𐑉𐐨-𐐷𐐭𐑌𐐴𐐻𐐯𐐼 𐐰𐐻 𐐶𐐲𐑌𐑅, 𐑄 𐐶𐐮𐐿𐐯𐐼 𐐰𐑆 𐐶𐐯𐑊 𐐰𐑆 𐑄 𐑉𐐴𐐽𐐲𐑅, 𐐌 𐐼𐐭 𐑌𐐱𐐻 𐑅𐐩; 𐑊𐐯𐐻 𐐮𐐻 𐑅𐐲𐑁𐐴𐑅, 𐑄𐐰𐐻 𐐌 𐑅𐐩 𐑄𐐰𐐻 𐑄𐐩 𐐫𐑊 𐐿𐐲𐑋 𐑁𐐬𐑉𐑃; 𐐫𐑉 𐐮𐑌 𐐲𐑄𐐲𐑉 𐐶𐐲𐑉𐐼𐑆, 𐑄𐐯𐑉 𐑉𐐯𐑆𐐲𐑉𐐯𐐿𐑇𐐲𐑌 𐐿𐐲𐑋𐐯𐑃 𐐻𐐭 𐐹𐐰𐑅 𐐺𐐨𐑁𐐬𐑉 𐑄 𐑉𐐯𐑆𐐲𐑉𐐯𐐿𐑇𐐲𐑌 𐐱𐑂 𐑄𐐬𐑆 𐐸𐐭 𐐼𐐴 𐐰𐑁𐐻𐐲𐑉 𐑄 𐑉𐐯𐑆𐐲𐑉𐐯𐐿𐑇𐐲𐑌 𐐱𐑂 𐐗𐑉𐐴𐑅𐐻. 𐐤𐐵 𐑋𐐴 𐑅𐐲𐑌, 𐐌 𐐼𐐭 𐑌𐐱𐐻 𐑅𐐩 𐑄𐐰𐐻 𐑄𐐯𐑉 𐑉𐐯𐑆𐐲𐑉𐐯𐐿𐑇𐐲𐑌 𐐿𐐲𐑋𐐯𐑃 𐐰𐐻 𐑄 𐑉𐐯𐑆𐐲𐑉𐐯𐐿𐑇𐐲𐑌 𐐱𐑂 𐐗𐑉𐐴𐑅𐐻; 𐐺𐐲𐐻 𐐺𐐨𐐸𐐬𐑊𐐼, 𐐌 𐑀𐐮𐑂 𐐮𐐻 𐐰𐑆 𐑋𐐴 𐐬𐐹𐐮𐑌𐐷𐐲𐑌, 𐑄𐐰𐐻 𐑄 𐑅𐐬𐑊𐑆 𐐰𐑌𐐼 𐑄 𐐺𐐱𐐼𐐨𐑆 𐐪𐑉 𐑉𐐨-𐐷𐐭𐑌𐐴𐐻𐐯𐐼, 𐐱𐑂 𐑄 𐑉𐐴𐐽𐐲𐑅, 𐐰𐐻 𐑄 𐑉𐐯𐑆𐐲𐑉𐐯𐐿𐑇𐐲𐑌 𐐱𐑂 𐐗𐑉𐐴𐑅𐐻, 𐐰𐑌𐐼 𐐸𐐮𐑆 𐐰𐑅𐐯𐑌𐑇𐐲𐑌 𐐮𐑌𐐻𐐭 𐐸𐐯𐑂𐐲𐑌. 𐐒𐐲𐐻 𐐸𐐶𐐯𐑄𐐲𐑉 𐐮𐐻 𐐺𐐨 𐐰𐐻 𐐸𐐮𐑆 𐑉𐐯𐑆𐐲𐑉𐐯𐐿𐑇𐐲𐑌, 𐐫𐑉 𐐰𐑁𐐻𐐲𐑉, 𐐌 𐐼𐐭 𐑌𐐱𐐻 𐑅𐐩; 𐐺𐐲𐐻 𐑄𐐮𐑅 𐑋𐐲𐐽 𐐌 𐑅𐐩, 𐑄𐐰𐐻 𐑄𐐯𐑉 𐐮𐑆 𐐲 𐑅𐐹𐐩𐑅 𐐺𐐨𐐻𐐶𐐨𐑌 𐐼𐐯𐑃 𐐰𐑌𐐼 𐑄 𐑉𐐯𐑆𐐲𐑉𐐯𐐿𐑇𐐲𐑌 𐐱𐑂 𐑄 𐐺𐐱𐐼𐐨, 𐐰𐑌𐐼 𐐲 𐑅𐐻𐐩𐐻 𐐱𐑂 𐑄 𐑅𐐬𐑊 𐐮𐑌 𐐸𐐰𐐹𐐨𐑌𐐯𐑅 𐐫𐑉 𐐮𐑌 𐑋𐐮𐑆𐐲𐑉𐐨, 𐐲𐑌𐐻𐐮𐑊 𐑄 𐐻𐐴𐑋 𐐸𐐶𐐮𐐽 𐐮𐑆 𐐲𐐹𐐶𐑎𐑌𐐻𐐯𐐼 𐐱𐑂 𐐘𐐱𐐼, 𐑄𐐰𐐻 𐑄 𐐼𐐯𐐼 𐑇𐐰𐑊 𐐿𐐲𐑋 𐑁𐐬𐑉𐑃, 𐐰𐑌𐐼 𐐺𐐨 𐑉𐐨-𐐷𐐭𐑌𐐴𐐻𐐯𐐼, 𐐺𐐬𐑃 𐑅𐐬𐑊 𐐰𐑌𐐼 𐐺𐐱𐐼𐐨, 𐐰𐑌𐐼 𐐺𐐨 𐐺𐑉𐐫𐐻 𐐻𐐭 𐑅𐐻𐐰𐑌𐐼 𐐺𐐨𐑁𐐬𐑉 𐐘𐐱𐐼, 𐐰𐑌𐐼 𐐺𐐨 𐐾𐐲𐐾𐐼 𐐲𐐿𐐫𐑉𐐼𐐮𐑍 𐐻𐐭 𐑄𐐯𐑉 𐐶𐐲𐑉𐐿𐑅; 𐐷𐐩, 𐑄𐐮𐑅 𐐺𐑉𐐮𐑍𐐯𐑃 𐐲𐐺𐐵𐐻 𐑄 𐑉𐐯𐑅𐐻𐐬𐑉𐐩𐑇𐐲𐑌 𐐱𐑂 𐑄𐐬𐑆 𐑃𐐮𐑍𐑆 𐐱𐑂 𐐸𐐶𐐮𐐽 𐐸𐐰𐑆 𐐺𐐮𐑌 𐑅𐐹𐐬𐐿𐐲𐑌 𐐺𐐴 𐑄 𐑋𐐵𐑃𐑅 𐐱𐑂 𐑄 𐐹𐑉𐐱𐑁𐐯𐐻𐑅. 𐐜 𐑅𐐬𐑊 𐑇𐐰𐑊 𐐺𐐨 𐑉𐐨𐑅𐐻𐐬𐑉𐐼 𐐻𐐭 𐑄 𐐺𐐱𐐼𐐨, 𐐰𐑌𐐼 𐑄 𐐺𐐱𐐼𐐨 𐐻𐐭 𐑄 𐑅𐐬𐑊; 𐐷𐐩, 𐐰𐑌𐐼 𐐯𐑂𐐲𐑉𐐨 𐑊𐐮𐑋 𐐰𐑌𐐼 𐐾𐑎𐑌𐐻 𐑇𐐰𐑊 𐐺𐐨 𐑉𐐨𐑅𐐻𐐬𐑉𐐼 𐐻𐐭 𐐮𐐻𐑅 𐐺𐐱𐐼𐐨; 𐐷𐐩, 𐐨𐑂𐐲𐑌 𐐲 𐐸𐐯𐑉 𐐱𐑂 𐑄 𐐸𐐯𐐼 𐑇𐐰𐑊 𐑌𐐱𐐻 𐐺𐐨 𐑊𐐱𐑅𐐻, 𐐺𐐲𐐻 𐐫𐑊 𐑃𐐮𐑍𐑆 𐑇𐐰𐑊 𐐺𐐨 𐑉𐐨𐑅𐐻𐐬𐑉𐐼 𐐻𐐭 𐑄𐐯𐑉 𐐹𐑉𐐱𐐹𐐲𐑉 𐐰𐑌𐐼 𐐹𐐲𐑉𐑁𐐯𐐿𐐻 𐑁𐑉𐐩𐑋. 𐐈𐑌𐐼 𐑌𐐵 𐑋𐐴 𐑅𐐲𐑌, 𐑄𐐮𐑅 𐐮𐑆 𐑄 𐑉𐐯𐑅𐐻𐐬𐑉𐐩𐑇𐐲𐑌 𐐱𐑂 𐐸𐐶𐐮𐐽 𐐸𐐰𐑆 𐐺𐐮𐑌 𐑅𐐹𐐬𐐿𐐲𐑌 𐐺𐐴 𐑄 𐑋𐐵𐑃𐑅 𐐱𐑂 𐑄 𐐹𐑉𐐱𐑁𐐯𐐻𐑅: 𐐈𐑌𐐼 𐑄𐐯𐑌 𐑇𐐰𐑊 𐑄 𐑉𐐴𐐽𐐲𐑅 𐑇𐐴𐑌 𐑁𐐬𐑉𐑃 𐐮𐑌 𐑄 𐐿𐐮𐑍𐐼𐐲𐑋 𐐱𐑂 𐐘𐐱𐐼. 𐐒𐐲𐐻 𐐺𐐨𐐸𐐬𐑊𐐼, 𐐰𐑌 𐐫𐑁𐐳𐑊 𐐼𐐯𐑃 𐐿𐐲𐑋𐐯𐑃 𐐲𐐹𐐱𐑌 𐑄 𐐶𐐮𐐿𐐯𐐼; 𐑁𐐫𐑉 𐑄𐐩 𐐼𐐴 𐐰𐑆 𐐻𐐭 𐑃𐐮𐑍𐑆 𐐹𐐲𐑉𐐻𐐩𐑌𐐮𐑍 𐐻𐐭 𐑃𐐮𐑍𐑆 𐐱𐑂 𐑉𐐴𐐽𐐲𐑅𐑌𐐯𐑅; 𐑁𐐫𐑉 𐑄𐐩 𐐪𐑉 𐐲𐑌𐐿𐑊𐐨𐑌, 𐐰𐑌𐐼 𐑌𐐬 𐐲𐑌𐐿𐑊𐐨𐑌 𐑃𐐮𐑍 𐐿𐐰𐑌 𐐮𐑌𐐸𐐯𐑉𐐮𐐻 𐑄 𐐿𐐮𐑍𐐼𐐲𐑋 𐐱𐑂 𐐘𐐱𐐼; 𐐺𐐲𐐻 𐑄𐐩 𐐪𐑉 𐐿𐐰𐑅𐐻 𐐵𐐻, 𐐰𐑌𐐼 𐐿𐐱𐑌𐑅𐐴𐑌𐐼 𐐻𐐭 𐐹𐐪𐑉𐐻𐐩𐐿 𐐱𐑂 𐑄 𐑁𐑉𐐭𐐻𐑅 𐐱𐑂 𐑄𐐯𐑉 𐑊𐐩𐐺𐐲𐑉𐑆 𐐫𐑉 𐑄𐐯𐑉 𐐶𐐲𐑉𐐿𐑅, 𐐸𐐶𐐮𐐽 𐐸𐐰𐑂 𐐺𐐮𐑌 𐐨𐑂𐐮𐑊; 𐐰𐑌𐐼 𐑄𐐩 𐐼𐑉𐐮𐑍𐐿 𐑄 𐐼𐑉𐐯𐑀𐑆 𐐱𐑂 𐐲 𐐺𐐮𐐻𐐲𐑉 𐐿𐐲𐐹.

8. 𐐈𐑌𐐼 𐑌𐐵, 𐑋𐐴 𐑅𐐲𐑌, 𐐌 𐐸𐐰𐑂 𐑅𐐲𐑋𐐸𐐶𐐱𐐻 𐐻𐐭 𐑅𐐩 𐐿𐐱𐑌𐑅𐐲𐑉𐑌𐐮𐑍 𐑄 𐑉𐐯𐑅𐐻𐐬𐑉𐐩𐑇𐐲𐑌 𐐱𐑂 𐐸𐐶𐐮𐐽 𐐸𐐰𐑆 𐐺𐐮𐑌 𐑅𐐹𐐬𐐿𐐲𐑌; 𐑁𐐫𐑉 𐐺𐐨𐐸𐐬𐑊𐐼, 𐑅𐐲𐑋 𐐸𐐰𐑂 𐑉𐐯𐑅𐐻𐐯𐐼 𐑄 𐑅𐐿𐑉𐐮𐐹𐐽𐐲𐑉𐑆, 𐐰𐑌𐐼 𐐸𐐰𐑂 𐑀𐐫𐑌 𐑁𐐪𐑉 𐐲𐑅𐐻𐑉𐐩 𐐺𐐨𐐿𐐫𐑆 𐐱𐑂 𐑄𐐮𐑅 𐑃𐐮𐑍. 𐐈𐑌𐐼 𐐌 𐐹𐐲𐑉𐑅𐐨𐑂 𐑄𐐰𐐻 𐑄𐐴 𐑋𐐴𐑌𐐼 𐐸𐐰𐑆 𐐺𐐮𐑌 𐐶𐐲𐑉𐐨𐐼 𐐫𐑊𐑅𐐬 𐐿𐐱𐑌𐑅𐐲𐑉𐑌𐐮𐑍 𐑄𐐮𐑅 𐑃𐐮𐑍. 𐐒𐐲𐐻 𐐺𐐨𐐸𐐬𐑊𐐼, 𐐌 𐐶𐐮𐑊 𐐯𐐿𐑅𐐹𐑊𐐩𐑌 𐐮𐐻 𐐲𐑌𐐻𐐭 𐑄𐐨. 𐐌 𐑅𐐩 𐐲𐑌𐐻𐐭 𐑄𐐨, 𐑋𐐴 𐑅𐐲𐑌, 𐑄𐐰𐐻 𐑄 𐐹𐑊𐐰𐑌 𐐱𐑂 𐑉𐐯𐑅𐐻𐐬𐑉𐐩𐑇𐐲𐑌 𐐮𐑆 𐑉𐐯𐐿𐐶𐐮𐑆𐐮𐐻 𐐶𐐮𐑄 𐑄 𐐾𐐲𐑅𐐻𐐮𐑅 𐐱𐑂 𐐘𐐱𐐼; 𐑁𐐫𐑉 𐐮𐐻 𐐮𐑆 𐑉𐐯𐐿𐐶𐐮𐑆𐐮𐐻 𐑄𐐰𐐻 𐐫𐑊 𐑃𐐮𐑍𐑆 𐑇𐐳𐐼 𐐺𐐨 𐑉𐐨𐑅𐐻𐐬𐑉𐐼 𐐻𐐭 𐑄𐐯𐑉 𐐹𐑉𐐱𐐹𐐲𐑉 𐐫𐑉𐐼𐐲𐑉. 𐐒𐐨𐐸𐐬𐑊𐐼, 𐐮𐐻 𐐮𐑆 𐑉𐐯𐐿𐐶𐐮𐑆𐐮𐐻 𐐰𐑌𐐼 𐐾𐐲𐑅𐐻, 𐐲𐐿𐐫𐑉𐐼𐐮𐑍 𐐻𐐭 𐑄 𐐹𐐵𐐲𐑉 𐐰𐑌𐐼 𐑉𐐯𐑆𐐲𐑉𐐯𐐿𐑇𐐲𐑌 𐐱𐑂 𐐗𐑉𐐴𐑅𐐻, 𐑄𐐰𐐻 𐑄 𐑅𐐬𐑊 𐐱𐑂 𐑋𐐰𐑌 𐑇𐐳𐐼 𐐺𐐨 𐑉𐐨𐑅𐐻𐐬𐑉𐐼 𐐻𐐭 𐐮𐐻𐑅 𐐺𐐱𐐼𐐨, 𐐰𐑌𐐼 𐑄𐐰𐐻 𐐯𐑂𐐲𐑉𐐨 𐐹𐐪𐑉𐐻 𐐱𐑂 𐑄 𐐺𐐱𐐼𐐨 𐑇𐐳𐐼 𐐺𐐨 𐑉𐐨𐑅𐐻𐐬𐑉𐐼 𐐻𐐭 𐐮𐐻𐑅𐐯𐑊𐑁. 𐐈𐑌𐐼 𐐮𐐻 𐐮𐑆 𐑉𐐯𐐿𐐶𐐮𐑆𐐮𐐻 𐐶𐐮𐑄 𐑄 𐐾𐐲𐑅𐐻𐐮𐑅 𐐱𐑂 𐐘𐐱𐐼, 𐑄𐐰𐐻 𐑋𐐯𐑌 𐑇𐐳𐐼 𐐺𐐨 𐐾𐐲𐐾𐐼 𐐲𐐿𐐫𐑉𐐼𐐮𐑍 𐐻𐐭 𐑄𐐯𐑉 𐐶𐐲𐑉𐐿𐑅; 𐐰𐑌𐐼 𐐮𐑁 𐑄𐐯𐑉 𐐶𐐲𐑉𐐿𐑅 𐐶𐐲𐑉 𐑀𐐳𐐼 𐐮𐑌 𐑄𐐮𐑅 𐑊𐐴𐑁, 𐐰𐑌𐐼 𐑄 𐐼𐐯𐑆𐐴𐑉𐑆 𐐱𐑂 𐑄𐐯𐑉 𐐸𐐪𐑉𐐻𐑅 𐐶𐐲𐑉 𐑀𐐳𐐼, 𐑄𐐰𐐻 𐑄𐐩 𐑇𐐳𐐼 𐐫𐑊𐑅𐐬, 𐐰𐐻 𐑄 𐑊𐐰𐑅𐐻 𐐼𐐩, 𐐺𐐨 𐑉𐐨𐑅𐐻𐐬𐑉𐐼 𐐲𐑌𐐻𐐭 𐑄𐐰𐐻 𐐸𐐶𐐮𐐽 𐐮𐑆 𐑀𐐳𐐼; 𐐰𐑌𐐼 𐐮𐑁 𐑄𐐯𐑉 𐐶𐐲𐑉𐐿𐑅 𐐪𐑉 𐐨𐑂𐐮𐑊 𐑄𐐩 𐑇𐐰𐑊 𐐺𐐨 𐑉𐐨𐑅𐐻𐐬𐑉𐐼 𐐲𐑌𐐻𐐭 𐑄𐐯𐑌 𐑁𐐫𐑉 𐐨𐑂𐐮𐑊; 𐑄𐐯𐑉𐑁𐐬𐑉 𐐫𐑊 𐑃𐐮𐑍𐑆 𐑇𐐰𐑊

𐐺 𐑉𐐨𐑅𐐻𐐬𐑉𐐼 𐐻𐐭 𐑄𐐩𐑉 𐐹𐑉𐐱𐐹𐐲𐑉 𐐫𐑉𐐼𐐲𐑉; 𐐯𐑂𐑉𐐨 𐑃𐐮𐑍 𐐻𐐭 𐐮𐐻𐑅 𐑌𐐰𐐽𐐲𐑉𐐲𐑊 𐑁𐑉𐐩𐑋; 𐑋𐐫𐑉𐐻𐐰𐑊𐐮𐐻𐐨 𐑉𐐩𐑆𐐼 𐐻𐐭 𐐮𐑋𐐫𐑉𐐻𐐰𐑊𐐮𐐻𐐨; 𐐿𐐫𐑉𐐲𐐹𐑇𐐲𐑌 𐐻𐐭 𐐮𐑌𐐿𐐫𐑉𐐲𐐹𐑇𐐲𐑌; 𐑉𐐩𐑆𐐼 𐐻𐐭 𐐯𐑌𐐼𐑊𐐯𐑅 𐐸𐐰𐐹𐐨𐑌𐐯𐑅, 𐐻𐐭 𐐮𐑌𐐸𐐯𐑉𐐮𐐻 𐑄 𐐿𐐮𐑍𐐼𐐲𐑋 𐐱𐑂 𐐘𐐱𐐼, 𐐫𐑉 𐐻𐐭 𐐯𐑌𐐼𐑊𐐯𐑅 𐑋𐐮𐑆𐐲𐑉𐐨 𐐻𐐭 𐐮𐑌𐐸𐐯𐑉𐐮𐐻 𐑄 𐐿𐐮𐑍𐐼𐐲𐑋 𐐱𐑂 𐑄 𐐼𐐯𐑂𐐲𐑊, 𐑄 𐐶𐐲𐑌 𐐱𐑌 𐐶𐐲𐑌 𐐸𐐰𐑌𐐼, 𐑄 𐐲𐑄𐐲𐑉 𐐱𐑌 𐑄 𐐲𐑄𐐲𐑉; 𐑄 𐐶𐐲𐑌 𐑉𐐩𐑆𐐼 𐐻𐐭 𐐸𐐰𐐹𐐨𐑌𐐯𐑅, 𐐰𐐿𐐫𐑉𐐼𐐮𐑍 𐐻𐐭 𐐸𐐮𐑆 𐐼𐐨𐑆𐐴𐑉𐑆 𐐱𐑂 𐐸𐐰𐐹𐐨𐑌𐐯𐑅; 𐐫𐑉 𐑀𐐳𐐼, 𐐰𐐿𐐫𐑉𐐼𐐮𐑍 𐐻𐐭 𐐸𐐮𐑆 𐐼𐐨𐑆𐐴𐑉𐑆 𐐱𐑂 𐑀𐐳𐐼; 𐐰𐑌𐐼 𐑄 𐐲𐑄𐐲𐑉 𐐻𐐭 𐐨𐑂𐐲𐑊, 𐐰𐐿𐐫𐑉𐐼𐐮𐑍 𐐻𐐭 𐐸𐐮𐑆 𐐼𐐨𐑆𐐴𐑉𐑆 𐐱𐑂 𐐨𐑂𐐲𐑊; 𐑁𐐫𐑉 𐐰𐑆 𐐸𐐨 𐐸𐐰𐑆 𐐼𐐨𐑆𐐴𐑉𐐼 𐐻𐐭 𐐼𐐭 𐐨𐑂𐐲𐑊 𐐫𐑊 𐑄 𐐼𐐩, 𐐨𐑂𐐲𐑌 𐑅𐐬 𐑇𐐰𐑊 𐐸𐐨 𐐸𐐰𐑂 𐐸𐐮𐑆 𐑉𐐨𐐶𐐫𐑉𐐼 𐐱𐑂 𐐨𐑂𐐲𐑊 𐐸𐐶𐐯𐑌 𐑄 𐑌𐐴𐐻 𐐿𐐲𐑋𐐯𐑃. 𐐈𐑌𐐼 𐑅𐐬 𐐮𐐻 𐐮𐑆 𐐱𐑌 𐑄 𐐲𐑄𐐲𐑉 𐐸𐐰𐑌𐐼. 𐐆𐑁 𐐸𐐨 𐐸𐐰𐑃 𐑉𐐨𐐹𐐯𐑌𐐻𐐯𐐼 𐐱𐑂 𐐸𐐮𐑆 𐑅𐐮𐑌𐑆, 𐐰𐑌𐐼 𐐼𐐨𐑆𐐴𐑉𐐼 𐑉𐐴𐐽𐐲𐑅𐑌𐐯𐑅 𐐲𐑌𐐻𐐮𐑊 𐑄 𐐯𐑌𐐼 𐐱𐑂 𐐸𐐮𐑆 𐐼𐐩𐑆, 𐐨𐑂𐐲𐑌 𐑅𐐬 𐐸𐐨 𐑇𐐰𐑊 𐐺𐐨 𐑉𐐨𐐶𐐫𐑉𐐼𐐯𐐼 𐐲𐑌𐐻𐐭 𐑉𐐴𐐽𐐲𐑅𐑌𐐯𐑅. 𐐜𐐨𐑆 𐐪𐑉 𐑄𐐩 𐑄𐐰𐐻 𐐪𐑉 𐑉𐐨𐐼𐐨𐑋𐐼 𐐱𐑂 𐑄 𐐢𐐫𐑉𐐼; 𐐷𐐩, 𐑄𐐨𐑆 𐐪𐑉 𐑄𐐩 𐑄𐐰𐐻 𐐪𐑉 𐐻𐐩𐐿𐑌 𐐵𐐻, 𐑄𐐰𐐻 𐐪𐑉 𐐼𐐨𐑊𐐮𐑂𐐲𐑉𐐼 𐑁𐑉𐐱𐑋 𐑄𐐰𐐻 𐐯𐑌𐐼𐑊𐐯𐑅 𐑌𐐴𐐻 𐐱𐑂 𐐼𐐪𐑉𐐿𐑌𐐯𐑅; 𐐰𐑌𐐼 𐑄𐐲𐑅 𐑄𐐩 𐑅𐐻𐐰𐑌𐐼 𐐫𐑉 𐑁𐐫𐑊; 𐑁𐐫𐑉 𐐺𐐨𐐸𐐬𐑊𐐼, 𐑄𐐩 𐐪𐑉 𐑄𐐩𐑉 𐐬𐑌 𐐾𐐲𐐾𐐯𐑆, 𐐸𐐶𐐯𐑄𐐲𐑉 𐐻𐐭 𐐼𐐭 𐑀𐐳𐐼 𐐫𐑉 𐐼𐐭 𐐨𐑂𐐲𐑊. 𐐤𐐵 𐑄 𐐼𐐨𐐿𐑉𐐨𐑆 𐐱𐑂 𐐘𐐱𐐼 𐐪𐑉 𐐲𐑌𐐫𐑊𐐻𐐲𐑉𐐲𐐺𐐲𐑊; 𐑄𐐯𐑉𐑁𐐬𐑉, 𐑄 𐐶𐐩 𐐮𐑆 𐐹𐑉𐐨𐐹𐐩𐑉𐐼, 𐑄𐐰𐐻 𐐸𐐭𐑅𐐬𐐯𐑂𐐲𐑉 𐐶𐐮𐑊 𐑋𐐩 𐐶𐐫𐐿 𐑄𐐯𐑉𐐮𐑌 𐐰𐑌𐐼 𐐺𐐨 𐑅𐐩𐑂𐐼. 𐐈𐑌𐐼 𐑌𐐵 𐐺𐐨𐐸𐐬𐑊𐐼, 𐑋𐐴 𐑅𐐲𐑌, 𐐼𐐭 𐑌𐐱𐐻 𐑉𐐮𐑅𐐿 𐐶𐐲𐑌 𐑋𐐬𐑉 𐐱𐑁𐐯𐑌𐑅 𐐰𐑀𐐯𐑌𐑅𐐻 𐐷𐐭𐑉 𐐘𐐱𐐼 𐐲𐐹𐐱𐑌 𐑄𐐬𐑆 𐐹𐑎𐑌𐐻𐑅 𐐱𐑂 𐐼𐐱𐐿𐐻𐑉𐐮𐑌, 𐐸𐐶𐐮𐐽 𐐷𐐨 𐐸𐐰𐑂 𐐸𐐮𐑄𐐲𐑉𐐻𐐭 𐑉𐐮𐑅𐐿𐐻 𐐻𐐭 𐐿𐐱𐑋𐐮𐐻 𐑅𐐮𐑌. 𐐔𐐭 𐑌𐐱𐐻 𐑅𐐲𐐹𐐬𐑆, 𐐺𐐨𐐿𐐫𐑆 𐐮𐐻 𐐸𐐰𐑆 𐐺𐐮𐑌 𐑅𐐹𐐬𐐿𐑌 𐐿𐐱𐑌𐑅𐐲𐑉𐑌𐐮𐑍 𐑉𐐯𐑅𐐻𐐬𐑉𐐩𐑇𐐲𐑌, 𐑄𐐰𐐻 𐐷𐐨 𐑇𐐰𐑊 𐐺𐐨 𐑉𐐨𐑅𐐻𐐬𐑉𐐼 𐑁𐑉𐐱𐑋 𐑅𐐮𐑌 𐐻𐐭 𐐸𐐰𐐹𐐨𐑌𐐯𐑅. 𐐒𐐨𐐸𐐬𐑊𐐼, 𐐌 𐑅𐐩 𐐲𐑌𐐻𐐭 𐐷𐐭, 𐐶𐐮𐐿𐐯𐐼𐑌𐐯𐑅 𐑌𐐯𐑂𐐲𐑉 𐐶𐐱𐑆 𐐸𐐰𐐹𐐨𐑌𐐯𐑅.

9. 𐐈𐑌𐐼 𐑌𐐵, 𐑋𐐴 𐑅𐐲𐑌, 𐐫𐑊 𐑋𐐯𐑌 𐑄𐐰𐐻 𐐪𐑉 𐐮𐑌 𐐩 𐑅𐐻𐐩𐐻 𐐱𐑂 𐑌𐐩𐐽𐐲𐑉, 𐐫𐑉 𐐌 𐐶𐐳𐐼 𐑅𐐩, 𐐮𐑌 𐐩 𐐿𐐪𐑉𐑌𐐲𐑊 𐑅𐐻𐐩𐐻, 𐐪𐑉 𐐮𐑌 𐑄 𐑀𐐫𐑊 𐐱𐑂 𐐺𐐮𐐻𐐲𐑉𐑌𐐯𐑅, 𐐰𐑌𐐼 𐐮𐑌 𐑄 𐐺𐐱𐑌𐐼𐑆 𐐱𐑂 𐐮𐑌𐐮𐐿𐐶𐐮𐐻𐐨; 𐑄𐐩 𐐪𐑉 𐐶𐐮𐑄𐐵𐐻 𐐘𐐱𐐼 𐐮𐑌 𐑄 𐐶𐐲𐑉𐑊𐐼, 𐐰𐑌𐐼 𐑄𐐩 𐐸𐐰𐑂 𐑀𐐱𐑌 𐐿𐐱𐑌𐐻𐑉𐐯𐑉𐐨 𐐻𐐭 𐑄 𐑌𐐩𐐽𐐲𐑉 𐐱𐑂 𐐘𐐱𐐼; 𐑄𐐯𐑉𐑁𐐬𐑉, 𐑄𐐩 𐐪𐑉 𐐮𐑌 𐐩 𐑅𐐻𐐩𐐻 𐐿𐐱𐑌𐐻𐑉𐐯𐑉𐐨 𐐻𐐭 𐑄 𐑌𐐩𐐽𐐲𐑉 𐐱𐑂 𐐸𐐰𐐹𐐨𐑌𐐯𐑅. 𐐈𐑌𐐼 𐑌𐐵 𐐺𐐨𐐸𐐬𐑊𐐼, 𐐮𐑆 𐑄 𐑋𐐨𐑌𐐮𐑍 𐐱𐑂 𐑄 𐐶𐐲𐑉𐐼 𐑉𐐯𐑅𐐻𐐬𐑉𐐩𐑇𐐲𐑌, 𐐻𐐭 𐐻𐐩𐐿 𐐩 𐑃𐐮𐑍 𐐱𐑂 𐐩 𐑌𐐰𐐽𐐲𐑉𐐲𐑊 𐑅𐐻𐐩𐐻, 𐐰𐑌𐐼 𐐹𐑊𐐩𐑅 𐐮𐐻 𐐮𐑌 𐐰𐑌 𐐲𐑌𐑌𐐰𐐽𐐲𐑉𐐲𐑊 𐑅𐐻𐐩𐐻, 𐐫𐑉 𐐻𐐭 𐐹𐑊𐐩𐑅 𐐮𐐻 𐐮𐑌 𐐩 𐑅𐐻𐐩𐐻 𐐱𐐹𐐬𐑆𐐮𐐻 𐐻𐐭 𐐮𐐻𐑅 𐑌𐐩𐐽𐐲𐑉? 𐐉, 𐑋𐐴 𐑅𐐲𐑌, 𐑄𐐮𐑅 𐐮𐑆 𐑌𐐱𐐻 𐑄 𐐿𐐩𐑅; 𐐺𐐲𐐻 𐑄 𐑋𐐨𐑌𐐮𐑍 𐐱𐑂 𐑄 𐐶𐐲𐑉𐐼 𐑉𐐯𐑅𐐻𐐬𐑉𐐩𐑇𐐲𐑌, 𐐮𐑆 𐐻𐐭 𐐺𐑉𐐮𐑍 𐐺𐐰𐐿 𐐰𐑀𐐯𐑌 𐐨𐑂𐐲𐑊 𐑁𐐫𐑉 𐐨𐑂𐐲𐑊, 𐐫𐑉 𐐿𐐪𐑉𐑌𐐲𐑊 𐑁𐐫𐑉 𐐿𐐪𐑉𐑌𐐲𐑊, 𐐫𐑉 𐐼𐐯𐑂𐐲𐑊𐐮𐑇 𐑁𐐫𐑉 𐐼𐐯𐑂𐐲𐑊𐐮𐑇; 𐑀𐐳𐐼 𐑁𐐫𐑉 𐑄𐐰𐐻 𐐸𐐶𐐮𐐽 𐐮𐑆 𐑀𐐳𐐼; 𐑉𐐴𐐽𐐲𐑅 𐑁𐐫𐑉 𐑄𐐰𐐻 𐐸𐐶𐐮𐐽 𐐮𐑆 𐑉𐐴𐐽𐐲𐑅; 𐐾𐐲𐑅𐐻 𐑁𐐫𐑉 𐑄𐐰𐐻 𐐸𐐶𐐮𐐽 𐐮𐑆 𐐾𐐲𐑅𐐻; 𐑋𐐲𐑉𐑅𐐮𐑁𐐳𐑊 𐑁𐐫𐑉 𐑄𐐰𐐻 𐐸𐐶𐐮𐐽 𐐮𐑆 𐑋𐐲𐑉𐑅𐐮𐑁𐐳𐑊; 𐑄𐐯𐑉𐑁𐐬𐑉, 𐑋𐐴 𐑅𐐲𐑌, 𐑅𐐨 𐑄𐐰𐐻 𐐷𐐭 𐐪𐑉 𐑋𐐲𐑉𐑅𐐮𐑁𐐳𐑊 𐐲𐑌𐐻𐐭 𐐷𐐭𐑉 𐐺𐑉𐐯𐑄𐑉𐐯𐑌; 𐐼𐐨𐑊 𐐾𐐲𐑅𐐻𐑊𐐨, 𐐾𐐲𐐾 𐑉𐐴𐐽𐐲𐑅𐑊𐐨, 𐐰𐑌𐐼 𐐼𐐭 𐑀𐐳𐐼 𐐿𐐱𐑌𐐻𐐮𐑌𐐷𐐭𐐰𐑊𐐨; 𐐰𐑌𐐼 𐐮𐑁 𐐷𐐨 𐐼𐐭 𐐫𐑊 𐑄𐐨𐑆 𐑃𐐮𐑍𐑆, 𐑄𐐯𐑌 𐑇𐐰𐑊 𐐷𐐨 𐑉𐐨𐑅𐐨𐑂 𐐷𐐭𐑉 𐑉𐐨𐐶𐐫𐑉𐐼; 𐐷𐐩, 𐐷𐐨 𐑇𐐰𐑊 𐐸𐐰𐑂 𐑋𐐲𐑉𐑅𐐨 𐑉𐐨𐑅𐐻𐐬𐑉𐐼 𐐲𐑌𐐻𐐭 𐐷𐐭 𐐰𐑀𐐯𐑌; 𐐷𐐨 𐑇𐐰𐑊 𐐸𐐰𐑂 𐐾𐐲𐑅𐐻𐐮𐑅 𐑉𐐨𐑅𐐻𐐬𐑉𐐼 𐐲𐑌𐐻𐐭 𐐷𐐭 𐐰𐑀𐐯𐑌; 𐐷𐐨 𐑇𐐰𐑊 𐐸𐐰𐑂 𐐩 𐑉𐐴𐐽𐐲𐑅 𐐾𐐲𐐾𐑋𐐯𐑌𐐻 𐑉𐐨𐑅𐐻𐐬𐑉𐐼 𐐲𐑌𐐻𐐭 𐐷𐐭 𐐰𐑀𐐯𐑌; 𐐰𐑌𐐼 𐐷𐐨 𐑇𐐰𐑊 𐐸𐐰𐑂 𐑀𐐳𐐼 𐑉𐐨𐐶𐐫𐑉𐐼𐐯𐐼 𐐲𐑌𐐻𐐭 𐐷𐐭 𐐰𐑀𐐯𐑌; 𐑁𐐫𐑉 𐑄𐐰𐐻 𐐸𐐶𐐮𐐽 𐐷𐐨 𐐼𐐭 𐑅𐐯𐑌𐐼 𐐵𐐻 𐑇𐐰𐑊 𐑉𐐨𐐻𐐲𐑉𐑌 𐐲𐑌𐐻𐐭 𐐷𐐭 𐐰𐑀𐐯𐑌, 𐐰𐑌𐐼 𐐺𐐨 𐑉𐐨𐑅𐐻𐐬𐑉𐐼; 𐑄𐐯𐑉𐑁𐐬𐑉 𐑄 𐐶𐐲𐑉𐐼 𐑉𐐯𐑅𐐻𐐬𐑉𐐩𐑇𐐲𐑌 𐑋𐐬𐑉 𐑁𐐳𐑊𐐨 𐐿𐐱𐑌𐐼𐐯𐑋𐑌𐐯𐑃 𐑄 𐑅𐐮𐑌𐐲𐑉, 𐐰𐑌𐐼 𐐾𐐲𐑅𐐻𐐮𐑁𐐴𐐯𐑃 𐐸𐐮𐑋 𐑌𐐱𐐻 𐐰𐐻 𐐫𐑊.

10. 𐐈𐑌𐐼 𐑌𐐵, 𐑋𐐴 𐑅𐐲𐑌, 𐐌 𐐹𐐲𐑉𐑅𐐨𐑂 𐑄𐐯𐑉 𐐮𐑆 𐑅𐐲𐑋𐐶𐐱𐐻 𐑋𐐬𐑉 𐐸𐐶𐐮𐐽 𐐼𐐲𐑃 𐐶𐐲𐑉𐐨 𐐷𐐭𐑉 𐑋𐐴𐑌𐐼, 𐐸𐐶𐐮𐐽 𐐷𐐨 𐐿𐐰𐑌𐐱𐐻 𐐲𐑌𐐼𐐲𐑉𐑅𐐻𐐰𐑌𐐼, 𐐸𐐶𐐮𐐽 𐐮𐑆 𐐿𐐱𐑌𐑅𐐲𐑉𐑌𐐮𐑍 𐑄 𐐾𐐲𐑅𐐻𐐮𐑅 𐐱𐑂 𐐘𐐱𐐼 𐐮𐑌 𐑄 𐐹𐐲𐑌𐐮𐑇𐑋𐐯𐑌𐐻 𐐱𐑂 𐑄 𐑅𐐮𐑌𐐲𐑉; 𐑁𐐫𐑉 𐐷𐐨 𐐼𐐭 𐐻𐑉𐐴 𐐻𐐭 𐑅𐐲𐐹𐐬𐑆 𐑄𐐰𐐻 𐐮𐐻 𐐮𐑆 𐐮𐑌𐐾𐐲𐑅𐐻𐐮𐑅 𐑄𐐰𐐻 𐑄 𐑅𐐮𐑌𐐲𐑉 𐑇𐐳𐐼 𐐺𐐨 𐐿𐐱𐑌𐑅𐐴𐑌𐐼 𐐻𐐭 𐐩 𐑅𐐻𐐩𐐻 𐐱𐑂 𐑋𐐮𐑆𐐲𐑉𐐨. 𐐤𐐵 𐐺𐐨𐐸𐐬𐑊𐐼, 𐑋𐐴 𐑅𐐲𐑌, 𐐌 𐐶𐐮𐑊 𐐯𐐿𐑅𐐹𐑊𐐩𐑌 𐑄𐐮𐑅 𐑃𐐮𐑍 𐐲𐑌𐐻𐐭 𐑄𐐨: 𐑁𐐫𐑉 𐐺𐐨𐐸𐐬𐑊𐐼, 𐐰𐑁𐐻𐐲𐑉 𐑄 𐐢𐐫𐑉𐐼 𐐘𐐱𐐼 𐑅𐐯𐑌𐐻 𐐵𐑉 𐑁𐐲𐑉𐑅𐐻 𐐹𐐩𐑉𐐯𐑌𐐻𐑅 𐑁𐐬𐑉𐑃 𐑁𐑉𐐱𐑋 𐑄 𐑀𐐪𐑉𐐼𐑌 𐐱𐑂 𐐀𐐼𐐯𐑌, 𐐻𐐭 𐐻𐐮𐑊 𐑄 𐑀𐑉𐐵𐑌𐐼, 𐑁𐑉𐐱𐑋 𐐸𐐶𐐯𐑌𐑅 𐑄𐐩 𐐶𐐲𐑉 𐐻𐐩𐐿𐑌; 𐐷𐐩, 𐐸𐐨 𐐼𐑉𐐭 𐐵𐐻 𐑄 𐑋𐐰𐑌, 𐐰𐑌𐐼 𐐸𐐨 𐐹𐑊𐐩𐑅𐐻 𐐰𐐻 𐑄 𐐨𐑅𐐻 𐐯𐑌𐐼 𐐱𐑂 𐑄 𐑀𐐪𐑉𐐼𐑌 𐐱𐑂 𐐀𐐼𐐯𐑌, 𐐗𐐯𐑉𐐲𐐺𐐮𐑋 𐐰𐑌𐐼 𐐩 𐑁𐑊𐐩𐑋𐐮𐑍 𐑅𐐫𐑉𐐼 𐐸𐐶𐐮𐐽 𐐻𐐲𐑉𐑌𐐼 𐐯𐑂𐑉𐐨 𐐶𐐩, 𐐻𐐭 𐐿𐐨𐐹 𐑄 𐐻𐑉𐐨 𐐱𐑂 𐑊𐐴𐑁. 𐐤𐐵 𐐶𐐨 𐑅𐐨 𐑄𐐰𐐻 𐑄 𐑋𐐰𐑌 𐐸𐐰𐐼 𐐺𐐨𐐿𐐲𐑋 𐐰𐑆 𐑄 𐐘𐐱𐐼

𐐘𐐱𐐼, 𐑌𐐬𐐮𐑍 𐑀𐐳𐐼 𐐰𐑌𐐼 𐐨𐑂𐐮𐑊; 𐐰𐑌𐐼 𐑊𐐯𐑅𐐻 𐐸𐐨 𐑇𐐳𐐼 𐐹𐐳𐐻 𐑁𐐫𐑉𐑃 𐐸𐐮𐑆 𐐸𐐰𐑌𐐼, 𐐰𐑌𐐼 𐐻𐐩𐐿 𐐫𐑊𐑅𐐬 𐐱𐑂 𐑄 𐐻𐑉𐐨 𐐱𐑂 𐑊𐐴𐑁, 𐐰𐑌𐐼 𐐨𐐻 𐐰𐑌𐐼 𐑊𐐮𐑂 𐑁𐐫𐑉𐐯𐑂𐐲𐑉, 𐑄 𐐢𐐫𐑉𐐼 𐐘𐐱𐐼 𐐹𐑊𐐩𐑅𐐻 𐐽𐐯𐑉𐐭𐐺𐐮𐑋 𐐰𐑌𐐼 𐑄 𐑁𐑊𐐩𐑋𐐮𐑍 𐑅𐐫𐑉𐐼, 𐑄𐐰𐐻 𐐸𐐨 𐑇𐐳𐐼 𐑌𐐱𐐻 𐐹𐐪𐑉𐐻𐐩𐐿 𐐱𐑂 𐑄 𐑁𐑉𐐭𐐻; 𐐰𐑌𐐼 𐑄𐐲𐑅 𐐶𐐨 𐑅𐐨 𐑄𐐰𐐻 𐑄𐐯𐑉 𐐶𐐱𐑆 𐐰 𐐻𐐴𐑋 𐑀𐑉𐐪𐑌𐐻𐐯𐐼 𐐲𐑌𐐻𐐭 𐑋𐐰𐑌 𐐻𐐭 𐑉𐐨𐐹𐐯𐑌𐐻, 𐐷𐐩, 𐐰 𐐹𐑉𐐬𐐺𐐩𐑇𐐲𐑌𐐯𐑉𐐨 𐐻𐐴𐑋, 𐐰 𐐻𐐴𐑋 𐐻𐐭 𐑉𐐨𐐹𐐯𐑌𐐻 𐐰𐑌𐐼 𐑅𐐲𐑉𐑂 𐐘𐐱𐐼. 𐐙𐐫𐑉 𐐺𐐨𐐸𐐬𐑊𐐼, 𐐮𐑁 𐐈𐐼𐐲𐑋 𐐸𐐰𐐼 𐐹𐐳𐐻 𐑁𐐫𐑉𐑃 𐐸𐐮𐑆 𐐸𐐰𐑌𐐼 𐐮𐑋𐐨𐐼𐐨𐐲𐐻𐑊𐐨, 𐐰𐑌𐐼 𐐹𐐪𐑉𐐻𐐩𐐿𐐲𐑌 𐐱𐑂 𐑄 𐐻𐑉𐐨 𐐱𐑂 𐑊𐐴𐑁, 𐐸𐐨 𐐶𐐳𐐼 𐐸𐐰𐑂 𐑊𐐮𐑂𐐼 𐑁𐐫𐑉𐐯𐑂𐐲𐑉, 𐐲𐐿𐐫𐑉𐐼𐐮𐑍 𐐻𐐭 𐑄 𐐶𐐲𐑉𐐼 𐐱𐑂 𐐘𐐱𐐼, 𐐸𐐰𐑂𐐮𐑍 𐑌𐐬 𐑅𐐹𐐩𐑅 𐑁𐐫𐑉 𐑉𐐨𐐹𐐯𐑌𐐻𐐲𐑌𐑅; 𐐷𐐩, 𐐰𐑌𐐼 𐐫𐑊𐑅𐐬 𐑄 𐐶𐐲𐑉𐐼 𐐱𐑂 𐐘𐐱𐐼 𐐶𐐳𐐼 𐐸𐐰𐑂 𐐺𐐮𐑌 𐑂𐐱𐐮𐐼, 𐐰𐑌𐐼 𐑄 𐑀𐑉𐐩𐐻 𐐹𐑊𐐰𐑌 𐐱𐑂 𐑅𐐰𐑊𐑂𐐩𐑇𐐲𐑌 𐐶𐐳𐐼 𐐸𐐰𐑂 𐐺𐐮𐑌 𐑁𐑉𐐲𐑅𐐻𐑉𐐩𐐻𐐯𐐼. 𐐒𐐲𐐻 𐐺𐐨𐐸𐐬𐑊𐐼, 𐐮𐐻 𐐶𐐱𐑆 𐐰𐐹𐐱𐐮𐑌𐐻𐐯𐐼 𐐲𐑌𐐻𐐭 𐑋𐐰𐑌 𐐻𐐭 𐐼𐐴; 𐑄𐐯𐑉𐑁𐐫𐑉, 𐐰𐑆 𐑄𐐩 𐐶𐐲𐑉 𐐿𐐲𐐻 𐐱𐑁 𐑁𐑉𐐱𐑋 𐑄 𐐻𐑉𐐨 𐐱𐑂 𐑊𐐴𐑁 𐑄𐐩 𐑇𐐳𐐼 𐐺𐐨 𐐿𐐲𐐻 𐐱𐑁 𐑁𐑉𐐱𐑋 𐑄 𐑁𐐩𐑅 𐐱𐑂 𐑄 𐐲𐑉𐑃; 𐐰𐑌𐐼 𐑋𐐰𐑌 𐐺𐐨𐐿𐐩𐑋 𐑊𐐱𐑅𐐻 𐑁𐐫𐑉𐐯𐑂𐐲𐑉; 𐐷𐐩, 𐑄𐐩 𐐺𐐨𐐿𐐩𐑋 𐑁𐐫𐑊𐐲𐑌 𐑋𐐰𐑌.

11. 𐐈𐑌𐐼 𐑌𐐵 𐐶𐐨 𐑅𐐨 𐐺𐐴 𐑄𐐮𐑅, 𐑄𐐰𐐻 𐐵𐑉 𐑁𐐲𐑉𐑅𐐻 𐐹𐐯𐑉𐐲𐑌𐐻𐑅 𐐶𐐲𐑉 𐐿𐐲𐐻 𐐱𐑁 𐐺𐐬𐑃 𐐻𐐯𐑋𐐹𐐬𐑉𐐲𐑊𐐨 𐐰𐑌𐐼 𐑅𐐹𐐮𐑉𐐮𐐻𐐷𐐭𐐲𐑊𐐨 𐑁𐑉𐐱𐑋 𐑄 𐐹𐑉𐐯𐑆𐐯𐑌𐑅 𐐱𐑂 𐑄 𐐢𐐫𐑉𐐼; 𐐰𐑌𐐼 𐑄𐐲𐑅 𐐶𐐨 𐑅𐐨 𐑄𐐩 𐐺𐐨𐐿𐐩𐑋 𐑅𐐲𐐺𐐾𐐯𐐿𐐻𐑅 𐐻𐐭 𐑁𐐱𐑊𐐬 𐐰𐑁𐐻𐐲𐑉 𐑄𐐩𐑉 𐐬𐑌 𐐶𐐮𐑊. 𐐤𐐵 𐐺𐐨𐐸𐐬𐑊𐐼, 𐐮𐐻 𐐶𐐱𐑆 𐑌𐐱𐐻 𐐯𐐿𐑅𐐹𐐨𐐼𐐨𐐲𐑌𐐻 𐑄𐐰𐐻 𐑋𐐰𐑌 𐑇𐐳𐐼 𐐺𐐨 𐑉𐐨𐐿𐑊𐐩𐑋𐐼 𐑁𐑉𐐱𐑋 𐑄𐐮𐑅 𐐻𐐯𐑋𐐹𐐬𐑉𐐲𐑊 𐐼𐐯𐑃, 𐑁𐐫𐑉 𐑄𐐰𐐻 𐐶𐐳𐐼 𐐼𐐨𐑅𐐻𐑉𐐱𐐮 𐑄 𐑀𐑉𐐩𐐻 𐐹𐑊𐐰𐑌 𐐱𐑂 𐐸𐐰𐐹𐐨𐑌𐐯𐑅; 𐑄𐐯𐑉𐑁𐐫𐑉, 𐐰𐑆 𐑄 𐑅𐐬𐑊 𐐿𐐳𐐼 𐑌𐐯𐑂𐐲𐑉 𐐼𐐴, 𐐰𐑌𐐼 𐑄 𐑁𐐫𐑊 𐐸𐐰𐐼 𐐺𐑉𐐫𐐻 𐐲𐐹𐐱𐑌 𐐫𐑊 𐑋𐐰𐑌𐐿𐐴𐑌𐐼 𐐰 𐑅𐐹𐐮𐑉𐐮𐐻𐐷𐐭𐐲𐑊 𐐼𐐯𐑃 𐐰𐑆 𐐶𐐯𐑊 𐐰𐑆 𐐰 𐐻𐐯𐑋𐐹𐐬𐑉𐐲𐑊; 𐑄𐐰𐐻 𐐮𐑆, 𐑄𐐩 𐐶𐐲𐑉 𐐿𐐲𐐻 𐐱𐑁 𐑁𐑉𐐱𐑋 𐑄 𐐹𐑉𐐯𐑆𐐯𐑌𐑅 𐐱𐑂 𐑄 𐐢𐐫𐑉𐐼; 𐐮𐐻 𐐶𐐱𐑆 𐐯𐐿𐑅𐐹𐐨𐐼𐐨𐐲𐑌𐐻 𐑄𐐰𐐻 𐑋𐐰𐑌𐐿𐐴𐑌𐐼 𐑇𐐳𐐼 𐐺𐐨 𐑉𐐨𐐿𐑊𐐩𐑋𐐼 𐑁𐑉𐐱𐑋 𐑄𐐮𐑅 𐑅𐐹𐐮𐑉𐐮𐐻𐐷𐐭𐐲𐑊 𐐼𐐯𐑃; 𐑄𐐯𐑉𐑁𐐫𐑉, 𐐰𐑆 𐑄𐐩 𐐸𐐰𐐼 𐐺𐐨𐐿𐐲𐑋 𐐿𐐪𐑉𐑌𐐲𐑊, 𐑅𐐯𐑌𐑇𐐭𐐲𐑊, 𐐰𐑌𐐼 𐐼𐐯𐑂𐐮𐑊𐐮𐑇, 𐐺𐐴 𐑌𐐩𐐽𐐲𐑉, 𐑄𐐮𐑅 𐐹𐑉𐐬𐐺𐐩𐑇𐐲𐑌𐐯𐑉𐐨 𐑅𐐻𐐩𐐻 𐐺𐐨𐐿𐐩𐑋 𐐰 𐑅𐐻𐐩𐐻 𐑁𐐫𐑉 𐑄𐐯𐑋 𐐻𐐭 𐐹𐑉𐐨𐐹𐐩𐑉; 𐐮𐐻 𐐺𐐨𐐿𐐩𐑋 𐐰 𐐹𐑉𐐨𐐹𐐰𐑉𐐲𐐻𐐲𐑉𐐨 𐑅𐐻𐐩𐐻. 𐐈𐑌𐐼 𐑌𐐵 𐑉𐐨𐑋𐐯𐑋𐐺𐐲𐑉, 𐑋𐐴 𐑅𐐲𐑌, 𐐮𐑁 𐐮𐐻 𐐶𐐲𐑉 𐑌𐐱𐐻 𐑁𐐫𐑉 𐑄 𐐹𐑊𐐰𐑌 𐐱𐑂 𐑉𐐨𐐼𐐯𐑋𐑇𐐲𐑌, (𐑊𐐩𐐮𐑍 𐐮𐐻 𐐰𐑅𐐴𐐼,) 𐐰𐑆 𐑅𐐭𐑌 𐐰𐑆 𐑄𐐩 𐐶𐐲𐑉 𐐼𐐯𐐼, 𐑄𐐩𐑉 𐑅𐐬𐑊𐑆 𐐶𐐲𐑉 𐑋𐐮𐑆𐐲𐑉𐐲𐐺𐑊, 𐐺𐐨𐐮𐑍 𐐿𐐲𐐻 𐐱𐑁 𐑁𐑉𐐱𐑋 𐑄 𐐹𐑉𐐯𐑆𐐯𐑌𐑅 𐐱𐑂 𐑄 𐐢𐐫𐑉𐐼. 𐐈𐑌𐐼 𐑌𐐵 𐑄𐐯𐑉 𐐶𐐱𐑆 𐑌𐐬 𐑋𐐨𐑌𐑆 𐐻𐐭 𐑉𐐨𐐿𐑊𐐩𐑋 𐑋𐐯𐑌 𐑁𐑉𐐱𐑋 𐑄𐐮𐑅 𐑁𐐫𐑊𐐲𐑌 𐑅𐐻𐐩𐐻, 𐐸𐐶𐐮𐐽 𐑋𐐰𐑌 𐐸𐐰𐐼 𐐺𐑉𐐫𐐻 𐐲𐐹𐐱𐑌 𐐸𐐮𐑋𐑅𐐯𐑊𐑁 𐐺𐐨𐐿𐐫𐑆 𐐱𐑂 𐐸𐐮𐑆 𐐬𐑌 𐐼𐐮𐑅𐐬𐐺𐐨𐐼𐐨𐐯𐑌𐑅; 𐑄𐐯𐑉𐑁𐐫𐑉, 𐐲𐐿𐐫𐑉𐐼𐐮𐑍 𐐻𐐭 𐐾𐐲𐑅𐐻𐐮𐑅, 𐑄 𐐹𐑊𐐰𐑌 𐐱𐑂 𐑉𐐨𐐼𐐯𐑋𐑇𐐲𐑌 𐐿𐐳𐐼 𐑌𐐱𐐻 𐐺𐐨 𐐺𐑉𐐫𐐻 𐐲𐐺𐐵𐐻, 𐐬𐑌𐑊𐐨 𐐱𐑌 𐐿𐐲𐑌𐐼𐐮𐑇𐐲𐑌𐑆 𐐱𐑂 𐑉𐐨𐐹𐐯𐑌𐐻𐐲𐑌𐑅 𐐱𐑂 𐑋𐐯𐑌 𐐮𐑌 𐑄𐐮𐑅 𐐹𐑉𐐬𐐺𐐩𐑇𐐲𐑌𐐯𐑉𐐨 𐑅𐐻𐐩𐐻, 𐐷𐐩, 𐑄𐐮𐑅 𐐹𐑉𐐨𐐹𐐰𐑉𐐲𐐻𐐲𐑉𐐨 𐑅𐐻𐐩𐐻; 𐑁𐐫𐑉 𐐯𐐿𐑅𐐯𐐹𐐻 𐐮𐐻 𐐶𐐲𐑉 𐑁𐐫𐑉 𐑄𐐨𐑆 𐐿𐐲𐑌𐐼𐐮𐑇𐐲𐑌𐑆, 𐑋𐐲𐑉𐑅𐐨 𐐿𐐳𐐼 𐑌𐐱𐐻 𐐻𐐩𐐿 𐐯𐑁𐐯𐐿𐐻 𐐯𐐿𐑅𐐯𐐹𐐻 𐐮𐐻 𐑇𐐳𐐼 𐐼𐐨𐑅𐐻𐑉𐐱𐐮 𐑄 𐐶𐐲𐑉𐐿 𐐱𐑂 𐐾𐐲𐑅𐐻𐐮𐑅. 𐐤𐐵 𐑄 𐐶𐐲𐑉𐐿 𐐱𐑂 𐐾𐐲𐑅𐐻𐐮𐑅 𐐿𐐳𐐼 𐑌𐐱𐐻 𐐺𐐨 𐐼𐐨𐑅𐐻𐑉𐐱𐐮𐐼; 𐐮𐑁 𐑅𐐬, 𐐘𐐱𐐼 𐐶𐐳𐐼 𐑅𐐨𐑅 𐐻𐐭 𐐺𐐨 𐐘𐐱𐐼.

12. 𐐈𐑌𐐼 𐑄𐐲𐑅 𐐶𐐨 𐑅𐐨 𐑄𐐰𐐻 𐐫𐑊 𐑋𐐰𐑌𐐿𐐴𐑌𐐼 𐐶𐐲𐑉 𐑁𐐫𐑊𐐲𐑌, 𐐰𐑌𐐼 𐑄𐐩 𐐶𐐲𐑉 𐐮𐑌 𐑄 𐑀𐑉𐐪𐑅𐐹 𐐱𐑂 𐐾𐐲𐑅𐐻𐐮𐑅; 𐐷𐐩, 𐑄 𐐾𐐲𐑅𐐻𐐮𐑅 𐐱𐑂 𐐘𐐱𐐼, 𐐸𐐶𐐮𐐽 𐐿𐐱𐑌𐑅𐐴𐑌𐐼 𐑄𐐯𐑋 𐑁𐐫𐑉𐐯𐑂𐐲𐑉 𐐻𐐭 𐐺𐐨 𐐿𐐲𐐻 𐐱𐑁 𐑁𐑉𐐱𐑋 𐐸𐐮𐑆 𐐹𐑉𐐯𐑆𐐯𐑌𐑅. 𐐈𐑌𐐼 𐑌𐐵 𐑄 𐐹𐑊𐐰𐑌 𐐱𐑂 𐑋𐐲𐑉𐑅𐐨 𐐿𐐳𐐼 𐑌𐐱𐐻 𐐺𐐨 𐐺𐑉𐐫𐐻 𐐲𐐺𐐵𐐻 𐐯𐐿𐑅𐐯𐐹𐐻 𐐰𐑌 𐐰𐐻𐐬𐑌𐑋𐐯𐑌𐐻 𐑇𐐳𐐼 𐐺𐐨 𐑋𐐩𐐼; 𐑄𐐯𐑉𐑁𐐫𐑉 𐐘𐐱𐐼 𐐸𐐮𐑋𐑅𐐯𐑊𐑁 𐐰𐐻𐐬𐑌𐐯𐑃 𐑁𐐫𐑉 𐑄 𐑅𐐮𐑌𐑆 𐐱𐑂 𐑄 𐐶𐐲𐑉𐑊𐐼, 𐐻𐐭 𐐺𐑉𐐮𐑍 𐐲𐐺𐐵𐐻 𐑄 𐐹𐑊𐐰𐑌 𐐱𐑂 𐑋𐐲𐑉𐑅𐐨, 𐐻𐐭 𐐰𐐹𐐨𐑆 𐑄 𐐼𐐨𐑋𐐰𐑌𐐼𐑆 𐐱𐑂 𐐾𐐲𐑅𐐻𐐮𐑅, 𐑄𐐰𐐻 𐐘𐐱𐐼 𐑋𐐴𐐻 𐐺𐐨 𐐰 𐐹𐐲𐑉𐑁𐐯𐐿𐐻, 𐐾𐐲𐑅𐐻 𐐘𐐱𐐼, 𐐰𐑌𐐼 𐐰 𐑋𐐲𐑉𐑅𐐨𐑁𐐳𐑊 𐐘𐐱𐐼 𐐫𐑊𐑅𐐬. 𐐤𐐵 𐑉𐐨𐐹𐐯𐑌𐐻𐐲𐑌𐑅 𐐿𐐳𐐼 𐑌𐐱𐐻 𐐿𐐲𐑋 𐐲𐑌𐐻𐐭 𐑋𐐯𐑌 𐐯𐐿𐑅𐐯𐐹𐐻 𐑄𐐯𐑉 𐐶𐐲𐑉 𐐰 𐐹𐐲𐑌𐐮𐑇𐑋𐐯𐑌𐐻, 𐐸𐐶𐐮𐐽 𐐫𐑊𐑅𐐬 𐐶𐐱𐑆 𐐨𐐻𐐲𐑉𐑌𐐲𐑊 𐐰𐑆 𐑄 𐑊𐐴𐑁 𐐱𐑂 𐑄 𐑅𐐬𐑊 𐑇𐐳𐐼 𐐺𐐨, 𐐰𐑁𐐮𐐿𐑅𐐻 𐐱𐐹𐐬𐑆𐐮𐐻 𐐻𐐭 𐑄 𐐹𐑊𐐰𐑌 𐐱𐑂 𐐸𐐰𐐹𐐨𐑌𐐯𐑅, 𐐸𐐶𐐮𐐽 𐐶𐐱𐑆 𐐰𐑆 𐐨𐐻𐐲𐑉𐑌𐐲𐑊 𐐫𐑊𐑅𐐬 𐐰𐑆 𐑄 𐑊𐐴𐑁 𐐱𐑂 𐑄 𐑅𐐬𐑊. 𐐤𐐵, 𐐸𐐵 𐐿𐐳𐐼 𐐰 𐑋𐐰𐑌 𐑉𐐨𐐹𐐯𐑌𐐻 𐐯𐐿𐑅𐐯𐐹𐐻 𐐸𐐨 𐑇𐐳𐐼 𐑅𐐮𐑌? 𐐐𐐵 𐐿𐐳𐐼 𐐸𐐨 𐑅𐐮𐑌, 𐐮𐑁 𐑄𐐯𐑉 𐐶𐐱𐑆 𐑌𐐬 𐑊𐐫, 𐐸𐐵 𐐿𐐳𐐼 𐑄𐐯𐑉 𐐺𐐨 𐐰 𐑊𐐫, 𐑅𐐩𐑂 𐑄𐐯𐑉 𐐶𐐱𐑆 𐐰 𐐹𐐲𐑌𐐮𐑇𐑋𐐯𐑌𐐻? 𐐤𐐵 𐑄𐐯𐑉 𐐶𐐱𐑆 𐐰 𐐹𐐲𐑌𐐮𐑇𐑋𐐯𐑌𐐻 𐐰𐑁𐐮𐐿𐑅𐐻, 𐐰𐑌𐐼 𐐰 𐐾𐐲𐑅𐐻 𐑊𐐫 𐑀𐐮𐑂𐐲𐑌, 𐐸𐐶𐐮𐐽 𐐺𐑉𐐫𐐻 𐑉𐐨𐑋𐐫𐑉𐑅 𐐱𐑂 𐐿𐐱𐑌𐑇𐐯𐑌𐑅 𐐲𐑌𐐻𐐭 𐑋𐐰𐑌. 𐐤𐐵, 𐐮𐑁 𐑄𐐯𐑉 𐐶𐐱𐑆 𐑌𐐬 𐑊𐐫 𐑀𐐮𐑂𐐲𐑌,—𐐮𐑁 𐐰 𐑋𐐰𐑌 𐑋𐐲𐑉𐐼𐐲𐑉𐐼, 𐐸𐐨 𐑇𐐳𐐼 𐐼𐐴,—𐐶𐐳𐐼 𐐸𐐨 𐐺𐐨 𐐰𐑁𐑉𐐩𐐼 𐐸𐐨 𐐶𐐳𐐼 𐐼𐐴 𐐮𐑁 𐐸𐐨 𐑇𐐳𐐼 𐑋𐐲𐑉𐐼𐐲𐑉? 𐐈𐑌𐐼 𐐫𐑊𐑅𐐬, 𐐮𐑁 𐑄𐐯𐑉 𐐶𐐱𐑆 𐑌𐐬 𐑊𐐫 𐑀𐐮𐑂𐐲𐑌 𐐲𐑀𐐯𐑌𐑅𐐻 𐑅𐐮𐑌, 𐑋𐐯𐑌 𐐶𐐳𐐼 𐑌𐐱𐐻

𐐺 𐐰𐑁𐑉𐐩𐐼 𐐻𐐭 𐑅𐐮𐑌. 𐐈𐑌𐐼 𐐮𐑁 𐑄𐐩𐑉 𐐶𐐱𐑆 𐑌𐐬 𐑊𐐫 𐑀𐐮𐑂𐑌 𐐮𐑁 𐑋𐐯𐑌 𐑅𐐮𐑌𐐼, 𐐸𐐶𐐱𐐻 𐐿𐐳𐐼 𐐾𐐲𐑅𐐻𐐮𐑅 𐐼𐐭, 𐐫𐑉 𐑋𐐲𐑉𐑅𐐮 𐐨𐑄𐐲𐑉; 𐑁𐐫𐑉 𐑄𐐩 𐐶𐐳𐐼 𐐸𐐰𐑂 𐑌𐐬 𐐿𐑊𐐩𐑋 𐐲𐐹𐐱𐑌 𐑄 𐐿𐑉𐐨𐐻𐐷𐐭𐑉? 𐐒𐐲𐐻 𐑄𐐩𐑉 𐐮𐑆 𐐩 𐑊𐐫 𐑀𐐮𐑂𐑌, 𐐰𐑌𐐼 𐐩 𐐹𐐲𐑌𐐮𐑇𐑋𐐯𐑌𐐻 𐐰𐑁𐐮𐐿𐑅𐐻, 𐐰𐑌𐐼 𐐩 𐑉𐐨𐐹𐐯𐑌𐐻𐐰𐑌𐑅 𐑀𐑉𐐰𐑌𐐻𐐮𐐼; 𐐸𐐶𐐮𐐽 𐑉𐐨𐐹𐐯𐑌𐐻𐐰𐑌𐑅, 𐑋𐐲𐑉𐑅𐐮 𐐿𐑊𐐩𐑋𐐯𐑃; 𐐲𐑄𐐲𐑉𐐶𐐴𐑆, 𐐾𐐲𐑅𐐻𐐮𐑅 𐐿𐑊𐐩𐑋𐐯𐑃 𐑄 𐐿𐑉𐐨𐐻𐐷𐐭𐑉, 𐐰𐑌𐐼 𐐯𐑀𐑆𐐯𐐿𐐷𐐭𐐻𐐯𐑃 𐑄 𐑊𐐫, 𐐰𐑌𐐼 𐑄 𐑊𐐫 𐐮𐑌𐑁𐑊𐐮𐐿𐐻𐐯𐑃 𐑄 𐐹𐐲𐑌𐐮𐑇𐑋𐐯𐑌𐐻; 𐐮𐑁 𐑌𐐱𐐻 𐑅𐐬, 𐑄 𐐶𐐲𐑉𐐿𐑅 𐐱𐑂 𐐾𐐲𐑅𐐻𐐮𐑅 𐐶𐐳𐐼 𐐺 𐐼𐐯𐑅𐐻𐑉𐐱𐐮𐐼, 𐐰𐑌𐐼 𐐘𐐱𐐼 𐐶𐐳𐐼 𐑅𐐨𐑅 𐐻𐐭 𐐺 𐐘𐐱𐐼. 𐐒𐐲𐐻 𐐘𐐱𐐼 𐑅𐐨𐑅𐐯𐑃 𐑌𐐱𐐻 𐐻𐐭 𐐺 𐐘𐐱𐐼, 𐐰𐑌𐐼 𐑋𐐲𐑉𐑅𐐮 𐐿𐑊𐐩𐑋𐐯𐑃 𐑄 𐐹𐐯𐑌𐐮𐐻𐐯𐑌𐐻, 𐐰𐑌𐐼 𐑋𐐲𐑉𐑅𐐮 𐐿𐐲𐑋𐐯𐑃 𐐺𐐿𐐫𐑆 𐐱𐑂 𐑄 𐐰𐐻𐐬𐑌𐑋𐐯𐑌𐐻; 𐐰𐑌𐐼 𐑄 𐐰𐐻𐐬𐑌𐑋𐐯𐑌𐐻 𐐺𐑉𐐮𐑍𐐯𐑃 𐐻𐐭 𐐹𐐰𐑅 𐑄 𐑉𐐯𐑆𐐲𐑉𐐯𐐿𐑇𐐲𐑌 𐐱𐑂 𐑄 𐐼𐐯𐐼; 𐐰𐑌𐐼 𐑄 𐑉𐐯𐑆𐐲𐑉𐐯𐐿𐑇𐐲𐑌 𐐱𐑂 𐑄 𐐼𐐯𐐼 𐐺𐑉𐐮𐑍𐐯𐑃 𐐺𐐰𐐿 𐑋𐐯𐑌 𐐮𐑌𐐻𐐭 𐑄 𐐹𐑉𐐯𐑆𐐯𐑌𐑅 𐐱𐑂 𐐘𐐱𐐼; 𐐰𐑌𐐼 𐑄𐐲𐑅 𐑄𐐩 𐐪𐑉 𐑉𐐯𐑅𐐻𐐬𐑉𐐼 𐐮𐑌𐐻𐐭 𐐸𐐮𐑆 𐐹𐑉𐐯𐑆𐐯𐑌𐑅, 𐐻𐐭 𐐺 𐐾𐐲𐐾𐐼 𐐰𐐿𐐫𐑉𐐼𐐮𐑍 𐐻𐐭 𐑄𐐩𐑉 𐐶𐐲𐑉𐐿𐑅, 𐐰𐐿𐐫𐑉𐐼𐐮𐑍 𐐻𐐭 𐑄 𐑊𐐫 𐐰𐑌𐐼 𐐾𐐲𐑅𐐻𐐮𐑅; 𐑁𐐫𐑉 𐐺𐐸𐐬𐑊𐐼, 𐐾𐐲𐑅𐐻𐐮𐑅 𐐯𐐿𐑅𐐲𐑉𐑅𐐴𐑆𐐯𐑃 𐐫𐑊 𐐸𐐮𐑆 𐐼𐐨𐑋𐐰𐑌𐐼𐑆, 𐐰𐑌𐐼 𐐫𐑊𐑅𐐬 𐑋𐐲𐑉𐑅𐐮 𐐿𐑊𐐩𐑋𐐯𐑃 𐐫𐑊 𐐸𐐶𐐮𐐽 𐐮𐑆 𐐸𐐲𐑉 𐐬𐑌; 𐐰𐑌𐐼 𐑄𐐲𐑅, 𐑌𐐲𐑌 𐐺𐐲𐐻 𐑄 𐐻𐑉𐐭𐑊𐐨 𐐹𐐯𐑌𐐮𐐻𐐯𐑌𐐻 𐐪𐑉 𐑅𐐩𐑂𐐼.

13. 𐐐𐐶𐐱𐐻! 𐐼𐐭 𐐷 𐑅𐐲𐐹𐐬𐑆 𐑄𐐰𐐻 𐑋𐐲𐑉𐑅𐐮 𐐿𐐰𐑌 𐑉𐐱𐐺 𐐾𐐲𐑅𐐻𐐮𐑅? 𐐌 𐑅𐐩 𐐲𐑌𐐻𐐭 𐐷𐐭, 𐑌𐐩; 𐑌𐐱𐐻 𐐶𐐲𐑌 𐐸𐐶𐐮𐐻. 𐐆𐑁 𐑅𐐬, 𐐘𐐱𐐼 𐐶𐐳𐐼 𐑅𐐨𐑅 𐐻𐐭 𐐺 𐐘𐐱𐐼. 𐐈𐑌𐐼 𐑄𐐲𐑅 𐐘𐐱𐐼 𐐺𐑉𐐮𐑍𐐯𐑃 𐐰𐐺𐐵𐐻 𐐸𐐮𐑆 𐑀𐑉𐐩𐐻 𐐰𐑌𐐼 𐐨𐐻𐐲𐑉𐑌𐐲𐑊 𐐹𐐲𐑉𐐹𐐲𐑅𐐯𐑆, 𐐸𐐶𐐮𐐽 𐐶𐐲𐑉 𐐹𐑉𐐨𐐹𐐩𐑉𐐼 𐑁𐑉𐐱𐑋 𐑄 𐑁𐐵𐑌𐐼𐐩𐑇𐐲𐑌 𐐱𐑂 𐑄 𐐶𐐲𐑉𐑊𐐼. 𐐈𐑌𐐼 𐑄𐐲𐑅 𐐿𐐲𐑋𐐯𐑃 𐐰𐐺𐐵𐐻 𐑄 𐑅𐐰𐑊𐑂𐐩𐑇𐐲𐑌 𐐰𐑌𐐼 𐑄 𐑉𐐨𐐼𐐲𐑋𐑇𐐲𐑌 𐐱𐑂 𐑋𐐯𐑌, 𐐰𐑌𐐼 𐐫𐑊𐑅𐐬 𐑄𐐩𐑉 𐐼𐐨𐑅𐐻𐑉𐐲𐐿𐑇𐐲𐑌 𐐰𐑌𐐼 𐑋𐐮𐑆𐐲𐑉𐐨; 𐑄𐐯𐑉𐑁𐐬𐑉, 𐐄 𐑋𐐴 𐑅𐐲𐑌, 𐐸𐐭𐑅𐐬𐐯𐑂𐐲𐑉 𐐶𐐮𐑊 𐐿𐐲𐑋, 𐑋𐐩 𐐿𐐲𐑋, 𐐰𐑌𐐼 𐐹𐐪𐑉𐐻𐐩𐐿 𐐱𐑂 𐑄 𐐶𐐫𐐻𐐲𐑉𐑆 𐐱𐑂 𐑊𐐴𐑁 𐑁𐑉𐐨𐑊𐐨: 𐐰𐑌𐐼 𐐸𐐭𐑅𐐬𐐯𐑂𐐲𐑉 𐐶𐐮𐑊 𐑌𐐱𐐻 𐐿𐐲𐑋, 𐑄 𐑅𐐩𐑋 𐐮𐑆 𐑌𐐱𐐻 𐐿𐐲𐑋𐐹𐐯𐑊𐐼 𐐻𐐭 𐐿𐐲𐑋; 𐐺𐐲𐐻 𐐮𐑌 𐑄 𐑊𐐰𐑅𐐻 𐐼𐐩, 𐐮𐐻 𐑇𐐰𐑊 𐐺 𐑉𐐯𐑅𐐻𐐬𐑉𐐼 𐐲𐑌𐐻𐐭 𐐸𐐮𐑋 𐐰𐐿𐐫𐑉𐐼𐐮𐑍 𐐻𐐭 𐐸𐐮𐑆 𐐼𐐨𐐼𐑆. 𐐆𐑁 𐐸𐐨 𐐸𐐰𐑆 𐐼𐐯𐑆𐐴𐑉𐐼 𐐻𐐭 𐐼𐐭 𐐨𐑂𐐲𐑊, 𐐰𐑌𐐼 𐐸𐐰𐑆 𐑌𐐱𐐻 𐑉𐐨𐐹𐐯𐑌𐐻𐐯𐐼 𐐮𐑌 𐐸𐐮𐑆 𐐼𐐩𐑆, 𐐺𐐸𐐬𐑊𐐼, 𐐨𐑂𐐲𐑊 𐑇𐐰𐑊 𐐺 𐐼𐐲𐑌 𐐲𐑌𐐻𐐭 𐐸𐐮𐑋, 𐐰𐐿𐐫𐑉𐐼𐐮𐑍 𐐻𐐭 𐑄 𐑉𐐯𐑅𐐻𐐬𐑉𐐩𐑇𐐲𐑌 𐐱𐑂 𐐘𐐱𐐼. 𐐈𐑌𐐼 𐑌𐐵, 𐑋𐐴 𐑅𐐲𐑌, 𐐌 𐐼𐐯𐑆𐐴𐑉 𐑄𐐰𐐻 𐐷 𐑇𐐳𐐼 𐑊𐐯𐐻 𐑄𐐨𐑆 𐑃𐐮𐑍𐑆 𐐻𐑉𐐲𐐺𐑊 𐐷𐐭 𐑌𐐬 𐑋𐐬𐑉, 𐐰𐑌𐐼 𐐬𐑌𐑊𐐨 𐑊𐐯𐐻 𐐷𐐭𐑉 𐑅𐐮𐑌𐑆 𐐻𐑉𐐲𐐺𐑊 𐐷𐐭, 𐐶𐐮𐑄 𐑄𐐰𐐻 𐐻𐑉𐐲𐐺𐑊 𐐸𐐶𐐮𐐽 𐑇𐐰𐑊 𐐺𐑉𐐮𐑍 𐐷𐐭 𐐼𐐵𐑌 𐐲𐑌𐐻𐐭 𐑉𐐨𐐹𐐯𐑌𐐻𐐰𐑌𐑅. 𐐄 𐑋𐐴 𐑅𐐲𐑌, 𐐌 𐐼𐐯𐑆𐐴𐑉 𐑄𐐰𐐻 𐐷 𐑇𐐳𐐼 𐐼𐐯𐑌𐐴 𐑄 𐐾𐐲𐑅𐐻𐐮𐑅 𐐱𐑂 𐐘𐐱𐐼 𐑌𐐬 𐑋𐐬𐑉. 𐐔𐐭 𐑌𐐱𐐻 𐐯𐑌𐐼𐐯𐑂𐐲𐑉 𐐻𐐭 𐐯𐐿𐑅𐐿𐐷𐐭𐑆 𐐷𐐭𐑉𐑅𐐯𐑊𐑁 𐐮𐑌 𐑄 𐑊𐐨𐑅𐐻 𐐹𐐱𐐮𐑌𐐻 𐐺𐐿𐐫𐑆 𐐱𐑂 𐐷𐐭𐑉 𐑅𐐮𐑌𐑆, 𐐺𐐴 𐐼𐐯𐑌𐐴𐐮𐑍 𐑄 𐐾𐐲𐑅𐐻𐐮𐑅 𐐱𐑂 𐐘𐐱𐐼; 𐐺𐐲𐐻 𐐼𐐭 𐐷𐐭 𐑊𐐯𐐻 𐑄 𐐾𐐲𐑅𐐻𐐮𐑅 𐐱𐑂 𐐘𐐱𐐼, 𐐰𐑌𐐼 𐐸𐐮𐑆 𐑋𐐲𐑉𐑅𐐮, 𐐰𐑌𐐼 𐐸𐐮𐑆 𐑊𐐱𐑍-𐑅𐐲𐑁𐐲𐑉𐐮𐑍, 𐐸𐐰𐑂 𐑁𐐳𐑊 𐑅𐐶𐐩 𐐮𐑌 𐐷𐐭𐑉 𐐸𐐪𐑉𐐻; 𐐰𐑌𐐼 𐑊𐐯𐐻 𐐮𐐻 𐐺𐑉𐐮𐑍 𐐷𐐭 𐐼𐐵𐑌 𐐻𐐭 𐑄 𐐼𐐲𐑅𐐻 𐐮𐑌 𐐸𐐷𐐭𐑋𐐮𐑊𐐮𐐻𐐨. 𐐈𐑌𐐼 𐑌𐐵, 𐐄 𐑋𐐴 𐑅𐐲𐑌, 𐐷 𐐪𐑉 𐐿𐐫𐑊𐐼 𐐱𐑂 𐐘𐐱𐐼 𐐻𐐭 𐐹𐑉𐐨𐐽 𐑄 𐐶𐐲𐑉𐐼 𐐲𐑌𐐻𐐭 𐑄𐐮𐑅 𐐹𐐨𐐹𐑊. 𐐈𐑌𐐼 𐑌𐐵, 𐑋𐐴 𐑅𐐲𐑌, 𐑀𐐬 𐑄𐐴 𐐶𐐩, 𐐼𐐨𐐿𐑊𐐩𐑉 𐑄 𐐶𐐲𐑉𐐼 𐐶𐐮𐑄 𐐻𐑉𐐭𐑃 𐐰𐑌𐐼 𐑅𐐬𐐺𐐲𐑉𐑌𐐯𐑅, 𐑄𐐰𐐻 𐑄𐐵 𐑋𐐩𐐯𐑅𐐻 𐐺𐑉𐐮𐑍 𐑅𐐬𐑊𐑆 𐐲𐑌𐐻𐐭 𐑉𐐨𐐹𐐯𐑌𐐻𐐰𐑌𐑅, 𐑄𐐰𐐻 𐑄 𐑀𐑉𐐩𐐻 𐐹𐑊𐐰𐑌 𐐱𐑂 𐑋𐐲𐑉𐑅𐐮 𐑋𐐩 𐐸𐐰𐑂 𐐿𐑊𐐩𐑋 𐐲𐐹𐐱𐑌 𐑄𐐯𐑋. 𐐈𐑌𐐼 𐑋𐐩 𐐘𐐱𐐼 𐑀𐑉𐐰𐑌𐐻 𐐲𐑌𐐻𐐭 𐐷𐐭 𐐨𐑂𐐲𐑌 𐐰𐐿𐐫𐑉𐐼𐐮𐑍 𐐻𐐭 𐑋𐐴 𐐶𐐲𐑉𐐼𐑆. 𐐁𐑋𐐯𐑌.

𐐕𐐈𐐑𐐓𐐊𐐡 XX.

1. 𐐈𐑌𐐼 𐑌𐐵 𐐮𐐻 𐐿𐐩𐑋 𐐻𐐭 𐐹𐐰𐑅, 𐑄𐐰𐐻 𐑄 𐑅𐐲𐑌𐑆 𐐱𐑂 𐐈𐑊𐑋𐐲 𐐼𐐮𐐼 𐑀𐐬 𐑁𐐫𐑉𐑃 𐐲𐑋𐐲𐑍 𐑄 𐐹𐐨𐐹𐑊, 𐐻𐐭 𐐼𐐨𐐿𐑊𐐩𐑉 𐑄 𐐶𐐲𐑉𐐼 𐐲𐑌𐐻𐐭 𐑄𐐯𐑋. 𐐈𐑌𐐼 𐐈𐑊𐑋𐐲, 𐐫𐑊𐑅𐐬, 𐐸𐐮𐑋𐑅𐐯𐑊𐑁, 𐐿𐐳𐐼 𐑌𐐱𐐻 𐑉𐐯𐑅𐐻, 𐐰𐑌𐐼 𐐸𐐨 𐐫𐑊𐑅𐐬 𐐶𐐯𐑌𐐻 𐑁𐐫𐑉𐑃. 𐐤𐐵 𐐶𐐨 𐑇𐐰𐑊 𐑅𐐩 𐑌𐐬 𐑋𐐬𐑉 𐐿𐐲𐑌𐑅𐐲𐑉𐑌𐐮𐑍 𐑄𐐩𐑉 𐐹𐑉𐐨𐐽𐐮𐑍, 𐐲𐐿𐑅𐐯𐐹𐐻 𐑄𐐰𐐻 𐑄𐐩 𐐹𐑉𐐨𐐽𐐻 𐑄 𐐶𐐲𐑉𐐼, 𐐰𐑌𐐼 𐑄 𐐻𐑉𐐭𐑃, 𐐰𐐿𐐫𐑉𐐼𐐮𐑍 𐐻𐐭 𐑄 𐑅𐐹𐐮𐑉𐐮𐐻 𐐱𐑂 𐐹𐑉𐐱𐑁𐐯𐑅𐐨 𐐰𐑌𐐼 𐑉𐐯𐑂𐐯𐑊𐐩𐑇𐐲𐑌; 𐐰𐑌𐐼 𐑄𐐩 𐐹𐑉𐐨𐐽𐐻 𐐰𐑁𐐻𐐲𐑉 𐑄 𐐸𐐬𐑊𐐨 𐐫𐑉𐐼𐐲𐑉 𐐱𐑂 𐐘𐐱𐐼, 𐐺𐐴 𐐸𐐶𐐮𐐽 𐑄𐐩 𐐶𐐲𐑉 𐐿𐐱𐑊𐐼.

2. 𐐈𐑌𐐼 𐑌𐐵 𐐌 𐑉𐐨𐐻𐐲𐑉𐑌 𐐻𐐭 𐐰𐑌 𐐰𐐿𐐵𐑌𐐻 𐐱𐑂 𐑄 𐐶𐐫𐑉𐑆 𐐺𐐯𐐻𐐶𐐨𐑌 𐑄 𐐤𐐨𐑁𐐴𐐻𐑅 𐐰𐑌𐐼 𐑄 𐐢𐐩𐑋𐐲𐑌-

𐐴𐐻𐑅, 𐐮𐑌 𐑄 𐐩𐐻𐐨𐑌𐑃 𐐷𐐨𐑉 𐐱𐑂 𐑄 𐑉𐐩𐑌 𐐱𐑂 𐑄 𐐾𐐲𐐾𐐯𐑆. 𐐙𐐫𐑉 𐐺𐐨𐐸𐐬𐑊𐐼, 𐐮𐐻 𐐿𐐩𐑋 𐐻𐐭 𐐹𐐰𐑅 𐑄𐐰𐐻 𐑄 𐐞𐐬𐑉𐐲𐑋𐐴𐐻𐑅 𐐺𐐨𐐿𐐩𐑋 𐐢𐐰𐑋𐐲𐑌𐐴𐐻𐑅; 𐑄𐐯𐑉𐑁𐐫𐑉, 𐐮𐑌 𐑄 𐐿𐐲𐑋𐐯𐑌𐑅𐑋𐐲𐑌𐐻 𐐱𐑂 𐑄 𐐩𐐻𐐨𐑌𐑃 𐐷𐐨𐑉, 𐑄 𐐹𐐨𐐹𐑊 𐐱𐑂 𐑄 𐐤𐐨𐑁𐐴𐐻𐑅 𐑅𐐫 𐑄𐐰𐐻 𐑄 𐐢𐐰𐑋𐐲𐑌𐐴𐐻𐑅 𐐶𐐲𐑉 𐐿𐐲𐑋𐐮𐑍 𐐲𐐹𐐱𐑌 𐑄𐐯𐑋; 𐑄𐐯𐑉𐑁𐐫𐑉 𐑄𐐩 𐑋𐐩𐐼 𐐹𐑉𐐯𐐹𐐲𐑉𐐩𐑇𐐲𐑌𐑆 𐑁𐐫𐑉 𐐶𐐫𐑉; 𐐷𐐩, 𐑄𐐩 𐑀𐐰𐑄𐐲𐑉𐐼 𐐻𐐭𐑀𐐯𐑄𐐲𐑉 𐑄𐐩𐑉 𐐪𐑉𐑋𐐨𐑆 𐐮𐑌 𐑄 𐑊𐐰𐑌𐐼 𐐱𐑂 𐐖𐐲𐑉𐑇𐐲𐑌. 𐐈𐑌𐐼 𐐮𐐻 𐐿𐐩𐑋 𐐻𐐭 𐐹𐐰𐑅 𐑄𐐰𐐻 𐑄 𐐢𐐰𐑋𐐲𐑌𐐴𐐻𐑅 𐐿𐐩𐑋 𐐶𐐮𐑄 𐑄𐐩𐑉 𐑃𐐵𐑆𐐲𐑌𐐼𐑆; 𐐰𐑌𐐼 𐑄𐐩 𐐿𐐩𐑋 𐐮𐑌𐐻𐐭 𐑄 𐑊𐐰𐑌𐐼 𐐱𐑂 𐐈𐑌𐐻𐐨𐐬𐑌𐐲𐑋, 𐐸𐐶𐐮𐐽 𐐮𐑆 𐑄 𐑊𐐰𐑌𐐼 𐐱𐑂 𐑄 𐐞𐐬𐑉𐐲𐑋𐐴𐐻𐑅; 𐐰𐑌𐐼 𐐲 𐑋𐐰𐑌 𐐺𐐴 𐑄 𐑌𐐩𐑋 𐐱𐑂 𐐞𐐯𐑉𐐲𐐸𐐯𐑋𐑌𐐲 𐐶𐐱𐑆 𐑄𐐩𐑉 𐑊𐐨𐐼𐐲𐑉. 𐐈𐑌𐐼 𐑌𐐵 𐐰𐑆 𐑄 𐐈𐑋𐐰𐑊𐐯𐐿𐐴𐐻𐑅 𐐶𐐲𐑉 𐐱𐑂 𐐲 𐑋𐐬𐑉 𐐶𐐮𐐿𐐯𐐼 𐐰𐑌𐐼 𐑋𐐲𐑉𐐼𐐲𐑉𐐲𐑅 𐐼𐐮𐑅𐐹𐐬𐑆𐐮𐑇𐐲𐑌 𐑄𐐰𐑌 𐑄 𐐢𐐰𐑋𐐲𐑌𐐴𐐻𐑅 𐐶𐐲𐑉, 𐐮𐑌 𐐰𐑌𐐼 𐐱𐑂 𐑄𐐯𐑋𐑅𐐯𐑊𐑂𐑆, 𐑄𐐯𐑉𐑁𐐫𐑉, 𐐞𐐯𐑉𐐲𐐸𐐯𐑋𐑌𐐲 𐐲𐐹𐐱𐐮𐑌𐐻𐐯𐐼 𐐽𐐨𐑁 𐐿𐐰𐐹𐐻𐐮𐑌𐑆 𐐬𐑂𐐲𐑉 𐑄 𐐢𐐰𐑋𐐲𐑌𐐴𐐻𐑅, 𐐰𐑌𐐼 𐑄𐐩 𐐶𐐲𐑉 𐐫𐑊 𐐈𐑋𐐰𐑊𐐯𐐿𐐴𐐻𐑅 𐐰𐑌𐐼 𐐞𐐬𐑉𐐲𐑋𐐴𐐻𐑅. 𐐤𐐵 𐑄𐐮𐑅 𐐸𐐨 𐐼𐐮𐐼, 𐑄𐐰𐐻 𐐸𐐨 𐑋𐐴𐐻 𐐹𐑉𐐯𐑆𐐲𐑉𐑂 𐑄𐐩𐑉 𐐸𐐩𐐻𐑉𐐯𐐼 𐐻𐐬𐑉𐐼𐑆 𐑄 𐐤𐐨𐑁𐐴𐐻𐑅; 𐑄𐐰𐐻 𐐸𐐨 𐑋𐐴𐐻 𐐺𐑉𐐮𐑍 𐑄𐐯𐑋 𐐮𐑌𐐻𐐭 𐑅𐐲𐐺𐐾𐐯𐐿𐑇𐐲𐑌 𐐻𐐭 𐑄 𐐰𐐿𐐱𐑋𐐹𐑊𐐮𐑇𐑋𐐲𐑌𐐻 𐐱𐑂 𐐸𐐮𐑆 𐐼𐐯𐑆𐐴𐑌𐑆: 𐑁𐐫𐑉 𐐺𐐨𐐸𐐬𐑊𐐼, 𐐸𐐮𐑆 𐐼𐐯𐑆𐐴𐑌𐑆 𐐶𐐲𐑉 𐐻𐐭 𐑅𐐻𐐲𐑉 𐐲𐐹 𐑄 𐐢𐐰𐑋𐐲𐑌𐐴𐐻𐑅 𐐻𐐭 𐐰𐑍𐑀𐐲𐑉 𐐲𐑀𐐯𐑌𐑅𐐻 𐑄 𐐤𐐨𐑁𐐴𐐻𐑅; 𐑄𐐮𐑅 𐐸𐐨 𐐼𐐮𐐼 𐑄𐐰𐐻 𐐸𐐨 𐑋𐐴𐐻 𐐷𐐭𐑆𐐲𐑉𐐹 𐑀𐑉𐐩𐐻 𐐹𐐵𐑉 𐐬𐑂𐐲𐑉 𐑄𐐯𐑋, 𐐰𐑌𐐼 𐐫𐑊𐑅𐐬 𐑄𐐰𐐻 𐐸𐐨 𐑋𐐴𐐻 𐑀𐐩𐑌 𐐹𐐵𐑉 𐐬𐑂𐐲𐑉 𐑄 𐐤𐐨𐑁𐐴𐐻𐑅 𐐺𐐴 𐐺𐑉𐐮𐑍𐐮𐑍 𐑄𐐯𐑋 𐐮𐑌𐐻𐐭 𐐺𐐱𐑌𐐼𐐩𐐾, 𐐯𐐻𐑅. 𐐈𐑌𐐼 𐑌𐐵 𐑄 𐐼𐐯𐑆𐐴𐑌 𐐱𐑂 𐑄 𐐤𐐨𐑁𐐴𐐻𐑅 𐐶𐐱𐑆 𐐻𐐭 𐑅𐐲𐐹𐐬𐑉𐐻 𐑄𐐩𐑉 𐑊𐐰𐑌𐐼𐑆, 𐐰𐑌𐐼 𐑄𐐩𐑉 𐐸𐐵𐑆𐐯𐑆, 𐐰𐑌𐐼 𐑄𐐩𐑉 𐐶𐐴𐑂𐑆, 𐐰𐑌𐐼 𐑄𐐩𐑉 𐐽𐐮𐑊𐐼𐑉𐐯𐑌, 𐑄𐐰𐐻 𐑄𐐩 𐑋𐐴𐐻 𐐹𐑉𐐯𐑆𐐲𐑉𐑂 𐑄𐐯𐑋 𐑁𐑉𐐱𐑋 𐑄 𐐸𐐰𐑌𐐼𐑆 𐐱𐑂 𐑄𐐩𐑉 𐐯𐑌𐐯𐑋𐐨𐑆; 𐐰𐑌𐐼 𐐫𐑊𐑅𐐬 𐑄𐐰𐐻 𐑄𐐩 𐑋𐐴𐐻 𐐹𐑉𐐯𐑆𐐲𐑉𐑂 𐑄𐐩𐑉 𐑉𐐴𐐻𐑅 𐐰𐑌𐐼 𐑄𐐩𐑉 𐐹𐑉𐐮𐑂𐐮𐑊𐐯𐐾𐐯𐑆; 𐐷𐐩, 𐐰𐑌𐐼 𐐫𐑊𐑅𐐬 𐑄𐐩𐑉 𐑊𐐮𐐺𐐲𐑉𐐻𐐨, 𐑄𐐰𐐻 𐑄𐐩 𐑋𐐴𐐻 𐐶𐐲𐑉𐑇𐐮𐐹 𐐘𐐱𐐼 𐐰𐐿𐐫𐑉𐐼𐐮𐑍 𐐻𐐭 𐑄𐐩𐑉 𐐼𐐯𐑆𐐴𐑉𐑆; 𐑁𐐫𐑉 𐑄𐐩 𐑌𐐷𐐭 𐑄𐐰𐐻 𐐮𐑁 𐑄𐐩 𐑇𐐳𐐼 𐑁𐐫𐑊 𐐮𐑌𐐻𐐭 𐑄 𐐸𐐰𐑌𐐼𐑆 𐐱𐑂 𐑄 𐐢𐐰𐑋𐐲𐑌𐐴𐐻𐑅, 𐑄𐐰𐐻 𐐸𐐭𐑅𐐬𐐯𐑂𐐲𐑉 𐑇𐐳𐐼 𐐶𐐲𐑉𐑇𐐮𐐹 𐐘𐐱𐐼 𐐮𐑌 𐑅𐐹𐐮𐑉𐐮𐐻 𐐰𐑌𐐼 𐐮𐑌 𐐻𐑉𐐭𐑃, 𐑄 𐐻𐑉𐐭 𐐰𐑌𐐼 𐑄 𐑊𐐮𐑂𐐮𐑍 𐐘𐐱𐐼, 𐑄 𐐢𐐰𐑋𐐲𐑌𐐴𐐻𐑅 𐐶𐐳𐐼 𐐼𐐯𐑅𐐻𐑉𐐦; 𐐷𐐩, 𐐰𐑌𐐼 𐑄𐐩 𐐫𐑊𐑅𐐬 𐑌𐐷𐐭 𐑄 𐐯𐐿𐑅𐐻𐑉𐐨𐑋 𐐸𐐩𐐻𐑉𐐯𐐼 𐐱𐑂 𐑄 𐐢𐐰𐑋𐐲𐑌𐐴𐐻𐑅 𐐻𐐬𐑉𐐼𐑆 𐑄𐐩𐑉 𐐺𐑉𐐯𐑄𐑉𐐯𐑌, 𐐸𐐭 𐐶𐐲𐑉 𐑄 𐐹𐐨𐐹𐑊 𐐱𐑂 𐐈𐑌𐐻𐐴-𐐤𐐨𐑁𐐴-𐐢𐐨𐐸𐐴, 𐐸𐐭 𐐶𐐲𐑉 𐐿𐐫𐑊𐐼 𐑄 𐐹𐐨𐐹𐑊 𐐱𐑂 𐐈𐑋𐐲𐑌; 𐐰𐑌𐐼 𐑄𐐩 𐐶𐐳𐐼 𐑌𐐱𐐻 𐐻𐐩𐐿 𐐲𐐹 𐐪𐑉𐑋𐑆; 𐐷𐐩, 𐑄𐐩 𐐸𐐰𐐼 𐐯𐑌𐐻𐐲𐑉𐐼 𐐮𐑌𐐻𐐭 𐐲 𐐿𐐲𐑂𐐯𐑌𐐲𐑌𐐻 𐐰𐑌𐐼 𐑄𐐩 𐐶𐐳𐐼 𐑌𐐱𐐻 𐐺𐑉𐐩𐐿 𐐮𐐻; 𐑄𐐯𐑉𐑁𐐫𐑉, 𐐮𐑁 𐑄𐐩 𐑇𐐳𐐼 𐑁𐐫𐑊 𐐮𐑌𐐻𐐭 𐑄 𐐸𐐰𐑌𐐼𐑆 𐐱𐑂 𐑄 𐐢𐐰𐑋𐐲𐑌𐐴𐐻𐑅, 𐑄𐐩 𐐶𐐳𐐼 𐐺𐐨 𐐼𐐯𐑅𐐻𐑉𐐦𐐼. 𐐈𐑌𐐼 𐑄 𐐤𐐨𐑁𐐴𐐻𐑅 𐐶𐐳𐐼 𐑌𐐱𐐻 𐑅𐐲𐑁𐐲𐑉 𐑄𐐰𐐻 𐑄𐐩 𐑇𐐳𐐼 𐐺𐐨 𐐼𐐯𐑅𐐻𐑉𐐦𐐼; 𐑄𐐯𐑉𐑁𐐫𐑉 𐑄𐐩 𐑀𐐩𐑂 𐑄𐐯𐑋 𐑊𐐰𐑌𐐼𐑆 𐑁𐐫𐑉 𐑄𐐩𐑉 𐐮𐑌𐐸𐐯𐑉𐐮𐐻𐐲𐑌𐑅. 𐐈𐑌𐐼 𐑄 𐐹𐐨𐐹𐑊 𐐱𐑂 𐐈𐑋𐐲𐑌 𐐼𐐮𐐼 𐑀𐐮𐑂 𐐲𐑌𐐻𐐭 𐑄 𐐤𐐨𐑁𐐴𐐻𐑅 𐐲 𐑊𐐪𐑉𐐾 𐐹𐐬𐑉𐑇𐐲𐑌 𐐱𐑂 𐑄𐐩𐑉 𐑅𐐲𐐺𐑅𐐻𐐲𐑌𐑅 𐐻𐐭 𐑅𐐲𐐹𐐬𐑉𐐻 𐑄𐐩𐑉 𐐪𐑉𐑋𐐨𐑆; 𐐰𐑌𐐼 𐑄𐐲𐑅 𐑄 𐐤𐐨𐑁𐐴𐐻𐑅 𐐶𐐲𐑉 𐐿𐐲𐑋𐐹𐐯𐑊𐐼, 𐐲𐑊𐐬𐑌, 𐐻𐐭 𐐶𐐮𐑄𐑅𐐻𐐰𐑌𐐼 𐐲𐑀𐐯𐑌𐑅𐐻 𐑄 𐐢𐐰𐑋𐐲𐑌𐐴𐐻𐑅, 𐐸𐐭 𐐶𐐲𐑉 𐐲 𐐿𐐱𐑋𐐹𐐵𐑌𐐼 𐐱𐑂 𐐢𐐩𐑋𐐲𐑌 𐐰𐑌𐐼 𐐢𐐯𐑋𐐷𐐭𐐯𐑊, 𐐰𐑌𐐼 𐑄 𐑅𐐲𐑌𐑆 𐐱𐑂 𐐌𐑇𐑋𐐩𐐯𐑊, 𐐰𐑌𐐼 𐐫𐑊 𐑄𐐬𐑆 𐐸𐐭 𐐸𐐰𐐼 𐐼𐐮𐑅𐐯𐑌𐐻𐐯𐐼 𐑁𐑉𐐱𐑋 𐑄 𐐤𐐨𐑁𐐴𐐻𐑅, 𐐸𐐭 𐐶𐐲𐑉 𐐈𐑋𐐰𐑊𐐯𐐿𐐴𐐻𐑅 𐐰𐑌𐐼 𐐞𐐬𐑉𐐲𐑋𐐴𐐻𐑅, 𐐰𐑌𐐼 𐑄 𐐼𐐯𐑅𐐯𐑌𐐼𐐲𐑌𐐻𐑅 𐐱𐑂 𐑄 𐐹𐑉𐐨𐑅𐐻𐑅 𐐱𐑂 𐐤𐐬𐐲. 𐐤𐐵 𐑄𐐬𐑆 𐐼𐐯𐑅𐐯𐑌𐐼𐐲𐑌𐐻𐑅 𐐶𐐲𐑉 𐐰𐑆 𐑌𐐧𐑋𐐲𐑉𐐲𐑅, 𐑌𐐨𐑉𐑊𐐨, 𐐰𐑆 𐐶𐐲𐑉 𐑄 𐐤𐐨𐑁𐐴𐐻𐑅; 𐐰𐑌𐐼 𐑄𐐲𐑅 𐑄 𐐤𐐨𐑁𐐴𐐻𐑅 𐐶𐐲𐑉 𐐱𐐺𐑊𐐴𐐾𐐼 𐐻𐐭 𐐿𐐲𐑌𐐻𐐯𐑌𐐼 𐐶𐐮𐑄 𐑄𐐩𐑉 𐐺𐑉𐐯𐑄𐑉𐐯𐑌, 𐐨𐑂𐐯𐑌 𐐲𐑌𐐻𐐭 𐐺𐑊𐐲𐐼𐑇𐐯𐐼.

3. 𐐈𐑌𐐼 𐐮𐐻 𐐿𐐩𐑋 𐐻𐐭 𐐹𐐰𐑅 𐐰𐑆 𐑄 𐐪𐑉𐑋𐐨𐑆 𐐱𐑂 𐑄 𐐢𐐰𐑋𐐲𐑌𐐴𐐻𐑅 𐐸𐐰𐐼 𐑀𐐰𐑄𐐲𐑉𐐼 𐐻𐐭𐑀𐐯𐑄𐐲𐑉 𐐮𐑌 𐑄 𐑊𐐰𐑌𐐼 𐐱𐑂 𐐈𐑌𐐻𐐨𐐬𐑌𐐲𐑋, 𐐺𐐨𐐸𐐬𐑊𐐼, 𐑄 𐐪𐑉𐑋𐐨𐑆 𐐱𐑂 𐑄 𐐤𐐨𐑁𐐴𐐻𐑅 𐐶𐐲𐑉 𐐹𐑉𐐨𐐹𐐯𐑉𐐼 𐐻𐐭 𐑋𐐨𐐻 𐑄𐐯𐑋 𐐮𐑌 𐑄 𐑊𐐰𐑌𐐼 𐐱𐑂 𐐖𐐲𐑉𐑇𐐲𐑌. 𐐤𐐵 𐑄 𐑊𐐨𐐼𐐲𐑉 𐐱𐑂 𐑄 𐐤𐐨𐑁𐐴𐐻𐑅, 𐐫𐑉 𐑄 𐑋𐐰𐑌 𐐸𐐭 𐐸𐐰𐐼 𐐺𐐨𐑌 𐐲𐐹𐐱𐐮𐑌𐐻𐐯𐐼 𐐻𐐭 𐐺 𐑄 𐐽𐐨𐑁 𐐿𐐰𐐹𐐻𐐮𐑌 𐐬𐑂𐐲𐑉 𐑄 𐐤𐐨𐑁𐐴𐐻𐑅; 𐑌𐐵 𐑄 𐐽𐐨𐑁 𐐿𐐰𐐹𐐻𐐮𐑌 𐐻𐐳𐐿 𐑄 𐐿𐐲𐑋𐐰𐑌𐐼 𐐱𐑂 𐐫𐑊 𐑄 𐐪𐑉𐑋𐐨𐑆 𐐱𐑂 𐑄 𐐤𐐨𐑁𐐴𐐻𐑅, 𐐰𐑌𐐼 𐐸𐐮𐑆 𐑌𐐩𐑋 𐐶𐐱𐑆 𐐣𐐬𐑉𐐬𐑌𐐴; 𐐰𐑌𐐼 𐐣𐐬𐑉𐐬𐑌𐐴 𐐻𐐳𐐿 𐐫𐑊 𐑄 𐐿𐐲𐑋𐐰𐑌𐐼, 𐐰𐑌𐐼 𐑄 𐑀𐐲𐑂𐐲𐑉𐑌𐑋𐐲𐑌𐐻 𐐱𐑂 𐑄𐐩𐑉 𐐶𐐫𐑉𐑆. 𐐈𐑌𐐼 𐐸𐐨 𐐶𐐱𐑆 𐐬𐑌𐑊𐐨 𐐻𐐶𐐯𐑌𐐻𐐨 𐐰𐑌𐐼 𐑁𐐴𐑂 𐐷𐐨𐑉𐑆 𐐬𐑊𐐼 𐐸𐐶𐐯𐑌 𐐸𐐨 𐐶𐐱𐑆 𐐲𐐹𐐱𐐮𐑌𐐻𐐯𐐼 𐐽𐐨𐑁 𐐿𐐰𐐹𐐻𐐮𐑌 𐐬𐑂𐐲𐑉 𐑄 𐐪𐑉𐑋𐐨𐑆 𐐱𐑂 𐑄 𐐤𐐨𐑁𐐴𐐻𐑅.

4. 𐐈𐑌𐐼 𐐮𐐻 𐐿𐐩𐑋 𐐻𐐭 𐐹𐐰𐑅 𐑄𐐰𐐻 𐐸𐐨 𐑋𐐯𐐻 𐑄 𐐢𐐰𐑋𐐲𐑌𐐴𐐻𐑅 𐐮𐑌 𐑄 𐐺𐐫𐑉𐐼𐐲𐑉𐑆 𐐱𐑂 𐐖𐐲𐑉𐑇𐐲𐑌, 𐐰𐑌𐐼 𐐸𐐮𐑆 𐐹𐐨𐐹𐑊 𐐶𐐲𐑉 𐐪𐑉𐑋𐐼 𐐶𐐮𐑄 𐑅𐐫𐑉𐐼𐑆, 𐐰𐑌𐐼 𐐶𐐮𐑄 𐑅𐐮𐑋𐐮𐐻𐐲𐑉𐑆, 𐐰𐑌𐐼 𐐫𐑊 𐑋𐐰𐑌𐐲𐑉 𐐱𐑂 𐐶𐐯𐐹𐐲𐑌𐑆 𐐱𐑂

𐐶𐐫𐑉. 𐐈𐑌𐐼 𐐸𐐶𐐯𐑌 𐐜 𐐪𐑉𐑋𐐨𐑆 𐐱𐑂 𐐜 𐐢𐐩𐑋𐐲𐑌𐐴𐐻𐑅 𐑅𐐫 𐑄𐐰𐐻 𐐜 𐐹𐐨𐐹𐑊 𐐱𐑂 𐐤𐐨𐑁𐐴, 𐐫𐑉 𐑄𐐰𐐻 𐐣𐐬𐑉𐐬𐑌𐐴, 𐐸𐐰𐐼 𐐹𐑉𐐨𐐹𐐩𐑉𐐼 𐐸𐐮𐑆 𐐹𐐨𐐹𐑊 𐐶𐐮𐑄 𐐺𐑉𐐯𐑅𐐻𐐹𐑊𐐩𐐻𐑅, 𐐰𐑌𐐼 𐐶𐐮𐑄 𐐪𐑉𐑋-𐑇𐐨𐑊𐐼𐑆; 𐐷𐐩, 𐐰𐑌𐐼 𐐫𐑊𐑅𐐬 𐑇𐐨𐑊𐐼𐑆 𐐻𐐭 𐐼𐐨𐑁𐐯𐑌𐐼 𐑄𐐩𐑉 𐐸𐐯𐐼𐑆; 𐐰𐑌𐐼 𐐫𐑊𐑅𐐬 𐑄𐐩 𐐶𐐲𐑉 𐐼𐑉𐐯𐑅𐐻 𐐶𐐮𐑄 𐑃𐐮𐐿 𐐿𐑊𐐬𐑄𐐮𐑍. 𐐤𐐵 𐐜 𐐪𐑉𐑋𐐨 𐐱𐑂 𐐞𐐨𐑉𐐰𐐸𐐯𐑋𐑌𐐲 𐐶𐐱𐑆 𐑌𐐱𐐻 𐐹𐑉𐐨𐐹𐐩𐑉𐐼 𐐶𐐮𐑄 𐐯𐑌𐐨 𐑅𐐲𐐽 𐑃𐐮𐑍. 𐐜𐐩 𐐸𐐰𐐼 𐐬𐑌𐑊𐐨 𐑄𐐩𐑉 𐑅𐐬𐑉𐐼𐑆 𐐰𐑌𐐼 𐑄𐐩𐑉 𐑅𐐮𐑋𐐨𐐻𐐲𐑉𐑆, 𐑄𐐩𐑉 𐐺𐐬𐑆 𐐰𐑌𐐼 𐑄𐐩𐑉 𐐰𐑉𐐬𐑆, 𐑄𐐩𐑉 𐑅𐐻𐐬𐑌𐑆 𐐰𐑌𐐼 𐑄𐐩𐑉 𐑅𐑊𐐮𐑍𐑆; 𐐒𐐲𐐻 𐑄𐐩 𐐶𐐲𐑉 𐑌𐐩𐐿𐐯𐐼, 𐑅𐐩𐑂 𐐮𐐻 𐐶𐐲𐑉 𐐲 𐑅𐐿𐐮𐑌 𐐸𐐶𐐮𐐽 𐐶𐐱𐑆 𐑀𐐲𐑉𐐼𐐯𐐼 𐐲𐐺𐐵𐐻 𐑄𐐩𐑉 𐑊𐐦𐑌𐑆; 𐐷𐐩, 𐐫𐑊 𐐶𐐲𐑉 𐑌𐐩𐐿𐐯𐐼, 𐑅𐐩𐑂 𐐮𐐻 𐐶𐐲𐑉 𐐜 𐐞𐐬𐑉𐐲𐑋𐐴𐐻𐑅 𐐰𐑌𐐼 𐐜 𐐈𐑋𐐰𐑊𐐯𐐿𐐴𐐻𐑅. 𐐒𐐲𐐻 𐑄𐐩 𐐶𐐲𐑉 𐑌𐐱𐐻 𐐪𐑉𐑋𐐼 𐐶𐐮𐑄 𐐺𐑉𐐯𐑅𐐻𐐹𐑊𐐩𐐻𐑅, 𐑌𐐫𐑉 𐑇𐐨𐑊𐐼𐑆; 𐑄𐐩𐑉𐑁𐐬𐑉 𐑄𐐩 𐐶𐐲𐑉 𐐯𐐿𐑅𐐨𐐼𐐮𐑍𐑊𐐨 𐐰𐑁𐑉𐐩𐐼 𐐱𐑂 𐐜 𐐪𐑉𐑋𐐨𐑆 𐐱𐑂 𐐜 𐐤𐐨𐑁𐐴𐐻𐑅, 𐐺𐐨𐐿𐐫𐑆 𐐱𐑂 𐑄𐐩𐑉 𐐪𐑉𐑋𐐲𐑉, 𐑌𐐱𐐻𐐶𐐮𐑄𐑅𐐻𐐰𐑌𐐼𐐮𐑍 𐑄𐐩𐑉 𐑌𐐲𐑋𐐺𐐲𐑉 𐐺𐐨𐐮𐑍 𐑅𐐬 𐑋𐐲𐐽 𐑀𐑉𐐩𐐻𐐲𐑉 𐑄𐐰𐑌 𐐜 𐐤𐐨𐑁𐐴𐐻𐑅.

5. 𐐒𐐨𐐸𐐬𐑊𐐼, 𐑌𐐵 𐐮𐐻 𐐿𐐩𐑋 𐐻𐐭 𐐹𐐰𐑅 𐑄𐐰𐐻 𐑄𐐩 𐐼𐐲𐑉𐑅𐐻 𐑌𐐱𐐻 𐐿𐐲𐑋 𐐰𐑀𐐯𐑌𐑅𐐻 𐐜 𐐤𐐨𐑁𐐴𐐻𐑅 𐐮𐑌 𐐜 𐐺𐐫𐑉𐐼𐐲𐑉𐑆 𐐱𐑂 𐐖𐐲𐑉𐑇𐐲𐑌: 𐑄𐐩𐑉𐑁𐐬𐑉 𐑄𐐩 𐐼𐐨𐐹𐐪𐑉𐐻𐐯𐐼 𐐵𐐻 𐐱𐑂 𐐜 𐑊𐐰𐑌𐐼 𐐱𐑂 𐐈𐑌𐐻𐐨𐐬𐑌𐐲𐑋 𐐮𐑌𐐻𐐭 𐐜 𐐶𐐮𐑊𐐼𐐲𐑉𐑌𐐲𐑅, 𐐰𐑌𐐼 𐐻𐐳𐐿 𐑄𐐩𐑉 𐐖𐐲𐑉𐑌𐐨 𐑉𐐵𐑌𐐼 𐐲𐐺𐐵𐐻 𐐮𐑌 𐐜 𐐶𐐮𐑊𐐼𐐲𐑉𐑌𐐲𐑅, 𐐲𐐶𐐩 𐐺𐐴 𐐜 𐐸𐐯𐐼 𐐱𐑂 𐐜 𐑉𐐮𐑂𐐲𐑉 𐐝𐐴𐐼𐐲𐑌, 𐑄𐐰𐐻 𐑄𐐩 𐑋𐐴𐐻 𐐿𐐲𐑋 𐐮𐑌𐐻𐐭 𐐜 𐑊𐐰𐑌𐐼 𐐱𐑂 𐐣𐐰𐑌𐐻𐐴, 𐐰𐑌𐐼 𐐻𐐩𐐿 𐐹𐐲𐑆𐐯𐑇𐐲𐑌 𐐱𐑂 𐐜 𐑊𐐰𐑌𐐼; 𐑁𐐫𐑉 𐑄𐐩 𐐼𐐮𐐼 𐑌𐐱𐐻 𐑅𐐲𐐹𐐬𐑆 𐑄𐐰𐐻 𐐜 𐐪𐑉𐑋𐐨𐑆 𐐱𐑂 𐐣𐐬𐑉𐐬𐑌𐐴 𐐶𐐳𐐼 𐑌𐐬 𐐸𐐶𐐮𐑄𐐲𐑉 𐑄𐐩 𐐸𐐰𐐼 𐑀𐐱𐑌. 𐐒𐐲𐐻 𐐮𐐻 𐐿𐐩𐑋 𐐻𐐭 𐐹𐐰𐑅 𐐰𐑆 𐑅𐐭𐑌 𐐰𐑆 𐑄𐐩 𐐸𐐰𐐼 𐐼𐐨𐐹𐐪𐑉𐐻𐐯𐐼 𐐮𐑌𐐻𐐭 𐐜 𐐶𐐮𐑊𐐼𐐲𐑉𐑌𐐲𐑅, 𐐣𐐬𐑉𐐬𐑌𐐴 𐑅𐐯𐑌𐐻 𐑅𐐹𐐴𐑆 𐐮𐑌𐐻𐐭 𐐜 𐐶𐐮𐑊𐐼𐐲𐑉𐑌𐐲𐑅 𐐻𐐭 𐐶𐐱𐐽 𐑄𐐩𐑉 𐐿𐐰𐑋𐐹; 𐐰𐑌𐐼 𐐣𐐬𐑉𐐬𐑌𐐴, 𐐫𐑊𐑅𐐬, 𐑌𐐬𐐮𐑍 𐐱𐑂 𐐜 𐐹𐑉𐐱𐑁𐐯𐑅𐐨𐑆 𐐱𐑂 𐐈𐑊𐑋𐐲, 𐑅𐐯𐑌𐐻 𐑅𐐲𐑉𐐻𐐯𐑌 𐑋𐐯𐑌 𐐲𐑌𐐻𐐭 𐐸𐐮𐑋, 𐐼𐐨𐑆𐐴𐑉𐐮𐑍 𐐸𐐮𐑋 𐑄𐐰𐐻 𐐸𐐨 𐑇𐐳𐐼 𐐮𐑌𐐿𐐶𐐴𐑉 𐐱𐑂 𐐜 𐐢𐐫𐑉𐐼, 𐐸𐐶𐐮𐑄𐐲𐑉 𐐜 𐐪𐑉𐑋𐐨𐑆 𐐱𐑂 𐐜 𐐤𐐨𐑁𐐴𐐻𐑅 𐑇𐐳𐐼 𐑀𐐬, 𐐻𐐭 𐐼𐐨𐑁𐐯𐑌𐐼 𐑄𐐯𐑋𐑅𐐯𐑊𐑂𐑆 𐐰𐑀𐐯𐑌𐑅𐐻 𐐜 𐐢𐐩𐑋𐐲𐑌𐐴𐐻𐑅. 𐐈𐑌𐐼 𐐮𐐻 𐐿𐐩𐑋 𐐻𐐭 𐐹𐐰𐑅 𐑄𐐰𐐻 𐐜 𐐶𐐲𐑉𐐼 𐐱𐑂 𐐜 𐐢𐐫𐑉𐐼 𐐿𐐩𐑋 𐐲𐑌𐐻𐐭 𐐈𐑊𐑋𐐲, 𐐰𐑌𐐼 𐐈𐑊𐑋𐐲 𐐮𐑌𐑁𐐫𐑉𐑋𐐼 𐐜 𐑋𐐯𐑅𐐯𐑌𐐾𐐲𐑉𐑆 𐐱𐑂 𐐣𐐬𐑉𐐬𐑌𐐴 𐑄𐐰𐐻 𐐜 𐐪𐑉𐑋𐐨𐑆 𐐱𐑂 𐐜 𐐢𐐩𐑋𐐲𐑌𐐴𐐻𐑅 𐐶𐐲𐑉 𐑋𐐪𐑉𐐽𐐮𐑍 𐑉𐐵𐑌𐐼 𐐲𐐺𐐵𐐻 𐐮𐑌 𐐜 𐐶𐐮𐑊𐐼𐐲𐑉𐑌𐐲𐑅, 𐑄𐐰𐐻 𐑄𐐩 𐑋𐐴𐐻 𐐿𐐲𐑋 𐐬𐑂𐐲𐑉 𐐮𐑌𐐻𐐭 𐐜 𐑊𐐰𐑌𐐼 𐐱𐑂 𐐣𐐰𐑌𐐻𐐴, 𐑄𐐰𐐻 𐑄𐐩 𐑋𐐴𐐻 𐐿𐐲𐑋𐐯𐑌𐑅 𐐰𐑌 𐐰𐐻𐐰𐐿 𐐲𐐹𐐱𐑌 𐐜 𐐶𐐨𐐿𐐲𐑉 𐐹𐐪𐑉𐐻 𐐱𐑂 𐐜 𐐹𐐨𐐹𐑊. 𐐈𐑌𐐼 𐑄𐐬𐑆 𐑋𐐯𐑅𐐯𐑌𐐾𐐲𐑉𐑆 𐐶𐐯𐑌𐐻 𐐰𐑌𐐼 𐐼𐐨𐑊𐐮𐑂𐐲𐑉𐐼 𐐜 𐑋𐐯𐑅𐐯𐐾 𐐲𐑌𐐻𐐭 𐐣𐐬𐑉𐐬𐑌𐐴.

6. 𐐤𐐵 𐐣𐐬𐑉𐐬𐑌𐐴, 𐑊𐐨𐑂𐐮𐑍 𐐲 𐐹𐐪𐑉𐐻 𐐱𐑂 𐐸𐐮𐑆 𐐪𐑉𐑋𐐨 𐐮𐑌 𐐜 𐑊𐐰𐑌𐐼 𐐱𐑂 𐐖𐐲𐑉𐑇𐐲𐑌, 𐑊𐐯𐑅𐐻 𐐺𐐴 𐐯𐑌𐐨 𐑋𐐨𐑌𐑆 𐐲 𐐹𐐪𐑉𐐻 𐐱𐑂 𐐜 𐐢𐐩𐑋𐐲𐑌𐐴𐐻𐑅 𐑇𐐳𐐼 𐐿𐐲𐑋 𐐮𐑌𐐻𐐭 𐑄𐐰𐐻 𐑊𐐰𐑌𐐼 𐐰𐑌𐐼 𐐻𐐩𐐿 𐐹𐐲𐑆𐐯𐑇𐐲𐑌 𐐱𐑂 𐐜 𐑅𐐮𐐻𐐨, 𐐻𐐳𐐿 𐐜 𐑉𐐨𐑋𐐩𐑌𐐮𐑍 𐐹𐐪𐑉𐐻 𐐱𐑂 𐐸𐐮𐑆 𐐪𐑉𐑋𐐨 𐐰𐑌𐐼 𐑋𐐪𐑉𐐽𐐻 𐐬𐑂𐐲𐑉 𐐮𐑌𐐻𐐭 𐐜 𐑊𐐰𐑌𐐼 𐐱𐑂 𐐣𐐰𐑌𐐻𐐴. 𐐈𐑌𐐼 𐐸𐐨 𐐿𐐫𐑆𐐼 𐑄𐐰𐐻 𐐫𐑊 𐐜 𐐹𐐨𐐹𐑊 𐐮𐑌 𐑄𐐰𐐻 𐐿𐐶𐐫𐑉𐐻𐐲𐑉 𐐱𐑂 𐐜 𐑊𐐰𐑌𐐼 𐑇𐐳𐐼 𐑀𐐰𐑄𐐲𐑉 𐑄𐐯𐑋𐑅𐐯𐑊𐑂𐑆 𐐻𐐭𐑀𐐯𐑄𐐲𐑉 𐐻𐐭 𐐺𐐰𐐻𐑊, 𐐰𐑀𐐯𐑌𐑅𐐻 𐐜 𐐢𐐩𐑋𐐲𐑌𐐴𐐻𐑅, 𐐻𐐭 𐐼𐐨𐑁𐐯𐑌𐐼 𐑄𐐩𐑉 𐑊𐐰𐑌𐐼𐑆 𐐰𐑌𐐼 𐑄𐐩𐑉 𐐿𐐲𐑌𐐻𐑉𐐨, 𐑄𐐩𐑉 𐑉𐐴𐐻𐑅 𐐰𐑌𐐼 𐑄𐐩𐑉 𐑊𐐮𐐺𐐲𐑉𐐻𐐨𐑆; 𐑄𐐩𐑉𐑁𐐬𐑉 𐑄𐐩 𐐶𐐲𐑉 𐐹𐑉𐐨𐐹𐐩𐑉𐐼 𐐰𐑀𐐯𐑌𐑅𐐻 𐐜 𐐻𐐴𐑋 𐐱𐑂 𐐜 𐐿𐐲𐑋𐐮𐑍 𐐱𐑂 𐐜 𐐢𐐩𐑋𐐲𐑌𐐴𐐻𐑅. 𐐈𐑌𐐼 𐐮𐐻 𐐿𐐩𐑋 𐐻𐐭 𐐹𐐰𐑅 𐑄𐐰𐐻 𐐣𐐬𐑉𐐬𐑌𐐴 𐐿𐐫𐑆𐐼 𐑄𐐰𐐻 𐐸𐐮𐑆 𐐪𐑉𐑋𐐨 𐑇𐐳𐐼 𐐺𐐨 𐑅𐐨𐐿𐑉𐐨𐐻𐐯𐐼 𐐮𐑌 𐐜 𐑂𐐰𐑊𐐨 𐐸𐐶𐐮𐐽 𐐶𐐱𐑆 𐑌𐐨𐑉 𐐜 𐐺𐐰𐑍𐐿 𐐱𐑂 𐐜 𐑉𐐮𐑂𐐲𐑉 𐐝𐐴𐐼𐐲𐑌, 𐐸𐐶𐐮𐐽 𐐶𐐱𐑆 𐐱𐑌 𐐜 𐐶𐐯𐑅𐐻 𐐱𐑂 𐐜 𐑉𐐮𐑂𐐲𐑉 𐐝𐐴𐐼𐐲𐑌 𐐮𐑌 𐐜 𐐶𐐮𐑊𐐼𐐲𐑉𐑌𐐲𐑅. 𐐈𐑌𐐼 𐐣𐐬𐑉𐐬𐑌𐐴 𐐹𐑊𐐩𐑅𐐻 𐑅𐐹𐐴𐑆 𐑉𐐵𐑌𐐼 𐐲𐐺𐐵𐐻, 𐑄𐐰𐐻 𐐸𐐨 𐑋𐐴𐐻 𐑌𐐬 𐐸𐐶𐐯𐑌 𐐜 𐐿𐐰𐑋𐐹 𐐱𐑂 𐐜 𐐢𐐩𐑋𐐲𐑌𐐴𐐻𐑅 𐑇𐐳𐐼 𐐿𐐲𐑋.

7. 𐐈𐑌𐐼 𐑌𐐵 𐐰𐑆 𐐣𐐬𐑉𐐬𐑌𐐴 𐑌𐐭 𐐜 𐐮𐑌𐐻𐐯𐑌𐑇𐐲𐑌 𐐱𐑂 𐐜 𐐢𐐩𐑋𐐲𐑌𐐴𐐻𐑅, 𐑄𐐰𐐻 𐐮𐐻 𐐶𐐱𐑆 𐑄𐐩𐑉 𐐮𐑌𐐻𐐯𐑌𐑇𐐲𐑌 𐐻𐐭 𐐼𐐨𐑅𐐻𐑉𐐦 𐑄𐐩𐑉 𐐺𐑉𐐯𐑄𐑉𐐯𐑌, 𐐫𐑉 𐐻𐐭 𐑅𐐲𐐺𐐾𐐯𐐿𐐻 𐑄𐐯𐑋 𐐰𐑌𐐼 𐐺𐑉𐐮𐑍 𐑄𐐯𐑋 𐐮𐑌𐐻𐐭 𐐺𐐱𐑌𐐼𐐮𐐾 𐑄𐐰𐐻 𐑄𐐩 𐑋𐐴𐐻 𐐯𐑅𐐻𐐰𐐺𐑊𐐮𐑇 𐐲 𐐿𐐮𐑍𐐼𐐲𐑋 𐐲𐑌𐐻𐐭 𐑄𐐯𐑋𐑅𐐯𐑊𐑂𐑆, 𐐬𐑂𐐲𐑉 𐐫𐑊 𐐜 𐑊𐐰𐑌𐐼; 𐐰𐑌𐐼 𐐸𐐨 𐐫𐑊𐑅𐐬 𐑌𐐬𐐮𐑍 𐑄𐐰𐐻 𐐮𐐻 𐐶𐐱𐑆 𐐜 𐐬𐑌𐑊𐐨 𐐼𐐨𐑆𐐴𐑉 𐐱𐑂 𐐜 𐐤𐐨𐑁𐐴𐐻𐑅, 𐐻𐐭 𐐹𐑉𐐨𐑆𐐲𐑉𐑂 𐑄𐐩𐑉 𐑊𐐰𐑌𐐼𐑆, 𐐰𐑌𐐼 𐑄𐐩𐑉 𐑊𐐮𐐺𐐲𐑉𐐻𐐨, 𐐰𐑌𐐼 𐑄𐐩𐑉 𐐕𐐲𐑉𐐽, 𐑄𐐩𐑉𐑁𐐬𐑉 𐐸𐐨 𐑃𐐫𐐻 𐐮𐐻 𐑌𐐬 𐑅𐐮𐑌 𐑄𐐰𐐻 𐐸𐐨 𐑇𐐳𐐼 𐐼𐐨𐑁𐐯𐑌𐐼 𐑄𐐯𐑋 𐐺𐐴 𐑅𐐻𐑉𐐰𐐻𐐲𐐾𐐯𐑋; 𐑄𐐩𐑉𐑁𐐬𐑉 𐐸𐐨 𐑁𐐵𐑌𐐼 𐐺𐐴 𐐸𐐮𐑆 𐑅𐐹𐐴𐑆, 𐐸𐐶𐐮𐐽 𐐿𐐬𐑉𐑅 𐐜 𐐢𐐩𐑋𐐲𐑌𐐴𐐻𐑅 𐐶𐐲𐑉 𐐻𐐭 𐐻𐐩𐐿. 𐐜𐐩𐑉𐑁𐐬𐑉 𐐸𐐨 𐐼𐐮𐑂𐐴𐐼𐐯𐐼 𐐸𐐮𐑆 𐐪𐑉𐑋𐐨, 𐐰𐑌𐐼 𐐺𐑉𐐫𐐻 𐐲 𐐹𐐪𐑉𐐻 𐐬𐑂𐐲𐑉 𐐮𐑌𐐻𐐭 𐐜 𐑂𐐰𐑊𐐨, 𐐰𐑌𐐼 𐐿𐐲𐑌𐑅𐐨𐑊𐐼 𐑄𐐯𐑋 𐐱𐑌 𐐜 𐐨𐑅𐐻,

𐐰𐑌𐐼 𐐱𐑌 𐑄 𐑅𐐵𐑃 𐐲𐑂 𐑄 𐐸𐐮𐑊 𐐡𐐮𐐹𐑊𐐲; 𐐰𐑌𐐼 𐑄 𐑉𐐨𐑋𐐩𐑌𐐼𐐲𐑉 𐐸𐐨 𐐿𐐲𐑌𐑅𐐨𐑊𐐼 𐐮𐑌 𐑄 𐐶𐐯𐑅𐐻 𐑂𐐰𐑊𐐮, 𐐱𐑌 𐑄 𐐶𐐯𐑅𐐻 𐐲𐑂 𐑄 𐑉𐐮𐑂𐐲𐑉 𐐝𐐴𐐼𐐲𐑌, 𐐰𐑌𐐼 𐑅𐐬 𐐼𐐵𐑌 𐐮𐑌𐐻𐐭 𐑄 𐐺𐐫𐑉𐐼𐐲𐑉𐑆 𐐲𐑂 𐑄 𐑊𐐰𐑌𐐼 𐐣𐐰𐑌𐐻𐐴. 𐐈𐑌𐐼 𐑄𐐲𐑅 𐐸𐐰𐑂𐐮𐑍 𐐹𐑊𐐩𐑅𐐻 𐐸𐐮𐑆 𐐪𐑉𐑋𐐨 𐐰𐐿𐐫𐑉𐐼𐐮𐑍 𐐻𐐭 𐐸𐐮𐑆 𐐼𐐨𐑆𐐴𐑉, 𐐸𐐨 𐐶𐐱𐑆 𐐹𐑉𐐨𐐹𐐩𐑉𐐼 𐐻𐐭 𐑋𐐨𐐻 𐑄𐐯𐑋.

8. 𐐈𐑌𐐼 𐐮𐐻 𐐿𐐩𐑋 𐐻𐐭 𐐹𐐰𐑅 𐑄𐐰𐐻 𐑄 𐐢𐐩𐑋𐐲𐑌𐐴𐐻𐑅 𐐿𐐩𐑋 𐐲𐐹 𐐱𐑌 𐑄 𐑌𐐫𐑉𐑃 𐐲𐑂 𐑄 𐐸𐐮𐑊, 𐐸𐐶𐐯𐑉 𐐲 𐐹𐐪𐑉𐐻 𐐲𐑂 𐑄 𐐪𐑉𐑋𐐨 𐐲𐑂 𐐣𐐬𐑉𐐬𐑌𐐴 𐐶𐐱𐑆 𐐿𐐲𐑌𐑅𐐨𐑊𐐼. 𐐈𐑌𐐼 𐐰𐑆 𐑄 𐐢𐐩𐑋𐐲𐑌𐐴𐐻𐑅 𐐸𐐰𐐼 𐐹𐐰𐑅𐐻 𐑄 𐐸𐐮𐑊 𐐡𐐮𐐹𐑊𐐲, 𐐰𐑌𐐼 𐐿𐐩𐑋 𐐮𐑌𐐻𐐭 𐑄 𐑂𐐰𐑊𐐮, 𐐰𐑌𐐼 𐐺𐐨𐑀𐐰𐑌 𐐻𐐭 𐐿𐑉𐐱𐑅 𐑄 𐑉𐐮𐑂𐐲𐑉 𐐝𐐴𐐼𐐲𐑌, 𐑄 𐐪𐑉𐑋𐐨 𐐸𐐶𐐮𐐽 𐐶𐐱𐑆 𐐿𐐲𐑌𐑅𐐨𐑊𐐼 𐐱𐑌 𐑄 𐑅𐐵𐑃 𐐲𐑂 𐑄 𐐸𐐮𐑊, 𐐸𐐶𐐮𐐽 𐐶𐐱𐑆 𐑊𐐯𐐼 𐐺𐐴 𐐲 𐑋𐐰𐑌 𐐸𐐭𐑆 𐑌𐐩𐑋 𐐶𐐱𐑆 𐐢𐐨𐐸𐐴; 𐐰𐑌𐐼 𐐸𐐨 𐑊𐐯𐐼 𐐸𐐮𐑆 𐐪𐑉𐑋𐐨 𐑁𐐬𐑉𐑃 𐐰𐑌𐐼 𐐯𐑌𐑅𐐲𐑉𐐿𐑊𐐼 𐑄 𐐢𐐩𐑋𐐲𐑌𐐴𐐻𐑅 𐐲𐐺𐐵𐐻 𐐱𐑌 𐑄 𐐨𐑅𐐻 𐐮𐑌 𐑄𐐩𐑉 𐑉𐐨𐑉.

9. 𐐈𐑌𐐼 𐐮𐐻 𐐿𐐩𐑋 𐐻𐐭 𐐹𐐰𐑅 𐑄𐐰𐐻 𐑄 𐐢𐐩𐑋𐐲𐑌𐐴𐐻𐑅, 𐐸𐐶𐐯𐑌 𐑄𐐩 𐑅𐐫 𐑄 𐐤𐐨𐑁𐐴𐐻𐑅 𐐿𐐲𐑋𐐮𐑍 𐐲𐐹𐐱𐑌 𐑄𐐯𐑋 𐐮𐑌 𐑄𐐩𐑉 𐑉𐐨𐑉, 𐐻𐐲𐑉𐑌𐐼 𐑄𐐯𐑋 𐐲𐐺𐐵𐐻, 𐐰𐑌𐐼 𐐺𐐨𐑀𐐰𐑌 𐐻𐐭 𐐿𐐲𐑌𐐻𐐯𐑌𐐼 𐐶𐐮𐑄 𐑄 𐐪𐑉𐑋𐐨 𐐲𐑂 𐐢𐐨𐐸𐐴; 𐐰𐑌𐐼 𐑄 𐐶𐐲𐑉𐐿 𐐲𐑂 𐐼𐐯𐑃 𐐿𐐲𐑋𐐯𐑌𐑅𐐻 𐐱𐑌 𐐺𐐬𐑃 𐑅𐐴𐐼𐑆, 𐐺𐐲𐐻 𐐮𐐻 𐐶𐐱𐑆 𐑋𐐬𐑉 𐐼𐑉𐐯𐐼𐑁𐐲𐑊 𐐱𐑌 𐑄 𐐹𐐪𐑉𐐻 𐐲𐑂 𐑄 𐐢𐐩𐑋𐐲𐑌𐐴𐐻𐑅, 𐑁𐐫𐑉 𐑄𐐩𐑉 𐑌𐐩𐐿𐐯𐐼𐑌𐐯𐑅 𐐶𐐱𐑆 𐐯𐐿𐑅𐐹𐐬𐑆𐐼 𐐻𐐭 𐑄 𐐸𐐯𐑂𐐨 𐐺𐑊𐐬𐑆 𐐲𐑂 𐑄 𐐤𐐨𐑁𐐴𐐻𐑅, 𐐶𐐮𐑄 𐑄𐐩𐑉 𐑅𐐫𐑉𐐼𐑆 𐐰𐑌𐐼 𐑄𐐩𐑉 𐑅𐐮𐑋𐐮𐐻𐐲𐑉𐑆, 𐐸𐐶𐐮𐐽 𐐺𐑉𐐫𐐻 𐐼𐐯𐑃 𐐫𐑊𐑋𐐬𐑅𐐻 𐐰𐐻 𐐯𐑂𐐲𐑉𐐨 𐑅𐐻𐑉𐐬𐐿; 𐐸𐐶𐐴𐑊 𐐱𐑌 𐑄 𐐲𐑄𐐲𐑉 𐐸𐐰𐑌𐐼 𐑄𐐩𐑉 𐐶𐐱𐑆 𐑌𐐵 𐐰𐑌𐐼 𐑄𐐯𐑌 𐐲 𐑋𐐰𐑌 𐑁𐐯𐑊 𐐲𐑋𐐲𐑍 𐑄 𐐤𐐨𐑁𐐴𐐻𐑅, 𐐺𐐴 𐑄𐐩𐑉 𐑅𐐫𐑉𐐼𐑆 𐐰𐑌𐐼 𐑄 𐑊𐐱𐑅 𐐲𐑂 𐐺𐑊𐐲𐐼; 𐑄𐐩 𐐺𐐨𐐮𐑍 𐑇𐐨𐑊𐐼𐐯𐐼 𐑁𐑉𐐱𐑋 𐑄 𐑋𐐬𐑉 𐑂𐐴𐐻𐐲𐑊 𐐹𐐪𐑉𐐻𐑅 𐐲𐑂 𐑄 𐐺𐐱𐐼𐐨, 𐐫𐑉 𐑄 𐑋𐐬𐑉 𐑂𐐴𐐻𐐲𐑊 𐐹𐐪𐑉𐐻𐑅 𐐲𐑂 𐑄 𐐺𐐱𐐼𐐨 𐐺𐐨𐐮𐑍 𐑇𐐨𐑊𐐼𐐯𐐼 𐑁𐑉𐐱𐑋 𐑄 𐑅𐐻𐑉𐐬𐐿𐑅 𐐲𐑂 𐑄 𐐢𐐩𐑋𐐲𐑌𐐴𐐻𐑅, 𐐺𐐴 𐑄𐐩𐑉 𐐺𐑉𐐯𐑅𐐻-𐐹𐑊𐐩𐐻𐑅, 𐐰𐑌𐐼 𐑄𐐩𐑉 𐐪𐑉𐑋-𐑇𐐨𐑊𐐼𐑆, 𐐰𐑌𐐼 𐑄𐐩𐑉 𐐸𐐯𐐼-𐐹𐑊𐐩𐐻𐑅: 𐐰𐑌𐐼 𐑄𐐲𐑅 𐑄 𐐤𐐨𐑁𐐴𐐻𐑅 𐐼𐐮𐐼 𐐿𐐰𐑉𐐨 𐐱𐑌 𐑄 𐐶𐐲𐑉𐐿 𐐲𐑂 𐐼𐐯𐑃 𐐲𐑋𐐲𐑍 𐑄 𐐢𐐩𐑋𐐲𐑌𐐴𐐻𐑅. 𐐈𐑌𐐼 𐐮𐐻 𐐿𐐩𐑋 𐐻𐐭 𐐹𐐰𐑅 𐑄𐐰𐐻 𐑄 𐐢𐐩𐑋𐐲𐑌𐐴𐐻𐑅 𐐺𐐨𐐿𐐩𐑋 𐑁𐑉𐐴𐐻𐑌𐐼, 𐐺𐐨𐐿𐐫𐑆 𐐲𐑂 𐑄 𐑀𐑉𐐩𐐻 𐐼𐐨𐑅𐐻𐑉𐐲𐐿𐑇𐐲𐑌 𐐲𐑋𐐲𐑍 𐑄𐐯𐑋, 𐐨𐑂𐐯𐑌 𐐲𐑌𐐻𐐮𐑊 𐑄𐐩 𐐺𐐨𐑀𐐰𐑌 𐐻𐐭 𐑁𐑊𐐨 𐐻𐐬𐑉𐐼𐑆 𐑄 𐑉𐐮𐑂𐐲𐑉 𐐝𐐴𐐼𐐲𐑌. 𐐈𐑌𐐼 𐑄𐐩 𐐶𐐲𐑉 𐐹𐐲𐑉𐑅𐐭𐐼 𐐺𐐴 𐐢𐐨𐐸𐐴 𐐰𐑌𐐼 𐐸𐐮𐑆 𐑋𐐯𐑌, 𐐰𐑌𐐼 𐑄𐐩 𐐶𐐲𐑉 𐐼𐑉𐐮𐑂𐐯𐑌 𐐺𐐴 𐐢𐐨𐐸𐐴 𐐮𐑌𐐻𐐭 𐑄 𐐶𐐫𐐻𐐲𐑉𐑆 𐐲𐑂 𐐝𐐴𐐼𐐲𐑌; 𐐰𐑌𐐼 𐑄𐐩 𐐿𐑉𐐱𐑅𐐻 𐑄 𐐶𐐫𐐻𐐲𐑉𐑆 𐐲𐑂 𐐝𐐴𐐼𐐲𐑌. 𐐈𐑌𐐼 𐐢𐐨𐐸𐐴 𐑉𐐨𐐻𐐩𐑌𐐼 𐐸𐐮𐑆 𐐪𐑉𐑋𐐨𐑆 𐐲𐐹𐐱𐑌 𐑄 𐐺𐐰𐑍𐐿 𐐲𐑂 𐑄 𐑉𐐮𐑂𐐲𐑉 𐐝𐐴𐐼𐐲𐑌, 𐑄𐐰𐐻 𐑄𐐩 𐑇𐐳𐐼 𐑌𐐱𐐻 𐐿𐑉𐐱𐑅.

10. 𐐈𐑌𐐼 𐐮𐐻 𐐿𐐩𐑋 𐐻𐐭 𐐹𐐰𐑅 𐑄𐐰𐐻 𐐣𐐬𐑉𐐬𐑌𐐴 𐐰𐑌𐐼 𐐸𐐮𐑆 𐐪𐑉𐑋𐐨 𐑋𐐯𐐻 𐑄 𐐢𐐩𐑋𐐲𐑌𐐴𐐻𐑅 𐐮𐑌 𐑄 𐑂𐐰𐑊𐐮, 𐐱𐑌 𐑄 𐐲𐑄𐐲𐑉 𐑅𐐴𐐼 𐐲𐑂 𐑄 𐑉𐐮𐑂𐐲𐑉 𐐝𐐴𐐼𐐲𐑌, 𐐰𐑌𐐼 𐐺𐐨𐑀𐐰𐑌 𐐻𐐭 𐑁𐐫𐑊 𐐲𐐹𐐱𐑌 𐑄𐐯𐑋 𐐰𐑌𐐼 𐐻𐐭 𐑅𐑊𐐩 𐑄𐐯𐑋. 𐐈𐑌𐐼 𐑄 𐐢𐐩𐑋𐐲𐑌𐐴𐐻𐑅 𐐼𐐮𐐼 𐑁𐑊𐐨 𐐲𐑀𐐯𐑌 𐐺𐐨𐑁𐐬𐑉 𐑄𐐯𐑋, 𐐻𐐬𐑉𐐼𐑆 𐑄 𐑊𐐰𐑌𐐼 𐐲𐑂 𐐣𐐰𐑌𐐻𐐴; 𐐰𐑌𐐼 𐑄𐐩 𐐶𐐲𐑉 𐑋𐐯𐐻 𐐲𐑀𐐯𐑌 𐐺𐐴 𐑄 𐐪𐑉𐑋𐐨𐑆 𐐲𐑂 𐐣𐐬𐑉𐐬𐑌𐐴. 𐐤𐐵 𐐮𐑌 𐑄𐐮𐑅 𐐿𐐩𐑅 𐑄 𐐢𐐩𐑋𐐲𐑌𐐴𐐻𐑅 𐐼𐐮𐐼 𐑁𐐴𐐻 𐐯𐐿𐑅𐐨𐐼𐐮𐑍𐑊𐐨; 𐐷𐐩, 𐑌𐐯𐑂𐐲𐑉 𐐸𐐰𐐼 𐑄 𐐢𐐩𐑋𐐲𐑌𐐴𐐻𐑅 𐐺𐐮𐑌 𐑌𐐬𐑌 𐐻𐐭 𐑁𐐴𐐻 𐐶𐐮𐑄 𐑅𐐲𐐽 𐐯𐐿𐑅𐐨𐐼𐐮𐑍 𐑀𐑉𐐩𐐻 𐑅𐐻𐑉𐐯𐑍𐑃 𐐰𐑌𐐼 𐐿𐐲𐑉𐐩𐐾, 𐑌𐐬, 𐑌𐐱𐐻 𐐨𐑂𐐯𐑌 𐑁𐑉𐐱𐑋 𐑄 𐐺𐐨𐑀𐐮𐑌𐐮𐑍; 𐐰𐑌𐐼 𐑄𐐩 𐐶𐐲𐑉 𐐮𐑌𐑅𐐹𐐴𐑉𐐼 𐐺𐐴 𐑄 𐐞𐐬𐑉𐐲𐑋𐐴𐐻𐑅 𐐰𐑌𐐼 𐑄 𐐈𐑋𐐰𐑊𐐯𐐿𐐴𐐻𐑅, 𐐸𐐭 𐐶𐐲𐑉 𐑄𐐩𐑉 𐐽𐐨𐑁 𐐿𐐰𐐹𐐻𐐯𐑌𐑆 𐐰𐑌𐐼 𐑊𐐨𐐼𐐲𐑉𐑆, 𐐰𐑌𐐼 𐐺𐐴 𐐞𐐯𐑉𐐲𐐸𐐯𐑋𐑌𐐲, 𐐸𐐭 𐐶𐐱𐑆 𐑄𐐩𐑉 𐐽𐐨𐑁 𐐿𐐰𐐹𐐻𐐯𐑌, 𐐫𐑉 𐑄𐐩𐑉 𐐽𐐨𐑁 𐑊𐐨𐐼𐐲𐑉 𐐰𐑌𐐼 𐐿𐐲𐑋𐐰𐑌𐐼𐐲𐑉; 𐐷𐐩, 𐑄𐐩 𐐼𐐮𐐼 𐑁𐐴𐐻 𐑊𐐴𐐿 𐐼𐑉𐐰𐑀𐐲𐑌𐑆, 𐐰𐑌𐐼 𐑋𐐯𐑌𐐨 𐐲𐑂 𐑄 𐐤𐐨𐑁𐐴𐐻𐑅 𐐶𐐲𐑉 𐑅𐑊𐐩𐑌 𐐺𐐴 𐑄𐐩𐑉 𐐸𐐰𐑌𐐼𐑆, 𐐷𐐩, 𐑁𐐫𐑉 𐑄𐐩 𐐼𐐮𐐼 𐑅𐑋𐐴𐐻 𐐮𐑌 𐐻𐐭 𐑋𐐯𐑌𐐨 𐐲𐑂 𐑄𐐩𐑉 𐐸𐐯𐐼-𐐹𐑊𐐩𐐻𐑅, 𐐰𐑌𐐼 𐑄𐐩 𐐼𐐮𐐼 𐐹𐐨𐑉𐑅 𐑋𐐯𐑌𐐨 𐐲𐑂 𐑄𐐩𐑉 𐐺𐑉𐐯𐑅𐐻-𐐹𐑊𐐩𐐻𐑅, 𐐰𐑌𐐼 𐑄𐐩 𐐼𐐮𐐼 𐑅𐑋𐐴𐐻 𐐫𐑁 𐑋𐐯𐑌𐐨 𐐲𐑂 𐑄𐐩𐑉 𐐪𐑉𐑋𐑆; 𐐰𐑌𐐼 𐑄𐐲𐑅 𐑄 𐐢𐐩𐑋𐐲𐑌𐐴𐐻𐑅 𐐼𐐮𐐼 𐑅𐑋𐐴𐐻 𐐮𐑌 𐑄𐐩𐑉 𐑁𐐨𐑉𐑅 𐐰𐑍𐑀𐐲𐑉. 𐐤𐐯𐑂𐐲𐑉𐑄𐐯𐑊𐐯𐑅, 𐑄 𐐤𐐨𐑁𐐴𐐻𐑅 𐐶𐐲𐑉 𐐮𐑌𐑅𐐹𐐴𐑉𐐼 𐐺𐐴 𐐲 𐐺𐐯𐐻𐐲𐑉 𐐿𐐫𐑆, 𐑁𐐫𐑉 𐑄𐐩 𐐶𐐲𐑉 𐑌𐐱𐐻 𐑁𐐴𐐻𐐮𐑍 𐑁𐐫𐑉 𐑋𐐱𐑌𐐲𐑉𐐿𐐨 𐑌𐐫𐑉 𐐹𐐵𐐲𐑉, 𐐺𐐲𐐻 𐑄𐐩 𐐶𐐲𐑉 𐑁𐐴𐐻𐐮𐑍 𐑁𐐫𐑉 𐑄𐐩𐑉 𐐸𐐬𐑋𐑆 𐐰𐑌𐐼 𐑄𐐩𐑉 𐑊𐐮𐐺𐐲𐑉𐐻𐐨𐑆, 𐑄𐐩𐑉 𐐶𐐴𐑂𐑆 𐐰𐑌𐐼 𐑄𐐩𐑉 𐐽𐐮𐑊𐐼𐑉𐐯𐑌, 𐐰𐑌𐐼 𐑄𐐩𐑉 𐐫𐑊; 𐐷𐐩, 𐑁𐐫𐑉 𐑄𐐩𐑉 𐑉𐐴𐐻𐑅 𐐲𐑂 𐐶𐐲𐑉𐑇𐐮𐐹 𐐰𐑌𐐼 𐑄𐐩𐑉 𐐽𐐲𐑉𐐽: 𐐰𐑌𐐼 𐑄𐐩 𐐶𐐲𐑉 𐐼𐐭𐐮𐑍 𐑄𐐰𐐻 𐐸𐐶𐐮𐐽 𐑄𐐩 𐑁𐐯𐑊𐐻 𐐶𐐱𐑆 𐑄 𐐼𐐧𐐻𐐨 𐐸𐐶𐐮𐐽 𐑄𐐩 𐐬𐐼 𐐻𐐭 𐑄𐐩𐑉 𐐘𐐱𐐼; 𐑁𐐫𐑉 𐑄 𐐢𐐫𐑉𐐼 𐐸𐐰𐐼 𐑅𐐯𐐼 𐐲𐑌𐐻𐐭 𐑄𐐯𐑋, 𐐰𐑌𐐼 𐐫𐑊𐑅𐐬 𐐲𐑌𐐻𐐭 𐑄𐐩𐑉 𐑁𐐪𐑄𐐲𐑉𐑆, 𐑄𐐰𐐻 𐐮𐑌𐐰𐑆𐑋𐐲𐐽 𐐰𐑆 𐐷𐐨 𐐪𐑉 𐑌𐐱𐐻 𐑀𐐮𐑊𐐻𐐨 𐐲𐑂 𐑄 𐑁𐐲𐑉𐑅𐐻 𐐱𐑁𐐯𐑌𐑅, 𐑌𐐨𐑄𐐲𐑉 𐑄 𐑅𐐯𐐿𐐲𐑌𐐼, 𐐷𐐨 𐑇𐐰𐑊 𐑌𐐱𐐻 𐑅𐐲𐑁𐐲𐑉 𐐷𐐫𐑉𐑅𐐯𐑊𐑂𐑆 𐐻𐐭 𐐺𐐨 𐑅𐑊𐐩𐑌 𐐺𐐴 𐑄 𐐸𐐰𐑌𐐼𐑆 𐐲𐑂 𐐷𐐫𐑉 𐐯𐑌𐐯𐑋𐐨𐑆. 𐐈𐑌𐐼 𐐲𐑀𐐯𐑌, 𐑄 𐐢𐐫𐑉𐐼 𐐸𐐰𐑆 𐑅𐐯𐐼 𐑄𐐰𐐻 𐐷𐐨 𐑇𐐰𐑊 𐐼𐐨𐑁𐐯𐑌𐐼 𐐷𐐫𐑉

𐑁𐐰𐑋𐐮𐑊𐐮𐑆 𐐨𐑂𐐲𐑌 𐐲𐑌𐐻𐐭 𐐺𐑊𐐲𐐼𐑇𐐯𐐼; 𐑄𐐩𐑉𐑁𐐬𐑉 𐑁𐐫𐑉 𐑄𐐮𐑅 𐐿𐐫𐑆 𐐶𐐲𐑉 𐑄 𐐤𐐨𐑁𐐴𐐻𐑅 𐐿𐐪𐑌𐐻𐐯𐑌𐐼𐐮𐑍 𐐶𐐮𐑄 𐑄 𐐢𐐰𐑋𐐲𐑌𐐴𐐻𐑅, 𐐻𐐭 𐐼𐐨𐑁𐐯𐑌𐐼 𐑄𐐯𐑋𐑅𐐯𐑊𐑂𐑆, 𐐰𐑌𐐼 𐑄𐐩𐑉 𐑁𐐰𐑋𐐮𐑊𐐮𐑆, 𐐰𐑌𐐼 𐑄𐐩𐑉 𐑊𐐰𐑌𐐼𐑆, 𐑄𐐩𐑉 𐐿𐐲𐑌𐐻𐑉𐐨, 𐐰𐑌𐐼 𐑄𐐩𐑉 𐑉𐐴𐐻𐑅, 𐐰𐑌𐐼 𐑄𐐩𐑉 𐑉𐐨𐑊𐐮𐐾𐐲𐑌.

11. 𐐈𐑌𐐼 𐐮𐐻 𐐿𐐩𐑋 𐐻𐐭 𐐹𐐰𐑅 𐑄𐐰𐐻 𐐸𐐶𐐯𐑌 𐑄 𐑋𐐯𐑌 𐐱𐑂 𐐣𐐬𐑉𐐬𐑌𐐴 𐑅𐐫 𐑄 𐑁𐐨𐑉𐑅𐑌𐐯𐑅 𐐰𐑌𐐼 𐑄 𐐰𐑍𐑀𐐲𐑉 𐐱𐑂 𐑄 𐐢𐐰𐑋𐐲𐑌𐐴𐐻𐑅, 𐑄𐐩 𐐶𐐲𐑉 𐐰𐐺𐐵𐐻 𐐻𐐭 𐑇𐑉𐐮𐑍𐐿 𐐰𐑌𐐼 𐑁𐑊𐐨 𐑁𐑉𐐪𐑋 𐑄𐐯𐑋. 𐐈𐑌𐐼 𐐣𐐬𐑉𐐬𐑌𐐴 𐐹𐐲𐑉𐑅𐐨𐑂𐐮𐑍 𐑄𐐩𐑉 𐐮𐑌𐐻𐐯𐑌𐐻, 𐑅𐐯𐑌𐐻 𐑁𐐬𐑉𐑃 𐐰𐑌𐐼 𐐮𐑌𐑅𐐹𐐴𐑉𐐼 𐑄𐐩𐑉 𐐸𐐪𐑉𐐻𐑅 𐐶𐐮𐑄 𐑄𐐨𐑆 𐑃𐐫𐐻𐑅—𐐷𐐩, 𐑄 𐑃𐐫𐐻𐑅 𐐱𐑂 𐑄𐐩𐑉 𐑊𐐰𐑌𐐼𐑆, 𐑄𐐩𐑉 𐑊𐐮𐐺𐐲𐑉𐐻𐐨, 𐐷𐐩, 𐑄𐐩𐑉 𐑁𐑉𐐨𐐼𐐲𐑋 𐑁𐑉𐐪𐑋 𐐺𐐪𐑌𐐼𐐩𐐾. 𐐈𐑌𐐼 𐐮𐐻 𐐿𐐩𐑋 𐐻𐐭 𐐹𐐰𐑅 𐑄𐐰𐐻 𐑄𐐩 𐐻𐐲𐑉𐑌𐐼 𐐲𐐹𐐪𐑌 𐑄 𐐢𐐰𐑋𐐲𐑌𐐴𐐻𐑅, 𐐰𐑌𐐼 𐑄𐐩 𐐿𐑉𐐴𐐼 𐐶𐐮𐑄 𐐶𐐲𐑌 𐑂𐑎𐑅 𐐲𐑌𐐻𐐭 𐑄 𐐢𐐫𐑉𐐼 𐑄𐐩𐑉 𐐘𐐪𐐼, 𐑁𐐫𐑉 𐑄𐐩𐑉 𐑊𐐮𐐺𐐲𐑉𐐻𐐨, 𐐰𐑌𐐼 𐑄𐐩𐑉 𐑁𐑉𐐨𐐼𐐲𐑋 𐑁𐑉𐐪𐑋 𐐺𐐪𐑌𐐼𐐩𐐾. 𐐈𐑌𐐼 𐑄𐐩 𐐺𐐨𐑀𐐰𐑌 𐐻𐐭 𐑅𐐻𐐰𐑌𐐼 𐐰𐑀𐐯𐑌𐑅𐐻 𐑄 𐐢𐐰𐑋𐐲𐑌𐐴𐐻𐑅 𐐶𐐮𐑄 𐐹𐐵𐐲𐑉: 𐐰𐑌𐐼 𐐮𐑌 𐑄𐐰𐐻 𐑅𐐯𐑊𐑁-𐑅𐐩𐑋 𐐵𐑉 𐑄𐐰𐐻 𐑄𐐩 𐐿𐑉𐐴𐐼 𐐲𐑌𐐻𐐭 𐑄 𐐢𐐫𐑉𐐼 𐑁𐐫𐑉 𐑄𐐩𐑉 𐑁𐑉𐐨𐐼𐐲𐑋, 𐑄 𐐢𐐰𐑋𐐲𐑌𐐴𐐻𐑅 𐐺𐐨𐑀𐐰𐑌 𐐻𐐭 𐑁𐑊𐐨 𐐺𐐨𐑁𐐬𐑉 𐑄𐐯𐑋; 𐐰𐑌𐐼 𐑄𐐩 𐑁𐑊𐐯𐐼 𐐨𐑂𐐲𐑌 𐐻𐐭 𐑄 𐐶𐐫𐐻𐐲𐑉𐑆 𐐱𐑂 𐐝𐐴𐐼𐐲𐑌. 𐐤𐐵 𐑄 𐐢𐐰𐑋𐐲𐑌𐐴𐐻𐑅 𐐶𐐲𐑉 𐑋𐐬𐑉 𐑌𐐭𐑋𐐲𐑉𐐲𐑅, 𐐷𐐩, 𐐺𐐴 𐑋𐐬𐑉 𐑄𐐰𐑌 𐐼𐐲𐐺𐑊 𐑄 𐑌𐐲𐑋𐐺𐐲𐑉 𐐱𐑂 𐑄 𐐤𐐨𐑁𐐴𐐻𐑅; 𐑌𐐯𐑂𐐲𐑉𐑄𐐲𐑊𐐯𐑅 𐑄𐐩 𐐶𐐲𐑉 𐐼𐑉𐐮𐑂𐐲𐑌 𐐮𐑌𐑅𐐬𐑋𐐲𐐽 𐑄𐐰𐐻 𐑄𐐩 𐐶𐐲𐑉 𐑀𐐰𐑄𐐲𐑉𐐼 𐐻𐐭𐑀𐐯𐑄𐐲𐑉 𐐮𐑌 𐐶𐐲𐑌 𐐺𐐪𐐼𐐨 𐐮𐑌 𐑄 𐑂𐐰𐑊𐐨, 𐐲𐐹𐐪𐑌 𐑄 𐐺𐐰𐑍𐐿 𐐺𐐴 𐑄 𐑉𐐮𐑂𐐲𐑉 𐐝𐐴𐐼𐐲𐑌: 𐑄𐐩𐑉𐑁𐐬𐑉 𐑄 𐐪𐑉𐑋𐐨𐑆 𐐱𐑂 𐐣𐐬𐑉𐐬𐑌𐐴 𐐯𐑌𐑅𐐲𐑉𐐿𐑊𐐼 𐑄𐐯𐑋 𐐰𐐺𐐵𐐻, 𐐷𐐩, 𐐨𐑂𐐲𐑌 𐐪𐑌 𐐺𐐬𐑃 𐑅𐐴𐐼𐑆 𐐱𐑂 𐑄 𐑉𐐮𐑂𐐲𐑉, 𐑁𐐫𐑉 𐐺𐐨𐐸𐐬𐑊𐐼, 𐐪𐑌 𐑄 𐐨𐑅𐐻 𐐶𐐲𐑉 𐑄 𐑋𐐯𐑌 𐐱𐑂 𐐢𐐨𐐸𐐴; 𐑄𐐩𐑉𐑁𐐬𐑉 𐐸𐐶𐐯𐑌 𐐞𐐯𐑉𐐰𐐸𐐯𐑋𐑌𐐪 𐑅𐐫 𐑄 𐑋𐐯𐑌 𐐱𐑂 𐐢𐐨𐐸𐐴 𐐪𐑌 𐑄 𐐨𐑅𐐻 𐐱𐑂 𐑄 𐑉𐐮𐑂𐐲𐑉 𐐝𐐴𐐼𐐲𐑌, 𐐰𐑌𐐼 𐑄 𐐪𐑉𐑋𐐨𐑆 𐐱𐑂 𐐣𐐬𐑉𐐬𐑌𐐴 𐐪𐑌 𐑄 𐐶𐐯𐑅𐐻 𐐱𐑂 𐑄 𐑉𐐮𐑂𐐲𐑉 𐐝𐐴𐐼𐐲𐑌, 𐑄𐐰𐐻 𐑄𐐩 𐐶𐐲𐑉 𐐯𐑌𐑅𐐲𐑉𐐿𐑊𐐼 𐐰𐐺𐐵𐐻 𐐺𐐴 𐑄 𐐤𐐨𐑁𐐴𐐻𐑅, 𐑄𐐩 𐐶𐐲𐑉 𐑅𐐻𐑉𐐲𐐿 𐐶𐐮𐑄 𐐻𐐯𐑉𐐲𐑉. 𐐤𐐵 𐐣𐐬𐑉𐐬𐑌𐐴, 𐐸𐐶𐐯𐑌 𐐸𐐨 𐑅𐐫 𐑄𐐩𐑉 𐐻𐐯𐑉𐐲𐑉, 𐐿𐐲𐑋𐐰𐑌𐐼𐐯𐐼 𐐸𐐮𐑆 𐑋𐐯𐑌 𐑄𐐰𐐻 𐑄𐐩 𐑇𐐳𐐼 𐑅𐐻𐐪𐐹 𐑇𐐯𐐼𐐮𐑍 𐑄𐐩𐑉 𐐺𐑊𐐲𐐼.

12. 𐐈𐑌𐐼 𐐮𐐻 𐐿𐐩𐑋 𐐻𐐭 𐐹𐐰𐑅 𐑄𐐰𐐻 𐑄𐐩 𐐼𐐮𐐼 𐑅𐐻𐐪𐐹 𐐰𐑌𐐼 𐐶𐐮𐑄𐐼𐑉𐐭 𐐩 𐐹𐐩𐑅 𐑁𐑉𐐪𐑋 𐑄𐐯𐑋. 𐐈𐑌𐐼 𐐣𐐬𐑉𐐬𐑌𐐴 𐑅𐐯𐐼 𐐲𐑌𐐻𐐭 𐐞𐐯𐑉𐐰𐐸𐐯𐑋𐑌𐐪, 𐐒𐐨𐐸𐐬𐑊𐐼, 𐐞𐐯𐑉𐐰𐐸𐐯𐑋𐑌𐐪, 𐑄𐐰𐐻 𐐶𐐨 𐐼𐐭 𐑌𐐪𐐻 𐐼𐐯𐑆𐐴𐑉 𐐻𐐭 𐐺 𐑋𐐯𐑌 𐐱𐑂 𐐺𐑊𐐲𐐼.—𐐏 𐑌𐐬 𐑄𐐰𐐻 𐐷 𐐪𐑉 𐐮𐑌 𐐵𐑉 𐐸𐐰𐑌𐐼𐑆, 𐐷𐐯𐐻 𐐶𐐨 𐐼𐐭 𐑌𐐪𐐻 𐐼𐐯𐑆𐐴𐑉 𐐻𐐭 𐑅𐑊𐐩 𐐷𐐭. 𐐒𐐨𐐸𐐬𐑊𐐼, 𐐶𐐨 𐐸𐐰𐑂 𐑌𐐪𐐻 𐐿𐐲𐑋 𐐵𐐻 𐐻𐐭 𐐺𐐰𐐻𐑊 𐐰𐑀𐐯𐑌𐑅𐐻 𐐷𐐭, 𐑄𐐰𐐻 𐐶𐐨 𐑋𐐴𐐻 𐑇𐐯𐐼 𐐷𐐭𐑉 𐐺𐑊𐐲𐐼 𐑁𐐫𐑉 𐐹𐐵𐐲𐑉; 𐑌𐐨𐑄𐐲𐑉 𐐼𐐭 𐐶𐐨 𐐼𐐯𐑆𐐴𐑉 𐐻𐐭 𐐺𐑉𐐮𐑍 𐐯𐑌𐐨 𐐶𐐲𐑌 𐐻𐐭 𐑄 𐐷𐐬𐐿 𐐱𐑂 𐐺𐐪𐑌𐐼𐐩𐐾. 𐐒𐐲𐐻 𐑄𐐮𐑅 𐐮𐑆 𐑄 𐑂𐐯𐑉𐐨 𐐿𐐫𐑆 𐑁𐐫𐑉 𐐸𐐶𐐮𐐽 𐐷 𐐸𐐰𐑂 𐐿𐐲𐑋 𐐰𐑀𐐯𐑌𐑅𐐻 𐐲𐑅; 𐐷𐐩, 𐐰𐑌𐐼 𐐷 𐐪𐑉 𐐰𐑍𐑀𐑉𐐨 𐐶𐐮𐑄 𐐲𐑅 𐐺𐐨𐐿𐐫𐑆 𐐱𐑂 𐐵𐑉 𐑉𐐨𐑊𐐮𐐾𐐲𐑌. 𐐒𐐲𐐻 𐑌𐐵 𐐷 𐐺𐐨𐐸𐐬𐑊𐐼 𐑄𐐰𐐻 𐑄 𐐢𐐫𐑉𐐼 𐐮𐑆 𐐶𐐮𐑄 𐐲𐑅; 𐐰𐑌𐐼 𐐷 𐐺𐐨𐐸𐐬𐑊𐐼 𐑄𐐰𐐻 𐐸𐐨 𐐸𐐰𐑆 𐐼𐐨𐑊𐐮𐑂𐐲𐑉𐐼 𐐷𐐭 𐐮𐑌𐐻𐐭 𐐵𐑉 𐐸𐐰𐑌𐐼𐑆. 𐐈𐑌𐐼 𐑌𐐵 𐐌 𐐶𐐳𐐼 𐑄𐐰𐐻 𐐷 𐑇𐐳𐐼 𐐲𐑌𐐼𐐲𐑉𐑅𐐻𐐰𐑌𐐼 𐑄𐐰𐐻 𐑄𐐮𐑅 𐐮𐑆 𐐼𐐲𐑌 𐐲𐑌𐐻𐐭 𐐲𐑅 𐐺𐐨𐐿𐐫𐑆 𐐱𐑂 𐐵𐑉 𐑉𐐨𐑊𐐮𐐾𐐲𐑌 𐐰𐑌𐐼 𐐵𐑉 𐑁𐐩𐑃 𐐮𐑌 𐐗𐑉𐐴𐑅𐐻. 𐐈𐑌𐐼 𐑌𐐵 𐐷 𐑅𐐨 𐑄𐐰𐐻 𐐷 𐐿𐐰𐑌𐐪𐐻 𐐼𐐯𐑅𐐻𐑉𐑎 𐑄𐐮𐑅 𐐵𐑉 𐑁𐐩𐑃. 𐐤𐐵 𐐷 𐑅𐐨 𐑄𐐰𐐻 𐑄𐐮𐑅 𐐮𐑆 𐑄 𐐻𐑉𐐭 𐑁𐐩𐑃 𐐱𐑂 𐐘𐐪𐐼; 𐐷𐐩, 𐐷 𐑅𐐨 𐑄𐐰𐐻 𐐘𐐪𐐼 𐐶𐐮𐑊 𐑅𐐲𐐹𐐬𐑉𐐻, 𐐰𐑌𐐼 𐐿𐐨𐐹, 𐐰𐑌𐐼 𐐹𐑉𐐨𐑆𐐲𐑉𐑂 𐐲𐑅, 𐑅𐐬 𐑊𐐫𐑍 𐐰𐑆 𐐶𐐨 𐐪𐑉 𐑁𐐩𐑃𐑁𐐳𐑊 𐐲𐑌𐐻𐐭 𐐸𐐮𐑋, 𐐰𐑌𐐼 𐐲𐑌𐐻𐐭 𐐵𐑉 𐑁𐐩𐑃, 𐐰𐑌𐐼 𐐵𐑉 𐑉𐐨𐑊𐐮𐐾𐐲𐑌; 𐐰𐑌𐐼 𐑌𐐯𐑂𐐲𐑉 𐐶𐐮𐑊 𐑄 𐐢𐐫𐑉𐐼 𐑅𐐲𐑁𐐲𐑉 𐑄𐐰𐐻 𐐶𐐨 𐑇𐐰𐑊 𐐺 𐐼𐐯𐑅𐐻𐑉𐑎𐐼, 𐐯𐐿𐑅𐐯𐐹𐐻 𐐶𐐨 𐑇𐐳𐐼 𐑁𐐫𐑊 𐐮𐑌𐐻𐐭 𐐻𐑉𐐰𐑌𐑅𐑀𐑉𐐯𐑇𐐲𐑌, 𐐰𐑌𐐼 𐐼𐐨𐑌𐐴 𐐵𐑉 𐑁𐐩𐑃. 𐐈𐑌𐐼 𐑌𐐵, 𐐞𐐯𐑉𐐰𐐸𐐯𐑋𐑌𐐪, 𐐌 𐐿𐐲𐑋𐐰𐑌𐐼 𐐷𐐭, 𐐮𐑌 𐑄 𐑌𐐩𐑋 𐐱𐑂 𐑄𐐰𐐻 𐐫𐑊-𐐹𐐵𐐲𐑉𐑁𐐳𐑊 𐐘𐐪𐐼, 𐐸𐐭 𐐸𐐰𐑆 𐑅𐐻𐑉𐐯𐑍𐑃𐑌𐐼 𐐵𐑉 𐐪𐑉𐑋𐑆 𐑄𐐰𐐻 𐐶𐐨 𐐸𐐰𐑂 𐑀𐐩𐑌𐐼 𐐹𐐵𐐲𐑉 𐐬𐑂𐐲𐑉 𐐷𐐭, 𐐺𐐴 𐐵𐑉 𐑁𐐩𐑃, 𐐺𐐴 𐐵𐑉 𐑉𐐨𐑊𐐮𐐾𐐲𐑌, 𐐰𐑌𐐼 𐐺𐐴 𐐵𐑉 𐑉𐐴𐐻𐑅 𐐱𐑂 𐐶𐐲𐑉𐑇𐐮𐐹, 𐐰𐑌𐐼 𐐺𐐴 𐐵𐑉 𐐽𐐲𐑉𐐽, 𐐰𐑌𐐼 𐐺𐐴 𐑄 𐑅𐐩𐐿𐑉𐐯𐐼 𐑅𐐲𐐹𐐬𐑉𐐻 𐐸𐐶𐐮𐐽 𐐶𐐨 𐐬 𐐻𐐭 𐐵𐑉 𐐶𐐴𐑂𐑆 𐐰𐑌𐐼 𐐵𐑉 𐐽𐐮𐑊𐐼𐑉𐐯𐑌, 𐐺𐐴 𐑄𐐰𐐻 𐑊𐐮𐐺𐐲𐑉𐐻𐐨 𐐸𐐶𐐮𐐽 𐐺𐐴𐑌𐐼𐑆 𐐲𐑅 𐐻𐐭 𐐵𐑉 𐑊𐐰𐑌𐐼𐑆 𐐰𐑌𐐼 𐐵𐑉 𐐿𐐲𐑌𐐻𐑉𐐨; 𐐷𐐩, 𐐰𐑌𐐼 𐐫𐑊𐑅𐐬 𐐺𐐴 𐑄 𐑋𐐩𐑌𐐻𐐯𐑌𐐰𐑌𐑅 𐐱𐑂 𐑄 𐑅𐐩𐐿𐑉𐐯𐐼 𐐶𐐲𐑉𐐼 𐐱𐑂 𐐘𐐪𐐼, 𐐻𐐭 𐐸𐐶𐐮𐐽 𐐶𐐨 𐐬 𐐫𐑊 𐐵𐑉 𐐸𐐰𐐹𐐨𐑌𐐯𐑅; 𐐰𐑌𐐼 𐐺𐐴 𐐫𐑊 𐑄𐐰𐐻 𐐮𐑆 𐑋𐐬𐑅𐐻 𐐼𐐨𐑉 𐐲𐑌𐐻𐐭 𐐲𐑅; 𐐷𐐩, 𐐰𐑌𐐼 𐑄𐐮𐑅 𐐮𐑆 𐑌𐐪𐐻 𐐫𐑊; 𐐌 𐐿𐐲𐑋𐐰𐑌𐐼 𐐷𐐭 𐐺𐐴 𐐫𐑊 𐑄 𐐼𐐯𐑆𐐴𐑉𐑆 𐐸𐐶𐐮𐐽 𐐷 𐐸𐐰𐑂 𐑁𐐫𐑉 𐑊𐐴𐑁, 𐑄𐐰𐐻 𐐷 𐐼𐐨𐑊𐐮𐑂𐐲𐑉 𐐲𐐹 𐐷𐐭𐑉 𐐶𐐯𐐹𐐲𐑌𐑆 𐐱𐑂 𐐶𐐫𐑉 𐐲𐑌𐐻𐐭 𐐲𐑅, 𐐰𐑌𐐼 𐐶𐐨 𐐶𐐮𐑊 𐑅𐐨𐐿 𐑌𐐪𐐻 𐐷𐐭𐑉 𐐺𐑊𐐲𐐼, 𐐺𐐲𐐻 𐐶𐐨 𐐶𐐮𐑊 𐑅𐐹𐐩𐑉 𐐷𐐭𐑉 𐑊𐐴𐑂𐑆 𐐮𐑁 𐐷 𐐶𐐮𐑊 𐑀𐐬 𐐷𐐭𐑉 𐐶𐐩, 𐐰𐑌𐐼 𐐿𐐲𐑋 𐑌𐐪𐐻 𐐰𐑀𐐯𐑌 𐐻𐐭 𐐶𐐫𐑉 𐐰𐑀𐐯𐑌𐑅𐐻 𐐲𐑅. 𐐈𐑌𐐼 𐑌𐐵, 𐐮𐑁 𐐷 𐐼𐐭 𐑌𐐪𐐻 𐑄𐐮𐑅, 𐐺𐐨𐐸𐐬𐑊𐐼, 𐐷 𐐪𐑉

𐐮𐑌 𐐵𐑉 𐐸𐐰𐑌𐐼𐑆, 𐐰𐑌𐐼 𐐌 𐐶𐐮𐑊 𐐿𐐱𐑋𐐰𐑌𐐼 𐑋𐐴 𐑋𐐯𐑌 𐑄𐐰𐐻 𐑄𐐩 𐑇𐐰𐑊 𐑁𐐫𐑊 𐐲𐐹𐐱𐑌 𐐷𐐭, 𐐰𐑌𐐼 𐐮𐑌𐑁𐑊𐐮𐐿𐐻 𐑄 𐐶𐐭𐑌𐐼𐑆 𐐲𐑂 𐐼𐐯𐑃 𐐮𐑌 𐐷𐐭𐑉 𐐺𐐱𐐼𐐨𐑆, 𐑄𐐰𐐻 𐐷𐐨 𐑋𐐩 𐐺𐐨𐐿𐐲𐑋 𐐯𐐿𐑅𐐻𐐮𐑍𐐿𐐻; 𐐰𐑌𐐼 𐑄𐐯𐑌 𐐶𐐨 𐐶𐐮𐑊 𐑅𐐨 𐐸𐐭 𐑇𐐰𐑊 𐐸𐐰𐑂 𐐹𐐵𐐲𐑉 𐐬𐑂𐐲𐑉 𐑄𐐮𐑅 𐐹𐐨𐐹𐑊; 𐐷𐐩, 𐐶𐐨 𐐶𐐮𐑊 𐑅𐐨 𐐸𐐭 𐑇𐐰𐑊 𐐺𐐨 𐐺𐑉𐐫𐐻 𐐮𐑌𐐻𐐭 𐐺𐐱𐑌𐐼𐐲𐐾.

13. 𐐈𐑌𐐼 𐑌𐐵 𐐮𐐻 𐐿𐐩𐑋 𐐻𐐭 𐐹𐐰𐑅 𐑄𐐰𐐻 𐐸𐐶𐐯𐑌 𐐞𐐯𐑉𐐲𐐸𐐯𐑋𐑌𐐲 𐐸𐐰𐐼 𐐸𐐲𐑉𐐼 𐑄𐐨𐑆 𐑅𐐩𐐮𐑍𐑆, 𐐸𐐨 𐐿𐐩𐑋 𐑁𐐫𐑉𐑃 𐐰𐑌𐐼 𐐼𐐮𐑊𐐮𐑂𐐲𐑉𐐼 𐐲𐐹 𐐸𐐮𐑆 𐑅𐐬𐑉𐐼, 𐐰𐑌𐐼 𐐸𐐮𐑆 𐑅𐐮𐑋𐐯𐐻𐐲𐑉, 𐐰𐑌𐐼 𐐸𐐮𐑆 𐐺𐐬 𐐮𐑌𐐻𐐭 𐑄 𐐸𐐰𐑌𐐼𐑆 𐐲𐑂 𐐣𐐬𐑉𐐬𐑌𐐴, 𐐰𐑌𐐼 𐑅𐐯𐐼 𐐲𐑌𐐻𐐭 𐐸𐐮𐑋, 𐐒𐐨𐐸𐐬𐑊𐐼, 𐐸𐐨𐑉 𐐪𐑉 𐐵𐑉 𐐶𐐯𐐹𐐲𐑌𐑆 𐐲𐑂 𐐶𐐫𐑉; 𐐶𐐨 𐐶𐐮𐑊 𐐼𐐮𐑊𐐮𐑂𐐲𐑉 𐑄𐐯𐑋 𐐲𐐹 𐐲𐑌𐐻𐐭 𐐷𐐭, 𐐺𐐲𐐻 𐐶𐐨 𐐶𐐮𐑊 𐑌𐐱𐐻 𐑅𐐲𐑁𐐲𐑉 𐐵𐑉𐑅𐐯𐑊𐑂𐑆 𐐻𐐭 𐐻𐐩𐐿 𐐰𐑌 𐐬𐑃 𐐲𐑌𐐻𐐭 𐐷𐐭, 𐐸𐐶𐐮𐐽 𐐶𐐨 𐑌𐐬 𐑄𐐰𐐻 𐐶𐐨 𐑇𐐰𐑊 𐐺𐑉𐐩𐐿, 𐐰𐑌𐐼 𐐫𐑊𐑅𐐬 𐐵𐑉 𐐽𐐮𐑊𐐼𐑉𐐯𐑌; 𐐺𐐲𐐻 𐐻𐐩𐐿 𐐵𐑉 𐐶𐐯𐐹𐐲𐑌𐑆 𐐲𐑂 𐐶𐐫𐑉, 𐐰𐑌𐐼 𐑅𐐲𐑁𐐲𐑉 𐑄𐐰𐐻 𐐶𐐨 𐑋𐐩 𐐼𐐨𐐹𐐪𐑉𐐻 𐐮𐑌𐐻𐐭 𐑄 𐐶𐐮𐑊𐐼𐐲𐑉𐑌𐐯𐑅; 𐐲𐑄𐐲𐑉𐐶𐐴𐑆 𐐶𐐨 𐐶𐐮𐑊 𐑉𐐨𐐻𐐩𐑌 𐐵𐑉 𐑅𐐬𐑉𐐼𐑆, 𐐰𐑌𐐼 𐐶𐐨 𐐶𐐮𐑊 𐐹𐐯𐑉𐐮𐑇 𐐫𐑉 𐐿𐐱𐑍𐐿𐐲𐑉. 𐐒𐐨𐐸𐐬𐑊𐐼, 𐐶𐐨 𐐪𐑉 𐑌𐐱𐐻 𐐲𐑂 𐐷𐐭𐑉 𐑁𐐩𐑃; 𐐶𐐨 𐐼𐐭 𐑌𐐱𐐻 𐐺𐐨𐑊𐐨𐑂 𐑄𐐰𐐻 𐐮𐐻 𐐮𐑆 𐐘𐐱𐐼 𐑄𐐰𐐻 𐐸𐐰𐑆 𐐼𐐮𐑊𐐮𐑂𐐲𐑉𐐼 𐐲𐑅 𐐮𐑌𐐻𐐭 𐐷𐐭𐑉 𐐸𐐰𐑌𐐼𐑆; 𐐺𐐲𐐻 𐐶𐐨 𐐺𐐨𐑊𐐨𐑂 𐑄𐐰𐐻 𐐮𐐻 𐐮𐑆 𐐷𐐭𐑉 𐐿𐐲𐑌𐐮𐑍 𐑄𐐰𐐻 𐐸𐐰𐑆 𐐹𐑉𐐨𐑆𐐲𐑉𐑂𐐼 𐐷𐐭 𐑁𐑉𐐱𐑋 𐐵𐑉 𐑅𐐬𐑉𐐼𐑆. 𐐒𐐨𐐸𐐬𐑊𐐼, 𐐮𐐻 𐐮𐑆 𐐷𐐭𐑉 𐐺𐑉𐐯𐑅𐐻𐐹𐑊𐐩𐐻𐑅 𐐰𐑌𐐼 𐐷𐐭𐑉 𐑇𐐨𐑊𐐼𐑆 𐑄𐐰𐐻 𐐸𐐰𐑂 𐐹𐑉𐐨𐑆𐐲𐑉𐑂𐐼 𐐷𐐭. 𐐈𐑌𐐼 𐑌𐐵 𐐸𐐶𐐯𐑌 𐐞𐐯𐑉𐐲𐐸𐐯𐑋𐑌𐐲 𐐸𐐰𐐼 𐑋𐐩𐐼 𐐰𐑌 𐐯𐑌𐐼 𐐲𐑂 𐑅𐐹𐐨𐐿𐐮𐑍 𐑄𐐨𐑆 𐐶𐐲𐑉𐐼𐑆, 𐐣𐐬𐑉𐐬𐑌𐐴 𐑉𐐨𐐻𐐲𐑉𐑌𐐼 𐑄 𐑅𐐬𐑉𐐼 𐐰𐑌𐐼 𐑄 𐐶𐐯𐐹𐐲𐑌𐑆 𐐲𐑂 𐐶𐐫𐑉, 𐐸𐐶𐐮𐐽 𐐸𐐨 𐐸𐐰𐐼 𐑉𐐨𐑅𐐨𐑂𐐼, 𐐲𐑌𐐻𐐭 𐐞𐐯𐑉𐐲𐐸𐐯𐑋𐑌𐐲, 𐑅𐐩𐐮𐑍, 𐐒𐐨𐐸𐐬𐑊𐐼, 𐐶𐐨 𐐶𐐮𐑊 𐐯𐑌𐐼 𐑄 𐐿𐐱𐑌𐑁𐑊𐐮𐐿𐐻. 𐐤𐐵 𐐌 𐐿𐐰𐑌𐑌𐐱𐐻 𐑉𐐨𐐿𐐫𐑊 𐑄 𐐶𐐲𐑉𐐼𐑆 𐐸𐐶𐐮𐐽 𐐌 𐐸𐐰𐑂 𐑅𐐹𐐬𐐿𐐲𐑌, 𐑄𐐯𐑉𐑁𐐬𐑉 𐐰𐑆 𐑄 𐐢𐐫𐑉𐐼 𐑊𐐮𐑂𐐯𐑃, 𐐷𐐨 𐑇𐐰𐑊 𐑌𐐱𐐻 𐐼𐐨𐐹𐐪𐑉𐐻 𐐯𐐿𐑅𐐯𐐹𐐻 𐐷𐐨 𐐼𐐨𐐹𐐪𐑉𐐻 𐐶𐐮𐑃 𐐰𐑌 𐐬𐑃 𐑄𐐰𐐻 𐐷𐐨 𐐶𐐮𐑊 𐑌𐐱𐐻 𐑉𐐨𐐻𐐲𐑉𐑌 𐐲𐑀𐐯𐑌 𐐲𐑀𐐯𐑌𐑅𐐻 𐐲𐑅 𐐻𐐭 𐐶𐐫𐑉. 𐐤𐐵 𐐰𐑆 𐐷𐐨 𐐪𐑉 𐐮𐑌 𐐵𐑉 𐐸𐐰𐑌𐐼𐑆 𐐶𐐨 𐐶𐐮𐑊 𐑅𐐹𐐮𐑊 𐐷𐐭𐑉 𐐺𐑊𐐲𐐼 𐐲𐐹𐐱𐑌 𐑄 𐑀𐑉𐐵𐑌𐐼, 𐐫𐑉 𐐷𐐨 𐑇𐐰𐑊 𐑅𐐲𐐺𐑋𐐮𐐻 𐐻𐐭 𐑄 𐐿𐐱𐑌𐐼𐐮𐑇𐐲𐑌𐑆 𐐸𐐶𐐮𐐽 𐐌 𐐸𐐰𐑂 𐐹𐑉𐐬𐐹𐐬𐑆𐐼. 𐐈𐑌𐐼 𐑌𐐵 𐐸𐐶𐐯𐑌 𐐣𐐬𐑉𐐬𐑌𐐴 𐐸𐐰𐐼 𐑅𐐯𐐼 𐑄𐐨𐑆 𐐶𐐲𐑉𐐼𐑆, 𐐞𐐯𐑉𐐲𐐸𐐯𐑋𐑌𐐲 𐑉𐐨𐐻𐐩𐑌𐐼 𐐸𐐮𐑆 𐑅𐐬𐑉𐐼, 𐐰𐑌𐐼 𐐸𐐨 𐐶𐐱𐑆 𐐰𐑍𐑀𐑉𐐨 𐐶𐐮𐑃 𐐣𐐬𐑉𐐬𐑌𐐴, 𐐰𐑌𐐼 𐐸𐐨 𐑉𐐲𐑇𐐻 𐑁𐐫𐑉𐐶𐐲𐑉𐐼 𐑄𐐰𐐻 𐐸𐐨 𐑋𐐴𐐻 𐑅𐑊𐐩 𐐣𐐬𐑉𐐬𐑌𐐴; 𐐺𐐲𐐻 𐐰𐑆 𐐸𐐨 𐑉𐐩𐑆𐐼 𐐸𐐮𐑆 𐑅𐐬𐑉𐐼, 𐐺𐐨𐐸𐐬𐑊𐐼, 𐐶𐐲𐑌 𐐲𐑂 𐐣𐐬𐑉𐐬𐑌𐐴'𐑅 𐑅𐐬𐑊𐐾𐐲𐑉𐑆 𐑅𐑋𐐬𐐻 𐐮𐐻 𐐨𐑂𐐲𐑌 𐐻𐐭 𐑄 𐐲𐑉𐑃; 𐐰𐑌𐐼 𐐮𐐻 𐐺𐑉𐐬𐐿 𐐺𐐴 𐑄 𐐸𐐮𐑊𐐻; 𐐰𐑌𐐼 𐐸𐐨 𐐫𐑊𐑅𐐬 𐑅𐑋𐐬𐐻 𐐞𐐯𐑉𐐲𐐸𐐯𐑋𐑌𐐲, 𐑄𐐰𐐻 𐐸𐐨 𐐻𐐳𐐿 𐐫𐑁 𐐸𐐮𐑆 𐑅𐐿𐐰𐑊𐐹, 𐐰𐑌𐐼 𐐮𐐻 𐑁𐐯𐑊 𐐻𐐭 𐑄 𐐲𐑉𐑃; 𐐰𐑌𐐼 𐐞𐐯𐑉𐐲𐐸𐐯𐑋𐑌𐐲 𐐶𐐮𐑃𐐼𐑉𐐭 𐑁𐑉𐐱𐑋 𐐺𐐨𐑁𐐬𐑉 𐑄𐐯𐑋 𐐮𐑌𐐻𐐭 𐑄 𐑋𐐮𐐼𐑅𐐻 𐐲𐑂 𐐸𐐮𐑆 𐑅𐐬𐑊𐐾𐐲𐑉𐑆.

14. 𐐈𐑌𐐼 𐐮𐐻 𐐿𐐩𐑋 𐐻𐐭 𐐹𐐰𐑅 𐑄𐐰𐐻 𐑄 𐑅𐐬𐑊𐐾𐐲𐑉 𐐸𐐭 𐑅𐐻𐐳𐐼 𐐺𐐴, 𐐸𐐭 𐑅𐑋𐐬𐐻 𐐫𐑁 𐑄 𐑅𐐿𐐰𐑊𐐹 𐐲𐑂 𐐞𐐯𐑉𐐲𐐸𐐯𐑋𐑌𐐲, 𐐻𐐳𐐿 𐐲𐐹 𐑄 𐑅𐐿𐐰𐑊𐐹 𐑁𐑉𐐱𐑋 𐐫𐑁 𐑄 𐑀𐑉𐐵𐑌𐐼 𐐺𐐴 𐑄 𐐸𐐩𐑉, 𐐰𐑌𐐼 𐑊𐐩𐐼 𐐮𐐻 𐐲𐐹𐐱𐑌 𐑄 𐐹𐑎𐑌𐐻 𐐲𐑂 𐐸𐐮𐑆 𐑅𐐬𐑉𐐼, 𐐰𐑌𐐼 𐑅𐐻𐑉𐐯𐐽𐐻 𐐮𐐻 𐑁𐐫𐑉𐑃 𐐲𐑌𐐻𐐭 𐑄𐐯𐑋, 𐑅𐐩𐐮𐑍 𐐲𐑌𐐻𐐭 𐑄𐐯𐑋 𐐶𐐮𐑃 𐐰 𐑊𐐵𐐼 𐑂𐑎𐑅, 𐐀𐑂𐐲𐑌 𐐰𐑆 𐑄𐐮𐑅 𐑅𐐿𐐰𐑊𐐹 𐐸𐐰𐑆 𐑁𐐫𐑊𐐲𐑌 𐐻𐐭 𐑄 𐐲𐑉𐑃, 𐐸𐐶𐐮𐐽 𐐮𐑆 𐑄 𐑅𐐿𐐰𐑊𐐹 𐐲𐑂 𐐷𐐭𐑉 𐐽𐐨𐑁, 𐑅𐐬 𐑇𐐰𐑊 𐐷𐐨 𐑁𐐫𐑊 𐐻𐐭 𐑄 𐐲𐑉𐑃, 𐐯𐐿𐑅𐐯𐐹𐐻 𐐷𐐨 𐐶𐐮𐑊 𐐼𐐮𐑊𐐮𐑂𐐲𐑉 𐐲𐐹 𐐷𐐭𐑉 𐐶𐐯𐐹𐐲𐑌𐑆 𐐲𐑂 𐐶𐐫𐑉 𐐰𐑌𐐼 𐐼𐐨𐐹𐐪𐑉𐐻 𐐶𐐮𐑃 𐐰 𐐿𐐲𐑂𐐯𐑌𐐲𐑌𐐻 𐐲𐑂 𐐹𐐨𐑅.

15. 𐐤𐐵 𐑄𐐯𐑉 𐐶𐐲𐑉 𐑋𐐯𐑌𐐨, 𐐸𐐶𐐯𐑌 𐑄𐐩 𐐸𐐲𐑉𐐼 𐑄𐐨𐑆 𐐶𐐲𐑉𐐼𐑆, 𐐰𐑌𐐼 𐑅𐐫 𐑄 𐑅𐐿𐐰𐑊𐐹 𐐸𐐶𐐮𐐽 𐐶𐐱𐑆 𐐲𐐹𐐱𐑌 𐑄 𐑅𐐬𐑉𐐼, 𐑄𐐰𐐻 𐐶𐐲𐑉 𐑅𐐻𐑉𐐲𐐿 𐐶𐐮𐑃 𐑁𐐨𐑉, 𐐰𐑌𐐼 𐑋𐐯𐑌𐐨 𐐿𐐩𐑋 𐑁𐐫𐑉𐑃 𐐰𐑌𐐼 𐑃𐑉𐐭 𐐼𐐵𐑌 𐑄𐐯𐑉 𐐶𐐯𐐹𐐲𐑌𐑆 𐐲𐑂 𐐶𐐫𐑉 𐐰𐐻 𐑄 𐑁𐐨𐐻 𐐲𐑂 𐐣𐐬𐑉𐐬𐑌𐐴, 𐐰𐑌𐐼 𐐯𐑌𐐻𐐲𐑉𐐼 𐐮𐑌𐐻𐐭 𐐰 𐐿𐐲𐑂𐐯𐑌𐐲𐑌𐐻 𐐲𐑂 𐐹𐐨𐑅. 𐐈𐑌𐐼 𐐰𐑆 𐑋𐐯𐑌𐐨 𐐰𐑆 𐐯𐑌𐐻𐐲𐑉𐐼 𐐮𐑌𐐻𐐭 𐐰 𐐿𐐲𐑂𐐯𐑌𐐲𐑌𐐻 𐑄𐐩 𐑅𐐲𐑁𐐲𐑉𐐼 𐐻𐐭 𐐼𐐨𐐹𐐪𐑉𐐻 𐐮𐑌𐐻𐐭 𐑄 𐐶𐐮𐑊𐐼𐐲𐑉𐑌𐐯𐑅.

16. 𐐤𐐵 𐐮𐐻 𐐿𐐩𐑋 𐐻𐐭 𐐹𐐰𐑅 𐑄𐐰𐐻 𐐞𐐯𐑉𐐲𐐸𐐯𐑋𐑌𐐲 𐐶𐐱𐑆 𐐯𐐿𐑅𐐨𐐼𐐮𐑍𐑊𐐨 𐑉𐐱𐑃, 𐐰𐑌𐐼 𐐸𐐨 𐐼𐐮𐐼 𐑅𐐻𐐲𐑉 𐐲𐐹 𐑄 𐑉𐐨𐑋𐐩𐑌𐐼𐐲𐑉 𐐲𐑂 𐐸𐐮𐑆 𐑅𐐬𐑊𐐾𐐲𐑉𐑆 𐐻𐐭 𐐰𐑍𐑀𐐲𐑉, 𐐻𐐭 𐐿𐐱𐑌𐐻𐐯𐑌𐐼 𐑋𐐬𐑉 𐐹𐐵𐐲𐑉𐑁𐐳𐑊𐐨 𐐲𐑀𐐯𐑌𐑅𐐻 𐑄 𐐤𐐨𐑁𐐴𐐻𐑅. 𐐈𐑌𐐼 𐑌𐐵 𐐣𐐬𐑉𐐬𐑌𐐴 𐐶𐐱𐑆 𐐰𐑍𐑀𐑉𐐨 𐐺𐐨𐐿𐐫𐑆 𐐲𐑂 𐑄 𐑅𐐻𐐲𐐺𐐲𐑉𐑌𐐯𐑅 𐐲𐑂 𐑄 𐐢𐐰𐑋𐐲𐑌𐐴𐐻𐑅; 𐑄𐐯𐑉𐑁𐐬𐑉 𐐸𐐨 𐐿𐐱𐑋𐐰𐑌𐐼𐐯𐐼 𐐸𐐮𐑆 𐐹𐐨𐐹𐑊 𐑄𐐰𐐻 𐑄𐐩 𐑇𐐳𐐼 𐑁𐐫𐑊 𐐲𐐹𐐱𐑌 𐑄𐐯𐑋 𐐰𐑌𐐼 𐑅𐑊𐐩 𐑄𐐯𐑋. 𐐈𐑌𐐼 𐐮𐐻 𐐿𐐩𐑋 𐐻𐐭 𐐹𐐰𐑅 𐑄𐐰𐐻 𐑄𐐩 𐐺𐐨𐑀𐐰𐑌 𐐻𐐭 𐑅𐑊𐐩 𐑄𐐯𐑋; 𐐷𐐩, 𐐰𐑌𐐼 𐑄 𐐢𐐰𐑋𐐲𐑌𐐴𐐻𐑅 𐐼𐐮𐐼 𐐿𐐱𐑌𐐻𐐯𐑌𐐼 𐐶𐐮𐑃 𐑄𐐯𐑉 𐑅𐐬𐑉𐐼𐑆 𐐰𐑌𐐼 𐑄𐐯𐑉 𐑋𐐴𐐻. 𐐒𐐲𐐻 𐐺𐐨𐐸𐐬𐑊𐐼, 𐑄𐐯𐑉 𐑌𐐩𐐿𐐯𐐼 𐑅𐐿𐐮𐑌𐑆 𐐰𐑌𐐼 𐑄𐐯𐑉 𐐺𐐩𐑉 𐐸𐐯𐐼𐑆 𐐶𐐲𐑉 𐐯𐐿𐑅𐐹𐐬𐑆𐐼 𐐻𐐭 𐑄 𐑇𐐪𐑉𐐹 𐑅𐐬𐑉𐐼𐑆 𐐲𐑂 𐑄 𐐤𐐨𐑁𐐴𐐻𐑅; 𐐷𐐩, 𐐺𐐨𐐸𐐬𐑊𐐼 𐑄𐐩 𐐶𐐲𐑉 𐐹𐐨𐑉𐑅𐐻 𐐰𐑌𐐼 𐑅𐑋𐐮𐐻𐐲𐑌; 𐐷𐐩, 𐐰𐑌𐐼

𐐼𐐮𐐼 𐑁𐐫𐑊 𐐯𐐿𐑅𐐨𐐼𐐮𐑍 𐑁𐐪𐑅𐐻 𐐺𐐨𐑁𐐬𐑉 𐑄 𐑅𐐬𐑉𐐼𐑆 𐐱𐑂 𐑄 𐐤𐐨𐑁𐐴𐐻𐑅, 𐐰𐑌𐐼 𐑄𐐩 𐐺𐐨𐑀𐐰𐑌 𐐻𐐭 𐐺 𐑅𐐶𐐯𐐹𐐻 𐐼𐐵𐑌, 𐐨𐑂𐑌 𐐰𐑆 𐑄 𐑅𐐬𐑊𐐾𐐯𐑉 𐐱𐑂 𐐣𐐬𐑉𐐬𐑌𐐴 𐐸𐐰𐐼 𐐹𐑉𐐱𐑁𐐨𐑅𐐴𐐼. 𐐤𐐵 𐐞𐐨𐑉𐐰𐐸𐐯𐑋𐑌𐐪, 𐐸𐐶𐐯𐑌 𐐸𐐨 𐑅𐐫 𐑄𐐰𐐻 𐑄𐐩 𐐶𐐲𐑉 𐐫𐑊 𐐲𐐺𐐵𐐻 𐐻𐐭 𐐺 𐐼𐐨𐑅𐐻𐑉𐐱𐐮𐐼, 𐐿𐑉𐐴𐐼 𐑋𐐴𐐻𐐮𐑊𐐮 𐐲𐑌𐐻𐐭 𐐣𐐬𐑉𐐬𐑌𐐴, 𐐹𐑉𐐱𐑋𐐮𐑅𐐮𐑍 𐑄𐐰𐐻 𐐸𐐨 𐐶𐐳𐐼 𐐿𐐲𐑂𐐨𐑌𐐲𐑌𐐻, 𐐰𐑌𐐼 𐐫𐑊𐑅𐐬 𐐸𐐮𐑆 𐐹𐐨𐐹𐑊 𐐶𐐮𐑄 𐑄𐐯𐑋, 𐐮𐑁 𐑄𐐩 𐐶𐐳𐐼 𐑅𐐹𐐩𐑉 𐑄 𐑉𐐨𐑋𐐩𐑌𐐼𐐯𐑉 𐐱𐑂 𐑄𐐩𐑉 𐑊𐐴𐑂𐑆, 𐑄𐐰𐐻 𐑄𐐩 𐑌𐐯𐑂𐐯𐑉 𐐶𐐳𐐼 𐐿𐐲𐑋 𐐻𐐭 𐐶𐐫𐑉 𐐲𐑀𐐯𐑌 𐐲𐑀𐐯𐑌𐑅𐐻 𐑄𐐯𐑋. 𐐈𐑌𐐼 𐐮𐐻 𐐿𐐩𐑋 𐐻𐐭 𐐹𐐪𐑅 𐑄𐐰𐐻 𐐣𐐬𐑉𐐬𐑌𐐴 𐐿𐐫𐑆𐐼 𐑄𐐰𐐻 𐑄 𐐶𐐲𐑉𐐿 𐐱𐑂 𐐼𐐯𐑃 𐑇𐐳𐐼 𐑅𐐨𐑅 𐐲𐑀𐐯𐑌 𐐲𐑋𐐲𐑍 𐑄 𐐹𐐨𐐹𐑊. 𐐈𐑌𐐼 𐐸𐐨 𐐻𐐳𐐿 𐑄 𐐶𐐯𐐹𐐲𐑌𐑆 𐐱𐑂 𐐶𐐫𐑉 𐑁𐑉𐐱𐑋 𐑄 𐐢𐐩𐑋𐐲𐑌𐐴𐐻𐑅; 𐐰𐑌𐐼 𐐪𐑁𐐻𐐯𐑉 𐑄𐐩 𐐸𐐰𐐼 𐐯𐑌𐐻𐐯𐑉𐐼 𐐮𐑌𐐻𐐭 𐐪 𐐿𐐲𐑂𐐨𐑌𐐲𐑌𐐻 𐐶𐐮𐑄 𐐸𐐮𐑋 𐐱𐑂 𐐹𐐨𐑅, 𐑄𐐩 𐐶𐐲𐑉 𐑅𐐲𐑁𐐯𐑉𐐼 𐐻𐐭 𐐼𐐨𐐹𐐪𐑉𐐻 𐐮𐑌𐐻𐐭 𐑄 𐐶𐐮𐑊𐐼𐐯𐑉𐑌𐐯𐑅. 𐐤𐐵 𐑄 𐑌𐐲𐑋𐐺𐐯𐑉 𐐱𐑂 𐑄𐐩𐑉 𐐼𐐯𐐼 𐐶𐐲𐑉 𐑌𐐱𐐻 𐑌𐐲𐑋𐐺𐐯𐑉𐐼 𐐺𐐨𐐿𐐱𐑆 𐐱𐑂 𐑄 𐑀𐑉𐐩𐐻𐑌𐐯𐑅 𐐱𐑂 𐑄 𐑌𐐲𐑋𐐺𐐯𐑉; 𐐷𐐩, 𐑄 𐑌𐐲𐑋𐐺𐐯𐑉 𐐱𐑂 𐑄𐐩𐑉 𐐼𐐯𐐼 𐐶𐐲𐑉 𐐯𐐿𐑅𐐨𐐼𐐮𐑍 𐑀𐑉𐐩𐐻, 𐐺𐐬𐑃 𐐱𐑌 𐑄 𐐤𐐨𐑁𐐴𐐻𐑅 𐐰𐑌𐐼 𐐱𐑌 𐑄 𐐢𐐩𐑋𐐲𐑌𐐴𐐻𐑅. 𐐈𐑌𐐼 𐐮𐐻 𐐿𐐩𐑋 𐐻𐐭 𐐹𐐪𐑅 𐑄𐐰𐐻 𐑄𐐩 𐐼𐐮𐐼 𐐿𐐪𐑅𐐻 𐑄𐐩𐑉 𐐼𐐯𐐼 𐐮𐑌𐐻𐐭 𐑄 𐐶𐐫𐐻𐐯𐑉𐑆 𐐱𐑂 𐐝𐐴𐐼𐐲𐑌, 𐐰𐑌𐐼 𐑄𐐩 𐐸𐐰𐑂 𐑀𐐫𐑌 𐑁𐐬𐑉𐑃 𐐰𐑌𐐼 𐐪𐑉 𐐺𐐯𐑉𐐮𐐼 𐐮𐑌 𐑄 𐐼𐐯𐐹𐑃𐑅 𐐱𐑂 𐑄 𐑅𐐨. 𐐈𐑌𐐼 𐑄 𐐪𐑉𐑋𐐮𐑆 𐐱𐑂 𐑄 𐐤𐐨𐑁𐐴𐐻𐑅, 𐐫𐑉 𐐱𐑂 𐐣𐐬𐑉𐐬𐑌𐐴, 𐑉𐐨𐐻𐐲𐑉𐑌𐐼 𐐰𐑌𐐼 𐐿𐐩𐑋 𐐻𐐭 𐑄𐐩𐑉 𐐸𐐵𐑆𐐯𐑆 𐐰𐑌𐐼 𐑄𐐩𐑉 𐑊𐐰𐑌𐐼𐑆. 𐐈𐑌𐐼 𐑄𐐲𐑅 𐐯𐑌𐐼𐐯𐐼 𐑄 𐐩𐐻𐐨𐑌𐑃 𐐷𐐨𐑉 𐐱𐑂 𐑄 𐑉𐐩𐑌 𐐱𐑂 𐑄 𐐾𐐲𐐾𐐯𐑆 𐐬𐑂𐐯𐑉 𐑄 𐐹𐐨𐐹𐑊 𐐱𐑂 𐐤𐐨𐑁𐐴. 𐐈𐑌𐐼 𐑄𐐲𐑅 𐐯𐑌𐐼𐐯𐐼 𐑄 𐑉𐐯𐐿𐐲𐑉𐐼 𐐱𐑂 𐐈𐑊𐑋𐐰, 𐐸𐐶𐐮𐐽 𐐶𐐱𐑆 𐑉𐐮𐐻𐑌 𐐲𐐹𐐱𐑌 𐑄 𐐹𐑊𐐩𐐻𐑅 𐐱𐑂 𐐤𐐨𐑁𐐴.

𐐕𐐰𐐹𐐻𐐯𐑉 XXI.

𐐜 𐐲𐐿𐐵𐑌𐐻 𐐱𐑂 𐑄 𐐹𐐨𐐹𐑊 𐐱𐑂 𐐤𐐨𐑁𐐴, 𐐰𐑌𐐼 𐑄𐐩𐑉 𐐶𐐫𐑉𐑆 𐐰𐑌𐐼 𐐼𐐮𐑅𐐯𐑌𐑇𐐲𐑌𐑆, 𐐮𐑌 𐑄 𐐼𐐩𐑆 𐐱𐑂 𐐐𐐨𐑊𐐩𐑋𐐲𐑌, 𐐲𐐿𐐫𐑉𐐼𐐮𐑍 𐐻𐐭 𐑄 𐑉𐐯𐐿𐐲𐑉𐐼 𐐱𐑂 𐐐𐐨𐑊𐐩𐑋𐐲𐑌, 𐐸𐐶𐐮𐐽 𐐸𐐨 𐐿𐐯𐐹𐐻 𐐮𐑌 𐐸𐐮𐑆 𐐼𐐩𐑆.

1. 𐐒𐐨𐐸𐐬𐑊𐐼, 𐑌𐐵 𐐮𐐻 𐐿𐐩𐑋 𐐻𐐭 𐐹𐐪𐑅 𐑄𐐰𐐻 𐑄 𐐹𐐨𐐹𐑊 𐐱𐑂 𐐤𐐨𐑁𐐴 𐐶𐐲𐑉 𐐯𐐿𐑅𐐨𐐼𐐮𐑍 𐑉𐐨𐐾𐐱𐐮𐑅𐐻, 𐐺𐐨𐐿𐐱𐑆 𐑄 𐐢𐐫𐑉𐐼 𐐸𐐰𐐼 𐐲𐑀𐐯𐑌 𐐼𐐨𐑊𐐮𐑂𐐯𐑉𐐼 𐑄𐐯𐑋 𐐵𐐻 𐐱𐑂 𐑄 𐐸𐐰𐑌𐐼𐑆 𐐱𐑂 𐑄𐐩𐑉 𐐯𐑌𐐯𐑋𐐮𐑆; 𐑄𐐯𐑉𐑁𐐬𐑉 𐑄𐐩 𐑀𐐩𐑂 𐑃𐐰𐑍𐐿𐑅 𐐲𐑌𐐻𐐭 𐑄 𐐢𐐫𐑉𐐼 𐑄𐐩𐑉 𐐘𐐱𐐼; 𐐷𐐩, 𐐰𐑌𐐼 𐑄𐐩 𐐼𐐮𐐼 𐑁𐐪𐑅𐐻 𐑋𐐲𐐽 𐐰𐑌𐐼 𐐹𐑉𐐩 𐑋𐐲𐐽, 𐐰𐑌𐐼 𐑄𐐩 𐐼𐐮𐐼 𐐶𐐲𐑉𐑇𐐮𐐹 𐐘𐐱𐐼 𐐶𐐮𐑄 𐐯𐐿𐑅𐐨𐐼𐐮𐑍 𐑀𐑉𐐩𐐻 𐐾𐐱𐐮.

2. 𐐈𐑌𐐼 𐐮𐐻 𐐿𐐩𐑋 𐐻𐐭 𐐹𐐪𐑅 𐐮𐑌 𐑄 𐑌𐐴𐑌𐐻𐐨𐑌𐑃 𐐷𐐨𐑉 𐐱𐑂 𐑄 𐑉𐐩𐑌 𐐱𐑂 𐑄 𐐾𐐲𐐾𐐯𐑆 𐐬𐑂𐐯𐑉 𐑄 𐐹𐐨𐐹𐑊 𐐱𐑂 𐐤𐐨𐑁𐐴, 𐑄𐐰𐐻 𐐈𐑊𐑋𐐰 𐐿𐐩𐑋 𐐲𐑌𐐻𐐭 𐐸𐐮𐑆 𐑅𐐲𐑌 𐐐𐐨𐑊𐐩𐑋𐐲𐑌 𐐰𐑌𐐼 𐑅𐐯𐐼 𐐲𐑌𐐻𐐭 𐐸𐐮𐑋, 𐐒𐐨𐑊𐐨𐑂𐐯𐑅𐐻 𐑄𐐵 𐑄 𐐶𐐲𐑉𐐼𐑆 𐐸𐐶𐐮𐐽 𐐌 𐑅𐐹𐐩𐐿 𐐲𐑌𐐻𐐭 𐑄𐐨 𐐿𐐲𐑌𐑅𐐲𐑉𐑌𐐮𐑍 𐑄𐐬𐑆 𐑉𐐯𐐿𐐲𐑉𐐼𐑆 𐐸𐐶𐐮𐐽 𐐸𐐰𐑂 𐐺𐐮𐑌 𐐿𐐯𐐹𐐻? 𐐈𐑌𐐼 𐐐𐐨𐑊𐐩𐑋𐐲𐑌 𐑅𐐯𐐼 𐐲𐑌𐐻𐐭 𐐸𐐮𐑋, 𐐏𐐩, 𐐌 𐐺𐐨𐑊𐐨𐑂. 𐐈𐑌𐐼 𐐈𐑊𐑋𐐰 𐑅𐐯𐐼 𐐲𐑀𐐯𐑌, 𐐒𐐨𐑊𐐨𐑂𐐯𐑅𐐻 𐑄𐐵 𐐮𐑌 𐐖𐐨𐑆𐐲𐑅 𐐗𐑉𐐴𐑅𐐻, 𐐸𐐭 𐑇𐐰𐑊 𐐿𐐲𐑋? 𐐈𐑌𐐼 𐐸𐐨 𐑅𐐯𐐼, 𐐏𐐩, 𐐌 𐐺𐐨𐑊𐐨𐑂 𐐫𐑊 𐑄 𐐶𐐲𐑉𐐼𐑆 𐐸𐐶𐐮𐐽 𐑄𐐵 𐐸𐐰𐑅𐐻 𐑅𐐹𐐬𐐿𐑌. 𐐈𐑌𐐼 𐐈𐑊𐑋𐐰 𐑅𐐯𐐼 𐐲𐑌𐐻𐐭 𐐸𐐮𐑋 𐐲𐑀𐐯𐑌, 𐐎𐐮𐑊 𐐷 𐐿𐐨𐐹 𐑋𐐴 𐐿𐐲𐑋𐐰𐑌𐐼𐑋𐐯𐑌𐐻𐑅? 𐐈𐑌𐐼 𐐸𐐨 𐑅𐐯𐐼, 𐐏𐐩, 𐐌 𐐶𐐮𐑊 𐐿𐐨𐐹 𐑄𐐴 𐐿𐐲𐑋𐐰𐑌𐐼𐑋𐐯𐑌𐐻𐑅 𐐶𐐮𐑄 𐐫𐑊 𐑋𐐴 𐐸𐐪𐑉𐐻. 𐐜𐐯𐑌 𐐈𐑊𐑋𐐰 𐑅𐐯𐐼 𐐲𐑌𐐻𐐭 𐐸𐐮𐑋, 𐐒𐑊𐐯𐑅𐐯𐐼 𐐪𐑉𐐻 𐑄𐐵; 𐐰𐑌𐐼 𐑄 𐐢𐐫𐑉𐐼 𐑇𐐰𐑊 𐐹𐑉𐐱𐑅𐐹𐐯𐑉 𐑄𐐨 𐐮𐑌 𐑄𐐮𐑅 𐑊𐐰𐑌𐐼. 𐐒𐐲𐐻 𐐺𐐨𐐸𐐬𐑊𐐼, 𐐌 𐐸𐐰𐑂 𐑅𐐲𐑋𐐶𐐱𐐻 𐐻𐐭 𐐹𐑉𐐱𐑁𐐨𐑅𐐴 𐐲𐑌𐐻𐐭 𐑄𐐨; 𐐺𐐲𐐻 𐐶𐐱𐐻 𐐌 𐐹𐑉𐐱𐑁𐐨𐑅𐐴 𐐲𐑌𐐻𐐭 𐑄𐐨, 𐐷 𐑇𐐰𐑊 𐑌𐐱𐐻 𐑋𐐩𐐿 𐑌𐐬𐑌; 𐐷𐐩, 𐐶𐐱𐐻 𐐌 𐐹𐑉𐐱𐑁𐐨𐑅𐐴 𐐲𐑌𐐻𐐭 𐑄𐐨 𐑇𐐰𐑊 𐑌𐐱𐐻 𐐺 𐑋𐐩𐐼 𐑌𐐬𐑌, 𐐨𐑂𐑌 𐐲𐑌𐐻𐐮𐑊 𐑄 𐐹𐑉𐐱𐑁𐐯𐑅𐐮 𐐮𐑆 𐑁𐐳𐑊𐑁𐐮𐑊𐐼; 𐑄𐐯𐑉𐑁𐐬𐑉 𐑉𐐴𐐻 𐑄 𐐶𐐲𐑉𐐼𐑆 𐐸𐐶𐐮𐐽 𐐌 𐑇𐐰𐑊 𐑅𐐩. 𐐈𐑌𐐼 𐑄𐐨𐑆 𐐪𐑉 𐑄 𐐶𐐲𐑉𐐼𐑆: 𐐒𐐨𐐸𐐬𐑊𐐼, 𐐌 𐐹𐐲𐑉𐑅𐐨𐑂 𐑄𐐰𐐻 𐑄𐐮𐑅 𐑂𐐯𐑉𐐮 𐐹𐐨𐐹𐑊, 𐑄 𐐤𐐨𐑁𐐴𐐻𐑅, 𐐲𐐿𐐫𐑉𐐼𐐮𐑍 𐐻𐐭 𐑄 𐑅𐐹𐐮𐑉𐐮𐐻 𐐱𐑂 𐑉𐐯𐑂𐐯𐑊𐐩𐑇𐐲𐑌 𐐸𐐶𐐮𐐽 𐐮𐑆 𐐮𐑌 𐑋𐐨, 𐐮𐑌 𐑁𐐬𐑉 𐐸𐐲𐑌𐐼𐑉𐐯𐐼 𐐷𐐨𐑉𐑆 𐑁𐑉𐐱𐑋 𐑄 𐐻𐐴𐑋 𐑄𐐰𐐻 𐐖𐐨𐑆𐐲𐑅 𐐗𐑉𐐴𐑅𐐻 𐑇𐐰𐑊 𐑋𐐰𐑌𐐮𐑁𐐯𐑅𐐻 𐐸𐐮𐑋𐑅𐐯𐑊𐑁 𐐲𐑌𐐻𐐭 𐑄𐐯𐑋, 𐑇𐐰𐑊 𐐼𐐶𐐮𐑌𐐼𐑊 𐐮𐑌 𐐲𐑌𐐺𐐨𐑊𐐨𐑁; 𐐷𐐩, 𐐰𐑌𐐼 𐑄𐐯𐑌 𐑇𐐰𐑊 𐑄𐐩 𐑅𐐨 𐐶𐐫𐑉𐑆 𐐰𐑌𐐼 𐐹𐐯𐑅𐐻𐐮𐑊𐐯𐑌𐑅𐐯𐑆, 𐐷𐐩, 𐑁𐐰𐑋𐐮𐑌𐑆 𐐰𐑌𐐼 𐐺𐑊𐐲𐐼𐑇𐐯𐐼, 𐐨𐑂𐑌 𐐲𐑌𐐻𐐮𐑊 𐑄 𐐹𐐨𐐹𐑊 𐐱𐑂 𐐤𐐨𐑁𐐴 𐑇𐐰𐑊 𐐺𐐨𐐿𐐲𐑋 𐐯𐐿𐑅𐐻𐐮𐑍𐐿𐐻; 𐐷𐐩, 𐐰𐑌𐐼 𐑄𐐮𐑅 𐐺𐐨𐐿𐐱𐑆 𐑄𐐩 𐑇𐐰𐑊 𐐼𐐶𐐮𐑌𐐼𐑊 𐐮𐑌 𐐲𐑌𐐺𐐨𐑊𐐨𐑁, 𐐰𐑌𐐼

𐑁𐐫𐑊 𐐮𐑌𐐻𐐭 𐑄 𐐶𐐲𐑉𐐿𐑅 𐐱𐑂 𐐼𐐪𐑉𐐿𐑌𐐯𐑅, 𐐰𐑌𐐼 𐑊𐐰𐑅𐐮𐑂𐐨𐐲𐑅𐑌𐐯𐑅, 𐐰𐑌𐐼 𐐫𐑊 𐑋𐐰𐑌𐐲𐑉 𐐱𐑂 𐐮𐑌𐐮𐐿𐐶𐐮𐐻𐐨𐑆; 𐐷𐐩, 𐐌 𐑅𐐩 𐐲𐑌𐐻𐐭 𐐷𐐭, 𐑄𐐰𐐻 𐐺𐐨𐐿𐐫𐑆 𐑄𐐩 𐑇𐐰𐑊 𐑅𐐮𐑌 𐐲𐑀𐐯𐑌𐑅𐐻 𐑅𐐬 𐑀𐑉𐐩𐐻 𐑊𐐴𐐻 𐐰𐑌𐐼 𐑌𐐱𐑊𐐯𐐾; 𐐷𐐩, 𐐌 𐑅𐐩 𐐲𐑌𐐻𐐭 𐐷𐐭, 𐑄𐐰𐐻 𐑁𐑉𐐱𐑋 𐑄𐐰𐐻 𐐼𐐩, 𐐨𐑂𐐲𐑌 𐑄 𐑁𐐬𐑉𐑃 𐐾𐐯𐑌𐐲𐑉𐐩𐑇𐐲𐑌 𐑇𐐰𐑊 𐑌𐐱𐐻 𐐫𐑊 𐐹𐐰𐑅 𐐲𐐶𐐩, 𐐺𐐨𐑁𐐬𐑉 𐑄𐐮𐑅 𐑀𐑉𐐩𐐻 𐐮𐑌𐐮𐐿𐐶𐐮𐐻𐐨 𐑇𐐰𐑊 𐐿𐐲𐑋; 𐐰𐑌𐐼 𐐸𐐶𐐯𐑌 𐑄𐐰𐐻 𐑀𐑉𐐩𐐻 𐐼𐐩 𐐿𐐲𐑋𐐯𐑃, 𐐺𐐨𐐸𐐬𐑊𐐼, 𐑄 𐐻𐐴𐑋 𐑂𐐯𐑉𐐨 𐑅𐐭𐑌 𐐿𐐲𐑋𐐯𐑃 𐑄𐐰𐐻 𐑄𐐬𐑆 𐐸𐐭 𐐪𐑉 𐑌𐐵, 𐐫𐑉 𐑄 𐑅𐐨𐐼 𐐱𐑂 𐑄𐐬𐑆 𐐸𐐭 𐐪𐑉 𐑌𐐵 𐑌𐐲𐑋𐐺𐐲𐑉𐐼 𐐲𐑋𐐲𐑍 𐑄 𐐹𐐨𐐹𐑊 𐐱𐑂 𐐤𐐨𐑁𐐴, 𐑇𐐰𐑊 𐑌𐐬 𐑋𐐬𐑉 𐐺𐐨 𐑌𐐲𐑋𐐺𐐲𐑉𐐼 𐐲𐑋𐐲𐑍 𐑄 𐐹𐐨𐐹𐑊 𐐱𐑂 𐐤𐐨𐑁𐐴; 𐐺𐐲𐐻 𐐸𐐭𐑅𐐬𐐯𐑂𐐲𐑉 𐑉𐐨𐑋𐐩𐑌𐐯𐑃, 𐐰𐑌𐐼 𐐮𐑆 𐑌𐐱𐐻 𐐼𐐯𐑅𐐻𐑉𐐱𐐮𐐼 𐐮𐑌 𐑄𐐰𐐻 𐑀𐑉𐐩𐐻 𐐰𐑌𐐼 𐐼𐑉𐐯𐐼𐑁𐐳𐑊 𐐼𐐩, 𐑇𐐰𐑊 𐐺𐐨 𐑌𐐲𐑋𐐺𐐲𐑉𐐼 𐐲𐑋𐐲𐑍 𐑄 𐐢𐐰𐑋𐐲𐑌𐐴𐐻𐑅, 𐐰𐑌𐐼 𐑇𐐰𐑊 𐐺𐐨𐐿𐐲𐑋 𐑊𐐴𐐿 𐐲𐑌𐐻𐐭 𐑄𐐯𐑋, 𐐫𐑊, 𐑅𐐩𐑂 𐐮𐐻 𐐺𐐨 𐐲 𐑁𐐷𐐭, 𐐸𐐭 𐑇𐐰𐑊 𐐺𐐨 𐐿𐐫𐑊𐐼 𐑄 𐐼𐐮𐑅𐐴𐐹𐑊𐑆 𐐱𐑂 𐑄 𐐢𐐫𐑉𐐼; 𐐰𐑌𐐼 𐑄𐐯𐑋 𐑇𐐰𐑊 𐑄 𐐢𐐰𐑋𐐲𐑌𐐴𐐻𐑅 𐐹𐐲𐑉𐑅𐐭, 𐐨𐑂𐐲𐑌 𐐲𐑌𐐻𐐮𐑊 𐑄𐐩 𐑇𐐰𐑊 𐐺𐐨𐐿𐐲𐑋 𐐯𐐿𐑅𐐻𐐮𐑍𐐿𐐻. 𐐈𐑌𐐼 𐑌𐐵, 𐐺𐐨𐐿𐐫𐑆 𐐱𐑂 𐐮𐑌𐐮𐐿𐐶𐐮𐐻𐐨, 𐑄𐐮𐑅 𐐹𐑉𐐱𐑁𐐯𐑅𐐨 𐑇𐐰𐑊 𐐺𐐨 𐑁𐐳𐑊𐑁𐐮𐑊𐐼.

3. 𐐈𐑌𐐼 𐐮𐐻 𐐿𐐩𐑋 𐐻𐐭 𐐹𐐰𐑅 𐑄𐐰𐐻 𐐰𐑁𐐻𐐲𐑉 𐐈𐑊𐑋𐐲 𐐸𐐰𐐼 𐑅𐐯𐐼 𐑄𐐨𐑆 𐐶𐐲𐑉𐐼𐑆 𐐻𐐭 𐐐𐐯𐑊𐐲𐑋𐐲𐑌, 𐐸𐐨 𐐺𐑊𐐯𐑅𐐻 𐐸𐐮𐑋, 𐐰𐑌𐐼 𐐫𐑊𐑅𐐬 𐐸𐐮𐑆 𐐲𐑄𐐲𐑉 𐑅𐐲𐑌𐑆; 𐐰𐑌𐐼 𐐸𐐨 𐐫𐑊𐑅𐐬 𐐺𐑊𐐯𐑅𐐻 𐑄 𐐲𐑉𐑃 𐑁𐐬𐑉 𐑄 𐑉𐐴𐐽𐐲𐑅 𐑅𐐩𐐿. 𐐈𐑌𐐼 𐐸𐐨 𐑅𐐯𐐼, 𐑄𐐲𐑅 𐑅𐐯𐑃 𐑄 𐐢𐐫𐑉𐐼 𐐘𐐱𐐼: 𐐗𐐲𐑉𐑅𐐯𐐼 𐑇𐐰𐑊 𐐺𐐨 𐑄 𐑊𐐰𐑌𐐼, 𐐷𐐩, 𐑄𐐮𐑅 𐑊𐐰𐑌𐐼, 𐐲𐑌𐐻𐐭 𐐯𐑂𐐲𐑉𐐨 𐑌𐐩𐑇𐐲𐑌, 𐐿𐐮𐑌𐐼𐑉𐐯𐐼, 𐐻𐐲𐑍, 𐐰𐑌𐐼 𐐹𐐨𐐹𐑊, 𐐲𐑌𐐻𐐭 𐐼𐐯𐑅𐐻𐑉𐐲𐐿𐑇𐐲𐑌, 𐐸𐐶𐐮𐐽 𐐼𐐭 𐐶𐐮𐐿𐐯𐐼𐑊𐐨, 𐐸𐐶𐐯𐑌 𐑄𐐩 𐐪𐑉 𐑁𐐳𐑊𐐨 𐑉𐐴𐐹; 𐐰𐑌𐐼 𐐰𐑆 𐐌 𐐸𐐰𐑂 𐑅𐐯𐐼, 𐑅𐐬 𐑇𐐰𐑊 𐐮𐐻 𐐺𐐨; 𐑁𐐫𐑉 𐑄𐐮𐑅 𐐮𐑆 𐑄 𐐿𐐲𐑉𐑅𐐮𐑍 𐐰𐑌𐐼 𐑄 𐐺𐑊𐐯𐑅𐐮𐑍 𐐱𐑂 𐐘𐐱𐐼 𐐲𐐹𐐱𐑌 𐑄 𐑊𐐰𐑌𐐼, 𐑁𐐫𐑉 𐑄 𐐢𐐫𐑉𐐼 𐐿𐐰𐑌𐐱𐐻 𐑊𐐳𐐿 𐐲𐐹𐐱𐑌 𐑅𐐮𐑌 𐐶𐐮𐑄 𐑄 𐑊𐐨𐑅𐐻 𐐼𐐨𐑀𐑉𐐨 𐐱𐑂 𐐰𐑊𐐵𐐲𐑌𐑅. 𐐈𐑌𐐼 𐑌𐐵, 𐐸𐐶𐐯𐑌 𐐈𐑊𐑋𐐲 𐐸𐐰𐐼 𐑅𐐯𐐼 𐑄𐐨𐑆 𐐶𐐲𐑉𐐼𐑆 𐐸𐐨 𐐺𐑊𐐯𐑅𐐻 𐑄 𐐽𐐲𐑉𐐽, 𐐷𐐩, 𐐫𐑊 𐑄𐐬𐑆 𐐸𐐭 𐑇𐐳𐐼 𐑅𐐻𐐰𐑌𐐼 𐑁𐐰𐑅𐐻 𐐮𐑌 𐑄 𐑁𐐩𐑃 𐑁𐑉𐐱𐑋 𐑄𐐰𐐻 𐐻𐐴𐑋 𐐸𐐯𐑌𐑅𐑁𐐬𐑉𐑃; 𐐰𐑌𐐼 𐐸𐐶𐐯𐑌 𐐈𐑊𐑋𐐲 𐐸𐐰𐐼 𐐼𐐲𐑌 𐑄𐐮𐑅 𐐸𐐨 𐐼𐐨𐐹𐐪𐑉𐐻𐐯𐐼 𐐵𐐻 𐐱𐑂 𐑄 𐑊𐐰𐑌𐐼 𐐱𐑂 𐐞𐐰𐑉𐐲𐐸𐐯𐑋𐑊𐐲, 𐐰𐑆 𐐮𐑁 𐐻𐐭 𐑀𐐬 𐐮𐑌𐐻𐐭 𐑄 𐑊𐐰𐑌𐐼 𐐱𐑂 𐐣𐐯𐑊𐐯𐐿. 𐐈𐑌𐐼 𐐮𐐻 𐐿𐐩𐑋 𐐻𐐭 𐐹𐐰𐑅 𐑄𐐰𐐻 𐐸𐐨 𐐶𐐱𐑆 𐑌𐐯𐑂𐐲𐑉 𐐸𐐲𐑉𐐼 𐐱𐑂 𐑋𐐬𐑉; 𐐰𐑆 𐐻𐐭 𐐸𐐮𐑆 𐐼𐐯𐑃 𐐫𐑉 𐐺𐐯𐑉𐐨𐐲𐑊 𐐶𐐨 𐑌𐐬 𐑌𐐱𐐻 𐐱𐑂. 𐐒𐐨𐐸𐐬𐑊𐐼, 𐑄𐐮𐑅 𐐶𐐨 𐑌𐐬, 𐑄𐐰𐐻 𐐸𐐨 𐐶𐐱𐑆 𐐲 𐑉𐐴𐐽𐐲𐑅 𐑋𐐰𐑌; 𐐰𐑌𐐼 𐑄 𐑅𐐩𐐮𐑍 𐐶𐐯𐑌𐐻 𐐲𐐺𐑉𐐫𐐼 𐐮𐑌 𐑄 𐐽𐐲𐑉𐐽 𐑄𐐰𐐻 𐐸𐐨 𐐶𐐱𐑆 𐐻𐐩𐐿𐑌 𐐲𐐹 𐐺𐐴 𐑄 𐐝𐐹𐐮𐑉𐐮𐐻, 𐐫𐑉 𐐺𐐯𐑉𐐨𐐼 𐐺𐐴 𐑄 𐐸𐐰𐑌𐐼 𐐱𐑂 𐑄 𐐢𐐫𐑉𐐼, 𐐨𐑂𐐲𐑌 𐐰𐑆 𐐣𐐬𐑆𐐯𐑆. 𐐒𐐲𐐻 𐐺𐐨𐐸𐐬𐑊𐐼, 𐑄 𐑅𐐿𐑉𐐮𐐹𐐽𐐲𐑉𐑆 𐑅𐐯𐑃 𐑄 𐐢𐐫𐑉𐐼 𐐻𐐳𐐿 𐐣𐐬𐑆𐐯𐑆 𐐲𐑌𐐻𐐭 𐐸𐐮𐑋𐑅𐐯𐑊𐑁; 𐐰𐑌𐐼 𐐶𐐨 𐑅𐐲𐐹𐐬𐑆 𐑄𐐰𐐻 𐐸𐐨 𐐸𐐰𐑆 𐐫𐑊𐑅𐐬 𐑉𐐨𐑅𐐨𐑂𐐼 𐐈𐑊𐑋𐐲 𐐮𐑌 𐑄 𐑅𐐹𐐮𐑉𐐮𐐻, 𐐲𐑌𐐻𐐭 𐐸𐐮𐑋𐑅𐐯𐑊𐑁: 𐑄𐐯𐑉𐑁𐐬𐑉, 𐑁𐐫𐑉 𐑄𐐮𐑅 𐐿𐐫𐑆, 𐐶𐐨 𐑌𐐬 𐑌𐐲𐑃𐐮𐑍 𐐿𐐱𐑌𐑅𐐲𐑉𐑌𐐮𐑍 𐐸𐐮𐑆 𐐼𐐯𐑃 𐐰𐑌𐐼 𐐺𐐯𐑉𐐨𐐲𐑊.

4. 𐐈𐑌𐐼 𐐮𐐻 𐐿𐐩𐑋 𐐻𐐭 𐐹𐐰𐑅 𐐮𐑌 𐑄 𐐿𐐱𐑋𐐯𐑌𐑅𐑋𐐯𐑌𐐻 𐐱𐑂 𐑄 𐑌𐐴𐑌𐐻𐐨𐑌𐑃 𐐷𐐨𐑉 𐐱𐑂 𐑄 𐑉𐐩𐑌 𐐱𐑂 𐑄 𐐾𐐲𐐾𐐯𐑆 𐐬𐑂𐐲𐑉 𐑄 𐐹𐐨𐐹𐑊 𐐱𐑂 𐐤𐐨𐑁𐐴, 𐑄𐐰𐐻 𐐐𐐯𐑊𐐲𐑋𐐲𐑌 𐐶𐐯𐑌𐐻 𐑁𐐬𐑉𐑃 𐐲𐑋𐐲𐑍 𐑄 𐐹𐐨𐐹𐑊 𐐻𐐭 𐐼𐐨𐐿𐑊𐐯𐑉 𐑄 𐐶𐐲𐑉𐐼 𐐲𐑌𐐻𐐭 𐑄𐐯𐑋: 𐑁𐐫𐑉 𐐺𐐨𐐸𐐬𐑊𐐼, 𐐺𐐨𐐿𐐫𐑆 𐐱𐑂 𐑄𐐯𐑉 𐐶𐐫𐑉𐑆 𐐶𐐮𐑄 𐑄 𐐢𐐰𐑋𐐲𐑌𐐴𐐻𐑅, 𐐰𐑌𐐼 𐑄 𐑋𐐯𐑌𐐨 𐑊𐐮𐐻𐑊 𐐼𐐮𐑅𐐯𐑌𐑇𐐲𐑌𐑆 𐐰𐑌𐐼 𐐼𐐮𐑅𐐻𐐲𐑉𐐺𐐲𐑌𐑅𐐯𐑆 𐐸𐐶𐐮𐐽 𐐸𐐰𐐼 𐐺𐐮𐑌 𐐲𐑋𐐲𐑍 𐑄 𐐹𐐨𐐹𐑊, 𐐮𐐻 𐐺𐐨𐐿𐐩𐑋 𐐯𐐿𐑅𐐹𐐨𐐼𐐨𐐲𐑌𐐻 𐑄𐐰𐐻 𐑄 𐐶𐐲𐑉𐐼 𐐱𐑂 𐐘𐐱𐐼 𐑇𐐳𐐼 𐐺𐐨 𐐼𐐨𐐿𐑊𐐯𐑉𐐼 𐐲𐑋𐐲𐑍 𐑄𐐯𐑋; 𐐷𐐩, 𐐰𐑌𐐼 𐑄𐐰𐐻 𐐲 𐑉𐐯𐑀𐐷𐐭𐑊𐐩𐑇𐐲𐑌 𐑇𐐳𐐼 𐐺𐐨 𐑋𐐩𐐼 𐑃𐑉𐐭𐐵𐐻 𐑄 𐐽𐐲𐑉𐐽; 𐑄𐐯𐑉𐑁𐐬𐑉, 𐐐𐐯𐑊𐐲𐑋𐐲𐑌 𐐰𐑌𐐼 𐐸𐐮𐑆 𐐺𐑉𐐯𐑄𐑉𐐯𐑌 𐐶𐐯𐑌𐐻 𐑁𐐬𐑉𐑃 𐐻𐐭 𐐯𐑅𐐻𐐰𐐺𐑊𐐮𐑇 𐑄 𐐽𐐲𐑉𐐽 𐐲𐑀𐐯𐑌 𐐮𐑌 𐐫𐑊 𐑄 𐑊𐐰𐑌𐐼, 𐐷𐐩, 𐐮𐑌 𐐯𐑂𐐲𐑉𐐨 𐑅𐐮𐐻𐐨 𐑃𐑉𐐭𐐵𐐻 𐐫𐑊 𐑄 𐑊𐐰𐑌𐐼 𐐸𐐶𐐮𐐽 𐐶𐐱𐑆 𐐹𐐲𐑆𐐯𐑅𐐻 𐐺𐐴 𐑄 𐐹𐐨𐐹𐑊 𐐱𐑂 𐐤𐐨𐑁𐐴. 𐐈𐑌𐐼 𐐮𐐻 𐐿𐐩𐑋 𐐻𐐭 𐐹𐐰𐑅 𐑄𐐰𐐻 𐑄𐐩 𐐼𐐮𐐼 𐐲𐐹𐐱𐐮𐑌𐐻 𐐹𐑉𐐨𐑅𐐻𐑅 𐐰𐑌𐐼 𐐻𐐨𐐽𐐲𐑉𐑆 𐑃𐑉𐐭𐐵𐐻 𐐫𐑊 𐑄 𐑊𐐰𐑌𐐼, 𐐬𐑂𐐲𐑉 𐐫𐑊 𐑄 𐐽𐐲𐑉𐐽𐐯𐑆.

5. 𐐈𐑌𐐼 𐑌𐐵 𐐮𐐻 𐐿𐐩𐑋 𐐻𐐭 𐐹𐐰𐑅 𐑄𐐰𐐻 𐐰𐑁𐐻𐐲𐑉 𐐐𐐯𐑊𐐲𐑋𐐲𐑌 𐐰𐑌𐐼 𐐸𐐮𐑆 𐐺𐑉𐐯𐑄𐑉𐐯𐑌 𐐸𐐰𐐼 𐐲𐐹𐐱𐐮𐑌𐐻𐐯𐐼 𐐹𐑉𐐨𐑅𐐻𐑅 𐐰𐑌𐐼 𐐻𐐨𐐽𐐲𐑉𐑆 𐐬𐑂𐐲𐑉 𐑄 𐐽𐐲𐑉𐐽𐐯𐑆, 𐑄𐐰𐐻 𐑄𐐯𐑉 𐐲𐑉𐐬𐑆 𐐲 𐐼𐐮𐑅𐐯𐑌𐑇𐐲𐑌 𐐲𐑋𐐲𐑍 𐑄𐐯𐑋, 𐐰𐑌𐐼 𐑄𐐩 𐐶𐐳𐐼 𐑌𐐱𐐻 𐑀𐐮𐑂 𐐸𐐨𐐼 𐐻𐐭 𐑄 𐐶𐐲𐑉𐐼𐑆 𐐱𐑂 𐐐𐐯𐑊𐐲𐑋𐐲𐑌 𐐰𐑌𐐼 𐐸𐐮𐑆 𐐺𐑉𐐯𐑄𐑉𐐯𐑌; 𐐺𐐲𐐻 𐑄𐐩 𐑀𐑉𐐭 𐐹𐑉𐐵𐐼, 𐐺𐐨𐐮𐑍 𐑊𐐮𐑁𐐻𐐯𐐼 𐐲𐐹 𐐮𐑌 𐑄𐐯𐑉 𐐸𐐪𐑉𐐻𐑅, 𐐺𐐨𐐿𐐫𐑆 𐐱𐑂 𐑄𐐯𐑉 𐐯𐐿𐑅𐐨𐐼𐐮𐑍𐑊𐐨 𐑀𐑉𐐩𐐻 𐑉𐐮𐐽𐐯𐑆; 𐑄𐐯𐑉𐑁𐐬𐑉 𐑄𐐩 𐑀𐑉𐐭 𐑉𐐮𐐽 𐐮𐑌 𐑄𐐯𐑉 𐐬𐑌 𐐴𐑆, 𐐰𐑌𐐼 𐐶𐐳𐐼 𐑌𐐱𐐻 𐑀𐐮𐑂 𐐸𐐨𐐼 𐐻𐐭 𐑄𐐯𐑉 𐐶𐐲𐑉𐐼𐑆, 𐐻𐐭 𐐶𐐫𐐿 𐐲𐐹𐑉𐐴𐐻𐑊𐐨 𐐺𐐨𐑁𐐬𐑉 𐐘𐐱𐐼.

6. 𐐈𐑌𐐼 𐐮𐐻 𐐿𐐩𐑋 𐐻𐐭 𐐹𐐰𐑅 𐑄𐐰𐐻 𐐰𐑆 𐑋𐐯𐑌𐐨 𐐰𐑆 𐐶𐐳𐐼 𐑌𐐱𐐻 𐐸𐐪𐑉𐐿𐐲𐑌 𐐻𐐭 𐑄 𐐶𐐲𐑉𐐼𐑆 𐐱𐑂 𐐐𐐯𐑊𐐲𐑋𐐲𐑌 𐐰𐑌𐐼 𐐸𐐮𐑆 𐐺𐑉𐐯𐑄𐑉𐐯𐑌, 𐐶𐐲𐑉 𐑀𐐰𐑄𐐲𐑉𐐼 𐐻𐐭𐑀𐐯𐑄𐐲𐑉 𐐰𐑀𐐯𐑌𐑅𐐻 𐑄𐐩𐑉 𐐺𐑉𐐯𐑄𐑉𐐯𐑌. 𐐈𐑌𐐼 𐑌𐐵 𐐺𐐨𐐸𐐬𐑊𐐼, 𐑄𐐩 𐐶𐐲𐑉 𐐯𐐿𐑅𐐨𐐼𐐮𐑍𐑊𐐨 𐑉𐐫𐑃, 𐐮𐑌𐑅𐐬𐑋𐐲𐐽 𐑄𐐰𐐻 𐑄𐐩 𐐶𐐲𐑉 𐐼𐐨𐐻𐐲𐑉𐑋𐐮𐑌𐐼 𐐻𐐭 𐑅𐑊𐐩 𐑄𐐯𐑋. 𐐤𐐵 𐑄 𐑊𐐨𐐼𐐲𐑉 𐐱𐑂 𐑄𐐬𐑆 𐐸𐐭 𐐶𐐲𐑉 𐑉𐐫𐑃 𐐰𐑀𐐯𐑌𐑅𐐻 𐑄𐐩𐑉 𐐺𐑉𐐯𐑄𐑉𐐯𐑌, 𐐶𐐱𐑆 𐐲 𐑊𐐪𐑉𐐾 𐐰𐑌𐐼 𐐲 𐑅𐐻𐑉𐐱𐑍 𐑋𐐰𐑌; 𐐰𐑌𐐼 𐐸𐐮𐑆 𐑌𐐩𐑋 𐐶𐐱𐑆 𐐈𐑋𐐲𐑊𐐮𐐿𐐴𐐲. 𐐈𐑌𐐼 𐐈𐑋𐐲𐑊𐐮𐐿𐐴𐐲 𐐶𐐱𐑆 𐐼𐐨𐑆𐐴𐑉𐐲𐑅 𐐻𐐭 𐐺 𐐲 𐐿𐐮𐑍: 𐐰𐑌𐐼 𐑄𐐬𐑆 𐐹𐐨𐐹𐐲𐑊 𐐸𐐭 𐐶𐐲𐑉 𐑉𐐫𐑃, 𐐶𐐲𐑉 𐐫𐑊𐑅𐐬 𐐼𐐨𐑆𐐴𐑉𐐲𐑅 𐑄𐐰𐐻 𐐸𐐨 𐑇𐐳𐐼 𐐺 𐑄𐐩𐑉 𐐿𐐮𐑍: 𐐰𐑌𐐼 𐑄𐐩 𐐶𐐲𐑉 𐑄 𐑀𐑉𐐩𐐻𐐲𐑉 𐐹𐐪𐑉𐐻 𐐱𐑂 𐑄𐐯𐑋 𐑄 𐑊𐐬𐐲𐑉 𐐾𐐲𐐾𐐯𐑆 𐐱𐑂 𐑄 𐑊𐐰𐑌𐐼: 𐐰𐑌𐐼 𐑄𐐩 𐐶𐐲𐑉 𐑅𐐨𐐿𐐮𐑍 𐑁𐐫𐑉 𐐹𐐵𐐲𐑉. 𐐈𐑌𐐼 𐑄𐐩 𐐸𐐰𐐼 𐐺𐐮𐑌 𐑊𐐯𐐼 𐐺𐐴 𐑄 𐑁𐑊𐐰𐐻𐐲𐑉𐐨𐑆 𐐱𐑂 𐐈𐑋𐐲𐑊𐐮𐐿𐐴𐐲, 𐑄𐐰𐐻 𐐮𐑁 𐑄𐐩 𐐶𐐳𐐼 𐑅𐐲𐐹𐐬𐑉𐐻 𐐸𐐮𐑋 𐐰𐑌𐐼 𐐯𐑅𐐻𐐰𐐺𐑊𐐮𐑇 𐐸𐐮𐑋 𐐻𐐭 𐐺 𐑄𐐩𐑉 𐐿𐐮𐑍, 𐑄𐐰𐐻 𐐸𐐨 𐐶𐐳𐐼 𐑋𐐩𐐿 𐑄𐐯𐑋 𐑉𐐭𐑊𐐲𐑉𐑆 𐐬𐑂𐐲𐑉 𐑄 𐐹𐐨𐐹𐐲𐑊. 𐐜𐐲𐑅 𐑄𐐩 𐐶𐐲𐑉 𐑊𐐯𐐼 𐐲𐐶𐐩 𐐺𐐴 𐐈𐑋𐐲𐑊𐐮𐐿𐐴𐐲 𐐻𐐭 𐐼𐐮𐑅𐐯𐑌𐑇𐐲𐑌𐑆, 𐑌𐐱𐐻𐐶𐐮𐑃𐑅𐐻𐐰𐑌𐐼𐐮𐑍 𐑄 𐐹𐑉𐐨𐐽𐐮𐑍 𐐱𐑂 𐐐𐐯𐑊𐐲𐑋𐐲𐑌 𐐰𐑌𐐼 𐐸𐐮𐑆 𐐺𐑉𐐯𐑄𐑉𐐯𐑌; 𐐷𐐩, 𐑌𐐱𐐻𐐶𐐮𐑃𐑅𐐻𐐰𐑌𐐼𐐮𐑍 𐑄𐐩𐑉 𐐯𐐿𐑅𐐨𐐼𐐮𐑍 𐑀𐑉𐐩𐐻 𐐿𐐩𐑉 𐐬𐑂𐐲𐑉 𐑄 𐐽𐐲𐑉𐐽, 𐑁𐐫𐑉 𐑄𐐩 𐐶𐐲𐑉 𐐸𐐴 𐐹𐑉𐐨𐑅𐐻𐑅 𐐬𐑂𐐲𐑉 𐑄 𐐽𐐲𐑉𐐽. 𐐈𐑌𐐼 𐑄𐐩𐑉 𐐶𐐲𐑉 𐑋𐐯𐑌𐐨 𐐮𐑌 𐑄 𐐽𐐲𐑉𐐽 𐐸𐐭 𐐺𐐨𐑊𐐨𐑂𐐼 𐐮𐑌 𐑄 𐑁𐑊𐐰𐐻𐐲𐑉𐐮𐑍 𐐶𐐲𐑉𐐼𐑆 𐐱𐑂 𐐈𐑋𐐲𐑊𐐮𐐿𐐴𐐲; 𐑄𐐩𐑉𐑁𐐬𐑉 𐑄𐐩 𐐼𐐮𐑅𐐯𐑌𐐻𐐯𐐼 𐐨𐑂𐐯𐑌 𐑁𐑉𐐱𐑋 𐑄 𐐽𐐲𐑉𐐽; 𐐰𐑌𐐼 𐑄𐐲𐑅 𐐶𐐲𐑉 𐑄 𐐰𐑁𐐩𐑉𐑆 𐐱𐑂 𐑄 𐐹𐐨𐐹𐐲𐑊 𐐱𐑂 𐐤𐐨𐑁𐐴 𐐯𐐿𐑅𐐨𐐼𐐮𐑍 𐐹𐑉𐐨𐐿𐐩𐑉𐐨𐐲𐑅 𐐰𐑌𐐼 𐐼𐐩𐑌𐐾𐐲𐑉𐐲𐑅, 𐑌𐐱𐐻𐐶𐐮𐑃𐑅𐐻𐐰𐑌𐐼𐐮𐑍 𐑄𐐩𐑉 𐑀𐑉𐐩𐐻 𐑂𐐮𐐿𐐻𐐬𐑉𐐨 𐐸𐐶𐐮𐐽 𐑄𐐩 𐐸𐐰𐐼 𐐸𐐰𐐼 𐐬𐑂𐐲𐑉 𐑄 𐐢𐐩𐑋𐐲𐑌𐐴𐐻𐑅, 𐐰𐑌𐐼 𐑄𐐩𐑉 𐑀𐑉𐐩𐐻 𐑉𐐨𐐾𐑎𐑅𐐮𐑍𐑆 𐐸𐐶𐐮𐐽 𐑄𐐩 𐐸𐐰𐐼 𐐸𐐰𐐼, 𐐺𐐨𐐿𐐫𐑆 𐐱𐑂 𐑄𐐩𐑉 𐐼𐐨𐑊𐐮𐑂𐐲𐑉𐐲𐑌𐑅 𐐺𐐴 𐑄 𐐸𐐰𐑌𐐼 𐐱𐑂 𐑄 𐐢𐐫𐑉𐐼. 𐐜𐐲𐑅 𐐶𐐨 𐑅𐐨 𐐸𐐵 𐐿𐐶𐐮𐐿 𐑄 𐐽𐐮𐑊𐐼𐑉𐐯𐑌 𐐱𐑂 𐑋𐐯𐑌 𐐼𐐭 𐑁𐐫𐑉𐑀𐐯𐐻 𐑄 𐐢𐐫𐑉𐐼 𐑄𐐩𐑉 𐐘𐐱𐐼: 𐐷𐐩, 𐐸𐐵 𐐿𐐶𐐮𐐿 𐐻𐐭 𐐼𐐭 𐐮𐑌𐐮𐐿𐐶𐐮𐐻𐐨, 𐐰𐑌𐐼 𐐻𐐭 𐐺 𐑊𐐯𐐼 𐐲𐐶𐐩 𐐺𐐴 𐑄 𐐨𐑂𐐮𐑊 𐐶𐐲𐑌: 𐐷𐐩, 𐐰𐑌𐐼 𐐶𐐨 𐐫𐑊𐑅𐐬 𐑅𐐨 𐑄 𐑀𐑉𐐩𐐻 𐐶𐐮𐐿𐐯𐐼𐑌𐐯𐑅 𐐶𐐲𐑌 𐑂𐐯𐑉𐐨 𐐶𐐮𐐿𐐯𐐼 𐑋𐐰𐑌 𐐿𐐰𐑌 𐐿𐐫𐑆 𐐻𐐭 𐐻𐐩𐐿 𐐹𐑊𐐩𐑅 𐐰𐑋𐐲𐑍 𐑄 𐐽𐐮𐑊𐐼𐑉𐐯𐑌 𐐱𐑂 𐑋𐐯𐑌: 𐐷𐐩, 𐐶𐐨 𐑅𐐨 𐑄𐐰𐐻 𐐈𐑋𐐲𐑊𐐮𐐿𐐴𐐲 𐐺𐐨𐐿𐐫𐑆 𐐸𐐨 𐐶𐐱𐑆 𐐲 𐑋𐐰𐑌 𐐱𐑂 𐐿𐐲𐑌𐐮𐑍 𐐼𐐨𐑂𐐴𐑅, 𐐰𐑌𐐼 𐐲 𐑋𐐰𐑌 𐐱𐑂 𐑋𐐯𐑌𐐨 𐑁𐑊𐐰𐐻𐐲𐑉𐐮𐑍 𐐶𐐲𐑉𐐼𐑆, 𐑄𐐰𐐻 𐐸𐐨 𐑊𐐯𐐼 𐐲𐐶𐐩 𐑄 𐐸𐐪𐑉𐐻𐑅 𐐱𐑂 𐑋𐐯𐑌𐐨 𐐹𐐨𐐹𐐲𐑊 𐐻𐐭 𐐼𐐭 𐐶𐐮𐐿𐐯𐐼𐑊𐐨: 𐐷𐐩, 𐐰𐑌𐐼 𐐻𐐭 𐑅𐐨𐐿 𐐻𐐭 𐐼𐐨𐑅𐐻𐑉𐑎 𐑄 𐐽𐐲𐑉𐐽 𐐱𐑂 𐐘𐐱𐐼, 𐐰𐑌𐐼 𐐻𐐭 𐐼𐐨𐑅𐐻𐑉𐑎 𐑄 𐑁𐐵𐑌𐐼𐐩𐑇𐐲𐑌 𐐱𐑂 𐑊𐐮𐐺𐐲𐑉𐐻𐐨 𐐸𐐶𐐮𐐽 𐐘𐐱𐐼 𐐸𐐰𐐼 𐑀𐑉𐐰𐑌𐐻𐐯𐐼 𐐲𐑌𐐻𐐭 𐑄𐐯𐑋, 𐐫𐑉 𐐸𐐶𐐮𐐽 𐐺𐑊𐐯𐑅𐐮𐑍 𐐘𐐱𐐼 𐐸𐐰𐐼 𐑅𐐯𐑌𐐻 𐐲𐐹𐐱𐑌 𐑄 𐑁𐐩𐑅 𐐱𐑂 𐑄 𐑊𐐰𐑌𐐼 𐑁𐐫𐑉 𐑄 𐑉𐐴𐐽𐐲𐑅' 𐑅𐐩𐐿.

7. 𐐈𐑌𐐼 𐑌𐐵 𐐮𐐻 𐐿𐐩𐑋 𐐻𐐭 𐐹𐐰𐑅 𐑄𐐰𐐻 𐐸𐐶𐐯𐑌 𐐣𐐫𐑉𐐬𐑌𐐴, 𐐸𐐭 𐐶𐐱𐑆 𐑄 𐐽𐐨𐑁 𐐿𐐱𐑋𐐰𐑌𐐼𐐲𐑉 𐐱𐑂 𐑄 𐐪𐑉𐑋𐐨𐑆 𐐱𐑂 𐑄 𐐤𐐨𐑁𐐴𐐻𐑅, 𐐸𐐰𐐼 𐐸𐐲𐑉𐐼 𐐱𐑂 𐑄𐐨𐑆 𐐼𐐮𐑅𐐯𐑌𐑇𐐲𐑌𐑆, 𐐸𐐨 𐐶𐐱𐑆 𐐰𐑍𐑀𐑉𐐨 𐐶𐐮𐑃 𐐈𐑋𐐲𐑊𐐮𐐿𐐴𐐲. 𐐈𐑌𐐼 𐐮𐐻 𐐿𐐩𐑋 𐐻𐐭 𐐹𐐰𐑅 𐑄𐐰𐐻 𐐸𐐨 𐑉𐐯𐑌𐐻 𐐸𐐮𐑆 𐐿𐐬𐐻; 𐐰𐑌𐐼 𐐸𐐨 𐐻𐐳𐐿 𐐲 𐐹𐐨𐑅 𐑄𐐩𐑉𐐱𐑂, 𐐰𐑌𐐼 𐑉𐐬𐐻 𐐲𐐹𐐱𐑌 𐐮𐐻, 𐐆𐑌 𐑋𐐯𐑋𐐬𐑉𐐨 𐐱𐑂 𐐵𐑉 𐐘𐐱𐐼, 𐐵𐑉 𐑉𐐨𐑊𐐮𐐾𐐲𐑌, 𐐰𐑌𐐼 𐑁𐑉𐐨𐐼𐐲𐑋, 𐐰𐑌𐐼 𐐵𐑉 𐐹𐐨𐑅, 𐐵𐑉 𐐶𐐴𐑂𐑆, 𐐰𐑌𐐼 𐐵𐑉 𐐽𐐮𐑊𐐼𐑉𐐯𐑌; 𐐰𐑌𐐼 𐐸𐐨 𐑁𐐰𐑅𐐲𐑌𐐼 𐐮𐐻 𐐲𐐹𐐱𐑌 𐑄 𐐯𐑌𐐼 𐐱𐑂 𐐲 𐐹𐐬𐑊 𐑄𐐩𐑉𐐱𐑂. 𐐈𐑌𐐼 𐐸𐐨 𐑁𐐰𐑅𐐲𐑌𐐼 𐐱𐑌 𐐸𐐮𐑆 𐐸𐐯𐐼-𐐹𐑊𐐩𐐻, 𐐰𐑌𐐼 𐐸𐐮𐑆 𐐺𐑉𐐯𐑅𐐻-𐐹𐑊𐐩𐐻, 𐐰𐑌𐐼 𐐸𐐮𐑆 𐑇𐐨𐑊𐐼𐑆, 𐐰𐑌𐐼 𐑀𐐲𐑉𐐼𐐯𐐼 𐐱𐑌 𐐸𐐮𐑆 𐐪𐑉𐑋𐐲𐑉 𐐲𐐺𐐵𐐻 𐐸𐐮𐑆 𐑊𐑎𐑌𐑆; 𐐰𐑌𐐼 𐐸𐐨 𐐻𐐳𐐿 𐑄 𐐹𐐬𐑊, 𐐸𐐶𐐮𐐽 𐐸𐐰𐐼 𐐱𐑌 𐑄 𐐯𐑌𐐼 𐑄𐐩𐑉𐐱𐑂 𐐸𐐮𐑆 𐑉𐐯𐑌𐐻 𐐿𐐬𐐻, (𐐰𐑌𐐼 𐐸𐐨 𐐿𐐫𐑊𐐼 𐐮𐐻 𐑄 𐐻𐐴𐐻𐐲𐑊 𐐱𐑂 𐑊𐐮𐐺𐐲𐑉𐐻𐐨,) 𐐰𐑌𐐼 𐐸𐐨 𐐺𐐵𐐼 𐐸𐐮𐑋𐑅𐐯𐑊𐑁 𐐻𐐭 𐑄 𐐲𐑉𐑃, 𐐰𐑌𐐼 𐐸𐐨 𐐹𐑉𐐩𐐼 𐑋𐐴𐐻𐐮𐑊𐐨 𐐲𐑌𐐻𐐭 𐐸𐐮𐑆 𐐘𐐱𐐼, 𐑁𐐫𐑉 𐑄 𐐺𐑊𐐯𐑅𐐮𐑍𐑆 𐐱𐑂 𐑊𐐮𐐺𐐲𐑉𐐻𐐨 𐐻𐐭 𐑉𐐯𐑅𐐻 𐐲𐐹𐐱𐑌 𐐸𐐮𐑆 𐐺𐑉𐐯𐑄𐑉𐐯𐑌 𐑅𐐬 𐑊𐐱𐑍 𐐰𐑆 𐑄𐐩𐑉 𐑇𐐳𐐼 𐐲 𐐺𐐰𐑌𐐼 𐐱𐑂 𐐗𐑉𐐮𐑅𐐽𐐲𐑌𐑆 𐑉𐐨𐑋𐐩𐑌 𐐻𐐭 𐐹𐐱𐑆𐐯𐑅 𐑄 𐑊𐐰𐑌𐐼: 𐑁𐐫𐑉 𐑄𐐲𐑅 𐐶𐐲𐑉 𐐫𐑊 𐑄 𐐻𐑉𐐭 𐐺𐐨𐑊𐐨𐑂𐐲𐑉𐑆 𐐱𐑂 𐐗𐑉𐐴𐑅𐐻, 𐐸𐐭 𐐺𐐨𐑊𐐱𐑍𐐼 𐐻𐐭 𐑄 𐐽𐐲𐑉𐐽 𐐱𐑂 𐐘𐐱𐐼, 𐐿𐐫𐑊𐐼 𐐺𐐴 𐑄𐐬𐑆 𐐸𐐭 𐐼𐐮𐐼 𐑌𐐱𐐻 𐐺𐐨𐑊𐐱𐑍 𐐻𐐭 𐑄 𐐽𐐲𐑉𐐽; 𐐰𐑌𐐼 𐑄𐐬𐑆 𐐸𐐭 𐐼𐐮𐐼 𐐺𐐨𐑊𐐱𐑍 𐐻𐐭 𐑄 𐐽𐐲𐑉𐐽 𐐶𐐲𐑉 𐑁𐐩𐑃𐑁𐐳𐑊; 𐐷𐐩, 𐐫𐑊 𐑄𐐬𐑆 𐐸𐐭 𐐶𐐲𐑉 𐐻𐑉𐐭 𐐺𐐨𐑊𐐨𐑂𐐲𐑉𐑆 𐐮𐑌 𐐗𐑉𐐴𐑅𐐻, 𐐻𐐳𐐿 𐐲𐐹𐐱𐑌 𐑄𐐯𐑋, 𐑀𐑊𐐰𐐼𐑊𐐨, 𐑄 𐑌𐐩𐑋 𐐱𐑂 𐐗𐑉𐐴𐑅𐐻, 𐐫𐑉 𐐗𐑉𐐮𐑅𐐽𐐲𐑌𐑆, 𐐰𐑆 𐑄𐐩 𐐶𐐲𐑉 𐐿𐐫𐑊𐐼, 𐐺𐐨𐐿𐐫𐑆 𐐱𐑂 𐑄𐐩𐑉 𐐺𐐨𐑊𐐨𐑁 𐐮𐑌 𐐗𐑉𐐴𐑅𐐻, 𐐸𐐭 𐑇𐐳𐐼 𐐿𐐲𐑋: 𐐰𐑌𐐼 𐑄𐐩𐑉𐑁𐐬𐑉, 𐐰𐐻 𐑄𐐮𐑅 𐐻𐐴𐑋, 𐐣𐐫𐑉𐐬𐑌𐐴 𐐹𐑉𐐩𐐼, 𐑄𐐰𐐻 𐑄 𐐿𐐫𐑆 𐐱𐑂 𐑄 𐐗𐑉𐐮𐑅𐐽𐐲𐑌𐑆, 𐐰𐑌𐐼 𐑄 𐑁𐑉𐐨𐐼𐐲𐑋 𐐱𐑂 𐑄 𐑊𐐰𐑌𐐼 𐑋𐐴𐐻 𐐺 𐑁𐐩𐑂𐐲𐑉𐐼.

8. 𐐈𐑌𐐼 𐐮𐐻 𐐿𐐩𐑋 𐐻𐐭 𐐹𐐰𐑅 𐑄𐐰𐐻 𐐸𐐶𐐯𐑌 𐐸𐐨 𐐸𐐰𐐼 𐐹𐐬𐑉𐐼 𐐵𐐻 𐐸𐐮𐑆 𐑅𐐬𐑊 𐐻𐐭 𐐘𐐱𐐼, 𐐸𐐨 𐑌𐐩𐑋𐐼 𐐫𐑊

𐑄 𐑊𐐰𐑌𐐼 𐐸𐐶𐐮𐐽 𐐶𐐱𐑆 𐑅𐐵𐑃 𐐱𐑂 𐑄 𐑊𐐰𐑌𐐼 𐐔𐐯𐑆𐐬𐑊𐐩𐑇𐐲𐑌: 𐐷𐐩, 𐐰𐑌𐐼 𐐮𐑌 𐑁𐐴𐑌, 𐐫𐑊 𐑄 𐑊𐐰𐑌𐐼, 𐐺𐐬𐑃 𐐱𐑌 𐑄 𐑌𐐫𐑉𐑃 𐐰𐑌𐐼 𐐱𐑌 𐑄 𐑅𐐵𐑃, 𐐩 𐐽𐐬𐑆𐑌 𐑊𐐰𐑌𐐼, 𐐰𐑌𐐼 𐑄 𐑊𐐰𐑌𐐼 𐐱𐑂 𐑊𐐮𐐺𐐲𐑉𐐻𐐮. 𐐈𐑌𐐼 𐐸𐐨 𐑅𐐯𐐼, 𐐟𐐳𐑉𐑊𐐮 𐐘𐐱𐐼 𐑇𐐰𐑊 𐑌𐐱𐐻 𐑅𐐲𐑁𐐲𐑉 𐑄𐐰𐐻 𐐶𐐨, 𐐸𐐭 𐐪𐑉 𐐼𐐨𐑅𐐹𐐴𐑆𐐼 𐐺𐐨𐐿𐐫𐑆 𐐶𐐨 𐐻𐐩𐐿 𐐲𐐹𐐱𐑌 𐐲𐑅 𐑄 𐑌𐐩𐑋 𐐱𐑂 𐐗𐑉𐐴𐑅𐐻, 𐑇𐐰𐑊 𐐺 𐐻𐑉𐐱𐐼𐐲𐑌 𐐼𐐵𐑌 𐐰𐑌𐐼 𐐼𐐨𐑅𐐻𐑉𐐫𐐮𐐼, 𐐲𐑌𐐻𐐮𐑊 𐐶𐐨 𐐺𐑉𐐮𐑍 𐐮𐐻 𐐲𐐹𐐱𐑌 𐐲𐑅 𐐺𐐴 𐐵𐑉 𐐬𐑌 𐐻𐑉𐐰𐑌𐑅𐑀𐑉𐐯𐑇𐐲𐑌𐑆. 𐐈𐑌𐐼 𐐸𐐶𐐯𐑌 𐐣𐐫𐑉𐐬𐑌𐐴 𐐸𐐰𐐼 𐑅𐐯𐐼 𐑄𐐨𐑆 𐐶𐐲𐑉𐐼𐑆, 𐐸𐐨 𐐶𐐯𐑌𐐻 𐑁𐐫𐑉𐑃 𐐰𐑋𐐲𐑍 𐑄 𐐹𐐨𐐹𐐲𐑊, 𐐶𐐩𐑂𐐮𐑍 𐑄 𐑉𐐯𐑌𐐻 𐐱𐑂 𐐸𐐮𐑆 𐑀𐐪𐑉𐑋𐐯𐑌𐐻 𐐮𐑌 𐑄 𐐩𐑉, 𐑄𐐰𐐻 𐐫𐑊 𐑋𐐴𐐻 𐑅𐐨 𐑄 𐑉𐐴𐐻𐐮𐑍 𐐸𐐶𐐮𐐽 𐐸𐐨 𐐸𐐰𐐼 𐑉𐐬𐐻 𐐲𐐹𐐱𐑌 𐑄 𐑉𐐯𐑌𐐻, 𐐰𐑌𐐼 𐐿𐑉𐐴𐐮𐑍 𐐶𐐮𐑄 𐐩 𐑊𐐵𐐼 𐑂𐐱𐐮𐑅, 𐑅𐐩𐐮𐑍, 𐐒𐐨𐐸𐐬𐑊𐐼, 𐐸𐐭𐑅𐐬𐐯𐑂𐐲𐑉 𐐶𐐮𐑊 𐑋𐐩𐑌𐐻𐐩𐑌 𐑄𐐮𐑅 𐐻𐐴𐐻𐐲𐑊 𐐲𐐹𐐱𐑌 𐑄 𐑊𐐰𐑌𐐼, 𐑊𐐯𐐻 𐑄𐐯𐑋 𐐿𐐲𐑋 𐑁𐐫𐑉𐑃 𐐮𐑌 𐑄 𐑅𐐻𐑉𐐯𐑍𐑃 𐐱𐑂 𐑄 𐐢𐐫𐑉𐐼, 𐐰𐑌𐐼 𐐯𐑌𐐻𐐲𐑉 𐐮𐑌𐐻𐐭 𐐩 𐐿𐐲𐑂𐐯𐑌𐐲𐑌𐐻 𐑄𐐰𐐻 𐑄𐐩 𐐶𐐮𐑊 𐑋𐐩𐑌𐐻𐐩𐑌 𐑄𐐩𐑉 𐑉𐐴𐐻𐑅, 𐐰𐑌𐐼 𐑄𐐩𐑉 𐑉𐐨𐑊𐐮𐐾𐐲𐑌, 𐑄𐐰𐐻 𐑄 𐐢𐐫𐑉𐐼 𐐘𐐱𐐼 𐑋𐐩 𐐺𐑊𐐯𐑅 𐑄𐐯𐑋.

9. 𐐈𐑌𐐼 𐐮𐐻 𐐿𐐩𐑋 𐐻𐐭 𐐹𐐰𐑅 𐑄𐐰𐐻 𐐸𐐶𐐯𐑌 𐐣𐐫𐑉𐐬𐑌𐐴 𐐸𐐰𐐼 𐐹𐑉𐐬𐐿𐑊𐐩𐑋𐐼 𐑄𐐨𐑆 𐐶𐐲𐑉𐐼𐑆, 𐐺𐐨𐐸𐐬𐑊𐐼 𐑄 𐐹𐐨𐐹𐐲𐑊 𐐿𐐩𐑋 𐑉𐐲𐑌𐐮𐑍 𐐻𐐳𐑀𐐯𐑄𐐲𐑉 𐐶𐐮𐑄 𐑄𐐩𐑉 𐐪𐑉𐑋𐐲𐑉 𐑀𐐲𐑉𐐼𐐯𐐼 𐐰𐐺𐐵𐐻 𐑄𐐩𐑉 𐑊𐐱𐐮𐑌𐑆, 𐑉𐐯𐑌𐐼𐐮𐑍 𐑄𐐩𐑉 𐑀𐐪𐑉𐑋𐐯𐑌𐐻𐑅 𐐮𐑌 𐐻𐐬𐐿𐑌, 𐐫𐑉 𐐰𐑆 𐐩 𐐿𐐲𐑂𐐯𐑌𐐲𐑌𐐻, 𐑄𐐰𐐻 𐑄𐐩 𐐶𐐳𐐼 𐑌𐐱𐐻 𐑁𐐫𐑉𐑅𐐩𐐿 𐑄 𐐢𐐫𐑉𐐼 𐑄𐐩𐑉 𐐘𐐱𐐼, 𐐫𐑉, 𐐮𐑌 𐐲𐑄𐐲𐑉 𐐶𐐲𐑉𐐼𐑆, 𐐮𐑁 𐑄𐐩 𐑇𐐳𐐼 𐐻𐑉𐐰𐑌𐑅𐑀𐑉𐐯𐑅 𐑄 𐐿𐐲𐑋𐐰𐑌𐐼𐑋𐐯𐑌𐐻𐑅 𐐱𐑂 𐐘𐐱𐐼, 𐐫𐑉 𐑁𐐫𐑊 𐐮𐑌𐐻𐐭 𐐻𐑉𐐰𐑌𐑅𐑀𐑉𐐯𐑇𐐲𐑌, 𐐰𐑌𐐼 𐐺 𐐰𐑇𐐩𐑋𐐼 𐐻𐐭 𐐻𐐩𐐿 𐐲𐐹𐐱𐑌 𐑄𐐯𐑋 𐑄 𐑌𐐩𐑋 𐐱𐑂 𐐗𐑉𐐴𐑅𐐻, 𐑄 𐐢𐐫𐑉𐐼 𐑇𐐳𐐼 𐑉𐐯𐑌𐐼 𐑄𐐯𐑋 𐐨𐑂𐑌 𐐰𐑆 𐑄𐐩 𐐸𐐰𐐼 𐑉𐐯𐑌𐐻 𐑄𐐩𐑉 𐑀𐐪𐑉𐑋𐐯𐑌𐐻𐑅. 𐐤𐐵 𐑄𐐮𐑅 𐐶𐐱𐑆 𐑄 𐐿𐐲𐑂𐐯𐑌𐐲𐑌𐐻 𐐸𐐶𐐮𐐽 𐑄𐐩 𐑋𐐩𐐼: 𐐰𐑌𐐼 𐑄𐐩 𐐿𐐪𐑅𐐻 𐑄𐐩𐑉 𐑀𐐪𐑉𐑋𐐯𐑌𐐻𐑅 𐐰𐐻 𐑄 𐑁𐐨𐐻 𐐱𐑂 𐐣𐐫𐑉𐐬𐑌𐐴, 𐑅𐐩𐐮𐑍, 𐐎𐐨 𐐿𐐲𐑂𐐯𐑌𐐲𐑌𐐻 𐐶𐐮𐑄 𐐵𐑉 𐐘𐐱𐐼, 𐑄𐐰𐐻 𐐶𐐨 𐑇𐐰𐑊 𐐺 𐐼𐐨𐑅𐐻𐑉𐐫𐐮𐐼, 𐐨𐑂𐑌 𐐰𐑆 𐐵𐑉 𐐺𐑉𐐯𐑄𐑉𐐯𐑌 𐐮𐑌 𐑄 𐑊𐐰𐑌𐐼 𐑌𐐫𐑉𐑃𐐶𐐲𐑉𐐼, 𐐮𐑁 𐐶𐐨 𐑇𐐰𐑊 𐑁𐐫𐑊 𐐮𐑌𐐻𐐭 𐐻𐑉𐐰𐑌𐑅𐑀𐑉𐐯𐑇𐐲𐑌: 𐐷𐐩, 𐐸𐐨 𐑋𐐩 𐐿𐐪𐑅𐐻 𐐲𐑅 𐐰𐐻 𐑄 𐑁𐐨𐐻 𐐱𐑂 𐐵𐑉 𐐯𐑌𐐨𐑋𐐮𐑆, 𐐨𐑂𐑌 𐐰𐑆 𐐶𐐨 𐐸𐐰𐑂 𐐿𐐪𐑅𐐻 𐐵𐑉 𐑀𐐪𐑉𐑋𐐯𐑌𐐻𐑅 𐐰𐐻 𐑄𐐴 𐑁𐐨𐐻, 𐐻𐐭 𐐺 𐐻𐑉𐐱𐐼𐐲𐑌 𐐲𐑌𐐼𐐲𐑉 𐑁𐐳𐐻, 𐐮𐑁 𐐶𐐨 𐑇𐐰𐑊 𐑁𐐫𐑊 𐐮𐑌𐐻𐐭 𐐻𐑉𐐰𐑌𐑅𐑀𐑉𐐯𐑇𐐲𐑌. 𐐣𐐫𐑉𐐬𐑌𐐴 𐑅𐐯𐐼 𐐲𐑌𐐻𐐭 𐑄𐐯𐑋, 𐐒𐐨𐐸𐐬𐑊𐐼, 𐐶𐐨 𐐪𐑉 𐐩 𐑉𐐯𐑋𐑌𐐲𐑌𐐻 𐐱𐑂 𐑄 𐑅𐐨𐐼 𐐱𐑂 𐐖𐐩𐐿𐐲𐐺: 𐐷𐐩, 𐐶𐐨 𐐪𐑉 𐐩 𐑉𐐯𐑋𐑌𐐲𐑌𐐻 𐐱𐑂 𐑄 𐑅𐐨𐐼 𐐱𐑂 𐐖𐐬𐑆𐐯𐑁, 𐐸𐐭𐑆 𐐿𐐬𐐻 𐐶𐐱𐑆 𐑉𐐯𐑌𐐻 𐐺𐐴 𐐸𐐮𐑆 𐐺𐑉𐐯𐑄𐑉𐐯𐑌 𐐮𐑌𐐻𐐭 𐑋𐐯𐑌𐐮 𐐹𐐨𐑅𐐯𐑆: 𐐷𐐩, 𐐰𐑌𐐼 𐑌𐐵 𐐺𐐨𐐸𐐬𐑊𐐼, 𐑊𐐯𐐻 𐐲𐑅 𐑉𐐨𐑋𐐯𐑋𐐺𐐲𐑉 𐐻𐐭 𐐿𐐨𐐹 𐑄 𐐿𐐲𐑋𐐰𐑌𐐼𐑋𐐯𐑌𐐻𐑅 𐐱𐑂 𐐘𐐱𐐼, 𐐫𐑉 𐐵𐑉 𐑀𐐪𐑉𐑋𐐯𐑌𐐻𐑅 𐑇𐐰𐑊 𐐺 𐑉𐐯𐑌𐐻 𐐺𐐴 𐐵𐑉 𐐺𐑉𐐯𐑄𐑉𐐯𐑌, 𐐰𐑌𐐼 𐐶𐐨 𐐺 𐐿𐐪𐑅𐐻 𐐮𐑌𐐻𐐭 𐐹𐑉𐐮𐑆𐐲𐑌, 𐐫𐑉 𐐺 𐑅𐐬𐑊𐐼, 𐐫𐑉 𐐺 𐑅𐑊𐐩𐑌: 𐐷𐐩, 𐑊𐐯𐐻 𐐲𐑅 𐐹𐑉𐐨𐑆𐐲𐑉𐑂 𐐵𐑉 𐑊𐐮𐐺𐐲𐑉𐐻𐐮, 𐐰𐑆 𐐩 𐑉𐐯𐑋𐑌𐐲𐑌𐐻 𐐱𐑂 𐐖𐐬𐑆𐐯𐑁: 𐐷𐐩, 𐑊𐐯𐐻 𐐲𐑅 𐑉𐐨𐑋𐐯𐑋𐐺𐐲𐑉 𐑄 𐐶𐐲𐑉𐐼𐑆 𐐱𐑂 𐐖𐐩𐐿𐐲𐐺, 𐐺𐐨𐑁𐐬𐑉 𐐸𐐮𐑆 𐐼𐐯𐑃: 𐑁𐐫𐑉 𐐺𐐨𐐸𐐬𐑊𐐼, 𐐸𐐨 𐑅𐐫 𐑄𐐰𐐻 𐐩 𐐹𐐪𐑉𐐻 𐐱𐑂 𐑄 𐑉𐐯𐑋𐑌𐐲𐑌𐐻 𐐱𐑂 𐑄 𐐿𐐬𐐻 𐐱𐑂 𐐖𐐬𐑆𐐯𐑁 𐐶𐐱𐑆 𐐹𐑉𐐨𐑆𐐲𐑉𐑂𐐼, 𐐰𐑌𐐼 𐐸𐐰𐐼 𐑌𐐱𐐻 𐐼𐐨𐐿𐐩𐐼. 𐐈𐑌𐐼 𐐸𐐨 𐑅𐐯𐐼, 𐐀𐑂𐑌 𐐰𐑆 𐑄𐐮𐑅 𐑉𐐯𐑋𐑌𐐲𐑌𐐻 𐐱𐑂 𐑀𐐪𐑉𐑋𐐯𐑌𐐻 𐐱𐑂 𐑋𐐴 𐑅𐐲𐑌 𐐸𐐰𐑃 𐐺𐐨𐑌 𐐹𐑉𐐨𐑆𐐲𐑉𐑂𐐼, 𐑅𐐬 𐑇𐐰𐑊 𐐩 𐑉𐐯𐑋𐑌𐐲𐑌𐐻 𐐱𐑂 𐑄 𐑅𐐨𐐼 𐐱𐑂 𐑋𐐴 𐑅𐐲𐑌 𐐺 𐐹𐑉𐐨𐑆𐐲𐑉𐑂𐐼 𐐺𐐴 𐑄 𐐸𐐰𐑌𐐼 𐐱𐑂 𐐘𐐱𐐼, 𐐰𐑌𐐼 𐐺 𐐻𐐩𐐿𐑌 𐐲𐑌𐐻𐐭 𐐸𐐮𐑋𐑅𐐯𐑊𐑁, 𐐸𐐶𐐴𐑊 𐑄 𐑉𐐨𐑋𐐩𐑌𐐼𐐲𐑉 𐐱𐑂 𐑄 𐑅𐐨𐐼 𐐱𐑂 𐐖𐐬𐑆𐐯𐑁 𐑇𐐰𐑊 𐐹𐐲𐑉𐐮𐑇, 𐐨𐑂𐑌 𐐰𐑆 𐑄 𐑉𐐯𐑋𐑌𐐲𐑌𐐻 𐐱𐑂 𐐸𐐮𐑆 𐑀𐐪𐑉𐑋𐐯𐑌𐐻. 𐐤𐐵 𐐺𐐨𐐸𐐬𐑊𐐼, 𐑄𐐮𐑅 𐑀𐐮𐑂𐐯𐑃 𐑋𐐴 𐑅𐐬𐑊 𐑅𐐱𐑉𐐬: 𐑌𐐯𐑂𐐲𐑉𐑄𐐯𐑊𐐯𐑅, 𐑋𐐴 𐑅𐐬𐑊 𐐸𐐰𐑃 𐐾𐐱𐐮 𐐮𐑌 𐑋𐐴 𐑅𐐲𐑌, 𐐺𐐨𐐿𐐫𐑆 𐐱𐑂 𐑄𐐰𐐻 𐐹𐐪𐑉𐐻 𐐱𐑂 𐐸𐐮𐑆 𐑅𐐨𐐼 𐐸𐐶𐐮𐐽 𐑇𐐰𐑊 𐐺 𐐻𐐩𐐿𐑌 𐐲𐑌𐐻𐐭 𐐘𐐱𐐼. 𐐤𐐵 𐐺𐐨𐐸𐐬𐑊𐐼, 𐑄𐐮𐑅 𐐶𐐱𐑆 𐑄 𐑊𐐰𐑍𐑀𐐶𐐯𐐾 𐐱𐑂 𐐖𐐩𐐿𐐲𐐺. 𐐈𐑌𐐼 𐑌𐐵 𐐸𐐭 𐑌𐐬𐐯𐑃 𐐺𐐲𐐻 𐐸𐐶𐐱𐐻 𐑄 𐑉𐐯𐑋𐑌𐐲𐑌𐐻 𐐱𐑂 𐑄 𐑅𐐨𐐼 𐐱𐑂 𐐖𐐬𐑆𐐯𐑁, 𐐸𐐶𐐮𐐽 𐑇𐐰𐑊 𐐹𐐲𐑉𐐮𐑇 𐐰𐑆 𐐸𐐮𐑆 𐑀𐐪𐑉𐑋𐐯𐑌𐐻, 𐐪𐑉 𐑄𐐬𐑆 𐐸𐐭 𐐸𐐰𐑂 𐐼𐐮𐑅𐐯𐑌𐐻𐐯𐐼 𐑁𐑉𐐲𐑋 𐐲𐑅: 𐐷𐐩, 𐐰𐑌𐐼 𐐨𐑂𐑌 𐐮𐐻 𐑇𐐰𐑊 𐐺 𐐵𐑉𐑅𐐯𐑊𐑂𐑆, 𐐮𐑁 𐐶𐐨 𐐼𐐭 𐑌𐐱𐐻 𐑅𐐻𐐰𐑌𐐼 𐑁𐐰𐑅𐐻 𐐮𐑌 𐑄 𐑁𐐩𐑃 𐐱𐑂 𐐗𐑉𐐴𐑅𐐻.

10. 𐐈𐑌𐐼 𐑌𐐵 𐐮𐐻 𐐿𐐩𐑋 𐐻𐐭 𐐹𐐰𐑅 𐑄𐐰𐐻 𐐸𐐶𐐯𐑌 𐐣𐐫𐑉𐐬𐑌𐐴 𐐸𐐰𐐼 𐑅𐐯𐐼 𐑄𐐨𐑆 𐐶𐐲𐑉𐐼𐑆, 𐐸𐐨 𐐶𐐯𐑌𐐻 𐑁𐐫𐑉𐑃, 𐐰𐑌𐐼 𐐫𐑊𐑅𐐬 𐑅𐐯𐑌𐐻 𐑁𐐫𐑉𐑃 𐐮𐑌 𐐫𐑊 𐑄 𐐹𐐪𐑉𐐻𐑅 𐐱𐑂 𐑄 𐑊𐐰𐑌𐐼 𐐸𐐶𐐯𐑉 𐑄𐐩𐑉 𐐶𐐲𐑉 𐐼𐐮𐑅𐐯𐑌𐑇𐐲𐑌𐑆, 𐐰𐑌𐐼 𐑀𐐰𐑄𐐲𐑉𐐼 𐐻𐐳𐑀𐐯𐑄𐐲𐑉 𐐫𐑊 𐑄 𐐹𐐨𐐹𐐲𐑊 𐐸𐐭 𐐶𐐲𐑉 𐐼𐐨𐑆𐐴𐑉𐐲𐑅 𐐻𐐭 𐑋𐐩𐑌𐐻𐐩𐑌 𐑄𐐩𐑉 𐑊𐐮𐐺𐐲𐑉𐐻𐐮, 𐐻𐐭 𐑅𐐻𐐰𐑌𐐼 𐐲𐑀𐐯𐑌𐑅𐐻 𐐈𐑋𐐲𐑊𐐮𐐿𐐴𐐲, 𐐰𐑌𐐼 𐑄𐐬𐑆 𐐸𐐭 𐐸𐐰𐐼 𐐼𐐮𐑅𐐯𐑌𐐻𐐯𐐼, 𐐸𐐭 𐐶𐐲𐑉 𐐿𐐫𐑊𐐼 𐐈𐑋𐐲𐑊𐐮𐐿𐐴𐐲𐐴𐐻𐑅.

11. 𐐈𐑌𐐼 𐐮𐐻 𐐿𐐩𐑋 𐐻𐐭 𐐹𐐰𐑅 𐑄𐐰𐐻 𐐸𐐶𐐯𐑌 𐐈𐑋𐐲𐑊𐐮𐐿𐐴𐐲 𐑅𐐫 𐑄𐐰𐐻 𐑄 𐐹𐐨𐐹𐐲𐑊 𐐱𐑂 𐐣𐐫𐑉𐐬𐑌𐐴 𐐶𐐲𐑉 𐑋𐐬𐑉 𐑌𐐭𐑋𐐲𐑉𐐲𐑅 𐑄𐐰𐑌 𐑄 𐐈𐑋𐐲𐑊𐐮𐐿𐐴𐐲𐐴𐐻𐑅; 𐐰𐑌𐐼 𐐸𐐨 𐐫𐑊𐑅𐐬 𐑅𐐫 𐑄𐐰𐐻 𐐸𐐮𐑆 𐐹𐐨𐐹𐐲𐑊 𐐶𐐲𐑉 𐐼𐐵𐐻𐑁𐐳𐑊

𐐿𐐲𐑌𐑅𐐲𐑉𐑌𐐮𐑍 𐑄 𐐾𐐲𐑅𐐻𐐮𐑅 𐐱𐑂 𐑄 𐐿𐐫𐑆 𐐮𐑌 𐐸𐐶𐐮𐐽 𐑄𐐩 𐐸𐐰𐐼 𐐲𐑌𐐼𐐲𐑉𐐻𐐩𐐿𐑌; 𐑄𐐩𐑉𐑁𐐬𐑉, 𐑁𐐨𐑉𐐮𐑍 𐑄𐐰𐐻 𐐸𐐨 𐑇𐐳𐐼 𐑌𐐱𐐻 𐑀𐐩𐑌 𐑄 𐐹𐐱𐐮𐑌𐐻, 𐐸𐐨 𐐻𐐳𐐿 𐑄𐐬𐑆 𐐱𐑂 𐐸𐐮𐑆 𐐹𐐨𐐹𐑊 𐐸𐐭 𐐶𐐳𐐼, 𐐰𐑌𐐼 𐐼𐐨𐐹𐐪𐑉𐐻𐐯𐐼 𐐮𐑌𐐻𐐭 𐑄 𐑊𐐰𐑌𐐼 𐐱𐑂 𐐤𐐨𐑁𐐴.

12. 𐐤𐐵 𐐣𐐬𐑉𐐬𐑌𐐴 𐑃𐐫𐐻 𐐮𐐻 𐐶𐐱𐑆 𐑌𐐱𐐻 𐐯𐐿𐑅𐐹𐐨𐐼𐐮𐐲𐑌𐐻 𐑄𐐰𐐻 𐑄 𐐢𐐩𐑋𐐲𐑌𐐴𐐻𐑅 𐑇𐐳𐐼 𐐸𐐰𐑂 𐐯𐑌𐐮 𐑋𐐬𐑉 𐑅𐐻𐑉𐐯𐑍𐑃: 𐑄𐐩𐑉𐑁𐐬𐑉 𐐸𐐨 𐑃𐐫𐐻 𐐻𐐭 𐐿𐐲𐐻 𐐫𐑁 𐑄 𐐹𐐨𐐹𐑊 𐐱𐑂 𐐈𐑋𐐰𐑊𐐮𐐿𐐴𐐲, 𐐫𐑉 𐐻𐐭 𐐻𐐩𐐿 𐑄𐐯𐑋 𐐰𐑌𐐼 𐐺𐑉𐐮𐑍 𐑄𐐯𐑋 𐐺𐐰𐐿, 𐐰𐑌𐐼 𐐹𐐳𐐻 𐐈𐑋𐐰𐑊𐐮𐐿𐐴𐐲 𐐻𐐭 𐐼𐐯𐑃: 𐐷𐐩, 𐑁𐐫𐑉 𐐸𐐨 𐑌𐐮𐐭 𐑄𐐰𐐻 𐐸𐐨 𐐶𐐳𐐼 𐑅𐐻𐐲𐑉 𐐲𐐹 𐑄 𐐢𐐩𐑋𐐲𐑌𐐴𐐻𐑅 𐐻𐐭 𐐰𐑍𐑀𐐲𐑉 𐐰𐑀𐐯𐑌𐑅𐐻 𐑄𐐯𐑋, 𐐰𐑌𐐼 𐐿𐐫𐑆 𐑄𐐯𐑋 𐐻𐐭 𐐿𐐲𐑋 𐐻𐐭 𐐺𐐰𐐻𐑊 𐐰𐑀𐐯𐑌𐑅𐐻 𐑄𐐯𐑋: 𐐰𐑌𐐼 𐑄𐐮𐑅 𐐸𐐨 𐑌𐐮𐐭 𐑄𐐰𐐻 𐐈𐑋𐐰𐑊𐐮𐐿𐐴𐐲 𐐶𐐳𐐼 𐐼𐐭, 𐑄𐐰𐐻 𐐸𐐨 𐑋𐐴𐐻 𐐱𐐺𐐻𐐩𐑌 𐐸𐐮𐑆 𐐹𐐲𐑉𐐹𐐲𐑅𐐯𐑆: 𐑄𐐩𐑉𐑁𐐬𐑉 𐐣𐐬𐑉𐐬𐑌𐐴 𐑃𐐫𐐻 𐐮𐐻 𐐶𐐱𐑆 𐐯𐐿𐑅𐐹𐐨𐐼𐐮𐐲𐑌𐐻 𐑄𐐰𐐻 𐐸𐐨 𐑇𐐳𐐼 𐐻𐐩𐐿 𐐸𐐮𐑆 𐐪𐑉𐑋𐐮𐑆, 𐐸𐐭 𐐸𐐰𐐼 𐑀𐐰𐑄𐐲𐑉𐐼 𐑄𐐯𐑋𐑅𐐯𐑊𐑂𐑆 𐐻𐐳𐑀𐐯𐑄𐐲𐑉, 𐐰𐑌𐐼 𐐪𐑉𐑋𐐼 𐑄𐐯𐑋𐑅𐐯𐑊𐑂𐑆, 𐐰𐑌𐐼 𐐯𐑌𐐻𐐲𐑉𐐼 𐐮𐑌𐐻𐐭 𐐲 𐐿𐐲𐑂𐐨𐑌𐐲𐑌𐐻 𐐻𐐭 𐐿𐐨𐐹 𐑄 𐐹𐐨𐑅: 𐐰𐑌𐐼 𐐮𐐻 𐐿𐐩𐑋 𐐻𐐭 𐐹𐐰𐑅 𐑄𐐰𐐻 𐐸𐐨 𐐻𐐳𐐿 𐐸𐐮𐑆 𐐪𐑉𐑋𐐮, 𐐰𐑌𐐼 𐑋𐐪𐑉𐐽𐐻 𐐵𐐻 𐐮𐑌𐐻𐐭 𐑄 𐐶𐐮𐑊𐐼𐐲𐑉𐑌𐐯𐑅, 𐐻𐐭 𐐿𐐲𐐻 𐐫𐑁 𐑄 𐐿𐐬𐑉𐑅 𐐱𐑂 𐐈𐑋𐐰𐑊𐐮𐐿𐐴𐐲 𐐮𐑌 𐑄 𐐶𐐮𐑊𐐼𐐲𐑉𐑌𐐯𐑅.

13. 𐐈𐑌𐐼 𐐮𐐻 𐐿𐐩𐑋 𐐻𐐭 𐐹𐐰𐑅 𐑄𐐰𐐻 𐐸𐐨 𐐼𐐮𐐼 𐐰𐐿𐐫𐑉𐐼𐐮𐑍 𐐻𐐭 𐐸𐐮𐑆 𐐼𐐨𐑆𐐴𐑉𐑆 𐐰𐑌𐐼 𐑋𐐪𐑉𐐽𐐻 𐑁𐐬𐑉𐑃 𐐮𐑌𐐻𐐭 𐑄 𐐶𐐮𐑊𐐼𐐲𐑉𐑌𐐯𐑅, 𐐰𐑌𐐼 𐐸𐐯𐐼𐐯𐐼 𐑄 𐐪𐑉𐑋𐐮𐑆 𐐱𐑂 𐐈𐑋𐐰𐑊𐐮𐐿𐐴𐐲. 𐐈𐑌𐐼 𐐮𐐻 𐐿𐐩𐑋 𐐻𐐭 𐐹𐐰𐑅 𐑄𐐰𐐻 𐐈𐑋𐐰𐑊𐐮𐐿𐐴𐐲 𐑁𐑊𐐯𐐼 𐐶𐐮𐑄 𐐲 𐑅𐑋𐐫𐑊 𐑌𐐲𐑋𐐺𐐲𐑉 𐐱𐑂 𐐸𐐮𐑆 𐑋𐐯𐑌, 𐐰𐑌𐐼 𐑄 𐑉𐐨𐑋𐐩𐑌𐐼𐐲𐑉 𐐶𐐲𐑉 𐐼𐐨𐑊𐐮𐑂𐐲𐑉𐐼 𐐲𐐹 𐐮𐑌𐐻𐐭 𐑄 𐐸𐐰𐑌𐐼𐑆 𐐱𐑂 𐐣𐐬𐑉𐐬𐑌𐐴, 𐐰𐑌𐐼 𐐶𐐲𐑉 𐐻𐐩𐐿𐑌 𐐺𐐰𐐿 𐐮𐑌𐐻𐐭 𐑄 𐑊𐐰𐑌𐐼 𐐱𐑂 𐐞𐐩𐑉𐐰𐐸𐐯𐑋𐑊𐐰. 𐐤𐐵 𐐣𐐬𐑉𐐬𐑌𐐴 𐐺𐐨𐐮𐑍 𐐲 𐑋𐐰𐑌 𐐸𐐭 𐐶𐐱𐑆 𐐲𐐹𐐱𐐮𐑌𐐻𐐯𐐼 𐐺𐐴 𐑄 𐐽𐐨𐑁 𐐾𐐲𐐾𐐯𐑆 𐐰𐑌𐐼 𐑄 𐑂𐐱𐐮𐑅 𐐱𐑂 𐑄 𐐹𐐨𐐹𐑊, 𐑄𐐩𐑉𐑁𐐬𐑉 𐐸𐐨 𐐸𐐰𐐼 𐐹𐐵𐐲𐑉 𐐰𐐿𐐫𐑉𐐼𐐮𐑍 𐐻𐐭 𐐸𐐮𐑆 𐐶𐐮𐑊 𐐶𐐮𐑄 𐑄 𐐪𐑉𐑋𐐮𐑆 𐐱𐑂 𐑄 𐐤𐐨𐑁𐐴𐐻𐑅, 𐐻𐐭 𐐯𐑅𐐻𐐰𐐺𐑊𐐮𐑇 𐐰𐑌𐐼 𐐻𐐭 𐐯𐐿𐑅𐐲𐑉𐑅𐐴𐑆 𐐫𐑃𐐱𐑉𐐮𐐻𐐮 𐐬𐑂𐐲𐑉 𐑄𐐯𐑋.

14. 𐐈𐑌𐐼 𐐮𐐻 𐐿𐐩𐑋 𐐻𐐭 𐐹𐐰𐑅 𐑄𐐰𐐻 𐐸𐐭𐑅𐐬𐐯𐑂𐐲𐑉 𐐱𐑂 𐑄 𐐈𐑋𐐰𐑊𐐮𐐿𐐴𐐲𐐴𐐻𐑅 𐑄𐐰𐐻 𐐶𐐳𐐼 𐑌𐐱𐐻 𐐯𐑌𐐻𐐲𐑉 𐐮𐑌𐐻𐐭 𐐲 𐐿𐐲𐑂𐐨𐑌𐐲𐑌𐐻 𐐻𐐭 𐑅𐐲𐐹𐐬𐑉𐐻 𐑄 𐐿𐐫𐑆 𐐱𐑂 𐑁𐑉𐐨𐐼𐐲𐑋, 𐑄𐐰𐐻 𐑄𐐩 𐑋𐐴𐐻 𐑋𐐩𐑌𐐻𐐩𐑌 𐐲 𐑁𐑉𐐨 𐑀𐐲𐑂𐐲𐑉𐑌𐑋𐐯𐑌𐐻, 𐐸𐐨 𐐿𐐫𐑆𐐼 𐐻𐐭 𐐺 𐐹𐐳𐐻 𐐻𐐭 𐐼𐐯𐑃; 𐐰𐑌𐐼 𐑄𐐩𐑉 𐐶𐐱𐑆 𐐺𐐲𐐻 𐑁𐐮𐐭 𐐸𐐭 𐐼𐐨𐑌𐐴𐐼 𐑄 𐐿𐐲𐑂𐐨𐑌𐐲𐑌𐐻 𐐱𐑂 𐑁𐑉𐐨𐐼𐐲𐑋.

15. 𐐈𐑌𐐼 𐐮𐐻 𐐿𐐩𐑋 𐐻𐐭 𐐹𐐰𐑅 𐐫𐑊𐑅𐐬, 𐑄𐐰𐐻 𐐸𐐨 𐐿𐐫𐑆𐐼 𐑄 𐐻𐐴𐐻𐑊 𐐱𐑂 𐑊𐐮𐐺𐐲𐑉𐐻𐐮 𐐻𐐭 𐐺 𐐸𐐱𐐮𐑅𐐻𐐯𐐼 𐐲𐐹𐐱𐑌 𐐯𐑂𐐲𐑉𐐮 𐐻𐐵𐑉 𐐸𐐶𐐮𐐽 𐐶𐐱𐑆 𐐮𐑌 𐐫𐑊 𐑄 𐑊𐐰𐑌𐐼, 𐐸𐐶𐐮𐐽 𐐶𐐱𐑆 𐐹𐐲𐑅𐐯𐑅𐐻 𐐺𐐴 𐑄 𐐤𐐨𐑁𐐴𐐻𐑅; 𐐰𐑌𐐼 𐑄𐐲𐑅 𐐣𐐬𐑉𐐬𐑌𐐴 𐐹𐑊𐐰𐑌𐐻𐐯𐐼 𐑄 𐑅𐐻𐐰𐑌𐐼𐐲𐑉𐐼 𐐱𐑂 𐑊𐐮𐐺𐐲𐑉𐐻𐐮 𐐰𐑋𐐲𐑍 𐑄 𐐤𐐨𐑁𐐴𐐻𐑅. 𐐈𐑌𐐼 𐑄𐐩 𐐺𐐨𐑀𐐰𐑌 𐐻𐐭 𐐸𐐰𐑂 𐐹𐐨𐑅 𐐰𐑀𐐯𐑌 𐐮𐑌 𐑄 𐑊𐐰𐑌𐐼; 𐐰𐑌𐐼 𐑄𐐲𐑅 𐑄𐐩 𐐼𐐮𐐼 𐑋𐐩𐑌𐐻𐐩𐑌 𐐹𐐨𐑅 𐐮𐑌 𐑄 𐑊𐐰𐑌𐐼, 𐐲𐑌𐐻𐐮𐑊 𐑌𐐨𐑉𐑊𐐮 𐑄 𐐯𐑌𐐼 𐐱𐑂 𐑄 𐑌𐐴𐑌𐐻𐐨𐑌𐑃 𐐷𐐨𐑉 𐐱𐑂 𐑄 𐑉𐐩𐑌 𐐱𐑂 𐑄 𐐾𐐲𐐾𐐯𐑆. 𐐈𐑌𐐼 𐐐𐐨𐑊𐐩𐑋𐐲𐑌 𐐰𐑌𐐼 𐑄 𐐸𐐴 𐐹𐑉𐐨𐑅𐐻𐑅 𐐼𐐮𐐼 𐐫𐑊𐑅𐐬 𐑋𐐩𐑌𐐻𐐩𐑌 𐐫𐑉𐐼𐐲𐑉 𐐮𐑌 𐑄 𐐽𐐲𐑉𐐽; 𐐷𐐩, 𐐨𐑂𐑌 𐑁𐐫𐑉 𐑄 𐑅𐐹𐐩𐑅 𐐱𐑂 𐑁𐐬𐑉 𐐷𐐨𐑉𐑆 𐐼𐐮𐐼 𐑄𐐩 𐐸𐐰𐑂 𐑋𐐲𐐽 𐐹𐐨𐑅 𐐰𐑌𐐼 𐑉𐐨𐐾𐐱𐐮𐑅𐐮𐑍 𐐮𐑌 𐑄 𐐽𐐲𐑉𐐽.

16. 𐐈𐑌𐐼 𐐮𐐻 𐐿𐐩𐑋 𐐻𐐭 𐐹𐐰𐑅 𐑄𐐰𐐻 𐑄𐐩𐑉 𐐶𐐲𐑉 𐑋𐐯𐑌𐐮 𐐸𐐭 𐐼𐐴𐐼, 𐑁𐐲𐑉𐑋𐑊𐐮 𐐺𐐨𐑊𐐨𐑂𐐮𐑍 𐑄𐐰𐐻 𐑄𐐩𐑉 𐑅𐐬𐑊𐑆 𐐶𐐲𐑉 𐑉𐐨𐐼𐐨𐑋𐐼 𐐺𐐴 𐑄 𐐢𐐫𐑉𐐼 𐐖𐐨𐑆𐐲𐑅 𐐗𐑉𐐴𐑅𐐻; 𐑄𐐲𐑅 𐑄𐐩 𐐶𐐯𐑌𐐻 𐐵𐐻 𐐱𐑂 𐑄 𐐶𐐲𐑉𐑊𐐼 𐑉𐐨𐐾𐐱𐐮𐑅𐐮𐑍. 𐐈𐑌𐐼 𐑄𐐩𐑉 𐐶𐐲𐑉 𐑅𐐲𐑋 𐐸𐐭 𐐼𐐴𐐼 𐐶𐐮𐑄 𐑁𐐨𐑂𐐲𐑉𐑆, 𐐸𐐶𐐮𐐽 𐐰𐐻 𐑅𐐲𐑋 𐑅𐐨𐑆𐑌𐑆 𐐱𐑂 𐑄 𐐷𐐨𐑉 𐐶𐐱𐑆 𐑂𐐯𐑉𐐮 𐑁𐑉𐐨𐐿𐐶𐐯𐑌𐐻 𐐮𐑌 𐑄 𐑊𐐰𐑌𐐼; 𐐺𐐲𐐻 𐑌𐐱𐐻 𐑅𐐬 𐑋𐐲𐐽 𐐶𐐮𐑄 𐑁𐐨𐑂𐐲𐑉𐑆, 𐐺𐐨𐐿𐐫𐑆 𐐱𐑂 𐑄 𐐯𐐿𐑅𐐯𐑊𐐯𐑌𐐻 𐐿𐐶𐐱𐑊𐐮𐐻𐐮𐑆 𐐱𐑂 𐑄 𐑋𐐯𐑌𐐮 𐐹𐑊𐐰𐑌𐐻𐑅 𐐰𐑌𐐼 𐑉𐐭𐐻𐑅 𐐸𐐶𐐮𐐽 𐐘𐐱𐐼 𐐸𐐰𐐼 𐐹𐑉𐐨𐐹𐐩𐑉𐐯𐐼 𐐻𐐭 𐑉𐐨𐑋𐐭𐑂 𐑄 𐐿𐐫𐑆 𐐱𐑂 𐐼𐐨𐑆𐐨𐑆𐐯𐑆, 𐐻𐐭 𐐸𐐶𐐮𐐽 𐑋𐐯𐑌 𐐶𐐲𐑉 𐑅𐐲𐐺𐐾𐐯𐐿𐐻 𐐺𐐴 𐑄 𐑌𐐩𐐽𐐲𐑉 𐐱𐑂 𐑄 𐐿𐑊𐐴𐑋𐐯𐐻. 𐐒𐐲𐐻 𐑄𐐩𐑉 𐐶𐐲𐑉 𐑋𐐯𐑌𐐮 𐐸𐐭 𐐼𐐴𐐼 𐐶𐐮𐑄 𐐬𐑊𐐼 𐐩𐐾; 𐐰𐑌𐐼 𐑄𐐬𐑆 𐐸𐐭 𐐼𐐴𐐼 𐐮𐑌 𐑄 𐑁𐐩𐑃 𐐱𐑂 𐐗𐑉𐐴𐑅𐐻 𐐪𐑉 𐐸𐐰𐐹𐐮 𐐮𐑌 𐐸𐐮𐑋, 𐐰𐑆 𐐶𐐨 𐑋𐐲𐑅𐐻 𐑌𐐨𐐼𐑆 𐑅𐐲𐐹𐐬𐑆. 𐐤𐐵 𐐶𐐨 𐐶𐐮𐑊 𐑉𐐨𐐻𐐲𐑉𐑌 𐐮𐑌 𐐵𐐲𐑉 𐑉𐐨𐐿𐐫𐑉𐐼 𐐻𐐭 𐐈𐑋𐐰𐑊𐐮𐐿𐐴𐐲, 𐐰𐑌𐐼 𐑄𐐬𐑆 𐐸𐐭 𐐸𐐰𐐼 𐑁𐑊𐐯𐐼 𐐶𐐮𐑄 𐐸𐐮𐑋 𐐮𐑌𐐻𐐭 𐑄 𐐶𐐮𐑊𐐼𐐲𐑉𐑌𐐯𐑅; 𐑁𐐫𐑉 𐐺𐐨𐐸𐐬𐑊𐐼 𐐸𐐨 𐐸𐐰𐐼 𐐻𐐩𐐿𐑌 𐑄𐐬𐑆 𐐸𐐭 𐐶𐐯𐑌𐐻 𐐶𐐮𐑄 𐐸𐐮𐑋, 𐐰𐑌𐐼 𐐶𐐯𐑌𐐻 𐐲𐐹 𐐮𐑌 𐑄 𐑊𐐰𐑌𐐼 𐐱𐑂 𐐤𐐨𐑁𐐴 𐐰𐑋𐐲𐑍 𐑄 𐐢𐐩𐑋𐐲𐑌𐐴𐐻𐑅, 𐐰𐑌𐐼 𐐼𐐮𐐼 𐑅𐐻𐐲𐑉 𐐲𐐹 𐑄 𐐢𐐩𐑋𐐲𐑌𐐴𐐻𐑅 𐐻𐐭 𐐰𐑍𐑀𐐲𐑉 𐐰𐑀𐐯𐑌𐑅𐐻 𐑄 𐐹𐐨𐐹𐑊 𐐱𐑂 𐐤𐐨𐑁𐐴, 𐐮𐑌𐑅𐐬𐑋𐐲𐐽 𐑄𐐰𐐻 𐑄 𐐿𐐮𐑍 𐐱𐑂 𐑄 𐐢𐐩𐑋𐐲𐑌𐐴𐐻𐑅

𐑅𐐯𐑌𐐻 𐐰 𐐹𐑉𐐪𐐿𐑊𐐲𐑋𐐩𐑇𐐲𐑌 𐑃𐑉𐐭𐐵𐐻 𐐫𐑊 𐐸𐐮𐑆 𐑊𐐰𐑌𐐼, 𐐲𐑋𐐲𐑍 𐐫𐑊 𐐸𐐮𐑆 𐐹𐐨𐐹𐑊, 𐑄𐐰𐐻 𐑄𐐩 𐑇𐐳𐐼 𐑀𐐰𐑄𐐲𐑉 𐑄𐐯𐑋𐑅𐐯𐑊𐑂𐑆 𐐻𐐭𐑀𐐯𐑄𐐲𐑉 𐐲𐑀𐐯𐑌, 𐐻𐐭 𐑀𐐬 𐐻𐐭 𐐺𐐰𐐻𐑊 𐐲𐑀𐐯𐑌𐑅𐐻 𐑄 𐐤𐐨𐑁𐐴𐐻𐑅.

17. 𐐈𐑌𐐼 𐐮𐐻 𐐿𐐩𐑋 𐐻𐐭 𐐹𐐪𐑅 𐑄𐐰𐐻 𐐸𐐶𐐯𐑌 𐑄 𐐹𐑉𐐪𐐿𐑊𐐲𐑋𐐩𐑇𐐲𐑌 𐐸𐐰𐐼 𐑀𐐱𐑌 𐑁𐐬𐑉𐑃 𐐲𐑋𐐲𐑍 𐑄𐐯𐑋, 𐑄𐐩 𐐶𐐲𐑉 𐐯𐐿𐑅𐐨𐐼𐐮𐑍𐑊𐐨 𐐲𐑁𐑉𐐩𐐼; 𐐷𐐩, 𐑄𐐩 𐑁𐐨𐑉𐐼 𐐻𐐭 𐐼𐐮𐑅𐐹𐑊𐐨𐑆 𐑄 𐐿𐐮𐑍, 𐐰𐑌𐐼 𐑄𐐩 𐐫𐑊𐑅𐐬 𐑁𐐨𐑉𐐼 𐐻𐐭 𐑀𐐬 𐐻𐐭 𐐺𐐰𐐻𐑊 𐐲𐑀𐐯𐑌𐑅𐐻 𐑄 𐐤𐐨𐑁𐐴𐐻𐑅, 𐑊𐐯𐑅𐐻 𐑄𐐩 𐑇𐐳𐐼 𐑊𐐭𐑆 𐑄𐐩𐑉 𐑊𐐴𐑂𐑆. 𐐈𐑌𐐼 𐐮𐐻 𐐿𐐩𐑋 𐐻𐐭 𐐹𐐪𐑅 𐑄𐐰𐐻 𐑄𐐩 𐐶𐐳𐐼 𐑌𐐱𐐻, 𐐫𐑉 𐑄 𐑋𐐬𐑉 𐐹𐐪𐑉𐐻 𐐱𐑂 𐑄𐐯𐑋 𐐶𐐳𐐼 𐑌𐐱𐐻, 𐐬𐐺𐐩 𐑄 𐐿𐐱𐑋𐐰𐑌𐐼𐑋𐐯𐑌𐐻𐑅 𐐱𐑂 𐑄 𐐿𐐮𐑍.

18. 𐐈𐑌𐐼 𐑌𐐵 𐐮𐐻 𐐿𐐩𐑋 𐐻𐐭 𐐹𐐪𐑅 𐑄𐐰𐐻 𐑄 𐐿𐐮𐑍 𐐶𐐱𐑆 𐑉𐐫𐑃 𐐺𐐨𐐿𐐫𐑆 𐐱𐑂 𐑄𐐩𐑉 𐐼𐐮𐑅𐐬𐐺𐐨𐐼𐐨𐐯𐑌𐑅; 𐑄𐐯𐑉𐑁𐐬𐑉 𐐸𐐨 𐑀𐐩𐑂 𐐈𐑋𐐰𐑊𐐮𐐿𐐴𐐲 𐑄 𐐿𐐱𐑋𐐰𐑌𐐼 𐐱𐑂 𐑄𐐰𐐻 𐐹𐐪𐑉𐐻 𐐱𐑂 𐐸𐐮𐑆 𐐪𐑉𐑋𐐨 𐐸𐐶𐐮𐐽 𐐶𐐱𐑆 𐐬𐐺𐐨𐐼𐐨𐐯𐑌𐐻 𐐲𐑌𐐻𐐭 𐐸𐐮𐑆 𐐿𐐱𐑋𐐰𐑌𐐼𐑆, 𐐰𐑌𐐼 𐐿𐐱𐑋𐐰𐑌𐐼𐐯𐐼 𐐸𐐮𐑋 𐑄𐐰𐐻 𐐸𐐨 𐑇𐐳𐐼 𐑀𐐬 𐑁𐐬𐑉𐑃 𐐰𐑌𐐼 𐐿𐐱𐑋𐐹𐐯𐑊 𐑄𐐯𐑋 𐐻𐐭 𐐪𐑉𐑋𐑆. 𐐤𐐵 𐐺𐐨𐐸𐐬𐑊𐐼, 𐑄𐐮𐑅 𐐶𐐱𐑆 𐑄 𐐼𐐨𐑆𐐴𐑉 𐐱𐑂 𐐈𐑋𐐰𐑊𐐮𐐿𐐴𐐲; 𐑁𐐫𐑉 𐐸𐐨 𐐺𐐨𐐮𐑍 𐐰 𐑂𐐯𐑉𐐨 𐑅𐐲𐐻𐑊 𐑋𐐰𐑌 𐐻𐐭 𐐼𐐭 𐐨𐑂𐑊, 𐑄𐐯𐑉𐑁𐐬𐑉 𐐸𐐨 𐑊𐐩𐐼 𐑄 𐐹𐑊𐐰𐑌 𐐮𐑌 𐐸𐐮𐑆 𐐸𐐪𐑉𐐻 𐐻𐐭 𐐼𐐨𐑃𐑉𐐬𐑌 𐑄 𐐿𐐮𐑍 𐐱𐑂 𐑄 𐐢𐐩𐑋𐐲𐑌𐐴𐐻𐑅. 𐐈𐑌𐐼 𐑌𐐵 𐐸𐐨 𐐸𐐰𐐼 𐑀𐐱𐐻 𐑄 𐐿𐐱𐑋𐐰𐑌𐐼 𐐱𐑂 𐑄𐐬𐑆 𐐹𐐪𐑉𐐻𐑅 𐐱𐑂 𐑄 𐐢𐐩𐑋𐐲𐑌𐐴𐐻𐑅 𐐸𐐭 𐐶𐐲𐑉 𐐮𐑌 𐑁𐐩𐑂𐐲𐑉 𐐱𐑂 𐑄 𐐿𐐮𐑍; 𐐰𐑌𐐼 𐐸𐐨 𐑅𐐫𐐻 𐐻𐐭 𐑀𐐩𐑌 𐑁𐐩𐑂𐐲𐑉 𐐱𐑂 𐑄𐐬𐑆 𐐸𐐭 𐐶𐐲𐑉 𐑌𐐱𐐻 𐐬𐐺𐐨𐐼𐐨𐐯𐑌𐐻; 𐑄𐐯𐑉𐑁𐐬𐑉 𐐸𐐨 𐐶𐐯𐑌𐐻 𐑁𐐫𐑉𐐶𐐲𐑉𐐼 𐐻𐐭 𐑄 𐐹𐑊𐐩𐑅 𐐸𐐶𐐮𐐽 𐐶𐐱𐑆 𐐿𐐫𐑊𐐼 𐐄𐑌𐐴𐐼𐐲, 𐑁𐐫𐑉 𐑄𐐮𐑄𐐲𐑉 𐐸𐐰𐐼 𐐫𐑊 𐑄 𐐢𐐩𐑋𐐲𐑌𐐴𐐻𐑅 𐑁𐑊𐐯𐐼; 𐑁𐐫𐑉 𐑄𐐩 𐐼𐐮𐑅𐐿𐐲𐑂𐐲𐑉𐐼 𐑄 𐐪𐑉𐑋𐐨 𐐿𐐲𐑋𐐮𐑍, 𐐰𐑌𐐼 𐑅𐐲𐐹𐐬𐑆𐐮𐑍 𐑄𐐰𐐻 𐑄𐐩 𐐶𐐲𐑉 𐐿𐐲𐑋𐐮𐑍 𐐻𐐭 𐐼𐐯𐑅𐐻𐑉𐑎 𐑄𐐯𐑋, 𐑄𐐯𐑉𐑁𐐬𐑉 𐑄𐐩 𐑁𐑊𐐯𐐼 𐐻𐐭 𐐄𐑌𐐴𐐼𐐲, 𐐻𐐭 𐑄 𐐹𐑊𐐩𐑅 𐐱𐑂 𐐪𐑉𐑋𐑆. 𐐈𐑌𐐼 𐑄𐐩 𐐸𐐰𐐼 𐐲𐐹𐑎𐑌𐐻𐐯𐐼 𐐰 𐑋𐐰𐑌 𐐻𐐭 𐐺𐐨 𐐰 𐐿𐐮𐑍 𐐰𐑌𐐼 𐐰 𐑊𐐨𐐼𐐲𐑉 𐐬𐑂𐐲𐑉 𐑄𐐯𐑋, 𐐺𐐨𐐮𐑍 𐑁𐐮𐐿𐑅𐐻 𐐮𐑌 𐑄𐐩𐑉 𐑋𐐴𐑌𐐼𐑆 𐐶𐐮𐑄 𐐰 𐐼𐐨𐐻𐐲𐑉𐑋𐐮𐑌𐐼 𐑉𐐯𐑆𐐬𐑊𐐭𐑇𐐲𐑌 𐑄𐐰𐐻 𐑄𐐩 𐐶𐐳𐐼 𐑌𐐱𐐻 𐐺𐐨 𐑅𐐲𐐺𐐾𐐯𐐿𐐻𐐯𐐼 𐐻𐐭 𐑀𐐬 𐐲𐑀𐐯𐑌𐑅𐐻 𐑄 𐐤𐐨𐑁𐐴𐐻𐑅.

19. 𐐈𐑌𐐼 𐐮𐐻 𐐿𐐩𐑋 𐐻𐐭 𐐹𐐪𐑅 𐑄𐐰𐐻 𐑄𐐩 𐐸𐐰𐐼 𐑀𐐰𐑄𐐲𐑉𐐼 𐑄𐐯𐑋𐑅𐐯𐑊𐑂𐑆 𐐻𐐭𐑀𐐯𐑄𐐲𐑉 𐐲𐐹𐐱𐑌 𐑄 𐐻𐐱𐐹 𐐱𐑂 𐑄 𐑋𐐵𐑌𐐻 𐐸𐐶𐐮𐐽 𐐶𐐱𐑆 𐐿𐐫𐑊𐐼 𐐈𐑌𐐻𐐮𐐹𐐲𐑅, 𐐮𐑌 𐐹𐑉𐐯𐐹𐐲𐑉𐐩𐑇𐐲𐑌 𐐻𐐭 𐐺𐐰𐐻𐑊. 𐐤𐐵 𐐮𐐻 𐐶𐐱𐑆 𐑌𐐱𐐻 𐐈𐑋𐐰𐑊𐐮𐐿𐐴𐐲'𐑆 𐐮𐑌𐐻𐐯𐑌𐑇𐐲𐑌 𐐻𐐭 𐑀𐐮𐑂 𐑄𐐯𐑋 𐐺𐐰𐐻𐑊, 𐐲𐐿𐐫𐑉𐐼𐐮𐑍 𐐻𐐭 𐑄 𐐿𐐱𐑋𐐰𐑌𐐼𐑋𐐯𐑌𐐻𐑅 𐐱𐑂 𐑄 𐐿𐐮𐑍; 𐐺𐐲𐐻 𐐺𐐨𐐸𐐬𐑊𐐼, 𐐮𐐻 𐐶𐐱𐑆 𐐸𐐮𐑆 𐐮𐑌𐐻𐐯𐑌𐑇𐐲𐑌 𐐻𐐭 𐑀𐐩𐑌 𐑁𐐩𐑂𐐲𐑉 𐐶𐐮𐑄 𐑄 𐐪𐑉𐑋𐐨𐑆 𐐱𐑂 𐑄 𐐢𐐩𐑋𐐲𐑌𐐴𐐻𐑅, 𐑄𐐰𐐻 𐐸𐐨 𐑋𐐴𐐻 𐐹𐑊𐐩𐑅 𐐸𐐮𐑋𐑅𐐯𐑊𐑁 𐐰𐐻 𐑄𐐩𐑉 𐐸𐐯𐐼 𐐰𐑌𐐼 𐐼𐐨𐑃𐑉𐐬𐑌 𐑄 𐐿𐐮𐑍, 𐐰𐑌𐐼 𐐻𐐩𐐿 𐐹𐐲𐑆𐐯𐑇𐐲𐑌 𐐱𐑂 𐑄 𐐿𐐮𐑍𐐼𐐲𐑋. 𐐈𐑌𐐼 𐐺𐐨𐐸𐐬𐑊𐐼, 𐐮𐐻 𐐿𐐩𐑋 𐐻𐐭 𐐹𐐪𐑅 𐑄𐐰𐐻 𐐸𐐨 𐐿𐐫𐑆𐐼 𐐸𐐮𐑆 𐐪𐑉𐑋𐐨 𐐻𐐭 𐐹𐐮𐐽 𐑄𐐩𐑉 𐐻𐐯𐑌𐐻𐑅 𐐮𐑌 𐑄 𐑂𐐰𐑊𐐨 𐐸𐐶𐐮𐐽 𐐶𐐱𐑆 𐑌𐐨𐑉 𐑄 𐑋𐐵𐑌𐐻 𐐈𐑌𐐻𐐮𐐹𐐲𐑅. 𐐈𐑌𐐼 𐐮𐐻 𐐿𐐩𐑋 𐐻𐐭 𐐹𐐪𐑅 𐑄𐐰𐐻 𐐸𐐶𐐯𐑌 𐐮𐐻 𐐶𐐱𐑆 𐑌𐐴𐐻, 𐐸𐐨 𐑅𐐯𐑌𐐻 𐐰 𐑅𐐨𐐿𐑉𐐯𐐻 𐐯𐑋𐐺𐐲𐑅𐐨 𐐮𐑌𐐻𐐭 𐑄 𐑋𐐵𐑌𐐻 𐐈𐑌𐐻𐐮𐐹𐐲𐑅, 𐐼𐐨𐑆𐐴𐑉𐐮𐑍 𐑄𐐰𐐻 𐑄 𐑊𐐨𐐼𐐲𐑉 𐐱𐑂 𐑄𐐬𐑆 𐐸𐐭 𐐶𐐲𐑉 𐐲𐐹𐐱𐑌 𐑄 𐑋𐐵𐑌𐐻, 𐐸𐐭𐑆 𐑌𐐩𐑋 𐐶𐐱𐑆 𐐢𐐨𐐸𐐱𐑌𐐻𐐴, 𐑄𐐰𐐻 𐐸𐐨 𐑇𐐳𐐼 𐐿𐐲𐑋 𐐼𐐵𐑌 𐐻𐐭 𐑄 𐑁𐐳𐐻 𐐱𐑂 𐑄 𐑋𐐵𐑌𐐻, 𐑁𐐫𐑉 𐐸𐐨 𐐼𐐨𐑆𐐴𐑉𐐼 𐐻𐐭 𐑅𐐹𐐨𐐿 𐐶𐐮𐑄 𐐸𐐮𐑋.

20. 𐐈𐑌𐐼 𐐮𐐻 𐐿𐐩𐑋 𐐻𐐭 𐐹𐐪𐑅 𐑄𐐰𐐻 𐐸𐐶𐐯𐑌 𐐢𐐨𐐸𐐱𐑌𐐻𐐴 𐑉𐐨𐑅𐐨𐑂𐐼 𐑄 𐑋𐐯𐑅𐐯𐐾, 𐐸𐐨 𐐼𐐲𐑉𐑅𐐻 𐑌𐐱𐐻 𐑀𐐬 𐐼𐐵𐑌 𐐻𐐭 𐑄 𐑁𐐳𐐻 𐐱𐑂 𐑄 𐑋𐐵𐑌𐐻. 𐐈𐑌𐐼 𐐮𐐻 𐐿𐐩𐑋 𐐻𐐭 𐐹𐐪𐑅 𐑄𐐰𐐻 𐐈𐑋𐐰𐑊𐐮𐐿𐐴𐐲 𐑅𐐯𐑌𐐻 𐐲𐑀𐐯𐑌 𐑄 𐑅𐐯𐐿𐐲𐑌𐐼 𐐻𐐴𐑋, 𐐼𐐨𐑆𐐴𐑉𐐮𐑍 𐐸𐐮𐑋 𐐻𐐭 𐐿𐐲𐑋 𐐼𐐵𐑌. 𐐈𐑌𐐼 𐐮𐐻 𐐿𐐩𐑋 𐐻𐐭 𐐹𐐪𐑅 𐑄𐐰𐐻 𐐢𐐨𐐸𐐱𐑌𐐻𐐴 𐐶𐐳𐐼 𐑌𐐱𐐻; 𐐰𐑌𐐼 𐐸𐐨 𐑅𐐯𐑌𐐻 𐐲𐑀𐐯𐑌 𐑄 𐑃𐐲𐑉𐐼 𐐻𐐴𐑋. 𐐈𐑌𐐼 𐐮𐐻 𐐿𐐩𐑋 𐐻𐐭 𐐹𐐪𐑅 𐑄𐐰𐐻 𐐸𐐶𐐯𐑌 𐐈𐑋𐐰𐑊𐐮𐐿𐐴𐐲 𐑁𐐵𐑌𐐼 𐑄𐐰𐐻 𐐸𐐨 𐐿𐐳𐐼 𐑌𐐱𐐻 𐑀𐐯𐐻 𐐢𐐨𐐸𐐱𐑌𐐻𐐴 𐐻𐐭 𐐿𐐲𐑋 𐐼𐐵𐑌 𐐫𐑁 𐑁𐑉𐐱𐑋 𐑄 𐑋𐐵𐑌𐐻, 𐐸𐐨 𐐶𐐯𐑌𐐻 𐐲𐐹 𐐮𐑌𐐻𐐭 𐑄 𐑋𐐵𐑌𐐻, 𐑌𐐨𐑉𐑊𐐨 𐐻𐐭 𐐢𐐨𐐸𐐱𐑌𐐻𐐴'𐑆 𐐿𐐰𐑋𐐹; 𐐰𐑌𐐼 𐐸𐐨 𐑅𐐯𐑌𐐻 𐐲𐑀𐐯𐑌 𐑄 𐑁𐐬𐑉𐑃 𐐻𐐴𐑋 𐐸𐐮𐑆 𐑋𐐯𐑅𐐯𐐾 𐐲𐑌𐐻𐐭 𐐢𐐨𐐸𐐱𐑌𐐻𐐴, 𐐼𐐨𐑆𐐴𐑉𐐮𐑍 𐑄𐐰𐐻 𐐸𐐨 𐐶𐐳𐐼 𐐿𐐲𐑋 𐐼𐐵𐑌, 𐐰𐑌𐐼 𐑄𐐰𐐻 𐐸𐐨 𐐶𐐳𐐼 𐐺𐑉𐐮𐑍 𐐸𐐮𐑆 𐑀𐐪𐑉𐐼𐑆 𐐶𐐮𐑄 𐐸𐐮𐑋.

21. 𐐈𐑌𐐼 𐐮𐐻 𐐿𐐩𐑋 𐐻𐐭 𐐹𐐪𐑅 𐑄𐐰𐐻 𐐸𐐶𐐯𐑌 𐐢𐐨𐐸𐐱𐑌𐐻𐐴 𐐸𐐰𐐼 𐐿𐐲𐑋 𐐼𐐵𐑌 𐐶𐐮𐑄 𐐸𐐮𐑆 𐑀𐐪𐑉𐐼𐑆 𐐻𐐭 𐐈𐑋𐐰𐑊𐐮𐐿𐐴𐐲, 𐑄𐐰𐐻 𐐈𐑋𐐰𐑊𐐮𐐿𐐴𐐲 𐐼𐐨𐑆𐐴𐑉𐐼 𐐸𐐮𐑋 𐐻𐐭 𐐿𐐲𐑋 𐐼𐐵𐑌 𐐶𐐮𐑄 𐐸𐐮𐑆 𐐪𐑉𐑋𐐨 𐐮𐑌 𐑄 𐑌𐐴𐐻-𐐻𐐴𐑋, 𐐰𐑌𐐼 𐑅𐐲𐑉𐐵𐑌𐐼 𐑄𐐬𐑆 𐑋𐐯𐑌 𐐮𐑌 𐑄𐐩𐑉 𐐿𐐰𐑋𐐹𐑅 𐐬𐑂𐐲𐑉 𐐸𐐭𐑋 𐑄 𐐿𐐮𐑍 𐐸𐐰𐐼 𐑀𐐮𐑂𐑌 𐐸𐐮𐑋 𐐿𐐱𐑋𐐰𐑌𐐼, 𐐰𐑌𐐼 𐑄𐐰𐐻 𐐸𐐨 𐐶𐐳𐐼 𐐼𐐨𐑊𐐮𐑂𐐲𐑉 𐑄𐐯𐑋 𐐲𐐹 𐐮𐑌𐐻𐐭 𐐢𐐨𐐸𐐱𐑌𐐻𐐴'𐑆 𐐸𐐰𐑌𐐼𐑆, 𐐮𐑁 𐐸𐐨 𐐶𐐳𐐼 𐑋𐐩𐐿 𐐸𐐮𐑋 (𐐈𐑋𐐰𐑊𐐮𐐿𐐴𐐲) 𐐰 𐑅𐐯𐐿𐐲𐑌𐐼 𐑊𐐨𐐼𐐲𐑉 𐐬𐑂𐐲𐑉 𐑄 𐐸𐐬𐑊 𐐪𐑉𐑋𐐨.

22. 𐐈𐑌𐐔 𐐮𐐻 𐐿𐐩𐑋 𐐻𐐭 𐐹𐐰𐑅 𐑄𐐰𐐻 𐐢𐐨𐐸𐐱𐑌𐐻𐐴 𐐿𐐩𐑋 𐐼𐐵𐑌 𐐶𐐮𐑄 𐐸𐐮𐑆 𐑋𐐯𐑌, 𐐰𐑌𐐼 𐑅𐐲𐑉𐐵𐑌𐐼𐐯𐐼 𐑄 𐑋𐐯𐑌 𐐱𐑂 𐐈𐑋𐐰𐑊𐐮𐐿𐐴𐐲, 𐑅𐐬 𐑄𐐰𐐻 𐐺𐐨𐑁𐐬𐑉 𐑄𐐩 𐐲𐐶𐐬𐐿 𐐰𐐻 𐑄 𐐼𐐫𐑌 𐐱𐑂 𐑄 𐐼𐐩 𐑄𐐩 𐐶𐐲𐑉 𐑅𐐲𐑉𐐵𐑌𐐼𐐯𐐼 𐐺𐐴 𐑄 𐐪𐑉𐑋𐐨𐑆 𐐱𐑂 𐐢𐐨𐐸𐐱𐑌𐐻𐐴. 𐐈𐑌𐐔 𐐮𐐻 𐐿𐐩𐑋 𐐻𐐭 𐐹𐐰𐑅 𐑄𐐰𐐻 𐐸𐐶𐐯𐑌 𐑄𐐩 𐑅𐐫 𐑄𐐰𐐻 𐑄𐐩 𐐶𐐲𐑉 𐑅𐐲𐑉𐐵𐑌𐐼𐐯𐐼, 𐑄𐐩 𐐹𐑊𐐯𐐼 𐐶𐐮𐑄 𐐈𐑋𐐰𐑊𐐮𐐿𐐴𐐲 𐑄𐐰𐐻 𐐸𐐨 𐐶𐐳𐐼 𐑅𐐲𐑁𐐲𐑉 𐑄𐐯𐑋 𐐻𐐭 𐑁𐐫𐑊 𐐮𐑌 𐐶𐐮𐑄 𐑄𐐩𐑉 𐐺𐑉𐐯𐑄𐑉𐐯𐑌, 𐑄𐐰𐐻 𐑄𐐩 𐑋𐐴𐐻 𐑌𐐱𐐻 𐐺 𐐼𐐨𐑅𐐻𐑉𐐱𐐮𐐼. 𐐤𐐵 𐑄𐐮𐑅 𐐶𐐱𐑆 𐑄 𐑂𐐯𐑉𐐨 𐑃𐐮𐑍 𐐸𐐶𐐮𐐽 𐐈𐑋𐐰𐑊𐐮𐐿𐐴𐐲 𐐼𐐨𐑆𐐴𐑉𐐼.

23. 𐐈𐑌𐐔 𐐮𐐻 𐐿𐐩𐑋 𐐻𐐭 𐐹𐐰𐑅 𐑄𐐰𐐻 𐐸𐐨 𐐼𐐨𐑊𐐮𐑂𐐲𐑉𐐼 𐐸𐐮𐑆 𐑋𐐯𐑌, 𐐿𐐱𐑌𐐻𐑉𐐯𐑉𐐨 𐐻𐐭 𐑄 𐐿𐐲𐑋𐐰𐑌𐐼𐑆 𐐱𐑂 𐑄 𐐿𐐮𐑍. 𐐤𐐵 𐑄𐐮𐑅 𐐶𐐱𐑆 𐑄 𐑃𐐮𐑍 𐑄𐐰𐐻 𐐈𐑋𐐰𐑊𐐮𐐿𐐴𐐲 𐐼𐐨𐑆𐐴𐑉𐐼, 𐑄𐐰𐐻 𐐸𐐨 𐑋𐐴𐐻 𐐰𐐿𐐱𐑋𐐹𐑊𐐮𐑇 𐐸𐐮𐑆 𐐼𐐨𐑆𐐴𐑌𐑆 𐐮𐑌 𐐼𐐨𐑃𐑉𐐬𐑌𐐮𐑍 𐑄 𐐿𐐮𐑍. 𐐤𐐵 𐐮𐐻 𐐶𐐱𐑆 𐑄 𐐿𐐲𐑅𐐻𐐲𐑋 𐐲𐑋𐐲𐑍 𐑄 𐐢𐐩𐑋𐐲𐑌𐐴𐐻𐑅, 𐐮𐑁 𐑄𐐩𐑉 𐐽𐐨𐑁 𐑊𐐨𐐼𐐲𐑉 𐐶𐐱𐑆 𐐿𐐮𐑊𐐼, 𐐻𐐭 𐐲𐐹𐐱𐐮𐑌𐐻 𐑄 𐑅𐐯𐐿𐐲𐑌𐐼 𐑊𐐨𐐼𐐲𐑉 𐐻𐐭 𐐺 𐑄𐐩𐑉 𐐽𐐨𐑁 𐑊𐐨𐐼𐐲𐑉.

24. 𐐈𐑌𐐔 𐐮𐐻 𐐿𐐩𐑋 𐐻𐐭 𐐹𐐰𐑅 𐑄𐐰𐐻 𐐈𐑋𐐰𐑊𐐮𐐿𐐴𐐲 𐐿𐐫𐑆𐐼 𐑄𐐰𐐻 𐐶𐐲𐑌 𐐱𐑂 𐐸𐐮𐑆 𐑅𐐲𐑉𐑂𐐰𐑌𐐻𐑅 𐑇𐐳𐐼 𐐰𐐼𐑋𐐮𐑌𐐮𐑅𐐻𐐲𐑉 𐐹𐐱𐐮𐑆𐐲𐑌 𐐺𐐴 𐐼𐐨𐑀𐑉𐐨𐑆 𐐻𐐭 𐐢𐐨𐐸𐐱𐑌𐐻𐐴, 𐑄𐐰𐐻 𐐸𐐨 𐐼𐐴𐐼. 𐐤𐐵 𐐸𐐶𐐯𐑌 𐐢𐐨𐐸𐐱𐑌𐐻𐐴 𐐶𐐱𐑆 𐐼𐐯𐐼, 𐑄 𐐢𐐩𐑋𐐲𐑌𐐴𐐻𐑅 𐐲𐐹𐐱𐐮𐑌𐐻𐐯𐐼 𐐈𐑋𐐰𐑊𐐮𐐿𐐴𐐲 𐐻𐐭 𐐺 𐑄𐐩𐑉 𐑊𐐨𐐼𐐲𐑉 𐐰𐑌𐐼 𐑄𐐩𐑉 𐐽𐐨𐑁 𐐿𐐲𐑋𐐰𐑌𐐼𐐲𐑉. 𐐈𐑌𐐔 𐐮𐐻 𐐿𐐩𐑋 𐐻𐐭 𐐹𐐰𐑅 𐑄𐐰𐐻 𐐈𐑋𐐰𐑊𐐮𐐿𐐴𐐲 𐑋𐐪𐑉𐐽𐐻 𐐶𐐮𐑄 𐐸𐐮𐑆 𐐪𐑉𐑋𐐨𐑆 (𐑁𐐫𐑉 𐐸𐐨 𐐸𐐰𐐼 𐑀𐐩𐑌𐐼 𐐸𐐮𐑆 𐐼𐐨𐑆𐐴𐑉𐑆) 𐐻𐐭 𐑄 𐑊𐐰𐑌𐐼 𐐱𐑂 𐐤𐐨𐑁𐐴, 𐐻𐐭 𐑄 𐑅𐐮𐐻𐐨 𐐱𐑂 𐐤𐐨𐑁𐐴, 𐐸𐐶𐐮𐐽 𐐶𐐱𐑆 𐑄 𐐽𐐨𐑁 𐑅𐐮𐐻𐐨. 𐐈𐑌𐐔 𐑄 𐐿𐐮𐑍 𐐿𐐩𐑋 𐐵𐐻 𐐻𐐭 𐑋𐐨𐐻 𐐸𐐮𐑋 𐐶𐐮𐑄 𐐸𐐮𐑆 𐑀𐐪𐑉𐐼𐑆, 𐑁𐐫𐑉 𐐸𐐨 𐑅𐐲𐐹𐐬𐑆𐐼 𐑄𐐰𐐻 𐐈𐑋𐐰𐑊𐐮𐐿𐐴𐐲 𐐸𐐰𐐼 𐑁𐐳𐑊𐑁𐐮𐑊𐐼 𐐸𐐮𐑆 𐐿𐐲𐑋𐐰𐑌𐐼𐑆, 𐐰𐑌𐐼 𐑄𐐰𐐻 𐐈𐑋𐐰𐑊𐐮𐐿𐐴𐐲 𐐸𐐰𐐼 𐑀𐐰𐑄𐐲𐑉𐐼 𐐻𐐭𐑀𐐯𐑄𐐲𐑉 𐑅𐐬 𐑀𐑉𐐩𐐻 𐐰𐑌 𐐪𐑉𐑋𐐨 𐐻𐐭 𐑀𐐬 𐐲𐑀𐐯𐑌𐑅𐐻 𐑄 𐐤𐐨𐑁𐐴𐐻𐑅 𐐻𐐭 𐐺𐐰𐐻𐑊. 𐐒𐐲𐐻 𐐺𐐨𐐸𐐬𐑊𐐼, 𐐰𐑆 𐑄 𐐿𐐮𐑍 𐐿𐐩𐑋 𐐵𐐻 𐐻𐐭 𐑋𐐨𐐻 𐐸𐐮𐑋, 𐐈𐑋𐐰𐑊𐐮𐐿𐐴𐐲 𐐿𐐫𐑆𐐼 𐑄𐐰𐐻 𐐸𐐮𐑆 𐑅𐐲𐑉𐑂𐐰𐑌𐐻𐑅 𐑇𐐳𐐼 𐑀𐐬 𐑁𐐬𐑉𐑃 𐐻𐐭 𐑋𐐨𐐻 𐑄 𐐿𐐮𐑍. 𐐈𐑌𐐔 𐑄𐐩 𐐶𐐯𐑌𐐻 𐐰𐑌𐐼 𐐺𐐵𐐼 𐑄𐐯𐑋𐑅𐐯𐑊𐑂𐑆 𐐺𐐨𐑁𐐬𐑉 𐑄 𐐿𐐮𐑍, 𐐰𐑆 𐐮𐑁 𐐻𐐭 𐑉𐐯𐑂𐐲𐑉𐐯𐑌𐑅 𐐸𐐮𐑋, 𐐺𐐨𐐿𐐫𐑆 𐐱𐑂 𐐸𐐮𐑆 𐑀𐑉𐐩𐐻𐑌𐐯𐑅. 𐐈𐑌𐐔 𐐮𐐻 𐐿𐐩𐑋 𐐻𐐭 𐐹𐐰𐑅 𐑄𐐰𐐻 𐑄 𐐿𐐮𐑍 𐐹𐐳𐐻 𐑁𐐬𐑉𐑃 𐐸𐐮𐑆 𐐸𐐰𐑌𐐼 𐐻𐐭 𐑉𐐩𐑆 𐑄𐐯𐑋, 𐐰𐑆 𐐶𐐱𐑆 𐑄 𐐿𐐲𐑅𐐻𐐲𐑋 𐐶𐐮𐑄 𐑄 𐐢𐐩𐑋𐐲𐑌𐐴𐐻𐑅, 𐐰𐑆 𐐲 𐐻𐐬𐐿𐐲𐑌 𐐱𐑂 𐐹𐐨𐑅, 𐐸𐐶𐐮𐐽 𐐿𐐲𐑅𐐻𐐲𐑋 𐑄𐐩 𐐸𐐰𐐼 𐐻𐐩𐐿𐐲𐑌 𐑁𐑉𐐱𐑋 𐑄 𐐤𐐨𐑁𐐴𐐻𐑅. 𐐈𐑌𐐔 𐐮𐐻 𐐿𐐩𐑋 𐐻𐐭 𐐹𐐰𐑅 𐑄𐐰𐐻 𐐸𐐶𐐯𐑌 𐐸𐐨 𐐸𐐰𐐼 𐑉𐐩𐑆𐐼 𐑄 𐑁𐐲𐑉𐑅𐐻 𐑁𐑉𐐱𐑋 𐑄 𐑀𐑉𐐵𐑌𐐼, 𐐺𐐨𐐸𐐬𐑊𐐼 𐐸𐐨 𐑅𐐻𐐰𐐺𐐼 𐑄 𐐿𐐮𐑍 𐐻𐐭 𐑄 𐐸𐐪𐑉𐐻; 𐐰𐑌𐐼 𐐸𐐨 𐑁𐐯𐑊 𐐻𐐭 𐑄 𐐲𐑉𐑃. 𐐤𐐵 𐑄 𐑅𐐲𐑉𐑂𐐰𐑌𐐻𐑅 𐐱𐑂 𐑄 𐐿𐐮𐑍 𐑁𐑊𐐯𐐼; 𐐰𐑌𐐼 𐑄 𐑅𐐲𐑉𐑂𐐰𐑌𐐻𐑅 𐐱𐑂 𐐈𐑋𐐰𐑊𐐮𐐿𐐴𐐲 𐑉𐐩𐑆𐐼 𐐲 𐐿𐑉𐐴, 𐑅𐐩𐐮𐑍, 𐐒𐐨𐐸𐐬𐑊𐐼 𐑄 𐑅𐐲𐑉𐑂𐐰𐑌𐐻𐑅 𐐱𐑂 𐑄 𐐿𐐮𐑍 𐐸𐐰𐑂 𐑅𐐻𐐰𐐺𐐼 𐐸𐐮𐑋 𐐻𐐭 𐑄 𐐸𐐪𐑉𐐻, 𐐰𐑌𐐼 𐐸𐐨 𐐸𐐰𐑆 𐑁𐐫𐑊𐐲𐑌 𐐰𐑌𐐼 𐑄𐐩 𐐸𐐰𐑂 𐑁𐑊𐐯𐐼; 𐐺𐐨𐐸𐐬𐑊𐐼, 𐐿𐐲𐑋 𐐰𐑌𐐼 𐑅𐐨.

25. 𐐈𐑌𐐔 𐐮𐐻 𐐿𐐩𐑋 𐐻𐐭 𐐹𐐰𐑅 𐑄𐐰𐐻 𐐈𐑋𐐰𐑊𐐮𐐿𐐴𐐲 𐐿𐐲𐑋𐐰𐑌𐐼𐐯𐐼 𐑄𐐰𐐻 𐐸𐐮𐑆 𐐪𐑉𐑋𐐨𐑆 𐑇𐐳𐐼 𐑋𐐪𐑉𐐽 𐑁𐐬𐑉𐑃, 𐐰𐑌𐐼 𐑅𐐨 𐐸𐐶𐐱𐐻 𐐸𐐰𐐼 𐐸𐐰𐐹𐐲𐑌𐐼 𐐻𐐭 𐑄 𐐿𐐮𐑍; 𐐰𐑌𐐼 𐐸𐐶𐐯𐑌 𐑄𐐩 𐐸𐐰𐐼 𐐿𐐲𐑋 𐐻𐐭 𐑄 𐑅𐐹𐐱𐐻, 𐐰𐑌𐐼 𐑁𐐵𐑌𐐼 𐑄 𐐿𐐮𐑍 𐑊𐐴𐐮𐑍 𐐮𐑌 𐐸𐐮𐑆 𐑀𐐬𐑉, 𐐈𐑋𐐰𐑊𐐮𐐿𐐴𐐲 𐐹𐑉𐐨𐐻𐐯𐑌𐐼𐐯𐐼 𐐻𐐭 𐐺 𐑉𐐫𐑃, 𐐰𐑌𐐼 𐑅𐐯𐐼, 𐐐𐐭𐑅𐐬𐐯𐑂𐐲𐑉 𐑊𐐲𐑂𐐼 𐑄 𐐿𐐮𐑍, 𐑊𐐯𐐻 𐐸𐐮𐑋 𐑀𐐬 𐑁𐐬𐑉𐑃, 𐐰𐑌𐐼 𐐹𐐲𐑉𐑅𐐭 𐐸𐐮𐑆 𐑅𐐲𐑉𐑂𐐰𐑌𐐻𐑅 𐑄𐐰𐐻 𐑄𐐩 𐑋𐐩 𐐺 𐑅𐑊𐐩𐑌.

26. 𐐈𐑌𐐔 𐐮𐐻 𐐿𐐩𐑋 𐐻𐐭 𐐹𐐰𐑅 𐑄𐐰𐐻 𐐫𐑊 𐑄𐐩 𐐸𐐭 𐑊𐐲𐑂𐐼 𐑄 𐐿𐐮𐑍, 𐐸𐐶𐐯𐑌 𐑄𐐩 𐐸𐐲𐑉𐐼 𐑄𐐨𐑆 𐐶𐐲𐑉𐐼𐑆, 𐐿𐐩𐑋 𐑁𐐬𐑉𐑃 𐐰𐑌𐐼 𐐹𐐲𐑉𐑅𐐭𐐼 𐐰𐑁𐐻𐐲𐑉 𐑄 𐑅𐐲𐑉𐑂𐐰𐑌𐐻𐑅 𐐱𐑂 𐑄 𐐿𐐮𐑍. 𐐤𐐵 𐐸𐐶𐐯𐑌 𐑄 𐑅𐐲𐑉𐑂𐐰𐑌𐐻𐑅 𐐱𐑂 𐑄 𐐿𐐮𐑍 𐑅𐐫 𐐰𐑌 𐐪𐑉𐑋𐐨 𐐹𐐲𐑉𐑅𐐭𐐮𐑍 𐐰𐑁𐐻𐐲𐑉 𐑄𐐯𐑋, 𐑄𐐩 𐐶𐐲𐑉 𐑁𐑉𐐴𐐻𐐲𐑌𐐼 𐐲𐑀𐐯𐑌 𐐰𐑌𐐼 𐑁𐑊𐐯𐐼 𐐮𐑌𐐻𐐭 𐑄 𐐶𐐮𐑊𐐼𐐲𐑉𐑌𐐯𐑅, 𐐰𐑌𐐼 𐐿𐐩𐑋 𐐬𐑂𐐲𐑉 𐐮𐑌𐐻𐐭 𐑄 𐑊𐐰𐑌𐐼 𐐱𐑂 𐐞𐐰𐑉𐐲𐐸𐐯𐑋𐑊𐐲 𐐰𐑌𐐼 𐐾𐐱𐐮𐑌𐐼 𐑄 𐐹𐐨𐐹𐑊 𐐱𐑂 𐐈𐑋𐐲𐑌; 𐐰𐑌𐐼 𐑄 𐐪𐑉𐑋𐐨 𐐸𐐶𐐮𐐽 𐐹𐐲𐑉𐑅𐐭𐐼 𐐰𐑁𐐻𐐲𐑉 𐑄𐐯𐑋 𐑉𐐨𐐻𐐲𐑉𐑌𐐼, 𐐸𐐰𐑂𐐮𐑍 𐐹𐐲𐑉𐑅𐐭𐐼 𐐰𐑁𐐻𐐲𐑉 𐑄𐐯𐑋 𐐮𐑌 𐑂𐐩𐑌; 𐐰𐑌𐐼 𐑄𐐲𐑅 𐐈𐑋𐐰𐑊𐐮𐐿𐐴𐐲, 𐐺𐐴 𐐸𐐮𐑆 𐑁𐑉𐐫𐐼, 𐑀𐐩𐑌𐐼 𐑄 𐐸𐐪𐑉𐐻𐑅 𐐱𐑂 𐑄 𐐹𐐨𐐹𐑊.

27. 𐐈𐑌𐐔 𐐮𐐻 𐐿𐐩𐑋 𐐻𐐭 𐐹𐐰𐑅 𐐱𐑌 𐑄 𐑋𐐱𐑉𐐬, 𐐸𐐨 𐐯𐑌𐐻𐐲𐑉𐐼 𐑄 𐑅𐐮𐐻𐐨 𐐤𐐨𐑁𐐴 𐐶𐐮𐑄 𐐸𐐮𐑆 𐐪𐑉𐑋𐐨𐑆, 𐐰𐑌𐐼 𐐻𐐳𐐿 𐐹𐐲𐑆𐐯𐑇𐐲𐑌 𐐱𐑂 𐑄 𐑅𐐮𐐻𐐨. 𐐈𐑌𐐔 𐑌𐐵 𐐮𐐻 𐐿𐐩𐑋 𐐻𐐭 𐐹𐐰𐑅 𐑄𐐰𐐻 𐑄 𐐿𐐶𐐨𐑌, 𐐸𐐶𐐯𐑌 𐑇𐐨 𐐸𐐰𐐼 𐐸𐐲𐑉𐐼 𐑄𐐰𐐻 𐑄 𐐿𐐮𐑍 𐐶𐐱𐑆 𐑅𐑊𐐩𐑌, 𐑁𐐫𐑉 𐐈𐑋𐐰𐑊𐐮𐐿𐐴𐐲 𐐸𐐰𐐼 𐑅𐐯𐑌𐐻 𐐰𐑌 𐐯𐑋𐐺𐐲𐑅𐐨 𐐻𐐭 𐑄 𐐿𐐶𐐨𐑌, 𐐮𐑌𐑁𐐫𐑉𐑋𐐮𐑍 𐐸𐐲𐑉 𐑄𐐰𐐻 𐑄 𐐿𐐮𐑍 𐐸𐐰𐐼 𐐺𐐨𐑌 𐑅𐑊𐐩𐑌 𐐺𐐴 𐐸𐐮𐑆 𐑅𐐲𐑉𐑂𐐰𐑌𐐻𐑅; 𐑄𐐰𐐻 𐐸𐐨 𐐸𐐰𐐼 𐐹𐐲𐑉𐑅𐐭𐐼 𐑄𐐯𐑋 𐐶𐐮𐑄 𐐸𐐮𐑆 𐐪𐑉𐑋𐐨, 𐐺𐐲𐐻 𐐮𐐻 𐐶𐐱𐑆 𐐮𐑌 𐑂𐐩𐑌, 𐐰𐑌𐐼 𐑄𐐩 𐐸𐐰𐐼 𐑋𐐩𐐼 𐑄𐐩𐑉 𐐯𐑅𐐿𐐩𐐹, 𐑄𐐯𐑉𐑁𐐬𐑉 𐐸𐐶𐐯𐑌 𐑄 𐐿𐐶𐐨𐑌 𐐸𐐰𐐼

𐑉𐐨𐑅𐐨𐑂𐐼 𐑄𐐮𐑅 𐑋𐐯𐑅𐐯𐐾, 𐑇𐐨 𐑅𐐯𐑌𐐻 𐐲𐑌𐐻𐐭 𐐈𐑋𐐲𐑊𐐮𐐿𐐴𐐲, 𐐼𐐨𐑆𐐴𐑉𐐮𐑍 𐐸𐐮𐑋 𐑄𐐰𐐻 𐐸𐐨 𐐶𐐳𐐼 𐑅𐐹𐐩𐑉 𐑄 𐐹𐐨𐐹𐐲𐑊 𐐱𐑂 𐑄 𐑅𐐮𐐻𐐨; 𐐰𐑌𐐼 𐑇𐐨 𐐫𐑊𐑅𐐬 𐐼𐐨𐑆𐐴𐑉𐐼 𐐸𐐮𐑋 𐑄𐐰𐐻 𐐸𐐨 𐑇𐐳𐐼 𐐿𐐲𐑋 𐐮𐑌 𐐲𐑌𐐻𐐭 𐐸𐐲𐑉; 𐐰𐑌𐐼 𐑇𐐨 𐐫𐑊𐑅𐐬 𐐼𐐨𐑆𐐴𐑉𐐼 𐐸𐐮𐑋 𐑄𐐰𐐻 𐐸𐐨 𐑇𐐳𐐼 𐐺𐑉𐐮𐑍 𐐶𐐮𐐻𐑌𐐯𐑅𐐯𐑆 𐐶𐐮𐑄 𐐸𐐮𐑋, 𐐻𐐭 𐐻𐐯𐑅𐐻𐐮𐑁𐐴 𐐿𐐪𐑌𐑅𐐲𐑉𐑌𐐮𐑍 𐑄 𐐼𐐯𐑃 𐐱𐑂 𐑄 𐐿𐐮𐑍.

28. 𐐈𐑌𐐼 𐐮𐐻 𐐿𐐩𐑋 𐐻𐐭 𐐹𐐪𐑅 𐑄𐐰𐐻 𐐈𐑋𐐲𐑊𐐮𐐿𐐴𐐲 𐐻𐐳𐐿 𐑄 𐑅𐐩𐑋 𐑅𐐲𐑉𐑂𐐲𐑌𐐻𐑅 𐑄𐐰𐐻 𐑅𐑊𐐭 𐑄 𐐿𐐮𐑍, 𐐰𐑌𐐼 𐐫𐑊 𐑄𐐯𐑋 𐑄𐐰𐐻 𐐶𐐲𐑉 𐐶𐐮𐑄 𐐸𐐮𐑋, 𐐰𐑌𐐼 𐐶𐐯𐑌𐐻 𐐮𐑌 𐐲𐑌𐐻𐐭 𐑄 𐐿𐐶𐐨𐑌, 𐐲𐑌𐐻𐐭 𐑄 𐐹𐑊𐐩𐑅 𐐸𐐶𐐩𐑉 𐑇𐐨 𐑅𐐰𐐻; 𐐰𐑌𐐼 𐑄𐐩 𐐫𐑊 𐐻𐐯𐑅𐐻𐐮𐑁𐐴𐐼 𐐲𐑌𐐻𐐭 𐐸𐐲𐑉 𐑄𐐰𐐻 𐑄 𐐿𐐮𐑍 𐐶𐐪𐑆 𐑅𐑊𐐩𐑌 𐐺𐐴 𐐸𐐮𐑆 𐐬𐑌 𐑅𐐲𐑉𐑂𐐲𐑌𐐻𐑅; 𐐰𐑌𐐼 𐑄𐐩 𐑅𐐯𐐼 𐐫𐑊𐑅𐐬, 𐐜𐐩 𐐸𐐰𐑂 𐑁𐑊𐐯𐐼; 𐐼𐐲𐑆 𐑌𐐪𐐻 𐑄𐐮𐑅 𐐻𐐯𐑅𐐻𐐮𐑁𐐴 𐐲𐑀𐐯𐑌𐑅𐐻 𐑄𐐯𐑋? 𐐈𐑌𐐼 𐑄𐐲𐑅 𐑄𐐩 𐑅𐐰𐐻𐐮𐑅𐑁𐐴𐐼 𐑄 𐐿𐐶𐐨𐑌 𐐿𐐪𐑌𐑅𐐲𐑉𐑌𐐮𐑍 𐑄 𐐼𐐯𐑃 𐐱𐑂 𐑄 𐐿𐐮𐑍.

29. 𐐈𐑌𐐼 𐐮𐐻 𐐿𐐩𐑋 𐐻𐐭 𐐹𐐪𐑅 𐑄𐐰𐐻 𐐈𐑋𐐲𐑊𐐮𐐿𐐴𐐲 𐑅𐐫𐐻 𐑄 𐑁𐐩𐑂𐐲𐑉 𐐱𐑂 𐑄 𐐿𐐶𐐨𐑌, 𐐰𐑌𐐼 𐐻𐐳𐐿 𐐸𐐲𐑉 𐐲𐑌𐐻𐐭 𐐸𐐮𐑋 𐐻𐐭 𐐶𐐴𐑁; 𐐰𐑌𐐼 𐑄𐐲𐑅 𐐺𐐴 𐐸𐐮𐑆 𐑁𐑉𐐫𐐼, 𐐰𐑌𐐼 𐐺𐐴 𐑄 𐐰𐑅𐐮𐑅𐐻𐐰𐑌𐑅 𐐱𐑂 𐐸𐐮𐑆 𐐿𐐲𐑌𐐮𐑍 𐑅𐐲𐑉𐑂𐐲𐑌𐐻𐑅, 𐐸𐐨 𐐪𐐺𐐻𐐩𐑌𐐼 𐑄 𐐿𐐮𐑍𐐼𐐲𐑋; 𐐷𐐩, 𐐸𐐨 𐐶𐐪𐑆 𐐰𐐿𐑌𐐪𐑊𐐯𐐾𐐼 𐐿𐐮𐑍 𐑃𐑉𐐭𐐵𐐻 𐐫𐑊 𐑄 𐑊𐐰𐑌𐐼, 𐐲𐑋𐐲𐑍 𐐫𐑊 𐑄 𐐹𐐨𐐹𐐲𐑊 𐐱𐑂 𐑄 𐐢𐐰𐑋𐐲𐑌𐐴𐐻𐑅, 𐐸𐐭 𐐶𐐲𐑉 𐐿𐐪𐑋𐐹𐐬𐑆𐐼 𐐱𐑂 𐑄 𐐢𐐰𐑋𐐲𐑌𐐴𐐻𐑅 𐐰𐑌𐐼 𐑄 𐐢𐐯𐑋𐐷𐐭𐐯𐑊𐐴𐐻𐑅, 𐐰𐑌𐐼 𐑄 𐐆𐑇𐑋𐐩𐐯𐑊𐐴𐐻𐑅, 𐐰𐑌𐐼 𐐫𐑊 𐑄 𐐼𐐮𐑅𐐯𐑌𐐻𐐲𐑉𐑆 𐐱𐑂 𐑄 𐐤𐐨𐑁𐐴𐐻𐑅, 𐑁𐑉𐐪𐑋 𐑄 𐑉𐐩𐑌 𐐱𐑂 𐐤𐐨𐑁𐐴 𐐼𐐵𐑌 𐐻𐐭 𐑄 𐐹𐑉𐐯𐑆𐐯𐑌𐐻 𐐻𐐴𐑋. 𐐤𐐵 𐑄𐐨𐑆 𐐼𐐮𐑅𐐯𐑌𐐻𐐲𐑉𐑆, 𐐸𐐰𐑂𐐮𐑍 𐑄 𐑅𐐩𐑋 𐐮𐑌𐑅𐐻𐑉𐐲𐐿𐑇𐐲𐑌 𐐰𐑌𐐼 𐑄 𐑅𐐩𐑋 𐐮𐑌𐑁𐐫𐑉𐑋𐐩𐑇𐐲𐑌 𐐱𐑂 𐑄 𐐤𐐨𐑁𐐴𐐻𐑅, 𐐷𐐩, 𐐸𐐰𐑂𐐮𐑍 𐐺𐐮𐑌 𐐮𐑌𐑅𐐻𐑉𐐲𐐿𐐻𐐯𐐼 𐐮𐑌 𐑄 𐑅𐐩𐑋 𐑌𐐪𐑊𐐯𐐾 𐐱𐑂 𐑄 𐐢𐐫𐑉𐐼, 𐑌𐐯𐑂𐐲𐑉𐑄𐐯𐑊𐐯𐑅, 𐐮𐐻 𐐮𐑆 𐑅𐐻𐑉𐐩𐑌𐐾 𐐻𐐭 𐑉𐐨𐑊𐐩𐐻, 𐑌𐐪𐐻 𐑊𐐫𐑍 𐐰𐑁𐐻𐐲𐑉 𐑄𐐩𐑉 𐐼𐐮𐑅𐐯𐑌𐑇𐐲𐑌𐑆 𐑄𐐩 𐐺𐐨𐐿𐐩𐑋 𐑋𐐬𐑉 𐐸𐐪𐑉𐐼𐐲𐑌𐐼 𐐰𐑌𐐼 𐐮𐑋𐐹𐐯𐑌𐐮𐐻𐐯𐑌𐐻, 𐐰𐑌𐐼 𐑋𐐬𐑉 𐐶𐐴𐑊𐐼, 𐐶𐐮𐐿𐐯𐐼, 𐐰𐑌𐐼 𐑁𐐨𐑉𐐬𐑇𐐲𐑅 𐑄𐐰𐑌 𐑄 𐐢𐐰𐑋𐐲𐑌𐐴𐐻𐑅; 𐐼𐑉𐐮𐑍𐐿𐐮𐑍 𐐮𐑌 𐐶𐐮𐑄 𐑄 𐐻𐑉𐐲𐐼𐐮𐑇𐐲𐑌𐑆 𐐱𐑂 𐑄 𐐢𐐰𐑋𐐲𐑌𐐴𐐻𐑅; 𐑀𐐮𐑂𐐮𐑍 𐐶𐐩 𐐻𐐭 𐐮𐑌𐐼𐐬𐑊𐐯𐑌𐑅, 𐐰𐑌𐐼 𐐫𐑊 𐑋𐐰𐑌𐐲𐑉 𐐱𐑂 𐑊𐐰𐑅𐐮𐑂𐐨𐐲𐑅𐑌𐐯𐑅; 𐐷𐐩, 𐐯𐑌𐐻𐐴𐑉𐑊𐐨 𐑁𐐫𐑉𐑀𐐯𐐻𐐮𐑍 𐑄 𐐢𐐫𐑉𐐼 𐑄𐐩𐑉 𐐘𐐪𐐼.

30. 𐐈𐑌𐐼 𐑌𐐵 𐐮𐐻 𐐿𐐩𐑋 𐐻𐐭 𐐹𐐪𐑅 𐑄𐐰𐐻 𐐰𐑆 𐑅𐐭𐑌 𐐰𐑆 𐐈𐑋𐐲𐑊𐐮𐐿𐐴𐐲 𐐸𐐰𐐼 𐐪𐐺𐐻𐐩𐑌𐐼 𐑄 𐐿𐐮𐑍𐐼𐐲𐑋, 𐐸𐐨 𐐺𐐨𐑀𐐰𐑌 𐐻𐐭 𐐮𐑌𐑅𐐹𐐴𐑉 𐑄 𐐸𐐪𐑉𐐻𐑅 𐐱𐑂 𐑄 𐐢𐐰𐑋𐐲𐑌𐐴𐐻𐑅 𐐲𐑀𐐯𐑌𐑅𐐻 𐑄 𐐹𐐨𐐹𐐲𐑊 𐐱𐑂 𐐤𐐨𐑁𐐴; 𐐷𐐩, 𐐸𐐨 𐐼𐐮𐐼 𐐲𐐹𐑎𐑌𐐻 𐑋𐐯𐑌 𐐻𐐭 𐑅𐐹𐐨𐐿 𐐲𐑌𐐻𐐭 𐑄 𐐢𐐰𐑋𐐲𐑌𐐴𐐻𐑅 𐑁𐑉𐐪𐑋 𐑄𐐩𐑉 𐐻𐐵𐐲𐑉𐑆, 𐐲𐑀𐐯𐑌𐑅𐐻 𐑄 𐐤𐐨𐑁𐐴𐐻𐑅. 𐐈𐑌𐐼 𐑄𐐲𐑅 𐐸𐐨 𐐼𐐮𐐼 𐐮𐑌𐑅𐐹𐐴𐑉 𐑄𐐩𐑉 𐐸𐐪𐑉𐐻𐑅 𐐲𐑀𐐯𐑌𐑅𐐻 𐑄 𐐤𐐨𐑁𐐴𐐻𐑅, 𐐮𐑌𐑅𐐬𐑋𐐲𐐽 𐑄𐐰𐐻 𐐮𐑌 𐑄 𐑊𐐰𐐻𐐲𐑉 𐐯𐑌𐐼 𐐱𐑂 𐑄 𐑌𐐴𐑌𐐻𐐨𐑌𐑃 𐐷𐐨𐑉 𐐱𐑂 𐑄 𐑉𐐩𐑌 𐐱𐑂 𐑄 𐐖𐐲𐐾𐐯𐑆, 𐐸𐐨 𐐸𐐰𐑂𐐮𐑍 𐐰𐐿𐐪𐑋𐐹𐑊𐐮𐑇𐐻 𐐸𐐮𐑆 𐐼𐐨𐑆𐐴𐑌𐑆 𐑄𐐲𐑅 𐑁𐐪𐑉; 𐐷𐐩, 𐐸𐐰𐑂𐐮𐑍 𐐺𐐮𐑌 𐑋𐐩𐐼 𐐿𐐮𐑍 𐐬𐑂𐐲𐑉 𐑄 𐐢𐐰𐑋𐐲𐑌𐐴𐐻𐑅, 𐐸𐐨 𐑅𐐫𐐻 𐐫𐑊𐑅𐐬 𐐻𐐭 𐑉𐐩𐑌 𐐬𐑂𐐲𐑉 𐐫𐑊 𐑄 𐑊𐐰𐑌𐐼; 𐐷𐐩, 𐐰𐑌𐐼 𐐫𐑊 𐑄 𐐹𐐨𐐹𐐲𐑊 𐐸𐐶𐐮𐐽 𐐶𐐲𐑉 𐐮𐑌 𐑄 𐑊𐐰𐑌𐐼, 𐑄 𐐤𐐨𐑁𐐴𐐻𐑅 𐐰𐑆 𐐶𐐯𐑊 𐐰𐑆 𐑄 𐐢𐐰𐑋𐐲𐑌𐐴𐐻𐑅. 𐐜𐐩𐑉𐑁𐐬𐑉 𐐸𐐨 𐐸𐐰𐐼 𐐰𐐿𐐪𐑋𐐹𐑊𐐮𐑇𐐻 𐐸𐐮𐑆 𐐼𐐨𐑆𐐴𐑌, 𐑁𐐫𐑉 𐐸𐐨 𐐸𐐰𐐼 𐐸𐐪𐑉𐐼𐐲𐑌𐐼 𐑄 𐐸𐐪𐑉𐐻𐑅 𐐱𐑂 𐑄 𐐢𐐰𐑋𐐲𐑌𐐴𐐻𐑅, 𐐰𐑌𐐼 𐐺𐑊𐐴𐑌𐐼𐐯𐐼 𐑄𐐩𐑉 𐑋𐐴𐑌𐐼𐑆, 𐐰𐑌𐐼 𐑅𐐻𐐲𐑉𐐼 𐑄𐐯𐑋 𐐲𐐹 𐐻𐐭 𐐰𐑍𐑀𐐲𐑉, 𐐮𐑌𐑅𐐬𐑋𐐲𐐽 𐑄𐐰𐐻 𐐸𐐨 𐐸𐐰𐐼 𐑀𐐰𐑄𐐲𐑉𐐼 𐐻𐐭𐑀𐐯𐑄𐐲𐑉 𐐩 𐑌𐐷𐐭𐑋𐐲𐑉𐐲𐑅 𐐸𐐬𐑅𐐻, 𐐻𐐭 𐑀𐐬 𐐻𐐭 𐐺𐐰𐐻𐑊 𐐲𐑀𐐯𐑌𐑅𐐻 𐑄 𐐤𐐨𐑁𐐴𐐻𐑅. 𐐙𐐫𐑉 𐐸𐐨 𐐶𐐪𐑆 𐐼𐐨𐐻𐐲𐑉𐑋𐐮𐑌𐐼, 𐐺𐐨𐐿𐐫𐑆 𐐱𐑂 𐑄 𐑀𐑉𐐩𐐻𐑌𐐯𐑅 𐐱𐑂 𐑄 𐑌𐐲𐑋𐐺𐐲𐑉 𐐱𐑂 𐐸𐐮𐑆 𐐹𐐨𐐹𐐲𐑊, 𐐻𐐭 𐐬𐑂𐐲𐑉𐐹𐐵𐐲𐑉 𐑄 𐐤𐐨𐑁𐐴𐐻𐑅, 𐐰𐑌𐐼 𐐻𐐭 𐐺𐑉𐐮𐑍 𐑄𐐯𐑋 𐐮𐑌𐐻𐐭 𐐺𐐪𐑌𐐼𐐩𐐾; 𐐰𐑌𐐼 𐑄𐐲𐑅 𐐸𐐨 𐐼𐐮𐐼 𐐲𐐹𐑎𐑌𐐻 𐐽𐐨𐑁 𐐿𐐰𐐹𐐻𐐩𐑌𐑆 𐐱𐑂 𐑄 𐐞𐐬𐑉𐐲𐑋𐐴𐐻𐑅, 𐑄𐐩 𐐺𐐨𐐮𐑍 𐑄 𐑋𐐬𐑅𐐻 𐐰𐐿𐐶𐐩𐑌𐐻𐐯𐐼 𐐶𐐮𐑄 𐑄 𐑅𐐻𐑉𐐯𐑍𐑃 𐐱𐑂 𐑄 𐐤𐐨𐑁𐐴𐐻𐑅, 𐐰𐑌𐐼 𐑄𐐩𐑉 𐐹𐑊𐐩𐑅𐐯𐑆 𐐱𐑂 𐑉𐐨𐑆𐐫𐑉𐐻, 𐐰𐑌𐐼 𐑄 𐐶𐐨𐐿𐐯𐑅𐐻 𐐹𐐪𐑉𐐻𐑅 𐐱𐑂 𐑄𐐩𐑉 𐑅𐐮𐐻𐐨𐑆; 𐑄𐐩𐑉𐑁𐐬𐑉 𐐸𐐨 𐐲𐐹𐑎𐑌𐐻𐐯𐐼 𐑄𐐯𐑋 𐐻𐐭 𐐺𐐨 𐐽𐐨𐑁 𐐿𐐰𐐹𐐻𐐩𐑌𐑆 𐐬𐑂𐐲𐑉 𐐸𐐮𐑆 𐐪𐑉𐑋𐐨𐑆.

31. 𐐈𐑌𐐼 𐐮𐐻 𐐿𐐩𐑋 𐐻𐐭 𐐹𐐪𐑅 𐑄𐐰𐐻 𐑄𐐩 𐐻𐐳𐐿 𐑄𐐩𐑉 𐐿𐐰𐑋𐐹, 𐐰𐑌𐐼 𐑋𐐭𐑂𐐼 𐑁𐐬𐑉𐑃 𐐻𐐬𐑉𐐼 𐑄 𐑊𐐰𐑌𐐼 𐐱𐑂 𐐞𐐰𐑉𐐲𐐸𐐯𐑋𐑊𐐲 𐐮𐑌 𐑄 𐐶𐐮𐑊𐐼𐐲𐑉𐑌𐐯𐑅. 𐐤𐐵 𐐮𐐻 𐐿𐐩𐑋 𐐻𐐭 𐐹𐐪𐑅 𐑄𐐰𐐻 𐐸𐐶𐐴𐑊 𐐈𐑋𐐲𐑊𐐮𐐿𐐴𐐲 𐐸𐐰𐐼 𐑄𐐲𐑅 𐐺𐐮𐑌 𐐪𐐺𐐻𐐩𐑌𐐮𐑍 𐐹𐐵𐐲𐑉 𐐺𐐴 𐑁𐑉𐐫𐐼 𐐰𐑌𐐼 𐐼𐐨𐑅𐐨𐐻, 𐐣𐐬𐑉𐐬𐑌𐐴, 𐐪𐑌 𐑄 𐐲𐑄𐐲𐑉 𐐸𐐰𐑌𐐼, 𐐸𐐰𐐼 𐐺𐐮𐑌 𐐹𐑉𐐨𐐹𐐩𐑉𐐮𐑍 𐑄 𐑋𐐴𐑌𐐼𐑆 𐐱𐑂 𐑄 𐐹𐐨𐐹𐐲𐑊 𐐻𐐭 𐐺𐐨 𐑁𐐩𐑃𐑁𐐳𐑊 𐐲𐑌𐐻𐐭 𐑄 𐐢𐐫𐑉𐐼 𐑄𐐩𐑉 𐐘𐐪𐐼; 𐐷𐐩, 𐐸𐐨 𐐸𐐰𐐼 𐐺𐐮𐑌 𐑅𐐻𐑉𐐯𐑍𐑃𐐲𐑌𐐮𐑍 𐑄 𐐪𐑉𐑋𐐨𐑆 𐐱𐑂 𐑄 𐐤𐐨𐑁𐐴𐐻𐑅, 𐐰𐑌𐐼 𐐨𐑉𐐯𐐿𐐻𐐮𐑍 𐑅𐑋𐐫𐑊 𐑁𐐬𐑉𐐻𐑅, 𐐫𐑉 𐐹𐑊𐐩𐑅𐐯𐑆 𐐱𐑂 𐑉𐐨𐑆𐐫𐑉𐐻; 𐑃𐑉𐐬𐐮𐑍 𐐲𐐹 𐐺𐐰𐑍𐐿𐑅 𐐱𐑂 𐐲𐑉𐑃 𐑉𐐵𐑌𐐼 𐐲𐐺𐐵𐐻, 𐐻𐐭 𐐯𐑌𐐿𐑊𐐬𐑆 𐐸𐐮𐑆 𐐪𐑉𐑋𐐨𐑆, 𐐰𐑌𐐼 𐐫𐑊𐑅𐐬 𐐺𐐮𐑊𐐼𐐮𐑍 𐐶𐐫𐑊𐑆 𐐱𐑂 𐑅𐐻𐐬𐑌

𐐻𐐭 𐐯𐑌𐐿𐑊𐐬𐑆 𐐸𐐮𐑆 𐐪𐑉𐑋𐐨𐑆, 𐐰𐑌𐐼 𐐫𐑊𐑅𐐬 𐐺𐐮𐑊𐐼𐐮𐑍 𐐶𐐫𐑊𐑆 𐐱𐑂 𐑅𐐻𐐬𐑌 𐐻𐐭 𐐯𐑌𐑅𐐲𐑉𐐿𐑊 𐑄𐐯𐑋 𐐲𐐺𐐵𐐻, 𐑉𐐵𐑌𐐼 𐐲𐐺𐐵𐐻 𐑄𐐯𐑉 𐑅𐐮𐐻𐐮𐑆, 𐐰𐑌𐐼 𐑄 𐐺𐐫𐑉𐐼𐐲𐑉𐑆 𐐱𐑂 𐑄𐐯𐑉 𐑊𐐰𐑌𐐼𐑆; 𐐷𐐩, 𐐫𐑊 𐑉𐐵𐑌𐐼 𐐲𐐺𐐵𐐻 𐑄 𐑊𐐰𐑌𐐼; 𐐰𐑌𐐼 𐐮𐑌 𐑄𐐯𐑉 𐐶𐐨𐐿𐐯𐑅𐐻 𐑁𐐫𐑉𐐻𐐮𐑁𐐮𐐿𐐩𐑇𐐲𐑌𐑆, 𐐸𐐨 𐐼𐐮𐐼 𐐹𐑊𐐩𐑅 𐑄 𐑀𐑉𐐩𐐻𐐲𐑉 𐑌𐐲𐑋𐐺𐐲𐑉 𐐱𐑂 𐑋𐐯𐑌; 𐐰𐑌𐐼 𐑄𐐲𐑅 𐐸𐐨 𐐼𐐮𐐼 𐑁𐐫𐑉𐐻𐐮𐑁𐐴 𐐰𐑌𐐼 𐑅𐐻𐑉𐐯𐑍𐑃𐐲𐑌 𐑄 𐑊𐐰𐑌𐐼 𐐸𐐶𐐮𐐽 𐐶𐐱𐑆 𐐹𐐲𐑆𐐯𐑅𐐻 𐐺𐐴 𐑄 𐑌𐐨𐑁𐐴𐐻𐑅. 𐐈𐑌𐐼 𐑄𐐲𐑅 𐐸𐐨 𐐶𐐱𐑆 𐐹𐑉𐐨𐐹𐐯𐑉𐐮𐑍 𐐻𐐭 𐑅𐐲𐐹𐐬𐑉𐐻 𐑄𐐯𐑉 𐑊𐐮𐐺𐐲𐑉𐐻𐐨, 𐑄𐐯𐑉 𐑊𐐰𐑌𐐼𐑆, 𐑄𐐯𐑉 𐐶𐐴𐑂𐑆, 𐐰𐑌𐐼 𐑄𐐯𐑉 𐐽𐐮𐑊𐐼𐑉𐐯𐑌, 𐐰𐑌𐐼 𐑄𐐯𐑉 𐐹𐐨𐑅, 𐐰𐑌𐐼 𐑄𐐰𐐻 𐑄𐐩 𐑋𐐴𐐻 𐑊𐐮𐑂 𐐲𐑌𐐻𐐭 𐑄 𐐢𐐫𐑉𐐼 𐑄𐐯𐑉 𐐘𐐪𐐼, 𐐰𐑌𐐼 𐑄𐐰𐐻 𐑄𐐩 𐑋𐐴𐐻 𐑋𐐩𐑌𐐻𐐩𐑌 𐑄𐐰𐐻 𐐸𐐶𐐮𐐽 𐐶𐐱𐑆 𐐿𐐫𐑊𐐼 𐐺𐐴 𐑄𐐯𐑉 𐐯𐑌𐐯𐑋𐐨𐑆 𐑄 𐐿𐐫𐑆 𐐱𐑂 𐐗𐑉𐐮𐑅𐐽𐐲𐑌𐑆. 𐐈𐑌𐐼 𐐣𐐬𐑉𐐬𐑌𐐴 𐐶𐐱𐑆 𐐩 𐑅𐐻𐑉𐐪𐑍 𐐰𐑌𐐼 𐐩 𐑋𐐴𐐻𐐨 𐑋𐐰𐑌; 𐐸𐐨 𐐶𐐱𐑆 𐐩 𐑋𐐰𐑌 𐐱𐑂 𐐩 𐐹𐐲𐑉𐑁𐐯𐐿𐐻 𐐲𐑌𐐼𐐲𐑉𐑅𐐻𐐰𐑌𐐼𐐮𐑍; 𐐷𐐩, 𐐩 𐑋𐐰𐑌 𐑄𐐰𐐻 𐐼𐐮𐐼 𐑌𐐪𐐻 𐐼𐐨𐑊𐐴𐐻 𐐮𐑌 𐐺𐑊𐐲𐐼𐑇𐐯𐐼; 𐐩 𐑋𐐰𐑌 𐐸𐐭𐑆 𐑅𐐬𐑊 𐐼𐐮𐐼 𐐾𐐱𐐮 𐐮𐑌 𐑄 𐑊𐐮𐐺𐐲𐑉𐐻𐐨 𐐰𐑌𐐼 𐑄 𐑁𐑉𐐨𐐼𐐲𐑋 𐐱𐑂 𐐸𐐮𐑆 𐐿𐐲𐑌𐐻𐑉𐐨, 𐐰𐑌𐐼 𐐸𐐮𐑆 𐐺𐑉𐐯𐑄𐑉𐐯𐑌 𐑁𐑉𐐱𐑋 𐐺𐐪𐑌𐐼𐐩𐐾 𐐰𐑌𐐼 𐑅𐑊𐐩𐑂𐐲𐑉𐐨; 𐐷𐐩, 𐐩 𐑋𐐰𐑌 𐐸𐐭𐑆 𐐸𐐪𐑉𐐻 𐐼𐐮𐐼 𐑅𐐶𐐯𐑊 𐐶𐐮𐑄 𐑃𐐰𐑍𐐿𐑅𐑀𐐮𐑂𐐮𐑍 𐐻𐐭 𐐸𐐮𐑆 𐐘𐐪𐐼, 𐑁𐐫𐑉 𐑄 𐑋𐐯𐑌𐐨 𐐹𐑉𐐮𐑂𐐮𐑊𐐯𐐾𐐯𐑆 𐐰𐑌𐐼 𐐺𐑊𐐯𐑅𐐮𐑍𐑆 𐐸𐐶𐐮𐐽 𐐸𐐨 𐐺𐐨𐑅𐐻𐐬𐐼 𐐲𐐹𐐪𐑌 𐐸𐐮𐑆 𐐹𐐨𐐹𐑊; 𐐩 𐑋𐐰𐑌 𐐸𐐭 𐐼𐐮𐐼 𐑊𐐩𐐺𐐲𐑉 𐐯𐐿𐑅𐐨𐐼𐐮𐑍𐑊𐐨 𐑁𐐫𐑉 𐑄 𐐶𐐯𐑊𐑁𐐩𐑉 𐐰𐑌𐐼 𐑅𐐩𐑁𐐻𐐨 𐐱𐑂 𐐸𐐮𐑆 𐐹𐐨𐐹𐑊; 𐐷𐐩, 𐐰𐑌𐐼 𐐸𐐨 𐐶𐐱𐑆 𐐩 𐑋𐐰𐑌 𐐸𐐭 𐐶𐐱𐑆 𐑁𐐲𐑉𐑋 𐐮𐑌 𐑄 𐑁𐐩𐑃 𐐱𐑂 𐐗𐑉𐐴𐑅𐐻, 𐐰𐑌𐐼 𐐸𐐨 𐐸𐐰𐐼 𐑅𐐶𐐫𐑉𐑌 𐐶𐐮𐑄 𐐰𐑌 𐐬𐑃 𐐻𐐭 𐐼𐐨𐑁𐐯𐑌𐐼 𐐸𐐮𐑆 𐐹𐐨𐐹𐑊, 𐐸𐐮𐑆 𐑉𐐴𐐻𐑅, 𐐰𐑌𐐼 𐐸𐐮𐑆 𐐿𐐲𐑌𐐻𐑉𐐨, 𐐰𐑌𐐼 𐐸𐐮𐑆 𐑉𐐨𐑊𐐮𐐾𐐲𐑌, 𐐨𐑂𐐲𐑌 𐐻𐐭 𐑄 𐑊𐐱𐑅 𐐱𐑂 𐐸𐐮𐑆 𐐺𐑊𐐲𐐼.

32. 𐐤𐐵 𐑄 𐑌𐐨𐑁𐐴𐐻𐑅 𐐶𐐲𐑉 𐐻𐐫𐐻 𐐻𐐭 𐐼𐐨𐑁𐐯𐑌𐐼 𐑄𐐯𐑋𐑅𐐯𐑊𐑂𐑆 𐐲𐑀𐐯𐑌𐑅𐐻 𐑄𐐯𐑉 𐐯𐑌𐐯𐑋𐐨𐑆, 𐐨𐑂𐐲𐑌 𐐻𐐭 𐑄 𐑇𐐯𐐼𐐮𐑍 𐐱𐑂 𐐺𐑊𐐲𐐼, 𐐮𐑁 𐐮𐐻 𐐶𐐲𐑉 𐑌𐐯𐑅𐐯𐑅𐐯𐑉𐐨; 𐐷𐐩, 𐐰𐑌𐐼 𐑄𐐩 𐐶𐐲𐑉 𐐫𐑊𐑅𐐬 𐐻𐐫𐐻 𐑌𐐯𐑂𐐲𐑉 𐐻𐐭 𐑀𐐮𐑂 𐐰𐑌 𐐱𐑁𐐯𐑌𐑅; 𐐷𐐩, 𐐰𐑌𐐼 𐑌𐐯𐑂𐐲𐑉 𐐻𐐭 𐑉𐐩𐑆 𐑄 𐑅𐐬𐑉𐐼, 𐐯𐐿𐑅𐐯𐐹𐐻 𐐮𐐻 𐐶𐐲𐑉 𐐲𐑀𐐯𐑌𐑅𐐻 𐐰𐑌 𐐯𐑌𐐯𐑋𐐨, 𐐯𐐿𐑅𐐯𐐹𐐻 𐐮𐐻 𐐶𐐲𐑉 𐐻𐐭 𐐹𐑉𐐨𐑆𐐲𐑉𐑂 𐑄𐐯𐑉 𐑊𐐴𐑂𐑆; 𐐰𐑌𐐼 𐑄𐐮𐑅 𐐶𐐱𐑆 𐑄𐐯𐑉 𐑁𐐩𐑃, 𐑄𐐰𐐻 𐐺𐐴 𐑅𐐬 𐐼𐐭𐐮𐑍, 𐐘𐐪𐐼 𐐶𐐳𐐼 𐐹𐑉𐐱𐑅𐐹𐐲𐑉 𐑄𐐯𐑋 𐐮𐑌 𐑄 𐑊𐐰𐑌𐐼; 𐐫𐑉 𐐮𐑌 𐐲𐑄𐐲𐑉 𐐶𐐲𐑉𐐼𐑆, 𐐮𐑁 𐑄𐐩 𐐶𐐲𐑉 𐑁𐐩𐑃𐑁𐐳𐑊 𐐮𐑌 𐐿𐐨𐐹𐐮𐑍 𐑄 𐐿𐐱𐑋𐐰𐑌𐐼𐑋𐐯𐑌𐐻𐑅 𐐱𐑂 𐐘𐐪𐐼, 𐑄𐐰𐐻 𐐸𐐨 𐐶𐐳𐐼 𐐹𐑉𐐱𐑅𐐹𐐲𐑉 𐑄𐐯𐑋 𐐮𐑌 𐑄 𐑊𐐰𐑌𐐼; 𐐷𐐩, 𐐶𐐫𐑉𐑌 𐑄𐐯𐑋 𐐻𐐭 𐑁𐑊𐐨, 𐐫𐑉 𐐻𐐭 𐐹𐑉𐐨𐐹𐐩𐑉 𐑁𐐫𐑉 𐐶𐐫𐑉, 𐐰𐐿𐐫𐑉𐐼𐐮𐑍 𐐻𐐭 𐑄𐐯𐑉 𐐼𐐩𐑌𐐾𐐲𐑉; 𐐰𐑌𐐼 𐐫𐑊𐑅𐐬 𐑄𐐰𐐻 𐐘𐐪𐐼 𐐶𐐳𐐼 𐑋𐐩𐐿 𐐮𐐻 𐑌𐐬𐑌 𐐲𐑌𐐻𐐭 𐑄𐐯𐑋 𐐸𐐶𐐮𐑄𐐲𐑉 𐑄𐐩 𐑇𐐳𐐼 𐑀𐐬 𐐻𐐭 𐐼𐐨𐑁𐐯𐑌𐐼 𐑄𐐯𐑋𐑅𐐯𐑊𐑂𐑆 𐐲𐑀𐐯𐑌𐑅𐐻 𐑄𐐯𐑉 𐐯𐑌𐐯𐑋𐐨𐑆; 𐐰𐑌𐐼 𐐺𐐴 𐑅𐐬 𐐼𐐭𐐮𐑍, 𐑄 𐐢𐐫𐑉𐐼 𐐶𐐳𐐼 𐐼𐐨𐑊𐐮𐑂𐐲𐑉 𐑄𐐯𐑋; 𐐰𐑌𐐼 𐑄𐐮𐑅 𐐶𐐱𐑆 𐑄 𐑁𐐩𐑃 𐐱𐑂 𐐣𐐬𐑉𐐬𐑌𐐴, 𐐰𐑌𐐼 𐐸𐐮𐑆 𐐸𐐪𐑉𐐻 𐐼𐐮𐐼 𐑀𐑊𐐬𐑉𐐨 𐐮𐑌 𐐮𐐻; 𐑌𐐪𐐻 𐐮𐑌 𐑄 𐑇𐐯𐐼𐐮𐑍 𐐱𐑂 𐐺𐑊𐐲𐐼, 𐐺𐐲𐐻 𐐮𐑌 𐐼𐐭𐐮𐑍 𐑀𐐳𐐼, 𐐮𐑌 𐐹𐑉𐐨𐑆𐐲𐑉𐑂𐐮𐑍 𐐸𐐮𐑆 𐐹𐐨𐐹𐑊; 𐐷𐐩, 𐐮𐑌 𐐿𐐨𐐹𐐮𐑍 𐑄 𐐿𐐱𐑋𐐰𐑌𐐼𐑋𐐯𐑌𐐻𐑅 𐐱𐑂 𐐘𐐪𐐼; 𐐷𐐩, 𐐰𐑌𐐼 𐑉𐐨𐑆𐐮𐑅𐐻𐐮𐑍 𐐮𐑌𐐮𐐿𐐶𐐮𐐻𐐨. 𐐏𐐩, 𐑂𐐯𐑉𐐮𐑊𐐨, 𐑂𐐯𐑉𐐮𐑊𐐨, 𐐌 𐑅𐐩 𐐲𐑌𐐻𐐭 𐐷𐐭, 𐐮𐑁 𐐫𐑊 𐑋𐐯𐑌 𐐸𐐰𐐼 𐐺𐐮𐑌, 𐐰𐑌𐐼 𐐶𐐲𐑉, 𐐰𐑌𐐼 𐐯𐑂𐐲𐑉 𐐶𐐳𐐼 𐐺𐐨, 𐑊𐐴𐐿 𐐲𐑌𐐻𐐭 𐐣𐐬𐑉𐐬𐑌𐐴, 𐐺𐐨𐐸𐐬𐑊𐐼, 𐑄 𐑂𐐯𐑉𐐨 𐐹𐐵𐐲𐑉𐑆 𐐱𐑂 𐐸𐐯𐑊 𐐶𐐳𐐼 𐐸𐐰𐑂 𐐺𐐮𐑌 𐑇𐐩𐐿𐐲𐑌 𐑁𐐫𐑉 𐐯𐑂𐐲𐑉; 𐐷𐐩, 𐑄 𐐼𐐯𐑂𐐮𐑊 𐐶𐐳𐐼 𐑌𐐯𐑂𐐲𐑉 𐐸𐐰𐑂 𐐹𐐵𐐲𐑉 𐐬𐑂𐐲𐑉 𐑄 𐐸𐐪𐑉𐐻𐑅 𐐱𐑂 𐑄 𐐽𐐮𐑊𐐼𐑉𐐯𐑌 𐐱𐑂 𐑋𐐯𐑌. 𐐒𐐨𐐸𐐬𐑊𐐼, 𐐸𐐨 𐐶𐐱𐑆 𐐩 𐑋𐐰𐑌 𐑊𐐴𐐿 𐐲𐑌𐐻𐐭 𐐈𐑋𐐲𐑌, 𐑄 𐑅𐐲𐑌 𐐱𐑂 𐐣𐐬𐑆𐐴𐐲, 𐐷𐐩, 𐐰𐑌𐐼 𐐨𐑂𐐲𐑌 𐑄 𐐲𐑄𐐲𐑉 𐑅𐐲𐑌𐑆 𐐱𐑂 𐐣𐐬𐑆𐐴𐐲; 𐐷𐐩, 𐐰𐑌𐐼 𐐫𐑊𐑅𐐬 𐐈𐑊𐑋𐐲 𐐰𐑌𐐼 𐐸𐐮𐑆 𐑅𐐲𐑌𐑆, 𐑁𐐫𐑉 𐑄𐐩 𐐶𐐲𐑉 𐐫𐑊 𐑋𐐯𐑌 𐐱𐑂 𐐘𐐪𐐼. 𐐤𐐵 𐐺𐐨𐐸𐐬𐑊𐐼, 𐐐𐐨𐑊𐐲𐑋𐐲𐑌 𐐰𐑌𐐼 𐐸𐐮𐑆 𐐺𐑉𐐯𐑄𐑉𐐯𐑌 𐐶𐐲𐑉 𐑌𐐬 𐑊𐐯𐑅 𐑅𐐲𐑉𐑂𐐮𐑅𐐲𐐺𐑊 𐐲𐑌𐐻𐐭 𐑄 𐐹𐐨𐐹𐑊 𐑄𐐰𐑌 𐐶𐐱𐑆 𐐣𐐬𐑉𐐬𐑌𐐴: 𐑁𐐫𐑉 𐑄𐐩 𐐼𐐮𐐼 𐐹𐑉𐐨𐐽 𐑄 𐐶𐐲𐑉𐐼 𐐱𐑂 𐐘𐐪𐐼, 𐐰𐑌𐐼 𐑄𐐩 𐐼𐐮𐐼 𐐺𐐰𐐹𐐻𐐴𐑆 𐐲𐑌𐐻𐐭 𐑉𐐨𐐹𐐯𐑌𐐻𐐰𐑌𐑅 𐐫𐑊 𐑋𐐯𐑌 𐐸𐐭𐑅𐐬𐐯𐑂𐐲𐑉 𐐶𐐳𐐼 𐐸𐐪𐑉𐐿𐐲𐑌 𐐲𐑌𐐻𐐭 𐑄𐐯𐑉 𐐶𐐲𐑉𐐼𐑆.

33. 𐐈𐑌𐐼 𐑄𐐲𐑅 𐑄𐐩 𐐶𐐯𐑌𐐻 𐑁𐐫𐑉𐑃, 𐐰𐑌𐐼 𐑄 𐐹𐐨𐐹𐑊 𐐼𐐮𐐼 𐐸𐐲𐑋𐐺𐑊 𐑄𐐯𐑋𐑅𐐯𐑊𐑂𐑆 𐐺𐐨𐐿𐐫𐑆 𐐱𐑂 𐑄𐐯𐑉 𐐶𐐲𐑉𐐼𐑆, 𐐮𐑌𐑅𐐬𐑋𐐲𐐽 𐑄𐐰𐐻 𐑄𐐩 𐐶𐐲𐑉 𐐸𐐴𐑊𐐨 𐑁𐐩𐑂𐐲𐑉𐐼 𐐱𐑂 𐑄 𐐢𐐫𐑉𐐼, 𐐰𐑌𐐼 𐑄𐐲𐑅 𐑄𐐩 𐐶𐐲𐑉 𐑁𐑉𐐨 𐑁𐑉𐐱𐑋 𐐶𐐫𐑉𐑆 𐐰𐑌𐐼 𐐿𐐱𐑌𐐻𐐯𐑌𐑇𐐲𐑌𐑆 𐐲𐑋𐐲𐑍 𐑄𐐯𐑋𐑅𐐯𐑊𐑂𐑆; 𐐷𐐩, 𐐨𐑂𐐲𐑌 𐑁𐐫𐑉 𐑄 𐑅𐐹𐐩𐑅 𐐱𐑂 𐑁𐐬𐑉 𐐷𐐨𐑉𐑆: 𐐺𐐲𐐻 𐐰𐑆 𐐌 𐐸𐐰𐑂 𐑅𐐯𐐼, 𐐮𐑌 𐑄 𐑊𐐰𐐻𐐲𐑉 𐐯𐑌𐐼 𐐱𐑂 𐑄 𐑌𐐴𐑌𐐻𐐨𐑌𐑃 𐐷𐐨𐑉, 𐐷𐐩, 𐑌𐐪𐐻𐐶𐐮𐑃𐑅𐐻𐐰𐑌𐐼𐐮𐑍 𐑄𐐯𐑉 𐐹𐐨𐑅 𐐲𐑋𐐲𐑍𐑅𐐻 𐑄𐐯𐑋𐑅𐐯𐑊𐑂𐑆, 𐑄𐐩 𐐶𐐲𐑉 𐐿𐐱𐑋𐐹𐐯𐑊𐐼 𐑉𐐨𐑊𐐲𐐿𐐻𐐰𐑌𐐻𐑊𐐨 𐐻𐐭 𐐿𐐱𐑌𐐻𐐯𐑌𐐼 𐐶𐐮𐑄 𐑄𐐯𐑉 𐐺𐑉𐐯𐑄𐑉𐐯𐑌, 𐑄 𐐢𐐩𐑋𐐲𐑌𐐴𐐻𐑅; 𐐷𐐩, 𐐰𐑌𐐼 𐐮𐑌 𐑁𐐴𐑌, 𐑄𐐯𐑉 𐐶𐐫𐑉𐑆 𐑌𐐯𐑂𐐲𐑉 𐐼𐐮𐐼 𐑅𐐨𐑅 𐑁𐐫𐑉 𐑄 𐑅𐐹𐐩𐑅 𐐱𐑂 𐑋𐐯𐑌𐐨 𐐷𐐨𐑉𐑆 𐐶𐐮𐑄 𐑄 𐐢𐐩𐑋𐐲𐑌𐐴𐐻𐑅, 𐑌𐐪𐐻𐐶𐐮𐑃𐑅𐐻𐐰𐑌𐐼𐐮𐑍 𐑄𐐯𐑉 𐑋𐐲𐐽 𐑉𐐨𐑊𐐲𐐿𐐻𐐰𐑌𐑅. 𐐤𐐵 𐑄𐐩 𐐶𐐲𐑉 𐑅𐐪𐑉𐐨 𐐻𐐭 𐐻𐐩𐐿 𐐲𐐹 𐐪𐑉𐑋𐑆 𐐲𐑀𐐯𐑌𐑅𐐻 𐑄 𐐢𐐩𐑋𐐲𐑌𐐴𐐻𐑅, 𐐺𐐨𐐿𐐫𐑆 𐑄𐐩 𐐼𐐮𐐼 𐑌𐐪𐐻 𐐼𐐨𐑊𐐴𐐻 𐐮𐑌 𐑄 𐑇𐐯𐐼𐐮𐑍 𐐱𐑂 𐐺𐑊𐐲𐐼; 𐐷𐐩, 𐐰𐑌𐐼

𐑄𐐮𐑅 𐐶𐐱𐑆 𐑌𐐱𐐻 𐐫𐑊; 𐑄𐐩 𐐶𐐲𐑉 𐑅𐐱𐑉𐐨 𐐻𐐭 𐐺𐐨 𐑄 𐑋𐐨𐑌𐑆 𐐱𐑂 𐑅𐐯𐑌𐐼𐐮𐑍 𐑅𐐬 𐑋𐐯𐑌𐐨 𐐱𐑂 𐑄𐐩𐑉 𐐺𐑉𐐯𐑄𐑉𐐯𐑌 𐐵𐐻 𐐱𐑂 𐑄𐐮𐑅 𐐶𐐲𐑉𐑊𐐼 𐐮𐑌𐐻𐐭 𐐰𐑌 𐐨𐐻𐐲𐑉𐑌𐐲𐑊 𐐶𐐲𐑉𐑊𐐼 𐐲𐑌𐐹𐑉𐐨𐐹𐐩𐑉𐐼 𐐻𐐭 𐑋𐐨𐐻 𐑄𐐩𐑉 𐐘𐐱𐐼; 𐑌𐐯𐑂𐐲𐑉𐑄𐐲𐑊𐐯𐑅 𐑄𐐩 𐐿𐐳𐐼 𐑌𐐱𐐻 𐑅𐐲𐑁𐐲𐑉 𐐻𐐭 𐑊𐐩 𐐼𐐵𐑌 𐑄𐐩𐑉 𐑊𐐴𐑂𐑆, 𐑄𐐰𐐻 𐑄𐐩𐑉 𐐶𐐴𐑂𐑆 𐐰𐑌𐐼 𐑄𐐩𐑉 𐐽𐐮𐑊𐐼𐑉𐐯𐑌 𐑇𐐳𐐼 𐐺𐐨 𐑋𐐰𐑅𐐲𐐿𐐲𐑉𐐼 𐐺𐐴 𐑄 𐐺𐐪𐑉𐐺𐐲𐑉𐐲𐑅 𐐿𐑉𐐭𐐲𐑊𐐻𐐨 𐐱𐑂 𐑄𐐬𐑆 𐐸𐐭 𐐶𐐲𐑉 𐐶𐐲𐑌𐑅 𐑄𐐩𐑉 𐐺𐑉𐐯𐑄𐑉𐐯𐑌, 𐐷𐐩, 𐐰𐑌𐐼 𐐸𐐰𐐼 𐐼𐐮𐑅𐐯𐑌𐐻𐐯𐐼 𐑁𐑉𐐱𐑋 𐑄𐐩𐑉 𐐽𐐲𐑉𐐽, 𐐰𐑌𐐼 𐐸𐐰𐐼 𐑊𐐯𐑁𐐻 𐑄𐐯𐑋, 𐐰𐑌𐐼 𐐸𐐰𐐼 𐑀𐐱𐑌 𐐻𐐭 𐐼𐐯𐑅𐐻𐑉𐐦 𐑄𐐯𐑋 𐐺𐐴 𐐾𐐦𐑌𐐮𐑍 𐑄 𐐢𐐩𐑋𐐲𐑌𐐴𐐻𐑅; 𐐷𐐩, 𐑄𐐩 𐐿𐐳𐐼 𐑌𐐱𐐻 𐐺𐐩𐑉 𐑄𐐰𐐻 𐑄𐐩𐑉 𐐺𐑉𐐯𐑄𐑉𐐯𐑌 𐑇𐐳𐐼 𐑉𐐨𐐾𐐦𐑅 𐐬𐑂𐐲𐑉 𐑄 𐐺𐑊𐐲𐐼 𐐱𐑂 𐑄 𐐤𐐨𐑁𐐴𐐻𐑅, 𐑅𐐬 𐑊𐐱𐑍 𐐰𐑆 𐑄𐐩𐑉 𐐶𐐲𐑉 𐐯𐑌𐐨 𐐸𐐭 𐑇𐐳𐐼 𐐿𐐨𐐹 𐑄 𐐿𐐲𐑋𐐰𐑌𐐼𐑋𐐯𐑌𐐻𐑅 𐐱𐑂 𐐘𐐱𐐼, 𐑁𐐫𐑉 𐑄 𐐹𐑉𐐱𐑋𐐮𐑅 𐐱𐑂 𐑄 𐐢𐐫𐑉𐐼 𐐶𐐱𐑆, 𐐮𐑁 𐑄𐐩 𐑇𐐳𐐼 𐐿𐐨𐐹 𐐸𐐮𐑆 𐐿𐐲𐑋𐐰𐑌𐐼𐑋𐐯𐑌𐐻𐑅, 𐑄𐐩 𐑇𐐳𐐼 𐐹𐑉𐐱𐑅𐐹𐐲𐑉 𐐮𐑌 𐑄 𐑊𐐰𐑌𐐼.

34. 𐐈𐑌𐐼 𐑌𐐵 𐐮𐐻 𐐿𐐩𐑋 𐐻𐐭 𐐹𐐰𐑅, 𐐮𐑌 𐑄 𐐮𐑊𐐯𐑂𐐲𐑌𐑃 𐑋𐐲𐑌𐑃 𐐱𐑂 𐑄 𐑌𐐴𐑌𐐻𐐨𐑌𐑃 𐐷𐐨𐑉, 𐐱𐑌 𐑄 𐐻𐐯𐑌𐑃 𐐼𐐩 𐐱𐑂 𐑄 𐑋𐐲𐑌𐑃, 𐑄 𐐪𐑉𐑋𐐨𐑆 𐐱𐑂 𐑄 𐐢𐐩𐑋𐐲𐑌𐐴𐐻𐑅 𐐶𐐲𐑉 𐑅𐐨𐑌 𐐲𐐹𐑉𐐬𐐽𐐮𐑍 𐐻𐐬𐑉𐐼𐑆 𐑄 𐑊𐐰𐑌𐐼 𐐱𐑂 𐐈𐑋𐐱𐑌𐐴𐐸𐐪. 𐐈𐑌𐐼 𐐺𐐨𐐸𐐬𐑊𐐼, 𐑄 𐑅𐐮𐐻𐐨 𐐸𐐰𐐼 𐐺𐐮𐑌 𐑉𐐨-𐐺𐐮𐑊𐐻, 𐐰𐑌𐐼 𐐣𐐬𐑉𐐬𐑌𐐴 𐐸𐐰𐐼 𐑅𐐻𐐩𐑇𐐲𐑌𐐼 𐐰𐑌 𐐪𐑉𐑋𐐨 𐐺𐐴 𐑄 𐐺𐐫𐑉𐐼𐐲𐑉𐑆 𐐱𐑂 𐑄 𐑅𐐮𐐻𐐨, 𐐰𐑌𐐼 𐑄𐐩 𐐸𐐰𐐼 𐐿𐐰𐑅𐐻 𐐲𐐹 𐐼𐐲𐑉𐐻 𐑉𐐵𐑌𐐼 𐐲𐐺𐐵𐐻, 𐐻𐐭 𐑇𐐨𐑊𐐼 𐑄𐐯𐑋 𐑁𐑉𐐱𐑋 𐑄 𐐰𐑉𐐬𐑆 𐐰𐑌𐐼 𐑄 𐑅𐐻𐐬𐑌𐑆 𐐱𐑂 𐑄 𐐢𐐩𐑋𐐲𐑌𐐴𐐻𐑅; 𐑁𐐫𐑉 𐐺𐐨𐐸𐐬𐑊𐐼, 𐑄𐐩 𐑁𐐫𐐻 𐐶𐐮𐑄 𐑅𐐻𐐬𐑌𐑆, 𐐰𐑌𐐼 𐐶𐐮𐑄 𐐰𐑉𐐬𐑆. 𐐒𐐨𐐸𐐬𐑊𐐼, 𐐌 𐑅𐐯𐐼 𐑄𐐰𐐻 𐑄 𐑅𐐮𐐻𐐨 𐐱𐑂 𐐈𐑋𐐱𐑌𐐴𐐸𐐪 𐐸𐐰𐐼 𐐺𐐮𐑌 𐑉𐐨-𐐺𐐮𐑊𐐻. 𐐌 𐑅𐐩 𐐲𐑌𐐻𐐭 𐐷𐐭, 𐐏𐐩, 𐑄𐐰𐐻 𐐮𐐻 𐐶𐐱𐑆 𐐮𐑌 𐐹𐐪𐑉𐐻 𐑉𐐨-𐐺𐐮𐑊𐐻, 𐐰𐑌𐐼 𐐺𐐨𐐿𐐫𐑆 𐑄 𐐢𐐩𐑋𐐲𐑌𐐴𐐻𐑅 𐐸𐐰𐐼 𐐼𐐯𐑅𐐻𐑉𐐦𐐼 𐐮𐐻 𐐶𐐲𐑌𐑅 𐐺𐐨𐐿𐐫𐑆 𐐱𐑂 𐑄 𐐮𐑌𐐮𐐿𐐶𐐮𐐻𐐨 𐐱𐑂 𐑄 𐐹𐐨𐐹𐐲𐑊, 𐑄𐐩 𐑅𐐲𐐹𐐬𐑆𐐼 𐑄𐐰𐐻 𐐮𐐻 𐐶𐐳𐐼 𐐲𐑀𐐯𐑌 𐐺𐐨𐐿𐐲𐑋 𐐰𐑌 𐐨𐑆𐐨 𐐹𐑉𐐩 𐑁𐐫𐑉 𐑄𐐯𐑋. 𐐒𐐲𐐻 𐐺𐐨𐐸𐐬𐑊𐐼, 𐐸𐐵 𐑀𐑉𐐩𐐻 𐐶𐐱𐑆 𐑄𐐩𐑉 𐐼𐐮𐑅𐐲𐐹𐐦𐑌𐐻𐑋𐐯𐑌𐐻: 𐑁𐐫𐑉 𐐺𐐨𐐸𐐬𐑊𐐼, 𐑄 𐐤𐐨𐑁𐐴𐐻𐑅 𐐸𐐰𐐼 𐐼𐐲𐑀 𐐲𐐹 𐐲 𐑉𐐮𐐾 𐐱𐑂 𐐲𐑉𐑃 𐑉𐐵𐑌𐐼 𐐲𐐺𐐵𐐻 𐑄𐐯𐑋, 𐐸𐐶𐐮𐐽 𐐶𐐱𐑆 𐑅𐐬 𐐸𐐴 𐑄𐐰𐐻 𐑄 𐐢𐐩𐑋𐐲𐑌𐐴𐐻𐑅 𐐿𐐳𐐼 𐑌𐐱𐐻 𐐿𐐰𐑅𐐻 𐑄𐐩𐑉 𐑅𐐻𐐬𐑌𐑆 𐐰𐑌𐐼 𐑄𐐩𐑉 𐐰𐑉𐐬𐑆 𐐰𐐻 𐑄𐐯𐑋, 𐑄𐐰𐐻 𐑄𐐩 𐑋𐐴𐐻 𐐻𐐩𐐿 𐐯𐑁𐐯𐐿𐐻, 𐑌𐐨𐑄𐐲𐑉 𐐿𐐳𐐼 𐑄𐐩 𐐿𐐲𐑋 𐐲𐐹𐐱𐑌 𐑄𐐯𐑋, 𐑅𐐩𐑂 𐐮𐐻 𐐶𐐱𐑆 𐐺𐐴 𐑄𐐩𐑉 𐐹𐑊𐐩𐑅 𐐱𐑂 𐐯𐑌𐐻𐑉𐐲𐑌𐑅. 𐐤𐐵 𐐰𐐻 𐑄𐐮𐑅 𐐻𐐴𐑋 𐑄 𐐽𐐨𐑁 𐐿𐐰𐐹𐐻𐐲𐑌𐑆 𐐱𐑂 𐑄 𐐢𐐩𐑋𐐲𐑌𐐴𐐻𐑅 𐐶𐐲𐑉 𐐲𐑅𐐻𐐱𐑌𐐮𐑇𐐻 𐐯𐐿𐑅𐐨𐐼𐐮𐑍𐑊𐐨, 𐐺𐐨𐐿𐐫𐑆 𐐱𐑂 𐑄 𐐶𐐮𐑆𐐼𐐲𐑋 𐐱𐑂 𐑄 𐐤𐐨𐑁𐐴𐐻𐑅 𐐮𐑌 𐐹𐑉𐐨𐐹𐐩𐑉𐐮𐑍 𐑄𐐩𐑉 𐐹𐑊𐐩𐑅𐐯𐑆 𐐱𐑂 𐑅𐐨𐐿𐐷𐐭𐑉𐐮𐐻𐐨. 𐐤𐐵 𐑄 𐑊𐐨𐐼𐐲𐑉𐑆 𐐱𐑂 𐑄 𐐢𐐩𐑋𐐲𐑌𐐴𐐻𐑅 𐐸𐐰𐐼 𐑅𐐲𐐹𐐬𐑆𐐼, 𐐺𐐨𐐿𐐫𐑆 𐐱𐑂 𐑄 𐑀𐑉𐐩𐐻𐑌𐐯𐑅 𐐱𐑂 𐑄𐐩𐑉 𐑌𐐲𐑋𐐺𐐲𐑉𐑆, 𐐷𐐩, 𐑄𐐩 𐑅𐐲𐐹𐐬𐑆𐐼 𐑄𐐰𐐻 𐑄𐐩 𐑇𐐳𐐼 𐐺𐐨 𐐹𐑉𐐮𐑂𐐮𐑊𐐯𐐾𐐼 𐐻𐐭 𐐿𐐲𐑋 𐐲𐐹𐐱𐑌 𐑄𐐯𐑋 𐐰𐑆 𐑄𐐩 𐐸𐐰𐐼 𐐸𐐮𐑄𐐲𐑉𐐻𐐭 𐐼𐐲𐑌; 𐐷𐐩, 𐐰𐑌𐐼 𐑄𐐩 𐐸𐐰𐐼 𐐫𐑊𐑅𐐬 𐐹𐑉𐐨𐐹𐐩𐑉𐐼 𐑄𐐯𐑋𐑅𐐯𐑊𐑂𐑆 𐐶𐐮𐑄 𐑇𐐨𐑊𐐼𐑆, 𐐰𐑌𐐼 𐐶𐐮𐑄 𐐺𐑉𐐯𐑅𐐻-𐐹𐑊𐐩𐐻𐑅; 𐐰𐑌𐐼 𐑄𐐩 𐐸𐐰𐐼 𐐫𐑊𐑅𐐬 𐐹𐑉𐐨𐐹𐐩𐑉𐐼 𐑄𐐯𐑋𐑅𐐯𐑊𐑂𐑆 𐐶𐐮𐑄 𐑀𐐪𐑉𐑋𐐯𐑌𐐻𐑅 𐐱𐑂 𐑅𐐿𐐮𐑌𐑆; 𐐷𐐩, 𐑂𐐯𐑉𐐨 𐑃𐐮𐐿 𐑀𐐪𐑉𐑋𐐯𐑌𐐻𐑅 𐐻𐐭 𐐿𐐲𐑂𐐲𐑉 𐑄𐐩𐑉 𐑌𐐩𐐿𐐯𐐼𐑌𐐯𐑅. 𐐈𐑌𐐼 𐐺𐐨𐐮𐑍 𐑄𐐲𐑅 𐐹𐑉𐐨𐐹𐐩𐑉𐐼, 𐑄𐐩 𐑅𐐲𐐹𐐬𐑆𐐼 𐑄𐐰𐐻 𐑄𐐩 𐑇𐐳𐐼 𐐨𐑆𐐮𐑊𐐨 𐐬𐑂𐐲𐑉𐐹𐐵𐐲𐑉 𐐰𐑌𐐼 𐑅𐐲𐐺𐐾𐐯𐐿𐐻 𐑄𐐩𐑉 𐐺𐑉𐐯𐑄𐑉𐐯𐑌 𐐻𐐭 𐑄 𐐷𐐬𐐿 𐐱𐑂 𐐺𐐱𐑌𐐼𐐩𐐾, 𐐫𐑉 𐑅𐑊𐐩 𐐰𐑌𐐼 𐑋𐐰𐑅𐐲𐐿𐐲𐑉 𐑄𐐯𐑋 𐐰𐐿𐐫𐑉𐐼𐐮𐑍 𐐻𐐭 𐑄𐐩𐑉 𐐹𐑊𐐯𐑠𐐲𐑉. 𐐒𐐲𐐻 𐐺𐐨𐐸𐐬𐑊𐐼, 𐐻𐐭 𐑄𐐩𐑉 𐐲𐐻𐐲𐑉𐑋𐐬𐑅𐐻 𐐲𐑅𐐻𐐱𐑌𐐮𐑇𐑋𐐯𐑌𐐻, 𐑄𐐩 𐐶𐐲𐑉 𐐹𐑉𐐨𐐹𐐩𐑉𐐼 𐑁𐐫𐑉 𐑄𐐯𐑋, 𐐮𐑌 𐐲 𐑋𐐰𐑌𐐲𐑉 𐐸𐐶𐐮𐐽 𐑌𐐯𐑂𐐲𐑉 𐐸𐐰𐐼 𐐺𐐮𐑌 𐑌𐐬𐑌 𐐲𐑋𐐲𐑍 𐑄 𐐽𐐮𐑊𐐼𐑉𐐯𐑌 𐐱𐑂 𐐢𐐨𐐸𐐴. 𐐤𐐵 𐑄𐐩 𐐶𐐲𐑉 𐐹𐑉𐐨𐐹𐐩𐑉𐐼 𐑁𐐫𐑉 𐑄 𐐢𐐩𐑋𐐲𐑌𐐴𐐻𐑅, 𐐻𐐭 𐐺𐐰𐐻𐐲𐑊 𐐰𐑁𐐻𐐲𐑉 𐑄 𐑋𐐰𐑌𐐲𐑉 𐐱𐑂 𐑄 𐐮𐑌𐑅𐐻𐑉𐐲𐐿𐑇𐐲𐑌𐑆 𐐱𐑂 𐐣𐐬𐑉𐐬𐑌𐐴.

35. 𐐈𐑌𐐼 𐐮𐐻 𐐿𐐩𐑋 𐐻𐐭 𐐹𐐰𐑅 𐑄𐐰𐐻 𐑄 𐐢𐐩𐑋𐐲𐑌𐐴𐐻𐑅, 𐐫𐑉 𐑄 𐐈𐑋𐐲𐑊𐐮𐐿𐐴𐐲𐐸𐐴𐐻𐑅, 𐐶𐐲𐑉 𐐯𐐿𐑅𐐨𐐼𐐮𐑍𐑊𐐨 𐐲𐑅𐐻𐐱𐑌𐐮𐑇𐐻 𐐰𐐻 𐑄𐐩𐑉 𐑋𐐰𐑌𐐲𐑉 𐐱𐑂 𐐹𐑉𐐯𐐹𐐲𐑉𐐩𐑇𐐲𐑌 𐑁𐐫𐑉 𐐶𐐫𐑉. 𐐤𐐵 𐐮𐑁 𐐿𐐮𐑍 𐐈𐑋𐐲𐑊𐐮𐐿𐐴𐐲 𐐸𐐰𐐼 𐐿𐐲𐑋 𐐼𐐵𐑌 𐐵𐐻 𐐱𐑂 𐑄 𐑊𐐰𐑌𐐼 𐐱𐑂 𐐤𐐨𐑁𐐴, 𐐰𐐻 𐑄 𐐸𐐯𐐼 𐐱𐑂 𐐸𐐮𐑆 𐐪𐑉𐑋𐐨, 𐐹𐐲𐑉𐐸𐐰𐐹𐑅 𐐸𐐨 𐐶𐐳𐐼 𐐸𐐰𐑂 𐐿𐐫𐑆𐐼 𐑄 𐐢𐐩𐑋𐐲𐑌𐐴𐐻𐑅 𐐻𐐭 𐐸𐐰𐑂 𐐲𐐻𐐰𐐿𐐻 𐑄 𐐤𐐨𐑁𐐴𐐻𐑅 𐐰𐐻 𐑄 𐑅𐐮𐐻𐐨 𐐱𐑂 𐐈𐑋𐐱𐑌𐐴𐐸𐐪; 𐑁𐐫𐑉 𐐺𐐨𐐸𐐬𐑊𐐼, 𐐸𐐨 𐐼𐐮𐐼 𐐿𐐩𐑉 𐑌𐐱𐐻 𐑁𐐫𐑉 𐑄 𐐺𐑊𐐲𐐼 𐐱𐑂 𐐸𐐮𐑆 𐐹𐐨𐐹𐐲𐑊. 𐐒𐐲𐐻 𐐺𐐨𐐸𐐬𐑊𐐼, 𐐈𐑋𐐲𐑊𐐮𐐿𐐴𐐲 𐐼𐐮𐐼 𐑌𐐱𐐻 𐐿𐐲𐑋 𐐼𐐵𐑌 𐐸𐐮𐑋𐑅𐐯𐑊𐑁 𐐻𐐭 𐐺𐐰𐐻𐐲𐑊. 𐐈𐑌𐐼 𐐺𐐨𐐸𐐬𐑊𐐼, 𐐸𐐮𐑆 𐐽𐐨𐑁 𐐿𐐰𐐹𐐻𐐲𐑌𐑆 𐐼𐐲𐑉𐑅𐐻 𐑌𐐱𐐻 𐐲𐐻𐐰𐐿 𐑄 𐐤𐐨𐑁𐐴𐐻𐑅 𐐰𐐻 𐑄 𐑅𐐮𐐻𐐨 𐐱𐑂 𐐈𐑋𐐱𐑌𐐴𐐸𐐪, 𐑁𐐫𐑉 𐐣𐐬𐑉𐐬𐑌𐐴 𐐸𐐰𐐼 𐐫𐑊𐐻𐐲𐑉𐐼 𐑄 𐑋𐐰𐑌𐐲𐐾𐑋𐐯𐑌𐐻 𐐱𐑂 𐐰𐑁𐐩𐑉𐑆 𐐲𐑋𐐲𐑍 𐑄 𐐤𐐨𐑁𐐴𐐻𐑅, 𐐮𐑌𐑅𐐬𐑋𐐲𐐽 𐑄𐐰𐐻 𐑄 𐐢𐐩𐑋𐐲𐑌𐐴𐐻𐑅 𐐶𐐲𐑉 𐐼𐐮𐑅𐐲𐐹𐐦𐑌𐐻𐐯𐐼 𐐮𐑌 𐑄𐐩𐑉 𐐹𐑊𐐩𐑅𐐯𐑆 𐐱𐑂 𐑉𐐨𐐻𐑉𐐨𐐻, 𐐰𐑌𐐼 𐑄𐐩 𐐿𐐳𐐼 𐑌𐐱𐐻 𐐿𐐲𐑋 𐐲𐐹𐐱𐑌 𐑄𐐯𐑋; 𐑄𐐩𐑉𐑁𐐬𐑉 𐑄𐐩 𐑉𐐨𐐻𐑉𐐨𐐻𐐯𐐼 𐐮𐑌𐐻𐐭 𐑄 𐐶𐐮𐑊𐐼𐐲𐑉𐑌𐐯𐑅, 𐐰𐑌𐐼 𐐻𐐳𐐿 𐑄𐐩𐑉

𐐿𐐰𐑋𐐹, 𐐰𐑌𐐼 𐑋𐐪𐑉𐐽𐐻 𐐻𐐬𐑉𐐼𐑆 𐑄 𐑊𐐰𐑌𐐼 𐐱𐑂 𐐤𐐬𐐲, 𐑅𐐲𐐹𐐬𐑆𐐮𐑍 𐑄𐐰𐐻 𐐻𐐭 𐐺𐐨 𐑄 𐑌𐐯𐐿𐑅𐐻 𐐺𐐯𐑅𐐻 𐐹𐑊𐐩𐑅 𐑁𐐫𐑉 𐑄𐐯𐑋 𐐻𐐭 𐐿𐐲𐑋 𐐲𐑀𐐯𐑌𐑅𐐻 𐑄 𐐤𐐨𐑁𐐴𐐻𐑅; 𐑁𐐫𐑉 𐑄𐐩 𐑌𐐭 𐑌𐐱𐐻 𐑄𐐰𐐻 𐐣𐐫𐑉𐐬𐑌𐐴 𐐸𐐰𐐼 𐑁𐐫𐑉𐐻𐐮𐑁𐐴𐐼, 𐐫𐑉 𐐸𐐰𐐼 𐐺𐐮𐑊𐐻 𐑁𐐫𐑉𐐻𐑅 𐐱𐑂 𐑅𐐨𐐿𐐷𐐭𐑉𐐮𐐻𐐨, 𐑁𐐫𐑉 𐐯𐑂𐐲𐑉𐐨 𐑅𐐮𐐻𐐨 𐐮𐑌 𐐫𐑊 𐑄 𐑊𐐰𐑌𐐼 𐑉𐐵𐑌𐐼 𐐲𐐺𐐵𐐻; 𐑄𐐯𐑉𐑁𐐬𐑉, 𐑄𐐩 𐑋𐐪𐑉𐐽𐐻 𐑁𐐫𐑉𐐶𐐲𐑉𐐼 𐐻𐐭 𐑄 𐑊𐐰𐑌𐐼 𐐱𐑂 𐐤𐐬𐐲 𐐶𐐮𐑄 𐐲 𐑁𐐲𐑉𐑋 𐐼𐐨𐐻𐐲𐑉𐑋𐐮𐑌𐐩𐑇𐐲𐑌; 𐐷𐐩, 𐑄𐐩𐑉 𐐽𐐨𐑁 𐐿𐐰𐐹𐐻𐐮𐑌𐑆 𐐿𐐩𐑋 𐑁𐐫𐑉𐐶𐐲𐑉𐐼 𐐰𐑌𐐼 𐐻𐐳𐐿 𐐰𐑌 𐐬𐑃 𐑄𐐰𐐻 𐑄𐐩 𐐶𐐳𐐼 𐐼𐐨𐑅𐐻𐑉𐑎 𐑄 𐐹𐐨𐐹𐑊 𐐱𐑂 𐑄𐐰𐐻 𐑅𐐮𐐻𐐨. 𐐒𐐲𐐻, 𐐺𐐨𐐸𐐬𐑊𐐼, 𐐻𐐭 𐑄𐐩𐑉 𐐲𐑅𐐻𐐱𐑌𐐮𐑇𐑋𐐯𐑌𐐻, 𐑄 𐑅𐐮𐐻𐐨 𐐱𐑂 𐐤𐐬𐐲, 𐐸𐐶𐐮𐐽 𐐸𐐰𐐼 𐐸𐐮𐑄𐐲𐑉𐐻𐐭 𐐺𐐮𐑌 𐐲 𐐶𐐨𐐿 𐐹𐑊𐐩𐑅, 𐐸𐐰𐐼 𐑌𐐵, 𐐺𐐴 𐑄 𐑋𐐨𐑌𐑆 𐐱𐑂 𐐣𐐫𐑉𐐬𐑌𐐴, 𐐺𐐨𐐿𐐲𐑋 𐑅𐐻𐑉𐐫𐑍; 𐐷𐐩, 𐐨𐑂𐐲𐑌 𐐻𐐭 𐐯𐐿𐑅𐐨𐐼 𐑄 𐑅𐐻𐑉𐐯𐑍𐑃 𐐱𐑂 𐑄 𐑅𐐮𐐻𐐨 𐐈𐑋𐐱𐑌𐐴𐐸𐐪. 𐐈𐑌𐐼 𐑌𐐵, 𐐺𐐨𐐸𐐬𐑊𐐼, 𐑄𐐮𐑅 𐐶𐐱𐑆 𐐶𐐮𐑆𐐼𐐲𐑋 𐐮𐑌 𐐣𐐫𐑉𐐬𐑌𐐴; 𐑁𐐫𐑉 𐐸𐐨 𐐸𐐰𐐼 𐑅𐐲𐐹𐐬𐑆𐐼 𐑄𐐰𐐻 𐑄𐐩 𐐶𐐳𐐼 𐐺𐐨 𐑁𐑉𐐴𐐻𐐲𐑌𐐼 𐐰𐐻 𐑄 𐑅𐐮𐐻𐐨 𐐈𐑋𐐱𐑌𐐴𐐸𐐪; 𐐰𐑌𐐼 𐐰𐑆 𐑄 𐑅𐐮𐐻𐐨 𐐱𐑂 𐐤𐐬𐐲 𐐸𐐰𐐼 𐐸𐐮𐑄𐐲𐑉𐐻𐐭 𐐺𐐮𐑌 𐑄 𐐶𐐨𐐿𐐯𐑅𐐻 𐐹𐐪𐑉𐐻 𐐱𐑂 𐑄 𐑊𐐰𐑌𐐼, 𐑄𐐯𐑉𐑁𐐬𐑉 𐑄𐐩 𐐶𐐳𐐼 𐑋𐐪𐑉𐐽 𐑄𐐮𐑄𐐲𐑉 𐐻𐐭 𐐺𐐰𐐻𐑊; 𐐰𐑌𐐼 𐑄𐐲𐑅 𐐮𐐻 𐐶𐐱𐑆 𐐰𐐿𐐫𐑉𐐼𐐮𐑍 𐐻𐐭 𐐸𐐮𐑆 𐐼𐐨𐑆𐐴𐑉𐑆. 𐐈𐑌𐐼, 𐐺𐐨𐐸𐐬𐑊𐐼, 𐐣𐐫𐑉𐐬𐑌𐐴 𐐸𐐰𐐼 𐐲𐐹𐑎𐑌𐐻𐐯𐐼 𐐢𐐨𐐸𐐴 𐐻𐐭 𐐺𐐨 𐐽𐐨𐑁 𐐿𐐰𐐹𐐻𐐮𐑌 𐐬𐑂𐐲𐑉 𐑄 𐑋𐐯𐑌 𐐱𐑂 𐑄𐐰𐐻 𐑅𐐮𐐻𐐨; 𐐰𐑌𐐼 𐐮𐐻 𐐶𐐱𐑆 𐑄𐐰𐐻 𐑅𐐩𐑋 𐐢𐐨𐐸𐐴 𐐸𐐭 𐑁𐐫𐐻 𐐶𐐮𐑄 𐑄 𐐢𐐰𐑋𐐲𐑌𐐴𐐻𐑅 𐐮𐑌 𐑄 𐑂𐐰𐑊𐐨 𐐱𐑌 𐑄 𐐨𐑅𐐻 𐐱𐑂 𐑄 𐑉𐐮𐑂𐐲𐑉 𐐝𐐴𐐼𐐲𐑌.

36. 𐐈𐑌𐐼 𐑌𐐵 𐐺𐐨𐐸𐐬𐑊𐐼 𐐮𐐻 𐐿𐐩𐑋 𐐻𐐭 𐐹𐐪𐑅, 𐑄𐐰𐐻 𐐸𐐶𐐯𐑌 𐑄 𐐢𐐰𐑋𐐲𐑌𐐴𐐻𐑅 𐐸𐐰𐐼 𐑁𐐵𐑌𐐼 𐑄𐐰𐐻 𐐢𐐨𐐸𐐴 𐐿𐐲𐑋𐐰𐑌𐐼𐐯𐐼 𐑄 𐑅𐐮𐐻𐐨, 𐑄𐐩 𐐶𐐲𐑉 𐐲𐑀𐐯𐑌 𐐼𐐮𐑅𐐲𐐹𐑎𐑌𐐻𐐯𐐼, 𐑁𐐫𐑉 𐑄𐐩 𐑁𐐨𐑉𐐼 𐐢𐐨𐐸𐐴 𐐯𐐿𐑅𐐨𐐼𐐮𐑍𐑊𐐨; 𐑌𐐯𐑂𐐲𐑉𐑄𐐲𐑊𐐯𐑅 𐑄𐐩𐑉 𐐽𐐨𐑁 𐐿𐐰𐐹𐐻𐐮𐑌𐑆 𐐸𐐰𐐼 𐑅𐐶𐐫𐑉𐑌 𐐶𐐮𐑄 𐐰𐑌 𐐬𐑃 𐐻𐐭 𐐲𐐻𐐰𐐿 𐑄 𐑅𐐮𐐻𐐨; 𐑄𐐯𐑉𐑁𐐬𐑉, 𐑄𐐩 𐐺𐑉𐐫𐐻 𐐲𐐹 𐑄𐐩𐑉 𐐪𐑉𐑋𐐨𐑆. 𐐤𐐵 𐐺𐐨𐐸𐐬𐑊𐐼, 𐑄 𐐢𐐰𐑋𐐲𐑌𐐴𐐻𐑅 𐐿𐐳𐐼 𐑌𐐱𐐻 𐑀𐐯𐐻 𐐮𐑌𐐻𐐭 𐑄𐐩𐑉 𐑁𐐫𐑉𐐻𐑅 𐐱𐑂 𐑅𐐨𐐿𐐷𐐭𐑉𐐮𐐻𐐨, 𐐺𐐴 𐐯𐑌𐐨 𐐲𐑄𐐲𐑉 𐐶𐐩 𐑅𐐩𐑂 𐐺𐐴 𐑄 𐐯𐑌𐐻𐑉𐐲𐑌𐑅, 𐐺𐐨𐐿𐐫𐑆 𐐱𐑂 𐑄 𐐸𐐴𐑌𐐯𐑅 𐐱𐑂 𐑄 𐐺𐐰𐑍𐐿 𐐸𐐶𐐮𐐽 𐐸𐐰𐐼 𐐺𐐮𐑌 𐑃𐑉𐐬𐑌 𐐲𐐹, 𐐰𐑌𐐼 𐑄 𐐼𐐯𐐹𐑃 𐐱𐑂 𐑄 𐐼𐐮𐐽 𐐸𐐶𐐮𐐽 𐐸𐐰𐐼 𐐺𐐮𐑌 𐐼𐐲𐑀 𐑉𐐵𐑌𐐼 𐐲𐐺𐐵𐐻, 𐑅𐐩𐑂 𐐮𐐻 𐐶𐐲𐑉 𐐺𐐴 𐑄 𐐯𐑌𐐻𐑉𐐲𐑌𐑅. 𐐈𐑌𐐼 𐑄𐐲𐑅 𐐶𐐲𐑉 𐑄 𐐤𐐨𐑁𐐴𐐻𐑅 𐐹𐑉𐐨𐐹𐐩𐑉𐐼 𐐻𐐭 𐐼𐐨𐑅𐐻𐑉𐑎 𐐫𐑊 𐑅𐐲𐐽 𐐰𐑆 𐑇𐐳𐐼 𐐲𐐻𐐯𐑋𐐹𐐻 𐐻𐐭 𐐿𐑊𐐴𐑋 𐐲𐐹 𐐻𐐭 𐐯𐑌𐐻𐐲𐑉 𐑄 𐑁𐐫𐑉𐐻 𐐺𐐴 𐐯𐑌𐐨 𐐲𐑄𐐲𐑉 𐐶𐐩, 𐐺𐐴 𐐿𐐰𐑅𐐻𐐮𐑍 𐐬𐑂𐐲𐑉 𐑅𐐻𐐬𐑌𐑆 𐐰𐑌𐐼 𐐰𐑉𐐬𐑆 𐐰𐐻 𐑄𐐯𐑋. 𐐜𐐲𐑅 𐑄𐐩 𐐶𐐲𐑉 𐐹𐑉𐐨𐐹𐐩𐑉𐐼; 𐐷𐐩, 𐐲 𐐺𐐱𐐼𐐨 𐐱𐑂 𐑄𐐩𐑉 𐑅𐐻𐑉𐐫𐑍𐐯𐑅𐐻 𐑋𐐯𐑌, 𐐶𐐮𐑄 𐑄𐐩𐑉 𐑅𐐬𐑉𐐼𐑆 𐐰𐑌𐐼 𐑄𐐩𐑉 𐑅𐑊𐐮𐑍𐑆, 𐐻𐐭 𐑅𐑋𐐴𐐻 𐐼𐐵𐑌 𐐫𐑊 𐐸𐐭 𐑇𐐳𐐼 𐐲𐐻𐐯𐑋𐐹𐐻 𐐻𐐭 𐐿𐐲𐑋 𐐮𐑌𐐻𐐭 𐑄𐐩𐑉 𐐹𐑊𐐩𐑅 𐐱𐑂 𐑅𐐨𐐿𐐷𐐭𐑉𐐮𐐻𐐨 𐐺𐐴 𐑄 𐐹𐑊𐐩𐑅 𐐱𐑂 𐐯𐑌𐐻𐑉𐐲𐑌𐑅; 𐐰𐑌𐐼 𐑄𐐲𐑅 𐐶𐐲𐑉 𐑄𐐩 𐐹𐑉𐐨𐐹𐐩𐑉𐐼 𐐻𐐭 𐐼𐐨𐑁𐐯𐑌𐐼 𐑄𐐯𐑋𐑅𐐯𐑊𐑂𐑆 𐐲𐑀𐐯𐑌𐑅𐐻 𐑄 𐐢𐐰𐑋𐐲𐑌𐐴𐐻𐑅.

37. 𐐈𐑌𐐼 𐐮𐐻 𐐿𐐩𐑋 𐐻𐐭 𐐹𐐪𐑅 𐑄𐐰𐐻 𐑄 𐐿𐐰𐐹𐐻𐐮𐑌𐑆 𐐱𐑂 𐑄 𐐢𐐰𐑋𐐲𐑌𐐴𐐻𐑅 𐐺𐑉𐐫𐐻 𐐲𐐹 𐑄𐐩𐑉 𐐪𐑉𐑋𐐨𐑆 𐐺𐐨𐑁𐐬𐑉 𐑄 𐐹𐑊𐐩𐑅 𐐱𐑂 𐐯𐑌𐐻𐑉𐐲𐑌𐑅, 𐐰𐑌𐐼 𐐺𐐨𐑀𐐰𐑌 𐐻𐐭 𐐿𐐱𐑌𐐻𐐯𐑌𐐼 𐐶𐐮𐑄 𐑄 𐐤𐐨𐑁𐐴𐐻𐑅, 𐐻𐐭 𐑀𐐯𐐻 𐐮𐑌𐐻𐐭 𐑄𐐩𐑉 𐐹𐑊𐐩𐑅 𐐱𐑂 𐑅𐐨𐐿𐐷𐐭𐑉𐐮𐐻𐐨; 𐐺𐐲𐐻 𐐺𐐨𐐸𐐬𐑊𐐼, 𐑄𐐩 𐐶𐐲𐑉 𐐼𐑉𐐮𐑂𐐲𐑌 𐐺𐐰𐐿 𐑁𐑉𐐱𐑋 𐐻𐐴𐑋 𐐻𐐭 𐐻𐐴𐑋, 𐐮𐑌𐑅𐐬𐑋𐐲𐐽 𐑄𐐰𐐻 𐑄𐐩 𐐶𐐲𐑉 𐑅𐑊𐐩𐑌 𐐶𐐮𐑄 𐐰𐑌 𐐮𐑋𐐯𐑌𐑅 𐑅𐑊𐐫𐐻𐐲𐑉. 𐐤𐐵 𐐸𐐶𐐯𐑌 𐑄𐐩 𐑁𐐵𐑌𐐼 𐑄𐐰𐐻 𐑄𐐩 𐐿𐐳𐐼 𐑌𐐱𐐻 𐐱𐐺𐐻𐐩𐑌 𐐹𐐵𐐲𐑉 𐐬𐑂𐐲𐑉 𐑄 𐐤𐐨𐑁𐐴𐐻𐑅 𐐺𐐴 𐑄 𐐹𐐪𐑅, 𐑄𐐩 𐐺𐐨𐑀𐐰𐑌 𐐻𐐭 𐐼𐐮𐑀 𐐼𐐵𐑌 𐑄𐐩𐑉 𐐺𐐰𐑍𐐿𐑅 𐐱𐑂 𐐲𐑉𐑃, 𐑄𐐰𐐻 𐑄𐐩 𐑋𐐴𐐻 𐐱𐐺𐐻𐐩𐑌 𐐲 𐐹𐐪𐑅 𐐻𐐭 𐑄𐐩𐑉 𐐪𐑉𐑋𐐨𐑆, 𐑄𐐰𐐻 𐑄𐐩 𐑋𐐴𐐻 𐐸𐐰𐑂 𐐰𐑌 𐐨𐐿𐐶𐐲𐑊 𐐽𐐰𐑌𐑅 𐐻𐐭 𐑁𐐴𐐻; 𐐺𐐲𐐻 𐐺𐐨𐐸𐐬𐑊𐐼, 𐐮𐑌 𐑄𐐨𐑆 𐐲𐐻𐐯𐑋𐐹𐐻𐑅 𐑄𐐩 𐐶𐐲𐑉 𐑅𐐶𐐯𐐹𐐻 𐐫𐑁 𐐺𐐴 𐑄 𐑅𐐻𐐬𐑌𐑆 𐐰𐑌𐐼 𐐰𐑉𐐬𐑆 𐐸𐐶𐐮𐐽 𐐶𐐲𐑉 𐑃𐑉𐐬𐑌 𐐰𐐻 𐑄𐐯𐑋; 𐐰𐑌𐐼 𐐮𐑌𐑅𐐻𐐯𐐼 𐐱𐑂 𐑁𐐮𐑊𐐮𐑍 𐐲𐐹 𐑄𐐩𐑉 𐐼𐐮𐐽𐐯𐑆 𐐺𐐴 𐐹𐐳𐑊𐐮𐑍 𐐼𐐵𐑌 𐑄 𐐺𐐰𐑍𐐿𐑅 𐐱𐑂 𐐲𐑉𐑃, 𐑄𐐩 𐐶𐐲𐑉 𐑁𐐮𐑊𐐼 𐐲𐐹 𐐮𐑌 𐐲 𐑋𐐯𐑈𐐲𐑉 𐐶𐐮𐑄 𐑄𐐩𐑉 𐐼𐐯𐐼 𐐰𐑌𐐼 𐐶𐐭𐑌𐐼𐐯𐐼 𐐺𐐱𐐼𐐨𐑆. 𐐜𐐲𐑅 𐑄 𐐤𐐨𐑁𐐴𐐻𐑅 𐐸𐐰𐐼 𐐫𐑊 𐐹𐐵𐐲𐑉 𐐬𐑂𐐲𐑉 𐑄𐐩𐑉 𐐯𐑌𐐯𐑋𐐨𐑆; 𐐰𐑌𐐼 𐑄𐐲𐑅 𐑄 𐐢𐐰𐑋𐐲𐑌𐐴𐐻𐑅 𐐼𐐮𐐼 𐐲𐐻𐐯𐑋𐐹𐐻 𐐻𐐭 𐐼𐐨𐑅𐐻𐑉𐑎 𐑄 𐐤𐐨𐑁𐐴𐐻𐑅 𐐲𐑌𐐻𐐮𐑊 𐑄𐐩𐑉 𐐽𐐨𐑁 𐐿𐐰𐐹𐐻𐐮𐑌𐑆 𐐶𐐲𐑉 𐐫𐑊 𐑅𐑊𐐩𐑌; 𐐷𐐩, 𐐰𐑌𐐼 𐑋𐐬𐑉 𐑄𐐰𐑌 𐐲 𐑃𐐵𐑆𐐲𐑌𐐼 𐐱𐑂 𐑄 𐐢𐐰𐑋𐐲𐑌𐐴𐐻𐑅 𐐶𐐲𐑉 𐑅𐑊𐐩𐑌; 𐐸𐐶𐐴𐑊, 𐐱𐑌 𐑄 𐐲𐑄𐐲𐑉 𐐸𐐰𐑌𐐼, 𐑄𐐯𐑉 𐐶𐐱𐑆 𐑌𐐱𐐻 𐐲 𐑅𐐮𐑍𐑀𐑊 𐑅𐐬𐑊 𐐱𐑂 𐑄 𐐤𐐨𐑁𐐴𐐻𐑅 𐐸𐐶𐐮𐐽 𐐶𐐱𐑆 𐑅𐑊𐐩𐑌. 𐐜𐐯𐑉 𐐶𐐲𐑉 𐐲𐐺𐐵𐐻 𐑁𐐮𐑁𐐻𐐨 𐐸𐐭 𐐶𐐲𐑉 𐐶𐐭𐑌𐐼𐐯𐐼, 𐐸𐐭 𐐸𐐰𐐼 𐐺𐐮𐑌 𐐯𐐿𐑅𐐹𐐬𐑆𐐼 𐐻𐐭 𐑄 𐐰𐑉𐐬𐑆 𐐱𐑂 𐑄 𐐢𐐰𐑋𐐲𐑌𐐴𐐻𐑅 𐑃𐑉𐐭 𐑄 𐐹𐐪𐑅, 𐐺𐐲𐐻 𐑄𐐩 𐐶𐐲𐑉 𐑇𐐨𐑊𐐼𐐯𐐼 𐐺𐐴 𐑄𐐩𐑉 𐑇𐐨𐑊𐐼𐑆, 𐐰𐑌𐐼 𐑄𐐩𐑉 𐐺𐑉𐐯𐑅𐐻-𐐹𐑊𐐩𐐻𐑅, 𐐰𐑌𐐼 𐑄𐐩𐑉 𐐸𐐯𐐼-𐐹𐑊𐐩𐐻𐑅, 𐐮𐑌𐑅𐐬𐑋𐐲𐐽 𐑄𐐰𐐻 𐑄𐐩𐑉 𐐶𐐭𐑌𐐼𐑆 𐐶𐐲𐑉 𐐲𐐹𐐱𐑌 𐑄𐐩𐑉 𐑊𐐯𐑀𐑆, 𐑋𐐯𐑌𐐨 𐐱𐑂 𐐸𐐶𐐮𐐽 𐐶𐐲𐑉 𐑂𐐯𐑉𐐨 𐑅𐐨𐑂𐐨𐑉.

38. 𐐈𐑌𐐼 𐐮𐐻 𐐗𐐩𐑋 𐐻𐐭 𐐹𐐰𐑅, 𐑄𐐰𐐻 𐐸𐐶𐐯𐑌 𐑄 𐐢𐐰𐑋𐐲𐑌𐐴𐐻𐑅 𐑅𐐫 𐑄𐐰𐐻 𐑄𐐯𐑉 𐐽𐐨𐑁 𐐗𐐰𐐹𐐻𐐲𐑌𐑆 𐐶𐐲𐑉 𐐫𐑊 𐑅𐑊𐐩𐑌 𐑄𐐩 𐑁𐑊𐐯𐐼 𐐮𐑌𐐻𐐭 𐑄 𐐶𐐮𐑊𐐼𐐲𐑉𐑌𐐯𐑅. 𐐈𐑌𐐼 𐐮𐐻 𐐗𐐩𐑋 𐐻𐐭 𐐹𐐰𐑅 𐑄𐐰𐐻 𐑄𐐩 𐑉𐐨𐐻𐐲𐑉𐑌𐐼 𐐻𐐭 𐑄 𐑊𐐰𐑌𐐼 𐐱𐑂 𐐤𐐨𐑁𐐴, 𐐻𐐭 𐐮𐑌𐑁𐐫𐑉𐑋 𐑄𐐯𐑉 𐐗𐐮𐑍, 𐐈𐑋𐐰𐑊𐐮𐐗𐐴𐐲, 𐐸𐐭 𐐶𐐱𐑆 𐐩 𐐤𐐨𐑁𐐴𐐻 𐐺𐐴 𐐺𐐲𐑉𐑃, 𐐗𐐱𐑌𐑅𐐲𐑉𐑌𐐮𐑍 𐑄𐐯𐑉 𐑀𐑉𐐩𐐻 𐑊𐐱𐑅. 𐐈𐑌𐐼 𐐮𐐻 𐐗𐐩𐑋 𐐻𐐭 𐐹𐐰𐑅 𐑄𐐰𐐻 𐐸𐐨 𐐶𐐱𐑆 𐐯𐐗𐑅𐐨𐐼𐐮𐑍𐑊𐐨 𐐰𐑍𐑀𐑉𐐨 𐐶𐐮𐑄 𐐸𐐮𐑆 𐐹𐐨𐐹𐑊, 𐐺𐐨𐐗𐐫𐑆 𐐸𐐨 𐐸𐐰𐐼 𐑌𐐱𐐻 𐐱𐐺𐐻𐐩𐑌𐐼 𐐸𐐮𐑆 𐐼𐐨𐑆𐐴𐑉 𐐬𐑂𐐲𐑉 𐑄 𐐤𐐨𐑁𐐴𐐻𐑅; 𐐸𐐨 𐐸𐐰𐐼 𐑌𐐱𐐻 𐑅𐐲𐐺𐐾𐐯𐐗𐐻𐐯𐐼 𐑄𐐯𐑋 𐐻𐐭 𐑄 𐐷𐐬𐐗 𐐱𐑂 𐐺𐐱𐑌𐐼𐐩𐐾; 𐐷𐐩, 𐐸𐐨 𐐶𐐱𐑆 𐐯𐐗𐑅𐐨𐐼𐐮𐑍𐑊𐐨 𐑉𐐫𐑃, 𐐰𐑌𐐼 𐐸𐐨 𐐼𐐮𐐼 𐐗𐐲𐑉𐑅 𐐘𐐱𐐼, 𐐰𐑌𐐼 𐐫𐑊𐑅𐐬 𐐣𐐫𐑉𐐬𐑌𐐴, 𐐰𐑌𐐼 𐑅𐐶𐐯𐑉𐐮𐑍 𐐶𐐮𐑄 𐐰𐑌 𐐬𐑃 𐑄𐐰𐐻 𐐸𐐨 𐐶𐐳𐐼 𐐼𐑉𐐮𐑍𐐗 𐐸𐐮𐑆 𐐺𐑊𐐲𐐼; 𐐰𐑌𐐼 𐑄𐐮𐑅 𐐺𐐨𐐗𐐫𐑆 𐐣𐐫𐑉𐐬𐑌𐐴 𐐸𐐰𐐼 𐐗𐐯𐐹𐐻 𐑄 𐐗𐐱𐑋𐐰𐑌𐐼𐑋𐐯𐑌𐐻𐑅 𐐱𐑂 𐐘𐐱𐐼 𐐮𐑌 𐐹𐑉𐐨𐐹𐐯𐑉𐐮𐑍 𐑁𐐫𐑉 𐑄 𐑅𐐩𐑁𐐻𐐨 𐐱𐑂 𐐸𐐮𐑆 𐐹𐐨𐐹𐑊. 𐐈𐑌𐐼 𐐮𐐻 𐐗𐐩𐑋 𐐻𐐭 𐐹𐐰𐑅, 𐑄𐐰𐐻 𐐱𐑌 𐑄 𐐲𐑄𐐲𐑉 𐐸𐐰𐑌𐐼, 𐑄 𐐹𐐨𐐹𐑊 𐐱𐑂 𐐤𐐨𐑁𐐴 𐐼𐐮𐐼 𐑃𐐰𐑍𐐗 𐑄 𐐢𐐫𐑉𐐼 𐑄𐐯𐑉 𐐘𐐱𐐼, 𐐺𐐨𐐗𐐫𐑆 𐐱𐑂 𐐸𐐮𐑆 𐑋𐐰𐐽𐑊𐐯𐑅 𐐹𐐵𐐲𐑉 𐐮𐑌 𐐼𐐨𐑊𐐮𐑂𐐲𐑉𐐮𐑍 𐑄𐐯𐑋 𐑁𐑉𐐱𐑋 𐑄 𐐸𐐰𐑌𐐼𐑆 𐐱𐑂 𐑄𐐯𐑉 𐐯𐑌𐐯𐑋𐐨𐑆. 𐐈𐑌𐐼 𐑄𐐲𐑅 𐐯𐑌𐐼𐐯𐐼 𐑄 𐑌𐐴𐑌𐐻𐐨𐑌𐑃 𐐷𐐨𐑉 𐐱𐑂 𐑄 𐑉𐐩𐑌 𐐱𐑂 𐑄 𐐾𐐲𐐾𐐯𐑆 𐐬𐑂𐐲𐑉 𐑄 𐐹𐐨𐐹𐑊 𐐱𐑂 𐐤𐐨𐑁𐐴: 𐐷𐐩, 𐐰𐑌𐐼 𐑄𐐯𐑉 𐐶𐐱𐑆 𐐗𐐱𐑌𐐻𐐮𐑌𐐷𐐭𐐲𐑊 𐐹𐐨𐑅 𐐲𐑋𐐲𐑍 𐑄𐐯𐑋, 𐐰𐑌𐐼 𐐯𐐗𐑅𐐨𐐼𐐮𐑍𐑊𐐨 𐑀𐑉𐐩𐐻 𐐹𐑉𐐱𐑅𐐹𐐯𐑉𐐮𐐻𐐨 𐐮𐑌 𐑄 𐐽𐐲𐑉𐐽 𐐺𐐨𐐗𐐫𐑆 𐐱𐑂 𐑄𐐯𐑉 𐐸𐐨𐐼 𐐰𐑌𐐼 𐐼𐐮𐑊𐐮𐐾𐐯𐑌𐑅 𐐸𐐶𐐮𐐽 𐑄𐐩 𐑀𐐩𐑂 𐐲𐑌𐐻𐐭 𐑄 𐐶𐐲𐑉𐐼 𐐱𐑂 𐐘𐐱𐐼, 𐐸𐐶𐐮𐐽 𐐶𐐱𐑆 𐐼𐐨𐐗𐑊𐐩𐑉𐐼 𐐲𐑌𐐻𐐭 𐑄𐐯𐑋 𐐺𐐴 𐐐𐐨𐑊𐐲𐑋𐐲𐑌, 𐐰𐑌𐐼 𐐟𐐮𐐺𐑊𐐱𐑌, 𐐰𐑌𐐼 𐐗𐐫𐑉𐐨𐐰𐑌𐐻𐐱𐑌, 𐐰𐑌𐐼 𐐈𐑋𐐲𐑌 𐐰𐑌𐐼 𐐸𐐮𐑆 𐐺𐑉𐐯𐑄𐑉𐐯𐑌, 𐐯𐐻𐑅.: 𐐷𐐩, 𐐰𐑌𐐼 𐐺𐐴 𐐫𐑊 𐑄𐐬𐑆 𐐸𐐭 𐐸𐐰𐐼 𐐺𐐮𐑌 𐐫𐑉𐐼𐐩𐑌𐐼 𐐺𐐴 𐑄 𐐸𐐬𐑊𐐨 𐐫𐑉𐐼𐐲𐑉 𐐱𐑂 𐐘𐐱𐐼, 𐐺𐐨𐐮𐑍 𐐺𐐰𐐹𐐻𐐴𐑆𐐼 𐐲𐑌𐐻𐐭 𐑉𐐨𐐹𐐯𐑌𐐻𐐲𐑌𐑅, 𐐰𐑌𐐼 𐑅𐐯𐑌𐐻 𐑁𐐬𐑉𐑃 𐐻𐐭 𐐹𐑉𐐨𐐽 𐐲𐑋𐐲𐑍 𐑄 𐐹𐐨𐐹𐑊, 𐐯𐐻𐑅.

𐐗𐐰𐐹𐐻𐐲𐑉 XXII.

1. 𐐈𐑌𐐼 𐑌𐐵 𐐮𐐻 𐐗𐐩𐑋 𐐻𐐭 𐐹𐐰𐑅 𐑄𐐰𐐻 𐐣𐐫𐑉𐐬𐑌𐐴 𐐼𐐮𐐼 𐑌𐐱𐐻 𐑅𐐻𐐱𐐹 𐑋𐐩𐐗𐐮𐑍 𐐹𐑉𐐯𐐹𐐲𐑉𐐩𐑇𐐲𐑌𐑆 𐑁𐐫𐑉 𐐶𐐫𐑉, 𐐫𐑉 𐐻𐐭 𐐼𐐨𐑁𐐯𐑌𐐼 𐐸𐐮𐑆 𐐹𐐨𐐹𐑊 𐐲𐑀𐐯𐑌𐑅𐐻 𐑄 𐐢𐐰𐑋𐐲𐑌𐐴𐐻𐑅; 𐑁𐐫𐑉 𐐸𐐨 𐐗𐐫𐑆𐐼 𐑄𐐰𐐻 𐐸𐐮𐑆 𐐪𐑉𐑋𐐨𐑆 𐑇𐐳𐐼 𐐗𐐱𐑋𐐯𐑌𐑅 𐐮𐑌 𐑄 𐐗𐐱𐑋𐐯𐑌𐑅𐑋𐐯𐑌𐐻 𐐱𐑂 𐑄 𐐻𐐶𐐯𐑌𐐻𐐨𐐯𐑃 𐐷𐐨𐑉 𐐱𐑂 𐑄 𐑉𐐩𐑌 𐐱𐑂 𐑄 𐐾𐐲𐐾𐐯𐑆, 𐑄𐐰𐐻 𐑄𐐩 𐑇𐐳𐐼 𐐗𐐱𐑋𐐯𐑌𐑅 𐐮𐑌 𐐼𐐮𐑀𐐮𐑍 𐐲𐐹 𐐸𐐨𐐹𐑅 𐐱𐑂 𐐲𐑉𐑃 𐑉𐐵𐑌𐐼 𐐲𐐺𐐵𐐻 𐐫𐑊 𐑄 𐑅𐐮𐐻𐐨𐑆, 𐑃𐑉𐐭𐐵𐐻 𐐫𐑊 𐑄 𐑊𐐰𐑌𐐼 𐐸𐐶𐐮𐐽 𐐶𐐱𐑆 𐐹𐐱𐑆𐐯𐑅𐐻 𐐺𐐴 𐑄 𐐤𐐨𐑁𐐴𐐻𐑅; 𐐰𐑌𐐼 𐐲𐐹𐐱𐑌 𐑄 𐐻𐐱𐐹 𐐱𐑂 𐑄𐐨𐑆 𐑉𐐮𐐾𐐯𐑆 𐐱𐑂 𐐲𐑉𐑃 𐐸𐐨 𐐗𐐫𐑆𐐼 𐑄𐐰𐐻 𐑄𐐯𐑉 𐑇𐐳𐐼 𐐺𐐨 𐐻𐐮𐑋𐐺𐐲𐑉𐑆; 𐐷𐐩, 𐐶𐐲𐑉𐐿𐑅 𐐱𐑂 𐐻𐐮𐑋𐐺𐐲𐑉𐑆 𐐺𐐮𐑊𐐻 𐐲𐐹 𐐻𐐭 𐑄 𐐸𐐴𐐻 𐐱𐑂 𐐩 𐑋𐐰𐑌, 𐑉𐐵𐑌𐐼 𐐲𐐺𐐵𐐻 𐑄 𐑅𐐮𐐻𐐨𐑆. 𐐈𐑌𐐼 𐐸𐐨 𐐗𐐫𐑆𐐼 𐑄𐐰𐐻 𐐲𐐹𐐱𐑌 𐑄𐐬𐑆 𐐶𐐲𐑉𐐿𐑅 𐐱𐑂 𐐻𐐮𐑋𐐺𐐲𐑉𐑆, 𐑄𐐯𐑉 𐑇𐐳𐐼 𐐺𐐨 𐐩 𐑁𐑉𐐩𐑋 𐐱𐑂 𐐹𐐮𐐗𐐯𐐻𐑅 𐐺𐐮𐑊𐐻 𐐲𐐹𐐱𐑌 𐑄 𐐻𐐮𐑋𐐺𐐲𐑉𐑆 𐑉𐐵𐑌𐐼 𐐲𐐺𐐵𐐻; 𐐰𐑌𐐼 𐑄𐐩 𐐶𐐲𐑉 𐑅𐐻𐑉𐐱𐑍 𐐰𐑌𐐼 𐐸𐐴; 𐐰𐑌𐐼 𐐸𐐨 𐐗𐐫𐑆𐐼 𐐻𐐵𐐲𐑉𐑆 𐐻𐐭 𐐺𐐨 𐐨𐑉𐐯𐐗𐐻𐐯𐐼 𐑄𐐰𐐻 𐐬𐑂𐐲𐑉𐑊𐐳𐐿𐐻 𐑄𐐬𐑆 𐐶𐐲𐑉𐐿𐑅 𐐱𐑂 𐐹𐐮𐐗𐐯𐐻𐑅, 𐐰𐑌𐐼 𐐸𐐨 𐐗𐐫𐑆𐐼 𐐹𐑊𐐩𐑅𐐯𐑆 𐐱𐑂 𐑅𐐨𐐗𐐷𐐭𐑉𐐮𐐻𐐨 𐐻𐐭 𐐺𐐨 𐐺𐐮𐑊𐐻 𐐲𐐹𐐱𐑌 𐑄𐐬𐑆 𐐻𐐵𐐲𐑉𐑆, 𐑄𐐰𐐻 𐑄 𐑅𐐻𐐬𐑌𐑆 𐐰𐑌𐐼 𐑄 𐐰𐑉𐐬𐑆 𐐱𐑂 𐑄 𐐢𐐰𐑋𐐲𐑌𐐴𐐻𐑅 𐐗𐐳𐐼 𐑌𐐱𐐻 𐐸𐐲𐑉𐐻 𐑄𐐯𐑋. 𐐈𐑌𐐼 𐑄𐐩 𐐶𐐲𐑉 𐐹𐑉𐐨𐐹𐐩𐑉𐐼, 𐑄𐐰𐐻 𐑄𐐩 𐐗𐐳𐐼 𐐗𐐰𐑅𐐻 𐑅𐐻𐐬𐑌𐑆 𐑁𐑉𐐱𐑋 𐑄 𐐻𐐱𐐹 𐑄𐐯𐑉𐐱𐑂, 𐐰𐐗𐐫𐑉𐐼𐐮𐑍 𐐻𐐭 𐑄𐐯𐑉 𐐹𐑊𐐯𐑠𐐲𐑉 𐐰𐑌𐐼 𐑄𐐯𐑉 𐑅𐐻𐑉𐐯𐑍𐑃, 𐐰𐑌𐐼 𐑅𐑊𐐩 𐐸𐐮𐑋 𐐸𐐭 𐑇𐐳𐐼 𐐰𐐻𐐯𐑋𐐹𐐻 𐐻𐐭 𐐰𐐹𐑉𐐬𐐽 𐑌𐐨𐑉 𐑄 𐐶𐐫𐑊𐑆 𐐱𐑂 𐑄 𐑅𐐮𐐻𐐨. 𐐜𐐲𐑅 𐐣𐐫𐑉𐐬𐑌𐐴 𐐼𐐮𐐼 𐐹𐑉𐐨𐐹𐐩𐑉 𐑅𐐻𐑉𐐱𐑍𐐸𐐬𐑊𐐼𐑆 𐐲𐑀𐐯𐑌𐑅𐐻 𐑄 𐐗𐐲𐑋𐐮𐑍 𐐱𐑂 𐑄𐐯𐑉 𐐯𐑌𐐯𐑋𐐨𐑆, 𐑉𐐵𐑌𐐼 𐐲𐐺𐐵𐐻 𐐯𐑂𐐲𐑉𐐨 𐑅𐐮𐐻𐐨 𐐮𐑌 𐐫𐑊 𐑄 𐑊𐐰𐑌𐐼.

2. 𐐈𐑌𐐼 𐐮𐐻 𐐗𐐩𐑋 𐐻𐐭 𐐹𐐰𐑅 𐑄𐐰𐐻 𐐣𐐫𐑉𐐬𐑌𐐴 𐐗𐐫𐑆𐐼 𐑄𐐰𐐻 𐐸𐐮𐑆 𐐪𐑉𐑋𐐨𐑆 𐑇𐐳𐐼 𐑀𐐬 𐑁𐐬𐑉𐑃 𐐮𐑌𐐻𐐭 𐑄 𐐨𐑅𐐻 𐐶𐐮𐑊𐐼𐐲𐑉𐑌𐐯𐑅; 𐐷𐐩, 𐐰𐑌𐐼 𐑄𐐩 𐐶𐐯𐑌𐐻 𐑁𐐬𐑉𐑃 𐐰𐑌𐐼 𐐼𐑉𐐬𐑂 𐐫𐑊 𐑄 𐐢𐐰𐑋𐐲𐑌𐐴𐐻𐑅 𐐸𐐭 𐐶𐐲𐑉 𐐮𐑌 𐑄 𐐨𐑅𐐻 𐐶𐐮𐑊𐐼𐐲𐑉𐑌𐐯𐑅 𐐮𐑌𐐻𐐭 𐑄𐐯𐑉 𐐬𐑌 𐑊𐐰𐑌𐐼𐑆, 𐐸𐐶𐐮𐐽 𐐶𐐲𐑉 𐑅𐐵𐑃 𐐱𐑂 𐑄 𐑊𐐰𐑌𐐼 𐐱𐑂 𐐞𐐰𐑉𐐲𐐸𐐯𐑋𐑊𐐲; 𐐰𐑌𐐼 𐑄 𐑊𐐰𐑌𐐼 𐐱𐑂 𐐤𐐨𐑁𐐴 𐐼𐐮𐐼 𐑉𐐲𐑌 𐐮𐑌 𐐩 𐑅𐐻𐑉𐐩𐐻 𐐗𐐬𐑉𐑅 𐑁𐑉𐐱𐑋 𐑄 𐐨𐑅𐐻 𐑅𐐨 𐐻𐐭 𐑄 𐐶𐐯𐑅𐐻. 𐐈𐑌𐐼 𐐮𐐻 𐐗𐐩𐑋 𐐻𐐭 𐐹𐐰𐑅 𐑄𐐰𐐻 𐐸𐐶𐐯𐑌 𐐣𐐫𐑉𐐬𐑌𐐴 𐐸𐐰𐐼 𐐼𐑉𐐮𐑂𐐲𐑌 𐐫𐑊 𐑄 𐐢𐐰𐑋𐐲𐑌𐐴𐐻𐑅 𐐵𐐻 𐐱𐑂 𐑄 𐐨𐑅𐐻 𐐶𐐮𐑊𐐼𐐲𐑉𐑌𐐯𐑅, 𐐸𐐶𐐮𐐽 𐐶𐐱𐑆 𐑌𐐫𐑉𐑃 𐐱𐑂 𐑄 𐑊𐐰𐑌𐐼𐑆 𐐱𐑂 𐑄𐐯𐑉 𐐬𐑌 𐐹𐐱𐑆𐐯𐑇𐐲𐑌𐑆, 𐐸𐐨 𐐗𐐫𐑆𐐼 𐑄𐐰𐐻 𐑄 𐐮𐑌𐐸𐐰𐐺𐐮𐐻𐐲𐑌𐐻𐑅 𐐸𐐭 𐐶𐐲𐑉 𐐮𐑌 𐑄 𐑊𐐰𐑌𐐼 𐐱𐑂 𐐞𐐰𐑉𐐲𐐸𐐯𐑋𐑊𐐲, 𐐰𐑌𐐼 𐐮𐑌 𐑄 𐑊𐐰𐑌𐐼 𐑉𐐵𐑌𐐼 𐐲𐐺𐐵𐐻, 𐑇𐐳𐐼 𐑀𐐬 𐑁𐐬𐑉𐑃 𐐮𐑌𐐻𐐭 𐑄 𐐨𐑅𐐻

𐐶𐐮𐑊𐐼𐐲𐑉𐑌𐐯𐑅, 𐐨𐑂𐐲𐑌 𐐻𐐭 𐑄 𐐺𐐫𐑉𐐼𐐲𐑉𐑆 𐐺𐐴 𐑄 𐑅𐐨 𐐨𐑅𐐻, 𐐰𐑌𐐼 𐐹𐐲𐑆𐐯𐑅 𐑄 𐑊𐐰𐑌𐐼. 𐐈𐑌𐐼 𐐸𐐨 𐐫𐑊𐑅𐐬 𐐹𐑊𐐩𐑅𐐻 𐐪𐑉𐑋𐐨𐑆 𐐱𐑌 𐑄 𐑅𐐵𐑃, 𐐮𐑌 𐑄 𐐺𐐫𐑉𐐼𐐲𐑉𐑆 𐐱𐑂 𐑄𐐩𐑉 𐐹𐐲𐑆𐐯𐑇𐐲𐑌𐑆, 𐐰𐑌𐐼 𐐿𐐫𐑆𐐼 𐑄𐐯𐑋 𐐻𐐭 𐐨𐑉𐐯𐐿𐐻 𐑁𐐫𐑉𐐻𐐮𐑁𐐮𐐿𐐩𐑇𐐲𐑌𐑆, 𐑄𐐰𐐻 𐑄𐐩 𐑋𐐴𐐻 𐑅𐐨𐐿𐐷𐐭𐑉 𐑄𐐩𐑉 𐐪𐑉𐑋𐐨𐑆 𐐰𐑌𐐼 𐑄𐐩𐑉 𐐹𐐨𐐹𐐲𐑊 𐑁𐑉𐐱𐑋 𐑄 𐐸𐐰𐑌𐐼𐑆 𐐱𐑂 𐑄𐐩𐑉 𐐯𐑌𐐯𐑋𐐨𐑆. 𐐈𐑌𐐼 𐑄𐐲𐑅 𐐸𐐨 𐐿𐐲𐐻 𐐫𐑁 𐐫𐑊 𐑄 𐑅𐐻𐑉𐐫𐑍𐐸𐐬𐑊𐐼𐑆 𐐱𐑂 𐑄 𐐢𐐰𐑋𐐲𐑌𐐴𐐻𐑅, 𐐮𐑌 𐑄 𐐨𐑅𐐻 𐐶𐐮𐑊𐐼𐐲𐑉𐑌𐐯𐑅; 𐐷𐐩, 𐐰𐑌𐐼 𐐫𐑊𐑅𐐬 𐐱𐑌 𐑄 𐐶𐐯𐑅𐐻, 𐑁𐐫𐑉𐐻𐐮𐑁𐐴𐐮𐑍 𐑄 𐑊𐐴𐑌 𐐺𐐨𐐻𐐶𐐨𐑌 𐑄 𐐤𐐨𐑁𐐴𐐻𐑅 𐐰𐑌𐐼 𐑄 𐐢𐐰𐑋𐐲𐑌𐐴𐐻𐑅, 𐐺𐐨𐐻𐐶𐐨𐑌 𐑄 𐑊𐐰𐑌𐐼 𐐱𐑂 𐐞𐐰𐑉𐐲𐐸𐐯𐑋𐑊𐐲 𐐰𐑌𐐼 𐑄 𐑊𐐰𐑌𐐼 𐐱𐑂 𐐤𐐨𐑁𐐴; 𐑁𐑉𐐱𐑋 𐑄 𐐶𐐯𐑅𐐻 𐑅𐐨, 𐑉𐐲𐑌𐐮𐑍 𐐺𐐴 𐑄 𐐸𐐯𐐼 𐐱𐑂 𐑄 𐑉𐐮𐑂𐐲𐑉 𐐝𐐴𐐼𐐲𐑌; 𐑄 𐐤𐐨𐑁𐐴𐐻𐑅 𐐹𐐲𐑆𐐯𐑅𐐮𐑍 𐐫𐑊 𐑄 𐑊𐐰𐑌𐐼 𐑌𐐫𐑉𐑃𐐶𐐲𐑉𐐼; 𐐷𐐩, 𐐨𐑂𐐲𐑌 𐐫𐑊 𐑄 𐑊𐐰𐑌𐐼 𐐸𐐶𐐮𐐽 𐐶𐐱𐑆 𐑌𐐫𐑉𐑃𐐶𐐲𐑉𐐼 𐐱𐑂 𐑄 𐑊𐐰𐑌𐐼 𐐒𐐵𐑌𐐻𐐮𐑁𐐳𐑊, 𐐰𐐿𐐫𐑉𐐼𐐮𐑍 𐐻𐐭 𐑄𐐩𐑉 𐐹𐑊𐐯𐑈𐐲𐑉. 𐐜𐐲𐑅 𐐣𐐬𐑉𐐬𐑌𐐴, 𐐶𐐮𐑄 𐐸𐐮𐑆 𐐪𐑉𐑋𐐨𐑆, 𐐸𐐶𐐮𐐽 𐐼𐐮𐐼 𐐮𐑌𐐿𐑉𐐨𐑅 𐐼𐐩𐑊𐐨 𐐺𐐨𐐿𐐫𐑆 𐐱𐑂 𐑄 𐐰𐑇𐐭𐑉𐐲𐑌𐑅 𐐱𐑂 𐐹𐑉𐐬𐐻𐐯𐐿𐑇𐐲𐑌 𐐸𐐶𐐮𐐽 𐐸𐐮𐑆 𐐶𐐲𐑉𐐿𐑅 𐐼𐐮𐐼 𐐺𐑉𐐮𐑍 𐑁𐐬𐑉𐑃 𐐲𐑌𐐻𐐭 𐑄𐐯𐑋; 𐑄𐐩𐑉𐑁𐐬𐑉 𐐸𐐨 𐐼𐐮𐐼 𐑅𐐨𐐿 𐐻𐐭 𐐿𐐲𐐻 𐐫𐑁 𐑄 𐑅𐐻𐑉𐐯𐑍𐑃 𐐰𐑌𐐼 𐑄 𐐹𐐵𐐲𐑉 𐐱𐑂 𐑄 𐐢𐐰𐑋𐐲𐑌𐐴𐐻𐑅, 𐑁𐑉𐐱𐑋 𐐫𐑁 𐑄 𐑊𐐰𐑌𐐼𐑆 𐐱𐑂 𐑄𐐩𐑉 𐐹𐐲𐑆𐐯𐑇𐐲𐑌𐑆, 𐑄𐐰𐐻 𐑄𐐩 𐑇𐐳𐐼 𐐸𐐰𐑂 𐑌𐐬 𐐹𐐵𐐲𐑉 𐐲𐐹𐐱𐑌 𐑄 𐑊𐐰𐑌𐐼𐑆 𐐱𐑂 𐑄𐐩𐑉 𐐹𐐲𐑆𐐯𐑇𐐲𐑌.

3. 𐐈𐑌𐐼 𐐮𐐻 𐐿𐐩𐑋 𐐻𐐭 𐐹𐐰𐑅 𐑄𐐰𐐻 𐑄 𐐤𐐨𐑁𐐴𐐻𐑅 𐐺𐐨𐑀𐐰𐑌 𐑄 𐑁𐐵𐑌𐐼𐐩𐑇𐐲𐑌 𐐱𐑂 𐐩 𐑅𐐮𐐻𐐨; 𐐰𐑌𐐼 𐑄𐐩 𐐿𐐫𐑊𐐼 𐑄 𐑌𐐩𐑋 𐐱𐑂 𐑄 𐑅𐐮𐐻𐐨 𐐣𐐬𐑉𐐬𐑌𐐴; 𐐰𐑌𐐼 𐐮𐐻 𐐶𐐱𐑆 𐐺𐐴 𐑄 𐐨𐑅𐐻 𐑅𐐨; 𐐰𐑌𐐼 𐐮𐐻 𐐶𐐱𐑆 𐐱𐑌 𐑄 𐑅𐐵𐑃 𐐺𐐴 𐑄 𐑊𐐴𐑌 𐐱𐑂 𐑄 𐐹𐐲𐑆𐐯𐑇𐐲𐑌𐑆 𐐱𐑂 𐑄 𐐢𐐰𐑋𐐲𐑌𐐴𐐻𐑅. 𐐈𐑌𐐼 𐑄𐐩 𐐫𐑊𐑅𐐬 𐐺𐐨𐑀𐐰𐑌 𐐩 𐑁𐐵𐑌𐐼𐐩𐑇𐐲𐑌 𐑁𐐫𐑉 𐐩 𐑅𐐮𐐻𐐨 𐐺𐐨𐐻𐐶𐐨𐑌 𐑄 𐑅𐐮𐐻𐐨 𐐱𐑂 𐐣𐐬𐑉𐐬𐑌𐐴 𐐰𐑌𐐼 𐑄 𐑅𐐮𐐻𐐨 𐐱𐑂 𐐁𐑉𐐲𐑌, 𐐾𐑎𐑌𐐮𐑍 𐑄 𐐺𐐫𐑉𐐼𐐲𐑉𐑆 𐐱𐑂 𐐁𐑉𐐲𐑌 𐐰𐑌𐐼 𐐣𐐬𐑉𐐬𐑌𐐴; 𐐰𐑌𐐼 𐑄𐐩 𐐿𐐫𐑊𐐼 𐑄 𐑌𐐩𐑋 𐐱𐑂 𐑄 𐑅𐐮𐐻𐐨, 𐐫𐑉 𐑄 𐑊𐐰𐑌𐐼, 𐐤𐐨𐑁𐐴𐐸𐐪. 𐐈𐑌𐐼 𐑄𐐩 𐐫𐑊𐑅𐐬 𐐺𐐨𐑀𐐰𐑌 𐐮𐑌 𐑄𐐰𐐻 𐑅𐐩𐑋 𐐷𐐨𐑉, 𐐻𐐭 𐐺𐐮𐑊𐐼 𐑋𐐯𐑌𐐨 𐑅𐐮𐐻𐐨𐑆 𐐱𐑌 𐑄 𐑌𐐫𐑉𐑃; 𐐶𐐲𐑌 𐐮𐑌 𐐩 𐐹𐐲𐑉𐐻𐐮𐐿𐐷𐐭𐑊𐐲𐑉 𐑋𐐰𐑌𐐲𐑉 𐐸𐐶𐐮𐐽 𐑄𐐩 𐐿𐐫𐑊𐐼 𐐢𐐨𐐸𐐴, 𐐸𐐶𐐮𐐽 𐐶𐐱𐑆 𐐮𐑌 𐑄 𐑌𐐫𐑉𐑃, 𐐺𐐴 𐑄 𐐺𐐫𐑉𐐼𐐲𐑉𐑆 𐐱𐑂 𐑄 𐑅𐐨 𐑇𐐬𐑉. 𐐈𐑌𐐼 𐑄𐐲𐑅 𐐯𐑌𐐼𐐯𐐼 𐑄 𐐻𐐶𐐯𐑌𐐻𐐨𐐯𐑃 𐐷𐐨𐑉. 𐐈𐑌𐐼 𐐮𐑌 𐑄𐐨𐑆 𐐹𐑉𐐱𐑅𐐹𐐲𐑉𐐲𐑅 𐑅𐐲𐑉𐐿𐐲𐑋𐑅𐐻𐐰𐑌𐑅𐐯𐑆 𐐶𐐲𐑉 𐑄 𐐹𐐨𐐹𐐲𐑊 𐐱𐑂 𐐤𐐨𐑁𐐴 𐐮𐑌 𐑄 𐐿𐐱𐑋𐐯𐑌𐑅𐑋𐐯𐑌𐐻 𐐱𐑂 𐑄 𐐻𐐶𐐯𐑌𐐻𐐨 𐐰𐑌𐐼 𐑁𐐲𐑉𐑅𐐻 𐐷𐐨𐑉 𐐱𐑂 𐑄 𐑉𐐩𐑌 𐐱𐑂 𐑄 𐐾𐐲𐐾𐐯𐑆 𐐬𐑂𐐲𐑉 𐑄 𐐹𐐨𐐹𐐲𐑊 𐐱𐑂 𐐤𐐨𐑁𐐴. 𐐈𐑌𐐼 𐑄𐐩 𐐼𐐮𐐼 𐐹𐑉𐐱𐑅𐐹𐐲𐑉 𐐯𐐿𐑅𐐨𐐼𐐮𐑍𐑊𐐨, 𐐰𐑌𐐼 𐑄𐐩 𐐺𐐨𐐿𐐩𐑋 𐐯𐐿𐑅𐐨𐐼𐐮𐑍𐑊𐐨 𐑉𐐮𐐽; 𐐷𐐩, 𐐰𐑌𐐼 𐑄𐐩 𐐼𐐮𐐼 𐑋𐐲𐑊𐐻𐐮𐐹𐑊𐐴, 𐐰𐑌𐐼 𐐶𐐰𐐿𐑅 𐑅𐐻𐑉𐐫𐑍 𐐮𐑌 𐑄 𐑊𐐰𐑌𐐼. 𐐈𐑌𐐼 𐑄𐐲𐑅 𐐶𐐨 𐑅𐐨 𐐸𐐵 𐑋𐐲𐑉𐑅𐐮𐑁𐐳𐑊 𐐰𐑌𐐼 𐐾𐐲𐑅𐐻 𐐪𐑉 𐐫𐑊 𐑄 𐐼𐐨𐑊𐐮𐑍𐑆 𐐱𐑂 𐑄 𐐢𐐫𐑉𐐼, 𐐻𐐭 𐑄 𐑁𐐳𐑊𐑁𐐮𐑊𐐮𐑍 𐐱𐑂 𐐫𐑊 𐐸𐐮𐑆 𐐶𐐲𐑉𐐼𐑆 𐐲𐑌𐐻𐐭 𐑄 𐐽𐐮𐑊𐐼𐑉𐐯𐑌 𐐱𐑂 𐑋𐐯𐑌: 𐐷𐐩, 𐐶𐐨 𐐿𐐰𐑌 𐐺𐐨𐐸𐐬𐑊𐐼 𐑄𐐰𐐻 𐐸𐐮𐑆 𐐶𐐲𐑉𐐼𐑆 𐐪𐑉 𐑂𐐯𐑉𐐮𐑁𐐴𐐼, 𐐨𐑂𐐲𐑌 𐐰𐐻 𐑄𐐮𐑅 𐐻𐐴𐑋, 𐐸𐐶𐐮𐐽 𐐸𐐨 𐑅𐐹𐐩𐐿 𐐲𐑌𐐻𐐭 𐐢𐐨𐐸𐐴, 𐑅𐐩𐐮𐑍, 𐐒𐑊𐐯𐑅𐐯𐐼 𐐪𐑉𐐻 𐑄𐐵 𐐰𐑌𐐼 𐑄𐐴 𐐽𐐮𐑊𐐼𐑉𐐯𐑌; 𐐰𐑌𐐼 𐑄𐐩 𐑇𐐰𐑊 𐐺𐐨 𐐺𐑊𐐯𐑅𐐯𐐼, 𐐮𐑌𐐰𐑆𐑋𐐲𐐽 𐐰𐑆 𐑄𐐩 𐑇𐐰𐑊 𐐿𐐨𐐹 𐑋𐐴 𐐿𐐱𐑋𐐰𐑌𐐼𐑋𐐯𐑌𐐻𐑅, 𐑄𐐩 𐑇𐐰𐑊 𐐹𐑉𐐱𐑅𐐹𐐲𐑉 𐐮𐑌 𐑄 𐑊𐐰𐑌𐐼. 𐐒𐐲𐐻 𐑉𐐨𐑋𐐯𐑋𐐺𐐲𐑉, 𐐮𐑌𐐰𐑆𐑋𐐲𐐽 𐐰𐑆 𐑄𐐩 𐐶𐐮𐑊 𐑌𐐱𐐻 𐐿𐐨𐐹 𐑋𐐴 𐐿𐐱𐑋𐐰𐑌𐐼𐑋𐐯𐑌𐐻𐑅, 𐑄𐐩 𐑇𐐰𐑊 𐐺𐐨 𐐿𐐲𐐻 𐐫𐑁 𐑁𐑉𐐱𐑋 𐑄 𐐹𐑉𐐯𐑆𐐯𐑌𐑅 𐐱𐑂 𐑄 𐐢𐐫𐑉𐐼. 𐐈𐑌𐐼 𐐶𐐨 𐑅𐐨 𐑄𐐰𐐻 𐑄𐐨𐑆 𐐹𐑉𐐱𐑋𐐮𐑅𐐯𐑆 𐐸𐐰𐑂 𐐺𐐮𐑌 𐑂𐐯𐑉𐐮𐑁𐐴𐐼 𐐻𐐭 𐑄 𐐹𐐨𐐹𐐲𐑊 𐐱𐑂 𐐤𐐨𐑁𐐴; 𐑁𐐫𐑉 𐐮𐐻 𐐸𐐰𐑆 𐐺𐐮𐑌 𐑄𐐩𐑉 𐐿𐐶𐐱𐑉𐐯𐑊𐐮𐑍𐑆 𐐰𐑌𐐼 𐑄𐐩𐑉 𐐿𐐱𐑌𐐻𐐯𐑌𐑇𐐲𐑌𐑆, 𐐷𐐩, 𐑄𐐩𐑉 𐑋𐐲𐑉𐐼𐐲𐑉𐐮𐑍𐑆, 𐐰𐑌𐐼 𐑄𐐩𐑉 𐐹𐑊𐐲𐑌𐐼𐐲𐑉𐐮𐑍𐑆, 𐑄𐐩𐑉 𐐴𐐼𐐱𐑊𐐲𐐻𐑉𐐨, 𐑄𐐩𐑉 𐐸𐐬𐑉𐐼𐐲𐑋𐑆, 𐐰𐑌𐐼 𐑄𐐩𐑉 𐐲𐐺𐐱𐑋𐐮𐑌𐐩𐑇𐐲𐑌𐑆, 𐐸𐐶𐐮𐐽 𐐶𐐲𐑉 𐐲𐑋𐐲𐑍 𐑄𐐯𐑋𐑅𐐯𐑊𐑂𐑆, 𐐸𐐶𐐮𐐽 𐐺𐑉𐐫𐐻 𐐲𐐹𐐱𐑌 𐑄𐐯𐑋 𐑄𐐩𐑉 𐐶𐐫𐑉𐑆 𐐰𐑌𐐼 𐑄𐐩𐑉 𐐼𐐯𐑅𐐻𐑉𐐲𐐿𐑇𐐲𐑌𐑆. 𐐈𐑌𐐼 𐑄𐐬𐑆 𐐸𐐭 𐐶𐐲𐑉 𐑁𐐩𐑃𐑁𐐳𐑊 𐐮𐑌 𐐿𐐨𐐹𐐮𐑍 𐑄 𐐿𐐱𐑋𐐰𐑌𐐼𐑋𐐯𐑌𐐻𐑅 𐐱𐑂 𐑄 𐐢𐐫𐑉𐐼, 𐐶𐐲𐑉 𐐼𐐯𐑊𐐮𐑂𐐲𐑉𐐼 𐐰𐐻 𐐫𐑊 𐐻𐐴𐑋𐑆, 𐐸𐐶𐐴𐑊𐑅𐐻 𐑃𐐵𐑆𐐲𐑌𐐼𐑆 𐐱𐑂 𐑄𐐩𐑉 𐐶𐐮𐐿𐐯𐐼 𐐺𐑉𐐯𐑄𐑉𐐯𐑌 𐐸𐐰𐑂 𐐺𐐮𐑌 𐐿𐐱𐑌𐑅𐐴𐑌𐐼 𐐻𐐭 𐐺𐐱𐑌𐐼𐐩𐐾, 𐐫𐑉 𐐻𐐭 𐐹𐐯𐑉𐐮𐑇 𐐺𐐴 𐑄 𐑅𐐫𐑉𐐼, 𐐫𐑉 𐐻𐐭 𐐼𐐶𐐮𐑌𐐼𐐲𐑊 𐐮𐑌 𐐲𐑌𐐺𐐨𐑊𐐨𐑁, 𐐰𐑌𐐼 𐑋𐐮𐑍𐑀𐐲𐑊 𐐶𐐮𐑄 𐑄 𐐢𐐰𐑋𐐲𐑌𐐴𐐻𐑅. 𐐒𐐲𐐻 𐐺𐐨𐐸𐐬𐑊𐐼 𐑄𐐩𐑉 𐑌𐐯𐑂𐐲𐑉 𐐶𐐱𐑆 𐐩 𐐸𐐰𐐹𐐨𐐲𐑉 𐐻𐐴𐑋 𐐲𐑋𐐲𐑍 𐑄 𐐹𐐨𐐹𐐲𐑊 𐐱𐑂 𐐤𐐨𐑁𐐴, 𐑅𐐮𐑌𐑅 𐑄 𐐼𐐩𐑆 𐐱𐑂 𐐤𐐨𐑁𐐴, 𐑄𐐰𐑌 𐐮𐑌 𐑄 𐐼𐐩𐑆 𐐱𐑂 𐐣𐐬𐑉𐐬𐑌𐐴; 𐐷𐐩, 𐐨𐑂𐐲𐑌 𐐰𐐻 𐑄𐐮𐑅 𐐻𐐴𐑋, 𐐮𐑌 𐑄 𐐻𐐶𐐯𐑌𐐻𐐨 𐐰𐑌𐐼 𐑁𐐲𐑉𐑅𐐻 𐐷𐐨𐑉 𐐱𐑂 𐑄 𐑉𐐩𐑌 𐐱𐑂 𐑄 𐐾𐐲𐐾𐐯𐑆. 𐐈𐑌𐐼 𐐮𐐻 𐐿𐐩𐑋 𐐻𐐭 𐐹𐐰𐑅 𐑄𐐰𐐻 𐑄 𐐻𐐶𐐯𐑌𐐻𐐨 𐐰𐑌𐐼 𐑅𐐯𐐿𐐲𐑌𐐼 𐐷𐐨𐑉 𐐱𐑂 𐑄 𐑉𐐩𐑌 𐐱𐑂 𐑄 𐐾𐐲𐐾𐐯𐑆 𐐫𐑊𐑅𐐬 𐐯𐑌𐐼𐐯𐐼 𐐮𐑌 𐐹𐐨𐑅; 𐐷𐐩, 𐐰𐑌𐐼 𐐫𐑊𐑅𐐬 𐑄 𐐻𐐶𐐯𐑌𐐻𐐨 𐐰𐑌𐐼 𐑃𐐲𐑉𐐼 𐐷𐐨𐑉.

4. 𐐈𐑌𐐼 𐐮𐐻 𐐿𐐩𐑋 𐐻𐐭 𐐹𐐰𐑅 𐑄𐐰𐐻 𐐮𐑌 𐑄 𐐿𐐱𐑋𐐯𐑌𐑅𐑋𐐯𐑌𐐻 𐐱𐑂 𐑄 𐐻𐐶𐐯𐑌𐐻𐐨 𐐰𐑌𐐼 𐑁𐐬𐑉𐑃 𐐷𐐨𐑉 𐐱𐑂 𐑄

𐑉𐐩𐑌 𐐲𐑂 𐑄 𐐾𐐲𐐾𐐯𐑆, 𐑄𐐩𐑉 𐐶𐐳𐐼 𐐫𐑊𐑅𐐬 𐐸𐐰𐑂 𐐺𐐮𐑌 𐐹𐐨𐑅 𐐲𐑋𐐲𐑍 𐑄 𐐹𐐨𐐹𐑊 𐐲𐑂 𐐤𐐨𐑁𐐴, 𐐸𐐰𐐼 𐐮𐐻 𐑌𐐱𐐻 𐐺𐐮𐑌 𐑁𐐫𐑉 𐐲 𐐿𐐲𐑌𐐻𐐯𐑌𐑇𐐲𐑌 𐐸𐐶𐐮𐐽 𐐻𐐳𐐿 𐐹𐑊𐐩𐑅 𐐲𐑋𐐲𐑍 𐑄𐐯𐑋 𐐿𐐲𐑌𐑅𐐲𐑉𐑌𐐮𐑍 𐑄 𐑊𐐰𐑌𐐼 𐐲𐑂 𐐢𐐨𐐸𐐴, 𐐰𐑌𐐼 𐑄 𐑊𐐰𐑌𐐼 𐐲𐑂 𐐣𐐬𐑉𐐴𐐰𐑌𐐻𐐲𐑌, 𐐸𐐶𐐮𐐽 𐐾𐐦𐑌𐐼 𐐲𐐹𐐱𐑌 𐑄 𐐺𐐫𐑉𐐼𐐲𐑉𐑆 𐐲𐑂 𐐢𐐨𐐸𐐴; 𐐺𐐬𐑃 𐐲𐑂 𐐸𐐶𐐮𐐽 𐐶𐐲𐑉 𐐱𐑌 𐑄 𐐺𐐫𐑉𐐼𐐲𐑉𐑆 𐐺𐐴 𐑄 𐑅𐐨 𐑇𐐬𐑉. 𐐙𐐫𐑉 𐐺𐐨𐐸𐐬𐑊𐐼 𐑄 𐐹𐐨𐐹𐑊 𐐸𐐭 𐐹𐐲𐑆𐐯𐑅𐐻 𐑄 𐑊𐐰𐑌𐐼 𐐲𐑂 𐐣𐐬𐑉𐐴𐐰𐑌𐐻𐐲𐑌, 𐐼𐐮𐐼 𐐿𐑊𐐩𐑋 𐐲 𐐹𐐪𐑉𐐻 𐐲𐑂 𐑄 𐑊𐐰𐑌𐐼 𐐲𐑂 𐐢𐐨𐐸𐐴; 𐑄𐐩𐑉𐑁𐐫𐑉 𐑄𐐩𐑉 𐐺𐐨𐑀𐐰𐑌 𐐻𐐭 𐐺𐐨 𐐲 𐐶𐐫𐑉𐑋 𐐿𐐲𐑌𐐻𐐯𐑌𐑇𐐲𐑌 𐐺𐐨𐐻𐐶𐐨𐑌 𐑄𐐯𐑋, 𐐮𐑌𐑅𐐲𐑋𐐲𐐽 𐑄𐐰𐐻 𐑄 𐐹𐐨𐐹𐑊 𐐲𐑂 𐐣𐐬𐑉𐐴𐐰𐑌𐐻𐐲𐑌 𐐻𐐳𐐿 𐐲𐐹 𐐪𐑉𐑋𐑆 𐐲𐑀𐐯𐑌𐑅𐐻 𐑄𐐩𐑉 𐐺𐑉𐐯𐑄𐑉𐐯𐑌, 𐐰𐑌𐐼 𐑄𐐩 𐐶𐐲𐑉 𐐼𐐨𐐻𐐲𐑉𐑋𐐮𐑌𐐼 𐐺𐐴 𐑄 𐑅𐐬𐑉𐐼 𐐻𐐭 𐑅𐑊𐐩 𐑄𐐯𐑋. 𐐒𐐲𐐻 𐐺𐐨𐐸𐐬𐑊𐐼 𐑄 𐐹𐐨𐐹𐑊 𐐸𐐭 𐐹𐐲𐑆𐐯𐑅𐐻 𐑄 𐑊𐐰𐑌𐐼 𐐲𐑂 𐐢𐐨𐐸𐐴, 𐑁𐑊𐐯𐐼 𐐻𐐭 𐑄 𐐿𐐰𐑋𐐹 𐐲𐑂 𐐣𐐬𐑉𐐬𐑌𐐴, 𐐰𐑌𐐼 𐐰𐐹𐐨𐑊𐐼 𐐲𐑌𐐻𐐭 𐐸𐐮𐑋 𐑁𐐫𐑉 𐐰𐑅𐐮𐑅𐐻𐐰𐑌𐑅; 𐑁𐐫𐑉 𐐺𐐨𐐸𐐬𐑊𐐼 𐑄𐐩 𐐶𐐲𐑉 𐑌𐐱𐐻 𐐮𐑌 𐑄 𐑉𐐫𐑍.

5. 𐐈𐑌𐐼 𐐮𐐻 𐐿𐐩𐑋 𐐻𐐭 𐐹𐐰𐑅 𐑄𐐰𐐻 𐐸𐐶𐐯𐑌 𐑄 𐐹𐐨𐐹𐑊 𐐲𐑂 𐐣𐐬𐑉𐐴𐐰𐑌𐐻𐐲𐑌, 𐐸𐐭 𐐶𐐲𐑉 𐑊𐐯𐐼 𐐺𐐴 𐐲 𐑋𐐰𐑌 𐐸𐐭𐑆 𐑌𐐩𐑋 𐐶𐐱𐑆 𐐣𐐬𐑉𐐴𐐰𐑌𐐻𐐲𐑌, 𐑁𐐵𐑌𐐼 𐑄𐐰𐐻 𐑄 𐐹𐐨𐐹𐑊 𐐲𐑂 𐐢𐐨𐐸𐐴 𐐸𐐰𐐼 𐑁𐑊𐐯𐐼 𐐻𐐭 𐑄 𐐿𐐰𐑋𐐹 𐐲𐑂 𐐣𐐬𐑉𐐬𐑌𐐴, 𐑄𐐩 𐐶𐐲𐑉 𐐯𐐿𐑅𐐨𐐼𐐮𐑍𐑊𐐨 𐑁𐐨𐑉𐑁𐐳𐑊 𐑊𐐯𐑅𐐻 𐑄 𐐪𐑉𐑋𐐨 𐐲𐑂 𐐣𐐬𐑉𐐬𐑌𐐴 𐑇𐐳𐐼 𐐿𐐲𐑋 𐐲𐐹𐐱𐑌 𐑄𐐯𐑋, 𐐰𐑌𐐼 𐐼𐐨𐑅𐐻𐑉𐐦 𐑄𐐯𐑋; 𐑄𐐩𐑉𐑁𐐫𐑉, 𐐣𐐬𐑉𐐴𐐰𐑌𐐻𐐲𐑌 𐐹𐐳𐐻 𐐮𐐻 𐐮𐑌𐐻𐐭 𐑄𐐩𐑉 𐐸𐐪𐑉𐐻𐑅 𐑄𐐰𐐻 𐑄𐐩 𐑇𐐳𐐼 𐑁𐑊𐐨 𐐻𐐭 𐑄 𐑊𐐰𐑌𐐼 𐐸𐐶𐐮𐐽 𐐶𐐱𐑆 𐑌𐐫𐑉𐑃𐐶𐐲𐑉𐐼, 𐐸𐐶𐐮𐐽 𐐶𐐱𐑆 𐐿𐐲𐑂𐐲𐑉𐐼 𐐶𐐮𐑄 𐑊𐐪𐑉𐑀 𐐺𐐱𐐼𐐮𐑆 𐐲𐑂 𐐶𐐫𐐻𐐲𐑉, 𐐰𐑌𐐼 𐐻𐐩𐐿 𐐹𐐲𐑆𐐯𐑇𐐲𐑌 𐐲𐑂 𐑄 𐑊𐐰𐑌𐐼 𐐸𐐶𐐮𐐽 𐐶𐐱𐑆 𐑌𐐫𐑉𐑃𐐶𐐲𐑉𐐼. 𐐈𐑌𐐼 𐐺𐐨𐐸𐐬𐑊𐐼, 𐑄𐐩 𐐶𐐳𐐼 𐐸𐐰𐑂 𐐿𐐰𐑉𐐮𐐼 𐑄𐐮𐑅 𐐹𐑊𐐰𐑌 𐐮𐑌𐐻𐐭 𐐯𐑁𐐯𐐿𐐻, (𐐸𐐶𐐮𐐽 𐐶𐐳𐐼 𐐸𐐰𐑂 𐐺𐐮𐑌 𐐲 𐐿𐐫𐑆 𐐻𐐭 𐐸𐐰𐑂 𐐺𐐮𐑌 𐑊𐐰𐑋𐐯𐑌𐐻𐐯𐐼,) 𐐺𐐲𐐻 𐐺𐐨𐐸𐐬𐑊𐐼 𐐣𐐬𐑉𐐴𐐰𐑌𐐻𐐲𐑌, 𐐺𐐨𐐮𐑍 𐐲 𐑋𐐰𐑌 𐐲𐑂 𐑋𐐲𐐽 𐐹𐐰𐑇𐐲𐑌, 𐑄𐐩𐑉𐑁𐐫𐑉 𐐸𐐨 𐐶𐐱𐑆 𐐰𐑍𐑀𐑉𐐨 𐐶𐐮𐑄 𐐶𐐲𐑌 𐐲𐑂 𐐸𐐮𐑆 𐑋𐐩𐐼-𐑅𐐲𐑉𐑂𐐲𐑌𐐻𐑅, 𐐰𐑌𐐼 𐐸𐐨 𐑁𐐯𐑊 𐐲𐐹𐐱𐑌 𐐸𐐲𐑉 𐐰𐑌𐐼 𐐺𐐨𐐻 𐐸𐐲𐑉 𐑋𐐲𐐽. 𐐈𐑌𐐼 𐐮𐐻 𐐿𐐩𐑋 𐐻𐐭 𐐹𐐰𐑅 𐑄𐐰𐐻 𐑇𐐨 𐑁𐑊𐐯𐐼, 𐐰𐑌𐐼 𐐿𐐩𐑋 𐐬𐑂𐐲𐑉 𐐻𐐭 𐑄 𐐿𐐰𐑋𐐹 𐐲𐑂 𐐣𐐬𐑉𐐬𐑌𐐴, 𐐰𐑌𐐼 𐐻𐐬𐑊𐐼 𐐣𐐬𐑉𐐬𐑌𐐴 𐐫𐑊 𐑃𐐮𐑍𐑆 𐐿𐐲𐑌𐑅𐐲𐑉𐑌𐐮𐑍 𐑄 𐑋𐐰𐐻𐐲𐑉; 𐐰𐑌𐐼 𐐫𐑊𐑅𐐬 𐐿𐐲𐑌𐑅𐐲𐑉𐑌𐐮𐑍 𐑄𐐩𐑉 𐐮𐑌𐐻𐐯𐑌𐑇𐐲𐑌𐑆 𐐻𐐭 𐑁𐑊𐐨 𐐮𐑌𐐻𐐭 𐑄 𐑊𐐰𐑌𐐼 𐑌𐐫𐑉𐑃𐐶𐐲𐑉𐐼. 𐐤𐐵 𐐺𐐨𐐸𐐬𐑊𐐼, 𐑄 𐐹𐐨𐐹𐑊 𐐸𐐭 𐐶𐐲𐑉 𐐮𐑌 𐑄 𐑊𐐰𐑌𐐼 𐐒𐐵𐑌𐐻𐐨𐑁𐐳𐑊, 𐐫𐑉 𐑉𐐰𐑄𐐲𐑉 𐐣𐐬𐑉𐐬𐑌𐐴, 𐑁𐐨𐑉𐐼 𐑄𐐰𐐻 𐑄𐐩 𐐶𐐳𐐼 𐐸𐐪𐑉𐐿𐐯𐑌 𐐻𐐭 𐑄 𐐶𐐲𐑉𐐼𐑆 𐐲𐑂 𐐣𐐬𐑉𐐴𐐰𐑌𐐻𐐲𐑌, 𐐰𐑌𐐼 𐐷𐐭𐑌𐐴𐐻 𐐶𐐮𐑄 𐐸𐐮𐑆 𐐹𐐨𐐹𐑊, 𐐰𐑌𐐼 𐑄𐐲𐑅 𐐸𐐨 𐐶𐐳𐐼 𐐱𐐺𐐻𐐩𐑌 𐐹𐐲𐑆𐐯𐑇𐐲𐑌 𐐲𐑂 𐑄𐐬𐑆 𐐹𐐪𐑉𐐻𐑅 𐐲𐑂 𐑄 𐑊𐐰𐑌𐐼 𐐸𐐶𐐮𐐽 𐐶𐐳𐐼 𐑊𐐩 𐐲 𐑁𐐵𐑌𐐼𐐩𐑇𐐲𐑌 𐑁𐐫𐑉 𐑅𐐨𐑉𐐨𐐲𐑅 𐐿𐐱𐑌𐑅𐐨𐐿𐐶𐐯𐑌𐑅𐐯𐑆 𐐲𐑋𐐲𐑍 𐑄 𐐹𐐨𐐹𐑊 𐐲𐑂 𐐤𐐨𐑁𐐴; 𐐷𐐩, 𐐸𐐶𐐮𐐽 𐐿𐐱𐑌𐑅𐐨𐐿𐐶𐐯𐑌𐑅𐐯𐑆 𐐶𐐳𐐼 𐑊𐐨𐐼 𐐻𐐭 𐑄 𐐬𐑂𐐲𐑉𐑃𐑉𐐬 𐐲𐑂 𐑄𐐩𐑉 𐑊𐐮𐐺𐐲𐑉𐐻𐐨; 𐑄𐐩𐑉𐑁𐐫𐑉 𐐣𐐬𐑉𐐬𐑌𐐴 𐑅𐐯𐑌𐐻 𐐰𐑌 𐐪𐑉𐑋𐐨, 𐐶𐐮𐑄 𐑄𐐩𐑉 𐐿𐐰𐑋𐐹, 𐐻𐐭 𐐸𐐯𐐼 𐑄 𐐹𐐨𐐹𐑊 𐐲𐑂 𐐣𐐬𐑉𐐴𐐰𐑌𐐻𐐲𐑌, 𐐻𐐭 𐑅𐐻𐐱𐐹 𐑄𐐩𐑉 𐑁𐑊𐐴𐐻 𐐮𐑌𐐻𐐭 𐑄 𐑊𐐰𐑌𐐼 𐑌𐐫𐑉𐑃𐐶𐐲𐑉𐐼. 𐐈𐑌𐐼 𐐮𐐻 𐐿𐐩𐑋 𐐻𐐭 𐐹𐐰𐑅 𐑄𐐰𐐻 𐑄𐐩 𐐼𐐮𐐼 𐑌𐐱𐐻 𐐸𐐯𐐼 𐑄𐐯𐑋, 𐐲𐑌𐐻𐐮𐑊 𐑄𐐩 𐐸𐐰𐐼 𐐿𐐲𐑋 𐐻𐐭 𐑄 𐐺𐐫𐑉𐐼𐐲𐑉𐑆 𐐲𐑂 𐑄 𐑊𐐰𐑌𐐼 𐐔𐐯𐑅𐐬𐑊𐐩𐑇𐐲𐑌; 𐐰𐑌𐐼 𐑄𐐩𐑉 𐑄𐐩 𐐼𐐮𐐼 𐐸𐐯𐐼 𐑄𐐯𐑋, 𐐺𐐴 𐑄 𐑌𐐰𐑉𐐬 𐐹𐐰𐑅 𐐸𐐶𐐮𐐽 𐑊𐐯𐐼 𐐺𐐴 𐑄 𐑅𐐨 𐐮𐑌𐐻𐐭 𐑄 𐑊𐐰𐑌𐐼 𐑌𐐫𐑉𐑃𐐶𐐲𐑉𐐼; 𐐷𐐩, 𐐺𐐴 𐑄 𐑅𐐨, 𐐱𐑌 𐑄 𐐶𐐯𐑅𐐻, 𐐰𐑌𐐼 𐐱𐑌 𐑄 𐐨𐑅𐐻.

6. 𐐈𐑌𐐼 𐐮𐐻 𐐿𐐩𐑋 𐐻𐐭 𐐹𐐰𐑅 𐑄𐐰𐐻 𐑄 𐐪𐑉𐑋𐐨 𐐸𐐶𐐮𐐽 𐐶𐐱𐑆 𐑅𐐯𐑌𐐻 𐐺𐐴 𐐣𐐬𐑉𐐬𐑌𐐴, 𐐸𐐶𐐮𐐽 𐐶𐐱𐑆 𐑊𐐯𐐼 𐐺𐐴 𐐲 𐑋𐐰𐑌 𐐸𐐭𐑆 𐑌𐐩𐑋 𐐶𐐱𐑆 𐐓𐐨𐐰𐑌𐐿𐐲𐑋, 𐐼𐐮𐐼 𐑋𐐨𐐻 𐑄 𐐹𐐨𐐹𐑊 𐐲𐑂 𐐣𐐬𐑉𐐴𐐰𐑌𐐻𐐲𐑌; 𐐰𐑌𐐼 𐑅𐐬 𐑅𐐻𐐲𐐺𐐲𐑉𐑌 𐐶𐐲𐑉 𐑄 𐐹𐐨𐐹𐑊 𐐲𐑂 𐐣𐐬𐑉𐐴𐐰𐑌𐐻𐐲𐑌, (𐐺𐐨𐐮𐑍 𐐮𐑌𐑅𐐹𐐴𐑉𐐼 𐐺𐐴 𐐸𐐮𐑆 𐐶𐐮𐐿𐐯𐐼𐑌𐐯𐑅 𐐰𐑌𐐼 𐑁𐑊𐐰𐐻𐐲𐑉𐐮𐑍 𐐶𐐲𐑉𐐼𐑆,) 𐑄𐐰𐐻 𐐲 𐐺𐐰𐐻𐐲𐑊 𐐿𐐲𐑋𐐯𐑌𐑅𐐻 𐐺𐐨𐐻𐐶𐐨𐑌 𐑄𐐯𐑋, 𐐮𐑌 𐑄 𐐸𐐶𐐮𐐽 𐐓𐐨𐐰𐑌𐐿𐐲𐑋 𐐼𐐮𐐼 𐑅𐑊𐐩 𐐣𐐬𐑉𐐴𐐰𐑌𐐻𐐲𐑌, 𐐰𐑌𐐼 𐐼𐐨𐑁𐐨𐐻 𐐸𐐮𐑆 𐐪𐑉𐑋𐐨, 𐐰𐑌𐐼 𐐻𐐳𐐿 𐑄𐐯𐑋 𐐹𐑉𐐮𐑆𐐲𐑌𐐲𐑉𐑆, 𐐰𐑌𐐼 𐑉𐐨𐐻𐐲𐑉𐑌𐐼 𐐻𐐭 𐑄 𐐿𐐰𐑋𐐹 𐐲𐑂 𐐣𐐬𐑉𐐬𐑌𐐴. 𐐈𐑌𐐼 𐑄𐐲𐑅 𐐯𐑌𐐼𐐯𐐼 𐑄 𐐻𐐶𐐯𐑌𐐻𐐨 𐐰𐑌𐐼 𐑁𐐬𐑉𐑃 𐐷𐐨𐑉 𐐲𐑂 𐑄 𐑉𐐩𐑌 𐐲𐑂 𐑄 𐐾𐐲𐐾𐐯𐑆 𐐬𐑂𐐲𐑉 𐑄 𐐹𐐨𐐹𐑊 𐐲𐑂 𐐤𐐨𐑁𐐴. 𐐈𐑌𐐼 𐑄𐐲𐑅 𐐶𐐲𐑉 𐑄 𐐹𐐨𐐹𐑊 𐐲𐑂 𐐣𐐬𐑉𐐴𐐰𐑌𐐻𐐲𐑌 𐐺𐑉𐐫𐐻 𐐺𐐰𐐿. 𐐈𐑌𐐼 𐐲𐐹𐐱𐑌 𐑄𐐩𐑉 𐐿𐐲𐑂𐐯𐑌𐐰𐑌𐐻𐐮𐑍 𐐻𐐭 𐐿𐐨𐐹 𐑄 𐐹𐐨𐑅, 𐑄𐐩 𐐶𐐲𐑉 𐑉𐐨𐑅𐐻𐐬𐑉𐐼 𐐻𐐭 𐑄 𐑊𐐰𐑌𐐼 𐐲𐑂 𐐣𐐬𐑉𐐴𐐰𐑌𐐻𐐲𐑌, 𐐰𐑌𐐼 𐐲 𐐷𐐭𐑌𐐷𐐲𐑌 𐐻𐐳𐐿 𐐹𐑊𐐩𐑅 𐐺𐐨𐐻𐐶𐐨𐑌 𐑄𐐯𐑋 𐐰𐑌𐐼 𐑄 𐐹𐐨𐐹𐑊 𐐲𐑂 𐐢𐐨𐐸𐐴; 𐐰𐑌𐐼 𐑄𐐩 𐐶𐐲𐑉 𐐫𐑊𐑅𐐬 𐑉𐐨𐑅𐐻𐐬𐑉𐐼 𐐻𐐭 𐑄𐐩𐑉 𐑊𐐰𐑌𐐼𐑆.

7. 𐐈𐑌𐐼 𐐮𐐻 𐐿𐐩𐑋 𐐻𐐭 𐐹𐐰𐑅 𐑄𐐰𐐻 𐐮𐑌 𐑄 𐑅𐐩𐑋 𐐷𐐨𐑉 𐑄𐐰𐐻 𐑄 𐐹𐐨𐐹𐑊 𐐲𐑂 𐐤𐐨𐑁𐐴 𐐸𐐰𐐼 𐐹𐐨𐑅 𐑉𐐨𐑅𐐻𐐬𐑉𐐼 𐐲𐑌𐐻𐐭 𐑄𐐯𐑋, 𐑄𐐰𐐻 𐐤𐐨𐑁𐐴𐐸𐐪, 𐑄 𐑅𐐯𐐿𐐲𐑌𐐼 𐐕𐐨𐑁 𐐖𐐲𐐾, 𐐼𐐴𐐼, 𐐸𐐰𐑂𐐮𐑍 𐑁𐐮𐑊𐐼 𐑄 𐐾𐐲𐐾𐑋𐐯𐑌𐐻-𐑅𐐨𐐻 𐐶𐐮𐑄 𐐹𐐲𐑉𐑁𐐯𐐿𐐻 𐐲𐐹𐑉𐐴𐐻𐑌𐐯𐑅 𐐺𐐨𐑁𐐬𐑉 𐐘𐐱𐐼; 𐑌𐐯𐑂𐐲𐑉𐑄𐐲𐑊𐐯𐑅, 𐐸𐐨 𐐸𐐰𐐼 𐑉𐐨𐑁𐐷𐐭𐑆𐐼 𐐈𐑊𐑋𐐲 𐐻𐐭 𐐻𐐩𐐿

𐐹𐐲𐑆𐐯𐑇𐐲𐑌 𐐱𐑂 𐑄𐐬𐑆 𐑉𐐯𐐿𐐲𐑉𐐼𐑆 𐐰𐑌𐐼 𐑄𐐬𐑆 𐑃𐐮𐑍𐑆 𐐸𐐶𐐮𐐽 𐐶𐐲𐑉 𐐯𐑅𐐻𐐨𐑋𐐼 𐐺𐐴 𐐈𐑊𐑋𐐲 𐐰𐑌𐐼 𐐸𐐮𐑆 𐑁𐐪𐑄𐐲𐑉𐑆 𐐻𐐭 𐐺 𐑋𐐬𐑅𐐻 𐑅𐐩𐐿𐑉𐐯𐐼: 𐑄𐐯𐑉𐑁𐐬𐑉 𐐈𐑊𐑋𐐲 𐐸𐐰𐐼 𐐿𐐲𐑌𐑁𐐲𐑉𐐼 𐑄𐐯𐑋 𐐲𐐹𐐱𐑌 𐐸𐐮𐑆 𐑅𐐲𐑌 𐐐𐐯𐑊𐐲𐑋𐐲𐑌.

8. 𐐒𐐨𐐸𐐬𐑊𐐼 𐐮𐐻 𐐿𐐩𐑋 𐐻𐐭 𐐹𐐪𐑅 𐑄𐐰𐐻 𐑄 𐑅𐐲𐑌 𐐱𐑂 𐐤𐐨𐑁𐐴𐐸𐐪 𐐶𐐱𐑆 𐐰𐐹𐐶𐐮𐑌𐐻𐐯𐐼 𐐻𐐭 𐑁𐐮𐑊 𐑄 𐐾𐐲𐐾𐑋𐐯𐑌𐐻 𐑅𐐨𐐻, 𐐮𐑌 𐑄 𐑅𐐻𐐯𐐼 𐐱𐑂 𐐸𐐮𐑆 𐑁𐐪𐑄𐐲𐑉; 𐐷𐐩, 𐐸𐐨 𐐶𐐱𐑆 𐐰𐐹𐐶𐐮𐑌𐐻𐐯𐐼 𐐽𐐨𐑁 𐐾𐐲𐐾 𐐰𐑌𐐼 𐑀𐐲𐑂𐐲𐑉𐑌𐐲𐑉 𐐬𐑂𐐲𐑉 𐑄 𐐹𐐨𐐹𐑊, 𐐶𐐮𐑄 𐐰𐑌 𐐬𐑃 𐐰𐑌𐐼 𐑅𐐩𐐿𐑉𐐯𐐼 𐐫𐑉𐐼𐐮𐑌𐐰𐑌𐑅 𐐻𐐭 𐐾𐐲𐐾 𐑉𐐴𐐽𐐲𐑅𐑊𐐨, 𐐰𐑌𐐼 𐐻𐐭 𐐿𐐨𐐹 𐑄 𐐹𐐨𐑅, 𐐰𐑌𐐼 𐑄 𐑁𐑉𐐨𐐼𐐲𐑋 𐐱𐑂 𐑄 𐐹𐐨𐐹𐑊, 𐐰𐑌𐐼 𐐻𐐭 𐑀𐑉𐐪𐑌𐐻 𐐲𐑌𐐻𐐭 𐑄𐐯𐑋 𐑄𐐩𐑉 𐑅𐐩𐐿𐑉𐐯𐐼 𐐹𐑉𐐮𐑂𐐮𐑊𐐯𐐾𐐯𐑆 𐐻𐐭 𐐶𐐲𐑉𐑇𐐮𐐹 𐑄 𐐢𐐫𐑉𐐼 𐑄𐐩𐑉 𐐘𐐱𐐼; 𐐷𐐩, 𐐻𐐭 𐑅𐐲𐐹𐐬𐑉𐐻 𐐰𐑌𐐼 𐑋𐐩𐑌𐐻𐐩𐑌 𐑄 𐐿𐐫𐑆 𐐱𐑂 𐐘𐐱𐐼 𐐫𐑊 𐐸𐐮𐑆 𐐼𐐩𐑆, 𐐰𐑌𐐼 𐐻𐐭 𐐺𐑉𐐮𐑍 𐑄 𐐶𐐮𐐿𐐯𐐼 𐐻𐐭 𐐾𐐲𐑅𐐻𐐮𐑅, 𐐰𐐿𐐫𐑉𐐼𐐮𐑍 𐐻𐐭 𐑄𐐩𐑉 𐐿𐑉𐐴𐑋. 𐐤𐐵 𐐺𐐨𐐸𐐬𐑊𐐼, 𐐸𐐮𐑆 𐑌𐐩𐑋 𐐶𐐱𐑆 𐐑𐐪𐐸𐐬𐑉𐐲𐑌. 𐐈𐑌𐐼 𐐑𐐪𐐸𐐬𐑉𐐲𐑌 𐐼𐐮𐐼 𐑁𐐮𐑊 𐑄 𐑅𐐨𐐻 𐐱𐑂 𐐸𐐮𐑆 𐑁𐐪𐑄𐐲𐑉, 𐐰𐑌𐐼 𐐼𐐮𐐼 𐐿𐐲𐑋𐐯𐑌𐑅 𐐸𐐮𐑆 𐑉𐐩𐑌 𐐮𐑌 𐑄 𐐯𐑌𐐼 𐐱𐑂 𐑄 𐐻𐐶𐐯𐑌𐐻𐐨 𐐰𐑌𐐼 𐑁𐐬𐑉𐑃 𐐷𐐨𐑉, 𐐬𐑂𐐲𐑉 𐑄 𐐹𐐨𐐹𐑊 𐐱𐑂 𐐤𐐨𐑁𐐴.

𐐗𐐰𐐹𐐻𐐲𐑉 XXIII.

1. 𐐈𐑌𐐼 𐑌𐐵 𐐮𐐻 𐐿𐐩𐑋 𐐻𐐭 𐐹𐐪𐑅 𐐮𐑌 𐑄 𐐿𐐲𐑋𐐯𐑌𐑅𐑋𐐯𐑌𐐻 𐐱𐑂 𐑄 𐐻𐐶𐐯𐑌𐐻𐐨 𐐰𐑌𐐼 𐑁𐐮𐑁𐑃 𐐷𐐨𐑉 𐐱𐑂 𐑄 𐑉𐐩𐑌 𐐱𐑂 𐑄 𐐾𐐲𐐾𐐯𐑆 𐐬𐑂𐐲𐑉 𐑄 𐐹𐐨𐐹𐑊 𐐱𐑂 𐐤𐐨𐑁𐐴, 𐑄𐐩 𐐸𐐰𐑂𐐮𐑍 𐐯𐑅𐐻𐐰𐐺𐑊𐐮𐑇𐐻 𐐹𐐨𐑅 𐐺𐐨𐐻𐐶𐐨𐑌 𐑄 𐐹𐐨𐐹𐑊 𐐱𐑂 𐐢𐐨𐐸𐐴 𐐰𐑌𐐼 𐑄 𐐹𐐨𐐹𐑊 𐐱𐑂 𐐣𐐬𐑉𐐨𐐰𐑌𐐻𐐲𐑌, 𐐿𐐲𐑌𐑅𐐲𐑉𐑌𐐮𐑍 𐑄𐐩𐑉 𐑊𐐰𐑌𐐼𐑆, 𐐰𐑌𐐼 𐐸𐐰𐑂𐐮𐑍 𐐿𐐲𐑋𐐯𐑌𐑅𐐻 𐑄 𐐻𐐶𐐯𐑌𐐻𐐨 𐐰𐑌𐐼 𐑁𐐮𐑁𐑃 𐐷𐐨𐑉 𐐮𐑌 𐐹𐐨𐑅; 𐑌𐐯𐑂𐐲𐑉𐑄𐐲𐑊𐐯𐑅, 𐑄𐐩 𐐼𐐮𐐼 𐑌𐐱𐐻 𐑊𐐱𐑍 𐑋𐐩𐑌𐐻𐐩𐑌 𐐰𐑌 𐐯𐑌𐐻𐐴𐑉 𐐹𐐨𐑅 𐐮𐑌 𐑄 𐑊𐐰𐑌𐐼, 𐑁𐐫𐑉 𐑄𐐩𐑉 𐐺𐐨𐑀𐐰𐑌 𐐻𐐭 𐐺 𐐩 𐐿𐐲𐑌𐐻𐐯𐑌𐑇𐐲𐑌 𐐲𐑋𐐲𐑍 𐑄 𐐹𐐨𐐹𐑊 𐐿𐐲𐑌𐑅𐐲𐑉𐑌𐐮𐑍 𐑄 𐐽𐐨𐑁 𐐾𐐲𐐾 𐐑𐐪𐐸𐐬𐑉𐐲𐑌; 𐑁𐐫𐑉 𐐺𐐨𐐸𐐬𐑊𐐼 𐑄𐐩𐑉 𐐶𐐲𐑉 𐐩 𐐹𐐪𐑉𐐻 𐐱𐑂 𐑄 𐐹𐐨𐐹𐑊 𐐸𐐭 𐐼𐐨𐑆𐐴𐑉𐐼 𐑄𐐰𐐻 𐐩 𐑁𐐷𐐭 𐐹𐐲𐑉𐐻𐐮𐐿𐐷𐐭𐑊𐐲𐑉 𐐹𐐦𐑌𐐻𐑅 𐐱𐑂 𐑄 𐑊𐐫 𐑇𐐳𐐼 𐐺 𐐫𐑊𐐻𐐲𐑉𐐼. 𐐒𐐲𐐻 𐐺𐐨𐐸𐐬𐑊𐐼, 𐐑𐐪𐐸𐐬𐑉𐐲𐑌 𐐶𐐳𐐼 𐑌𐐱𐐻 𐐫𐑊𐐻𐐲𐑉, 𐑌𐐫𐑉 𐑅𐐲𐑁𐐲𐑉 𐑄 𐑊𐐫 𐐻𐐭 𐐺 𐐫𐑊𐐻𐐲𐑉𐐼; 𐑄𐐯𐑉𐑁𐐬𐑉, 𐐸𐐨 𐐼𐐮𐐼 𐑌𐐱𐐻 𐐸𐐪𐑉𐐿𐐲𐑌 𐐻𐐭 𐑄𐐬𐑆 𐐸𐐭 𐐸𐐰𐐼 𐑅𐐯𐑌𐐻 𐐮𐑌 𐑄𐐩𐑉 𐑂𐐦𐑅𐐯𐑆 𐐶𐐮𐑄 𐑄𐐩𐑉 𐐹𐐯𐐻𐐮𐑇𐐲𐑌𐑆, 𐐿𐐲𐑌𐑅𐐲𐑉𐑌𐐮𐑍 𐑄 𐐫𐑊𐐻𐐲𐑉𐐮𐑍 𐐱𐑂 𐑄 𐑊𐐫; 𐑄𐐯𐑉𐑁𐐬𐑉, 𐑄𐐬𐑆 𐐸𐐭 𐐶𐐲𐑉 𐐼𐐯𐑆𐐴𐑉𐐲𐑅 𐑄𐐰𐐻 𐑄 𐑊𐐫 𐑇𐐳𐐼 𐐺 𐐫𐑊𐐻𐐲𐑉𐐼 𐐶𐐲𐑉 𐐰𐑍𐑀𐑉𐐨 𐐶𐐮𐑄 𐐸𐐮𐑋, 𐐰𐑌𐐼 𐐼𐐨𐑆𐐴𐑉𐐼 𐑄𐐰𐐻 𐐸𐐨 𐑇𐐳𐐼 𐑌𐐬 𐑊𐐱𐑍𐑀𐐲𐑉 𐐺 𐐽𐐨𐑁 𐐾𐐲𐐾 𐐬𐑂𐐲𐑉 𐑄 𐑊𐐰𐑌𐐼: 𐑄𐐯𐑉𐑁𐐬𐑉 𐑄𐐩𐑉 𐐲𐑉𐐬𐑆 𐐩 𐐶𐐫𐑉𐑋 𐐼𐐮𐑅𐐹𐐷𐐭𐐻 𐐿𐐲𐑌𐑅𐐲𐑉𐑌𐐮𐑍 𐑄 𐑋𐐰𐐻𐐲𐑉; 𐐺𐐲𐐻 𐑌𐐱𐐻 𐐲𐑌𐐻𐐭 𐐺𐑊𐐲𐐼𐑇𐐯𐐼.

2. 𐐈𐑌𐐼 𐐮𐐻 𐐿𐐩𐑋 𐐻𐐭 𐐹𐐪𐑅 𐑄𐐰𐐻 𐑄𐐬𐑆 𐐸𐐭 𐐶𐐲𐑉 𐐼𐐯𐑆𐐴𐑉𐐲𐑅 𐑄𐐰𐐻 𐐑𐐪𐐸𐐬𐑉𐐲𐑌 𐑇𐐳𐐼 𐐺 𐐼𐐨𐑃𐑉𐐬𐑌𐐼 𐑁𐑉𐐱𐑋 𐑄 𐐾𐐲𐐾𐑋𐐯𐑌𐐻 𐑅𐐨𐐻, 𐐶𐐲𐑉 𐐿𐐫𐑊𐐼 𐐿𐐮𐑍-𐑋𐐯𐑌, 𐑁𐐫𐑉 𐑄𐐩 𐐶𐐲𐑉 𐐼𐐯𐑆𐐴𐑉𐐲𐑅 𐑄𐐰𐐻 𐑄 𐑊𐐫 𐑇𐐳𐐼 𐐺 𐐫𐑊𐐻𐐲𐑉𐐼 𐐮𐑌 𐐩 𐑋𐐰𐑌𐐲𐑉 𐐻𐐭 𐐬𐑂𐐲𐑉𐑃𐑉𐐬 𐑄 𐑁𐑉𐐨 𐑀𐐲𐑂𐐲𐑉𐑌𐑋𐐯𐑌𐐻, 𐐰𐑌𐐼 𐐻𐐭 𐐯𐑅𐐻𐐰𐐺𐑊𐐮𐑇 𐐩 𐐿𐐮𐑍 𐐬𐑂𐐲𐑉 𐑄 𐑊𐐰𐑌𐐼. 𐐈𐑌𐐼 𐑄𐐬𐑆 𐐸𐐭 𐐶𐐲𐑉 𐐼𐐯𐑆𐐴𐑉𐐲𐑅 𐑄𐐰𐐻 𐐑𐐪𐐸𐐬𐑉𐐲𐑌 𐑇𐐳𐐼 𐑉𐐨𐑋𐐩𐑌 𐐽𐐨𐑁 𐐾𐐲𐐾 𐐬𐑂𐐲𐑉 𐑄 𐑊𐐰𐑌𐐼, 𐐻𐐳𐐿 𐐲𐐹𐐱𐑌 𐑄𐐯𐑋 𐑄 𐑌𐐩𐑋 𐐱𐑂 𐑁𐑉𐐨𐑋𐐯𐑌; 𐐰𐑌𐐼 𐑄𐐲𐑅 𐐶𐐱𐑆 𐑄 𐐼𐐮𐑂𐐮𐑈𐐲𐑌 𐐲𐑋𐐲𐑍 𐑄𐐯𐑋: 𐑁𐐫𐑉 𐑄 𐑁𐑉𐐨𐑋𐐯𐑌 𐐸𐐰𐐼 𐑅𐐶𐐬𐑉𐑌 𐐫𐑉 𐐿𐐲𐑂𐐯𐑌𐐰𐑌𐐻𐐯𐐼 𐐻𐐭 𐑋𐐩𐑌𐐻𐐩𐑌 𐑄𐐩𐑉 𐑉𐐴𐐻𐑅 𐐰𐑌𐐼 𐑄 𐐹𐑉𐐮𐑂𐐮𐑊𐐯𐐾𐐯𐑆 𐐱𐑂 𐑄𐐩𐑉 𐑉𐐨𐑊𐐮𐐾𐐲𐑌 𐐺𐐴 𐐩 𐑁𐑉𐐨 𐑀𐐲𐑂𐐲𐑉𐑌𐑋𐐯𐑌𐐻.

3. 𐐈𐑌𐐼 𐐮𐐻 𐐿𐐩𐑋 𐐻𐐭 𐐹𐐪𐑅 𐑄𐐰𐐻 𐑄𐐮𐑅 𐑋𐐰𐐻𐐲𐑉 𐐱𐑂 𐑄𐐩𐑉 𐐿𐐲𐑌𐐻𐐯𐑌𐑇𐐲𐑌 𐐶𐐱𐑆 𐑅𐐯𐐻𐑊𐐼 𐐺𐐴 𐑄 𐑂𐐦𐑅 𐐱𐑂 𐑄 𐐹𐐨𐐹𐑊. 𐐈𐑌𐐼 𐐮𐐻 𐐿𐐩𐑋 𐐻𐐭 𐐹𐐪𐑅 𐑄𐐰𐐻 𐑄 𐑂𐐦𐑅 𐐱𐑂 𐑄 𐐹𐐨𐐹𐑊 𐐿𐐩𐑋 𐐮𐑌 𐑁𐐩𐑂𐐲𐑉 𐐱𐑂 𐑄 𐑁𐑉𐐨𐑋𐐯𐑌, 𐐰𐑌𐐼 𐐑𐐪𐐸𐐬𐑉𐐲𐑌 𐑉𐐨𐐻𐐩𐑌𐐼 𐑄 𐐾𐐲𐐾𐑋𐐯𐑌𐐻 𐑅𐐨𐐻, 𐐸𐐶𐐮𐐽 𐐿𐐫𐑆𐐼 𐑋𐐲𐐽 𐑉𐐨𐐾𐐦𐑅𐐮𐑍 𐐲𐑋𐐲𐑍 𐑄 𐐺𐑉𐐯𐑄𐑉𐐯𐑌 𐐱𐑂 𐐑𐐪𐐸𐐬𐑉𐐲𐑌, 𐐰𐑌𐐼 𐐫𐑊𐑅𐐬 𐑋𐐯𐑌𐐨 𐐱𐑂 𐑄 𐐹𐐨𐐹𐑊 𐐱𐑂 𐑊𐐮𐐺𐐲𐑉𐐻𐐨; 𐐸𐐭 𐐫𐑊𐑅𐐬 𐐹𐐳𐐻 𐑄 𐐿𐐮𐑍-𐑋𐐯𐑌 𐐻𐐭 𐑅𐐴𐑊𐐯𐑌𐑅, 𐑄𐐰𐐻 𐑄𐐩 𐐼𐐲𐑉𐑅𐐻 𐑌𐐱𐐻 𐐱𐐹𐐬𐑆, 𐐺𐐲𐐻 𐐶𐐲𐑉 𐐬𐐺𐑊𐐴𐐾𐐼 𐐻𐐭 𐑋𐐩𐑌𐐻𐐩𐑌 𐑄 𐐿𐐫𐑆 𐐱𐑂 𐑁𐑉𐐨𐐼𐐲𐑋. 𐐤𐐵 𐑄𐐬𐑆 𐐸𐐭 𐐶𐐲𐑉 𐐮𐑌 𐑁𐐩𐑂𐐲𐑉 𐐱𐑂 𐐿𐐮𐑍𐑆 𐐶𐐲𐑉 𐑄𐐬𐑆 𐐱𐑂 𐐸𐐴 𐐺𐐲𐑉𐑃; 𐐰𐑌𐐼 𐑄𐐩 𐑅𐐫𐐻 𐐻𐐭 𐐺 𐐿𐐮𐑍𐑆; 𐐰𐑌𐐼 𐑄𐐩 𐐶𐐲𐑉 𐑅𐐲𐐹𐐬𐑉𐐻𐐯𐐼 𐐺𐐴 𐑄𐐬𐑆 𐐸𐐭 𐑅𐐫𐐻 𐐹𐐵𐐲𐑉 𐐰𐑌𐐼 𐐫𐑃𐐱𐑉𐐮𐐻𐐨 𐐬𐑂𐐲𐑉 𐑄 𐐹𐐨𐐹𐑊. 𐐒𐐲𐐻 𐐺𐐨𐐸𐐬𐑊𐐼, 𐑄𐐮𐑅 𐐶𐐱𐑆 𐐩 𐐿𐑉𐐮𐐻𐐮𐐿𐐲𐑊 𐐻𐐴𐑋 𐑁𐐫𐑉 𐑅𐐲𐐽 𐐿𐐲𐑌𐐻𐐯𐑌𐑇𐐲𐑌𐑆 𐐻𐐭 𐐺 𐐲𐑋𐐲𐑍 𐑄 𐐹𐐨𐐹𐑊

𐐱𐑂 𐐤𐐨𐑁𐐴: 𐑁𐐫𐑉 𐐺𐐨𐐸𐐬𐑊𐐼, 𐐈𐑋𐐲𐑊𐐮𐐿𐐴𐐲 𐐸𐐰𐐼 𐐲𐑀𐐯𐑌 𐑅𐐻𐐲𐑉𐐼 𐐲𐐹 𐑄 𐐸𐐪𐑉𐐻𐑅 𐐱𐑂 𐑄 𐐹𐐨𐐹𐑊 𐐱𐑂 𐑄 𐐢𐐰𐑋𐐲𐑌𐐴𐐻𐑅, 𐐲𐑀𐐯𐑌𐑅𐐻 𐑄 𐐹𐐨𐐹𐑊 𐐱𐑂 𐑄 𐐤𐐨𐑁𐐴𐐻𐑅, 𐐰𐑌𐐼 𐐸𐐨 𐐶𐐱𐑆 𐑀𐐰𐑄𐐲𐑉𐐮𐑍 𐐻𐐭𐑀𐐯𐑄𐐲𐑉 𐑅𐐬𐑊𐐾𐐲𐑉𐑆, 𐑁𐑉𐐱𐑋 𐐫𐑊 𐐹𐐪𐑉𐐻𐑅 𐐱𐑂 𐐸𐐮𐑆 𐑊𐐰𐑌𐐼, 𐐰𐑌𐐼 𐐪𐑉𐑋𐐮𐑍 𐑄𐐯𐑋, 𐐰𐑌𐐼 𐐹𐑉𐐨𐐹𐐩𐑉𐐮𐑍 𐑁𐐫𐑉 𐐶𐐫𐑉, 𐐶𐐮𐑄 𐐫𐑊 𐐼𐐮𐑊𐐮𐐾𐐯𐑌𐑅; 𐑁𐐫𐑉 𐐸𐐨 𐐸𐐰𐐼 𐑅𐐶𐐫𐑉𐑌 𐐻𐐭 𐐼𐑉𐐮𐑍𐐿 𐑄 𐐺𐑊𐐲𐐼 𐐱𐑂 𐐣𐐫𐑉𐐬𐑌𐐴. 𐐒𐐲𐐻 𐐺𐐨𐐸𐐬𐑊𐐼, 𐐶𐐨 𐑇𐐰𐑊 𐑅𐐨 𐑄𐐰𐐻 𐐸𐐮𐑆 𐐹𐑉𐐱𐑋𐐮𐑅 𐐸𐐶𐐮𐐽 𐐸𐐨 𐑋𐐩𐐼 𐐶𐐱𐑆 𐑉𐐰𐑇; 𐑌𐐯𐑂𐐲𐑉𐑄𐐲𐑊𐐯𐑅, 𐐸𐐨 𐐼𐐮𐐼 𐐹𐑉𐐨𐐹𐐩𐑉 𐐸𐐮𐑋𐑅𐐯𐑊𐑁 𐐰𐑌𐐼 𐐸𐐮𐑆 𐐪𐑉𐑋𐐨𐑆 𐐻𐐭 𐐿𐐲𐑋 𐐻𐐭 𐐺𐐰𐐻𐑊 𐐲𐑀𐐯𐑌𐑅𐐻 𐑄 𐐤𐐨𐑁𐐴𐐻𐑅. 𐐤𐐵 𐐸𐐮𐑆 𐐪𐑉𐑋𐐨𐑆 𐐶𐐲𐑉 𐑌𐐱𐐻 𐑅𐐬 𐑀𐑉𐐩𐐻 𐐰𐑆 𐑄𐐩 𐐸𐐰𐐼 𐐸𐐮𐑄𐐲𐑉𐐻𐐭 𐐺𐐮𐑌, 𐐺𐐨𐐿𐐫𐑆 𐐱𐑂 𐑄 𐑋𐐯𐑌𐐨 𐑃𐐵𐑆𐐲𐑌𐐼𐑆 𐐸𐐭 𐐸𐐰𐐼 𐐺𐐮𐑌 𐑅𐑊𐐩𐑌 𐐺𐐴 𐑄 𐐸𐐰𐑌𐐼 𐐱𐑂 𐑄 𐐤𐐨𐑁𐐴𐐻𐑅; 𐐺𐐲𐐻 𐑌𐐱𐐻𐐶𐐮𐑃𐑅𐐻𐐰𐑌𐐼𐐮𐑍 𐑄𐐯𐑉 𐑀𐑉𐐩𐐻 𐑊𐐱𐑅, 𐐈𐑋𐐲𐑊𐐮𐐿𐐴𐐲 𐐸𐐰𐐼 𐑀𐐰𐑄𐐲𐑉𐐼 𐐻𐐭𐑀𐐯𐑄𐐲𐑉 𐐲 𐐶𐐲𐑌𐐼𐐲𐑉𐑁𐐳𐑊𐐨 𐑀𐑉𐐩𐐻 𐐪𐑉𐑋𐐨, 𐐮𐑌𐑅𐐬𐑋𐐲𐐽 𐑄𐐰𐐻 𐐸𐐨 𐑁𐐨𐑉𐐼 𐑌𐐱𐐻 𐐻𐐭 𐐿𐐲𐑋 𐐼𐐵𐑌 𐐻𐐭 𐑄 𐑊𐐰𐑌𐐼 𐐱𐑂 𐐞𐐰𐑉𐐲𐐸𐐯𐑋𐑊𐐲. 𐐏𐐩, 𐐨𐑂𐐲𐑌 𐐈𐑋𐐲𐑊𐐮𐐿𐐴𐐲 𐐼𐐮𐐼 𐐸𐐮𐑋𐑅𐐯𐑊𐑁 𐐿𐐲𐑋 𐐼𐐵𐑌, 𐐰𐐻 𐑄 𐐸𐐯𐐼 𐐱𐑂 𐑄 𐐢𐐰𐑋𐐲𐑌𐐴𐐻𐑅. 𐐈𐑌𐐼 𐐮𐐻 𐐶𐐱𐑆 𐐮𐑌 𐑄 𐐻𐐶𐐯𐑌𐐻𐐨 𐐰𐑌𐐼 𐑁𐐮𐑁𐑃 𐐷𐐨𐑉 𐐱𐑂 𐑄 𐑉𐐩𐑌 𐐱𐑂 𐑄 𐐾𐐲𐐾𐐯𐑆; 𐐰𐑌𐐼 𐐮𐐻 𐐶𐐱𐑆 𐐰𐐻 𐑄 𐑅𐐩𐑋 𐐻𐐴𐑋 𐑄𐐰𐐻 𐑄𐐩 𐐸𐐰𐐼 𐐺𐐨𐑀𐐲𐑌 𐐻𐐭 𐑅𐐯𐐻𐑊 𐑄 𐐰𐑁𐐩𐑉𐑆 𐐱𐑂 𐑄𐐯𐑉 𐐿𐐱𐑌𐐻𐐯𐑌𐑇𐐲𐑌𐑆 𐐿𐐱𐑌𐑅𐐲𐑉𐑌𐐮𐑍 𐑄 𐐽𐐨𐑁 𐐾𐐲𐐾, 𐐑𐐪𐐸𐐬𐑉𐐲𐑌.

4. 𐐈𐑌𐐼 𐐮𐐻 𐐿𐐩𐑋 𐐻𐐭 𐐹𐐰𐑅 𐑄𐐰𐐻 𐐸𐐶𐐯𐑌 𐑄 𐑋𐐯𐑌 𐐸𐐭 𐐶𐐲𐑉 𐐿𐐫𐑊𐐼 𐐿𐐮𐑍-𐑋𐐯𐑌, 𐐸𐐰𐐼 𐐸𐐲𐑉𐐼 𐑄𐐰𐐻 𐑄 𐐢𐐰𐑋𐐲𐑌𐐴𐐻𐑅 𐐶𐐲𐑉 𐐿𐐲𐑋𐐮𐑍 𐐼𐐵𐑌 𐐻𐐭 𐐺𐐰𐐻𐑊 𐐲𐑀𐐯𐑌𐑅𐐻 𐑄𐐯𐑋, 𐑄𐐩 𐐶𐐲𐑉 𐑀𐑊𐐰𐐼 𐐮𐑌 𐑄𐐯𐑉 𐐸𐐪𐑉𐐻𐑅, 𐐰𐑌𐐼 𐑄𐐩 𐑉𐐨𐑁𐐷𐐭𐑆𐐼 𐐻𐐭 𐐻𐐩𐐿 𐐲𐐹 𐐪𐑉𐑋𐑆; 𐑁𐐫𐑉 𐑄𐐩 𐐶𐐲𐑉 𐑅𐐬 𐑉𐐫𐑃 𐐶𐐮𐑄 𐑄 𐐽𐐨𐑁 𐐾𐐲𐐾, 𐐰𐑌𐐼 𐐫𐑊𐑅𐐬 𐐶𐐮𐑄 𐑄 𐐹𐐨𐐹𐑊 𐐱𐑂 𐑊𐐮𐐺𐐲𐑉𐐻𐐨, 𐑄𐐰𐐻 𐑄𐐩 𐐶𐐳𐐼 𐑌𐐱𐐻 𐐻𐐩𐐿 𐐲𐐹 𐐪𐑉𐑋𐑆 𐐻𐐭 𐐼𐐨𐑁𐐯𐑌𐐼 𐑄𐐯𐑉 𐐿𐐲𐑌𐐻𐑉𐐨. 𐐈𐑌𐐼 𐐮𐐻 𐐿𐐩𐑋 𐐻𐐭 𐐹𐐰𐑅 𐑄𐐰𐐻 𐐸𐐶𐐯𐑌 𐐣𐐫𐑉𐐬𐑌𐐴 𐑅𐐫 𐑄𐐮𐑅, 𐐰𐑌𐐼 𐐫𐑊𐑅𐐬 𐑅𐐫 𐑄𐐰𐐻 𐑄 𐐢𐐰𐑋𐐲𐑌𐐴𐐻𐑅 𐐶𐐲𐑉 𐐿𐐲𐑋𐐮𐑍 𐐮𐑌𐐻𐐭 𐑄 𐐺𐐫𐑉𐐼𐐲𐑉𐑆 𐐱𐑂 𐑄 𐑊𐐰𐑌𐐼, 𐐸𐐨 𐐶𐐱𐑆 𐐯𐐿𐑅𐐨𐐼𐐮𐑍𐑊𐐨 𐑉𐐫𐑃, 𐐺𐐨𐐿𐐫𐑆 𐐱𐑂 𐑄 𐑅𐐻𐐲𐐺𐐲𐑉𐑌𐐯𐑅 𐐱𐑂 𐑄𐐬𐑆 𐐹𐐨𐐹𐑊 𐐸𐐭𐑋 𐐸𐐨 𐐸𐐰𐐼 𐑊𐐩𐐺𐐲𐑉𐐼 𐐶𐐮𐑄 𐑅𐐬 𐑋𐐲𐐽 𐐼𐐮𐑊𐐮𐐾𐐯𐑌𐑅 𐐻𐐭 𐐹𐑉𐐨𐑆𐐲𐑉𐑂; 𐐏𐐩, 𐐸𐐨 𐐶𐐱𐑆 𐐯𐐿𐑅𐐨𐐼𐐮𐑍𐑊𐐨 𐑉𐐫𐑃; 𐐸𐐮𐑆 𐑅𐐬𐑊 𐐶𐐱𐑆 𐑁𐐮𐑊𐐼 𐐶𐐮𐑄 𐐰𐑍𐑀𐐲𐑉 𐐲𐑀𐐯𐑌𐑅𐐻 𐑄𐐯𐑋. 𐐈𐑌𐐼 𐐮𐐻 𐐿𐐩𐑋 𐐻𐐭 𐐹𐐰𐑅 𐑄𐐰𐐻 𐐸𐐨 𐑅𐐯𐑌𐐻 𐐲 𐐹𐐨𐐻𐐮𐑇𐐲𐑌, 𐐶𐐮𐑄 𐑄 𐑂𐑎𐑅 𐐱𐑂 𐑄 𐐹𐐨𐐹𐑊, 𐐲𐑌𐐻𐐭 𐑄 𐑀𐐲𐑂𐐲𐑉𐑌𐐲𐑉 𐐱𐑂 𐑄 𐑊𐐰𐑌𐐼, 𐐼𐐨𐑆𐐴𐑉𐐮𐑍 𐑄𐐰𐐻 𐐸𐐨 𐑇𐐳𐐼 𐑉𐐨𐐼 𐐮𐐻, 𐐰𐑌𐐼 𐑀𐐮𐑂 𐐸𐐮𐑋, (𐐣𐐫𐑉𐐬𐑌𐐴,) 𐐹𐐵𐐲𐑉 𐐻𐐭 𐐿𐐱𐑋𐐹𐐯𐑊 𐑄𐐬𐑆 𐐼𐐮𐑅𐐯𐑌𐐻𐐲𐑉𐑆 𐐻𐐭 𐐼𐐨𐑁𐐯𐑌𐐼 𐑄𐐯𐑉 𐐿𐐲𐑌𐐻𐑉𐐨, 𐐫𐑉 𐐻𐐭 𐐹𐐳𐐻 𐑄𐐯𐑋 𐐻𐐭 𐐼𐐯𐑃: 𐑁𐐫𐑉 𐐮𐐻 𐐶𐐱𐑆 𐐸𐐮𐑆 𐑁𐐲𐑉𐑅𐐻 𐐿𐐩𐑉 𐐻𐐭 𐐹𐐳𐐻 𐐰𐑌 𐐯𐑌𐐼 𐐻𐐭 𐑅𐐲𐐽 𐐿𐐱𐑌𐐻𐐯𐑌𐑇𐐲𐑌𐑆, 𐐰𐑌𐐼 𐐼𐐮𐑅𐐯𐑌𐑇𐐲𐑌𐑆 𐐲𐑋𐐲𐑍 𐑄 𐐹𐐨𐐹𐑊; 𐑁𐐫𐑉 𐐺𐐨𐐸𐐬𐑊𐐼, 𐑄𐐮𐑅 𐐸𐐰𐐼 𐐺𐐮𐑌 𐐸𐐮𐑄𐐲𐑉𐐻𐐭 𐐲 𐐿𐐫𐑆 𐐱𐑂 𐐫𐑊 𐑄𐐯𐑉 𐐼𐐨𐑅𐐻𐑉𐐲𐐿𐑇𐐲𐑌. 𐐈𐑌𐐼 𐐮𐐻 𐐿𐐩𐑋 𐐻𐐭 𐐹𐐰𐑅 𐑄𐐰𐐻 𐐮𐐻 𐐶𐐱𐑆 𐑀𐑉𐐰𐑌𐐻𐐯𐐼, 𐐰𐐿𐐫𐑉𐐼𐐮𐑍 𐐻𐐭 𐑄 𐑂𐑎𐑅 𐐱𐑂 𐑄 𐐹𐐨𐐹𐑊.

5. 𐐈𐑌𐐼 𐐮𐐻 𐐿𐐩𐑋 𐐻𐐭 𐐹𐐰𐑅 𐑄𐐰𐐻 𐐣𐐫𐑉𐐬𐑌𐐴 𐐿𐐱𐑋𐐰𐑌𐐼𐐯𐐼 𐑄𐐰𐐻 𐐸𐐮𐑆 𐐪𐑉𐑋𐐨 𐑇𐐳𐐼 𐑀𐐬 𐐲𐑀𐐯𐑌𐑅𐐻 𐑄𐐬𐑆 𐐿𐐮𐑍-𐑋𐐯𐑌, 𐐻𐐭 𐐹𐐳𐑊 𐐼𐐵𐑌 𐑄𐐯𐑉 𐐹𐑉𐐴𐐼 𐐰𐑌𐐼 𐑄𐐯𐑉 𐑌𐐬𐐺𐐮𐑊𐐮𐐻𐐨, 𐐰𐑌𐐼 𐑊𐐯𐑂𐐲𐑊 𐑄𐐯𐑋 𐐶𐐮𐑄 𐑄 𐐲𐑉𐑃, 𐐫𐑉 𐑄𐐩 𐑇𐐳𐐼 𐐻𐐩𐐿 𐐲𐐹 𐐪𐑉𐑋𐑆 𐐰𐑌𐐼 𐑅𐐲𐐹𐐫𐑉𐐻 𐑄 𐐿𐐫𐑆 𐐱𐑂 𐑊𐐮𐐺𐐲𐑉𐐻𐐨. 𐐈𐑌𐐼 𐐮𐐻 𐐿𐐩𐑋 𐐻𐐭 𐐹𐐰𐑅 𐑄𐐰𐐻 𐑄 𐐪𐑉𐑋𐐨𐑆 𐐼𐐮𐐼 𐑋𐐪𐑉𐐽 𐑁𐐬𐑉𐑃 𐐲𐑀𐐯𐑌𐑅𐐻 𐑄𐐯𐑋; 𐐰𐑌𐐼 𐑄𐐩 𐐼𐐮𐐼 𐐹𐐳𐑊 𐐼𐐵𐑌 𐑄𐐯𐑉 𐐹𐑉𐐴𐐼 𐐰𐑌𐐼 𐑄𐐯𐑉 𐑌𐐬𐐺𐐮𐑊𐐮𐐻𐐨, 𐐮𐑌𐑅𐐬𐑋𐐲𐐽 𐑄𐐰𐐻 𐐰𐑆 𐑄𐐩 𐐼𐐮𐐼 𐑊𐐮𐑁𐐻 𐑄𐐯𐑉 𐐶𐐯𐐹𐐲𐑌𐑆 𐐱𐑂 𐐶𐐫𐑉 𐐻𐐭 𐑁𐐴𐐻 𐐲𐑀𐐯𐑌𐑅𐐻 𐑄 𐑋𐐯𐑌 𐐱𐑂 𐐣𐐫𐑉𐐬𐑌𐐴, 𐑄𐐩 𐐶𐐲𐑉 𐐸𐐷𐐭𐑌 𐐼𐐵𐑌 𐐰𐑌𐐼 𐑊𐐯𐑂𐐲𐑊𐐼 𐐻𐐭 𐑄 𐐲𐑉𐑃. 𐐈𐑌𐐼 𐐮𐐻 𐐿𐐩𐑋 𐐻𐐭 𐐹𐐰𐑅 𐑄𐐰𐐻 𐑄𐐯𐑉 𐐶𐐲𐑉 𐑁𐐬𐑉 𐑃𐐵𐑆𐐲𐑌𐐼 𐐱𐑂 𐑄𐐬𐑆 𐐼𐐮𐑅𐐯𐑌𐐻𐐲𐑉𐑆 𐐸𐐭 𐐶𐐲𐑉 𐐸𐐷𐐭𐑌 𐐼𐐵𐑌 𐐺𐐴 𐑄 𐑅𐐬𐑉𐐼; 𐐰𐑌𐐼 𐑄𐐬𐑆 𐐱𐑂 𐑄𐐯𐑉 𐑊𐐨𐐼𐐲𐑉𐑆 𐐸𐐭 𐐶𐐲𐑉 𐑌𐐱𐐻 𐑅𐑊𐐩𐑌 𐐮𐑌 𐐺𐐰𐐻𐑊 𐐶𐐲𐑉 𐐻𐐩𐐿𐑌 𐐰𐑌𐐼 𐐿𐐰𐑅𐐻 𐐮𐑌𐐻𐐭 𐐹𐑉𐐮𐑆𐑌, 𐑁𐐫𐑉 𐑄𐐯𐑉 𐐶𐐱𐑆 𐑌𐐬 𐐻𐐴𐑋 𐑁𐐫𐑉 𐑄𐐯𐑉 𐐻𐑉𐐴𐐲𐑊𐑆 𐐰𐐻 𐑄𐐮𐑅 𐐹𐐨𐑉𐐨𐐲𐐼; 𐐰𐑌𐐼 𐑄 𐑉𐐨𐑋𐐩𐑌𐐼𐐲𐑉 𐐱𐑂 𐑄𐐬𐑆 𐐼𐐮𐑅𐐯𐑌𐐻𐐲𐑉𐑆, 𐑉𐐰𐑄𐐲𐑉 𐑄𐐰𐑌 𐐺𐐨 𐑅𐑋𐐮𐐻𐑌 𐐼𐐵𐑌 𐐻𐐭 𐑄 𐐲𐑉𐑃 𐐺𐐴 𐑄 𐑅𐐬𐑉𐐼, 𐐷𐐨𐑊𐐼𐐯𐐼 𐐻𐐭 𐑄 𐑅𐐻𐐰𐑌𐐼𐐲𐑉𐐼 𐐱𐑂 𐑊𐐮𐐺𐐲𐑉𐐻𐐨, 𐐰𐑌𐐼 𐐶𐐲𐑉 𐐿𐐱𐑋𐐹𐐯𐑊𐐼 𐐻𐐭 𐐸𐑎𐑅𐐻 𐑄 𐐻𐐴𐐻𐑊 𐐱𐑂 𐑊𐐮𐐺𐐲𐑉𐐻𐐨 𐐲𐐹𐐱𐑌 𐑄𐐯𐑉 𐐻𐐵𐐲𐑉𐑆, 𐐰𐑌𐐼 𐐮𐑌 𐑄𐐯𐑉 𐑅𐐮𐐻𐐨𐑆, 𐐰𐑌𐐼 𐐻𐐭 𐐻𐐩𐐿 𐐲𐐹 𐐪𐑉𐑋𐑆 𐐮𐑌 𐐼𐐨𐑁𐐯𐑌𐑅 𐐱𐑂 𐑄𐐯𐑉 𐐿𐐲𐑌𐐻𐑉𐐨. 𐐈𐑌𐐼 𐑄𐐲𐑅 𐐣𐐫𐑉𐐬𐑌𐐴 𐐹𐐳𐐻 𐐰𐑌 𐐯𐑌𐐼 𐐻𐐭 𐑄𐐬𐑆 𐐿𐐮𐑍-𐑋𐐯𐑌, 𐑄𐐰𐐻 𐑄𐐯𐑉 𐐶𐐲𐑉 𐑌𐐱𐐻 𐐯𐑌𐐨 𐑌𐐬𐑌 𐐺𐐴 𐑄 𐐰𐐹𐐯𐑊𐐩𐑇𐐲𐑌 𐐱𐑂 𐐿𐐮𐑍-𐑋𐐯𐑌; 𐐰𐑌𐐼 𐑄𐐲𐑅 𐐸𐐨 𐐹𐐳𐐻 𐐰𐑌 𐐯𐑌𐐼 𐐻𐐭 𐑄 𐑅𐐻𐐲𐐺𐐲𐑉𐑌𐐯𐑅 𐐰𐑌𐐼 𐑄 𐐹𐑉𐐴𐐼 𐐱𐑂 𐑄𐐬𐑆 𐐹𐐨𐐹𐑊 𐐸𐐭 𐐹𐑉𐐬𐑁𐐯𐑅𐐻 𐑄 𐐺𐑊𐐲𐐼 𐐱𐑂

𐑌𐐬𐐺𐐮𐑊𐐮𐐻𐐨; 𐐺𐐲𐐻 𐑄𐐩 𐐶𐐲𐑉 𐐺𐑉𐐫𐐻 𐐼𐐵𐑌 𐐻𐐭 𐐸𐐲𐑋𐐺𐑊 𐑄𐐯𐑋𐑅𐐯𐑊𐑂𐑆 𐑊𐐴𐐿 𐐲𐑌𐐻𐐭 𐑄𐐯𐑉 𐐺𐑉𐐯𐑄𐑉𐐯𐑌, 𐐰𐑌𐐼 𐐻𐐭 𐑁𐐴𐐻 𐑂𐐰𐑊𐐷𐐲𐑌𐐻𐑊𐐨 𐑁𐐫𐑉 𐑄𐐯𐑉 𐑁𐑉𐐨𐐼𐐲𐑋 𐑁𐑉𐐱𐑋 𐐺𐐱𐑌𐐼𐐩𐐾.

6. 𐐒𐐨𐐸𐐬𐑊𐐼 𐐮𐐻 𐐿𐐩𐑋 𐐻𐐭 𐐹𐐰𐑅 𐑄𐐰𐐻 𐐸𐐶𐐴𐑊 𐐣𐐫𐑉𐐬𐑌𐐴 𐐶𐐲𐑆 𐑄𐐲𐑅 𐐺𐑉𐐩𐐿𐐮𐑍 𐐼𐐵𐑌 𐑄 𐐶𐐫𐑉𐑆 𐐰𐑌𐐼 𐐿𐐱𐑌𐐻𐐯𐑌𐑇𐐲𐑌𐑆 𐐲𐑋𐐲𐑍 𐐸𐐮𐑆 𐐬𐑌 𐐹𐐨𐐹𐑊, 𐐰𐑌𐐼 𐑅𐐲𐐺𐐾𐐯𐐿𐐻𐐮𐑍 𐑄𐐯𐑋 𐐻𐐭 𐐹𐐨𐑅 𐐰𐑌𐐼 𐑅𐐮𐑂𐐮𐑊𐐮𐑆𐐩𐑇𐐲𐑌, 𐐰𐑌𐐼 𐑋𐐩𐐿𐐮𐑍 𐑉𐐯𐑀𐐷𐐭𐑊𐐩𐑇𐐲𐑌𐑆 𐐻𐐭 𐐹𐑉𐐨𐐹𐐯𐑉 𐑁𐐫𐑉 𐐶𐐫𐑉 𐐲𐑀𐐯𐑌𐑅𐐻 𐑄 𐐢𐐩𐑋𐐲𐑌𐐴𐐻𐑅, 𐐺𐐨𐐸𐐬𐑊𐐼, 𐑄 𐐢𐐩𐑋𐐲𐑌𐐴𐐻𐑅 𐐸𐐰𐐼 𐐿𐐲𐑋 𐐮𐑌𐐻𐐭 𐑄 𐑊𐐰𐑌𐐼 𐐱𐑂 𐐣𐐫𐑉𐐬𐑌𐐴, 𐐸𐐶𐐮𐐽 𐐶𐐲𐑆 𐐮𐑌 𐑄 𐐺𐐫𐑉𐐼𐐲𐑉𐑆 𐐺𐐴 𐑄 𐑅𐐨 𐑇𐐬𐑉.

7. 𐐈𐑌𐐼 𐐮𐐻 𐐿𐐩𐑋 𐐻𐐭 𐐹𐐰𐑅 𐑄𐐰𐐻 𐑄 𐐤𐐨𐑁𐐴𐐻𐑅 𐐶𐐲𐑉 𐑌𐐱𐐻 𐑅𐐲𐑁𐐮𐑇𐐯𐑌𐐻𐑊𐐨 𐑅𐐻𐑉𐐱𐑍 𐐮𐑌 𐑄 𐑅𐐮𐐻𐐨 𐐱𐑂 𐐣𐐫𐑉𐐬𐑌𐐴; 𐑄𐐯𐑉𐑁𐐬𐑉 𐐈𐑋𐐰𐑊𐐮𐐿𐐴𐐲 𐐼𐐮𐐼 𐐼𐑉𐐴𐑂 𐑄𐐯𐑋, 𐑅𐑊𐐩𐐮𐑍 𐑋𐐯𐑌𐐨. 𐐈𐑌𐐼 𐐮𐐻 𐐿𐐩𐑋 𐐻𐐭 𐐹𐐰𐑅 𐑄𐐰𐐻 𐐈𐑋𐐰𐑊𐐮𐐿𐐴𐐲 𐐼𐐮𐐼 𐐻𐐩𐐿 𐐹𐐱𐑆𐐯𐑇𐐲𐑌 𐐱𐑂 𐑄 𐑅𐐮𐐻𐐨; 𐐷𐐩, 𐐹𐐱𐑆𐐯𐑇𐐲𐑌 𐐱𐑂 𐐫𐑊 𐑄𐐯𐑉 𐑁𐐫𐑉𐐻𐐮𐑁𐐮𐐿𐐩𐑇𐐲𐑌𐑆. 𐐈𐑌𐐼 𐑄𐐬𐑆 𐐸𐐭 𐑁𐑊𐐯𐐼 𐐵𐐻 𐐱𐑂 𐑄 𐑅𐐮𐐻𐐨 𐐱𐑂 𐐣𐐫𐑉𐐬𐑌𐐴, 𐐿𐐩𐑋 𐐻𐐭 𐑄 𐑅𐐮𐐻𐐨 𐐱𐑂 𐐤𐐨𐑁𐐴𐐸𐐲; 𐐰𐑌𐐼 𐐫𐑊𐑅𐐬 𐑄 𐐹𐐨𐐹𐑊 𐐱𐑂 𐑄 𐑅𐐮𐐻𐐨 𐐱𐑂 𐐢𐐨𐐸𐐴 𐑀𐐰𐑄𐐲𐑉𐐼 𐑄𐐯𐑋𐑅𐐯𐑊𐑂𐑆 𐐻𐐭𐑀𐐯𐑄𐐲𐑉, 𐐰𐑌𐐼 𐑋𐐩𐐼 𐐹𐑉𐐯𐐹𐐲𐑉𐐩𐑇𐐲𐑌𐑆, 𐐰𐑌𐐼 𐐶𐐲𐑉 𐑉𐐯𐐼𐐨 𐐻𐐭 𐑉𐐨𐑅𐐨𐑂 𐑄 𐐢𐐩𐑋𐐲𐑌𐐴𐐻𐑅 𐐻𐐭 𐐺𐐰𐐻𐑊.

8. 𐐒𐐲𐐻 𐐮𐐻 𐐿𐐩𐑋 𐐻𐐭 𐐹𐐰𐑅 𐑄𐐰𐐻 𐐈𐑋𐐰𐑊𐐮𐐿𐐴𐐲 𐐶𐐳𐐼 𐑌𐐱𐐻 𐑅𐐲𐑁𐐲𐑉 𐑄 𐐢𐐩𐑋𐐲𐑌𐐴𐐻𐑅 𐐻𐐭 𐑀𐐬 𐐲𐑀𐐯𐑌𐑅𐐻 𐑄 𐑅𐐮𐐻𐐨 𐐱𐑂 𐐤𐐨𐑁𐐴𐐸𐐲 𐐻𐐭 𐐺𐐰𐐻𐑊, 𐐺𐐲𐐻 𐐿𐐯𐐹𐐻 𐑄𐐯𐑋 𐐼𐐵𐑌 𐐺𐐴 𐑄 𐑅𐐨 𐑇𐐬𐑉, 𐑊𐐨𐑂𐐮𐑍 𐑋𐐯𐑌 𐐮𐑌 𐐯𐑂𐐲𐑉𐐨 𐑅𐐮𐐻𐐨 𐐻𐐭 𐑋𐐩𐑌𐐻𐐩𐑌 𐐰𐑌𐐼 𐐼𐐨𐑁𐐯𐑌𐐼 𐐮𐐻; 𐐰𐑌𐐼 𐑄𐐲𐑅 𐐸𐐨 𐐶𐐯𐑌𐐻 𐐱𐑌, 𐐻𐐩𐐿𐐮𐑍 𐐹𐐱𐑆𐐯𐑇𐐲𐑌 𐐱𐑂 𐑋𐐯𐑌𐐨 𐑅𐐮𐐻𐐨𐑆: 𐑄 𐑅𐐮𐐻𐐨 𐐱𐑂 𐐤𐐨𐑁𐐴𐐸𐐲, 𐐰𐑌𐐼 𐑄 𐑅𐐮𐐻𐐨 𐐱𐑂 𐐢𐐨𐐸𐐴, 𐐰𐑌𐐼 𐑄 𐑅𐐮𐐻𐐨 𐐱𐑂 𐐣𐐫𐑉𐐨𐐰𐑌𐐻𐐲𐑌, 𐐰𐑌𐐼 𐑄 𐑅𐐮𐐻𐐨 𐐱𐑂 𐐉𐑋𐑌𐐲𐑉, 𐐰𐑌𐐼 𐑄 𐑅𐐮𐐻𐐨 𐐱𐑂 𐐘𐐮𐐼, 𐐰𐑌𐐼 𐑄 𐑅𐐮𐐻𐐨 𐐱𐑂 𐐣𐐷𐐭𐑊𐐯𐐿, 𐐫𐑊 𐐱𐑂 𐐸𐐶𐐮𐐽 𐐶𐐲𐑉 𐐱𐑌 𐑄 𐐨𐑅𐐻 𐐺𐐫𐑉𐐼𐐲𐑉𐑆 𐐺𐐴 𐑄 𐑅𐐨 𐑇𐐬𐑉. 𐐈𐑌𐐼 𐑄𐐲𐑅 𐐸𐐰𐐼 𐑄 𐐢𐐩𐑋𐐲𐑌𐐴𐐻𐑅 𐐱𐐺𐐻𐐩𐑌𐐼, 𐐺𐐴 𐑄 𐐿𐐲𐑌𐐮𐑍 𐐱𐑂 𐐈𐑋𐐰𐑊𐐮𐐿𐐴𐐲, 𐑅𐐬 𐑋𐐯𐑌𐐨 𐑅𐐮𐐻𐐨𐑆, 𐐺𐐴 𐑄𐐯𐑉 𐑌𐐲𐑋𐐺𐐲𐑉𐑊𐐯𐑅 𐐸𐐬𐑅𐐻𐑅, 𐐫𐑊 𐐱𐑂 𐐸𐐶𐐮𐐽 𐐶𐐲𐑉 𐑅𐐻𐑉𐐱𐑍𐑊𐐨 𐑁𐐫𐑉𐐻𐐮𐑁𐐴𐐼 𐐰𐑁𐐻𐐲𐑉 𐑄 𐑋𐐰𐑌𐐲𐑉 𐐱𐑂 𐑄 𐑁𐐫𐑉𐐻𐐮𐑁𐐮𐐿𐐩𐑇𐐲𐑌𐑆 𐐱𐑂 𐐣𐐫𐑉𐐬𐑌𐐴; 𐐫𐑊 𐐱𐑂 𐐸𐐶𐐮𐐽 𐐰𐑁𐐬𐑉𐐼𐐯𐐼 𐑅𐐻𐑉𐐱𐑍𐐸𐐬𐑊𐐼𐑆 𐑁𐐫𐑉 𐑄 𐐢𐐩𐑋𐐲𐑌𐐴𐐻𐑅.

9. 𐐈𐑌𐐼 𐐮𐐻 𐐿𐐩𐑋 𐐻𐐭 𐐹𐐰𐑅 𐑄𐐰𐐻 𐑄𐐩 𐑋𐐪𐑉𐐽𐐻 𐐻𐐭 𐑄 𐐺𐐫𐑉𐐼𐐲𐑉𐑆 𐐱𐑂 𐑄 𐑊𐐰𐑌𐐼 𐐒𐐵𐑌𐐻𐐮𐑁𐐳𐑊, 𐐼𐑉𐐴𐑂𐐮𐑍 𐑄 𐐤𐐨𐑁𐐴𐐻𐑅 𐐺𐐨𐑁𐐬𐑉 𐑄𐐯𐑋, 𐐰𐑌𐐼 𐑅𐑊𐐩𐐮𐑍 𐑋𐐯𐑌𐐨. 𐐒𐐲𐐻 𐐮𐐻 𐐿𐐩𐑋 𐐻𐐭 𐐹𐐰𐑅 𐑄𐐰𐐻 𐑄𐐩 𐐶𐐲𐑉 𐑋𐐯𐐻 𐐺𐐴 𐐓𐐨𐐰𐑌𐐿𐐲𐑋, 𐐸𐐭 𐐸𐐰𐐼 𐑅𐑊𐐩𐑌 𐐣𐐫𐑉𐐨𐐰𐑌𐐻𐐲𐑌, 𐐰𐑌𐐼 𐐸𐐰𐐼 𐐸𐐯𐐼𐐯𐐼 𐐸𐐮𐑆 𐐹𐐨𐐹𐑊 𐐮𐑌 𐐸𐐮𐑆 𐑁𐑊𐐴𐐻. 𐐈𐑌𐐼 𐐮𐐻 𐐿𐐩𐑋 𐐻𐐭 𐐹𐐰𐑅 𐑄𐐰𐐻 𐐸𐐨 𐐸𐐯𐐼𐐯𐐼 𐐈𐑋𐐰𐑊𐐮𐐿𐐴𐐲 𐐫𐑊𐑅𐐬, 𐐰𐑆 𐐸𐐨 𐐶𐐲𐑆 𐑋𐐪𐑉𐐽𐐮𐑍 𐑁𐐬𐑉𐑃 𐐶𐐮𐑄 𐐸𐐮𐑆 𐑌𐐷𐐭𐑋𐐲𐑉𐐲𐑅 𐐪𐑉𐑋𐐨, 𐑄𐐰𐐻 𐐸𐐨 𐑋𐐴𐐻 𐐻𐐩𐐿 𐐹𐐱𐑆𐐯𐑇𐐲𐑌 𐐱𐑂 𐑄 𐑊𐐰𐑌𐐼 𐐒𐐵𐑌𐐻𐐮𐑁𐐳𐑊, 𐐰𐑌𐐼 𐐫𐑊𐑅𐐬 𐑄 𐑊𐐰𐑌𐐼 𐑌𐐫𐑉𐑃𐐶𐐲𐑉𐐼. 𐐒𐐲𐐻 𐐺𐐨𐐸𐐬𐑊𐐼, 𐐸𐐨 𐑋𐐯𐐻 𐐶𐐮𐑄 𐐲 𐐼𐐮𐑅𐐲𐐹𐐱𐐮𐑌𐐻𐑋𐐯𐑌𐐻, 𐐺𐐴 𐐺𐐨𐐮𐑍 𐑉𐐨𐐹𐐲𐑊𐑅𐐻 𐐺𐐴 𐐓𐐨𐐰𐑌𐐿𐐲𐑋 𐐰𐑌𐐼 𐐸𐐮𐑆 𐑋𐐯𐑌, 𐑁𐐫𐑉 𐑄𐐩 𐐶𐐲𐑉 𐑀𐑉𐐩𐐻 𐐶𐐫𐑉𐐷𐐲𐑉𐑆: 𐑁𐐫𐑉 𐐯𐑂𐐲𐑉𐐨 𐑋𐐰𐑌 𐐱𐑂 𐐓𐐨𐐰𐑌𐐿𐐲𐑋 𐐼𐐮𐐼 𐐯𐐿𐑅𐐨𐐼 𐑄 𐐢𐐩𐑋𐐲𐑌𐐴𐐻𐑅 𐐮𐑌 𐑄𐐯𐑉 𐑅𐐻𐑉𐐯𐑍𐑃, 𐐰𐑌𐐼 𐐮𐑌 𐑄𐐯𐑉 𐑅𐐿𐐮𐑊 𐐱𐑂 𐐶𐐫𐑉, 𐐮𐑌𐑅𐐬𐑋𐐲𐐽 𐑄𐐰𐐻 𐑄𐐩 𐐼𐐮𐐼 𐑀𐐩𐑌 𐐰𐐼𐑂𐐰𐑌𐐻𐐩𐐾 𐐬𐑂𐐲𐑉 𐑄 𐐢𐐩𐑋𐐲𐑌𐐴𐐻𐑅.

10. 𐐈𐑌𐐼 𐐮𐐻 𐐿𐐩𐑋 𐐻𐐭 𐐹𐐰𐑅 𐑄𐐰𐐻 𐑄𐐩 𐐼𐐮𐐼 𐐸𐐰𐑉𐐲𐑅 𐑄𐐯𐑋, 𐐮𐑌𐑅𐐬𐑋𐐲𐐽 𐑄𐐰𐐻 𐑄𐐩 𐐼𐐮𐐼 𐑅𐑊𐐩 𐑄𐐯𐑋 𐐨𐑂𐐲𐑌 𐐲𐑌𐐻𐐮𐑊 𐐮𐐻 𐐶𐐲𐑆 𐐼𐐪𐑉𐐿. 𐐈𐑌𐐼 𐐮𐐻 𐐿𐐩𐑋 𐐻𐐭 𐐹𐐰𐑅 𐑄𐐰𐐻 𐐓𐐨𐐰𐑌𐐿𐐲𐑋 𐐰𐑌𐐼 𐐸𐐮𐑆 𐑋𐐯𐑌 𐐼𐐮𐐼 𐐹𐐮𐐽 𐑄𐐯𐑉 𐐻𐐯𐑌𐐻𐑅 𐐮𐑌 𐑄 𐐺𐐫𐑉𐐼𐐲𐑉𐑆 𐐱𐑂 𐑄 𐑊𐐰𐑌𐐼 𐐒𐐵𐑌𐐻𐐮𐑁𐐳𐑊; 𐐰𐑌𐐼 𐐈𐑋𐐰𐑊𐐮𐐿𐐴𐐲 𐐼𐐮𐐼 𐐹𐐮𐐽 𐐸𐐮𐑆 𐐻𐐯𐑌𐐻𐑅 𐐮𐑌 𐑄 𐐺𐐫𐑉𐐼𐐲𐑉𐑆 𐐱𐑌 𐑄 𐐺𐐨𐐽 𐐺𐐴 𐑄 𐑅𐐨 𐑇𐐬𐑉, 𐐰𐑌𐐼 𐐰𐑁𐐻𐐲𐑉 𐑄𐐮𐑅 𐑋𐐰𐑌𐐲𐑉 𐐶𐐲𐑉 𐑄𐐩 𐐼𐑉𐐮𐑂𐐲𐑌.

11. 𐐈𐑌𐐼 𐐮𐐻 𐐿𐐩𐑋 𐐻𐐭 𐐹𐐰𐑅 𐑄𐐰𐐻 𐐸𐐶𐐯𐑌 𐑄 𐑌𐐴𐐻 𐐸𐐰𐐼 𐐿𐐲𐑋, 𐐓𐐨𐐰𐑌𐐿𐐲𐑋 𐐰𐑌𐐼 𐐸𐐮𐑆 𐑅𐐲𐑉𐑂𐐲𐑌𐐻 𐑅𐐻𐐬𐑊 𐑁𐐬𐑉𐑃 𐐰𐑌𐐼 𐐶𐐯𐑌𐐻 𐐵𐐻 𐐺𐐴 𐑌𐐴𐐻, 𐐰𐑌𐐼 𐐶𐐯𐑌𐐻 𐐮𐑌𐐻𐐭 𐑄 𐐿𐐰𐑋𐐹 𐐱𐑂 𐐈𐑋𐐰𐑊𐐮𐐿𐐴𐐲; 𐐰𐑌𐐼 𐐺𐐨𐐸𐐬𐑊𐐼, 𐑅𐑊𐐨𐐹 𐐸𐐰𐐼 𐐬𐑂𐐲𐑉𐐹𐐵𐐲𐑉𐐼 𐑄𐐯𐑋, 𐐺𐐨𐐿𐐫𐑆 𐐱𐑂 𐑄𐐯𐑉 𐑋𐐲𐐽 𐑁𐐲𐐻𐐨𐑀, 𐐸𐐶𐐮𐐽 𐐶𐐲𐑆 𐐿𐐫𐑆𐐼 𐐺𐐴 𐑄 𐑊𐐩𐐺𐐲𐑉𐑆 𐐰𐑌𐐼 𐐸𐐨𐐻 𐐱𐑂 𐑄 𐐼𐐩.

12. 𐐈𐑌𐐼 𐐮𐐻 𐐿𐐩𐑋 𐐻𐐭 𐐹𐐰𐑅 𐑄𐐰𐐻 𐐓𐐨𐐰𐑌𐐿𐐲𐑋 𐑅𐐻𐐬𐑊 𐐹𐑉𐐮𐑂𐐮𐑊𐐨 𐐮𐑌𐐻𐐭 𐑄 𐐻𐐯𐑌𐐻 𐐱𐑂 𐑄 𐐿𐐮𐑍, 𐐰𐑌𐐼 𐐹𐐳𐐻 𐐲 𐐾𐐰𐑂𐐯𐑊𐐮𐑌 𐐻𐐭 𐐸𐐮𐑆 𐐸𐐪𐑉𐐻; 𐐰𐑌𐐼 𐐸𐐨 𐐼𐐮𐐼 𐐿𐐫𐑆 𐑄 𐐼𐐯𐑃 𐐱𐑂 𐑄 𐐿𐐮𐑍 𐐮𐑋𐐨𐐼𐐨𐐲𐐻𐑊𐐨, 𐑄𐐰𐐻 𐐸𐐨 𐐼𐐮𐐼 𐑌𐐱𐐻 𐐲𐐶𐐩𐐿 𐐸𐐮𐑆 𐑅𐐲𐑉𐑂𐐲𐑌𐐻𐑅. 𐐈𐑌𐐼 𐐸𐐨 𐑉𐐨𐐻𐐲𐑉𐑌𐐼 𐐲𐑀𐐯𐑌 𐐹𐑉𐐮𐑂𐐮𐑊𐐨 𐐻𐐭 𐐸𐐮𐑆 𐐬𐑌 𐐿𐐰𐑋𐐹, 𐐰𐑌𐐼 𐐺𐐨-

𐐸𐐬𐑊𐐼 𐐸𐐮𐑆 𐑋𐐯𐑌 𐐶𐐲𐑉 𐐲𐑅𐑊𐐨𐐹; 𐐰𐑌𐐼 𐐸𐐨 𐐲𐐶𐐬𐐿 𐑄𐐯𐑋 𐐰𐑌𐐼 𐐻𐐬𐑊𐐼 𐑄𐐯𐑋 𐐫𐑊 𐑄 𐑃𐐮𐑍𐑆 𐑄𐐰𐐻 𐐸𐐨 𐐸𐐰𐐼 𐐼𐐲𐑌. 𐐈𐑌𐐼 𐐸𐐨 𐐿𐐫𐑆𐐼 𐑄𐐰𐐻 𐐸𐐮𐑆 𐐪𐑉𐑋𐐨𐑆 𐑇𐐳𐐼 𐑅𐐻𐐰𐑌𐐼 𐐮𐑌 𐑉𐐯𐐼𐐨𐑌𐐯𐑅, 𐑊𐐯𐑅𐐻 𐑄 𐐢𐐩𐑋𐐲𐑌𐐴𐐻𐑅 𐐸𐐰𐐼 𐐲𐐶𐐩𐐿𐐻, 𐐰𐑌𐐼 𐑇𐐳𐐼 𐐿𐐲𐑋 𐐲𐐹𐐱𐑌 𐑄𐐯𐑋. 𐐈𐑌𐐼 𐑄𐐲𐑅 𐐯𐑌𐐼𐐯𐐼 𐑄 𐐻𐐶𐐯𐑌𐐻𐐨 𐐰𐑌𐐼 𐑁𐐮𐑁𐑃 𐐷𐐨𐑉 𐐱𐑂 𐑄 𐑉𐐩𐑌 𐐱𐑂 𐑄 𐐾𐐲𐐾𐐯𐑆 𐐬𐑂𐐲𐑉 𐑄 𐐹𐐨𐐹𐐲𐑊 𐐱𐑂 𐐤𐐨𐑁𐐴; 𐐰𐑌𐐼 𐑄𐐲𐑅 𐐯𐑌𐐼𐐯𐐼 𐑄 𐐼𐐩𐑆 𐐱𐑂 𐐈𐑋𐐲𐑊𐐮𐐿𐐴𐐲.

𐐕𐐈𐐑𐐓𐐊𐐡 XXIV.

1. 𐐈𐑌𐐼 𐑌𐐵 𐐮𐐻 𐐿𐐩𐑋 𐐻𐐭 𐐹𐐪𐑅 𐑄𐐰𐐻 𐐮𐑌 𐑄 𐐻𐐶𐐯𐑌𐐻𐐨 𐐰𐑌𐐼 𐑅𐐮𐐿𐑅𐑃 𐐷𐐨𐑉 𐐱𐑂 𐑄 𐑉𐐩𐑌 𐐱𐑂 𐑄 𐐾𐐲𐐾𐐯𐑆 𐐬𐑂𐐲𐑉 𐑄 𐐹𐐨𐐹𐐲𐑊 𐐱𐑂 𐐤𐐨𐑁𐐴, 𐐺𐐨𐐸𐐬𐑊𐐼, 𐐸𐐶𐐯𐑌 𐑄 𐐢𐐩𐑋𐐲𐑌𐐴𐐻𐑅 𐐲𐐶𐐬𐐿 𐐱𐑌 𐑄 𐑁𐐲𐑉𐑅𐐻 𐑋𐐫𐑉𐑌𐐮𐑍 𐐱𐑂 𐑄 𐑁𐐲𐑉𐑅𐐻 𐑋𐐲𐑌𐑃, 𐐺𐐨𐐸𐐬𐑊𐐼, 𐑄𐐩 𐑁𐐵𐑌𐐼 𐐈𐑋𐐲𐑊𐐮𐐿𐐴𐐲 𐐶𐐱𐑆 𐐼𐐯𐐼 𐐮𐑌 𐐸𐐮𐑆 𐐬𐑌 𐐻𐐯𐑌𐐻; 𐐰𐑌𐐼 𐑄𐐩 𐐫𐑊𐑅𐐬 𐑅𐐫 𐑄𐐰𐐻 𐐓𐐨𐐰𐑌𐐿𐐲𐑋 𐐶𐐱𐑆 𐑉𐐯𐐼𐐨 𐐻𐐭 𐑀𐐮𐑂 𐑄𐐯𐑋 𐐺𐐰𐐻𐐲𐑊 𐐱𐑌 𐑄𐐰𐐻 𐐼𐐩. 𐐈𐑌𐐼 𐑌𐐵 𐐸𐐶𐐯𐑌 𐑄 𐐢𐐩𐑋𐐲𐑌𐐴𐐻𐑅 𐑅𐐫 𐑄𐐮𐑅, 𐑄𐐩 𐐶𐐲𐑉 𐐰𐑁𐑉𐐴𐐻𐐯𐐼; 𐐰𐑌𐐼 𐑄𐐩 𐐰𐐺𐐰𐑌𐐼𐐲𐑌𐐼 𐑄𐐩𐑉 𐐼𐐨𐑆𐐴𐑌 𐐮𐑌 𐑋𐐪𐑉𐐽𐐮𐑍 𐐮𐑌𐐻𐐭 𐑄 𐑊𐐰𐑌𐐼 𐑌𐐫𐑉𐑃𐐶𐐲𐑉𐐼, 𐐰𐑌𐐼 𐑉𐐨𐐻𐑉𐐨𐐻𐐯𐐼 𐐶𐐮𐑄 𐐫𐑊 𐑄𐐩𐑉 𐐪𐑉𐑋𐐨 𐐮𐑌𐐻𐐭 𐑄 𐑅𐐮𐐻𐐨 𐐱𐑂 𐐣𐐷𐐭𐑊𐐯𐐿, 𐐰𐑌𐐼 𐑅𐐫𐐻 𐐹𐑉𐐬𐐻𐐯𐐿𐑇𐐲𐑌 𐐮𐑌 𐑄𐐩𐑉 𐑁𐐫𐑉𐐻𐐮𐑁𐐮𐐿𐐩𐑇𐐲𐑌𐑆. 𐐈𐑌𐐼 𐐮𐐻 𐐿𐐩𐑋 𐐻𐐭 𐐹𐐪𐑅 𐑄𐐰𐐻 𐑄 𐐺𐑉𐐲𐑄𐐲𐑉 𐐱𐑂 𐐈𐑋𐐲𐑊𐐮𐐿𐐴𐐲 𐐶𐐱𐑆 𐐰𐐹𐑎𐑌𐐻𐐯𐐼 𐐿𐐮𐑍 𐐬𐑂𐐲𐑉 𐑄 𐐹𐐨𐐹𐐲𐑊; 𐐰𐑌𐐼 𐐸𐐮𐑆 𐑌𐐩𐑋 𐐶𐐱𐑆 𐐈𐑋𐐫𐑉𐐲𐑌; 𐑄𐐲𐑅 𐐿𐐮𐑍 𐐈𐑋𐐫𐑉𐐲𐑌, 𐑄 𐐺𐑉𐐲𐑄𐐲𐑉 𐐱𐑂 𐐿𐐮𐑍 𐐈𐑋𐐲𐑊𐐮𐐿𐐴𐐲, 𐐶𐐱𐑆 𐐰𐐹𐑎𐑌𐐻𐐯𐐼 𐐻𐐭 𐑉𐐩𐑌 𐐮𐑌 𐐸𐐮𐑆 𐑅𐐻𐐯𐐼.

2. 𐐈𐑌𐐼 𐐮𐐻 𐐿𐐩𐑋 𐐻𐐭 𐐹𐐪𐑅 𐑄𐐰𐐻 𐐸𐐨 𐐼𐐮𐐼 𐐿𐐲𐑋𐐪𐑌𐐼 𐑄𐐰𐐻 𐐸𐐮𐑆 𐐹𐐨𐐹𐐲𐑊 𐑇𐐳𐐼 𐑋𐐩𐑌𐐻𐐩𐑌 𐑄𐐬𐑆 𐑅𐐮𐐻𐐨𐑆 𐐸𐐶𐐮𐐽 𐑄𐐩 𐐸𐐰𐐼 𐐻𐐩𐐿𐐲𐑌 𐐺𐐴 𐑄 𐑇𐐯𐐼𐐮𐑍 𐐱𐑂 𐐺𐑊𐐲𐐼; 𐑁𐐫𐑉 𐑄𐐩 𐐸𐐰𐐼 𐑌𐐱𐐻 𐐻𐐩𐐿𐐲𐑌 𐐯𐑌𐐨 𐑅𐐮𐐻𐐨𐑆, 𐑅𐐩𐑂 𐑄𐐩 𐐸𐐰𐐼 𐑊𐐱𐑅𐐻 𐑋𐐲𐐽 𐐺𐑊𐐲𐐼. 𐐈𐑌𐐼 𐑌𐐵 𐐓𐐨𐐰𐑌𐐿𐐲𐑋 𐑅𐐫 𐑄𐐰𐐻 𐑄 𐐢𐐩𐑋𐐲𐑌𐐴𐐻𐑅 𐐶𐐲𐑉 𐐼𐐨𐐻𐐲𐑉𐑋𐐮𐑌𐐼 𐐻𐐭 𐑋𐐩𐑌𐐻𐐩𐑌 𐑄𐐬𐑆 𐑅𐐮𐐻𐐨𐑆 𐐸𐐶𐐮𐐽 𐑄𐐩 𐐸𐐰𐐼 𐐻𐐩𐐿𐐲𐑌, 𐐰𐑌𐐼 𐑄𐐬𐑆 𐐹𐐪𐑉𐐻𐑅 𐐱𐑂 𐑄 𐑊𐐰𐑌𐐼 𐐸𐐶𐐮𐐽 𐑄𐐩 𐐸𐐰𐐼 𐐱𐐺𐐻𐐩𐑌𐐼 𐐹𐐲𐑆𐐯𐑇𐐲𐑌 𐐱𐑂; 𐐰𐑌𐐼 𐐫𐑊𐑅𐐬 𐑅𐐨𐐮𐑍 𐑄 𐐨𐑌𐐫𐑉𐑋𐐮𐐻𐐨 𐐱𐑂 𐑄𐐩𐑉 𐑌𐐲𐑋𐐺𐐲𐑉, 𐐓𐐨𐐰𐑌𐐿𐐲𐑋 𐑃𐐫𐐻 𐐮𐐻 𐐶𐐱𐑆 𐑌𐐱𐐻 𐐯𐐿𐑅𐐹𐐨𐐼𐐨𐐯𐑌𐐻 𐑄𐐰𐐻 𐐸𐐨 𐑇𐐳𐐼 𐐰𐐻𐐯𐑋𐐹𐐻 𐐻𐐭 𐐰𐐻𐐰𐐿 𐑄𐐯𐑋 𐐮𐑌 𐑄𐐩𐑉 𐑁𐐫𐑉𐐻𐑅; 𐐺𐐲𐐻 𐐸𐐨 𐐿𐐯𐐹𐐻 𐐸𐐮𐑆 𐑋𐐯𐑌 𐑉𐐵𐑌𐐼 𐐲𐐺𐐵𐐻, 𐐰𐑆 𐐮𐑁 𐑋𐐩𐐿𐐮𐑍 𐐹𐑉𐐯𐐹𐐲𐑉𐐩𐑇𐐲𐑌𐑆 𐑁𐐫𐑉 𐐶𐐫𐑉; 𐐷𐐩, 𐐰𐑌𐐼 𐐻𐑉𐐭𐑊𐐨 𐐸𐐨 𐐶𐐱𐑆 𐐹𐑉𐐨𐐹𐐩𐑉𐐮𐑍 𐐻𐐭 𐐼𐐨𐑁𐐯𐑌𐐼 𐐸𐐮𐑋𐑅𐐯𐑊𐑁 𐐰𐑀𐐯𐑌𐑅𐐻 𐑄𐐯𐑋, 𐐺𐐴 𐐿𐐪𐑅𐐻𐐮𐑍 𐐲𐐹 𐐶𐐫𐑊𐑆 𐑉𐐵𐑌𐐼 𐐲𐐺𐐵𐐻, 𐐰𐑌𐐼 𐐹𐑉𐐨𐐹𐐩𐑉𐐮𐑍 𐐹𐑊𐐩𐑅𐐯𐑆 𐐱𐑂 𐑉𐐨𐑆𐐫𐑉𐐻.

3. 𐐈𐑌𐐼 𐐮𐐻 𐐿𐐩𐑋 𐐻𐐭 𐐹𐐪𐑅 𐑄𐐰𐐻 𐐸𐐨 𐐿𐐯𐐹𐐻 𐑄𐐲𐑅 𐐹𐑉𐐨𐐹𐐩𐑉𐐮𐑍 𐑁𐐫𐑉 𐐶𐐫𐑉, 𐐲𐑌𐐻𐐮𐑊 𐐣𐐬𐑉𐐬𐑌𐐴 𐐸𐐰𐐼 𐑅𐐯𐑌𐐻 𐐩 𐑊𐐪𐑉𐐾 𐑌𐐲𐑋𐐺𐐲𐑉 𐐱𐑂 𐑋𐐯𐑌 𐐻𐐭 𐑅𐐻𐑉𐐯𐑍𐑃𐐲𐑌 𐐸𐐮𐑆 𐐪𐑉𐑋𐐨. 𐐈𐑌𐐼 𐐣𐐬𐑉𐐬𐑌𐐴 𐐫𐑊𐑅𐐬 𐑅𐐯𐑌𐐻 𐐫𐑉𐐼𐐲𐑉𐑆 𐐲𐑌𐐻𐐭 𐐸𐐮𐑋, 𐑄𐐰𐐻 𐐸𐐨 𐑇𐐳𐐼 𐑉𐐨𐐻𐐩𐑌 𐐫𐑊 𐑄 𐐹𐑉𐐮𐑆𐐲𐑌𐐲𐑉𐑆 𐐸𐐭 𐑁𐐯𐑊 𐐮𐑌𐐻𐐭 𐐸𐐮𐑆 𐐸𐐰𐑌𐐼𐑆; 𐑁𐐫𐑉 𐐰𐑆 𐑄 𐐢𐐩𐑋𐐲𐑌𐐴𐐻𐑅 𐐸𐐰𐐼 𐐻𐐩𐐿𐐲𐑌 𐑋𐐯𐑌𐐨 𐐹𐑉𐐮𐑆𐐲𐑌𐐲𐑉𐑆, 𐑄𐐰𐐻 𐐸𐐨 𐑇𐐳𐐼 𐑉𐐨𐐻𐐩𐑌 𐐫𐑊 𐑄 𐐹𐑉𐐮𐑆𐐲𐑌𐐲𐑉𐑆 𐐱𐑂 𐑄 𐐢𐐩𐑋𐐲𐑌𐐴𐐻𐑅, 𐐰𐑆 𐐩 𐑉𐐰𐑌𐑅𐐲𐑋 𐑁𐐫𐑉 𐑄𐐬𐑆 𐐸𐐭𐑋 𐑄 𐐢𐐩𐑋𐐲𐑌𐐴𐐻𐑅 𐐸𐐰𐐼 𐐻𐐩𐐿𐐲𐑌. 𐐈𐑌𐐼 𐐸𐐨 𐐫𐑊𐑅𐐬 𐑅𐐯𐑌𐐻 𐐫𐑉𐐼𐐲𐑉𐑆 𐐲𐑌𐐻𐐭 𐐸𐐮𐑋, 𐑄𐐰𐐻 𐐸𐐨 𐑇𐐳𐐼 𐑁𐐫𐑉𐐻𐐮𐑁𐐴 𐑄 𐑊𐐰𐑌𐐼 𐐒𐐵𐑌𐐻𐐮𐑁𐐳𐑊, 𐐰𐑌𐐼 𐑅𐐨𐐿𐐷𐐭𐑉 𐑄 𐑌𐐰𐑉𐐬 𐐹𐐪𐑅 𐐸𐐶𐐮𐐽 𐑊𐐯𐐼 𐐮𐑌𐐻𐐭 𐑄 𐑊𐐰𐑌𐐼 𐑌𐐫𐑉𐑃𐐶𐐲𐑉𐐼, 𐑊𐐯𐑅𐐻 𐑄 𐐢𐐩𐑋𐐲𐑌𐐴𐐻𐑅 𐑇𐐳𐐼 𐐱𐐺𐐻𐐩𐑌 𐑄𐐰𐐻 𐐹𐑎𐑌𐐻, 𐐰𐑌𐐼 𐑇𐐳𐐼 𐐸𐐰𐑂 𐐹𐐵𐐲𐑉 𐐻𐐭 𐐸𐐰𐑉𐐲𐑅 𐑄𐐯𐑋 𐐱𐑌 𐐯𐑂𐐲𐑉𐐨 𐑅𐐴𐐼. 𐐈𐑌𐐼 𐐣𐐬𐑉𐐬𐑌𐐴 𐐫𐑊𐑅𐐬 𐑅𐐯𐑌𐐻 𐐲𐑌𐐻𐐭 𐐸𐐮𐑋, 𐐼𐐨𐑆𐐴𐑉𐐮𐑍 𐐸𐐮𐑋 𐑄𐐰𐐻 𐐸𐐨 𐐶𐐳𐐼 𐐺𐐨 𐑁𐐩𐑃𐑁𐐳𐑊 𐐮𐑌 𐑋𐐩𐑌𐐻𐐩𐑌𐐮𐑍 𐑄𐐰𐐻 𐐿𐐶𐐫𐑉𐐻𐐲𐑉 𐐱𐑂 𐑄 𐑊𐐰𐑌𐐼, 𐐰𐑌𐐼 𐑄𐐰𐐻 𐐸𐐨 𐐶𐐳𐐼 𐑅𐐨𐐿 𐐯𐑂𐐲𐑉𐐨 𐐱𐐹𐐲𐑉𐐻𐐷𐐭𐑌𐐮𐐻𐐨 𐐻𐐭 𐑅𐐿𐐲𐑉𐐾 𐑄 𐐢𐐩𐑋𐐲𐑌𐐴𐐻𐑅 𐐮𐑌 𐑄𐐰𐐻 𐐿𐐶𐐫𐑉𐐻𐐲𐑉, 𐐰𐑆 𐑋𐐲𐐽 𐐰𐑆 𐐶𐐱𐑆 𐐮𐑌 𐐸𐐮𐑆 𐐹𐐵𐐲𐑉, 𐑄𐐰𐐻 𐐹𐐲𐑉𐐸𐐰𐐹𐑅 𐐸𐐨 𐑋𐐴𐐻 𐐻𐐩𐐿 𐐲𐑀𐐯𐑌 𐐺𐐴 𐑅𐐻𐑉𐐰𐐻𐐲𐐾𐐯𐑋 𐐫𐑉 𐑅𐐲𐑋 𐐲𐑄𐐲𐑉 𐐶𐐩, 𐑄𐐬𐑆 𐑅𐐮𐐻𐐨𐑆 𐐸𐐶𐐮𐐽 𐐸𐐰𐐼 𐐺𐐮𐑌 𐐻𐐩𐐿𐐲𐑌 𐐵𐐻 𐐱𐑂 𐑄𐐩𐑉 𐐸𐐰𐑌𐐼𐑆; 𐐰𐑌𐐼 𐑄𐐰𐐻 𐐸𐐨 𐐫𐑊𐑅𐐬 𐐶𐐳𐐼 𐑁𐐫𐑉𐐻𐐮𐑁𐐴 𐐰𐑌𐐼 𐑅𐐻𐑉𐐯𐑍𐑃𐐲𐑌 𐑄 𐑅𐐮𐐻𐐨𐑆 𐑉𐐵𐑌𐐼 𐐲𐐺𐐵𐐻, 𐐸𐐶𐐮𐐽 𐐸𐐰𐐼 𐑌𐐱𐐻 𐑁𐐫𐑊𐐲𐑌 𐐮𐑌𐐻𐐭 𐑄 𐐸𐐰𐑌𐐼𐑆 𐐱𐑂 𐑄 𐐢𐐩𐑋𐐲𐑌𐐴𐐻𐑅. 𐐈𐑌𐐼 𐐸𐐨 𐐫𐑊𐑅𐐬 𐑅𐐯𐐼 𐐲𐑌𐐻𐐭 𐐸𐐮𐑋, 𐐌 𐐶𐐳𐐼 𐐿𐐲𐑋 𐐲𐑌𐐻𐐭 𐐷𐐭, 𐐺𐐲𐐻 𐐺𐐨𐐸𐐬𐑊𐐼 𐑄 𐐢𐐩𐑋𐐲𐑌𐐴𐐻𐑅 𐐪𐑉

𐐲𐐹𐐱𐑌 𐐲𐑅 𐐮𐑌 𐑄 𐐺𐐫𐑉𐐼𐐲𐑉𐑆 𐐲𐑂 𐑄 𐑊𐐰𐑌𐐼 𐐺𐐴 𐑄 𐐶𐐯𐑅𐐻 𐑅𐐨; 𐐰𐑌𐐼 𐐺𐐨𐐸𐐬𐑊𐐼, 𐐌 𐑀𐐬 𐐰𐑀𐐯𐑌𐑅𐐻 𐑄𐐯𐑋, 𐑄𐐯𐑉𐑁𐐬𐑉 𐐌 𐐿𐐰𐑌𐐱𐐻 𐐿𐐲𐑋 𐐲𐑌𐐻𐐭 𐐷𐐭.

4. 𐐤𐐵 𐑄 𐐿𐐮𐑍 (𐐈𐑋𐐬𐑉𐐱𐑌) 𐐸𐐰𐐼 𐐼𐐨𐐹𐐪𐑉𐐻𐐯𐐼 𐐵𐐻 𐐲𐑂 𐑄 𐑊𐐰𐑌𐐼 𐐲𐑂 𐐞𐐰𐑉𐐰𐐸𐐯𐑋𐑊𐐪, 𐐰𐑌𐐼 𐐸𐐰𐐼 𐑋𐐩𐐼 𐑌𐐬𐑌 𐐲𐑌𐐻𐐭 𐑄 𐐿𐐶𐐨𐑌 𐐿𐐲𐑌𐑅𐐲𐑉𐑌𐐮𐑍 𐑄 𐐼𐐯𐑃 𐐲𐑂 𐐸𐐮𐑆 𐐺𐑉𐐲𐑄𐐲𐑉, 𐐰𐑌𐐼 𐐸𐐰𐐼 𐑀𐐰𐑄𐐲𐑉𐐼 𐐻𐐭𐑀𐐯𐑄𐐲𐑉 𐐩 𐑊𐐪𐑉𐐾 𐑌𐐲𐑋𐐺𐐲𐑉 𐐲𐑂 𐑋𐐯𐑌, 𐐰𐑌𐐼 𐐸𐐰𐐼 𐑋𐐪𐑉𐐽𐐻 𐑁𐐫𐑉𐑃 𐐰𐑀𐐯𐑌𐑅𐐻 𐑄 𐐤𐐨𐑁𐐴𐐻𐑅, 𐐫𐑌 𐑄 𐐺𐐫𐑉𐐼𐐲𐑉𐑆 𐐺𐐴 𐑄 𐐶𐐯𐑅𐐻 𐑅𐐨; 𐐰𐑌𐐼 𐑄𐐲𐑅 𐐸𐐨 𐐶𐐱𐑆 𐐯𐑌𐐼𐐯𐑂𐐲𐑉𐐮𐑍 𐐻𐐭 𐐸𐐰𐑉𐐲𐑅 𐑄 𐐤𐐨𐑁𐐴𐐻𐑅, 𐐰𐑌𐐼 𐐻𐐭 𐐼𐑉𐐫 𐐲𐐶𐐩 𐐩 𐐹𐐪𐑉𐐻 𐐲𐑂 𐑄𐐯𐑉 𐑁𐐫𐑉𐑅𐐯𐑆 𐐻𐐭 𐑄𐐰𐐻 𐐹𐐪𐑉𐐻 𐐲𐑂 𐑄 𐑊𐐰𐑌𐐼, 𐐸𐐶𐐴𐑊 𐐸𐐨 𐐸𐐰𐐼 𐐿𐐲𐑋𐐰𐑌𐐼𐐯𐐼 𐑄𐐬𐑆 𐐸𐐭𐑋 𐐸𐐨 𐐸𐐰𐐼 𐑊𐐯𐑁𐐻 𐐻𐐭 𐐹𐐲𐑆𐐯𐑅 𐑄 𐑅𐐮𐐻𐐨𐑆 𐐸𐐶𐐮𐐽 𐐸𐐨 𐐸𐐰𐐼 𐐻𐐩𐐿𐑌, 𐑄𐐰𐐻 𐑄𐐩 𐑇𐐳𐐼 𐐫𐑊𐑅𐐬 𐐸𐐰𐑉𐐲𐑅 𐑄 𐐤𐐨𐑁𐐴𐐻𐑅 𐐫𐑌 𐑄 𐐺𐐫𐑉𐐼𐐲𐑉𐑆 𐐺𐐴 𐑄 𐐨𐑅𐐻 𐑅𐐨; 𐐰𐑌𐐼 𐑇𐐳𐐼 𐐻𐐩𐐿 𐐹𐐲𐑆𐐯𐑇𐐲𐑌 𐐲𐑂 𐑄𐐯𐑉 𐑊𐐰𐑌𐐼𐑆 𐐰𐑆 𐑋𐐲𐐽 𐐰𐑆 𐐮𐐻 𐐶𐐱𐑆 𐐮𐑌 𐑄𐐯𐑉 𐐹𐐵𐐲𐑉, 𐐲𐐿𐐫𐑉𐐼𐐮𐑍 𐐻𐐭 𐑄 𐐹𐐵𐐲𐑉 𐐲𐑂 𐑄𐐯𐑉 𐐪𐑉𐑋𐐨𐑆. 𐐈𐑌𐐼 𐑄𐐲𐑅 𐐶𐐲𐑉 𐑄 𐐤𐐨𐑁𐐴𐐻𐑅 𐐮𐑌 𐑄𐐬𐑆 𐐼𐐩𐑌𐐾𐐲𐑉𐐲𐑅 𐑅𐐲𐑉𐐿𐐲𐑋𐑅𐐻𐐰𐑌𐑅𐐯𐑆, 𐐮𐑌 𐑄 𐐯𐑌𐐼𐐮𐑍 𐐲𐑂 𐑄 𐐻𐐶𐐯𐑌𐐻𐐨 𐐰𐑌𐐼 𐑅𐐮𐐿𐑅𐑃 𐐷𐐨𐑉 𐐲𐑂 𐑄 𐑉𐐩𐑌 𐐲𐑂 𐑄 𐐾𐐲𐐾𐐯𐑆 𐐬𐑂𐐲𐑉 𐑄 𐐹𐐨𐐹𐑊 𐐲𐑂 𐐤𐐨𐑁𐐴.

5. 𐐒𐐲𐐻 𐐺𐐨𐐸𐐬𐑊𐐼, 𐐮𐐻 𐐿𐐩𐑋 𐐻𐐭 𐐹𐐰𐑅 𐐮𐑌 𐑄 𐐻𐐶𐐯𐑌𐐻𐐨 𐐰𐑌𐐼 𐑅𐐯𐑂𐐲𐑌𐑃 𐐷𐐨𐑉 𐐲𐑂 𐑄 𐑉𐐩𐑌 𐐲𐑂 𐑄 𐐾𐐲𐐾𐐯𐑆, 𐑄𐐰𐐻 𐐓𐐨𐐰𐑍𐐿𐐲𐑋, 𐐺𐐴 𐑄 𐐿𐐲𐑋𐐰𐑌𐐼 𐐲𐑂 𐐣𐐫𐑉𐐬𐑌𐐴, 𐐸𐐭 𐐸𐐰𐐼 𐐯𐑅𐐻𐐰𐐺𐑊𐐮𐑇𐐻 𐐪𐑉𐑋𐐨𐑆 𐐻𐐭 𐐹𐑉𐐬𐐻𐐯𐐿𐐻 𐑄 𐑅𐐵𐑃 𐐰𐑌𐐼 𐑄 𐐶𐐯𐑅𐐻 𐐺𐐫𐑉𐐼𐐲𐑉𐑆 𐐲𐑂 𐑄 𐑊𐐰𐑌𐐼, 𐐰𐑌𐐼 𐐸𐐰𐐼 𐐺𐐨𐑀𐐲𐑌 𐐸𐐮𐑆 𐑋𐐪𐑉𐐽 𐐻𐐬𐑉𐐲𐑉𐐼𐑆 𐑄 𐑊𐐰𐑌𐐼 𐐒𐐵𐑌𐐻𐐮𐑁𐐳𐑊, 𐑄𐐰𐐻 𐐸𐐨 𐑋𐐴𐐻 𐐰𐑅𐐮𐑅𐐻 𐐓𐐨𐐰𐑍𐐿𐐲𐑋 𐐶𐐮𐑄 𐐸𐐮𐑆 𐑋𐐯𐑌 𐐮𐑌 𐑉𐐨𐐻𐐩𐐿𐐮𐑍 𐑄 𐑅𐐮𐐻𐐨𐑆 𐐸𐐶𐐮𐐽 𐑄𐐩 𐐸𐐰𐐼 𐑊𐐱𐑅𐐻. 𐐈𐑌𐐼 𐐮𐐻 𐐿𐐩𐑋 𐐻𐐭 𐐹𐐰𐑅 𐑄𐐰𐐻 𐐓𐐨𐐰𐑍𐐿𐐲𐑋 𐐸𐐰𐐼 𐑉𐐨𐑅𐐨𐑂𐐼 𐐫𐑉𐐼𐐲𐑉𐑆 𐐻𐐭 𐑋𐐩𐐿 𐐰𐑌 𐐰𐐻𐐰𐐿 𐐲𐐹𐐱𐑌 𐑄 𐑅𐐮𐐻𐐨 𐐲𐑂 𐐣𐐷𐐭𐑊𐐯𐐿, 𐐰𐑌𐐼 𐑉𐐨𐐻𐐩𐐿 𐐮𐐻 𐐮𐑁 𐐮𐐻 𐐶𐐲𐑉 𐐹𐐱𐑅𐐮𐐺𐑊.

6. 𐐈𐑌𐐼 𐐮𐐻 𐐿𐐩𐑋 𐐻𐐭 𐐹𐐰𐑅 𐑄𐐰𐐻 𐐓𐐨𐐰𐑍𐐿𐐲𐑋 𐑋𐐩𐐼 𐐹𐑉𐐯𐐹𐐲𐑉𐐩𐑇𐐲𐑌𐑆 𐐻𐐭 𐑋𐐩𐐿 𐐰𐑌 𐐰𐐻𐐰𐐿 𐐲𐐹𐐱𐑌 𐑄 𐑅𐐮𐐻𐐨 𐐲𐑂 𐐣𐐷𐐭𐑊𐐯𐐿, 𐐰𐑌𐐼 𐑋𐐪𐑉𐐽 𐑁𐐫𐑉𐑃 𐐶𐐮𐑄 𐐸𐐮𐑆 𐐪𐑉𐑋𐐨 𐐰𐑀𐐯𐑌𐑅𐐻 𐑄 𐐢𐐰𐑋𐐲𐑌𐐴𐐻𐑅; 𐐺𐐲𐐻 𐐸𐐨 𐑅𐐫 𐑄𐐰𐐻 𐐮𐐻 𐐶𐐱𐑆 𐐮𐑋𐐹𐐱𐑅𐐮𐐺𐑊 𐑄𐐰𐐻 𐐸𐐨 𐐿𐐳𐐼 𐐬𐑂𐐲𐑉𐐹𐐵𐐲𐑉 𐑄𐐯𐑋 𐐸𐐶𐐴𐑊 𐑄𐐩 𐐶𐐲𐑉 𐐮𐑌 𐑄𐐯𐑉 𐑁𐐫𐑉𐐻𐐮𐑁𐐮𐐿𐐩𐑇𐐲𐑌𐑆; 𐑄𐐯𐑉𐑁𐐬𐑉 𐐸𐐨 𐐲𐐺𐐰𐑌𐐼𐐲𐑌𐐼 𐐸𐐮𐑆 𐐼𐐨𐑆𐐴𐑌𐑆, 𐐰𐑌𐐼 𐑉𐐨𐐻𐐲𐑉𐑌𐐼 𐐲𐑀𐐯𐑌 𐐻𐐭 𐑄 𐑅𐐮𐐻𐐨 𐐒𐐵𐑌𐐻𐐮𐑁𐐳𐑊, 𐐻𐐭 𐐶𐐩𐐻 𐑁𐐫𐑉 𐑄 𐐿𐐲𐑋𐐮𐑍 𐐲𐑂 𐐣𐐫𐑉𐐬𐑌𐐴, 𐑄𐐰𐐻 𐐸𐐨 𐑋𐐴𐐻 𐑉𐐨𐑅𐐨𐑂 𐑅𐐻𐑉𐐯𐑍𐑃 𐐻𐐭 𐐸𐐮𐑆 𐐪𐑉𐑋𐐨.

7. 𐐈𐑌𐐼 𐐮𐐻 𐐿𐐩𐑋 𐐻𐐭 𐐹𐐰𐑅 𐑄𐐰𐐻 𐐣𐐫𐑉𐐬𐑌𐐴 𐐼𐐮𐐼 𐐲𐑉𐐴𐑂 𐐶𐐮𐑄 𐐸𐐮𐑆 𐐪𐑉𐑋𐐨 𐐰𐐻 𐑄 𐑊𐐰𐑌𐐼 𐐲𐑂 𐐒𐐵𐑌𐐻𐐮𐑁𐐳𐑊, 𐐮𐑌 𐑄 𐑊𐐰𐐻𐐲𐑉 𐐯𐑌𐐼 𐐲𐑂 𐑄 𐐻𐐶𐐯𐑌𐐻𐐨 𐐰𐑌𐐼 𐑅𐐯𐑂𐐲𐑌𐑃 𐐷𐐨𐑉 𐐲𐑂 𐑄 𐑉𐐩𐑌 𐐲𐑂 𐑄 𐐾𐐲𐐾𐐯𐑆 𐐬𐑂𐐲𐑉 𐑄 𐐹𐐨𐐹𐑊 𐐲𐑂 𐐤𐐨𐑁𐐴. 𐐈𐑌𐐼 𐐮𐑌 𐑄 𐐿𐐲𐑋𐐯𐑌𐑅𐑋𐐯𐑌𐐻 𐐲𐑂 𐑄 𐐻𐐶𐐯𐑌𐐻𐐨 𐐰𐑌𐐼 𐐩𐐻𐑃 𐐷𐐨𐑉, 𐐣𐐫𐑉𐐬𐑌𐐴 𐐰𐑌𐐼 𐐓𐐨𐐰𐑍𐐿𐐲𐑋, 𐐰𐑌𐐼 𐑋𐐯𐑌𐐨 𐐲𐑂 𐑄 𐐽𐐨𐑁 𐐿𐐰𐐹𐐻𐐲𐑌𐑆, 𐐸𐐯𐑊𐐼 𐐩 𐐿𐐵𐑌𐑅𐐮𐑊 𐐲𐑂 𐐶𐐫𐑉, 𐐸𐐶𐐱𐐻 𐑄𐐩 𐑇𐐳𐐼 𐐼𐐭 𐐻𐐭 𐐿𐐫𐑆 𐑄 𐐢𐐰𐑋𐐲𐑌𐐴𐐻𐑅 𐐻𐐭 𐐿𐐲𐑋 𐐵𐐻 𐐰𐑀𐐯𐑌𐑅𐐻 𐑄𐐯𐑋 𐐻𐐭 𐐺𐐰𐐻𐑊; 𐐫𐑉 𐑄𐐰𐐻 𐑄𐐩 𐑋𐐴𐐻 𐐺𐐴 𐑅𐐲𐑋 𐑋𐐨𐑌𐑆 𐑁𐑊𐐰𐐻𐐲𐑉 𐑄𐐯𐑋 𐐵𐐻 𐐲𐑂 𐑄𐐯𐑉 𐑅𐐻𐑉𐐱𐑍 𐐸𐐬𐑊𐐼𐑆, 𐑄𐐰𐐻 𐑄𐐩 𐑋𐐴𐐻 𐑀𐐩𐑌 𐐰𐐼𐑂𐐰𐑌𐐻𐐲𐐾 𐐬𐑂𐐲𐑉 𐑄𐐯𐑋 𐐰𐑌𐐼 𐐻𐐩𐐿 𐐲𐑀𐐯𐑌 𐑄 𐑅𐐮𐐻𐐨 𐐲𐑂 𐐣𐐷𐐭𐑊𐐯𐐿.

8. 𐐈𐑌𐐼 𐐮𐐻 𐐿𐐩𐑋 𐐻𐐭 𐐹𐐰𐑅 𐑄𐐩 𐑅𐐯𐑌𐐻 𐐯𐑋𐐺𐐰𐑅𐐨𐑆 𐐻𐐭 𐑄 𐐪𐑉𐑋𐐨 𐐲𐑂 𐑄 𐐢𐐰𐑋𐐲𐑌𐐴𐐻𐑅, 𐐸𐐶𐐮𐐽 𐐹𐑉𐐬𐐻𐐯𐐿𐐻𐐲𐐼 𐑄 𐑅𐐮𐐻𐐨 𐐲𐑂 𐐣𐐷𐐭𐑊𐐯𐐿, 𐐻𐐭 𐑄𐐯𐑉 𐑊𐐨𐐼𐐲𐑉, 𐐸𐐭𐑆 𐑌𐐩𐑋 𐐶𐐱𐑆 𐐖𐐩𐐿𐐲𐐺, 𐐼𐐯𐑆𐐴𐑉𐐮𐑍 𐐸𐐮𐑋 𐑄𐐰𐐻 𐐸𐐨 𐐶𐐳𐐼 𐐿𐐲𐑋 𐐵𐐻 𐐶𐐮𐑄 𐐸𐐮𐑆 𐐪𐑉𐑋𐐨𐑆 𐐻𐐭 𐑋𐐨𐐻 𐑄𐐯𐑋 𐐲𐐹𐐱𐑌 𐑄 𐐹𐑊𐐩𐑌𐑆, 𐐺𐐨𐐻𐐶𐐨𐑌 𐑄 𐐻𐐭 𐑅𐐮𐐻𐐨𐑆. 𐐒𐐲𐐻 𐐺𐐨𐐸𐐬𐑊𐐼, 𐐖𐐩𐐿𐐲𐐺, 𐐸𐐭 𐐶𐐱𐑆 𐐩 𐐞𐐫𐑉𐐲𐑋𐐴𐐻, 𐐶𐐳𐐼 𐑌𐐱𐐻 𐐿𐐲𐑋 𐐵𐐻 𐐶𐐮𐑄 𐐸𐐮𐑆 𐐪𐑉𐑋𐐨 𐐻𐐭 𐑋𐐨𐐻 𐑄𐐯𐑋 𐐲𐐹𐐱𐑌 𐑄 𐐹𐑊𐐩𐑌𐑆.

9. 𐐈𐑌𐐼 𐐮𐐻 𐐿𐐩𐑋 𐐻𐐭 𐐹𐐰𐑅 𐑄𐐰𐐻 𐐣𐐫𐑉𐐬𐑌𐐴, 𐐸𐐰𐑂𐐮𐑍 𐑌𐐬 𐐸𐐬𐐹𐑅 𐐲𐑂 𐑋𐐨𐐻𐐮𐑍 𐑄𐐯𐑋 𐐲𐐹𐐱𐑌 𐑁𐐩𐑉 𐑀𐑉𐐵𐑌𐐼𐑆, 𐑄𐐯𐑉𐑁𐐬𐑉, 𐐸𐐨 𐑉𐐨𐑆𐐱𐑊𐑂𐐼 𐐲𐐹𐐱𐑌 𐐩 𐐹𐑊𐐰𐑌 𐑄𐐰𐐻 𐐸𐐨 𐑋𐐴𐐻 𐐼𐐨𐐿𐐱𐐮 𐑄 𐐢𐐰𐑋𐐲𐑌𐐴𐐻𐑅 𐐵𐐻 𐐲𐑂 𐑄𐐯𐑉 𐑅𐐻𐑉𐐱𐑍 𐐸𐐬𐑊𐐼𐑆. 𐐜𐐯𐑉𐑁𐐬𐑉, 𐐸𐐨 𐐿𐐫𐑆𐐼 𐑄𐐰𐐻 𐐓𐐨𐐰𐑍𐐿𐐲𐑋 𐑇𐐳𐐼 𐐻𐐩𐐿 𐐩 𐑅𐑋𐐫𐑊 𐑌𐐲𐑋𐐺𐐲𐑉 𐐲𐑂 𐑋𐐯𐑌 𐐰𐑌𐐼 𐑋𐐪𐑉𐐽 𐐼𐐵𐑌 𐑌𐐨𐑉 𐑄 𐑅𐐨 𐑇𐐬𐑉; 𐐰𐑌𐐼 𐐣𐐫𐑉𐐬𐑌𐐴 𐐰𐑌𐐼 𐐸𐐮𐑆 𐐪𐑉𐑋𐐨, 𐐺𐐴 𐑌𐐴𐐻, 𐑋𐐪𐑉𐐽𐐻 𐐮𐑌 𐑄 𐐶𐐮𐑊𐐼𐐲𐑉𐑌𐐯𐑅, 𐐫𐑌 𐑄 𐐶𐐯𐑅𐐻 𐐲𐑂 𐑄 𐑅𐐮𐐻𐐨 𐐣𐐷𐐭𐑊𐐯𐐿; 𐐰𐑌𐐼 𐑄𐐲𐑅, 𐐫𐑌 𐑄 𐑋𐐱𐑉𐐬, 𐐸𐐶𐐯𐑌 𐑄 𐑀𐐪𐑉𐐼𐑆 𐐲𐑂 𐑄 𐐢𐐰𐑋𐐲𐑌𐐴𐐻𐑅 𐐸𐐰𐐼 𐐼𐐮𐑅𐐿𐐲𐑂𐐲𐑉𐐼 𐐓𐐨𐐰𐑍𐐿𐐲𐑋, 𐑄𐐩 𐑉𐐰𐑌 𐐰𐑌𐐼 𐐻𐐬𐑊𐐼 𐐮𐐻 𐐲𐑌𐐻𐐭 𐐖𐐩𐐿𐐲𐐺, 𐑄𐐯𐑉 𐑊𐐨𐐼𐐲𐑉.

10. 𐐈𐑌𐐼 𐐮𐐻 𐐗𐐩𐑋 𐐻𐐭 𐐹𐐰𐑅 𐑄𐐰𐐻 𐑄 𐐪𐑉𐑋𐐨𐑆 𐐱𐑂 𐑄 𐐢𐐰𐑋𐐲𐑌𐐴𐐻𐑅 𐐼𐐮𐐼 𐑋𐐪𐑉𐐽 𐑁𐐫𐑉𐑃 𐐲𐑀𐐯𐑌𐑅𐐻 𐐓𐐨𐐰𐑌𐐿𐐲𐑋, 𐑅𐐲𐐹𐐬𐑆𐐮𐑍 𐐺𐐴 𐑄𐐩𐑉 𐑌𐐲𐑋𐐺𐐲𐑉𐑆 𐐻𐐭 𐐬𐑂𐐲𐑉𐐹𐐵𐐲𐑉 𐐓𐐨𐐰𐑌𐐿𐐲𐑋, 𐐺𐐨𐐿𐐫𐑆 𐐱𐑂 𐑄 𐑅𐑋𐐫𐑊𐑌𐐯𐑅 𐐱𐑂 𐐸𐐮𐑆 𐑌𐐲𐑋𐐺𐐲𐑉𐑆. 𐐈𐑌𐐼 𐐰𐑆 𐐓𐐨𐐰𐑌𐐿𐐲𐑋 𐑅𐐫 𐑄 𐐪𐑉𐑋𐐨𐑆 𐐱𐑂 𐑄 𐐢𐐰𐑋𐐲𐑌𐐴𐐻𐑅 𐐿𐐲𐑋𐐮𐑍 𐐵𐐻 𐐲𐑀𐐯𐑌𐑅𐐻 𐐸𐐮𐑋 𐐸𐐨 𐐺𐐨𐑀𐐰𐑌 𐐻𐐭 𐑉𐐨𐐻𐑉𐐨𐐻 𐐼𐐵𐑌 𐐺𐐴 𐑄 𐑅𐐨 𐑇𐐬𐑉, 𐑌𐐫𐑉𐑃𐐶𐐲𐑉𐐼.

11. 𐐈𐑌𐐼 𐐮𐐻 𐐗𐐩𐑋 𐐻𐐭 𐐹𐐰𐑅 𐑄𐐰𐐻 𐐸𐐶𐐯𐑌 𐑄 𐐢𐐰𐑋𐐲𐑌𐐴𐐻𐑅 𐑅𐐫 𐑄𐐰𐐻 𐐸𐐨 𐐺𐐨𐑀𐐰𐑌 𐐻𐐭 𐑁𐑊𐐨, 𐑄𐐩 𐐻𐐳𐐿 𐐿𐐲𐑉𐐲𐐾 𐐰𐑌𐐼 𐐹𐐲𐑉𐑅𐐷𐐭𐐼 𐑄𐐯𐑋 𐐶𐐮𐑄 𐑂𐐮𐑀𐐲𐑉. 𐐈𐑌𐐼 𐐸𐐶𐐴𐑊 𐐓𐐨𐐰𐑌𐐿𐐲𐑋 𐐶𐐱𐑆 𐑄𐐲𐑅 𐑊𐐨𐐼𐐮𐑍 𐐲𐐶𐐩 𐑄 𐐢𐐰𐑋𐐲𐑌𐐴𐐻𐑅 𐐸𐐭 𐐶𐐲𐑉 𐐹𐐲𐑉𐑅𐐷𐐭𐐮𐑍 𐑄𐐯𐑋 𐐮𐑌 𐑂𐐩𐑌, 𐐺𐐨𐐸𐐬𐑊𐐼, 𐐣𐐬𐑉𐐬𐑌𐐴 𐐿𐐱𐑋𐐰𐑌𐐼𐐯𐐼 𐑄𐐰𐐻 𐐩 𐐹𐐪𐑉𐐻 𐐱𐑂 𐐸𐐮𐑆 𐐪𐑉𐑋𐐨 𐐸𐐭 𐐶𐐲𐑉 𐐶𐐮𐑄 𐐸𐐮𐑋 𐑇𐐳𐐼 𐑋𐐪𐑉𐐽 𐑁𐐫𐑉𐑃 𐐮𐑌𐐻𐐭 𐑄 𐑅𐐮𐐻𐐨, 𐐰𐑌𐐼 𐐻𐐩𐐿 𐐹𐐱𐑆𐐯𐑇𐐲𐑌 𐐱𐑂 𐐮𐐻. 𐐈𐑌𐐼 𐑄𐐲𐑅 𐑄𐐩 𐐼𐐮𐐼, 𐐰𐑌𐐼 𐑅𐑊𐐭 𐐫𐑊 𐑄𐐬𐑆 𐐸𐐭 𐐸𐐰𐐼 𐐺𐐮𐑌 𐑊𐐯𐑁𐐻 𐐻𐐭 𐐹𐑉𐐬𐐻𐐯𐐿𐐻 𐑄 𐑅𐐮𐐻𐐨; 𐐷𐐩, 𐐫𐑊 𐑄𐐬𐑆 𐐸𐐭 𐐶𐐳𐐼 𐑌𐐱𐐻 𐐷𐐨𐑊𐐼 𐐲𐐹 𐑄𐐩𐑉 𐐶𐐯𐐹𐐲𐑌𐑆 𐐱𐑂 𐐶𐐫𐑉. 𐐈𐑌𐐼 𐑄𐐲𐑅 𐐣𐐬𐑉𐐬𐑌𐐴 𐐸𐐰𐐼 𐐱𐐺𐐻𐐩𐑌𐐼 𐐹𐐱𐑆𐐯𐑇𐐲𐑌 𐐱𐑂 𐑄 𐑅𐐮𐐻𐐨 𐐣𐐭𐑊𐐯𐐿, 𐐶𐐮𐑄 𐐩 𐐹𐐪𐑉𐐻 𐐱𐑂 𐐸𐐮𐑆 𐐪𐑉𐑋𐐨, 𐐸𐐶𐐴𐑊 𐐸𐐨 𐑋𐐪𐑉𐐽𐐻 𐐶𐐮𐑄 𐑄 𐑉𐐨𐑋𐐩𐑌𐐼𐐲𐑉 𐐻𐐭 𐑋𐐨𐐻 𐑄 𐐢𐐰𐑋𐐲𐑌𐐴𐐻𐑅, 𐐸𐐶𐐯𐑌 𐑄𐐩 𐑇𐐳𐐼 𐑉𐐨𐐻𐐲𐑉𐑌 𐑁𐑉𐐱𐑋 𐑄 𐐹𐐲𐑉𐑅𐐷𐐭𐐻 𐐱𐑂 𐐓𐐨𐐰𐑌𐐿𐐲𐑋.

12. 𐐈𐑌𐐼 𐐮𐐻 𐐗𐐩𐑋 𐐻𐐭 𐐹𐐰𐑅 𐑄𐐰𐐻 𐑄 𐐢𐐰𐑋𐐲𐑌𐐴𐐻𐑅 𐐼𐐮𐐼 𐐹𐐲𐑉𐑅𐐷𐐭 𐐓𐐨𐐰𐑌𐐿𐐲𐑋 𐐲𐑌𐐻𐐮𐑊 𐑄𐐩 𐐗𐐩𐑋 𐑌𐐨𐑉 𐑄 𐑅𐐮𐐻𐐨 𐐒𐐵𐑌𐐻𐐮𐑁𐐳𐑊, 𐐰𐑌𐐼 𐑄𐐯𐑌 𐑄𐐩 𐐶𐐲𐑉 𐑋𐐯𐐻 𐐺𐐴 𐐢𐐨𐐸𐐴, 𐐰𐑌𐐼 𐐩 𐑅𐑋𐐫𐑊 𐐪𐑉𐑋𐐨, 𐐸𐐶𐐮𐐽 𐐸𐐰𐐼 𐐺𐐮𐑌 𐑊𐐯𐑁𐐻 𐐻𐐭 𐐹𐑉𐐬𐐻𐐯𐐿𐐻 𐑄 𐑅𐐮𐐻𐐨 𐐒𐐵𐑌𐐻𐐮𐑁𐐳𐑊. 𐐈𐑌𐐼 𐑌𐐵 𐐺𐐨𐐸𐐬𐑊𐐼, 𐐸𐐶𐐯𐑌 𐑄 𐐽𐐨𐑁 𐐿𐐰𐐹𐐻𐐮𐑌𐑆 𐐱𐑂 𐑄 𐐢𐐰𐑋𐐲𐑌𐐴𐐻𐑅 𐐸𐐰𐐼 𐐺𐐨𐐸𐐯𐑊𐐼 𐐢𐐨𐐸𐐴 𐐶𐐮𐑄 𐐸𐐮𐑆 𐐪𐑉𐑋𐐨 𐐿𐐲𐑋𐐮𐑍 𐐲𐑀𐐯𐑌𐑅𐐻 𐑄𐐯𐑋, 𐑄𐐩 𐑁𐑊𐐯𐐼 𐐮𐑌 𐑋𐐲𐐽 𐐿𐐱𐑌𐑁𐐷𐐭𐑈𐐲𐑌, 𐑊𐐯𐑅𐐻 𐐹𐐲𐑉𐐸𐐰𐐹𐑅 𐑄𐐩 𐑇𐐳𐐼 𐑌𐐱𐐻 𐐱𐐺𐐻𐐩𐑌 𐑄 𐑅𐐮𐐻𐐨 𐐣𐐭𐑊𐐯𐐿, 𐐺𐐨𐑁𐐬𐑉 𐐢𐐨𐐸𐐴 𐑇𐐳𐐼 𐐬𐑂𐐲𐑉𐐻𐐩𐐿 𐑄𐐯𐑋; 𐑁𐐫𐑉 𐑄𐐩 𐐶𐐲𐑉 𐐶𐐨𐑉𐐨𐐼 𐐺𐐨𐐿𐐫𐑆 𐐱𐑂 𐑄𐐩𐑉 𐑋𐐪𐑉𐐽, 𐐰𐑌𐐼 𐑄 𐑋𐐯𐑌 𐐱𐑂 𐐢𐐨𐐸𐐴 𐐶𐐲𐑉 𐑁𐑉𐐯𐑇. 𐐤𐐵 𐑄 𐐢𐐰𐑋𐐲𐑌𐐴𐐻𐑅 𐐼𐐮𐐼 𐑌𐐱𐐻 𐑌𐐬 𐑄𐐰𐐻 𐐣𐐬𐑉𐐬𐑌𐐴 𐐸𐐰𐐼 𐐺𐐮𐑌 𐐮𐑌 𐑄𐐩𐑉 𐑉𐐨𐑉 𐐶𐐮𐑄 𐐸𐐮𐑆 𐐪𐑉𐑋𐐨; 𐐰𐑌𐐼 𐐫𐑊 𐑄𐐩 𐑁𐐨𐑉𐐼 𐐶𐐱𐑆 𐐢𐐨𐐸𐐴 𐐰𐑌𐐼 𐐸𐐮𐑆 𐑋𐐯𐑌. 𐐤𐐵 𐐢𐐨𐐸𐐴 𐐶𐐱𐑆 𐑌𐐱𐐻 𐐼𐐨𐑆𐐴𐑉𐐲𐑅 𐐻𐐭 𐐬𐑂𐐲𐑉𐐻𐐩𐐿 𐑄𐐯𐑋 𐐻𐐮𐑊 𐑄𐐩 𐑇𐐳𐐼 𐑋𐐨𐐻 𐐣𐐬𐑉𐐬𐑌𐐴 𐐰𐑌𐐼 𐐸𐐮𐑆 𐐪𐑉𐑋𐐨. 𐐈𐑌𐐼 𐐮𐐻 𐐗𐐩𐑋 𐐻𐐭 𐐹𐐰𐑅 𐑄𐐰𐐻 𐐺𐐨𐑁𐐬𐑉 𐑄 𐐢𐐰𐑋𐐲𐑌𐐴𐐻𐑅 𐐸𐐰𐐼 𐑉𐐨𐐻𐑉𐐨𐐻𐐯𐐼 𐑁𐐪𐑉 𐑄𐐩 𐐶𐐲𐑉 𐑅𐐲𐑉𐐵𐑌𐐼𐐯𐐼 𐐺𐐴 𐑄 𐐤𐐨𐑁𐐴𐐻𐑅, 𐐺𐐴 𐑄 𐑋𐐯𐑌 𐐱𐑂 𐐣𐐬𐑉𐐬𐑌𐐴 𐐱𐑌 𐐶𐐲𐑌 𐐸𐐰𐑌𐐼, 𐐰𐑌𐐼 𐑄 𐑋𐐯𐑌 𐐱𐑂 𐐢𐐨𐐸𐐴 𐐱𐑌 𐑄 𐐲𐑄𐐲𐑉, 𐐫𐑊 𐐱𐑂 𐐸𐐭𐑋 𐐶𐐲𐑉 𐑁𐑉𐐯𐑇 𐐰𐑌𐐼 𐑁𐐳𐑊 𐐱𐑂 𐑅𐐻𐑉𐐯𐑍𐑃; 𐐺𐐲𐐻 𐑄 𐐢𐐰𐑋𐐲𐑌𐐴𐐻𐑅 𐐶𐐲𐑉 𐐶𐐨𐑉𐐨𐐼 𐐺𐐨𐐿𐐫𐑆 𐐱𐑂 𐑄𐐩𐑉 𐑊𐐱𐑍 𐑋𐐪𐑉𐐽. 𐐈𐑌𐐼 𐐣𐐬𐑉𐐬𐑌𐐴 𐐿𐐱𐑋𐐰𐑌𐐼𐐯𐐼 𐐸𐐮𐑆 𐑋𐐯𐑌 𐑄𐐰𐐻 𐑄𐐩 𐑇𐐳𐐼 𐑁𐐫𐑊 𐐲𐐹𐐱𐑌 𐑄𐐯𐑋 𐐲𐑌𐐻𐐮𐑊 𐑄𐐩 𐐸𐐰𐐼 𐑀𐐮𐑂𐐲𐑌 𐐲𐐹 𐑄𐐩𐑉 𐐶𐐯𐐹𐐲𐑌𐑆 𐐱𐑂 𐐶𐐫𐑉.

13. 𐐈𐑌𐐼 𐐮𐐻 𐐗𐐩𐑋 𐐻𐐭 𐐹𐐰𐑅 𐑄𐐰𐐻 𐐖𐐩𐐿𐐲𐐺, 𐐺𐐨𐐮𐑍 𐑄𐐩𐑉 𐑊𐐨𐐼𐐲𐑉, 𐐺𐐨𐐮𐑍 𐐫𐑊𐑅𐐬 𐐩 𐐞𐐬𐑉𐐲𐑋𐐴𐐻, 𐐰𐑌𐐼 𐐸𐐰𐑂𐐮𐑍 𐐰𐑌 𐐲𐑌𐐿𐐱𐑍𐐿𐐲𐑉𐐲𐐺𐑊 𐑅𐐹𐐮𐑉𐐮𐐻, 𐐸𐐨 𐑊𐐯𐐼 𐑄 𐐢𐐰𐑋𐐲𐑌𐐴𐐻𐑅 𐑁𐐫𐑉𐑃 𐐻𐐭 𐐺𐐰𐐻𐑊, 𐐶𐐮𐑄 𐐯𐐿𐑅𐐨𐐼𐐮𐑍 𐑁𐐷𐐭𐑉𐐨 𐐲𐑀𐐯𐑌𐑅𐐻 𐐣𐐬𐑉𐐬𐑌𐐴. 𐐣𐐬𐑉𐐬𐑌𐐴 𐐺𐐨𐐮𐑍 𐐮𐑌 𐑄𐐩𐑉 𐐿𐐬𐑉𐑅 𐐱𐑂 𐑋𐐪𐑉𐐽, 𐑄𐐯𐑉𐑁𐐬𐑉 𐐖𐐩𐐿𐐲𐐺 𐐶𐐱𐑆 𐐼𐐨𐐻𐐲𐑉𐑋𐐮𐑌𐐼 𐐻𐐭 𐑅𐑊𐐩 𐑄𐐯𐑋, 𐐰𐑌𐐼 𐐿𐐲𐐻 𐐸𐐮𐑆 𐐶𐐩 𐑃𐑉𐐭 𐐻𐐭 𐑄 𐑅𐐮𐐻𐐨 𐐱𐑂 𐐣𐐭𐑊𐐯𐐿. 𐐒𐐲𐐻 𐐺𐐨𐐸𐐬𐑊𐐼, 𐐣𐐬𐑉𐐬𐑌𐐴 𐐰𐑌𐐼 𐐸𐐮𐑆 𐑋𐐯𐑌 𐐶𐐲𐑉 𐑋𐐬𐑉 𐐹𐐵𐐲𐑉𐑁𐐳𐑊; 𐑄𐐯𐑉𐑁𐐬𐑉 𐑄𐐩 𐐼𐐮𐐼 𐑌𐐱𐐻 𐑀𐐮𐑂 𐐶𐐩 𐐺𐐨𐑁𐐬𐑉 𐑄 𐐢𐐰𐑋𐐲𐑌𐐴𐐻𐑅.

14. 𐐈𐑌𐐼 𐐮𐐻 𐐗𐐩𐑋 𐐻𐐭 𐐹𐐰𐑅 𐑄𐐰𐐻 𐑄𐐩 𐑁𐐫𐐻 𐐱𐑌 𐐺𐐬𐑃 𐐸𐐰𐑌𐐼𐑆 𐐶𐐮𐑄 𐐯𐐿𐑅𐐨𐐼𐐮𐑍 𐑁𐐷𐐭𐑉𐐨; 𐐰𐑌𐐼 𐑄𐐩𐑉 𐐶𐐲𐑉 𐑋𐐯𐑌𐐨 𐑅𐑊𐐩𐑌 𐐱𐑌 𐐺𐐬𐑃 𐑅𐐴𐐼𐑆; 𐐷𐐩, 𐐰𐑌𐐼 𐐣𐐬𐑉𐐬𐑌𐐴 𐐶𐐱𐑆 𐐶𐐭𐑌𐐼𐐯𐐼, 𐐰𐑌𐐼 𐐖𐐩𐐿𐐲𐐺 𐐶𐐱𐑆 𐐿𐐮𐑊𐐼. 𐐈𐑌𐐼 𐐢𐐨𐐸𐐴 𐐹𐑉𐐯𐑅𐐻 𐐲𐐹𐐱𐑌 𐑄𐐩𐑉 𐑉𐐨𐑉 𐐶𐐮𐑄 𐑅𐐲𐐽 𐑁𐐷𐐭𐑉𐐨 𐐶𐐮𐑄 𐐸𐐮𐑆 𐑅𐐻𐑉𐐱𐑍 𐑋𐐯𐑌, 𐑄𐐰𐐻 𐑄 𐐢𐐰𐑋𐐲𐑌𐐴𐐻𐑅 𐐮𐑌 𐑄 𐑉𐐨𐑉 𐐼𐐨𐑊𐐮𐑂𐐲𐑉𐐼 𐐲𐐹 𐑄𐐩𐑉 𐐶𐐯𐐹𐐲𐑌𐑆 𐐱𐑂 𐐶𐐫𐑉; 𐐰𐑌𐐼 𐑄 𐑉𐐨𐑋𐐩𐑌𐐼𐐲𐑉 𐐱𐑂 𐑄𐐯𐑋, 𐐺𐐨𐐮𐑍 𐑋𐐲𐐽 𐐿𐐱𐑌𐑁𐐷𐐭𐑆𐐼, 𐑌𐐭 𐑌𐐱𐐻 𐐸𐐶𐐮𐑄𐐲𐑉 𐐻𐐭 𐑀𐐬 𐐫𐑉 𐐻𐐭 𐑅𐐻𐑉𐐴𐐿. 𐐤𐐵 𐐣𐐬𐑉𐐬𐑌𐐴 𐑅𐐨𐐮𐑍 𐑄𐐩𐑉 𐐿𐐱𐑌𐑁𐐷𐐭𐑈𐐲𐑌, 𐐸𐐨 𐑅𐐯𐐼 𐐲𐑌𐐻𐐭 𐑄𐐯𐑋, 𐐆𐑁 𐐷𐐨 𐐶𐐮𐑊 𐐺𐑉𐐮𐑍 𐑁𐐫𐑉𐑃 𐐷𐐳𐑉 𐐶𐐯𐐹𐐲𐑌𐑆 𐐱𐑂 𐐶𐐫𐑉, 𐐰𐑌𐐼 𐐼𐐨𐑊𐐮𐑂𐐲𐑉 𐑄𐐯𐑋 𐐲𐐹, 𐐺𐐨𐐸𐐬𐑊𐐼 𐐶𐐨 𐐶𐐮𐑊 𐑁𐐫𐑉𐐺𐐩𐑉 𐐻𐐭 𐑇𐐯𐐼 𐐷𐐳𐑉 𐐺𐑊𐐲𐐼. 𐐈𐑌𐐼 𐐮𐐻 𐐗𐐩𐑋 𐐻𐐭 𐐹𐐰𐑅 𐑄𐐰𐐻 𐐸𐐶𐐯𐑌 𐑄 𐐢𐐰𐑋𐐲𐑌𐐴𐐻𐑅 𐐸𐐰𐐼 𐐸𐐲𐑉𐐼 𐑄𐐨𐑆 𐐶𐐲𐑉𐐼𐑆, 𐑄𐐩𐑉 𐐽𐐨𐑁 𐐿𐐰𐐹𐐻𐐮𐑌𐑆, 𐐫𐑊 𐑄𐐬𐑆 𐐸𐐭 𐐶𐐲𐑉 𐑌𐐱𐐻 𐑅𐑊𐐩𐑌, 𐐗𐐩𐑋 𐑁𐐫𐑉𐑃 𐐰𐑌𐐼 𐑃𐑉𐐭 𐐼𐐵𐑌 𐑄𐐩𐑉 𐐶𐐯𐐹𐐲𐑌𐑆 𐐱𐑂 𐐶𐐫𐑉 𐐰𐐻 𐑄 𐑁𐐨𐐻 𐐱𐑂 𐐣𐐬𐑉𐐬𐑌𐐴, 𐐰𐑌𐐼 𐐫𐑊𐑅𐐬

𐐿𐐱𐑋𐐰𐑌𐐼𐐲𐐼 𐑄𐐩𐑉 𐑋𐐯𐑌 𐑄𐐰𐐻 𐑄𐐩 𐑇𐐳𐐼 𐐼𐐭 𐑄 𐑅𐐩𐑋; 𐐺𐐲𐐻 𐐺𐐨𐐸𐐬𐑊𐐼, 𐑄𐐩𐑉 𐐶𐐲𐑉 𐑋𐐯𐑌𐐨 𐑄𐐰𐐻 𐐶𐐳𐐼 𐑌𐐱𐐻; 𐐰𐑌𐐼 𐑄𐐬𐑆 𐐸𐐭 𐐶𐐳𐐼 𐑌𐐱𐐻 𐐼𐐯𐑊𐐮𐑂𐐲𐑉 𐐲𐐹 𐑄𐐩𐑉 𐑅𐐫𐑉𐐼𐑆, 𐐶𐐲𐑉 𐐻𐐩𐐿𐑌 𐐰𐑌𐐼 𐐺𐐵𐑌𐐼, 𐐰𐑌𐐼 𐑄𐐩𐑉 𐐶𐐯𐐹𐐲𐑌𐑆 𐐱𐑂 𐐶𐐫𐑉 𐐶𐐲𐑉 𐐻𐐩𐐿𐑌 𐑁𐑉𐐱𐑋 𐑄𐐯𐑋, 𐐰𐑌𐐼 𐑄𐐩 𐐶𐐲𐑉 𐐿𐐱𐑋𐐹𐐯𐑊𐐼 𐐻𐐭 𐑋𐐪𐑉𐐽 𐐶𐐮𐑃 𐑄𐐩𐑉 𐐺𐑉𐐯𐑄𐑉𐐯𐑌 𐑁𐐫𐑉𐑃 𐐮𐑌𐐻𐐭 𐑄 𐑊𐐰𐑌𐐼 𐐒𐐵𐑌𐐻𐐮𐑁𐐳𐑊. 𐐈𐑌𐐼 𐑌𐐵 𐑄 𐑌𐐲𐑋𐐺𐐲𐑉 𐐱𐑂 𐐹𐑉𐐮𐑆𐑌𐐲𐑉𐑆 𐐸𐐭 𐐶𐐲𐑉 𐐻𐐩𐐿𐑌 𐐯𐐿𐑅𐐨𐐼𐐯𐐼 𐑋𐐫𐑉 𐑄𐐰𐑌 𐑄 𐑌𐐲𐑋𐐺𐐲𐑉 𐐱𐑂 𐑄𐐬𐑆 𐐸𐐭 𐐸𐐰𐐼 𐐺𐐮𐑌 𐑅𐑊𐐩𐑌; 𐐷𐐩, 𐑋𐐫𐑉 𐑄𐐰𐑌 𐑄𐐬𐑆 𐐸𐐭 𐐸𐐰𐐼 𐐺𐐮𐑌 𐑅𐑊𐐩𐑌 𐐱𐑌 𐐺𐐬𐑃 𐑅𐐴𐐼𐑆.

15. 𐐈𐑌𐐼 𐐮𐐻 𐐿𐐩𐑋 𐐻𐐭 𐐹𐐰𐑅 𐑄𐐰𐐻 𐑄𐐩 𐐼𐐮𐐼 𐑅𐐯𐐻 𐑀𐐪𐑉𐐼𐑆 𐐬𐑂𐐲𐑉 𐑄 𐐹𐑉𐐮𐑆𐑌𐐲𐑉𐑆 𐐱𐑂 𐑄 𐐢𐐰𐑋𐐲𐑌𐐴𐐻𐑅, 𐐰𐑌𐐼 𐐼𐐮𐐼 𐐿𐐱𐑋𐐹𐐯𐑊 𐑄𐐯𐑋 𐐻𐐭 𐑀𐐬 𐑁𐐫𐑉𐑃 𐐰𐑌𐐼 𐐺𐐯𐑉𐐨 𐑄𐐩𐑉 𐐼𐐯𐐼; 𐐷𐐩, 𐐰𐑌𐐼 𐐫𐑊𐑅𐐬 𐑄 𐐼𐐯𐐼 𐐱𐑂 𐑄 𐐤𐐨𐑁𐐴𐐻𐑅 𐐸𐐭 𐐶𐐲𐑉 𐑅𐑊𐐩𐑌; 𐐰𐑌𐐼 𐐣𐐬𐑉𐐬𐑌𐐴 𐐹𐑊𐐩𐑅𐐻 𐑋𐐯𐑌 𐐬𐑂𐐲𐑉 𐑄𐐯𐑋 𐐻𐐭 𐑀𐐪𐑉𐐼 𐑄𐐯𐑋 𐐸𐐶𐐴𐑊 𐑄𐐩 𐑇𐐳𐐼 𐐹𐐲𐑉𐑁𐐫𐑉𐑋 𐑄𐐩𐑉 𐑊𐐩𐐺𐐲𐑉𐑆. 𐐈𐑌𐐼 𐐣𐐬𐑉𐐬𐑌𐐴 𐐶𐐯𐑌𐐻 𐐻𐐭 𐑄 𐑅𐐮𐐻𐐨 𐐱𐑂 𐐣𐐷𐐭𐑊𐐯𐐿 𐐶𐐮𐑃 𐐢𐐨𐐸𐐴, 𐐰𐑌𐐼 𐐻𐐳𐐿 𐐿𐐱𐑋𐐰𐑌𐐼 𐐱𐑂 𐑄 𐑅𐐮𐐻𐐨, 𐐰𐑌𐐼 𐑀𐐩𐑂 𐐮𐐻 𐐲𐑌𐐻𐐭 𐐢𐐨𐐸𐐴. 𐐤𐐵 𐐺𐐨𐐸𐐬𐑊𐐼, 𐑄𐐮𐑅 𐐢𐐨𐐸𐐴 𐐶𐐱𐑆 𐐲 𐑋𐐰𐑌 𐐸𐐭 𐐸𐐰𐐼 𐐺𐐮𐑌 𐐶𐐮𐑃 𐐣𐐬𐑉𐐬𐑌𐐴 𐐮𐑌 𐑄 𐑋𐐫𐑉 𐐹𐐪𐑉𐐻 𐐱𐑂 𐐫𐑊 𐐸𐐮𐑆 𐐺𐐰𐐻𐑊𐑆; 𐐰𐑌𐐼 𐐸𐐨 𐐶𐐱𐑆 𐐲 𐑋𐐰𐑌 𐑊𐐴𐐿 𐐲𐑌𐐻𐐭 𐐣𐐬𐑉𐐬𐑌𐐴; 𐐰𐑌𐐼 𐑄𐐩 𐑉𐐨𐐾𐑎𐑅𐐻 𐐮𐑌 𐐨𐐽 𐐲𐑄𐐲𐑉𐑆 𐑅𐐩𐑁𐐻𐐨; 𐐷𐐩, 𐑄𐐩 𐐶𐐲𐑉 𐐺𐐨𐑊𐐲𐑂𐐯𐐼 𐐺𐐴 𐐨𐐽 𐐲𐑄𐐲𐑉, 𐐰𐑌𐐼 𐐫𐑊𐑅𐐬 𐐺𐐨𐑊𐐲𐑂𐐯𐐼 𐐺𐐴 𐐫𐑊 𐑄 𐐹𐐨𐐹𐑊 𐐱𐑂 𐐤𐐨𐑁𐐴.

16. 𐐈𐑌𐐼 𐐮𐐻 𐐿𐐩𐑋 𐐻𐐭 𐐹𐐰𐑅 𐑄𐐰𐐻 𐐰𐑁𐐻𐐲𐑉 𐑄 𐐢𐐰𐑋𐐲𐑌𐐴𐐻𐑅 𐐸𐐰𐐼 𐑁𐐮𐑌𐐮𐑇𐐻 𐐺𐐯𐑉𐐨𐐮𐑍 𐑄𐐩𐑉 𐐼𐐯𐐼, 𐐰𐑌𐐼 𐐫𐑊𐑅𐐬 𐑄 𐐼𐐯𐐼 𐐱𐑂 𐑄 𐐤𐐨𐑁𐐴𐐻𐑅, 𐑄𐐩 𐐶𐐲𐑉 𐑋𐐪𐑉𐐽𐐻 𐐺𐐰𐐿 𐐮𐑌𐐻𐐭 𐑄 𐑊𐐰𐑌𐐼 𐐒𐐵𐑌𐐻𐐮𐑁𐐳𐑊; 𐐰𐑌𐐼 𐐓𐐨𐐰𐑌𐐿𐐲𐑋, 𐐺𐐴 𐑄 𐐫𐑉𐐼𐐲𐑉𐑆 𐐱𐑂 𐐣𐐬𐑉𐐬𐑌𐐴, 𐐿𐐫𐑆𐐼 𐑄𐐰𐐻 𐑄𐐩 𐑇𐐳𐐼 𐐿𐐱𐑋𐐯𐑌𐑅 𐑊𐐩𐐺𐐲𐑉𐐮𐑍 𐐮𐑌 𐐼𐐮𐑀𐐮𐑍 𐐲 𐐼𐐮𐐽 𐑉𐐵𐑌𐐼 𐐲𐐺𐐵𐐻 𐑄 𐑊𐐰𐑌𐐼, 𐐫𐑉 𐑄 𐑅𐐮𐐻𐐨 𐐒𐐵𐑌𐐻𐐮𐑁𐐳𐑊; 𐐰𐑌𐐼 𐐸𐐨 𐐿𐐫𐑆𐐼 𐑄𐐰𐐻 𐑄𐐩 𐑇𐐳𐐼 𐐺𐐮𐑊𐐼 𐐲 𐐺𐑉𐐯𐑅𐐻𐐶𐐲𐑉𐐿 𐐱𐑂 𐐻𐐮𐑋𐐺𐐲𐑉𐑆 𐐲𐐹𐐱𐑌 𐑄 𐐮𐑌𐐲𐑉 𐐺𐐰𐑍𐐿 𐐱𐑂 𐑄 𐐼𐐮𐐽; 𐐰𐑌𐐼 𐑄𐐩 𐐿𐐰𐑅𐐻 𐐲𐐹 𐐼𐐲𐑉𐐻 𐐵𐐻 𐐱𐑂 𐑄 𐐼𐐮𐐽 𐐲𐑀𐐯𐑌𐑅𐐻 𐑄 𐐺𐑉𐐯𐑅𐐻𐐶𐐲𐑉𐐿 𐐱𐑂 𐐻𐐮𐑋𐐺𐐲𐑉𐑆; 𐐰𐑌𐐼 𐑄𐐲𐑅 𐑄𐐩 𐐼𐐮𐐼 𐐿𐐫𐑆 𐑄 𐐢𐐰𐑋𐐲𐑌𐐴𐐻𐑅 𐐻𐐭 𐑊𐐩𐐺𐐲𐑉 𐐲𐑌𐐻𐐮𐑊 𐑄𐐩 𐐸𐐰𐐼 𐐯𐑌𐑅𐐲𐑉𐐿𐑊𐐼 𐑄 𐑅𐐮𐐻𐐨 𐐱𐑂 𐐒𐐵𐑌𐐻𐐮𐑁𐐳𐑊 𐑉𐐵𐑌𐐼 𐐲𐐺𐐵𐐻 𐐶𐐮𐑃 𐐲 𐑅𐐻𐑉𐐱𐑍 𐐶𐐫𐑊 𐐱𐑂 𐐻𐐮𐑋𐐺𐐲𐑉𐑆 𐐰𐑌𐐼 𐐲𐑉𐑃, 𐐻𐐭 𐐰𐑌 𐐯𐐿𐑅𐐨𐐼𐐮𐑍 𐐸𐐴𐐻. 𐐈𐑌𐐼 𐑄𐐮𐑅 𐑅𐐮𐐻𐐨 𐐺𐐨𐐿𐐩𐑋 𐐰𐑌 𐐯𐐿𐑅𐐨𐐼𐐮𐑍 𐑅𐐻𐑉𐐱𐑍𐐸𐐬𐑊𐐼 𐐯𐑂𐐲𐑉 𐐰𐑁𐐻𐐲𐑉; 𐐰𐑌𐐼 𐐮𐑌 𐑄𐐮𐑅 𐑅𐐮𐐻𐐨 𐑄𐐩 𐐼𐐮𐐼 𐑀𐐪𐑉𐐼 𐑄 𐐹𐑉𐐮𐑆𐑌𐐲𐑉𐑆 𐐱𐑂 𐑄 𐐢𐐰𐑋𐐲𐑌𐐴𐐻𐑅; 𐐷𐐩, 𐐨𐑂𐑌 𐐶𐐮𐑃𐐮𐑌 𐐲 𐐶𐐫𐑊, 𐐸𐐶𐐮𐐽 𐑄𐐩 𐐸𐐰𐐼 𐐿𐐫𐑆𐐼 𐑄𐐯𐑋 𐐻𐐭 𐐺𐐮𐑊𐐼 𐐶𐐮𐑃 𐑄𐐩𐑉 𐐬𐑌 𐐸𐐰𐑌𐐼𐑆. 𐐤𐐵 𐐣𐐬𐑉𐐬𐑌𐐴 𐐶𐐱𐑆 𐐿𐐱𐑋𐐹𐐯𐑊𐐼 𐐻𐐭 𐐿𐐫𐑆 𐑄 𐐢𐐰𐑋𐐲𐑌𐐴𐐻𐑅 𐐻𐐭 𐑊𐐩𐐺𐐲𐑉, 𐐺𐐨𐐿𐐫𐑆 𐐮𐐻 𐐶𐐱𐑆 𐐨𐑆𐐨 𐐻𐐭 𐑀𐐪𐑉𐐼 𐑄𐐯𐑋 𐐸𐐶𐐴𐑊 𐐰𐐻 𐑄𐐩𐑉 𐑊𐐩𐐺𐐲𐑉; 𐐰𐑌𐐼 𐐸𐐨 𐐼𐐨𐑆𐐴𐑉𐐼 𐐫𐑊 𐐸𐐮𐑆 𐑁𐐫𐑉𐑅𐐯𐑆 𐐸𐐶𐐯𐑌 𐐸𐐨 𐑇𐐳𐐼 𐑋𐐩𐐿 𐐰𐑌 𐐰𐐻𐐰𐐿 𐐲𐐹𐐱𐑌 𐑄 𐐢𐐰𐑋𐐲𐑌𐐴𐐻𐑅.

17. 𐐈𐑌𐐼 𐐮𐐻 𐐿𐐩𐑋 𐐻𐐭 𐐹𐐰𐑅 𐑄𐐰𐐻 𐐣𐐬𐑉𐐬𐑌𐐴 𐐸𐐰𐐼 𐑄𐐲𐑅 𐑀𐐩𐑌𐐼 𐐲 𐑂𐐮𐐿𐐻𐐲𐑉𐐨 𐐬𐑂𐐲𐑉 𐐶𐐲𐑌 𐐱𐑂 𐑄 𐑀𐑉𐐩𐐻𐐯𐑅𐐻 𐐱𐑂 𐑄 𐐪𐑉𐑋𐐨𐑆 𐐱𐑂 𐑄 𐐢𐐰𐑋𐐲𐑌𐐴𐐻𐑅, 𐐰𐑌𐐼 𐐸𐐰𐐼 𐐱𐐺𐐻𐐩𐑌𐐼 𐐹𐐱𐑆𐐯𐑇𐐲𐑌 𐐱𐑂 𐑄 𐑅𐐮𐐻𐐨 𐐱𐑂 𐐣𐐷𐐭𐑊𐐯𐐿, 𐐸𐐶𐐮𐐽 𐐶𐐱𐑆 𐐶𐐲𐑌 𐐱𐑂 𐑄 𐑅𐐻𐑉𐐱𐑍𐑀𐐯𐑅𐐻 𐐸𐐬𐑊𐐼𐑆 𐐱𐑂 𐑄 𐐢𐐰𐑋𐐲𐑌𐐴𐐻𐑅 𐐮𐑌 𐑄 𐑊𐐰𐑌𐐼 𐐱𐑂 𐐤𐐨𐑁𐐴; 𐐰𐑌𐐼 𐑄𐐲𐑅 𐐸𐐨 𐐸𐐰𐐼 𐐫𐑊𐑅𐐬 𐐺𐐮𐑊𐐻 𐐲 𐑅𐐻𐑉𐐱𐑍𐐸𐐬𐑊𐐼 𐐻𐐭 𐑉𐐨𐐻𐐩𐑌 𐐸𐐮𐑆 𐐹𐑉𐐮𐑆𐑌𐐲𐑉𐑆. 𐐈𐑌𐐼 𐐮𐐻 𐐿𐐩𐑋 𐐻𐐭 𐐹𐐰𐑅 𐑄𐐰𐐻 𐐸𐐨 𐐼𐐮𐐼 𐑌𐐬 𐑋𐐫𐑉 𐐰𐐻𐐯𐑋𐐹𐐻 𐐲 𐐺𐐰𐐻𐑊 𐐶𐐮𐑃 𐑄 𐐢𐐰𐑋𐐲𐑌𐐴𐐻𐑅 𐐮𐑌 𐑄𐐰𐐻 𐐷𐐨𐑉, 𐐺𐐲𐐻 𐐸𐐨 𐐼𐐮𐐼 𐐯𐑋𐐹𐑊𐑎 𐐸𐐮𐑆 𐑋𐐯𐑌 𐐮𐑌 𐐹𐑉𐐨𐐹𐐩𐑉𐐮𐑍 𐑁𐐫𐑉 𐐶𐐫𐑉; 𐐷𐐩, 𐐰𐑌𐐼 𐐮𐑌 𐑋𐐩𐐿𐐮𐑍 𐑁𐐫𐑉𐐻𐐮𐑁𐐮𐐿𐐩𐑇𐐲𐑌𐑆 𐐻𐐭 𐑀𐐪𐑉𐐼 𐐲𐑀𐐯𐑌𐑅𐐻 𐑄 𐐢𐐰𐑋𐐲𐑌𐐴𐐻𐑅; 𐐷𐐩, 𐐰𐑌𐐼 𐐫𐑊𐑅𐐬 𐐼𐐯𐑊𐐮𐑂𐐲𐑉𐐮𐑍 𐑄𐐩𐑉 𐐶𐐮𐑋𐐯𐑌 𐐰𐑌𐐼 𐑄𐐩𐑉 𐐽𐐮𐑊𐐼𐑉𐐯𐑌 𐑁𐑉𐐱𐑋 𐑁𐐰𐑋𐐮𐑌 𐐰𐑌𐐼 𐐰𐑁𐑊𐐮𐐿𐑇𐐲𐑌, 𐐰𐑌𐐼 𐐹𐑉𐐬𐑂𐐴𐐼𐐮𐑍 𐑁𐐭𐐼 𐑁𐐫𐑉 𐑄𐐩𐑉 𐐪𐑉𐑋𐐨𐑆.

18. 𐐈𐑌𐐼 𐑌𐐵 𐐮𐐻 𐐿𐐩𐑋 𐐻𐐭 𐐹𐐰𐑅 𐑄𐐰𐐻 𐑄 𐐪𐑉𐑋𐐨𐑆 𐐱𐑂 𐑄 𐐢𐐰𐑋𐐲𐑌𐐴𐐻𐑅, 𐐱𐑌 𐑄 𐐎𐐯𐑅𐐻 𐑅𐐨, 𐑅𐐵𐑃, 𐐸𐐶𐐴𐑊 𐐮𐑌 𐑄 𐐰𐐺𐑅𐐯𐑌𐑅 𐐱𐑂 𐐣𐐬𐑉𐐬𐑌𐐴, 𐐱𐑌 𐐲𐐿𐐵𐑌𐐻 𐐱𐑂 𐑅𐐲𐑋 𐐮𐑌𐐻𐑉𐐨𐑀 𐐲𐑋𐐲𐑍𐑅𐐻 𐑄 𐐤𐐨𐑁𐐴𐐻𐑅, 𐐸𐐶𐐮𐐽 𐐿𐐫𐑆𐐼 𐐼𐐮𐑅𐐯𐑌𐑇𐐲𐑌𐑆 𐐲𐑋𐐲𐑍𐑅𐐻 𐑄𐐯𐑋, 𐐸𐐰𐐼 𐑀𐐩𐑌𐐼 𐑅𐐲𐑋 𐑀𐑉𐐵𐑌𐐼 𐐬𐑂𐐲𐑉 𐑄 𐐤𐐨𐑁𐐴𐐻𐑅, 𐐷𐐩, 𐐮𐑌𐑅𐐬𐑋𐐲𐐽 𐑄𐐰𐐻 𐑄𐐩 𐐸𐐰𐐼 𐐱𐐺𐐻𐐩𐑌𐐼 𐐹𐐱𐑆𐐯𐑇𐐲𐑌 𐐱𐑂 𐐲 𐑌𐐲𐑋𐐺𐐲𐑉 𐐱𐑂 𐑄𐐩𐑉 𐑅𐐮𐐻𐐨𐑆 𐐮𐑌 𐑄𐐰𐐻 𐐹𐐪𐑉𐐻 𐐱𐑂 𐑄 𐑊𐐰𐑌𐐼; 𐐰𐑌𐐼 𐑄𐐲𐑅 𐐺𐐨𐐿𐐫𐑆 𐐱𐑂 𐐮𐑌𐐮𐐿𐐶𐐮𐐻𐐨 𐐲𐑋𐐲𐑍𐑅𐐻 𐑄𐐯𐑋𐑅𐐯𐑊𐑂𐑆, 𐐷𐐩, 𐐺𐐨𐐿𐐫𐑆 𐐱𐑂 𐐼𐐮𐑅𐐯𐑌𐑇𐐲𐑌𐑆 𐐰𐑌𐐼 𐐮𐑌𐐻𐑉𐐨𐑀 𐐲𐑋𐐲𐑍 𐑄𐐯𐑋𐑅𐐯𐑊𐑂𐑆, 𐑄𐐩 𐐶𐐲𐑉 𐐹𐑊𐐩𐑅𐐻 𐐮𐑌 𐑄 𐑋𐐬𐑅𐐻 𐐼𐐩𐑌𐐾𐐲𐑉𐐲𐑅 𐑅𐐲𐑉𐐿𐐲𐑋𐑅𐐻𐐰𐑌𐑅𐐯𐑆.

19. 𐐈𐑌𐐼 𐑌𐐵 𐐺𐐨𐐸𐐬𐑊𐐼, 𐐴 𐐸𐐰𐑂 𐑅𐐲𐑋𐐸𐐶𐐱𐐻 𐐻𐐭 𐑅𐐩 𐐿𐐱𐑌𐑅𐐲𐑉𐑌𐐮𐑍 𐑄 𐐹𐐨𐐹𐑊 𐐱𐑂 𐐈𐑋𐐲𐑌, 𐐸𐐭, 𐐮𐑌 𐑄 𐐺𐐨𐑀𐐮𐑌𐐮𐑍, 𐐶𐐲𐑉 𐐢𐐩𐑋𐐲𐑌𐐴𐐻𐑅; 𐐺𐐲𐐻 𐐺𐐴 𐐈𐑋𐐲𐑌 𐐰𐑌𐐼 𐐸𐐮𐑆 𐐺𐑉𐐯𐑄𐑉𐐯𐑌, 𐐫𐑉 𐑉𐐰𐑄𐐲𐑉 𐐺𐐴 𐑄 𐐹𐐵𐐲𐑉 𐐰𐑌𐐼 𐐶𐐲𐑉𐐼 𐐱𐑂 𐐘𐐱𐐼, 𐑄𐐩 𐐸𐐰𐐼 𐐺𐐮𐑌 𐐿𐐱𐑌𐑂𐐲𐑉𐐻𐐯𐐼 𐐲𐑌𐐻𐐭 𐑄 𐐢𐐫𐑉𐐼: 𐐰𐑌𐐼 𐑄𐐩 𐐸𐐰𐐼 𐐺𐐮𐑌 𐐺𐑉𐐫𐐻 𐐼𐐵𐑌 𐐮𐑌𐐻𐐭 𐑄 𐑊𐐰𐑌𐐼 𐐱𐑂 𐐞𐐯𐑉𐐲𐐸𐐯𐑋𐑊𐐲, 𐐰𐑌𐐼 𐐸𐐰𐐼 𐐯𐑂𐐲𐑉 𐑅𐐮𐑌𐑅 𐐺𐐮𐑌 𐐹𐑉𐐬𐐻𐐯𐐿𐐻𐐯𐐼 𐐺𐐴 𐑄 𐐤𐐨𐑁𐐴𐐻𐑅; 𐐰𐑌𐐼 𐐺𐐨𐐿𐐱𐑆 𐐱𐑂 𐑄𐐩𐑉 𐐬𐑃, 𐑄𐐩 𐐸𐐰𐐼 𐐺𐐮𐑌 𐐿𐐯𐐹𐐻 𐑁𐑉𐐱𐑋 𐐻𐐩𐐿𐐮𐑍 𐐲𐐹 𐐪𐑉𐑋𐑆 𐐰𐑀𐐯𐑌𐑅𐐻 𐑄𐐩𐑉 𐐺𐑉𐐯𐑄𐑉𐐯𐑌; 𐑁𐐫𐑉 𐑄𐐩 𐐸𐐰𐐼 𐐻𐐩𐐿𐐲𐑌 𐐰𐑌 𐐬𐑃, 𐑄𐐰𐐻 𐑄𐐩 𐑌𐐯𐑂𐐲𐑉 𐐶𐐳𐐼 𐑇𐐯𐐼 𐐺𐑊𐐲𐐼 𐑋𐐬𐑉: 𐐰𐑌𐐼 𐐰𐐿𐐫𐑉𐐼𐐮𐑍 𐐻𐐭 𐑄𐐩𐑉 𐐬𐑃 𐑄𐐩 𐐶𐐳𐐼 𐐸𐐰𐑂 𐐹𐐯𐑉𐐮𐑇𐐻; 𐐷𐐩, 𐑄𐐩 𐐶𐐳𐐼 𐐸𐐰𐑂 𐑅𐐲𐑁𐐲𐑉𐐼 𐑄𐐯𐑋𐑅𐐯𐑊𐑂𐑆 𐐻𐐭 𐐸𐐰𐑂 𐑁𐐫𐑊𐑌 𐐮𐑌𐐻𐐭 𐑄 𐐸𐐰𐑌𐐼𐑆 𐐱𐑂 𐑄𐐩𐑉 𐐺𐑉𐐯𐑄𐑉𐐯𐑌, 𐐸𐐰𐐼 𐐮𐐻 𐑌𐐱𐐻 𐐺𐐮𐑌 𐑁𐐫𐑉 𐑄 𐐹𐐮𐐻𐐨 𐐰𐑌𐐼 𐑄 𐐯𐐿𐑅𐐨𐐼𐐮𐑍 𐑊𐐲𐑂 𐐸𐐶𐐮𐐽 𐐈𐑋𐐲𐑌 𐐰𐑌𐐼 𐐸𐐮𐑆 𐐺𐑉𐐯𐑄𐑉𐐯𐑌 𐐸𐐰𐐼 𐐸𐐰𐐼 𐑁𐐫𐑉 𐑄𐐯𐑋; 𐐰𐑌𐐼 𐑁𐐫𐑉 𐑄𐐮𐑅 𐐿𐐫𐑆, 𐑄𐐩 𐐶𐐲𐑉 𐐺𐑉𐐫𐐻 𐐼𐐵𐑌 𐐮𐑌𐐻𐐭 𐑄 𐑊𐐰𐑌𐐼 𐐱𐑂 𐐞𐐯𐑉𐐲𐐸𐐯𐑋𐑊𐐲; 𐐰𐑌𐐼 𐑄𐐩 𐐯𐑂𐐲𐑉 𐐸𐐰𐐼 𐐺𐐮𐑌 𐐹𐑉𐐬𐐻𐐯𐐿𐐻𐐯𐐼 𐐺𐐴 𐑄 𐐤𐐨𐑁𐐴𐐻𐑅.

20. 𐐒𐐲𐐻 𐐮𐐻 𐐿𐐩𐑋 𐐻𐐭 𐐹𐐪𐑅 𐑄𐐰𐐻 𐐸𐐶𐐯𐑌 𐑄𐐩 𐑅𐐫 𐑄 𐐼𐐩𐑌𐐾𐐲𐑉, 𐐰𐑌𐐼 𐑄 𐑋𐐯𐑌𐐨 𐐰𐑁𐑊𐐮𐐿𐑇𐐲𐑌𐑆 𐐰𐑌𐐼 𐐻𐑉𐐮𐐺𐐷𐐭𐑊𐐩𐑇𐐲𐑌𐑆 𐐸𐐶𐐮𐐽 𐑄 𐐤𐐨𐑁𐐴𐐻𐑅 𐐺𐐫𐑉 𐑁𐐫𐑉 𐑄𐐯𐑋, 𐑄𐐩 𐐶𐐲𐑉 𐑋𐐭𐑂𐐼 𐐶𐐮𐑃 𐐿𐐲𐑋𐐹𐐰𐑇𐐲𐑌, 𐐰𐑌𐐼 𐐶𐐲𐑉 𐐼𐐯𐑆𐐴𐑉𐐲𐑅 𐐻𐐭 𐐻𐐩𐐿 𐐲𐐹 𐐪𐑉𐑋𐑆 𐐮𐑌 𐑄 𐐼𐐯𐑁𐐯𐑌𐑅 𐐱𐑂 𐑄𐐩𐑉 𐐿𐐲𐑌𐐻𐑉𐐨. 𐐒𐐲𐐻 𐐺𐐨𐐸𐐬𐑊𐐼, 𐐰𐑆 𐑄𐐩 𐐶𐐲𐑉 𐐲𐐺𐐵𐐻 𐐻𐐭 𐐻𐐩𐐿 𐑄𐐩𐑉 𐐶𐐯𐐹𐐲𐑌𐑆 𐐱𐑂 𐐶𐐫𐑉, 𐑄𐐩 𐐶𐐲𐑉 𐐬𐑂𐐲𐑉𐐹𐐵𐐲𐑉𐐼 𐐺𐐴 𐑄 𐐹𐐲𐑉𐑅𐐶𐐩𐑈𐐲𐑌𐑆 𐐱𐑂 𐐐𐐨𐑊𐐲𐑋𐐲𐑌 𐐰𐑌𐐼 𐐸𐐮𐑆 𐐺𐑉𐐯𐑄𐑉𐐯𐑌, 𐑁𐐫𐑉 𐑄𐐩 𐐶𐐲𐑉 𐐲𐐺𐐵𐐻 𐐻𐐭 𐐺𐑉𐐩𐐿 𐑄 𐐬𐑃 𐐸𐐶𐐮𐐽 𐑄𐐩 𐐸𐐰𐐼 𐑋𐐩𐐼; 𐐰𐑌𐐼 𐐐𐐨𐑊𐐲𐑋𐐲𐑌 𐑁𐐨𐑉𐐼 𐑊𐐯𐑅𐐻 𐐺𐐴 𐑅𐐬 𐐼𐐭𐐮𐑍, 𐑄𐐩 𐑇𐐳𐐼 𐑊𐐭𐑆 𐑄𐐩𐑉 𐑅𐐬𐑊𐑆; 𐑄𐐯𐑉𐑁𐐫𐑉 𐐫𐑊 𐑄𐐬𐑆 𐐸𐐭 𐐸𐐰𐐼 𐐯𐑌𐐻𐐲𐑉𐐼 𐐮𐑌𐐻𐐭 𐑄𐐮𐑅 𐐿𐐲𐑂𐐲𐑌𐐲𐑌𐐻, 𐐶𐐲𐑉 𐐿𐐲𐑋𐐹𐐯𐑊𐐼 𐐻𐐭 𐐺𐐨𐐸𐐬𐑊𐐼 𐑄𐐩𐑉 𐐺𐑉𐐯𐑄𐑉𐐯𐑌 𐐶𐐩𐐼 𐑃𐑉𐐭 𐑄𐐩𐑉 𐐰𐑁𐑊𐐮𐐿𐑇𐐲𐑌𐑆, 𐐮𐑌 𐑄𐐩𐑉 𐐼𐐩𐑌𐐾𐐲𐑉𐐲𐑅 𐑅𐐲𐑉𐐿𐐲𐑋𐑅𐐻𐐰𐑌𐑅𐐯𐑆, 𐐰𐐻 𐑄𐐮𐑅 𐐻𐐴𐑋. 𐐒𐐲𐐻 𐐺𐐨𐐸𐐬𐑊𐐼, 𐐮𐐻 𐐿𐐩𐑋 𐐻𐐭 𐐹𐐪𐑅 𐑄𐐩 𐐸𐐰𐐼 𐑋𐐯𐑌𐐨 𐑅𐐲𐑌𐑆, 𐐸𐐭 𐐸𐐰𐐼 𐑌𐐱𐐻 𐐯𐑌𐐻𐐲𐑉𐐼 𐐮𐑌𐐻𐐭 𐐩 𐐿𐐲𐑂𐐲𐑌𐐲𐑌𐐻 𐑄𐐰𐐻 𐑄𐐩 𐐶𐐳𐐼 𐑌𐐱𐐻 𐐻𐐩𐐿 𐑄𐐩𐑉 𐐶𐐯𐐹𐐲𐑌𐑆 𐐱𐑂 𐐶𐐫𐑉 𐐻𐐭 𐐼𐐯𐑁𐐯𐑌𐐼 𐑄𐐯𐑋𐑅𐐯𐑊𐑂𐑆 𐐰𐑀𐐯𐑌𐑅𐐻 𐑄𐐩𐑉 𐐯𐑌𐐲𐑋𐐨𐑆; 𐑄𐐯𐑉𐑁𐐫𐑉 𐑄𐐩 𐐼𐐮𐐼 𐐰𐑅𐐯𐑋𐐺𐑊 𐑄𐐯𐑋𐑅𐐯𐑊𐑂𐑆 𐐻𐐲𐑀𐐯𐑄𐐲𐑉 𐐰𐐻 𐑄𐐮𐑅 𐐻𐐴𐑋, 𐐰𐑆 𐑋𐐯𐑌𐐨 𐐰𐑆 𐐶𐐲𐑉 𐐩𐐺𐑊 𐐻𐐭 𐐻𐐩𐐿 𐐲𐐹 𐐪𐑉𐑋𐑆; 𐐰𐑌𐐼 𐑄𐐩 𐐿𐐫𐑊𐐼 𐑄𐐯𐑋𐑅𐐯𐑊𐑂𐑆 𐐤𐐨𐑁𐐴𐐻𐑅; 𐐰𐑌𐐼 𐑄𐐩 𐐯𐑌𐐻𐐲𐑉𐐼 𐐮𐑌𐐻𐐭 𐐩 𐐿𐐲𐑂𐐲𐑌𐐲𐑌𐐻 𐐻𐐭 𐑁𐐴𐐻 𐑁𐐫𐑉 𐑄 𐑊𐐮𐐺𐐲𐑉𐐻𐐨 𐐱𐑂 𐑄 𐐤𐐨𐑁𐐴𐐻𐑅; 𐐷𐐩, 𐐻𐐭 𐐹𐑉𐐬𐐻𐐯𐐿𐐻 𐑄 𐑊𐐰𐑌𐐼 𐐲𐑌𐐻𐐭 𐑄 𐑊𐐩𐐮𐑍 𐐼𐐵𐑌 𐐱𐑂 𐑄𐐩𐑉 𐑊𐐴𐑂𐑆; 𐐷𐐩, 𐐨𐑂𐐲𐑌 𐑄𐐩 𐐿𐐲𐑂𐐲𐑌𐐲𐑌𐐻𐐯𐐼 𐑄𐐰𐐻 𐑄𐐩 𐑌𐐯𐑂𐐲𐑉 𐐶𐐳𐐼 𐑀𐐮𐑂 𐐲𐐹 𐑄𐐩𐑉 𐑊𐐮𐐺𐐲𐑉𐐻𐐨, 𐐺𐐲𐐻 𐑄𐐩 𐐶𐐳𐐼 𐑁𐐴𐐻 𐐮𐑌 𐐫𐑊 𐐿𐐩𐑅𐐯𐑆 𐐻𐐭 𐐹𐑉𐐬𐐻𐐯𐐿𐐻 𐑄 𐐤𐐨𐑁𐐴𐐻𐑅 𐐰𐑌𐐼 𐑄𐐯𐑋𐑅𐐯𐑊𐑂𐑆 𐑁𐑉𐐱𐑋 𐐺𐐱𐑌𐐼𐐮𐐾.

21. 𐐤𐐵 𐐺𐐨𐐸𐐬𐑊𐐼, 𐑄𐐯𐑉 𐐶𐐲𐑉 𐐻𐐭 𐑃𐐵𐑆𐐲𐑌𐐼 𐐱𐑂 𐑄𐐬𐑆 𐐷𐐲𐑍 𐑋𐐯𐑌, 𐐸𐐭 𐐯𐑌𐐻𐐲𐑉𐐼 𐐮𐑌𐐻𐐭 𐑄𐐮𐑅 𐐿𐐲𐑂𐐲𐑌𐐲𐑌𐐻, 𐐰𐑌𐐼 𐐻𐐩𐐿 𐑄𐐩𐑉 𐐶𐐯𐐹𐐲𐑌𐑆 𐐱𐑂 𐐶𐐫𐑉 𐐻𐐭 𐐼𐐯𐑁𐐯𐑌𐐼 𐑄𐐩𐑉 𐐿𐐲𐑌𐐻𐑉𐐨. 𐐈𐑌𐐼 𐑌𐐵 𐐺𐐨𐐸𐐬𐑊𐐼, 𐐰𐑆 𐑄𐐩 𐑌𐐯𐑂𐐲𐑉 𐐸𐐰𐐼 𐐸𐐮𐑄𐐲𐑉𐐻𐐭 𐐺𐐮𐑌 𐐩 𐐼𐐮𐑅𐐰𐐼𐑂𐐰𐑌𐐻𐐩𐐾 𐐻𐐭 𐑄 𐐤𐐨𐑁𐐴𐐻𐑅, 𐑄𐐩 𐐺𐐨𐐿𐐩𐑋 𐑌𐐵 𐐰𐐻 𐑄𐐮𐑅 𐐹𐐨𐑉𐐨𐐲𐐼 𐐱𐑂 𐐻𐐴𐑋 𐐫𐑊𐑅𐐬 𐐩 𐑀𐑉𐐩𐐻 𐑅𐐲𐐹𐐬𐑉𐐻; 𐑁𐐫𐑉 𐑄𐐩 𐐻𐐩𐐿 𐑄𐐩𐑉 𐐶𐐯𐐹𐐲𐑌𐑆 𐐱𐑂 𐐶𐐫𐑉, 𐐰𐑌𐐼 𐑄𐐩 𐐶𐐳𐐼 𐑄𐐰𐐻 𐐐𐐨𐑊𐐲𐑋𐐲𐑌 𐑇𐐳𐐼 𐐺𐐨 𐑄𐐩𐑉 𐑊𐐨𐐼𐐲𐑉. 𐐈𐑌𐐼 𐑄𐐩 𐐶𐐲𐑉 𐐫𐑊 𐐷𐐲𐑍 𐑋𐐯𐑌, 𐐰𐑌𐐼 𐑄𐐩 𐐶𐐲𐑉 𐐯𐐿𐑅𐐨𐐼𐐮𐑍𐑊𐐨 𐑂𐐰𐑊𐐷𐐲𐑌𐐻 𐑁𐐫𐑉 𐐿𐐲𐑉𐐩𐐾, 𐐰𐑌𐐼 𐐫𐑊𐑅𐐬 𐑁𐐫𐑉 𐑅𐐻𐑉𐐯𐑍𐑃 𐐰𐑌𐐼 𐐰𐐿𐐻𐐮𐑂𐐮𐐻𐐨; 𐐺𐐲𐐻 𐐺𐐨𐐸𐐬𐑊𐐼, 𐑄𐐮𐑅 𐐶𐐱𐑆 𐑌𐐱𐐻 𐐫𐑊: 𐑄𐐩 𐐶𐐲𐑉 𐑋𐐯𐑌 𐐸𐐭 𐐶𐐲𐑉 𐐻𐑉𐐭 𐐰𐐻 𐐫𐑊 𐐻𐐴𐑋𐑆 𐐮𐑌 𐐸𐐶𐐲𐐻𐑅𐐬𐐯𐑂𐐲𐑉 𐑃𐐮𐑍 𐑄𐐩 𐐶𐐲𐑉 𐐯𐑌𐐻𐑉𐐲𐑅𐐻𐐯𐐼; 𐐷𐐩, 𐑄𐐩 𐐶𐐲𐑉 𐑋𐐯𐑌 𐐱𐑂 𐐻𐑉𐐭𐑃 𐐰𐑌𐐼 𐑅𐐬𐐺𐐲𐑉𐑌𐐯𐑅, 𐑁𐐫𐑉 𐑄𐐩 𐐸𐐰𐐼 𐐺𐐮𐑌 𐐻𐐫𐐻 𐐻𐐭 𐐿𐐨𐐹 𐑄 𐐿𐐲𐑋𐐰𐑌𐐼𐑋𐐲𐑌𐐻𐑅 𐐱𐑂 𐐘𐐱𐐼, 𐐰𐑌𐐼 𐐻𐐭 𐐶𐐫𐐿 𐐲𐐹𐑉𐐴𐐻𐑊𐐨 𐐺𐐨𐑁𐐫𐑉 𐐸𐐮𐑋.

22. 𐐈𐑌𐐼 𐑌𐐵 𐐮𐐻 𐐿𐐩𐑋 𐐻𐐭 𐐹𐐪𐑅 𐑄𐐰𐐻 𐐐𐐨𐑊𐐲𐑋𐐲𐑌 𐐼𐐮𐐼 𐑋𐐪𐑉𐐽 𐐰𐐻 𐑄 𐐸𐐯𐐼 𐐱𐑂 𐐸𐐮𐑆 𐐻𐐭 𐑃𐐵𐑆𐐲𐑌𐐼 𐑅𐐻𐑉𐐮𐐹𐑊𐐮𐑍 𐑅𐐬𐑊𐐾𐐲𐑉𐑆, 𐐻𐐭 𐑄 𐑅𐐲𐐹𐐬𐑉𐐻 𐐱𐑂 𐑄 𐐹𐐨𐐹𐑊 𐐮𐑌 𐑄 𐐺𐐫𐑉𐐼𐐲𐑉𐑆 𐐱𐑂 𐑄 𐑊𐐰𐑌𐐼 𐐱𐑌 𐑄 𐑅𐐵𐑃 𐐺𐐴 𐑄 𐐎𐐯𐑅𐐻 𐑅𐐨. 𐐈𐑌𐐼 𐑄𐐲𐑅 𐐯𐑌𐐼𐐯𐐼 𐑄 𐐻𐐶𐐯𐑌𐐻𐐨 𐐰𐑌𐐼 𐐩𐐻𐑃 𐐷𐐨𐑉 𐐱𐑂 𐑄 𐑉𐐩𐑌 𐐱𐑂 𐑄 𐐖𐐲𐐾𐐯𐑆 𐐬𐐲𐑂𐐲𐑉 𐑄 𐐹𐐨𐐹𐑊 𐐱𐑂 𐐤𐐨𐑁𐐴, 𐐯𐐻𐑅.

𐐗𐐰𐐹𐐻𐐲𐑉 XXV.

1. 𐐈𐑌𐐼 𐑌𐐵 𐐮𐐻 𐐿𐐩𐑋 𐐻𐐭 𐐹𐐰𐑅 𐐮𐑌 𐑄 𐐻𐐶𐐯𐑌𐐻𐐮 𐐰𐑌𐐼 𐑌𐐴𐑌𐑃 𐐷𐐨𐑉 𐐱𐑂 𐑄 𐐾𐐲𐐾𐐯𐑆, 𐑄𐐰𐐻 𐐈𐑋𐐬𐑉𐐲𐑌
𐑅𐐯𐑌𐐻 𐐲𐑌𐐻𐐭 𐐣𐐬𐑉𐐬𐑌𐐴, 𐐼𐐯𐑆𐐴𐑉𐐮𐑍 𐑄𐐰𐐻 𐐸𐐨 𐐶𐐳𐐼 𐐯𐐿𐑅𐐽𐐩𐑌𐐾 𐐹𐑉𐐮𐑆𐐲𐑌𐐲𐑉𐑆. 𐐈𐑌𐐼 𐐮𐐻 𐐿𐐩𐑋 𐐻𐐭 𐐹𐐰𐑅
𐑄𐐰𐐻 𐐣𐐬𐑉𐐬𐑌𐐴 𐑁𐐯𐑊𐐻 𐐻𐐭 𐑉𐐯𐐾𐐫𐐮𐑅 𐐯𐐿𐑅𐐨𐐼𐐮𐑍𐑊𐐮 𐐰𐐻 𐑄𐐮𐑅 𐑉𐐯𐐿𐐶𐐯𐑅𐐻, 𐑁𐐬𐑉 𐐸𐐨 𐐼𐐯𐑆𐐴𐑉𐐼 𐑄 𐐹𐑉𐐬-𐑂𐐮𐑈𐐲𐑌𐑆 𐐸𐐶𐐮𐐽 𐐶𐐲𐑉 𐐮𐑋𐐹𐐪𐑉𐐻𐐯𐐼 𐑁𐐬𐑉 𐑄 𐑅𐐲𐐹𐐬𐑉𐐻 𐐱𐑂 𐑄 𐐢𐐰𐑋𐐲𐑌𐐴𐐻 𐐹𐑉𐐮𐑆𐐲𐑌𐐲𐑉𐑆 𐑁𐐬𐑉 𐑄 𐑅𐐲𐐹𐐬𐑉𐐻 𐐱𐑂
𐐸𐐮𐑆 𐐬𐑌 𐐹𐐨𐐹𐑊; 𐐰𐑌𐐼 𐐸𐐨 𐐫𐑊𐑅𐐬 𐐼𐐯𐑆𐐴𐑉𐐼 𐐸𐐮𐑆 𐐬𐑌 𐐹𐐨𐐹𐑊 𐑁𐐬𐑉 𐑄 𐑅𐐻𐑉𐐯𐑍𐑃𐐲𐑌𐐮𐑍 𐐱𐑂 𐐸𐐮𐑆 𐐪𐑉𐑋𐐮.
𐐤𐐵 𐑄 𐐢𐐰𐑋𐐲𐑌𐐴𐐻𐑅 𐐸𐐰𐐼 𐐻𐐩𐐿𐐲𐑌 𐑋𐐯𐑌𐐮 𐐶𐐮𐑋𐐯𐑌 𐐰𐑌𐐼 𐐽𐐮𐑊𐐼𐑉𐐯𐑌, 𐐰𐑌𐐼 𐑄𐐯𐑉 𐐶𐐱𐑆 𐑌𐐱𐐻 𐐵 𐐶𐐳𐑋𐐲𐑌 𐑌𐐬𐑉 𐐵
𐐽𐐴𐑊𐐼 𐐲𐑋𐐲𐑍 𐐫𐑊 𐑄 𐐹𐑉𐐮𐑆𐐲𐑌𐐲𐑉𐑆 𐐱𐑂 𐐣𐐬𐑉𐐬𐑌𐐴, 𐐬𐑉 𐑄 𐐹𐑉𐐮𐑆𐐲𐑌𐐲𐑉𐑆 𐐸𐐭𐑋 𐐣𐐬𐑉𐐬𐑌𐐴 𐐸𐐰𐐼 𐐻𐐩𐐿𐐲𐑌; 𐑄𐐯𐑉-𐑁𐐬𐑉 𐐣𐐬𐑉𐐬𐑌𐐴 𐑉𐐯𐑆𐐱𐑊𐑂𐐼 𐐲𐐹𐐱𐑌 𐐵 𐑅𐐻𐑉𐐰𐐻𐐲𐐾𐐯𐑋 𐐻𐐭 𐐱𐐺𐐻𐐩𐑌 𐐰𐑆 𐑋𐐯𐑌𐐮 𐐹𐑉𐐮𐑆𐐲𐑌𐐲𐑉𐑆 𐐱𐑂 𐑄 𐐤𐐨𐑁𐐴𐐻𐑅
𐑁𐑉𐐱𐑋 𐑄 𐐢𐐰𐑋𐐲𐑌𐐴𐐻𐑅 𐐰𐑆 𐐮𐐻 𐐶𐐲𐑉 𐐹𐐱𐑅𐐮𐐺𐑊; 𐑄𐐯𐑉𐑁𐐬𐑉 𐐸𐐨 𐑉𐐬𐐻 𐐰𐑌 𐐯𐐹𐐮𐑅𐑊 𐐰𐑌𐐼 𐑅𐐯𐑌𐐻 𐐮𐐻 𐐺𐐴 𐑄
𐑅𐐲𐑉𐑂𐐰𐑌𐐻 𐐱𐑂 𐐈𐑋𐐬𐑉𐐲𐑌, 𐑄 𐑅𐐩𐑋 𐐸𐐭 𐐸𐐰𐐼 𐐺𐑉𐐫𐐻 𐐰𐑌 𐐯𐐹𐐮𐑅𐑊 𐐻𐐭 𐐣𐐬𐑉𐐬𐑌𐐴. 𐐤𐐵 𐑄𐐨𐑆 𐐪𐑉 𐑄
𐐶𐐲𐑉𐐼𐑆 𐐸𐐶𐐮𐐽 𐐸𐐨 𐑉𐐬𐐻 𐐲𐑌𐐻𐐭 𐐈𐑋𐐬𐑉𐐲𐑌, 𐑅𐐩𐐮𐑍, 𐐒𐐨𐐸𐐬𐑊𐐼, 𐐈𐑋𐐬𐑉𐐲𐑌, 𐐌 𐐸𐐰𐑂 𐑉𐐮𐐻𐑌 𐐲𐑌𐐻𐐭 𐐷𐐭
𐑅𐐲𐑋𐐸𐐶𐐱𐐻 𐐿𐐱𐑌𐑅𐐲𐑉𐑌𐐮𐑍 𐑄𐐮𐑅 𐐶𐐫𐑉 𐐸𐐶𐐮𐐽 𐐷𐐨 𐐸𐐰𐑂 𐐶𐐩𐐾𐐼 𐐲𐑀𐐯𐑌𐑅𐐻 𐑋𐐴 𐐹𐐨𐐹𐑊, 𐐬𐑉 𐑉𐐰𐑄𐐲𐑉 𐐸𐐶𐐮𐐽
𐑄𐐴 𐐺𐑉𐐲𐑄𐐲𐑉 𐐸𐐰𐑃 𐐶𐐩𐐾𐐼 𐐲𐑀𐐯𐑌𐑅𐐻 𐑄𐐯𐑋, 𐐰𐑌𐐼 𐐸𐐶𐐮𐐽 𐐷𐐨 𐐪𐑉 𐑅𐐻𐐮𐑊 𐐼𐐯𐐻𐐲𐑉𐑋𐐮𐑌𐐼 𐐻𐐭 𐐿𐐰𐑉𐐮 𐐱𐑌 𐐰𐑁𐐻𐐲𐑉
𐐸𐐮𐑆 𐐼𐐯𐑃. 𐐒𐐨𐐸𐐬𐑊𐐼, 𐐌 𐐶𐐳𐐼 𐐻𐐯𐑊 𐐷𐐭 𐑅𐐲𐑋𐐸𐐶𐐱𐐻 𐐿𐐱𐑌𐑅𐐲𐑉𐑌𐐮𐑍 𐑄 𐐾𐐲𐑅𐐻𐐮𐑅 𐐱𐑂 𐐘𐐱𐐼, 𐐰𐑌𐐼 𐑄
𐑅𐐬𐑉𐐼 𐐱𐑂 𐐸𐐮𐑆 𐐫𐑊𐑋𐐴𐐻𐐮 𐑉𐐰𐑃, 𐐸𐐶𐐮𐐽 𐐼𐐲𐑃 𐐸𐐰𐑍 𐐬𐑂𐐲𐑉 𐐷𐐭, 𐐯𐐿𐑅𐐯𐐹𐐻 𐐷𐐨 𐑉𐐯𐐹𐐯𐑌𐐻 𐐰𐑌𐐼 𐐶𐐮𐑄𐐼𐑉𐐫
𐐷𐐬𐑉 𐐪𐑉𐑋𐐮𐑆 𐐮𐑌𐐻𐐭 𐐷𐐬𐑉 𐐬𐑌 𐑊𐐰𐑌𐐼𐑆, 𐐬𐑉 𐑄 𐑊𐐰𐑌𐐼 𐐱𐑂 𐐷𐐬𐑉 𐐹𐐲𐑆𐐯𐑇𐐲𐑌𐑆, 𐐸𐐶𐐮𐐽 𐐮𐑆 𐑄 𐑊𐐰𐑌𐐼 𐐱𐑂
𐐤𐐨𐑁𐐴; 𐐷𐐩, 𐐌 𐐶𐐳𐐼 𐐻𐐯𐑊 𐐷𐐭 𐑄𐐨𐑆 𐑃𐐮𐑍𐑆, 𐐮𐑁 𐐷𐐨 𐐶𐐲𐑉 𐐿𐐩𐐹𐐲𐐺𐑊 𐐱𐑂 𐐸𐐪𐑉𐐿𐐲𐑌𐐮𐑍 𐐲𐑌𐐻𐐭 𐑄𐐯𐑋; 𐐷𐐩, 𐐌
𐐶𐐳𐐼 𐐻𐐯𐑊 𐐷𐐭 𐐿𐐱𐑌𐑅𐐲𐑉𐑌𐐮𐑍 𐑄𐐰𐐻 𐐫𐑁𐐳𐑊 𐐸𐐯𐑊 𐑄𐐰𐐻 𐐲𐐶𐐩𐐻𐑅 𐐻𐐭 𐑉𐐯𐑅𐐨𐑂 𐑅𐐲𐐽 𐑋𐐲𐑉𐐼𐐲𐑉𐐲𐑉𐑆 𐐰𐑆 𐑄𐐵
𐐰𐑌𐐼 𐑄𐐴 𐐺𐑉𐐲𐑄𐐲𐑉 𐐸𐐰𐑂 𐐺𐐮𐑌, 𐐯𐐿𐑅𐐯𐐹𐐻 𐐷𐐨 𐑉𐐯𐐹𐐯𐑌𐐻 𐐰𐑌𐐼 𐐶𐐮𐑄𐐼𐑉𐐫 𐐷𐐬𐑉 𐑋𐐲𐑉𐐼𐐲𐑉𐐲𐑅 𐐹𐐲𐑉𐐹𐐲𐑅𐐯𐑆,
𐐰𐑌𐐼 𐑉𐐯𐐻𐐲𐑉𐑌 𐐶𐐮𐑄 𐐷𐐬𐑉 𐐪𐑉𐑋𐐮𐑆 𐐻𐐭 𐐷𐐬𐑉 𐐬𐑌 𐑊𐐰𐑌𐐼𐑆; 𐐺𐐲𐐻 𐐰𐑆 𐐷𐐨 𐐸𐐰𐑂 𐐶𐐲𐑌𐑅 𐑉𐐯𐐾𐐯𐐿𐐻𐐯𐐼 𐑄𐐨𐑆 𐑃𐐮𐑍𐑆,
𐐰𐑌𐐼 𐐸𐐰𐑂 𐑁𐐫𐐻 𐐲𐑀𐐯𐑌𐑅𐐻 𐑄 𐐹𐐨𐐹𐑊 𐐱𐑂 𐑄 𐐢𐐬𐑉𐐼, 𐐨𐑂𐐲𐑌 𐑅𐐬 𐐌 𐑋𐐩 𐐯𐐿𐑅𐐹𐐯𐐿𐐻 𐐷𐐭 𐐶𐐮𐑊 𐐼𐐭 𐐮𐐻
𐐲𐑀𐐯𐑌.

2. 𐐈𐑌𐐼 𐑌𐐵 𐐺𐐨𐐸𐐬𐑊𐐼, 𐐶𐐨 𐐪𐑉 𐐹𐑉𐐯𐐹𐐩𐑉𐐼 𐐻𐐭 𐑉𐐯𐑅𐐨𐑂 𐐷𐐭; 𐐷𐐩, 𐐰𐑌𐐼 𐐯𐐿𐑅𐐯𐐹𐐻 𐐷𐐭 𐐶𐐮𐑄𐐼𐑉𐐫
𐐷𐐬𐑉 𐐹𐐲𐑉𐐹𐐲𐑅𐐯𐑆, 𐐺𐐨𐐸𐐬𐑊𐐼 𐐷𐐨 𐐶𐐮𐑊 𐐹𐐳𐑊 𐐼𐐵𐑌 𐑄 𐑉𐐰𐑃 𐐱𐑂 𐑄𐐰𐐻 𐐘𐐱𐐼 𐐸𐐭𐑋 𐐷𐐭 𐐸𐐰𐑂 𐑉𐐯𐐾𐐯𐐿𐐻𐐯𐐼
𐐲𐐹𐐱𐑌 𐐷𐐭, 𐐨𐑂𐐲𐑌 𐐻𐐭 𐐷𐐬𐑉 𐐲𐐻𐐲𐑉 𐐼𐐯𐑅𐐻𐑉𐐲𐐿𐑇𐐲𐑌; 𐐺𐐲𐐻 𐐰𐑆 𐑄 𐐢𐐬𐑉𐐼 𐑊𐐮𐑂𐐯𐑃, 𐐵𐑉 𐐪𐑉𐑋𐐮𐑆 𐑇𐐰𐑊 𐐿𐐲𐑋
𐐲𐐹𐐱𐑌 𐐷𐐭, 𐐯𐐿𐑅𐐯𐐹𐐻 𐐷𐐨 𐐶𐐮𐑄𐐼𐑉𐐫, 𐐰𐑌𐐼 𐐷𐐨 𐑇𐐰𐑊 𐑅𐐭𐑌 𐐺𐐨 𐑂𐐮𐑆𐐮𐐻𐐯𐐼 𐐶𐐮𐑄 𐐼𐐯𐑃, 𐑁𐐬𐑉 𐐶𐐨 𐐶𐐮𐑊 𐑉𐐯-𐐻𐐩𐑌 𐐵𐑉 𐑅𐐮𐐻𐐮𐑆 𐐰𐑌𐐼 𐐵𐑉 𐑊𐐰𐑌𐐼𐑆; 𐐷𐐩, 𐐰𐑌𐐼 𐐶𐐨 𐐶𐐮𐑊 𐑋𐐩𐑌𐐻𐐩𐑌 𐐵𐑉 𐑉𐐯𐑊𐐮𐐾𐐲𐑌 𐐰𐑌𐐼 𐑄 𐐿𐐫𐑆 𐐱𐑂 𐐵𐑉
𐐘𐐱𐐼. 𐐒𐐲𐐻 𐐺𐐨𐐸𐐬𐑊𐐼, 𐐮𐐻 𐑅𐐲𐐹𐐬𐑆𐐯𐑃 𐑋𐐨 𐑄𐐰𐐻 𐐌 𐐻𐐫𐐿 𐐻𐐭 𐐷𐐭 𐐿𐐱𐑌𐑅𐐲𐑉𐑌𐐮𐑍 𐑄𐐨𐑆 𐑃𐐮𐑍𐑆 𐐮𐑌
𐑂𐐩𐑌; 𐐬𐑉 𐐮𐐻 𐑅𐐲𐐹𐐬𐑆𐐯𐑃 𐑋𐐨 𐑄𐐰𐐻 𐑄𐐵 𐐪𐑉𐐻 𐐵 𐐽𐐴𐑊𐐼 𐐱𐑂 𐐸𐐯𐑊; 𐑄𐐯𐑉𐑁𐐬𐑉 𐐌 𐐶𐐮𐑊 𐐿𐑊𐐬𐑆 𐑋𐐴 𐐯𐐹𐐮𐑅𐑊
𐐺𐐴 𐐻𐐯𐑊𐐮𐑍 𐐷𐐭 𐑄𐐰𐐻 𐐌 𐐶𐐮𐑊 𐑌𐐱𐐻 𐐯𐐿𐑅𐐽𐐩𐑌𐐾 𐐹𐑉𐐮𐑆𐐲𐑌𐐲𐑉𐑆, 𐑅𐐩𐑂 𐐮𐐻 𐐺𐐨 𐐱𐑌 𐐿𐐲𐑌𐐼𐐮𐑇𐐲𐑌𐑆 𐑄𐐰𐐻 𐐷𐐨 𐐶𐐮𐑊
𐐼𐐯𐑊𐐮𐑂𐐲𐑉 𐐲𐐹 𐐵 𐑋𐐰𐑌 𐐰𐑌𐐼 𐐸𐐮𐑆 𐐶𐐴𐑁, 𐐰𐑌𐐼 𐐸𐐮𐑆 𐐽𐐮𐑊𐐼𐑉𐐯𐑌, 𐑁𐐬𐑉 𐐶𐐲𐑌 𐐹𐑉𐐮𐑆𐐲𐑌𐐲𐑉; 𐐮𐑁 𐑄𐐮𐑅 𐐺𐐨 𐑄 𐐿𐐩𐑅
𐑄𐐰𐐻 𐐷𐐨 𐐶𐐮𐑊 𐐼𐐭 𐐮𐐻, 𐐌 𐐶𐐮𐑊 𐐯𐐿𐑅𐐽𐐩𐑌𐐾. 𐐈𐑌𐐼 𐐺𐐨𐐸𐐬𐑊𐐼, 𐐮𐑁 𐐷𐐨 𐐼𐐭 𐑌𐐱𐐻 𐑄𐐮𐑅, 𐐌 𐐶𐐮𐑊 𐐿𐐲𐑋
𐐲𐑀𐐯𐑌𐑅𐐻 𐐷𐐭 𐐶𐐮𐑄 𐑋𐐴 𐐪𐑉𐑋𐐮𐑆; 𐐷𐐩, 𐐨𐑂𐐲𐑌 𐐌 𐐶𐐮𐑊 𐐪𐑉𐑋 𐑋𐐴 𐐶𐐮𐑋𐐯𐑌 𐐰𐑌𐐼 𐑋𐐴 𐐽𐐮𐑊𐐼𐑉𐐯𐑌, 𐐰𐑌𐐼 𐐌 𐐶𐐮𐑊
𐐿𐐲𐑋 𐐲𐑀𐐯𐑌𐑅𐐻 𐐷𐐭, 𐐰𐑌𐐼 𐐌 𐐶𐐮𐑊 𐑁𐐱𐑊𐐬 𐐷𐐭 𐐨𐑂𐐲𐑌 𐐮𐑌𐐻𐐭 𐐷𐐬𐑉 𐐬𐑌 𐑊𐐰𐑌𐐼, 𐐸𐐶𐐮𐐽 𐐮𐑆 𐑄 𐑊𐐰𐑌𐐼 𐐱𐑂 𐐵𐑉
𐑁𐐲𐑉𐑅𐐻 𐐮𐑌𐐸𐐯𐑉𐐮𐐻𐐲𐑌𐑅; 𐐷𐐩, 𐐰𐑌𐐼 𐐮𐐻 𐑇𐐰𐑊 𐐺𐐨 𐐺𐑊𐐲𐐼 𐑁𐐬𐑉 𐐺𐑊𐐲𐐼; 𐐷𐐩, 𐑊𐐴𐑁 𐑁𐐬𐑉 𐑊𐐴𐑁; 𐐰𐑌𐐼 𐐌 𐐶𐐮𐑊
𐑀𐐮𐑂 𐐷𐐭 𐐺𐐰𐐻𐑊, 𐐨𐑂𐐲𐑌 𐐲𐑌𐐻𐐮𐑊 𐐷𐐭 𐐪𐑉 𐐼𐐯𐑅𐐻𐑉𐐱𐐮𐐼 𐑁𐑉𐐱𐑋 𐐫𐑁 𐑄 𐑁𐐩𐑅 𐐱𐑂 𐑄 𐐲𐑉𐑃. 𐐒𐐨𐐸𐐬𐑊𐐼, 𐐌
𐐰𐑋 𐐮𐑌 𐑋𐐴 𐐰𐑍𐑀𐐲𐑉, 𐐰𐑌𐐼 𐐫𐑊𐑅𐐬 𐑋𐐴 𐐹𐐨𐐹𐑊; 𐐷𐐨 𐐸𐐰𐑂 𐑅𐐫𐐻 𐐻𐐭 𐑋𐐲𐑉𐐼𐐲𐑉 𐐲𐑅, 𐐰𐑌𐐼 𐐶𐐨 𐐸𐐰𐑂 𐐬𐑌𐑊𐐮

𐑅𐐫𐐻 𐐻𐐭 𐐼𐐨𐑁𐐯𐑌𐐼 𐐵𐑉𐑅𐐯𐑊𐑂𐑆. 𐐒𐐲𐐻 𐐺𐐨𐐸𐐬𐑊𐐼, 𐐮𐑁 𐐷𐐨 𐑅𐐨𐐿 𐐻𐐭 𐐼𐐨𐑅𐐻𐑉𐐱𐐮 𐐲𐑅 𐑋𐐬𐑉, 𐐶𐐨 𐐶𐐮𐑊 𐑅𐐨𐐿 𐐻𐐭 𐐼𐐨𐑅𐐻𐑉𐐱𐐮 𐐷𐐭; 𐐷𐐩, 𐐰𐑌𐐼 𐐶𐐨 𐐶𐐮𐑊 𐑅𐐨𐐿 𐐵𐑉 𐑊𐐰𐑌𐐼, 𐑄 𐑊𐐰𐑌𐐼 𐐱𐑂 𐐵𐑉 𐑁𐐲𐑉𐑅𐐻 𐐮𐑌𐐸𐐯𐑉𐐮𐐻𐐰𐑌𐑅. 𐐤𐐵 𐐌 𐐿𐑊𐐬𐑆 𐑋𐐴 𐐯𐐹𐐮𐑅𐑊. 𐐌 𐐰𐑋 𐐣𐐬𐑉𐐬𐑌𐐴; 𐐌 𐐰𐑋 𐐲 𐑊𐐨𐐼𐐲𐑉 𐐱𐑂 𐑄 𐐹𐐨𐐹𐑊 𐐱𐑂 𐑄 𐐤𐐨𐑁𐐴𐐻𐑅.

3. 𐐤𐐵 𐐮𐐻 𐐿𐐩𐑋 𐐻𐐭 𐐹𐐰𐑅 𐑄𐐰𐐻 𐐈𐑋𐐬𐑉𐐱𐑌, 𐐸𐐶𐐯𐑌 𐐸𐐨 𐐸𐐰𐐼 𐑉𐐨𐑅𐐨𐑂𐐼 𐑄𐐮𐑅 𐐯𐐹𐐮𐑅𐑊, 𐐸𐐨 𐐶𐐱𐑆 𐐰𐑍𐑀𐑉𐐨; 𐐰𐑌𐐼 𐐸𐐨 𐑉𐐬𐐻 𐐰𐑌𐐲𐑄𐐲𐑉 𐐯𐐹𐐮𐑅𐑊 𐐲𐑌𐐻𐐭 𐐣𐐬𐑉𐐬𐑌𐐴, 𐐰𐑌𐐼 𐑄𐐨𐑆 𐐪𐑉 𐑄 𐐶𐐲𐑉𐐼𐑆 𐐸𐐶𐐮𐐽 𐐸𐐨 𐑉𐐬𐐻, 𐑅𐐩𐐮𐑍, 𐐌 𐐰𐑋 𐐈𐑋𐐬𐑉𐐱𐑌, 𐑄 𐐿𐐮𐑍 𐐱𐑂 𐑄 𐐢𐐩𐑋𐐲𐑌𐐴𐐻𐑅; 𐐌 𐐰𐑋 𐑄 𐐺𐑉𐐲𐑄𐐲𐑉 𐐱𐑂 𐐈𐑋𐐰𐑊𐐮𐐿𐐴𐐲 𐐸𐐭𐑋 𐐷𐐨 𐐸𐐰𐑂 𐑋𐐲𐑉𐐼𐐲𐑉𐐼. 𐐒𐐨𐐸𐐬𐑊𐐼, 𐐌 𐐶𐐮𐑊 𐐲𐑂𐐯𐑌𐐾 𐐸𐐮𐑆 𐐺𐑊𐐲𐐼 𐐲𐐹𐐱𐑌 𐐷𐐭, 𐐷𐐩, 𐐰𐑌𐐼 𐐌 𐐶𐐮𐑊 𐐿𐐲𐑋 𐐲𐐹𐐱𐑌 𐐷𐐭 𐐶𐐮𐑄 𐑋𐐴 𐐪𐑉𐑋𐐨𐑆, 𐑁𐐫𐑉 𐐌 𐑁𐐨𐑉 𐑌𐐱𐐻 𐐷𐐭𐑉 𐑃𐑉𐐯𐐻𐐲𐑌𐐮𐑍𐑆; 𐑁𐐫𐑉 𐐺𐐨𐐸𐐬𐑊𐐼, 𐐷𐐭𐑉 𐑁𐐪𐑄𐐲𐑉𐑆 𐐼𐐮𐐼 𐑉𐐱𐑍 𐑄𐐩𐑉 𐐺𐑉𐐯𐑄𐑉𐐯𐑌, 𐐮𐑌𐑅𐐬𐑋𐐲𐐽 𐑄𐐰𐐻 𐑄𐐩 𐐼𐐮𐐼 𐑉𐐱𐐺 𐑄𐐯𐑋 𐐱𐑂 𐑄𐐩𐑉 𐑉𐐴𐐻 𐐻𐐭 𐑄 𐑀𐐲𐑂𐐲𐑉𐑌𐑋𐐯𐑌𐐻, 𐐸𐐶𐐯𐑌 𐐮𐐻 𐑉𐐴𐐻𐑊𐐨 𐐺𐐨𐑊𐐱𐑍𐐼 𐐲𐑌𐐻𐐭 𐑄𐐯𐑋. 𐐈𐑌𐐼 𐑌𐐵 𐐺𐐨𐐸𐐬𐑊𐐼, 𐐮𐑁 𐐷𐐨 𐐶𐐮𐑊 𐑊𐐩 𐐼𐐵𐑌 𐐷𐐭𐑉 𐐪𐑉𐑋𐑆, 𐐰𐑌𐐼 𐑅𐐲𐐺𐐾𐐯𐐿𐐻 𐐷𐐭𐑉𐑅𐐯𐑊𐑂𐑆 𐐻𐐭 𐐺𐐨 𐑀𐐲𐑂𐐲𐑉𐑌𐐼 𐐺𐐴 𐑄𐐬𐑆 𐐻𐐭 𐐸𐐭𐑋 𐑄 𐑀𐐲𐑂𐐲𐑉𐑌𐑋𐐯𐑌𐐻 𐐼𐐲𐑃 𐑉𐐴𐐻𐑊𐐨 𐐺𐐨𐑊𐐱𐑍, 𐑄𐐯𐑌 𐐶𐐮𐑊 𐐌 𐐿𐐫𐑆 𐑄𐐰𐐻 𐑋𐐴 𐐹𐐨𐐹𐑊 𐑇𐐰𐑊 𐑊𐐩 𐐼𐐵𐑌 𐑄𐐩𐑉 𐐶𐐯𐐹𐐲𐑌𐑆, 𐐰𐑌𐐼 𐑇𐐰𐑊 𐐺𐐨 𐐰𐐻 𐐶𐐫𐑉 𐑌𐐬 𐑋𐐬𐑉. 𐐒𐐨𐐸𐐬𐑊𐐼, 𐐷𐐨 𐐸𐐰𐑂 𐐺𐑉𐐨𐑄𐐼 𐐵𐐻 𐑋𐐯𐑌𐐨 𐑃𐑉𐐯𐐻𐐲𐑌𐐮𐑍𐑆 𐐲𐑀𐐯𐑌𐑅𐐻 𐑋𐐨 𐐰𐑌𐐼 𐑋𐐴 𐐹𐐨𐐹𐑊; 𐐺𐐲𐐻 𐐺𐐨𐐸𐐬𐑊𐐼, 𐐶𐐨 𐑁𐐨𐑉 𐑌𐐱𐐻 𐐷𐐭𐑉 𐑃𐑉𐐯𐐻𐐲𐑌𐐮𐑍𐑆; 𐑌𐐯𐑂𐐲𐑉𐑄𐐲𐑊𐐯𐑅, 𐐌 𐐶𐐮𐑊 𐑀𐑉𐐰𐑌𐐻 𐐻𐐭 𐐯𐐿𐑅𐐽𐐩𐑌𐐾 𐐹𐑉𐐮𐑆𐐲𐑌𐐲𐑉𐑆 𐐰𐐿𐐫𐑉𐐼𐐮𐑍 𐐻𐐭 𐐷𐐭𐑉 𐑉𐐨𐐿𐐶𐐯𐑅𐐻, 𐑀𐑊𐐰𐐼𐑊𐐨, 𐑄𐐰𐐻 𐐌 𐑋𐐩 𐐹𐑉𐐨𐑆𐐲𐑉𐑂 𐑋𐐴 𐑁𐐭𐐼 𐑁𐐫𐑉 𐑋𐐴 𐑋𐐯𐑌 𐐱𐑂 𐐶𐐫𐑉; 𐐰𐑌𐐼 𐐶𐐨 𐐶𐐮𐑊 𐐶𐐩𐐾 𐐲 𐐶𐐫𐑉 𐐸𐐶𐐮𐐽 𐑇𐐰𐑊 𐐺𐐨 𐐨𐐻𐐲𐑉𐑌𐐲𐑊, 𐐨𐑄𐐲𐑉 𐐻𐐭 𐑄 𐑅𐐲𐐺𐐾𐐯𐐿𐐻𐐮𐑍 𐑄 𐐤𐐨𐑁𐐴𐐻𐑅 𐐻𐐭 𐐵𐑉 𐐫𐑃𐐱𐑉𐐮𐐻𐐨, 𐐫𐑉 𐐻𐐭 𐑄𐐩𐑉 𐐨𐐻𐐲𐑉𐑌𐐲𐑊 𐐯𐐿𐑅𐐻𐐮𐑍𐐿𐑇𐐲𐑌. 𐐈𐑌𐐼 𐐰𐑆 𐐿𐐱𐑌𐑅𐐲𐑉𐑌𐐮𐑍 𐑄𐐰𐐻 𐐘𐐱𐐼 𐐸𐐭𐑋 𐐷𐐨 𐑅𐐩 𐐶𐐨 𐐸𐐰𐑂 𐑉𐐨𐐾𐐯𐐿𐐻𐐯𐐼, 𐐺𐐨𐐸𐐬𐑊𐐼, 𐐶𐐨 𐑌𐐬 𐑌𐐱𐐻 𐑅𐐲𐐽 𐐲 𐐺𐐨𐐮𐑍; 𐑌𐐨𐑄𐐲𐑉 𐐼𐐭 𐐷𐐨; 𐐺𐐲𐐻 𐐮𐑁 𐐮𐐻 𐑅𐐬 𐐺𐐨 𐑄𐐰𐐻 𐑄𐐯𐑉 𐐮𐑆 𐑅𐐲𐐽 𐐲 𐐺𐐨𐐮𐑍, 𐐶𐐨 𐑌𐐬 𐑌𐐱𐐻 𐐺𐐲𐐻 𐑄𐐰𐐻 𐐸𐐨 𐐸𐐰𐑃 𐑋𐐩𐐼 𐐲𐑅 𐐰𐑆 𐐶𐐯𐑊 𐐰𐑆 𐐷𐐭; 𐐰𐑌𐐼 𐐮𐑁 𐐮𐐻 𐑅𐐬 𐐺𐐨 𐑄𐐰𐐻 𐑄𐐯𐑉 𐐮𐑆 𐐲 𐐼𐐯𐑂𐐮𐑊 𐐰𐑌𐐼 𐐲 𐐸𐐯𐑊, 𐐺𐐨𐐸𐐬𐑊𐐼, 𐐶𐐮𐑊 𐐸𐐨 𐑌𐐱𐐻 𐑅𐐯𐑌𐐼 𐐷𐐭 𐑄𐐯𐑉 𐐻𐐭 𐐼𐐶𐐯𐑊 𐐶𐐮𐑄 𐑋𐐴 𐐺𐑉𐐲𐑄𐐲𐑉 𐐸𐐭𐑋 𐐷𐐨 𐐸𐐰𐑂 𐑋𐐲𐑉𐐼𐐲𐑉𐐼, 𐐸𐐭𐑋 𐐷𐐨 𐐸𐐰𐑂 𐐸𐐮𐑌𐐻𐐯𐐼 𐑄𐐰𐐻 𐐸𐐨 𐐸𐐰𐑃 𐑀𐐱𐑌 𐐻𐐭 𐑅𐐲𐐽 𐐲 𐐹𐑊𐐩𐑅? 𐐒𐐲𐐻 𐐺𐐨𐐸𐐬𐑊𐐼, 𐑄𐐨𐑆 𐑃𐐮𐑍𐑆 𐑋𐐰𐐻𐐲𐑉 𐑌𐐱𐐻. 𐐌 𐐰𐑋 𐐈𐑋𐐬𐑉𐐱𐑌, 𐐰𐑌𐐼 𐐲 𐐼𐐨𐑅𐐯𐑌𐐼𐐰𐑌𐐻 𐐱𐑂 𐐞𐐬𐑉𐐰𐑋, 𐐸𐐭𐑋 𐐷𐐭𐑉 𐑁𐐪𐑄𐐲𐑉𐑆 𐐹𐑉𐐯𐑅𐐻 𐐰𐑌𐐼 𐐺𐑉𐐫𐐻 𐐵𐐻 𐐱𐑂 𐐖𐐨𐑉𐐭𐑅𐐲𐑊𐐯𐑋. 𐐈𐑌𐐼 𐐺𐐨𐐸𐐬𐑊𐐼 𐑌𐐵, 𐐌 𐐰𐑋 𐐲 𐐺𐐬𐑊𐐼 𐐢𐐩𐑋𐐲𐑌𐐴𐐻; 𐐺𐐨𐐸𐐬𐑊𐐼, 𐑄𐐮𐑅 𐐶𐐫𐑉 𐐸𐐰𐑃 𐐺𐐮𐑌 𐐶𐐩𐐾𐐼 𐐻𐐭 𐐲𐑂𐐯𐑌𐐾 𐑄𐐩𐑉 𐑉𐐱𐑍𐑆, 𐐰𐑌𐐼 𐐻𐐭 𐑋𐐩𐑌𐐻𐐩𐑌, 𐐰𐑌𐐼 𐐻𐐭 𐐱𐐺𐐻𐐩𐑌 𐑄𐐩𐑉 𐑉𐐴𐐻𐑅 𐐻𐐭 𐑄 𐑀𐐲𐑂𐐲𐑉𐑌𐑋𐐯𐑌𐐻; 𐐰𐑌𐐼 𐐌 𐐿𐑊𐐬𐑆 𐑋𐐴 𐐯𐐹𐐮𐑅𐑊 𐐻𐐭 𐐣𐐬𐑉𐐬𐑌𐐴.

4. 𐐤𐐵 𐐮𐐻 𐐿𐐩𐑋 𐐻𐐭 𐐹𐐰𐑅 𐑄𐐰𐐻 𐐸𐐶𐐯𐑌 𐐣𐐬𐑉𐐬𐑌𐐴 𐐸𐐰𐐼 𐑉𐐨𐑅𐐨𐑂𐐼 𐑄𐐮𐑅 𐐯𐐹𐐮𐑅𐑊, 𐐸𐐨 𐐶𐐱𐑆 𐑋𐐬𐑉 𐐰𐑍𐑀𐑉𐐨, 𐐺𐐨𐐿𐐫𐑆 𐐸𐐨 𐑌𐐭 𐑄𐐰𐐻 𐐈𐑋𐐬𐑉𐐱𐑌 𐐸𐐰𐐼 𐐲 𐐹𐐲𐑉𐑁𐐯𐐿𐐻 𐑌𐐱𐑊𐐯𐐾 𐐱𐑂 𐐸𐐮𐑆 𐑁𐑉𐐫𐐼; 𐐷𐐩, 𐐸𐐨 𐑌𐐭 𐑄𐐰𐐻 𐐈𐑋𐐬𐑉𐐱𐑌 𐑌𐐭 𐑄𐐰𐐻 𐐮𐐻 𐐶𐐱𐑆 𐑌𐐱𐐻 𐐲 𐐾𐐲𐑅𐐻 𐐿𐐫𐑆 𐑄𐐰𐐻 𐐸𐐰𐐼 𐐿𐐫𐑆𐐼 𐐸𐐮𐑋 𐐻𐐭 𐐶𐐩𐐾 𐐲 𐐶𐐫𐑉 𐐲𐑀𐐯𐑌𐑅𐐻 𐑄 𐐹𐐨𐐹𐑊 𐐱𐑂 𐐤𐐨𐑁𐐴. 𐐈𐑌𐐼 𐐸𐐨 𐑅𐐯𐐼, 𐐒𐐨𐐸𐐬𐑊𐐼, 𐐌 𐐶𐐮𐑊 𐑌𐐱𐐻 𐐯𐐿𐑅𐐽𐐩𐑌𐐾 𐐹𐑉𐐮𐑆𐐲𐑌𐐲𐑉𐑆 𐐶𐐮𐑄 𐐈𐑋𐐬𐑉𐐱𐑌, 𐑅𐐩𐑂 𐐸𐐨 𐐶𐐮𐑊 𐐶𐐮𐑄𐐼𐑉𐐫 𐐸𐐮𐑆 𐐹𐐲𐑉𐐹𐐲𐑅, 𐐰𐑆 𐐌 𐐸𐐰𐑂 𐑅𐐻𐐩𐐻𐐯𐐼 𐐮𐑌 𐑋𐐴 𐐯𐐹𐐮𐑅𐑊; 𐑁𐐫𐑉 𐐌 𐐶𐐮𐑊 𐑌𐐱𐐻 𐑀𐑉𐐰𐑌𐐻 𐐲𐑌𐐻𐐭 𐐸𐐮𐑋 𐑄𐐰𐐻 𐐸𐐨 𐑇𐐰𐑊 𐐸𐐰𐑂 𐐯𐑌𐐨 𐑋𐐬𐑉 𐐹𐐵𐐲𐑉 𐑄𐐰𐑌 𐐸𐐶𐐱𐐻 𐐸𐐨 𐐸𐐰𐑃 𐑀𐐱𐐻. 𐐒𐐨𐐸𐐬𐑊𐐼, 𐐌 𐑌𐐬 𐑄 𐐹𐑊𐐩𐑅 𐐸𐐶𐐩𐑉 𐑄 𐐢𐐩𐑋𐐲𐑌𐐴𐐻𐑅 𐐼𐐭 𐑀𐐪𐑉𐐼 𐑋𐐴 𐐹𐐨𐐹𐑊 𐐸𐐭𐑋 𐑄𐐩 𐐸𐐰𐑂 𐐻𐐩𐐿𐑌 𐐹𐑉𐐮𐑆𐐲𐑌𐐲𐑉𐑆; 𐐰𐑌𐐼 𐐰𐑆 𐐈𐑋𐐬𐑉𐐱𐑌 𐐶𐐳𐐼 𐑌𐐱𐐻 𐑀𐑉𐐰𐑌𐐻 𐐲𐑌𐐻𐐭 𐑋𐐨 𐑋𐐴𐑌 𐐯𐐹𐐮𐑅𐑊, 𐐺𐐨𐐸𐐬𐑊𐐼, 𐐌 𐐶𐐮𐑊 𐑀𐐮𐑂 𐐲𐑌𐐻𐐭 𐐸𐐮𐑋 𐐰𐐿𐐫𐑉𐐼𐐮𐑍 𐐻𐐭 𐑋𐐴 𐐶𐐲𐑉𐐼𐑆; 𐐷𐐩, 𐐌 𐐶𐐮𐑊 𐑅𐐨𐐿 𐐼𐐯𐑃 𐐲𐑋𐐲𐑍 𐑄𐐯𐑋, 𐐲𐑌𐐻𐐮𐑊 𐑄𐐩 𐑇𐐰𐑊 𐑅𐐭 𐑁𐐫𐑉 𐐹𐐨𐑅. 𐐈𐑌𐐼 𐐮𐐻 𐐿𐐩𐑋 𐐻𐐭 𐐹𐐰𐑅 𐑄𐐰𐐻 𐐸𐐶𐐯𐑌 𐐣𐐬𐑉𐐬𐑌𐐴 𐐸𐐰𐐼 𐑅𐐯𐐼 𐑄𐐨𐑆 𐐶𐐲𐑉𐐼𐑆, 𐐸𐐨 𐐿𐐫𐑆𐐼 𐑄𐐰𐐻 𐐲 𐑅𐐲𐑉𐐽 𐑇𐐳𐐼 𐐺𐐨 𐑋𐐩𐐼 𐐲𐑋𐐲𐑍 𐐸𐐮𐑆 𐑋𐐯𐑌, 𐑄𐐰𐐻 𐐹𐐲𐑉𐐸𐐰𐐹𐑅 𐐸𐐨 𐑋𐐴𐐻 𐑁𐐴𐑌𐐼 𐐲 𐑋𐐰𐑌 𐐸𐐭 𐐶𐐱𐑆 𐐲 𐐼𐐨𐑅𐐯𐑌𐐼𐐰𐑌𐐻 𐐱𐑂 𐐢𐐩𐑋𐐲𐑌 𐐲𐑋𐐲𐑍 𐑄𐐯𐑋.

5. 𐐈𐑌𐐼 𐐮𐐻 𐐿𐐩𐑋 𐐻𐐭 𐐹𐐰𐑅 𐑄𐐰𐐻 𐑄𐐩 𐑁𐐵𐑌𐐼 𐐶𐐲𐑌, 𐐸𐐭𐑆 𐑌𐐩𐑋 𐐶𐐱𐑆 𐐢𐐩𐑋𐐲𐑌; 𐐰𐑌𐐼 𐐸𐐨 𐐶𐐱𐑆 𐐶𐐲𐑌 𐐱𐑂 𐑄 𐑅𐐲𐑉𐑂𐐲𐑌𐐻𐑅 𐐱𐑂 𐑄 𐐿𐐮𐑍 𐐸𐐭 𐐶𐐱𐑆 𐑋𐐲𐑉𐐼𐐲𐑉𐐼 𐐺𐐴 𐐈𐑋𐐰𐑊𐐮𐐿𐐴𐐲. 𐐤𐐵 𐐣𐐬𐑉𐐬𐑌𐐴 𐐿𐐫𐑆𐐼 𐑄𐐰𐐻 𐐢𐐩𐑋𐐲𐑌 𐐰𐑌𐐼 𐐲 𐑅𐑋𐐫𐑊 𐑌𐐲𐑋𐐺𐐲𐑉 𐐱𐑂 𐐸𐐮𐑆 𐑋𐐯𐑌 𐑇𐐳𐐼 𐑀𐐬 𐑁𐐬𐑉𐑃 𐐲𐑌𐐻𐐭 𐑄 𐑀𐐪𐑉𐐼𐑆 𐐸𐐭 𐐶𐐲𐑉

𐐬𐑂𐐲𐑉 𐑄 𐐤𐐨𐑁𐐴𐐻𐑅. 𐐤𐐵 𐑄 𐐤𐐨𐑁𐐴𐐻𐑅 𐐶𐐲𐑉 𐑀𐐪𐑉𐐼𐐯𐐼 𐐮𐑌 𐑄 𐑅𐐮𐐻𐐨 𐐱𐑂 𐐘𐐮𐐼; 𐑄𐐯𐑉𐑁𐐬𐑉 𐐣𐐬𐑉𐐬𐑌𐐴 𐐰𐐹𐑎𐑌𐐻𐐯𐐼 𐐢𐐩𐑋𐐲𐑌 𐐰𐑌𐐼 𐐿𐐫𐑆𐐼 𐑄𐐰𐐻 𐐲 𐑅𐑋𐐫𐑊 𐑌𐐲𐑋𐐺𐐲𐑉 𐐱𐑂 𐑋𐐯𐑌 𐑇𐐳𐐼 𐑀𐐬 𐐶𐐮𐑄 𐐸𐐮𐑋.

6. 𐐈𐑌𐐼 𐐸𐐶𐐯𐑌 𐐮𐐻 𐐶𐐱𐑆 𐐨𐑂𐑌𐐮𐑍, 𐐢𐐩𐑋𐐲𐑌 𐐶𐐯𐑌𐐻 𐐻𐐭 𐑄 𐑀𐐪𐑉𐐼𐑆 𐐸𐐭 𐐶𐐲𐑉 𐐬𐑂𐐲𐑉 𐑄 𐐤𐐨𐑁𐐴𐐻𐑅, 𐐰𐑌𐐼 𐐺𐐨𐐸𐐬𐑊𐐼, 𐑄𐐩 𐑅𐐫 𐐸𐐮𐑋 𐐿𐐲𐑋𐐮𐑍, 𐐰𐑌𐐼 𐑄𐐩 𐐸𐐩𐑊𐐼 𐐸𐐮𐑋; 𐐺𐐲𐐻 𐐸𐐨 𐑅𐐯𐑃 𐐲𐑌𐐻𐐭 𐑄𐐯𐑋, 𐐙𐐨𐑉 𐑌𐐱𐐻, 𐐺𐐨𐐸𐐬𐑊𐐼, 𐐌 𐐰𐑋 𐐲 𐐢𐐩𐑋𐐲𐑌𐐴𐐻. 𐐒𐐨𐐸𐐬𐑊𐐼, 𐐶𐐨 𐐸𐐰𐑂 𐐯𐑅𐐿𐐩𐐹𐐻 𐑁𐑉𐐱𐑋 𐑄 𐐤𐐨𐑁𐐴𐐻𐑅, 𐐰𐑌𐐼 𐑄𐐩 𐑅𐑊𐐨𐐹; 𐐰𐑌𐐼 𐐺𐐨𐐸𐐬𐑊𐐼 𐐶𐐨 𐐸𐐰𐑂 𐐻𐐩𐐿𐐲𐑌 𐐱𐑂 𐑄𐐩𐑉 𐐶𐐴𐑌, 𐐰𐑌𐐼 𐐺𐑉𐐫𐐻 𐐶𐐮𐑄 𐐲𐑅. 𐐤𐐵 𐐸𐐶𐐯𐑌 𐑄 𐐢𐐩𐑋𐐲𐑌𐐴𐐻𐑅 𐐸𐐲𐑉𐐼 𐑄𐐨𐑆 𐐶𐐲𐑉𐐼𐑆 𐑄𐐩 𐑉𐐨𐑅𐐨𐑂𐐼 𐐸𐐮𐑋 𐐶𐐮𐑄 𐐾𐑎; 𐐰𐑌𐐼 𐑄𐐩 𐑅𐐯𐐼 𐐲𐑌𐐻𐐭 𐐸𐐮𐑋, 𐐘𐐮𐑂 𐐲𐑅 𐐱𐑂 𐐷𐐭𐑉 𐐶𐐴𐑌, 𐑄𐐰𐐻 𐐶𐐨 𐑋𐐩 𐐼𐑉𐐮𐑍𐐿; 𐐶𐐨 𐐪𐑉 𐑀𐑊𐐰𐐼 𐑄𐐰𐐻 𐐷𐐨 𐐸𐐰𐑂 𐑄𐐲𐑅 𐐻𐐩𐐿𐐲𐑌 𐐶𐐴𐑌 𐐶𐐮𐑄 𐐷𐐭, 𐑁𐐫𐑉 𐐶𐐨 𐐪𐑉 𐐶𐐨𐑉𐐨. 𐐒𐐲𐐻 𐐢𐐩𐑋𐐲𐑌 𐑅𐐯𐐼 𐐲𐑌𐐻𐐭 𐑄𐐯𐑋, 𐐢𐐯𐐻 𐐲𐑅 𐐿𐐨𐐹 𐐱𐑂 𐐵𐑉 𐐶𐐴𐑌 𐐻𐐮𐑊 𐐶𐐨 𐑀𐐬 𐐲𐑀𐐯𐑌𐑅𐐻 𐑄 𐐤𐐨𐑁𐐴𐐻𐑅 𐐻𐐭 𐐺𐐰𐐻𐑊. 𐐒𐐲𐐻 𐑄𐐮𐑅 𐑅𐐩𐐮𐑍 𐐬𐑌𐑊𐐨 𐑋𐐩𐐼 𐑄𐐯𐑋 𐑋𐐬𐑉 𐐼𐐨𐑆𐐴𐑉𐐲𐑅 𐐻𐐭 𐐼𐑉𐐮𐑍𐐿 𐐱𐑂 𐑄 𐐶𐐴𐑌; 𐐙𐐫𐑉, 𐑅𐐯𐐼 𐑄𐐩, 𐐶𐐨 𐐪𐑉 𐐶𐐨𐑉𐐨, 𐑄𐐯𐑉𐑁𐐬𐑉 𐑊𐐯𐐻 𐐲𐑅 𐐻𐐩𐐿 𐐱𐑂 𐑄 𐐶𐐴𐑌, 𐐰𐑌𐐼 𐐺𐐴 𐐰𐑌𐐼 𐐺𐐴 𐐶𐐨 𐑇𐐰𐑊 𐑉𐐨𐑅𐐨𐑂 𐐶𐐴𐑌 𐑁𐐫𐑉 𐐵𐑉 𐑉𐐩𐑇𐐲𐑌𐑆, 𐐸𐐶𐐮𐐽 𐐶𐐮𐑊 𐑅𐐻𐑉𐐯𐑍𐑃𐐲𐑌 𐐲𐑅 𐐻𐐭 𐑀𐐬 𐐲𐑀𐐯𐑌𐑅𐐻 𐑄 𐐤𐐨𐑁𐐴𐐻𐑅. 𐐈𐑌𐐼 𐐢𐐩𐑋𐐲𐑌 𐑅𐐯𐐼 𐐲𐑌𐐻𐐭 𐑄𐐯𐑋, 𐐏𐐭 𐑋𐐩 𐐼𐐭 𐐰𐐿𐐫𐑉𐐼𐐮𐑍 𐐻𐐭 𐐷𐐭𐑉 𐐼𐐨𐑆𐐴𐑉𐑆. 𐐈𐑌𐐼 𐐮𐐻 𐐿𐐩𐑋 𐐻𐐭 𐐹𐐪𐑅 𐑄𐐰𐐻 𐑄𐐩 𐐼𐐮𐐼 𐐻𐐩𐐿 𐐱𐑂 𐑄 𐐶𐐴𐑌 𐑁𐑉𐐨𐑊𐐨; 𐐰𐑌𐐼 𐐮𐐻 𐐶𐐱𐑆 𐐹𐑊𐐯𐑆𐐲𐑌𐐻 𐐻𐐭 𐑄𐐩𐑉 𐐻𐐩𐑅𐐻, 𐑄𐐯𐑉𐑁𐐬𐑉 𐑄𐐩 𐐻𐐳𐐿 𐐱𐑂 𐐮𐐻 𐑋𐐬𐑉 𐑁𐑉𐐨𐑊𐐨; 𐐰𐑌𐐼 𐐮𐐻 𐐶𐐱𐑆 𐑅𐐻𐑉𐐫𐑍, 𐐸𐐰𐑂𐐮𐑍 𐐺𐐮𐑌 𐐹𐑉𐐨𐐹𐐩𐑉𐐼 𐐮𐑌 𐐮𐐻𐑅 𐑅𐐻𐑉𐐯𐑍𐑃.

7. 𐐈𐑌𐐼 𐐮𐐻 𐐿𐐩𐑋 𐐻𐐭 𐐹𐐪𐑅 𐑄𐐩 𐐼𐐮𐐼 𐐼𐑉𐐮𐑍𐐿 𐐰𐑌𐐼 𐐶𐐲𐑉 𐑋𐐯𐑉𐐨, 𐐰𐑌𐐼 𐐺𐐴 𐐰𐑌𐐼 𐐺𐐴 𐑄𐐩 𐐶𐐲𐑉 𐐫𐑊 𐐼𐑉𐐲𐑍𐐿𐐲𐑌. 𐐈𐑌𐐼 𐑌𐐵 𐐸𐐶𐐯𐑌 𐐢𐐩𐑋𐐲𐑌 𐐰𐑌𐐼 𐐸𐐮𐑆 𐑋𐐯𐑌 𐑅𐐫 𐑄𐐰𐐻 𐑄𐐩 𐐶𐐲𐑉 𐐫𐑊 𐐼𐑉𐐲𐑍𐐿𐐲𐑌, 𐐰𐑌𐐼 𐐶𐐲𐑉 𐐮𐑌 𐐲 𐐼𐐨𐐹 𐑅𐑊𐐨𐐹, 𐑄𐐩 𐑉𐐨𐐻𐐲𐑉𐑌𐐼 𐐻𐐭 𐐣𐐬𐑉𐐬𐑌𐐴, 𐐰𐑌𐐼 𐐻𐐬𐑊𐐼 𐐸𐐮𐑋 𐐫𐑊 𐑄 𐑃𐐮𐑍𐑆 𐑄𐐰𐐻 𐐸𐐰𐐼 𐐸𐐰𐐹𐐲𐑌𐐼. 𐐈𐑌𐐼 𐑌𐐵 𐑄𐐮𐑅 𐐶𐐱𐑆 𐐰𐐿𐐫𐑉𐐼𐐮𐑍 𐐻𐐭 𐑄 𐐼𐐨𐑆𐐴𐑌 𐐱𐑂 𐐣𐐬𐑉𐐬𐑌𐐴. 𐐈𐑌𐐼 𐐣𐐬𐑉𐐬𐑌𐐴 𐐸𐐰𐐼 𐐹𐑉𐐨𐐹𐐩𐑉𐐼 𐐸𐐮𐑆 𐑋𐐯𐑌 𐐶𐐮𐑄 𐐶𐐯𐐹𐐲𐑌𐑆 𐐱𐑂 𐐶𐐫𐑉; 𐐰𐑌𐐼 𐐸𐐨 𐐶𐐯𐑌𐐻 𐐻𐐭 𐑄 𐑅𐐮𐐻𐐨 𐐘𐐮𐐼, 𐐸𐐶𐐴𐑊 𐑄 𐐢𐐩𐑋𐐲𐑌𐐴𐐻𐑅 𐐶𐐲𐑉 𐐮𐑌 𐐲 𐐼𐐨𐐹 𐑅𐑊𐐨𐐹, 𐐰𐑌𐐼 𐐼𐑉𐐲𐑍𐐿𐐲𐑌, 𐐰𐑌𐐼 𐐿𐐪𐑅𐐻 𐐮𐑌 𐐶𐐯𐐹𐐲𐑌𐑆 𐐱𐑂 𐐶𐐫𐑉 𐐲𐑌𐐻𐐭 𐑄 𐐹𐑉𐐮𐑆𐐲𐑌𐐲𐑉𐑆, 𐐮𐑌𐑅𐐬𐑋𐐲𐐽 𐑄𐐰𐐻 𐑄𐐩 𐐶𐐲𐑉 𐐫𐑊 𐐪𐑉𐑋𐐼; 𐐷𐐩, 𐐨𐑂𐐲𐑌 𐐻𐐭 𐑄𐐩𐑉 𐐶𐐮𐑋𐐯𐑌, 𐐰𐑌𐐼 𐐫𐑊 𐑄𐐬𐑆 𐐱𐑂 𐑄𐐩𐑉 𐐽𐐮𐑊𐐼𐑉𐐯𐑌, 𐐰𐑆 𐑋𐐯𐑌𐐨 𐐰𐑆 𐐶𐐲𐑉 𐐩𐐺𐑊 𐐻𐐭 𐐷𐐭𐑆 𐐲 𐐶𐐯𐐹𐐲𐑌 𐐱𐑂 𐐶𐐫𐑉, 𐐸𐐶𐐯𐑌 𐐣𐐬𐑉𐐬𐑌𐐴 𐐸𐐰𐐼 𐐪𐑉𐑋𐐼 𐐫𐑊 𐑄𐐬𐑆 𐐹𐑉𐐮𐑆𐐲𐑌𐐲𐑉𐑆: 𐐰𐑌𐐼 𐐫𐑊 𐑄𐐬𐑆 𐑃𐐮𐑍𐑆 𐐶𐐲𐑉 𐐼𐐲𐑌 𐐮𐑌 𐐲 𐐹𐑉𐐬𐑁𐐵𐑌𐐼 𐑅𐐴𐑊𐐯𐑌𐑅. 𐐒𐐲𐐻 𐐸𐐰𐐼 𐑄𐐩 𐐲𐐶𐐩𐐿𐐲𐑌𐐼 𐑄 𐐢𐐩𐑋𐐲𐑌𐐴𐐻𐑅, 𐐺𐐨𐐸𐐬𐑊𐐼 𐑄𐐩 𐐶𐐲𐑉 𐐼𐑉𐐲𐑍𐐿𐐲𐑌, 𐐰𐑌𐐼 𐑄 𐐤𐐨𐑁𐐴𐐻𐑅 𐐿𐐳𐐼 𐐸𐐰𐑂 𐑅𐑊𐐩𐑌 𐑄𐐯𐑋. 𐐒𐐲𐐻 𐐺𐐨𐐸𐐬𐑊𐐼, 𐑄𐐮𐑅 𐐶𐐱𐑆 𐑌𐐱𐐻 𐑄 𐐼𐐨𐑆𐐴𐑉 𐐱𐑂 𐐣𐐬𐑉𐐬𐑌𐐴: 𐐸𐐨 𐐼𐐮𐐼 𐑌𐐱𐐻 𐐼𐐨𐑊𐐴𐐻 𐐮𐑌 𐑋𐐲𐑉𐐼𐐲𐑉 𐐫𐑉 𐐺𐑊𐐲𐐼𐑇𐐯𐐼, 𐐺𐐲𐐻 𐐸𐐨 𐐼𐐨𐑊𐐴𐐻𐐯𐐼 𐐮𐑌 𐑄 𐑅𐐩𐑂𐐮𐑍 𐐱𐑂 𐐸𐐮𐑆 𐐹𐐨𐐹𐑊 𐑁𐑉𐐱𐑋 𐐼𐐨𐑅𐐻𐑉𐐲𐐿𐑇𐐲𐑌; 𐐰𐑌𐐼 𐑁𐐫𐑉 𐑄𐐮𐑅 𐐿𐐫𐑆 𐐸𐐨 𐑋𐐴𐐻 𐑌𐐱𐐻 𐐺𐑉𐐮𐑍 𐐲𐐹𐐱𐑌 𐐸𐐮𐑋 𐐮𐑌𐐾𐐲𐑅𐐻𐐮𐑅, 𐐸𐐨 𐐶𐐳𐐼 𐑌𐐱𐐻 𐑁𐐫𐑊 𐐲𐐹𐐱𐑌 𐑄 𐐢𐐩𐑋𐐲𐑌𐐴𐐻𐑅 𐐰𐑌𐐼 𐐼𐐨𐑅𐐻𐑉𐑎 𐑄𐐯𐑋 𐐮𐑌 𐑄𐐩𐑉 𐐼𐑉𐐲𐑍𐐿𐐲𐑌𐑌𐐯𐑅. 𐐒𐐲𐐻 𐐸𐐨 𐐸𐐰𐐼 𐐱𐐺𐐻𐐩𐑌𐐼 𐐸𐐮𐑆 𐐼𐐨𐑆𐐴𐑉𐑆; 𐑁𐐫𐑉 𐐸𐐨 𐐸𐐰𐐼 𐐪𐑉𐑋𐐼 𐑄𐐬𐑆 𐐹𐑉𐐮𐑆𐐲𐑌𐐲𐑉𐑆 𐐱𐑂 𐑄 𐐤𐐨𐑁𐐴𐐻𐑅 𐐸𐐭 𐐶𐐲𐑉 𐐶𐐮𐑄𐐮𐑌 𐑄 𐐶𐐫𐑊 𐐱𐑂 𐑄 𐑅𐐮𐐻𐐨, 𐐰𐑌𐐼 𐐸𐐰𐐼 𐑀𐐮𐑂𐐲𐑌 𐑄𐐯𐑋 𐐹𐐵𐐲𐑉 𐐻𐐭 𐑀𐐩𐑌 𐐹𐐱𐑆𐐯𐑇𐐲𐑌 𐐱𐑂 𐑄𐐬𐑆 𐐹𐐪𐑉𐐻𐑅 𐐸𐐶𐐮𐐽 𐐶𐐲𐑉 𐐶𐐮𐑄𐐮𐑌 𐑄 𐐶𐐫𐑊𐑆; 𐐰𐑌𐐼 𐑄𐐯𐑌 𐐸𐐨 𐐿𐐫𐑆𐐼 𐑄 𐑋𐐯𐑌 𐐸𐐭 𐐶𐐲𐑉 𐐶𐐮𐑄 𐐸𐐮𐑋 𐐻𐐭 𐐶𐐮𐑄𐐼𐑉𐐫 𐐲 𐐹𐐩𐑅 𐑁𐑉𐐱𐑋 𐑄𐐯𐑋, 𐐰𐑌𐐼 𐑅𐐲𐑉𐐵𐑌𐐼 𐑄 𐐪𐑉𐑋𐐨𐑆 𐐱𐑂 𐑄 𐐢𐐩𐑋𐐲𐑌𐐴𐐻𐑅. 𐐤𐐵 𐐺𐐨𐐸𐐬𐑊𐐼 𐑄𐐮𐑅 𐐶𐐱𐑆 𐐼𐐲𐑌 𐐮𐑌 𐑄 𐑌𐐴𐐻-𐐻𐐴𐑋, 𐑅𐐬 𐑄𐐰𐐻 𐐸𐐶𐐯𐑌 𐑄 𐐢𐐩𐑋𐐲𐑌𐐴𐐻𐑅 𐐲𐐶𐐬𐐿 𐐮𐑌 𐑄 𐑋𐐫𐑉𐑌𐐮𐑍, 𐑄𐐩 𐐺𐐨𐐸𐐯𐑊𐐼 𐑄𐐰𐐻 𐑄𐐩 𐐶𐐲𐑉 𐑅𐐲𐑉𐐵𐑌𐐼𐐯𐐼 𐐺𐐴 𐑄 𐐤𐐨𐑁𐐴𐐻𐑅 𐐶𐐮𐑄𐐵𐐻, 𐐰𐑌𐐼 𐑄𐐰𐐻 𐑄𐐩𐑉 𐐹𐑉𐐮𐑆𐐲𐑌𐐲𐑉𐑆 𐐶𐐲𐑉 𐐪𐑉𐑋𐐼 𐐶𐐮𐑄𐐮𐑌. 𐐈𐑌𐐼 𐑄𐐲𐑅 𐑄𐐩 𐑅𐐫 𐑄𐐰𐐻 𐑄 𐐤𐐨𐑁𐐴𐐻𐑅 𐐸𐐰𐐼 𐐹𐐵𐐲𐑉 𐐬𐑂𐐲𐑉 𐑄𐐯𐑋; 𐐰𐑌𐐼 𐐮𐑌 𐑄𐐨𐑆 𐑅𐐲𐑉𐐿𐐲𐑋𐑅𐐻𐐰𐑌𐑅𐐯𐑆 𐑄𐐩 𐑁𐐵𐑌𐐼 𐑄𐐰𐐻 𐐮𐐻 𐐶𐐱𐑆 𐑌𐐱𐐻 𐐯𐐿𐑅𐐹𐐨𐐼𐐨𐐯𐑌𐐻 𐑄𐐰𐐻 𐑄𐐩 𐑇𐐳𐐼 𐑁𐐴𐐻 𐐶𐐮𐑄 𐑄 𐐤𐐨𐑁𐐴𐐻𐑅; 𐑄𐐯𐑉𐑁𐐬𐑉 𐑄𐐩𐑉 𐐽𐐨𐑁 𐐿𐐰𐐹𐐻𐐯𐑌𐑆 𐐼𐐨𐑋𐐰𐑌𐐼𐐯𐐼 𐑄𐐩𐑉 𐐶𐐯𐐹𐐲𐑌𐑆 𐐱𐑂 𐐶𐐫𐑉, 𐐰𐑌𐐼 𐑄𐐩 𐐺𐑉𐐫𐐻 𐑄𐐯𐑋 𐑁𐐬𐑉𐑃 𐐰𐑌𐐼 𐐿𐐪𐑅𐐻 𐑄𐐯𐑋 𐐰𐐻 𐑄 𐑁𐐨𐐻 𐐱𐑂 𐑄 𐐤𐐨𐑁𐐴𐐻𐑅, 𐐹𐑊𐐨𐐼𐐮𐑍 𐑁𐐫𐑉 𐑋𐐲𐑉𐑅𐐨. 𐐤𐐵 𐐺𐐨𐐸𐐬𐑊𐐼, 𐑄𐐮𐑅 𐐶𐐱𐑆 𐑄 𐐼𐐨𐑆𐐴𐑉 𐐱𐑂 𐐣𐐬𐑉𐐬𐑌𐐴. 𐐐𐐨 𐐻𐐳𐐿 𐑄𐐯𐑋 𐐹𐑉𐐮𐑆𐐲𐑌𐐲𐑉𐑆 𐐱𐑂 𐐶𐐫𐑉, 𐐰𐑌𐐼 𐐻𐐳𐐿 𐐹𐐱𐑆𐐯𐑇𐐲𐑌 𐐱𐑂 𐑄 𐑅𐐮𐐻𐐨, 𐐰𐑌𐐼 𐐿𐐫𐑆𐐼 𐑄𐐰𐐻 𐐫𐑊 𐑄 𐐹𐑉𐐮𐑆𐐲𐑌𐐲𐑉𐑆 𐑇𐐳𐐼 𐐺𐐨 𐑊𐐮𐐺𐐲𐑉𐐩𐐻𐐯𐐼,

𐐸𐐭 𐐶𐐲𐑉 𐐤𐐨𐑁𐐴𐐻𐑅; 𐐰𐑌𐐼 𐑄𐐩 𐐼𐐮𐐼 𐐾𐐦𐑌 𐑄 𐐪𐑉𐑋𐐨 𐐱𐑂 𐐣𐐬𐑉𐐬𐑌𐐴, 𐐰𐑌𐐼 𐐶𐐲𐑉 𐐲 𐑀𐑉𐐩𐐻 𐑅𐐻𐑉𐐯𐑍𐑃 𐐻𐐭 𐐸𐐮𐑆 𐐪𐑉𐑋𐐨.

8. 𐐈𐑌𐐼 𐐮𐐻 𐐿𐐩𐑋 𐐻𐐭 𐐹𐐰𐑅 𐑄𐐰𐐻 𐐸𐐨 𐐼𐐮𐐼 𐐿𐐫𐑆 𐑄 𐐢𐐩𐑋𐐲𐑌𐐴𐐻𐑅 𐐸𐐭𐑋 𐐸𐐨 𐐸𐐰𐐼 𐐻𐐩𐐿𐐲𐑌 𐐹𐑉𐐮𐑆𐐲𐑌𐐲𐑉𐑆, 𐑄𐐰𐐻 𐑄𐐩 𐑇𐐳𐐼 𐐿𐐱𐑋𐐯𐑌𐑅 𐐲 𐑊𐐩𐐺𐐲𐑉 𐐮𐑌 𐑅𐐻𐑉𐐯𐑍𐑃𐐲𐑌𐐮𐑍 𐑄 𐑁𐐫𐑉𐐻𐐮𐑁𐐮𐐿𐐩𐑇𐐲𐑌𐑆 𐑉𐐵𐑌𐐼 𐐲𐐺𐐵𐐻 𐑄 𐑅𐐮𐐻𐐨 𐐘𐐮𐐼. 𐐈𐑌𐐼 𐐮𐐻 𐐿𐐩𐑋 𐐻𐐭 𐐹𐐰𐑅 𐑄𐐰𐐻 𐐸𐐶𐐯𐑌 𐐸𐐨 𐐸𐐰𐐼 𐑁𐐫𐑉𐐻𐐮𐑁𐐴𐐼 𐑄 𐑅𐐮𐐻𐐨 𐐘𐐮𐐼, 𐐰𐐿𐐫𐑉𐐼𐐮𐑍 𐐻𐐭 𐐸𐐮𐑆 𐐼𐐨𐑆𐐴𐑉𐑆, 𐐸𐐨 𐐿𐐫𐑆𐐼 𐑄𐐰𐐻 𐐸𐐮𐑆 𐐹𐑉𐐮𐑆𐐲𐑌𐐲𐑉𐑆 𐑇𐐳𐐼 𐐺 𐐻𐐩𐐿𐐲𐑌 𐐻𐐭 𐑄 𐑅𐐮𐐻𐐨 𐐒𐐵𐑌𐐻𐐮𐑁𐐳𐑊; 𐐰𐑌𐐼 𐐸𐐨 𐐫𐑊𐑅𐐬 𐑀𐐪𐑉𐐼𐐯𐐼 𐑄𐐰𐐻 𐑅𐐮𐐻𐐨 𐐶𐐮𐑄 𐐰𐑌 𐐯𐐿𐑅𐐨𐐼𐐮𐑍𐑊𐐨 𐑅𐐻𐑉𐐫𐑍 𐑁𐐬𐑉𐑅. 𐐈𐑌𐐼 𐐮𐐻 𐐿𐐩𐑋 𐐻𐐭 𐐹𐐰𐑅 𐑄𐐰𐐻 𐑄𐐩 𐐼𐐮𐐼, 𐑌𐐱𐐻𐐶𐐮𐑄𐑅𐐻𐐰𐑌𐐼𐐮𐑍 𐐫𐑊 𐑄 𐐮𐑌𐐻𐑉𐐨𐑀𐑆 𐐱𐑂 𐑄 𐐢𐐩𐑋𐐲𐑌𐐴𐐻𐑅, 𐐿𐐨𐐹 𐐰𐑌𐐼 𐐹𐑉𐐬𐐻𐐯𐐿𐐻 𐐫𐑊 𐑄 𐐹𐑉𐐮𐑆𐐲𐑌𐐲𐑉𐑆 𐐸𐐭𐑋 𐑄𐐩 𐐸𐐰𐐼 𐐻𐐩𐐿𐐲𐑌, 𐐰𐑌𐐼 𐐫𐑊𐑅𐐬 𐑋𐐩𐑌𐐻𐐩𐑌 𐐫𐑊 𐑄 𐑀𐑉𐐵𐑌𐐼 𐐰𐑌𐐼 𐑄 𐐰𐐼𐑂𐐰𐑌𐐻𐐯𐐾 𐐸𐐶𐐮𐐽 𐑄𐐩 𐐸𐐰𐐼 𐑉𐐨-𐐻𐐩𐐿𐐲𐑌. 𐐈𐑌𐐼 𐐮𐐻 𐐿𐐩𐑋 𐐻𐐭 𐐹𐐰𐑅 𐑄𐐰𐐻 𐑄 𐐤𐐨𐑁𐐴𐐻𐑅 𐐺𐐨𐑀𐐰𐑌 𐐰𐑀𐐯𐑌 𐐻𐐭 𐐺 𐑂𐐮𐐿𐐻𐐬𐑉𐐨𐐲𐑅, 𐐰𐑌𐐼 𐐻𐐭 𐑉𐐨𐐿𐑊𐐩𐑋 𐑄𐐩𐑉 𐑉𐐴𐐻𐑅 𐐰𐑌𐐼 𐑄𐐩𐑉 𐐹𐑉𐐮𐑂𐐮𐑊𐐯𐐾𐐯𐑆. 𐐣𐐯𐑌𐐨 𐐻𐐴𐑋𐑆 𐐼𐐮𐐼 𐑄 𐐢𐐩𐑋𐐲𐑌𐐴𐐻𐑅 𐐰𐐻𐐯𐑋𐐹𐐻 𐐻𐐭 𐐯𐑌𐑅𐐲𐑉𐐿𐑊 𐑄𐐯𐑋 𐐲𐐺𐐵𐐻 𐐺𐐴 𐑌𐐴𐐻, 𐐺𐐲𐐻 𐐮𐑌 𐑄𐐨𐑆 𐐰𐐻𐐯𐑋𐐹𐐻𐑅 𐑄𐐩 𐐼𐐮𐐼 𐑊𐐭𐑆 𐑋𐐯𐑌𐐨 𐐹𐑉𐐮𐑆𐐲𐑌𐐲𐑉𐑆. 𐐈𐑌𐐼 𐑋𐐯𐑌𐐨 𐐻𐐴𐑋𐑆 𐐼𐐮𐐼 𐑄𐐩 𐐰𐐻𐐯𐑋𐐹𐐻 𐐻𐐭 𐐰𐐼𐑋𐐮𐑌𐐮𐑅𐐻𐐲𐑉 𐐱𐑂 𐑄𐐩𐑉 𐐶𐐴𐑌 𐐻𐐭 𐑄 𐐤𐐨𐑁𐐴𐐻𐑅, 𐑄𐐰𐐻 𐑄𐐩 𐑋𐐴𐐻 𐐼𐐯𐑅𐐻𐑉𐐦 𐑄𐐯𐑋 𐐶𐐮𐑄 𐐹𐐦𐑆𐐲𐑌 𐐫𐑉 𐐶𐐮𐑄 𐐼𐑉𐐲𐑍𐐿𐐲𐑌𐐯𐑅. 𐐒𐐲𐐻 𐐺𐐨𐐸𐐬𐑊𐐼, 𐑄 𐐤𐐨𐑁𐐴𐐻𐑅 𐐶𐐲𐑉 𐑌𐐱𐐻 𐑅𐑊𐐬 𐐻𐐭 𐑉𐐨𐑋𐐯𐑋𐐺𐐲𐑉 𐑄 𐐢𐐫𐑉𐐼 𐑄𐐩𐑉 𐐘𐐱𐐼, 𐐮𐑌 𐑄𐐮𐑅 𐑄𐐩𐑉 𐐻𐐴𐑋 𐐱𐑂 𐐰𐑁𐑊𐐮𐐿𐑇𐐲𐑌. 𐐜𐐩 𐐿𐐳𐐼 𐑌𐐱𐐻 𐐺 𐐻𐐩𐐿𐐲𐑌 𐐮𐑌 𐑄𐐩𐑉 𐑅𐑌𐐩𐑉𐑆; 𐐷𐐩, 𐑄𐐩 𐐶𐐳𐐼 𐑌𐐱𐐻 𐐹𐐪𐑉𐐻𐐩𐐿 𐐱𐑂 𐑄𐐩𐑉 𐐶𐐴𐑌, 𐑅𐐩𐑂 𐑄𐐩 𐐸𐐰𐐼 𐑁𐐲𐑉𐑅𐐻 𐑀𐐮𐑂𐐲𐑌 𐐮𐐻 𐐻𐐭 𐑅𐐲𐑋 𐐱𐑂 𐑄 𐐢𐐩𐑋𐐲𐑌𐐴𐐻 𐐹𐑉𐐮𐑆𐐲𐑌𐐲𐑉𐑆. 𐐈𐑌𐐼 𐑄𐐩 𐐶𐐲𐑉 𐑄𐐲𐑅 𐐿𐐫𐑇𐐲𐑅 𐑄𐐰𐐻 𐑌𐐬 𐐹𐐦𐑆𐐲𐑌 𐑇𐐳𐐼 𐐺 𐐰𐐼𐑋𐐮𐑌𐐮𐑅𐐻𐐲𐑉𐐼 𐐲𐑋𐐲𐑍 𐑄𐐯𐑋; 𐑁𐐫𐑉 𐐮𐑁 𐑄𐐩𐑉 𐐶𐐴𐑌 𐐶𐐳𐐼 𐐹𐐦𐑆𐐲𐑌 𐐲 𐐢𐐩𐑋𐐲𐑌𐐴𐐻, 𐐮𐐻 𐐶𐐳𐐼 𐐫𐑊𐑅𐐬 𐐹𐐦𐑆𐐲𐑌 𐐲 𐐤𐐨𐑁𐐴𐐻; 𐐰𐑌𐐼 𐑄𐐲𐑅 𐑄𐐩 𐐼𐐮𐐼 𐐻𐑉𐐴 𐐫𐑊 𐑄𐐩𐑉 𐑊𐐮𐐿𐐲𐑉𐑆. 𐐈𐑌𐐼 𐑌𐐵 𐐮𐐻 𐐿𐐩𐑋 𐐻𐐭 𐐹𐐰𐑅 𐑄𐐰𐐻 𐐮𐐻 𐐶𐐱𐑆 𐐯𐐿𐑅𐐹𐐨𐐼𐐨𐐲𐑌𐐻 𐑁𐐫𐑉 𐐣𐐬𐑉𐐬𐑌𐐴 𐐻𐐭 𐑋𐐩𐐿 𐐹𐑉𐐯𐐹𐐲𐑉𐐩𐑇𐐲𐑌𐑆 𐐻𐐭 𐐰𐐻𐐰𐐿 𐑄 𐑅𐐮𐐻𐐨 𐐣𐐬𐑉𐐨𐐰𐑌𐐻𐐲𐑌; 𐑁𐐫𐑉 𐐺𐐨𐐸𐐬𐑊𐐼, 𐑄 𐐢𐐩𐑋𐐲𐑌𐐴𐐻𐑅 𐐸𐐰𐐼, 𐐺𐐴 𐑄𐐩𐑉 𐑊𐐩𐐺𐐲𐑉𐑆, 𐑁𐐫𐑉𐐻𐐮𐑁𐐴𐐼 𐑄 𐑅𐐮𐐻𐐨 𐐣𐐬𐑉𐐨𐐰𐑌𐐻𐐲𐑌, 𐐲𐑌𐐻𐐮𐑊 𐐮𐐻 𐐸𐐰𐐼 𐐺𐐨𐐿𐐲𐑋 𐐰𐑌 𐐯𐐿𐑅𐐨𐐼𐐮𐑍 𐑅𐐻𐑉𐐫𐑍𐐸𐐬𐑊𐐼. 𐐈𐑌𐐼 𐑄𐐩 𐐶𐐲𐑉 𐐿𐐱𐑌𐐻𐐮𐑌𐐷𐐭𐐲𐑊𐐨 𐐺𐑉𐐮𐑍𐐮𐑍 𐑌𐐧 𐑁𐐬𐑉𐑅𐐯𐑆 𐐮𐑌𐐻𐐭 𐑄𐐰𐐻 𐑅𐐮𐐻𐐨, 𐐰𐑌𐐼 𐐫𐑊𐑅𐐬 𐑌𐐧 𐑅𐐲𐐹𐑊𐐴𐑆 𐐱𐑂 𐐹𐑉𐐬𐑂𐐮𐑠𐐲𐑌𐑆. 𐐈𐑌𐐼 𐑄𐐲𐑅 𐐯𐑌𐐼𐐯𐐼 𐑄 𐐻𐐶𐐯𐑌𐐻𐐨 𐐰𐑌𐐼 𐑌𐐴𐑌𐑃 𐐷𐐨𐑉 𐐱𐑂 𐑄 𐑉𐐩𐑌 𐐱𐑂 𐑄 𐐾𐐲𐐾𐐯𐑆 𐐬𐑂𐐲𐑉 𐑄 𐐹𐐨𐐹𐑊 𐐱𐑂 𐐤𐐨𐑁𐐴.

𐐕𐐈𐐑𐐻𐐲𐑉 XXVI.

1. 𐐈𐑌𐐼 𐑌𐐵 𐐮𐐻 𐐿𐐩𐑋 𐐻𐐭 𐐹𐐰𐑅 𐐮𐑌 𐑄 𐐿𐐱𐑋𐐯𐑌𐑅𐑋𐐲𐑌𐐻 𐐱𐑂 𐑄 𐑃𐐲𐑉𐐻𐐨𐐯𐑃 𐐷𐐨𐑉 𐐱𐑂 𐑄 𐑉𐐩𐑌 𐐱𐑂 𐑄 𐐾𐐲𐐾𐐯𐑆, 𐐮𐑌 𐑄 𐑅𐐯𐐿𐐲𐑌𐐼 𐐼𐐩, 𐐮𐑌 𐑄 𐑁𐐲𐑉𐑅𐐻 𐑋𐐲𐑌𐑃, 𐐣𐐬𐑉𐐬𐑌𐐴 𐑉𐐨𐑅𐐨𐑂𐐼 𐐰𐑌 𐐨𐐹𐐮𐑅𐑊 𐑁𐑉𐐱𐑋 𐐐𐐨𐑊𐐩𐑋𐐲𐑌, 𐑅𐐻𐐩𐐻𐐮𐑍 𐑄 𐐰𐑁𐐩𐑉𐑆 𐐱𐑂 𐑄 𐐹𐐨𐐹𐑊 𐐮𐑌 𐑄𐐰𐐻 𐐿𐐶𐐫𐑉𐐻𐐲𐑉 𐐱𐑂 𐑄 𐑊𐐰𐑌𐐼. 𐐈𐑌𐐼 𐑄𐐨𐑆 𐐪𐑉 𐑄 𐐶𐐲𐑉𐐼𐑆 𐐸𐐶𐐮𐐽 𐐸𐐨 𐑉𐐬𐐻, 𐑅𐐩𐐮𐑍, 𐐣𐐴 𐐼𐐨𐑉𐑊𐐨 𐐺𐐨𐑊𐐲𐑂𐐯𐐼 𐐺𐑉𐐲𐑄𐐲𐑉, 𐐣𐐬𐑉𐐬𐑌𐐴, 𐐰𐑆 𐐶𐐯𐑊 𐐮𐑌 𐑄 𐐢𐐫𐑉𐐼 𐐰𐑆 𐐮𐑌 𐑄 𐐻𐑉𐐮𐐺𐐷𐐭𐑊𐐩𐑇𐐲𐑌𐑆 𐐱𐑂 𐐵𐑉 𐐶𐐫𐑉𐑁𐐩𐑉; 𐐺𐐨𐐸𐐬𐑊𐐼, 𐑋𐐴 𐐺𐐨𐑊𐐲𐑂𐐯𐐼 𐐺𐑉𐐲𐑄𐐲𐑉, 𐐌 𐐸𐐰𐑂 𐑅𐐲𐑋𐐸𐐶𐐱𐐻 𐐻𐐭 𐐻𐐯𐑊 𐐷𐐭 𐐿𐐱𐑌𐑅𐐲𐑉𐑌𐐮𐑍 𐐵𐑉 𐐶𐐫𐑉𐑁𐐩𐑉 𐐮𐑌 𐑄𐐮𐑅 𐐹𐐪𐑉𐐻 𐐱𐑂 𐑄 𐑊𐐰𐑌𐐼. 𐐒𐐨𐐸𐐬𐑊𐐼, 𐐻𐐭 𐑃𐐵𐑆𐐲𐑌𐐼 𐐱𐑂 𐑄 𐑅𐐲𐑌𐑆 𐐱𐑂 𐑄𐐬𐑆 𐑋𐐯𐑌 𐐸𐐭𐑋 𐐈𐑋𐐲𐑌 𐐺𐑉𐐫𐐻 𐐼𐐵𐑌 𐐵𐐻 𐐱𐑂 𐑄 𐑊𐐰𐑌𐐼 𐐱𐑂 𐐤𐐨𐑁𐐴. 𐐤𐐵 𐐷 𐐸𐐰𐑂 𐑌𐐬𐑌 𐑄𐐰𐐻 𐑄𐐨𐑆 𐐶𐐲𐑉 𐐼𐐨𐑅𐐯𐑌𐐼𐐲𐑌𐐻𐑅 𐐱𐑂 𐐢𐐩𐑋𐐲𐑌, 𐐸𐐭 𐐶𐐱𐑆 𐑄 𐐯𐑊𐐼𐐯𐑅𐐻 𐑅𐐲𐑌 𐐱𐑂 𐐵𐑉 𐑁𐐪𐑄𐐲𐑉 𐐢𐐨𐐸𐐴. 𐐤𐐵 𐐌 𐑌𐐨𐐼 𐑌𐐱𐐻 𐑉𐐨𐐸𐐲𐑉𐑅 𐐲𐑌𐐻𐐭 𐐷𐐭 𐐿𐐱𐑌𐑅𐐲𐑉𐑌𐐮𐑍 𐑄𐐩𐑉 𐐻𐑉𐐲𐐼𐐮𐑇𐐲𐑌𐑆 𐐫𐑉 𐑄𐐩𐑉 𐐲𐑌𐐺𐐨𐑊𐐨𐑁, 𐑁𐐫𐑉 𐑄𐐵 𐑌𐐬𐐯𐑅𐐻 𐐿𐐱𐑌𐑅𐐲𐑉𐑌𐐮𐑍 𐐫𐑊 𐑄𐐨𐑆 𐑃𐐮𐑍𐑆; 𐑄𐐩𐑉𐑁𐐫𐑉 𐐮𐐻 𐑅𐐲𐑁𐐴𐑅𐐯𐑃 𐑋𐐨 𐑄𐐰𐐻 𐐌 𐐻𐐯𐑊 𐐷𐐭 𐑄𐐰𐐻 𐐻𐐭 𐑃𐐵𐑆𐐲𐑌𐐼 𐐱𐑂 𐑄𐐨𐑆 𐐷𐐲𐑍 𐑋𐐯𐑌 𐐸𐐰𐑂 𐐻𐐩𐐿𐐲𐑌 𐑄𐐩𐑉 𐐶𐐯𐐹𐐲𐑌𐑆 𐐱𐑂 𐐶𐐫𐑉, 𐐰𐑌𐐼 𐐶𐐳𐐼 𐑄𐐰𐐻 𐐌 𐑇𐐳𐐼 𐐺 𐑄𐐩𐑉 𐑊𐐨𐐼𐐲𐑉; 𐐰𐑌𐐼 𐐶𐐨 𐐸𐐰𐑂 𐐿𐐲𐑋 𐑁𐐫𐑉𐑃 𐐻𐐭 𐐼𐐨𐑁𐐯𐑌𐐼 𐐵𐑉 𐐿𐐲𐑌𐐻𐑉𐐨. 𐐈𐑌𐐼 𐑌𐐵 𐐷 𐐫𐑊𐑅𐐬 𐑌𐐬 𐐿𐐱𐑌𐑅𐐲𐑉𐑌𐐮𐑍 𐑄 𐐿𐐲𐑂𐐲𐑌𐐲𐑌𐐻 𐐸𐐶𐐮𐐽 𐑄𐐩𐑉 𐑁𐐪𐑄𐐲𐑉𐑆 𐑋𐐩𐐼, 𐑄𐐰𐐻 𐑄𐐩 𐐶𐐳𐐼 𐑌𐐱𐐻 𐐻𐐩𐐿 𐐲𐐹 𐑄𐐩𐑉 𐐶𐐯𐐹𐐲𐑌𐑆 𐐱𐑂

𐐶𐐫𐑉 𐐲𐑀𐐯𐑌𐑅𐐻 𐑄𐐩𐑉 𐐺𐑉𐐯𐑄𐑉𐐯𐑌 𐐻𐐭 𐑇𐐯𐐼 𐐺𐑊𐐲𐐼. 𐐒𐐲𐐻 𐐮𐑌 𐑄 𐐻𐐶𐐯𐑌𐐻𐐨 𐐰𐑌𐐼 𐑅𐐮𐐿𐑅𐑃 𐐷𐐨𐑉, 𐐸𐐶𐐯𐑌 𐑄𐐩 𐑅𐐫 𐐵𐑉 𐐲𐑁𐑊𐐮𐐿𐑇𐐲𐑌𐑆 𐐰𐑌𐐼 𐐵𐑉 𐐻𐑉𐐮𐐺𐐷𐐭𐑊𐐩𐑇𐐲𐑌𐑆 𐑁𐐫𐑉 𐑄𐐯𐑋, 𐑄𐐩 𐐶𐐲𐑉 𐐲𐐺𐐵𐐻 𐐻𐐭 𐐺𐑉𐐩𐐿 𐑄 𐐿𐐲𐑂𐐯𐑌𐐲𐑌𐐻 𐐸𐐶𐐮𐐽 𐑄𐐩 𐐸𐐰𐐼 𐑋𐐩𐐼, 𐐰𐑌𐐼 𐐻𐐩𐐿 𐐲𐐹 𐑄𐐩𐑉 𐐶𐐯𐐹𐐲𐑌𐑆 𐐲𐑂 𐐶𐐫𐑉 𐐮𐑌 𐐵𐑉 𐐼𐐯𐑁𐐯𐑌𐑅. 𐐒𐐲𐐻 𐐌 𐐶𐐳𐐼 𐑌𐐱𐐻 𐑅𐐲𐑁𐐲𐑉 𐑄𐐯𐑋 𐑄𐐰𐐻 𐑄𐐩 𐑇𐐳𐐼 𐐺𐑉𐐩𐐿 𐑄𐐮𐑅 𐐿𐐲𐑂𐐯𐑌𐐲𐑌𐐻 𐐸𐐶𐐮𐐽 𐑄𐐩 𐐸𐐰𐐼 𐑋𐐩𐐼, 𐑅𐐲𐐹𐐬𐑆𐐮𐑍 𐑄𐐰𐐻 𐐘𐐱𐐼 𐐶𐐳𐐼 𐑅𐐻𐑉𐐯𐑍𐑃𐐲𐑌 𐐲𐑅, 𐐮𐑌𐑅𐐬𐑋𐐲𐐽 𐑄𐐰𐐻 𐐶𐐨 𐑇𐐳𐐼 𐑌𐐱𐐻 𐑅𐐲𐑁𐐲𐑉 𐑋𐐬𐑉 𐐺𐐨𐐿𐐫𐑆 𐐲𐑂 𐑄 𐑁𐐳𐑊𐑁𐐮𐑊𐐮𐑍 𐑄 𐐬𐑃 𐐸𐐶𐐮𐐽 𐑄𐐩 𐐸𐐰𐐼 𐐻𐐩𐐿𐐲𐑌. 𐐒𐐲𐐻 𐐺𐐨𐐸𐐬𐑊𐐼, 𐐸𐐨𐑉 𐐮𐑆 𐐶𐐲𐑌 𐑃𐐮𐑍 𐐮𐑌 𐐸𐐶𐐮𐐽 𐐶𐐨 𐑋𐐩 𐐸𐐰𐑂 𐑀𐑉𐐩𐐻 𐐾𐐱𐐮. 𐐙𐐫𐑉 𐐺𐐨𐐸𐐬𐑊𐐼, 𐐮𐑌 𐑄 𐐻𐐶𐐯𐑌𐐻𐐨 𐐰𐑌𐐼 𐑅𐐮𐐿𐑅𐑃 𐐷𐐨𐑉, 𐐌, 𐐐𐐨𐑊𐐲𐑋𐐲𐑌, 𐐼𐐮𐐼 𐑋𐐪𐑉𐐽 𐐰𐐻 𐑄 𐐸𐐯𐐼 𐐲𐑂 𐑄𐐨𐑆 𐐻𐐭 𐑃𐐵𐑆𐐲𐑌𐐼 𐐷𐐲𐑍 𐑋𐐯𐑌 𐐻𐐭 𐑄 𐑅𐐮𐐻𐐨 𐐲𐑂 𐐖𐐭𐐼𐐨𐐲, 𐐻𐐭 𐐲𐑅𐐮𐑅𐐻 𐐈𐑌𐐻𐐮𐐹𐐲𐑅, 𐐸𐐭𐑋 𐐷𐐨 𐐸𐐰𐐼 𐐲𐐹𐐱𐐮𐑌𐐻𐐯𐐼 𐐲 𐑊𐐨𐐼𐐲𐑉 𐐬𐑂𐐲𐑉 𐑄 𐐹𐐨𐐹𐑊 𐐲𐑂 𐑄𐐰𐐻 𐐹𐐪𐑉𐐻 𐐲𐑂 𐑄 𐑊𐐰𐑌𐐼. 𐐈𐑌𐐼 𐐌 𐐼𐐮𐐼 𐐾𐐱𐐮𐑌 𐑋𐐴 𐐻𐐭 𐑃𐐵𐑆𐐲𐑌𐐼 𐑅𐐲𐑌𐑆, (𐑁𐐫𐑉 𐑄𐐩 𐐪𐑉 𐐶𐐲𐑉𐑄𐐨 𐐻𐐭 𐐺𐐨 𐐿𐐫𐑊𐐼 𐑅𐐲𐑌𐑆,) 𐐻𐐭 𐑄 𐐪𐑉𐑋𐐨 𐐲𐑂 𐐈𐑌𐐻𐐮𐐹𐐲𐑅, 𐐮𐑌 𐐸𐐶𐐮𐐽 𐑅𐐻𐑉𐐯𐑍𐑃 𐐈𐑌𐐻𐐮𐐹𐐲𐑅 𐐼𐐮𐐼 𐑉𐐨𐐾𐐱𐐮𐑅 𐐯𐐿𐑅𐐨𐐼𐐮𐑍𐑊𐐨; 𐑁𐐫𐑉 𐐺𐐨𐐸𐐬𐑊𐐼, 𐐸𐐮𐑆 𐐪𐑉𐑋𐐨 𐐸𐐰𐐼 𐐺𐐮𐑌 𐑉𐐨𐐼𐐷𐐭𐑅𐐼 𐐺𐐴 𐑄 𐐢𐐰𐑋𐐲𐑌𐐴𐐻𐑅, 𐐺𐐨𐐿𐐫𐑆 𐑄𐐩𐑉 𐑁𐐬𐑉𐑅𐐯𐑆 𐐸𐐰𐐼 𐑅𐑊𐐩𐑌 𐐲 𐑂𐐪𐑅𐐻 𐑌𐐲𐑋𐐺𐐲𐑉 𐐲𐑂 𐐵𐑉 𐑋𐐯𐑌, 𐑁𐐫𐑉 𐐸𐐶𐐮𐐽 𐐿𐐫𐑆 𐐶𐐨 𐐸𐐰𐑂 𐐻𐐭 𐑋𐐬𐑉𐑌. 𐐤𐐯𐑂𐐲𐑉𐑄𐐲𐑊𐐯𐑅 𐐶𐐨 𐑋𐐩 𐐿𐐱𐑌𐑅𐐬𐑊 𐐵𐑉𐑅𐐯𐑊𐑂𐑆 𐐮𐑌 𐑄𐐮𐑅 𐐹𐐱𐐮𐑌𐐻, 𐑄𐐰𐐻 𐑄𐐩 𐐸𐐰𐑂 𐐼𐐴𐐼 𐐮𐑌 𐑄 𐐿𐐫𐑆 𐐲𐑂 𐑄𐐩𐑉 𐐿𐐲𐑌𐐻𐑉𐐨 𐐰𐑌𐐼 𐐲𐑂 𐑄𐐩𐑉 𐐘𐐱𐐼, 𐐷𐐩, 𐐰𐑌𐐼 𐑄𐐩 𐐪𐑉 𐐸𐐰𐐹𐐨. 𐐈𐑌𐐼 𐑄 𐐢𐐰𐑋𐐲𐑌𐐴𐐻𐑅 𐐸𐐰𐐼 𐐫𐑊𐑅𐐬 𐑉𐐨𐐻𐐩𐑌𐐼 𐑋𐐯𐑌𐐨 𐐹𐑉𐐮𐑆𐐲𐑌𐐲𐑉𐑆, 𐐫𐑊 𐐲𐑂 𐐸𐐭𐑋 𐐪𐑉 𐐽𐐨𐑁 𐐿𐐰𐐹𐐻𐐩𐑌𐑆, 𐑁𐐫𐑉 𐑌𐐲𐑌 𐐲𐑄𐐲𐑉 𐐸𐐰𐑂 𐑄𐐩 𐑅𐐹𐐩𐑉𐐼 𐐲𐑊𐐴𐑂. 𐐈𐑌𐐼 𐐶𐐨 𐑅𐐲𐐹𐐬𐑆 𐑄𐐰𐐻 𐑄𐐩 𐐪𐑉 𐑌𐐵 𐐰𐐻 𐑄𐐮𐑅 𐐻𐐴𐑋 𐐮𐑌 𐑄 𐑊𐐰𐑌𐐼 𐐲𐑂 𐐤𐐨𐑁𐐴; 𐐮𐐻 𐐮𐑆 𐑅𐐬 𐐮𐑁 𐑄𐐩 𐐪𐑉 𐑌𐐱𐐻 𐑅𐑊𐐩𐑌.

2. 𐐈𐑌𐐼 𐑌𐐵 𐑄𐐨𐑆 𐐪𐑉 𐑄 𐑅𐐮𐐻𐐨𐑆 𐐸𐐶𐐮𐐽 𐑄 𐐢𐐰𐑋𐐲𐑌𐐴𐐻𐑅 𐐸𐐰𐑂 𐐱𐐺𐐻𐐩𐑌𐐼 𐐹𐐲𐑆𐐯𐑇𐐲𐑌 𐐲𐑂 𐐺𐐴 𐑄 𐑇𐐯𐐼𐐮𐑍 𐐲𐑂 𐑄 𐐺𐑊𐐲𐐼 𐐲𐑂 𐑅𐐬 𐑋𐐯𐑌𐐨 𐐲𐑂 𐐵𐑉 𐑂𐐰𐑊𐐷𐐲𐑌𐐻 𐑋𐐯𐑌:—𐐜 𐑊𐐰𐑌𐐼 𐐲𐑂 𐐣𐐰𐑌𐐻𐐴, 𐐫𐑉 𐑄 𐑅𐐮𐐻𐐨 𐐲𐑂 𐐣𐐰𐑌𐐻𐐴, 𐐰𐑌𐐼 𐑄 𐑅𐐮𐐻𐐨 𐐲𐑂 𐐞𐐨𐑆𐑉𐐱𐑋, 𐐰𐑌𐐼 𐑄 𐑅𐐮𐐻𐐨 𐐲𐑂 𐐗𐐷𐐭𐑋𐐯𐑌𐐴, 𐐰𐑌𐐼 𐑄 𐑅𐐮𐐻𐐨 𐐲𐑂 𐐈𐑌𐐻𐐮𐐹𐐰𐑉𐐲. 𐐈𐑌𐐼 𐑄𐐨𐑆 𐐪𐑉 𐑄 𐑅𐐮𐐻𐐨𐑆 𐐸𐐶𐐮𐐽 𐑄𐐩 𐐹𐐲𐑆𐐯𐑅𐐻 𐐸𐐶𐐯𐑌 𐐌 𐐲𐑉𐐴𐑂𐐼 𐐰𐐻 𐑄 𐑅𐐮𐐻𐐨 𐐲𐑂 𐐖𐐭𐐼𐐨𐐲; 𐐰𐑌𐐼 𐐌 𐑁𐐵𐑌𐐼 𐐈𐑌𐐻𐐮𐐹𐐲𐑅 𐐰𐑌𐐼 𐐸𐐮𐑆 𐑋𐐯𐑌 𐐻𐐱𐐮𐑊𐐮𐑍 𐐶𐐮𐑄 𐑄𐐩𐑉 𐑋𐐴𐐻 𐐻𐐭 𐑁𐐫𐑉𐐻𐐮𐑁𐐴 𐑄 𐑅𐐮𐐻𐐨; 𐐷𐐩, 𐐰𐑌𐐼 𐑄𐐩 𐐶𐐲𐑉 𐐼𐐯𐐹𐑉𐐯𐑅𐐻 𐐮𐑌 𐐺𐐱𐐼𐐨 𐐰𐑆 𐐶𐐯𐑊 𐐰𐑆 𐐮𐑌 𐑅𐐹𐐮𐑉𐐮𐐻, 𐑁𐐫𐑉 𐑄𐐩 𐐸𐐰𐐼 𐑁𐐫𐐻 𐑂𐐰𐑊𐐷𐐲𐑌𐐻𐑊𐐨 𐐺𐐴 𐐼𐐩 𐐰𐑌𐐼 𐐻𐐱𐐮𐑊𐐼 𐐺𐐴 𐑌𐐴𐐻 𐐻𐐭 𐑋𐐩𐑌𐐻𐐩𐑌 𐑄𐐩𐑉 𐑅𐐮𐐻𐐨𐑆; 𐐰𐑌𐐼 𐑄𐐲𐑅 𐑄𐐩 𐐸𐐰𐐼 𐑅𐐲𐑁𐐲𐑉𐐼 𐑀𐑉𐐩𐐻 𐐲𐑁𐑊𐐮𐐿𐑇𐐲𐑌𐑆 𐐲𐑂 𐐯𐑂𐐲𐑉𐐨 𐐿𐐴𐑌𐐼. 𐐈𐑌𐐼 𐑌𐐵 𐑄𐐩 𐐶𐐲𐑉 𐐼𐐨𐐻𐐲𐑉𐑋𐐮𐑌𐐼 𐐻𐐭 𐐿𐐱𐑍𐐿𐐲𐑉 𐐮𐑌 𐑄𐐮𐑅 𐐹𐑊𐐩𐑅 𐐫𐑉 𐐼𐐴; 𐑄𐐯𐑉𐑁𐐬𐑉 𐐷𐐭 𐑋𐐩 𐐶𐐯𐑊 𐑅𐐲𐐹𐐬𐑆 𐑄𐐰𐐻 𐑄𐐮𐑅 𐑊𐐮𐐻𐑊 𐑁𐐬𐑉𐑅 𐐸𐐶𐐮𐐽 𐐌 𐐺𐑉𐐫𐐻 𐐶𐐮𐑄 𐑋𐐨, 𐐷𐐩, 𐑄𐐬𐑆 𐑅𐐲𐑌𐑆 𐐲𐑂 𐑋𐐴𐑌, 𐑀𐐩𐑂 𐑄𐐯𐑋 𐑀𐑉𐐩𐐻 𐐸𐐬𐐹𐑅 𐐰𐑌𐐼 𐑋𐐲𐐽 𐐾𐐱𐐮.

3. 𐐈𐑌𐐼 𐑌𐐵 𐐮𐐻 𐐿𐐩𐑋 𐐻𐐭 𐐹𐐰𐑅 𐑄𐐰𐐻 𐐸𐐶𐐯𐑌 𐑄 𐐢𐐰𐑋𐐲𐑌𐐴𐐻𐑅 𐑅𐐫 𐑄𐐰𐐻 𐐈𐑌𐐻𐐮𐐹𐐲𐑅 𐐸𐐰𐐼 𐑉𐐨𐑅𐐨𐑂𐐼 𐐲 𐑀𐑉𐐩𐐻𐐲𐑉 𐑅𐐻𐑉𐐯𐑍𐑃 𐐻𐐭 𐐸𐐮𐑆 𐐪𐑉𐑋𐐨, 𐑄𐐩 𐐶𐐲𐑉 𐐿𐐲𐑋𐐹𐐯𐑊𐐼 𐐺𐐴 𐑄 𐐫𐑉𐐼𐐲𐑉𐑆 𐐲𐑂 𐐈𐑋𐐬𐑉𐐲𐑌 𐐻𐐭 𐑌𐐱𐐻 𐐿𐐲𐑋 𐐲𐑀𐐯𐑌𐑅𐐻 𐑄 𐑅𐐮𐐻𐐨 𐐲𐑂 𐐖𐐭𐐼𐐨𐐲, 𐐫𐑉 𐐲𐑀𐐯𐑌𐑅𐐻 𐐲𐑅, 𐐻𐐭 𐐺𐐰𐐻𐑊. 𐐈𐑌𐐼 𐑄𐐲𐑅 𐐶𐐲𐑉 𐐶𐐨 𐑁𐐩𐑂𐐲𐑉𐐼 𐐲𐑂 𐑄 𐐢𐐫𐑉𐐼; 𐑁𐐫𐑉 𐐸𐐰𐐼 𐑄𐐩 𐐿𐐲𐑋 𐐲𐐹𐐱𐑌 𐐲𐑅 𐐮𐑌 𐑄𐐮𐑅 𐐵𐑉 𐐶𐐨𐐿𐑌𐐯𐑅, 𐑄𐐩 𐑋𐐴𐐻 𐐸𐐰𐑂 𐐹𐐲𐑉𐐸𐐰𐐹𐑅 𐐼𐐯𐑅𐐻𐑉𐐱𐐮𐐼 𐐵𐑉 𐑊𐐮𐐻𐑊 𐐪𐑉𐑋𐐨; 𐐺𐐲𐐻 𐑄𐐲𐑅 𐐶𐐲𐑉 𐐶𐐨 𐐹𐑉𐐨𐑆𐐲𐑉𐑂𐐼. 𐐜𐐩 𐐶𐐲𐑉 𐐿𐐲𐑋𐐰𐑌𐐼𐐯𐐼 𐐺𐐴 𐐈𐑋𐐬𐑉𐐲𐑌 𐐻𐐭 𐑋𐐩𐑌𐐻𐐩𐑌 𐑄𐐬𐑆 𐑅𐐮𐐻𐐨𐑆 𐐸𐐶𐐮𐐽 𐑄𐐩 𐐸𐐰𐐼 𐐻𐐩𐐿𐐲𐑌. 𐐈𐑌𐐼 𐑄𐐲𐑅 𐐯𐑌𐐼𐐯𐐼 𐑄 𐐻𐐶𐐯𐑌𐐻𐐨 𐐰𐑌𐐼 𐑅𐐮𐐿𐑅𐑃 𐐷𐐨𐑉. 𐐈𐑌𐐼 𐐮𐑌 𐑄 𐐿𐐲𐑋𐐯𐑌𐑅𐑋𐐯𐑌𐐻 𐐲𐑂 𐑄 𐐻𐐶𐐯𐑌𐐻𐐨 𐐰𐑌𐐼 𐑅𐐯𐑂𐐲𐑌𐑃 𐐷𐐨𐑉, 𐐶𐐨 𐐸𐐰𐐼 𐐹𐑉𐐨𐐹𐐩𐑉𐐼 𐐵𐑉 𐑅𐐮𐐻𐐨 𐐰𐑌𐐼 𐐵𐑉𐑅𐐯𐑊𐑂𐑆 𐑁𐐫𐑉 𐐼𐐯𐑁𐐯𐑌𐑅. 𐐤𐐵 𐐶𐐨 𐐶𐐲𐑉 𐐼𐐯𐑆𐐴𐑉𐐲𐑅 𐑄𐐰𐐻 𐑄 𐐢𐐰𐑋𐐲𐑌𐐴𐐻𐑅 𐑇𐐳𐐼 𐐿𐐲𐑋 𐐲𐐹𐐱𐑌 𐐲𐑅; 𐑁𐐫𐑉 𐐶𐐨 𐐶𐐲𐑉 𐑌𐐱𐐻 𐐼𐐯𐑆𐐴𐑉𐐲𐑅 𐐻𐐭 𐑋𐐩𐐿 𐐰𐑌 𐐲𐐻𐐰𐐿 𐐲𐐹𐐱𐑌 𐑄𐐯𐑋 𐐮𐑌 𐑄𐐩𐑉 𐑅𐐻𐑉𐐱𐑍𐐸𐐬𐑊𐐼𐑆. 𐐈𐑌𐐼 𐐮𐐻 𐐿𐐩𐑋 𐐻𐐭 𐐹𐐰𐑅 𐑄𐐰𐐻 𐐶𐐨 𐐿𐐯𐐹𐐻 𐑅𐐹𐐴𐑆 𐐵𐐻 𐑉𐐵𐑌𐐼 𐐲𐐺𐐵𐐻, 𐐻𐐭 𐐶𐐱𐐽 𐑄 𐑋𐐭𐑂𐑋𐐯𐑌𐐻𐑅 𐐲𐑂 𐑄 𐐢𐐰𐑋𐐲𐑌𐐴𐐻𐑅, 𐑄𐐰𐐻 𐑄𐐩 𐑋𐐴𐐻 𐑌𐐱𐐻 𐐹𐐰𐑅 𐐲𐑅 𐐺𐐴 𐑌𐐴𐐻 𐑌𐐫𐑉 𐐺𐐴 𐐼𐐩, 𐐻𐐭 𐑋𐐩𐐿 𐐰𐑌 𐐲𐐻𐐰𐐿 𐐲𐐹𐐱𐑌 𐐵𐑉 𐐲𐑄𐐲𐑉 𐑅𐐮𐐻𐐨𐑆 𐐸𐐶𐐮𐐽 𐐶𐐲𐑉 𐐱𐑌 𐑄 𐑌𐐫𐑉𐑃𐐶𐐲𐑉𐐼; 𐑁𐐫𐑉 𐐶𐐨 𐑌𐐭 𐐮𐑌 𐑄𐐬𐑆 𐑅𐐮𐐻𐐨𐑆 𐑄𐐩 𐐶𐐲𐑉 𐑌𐐱𐐻 𐑅𐐲𐑁𐐮𐑇𐐲𐑌𐐻𐑊𐐨 𐑅𐐻𐑉𐐱𐑍 𐐻𐐭 𐑋𐐨𐐻 𐑄𐐯𐑋; 𐑄𐐯𐑉𐑁𐐬𐑉 𐐶𐐨 𐐶𐐲𐑉 𐐼𐐯𐑆𐐴𐑉𐐲𐑅, 𐐮𐑁 𐑄𐐩 𐑇𐐳𐐼 𐐹𐐰𐑅 𐐺𐐴 𐐲𐑅, 𐐻𐐭 𐑁𐐫𐑊 𐐲𐐹𐐱𐑌 𐑄𐐯𐑋 𐐮𐑌 𐑄𐐩𐑉 𐑉𐐨𐑉, 𐐰𐑌𐐼 𐑄𐐲𐑅 𐐺𐑉𐐮𐑍 𐑄𐐯𐑋 𐐲𐐹 𐐮𐑌 𐑄 𐑉𐐨𐑉 𐐰𐐻 𐑄 𐑅𐐩𐑋 𐐻𐐴𐑋 𐑄𐐩 𐐶𐐲𐑉 𐑋𐐯𐐻

𐐮𐑌 𐑄 𐑁𐑉𐐲𐑌𐐻. 𐐎𐐨 𐑅𐐲𐐹𐐬𐑆𐐼 𐑄𐐰𐐻 𐐶𐐨 𐐿𐐳𐐼 𐐬𐑂𐐲𐑉𐐹𐐵𐐲𐑉 𐑄𐐯𐑋; 𐐺𐐲𐐻 𐐺𐐨𐐸𐐬𐑊𐐼, 𐐶𐐨 𐐶𐐲𐑉 𐐼𐐮𐑅𐐲𐐹𐐱𐐮𐑌𐐻𐐯𐐼 𐐮𐑌 𐑄𐐮𐑅 𐐵𐑉 𐐼𐐨𐑆𐐴𐑉. 𐐜𐐩 𐐼𐐲𐑉𐑅𐐻 𐑌𐐱𐐻 𐐹𐐪𐑅 𐐺𐐴 𐐲𐑅 𐐶𐐮𐑄 𐑄𐐯𐑉 𐐸𐐬𐑊 𐐪𐑉𐑋𐐨, 𐑌𐐨𐑄𐐲𐑉 𐐼𐐲𐑉𐑅𐐻 𐑄𐐩 𐐶𐐮𐑄 𐐲 𐐹𐐪𐑉𐐻, 𐑊𐐯𐑅𐐻 𐑄𐐩 𐑇𐐳𐐼 𐑌𐐱𐐻 𐐺𐐨 𐑅𐐲𐑁𐐮𐑇𐐲𐑌𐐻𐑊𐐨 𐑅𐐻𐑉𐐱𐑍, 𐐰𐑌𐐼 𐑄𐐩 𐑇𐐳𐐼 𐑁𐐪𐑊. 𐐤𐐨𐑄𐐲𐑉 𐐼𐐲𐑉𐑅𐐻 𐑄𐐩 𐑋𐐪𐑉𐐽 𐐼𐐵𐑌 𐐲𐑀𐐯𐑌𐑅𐐻 𐑄 𐑅𐐮𐐻𐐨 𐐱𐑂 𐐞𐐪𐑉𐐲𐐸𐐯𐑋𐑊𐐲; 𐑌𐐨𐑄𐐲𐑉 𐐼𐐲𐑉𐑅𐐻 𐑄𐐩 𐐿𐑉𐐱𐑅 𐑄 𐐸𐐯𐐼 𐐱𐑂 𐐝𐐴𐐼𐐲𐑌, 𐐬𐑂𐐲𐑉 𐐻𐐭 𐑄 𐑅𐐮𐐻𐐨 𐐱𐑂 𐐤𐐨𐑁𐐴𐐸𐐪. 𐐈𐑌𐐼 𐑄𐐲𐑅, 𐐶𐐮𐑄 𐑄𐐯𐑉 𐑁𐐬𐑉𐑅𐐯𐑆, 𐑄𐐩 𐐶𐐲𐑉 𐐼𐐨𐐻𐐲𐑉𐑋𐐮𐑌𐐼 𐐻𐐭 𐑋𐐩𐑌𐐻𐐩𐑌 𐑄𐐬𐑆 𐑅𐐮𐐻𐐨𐑆 𐐸𐐶𐐮𐐽 𐑄𐐩 𐐸𐐰𐐼 𐐻𐐩𐐿𐐲𐑌.

4. 𐐈𐑌𐐼 𐑌𐐵 𐐮𐐻 𐐿𐐩𐑋 𐐻𐐭 𐐹𐐪𐑅, 𐐮𐑌 𐑄 𐑅𐐯𐐿𐐲𐑌𐐼 𐑋𐐲𐑌𐑃 𐐱𐑂 𐑄𐐮𐑅 𐐷𐐨𐑉, 𐑄𐐯𐑉 𐐶𐐱𐑆 𐐺𐑉𐐫𐐻 𐐲𐑌𐐻𐐭 𐐲𐑅 𐑋𐐯𐑌𐐨 𐐹𐑉𐐬𐑂𐐮𐑈𐐲𐑌𐑆 𐑁𐑉𐐱𐑋 𐑄 𐑁𐐪𐑄𐐲𐑉𐑆 𐐱𐑂 𐑄𐐬𐑆 𐑋𐐴 𐐻𐐭 𐑃𐐵𐑆𐐲𐑌𐐼 𐑅𐐲𐑌𐑆. 𐐈𐑌𐐼 𐐫𐑊𐑅𐐬 𐑄𐐯𐑉 𐐶𐐲𐑉 𐑅𐐯𐑌𐐻 𐐻𐐭 𐑃𐐵𐑆𐐲𐑌𐐼 𐑋𐐯𐑌 𐐲𐑌𐐻𐐭 𐐲𐑅 𐑁𐑉𐐱𐑋 𐑄 𐑊𐐰𐑌𐐼 𐐱𐑂 𐐞𐐪𐑉𐐲𐐸𐐯𐑋𐑊𐐲. 𐐈𐑌𐐼 𐑄𐐲𐑅 𐐶𐐨 𐐶𐐲𐑉 𐐹𐑉𐐨𐐹𐐯𐑉𐐼 𐐶𐐮𐑄 𐐻𐐯𐑌 𐑃𐐵𐑆𐐲𐑌𐐼 𐑋𐐯𐑌, 𐐰𐑌𐐼 𐐹𐑉𐐬𐑂𐐮𐑈𐐲𐑌𐑆 𐑁𐐫𐑉 𐑄𐐯𐑋, 𐐰𐑌𐐼 𐐫𐑊𐑅𐐬 𐑁𐐫𐑉 𐑄𐐯𐑉 𐐶𐐴𐑂𐑆 𐐰𐑌𐐼 𐑄𐐯𐑉 𐐽𐐮𐑊𐐼𐑉𐐯𐑌. 𐐈𐑌𐐼 𐑄 𐐢𐐰𐑋𐐲𐑌𐐴𐐻𐑅, 𐑄𐐲𐑅 𐑅𐐨𐐮𐑍 𐐵𐑉 𐑁𐐬𐑉𐑅𐐯𐑆 𐐮𐑌𐐿𐑉𐐨𐑅 𐐼𐐩𐑊𐐨, 𐐰𐑌𐐼 𐐹𐑉𐐬𐑂𐐮𐑈𐐲𐑌𐑆 𐐲𐑉𐐴𐑂 𐑁𐐫𐑉 𐐵𐑉 𐑅𐐲𐐹𐐬𐑉𐐻, 𐑄𐐩 𐐺𐐨𐑀𐐰𐑌 𐐻𐐭 𐐺𐐨 𐑁𐐨𐑉𐑁𐐳𐑊, 𐐰𐑌𐐼 𐐺𐐨𐑀𐐰𐑌 𐐻𐐭 𐑅𐐰𐑊𐐨 𐑁𐐬𐑉𐑃, 𐐮𐑁 𐐮𐐻 𐐶𐐲𐑉 𐐹𐐱𐑅𐐮𐐺𐑊, 𐐻𐐭 𐐹𐐳𐐻 𐐰𐑌 𐐯𐑌𐐼 𐐻𐐭 𐐵𐑉 𐑉𐐨𐑅𐐨𐑂𐐮𐑍 𐐹𐑉𐐬𐑂𐐮𐑈𐐲𐑌𐑆 𐐰𐑌𐐼 𐑅𐐻𐑉𐐯𐑍𐑃. 𐐤𐐵 𐐸𐐶𐐯𐑌 𐐶𐐨 𐑅𐐫 𐑄𐐰𐐻 𐑄 𐐢𐐰𐑋𐐲𐑌𐐴𐐻𐑅 𐐺𐐨𐑀𐐰𐑌 𐐻𐐭 𐑀𐑉𐐬 𐐲𐑌𐐨𐑆𐐨 𐐱𐑌 𐑄𐐮𐑅 𐐶𐐴𐑆, 𐐶𐐨 𐐶𐐲𐑉 𐐼𐐨𐑆𐐴𐑉𐐲𐑅 𐐻𐐭 𐐺𐑉𐐮𐑍 𐐲 𐑅𐐻𐑉𐐰𐐻𐐲𐐾𐐯𐑋 𐐮𐑌𐐻𐐭 𐐯𐑁𐐯𐐿𐐻 𐐲𐐹𐐱𐑌 𐑄𐐯𐑋; 𐑄𐐯𐑉𐑁𐐬𐑉 𐐈𐑌𐐻𐐮𐐹𐐲𐑅 𐐫𐑉𐐼𐐲𐑉𐐼 𐑄𐐰𐐻 𐐌 𐑇𐐳𐐼 𐑋𐐪𐑉𐐽 𐑁𐐬𐑉𐑃 𐐶𐐮𐑄 𐑋𐐴 𐑊𐐮𐐻𐑊 𐑅𐐲𐑌𐑆 𐐻𐐭 𐐲 𐑌𐐩𐐺𐐲𐑉𐐮𐑍 𐑅𐐮𐐻𐐨, 𐐰𐑆 𐐮𐑁 𐐶𐐨 𐐶𐐲𐑉 𐐿𐐰𐑉𐐨𐐮𐑍 𐐹𐑉𐐬𐑂𐐮𐑈𐐲𐑌𐑆 𐐻𐐭 𐐲 𐑌𐐩𐐺𐐲𐑉𐐮𐑍 𐑅𐐮𐐻𐐨. 𐐈𐑌𐐼 𐐶𐐨 𐐶𐐲𐑉 𐐻𐐭 𐑋𐐪𐑉𐐽 𐑌𐐨𐑉 𐑄 𐑅𐐮𐐻𐐨 𐐱𐑂 𐐈𐑌𐐻𐐨𐐹𐐯𐑉𐐲, 𐐰𐑆 𐐮𐑁 𐐶𐐨 𐐶𐐲𐑉 𐑀𐐬𐐮𐑍 𐐻𐐭 𐑄 𐑅𐐮𐐻𐐨 𐐺𐐨𐐷𐐱𐑌𐐼, 𐐮𐑌 𐑄 𐐺𐐫𐑉𐐼𐐲𐑉𐑆 𐐺𐐴 𐑄 𐑅𐐨𐑇𐐬𐑉. 𐐈𐑌𐐼 𐐮𐐻 𐐿𐐩𐑋 𐐻𐐭 𐐹𐐪𐑅 𐑄𐐰𐐻 𐐶𐐨 𐐼𐐮𐐼 𐑋𐐪𐑉𐐽 𐑁𐐬𐑉𐑃, 𐐰𐑆 𐐮𐑁 𐐶𐐮𐑄 𐐵𐑉 𐐹𐑉𐐬𐑂𐐮𐑈𐐲𐑌𐑆, 𐐻𐐭 𐑀𐐬 𐐻𐐭 𐑄𐐰𐐻 𐑅𐐮𐐻𐐨. 𐐈𐑌𐐼 𐐮𐐻 𐐿𐐩𐑋 𐐻𐐭 𐐹𐐪𐑅 𐑄𐐰𐐻 𐐈𐑌𐐻𐐮𐐹𐐲𐑅 𐐼𐐮𐐼 𐑋𐐪𐑉𐐽 𐑁𐐬𐑉𐑃, 𐐶𐐮𐑄 𐐲 𐐹𐐪𐑉𐐻 𐐱𐑂 𐐸𐐮𐑆 𐐪𐑉𐑋𐐨, 𐑊𐐨𐑂𐐮𐑍 𐑄 𐑉𐐨𐑋𐐩𐑌𐐼𐐲𐑉 𐐻𐐭 𐑋𐐩𐑌𐐻𐐩𐑌 𐑄 𐑅𐐮𐐻𐐨. 𐐒𐐲𐐻 𐐸𐐨 𐐼𐐮𐐼 𐑌𐐱𐐻 𐑋𐐪𐑉𐐽 𐑁𐐬𐑉𐑃, 𐐲𐑌𐐻𐐮𐑊 𐐌 𐐸𐐰𐐼 𐑀𐐱𐑌 𐑁𐐬𐑉𐑃 𐐶𐐮𐑄 𐑋𐐴 𐑊𐐮𐐻𐑊 𐐪𐑉𐑋𐐨, 𐐰𐑌𐐼 𐐿𐐩𐑋 𐑌𐐨𐑉 𐑄 𐑅𐐮𐐻𐐨 𐐈𐑌𐐻𐐨𐐹𐐯𐑉𐐲. 𐐈𐑌𐐼 𐑌𐐵 𐐮𐑌 𐑄 𐑅𐐮𐐻𐐨 𐐈𐑌𐐻𐐨𐐹𐐯𐑉𐐲 𐐶𐐲𐑉 𐑅𐐻𐐩𐑇𐐲𐑌𐐼 𐑄 𐑅𐐻𐑉𐐱𐑍𐐯𐑅𐐻 𐐪𐑉𐑋𐐨 𐐱𐑂 𐑄 𐐢𐐰𐑋𐐲𐑌𐐴𐐻𐑅; 𐐷𐐩, 𐑄 𐑋𐐬𐑅𐐻 𐑌𐐭𐑋𐐲𐑉𐐲𐑅. 𐐈𐑌𐐼 𐐮𐐻 𐐿𐐩𐑋 𐐻𐐭 𐐹𐐪𐑅 𐑄𐐰𐐻 𐐸𐐶𐐯𐑌 𐑄𐐩 𐐸𐐰𐐼 𐐺𐐮𐑌 𐐮𐑌𐑁𐐫𐑉𐑋𐐼 𐐺𐐴 𐑄𐐯𐑉 𐑅𐐹𐐴𐑆, 𐑄𐐩 𐐿𐐩𐑋 𐑁𐐬𐑉𐑃 𐐶𐐮𐑄 𐑄𐐯𐑉 𐐪𐑉𐑋𐐨, 𐐰𐑌𐐼 𐑋𐐪𐑉𐐽𐐻 𐐲𐑀𐐯𐑌𐑅𐐻 𐐲𐑅.

5. 𐐈𐑌𐐼 𐐮𐐻 𐐿𐐩𐑋 𐐻𐐭 𐐹𐐪𐑅 𐑄𐐰𐐻 𐐶𐐨 𐐼𐐮𐐼 𐑁𐑊𐐨 𐐺𐐨𐑁𐐬𐑉 𐑄𐐯𐑋, 𐑌𐐫𐑉𐑃𐐶𐐲𐑉𐐼. 𐐈𐑌𐐼 𐑄𐐲𐑅 𐐶𐐨 𐐼𐐮𐐼 𐑊𐐨𐐼 𐐲𐐶𐐩 𐑄 𐑋𐐬𐑅𐐻 𐐹𐐵𐐲𐑉𐑁𐐳𐑊 𐐪𐑉𐑋𐐨 𐐱𐑂 𐑄 𐐢𐐰𐑋𐐲𐑌𐐴𐐻𐑅; 𐐷𐐩, 𐐨𐑂𐐲𐑌 𐐻𐐭 𐐲 𐐿𐐱𐑌𐑅𐐮𐐼𐐲𐑉𐐲𐐺𐑊 𐐼𐐮𐑅𐐻𐐲𐑌𐑅, 𐐮𐑌𐑅𐐬𐑋𐐲𐐽 𐑄𐐰𐐻 𐐸𐐶𐐯𐑌 𐑄𐐩 𐑅𐐫 𐑄 𐐪𐑉𐑋𐐨 𐐱𐑂 𐐈𐑌𐐻𐐮𐐹𐐲𐑅 𐐹𐐲𐑉𐑅𐐭𐐮𐑍 𐑄𐐯𐑋, 𐐶𐐮𐑄 𐑄𐐯𐑉 𐑋𐐴𐐻, 𐑄𐐩 𐐼𐐮𐐼 𐑌𐐱𐐻 𐐻𐐲𐑉𐑌 𐐻𐐭 𐑄 𐑉𐐴𐐻 𐑌𐐫𐑉 𐐻𐐭 𐑄 𐑊𐐯𐑁𐐻, 𐐺𐐲𐐻 𐐹𐐲𐑉𐑅𐐭𐐼 𐑄𐐯𐑉 𐑋𐐪𐑉𐐽 𐐮𐑌 𐐲 𐑅𐐻𐑉𐐩𐐻 𐐿𐐬𐑉𐑅 𐐰𐑁𐐻𐐲𐑉 𐐲𐑅; 𐐰𐑌𐐼, 𐐰𐑆 𐐶𐐨 𐑅𐐲𐐹𐐬𐑆, 𐐮𐐻 𐐶𐐱𐑆 𐑄𐐯𐑉 𐐮𐑌𐐻𐐯𐑌𐐻 𐐻𐐭 𐑅𐑊𐐩 𐐲𐑅 𐐺𐐨𐑁𐐬𐑉 𐐈𐑌𐐻𐐮𐐹𐐲𐑅 𐑇𐐳𐐼 𐐬𐑂𐐲𐑉𐐻𐐩𐐿 𐑄𐐯𐑋, 𐐰𐑌𐐼 𐑄𐐮𐑅 𐑄𐐰𐐻 𐑄𐐩 𐑋𐐴𐐻 𐑌𐐱𐐻 𐐺𐐨 𐑅𐐲𐑉𐐵𐑌𐐼𐐯𐐼 𐐺𐐴 𐐵𐑉 𐐹𐐨𐐹𐑊. 𐐈𐑌𐐼 𐑌𐐵 𐐈𐑌𐐻𐐮𐐹𐐲𐑅, 𐐺𐐨𐐸𐐬𐑊𐐼𐐮𐑍 𐐵𐑉 𐐼𐐩𐑌𐐾𐐲𐑉, 𐐼𐐮𐐼 𐑅𐐹𐐨𐐼 𐑄 𐑋𐐪𐑉𐐽 𐐱𐑂 𐐸𐐮𐑆 𐐪𐑉𐑋𐐨. 𐐒𐐲𐐻 𐐺𐐨𐐸𐐬𐑊𐐼, 𐐮𐐻 𐐶𐐱𐑆 𐑌𐐴𐐻; 𐑄𐐯𐑉𐑁𐐬𐑉 𐑄𐐩 𐐼𐐮𐐼 𐑌𐐱𐐻 𐐬𐑂𐐲𐑉𐐻𐐩𐐿 𐐲𐑅, 𐑌𐐨𐑄𐐲𐑉 𐐼𐐮𐐼 𐐈𐑌𐐻𐐮𐐹𐐲𐑅 𐐬𐑂𐐲𐑉𐐻𐐩𐐿 𐑄𐐯𐑋; 𐑄𐐯𐑉𐑁𐐬𐑉 𐐶𐐨 𐐼𐐮𐐼 𐐿𐐰𐑋𐐹 𐑁𐐫𐑉 𐑄 𐑌𐐴𐐻.

6. 𐐈𐑌𐐼 𐐮𐐻 𐐿𐐩𐑋 𐐻𐐭 𐐹𐐪𐑅 𐑄𐐰𐐻 𐐺𐐨𐑁𐐬𐑉 𐑄 𐐼𐐫𐑌 𐐱𐑂 𐑄 𐑋𐐫𐑉𐑌𐐮𐑍, 𐐺𐐨𐐸𐐬𐑊𐐼, 𐑄 𐐢𐐰𐑋𐐲𐑌𐐴𐐻𐑅 𐐶𐐲𐑉 𐐹𐐲𐑉𐑅𐐭𐐮𐑍 𐐲𐑅. 𐐤𐐵 𐐶𐐨 𐐶𐐲𐑉 𐑌𐐱𐐻 𐑅𐐲𐑁𐐮𐑇𐐲𐑌𐐻𐑊𐐨 𐑅𐐻𐑉𐐱𐑍 𐐻𐐭 𐐿𐐱𐑌𐐻𐐯𐑌𐐼 𐐶𐐮𐑄 𐑄𐐯𐑋; 𐐷𐐩, 𐐌 𐐶𐐳𐐼 𐑌𐐱𐐻 𐑅𐐲𐑁𐐲𐑉 𐑄𐐰𐐻 𐑋𐐴 𐑊𐐮𐐻𐑊 𐑅𐐲𐑌𐑆 𐑇𐐳𐐼 𐑁𐐪𐑊 𐐮𐑌𐐻𐐭 𐑄𐐯𐑉 𐐸𐐰𐑌𐐼𐑆; 𐑄𐐯𐑉𐑁𐐬𐑉 𐐶𐐨 𐐼𐐮𐐼 𐐿𐐱𐑌𐐻𐐮𐑌𐐷𐐭 𐐵𐑉 𐑋𐐪𐑉𐐽, 𐐰𐑌𐐼 𐐶𐐨 𐐻𐐳𐐿 𐐵𐑉 𐑋𐐪𐑉𐐽 𐐮𐑌𐐻𐐭 𐑄 𐐶𐐮𐑊𐐼𐐲𐑉𐑌𐐯𐑅. 𐐤𐐵 𐑄𐐩 𐐼𐐲𐑉𐑅𐐻 𐑌𐐱𐐻 𐐻𐐲𐑉𐑌 𐐻𐐭 𐑄 𐑉𐐴𐐻 𐑌𐐫𐑉 𐐻𐐭 𐑄 𐑊𐐯𐑁𐐻, 𐑊𐐯𐑅𐐻 𐑄𐐩 𐑇𐐳𐐼 𐐺𐐨 𐑅𐐲𐑉𐐵𐑌𐐼𐐯𐐼; 𐑌𐐨𐑄𐐲𐑉 𐐶𐐳𐐼 𐐌 𐐻𐐲𐑉𐑌 𐐻𐐭 𐑄 𐑉𐐴𐐻 𐑌𐐫𐑉 𐐻𐐭 𐑄 𐑊𐐯𐑁𐐻, 𐑊𐐯𐑅𐐻 𐑄𐐩 𐑇𐐳𐐼 𐐬𐑂𐐲𐑉𐐻𐐩𐐿 𐑋𐐨, 𐐰𐑌𐐼 𐐶𐐨 𐐿𐐳𐐼 𐑌𐐱𐐻 𐑅𐐻𐐰𐑌𐐼 𐐲𐑀𐐯𐑌𐑅𐐻 𐑄𐐯𐑋, 𐐺𐐲𐐻 𐐺𐐨 𐑅𐑊𐐩𐑌, 𐐰𐑌𐐼 𐑄𐐩 𐐶𐐳𐐼 𐑋𐐩𐐿 𐑄𐐯𐑉 𐐯𐑅𐐿𐐩𐐹; 𐐰𐑌𐐼 𐑄𐐲𐑅 𐐶𐐨 𐐼𐐮𐐼 𐑁𐑊𐐨 𐐫𐑊 𐑄𐐰𐐻 𐐼𐐩 𐐮𐑌𐐻𐐭 𐑄 𐐶𐐮𐑊𐐼𐐲𐑉𐑌𐐯𐑅, 𐐨𐑂𐐲𐑌 𐐲𐑌𐐻𐐮𐑊 𐐮𐐻 𐐶𐐱𐑆 𐐼𐐪𐑉𐐿.

7. 𐐈𐑌𐐼 𐐮𐐻 𐐿𐐩𐑋 𐐻𐐭 𐐹𐐰𐑅 𐑄𐐰𐐻 𐐲𐑀𐐯𐑌 𐐸𐐶𐐯𐑌 𐑄 𐑊𐐴𐐻 𐐱𐑂 𐑄 𐑋𐐱𐑉𐐬 𐐿𐐩𐑋, 𐐶𐐨 𐑅𐐫 𐑄 𐐢𐐩𐑋𐐲𐑌𐐴𐐻𐑅 𐐲𐐹𐐱𐑌 𐐲𐑅, 𐐰𐑌𐐼 𐐶𐐨 𐐼𐐮𐐼 𐑁𐑊𐐨 𐐺𐐨𐑁𐐬𐑉 𐑄𐐯𐑋. 𐐒𐐲𐐻 𐐮𐐻 𐐿𐐩𐑋 𐐻𐐭 𐐹𐐰𐑅 𐑄𐐰𐐻 𐑄𐐩 𐐼𐐮𐐼 𐑌𐐱𐐻 𐐹𐐲𐑉𐑅𐐭 𐐲𐑅 𐑁𐐪𐑉, 𐐺𐐨𐑁𐐬𐑉 𐑄𐐩 𐐸𐐫𐑊𐐻𐐯𐐼; 𐐰𐑌𐐼 𐐮𐐻 𐐶𐐱𐑆 𐐮𐑌 𐑄 𐑋𐐫𐑉𐑌𐐮𐑍 𐐱𐑂 𐑄 𐑃𐐲𐑉𐐼 𐐼𐐩 𐐱𐑂 𐑄 𐑅𐐯𐑂𐐲𐑌𐑃 𐑋𐐲𐑌𐑃. 𐐈𐑌𐐼 𐑌𐐵 𐐸𐐶𐐯𐑄𐐲𐑉 𐑄𐐩 𐐶𐐲𐑉 𐐬𐑂𐐲𐑉𐐻𐐩𐐿𐐲𐑌 𐐺𐐴 𐐈𐑌𐐻𐐮𐐹𐐲𐑅, 𐐶𐐨 𐑌𐐭 𐑌𐐱𐐻, 𐐺𐐲𐐻 𐐌 𐑅𐐯𐐼 𐐲𐑌𐐻𐐭 𐑋𐐴 𐑋𐐯𐑌, 𐐒𐐨𐐸𐐬𐑊𐐼, 𐐶𐐨 𐑌𐐬 𐑌𐐱𐐻 𐐺𐐲𐐻 𐑄𐐩 𐐸𐐰𐑂 𐐸𐐫𐑊𐐻𐐯𐐼 𐑁𐐫𐑉 𐑄 𐐹𐐲𐑉𐐹𐐲𐑅 𐑄𐐰𐐻 𐐶𐐨 𐑇𐐳𐐼 𐐿𐐲𐑋 𐐲𐑀𐐯𐑌𐑅𐐻 𐑄𐐯𐑋, 𐑄𐐰𐐻 𐑄𐐩 𐑋𐐴𐐻 𐐿𐐰𐐽 𐐲𐑅 𐐮𐑌 𐑄𐐩𐑉 𐑅𐑌𐐩𐑉; 𐑄𐐩𐑉𐑁𐐫𐑉 𐐸𐐶𐐱𐐻 𐑅𐐩 𐐷𐐨, 𐑋𐐴 𐑅𐐲𐑌𐑆, 𐐶𐐮𐑊 𐐷𐐨 𐑀𐐬 𐐲𐑀𐐯𐑌𐑅𐐻 𐑄𐐯𐑋 𐐻𐐭 𐐺𐐰𐐻𐑊? 𐐈𐑌𐐼 𐑌𐐵 𐐌 𐑅𐐩 𐐲𐑌𐐻𐐭 𐐷𐐭, 𐑋𐐴 𐐺𐐨𐑊𐐲𐑂𐐯𐐼 𐐺𐑉𐐲𐑄𐐲𐑉 𐐣𐐬𐑉𐐬𐑌𐐴, 𐑄𐐰𐐻 𐑌𐐯𐑂𐐲𐑉 𐐸𐐰𐐼 𐐌 𐑅𐐨𐑌 𐑅𐐬 𐑀𐑉𐐩𐐻 𐐿𐐲𐑉𐐲𐐾, 𐑌𐐩, 𐑌𐐱𐐻 𐐲𐑋𐐲𐑍𐑅𐐻 𐐫𐑊 𐑄 𐐤𐐨𐑁𐐴𐐻𐑅. 𐐙𐐫𐑉 𐐰𐑆 𐐌 𐐸𐐰𐐼 𐐯𐑂𐐲𐑉 𐐿𐐫𐑊𐐼 𐑄𐐯𐑋 𐑋𐐴 𐑅𐐲𐑌𐑆, (𐑁𐐫𐑉 𐑄𐐩 𐐶𐐲𐑉 𐐫𐑊 𐐱𐑂 𐑄𐐯𐑋 𐑂𐐯𐑉𐐨 𐐷𐐲𐑍,) 𐐨𐑂𐐲𐑌 𐑅𐐬 𐑄𐐩 𐑅𐐯𐐼 𐐲𐑌𐐻𐐭 𐑋𐐨, 𐐙𐐪𐑄𐐲𐑉, 𐐺𐐨𐐸𐐬𐑊𐐼 𐐵𐑉 𐐘𐐱𐐼 𐐮𐑆 𐐶𐐮𐑄 𐐲𐑅, 𐐰𐑌𐐼 𐐸𐐨 𐐶𐐮𐑊 𐑌𐐱𐐻 𐑅𐐲𐑁𐐲𐑉 𐑄𐐰𐐻 𐐶𐐨 𐑇𐐰𐑊 𐑁𐐫𐑊; 𐑄𐐯𐑌 𐑊𐐯𐐻 𐐲𐑅 𐑀𐐬 𐑁𐐬𐑉𐑃; 𐐶𐐨 𐐶𐐳𐐼 𐑌𐐱𐐻 𐑅𐑊𐐩 𐐵𐑉 𐐺𐑉𐐯𐑄𐑉𐐯𐑌, 𐐮𐑁 𐑄𐐩 𐐶𐐳𐐼 𐑊𐐯𐐻 𐐲𐑅 𐐰𐑊𐐬𐑌; 𐑄𐐩𐑉𐑁𐐫𐑉 𐑊𐐯𐐻 𐐲𐑅 𐑀𐐬, 𐑊𐐯𐑅𐐻 𐑄𐐩 𐑇𐐳𐐼 𐐬𐑂𐐲𐑉𐐹𐐵𐐲𐑉 𐑄 𐐪𐑉𐑋𐐨 𐐱𐑂 𐐈𐑌𐐻𐐮𐐹𐐲𐑅. 𐐤𐐵 𐑄𐐩 𐑌𐐯𐑂𐐲𐑉 𐐸𐐰𐐼 𐑁𐐫𐐻, 𐐷𐐯𐐻 𐑄𐐩 𐐼𐐮𐐼 𐑌𐐱𐐻 𐑁𐐨𐑉 𐐼𐐯𐑃; 𐐰𐑌𐐼 𐑄𐐩 𐐼𐐮𐐼 𐑃𐐮𐑍𐐿 𐑋𐐬𐑉 𐐲𐐹𐐱𐑌 𐑄 𐑊𐐮𐐺𐐲𐑉𐐻𐐨 𐐱𐑂 𐑄𐐩𐑉 𐑁𐐪𐑄𐐲𐑉𐑆 𐑄𐐰𐑌 𐑄𐐩 𐐼𐐮𐐼 𐐲𐐹𐐱𐑌 𐑄𐐩𐑉 𐑊𐐴𐑂𐑆; 𐐷𐐩, 𐑄𐐩 𐐸𐐰𐐼 𐐺𐐮𐑌 𐐻𐐫𐐻 𐐺𐐴 𐑄𐐩𐑉 𐑋𐐲𐑄𐐲𐑉𐑆, 𐑄𐐰𐐻 𐐮𐑁 𐑄𐐩 𐐼𐐮𐐼 𐑌𐐱𐐻 𐐼𐐵𐐻, 𐐘𐐱𐐼 𐐶𐐳𐐼 𐐼𐐮𐑊𐐮𐑂𐐲𐑉 𐑄𐐯𐑋. 𐐈𐑌𐐼 𐑄𐐩 𐑉𐐨𐐸𐐲𐑉𐑅𐐻 𐐲𐑌𐐻𐐭 𐑋𐐨 𐑄 𐐶𐐲𐑉𐐼𐑆 𐐱𐑂 𐑄𐐩𐑉 𐑋𐐲𐑄𐐲𐑉𐑆, 𐑅𐐩𐐮𐑍, 𐐎𐐨 𐐼𐐭 𐑌𐐱𐐻 𐐼𐐵𐐻 𐐵𐑉 𐑋𐐲𐑄𐐲𐑉𐑆 𐑌𐐭 𐐮𐐻.

8. 𐐈𐑌𐐼 𐐮𐐻 𐐿𐐩𐑋 𐐻𐐭 𐐹𐐰𐑅 𐑄𐐰𐐻 𐐌 𐐼𐐮𐐼 𐑉𐐨𐐻𐐲𐑉𐑌 𐐶𐐮𐑄 𐑋𐐴 𐐻𐐭 𐑃𐐵𐑆𐐲𐑌𐐼, 𐐲𐑀𐐯𐑌𐑅𐐻 𐑄𐐨𐑆 𐐢𐐩𐑋𐐲𐑌𐐴𐐻𐑅 𐐸𐐭 𐐸𐐰𐐼 𐐹𐐲𐑉𐑅𐐭𐐼 𐐲𐑅. 𐐈𐑌𐐼 𐑌𐐵 𐐺𐐨𐐸𐐬𐑊𐐼, 𐑄 𐐪𐑉𐑋𐐨𐑆 𐐱𐑂 𐐈𐑌𐐻𐐮𐐹𐐲𐑅 𐐸𐐰𐐼 𐐬𐑂𐐲𐑉𐐻𐐩𐐿𐐲𐑌 𐑄𐐯𐑋, 𐐰𐑌𐐼 𐐲 𐐻𐐯𐑉𐐲𐐺𐑊 𐐺𐐰𐐻𐑊 𐐸𐐰𐐼 𐐿𐐱𐑋𐐯𐑌𐑅𐐻. 𐐜 𐐪𐑉𐑋𐐨 𐐱𐑂 𐐈𐑌𐐻𐐮𐐹𐐲𐑅 𐐺𐐨𐐮𐑍 𐐶𐐨𐑉𐐨, 𐐺𐐨𐐿𐐫𐑆 𐐱𐑂 𐑄𐐩𐑉 𐑊𐐱𐑍 𐑋𐐪𐑉𐐽 𐐮𐑌 𐑅𐐬 𐑇𐐫𐑉𐐻 𐐲 𐑅𐐹𐐩𐑅 𐐱𐑂 𐐻𐐴𐑋, 𐐶𐐲𐑉 𐐲𐐺𐐵𐐻 𐐻𐐭 𐑁𐐫𐑊 𐐮𐑌𐐻𐐭 𐑄 𐐸𐐰𐑌𐐼𐑆 𐐱𐑂 𐑄 𐐢𐐩𐑋𐐲𐑌𐐴𐐻𐑅; 𐐰𐑌𐐼 𐐸𐐰𐐼 𐐌 𐑌𐐱𐐻 𐑉𐐨𐐻𐐲𐑉𐑌𐐼 𐐶𐐮𐑄 𐑋𐐴 𐐻𐐭 𐑃𐐵𐑆𐐲𐑌𐐼 𐑄𐐩 𐐶𐐳𐐼 𐐸𐐰𐑂 𐐱𐐺𐐻𐐩𐑌𐐼 𐑄𐐩𐑉 𐐹𐐲𐑉𐐹𐐲𐑅. 𐐙𐐫𐑉 𐐈𐑌𐐻𐐮𐐹𐐲𐑅 𐐸𐐰𐐼 𐑁𐐫𐑊𐐲𐑌 𐐺𐐴 𐑄 𐑅𐐬𐑉𐐼, 𐐰𐑌𐐼 𐑋𐐯𐑌𐐨 𐐱𐑂 𐐸𐐮𐑆 𐑊𐐨𐐼𐐲𐑉𐑆, 𐐺𐐨𐐿𐐫𐑆 𐐱𐑂 𐑄𐐩𐑉 𐐶𐐨𐑉𐐨𐑌𐐯𐑅, 𐐸𐐶𐐮𐐽 𐐶𐐱𐑆 𐐱𐐿𐐩𐑈𐐲𐑌𐐼 𐐺𐐴 𐑄 𐑅𐐹𐐨𐐼 𐐱𐑂 𐑄𐐩𐑉 𐑋𐐪𐑉𐐽; 𐑄𐐩𐑉𐑁𐐫𐑉 𐑄 𐑋𐐯𐑌 𐐱𐑂 𐐈𐑌𐐻𐐮𐐹𐐲𐑅 𐐺𐐨𐐮𐑍 𐐿𐐱𐑌𐑁𐐷𐐭𐑆𐐼, 𐐺𐐨𐐿𐐫𐑆 𐐱𐑂 𐑄 𐑁𐐫𐑊 𐐱𐑂 𐑄𐐩𐑉 𐑊𐐨𐐼𐐲𐑉𐑆, 𐐺𐐯𐑀𐐰𐑌 𐐻𐐭 𐑀𐐮𐑂 𐐶𐐩 𐐺𐐨𐑁𐐬𐑉 𐑄 𐐢𐐩𐑋𐐲𐑌𐐴𐐻𐑅.

9. 𐐈𐑌𐐼 𐐮𐐻 𐐿𐐩𐑋 𐐻𐐭 𐐹𐐰𐑅 𐑄𐐰𐐻 𐑄 𐐢𐐩𐑋𐐲𐑌𐐴𐐻𐑅 𐐻𐐳𐐿 𐐿𐐲𐑉𐐲𐐾, 𐐰𐑌𐐼 𐐺𐐯𐑀𐐰𐑌 𐐻𐐭 𐐹𐐲𐑉𐑅𐐭 𐑄𐐯𐑋; 𐐰𐑌𐐼 𐑄𐐲𐑅 𐐶𐐲𐑉 𐑄 𐐢𐐩𐑋𐐲𐑌𐐴𐐻𐑅 𐐹𐐲𐑉𐑅𐐭𐐮𐑍 𐑄𐐯𐑋 𐐶𐐮𐑄 𐑀𐑉𐐩𐐻 𐑂𐐮𐑀𐐲𐑉 𐐸𐐶𐐯𐑌 𐐐𐐨𐑊𐐲𐑋𐐲𐑌 𐐿𐐩𐑋 𐐲𐐹𐐱𐑌 𐑄𐐩𐑉 𐑉𐐨𐑉 𐐶𐐮𐑄 𐐸𐐮𐑆 𐐻𐐭 𐑃𐐵𐑆𐐲𐑌𐐼, 𐐰𐑌𐐼 𐐺𐐯𐑀𐐰𐑌 𐐻𐐭 𐑅𐑊𐐩 𐑄𐐯𐑋 𐐯𐐿𐑅𐐨𐐼𐐮𐑍𐑊𐐨, 𐐮𐑌𐑅𐐬𐑋𐐲𐐽 𐑄𐐰𐐻 𐑄 𐐸𐐬𐑊 𐐪𐑉𐑋𐐨 𐐱𐑂 𐑄 𐐢𐐩𐑋𐐲𐑌𐐴𐐻𐑅 𐐸𐐫𐑊𐐻𐐯𐐼, 𐐰𐑌𐐼 𐐻𐐲𐑉𐑌𐐼 𐐲𐐹𐐱𐑌 𐐐𐐨𐑊𐐲𐑋𐐲𐑌. 𐐤𐐵 𐐸𐐶𐐯𐑌 𐑄 𐐹𐐨𐐹𐑊 𐐱𐑂 𐐈𐑌𐐻𐐮𐐹𐐲𐑅 𐑅𐐫 𐑄𐐰𐐻 𐑄 𐐢𐐩𐑋𐐲𐑌𐐴𐐻𐑅 𐐸𐐰𐐼 𐐻𐐲𐑉𐑌𐐼 𐑄𐐯𐑋 𐐲𐐺𐐵𐐻, 𐑄𐐩 𐑀𐐰𐑄𐐲𐑉𐐼 𐐻𐐭𐑀𐐯𐑄𐐲𐑉 𐑄𐐩𐑉 𐑋𐐯𐑌, 𐐰𐑌𐐼 𐐿𐐩𐑋 𐐲𐑀𐐯𐑌 𐐲𐐹𐐱𐑌 𐑄 𐑉𐐨𐑉 𐐱𐑂 𐑄 𐐢𐐩𐑋𐐲𐑌𐐴𐐻𐑅.

10. 𐐈𐑌𐐼 𐑌𐐵 𐐮𐐻 𐐿𐐩𐑋 𐐻𐐭 𐐹𐐰𐑅 𐑄𐐰𐐻 𐐶𐐨, 𐑄 𐐹𐐨𐐹𐑊 𐐱𐑂 𐐤𐐨𐑁𐐴, 𐑄 𐐹𐐨𐐹𐑊 𐐱𐑂 𐐈𐑌𐐻𐐮𐐹𐐲𐑅, 𐐰𐑌𐐼 𐐌 𐐶𐐮𐑄 𐑋𐐴 𐐻𐐭 𐑃𐐵𐑆𐐲𐑌𐐼, 𐐼𐐮𐐼 𐑅𐐲𐑉𐐵𐑌𐐼 𐑄 𐐢𐐩𐑋𐐲𐑌𐐴𐐻𐑅, 𐐰𐑌𐐼 𐐼𐐮𐐼 𐑅𐑊𐐩 𐑄𐐯𐑋; 𐐷𐐩, 𐐮𐑌𐑅𐐬𐑋𐐲𐐽 𐑄𐐰𐐻 𐑄𐐩 𐐶𐐲𐑉 𐐿𐐱𐑋𐐹𐐯𐑊𐐼 𐐻𐐭 𐐼𐐮𐑊𐐮𐑂𐐲𐑉 𐐲𐐹 𐑄𐐩𐑉 𐐶𐐯𐐹𐐲𐑌𐑆 𐐱𐑂 𐐶𐐫𐑉, 𐐰𐑌𐐼 𐐫𐑊𐑅𐐬 𐑄𐐯𐑋𐑅𐐯𐑊𐑂𐑆 𐐰𐑆 𐐹𐑉𐐮𐑆𐐲𐑌𐐲𐑉𐑆 𐐱𐑂 𐐶𐐫𐑉.

11. 𐐈𐑌𐐼 𐑌𐐵 𐐮𐐻 𐐿𐐩𐑋 𐐻𐐭 𐐹𐐰𐑅 𐑄𐐰𐐻 𐐸𐐶𐐯𐑌 𐑄𐐩 𐐸𐐰𐐼 𐑅𐐲𐑉𐐯𐑌𐐼𐐲𐑉𐐼 𐑄𐐯𐑋𐑅𐐯𐑊𐑂𐑆 𐐲𐐹 𐐲𐑌𐐻𐐭 𐐲𐑅, 𐐺𐐨𐐸𐐬𐑊𐐼 𐐌 𐑌𐐲𐑋𐐺𐐲𐑉𐐼 𐑄𐐬𐑆 𐐷𐐲𐑍 𐑋𐐯𐑌 𐐸𐐭 𐐸𐐰𐐼 𐑁𐐫𐐻 𐐶𐐮𐑄 𐑋𐐨, 𐑁𐐨𐑉𐐮𐑍 𐑊𐐯𐑅𐐻 𐑄𐐩𐑉 𐐶𐐲𐑉 𐑋𐐯𐑌𐐨 𐐱𐑂 𐑄𐐯𐑋 𐑅𐑊𐐩𐑌. 𐐒𐐲𐐻 𐐺𐐨𐐸𐐬𐑊𐐼, 𐐻𐐭 𐑋𐐴 𐑀𐑉𐐩𐐻 𐐾𐐱𐐴, 𐑄𐐩𐑉 𐐸𐐰𐐼 𐑌𐐱𐐻 𐐶𐐲𐑌 𐑅𐐬𐑊 𐐱𐑂 𐑄𐐯𐑋 𐑁𐐫𐑊𐐲𐑌 𐐻𐐭 𐑄 𐐲𐑉𐑃; 𐐷𐐩, 𐐰𐑌𐐼 𐑄𐐩 𐐸𐐰𐐼 𐑁𐐫𐐻 𐐰𐑆 𐐮𐑁 𐐶𐐮𐑄 𐑄 𐑅𐐻𐑉𐐯𐑍𐑃 𐐱𐑂 𐐘𐐱𐐼; 𐐷𐐩, 𐑌𐐯𐑂𐐲𐑉 𐐶𐐲𐑉 𐑋𐐯𐑌 𐑌𐐬𐑌 𐐻𐐭 𐐸𐐰𐑂 𐑁𐐫𐐻 𐐶𐐮𐑄 𐑅𐐲𐐽 𐑋𐐮𐑉𐐰𐐿𐐷𐐲𐑊𐐲𐑅 𐑅𐐻𐑉𐐯𐑍𐑃; 𐐰𐑌𐐼 𐐶𐐮𐑄 𐑅𐐲𐐽 𐑋𐐴𐐻𐐨 𐐹𐐵𐐲𐑉 𐐼𐐮𐐼 𐑄𐐩 𐑁𐐫𐑊

𐐲𐐹𐐱𐑌 𐑄 𐐢𐐰𐑋𐐲𐑌𐐴𐐻𐑅, 𐑄𐐰𐐻 𐑄𐐩 𐐼𐐮𐐼 𐑁𐑉𐐴𐐻𐑌 𐑄𐐯𐑋; 𐐰𐑌𐐼 𐑁𐐫𐑉 𐑄𐐮𐑅 𐐿𐐫𐑆 𐐼𐐮𐐼 𐑄 𐐢𐐰𐑋𐐲𐑌𐐴𐐻𐑅 𐐼𐐯𐑊𐐮𐑂𐐲𐑉 𐑄𐐯𐑋𐑅𐐯𐑊𐑂𐑆 𐐲𐐹 𐐰𐑆 𐐹𐑉𐐮𐑆𐑌𐐲𐑉𐑆 𐐱𐑂 𐐶𐐫𐑉. 𐐈𐑌𐐼 𐐰𐑆 𐐶𐐨 𐐸𐐰𐐼 𐑌𐐬 𐐹𐑊𐐩𐑅 𐑁𐐫𐑉 𐐵𐑉 𐐹𐑉𐐮𐑆𐑌𐐲𐑉𐑆, 𐑄𐐰𐐻 𐐶𐐨 𐐿𐐳𐐼 𐑀𐐪𐑉𐐼 𐑄𐐯𐑋 𐐻𐐭 𐐿𐐨𐐹 𐑄𐐯𐑋 𐑁𐑉𐐱𐑋 𐑄 𐐪𐑉𐑋𐐨𐑆 𐐱𐑂 𐑄 𐐢𐐰𐑋𐐲𐑌𐐴𐐻𐑅, 𐑄𐐯𐑉𐑁𐐬𐑉 𐐶𐐨 𐑅𐐯𐑌𐐻 𐑄𐐯𐑋 𐐻𐐭 𐑄 𐑊𐐰𐑌𐐼 𐐱𐑂 𐐞𐐩𐑉𐐲𐐸𐐯𐑋𐑊𐐲, 𐐰𐑌𐐼 𐐲 𐐹𐐪𐑉𐐻 𐐱𐑂 𐑄𐐬𐑆 𐑋𐐯𐑌 𐐸𐐭 𐐶𐐲𐑉 𐑌𐐱𐐻 𐑅𐑊𐐩𐑌 𐐱𐑂 𐐈𐑌𐐻𐐮𐐹𐐲𐑅, 𐐶𐐮𐑄 𐑄𐐯𐑋; 𐐰𐑌𐐼 𐑄 𐑉𐐨𐑋𐐩𐑌𐐼𐐲𐑉 𐐌 𐐻𐐳𐐿 𐐰𐑌𐐼 𐐾𐐱𐐮𐑌𐐼 𐑄𐐯𐑋 𐐻𐐭 𐑋𐐴 𐑅𐐻𐑉𐐴𐐹𐑊𐐮𐑍 𐐈𐑋𐐲𐑌𐐴𐐻𐑅, 𐐰𐑌𐐼 𐐻𐐳𐐿 𐐵𐑉 𐑋𐐪𐑉𐐽 𐐺𐐰𐐿 𐐻𐐭 𐑄 𐑅𐐮𐐻𐐨 𐐱𐑂 𐐖𐐭𐐼𐐨𐐲.

12. 𐐈𐑌𐐼 𐑌𐐵 𐐮𐐻 𐐿𐐩𐑋 𐐻𐐭 𐐹𐐰𐑅 𐑄𐐰𐐻 𐐌 𐑉𐐨𐑅𐐨𐑂𐐼 𐐰𐑌 𐐨𐐹𐐮𐑅𐐲𐑊 𐑁𐑉𐐱𐑋 𐐈𐑋𐐫𐑉𐐱𐑌, 𐑄 𐐿𐐮𐑍, 𐑅𐐻𐐩𐐻𐐮𐑍 𐑄𐐰𐐻 𐐮𐑁 𐐌 𐐶𐐳𐐼 𐐼𐐯𐑊𐐮𐑂𐐲𐑉 𐐲𐐹 𐑄𐐬𐑆 𐐹𐑉𐐮𐑆𐑌𐐲𐑉𐑆 𐐱𐑂 𐐶𐐫𐑉 𐐸𐐭𐑋 𐐶𐐨 𐐸𐐰𐐼 𐐻𐐩𐐿𐑌, 𐑄𐐰𐐻 𐐸𐐨 𐐶𐐳𐐼 𐐼𐐯𐑊𐐮𐑂𐐲𐑉 𐐲𐐹 𐑄 𐑅𐐮𐐻𐐨 𐐱𐑂 𐐈𐑌𐐻𐐨𐐹𐐪𐑉𐐲 𐐲𐑌𐐻𐐭 𐐲𐑅. 𐐒𐐲𐐻 𐐌 𐑅𐐯𐑌𐐻 𐐰𐑌 𐐨𐐹𐐮𐑅𐐲𐑊 𐐲𐑌𐐻𐐭 𐑄 𐐿𐐮𐑍, 𐑄𐐰𐐻 𐐶𐐨 𐐶𐐲𐑉 𐑇𐐭𐑉 𐐵𐑉 𐑁𐐬𐑉𐑅𐐯𐑆 𐐶𐐲𐑉 𐑅𐐲𐑁𐐮𐑇𐐯𐑌𐐻 𐐻𐐭 𐐻𐐩𐐿 𐑄 𐑅𐐮𐐻𐐨 𐐱𐑂 𐐈𐑌𐐻𐐨𐐹𐐪𐑉𐐲 𐐺𐐴 𐐵𐑉 𐑁𐐬𐑉𐑅; 𐐰𐑌𐐼 𐐺𐐴 𐐼𐐯𐑊𐐮𐑂𐐲𐑉𐐮𐑍 𐐲𐐹 𐑄 𐐹𐑉𐐮𐑆𐑌𐐲𐑉𐑆 𐑁𐐫𐑉 𐑄𐐰𐐻 𐑅𐐮𐐻𐐨, 𐐶𐐨 𐑇𐐳𐐼 𐑅𐐲𐐹𐐬𐑆 𐐵𐑉𐑅𐐯𐑊𐑂𐑆 𐐲𐑌𐐶𐐴𐑆, 𐐰𐑌𐐼 𐑄𐐰𐐻 𐐶𐐨 𐐶𐐳𐐼 𐐬𐑌𐑊𐐨 𐐼𐐯𐑊𐐮𐑂𐐲𐑉 𐐵𐑉 𐐹𐑉𐐮𐑆𐑌𐐲𐑉𐑆 𐐱𐑌 𐐯𐐿𐑅𐐽𐐩𐑌𐐾. 𐐈𐑌𐐼 𐐈𐑋𐐫𐑉𐐱𐑌 𐑉𐐨𐑁𐐷𐐭𐑆𐐼 𐑋𐐴𐑌 𐐨𐐹𐐮𐑅𐐲𐑊, 𐑁𐐫𐑉 𐐸𐐨 𐐶𐐳𐐼 𐑌𐐱𐐻 𐐯𐐿𐑅𐐽𐐩𐑌𐐾 𐐹𐑉𐐮𐑆𐑌𐐲𐑉𐑆; 𐑄𐐯𐑉𐑁𐐬𐑉 𐐶𐐨 𐐺𐐨𐑀𐐰𐑌 𐐻𐐭 𐑋𐐩𐐿 𐐹𐑉𐐯𐐹𐐪𐑉𐐩𐑇𐐲𐑌𐑆 𐐻𐐭 𐑀𐐬 𐐲𐑀𐐯𐑌𐑅𐐻 𐑄 𐑅𐐮𐐻𐐨 𐐱𐑂 𐐈𐑌𐐻𐐨𐐹𐐪𐑉𐐲. 𐐒𐐲𐐻 𐑄 𐐹𐐨𐐹𐑊 𐐱𐑂 𐐈𐑌𐐻𐐨𐐹𐐪𐑉𐐲 𐐼𐐮𐐼 𐑊𐐨𐑂 𐑄 𐑅𐐮𐐻𐐨, 𐐰𐑌𐐼 𐑁𐑊𐐯𐐼 𐐻𐐭 𐑄𐐩𐑉 𐐲𐑄𐐲𐑉 𐑅𐐮𐐻𐐨𐑆, 𐐸𐐶𐐮𐐽 𐑄𐐩 𐐸𐐰𐐼 𐐹𐐱𐑆𐐯𐑇𐐲𐑌 𐐱𐑂, 𐐻𐐭 𐑁𐐫𐑉𐐻𐐮𐑁𐐴 𐑄𐐯𐑋; 𐐰𐑌𐐼 𐑄𐐲𐑅 𐑄 𐑅𐐮𐐻𐐨 𐐱𐑂 𐐈𐑌𐐻𐐨𐐹𐐪𐑉𐐲 𐑁𐐯𐑊 𐐮𐑌𐐻𐐭 𐐵𐑉 𐐸𐐰𐑌𐐼𐑆. 𐐈𐑌𐐼 𐑄𐐲𐑅 𐐯𐑌𐐼𐐯𐐼 𐑄 𐐻𐐶𐐯𐑌𐐻𐐨 𐐰𐑌𐐼 𐐩𐐻𐑃 𐐷𐐨𐑉 𐐱𐑂 𐑄 𐑉𐐩𐑌 𐐱𐑂 𐑄 𐐖𐐲𐐾𐐯𐑆.

13. 𐐈𐑌𐐼 𐐮𐐻 𐐿𐐩𐑋 𐐻𐐭 𐐹𐐰𐑅 𐐮𐑌 𐑄 𐐿𐐱𐑋𐐯𐑌𐑅𐑋𐐯𐑌𐐻 𐐱𐑂 𐑄 𐐻𐐶𐐯𐑌𐐻𐐨 𐐰𐑌𐐼 𐑌𐐴𐑌𐑃 𐐷𐐨𐑉, 𐐶𐐨 𐑉𐐨𐑅𐐨𐑂𐐼 𐐲 𐑅𐐲𐐹𐑊𐐴 𐐱𐑂 𐐹𐑉𐐬𐑂𐐮𐑈𐐲𐑌𐑆, 𐐰𐑌𐐼 𐐫𐑊𐑅𐐬 𐐰𐑌 𐐰𐐼𐐮𐑇𐐲𐑌 𐐻𐐭 𐐵𐑉 𐐪𐑉𐑋𐐨, 𐑁𐑉𐐱𐑋 𐑄 𐑊𐐰𐑌𐐼 𐐱𐑂 𐐞𐐩𐑉𐐲𐐸𐐯𐑋𐑊𐐲, 𐐰𐑌𐐼 𐑁𐑉𐐱𐑋 𐑄 𐑊𐐰𐑌𐐼 𐑉𐐵𐑌𐐼 𐐲𐐺𐐵𐐻, 𐐻𐐭 𐑄 𐑌𐐲𐑋𐐺𐐲𐑉 𐐱𐑂 𐑅𐐮𐐿𐑅 𐑃𐐵𐑆𐐰𐑌𐐼 𐑋𐐯𐑌, 𐐺𐐨𐑅𐐴𐐼𐑆 𐑅𐐮𐐿𐑅𐐻𐐨 𐐱𐑂 𐑄 𐑅𐐲𐑌𐑆 𐐱𐑂 𐑄 𐐈𐑋𐐲𐑌𐐴𐐻𐑅, 𐐸𐐭 𐐸𐐰𐐼 𐐿𐐲𐑋 𐐻𐐭 𐐾𐐱𐐮𐑌 𐑄𐐩𐑉 𐐺𐑉𐐯𐑄𐑉𐐯𐑌, 𐑋𐐴 𐑊𐐮𐐻𐑊 𐐺𐐰𐑌𐐼 𐐱𐑂 𐐻𐐭 𐑃𐐵𐑆𐐰𐑌𐐼. 𐐈𐑌𐐼 𐑌𐐵 𐐺𐐨𐐸𐐬𐑊𐐼, 𐐶𐐨 𐐶𐐲𐑉 𐑅𐐻𐑉𐐱𐑍, 𐐷𐐩, 𐐰𐑌𐐼 𐐶𐐨 𐐸𐐰𐐼 𐐫𐑊𐑅𐐬 𐐲 𐐹𐑊𐐯𐑌𐐻𐐨 𐐱𐑂 𐐹𐑉𐐬𐑂𐐮𐑈𐐲𐑌𐑆 𐐺𐑉𐐫𐐻 𐐲𐑌𐐻𐐭 𐐲𐑅.

14. 𐐈𐑌𐐼 𐐮𐐻 𐐿𐐩𐑋 𐐻𐐭 𐐹𐐰𐑅 𐑄𐐰𐐻 𐐮𐐻 𐐶𐐱𐑆 𐐵𐑉 𐐼𐐨𐑆𐐴𐑉 𐐻𐐭 𐐶𐐩𐐾 𐐲 𐐺𐐰𐐻𐑊 𐐶𐐮𐑄 𐑄 𐐪𐑉𐑋𐐨 𐐸𐐶𐐮𐐽 𐐶𐐱𐑆 𐐹𐑊𐐩𐑅𐐻 𐐻𐐭 𐐹𐑉𐐬𐐻𐐯𐐿𐐻 𐑄 𐑅𐐮𐐻𐐨 𐐗𐐭𐑋𐐨𐑌𐐴. 𐐈𐑌𐐼 𐑌𐐵 𐐺𐐨𐐸𐐬𐑊𐐼, 𐐌 𐐶𐐮𐑊 𐑇𐐬 𐐲𐑌𐐻𐐭 𐐷𐐭 𐑄𐐰𐐻 𐐶𐐨 𐑅𐐭𐑌 𐐰𐐿𐐱𐑋𐐹𐑊𐐮𐑇𐐻 𐐵𐑉 𐐼𐐨𐑆𐐴𐑉; 𐐷𐐩, 𐐶𐐮𐑄 𐐵𐑉 𐑅𐐻𐑉𐐱𐑍 𐑁𐐬𐑉𐑅, 𐐫𐑉 𐐶𐐮𐑄 𐐲 𐐹𐐪𐑉𐐻 𐐱𐑂 𐐵𐑉 𐑅𐐻𐑉𐐱𐑍 𐑁𐐬𐑉𐑅, 𐐶𐐨 𐐼𐐮𐐼 𐑅𐐲𐑉𐐵𐑌𐐼, 𐐺𐐴 𐑌𐐴𐐻, 𐑄 𐑅𐐮𐐻𐐨 𐐗𐐭𐑋𐐨𐑌𐐴, 𐐲 𐑊𐐮𐐻𐑊 𐐺𐐨𐑁𐐬𐑉 𐑄𐐩 𐐶𐐲𐑉 𐐻𐐭 𐑉𐐨𐑅𐐨𐑂 𐐲 𐑅𐐲𐐹𐑊𐐴 𐐱𐑂 𐐹𐑉𐐬𐑂𐐮𐑈𐐲𐑌𐑆. 𐐈𐑌𐐼 𐐮𐐻 𐐿𐐩𐑋 𐐻𐐭 𐐹𐐰𐑅 𐑄𐐰𐐻 𐐶𐐨 𐐼𐐮𐐼 𐐿𐐰𐑋𐐹 𐑉𐐵𐑌𐐼 𐐲𐐺𐐵𐐻 𐑄 𐑅𐐮𐐻𐐨 𐑁𐐫𐑉 𐑋𐐯𐑌𐐨 𐑌𐐴𐐻𐑅; 𐐺𐐲𐐻 𐐶𐐨 𐐼𐐮𐐼 𐑅𐑊𐐨𐐹 𐐲𐐹𐐱𐑌 𐐵𐑉 𐑅𐐬𐑉𐐼𐑆, 𐐰𐑌𐐼 𐐿𐐨𐐹 𐑀𐐪𐑉𐐼𐑆, 𐑄𐐰𐐻 𐑄 𐐢𐐰𐑋𐐲𐑌𐐴𐐻𐑅 𐐿𐐳𐐼 𐑌𐐱𐐻 𐐿𐐲𐑋 𐐲𐐹𐐱𐑌 𐐲𐑅 𐐺𐐴 𐑌𐐴𐐻 𐐰𐑌𐐼 𐑅𐑊𐐩 𐐲𐑅, 𐐸𐐶𐐮𐐽 𐑄𐐩 𐐰𐐻𐐯𐑋𐐹𐐻𐐯𐐼 𐑋𐐯𐑌𐐨 𐐻𐐴𐑋𐑆; 𐐺𐐲𐐻 𐐰𐑆 𐑋𐐯𐑌𐐨 𐐻𐐴𐑋𐑆 𐐰𐑆 𐑄𐐩 𐐰𐐻𐐯𐑋𐐹𐐻𐐯𐐼 𐑄𐐮𐑅, 𐑄𐐩𐑉 𐐺𐑊𐐲𐐼 𐐶𐐱𐑆 𐑅𐐹𐐮𐑊𐐻. 𐐈𐐻 𐑊𐐯𐑍𐑃 𐑄𐐩𐑉 𐐹𐑉𐐬𐑂𐐮𐑈𐐲𐑌𐑆 𐐼𐐮𐐼 𐐲𐑉𐐴𐑂, 𐐰𐑌𐐼 𐑄𐐩 𐐶𐐲𐑉 𐐲𐐺𐐵𐐻 𐐻𐐭 𐐯𐑌𐐻𐐲𐑉 𐑄 𐑅𐐮𐐻𐐨 𐐺𐐴 𐑌𐐴𐐻. 𐐈𐑌𐐼 𐐶𐐨, 𐐮𐑌𐑅𐐻𐐯𐐼 𐐱𐑂 𐐺𐐨𐐮𐑍 𐐢𐐰𐑋𐐲𐑌𐐴𐐻𐑅, 𐐶𐐲𐑉 𐐤𐐨𐑁𐐴𐐻𐑅; 𐑄𐐯𐑉𐑁𐐬𐑉, 𐐶𐐨 𐐼𐐮𐐼 𐐻𐐩𐐿 𐑄𐐯𐑋 𐐰𐑌𐐼 𐑄𐐩𐑉 𐐹𐑉𐐬𐑂𐐮𐑈𐐲𐑌𐑆. 𐐈𐑌𐐼 𐑌𐐱𐐻𐐶𐐮𐑄𐑅𐐻𐐰𐑌𐐼𐐮𐑍 𐑄 𐐢𐐰𐑋𐐲𐑌𐐴𐐻𐑅 𐐺𐐨𐐮𐑍 𐐿𐐲𐐻 𐐫𐑁 𐑁𐑉𐐱𐑋 𐑄𐐩𐑉 𐑅𐐲𐐹𐐬𐑉𐐻 𐐰𐑁𐐻𐐲𐑉 𐑄𐐮𐑅 𐑋𐐰𐑌𐐲𐑉, 𐑄𐐩 𐐶𐐲𐑉 𐑅𐐻𐐮𐑊 𐐼𐐨𐐻𐐲𐑉𐑋𐐮𐑌𐐼 𐐻𐐭 𐑋𐐩𐑌𐐻𐐩𐑌 𐑄 𐑅𐐮𐐻𐐨; 𐑄𐐯𐑉𐑁𐐬𐑉 𐐮𐐻 𐐺𐐨𐐿𐐩𐑋 𐐯𐐿𐑅𐐹𐐨𐐼𐐨𐐯𐑌𐐻 𐑄𐐰𐐻 𐐶𐐨 𐑇𐐳𐐼 𐐻𐐩𐐿 𐑄𐐬𐑆 𐐹𐑉𐐬𐑂𐐮𐑈𐐲𐑌𐑆 𐐰𐑌𐐼 𐑅𐐯𐑌𐐼 𐑄𐐯𐑋 𐐻𐐭 𐐖𐐭𐐼𐐨𐐲, 𐐰𐑌𐐼 𐐵𐑉 𐐹𐑉𐐮𐑆𐑌𐐲𐑉𐑆 𐐻𐐭 𐑄 𐑊𐐰𐑌𐐼 𐐱𐑂 𐐞𐐩𐑉𐐲𐐸𐐯𐑋𐑊𐐲.

15. 𐐈𐑌𐐼 𐐮𐐻 𐐿𐐩𐑋 𐐻𐐭 𐐹𐐰𐑅 𐑄𐐰𐐻 𐑌𐐱𐐻 𐑋𐐯𐑌𐐨 𐐼𐐩𐑆 𐐸𐐰𐐼 𐐹𐐰𐑅𐐻 𐐲𐐶𐐩 𐐺𐐨𐑁𐐬𐑉 𐑄 𐐢𐐰𐑋𐐲𐑌𐐴𐐻𐑅 𐐺𐐨𐑀𐐰𐑌 𐐻𐐭 𐑊𐐭𐑆 𐐫𐑊 𐐸𐐬𐐹𐑅 𐐱𐑂 𐑅𐐲𐐿𐐲𐑉; 𐑄𐐯𐑉𐑁𐐬𐑉 𐑄𐐩 𐐷𐐨𐑊𐐼𐐯𐐼 𐐲𐐹 𐑄 𐑅𐐮𐐻𐐨 𐐲𐑌𐐻𐐭 𐐵𐑉 𐐸𐐰𐑌𐐼𐑆; 𐐰𐑌𐐼 𐑄𐐲𐑅 𐐶𐐨 𐐸𐐰𐐼 𐐰𐐿𐐱𐑋𐐹𐑊𐐮𐑇𐐻 𐐵𐑉 𐐼𐐨𐑆𐐴𐑌𐑆 𐐮𐑌 𐐱𐐺𐐻𐐩𐑌𐐮𐑍 𐑄 𐑅𐐮𐐻𐐨 𐐗𐐭𐑋𐐨𐑌𐐴. 𐐒𐐲𐐻 𐐮𐐻 𐐿𐐩𐑋 𐐻𐐭 𐐹𐐰𐑅 𐑄𐐰𐐻 𐐵𐑉 𐐹𐑉𐐮𐑆𐑌𐐲𐑉𐑆 𐐶𐐲𐑉 𐑅𐐬 𐑌𐐷𐐭𐑋𐐲𐑉𐐲𐑅, 𐑄𐐰𐐻 𐑌𐐱𐐻𐐶𐐮𐑄𐑅𐐻𐐰𐑌𐐼𐐮𐑍 𐑄 𐐨𐑌𐐫𐑉𐑋𐐮𐐻𐐨 𐐱𐑂 𐐵𐑉

𐑌𐐲𐑋𐐺𐐲𐑉𐑆, 𐐶𐐨 𐐶𐐲𐑉 𐐬𐐺𐑊𐐴𐐾𐐼 𐐻𐐭 𐐯𐑋𐐹𐑊𐐦 𐐫𐑊 𐐵𐑉 𐑁𐐬𐑉𐑅 𐐻𐐭 𐑀𐐪𐑉𐐼 𐑄𐐯𐑋, 𐐫𐑉 𐐻𐐭 𐐹𐐳𐐻 𐑄𐐯𐑋 𐐻𐐭 𐐼𐐯𐑃. 𐐙𐐫𐑉 𐐺𐐨𐐸𐐬𐑊𐐼, 𐑄𐐩 𐐶𐐳𐐼 𐐺𐑉𐐩𐐿 𐐵𐐻 𐐮𐑌 𐑀𐑉𐐩𐐻 𐑌𐐲𐑋𐐺𐐲𐑉𐑆, 𐐰𐑌𐐼 𐐶𐐳𐐼 𐑁𐐴𐐻 𐐶𐐮𐑄 𐑅𐐻𐐬𐑌𐑆, 𐐰𐑌𐐼 𐐶𐐮𐑄 𐐿𐑊𐐲𐐺𐑆, 𐐫𐑉 𐐸𐐶𐐱𐐻𐑅𐐬𐐯𐑂𐐲𐑉 𐑃𐐮𐑍 𐑄𐐩 𐐿𐐳𐐼 𐑀𐐯𐐻 𐐮𐑌𐐻𐐭 𐑄𐐯𐑉 𐐸𐐰𐑌𐐼𐑆, 𐐮𐑌𐑅𐐬𐑋𐐲𐐽 𐑄𐐰𐐻 𐐶𐐨 𐐼𐐮𐐼 𐑅𐑊𐐩 𐐲𐐹𐐶𐐲𐑉𐐼𐑆 𐐱𐑂 𐐻𐐭 𐑃𐐵𐑆𐐰𐑌𐐼 𐐱𐑂 𐑄𐐯𐑋, 𐐰𐑁𐐻𐐲𐑉 𐑄𐐩 𐐸𐐰𐐼 𐑅𐐲𐑉𐐯𐑌𐐼𐐲𐑉𐐼 𐑄𐐯𐑋𐑅𐐯𐑊𐑂𐑆 𐐹𐑉𐐮𐑆𐐲𐑌𐐲𐑉𐑆 𐐱𐑂 𐐶𐐫𐑉. 𐐜𐐯𐑉𐑁𐐬𐑉 𐐮𐐻 𐐺𐐨𐐿𐐩𐑋 𐐯𐐿𐑅𐐹𐐨𐐼𐐨𐐯𐑌𐐻 𐑁𐐫𐑉 𐐲𐑅, 𐑄𐐰𐐻 𐐶𐐨 𐑇𐐳𐐼 𐐹𐐳𐐻 𐐰𐑌 𐐯𐑌𐐼 𐐻𐐭 𐑄𐐯𐑉 𐑊𐐴𐑂𐑆, 𐐫𐑉 𐑀𐐪𐑉𐐼 𐑄𐐯𐑋, 𐑅𐐬𐑉𐐼 𐐮𐑌 𐐸𐐰𐑌𐐼, 𐐼𐐵𐑌 𐐻𐐭 𐑄 𐑊𐐰𐑌𐐼 𐐱𐑂 𐐞𐐯𐑉𐐲𐐸𐐯𐑋𐑊𐐲; 𐐰𐑌𐐼 𐐫𐑊𐑅𐐬 𐐵𐑉 𐐹𐑉𐐬𐑂𐐮𐑈𐐲𐑌𐑆 𐐶𐐲𐑉 𐑌𐐱𐐻 𐐯𐑌𐐨 𐑋𐐬𐑉 𐑄𐐰𐑌 𐑅𐐲𐑁𐐮𐑇𐐯𐑌𐐻 𐑁𐐫𐑉 𐐵𐑉 𐐬𐑌 𐐹𐐨𐐹𐑊, 𐑌𐐱𐐻𐐶𐐮𐑃𐑅𐐻𐐰𐑌𐐼𐐮𐑍 𐑄𐐰𐐻 𐐸𐐶𐐮𐐽 𐐶𐐨 𐐸𐐰𐐼 𐐻𐐩𐐿𐐯𐑌 𐑁𐑉𐐱𐑋 𐑄 𐐢𐐰𐑋𐐲𐑌𐐴𐐻𐑅. 𐐈𐑌𐐼 𐑌𐐵, 𐐮𐑌 𐑄𐐬𐑆 𐐿𐑉𐐮𐐻𐐮𐐿𐐲𐑊 𐑅𐐲𐑉𐐿𐐲𐑋𐑅𐐻𐐰𐑌𐑅𐐯𐑆, 𐐮𐐻 𐐺𐐨𐐿𐐩𐑋 𐐲 𐑂𐐯𐑉𐐨 𐑅𐐨𐑉𐐨𐐲𐑅 𐑋𐐰𐐻𐐲𐑉 𐐻𐐭 𐐼𐐨𐐻𐐲𐑉𐑋𐐮𐑌 𐐿𐐱𐑌𐑅𐐲𐑉𐑌𐐮𐑍 𐑄𐐨𐑆 𐐹𐑉𐐮𐑆𐐲𐑌𐐲𐑉𐑆 𐐱𐑂 𐐶𐐫𐑉; 𐑌𐐯𐑂𐐲𐑉𐑄𐐯𐑊𐐯𐑅, 𐐶𐐨 𐐼𐐮𐐼 𐑉𐐨𐑆𐐱𐑊𐑂 𐐻𐐭 𐑅𐐯𐑌𐐼 𐑄𐐯𐑋 𐐼𐐵𐑌 𐐻𐐭 𐑄 𐑊𐐰𐑌𐐼 𐐱𐑂 𐐞𐐯𐑉𐐲𐐸𐐯𐑋𐑊𐐲; 𐑄𐐯𐑉𐑁𐐬𐑉 𐐶𐐨 𐑅𐐨𐑊𐐯𐐿𐐻𐐯𐐼 𐐲 𐐹𐐪𐑉𐐻 𐐱𐑂 𐐵𐑉 𐑋𐐯𐑌, 𐐰𐑌𐐼 𐑀𐐩𐑂 𐑄𐐯𐑋 𐐽𐐪𐑉𐐾 𐐬𐑂𐐲𐑉 𐐵𐑉 𐐹𐑉𐐮𐑆𐐲𐑌𐐲𐑉𐑆 𐐻𐐭 𐑀𐐬 𐐼𐐵𐑌 𐐻𐐭 𐑄 𐑊𐐰𐑌𐐼 𐐱𐑂 𐐞𐐯𐑉𐐲𐐸𐐯𐑋𐑊𐐲.

16. 𐐒𐐲𐐻 𐐮𐐻 𐐿𐐩𐑋 𐐻𐐭 𐐹𐐰𐑅 𐑄𐐰𐐻 𐐱𐑌 𐑄 𐑋𐐱𐑉𐐬 𐑄𐐩 𐐼𐐮𐐼 𐑉𐐨𐐻𐐲𐑉𐑌. 𐐈𐑌𐐼 𐑌𐐵 𐐺𐐨𐐸𐐬𐑊𐐼, 𐐶𐐨 𐐼𐐭 𐑌𐐱𐐻 𐐮𐑌𐐿𐐶𐐴𐑉 𐐿𐐱𐑌𐑅𐐲𐑉𐑌𐐮𐑍 𐑄 𐐹𐑉𐐮𐑆𐐲𐑌𐐲𐑉𐑆; 𐑁𐐫𐑉 𐐺𐐨𐐸𐐬𐑊𐐼, 𐑄 𐐢𐐰𐑋𐐲𐑌𐐴𐐻𐑅 𐐶𐐲𐑉 𐐲𐐹𐐱𐑌 𐐲𐑅, 𐐰𐑌𐐼 𐑄𐐩 𐑉𐐨𐐻𐐲𐑉𐑌𐐼 𐐮𐑌 𐑅𐐨𐑆𐐲𐑌 𐐻𐐭 𐑅𐐩𐑂 𐐲𐑅 𐑁𐑉𐐱𐑋 𐑁𐐫𐑊𐐮𐑍 𐐮𐑌𐐻𐐭 𐑄𐐯𐑉 𐐸𐐰𐑌𐐼𐑆. 𐐙𐐫𐑉 𐐺𐐨𐐸𐐬𐑊𐐼, 𐐈𐑋𐐬𐑉𐐱𐑌 𐐸𐐰𐐼 𐑅𐐯𐑌𐐻 𐐻𐐭 𐑄𐐯𐑉 𐑅𐐲𐐹𐐬𐑉𐐻 𐐲 𐑌𐐧 𐑅𐐲𐐹𐑊𐐴 𐐱𐑂 𐐹𐑉𐐬𐑂𐐮𐑈𐐲𐑌𐑆, 𐐰𐑌𐐼 𐐫𐑊𐑅𐐬 𐐲 𐑌𐐧𐑋𐐲𐑉𐐲𐑅 𐐪𐑉𐑋𐐨 𐐱𐑂 𐑋𐐯𐑌.

17. 𐐈𐑌𐐼 𐐮𐐻 𐐿𐐩𐑋 𐐻𐐭 𐐹𐐰𐑅 𐑄𐐰𐐻 𐑄𐐬𐑆 𐑋𐐯𐑌 𐐸𐐭𐑋 𐐶𐐨 𐑅𐐯𐑌𐐻 𐐶𐐮𐑄 𐑄 𐐹𐑉𐐮𐑆𐐲𐑌𐐲𐑉𐑆, 𐐼𐐮𐐼 𐐲𐑉𐐴𐑂 𐐮𐑌 𐑅𐐨𐑆𐐲𐑌 𐐻𐐭 𐐽𐐯𐐿 𐑄𐐯𐑋, 𐐰𐑆 𐑄𐐩 𐐶𐐲𐑉 𐐲𐐺𐐵𐐻 𐐻𐐭 𐐬𐑂𐐲𐑉𐐹𐐵𐐲𐑉 𐐲𐑅. 𐐒𐐲𐐻 𐐺𐐨𐐸𐐬𐑊𐐼, 𐑋𐐴 𐑊𐐮𐐻𐑊 𐐺𐐰𐑌𐐼 𐐱𐑂 𐐻𐐭 𐑃𐐵𐑆𐐰𐑌𐐼 𐐰𐑌𐐼 𐑅𐐮𐐿𐑅𐐻𐐨, 𐑁𐐫𐐻 𐑋𐐬𐑅𐐻 𐐼𐐯𐑅𐐹𐐲𐑉𐐩𐐻𐑊𐐨; 𐐷𐐩, 𐑄𐐩 𐐶𐐲𐑉 𐑁𐐲𐑉𐑋 𐐺𐐨𐑁𐐬𐑉 𐑄 𐐢𐐰𐑋𐐲𐑌𐐴𐐻𐑅, 𐐰𐑌𐐼 𐐼𐐮𐐼 𐐰𐐼𐑋𐐮𐑌𐐮𐑅𐐻𐐲𐑉 𐐼𐐯𐑃 𐐲𐑌𐐻𐐭 𐐫𐑊 𐑄𐐬𐑆 𐐸𐐭 𐐱𐐹𐐬𐑆𐐼 𐑄𐐯𐑋; 𐐰𐑌𐐼 𐐰𐑆 𐑄 𐑉𐐨𐑋𐐩𐑌𐐼𐐲𐑉 𐐱𐑂 𐐵𐑉 𐐪𐑉𐑋𐐨 𐐶𐐲𐑉 𐐲𐐺𐐵𐐻 𐐻𐐭 𐑀𐐮𐑂 𐐶𐐩 𐐺𐐨𐑁𐐬𐑉 𐑄 𐐢𐐰𐑋𐐲𐑌𐐴𐐻𐑅, 𐐺𐐨𐐸𐐬𐑊𐐼, 𐑄𐐬𐑆 𐐻𐐭 𐑃𐐵𐑆𐐰𐑌𐐼 𐐰𐑌𐐼 𐑅𐐮𐐿𐑅𐐻𐐨 𐐶𐐲𐑉 𐑁𐐲𐑉𐑋 𐐰𐑌𐐼 𐐲𐑌𐐼𐐫𐑌𐐻𐐯𐐼; 𐐷𐐩, 𐐰𐑌𐐼 𐑄𐐩 𐐼𐐮𐐼 𐐬𐐺𐐩 𐐰𐑌𐐼 𐐱𐐺𐑆𐐲𐑉𐑂 𐐻𐐭 𐐹𐐲𐑉𐑁𐐫𐑉𐑋 𐐯𐑂𐐲𐑉𐐨 𐐶𐐲𐑉𐐼 𐐱𐑂 𐐿𐐱𐑋𐐰𐑌𐐼 𐐶𐐮𐑄 𐐯𐑀𐑆𐐰𐐿𐐻𐑌𐐯𐑅; 𐐷𐐩, 𐐰𐑌𐐼 𐐨𐑂𐐲𐑌 𐐰𐐿𐐫𐑉𐐼𐐮𐑍 𐐻𐐭 𐑄𐐯𐑉 𐑁𐐩𐑃 𐐮𐐻 𐐶𐐱𐑆 𐐼𐐲𐑌 𐐲𐑌𐐻𐐭 𐑄𐐯𐑋; 𐐰𐑌𐐼 𐐌 𐐼𐐮𐐼 𐑉𐐨𐑋𐐯𐑋𐐺𐐲𐑉 𐑄 𐐶𐐲𐑉𐐼𐑆 𐐸𐐶𐐮𐐽 𐑄𐐩 𐑅𐐯𐐼 𐐲𐑌𐐻𐐭 𐑋𐐨, 𐑄𐐰𐐻 𐑄𐐯𐑉 𐑋𐐲𐑄𐐲𐑉𐑆 𐐸𐐰𐐼 𐐻𐐫𐐻 𐑄𐐯𐑋. 𐐈𐑌𐐼 𐑌𐐵 𐐺𐐨𐐸𐐬𐑊𐐼, 𐐮𐐻 𐐶𐐱𐑆 𐐻𐐭 𐑄𐐨𐑆 𐑋𐐴 𐑅𐐲𐑌𐑆, 𐐰𐑌𐐼 𐑄𐐬𐑆 𐑋𐐯𐑌 𐐸𐐭 𐐸𐐰𐐼 𐐺𐐮𐑌 𐑅𐐨𐑊𐐯𐐿𐐻𐐯𐐼 𐐻𐐭 𐐿𐐱𐑌𐑂𐐩 𐑄 𐐹𐑉𐐮𐑆𐐲𐑌𐐲𐑉𐑆, 𐐻𐐭 𐐸𐐭𐑋 𐐶𐐨 𐐬 𐑄𐐮𐑅 𐑀𐑉𐐩𐐻 𐑂𐐮𐐿𐐻𐐬𐑉𐐨; 𐑁𐐫𐑉 𐐮𐐻 𐐶𐐱𐑆 𐑄𐐩 𐐸𐐭 𐐼𐐮𐐼 𐐺𐐨𐐻 𐑄 𐐢𐐰𐑋𐐲𐑌𐐴𐐻𐑅; 𐑄𐐯𐑉𐑁𐐬𐑉, 𐑄𐐩 𐐶𐐲𐑉 𐐼𐑉𐐮𐑂𐐲𐑌 𐐺𐐰𐐿 𐐻𐐭 𐑄 𐑅𐐮𐐻𐐨 𐐱𐑂 𐐣𐐰𐑌𐐻𐐴. 𐐈𐑌𐐼 𐐶𐐨 𐑉𐐨𐐻𐐩𐑌𐐼 𐐵𐑉 𐑅𐐮𐐻𐐨 𐐗𐐷𐐭𐑋𐐯𐑌𐐴, 𐐰𐑌𐐼 𐐶𐐲𐑉 𐑌𐐱𐐻 𐐫𐑊 𐐼𐐯𐑅𐐻𐑉𐐦𐐼 𐐺𐐴 𐑄 𐑅𐐬𐑉𐐼; 𐑌𐐯𐑂𐐲𐑉𐑄𐐯𐑊𐐯𐑅, 𐐶𐐨 𐐸𐐰𐐼 𐑅𐐲𐑁𐐲𐑉𐐼 𐑀𐑉𐐩𐐻 𐑊𐐱𐑅.

18. 𐐈𐑌𐐼 𐐮𐐻 𐐿𐐩𐑋 𐐻𐐭 𐐹𐐰𐑅 𐑄𐐰𐐻 𐐰𐑁𐐻𐐲𐑉 𐑄 𐐢𐐰𐑋𐐲𐑌𐐴𐐻𐑅 𐐸𐐰𐐼 𐑁𐑊𐐯𐐼, 𐐌 𐐮𐑋𐐨𐐼𐐨𐐯𐐻𐑊𐐨 𐑀𐐩𐑂 𐐫𐑉𐐼𐐲𐑉𐑆 𐑄𐐰𐐻 𐑋𐐴 𐑋𐐯𐑌 𐐸𐐭 𐐸𐐰𐐼 𐐺𐐮𐑌 𐐶𐐭𐑌𐐼𐐯𐐼 𐑇𐐳𐐼 𐐺𐐨 𐐻𐐩𐐿𐐲𐑌 𐑁𐑉𐐱𐑋 𐐲𐑋𐐲𐑍 𐑄 𐐼𐐯𐐼, 𐐰𐑌𐐼 𐐿𐐫𐑆𐐼 𐑄𐐰𐐻 𐑄𐐯𐑉 𐐶𐐭𐑌𐐼𐑆 𐑇𐐳𐐼 𐐺𐐨 𐐼𐑉𐐯𐑅𐐻. 𐐈𐑌𐐼 𐐮𐐻 𐐿𐐩𐑋 𐐻𐐭 𐐹𐐰𐑅 𐑄𐐰𐐻 𐑄𐐯𐑉 𐐶𐐲𐑉 𐐻𐐭 𐐸𐐲𐑌𐐼𐑉𐐯𐐼, 𐐵𐐻 𐐱𐑂 𐑋𐐴 𐐻𐐭 𐑃𐐵𐑆𐐰𐑌𐐼 𐐰𐑌𐐼 𐑅𐐮𐐿𐑅𐐻𐐨, 𐐸𐐭 𐐸𐐰𐐼 𐑁𐐩𐑌𐐻𐐯𐐼 𐐺𐐨𐐿𐐫𐑆 𐐱𐑂 𐑄 𐑊𐐱𐑅 𐐱𐑂 𐐺𐑊𐐲𐐼; 𐑌𐐯𐑂𐐲𐑉𐑄𐐯𐑊𐐯𐑅, 𐐰𐐿𐐫𐑉𐐼𐐮𐑍 𐐻𐐭 𐑄 𐑀𐐳𐐼𐑌𐐯𐑅 𐐱𐑂 𐐘𐐱𐐼, 𐐰𐑌𐐼 𐐻𐐭 𐐵𐑉 𐑀𐑉𐐩𐐻 𐐲𐑅𐐻𐐱𐑌𐐮𐑇𐑋𐐯𐑌𐐻, 𐐰𐑌𐐼 𐐫𐑊𐑅𐐬 𐑄 𐐾𐐦 𐐱𐑂 𐐵𐑉 𐐸𐐬𐑊 𐐪𐑉𐑋𐐨, 𐑄𐐯𐑉 𐐶𐐱𐑆 𐑌𐐱𐐻 𐐶𐐲𐑌 𐑅𐐬𐑊 𐐱𐑂 𐑄𐐯𐑋 𐐸𐐭 𐐼𐐮𐐼 𐐹𐐯𐑉𐐮𐑇; 𐐷𐐩, 𐐰𐑌𐐼 𐑌𐐨𐑄𐐲𐑉 𐐶𐐱𐑆 𐑄𐐯𐑉 𐐶𐐲𐑌 𐑅𐐬𐑊 𐐲𐑋𐐲𐑍 𐑄𐐯𐑋 𐐸𐐭 𐐸𐐰𐐼 𐑌𐐱𐐻 𐑉𐐨𐑅𐐨𐑂𐐼 𐑋𐐯𐑌𐐨 𐐶𐐭𐑌𐐼𐑆. 𐐈𐑌𐐼 𐑌𐐵, 𐑄𐐯𐑉 𐐹𐑉𐐯𐑆𐐲𐑉𐑂𐐩𐑇𐐲𐑌 𐐶𐐱𐑆 𐐲𐑅𐐻𐐱𐑌𐐮𐑇𐐮𐑍 𐐻𐐭 𐐵𐑉 𐐸𐐬𐑊 𐐪𐑉𐑋𐐨; 𐐷𐐩, 𐑄𐐰𐐻 𐑄𐐩 𐑇𐐳𐐼 𐐺𐐨 𐑅𐐹𐐯𐑉𐐼, 𐐸𐐶𐐴𐑊 𐑄𐐯𐑉 𐐶𐐱𐑆 𐐲 𐑃𐐵𐑆𐐰𐑌𐐼 𐐱𐑂 𐐵𐑉 𐐺𐑉𐐯𐑃𐑉𐐯𐑌 𐐸𐐭 𐐶𐐲𐑉 𐑅𐑊𐐩𐑌. 𐐈𐑌𐐼 𐐶𐐨 𐐼𐐭 𐐾𐐲𐑅𐐻𐑊𐐨 𐐰𐑅𐐿𐑉𐐴𐐺 𐐮𐐻 𐐻𐐭 𐑄 𐑋𐐮𐑉𐐰𐐿𐐷𐐭𐑊𐐲𐑅 𐐹𐐵𐐲𐑉 𐐱𐑂 𐐘𐐱𐐼, 𐐺𐐨𐐿𐐫𐑆 𐐱𐑂 𐑄𐐯𐑉 𐐯𐐿𐑅𐐨𐐼𐐮𐑍 𐑁𐐩𐑃 𐐮𐑌 𐑄𐐰𐐻 𐐸𐐶𐐮𐐽 𐑄𐐩 𐐸𐐰𐐼 𐐺𐐮𐑌 𐐻𐐫𐐻 𐐻𐐭 𐐺𐐨𐑊𐐨𐑂, 𐑄𐐰𐐻 𐑄𐐯𐑉 𐐶𐐱𐑆 𐐲 𐐾𐐲𐑅𐐻 𐐘𐐱𐐼; 𐐰𐑌𐐼 𐐸𐐭𐑅𐐬𐐯𐑂𐐲𐑉 𐐼𐐮𐐼 𐑌𐐱𐐻 𐐼𐐵𐐻, 𐑄𐐰𐐻 𐑄𐐩 𐑇𐐳𐐼 𐐺𐐨

𐐹𐑉𐐨𐑆𐐲𐑉𐑂𐐼 𐐺𐐴 𐐸𐐮𐑆 𐑋𐐪𐑉𐑂𐐯𐑊𐐲𐑅 𐐹𐐵𐐲𐑉. 𐐤𐐵 𐑄𐐮𐑅 𐐶𐐲𐑆 𐑄 𐑁𐐩𐑃 𐐲𐑂 𐑄𐐨𐑆 𐐲𐑂 𐐸𐐭𐑋 𐐌 𐐸𐐰𐑂 𐑅𐐹𐐬𐐿𐐲𐑌; 𐑄𐐩 𐐪𐑉 𐐷𐐲𐑍, 𐐰𐑌𐐼 𐑄𐐩𐑉 𐑋𐐴𐑌𐐼𐑆 𐐪𐑉 𐑁𐐲𐑉𐑋; 𐐰𐑌𐐼 𐑄𐐩 𐐼𐐭 𐐹𐐳𐐻 𐑄𐐩𐑉 𐐻𐑉𐐲𐑅𐐻 𐐮𐑌 𐐘𐐱𐐼 𐐿𐐪𐑌𐐻𐐮𐑌𐐷𐐭𐐲𐑊𐐨.

19. 𐐈𐑌𐐼 𐑌𐐵 𐐮𐐻 𐐿𐐩𐑋 𐐻𐐭 𐐹𐐰𐑅 𐑄𐐰𐐻 𐐰𐑁𐐻𐐲𐑉 𐐶𐐨 𐐸𐐰𐐼 𐑄𐐲𐑅 𐐻𐐩𐐿𐐲𐑌 𐐿𐐩𐑉 𐐲𐑂 𐐵𐑉 𐐶𐐭𐑌𐐼𐐯𐐼 𐑋𐐯𐑌, 𐐰𐑌𐐼 𐐸𐐰𐐼 𐐺𐐯𐑉𐐨𐐼 𐐵𐑉 𐐼𐐯𐐼, 𐐰𐑌𐐼 𐐫𐑊𐑅𐐬 𐑄 𐐼𐐯𐐼 𐐲𐑂 𐑄 𐐢𐐩𐑋𐐲𐑌𐐴𐐻𐑅, 𐐸𐐭 𐐶𐐲𐑉 𐑋𐐯𐑌𐐨, 𐐺𐐨𐐸𐐬𐑊𐐼, 𐐶𐐨 𐐼𐐮𐐼 𐐮𐑌𐐿𐐶𐐴𐑉 𐐲𐑂 𐐘𐐮𐐼 𐐿𐐪𐑌𐑅𐐲𐑉𐑌𐐮𐑍 𐑄 𐐹𐑉𐐮𐑆𐐲𐑌𐐲𐑉𐑆 𐐸𐐭𐑋 𐑄𐐩 𐐸𐐰𐐼 𐑅𐐻𐐪𐑉𐐻𐐯𐐼 𐐻𐐭 𐑀𐐬 𐐼𐐵𐑌 𐐻𐐭 𐑄 𐑊𐐰𐑌𐐼 𐐲𐑂 𐐞𐐰𐑉𐐲𐐸𐐯𐑋𐑊𐐲 𐐶𐐮𐑄. 𐐤𐐵 𐐘𐐮𐐼 𐐶𐐲𐑆 𐑄 𐐽𐐨𐑁 𐐿𐐰𐐹𐐻𐐮𐑌 𐐬𐑂𐐲𐑉 𐑄 𐐺𐐰𐑌𐐼 𐐸𐐭 𐐶𐐲𐑆 𐐲𐐹𐐱𐐮𐑌𐐻𐐯𐐼 𐐻𐐭 𐑀𐐪𐑉𐐼 𐑄𐐯𐑋 𐐼𐐵𐑌 𐐻𐐭 𐑄 𐑊𐐰𐑌𐐼. 𐐈𐑌𐐼 𐑌𐐵, 𐑄𐐨𐑆 𐐪𐑉 𐑄 𐐶𐐲𐑉𐐼𐑆 𐐸𐐶𐐮𐐽 𐐘𐐮𐐼 𐑅𐐯𐐼 𐐲𐑌𐐻𐐭 𐑋𐐨, 𐐒𐐨𐐸𐐬𐑊𐐼, 𐐶𐐨 𐐼𐐮𐐼 𐑅𐐻𐐪𐑉𐐻 𐐻𐐭 𐑀𐐬 𐐼𐐵𐑌 𐐻𐐭 𐑄 𐑊𐐰𐑌𐐼 𐐲𐑂 𐐞𐐰𐑉𐐲𐐸𐐯𐑋𐑊𐐲 𐐶𐐮𐑄 𐐵𐑉 𐐹𐑉𐐮𐑆𐐲𐑌𐐲𐑉𐑆. 𐐈𐑌𐐼 𐐮𐐻 𐐿𐐩𐑋 𐐻𐐭 𐐹𐐰𐑅 𐑄𐐰𐐻 𐐶𐐨 𐐼𐐮𐐼 𐑋𐐨𐐻 𐑄 𐑅𐐹𐐴𐑆 𐐲𐑂 𐐵𐑉 𐐪𐑉𐑋𐐨𐑆, 𐐸𐐭 𐐸𐐰𐐼 𐐺𐐮𐑌 𐑅𐐯𐑌𐐻 𐐵𐐻 𐐻𐐭 𐐶𐐱𐐽 𐑄 𐐿𐐰𐑋𐐹 𐐲𐑂 𐑄 𐐢𐐩𐑋𐐲𐑌𐐴𐐻𐑅. 𐐈𐑌𐐼 𐑄𐐩 𐐿𐑉𐐴𐐼 𐐲𐑌𐐻𐐭 𐐲𐑅, 𐑅𐐩𐐮𐑍, 𐐒𐐨𐐸𐐬𐑊𐐼, 𐑄 𐐪𐑉𐑋𐐨𐑆 𐐲𐑂 𐑄 𐐢𐐩𐑋𐐲𐑌𐐴𐐻𐑅 𐐪𐑉 𐑋𐐪𐑉𐐽𐐮𐑍 𐐻𐐬𐐲𐑉𐐼𐑆 𐑄 𐑅𐐮𐐻𐐨 𐐲𐑂 𐐗𐐷𐐭𐑋𐐨𐑌𐐴; 𐐰𐑌𐐼 𐐺𐐨𐐸𐐬𐑊𐐼, 𐑄𐐩 𐐶𐐮𐑊 𐑁𐐫𐑊 𐐲𐐹𐐪𐑌 𐑄𐐯𐑋, 𐐷𐐩, 𐐰𐑌𐐼 𐐶𐐮𐑊 𐐼𐐯𐑅𐐻𐑉𐐱𐐮 𐐵𐑉 𐐹𐐨𐐹𐑊.

20. 𐐈𐑌𐐼 𐐮𐐻 𐐿𐐩𐑋 𐐻𐐭 𐐹𐐰𐑅 𐑄𐐰𐐻 𐐵𐑉 𐐹𐑉𐐮𐑆𐐲𐑌𐐲𐑉𐑆 𐐼𐐮𐐼 𐐸𐐨𐑉 𐑄𐐩𐑉 𐐿𐑉𐐴𐑆, 𐐸𐐶𐐮𐐽 𐐿𐐫𐑆𐐼 𐑄𐐯𐑋 𐐻𐐭 𐐻𐐩𐐿 𐐿𐐲𐑉𐐩𐐾; 𐐰𐑌𐐼 𐑄𐐩 𐐼𐐮𐐼 𐑉𐐴𐑆 𐐲𐐹 𐐮𐑌 𐑉𐐯𐐺𐐯𐑊𐐷𐐲𐑌 𐐰𐑀𐐯𐑌𐑅𐐻 𐐲𐑅. 𐐈𐑌𐐼 𐐮𐐻 𐐿𐐩𐑋 𐐻𐐭 𐐹𐐰𐑅 𐐺𐐨𐐿𐐫𐑆 𐐲𐑂 𐑄𐐩𐑉 𐑉𐐯𐐺𐐯𐑊𐐷𐐲𐑌, 𐐶𐐨 𐐼𐐮𐐼 𐐿𐐫𐑆 𐑄𐐰𐐻 𐐵𐑉 𐑅𐐬𐑉𐐼𐑆 𐑇𐐳𐐼 𐐿𐐲𐑋 𐐲𐐹𐐪𐑌 𐑄𐐯𐑋. 𐐈𐑌𐐼 𐐮𐐻 𐐿𐐩𐑋 𐐻𐐭 𐐹𐐰𐑅 𐑄𐐰𐐻 𐑄𐐩 𐐼𐐮𐐼 𐐮𐑌 𐐩 𐐺𐐱𐐼𐐨 𐑉𐐲𐑌 𐐲𐐹𐐪𐑌 𐐵𐑉 𐑅𐐬𐑉𐐼𐑆, 𐐮𐑌 𐑄 𐐸𐐶𐐮𐐽 𐑄 𐑀𐑉𐐩𐐻𐐲𐑉 𐑌𐐲𐑋𐐺𐐲𐑉 𐐲𐑂 𐑄𐐯𐑋 𐐶𐐲𐑉 𐑅𐑊𐐩𐑌; 𐐰𐑌𐐼 𐑄 𐑉𐐨𐑋𐐩𐑌𐐼𐐲𐑉 𐐲𐑂 𐑄𐐯𐑋 𐐺𐑉𐐬𐐿 𐑃𐑉𐐭 𐐰𐑌𐐼 𐑁𐑊𐐯𐐼 𐑁𐑉𐐱𐑋 𐐲𐑅. 𐐈𐑌𐐼 𐐺𐐨𐐸𐐬𐑊𐐼, 𐐸𐐶𐐯𐑌 𐑄𐐩 𐐸𐐰𐐼 𐑁𐑊𐐯𐐼, 𐐰𐑌𐐼 𐐶𐐨 𐐿𐐳𐐼 𐑌𐐱𐐻 𐐬𐑂𐐲𐑉𐐻𐐩𐐿 𐑄𐐯𐑋, 𐐶𐐨 𐐻𐐳𐐿 𐐵𐑉 𐑋𐐪𐑉𐐽 𐐶𐐮𐑄 𐑅𐐹𐐨𐐼 𐐻𐐬𐐲𐑉𐐼𐑆 𐑄 𐑅𐐮𐐻𐐨 𐐲𐑂 𐐗𐐷𐐭𐑋𐐨𐑌𐐴; 𐐰𐑌𐐼 𐐺𐐨𐐸𐐬𐑊𐐼, 𐐶𐐨 𐐼𐐮𐐼 𐐲𐑉𐐴𐑂 𐐮𐑌 𐐻𐐴𐑋 𐑄𐐰𐐻 𐐶𐐨 𐑋𐐴𐐻 𐐲𐑅𐐮𐑅𐐻 𐐵𐑉 𐐺𐑉𐐯𐑄𐑉𐐯𐑌 𐐮𐑌 𐐹𐑉𐐨𐑆𐐲𐑉𐑂𐐮𐑍 𐑄 𐑅𐐮𐐻𐐨. 𐐈𐑌𐐼 𐐺𐐨𐐸𐐬𐑊𐐼, 𐐶𐐨 𐐪𐑉 𐐲𐑀𐐯𐑌 𐐼𐐨𐑊𐐮𐑂𐐲𐑉𐐼 𐐵𐐻 𐐲𐑂 𐑄 𐐸𐐰𐑌𐐼𐑆 𐐲𐑂 𐐵𐑉 𐐯𐑌𐐯𐑋𐐨𐑆. 𐐈𐑌𐐼 𐐺𐑊𐐯𐑅𐐯𐐼 𐐮𐑆 𐑄 𐑌𐐩𐑋 𐐲𐑂 𐐵𐑉 𐐘𐐱𐐼; 𐑁𐐫𐑉 𐐺𐐨𐐸𐐬𐑊𐐼, 𐐮𐐻 𐐮𐑆 𐐸𐐨 𐑄𐐰𐐻 𐐸𐐰𐑆 𐐼𐐨𐑊𐐮𐑂𐐲𐑉𐐼 𐐲𐑅; 𐐷𐐩, 𐑄𐐰𐐻 𐐸𐐰𐑆 𐐼𐐲𐑌 𐑄𐐮𐑅 𐑀𐑉𐐩𐐻 𐑃𐐮𐑍 𐑁𐐫𐑉 𐐲𐑅.

21. 𐐤𐐵 𐐮𐐻 𐐿𐐩𐑋 𐐻𐐭 𐐹𐐰𐑅 𐑄𐐰𐐻 𐐸𐐶𐐯𐑌 𐐌, 𐐐𐐯𐑊𐐲𐑋𐐲𐑌, 𐐸𐐰𐐼 𐐸𐐲𐑉𐐼 𐑄𐐨𐑆 𐐶𐐲𐑉𐐼𐑆 𐐲𐑂 𐐘𐐮𐐼, 𐐌 𐐶𐐲𐑆 𐑁𐐮𐑊𐐼 𐐶𐐮𐑄 𐐯𐐿𐑅𐐨𐐼𐐮𐑍 𐐾𐐱𐐮, 𐐺𐐨𐐿𐐫𐑆 𐐲𐑂 𐑄 𐑀𐐳𐐼𐑌𐐯𐑅 𐐲𐑂 𐐘𐐱𐐼 𐐮𐑌 𐐹𐑉𐐨𐑆𐐲𐑉𐑂𐐮𐑍 𐐲𐑅, 𐑄𐐰𐐻 𐐶𐐨 𐑋𐐴𐐻 𐑌𐐱𐐻 𐐫𐑊 𐐹𐐯𐑉𐐮𐑇; 𐐷𐐩, 𐐰𐑌𐐼 𐐌 𐐻𐑉𐐲𐑅𐐻 𐑄𐐰𐐻 𐑄 𐑅𐐬𐑊𐑆 𐐲𐑂 𐑄𐐯𐑋 𐐸𐐭 𐐸𐐰𐑂 𐐺𐐮𐑌 𐑅𐑊𐐩𐑌, 𐐸𐐰𐑂 𐐯𐑌𐐻𐐲𐑉𐐼 𐐮𐑌𐐻𐐭 𐑄 𐑉𐐯𐑅𐐻 𐐲𐑂 𐑄𐐩𐑉 𐐘𐐱𐐼.

22. 𐐈𐑌𐐼 𐐺𐐨𐐸𐐬𐑊𐐼, 𐑌𐐵 𐐮𐐻 𐐿𐐩𐑋 𐐻𐐭 𐐹𐐰𐑅 𐑄𐐰𐐻 𐐵𐑉 𐑌𐐯𐐿𐑅𐐻 𐑋𐐭𐑂𐑋𐐯𐑌𐐻 𐐶𐐲𐑆 𐐻𐐭 𐐱𐐺𐐻𐐩𐑌 𐑄 𐑅𐐮𐐻𐐨 𐐲𐑂 𐐣𐐰𐑌𐐻𐐴; 𐐺𐐲𐐻 𐐺𐐨𐐸𐐬𐑊𐐼, 𐑄𐐩𐑉 𐐶𐐲𐑆 𐑌𐐬 𐐶𐐩 𐑄𐐰𐐻 𐐶𐐨 𐐿𐐳𐐼 𐑊𐐨𐐼 𐑄𐐯𐑋 𐐵𐐻 𐐲𐑂 𐑄 𐑅𐐮𐐻𐐨 𐐺𐐴 𐐵𐑉 𐑅𐑋𐐫𐑊 𐐺𐐰𐑌𐐼𐑆. 𐐙𐐫𐑉 𐐺𐐨𐐸𐐬𐑊𐐼 𐑄𐐩 𐑉𐐨𐑋𐐯𐑋𐐺𐐲𐑉𐐼 𐑄𐐰𐐻 𐐸𐐶𐐮𐐽 𐐶𐐨 𐐸𐐰𐐼 𐐸𐐮𐑄𐐲𐑉𐐻𐐭 𐐼𐐲𐑌; 𐑄𐐩𐑉𐑁𐐬𐑉 𐐶𐐨 𐐿𐐳𐐼 𐑌𐐱𐐻 𐐼𐐨𐐿𐐱𐐮 𐑄𐐯𐑋 𐐲𐐶𐐩 𐑁𐑉𐐱𐑋 𐑄𐐩𐑉 𐑅𐐻𐑉𐐱𐑍𐐸𐐬𐑊𐐼𐑆; 𐐰𐑌𐐼 𐑄𐐩 𐐶𐐲𐑉 𐑅𐐬 𐑋𐐲𐐽 𐑋𐐬𐑉 𐑌𐐷𐐭𐑋𐐲𐑉𐐲𐑅 𐑄𐐰𐑌 𐐶𐐲𐑆 𐐵𐑉 𐐪𐑉𐑋𐐨, 𐑄𐐰𐐻 𐐶𐐨 𐐼𐐲𐑉𐑅𐐻 𐑌𐐱𐐻 𐑀𐐬 𐑁𐐬𐑉𐑃 𐐰𐑌𐐼 𐐲𐐻𐐰𐐿 𐑄𐐯𐑋 𐐮𐑌 𐑄𐐩𐑉 𐑅𐐻𐑉𐐱𐑍𐐸𐐬𐑊𐐼𐑆. 𐐏𐐩, 𐐰𐑌𐐼 𐐮𐐻 𐐺𐐨𐐿𐐩𐑋 𐐯𐐿𐑅𐐹𐐨𐐼𐐨𐐯𐑌𐐻 𐑄𐐰𐐻 𐐶𐐨 𐑇𐐳𐐼 𐐯𐑋𐐹𐑊𐐱𐐮 𐐵𐑉 𐑋𐐯𐑌, 𐐻𐐭 𐑄 𐑋𐐩𐑌𐐻𐐩𐑌𐐮𐑍 𐑄𐐬𐑆 𐐹𐐪𐑉𐐻𐑅 𐐲𐑂 𐑄 𐑊𐐰𐑌𐐼, 𐐲𐑂 𐑄 𐐸𐐶𐐮𐐽 𐐶𐐨 𐐸𐐰𐐼 𐑉𐐨𐑀𐐩𐑌𐐼 𐐲𐑂 𐐵𐑉 𐐹𐐲𐑆𐐯𐑇𐐲𐑌𐑆; 𐑄𐐩𐑉𐑁𐐬𐑉 𐐮𐐻 𐐺𐐨𐐿𐐩𐑋 𐐯𐐿𐑅𐐹𐐨𐐼𐐨𐐯𐑌𐐻 𐑄𐐰𐐻 𐐶𐐨 𐑇𐐳𐐼 𐐶𐐩𐐻, 𐑄𐐰𐐻 𐐶𐐨 𐑋𐐴𐐻 𐑉𐐨𐑅𐐨𐑂 𐑋𐐬𐑉 𐑅𐐻𐑉𐐯𐑍𐑃 𐑁𐑉𐐱𐑋 𐑄 𐑊𐐰𐑌𐐼 𐐲𐑂 𐐞𐐰𐑉𐐲𐐸𐐯𐑋𐑊𐐲, 𐐰𐑌𐐼 𐐫𐑊𐑅𐐬 𐐩 𐑌𐐷𐐭 𐑅𐐲𐐹𐑊𐐴 𐐲𐑂 𐐹𐑉𐐬𐑂𐐮𐑠𐐲𐑌𐑆.

23. 𐐈𐑌𐐼 𐐮𐐻 𐐿𐐩𐑋 𐐻𐐭 𐐹𐐰𐑅 𐑄𐐰𐐻 𐐌 𐑄𐐲𐑅 𐐼𐐮𐐼 𐑅𐐯𐑌𐐼 𐐰𐑌 𐐯𐑋𐐺𐐲𐑅𐐨 𐐻𐐭 𐑄 𐑀𐐲𐑂𐐲𐑉𐑌𐐲𐑉 𐐲𐑂 𐐵𐑉 𐑊𐐰𐑌𐐼, 𐐻𐐭 𐐰𐐿𐐶𐐩𐑌𐐻 𐐸𐐮𐑋 𐐿𐐪𐑌𐑅𐐲𐑉𐑌𐐮𐑍 𐑄 𐐰𐑁𐐩𐑉𐑆 𐐲𐑂 𐐵𐑉 𐐹𐐨𐐹𐑊. 𐐈𐑌𐐼 𐐮𐐻 𐐿𐐩𐑋 𐐻𐐭 𐐹𐐰𐑅 𐑄𐐰𐐻 𐐶𐐨 𐐼𐐮𐐼 𐐶𐐩𐐻 𐐻𐐭 𐑉𐐨𐑅𐐨𐑂 𐐹𐑉𐐬𐑂𐐮𐑠𐐲𐑌𐑆 𐐰𐑌𐐼 𐑅𐐻𐑉𐐯𐑍𐑃, 𐑁𐑉𐐱𐑋 𐑄 𐑊𐐰𐑌𐐼 𐐲𐑂 𐐞𐐰𐑉𐐲𐐸𐐯𐑋𐑊𐐲. 𐐒𐐲𐐻 𐐺𐐨𐐸𐐬𐑊𐐼, 𐑄𐐮𐑅 𐐼𐐮𐐼 𐐹𐑉𐐱𐑁𐐮𐐻 𐐲𐑅 𐐺𐐲𐐻 𐑊𐐮𐐻𐑊; 𐑁𐐫𐑉 𐑄 𐐢𐐩𐑋𐐲𐑌𐐴𐐻𐑅 𐐶𐐲𐑉 𐐫𐑊𐑅𐐬 𐑉𐐨𐑅𐐨𐑂𐐮𐑍 𐑀𐑉𐐩𐐻 𐑅𐐻𐑉𐐯𐑍𐑃, 𐑁𐑉𐐱𐑋 𐐼𐐩 𐐻𐐭 𐐼𐐩, 𐐰𐑌𐐼 𐐫𐑊𐑅𐐬 𐑋𐐯𐑌𐐨 𐐹𐑉𐐬𐑂𐐮𐑠𐐲𐑌𐑆; 𐐰𐑌𐐼 𐑄𐐲𐑅 𐐶𐐲𐑉 𐐵𐑉 𐑅𐐲𐑉-

𐐿𐐲𐑋𐑅𐐻𐐰𐑌𐑅𐐯𐑆 𐐰𐐻 𐑄𐐮𐑅 𐐹𐐨𐑉𐐨𐐲𐐼 𐐲𐑂 𐐻𐐴𐑋. 𐐰𐑌𐐼 𐑄 𐐢𐐰𐑋𐐲𐑌𐐴𐐻𐑅 𐐶𐐯𐑉 𐑅𐐰𐑊𐐨𐐮𐑍 𐑁𐐬𐑉𐑃 𐐲𐑀𐐯𐑌𐑅𐐻 𐐲𐑅, 𐑁𐑉𐐲𐑋 𐐻𐐴𐑋 𐐻𐐭 𐐻𐐴𐑋, 𐑉𐐯𐑆𐐮𐑅𐐻𐐮𐑍 𐐺𐐴 𐑅𐐻𐑉𐐰𐐻𐐲𐐾𐐲𐑋 𐐻𐐭 𐐼𐐯𐑅𐐻𐑉𐐫𐐶 𐐲𐑅; 𐑌𐐯𐑂𐐲𐑉𐑄𐐲𐑊𐐯𐑅 𐐶𐐨 𐐿𐐳𐐼 𐑌𐐪𐐻 𐐿𐐲𐑋 𐐻𐐭 𐐺𐐰𐐻𐑊 𐐶𐐮𐑄 𐑄𐐯𐑋, 𐐺𐐨𐐿𐐪𐑆 𐐲𐑂 𐑄𐐯𐑉 𐑉𐐨𐐻𐑉𐐨𐐻𐑅 𐐰𐑌𐐼 𐑄𐐯𐑉 𐑅𐐻𐑉𐐱𐑍𐐸𐐬𐑊𐐼𐑆.

24. 𐐰𐑌𐐼 𐐮𐐻 𐐿𐐩𐑋 𐐻𐐭 𐐹𐐰𐑅 𐑄𐐰𐐻 𐐶𐐨 𐐼𐐮𐐼 𐐶𐐩𐐻 𐐮𐑌 𐑄𐐨𐑆 𐐼𐐮𐑁𐐮𐐿𐐲𐑊𐐻 𐑅𐐲𐑉𐐿𐐲𐑋𐑅𐐻𐐰𐑌𐑅𐐯𐑆, 𐑁𐐫𐑉 𐑄 𐑅𐐹𐐩𐑅 𐐲𐑂 𐑋𐐯𐑌𐐨 𐑋𐐲𐑌𐑃𐑅, 𐐨𐑂𐐲𐑌 𐐲𐑌𐐻𐐮𐑊 𐐶𐐨 𐐶𐐯𐑉 𐐲𐐺𐐵𐐻 𐐻𐐭 𐐹𐐲𐑉𐐮𐑇 𐑁𐐫𐑉 𐑄 𐐶𐐪𐑌𐐻 𐐲𐑂 𐑁𐐭𐐼. 𐐒𐐲𐐻 𐐮𐐻 𐐿𐐩𐑋 𐐻𐐭 𐐹𐐰𐑅 𐑄𐐰𐐻 𐐶𐐨 𐐼𐐮𐐼 𐑉𐐯𐑅𐐨𐑂 𐑁𐐭𐐼, 𐐸𐐶𐐮𐐽 𐐶𐐲𐑆 𐑀𐐪𐑉𐐼𐐲𐐼 𐐻𐐭 𐐲𐑅 𐐺𐐴 𐐰𐑌 𐐪𐑉𐑋𐐨 𐐲𐑂 𐐻𐐭 𐑃𐐵𐑆𐐲𐑌𐐼 𐑋𐐯𐑌 𐐻𐐭 𐐵𐑉 𐐰𐑅𐐮𐑅𐐻𐐲𐑌𐑅; 𐐰𐑌𐐼 𐑄𐐮𐑅 𐐮𐑆 𐐫𐑊 𐑄 𐐰𐑅𐐮𐑅𐐻𐐲𐑌𐑅 𐐸𐐶𐐮𐐽 𐐶𐐨 𐐼𐐮𐐼 𐑉𐐯𐑅𐐨𐑂, 𐐻𐐭 𐐼𐐯𐑁𐐯𐑌𐐼 𐐵𐑉𐑅𐐯𐑊𐑂𐑆 𐐰𐑌𐐼 𐐵𐑉 𐐿𐐲𐑌𐐻𐑉𐐨 𐑁𐑉𐐲𐑋 𐑁𐐫𐑊𐐮𐑍 𐐮𐑌𐐻𐐭 𐑄 𐐸𐐰𐑌𐐼𐑆 𐐲𐑂 𐐵𐑉 𐐯𐑌𐐲𐑋𐐨𐑆; 𐐷𐐩, 𐐻𐐭 𐐿𐐪𐑌𐐻𐐯𐑌𐐼 𐐶𐐮𐑄 𐐰𐑌 𐐯𐑌𐐲𐑋𐐨 𐐸𐐶𐐮𐐽 𐐶𐐲𐑆 𐐮𐑌𐐭𐑋𐐲𐑉𐐲𐐺𐑊. 𐐰𐑌𐐼 𐑌𐐵 𐑄 𐐿𐐫𐑆 𐐲𐑂 𐑄𐐨𐑆 𐐵𐑉 𐐯𐑋𐐺𐐰𐑉𐐲𐑅𐑋𐐲𐑌𐐻𐑅, 𐐫𐑉 𐑄 𐐿𐐫𐑆 𐐸𐐶𐐴 𐑄𐐩 𐐼𐐮𐐼 𐑌𐐪𐐻 𐑅𐐯𐑌𐐼 𐑋𐐬𐑉 𐑅𐐻𐑉𐐯𐑍𐑃 𐐲𐑌𐐻𐐭 𐐲𐑅, 𐐶𐐨 𐑌𐐬 𐑌𐐪𐐻; 𐑄𐐯𐑉𐑁𐐬𐑉 𐐶𐐨 𐐪𐑉 𐑀𐑉𐐨𐑂𐐼, 𐐰𐑌𐐼 𐐫𐑊𐑅𐐬 𐑁𐐮𐑊𐐼 𐐶𐐮𐑄 𐑁𐐨𐑉, 𐑊𐐯𐑅𐐻 𐐺𐐴 𐐯𐑌𐐨 𐑋𐐨𐑌𐑆 𐑄 𐐾𐐲𐐾𐑋𐐲𐑌𐐻𐑅 𐐲𐑂 𐐘𐐪𐐼 𐑇𐐳𐐼 𐐿𐐲𐑋 𐐲𐐹𐐪𐑌 𐐵𐑉 𐑊𐐰𐑌𐐼, 𐐻𐐭 𐐵𐑉 𐐬𐑂𐐲𐑉𐑃𐑉𐐬 𐐰𐑌𐐼 𐐲𐐻𐐲𐑉 𐐰𐑌𐐴𐐲𐑊𐐩𐑇𐐲𐑌; 𐑄𐐯𐑉𐑁𐐬𐑉 𐐶𐐨 𐐼𐐮𐐼 𐐹𐐬𐑉 𐐵𐐻 𐐵𐑉 𐑅𐐬𐑊𐑆 𐐮𐑌 𐐹𐑉𐐯𐑉 𐐻𐐭 𐐘𐐪𐐼, 𐑄𐐰𐐻 𐐸𐐨 𐐶𐐳𐐼 𐑅𐐻𐑉𐐯𐑍𐑃𐐲𐑌 𐐲𐑅 𐐰𐑌𐐼 𐐼𐐯𐑊𐐮𐑂𐐲𐑉 𐐲𐑅 𐐵𐐻 𐐲𐑂 𐑄 𐐸𐐰𐑌𐐼𐑆 𐐲𐑂 𐐵𐑉 𐐯𐑌𐐲𐑋𐐨𐑆; 𐐷𐐩, 𐐰𐑌𐐼 𐐫𐑊𐑅𐐬 𐑀𐐮𐑂 𐐲𐑅 𐑅𐐻𐑉𐐯𐑍𐑃 𐑄𐐰𐐻 𐐶𐐨 𐑋𐐴𐐻 𐑉𐐨𐐻𐐩𐑌 𐐵𐑉 𐑅𐐮𐐻𐐨𐑆, 𐐰𐑌𐐼 𐐵𐑉 𐑊𐐰𐑌𐐼𐑆, 𐐰𐑌𐐼 𐐵𐑉 𐐹𐐲𐑆𐐯𐑇𐐲𐑌𐑆, 𐑁𐐫𐑉 𐑄 𐑅𐐲𐐹𐐬𐑉𐐻 𐐲𐑂 𐐵𐑉 𐐹𐐨𐐹𐑊. 𐐏𐐩, 𐐰𐑌𐐼 𐐮𐐻 𐐿𐐩𐑋 𐐻𐐭 𐐹𐐰𐑅 𐑄𐐰𐐻 𐑄 𐐢𐐪𐑉𐐼 𐐵𐑉 𐐘𐐪𐐼 𐐼𐐮𐐼 𐑂𐐮𐑆𐐮𐐻 𐐲𐑅 𐐶𐐮𐑄 𐐰𐑇𐐭𐑉𐐲𐑌𐑅𐐯𐑆, 𐑄𐐰𐐻 𐐸𐐨 𐐶𐐳𐐼 𐐼𐐯𐑊𐐮𐑂𐐲𐑉 𐐲𐑅; 𐐷𐐩, 𐐮𐑌𐑅𐐬𐑋𐐲𐐽 𐑄𐐰𐐻 𐐸𐐨 𐐼𐐮𐐼 𐑅𐐹𐐨𐐿 𐐹𐐨𐑅 𐐻𐐭 𐐵𐑉 𐑅𐐬𐑊𐑆, 𐐰𐑌𐐼 𐐼𐐮𐐼 𐑀𐑉𐐰𐑌𐐻 𐐲𐑌𐐻𐐭 𐐲𐑅 𐑀𐑉𐐩𐐻 𐑁𐐩𐑃, 𐐰𐑌𐐼 𐐼𐐮𐐼 𐐿𐐫𐑆 𐐲𐑅 𐑄𐐰𐐻 𐐶𐐨 𐑇𐐳𐐼 𐐸𐐬𐐹 𐑁𐐫𐑉 𐐵𐑉 𐐼𐐯𐑊𐐮𐑂𐐲𐑉𐐲𐑌𐑅 𐐮𐑌 𐐸𐐮𐑋; 𐐰𐑌𐐼 𐐶𐐨 𐐼𐐮𐐼 𐐻𐐩𐐿 𐐿𐐲𐑉𐐩𐐾 𐐶𐐮𐑄 𐐵𐑉 𐑅𐑋𐐫𐑊 𐑁𐐬𐑉𐑅 𐐸𐐶𐐮𐐽 𐐶𐐨 𐐸𐐰𐐼 𐑉𐐯𐑅𐐨𐑂𐐼, 𐐰𐑌𐐼 𐐶𐐯𐑉 𐑁𐐮𐐿𐑅𐐻 𐐶𐐮𐑄 𐐩 𐐼𐐯𐐻𐐲𐑉𐑋𐐮𐑌𐐩𐑇𐐲𐑌 𐐻𐐭 𐐿𐐪𐑍𐐿𐐲𐑉 𐐵𐑉 𐐯𐑌𐐲𐑋𐐨𐑆, 𐐰𐑌𐐼 𐐻𐐭 𐑋𐐩𐑌𐐻𐐩𐑌 𐐵𐑉 𐑊𐐰𐑌𐐼𐑆, 𐐰𐑌𐐼 𐐵𐑉 𐐹𐐲𐑆𐐯𐑇𐐲𐑌𐑆, 𐐰𐑌𐐼 𐐵𐑉 𐐶𐐴𐑂𐑆, 𐐰𐑌𐐼 𐐵𐑉 𐐽𐐮𐑊𐐼𐑉𐐯𐑌, 𐐰𐑌𐐼 𐑄 𐐿𐐫𐑆 𐐲𐑂 𐐵𐑉 𐑊𐐮𐐺𐐲𐑉𐐻𐐨. 𐐰𐑌𐐼 𐑄𐐲𐑅 𐐶𐐨 𐐼𐐮𐐼 𐑀𐐬 𐑁𐐬𐑉𐑃 𐐶𐐮𐑄 𐐫𐑊 𐐵𐑉 𐑋𐐴𐐻 𐐲𐑀𐐯𐑌𐑅𐐻 𐑄 𐐢𐐰𐑋𐐲𐑌𐐴𐐻𐑅, 𐐸𐐭 𐐶𐐯𐑉 𐐮𐑌 𐑄 𐑅𐐮𐐻𐐨 𐐲𐑂 𐐣𐐰𐑌𐐻𐐴; 𐐰𐑌𐐼 𐐶𐐨 𐐼𐐮𐐼 𐐹𐐮𐐽 𐐵𐑉 𐐻𐐯𐑌𐐻𐑅 𐐺𐐴 𐑄 𐐶𐐮𐑊𐐼𐐲𐑉𐑌𐐯𐑅 𐑅𐐴𐐼, 𐐸𐐶𐐮𐐽 𐐶𐐲𐑆 𐑌𐐨𐑉 𐐻𐐭 𐑄 𐑅𐐮𐐻𐐨. 𐐰𐑌𐐼 𐐮𐐻 𐐿𐐩𐑋 𐐻𐐭 𐐹𐐰𐑅 𐑄𐐰𐐻 𐐪𐑌 𐑄 𐑋𐐪𐑉𐐬, 𐑄𐐰𐐻 𐐸𐐶𐐯𐑌 𐑄 𐐢𐐰𐑋𐐲𐑌𐐴𐐻𐑅 𐑅𐐫 𐑄𐐰𐐻 𐐶𐐨 𐐶𐐯𐑉 𐐮𐑌 𐑄 𐐺𐐫𐑉𐐼𐐲𐑉𐑆 𐐺𐐴 𐑄 𐐶𐐮𐑊𐐼𐐲𐑉𐑌𐐯𐑅 𐐸𐐶𐐮𐐽 𐐶𐐲𐑆 𐑌𐐨𐑉 𐑄 𐑅𐐮𐐻𐐨, 𐑄𐐰𐐻 𐑄𐐩 𐑅𐐯𐑌𐐻 𐐵𐐻 𐑄𐐯𐑉 𐑅𐐹𐐴𐑆 𐑉𐐵𐑌𐐼 𐐲𐐺𐐵𐐻 𐐲𐑅, 𐑄𐐰𐐻 𐑄𐐩 𐑋𐐴𐐻 𐐼𐐮𐑅𐐿𐐲𐑂𐐲𐑉 𐑄 𐑌𐐲𐑋𐐺𐐲𐑉 𐐰𐑌𐐼 𐑄 𐑅𐐻𐑉𐐯𐑍𐑃 𐐲𐑂 𐐵𐑉 𐐪𐑉𐑋𐐨.

25. 𐐰𐑌𐐼 𐐮𐐻 𐐿𐐩𐑋 𐐻𐐭 𐐹𐐰𐑅 𐑄𐐰𐐻 𐐸𐐶𐐯𐑌 𐑄𐐩 𐑅𐐫 𐑄𐐰𐐻 𐐶𐐨 𐐶𐐯𐑉 𐑌𐐪𐐻 𐑅𐐻𐑉𐐱𐑍, 𐐰𐐿𐐫𐑉𐐼𐐮𐑍 𐐻𐐭 𐐵𐑉 𐑌𐐲𐑋𐐺𐐲𐑉𐑆, 𐐰𐑌𐐼 𐑁𐐨𐑉𐐮𐑍 𐑄𐐰𐐻 𐐶𐐨 𐑇𐐳𐐼 𐐿𐐲𐐻 𐑄𐐯𐑋 𐐫𐑁 𐑁𐑉𐐲𐑋 𐑄𐐯𐑉 𐑅𐐲𐐹𐐬𐑉𐐻, 𐐯𐐿𐑅𐐯𐐹𐐻 𐑄𐐩 𐑇𐐳𐐼 𐐿𐐲𐑋 𐐵𐐻 𐐻𐐭 𐐺𐐰𐐻𐑊 𐐲𐑀𐐯𐑌𐑅𐐻 𐐲𐑅, 𐐰𐑌𐐼 𐐿𐐮𐑊 𐐲𐑅; 𐐰𐑌𐐼 𐐫𐑊𐑅𐐬 𐑅𐐲𐐹𐐬𐑆𐐮𐑍 𐑄𐐰𐐻 𐑄𐐩 𐐿𐐳𐐼 𐐨𐑆𐐮𐑊𐐨 𐐼𐐯𐑅𐐻𐑉𐐫𐐶 𐐲𐑅 𐐶𐐮𐑄 𐑄𐐯𐑉 𐑌𐐭𐑋𐐲𐑉𐐲𐑅 𐐸𐐬𐑅𐐻𐑅, 𐑄𐐯𐑉𐑁𐐬𐑉 𐑄𐐩 𐐺𐐨𐑀𐐰𐑌 𐐻𐐭 𐑋𐐩𐐿 𐐹𐑉𐐯𐐹𐐲𐑉𐐩𐑇𐐲𐑌𐑆 𐐻𐐭 𐐿𐐲𐑋 𐐵𐐻 𐐲𐑀𐐯𐑌𐑅𐐻 𐐲𐑅 𐐻𐐭 𐐺𐐰𐐻𐑊. 𐐰𐑌𐐼 𐐸𐐶𐐯𐑌 𐐶𐐨 𐑅𐐫 𐑄𐐰𐐻 𐑄𐐩 𐐶𐐯𐑉 𐑋𐐩𐐿𐐮𐑍 𐐹𐑉𐐯𐐹𐐲𐑉𐐩𐑇𐐲𐑌𐑆 𐐻𐐭 𐐿𐐲𐑋 𐐵𐐻 𐐲𐑀𐐯𐑌𐑅𐐻 𐐲𐑅, 𐐺𐐨𐐸𐐬𐑊𐐼, 𐐌 𐐿𐐫𐑆𐐼 𐑄𐐰𐐻 𐐘𐐮𐐼, 𐐶𐐮𐑄 𐐩 𐑅𐑋𐐫𐑊 𐑌𐐲𐑋𐐺𐐲𐑉 𐐲𐑂 𐑋𐐯𐑌, 𐑇𐐳𐐼 𐑅𐐨𐐿𐑉𐐨𐐻 𐐸𐐮𐑋𐑅𐐯𐑊𐑁 𐐮𐑌 𐑄 𐐶𐐮𐑊𐐼𐐲𐑉𐑌𐐯𐑅, 𐐰𐑌𐐼 𐐫𐑊𐑅𐐬 𐑄𐐰𐐻 𐐓𐐨𐐪𐑋𐑌𐐲𐑉 𐐰𐑌𐐼 𐐩 𐑅𐑋𐐫𐑊 𐑌𐐲𐑋𐐺𐐲𐑉 𐐲𐑂 𐑋𐐯𐑌, 𐑇𐐳𐐼 𐑅𐐨𐐿𐑉𐐨𐐻 𐑄𐐯𐑋𐑅𐐯𐑊𐑂𐑆 𐐫𐑊𐑅𐐬 𐐮𐑌 𐑄 𐐶𐐮𐑊𐐼𐐲𐑉𐑌𐐯𐑅. 𐐤𐐵 𐐘𐐮𐐼 𐐰𐑌𐐼 𐐸𐐮𐑆 𐑋𐐯𐑌 𐐶𐐯𐑉 𐐪𐑌 𐑄 𐑉𐐴𐐻, 𐐰𐑌𐐼 𐑄 𐐲𐑄𐐲𐑉𐑆 𐐪𐑌 𐑄 𐑊𐐯𐑁𐐻; 𐐰𐑌𐐼 𐐸𐐶𐐯𐑌 𐑄𐐩 𐐸𐐰𐐼 𐑄𐐲𐑅 𐑅𐐨𐐿𐑉𐐨𐐻𐐲𐐼 𐑄𐐯𐑋𐑅𐐯𐑊𐑂𐑆, 𐐺𐐨𐐸𐐬𐑊𐐼, 𐐌 𐑉𐐨𐑋𐐩𐑌𐐼 𐐶𐐮𐑄 𐑄 𐑉𐐨𐑋𐐩𐑌𐐼𐐲𐑉 𐐲𐑂 𐑋𐐴 𐐪𐑉𐑋𐐨 𐐮𐑌 𐑄𐐰𐐻 𐑅𐐩𐑋 𐐹𐑊𐐩𐑅 𐐸𐐶𐐯𐑉 𐐶𐐨 𐐸𐐰𐐼 𐑁𐐲𐑉𐑅𐐻 𐐹𐐮𐐽𐐻 𐐵𐑉 𐐻𐐯𐑌𐐻𐑅, 𐐲𐑀𐐯𐑌𐑅𐐻 𐑄 𐐻𐐴𐑋 𐑄𐐰𐐻 𐑄 𐐢𐐰𐑋𐐲𐑌𐐴𐐻𐑅 𐑇𐐳𐐼 𐐿𐐲𐑋 𐐵𐐻 𐐻𐐭 𐐺𐐰𐐻𐑊.

26. 𐐰𐑌𐐼 𐐮𐐻 𐐿𐐩𐑋 𐐻𐐭 𐐹𐐰𐑅 𐑄𐐰𐐻 𐑄 𐐢𐐰𐑋𐐲𐑌𐐴𐐻𐑅 𐐼𐐮𐐼 𐐿𐐲𐑋 𐐵𐐻 𐐶𐐮𐑄 𐑄𐐯𐑉 𐑌𐐭𐑋𐐲𐑉𐐲𐑅 𐐪𐑉𐑋𐐨 𐐲𐑀𐐯𐑌𐑅𐐻 𐐲𐑅. 𐐰𐑌𐐼 𐐸𐐶𐐯𐑌 𐑄𐐩 𐐸𐐰𐐼 𐐿𐐲𐑋 𐐰𐑌𐐼 𐐶𐐯𐑉 𐐲𐐺𐐵𐐻 𐐻𐐭 𐑁𐐫𐑊 𐐲𐐹𐐪𐑌 𐐲𐑅 𐐶𐐮𐑄 𐑄 𐑅𐐬𐑉𐐼, 𐐌 𐐿𐐫𐑆𐐼 𐑄𐐰𐐻 𐑋𐐴 𐑋𐐯𐑌, 𐑄𐐬𐑆 𐐸𐐭 𐐶𐐯𐑉 𐐶𐐮𐑄 𐑋𐐨, 𐑇𐐳𐐼 𐑉𐐨𐐻𐑉𐐨𐐻 𐐮𐑌𐐻𐐭 𐑄 𐐶𐐮𐑊𐐼𐐲𐑉𐑌𐐯𐑅.

27. 𐐰𐑌𐐼 𐐮𐐻 𐐿𐐩𐑋 𐐻𐐭 𐐹𐐰𐑅 𐑄𐐰𐐻 𐑄 𐐢𐐰𐑋𐐲𐑌𐐴𐐻𐑅 𐐼𐐮𐐼 𐑁𐐪𐑊𐐬 𐐰𐑁𐐻𐐲𐑉 𐐲𐑅 𐐶𐐮𐑄 𐑀𐑉𐐩𐐻 𐑅𐐹𐐨𐐼,

𐑁𐐫𐑉 𐑄𐐩 𐐶𐐲𐑉 𐐯𐐿𐑅𐐨𐐼𐐮𐑍𐑊𐐨 𐐼𐐮𐑆𐐴𐑉𐐲𐑅 𐐻𐐭 𐐬𐑂𐐲𐑉𐐻𐐩𐐿 𐐲𐑅, 𐑄𐐰𐐻 𐑄𐐩 𐑋𐐴𐐻 𐑅𐑊𐐩 𐐲𐑅; 𐑄𐐩𐑉𐑁𐐬𐑉 𐑄𐐩 𐐼𐐮𐐼 𐑁𐐱𐑊𐐬 𐐲𐑅 𐐮𐑌𐐻𐐭 𐑄 𐐶𐐮𐑊𐐼𐐲𐑉𐑌𐐯𐑅; 𐐰𐑌𐐼 𐐶𐐨 𐐼𐐮𐐼 𐐹𐐰𐑅 𐐺𐐴 𐐮𐑌 𐑄 𐑋𐐮𐐼𐑅𐐻 𐐱𐑂 𐐘𐐮𐐼 𐐰𐑌𐐼 𐐓𐐨𐐱𐑋𐑌𐐲𐑉, 𐐮𐑌𐑅𐐬𐑋𐐲𐐽 𐑄𐐰𐐻 𐑄𐐩 𐐶𐐲𐑉 𐑌𐐱𐐻 𐐼𐐮𐑅𐐿𐐲𐑂𐐲𐑉𐐼 𐐺𐐴 𐑄 𐐢𐐰𐑋𐐲𐑌𐐴𐐻𐑅.

28. 𐐈𐑌𐐼 𐐮𐐻 𐐿𐐩𐑋 𐐻𐐭 𐐹𐐰𐑅 𐑄𐐰𐐻 𐐸𐐶𐐯𐑌 𐑄 𐐢𐐰𐑋𐐲𐑌𐐴𐐻𐑅 𐐸𐐰𐐼 𐐹𐐰𐑅𐐻 𐐺𐐴, 𐐫𐑉 𐐸𐐶𐐯𐑌 𐑄 𐐪𐑉𐑋𐐨 𐐸𐐰𐐼 𐐹𐐰𐑅𐐻 𐐺𐐴, 𐐘𐐮𐐼 𐐰𐑌𐐼 𐐓𐐨𐐱𐑋𐑌𐐲𐑉 𐐼𐐮𐐼 𐑉𐐴𐑆 𐐲𐐹 𐑁𐑉𐐱𐑋 𐑄𐐩𐑉 𐑅𐐨𐐿𐑉𐐯𐐻 𐐹𐑊𐐩𐑅𐐯𐑆, 𐐰𐑌𐐼 𐐼𐐮𐐼 𐐿𐐲𐐻 𐐫𐑁 𐑄 𐑅𐐹𐐴𐑆 𐐱𐑂 𐑄 𐐢𐐰𐑋𐐲𐑌𐐴𐐻𐑅, 𐑄𐐰𐐻 𐑄𐐩 𐑇𐐳𐐼 𐑌𐐱𐐻 𐑉𐐨𐐻𐐲𐑉𐑌 𐐻𐐭 𐑄 𐑅𐐮𐐻𐐨. 𐐈𐑌𐐼 𐐮𐐻 𐐿𐐩𐑋 𐐻𐐭 𐐹𐐰𐑅 𐑄𐐰𐐻 𐐸𐐶𐐯𐑌 𐑄𐐩 𐐸𐐰𐐼 𐐿𐐲𐐻 𐑄𐐯𐑋 𐐫𐑁, 𐑄𐐩 𐑉𐐰𐑌 𐐻𐐭 𐑄 𐑅𐐮𐐻𐐨, 𐐰𐑌𐐼 𐑁𐐯𐑊 𐐲𐐹𐐱𐑌 𐑄 𐑀𐐪𐑉𐐼𐑆 𐐸𐐭 𐐶𐐲𐑉 𐑊𐐯𐑁𐐻 𐐻𐐭 𐑀𐐪𐑉𐐼 𐑄 𐑅𐐮𐐻𐐨, 𐐮𐑌𐑅𐐬𐑋𐐲𐐽 𐑄𐐰𐐻 𐑄𐐩 𐐼𐐮𐐼 𐐼𐐯𐑅𐐻𐑉𐐱𐐮 𐑄𐐯𐑋, 𐐰𐑌𐐼 𐐼𐐮𐐼 𐐻𐐩𐐿 𐐹𐐲𐑆𐐯𐑇𐐲𐑌 𐐱𐑂 𐑄 𐑅𐐮𐐻𐐨. 𐐤𐐵 𐑄𐐮𐑅 𐐶𐐱𐑆 𐐼𐐲𐑌 𐐺𐐨𐐿𐐫𐑆 𐑄 𐐢𐐰𐑋𐐲𐑌𐐴𐐻𐑅 𐐼𐐮𐐼 𐑅𐐲𐑁𐐲𐑉 𐑄𐐩𐑉 𐐸𐐬𐑊 𐐪𐑉𐑋𐐨, 𐑅𐐩𐑂 𐐩 𐑁𐐧 𐑀𐐪𐑉𐐼𐑆 𐐬𐑌𐑊𐐨, 𐐻𐐭 𐐺𐐨 𐑊𐐯𐐼 𐐰𐐶𐐩 𐐮𐑌𐐻𐐭 𐑄 𐐶𐐮𐑊𐐼𐐲𐑉𐑌𐐯𐑅.

29. 𐐈𐑌𐐼 𐐮𐐻 𐐿𐐩𐑋 𐐻𐐭 𐐹𐐰𐑅 𐑄𐐰𐐻 𐐘𐐮𐐼 𐐰𐑌𐐼 𐐓𐐨𐐱𐑋𐑌𐐲𐑉 𐐺𐐴 𐑄𐐮𐑅 𐑋𐐨𐑌𐑆 𐐸𐐰𐐼 𐐱𐐺𐐻𐐩𐑌𐐼 𐐹𐐲𐑆-𐐯𐑇𐐲𐑌 𐐱𐑂 𐑄𐐩𐑉 𐑅𐐻𐑉𐐱𐑍𐐸𐐬𐑊𐐼𐑆. 𐐈𐑌𐐼 𐐮𐐻 𐐿𐐩𐑋 𐐻𐐭 𐐹𐐰𐑅 𐑄𐐰𐐻 𐐶𐐨 𐐻𐐳𐐿 𐐵𐑉 𐐿𐐬𐑉𐑅, 𐐰𐑁𐐻𐐲𐑉 𐐸𐐰𐑂𐐮𐑍 𐐻𐑉𐐰𐑂𐐯𐑊𐐼 𐑋𐐲𐐽 𐐮𐑌 𐑄 𐐶𐐮𐑊𐐼𐐲𐑉𐑌𐐯𐑅, 𐐻𐐬𐑉𐐼𐑆 𐑄 𐑊𐐰𐑌𐐼 𐐱𐑂 𐐞𐐰𐑉𐐲𐐸𐐯𐑋𐑊𐐲. 𐐈𐑌𐐼 𐐸𐐶𐐯𐑌 𐑄 𐐢𐐰𐑋𐐲𐑌𐐴𐐻𐑅 𐑅𐐫 𐑄𐐰𐐻 𐑄𐐩 𐐶𐐲𐑉 𐑋𐐪𐑉𐐽𐐮𐑍 𐐻𐐬𐑉𐐼𐑆 𐑄 𐑊𐐰𐑌𐐼 𐐱𐑂 𐐞𐐰𐑉𐐲𐐸𐐯𐑋𐑊𐐲, 𐑄𐐩 𐐶𐐲𐑉 𐐯𐐿𐑅𐐨𐐼𐐮𐑍𐑊𐐨 𐐲𐑁𐑉𐐩𐐼, 𐑊𐐯𐑅𐐻 𐑄𐐩𐑉 𐐶𐐱𐑆 𐐩 𐐹𐑊𐐰𐑌 𐑊𐐩𐐼 𐐻𐐭 𐑊𐐨𐐼 𐑄𐐯𐑋 𐐱𐑌 𐐻𐐭 𐐼𐐯𐑅𐐻𐑉𐐲𐐿𐑇𐐲𐑌; 𐑄𐐩𐑉𐑁𐐬𐑉 𐑄𐐩 𐐺𐐨-𐑀𐐰𐑌 𐐻𐐭 𐑉𐐨𐐻𐑉𐐨𐐻 𐐮𐑌𐐻𐐭 𐑄 𐐶𐐮𐑊𐐼𐐲𐑉𐑌𐐯𐑅 𐐲𐑀𐐯𐑌, 𐐷𐐩, 𐐨𐑂𐐲𐑌 𐐺𐐰𐐿 𐐺𐐴 𐑄 𐑅𐐩𐑋 𐐶𐐩 𐐸𐐶𐐮𐐽 𐑄𐐩 𐐸𐐰𐐼 𐐿𐐲𐑋. 𐐈𐑌𐐼 𐐺𐐨𐐸𐐬𐑊𐐼, 𐐮𐐻 𐐶𐐱𐑆 𐑌𐐴𐐻, 𐐰𐑌𐐼 𐑄𐐩 𐐼𐐮𐐼 𐐹𐐮𐐽 𐑄𐐩𐑉 𐐻𐐯𐑌𐐻𐑅, 𐑁𐐫𐑉 𐑄 𐐽𐐨𐑁 𐐿𐐰𐐹𐐻𐐲𐑌𐑆 𐐱𐑂 𐑄 𐐢𐐰𐑋𐐲𐑌𐐴𐐻𐑅 𐐸𐐰𐐼 𐑅𐐲𐐹𐐬𐑆𐐼 𐑄𐐰𐐻 𐑄 𐐤𐐨𐑁𐐴𐐻𐑅 𐐶𐐲𐑉 𐐶𐐨𐑉𐐨 𐐺𐐨𐐿𐐫𐑆 𐐱𐑂 𐑄𐐩𐑉 𐑋𐐪𐑉𐐽; 𐐰𐑌𐐼 𐑅𐐲𐐹𐐬𐑆𐐮𐑍 𐑄𐐰𐐻 𐑄𐐩 𐐸𐐰𐐼 𐐼𐑉𐐮𐑂𐐲𐑌 𐑄𐐩𐑉 𐐸𐐬𐑊 𐐪𐑉𐑋𐐨, 𐑄𐐩𐑉𐑁𐐬𐑉 𐑄𐐩 𐐻𐐳𐐿 𐑌𐐬 𐑃𐐫𐐻 𐐿𐐱𐑌𐑅𐐲𐑉𐑌𐐮𐑍 𐑄 𐑅𐐮𐐻𐐨 𐐱𐑂 𐐣𐐰𐑌𐐻𐐴.

30. 𐐤𐐵 𐐮𐐻 𐐿𐐩𐑋 𐐻𐐭 𐐹𐐰𐑅 𐑄𐐰𐐻 𐐸𐐶𐐯𐑌 𐐮𐐻 𐐶𐐱𐑆 𐑌𐐴𐐻, 𐑄𐐰𐐻 𐐌 𐐿𐐫𐑆𐐼 𐑄𐐰𐐻 𐑋𐐴 𐑋𐐯𐑌 𐑇𐐳𐐼 𐑌𐐱𐐻 𐑅𐑊𐐨𐐹, 𐐺𐐲𐐻 𐑄𐐰𐐻 𐑄𐐩 𐑇𐐳𐐼 𐑋𐐪𐑉𐐽 𐑁𐐫𐑉𐐶𐐲𐑉𐐼 𐐺𐐴 𐐰𐑌𐐲𐑄𐐲𐑉 𐐶𐐩, 𐐻𐐬𐑉𐐼𐑆 𐑄 𐑊𐐰𐑌𐐼 𐐱𐑂 𐐣𐐰𐑌𐐻𐐴. 𐐈𐑌𐐼 𐐺𐐨𐐿𐐫𐑆 𐐱𐑂 𐑄𐐮𐑅 𐐵𐑉 𐑋𐐪𐑉𐐽 𐐮𐑌 𐑄 𐑌𐐴𐐻 𐐻𐐴𐑋, 𐐺𐐨𐐸𐐬𐑊𐐼, 𐐱𐑌 𐑄 𐑋𐐫𐑉𐐬 𐐶𐐨 𐐶𐐲𐑉 𐐺𐐨𐐷𐐱𐑌𐐼 𐑄 𐐢𐐰𐑋𐐲𐑌𐐴𐐻𐑅, 𐐮𐑌𐑅𐐬𐑋𐐲𐐽 𐑄𐐰𐐻 𐐶𐐨 𐐼𐐮𐐼 𐐲𐑉𐐴𐑂 𐐺𐐨𐑁𐐬𐑉 𐑄𐐯𐑋 𐐰𐐻 𐑄 𐑅𐐮𐐻𐐨 𐐱𐑂 𐐣𐐰𐑌𐐻𐐴. 𐐈𐑌𐐼 𐑄𐐲𐑅 𐐮𐐻 𐐿𐐩𐑋 𐐻𐐭 𐐹𐐰𐑅, 𐑄𐐰𐐻 𐐺𐐴 𐑄𐐮𐑅 𐑅𐐻𐑉𐐰𐐻𐐲𐐾𐐯𐑋 𐐶𐐨 𐐼𐐮𐐼 𐐻𐐩𐐿 𐐹𐐲𐑆𐐯𐑇𐐲𐑌 𐐱𐑂 𐑄 𐑅𐐮𐐻𐐨 𐐱𐑂 𐐣𐐰𐑌𐐻𐐴 𐐶𐐮𐑄𐐵𐐻 𐑄 𐑇𐐯𐐼𐐮𐑍 𐐱𐑂 𐐺𐑊𐐲𐐼.

31. 𐐈𐑌𐐼 𐐮𐐻 𐐿𐐩𐑋 𐐻𐐭 𐐹𐐰𐑅 𐑄𐐰𐐻 𐐸𐐶𐐯𐑌 𐑄 𐐪𐑉𐑋𐐨𐑆 𐐱𐑂 𐑄 𐐢𐐰𐑋𐐲𐑌𐐴𐐻𐑅 𐐼𐐮𐐼 𐐲𐑉𐐴𐑂 𐑌𐐨𐑉 𐑄 𐑅𐐮𐐻𐐨, 𐐰𐑌𐐼 𐑅𐐫 𐑄𐐰𐐻 𐐶𐐨 𐐶𐐲𐑉 𐐹𐑉𐐨𐐹𐐩𐑉𐐼 𐐻𐐭 𐑋𐐨𐐻 𐑄𐐯𐑋, 𐑄𐐩 𐐶𐐲𐑉 𐐰𐑅𐐻𐐱𐑌𐐮𐑇𐐻 𐐯𐐿𐑅𐐨𐐼𐐮𐑍𐑊𐐨, 𐐰𐑌𐐼 𐑅𐐻𐑉𐐲𐐿 𐐶𐐮𐑄 𐑀𐑉𐐩𐐻 𐑁𐐨𐑉, 𐐮𐑌𐑅𐐬𐑋𐐲𐐽 𐑄𐐰𐐻 𐑄𐐩 𐐼𐐮𐐼 𐑁𐑊𐐨 𐐮𐑌𐐻𐐭 𐑄 𐐶𐐮𐑊𐐼𐐲𐑉𐑌𐐯𐑅. 𐐏𐐩, 𐐰𐑌𐐼 𐐮𐐻 𐐿𐐩𐑋 𐐻𐐭 𐐹𐐰𐑅 𐑄𐐰𐐻 𐑄 𐐪𐑉𐑋𐐨𐑆 𐐱𐑂 𐑄 𐐢𐐰𐑋𐐲𐑌𐐴𐐻𐑅 𐐼𐐮𐐼 𐑁𐑊𐐨 𐐵𐐻 𐐱𐑂 𐐫𐑊 𐑄𐐮𐑅 𐐿𐐶𐐫𐑉𐐻𐐲𐑉 𐐱𐑂 𐑄 𐑊𐐰𐑌𐐼. 𐐒𐐲𐐻 𐐺𐐨𐐸𐐬𐑊𐐼, 𐑄𐐩 𐐸𐐰𐑂 𐐿𐐰𐑉𐐨𐐼 𐐶𐐮𐑄 𐑄𐐯𐑋 𐑋𐐯𐑌𐐨 𐐶𐐮𐑋𐐯𐑌 𐐰𐑌𐐼 𐐽𐐮𐑊𐐼𐑉𐐯𐑌 𐐵𐐻 𐐱𐑂 𐑄 𐑊𐐰𐑌𐐼. 𐐈𐑌𐐼 𐑄𐐬𐑆 𐑅𐐮𐐻𐐨𐑆 𐐸𐐶𐐮𐐽 𐐸𐐰𐐼 𐐺𐐮𐑌 𐐻𐐩𐐿𐐲𐑌 𐐺𐐴 𐑄 𐐢𐐰𐑋𐐲𐑌𐐴𐐻𐑅, 𐐫𐑊 𐐱𐑂 𐑄𐐯𐑋 𐐪𐑉 𐐰𐐻 𐑄𐐮𐑅 𐐹𐐨𐑉𐐨𐐲𐐼 𐐱𐑂 𐐻𐐴𐑋 𐐮𐑌 𐐵𐑉 𐐹𐐲𐑆𐐯𐑇𐐲𐑌; 𐐰𐑌𐐼 𐐵𐑉 𐑁𐐪𐑄𐐲𐑉𐑆, 𐐰𐑌𐐼 𐐵𐑉 𐐶𐐮𐑋𐐯𐑌, 𐐰𐑌𐐼 𐐵𐑉 𐐽𐐮𐑊𐐼𐑉𐐯𐑌, 𐐪𐑉 𐑉𐐨𐐻𐐲𐑉𐑌𐐮𐑍 𐐻𐐭 𐑄𐐩𐑉 𐐸𐐬𐑋𐑆, 𐐫𐑊 𐑅𐐩𐑂 𐐮𐐻 𐐺𐐨 𐑄𐐬𐑆 𐐸𐐭 𐐸𐐰𐑂 𐐺𐐮𐑌 𐐻𐐩𐐿𐐲𐑌 𐐹𐑉𐐮𐑆𐐲𐑌𐐲𐑉𐑆 𐐰𐑌𐐼 𐐿𐐰𐑉𐐨𐐼 𐐫𐑁 𐐺𐐴 𐑄 𐐢𐐰𐑋𐐲𐑌𐐴𐐻𐑅. 𐐒𐐲𐐻 𐐺𐐨𐐸𐐬𐑊𐐼, 𐐵𐑉 𐐪𐑉𐑋𐐨𐑆 𐐪𐑉 𐑅𐑋𐐫𐑊 𐐻𐐭 𐑋𐐩𐑌𐐻𐐩𐑌 𐑅𐐬 𐑀𐑉𐐩𐐻 𐐩 𐑌𐐲𐑋𐐺𐐲𐑉 𐐱𐑂 𐑅𐐮𐐻𐐨𐑆, 𐐰𐑌𐐼 𐑅𐐬 𐑀𐑉𐐩𐐻 𐐹𐐲𐑆𐐯𐑇𐐲𐑌𐑆. 𐐒𐐲𐐻 𐐺𐐨𐐸𐐬𐑊𐐼, 𐐶𐐨 𐐻𐑉𐐲𐑅𐐻 𐐮𐑌 𐐵𐑉 𐐘𐐱𐐼 𐐸𐐭 𐐸𐐰𐑆 𐑀𐐮𐑂𐐲𐑌 𐐲𐑅 𐑂𐐮𐐿𐐻𐐬𐑉𐐨 𐐬𐑂𐐲𐑉 𐑄𐐬𐑆 𐑊𐐰𐑌𐐼𐑆, 𐐮𐑌𐑅𐐬𐑋𐐲𐐽 𐑄𐐰𐐻 𐐶𐐨 𐐸𐐰𐑂 𐐱𐐺𐐻𐐩𐑌𐐼 𐑄𐐬𐑆 𐑅𐐮𐐻𐐨𐑆 𐐰𐑌𐐼 𐑄𐐬𐑆 𐑊𐐰𐑌𐐼𐑆, 𐐸𐐶𐐮𐐽 𐐶𐐲𐑉 𐐵𐑉 𐐬𐑌. 𐐤𐐵 𐐶𐐨 𐐼𐐭 𐑌𐐱𐐻 𐑌𐐬 𐑄 𐐿𐐫𐑆 𐑄𐐰𐐻 𐑄 𐑀𐐲𐑂𐐲𐑉𐑌𐑋𐐯𐑌𐐻 𐐼𐐲𐑆 𐑌𐐱𐐻 𐑀𐑉𐐪𐑌𐐻 𐐲𐑅 𐑋𐐬𐑉 𐑅𐐻𐑉𐐯𐑍𐑃; 𐑌𐐨𐑄𐐲𐑉 𐐼𐐭 𐑄𐐬𐑆 𐑋𐐯𐑌 𐐸𐐭 𐐿𐐩𐑋 𐐲𐐹 𐐲𐑌𐐻𐐭 𐐲𐑅 𐑌𐐬 𐐸𐐶𐐴 𐐶𐐨 𐐸𐐰𐑂 𐑌𐐱𐐻 𐑉𐐨𐑅𐐨𐑂𐐼 𐑀𐑉𐐩𐐻𐐲𐑉 𐑅𐐻𐑉𐐯𐑍𐑃. 𐐒𐐨𐐸𐐬𐑊𐐼, 𐐶𐐨 𐐼𐐭 𐑌𐐱𐐻 𐑌𐐬 𐐺𐐲𐐻 𐐸𐐶𐐱𐐻 𐐷𐐨 𐐪𐑉 𐐲𐑌𐑅𐐲𐐿𐑅𐐯𐑅𐑁𐐳𐑊, 𐐰𐑌𐐼 𐐷𐐨 𐐸𐐰𐑂 𐐼𐑉𐐫𐑌 𐐰𐐶𐐩 𐑄 𐑁𐐬𐑉𐑅𐐯𐑆 𐐮𐑌𐐻𐐭 𐑄𐐰𐐻 𐐿𐐶𐐫𐑉𐐻𐐲𐑉 𐐱𐑂 𐑄 𐑊𐐰𐑌𐐼; 𐐮𐑁 𐑅𐐬, 𐐶𐐨 𐐼𐐭 𐑌𐐱𐐻 𐐼𐐮𐑆𐐴𐑉

𐐻𐐭 𐐹𐐲𐑉𐑁𐐫𐑉𐑋. 𐐈𐑌𐐼 𐐮𐑁 𐐮𐐻 𐐮𐑆 𐑌𐐪𐐻 𐑅𐐬, 𐐒𐐨𐐸𐐬𐑊𐐼, 𐐶𐐨 𐑁𐐨𐑉 𐑄𐐰𐐻 𐑄𐐩𐑉 𐐮𐑆 𐑅𐐲𐑋 𐑁𐐰𐐿𐑇𐐲𐑌 𐐮𐑌 𐑄 𐑀𐐲𐑂𐐲𐑉𐑌𐑋𐐯𐑌𐐻, 𐑄𐐰𐐻 𐑄𐐩 𐐼𐐭 𐑌𐐪𐐻 𐑅𐐯𐑌𐐼 𐑋𐐬𐑉 𐑋𐐯𐑌 𐐻𐐭 𐐵𐑉 𐐰𐑅𐐮𐑅𐐻𐐲𐑌𐑅; 𐑁𐐫𐑉 𐐶𐐨 𐑌𐐬 𐑄𐐰𐐻 𐑄𐐩 𐐪𐑉 𐑋𐐬𐑉 𐑌𐐷𐐭𐑋𐐲𐑉𐐲𐑅 𐑄𐐰𐑌 𐑄𐐰𐐻 𐐸𐐶𐐮𐐽 𐑄𐐩 𐐸𐐰𐑂 𐑅𐐯𐑌𐐻. 𐐒𐐲𐐻 𐐺𐐨𐐸𐐬𐑊𐐼, 𐐮𐐻 𐑋𐐰𐐻𐐲𐑉𐐯𐑃 𐑌𐐪𐐻: 𐐶𐐨 𐐻𐑉𐐲𐑅𐐻 𐐘𐐪𐐼 𐐶𐐮𐑊 𐐼𐐯𐑊𐐮𐑂𐐲𐑉 𐐲𐑅, 𐑌𐐪𐐻𐐶𐐮𐑃𐑅𐐻𐐰𐑌𐐼𐐮𐑍 𐑄 𐐶𐐨𐐿𐑌𐐯𐑅 𐐱𐑂 𐐵𐑉 𐐪𐑉𐑋𐐨𐑆, 𐐷𐐩, 𐐰𐑌𐐼 𐐼𐐯𐑊𐐮𐑂𐐲𐑉 𐐲𐑅 𐐵𐐻 𐐱𐑂 𐑄 𐐸𐐰𐑌𐐼𐑆 𐐱𐑂 𐐵𐑉 𐐯𐑌𐐯𐑋𐐨𐑆.

32. 𐐒𐐨𐐸𐐬𐑊𐐼, 𐑄𐐮𐑅 𐐮𐑆 𐑄 𐐻𐐶𐐯𐑌𐐻𐐨 𐐰𐑌𐐼 𐑌𐐴𐑌𐑃 𐐷𐐨𐑉 𐐮𐑌 𐑄 𐑊𐐰𐐻𐐲𐑉 𐐯𐑌𐐼, 𐐰𐑌𐐼 𐐶𐐨 𐐪𐑉 𐐮𐑌 𐑄 𐐹𐐲𐑆𐐯𐑇𐐲𐑌 𐐱𐑂 𐐵𐑉 𐑊𐐰𐑌𐐼𐑆; 𐐰𐑌𐐼 𐑄 𐐢𐐩𐑋𐐲𐑌𐐴𐐻𐑅 𐐸𐐰𐑂 𐑁𐑊𐐯𐐼 𐐻𐐭 𐑄 𐑊𐐰𐑌𐐼 𐐱𐑂 𐐤𐐨𐑁𐐴. 𐐈𐑌𐐼 𐑄𐐬𐑆 𐑅𐐲𐑌𐑆 𐐱𐑂 𐑄 𐐹𐐨𐐹𐑊 𐐱𐑂 𐐈𐑋𐐲𐑌, 𐐱𐑂 𐐸𐐭𐑋 𐐌 𐐸𐐰𐑂 𐑅𐐬 𐐸𐐴𐑊𐐨 𐑅𐐹𐐬𐐿𐐲𐑌, 𐐪𐑉 𐐶𐐮𐑄 𐑋𐐨 𐐮𐑌 𐑄 𐑅𐐮𐐻𐐨 𐐱𐑂 𐐣𐐰𐑌𐐻𐐴; 𐐰𐑌𐐼 𐑄 𐐢𐐫𐑉𐐼 𐐸𐐰𐑆 𐑅𐐲𐐹𐐬𐑉𐐻𐐲𐐼 𐑄𐐯𐑋, 𐐷𐐩, 𐐰𐑌𐐼 𐐿𐐯𐐹𐐻 𐑄𐐯𐑋 𐑁𐑉𐐲𐑋 𐑁𐐫𐑊𐐮𐑍 𐐺𐐴 𐑄 𐑅𐐬𐑉𐐼, 𐐮𐑌𐑅𐐲𐐽 𐑄𐐰𐐻 𐐨𐑂𐐲𐑌 𐐶𐐲𐑌 𐑅𐐬𐑊 𐐸𐐰𐑆 𐑌𐐪𐐻 𐐺𐐨𐑌 𐑅𐑊𐐩𐑌. 𐐒𐐲𐐻 𐐺𐐨𐐸𐐬𐑊𐐼, 𐑄𐐩 𐐸𐐰𐑂 𐑉𐐨𐑅𐐨𐑂𐐼 𐑋𐐯𐑌𐐨 𐐶𐐭𐑌𐐼𐑆; 𐑌𐐯𐑂𐐲𐑉𐑄𐐯𐑊𐐯𐑅 𐑄𐐩 𐑅𐐻𐐰𐑌𐐼 𐑁𐐰𐑅𐐻 𐐮𐑌 𐑄𐐰𐐻 𐑊𐐮𐐺𐐲𐑉𐐻𐐨 𐐸𐐶𐐯𐑉𐐶𐐮𐑃 𐐘𐐪𐐼 𐐸𐐰𐑆 𐑋𐐩𐐼 𐑄𐐯𐑋 𐑁𐑉𐐨; 𐐰𐑌𐐼 𐑄𐐩 𐐪𐑉 𐑅𐐻𐑉𐐮𐐿𐐻 𐐻𐐭 𐑉𐐨𐑋𐐯𐑋𐐺𐐲𐑉 𐑄 𐐢𐐫𐑉𐐼 𐑄𐐩𐑉 𐐘𐐪𐐼 𐑁𐑉𐐲𐑋 𐐼𐐩 𐐻𐐭 𐐼𐐩; 𐐷𐐩, 𐑄𐐩 𐐼𐐭 𐐱𐐺𐑆𐐲𐑉𐑂 𐐻𐐭 𐐿𐐨𐐹 𐐸𐐮𐑆 𐑅𐐻𐐰𐐽𐐭𐐻𐑅, 𐐰𐑌𐐼 𐐸𐐮𐑆 𐐾𐐲𐐾𐑋𐐯𐑌𐐻𐑅, 𐐰𐑌𐐼 𐐸𐐮𐑆 𐐿𐐱𐑋𐐰𐑌𐐼𐑋𐐯𐑌𐐻𐑅 𐐿𐐱𐑌𐐻𐐮𐑌𐐷𐐭𐐲𐑊𐐨; 𐐰𐑌𐐼 𐑄𐐩𐑉 𐑁𐐩𐑃 𐐮𐑆 𐑅𐐻𐑉𐐱𐑍 𐐮𐑌 𐑄 𐐹𐑉𐐱𐑁𐐯𐑅𐐨𐑆 𐐿𐐱𐑌𐑅𐐲𐑉𐑌𐐮𐑍 𐑄𐐰𐐻 𐐸𐐶𐐮𐐽 𐐮𐑆 𐐻𐐭 𐐿𐐲𐑋. 𐐈𐑌𐐼 𐑌𐐵, 𐑋𐐴 𐐺𐐨𐑊𐐲𐑂𐐯𐐼 𐐺𐑉𐐲𐑄𐐲𐑉 𐐣𐐫𐑉𐐬𐑌𐐴, 𐑋𐐩 𐑄 𐐢𐐫𐑉𐐼 𐐵𐑉 𐐘𐐪𐐼, 𐐸𐐭 𐐸𐐰𐑆 𐑉𐐨𐐼𐐨𐑋𐐼 𐐲𐑅 𐐰𐑌𐐼 𐑋𐐩𐐼 𐐲𐑅 𐑁𐑉𐐨, 𐐿𐐨𐐹 𐐷𐐭 𐐿𐐱𐑌𐐻𐐮𐑌𐐷𐐭𐐲𐑊𐐨 𐐮𐑌 𐐸𐐮𐑆 𐐹𐑉𐐯𐑆𐐯𐑌𐑅; 𐐷𐐩, 𐐰𐑌𐐼 𐑋𐐩 𐐸𐐨 𐑁𐐩𐑂𐐲𐑉 𐑄𐐮𐑅 𐐹𐐨𐐹𐑊, 𐐨𐑂𐐲𐑌 𐑄𐐰𐐻 𐐷𐐨 𐑋𐐩 𐐸𐐰𐑂 𐑅𐐲𐐿𐑅𐐯𐑅 𐐮𐑌 𐐱𐐺𐐻𐐩𐑌𐐮𐑍 𐑄 𐐹𐐲𐑆𐐯𐑇𐐲𐑌 𐐱𐑂 𐐫𐑊 𐑄𐐰𐐻 𐐸𐐶𐐮𐐽 𐑄 𐐢𐐩𐑋𐐲𐑌𐐴𐐻𐑅 𐐸𐐰𐑂 𐐻𐐩𐐿𐑌 𐑁𐑉𐐲𐑋 𐐲𐑅, 𐐸𐐶𐐮𐐽 𐐶𐐪𐑆 𐑁𐐫𐑉 𐐵𐑉 𐑅𐐲𐐹𐐬𐑉𐐻. 𐐈𐑌𐐼 𐑌𐐵, 𐐺𐐨𐐸𐐬𐑊𐐼, 𐐌 𐐿𐑊𐐬𐑆 𐑋𐐴𐑌 𐐯𐐹𐐮𐑅𐑊. 𐐌 𐐰𐑋 𐐐𐐯𐑊𐐲𐑋𐐲𐑌, 𐑄 𐑅𐐲𐑌 𐐱𐑂 𐐈𐑊𐑋𐐲.

𐐕𐐰𐐹𐐻𐐲𐑉 XXVII.

1. 𐐤𐐵 𐐮𐐻 𐐿𐐩𐑋 𐐻𐐭 𐐹𐐰𐑅 𐐮𐑌 𐑄 𐑃𐐲𐑉𐐻𐐨𐐯𐑃 𐐷𐐨𐑉 𐐱𐑂 𐑄 𐑉𐐩𐑌 𐐱𐑂 𐑄 𐐾𐐲𐐾𐐯𐑆 𐐬𐑂𐐲𐑉 𐑄 𐐹𐐨𐐹𐑊 𐐱𐑂 𐐤𐐨𐑁𐐴, 𐐰𐑁𐐻𐐲𐑉 𐐣𐐫𐑉𐐬𐑌𐐴 𐐸𐐰𐐼 𐑉𐐨𐑅𐐨𐑂𐐼 𐐰𐑌𐐼 𐐸𐐰𐐼 𐑉𐐯𐐼 𐐐𐐯𐑊𐐲𐑋𐐲𐑌'𐑆 𐐯𐐹𐐮𐑅𐑊, 𐐸𐐨 𐐶𐐪𐑆 𐐯𐐿𐑅𐐨𐐼𐐮𐑍𐑊𐐨 𐑉𐐨𐐾𐐦𐑅𐐻 𐐺𐐨𐐿𐐫𐑆 𐐱𐑂 𐑄 𐐶𐐯𐑊𐑁𐐩𐑉, 𐐷𐐩, 𐑄 𐐯𐐿𐑅𐐨𐐼𐐮𐑍 𐑅𐐲𐐿𐑅𐐯𐑅 𐐸𐐶𐐮𐐽 𐐐𐐯𐑊𐐲𐑋𐐲𐑌 𐐸𐐰𐐼 𐐸𐐰𐐼, 𐐮𐑌 𐐱𐐺𐐻𐐩𐑌𐐮𐑍 𐑄𐐬𐑆 𐑊𐐰𐑌𐐼𐑆 𐐸𐐶𐐮𐐽 𐐶𐐲𐑉 𐑊𐐱𐑅𐐻; 𐐷𐐩, 𐐰𐑌𐐼 𐐸𐐨 𐐼𐐮𐐼 𐑋𐐩𐐿 𐐮𐐻 𐑌𐐬𐑌 𐐲𐑌𐐻𐐭 𐐫𐑊 𐐸𐐮𐑆 𐐹𐐨𐐹𐑊, 𐐮𐑌 𐐫𐑊 𐑄 𐑊𐐰𐑌𐐼 𐑉𐐵𐑌𐐼 𐐰𐐺𐐵𐐻 𐐮𐑌 𐑄𐐰𐐻 𐐹𐐪𐑉𐐻 𐐸𐐶𐐯𐑉 𐐸𐐨 𐐶𐐪𐑆, 𐑄𐐰𐐻 𐑄𐐩 𐑋𐐴𐐻 𐑉𐐨𐐾𐐦𐑅 𐐫𐑊𐑅𐐬.

2. 𐐈𐑌𐐼 𐐮𐐻 𐐿𐐩𐑋 𐐻𐐭 𐐹𐐰𐑅 𐑄𐐰𐐻 𐐸𐐨 𐐮𐑋𐐨𐐼𐐨𐐲𐐻𐑊𐐨 𐑅𐐯𐑌𐐻 𐐰𐑌 𐐯𐐹𐐮𐑅𐑊 𐐻𐐭 𐐑𐐩𐐸𐐬𐑉𐐲𐑌, 𐐼𐐨𐑆𐐴𐑉𐐮𐑍 𐑄𐐰𐐻 𐐸𐐨 𐑇𐐳𐐼 𐐿𐐫𐑆 𐑋𐐯𐑌 𐐻𐐭 𐐺𐐨 𐑀𐐰𐑄𐐲𐑉𐐼 𐐻𐐭𐑀𐐯𐑄𐐲𐑉 𐐻𐐭 𐑅𐐻𐑉𐐯𐑍𐑃𐐲𐑌 𐐐𐐯𐑊𐐲𐑋𐐲𐑌, 𐐫𐑉 𐑄 𐐪𐑉𐑋𐐨𐑆 𐐱𐑂 𐐐𐐯𐑊𐐲𐑋𐐲𐑌, 𐐮𐑌𐑅𐐲𐐽 𐑄𐐰𐐻 𐐸𐐨 𐑋𐐴𐐻 𐐶𐐮𐑄 𐐨𐑆 𐑋𐐩𐑌𐐻𐐩𐑌 𐑄𐐰𐐻 𐐹𐐪𐑉𐐻 𐐱𐑂 𐑄 𐑊𐐰𐑌𐐼 𐐸𐐶𐐮𐐽 𐐸𐐨 𐐸𐐰𐐼 𐐺𐐨𐑌 𐑅𐐬 𐑋𐐮𐑉𐐰𐐿𐐷𐐭𐑊𐐲𐑅𐑊𐐨 𐐹𐑉𐐱𐑅𐐹𐐲𐑉𐐼 𐐮𐑌 𐑉𐐨𐑀𐐩𐑌𐐮𐑍. 𐐈𐑌𐐼 𐐮𐐻 𐐿𐐩𐑋 𐐻𐐭 𐐹𐐰𐑅 𐐸𐐶𐐯𐑌 𐐣𐐫𐑉𐐬𐑌𐐴 𐐸𐐰𐐼 𐑅𐐯𐑌𐐻 𐑄𐐮𐑅 𐐯𐐹𐐮𐑅𐑊 𐐻𐐭 𐑄 𐑊𐐰𐑌𐐼 𐐱𐑂 𐐞𐐪𐑉𐐲𐐸𐐯𐑋𐑊𐐲, 𐐸𐐨 𐐺𐐨𐑀𐐰𐑌 𐐲𐑀𐐯𐑌 𐐻𐐭 𐑊𐐩 𐐰 𐐹𐑊𐐰𐑌 𐑄𐐰𐐻 𐐸𐐨 𐑋𐐴𐐻 𐐱𐐺𐐻𐐩𐑌 𐑄 𐑉𐐨𐑋𐐩𐑌𐐼𐐲𐑉 𐐱𐑂 𐑄𐐬𐑆 𐐹𐐲𐑆𐐯𐑇𐐲𐑌𐑆 𐐰𐑌𐐼 𐑅𐐮𐐻𐐨𐑆 𐐸𐐶𐐮𐐽 𐑄 𐐢𐐩𐑋𐐲𐑌𐐴𐐻𐑅 𐐸𐐰𐐼 𐐻𐐩𐐿𐑌 𐑁𐑉𐐲𐑋 𐑄𐐯𐑋.

3. 𐐈𐑌𐐼 𐐮𐐻 𐐿𐐩𐑋 𐐻𐐭 𐐹𐐰𐑅 𐑄𐐰𐐻 𐐸𐐶𐐴𐑊 𐐣𐐫𐑉𐐬𐑌𐐴 𐐶𐐪𐑆 𐑄𐐲𐑅 𐑋𐐩𐐿𐐮𐑍 𐐹𐑉𐐯𐐹𐐲𐑉𐐩𐑇𐐲𐑌𐑆 𐐻𐐭 𐑀𐐬 𐐲𐑀𐐯𐑌𐑅𐐻 𐑄 𐐢𐐩𐑋𐐲𐑌𐐴𐐻𐑅 𐐻𐐭 𐐺𐐰𐐻𐑊, 𐐺𐐨𐐸𐐬𐑊𐐼, 𐑄 𐐹𐐨𐐹𐑊 𐐱𐑂 𐐤𐐨𐑁𐐴𐐸𐐪, 𐐸𐐭 𐐶𐐲𐑉 𐑀𐐰𐑄𐐲𐑉𐐼 𐐻𐐭𐑀𐐯𐑄𐐲𐑉 𐑁𐑉𐐲𐑋 𐑄 𐑅𐐮𐐻𐐨 𐐱𐑂 𐐣𐐫𐑉𐐬𐑌𐐴, 𐐰𐑌𐐼 𐑄 𐑅𐐮𐐻𐐨 𐐱𐑂 𐐢𐐨𐐸𐐴, 𐐰𐑌𐐼 𐑄 𐑅𐐮𐐻𐐨 𐐱𐑂 𐐣𐐫𐑉𐐬𐑌𐐴𐐸𐐪, 𐐶𐐲𐑉 𐐲𐐻𐐰𐐿𐐻 𐐺𐐴 𐑄 𐐢𐐩𐑋𐐲𐑌𐐴𐐻𐑅; 𐐷𐐩, 𐐨𐑂𐐲𐑌 𐑄𐐬𐑆 𐐸𐐭 𐐸𐐰𐐼 𐐺𐐨𐑌 𐐿𐐲𐑋𐐹𐐯𐑊𐐼 𐐻𐐭 𐑁𐑊𐐨 𐑁𐑉𐐲𐑋 𐑄 𐑊𐐰𐑌𐐼 𐐱𐑂 𐐣𐐰𐑌𐐻𐐴, 𐐰𐑌𐐼 𐑁𐑉𐐲𐑋 𐑄 𐑊𐐰𐑌𐐼 𐑉𐐵𐑌𐐼 𐐰𐐺𐐵𐐻, 𐐸𐐰𐐼 𐐿𐐲𐑋 𐐬𐑂𐐲𐑉 𐐰𐑌𐐼 𐐾𐐦𐑌𐐼 𐑄 𐐢𐐩𐑋𐐲𐑌𐐴𐐻𐑅 𐐮𐑌 𐑄𐐮𐑅 𐐹𐐪𐑉𐐻 𐐱𐑂 𐑄 𐑊𐐰𐑌𐐼; 𐐰𐑌𐐼 𐑄𐐲𐑅 𐐺𐐨𐐮𐑍 𐐯𐐿𐑅𐐨𐐼𐐮𐑍𐑊𐐨 𐑌𐐷𐐭𐑋𐐲𐑉𐐲𐑅, 𐐷𐐩, 𐐰𐑌𐐼 𐑉𐐨𐑅𐐨𐑂𐐮𐑍 𐑅𐐻𐑉𐐯𐑍𐑃

𐑁𐑉𐐱𐑋 𐐼𐐩 𐐻𐐭 𐐼𐐩, 𐐺𐐴 𐑄 𐐿𐐲𐑋𐐰𐑌𐐼 𐐲𐑂 𐐈𐑋𐐬𐑉𐐱𐑌 𐑄𐐩 𐐿𐐩𐑋 𐑁𐐫𐑉𐑃 𐐲𐑀𐐯𐑌𐑅𐐻 𐑄 𐐹𐐨𐐹𐑊 𐐲𐑂 𐐤𐐨𐑁𐐴𐐸𐐪, 𐐰𐑌𐐼 𐑄𐐩 𐐼𐐮𐐼 𐐺𐐨𐑀𐐮𐑌 𐐻𐐭 𐑅𐑊𐐩 𐑄𐐯𐑋 𐐶𐐮𐑄 𐐰𐑌 𐐯𐐿𐑅𐐨𐐼𐐮𐑍𐑊𐐨 𐑀𐑉𐐩𐐻 𐑅𐑊𐐫𐐻𐐲𐑉. 𐐈𐑌𐐼 𐑄𐐩𐑉 𐐪𐑉𐑋𐐨𐑆 𐐶𐐲𐑉 𐑅𐐬 𐑌𐐭𐑋𐐲𐑉𐐲𐑅 𐑄𐐰𐐻 𐑄 𐑉𐐨𐑋𐐩𐑌𐐼𐐲𐑉 𐐲𐑂 𐑄 𐐹𐐨𐐹𐑊 𐐲𐑂 𐐤𐐨𐑁𐐴𐐸𐐪 𐐶𐐲𐑉 𐐬𐐺𐑊𐐴𐐾𐐼 𐐻𐐭 𐑁𐑊𐐨 𐐺𐐨𐑁𐐬𐑉 𐑄𐐯𐑋; 𐐰𐑌𐐼 𐑄𐐩 𐐿𐐩𐑋 𐐨𐑂𐑌 𐐰𐑌𐐼 𐐾𐑎𐑌𐐼 𐑄 𐐪𐑉𐑋𐐨 𐐲𐑂 𐐣𐐬𐑉𐐬𐑌𐐴. 𐐈𐑌𐐼 𐑌𐐵 𐐰𐑆 𐐣𐐬𐑉𐐬𐑌𐐴 𐐸𐐰𐐼 𐑅𐐲𐐹𐐬𐑆𐐼 𐑄𐐰𐐻 𐑄𐐯𐑉 𐑇𐐳𐐼 𐐺𐐨 𐑋𐐯𐑌 𐑅𐐯𐑌𐐻 𐐻𐐭 𐑄 𐑅𐐮𐐻𐐨 𐐲𐑂 𐐤𐐨𐑁𐐴𐐸𐐪, 𐐻𐐭 𐑄 𐐲𐑅𐐮𐑅𐐻𐐲𐑌𐑅 𐐲𐑂 𐑄 𐐹𐐨𐐹𐑊 𐐻𐐭 𐑋𐐩𐑌𐐻𐐩𐑌 𐑄𐐰𐐻 𐑅𐐮𐐻𐐨, 𐐰𐑌𐐼 𐑌𐐬𐐮𐑍 𐑄𐐰𐐻 𐐮𐐻 𐐶𐐱𐑆 𐐨𐑆𐐨𐐲𐑉 𐐻𐐭 𐐿𐐨𐐹 𐑄 𐑅𐐮𐐻𐐨 𐑁𐑉𐐱𐑋 𐑁𐐫𐑊𐐮𐑍 𐐮𐑌𐐻𐐭 𐑄 𐐸𐐰𐑌𐐼𐑆 𐐲𐑂 𐑄 𐐢𐐰𐑋𐐲𐑌𐐴𐐻𐑅 𐑄𐐰𐑌 𐐻𐐭 𐑉𐐨𐐻𐐩𐐿 𐐮𐐻 𐑁𐑉𐐱𐑋 𐑄𐐯𐑋, 𐐸𐐨 𐑅𐐲𐐹𐐬𐑆𐐼 𐑄𐐰𐐻 𐑄𐐩 𐐶𐐳𐐼 𐐨𐑆𐐮𐑊𐐨 𐑋𐐩𐑌𐐻𐐩𐑌 𐑄𐐰𐐻 𐑅𐐮𐐻𐐨; 𐑄𐐯𐑉𐑁𐐬𐑉 𐐸𐐨 𐑉𐐨𐐻𐐩𐑌𐐼 𐐫𐑊 𐐸𐐮𐑆 𐑁𐐬𐑉𐑅 𐐻𐐭 𐑋𐐩𐑌𐐻𐐩𐑌 𐑄𐐬𐑆 𐐹𐑊𐐩𐑅𐐯𐑆 𐐸𐐶𐐮𐐽 𐐸𐐨 𐐸𐐰𐐼 𐑉𐐨𐐿𐐲𐑂𐐲𐑉𐐼.

4\. 𐐈𐑌𐐼 𐑌𐐵 𐐸𐐶𐐯𐑌 𐐣𐐬𐑉𐐬𐑌𐐴 𐑅𐐫 𐑄𐐰𐐻 𐑄 𐑅𐐮𐐻𐐨 𐐲𐑂 𐐤𐐨𐑁𐐴𐐸𐐪 𐐶𐐱𐑆 𐑊𐐱𐑅𐐻, 𐐸𐐨 𐐶𐐱𐑆 𐐯𐐿𐑅𐐨𐐼𐐮𐑍𐑊𐐨 𐑅𐐱𐑉𐐬𐑁𐐳𐑊, 𐐰𐑌𐐼 𐐺𐐨𐑀𐐰𐑌 𐐻𐐭 𐐼𐐵𐐻, 𐐺𐐨𐐿𐐫𐑆 𐐲𐑂 𐑄 𐐶𐐮𐐿𐐯𐐼𐑌𐐯𐑅 𐐲𐑂 𐑄 𐐹𐐨𐐹𐑊, 𐐸𐐶𐐯𐑄𐐲𐑉 𐑄𐐩 𐑇𐐳𐐼 𐑌𐐱𐐻 𐑁𐐫𐑊 𐐮𐑌𐐻𐐭 𐑄 𐐸𐐰𐑌𐐼𐑆 𐐲𐑂 𐑄𐐩𐑉 𐐺𐑉𐐯𐑄𐑉𐐯𐑌. 𐐤𐐵 𐑄𐐮𐑅 𐐶𐐱𐑆 𐑄 𐐿𐐩𐑅 𐐶𐐮𐑄 𐐫𐑊 𐐸𐐮𐑆 𐐽𐐨𐑁 𐐿𐐰𐐹𐐻𐐯𐑌𐑆. 𐐜𐐩 𐐼𐐵𐐻𐐯𐐼 𐐰𐑌𐐼 𐑋𐐪𐑉𐑂𐐯𐑊𐐼 𐐫𐑊𐑅𐐬, 𐐺𐐨𐐿𐐫𐑆 𐐲𐑂 𐑄 𐐶𐐮𐐿𐐯𐐼𐑌𐐯𐑅 𐐲𐑂 𐑄 𐐹𐐨𐐹𐑊; 𐐰𐑌𐐼 𐑄𐐮𐑅 𐐺𐐨𐐿𐐫𐑆 𐐲𐑂 𐑄 𐑅𐐲𐐿𐑅𐐯𐑅 𐐲𐑂 𐑄 𐐢𐐰𐑋𐐲𐑌𐐴𐐻𐑅 𐐬𐑂𐐲𐑉 𐑄𐐯𐑋. 𐐈𐑌𐐼 𐐮𐐻 𐐿𐐩𐑋 𐐻𐐭 𐐹𐐰𐑅 𐑄𐐰𐐻 𐐣𐐬𐑉𐐬𐑌𐐴 𐐶𐐱𐑆 𐐰𐑍𐑀𐑉𐐨 𐐶𐐮𐑄 𐑄 𐑀𐐲𐑂𐐲𐑉𐑌𐑋𐐯𐑌𐐻, 𐐺𐐨𐐿𐐫𐑆 𐐲𐑂 𐑄𐐩𐑉 𐐮𐑌𐐼𐐮𐑁𐐲𐑉𐐯𐑌𐑅 𐐿𐐱𐑌𐑅𐐲𐑉𐑌𐐮𐑍 𐑄 𐑁𐑉𐐨𐐼𐐲𐑋 𐐲𐑂 𐑄𐐩𐑉 𐐿𐐲𐑌𐐻𐑉𐐨.

5\. 𐐈𐑌𐐼 𐐮𐐻 𐐿𐐩𐑋 𐐻𐐭 𐐹𐐰𐑅 𐑄𐐰𐐻 𐐸𐐨 𐑉𐐬𐐻 𐐲𐑀𐐯𐑌 𐐻𐐭 𐑄 𐐘𐐲𐑂𐐲𐑉𐑌𐐲𐑉 𐐲𐑂 𐑄 𐑊𐐰𐑌𐐼, 𐐸𐐭 𐐶𐐱𐑆 𐐑𐐩𐐸𐐬𐑉𐐰𐑌, 𐐰𐑌𐐼 𐑄𐐨𐑆 𐐪𐑉 𐑄 𐐶𐐲𐑉𐐼𐑆 𐐸𐐶𐐮𐐽 𐐸𐐨 𐑉𐐬𐐻, 𐑅𐐩𐐮𐑍: 𐐒𐐨𐐸𐐬𐑊𐐼, 𐐌 𐐼𐐴𐑉𐐯𐐿𐐻 𐑋𐐴𐑌 𐐯𐐹𐐮𐑅𐑊 𐐻𐐭 𐐑𐐩𐐸𐐬𐑉𐐰𐑌, 𐐮𐑌 𐑄 𐑅𐐮𐐻𐐨 𐐲𐑂 𐐞𐐰𐑉𐐲𐐸𐐯𐑋𐑊𐐲, 𐐸𐐭 𐐮𐑆 𐑄 𐐕𐐨𐑁 𐐖𐐲𐐾 𐐰𐑌𐐼 𐑄 𐐘𐐲𐑂𐐲𐑉𐑌𐐲𐑉 𐐬𐑂𐐲𐑉 𐑄 𐑊𐐰𐑌𐐼, 𐐰𐑌𐐼 𐐫𐑊𐑅𐐬 𐐻𐐭 𐐫𐑊 𐑄𐐬𐑆 𐐸𐐭 𐐸𐐰𐑂 𐐺𐐮𐑌 𐐽𐐬𐑆𐑌 𐐺𐐴 𐑄𐐮𐑅 𐐹𐐨𐐹𐑊 𐐻𐐭 𐑀𐐲𐑂𐐲𐑉𐑌 𐐰𐑌𐐼 𐑋𐐰𐑌𐐩𐐾 𐑄 𐐲𐑁𐐩𐑉𐑆 𐐲𐑂 𐑄𐐮𐑅 𐐶𐐫𐑉; 𐑁𐐫𐑉 𐐺𐐨𐐸𐐬𐑊𐐼, 𐐌 𐐸𐐰𐑂 𐑅𐐲𐑋𐐸𐐶𐐱𐐻 𐐻𐐭 𐑅𐐩 𐐲𐑌𐐻𐐭 𐑄𐐯𐑋 𐐺𐐴 𐑄 𐐶𐐩 𐐲𐑂 𐐿𐐱𐑌𐐼𐐯𐑋𐑌𐐩𐑇𐐲𐑌; 𐑁𐐫𐑉 𐐺𐐨𐐸𐐬𐑊𐐼, 𐐷𐐨 𐐷𐐭𐑉𐑅𐐯𐑊𐑂𐑆 𐑌𐐬 𐑄𐐰𐐻 𐐷𐐨 𐐸𐐰𐑂 𐐺𐐮𐑌 𐐰𐐹𐑎𐑌𐐻𐐯𐐼 𐐻𐐭 𐑀𐐰𐑄𐐲𐑉 𐐻𐐭𐑀𐐯𐑄𐐲𐑉 𐑋𐐯𐑌, 𐐰𐑌𐐼 𐐪𐑉𐑋 𐑄𐐯𐑋 𐐶𐐮𐑄 𐑅𐐬𐑉𐐼𐑆, 𐐰𐑌𐐼 𐐶𐐮𐑄 𐑅𐐮𐑋𐐯𐐻𐐲𐑉𐑆, 𐐰𐑌𐐼 𐐫𐑊 𐑋𐐰𐑌𐐲𐑉 𐐲𐑂 𐐶𐐯𐐹𐐲𐑌𐑆 𐐲𐑂 𐐶𐐫𐑉 𐐲𐑂 𐐯𐑂𐐲𐑉𐐨 𐐿𐐴𐑌𐐼, 𐐰𐑌𐐼 𐑅𐐯𐑌𐐼 𐑁𐐫𐑉𐑃 𐐲𐑀𐐯𐑌𐑅𐐻 𐑄 𐐢𐐰𐑋𐐲𐑌𐐴𐐻𐑅, 𐐮𐑌 𐐸𐐶𐐱𐐻𐑅𐐬𐐯𐑂𐐲𐑉 𐐹𐐪𐑉𐐻𐑅 𐑄𐐩 𐑇𐐳𐐼 𐐿𐐲𐑋 𐐮𐑌𐐻𐐭 𐐵𐑉 𐑊𐐰𐑌𐐼. 𐐈𐑌𐐼 𐑌𐐵 𐐺𐐨𐐸𐐬𐑊𐐼, 𐐌 𐑅𐐩 𐐲𐑌𐐻𐐭 𐐷𐐭 𐑄𐐰𐐻 𐑋𐐴𐑅𐐯𐑊𐑁, 𐐰𐑌𐐼 𐐫𐑊𐑅𐐬 𐑋𐐴 𐑋𐐯𐑌, 𐐰𐑌𐐼 𐐫𐑊𐑅𐐬 𐐐𐐨𐑊𐐰𐑋𐐲𐑌 𐐰𐑌𐐼 𐐸𐐮𐑆 𐑋𐐯𐑌, 𐐸𐐰𐑂 𐑅𐐲𐑁𐐲𐑉𐐼 𐐯𐐿𐑅𐐨𐐼𐐮𐑍𐑊𐐨 𐑀𐑉𐐩𐐻 𐑅𐐲𐑁𐐲𐑉𐐮𐑍𐑆; 𐐷𐐩, 𐐨𐑂𐑌 𐐸𐐲𐑍𐑀𐐲𐑉, 𐑃𐐲𐑉𐑅𐐻, 𐐰𐑌𐐼 𐑁𐐲𐐻𐐨𐑀, 𐐰𐑌𐐼 𐐫𐑊 𐑋𐐰𐑌𐐲𐑉 𐐲𐑂 𐐲𐑁𐑊𐐮𐐿𐑇𐐲𐑌𐑆 𐐲𐑂 𐐯𐑂𐐲𐑉𐐨 𐐿𐐴𐑌𐐼. 𐐒𐐲𐐻 𐐺𐐨𐐸𐐬𐑊𐐼, 𐐶𐐲𐑉 𐑄𐐮𐑅 𐐫𐑊 𐐶𐐨 𐐸𐐰𐐼 𐑅𐐲𐑁𐐲𐑉𐐼, 𐐶𐐨 𐐶𐐳𐐼 𐑌𐐱𐐻 𐑋𐐲𐑉𐑋𐐲𐑉 𐑌𐐫𐑉 𐐿𐐱𐑋𐐹𐑊𐐩𐑌; 𐐺𐐲𐐻 𐐺𐐨𐐸𐐬𐑊𐐼, 𐑀𐑉𐐩𐐻 𐐸𐐰𐑆 𐐺𐐮𐑌 𐑄 𐑅𐑊𐐫𐐻𐐲𐑉 𐐲𐑋𐐲𐑍 𐐵𐑉 𐐹𐐨𐐹𐑊; 𐐷𐐩, 𐑃𐐵𐑆𐐲𐑌𐐼𐑆 𐐸𐐰𐑂 𐑁𐐫𐑊𐑌 𐐺𐐴 𐑄 𐑅𐐬𐑉𐐼, 𐐸𐐶𐐴𐑊 𐐮𐐻 𐑋𐐴𐐻 𐐸𐐰𐑂 𐐲𐑄𐐲𐑉𐐶𐐴𐑆 𐐺𐐮𐑌 𐐮𐑁 𐐷𐐨 𐐸𐐰𐐼 𐑉𐐯𐑌𐐼𐐲𐑉𐐼 𐐲𐑌𐐻𐐭 𐐵𐑉 𐐪𐑉𐑋𐐨𐑆 𐑅𐐲𐑁𐐮𐑇𐐯𐑌𐐻 𐑅𐐻𐑉𐐯𐑍𐑃 𐐰𐑌𐐼 𐑅𐐲𐐿𐐲𐑉 𐑁𐐫𐑉 𐑄𐐯𐑋. 𐐏𐐩, 𐑀𐑉𐐩𐐻 𐐸𐐰𐑆 𐐺𐐮𐑌 𐐷𐐭𐑉 𐑌𐐯𐑀𐑊𐐯𐐿𐐻 𐐻𐐬𐑉𐐼𐑆 𐐲𐑅. 𐐈𐑌𐐼 𐑌𐐵 𐐺𐐨𐐸𐐬𐑊𐐼, 𐐶𐐨 𐐼𐐨𐑆𐐴𐑉 𐐻𐐭 𐑌𐐬 𐑄 𐐿𐐫𐑆 𐐲𐑂 𐑄𐐮𐑅 𐐯𐐿𐑅𐐨𐐼𐐮𐑍𐑊𐐨 𐑀𐑉𐐩𐐻 𐑌𐐯𐑀𐑊𐐯𐐿𐐻; 𐐷𐐩, 𐐶𐐨 𐐼𐐨𐑆𐐴𐑉 𐐻𐐭 𐑌𐐬 𐑄 𐐿𐐫𐑆 𐐲𐑂 𐐷𐐭𐑉 𐑃𐐫𐐻𐑊𐐯𐑅 𐑅𐐻𐐩𐐻. 𐐗𐐰𐑌 𐐷𐐭 𐑃𐐮𐑍𐐿 𐐻𐐭 𐑅𐐮𐐻 𐐲𐐹𐐱𐑌 𐐷𐐭𐑉 𐑃𐑉𐐬𐑌𐑆 𐐮𐑌 𐐲 𐑅𐐻𐐩𐐻 𐐲𐑂 𐑃𐐫𐐻𐑊𐐯𐑅 𐑅𐐻𐐭𐐹𐐲𐑉, 𐐸𐐶𐐴𐑊 𐐷𐐭𐑉 𐐯𐑌𐐯𐑋𐐨𐑆 𐐪𐑉 𐑅𐐹𐑉𐐯𐐼𐐮𐑍 𐑄 𐐶𐐲𐑉𐐿 𐐲𐑂 𐐼𐐯𐑃 𐐲𐑉𐐵𐑌𐐼 𐐷𐐭? 𐐏𐐩, 𐐸𐐶𐐴𐑊 𐑄𐐩 𐐪𐑉 𐑋𐐲𐑉𐐼𐐲𐑉𐐮𐑍 𐑃𐐵𐑆𐐲𐑌𐐼𐑆 𐐲𐑂 𐐷𐐭𐑉 𐐺𐑉𐐯𐑄𐑉𐐯𐑌; 𐐷𐐩, 𐐨𐑂𐑌 𐑄𐐩 𐐸𐐭 𐐸𐐰𐑂 𐑊𐐳𐐿𐐻 𐐲𐐹 𐐻𐐭 𐐷𐐭 𐑁𐐫𐑉 𐐹𐑉𐐬𐐻𐐯𐐿𐑇𐐲𐑌, 𐐷𐐩, 𐐸𐐰𐑂 𐐹𐑊𐐩𐑅𐐻 𐐷𐐭 𐐮𐑌 𐐲 𐑅𐐮𐐻𐐷𐐭𐐩𐑇𐐲𐑌 𐑄𐐰𐐻 𐐷𐐨 𐑋𐐴𐐻 𐐸𐐰𐑂 𐑅𐐲𐐿𐐲𐑉𐐼 𐑄𐐯𐑋; 𐐷𐐩, 𐐷𐐨 𐑋𐐴𐐻 𐐸𐐰𐑂 𐑅𐐯𐑌𐐻 𐐪𐑉𐑋𐐨𐑆 𐐲𐑌𐐻𐐭 𐑄𐐯𐑋, 𐐻𐐭 𐐸𐐰𐑂 𐑅𐐻𐑉𐐯𐑍𐑃𐑌𐐼 𐑄𐐯𐑋, 𐐰𐑌𐐼 𐐸𐐰𐑂 𐑅𐐩𐑂𐐼 𐑃𐐵𐑆𐐲𐑌𐐼𐑆 𐐲𐑂 𐑄𐐯𐑋 𐑁𐑉𐐱𐑋 𐑁𐐫𐑊𐐮𐑍 𐐺𐐴 𐑄 𐑅𐐬𐑉𐐼. 𐐒𐐲𐐻 𐐺𐐨𐐸𐐬𐑊𐐼, 𐑄𐐮𐑅 𐐮𐑆 𐑌𐐱𐐻 𐐫𐑊, 𐐷𐐨 𐐸𐐰𐑂 𐐶𐐮𐑄𐐸𐐯𐑊𐐼 𐐷𐐭𐑉 𐐹𐑉𐐬𐑂𐐮𐑈𐐲𐑌𐑆 𐑁𐑉𐐱𐑋 𐑄𐐯𐑋, 𐐮𐑌𐑅𐐬𐑋𐐲𐐽 𐑄𐐰𐐻 𐑋𐐯𐑌𐐨 𐐸𐐰𐑂 𐑁𐐫𐐻 𐐰𐑌𐐼 𐐺𐑊𐐯𐐼 𐐵𐐻 𐑄𐐩𐑉 𐑊𐐴𐑂𐑆 𐐺𐐨𐐿𐐫𐑆 𐐲𐑂 𐑄𐐩𐑉 𐑀𐑉𐐩𐐻 𐐼𐐨𐑆𐐴𐑉𐑆 𐐸𐐶𐐮𐐽 𐑄𐐩 𐐸𐐰𐐼 𐑁𐐫𐑉 𐑄 𐐶𐐯𐑊𐑁𐐩𐑉 𐐲𐑂 𐑄𐐮𐑅 𐐹𐐨𐐹𐑊; 𐐷𐐩, 𐐰𐑌𐐼 𐑄𐐮𐑅 𐑄𐐩 𐐸𐐰𐑂 𐐼𐐲𐑌 𐐸𐐶𐐯𐑌 𐑄𐐩 𐐶𐐲𐑉 𐐲𐐺𐐵𐐻 𐐻𐐭 𐐹𐐯𐑉𐐮𐑇 𐐶𐐮𐑄 𐐸𐐲𐑍𐑀𐐲𐑉, 𐐺𐐨𐐿𐐫𐑆 𐐲𐑂 𐐷𐐭𐑉 𐐯𐐿𐑅𐐨𐐼𐐮𐑍𐑊𐐨 𐑀𐑉𐐩𐐻 𐑌𐐯𐑀𐑊𐐯𐐿𐐻 𐐻𐐬𐑉𐐼𐑆 𐑄𐐯𐑋.

6. 𐐈𐑌𐐼 𐑌𐐵, 𐑋𐐴 𐐺𐐮𐑊𐐲𐑂𐐯𐐼 𐐺𐑉𐐯𐑄𐑉𐐯𐑌, 𐑁𐐫𐑉 𐐷 𐐸𐐰𐐼 𐐫𐐻 𐐻𐐭 𐐺 𐐺𐐮𐑊𐐲𐑂𐐯𐐼; 𐐷𐐩, 𐐰𐑌𐐼 𐐷 𐐸𐐰𐐼 𐐫𐐻 𐐻𐐭 𐐸𐐰𐑂 𐑅𐐻𐐲𐑉𐐼 𐐷𐐭𐑉𐑅𐐯𐑊𐑂𐑆 𐑋𐐬𐑉 𐐼𐐮𐑊𐐮𐐾𐐯𐑌𐐻𐑊𐐨 𐑁𐐫𐑉 𐑄 𐐶𐐯𐑊𐑁𐐯𐑉 𐐰𐑌𐐼 𐑄 𐑁𐑉𐐨𐐼𐐲𐑋 𐐲𐑂 𐑄𐐮𐑅 𐐹𐐨𐐹𐑊; 𐐺𐐲𐐻 𐐺𐐨𐐸𐐬𐑊𐐼, 𐐷 𐐸𐐰𐑂 𐑌𐐯𐑀𐑊𐐯𐐿𐐻𐐯𐐼 𐑄𐐯𐑋, 𐐮𐑌𐑅𐐬𐑋𐐲𐐽 𐑄𐐰𐐻 𐑄 𐐺𐑊𐐲𐐼 𐐲𐑂 𐑃𐐵𐑆𐐲𐑌𐐼𐑆 𐑇𐐰𐑊 𐐿𐐲𐑋 𐐲𐐹𐐱𐑌 𐐷𐐭𐑉 𐐸𐐯𐐼𐑆 𐑁𐐫𐑉 𐑂𐐯𐑌𐐾𐐲𐑌𐑅; 𐐷𐐩, 𐑁𐐫𐑉 𐑌𐐬𐑌 𐐲𐑌𐐻𐐭 𐐘𐐱𐐼 𐐶𐐲𐑉 𐐫𐑊 𐑄𐐩𐑉 𐐿𐑉𐐴𐑆, 𐐰𐑌𐐼 𐐫𐑊 𐑄𐐩𐑉 𐑅𐐲𐑁𐐲𐑉𐐨𐑍𐑆. 𐐒𐐨𐐸𐐬𐑊𐐼, 𐐿𐐳𐐼 𐐷 𐑅𐐲𐐹𐐬𐑆 𐑄𐐰𐐻 𐐷 𐐿𐐳𐐼 𐑅𐐮𐐻 𐐲𐐹𐐱𐑌 𐐷𐐭𐑉 𐑃𐑉𐐬𐑌𐑆, 𐐰𐑌𐐼 𐐺𐐨𐐿𐐫𐑆 𐐲𐑂 𐑄 𐐯𐐿𐑅𐐨𐐼𐐮𐑍 𐑀𐐳𐐼𐑌𐐯𐑅 𐐲𐑂 𐐘𐐱𐐼 𐐷 𐐿𐐳𐐼 𐐼𐐭 𐑌𐐲𐑃𐐮𐑍, 𐐰𐑌𐐼 𐐸𐐨 𐐶𐐳𐐼 𐐼𐐮𐑊𐐮𐑂𐐲𐑉 𐐷𐐭? 𐐒𐐨𐐸𐐬𐑊𐐼, 𐐮𐑁 𐐷 𐐸𐐰𐑂 𐑅𐐲𐐹𐐬𐑆𐐼 𐑄𐐮𐑅, 𐐷 𐐸𐐰𐑂 𐑅𐐲𐐹𐐬𐑆𐐼 𐐮𐑌 𐑂𐐩𐑌:—𐐔𐐭 𐐷 𐑅𐐲𐐹𐐬𐑆 𐑄𐐰𐐻, 𐐺𐐨𐐿𐐫𐑆 𐑅𐐬 𐑋𐐯𐑌𐐨 𐐲𐑂 𐐷𐐭𐑉 𐐺𐑉𐐯𐑄𐑉𐐯𐑌 𐐸𐐰𐑂 𐐺𐐮𐑌 𐐿𐐮𐑊𐐼, 𐐮𐐻 𐐮𐑆 𐐺𐐨𐐿𐐫𐑆 𐐲𐑂 𐑄𐐩𐑉 𐐶𐐮𐐿𐐯𐐼𐑌𐐯𐑅? 𐐌 𐑅𐐩 𐐲𐑌𐐻𐐭 𐐷𐐭, 𐐮𐑁 𐐷 𐐸𐐰𐑂 𐑅𐐲𐐹𐐬𐑆𐐼 𐑄𐐮𐑅, 𐐷 𐐸𐐰𐑂 𐑅𐐲𐐹𐐬𐑆𐐼 𐐮𐑌 𐑂𐐩𐑌: 𐑁𐐫𐑉 𐐌 𐑅𐐩 𐐲𐑌𐐻𐐭 𐐷𐐭, 𐑄𐐯𐑉 𐐪𐑉 𐑋𐐯𐑌𐐨 𐐸𐐶𐐮𐐽 𐐸𐐰𐑂 𐑁𐐫𐑊𐑌 𐐺𐐴 𐑄 𐑅𐐬𐑉𐐼; 𐐰𐑌𐐼 𐐺𐐨𐐸𐐬𐑊𐐼 𐐮𐐻 𐐮𐑆 𐐻𐐭 𐐷𐐭𐑉 𐐿𐐱𐑌𐐼𐐯𐑋𐑌𐐩𐑇𐐲𐑌; 𐑁𐐫𐑉 𐑄 𐐢𐐫𐑉𐐼 𐑅𐐲𐑁𐐲𐑉𐐯𐑃 𐑄 𐑉𐐴𐐽𐐲𐑅 𐐻𐐭 𐐺 𐑅𐑊𐐩𐑌 𐑄𐐰𐐻 𐐸𐐮𐑆 𐐾𐐲𐑅𐐻𐐮𐑅 𐐰𐑌𐐼 𐐾𐐲𐐾𐑋𐐯𐑌𐐻 𐑋𐐩 𐐿𐐲𐑋 𐐲𐐹𐐱𐑌 𐑄 𐐶𐐮𐐿𐐯𐐼; 𐑄𐐯𐑉𐑁𐐫𐑉 𐐷 𐑌𐐨𐐼 𐑌𐐱𐐻 𐑅𐐲𐐹𐐬𐑆 𐑄𐐰𐐻 𐑄 𐑉𐐴𐐽𐐲𐑅 𐐪𐑉 𐑊𐐱𐑅𐐻 𐐺𐐨𐐿𐐫𐑆 𐑄𐐩 𐐪𐑉 𐑅𐑊𐐩𐑌; 𐐺𐐲𐐻 𐐺𐐨𐐸𐐬𐑊𐐼, 𐑄𐐩 𐐼𐐭 𐐯𐑌𐐻𐐲𐑉 𐐮𐑌𐐻𐐭 𐑄 𐑉𐐯𐑅𐐻 𐐲𐑂 𐑄 𐐢𐐫𐑉𐐼 𐑄𐐩𐑉 𐐘𐐱𐐼.

7. 𐐈𐑌𐐼 𐑌𐐵 𐐺𐐨𐐸𐐬𐑊𐐼, 𐐌 𐑅𐐩 𐐲𐑌𐐻𐐭 𐐷𐐭, 𐐌 𐑁𐐨𐑉 𐐯𐐿𐑅𐐨𐐼𐐮𐑍𐑊𐐨 𐑄𐐰𐐻 𐑄 𐐾𐐲𐐾𐑋𐐯𐑌𐐻𐑅 𐐲𐑂 𐐘𐐱𐐼 𐐶𐐮𐑊 𐐿𐐲𐑋 𐐲𐐹𐐱𐑌 𐑄𐐮𐑅 𐐹𐐨𐐹𐑊, 𐐺𐐨𐐿𐐫𐑆 𐐲𐑂 𐑄𐐩𐑉 𐐯𐐿𐑅𐐨𐐼𐐮𐑍 𐑅𐑊𐐬𐑃𐑁𐐳𐑊𐑌𐐯𐑅; 𐐷𐐩, 𐐨𐑂𐐲𐑌 𐑄 𐑅𐑊𐐬𐑃𐑁𐐳𐑊𐑌𐐯𐑅 𐐲𐑂 𐐵𐑉 𐑀𐐲𐑂𐐲𐑉𐑌𐑋𐐯𐑌𐐻, 𐐰𐑌𐐼 𐑄𐐩𐑉 𐐯𐐿𐑅𐐨𐐼𐐮𐑍 𐑀𐑉𐐩𐐻 𐑌𐐯𐑀𐑊𐐯𐐿𐐻 𐐻𐐬𐑉𐐼𐑆 𐑄𐐩𐑉 𐐺𐑉𐐯𐑄𐑉𐐯𐑌, 𐐷𐐩, 𐐻𐐬𐑉𐐼𐑆 𐑄𐐬𐑆 𐐸𐐶𐐮𐐽 𐐸𐐰𐑂 𐐺𐐮𐑌 𐑅𐑊𐐩𐑌: 𐑁𐐫𐑉 𐐶𐐲𐑉 𐐮𐐻 𐑌𐐱𐐻 𐑁𐐫𐑉 𐑄 𐐶𐐮𐐿𐐯𐐼𐑌𐐯𐑅 𐐸𐐶𐐮𐐽 𐑁𐐲𐑉𐑅𐐻 𐐿𐐱𐑋𐐯𐑌𐑅𐐻 𐐰𐐻 𐐵𐑉 𐐸𐐯𐐼, 𐐶𐐨 𐐿𐐳𐐼 𐐸𐐰𐑂 𐐶𐐮𐑄𐑅𐐻𐐳𐐼 𐐵𐑉 𐐯𐑌𐐯𐑋𐐨𐑆, 𐑄𐐰𐐻 𐑄𐐩 𐐿𐐳𐐼 𐐸𐐰𐑂 𐑀𐐩𐑌𐐼 𐑌𐐬 𐐹𐐵𐐲𐑉 𐐬𐑂𐐲𐑉 𐐲𐑅: 𐐷𐐩, 𐐸𐐰𐐼 𐐮𐐻 𐑌𐐱𐐻 𐐺𐐮𐑌 𐑁𐐫𐑉 𐑄 𐐶𐐫𐑉 𐐸𐐶𐐮𐐽 𐐺𐑉𐐬𐐿 𐐵𐐻 𐐲𐑋𐐲𐑍 𐐵𐑉𐑅𐐯𐑊𐑂𐑆; 𐐷𐐩, 𐐶𐐲𐑉 𐐮𐐻 𐑌𐐱𐐻 𐑁𐐫𐑉 𐑄𐐨𐑆 𐐿𐐮𐑍-𐑋𐐯𐑌, 𐐸𐐶𐐮𐐽 𐐿𐐫𐑆𐐼 𐑅𐐬 𐑋𐐲𐐽 𐐺𐑊𐐲𐐼𐑇𐐯𐐼 𐐲𐑋𐐲𐑍 𐐵𐑉𐑅𐐯𐑊𐑂𐑆; 𐐷𐐩, 𐐰𐐻 𐑄 𐐻𐐴𐑋 𐐶𐐨 𐐶𐐲𐑉 𐐿𐐱𐑌𐐻𐐯𐑌𐐼𐐮𐑍 𐐲𐑋𐐲𐑍 𐐵𐑉𐑅𐐯𐑊𐑂𐑆, 𐐮𐑁 𐐶𐐨 𐐸𐐰𐐼 𐐷𐐭𐑌𐐴𐐻𐐯𐐼 𐐵𐑉 𐑅𐐻𐑉𐐯𐑍𐑃 𐐰𐑆 𐐶𐐨 𐐸𐐮𐑄𐐲𐑉𐐻𐐭 𐐸𐐰𐑂 𐐼𐐲𐑌; 𐐷𐐩, 𐐸𐐰𐐼 𐐮𐐻 𐑌𐐱𐐻 𐐺𐐮𐑌 𐑁𐐫𐑉 𐑄 𐐼𐐨𐑆𐐴𐑉 𐐲𐑂 𐐹𐐵𐐲𐑉 𐐰𐑌𐐼 𐐫𐑃𐐱𐑉𐐮𐐻𐐨 𐐸𐐶𐐮𐐽 𐑄𐐬𐑆 𐐿𐐮𐑍-𐑋𐐯𐑌 𐐸𐐰𐐼 𐐬𐑂𐐲𐑉 𐐲𐑅; 𐐸𐐰𐐼 𐑄𐐩 𐐺𐐮𐑌 𐐻𐑉𐐭 𐐻𐐭 𐑄 𐐿𐐫𐑆 𐐲𐑂 𐐵𐑉 𐑁𐑉𐐨𐐼𐐲𐑋, 𐐰𐑌𐐼 𐐷𐐭𐑌𐐴𐐻𐐯𐐼 𐐶𐐮𐑄 𐐲𐑅, 𐐰𐑌𐐼 𐑀𐐱𐑌 𐑁𐐬𐑉𐑃 𐐲𐑀𐐯𐑌𐑅𐐻 𐐵𐑉 𐐯𐑌𐐯𐑋𐐨𐑆, 𐐮𐑌𐑅𐐻𐐯𐐼 𐐲𐑂 𐐻𐐩𐐿𐐮𐑍 𐐲𐐹 𐑄𐐩𐑉 𐑅𐐬𐑉𐐼𐑆 𐐲𐑀𐐯𐑌𐑅𐐻 𐐲𐑅, 𐐸𐐶𐐮𐐽 𐐶𐐱𐑆 𐑄 𐐿𐐫𐑆 𐐲𐑂 𐑅𐐬 𐑋𐐲𐐽 𐐺𐑊𐐲𐐼𐑇𐐯𐐼 𐐲𐑋𐐲𐑍 𐐵𐑉𐑅𐐯𐑊𐑂𐑆; 𐐷𐐩, 𐐮𐑁 𐐶𐐨 𐐸𐐰𐐼 𐑀𐐱𐑌 𐑁𐐬𐑉𐑃 𐐲𐑀𐐯𐑌𐑅𐐻 𐑄𐐯𐑋 𐐮𐑌 𐑄 𐑅𐐻𐑉𐐯𐑍𐑃 𐐲𐑂 𐑄 𐐢𐐫𐑉𐐼, 𐐶𐐨 𐑇𐐳𐐼 𐐸𐐰𐑂 𐐼𐐮𐑅𐐹𐐲𐑉𐑅𐐻 𐐵𐑉 𐐯𐑌𐐯𐑋𐐨𐑆; 𐑁𐐫𐑉 𐐮𐐻 𐐶𐐳𐐼 𐐸𐐰𐑂 𐐺𐐮𐑌 𐐼𐐲𐑌 𐐰𐐿𐐫𐑉𐐼𐐮𐑍 𐐻𐐭 𐑄 𐑁𐐳𐑊𐑁𐐮𐑊𐐮𐑍 𐐲𐑂 𐐸𐐮𐑆 𐐶𐐲𐑉𐐼. 𐐒𐐲𐐻 𐐺𐐨𐐸𐐬𐑊𐐼, 𐑌𐐵 𐑄 𐐢𐐩𐑋𐐲𐑌𐐴𐐻𐑅 𐐪𐑉 𐐿𐐲𐑋𐐮𐑍 𐐲𐐹𐐱𐑌 𐐲𐑅, 𐐻𐐩𐐿𐐮𐑍 𐐹𐐲𐑆𐐯𐑇𐐲𐑌 𐐲𐑂 𐐵𐑉 𐑊𐐰𐑌𐐼𐑆, 𐐰𐑌𐐼 𐑄𐐩 𐐪𐑉 𐑋𐐲𐑉𐐼𐐲𐑉𐐮𐑍 𐐵𐑉 𐐹𐐨𐐹𐑊 𐐶𐐮𐑄 𐑄 𐑅𐐬𐑉𐐼: 𐐷𐐩, 𐐵𐑉 𐐶𐐮𐑋𐐯𐑌 𐐰𐑌𐐼 𐐵𐑉 𐐽𐐮𐑊𐐼𐑉𐐯𐑌: 𐐰𐑌𐐼 𐐫𐑊𐑅𐐬 𐐿𐐰𐑉𐐨𐐮𐑍 𐑄𐐯𐑋 𐐲𐐶𐐩 𐐿𐐰𐐹𐐻𐐮𐑂; 𐐿𐐫𐑆𐐮𐑍 𐑄𐐯𐑋 𐑄𐐰𐐻 𐑄𐐩 𐑇𐐳𐐼 𐑅𐐲𐑁𐐲𐑉 𐐫𐑊 𐑋𐐰𐑌𐐲𐑉 𐐲𐑂 𐐰𐑁𐑊𐐮𐐿𐑇𐐲𐑌𐑆; 𐐰𐑌𐐼 𐑄𐐮𐑅 𐐺𐐨𐐿𐐫𐑆 𐐲𐑂 𐑄 𐑀𐑉𐐩𐐻 𐐶𐐮𐐿𐐯𐐼𐑌𐐯𐑅 𐐲𐑂 𐑄𐐬𐑆 𐐸𐐶𐐮𐐽 𐐪𐑉 𐑅𐐨𐐿𐐮𐑍 𐑁𐐫𐑉 𐐹𐐵𐐲𐑉 𐐰𐑌𐐼 𐐫𐑃𐐱𐑉𐐮𐐻𐐨; 𐐷𐐩, 𐐨𐑂𐐲𐑌 𐑄𐐬𐑆 𐐿𐐮𐑍-𐑋𐐯𐑌. 𐐒𐐲𐐻 𐐸𐐶𐐴 𐑇𐐳𐐼 𐐌 𐑅𐐩 𐑋𐐲𐐽 𐐿𐐱𐑌𐑅𐐲𐑉𐑌𐐮𐑍 𐑄𐐮𐑅 𐑋𐐰𐐻𐐲𐑉, 𐑁𐐫𐑉 𐐶𐐨 𐑌𐐬 𐑌𐐱𐐻 𐐺𐐲𐐻 𐐸𐐶𐐱𐐻 𐐷 𐐷𐐭𐑉𐑅𐐯𐑊𐑂𐑆 𐐪𐑉 𐑅𐐨𐐿𐐮𐑍 𐑁𐐫𐑉 𐐫𐑃𐐱𐑉𐐮𐐻𐐨? 𐐎𐐨 𐑌𐐬 𐑌𐐱𐐻 𐐺𐐲𐐻 𐐸𐐶𐐱𐐻 𐐷 𐐪𐑉 𐐫𐑊𐑅𐐬 𐐻𐑉𐐩𐐻𐐲𐑉𐑆 𐐻𐐭 𐐷𐐭𐑉 𐐿𐐲𐑌𐐻𐑉𐐨. 𐐉𐑉 𐐮𐑆 𐐮𐐻 𐑄𐐰𐐻 𐐷 𐐸𐐰𐑂 𐑌𐐯𐑀𐑊𐐯𐐿𐐻𐐯𐐼 𐐲𐑅 𐐺𐐨𐐿𐐫𐑆 𐐷 𐐪𐑉 𐐮𐑌 𐑄 𐐸𐐪𐑉𐐻 𐐲𐑂 𐐵𐑉 𐐿𐐲𐑌𐐻𐑉𐐨, 𐐰𐑌𐐼 𐐷 𐐪𐑉 𐑅𐐲𐑉𐐵𐑌𐐼𐐯𐐼 𐐺𐐴 𐑅𐐨𐐿𐐷𐐭𐑉𐐮𐐻𐐨, 𐑄𐐰𐐻 𐐷 𐐼𐐭 𐑌𐐱𐐻 𐐿𐐫𐑆 𐑁𐐳𐐼 𐐻𐐭 𐐺 𐑅𐐯𐑌𐐻 𐐲𐑌𐐻𐐭 𐐲𐑅, 𐐰𐑌𐐼 𐐫𐑊𐑅𐐬 𐑋𐐯𐑌 𐐻𐐭 𐑅𐐻𐑉𐐯𐑍𐑃𐐲𐑌 𐐵𐑉 𐐪𐑉𐑋𐐨𐑆? 𐐐𐐰𐑂 𐐷 𐑁𐐲𐑉𐑀𐐱𐐻𐑌 𐑄 𐐿𐐱𐑋𐐰𐑌𐐼𐑋𐐯𐑌𐐻𐑅 𐐲𐑂 𐑄 𐐢𐐫𐑉𐐼 𐐷𐐭𐑉 𐐘𐐱𐐼? 𐐏𐐩, 𐐸𐐰𐑂 𐐷 𐑁𐐲𐑉𐑀𐐱𐐻𐑌 𐑄 𐐿𐐰𐐹𐐻𐐮𐑂𐐮𐐻𐐨 𐐲𐑂 𐐵𐑉 𐑁𐐪𐑄𐐲𐑉𐑆? 𐐐𐐰𐑂 𐐷 𐑁𐐲𐑉𐑀𐐱𐐻𐑌 𐑄 𐑋𐐯𐑌𐐨 𐐻𐐴𐑋𐑆 𐐶𐐨 𐐸𐐰𐑂 𐐺𐐮𐑌 𐐼𐐮𐑊𐐮𐑂𐐲𐑉𐐼 𐐵𐐻 𐐲𐑂 𐑄 𐐸𐐰𐑌𐐼𐑆 𐐲𐑂 𐐵𐑉 𐐯𐑌𐐯𐑋𐐨𐑆? 𐐉𐑉 𐐼𐐭 𐐷 𐑅𐐲𐐹𐐬𐑆 𐑄𐐰𐐻 𐑄 𐐢𐐫𐑉𐐼 𐐶𐐮𐑊 𐑅𐐻𐐮𐑊 𐐼𐐮𐑊𐐮𐑂𐐲𐑉 𐐲𐑅 𐐸𐐶𐐴𐑊 𐐶𐐨 𐑅𐐮𐐻 𐐲𐐹𐐱𐑌 𐐵𐑉 𐑃𐑉𐐬𐑌𐑆, 𐐰𐑌𐐼 𐐼𐐭 𐑌𐐱𐐻 𐑋𐐩𐐿 𐐷𐐭𐑅 𐐲𐑂 𐑄 𐑋𐐨𐑌𐑆 𐐸𐐶𐐮𐐽 𐑄 𐐢𐐫𐑉𐐼 𐐸𐐰𐑆 𐐹𐑉𐐬𐑂𐐴𐐼𐐯𐐼 𐑁𐐫𐑉 𐐲𐑅? 𐐏𐐩, 𐐶𐐮𐑊 𐐷 𐑅𐐮𐐻 𐐮𐑌 𐐴𐐼𐑊𐑌𐐯𐑅 𐐸𐐶𐐴𐑊 𐐷 𐐪𐑉 𐑅𐐲𐑉𐐵𐑌𐐼𐐯𐐼 𐐶𐐮𐑄 𐑃𐐵𐑆𐐲𐑌𐐼𐑆 𐐲𐑂 𐑄𐐬𐑆, 𐐷𐐩, 𐐰𐑌𐐼 𐐻𐐯𐑌𐑆 𐐲𐑂

𐑃𐐵𐑆𐐲𐑌𐐼𐑆, 𐐸𐐭 𐐼𐐭 𐐫𐑊𐑅𐐬 𐑅𐐮𐐻 𐐮𐑌 𐐴𐐼𐑊𐑌𐐯𐑅, 𐐸𐐶𐐴𐑊 𐑄𐐩𐑉 𐐪𐑉 𐑃𐐵𐑆𐐲𐑌𐐼𐑆 𐑉𐐵𐑌𐐼 𐐲𐐺𐐵𐐻 𐐮𐑌 𐑄 𐐺𐐫𐑉𐐼𐐲𐑉𐑆 𐐱𐑂 𐑄 𐑊𐐰𐑌𐐼 𐐸𐐭 𐐪𐑉 𐑁𐐫𐑊𐐮𐑍 𐐺𐐴 𐑄 𐑅𐐬𐑉𐐼, 𐐷𐐩, 𐐶𐐭𐑌𐐼𐐯𐐼 𐐰𐑌𐐼 𐐺𐑊𐐨𐐼𐐮𐑍? 𐐔𐐭 𐐷 𐑅𐐲𐐹𐐬𐑆 𐑄𐐰𐐻 𐐘𐐱𐐼 𐐶𐐮𐑊 𐑊𐐳𐐿 𐐲𐐹𐐱𐑌 𐐷𐐭 𐐰𐑆 𐑀𐐮𐑊𐐻𐑊𐐯𐑅 𐐸𐐶𐐴𐑊 𐐷 𐑅𐐮𐐻 𐑅𐐻𐐮𐑊 𐐰𐑌𐐼 𐐺𐐨𐐸𐐬𐑊𐐼 𐑄𐐨𐑆 𐑃𐐮𐑍𐑆? 𐐒𐐨𐐸𐐬𐑊𐐼 𐐌 𐑅𐐩 𐐲𐑌𐐻𐐭 𐐷𐐭, 𐐤𐐩. 𐐤𐐵 𐐌 𐐶𐐳𐐼 𐑄𐐰𐐻 𐐷 𐑇𐐳𐐼 𐑉𐐨𐑋𐐯𐑋𐐺𐐲𐑉 𐑄𐐰𐐻 𐐘𐐱𐐼 𐐸𐐰𐑆 𐑅𐐯𐐼 𐑄𐐰𐐻 𐑄 𐐮𐑌𐐶𐐲𐑉𐐼 𐑂𐐯𐑅𐐯𐑊 𐑇𐐰𐑊 𐐺𐐨 𐐿𐑊𐐯𐑌𐑆𐐼 𐑁𐐲𐑉𐑅𐐻, 𐐰𐑌𐐼 𐑄𐐯𐑌 𐑇𐐰𐑊 𐑄 𐐵𐐻𐐲𐑉 𐑂𐐯𐑅𐐯𐑊 𐐺𐐨 𐐿𐑊𐐯𐑌𐑆𐐼 𐐫𐑊𐑅𐐬.

8. 𐐈𐑌𐐼 𐑌𐐵, 𐐯𐐿𐑅𐐯𐐹𐐻 𐐷 𐐼𐐭 𐑉𐐨𐐹𐐯𐑌𐐻 𐐱𐑂 𐑄𐐰𐐻 𐐸𐐶𐐮𐐽 𐐷 𐐸𐐰𐑂 𐐼𐐲𐑌, 𐐰𐑌𐐼 𐐺𐐨𐑀𐐮𐑌 𐐻𐐭 𐐺𐐨 𐐲𐐹 𐐰𐑌𐐼 𐐼𐐭𐐮𐑍, 𐐰𐑌𐐼 𐑅𐐯𐑌𐐼 𐑁𐐬𐑉𐑃 𐑁𐐭𐐼 𐐰𐑌𐐼 𐑋𐐯𐑌 𐐲𐑌𐐻𐐭 𐐲𐑅, 𐐰𐑌𐐼 𐐫𐑊𐑅𐐬 𐐲𐑌𐐻𐐭 𐐐𐐨𐑊𐐰𐑋𐐲𐑌, 𐑄𐐰𐐻 𐐸𐐨 𐑋𐐩 𐑅𐐲𐐹𐐬𐑉𐐻 𐑄𐐬𐑆 𐐹𐐪𐑉𐐻𐑅 𐐱𐑂 𐐵𐑉 𐐿𐐲𐑌𐐻𐑉𐐨 𐐸𐐶𐐮𐐽 𐐸𐐨 𐐸𐐰𐑃 𐑉𐐨𐑀𐐩𐑌𐐼, 𐐰𐑌𐐼 𐑄𐐰𐐻 𐐶𐐨 𐑋𐐩 𐐫𐑊𐑅𐐬 𐑉𐐨𐐿𐐲𐑂𐐲𐑉 𐑄 𐑉𐐨𐑋𐐩𐑌𐐼𐐲𐑉 𐐱𐑂 𐐵𐑉 𐐹𐐱𐑆𐐯𐑇𐐲𐑌𐑆 𐐮𐑌 𐑄𐐨𐑆 𐐹𐐪𐑉𐐻𐑅, 𐐺𐐨𐐸𐐬𐑊𐐼 𐐮𐐻 𐐶𐐮𐑊 𐐺𐐨 𐐯𐐿𐑅𐐹𐐨𐐼𐐨𐐯𐑌𐐻 𐑄𐐰𐐻 𐐶𐐨 𐐿𐐱𐑌𐐻𐐯𐑌𐐼 𐑌𐐬 𐑋𐐬𐑉 𐐶𐐮𐑄 𐑄 𐐢𐐰𐑋𐐲𐑌𐐴𐐻𐑅 𐐲𐑌𐐻𐐮𐑊 𐐶𐐨 𐐸𐐰𐑂 𐑁𐐲𐑉𐑅𐐻 𐐿𐑊𐐯𐑌𐑆𐐼 𐐵𐑉 𐐮𐑌𐐶𐐲𐑉𐐼 𐑂𐐯𐑅𐐯𐑊; 𐐷𐐩, 𐐨𐑂𐐯𐑌 𐑄 𐑀𐑉𐐩𐐻 𐐸𐐯𐐼 𐐱𐑂 𐐵𐑉 𐑀𐐲𐑂𐐲𐑉𐑌𐑋𐐯𐑌𐐻; 𐐰𐑌𐐼 𐐯𐐿𐑅𐐯𐐹𐐻 𐐷 𐑀𐑉𐐰𐑌𐐻 𐑋𐐴𐑌 𐐨𐐹𐐮𐑅𐑊, 𐐰𐑌𐐼 𐐿𐐲𐑋 𐐵𐐻 𐐰𐑌𐐼 𐑇𐐬 𐐲𐑌𐐻𐐭 𐑋𐐨 𐐲 𐐻𐑉𐐭 𐑅𐐹𐐮𐑉𐐮𐐻 𐐱𐑂 𐑁𐑉𐐨𐐼𐐲𐑋, 𐐰𐑌𐐼 𐑅𐐻𐑉𐐴𐑂 𐐻𐐭 𐑅𐐻𐑉𐐯𐑍𐑃𐐯𐑌 𐐰𐑌𐐼 𐑁𐐫𐑉𐐻𐐮𐑁𐐴 𐐵𐑉 𐐪𐑉𐑋𐐨𐑆, 𐐰𐑌𐐼 𐑀𐑉𐐰𐑌𐐻 𐐲𐑌𐐻𐐭 𐑄𐐯𐑋 𐑁𐐭𐐼 𐑁𐐫𐑉 𐑄𐐩𐑉 𐑅𐐲𐐹𐐬𐑉𐐻, 𐐺𐐨𐐸𐐬𐑊𐐼, 𐐌 𐐶𐐮𐑊 𐑊𐐨𐑂 𐐲 𐐹𐐪𐑉𐐻 𐐱𐑂 𐑋𐐴 𐑁𐑉𐐨𐑋𐐯𐑌 𐐻𐐭 𐑋𐐩𐑌𐐻𐐩𐑌 𐑄𐐮𐑅 𐐹𐐪𐑉𐐻 𐐱𐑂 𐐵𐑉 𐑊𐐰𐑌𐐼, 𐐰𐑌𐐼 𐐌 𐐶𐐮𐑊 𐑊𐐨𐑂 𐑄 𐑅𐐻𐑉𐐯𐑍𐑃 𐐰𐑌𐐼 𐑄 𐐺𐑊𐐯𐑅𐐮𐑍𐑆 𐐱𐑂 𐐘𐐱𐐼 𐐲𐐹𐐱𐑌 𐑄𐐯𐑋, 𐑄𐐰𐐻 𐑌𐐲𐑌 𐐲𐑄𐐲𐑉 𐐹𐐵𐐲𐑉 𐐿𐐰𐑌 𐐱𐐹𐐲𐑉𐐩𐐻 𐐲𐑀𐐯𐑌𐑅𐐻 𐑄𐐯𐑋; 𐐰𐑌𐐼 𐑄𐐮𐑅 𐐺𐐨𐐿𐐫𐑆 𐐱𐑂 𐑄𐐩𐑉 𐐯𐐿𐑅𐐨𐐼𐐮𐑍 𐑁𐐩𐑃, 𐐰𐑌𐐼 𐑄𐐩𐑉 𐐹𐐩𐑇𐐯𐑌𐑅 𐐮𐑌 𐑄𐐩𐑉 𐐻𐑉𐐮𐐺𐐷𐐭𐑊𐐩𐑇𐐲𐑌𐑆; 𐐰𐑌𐐼 𐐌 𐐶𐐮𐑊 𐐿𐐲𐑋 𐐲𐑌𐐻𐐭 𐐷𐐭, 𐐰𐑌𐐼 𐐮𐑁 𐑄𐐩𐑉 𐐺𐐨 𐐯𐑌𐐨 𐐲𐑋𐐲𐑍 𐐷𐐭 𐑄𐐰𐐻 𐐸𐐰𐑃 𐐲 𐐼𐐨𐑆𐐴𐑉 𐑁𐐫𐑉 𐑁𐑉𐐨𐐼𐐲𐑋, 𐐷𐐩, 𐐮𐑁 𐑄𐐩𐑉 𐐺𐐨 𐐨𐑂𐐯𐑌 𐐲 𐑅𐐹𐐪𐑉𐐿 𐐱𐑂 𐑁𐑉𐐨𐐼𐐲𐑋 𐑉𐐨𐑋𐐩𐑌𐐮𐑍, 𐐺𐐨𐐸𐐬𐑊𐐼 𐐌 𐐶𐐮𐑊 𐑅𐐻𐐲𐑉 𐐲𐐹 𐐮𐑌𐑅𐐲𐑉𐐯𐐿𐑇𐐲𐑌𐑆 𐐲𐑋𐐲𐑍 𐐷𐐭, 𐐨𐑂𐐯𐑌 𐐲𐑌𐐻𐐮𐑊 𐑄𐐬𐑆 𐐸𐐭 𐐸𐐰𐑂 𐐼𐐨𐑆𐐴𐑉𐑆 𐐻𐐭 𐐷𐐭𐑆𐐲𐑉𐐹 𐐹𐐵𐐲𐑉 𐐰𐑌𐐼 𐐫𐑃𐐱𐑉𐐮𐐻𐐨 𐑇𐐰𐑊 𐐺𐐨𐐿𐐲𐑋 𐐯𐐿𐑅𐐻𐐮𐑍𐐿𐐻; 𐐷𐐩, 𐐺𐐨𐐸𐐬𐑊𐐼 𐐌 𐐼𐐭 𐑌𐐱𐐻 𐑁𐐨𐑉 𐐷𐐬𐑉 𐐹𐐵𐐲𐑉 𐑌𐐫𐑉 𐐷𐐬𐑉 𐐫𐑃𐐱𐑉𐐮𐐻𐐨, 𐐺𐐲𐐻 𐐮𐐻 𐐮𐑆 𐑋𐐴 𐐘𐐱𐐼 𐐸𐐭𐑋 𐐌 𐑁𐐨𐑉, 𐐰𐑌𐐼 𐐮𐐻 𐐮𐑆 𐐰𐐿𐐫𐑉𐐼𐐮𐑍 𐐻𐐭 𐐸𐐮𐑆 𐐿𐐱𐑋𐐰𐑌𐐼𐑋𐐯𐑌𐐻𐑅 𐑄𐐰𐐻 𐐌 𐐼𐐭 𐐻𐐩𐐿 𐑋𐐴 𐑅𐐬𐑉𐐼 𐐻𐐭 𐐿𐐲𐑋 𐐻𐐭 𐑄 𐐼𐐨𐑁𐐯𐑌𐑅 𐐱𐑂 𐑋𐐴 𐐿𐐲𐑌𐐻𐑉𐐨, 𐐰𐑌𐐼 𐐮𐐻 𐐮𐑆 𐐺𐐨𐐿𐐫𐑆 𐐱𐑂 𐐷𐐬𐑉 𐐮𐑌𐐮𐐿𐐶𐐮𐐻𐐨 𐑄𐐰𐐻 𐐶𐐨 𐐸𐐰𐑂 𐑅𐐲𐑁𐐲𐑉𐐼 𐑅𐐬 𐑋𐐲𐐽 𐑊𐐫𐑅. 𐐒𐐨𐐸𐐬𐑊𐐼, 𐐮𐐻 𐐮𐑆 𐐻𐐴𐑋, 𐐷𐐩, 𐑄 𐐻𐐴𐑋 𐐮𐑆 𐑌𐐵 𐐰𐐻 𐐸𐐰𐑌𐐼, 𐑄𐐰𐐻 𐐯𐐿𐑅𐐯𐐹𐐻 𐐷 𐐼𐐭 𐐺𐐨𐑅𐐻𐐲𐑉 𐐷𐐬𐑉𐑅𐐯𐑊𐑂𐑆 𐐮𐑌 𐑄 𐐼𐐨𐑁𐐯𐑌𐑅 𐐱𐑂 𐐷𐐬𐑉 𐐿𐐲𐑌𐐻𐑉𐐨 𐐰𐑌𐐼 𐐷𐐬𐑉 𐑊𐐮𐐻𐑊 𐐶𐐲𐑌𐑆, 𐑄 𐑅𐐬𐑉𐐼 𐐱𐑂 𐐾𐐲𐑅𐐻𐐮𐑅 𐐼𐐲𐑃 𐐸𐐰𐑍 𐐬𐑂𐐲𐑉 𐐷𐐭; 𐐷𐐩, 𐐰𐑌𐐼 𐐮𐐻 𐑇𐐰𐑊 𐑁𐐫𐑊 𐐲𐐹𐐱𐑌 𐐷𐐭 𐐰𐑌𐐼 𐑂𐐮𐑆𐐮𐐻 𐐷𐐭 𐐨𐑂𐐯𐑌 𐐻𐐭 𐐷𐐬𐑉 𐐲𐐻𐐲𐑉 𐐼𐐯𐑅𐐻𐑉𐐲𐐿𐑇𐐲𐑌. 𐐒𐐨𐐸𐐬𐑊𐐼, 𐐌 𐐶𐐩𐐻 𐑁𐐫𐑉 𐐰𐑅𐐮𐑅𐐻𐐰𐑌𐑅 𐑁𐑉𐐱𐑋 𐐷𐐭, 𐐰𐑌𐐼, 𐐯𐐿𐑅𐐯𐐹𐐻 𐐷 𐐼𐐭 𐐰𐐼𐑋𐐮𐑌𐐮𐑅𐐻𐐲𐑉 𐐲𐑌𐐻𐐭 𐐵𐑉 𐑉𐐨𐑊𐐨𐑁, 𐐺𐐨𐐸𐐬𐑊𐐼 𐐌 𐐿𐐲𐑋 𐐲𐑌𐐻𐐭 𐐷𐐭, 𐐨𐑂𐐯𐑌 𐐮𐑌 𐑄 𐑊𐐰𐑌𐐼 𐐱𐑂 𐐞𐐰𐑉𐐲𐐸𐐯𐑋𐑊𐐲, 𐐰𐑌𐐼 𐑅𐑋𐐴𐐻 𐐷𐐭 𐐶𐐮𐑄 𐑄 𐑅𐐬𐑉𐐼, 𐐮𐑌𐑅𐐬𐑋𐐲𐐽 𐑄𐐰𐐻 𐐷 𐐿𐐰𐑌 𐐸𐐰𐑂 𐑌𐐬 𐑋𐐬𐑉 𐐹𐐵𐐲𐑉 𐐻𐐭 𐐮𐑋𐐹𐐨𐐼 𐑄 𐐹𐑉𐐱𐑀𐑉𐐯𐑅 𐐱𐑂 𐑄𐐮𐑅 𐐹𐐨𐐹𐑊 𐐮𐑌 𐑄 𐐿𐐫𐑆 𐐱𐑂 𐐵𐑉 𐑁𐑉𐐨𐐼𐐲𐑋; 𐑁𐐫𐑉 𐐺𐐨𐐸𐐬𐑊𐐼, 𐑄 𐐢𐐫𐑉𐐼 𐐶𐐮𐑊 𐑌𐐱𐐻 𐑅𐐲𐑁𐐲𐑉 𐑄𐐰𐐻 𐐷 𐑇𐐰𐑊 𐑊𐐮𐑂 𐐰𐑌𐐼 𐐶𐐰𐐿𐑅 𐑅𐐻𐑉𐐫𐑍 𐐮𐑌 𐐷𐐬𐑉 𐐮𐑌𐐮𐐿𐐶𐐮𐐻𐐨𐑆 𐐻𐐭 𐐼𐐯𐑅𐐻𐑉𐐱𐐮 𐐸𐐮𐑆 𐑉𐐴𐐽𐐲𐑅 𐐹𐐨𐐹𐑊. 𐐒𐐨𐐸𐐬𐑊𐐼, 𐐿𐐰𐑌 𐐷𐐭 𐑅𐐲𐐹𐐬𐑆 𐑄𐐰𐐻 𐑄 𐐢𐐫𐑉𐐼 𐐶𐐮𐑊 𐑅𐐹𐐩𐑉 𐐷𐐭, 𐐰𐑌𐐼 𐐿𐐲𐑋 𐐵𐐻 𐐮𐑌 𐐾𐐲𐐾𐑋𐐯𐑌𐐻 𐐲𐑀𐐯𐑌𐑅𐐻 𐑄 𐐢𐐰𐑋𐐲𐑌𐐴𐐻𐑅, 𐐸𐐶𐐯𐑌 𐐮𐐻 𐐮𐑆 𐑄 𐐻𐑉𐐰𐐼𐐮𐑇𐐲𐑌 𐐱𐑂 𐑄𐐩𐑉 𐑁𐐪𐑄𐐲𐑉𐑆 𐑄𐐰𐐻 𐐸𐐰𐑆 𐐿𐐫𐑆𐐼 𐑄𐐩𐑉 𐐸𐐩𐐻𐑉𐐯𐐼, 𐐷𐐩, 𐐰𐑌𐐼 𐐮𐐻 𐐸𐐰𐑆 𐐺𐐮𐑌 𐑉𐐨𐐼𐐲𐐺𐑊𐐼 𐐺𐐴 𐑄𐐬𐑆 𐐸𐐭 𐐸𐐰𐑂 𐐼𐐮𐑅𐐯𐑌𐐻𐐯𐐼 𐑁𐑉𐐱𐑋 𐐲𐑅; 𐐸𐐶𐐴𐑊 𐐷𐐬𐑉 𐐮𐑌𐐮𐐿𐐶𐐮𐐻𐐨 𐐮𐑆 𐑁𐐫𐑉 𐑄 𐐿𐐫𐑆 𐐱𐑂 𐐷𐐬𐑉 𐑊𐐲𐑂 𐐱𐑂 𐑀𐑊𐐬𐑉𐐨 𐐰𐑌𐐼 𐑄 𐑂𐐩𐑌 𐑃𐐮𐑍𐑆 𐐱𐑂 𐑄 𐐶𐐲𐑉𐑊𐐼? 𐐏 𐑌𐐬 𐑄𐐰𐐻 𐐷 𐐼𐐭 𐐻𐑉𐐰𐑌𐑆𐑀𐑉𐐯𐑅 𐑄 𐑊𐐫𐑆 𐐱𐑂 𐐘𐐱𐐼, 𐐰𐑌𐐼 𐐷 𐐼𐐭 𐑌𐐬 𐑄𐐰𐐻 𐐷 𐐼𐐭 𐐻𐑉𐐰𐑋𐐹𐑊 𐑄𐐯𐑋 𐐲𐑌𐐼𐐲𐑉 𐐷𐐬𐑉 𐑁𐐨𐐻. 𐐒𐐨𐐸𐐬𐑊𐐼, 𐑄 𐐢𐐫𐑉𐐼 𐑅𐐯𐑃 𐐲𐑌𐐻𐐭 𐑋𐐨, 𐐆𐑁 𐑄𐐬𐑆 𐐸𐐭𐑋 𐐷 𐐸𐐰𐑂 𐐰𐐹𐐱𐐮𐑌𐐻𐐯𐐼 𐐷𐐬𐑉 𐑀𐐲𐑂𐐲𐑉𐑌𐐲𐑉𐑆 𐐼𐐭 𐑌𐐱𐐻 𐑉𐐨𐐹𐐯𐑌𐐻 𐐱𐑂 𐑄𐐩𐑉 𐑅𐐮𐑌𐑆 𐐰𐑌𐐼 𐐮𐑌𐐮𐐿𐐶𐐮𐐻𐐨𐑆, 𐐷 𐑇𐐰𐑊 𐑀𐐬 𐐲𐐹 𐐻𐐭 𐐺𐐰𐐻𐑊 𐐲𐑀𐐯𐑌𐑅𐐻 𐑄𐐯𐑋.

9. 𐐈𐑌𐐼 𐑌𐐵 𐐺𐐨𐐸𐐬𐑊𐐼, 𐐌, 𐐣𐐬𐑉𐐬𐑌𐐴, 𐐰𐑋 𐐿𐐱𐑌𐑅𐐻𐑉𐐩𐑌𐐼, 𐐰𐐿𐐫𐑉𐐼𐐮𐑍 𐐻𐐭 𐑄 𐐿𐐲𐑂𐐯𐑌𐐰𐑌𐐻 𐐸𐐶𐐮𐐽 𐐌 𐐸𐐰𐑂 𐑋𐐩𐐼 𐐻𐐭 𐐿𐐨𐐹 𐑄 𐐿𐐱𐑋𐐰𐑌𐐼𐑋𐐯𐑌𐐻𐑅 𐐱𐑂 𐑋𐐴 𐐘𐐱𐐼; 𐑄𐐯𐑉𐑁𐐬𐑉 𐐌 𐐶𐐳𐐼 𐑄𐐰𐐻 𐐷 𐑇𐐳𐐼 𐐰𐐼𐐸𐐨𐑉

𐐻𐐭 𐑄 𐐶𐐲𐑉𐐼 𐐱𐑂 𐐘𐐱𐐼, 𐐰𐑌𐐼 𐑅𐐯𐑌𐐼 𐑅𐐹𐐨𐐼𐐮𐑊𐐨 𐐲𐑌𐐻𐐭 𐑋𐐨 𐐱𐑂 𐐷𐐬𐑉 𐐹𐑉𐐬𐑂𐐮𐑈𐐲𐑌𐑆 𐐰𐑌𐐼 𐐱𐑂 𐐷𐐬𐑉 𐑋𐐯𐑌, 𐐰𐑌𐐼 𐐫𐑊𐑅𐐬 𐐻𐐭 𐐐𐐯𐑊𐐲𐑋𐐲𐑌. 𐐈𐑌𐐼 𐐺𐐨𐐸𐐬𐑊𐐼, 𐐮𐑁 𐐷𐐨 𐐶𐐮𐑊 𐑌𐐱𐐻 𐐼𐐭 𐑄𐐮𐑅 𐐌 𐐿𐐲𐑋 𐐲𐑌𐐻𐐭 𐐷𐐭 𐑅𐐹𐐨𐐼𐐮𐑊𐐨; 𐑁𐐫𐑉 𐐺𐐨𐐸𐐬𐑊𐐼, 𐐘𐐱𐐼 𐐶𐐮𐑊 𐑌𐐱𐐻 𐑅𐐲𐑁𐐲𐑉 𐑄𐐰𐐻 𐐶𐐨 𐑇𐐳𐐼 𐐹𐐯𐑉𐐮𐑇 𐐶𐐮𐑄 𐐸𐐲𐑍𐑀𐐲𐑉; 𐑄𐐯𐑉𐑁𐐫𐑉 𐐸𐐨 𐐶𐐮𐑊 𐑀𐐮𐑂 𐐲𐑌𐐻𐐭 𐐲𐑅 𐐱𐑂 𐐷𐐬𐑉 𐑁𐐭𐐼, 𐐨𐑂𐐲𐑌 𐐮𐑁 𐐮𐐻 𐑋𐐲𐑅𐐻 𐐺𐐨 𐐺𐐴 𐑄 𐑅𐐬𐑉𐐼. 𐐤𐐵 𐑅𐐨 𐑄𐐰𐐻 𐐷𐐨 𐑁𐐳𐑊𐑁𐐮𐑊 𐑄 𐐶𐐲𐑉𐐼 𐐱𐑂 𐐘𐐱𐐼. 𐐒𐐨𐐸𐐬𐑊𐐼, 𐐌 𐐰𐑋 𐐣𐐬𐑉𐐬𐑌𐐴, 𐐷𐐬𐑉 𐐽𐐨𐑁 𐐿𐐰𐐹𐐻𐐯𐑌. 𐐌 𐑅𐐨𐐿 𐑌𐐱𐐻 𐑁𐐫𐑉 𐐹𐐵𐐲𐑉, 𐐺𐐲𐐻 𐐻𐐭 𐐹𐐳𐑊 𐐮𐐻 𐐼𐐵𐑌. 𐐌 𐑅𐐨𐐿 𐑌𐐱𐐻 𐑁𐐫𐑉 𐐱𐑌𐐲𐑉 𐐱𐑂 𐑄 𐐶𐐲𐑉𐑊𐐼, 𐐺𐐲𐐻 𐑁𐐫𐑉 𐑄 𐑀𐑊𐐬𐑉𐐨 𐐱𐑂 𐑋𐐴 𐐘𐐱𐐼, 𐐰𐑌𐐼 𐑄 𐑁𐑉𐐨𐐼𐐲𐑋 𐐰𐑌𐐼 𐐶𐐯𐑊𐑁𐐩𐑉 𐐱𐑂 𐑋𐐴 𐐿𐐲𐑌𐐻𐑉𐐨. 𐐈𐑌𐐼 𐑄𐐲𐑅 𐐌 𐐿𐑊𐐬𐑆 𐑋𐐴𐑌 𐐯𐐹𐐮𐑅𐑊.

𐐕𐐰𐐹𐐻𐐲𐑉 XXVIII.

1. 𐐒𐐨𐐸𐐬𐑊𐐼, 𐑌𐐵 𐐮𐐻 𐐿𐐩𐑋 𐐻𐐭 𐐹𐐰𐑅 𐑄𐐰𐐻 𐑅𐐭𐑌 𐐰𐑁𐐻𐐲𐑉 𐐣𐐬𐑉𐐬𐑌𐐴 𐐸𐐰𐐼 𐑅𐐯𐑌𐐻 𐐸𐐮𐑆 𐐯𐐹𐐮𐑅𐑊 𐐲𐑌𐐻𐐭 𐑄 𐐽𐐨𐑁 𐑀𐐲𐑂𐐲𐑉𐑌𐐲𐑉, 𐐸𐐨 𐑉𐐨𐑅𐐨𐑂𐐼 𐐰𐑌 𐐯𐐹𐐮𐑅𐑊 𐑁𐑉𐐱𐑋 𐐑𐐰𐐸𐐬𐑉𐐲𐑌, 𐑄 𐐽𐐨𐑁 𐑀𐐲𐑂𐐲𐑉𐑌𐐲𐑉. 𐐈𐑌𐐼 𐑄𐐨𐑆 𐐪𐑉 𐑄 𐐶𐐲𐑉𐐼𐑆 𐐸𐐶𐐮𐐽 𐐸𐐨 𐑉𐐨𐑅𐐨𐑂𐐼:—𐐌, 𐐑𐐰𐐸𐐬𐑉𐐲𐑌, 𐐸𐐭 𐐰𐑋 𐑄 𐐽𐐨𐑁 𐑀𐐲𐑂𐐲𐑉𐑌𐐲𐑉 𐐱𐑂 𐑄𐐮𐑅 𐑊𐐰𐑌𐐼, 𐐼𐐭 𐑅𐐯𐑌𐐼 𐑄𐐨𐑆 𐐶𐐲𐑉𐐼𐑆 𐐲𐑌𐐻𐐭 𐐣𐐬𐑉𐐬𐑌𐐴, 𐑄 𐐽𐐨𐑁 𐐿𐐰𐐹𐐻𐐯𐑌 𐐬𐑂𐐲𐑉 𐑄 𐐪𐑉𐑋𐐨. 𐐒𐐨𐐸𐐬𐑊𐐼, 𐐌 𐑅𐐩 𐐲𐑌𐐻𐐭 𐐷𐐭, 𐐣𐐬𐑉𐐬𐑌𐐴, 𐑄𐐰𐐻 𐐌 𐐼𐐭 𐑌𐐱𐐻 𐐾𐑎 𐐮𐑌 𐐷𐐬𐑉 𐑀𐑉𐐩𐐻 𐐰𐑁𐑊𐐮𐐿𐑇𐐲𐑌𐑆; 𐐷𐐩, 𐐮𐐻 𐑀𐑉𐐨𐑂𐑆 𐑋𐐴 𐑅𐐬𐑊. 𐐒𐐲𐐻 𐐺𐐨𐐸𐐬𐑊𐐼, 𐑄𐐩𐑉 𐐪𐑉 𐑄𐐬𐑆 𐐸𐐭 𐐼𐐭 𐐾𐑎 𐐮𐑌 𐐷𐐬𐑉 𐐰𐑁𐑊𐐮𐐿𐑇𐐲𐑌𐑆; 𐐷𐐩, 𐐮𐑌𐑅𐐬𐑋𐐲𐐽 𐑄𐐰𐐻 𐑄𐐩 𐐸𐐰𐑂 𐑉𐐮𐑆𐐲𐑌 𐐲𐐹 𐐮𐑌 𐑉𐐯𐐺𐐯𐑊𐐷𐐲𐑌 𐐰𐑀𐐯𐑌𐑅𐐻 𐑋𐐨, 𐐰𐑌𐐼 𐐫𐑊𐑅𐐬 𐑄𐐬𐑆 𐐱𐑂 𐑋𐐴 𐐹𐐨𐐹𐑊 𐐸𐐭 𐐪𐑉 𐑁𐑉𐐨𐑋𐐯𐑌; 𐐷𐐩, 𐐰𐑌𐐼 𐑄𐐬𐑆 𐐸𐐭 𐐸𐐰𐑂 𐑉𐐮𐑆𐐲𐑌 𐐲𐐹 𐐪𐑉 𐐯𐐿𐑅𐐨𐐼𐐮𐑍𐑊𐐨 𐑌𐐭𐑋𐐲𐑉𐐲𐑅; 𐐰𐑌𐐼 𐐮𐐻 𐐮𐑆 𐑄𐐬𐑆 𐐸𐐭 𐐸𐐰𐑂 𐑅𐐫𐐻 𐐻𐐭 𐐻𐐩𐐿 𐐰𐐶𐐩 𐑄 𐐾𐐲𐐾𐑋𐐯𐑌𐐻 𐑅𐐨𐐻 𐑁𐑉𐐱𐑋 𐑋𐐨, 𐑄𐐰𐐻 𐐸𐐰𐑂 𐐺𐐮𐑌 𐑄 𐐿𐐫𐑆 𐐱𐑂 𐑄𐐮𐑅 𐑀𐑉𐐩𐐻 𐐮𐑌𐐮𐐿𐐶𐐮𐐻𐐨; 𐑁𐐫𐑉 𐑄𐐩 𐐸𐐰𐑂 𐐷𐐭𐑆𐐼 𐑀𐑉𐐩𐐻 𐑁𐑊𐐰𐐻𐐲𐑉𐐨, 𐐰𐑌𐐼 𐑄𐐩 𐐸𐐰𐑂 𐑊𐐯𐐼 𐐰𐐶𐐩 𐑄 𐐸𐐪𐑉𐐻𐑅 𐐱𐑂 𐑋𐐯𐑌𐐨 𐐹𐐨𐐹𐑊, 𐐸𐐶𐐮𐐽 𐐶𐐮𐑊 𐐺𐐨 𐑄 𐐿𐐫𐑆 𐐱𐑂 𐑅𐐬𐑉 𐐰𐑁𐑊𐐮𐐿𐑇𐐲𐑌 𐐰𐑋𐐲𐑍 𐐲𐑅; 𐑄𐐩 𐐸𐐰𐑂 𐐶𐐮𐑄𐐸𐐯𐑊𐐼 𐐵𐐲𐑉 𐐹𐑉𐐬𐑂𐐮𐑈𐐲𐑌𐑆, 𐐰𐑌𐐼 𐐸𐐰𐑂 𐐼𐐫𐑌𐐻𐐯𐐼 𐐵𐐲𐑉 𐑁𐑉𐐨𐑋𐐯𐑌 𐑄𐐰𐐻 𐑄𐐩 𐐸𐐰𐑂 𐑌𐐱𐐻 𐐿𐐲𐑋 𐐲𐑌𐐻𐐭 𐐷𐐭. 𐐈𐑌𐐼 𐐺𐐨𐐸𐐬𐑊𐐼, 𐑄𐐩 𐐸𐐰𐑂 𐐼𐑉𐐮𐑂𐐲𐑌 𐑋𐐨 𐐵𐐻 𐐺𐐨𐑁𐐬𐑉 𐑄𐐯𐑋, 𐐰𐑌𐐼 𐐌 𐐸𐐰𐑂 𐑁𐑊𐐯𐐼 𐐻𐐭 𐑄 𐑊𐐰𐑌𐐼 𐐱𐑂 𐐘𐐮𐐼𐐨𐐲𐑌, 𐐶𐐮𐑄 𐐰𐑆 𐑋𐐯𐑌𐐨 𐑋𐐯𐑌 𐐰𐑆 𐐮𐐻 𐐶𐐲𐑉 𐐹𐐱𐑅𐐮𐐺𐑊 𐑄𐐰𐐻 𐐌 𐐿𐐳𐐼 𐑀𐐯𐐻. 𐐈𐑌𐐼 𐐺𐐨𐐸𐐬𐑊𐐼, 𐐌 𐐸𐐰𐑂 𐑅𐐯𐑌𐐻 𐐰 𐐹𐑉𐐱𐐿𐑊𐐲𐑋𐐩𐑇𐐲𐑌 𐑃𐑉𐐭𐐵𐐻 𐑄𐐮𐑅 𐐹𐐪𐑉𐐻 𐐱𐑂 𐑄 𐑊𐐰𐑌𐐼; 𐐰𐑌𐐼 𐐺𐐨𐐸𐐬𐑊𐐼, 𐑄𐐩 𐐪𐑉 𐑁𐑊𐐱𐐿𐐮𐑍 𐐻𐐭 𐐲𐑅 𐐼𐐩𐑊𐐨, 𐐻𐐭 𐑄𐐩𐑉 𐐪𐑉𐑋𐑆, 𐐮𐑌 𐑄 𐐼𐐨𐑁𐐯𐑌𐑅 𐐱𐑂 𐑄𐐩𐑉 𐐿𐐲𐑌𐐻𐑉𐐨 𐐰𐑌𐐼 𐑄𐐩𐑉 𐑁𐑉𐐨𐐼𐐲𐑋, 𐐰𐑌𐐼 𐐻𐐭 𐐰𐑂𐐯𐑌𐐾 𐐵𐐲𐑉 𐑉𐐱𐑍𐑆. 𐐈𐑌𐐼 𐑄𐐩 𐐸𐐰𐑂 𐐿𐐲𐑋 𐐲𐑌𐐻𐐭 𐐲𐑅, 𐐮𐑌𐑅𐐬𐑋𐐲𐐽 𐑄𐐰𐐻 𐑄𐐬𐑆 𐐸𐐭 𐐸𐐰𐑂 𐑉𐐮𐑆𐐲𐑌 𐐲𐐹 𐐮𐑌 𐑉𐐯𐐺𐐯𐑊𐐷𐐲𐑌 𐐰𐑀𐐯𐑌𐑅𐐻 𐐲𐑅, 𐐪𐑉 𐑅𐐯𐐻 𐐰𐐻 𐐼𐐨𐑁𐐴𐐰𐑌𐑅; 𐐷𐐩, 𐐮𐑌𐑅𐐬𐑋𐐲𐐽 𐑄𐐰𐐻 𐑄𐐩 𐐼𐐭 𐑁𐐨𐑉 𐐲𐑅, 𐐰𐑌𐐼 𐐼𐐲𐑉𐑅𐐻 𐑌𐐱𐐻 𐐿𐐲𐑋 𐐵𐐻 𐐰𐑀𐐯𐑌𐑅𐐻 𐐲𐑅 𐐻𐐭 𐐺𐐰𐐻𐑊. 𐐜𐐩 𐐸𐐰𐑂 𐑀𐐱𐐻 𐐹𐐲𐑆𐐯𐑇𐐲𐑌 𐐱𐑂 𐑄 𐑊𐐰𐑌𐐼, 𐐫𐑉 𐑄 𐑅𐐮𐐻𐐨 𐐱𐑂 𐐞𐐯𐑉𐐲𐐸𐐯𐑋𐑊𐐲; 𐑄𐐩 𐐸𐐰𐑂 𐐲𐐹𐑎𐑌𐐻𐐯𐐼 𐐰 𐐿𐐮𐑍 𐐬𐑂𐐲𐑉 𐑄𐐯𐑋, 𐐰𐑌𐐼 𐐸𐐨 𐐸𐐰𐑃 𐑉𐐮𐐻𐐲𐑌 𐐲𐑌𐐻𐐭 𐑄 𐐿𐐮𐑍 𐐱𐑂 𐑄 𐐢𐐩𐑋𐐲𐑌𐐴𐐻𐑅, 𐐮𐑌 𐑄 𐐸𐐶𐐮𐐽 𐐸𐐨 𐐸𐐰𐑃 𐐾𐑎𐑌𐐼 𐐰𐑌 𐐰𐑊𐐴𐐲𐑌𐑅 𐐶𐐮𐑄 𐐸𐐮𐑋; 𐐮𐑌 𐑄 𐐸𐐶𐐮𐐽 𐐰𐑊𐐴𐐲𐑌𐑅 𐐸𐐨 𐐸𐐰𐑃 𐐲𐑀𐑉𐐨𐐼 𐐻𐐭 𐑋𐐩𐑌𐐻𐐩𐑌 𐑄 𐑅𐐮𐐻𐐨 𐐱𐑂 𐐞𐐯𐑉𐐲𐐸𐐯𐑋𐑊𐐲, 𐐸𐐶𐐮𐐽 𐑋𐐩𐑌𐐻𐐲𐑌𐐰𐑌𐑅 𐐸𐐨 𐑅𐐲𐐹𐐬𐑆𐐯𐑃 𐐶𐐮𐑊 𐐯𐑌𐐩𐐺𐑊 𐑄 𐐢𐐩𐑋𐐲𐑌𐐴𐐻𐑅 𐐻𐐭 𐐿𐐱𐑍𐐿𐐲𐑉 𐑄 𐑉𐐨𐑋𐐩𐑌𐐼𐐲𐑉 𐐱𐑂 𐑄 𐑊𐐰𐑌𐐼, 𐐰𐑌𐐼 𐐸𐐨 𐑇𐐰𐑊 𐐺𐐨 𐐹𐑊𐐩𐑅𐐻 𐐿𐐮𐑍 𐐬𐑂𐐲𐑉 𐑄𐐮𐑅 𐐹𐐨𐐹𐑊, 𐐸𐐶𐐯𐑌 𐑄𐐩 𐑇𐐰𐑊 𐐺𐐨 𐐿𐐱𐑍𐐿𐐲𐑉𐐼 𐐲𐑌𐐼𐐲𐑉 𐑄 𐐢𐐩𐑋𐐲𐑌𐐴𐐻𐑅. 𐐈𐑌𐐼 𐑌𐐵 𐐮𐑌 𐐷𐐬𐑉 𐐯𐐹𐐮𐑅𐑊 𐐷𐐭 𐐸𐐰𐑂 𐑅𐐯𐑌𐑇𐐲𐑉𐐼 𐑋𐐨, 𐐺𐐲𐐻 𐐮𐐻 𐑋𐐰𐐻𐐲𐑉𐐯𐑃 𐑌𐐱𐐻; 𐐌 𐐰𐑋 𐑌𐐱𐐻 𐐰𐑍𐑀𐑉𐐨, 𐐺𐐲𐐻 𐐼𐐭 𐑉𐐨𐐾𐑎𐑅 𐐮𐑌 𐑄 𐑀𐑉𐐩𐐻𐑌𐐯𐑅 𐐱𐑂 𐐷𐐬𐑉 𐐸𐐪𐑉𐐻. 𐐌, 𐐑𐐰𐐸𐐬𐑉𐐲𐑌, 𐐼𐐭 𐑌𐐱𐐻 𐑅𐐨𐐿 𐑁𐐫𐑉 𐐹𐐵𐐲𐑉, 𐑅𐐩𐑂 𐐬𐑌𐑊𐐨 𐐻𐐭 𐑉𐐨𐐻𐐩𐑌 𐑋𐐴 𐐾𐐲𐐾𐑋𐐯𐑌𐐻 𐑅𐐨𐐻, 𐑄𐐰𐐻 𐐌 𐑋𐐩 𐐹𐑉𐐨𐑆𐐲𐑉𐑂 𐑄 𐑉𐐴𐐻𐑅 𐐰𐑌𐐼 𐑄 𐑊𐐮𐐺𐐲𐑉𐐻𐐨 𐐱𐑂 𐑋𐐴 𐐹𐐨𐐹𐑊. 𐐣𐐴 𐑅𐐬𐑊 𐑅𐐻𐐰𐑌𐐼𐐯𐑃 𐑁𐐰𐑅𐐻 𐐮𐑌 𐑄𐐰𐐻 𐑊𐐮𐐺𐐲𐑉𐐻𐐨, 𐐮𐑌 𐑄 𐐸𐐶𐐮𐐽 𐐘𐐱𐐼 𐐸𐐰𐑃 𐑋𐐩𐐼 𐐲𐑅 𐑁𐑉𐐨.

2. 𐐈𐑌𐐼 𐑌𐐵, 𐐺𐐨𐐸𐐬𐑊𐐼, 𐐶𐐨 𐐶𐐮𐑊 𐑉𐐨𐑆𐐮𐑅𐐻 𐐶𐐮𐐿𐐯𐐼𐑌𐐯𐑅 𐐨𐑂𐑌 𐐲𐑌𐐻𐐭 𐐺𐑊𐐲𐐼𐑖𐐯𐐼. 𐐎𐐨 𐐶𐐳𐐼 𐑌𐐱𐐻 𐑖𐐯𐐼 𐑄 𐐺𐑊𐐲𐐼 𐐱𐑂 𐑄 𐐢𐐩𐑋𐐲𐑌𐐴𐐻𐑅 𐐮𐑁 𐑄𐐩 𐐶𐐳𐐼 𐑅𐐻𐐩 𐐮𐑌 𐑄𐐩𐑉 𐐬𐑌 𐑊𐐰𐑌𐐼. 𐐎𐐨 𐐶𐐳𐐼 𐑌𐐱𐐻 𐑖𐐯𐐼 𐑄 𐐺𐑊𐐲𐐼 𐐱𐑂 𐐵𐑉 𐐺𐑉𐐯𐑄𐑉𐐯𐑌, 𐐮𐑁 𐑄𐐩 𐐶𐐳𐐼 𐑌𐐱𐐻 𐑉𐐴𐑆 𐐲𐐹 𐐮𐑌 𐑉𐐨𐐺𐐯𐑊𐐷𐐲𐑌 𐐰𐑌𐐼 𐐻𐐩𐐿 𐑄 𐑅𐐬𐑉𐐼 𐐲𐑀𐐯𐑌𐑅𐐻 𐐲𐑅. 𐐎𐐨 𐐶𐐳𐐼 𐑅𐐲𐐺𐐾𐐯𐐿𐐻 𐐵𐑉𐑅𐐯𐑊𐑂𐑆 𐐻𐐭 𐑄 𐐷𐐬𐐿 𐐱𐑂 𐐺𐐱𐑌𐐼𐐯𐐾, 𐐮𐑁 𐐮𐐻 𐐶𐐲𐑉 𐑉𐐯𐐿𐐶𐐮𐑆𐐮𐐻 𐐶𐐮𐑄 𐑄 𐐾𐐲𐑅𐐻𐐮𐑅 𐐱𐑂 𐐘𐐱𐐼, 𐐫𐑉 𐐮𐑁 𐐸𐐨 𐑖𐐳𐐼 𐐿𐐱𐑋𐐰𐑌𐐼 𐐲𐑅 𐑅𐐬 𐐻𐐭 𐐼𐐭. 𐐒𐐲𐐻 𐐺𐐨𐐸𐐬𐑊𐐼 𐐸𐐨 𐐼𐐲𐑃 𐑌𐐱𐐻 𐐿𐐱𐑋𐐰𐑌𐐼 𐐲𐑅 𐑄𐐰𐐻 𐐶𐐨 𐑖𐐰𐑊 𐑅𐐲𐐺𐐾𐐯𐐿𐐻 𐐵𐑉𐑅𐐯𐑊𐑂𐑆 𐐻𐐭 𐐵𐑉 𐐯𐑌𐐯𐑋𐐨𐑆, 𐐺𐐲𐐻 𐑄𐐰𐐻 𐐶𐐨 𐑖𐐳𐐼 𐐹𐐳𐐻 𐐵𐑉 𐐻𐑉𐐲𐑅𐐻 𐐮𐑌 𐐸𐐮𐑋, 𐐰𐑌𐐼 𐐸𐐨 𐐶𐐮𐑊 𐐼𐐨𐑊𐐮𐑂𐐲𐑉 𐐲𐑅; 𐑄𐐯𐑉𐑁𐐬𐑉, 𐑋𐐴 𐐺𐐨𐑊𐐲𐑂𐐯𐐼 𐐺𐑉𐐲𐑄𐐲𐑉, 𐐣𐐫𐑉𐐬𐑌𐐴, 𐑊𐐯𐐻 𐐲𐑅 𐑉𐐨𐑆𐐮𐑅𐐻 𐐨𐑂𐑊, 𐐰𐑌𐐼 𐐸𐐶𐐱𐐻𐑅𐐬𐐯𐑂𐐲𐑉 𐐨𐑂𐑊 𐐶𐐨 𐐿𐐰𐑌𐐱𐐻 𐑉𐐨𐑆𐐮𐑅𐐻 𐐶𐐮𐑄 𐐵𐑉 𐐶𐐲𐑉𐐼𐑆, 𐐷𐐩, 𐑅𐐲𐐽 𐐰𐑆 𐑉𐐨𐐺𐐯𐑊𐐷𐐲𐑌𐑆 𐐰𐑌𐐼 𐐼𐐮𐑅𐐯𐑌𐑖𐐲𐑌𐑆, 𐑊𐐯𐐻 𐐲𐑅 𐑉𐐨𐑆𐐮𐑅𐐻 𐑄𐐯𐑋 𐐶𐐮𐑄 𐐵𐑉 𐑅𐐬𐑉𐐼𐑆, 𐑄𐐰𐐻 𐐶𐐨 𐑋𐐩 𐑉𐐨𐐻𐐩𐑌 𐐵𐑉 𐑁𐑉𐐨𐐼𐐲𐑋, 𐑄𐐰𐐻 𐐶𐐨 𐑋𐐩 𐑉𐐨𐐾𐐦𐑅 𐐮𐑌 𐑄 𐑀𐑉𐐩𐐻 𐐹𐑉𐐮𐑂𐐮𐑊𐐯𐐾 𐐱𐑂 𐐵𐑉 𐐽𐐲𐑉𐐽, 𐐰𐑌𐐼 𐐮𐑌 𐑄 𐐿𐐫𐑆 𐐱𐑂 𐐵𐑉 𐐡𐐨𐐼𐐨𐑋𐐲𐑉 𐐰𐑌𐐼 𐐵𐑉 𐐘𐐱𐐼. 𐐜𐐯𐑉𐑁𐐬𐑉, 𐐿𐐲𐑋 𐐲𐑌𐐻𐐭 𐑋𐐨 𐑅𐐹𐐨𐐼𐐮𐑊𐐨 𐐶𐐮𐑄 𐐩 𐑁𐐧 𐐱𐑂 𐐷𐐭𐑉 𐑋𐐯𐑌, 𐐰𐑌𐐼 𐑊𐐨𐑂 𐑄 𐑉𐐨𐑋𐐩𐑌𐐼𐐲𐑉 𐐮𐑌 𐑄 𐐽𐐪𐑉𐐾 𐐱𐑂 𐐢𐐨𐐸𐐴 𐐰𐑌𐐼 𐐓𐐨𐐰𐑍𐐿𐐲𐑋; 𐑀𐐮𐑂 𐐲𐑌𐐻𐐭 𐑄𐐯𐑋 𐐹𐐵𐐲𐑉 𐐻𐐭 𐐿𐐱𐑌𐐼𐐲𐐿𐐻 𐑄 𐐶𐐫𐑉 𐐮𐑌 𐑄𐐰𐐻 𐐹𐐪𐑉𐐻 𐐱𐑂 𐑄 𐑊𐐰𐑌𐐼, 𐐰𐐿𐐫𐑉𐐼𐐮𐑍 𐐻𐐭 𐑄 𐐝𐐹𐐮𐑉𐐮𐐻 𐐱𐑂 𐐘𐐱𐐼, 𐐸𐐶𐐮𐐽 𐐮𐑆 𐐫𐑊𐑅𐐬 𐑄 𐑅𐐹𐐮𐑉𐐮𐐻 𐐱𐑂 𐑁𐑉𐐨𐐼𐐲𐑋 𐐸𐐶𐐮𐐽 𐐮𐑆 𐐮𐑌 𐑄𐐯𐑋. 𐐒𐐨𐐸𐐬𐑊𐐼 𐐌 𐐸𐐰𐑂 𐑅𐐯𐑌𐐻 𐐩 𐑁𐐧 𐐹𐑉𐐬𐑂𐐮𐑠𐐲𐑌𐑆 𐐲𐑌𐐻𐐭 𐑄𐐯𐑋, 𐑄𐐰𐐻 𐑄𐐩 𐑋𐐩 𐑌𐐱𐐻 𐐹𐐯𐑉𐐮𐑖 𐐲𐑌𐐻𐐮𐑊 𐐷𐐨 𐐿𐐰𐑌 𐐿𐐲𐑋 𐐲𐑌𐐻𐐭 𐑋𐐨. 𐐘𐐰𐑄𐐲𐑉 𐐻𐐭𐑀𐐯𐑄𐐲𐑉 𐐸𐐶𐐱𐐻𐑅𐐬𐐯𐑂𐐲𐑉 𐑁𐐬𐑉𐑅 𐐷𐐨 𐐿𐐰𐑌 𐐲𐐹𐐱𐑌 𐐷𐐭𐑉 𐑋𐐪𐑉𐐽 𐐸𐐮𐑄𐐲𐑉, 𐐰𐑌𐐼 𐐶𐐨 𐐶𐐮𐑊 𐑀𐐬 𐑅𐐹𐐨𐐼𐐮𐑊𐐨 𐐲𐑀𐐯𐑌𐑅𐐻 𐑄𐐬𐑆 𐐼𐐮𐑅𐐯𐑌𐐻𐐲𐑉𐑆 𐐮𐑌 𐑄 𐑅𐐻𐑉𐐯𐑍𐑃 𐐱𐑂 𐐵𐑉 𐐘𐐱𐐼, 𐐰𐐿𐐫𐑉𐐼𐐮𐑍 𐐻𐐭 𐑄 𐑁𐐩𐑃 𐐸𐐶𐐮𐐽 𐐮𐑆 𐐮𐑌 𐐲𐑅. 𐐈𐑌𐐼 𐐶𐐨 𐐶𐐮𐑊 𐐻𐐩𐐿 𐐹𐐲𐑆𐐯𐑖𐐲𐑌 𐐱𐑂 𐑄 𐑅𐐮𐐻𐐨 𐐱𐑂 𐐞𐐰𐑉𐐲𐐸𐐯𐑋𐑊𐐲, 𐑄𐐰𐐻 𐐶𐐨 𐑋𐐩 𐐱𐐺𐐻𐐩𐑌 𐑋𐐬𐑉 𐑁𐐭𐐼 𐐻𐐭 𐑅𐐯𐑌𐐼 𐑁𐐬𐑉𐑃 𐐲𐑌𐐻𐐭 𐐢𐐨𐐸𐐴 𐐰𐑌𐐼 𐐓𐐨𐐰𐑍𐐿𐐲𐑋; 𐐷𐐩, 𐐶𐐨 𐐶𐐮𐑊 𐑀𐐬 𐑁𐐬𐑉𐑃 𐐲𐑀𐐯𐑌𐑅𐐻 𐑄𐐯𐑋 𐐮𐑌 𐑄 𐑅𐐻𐑉𐐯𐑍𐑃 𐐱𐑂 𐑄 𐐢𐐪𐑉𐐼, 𐐰𐑌𐐼 𐐶𐐨 𐐶𐐮𐑊 𐐹𐐳𐐻 𐐰𐑌 𐐯𐑌𐐼 𐐻𐐭 𐑄𐐮𐑅 𐑀𐑉𐐩𐐻 𐐮𐑌𐐮𐐿𐐶𐐮𐐻𐐨.

3. 𐐈𐑌𐐼 𐑌𐐵, 𐐣𐐫𐑉𐐬𐑌𐐴, 𐐌 𐐼𐐭 𐐾𐐦 𐐮𐑌 𐑉𐐨𐑅𐐨𐑂𐐮𐑍 𐐷𐐭𐑉 𐐨𐐹𐐮𐑅𐑊, 𐑁𐐫𐑉 𐐌 𐐶𐐪𐑆 𐑅𐐲𐑋𐐸𐐶𐐱𐐻 𐐶𐐲𐑉𐐨𐐼 𐐿𐐱𐑌𐑅𐐲𐑉𐑌𐐮𐑍 𐐸𐐶𐐱𐐻 𐐶𐐨 𐑖𐐳𐐼 𐐼𐐭, 𐐸𐐶𐐯𐑄𐐲𐑉 𐐮𐐻 𐑖𐐳𐐼 𐐺𐐨 𐐾𐐲𐑅𐐻 𐐮𐑌 𐐲𐑅 𐐻𐐭 𐑀𐐬 𐐲𐑀𐐯𐑌𐑅𐐻 𐐵𐑉 𐐺𐑉𐐯𐑄𐑉𐐯𐑌. 𐐒𐐲𐐻 𐐷𐐨 𐐸𐐰𐑂 𐑅𐐯𐐼, 𐐯𐐿𐑅𐐯𐐹𐐻 𐑄𐐩 𐑉𐐨𐐹𐐯𐑌𐐻 𐑄 𐐢𐐪𐑉𐐼 𐐸𐐰𐑃 𐐿𐐱𐑋𐐰𐑌𐐼𐐯𐐼 𐐷𐐭 𐑄𐐰𐐻 𐐷𐐨 𐑖𐐳𐐼 𐑀𐐬 𐐲𐑀𐐯𐑌𐑅𐐻 𐑄𐐯𐑋. 𐐝𐐨 𐑄𐐰𐐻 𐐷𐐨 𐑅𐐻𐑉𐐯𐑍𐑃𐑌 𐐢𐐨𐐸𐐴 𐐰𐑌𐐼 𐐓𐐨𐐰𐑍𐐿𐐲𐑋 𐐮𐑌 𐑄 𐐢𐐪𐑉𐐼: 𐐻𐐯𐑊 𐑄𐐯𐑋 𐐻𐐭 𐑁𐐨𐑉 𐑌𐐱𐐻, 𐑁𐐫𐑉 𐐘𐐱𐐼 𐐶𐐮𐑊 𐐼𐐨𐑊𐐮𐑂𐐲𐑉 𐑄𐐯𐑋; 𐐷𐐩, 𐐰𐑌𐐼 𐐫𐑊𐑅𐐬 𐐫𐑊 𐑄𐐬𐑆 𐐸𐐭 𐑅𐐻𐐰𐑌𐐼 𐑁𐐰𐑅𐐻 𐐮𐑌 𐑄𐐰𐐻 𐑊𐐮𐐺𐐲𐑉𐐻𐐨 𐐸𐐶𐐩𐑉𐐶𐐮𐑄 𐐘𐐱𐐼 𐐸𐐰𐑃 𐑋𐐩𐐼 𐑄𐐯𐑋 𐑁𐑉𐐨. 𐐈𐑌𐐼 𐑌𐐵 𐐌 𐐿𐑊𐐬𐑆 𐑋𐐴𐑌 𐐨𐐹𐐮𐑅𐑊 𐐻𐐭 𐑋𐐴 𐐺𐐨𐑊𐐲𐑂𐐯𐐼 𐐺𐑉𐐲𐑄𐐲𐑉 𐐣𐐫𐑉𐐬𐑌𐐴.

𐐕𐐰𐐹𐐻𐐲𐑉 XXIX.

1. 𐐈𐑌𐐼 𐑌𐐵 𐐮𐐻 𐐿𐐩𐑋 𐐻𐐭 𐐹𐐪𐑅 𐑄𐐰𐐻 𐐸𐐶𐐯𐑌 𐐣𐐫𐑉𐐬𐑌𐐴 𐐸𐐰𐐼 𐑉𐐨𐑅𐐨𐑂𐐼 𐑄𐐮𐑅 𐐨𐐹𐐮𐑅𐑊, 𐐸𐐮𐑆 𐐸𐐪𐑉𐐻 𐐼𐐮𐐼 𐐻𐐩𐐿 𐐿𐐲𐑉𐐯𐐾, 𐐰𐑌𐐼 𐐶𐐪𐑆 𐑁𐐮𐑊𐐼 𐐶𐐮𐑄 𐐯𐐿𐑅𐐨𐐼𐐮𐑍 𐑀𐑉𐐩𐐻 𐐾𐐦, 𐐺𐐨𐐿𐐫𐑆 𐐱𐑂 𐑄 𐑁𐐩𐑃𐑁𐐳𐑊𐑌𐐯𐑅 𐐱𐑂 𐐑𐐪𐐸𐐫𐑉𐐲𐑌, 𐑄𐐰𐐻 𐐸𐐨 𐐶𐐪𐑆 𐑌𐐱𐐻 𐐫𐑊𐑅𐐬 𐐩 𐐻𐑉𐐩𐐻𐐲𐑉 𐐻𐐭 𐑄 𐑁𐑉𐐨𐐼𐐲𐑋 𐐰𐑌𐐼 𐐿𐐫𐑆 𐐱𐑂 𐐸𐐮𐑆 𐐿𐐲𐑌𐐻𐑉𐐨. 𐐒𐐲𐐻 𐐸𐐨 𐐼𐐮𐐼 𐐫𐑊𐑅𐐬 𐑋𐐬𐑉𐑌 𐐯𐐿𐑅𐐨𐐼𐐮𐑍𐑊𐐨, 𐐺𐐨𐐿𐐫𐑆 𐐱𐑂 𐑄 𐐮𐑌𐐮𐐿𐐶𐐮𐐻𐐨 𐐱𐑂 𐑄𐐬𐑆 𐐸𐐭 𐐸𐐰𐐼 𐐼𐑉𐐮𐑂𐑌 𐐑𐐪𐐸𐐫𐑉𐐲𐑌 𐑁𐑉𐐱𐑋 𐑄 𐐾𐐲𐐾𐑋𐐯𐑌𐐻-𐑅𐐨𐐻; 𐐷𐐩, 𐐮𐑌 𐑁𐐴𐑌 𐐺𐐨𐐿𐐫𐑆 𐐱𐑂 𐑄𐐬𐑆 𐐸𐐭 𐐸𐐰𐐼 𐑉𐐨𐐺𐐯𐑊𐐼 𐐲𐑀𐐯𐑌𐑅𐐻 𐑄𐐩𐑉 𐐿𐐲𐑌𐐻𐑉𐐨 𐐰𐑌𐐼 𐐫𐑊𐑅𐐬 𐑄𐐩𐑉 𐐘𐐱𐐼.

2. 𐐈𐑌𐐼 𐐮𐐻 𐐿𐐩𐑋 𐐻𐐭 𐐹𐐪𐑅 𐑄𐐰𐐻 𐐣𐐫𐑉𐐬𐑌𐐴 𐐻𐐳𐐿 𐐩 𐑅𐑋𐐫𐑊 𐑌𐐲𐑋𐐺𐐲𐑉 𐐱𐑂 𐑋𐐯𐑌, 𐐰𐐿𐐫𐑉𐐼𐐮𐑍 𐐻𐐭 𐑄 𐐼𐐨𐑆𐐴𐑉 𐐱𐑂 𐐑𐐪𐐸𐐫𐑉𐐲𐑌, 𐐰𐑌𐐼 𐑀𐐩𐑂 𐐢𐐨𐐸𐐴 𐐰𐑌𐐼 𐐓𐐨𐐰𐑍𐐿𐐲𐑋 𐐿𐐱𐑋𐐰𐑌𐐼 𐐬𐑂𐐲𐑉 𐑄 𐑉𐐨𐑋𐐩𐑌𐐼𐐲𐑉 𐐱𐑂 𐐸𐐮𐑆 𐐪𐑉𐑋𐐨, 𐐰𐑌𐐼 𐐻𐐳𐐿 𐐸𐐮𐑆 𐑋𐐪𐑉𐐽 𐐻𐐬𐑉𐐼𐑆 𐑄 𐑊𐐰𐑌𐐼 𐐱𐑂 𐐘𐐮𐐼𐐨𐐲𐑌. 𐐈𐑌𐐼 𐐸𐐨 𐐼𐐮𐐼 𐑉𐐩𐑆 𐑄 𐑅𐐻𐐰𐑌𐐼𐐲𐑉𐐼

𐐱𐑂 𐑊𐐮𐐺𐐲𐑉𐐻𐐨 𐐮𐑌 𐐸𐐶𐐱𐐻𐑅𐐬𐐯𐑂𐐲𐑉 𐐹𐑊𐐩𐑅 𐐸𐐨 𐐼𐐮𐐼 𐐯𐑌𐐻𐐲𐑉, 𐐰𐑌𐐼 𐑀𐐩𐑌𐐼 𐐸𐐶𐐱𐐻𐑅𐐬𐐯𐑂𐐲𐑉 𐑁𐐬𐑉𐑅 𐐸𐐨 𐐿𐐳𐐼 𐐮𐑌 𐐫𐑊 𐐸𐐮𐑆 𐑋𐐪𐑉𐐽 𐐻𐐬𐑉𐐼𐑆 𐑄 𐑊𐐰𐑌𐐼 𐐱𐑂 𐐘𐐮𐐼𐐨𐐲𐑌.

3. 𐐈𐑌𐐼 𐐮𐐻 𐐿𐐩𐑋 𐐻𐐭 𐐹𐐪𐑅 𐑄𐐰𐐻 𐑃𐐵𐑆𐐲𐑌𐐼𐑆 𐐼𐐮𐐼 𐑁𐑊𐐱𐐿 𐐲𐑌𐐻𐐭 𐐸𐐮𐑆 𐑅𐐻𐐰𐑌𐐼𐐲𐑉𐐼, 𐐰𐑌𐐼 𐐼𐐮𐐼 𐐻𐐩𐐿 𐐲𐐹 𐑄𐐯𐑉 𐑅𐐬𐑉𐐼𐑆 𐐮𐑌 𐑄 𐐼𐐨𐑁𐐯𐑌𐑅 𐐱𐑂 𐑄𐐯𐑉 𐑁𐑉𐐨𐐼𐐲𐑋, 𐑄𐐰𐐻 𐑄𐐩 𐑋𐐴𐐻 𐑌𐐱𐐻 𐐿𐐲𐑋 𐐮𐑌𐐻𐐭 𐐺𐐱𐑌𐐼𐐩𐐾; 𐐰𐑌𐐼 𐑄𐐲𐑅 𐐸𐐶𐐯𐑌 𐐣𐐬𐑉𐐬𐑌𐐴 𐐸𐐰𐐼 𐑀𐐰𐑄𐐲𐑉𐐼 𐐻𐐭𐑀𐐯𐑄𐐲𐑉 𐐸𐐶𐐱𐐻𐑅𐐬𐐯𐑂𐐲𐑉 𐑋𐐯𐑌 𐐸𐐨 𐐿𐐳𐐼 𐐮𐑌 𐐫𐑊 𐐸𐐮𐑆 𐑋𐐪𐑉𐐽, 𐐸𐐨 𐐿𐐩𐑋 𐐻𐐭 𐑄 𐑊𐐰𐑌𐐼 𐐱𐑂 𐐘𐐮𐐼𐐨𐐲𐑌; 𐐰𐑌𐐼 𐐧𐑌𐐴𐐻𐐮𐑍 𐐸𐐮𐑆 𐑁𐐬𐑉𐑅𐐯𐑆 𐐶𐐮𐑃 𐑄𐐬𐑆 𐐱𐑂 𐐑𐐩𐐸𐐬𐑉𐐲𐑌, 𐑄𐐩 𐐺𐐨𐐿𐐩𐑋 𐐯𐐿𐑅𐐨𐐼𐐮𐑍𐑊𐐨 𐑅𐐻𐑉𐐱𐑍, 𐐨𐑂𐐲𐑌 𐑅𐐻𐑉𐐱𐑍𐐲𐑉 𐑄𐐰𐑌 𐑄 𐑋𐐯𐑌 𐐱𐑂 𐐑𐐩𐐿𐐲𐑅, 𐐸𐐭 𐐶𐐱𐑆 𐑄 𐐿𐐮𐑍 𐐱𐑂 𐑄𐐬𐑆 𐐼𐐮𐑅𐐯𐑌𐐻𐐲𐑉𐑆 𐐸𐐭 𐐸𐐰𐐼 𐐼𐑉𐐮𐑂𐐲𐑌 𐑄 𐑁𐑉𐐨𐑋𐐯𐑌 𐐵𐐻 𐐱𐑂 𐑄 𐑊𐐰𐑌𐐼 𐐱𐑂 𐐞𐐰𐑉𐐲𐐸𐐯𐑋𐑊𐐲, 𐐰𐑌𐐼 𐐸𐐰𐐼 𐐻𐐩𐐿𐐲𐑌 𐐹𐐱𐑆𐐯𐑇𐐲𐑌 𐐱𐑂 𐑄 𐑊𐐰𐑌𐐼.

4. 𐐈𐑌𐐼 𐐮𐐻 𐐿𐐩𐑋 𐐻𐐭 𐐹𐐪𐑅 𐑄𐐰𐐻 𐐣𐐬𐑉𐐬𐑌𐐴 𐐰𐑌𐐼 𐐑𐐩𐐸𐐬𐑉𐐲𐑌 𐐶𐐯𐑌𐐻 𐐼𐐵𐑌 𐐶𐐮𐑃 𐑄𐐯𐑉 𐐪𐑉𐑋𐐨𐑆 𐐮𐑌𐐻𐐭 𐑄 𐑊𐐰𐑌𐐼 𐐱𐑂 𐐞𐐰𐑉𐐲𐐸𐐯𐑋𐑊𐐲, 𐐰𐑌𐐼 𐐶𐐯𐑌𐐻 𐑁𐐬𐑉𐑃 𐐰𐑀𐐯𐑌𐑅𐐻 𐑄 𐑅𐐮𐐻𐐨, 𐐰𐑌𐐼 𐐼𐐮𐐼 𐑋𐐨𐐻 𐑄 𐑋𐐯𐑌 𐐱𐑂 𐐑𐐩𐐿𐐲𐑅, 𐐮𐑌𐑅𐐬𐑋𐐲𐐽 𐑄𐐰𐐻 𐑄𐐩 𐐼𐐮𐐼 𐐿𐐲𐑋 𐐻𐐭 𐐺𐐰𐐻𐑊. 𐐈𐑌𐐼 𐐺𐐨𐐸𐐬𐑊𐐼 𐐑𐐩𐐿𐐲𐑅 𐐶𐐱𐑆 𐑅𐑊𐐩𐑌, 𐐰𐑌𐐼 𐐸𐐮𐑆 𐑋𐐯𐑌 𐐶𐐲𐑉 𐐻𐐩𐐿𐐲𐑌 𐐹𐑉𐐮𐑆𐐲𐑌𐐲𐑉𐑆, 𐐰𐑌𐐼 𐐑𐐩𐐸𐐬𐑉𐐲𐑌 𐐶𐐱𐑆 𐑉𐐨𐑅𐐻𐐬𐑉𐐼 𐐻𐐭 𐐸𐐮𐑆 𐐾𐐲𐐾𐑋𐐯𐑌𐐻 𐑅𐐨𐐻. 𐐈𐑌𐐼 𐑄 𐑋𐐯𐑌 𐐱𐑂 𐐑𐐩𐐿𐐲𐑅 𐑉𐐨𐑅𐐨𐑂𐐼 𐑄𐐯𐑉 𐐻𐑉𐐴𐐲𐑊, 𐐰𐐿𐐬𐑉𐐼𐐮𐑍 𐐻𐐭 𐑄 𐑊𐐫, 𐐰𐑌𐐼 𐐫𐑊𐑅𐐬 𐑄𐐬𐑆 𐐿𐐮𐑍-𐑋𐐯𐑌 𐐸𐐭 𐐸𐐰𐐼 𐐺𐐮𐑌 𐐻𐐩𐐿𐐲𐑌 𐐰𐑌𐐼 𐐿𐐪𐑅𐐻 𐐮𐑌𐐻𐐭 𐐹𐑉𐐮𐑆𐐲𐑌; 𐐰𐑌𐐼 𐑄𐐩 𐐶𐐲𐑉 𐐯𐐿𐑅𐐯𐐿𐐷𐐭𐐻𐐯𐐼 𐐰𐐿𐐬𐑉𐐼𐐮𐑍 𐐻𐐭 𐑄 𐑊𐐫; 𐐷𐐩, 𐑄𐐬𐑆 𐑋𐐯𐑌 𐐱𐑂 𐐑𐐩𐐿𐐲𐑅, 𐐰𐑌𐐼 𐑄𐐬𐑆 𐐿𐐮𐑍-𐑋𐐯𐑌, 𐐸𐐭𐑅𐐬𐐯𐑂𐐲𐑉 𐐶𐐳𐐼 𐑌𐐱𐐻 𐐻𐐩𐐿 𐐲𐐹 𐐪𐑉𐑋𐑆 𐐮𐑌 𐑄 𐐼𐐨𐑁𐐯𐑌𐑅 𐐱𐑂 𐑄𐐯𐑉 𐐿𐐲𐑌𐐻𐑉𐐨, 𐐺𐐲𐐻 𐐶𐐳𐐼 𐑁𐐴𐐻 𐐰𐑀𐐯𐑌𐑅𐐻 𐐮𐐻, 𐐶𐐲𐑉 𐐹𐐳𐐻 𐐻𐐭 𐐼𐐯𐑃; 𐐰𐑌𐐼 𐑄𐐲𐑅 𐐮𐐻 𐐺𐐨-𐐿𐐩𐑋 𐐯𐐿𐑅𐐹𐐨𐐼𐐨𐐯𐑌𐐻 𐑄𐐰𐐻 𐑄𐐮𐑅 𐑊𐐫 𐑇𐐳𐐼 𐐺𐐨 𐑅𐐻𐑉𐐮𐐿𐐻𐑊𐐨 𐐱𐐺𐑆𐐲𐑉𐑂𐐼 𐑁𐐬𐑉 𐑄 𐑅𐐩𐑁𐐻𐐨 𐐱𐑂 𐑄𐐯𐑉 𐐿𐐲𐑌𐐻𐑉𐐨; 𐐷𐐩, 𐐰𐑌𐐼 𐐸𐐭𐑅𐐬𐐯𐑂𐐲𐑉 𐐶𐐱𐑆 𐑁𐐵𐑌𐐼 𐐼𐐨𐑌𐐴𐐮𐑍 𐑄𐐯𐑉 𐑁𐑉𐐨𐐼𐐲𐑋 𐐶𐐱𐑆 𐑅𐐹𐐨𐐼𐐮𐑊𐐨 𐐯𐐿𐑅𐐯𐐿𐐷𐐭𐐻𐐯𐐼 𐐰𐐿𐐬𐑉𐐼-𐐮𐑍 𐐻𐐭 𐑄 𐑊𐐫. 𐐈𐑌𐐼 𐑄𐐲𐑅 𐐯𐑌𐐼𐐯𐐼 𐑄 𐑃𐐲𐑉𐐻𐐨𐐯𐑃 𐐷𐐨𐑉 𐐱𐑂 𐑄 𐑉𐐩𐑌 𐐱𐑂 𐑄 𐐾𐐲𐐾𐐯𐑆 𐐬𐑂𐐲𐑉 𐑄 𐐹𐐨𐐹𐑊 𐐱𐑂 𐐤𐐨𐑁𐐴; 𐐣𐐬𐑉𐐬𐑌𐐴 𐐰𐑌𐐼 𐐑𐐩𐐸𐐬𐑉𐐲𐑌 𐐸𐐰𐑂𐐮𐑍 𐑉𐐨𐑅𐐻𐐬𐑉𐐼 𐐹𐐨𐑅 𐐻𐐭 𐑄 𐑊𐐰𐑌𐐼 𐐱𐑂 𐐞𐐰𐑉𐐲𐐸𐐯𐑋𐑊𐐲, 𐐲𐑋𐐲𐑍 𐑄𐐯𐑉 𐐬𐑌 𐐹𐐨𐐹𐑊, 𐐸𐐰𐑂𐐮𐑍 𐐮𐑌𐑁𐑊𐐮𐐿𐐻𐐯𐐼 𐐼𐐯𐑃 𐐲𐐹𐐱𐑌 𐐫𐑊 𐑄𐐬𐑆 𐐸𐐭 𐐶𐐲𐑉 𐑌𐐱𐐻 𐐻𐑉𐐭 𐐻𐐭 𐑄 𐐿𐐫𐑆 𐐱𐑂 𐑁𐑉𐐨𐐼𐐲𐑋.

5. 𐐈𐑌𐐼 𐐮𐐻 𐐿𐐩𐑋 𐐻𐐭 𐐹𐐪𐑅 𐐮𐑌 𐑄 𐐿𐐱𐑋𐐯𐑌𐑅𐑋𐐯𐑌𐐻 𐐱𐑂 𐑄 𐑃𐐲𐑉𐐻𐐨 𐐰𐑌𐐼 𐑁𐐲𐑉𐑅𐐻 𐐷𐐨𐑉 𐐱𐑂 𐑄 𐑉𐐩𐑌 𐐱𐑂 𐑄 𐐾𐐲𐐾𐐯𐑆 𐐬𐑂𐐲𐑉 𐑄 𐐹𐐨𐐹𐑊 𐐱𐑂 𐐤𐐨𐑁𐐴, 𐐣𐐬𐑉𐐬𐑌𐐴 𐐮𐑋𐐨𐐼𐐨𐐯𐐻𐑊𐐨 𐐿𐐫𐑆𐐼 𐑄𐐰𐐻 𐐹𐑉𐐬𐑂𐐮𐑈𐐲𐑌𐑆 𐑇𐐳𐐼 𐐺𐐨 𐑅𐐯𐑌𐐻, 𐐰𐑌𐐼 𐐫𐑊𐑅𐐬 𐐰𐑌 𐐪𐑉𐑋𐐨 𐐱𐑂 𐑅𐐮𐐿𐑅 𐑃𐐵𐑆𐐲𐑌𐐼 𐑋𐐯𐑌 𐑇𐐳𐐼 𐐺𐐨 𐑅𐐯𐑌𐐻 𐐲𐑌𐐻𐐭 𐐐𐐨𐑊𐐲𐑋𐐲𐑌 𐐻𐐭 𐐰𐑅𐐮𐑅𐐻 𐐸𐐮𐑋 𐐮𐑌 𐐹𐑉𐐨𐑆𐐲𐑉𐑂𐐮𐑍 𐑄𐐰𐐻 𐐹𐐪𐑉𐐻 𐐱𐑂 𐑄 𐑊𐐰𐑌𐐼; 𐐰𐑌𐐼 𐐸𐐨 𐐫𐑊𐑅𐐬 𐐿𐐫𐑆𐐼 𐑄𐐰𐐻 𐐰𐑌 𐐪𐑉𐑋𐐨 𐐱𐑂 𐑅𐐮𐐿𐑅 𐑃𐐵𐑆𐐲𐑌𐐼 𐑋𐐯𐑌, 𐐶𐐮𐑃 𐐲 𐑅𐐲𐑁𐐮𐑇𐐯𐑌𐐻 𐐿𐐶𐐱𐑌𐐻𐐮𐐻𐐨 𐐱𐑂 𐑁𐐭𐐼, 𐑇𐐳𐐼 𐐺𐐨 𐑅𐐯𐑌𐐻 𐐻𐐭 𐑄 𐐪𐑉𐑋𐐨𐑆 𐐱𐑂 𐐢𐐨𐐸𐐴 𐐰𐑌𐐼 𐐓𐐨𐐰𐑍𐐿𐐲𐑋. 𐐈𐑌𐐼 𐐮𐐻 𐐿𐐩𐑋 𐐻𐐭 𐐹𐐪𐑅 𐑄𐐰𐐻 𐑄𐐮𐑅 𐐶𐐱𐑆 𐐼𐐲𐑌 𐐻𐐭 𐑁𐐬𐑉𐐻𐐮𐑁𐐴 𐑄 𐑊𐐰𐑌𐐼 𐐰𐑀𐐯𐑌𐑅𐐻 𐑄 𐐢𐐰𐑋𐐲𐑌𐐴𐐻𐑅.

6. 𐐈𐑌𐐼 𐐮𐐻 𐐿𐐩𐑋 𐐻𐐭 𐐹𐐪𐑅 𐑄𐐰𐐻 𐐣𐐬𐑉𐐬𐑌𐐴 𐐰𐑌𐐼 𐐑𐐩𐐸𐐬𐑉𐐲𐑌, 𐑊𐐨𐑂𐐮𐑍 𐐲 𐑊𐐪𐑉𐐾 𐐺𐐱𐐼𐐨 𐐱𐑂 𐑋𐐯𐑌 𐐮𐑌 𐑄 𐑊𐐰𐑌𐐼 𐐱𐑂 𐐞𐐰𐑉𐐲𐐸𐐯𐑋𐑊𐐲, 𐐻𐐳𐐿 𐑄𐐯𐑉 𐑋𐐪𐑉𐐽 𐐶𐐮𐑃 𐐲 𐑊𐐪𐑉𐐾 𐐺𐐱𐐼𐐨 𐐱𐑂 𐑋𐐯𐑌 𐐻𐐬𐑉𐐼𐑆 𐑄 𐑊𐐰𐑌𐐼 𐐱𐑂 𐐤𐐨𐑁𐐴𐐸𐐪, 𐐺𐐨𐐮𐑍 𐐼𐐨𐐻𐐲𐑉𐑋𐐮𐑌𐐼 𐐻𐐭 𐐬𐑂𐐲𐑉𐑃𐑉𐐬 𐑄 𐐢𐐰𐑋𐐲𐑌𐐴𐐻𐑅 𐐮𐑌 𐑄𐐰𐐻 𐑅𐐮𐐻𐐨.

7. 𐐈𐑌𐐼 𐐮𐐻 𐐿𐐩𐑋 𐐻𐐭 𐐹𐐪𐑅 𐑄𐐰𐐻 𐐰𐑆 𐑄𐐩 𐐶𐐲𐑉 𐑋𐐪𐑉𐐽𐐮𐑍 𐐻𐐬𐑉𐐼𐑆 𐑄 𐑊𐐰𐑌𐐼, 𐑄𐐩 𐐻𐐳𐐿 𐐲 𐑊𐐪𐑉𐐾 𐐺𐐱𐐼𐐨 𐐱𐑂 𐑋𐐯𐑌 𐐱𐑂 𐑄 𐐢𐐰𐑋𐐲𐑌𐐴𐐻𐑅, 𐐰𐑌𐐼 𐑅𐑊𐐭 𐑋𐐯𐑌𐐨 𐐱𐑂 𐑄𐐯𐑋, 𐐰𐑌𐐼 𐐻𐐳𐐿 𐑄𐐯𐑉 𐐹𐑉𐐬𐑂𐐮𐑈𐐲𐑌𐑆 𐐰𐑌𐐼 𐑄𐐯𐑉 𐐶𐐯𐐹𐐲𐑌𐑆 𐐱𐑂 𐐶𐐫𐑉. 𐐈𐑌𐐼 𐐮𐐻 𐐿𐐩𐑋 𐐻𐐭 𐐹𐐪𐑅 𐐪𐑁𐐻𐐲𐑉 𐑄𐐩 𐐸𐐰𐐼 𐐻𐐩𐐿𐐲𐑌 𐑄𐐯𐑋, 𐑄𐐩 𐐿𐐫𐑆𐐼 𐑄𐐯𐑋 𐐻𐐭 𐐯𐑌𐐻𐐲𐑉 𐐮𐑌𐐻𐐭 𐐲 𐐿𐐲𐑂𐐯𐑌𐐰𐑌𐐻 𐑄𐐰𐐻 𐑄𐐩 𐐶𐐳𐐼 𐑌𐐬 𐑋𐐬𐑉 𐐻𐐩𐐿 𐐲𐐹 𐑄𐐯𐑉 𐐶𐐯𐐹𐐲𐑌𐑆 𐐱𐑂 𐐶𐐫𐑉 𐐰𐑀𐐯𐑌𐑅𐐻 𐑄 𐐤𐐨𐑁𐐴𐐻𐑅. 𐐈𐑌𐐼 𐐸𐐶𐐯𐑌 𐑄𐐩 𐐸𐐰𐐼 𐐯𐑌𐐻𐐲𐑉𐐼 𐐮𐑌𐐻𐐭 𐑄𐐮𐑅 𐐿𐐲𐑂𐐯𐑌𐐰𐑌𐐻, 𐑄𐐩 𐑅𐐯𐑌𐐻 𐑄𐐯𐑋 𐐻𐐭 𐐼𐐶𐐯𐑊 𐐶𐐮𐑃 𐑄 𐐹𐐨𐐹𐑊 𐐱𐑂 𐐈𐑋𐐲𐑌, 𐐰𐑌𐐼 𐑄𐐩 𐐶𐐲𐑉 𐐮𐑌 𐑌𐐲𐑋𐐺𐐲𐑉 𐐲𐐺𐐵𐐻 𐑁𐐬𐑉 𐑃𐐵𐑆𐐲𐑌𐐼, 𐐸𐐭 𐐸𐐰𐐼 𐑌𐐱𐐻 𐐺𐐮𐑌 𐑅𐑊𐐩𐑌.

8. 𐐈𐑌𐐼 𐐮𐐻 𐐿𐐩𐑋 𐐻𐐭 𐐹𐐪𐑅 𐑄𐐰𐐻 𐐸𐐶𐐯𐑌 𐑄𐐩 𐐸𐐰𐐼 𐑅𐐯𐑌𐐻 𐑄𐐯𐑋 𐐲𐐶𐐩 𐑄𐐩 𐐹𐐲𐑉𐑅𐐷𐐭𐐼 𐑄𐐯𐑉 𐑋𐐪𐑉𐐽

𐐻𐐬𐑉𐐼𐑆 𐑄 𐑊𐐰𐑌𐐼 𐐱𐑂 𐐤𐐨𐑁𐐴𐐸𐐪. 𐐈𐑌𐐼 𐐮𐐻 𐐿𐐩𐑋 𐐻𐐭 𐐹𐐰𐑅 𐑄𐐰𐐻 𐐸𐐶𐐯𐑌 𐑄𐐩 𐐸𐐰𐐼 𐐿𐐲𐑋 𐐻𐐭 𐑄 𐑅𐐮𐐻𐐮 𐐤𐐨𐑁𐐴𐐸𐐪, 𐑄𐐩 𐐼𐐮𐐼 𐐹𐐮𐐽 𐑄𐐯𐑉 𐐻𐐯𐑌𐐻𐑅 𐐮𐑌 𐑄 𐐹𐑊𐐩𐑌𐑆 𐐱𐑂 𐐤𐐨𐑁𐐴𐐸𐐪, 𐐸𐐶𐐮𐐽 𐐮𐑆 𐑌𐐨𐑉 𐑄 𐑅𐐮𐐻𐐮 𐐤𐐨𐑁𐐴𐐸𐐪. 𐐤𐐵 𐐣𐐬𐑉𐐬𐑌𐐴 𐐶𐐪𐑆 𐐼𐐨𐑆𐐴𐑉𐐲𐑅 𐑄𐐰𐐻 𐑄 𐐢𐐩𐑋𐐲𐑌𐐴𐐻𐑅 𐑇𐐳𐐼 𐐿𐐲𐑋 𐐵𐐻 𐐻𐐭 𐐺𐐰𐐻𐑊 𐐲𐑀𐐯𐑌𐑅𐐻 𐑄𐐯𐑋, 𐐲𐐹𐐱𐑌 𐑄 𐐹𐑊𐐩𐑌𐑆; 𐐺𐐲𐐻 𐑄 𐐢𐐩𐑋𐐲𐑌𐐴𐐻𐑅 𐑌𐐬𐐮𐑍 𐐱𐑂 𐑄𐐯𐑉 𐐯𐐿𐑅𐐨𐐼𐐮𐑍 𐑀𐑉𐐩𐐻 𐐿𐐲𐑉𐐲𐐾, 𐐰𐑌𐐼 𐐺𐐨𐐸𐐬𐑊𐐼𐐮𐑍 𐑄 𐑀𐑉𐐩𐐻𐑌𐐯𐑅 𐐱𐑂 𐑄𐐯𐑉 𐑌𐐲𐑋𐐺𐐲𐑉𐑆, 𐑄𐐯𐑉𐑁𐐬𐑉 𐑄𐐩 𐐼𐐲𐑉𐑅𐐻 𐑌𐐱𐐻 𐐿𐐲𐑋 𐐵𐐻 𐐲𐑀𐐯𐑌𐑅𐐻 𐑄𐐯𐑋; 𐑄𐐯𐑉𐑁𐐬𐑉 𐑄𐐩 𐐼𐐮𐐼 𐑌𐐱𐐻 𐐿𐐲𐑋 𐐻𐐭 𐐺𐐰𐐻𐑊 𐐮𐑌 𐑄𐐰𐐻 𐐼𐐩. 𐐈𐑌𐐼 𐐸𐐶𐐯𐑌 𐑄 𐑌𐐴𐐻 𐐿𐐩𐑋, 𐐣𐐬𐑉𐐬𐑌𐐴 𐐶𐐯𐑌𐐻 𐑁𐐬𐑉𐑃 𐐮𐑌 𐑄 𐐼𐐪𐑉𐐿𐑌𐐯𐑅 𐐱𐑂 𐑄 𐑌𐐴𐐻, 𐐰𐑌𐐼 𐐿𐐩𐑋 𐐲𐐹𐐱𐑌 𐑄 𐐻𐐱𐐹 𐐱𐑂 𐑄 𐐶𐐫𐑊 𐐻𐐭 𐑅𐐹𐐴 𐐵𐐻 𐐮𐑌 𐐸𐐶𐐱𐐻 𐐹𐐪𐑉𐐻 𐐱𐑂 𐑄 𐑅𐐮𐐻𐐮 𐑄 𐐢𐐩𐑋𐐲𐑌𐐴𐐻𐑅 𐐼𐐮𐐼 𐐿𐐰𐑋𐐹 𐐶𐐮𐑄 𐑄𐐯𐑉 𐐪𐑉𐑋𐐨.

9. 𐐈𐑌𐐼 𐐮𐐻 𐐿𐐩𐑋 𐐻𐐭 𐐹𐐰𐑅 𐑄𐐰𐐻 𐑄𐐩 𐐶𐐲𐑉 𐐱𐑌 𐑄 𐐨𐑅𐐻, 𐐺𐐴 𐑄 𐐯𐑌𐐻𐑉𐐲𐑌𐑅; 𐐰𐑌𐐼 𐑄𐐩 𐐶𐐲𐑉 𐐫𐑊 𐐲𐑅𐑊𐐨𐐹. 𐐈𐑌𐐼 𐑌𐐵 𐐣𐐬𐑉𐐬𐑌𐐴 𐑉𐐨𐐻𐐲𐑉𐑌𐐼 𐐻𐐭 𐐸𐐮𐑆 𐐪𐑉𐑋𐐨, 𐐰𐑌𐐼 𐐿𐐫𐑆𐐼 𐑄𐐰𐐻 𐑄𐐩 𐑇𐐳𐐼 𐐹𐑉𐐨𐐹𐐩𐑉 𐐮𐑌 𐐸𐐩𐑅𐐻 𐑅𐐻𐑉𐐫𐑍 𐐿𐐫𐑉𐐼𐑆 𐐰𐑌𐐼 𐑊𐐰𐐼𐐲𐑉𐑆, 𐐻𐐭 𐐺 𐑊𐐯𐐻 𐐼𐐵𐑌 𐑁𐑉𐐱𐑋 𐑄 𐐻𐐱𐐹 𐐱𐑂 𐑄 𐐶𐐫𐑊 𐐮𐑌𐐻𐐭 𐑄 𐐮𐑌𐐲𐑉 𐐹𐐪𐑉𐐻 𐐱𐑂 𐑄 𐐶𐐫𐑊.

10. 𐐈𐑌𐐼 𐐮𐐻 𐐿𐐩𐑋 𐐻𐐭 𐐹𐐰𐑅 𐑄𐐰𐐻 𐐣𐐬𐑉𐐬𐑌𐐴 𐐿𐐫𐑆𐐼 𐑄𐐰𐐻 𐐸𐐮𐑆 𐑋𐐯𐑌 𐑇𐐳𐐼 𐑋𐐪𐑉𐐽 𐑁𐐬𐑉𐑃 𐐰𐑌𐐼 𐐿𐐲𐑋 𐐲𐐹𐐱𐑌 𐑄 𐐻𐐱𐐹 𐐱𐑂 𐑄 𐐶𐐫𐑊, 𐐰𐑌𐐼 𐑊𐐯𐐻 𐑄𐐯𐑋𐑅𐐯𐑊𐑂𐑆 𐐼𐐵𐑌 𐐮𐑌𐐻𐐭 𐑄𐐰𐐻 𐐹𐐪𐑉𐐻 𐐱𐑂 𐑄 𐑅𐐮𐐻𐐮, 𐐷𐐩, 𐐨𐑂𐑌 𐐱𐑌 𐑄 𐐶𐐯𐑅𐐻, 𐐸𐐶𐐩𐑉 𐑄 𐐢𐐩𐑋𐐲𐑌𐐴𐐻𐑅 𐐼𐐮𐐼 𐑌𐐱𐐻 𐐿𐐰𐑋𐐹 𐐶𐐮𐑄 𐑄𐐯𐑉 𐐪𐑉𐑋𐐨𐑆.

11. 𐐈𐑌𐐼 𐐮𐐻 𐐿𐐩𐑋 𐐻𐐭 𐐹𐐰𐑅 𐑄𐐰𐐻 𐑄𐐩 𐐶𐐲𐑉 𐐫𐑊 𐑊𐐯𐐻 𐐼𐐵𐑌 𐐮𐑌𐐻𐐭 𐑄 𐑅𐐮𐐻𐐮 𐐺𐐴 𐑌𐐴𐐻, 𐐺𐐴 𐑄 𐑋𐐨𐑌𐑆 𐐱𐑂 𐑄𐐯𐑉 𐑅𐐻𐑉𐐫𐑍 𐐿𐐫𐑉𐐼𐑆 𐐰𐑌𐐼 𐑄𐐯𐑉 𐑊𐐰𐐼𐐲𐑉𐑆; 𐑄𐐲𐑅 𐐸𐐶𐐯𐑌 𐑄 𐑋𐐫𐑉𐑌𐐮𐑍 𐐿𐐩𐑋, 𐑄𐐩 𐐶𐐲𐑉 𐐫𐑊 𐐶𐐮𐑄𐐮𐑌 𐑄 𐐶𐐫𐑊𐑆 𐐱𐑂 𐑄 𐑅𐐮𐐻𐐮. 𐐈𐑌𐐼 𐑌𐐵 𐐸𐐶𐐯𐑌 𐑄 𐐢𐐩𐑋𐐲𐑌𐐴𐐻𐑅 𐐲𐐶𐐬𐐿, 𐐰𐑌𐐼 𐑅𐐫 𐑄𐐰𐐻 𐑄 𐐪𐑉𐑋𐐨𐑆 𐐱𐑂 𐐣𐐬𐑉𐐬𐑌𐐴 𐐶𐐲𐑉 𐐶𐐮𐑄𐐮𐑌 𐑄 𐐶𐐫𐑊𐑆, 𐑄𐐩 𐐶𐐲𐑉 𐐲𐑁𐑉𐐴𐐻𐐯𐐼 𐐯𐐿𐑅𐐨𐐼𐐮𐑍𐑊𐐨, 𐐮𐑌𐑅𐐬𐑋𐐲𐐽 𐑄𐐰𐐻 𐑄𐐩 𐐼𐐮𐐼 𐑁𐑊𐐨 𐐵𐐻 𐐺𐐴 𐑄 𐐹𐐰𐑅. 𐐈𐑌𐐼 𐑌𐐵 𐐸𐐶𐐯𐑌 𐐣𐐬𐑉𐐬𐑌𐐴 𐑅𐐫 𐑄𐐰𐐻 𐑄𐐩 𐐶𐐲𐑉 𐑁𐑊𐐨𐐮𐑍 𐐺𐐨𐑁𐐬𐑉 𐐸𐐮𐑋, 𐐸𐐨 𐐼𐐮𐐼 𐐿𐐫𐑆 𐑄𐐰𐐻 𐐸𐐮𐑆 𐑋𐐯𐑌 𐑇𐐳𐐼 𐑋𐐪𐑉𐐽 𐑁𐐬𐑉𐑃 𐐲𐑀𐐯𐑌𐑅𐐻 𐑄𐐯𐑋, 𐐰𐑌𐐼 𐑅𐑊𐐭 𐑋𐐯𐑌𐐨, 𐐰𐑌𐐼 𐑅𐐲𐑉𐐵𐑌𐐼𐐯𐐼 𐑋𐐯𐑌𐐨 𐐲𐑄𐐲𐑉𐑆, 𐐰𐑌𐐼 𐐻𐐳𐐿 𐑄𐐯𐑋 𐐹𐑉𐐮𐑆𐐲𐑌𐐲𐑉𐑆; 𐐰𐑌𐐼 𐑄 𐑉𐐨𐑋𐐩𐑌𐐼𐐲𐑉 𐐱𐑂 𐑄𐐯𐑋 𐑁𐑊𐐯𐐼 𐐮𐑌𐐻𐐭 𐑄 𐑊𐐰𐑌𐐼 𐐱𐑂 𐐣𐐬𐑉𐐬𐑌𐐴, 𐐸𐐶𐐮𐐽 𐐶𐐱𐑆 𐐮𐑌 𐑄 𐐺𐐫𐑉𐐼𐐲𐑉𐑆, 𐐺𐐴 𐑄 𐑅𐐨 𐑇𐐬𐑉. 𐐜𐐲𐑅 𐐸𐐰𐐼 𐐣𐐬𐑉𐐬𐑌𐐴 𐐰𐑌𐐼 𐐑𐐪-𐐸𐐬𐑉𐐲𐑌 𐑀𐐩𐑌𐐼 𐑄 𐐹𐐲𐑆𐐯𐑇𐐲𐑌 𐐱𐑂 𐑄 𐑅𐐮𐐻𐐮 𐐤𐐨𐑁𐐴𐐸𐐪, 𐐶𐐮𐑄𐐵𐐻 𐑄 𐑊𐐱𐑅 𐐱𐑂 𐐶𐐲𐑌 𐑅𐐬𐑊; 𐐰𐑌𐐼 𐑄𐐯𐑉 𐐶𐐲𐑉 𐑋𐐯𐑌𐐨 𐐱𐑂 𐑄 𐐢𐐩𐑋𐐲𐑌𐐴𐐻𐑅 𐐸𐐭 𐐶𐐲𐑉 𐑅𐑊𐐩𐑌.

12. 𐐤𐐵 𐐮𐐻 𐐿𐐩𐑋 𐐻𐐭 𐐹𐐰𐑅 𐑄𐐰𐐻 𐑋𐐯𐑌𐐨 𐐱𐑂 𐑄 𐐢𐐩𐑋𐐲𐑌𐐴𐐻𐑅 𐑄𐐰𐐻 𐐶𐐲𐑉 𐐹𐑉𐐮𐑆𐐲𐑌𐐲𐑉𐑆, 𐐶𐐲𐑉 𐐼𐐨𐑆𐐴𐑉𐐲𐑅 𐐻𐐭 𐐾𐐦𐑌 𐑄 𐐹𐐨𐐹𐑊 𐐱𐑂 𐐈𐑋𐐲𐑌, 𐐰𐑌𐐼 𐐺𐐨𐐿𐐲𐑋 𐐩 𐑁𐑉𐐨 𐐹𐐨𐐹𐑊. 𐐈𐑌𐐼 𐐮𐐻 𐐿𐐩𐑋 𐐻𐐭 𐐹𐐰𐑅 𐑄𐐰𐐻 𐐰𐑆 𐑋𐐯𐑌𐐨 𐐰𐑆 𐐶𐐲𐑉 𐐼𐐨𐑆𐐴𐑉𐐲𐑅, 𐐲𐑌𐐻𐐭 𐑄𐐯𐑋 𐐮𐐻 𐐶𐐱𐑆 𐑀𐑉𐐰𐑌𐐻𐐯𐐼, 𐐰𐐿𐐫𐑉𐐼𐐮𐑍 𐐻𐐭 𐑄𐐯𐑉 𐐼𐐨𐑆𐐴𐑉𐑆; 𐑄𐐯𐑉-𐑁𐐬𐑉, 𐐫𐑊 𐑄 𐐹𐑉𐐮𐑆𐐲𐑌𐐲𐑉𐑆 𐐱𐑂 𐑄 𐐢𐐩𐑋𐐲𐑌𐐴𐐻𐑅 𐐼𐐮𐐼 𐐾𐐦𐑌 𐑄 𐐹𐐨𐐹𐑊 𐐱𐑂 𐐈𐑋𐐲𐑌, 𐐰𐑌𐐼 𐐼𐐮𐐼 𐐺𐐨𐑀𐐮𐑌 𐐻𐐭 𐑊𐐩𐐺𐐲𐑉 𐐯𐐿𐑅𐐨𐐼𐐮𐑍𐑊𐐨, 𐐻𐐮𐑊𐐮𐑍 𐑄 𐑀𐑉𐐵𐑌𐐼, 𐑉𐐩𐑆𐐮𐑍 𐐫𐑊 𐑋𐐰𐑌𐐲𐑉 𐐱𐑂 𐑀𐑉𐐩𐑌, 𐐰𐑌𐐼 𐑁𐑊𐐱𐐿𐑅, 𐐰𐑌𐐼 𐐸𐐲𐑉𐐼𐑆 𐐱𐑂 𐐯𐑂𐐲𐑉𐐨 𐐿𐐴𐑌𐐼; 𐐰𐑌𐐼 𐑄𐐲𐑅 𐐶𐐲𐑉 𐑄 𐐤𐐨𐑁𐐴𐐻𐑅 𐑉𐐨𐑊𐐨𐑂𐐼 𐑁𐑉𐐱𐑋 𐐩 𐑀𐑉𐐩𐐻 𐐺𐐲𐑉𐐼𐐲𐑌; 𐐷𐐩, 𐐮𐑌𐑅𐐬-𐑋𐐲𐐽 𐑄𐐰𐐻 𐑄𐐩 𐐶𐐲𐑉 𐑉𐐨𐑊𐐨𐑂𐐼 𐑁𐑉𐐱𐑋 𐐫𐑊 𐑄 𐐹𐑉𐐮𐑆𐐲𐑌𐐲𐑉𐑆 𐐱𐑂 𐑄 𐐢𐐩𐑋𐐲𐑌𐐴𐐻𐑅.

13. 𐐤𐐵 𐐮𐐻 𐐿𐐩𐑋 𐐻𐐭 𐐹𐐰𐑅 𐑄𐐰𐐻 𐐣𐐬𐑉𐐬𐑌𐐴, 𐐰𐑁𐐻𐐲𐑉 𐐸𐐨 𐐸𐐰𐐼 𐐱𐐺𐐻𐐩𐑌𐐼 𐐹𐐲𐑆𐐯𐑇𐐲𐑌 𐐱𐑂 𐑄 𐑅𐐮𐐻𐐮 𐐤𐐨𐑁𐐴𐐸𐐪, 𐐸𐐰𐑂𐐮𐑍 𐐻𐐩𐐿𐐲𐑌 𐑋𐐯𐑌𐐨 𐐹𐑉𐐮𐑆𐐲𐑌𐐲𐑉𐑆, 𐐸𐐶𐐮𐐽 𐐼𐐮𐐼 𐑉𐐨𐐼𐐷𐐭𐑅 𐑄 𐐪𐑉𐑋𐐨𐑆 𐐱𐑂 𐑄 𐐢𐐩𐑋𐐲𐑌𐐴𐐻𐑅 𐐯𐐿-𐑅𐐨𐐼𐐮𐑍𐑊𐐨, 𐐰𐑌𐐼 𐐸𐐰𐑂𐐮𐑍 𐑉𐐨𐑀𐐩𐑌𐐼 𐑋𐐯𐑌𐐨 𐐱𐑂 𐑄 𐐤𐐨𐑁𐐴𐐻𐑅 𐐸𐐭 𐐸𐐰𐐼 𐐺𐐮𐑌 𐐻𐐩𐐿𐐲𐑌 𐐹𐑉𐐮𐑆𐐲𐑌𐐲𐑉𐑆, 𐐸𐐶𐐮𐐽 𐐼𐐮𐐼 𐑅𐐻𐑉𐐯𐑍𐑃𐐲𐑌 𐑄 𐐪𐑉𐑋𐐨 𐐱𐑂 𐐣𐐬𐑉𐐬𐑌𐐴 𐐯𐐿𐑅𐐨𐐼𐐮𐑍𐑊𐐨; 𐑄𐐯𐑉𐑁𐐬𐑉 𐐣𐐬𐑉𐐬𐑌𐐴 𐐶𐐯𐑌𐐻 𐑁𐐬𐑉𐑃 𐑁𐑉𐐱𐑋 𐑄 𐑊𐐰𐑌𐐼 𐐱𐑂 𐐤𐐨𐑁𐐴𐐸𐐪 𐐻𐐭 𐑄 𐑊𐐰𐑌𐐼 𐐱𐑂 𐐢𐐨𐐸𐐴.

14. 𐐈𐑌𐐼 𐐮𐐻 𐐿𐐩𐑋 𐐻𐐭 𐐹𐐰𐑅 𐑄𐐰𐐻 𐐸𐐶𐐯𐑌 𐑄 𐐢𐐩𐑋𐐲𐑌𐐴𐐻𐑅 𐑅𐐫 𐑄𐐰𐐻 𐐣𐐬𐑉𐐬𐑌𐐴 𐐶𐐱𐑆 𐐿𐐲𐑋𐐮𐑍 𐐲𐑀𐐯𐑌𐑅𐐻 𐑄𐐯𐑋, 𐑄𐐩 𐐶𐐲𐑉 𐐲𐑀𐐯𐑌 𐑁𐑉𐐴𐐻𐑌𐐼, 𐐰𐑌𐐼 𐑁𐑊𐐯𐐼 𐐺𐐨𐑁𐐬𐑉 𐑄 𐐪𐑉𐑋𐐨 𐐱𐑂 𐐣𐐬𐑉𐐬𐑌𐐴. 𐐈𐑌𐐼 𐐮𐐻 𐐿𐐩𐑋 𐐻𐐭 𐐹𐐰𐑅 𐑄𐐰𐐻 𐐣𐐬𐑉𐐬𐑌𐐴 𐐰𐑌𐐼 𐐸𐐮𐑆 𐐪𐑉𐑋𐐨 𐐼𐐮𐐼 𐐹𐐲𐑉𐑅𐐭 𐑄𐐯𐑋 𐑁𐑉𐐱𐑋 𐑅𐐮𐐻𐐮 𐐻𐐭 𐑅𐐮𐐻𐐮, 𐐲𐑌𐐻𐐮𐑊 𐑄𐐩 𐐶𐐲𐑉 𐑋𐐯𐐻 𐐺𐐴 𐐢𐐨𐐸𐐴 𐐰𐑌𐐼 𐐓𐐨𐐰𐑌𐐿𐐲𐑋. 𐐈𐑌𐐼 𐑄 𐐢𐐩𐑋𐐲𐑌𐐴𐐻𐑅 𐑁𐑊𐐯𐐼 𐑁𐑉𐐱𐑋 𐐢𐐨𐐸𐐴 𐐰𐑌𐐼 𐐓𐐨𐐰𐑌𐐿𐐲𐑋,

𐐨𐑂𐐲𐑌 𐐼𐐵𐑌 𐐲𐐹𐐱𐑌 𐑄 𐐺𐐫𐑉𐐼𐐲𐑉𐑆 𐐺𐐴 𐑄 𐑅𐐨 𐑇𐐬𐑉, 𐐲𐑌𐐻𐐮𐑊 𐑄𐐩 𐐿𐐩𐑋 𐐻𐐭 𐑄 𐑊𐐰𐑌𐐼 𐐱𐑂 𐐣𐐬𐑉𐐬𐑌𐐴. 𐐈𐑌𐐼 𐑄 𐐪𐑉𐑋𐐨𐑆 𐐱𐑂 𐑄 𐐢𐐩𐑋𐐲𐑌𐐴𐐻𐑅 𐐶𐐲𐑉 𐐫𐑊 𐑀𐐰𐑄𐐲𐑉𐐼 𐐻𐐳𐑀𐐯𐑄𐐲𐑉, 𐐮𐑌𐑅𐐬𐑋𐐲𐐽 𐑄𐐰𐐻 𐑄𐐩 𐐶𐐲𐑉 𐐫𐑊 𐐮𐑌 𐐶𐐲𐑌 𐐺𐐱𐐼𐐨, 𐐮𐑌 𐑄 𐑊𐐰𐑌𐐼 𐐱𐑂 𐐣𐐬𐑉𐐬𐑌𐐴. 𐐤𐐵 𐐈𐑋𐐬𐑉𐐲𐑌, 𐑄 𐐿𐐮𐑍 𐐱𐑂 𐑄 𐐢𐐩𐑋𐐲𐑌𐐴𐐻𐑅, 𐐶𐐱𐑆 𐐫𐑊𐑅𐐬 𐐶𐐮𐑄 𐑄𐐯𐑋.

15. 𐐈𐑌𐐼 𐐮𐐻 𐐿𐐩𐑋 𐐻𐐭 𐐹𐐰𐑅 𐑄𐐰𐐻 𐐣𐐬𐑉𐐬𐑌𐐴, 𐐰𐑌𐐼 𐐢𐐨𐐸𐐴, 𐐰𐑌𐐼 𐐓𐐨𐐰𐑌𐐿𐐲𐑋 𐐼𐐮𐐼 𐐯𐑌𐐿𐐰𐑋𐐹 𐐶𐐮𐑄 𐑄𐐯𐑉 𐐪𐑉𐑋𐐨𐑆 𐑉𐐵𐑌𐐼 𐐲𐐺𐐵𐐻 𐐮𐑌 𐑄 𐐺𐐫𐑉𐐼𐐲𐑉𐑆 𐐱𐑂 𐑄 𐑊𐐰𐑌𐐼 𐐱𐑂 𐐣𐐬𐑉𐐬𐑌𐐴, 𐐮𐑌𐑅𐐬𐑋𐐲𐐽 𐑄𐐰𐐻 𐑄 𐐢𐐩𐑋𐐲𐑌𐐴𐐻𐑅 𐐶𐐲𐑉 𐐯𐑌𐑅𐐲𐑉𐐿𐑊𐐼 𐐲𐐺𐐵𐐻 𐐮𐑌 𐑄 𐐺𐐫𐑉𐐼𐐲𐑉𐑆 𐐺𐐴 𐑄 𐐶𐐮𐑊𐐼𐐲𐑉𐑌𐐯𐑅, 𐐫𐑌 𐑄 𐑅𐐵𐑃, 𐐰𐑌𐐼 𐐮𐑌 𐑄 𐐺𐐫𐑉𐐼𐐲𐑉𐑆 𐐺𐐴 𐑄 𐐶𐐮𐑊𐐼𐐲𐑉𐑌𐐯𐑅, 𐐫𐑌 𐑄 𐐨𐑅𐐻; 𐐰𐑌𐐼 𐑄𐐲𐑅 𐑄𐐩 𐐼𐐮𐐼 𐐯𐑌𐐿𐐰𐑋𐐹 𐑁𐐫𐑉 𐑄 𐑌𐐴𐐻. 𐐙𐐫𐑉 𐐺𐐨𐐸𐐬𐑊𐐼, 𐑄 𐐤𐐨𐑁𐐴𐐻𐑅 𐐰𐑌𐐼 𐑄 𐐢𐐩𐑋𐐲𐑌𐐴𐐻𐑅 𐐫𐑊𐑅𐐬, 𐐶𐐲𐑉 𐐶𐐨𐑉𐐨 𐐺𐐨𐐿𐐫𐑆 𐐱𐑂 𐑄 𐑀𐑉𐐩𐐻𐑌𐐯𐑅 𐐱𐑂 𐑄 𐑋𐐪𐑉𐐽; 𐑄𐐯𐑉𐑁𐐬𐑉 𐑄𐐩 𐐼𐐮𐐼 𐑌𐐱𐐻 𐑉𐐨𐑆𐐱𐑊𐑂 𐐲𐐹𐐱𐑌 𐐯𐑌𐐨 𐑅𐐻𐑉𐐰𐐻𐐲𐐾𐐯𐑋 𐐮𐑌 𐑄 𐑌𐐴𐐻-𐐻𐐴𐑋, 𐑅𐐩𐑂 𐐮𐐻 𐐶𐐲𐑉 𐐓𐐨𐐰𐑌𐐿𐐲𐑋; 𐑁𐐫𐑉 𐐸𐐨 𐐶𐐱𐑆 𐐯𐐿𐑅𐐨𐐼𐐮𐑍𐑊𐐨 𐐰𐑍𐑀𐑉𐐨 𐐶𐐮𐑄 𐐈𐑋𐐬𐑉𐐲𐑌, 𐐮𐑌𐑅𐐬𐑋𐐲𐐽 𐑄𐐰𐐻 𐐸𐐨 𐐿𐐲𐑌𐑅𐐮𐐼𐐲𐑉𐐼 𐑄𐐰𐐻 𐐈𐑋𐐬𐑉𐐲𐑌, 𐐰𐑌𐐼 𐐈𐑋𐐲𐑊𐐮𐐿𐐴𐐲 𐐸𐐰𐐼 𐐺𐐮𐑌 𐑄 𐐿𐐫𐑆 𐐱𐑂 𐑄𐐮𐑅 𐑀𐑉𐐩𐐻 𐐰𐑌𐐼 𐑊𐐰𐑅𐐻𐐮𐑍 𐐶𐐫𐑉 𐐺𐐨𐐻𐐶𐐨𐑌 𐑄𐐯𐑋 𐐰𐑌𐐼 𐑄 𐐢𐐩𐑋𐐲𐑌𐐴𐐻𐑅, 𐐸𐐶𐐮𐐽 𐐸𐐰𐐼 𐐺𐐮𐑌 𐑄 𐐿𐐫𐑆 𐐱𐑂 𐑅𐐬 𐑋𐐲𐐽 𐐶𐐫𐑉 𐐰𐑌𐐼 𐐺𐑊𐐲𐐼𐑇𐐯𐐼, 𐐷𐐩, 𐐰𐑌𐐼 𐑅𐐬 𐑋𐐲𐐽 𐑁𐐰𐑋𐐮𐑌.

16. 𐐈𐑌𐐼 𐐮𐐻 𐐿𐐩𐑋 𐐻𐐭 𐐹𐐰𐑅 𐑄𐐰𐐻 𐐓𐐨𐐰𐑌𐐿𐐲𐑋 𐐮𐑌 𐐸𐐮𐑆 𐐰𐑍𐑀𐐲𐑉 𐐼𐐮𐐼 𐑀𐐬 𐑁𐐬𐑉𐑃 𐐮𐑌𐐻𐐭 𐑄 𐐿𐐰𐑋𐐹 𐐱𐑂 𐑄 𐐢𐐩𐑋𐐲𐑌𐐴𐐻𐑅, 𐐰𐑌𐐼 𐐼𐐮𐐼 𐑊𐐯𐐻 𐐸𐐮𐑋𐑅𐐯𐑊𐑁 𐐼𐐵𐑌 𐐬𐑂𐐲𐑉 𐑄 𐐶𐐫𐑊𐑆 𐐱𐑂 𐑄 𐑅𐐮𐐻𐐨. 𐐈𐑌𐐼 𐐸𐐨 𐐶𐐯𐑌𐐻 𐑁𐐬𐑉𐑃 𐐶𐐮𐑄 𐐲 𐐿𐐫𐑉𐐼, 𐑁𐑉𐐲𐑋 𐐹𐑊𐐩𐑅 𐐻𐐭 𐐹𐑊𐐩𐑅, 𐐮𐑌𐑅𐐬𐑋𐐲𐐽 𐑄𐐰𐐻 𐐸𐐨 𐐼𐐮𐐼 𐑁𐐴𐑌𐐼 𐑄 𐐿𐐮𐑍; 𐐰𐑌𐐼 𐐸𐐨 𐐼𐐮𐐼 𐐿𐐰𐑅𐐻 𐐲 𐐾𐐰𐑂𐐲𐑊𐐮𐑌 𐐰𐐻 𐐸𐐮𐑋, 𐐸𐐶𐐮𐐽 𐐼𐐮𐐼 𐐹𐐨𐑉𐑅 𐐸𐐮𐑋 𐑌𐐨𐑉 𐑄 𐐸𐐪𐑉𐐻. 𐐒𐐲𐐻 𐐺𐐨𐐸𐐬𐑊𐐼, 𐑄 𐐿𐐮𐑍 𐐼𐐮𐐼 𐐲𐐶𐐩𐐿𐐲𐑌 𐐸𐐮𐑆 𐑅𐐲𐑉𐑂𐐲𐑌𐐻𐑅 𐐺𐐨𐑁𐐬𐑉 𐐸𐐨 𐐼𐐴𐐼, 𐐮𐑌𐑅𐐬𐑋𐐲𐐽 𐑄𐐰𐐻 𐑄𐐩 𐐼𐐮𐐼 𐐹𐐲𐑉𐑅𐐭 𐐓𐐨𐐰𐑌𐐿𐐲𐑋, 𐐰𐑌𐐼 𐑅𐑊𐐭 𐐸𐐮𐑋.

17. 𐐤𐐵 𐐮𐐻 𐐿𐐩𐑋 𐐻𐐭 𐐹𐐰𐑅 𐑄𐐰𐐻 𐐸𐐶𐐯𐑌 𐐢𐐨𐐸𐐴 𐐰𐑌𐐼 𐐣𐐬𐑉𐐬𐑌𐐴 𐑌𐐭 𐑄𐐰𐐻 𐐓𐐨𐐰𐑌𐐿𐐲𐑋 𐐶𐐱𐑆 𐐼𐐯𐐼, 𐑄𐐩 𐐶𐐲𐑉 𐐯𐐿𐑅𐐨𐐼𐐮𐑍𐑊𐐨 𐑅𐐱𐑉𐐬𐑁𐐳𐑊: 𐑁𐐫𐑉 𐐺𐐨𐐸𐐬𐑊𐐼, 𐐸𐐨 𐐸𐐰𐐼 𐐺𐐮𐑌 𐐲 𐑋𐐰𐑌 𐐸𐐭 𐐸𐐰𐐼 𐑁𐐫𐐻 𐑂𐐰𐑊𐐨𐐲𐑌𐐻𐑊𐐨 𐑁𐐫𐑉 𐐸𐐮𐑆 𐐿𐐲𐑌𐐻𐑉𐐨, 𐐷𐐩, 𐐲 𐐻𐑉𐐭 𐑁𐑉𐐯𐑌𐐼 𐐻𐐭 𐑊𐐮𐐺𐐲𐑉𐐻𐐨; 𐐰𐑌𐐼 𐐸𐐨 𐐸𐐰𐐼 𐑅𐐲𐑁𐐲𐑉𐐼 𐑂𐐯𐑉𐐨 𐑋𐐯𐑌𐐨 𐐯𐐿𐑅𐐨𐐼𐐮𐑍𐑊𐐨 𐑅𐐬𐑉 𐐰𐑁𐑊𐐮𐐿𐑇𐐲𐑌𐑆. 𐐒𐐲𐐻 𐐺𐐨𐐸𐐬𐑊𐐼, 𐐸𐐨 𐐶𐐱𐑆 𐐼𐐯𐐼, 𐐰𐑌𐐼 𐐸𐐰𐐼 𐑀𐐫𐑌 𐑄 𐐶𐐩 𐐱𐑂 𐐫𐑊 𐑄 𐐲𐑉𐑃.

18. 𐐤𐐵 𐐮𐐻 𐐿𐐩𐑋 𐐻𐐭 𐐹𐐰𐑅 𐑄𐐰𐐻 𐐣𐐬𐑉𐐬𐑌𐐴 𐑋𐐪𐑉𐐽𐐻 𐑁𐐬𐑉𐑃 𐐫𐑌 𐑄 𐑋𐐱𐑉𐐬, 𐐰𐑌𐐼 𐐿𐐩𐑋 𐐲𐐹𐐱𐑌 𐑄 𐐢𐐩𐑋𐐲𐑌𐐴𐐻𐑅, 𐐮𐑌𐑅𐐬𐑋𐐲𐐽 𐑄𐐰𐐻 𐑄𐐩 𐐼𐐮𐐼 𐑅𐑊𐐩 𐑄𐐯𐑋 𐐶𐐮𐑄 𐐲 𐑀𐑉𐐩𐐻 𐑅𐑊𐐫𐐻𐐲𐑉; 𐐰𐑌𐐼 𐑄𐐩 𐐼𐐮𐐼 𐐼𐑉𐐴𐑂 𐑄𐐯𐑋 𐐵𐐻 𐐱𐑂 𐑄 𐑊𐐰𐑌𐐼; 𐐰𐑌𐐼 𐑄𐐩 𐐼𐐮𐐼 𐑁𐑊𐐨, 𐐨𐑂𐐲𐑌 𐑄𐐰𐐻 𐑄𐐩 𐐼𐐮𐐼 𐑌𐐱𐐻 𐑉𐐨𐐻𐐲𐑉𐑌 𐐰𐐻 𐑄𐐰𐐻 𐐻𐐴𐑋 𐐲𐑀𐐯𐑌𐑅𐐻 𐑄 𐐤𐐨𐑁𐐴𐐻𐑅. 𐐈𐑌𐐼 𐑄𐐲𐑅 𐐯𐑌𐐼𐐯𐐼 𐑄 𐑃𐐲𐑉𐐻𐐨 𐐰𐑌𐐼 𐑁𐐲𐑉𐑅𐐻 𐐷𐐨𐑉 𐐱𐑂 𐑄 𐑉𐐩𐑌 𐐱𐑂 𐑄 𐐾𐐲𐐾𐐯𐑆 𐐬𐑂𐐲𐑉 𐑄 𐐹𐐨𐐹𐑊 𐐱𐑂 𐐤𐐨𐑁𐐴; 𐐰𐑌𐐼 𐑄𐐲𐑅 𐑄𐐩 𐐸𐐰𐐼 𐐸𐐰𐐼 𐐶𐐫𐑉𐑆, 𐐰𐑌𐐼 𐐺𐑊𐐲𐐼𐑇𐐯𐐼𐑆, 𐐰𐑌𐐼 𐑁𐐰𐑋𐐮𐑌, 𐐰𐑌𐐼 𐐰𐑁𐑊𐐮𐐿𐑇𐐲𐑌, 𐑁𐐫𐑉 𐑄 𐑅𐐹𐐩𐑅 𐐱𐑂 𐑋𐐯𐑌𐐨 𐐷𐐨𐑉𐑆. 𐐈𐑌𐐼 𐑄𐐯𐑉 𐐸𐐰𐐼 𐐺𐐮𐑌 𐑋𐐲𐑉𐐼𐐲𐑉𐑆, 𐐰𐑌𐐼 𐐿𐐱𐑌𐐻𐐯𐑌𐑇𐐲𐑌𐑆, 𐐰𐑌𐐼 𐐼𐐮𐑅𐐯𐑌𐑇𐐲𐑌𐑆, 𐐰𐑌𐐼 𐐫𐑊 𐑋𐐰𐑌𐐲𐑉 𐐱𐑂 𐐮𐑌𐐮𐐿𐐶𐐮𐐻𐐨 𐐲𐑋𐐲𐑍 𐑄 𐐹𐐨𐐹𐑊 𐐱𐑂 𐐤𐐨𐑁𐐴; 𐑌𐐯𐑂𐐲𐑉𐑄𐐨𐑊𐐯𐑅 𐑁𐐫𐑉 𐑄 𐑉𐐴𐐽𐐲𐑅𐐯𐑅' 𐑅𐐩𐐿, 𐐷𐐩, 𐐺𐐨𐐿𐐫𐑆 𐐱𐑂 𐑄 𐐹𐑉𐐯𐑉𐑆 𐐱𐑂 𐑄 𐑉𐐴𐐽𐐲𐑅, 𐑄𐐩 𐐶𐐲𐑉 𐑅𐐹𐐯𐑉𐐼. 𐐒𐐲𐐻 𐐺𐐨𐐸𐐬𐑊𐐼, 𐐺𐐨𐐿𐐫𐑆 𐐱𐑂 𐑄 𐐯𐐿𐑅𐐨𐐼𐐮𐑍𐑊𐐨 𐑀𐑉𐐩𐐻 𐑊𐐯𐑍𐑃 𐐱𐑂 𐑄 𐐶𐐫𐑉 𐐺𐐨𐐻𐐶𐐨𐑌 𐑄 𐐤𐐨𐑁𐐴𐐻𐑅 𐐰𐑌𐐼 𐑄 𐐢𐐩𐑋𐐲𐑌𐐴𐐻𐑅, 𐑋𐐯𐑌𐐨 𐐸𐐰𐐼 𐐺𐐨𐐿𐐲𐑋 𐐸𐐪𐑉𐐼𐐲𐑌𐐼, 𐐺𐐨𐐿𐐫𐑆 𐐱𐑂 𐑄 𐐯𐐿𐑅𐐨𐐼𐐮𐑍𐑊𐐨 𐑀𐑉𐐩𐐻 𐑊𐐯𐑍𐑃 𐐱𐑂 𐑄 𐐶𐐫𐑉; 𐐰𐑌𐐼 𐑋𐐯𐑌𐐨 𐐶𐐲𐑉 𐑅𐐫𐑁𐐲𐑌𐐼, 𐐺𐐨𐐿𐐫𐑆 𐐱𐑂 𐑄𐐯𐑉 𐐰𐑁𐑊𐐮𐐿𐑇𐐲𐑌𐑆, 𐐮𐑌𐑅𐐬𐑋𐐲𐐽 𐑄𐐰𐐻 𐑄𐐩 𐐼𐐮𐐼 𐐸𐐲𐑋𐐺𐑊 𐑄𐐯𐑋𐑅𐐯𐑊𐑂𐑆 𐐺𐐨𐑁𐐬𐑉 𐐘𐐱𐐼, 𐐨𐑂𐐲𐑌 𐐮𐑌 𐑄 𐐼𐐯𐐹𐑃 𐐱𐑂 𐐸𐐷𐐭𐑋𐐮𐑊𐐮𐐻𐐨.

19. 𐐈𐑌𐐼 𐐮𐐻 𐐿𐐩𐑋 𐐻𐐭 𐐹𐐰𐑅 𐑄𐐰𐐻 𐐰𐑁𐐻𐐲𐑉 𐐣𐐬𐑉𐐬𐑌𐐴 𐐸𐐰𐐼 𐑁𐐫𐑉𐐻𐐮𐑁𐐴𐐼 𐑄𐐬𐑆 𐐹𐐪𐑉𐐻𐑅 𐐱𐑂 𐑄 𐑊𐐰𐑌𐐼 𐐸𐐶𐐮𐐽 𐐶𐐲𐑉 𐑋𐐬𐑅𐐻 𐐯𐐿𐑅𐐹𐐬𐑆𐐼 𐐻𐐭 𐑄 𐐢𐐩𐑋𐐲𐑌𐐴𐐻𐑅, 𐐲𐑌𐐻𐐮𐑊 𐑄𐐩 𐐶𐐲𐑉 𐑅𐐲𐑁𐐮𐑇𐐲𐑌𐐻𐑊𐐨 𐑅𐐻𐑉𐐱𐑍, 𐐸𐐨 𐑉𐐨𐐻𐐲𐑉𐑌𐐼 𐐻𐐭 𐑄 𐑅𐐮𐐻𐐨 𐐱𐑂 𐐞𐐪𐑉𐐲𐐸𐐯𐑋𐑊𐐲; 𐐰𐑌𐐼 𐐫𐑊𐑅𐐬 𐐐𐐨𐑊𐐲𐑋𐐲𐑌 𐑉𐐨𐐻𐐲𐑉𐑌𐐼 𐐻𐐭 𐑄 𐐹𐑊𐐩𐑅 𐐱𐑂 𐐸𐐮𐑆 𐐮𐑌𐐸𐐯𐑉𐐮𐐻𐐲𐑌𐑅; 𐐰𐑌𐐼 𐑄𐐯𐑉 𐐶𐐱𐑆 𐐶𐐲𐑌𐑅 𐑋𐐬𐑉 𐐹𐐨𐑅 𐐯𐑅𐐻𐐰𐐺𐑊𐐮𐑇𐐻 𐐲𐑋𐐲𐑍 𐑄 𐐹𐐨𐐹𐑊 𐐱𐑂 𐐤𐐨𐑁𐐴. 𐐈𐑌𐐼 𐐣𐐬𐑉𐐬𐑌𐐴

𐐷𐐨𐑊𐐼𐐲𐐼 𐐲𐐹 𐑄 𐐿𐐲𐑋𐐰𐑌𐐼 𐐱𐑂 𐐸𐐮𐑆 𐐪𐑉𐑋𐐨𐑆 𐐮𐑌𐐻𐐭 𐑄 𐐸𐐰𐑌𐐼𐑆 𐐱𐑂 𐐸𐐮𐑆 𐑅𐐲𐑌, 𐐸𐐭𐑆 𐑌𐐩𐑋 𐐶𐐱𐑆 𐐣𐐬𐑉𐐬𐑌𐐴𐐸𐐪; 𐐰𐑌𐐼 𐐸𐐨 𐑉𐐨𐐻𐐴𐑉𐐼 𐐻𐐭 𐐸𐐮𐑆 𐐬𐑌 𐐸𐐵𐑅 𐑄𐐰𐐻 𐐸𐐨 𐑋𐐴𐐻 𐑅𐐹𐐯𐑌𐐼 𐑄 𐑉𐐨𐑋𐐩𐑌𐐼𐐲𐑉 𐐱𐑂 𐐸𐐮𐑆 𐐼𐐩𐑆 𐐮𐑌 𐐹𐐨𐑅. 𐐈𐑌𐐼 𐐑𐐩𐐸𐐬𐑉𐐲𐑌 𐐼𐐮𐐼 𐑉𐐨𐐻𐐲𐑉𐑌 𐐻𐐭 𐐸𐐮𐑆 𐐾𐐲𐐾𐑋𐐲𐑌𐐻 𐑅𐐨𐐻; 𐐰𐑌𐐼 𐐐𐐨𐑊𐐲𐑋𐐲𐑌 𐐼𐐮𐐼 𐐻𐐩𐐿 𐐲𐐹𐐱𐑌 𐐸𐐮𐑋 𐐲𐑀𐐯𐑌 𐐻𐐭 𐐹𐑉𐐨𐐽 𐐲𐑌𐐻𐐭 𐑄 𐐹𐐨𐐹𐐲𐑊 𐑄 𐐶𐐲𐑉𐐼 𐐱𐑂 𐐘𐐪𐐼: 𐑁𐐫𐑉 𐐺𐐨𐐿𐐫𐑆 𐐱𐑂 𐑅𐐬 𐑋𐐰𐑌𐐨 𐐶𐐫𐑉𐑆 𐐰𐑌𐐼 𐐿𐐲𐑌𐐻𐐯𐑌𐑇𐐲𐑌𐑆, 𐐮𐐻 𐐸𐐰𐐼 𐐺𐐨𐐿𐐲𐑋 𐐯𐐿𐑅𐐹𐐨𐐼𐐨𐐲𐑌𐐻 𐑄𐐰𐐻 𐐲 𐑉𐐯𐑀𐐷𐐲𐑊𐐩𐑇𐐲𐑌 𐑇𐐳𐐼 𐐺𐐨 𐑋𐐩𐐼 𐐲𐑀𐐯𐑌 𐐮𐑌 𐑄 𐐕𐐲𐑉𐐽: 𐑄𐐯𐑉𐑁𐐬𐑉 𐐐𐐨𐑊𐐲𐑋𐐲𐑌 𐐰𐑌𐐼 𐐸𐐮𐑆 𐐺𐑉𐐯𐑄𐑉𐐯𐑌 𐐶𐐯𐑌𐐻 𐑁𐐬𐑉𐑃, 𐐰𐑌𐐼 𐐼𐐮𐐼 𐐼𐐨𐐿𐑊𐐩𐑉 𐑄 𐐶𐐲𐑉𐐼 𐐱𐑂 𐐘𐐪𐐼 𐐶𐐮𐑃 𐑋𐐲𐐽 𐐹𐐵𐐲𐑉, 𐐲𐑌𐐻𐐭 𐑄 𐐿𐐲𐑌𐑂𐐮𐑌𐑅𐐮𐑍 𐐱𐑂 𐑋𐐯𐑌𐐨 𐐹𐐨𐐹𐐲𐑊 𐐱𐑂 𐑄𐐯𐑉 𐐶𐐮𐐿𐐯𐐼𐑌𐐯𐑅, 𐐸𐐶𐐮𐐽 𐐼𐐮𐐼 𐐿𐐫𐑆 𐑄𐐯𐑋 𐐻𐐭 𐑉𐐨𐐹𐐯𐑌𐐻 𐐱𐑂 𐑄𐐯𐑉 𐑅𐐮𐑌𐑆, 𐐰𐑌𐐼 𐐻𐐭 𐐺𐐨 𐐺𐐰𐐹𐐻𐐴𐑆𐐼 𐐲𐑌𐐻𐐭 𐑄 𐐢𐐫𐑉𐐼 𐑄𐐯𐑉 𐐘𐐪𐐼.

20. 𐐈𐑌𐐼 𐐮𐐻 𐐿𐐩𐑋 𐐻𐐭 𐐹𐐰𐑅 𐑄𐐰𐐻 𐑄𐐩 𐐼𐐮𐐼 𐐯𐑅𐐻𐐰𐐺𐑊𐐮𐑇 𐐲𐑀𐐯𐑌 𐑄 𐐕𐐲𐑉𐐽 𐐱𐑂 𐐘𐐪𐐼, 𐑃𐑉𐐭𐐵𐐻 𐐫𐑊 𐑄 𐑊𐐰𐑌𐐼; 𐐷𐐩, 𐐰𐑌𐐼 𐑉𐐯𐑀𐐷𐐲𐑊𐐩𐑇𐐲𐑌𐑆 𐐶𐐲𐑉 𐑋𐐩𐐼 𐐿𐐲𐑌𐑅𐐲𐑉𐑌𐐮𐑍 𐑄 𐑊𐐫. 𐐈𐑌𐐼 𐑄𐐯𐑉 𐐾𐐲𐐾𐐯𐑆 𐐰𐑌𐐼 𐑄𐐯𐑉 𐐽𐐨𐑁 𐐾𐐲𐐾𐐯𐑆 𐐶𐐲𐑉 𐐽𐐬𐑆𐑌. 𐐈𐑌𐐼 𐑄 𐐹𐐨𐐹𐐲𐑊 𐐱𐑂 𐐤𐐨𐑁𐐴 𐐺𐐨𐑀𐐰𐑌 𐐻𐐭 𐐹𐑉𐐱𐑅𐐹𐐲𐑉 𐐲𐑀𐐯𐑌 𐐮𐑌 𐑄 𐑊𐐰𐑌𐐼, 𐐰𐑌𐐼 𐐺𐐨𐑀𐐰𐑌 𐐻𐐭 𐑋𐐲𐑊𐐻𐐮𐐹𐑊𐐴 𐐰𐑌𐐼 𐐻𐐭 𐐶𐐰𐐿𐑅 𐐯𐐿𐑅𐐨𐐼𐐮𐑍 𐑅𐐻𐑉𐐫𐑍 𐐲𐑀𐐯𐑌 𐐮𐑌 𐑄 𐑊𐐰𐑌𐐼. 𐐈𐑌𐐼 𐑄𐐩 𐐺𐐨𐑀𐐰𐑌 𐐻𐐭 𐑀𐑉𐐬 𐐯𐐿𐑅𐐨𐐼𐐮𐑍 𐑉𐐮𐐽; 𐐺𐐲𐐻 𐑌𐐱𐐻𐐶𐐮𐑄𐑅𐐻𐐰𐑌𐐼𐐮𐑍 𐑄𐐯𐑉 𐑉𐐮𐐽𐐯𐑆, 𐐬𐑉 𐑄𐐯𐑉 𐑅𐐻𐑉𐐯𐑍𐑃, 𐐬𐑉 𐑄𐐯𐑉 𐐹𐑉𐐱𐑅𐐹𐐯𐑉𐐮𐐻𐐨, 𐑄𐐩 𐐶𐐲𐑉 𐑌𐐱𐐻 𐑊𐐮𐑁𐐻𐐯𐐼 𐐲𐐹 𐐮𐑌 𐑄 𐐹𐑉𐐴𐐼 𐐱𐑂 𐑄𐐯𐑉 𐐴𐑆; 𐑌𐐨𐑄𐐲𐑉 𐐶𐐲𐑉 𐑄𐐩 𐑅𐑊𐐬 𐐻𐐭 𐑉𐐨𐑋𐐯𐑋𐐺𐐲𐑉 𐑄 𐐢𐐫𐑉𐐼 𐑄𐐯𐑉 𐐘𐐪𐐼; 𐐺𐐲𐐻 𐑄𐐩 𐐼𐐮𐐼 𐐸𐐲𐑋𐐺𐑊 𐑄𐐯𐑋𐑅𐐯𐑊𐑂𐑆 𐐯𐐿𐑅𐐨𐐼𐐮𐑍𐑊𐐨 𐐺𐐨𐑁𐐬𐑉 𐐸𐐮𐑋; 𐐷𐐩, 𐑄𐐩 𐐼𐐮𐐼 𐑉𐐨𐑋𐐯𐑋𐐺𐐲𐑉 𐐸𐐵 𐑀𐑉𐐩𐐻 𐑃𐐮𐑍𐑆 𐑄 𐐢𐐫𐑉𐐼 𐐸𐐰𐐼 𐐼𐐲𐑌 𐑁𐐫𐑉 𐑄𐐯𐑋, 𐑄𐐰𐐻 𐐸𐐨 𐐸𐐰𐐼 𐐼𐐮𐑊𐐮𐑂𐐲𐑉𐐼 𐑄𐐯𐑋 𐑁𐑉𐐱𐑋 𐐼𐐯𐑃, 𐐰𐑌𐐼 𐑁𐑉𐐱𐑋 𐐺𐐱𐑌𐐼𐑆, 𐐰𐑌𐐼 𐑁𐑉𐐱𐑋 𐐹𐑉𐐮𐑆𐐲𐑌𐑆, 𐐰𐑌𐐼 𐑁𐑉𐐱𐑋 𐐫𐑊 𐑋𐐰𐑌𐐲𐑉 𐐱𐑂 𐐰𐑁𐑊𐐮𐐿𐑇𐐲𐑌𐑆; 𐐰𐑌𐐼 𐐸𐐨 𐐸𐐰𐐼 𐐼𐐮𐑊𐐮𐑂𐐲𐑉𐐼 𐑄𐐯𐑋 𐐵𐐻 𐐱𐑂 𐑄 𐐸𐐰𐑌𐐼𐑆 𐐱𐑂 𐑄𐐯𐑉 𐐯𐑌𐐯𐑋𐐨𐑆. 𐐈𐑌𐐼 𐑄𐐩 𐐼𐐮𐐼 𐐹𐑉𐐩 𐐲𐑌𐐻𐐭 𐑄 𐐢𐐫𐑉𐐼 𐑄𐐯𐑉 𐐘𐐪𐐼 𐐿𐐲𐑌𐐻𐐮𐑌𐐷𐐭𐐲𐑊𐐨, 𐐮𐑌𐑅𐐬𐑋𐐲𐐽 𐑄𐐰𐐻 𐑄 𐐢𐐫𐑉𐐼 𐐼𐐮𐐼 𐐺𐑊𐐯𐑅 𐑄𐐯𐑋, 𐐰𐐿𐐫𐑉𐐼𐐮𐑍 𐐻𐐭 𐐸𐐮𐑆 𐐶𐐲𐑉𐐼, 𐑅𐐬 𐑄𐐰𐐻 𐑄𐐩 𐐼𐐮𐐼 𐐶𐐰𐐿𐑅 𐑅𐐻𐑉𐐫𐑍, 𐐰𐑌𐐼 𐐹𐑉𐐱𐑅𐐹𐐲𐑉 𐐮𐑌 𐑄 𐑊𐐰𐑌𐐼. 𐐈𐑌𐐼 𐐮𐐻 𐐿𐐩𐑋 𐐻𐐭 𐐹𐐰𐑅 𐑄𐐰𐐻 𐐫𐑊 𐑄𐐨𐑆 𐑃𐐮𐑍𐑆 𐐶𐐲𐑉 𐐼𐐲𐑌. 𐐈𐑌𐐼 𐐐𐐨𐑊𐐲𐑋𐐲𐑌 𐐼𐐴𐐼, 𐐮𐑌 𐑄 𐑃𐐲𐑉𐐻𐐨 𐐰𐑌𐐼 𐑁𐐮𐑁𐑃 𐐷𐐨𐑉 𐐱𐑂 𐑄 𐑉𐐩𐑌 𐐱𐑂 𐑄 𐐾𐐲𐐾𐐯𐑆 𐐬𐑂𐐲𐑉 𐑄 𐐹𐐨𐐹𐐲𐑊 𐐱𐑂 𐐤𐐨𐑁𐐴.

𐐕𐐰𐐹𐐻𐐲𐑉 XXX.

1. 𐐈𐑌𐐼 𐐮𐐻 𐐿𐐩𐑋 𐐻𐐭 𐐹𐐰𐑅 𐐮𐑌 𐑄 𐐿𐐲𐑋𐐯𐑌𐑅𐑋𐐲𐑌𐐻 𐐱𐑂 𐑄 𐑃𐐲𐑉𐐻𐐨 𐐰𐑌𐐼 𐑅𐐮𐐿𐑅𐑃 𐐷𐐨𐑉 𐐱𐑂 𐑄 𐑉𐐩𐑌 𐐱𐑂 𐑄 𐐾𐐲𐐾𐐯𐑆 𐐬𐑂𐐲𐑉 𐑄 𐐹𐐨𐐹𐐲𐑊 𐐱𐑂 𐐤𐐨𐑁𐐴, 𐑄𐐰𐐻 𐐟𐐮𐐺𐑊𐐲𐑌 𐐻𐐳𐐿 𐐹𐐲𐑆𐐯𐑇𐐲𐑌 𐐱𐑂 𐑄𐐬𐑆 𐑅𐐩𐐿𐑉𐐯𐐼 𐑃𐐮𐑍𐑆 𐐸𐐶𐐮𐐽 𐐸𐐰𐐼 𐐺𐐮𐑌 𐐼𐐮𐑊𐐮𐑂𐐲𐑉𐐼 𐐲𐑌𐐻𐐭 𐐐𐐨𐑊𐐲𐑋𐐲𐑌 𐐺𐐴 𐐈𐑊𐑋𐐲; 𐐰𐑌𐐼 𐐸𐐨 𐐶𐐱𐑆 𐐲 𐐾𐐲𐑅𐐻 𐑋𐐰𐑌, 𐐰𐑌𐐼 𐐸𐐨 𐐼𐐮𐐼 𐐶𐐫𐐿 𐐲𐐹𐑉𐐴𐐻𐑊𐐨 𐐺𐐨𐑁𐐬𐑉 𐐘𐐪𐐼; 𐐰𐑌𐐼 𐐸𐐨 𐐼𐐮𐐼 𐐱𐐺𐑆𐐲𐑉𐑂 𐐻𐐭 𐐼𐐭 𐑀𐐳𐐼 𐐿𐐱𐑌𐐻𐐮𐑌𐐷𐐭𐐲𐑊𐐨, 𐐻𐐭 𐐿𐐨𐐹 𐑄 𐐿𐐲𐑋𐐰𐑌𐐼𐑋𐐲𐑌𐐻𐑅 𐐱𐑂 𐑄 𐐢𐐫𐑉𐐼 𐐸𐐮𐑆 𐐘𐐪𐐼; 𐐰𐑌𐐼 𐐫𐑊𐑅𐐬 𐐼𐐮𐐼 𐐸𐐮𐑆 𐐺𐑉𐐲𐑄𐐲𐑉.

2. 𐐈𐑌𐐼 𐐮𐐻 𐐿𐐩𐑋 𐐻𐐭 𐐹𐐰𐑅 𐑄𐐰𐐻 𐐣𐐬𐑉𐐬𐑌𐐴 𐐼𐐴𐐼 𐐫𐑊𐑅𐐬: 𐐰𐑌𐐼 𐑄𐐲𐑅 𐐯𐑌𐐼𐐯𐐼 𐑄 𐑃𐐲𐑉𐐻𐐨 𐐰𐑌𐐼 𐑅𐐮𐐿𐑅𐑃 𐐷𐐨𐑉 𐐱𐑂 𐑄 𐑉𐐩𐑌 𐐱𐑂 𐑄 𐐾𐐲𐐾𐐯𐑆. 𐐈𐑌𐐼 𐐮𐐻 𐐿𐐩𐑋 𐐻𐐭 𐐹𐐰𐑅 𐑄𐐰𐐻 𐐮𐑌 𐑄 𐑃𐐲𐑉𐐻𐐨 𐐰𐑌𐐼 𐑅𐐯𐑂𐐲𐑌𐑃 𐐷𐐨𐑉 𐐱𐑂 𐑄 𐑉𐐩𐑌 𐐱𐑂 𐑄 𐐾𐐲𐐾𐐯𐑆, 𐑄𐐯𐑉 𐐶𐐱𐑆 𐐲 𐑊𐐪𐑉𐐾 𐐿𐐲𐑋𐐹𐐲𐑌𐐨 𐐱𐑂 𐑋𐐯𐑌, 𐐨𐑂𐐲𐑌 𐐻𐐭 𐑄 𐐲𐑋𐐵𐑌𐐻 𐐱𐑂 𐑁𐐴𐑂 𐑃𐐵𐑆𐐲𐑌𐐼 𐐰𐑌𐐼 𐑁𐐬𐑉 𐐸𐐲𐑌𐐼𐑉𐐯𐐼 𐑋𐐯𐑌, 𐐶𐐮𐑃 𐑄𐐯𐑉 𐐶𐐴𐑂𐑆 𐐰𐑌𐐼 𐑄𐐯𐑉 𐐽𐐮𐑊𐐼𐑉𐐯𐑌, 𐐼𐐨𐐹𐐪𐑉𐐻𐐯𐐼 𐐵𐐻 𐐱𐑂 𐑄 𐑊𐐰𐑌𐐼 𐐱𐑂 𐐞𐐰𐑉𐐲𐐸𐐯𐑋𐑊𐐲, 𐐮𐑌𐐻𐐭 𐑄 𐑊𐐰𐑌𐐼 𐐸𐐶𐐮𐐽 𐐶𐐱𐑆 𐑌𐐫𐑉𐑃𐐶𐐲𐑉𐐼.

3. 𐐈𐑌𐐼 𐐮𐐻 𐐿𐐩𐑋 𐐻𐐭 𐐹𐐰𐑅 𐑄𐐰𐐻 𐐐𐐩𐑀𐐱𐑃, 𐐸𐐨 𐐺𐐨𐐮𐑍 𐐰𐑌 𐐯𐐿𐑅𐐨𐐼𐐮𐑍 𐐿𐐷𐐭𐑉𐐨𐐲𐑅 𐑋𐐰𐑌, 𐑄𐐯𐑉𐑁𐐬𐑉 𐐸𐐨 𐐶𐐯𐑌𐐻 𐑁𐐬𐑉𐑃 𐐰𐑌𐐼 𐐺𐐮𐑊𐐻 𐐸𐐮𐑋 𐐰𐑌 𐐯𐐿𐑅𐐨𐐼𐐮𐑍 𐑊𐐪𐑉𐐾 𐑇𐐮𐐹, 𐐱𐑌 𐑄 𐐺𐐫𐑉𐐼𐐲𐑉𐑆 𐐱𐑂 𐑄 𐑊𐐰𐑌𐐼 𐐒𐐵𐑌𐐻𐐮𐑁𐐳𐑊, 𐐺𐐴 𐑄 𐑊𐐰𐑌𐐼 𐐔𐐯𐑅𐐬𐑊𐐩𐑇𐐲𐑌, 𐐰𐑌𐐼 𐑊𐐫𐑌𐐽𐐻 𐐮𐐻 𐑁𐐬𐑉𐑃 𐐮𐑌𐐻𐐭 𐑄 𐐶𐐯𐑅𐐻 𐑅𐐨, 𐐺𐐴 𐑄 𐑌𐐰𐑉𐐬 𐑌𐐯𐐿 𐐸𐐶𐐮𐐽 𐑊𐐯𐐼 𐐮𐑌𐐻𐐭 𐑄 𐑊𐐰𐑌𐐼 𐑌𐐫𐑉𐑃𐐶𐐲𐑉𐐼. 𐐈𐑌𐐼 𐐺𐐨𐐸𐐬𐑊𐐼, 𐑄𐐯𐑉 𐐶𐐲𐑉 𐑋𐐯𐑌𐐨 𐐱𐑂 𐑄 𐐤𐐨𐑁𐐴𐐻𐑅 𐐸𐐭

𐐼𐐮𐐼 𐑅𐐩𐑊 𐑁𐐬𐑉𐑃 𐐶𐐮𐑃 𐑋𐐲𐐽 𐐹𐑉𐐬𐑂𐐮𐑈𐐲𐑌𐑆, 𐐰𐑌𐐼 𐐫𐑊𐑅𐐬 𐑋𐐯𐑌𐐨 𐐶𐐮𐑋𐐯𐑌 𐐰𐑌𐐼 𐐽𐐮𐑊𐐼𐑉𐐯𐑌; 𐐰𐑌𐐼 𐑄𐐩 𐐻𐐳𐐿 𐑄𐐯𐑉 𐐿𐐬𐑉𐑅 𐑌𐐫𐑉𐑃𐐶𐐲𐑉𐐼. 𐐈𐑌𐐼 𐑄𐐲𐑅 𐐯𐑌𐐼𐐯𐐼 𐑄 𐑃𐐲𐑉𐐻𐐨 𐐰𐑌𐐼 𐑅𐐯𐑂𐐯𐑌𐑃 𐐷𐐨𐑉. 𐐈𐑌𐐼 𐐮𐑌 𐑄 𐑃𐐲𐑉𐐻𐐨 𐐰𐑌𐐼 𐐩𐐻𐑃 𐐷𐐨𐑉, 𐑄𐐮𐑅 𐑋𐐰𐑌 𐐺𐐮𐑊𐐻 𐐲𐑄𐐲𐑉 𐑇𐐮𐐹𐑅. 𐐈𐑌𐐼 𐑄 𐑁𐐲𐑉𐑅𐐻 𐑇𐐮𐐹 𐐼𐐮𐐼 𐐫𐑊𐑅𐐬 𐑉𐐨𐐻𐐲𐑉𐑌, 𐐰𐑌𐐼 𐑋𐐯𐑌𐐨 𐑋𐐬𐑉 𐐹𐐨𐐹𐑊 𐐼𐐮𐐼 𐐯𐑌𐐻𐐲𐑉 𐐮𐑌𐐻𐐭 𐐮𐐻; 𐐰𐑌𐐼 𐑄𐐩 𐐫𐑊𐑅𐐬 𐐻𐐳𐐿 𐑋𐐲𐐽 𐐹𐑉𐐬𐑂𐐮𐑈𐐲𐑌𐑆, 𐐰𐑌𐐼 𐑅𐐯𐐻 𐐵𐐻 𐐲𐑀𐐯𐑌 𐐻𐐭 𐑄 𐑊𐐰𐑌𐐼 𐑌𐐫𐑉𐑃𐐶𐐲𐑉𐐼.

4. 𐐈𐑌𐐼 𐐮𐐻 𐐗𐐩𐑋 𐐻𐐭 𐐹𐐰𐑅 𐑄𐐰𐐻 𐑄𐐩 𐐶𐐲𐑉 𐑌𐐯𐑂𐐲𐑉 𐐸𐐲𐑉𐐼 𐐱𐑂 𐑋𐐬𐑉. 𐐈𐑌𐐼 𐐶𐐨 𐑅𐐲𐐹𐐬𐑆 𐑄𐐰𐐻 𐑄𐐩 𐐶𐐲𐑉 𐐼𐑉𐐵𐑌𐐼 𐐮𐑌 𐑄 𐐼𐐯𐐹𐑃𐑅 𐐱𐑂 𐑄 𐑅𐐨. 𐐈𐑌𐐼 𐐮𐐻 𐐗𐐩𐑋 𐐻𐐭 𐐹𐐰𐑅 𐑄𐐰𐐻 𐐶𐐲𐑌 𐐲𐑄𐐲𐑉 𐑇𐐮𐐹 𐐫𐑊𐑅𐐬 𐐼𐐮𐐼 𐑅𐐩𐑊 𐑁𐐬𐑉𐑃; 𐐰𐑌𐐼 𐐸𐐶𐐮𐑄𐐲𐑉 𐑇𐐨 𐐼𐐮𐐼 𐑀𐐬, 𐐶𐐨 𐑌𐐬 𐑌𐐱𐐻. 𐐈𐑌𐐼 𐐮𐐻 𐐗𐐩𐑋 𐐻𐐭 𐐹𐐰𐑅 𐑄𐐰𐐻 𐐮𐑌 𐑄𐐮𐑅 𐐷𐐨𐑉 𐑄𐐯𐑉 𐐶𐐲𐑉 𐑋𐐯𐑌𐐨 𐐹𐐨𐐹𐑊 𐐸𐐭 𐐶𐐯𐑌𐐻 𐑁𐐬𐑉𐑃 𐐮𐑌𐐻𐐭 𐑄 𐑊𐐰𐑌𐐼 𐑌𐐫𐑉𐑃𐐶𐐲𐑉𐐼. 𐐈𐑌𐐼 𐑄𐐲𐑅 𐐯𐑌𐐼𐐯𐐼 𐑄 𐑃𐐲𐑉𐐻𐐨 𐐰𐑌𐐼 𐐩𐐻𐑃 𐐷𐐨𐑉.

5. 𐐈𐑌𐐼 𐐮𐐻 𐐗𐐩𐑋 𐐻𐐭 𐐹𐐰𐑅 𐐮𐑌 𐑄 𐑃𐐲𐑉𐐻𐐨 𐐰𐑌𐐼 𐑌𐐴𐑌𐑃 𐐷𐐨𐑉 𐐱𐑂 𐑄 𐑉𐐩𐑌 𐐱𐑂 𐑄 𐐖𐐲𐐾𐐯𐑆, 𐐟𐐮𐐺𐑊𐐲𐑌 𐐼𐐴𐐼 𐐫𐑊𐑅𐐬, 𐐰𐑌𐐼 𐐗𐐬𐑉𐐨𐐰𐑌𐐻𐐲𐑌 𐐸𐐰𐐼 𐑀𐐱𐑌 𐑁𐐬𐑉𐑃 𐐻𐐭 𐑄 𐑊𐐰𐑌𐐼 𐑌𐐫𐑉𐑃𐐶𐐲𐑉𐐼, 𐐮𐑌 𐐲 𐑇𐐮𐐹, 𐐻𐐭 𐐿𐐯𐑉𐐨 𐑁𐐬𐑉𐑃 𐐹𐑉𐐬𐑂𐐮𐑈𐐲𐑌𐑆 𐐲𐑌𐐻𐐭 𐑄 𐐹𐐨𐐹𐑊 𐐸𐐭 𐐸𐐰𐐼 𐑀𐐱𐑌 𐑁𐐬𐑉𐑃 𐐮𐑌𐐻𐐭 𐑄𐐰𐐻 𐑊𐐰𐑌𐐼; 𐑄𐐯𐑉𐑁𐐬𐑉 𐐮𐐻 𐐺𐐨𐐿𐐩𐑋 𐐯𐐿𐑅𐐹𐐨𐐼𐐨𐐲𐑌𐐻 𐑁𐐬𐑉 𐐟𐐮𐐺𐑊𐐲𐑌 𐐻𐐭 𐐿𐐱𐑌𐑁𐐲𐑉 𐑄𐐬𐑆 𐑅𐐩𐐿𐑉𐐯𐐼 𐑃𐐮𐑍𐑆, 𐐺𐐨𐑁𐐬𐑉 𐐸𐐮𐑆 𐐼𐐯𐑃, 𐐲𐐹𐐱𐑌 𐑄 𐑅𐐲𐑌 𐐱𐑂 𐐐𐐨𐑊𐐲𐑋𐐲𐑌, 𐐸𐐭 𐐶𐐲𐑆 𐐿𐐫𐑊𐐼 𐐐𐐨𐑊𐐲𐑋𐐲𐑌, 𐐺𐐨𐐮𐑍 𐐿𐐫𐑊𐐼 𐐰𐑁𐐻𐐲𐑉 𐑄 𐑌𐐩𐑋 𐐱𐑂 𐐸𐐮𐑆 𐑁𐐪𐑄𐐲𐑉. 𐐤𐐵 𐐺𐐨𐐸𐐬𐑊𐐼, 𐐫𐑊 𐑄𐐬𐑆 𐐯𐑌𐑀𐑉𐐩𐑂𐐮𐑍𐑆 𐐸𐐶𐐮𐐽 𐐶𐐲𐑉 𐐮𐑌 𐑄 𐐹𐐲𐑆𐐯𐑇𐐲𐑌 𐐱𐑂 𐐐𐐨𐑊𐐲𐑋𐐲𐑌, 𐐶𐐲𐑉 𐑉𐐮𐐻𐐲𐑌 𐐰𐑌𐐼 𐑅𐐯𐑌𐐻 𐑁𐐬𐑉𐑃 𐐲𐑋𐐲𐑍 𐑄 𐐽𐐮𐑊𐐼𐑉𐐯𐑌 𐐱𐑂 𐑋𐐯𐑌 𐑃𐑉𐐭𐐵𐐻 𐐫𐑊 𐑄 𐑊𐐰𐑌𐐼, 𐑅𐐩𐑂 𐐮𐐻 𐐶𐐲𐑉 𐑄𐐬𐑆 𐐹𐐪𐑉𐐻𐑅 𐐸𐐶𐐮𐐽 𐐸𐐰𐐼 𐐺𐐨𐑌 𐐿𐐲𐑋𐐰𐑌𐐼𐐯𐐼 𐐺𐐴 𐐈𐑊𐑋𐐲 𐑇𐐳𐐼 𐑌𐐱𐐻 𐑀𐐬 𐑁𐐬𐑉𐑃. 𐐤𐐯𐑂𐐲𐑉𐑄𐐯𐑊𐐯𐑅, 𐑄𐐨𐑆 𐑃𐐮𐑍𐑆 𐐶𐐲𐑉 𐐻𐐭 𐐺𐐨 𐐿𐐯𐐹𐐻 𐑅𐐩𐐿𐑉𐐯𐐼, 𐐰𐑌𐐼 𐐸𐐰𐑌𐐼𐐯𐐼 𐐼𐐵𐑌 𐑁𐑉𐐱𐑋 𐐶𐐲𐑌 𐐾𐐯𐑌𐐲𐑉𐐩𐑇𐐲𐑌 𐐻𐐭 𐐲𐑌𐐲𐑄𐐲𐑉; 𐑄𐐯𐑉𐑁𐐬𐑉, 𐐮𐑌 𐑄𐐮𐑅 𐐷𐐨𐑉, 𐑄𐐩 𐐸𐐰𐐼 𐐺𐐨𐑌 𐐿𐐱𐑌𐑁𐐲𐑉𐐼 𐐲𐐹𐐱𐑌 𐐐𐐨𐑊𐐲𐑋𐐲𐑌, 𐐺𐐨𐑁𐐬𐑉 𐑄 𐐼𐐯𐑃 𐐱𐑂 𐐟𐐮𐐺𐑊𐐲𐑌. 𐐈𐑌𐐼 𐐮𐐻 𐐗𐐩𐑋 𐐻𐐭 𐐹𐐰𐑅 𐐫𐑊𐑅𐐬 𐐮𐑌 𐑄𐐮𐑅 𐐷𐐨𐑉, 𐑄𐐰𐐻 𐑄𐐯𐑉 𐐶𐐲𐑉 𐑅𐐲𐑋 𐐼𐐮𐑅𐐯𐑌𐐻𐐲𐑉𐑆 𐐸𐐭 𐐸𐐰𐐼 𐑀𐐱𐑌 𐑁𐐬𐑉𐑃 𐐲𐑌𐐻𐐭 𐑄 𐐢𐐩𐑋𐐲𐑌𐐴𐐻𐑅; 𐐰𐑌𐐼 𐑄𐐩 𐐶𐐲𐑉 𐑅𐐻𐐲𐑉𐐼 𐐲𐐹 𐐲𐑀𐐯𐑌 𐐻𐐭 𐐰𐑍𐑀𐐲𐑉 𐐲𐑀𐐯𐑌𐑅𐐻 𐑄 𐐤𐐨𐑁𐐴𐐻𐑅. 𐐈𐑌𐐼 𐐫𐑊𐑅𐐬 𐐮𐑌 𐑄𐐮𐑅 𐑅𐐩𐑋 𐐷𐐨𐑉, 𐑄𐐩 𐐗𐐩𐑋 𐐼𐐵𐑌 𐐶𐐮𐑃 𐐲 𐑌𐐭𐑋𐐲𐑉𐐲𐑅 𐐪𐑉𐑋𐐨 𐐻𐐭 𐐶𐐫𐑉 𐐲𐑀𐐯𐑌𐑅𐐻 𐑄 𐐹𐐨𐐹𐑊 𐐱𐑂 𐐣𐐬𐑉𐐬𐑌𐐴𐐸𐐪, 𐐫𐑉 𐐲𐑀𐐯𐑌𐑅𐐻 𐑄 𐐪𐑉𐑋𐐨 𐐱𐑂 𐐣𐐬𐑉𐐬𐑌𐐴𐐸𐐪, 𐐮𐑌 𐑄 𐐸𐐶𐐮𐐽 𐑄𐐩 𐐶𐐲𐑉 𐐺𐐨𐐻𐐲𐑌, 𐐰𐑌𐐼 𐐼𐑉𐐮𐑂𐐲𐑌 𐐺𐐰𐐿 𐐲𐑀𐐯𐑌 𐐻𐐭 𐑄𐐯𐑉 𐐬𐑌 𐑊𐐰𐑌𐐼𐑆, 𐑅𐐲𐑁𐐲𐑉𐐮𐑍 𐑀𐑉𐐩𐐻 𐑊𐐱𐑅. 𐐈𐑌𐐼 𐑄𐐲𐑅 𐐯𐑌𐐼𐐯𐐼 𐑄 𐑃𐐲𐑉𐐻𐐨 𐐰𐑌𐐼 𐑌𐐴𐑌𐑃 𐐷𐐨𐑉 𐐱𐑂 𐑄 𐑉𐐩𐑌 𐐱𐑂 𐑄 𐐖𐐲𐐾𐐯𐑆 𐐬𐑂𐐲𐑉 𐑄 𐐹𐐨𐐹𐑊 𐐱𐑂 𐐤𐐨𐑁𐐴. 𐐈𐑌𐐼 𐑄𐐲𐑅 𐐯𐑌𐐼𐐯𐐼 𐑄 𐐲𐐿𐐵𐑌𐐻 𐐱𐑂 𐐈𐑊𐑋𐐲, 𐐰𐑌𐐼 𐐐𐐨𐑊𐐲𐑋𐐲𐑌 𐐸𐐮𐑆 𐑅𐐲𐑌, 𐐰𐑌𐐼 𐐫𐑊𐑅𐐬 𐐟𐐮𐐺𐑊𐐲𐑌, 𐐸𐐭 𐐶𐐲𐑆 𐐸𐐮𐑆 𐑅𐐲𐑌.

𐐜 𐐒𐐳𐐿 𐐱𐑂 𐐐𐐨𐑊𐐰𐑋𐐲𐑌.

𐐕𐐈𐐑𐐓𐐊𐐡 I.

𐐈𐑌 𐐰𐐿𐐵𐑌𐐻 𐐱𐑂 𐑄 𐐤𐐨𐑁𐐴𐐻𐑅. 𐐜𐐯𐑉 𐐶𐐫𐑉𐑆 𐐰𐑌𐐼 𐐿𐐱𐑌𐐻𐐯𐑌𐑇𐐲𐑌𐑆, 𐐰𐑌𐐼 𐑄𐐯𐑉 𐐼𐐮𐑅𐐯𐑌𐑇𐐲𐑌𐑆. 𐐈𐑌𐐼 𐐫𐑊𐑅𐐬 𐑄 𐐹𐑉𐐱𐑁𐐯𐑅𐐨𐑆 𐐱𐑂 𐑋𐐯𐑌𐐨 𐐸𐐬𐑊𐐨 𐐹𐑉𐐱𐑁𐐯𐐻𐑅, 𐐺𐐨𐑁𐐬𐑉 𐑄 𐐿𐐲𐑋𐐮𐑍 𐐱𐑂 𐐗𐑉𐐴𐑅𐐻, 𐐰𐐿𐐬𐑉𐐼𐐮𐑍 𐐻𐐭 𐑄 𐑉𐐯𐐿𐐲𐑉𐐼𐑆 𐐱𐑂 𐐐𐐨𐑊𐐰𐑋𐐲𐑌, 𐐸𐐭 𐐶𐐱𐑆 𐑄 𐑅𐐲𐑌 𐐱𐑂 𐐐𐐨𐑊𐐰𐑋𐐲𐑌, 𐐰𐑌𐐼 𐐫𐑊𐑅𐐬 𐐰𐐿𐐬𐑉𐐼𐐮𐑍 𐐻𐐭 𐑄 𐑉𐐯𐐿𐐲𐑉𐐼𐑆 𐐱𐑂 𐐸𐐮𐑆 𐑅𐐲𐑌𐑆, 𐐨𐑂𐐲𐑌 𐐼𐐵𐑌 𐐻𐐭 𐑄 𐐿𐐲𐑋𐐮𐑍 𐐱𐑂 𐐗𐑉𐐴𐑅𐐻. 𐐈𐑌𐐼 𐐫𐑊𐑅𐐬 𐑋𐐯𐑌𐐨 𐐱𐑂 𐑄 𐐢𐐩𐑋𐐲𐑌𐐴𐐻𐑅 𐐪𐑉 𐐿𐐱𐑌𐑂𐐲𐑉𐐻𐐯𐐼. 𐐈𐑌 𐐰𐐿𐐵𐑌𐐻 𐐱𐑂 𐑄𐐯𐑉 𐐿𐐱𐑌𐑂𐐲𐑉𐑇𐐲𐑌. 𐐈𐑌 𐐰𐐿𐐵𐑌𐐻 𐐱𐑂 𐑄 𐑉𐐴𐐽𐐲𐑅𐑌𐐯𐑅 𐐱𐑂 𐑄 𐐢𐐩𐑋𐐲𐑌𐐴𐐻𐑅, 𐐰𐑌𐐼 𐑄 𐐶𐐮𐐿𐐯𐐼𐑌𐐯𐑅 𐐰𐑌𐐼 𐐲𐐺𐐱𐑋𐐮𐑌𐐩𐑇𐐲𐑌𐑆 𐐱𐑂 𐑄 𐐤𐐨𐑁𐐴𐐻𐑅, 𐐰𐐿𐐬𐑉𐐼𐐮𐑍 𐐻𐐭 𐑄 𐑉𐐯𐐿𐐲𐑉𐐼 𐐱𐑂 𐐐𐐨𐑊𐐰𐑋𐐲𐑌 𐐰𐑌𐐼 𐐸𐐮𐑆 𐑅𐐲𐑌𐑆, 𐐨𐑂𐐲𐑌 𐐼𐐵𐑌 𐐻𐐭 𐑄 𐐿𐐲𐑋𐐮𐑍 𐐱𐑂 𐐗𐑉𐐴𐑅𐐻, 𐐸𐐶𐐮𐐽 𐐮𐑆 𐐿𐐫𐑊𐐼 𐑄 𐐺𐐳𐐿 𐐱𐑂 𐐐𐐨𐑊𐐰𐑋𐐲𐑌, 𐐯𐐻𐑅.

1. 𐐈𐑌𐐼 𐑌𐐵 𐐺𐐨𐐸𐐬𐑊𐐼, 𐐮𐐻 𐐿𐐩𐑋 𐐻𐐭 𐐹𐐰𐑅 𐐮𐑌 𐑄 𐐿𐐱𐑋𐐯𐑌𐑅𐑋𐐯𐑌𐐻 𐐱𐑂 𐑄 𐑁𐐫𐑉𐐻𐐨𐐯𐑃 𐐷𐐨𐑉 𐐱𐑂 𐑄 𐑉𐐩𐑌 𐐱𐑂 𐑄 𐐾𐐲𐐾𐐯𐑆 𐐬𐑂𐐲𐑉 𐑄 𐐹𐐨𐐹𐑊 𐐱𐑂 𐐤𐐨𐑁𐐴, 𐑄𐐯𐑉 𐐺𐐨𐑀𐐰𐑌 𐐻𐐭 𐐺𐐨 𐐩 𐑅𐐨𐑉𐐨𐐲𐑅 𐐼𐐮𐑁𐐮𐐿𐐲𐑊𐐻𐐨 𐐲𐑋𐐲𐑍 𐑄 𐐹𐐨𐐹𐑊 𐐱𐑂 𐑄 𐐤𐐨𐑁𐐴𐐻𐑅. 𐐙𐐫𐑉 𐐺𐐨𐐸𐐬𐑊𐐼, 𐐑𐐩𐐸𐐬𐑉𐐲𐑌 𐐸𐐰𐐼 𐐼𐐴𐐼, 𐐰𐑌𐐼 𐑀𐐱𐑌 𐑄 𐐶𐐩 𐐱𐑂 𐐫𐑊 𐑄 𐐲𐑉𐑃; 𐑄𐐯𐑉𐑁𐐬𐑉 𐑄𐐯𐑉 𐐺𐐨𐑀𐐰𐑌 𐐻𐐭 𐐺𐐨 𐐩 𐑅𐐨𐑉𐐨𐐲𐑅 𐐿𐐱𐑌𐐻𐐯𐑌𐑇𐐲𐑌 𐐿𐐱𐑌𐑅𐐲𐑉𐑌𐐮𐑍 𐐸𐐭 𐑇𐐳𐐼 𐐸𐐰𐑂 𐑄 𐐾𐐲𐐾𐑋𐐯𐑌𐐻-𐑅𐐨𐐻 𐐲𐑋𐐲𐑍 𐑄 𐐺𐑉𐐯𐑄𐑉𐐯𐑌, 𐐸𐐭 𐐶𐐲𐑉 𐑄 𐑅𐐲𐑌𐑆 𐐱𐑂 𐐑𐐩𐐸𐐬𐑉𐐲𐑌. 𐐤𐐵 𐑄𐐨𐑆 𐐪𐑉 𐑄𐐯𐑉 𐑌𐐩𐑋𐑆 𐐸𐐭 𐐼𐐮𐐼 𐐿𐐱𐑌𐐻𐐯𐑌𐐼 𐑁𐐫𐑉 𐑄 𐐾𐐲𐐾𐑋𐐯𐑌𐐻-𐑅𐐨𐐻, 𐐸𐐭 𐐼𐐮𐐼 𐐫𐑊𐑅𐐬 𐐿𐐫𐑆 𐑄 𐐹𐐨𐐹𐑊 𐐻𐐭 𐐿𐐱𐑌𐐻𐐯𐑌𐐼: 𐐑𐐩𐐸𐐬𐑉𐐲𐑌, 𐐑𐐩𐐰𐑌𐐿𐐴, 𐐑𐐰𐐿𐐷𐐭𐑋𐐯𐑌𐐴. 𐐤𐐵 𐑄𐐨𐑆 𐐪𐑉 𐑌𐐱𐐻 𐐫𐑊 𐑄 𐑅𐐲𐑌𐑆 𐐱𐑂 𐐑𐐩𐐸𐐬𐑉𐐲𐑌, (𐑁𐐫𐑉 𐐸𐐨 𐐸𐐰𐐼 𐑋𐐯𐑌𐐨,) 𐐺𐐲𐐻 𐑄𐐨𐑆 𐐪𐑉 𐑄𐐩 𐐸𐐭 𐐼𐐮𐐼 𐐿𐐱𐑌𐐻𐐯𐑌𐐼 𐑁𐐫𐑉 𐑄 𐐾𐐲𐐾𐑋𐐯𐑌𐐻-𐑅𐐨𐐻; 𐑄𐐯𐑉𐑁𐐬𐑉, 𐑄𐐩 𐐼𐐮𐐼 𐐿𐐫𐑆 𐑃𐑉𐐨 𐐼𐐮𐑂𐐮𐑈𐐲𐑌𐑆 𐐲𐑋𐐲𐑍 𐑄 𐐹𐐨𐐹𐑊. 𐐤𐐯𐑂𐐲𐑉𐑄𐐲𐑊𐐯𐑅, 𐐮𐐻 𐐿𐐩𐑋 𐐻𐐭 𐐹𐐰𐑅 𐑄𐐰𐐻 𐐑𐐩𐐸𐐬𐑉𐐲𐑌 𐐶𐐱𐑆 𐐲𐐹𐐱𐐮𐑌𐐻𐐯𐐼 𐐺𐐴 𐑄 𐑂𐐱𐐮𐑅 𐐱𐑂 𐑄 𐐹𐐨𐐹𐑊 𐐻𐐭 𐐺𐐨 𐐽𐐨𐑁 𐐾𐐲𐐾 𐐰𐑌𐐼 𐐩 𐑀𐐲𐑂𐐲𐑉𐑌𐐲𐑉 𐐬𐑂𐐲𐑉 𐑄 𐐹𐐨𐐹𐑊 𐐱𐑂 𐐤𐐨𐑁𐐴.

2. 𐐈𐑌𐐼 𐐮𐐻 𐐿𐐩𐑋 𐐻𐐭 𐐹𐐰𐑅 𐑄𐐰𐐻 𐐑𐐰𐐿𐐷𐐭𐑋𐐯𐑌𐐴, 𐐸𐐶𐐯𐑌 𐐸𐐨 𐑅𐐫 𐑄𐐰𐐻 𐐸𐐨 𐐿𐐳𐐼 𐑌𐐱𐐻 𐐱𐐺𐐻𐐩𐑌 𐑄 𐐾𐐲𐐾𐑋𐐯𐑌𐐻-𐑅𐐨𐐻, 𐐸𐐨 𐐼𐐮𐐼 𐐷𐐭𐑌𐐴𐐻 𐐶𐐮𐑄 𐑄 𐑂𐐱𐐮𐑅 𐐱𐑂 𐑄 𐐹𐐨𐐹𐑊. 𐐒𐐲𐐻 𐐺𐐨𐐸𐐬𐑊𐐼, 𐐑𐐩𐐰𐑌𐐿𐐴, 𐐰𐑌𐐼 𐑄𐐰𐐻 𐐹𐐪𐑉𐐻 𐐱𐑂 𐑄 𐐹𐐨𐐹𐑊 𐑄𐐰𐐻 𐐶𐐲𐑉 𐐼𐐯𐑆𐐴𐑉𐐲𐑅 𐑄𐐰𐐻 𐐸𐐨 𐑇𐐳𐐼 𐐺𐐨 𐑄𐐯𐑉 𐑀𐐲𐑂𐐲𐑉𐑌𐐲𐑉, 𐐶𐐱𐑆 𐐯𐐿𐑅𐐨𐐼𐐮𐑍𐑊𐐨 𐑉𐐱𐑃; 𐑄𐐯𐑉𐑁𐐬𐑉, 𐐸𐐨 𐐶𐐱𐑆 𐐲𐐺𐐵𐐻 𐐻𐐭 𐑁𐑊𐐰𐐻𐐲𐑉 𐐲𐐶𐐩 𐑄𐐬𐑆 𐐹𐐨𐐹𐑊 𐐻𐐭 𐑉𐐴𐑆 𐐲𐐹 𐐮𐑌 𐑉𐐯𐐺𐐯𐑊𐐷𐐲𐑌 𐐲𐑀𐐯𐑌𐑅𐐻 𐑄𐐯𐑉 𐐺𐑉𐐯𐑄𐑉𐐯𐑌.

3. 𐐈𐑌𐐼 𐐮𐐻 𐐿𐐩𐑋 𐐻𐐭 𐐹𐐰𐑅, 𐐰𐑆 𐐸𐐨 𐐶𐐱𐑆 𐐲𐐺𐐵𐐻 𐐻𐐭 𐐼𐐭 𐑄𐐮𐑅, 𐐺𐐨𐐸𐐬𐑊𐐼, 𐐸𐐨 𐐶𐐱𐑆 𐐻𐐩𐐿𐑌, 𐐰𐑌𐐼 𐐶𐐱𐑆 𐐻𐑉𐐴𐐼 𐐰𐐿𐐬𐑉𐐼𐐮𐑍 𐐻𐐭 𐑄 𐑂𐐱𐐮𐑅 𐐱𐑂 𐑄 𐐹𐐨𐐹𐑊, 𐐰𐑌𐐼 𐐿𐐱𐑌𐐼𐐯𐑋𐐼 𐐲𐑌𐐻𐐭 𐐼𐐯𐑃; 𐑁𐐫𐑉 𐐸𐐨 𐐸𐐰𐐼 𐑉𐐩𐑆𐐼 𐐲𐐹 𐐮𐑌 𐑉𐐯𐐺𐐯𐑊𐐷𐐲𐑌 𐐰𐑌𐐼 𐑅𐐫𐐻 𐐻𐐭 𐐼𐐯𐑅𐐻𐑉𐐱𐐮 𐑄 𐑊𐐮𐐺𐐲𐑉𐐻𐐨 𐐱𐑂 𐑄 𐐹𐐨𐐹𐑊. 𐐤𐐵 𐐸𐐶𐐯𐑌 𐑄𐐬𐑆 𐐹𐐨𐐹𐑊 𐐸𐐭 𐐶𐐲𐑉 𐐼𐐯𐑆𐐴𐑉𐐲𐑅 𐑄𐐰𐐻 𐐸𐐨 𐑇𐐳𐐼 𐐺𐐨 𐑄𐐯𐑉 𐑀𐐲𐑂𐐲𐑉𐑌𐐲𐑉 𐑅𐐫 𐑄𐐰𐐻 𐐸𐐨 𐐶𐐱𐑆 𐐿𐐱𐑌𐐼𐐯𐑋𐐼 𐐲𐑌𐐻𐐭 𐐼𐐯𐑃, 𐑄𐐯𐑉𐑁𐐬𐑉 𐑄𐐩 𐐶𐐲𐑉 𐐰𐑍𐑀𐑉𐐨, 𐐰𐑌𐐼 𐐺𐐨𐐸𐐬𐑊𐐼, 𐑄𐐩 𐑅𐐯𐑌𐐻 𐑁𐐬𐑉𐑃 𐐶𐐲𐑌 𐐗𐐮𐑇𐐿𐐷𐐭𐑋𐐯𐑌, 𐐨𐑂𐐲𐑌 𐐻𐐭 𐑄 𐐾𐐲𐐾𐑋𐐯𐑌𐐻-𐑅𐐨𐐻 𐐱𐑂 𐐑𐐩𐐸𐐬𐑉𐐲𐑌, 𐐰𐑌𐐼 𐑋𐐲𐑉𐐼𐐲𐑉𐐼 𐐑𐐩𐐸𐐬𐑉𐐲𐑌 𐐰𐑆 𐐸𐐨 𐑅𐐰𐐻 𐐲𐐹𐐱𐑌 𐑄 𐐾𐐲𐐾𐑋𐐯𐑌𐐻-𐑅𐐨𐐻. 𐐈𐑌𐐼 𐐸𐐨 𐐶𐐱𐑆 𐐹𐐲𐑉𐑅𐐷𐐭𐐼 𐐺𐐴 𐑄 𐑅𐐲𐑉𐑂𐐲𐑌𐐻𐑅 𐐱𐑂 𐐑𐐩𐐸𐐬𐑉𐐲𐑌; 𐐺𐐲𐐻 𐐺𐐨𐐸𐐬𐑊𐐼, 𐑅𐐬 𐑅𐐹𐐨𐐼𐐨

𐐶𐐱𐑆 𐑄 𐑁𐑊𐐴𐐻 𐐱𐑂 𐐗𐐮𐑇𐐿𐐷𐐭𐑋𐐯𐑌, 𐑄𐐰𐐻 𐑌𐐬 𐑋𐐰𐑌 𐐿𐐳𐐼 𐐬𐑂𐐲𐑉𐐻𐐩𐐿 𐐸𐐮𐑋. 𐐈𐑌𐐼 𐐸𐐨 𐐶𐐯𐑌𐐻 𐐲𐑌𐐻𐐭 𐑄𐐬𐑆 𐑄𐐰𐐻 𐑅𐐯𐑌𐐻 𐐸𐐮𐑋, 𐐰𐑌𐐼 𐑄𐐩 𐐫𐑊 𐐯𐑌𐐻𐐲𐑉𐐼 𐐮𐑌𐐻𐐭 𐐲 𐐿𐐲𐑂𐐯𐑌𐐰𐑌𐐻, 𐐷𐐩, 𐑅𐐶𐐯𐑉𐐮𐑍 𐐺𐐴 𐑄𐐩𐑉 𐐯𐑂𐐲𐑉𐑊𐐰𐑅𐐻𐐮𐑍 𐐣𐐩𐐿𐐲𐑉, 𐑄𐐰𐐻 𐑄𐐩 𐐶𐐳𐐼 𐐻𐐯𐑊 𐑌𐐬 𐑋𐐰𐑌 𐑄𐐰𐐻 𐐗𐐮𐑇𐐿𐐷𐐭𐑋𐐯𐑌 𐐸𐐰𐐼 𐑋𐐲𐑉𐐼𐐲𐑉𐐼 𐐑𐐩𐐸𐐬𐑉𐐲𐑌; 𐑄𐐯𐑉𐑁𐐬𐑉 𐐗𐐮𐑇𐐿𐐷𐐭𐑋𐐯𐑌 𐐶𐐱𐑆 𐑌𐐱𐐻 𐑌𐐬𐑌 𐐲𐑋𐐲𐑍 𐑄 𐐹𐐨𐐹𐐲𐑊 𐐱𐑂 𐐤𐐨𐑁𐐴, 𐑁𐐫𐑉 𐐸𐐨 𐐶𐐱𐑆 𐐮𐑌 𐐼𐐮𐑅𐑀𐐴𐑆 𐐰𐐻 𐑄 𐐻𐐴𐑋 𐑄𐐰𐐻 𐐸𐐨 𐑋𐐲𐑉𐐼𐐲𐑉𐐼 𐐑𐐩𐐸𐐬𐑉𐐲𐑌. 𐐈𐑌𐐼 𐐗𐐮𐑇𐐿𐐷𐐭𐑋𐐯𐑌, 𐐰𐑌𐐼 𐐸𐐮𐑆 𐐺𐐰𐑌𐐼 𐐸𐐭 𐐸𐐰𐐼 𐐿𐐲𐑂𐐯𐑌𐐰𐑌𐐻𐐯𐐼 𐐶𐐮𐑄 𐐸𐐮𐑋, 𐐼𐐮𐐼 𐑋𐐮𐑍𐑀𐐲𐑊 𐑄𐐯𐑋𐑅𐐯𐑊𐑂𐑆 𐐲𐑋𐐲𐑍 𐑄 𐐹𐐨𐐹𐐲𐑊, 𐐮𐑌 𐐲 𐑋𐐰𐑌𐐲𐑉 𐑄𐐰𐐻 𐑄𐐩 𐐫𐑊 𐐿𐐳𐐼 𐑌𐐱𐐻 𐐺𐐨 𐑁𐐵𐑌𐐼; 𐐺𐐲𐐻 𐐰𐑆 𐑋𐐯𐑌𐐨 𐐰𐑆 𐐶𐐲𐑉 𐑁𐐵𐑌𐐼, 𐐶𐐲𐑉 𐐿𐐱𐑌𐐼𐐯𐑋𐐼 𐐲𐑌𐐻𐐭 𐐼𐐯𐑃. 𐐈𐑌𐐼 𐑌𐐵 𐐺𐐨𐐸𐐬𐑊𐐼, 𐐑𐐰𐐿𐐷𐐭𐑋𐐯𐑌𐐨 𐐶𐐱𐑆 𐐲𐐹𐑎𐑌𐐻𐐯𐐼, 𐐰𐐿𐐫𐑉𐐼𐐮𐑍 𐐻𐐭 𐑄 𐑂𐑎𐑅 𐐱𐑂 𐑄 𐐹𐐨𐐹𐐲𐑊, 𐐻𐐭 𐐺𐐨 𐐲 𐐽𐐨𐑁 𐐾𐐲𐐾 𐐰𐑌𐐼 𐐲 𐑀𐐲𐑂𐐲𐑉𐑌𐐲𐑉 𐐬𐑂𐐲𐑉 𐑄 𐐹𐐨𐐹𐐲𐑊, 𐐻𐐭 𐑉𐐩𐑌 𐐮𐑌 𐑄 𐑅𐐻𐐯𐐼 𐐱𐑂 𐐸𐐮𐑆 𐐺𐑉𐐲𐑄𐐲𐑉 𐐑𐐩𐐸𐐬𐑉𐐲𐑌; 𐐰𐑌𐐼 𐐮𐐻 𐐶𐐱𐑆 𐐰𐐿𐐫𐑉𐐼𐐮𐑍 𐐻𐐭 𐐸𐐮𐑆 𐑉𐐴𐐻. 𐐈𐑌𐐼 𐐫𐑊 𐑄𐐮𐑅 𐐶𐐱𐑆 𐐼𐐲𐑌 𐐮𐑌 𐑄 𐑁𐐫𐑉𐐻𐐨𐐯𐑃 𐐷𐐨𐑉 𐐱𐑂 𐑄 𐑉𐐩𐑌 𐐱𐑂 𐑄 𐐾𐐲𐐾𐐯𐑆; 𐐰𐑌𐐼 𐐮𐐻 𐐸𐐰𐐼 𐐰𐑌 𐐯𐑌𐐼.

4\. 𐐈𐑌𐐼 𐐮𐐻 𐐿𐐩𐑋 𐐻𐐭 𐐹𐐰𐑅 𐐮𐑌 𐑄 𐑁𐐫𐑉𐐻𐐨 𐐰𐑌𐐼 𐑁𐐲𐑉𐑅𐐻 𐐷𐐨𐑉 𐐱𐑂 𐑄 𐑉𐐩𐑌 𐐱𐑂 𐑄 𐐾𐐲𐐾𐐯𐑆 𐑄𐐰𐐻 𐑄 𐐢𐐰𐑋𐐲𐑌𐐴𐐻𐑅 𐐸𐐰𐐼 𐑀𐐰𐑄𐐲𐑉𐐼 𐐻𐐭𐑀𐐯𐑄𐐲𐑉 𐐰𐑌 𐐮𐑌𐐷𐐭𐑋𐐲𐑉𐐲𐐺𐑊 𐐪𐑉𐑋𐐨 𐐱𐑂 𐑋𐐯𐑌, 𐐰𐑌𐐼 𐐪𐑉𐑋𐐼 𐑄𐐯𐑋 𐐶𐐮𐑄 𐑅𐐬𐑉𐐼𐑆, 𐐰𐑌𐐼 𐐶𐐮𐑄 𐑅𐐮𐑋𐐲𐐻𐐲𐑉𐑆, 𐐰𐑌𐐼 𐐶𐐮𐑄 𐐺𐐬𐑆, 𐐰𐑌𐐼 𐐶𐐮𐑄 𐐰𐑉𐐬𐑆, 𐐰𐑌𐐼 𐐶𐐮𐑄 𐐸𐐯𐐼-𐐹𐑊𐐩𐐻𐑅, 𐐰𐑌𐐼 𐐶𐐮𐑄 𐐺𐑉𐐯𐑅𐐻-𐐹𐑊𐐩𐐻𐑅, 𐐰𐑌𐐼 𐐶𐐮𐑄 𐐫𐑊 𐑋𐐰𐑌𐐲𐑉 𐐱𐑂 𐑇𐐨𐑊𐐼𐑆 𐐱𐑂 𐐯𐑂𐐲𐑉𐐨 𐐿𐐴𐑌𐐼; 𐐰𐑌𐐼 𐑄𐐩 𐐿𐐩𐑋 𐐼𐐵𐑌 𐐲𐑀𐐯𐑌, 𐑄𐐰𐐻 𐑄𐐩 𐑋𐐴𐐻 𐐹𐐮𐐽 𐐺𐐰𐐻𐑊 𐐲𐑀𐐯𐑌𐑅𐐻 𐑄 𐐤𐐨𐑁𐐴𐐻𐑅. 𐐈𐑌𐐼 𐑄𐐩 𐐶𐐲𐑉 𐑊𐐯𐐼 𐐺𐐴 𐐲 𐑋𐐰𐑌 𐐸𐐭𐑆 𐑌𐐩𐑋 𐐶𐐱𐑆 𐐗𐐬𐑉𐐨𐐰𐑌𐐻𐐲𐑋𐐲𐑉; 𐐰𐑌𐐼 𐐸𐐨 𐐶𐐱𐑆 𐐲 𐐼𐐨𐑅𐐯𐑌𐐼𐐰𐑌𐐻 𐐱𐑂 𐐞𐐩𐑉𐐲𐐸𐐯𐑋𐑊𐐲; 𐐰𐑌𐐼 𐐸𐐨 𐐶𐐱𐑆 𐐲 𐐼𐐮𐑅𐐯𐑌𐐻𐐲𐑉 𐑁𐑉𐐱𐑋 𐐲𐑋𐐲𐑍 𐑄 𐐤𐐨𐑁𐐴𐐻𐑅; 𐐰𐑌𐐼 𐐸𐐨 𐐶𐐱𐑆 𐐲 𐑊𐐪𐑉𐐾 𐐰𐑌𐐼 𐐲 𐑋𐐴𐐻𐐨 𐑋𐐰𐑌; 𐑄𐐯𐑉𐑁𐐬𐑉, 𐑄 𐐿𐐮𐑍 𐐱𐑂 𐑄 𐐢𐐰𐑋𐐲𐑌𐐴𐐻𐑅, 𐐸𐐭𐑆 𐑌𐐩𐑋 𐐶𐐱𐑆 𐐓𐐭𐐺𐐰𐑊𐐱𐑃, 𐐸𐐭 𐐶𐐱𐑆 𐑄 𐑅𐐲𐑌 𐐱𐑂 𐐈𐑋𐐬𐑉𐐱𐑌, 𐑅𐐲𐐹𐐬𐑆𐐮𐑍 𐑄𐐰𐐻 𐐗𐐬𐑉𐐨𐐰𐑌𐐻𐐲𐑋𐐲𐑉, 𐐺𐐨𐐮𐑍 𐐲 𐑋𐐴𐐻𐐨 𐑋𐐰𐑌, 𐐿𐐳𐐼 𐑅𐐻𐐰𐑌𐐼 𐐲𐑀𐐯𐑌𐑅𐐻 𐑄 𐐤𐐨𐑁𐐴𐐻𐑅, 𐐮𐑌𐑅𐐬𐑋𐐲𐐽 𐐶𐐮𐑄 𐐸𐐮𐑆 𐑅𐐻𐑉𐐯𐑍𐑃, 𐐰𐑌𐐼 𐐫𐑊𐑅𐐬 𐐶𐐮𐑄 𐐸𐐮𐑆 𐑀𐑉𐐩𐐻 𐐶𐐮𐑆𐐼𐐲𐑋, 𐑄𐐰𐐻 𐐺𐐴 𐑅𐐯𐑌𐐼𐐮𐑍 𐐸𐐮𐑋 𐑁𐐬𐑉𐑃 𐐸𐐨 𐑇𐐳𐐼 𐑀𐐩𐑌 𐐹𐐵𐐲𐑉 𐐬𐑂𐐲𐑉 𐑄 𐐤𐐨𐑁𐐴𐐻𐑅; 𐑄𐐯𐑉𐑁𐐬𐑉 𐐸𐐨 𐐼𐐮𐐼 𐑅𐐻𐐲𐑉 𐑄𐐯𐑋 𐐲𐐹 𐐻𐐭 𐐰𐑍𐑀𐐲𐑉, 𐐰𐑌𐐼 𐐸𐐨 𐐼𐐮𐐼 𐑀𐐰𐑄𐐲𐑉 𐐻𐐭𐑀𐐯𐑄𐐲𐑉 𐐸𐐮𐑆 𐐪𐑉𐑋𐐨𐑆, 𐐰𐑌𐐼 𐐸𐐨 𐐼𐐮𐐼 𐐲𐐹𐑎𐑌𐐻 𐐗𐐬𐑉𐐨𐐰𐑌𐐻𐐲𐑋𐐲𐑉 𐐻𐐭 𐐺𐐨 𐑄𐐩𐑉 𐑊𐐨𐐼𐐲𐑉, 𐐰𐑌𐐼 𐐼𐐮𐐼 𐐿𐐫𐑆 𐑄𐐰𐐻 𐑄𐐩 𐑇𐐳𐐼 𐑋𐐪𐑉𐐽 𐐼𐐵𐑌 𐐻𐐭 𐑄 𐑊𐐰𐑌𐐼 𐐱𐑂 𐐞𐐩𐑉𐐲𐐸𐐯𐑋𐑊𐐲, 𐐻𐐭 𐐺𐐰𐐻𐑊 𐐲𐑀𐐯𐑌𐑅𐐻 𐑄 𐐤𐐨𐑁𐐴𐐻𐑅.

5\. 𐐈𐑌𐐼 𐐮𐐻 𐐿𐐩𐑋 𐐻𐐭 𐐹𐐰𐑅 𐑄𐐰𐐻 𐐺𐐨𐐿𐐫𐑆 𐐱𐑂 𐑅𐐬 𐑋𐐲𐐽 𐐿𐐱𐑌𐐻𐐯𐑌𐑇𐐲𐑌, 𐐰𐑌𐐼 𐑅𐐬 𐑋𐐲𐐽 𐐼𐐮𐑁𐐮𐐿𐐲𐑊𐐻𐐨 𐐮𐑌 𐑄 𐑀𐐲𐑂𐐲𐑉𐑌𐑋𐐯𐑌𐐻, 𐑄𐐰𐐻 𐑄𐐩 𐐸𐐰𐐼 𐑌𐐱𐐻 𐐿𐐯𐐹𐐻 𐑅𐐲𐑁𐐮𐑇𐐯𐑌𐐻 𐑀𐐪𐑉𐐼𐑆 𐐮𐑌 𐑄 𐑊𐐰𐑌𐐼 𐐱𐑂 𐐞𐐩𐑉𐐲𐐸𐐯𐑋𐑊𐐲; 𐑁𐐫𐑉 𐑄𐐩 𐐸𐐰𐐼 𐑅𐐲𐐹𐐬𐑆𐐼 𐑄𐐰𐐻 𐑄 𐐢𐐰𐑋𐐲𐑌𐐴𐐻𐑅 𐐼𐐲𐑉𐑅𐐻 𐑌𐐱𐐻 𐐿𐐲𐑋 𐐮𐑌𐐻𐐭 𐑄 𐐸𐐪𐑉𐐻 𐐱𐑂 𐑄𐐩𐑉 𐑊𐐰𐑌𐐼𐑆 𐐻𐐭 𐐰𐐻𐐰𐐿 𐑄𐐰𐐻 𐑀𐑉𐐩𐐻 𐑅𐐮𐐻𐐨 𐐞𐐩𐑉𐐲𐐸𐐯𐑋𐑊𐐲. 𐐒𐐲𐐻 𐐮𐐻 𐐿𐐩𐑋 𐐻𐐭 𐐹𐐰𐑅 𐑄𐐰𐐻 𐐗𐐬𐑉𐐨𐐰𐑌𐐻𐐲𐑋𐐲𐑉 𐐼𐐮𐐼 𐑋𐐪𐑉𐐽 𐑁𐐬𐑉𐑃 𐐰𐐻 𐑄 𐐸𐐯𐐼 𐐱𐑂 𐐸𐐮𐑆 𐑌𐐷𐐭𐑋𐐲𐑉𐐲𐑅 𐐸𐐬𐑅𐐻, 𐐰𐑌𐐼 𐐿𐐩𐑋 𐐲𐐹𐐱𐑌 𐑄 𐐮𐑌𐐸𐐰𐐺𐐮𐐻𐐲𐑌𐐻𐑅 𐐱𐑂 𐑄 𐑅𐐮𐐻𐐨, 𐐰𐑌𐐼 𐑄𐐩𐑉 𐑋𐐪𐑉𐐽 𐐶𐐱𐑆 𐐶𐐮𐑄 𐑅𐐲𐐽 𐐯𐐿𐑅𐐨𐐼𐐮𐑍 𐑀𐑉𐐩𐐻 𐑅𐐹𐐨𐐼, 𐑄𐐰𐐻 𐑄𐐯𐑉 𐐶𐐱𐑆 𐑌𐐬 𐐻𐐴𐑋 𐑁𐐫𐑉 𐑄 𐐤𐐨𐑁𐐴𐐻𐑅 𐐻𐐭 𐑀𐐰𐑄𐐲𐑉 𐐻𐐭𐑀𐐯𐑄𐐲𐑉 𐑄𐐩𐑉 𐐪𐑉𐑋𐐨𐑆; 𐑄𐐯𐑉𐑁𐐬𐑉 𐐗𐐬𐑉𐐨𐐰𐑌𐐻𐐲𐑋𐐲𐑉 𐐼𐐮𐐼 𐐿𐐲𐐻 𐐼𐐵𐑌 𐑄 𐐶𐐱𐐽 𐐺𐐴 𐑄 𐐯𐑌𐐻𐑉𐐲𐑌𐑅 𐐱𐑂 𐑄 𐑅𐐮𐐻𐐨, 𐐰𐑌𐐼 𐐼𐐮𐐼 𐑋𐐪𐑉𐐽 𐑁𐐬𐑉𐑃 𐐶𐐮𐑄 𐐸𐐮𐑆 𐐸𐐬𐑊 𐐪𐑉𐑋𐐨 𐐮𐑌𐐻𐐭 𐑄 𐑅𐐮𐐻𐐨, 𐐰𐑌𐐼 𐑄𐐩 𐐼𐐮𐐼 𐑅𐑊𐐩 𐐯𐑂𐐲𐑉𐐨 𐐶𐐲𐑌 𐐸𐐭 𐐼𐐮𐐼 𐐲𐐹𐐬𐑆 𐑄𐐯𐑋, 𐐮𐑌𐑅𐐬𐑋𐐲𐐽 𐑄𐐰𐐻 𐑄𐐩 𐐼𐐮𐐼 𐐻𐐩𐐿 𐐹𐐲𐑆𐐯𐑇𐐲𐑌 𐐱𐑂 𐑄 𐐸𐐬𐑊 𐑅𐐮𐐻𐐨. 𐐈𐑌𐐼 𐐮𐐻 𐐿𐐩𐑋 𐐻𐐭 𐐹𐐰𐑅 𐑄𐐰𐐻 𐐑𐐰𐐿𐐷𐐭𐑋𐐯𐑌𐐨, 𐐸𐐭 𐐶𐐱𐑆 𐑄 𐐽𐐨𐑁 𐐾𐐲𐐾, 𐐼𐐮𐐼 𐑁𐑊𐐨 𐐺𐐨𐑁𐐬𐑉 𐐗𐐬𐑉𐐨𐐰𐑌𐐻𐐲𐑋𐐲𐑉, 𐐨𐑂𐐲𐑌 𐐻𐐭 𐑄 𐐶𐐫𐑊𐑆 𐐱𐑂 𐑄 𐑅𐐮𐐻𐐨. 𐐈𐑌𐐼 𐐮𐐻 𐐿𐐩𐑋 𐐻𐐭 𐐹𐐰𐑅 𐑄𐐰𐐻 𐐗𐐬𐑉𐐨𐐰𐑌𐐻𐐲𐑋𐐲𐑉 𐐼𐐮𐐼 𐑅𐑋𐐴𐐻 𐐸𐐮𐑋 𐐲𐑀𐐯𐑌𐑅𐐻 𐑄 𐐶𐐫𐑊, 𐐮𐑌𐑅𐐬𐑋𐐲𐐽 𐑄𐐰𐐻 𐐸𐐨 𐐼𐐴𐐼. 𐐈𐑌𐐼 𐑄𐐲𐑅 𐐯𐑌𐐼𐐯𐐼 𐑄 𐐼𐐩𐑆 𐐱𐑂 𐐑𐐰𐐿𐐷𐐭𐑋𐐯𐑌𐐨.

6\. 𐐈𐑌𐐼 𐑌𐐵 𐐸𐐶𐐯𐑌 𐐗𐐬𐑉𐐨𐐰𐑌𐐻𐐲𐑋𐐲𐑉 𐑅𐐫 𐑄𐐰𐐻 𐐸𐐨 𐐶𐐱𐑆 𐐮𐑌 𐐹𐐲𐑆𐐯𐑇𐐲𐑌 𐐱𐑂 𐑄 𐑅𐐮𐐻𐐨 𐐱𐑂 𐐞𐐩𐑉𐐲𐐸𐐯𐑋𐑊𐐲, 𐐰𐑌𐐼 𐑅𐐫 𐑄𐐰𐐻 𐑄 𐐤𐐨𐑁𐐴𐐻𐑅 𐐸𐐰𐐼 𐑁𐑊𐐯𐐼 𐐺𐐨𐑁𐐬𐑉 𐑄𐐯𐑋, 𐐰𐑌𐐼 𐐶𐐲𐑉 𐑅𐑊𐐩𐑌, 𐐰𐑌𐐼 𐐶𐐲𐑉 𐐻𐐩𐐿𐐲𐑌, 𐐰𐑌𐐼 𐐶𐐲𐑉 𐐿𐐪𐑅𐐻 𐐮𐑌𐐻𐐭 𐐹𐑉𐐮𐑆𐐲𐑌, 𐐰𐑌𐐼 𐑄𐐰𐐻 𐐸𐐨 𐐸𐐰𐐼 𐐱𐐺𐐻𐐩𐑌𐐼 𐑄 𐐹𐐲𐑆𐐯𐑇𐐲𐑌 𐐱𐑂 𐑄 𐑅𐐻𐑉𐐱𐑍𐑀𐐯𐑅𐐻 𐐸𐐬𐑊𐐼 𐐮𐑌 𐐫𐑊 𐑄 𐑊𐐰𐑌𐐼, 𐐸𐐮𐑆 𐐸𐐪𐑉𐐻 𐐻𐐳𐐿 𐐿𐐲𐑉𐐩𐐾, 𐐮𐑌𐑅𐐬𐑋𐐲𐐽 𐑄𐐰𐐻 𐐸𐐨 𐐶𐐱𐑆 𐐲𐐺𐐵𐐻 𐐻𐐭 𐑀𐐬 𐑁𐐬𐑉𐑃 𐐰𐑀𐐯𐑌𐑅𐐻 𐐫𐑊 𐐜 𐑊𐐰𐑌𐐼. 𐐈𐑌𐐼 𐑌𐐵 𐐸𐐨 𐐼𐐮𐐼 𐑌𐐱𐐻 𐐻𐐰𐑉𐐨 𐐮𐑌 𐐜 𐑊𐐰𐑌𐐼 𐐱𐑂 𐐞𐐯𐑉𐐲𐐸𐐯𐑋𐑊𐐲, 𐐺𐐲𐐻 𐐸𐐨 𐐼𐐮𐐼 𐑋𐐪𐑉𐐽 𐑁𐐬𐑉𐑃 𐐶𐐮𐑃 𐐲 𐑊𐐪𐑉𐐾 𐐪𐑉𐑋𐐨, 𐐨𐑂𐐲𐑌 𐐻𐐬𐑉𐐼𐑆 𐐜 𐑅𐐮𐐻𐐨 𐐱𐑂 𐐒𐐵𐑌𐐻𐐨𐑁𐐳𐑊; 𐑁𐐫𐑉 𐐮𐐻 𐐶𐐱𐑆 𐐸𐐮𐑆 𐐼𐐨𐐻𐐲𐑉𐑋𐐮𐑌𐐩𐑇𐐲𐑌 𐐻𐐭 𐑀𐐬 𐑁𐐬𐑉𐑃 𐐰𐑌𐐼 𐐿𐐲𐐻 𐐸𐐮𐑆 𐐶𐐩 𐑃𐑉𐐭 𐐶𐐮𐑃 𐐜 𐑅𐐬𐑉𐐼, 𐑄𐐰𐐻 𐐸𐐨 𐑋𐐴𐐻 𐐱𐐺𐐻𐐩𐑌 𐐜 𐑌𐐫𐑉𐑃 𐐹𐐪𐑉𐐻𐑅 𐐱𐑂 𐐜 𐑊𐐰𐑌𐐼; 𐐰𐑌𐐼 𐑅𐐲𐐹𐐬𐑆𐐮𐑍 𐑄𐐰𐐻 𐑄𐐯𐑉 𐑀𐑉𐐩𐐻𐐯𐑅𐐻 𐑅𐐻𐑉𐐯𐑍𐑃 𐐶𐐱𐑆 𐐮𐑌 𐐜 𐑅𐐯𐑌𐐻𐐲𐑉 𐐱𐑂 𐐜 𐑊𐐰𐑌𐐼, 𐑄𐐯𐑉𐑁𐐬𐑉 𐐸𐐨 𐐼𐐮𐐼 𐑋𐐪𐑉𐐽 𐑁𐐬𐑉𐑃, 𐑀𐐮𐑂𐐮𐑍 𐑄𐐯𐑋 𐑌𐐬 𐐻𐐴𐑋 𐐻𐐭 𐐰𐑅𐐯𐑋𐐺𐐲𐑊 𐑄𐐯𐑋𐑅𐐯𐑊𐑂𐑆 𐐻𐐭𐑀𐐯𐑄𐐲𐑉 𐑅𐐩𐑂 𐐮𐐻 𐐶𐐲𐑉 𐐮𐑌 𐑅𐑋𐐫𐑊 𐐺𐐱𐐼𐐨𐑆: 𐐰𐑌𐐼 𐐮𐑌 𐑄𐐮𐑅 𐑋𐐰𐑌𐐲𐑉 𐑄𐐩 𐐼𐐮𐐼 𐑁𐐫𐑊 𐐲𐐹𐐱𐑌 𐑄𐐯𐑋 𐐰𐑌𐐼 𐐿𐐲𐐻 𐑄𐐯𐑋 𐐼𐐵𐑌 𐐻𐐭 𐐜 𐐲𐑉𐑃. 𐐒𐐲𐐻 𐐺𐐨𐐸𐐬𐑊𐐼, 𐑄𐐮𐑅 𐑋𐐪𐑉𐐽 𐐱𐑂 𐐗𐐬𐑉𐐨𐐰𐑌𐐻𐐲𐑋𐐲𐑉 𐑃𐑉𐐭 𐐜 𐑅𐐯𐑌𐐻𐐲𐑉 𐐱𐑂 𐐜 𐑊𐐰𐑌𐐼, 𐑀𐐩𐑂 𐐣𐐬𐑉𐐱𐑌𐐴𐐸𐐪 𐑀𐑉𐐩𐐻 𐐰𐐼𐑂𐐰𐑌𐐻𐐩𐐾 𐐬𐑂𐐲𐑉 𐑄𐐯𐑋, 𐑌𐐱𐐻𐐶𐐮𐑄𐑅𐐻𐐰𐑌𐐼𐐮𐑍 𐐜 𐑀𐑉𐐩𐐻𐑌𐐯𐑅 𐐱𐑂 𐐜 𐑌𐐲𐑋𐐺𐐲𐑉 𐐱𐑂 𐐜 𐐤𐐨𐑁𐐴𐐻𐑅 𐐸𐐭 𐐶𐐲𐑉 𐑅𐑊𐐩𐑌; 𐑁𐐫𐑉 𐐺𐐨𐐸𐐬𐑊𐐼, 𐐣𐐬𐑉𐐱𐑌𐐴𐐸𐐪 𐐸𐐰𐐼 𐑅𐐲𐐹𐐬𐑆𐐼 𐑄𐐰𐐻 𐐜 𐐢𐐩𐑋𐐲𐑌𐐴𐐻𐑅 𐐼𐐲𐑉𐑅𐐻 𐑌𐐱𐐻 𐐿𐐲𐑋 𐐮𐑌𐐻𐐭 𐐜 𐑅𐐯𐑌𐐻𐐲𐑉 𐐱𐑂 𐐜 𐑊𐐰𐑌𐐼, 𐐺𐐲𐐻 𐑄𐐰𐐻 𐑄𐐩 𐐶𐐳𐐼 𐐰𐐻𐐰𐐿 𐐜 𐑅𐐮𐐻𐐨𐑆 𐑉𐐵𐑌𐐼 𐐲𐐺𐐵𐐻 𐐮𐑌 𐐜 𐐺𐐫𐑉𐐼𐐲𐑉𐑆 𐐰𐑆 𐑄𐐩 𐐸𐐰𐐼 𐐸𐐮𐑄𐐲𐑉𐐻𐐭 𐐼𐐲𐑌; 𐑄𐐯𐑉𐑁𐐬𐑉 𐐣𐐬𐑉𐐱𐑌𐐴𐐸𐐪 𐐸𐐰𐐼 𐐿𐐫𐑆𐐼 𐑄𐐰𐐻 𐑄𐐯𐑉 𐑅𐐻𐑉𐐱𐑍 𐐪𐑉𐑋𐐨𐑆 𐑇𐐳𐐼 𐑋𐐩𐑌𐐻𐐩𐑌 𐑄𐐬𐑆 𐐹𐐪𐑉𐐻𐑅 𐑉𐐵𐑌𐐼 𐐲𐐺𐐵𐐻 𐐺𐐴 𐐜 𐐺𐐫𐑉𐐼𐐲𐑉𐑆. 𐐒𐐲𐐻 𐐺𐐨𐐸𐐬𐑊𐐼, 𐐜 𐐢𐐩𐑋𐐲𐑌𐐴𐐻𐑅 𐐶𐐲𐑉 𐑌𐐱𐐻 𐑁𐑉𐐴𐐻𐐲𐑌𐐼 𐐰𐐿𐐫𐑉𐐼𐐮𐑍 𐐻𐐭 𐐸𐐮𐑆 𐐼𐐨𐑆𐐴𐑉, 𐐺𐐲𐐻 𐑄𐐩 𐐸𐐰𐐼 𐐿𐐲𐑋 𐐮𐑌𐐻𐐭 𐐜 𐑅𐐯𐑌𐐻𐐲𐑉 𐐱𐑂 𐐜 𐑊𐐰𐑌𐐼, 𐐰𐑌𐐼 𐐸𐐰𐐼 𐐻𐐩𐐿𐐲𐑌 𐐜 𐐿𐐰𐐹𐐮𐐻𐐲𐑊 𐑅𐐮𐐻𐐨 𐐸𐐶𐐮𐐽 𐐶𐐱𐑆 𐐜 𐑅𐐮𐐻𐐨 𐐱𐑂 𐐞𐐯𐑉𐐲𐐸𐐯𐑋𐑊𐐲, 𐐰𐑌𐐼 𐐶𐐲𐑉 𐑋𐐪𐑉𐐽𐐮𐑍 𐑃𐑉𐐭 𐐜 𐑋𐐬𐑅𐐻 𐐿𐐰𐐹𐐮𐐻𐐲𐑊 𐐹𐐪𐑉𐐻𐑅 𐐱𐑂 𐐜 𐑊𐐰𐑌𐐼, 𐑅𐑊𐐩𐐮𐑍 𐐜 𐐹𐐨𐐹𐑊 𐐶𐐮𐑃 𐐲 𐑀𐑉𐐩𐐻 𐑅𐑊𐐫𐐻𐐲𐑉, 𐐺𐐬𐑃 𐑋𐐯𐑌, 𐐶𐐮𐑋𐐯𐑌, 𐐰𐑌𐐼 𐐽𐐮𐑊𐐼𐑉𐐯𐑌, 𐐻𐐩𐐿𐐮𐑍 𐐹𐐱𐑆𐐯𐑇𐐲𐑌 𐐱𐑂 𐑋𐐯𐑌𐐨 𐑅𐐮𐐻𐐨𐑆 𐐰𐑌𐐼 𐐱𐑂 𐑋𐐯𐑌𐐨 𐑅𐐻𐑉𐐱𐑍𐐸𐐬𐑊𐐼𐑆. 𐐒𐐲𐐻 𐐸𐐶𐐯𐑌 𐐣𐐬𐑉𐐱𐑌𐐴𐐸𐐪 𐐸𐐰𐐼 𐐼𐐮𐑅𐐿𐐲𐑂𐐲𐑉𐐼 𐑄𐐮𐑅, 𐐸𐐨 𐐮𐑋𐐨𐐼𐐨𐐲𐐻𐑊𐐨 𐑅𐐯𐑌𐐻 𐑁𐐬𐑉𐑃 𐐢𐐨𐐸𐐴 𐐶𐐮𐑃 𐐰𐑌 𐐪𐑉𐑋𐐨 𐑉𐐵𐑌𐐼 𐐲𐐺𐐵𐐻 𐐻𐐭 𐐸𐐯𐐼 𐑄𐐯𐑋 𐐺𐐨𐑁𐐬𐑉 𐑄𐐩 𐑇𐐳𐐼 𐐿𐐲𐑋 𐐻𐐭 𐐜 𐑊𐐰𐑌𐐼 𐐒𐐵𐑌𐐻𐐨𐑁𐐳𐑊. 𐐈𐑌𐐼 𐑄𐐲𐑅 𐐸𐐨 𐐼𐐮𐐼; 𐐰𐑌𐐼 𐐸𐐨 𐐼𐐮𐐼 𐐸𐐯𐐼 𐑄𐐯𐑋 𐐺𐐨𐑁𐐬𐑉 𐑄𐐩 𐐿𐐩𐑋 𐐻𐐭 𐐜 𐑊𐐰𐑌𐐼 𐐒𐐵𐑌𐐻𐐨𐑁𐐳𐑊, 𐐰𐑌𐐼 𐑀𐐩𐑂 𐐲𐑌𐐻𐐭 𐑄𐐯𐑋 𐐺𐐰𐐻𐐲𐑊, 𐐮𐑌𐑅𐐬𐑋𐐲𐐽 𐑄𐐰𐐻 𐑄𐐩 𐐺𐐨𐑀𐐰𐑌 𐐻𐐭 𐑉𐐨𐐻𐑉𐐨𐐻 𐐺𐐰𐐿 𐐻𐐬𐑉𐐼𐑆 𐐜 𐑊𐐰𐑌𐐼 𐐱𐑂 𐐞𐐯𐑉𐐲𐐸𐐯𐑋𐑊𐐲. 𐐈𐑌𐐼 𐐮𐐻 𐐿𐐩𐑋 𐐻𐐭 𐐹𐐰𐑅 𐑄𐐰𐐻 𐐣𐐬𐑉𐐱𐑌𐐴𐐸𐐪 𐐼𐐮𐐼 𐐸𐐯𐐼 𐑄𐐯𐑋 𐐮𐑌 𐑄𐐯𐑉 𐑉𐐨𐐻𐑉𐐨𐐻, 𐐰𐑌𐐼 𐐼𐐮𐐼 𐑀𐐮𐑂 𐐲𐑌𐐻𐐭 𐑄𐐯𐑋 𐐺𐐰𐐻𐐲𐑊, 𐐮𐑌𐑅𐐬𐑋𐐲𐐽 𐑄𐐰𐐻 𐐮𐐻 𐐺𐐨𐐿𐐩𐑋 𐐰𐑌 𐐯𐐿𐑅𐐨𐐼𐐮𐑍 𐐺𐑊𐐲𐐼𐐨 𐐺𐐰𐐻𐐲𐑊; 𐐷𐐩, 𐑋𐐯𐑌𐐨 𐐶𐐲𐑉 𐑅𐑊𐐩𐑌, 𐐰𐑌𐐼 𐐲𐑋𐐲𐑍 𐐜 𐑌𐐲𐑋𐐺𐐲𐑉 𐐸𐐭 𐐶𐐲𐑉 𐑅𐑊𐐩𐑌, 𐐗𐐬𐑉𐐨𐐰𐑌𐐻𐐲𐑋𐐲𐑉 𐐶𐐱𐑆 𐐫𐑊𐑅𐐬 𐑁𐐵𐑌𐐼. 𐐈𐑌𐐼 𐑌𐐵 𐐺𐐨𐐸𐐬𐑊𐐼, 𐐜 𐐢𐐩𐑋𐐲𐑌𐐴𐐻𐑅 𐐿𐐳𐐼 𐑌𐐱𐐻 𐑉𐐨𐐻𐑉𐐨𐐻 𐐨𐑄𐐲𐑉 𐐶𐐩, 𐑌𐐨𐑄𐐲𐑉 𐐱𐑌 𐐜 𐑌𐐫𐑉𐑃, 𐑌𐐫𐑉 𐐱𐑌 𐐜 𐑅𐐵𐑃, 𐑌𐐫𐑉 𐐱𐑌 𐐜 𐐨𐑅𐐻, 𐑌𐐫𐑉 𐐱𐑌 𐐜 𐐶𐐯𐑅𐐻, 𐑁𐐫𐑉 𐑄𐐩 𐐶𐐲𐑉 𐑅𐐲𐑉𐐵𐑌𐐼𐐯𐐼 𐐱𐑌 𐐯𐑂𐐲𐑉𐐨 𐐸𐐰𐑌𐐼 𐐺𐐴 𐐜 𐐤𐐨𐑁𐐴𐐻𐑅: 𐐰𐑌𐐼 𐑄𐐲𐑅 𐐸𐐰𐐼 𐐗𐐬𐑉𐐨𐐰𐑌𐐻𐐲𐑋𐐲𐑉 𐐹𐑊𐐲𐑌𐐾𐐼 𐐜 𐐢𐐩𐑋𐐲𐑌𐐴𐐻𐑅 𐐮𐑌𐐻𐐭 𐐜 𐑋𐐮𐐼𐑅𐐻 𐐱𐑂 𐐜 𐐤𐐨𐑁𐐴𐐻𐑅, 𐐮𐑌𐑅𐐬𐑋𐐲𐐽 𐑄𐐰𐐻 𐑄𐐩 𐐶𐐲𐑉 𐐮𐑌 𐐜 𐐹𐐵𐐲𐑉 𐐱𐑂 𐐜 𐐤𐐨𐑁𐐴𐐻𐑅, 𐐰𐑌𐐼 𐐸𐐨 𐐸𐐮𐑋𐑅𐐯𐑊𐑁 𐐶𐐱𐑆 𐑅𐑊𐐩𐑌, 𐐰𐑌𐐼 𐐜 𐐢𐐩𐑋𐐲𐑌𐐴𐐻𐑅 𐐼𐐮𐐼 𐐷𐐨𐑊𐐼 𐑄𐐯𐑋𐑅𐐯𐑊𐑂𐑆 𐐮𐑌𐐻𐐭 𐐜 𐐸𐐰𐑌𐐼𐑆 𐐱𐑂 𐐜 𐐤𐐨𐑁𐐴𐐻𐑅.

7. 𐐈𐑌𐐼 𐐮𐐻 𐐿𐐩𐑋 𐐻𐐭 𐐹𐐰𐑅 𐑄𐐰𐐻 𐐣𐐬𐑉𐐱𐑌𐐴𐐸𐐪 𐐻𐐳𐐿 𐐹𐐱𐑆𐐯𐑇𐐲𐑌 𐐱𐑂 𐐜 𐑅𐐮𐐻𐐨 𐐱𐑂 𐐞𐐯𐑉𐐲𐐸𐐯𐑋𐑊𐐲 𐐲𐑀𐐯𐑌, 𐐰𐑌𐐼 𐐿𐐫𐑆𐐼 𐑄𐐰𐐻 𐐜 𐐢𐐩𐑋𐐲𐑌𐐴𐐻𐑅 𐐸𐐭 𐐸𐐰𐐼 𐐺𐐨𐑌 𐐻𐐩𐐿𐐲𐑌 𐐹𐑉𐐮𐑆𐐲𐑌𐐲𐑉𐑆 𐑇𐐳𐐼 𐐼𐐨𐐹𐐪𐑉𐐻 𐐵𐐻 𐐱𐑂 𐐜 𐑊𐐰𐑌𐐼 𐐮𐑌 𐐹𐐨𐑅. 𐐈𐑌𐐼 𐑄𐐲𐑅 𐐯𐑌𐐼𐐯𐐼 𐐜 𐑁𐐫𐑉𐐻𐐨 𐐰𐑌𐐼 𐑁𐐲𐑉𐑅𐐻 𐐷𐐨𐑉 𐐱𐑂 𐐜 𐑉𐐩𐑌 𐐱𐑂 𐐜 𐐾𐐲𐐾𐐯𐑆.

8. 𐐈𐑌𐐼 𐐮𐐻 𐐿𐐩𐑋 𐐻𐐭 𐐹𐐰𐑅 𐐮𐑌 𐐜 𐑁𐐫𐑉𐐻𐐨 𐐰𐑌𐐼 𐑅𐐯𐐿𐐲𐑌𐐼 𐐷𐐨𐑉 𐐱𐑂 𐐜 𐑉𐐩𐑌 𐐱𐑂 𐐜 𐐾𐐲𐐾𐐯𐑆, 𐐰𐑁𐐻𐐲𐑉 𐐣𐐬𐑉𐐱𐑌𐐴𐐸𐐪 𐐸𐐰𐐼 𐐯𐑅𐐻𐐰𐐺𐑊𐐮𐑇𐐻 𐐲𐑀𐐯𐑌 𐐹𐐨𐑅 𐐺𐐨𐐻𐐶𐐨𐑌 𐐜 𐐤𐐨𐑁𐐴𐐻𐑅 𐐰𐑌𐐼 𐐜 𐐢𐐩𐑋𐐲𐑌𐐴𐐻𐑅, 𐐺𐐨𐐸𐐬𐑊𐐼 𐑄𐐯𐑉 𐐶𐐱𐑆 𐑌𐐬 𐐶𐐲𐑌 𐐻𐐭 𐑁𐐮𐑊 𐐜 𐐾𐐲𐐾𐑋𐐯𐑌𐐻-𐑅𐐨𐐻; 𐑄𐐯𐑉𐑁𐐬𐑉 𐑄𐐯𐑉 𐐺𐐨𐑀𐐰𐑌 𐐻𐐭 𐐺𐐨 𐐲 𐐿𐐱𐑌𐐻𐐯𐑌𐑇𐐲𐑌 𐐲𐑀𐐯𐑌 𐐲𐑋𐐲𐑍 𐐜 𐐹𐐨𐐹𐑊 𐐿𐐱𐑌𐑅𐐲𐑉𐑌𐐮𐑍 𐐸𐐭 𐑇𐐳𐐼 𐑁𐐮𐑊 𐐜 𐐾𐐲𐐾𐑋𐐯𐑌𐐻-𐑅𐐨𐐻. 𐐈𐑌𐐼 𐐮𐐻 𐐿𐐩𐑋 𐐻𐐭 𐐹𐐰𐑅 𐑄𐐰𐐻 𐐐𐐨𐑊𐐲𐑋𐐲𐑌, 𐐸𐐭 𐐶𐐱𐑆 𐐜 𐑅𐐲𐑌 𐐱𐑂 𐐐𐐨𐑊𐐲𐑋𐐲𐑌, 𐐶𐐱𐑆 𐐲𐐹𐐱𐐮𐑌𐐻𐐯𐐼 𐐻𐐭 𐑁𐐮𐑊 𐐜 𐐾𐐲𐐾𐑋𐐯𐑌𐐻-𐑅𐐨𐐻, 𐐺𐐴 𐐜 𐑂𐐱𐐮𐑅 𐐱𐑂 𐐜 𐐹𐐨𐐹𐑊; 𐐺𐐲𐐻 𐐺𐐨𐐸𐐬𐑊𐐼, 𐐗𐐮𐑇𐐿𐐭𐑋𐐯𐑌, 𐐸𐐭 𐐸𐐰𐐼 𐑋𐐲𐑉𐐼𐐲𐑉𐐼 𐐑𐐰𐐸𐐬𐑉𐐰𐑌, 𐐼𐐮𐐼 𐑊𐐩 𐐶𐐩𐐻 𐐻𐐭 𐐼𐐯𐑅𐐻𐑉𐐱𐐮 𐐐𐐨𐑊𐐲𐑋𐐲𐑌 𐐫𐑊𐑅𐐬; 𐐰𐑌𐐼 𐐸𐐨 𐐶𐐱𐑆 𐐲𐐹𐐸𐐯𐑊𐐼 𐐺𐐴 𐐸𐐮𐑆 𐐺𐐰𐑌𐐼, 𐐸𐐭 𐐸𐐰𐐼 𐐯𐑌𐐻𐐲𐑉𐐼 𐐮𐑌𐐻𐐭 𐐲 𐐿𐐲𐑂𐐯𐑌𐐰𐑌𐐻 𐑄𐐰𐐻 𐑌𐐬 𐐶𐐲𐑌 𐑇𐐳𐐼 𐑌𐐬 𐐸𐐮𐑆 𐐶𐐮𐐿𐐯𐐼𐑌𐐯𐑅; 𐑁𐐫𐑉 𐑄𐐯𐑉 𐐶𐐱𐑆 𐐶𐐲𐑌 𐐘𐐰𐐼𐐨𐐰𐑌𐐻𐐲𐑌 𐐸𐐭 𐐶𐐱𐑆 𐐯𐐿𐑅𐐨𐐼𐐮𐑍 𐐯𐐿𐑅𐐹𐐲𐑉𐐻 𐐮𐑌 𐑋𐐯𐑌𐐨 𐐶𐐲𐑉𐐼𐑆, 𐐰𐑌𐐼 𐐫𐑊𐑅𐐬 𐐮𐑌 𐐸𐐮𐑆 𐐿𐑉𐐰𐑁𐐻, 𐐻𐐭

𐐿𐐰𐑉𐐨 𐐱𐑌 𐑄 𐑅𐐨𐐿𐑉𐐯𐐻 𐐶𐐲𐑉𐐿 𐐱𐑂 𐑋𐐲𐑉𐐼𐐲𐑉 𐐰𐑌𐐼 𐐱𐑂 𐑉𐐱𐐺𐐲𐑉𐐨; 𐑄𐐩𐑉𐑁𐐬𐑉 𐐸𐐨 𐐺𐐨𐐿𐐩𐑋 𐑄 𐑊𐐨𐐼𐐲𐑉 𐐱𐑂 𐑄 𐐺𐐰𐑌𐐼 𐐱𐑂 𐐗𐐮𐑇𐐿𐐭𐑋𐐯𐑌; 𐑄𐐩𐑉𐑁𐐬𐑉 𐐸𐐨 𐐼𐐮𐐼 𐑁𐑊𐐰𐐻𐐲𐑉 𐑄𐐯𐑋, 𐐰𐑌𐐼 𐐫𐑊𐑅𐐬 𐐗𐐮𐑇𐐿𐐭𐑋𐐯𐑌, 𐑄𐐰𐐻 𐐮𐑁 𐑄𐐩 𐐶𐐳𐐼 𐐹𐑊𐐩𐑅 𐐸𐐮𐑋 𐐮𐑌 𐑄 𐐾𐐲𐐾𐑋𐐯𐑌𐐻 𐑅𐐨𐐻, 𐐸𐐨 𐐶𐐳𐐼 𐑀𐑉𐐰𐑌𐐻 𐐲𐑌𐐻𐐭 𐑄𐐬𐑆 𐐸𐐭 𐐺𐐨𐑊𐐫𐑍𐐼 𐐻𐐭 𐐸𐐮𐑆 𐐺𐐰𐑌𐐼 𐑄𐐰𐐻 𐑄𐐩 𐑇𐐳𐐼 𐐺𐐨 𐐹𐑊𐐩𐑅𐐻 𐐮𐑌 𐐹𐐵𐐲𐑉 𐐰𐑌𐐼 𐐫𐑃𐐱𐑉𐐮𐐻𐐨 𐐲𐑋𐐲𐑍 𐑄 𐐹𐐨𐐹𐑊; 𐑄𐐩𐑉𐑁𐐬𐑉 𐐗𐐮𐑇𐐿𐐭𐑋𐐯𐑌 𐑅𐐫𐐻 𐐻𐐭 𐐼𐐯𐑅𐐻𐑉𐐱𐐨 𐐐𐐨𐑊𐐲𐑋𐐲𐑌.

9. 𐐈𐑌𐐼 𐐮𐐻 𐐿𐐩𐑋 𐐻𐐭 𐐹𐐰𐑅 𐐰𐑆 𐐸𐐨 𐐶𐐯𐑌𐐻 𐑁𐐬𐑉𐑃 𐐻𐐭𐐶𐐫𐑉𐐼𐑆 𐑄 𐐾𐐲𐐾𐑋𐐯𐑌𐐻 𐑅𐐨𐐻, 𐐻𐐭 𐐼𐐯𐑅𐐻𐑉𐐱𐐨 𐐐𐐨𐑊𐐲𐑋𐐲𐑌, 𐐺𐐨𐐸𐐬𐑊𐐼 𐐶𐐲𐑌 𐐱𐑂 𐑄 𐑅𐐲𐑉𐑂𐐲𐑌𐐻𐑅 𐐱𐑂 𐐐𐐨𐑊𐐲𐑋𐐲𐑌, 𐐸𐐰𐑂𐐮𐑍 𐐺𐐨𐑌 𐐵𐐻 𐐺𐐴 𐑌𐐴𐐻, 𐐰𐑌𐐼 𐐸𐐰𐑂𐐮𐑍 𐐱𐐺𐐻𐐩𐑌𐐼, 𐑃𐑉𐐭 𐐼𐐮𐑅𐑀𐐴𐑆, 𐐲 𐑌𐐱𐑊𐐮𐐾 𐐱𐑂 𐑄𐐬𐑆 𐐹𐑊𐐰𐑌𐑆 𐐸𐐶𐐮𐐽 𐐸𐐰𐐼 𐐺𐐨𐑌 𐑊𐐩𐐼 𐐺𐐴 𐑄𐐮𐑅 𐐺𐐰𐑌𐐼 𐐻𐐭 𐐼𐐯𐑅𐐻𐑉𐐱𐐨 𐐐𐐨𐑊𐐲𐑋𐐲𐑌. 𐐈𐑌𐐼 𐐮𐐻 𐐿𐐩𐑋 𐐻𐐭 𐐹𐐰𐑅 𐑄𐐰𐐻 𐐸𐐨 𐑋𐐯𐐻 𐐗𐐮𐑇𐐿𐐭𐑋𐐯𐑌, 𐐰𐑌𐐼 𐐸𐐨 𐑀𐐩𐑂 𐐲𐑌𐐻𐐭 𐐸𐐮𐑋 𐐲 𐑅𐐴𐑌; 𐑄𐐩𐑉𐑁𐐬𐑉 𐐗𐐮𐑇𐐿𐐭𐑋𐐯𐑌 𐑋𐐩𐐼 𐑌𐐬𐑌 𐐲𐑌𐐻𐐭 𐐸𐐮𐑋 𐑄 𐐱𐐺𐐾𐐯𐐿𐐻 𐐱𐑂 𐐸𐐮𐑆 𐐼𐐯𐑆𐐴𐑉, 𐐼𐐯𐑆𐐴𐑉𐐮𐑍 𐑄𐐰𐐻 𐐸𐐨 𐐶𐐳𐐼 𐐿𐐱𐑌𐐼𐐲𐐿𐐻 𐐸𐐮𐑋 𐐻𐐭 𐑄 𐐾𐐲𐐾𐑋𐐯𐑌𐐻 𐑅𐐨𐐻, 𐑄𐐰𐐻 𐐸𐐨 𐑋𐐴𐐻 𐑋𐐲𐑉𐐼𐐲𐑉 𐐐𐐨𐑊𐐲𐑋𐐲𐑌; 𐐰𐑌𐐼 𐐸𐐶𐐯𐑌 𐑄 𐑅𐐲𐑉𐑂𐐲𐑌𐐻 𐐱𐑂 𐐐𐐨𐑊𐐲𐑋𐐲𐑌 𐐸𐐰𐐼 𐑌𐐬𐑌 𐐫𐑊 𐑄 𐐸𐐪𐑉𐐻 𐐱𐑂 𐐗𐐮𐑇𐐿𐐭𐑋𐐯𐑌, 𐐰𐑌𐐼 𐐸𐐵 𐑄𐐰𐐻 𐐮𐐻 𐐶𐐱𐑆 𐐸𐐮𐑆 𐐱𐐺𐐾𐐯𐐿𐐻 𐐻𐐭 𐑋𐐲𐑉𐐼𐐲𐑉, 𐐰𐑌𐐼 𐐫𐑊𐑅𐐬 𐑄𐐰𐐻 𐐮𐐻 𐐶𐐱𐑆 𐑄 𐐱𐐺𐐾𐐯𐐿𐐻 𐐱𐑂 𐐫𐑊 𐑄𐐬𐑆 𐐸𐐭 𐐺𐐨𐑊𐐫𐑍𐐼 𐐻𐐭 𐐸𐐮𐑆 𐐺𐐰𐑌𐐼 𐐻𐐭 𐑋𐐲𐑉𐐼𐐲𐑉, 𐐰𐑌𐐼 𐐻𐐭 𐑉𐐱𐐺, 𐐰𐑌𐐼 𐐻𐐭 𐑀𐐩𐑌 𐐹𐐵𐐲𐑉, (𐐰𐑌𐐼 𐑄𐐮𐑅 𐐶𐐱𐑆 𐑄𐐩𐑉 𐑅𐐨𐐿𐑉𐐯𐐻 𐐹𐑊𐐰𐑌, 𐐰𐑌𐐼 𐑄𐐩𐑉 𐐿𐐱𐑋𐐺𐐮𐑌𐐩𐑇𐐲𐑌,) 𐑄 𐑅𐐲𐑉𐑂𐐲𐑌𐐻 𐐱𐑂 𐐐𐐨𐑊𐐲𐑋𐐲𐑌 𐑅𐐯𐐼 𐐲𐑌𐐻𐐭 𐐗𐐮𐑇𐐿𐐭𐑋𐐯𐑌, 𐐢𐐯𐐻 𐐲𐑅 𐑀𐐬 𐑁𐐬𐑉𐑃 𐐲𐑌𐐻𐐭 𐑄 𐐾𐐲𐐾𐑋𐐯𐑌𐐻 𐑅𐐨𐐻. 𐐤𐐵 𐑄𐐮𐑅 𐐼𐐮𐐼 𐐹𐑊𐐨𐑆 𐐗𐐮𐑇𐐿𐐭𐑋𐐯𐑌 𐐯𐐿𐑅𐐨𐐼𐐮𐑍𐑊𐐨 𐑁𐐫𐑉 𐐸𐐨 𐐼𐐮𐐼 𐑅𐐲𐐹𐐬𐑆 𐑄𐐰𐐻 𐐸𐐨 𐑇𐐳𐐼 𐐰𐐿𐐱𐑋𐐹𐑊𐐮𐑇 𐐸𐐮𐑆 𐐼𐐨𐑆𐐴𐑌; 𐐺𐐲𐐻 𐐺𐐨𐐸𐐬𐑊𐐼, 𐑄 𐑅𐐲𐑉𐑂𐐲𐑌𐐻 𐐱𐑂 𐐐𐐨𐑊𐐲𐑋𐐲𐑌, 𐐰𐑆 𐑄𐐩 𐐶𐐲𐑉 𐑀𐐬𐐮𐑍 𐑁𐐬𐑉𐑃 𐐲𐑌𐐻𐐭 𐑄 𐐾𐐲𐐾𐑋𐐯𐑌𐐻 𐑅𐐨𐐻, 𐐼𐐮𐐼 𐑅𐐻𐐰𐐺 𐐗𐐮𐑇𐐿𐐭𐑋𐐯𐑌 𐐨𐑂𐐲𐑌 𐐻𐐭 𐑄 𐐸𐐪𐑉𐐻, 𐑄𐐰𐐻 𐐸𐐨 𐑁𐐯𐑊 𐐼𐐯𐐼 𐐶𐐮𐑄𐐵𐐻 𐐲 𐑀𐑉𐐬𐑌. 𐐈𐑌𐐼 𐐸𐐨 𐑉𐐰𐑌 𐐰𐑌𐐼 𐐻𐐬𐑊𐐼 𐐐𐐨𐑊𐐲𐑋𐐲𐑌 𐐫𐑊 𐑄 𐑃𐐮𐑍𐑆 𐐸𐐶𐐮𐐽 𐐸𐐨 𐐸𐐰𐐼 𐑅𐐨𐑌, 𐐰𐑌𐐼 𐐸𐐲𐑉𐐼, 𐐰𐑌𐐼 𐐼𐐲𐑌.

10. 𐐈𐑌𐐼 𐐮𐐻 𐐿𐐩𐑋 𐐻𐐭 𐐹𐐰𐑅 𐑄𐐰𐐻 𐐐𐐨𐑊𐐲𐑋𐐲𐑌 𐐼𐐮𐐼 𐑅𐐯𐑌𐐼 𐑁𐐬𐑉𐑃 𐐻𐐭 𐐻𐐩𐐿 𐑄𐐮𐑅 𐐺𐐰𐑌𐐼 𐐱𐑂 𐑉𐐱𐐺𐐲𐑉𐑆 𐐰𐑌𐐼 𐑅𐐨𐐿𐑉𐐯𐐻 𐑋𐐲𐑉𐐼𐐲𐑉𐐲𐑉𐑆, 𐑄𐐰𐐻 𐑄𐐩 𐑋𐐴𐐻 𐐺𐐨 𐐯𐐿𐑅𐐯𐐿𐐷𐐭𐐻𐐯𐐼 𐐰𐐿𐐬𐑉𐐼𐐮𐑍 𐐻𐐭 𐑄 𐑊𐐫. 𐐒𐐲𐐻 𐐺𐐨𐐸𐐬𐑊𐐼, 𐐸𐐶𐐯𐑌 𐐘𐐰𐐼𐐨𐐰𐑌𐐻𐐲𐑌 𐐸𐐰𐐼 𐑁𐐵𐑌𐐼 𐑄𐐰𐐻 𐐗𐐮𐑇𐐿𐐭𐑋𐐯𐑌 𐐼𐐮𐐼 𐑌𐐱𐐻 𐑉𐐨𐐻𐐲𐑉𐑌, 𐐸𐐨 𐑁𐐨𐑉𐐼 𐑊𐐯𐑅𐐻 𐑄𐐰𐐻 𐐸𐐨 𐑇𐐳𐐼 𐐺𐐨 𐐼𐐯𐑅𐐻𐑉𐐱𐐮𐐼; 𐑄𐐩𐑉𐑁𐐬𐑉 𐐸𐐨 𐐿𐐫𐑆𐐼 𐑄𐐰𐐻 𐐸𐐮𐑆 𐐺𐐰𐑌𐐼 𐑇𐐳𐐼 𐑁𐐱𐑊𐐬 𐐸𐐮𐑋. 𐐈𐑌𐐼 𐑄𐐩 𐐻𐐳𐐿 𐑄𐐩𐑉 𐑁𐑊𐐴𐐻 𐐵𐐻 𐐱𐑂 𐑄 𐑊𐐰𐑌𐐼, 𐐺𐐴 𐐲 𐑅𐐨𐐿𐑉𐐯𐐻 𐐶𐐩, 𐐮𐑌𐐻𐐭 𐑄 𐐶𐐮𐑊𐐼𐐲𐑉𐑌𐐯𐑅; 𐐰𐑌𐐼 𐑄𐐲𐑅 𐐸𐐶𐐯𐑌 𐐐𐐨𐑊𐐲𐑋𐐲𐑌 𐑅𐐯𐑌𐐻 𐑁𐐬𐑉𐑃 𐐻𐐭 𐐻𐐩𐐿 𐑄𐐯𐑋 𐑄𐐩 𐐿𐐳𐐼 𐑌𐐬𐐸𐐶𐐩𐑉 𐐺𐐨 𐑁𐐵𐑌𐐼. 𐐈𐑌𐐼 𐑋𐐬𐑉 𐐱𐑂 𐑄𐐮𐑅 𐐘𐐰𐐼𐐨𐐰𐑌𐐻𐐲𐑌 𐑇𐐰𐑊 𐐺𐐨 𐑅𐐹𐐬𐐿𐐲𐑌 𐐸𐐨𐑉𐐰𐑁𐐻𐐲𐑉. 𐐈𐑌𐐼 𐑄𐐲𐑅 𐐯𐑌𐐼𐐯𐐼 𐑄 𐑁𐐫𐑉𐐻𐐨 𐐰𐑌𐐼 𐑅𐐯𐐿𐐲𐑌𐐼 𐐷𐐨𐑉 𐐱𐑂 𐑄 𐑉𐐩𐑌 𐐱𐑂 𐑄 𐐾𐐲𐐾𐐯𐑆 𐐬𐑂𐐲𐑉 𐑄 𐐹𐐨𐐹𐑊 𐐱𐑂 𐐤𐐨𐑁𐐴. 𐐈𐑌𐐼 𐐺𐐨𐐸𐐬𐑊𐐼, 𐐮𐑌 𐑄 𐐯𐑌𐐼 𐐱𐑂 𐑄𐐮𐑅 𐐺𐐳𐐿, 𐐷𐐨 𐑇𐐰𐑊 𐑅𐐨 𐑄𐐰𐐻 𐑄𐐮𐑅 𐐘𐐰𐐼𐐨𐐰𐑌𐐻𐐲𐑌 𐐼𐐮𐐼 𐐹𐑉𐐭𐑂 𐑄 𐐬𐑂𐐲𐑉𐑃𐑉𐐬, 𐐷𐐩, 𐐫𐑊𐑋𐐬𐑅𐐻 𐑄 𐐯𐑌𐐻𐐴𐑉 𐐼𐐯𐑅𐐻𐑉𐐲𐐿𐑇𐐲𐑌 𐐱𐑂 𐑄 𐐹𐐨𐐹𐑊 𐐱𐑂 𐐤𐐨𐑁𐐴. 𐐒𐐨𐐸𐐬𐑊𐐼 𐐌 𐐼𐐭 𐑌𐐱𐐻 𐑋𐐨𐑌 𐑄 𐐯𐑌𐐼 𐐱𐑂 𐑄 𐐺𐐳𐐿 𐐱𐑂 𐐐𐐨𐑊𐐲𐑋𐐲𐑌, 𐐺𐐲𐐻 𐐌 𐑋𐐨𐑌 𐑄 𐐯𐑌𐐼 𐐱𐑂 𐑄 𐐺𐐳𐐿 𐐱𐑂 𐐤𐐨𐑁𐐴, 𐑁𐑉𐐱𐑋 𐐸𐐶𐐮𐐽 𐐌 𐐸𐐰𐑂 𐐻𐐩𐐿𐐲𐑌 𐐫𐑊 𐑄 𐐰𐐿𐐵𐑌𐐻 𐐸𐐶𐐮𐐽 𐐌 𐐸𐐰𐑂 𐑉𐐮𐐻𐐲𐑌.

𐐕𐐰𐐹𐐻𐐲𐑉 II.

1. 𐐈𐑌𐐼 𐑌𐐵 𐐮𐐻 𐐿𐐩𐑋 𐐻𐐭 𐐹𐐰𐑅 𐐮𐑌 𐑄 𐑁𐐫𐑉𐐻𐐨 𐐰𐑌𐐼 𐑃𐐲𐑉𐐼 𐐷𐐨𐑉 𐐱𐑂 𐑄 𐑉𐐩𐑌 𐐱𐑂 𐑄 𐐾𐐲𐐾𐐯𐑆, 𐑄𐐩𐑉 𐐶𐐱𐑆 𐑌𐐬 𐐿𐐱𐑌𐐻𐐯𐑌𐑇𐐲𐑌 𐐲𐑋𐐲𐑍 𐑄 𐐹𐐨𐐹𐑊 𐐱𐑂 𐐤𐐨𐑁𐐴, 𐑅𐐩𐑂 𐐮𐐻 𐐶𐐲𐑉 𐐲 𐑊𐐮𐐻𐑊 𐐹𐑉𐐴𐐼 𐐸𐐶𐐮𐐽 𐐶𐐱𐑆 𐐮𐑌 𐑄 𐐽𐐲𐑉𐐽, 𐐸𐐶𐐮𐐽 𐐼𐐮𐐼 𐐿𐐫𐑆 𐑅𐐲𐑋 𐑊𐐮𐐻𐑊 𐐼𐐮𐑅𐐯𐑌𐑇𐐲𐑌𐑆 𐐲𐑋𐐲𐑍 𐑄 𐐹𐐨𐐹𐑊, 𐐸𐐶𐐮𐐽 𐐰𐑁𐐩𐑉𐑆 𐐶𐐲𐑉 𐑅𐐯𐐻𐑊𐐼 𐐮𐑌 𐑄 𐐯𐑌𐐼𐐮𐑍 𐐱𐑂 𐑄 𐑁𐐫𐑉𐐻𐐨 𐐰𐑌𐐼 𐑃𐐲𐑉𐐼 𐐷𐐨𐑉. 𐐈𐑌𐐼 𐑄𐐩𐑉 𐐶𐐱𐑆 𐑌𐐬 𐐿𐐱𐑌𐐻𐐯𐑌𐑇𐐲𐑌 𐐲𐑋𐐲𐑍 𐑄 𐐹𐐨𐐹𐑊 𐐮𐑌 𐑄 𐑁𐐫𐑉𐐻𐐨 𐐰𐑌𐐼 𐑁𐐬𐑉𐑃 𐐷𐐨𐑉; 𐑌𐐨𐑄𐐲𐑉 𐐶𐐱𐑆 𐑄𐐩𐑉 𐑋𐐲𐐽 𐐿𐐱𐑌𐐻𐐯𐑌𐑇𐐲𐑌 𐐮𐑌 𐑄 𐑁𐐫𐑉𐐻𐐨 𐐰𐑌𐐼 𐑁𐐮𐑁𐑃 𐐷𐐨𐑉. 𐐈𐑌𐐼 𐐮𐐻 𐐿𐐩𐑋 𐐻𐐭 𐐹𐐰𐑅 𐐮𐑌 𐑄 𐑁𐐫𐑉𐐻𐐨 𐐰𐑌𐐼 𐑅𐐮𐐿𐑅𐑃, 𐐷𐐩, 𐑄𐐩𐑉 𐐶𐐱𐑆 𐑋𐐲𐐽 𐐿𐐱𐑌𐐻𐐯𐑌𐑇𐐲𐑌 𐐰𐑌𐐼 𐑋𐐯𐑌𐐨

𐐼𐐮𐑅𐐯𐑌𐑇𐐲𐑌𐑆; 𐐮𐑌 𐑄 𐐸𐐶𐐮𐐽 𐑄𐐯𐑉 𐐶𐐲𐑉 𐐰𐑌 𐐯𐐿𐑅𐐨𐐼𐐮𐑍𐑊𐐨 𐑀𐑉𐐩𐐻 𐑋𐐯𐑌𐐨 𐐸𐐭 𐐼𐐨𐐹𐐪𐑉𐐻𐐯𐐼 𐐵𐐻 𐐱𐑂 𐑄 𐑊𐐰𐑌𐐼 𐐱𐑂 𐐞𐐪𐑉𐐲𐐸𐐯𐑋𐑊𐐲, 𐐰𐑌𐐼 𐐶𐐯𐑌𐐻 𐑁𐐫𐑉𐑃 𐐲𐑌𐐻𐐭 𐑄 𐑊𐐰𐑌𐐼 𐑌𐐫𐑉𐑃𐐶𐐲𐑉𐐼, 𐐻𐐭 𐐮𐑌𐐸𐐯𐑉𐐮𐐻 𐑄 𐑊𐐰𐑌𐐼; 𐐰𐑌𐐼 𐑄𐐩 𐐼𐐮𐐼 𐐻𐑉𐐰𐑂𐐯𐑊 𐐻𐐭 𐐰𐑌 𐐯𐐿𐑅𐐨𐐼𐐮𐑍𐑊𐐨 𐑀𐑉𐐩𐐻 𐐼𐐮𐑅𐐻𐐲𐑌𐑅, 𐐮𐑌𐑅𐐬𐑋𐐲𐐽 𐑄𐐰𐐻 𐑄𐐩 𐐿𐐩𐑋 𐐻𐐭 𐑊𐐪𐑉𐐾 𐐺𐐱𐐼𐐨𐑆 𐐱𐑂 𐐶𐐫𐐻𐐲𐑉, 𐐰𐑌𐐼 𐑋𐐯𐑌𐐨 𐑉𐐮𐑂𐐲𐑉𐑆; 𐐷𐐩, 𐐰𐑌𐐼 𐐨𐑂𐐲𐑌 𐑄𐐩 𐐼𐐮𐐼 𐑅𐐹𐑉𐐯𐐼 𐑁𐐫𐑉𐑃 𐐮𐑌𐐻𐐭 𐐫𐑊 𐐹𐐪𐑉𐐻𐑅 𐐱𐑂 𐑄 𐑊𐐰𐑌𐐼, 𐐮𐑌𐐻𐐭 𐐸𐐶𐐱𐐻𐐯𐑂𐐲𐑉 𐐹𐐪𐑉𐐻𐑅 𐐮𐐻 𐐸𐐰𐐼 𐑌𐐱𐐻 𐐺𐐮𐑌 𐑉𐐯𐑌𐐼𐐲𐑉𐐼 𐐼𐐯𐑅𐐬𐑊𐐩𐐻, 𐐰𐑌𐐼 𐐶𐐮𐑃𐐵𐐻 𐐻𐐮𐑋𐐺𐐲𐑉, 𐐺𐐨𐐿𐐫𐑆 𐐱𐑂 𐑄 𐑋𐐯𐑌𐐨 𐐮𐑌𐐸𐐰𐐺𐐮𐐻𐐲𐑌𐐻𐑅 𐐸𐐭 𐐸𐐰𐐼 𐐺𐐨𐑁𐐬𐑉 𐐮𐑌𐐸𐐯𐑉𐐮𐐻𐐯𐐼 𐑄 𐑊𐐰𐑌𐐼. 𐐈𐑌𐐼 𐑌𐐵 𐑌𐐬 𐐹𐐪𐑉𐐻 𐐱𐑂 𐑄 𐑊𐐰𐑌𐐼 𐐶𐐱𐑆 𐐼𐐯𐑅𐐬𐑊𐐩𐐻, 𐑅𐐩𐑂 𐐮𐐻 𐐶𐐲𐑉 𐑁𐐫𐑉 𐐻𐐮𐑋𐐺𐐲𐑉, 𐐯𐐻𐑅.; 𐐺𐐲𐐻 𐐺𐐨𐐿𐐫𐑆 𐐱𐑂 𐑄 𐑀𐑉𐐩𐐻𐑌𐐯𐑅 𐐱𐑂 𐑄 𐐼𐐯𐑅𐐻𐑉𐐲𐐿𐑇𐐲𐑌 𐐱𐑂 𐑄 𐐹𐐨𐐹𐑊 𐐸𐐭 𐐸𐐰𐐼 𐐺𐐨𐑁𐐬𐑉 𐐮𐑌𐐸𐐰𐐺𐐮𐐻𐐯𐐼 𐑄 𐑊𐐰𐑌𐐼, 𐐮𐐻 𐐶𐐱𐑆 𐐿𐐫𐑊𐐼 𐐼𐐯𐑅𐐬𐑊𐐩𐐻. 𐐈𐑌𐐼 𐑄𐐯𐑉 𐐺𐐨𐐮𐑍 𐐺𐐲𐐻 𐑊𐐮𐐻𐐲𐑊 𐐻𐐮𐑋𐐺𐐲𐑉 𐐲𐐹𐐱𐑌 𐑄 𐑁𐐩𐑅 𐐱𐑂 𐑄 𐑊𐐰𐑌𐐼, 𐑌𐐯𐑂𐐲𐑉𐑄𐐯𐑊𐐯𐑅 𐑄 𐐹𐐨𐐹𐑊 𐐸𐐭 𐐶𐐯𐑌𐐻 𐑁𐐫𐑉𐑃 𐐺𐐨𐐿𐐩𐑋 𐐯𐐿𐑅𐐨𐐼𐐮𐑍𐑊𐐨 𐐯𐐿𐑅𐐹𐐲𐑉𐐻 𐐮𐑌 𐑄 𐐶𐐲𐑉𐐿𐐮𐑍 𐐱𐑂 𐑅𐐯𐑋𐐯𐑌𐐻; 𐑄𐐯𐑉𐑁𐐬𐑉 𐑄𐐩 𐐼𐐮𐐼 𐐺𐐮𐑊𐐼 𐐸𐐵𐑆𐐯𐑆 𐐱𐑂 𐑅𐐯𐑋𐐯𐑌𐐻, 𐐮𐑌 𐑄 𐐸𐐶𐐮𐐽 𐑄𐐩 𐐼𐐮𐐼 𐐼𐐶𐐯𐑊.

2. 𐐈𐑌𐐼 𐐮𐐻 𐐿𐐩𐑋 𐐻𐐭 𐐹𐐪𐑅 𐑄𐐰𐐻 𐑄𐐩 𐐼𐐮𐐼 𐑋𐐲𐑊𐐻𐐮𐐹𐑊𐐴 𐐰𐑌𐐼 𐑅𐐹𐑉𐐯𐐼, 𐐰𐑌𐐼 𐐼𐐮𐐼 𐑀𐐬 𐑁𐐫𐑉𐑃 𐑁𐑉𐐱𐑋 𐑄 𐑊𐐰𐑌𐐼 𐑅𐐵𐑃𐐶𐐲𐑉𐐼 𐐻𐐭 𐑄 𐑊𐐰𐑌𐐼 𐑌𐐫𐑉𐑃𐐶𐐲𐑉𐐼, 𐐰𐑌𐐼 𐐼𐐮𐐼 𐑅𐐹𐑉𐐯𐐼 𐐮𐑌𐑅𐐬𐑋𐐲𐐽 𐑄𐐰𐐻 𐑄𐐩 𐐺𐐨𐑀𐐰𐑌 𐐻𐐭 𐐿𐐲𐑂𐐲𐑉 𐑄 𐑁𐐩𐑅 𐐱𐑂 𐑄 𐐸𐐬𐑊 𐐲𐑉𐑃, 𐑁𐑉𐐱𐑋 𐑄 𐑅𐐨 𐑅𐐵𐑃 𐐻𐐭 𐑄 𐑅𐐨 𐑌𐐫𐑉𐑃, 𐑁𐑉𐐱𐑋 𐑄 𐑅𐐨 𐐶𐐯𐑅𐐻 𐐻𐐭 𐑄 𐑅𐐨 𐐨𐑅𐐻. 𐐈𐑌𐐼 𐑄 𐐹𐐨𐐹𐑊 𐐸𐐭 𐐶𐐲𐑉 𐐮𐑌 𐑄 𐑊𐐰𐑌𐐼 𐑌𐐫𐑉𐑃𐐶𐐲𐑉𐐼, 𐐼𐐮𐐼 𐐼𐐶𐐯𐑊 𐐮𐑌 𐐻𐐯𐑌𐐻𐑅, 𐐰𐑌𐐼 𐐮𐑌 𐐸𐐵𐑆𐐯𐑆 𐐱𐑂 𐑅𐐯𐑋𐐯𐑌𐐻, 𐐰𐑌𐐼 𐑄𐐩 𐐼𐐮𐐼 𐑅𐐲𐑁𐐲𐑉 𐐸𐐶𐐱𐐻𐑅𐐬𐐯𐑂𐐲𐑉 𐐻𐑉𐐨 𐑇𐐳𐐼 𐑅𐐹𐑉𐐮𐑍 𐐲𐐹 𐐲𐐹𐐱𐑌 𐑄 𐑁𐐩𐑅 𐐱𐑂 𐑄 𐑊𐐰𐑌𐐼, 𐑄𐐰𐐻 𐐮𐐻 𐑇𐐳𐐼 𐑀𐑉𐐬 𐐲𐐹, 𐑄𐐰𐐻 𐐮𐑌 𐐻𐐴𐑋 𐑄𐐩 𐑋𐐴𐐻 𐐸𐐰𐑂 𐐻𐐮𐑋𐐺𐐲𐑉 𐐻𐐭 𐐺𐐮𐑊𐐼 𐑄𐐩𐑉 𐐸𐐵𐑆𐐯𐑆, 𐐷𐐩, 𐑄𐐩𐑉 𐑅𐐮𐐻𐐨𐑆, 𐐰𐑌𐐼 𐑄𐐩𐑉 𐐻𐐯𐑋𐐹𐑊𐑆, 𐐰𐑌𐐼 𐑄𐐩𐑉 𐑅𐐮𐑌𐐲𐑀𐐱𐑀𐑆, 𐐰𐑌𐐼 𐑄𐐩𐑉 𐑅𐐰𐑍𐐿𐐻𐐷𐐭𐐯𐑉𐐨𐑆, 𐐰𐑌𐐼 𐐫𐑊 𐑋𐐰𐑌𐐲𐑉 𐐱𐑂 𐑄𐐩𐑉 𐐺𐐮𐑊𐐼𐐮𐑍𐑆.

3. 𐐈𐑌𐐼 𐐮𐐻 𐐿𐐩𐑋 𐐻𐐭 𐐹𐐪𐑅 𐐰𐑆 𐐻𐐮𐑋𐐺𐐲𐑉 𐐶𐐱𐑆 𐐯𐐿𐑅𐐨𐐼𐐮𐑍𐑊𐐨 𐑅𐐿𐐩𐑉𐑅 𐐮𐑌 𐑄 𐑊𐐰𐑌𐐼 𐑌𐐫𐑉𐑃𐐶𐐲𐑉𐐼, 𐑄𐐩 𐐼𐐮𐐼 𐑅𐐯𐑌𐐼 𐑁𐐫𐑉𐑃 𐑋𐐲𐐽 𐐺𐐴 𐑄 𐐶𐐩 𐐱𐑂 𐑇𐐮𐐹𐐮𐑍; 𐐰𐑌𐐼 𐑄𐐲𐑅 𐑄𐐩 𐐼𐐮𐐼 𐐯𐑌𐐩𐐺𐑊 𐑄 𐐹𐐨𐐹𐑊 𐐮𐑌 𐑄 𐑊𐐰𐑌𐐼 𐑌𐐫𐑉𐑃𐐶𐐲𐑉𐐼, 𐑄𐐰𐐻 𐑄𐐩 𐑋𐐴𐐻 𐐺𐐮𐑊𐐼 𐑋𐐯𐑌𐐨 𐑅𐐮𐐻𐐨𐑆, 𐐺𐐬𐑃 𐐱𐑂 𐐶𐐳𐐼 𐐰𐑌𐐼 𐐱𐑂 𐑅𐐯𐑋𐐯𐑌𐐻. 𐐈𐑌𐐼 𐐮𐐻 𐐿𐐩𐑋 𐐻𐐭 𐐹𐐪𐑅 𐑄𐐰𐐻 𐑄𐐯𐑉 𐐶𐐲𐑉 𐑋𐐯𐑌𐐨 𐐱𐑂 𐑄 𐐹𐐨𐐹𐑊 𐐱𐑂 𐐁𐑋𐐲𐑌, 𐐸𐐭 𐐶𐐲𐑉 𐐢𐐩𐑋𐐲𐑌𐐴𐐻𐑅 𐐺𐐴 𐐺𐐲𐑉𐑃, 𐐼𐐮𐐼 𐐫𐑊𐑅𐐬 𐑀𐐬 𐑁𐐫𐑉𐑃 𐐮𐑌𐐻𐐭 𐑄𐐮𐑅 𐑊𐐰𐑌𐐼.

4. 𐐈𐑌𐐼 𐑌𐐵 𐑄𐐯𐑉 𐐪𐑉 𐑋𐐯𐑌𐐨 𐑉𐐯𐐿𐐲𐑉𐐼𐑆 𐐿𐐯𐐹𐐻 𐐱𐑂 𐑄 𐐹𐑉𐐬𐑅𐐨𐐼𐐮𐑍𐑆 𐐱𐑂 𐑄𐐮𐑅 𐐹𐐨𐐹𐑊, 𐐺𐐴 𐑋𐐯𐑌𐐨 𐐱𐑂 𐑄𐐮𐑅 𐐹𐐨𐐹𐑊, 𐐸𐐶𐐮𐐽 𐐪𐑉 𐐹𐐪𐑉𐐻𐐮𐐿𐐷𐐭𐑊𐐲𐑉 𐐰𐑌𐐼 𐑂𐐯𐑉𐐨 𐑊𐐪𐑉𐐾, 𐐿𐐱𐑌𐑅𐐲𐑉𐑌𐐮𐑍 𐑄𐐯𐑋; 𐐺𐐲𐐻 𐐺𐐨𐐸𐐬𐑊𐐼, 𐐰 𐐸𐐲𐑌𐐼𐑉𐐯𐐼𐑃 𐐹𐐪𐑉𐐻 𐐱𐑂 𐑄 𐐹𐑉𐐬𐑅𐐨𐐼𐐮𐑍𐑆 𐐱𐑂 𐑄𐐮𐑅 𐐹𐐨𐐹𐑊, 𐐷𐐩, 𐑄 𐐲𐐿𐐵𐑌𐐻 𐐱𐑂 𐑄 𐐢𐐩𐑋𐐲𐑌𐐴𐐻𐑅, 𐐰𐑌𐐼 𐐱𐑂 𐑄 𐐤𐐨𐑁𐐴𐐻𐑅, 𐐰𐑌𐐼 𐑄𐐩𐑉 𐐶𐐫𐑉𐑆, 𐐰𐑌𐐼 𐐿𐐱𐑌𐐻𐐯𐑌𐑇𐐲𐑌𐑆, 𐐰𐑌𐐼 𐐼𐐮𐑅𐐯𐑌𐑇𐐲𐑌𐑆, 𐐰𐑌𐐼 𐑄𐐩𐑉 𐐹𐑉𐐨𐐽𐐮𐑍, 𐐰𐑌𐐼 𐑄𐐩𐑉 𐐹𐑉𐐱𐑁𐐯𐑅𐐨𐑆, 𐐰𐑌𐐼 𐑄𐐩𐑉 𐑇𐐮𐐹𐐮𐑍, 𐐰𐑌𐐼 𐑄𐐩𐑉 𐐺𐐮𐑊𐐼𐐮𐑍 𐐱𐑂 𐑇𐐮𐐹𐑅, 𐐰𐑌𐐼 𐑄𐐩𐑉 𐐺𐐮𐑊𐐼𐐮𐑍 𐐱𐑂 𐐻𐐯𐑋𐐹𐑊𐑆, 𐐰𐑌𐐼 𐐱𐑂 𐑅𐐮𐑌𐐲𐑀𐐱𐑀𐑆, 𐐰𐑌𐐼 𐑄𐐩𐑉 𐑅𐐰𐑍𐐿𐐻𐐷𐐭𐐯𐑉𐐨𐑆, 𐐰𐑌𐐼 𐑄𐐩𐑉 𐑉𐐴𐐽𐐲𐑅𐑌𐐯𐑅, 𐐰𐑌𐐼 𐑄𐐩𐑉 𐐶𐐮𐐿𐐯𐐼𐑌𐐯𐑅, 𐐰𐑌𐐼 𐑄𐐩𐑉 𐑋𐐲𐑉𐐼𐐲𐑉𐑆, 𐐰𐑌𐐼 𐑄𐐩𐑉 𐑉𐐱𐐺𐐮𐑍𐑆, 𐐰𐑌𐐼 𐑄𐐩𐑉 𐐹𐑊𐐲𐑌𐐼𐐲𐑉𐐮𐑍, 𐐰𐑌𐐼 𐐫𐑊 𐑋𐐰𐑌𐐲𐑉 𐐱𐑂 𐐲𐐺𐐱𐑋𐐮𐑌𐐩𐑇𐐲𐑌𐑆 𐐰𐑌𐐼 𐐸𐐬𐑉𐐼𐐲𐑋𐑆, 𐐿𐐰𐑌𐐱𐐻 𐐺𐐨 𐐿𐐱𐑌𐐻𐐩𐑌𐐯𐐼 𐐮𐑌 𐑄𐐮𐑅 𐐶𐐲𐑉𐐿; 𐐺𐐲𐐻 𐐺𐐨𐐸𐐬𐑊𐐼, 𐑄𐐯𐑉 𐐪𐑉 𐑋𐐯𐑌𐐨 𐐺𐐳𐐿𐑅 𐐰𐑌𐐼 𐑋𐐯𐑌𐐨 𐑉𐐯𐐿𐐲𐑉𐐼𐑆 𐐱𐑂 𐐯𐑂𐐲𐑉𐐨 𐐿𐐴𐑌𐐼, 𐐰𐑌𐐼 𐑄𐐩 𐐸𐐰𐑂 𐐺𐐮𐑌 𐐿𐐯𐐹𐐻 𐐽𐐨𐑁𐑊𐐨 𐐺𐐴 𐑄 𐐤𐐨𐑁𐐴𐐻𐑅; 𐐰𐑌𐐼 𐑄𐐩 𐐸𐐰𐑂 𐐺𐐮𐑌 𐐸𐐰𐑌𐐼𐐯𐐼 𐐼𐐵𐑌 𐑁𐑉𐐱𐑋 𐐶𐐲𐑌 𐐾𐐯𐑌𐐲𐑉𐐩𐑇𐐲𐑌 𐐻𐐭 𐐲𐑌𐐲𐑄𐐲𐑉 𐐺𐐴 𐑄 𐐤𐐨𐑁𐐴𐐻𐑅, 𐐨𐑂𐐲𐑌 𐐲𐑌𐐻𐐮𐑊 𐑄𐐩 𐐸𐐰𐑂 𐑁𐐫𐑊𐐲𐑌 𐐮𐑌𐐻𐐭 𐐻𐑉𐐰𐑌𐑆𐑀𐑉𐐯𐑇𐐲𐑌, 𐐰𐑌𐐼 𐐸𐐰𐑂 𐐺𐐮𐑌 𐑋𐐲𐑉𐐼𐐲𐑉𐐼, 𐐹𐑊𐐲𐑌𐐼𐐲𐑉𐐼, 𐐰𐑌𐐼 𐐸𐐲𐑌𐐻𐐯𐐼, 𐐰𐑌𐐼 𐐼𐑉𐐮𐑂𐐲𐑌 𐑁𐐫𐑉𐑃, 𐐰𐑌𐐼 𐑅𐑊𐐩𐑌, 𐐰𐑌𐐼 𐑅𐐿𐐰𐐻𐐲𐑉𐐼 𐐲𐐹𐐱𐑌 𐑄 𐑁𐐩𐑅 𐐱𐑂 𐑄 𐐲𐑉𐑃, 𐐰𐑌𐐼 𐑋𐐮𐐿𐑅𐐻 𐐶𐐮𐑄 𐑄 𐐢𐐩𐑋𐐲𐑌𐐴𐐻𐑅, 𐐲𐑌𐐻𐐮𐑊 𐑄𐐩 𐐪𐑉 𐑌𐐬 𐑋𐐬𐑉 𐐿𐐫𐑊𐐼 𐑄 𐐤𐐨𐑁𐐴𐐻𐑅, 𐐺𐐨𐐿𐐲𐑋𐐮𐑍 𐐶𐐮𐐿𐐯𐐼, 𐐰𐑌𐐼 𐐶𐐴𐑊𐐼, 𐐰𐑌𐐼 𐑁𐐨𐑉𐐬𐑇𐐲𐑅, 𐐷𐐩, 𐐨𐑂𐐲𐑌 𐐺𐐨𐐿𐐲𐑋𐐮𐑍 𐐢𐐩𐑋𐐲𐑌𐐴𐐻𐑅.

5. 𐐈𐑌𐐼 𐑌𐐵 𐐌 𐑉𐐨𐐻𐐲𐑉𐑌 𐐲𐑀𐐯𐑌 𐐻𐐭 𐑋𐐴𐑌 𐐲𐐿𐐵𐑌𐐻; 𐑄𐐯𐑉𐑁𐐬𐑉 𐐸𐐶𐐱𐐻 𐐌 𐐸𐐰𐑂 𐑅𐐹𐐬𐐿𐐲𐑌 𐐸𐐰𐐼 𐐹𐐰𐑅𐐻 𐐰𐑁𐐻𐐲𐑉 𐑄𐐯𐑉 𐐸𐐰𐐼 𐐺𐐮𐑌 𐑀𐑉𐐩𐐻 𐐿𐐱𐑌𐐻𐐯𐑌𐑇𐐲𐑌𐑆, 𐐰𐑌𐐼 𐐼𐐮𐑅𐐻𐐲𐑉𐐺𐐲𐑌𐑅𐐯𐑆, 𐐰𐑌𐐼 𐐶𐐫𐑉𐑆, 𐐰𐑌𐐼 𐐼𐐮𐑅𐐯𐑌𐑇𐐲𐑌𐑆, 𐐲𐑋𐐲𐑍 𐑄 𐐹𐐨𐐹𐑊 𐐱𐑂 𐐤𐐨𐑁𐐴. 𐐜 𐑁𐐫𐑉𐐻𐐨 𐐰𐑌𐐼 𐑅𐐮𐐿𐑅𐑃 𐐷𐐨𐑉 𐐱𐑂 𐑄 𐑉𐐩𐑌 𐐱𐑂 𐑄 𐐖𐐲𐐾𐐯𐑆

𐐤𐐨𐑁𐐴𐐻𐑅. 𐐈𐑌𐐼 𐐮𐐻 𐐿𐐩𐑋 𐐻𐐭 𐐹𐐰𐑅 𐑄𐐰𐐻 𐑄𐐯𐑉 𐐶𐐱𐑆 𐑅𐐻𐐮𐑊 𐑀𐑉𐐩𐐻 𐐿𐐱𐑌𐐻𐐯𐑌𐑇𐐲𐑌 𐐮𐑌 𐑄 𐑊𐐰𐑌𐐼, 𐐷𐐩, 𐐨𐑂𐐲𐑌 𐐮𐑌 𐑄 𐑁𐐫𐑉𐐻𐐨 𐐰𐑌𐐼 𐑅𐐯𐑂𐐲𐑌𐑃 𐐷𐐨𐑉, 𐐰𐑌𐐼 𐐫𐑊𐑅𐐬 𐐮𐑌 𐑄 𐑁𐐫𐑉𐐻𐐨 𐐰𐑌𐐼 𐐩𐐻𐑃 𐐷𐐨𐑉; 𐑌𐐯𐑂𐐲𐑉𐑄𐐲𐑊𐐯𐑅, 𐐐𐐨𐑊𐐪𐑋𐐲𐑌 𐐼𐐮𐐼 𐑁𐐮𐑊 𐑄 𐐾𐐲𐐾𐑋𐐯𐑌𐐻-𐑅𐐨𐐻 𐐶𐐮𐑃 𐐾𐐲𐑅𐐻𐐮𐑅 𐐰𐑌𐐼 𐐯𐐿𐐶𐐮𐐻𐐨; 𐐷𐐩, 𐐸𐐨 𐐼𐐮𐐼 𐐱𐐺𐑆𐐲𐑉𐑂 𐐻𐐭 𐐿𐐨𐐹 𐑄 𐑅𐐻𐐰𐐽𐐭𐐻𐑅, 𐐰𐑌𐐼 𐑄 𐐾𐐲𐐾𐑋𐐯𐑌𐐻𐑅, 𐐰𐑌𐐼 𐑄 𐐿𐐱𐑋𐐰𐑌𐐼𐑋𐐯𐑌𐐻𐑅 𐐱𐑂 𐐘𐐱𐐼; 𐐰𐑌𐐼 𐐸𐐨 𐐼𐐮𐐼 𐐼𐐭 𐑄𐐰𐐻 𐐸𐐶𐐮𐐽 𐐶𐐱𐑆 𐑉𐐴𐐻 𐐮𐑌 𐑄 𐑅𐐴𐐻 𐐱𐑂 𐐘𐐱𐐼 𐐿𐐱𐑌𐐻𐐮𐑌𐐷𐐳𐐲𐑊𐐨; 𐐰𐑌𐐼 𐐸𐐨 𐐼𐐮𐐼 𐐶𐐫𐐿 𐐰𐑁𐐻𐐲𐑉 𐑄 𐐶𐐩𐑆 𐐱𐑂 𐐸𐐮𐑆 𐑁𐐪𐑄𐐲𐑉, 𐐮𐑌𐑅𐐬𐑋𐐲𐐽 𐑄𐐰𐐻 𐐸𐐨 𐐼𐐮𐐼 𐐹𐑉𐐱𐑅𐐹𐐲𐑉 𐐮𐑌 𐑄 𐑊𐐰𐑌𐐼. 𐐈𐑌𐐼 𐐮𐐻 𐐿𐐩𐑋 𐐻𐐭 𐐹𐐰𐑅 𐑄𐐰𐐻 𐐸𐐨 𐐸𐐰𐐼 𐐻𐐭 𐑅𐐲𐑌𐑆. 𐐐𐐨 𐑀𐐩𐑂 𐐲𐑌𐐻𐐭 𐑄 𐐯𐑊𐐼𐐯𐑅𐐻 𐑄 𐑌𐐩𐑋 𐐱𐑂 𐐤𐐨𐑁𐐴, 𐐰𐑌𐐼 𐐲𐑌𐐻𐐭 𐑄 𐐷𐐲𐑍𐑀𐐯𐑅𐐻, 𐑄 𐑌𐐩𐑋 𐐱𐑂 𐐢𐐨𐐸𐐴. 𐐈𐑌𐐼 𐑄𐐩 𐐺𐐨𐑀𐐰𐑌 𐐻𐐭 𐑀𐑉𐐬 𐐲𐐹 𐐲𐑌𐐻𐐭 𐑄 𐐢𐐫𐑉𐐼. 𐐈𐑌𐐼 𐐮𐐻 𐐿𐐩𐑋 𐐻𐐭 𐐹𐐰𐑅 𐑄𐐰𐐻 𐑄 𐐶𐐫𐑉𐑆 𐐰𐑌𐐼 𐐿𐐱𐑌𐐻𐐯𐑌𐑇𐐲𐑌𐑆 𐐺𐐨𐑀𐐰𐑌 𐐻𐐭 𐑅𐐨𐑅, 𐐮𐑌 𐐰 𐑅𐑋𐐫𐑊 𐐼𐐨𐑀𐑉𐐨, 𐐲𐑋𐐲𐑍 𐑄 𐐹𐐨𐐹𐐲𐑊 𐐱𐑂 𐑄 𐐤𐐨𐑁𐐴𐐻𐑅, 𐐮𐑌 𐑄 𐑊𐐰𐐻𐐲𐑉 𐐯𐑌𐐼 𐐱𐑂 𐑄 𐑁𐐫𐑉𐐻𐐨 𐐰𐑌𐐼 𐐩𐐻𐑃 𐐷𐐨𐑉 𐐱𐑂 𐑄 𐑉𐐩𐑌 𐐱𐑂 𐑄 𐐾𐐲𐐾𐐯𐑆 𐐬𐑂𐐲𐑉 𐑄 𐐹𐐨𐐹𐐲𐑊 𐐱𐑂 𐐤𐐨𐑁𐐴. 𐐈𐑌𐐼 𐐮𐐻 𐐿𐐩𐑋 𐐻𐐭 𐐹𐐰𐑅 𐐮𐑌 𐑄 𐑁𐐫𐑉𐐻𐐨 𐐰𐑌𐐼 𐑌𐐴𐑌𐑃 𐐷𐐨𐑉 𐐱𐑂 𐑄 𐑉𐐩𐑌 𐐱𐑂 𐑄 𐐾𐐲𐐾𐐯𐑆, 𐑄𐐯𐑉 𐐶𐐱𐑆 𐐿𐐱𐑌𐐻𐐮𐑌𐐷𐐳𐐲𐑊 𐐹𐐨𐑅 𐐯𐑅𐐻𐐰𐐺𐑊𐐮𐑇𐐻 𐐮𐑌 𐑄 𐑊𐐰𐑌𐐼, 𐐫𐑊 𐑅𐐩𐑂 𐐮𐐻 𐐶𐐲𐑉 𐑄 𐑅𐐨𐐿𐑉𐐯𐐻 𐐿𐐱𐑋𐐺𐐮𐑌𐐩𐑇𐐲𐑌𐑆 𐐸𐐶𐐮𐐽 𐐘𐐰𐐼𐐨𐐰𐑌𐐻𐐲𐑌 𐑄 𐑉𐐱𐐺𐐲𐑉 𐐸𐐰𐐼 𐐯𐑅𐐻𐐰𐐺𐑊𐐮𐑇𐐻 𐐮𐑌 𐑄 𐑋𐐬𐑉 𐑅𐐯𐐻𐐲𐑊𐐼 𐐹𐐪𐑉𐐻𐑅 𐐱𐑂 𐑄 𐑊𐐰𐑌𐐼, 𐐸𐐶𐐮𐐽 𐐰𐐻 𐑄𐐰𐐻 𐐻𐐴𐑋 𐐶𐐲𐑉 𐑌𐐱𐐻 𐑌𐐬𐑌 𐐲𐑌𐐻𐐭 𐑄𐐬𐑆 𐐸𐐭 𐐶𐐲𐑉 𐐰𐐻 𐑄 𐐸𐐯𐐼 𐐱𐑂 𐑀𐐲𐑂𐐲𐑉𐑌𐑋𐐯𐑌𐐻; 𐑄𐐯𐑉𐑁𐐬𐑉 𐑄𐐩 𐐶𐐲𐑉 𐑌𐐱𐐻 𐐼𐐯𐑅𐐻𐑉𐐱𐐮𐐼 𐐵𐐻 𐐱𐑂 𐑄 𐑊𐐰𐑌𐐼.

6. 𐐈𐑌𐐼 𐐮𐐻 𐐿𐐩𐑋 𐐻𐐭 𐐹𐐰𐑅 𐑄𐐰𐐻 𐐮𐑌 𐑄𐐮𐑅 𐑅𐐩𐑋 𐐷𐐨𐑉 𐑄𐐯𐑉 𐐶𐐱𐑆 𐐯𐐿𐑅𐐨𐐼𐐮𐑍𐑊𐐨 𐑀𐑉𐐩𐐻 𐐹𐑉𐐱𐑅𐐹𐐯𐑉𐐮𐐻𐐨 𐐮𐑌 𐑄 𐐽𐐲𐑉𐐽, 𐐮𐑌𐑅𐐬𐑋𐐲𐐽 𐑄𐐰𐐻 𐑄𐐯𐑉 𐐶𐐲𐑉 𐑃𐐵𐑆𐐲𐑌𐐼𐑆 𐐸𐐭 𐐼𐐮𐐼 𐐾𐐱𐐮𐑌 𐑄𐐯𐑋𐑅𐐯𐑊𐑂𐑆 𐐲𐑌𐐻𐐭 𐑄 𐐽𐐲𐑉𐐽, 𐐰𐑌𐐼 𐐶𐐲𐑉 𐐺𐐰𐐹𐐻𐐴𐑆𐐼 𐐲𐑌𐐻𐐭 𐑉𐐨𐐹𐐯𐑌𐐻𐐲𐑌𐑅; 𐐰𐑌𐐼 𐑅𐐬 𐑀𐑉𐐩𐐻 𐐶𐐱𐑆 𐑄 𐐹𐑉𐐱𐑅𐐹𐐯𐑉𐐮𐐻𐐨 𐐱𐑂 𐑄 𐐽𐐲𐑉𐐽, 𐐰𐑌𐐼 𐑅𐐬 𐑋𐐯𐑌𐐨 𐑄 𐐺𐑊𐐯𐑅𐐮𐑍𐑆 𐐸𐐶𐐮𐐽 𐐶𐐲𐑉 𐐹𐐬𐑉𐐼 𐐵𐐻 𐐲𐐹𐐱𐑌 𐑄 𐐹𐐨𐐹𐐲𐑊, 𐑄𐐰𐐻 𐐨𐑂𐐲𐑌 𐑄 𐐸𐐴 𐐹𐑉𐐨𐑅𐐻𐑅 𐐰𐑌𐐼 𐑄 𐐻𐐨𐐽𐐲𐑉𐑆 𐐶𐐲𐑉 𐑄𐐯𐑋𐑅𐐯𐑊𐑂𐑆 𐐲𐑅𐐻𐐱𐑌𐐮𐑇𐐻 𐐺𐐨𐐷𐐱𐑌𐐼 𐑋𐐯𐑈𐐲𐑉. 𐐈𐑌𐐼 𐐮𐐻 𐐿𐐩𐑋 𐐻𐐭 𐐹𐐰𐑅 𐑄𐐰𐐻 𐑄 𐐶𐐲𐑉𐐿 𐐱𐑂 𐑄 𐐢𐐫𐑉𐐼 𐐼𐐮𐐼 𐐹𐑉𐐱𐑅𐐹𐐲𐑉 𐐲𐑌𐐻𐐭 𐑄 𐐺𐐰𐐹𐐻𐐴𐑆𐐮𐑍 𐐰𐑌𐐼 𐐷𐐭𐑌𐐴𐐻𐐮𐑍 𐐻𐐭 𐑄 𐐽𐐲𐑉𐐽 𐐱𐑂 𐐘𐐱𐐼, 𐑋𐐯𐑌𐐨 𐑅𐐬𐑊𐑆; 𐐷𐐩, 𐐨𐑂𐐲𐑌 𐐻𐐯𐑌𐑆 𐐱𐑂 𐑃𐐵𐑆𐐲𐑌𐐼𐑆. 𐐜𐐲𐑅 𐐶𐐨 𐑋𐐩 𐑅𐐨 𐑄𐐰𐐻 𐑄 𐐢𐐫𐑉𐐼 𐐮𐑆 𐑋𐐲𐑉𐑅𐐮𐑁𐐳𐑊 𐐲𐑌𐐻𐐭 𐐫𐑊 𐐸𐐭 𐐶𐐮𐑊, 𐐮𐑌 𐑄 𐑅𐐮𐑌𐑅𐐯𐑉𐐮𐐻𐐨 𐐱𐑂 𐑄𐐯𐑉 𐐸𐐪𐑉𐐻𐑅, 𐐿𐐫𐑊 𐐲𐐹𐐱𐑌 𐐸𐐮𐑆 𐐸𐐬𐑊𐐨 𐑌𐐩𐑋; 𐐷𐐩, 𐑄𐐲𐑅 𐐶𐐨 𐑅𐐨 𐑄𐐰𐐻 𐑄 𐑀𐐩𐐻 𐐱𐑂 𐐸𐐯𐑂𐐲𐑌 𐐮𐑆 𐐬𐐹𐐲𐑌 𐐲𐑌𐐻𐐭 𐐫𐑊, 𐐨𐑂𐐲𐑌 𐐻𐐭 𐑄𐐬𐑆 𐐸𐐭 𐐶𐐮𐑊 𐐺𐐨𐑊𐐨𐑂 𐐱𐑌 𐑄 𐑌𐐩𐑋 𐐱𐑂 𐐖𐐨𐑆𐐲𐑅 𐐗𐑉𐐴𐑅𐐻, 𐐸𐐭 𐐮𐑆 𐑄 𐐝𐐲𐑌 𐐱𐑂 𐐘𐐱𐐼; 𐐷𐐩, 𐐶𐐨 𐑅𐐨 𐑄𐐰𐐻 𐐸𐐭𐑅𐐬𐐯𐑂𐐲𐑉 𐐶𐐮𐑊 𐑋𐐩 𐑊𐐩 𐐸𐐬𐑊𐐼 𐐲𐐹𐐱𐑌 𐑄 𐐶𐐲𐑉𐐼 𐐱𐑂 𐐘𐐱𐐼, 𐐸𐐶𐐮𐐽 𐐮𐑆 𐐿𐐶𐐮𐐿 𐐰𐑌𐐼 𐐹𐐵𐐲𐑉𐑁𐐳𐑊, 𐐸𐐶𐐮𐐽 𐑇𐐰𐑊 𐐼𐐮𐑂𐐴𐐼 𐐰𐑅𐐲𐑌𐐼𐐲𐑉 𐐫𐑊 𐑄 𐐿𐐲𐑌𐐮𐑍, 𐐰𐑌𐐼 𐑄 𐑅𐑌𐐩𐑉𐑆, 𐐰𐑌𐐼 𐑄 𐐶𐐴𐑊𐑆 𐐱𐑂 𐑄 𐐼𐐯𐑂𐐮𐑊, 𐐰𐑌𐐼 𐑊𐐨𐐼 𐑄 𐑋𐐰𐑌 𐐱𐑂 𐐗𐑉𐐴𐑅𐐻 𐐮𐑌 𐐰 𐑅𐐻𐑉𐐩𐐻 𐐰𐑌𐐼 𐑌𐐰𐑉𐐬 𐐿𐐬𐑉𐑅 𐐲𐐿𐑉𐐱𐑅 𐑄𐐰𐐻 𐐯𐑂𐐲𐑉𐑊𐐰𐑅𐐻𐐮𐑍 𐑀𐐲𐑊𐑁 𐐱𐑂 𐑋𐐮𐑆𐐲𐑉𐐨 𐐸𐐶𐐮𐐽 𐐮𐑆 𐐹𐑉𐐨𐐹𐐩𐑉𐐼 𐐻𐐭 𐐯𐑌𐑀𐐲𐑊𐑁 𐑄 𐐶𐐮𐐿𐐯𐐼, 𐐰𐑌𐐼 𐑊𐐰𐑌𐐼 𐑄𐐯𐑉 𐑅𐐬𐑊𐑆, 𐐷𐐩, 𐑄𐐯𐑉 𐐮𐑋𐐫𐑉𐐻𐐲𐑊 𐑅𐐬𐑊𐑆, 𐐰𐐻 𐑄 𐑉𐐴𐐻 𐐸𐐰𐑌𐐼 𐐱𐑂 𐐘𐐱𐐼, 𐐮𐑌 𐑄 𐐿𐐮𐑍𐐼𐐲𐑋 𐐱𐑂 𐐸𐐯𐑂𐐲𐑌, 𐐻𐐭 𐑅𐐮𐐻 𐐼𐐵𐑌 𐐶𐐮𐑃 𐐁𐐺𐑉𐐲𐐸𐐰𐑋, 𐐰𐑌𐐼 𐐌𐑆𐐲𐐿, 𐐰𐑌𐐼 𐐶𐐮𐑃 𐐖𐐩𐐿𐐲𐐺, 𐐰𐑌𐐼 𐐶𐐮𐑃 𐐫𐑊 𐐵𐑉 𐐸𐐬𐑊𐐨 𐑁𐐪𐑄𐐲𐑉𐑆, 𐐻𐐭 𐑀𐐬 𐑌𐐬 𐑋𐐬𐑉 𐐵𐐻. 𐐈𐑌𐐼 𐐮𐑌 𐑄𐐮𐑅 𐐷𐐨𐑉 𐑄𐐯𐑉 𐐶𐐱𐑆 𐐿𐐱𐑌𐐻𐐮𐑌𐐷𐐳𐐲𐑊 𐑉𐐨𐐾𐐱𐐮𐑅𐐮𐑍 𐐮𐑌 𐑄 𐑊𐐰𐑌𐐼 𐐱𐑂 𐐞𐐰𐑉𐐲𐐸𐐯𐑋𐑊𐐲, 𐐰𐑌𐐼 𐐮𐑌 𐐫𐑊 𐑄 𐑉𐐨𐐾𐐲𐑌𐑆 𐑉𐐵𐑌𐐼 𐐲𐐺𐐵𐐻, 𐐨𐑂𐐲𐑌 𐐮𐑌 𐐫𐑊 𐑄 𐑊𐐰𐑌𐐼 𐐸𐐶𐐮𐐽 𐐶𐐱𐑆 𐐹𐐲𐑆𐐯𐑅𐐻 𐐺𐐴 𐑄 𐐤𐐨𐑁𐐴𐐻𐑅. 𐐈𐑌𐐼 𐐮𐐻 𐐿𐐩𐑋 𐐻𐐭 𐐹𐐰𐑅 𐑄𐐰𐐻 𐑄𐐯𐑉 𐐶𐐱𐑆 𐐹𐐨𐑅 𐐰𐑌𐐼 𐐯𐐿𐑅𐐨𐐼𐐮𐑍𐑊𐐨 𐑀𐑉𐐩𐐻 𐐾𐐱𐐮 𐐮𐑌 𐑄 𐑉𐐨𐑋𐐩𐑌𐐼𐐲𐑉 𐐱𐑂 𐑄 𐑁𐐫𐑉𐐻𐐨 𐐰𐑌𐐼 𐑌𐐴𐑌𐑃 𐐷𐐨𐑉; 𐐷𐐩, 𐐰𐑌𐐼 𐐫𐑊𐑅𐐬 𐑄𐐯𐑉 𐐶𐐱𐑆 𐐿𐐱𐑌𐐻𐐮𐑌𐐷𐐳𐐲𐑊 𐐹𐐨𐑅 𐐰𐑌𐐼 𐑀𐑉𐐩𐐻 𐐾𐐱𐐮 𐐮𐑌 𐑄 𐑁𐐮𐑁𐐻𐐨𐐯𐑃 𐐷𐐨𐑉 𐐱𐑂 𐑄 𐑉𐐩𐑌 𐐱𐑂 𐑄 𐐾𐐲𐐾𐐯𐑆. 𐐈𐑌𐐼 𐐮𐑌 𐑄 𐑁𐐮𐑁𐐻𐐨 𐐰𐑌𐐼 𐑁𐐲𐑉𐑅𐐻 𐐷𐐨𐑉 𐐱𐑂 𐑄 𐑉𐐩𐑌 𐐱𐑂 𐑄 𐐾𐐲𐐾𐐯𐑆 𐑄𐐯𐑉 𐐶𐐱𐑆 𐐹𐐨𐑅 𐐫𐑊𐑅𐐬, 𐑅𐐩𐑂 𐐮𐐻 𐐶𐐲𐑉 𐑄 𐐹𐑉𐐴𐐼 𐐸𐐶𐐮𐐽 𐐺𐐨𐑀𐐰𐑌 𐐻𐐭 𐐯𐑌𐐻𐐲𐑉 𐐮𐑌𐐻𐐭 𐑄 𐐽𐐲𐑉𐐽; 𐑌𐐱𐐻 𐐮𐑌𐐻𐐭 𐑄 𐐽𐐲𐑉𐐽 𐐱𐑂 𐐘𐐱𐐼, 𐐺𐐲𐐻 𐐮𐑌𐐻𐐭 𐑄 𐐸𐐪𐑉𐐻𐑅 𐐱𐑂 𐑄 𐐹𐐨𐐹𐐲𐑊 𐐸𐐭 𐐹𐑉𐐬𐑁𐐯𐑅𐐻 𐐻𐐭 𐐺𐐨𐑊𐐱𐑍 𐐻𐐭 𐑄 𐐽𐐲𐑉𐐽 𐐱𐑂 𐐘𐐱𐐼; 𐐰𐑌𐐼 𐑄𐐩 𐐶𐐲𐑉 𐑊𐐮𐑁𐐻𐐯𐐼 𐐲𐐹 𐐮𐑌 𐐹𐑉𐐴𐐼, 𐐨𐑂𐐲𐑌 𐐻𐐭 𐑄 𐐹𐐲𐑉𐑅𐐨𐐿𐐷𐐭𐑇𐐲𐑌 𐐱𐑂 𐑋𐐯𐑌𐐨 𐐱𐑂 𐑄𐐯𐑉 𐐺𐑉𐐯𐑄𐑉𐐯𐑌. 𐐤𐐵 𐑄𐐮𐑅 𐐶𐐱𐑆 𐐰 𐑀𐑉𐐩𐐻 𐐨𐑂𐐲𐑊, 𐐸𐐶𐐮𐐽 𐐼𐐮𐐼 𐐿𐐫𐑆 𐑄 𐑋𐐬𐑉 𐐸𐐲𐑋𐐺𐐲𐑊 𐐹𐐪𐑉𐐻 𐐱𐑂 𐑄 𐐹𐐨𐐹𐐲𐑊 𐐻𐐭 𐑅𐐲𐑁𐐲𐑉 𐑀𐑉𐐩𐐻 𐐹𐐲𐑉𐑅𐐨𐐿𐐷𐐭𐑇𐐲𐑌𐑆, 𐐰𐑌𐐼 𐐻𐐭 𐐶𐐩𐐼 𐑃𐑉𐐭 𐑋𐐲𐐽 𐐰𐑁𐑊𐐮𐐿𐑇𐐲𐑌; 𐑌𐐯𐑂𐐲𐑉𐑄𐐲𐑊𐐯𐑅 𐑄𐐩 𐐼𐐮𐐼 𐑁𐐰𐑅𐐻 𐐰𐑌𐐼

𐐹𐑉𐐩 𐐫𐑁𐐻, 𐐰𐑌𐐼 𐐼𐐮𐐼 𐐶𐐰𐐿𐑅 𐑅𐐻𐑉𐐫𐑍𐑀𐐲𐑉 𐐰𐑌𐐼 𐑅𐐻𐑉𐐫𐑍𐑀𐐲𐑉 𐐮𐑌 𐑄𐐩𐑉 𐐸𐐷𐐭𐑋𐐮𐑊𐐮𐐻𐐨, 𐐰𐑌𐐼 𐑁𐐲𐑉𐑋𐐲𐑉 𐐰𐑌𐐼 𐑁𐐲𐑉𐑋𐐲𐑉 𐐮𐑌 𐑄 𐑁𐐩𐑃 𐐲𐑂 𐐗𐑉𐐴𐑅𐐻, 𐐲𐑌𐐻𐐭 𐑄 𐑁𐐮𐑊𐐮𐑍 𐑄𐐩𐑉 𐑅𐐬𐑊𐑆 𐐶𐐮𐑄 𐐾𐑎 𐐰𐑌𐐼 𐐿𐐱𐑌𐑅𐐬𐑊𐐩𐑇𐐲𐑌, 𐐷𐐩, 𐐨𐑂𐐲𐑌 𐐻𐐭 𐑄 𐐹𐐷𐐭𐑉𐐮𐑁𐐴𐐮𐑍 𐐰𐑌𐐼 𐑄 𐑅𐐰𐑍𐐿𐐻𐐮𐑁𐐮𐐿𐐩𐑇𐐲𐑌 𐐲𐑂 𐑄𐐩𐑉 𐐸𐐪𐑉𐐻𐑅, 𐐸𐐶𐐮𐐽 𐑅𐐰𐑍𐐿𐐻𐐮𐑁𐐮𐐿𐐩𐑇𐐲𐑌 𐐿𐐲𐑋𐐯𐑃 𐐺𐐨𐐿𐐫𐑆 𐐲𐑂 𐑄𐐩𐑉 𐐷𐐨𐑊𐐼𐐮𐑍 𐑄𐐩𐑉 𐐸𐐪𐑉𐐻𐑅 𐐲𐑌𐐻𐐭 𐐘𐐱𐐼. 𐐈𐑌𐐼 𐐮𐐻 𐐿𐐩𐑋 𐐻𐐭 𐐹𐐰𐑅 𐑄𐐰𐐻 𐑄 𐑁𐐮𐑁𐐻𐐨 𐐰𐑌𐐼 𐑅𐐯𐐿𐐲𐑌𐐼 𐐷𐐨𐑉 𐐯𐑌𐐼𐐯𐐼 𐐮𐑌 𐐹𐐨𐑅 𐐫𐑊𐑅𐐬, 𐑅𐐩𐑂 𐐮𐐻 𐐶𐐲𐑉 𐑄 𐐯𐐿𐑅𐐨𐐼𐐮𐑍 𐑀𐑉𐐩𐐻 𐐹𐑉𐐴𐐼 𐐸𐐶𐐮𐐽 𐐸𐐰𐐼 𐑀𐐱𐐻𐐲𐑌 𐐮𐑌𐐻𐐭 𐑄 𐐸𐐪𐑉𐐻𐑅 𐐲𐑂 𐑄 𐐹𐐨𐐹𐐲𐑊; 𐐰𐑌𐐼 𐐮𐐻 𐐶𐐱𐑆 𐐺𐐨𐐿𐐫𐑆 𐐲𐑂 𐑄𐐩𐑉 𐐯𐐿𐑅𐐨𐐼𐐮𐑍 𐑀𐑉𐐩𐐻 𐑉𐐮𐐽𐐯𐑆 𐐰𐑌𐐼 𐑄𐐩𐑉 𐐹𐑉𐐱𐑅𐐹𐐯𐑉𐐮𐐻𐐨 𐐮𐑌 𐑄 𐑊𐐰𐑌𐐼; 𐐰𐑌𐐼 𐐮𐐻 𐐼𐐮𐐼 𐑀𐑉𐐬 𐐲𐐹𐐱𐑌 𐑄𐐯𐑋 𐑁𐑉𐐱𐑋 𐐼𐐩 𐐻𐐭 𐐼𐐩.

7. 𐐈𐑌𐐼 𐐮𐐻 𐐿𐐩𐑋 𐐻𐐭 𐐹𐐰𐑅 𐐮𐑌 𐑄 𐑁𐐮𐑁𐐻𐐨 𐐰𐑌𐐼 𐑃𐐲𐑉𐐼 𐐷𐐨𐑉 𐐲𐑂 𐑄 𐑉𐐩𐑌 𐐲𐑂 𐑄 𐐾𐐲𐐾𐐯𐑆, 𐐐𐐨𐑊𐐲𐑋𐐲𐑌 𐐼𐐴𐐼, 𐐰𐑌𐐼 𐐸𐐮𐑆 𐐯𐑊𐐼𐐯𐑅𐐻 𐑅𐐲𐑌 𐐤𐐨𐑁𐐴 𐐺𐐨𐑀𐐰𐑌 𐐻𐐭 𐑉𐐩𐑌 𐐮𐑌 𐐸𐐮𐑆 𐑅𐐻𐐯𐐼. 𐐈𐑌𐐼 𐐮𐐻 𐐿𐐩𐑋 𐐻𐐭 𐐹𐐰𐑅 𐑄𐐰𐐻 𐐸𐐨 𐐼𐐮𐐼 𐑁𐐮𐑊 𐑄 𐐾𐐲𐐾𐑋𐐯𐑌𐐻-𐑅𐐨𐐻 𐐶𐐮𐑄 𐐾𐐲𐑅𐐻𐐮𐑅 𐐰𐑌𐐼 𐐯𐐿𐐶𐐮𐐻𐐨; 𐐷𐐩, 𐐸𐐨 𐐼𐐮𐐼 𐐿𐐨𐐹 𐑄 𐐿𐐱𐑋𐑋𐐰𐑌𐐼𐑋𐐯𐑌𐐻𐑅 𐐲𐑂 𐐘𐐱𐐼, 𐐰𐑌𐐼 𐐼𐐮𐐼 𐐶𐐫𐐿 𐐮𐑌 𐑄 𐐶𐐩𐑆 𐐲𐑂 𐐸𐐮𐑆 𐑁𐐪𐑄𐐲𐑉. 𐐈𐑌𐐼 𐐮𐐻 𐐿𐐩𐑋 𐐻𐐭 𐐹𐐰𐑅 𐐮𐑌 𐑄 𐑁𐐮𐑁𐐻𐐨 𐐰𐑌𐐼 𐑁𐐬𐑉𐑃 𐐷𐐨𐑉 𐑄𐐩𐑉 𐐶𐐲𐑉 𐑋𐐯𐑌𐐨 𐐼𐐮𐑅𐐯𐑌𐑇𐐲𐑌𐑆 𐐮𐑌 𐑄 𐐽𐐲𐑉𐐽, 𐐰𐑌𐐼 𐑄𐐩𐑉 𐐶𐐱𐑆 𐐫𐑊𐑅𐐬 𐐲 𐐿𐐱𐑌𐐻𐐯𐑌𐑇𐐲𐑌 𐐲𐑋𐐲𐑍 𐑄 𐐹𐐨𐐹𐐲𐑊, 𐐮𐑌𐑅𐐬𐑋𐐲𐐽 𐑄𐐰𐐻 𐑄𐐩𐑉 𐐶𐐱𐑆 𐑋𐐲𐐽 𐐺𐑊𐐲𐐼𐑇𐐯𐐼; 𐐰𐑌𐐼 𐑄 𐑉𐐨𐐺𐐯𐑊𐐷𐐲𐑅 𐐹𐐪𐑉𐐻 𐐶𐐲𐑉 𐑅𐑊𐐩𐑌 𐐰𐑌𐐼 𐐼𐑉𐐮𐑂𐐲𐑌 𐐵𐐻 𐐲𐑂 𐑄 𐑊𐐰𐑌𐐼, 𐐰𐑌𐐼 𐑄𐐩 𐐼𐐮𐐼 𐑀𐐬 𐐲𐑌𐐻𐐭 𐑄 𐐿𐐮𐑍 𐐲𐑂 𐑄 𐐢𐐰𐑋𐐲𐑌𐐴𐐻𐑅.

8. 𐐈𐑌𐐼 𐐮𐐻 𐐿𐐩𐑋 𐐻𐐭 𐐹𐐰𐑅 𐑄𐐰𐐻 𐑄𐐩 𐐼𐐮𐐼 𐐯𐑌𐐼𐐯𐑂𐐲𐑉 𐐻𐐭 𐑅𐐻𐐲𐑉 𐐲𐐹 𐑄 𐐢𐐰𐑋𐐲𐑌𐐴𐐻𐑅 𐐻𐐭 𐐶𐐫𐑉 𐐲𐑀𐐯𐑌𐑅𐐻 𐑄 𐐤𐐨𐑁𐐴𐐻𐑅; 𐐺𐐲𐐻 𐐺𐐨𐐸𐐬𐑊𐐼 𐑄 𐐢𐐰𐑋𐐲𐑌𐐴𐐻𐑅 𐐶𐐲𐑉 𐐯𐐿𐑅𐐨𐐼𐐮𐑍𐑊𐐨 𐐲𐑁𐑉𐐩𐐼, 𐐮𐑌𐑅𐐬𐑋𐐲𐐽 𐑄𐐰𐐻 𐑄𐐩 𐐶𐐳𐐼 𐑌𐐱𐐻 𐐸𐐪𐑉𐐿𐐲𐑌 𐐻𐐭 𐑄 𐐶𐐲𐑉𐐼𐑆 𐐲𐑂 𐑄𐐬𐑆 𐐼𐐮𐑅𐐯𐑌𐐻𐐲𐑉𐑆. 𐐒𐐲𐐻 𐐮𐐻 𐐿𐐩𐑋 𐐻𐐭 𐐹𐐰𐑅 𐐮𐑌 𐑄 𐑁𐐮𐑁𐐻𐐨 𐐰𐑌𐐼 𐑅𐐮𐐿𐑅𐑃 𐐷𐐨𐑉 𐐲𐑂 𐑄 𐑉𐐩𐑌 𐐲𐑂 𐑄 𐐾𐐲𐐾𐐯𐑆, 𐑄𐐩𐑉 𐐶𐐲𐑉 𐐼𐐮𐑅𐐯𐑌𐐻𐐲𐑉𐑆 𐐸𐐭 𐐶𐐯𐑌𐐻 𐐲𐐹 𐑁𐑉𐐱𐑋 𐑄 𐐤𐐨𐑁𐐴𐐻𐑅 𐐲𐑌𐐻𐐭 𐑄 𐐢𐐰𐑋𐐲𐑌𐐴𐐻𐑅; 𐐰𐑌𐐼 𐑄𐐩 𐑅𐐲𐐿𐑅𐐨𐐼𐐯𐐼 𐐶𐐮𐑄 𐑄𐐬𐑆 𐐲𐑄𐐲𐑉𐑆 𐐮𐑌 𐑅𐐻𐐲𐑉𐐮𐑍 𐑄𐐯𐑋 𐐲𐐹 𐐻𐐭 𐐰𐑍𐑀𐐲𐑉 𐐲𐑀𐐯𐑌𐑅𐐻 𐑄 𐐤𐐨𐑁𐐴𐐻𐑅; 𐐰𐑌𐐼 𐑄𐐩 𐐶𐐲𐑉 𐐫𐑊 𐑄𐐰𐐻 𐐷𐐨𐑉 𐐹𐑉𐐨𐐹𐐩𐑉𐐮𐑍 𐑁𐐫𐑉 𐐶𐐫𐑉. 𐐈𐑌𐐼 𐐮𐑌 𐑄 𐑁𐐮𐑁𐐻𐐨 𐐰𐑌𐐼 𐑅𐐯𐑂𐐲𐑌𐑃 𐐷𐐨𐑉 𐑄𐐩 𐐼𐐮𐐼 𐐿𐐲𐑋 𐐼𐐵𐑌 𐐲𐑀𐐯𐑌𐑅𐐻 𐑄 𐐤𐐨𐑁𐐴𐐻𐑅 𐐻𐐭 𐐺𐐰𐐻𐐲𐑊, 𐐰𐑌𐐼 𐑄𐐩 𐐼𐐮𐐼 𐐿𐐱𐑋𐑋𐐯𐑌𐑅 𐑄 𐐶𐐲𐑉𐐿 𐐲𐑂 𐐼𐐯𐑃; 𐐷𐐩, 𐐮𐑌𐑅𐐬𐑋𐐲𐐽 𐑄𐐰𐐻 𐐮𐑌 𐑄 𐑁𐐮𐑁𐐻𐐨 𐐰𐑌𐐼 𐐩𐐻𐑃 𐐷𐐨𐑉 𐐲𐑂 𐑄 𐑉𐐩𐑌 𐐲𐑂 𐑄 𐐾𐐲𐐾𐐯𐑆, 𐑄𐐩 𐑅𐐲𐐿𐑅𐐨𐐼𐐯𐐼 𐐮𐑌 𐐱𐐺𐐻𐐩𐑌𐐮𐑍 𐐹𐐱𐑆𐐯𐑇𐐲𐑌 𐐲𐑂 𐑄 𐑊𐐰𐑌𐐼 𐐲𐑂 𐐞𐐯𐑉𐐲𐐸𐐯𐑋𐑊𐐲; 𐐷𐐩, 𐐰𐑌𐐼 𐐫𐑊𐑅𐐬 𐐫𐑊 𐑄 𐑊𐐰𐑌𐐼𐑆, 𐐨𐑂𐐲𐑌 𐐲𐑌𐐻𐐭 𐑄 𐑊𐐰𐑌𐐼 𐐸𐐶𐐮𐐽 𐐶𐐱𐑆 𐑌𐐨𐑉 𐑄 𐑊𐐰𐑌𐐼 𐐒𐐵𐑌𐐻𐐮𐑁𐐳𐑊; 𐐰𐑌𐐼 𐑄 𐐤𐐨𐑁𐐴𐐻𐑅, 𐐰𐑌𐐼 𐑄 𐐪𐑉𐑋𐐨𐑆 𐐲𐑂 𐐣𐐬𐑉𐐬𐑌𐐴𐐸𐐪, 𐐶𐐲𐑉 𐐼𐑉𐐮𐑂𐐲𐑌 𐐨𐑂𐐲𐑌 𐐮𐑌𐐻𐐭 𐑄 𐑊𐐰𐑌𐐼 𐐲𐑂 𐐒𐐵𐑌𐐻𐐮𐑁𐐳𐑊; 𐐰𐑌𐐼 𐑄𐐩𐑉 𐑄𐐩 𐐼𐐮𐐼 𐑁𐐫𐑉𐐻𐐮𐑁𐐴 𐐲𐑀𐐯𐑌𐑅𐐻 𐑄 𐐢𐐰𐑋𐐲𐑌𐐴𐐻𐑅, 𐑁𐑉𐐱𐑋 𐑄 𐐶𐐯𐑅𐐻 𐑅𐐨, 𐐨𐑂𐐲𐑌 𐐲𐑌𐐻𐐭 𐑄 𐐨𐑅𐐻; 𐐮𐐻 𐐺𐐨𐐮𐑍 𐐲 𐐼𐐩'𐑆 𐐾𐐲𐑉𐑌𐐨 𐑁𐐫𐑉 𐐲 𐐤𐐨𐑁𐐴𐐻, 𐐱𐑌 𐑄 𐑊𐐴𐑌 𐐸𐐶𐐮𐐽 𐑄𐐩 𐐸𐐰𐐼 𐑁𐐫𐑉𐐻𐐮𐑁𐐴𐐼 𐐰𐑌𐐼 𐑅𐐻𐐩𐑇𐐲𐑌𐐼 𐑄𐐩𐑉 𐐪𐑉𐑋𐐨𐑆 𐐻𐐭 𐐼𐐨𐑁𐐯𐑌𐐼 𐑄𐐩𐑉 𐑌𐐫𐑉𐑃 𐐿𐐲𐑌𐐻𐑉𐐨. 𐐈𐑌𐐼 𐑄𐐲𐑅 𐑄𐐬𐑆 𐐼𐐮𐑅𐐯𐑌𐐻𐐲𐑉𐑆 𐐲𐑂 𐑄 𐐤𐐨𐑁𐐴𐐻𐑅, 𐐶𐐮𐑄 𐑄 𐐸𐐯𐑊𐐹 𐐲𐑂 𐐲 𐑌𐐷𐐭𐑋𐐲𐑉𐐲𐑅 𐐪𐑉𐑋𐐨 𐐲𐑂 𐑄 𐐢𐐰𐑋𐐲𐑌𐐴𐐻𐑅, 𐐸𐐰𐐼 𐐱𐐺𐐻𐐩𐑌𐐼 𐐫𐑊 𐑄 𐐹𐐱𐑆𐐯𐑇𐐲𐑌 𐐲𐑂 𐑄 𐐤𐐨𐑁𐐴𐐻𐑅 𐐸𐐶𐐮𐐽 𐐶𐐱𐑆 𐐮𐑌 𐑄 𐑊𐐰𐑌𐐼 𐑅𐐵𐑃𐐶𐐲𐑉𐐼. 𐐈𐑌𐐼 𐐫𐑊 𐑄𐐮𐑅 𐐶𐐱𐑆 𐐼𐐲𐑌 𐐮𐑌 𐑄 𐑁𐐮𐑁𐐻𐐨 𐐰𐑌𐐼 𐐩𐐻𐑃 𐐰𐑌𐐼 𐑌𐐴𐑌𐑃 𐐷𐐨𐑉𐑆 𐐲𐑂 𐑄 𐑉𐐩𐑌 𐐲𐑂 𐑄 𐐾𐐲𐐾𐐯𐑆.

9. 𐐈𐑌𐐼 𐐮𐐻 𐐿𐐩𐑋 𐐻𐐭 𐐹𐐰𐑅 𐐮𐑌 𐑄 𐑅𐐮𐐿𐑅𐐻𐐨𐐯𐑃 𐐷𐐨𐑉 𐐲𐑂 𐑄 𐑉𐐩𐑌 𐐲𐑂 𐑄 𐐾𐐲𐐾𐐯𐑆, 𐐣𐐬𐑉𐐬𐑌𐐴𐐸𐐪 𐐼𐐮𐐼 𐑅𐐲𐐿𐑅𐐨𐐼 𐐶𐐮𐑄 𐐸𐐮𐑆 𐐪𐑉𐑋𐐨𐑆 𐐮𐑌 𐐱𐐺𐐻𐐩𐑌𐐮𐑍 𐑋𐐯𐑌𐐨 𐐹𐐪𐑉𐐻𐑅 𐐲𐑂 𐑄 𐑊𐐰𐑌𐐼; 𐐷𐐩, 𐑄𐐩 𐑉𐐨𐑀𐐩𐑌𐐼 𐑋𐐯𐑌𐐨 𐑅𐐮𐐻𐐨𐑆 𐐸𐐶𐐮𐐽 𐐸𐐰𐐼 𐑁𐐫𐑊𐐲𐑌 𐐮𐑌𐐻𐐭 𐑄 𐐸𐐰𐑌𐐼𐑆 𐐲𐑂 𐑄 𐐢𐐰𐑋𐐲𐑌𐐴𐐻𐑅.

10. 𐐈𐑌𐐼 𐐮𐐻 𐐿𐐩𐑋 𐐻𐐭 𐐹𐐰𐑅 𐐮𐑌 𐑄 𐑅𐐮𐐿𐑅𐐻𐐨 𐐰𐑌𐐼 𐑁𐐲𐑉𐑅𐐻 𐐷𐐨𐑉 𐐲𐑂 𐑄 𐑉𐐩𐑌 𐐲𐑂 𐑄 𐐾𐐲𐐾𐐯𐑆, 𐑄𐐩 𐑅𐐲𐐿𐑅𐐨𐐼𐐯𐐼 𐐮𐑌 𐑉𐐨𐑀𐐩𐑌𐐮𐑍 𐐨𐑂𐐲𐑌 𐑄 𐐸𐐪𐑁 𐐲𐑂 𐐫𐑊 𐑄𐐩𐑉 𐐹𐐱𐑆𐐯𐑇𐐲𐑌𐑆. 𐐤𐐵 𐑄𐐮𐑅 𐑀𐑉𐐩𐐻 𐑊𐐫𐑅 𐐲𐑂 𐑄 𐐤𐐨𐑁𐐴𐐻𐑅, 𐐰𐑌𐐼 𐑄 𐑀𐑉𐐩𐐻 𐑅𐑊𐐫𐐻𐐲𐑉 𐐸𐐶𐐮𐐽 𐐶𐐱𐑆 𐐲𐑋𐐲𐑍 𐑄𐐯𐑋, 𐐶𐐳𐐼 𐑌𐐱𐐻 𐐸𐐰𐑂 𐐸𐐰𐐹𐐲𐑌𐐼, 𐐸𐐰𐐼 𐐮𐐻 𐑌𐐱𐐻 𐐺𐐮𐑌 𐑁𐐫𐑉 𐑄𐐩𐑉 𐐶𐐮𐐿𐐯𐐼𐑌𐐯𐑅 𐐰𐑌𐐼 𐑄𐐩𐑉 𐐲𐐺𐐱𐑋𐐮𐑌𐐩𐑇𐐲𐑌 𐐸𐐶𐐮𐐽 𐐶𐐱𐑆 𐐲𐑋𐐲𐑍 𐑄𐐯𐑋; 𐐷𐐩, 𐐰𐑌𐐼 𐐮𐐻 𐐶𐐱𐑆 𐐲𐑋𐐲𐑍 𐑄𐐬𐑆 𐐫𐑊𐑅𐐬 𐐸𐐭 𐐹𐑉𐐬𐑁𐐯𐑅𐐻 𐐻𐐭 𐐺𐐨𐑊𐐫𐑍 𐐻𐐭 𐑄 𐐽𐐲𐑉𐐽 𐐲𐑂 𐐘𐐱𐐼; 𐐰𐑌𐐼 𐐮𐐻 𐐶𐐱𐑆 𐐺𐐨𐐿𐐫𐑆 𐐲𐑂 𐑄 𐐹𐑉𐐴𐐼 𐐲𐑂 𐑄𐐩𐑉 𐐸𐐪𐑉𐐻𐑅, 𐐺𐐨𐐿𐐫𐑆 𐐲𐑂 𐑄𐐩𐑉 𐐯𐐿𐑅𐐨𐐼𐐮𐑍 𐑉𐐮𐐽𐐯𐑆, 𐐷𐐩, 𐐮𐐻 𐐶𐐱𐑆 𐐺𐐨𐐿𐐫𐑆 𐐲𐑂 𐑄𐐩𐑉

𐐱𐐹𐑉𐐯𐑇𐐲𐑌 𐐻𐐭 𐑄 𐐹𐐭𐑉, 𐐶𐐮𐑄𐐸𐐬𐑊𐐼𐐮𐑍 𐑄𐐯𐑉 𐑁𐐭𐐼 𐑁𐑉𐐱𐑋 𐑄 𐐸𐐲𐑍𐑀𐑉𐐨, 𐐶𐐮𐑄𐐸𐐬𐑊𐐼𐐮𐑍 𐑄𐐯𐑉 𐐿𐑊𐐬𐑄𐐮𐑍 𐑁𐑉𐐱𐑋 𐑄 𐑌𐐩𐐿𐐯𐐼, 𐐰𐑌𐐼 𐑅𐑋𐐴𐐻𐐮𐑍 𐑄𐐯𐑉 𐐸𐐲𐑋𐐺𐐲𐑊 𐐺𐑉𐐯𐑄𐑉𐐯𐑌 𐐲𐐹𐐱𐑌 𐑄 𐐽𐐨𐐿, 𐑋𐐩𐐿𐐮𐑍 𐐩 𐑋𐐱𐐿 𐐱𐑂 𐑄𐐰𐐻 𐐸𐐶𐐮𐐽 𐐶𐐱𐑆 𐑅𐐩𐐿𐑉𐐯𐐼, 𐐼𐐨𐑌𐐴𐐮𐑍 𐑄 𐑅𐐹𐐮𐑉𐐮𐐻 𐐱𐑂 𐐹𐑉𐐱𐑁𐐯𐑅𐐨 𐐰𐑌𐐼 𐐱𐑂 𐑉𐐯𐑂𐐯𐑊𐐩𐑇𐐲𐑌, 𐑋𐐲𐑉𐐼𐐲𐑉𐐮𐑍, 𐐹𐑊𐐲𐑌𐐼𐐲𐑉𐐮𐑍, 𐑊𐐴𐐮𐑍, 𐑅𐐻𐐨𐑊𐐮𐑍, 𐐿𐐱𐑋𐐮𐐻𐐮𐑍 𐐰𐐼𐐲𐑊𐐻𐐲𐑉𐐨, 𐑉𐐴𐑆𐐮𐑍 𐐲𐐹 𐐮𐑌 𐑀𐑉𐐩𐐻 𐐿𐐱𐑌𐐻𐐯𐑌𐑇𐐲𐑌𐑆, 𐐰𐑌𐐼 𐐼𐐯𐑆𐐲𐑉𐐻𐐮𐑍 𐐲𐐶𐐩 𐐮𐑌𐐻𐐭 𐑄 𐑊𐐰𐑌𐐼 𐐱𐑂 𐐤𐐨𐑁𐐴, 𐐲𐑋𐐲𐑍 𐑄 𐐢𐐩𐑋𐐲𐑌𐐴𐐻𐑅; 𐐰𐑌𐐼 𐐺𐐨𐐿𐐫𐑆 𐐱𐑂 𐑄𐐮𐑅 𐑄𐐯𐑉 𐑀𐑉𐐩𐐻 𐐶𐐮𐐿𐐯𐐼𐑌𐐯𐑅, 𐐰𐑌𐐼 𐑄𐐯𐑉 𐐺𐐬𐑅𐐻𐐮𐑍𐑆 𐐮𐑌 𐑄𐐯𐑉 𐐬𐑌 𐑅𐐻𐑉𐐯𐑍𐑃, 𐑄𐐩 𐐶𐐲𐑉 𐑊𐐯𐑁𐐻 𐐮𐑌 𐑄𐐯𐑉 𐐬𐑌 𐑅𐐻𐑉𐐯𐑍𐑃; 𐑄𐐯𐑉𐑁𐐬𐑉 𐑄𐐩 𐐼𐐮𐐼 𐑌𐐱𐐻 𐐹𐑉𐐱𐑅𐐹𐐲𐑉, 𐐺𐐲𐐻 𐐶𐐲𐑉 𐐰𐑁𐑊𐐮𐐿𐐻𐐯𐐼 𐐰𐑌𐐼 𐑅𐑋𐐮𐐻𐐲𐑌, 𐐰𐑌𐐼 𐐼𐑉𐐮𐑂𐐯𐑌 𐐺𐐨𐑁𐐬𐑉 𐑄 𐐢𐐩𐑋𐐲𐑌𐐴𐐻𐑅, 𐐲𐑌𐐻𐐮𐑊 𐑄𐐩 𐐸𐐰𐐼 𐑊𐐱𐑅𐐻 𐐹𐐱𐑆𐐯𐑇𐐲𐑌 𐐱𐑂 𐐫𐑊𐑋𐐬𐑅𐐻 𐐫𐑊 𐑄𐐯𐑉 𐑊𐐰𐑌𐐼𐑆. 𐐒𐐲𐐻 𐐺𐐨𐐸𐐬𐑊𐐼, 𐐣𐐱𐑉𐐱𐑌𐐴𐐸𐐪 𐐼𐐮𐐼 𐐹𐑉𐐨𐐽 𐑋𐐯𐑌𐐨 𐑃𐐮𐑍𐑆 𐐲𐑌𐐻𐐭 𐑄 𐐹𐐨𐐹𐐲𐑊 𐐺𐐨𐐿𐐫𐑆 𐐱𐑂 𐑄𐐯𐑉 𐐮𐑌𐐮𐐿𐐶𐐮𐐻𐐨, 𐐰𐑌𐐼 𐐫𐑊𐑅𐐬 𐐤𐐨𐑁𐐴 𐐰𐑌𐐼 𐐢𐐨𐐸𐐴, 𐐸𐐭 𐐶𐐲𐑉 𐑄 𐑅𐐲𐑌𐑆 𐐱𐑂 𐐐𐐯𐑊𐐲𐑋𐐲𐑌, 𐐼𐐮𐐼 𐐹𐑉𐐨𐐽 𐑋𐐯𐑌𐐨 𐑃𐐮𐑍𐑆 𐐲𐑌𐐻𐐭 𐑄 𐐹𐐨𐐹𐐲𐑊; 𐐷𐐩, 𐐰𐑌𐐼 𐐼𐐮𐐼 𐐹𐑉𐐱𐑁𐐯𐑅𐐴 𐑋𐐯𐑌𐐨 𐑃𐐮𐑍𐑆 𐐲𐑌𐐻𐐭 𐑄𐐯𐑋 𐐿𐐱𐑌𐑅𐐲𐑉𐑌𐐮𐑍 𐑄𐐯𐑉 𐐮𐑌𐐮𐐿𐐶𐐮𐐻𐐨𐑆, 𐐰𐑌𐐼 𐐸𐐶𐐱𐐻 𐑇𐐳𐐼 𐐿𐐲𐑋 𐐲𐑌𐐻𐐭 𐑄𐐯𐑋 𐐮𐑁 𐑄𐐩 𐐼𐐮𐐼 𐑌𐐱𐐻 𐑉𐐨𐐹𐐯𐑌𐐻 𐐱𐑂 𐑄𐐯𐑉 𐑅𐐮𐑌𐑆. 𐐈𐑌𐐼 𐐮𐐻 𐐿𐐩𐑋 𐐻𐐭 𐐹𐐰𐑅 𐑄𐐰𐐻 𐑄𐐩 𐐼𐐮𐐼 𐑉𐐨𐐹𐐯𐑌𐐻, 𐐰𐑌𐐼 𐐮𐑌𐐰𐑆𐑋𐐲𐐽 𐐰𐑆 𐑄𐐩 𐐼𐐮𐐼 𐑉𐐨𐐹𐐯𐑌𐐻 𐑄𐐩 𐐼𐐮𐐼 𐐺𐐨𐑀𐐮𐑌 𐐻𐐭 𐐹𐑉𐐱𐑅𐐹𐐲𐑉; 𐑁𐐫𐑉 𐐸𐐶𐐯𐑌 𐐣𐐱𐑉𐐱𐑌𐐴𐐸𐐪 𐑅𐐫 𐑄𐐰𐐻 𐑄𐐩 𐐼𐐮𐐼 𐑉𐐨𐐹𐐯𐑌𐐻, 𐐸𐐨 𐐼𐐮𐐼 𐑂𐐯𐑌𐐽𐐲𐑉 𐐻𐐭 𐑊𐐨𐐼 𐑄𐐯𐑋 𐑁𐐬𐑉𐑃 𐑁𐑉𐐱𐑋 𐐹𐑊𐐩𐑅 𐐻𐐭 𐐹𐑊𐐩𐑅, 𐐰𐑌𐐼 𐑁𐑉𐐱𐑋 𐑅𐐮𐐻𐐨 𐐻𐐭 𐑅𐐮𐐻𐐨, 𐐨𐑂𐐯𐑌 𐐲𐑌𐐻𐐮𐑊 𐑄𐐩 𐐸𐐰𐐼 𐑉𐐨𐑀𐐩𐑌𐐼 𐑄 𐐶𐐲𐑌-𐐸𐐪𐑁 𐐱𐑂 𐑄𐐯𐑉 𐐹𐑉𐐱𐐹𐐲𐑉𐐻𐐨, 𐐰𐑌𐐼 𐑄 𐐶𐐲𐑌-𐐸𐐪𐑁 𐐱𐑂 𐐫𐑊 𐑄𐐯𐑉 𐑊𐐰𐑌𐐼𐑆. 𐐈𐑌𐐼 𐑄𐐲𐑅 𐐯𐑌𐐼𐐯𐐼 𐑄 𐑅𐐮𐐿𐑅𐐻𐐨 𐐰𐑌𐐼 𐑁𐐲𐑉𐑅𐐻 𐐷𐐨𐑉 𐐱𐑂 𐑄 𐑉𐐩𐑌 𐐱𐑂 𐑄 𐐖𐐲𐐾𐐯𐑆.

11. 𐐈𐑌𐐼 𐐮𐐻 𐐿𐐩𐑋 𐐻𐐭 𐐹𐐰𐑅 𐐮𐑌 𐑄 𐑅𐐮𐐿𐑅𐐻𐐨 𐐰𐑌𐐼 𐑅𐐯𐐿𐐲𐑌𐐼 𐐷𐐨𐑉 𐐱𐑂 𐑄 𐑉𐐩𐑌 𐐱𐑂 𐑄 𐐖𐐲𐐾𐐯𐑆, 𐑄𐐰𐐻 𐐣𐐱𐑉𐐱𐑌𐐴𐐸𐐪 𐐿𐐳𐐼 𐐱𐐺𐐻𐐩𐑌 𐑌𐐬 𐑋𐐬𐑉 𐐹𐐱𐑆𐐯𐑇𐐲𐑌𐑆 𐐬𐑂𐐲𐑉 𐑄 𐐢𐐩𐑋𐐲𐑌𐐴𐐻𐑅; 𐑄𐐯𐑉𐑁𐐬𐑉 𐑄𐐩 𐐼𐐮𐐼 𐐲𐐺𐐰𐑌𐐼𐐲𐑌 𐑄𐐯𐑉 𐐼𐐯𐑆𐐴𐑌 𐐻𐐭 𐐱𐐺𐐻𐐩𐑌 𐑄 𐑉𐐨𐑋𐐩𐑌𐐼𐐲𐑉 𐐱𐑂 𐑄𐐯𐑉 𐑊𐐰𐑌𐐼𐑆, 𐑁𐐫𐑉 𐑅𐐬 𐑌𐐭𐑋𐐲𐑉𐐲𐑅 𐐶𐐲𐑉 𐑄 𐐢𐐩𐑋𐐲𐑌𐐴𐐻𐑅 𐑄𐐰𐐻 𐐮𐐻 𐐺𐐨𐐿𐐩𐑋 𐐮𐑋𐐹𐐱𐑅𐐮𐐺𐐲𐑊 𐑁𐐫𐑉 𐑄 𐐤𐐨𐑁𐐴𐐻𐑅 𐐻𐐭 𐐱𐐺𐐻𐐩𐑌 𐑋𐐬𐑉 𐐹𐐵𐐲𐑉 𐐬𐑂𐐲𐑉 𐑄𐐯𐑋; 𐑄𐐯𐑉𐑁𐐬𐑉 𐐣𐐱𐑉𐐱𐑌𐐴𐐸𐐪 𐐼𐐮𐐼 𐐯𐑋𐐹𐑊𐐫𐐮 𐐫𐑊 𐐸𐐮𐑆 𐐪𐑉𐑋𐐨𐑆 𐐮𐑌 𐑋𐐩𐑌𐐻𐐩𐑌𐐮𐑍 𐑄𐐬𐑆 𐐹𐐪𐑉𐐻𐑅 𐐸𐐶𐐮𐐽 𐐸𐐨 𐐸𐐰𐐼 𐐻𐐩𐐿𐐯𐑌.

12. 𐐈𐑌𐐼 𐐮𐐻 𐐿𐐩𐑋 𐐻𐐭 𐐹𐐰𐑅, 𐐺𐐨𐐿𐐫𐑆 𐐱𐑂 𐑄 𐑀𐑉𐐩𐐻𐑌𐐯𐑅 𐐱𐑂 𐑄 𐑌𐐲𐑋𐐺𐐲𐑉 𐐱𐑂 𐑄 𐐢𐐩𐑋𐐲𐑌𐐴𐐻𐑅, 𐑄 𐐤𐐨𐑁𐐴𐐻𐑅 𐐶𐐲𐑉 𐐮𐑌 𐑀𐑉𐐩𐐻 𐑁𐐨𐑉, 𐑊𐐯𐑅𐐻 𐑄𐐩 𐑇𐐳𐐼 𐐺𐐨 𐐬𐑂𐐲𐑉𐐹𐐵𐐲𐑉𐐼, 𐐰𐑌𐐼 𐐻𐑉𐐱𐐼𐐲𐑌 𐐼𐐵𐑌, 𐐰𐑌𐐼 𐑅𐑊𐐩𐑌, 𐐰𐑌𐐼 𐐼𐐯𐑅𐐻𐑉𐐫𐐮𐐼; 𐐷𐐩, 𐑄𐐩 𐐺𐐨𐑀𐐰𐑌 𐐻𐐭 𐑉𐐨𐑋𐐯𐑋𐐺𐐲𐑉 𐑄 𐐹𐑉𐐱𐑁𐐯𐑅𐐨𐑆 𐐱𐑂 𐐈𐑊𐑋𐐲, 𐐰𐑌𐐼 𐐫𐑊𐑅𐐬 𐑄 𐐶𐐲𐑉𐐼𐑆 𐐱𐑂 𐐣𐐬𐑆𐐴𐐲; 𐐰𐑌𐐼 𐑄𐐩 𐑅𐐫 𐑄𐐰𐐻 𐑄𐐩 𐐸𐐰𐐼 𐐺𐐮𐑌 𐐩 𐑅𐐻𐐮𐑁𐑌𐐯𐐿𐐻 𐐹𐐨𐐹𐐲𐑊, 𐐰𐑌𐐼 𐑄𐐰𐐻 𐑄𐐩 𐐸𐐰𐐼 𐑅𐐯𐐻 𐐰𐐻 𐑌𐐫𐐻 𐑄 𐐿𐐱𐑋𐐰𐑌𐐼𐑋𐐯𐑌𐐻𐑅 𐐱𐑂 𐐘𐐱𐐼; 𐐰𐑌𐐼 𐑄𐐰𐐻 𐑄𐐩 𐐸𐐰𐐼 𐐫𐑊𐐻𐐲𐑉𐐼 𐐰𐑌𐐼 𐐻𐑉𐐰𐑋𐐹𐐲𐑊𐐼 𐐲𐑌𐐼𐐲𐑉 𐑄𐐯𐑉 𐑁𐐨𐐻 𐑄 𐑊𐐫𐑆 𐐱𐑂 𐐣𐐬𐑆𐐴𐐲, 𐐫𐑉 𐑄𐐰𐐻 𐐸𐐶𐐮𐐽 𐑄 𐐢𐐫𐑉𐐼 𐐿𐐱𐑋𐐰𐑌𐐼𐐯𐐼 𐐸𐐮𐑋 𐐻𐐭 𐑀𐐮𐑂 𐐲𐑌𐐻𐐭 𐑄 𐐹𐐨𐐹𐐲𐑊; 𐐰𐑌𐐼 𐑄𐐲𐑅 𐑅𐐨𐐮𐑍 𐑄𐐰𐐻 𐑄𐐯𐑉 𐑊𐐫𐑆 𐐸𐐰𐐼 𐐺𐐨𐐿𐐲𐑋 𐐿𐐱𐑉𐐲𐐹𐐻𐐯𐐼, 𐐰𐑌𐐼 𐑄𐐰𐐻 𐑄𐐩 𐐸𐐰𐐼 𐐺𐐨𐐿𐐲𐑋 𐐩 𐐶𐐮𐐿𐐯𐐼 𐐹𐐨𐐹𐐲𐑊, 𐐮𐑌𐑅𐐬𐑋𐐲𐐽 𐑄𐐰𐐻 𐑄𐐩 𐐶𐐲𐑉 𐐶𐐮𐐿𐐯𐐼 𐐨𐑂𐐯𐑌 𐑊𐐴𐐿 𐐲𐑌𐐻𐐭 𐑄 𐐢𐐩𐑋𐐲𐑌𐐴𐐻𐑅. 𐐈𐑌𐐼 𐐺𐐨𐐿𐐫𐑆 𐐱𐑂 𐑄𐐯𐑉 𐐮𐑌𐐮𐐿𐐶𐐮𐐻𐐨, 𐑄 𐐽𐐲𐑉𐐽 𐐸𐐰𐐼 𐐺𐐨𐑀𐐲𐑌 𐐻𐐭 𐐼𐐶𐐮𐑌𐐼𐐲𐑊; 𐐰𐑌𐐼 𐑄𐐩 𐐺𐐨𐑀𐐰𐑌 𐐻𐐭 𐐼𐐮𐑅𐐺𐐨𐑊𐐨𐑂 𐐮𐑌 𐑄 𐑅𐐹𐐮𐑉𐐮𐐻 𐐱𐑂 𐐹𐑉𐐱𐑁𐐯𐑅𐐨, 𐐰𐑌𐐼 𐐮𐑌 𐑄 𐑅𐐹𐐮𐑉𐐮𐐻 𐐱𐑂 𐑉𐐯𐑂𐐯𐑊𐐩𐑇𐐲𐑌; 𐐰𐑌𐐼 𐑄 𐐾𐐲𐐾𐑋𐐯𐑌𐐻𐑅 𐐱𐑂 𐐘𐐱𐐼 𐐼𐐮𐐼 𐑅𐐻𐐩𐑉 𐑄𐐯𐑋 𐐮𐑌 𐑄 𐑁𐐩𐑅. 𐐈𐑌𐐼 𐑄𐐩 𐑅𐐫 𐑄𐐰𐐻 𐑄𐐩 𐐸𐐰𐐼 𐐺𐐨𐐿𐐲𐑋 𐐶𐐨𐐿, 𐑊𐐴𐐿 𐐲𐑌𐐻𐐭 𐑄𐐯𐑉 𐐺𐑉𐐯𐑄𐑉𐐯𐑌, 𐑄 𐐢𐐩𐑋𐐲𐑌𐐴𐐻𐑅, 𐐰𐑌𐐼 𐑄𐐰𐐻 𐑄 𐐝𐐹𐐮𐑉𐐮𐐻 𐐱𐑂 𐑄 𐐢𐐫𐑉𐐼 𐐼𐐮𐐼 𐑌𐐬 𐑋𐐬𐑉 𐐹𐑉𐐨𐑆𐐲𐑉𐑂 𐑄𐐯𐑋; 𐐷𐐩, 𐐮𐐻 𐐸𐐰𐐼 𐐶𐐮𐑄𐐼𐑉𐐫𐑌 𐑁𐑉𐐱𐑋 𐑄𐐯𐑋 𐐺𐐨𐐿𐐫𐑆 𐑄 𐐝𐐹𐐮𐑉𐐮𐐻 𐐱𐑂 𐑄 𐐢𐐫𐑉𐐼 𐐼𐐲𐑃 𐑌𐐱𐐻 𐐼𐐶𐐯𐑊 𐐮𐑌 𐐲𐑌𐐸𐐬𐑊𐐨 𐐻𐐯𐑋𐐹𐐲𐑊𐑆; 𐑄𐐯𐑉𐑁𐐬𐑉 𐑄 𐐢𐐫𐑉𐐼 𐐼𐐮𐐼 𐑅𐐨𐑅 𐐻𐐭 𐐹𐑉𐐨𐑆𐐲𐑉𐑂 𐑄𐐯𐑋 𐐺𐐴 𐐸𐐮𐑆 𐑋𐐮𐑉𐐰𐐿𐐷𐐭𐑊𐐲𐑅 𐐰𐑌𐐼 𐑋𐐰𐐽𐑊𐐯𐑅 𐐹𐐵𐐲𐑉, 𐑁𐐫𐑉 𐑄𐐩 𐐸𐐰𐐼 𐑁𐐫𐑊𐐯𐑌 𐐮𐑌𐐻𐐭 𐐩 𐑅𐐻𐐩𐐻 𐐱𐑂 𐐲𐑌𐐺𐐨𐑊𐐨𐑁 𐐰𐑌𐐼 𐐫𐑁𐐳𐑊 𐐶𐐮𐐿𐐯𐐼𐑌𐐯𐑅; 𐐰𐑌𐐼 𐑄𐐩 𐑅𐐫 𐑄𐐰𐐻 𐑄 𐐢𐐩𐑋𐐲𐑌𐐴𐐻𐑅 𐐶𐐲𐑉 𐐯𐐿𐑅𐐨𐐼𐐮𐑍𐑊𐐨 𐑋𐐬𐑉 𐑌𐐭𐑋𐐲𐑉𐐲𐑅 𐑄𐐰𐑌 𐑄𐐩, 𐐰𐑌𐐼 𐐯𐐿𐑅𐐯𐐹𐐻 𐑄𐐩 𐑇𐐳𐐼 𐐿𐑊𐐨𐑂 𐐲𐑌𐐻𐐭 𐑄 𐐢𐐫𐑉𐐼 𐑄𐐯𐑉 𐐘𐐱𐐼, 𐑄𐐩 𐑋𐐲𐑅𐐻 𐐲𐑌𐐲𐑂𐐫𐐮𐐼𐐲𐐺𐑊𐐨 𐐹𐐯𐑉𐐮𐑇. 𐐙𐐫𐑉 𐐺𐐨𐐸𐐬𐑊𐐼, 𐑄𐐩 𐑅𐐫 𐑄𐐰𐐻 𐑄 𐑅𐐻𐑉𐐯𐑍𐑃 𐐱𐑂 𐑄 𐐢𐐩𐑋𐐲𐑌𐐴𐐻𐑅 𐐶𐐱𐑆 𐐰𐑆 𐑀𐑉𐐩𐐻 𐐰𐑆 𐑄𐐯𐑉 𐑅𐐻𐑉𐐯𐑍𐑃, 𐐨𐑂𐐯𐑌 𐑋𐐰𐑌 𐑁𐐫𐑉 𐑋𐐰𐑌.

𐐰𐑌𐐼 𐑄𐐲𐑅 𐐸𐐰𐐼 𐑄𐐩 𐑁𐐫𐑊𐑌 𐐮𐑌𐐻𐐭 𐑄𐐮𐑅 𐑀𐑉𐐩𐐻 𐐻𐑉𐐰𐑌𐑅𐑀𐑉𐐯𐑇𐐲𐑌; 𐐷𐐩, 𐑄𐐲𐑅 𐐸𐐰𐐼 𐑄𐐩 𐐺𐐨𐐿𐐲𐑋 𐐶𐐨𐐿, 𐐺𐐨𐐿𐐱𐑆 𐐱𐑂 𐑄𐐯𐑉 𐐻𐑉𐐰𐑌𐑅𐑀𐑉𐐯𐑇𐐲𐑌, 𐐮𐑌 𐑄 𐑅𐐹𐐩𐑅 𐐱𐑂 𐑌𐐱𐐻 𐑋𐐯𐑌𐐨 𐐷𐐨𐑉𐑆.

13. 𐐰𐑌𐐼 𐐮𐐻 𐐿𐐩𐐶 𐐻𐐭 𐐹𐐰𐑅 𐑄𐐰𐐻 𐐮𐑌 𐑄𐐮𐑅 𐑅𐐩𐑋 𐐷𐐨𐑉, 𐐺𐐨𐐸𐐬𐑊𐐼, 𐐤𐐨𐑁𐐴 𐐼𐐮𐑊𐐮𐑂𐐲𐑉𐐼 𐐲𐐹 𐑄 𐐾𐐲𐐾𐑋𐐲𐑌𐐻-𐑅𐐨𐐻 𐐻𐐭 𐐩 𐑋𐐰𐑌 𐐸𐐭𐑆 𐑌𐐩𐑋 𐐶𐐱𐑆 𐐝𐐨𐑆𐐬𐑉𐐲𐑋. 𐐙𐐬𐑉 𐐰𐑆 𐑄𐐯𐑉 𐑊𐐫𐑆 𐐰𐑌𐐼 𐑄𐐯𐑉 𐑀𐐲𐑂𐐲𐑉𐑌𐑋𐐯𐑌𐐻𐑅 𐐶𐐲𐑉 𐐯𐑅𐐻𐐰𐐺𐑊𐐮𐑇𐐻 𐐺𐐴 𐑄 𐑂𐐶𐐰𐑅 𐐱𐑂 𐑄 𐐹𐐨𐐹𐑊, 𐐰𐑌𐐼 𐑄𐐩 𐐸𐐭 𐐽𐐬𐑆 𐐨𐑂𐐮𐑊 𐐶𐐲𐑉 𐑋𐐬𐑉 𐑌𐐭𐑋𐐲𐑉𐐲𐑅 𐑄𐐰𐑌 𐑄𐐩 𐐸𐐭 𐐽𐐬𐑆 𐑀𐐳𐐼, 𐑄𐐯𐑉𐑁𐐬𐑉 𐑄𐐩 𐐶𐐲𐑉 𐑉𐐴𐐹𐐲𐑌𐐮𐑍 𐑁𐐬𐑉 𐐼𐐯𐑅𐐻𐑉𐐲𐐿𐑇𐐲𐑌, 𐑁𐐬𐑉 𐑄 𐑊𐐫𐑆 𐐸𐐰𐐼 𐐺𐐨𐐿𐐲𐑋 𐐿𐐲𐑉𐐲𐐹𐐻𐐯𐐼; 𐐷𐐩, 𐐰𐑌𐐼 𐑄𐐮𐑅 𐐶𐐱𐑆 𐑌𐐱𐐻 𐐫𐑊; 𐑄𐐩 𐐶𐐲𐑉 𐐩 𐑅𐐻𐐮𐑁𐑌𐐯𐐿𐐻 𐐹𐐨𐐹𐑊, 𐐮𐑌𐑅𐐬𐑋𐐲𐐽 𐑄𐐰𐐻 𐑄𐐩 𐐿𐐳𐐼 𐑌𐐱𐐻 𐐺𐐨 𐑀𐐲𐑂𐐲𐑉𐑌𐐼 𐐺𐐴 𐑄 𐑊𐐫 𐑌𐐬𐑉 𐐾𐐲𐑅𐐻𐐮𐑅, 𐑅𐐩𐑂 𐐮𐐻 𐐶𐐲𐑉 𐐻𐐭 𐑄𐐯𐑉 𐐼𐐯𐑅𐐻𐑉𐐲𐐿𐑇𐐲𐑌.

14. 𐐰𐑌𐐼 𐐮𐐻 𐐿𐐩𐐶 𐐻𐐭 𐐹𐐰𐑅 𐑄𐐰𐐻 𐐤𐐨𐑁𐐴 𐐸𐐰𐐼 𐐺𐐨𐐿𐐲𐑋 𐐶𐐨𐑉𐐨 𐐺𐐨𐐿𐐫𐑆 𐐱𐑂 𐑄𐐯𐑉 𐐮𐑌𐐮𐐿𐐶𐐮𐐻𐐨; 𐐰𐑌𐐼 𐐸𐐨 𐐷𐐨𐑊𐐼𐐯𐐼 𐐲𐐹 𐑄 𐐾𐐲𐐾𐑋𐐲𐑌𐐻-𐑅𐐨𐐻, 𐐰𐑌𐐼 𐐻𐐳𐐿 𐐮𐐻 𐐲𐐹𐐱𐑌 𐐸𐐮𐑋 𐐻𐐭 𐐹𐑉𐐨𐐽 𐑄 𐐶𐐲𐑉𐐼 𐐱𐑂 𐐘𐐱𐐼 𐐫𐑊 𐑄 𐑉𐐨𐑋𐐩𐑌𐐼𐐲𐑉 𐐱𐑂 𐐸𐐮𐑆 𐐼𐐩𐑆, 𐐰𐑌𐐼 𐐸𐐮𐑆 𐐺𐑉𐐲𐑄𐐲𐑉 𐐢𐐨𐐸𐐴 𐐫𐑊𐑅𐐬, 𐐫𐑊 𐑄 𐑉𐐨𐑋𐐩𐑌𐐼𐐲𐑉 𐐱𐑂 𐐸𐐮𐑆 𐐼𐐩𐑆; 𐑁𐐬𐑉 𐑄𐐩 𐑉𐐨𐑋𐐯𐑋𐐺𐐲𐑉𐐼 𐑄 𐐶𐐲𐑉𐐼𐑆 𐐸𐐶𐐮𐐽 𐑄𐐯𐑉 𐑁𐐪𐑄𐐲𐑉 𐐐𐐨𐑊𐐲𐑋𐐲𐑌 𐑅𐐹𐐪𐐿 𐐲𐑌𐐻𐐭 𐑄𐐯𐑋. 𐐰𐑌𐐼 𐑄𐐨𐑆 𐐪𐑉 𐑄 𐐶𐐲𐑉𐐼𐑆 𐐸𐐶𐐮𐐽 𐐸𐐨 𐑅𐐹𐐪𐐿: 𐐒𐐨𐐸𐐬𐑊𐐼, 𐑋𐐴 𐑅𐐲𐑌𐑆, 𐐌 𐐼𐐯𐑆𐐴𐑉 𐑄𐐰𐐻 𐐷𐐨 𐑇𐐳𐐼 𐑉𐐨𐑋𐐯𐑋𐐺𐐲𐑉 𐐻𐐭 𐐿𐐨𐐹 𐑄 𐐿𐐱𐑋𐐰𐑌𐐼𐑋𐐯𐑌𐐻𐑅 𐐱𐑂 𐐘𐐱𐐼; 𐐰𐑌𐐼 𐐌 𐐶𐐳𐐼 𐑄𐐰𐐻 𐐷𐐨 𐑇𐐳𐐼 𐐼𐐨𐐿𐑊𐐯𐑉 𐑄𐐨𐑆 𐐶𐐲𐑉𐐼𐑆 𐐲𐑌𐐻𐐭 𐑄 𐐹𐐨𐐹𐑊. 𐐒𐐨𐐸𐐬𐑊𐐼, 𐐌 𐐸𐐰𐑂 𐑀𐐮𐑂𐐲𐑌 𐐲𐑌𐐻𐐭 𐐷𐐭 𐑄 𐑌𐐩𐑋𐑆 𐐱𐑂 𐐵𐑉 𐑁𐐲𐑉𐑅𐐻 𐐹𐐯𐑉𐐲𐑌𐐻𐑅 𐐸𐐭 𐐿𐐩𐐶 𐐵𐐻 𐐱𐑂 𐑄 𐑊𐐰𐑌𐐼 𐐱𐑂 𐐖𐐲𐑉𐐭𐑅𐐲𐑊𐐲𐑋; 𐐰𐑌𐐼 𐑄𐐮𐑅 𐐌 𐐸𐐰𐑂 𐐼𐐲𐑌 𐑄𐐰𐐻 𐐸𐐶𐐯𐑌 𐐷𐐭 𐑉𐐨𐑋𐐯𐑋𐐺𐐲𐑉 𐐷𐐬𐑉 𐑌𐐩𐑋𐑆, 𐐷𐐨 𐑋𐐩 𐑉𐐨𐑋𐐯𐑋𐐺𐐲𐑉 𐑄𐐯𐑋: 𐐰𐑌𐐼 𐐸𐐶𐐯𐑌 𐐷𐐨 𐑉𐐨𐑋𐐯𐑋𐐺𐐲𐑉 𐑄𐐯𐑋, 𐐷𐐨 𐑋𐐩 𐑉𐐨𐑋𐐯𐑋𐐺𐐲𐑉 𐑄𐐯𐑉 𐐶𐐲𐑉𐐿𐑅; 𐐰𐑌𐐼 𐐸𐐶𐐯𐑌 𐐷𐐨 𐑉𐐨𐑋𐐯𐑋𐐺𐐲𐑉 𐑄𐐯𐑉 𐐶𐐲𐑉𐐿𐑅, 𐐷𐐨 𐑋𐐩 𐑌𐐬 𐐸𐐵 𐑄𐐰𐐻 𐐮𐐻 𐐮𐑆 𐑅𐐯𐐼, 𐐰𐑌𐐼 𐐫𐑊𐑅𐐬 𐑉𐐮𐐻𐐲𐑌, 𐑄𐐰𐐻 𐑄𐐩 𐐶𐐲𐑉 𐑀𐐳𐐼; 𐑄𐐯𐑉𐑁𐐬𐑉, 𐑋𐐴 𐑅𐐲𐑌𐑆, 𐐌 𐐶𐐳𐐼 𐑄𐐰𐐻 𐐷𐐨 𐑇𐐳𐐼 𐐼𐐭 𐑄𐐰𐐻 𐐸𐐶𐐮𐐽 𐐮𐑆 𐑀𐐳𐐼, 𐑄𐐰𐐻 𐐮𐐻 𐑋𐐩 𐐺𐐨 𐑅𐐯𐐼 𐐱𐑂 𐐷𐐭, 𐐰𐑌𐐼 𐐫𐑊𐑅𐐬 𐑉𐐮𐐻𐐲𐑌, 𐐨𐑂𐑌 𐐰𐑆 𐐮𐐻 𐐸𐐰𐑆 𐐺𐐨𐑌 𐑅𐐯𐐼 𐐰𐑌𐐼 𐑉𐐮𐐻𐐲𐑌 𐐱𐑂 𐑄𐐯𐑋. 𐐰𐑌𐐼 𐑌𐐵, 𐑋𐐴 𐑅𐐲𐑌𐑆, 𐐺𐐨𐐸𐐬𐑊𐐼 𐐌 𐐸𐐰𐑂 𐑅𐐲𐑋𐐶𐐱𐐻 𐑋𐐬𐑉 𐐻𐐭 𐐼𐐯𐑆𐐴𐑉 𐐱𐑂 𐐷𐐭, 𐐸𐐶𐐮𐐽 𐐼𐐯𐑆𐐴𐑉 𐐮𐑆, 𐑄𐐰𐐻 𐐷𐐨 𐑋𐐩 𐑌𐐱𐐻 𐐼𐐭 𐑄𐐨𐑆 𐑃𐐮𐑍𐑆 𐑄𐐰𐐻 𐐷𐐨 𐑋𐐩 𐐺𐐬𐑅𐐻, 𐐺𐐲𐐻 𐑄𐐰𐐻 𐐷𐐨 𐑋𐐩 𐐼𐐭 𐑄𐐨𐑆 𐑃𐐮𐑍𐑆 𐐻𐐭 𐑊𐐩 𐐲𐐹 𐑁𐐬𐑉 𐐷𐐬𐑉𐑅𐐯𐑊𐑂𐑆 𐐩 𐐻𐑉𐐯𐑈𐐲𐑉 𐐮𐑌 𐐸𐐯𐑂𐐲𐑌, 𐐷𐐩, 𐐸𐐶𐐮𐐽 𐐮𐑆 𐐨𐐻𐐲𐑉𐑌𐐲𐑊, 𐐰𐑌𐐼 𐐸𐐶𐐮𐐽 𐑁𐐩𐐼𐐯𐑃 𐑌𐐱𐐻 𐐲𐐶𐐩; 𐐷𐐩, 𐑄𐐰𐐻 𐐷𐐨 𐑋𐐩 𐐸𐐰𐑂 𐑄𐐰𐐻 𐐹𐑉𐐯𐑇𐐲𐑅 𐑀𐐮𐑁𐐻 𐐱𐑂 𐐨𐐻𐐲𐑉𐑌𐐲𐑊 𐑊𐐴𐑁, 𐐸𐐶𐐮𐐽 𐐶𐐨 𐐸𐐰𐑂 𐑉𐐨𐑆𐐲𐑌 𐐻𐐭 𐑅𐐲𐐹𐐬𐑆 𐐸𐐰𐑃 𐐺𐐨𐑌 𐑀𐐮𐑂𐐲𐑌 𐐻𐐭 𐐵𐑉 𐑁𐐪𐑄𐐲𐑉𐑆.

15. 𐐄 𐑉𐐨𐑋𐐯𐑋𐐺𐐲𐑉, 𐑉𐐨𐑋𐐯𐑋𐐺𐐲𐑉, 𐑋𐐴 𐑅𐐲𐑌𐑆, 𐑄 𐐶𐐲𐑉𐐼𐑆 𐐸𐐶𐐮𐐽 𐐿𐐮𐑍 𐐒𐐯𐑌𐐾𐐲𐑋𐐲𐑌 𐑅𐐹𐐪𐐿 𐐲𐑌𐐻𐐭 𐐸𐐮𐑆 𐐹𐐨𐐹𐑊; 𐐷𐐩, 𐑉𐐨𐑋𐐯𐑋𐐺𐐲𐑉 𐑄𐐰𐐻 𐑄𐐯𐑉 𐐮𐑆 𐑌𐐬 𐐲𐑄𐐲𐑉 𐐶𐐩 𐑌𐐬𐑉 𐑋𐐨𐑌𐑆 𐐸𐐶𐐯𐑉𐐺𐐴 𐑋𐐰𐑌 𐐿𐐰𐑌 𐐺𐐨 𐑅𐐩𐑂𐐼, 𐐬𐑌𐑊𐐨 𐑃𐑉𐐭 𐑄 𐐲𐐻𐐬𐑌𐐮𐑍 𐐺𐑊𐐲𐐼 𐐱𐑂 𐐖𐐨𐑆𐐲𐑅 𐐗𐑉𐐴𐑅𐐻, 𐐸𐐭 𐑇𐐰𐑊 𐐿𐐲𐑋; 𐐷𐐩, 𐑉𐐨𐑋𐐯𐑋𐐺𐐲𐑉 𐑄𐐰𐐻 𐐸𐐨 𐐿𐐲𐑋𐐯𐑃 𐐻𐐭 𐑉𐐨𐐼𐐨𐑋 𐑄 𐐶𐐲𐑉𐑊𐐼. 𐐰𐑌𐐼 𐑉𐐨𐑋𐐯𐑋𐐺𐐲𐑉 𐐫𐑊𐑅𐐬 𐑄 𐐶𐐲𐑉𐐼𐑆 𐐸𐐶𐐮𐐽 𐐈𐑋𐐷𐐭𐑊𐐯𐐿 𐑅𐐹𐐪𐐿 𐐲𐑌𐐻𐐭 𐐞𐐨𐐯𐑆𐑉𐐲𐑋, 𐐮𐑌 𐑄 𐑅𐐮𐐻𐐨 𐐱𐑂 𐐈𐑋𐐲𐑌𐐴𐐲; 𐑁𐐬𐑉 𐐸𐐨 𐑅𐐯𐐼 𐐲𐑌𐐻𐐭 𐐸𐐮𐑋 𐑄𐐰𐐻 𐑄 𐐢𐐫𐑉𐐼 𐑇𐐳𐑉𐑊𐐨 𐑇𐐳𐐼 𐐿𐐲𐑋 𐐻𐐭 𐑉𐐨𐐼𐐨𐑋 𐐸𐐮𐑆 𐐹𐐨𐐹𐑊; 𐐺𐐲𐐻 𐑄𐐰𐐻 𐐸𐐨 𐑇𐐳𐐼 𐑌𐐱𐐻 𐐿𐐲𐑋 𐐻𐐭 𐑉𐐨𐐼𐐨𐑋 𐑄𐐯𐑋 𐐮𐑌 𐑄𐐯𐑉 𐑅𐐮𐑌𐑆, 𐐺𐐲𐐻 𐐻𐐭 𐑉𐐨𐐼𐐨𐑋 𐑄𐐯𐑋 𐑁𐑉𐐱𐑋 𐑄𐐯𐑉 𐑅𐐮𐑌𐑆. 𐐰𐑌𐐼 𐐸𐐨 𐐸𐐰𐑃 𐐹𐐵𐐲𐑉 𐑀𐐮𐑂𐐲𐑌 𐐲𐑌𐐻𐐭 𐐸𐐮𐑋 𐑁𐑉𐐱𐑋 𐑄 𐐙𐐪𐑄𐐲𐑉, 𐐻𐐭 𐑉𐐨𐐼𐐨𐑋 𐑄𐐯𐑋 𐑁𐑉𐐱𐑋 𐑄𐐯𐑉 𐑅𐐮𐑌𐑆, 𐐺𐐨𐐿𐐫𐑆 𐐱𐑂 𐑉𐐨𐐹𐐯𐑌𐐻𐐲𐑌𐑅; 𐑄𐐯𐑉𐑁𐐬𐑉 𐐸𐐨 𐐸𐐰𐑃 𐑅𐐯𐑌𐐻 𐐸𐐮𐑆 𐐩𐑌𐐾𐐯𐑊𐑆 𐐻𐐭 𐐼𐐨𐐿𐑊𐐯𐑉 𐑄 𐐻𐐴𐐼𐐮𐑍𐑆 𐐱𐑂 𐑄 𐐿𐐱𐑌𐐼𐐮𐑇𐐲𐑌𐑆 𐐱𐑂 𐑉𐐨𐐹𐐯𐑌𐐻𐐲𐑌𐑅, 𐐸𐐶𐐮𐐽 𐐺𐑉𐐮𐑍𐐯𐑃 𐐲𐑌𐐻𐐭 𐑄 𐐹𐐵𐐲𐑉 𐐱𐑂 𐑄 𐐡𐐨𐐼𐐨𐑋𐐲𐑉, 𐐲𐑌𐐻𐐭 𐑄 𐑅𐐰𐑊𐑂𐐩𐑇𐐲𐑌 𐐱𐑂 𐑄𐐯𐑉 𐑅𐐬𐑊𐑆. 𐐰𐑌𐐼 𐑌𐐵, 𐑋𐐴 𐑅𐐲𐑌𐑆, 𐑉𐐨𐑋𐐯𐑋𐐺𐐲𐑉, 𐑉𐐨𐑋𐐯𐑋𐐺𐐲𐑉 𐑄𐐰𐐻 𐐮𐐻 𐐮𐑆 𐐲𐐹𐐱𐑌 𐑄 𐑉𐐱𐐿 𐐱𐑂 𐐵𐑉 𐐡𐐨𐐼𐐨𐑋𐐲𐑉, 𐐸𐐭 𐐮𐑆 𐐗𐑉𐐴𐑅𐐻, 𐑄 𐐝𐐲𐑌 𐐱𐑂 𐐘𐐱𐐼, 𐑄𐐰𐐻 𐐷𐐨 𐑋𐐲𐑅𐐻 𐐺𐐮𐑊𐐼 𐐷𐐬𐑉 𐑁𐐵𐑌𐐼𐐩𐑇𐐲𐑌; 𐑄𐐰𐐻 𐐸𐐶𐐯𐑌 𐑄 𐐼𐐯𐑂𐐮𐑊 𐑇𐐰𐑊 𐑅𐐯𐑌𐐼 𐑁𐐬𐑉𐑃 𐐸𐐮𐑆 𐑋𐐴𐐻𐐨 𐐶𐐮𐑌𐐼𐑆, 𐐷𐐩, 𐐸𐐮𐑆 𐑇𐐪𐑁𐐻𐑅 𐐮𐑌 𐑄 𐐸𐐶𐐲𐑉𐑊𐐶𐐮𐑌𐐼; 𐐷𐐩, 𐐸𐐶𐐯𐑌 𐐫𐑊 𐐸𐐮𐑆 𐐸𐐩𐑊 𐐰𐑌𐐼 𐐸𐐮𐑆 𐑋𐐴𐐻𐐨 𐑅𐐻𐐬𐑉𐑋 𐑇𐐰𐑊 𐐺𐐨𐐻 𐐲𐐹𐐱𐑌 𐐷𐐭, 𐐮𐐻 𐑇𐐰𐑊 𐐸𐐰𐑂 𐑌𐐬 𐐹𐐵𐐲𐑉 𐐬𐑂𐐲𐑉 𐐷𐐭, 𐐻𐐭 𐐼𐑉𐐰𐑀 𐐷𐐭 𐐼𐐵𐑌 𐐻𐐭 𐑄 𐑀𐐲𐑊𐑁 𐐱𐑂 𐑋𐐮𐑆𐐲𐑉𐐨 𐐰𐑌𐐼 𐐯𐑌𐐼𐑊𐐯𐑅 𐐶𐐬, 𐐺𐐨𐐿𐐫𐑆 𐐱𐑂 𐑄 𐑉𐐱𐐿 𐐲𐐹𐐱𐑌 𐐸𐐶𐐮𐐽 𐐷𐐨 𐐪𐑉 𐐺𐐮𐑊𐐻, 𐐸𐐶𐐮𐐽 𐐮𐑆 𐐩 𐑇𐐳𐑉 𐑁𐐵𐑌𐐼𐐩𐑇𐐲𐑌, 𐐩 𐑁𐐵𐑌𐐼𐐩𐑇𐐲𐑌 𐐸𐐶𐐯𐑉𐐱𐑌 𐐮𐑁 𐑋𐐯𐑌 𐐺𐐮𐑊𐐼 𐑄𐐩 𐐿𐐰𐑌𐐱𐐻 𐑁𐐫𐑊.

16. 𐐈𐑌𐐼 𐐮𐐻 𐐿𐐩𐑋 𐐻𐐭 𐐹𐐰𐑅 𐑄𐐰𐐻 𐑄𐐨𐑆 𐐶𐐲𐑉 𐑄 𐐶𐐲𐑉𐐼𐑆 𐐸𐐶𐐮𐐽 𐐐𐐨𐑊𐐩𐑋𐐲𐑌 𐐻𐐫𐐻 𐐻𐐭 𐐸𐐮𐑆 𐑅𐐲𐑌𐑆; 𐐷𐐩, 𐐸𐐨 𐐼𐐮𐐼 𐐻𐐨𐐽 𐑄𐐯𐑋 𐑋𐐯𐑌𐐨 𐑃𐐮𐑍𐑆 𐐸𐐶𐐮𐐽 𐐪𐑉 𐑌𐐱𐐻 𐑉𐐮𐐻𐐲𐑌, 𐐰𐑌𐐼 𐐫𐑊𐑅𐐬 𐑋𐐯𐑌𐐨 𐑃𐐮𐑍𐑆 𐐸𐐶𐐮𐐽 𐐪𐑉 𐑉𐐮𐐻𐐲𐑌. 𐐈𐑌𐐼 𐑄𐐩 𐐼𐐮𐐼 𐑉𐐨𐑋𐐯𐑋𐐺𐐲𐑉 𐐸𐐮𐑆 𐐶𐐲𐑉𐐼𐑆; 𐐰𐑌𐐼 𐑄𐐯𐑉𐑁𐐬𐑉 𐑄𐐩 𐐶𐐯𐑌𐐻 𐑁𐐫𐑉𐑃, 𐐿𐐨𐐹𐐮𐑍 𐑄 𐐿𐐱𐑋𐐰𐑌𐐼𐑋𐐯𐑌𐐻𐑅 𐐲𐑂 𐐘𐐱𐐼 𐐻𐐭 𐐻𐐨𐐽 𐑄 𐐶𐐲𐑉𐐼 𐐲𐑂 𐐘𐐱𐐼 𐐲𐑋𐐲𐑍 𐐫𐑊 𐑄 𐐹𐐨𐐹𐑊 𐐲𐑂 𐐤𐐨𐑁𐐴, 𐐺𐐨𐑀𐐮𐑌𐐮𐑍 𐐰𐐻 𐑄 𐑅𐐮𐐻𐐨 𐐒𐐵𐑌𐐻𐐮𐑁𐐳𐑊; 𐐰𐑌𐐼 𐑁𐑉𐐱𐑋 𐑄𐐯𐑌𐑅𐑁𐐫𐑉𐑃 𐐻𐐭 𐑄 𐑅𐐮𐐻𐐨 𐐲𐑂 𐐘𐐮𐐼; 𐐰𐑌𐐼 𐑁𐑉𐐱𐑋 𐑄 𐑅𐐮𐐻𐐨 𐐲𐑂 𐐘𐐮𐐼 𐐻𐐭 𐑄 𐑅𐐮𐐻𐐨 𐐲𐑂 𐐣𐐭𐑊𐐯𐐿; 𐐰𐑌𐐼 𐐨𐑂𐐲𐑌 𐑁𐑉𐐱𐑋 𐐶𐐲𐑌 𐑅𐐮𐐻𐐨 𐐻𐐭 𐐰𐑌𐐲𐑄𐐲𐑉, 𐐲𐑌𐐻𐐮𐑊 𐑄𐐩 𐐸𐐰𐐼 𐑀𐐫𐑌 𐑁𐐫𐑉𐑃 𐐲𐑋𐐲𐑍 𐐫𐑊 𐑄 𐐹𐐨𐐹𐑊 𐐲𐑂 𐐤𐐨𐑁𐐴 𐐸𐐭 𐐶𐐲𐑉 𐐮𐑌 𐑄 𐑊𐐰𐑌𐐼 𐑅𐐵𐑃𐐶𐐲𐑉𐐼; 𐐰𐑌𐐼 𐑁𐑉𐐱𐑋 𐑄𐐯𐑌𐑅 𐐮𐑌𐐻𐐭 𐑄 𐑊𐐰𐑌𐐼 𐐲𐑂 𐐞𐐰𐑉𐐲𐐸𐐯𐑋𐑊𐐲, 𐐲𐑋𐐲𐑍 𐑄 𐐢𐐩𐑋𐐲𐑌𐐴𐐻𐑅.

17. 𐐈𐑌𐐼 𐐮𐐻 𐐿𐐩𐑋 𐐻𐐭 𐐹𐐰𐑅 𐑄𐐰𐐻 𐑄𐐩 𐐼𐐮𐐼 𐐹𐑉𐐨𐐽 𐐶𐐮𐑄 𐑀𐑉𐐩𐐻 𐐹𐐵𐐲𐑉, 𐐮𐑌𐑅𐐬𐑋𐐲𐐽 𐑄𐐰𐐻 𐑄𐐩 𐐼𐐮𐐼 𐐿𐐱𐑌𐑁𐐵𐑌𐐼 𐑋𐐯𐑌𐐨 𐐲𐑂 𐑄𐐬𐑆 𐐼𐐮𐑅𐐯𐑌𐐻𐐲𐑉𐑆 𐐸𐐭 𐐸𐐰𐐼 𐑀𐐫𐑌 𐐬𐑂𐐲𐑉 𐑁𐑉𐐱𐑋 𐑄 𐐤𐐨𐑁𐐴𐐻𐑅, 𐐮𐑌𐑅𐐬𐑋𐐲𐐽 𐑄𐐰𐐻 𐑄𐐩 𐐿𐐩𐑋 𐑁𐐫𐑉𐑃 𐐰𐑌𐐼 𐐼𐐮𐐼 𐐿𐐱𐑌𐑁𐐯𐑅 𐑄𐐩𐑉 𐑅𐐮𐑌𐑆, 𐐰𐑌𐐼 𐐶𐐲𐑉 𐐺𐐰𐐹𐐻𐐴𐑆𐐼 𐐲𐑌𐐻𐐭 𐑉𐐨𐐹𐐯𐑌𐐻𐐲𐑌𐑅, 𐐰𐑌𐐼 𐐮𐑋𐐨𐐼𐐨𐐲𐐻𐑊𐐨 𐑉𐐨𐐻𐐲𐑉𐑌𐐼 𐐻𐐭 𐑄 𐐤𐐨𐑁𐐴𐐻𐑅 𐐻𐐭 𐐯𐑌𐐼𐐯𐑂𐐲𐑉 𐐻𐐭 𐑉𐐨𐐹𐐩𐑉 𐐲𐑌𐐻𐐭 𐑄𐐯𐑋 𐑄 𐑉𐐱𐑍𐑆 𐐸𐐶𐐮𐐽 𐑄𐐩 𐐸𐐰𐐼 𐐼𐐲𐑌. 𐐈𐑌𐐼 𐐮𐐻 𐐿𐐩𐑋 𐐻𐐭 𐐹𐐰𐑅 𐑄𐐰𐐻 𐐤𐐨𐑁𐐴 𐐰𐑌𐐼 𐐢𐐨𐐸𐐴 𐐼𐐮𐐼 𐐹𐑉𐐨𐐽 𐐲𐑌𐐻𐐭 𐑄 𐐢𐐩𐑋𐐲𐑌𐐴𐐻𐑅 𐐶𐐮𐑄 𐑅𐐲𐐽 𐑀𐑉𐐩𐐻 𐐹𐐵𐐲𐑉 𐐰𐑌𐐼 𐐫𐑃𐐱𐑉𐐮𐐻𐐨, 𐑁𐐫𐑉 𐑄𐐩 𐐸𐐰𐐼 𐐹𐐵𐐲𐑉 𐐰𐑌𐐼 𐐫𐑃𐐱𐑉𐐮𐐻𐐨 𐑀𐐮𐑂𐐲𐑌 𐐲𐑌𐐻𐐭 𐑄𐐯𐑋 𐑄𐐰𐐻 𐑄𐐩 𐑋𐐴𐐻 𐑅𐐹𐐨𐐿, 𐐰𐑌𐐼 𐑄𐐩 𐐫𐑊𐑅𐐬 𐐸𐐰𐐼 𐐸𐐶𐐱𐐻 𐑄𐐩 𐑇𐐳𐐼 𐑅𐐹𐐨𐐿 𐑀𐐮𐑂𐐲𐑌 𐐲𐑌𐐻𐐭 𐑄𐐯𐑋; 𐑄𐐯𐑉𐑁𐐬𐑉 𐑄𐐩 𐐼𐐮𐐼 𐑅𐐹𐐨𐐿 𐐲𐑌𐐻𐐭 𐑄 𐑀𐑉𐐩𐐻 𐐰𐑅𐐻𐐱𐑌𐐮𐑇𐑋𐐯𐑌𐐻 𐐲𐑂 𐑄 𐐢𐐩𐑋𐐲𐑌𐐴𐐻𐑅, 𐐻𐐭 𐑄 𐐿𐐱𐑌𐑂𐐮𐑌𐑅𐐮𐑍 𐑄𐐯𐑋, 𐐮𐑌𐑅𐐬𐑋𐐲𐐽 𐑄𐐰𐐻 𐑄𐐩𐑉 𐐶𐐲𐑉 𐐩𐐻 𐑃𐐵𐑆𐐲𐑌𐐼 𐐲𐑂 𐑄 𐐢𐐩𐑋𐐲𐑌𐐴𐐻𐑅 𐐸𐐭 𐐶𐐲𐑉 𐐮𐑌 𐑄 𐑊𐐰𐑌𐐼 𐐲𐑂 𐐞𐐰𐑉𐐲𐐸𐐯𐑋𐑊𐐲 𐐰𐑌𐐼 𐑉𐐵𐑌𐐼 𐐲𐐺𐐵𐐻, 𐐺𐐰𐐹𐐻𐐴𐑆𐐼 𐐲𐑌𐐻𐐭 𐑉𐐨𐐹𐐯𐑌𐐻𐐲𐑌𐑅, 𐐰𐑌𐐼 𐐶𐐲𐑉 𐐿𐐱𐑌𐑂𐐮𐑌𐑅𐐻 𐐲𐑂 𐑄 𐐶𐐮𐐿𐐯𐐼𐑌𐐯𐑅 𐐲𐑂 𐑄 𐐻𐑉𐐲𐐼𐐮𐑇𐐲𐑌𐑆 𐐲𐑂 𐑄𐐩𐑉 𐑁𐐪𐑄𐐲𐑉𐑆.

18. 𐐈𐑌𐐼 𐐮𐐻 𐐿𐐩𐑋 𐐻𐐭 𐐹𐐰𐑅 𐑄𐐰𐐻 𐐤𐐨𐑁𐐴 𐐰𐑌𐐼 𐐢𐐨𐐸𐐴 𐐼𐐮𐐼 𐐹𐑉𐐬𐑅𐐨𐐼 𐑁𐑉𐐱𐑋 𐑄𐐯𐑌𐑅 𐐻𐐭 𐑀𐐬 𐐻𐐭 𐑄 𐑊𐐰𐑌𐐼 𐐲𐑂 𐐤𐐨𐑁𐐴. 𐐈𐑌𐐼 𐐮𐐻 𐐿𐐩𐑋 𐐻𐐭 𐐹𐐰𐑅 𐑄𐐰𐐻 𐑄𐐩 𐐶𐐲𐑉 𐐻𐐩𐐿𐐲𐑌 𐐺𐐴 𐐰𐑌 𐐪𐑉𐑋𐐨 𐐲𐑂 𐑄 𐐢𐐩𐑋𐐲𐑌𐐴𐐻𐑅 𐐰𐑌𐐼 𐐿𐐰𐑅𐐻 𐐮𐑌𐐻𐐭 𐐹𐑉𐐮𐑆𐐲𐑌; 𐐷𐐩, 𐐨𐑂𐐲𐑌 𐐮𐑌 𐑄𐐰𐐻 𐑅𐐩𐑋 𐐹𐑉𐐮𐑆𐐲𐑌 𐐮𐑌 𐐸𐐶𐐮𐐽 𐐈𐑋𐐲𐑌 𐐰𐑌𐐼 𐐸𐐮𐑆 𐐺𐑉𐐯𐑄𐑉𐐯𐑌 𐐶𐐲𐑉 𐐿𐐰𐑅𐐻 𐐺𐐴 𐑄 𐑅𐐲𐑉𐑂𐐲𐑌𐐻𐑅 𐐲𐑂 𐐢𐐮𐑋𐐸𐐴. 𐐈𐑌𐐼 𐐰𐑁𐐻𐐲𐑉 𐑄𐐩 𐐸𐐰𐐼 𐐺𐐮𐑌 𐐿𐐰𐑅𐐻 𐐮𐑌𐐻𐐭 𐐹𐑉𐐮𐑆𐐲𐑌 𐑋𐐯𐑌𐐨 𐐼𐐩𐑆 𐐶𐐮𐑄𐐵𐐻 𐑁𐐭𐐼, 𐐺𐐨𐐸𐐬𐑊𐐼 𐑄𐐩 𐐶𐐯𐑌𐐻 𐑁𐐫𐑉𐑃 𐐮𐑌𐐻𐐭 𐑄 𐐹𐑉𐐮𐑆𐐲𐑌 𐐻𐐭 𐐻𐐩𐐿 𐑄𐐯𐑋 𐑄𐐰𐐻 𐑄𐐩 𐑋𐐴𐐻 𐑅𐑊𐐩 𐑄𐐯𐑋. 𐐈𐑌𐐼 𐐮𐐻 𐐿𐐩𐑋 𐐻𐐭 𐐹𐐰𐑅 𐑄𐐰𐐻 𐐤𐐨𐑁𐐴 𐐰𐑌𐐼 𐐢𐐨𐐸𐐴 𐐶𐐲𐑉 𐐯𐑌𐑅𐐲𐑉𐐿𐑊𐐼 𐐲𐐺𐐵𐐻 𐐰𐑆 𐐮𐑁 𐐺𐐴 𐑁𐐴𐐲𐑉, 𐐨𐑂𐐲𐑌 𐐮𐑌𐑅𐐬𐑋𐐲𐐽 𐑄𐐰𐐻 𐑄𐐩 𐐼𐐲𐑉𐑅𐐻 𐑌𐐱𐐻 𐑊𐐩 𐑄𐐩𐑉 𐐸𐐰𐑌𐐼𐑆 𐐲𐐹𐐱𐑌 𐑄𐐯𐑋 𐑁𐐫𐑉 𐑁𐐨𐑉 𐑊𐐯𐑅𐐻 𐑄𐐩 𐑇𐐳𐐼 𐐺𐐨 𐐺𐐲𐑉𐑌𐐼. 𐐤𐐯𐑂𐐲𐑉𐑄𐐯𐑊𐐯𐑅, 𐐤𐐨𐑁𐐴 𐐰𐑌𐐼 𐐢𐐨𐐸𐐴 𐐶𐐲𐑉 𐑌𐐱𐐻 𐐺𐐲𐑉𐑌𐐼; 𐐰𐑌𐐼 𐑄𐐩 𐐶𐐲𐑉 𐐰𐑆 𐑅𐐻𐐰𐑌𐐼𐐮𐑍 𐐮𐑌 𐑄 𐑋𐐮𐐼𐑅𐐻 𐐲𐑂 𐑁𐐴𐐲𐑉, 𐐰𐑌𐐼 𐐶𐐲𐑉 𐑌𐐱𐐻 𐐺𐐲𐑉𐑌𐐼. 𐐈𐑌𐐼 𐐸𐐶𐐯𐑌 𐑄𐐩 𐑅𐐫 𐑄𐐰𐐻 𐑄𐐩 𐐶𐐲𐑉 𐐯𐑌𐑅𐐲𐑉𐐿𐑊𐐼 𐐲𐐺𐐵𐐻 𐐶𐐮𐑄 𐐰 𐐹𐐮𐑊𐐲𐑉 𐐲𐑂 𐑁𐐴𐐲𐑉, 𐐰𐑌𐐼 𐑄𐐰𐐻 𐐮𐐻 𐐺𐐲𐑉𐑌𐐼 𐑄𐐯𐑋 𐑌𐐱𐐻, 𐑄𐐩𐑉 𐐸𐐪𐑉𐐻𐑅 𐐼𐐮𐐼 𐐻𐐩𐐿 𐐿𐐲𐑉𐐩𐐾. 𐐙𐐫𐑉 𐑄𐐩 𐑅𐐫 𐑄𐐰𐐻 𐑄 𐐢𐐩𐑋𐐲𐑌𐐴𐐻𐑅 𐐼𐐲𐑉𐑅𐐻 𐑌𐐱𐐻 𐑊𐐩 𐑄𐐩𐑉 𐐸𐐰𐑌𐐼𐑆 𐐲𐐹𐐱𐑌 𐑄𐐯𐑋; 𐑌𐐨𐑄𐐲𐑉 𐐼𐐲𐑉𐑅𐐻 𐑄𐐩 𐐿𐐲𐑋 𐑌𐐨𐑉 𐐲𐑌𐐻𐐭 𐑄𐐯𐑋, 𐐺𐐲𐐻 𐑅𐐻𐐳𐐼 𐐰𐑆 𐐮𐑁 𐑄𐐩 𐐶𐐲𐑉 𐑅𐐻𐑉𐐲𐐿 𐐼𐐲𐑋 𐐶𐐮𐑄 𐐰𐑋𐐩𐑆𐑋𐐯𐑌𐐻.

19. 𐐈𐑌𐐼 𐐮𐐻 𐐿𐐩𐑋 𐐻𐐭 𐐹𐐰𐑅 𐑄𐐰𐐻 𐐤𐐨𐑁𐐴 𐐰𐑌𐐼 𐐢𐐨𐐸𐐴 𐐼𐐮𐐼 𐑅𐐻𐐰𐑌𐐼 𐑁𐐫𐑉𐑃, 𐐰𐑌𐐼 𐐺𐐨𐑀𐐰𐑌 𐐻𐐭 𐑅𐐹𐐨𐐿 𐐲𐑌𐐻𐐭 𐑄𐐯𐑋, 𐑅𐐩𐐮𐑍, 𐐙𐐨𐑉 𐑌𐐱𐐻, 𐑁𐐫𐑉 𐐺𐐨𐐸𐐬𐑊𐐼, 𐐮𐐻 𐐮𐑆 𐐘𐐱𐐼 𐑄𐐰𐐻 𐐸𐐰𐑃 𐑇𐐬𐑌 𐐲𐑌𐐻𐐭 𐐷𐐭 𐑄𐐮𐑅 𐑋𐐪𐑉𐑂𐐯𐑊𐐲𐑅 𐑃𐐮𐑍, 𐐮𐑌 𐑄 𐐸𐐶𐐮𐐽 𐐮𐑆 𐑇𐐬𐑌 𐐲𐑌𐐻𐐭 𐐷𐐭 𐑄𐐰𐐻 𐐷𐐨 𐐿𐐰𐑌𐐱𐐻 𐑊𐐩 𐐷𐐭𐑉 𐐸𐐰𐑌𐐼𐑆 𐐱𐑌 𐐲𐑅 𐐻𐐭 𐑅𐑊𐐩 𐐲𐑅. 𐐈𐑌𐐼 𐐺𐐨𐐸𐐬𐑊𐐼, 𐐸𐐶𐐯𐑌 𐑄𐐩 𐐸𐐰𐐼 𐑅𐐯𐐼 𐑄𐐨𐑆 𐐶𐐲𐑉𐐼𐑆, 𐑄 𐐲𐑉𐑃 𐑇𐐳𐐿 𐐯𐐿𐑅𐐨𐐼𐐮𐑍𐑊𐐨, 𐐰𐑌𐐼 𐑄 𐐶𐐫𐑊𐑆 𐐲𐑂 𐑄 𐐹𐑉𐐮𐑆𐐲𐑌 𐐼𐐮𐐼 𐑇𐐩𐐿 𐐰𐑆 𐐮𐑁 𐑄𐐩 𐐶𐐲𐑉 𐐲𐐺𐐵𐐻 𐐻𐐭 𐐻𐐲𐑋𐐺𐑊 𐐻𐐭 𐑄 𐐲𐑉𐑃; 𐐺𐐲𐐻 𐐺𐐨𐐸𐐬𐑊𐐼, 𐑄𐐩 𐐼𐐮𐐼 𐑌𐐱𐐻 𐑁𐐫𐑊. 𐐈𐑌𐐼 𐐺𐐨𐐸𐐬𐑊𐐼, 𐑄𐐩 𐑄𐐰𐐻 𐐶𐐲𐑉 𐐮𐑌 𐑄 𐐹𐑉𐐮𐑆𐐲𐑌 𐐶𐐲𐑉 𐐢𐐩𐑋𐐲𐑌𐐴𐐻𐑅 𐐰𐑌𐐼 𐐤𐐨𐑁𐐴𐐻𐑅 𐐸𐐭 𐐶𐐲𐑉 𐐼𐐮𐑅𐐯𐑌𐐻𐐲𐑉𐑆. 𐐈𐑌𐐼 𐐮𐐻 𐐿𐐩𐑋 𐐻𐐭 𐐹𐐰𐑅 𐑄𐐰𐐻 𐑄𐐩 𐐶𐐲𐑉 𐐬𐑂𐐲𐑉𐑇𐐰𐐼𐐬𐐼 𐐶𐐮𐑄 𐐰 𐐿𐑊𐐵𐐼 𐐲𐑂 𐐼𐐪𐑉𐐿𐑌𐐯𐑅, 𐐰𐑌𐐼 𐐰𐑌 𐐫𐑁𐐳𐑊 𐑅𐐱𐑊𐐯𐑋 𐑁𐐨𐑉 𐐿𐐩𐑋 𐐲𐐹𐐱𐑌 𐑄𐐯𐑋. 𐐈𐑌𐐼 𐐮𐐻 𐐿𐐩𐑋 𐐻𐐭 𐐹𐐰𐑅 𐑄𐐰𐐻 𐑄𐐩𐑉 𐐿𐐩𐑋 𐐰 𐑂𐐦𐑅 𐐰𐑆 𐐮𐑁 𐐮𐐻 𐐶𐐲𐑉 𐐲𐐺𐐲𐑂 𐑄 𐐿𐑊𐐵𐐼 𐐲𐑂 𐐼𐐪𐑉𐐿𐑌𐐯𐑅, 𐑅𐐩𐐮𐑍, 𐐡𐐨𐐹𐐯𐑌𐐻 𐐷𐐨, 𐑉𐐨-

𐐹𐐯𐑌𐐻 𐐷𐐨, 𐐰𐑌𐐼 𐑅𐐨𐐿 𐑌𐐬 𐑋𐐬𐑉 𐐻𐐭 𐐼𐐨𐑅𐐻𐑉𐐱𐐮 𐑋𐐴 𐑅𐐲𐑉𐑂𐐰𐑌𐐻𐑅 𐐸𐐭𐑋 𐐴 𐐸𐐰𐑂 𐑅𐐯𐑌𐐻 𐐲𐑌𐐻𐐭 𐐷𐐭 𐐻𐐭 𐐼𐐨𐐿𐑊𐐩𐑉 𐑀𐐳𐐼 𐐻𐐴𐐼𐐮𐑍𐑆.

20. 𐐈𐑌𐐼 𐐮𐐻 𐐿𐐩𐑋 𐐻𐐭 𐐹𐐰𐑅 𐐸𐐶𐐯𐑌 𐑄𐐩 𐐸𐐲𐑉𐐼 𐑄𐐮𐑅 𐑂𐐱𐐮𐑅, 𐐰𐑌𐐼 𐐺𐐨𐐸𐐯𐑊𐐼 𐑄𐐰𐐻 𐐮𐐻 𐐶𐐱𐑆 𐑌𐐱𐐻 𐐲 𐑂𐐱𐐮𐑅 𐐱𐑂 𐑃𐐲𐑌𐐼𐐲𐑉; 𐑌𐐨𐑄𐐲𐑉 𐐶𐐱𐑆 𐐮𐐻 𐐲 𐑂𐐱𐐮𐑅 𐐱𐑂 𐐲 𐑀𐑉𐐩𐐻 𐐻𐐭𐑋𐐲𐑊𐐻𐐷𐐭𐐲𐑅 𐑌𐐱𐐮𐑆; 𐐺𐐲𐐻 𐐺𐐨𐐸𐐬𐑊𐐼, 𐐮𐐻 𐐶𐐱𐑆 𐐲 𐑅𐐻𐐮𐑊 𐑂𐐱𐐮𐑅 𐐱𐑂 𐐹𐐲𐑉𐑁𐐯𐐿𐐻 𐑋𐐴𐑊𐐼𐑌𐐯𐑅, 𐐰𐑆 𐐮𐑁 𐐮𐐻 𐐸𐐰𐐼 𐐺𐐮𐑌 𐐲 𐐸𐐶𐐮𐑅𐐹𐐲𐑉, 𐐰𐑌𐐼 𐐮𐐻 𐐼𐐮𐐼 𐐹𐐨𐑉𐑅 𐐨𐑂𐐲𐑌 𐐻𐐭 𐑄 𐑂𐐯𐑉𐐨 𐑅𐐬𐑊. 𐐈𐑌𐐼 𐑌𐐱𐐻𐐶𐐮𐑃𐑅𐐻𐐰𐑌𐐼𐐮𐑍 𐑄 𐑋𐐴𐑊𐐼𐑌𐐯𐑅 𐐱𐑂 𐑄 𐑂𐐱𐐮𐑅, 𐐺𐐨𐐸𐐬𐑊𐐼 𐑄 𐐲𐑉𐑃 𐑇𐐳𐐿 𐐯𐐿𐑅𐐨𐐼𐐮𐑍𐑊𐐨, 𐐰𐑌𐐼 𐑄 𐐶𐐫𐑊𐑆 𐐱𐑂 𐑄 𐐹𐑉𐐮𐑆𐐲𐑌 𐐻𐑉𐐯𐑋𐐺𐐲𐑊𐐼 𐐲𐑀𐐯𐑌, 𐐰𐑆 𐐮𐑁 𐐮𐐻 𐐶𐐲𐑉 𐐲𐐺𐐵𐐻 𐐻𐐭 𐐻𐐲𐑋𐐺𐐲𐑊 𐐻𐐭 𐑄 𐐲𐑉𐑃; 𐐰𐑌𐐼 𐐺𐐨𐐸𐐬𐑊𐐼 𐑄 𐐿𐑊𐐵𐐼 𐐱𐑂 𐐼𐐪𐑉𐐿𐑌𐐯𐑅, 𐐸𐐶𐐮𐐽 𐐸𐐰𐐼 𐐬𐑂𐐲𐑉𐑇𐐰𐐼𐐬𐐼 𐑄𐐯𐑋, 𐐼𐐮𐐼 𐑌𐐱𐐻 𐐼𐐮𐑅𐐹𐐲𐑉𐑅. 𐐈𐑌𐐼 𐐺𐐨𐐸𐐬𐑊𐐼 𐑄 𐑂𐐱𐐮𐑅 𐐿𐐩𐑋 𐐲𐑀𐐯𐑌, 𐑅𐐩𐐮𐑍, 𐐡𐐨𐐹𐐯𐑌𐐻 𐐷𐐨, 𐑉𐐨𐐹𐐯𐑌𐐻 𐐷𐐨, 𐑁𐐫𐑉 𐑄 𐐿𐐮𐑍𐐼𐐲𐑋 𐐱𐑂 𐐸𐐯𐑂𐐲𐑌 𐐮𐑆 𐐰𐐻 𐐸𐐰𐑌𐐼; 𐐰𐑌𐐼 𐑅𐐨𐐿 𐑌𐐬 𐑋𐐬𐑉 𐐻𐐭 𐐼𐐨𐑅𐐻𐑉𐐱𐐮 𐑋𐐴 𐑅𐐲𐑉𐑂𐐰𐑌𐐻𐑅. 𐐈𐑌𐐼 𐐮𐐻 𐐿𐐩𐑋 𐐻𐐭 𐐹𐐰𐑅 𐑄𐐰𐐻 𐑄 𐐲𐑉𐑃 𐑇𐐳𐐿 𐐲𐑀𐐯𐑌, 𐐰𐑌𐐼 𐑄 𐐶𐐫𐑊𐑆 𐐻𐑉𐐯𐑋𐐺𐐲𐑊𐐼; 𐐰𐑌𐐼 𐐫𐑊𐑅𐐬 𐐲𐑀𐐯𐑌 𐑄 𐑃𐐲𐑉𐐼 𐐻𐐴𐑋 𐑄 𐑂𐐱𐐮𐑅 𐐿𐐩𐑋, 𐐰𐑌𐐼 𐐼𐐮𐐼 𐑅𐐹𐐨𐐿 𐐲𐑌𐐻𐐭 𐑄𐐯𐑋 𐑋𐐪𐑉𐑂𐐯𐑊𐐲𐑅 𐐶𐐲𐑉𐐼𐑆 𐐸𐐶𐐮𐐽 𐐿𐐰𐑌𐐱𐐻 𐐺𐐨 𐐲𐐻𐐲𐑉𐐼 𐐺𐐴 𐑋𐐰𐑌; 𐐰𐑌𐐼 𐑄 𐐶𐐫𐑊𐑆 𐐼𐐮𐐼 𐐻𐑉𐐯𐑋𐐺𐐲𐑊 𐐲𐑀𐐯𐑌, 𐐰𐑌𐐼 𐑄 𐐲𐑉𐑃 𐑇𐐳𐐿 𐐰𐑆 𐐮𐑁 𐐮𐐻 𐐶𐐲𐑉 𐐲𐐺𐐵𐐻 𐐻𐐭 𐐼𐐮𐑂𐐴𐐼 𐐰𐑅𐐲𐑌𐐼𐐲𐑉.

21. 𐐈𐑌𐐼 𐐮𐐻 𐐿𐐩𐑋 𐐻𐐭 𐐹𐐰𐑅 𐑄𐐰𐐻 𐑄 𐐢𐐰𐑋𐐲𐑌𐐴𐐻𐑅 𐐿𐐳𐐼 𐑌𐐱𐐻 𐑁𐑊𐐨 𐐺𐐨𐐿𐐫𐑆 𐐱𐑂 𐑄 𐐿𐑊𐐵𐐼 𐐱𐑂 𐐼𐐪𐑉𐐿𐑌𐐯𐑅 𐐸𐐶𐐮𐐽 𐐼𐐮𐐼 𐐬𐑂𐐲𐑉𐑇𐐰𐐼𐐬 𐑄𐐯𐑋; 𐐷𐐩, 𐐰𐑌𐐼 𐐫𐑊𐑅𐐬 𐑄𐐩 𐐶𐐲𐑉 𐐮𐑋𐐭𐑂𐐲𐐺𐐲𐑊 𐐺𐐨𐐿𐐫𐑆 𐐱𐑂 𐑄 𐑁𐐨𐑉 𐐸𐐶𐐮𐐽 𐐼𐐮𐐼 𐐿𐐲𐑋 𐐲𐐹𐐱𐑌 𐑄𐐯𐑋. 𐐤𐐵 𐑄𐐯𐑉 𐐶𐐱𐑆 𐐶𐐲𐑌 𐐲𐑋𐐲𐑍 𐑄𐐯𐑋 𐐸𐐭 𐐶𐐱𐑆 𐐲 𐐤𐐨𐑁𐐴𐐻 𐐺𐐴 𐐺𐐲𐑉𐑃, 𐐸𐐭 𐐸𐐰𐐼 𐐶𐐲𐑌𐑅 𐐺𐐨𐑊𐐱𐑍𐐼 𐐻𐐭 𐑄 𐐽𐐲𐑉𐐽 𐐱𐑂 𐐘𐐱𐐼, 𐐺𐐲𐐻 𐐸𐐰𐐼 𐐼𐐮𐑅𐐯𐑌𐐻𐐯𐐼 𐑁𐑉𐐱𐑋 𐑄𐐯𐑋. 𐐈𐑌𐐼 𐐮𐐻 𐐿𐐩𐑋 𐐻𐐭 𐐹𐐰𐑅 𐑄𐐰𐐻 𐐸𐐨 𐐻𐐲𐑉𐑌𐐼 𐐸𐐮𐑋 𐐲𐐺𐐵𐐻, 𐐰𐑌𐐼 𐐺𐐨𐐸𐐬𐑊𐐼 𐐸𐐨 𐑅𐐫 𐑃𐑉𐐭 𐑄 𐐿𐑊𐐵𐐼 𐐱𐑂 𐐼𐐪𐑉𐐿𐑌𐐯𐑅 𐑄 𐑁𐐩𐑅𐐯𐑆 𐐱𐑂 𐐤𐐨𐑁𐐴 𐐰𐑌𐐼 𐐢𐐨𐐸𐐴; 𐐰𐑌𐐼 𐐺𐐨𐐸𐐬𐑊𐐼 𐑄𐐩 𐐼𐐮𐐼 𐑇𐐴𐑌 𐐯𐐿𐑅𐐨𐐼𐐮𐑍𐑊𐐨, 𐐨𐑂𐐲𐑌 𐐰𐑆 𐑄 𐑁𐐩𐑅𐐯𐑆 𐐱𐑂 𐐩𐑌𐐾𐐯𐑊𐑆. 𐐈𐑌𐐼 𐐸𐐨 𐐺𐐨𐐸𐐯𐑊𐐼 𐑄𐐰𐐻 𐑄𐐩 𐐼𐐮𐐼 𐑊𐐮𐑁𐐻 𐑄𐐩𐑉 𐐴𐑆 𐐻𐐭 𐐸𐐯𐑂𐐲𐑌; 𐐰𐑌𐐼 𐑄𐐩 𐐶𐐲𐑉 𐐮𐑌 𐑄 𐐰𐐻𐐮𐐻𐐷𐐭𐐼 𐐰𐑆 𐐮𐑁 𐐻𐐫𐐿𐐮𐑍 𐐫𐑉 𐑊𐐮𐑁𐐻𐐮𐑍 𐑄𐐩𐑉 𐑂𐐱𐐮𐑅𐐯𐑆 𐐻𐐭 𐑅𐐲𐑋 𐐺𐐨𐐮𐑍 𐐸𐐭𐑋 𐑄𐐩 𐐺𐐨𐐸𐐯𐑊𐐼.

22. 𐐈𐑌𐐼 𐐮𐐻 𐐿𐐩𐑋 𐐻𐐭 𐐹𐐰𐑅 𐑄𐐰𐐻 𐑄𐐮𐑅 𐑋𐐰𐑌 𐐼𐐮𐐼 𐐿𐑉𐐴 𐐲𐑌𐐻𐐭 𐑄 𐑋𐐲𐑊𐐻𐐮𐐻𐐷𐐭𐐼, 𐑄𐐰𐐻 𐑄𐐩 𐑋𐐴𐐻 𐐻𐐲𐑉𐑌 𐐰𐑌𐐼 𐑊𐐳𐐿. 𐐈𐑌𐐼 𐐺𐐨𐐸𐐬𐑊𐐼, 𐑄𐐯𐑉 𐐶𐐱𐑆 𐐹𐐵𐐲𐑉 𐑀𐐮𐑂𐐲𐑌 𐐲𐑌𐐻𐐭 𐑄𐐯𐑋, 𐑄𐐰𐐻 𐑄𐐩 𐐼𐐮𐐼 𐐻𐐲𐑉𐑌 𐐰𐑌𐐼 𐑊𐐳𐐿; 𐐰𐑌𐐼 𐑄𐐩 𐐼𐐮𐐼 𐐺𐐨𐐸𐐬𐑊𐐼 𐑄 𐑁𐐩𐑅𐐯𐑆 𐐱𐑂 𐐤𐐨𐑁𐐴 𐐰𐑌𐐼 𐐢𐐨𐐸𐐴. 𐐈𐑌𐐼 𐑄𐐩 𐑅𐐯𐐼 𐐲𐑌𐐻𐐭 𐑄 𐑋𐐰𐑌, 𐐒𐐨𐐸𐐬𐑊𐐼, 𐐸𐐶𐐱𐐻 𐐼𐐭 𐐫𐑊 𐑄𐐨𐑆 𐑃𐐮𐑍𐑆 𐑋𐐨𐑌? 𐐰𐑌𐐼 𐐸𐐭 𐐮𐑆 𐐮𐐻 𐐶𐐮𐑄 𐐸𐐭𐑋 𐑄𐐨𐑆 𐑋𐐯𐑌 𐐼𐐭 𐐿𐐱𐑌𐑂𐐲𐑉𐑅? 𐐤𐐵 𐑄 𐑋𐐰𐑌'𐑆 𐑌𐐩𐑋 𐐶𐐱𐑆 𐐈𐑋𐐮𐑌𐐲𐐼𐐰𐐺. 𐐈𐑌𐐼 𐐈𐑋𐐮𐑌𐐲𐐼𐐰𐐺 𐑅𐐯𐐼 𐐲𐑌𐐻𐐭 𐑄𐐯𐑋, 𐐜𐐩 𐐼𐐭 𐐿𐐱𐑌𐑂𐐲𐑉𐑅 𐐶𐐮𐑄 𐑄 𐐩𐑌𐐾𐐯𐑊𐑆 𐐱𐑂 𐐘𐐱𐐼. 𐐈𐑌𐐼 𐐮𐐻 𐐿𐐩𐑋 𐐻𐐭 𐐹𐐰𐑅 𐑄𐐰𐐻 𐑄 𐐢𐐰𐑋𐐲𐑌𐐴𐐻𐑅 𐑅𐐯𐐼 𐐲𐑌𐐻𐐭 𐐸𐐮𐑋, 𐐐𐐶𐐱𐐻 𐑇𐐰𐑊 𐐶𐐨 𐐼𐐭, 𐑄𐐰𐐻 𐑄𐐮𐑅 𐐿𐑊𐐵𐐼 𐐱𐑂 𐐼𐐪𐑉𐐿𐑌𐐯𐑅 𐑋𐐩 𐐺𐐨 𐑉𐐨𐑋𐐭𐑂𐐼 𐑁𐑉𐐱𐑋 𐐬𐑂𐐲𐑉𐑇𐐰𐐼𐐬𐐮𐑍 𐐲𐑅? 𐐈𐑌𐐼 𐐈𐑋𐐮𐑌𐐲𐐼𐐰𐐺 𐑅𐐯𐐼 𐐲𐑌𐐻𐐭 𐑄𐐯𐑋, 𐐏𐐭 𐑋𐐲𐑅𐐻 𐑉𐐨𐐹𐐯𐑌𐐻, 𐐰𐑌𐐼 𐐿𐑉𐐴 𐐲𐑌𐐻𐐭 𐑄 𐑂𐐱𐐮𐑅, 𐐨𐑂𐐲𐑌 𐐲𐑌𐐻𐐮𐑊 𐐷𐐨 𐑇𐐰𐑊 𐐸𐐰𐑂 𐑁𐐩𐑃 𐐮𐑌 𐐗𐑉𐐴𐑅𐐻, 𐐸𐐭 𐐶𐐱𐑆 𐐻𐐫𐐻 𐐲𐑌𐐻𐐭 𐐷𐐭 𐐺𐐴 𐐈𐑊𐑋𐐲, 𐐰𐑌𐐼 𐐈𐑋𐐷𐐭𐑊𐐯𐐿, 𐐰𐑌𐐼 𐐞𐐨𐑆𐑉𐐱𐑋; 𐐰𐑌𐐼 𐐸𐐶𐐯𐑌 𐐷𐐨 𐑇𐐰𐑊 𐐼𐐭 𐑄𐐮𐑅, 𐑄 𐐿𐑊𐐵𐐼 𐐱𐑂 𐐼𐐪𐑉𐐿𐑌𐐯𐑅 𐑇𐐰𐑊 𐐺𐐨 𐑉𐐨𐑋𐐭𐑂𐐼 𐑁𐑉𐐱𐑋 𐐬𐑂𐐲𐑉𐑇𐐰𐐼𐐬𐐮𐑍 𐐷𐐭.

23. 𐐈𐑌𐐼 𐐮𐐻 𐐿𐐩𐑋 𐐻𐐭 𐐹𐐰𐑅 𐑄𐐰𐐻 𐑄𐐩 𐐫𐑊 𐐼𐐮𐐼 𐐺𐐨𐑀𐐮𐑌 𐐻𐐭 𐐿𐑉𐐴 𐐲𐑌𐐻𐐭 𐑄 𐑂𐐱𐐮𐑅 𐐱𐑂 𐐸𐐮𐑋 𐐸𐐭 𐐸𐐰𐐼 𐑇𐐩𐐿𐐲𐑌 𐑄 𐐲𐑉𐑃; 𐐷𐐩, 𐑄𐐩 𐐼𐐮𐐼 𐐿𐑉𐐴 𐐨𐑂𐐲𐑌 𐐲𐑌𐐻𐐮𐑊 𐑄 𐐿𐑊𐐵𐐼 𐐱𐑂 𐐼𐐪𐑉𐐿𐑌𐐯𐑅 𐐶𐐱𐑆 𐐼𐐮𐑅𐐹𐐲𐑉𐑅𐐻. 𐐈𐑌𐐼 𐐮𐐻 𐐿𐐩𐑋 𐐻𐐭 𐐹𐐰𐑅 𐑄𐐰𐐻 𐐸𐐶𐐯𐑌 𐑄𐐩 𐐿𐐰𐑅𐐻 𐑄𐐩𐑉 𐐴𐑆 𐐲𐐺𐐵𐐻, 𐐰𐑌𐐼 𐑅𐐫 𐑄𐐰𐐻 𐑄 𐐿𐑊𐐵𐐼 𐐱𐑂 𐐼𐐪𐑉𐐿𐑌𐐯𐑅 𐐶𐐱𐑆 𐐼𐐮𐑅𐐹𐐲𐑉𐑅𐐻 𐑁𐑉𐐱𐑋 𐐬𐑂𐐲𐑉𐑇𐐰𐐼𐐬𐐮𐑍 𐑄𐐯𐑋, 𐐰𐑌𐐼 𐐺𐐨𐐸𐐬𐑊𐐼, 𐑄𐐩 𐑅𐐫 𐑄𐐰𐐻 𐑄𐐩 𐐶𐐲𐑉 𐐯𐑌𐑅𐐲𐑉𐐿𐐲𐑊𐐼 𐐲𐐺𐐵𐐻, 𐐷𐐩, 𐐯𐑂𐐲𐑉𐐨 𐑅𐐬𐑊, 𐐺𐐴 𐐲 𐐹𐐮𐑊𐐲𐑉 𐐱𐑂 𐑁𐐴𐑉. 𐐈𐑌𐐼 𐐤𐐨𐑁𐐴 𐐰𐑌𐐼 𐐢𐐨𐐸𐐴 𐐶𐐲𐑉 𐐮𐑌 𐑄 𐑋𐐮𐐼𐑅𐐻 𐐱𐑂 𐑄𐐯𐑋; 𐐷𐐩, 𐑄𐐩 𐐶𐐲𐑉 𐐯𐑌𐑅𐐲𐑉𐐿𐐲𐑊𐐼 𐐲𐐺𐐵𐐻; 𐐷𐐩, 𐑄𐐩 𐐶𐐲𐑉 𐐰𐑆 𐐮𐑁 𐐮𐑌 𐑄 𐑋𐐮𐐼𐑅𐐻 𐐱𐑂 𐐲 𐑁𐑊𐐩𐑋𐐮𐑍 𐑁𐐴𐑉, 𐐷𐐯𐐻 𐐮𐐻 𐐼𐐮𐐼 𐐸𐐪𐑉𐑋 𐑄𐐯𐑋 𐑌𐐱𐐻, 𐑌𐐨𐑄𐐲𐑉 𐐼𐐮𐐼 𐐮𐐻 𐐻𐐩𐐿 𐐸𐐬𐑊𐐼 𐐲𐐹𐐱𐑌 𐑄 𐐶𐐫𐑊𐑆 𐐱𐑂 𐑄 𐐹𐑉𐐮𐑆𐐲𐑌; 𐐰𐑌𐐼 𐑄𐐩 𐐶𐐲𐑉 𐑁𐐮𐑊𐐼 𐐶𐐮𐑄 𐑄𐐰𐐻 𐐾𐐱𐐮 𐐸𐐶𐐮𐐽 𐐮𐑆 𐐲𐑌𐑅𐐹𐐨𐐿𐐲𐐺𐐲𐑊 𐐰𐑌𐐼 𐑁𐐳𐑊 𐐱𐑂 𐑀𐑊𐐬𐑉𐐨. 𐐈𐑌𐐼 𐐺𐐨𐐸𐐬𐑊𐐼 𐑄 𐐐𐐬𐑊𐐨 𐐝𐐹𐐮𐑉𐐮𐐻 𐐱𐑂 𐐘𐐱𐐼 𐐼𐐮𐐼 𐐿𐐲𐑋 𐐼𐐵𐑌 𐑁𐑉𐐱𐑋 𐐸𐐯𐑂𐐲𐑌, 𐐰𐑌𐐼 𐐼𐐮𐐼 𐐯𐑌𐐻𐐲𐑉 𐐮𐑌𐐻𐐭

𐑄𐐯𐑉 𐐸𐐪𐑉𐐻𐑅, 𐐰𐑌𐐼 𐑄𐐩 𐐶𐐲𐑉 𐑁𐐮𐑊𐐼 𐐰𐑆 𐐮𐑁 𐐶𐐮𐑄 𐑁𐐴𐑉, 𐐰𐑌𐐼 𐑄𐐩 𐐿𐐳𐐼 𐑅𐐹𐐨𐐿 𐑁𐐫𐑉𐑃 𐑋𐐪𐑉𐑂𐐯𐑊𐐲𐑅 𐐶𐐲𐑉𐐼𐑆.

24. 𐐈𐑌𐐼 𐐮𐐻 𐐿𐐩𐑋 𐐻𐐭 𐐹𐐪𐑅 𐑄𐐰𐐻 𐑄𐐯𐑉 𐐿𐐩𐑋 𐐲 𐑂𐑎𐑅 𐐲𐑌𐐻𐐭 𐑄𐐯𐑋, 𐐷𐐩, 𐐲 𐐹𐑊𐐯𐑆𐐲𐑌𐐻 𐑂𐑎𐑅, 𐐰𐑆 𐐮𐑁 𐐮𐐻 𐐶𐐲𐑉 𐐲 𐐸𐐶𐐮𐑅𐐹𐐲𐑉, 𐑅𐐩𐐮𐑍, 𐐑𐐨𐑅, 𐐹𐐨𐑅 𐐺 𐐲𐑌𐐻𐐭 𐐷𐐭, 𐐺𐐨𐐿𐐫𐑆 𐐱𐑂 𐐷𐐭𐑉 𐑁𐐩𐑃 𐐮𐑌 𐑋𐐴 𐐎𐐯𐑊 𐐒𐐨𐑊𐐲𐑂𐐯𐐼, 𐐸𐐭 𐐶𐐱𐑆 𐑁𐑉𐐱𐑋 𐑄 𐑁𐐵𐑌𐐼𐐩𐑇𐐲𐑌 𐐱𐑂 𐑄 𐐶𐐲𐑉𐑊𐐼. 𐐈𐑌𐐼 𐑌𐐵 𐐸𐐶𐐯𐑌 𐑄𐐩 𐐸𐐲𐑉𐐼 𐑄𐐮𐑅, 𐑄𐐩 𐐿𐐪𐑅𐐻 𐐲𐐹 𐑄𐐯𐑉 𐐴𐑆 𐐰𐑆 𐐮𐑁 𐐻𐐭 𐐺𐐨𐐸𐐬𐑊𐐼 𐑁𐑉𐐱𐑋 𐐸𐐶𐐯𐑌𐑅 𐑄 𐑂𐑎𐑅 𐐿𐐩𐑋; 𐐰𐑌𐐼 𐐺𐐨𐐸𐐬𐑊𐐼, 𐑄𐐩 𐑅𐐫 𐑄 𐐸𐐯𐑂𐐲𐑌𐑆 𐐬𐐹𐐲𐑌; 𐐰𐑌𐐼 𐐩𐑌𐐾𐐯𐑊𐑆 𐐿𐐩𐑋 𐐼𐐵𐑌 𐐵𐐻 𐐱𐑂 𐐸𐐯𐑂𐐲𐑌, 𐐰𐑌𐐼 𐑋𐐮𐑌𐐮𐑅𐐻𐐲𐑉𐐼 𐐲𐑌𐐻𐐭 𐑄𐐯𐑋. 𐐈𐑌𐐼 𐑄𐐯𐑉 𐐶𐐲𐑉 𐐲𐐺𐐵𐐻 𐑃𐑉𐐨 𐐸𐐲𐑌𐐼𐑉𐐯𐐼 𐑅𐐬𐑊𐑆 𐐸𐐭 𐑅𐐫 𐐰𐑌𐐼 𐐸𐐲𐑉𐐼 𐑄𐐨𐑆 𐑃𐐮𐑍𐑆; 𐐰𐑌𐐼 𐑄𐐩 𐐶𐐲𐑉 𐐺𐐮𐐼𐐲𐑌 𐐻𐐭 𐑀𐐬 𐑁𐐫𐑉𐑃 𐐰𐑌𐐼 𐑋𐐪𐑉𐑂𐐯𐑊 𐑌𐐱𐐻, 𐑌𐐨𐑄𐐲𐑉 𐑇𐐳𐐼 𐑄𐐩 𐐼𐐵𐐻. 𐐈𐑌𐐼 𐐮𐐻 𐐿𐐩𐑋 𐐻𐐭 𐐹𐐪𐑅 𐑄𐐰𐐻 𐑄𐐩 𐐼𐐮𐐼 𐑀𐐬 𐑁𐐫𐑉𐑃, 𐐰𐑌𐐼 𐐼𐐮𐐼 𐑋𐐮𐑌𐐮𐑅𐐻𐐲𐑉 𐐲𐑌𐐻𐐭 𐑄 𐐹𐐨𐐹𐑊, 𐐼𐐨𐐿𐑊𐐩𐑉𐐮𐑍 𐑃𐑉𐐭𐐵𐐻 𐐫𐑊 𐑄 𐑉𐐨𐐾𐐲𐑌𐑆 𐑉𐐵𐑌𐐼 𐐲𐐺𐐵𐐻 𐐫𐑊 𐑄 𐑃𐐮𐑍𐑆 𐐸𐐶𐐮𐐽 𐑄𐐩 𐐸𐐰𐐼 𐐸𐐲𐑉𐐼 𐐰𐑌𐐼 𐑅𐐨𐑌, 𐐮𐑌𐑅𐐬𐑋𐐲𐐽 𐑄𐐰𐐻 𐑄 𐑋𐐬𐑉 𐐹𐐪𐑉𐐻 𐐱𐑂 𐑄 𐐢𐐩𐑋𐐲𐑌𐐴𐐻𐑅 𐐶𐐲𐑉 𐐿𐐱𐑌𐑂𐐮𐑌𐑅𐐻 𐐱𐑂 𐑄𐐯𐑋, 𐐺𐐨𐐿𐐫𐑆 𐐱𐑂 𐑄 𐑀𐑉𐐩𐐻𐑌𐐯𐑅 𐐱𐑂 𐑄 𐐯𐑂𐐮𐐼𐐯𐑌𐑅𐐯𐑆 𐐸𐐶𐐮𐐽 𐑄𐐩 𐐸𐐰𐐼 𐑉𐐨𐑅𐐨𐑂𐐼; 𐐰𐑌𐐼 𐐰𐑆 𐑋𐐯𐑌𐐨 𐐰𐑆 𐐶𐐲𐑉 𐐿𐐱𐑌𐑂𐐮𐑌𐑅𐐻 𐐼𐐮𐐼 𐑊𐐩 𐐼𐐵𐑌 𐑄𐐯𐑉 𐐶𐐯𐐹𐐲𐑌𐑆 𐐱𐑂 𐐶𐐫𐑉, 𐐰𐑌𐐼 𐐫𐑊𐑅𐐬 𐑄𐐯𐑉 𐐸𐐩𐐻𐑉𐐯𐐼, 𐐰𐑌𐐼 𐑄 𐐻𐑉𐐲𐐼𐐮𐑇𐐲𐑌 𐐱𐑂 𐑄𐐯𐑉 𐑁𐐪𐑄𐐲𐑉𐑆. 𐐈𐑌𐐼 𐐮𐐻 𐐿𐐩𐑋 𐐻𐐭 𐐹𐐪𐑅 𐑄𐐰𐐻 𐑄𐐩 𐐼𐐮𐐼 𐐷𐐨𐑊𐐼 𐐲𐐹 𐐲𐑌𐐻𐐭 𐑄 𐐤𐐨𐑁𐐴𐐻𐑅 𐑄 𐑊𐐰𐑌𐐼𐑆 𐐱𐑂 𐑄𐐯𐑉 𐐹𐐲𐑆𐐯𐑇𐐲𐑌.

25. 𐐈𐑌𐐼 𐐮𐐻 𐐿𐐩𐑋 𐐻𐐭 𐐹𐐪𐑅 𐑄𐐰𐐻 𐐸𐐶𐐯𐑌 𐑄 𐑅𐐮𐐿𐑅𐐻𐐨 𐐰𐑌𐐼 𐑅𐐯𐐿𐐲𐑌𐐼 𐐷𐐨𐑉 𐐱𐑂 𐑄 𐑉𐐩𐑌 𐐱𐑂 𐑄 𐐾𐐲𐐾𐐯𐑆 𐐸𐐰𐐼 𐐯𐑌𐐼𐐯𐐼, 𐐫𐑊 𐑄𐐨𐑆 𐑃𐐮𐑍𐑆 𐐸𐐰𐐼 𐐸𐐰𐐹𐐲𐑌𐐼, 𐐰𐑌𐐼 𐑄 𐐢𐐩𐑋𐐲𐑌𐐴𐐻𐑅 𐐸𐐰𐐼 𐐺𐐨𐐿𐐲𐑋, 𐑄 𐑋𐐬𐑉 𐐹𐐪𐑉𐐻 𐐱𐑂 𐑄𐐯𐑋, 𐐲 𐑉𐐴𐐽𐐲𐑅 𐐹𐐨𐐹𐑊, 𐐮𐑌𐑅𐐬𐑋𐐲𐐽 𐑄𐐰𐐻 𐑄𐐯𐑉 𐑉𐐴𐐽𐐲𐑅𐑌𐐯𐑅 𐐼𐐮𐐼 𐐯𐐿𐑅𐐨𐐼 𐑄𐐰𐐻 𐐱𐑂 𐑄 𐐤𐐨𐑁𐐴𐐻𐑅, 𐐺𐐨𐐿𐐫𐑆 𐐱𐑂 𐑄𐐯𐑉 𐑁𐐲𐑉𐑋𐑌𐐯𐑅 𐐰𐑌𐐼 𐑄𐐯𐑉 𐑅𐐻𐐯𐐼𐐨𐑌𐐯𐑅 𐐮𐑌 𐑄 𐑁𐐩𐑃. 𐐙𐐫𐑉 𐐺𐐨𐐸𐐬𐑊𐐼, 𐑄𐐯𐑉 𐐶𐐲𐑉 𐑋𐐯𐑌𐐨 𐐱𐑂 𐑄 𐐤𐐨𐑁𐐴𐐻𐑅 𐐸𐐭 𐐸𐐰𐐼 𐐺𐐨𐐿𐐲𐑋 𐐸𐐪𐑉𐐼𐐲𐑌𐐼, 𐐰𐑌𐐼 𐐮𐑋𐐹𐐯𐑌𐐮𐐻𐐯𐑌𐐻, 𐐰𐑌𐐼 𐑀𐑉𐐬𐑅𐑊𐐨 𐐶𐐮𐐿𐐯𐐼, 𐐮𐑌𐑅𐐬𐑋𐐲𐐽 𐑄𐐰𐐻 𐑄𐐩 𐐼𐐮𐐼 𐑉𐐨𐐾𐐯𐐿𐐻 𐑄 𐐶𐐲𐑉𐐼 𐐱𐑂 𐐘𐐱𐐼, 𐐰𐑌𐐼 𐐫𐑊 𐑄 𐐹𐑉𐐨𐐽𐐮𐑍 𐐰𐑌𐐼 𐐹𐑉𐐱𐑁𐐯𐑅𐐴𐐮𐑍 𐐸𐐶𐐮𐐽 𐐼𐐮𐐼 𐐿𐐲𐑋 𐐲𐑋𐐲𐑍 𐑄𐐯𐑋. 𐐤𐐯𐑂𐐲𐑉𐑄𐐯𐑊𐐯𐑅 𐑄 𐐹𐐨𐐹𐑊 𐐱𐑂 𐑄 𐐽𐐲𐑉𐐽 𐐼𐐮𐐼 𐐸𐐰𐑂 𐑀𐑉𐐩𐐻 𐐾𐑎, 𐐺𐐨𐐿𐐫𐑆 𐐱𐑂 𐑄 𐐿𐐱𐑌𐑂𐐲𐑉𐑇𐐲𐑌 𐐱𐑂 𐑄 𐐢𐐩𐑋𐐲𐑌𐐴𐐻𐑅; 𐐷𐐩, 𐐺𐐨𐐿𐐫𐑆 𐐱𐑂 𐑄 𐐽𐐲𐑉𐐽 𐐱𐑂 𐐘𐐱𐐼, 𐐸𐐶𐐮𐐽 𐐸𐐰𐐼 𐐺𐐮𐑌 𐐯𐑅𐐻𐐰𐐺𐑊𐐮𐑇𐐻 𐐲𐑋𐐲𐑍 𐑄𐐯𐑋. 𐐈𐑌𐐼 𐑄𐐩 𐐼𐐮𐐼 𐑁𐐯𐑊𐐬𐑇𐐮𐐹 𐐶𐐲𐑌 𐐶𐐮𐑄 𐐰𐑌𐐲𐑄𐐲𐑉, 𐐰𐑌𐐼 𐐼𐐮𐐼 𐑉𐐨𐐾𐑎𐑅 𐐶𐐲𐑌 𐐶𐐮𐑄 𐐰𐑌𐐲𐑄𐐲𐑉, 𐐰𐑌𐐼 𐐼𐐮𐐼 𐐸𐐰𐑂 𐑀𐑉𐐩𐐻 𐐾𐑎. 𐐈𐑌𐐼 𐐮𐐻 𐐿𐐩𐑋 𐐻𐐭 𐐹𐐪𐑅 𐑄𐐰𐐻 𐑋𐐯𐑌𐐨 𐐱𐑂 𐑄 𐐢𐐩𐑋𐐲𐑌𐐴𐐻𐑅 𐐼𐐮𐐼 𐐿𐐲𐑋 𐐼𐐵𐑌 𐐮𐑌𐐻𐐭 𐑄 𐑊𐐰𐑌𐐼 𐐱𐑂 𐐞𐐩𐑉𐐲𐐸𐐯𐑋𐑊𐐲, 𐐰𐑌𐐼 𐐼𐐮𐐼 𐐼𐐨𐐿𐑊𐐩𐑉 𐐲𐑌𐐻𐐭 𐑄 𐐹𐐨𐐹𐑊 𐐱𐑂 𐑄 𐐤𐐨𐑁𐐴𐐻𐑅 𐑄 𐑋𐐰𐑌𐐲𐑉 𐐱𐑂 𐑄𐐯𐑉 𐐿𐐱𐑌𐑂𐐲𐑉𐑇𐐲𐑌, 𐐰𐑌𐐼 𐐼𐐮𐐼 𐐯𐑀𐑆𐐫𐑉𐐻 𐑄𐐯𐑋 𐐻𐐭 𐑁𐐩𐑃 𐐰𐑌𐐼 𐑉𐐨𐐹𐐯𐑌𐐻𐐲𐑌𐑅; 𐐷𐐩, 𐐰𐑌𐐼 𐑋𐐯𐑌𐐨 𐐼𐐮𐐼 𐐹𐑉𐐨𐐽 𐐶𐐮𐑄 𐐯𐐿𐑅𐐨𐐼𐐮𐑍𐑊𐐨 𐑀𐑉𐐩𐐻 𐐹𐐵𐐲𐑉 𐐰𐑌𐐼 𐐫𐑃𐐱𐑉𐐮𐐻𐐨, 𐐲𐑌𐐻𐐭 𐑄 𐐺𐑉𐐮𐑍𐐮𐑍 𐐼𐐵𐑌 𐑋𐐯𐑌𐐨 𐐱𐑂 𐑄𐐯𐑋 𐐮𐑌𐐻𐐭 𐑄 𐐼𐐯𐐹𐑃𐑅 𐐱𐑂 𐐸𐐷𐐭𐑋𐐮𐑊𐐮𐐻𐐨, 𐐻𐐭 𐐺 𐑄 𐐸𐐲𐑋𐐺𐑊 𐑁𐐱𐑊𐐬𐐲𐑉𐑆 𐐱𐑂 𐐘𐐱𐐼 𐐰𐑌𐐼 𐑄 𐐢𐐰𐑋.

26. 𐐈𐑌𐐼 𐐮𐐻 𐐿𐐩𐑋 𐐻𐐭 𐐹𐐪𐑅 𐑄𐐰𐐻 𐑋𐐯𐑌𐐨 𐐱𐑂 𐑄 𐐢𐐩𐑋𐐲𐑌𐐴𐐻𐑅 𐐼𐐮𐐼 𐑀𐐬 𐐮𐑌𐐻𐐭 𐑄 𐑊𐐰𐑌𐐼 𐑌𐐫𐑉𐑃𐐶𐐲𐑉𐐼; 𐐰𐑌𐐼 𐐫𐑊𐑅𐐬 𐐤𐐨𐑁𐐴 𐐰𐑌𐐼 𐐢𐐨𐐸𐐴 𐐶𐐯𐑌𐐻 𐐮𐑌𐐻𐐭 𐑄 𐑊𐐰𐑌𐐼 𐑌𐐫𐑉𐑃𐐶𐐲𐑉𐐼, 𐐻𐐭 𐐹𐑉𐐨𐐽 𐐲𐑌𐐻𐐭 𐑄 𐐹𐐨𐐹𐑊. 𐐈𐑌𐐼 𐑄𐐲𐑅 𐐯𐑌𐐼𐐯𐐼 𐑄 𐑅𐐮𐐿𐑅𐐻𐐨 𐐰𐑌𐐼 𐑃𐐲𐑉𐐼 𐐷𐐨𐑉. 𐐈𐑌𐐼 𐐺𐐨𐐸𐐬𐑊𐐼, 𐑄𐐯𐑉 𐐶𐐲𐑆 𐐹𐐨𐑅 𐐮𐑌 𐐫𐑊 𐑄 𐑊𐐰𐑌𐐼, 𐐮𐑌𐑅𐐬𐑋𐐲𐐽 𐑄𐐰𐐻 𐑄 𐐤𐐨𐑁𐐴𐐻𐑅 𐐼𐐮𐐼 𐑀𐐬 𐐮𐑌𐐻𐐭 𐐸𐐶𐐱𐐻𐑅𐐬𐐯𐑂𐐲𐑉 𐐹𐐪𐑉𐐻 𐐱𐑂 𐑄 𐑊𐐰𐑌𐐼 𐑄𐐩 𐐶𐐳𐐼, 𐐸𐐶𐐯𐑄𐐲𐑉 𐐲𐑋𐐲𐑍 𐑄 𐐤𐐨𐑁𐐴𐐻𐑅 𐐫𐑉 𐑄 𐐢𐐩𐑋𐐲𐑌𐐴𐐻𐑅. 𐐈𐑌𐐼 𐐮𐐻 𐐿𐐩𐑋 𐐻𐐭 𐐹𐐪𐑅 𐑄𐐰𐐻 𐑄 𐐢𐐩𐑋𐐲𐑌𐐴𐐻𐑅 𐐼𐐮𐐼 𐐫𐑊𐑅𐐬 𐑀𐐬 𐐸𐐶𐐮𐑄𐐲𐑉𐑅𐐬𐐯𐑂𐐲𐑉 𐑄𐐩 𐐶𐐳𐐼, 𐐸𐐶𐐯𐑄𐐲𐑉 𐐮𐐻 𐐶𐐲𐑉 𐐲𐑋𐐲𐑍 𐑄 𐐢𐐩𐑋𐐲𐑌𐐴𐐻𐑅 𐐫𐑉 𐐲𐑋𐐲𐑍 𐑄 𐐤𐐨𐑁𐐴𐐻𐑅; 𐐰𐑌𐐼 𐑄𐐲𐑅 𐑄𐐩 𐐼𐐮𐐼 𐐸𐐰𐑂 𐑁𐑉𐐨 𐐮𐑌𐐻𐐲𐑉𐐿𐐬𐑉𐑅 𐐶𐐲𐑌 𐐶𐐮𐑄 𐐰𐑌𐐲𐑄𐐲𐑉, 𐐻𐐭 𐐺𐐴 𐐰𐑌𐐼 𐐻𐐭 𐑅𐐯𐑊, 𐐰𐑌𐐼 𐐻𐐭 𐑀𐐯𐐻 𐑀𐐩𐑌, 𐐰𐐿𐐫𐑉𐐼𐐮𐑍 𐐻𐐭 𐑄𐐯𐑉 𐐼𐐨𐑆𐐴𐑉.

27. 𐐈𐑌𐐼 𐐮𐐻 𐐿𐐩𐑋 𐐻𐐭 𐐹𐐪𐑅 𐑄𐐰𐐻 𐑄𐐩 𐐺𐐨𐐿𐐩𐑋 𐐯𐐿𐑅𐐨𐐼𐐮𐑍𐑊𐐨 𐑉𐐮𐐽, 𐐺𐐬𐑃 𐑄 𐐢𐐩𐑋𐐲𐑌𐐴𐐻𐑅 𐐰𐑌𐐼 𐑄 𐐤𐐨𐑁𐐴𐐻𐑅; 𐐰𐑌𐐼 𐑄𐐩 𐐼𐐮𐐼 𐐸𐐰𐑂 𐐰𐑌 𐐯𐐿𐑅𐐨𐐼𐐮𐑍 𐐹𐑊𐐯𐑌𐐻𐐨 𐐱𐑂 𐑀𐐬𐑊𐐼, 𐐰𐑌𐐼 𐐱𐑂 𐑅𐐮𐑊𐑂𐐲𐑉, 𐐰𐑌𐐼 𐐱𐑂 𐐫𐑊 𐑋𐐰𐑌𐐲𐑉 𐐱𐑂 𐐹𐑉𐐯𐑇𐐲𐑅 𐑋𐐯𐐻𐐲𐑊𐑆, 𐐺𐐬𐑃 𐐮𐑌 𐑄 𐑊𐐰𐑌𐐼 𐑅𐐵𐑃, 𐐰𐑌𐐼 𐐮𐑌 𐑄 𐑊𐐰𐑌𐐼 𐑌𐐫𐑉𐑃. 𐐤𐐵 𐑄 𐑊𐐰𐑌𐐼

𐑅𐐵𐑃 𐐶𐐪𐑆 𐐿𐐫𐑊𐐼 𐐢𐐨𐐸𐐴, 𐐰𐑌𐐼 𐑄 𐑊𐐰𐑌𐐼 𐑌𐐫𐑉𐑃 𐐶𐐪𐑆 𐐿𐐫𐑊𐐼 𐐣𐐷𐐭𐑊𐐯𐐿, 𐐸𐐶𐐮𐐽 𐐶𐐪𐑆 𐐰𐑁𐐻𐐲𐑉 𐑄 𐑅𐐲𐑌 𐐱𐑂 𐐞𐐯𐐼𐐯𐐿𐐴𐐲; 𐑁𐐫𐑉 𐑄 𐐢𐐫𐑉𐐼 𐐼𐐮𐐼 𐐺𐑉𐐮𐑍 𐐣𐐷𐐭𐑊𐐯𐐿 𐐮𐑌𐐻𐐭 𐑄 𐑊𐐰𐑌𐐼 𐑌𐐫𐑉𐑃, 𐐰𐑌𐐼 𐐢𐐨𐐸𐐴 𐐮𐑌𐐻𐐭 𐑄 𐑊𐐰𐑌𐐼 𐑅𐐵𐑃. 𐐈𐑌𐐼 𐐺𐐨𐐸𐐬𐑊𐐼, 𐑄𐐯𐑉 𐐶𐐪𐑆 𐐫𐑊 𐑋𐐰𐑌𐐲𐑉 𐐱𐑂 𐑀𐐬𐑊𐐼 𐐮𐑌 𐐺𐐬𐑃 𐑄𐐨𐑆 𐑊𐐰𐑌𐐼𐑆, 𐐰𐑌𐐼 𐐱𐑂 𐑅𐐮𐑊𐑂𐐲𐑉, 𐐰𐑌𐐼 𐐱𐑂 𐐹𐑉𐐯𐑇𐐲𐑅 𐐬𐑉 𐐱𐑂 𐐯𐑂𐐲𐑉𐐨 𐐿𐐴𐑌𐐼: 𐐰𐑌𐐼 𐑄𐐯𐑉 𐐶𐐲𐑉 𐐫𐑊𐑅𐐬 𐐿𐐷𐐭𐑉𐐨𐐲𐑅 𐐶𐐲𐑉𐐿𐑋𐐲𐑌, 𐐸𐐭 𐐼𐐮𐐼 𐐶𐐲𐑉𐐿 𐐫𐑊 𐐿𐐴𐑌𐐼𐑆 𐐱𐑂 𐐬𐑉, 𐐰𐑌𐐼 𐐼𐐮𐐼 𐑉𐐨𐑁𐐴𐑌 𐐮𐐻; 𐐰𐑌𐐼 𐑄𐐲𐑅 𐑄𐐩 𐐼𐐮𐐼 𐐺𐐨𐐿𐐲𐑋 𐑉𐐮𐐽. 𐐜𐐩 𐐼𐐮𐐼 𐑉𐐩𐑆 𐑀𐑉𐐩𐑌 𐐮𐑌 𐐰𐐺𐐲𐑌𐐼𐐲𐑌𐑅, 𐐺𐐬𐑃 𐐮𐑌 𐑄 𐑌𐐫𐑉𐑃 𐐰𐑌𐐼 𐐮𐑌 𐑄 𐑅𐐵𐑃; 𐐰𐑌𐐼 𐑄𐐩 𐐼𐐮𐐼 𐑁𐑊𐐲𐑉𐐮𐑇 𐐯𐐿𐑅𐐨𐐼𐐮𐑍𐑊𐐨, 𐐺𐐬𐑃 𐐮𐑌 𐑄 𐑌𐐫𐑉𐑃 𐐰𐑌𐐼 𐐮𐑌 𐑄 𐑅𐐵𐑃. 𐐈𐑌𐐼 𐑄𐐩 𐐼𐐮𐐼 𐑋𐐲𐑊𐐻𐐮𐐹𐑊𐐴 𐐰𐑌𐐼 𐐶𐐰𐐿𐑅 𐐯𐐿𐑅𐐨𐐼𐐮𐑍𐑊𐐨 𐑅𐐻𐑉𐐪𐑍 𐐮𐑌 𐑄 𐑊𐐰𐑌𐐼. 𐐈𐑌𐐼 𐑄𐐩 𐐼𐐮𐐼 𐑉𐐩𐑆 𐑋𐐯𐑌𐐨 𐑁𐑊𐐪𐐿𐑅 𐐰𐑌𐐼 𐐸𐐲𐑉𐐼𐑆, 𐐷𐐩, 𐑋𐐯𐑌𐐨 𐑁𐐰𐐻𐑊𐐮𐑍𐑆. 𐐒𐐨𐐸𐐬𐑊𐐼, 𐑄𐐯𐑉 𐐶𐐮𐑋𐐲𐑌 𐐼𐐮𐐼 𐐻𐐱𐐮𐑊 𐐰𐑌𐐼 𐑅𐐹𐐮𐑌, 𐐰𐑌𐐼 𐐼𐐮𐐼 𐑋𐐩𐐿 𐐫𐑊 𐑋𐐰𐑌𐐲𐑉 𐐱𐑂 𐐿𐑊𐐱𐑃, 𐐱𐑂 𐑁𐐴𐑌 𐐻𐐶𐐴𐑌𐐼 𐑊𐐮𐑌𐐯𐑌, 𐐰𐑌𐐼 𐐿𐑊𐐱𐑃 𐐱𐑂 𐐯𐑂𐐲𐑉𐐨 𐐿𐐴𐑌𐐼, 𐐻𐐭 𐐿𐑊𐐬𐑄 𐑄𐐯𐑉 𐑌𐐩𐐿𐐯𐐼𐑌𐐯𐑅. 𐐈𐑌𐐼 𐑄𐐲𐑅 𐑄 𐑅𐐮𐐿𐑅𐐻𐐨 𐐰𐑌𐐼 𐑁𐐬𐑉𐑃 𐐷𐐨𐑉 𐐼𐐮𐐼 𐐹𐐰𐑅 𐐲𐐶𐐩 𐐮𐑌 𐐹𐐨𐑅. 𐐈𐑌𐐼 𐐮𐑌 𐑄 𐑅𐐮𐐿𐑅𐐻𐐨 𐐰𐑌𐐼 𐑁𐐮𐑁𐑃 𐐷𐐨𐑉 𐑄𐐩 𐐼𐐮𐐼 𐐫𐑊𐑅𐐬 𐐸𐐰𐑂 𐑀𐑉𐐩𐐻 𐐾𐐱𐐮 𐐰𐑌𐐼 𐐹𐐨𐑅; 𐐷𐐩, 𐑋𐐲𐐽 𐐹𐑉𐐨𐐽𐐮𐑍 𐐰𐑌𐐼 𐑋𐐯𐑌𐐨 𐐹𐑉𐐪𐑁𐐯𐑅𐐨𐑆 𐐿𐐱𐑌𐑅𐐲𐑉𐑌𐐮𐑍 𐑄𐐰𐐻 𐐸𐐶𐐮𐐽 𐐶𐐪𐑆 𐐻𐐭 𐐿𐐲𐑋. 𐐈𐑌𐐼 𐑄𐐲𐑅 𐐹𐐰𐑅𐐻 𐐲𐐶𐐩 𐑄 𐑅𐐮𐐿𐑅𐐻𐐨 𐐰𐑌𐐼 𐑁𐐮𐑁𐑃 𐐷𐐨𐑉.

28. 𐐈𐑌𐐼 𐐮𐐻 𐐿𐐩𐑋 𐐻𐐭 𐐹𐐰𐑅 𐑄𐐰𐐻 𐐮𐑌 𐑄 𐑅𐐮𐐿𐑅𐐻𐐨 𐐰𐑌𐐼 𐑅𐐮𐐿𐑅𐑃 𐐷𐐨𐑉 𐐱𐑂 𐑄 𐑉𐐩𐑌 𐐱𐑂 𐑄 𐐾𐐲𐐾𐐯𐑆, 𐐺𐐨𐐸𐐬𐑊𐐼, 𐐝𐐯𐑆𐐬𐑉𐐲𐑋 𐐶𐐪𐑆 𐑋𐐲𐑉𐐼𐐲𐑉𐐼 𐐺𐐴 𐐰𐑌 𐐲𐑌𐑌𐐬𐑌 𐐸𐐰𐑌𐐼 𐐰𐑆 𐐸𐐨 𐑅𐐰𐐻 𐐲𐐹𐐱𐑌 𐑄 𐐾𐐲𐐾𐑋𐐯𐑌𐐻 𐑅𐐨𐐻. 𐐈𐑌𐐼 𐐮𐐻 𐐿𐐩𐑋 𐐻𐐭 𐐹𐐰𐑅 𐑄𐐰𐐻 𐐮𐑌 𐑄 𐑅𐐩𐑋 𐐷𐐨𐑉, 𐑄𐐰𐐻 𐐸𐐮𐑆 𐑅𐐲𐑌, 𐐸𐐭 𐐸𐐰𐐼 𐐺𐐨𐑌 𐐲𐐹𐐱𐐮𐑌𐐻𐐯𐐼 𐐺𐐴 𐑄 𐐹𐐨𐐹𐑊 𐐮𐑌 𐐸𐐮𐑆 𐑅𐐻𐐯𐐼, 𐐶𐐪𐑆 𐐫𐑊𐑅𐐬 𐑋𐐲𐑉𐐼𐐲𐑉𐐼. 𐐈𐑌𐐼 𐑄𐐲𐑅 𐐯𐑌𐐼𐐯𐐼 𐑄 𐑅𐐮𐐿𐑅𐐻𐐨 𐐰𐑌𐐼 𐑅𐐮𐐿𐑅𐑃 𐐷𐐨𐑉. 𐐈𐑌𐐼 𐐮𐑌 𐑄 𐐿𐐱𐑋𐐯𐑌𐑅𐑋𐐯𐑌𐐻 𐐱𐑂 𐑄 𐑅𐐮𐐿𐑅𐐻𐐨 𐐰𐑌𐐼 𐑅𐐯𐑂𐐲𐑌𐑃 𐐷𐐨𐑉, 𐑄 𐐹𐐨𐐹𐑊 𐐺𐐨𐑀𐐰𐑌 𐐻𐐭 𐑀𐑉𐐬 𐐯𐐿𐑅𐐨𐐼𐐮𐑍𐑊𐐨 𐐶𐐮𐐿𐐯𐐼 𐐲𐑀𐐯𐑌. 𐐙𐐫𐑉 𐐺𐐨𐐸𐐬𐑊𐐼, 𐑄 𐐢𐐫𐑉𐐼 𐐸𐐰𐐼 𐐺𐑊𐐯𐑅𐐻 𐑄𐐯𐑋 𐑅𐐬 𐑊𐐱𐑍 𐐶𐐮𐑄 𐑄 𐑉𐐮𐐽𐐯𐑆 𐐱𐑂 𐑄 𐐶𐐲𐑉𐑊𐐼, 𐑄𐐰𐐻 𐑄𐐩 𐐸𐐰𐐼 𐑌𐐱𐐻 𐐺𐐨𐑌 𐑅𐐻𐐲𐑉𐐼 𐐲𐐹 𐐻𐐭 𐐰𐑍𐑀𐐲𐑉, 𐐻𐐭 𐐶𐐫𐑉𐑆, 𐑌𐐫𐑉 𐐻𐐭 𐐺𐑊𐐲𐐼𐑇𐐯𐐼; 𐑄𐐯𐑉𐑁𐐬𐑉 𐑄𐐩 𐐺𐐨𐑀𐐰𐑌 𐐻𐐭 𐑅𐐯𐐻 𐑄𐐯𐑉 𐐸𐐪𐑉𐐻𐑅 𐐲𐐹𐐱𐑌 𐑄𐐯𐑉 𐑉𐐮𐐽𐐯𐑆; 𐐷𐐩, 𐑄𐐩 𐐺𐐨𐑀𐐰𐑌 𐐻𐐭 𐑅𐐨𐐿 𐐻𐐭 𐑀𐐯𐐻 𐑀𐐩𐑌, 𐑄𐐰𐐻 𐑄𐐩 𐑋𐐴𐐻 𐐺𐐨 𐑊𐐮𐑁𐐻𐐯𐐼 𐐲𐐹 𐐶𐐲𐑌 𐐲𐐺𐐲𐑂 𐐲𐑌𐐲𐑄𐐲𐑉; 𐑄𐐯𐑉𐑁𐐬𐑉 𐑄𐐩 𐐺𐐨𐑀𐐰𐑌 𐐻𐐭 𐐿𐐱𐑋𐐮𐐻 𐑅𐐨𐐿𐑉𐐯𐐻 𐑋𐐲𐑉𐐼𐐲𐑉𐑆, 𐐰𐑌𐐼 𐐻𐐭 𐑉𐐱𐐺, 𐐰𐑌𐐼 𐐻𐐭 𐐹𐑊𐐲𐑌𐐼𐐲𐑉, 𐑄𐐰𐐻 𐑄𐐩 𐑋𐐴𐐻 𐑀𐐯𐐻 𐑀𐐩𐑌. 𐐈𐑌𐐼 𐑌𐐵 𐐺𐐨𐐸𐐬𐑊𐐼, 𐑄𐐬𐑆 𐑋𐐲𐑉𐐼𐐲𐑉𐐲𐑉𐑆 𐐰𐑌𐐼 𐐹𐑊𐐲𐑌𐐼𐐲𐑉𐐲𐑉𐑆 𐐶𐐲𐑉 𐐰 𐐺𐐰𐑌𐐼 𐐸𐐭 𐐸𐐰𐐼 𐐺𐐨𐑌 𐑁𐐫𐑉𐑋𐐼 𐐺𐐴 𐐗𐐮𐑇𐐿𐐲𐑋𐐯𐑌 𐐰𐑌𐐼 𐐘𐐰𐐼𐐨𐐰𐑌𐐻𐐲𐑌. 𐐈𐑌𐐼 𐑌𐐵 𐐮𐐻 𐐸𐐰𐐼 𐐿𐐲𐑋 𐐻𐐭 𐐹𐐰𐑅 𐑄𐐰𐐻 𐑄𐐯𐑉 𐐶𐐲𐑉 𐑋𐐯𐑌𐐨, 𐐨𐑂𐐲𐑌 𐐲𐑋𐐲𐑍 𐑄 𐐤𐐨𐑁𐐴𐐻𐑅, 𐐱𐑂 𐐘𐐰𐐼𐐨𐐰𐑌𐐻𐐲𐑌'𐑆 𐐺𐐰𐑌𐐼. 𐐒𐐲𐐻 𐐺𐐨𐐸𐐬𐑊𐐼, 𐑄𐐩 𐐶𐐲𐑉 𐑋𐐬𐑉 𐑌𐐭𐑋𐐲𐑉𐐲𐑅 𐐲𐑋𐐲𐑍 𐑄 𐑋𐐬𐑉 𐐶𐐮𐐿𐐯𐐼 𐐹𐐪𐑉𐐻 𐐱𐑂 𐑄 𐐢𐐩𐑋𐐲𐑌𐐴𐐻𐑅. 𐐈𐑌𐐼 𐑄𐐩 𐐶𐐲𐑉 𐐿𐐫𐑊𐐼 𐐘𐐰𐐼𐐨𐐰𐑌𐐻𐐲𐑌'𐑆 𐑉𐐱𐐺𐐲𐑉𐑆 𐐰𐑌𐐼 𐑋𐐲𐑉𐐼𐐲𐑉𐐲𐑉𐑆; 𐐰𐑌𐐼 𐐮𐐻 𐐶𐐪𐑆 𐑄𐐩 𐐸𐐭 𐐼𐐮𐐼 𐑋𐐲𐑉𐐼𐐲𐑉 𐑄 𐐽𐐨𐑁 𐐾𐐲𐐾 𐐝𐐯𐑆𐐬𐑉𐐲𐑋, 𐐰𐑌𐐼 𐐸𐐮𐑆 𐑅𐐲𐑌, 𐐸𐐶𐐴𐑊 𐐮𐑌 𐑄 𐐾𐐲𐐾𐑋𐐯𐑌𐐻-𐑅𐐨𐐻; 𐐰𐑌𐐼 𐐺𐐨𐐸𐐬𐑊𐐼, 𐑄𐐩 𐐶𐐲𐑉 𐑌𐐱𐐻 𐑁𐐵𐑌𐐼.

29. 𐐈𐑌𐐼 𐑌𐐵 𐐮𐐻 𐐿𐐩𐑋 𐐻𐐭 𐐹𐐰𐑅 𐑄𐐰𐐻 𐐸𐐶𐐯𐑌 𐑄 𐐢𐐩𐑋𐐲𐑌𐐴𐐻𐑅 𐑁𐐵𐑌𐐼 𐑄𐐰𐐻 𐑄𐐯𐑉 𐐶𐐲𐑉 𐑉𐐱𐐺𐐲𐑉𐑆 𐐲𐑋𐐲𐑍 𐑄𐐯𐑋, 𐑄𐐩 𐐶𐐲𐑉 𐐯𐐿𐑅𐐨𐐼𐐮𐑍𐑊𐐨 𐑅𐐱𐑉𐐬𐑁𐐳𐑊; 𐐰𐑌𐐼 𐑄𐐩 𐐼𐐮𐐼 𐐷𐐭𐑆 𐐯𐑂𐐲𐑉𐐨 𐑋𐐨𐑌𐑆 𐐮𐑌 𐑄𐐯𐑉 𐐹𐐵𐐲𐑉 𐐻𐐭 𐐼𐐯𐑅𐐻𐑉𐐱𐐮 𐑄𐐯𐑋 𐐫𐑁 𐑄 𐑁𐐩𐑅 𐐱𐑂 𐑄 𐐲𐑉𐑃. 𐐒𐐲𐐻 𐐺𐐨𐐸𐐬𐑊𐐼, 𐐝𐐩𐐻𐐲𐑌 𐐼𐐮𐐼 𐑅𐐻𐐲𐑉 𐐲𐐹 𐑄 𐐸𐐪𐑉𐐻𐑅 𐐱𐑂 𐑄 𐑋𐐬𐑉 𐐹𐐪𐑉𐐻 𐐱𐑂 𐑄 𐐤𐐨𐑁𐐴𐐻𐑅, 𐐮𐑌𐑅𐐲𐑋𐐲𐐽 𐑄𐐰𐐻 𐑄𐐩 𐐼𐐮𐐼 𐐷𐐭𐑌𐐴𐐻 𐐶𐐮𐑄 𐑄𐐬𐑆 𐐺𐐰𐑌𐐼𐑆 𐐱𐑂 𐑉𐐱𐐺𐐲𐑉𐑆, 𐐰𐑌𐐼 𐐼𐐮𐐼 𐐯𐑌𐐻𐐲𐑉 𐐮𐑌𐐻𐐭 𐑄𐐯𐑉 𐐿𐐲𐑂𐐯𐑌𐐲𐑌𐐻𐑅, 𐐰𐑌𐐼 𐑄𐐯𐑉 𐐬𐑃𐑅, 𐑄𐐰𐐻 𐑄𐐩 𐐶𐐲𐐼 𐐹𐑉𐐬𐐻𐐯𐐿𐐻 𐐰𐑌𐐼 𐐹𐑉𐐨𐑆𐐲𐑉𐑂 𐐶𐐲𐑌 𐐲𐑌𐐲𐑄𐐲𐑉 𐐮𐑌 𐐸𐐶𐐱𐐻𐑅𐐬𐐯𐑂𐐲𐑉 𐐼𐐮𐑁𐐮𐐿𐐲𐑊𐐻 𐑅𐐲𐑉𐐿𐐲𐑋𐑅𐐻𐐰𐑌𐑅𐐯𐑆 𐑄𐐩 𐑇𐐳𐐼 𐐺𐐨 𐐹𐑊𐐩𐑅𐐻, 𐑄𐐰𐐻 𐑄𐐩 𐑇𐐳𐐼 𐑌𐐱𐐻 𐑅𐐲𐑁𐐲𐑉 𐑁𐐫𐑉 𐑄𐐯𐑉 𐑋𐐲𐑉𐐼𐐲𐑉𐑆, 𐐰𐑌𐐼 𐑄𐐯𐑉 𐐹𐑊𐐲𐑌𐐼𐐲𐑉𐐮𐑍𐑆, 𐐰𐑌𐐼 𐑄𐐯𐑉 𐑅𐐻𐐨𐑊𐐮𐑍𐑆.

30. 𐐈𐑌𐐼 𐐮𐐻 𐐿𐐩𐑋 𐐻𐐭 𐐹𐐰𐑅 𐑄𐐰𐐻 𐑄𐐩 𐐼𐐮𐐼 𐐸𐐰𐑂 𐑄𐐯𐑉 𐑅𐐴𐑌𐑆, 𐐷𐐩, 𐑄𐐯𐑉 𐑅𐐨𐐿𐑉𐐯𐐻 𐑅𐐴𐑌𐑆, 𐐰𐑌𐐼 𐑄𐐯𐑉 𐑅𐐨𐐿𐑉𐐯𐐻 𐐶𐐲𐑉𐐼𐑆; 𐐰𐑌𐐼 𐑄𐐮𐑅 𐑄𐐰𐐻 𐑄𐐩 𐑋𐐴𐐻 𐐼𐐮𐑅𐐻𐐮𐑍𐑀𐐶𐐮𐑇 𐐰 𐐺𐑉𐐲𐑄𐐲𐑉 𐐸𐐭 𐐸𐐰𐐼 𐐯𐑌𐐻𐐲𐑉𐐼 𐐮𐑌𐐻𐐭 𐑄 𐐿𐐲𐑂𐐯𐑌𐐲𐑌𐐻, 𐑄𐐰𐐻 𐐸𐐶𐐱𐐻𐑅𐐬𐐯𐑂𐐲𐑉 𐐶𐐮𐐿𐐯𐐼𐑌𐐯𐑅 𐐸𐐮𐑆 𐐺𐑉𐐲𐑄𐐲𐑉 𐑇𐐳𐐼 𐐼𐐭, 𐐸𐐨 𐑇𐐳𐐼 𐑌𐐱𐐻 𐐺𐐨 𐐮𐑌𐐾𐐲𐑉𐐼 𐐺𐐴 𐐸𐐮𐑆 𐐺𐑉𐐲𐑄𐐲𐑉, 𐑌𐐫𐑉 𐐺𐐴 𐑄𐐬𐑆 𐐸𐐭 𐐼𐐮𐐼 𐐺𐐨𐑊𐐱𐑍 𐐻𐐭 𐐸𐐮𐑆 𐐺𐐰𐑌𐐼, 𐐸𐐭 𐐸𐐰𐐼 𐐻𐐩𐐿𐐲𐑌 𐑄𐐮𐑅 𐐿𐐲𐑂𐐯𐑌𐐲𐑌𐐻; 𐐰𐑌𐐼 𐑄𐐲𐑅 𐑄𐐩 𐑋𐐴𐐻 𐑋𐐲𐑉𐐼𐐲𐑉, 𐐰𐑌𐐼 𐐹𐑊𐐲𐑌𐐼𐐲𐑉, 𐐰𐑌𐐼 𐑅𐐻𐐨𐑊, 𐐰𐑌𐐼 𐐿𐐱𐑋𐐮𐐻 𐐸𐐬𐑉𐐼𐐲𐑋𐑆,

𐐰𐑌𐐼 𐐫𐑊 𐑋𐐰𐑌𐐲𐑉 𐐲𐑂 𐐶𐐮𐐿𐐯𐐼𐑌𐐯𐑅, 𐐿𐐱𐑌𐐻𐑉𐐯𐑉𐐨 𐐻𐐭 𐑄 𐑊𐐫𐑆 𐐲𐑂 𐑄𐐩𐑉 𐐿𐐲𐑌𐐻𐑉𐐨 𐐰𐑌𐐼 𐐫𐑊𐑅𐐬 𐑄 𐑊𐐫𐑆 𐐲𐑂 𐑄𐐩𐑉 𐐘𐐱𐐼; 𐐰𐑌𐐼 𐐸𐐭𐑅𐐬𐐯𐑂𐐲𐑉 𐐲𐑂 𐑄𐐬𐑆 𐐸𐐭 𐐺𐐨𐑊𐐱𐑍𐐼 𐐻𐐭 𐑄𐐩𐑉 𐐺𐐰𐑌𐐼, 𐑇𐐳𐐼 𐑉𐐨𐑂𐐨𐑊 𐐲𐑌𐐻𐐭 𐑄 𐐶𐐲𐑉𐑊𐐼 𐐲𐑂 𐑄𐐩𐑉 𐐶𐐮𐐿𐐯𐐼𐑌𐐯𐑅 𐐰𐑌𐐼 𐑄𐐩𐑉 𐐰𐐺𐐱𐑋𐐮𐑌𐐩𐑇𐐲𐑌𐑆, 𐑇𐐳𐐼 𐐺𐐨 𐐻𐑉𐐴𐐼, 𐑌𐐱𐐻 𐐰𐐿𐐫𐑉𐐼𐐮𐑍 𐐻𐐭 𐑄 𐑊𐐫𐑆 𐐲𐑂 𐑄𐐩𐑉 𐐿𐐲𐑌𐐻𐑉𐐨, 𐐺𐐲𐐻 𐐰𐐿𐐫𐑉𐐼𐐮𐑍 𐐻𐐭 𐑄 𐑊𐐫𐑆 𐐲𐑂 𐑄𐐩𐑉 𐐶𐐮𐐿𐐯𐐼𐑌𐐯𐑅, 𐐸𐐶𐐮𐐽 𐐸𐐰𐐼 𐐺𐐨𐑌 𐑀𐐮𐑂𐐲𐑌 𐐺𐐴 𐐘𐐰𐐼𐐨𐐰𐑌𐐻𐐲𐑌 𐐰𐑌𐐼 𐐗𐐮𐑇𐐿𐐭𐑋𐐯𐑌. 𐐤𐐵 𐐺𐐨𐐸𐐬𐑊𐐼, 𐐮𐐻 𐐮𐑆 𐑄𐐨𐑆 𐑅𐐨𐐿𐑉𐐯𐐻 𐐬𐑃𐑅 𐐰𐑌𐐼 𐐿𐐲𐑂𐐯𐑌𐐰𐑌𐐻𐑅, 𐐸𐐶𐐮𐐽 𐐈𐑊𐑋𐐲 𐐿𐐱𐑋𐐰𐑌𐐼𐐯𐐼 𐐸𐐮𐑆 𐑅𐐲𐑌 𐑇𐐳𐐼 𐑌𐐱𐐻 𐑀𐐬 𐑁𐐬𐑉𐑃 𐐲𐑌𐐻𐐭 𐑄 𐐶𐐲𐑉𐑊𐐼, 𐑊𐐯𐑅𐐻 𐑄𐐩 𐑇𐐳𐐼 𐐺𐐨 𐐩 𐑋𐐨𐑌𐑆 𐐲𐑂 𐐺𐑉𐐮𐑍𐐮𐑍 𐐼𐐵𐑌 𐑄 𐐹𐐨𐐹𐐲𐑊 𐐲𐑌𐐻𐐭 𐐼𐐯𐑅𐐻𐑉𐐲𐐿𐑇𐐲𐑌. 𐐤𐐵 𐐺𐐨𐐸𐐬𐑊𐐼, 𐑄𐐬𐑆 𐑅𐐨𐐿𐑉𐐯𐐻 𐐬𐑃𐑅 𐐰𐑌𐐼 𐐿𐐲𐑂𐐯𐑌𐐰𐑌𐐻𐑅 𐐼𐐮𐐼 𐑌𐐱𐐻 𐐿𐐲𐑋 𐑁𐐬𐑉𐑃 𐐲𐑌𐐻𐐭 𐐘𐐰𐐼𐐨𐐰𐑌𐐻𐐲𐑌 𐑁𐑉𐐱𐑋 𐑄 𐑉𐐯𐐿𐐲𐑉𐐼𐑆 𐐸𐐶𐐮𐐽 𐐶𐐲𐑉 𐐼𐐯𐑊𐐮𐑂𐐲𐑉𐐼 𐐲𐑌𐐻𐐭 𐐐𐐨𐑊𐐲𐑋𐐲𐑌; 𐐺𐐲𐐻 𐐺𐐨𐐸𐐬𐑊𐐼, 𐑄𐐩 𐐶𐐲𐑉 𐐹𐐳𐐻 𐐮𐑌𐐻𐐭 𐑄 𐐸𐐪𐑉𐐻 𐐲𐑂 𐐘𐐰𐐼𐐨𐐰𐑌𐐻𐐲𐑌 𐐺𐐴 𐑄𐐰𐐻 𐑅𐐩𐑋 𐐺𐐨𐐮𐑍 𐐸𐐭 𐐼𐐮𐐼 𐐯𐑌𐐻𐐴𐑅 𐐵𐑉 𐑁𐐲𐑉𐑅𐐻 𐐹𐐯𐑉𐐯𐑌𐐻𐑅 𐐻𐐭 𐐹𐐪𐑉𐐻𐐩𐐿 𐐲𐑂 𐑄 𐑁𐐫𐑉𐐺𐐮𐐼𐑌 𐑁𐑉𐐭𐐻; 𐐷𐐩, 𐑄𐐰𐐻 𐑅𐐩𐑋 𐐺𐐨𐐮𐑍 𐐸𐐭 𐐼𐐮𐐼 𐐹𐑊𐐱𐐻 𐐶𐐮𐑄 𐐗𐐩𐑌, 𐑄𐐰𐐻 𐐮𐑁 𐐸𐐨 𐐶𐐳𐐼 𐑋𐐲𐑉𐐼𐐲𐑉 𐐸𐐮𐑆 𐐺𐑉𐐲𐑄𐐲𐑉 𐐁𐐺𐐯𐑊 𐐮𐐻 𐑇𐐳𐐼 𐑌𐐱𐐻 𐐺𐐨 𐑌𐐬𐑌 𐐲𐑌𐐻𐐭 𐑄 𐐶𐐲𐑉𐑊𐐼. 𐐐𐑌𐐼 𐐸𐐨 𐐼𐐮𐐼 𐐹𐑊𐐱𐐻 𐐶𐐮𐑄 𐐗𐐩𐑌 𐐰𐑌𐐼 𐐸𐐮𐑆 𐑁𐐱𐑊𐐬𐐲𐑉𐑆 𐑁𐑉𐐱𐑋 𐑄𐐰𐐻 𐐻𐐴𐑋 𐑁𐐬𐑉𐑃. 𐐈𐑌𐐼 𐐫𐑊𐑅𐐬 𐐮𐐻 𐐮𐑆 𐑄𐐰𐐻 𐑅𐐩𐑋 𐐺𐐨𐐮𐑍 𐐸𐐭 𐐹𐐳𐐻 𐐮𐐻 𐐮𐑌𐐻𐐭 𐑄 𐐸𐐪𐑉𐐻𐑅 𐐲𐑂 𐑄 𐐹𐐨𐐹𐐲𐑊 𐐻𐐭 𐐺𐐮𐑊𐐼 𐐩 𐐻𐐵𐐲𐑉 𐑅𐐲𐑁𐐮𐑇𐐲𐑌𐐻𐑊𐐨 𐐸𐐴 𐑄𐐰𐐻 𐑄𐐩 𐑋𐐴𐐻 𐑀𐐯𐐻 𐐻𐐭 𐐸𐐯𐑂𐐲𐑌. 𐐈𐑌𐐼 𐐮𐐻 𐐶𐐱𐑆 𐑄𐐰𐐻 𐑅𐐩𐑋 𐐺𐐨𐐮𐑍 𐐸𐐭 𐑊𐐯𐐼 𐐱𐑌 𐑄 𐐹𐐨𐐹𐐲𐑊 𐐸𐐭 𐐿𐐩𐑋 𐑁𐑉𐐱𐑋 𐑄𐐰𐐻 𐐻𐐵𐐲𐑉 𐐮𐑌𐐻𐐭 𐑄𐐮𐑅 𐑊𐐰𐑌𐐼, 𐐸𐐭 𐑅𐐹𐑉𐐯𐐼 𐑄 𐐶𐐲𐑉𐐿𐑅 𐐲𐑂 𐐼𐐪𐑉𐐿𐑌𐐯𐑅 𐐰𐑌𐐼 𐐰𐐺𐐱𐑋𐐮𐑌𐐩𐑇𐐲𐑌𐑆 𐐬𐑂𐐲𐑉 𐐫𐑊 𐑄 𐑁𐐩𐑅 𐐲𐑂 𐑄 𐑊𐐰𐑌𐐼, 𐐲𐑌𐐻𐐮𐑊 𐐸𐐨 𐐼𐑉𐐰𐑀𐐼 𐑄 𐐹𐐨𐐹𐐲𐑊 𐐼𐐵𐑌 𐐻𐐭 𐐰𐑌 𐐯𐑌𐐻𐐴𐑉 𐐼𐐯𐑅𐐻𐑉𐐲𐐿𐑇𐐲𐑌 𐐰𐑌𐐼 𐐻𐐭 𐐰𐑌 𐐯𐑂𐐲𐑉𐑊𐐰𐑅𐐻𐐮𐑍 𐐸𐐯𐑊; 𐐷𐐩, 𐐮𐐻 𐐮𐑆 𐑄𐐰𐐻 𐑅𐐩𐑋 𐐺𐐨𐐮𐑍 𐐸𐐭 𐐹𐐳𐐻 𐐮𐐻 𐐮𐑌𐐻𐐭 𐑄 𐐸𐐪𐑉𐐻 𐐲𐑂 𐐘𐐰𐐼𐐨𐐰𐑌𐐻𐐲𐑌 𐐻𐐭 𐑅𐐻𐐮𐑊 𐐿𐐰𐑉𐐨 𐐱𐑌 𐑄 𐐶𐐲𐑉𐐿 𐐲𐑂 𐐼𐐪𐑉𐐿𐑌𐐯𐑅, 𐐰𐑌𐐼 𐐲𐑂 𐑅𐐨𐐿𐑉𐐯𐐻 𐑋𐐲𐑉𐐼𐐲𐑉; 𐐰𐑌𐐼 𐐸𐐨 𐐸𐐰𐑆 𐐺𐑉𐐫𐐻 𐐮𐐻 𐑁𐐬𐑉𐑃 𐑁𐑉𐐱𐑋 𐑄 𐐺𐐨𐑀𐐮𐑌𐐮𐑍 𐐲𐑂 𐑋𐐰𐑌, 𐐨𐑂𐐲𐑌 𐐼𐐵𐑌 𐐻𐐭 𐑄𐐮𐑅 𐐻𐐴𐑋. 𐐈𐑌𐐼 𐐺𐐨𐐸𐐬𐑊𐐼, 𐐮𐐻 𐐮𐑆 𐐸𐐨 𐐸𐐭 𐐮𐑆 𐑄 𐐫𐑃𐐲𐑉 𐐲𐑂 𐐫𐑊 𐑅𐐮𐑌. 𐐈𐑌𐐼 𐐺𐐨𐐸𐐬𐑊𐐼, 𐐸𐐨 𐐼𐐲𐑃 𐐿𐐰𐑉𐐨 𐐱𐑌 𐐸𐐮𐑆 𐐶𐐲𐑉𐐿𐑅 𐐲𐑂 𐐼𐐪𐑉𐐿𐑌𐐯𐑅 𐐰𐑌𐐼 𐑅𐐨𐐿𐑉𐐯𐐻 𐑋𐐲𐑉𐐼𐐲𐑉, 𐐰𐑌𐐼 𐐼𐐲𐑃 𐐸𐐰𐑌𐐼 𐐼𐐵𐑌 𐑄𐐩𐑉 𐐹𐑊𐐱𐐻𐑅, 𐐰𐑌𐐼 𐑄𐐩𐑉 𐐬𐑃𐑅, 𐐰𐑌𐐼 𐑄𐐩𐑉 𐐿𐐲𐑂𐐯𐑌𐐰𐑌𐐻𐑅, 𐐰𐑌𐐼 𐑄𐐩𐑉 𐐹𐑊𐐰𐑌𐑆 𐐲𐑂 𐐫𐑁𐐳𐑊 𐐶𐐮𐐿𐐯𐐼𐑌𐐯𐑅, 𐑁𐑉𐐱𐑋 𐐾𐐯𐑌𐐲𐑉𐐩𐑇𐐲𐑌 𐐻𐐭 𐐾𐐯𐑌𐐲𐑉𐐩𐑇𐐲𐑌, 𐐰𐐿𐐫𐑉𐐼𐐮𐑍 𐐰𐑆 𐐸𐐨 𐐿𐐰𐑌 𐑀𐐯𐐻 𐐸𐐬𐑊𐐼 𐐲𐐹𐐱𐑌 𐑄 𐐸𐐪𐑉𐐻𐑅 𐐲𐑂 𐑄 𐐽𐐮𐑊𐐼𐑉𐐯𐑌 𐐲𐑂 𐑋𐐯𐑌. 𐐈𐑌𐐼 𐑌𐐵 𐐺𐐨𐐸𐐬𐑊𐐼, 𐐸𐐨 𐐸𐐰𐐼 𐑀𐐱𐐻 𐑀𐑉𐐩𐐻 𐐸𐐬𐑊𐐼 𐐲𐐹𐐱𐑌 𐑄 𐐸𐐪𐑉𐐻𐑅 𐐲𐑂 𐑄 𐐤𐐨𐑁𐐴𐐻𐑅; 𐐷𐐩, 𐐮𐑌𐑅𐐬𐑋𐐲𐐽 𐑄𐐰𐐻 𐑄𐐩 𐐸𐐰𐐼 𐐺𐐨𐐿𐐲𐑋 𐐯𐐿𐑅𐐨𐐼𐐮𐑍𐑊𐐨 𐐶𐐮𐐿𐐯𐐼; 𐐷𐐩, 𐑄 𐑋𐐬𐑉 𐐹𐐪𐑉𐐻 𐐲𐑂 𐑄𐐯𐑋 𐐸𐐰𐐼 𐐻𐐲𐑉𐑌𐐼 𐐵𐐻 𐐲𐑂 𐑄 𐐶𐐩 𐐲𐑂 𐑉𐐴𐐽𐐲𐑅𐑌𐐯𐑅, 𐐰𐑌𐐼 𐐼𐐮𐐼 𐐻𐑉𐐰𐑋𐐹𐐲𐑊 𐐲𐑌𐐼𐐲𐑉 𐑄𐐩𐑉 𐑁𐐨𐐻 𐑄 𐐿𐐱𐑋𐐰𐑌𐐼𐑋𐐯𐑌𐐻𐑅 𐐲𐑂 𐐘𐐱𐐼, 𐐰𐑌𐐼 𐐼𐐮𐐼 𐐻𐐲𐑉𐑌 𐐲𐑌𐐻𐐭 𐑄𐐩𐑉 𐐬𐑌 𐐶𐐩𐑆, 𐐰𐑌𐐼 𐐼𐐮𐐼 𐐺𐐮𐑊𐐼 𐐲𐐹 𐐲𐑌𐐻𐐭 𐑄𐐯𐑋𐑅𐐯𐑊𐑂𐑆 𐐴𐐼𐐲𐑊𐑆 𐐲𐑂 𐑄𐐩𐑉 𐑀𐐬𐑊𐐼 𐐰𐑌𐐼 𐑄𐐩𐑉 𐑅𐐮𐑊𐑂𐐲𐑉.

31. 𐐈𐑌𐐼 𐐮𐐻 𐐿𐐩𐑋 𐐻𐐭 𐐹𐐰𐑅 𐑄𐐰𐐻 𐐫𐑊 𐑄𐐨𐑆 𐐮𐑌𐐮𐐿𐐶𐐮𐐻𐐨𐑆 𐐼𐐮𐐼 𐐿𐐲𐑋 𐐲𐑌𐐻𐐭 𐑄𐐯𐑋, 𐐮𐑌 𐑄 𐑅𐐹𐐩𐑅 𐐲𐑂 𐑌𐐱𐐻 𐑋𐐯𐑌𐐨 𐐷𐐨𐑉𐑆, 𐐮𐑌𐑅𐐬𐑋𐐲𐐽 𐑄𐐰𐐻 𐐩 𐑋𐐬𐑉 𐐹𐐪𐑉𐐻 𐐲𐑂 𐐮𐐻 𐐸𐐰𐐼 𐐿𐐲𐑋 𐐲𐑌𐐻𐐭 𐑄𐐯𐑋 𐐮𐑌 𐑄 𐑅𐐮𐐿𐑅𐐻𐐨 𐐰𐑌𐐼 𐑅𐐯𐑂𐐲𐑌𐑃 𐐷𐐨𐑉 𐐲𐑂 𐑄 𐑉𐐩𐑌 𐐲𐑂 𐑄 𐐾𐐲𐐾𐐯𐑆 𐐬𐑂𐐲𐑉 𐑄 𐐹𐐨𐐹𐐲𐑊 𐐲𐑂 𐐤𐐨𐑁𐐴. 𐐈𐑌𐐼 𐑄𐐩 𐐼𐐮𐐼 𐑀𐑉𐐬 𐐮𐑌 𐑄𐐩𐑉 𐐮𐑌𐐮𐐿𐐶𐐮𐐻𐐨𐑆 𐐮𐑌 𐑄 𐑅𐐮𐐿𐑅𐐻𐐨 𐐰𐑌𐐼 𐐩𐐻𐑃 𐐷𐐨𐑉 𐐫𐑊𐑅𐐬, 𐐻𐐭 𐑄 𐑀𐑉𐐩𐐻 𐑅𐐱𐑉𐐬 𐐰𐑌𐐼 𐑊𐐰𐑋𐐯𐑌𐐻𐐩𐑇𐐲𐑌 𐐲𐑂 𐑄 𐑉𐐴𐐽𐐲𐑅. 𐐈𐑌𐐼 𐑄𐐲𐑅 𐐶𐐨 𐑅𐐨 𐑄𐐰𐐻 𐑄 𐐤𐐨𐑁𐐴𐐻𐑅 𐐼𐐮𐐼 𐐺𐐨𐑀𐐮𐑌 𐐻𐐭 𐐼𐐶𐐮𐑌𐐼𐐲𐑊 𐐮𐑌 𐐲𐑌𐐺𐐨𐑊𐐨𐑁, 𐐰𐑌𐐼 𐑀𐑉𐐬 𐐮𐑌 𐐶𐐮𐐿𐐯𐐼𐑌𐐯𐑅 𐐰𐑌𐐼 𐐰𐐺𐐱𐑋𐐮𐑌𐐩𐑇𐐲𐑌𐑆, 𐐸𐐶𐐴𐑊 𐑄 𐐢𐐩𐑋𐐲𐑌𐐴𐐻𐑅 𐐺𐐨𐑀𐐰𐑌 𐐻𐐭 𐑀𐑉𐐬 𐐯𐐿𐑅𐐨𐐼𐐮𐑍𐑊𐐨 𐐮𐑌 𐑄 𐑌𐐱𐑊𐐯𐐾 𐐲𐑂 𐑄𐐩𐑉 𐐘𐐱𐐼; 𐐷𐐩, 𐑄𐐩 𐐼𐐮𐐼 𐐺𐐨𐑀𐐮𐑌 𐐻𐐭 𐐿𐐨𐐹 𐐸𐐮𐑆 𐑅𐐻𐐰𐐽𐐭𐐻𐑅 𐐰𐑌𐐼 𐐿𐐱𐑋𐐰𐑌𐐼𐑋𐐯𐑌𐐻𐑅, 𐐰𐑌𐐼 𐐻𐐭 𐐶𐐫𐐿 𐐮𐑌 𐐻𐑉𐐭𐑃 𐐰𐑌𐐼 𐐲𐐹𐑉𐐴𐐻𐑌𐐯𐑅 𐐺𐐨𐑁𐐬𐑉 𐐸𐐮𐑋. 𐐈𐑌𐐼 𐑄𐐲𐑅 𐐶𐐨 𐑅𐐨 𐑄𐐰𐐻 𐑄 𐐝𐐹𐐮𐑉𐐮𐐻 𐐲𐑂 𐑄 𐐢𐐫𐑉𐐼 𐐺𐐨𐑀𐐰𐑌 𐐻𐐭 𐐶𐐮𐑃𐐼𐑉𐐫 𐑁𐑉𐐱𐑋 𐑄 𐐤𐐨𐑁𐐴𐐻𐑅, 𐐺𐐨𐐿𐐫𐑆 𐐲𐑂 𐑄 𐐶𐐮𐐿𐐯𐐼𐑌𐐯𐑅 𐐰𐑌𐐼 𐑄 𐐸𐐪𐑉𐐼𐑌𐐯𐑅 𐐲𐑂 𐑄𐐩𐑉 𐐸𐐪𐑉𐐻𐑅. 𐐈𐑌𐐼 𐑄𐐲𐑅 𐐶𐐨 𐑅𐐨 𐑄𐐰𐐻 𐑄 𐐢𐐫𐑉𐐼 𐐺𐐨𐑀𐐰𐑌 𐐻𐐭 𐐹𐐬𐑉 𐐵𐐻 𐐸𐐮𐑆 𐐝𐐹𐐮𐑉𐐮𐐻 𐐲𐐹𐐱𐑌 𐑄 𐐢𐐩𐑋𐐲𐑌𐐴𐐻𐑅, 𐐺𐐨𐐿𐐫𐑆 𐐲𐑂 𐑄𐐩𐑉 𐐨𐑆𐐨𐑌𐐯𐑅 𐐰𐑌𐐼 𐐶𐐮𐑊𐐮𐑍𐑌𐐯𐑅 𐐻𐐭 𐐺𐐨𐑊𐐨𐑂 𐐮𐑌 𐐸𐐮𐑆 𐐶𐐲𐑉𐐼𐑆.

32. 𐐈𐑌𐐼 𐐮𐐻 𐐿𐐩𐑋 𐐻𐐭 𐐹𐐰𐑅 𐑄𐐰𐐻 𐑄 𐐢𐐩𐑋𐐲𐑌𐐴𐐻𐑅 𐐼𐐮𐐼 𐐸𐐲𐑌𐐻 𐑄 𐐺𐐰𐑌𐐼 𐐲𐑂 𐑉𐐱𐐺𐐲𐑉𐑆 𐐲𐑂 𐐘𐐰𐐼𐐨-

𐐰𐑌𐐻𐐲𐑌: 𐐰𐑌𐐼 𐑄𐐩 𐐼𐐮𐐼 𐐹𐑉𐐨𐐽 𐑄 𐐶𐐲𐑉𐐼 𐐱𐑂 𐐘𐐱𐐼 𐐲𐑋𐐲𐑍 𐑄 𐑋𐐬𐑉 𐐶𐐮𐐿𐐯𐐼 𐐹𐐪𐑉𐐻 𐐱𐑂 𐑄𐐯𐑋, 𐐮𐑌𐑅𐐬𐑋𐐲𐐽 𐑄𐐰𐐻 𐑄𐐮𐑅 𐐺𐐰𐑌𐐼 𐐱𐑂 𐑉𐐱𐐺𐐲𐑉𐑆 𐐶𐐲𐑆 𐐲𐐻𐐲𐑉𐑊𐐨 𐐼𐐯𐑅𐐻𐑉𐐱𐐮𐐼 𐑁𐑉𐐱𐑋 𐐲𐑋𐐲𐑍 𐑄 𐐢𐐩𐑋𐐲𐑌𐐴𐐻𐑅. 𐐈𐑌𐐼 𐐮𐐻 𐐿𐐩𐑋 𐐻𐐭 𐐹𐐰𐑅 𐐱𐑌 𐑄 𐐲𐑄𐐲𐑉 𐐸𐐰𐑌𐐼, 𐑄𐐰𐐻 𐑄 𐐤𐐨𐑁𐐴𐐻𐑅 𐐼𐐮𐐼 𐐺𐐮𐑊𐐼 𐑄𐐯𐑋 𐐲𐐹 𐐰𐑌𐐼 𐑅𐐲𐐹𐐬𐑉𐐻 𐑄𐐯𐑋, 𐐺𐐨𐑀𐐮𐑌𐐮𐑍 𐐰𐐻 𐑄 𐑋𐐬𐑉 𐐶𐐮𐐿𐐯𐐼 𐐹𐐪𐑉𐐻 𐐱𐑂 𐑄𐐯𐑋, 𐐲𐑌𐐻𐐮𐑊 𐑄𐐩 𐐸𐐰𐐼 𐐬𐑂𐐲𐑉𐑅𐐹𐑉𐐯𐐼 𐐫𐑊 𐑄 𐑊𐐰𐑌𐐼 𐐱𐑂 𐑄 𐐤𐐨𐑁𐐴𐐻𐑅, 𐐰𐑌𐐼 𐐸𐐰𐐼 𐑅𐐨𐐼𐐷𐐭𐑅𐐻 𐑄 𐑋𐐬𐑉 𐐹𐐪𐑉𐐻 𐐱𐑂 𐑄 𐑉𐐴𐐽𐐲𐑅, 𐐲𐑌𐐻𐐮𐑊 𐑄𐐩 𐐸𐐰𐐼 𐐿𐐲𐑋 𐐼𐐵𐑌 𐐻𐐭 𐐺𐐨𐑊𐐨𐑂 𐐮𐑌 𐑄𐐩𐑉 𐐶𐐲𐑉𐐿𐑅, 𐐰𐑌𐐼 𐐹𐐪𐑉𐐻𐐩𐐿 𐐱𐑂 𐑄𐐩𐑉 𐑅𐐹𐐱𐐮𐑊𐑆, 𐐰𐑌𐐼 𐐻𐐭 𐐾𐐱𐐮𐑌 𐐶𐐮𐑃 𐑄𐐯𐑋 𐐮𐑌 𐑄𐐩𐑉 𐑅𐐨𐐿𐑉𐐯𐐻 𐑋𐐲𐑉𐐼𐐲𐑉𐑆 𐐰𐑌𐐼 𐐿𐐱𐑋𐐺𐐮𐑌𐐩𐑇𐐲𐑌𐑆. 𐐈𐑌𐐼 𐑄𐐲𐑅 𐑄𐐩 𐐼𐐮𐐼 𐐱𐐺𐐻𐐩𐑌 𐑄 𐑅𐐬𐑊 𐑋𐐰𐑌𐐲𐐾𐑋𐐲𐑌𐐻 𐐱𐑂 𐑄 𐑀𐐲𐑂𐐲𐑉𐑌𐑋𐐲𐑌𐐻, 𐐮𐑌𐑅𐐬𐑋𐐲𐐽 𐑄𐐰𐐻 𐑄𐐩 𐐼𐐮𐐼 𐐻𐑉𐐰𐑋𐐹𐑊 𐐲𐑌𐐼𐐲𐑉 𐑄𐐩𐑉 𐑁𐐨𐐻, 𐐰𐑌𐐼 𐑅𐑋𐐴𐐻, 𐐰𐑌𐐼 𐑉𐐯𐑌𐐼, 𐐰𐑌𐐼 𐐻𐐲𐑉𐑌 𐑄𐐩𐑉 𐐺𐐰𐐿𐑅 𐐲𐐹𐐱𐑌 𐑄 𐐹𐐭𐑉, 𐐰𐑌𐐼 𐑄 𐑋𐐨𐐿, 𐐰𐑌𐐼 𐑄 𐐸𐐲𐑋𐐺𐑊 𐑁𐐱𐑊𐐬𐐲𐑉𐑆 𐐱𐑂 𐐘𐐱𐐼. 𐐈𐑌𐐼 𐑄𐐲𐑅 𐐶𐐨 𐑅𐐨 𐑄𐐰𐐻 𐑄𐐩 𐐶𐐲𐑉 𐐮𐑌 𐐰𐑌 𐐫𐑁𐐳𐑊 𐑅𐐻𐐩𐐻, 𐐰𐑌𐐼 𐑉𐐴𐐹𐐲𐑌𐐮𐑍 𐑁𐐬𐑉 𐐰𐑌 𐐯𐑂𐐲𐑉𐑊𐐰𐑅𐐻𐐮𐑍 𐐼𐐯𐑅𐐻𐑉𐐲𐐿𐑇𐐲𐑌. 𐐈𐑌𐐼 𐐮𐐻 𐐿𐐩𐑋 𐐻𐐭 𐐹𐐰𐑅 𐑄𐐰𐐻 𐑄𐐲𐑅 𐐯𐑌𐐼𐐯𐐼 𐑄 𐑅𐐮𐐿𐑅𐐻𐐨 𐐰𐑌𐐼 𐐩𐐻𐑃 𐐷𐐨𐑉 𐐱𐑂 𐑄 𐑉𐐩𐑌 𐐱𐑂 𐑄 𐐾𐐲𐐾𐐯𐑆 𐐬𐑂𐐲𐑉 𐑄 𐐹𐐨𐐹𐑊 𐐱𐑂 𐐤𐐨𐑁𐐴.

𐐕𐐈𐐑𐐓𐐊𐐡 III.

𐐜 𐐹𐑉𐐱𐑁𐐯𐑅𐐨 𐐱𐑂 𐐤𐐨𐑁𐐴 𐑄 𐑅𐐲𐑌 𐐱𐑂 𐐐𐐨𐑊𐐩𐑋𐐲𐑌.—𐐘𐐱𐐼 𐑃𐑉𐐯𐐻𐑌𐑆 𐑄 𐐹𐐨𐐹𐑊 𐐱𐑂 𐐤𐐨𐑁𐐴, 𐑄𐐰𐐻 𐐸𐐨 𐐶𐐮𐑊 𐑂𐐮𐑆𐐮𐐻 𐑄𐐯𐑋 𐐮𐑌 𐐸𐐮𐑆 𐐰𐑍𐑀𐐲𐑉, 𐐻𐐭 𐑄𐐩𐑉 𐐲𐐻𐐲𐑉 𐐼𐐯𐑅𐐻𐑉𐐲𐐿𐑇𐐲𐑌, 𐐯𐐿𐑅𐐯𐐹𐐻 𐑄𐐩 𐑉𐐨𐐹𐐯𐑌𐐻 𐐱𐑂 𐑄𐐩𐑉 𐐶𐐮𐐿𐐯𐐼𐑌𐐯𐑅. 𐐘𐐱𐐼 𐑅𐑋𐐴𐐻𐐯𐑃 𐑄 𐐹𐐨𐐹𐑊 𐐱𐑂 𐐤𐐨𐑁𐐴 𐐶𐐮𐑃 𐐹𐐯𐑅𐐻𐐮𐑊𐐯𐑌𐑅; 𐑄𐐩 𐑉𐐨𐐹𐐯𐑌𐐻 𐐰𐑌𐐼 𐐻𐐲𐑉𐑌 𐐲𐑌𐐻𐐭 𐐸𐐮𐑋. 𐐝𐐰𐑋𐐷𐐭𐐯𐑊, 𐐩 𐐢𐐩𐑋𐐲𐑌𐐴𐐻, 𐐹𐑉𐐱𐑁𐐯𐑅𐐴𐑆 𐐲𐑌𐐻𐐭 𐑄 𐐤𐐨𐑁𐐴𐐻𐑅.

1. 𐐒𐐨𐐸𐐬𐑊𐐼, 𐑌𐐵 𐐮𐐻 𐐿𐐩𐑋 𐐻𐐭 𐐹𐐰𐑅 𐐮𐑌 𐑄 𐑅𐐮𐐿𐑅𐐻𐐨 𐐰𐑌𐐼 𐑌𐐴𐑌𐑃 𐐷𐐨𐑉 𐐱𐑂 𐑄 𐑉𐐩𐑌 𐐱𐑂 𐑄 𐐾𐐲𐐾𐐯𐑆 𐐬𐑂𐐲𐑉 𐑄 𐐹𐐨𐐹𐑊 𐐱𐑂 𐑄 𐐤𐐨𐑁𐐴𐐻𐑅, 𐑄𐐰𐐻 𐐤𐐨𐑁𐐴, 𐑄 𐑅𐐲𐑌 𐐱𐑂 𐐐𐐨𐑊𐐩𐑋𐐲𐑌, 𐑉𐐨𐐻𐐲𐑉𐑌𐐼 𐐻𐐭 𐑄 𐑊𐐰𐑌𐐼 𐐱𐑂 𐐞𐐩𐑉𐐰𐐸𐐯𐑋𐑊𐐲, 𐑁𐑉𐐱𐑋 𐑄 𐑊𐐰𐑌𐐼 𐑌𐐫𐑉𐑃𐐶𐐲𐑉𐐼: 𐑁𐐫𐑉 𐐸𐐨 𐐸𐐰𐐼 𐐺𐐮𐑌 𐑁𐐫𐑉𐑃 𐐲𐑋𐐲𐑍 𐑄 𐐹𐐨𐐹𐑊 𐐸𐐭 𐐶𐐲𐑉 𐐮𐑌 𐑄 𐑊𐐰𐑌𐐼 𐑌𐐫𐑉𐑃𐐶𐐲𐑉𐐼, 𐐰𐑌𐐼 𐐼𐐮𐐼 𐐹𐑉𐐨𐐽 𐑄 𐐶𐐲𐑉𐐼 𐐱𐑂 𐐘𐐱𐐼 𐐲𐑌𐐻𐐭 𐑄𐐯𐑋, 𐐰𐑌𐐼 𐐼𐐮𐐼 𐐹𐑉𐐱𐑁𐐯𐑅𐐴 𐑋𐐯𐑌𐐨 𐑃𐐮𐑍𐑆 𐐲𐑌𐐻𐐭 𐑄𐐯𐑋; 𐐰𐑌𐐼 𐑄𐐩 𐐼𐐮𐐼 𐑉𐐨𐐾𐐯𐐿𐐻 𐐫𐑊 𐐸𐐮𐑆 𐐶𐐲𐑉𐐼𐑆, 𐐮𐑌𐑅𐐬𐑋𐐲𐐽 𐑄𐐰𐐻 𐐸𐐨 𐐿𐐳𐐼 𐑌𐐱𐐻 𐑅𐐻𐐩 𐐲𐑋𐐲𐑍 𐑄𐐯𐑋, 𐐺𐐲𐐻 𐑉𐐨𐐻𐐲𐑉𐑌𐐼 𐐲𐑀𐐯𐑌 𐐲𐑌𐐻𐐭 𐑄 𐑊𐐰𐑌𐐼 𐐱𐑂 𐐸𐐮𐑆 𐑌𐐩𐐻𐐮𐑂𐐮𐐻𐐮; 𐐰𐑌𐐼 𐑅𐐨𐐮𐑍 𐑄 𐐹𐐨𐐹𐑊 𐐮𐑌 𐐩 𐑅𐐻𐐩𐐻 𐐱𐑂 𐑅𐐲𐐽 𐐫𐑁𐐳𐑊 𐐶𐐮𐐿𐐯𐐼𐑌𐐯𐑅, 𐐰𐑌𐐼 𐑄𐐬𐑆 𐐘𐐰𐐼𐐨𐐰𐑌𐐻𐐲𐑌 𐑉𐐱𐐺𐐲𐑉𐑆 𐑁𐐮𐑊𐐮𐑍 𐑄 𐐾𐐲𐐾𐑋𐐯𐑌𐐻 𐑅𐐨𐐻𐑅; 𐐸𐐰𐑂𐐮𐑍 𐐷𐐭𐑆𐐲𐑉𐐹𐐻 𐑄 𐐹𐐵𐐲𐑉 𐐰𐑌𐐼 𐐫𐑃𐐱𐑉𐐮𐐻𐐨 𐐱𐑂 𐑄 𐑊𐐰𐑌𐐼; 𐑊𐐩𐐮𐑍 𐐲𐑅𐐴𐐼 𐑄 𐐿𐐲𐑋𐐰𐑌𐐼𐑋𐐯𐑌𐐻𐑅 𐐱𐑂 𐐘𐐱𐐼, 𐐰𐑌𐐼 𐑌𐐱𐐻 𐐮𐑌 𐑄 𐑊𐐨𐑅𐐻 𐐲𐑉𐐴𐐻 𐐺𐐨𐑁𐐬𐑉 𐐸𐐮𐑋; 𐐼𐐭𐐮𐑍 𐑌𐐬 𐐾𐐲𐑅𐐻𐐮𐑅 𐐲𐑌𐐻𐐭 𐑄 𐐽𐐮𐑊𐐼𐑉𐐯𐑌 𐐱𐑂 𐑋𐐯𐑌; 𐐿𐐱𐑌𐐼𐐯𐑋𐐮𐑍 𐑄 𐑉𐐴𐐽𐐲𐑅 𐐺𐐨𐐿𐐫𐑆 𐐱𐑂 𐑄𐐩𐑉 𐑉𐐴𐐽𐐲𐑅𐑌𐐯𐑅; 𐑊𐐯𐐻𐐮𐑍 𐑄 𐑀𐐮𐑊𐐻𐐨 𐐰𐑌𐐼 𐑄 𐐶𐐮𐐿𐐯𐐼 𐑀𐐬 𐐲𐑌𐐹𐐲𐑌𐐮𐑇𐐻, 𐐺𐐨𐐿𐐫𐑆 𐐱𐑂 𐑄𐐩𐑉 𐑋𐐲𐑌𐐨; 𐐰𐑌𐐼 𐑋𐐬𐑉𐐬𐑂𐐲𐑉 𐐻𐐭 𐐺 𐐸𐐯𐑊𐐼 𐐮𐑌 𐐫𐑁𐐮𐑅 𐐰𐐻 𐑄 𐐸𐐯𐐼 𐐱𐑂 𐑀𐐲𐑂𐐲𐑉𐑌𐑋𐐲𐑌𐐻, 𐐻𐐭 𐑉𐐭𐑊 𐐰𐑌𐐼 𐐼𐐭 𐐲𐐿𐐫𐑉𐐼𐐮𐑍 𐐻𐐭 𐑄𐐩𐑉 𐐶𐐮𐑊𐑆, 𐑄𐐰𐐻 𐑄𐐩 𐑋𐐴𐐻 𐑀𐐯𐐻 𐑀𐐩𐑌 𐐰𐑌𐐼 𐑀𐑊𐐬𐑉𐐨 𐐱𐑂 𐑄 𐐶𐐲𐑉𐑊𐐼; 𐐰𐑌𐐼 𐑋𐐬𐑉𐐬𐑂𐐲𐑉 𐑄𐐰𐐻 𐑄𐐩 𐑋𐐴𐐻 𐑄 𐑋𐐬𐑉 𐐨𐑆𐐮𐑊𐐨 𐐿𐐱𐑋𐐮𐐻 𐐲𐐼𐐲𐑊𐐻𐐲𐑉𐐨, 𐐰𐑌𐐼 𐑅𐐻𐐨𐑊, 𐐰𐑌𐐼 𐐿𐐮𐑊, 𐐰𐑌𐐼 𐐼𐐭 𐐲𐐿𐐫𐑉𐐼𐐮𐑍 𐐻𐐭 𐑄𐐩𐑉 𐐬𐑌 𐐶𐐮𐑊𐑆. 𐐤𐐵 𐑄𐐮𐑅 𐑀𐑉𐐩𐐻 𐐮𐑌𐐮𐐿𐐶𐐮𐐻𐐨 𐐸𐐰𐐼 𐐿𐐲𐑋 𐐲𐐹𐐱𐑌 𐑄 𐐤𐐨𐑁𐐴𐐻𐑅, 𐐮𐑌 𐑄 𐑅𐐹𐐩𐑅 𐐱𐑂 𐑌𐐱𐐻 𐑋𐐯𐑌𐐨 𐐷𐐨𐑉𐑆; 𐐰𐑌𐐼 𐐸𐐶𐐯𐑌 𐐤𐐨𐑁𐐴 𐑅𐐫 𐐮𐐻, 𐐸𐐮𐑆 𐐸𐐪𐑉𐐻 𐐶𐐲𐑆 𐑅𐐶𐐬𐑊𐐯𐑌 𐐶𐐮𐑃 𐑅𐐱𐑉𐐬 𐐶𐐮𐑃𐐮𐑌 𐐸𐐮𐑆 𐐺𐑉𐐯𐑅𐐻; 𐐰𐑌𐐼 𐐸𐐨 𐐼𐐮𐐼 𐐯𐐿𐑅𐐿𐑊𐐩𐑋 𐐮𐑌 𐑄 𐐰𐑀𐐲𐑌𐐨 𐐱𐑂 𐐸𐐮𐑆 𐑅𐐬𐑊, 𐐄, 𐑄𐐰𐐻 𐐌 𐐿𐐳𐐼 𐐸𐐰𐑂 𐐸𐐰𐐼 𐑋𐐴 𐐼𐐩𐑆 𐐮𐑌 𐑄 𐐼𐐩𐑆 𐐸𐐶𐐯𐑌 𐑋𐐴 𐑁𐐪𐑄𐐲𐑉 𐐤𐐨𐑁𐐴 𐑁𐐲𐑉𐑅𐐻 𐐿𐐩𐑋 𐐵𐐻 𐐱𐑂 𐑄 𐑊𐐰𐑌𐐼 𐐱𐑂 𐐖𐐨𐑉𐐭𐑅𐐰𐑊𐐯𐑋, 𐑄𐐰𐐻 𐐌 𐐿𐐳𐐼 𐐸𐐰𐑂 𐐾𐐱𐐮𐐼 𐐶𐐮𐑃 𐐸𐐮𐑋 𐐮𐑌 𐑄 𐐹𐑉𐐱𐑋𐐮𐑅𐐻 𐑊𐐰𐑌𐐼; 𐑄𐐯𐑌 𐐶𐐲𐑉 𐐸𐐮𐑆 𐐹𐐨𐐹𐑊 𐐨𐑆𐐨 𐐻𐐭 𐐺 𐐯𐑌𐐻𐑉𐐨𐐻𐐯𐐼, 𐑁𐐲𐑉𐑋 𐐻𐐭 𐐿𐐨𐐹 𐑄 𐐿𐐲𐑋𐐰𐑌𐐼𐑋𐐯𐑌𐐻𐑅 𐐱𐑂 𐐘𐐱𐐼, 𐐰𐑌𐐼 𐑅𐑊𐐬 𐐻𐐭 𐐺 𐑊𐐯𐐼 𐐻𐐭 𐐼𐐭 𐐮𐑌𐐮𐐿𐐶𐐮𐐻𐐨; 𐐰𐑌𐐼 𐑄𐐩 𐐶𐐲𐑉 𐐿𐐶𐐮𐐿 𐐻𐐭 𐐸𐐪𐑉𐐿𐐲𐑌 𐐲𐑌𐐻𐐭 𐑄 𐐶𐐲𐑉𐐼𐑆 𐐱𐑂 𐑄 𐐢𐐫𐑉𐐼;

𐐷𐐩, 𐐮𐑁 𐑋𐐴 𐐼𐐩𐑆 𐐿𐐳𐐼 𐐸𐐰𐑂 𐐺𐐮𐑌 𐐮𐑌 𐑄𐐯𐑋 𐐼𐐩𐑆, 𐑄𐐯𐑌 𐐶𐐳𐐼 𐑋𐐴 𐑅𐐬𐑊 𐐸𐐰𐑂 𐐸𐐰𐐼 𐐾𐑎 𐐮𐑌 𐑄 𐑉𐐴𐐽𐐲𐑅𐑌𐐯𐑅 𐐲𐑂 𐑋𐐴 𐐺𐑉𐐯𐑄𐑉𐐯𐑌. 𐐒𐐲𐐻 𐐺𐐨𐐸𐐬𐑊𐐼, 𐐌 𐐰𐑋 𐐿𐐱𐑌𐑅𐐴𐑌𐐼 𐑄𐐰𐐻 𐑄𐐨𐑆 𐐪𐑉 𐑋𐐴 𐐼𐐩𐑆, 𐐰𐑌𐐼 𐑄𐐰𐐻 𐑋𐐴 𐑅𐐬𐑊 𐑇𐐰𐑊 𐐺𐐨 𐑁𐐮𐑊𐐼 𐐶𐐮𐑄 𐑅𐐱𐑉𐐬, 𐐺𐐨𐐿𐐪𐑆 𐐲𐑂 𐑄𐐮𐑅 𐑄 𐐶𐐮𐐿𐐯𐐼𐑌𐐯𐑅 𐐲𐑂 𐑋𐐴 𐐺𐑉𐐯𐑄𐑉𐐯𐑌. 𐐈𐑌𐐼 𐐺𐐨𐐸𐐬𐑊𐐼, 𐑌𐐵 𐐮𐐻 𐐿𐐩𐑋 𐐻𐐭 𐐹𐐪𐑅 𐑄𐐰𐐻 𐐮𐐻 𐐶𐐱𐑆 𐐲𐐹𐐱𐑌 𐐩 𐐻𐐵𐐲𐑉, 𐐸𐐶𐐮𐐽 𐐶𐐱𐑆 𐐮𐑌 𐑄 𐑀𐐪𐑉𐐼𐐲𐑌 𐐲𐑂 𐐤𐐨𐑁𐐴, 𐐸𐐶𐐮𐐽 𐐶𐐱𐑆 𐐺𐐴 𐑄 𐐸𐐴𐐶𐐩 𐐸𐐶𐐮𐐽 𐑊𐐯𐐼 𐐻𐐭 𐑄 𐐽𐐨𐑁 𐑋𐐪𐑉𐐿𐐯𐐻, 𐐸𐐶𐐮𐐽 𐐶𐐱𐑆 𐐮𐑌 𐑄 𐑅𐐮𐐻𐐨 𐐲𐑂 𐐞𐐪𐑉𐐲𐐸𐐯𐑋𐑊𐐲; 𐑄𐐯𐑉𐑁𐐬𐑉 𐐤𐐨𐑁𐐴 𐐸𐐰𐐼 𐐺𐐵𐐼 𐐸𐐮𐑋𐑅𐐯𐑊𐑁 𐐲𐐹𐐱𐑌 𐑄 𐐻𐐵𐐲𐑉 𐐸𐐶𐐮𐐽 𐐶𐐱𐑆 𐐮𐑌 𐐸𐐮𐑆 𐑀𐐪𐑉𐐼𐐲𐑌, 𐐸𐐶𐐮𐐽 𐐻𐐵𐐲𐑉 𐐶𐐱𐑆 𐐫𐑊𐑅𐐬 𐑌𐐨𐑉 𐐲𐑌𐐻𐐭 𐑄 𐑀𐐪𐑉𐐼𐐲𐑌 𐑀𐐩𐐻 𐐺𐐴 𐐸𐐶𐐮𐐽 𐑊𐐯𐐼 𐑄 𐐸𐐴𐐶𐐩.

2. 𐐈𐑌𐐼 𐐮𐐻 𐐿𐐩𐑋 𐐻𐐭 𐐹𐐪𐑅 𐑄𐐰𐐻 𐑄𐐯𐑉 𐐶𐐯𐑉 𐑅𐐲𐑉𐐻𐐲𐑌 𐑋𐐯𐑌 𐐹𐐪𐑅𐐮𐑍 𐐺𐐴 𐐰𐑌𐐼 𐑅𐐫 𐐤𐐨𐑁𐐴 𐐰𐑆 𐐸𐐨 𐐶𐐱𐑆 𐐹𐐬𐑉𐐮𐑍 𐐵𐐻 𐐸𐐮𐑆 𐑅𐐬𐑊 𐐲𐑌𐐻𐐭 𐐘𐐱𐐼 𐐲𐐹𐐱𐑌 𐑄 𐐻𐐵𐐲𐑉, 𐐰𐑌𐐼 𐑄𐐩 𐑉𐐰𐑌 𐐰𐑌𐐼 𐐻𐐬𐑊𐐼 𐑄 𐐹𐐨𐐹𐑊 𐐸𐐶𐐱𐐻 𐑄𐐩 𐐸𐐰𐐼 𐑅𐐨𐑌, 𐐰𐑌𐐼 𐑄 𐐹𐐨𐐹𐑊 𐐿𐐩𐑋 𐐻𐐭𐑀𐐯𐑄𐐲𐑉 𐐮𐑌 𐑋𐐲𐑊𐐻𐐨𐐻𐐭𐐼𐑆 𐑄𐐰𐐻 𐑄𐐩 𐑋𐐴𐐻 𐑌𐐬 𐑄 𐐿𐐫𐑆 𐐲𐑂 𐑅𐐬 𐑀𐑉𐐩𐐻 𐑋𐐬𐑉𐑌𐐮𐑍 𐑁𐐫𐑉 𐑄 𐐶𐐮𐐿𐐯𐐼𐑌𐐯𐑅 𐐲𐑂 𐑄 𐐹𐐨𐐹𐑊. 𐐈𐑌𐐼 𐑌𐐵 𐐸𐐶𐐯𐑌 𐐤𐐨𐑁𐐴 𐐩𐑉𐐬𐑆 𐐸𐐨 𐐺𐐨𐐸𐐯𐑊𐐼 𐑄 𐑋𐐲𐑊𐐻𐐨𐐻𐐭𐐼𐑆 𐐲𐑂 𐐹𐐨𐐹𐑊 𐐸𐐭 𐐸𐐰𐐼 𐑀𐐰𐑄𐐲𐑉𐐼 𐐻𐐭𐑀𐐯𐑄𐐲𐑉. 𐐈𐑌𐐼 𐐮𐐻 𐐿𐐩𐑋 𐐻𐐭 𐐹𐐪𐑅 𐑄𐐰𐐻 𐐸𐐨 𐐬𐐹𐐯𐑌𐐼 𐐸𐐮𐑆 𐑋𐐵𐑃 𐐰𐑌𐐼 𐑅𐐯𐐼 𐐲𐑌𐐻𐐭 𐑄𐐯𐑋, 𐐒𐐨𐐸𐐬𐑊𐐼, 𐐸𐐶𐐴 𐐸𐐰𐑂 𐐷𐐨 𐑀𐐰𐑄𐐲𐑉𐐼 𐐷𐐭𐑉𐑅𐐯𐑊𐑂𐑆 𐐻𐐭𐑀𐐯𐑄𐐲𐑉? 𐐜𐐰𐐻 𐐌 𐑋𐐩 𐐻𐐯𐑊 𐐷𐐭 𐐲𐑂 𐐷𐐭𐑉 𐐮𐑌𐐮𐐿𐐶𐐮𐐻𐐨𐑆? 𐐏𐐩, 𐐺𐐨𐐿𐐪𐑆 𐐌 𐐸𐐰𐑂 𐑀𐐱𐐻 𐐲𐐹𐐱𐑌 𐑋𐐴 𐐻𐐵𐐲𐑉, 𐑄𐐰𐐻 𐐌 𐑋𐐴𐐻 𐐹𐐬𐑉 𐐵𐐻 𐑋𐐴 𐑅𐐬𐑊 𐐲𐑌𐐻𐐭 𐑋𐐴 𐐘𐐱𐐼, 𐐺𐐨𐐿𐐪𐑆 𐐲𐑂 𐑄 𐐯𐐿𐑅𐐨𐐼𐐮𐑍 𐑅𐐱𐑉𐐬 𐐲𐑂 𐑋𐐴 𐐸𐐪𐑉𐐻, 𐐸𐐶𐐮𐐽 𐐮𐑆 𐐺𐐨𐐿𐐪𐑆 𐐲𐑂 𐐷𐐭𐑉 𐐮𐑌𐐮𐐿𐐶𐐮𐐻𐐨𐑆? 𐐈𐑌𐐼 𐐺𐐨𐐿𐐪𐑆 𐐲𐑂 𐑋𐐴 𐑋𐐬𐑉𐑌𐐮𐑍 𐐰𐑌𐐼 𐑊𐐰𐑋𐐯𐑌𐐻𐐩𐑇𐐲𐑌, 𐐷𐐨 𐐸𐐰𐑂 𐑀𐐰𐑄𐐲𐑉𐐼 𐐷𐐭𐑉𐑅𐐯𐑊𐑂𐑆 𐐻𐐭𐑀𐐯𐑄𐐲𐑉, 𐐰𐑌𐐼 𐐼𐐭 𐑋𐐪𐑉𐑂𐐯𐑊; 𐐷𐐩, 𐐰𐑌𐐼 𐐷𐐨 𐐸𐐰𐑂 𐑀𐑉𐐩𐐻 𐑌𐐨𐐼 𐐻𐐭 𐑋𐐪𐑉𐑂𐐯𐑊; 𐐷𐐩, 𐐷𐐨 𐐫𐐻 𐐻𐐭 𐑋𐐪𐑉𐑂𐐯𐑊, 𐐺𐐨𐐿𐐪𐑆 𐐷𐐨 𐐪𐑉 𐑀𐐮𐑂𐐲𐑌 𐐲𐐶𐐩 𐑄𐐰𐐻 𐑄 𐐼𐐯𐑂𐐲𐑊 𐐸𐐰𐑆 𐑀𐐱𐐻 𐑅𐐬 𐑀𐑉𐐩𐐻 𐐸𐐬𐑊𐐼 𐐲𐐹𐐱𐑌 𐐷𐐭𐑉 𐐸𐐪𐑉𐐻𐑅; 𐐷𐐩, 𐐸𐐵 𐐿𐐳𐐼 𐐷𐐭 𐐸𐐰𐑂 𐑀𐐮𐑂𐐲𐑌 𐐶𐐩 𐐻𐐭 𐑄 𐐯𐑌𐐻𐐴𐑅𐐮𐑍 𐐲𐑂 𐐸𐐮𐑋 𐐸𐐭 𐐮𐑆 𐑅𐐨𐐿𐐮𐑍 𐐻𐐭 𐐸𐐲𐑉𐑊 𐐲𐐶𐐩 𐐷𐐭𐑉 𐑅𐐬𐑊𐑆 𐐼𐐵𐑌 𐐻𐐭 𐐯𐑂𐐲𐑉𐑊𐐰𐑅𐐻𐐮𐑍 𐑋𐐮𐑆𐐲𐑉𐐨 𐐰𐑌𐐼 𐐯𐑌𐐼𐑊𐐯𐑅 𐐶𐐬; 𐐄 𐑉𐐨𐐹𐐯𐑌𐐻 𐐷𐐨, 𐑉𐐨𐐹𐐯𐑌𐐻 𐐷𐐨! 𐐐𐐶𐐴 𐐶𐐮𐑊 𐐷𐐨 𐐼𐐴? 𐐓𐐲𐑉𐑌 𐐷𐐨, 𐐻𐐲𐑉𐑌 𐐷𐐨 𐐲𐑌𐐻𐐭 𐑄 𐐢𐐫𐑉𐐼 𐐷𐐭𐑉 𐐘𐐱𐐼. 𐐐𐐶𐐴 𐐸𐐰𐑆 𐐸𐐨 𐑁𐐫𐑉𐑅𐐩𐐿𐑌 𐐷𐐭? 𐐆𐐻 𐐮𐑆 𐐺𐐨𐐿𐐪𐑆 𐐷𐐭 𐐸𐐰𐑂 𐐸𐐪𐑉𐐼𐐲𐑌𐐼 𐐷𐐭𐑉 𐐸𐐪𐑉𐐻𐑅; 𐐷𐐩, 𐐷𐐨 𐐶𐐮𐑊 𐑌𐐱𐐻 𐐸𐐪𐑉𐐿𐐲𐑌 𐐲𐑌𐐻𐐭 𐑄 𐑂𐑎𐑅 𐐲𐑂 𐑄 𐑀𐐳𐐼 𐑇𐐯𐐹𐐲𐑉𐐼; 𐐷𐐩, 𐐷𐐨 𐐸𐐰𐑂 𐐹𐑉𐐬𐑂𐐬𐐿𐐻 𐐸𐐮𐑋 𐐻𐐭 𐐰𐑍𐑀𐐲𐑉 𐐲𐑀𐐯𐑌𐑅𐐻 𐐷𐐭. 𐐈𐑌𐐼 𐐺𐐨𐐸𐐬𐑊𐐼 𐐮𐑌𐑅𐐻𐐯𐐼 𐐲𐑂 𐑀𐐰𐑄𐐲𐑉𐐮𐑍 𐐷𐐭, 𐐯𐐿𐑅𐐯𐐹𐐻 𐐷𐐨 𐐶𐐮𐑊 𐑉𐐨𐐹𐐯𐑌𐐻, 𐐺𐐨𐐸𐐬𐑊𐐼 𐐸𐐨 𐑇𐐰𐑊 𐑅𐐿𐐰𐐻𐐲𐑉 𐐷𐐭 𐑁𐐬𐑉𐑃 𐑄𐐰𐐻 𐐷𐐨 𐑇𐐰𐑊 𐐺𐐨𐐿𐐲𐑋 𐑋𐐨𐐻 𐑁𐐫𐑉 𐐼𐐱𐑀𐑆 𐐰𐑌𐐼 𐐶𐐴𐑊𐐼 𐐺𐐨𐑅𐐻𐑅. 𐐄! 𐐸𐐵 𐐿𐐳𐐼 𐐷𐐭 𐐸𐐰𐑂 𐑁𐐫𐑉𐑀𐐱𐐻𐐲𐑌 𐐷𐐭𐑉 𐐘𐐱𐐼 𐐮𐑌 𐑄 𐑂𐐯𐑉𐐨 𐐼𐐩 𐑄𐐰𐐻 𐐸𐐨 𐐸𐐰𐑆 𐐼𐐮𐑊𐐮𐑂𐐲𐑉𐐼 𐐷𐐭? 𐐒𐐲𐐻 𐐺𐐨𐐸𐐬𐑊𐐼, 𐐮𐐻 𐐮𐑆 𐐻𐐭 𐑀𐐯𐐻 𐑀𐐩𐑌, 𐐻𐐭 𐐺𐐨 𐐹𐑉𐐩𐑆𐐼 𐐲𐑂 𐑋𐐯𐑌; 𐐷𐐩, 𐐰𐑌𐐼 𐑄𐐰𐐻 𐐷𐐨 𐑋𐐴𐐻 𐑀𐐯𐐻 𐑀𐐬𐑊𐐼 𐐰𐑌𐐼 𐑅𐐮𐑊𐑂𐐲𐑉. 𐐈𐑌𐐼 𐐷𐐨 𐐸𐐰𐑂 𐑅𐐯𐐻 𐐷𐐭𐑉 𐐸𐐪𐑉𐐻𐑅 𐐲𐐹𐐱𐑌 𐑄 𐑉𐐮𐐽𐐯𐑆 𐐰𐑌𐐼 𐑄 𐑂𐐩𐑌 𐑃𐐮𐑍𐑆 𐐲𐑂 𐑄𐐮𐑅 𐐶𐐲𐑉𐑊𐐼, 𐑁𐐫𐑉 𐑄 𐐸𐐶𐐮𐐽 𐐷𐐨 𐐼𐐭 𐑋𐐲𐑉𐐼𐐲𐑉, 𐐰𐑌𐐼 𐐹𐑊𐐲𐑌𐐼𐐲𐑉, 𐐰𐑌𐐼 𐑅𐐻𐐨𐑊, 𐐰𐑌𐐼 𐐺𐐯𐑉 𐑁𐐫𐑊𐑅 𐐶𐐮𐐻𐑌𐐯𐑅 𐐲𐑀𐐯𐑌𐑅𐐻 𐐷𐐭𐑉 𐑌𐐩𐐺𐐲𐑉, 𐐰𐑌𐐼 𐐼𐐭 𐐫𐑊 𐑋𐐰𐑌𐐲𐑉 𐐲𐑂 𐐮𐑌𐐮𐐿𐐶𐐮𐐻𐐨; 𐐰𐑌𐐼 𐑁𐐫𐑉 𐑄𐐮𐑅 𐐿𐐫𐑆 𐐶𐐬 𐑇𐐰𐑊 𐐿𐐲𐑋 𐐲𐑌𐐻𐐭 𐐷𐐭 𐐯𐐿𐑅𐐯𐐹𐐻 𐐷𐐨 𐑇𐐰𐑊 𐑉𐐨𐐹𐐯𐑌𐐻. 𐐙𐐫𐑉 𐐮𐑁 𐐷𐐨 𐐶𐐮𐑊 𐑌𐐱𐐻 𐑉𐐨𐐹𐐯𐑌𐐻, 𐐺𐐨𐐸𐐬𐑊𐐼 𐑄𐐮𐑅 𐑀𐑉𐐩𐐻 𐑅𐐮𐐻𐐨, 𐐰𐑌𐐼 𐐫𐑊𐑅𐐬 𐐫𐑊 𐑄𐐬𐑆 𐑀𐑉𐐩𐐻 𐑅𐐮𐐻𐐨𐑆 𐐸𐐶𐐮𐐽 𐐪𐑉 𐑉𐐵𐑌𐐼 𐐲𐐺𐐵𐐻, 𐐸𐐶𐐮𐐽 𐐪𐑉 𐐮𐑌 𐑄 𐑊𐐰𐑌𐐼 𐐲𐑂 𐐵𐑉 𐐹𐐱𐑆𐐯𐑇𐐲𐑌, 𐑇𐐰𐑊 𐐺𐐨 𐐻𐐩𐐿𐑌 𐐲𐐶𐐩, 𐑄𐐰𐐻 𐐷𐐨 𐑇𐐰𐑊 𐐸𐐰𐑂 𐑌𐐬 𐐹𐑊𐐩𐑅 𐐮𐑌 𐑄𐐯𐑋; 𐑁𐐫𐑉 𐐺𐐨𐐸𐐬𐑊𐐼, 𐑄 𐐢𐐫𐑉𐐼 𐐶𐐮𐑊 𐑌𐐱𐐻 𐑀𐑉𐐰𐑌𐐻 𐐲𐑌𐐻𐐭 𐐷𐐭 𐑅𐐻𐑉𐐯𐑍𐑃, 𐐰𐑆 𐐸𐐨 𐐸𐐰𐑆 𐐸𐐮𐑄𐐲𐑉𐐻𐐭 𐐼𐐲𐑌, 𐐻𐐭 𐐶𐐮𐑄𐑅𐐻𐐰𐑌𐐼 𐐲𐑀𐐯𐑌𐑅𐐻 𐐷𐐭𐑉 𐐯𐑌𐐯𐑋𐐨𐑆; 𐑁𐐫𐑉 𐐺𐐨𐐸𐐬𐑊𐐼, 𐑄𐐲𐑅 𐑅𐐯𐑃 𐑄 𐐢𐐫𐑉𐐼, 𐐌 𐐶𐐮𐑊 𐑌𐐱𐐻 𐑇𐐬 𐐲𐑌𐐻𐐭 𐑄 𐐶𐐮𐐿𐐯𐐼 𐐲𐑂 𐑋𐐴 𐑅𐐻𐑉𐐯𐑍𐑃, 𐐻𐐭 𐐶𐐲𐑌 𐑋𐐬𐑉 𐑄𐐰𐑌 𐑄 𐐲𐑄𐐲𐑉, 𐑅𐐩𐑂 𐐮𐐻 𐐺𐐨 𐐲𐑌𐐻𐐭 𐑄𐐬𐑆 𐐸𐐭 𐑉𐐨𐐹𐐯𐑌𐐻 𐐲𐑂 𐑄𐐯𐑉 𐑅𐐮𐑌𐑆, 𐐰𐑌𐐼 𐐸𐐪𐑉𐐿𐐲𐑌 𐐲𐑌𐐻𐐭 𐑋𐐴 𐐶𐐲𐑉𐐼𐑆. 𐐤𐐵 𐑄𐐯𐑉𐑁𐐬𐑉 𐐌 𐐶𐐳𐐼 𐑄𐐰𐐻 𐐷𐐨 𐑇𐐳𐐼 𐐺𐐨𐐸𐐬𐑊𐐼, 𐑋𐐴 𐐺𐑉𐐯𐑄𐑉𐐯𐑌, 𐑄𐐰𐐻 𐐮𐐻 𐑇𐐰𐑊 𐐺𐐨 𐐺𐐯𐐻𐐲𐑉 𐑁𐐫𐑉 𐑄 𐐢𐐩𐑋𐐲𐑌𐐴𐐻𐑆 𐑄𐐰𐑌 𐑁𐐫𐑉 𐐷𐐭, 𐐯𐐿𐑅𐐯𐐹𐐻 𐐷𐐨 𐑇𐐰𐑊 𐑉𐐨𐐹𐐯𐑌𐐻; 𐑁𐐫𐑉 𐐺𐐨𐐸𐐬𐑊𐐼 𐑄𐐩 𐐪𐑉 𐑋𐐬𐑉 𐑉𐐴𐐽𐐲𐑅 𐑄𐐰𐑌 𐐷𐐭, 𐑁𐐫𐑉 𐑄𐐩 𐐸𐐰𐑂 𐑌𐐱𐐻 𐑅𐐮𐑌𐐼 𐐲𐑀𐐯𐑌𐑅𐐻 𐑄𐐰𐐻 𐑀𐑉𐐩𐐻 𐑌𐐱𐑊𐐯𐐾 𐐸𐐶𐐮𐐽 𐐷𐐨 𐐸𐐰𐑂 𐑉𐐨𐑅𐐨𐑂𐐼; 𐑄𐐯𐑉𐑁𐐬𐑉 𐑄 𐐢𐐫𐑉𐐼 𐐶𐐮𐑊 𐐺𐐨 𐑋𐐲𐑉𐑅𐐮𐑁𐐳𐑊 𐐲𐑌𐐻𐐭 𐑄𐐯𐑋; 𐐷𐐩, 𐐸𐐨 𐐶𐐮𐑊 𐑊𐐯𐑍𐑃𐐲𐑌 𐐵𐐻 𐑄𐐯𐑉 𐐼𐐩𐑆 𐐰𐑌𐐼 𐐮𐑌𐐿𐑉𐐨𐑅 𐑄𐐯𐑉

𐑅𐐨𐐼, 𐐨𐑂𐐲𐑌 𐐸𐐶𐐯𐑌 𐑄𐐵 𐑇𐐰𐑊𐐻 𐐺𐐨 𐐲𐐻𐐲𐑉𐑊𐐨 𐐼𐐯𐑅𐐻𐑉𐑎𐐼, 𐐯𐐿𐑅𐐯𐐹𐐻 𐑄𐐵 𐑇𐐰𐑊𐐻 𐑉𐐨𐐹𐐯𐑌𐐻; 𐐷𐐩, 𐐶𐐬 𐐺𐐨 𐐲𐑌𐐻𐐭 𐐷𐐭 𐐺𐐨𐐿𐐫𐑆 𐐱𐑂 𐑄𐐰𐐻 𐑀𐑉𐐩𐐻 𐐲𐐺𐐱𐑋𐐮𐑌𐐩𐑇𐐲𐑌 𐐸𐐶𐐮𐐽 𐐸𐐰𐑆 𐐿𐐲𐑋 𐐲𐑋𐐲𐑍 𐐷𐐭; 𐐰𐑌𐐼 𐐷𐐨 𐐸𐐰𐑂 𐑏𐑌𐐴𐐻𐐯𐐼 𐐷𐐭𐑉𐑅𐐯𐑊𐑂𐑆 𐐲𐑌𐐻𐐭 𐐮𐐻; 𐐷𐐩, 𐐻𐐭 𐑄𐐰𐐻 𐑅𐐨𐐿𐑉𐐯𐐻 𐐺𐐰𐑌𐐼 𐐸𐐶𐐮𐐽 𐐶𐐱𐑆 𐐯𐑅𐐻𐐰𐐺𐑊𐐮𐑇𐐻 𐐺𐐴 𐐘𐐰𐐼𐐨𐐰𐑌𐐻𐐲𐑌; 𐐷𐐩, 𐐶𐐬 𐑇𐐰𐑊 𐐿𐐲𐑋 𐐲𐑌𐐻𐐭 𐐷𐐭 𐐺𐐨𐐿𐐫𐑆 𐐱𐑂 𐑄𐐰𐐻 𐐹𐑉𐐴𐐼 𐐸𐐶𐐮𐐽 𐐷𐐨 𐐸𐐰𐑂 𐑅𐐲𐑁𐐲𐑉𐐼 𐐻𐐭 𐐯𐑌𐐻𐐲𐑉 𐐷𐐭𐑉 𐐸𐐪𐑉𐐻𐑅, 𐐸𐐶𐐮𐐽 𐐸𐐰𐑆 𐑊𐐮𐑁𐐻𐐯𐐼 𐐷𐐭 𐐲𐐹 𐐺𐐨𐐷𐐱𐑌𐐼 𐑄𐐰𐐻 𐐸𐐶𐐮𐐽 𐐮𐑆 𐑀𐐳𐐼, 𐐺𐐨𐐿𐐫𐑆 𐐱𐑂 𐐷𐐭𐑉 𐐯𐐿𐑅𐐨𐐼𐐮𐑍𐑊𐐨 𐑀𐑉𐐩𐐻 𐑉𐐮𐐽𐐯𐑆; 𐐷𐐩, 𐐶𐐬 𐐺𐐨 𐐲𐑌𐐻𐐭 𐐷𐐭 𐐺𐐨𐐿𐐫𐑆 𐐱𐑂 𐐷𐐭𐑉 𐐶𐐮𐐿𐐯𐐼𐑌𐐯𐑅 𐐰𐑌𐐼 𐐲𐐺𐐱𐑋𐐮𐑌𐐩𐑇𐐲𐑌𐑆. 𐐈𐑌𐐼 𐐯𐐿𐑅𐐯𐐹𐐻 𐐷𐐨 𐑉𐐨𐐹𐐯𐑌𐐻 𐐷𐐨 𐑇𐐰𐑊 𐐹𐐯𐑉𐐮𐑇; 𐐷𐐩, 𐐨𐑂𐐲𐑌 𐐷𐐭𐑉 𐑊𐐰𐑌𐐼𐑆 𐑇𐐰𐑊 𐐺𐐨 𐐻𐐩𐐿𐐲𐑌 𐑁𐑉𐐱𐑋 𐐷𐐭, 𐐰𐑌𐐼 𐐷𐐨 𐑇𐐰𐑊 𐐺𐐨 𐐼𐐯𐑅𐐻𐑉𐑎𐐼 𐑁𐑉𐐱𐑋 𐐫𐑁 𐑄 𐑁𐐩𐑅 𐐱𐑂 𐑄 𐐲𐑉𐑃. 𐐒𐐨𐐸𐐬𐑊𐐼 𐑌𐐵, 𐐴 𐐼𐐭 𐑌𐐱𐐻 𐑅𐐩 𐑄𐐰𐐻 𐑄𐐨𐑆 𐑃𐐮𐑍𐑆 𐑇𐐰𐑊 𐐺𐐨, 𐐱𐑂 𐑋𐐴𐑅𐐯𐑊𐑁, 𐐺𐐨𐐿𐐫𐑆 𐐮𐐻 𐐮𐑆 𐑌𐐱𐐻 𐐱𐑂 𐑋𐐴𐑅𐐯𐑊𐑁 𐑄𐐰𐐻 𐐴 𐑌𐐬 𐑄𐐨𐑆 𐑃𐐮𐑍𐑆; 𐐺𐐲𐐻 𐐺𐐨𐐸𐐬𐑊𐐼, 𐐴 𐑌𐐬 𐑄𐐰𐐻 𐑄𐐨𐑆 𐑃𐐮𐑍𐑆 𐐪𐑉 𐐻𐑉𐐭 𐐺𐐨𐐿𐐫𐑆 𐑄 𐐢𐐫𐑉𐐼 𐐘𐐱𐐼 𐐸𐐰𐑆 𐑋𐐩𐐼 𐑄𐐯𐑋 𐑌𐐬𐑌 𐐲𐑌𐐻𐐭 𐑋𐐨, 𐑄𐐯𐑉𐑁𐐬𐑉 𐐴 𐐻𐐯𐑅𐐻𐐮𐑁𐐴 𐑄𐐰𐐻 𐑄𐐩 𐑇𐐰𐑊 𐐺𐐨.

3. 𐐈𐑌𐐼 𐑌𐐵 𐐮𐐻 𐐿𐐩𐑋 𐐻𐐭 𐐹𐐰𐑅 𐑄𐐰𐐻 𐐸𐐶𐐯𐑌 𐐤𐐨𐑁𐐴 𐐸𐐰𐐼 𐑅𐐯𐐼 𐑄𐐨𐑆 𐐶𐐲𐑉𐐼𐑆, 𐐺𐐨𐐸𐐬𐑊𐐼 𐑄𐐯𐑉 𐐶𐐲𐑉 𐑋𐐯𐑌 𐐸𐐶𐐮𐐽 𐐶𐐲𐑉 𐐾𐐲𐐾𐐯𐑆, 𐐸𐐶𐐮𐐽 𐐫𐑊𐑅𐐬 𐐺𐐨𐑊𐐱𐑍𐐼 𐐻𐐭 𐑄 𐑅𐐨𐐿𐑉𐐯𐐻 𐐺𐐰𐑌𐐼 𐐱𐑂 𐐘𐐰𐐼𐐨𐐰𐑌𐐻𐐲𐑌; 𐐰𐑌𐐼 𐑄𐐩 𐐶𐐲𐑉 𐐰𐑍𐑀𐑉𐐨, 𐐰𐑌𐐼 𐑄𐐩 𐐿𐑉𐐴𐐼 𐐵𐐻 𐐲𐑀𐐯𐑌𐑅𐐻 𐐸𐐮𐑋, 𐑅𐐩𐐮𐑍 𐐲𐑌𐐻𐐭 𐑄 𐐹𐐨𐐹𐑊, 𐐐𐐶𐐴 𐐼𐐭 𐐷𐐨 𐑌𐐱𐐻 𐑅𐐨𐑆 𐐲𐐹𐐱𐑌 𐑄𐐮𐑅 𐑋𐐰𐑌 𐐰𐑌𐐼 𐐺𐑉𐐮𐑍 𐐸𐐮𐑋 𐑁𐐬𐑉𐑃, 𐑄𐐰𐐻 𐐸𐐨 𐑋𐐩 𐐺𐐨 𐐿𐐱𐑌𐐼𐐯𐑋𐐼 𐐰𐐿𐐫𐑉𐐼𐐮𐑍 𐐻𐐭 𐑄 𐐿𐑉𐐴𐑋 𐐸𐐶𐐮𐐽 𐐸𐐨 𐐸𐐰𐑆 𐐼𐐲𐑌? 𐐐𐐶𐐴 𐑅𐐨𐐯𐑅𐐻 𐑄𐐵 𐑄𐐮𐑅 𐑋𐐰𐑌, 𐐰𐑌𐐼 𐐸𐐨𐑉𐐯𐑅𐐻 𐐸𐐮𐑋 𐑉𐐨𐑂𐐴𐑊 𐐲𐑀𐐯𐑌𐑅𐐻 𐑄𐐮𐑅 𐐹𐐨𐐹𐑊 𐐰𐑌𐐼 𐐲𐑀𐐯𐑌𐑅𐐻 𐐵𐑉 𐑊𐐫? 𐐙𐐬𐑉 𐐺𐐨𐐸𐐬𐑊𐐼, 𐐤𐐨𐑁𐐴 𐐸𐐰𐐼 𐑅𐐹𐐬𐐿𐐲𐑌 𐐲𐑌𐐻𐐭 𐑄𐐯𐑋 𐐿𐐱𐑌𐑅𐐲𐑉𐑌𐐮𐑍 𐑄 𐐿𐐱𐑉𐐲𐐹𐐻𐑌𐐯𐑅 𐐱𐑂 𐑄𐐯𐑉 𐑊𐐫; 𐐷𐐩, 𐑋𐐯𐑌𐐨 𐑃𐐮𐑍𐑆 𐐼𐐮𐐼 𐐤𐐨𐑁𐐴 𐑅𐐹𐐨𐐿 𐐸𐐶𐐮𐐽 𐐿𐐰𐑌𐐱𐐻 𐐺𐐨 𐑉𐐮𐐻𐐲𐑌; 𐐰𐑌𐐼 𐑌𐐲𐑃𐐮𐑍 𐐼𐐮𐐼 𐐸𐐨 𐑅𐐹𐐨𐐿 𐐸𐐶𐐮𐐽 𐐶𐐱𐑆 𐐿𐐱𐑌𐐻𐑉𐐯𐑉𐐨 𐐻𐐭 𐑄 𐐿𐐱𐑋𐐰𐑌𐐼𐑋𐐯𐑌𐐻𐑅 𐐱𐑂 𐐘𐐱𐐼. 𐐈𐑌𐐼 𐑄𐐬𐑆 𐐾𐐲𐐾𐐯𐑆 𐐶𐐲𐑉 𐐰𐑍𐑀𐑉𐐨 𐐶𐐮𐑄 𐐸𐐮𐑋 𐐺𐐨𐐿𐐫𐑆 𐐸𐐨 𐑅𐐹𐐩𐐿 𐐹𐑊𐐩𐑌𐑊𐐨 𐐲𐑌𐐻𐐭 𐑄𐐯𐑋 𐐿𐐱𐑌𐑅𐐲𐑉𐑌𐐮𐑍 𐑄𐐯𐑉 𐑅𐐨𐐿𐑉𐐯𐐻 𐐶𐐲𐑉𐐿𐑅 𐐱𐑂 𐐼𐐪𐑉𐐿𐑌𐐯𐑅; 𐑌𐐯𐑂𐐲𐑉𐑄𐐯𐑊𐐯𐑅 𐑄𐐩 𐐼𐐲𐑉𐑅𐐻 𐑌𐐱𐐻 𐑊𐐩 𐑄𐐯𐑉 𐐬𐑌 𐐸𐐰𐑌𐐼𐑆 𐐲𐐹𐐱𐑌 𐐸𐐮𐑋, 𐑁𐐬𐑉 𐑄𐐩 𐑁𐐨𐑉𐐼 𐑄 𐐹𐐨𐐹𐑊 𐑊𐐯𐑅𐐻 𐑄𐐩 𐑇𐐳𐐼 𐐿𐑉𐐴 𐐵𐐻 𐐲𐑀𐐯𐑌𐑅𐐻 𐑄𐐯𐑋; 𐑄𐐯𐑉𐑁𐐬𐑉 𐑄𐐩 𐐼𐐮𐐼 𐐿𐑉𐐴 𐐲𐑌𐐻𐐭 𐑄 𐐹𐐨𐐹𐑊, 𐑅𐐩𐐮𐑍, 𐐐𐐶𐐴 𐐼𐐭 𐐷𐐭 𐑅𐐲𐑁𐐲𐑉 𐑄𐐮𐑅 𐑋𐐰𐑌 𐐻𐐭 𐑉𐐨𐑂𐐴𐑊 𐐲𐑀𐐯𐑌𐑅𐐻 𐐲𐑅? 𐐙𐐬𐑉 𐐺𐐨𐐸𐐬𐑊𐐼 𐐸𐐨 𐐼𐐲𐑃 𐐿𐐱𐑌𐐼𐐯𐑋 𐐫𐑊 𐑄𐐮𐑅 𐐹𐐨𐐹𐑊, 𐐨𐑂𐐲𐑌 𐐲𐑌𐐻𐐭 𐐼𐐯𐑅𐐻𐑉𐐲𐐿𐑇𐐲𐑌; 𐐷𐐩, 𐐰𐑌𐐼 𐐫𐑊𐑅𐐬 𐑄𐐰𐐻 𐑄𐐨𐑆 𐐵𐑉 𐑀𐑉𐐩𐐻 𐑅𐐮𐐻𐐮𐑆 𐑇𐐰𐑊 𐐺𐐨 𐐻𐐩𐐿𐐲𐑌 𐑁𐑉𐐱𐑋 𐐲𐑅, 𐑄𐐰𐐻 𐐶𐐨 𐑇𐐰𐑊 𐐸𐐰𐑂 𐑌𐐬 𐐹𐑊𐐩𐑅 𐐮𐑌 𐑄𐐯𐑋. 𐐈𐑌𐐼 𐑌𐐵 𐐶𐐨 𐑌𐐬 𐑄𐐰𐐻 𐑄𐐮𐑅 𐐮𐑆 𐐮𐑋𐐹𐐱𐑅𐐮𐐺𐑊, 𐑁𐐬𐑉 𐐺𐐨𐐸𐐬𐑊𐐼, 𐐶𐐨 𐐪𐑉 𐐹𐐵𐐲𐑉𐑁𐐳𐑊, 𐐰𐑌𐐼 𐐵𐑉 𐑅𐐮𐐻𐐮𐑆 𐑀𐑉𐐩𐐻, 𐑄𐐯𐑉𐑁𐐬𐑉 𐐵𐑉 𐐯𐑌𐐯𐑋𐐮𐑆 𐐿𐐰𐑌 𐐸𐐰𐑂 𐑌𐐬 𐐹𐐵𐐲𐑉 𐐬𐑂𐐲𐑉 𐐲𐑅.

4. 𐐈𐑌𐐼 𐐮𐐻 𐐿𐐩𐑋 𐐻𐐭 𐐹𐐰𐑅 𐑄𐐰𐐻 𐑄𐐲𐑅 𐑄𐐩 𐐼𐐮𐐼 𐑅𐐻𐐲𐑉 𐐲𐐹 𐑄 𐐹𐐨𐐹𐑊 𐐻𐐭 𐐰𐑍𐑀𐐲𐑉 𐐲𐑀𐐯𐑌𐑅𐐻 𐐤𐐨𐑁𐐴, 𐐰𐑌𐐼 𐑉𐐩𐑆𐐼 𐐿𐐱𐑌𐐻𐐯𐑌𐑇𐐲𐑌𐑆 𐐲𐑋𐐲𐑍 𐑄𐐯𐑋; 𐑁𐐬𐑉 𐑄𐐯𐑉 𐐶𐐲𐑉 𐑅𐐲𐑋 𐐸𐐭 𐐼𐐮𐐼 𐐿𐑉𐐴 𐐵𐐻, 𐐢𐐯𐐻 𐑄𐐮𐑅 𐑋𐐰𐑌 𐐲𐑊𐐬𐑌, 𐑁𐐬𐑉 𐐸𐐨 𐐮𐑆 𐐲 𐑀𐐳𐐼 𐑋𐐰𐑌, 𐐰𐑌𐐼 𐑄𐐬𐑆 𐑃𐐮𐑍𐑆 𐐸𐐶𐐮𐐽 𐐸𐐨 𐑅𐐯𐑃 𐐶𐐮𐑊 𐑇𐐭𐑉𐑊𐐨 𐐿𐐲𐑋 𐐻𐐭 𐐹𐐰𐑅 𐐯𐐿𐑅𐐯𐐹𐐻 𐐶𐐨 𐑉𐐨𐐹𐐯𐑌𐐻; 𐐷𐐩, 𐐺𐐨𐐸𐐬𐑊𐐼, 𐐫𐑊 𐑄 𐐾𐐲𐐾𐑋𐐯𐑌𐐻𐑅 𐐶𐐮𐑊 𐐿𐐲𐑋 𐐲𐐹𐐱𐑌 𐐲𐑅 𐐸𐐶𐐮𐐽 𐐸𐐨 𐐸𐐰𐑆 𐐻𐐯𐑅𐐻𐐮𐑁𐐴𐐼 𐐲𐑌𐐻𐐭 𐐲𐑅; 𐑁𐐬𐑉 𐐶𐐨 𐑌𐐬 𐑄𐐰𐐻 𐐸𐐨 𐐸𐐰𐑆 𐐻𐐯𐑅𐐻𐐮𐑁𐐴𐐼 𐐲𐑉𐐴𐐻 𐐲𐑌𐐻𐐭 𐐲𐑅 𐐿𐐱𐑌𐑅𐐲𐑉𐑌𐐮𐑍 𐐵𐑉 𐐮𐑌𐐮𐐿𐐶𐐮𐐻𐐮𐑆. 𐐈𐑌𐐼 𐐺𐐨𐐸𐐬𐑊𐐼 𐑄𐐩 𐐪𐑉 𐑋𐐯𐑌𐐨, 𐐰𐑌𐐼 𐐸𐐨 𐑌𐐬𐐯𐑃 𐐰𐑆 𐐶𐐯𐑊 𐐫𐑊 𐑃𐐮𐑍𐑆 𐐸𐐶𐐮𐐽 𐑇𐐰𐑊 𐐺𐐨𐑁𐐫𐑊 𐐲𐑅 𐐰𐑆 𐐸𐐨 𐑌𐐬𐐯𐑃 𐐱𐑂 𐐵𐑉 𐐮𐑌𐐮𐐿𐐶𐐮𐐻𐐮𐑆; 𐐷𐐩, 𐐰𐑌𐐼 𐐺𐐨𐐸𐐬𐑊𐐼, 𐐮𐑁 𐐸𐐨 𐐸𐐰𐐼 𐑌𐐱𐐻 𐐺𐐮𐑌 𐐲 𐐹𐑉𐐱𐑁𐐯𐐻 𐐸𐐨 𐐿𐐳𐐼 𐑌𐐱𐐻 𐐸𐐰𐑂 𐐻𐐯𐑅𐐻𐐮𐑁𐐴𐐼 𐐿𐐱𐑌𐑅𐐲𐑉𐑌𐐮𐑍 𐑄𐐬𐑆 𐑃𐐮𐑍𐑆. 𐐈𐑌𐐼 𐐮𐐻 𐐿𐐩𐑋 𐐻𐐭 𐐹𐐰𐑅 𐑄𐐰𐐻 𐑄𐐬𐑆 𐐹𐐨𐐹𐑊 𐐸𐐭 𐑅𐐫𐐻 𐐻𐐭 𐐼𐐯𐑅𐐻𐑉𐑎 𐐤𐐨𐑁𐐴 𐐶𐐲𐑉 𐐿𐐱𐑋𐐹𐐯𐑊𐐼 𐐺𐐨𐐿𐐫𐑆 𐐱𐑂 𐑄𐐯𐑉 𐑁𐐨𐑉, 𐑄𐐰𐐻 𐑄𐐩 𐐼𐐮𐐼 𐑌𐐱𐐻 𐑊𐐩 𐑄𐐯𐑉 𐐸𐐰𐑌𐐼𐑆 𐐱𐑌 𐐸𐐮𐑋; 𐑄𐐯𐑉𐑁𐐬𐑉 𐐸𐐨 𐐺𐐨𐑀𐐰𐑌 𐐲𐑀𐐯𐑌 𐐻𐐭 𐑅𐐹𐐨𐐿 𐐲𐑌𐐻𐐭 𐑄𐐯𐑋, 𐑅𐐨𐐮𐑍 𐑄𐐰𐐻 𐐸𐐨 𐐸𐐰𐐼 𐑀𐐩𐑌𐐼 𐑁𐐩𐑂𐐲𐑉 𐐮𐑌 𐑄 𐐴𐑆 𐐱𐑂 𐑅𐐲𐑋, 𐐮𐑌𐑅𐐬𐑋𐐲𐐽 𐑄𐐰𐐻 𐑄 𐑉𐐨𐑋𐐩𐑌𐐼𐐲𐑉 𐐱𐑂 𐑄𐐯𐑋 𐐼𐐮𐐼 𐑁𐐨𐑉; 𐑄𐐯𐑉𐑁𐐬𐑉 𐐸𐐨 𐐶𐐱𐑆 𐐿𐐱𐑌𐑅𐐻𐑉𐐩𐑌𐐼 𐐻𐐭 𐑅𐐹𐐨𐐿 𐑋𐐬𐑉 𐐲𐑌𐐻𐐭 𐑄𐐯𐑋, 𐑅𐐩𐐮𐑍, 𐐒𐐨𐐸𐐬𐑊𐐼 𐑋𐐴 𐐺𐑉𐐯𐑄𐑉𐐯𐑌, 𐐸𐐰𐑂 𐐷𐐨 𐑌𐐱𐐻 𐑉𐐯𐐼 𐑄𐐰𐐻 𐐘𐐱𐐼 𐑀𐐩𐑂 𐐹𐐵𐐲𐑉 𐐲𐑌𐐻𐐭 𐐶𐐲𐑌 𐑋𐐰𐑌, 𐐨𐑂𐐲𐑌 𐐣𐐬𐑆𐐯𐑆, 𐐻𐐭 𐑅𐑋𐐴𐐻 𐐲𐐹𐐱𐑌 𐑄 𐐶𐐫𐐻𐐲𐑉𐑆 𐐱𐑂 𐑄 𐐡𐐯𐐼 𐐝𐐨, 𐐰𐑌𐐼 𐑄𐐩 𐐹𐐪𐑉𐐻𐐯𐐼 𐐸𐐮𐑄𐐲𐑉 𐐰𐑌𐐼 𐑄𐐮𐑄𐐲𐑉, 𐐮𐑌𐑅𐐬𐑋𐐲𐐽 𐑄𐐰𐐻 𐑄 𐐆𐑆𐑉𐐩𐐯𐑊-

𐐴𐐻𐑅, 𐐸𐐭 𐐶𐐲𐑉 𐐵𐑉 𐑁𐐪𐑄𐐲𐑉𐑆, 𐐿𐐩𐑋 𐑃𐑉𐐭 𐐲𐐹𐐱𐑌 𐐼𐑉𐐴 𐑀𐑉𐐵𐑌𐐼, 𐐰𐑌𐐼 𐑄 𐐶𐐫𐐻𐐲𐑉𐑆 𐐿𐑊𐐬𐑆𐐼 𐐲𐐹𐐱𐑌 𐑄 𐐪𐑉𐑋𐐨𐑆 𐐲𐑂 𐑄 𐐀𐐾𐐮𐐹𐑇𐐲𐑌𐑆 𐐰𐑌𐐼 𐑅𐐶𐐱𐑊𐐬𐐼 𐑄𐐯𐑋 𐐲𐐹?

5. 𐐈𐑌𐐼 𐑌𐐵 𐐺𐐨𐐸𐐬𐑊𐐼, 𐐮𐑁 𐐘𐐱𐐼 𐑀𐐩𐑂 𐐲𐑌𐐻𐐭 𐑄𐐮𐑅 𐑋𐐰𐑌 𐑅𐐲𐐽 𐐹𐐵𐐲𐑉, 𐑄𐐯𐑌 𐐸𐐶𐐴 𐑇𐐳𐐼 𐐷 𐐼𐐮𐑅𐐹𐐷𐐭𐐻 𐐲𐑋𐐲𐑍 𐐷𐐫𐑉𐑅𐐯𐑊𐑂𐑆, 𐐰𐑌𐐼 𐑅𐐩 𐑄𐐰𐐻 𐐸𐐨 𐐸𐐰𐑃 𐑀𐐮𐑂𐐲𐑌 𐐲𐑌𐐻𐐭 𐑋𐐨 𐑌𐐬 𐐹𐐵𐐲𐑉 𐐸𐐶𐐯𐑉𐐺𐐴 𐐌 𐑋𐐩 𐑌𐐬 𐐿𐐱𐑌𐑅𐐲𐑉𐑌𐐮𐑍 𐑄 𐐾𐐲𐐾𐑋𐐲𐑌𐐻𐑅 𐑄𐐰𐐻 𐑇𐐰𐑊 𐐿𐐲𐑋 𐐲𐐹𐐱𐑌 𐐷𐐭 𐐯𐐿𐑅𐐯𐐹𐐻 𐐷 𐑉𐐨𐐹𐐯𐑌𐐻? 𐐒𐐲𐐻, 𐐺𐐨𐐸𐐬𐑊𐐼, 𐐷 𐑌𐐱𐐻 𐐬𐑌𐑊𐐨 𐐼𐐨𐑌𐐴 𐑋𐐴 𐐶𐐲𐑉𐐼𐑆, 𐐺𐐲𐐻 𐐷 𐐫𐑊𐑅𐐬 𐐼𐐨𐑌𐐴 𐐫𐑊 𐑄 𐐶𐐲𐑉𐐼𐑆 𐐸𐐶𐐮𐐽 𐐸𐐰𐑂 𐐺𐐨𐑌 𐑅𐐹𐐬𐐿𐐲𐑌 𐐺𐐴 𐐵𐑉 𐑁𐐪𐑄𐐲𐑉𐑆, 𐐰𐑌𐐼 𐐫𐑊𐑅𐐬 𐑄 𐐶𐐲𐑉𐐼𐑆 𐐸𐐶𐐮𐐽 𐐶𐐲𐑉 𐑅𐐹𐐬𐐿𐐲𐑌 𐐺𐐴 𐑄𐐮𐑅 𐑋𐐰𐑌, 𐐣𐐬𐑆𐐯𐑆, 𐐸𐐭 𐐸𐐰𐐼 𐑅𐐲𐐽 𐑀𐑉𐐩𐐻 𐐹𐐵𐐲𐑉 𐑀𐐮𐑂𐐲𐑌 𐐲𐑌𐐻𐐭 𐐸𐐮𐑋; 𐐷𐐩, 𐑄 𐐶𐐲𐑉𐐼𐑆 𐐸𐐶𐐮𐐽 𐐸𐐨 𐐸𐐰𐑃 𐑅𐐹𐐬𐐿𐐲𐑌 𐐿𐐱𐑌𐑅𐐲𐑉𐑌𐐮𐑍 𐑄 𐐿𐐲𐑋𐐮𐑍 𐐲𐑂 𐑄 𐐣𐐯𐑅𐐴𐐲. 𐐏𐐩, 𐐼𐐮𐐼 𐐸𐐨 𐑌𐐱𐐻 𐐺𐐩𐑉 𐑉𐐯𐐿𐐲𐑉𐐼 𐑄𐐰𐐻 𐑄 𐐝𐐲𐑌 𐐲𐑂 𐐘𐐱𐐼 𐑇𐐳𐐼 𐐿𐐲𐑋? 𐐈𐑌𐐼 𐐰𐑆 𐐸𐐨 𐑊𐐮𐑁𐐻𐐲𐐼 𐐲𐐹 𐑄 𐐺𐑉𐐩𐑆𐐲𐑌 𐑅𐐲𐑉𐐹𐐲𐑌𐐻 𐐮𐑌 𐑄 𐐶𐐮𐑊𐐼𐐲𐑉𐑌𐐯𐑅, 𐐨𐑂𐐲𐑌 𐑅𐐬 𐑇𐐰𐑊 𐐸𐐨 𐐺𐐨 𐑊𐐮𐑁𐐻𐐲𐐼 𐐲𐐹 𐐸𐐭 𐑇𐐳𐐼 𐐿𐐲𐑋. 𐐈𐑌𐐼 𐐰𐑆 𐑋𐐯𐑌𐐨 𐐰𐑆 𐑇𐐳𐐼 𐑊𐐳𐐿 𐐲𐐹𐐱𐑌 𐑄𐐰𐐻 𐑅𐐲𐑉𐐹𐐲𐑌𐐻 𐑇𐐳𐐼 𐑊𐐮𐑂, 𐐨𐑂𐐲𐑌 𐑅𐐬 𐐰𐑆 𐑋𐐯𐑌𐐨 𐐰𐑆 𐑇𐐳𐐼 𐑊𐐳𐐿 𐐲𐐹𐐱𐑌 𐑄 𐐝𐐲𐑌 𐐲𐑂 𐐘𐐱𐐼 𐐶𐐮𐑄 𐑁𐐩𐑃, 𐐸𐐰𐑂𐐮𐑍 𐐩 𐐿𐐱𐑌𐐻𐑉𐐴𐐻 𐑅𐐹𐐮𐑉𐐮𐐻, 𐑋𐐴𐐻 𐑊𐐮𐑂, 𐐨𐑂𐐲𐑌 𐐲𐑌𐐻𐐭 𐑄𐐰𐐻 𐑊𐐴𐑁 𐐸𐐶𐐮𐐽 𐐮𐑆 𐐨𐐻𐐲𐑉𐑌𐐲𐑊.

6. 𐐈𐑌𐐼 𐑌𐐵 𐐺𐐨𐐸𐐬𐑊𐐼, 𐐣𐐬𐑆𐐯𐑆 𐐼𐐮𐐼 𐑌𐐱𐐻 𐐬𐑌𐑊𐐨 𐐻𐐯𐑅𐐻𐐮𐑁𐐴 𐐲𐑂 𐑄𐐨𐑆 𐑃𐐮𐑍𐑆, 𐐺𐐲𐐻 𐐫𐑊𐑅𐐬 𐐫𐑊 𐑄 𐐸𐐬𐑊𐐨 𐐹𐑉𐐱𐑁𐐲𐐻𐑅, 𐑁𐑉𐐱𐑋 𐐸𐐮𐑆 𐐼𐐩𐑆, 𐐨𐑂𐐲𐑌 𐐻𐐭 𐑄 𐐼𐐩𐑆 𐐲𐑂 𐐁𐐺𐑉𐐲𐐸𐐰𐑋. 𐐏𐐩, 𐐰𐑌𐐼 𐐺𐐨𐐸𐐬𐑊𐐼, 𐐁𐐺𐑉𐐲𐐸𐐰𐑋 𐑅𐐫 𐐲𐑂 𐐸𐐮𐑆 𐐿𐐲𐑋𐐮𐑍, 𐐰𐑌𐐼 𐐶𐐱𐑆 𐑁𐐮𐑊𐐼 𐐶𐐮𐑄 𐑀𐑊𐐰𐐼𐑌𐐯𐑅 𐐰𐑌𐐼 𐐼𐐮𐐼 𐑉𐐨𐐾𐐱𐐮𐑅. 𐐏𐐩, 𐐰𐑌𐐼 𐐺𐐨𐐸𐐬𐑊𐐼 𐐌 𐑅𐐩 𐐲𐑌𐐻𐐭 𐐷𐐭, 𐑄𐐰𐐻 𐐁𐐺𐑉𐐲𐐸𐐰𐑋 𐑌𐐱𐐻 𐐬𐑌𐑊𐐨 𐑌𐐭 𐐲𐑂 𐑄𐐨𐑆 𐑃𐐮𐑍𐑆, 𐐺𐐲𐐻 𐑄𐐯𐑉 𐐶𐐲𐑉 𐑋𐐯𐑌𐐨 𐐺𐐨𐑁𐐬𐑉 𐑄 𐐼𐐩𐑆 𐐲𐑂 𐐁𐐺𐑉𐐲𐐸𐐰𐑋, 𐐸𐐭 𐐶𐐲𐑉 𐐿𐐫𐑊𐐼 𐐺𐐴 𐑄 𐐫𐑉𐐼𐐲𐑉 𐐲𐑂 𐐘𐐱𐐼; 𐐷𐐩, 𐐨𐑂𐐲𐑌 𐐰𐑁𐐻𐐲𐑉 𐑄 𐐫𐑉𐐼𐐲𐑉 𐐲𐑂 𐐸𐐮𐑆 𐐝𐐲𐑌; 𐐰𐑌𐐼 𐑄𐐮𐑅 𐑄𐐰𐐻 𐐮𐐻 𐑇𐐳𐐼 𐐺𐐨 𐑇𐐬𐑌 𐐲𐑌𐐻𐐭 𐑄 𐐹𐐨𐐹𐑊 𐐩 𐑀𐑉𐐩𐐻 𐑋𐐯𐑌𐐨 𐑃𐐵𐑆𐐲𐑌𐐼 𐐷𐐨𐑉𐑆 𐐺𐐨𐑁𐐬𐑉 𐐸𐐮𐑆 𐐿𐐲𐑋𐐮𐑍, 𐑄𐐰𐐻 𐐨𐑂𐐲𐑌 𐑉𐐨𐐼𐐯𐑋𐑇𐐲𐑌 𐑇𐐳𐐼 𐐿𐐲𐑋 𐐲𐑌𐐻𐐭 𐑄𐐯𐑋. 𐐈𐑌𐐼 𐑌𐐵 𐐌 𐐶𐐳𐐼 𐑄𐐰𐐻 𐐷 𐑇𐐳𐐼 𐑌𐐬, 𐑄𐐰𐐻 𐐨𐑂𐐲𐑌 𐑅𐐮𐑌𐑅 𐑄 𐐼𐐩𐑆 𐐲𐑂 𐐁𐐺𐑉𐐲𐐸𐐰𐑋, 𐑄𐐯𐑉 𐐸𐐰𐑂 𐐺𐐨𐑌 𐑋𐐯𐑌𐐨 𐐹𐑉𐐱𐑁𐐲𐐻𐑅 𐑄𐐰𐐻 𐐸𐐰𐑃 𐐻𐐯𐑅𐐻𐐮𐑁𐐴𐐼 𐑄𐐨𐑆 𐑃𐐮𐑍𐑆; 𐐷𐐩, 𐐺𐐨𐐸𐐬𐑊𐐼, 𐑄 𐐹𐑉𐐱𐑁𐐲𐐻 𐐞𐐨𐑌𐐱𐑅 𐐼𐐮𐐼 𐐻𐐯𐑅𐐻𐐮𐑁𐐴 𐐺𐐬𐑊𐐼𐑊𐐨; 𐑁𐐫𐑉 𐑄 𐐸𐐶𐐮𐐽 𐐸𐐨 𐐶𐐱𐑆 𐑅𐑊𐐩𐑌. 𐐈𐑌𐐼 𐐺𐐨𐐸𐐬𐑊𐐼, 𐐫𐑊𐑅𐐬 𐐞𐐨𐑌𐐱𐐿, 𐐰𐑌𐐼 𐐫𐑊𐑅𐐬 𐐀𐑆𐐴𐐲𐑅, 𐐰𐑌𐐼 𐐫𐑊𐑅𐐬 𐐌𐑆𐐩𐐲, 𐐰𐑌𐐼 𐐖𐐯𐑉𐐯𐑋𐐴𐐲. (𐐖𐐯𐑉𐐯𐑋𐐴𐐲 𐐺𐐨𐐮𐑍 𐑄𐐰𐐻 𐑅𐐩𐑋 𐐹𐑉𐐱𐑁𐐲𐐻 𐐸𐐭 𐐻𐐯𐑅𐐻𐐮𐑁𐐴𐐼 𐐲𐑂 𐑄 𐐼𐐨𐑅𐐻𐑉𐐲𐐿𐑇𐐲𐑌 𐐲𐑂 𐐖𐐲𐑉𐐭𐑅𐐲𐑊𐐯𐑋.) 𐐈𐑌𐐼 𐑌𐐵 𐐶𐐨 𐑌𐐬 𐑄𐐰𐐻 𐐖𐐲𐑉𐐭𐑅𐐲𐑊𐐯𐑋 𐐶𐐱𐑆 𐐼𐐨𐑅𐐻𐑉𐐱𐐮𐐼 𐐲𐐿𐐫𐑉𐐼𐐮𐑍 𐐻𐐭 𐑄 𐐶𐐲𐑉𐐼𐑆 𐐲𐑂 𐐖𐐯𐑉𐐯𐑋𐐴𐐲. 𐐄 𐑄𐐯𐑌, 𐐸𐐶𐐴 𐑌𐐱𐐻 𐑄 𐐝𐐲𐑌 𐐲𐑂 𐐘𐐱𐐼 𐐿𐐲𐑋, 𐐲𐐿𐐫𐑉𐐼𐐮𐑍 𐐻𐐭 𐐸𐐮𐑆 𐐹𐑉𐐱𐑁𐐯𐑅𐐨? 𐐈𐑌𐐼 𐑌𐐵 𐐶𐐮𐑊 𐐷𐐭 𐐼𐐮𐑅𐐹𐐷𐐭𐐻 𐑄𐐰𐐻 𐐖𐐲𐑉𐐭𐑅𐐲𐑊𐐯𐑋 𐐶𐐱𐑆 𐐼𐐨𐑅𐐻𐑉𐐱𐐮𐐼? 𐐎𐐮𐑊 𐐷 𐑅𐐩 𐑄𐐰𐐻 𐑄 𐑅𐐲𐑌𐑆 𐐲𐑂 𐐞𐐯𐐼𐐯𐐿𐐴𐐲 𐐶𐐲𐑉 𐑌𐐱𐐻 𐑅𐑊𐐩𐑌, 𐐫𐑊 𐐯𐐿𐑅𐐯𐐹𐐻 𐐮𐐻 𐐶𐐲𐑉 𐐣𐐷𐐭𐑊𐐯𐐿? 𐐏𐐩, 𐐰𐑌𐐼 𐐼𐐭 𐐷 𐑌𐐱𐐻 𐐺𐐨𐐸𐐬𐑊𐐼 𐑄𐐰𐐻 𐑄 𐑅𐐨𐐼 𐐲𐑂 𐐞𐐯𐐼𐐯𐐿𐐴𐐲 𐐪𐑉 𐐶𐐮𐑄 𐐲𐑅, 𐐰𐑌𐐼 𐑄𐐩 𐐶𐐲𐑉 𐐼𐑉𐐮𐑂𐐲𐑌 𐐵𐐻 𐐲𐑂 𐑄 𐑊𐐰𐑌𐐼 𐐲𐑂 𐐖𐐲𐑉𐐭𐑅𐐲𐑊𐐯𐑋? 𐐒𐐲𐐻 𐐺𐐨𐐸𐐬𐑊𐐼, 𐑄𐐮𐑅 𐐮𐑆 𐑌𐐱𐐻 𐐫𐑊. 𐐆𐑉 𐑁𐐪𐑄𐐲𐑉 𐐢𐐨𐐸𐐴 𐐶𐐱𐑆 𐐼𐑉𐐮𐑂𐐲𐑌 𐐵𐐻 𐐲𐑂 𐐖𐐲𐑉𐐭𐑅𐐲𐑊𐐯𐑋 𐐺𐐨𐐿𐐫𐑆 𐐸𐐨 𐐻𐐯𐑅𐐻𐐮𐑁𐐴𐐼 𐐲𐑂 𐑄𐐨𐑆 𐑃𐐮𐑍𐑆. 𐐤𐐨𐑁𐐴 𐐫𐑊𐑅𐐬 𐐻𐐯𐑅𐐻𐐮𐑁𐐴𐐼 𐐲𐑂 𐑄𐐨𐑆 𐑃𐐮𐑍𐑆, 𐐰𐑌𐐼 𐐫𐑊𐑅𐐬 𐐫𐑊𐑋𐐬𐑅𐐻 𐐫𐑊 𐐲𐑂 𐐵𐑉 𐑁𐐪𐑄𐐲𐑉𐑆, 𐐨𐑂𐐲𐑌 𐐼𐐵𐑌 𐐻𐐭 𐑄𐐮𐑅 𐐻𐐴𐑋; 𐐷𐐩, 𐑄𐐩 𐐸𐐰𐑂 𐐻𐐯𐑅𐐻𐐮𐑁𐐴𐐼 𐐲𐑂 𐑄 𐐿𐐲𐑋𐐮𐑍 𐐲𐑂 𐐗𐑉𐐴𐑅𐐻, 𐐰𐑌𐐼 𐐸𐐰𐑂 𐑊𐐳𐐿𐐻 𐑁𐐫𐑉𐐶𐐲𐑉𐐼, 𐐰𐑌𐐼 𐐸𐐰𐑂 𐑉𐐨𐐾𐐱𐐮𐑅𐐻 𐐮𐑌 𐐸𐐮𐑆 𐐼𐐩 𐐸𐐶𐐮𐐽 𐐮𐑆 𐐻𐐭 𐐿𐐲𐑋. 𐐈𐑌𐐼 𐐺𐐨𐐸𐐬𐑊𐐼, 𐐸𐐨 𐐮𐑆 𐐘𐐱𐐼, 𐐰𐑌𐐼 𐐸𐐨 𐐮𐑆 𐐶𐐮𐑄 𐑄𐐯𐑋, 𐐰𐑌𐐼 𐐸𐐨 𐐼𐐮𐐼 𐑋𐐰𐑌𐐮𐑁𐐯𐑅𐐻 𐐸𐐮𐑋𐑅𐐯𐑊𐑁 𐐲𐑌𐐻𐐭 𐑄𐐯𐑋, 𐑄𐐰𐐻 𐑄𐐩 𐐶𐐲𐑉 𐑉𐐨𐐼𐐨𐑋𐐼 𐐺𐐴 𐐸𐐮𐑋; 𐐰𐑌𐐼 𐑄𐐩 𐑀𐐩𐑂 𐐲𐑌𐐻𐐭 𐐸𐐮𐑋 𐑀𐑊𐐬𐑉𐐨, 𐐺𐐨𐐿𐐫𐑆 𐐲𐑂 𐑄𐐰𐐻 𐐸𐐶𐐮𐐽 𐐮𐑆 𐐻𐐭 𐐿𐐲𐑋. 𐐈𐑌𐐼 𐑌𐐵 𐑅𐐨𐐮𐑍 𐐷 𐑌𐐬 𐑄𐐨𐑆 𐑃𐐮𐑍𐑆, 𐐰𐑌𐐼 𐐿𐐰𐑌𐐱𐐻 𐐼𐐨𐑌𐐴 𐑄𐐯𐑋, 𐐯𐐿𐑅𐐯𐐹𐐻 𐐷 𐑇𐐰𐑊 𐑊𐐴, 𐑄𐐯𐑉𐑁𐐬𐑉 𐐮𐑌 𐑄𐐮𐑅 𐐷 𐐸𐐰𐑂 𐑅𐐮𐑌𐐼, 𐑁𐐫𐑉 𐐷 𐐸𐐰𐑂 𐑉𐐨𐐾𐐯𐐿𐐻𐐲𐐼 𐐫𐑊 𐑄𐐨𐑆 𐑃𐐮𐑍𐑆, 𐑌𐐱𐐻𐐶𐐮𐑄𐑅𐐻𐐰𐑌𐐼𐐮𐑍 𐑅𐐬 𐑋𐐯𐑌𐐨 𐐯𐑂𐐮𐐼𐐯𐑌𐑅𐐯𐑆 𐐸𐐶𐐮𐐽 𐐷 𐐸𐐰𐑂 𐑉𐐨𐑅𐐨𐑂𐐼; 𐐷𐐩, 𐐨𐑂𐐲𐑌 𐐷 𐐸𐐰𐑂 𐑉𐐨𐑅𐐨𐑂𐐼 𐐫𐑊 𐑃𐐮𐑍𐑆, 𐐺𐐬𐑃 𐑃𐐮𐑍𐑆 𐐮𐑌 𐐸𐐯𐑂𐐲𐑌, 𐐰𐑌𐐼 𐐫𐑊 𐑃𐐮𐑍𐑆 𐐸𐐶𐐮𐐽 𐐪𐑉 𐐮𐑌 𐑄 𐐲𐑉𐑃, 𐐰𐑆 𐐩 𐐶𐐮𐐻𐑌𐐯𐑅 𐑄𐐰𐐻 𐑄𐐩 𐐪𐑉 𐐻𐑉𐐭. 𐐒𐐲𐐻 𐐺𐐨𐐸𐐬𐑊𐐼, 𐐷 𐐸𐐰𐑂 𐑉𐐨𐐾𐐯𐐿𐐻𐐲𐐼 𐑄 𐐻𐑉𐐭𐑃, 𐐰𐑌𐐼 𐑉𐐨𐐺𐐯𐑊𐐼 𐐲𐑀𐐯𐑌𐑅𐐻 𐐷𐐫𐑉 𐐸𐐬𐑊𐐨 𐐘𐐱𐐼; 𐐰𐑌𐐼 𐐨𐑂𐐲𐑌 𐐰𐐻 𐑄𐐮𐑅 𐐻𐐴𐑋, 𐐮𐑌𐑅𐐻𐐯𐐼 𐐲𐑂 𐑊𐐩𐐮𐑍 𐐲𐐹 𐑁𐐫𐑉 𐐷𐐫𐑉𐑅𐐯𐑊𐑂𐑆 𐐻𐑉𐐯𐑈𐐲𐑉𐑆

𐐮𐑌 𐐸𐐯𐑂𐑌, 𐐸𐐶𐐯𐑉 𐑌𐐲𐑃𐐮𐑍 𐐼𐐲𐑃 𐐿𐐱𐑉𐐲𐐹𐐻, 𐐰𐑌𐐼 𐐸𐐶𐐯𐑉 𐑌𐐲𐑃𐐮𐑍 𐐿𐐰𐑌 𐐿𐐲𐑋 𐐸𐐶𐐮𐐽 𐐮𐑆 𐐲𐑌𐐿𐑊𐐨𐑌, 𐐷𐐨 𐐪𐑉 𐐸𐐨𐐹𐐮𐑍 𐐲𐐹 𐑁𐐫𐑉 𐐷𐐭𐑉𐑅𐐯𐑊𐑂𐑆 𐑉𐐪𐑃 𐐲𐑀𐐯𐑌𐑅𐐻 𐑄 𐐼𐐩 𐐱𐑂 𐐾𐐲𐐾𐑋𐐲𐑌𐐻; 𐐷𐐩, 𐐨𐑂𐑌 𐐰𐐻 𐑄𐐮𐑅 𐐻𐐴𐑋 𐐷𐐨 𐐪𐑉 𐑉𐐴𐐹𐐲𐑌𐐮𐑍 𐐺𐐨𐐿𐐫𐑆 𐐱𐑂 𐐷𐐭𐑉 𐑋𐐲𐑉𐐼𐐲𐑉𐑆 𐐰𐑌𐐼 𐐷𐐭𐑉 𐑁𐐫𐑉𐑌𐐮𐐿𐐩𐑇𐐲𐑌 𐐰𐑌𐐼 𐐶𐐮𐐿𐐯𐐼𐑌𐐯𐑅, 𐑁𐐫𐑉 𐐯𐑂𐐲𐑉𐑊𐐰𐑅𐐻𐐮𐑍 𐐼𐐯𐑅𐐻𐑉𐐲𐐿𐑇𐐲𐑌; 𐐷𐐩, 𐐰𐑌𐐼 𐐯𐐿𐑅𐐯𐐹𐐻 𐐷𐐨 𐑉𐐨𐐹𐐯𐑌𐐻, 𐐮𐐻 𐐶𐐮𐑊 𐐿𐐲𐑋 𐐲𐑌𐐻𐐭 𐐷𐐭 𐑅𐐭𐑌; 𐐷𐐩, 𐐺𐐨𐐸𐐬𐑊𐐼 𐐮𐐻 𐐮𐑆 𐑌𐐵 𐐨𐑂𐑌 𐐰𐐻 𐐷𐐭𐑉 𐐼𐐬𐑉𐑆; 𐐷𐐩, 𐑀𐐬 𐐷𐐨 𐐮𐑌 𐐲𐑌𐐻𐐭 𐑄 𐐾𐐲𐐾𐑋𐐲𐑌𐐻-𐑅𐐨𐐻, 𐐰𐑌𐐼 𐑅𐐲𐑉𐐽; 𐐰𐑌𐐼 𐐺𐐨𐐸𐐬𐑊𐐼, 𐐷𐐭𐑉 𐐾𐐲𐐾 𐐮𐑆 𐑋𐐲𐑉𐐼𐐲𐑉𐐼, 𐐰𐑌𐐼 𐐸𐐨 𐑊𐐴𐐯𐑃 𐐮𐑌 𐐸𐐮𐑆 𐐺𐑊𐐲𐐼; 𐐰𐑌𐐼 𐐸𐐨 𐐸𐐰𐑃 𐐺𐐮𐑌 𐑋𐐲𐑉𐐼𐐲𐑉𐐼 𐐺𐐴 𐐸𐐮𐑆 𐐺𐑉𐐲𐑄𐐲𐑉, 𐐸𐐭 𐑅𐐨𐐿𐐯𐑃 𐐻𐐭 𐑅𐐮𐐻 𐐮𐑌 𐑄 𐐾𐐲𐐾𐑋𐐲𐑌𐐻-𐑅𐐨𐐻. 𐐈𐑌𐐼 𐐺𐐨𐐸𐐬𐑊𐐼 𐑄𐐩 𐐺𐐬𐑃 𐐺𐐨𐑊𐐱𐑍 𐐻𐐭 𐐷𐐭𐑉 𐑅𐐨𐐿𐑉𐐯𐐻 𐐺𐐰𐑌𐐼, 𐐸𐐭𐑆 𐐫𐑃𐐲𐑉 𐐮𐑆 𐐘𐐰𐐼𐐨𐐰𐑌𐐻𐐲𐑌 𐐰𐑌𐐼 𐑄 𐐨𐑂𐑊 𐐶𐐲𐑌 𐐸𐐭 𐑅𐐨𐐿𐐯𐑃 𐐻𐐭 𐐼𐐯𐑅𐐻𐑉𐐱𐐷 𐑄 𐑅𐐬𐑊𐑆 𐐱𐑂 𐑋𐐯𐑌.

7. 𐐒𐐨𐐸𐐬𐑊𐐼, 𐑌𐐵 𐐮𐐻 𐐿𐐩𐑋 𐐻𐐭 𐐹𐐰𐑅 𐑄𐐰𐐻 𐐸𐐶𐐯𐑌 𐐤𐐨𐑁𐐴 𐐸𐐰𐐼 𐑅𐐹𐐬𐐿𐑌 𐑄𐐨𐑆 𐐶𐐲𐑉𐐼𐑆, 𐑅𐐲𐑉𐐻𐐲𐑌 𐑋𐐯𐑌 𐐸𐐭 𐐶𐐲𐑉 𐐲𐑋𐐲𐑍 𐑄𐐯𐑋 𐑉𐐰𐑌 𐐻𐐭 𐑄 𐐾𐐲𐐾𐑋𐐲𐑌𐐻-𐑅𐐨𐐻; 𐐷𐐩, 𐐨𐑂𐑌 𐑄𐐯𐑉 𐐶𐐲𐑉 𐑁𐐴𐑂 𐐸𐐭 𐐶𐐯𐑌𐐻, 𐐰𐑌𐐼 𐑄𐐩 𐑅𐐯𐐼 𐐲𐑋𐐲𐑍 𐑄𐐯𐑋𐑅𐐯𐑊𐑂𐑆, 𐐰𐑆 𐑄𐐩 𐐶𐐯𐑌𐐻, 𐐒𐐨𐐸𐐬𐑊𐐼, 𐑌𐐵 𐐶𐐨 𐐶𐐮𐑊 𐑌𐐬 𐐱𐑂 𐐩 𐑇𐐳𐑉𐐮𐐻𐐨 𐐸𐐶𐐯𐑄𐐲𐑉 𐑄𐐮𐑅 𐑋𐐰𐑌 𐐺𐐨 𐐩 𐐹𐑉𐐱𐑁𐐯𐐻, 𐐰𐑌𐐼 𐐘𐐱𐐼 𐐸𐐰𐑃 𐐿𐐲𐑋𐐰𐑌𐐼𐐯𐐼 𐐸𐐮𐑋 𐐻𐐭 𐐹𐑉𐐱𐑁𐐯𐑅𐐴 𐑅𐐲𐐽 𐑋𐐪𐑉𐑂𐐯𐑊𐐲𐑅 𐑃𐐮𐑍𐑆 𐐲𐑌𐐻𐐭 𐐲𐑅. 𐐒𐐨𐐸𐐬𐑊𐐼, 𐐶𐐨 𐐼𐐭 𐑌𐐱𐐻 𐐺𐐨𐑊𐐨𐑂 𐑄𐐰𐐻 𐐸𐐨 𐐸𐐰𐑃; 𐐷𐐩, 𐐶𐐨 𐐼𐐭 𐑌𐐱𐐻 𐐺𐐨𐑊𐐨𐑂 𐑄𐐰𐐻 𐐸𐐨 𐐮𐑆 𐐩 𐐹𐑉𐐱𐑁𐐯𐐻; 𐑌𐐯𐑂𐐲𐑉𐑄𐐲𐑊𐐯𐑅, 𐐮𐑁 𐑄𐐮𐑅 𐑃𐐮𐑍 𐐸𐐶𐐮𐐽 𐐸𐐨 𐐸𐐰𐑆 𐑅𐐯𐐼 𐐿𐐱𐑌𐑅𐐲𐑉𐑌𐐮𐑍 𐑄 𐐽𐐨𐑁 𐐾𐐲𐐾 𐐺𐐨 𐐻𐑉𐐭, 𐑄𐐰𐐻 𐐸𐐨 𐐺𐐨 𐐼𐐯𐐼, 𐑄𐐯𐑌 𐐶𐐮𐑊 𐐶𐐨 𐐺𐐨𐑊𐐨𐑂 𐑄𐐰𐐻 𐑄 𐐲𐑄𐐲𐑉 𐐶𐐲𐑉𐐼𐑆 𐐸𐐶𐐮𐐽 𐐸𐐨 𐐸𐐰𐑆 𐑅𐐹𐐬𐐿𐑌 𐐪𐑉 𐐻𐑉𐐭. 𐐈𐑌𐐼 𐐮𐐻 𐐿𐐩𐑋 𐐻𐐭 𐐹𐐰𐑅 𐑄𐐰𐐻 𐑄𐐩 𐑉𐐰𐑌 𐐮𐑌 𐑄𐐩𐑉 𐑋𐐴𐐻, 𐐰𐑌𐐼 𐐿𐐩𐑋 𐐮𐑌 𐐲𐑌𐐻𐐭 𐑄 𐐾𐐲𐐾𐑋𐐲𐑌𐐻-𐑅𐐨𐐻; 𐐰𐑌𐐼 𐐺𐐨𐐸𐐬𐑊𐐼 𐑄 𐐽𐐨𐑁 𐐾𐐲𐐾 𐐸𐐰𐐼 𐑁𐐫𐑊𐑌 𐐻𐐭 𐑄 𐐲𐑉𐑃, 𐐰𐑌𐐼 𐐼𐐮𐐼 𐑊𐐴 𐐮𐑌 𐐸𐐮𐑆 𐐺𐑊𐐲𐐼. 𐐈𐑌𐐼 𐑌𐐵 𐐺𐐨𐐸𐐬𐑊𐐼, 𐐸𐐶𐐯𐑌 𐑄𐐩 𐑅𐐫 𐑄𐐮𐑅, 𐑄𐐩 𐐶𐐲𐑉 𐐰𐑅𐐻𐐱𐑌𐐮𐑇𐐻 𐐯𐐿𐑅𐐨𐐼𐐮𐑍𐑊𐐨, 𐐮𐑌𐑅𐐲𐑋𐐲𐐽 𐑄𐐰𐐻 𐑄𐐩 𐑁𐐯𐑊 𐐻𐐭 𐑄 𐐲𐑉𐑃; 𐑁𐐫𐑉 𐑄𐐩 𐐸𐐰𐐼 𐑌𐐱𐐻 𐐺𐐨𐑊𐐨𐑂𐐼 𐑄 𐐶𐐲𐑉𐐼𐑆 𐐸𐐶𐐮𐐽 𐐤𐐨𐑁𐐴 𐐸𐐰𐐼 𐑅𐐹𐐬𐐿𐑌 𐐿𐐱𐑌𐑅𐐲𐑉𐑌𐐮𐑍 𐑄 𐐽𐐨𐑁 𐐾𐐲𐐾. 𐐒𐐲𐐻 𐑌𐐵, 𐐸𐐶𐐯𐑌 𐑄𐐩 𐑅𐐫, 𐑄𐐩 𐐺𐐨𐑊𐐨𐑂𐐼, 𐐰𐑌𐐼 𐑁𐐨𐑉 𐐿𐐩𐑋 𐐲𐐹𐐱𐑌 𐑄𐐯𐑋 𐑊𐐯𐑅𐐻 𐐫𐑊 𐑄 𐐾𐐲𐐾𐑋𐐲𐑌𐐻𐑅 𐐸𐐶𐐮𐐽 𐐤𐐨𐑁𐐴 𐐸𐐰𐐼 𐑅𐐹𐐬𐐿𐑌 𐑇𐐳𐐼 𐐿𐐲𐑋 𐐲𐐹𐐱𐑌 𐑄 𐐹𐐨𐐹𐑊; 𐑄𐐯𐑉𐑁𐐬𐑉 𐑄𐐩 𐐼𐐮𐐼 𐐿𐐶𐐩𐐿, 𐐰𐑌𐐼 𐐸𐐰𐐼 𐑁𐐫𐑊𐑌 𐐻𐐭 𐑄 𐐲𐑉𐑃. 𐐤𐐵 𐐮𐑋𐐨𐐼𐐨𐐲𐐻𐑊𐐨 𐐸𐐶𐐯𐑌 𐑄 𐐾𐐲𐐾 𐐸𐐰𐐼 𐐺𐐮𐑌 𐑋𐐲𐑉𐐼𐐲𐑉𐐼, 𐐸𐐨 𐐺𐐨𐐮𐑍 𐑅𐐻𐐰𐐺𐐼 𐐺𐐴 𐐸𐐮𐑆 𐐺𐑉𐐲𐑄𐐲𐑉 𐐺𐐴 𐐩 𐑀𐐪𐑉𐐺 𐐱𐑂 𐑅𐐨𐐿𐑉𐐯𐑅𐐨, 𐐰𐑌𐐼 𐐸𐐨 𐑁𐑊𐐯𐐼, 𐐰𐑌𐐼 𐑄 𐑅𐐲𐑉𐑂𐐲𐑌𐐻𐑅 𐑉𐐰𐑌 𐐰𐑌𐐼 𐐻𐐬𐑊𐐼 𐑄 𐐹𐐨𐐹𐑊, 𐑉𐐩𐑆𐐮𐑍 𐑄 𐐿𐑉𐐴 𐐱𐑂 𐑋𐐲𐑉𐐼𐐲𐑉 𐐲𐑋𐐲𐑍 𐑄𐐯𐑋; 𐐰𐑌𐐼 𐐺𐐨𐐸𐐬𐑊𐐼 𐑄 𐐹𐐨𐐹𐑊 𐐼𐐮𐐼 𐑀𐐰𐑄𐐲𐑉 𐑄𐐯𐑋𐑅𐐯𐑊𐑂𐑆 𐐻𐐲𐑀𐐯𐑄𐐲𐑉 𐐲𐑌𐐻𐐭 𐑄 𐐹𐑊𐐩𐑅 𐐱𐑂 𐑄 𐐾𐐲𐐾𐑋𐐲𐑌𐐻-𐑅𐐨𐐻; 𐐰𐑌𐐼 𐐺𐐨𐐸𐐬𐑊𐐼, 𐐻𐐭 𐑄𐐩𐑉 𐐰𐑅𐐻𐐱𐑌𐐮𐑇𐑋𐐲𐑌𐐻 𐑄𐐩 𐑅𐐫 𐑄𐐬𐑆 𐑁𐐴𐑂 𐑋𐐯𐑌 𐐸𐐭 𐐸𐐰𐐼 𐑁𐐫𐑊𐑌 𐐻𐐭 𐑄 𐐲𐑉𐑃. 𐐈𐑌𐐼 𐑌𐐵 𐐺𐐨𐐸𐐬𐑊𐐼, 𐑄 𐐹𐐨𐐹𐑊 𐑌𐐷𐐭 𐑌𐐲𐑃𐐮𐑍 𐐿𐐱𐑌𐑅𐐲𐑉𐑌𐐮𐑍 𐑄 𐑋𐐲𐑊𐐻𐐨𐐻𐐭𐐼 𐐸𐐭 𐐸𐐰𐐼 𐑀𐐰𐑄𐐲𐑉𐐼 𐐻𐐲𐑀𐐯𐑄𐐲𐑉 𐐰𐐻 𐑄 𐑀𐐪𐑉𐐼𐑌 𐐱𐑂 𐐤𐐨𐑁𐐴; 𐑄𐐯𐑉𐑁𐐬𐑉 𐑄𐐩 𐑅𐐯𐐼 𐐲𐑋𐐲𐑍 𐑄𐐯𐑋𐑅𐐯𐑊𐑂𐑆, 𐐜𐐨𐑆 𐑋𐐯𐑌 𐐪𐑉 𐑄𐐩 𐐸𐐭 𐐸𐐰𐑂 𐑋𐐲𐑉𐐼𐐲𐑉𐐼 𐑄 𐐾𐐲𐐾, 𐐰𐑌𐐼 𐐘𐐱𐐼 𐐸𐐰𐑆 𐑅𐑋𐐮𐐻𐑌 𐑄𐐯𐑋 𐑄𐐰𐐻 𐑄𐐩 𐐿𐐳𐐼 𐑌𐐱𐐻 𐑁𐑊𐐨 𐑁𐑉𐐱𐑋 𐐲𐑅.

8. 𐐈𐑌𐐼 𐐮𐐻 𐐿𐐩𐑋 𐐻𐐭 𐐹𐐰𐑅 𐑄𐐰𐐻 𐑄𐐩 𐑊𐐩𐐼 𐐸𐐬𐑊𐐼 𐐱𐑌 𐑄𐐯𐑋, 𐐰𐑌𐐼 𐐺𐐵𐑌𐐼 𐑄𐐯𐑋, 𐐰𐑌𐐼 𐐿𐐰𐑅𐐻 𐑄𐐯𐑋 𐐮𐑌𐐻𐐭 𐐹𐑉𐐮𐑆𐐲𐑌. 𐐈𐑌𐐼 𐑄𐐯𐑉 𐐶𐐱𐑆 𐐩 𐐹𐑉𐐱𐐿𐑊𐐲𐑋𐐩𐑇𐐲𐑌 𐑅𐐯𐑌𐐻 𐐲𐐺𐑉𐐫𐐼 𐑄𐐰𐐻 𐑄 𐐾𐐲𐐾 𐐶𐐱𐑆 𐑅𐑊𐐩𐑌, 𐐰𐑌𐐼 𐑄𐐰𐐻 𐑄 𐑋𐐲𐑉𐐼𐐲𐑉𐐲𐑉𐑆 𐐸𐐰𐐼 𐐺𐐮𐑌 𐐻𐐩𐐿𐑌, 𐐰𐑌𐐼 𐐶𐐲𐑉 𐐿𐐰𐑅𐐻 𐐮𐑌𐐻𐐭 𐐹𐑉𐐮𐑆𐐲𐑌. 𐐈𐑌𐐼 𐐮𐐻 𐐿𐐩𐑋 𐐻𐐭 𐐹𐐰𐑅 𐑄𐐰𐐻 𐐱𐑌 𐑄 𐑋𐐱𐑉𐐬 𐑄 𐐹𐐨𐐹𐑊 𐐼𐐮𐐼 𐐲𐑅𐐯𐑋𐐺𐑊 𐑄𐐯𐑋𐑅𐐯𐑊𐑂𐑆 𐐻𐐲𐑀𐐯𐑄𐐲𐑉 𐐻𐐭 𐑋𐐬𐑉𐑌 𐐰𐑌𐐼 𐐻𐐭 𐑁𐐪𐑅𐐻, 𐐰𐐻 𐑄 𐐺𐐯𐑉𐐨𐐲𐑊 𐐱𐑂 𐑄 𐑀𐑉𐐩𐐻 𐐽𐐨𐑁 𐐾𐐲𐐾 𐐸𐐭 𐐸𐐰𐐼 𐐺𐐮𐑌 𐑅𐑊𐐩𐑌. 𐐈𐑌𐐼 𐑄𐐲𐑅 𐐫𐑊𐑅𐐬 𐑄𐐬𐑆 𐐾𐐲𐐾𐐯𐑆 𐐸𐐭 𐐶𐐲𐑉 𐐰𐐻 𐑄 𐑀𐐪𐑉𐐼𐑌 𐐱𐑂 𐐤𐐨𐑁𐐴, 𐐰𐑌𐐼 𐐸𐐲𐑉𐐼 𐐸𐐮𐑆 𐐶𐐲𐑉𐐼𐑆, 𐐶𐐲𐑉 𐐫𐑊𐑅𐐬 𐑀𐐰𐑄𐐲𐑉𐐼 𐐻𐐲𐑀𐐯𐑄𐐲𐑉 𐐰𐐻 𐑄 𐐺𐐯𐑉𐐨𐐲𐑊.

9. 𐐈𐑌𐐼 𐐮𐐻 𐐿𐐩𐑋 𐐻𐐭 𐐹𐐰𐑅 𐑄𐐰𐐻 𐑄𐐩 𐐮𐑌𐐿𐐶𐐴𐑉𐐼 𐐲𐑋𐐲𐑍 𐑄 𐐹𐐨𐐹𐑊, 𐑅𐐩𐐮𐑍, 𐐐𐐶𐐯𐑉 𐐪𐑉 𐑄 𐑁𐐴𐑂 𐐸𐐭 𐐶𐐲𐑉 𐑅𐐯𐑌𐐻 𐐻𐐭 𐐮𐑌𐐿𐐶𐐴𐑉 𐐿𐐱𐑌𐑅𐐲𐑉𐑌𐐮𐑍 𐑄 𐐽𐐨𐑁 𐐾𐐲𐐾 𐐸𐐶𐐯𐑄𐐲𐑉 𐐸𐐨 𐐶𐐱𐑆 𐐼𐐯𐐼? 𐐈𐑌𐐼 𐑄𐐩 𐐰𐑌𐑅𐐲𐑉𐐼 𐐰𐑌𐐼 𐑅𐐯𐐼, 𐐗𐐱𐑌𐑅𐐲𐑉𐑌𐐮𐑍 𐑄𐐮𐑅 𐑁𐐴𐑂 𐐸𐐭𐑋 𐐷𐐨 𐑅𐐩 𐐷𐐨 𐐸𐐰𐑂 𐑅𐐯𐑌𐐻, 𐐶𐐨 𐑌𐐬 𐑌𐐱𐐻; 𐐺𐐲𐐻 𐑄𐐯𐑉 𐐪𐑉 𐑁𐐴𐑂 𐐸𐐭 𐐪𐑉 𐑄 𐑋𐐲𐑉𐐼𐐲𐑉𐐲𐑉𐑆, 𐐸𐐭𐑋 𐐶𐐨 𐐸𐐰𐑂 𐐿𐐰𐑅𐐻 𐐮𐑌𐐻𐐭 𐐹𐑉𐐮𐑆𐐲𐑌. 𐐈𐑌𐐼 𐐮𐐻 𐐿𐐩𐑋 𐐻𐐭 𐐹𐐰𐑅 𐑄𐐰𐐻 𐑄

𐐾𐐲𐐾𐐯𐑆 𐐼𐐨𐑆𐐴𐑉𐐼 𐑄𐐰𐐻 𐑄𐐩 𐑇𐐳𐐼 𐐺 𐐺𐑉𐐫𐐻; 𐐰𐑌𐐼 𐑄𐐩 𐐶𐐲𐑉 𐐺𐑉𐐫𐐻, 𐐰𐑌𐐼 𐐺𐐨𐐸𐐬𐑊𐐼 𐑄𐐩 𐐶𐐲𐑉 𐑄 𐑁𐐴𐑂 𐐸𐐭 𐐶𐐲𐑉 𐑅𐐯𐑌𐐻. 𐐈𐑌𐐼 𐐺𐐨𐐸𐐬𐑊𐐼, 𐑄 𐐾𐐲𐐾𐐯𐑆 𐐮𐑌𐐿𐐶𐐴𐑉𐐼 𐐱𐑂 𐑄𐐯𐑋 𐐻𐐭 𐑌𐐬 𐐿𐐱𐑌𐑅𐐲𐑉𐑌𐐮𐑍 𐑄 𐑋𐐰𐐻𐐲𐑉, 𐐰𐑌𐐼 𐑄𐐩 𐐻𐐬𐑊𐐼 𐑄𐐯𐑋 𐐫𐑊 𐑄𐐰𐐻 𐑄𐐩 𐐸𐐰𐐼 𐐼𐐲𐑌, 𐑅𐐩𐐮𐑍, 𐐎𐐨 𐑉𐐰𐑌 𐐰𐑌𐐼 𐐿𐐩𐑋 𐐻𐐭 𐑄 𐐹𐑊𐐩𐑅 𐐱𐑂 𐑄 𐐾𐐲𐐾𐑋𐐯𐑌𐐻-𐑅𐐨𐐻, 𐐰𐑌𐐼 𐐸𐐶𐐯𐑌 𐐶𐐨 𐑅𐐫 𐐫𐑊 𐑃𐐮𐑍𐑆 𐐨𐑂𐐯𐑌 𐐰𐑆 𐐤𐐨𐑁𐐴 𐐸𐐰𐐼 𐐻𐐯𐑅𐐻𐐮𐑁𐐴𐐼, 𐐶𐐨 𐐶𐐲𐑉 𐐰𐑅𐐻𐐱𐑌𐐮𐑇𐐻, 𐐮𐑌𐑅𐐬𐑋𐐲𐐽 𐑄𐐰𐐻 𐐶𐐨 𐑁𐐯𐑊 𐐻𐐭 𐑄 𐐲𐑉𐑃; 𐐰𐑌𐐼 𐐸𐐶𐐯𐑌 𐐶𐐨 𐐶𐐲𐑉 𐑉𐐨𐐿𐐲𐑂𐐲𐑉𐐼 𐑁𐑉𐐱𐑋 𐐵𐑉 𐐰𐑅𐐻𐐱𐑌𐐮𐑇𐑋𐐯𐑌𐐻, 𐐺𐐨𐐸𐐬𐑊𐐼, 𐑄𐐩 𐐿𐐪𐑅𐐻 𐐲𐑅 𐐮𐑌𐐻𐐭 𐐹𐑉𐐮𐑆𐐲𐑌. 𐐤𐐵, 𐐰𐑆 𐑁𐐫𐑉 𐑄 𐑋𐐲𐑉𐐼𐐲𐑉 𐐱𐑂 𐑄𐐮𐑅 𐑋𐐰𐑌, 𐐶𐐨 𐑌𐐬 𐑌𐐱𐐻 𐐸𐐭 𐐸𐐰𐑆 𐐼𐐲𐑌 𐐮𐐻; 𐐰𐑌𐐼 𐐬𐑌𐑊𐐨 𐑄𐐮𐑅 𐑋𐐲𐐽 𐐶𐐨 𐑌𐐬, 𐐶𐐨 𐑉𐐰𐑌 𐐰𐑌𐐼 𐐿𐐩𐑋 𐐰𐐿𐐫𐑉𐐼𐐮𐑍 𐐰𐑆 𐐷 𐐼𐐨𐑆𐐴𐑉𐐼, 𐐰𐑌𐐼 𐐺𐐨𐐸𐐬𐑊𐐼 𐐸𐐨 𐐶𐐱𐑆 𐐼𐐯𐐼, 𐐰𐐿𐐫𐑉𐐼𐐮𐑍 𐐻𐐭 𐑄 𐐶𐐲𐑉𐐼𐑆 𐐱𐑂 𐐤𐐨𐑁𐐴.

10. 𐐈𐑌𐐼 𐑌𐐵 𐐮𐐻 𐐿𐐩𐑋 𐐻𐐭 𐐹𐐪𐑅 𐑄𐐰𐐻 𐑄 𐐾𐐲𐐾𐐯𐑆 𐐼𐐮𐐼 𐐯𐐿𐑅𐐹𐐵𐑌𐐼 𐑄 𐑋𐐰𐐻𐐲𐑉 𐐲𐑌𐐻𐐭 𐑄 𐐹𐐨𐐹𐐲𐑊, 𐐰𐑌𐐼 𐐼𐐮𐐼 𐐿𐑉𐐴 𐐵𐐻 𐐲𐑀𐐯𐑌𐑅𐐻 𐐤𐐨𐑁𐐴, 𐑅𐐩𐐮𐑍, 𐐒𐐨𐐸𐐬𐑊𐐼, 𐐶𐐨 𐑌𐐬 𐑄𐐰𐐻 𐑄𐐮𐑅 𐐤𐐨𐑁𐐴 𐑋𐐲𐑅𐐻 𐐸𐐰𐑂 𐐲𐑀𐑉𐐨𐐼 𐐶𐐮𐑄 𐑅𐐲𐑋 𐐶𐐲𐑌 𐐻𐐭 𐑅𐑊𐐩 𐑄 𐐾𐐲𐐾, 𐐰𐑌𐐼 𐑄𐐯𐑌 𐐸𐐨 𐑋𐐴𐐻 𐐼𐐨𐐿𐑊𐐩𐑉 𐐮𐐻 𐐲𐑌𐐻𐐭 𐐲𐑅, 𐑄𐐰𐐻 𐐸𐐨 𐑋𐐴𐐻 𐐿𐐱𐑌𐑂𐐲𐑉𐐻 𐐲𐑅 𐐲𐑌𐐻𐐭 𐐸𐐮𐑆 𐑁𐐩𐑃, 𐑄𐐰𐐻 𐐸𐐨 𐑋𐐴𐐻 𐑉𐐩𐑆 𐐸𐐮𐑋𐑅𐐯𐑊𐑁 𐐻𐐭 𐐺 𐐲 𐑀𐑉𐐩𐐻 𐑋𐐰𐑌, 𐐽𐐬𐑆𐐲𐑌 𐐱𐑂 𐐘𐐱𐐼, 𐐰𐑌𐐼 𐐲 𐐹𐑉𐐱𐑁𐐯𐐻; 𐐰𐑌𐐼 𐑌𐐵 𐐺𐐨𐐸𐐬𐑊𐐼, 𐐶𐐨 𐐶𐐮𐑊 𐐼𐐨𐐻𐐯𐐿𐐻 𐑄𐐮𐑅 𐑋𐐰𐑌, 𐐰𐑌𐐼 𐐸𐐨 𐑇𐐰𐑊 𐐿𐐱𐑌𐑁𐐯𐑅 𐐸𐐮𐑆 𐑁𐐫𐑊𐐻, 𐐰𐑌𐐼 𐑋𐐩𐐿 𐑌𐐬𐑌 𐐲𐑌𐐻𐐭 𐐲𐑅 𐑄 𐐻𐑉𐐭 𐑋𐐲𐑉𐐼𐐲𐑉𐐲𐑉 𐐱𐑂 𐑄𐐮𐑅 𐐾𐐲𐐾. 𐐈𐑌𐐼 𐐮𐐻 𐐿𐐩𐑋 𐐻𐐭 𐐹𐐪𐑅 𐑄𐐰𐐻 𐑄 𐑁𐐴𐑂 𐐶𐐲𐑉 𐑊𐐮𐐺𐐲𐑉𐐩𐐻𐐯𐐼 𐐱𐑌 𐑄 𐐼𐐩 𐐱𐑂 𐑄 𐐺𐐯𐑉𐐨𐐲𐑊. 𐐤𐐯𐑂𐐲𐑉𐑄𐐲𐑊𐐯𐑅, 𐑄𐐩 𐐼𐐮𐐼 𐑉𐐨𐐺𐐷𐐭𐐿 𐑄 𐐾𐐲𐐾𐐯𐑆 𐐮𐑌 𐑄 𐐶𐐲𐑉𐐼𐑆 𐐸𐐶𐐮𐐽 𐑄𐐩 𐐸𐐰𐐼 𐑅𐐹𐐬𐐿𐐲𐑌 𐐲𐑀𐐯𐑌𐑅𐐻 𐐤𐐨𐑁𐐴, 𐐰𐑌𐐼 𐐼𐐮𐐼 𐐿𐐱𐑌𐐻𐐯𐑌𐐼 𐐶𐐮𐑄 𐑄𐐯𐑋 𐐶𐐲𐑌 𐐺𐐴 𐐶𐐲𐑌, 𐐮𐑌𐑅𐐬𐑋𐐲𐐽 𐑄𐐰𐐻 𐑄𐐩 𐐼𐐮𐐼 𐐿𐐱𐑌𐑁𐐵𐑌𐐼 𐑄𐐯𐑋. 𐐤𐐯𐑂𐐲𐑉𐑄𐐲𐑊𐐯𐑅, 𐑄𐐩 𐐿𐐫𐑆𐐼 𐑄𐐰𐐻 𐐤𐐨𐑁𐐴 𐑇𐐳𐐼 𐐺 𐐻𐐩𐐿𐐲𐑌 𐐰𐑌𐐼 𐐺𐐵𐑌𐐼, 𐐰𐑌𐐼 𐐺𐑉𐐫𐐻 𐐺𐐨𐑁𐐬𐑉 𐑄 𐑋𐐲𐑊𐐻𐐮𐐻𐐷𐐭𐐼, 𐐰𐑌𐐼 𐑄𐐩 𐐺𐐨𐑀𐐰𐑌 𐐻𐐭 𐐿𐐶𐐯𐑅𐐽𐐲𐑌 𐐸𐐮𐑋 𐐮𐑌 𐐼𐐴𐑂𐐲𐑉𐑆 𐐶𐐩𐑆, 𐑄𐐰𐐻 𐑄𐐩 𐑋𐐴𐐻 𐐿𐑉𐐱𐑅 𐐸𐐮𐑋, 𐑄𐐰𐐻 𐑄𐐩 𐑋𐐴𐐻 𐐰𐐿𐐷𐐭𐑆 𐐸𐐮𐑋 𐐻𐐭 𐐼𐐯𐑃: 𐑅𐐩𐐮𐑍 𐐲𐑌𐐻𐐭 𐐸𐐮𐑋, 𐐜𐐵 𐐪𐑉𐐻 𐐿𐐱𐑌𐑁𐐯𐐼𐐲𐑉𐐩𐐻; 𐐸𐐭 𐐮𐑆 𐑄𐐮𐑅 𐑋𐐰𐑌 𐑄𐐰𐐻 𐐸𐐰𐑃 𐐼𐐲𐑌 𐑄𐐮𐑅 𐑋𐐲𐑉𐐼𐐲𐑉? 𐐤𐐵 𐐻𐐯𐑊 𐐲𐑅, 𐐰𐑌𐐼 𐐰𐐿𐑌𐐱𐑊𐐯𐐾 𐑄𐐴 𐑁𐐫𐑊𐐻, 𐑅𐐩𐐮𐑍, 𐐒𐐨𐐸𐐬𐑊𐐼 𐐸𐐨𐑉 𐐮𐑆 𐑋𐐲𐑌𐐨; 𐐰𐑌𐐼 𐐫𐑊𐑅𐐬 𐐶𐐨 𐐶𐐮𐑊 𐑀𐑉𐐰𐑌𐐻 𐐲𐑌𐐻𐐭 𐑄𐐨 𐑄𐐴 𐑊𐐴𐑁 𐐮𐑁 𐑄𐐵 𐐶𐐮𐑊𐐻 𐐻𐐯𐑊 𐐲𐑅, 𐐰𐑌𐐼 𐐰𐐿𐑌𐐱𐑊𐐯𐐾 𐑄 𐐲𐑀𐑉𐐨𐑋𐐯𐑌𐐻 𐐸𐐶𐐮𐐽 𐑄𐐵 𐐸𐐰𐑅𐐻 𐑋𐐩𐐼 𐐶𐐮𐑄 𐐸𐐮𐑋.

11. 𐐒𐐲𐐻 𐐤𐐨𐑁𐐴 𐑅𐐯𐐼 𐐲𐑌𐐻𐐭 𐑄𐐯𐑋, 𐐄 𐐷 𐑁𐐭𐑊𐑆, 𐐷 𐐲𐑌𐑅𐐲𐑉𐐿𐐲𐑋𐑅𐐴𐑆𐐼 𐐱𐑂 𐐸𐐪𐑉𐐻, 𐐷 𐐺𐑊𐐴𐑌𐐼, 𐐰𐑌𐐼 𐐷 𐑅𐐻𐐮𐑁-𐑌𐐯𐐿𐐻 𐐹𐐨𐐹𐐲𐑊, 𐐼𐐭 𐐷 𐑌𐐬 𐐸𐐵 𐑊𐐱𐑍 𐑄 𐐢𐐫𐑉𐐼 𐐷𐐬𐑉 𐐘𐐱𐐼 𐐶𐐮𐑊 𐑅𐐲𐑁𐐲𐑉 𐐷𐐭 𐑄𐐰𐐻 𐐷 𐑇𐐰𐑊 𐑀𐐬 𐐱𐑌 𐐮𐑌 𐑄𐐮𐑅 𐐷𐐬𐑉 𐐶𐐩 𐐱𐑂 𐑅𐐮𐑌? 𐐄 𐐷 𐑇𐐳𐐼 𐐫𐐻 𐐻𐐭 𐐺𐐨𐑀𐐮𐑌 𐐻𐐭 𐐸𐐵𐑊 𐐰𐑌𐐼 𐑋𐐬𐑉𐑌, 𐐺𐐨𐐿𐐫𐑆 𐐱𐑂 𐑄 𐑀𐑉𐐩𐐻 𐐼𐐯𐑅𐐻𐑉𐐲𐐿𐑇𐐲𐑌 𐐰𐐻 𐑄𐐮𐑅 𐐻𐐴𐑋 𐐸𐐶𐐮𐐽 𐐼𐐲𐑃 𐐲𐐶𐐩𐐻 𐐷𐐭, 𐐯𐐿𐑅𐐯𐐹𐐻 𐐷 𐑇𐐰𐑊 𐑉𐐨𐐹𐐯𐑌𐐻. 𐐒𐐨𐐸𐐬𐑊𐐼 𐐷 𐑅𐐩 𐑄𐐰𐐻 𐐌 𐐸𐐰𐑂 𐐲𐑀𐑉𐐨𐐼 𐐶𐐮𐑄 𐐲 𐑋𐐰𐑌, 𐑄𐐰𐐻 𐐸𐐨 𐑇𐐳𐐼 𐑋𐐲𐑉𐐼𐐲𐑉 𐐝𐐨𐑆𐐬𐑉𐐲𐑋, 𐐵𐑉 𐐽𐐨𐑁 𐐾𐐲𐐾. 𐐒𐐲𐐻 𐐺𐐨𐐸𐐬𐑊𐐼, 𐐌 𐑅𐐩 𐐲𐑌𐐻𐐭 𐐷𐐭, 𐑄𐐰𐐻 𐑄𐐮𐑅 𐐮𐑆 𐐺𐐨𐐿𐐫𐑆 𐐌 𐐸𐐰𐑂 𐐻𐐯𐑅𐐻𐐮𐑁𐐴𐐼 𐐲𐑌𐐻𐐭 𐐷𐐭, 𐑄𐐰𐐻 𐐷 𐑋𐐴𐐻 𐑌𐐬 𐐿𐐱𐑌𐑅𐐲𐑉𐑌𐐮𐑍 𐑄𐐮𐑅 𐑃𐐮𐑍; 𐐷𐐩, 𐐨𐑂𐐯𐑌 𐑁𐐫𐑉 𐐲 𐐶𐐮𐐻𐑌𐐯𐑅 𐐲𐑌𐐻𐐭 𐐷𐐭, 𐑄𐐰𐐻 𐐌 𐐼𐐮𐐼 𐑌𐐬 𐐱𐑂 𐑄 𐐶𐐮𐐿𐐯𐐼𐑌𐐯𐑅 𐐰𐑌𐐼 𐐲𐐺𐐱𐑋𐐮𐑌𐐩𐑇𐐲𐑌𐑆 𐐸𐐶𐐮𐐽 𐐪𐑉 𐐲𐑋𐐲𐑍 𐐷𐐭. 𐐈𐑌𐐼 𐐺𐐨𐐿𐐫𐑆 𐐌 𐐸𐐰𐑂 𐐼𐐲𐑌 𐑄𐐮𐑅, 𐐷 𐑅𐐩 𐑄𐐰𐐻 𐐌 𐐸𐐰𐑂 𐐲𐑀𐑉𐐨𐐼 𐐶𐐮𐑄 𐐲 𐑋𐐰𐑌 𐑄𐐰𐐻 𐐸𐐨 𐑇𐐳𐐼 𐐼𐐭 𐑄𐐮𐑅 𐑃𐐮𐑍; 𐐷𐐩, 𐐺𐐨𐐿𐐫𐑆 𐐌 𐑇𐐬𐐼 𐐲𐑌𐐻𐐭 𐐷𐐭 𐑄𐐮𐑅 𐑅𐐴𐑌, 𐐷 𐐪𐑉 𐐰𐑍𐑀𐑉𐐨 𐐶𐐮𐑄 𐑋𐐨, 𐐰𐑌𐐼 𐑅𐐨𐐿 𐐻𐐭 𐐼𐐯𐑅𐐻𐑉𐑎 𐑋𐐴 𐑊𐐴𐑁. 𐐈𐑌𐐼 𐑌𐐵 𐐺𐐨𐐸𐐬𐑊𐐼, 𐐌 𐐶𐐮𐑊 𐑇𐐬 𐐲𐑌𐐻𐐭 𐐷𐐭 𐐲𐑌𐐲𐑄𐐲𐑉 𐑅𐐴𐑌, 𐐰𐑌𐐼 𐑅𐐨 𐐮𐑁 𐐷 𐐶𐐮𐑊 𐐮𐑌 𐑄𐐮𐑅 𐑃𐐮𐑍 𐑅𐐨𐐿 𐐻𐐭 𐐼𐐯𐑅𐐻𐑉𐑎 𐑋𐐨. 𐐒𐐨𐐸𐐬𐑊𐐼 𐐌 𐑅𐐩 𐐲𐑌𐐻𐐭 𐐷𐐭, 𐐘𐐬 𐐻𐐭 𐑄 𐐸𐐵𐑅 𐐱𐑂 𐐝𐐨𐐰𐑌𐐻𐐲𐑋, 𐐸𐐭 𐐮𐑆 𐑄 𐐺𐑉𐐲𐑄𐐲𐑉 𐐱𐑂 𐐝𐐨𐑆𐐬𐑉𐐲𐑋, 𐐰𐑌𐐼 𐑅𐐩 𐐲𐑌𐐻𐐭 𐐸𐐮𐑋, 𐐐𐐰𐑆 𐐤𐐨𐑁𐐴, 𐑄 𐐹𐑉𐐨𐐻𐐯𐑌𐐼𐐯𐐼 𐐹𐑉𐐱𐑁𐐯𐐻, 𐐸𐐭 𐐼𐐲𐑃 𐐹𐑉𐐱𐑁𐐯𐑅𐐴 𐑅𐐬 𐑋𐐲𐐽 𐐨𐑂𐐮𐑊 𐐿𐐱𐑌𐑅𐐲𐑉𐑌𐐮𐑍 𐑄𐐮𐑅 𐐹𐐨𐐹𐐲𐑊, 𐐲𐑀𐑉𐐨𐐼 𐐶𐐮𐑄 𐑄𐐨, 𐐮𐑌 𐑄 𐐸𐐶𐐮𐐽 𐐷 𐐸𐐰𐑂 𐑋𐐲𐑉𐐼𐐲𐑉𐐼 𐐝𐐨𐑆𐐬𐑉𐐲𐑋, 𐐸𐐭 𐐮𐑆 𐐷𐐬𐑉 𐐺𐑉𐐲𐑄𐐲𐑉? 𐐈𐑌𐐼 𐐺𐐨𐐸𐐬𐑊𐐼, 𐐸𐐨 𐑇𐐰𐑊 𐑅𐐩 𐐲𐑌𐐻𐐭 𐐷𐐭, 𐐤𐐩. 𐐈𐑌𐐼 𐐷 𐑇𐐰𐑊 𐑅𐐩 𐐲𐑌𐐻𐐭 𐐸𐐮𐑋, 𐐐𐐰𐑂 𐐷 𐑋𐐲𐑉𐐼𐐲𐑉𐐼 𐐷𐐬𐑉 𐐺𐑉𐐲𐑄𐐲𐑉? 𐐈𐑌𐐼 𐐸𐐨 𐑇𐐰𐑊 𐑅𐐻𐐰𐑌𐐼 𐐶𐐮𐑄 𐑁𐐨𐑉 𐐰𐑌𐐼 𐐶𐐮𐑅𐐻 𐑌𐐱𐐻 𐐸𐐶𐐱𐐻 𐐻𐐭 𐑅𐐩. 𐐈𐑌𐐼 𐐺𐐨𐐸𐐬𐑊𐐼, 𐐸𐐨 𐑇𐐰𐑊 𐐼𐐨𐑌𐐴 𐐲𐑌𐐻𐐭 𐐷𐐭; 𐐰𐑌𐐼 𐐸𐐨 𐑇𐐰𐑊 𐑋𐐩𐐿 𐐰𐑆 𐐮𐑁 𐐸𐐨 𐐶𐐲𐑉 𐐰𐑅𐐻𐐱𐑌𐐮𐑇𐐻; 𐑌𐐯𐑂𐐲𐑉𐑄𐐲𐑊𐐯𐑅, 𐐸𐐨 𐑇𐐰𐑊 𐐼𐐨𐐿𐑊𐐩𐑉 𐐲𐑌𐐻𐐭 𐐷𐐭 𐑄𐐰𐐻 𐐸𐐨 𐐮𐑆 𐐮𐑌𐐬𐑅𐐯𐑌𐐻.

𐐒𐐲𐐻 𐐒𐐨𐐸𐐬𐑊𐐼, 𐐌 𐐶𐐮𐑊 𐑂𐐮𐑆𐐮𐐻 𐑄𐐯𐑋, 𐐰𐑌𐐼 𐐌 𐐶𐐮𐑊 𐑅𐑋𐐴𐐻 𐐲𐐹𐐱𐑌 𐑄 𐑅𐐲𐑌𐑆 𐐱𐑂 𐑄𐐯 𐑀𐐬𐑊𐐼. 𐐰𐑌𐐼 𐐸𐐶𐐯𐑌 𐐌 𐐸𐐰𐑂 𐑅𐐨𐑌 𐑄𐐮𐑅, 𐐌 𐐶𐐮𐑊 𐑅𐐩, 𐐸𐐭 𐐸𐐲𐑌 𐐸𐐨𐑉𐑆 𐐫𐑊𐑊 𐑄𐐮𐑅 𐐒𐐲𐐻? 𐐐𐐭 𐐶𐐲 𐐸𐐰𐐼 𐐸𐐲 𐑄𐐰𐐻 𐑄𐐮𐑅 𐐮𐑆 𐑄 𐐒𐐲𐐻 𐐱𐑂 𐐸𐐲𐑉 𐐒𐐲𐑉𐑄𐐲𐑉? 𐐰𐑌𐐼 𐑄𐐯𐑌 𐐶𐐮𐑊 𐐸𐐨 𐐻𐐲𐑉𐑌𐐲𐑉, 𐐰𐑌𐐼 𐐶𐐮𐑊 𐐮𐑌𐐼 𐐻𐐩𐐿, 𐐱𐑌 𐐰𐑆 𐐮𐑁 𐐶𐐲𐑊 𐐸𐐰𐐼 𐐫𐑊𐑌 𐐲𐑌𐐻𐐭 𐐸𐐮𐑋. 𐐰𐑌𐐼 𐑄𐐯𐑌 𐐶𐐮𐑊 𐐌 𐑅𐐩, 𐐒𐐲-𐐶𐐫𐑉 𐐱𐑂 𐑄𐐮𐑅 𐑁𐐫𐑉 𐐰𐑌𐐼 𐑄𐐮𐑅 𐐻𐐯𐑊𐐮𐑍𐑆 𐐸𐐶𐐮𐐽 𐐸𐐰𐑆 𐐫𐑊𐑌 𐐲𐑌𐐻𐐭 𐐸𐐭𐑉 𐑁𐐯𐑅, 𐐒𐐨𐐸𐐬𐑊𐐼, 𐐶𐐨 𐐸𐐬 𐑄𐐰𐐻 𐑄𐐨 𐐫𐑉 𐐶𐐮𐑊𐐻. 𐐰𐑌𐐼 𐑄𐐯𐑌 𐐶𐐮𐑊 𐐶𐐩𐐻𐐲𐑉 𐑁𐐫𐑉 𐐫𐑊𐑌 𐐲𐑌𐐻𐐭 𐐸𐐮𐑋; 𐐰𐑌𐐼 𐑄𐐯𐑌 𐐶𐐮𐑊 𐐸𐐨 𐐫𐑊𐑌-𐐹𐐰𐑅 𐐲𐑌𐐻𐐭 𐐸𐐮𐑋, 𐐰𐑌𐐼 𐐼𐐫𐑌𐐻 𐐸𐐬 𐑉𐐫𐐻 𐑄𐐰𐐻 𐐸𐐨 𐐸𐐰𐑆 𐐼𐐲𐑌 𐑄𐐮𐑅 𐐶𐐲𐑉𐐼𐐲𐑉. 𐐰𐑌𐐼 𐑄𐐯𐑌 𐐶𐐮𐑊 𐐸𐐨 𐑅𐐩 𐐲𐑌𐐻𐐭 𐐸𐐮𐑋, 𐑄𐐰𐐻 𐐌, 𐐤𐐨𐑁𐐴, 𐐸𐐬 𐐸𐐲𐑉𐐼𐐲𐑌 𐐫𐑌𐐸𐐱𐑌𐐲𐑋𐐲𐑌 𐑄 𐑉𐐲𐑌𐐲𐐻, 𐑅𐐯𐐼 𐐮𐐻 𐐶𐐲𐑉 𐐫𐑉𐐯𐑌 𐐲𐑌𐐻𐐭 𐑉𐐨 𐐒𐐴 𐑄 𐐹𐐵𐐲𐑉 𐐱𐑂 𐐘𐐱𐐼. 𐐰𐑌𐐼 𐑄𐐯𐑌 𐐶𐐮𐑊 𐐌 𐐸𐐬 𐑄𐐰𐐻 𐐌 𐐰𐑋 𐐰𐑌 𐐱𐑌𐐯𐑅𐐻 𐑉𐐲𐑌, 𐐰𐑌𐐼 𐑄𐐰𐐻 𐐌 𐐰𐑋 𐑅𐐲𐑌𐐻 𐐲𐑌𐐻𐐭 𐐸𐐮𐑋 𐑁𐑉𐐲𐑋 𐐘𐐱𐐼.

12. 𐐰𐑌𐐼 𐐮𐐻 𐐗𐐩𐑋 𐐻𐐭 𐐑𐐰𐑅 𐑄𐐰𐐻 𐑄𐐩 𐐶𐐲𐑌𐐻 𐐰𐑌𐐼 𐐼𐐮𐐼, 𐐨𐑂𐐯𐑌 𐐰𐐿𐐫𐑉𐐼𐐮𐑍 𐐰𐑆 𐐤𐐨𐑁𐐴 𐐸𐐰𐐼 𐑅𐐯𐐼 𐐲𐑌𐐻𐐭 𐑄𐐯𐑋. 𐐰𐑌𐐼 𐐒𐐨𐐸𐐬𐑊𐐼, 𐑄 𐐶𐐲𐑉𐐼𐐲𐑉 𐐸𐐶𐐮𐐽 𐐸𐐨 𐐸𐐰𐐼 𐑅𐐯𐐼, 𐐶𐐲𐑆 𐐻𐑉𐐭; 𐑁𐐫𐑉 𐐰𐐿𐐫𐑉𐐼𐐮𐑍 𐐻𐐭 𐑄 𐐶𐐲𐑉𐐼𐑆, 𐐸𐐨 𐐼𐐮𐐼 𐐼𐐴; 𐐰𐑌𐐼 𐐫𐑊𐑅𐐬 𐐰𐐿𐐫𐑉𐐼𐐮𐑍 𐐻𐐭 𐑄 𐐶𐐲𐑉𐐼𐑆 𐐸𐐨 𐐼𐐮𐐼 𐐫𐑌𐑅𐐲𐑉. 𐐰𐑌𐐼 𐐸𐐨 𐐶𐐲𐑆 𐐒𐑉𐐱𐐻 𐐻𐐭 𐐹𐑉𐐮𐑆𐐲𐑌 𐑄𐐰𐐻 𐐸𐐨 𐑁𐐮𐑉𐑅𐐲𐑊𐑁 𐐶𐐲𐑆 𐑄 𐐗𐐨𐑁 𐐾𐐲𐐼𐐲𐑉𐐨, 𐐸𐐶𐐮𐐽 𐑄𐐰𐐻 𐑄 𐑉𐐭𐑊 𐐶𐐲𐑉 𐑅𐐯𐐼 𐐮𐑌 𐑉𐐨𐐼𐐮𐑍𐐲𐑌; 𐐰𐑌𐐼 𐐫𐑊𐑅𐐬 𐐶𐐲𐑆 𐐤𐐨𐑁𐐴. 𐐰𐑌𐐼 𐑄𐐯𐑉 𐐶𐐲𐑉 𐑅𐐲𐑋 𐐱𐑂 𐑄 𐐤𐐨𐑁𐐴𐐻𐑅 𐐸𐐬 𐐒𐐨𐑊𐐨𐑂𐐼 𐐮𐑌 𐑄 𐐶𐐲𐑉𐐼𐑆 𐐱𐑂 𐐤𐐨𐑁𐐴; 𐐰𐑌𐐼 𐑄𐐯𐑉 𐐶𐐲𐑉 𐑅𐐲𐑋 𐐫𐑊𐑅𐐬, 𐐸𐐬 𐐒𐐨𐑊𐐨𐑂𐐼, 𐐒𐐨𐐿𐐱𐑆 𐐱𐑂 𐑄 𐐻𐐯𐑅𐐻𐐮-𐑋𐐲𐑌𐐨 𐐱𐑂 𐑄 𐑁𐐴𐑂, 𐑁𐐫𐑉 𐑄𐐩 𐐸𐐰𐐼 𐐒𐐨𐑌 𐐲𐐿𐐯𐑌𐐻𐐲𐐼 𐐸𐐶𐐮𐑊 𐑄𐐩 𐐶𐐲𐑉 𐐮𐑌 𐐹𐑉𐐮𐑆𐐲𐑌. 𐐰𐑌𐐼 𐑌𐐵 𐑄𐐯𐑉 𐐶𐐲𐑉 𐑅𐐲𐑋 𐐰𐑋𐐲𐑍 𐑄 𐐹𐑉𐐮𐑆𐐲𐑌, 𐐸𐐬 𐑅𐐯𐐼 𐑄𐐰𐐻 𐐤𐐨𐑁𐐴 𐐶𐐲𐑆 𐐩 𐐹𐑉𐐱𐑁𐐯𐐻; 𐐰𐑌𐐼 𐑄𐐯𐑉 𐐶𐐲𐑉 𐐲𐑄𐐲𐑉𐑆 𐐸𐐬 𐑅𐐯𐐼, 𐐒𐐨𐐸𐐬𐑊𐐼, 𐐸𐐨 𐐮𐑆 𐐩 𐐘𐐱𐐼, 𐑁𐐫𐑉 𐐲𐑊𐐯𐑅 𐐸𐐨 𐐶𐐲𐑆 𐐩 𐐘𐐱𐐼, 𐐸𐐨 𐐿𐐲𐐼 𐑌𐐱𐐻 𐐸𐐬 𐐱𐑂 𐐫𐑊 𐑔𐐮𐑍𐑆. 𐐙𐐫𐑉 𐐒𐐨𐐸𐐬𐑊𐐼, 𐐸𐐨 𐐸𐐰𐑆 𐐻𐐬𐑊𐐼 𐐲𐑆 𐑄 𐑔𐐫𐐻𐑅 𐐱𐑂 𐐵𐐲𐑉 𐐸𐐲𐑉𐐻𐑅, 𐐰𐑌𐐼 𐐫𐑊𐑅𐐬 𐐸𐐰𐑆 𐐻𐐬𐑊𐐼 𐐲𐑆 𐑔𐐮𐑍𐑆; 𐐰𐑌𐐼 𐐨𐑂𐐯𐑌 𐐸𐐨 𐐸𐐰𐑆 𐐒𐑉𐐱𐐻 𐐲𐑌𐐻𐐭 𐐵𐐲𐑉 𐑌𐐱𐑊𐐲𐐾 𐑄 𐐻𐑉𐐭 𐑋𐐲𐑉𐐼𐐲𐑉𐐲𐑉 𐐱𐑂 𐐵𐐲𐑉 𐐕𐐨𐑁 𐐖𐐲𐐾.

13. 𐐰𐑌𐐼 𐐮𐐻 𐐗𐐩𐑋 𐐻𐐭 𐐑𐐰𐑅 𐑄𐐰𐐻 𐑄𐐯𐑉 𐐲𐑉𐐬𐑆 𐐩 𐐼𐐮𐑂𐐮𐑈𐐲𐑌 𐐲𐑋𐐲𐑍 𐑄 𐐹𐐨𐐹𐐲𐑊, 𐐮𐑌𐑅𐐱𐑋𐐲𐐽 𐑄𐐰𐐻 𐑄𐐩 𐐼𐐮𐑂𐐴𐐼𐐲𐐼 𐐸𐐮𐑄𐐲𐑉 𐐰𐑌𐐼 𐑄𐐮𐑄𐐲𐑉, 𐐰𐑌𐐼 𐐶𐐲𐑌𐐻 𐑄𐐯𐑉 𐐶𐐩𐑆, 𐑊𐐨𐑂𐐮𐑍 𐐤𐐨𐑁𐐴 𐐰𐑊𐐬𐑌, 𐐰𐑆 𐐸𐐨 𐐶𐐲𐑆 𐑅𐐻𐐰𐑌𐐼-𐐮𐑍 𐐮𐑌 𐑄 𐑋𐐮𐐼𐑅𐐻 𐐱𐑂 𐑄𐐯𐑋. 𐐰𐑌𐐼 𐐮𐐻 𐐗𐐩𐑋 𐐻𐐭 𐐑𐐰𐑅 𐑄𐐰𐐻 𐐤𐐨𐑁𐐴 𐐶𐐲𐑌𐐻 𐐸𐐮𐑆 𐐶𐐩 𐐻𐐭𐐶𐐲𐑉𐐼𐑆 𐐸𐐮𐑆 𐐬𐑌 𐐸𐐵𐑅, 𐐹𐐱𐑌𐐼𐐲𐑉𐐮𐑍 𐐲𐐹𐐱𐑌 𐑄 𐑔𐐮𐑍𐑆 𐐸𐐶𐐮𐐽 𐑄 𐐢𐐫𐑉𐐼 𐐸𐐰𐐼 𐑇𐐬𐑌 𐐲𐑌𐐻𐐭 𐐸𐐮𐑋. 𐐰𐑌𐐼 𐐮𐐻 𐐗𐐩𐑋 𐐻𐐭 𐐑𐐰𐑅 𐐰𐑆 𐐸𐐨 𐐶𐐲𐑆 𐑄𐐲𐑆 𐐹𐐱𐑌𐐼𐐲𐑉𐐮𐑍,—𐐒𐐨𐐮𐑍 𐑋𐐲𐐽 𐐼𐐲𐑅𐐻 𐐲𐐸𐑌 𐐒𐐨𐐿𐐱𐑆 𐐱𐑂 𐑄 𐐶𐐮𐐿𐐲𐐼𐑌𐐲𐑅 𐐱𐑂 𐑄 𐐹𐐨𐐹𐐲𐑊 𐐱𐑂 𐑄 𐐤𐐨𐑁𐐴𐐻𐑅, 𐑄𐐯𐑉 𐑅𐐨𐐿𐑉𐐲𐐻 𐐶𐐲𐑉𐐿𐑅 𐐱𐑂 𐐼𐐲𐑉𐐿𐑌𐐲𐑅, 𐐰𐑌𐐼 𐑄𐐯𐑉 𐑋𐐲𐑉𐐼𐐲𐑉𐐮𐑍, 𐐰𐑌𐐼 𐑄𐐯𐑉 𐐹𐐲𐑉𐑌𐐼𐐲𐑉𐐮𐑍, 𐐰𐑌𐐼 𐐫𐑊 𐑋𐐲𐑌𐐲𐑉 𐐱𐑂 𐐮𐑌𐐮𐐿𐐶𐐮𐐻𐐨—𐐰𐑌𐐼 𐐮𐐻 𐐗𐐩𐑋 𐐻𐐭 𐐑𐐰𐑅 𐐰𐑆 𐐸𐐨 𐐶𐐲𐑆 𐑄𐐲𐑆 𐐹𐐱𐑌𐐼𐐲𐑉𐐮𐑍 𐐮𐑌 𐐸𐐮𐑆 𐐸𐐲𐑉𐐻, 𐐒𐐨𐐸𐐬𐑊𐐼, 𐐩 𐑂𐐶𐐮𐑅 𐐗𐐩𐑋 𐐲𐑌𐐻𐐭 𐐸𐐮𐑋 𐑅𐐩𐐮𐑍, 𐐒𐑊𐐯𐑅𐐲𐐼 𐐪𐑉𐐻 𐑄𐐵, 𐐤𐐨𐑁𐐴, 𐑁𐐫𐑉 𐑄𐐬𐑆 𐑔𐐮𐑍𐑆 𐐸𐐶𐐮𐐽 𐑄𐐵 𐐸𐐰𐑅𐐻 𐐼𐐲𐑌; 𐑁𐐫𐑉 𐐌 𐐸𐐰𐑂 𐐒𐐨𐐸𐐾𐐬𐑊𐐼 𐐸𐐵 𐑄𐐵 𐐸𐐰𐑅𐐻 𐐶𐐮𐑄 𐐲𐑌-𐐶𐐩𐑉𐐨𐐮𐑍𐑌𐐲𐑅 𐐼𐐨𐐿𐑊𐐯𐐩𐑉𐐼 𐑄 𐐶𐐲𐑉𐐼 𐐸𐐶𐐮𐐽 𐐌 𐐸𐐰𐑂 𐑀𐐮𐑂𐐲𐑌 𐐲𐑌𐐻𐐭 𐑄𐐨, 𐐲𐑌𐐻𐐭 𐑄𐐮𐑅 𐐹𐐨𐐹𐐲𐑊. 𐐰𐑌𐐼 𐑄𐐵 𐐸𐐰𐑅𐐻 𐑌𐐱𐐻 𐑁𐐨𐑉𐐼 𐑄𐐯𐑋, 𐐰𐑌𐐼 𐐸𐐰𐑅𐐻 𐑌𐐱𐐻 𐑅𐐫𐐻 𐑄𐐴𐑌 𐐬𐑌 𐑊𐐴𐑁, 𐐒𐐲𐐻 𐐸𐐰𐑅𐐻 𐑅𐐫𐐻 𐑋𐐴 𐐶𐐮𐑊, 𐐰𐑌𐐼 𐐻𐐭 𐐿𐐨𐐹 𐑋𐐴 𐐿𐐱𐑋𐐰𐑌𐐼𐑋𐐲𐑌𐐻𐑅. 𐐰𐑌𐐼 𐑌𐐵 𐐒𐐨𐐿𐐱𐑆 𐑄𐐵 𐐸𐐰𐑅𐐻 𐐼𐐲𐑌 𐑄𐐮𐑅 𐐶𐐮𐑄 𐑅𐐲𐐽 𐐲𐑌𐐶𐐯𐑉𐐨𐐮𐑍𐑌𐐲𐑅, 𐐒𐐨𐐸𐐬𐑊𐐼, 𐐌 𐐶𐐮𐑊 𐐒𐑊𐐯𐑅 𐑄𐐨 𐑁𐐫𐑉 𐐯𐑂𐐲𐑉; 𐐰𐑌𐐼 𐐌 𐐶𐐮𐑊 𐑋𐐩𐐿 𐑄𐐨 𐑋𐐴𐐻𐐨 𐐮𐑌 𐐶𐐲𐑉𐐼 𐐰𐑌𐐼 𐐮𐑌 𐐼𐐨𐐼, 𐐮𐑌 𐑁𐐩𐑔 𐐰𐑌𐐼 𐐮𐑌 𐐶𐐲𐑉𐐿𐑅; 𐐷𐐩, 𐐨𐑂𐐯𐑌 𐑄𐐰𐐻 𐐫𐑊 𐑔𐐮𐑍𐑆 𐑇𐐰𐑊 𐐒𐐨 𐐼𐐲𐑌 𐐲𐑌𐐻𐐭 𐑄 𐐰𐐿𐐫𐑉𐐼𐐮𐑍 𐐻𐐭 𐑄𐐴 𐐶𐐲𐑉𐐼, 𐑁𐐫𐑉 𐑄𐐵 𐑇𐐰𐑊𐐻 𐑌𐐱𐐻 𐐰𐑅𐐿 𐑄𐐰𐐻 𐐸𐐶𐐮𐐽 𐐮𐑆 𐐪𐑌𐐻𐑉𐐨𐐲𐐻 𐐻𐐭 𐑋𐐴 𐐶𐐮𐑊. 𐐒𐐨𐐸𐐬𐑊𐐼, 𐑄𐐵 𐐪𐑉𐐻 𐐤𐐨𐑁𐐴, 𐐰𐑌𐐼 𐐌 𐐰𐑋 𐐘𐐱𐐼. 𐐒𐐨𐐸𐐬𐑊𐐼, 𐐌 𐐼𐐮𐐿𐑊𐐯𐑉 𐐮𐐻 𐐲𐑌𐐻𐐭 𐑄 𐐮𐑌 𐑄 𐐹𐑉𐐯𐑆𐐲𐑌𐑅 𐐱𐑂 𐑋𐐴𐑌 𐐯𐑌𐐾𐐲𐑊𐑆, 𐑄𐐰𐐻 𐑄𐐵 𐑇𐐰𐑊𐐻 𐐸𐐰𐑂 𐐹𐐵𐐲𐑉 𐐬𐑂𐐲𐑉 𐑄𐐮𐑅 𐐹𐐨𐐹𐐲𐑊, 𐐰𐑌𐐼 𐑇𐐰𐑊𐐻 𐑅𐑋𐐴𐐻 𐑄 𐐲𐑉𐑔 𐐶𐐮𐑄 𐑁𐐰𐑋𐐮𐑌, 𐐰𐑌𐐼 𐐶𐐮𐑄 𐐹𐐯𐑅𐐻𐐲𐑊𐐲𐑌𐑅, 𐐰𐑌𐐼 𐐼𐐲𐑅𐐻𐑉𐐲𐐿𐑇𐐲𐑌, 𐐰𐐿𐐫𐑉𐐼𐐮𐑍 𐐻𐐭 𐑄 𐐶𐐮𐐿𐐲𐐼𐑌𐐲𐑅 𐐱𐑂 𐑄𐐮𐑅 𐐹𐐨𐐹𐐲𐑊. 𐐒𐐨𐐸𐐬𐑊𐐼, 𐐌 𐑀𐐮𐑂 𐐲𐑌𐐻𐐭 𐐷𐐭 𐐹𐐵𐐲𐑉, 𐑄𐐰𐐻 𐐸𐐶𐐫𐐻𐑅𐐬𐐯𐑂𐐲𐑉 𐐷𐐨 𐑇𐐰𐑊 𐑅𐐨𐑊 𐐱𐑌 𐐲𐑉𐑔, 𐑇𐐰𐑊 𐐒𐐨 𐑅𐐨𐑊𐐼 𐐮𐑌 𐐸𐐯𐑂𐐲𐑌; 𐐰𐑌𐐼 𐐸𐐶𐐫𐐻𐑅𐐬-𐐯𐑂𐐲𐑉 𐐷𐐨 𐑇𐐰𐑊 𐑊𐐭𐑆 𐐱𐑌 𐐲𐑉𐑔 𐑇𐐰𐑊 𐐒𐐨 𐑊𐐭𐑅𐐻 𐐮𐑌 𐐸𐐯𐑂𐐲𐑌; 𐐰𐑌𐐼 𐑄𐐲𐑆 𐑇𐐰𐑊 𐐷𐐨 𐐸𐐰𐑂 𐐹𐐵𐐲𐑉 𐐲𐑋𐐲𐑍 𐑄𐐮𐑅

𐐹𐐨𐐹𐑊. 𐐈𐑌𐐼 𐑌𐐵, 𐐮𐑁 𐐷𐐨 𐑇𐐰𐑊 𐑅𐐩 𐐲𐑌𐐻𐐭 𐑄𐐮𐑅 𐐻𐐯𐑋𐐹𐑊, 𐐮𐐻 𐑇𐐰𐑊 𐐺𐐨 𐑉𐐯𐑌𐐻 𐐮𐑌 𐐻𐐶𐐩𐑌, 𐐮𐐻 𐑇𐐰𐑊 𐐺𐐨 𐐼𐐲𐑌. 𐐈𐑌𐐼 𐐺𐐨𐐸𐐬𐑊𐐼 𐐮𐑁 𐐷𐐨 𐑇𐐰𐑊 𐑅𐐩, 𐑄𐐰𐐻 𐐘𐐱𐐼 𐑇𐐰𐑊 𐑅𐑋𐐴𐐻 𐑄𐐮𐑅 𐐹𐐨𐐹𐑊, 𐐮𐐻 𐑇𐐰𐑊 𐐿𐐲𐑋 𐐻𐐭 𐐹𐐰𐑅. 𐐈𐑌𐐼 𐑌𐐵 𐐺𐐨𐐸𐐬𐑊𐐼, 𐐌 𐐿𐐱𐑋𐐰𐑌𐐼 𐐷𐐭 𐑄𐐰𐐻 𐐷𐐨 𐑇𐐰𐑊 𐑀𐐬, 𐐰𐑌𐐼 𐐼𐐨𐐿𐑊𐐯𐑉 𐐲𐑌𐐻𐐭 𐑄𐐮𐑅 𐐹𐐨𐐹𐑊, 𐑄𐐰𐐻 𐑄𐐲𐑅 𐑅𐐯𐑃 𐑄 𐐢𐐫𐑉𐐼 𐐘𐐱𐐼, 𐐸𐐭 𐐮𐑆 𐑄 𐐉𐑊𐑋𐐴𐐻𐐨, 𐐇𐐿𐑅𐐯𐐹𐐻 𐐷𐐨 𐑉𐐨𐐹𐐯𐑌𐐻 𐐷𐐨 𐑇𐐰𐑊 𐐺𐐨 𐑅𐑋𐐮𐐻𐑌, 𐐨𐑂𐑌 𐐲𐑌𐐻𐐭 𐐼𐐯𐑅𐐻𐑉𐐲𐐿𐑇𐐲𐑌.

14. 𐐈𐑌𐐼 𐐺𐐨𐐸𐐬𐑊𐐼, 𐑌𐐵 𐐮𐐻 𐐿𐐩𐑋 𐐻𐐭 𐐹𐐰𐑅 𐑄𐐰𐐻 𐐸𐐶𐐯𐑌 𐑄 𐐢𐐫𐑉𐐼 𐐸𐐰𐐼 𐑅𐐹𐐬𐐿𐑌 𐑄𐐨𐑆 𐐶𐐲𐑉𐐼𐑆 𐐲𐑌𐐻𐐭 𐐤𐐨𐑁𐐴, 𐐸𐐨 𐐼𐐮𐐼 𐑅𐐻𐐱𐐹, 𐐰𐑌𐐼 𐐼𐐮𐐼 𐑌𐐱𐐻 𐑀𐐬 𐐲𐑌𐐻𐐭 𐐸𐐮𐑆 𐐬𐑌 𐐸𐐵𐑅, 𐐺𐐲𐐻 𐐼𐐮𐐼 𐑉𐐨𐐻𐐲𐑉𐑌 𐐲𐑌𐐻𐐭 𐑄 𐑋𐐲𐑊𐐻𐐨𐐻𐐭𐐼𐑆 𐐸𐐭 𐐶𐐲𐑉 𐑅𐐿𐐰𐐻𐐲𐑉𐐼 𐐰𐐺𐐵𐐻 𐐲𐐹𐐱𐑌 𐑄 𐑁𐐩𐑅 𐐱𐑂 𐑄 𐑊𐐰𐑌𐐼, 𐐰𐑌𐐼 𐐺𐐨𐑀𐐰𐑌 𐐻𐐭 𐐼𐐨𐐿𐑊𐐯𐑉 𐐲𐑌𐐻𐐭 𐑄𐐯𐑋 𐑄 𐐶𐐲𐑉𐐼 𐐱𐑂 𐑄 𐐢𐐫𐑉𐐼 𐐸𐐶𐐮𐐽 𐐸𐐰𐐼 𐐺𐐮𐑌 𐑅𐐹𐐬𐐿𐑌 𐐲𐑌𐐻𐐭 𐐸𐐮𐑋, 𐐿𐐱𐑌𐑅𐐲𐑉𐑌𐐮𐑍 𐑄𐐯𐑉 𐐼𐐯𐑅𐐻𐑉𐐲𐐿𐑇𐐲𐑌, 𐐮𐑁 𐑄𐐩 𐐼𐐮𐐼 𐑌𐐱𐐻 𐑉𐐨𐐹𐐯𐑌𐐻. 𐐤𐐵 𐐺𐐨𐐸𐐬𐑊𐐼, 𐑌𐐱𐐻𐐶𐐮𐑃𐑅𐐻𐐰𐑌𐐼𐐮𐑍 𐑄𐐰𐐻 𐑀𐑉𐐩𐐻 𐑋𐐮𐑉𐐲𐐿𐑊 𐐸𐐶𐐮𐐽 𐐤𐐨𐑁𐐴 𐐸𐐰𐐼 𐐼𐐲𐑌 𐐮𐑌 𐐻𐐯𐑊𐐮𐑍 𐑄𐐯𐑋 𐐿𐐱𐑌𐑅𐐲𐑉𐑌𐐮𐑍 𐑄 𐐼𐐯𐑃 𐐱𐑂 𐑄 𐐗𐐨𐑁 𐐖𐐲𐐾, 𐑄𐐩 𐐼𐐮𐐼 𐐸𐐪𐑉𐐼𐑌 𐑄𐐯𐑉 𐐸𐐪𐑉𐐻𐑅, 𐐰𐑌𐐼 𐐼𐐮𐐼 𐑌𐐱𐐻 𐐸𐐪𐑉𐐿𐑌 𐐲𐑌𐐻𐐭 𐑄 𐐶𐐲𐑉𐐼𐑆 𐐱𐑂 𐑄 𐐢𐐫𐑉𐐼; 𐑄𐐯𐑉𐑁𐐬𐑉 𐐤𐐨𐑁𐐴 𐐼𐐮𐐼 𐐼𐐨𐐿𐑊𐐯𐑉 𐐲𐑌𐐻𐐭 𐑄𐐯𐑋 𐑄 𐐶𐐲𐑉𐐼 𐐱𐑂 𐑄 𐐢𐐫𐑉𐐼, 𐑅𐐩𐐮𐑍, 𐐇𐐿𐑅𐐯𐐹𐐻 𐐷𐐨 𐑉𐐨𐐹𐐯𐑌𐐻, 𐑄𐐲𐑅 𐑅𐐯𐑃 𐑄 𐐢𐐫𐑉𐐼, 𐐷𐐨 𐑇𐐰𐑊 𐐺𐐨 𐑅𐑋𐐮𐐻𐑌 𐐨𐑂𐑌 𐐲𐑌𐐻𐐭 𐐼𐐯𐑅𐐻𐑉𐐲𐐿𐑇𐐲𐑌. 𐐈𐑌𐐼 𐐮𐐻 𐐿𐐩𐑋 𐐻𐐭 𐐹𐐰𐑅 𐑄𐐰𐐻 𐐸𐐶𐐯𐑌 𐐤𐐨𐑁𐐴 𐐸𐐰𐐼 𐐼𐐨𐐿𐑊𐐯𐑉𐐼 𐐲𐑌𐐻𐐭 𐑄𐐯𐑋 𐑄 𐐶𐐲𐑉𐐼, 𐐺𐐨𐐸𐐬𐑊𐐼, 𐑄𐐩 𐐼𐐮𐐼 𐑅𐐻𐐮𐑊 𐐸𐐪𐑉𐐼𐑌 𐑄𐐯𐑉 𐐸𐐪𐑉𐐻𐑅, 𐐰𐑌𐐼 𐐶𐐳𐐼 𐑌𐐱𐐻 𐐸𐐪𐑉𐐿𐑌 𐐲𐑌𐐻𐐭 𐐸𐐮𐑆 𐐶𐐲𐑉𐐼𐑆; 𐑄𐐯𐑉𐑁𐐬𐑉 𐑄𐐩 𐐼𐐮𐐼 𐑉𐐨𐑂𐐴𐑊 𐐰𐑀𐐯𐑌𐑅𐐻 𐐸𐐮𐑋, 𐐰𐑌𐐼 𐐼𐐮𐐼 𐑅𐐨𐐿 𐐻𐐭 𐑊𐐩 𐑄𐐯𐑉 𐐸𐐰𐑌𐐼𐑆 𐐲𐐹𐐱𐑌 𐐸𐐮𐑋, 𐑄𐐰𐐻 𐑄𐐩 𐑋𐐴𐐻 𐐿𐐰𐑅𐐻 𐐸𐐮𐑋 𐐮𐑌𐐻𐐭 𐐹𐑉𐐮𐑆𐑌. 𐐒𐐲𐐻 𐐺𐐨𐐸𐐬𐑊𐐼, 𐑄 𐐹𐐵𐐲𐑉 𐐱𐑂 𐐘𐐱𐐼 𐐶𐐱𐑆 𐐶𐐮𐑄 𐐸𐐮𐑋, 𐐰𐑌𐐼 𐑄𐐩 𐐿𐐳𐐼 𐑌𐐱𐐻 𐐻𐐩𐐿 𐐸𐐮𐑋 𐐻𐐭 𐐿𐐰𐑅𐐻 𐐸𐐮𐑋 𐐮𐑌𐐻𐐭 𐐹𐑉𐐮𐑆𐑌, 𐑁𐐫𐑉 𐐸𐐨 𐐶𐐱𐑆 𐐻𐐩𐐿𐑌 𐐺𐐴 𐑄 𐐝𐐹𐐮𐑉𐐮𐐻, 𐐰𐑌𐐼 𐐿𐐱𐑌𐑂𐐩𐐼 𐐰𐐶𐐩 𐐵𐐻 𐐱𐑂 𐑄 𐑋𐐮𐐼𐑅𐐻 𐐱𐑂 𐑄𐐯𐑋.

15. 𐐈𐑌𐐼 𐐮𐐻 𐐿𐐩𐑋 𐐻𐐭 𐐹𐐰𐑅 𐑄𐐰𐐻 𐑄𐐲𐑅 𐐸𐐨 𐐼𐐮𐐼 𐑀𐐬 𐑁𐐬𐑉𐑃 𐐮𐑌 𐑄 𐐝𐐹𐐮𐑉𐐮𐐻, 𐑁𐑉𐐱𐑋 𐑋𐐲𐑊𐐻𐐨𐐻𐐭𐐼 𐐻𐐭 𐑋𐐲𐑊𐐻𐐨𐐻𐐭𐐼, 𐐼𐐨𐐿𐑊𐐯𐑉𐐮𐑍 𐑄 𐐶𐐲𐑉𐐼 𐐱𐑂 𐐘𐐱𐐼, 𐐨𐑂𐑌 𐐲𐑌𐐻𐐮𐑊 𐐸𐐨 𐐸𐐰𐐼 𐐼𐐨𐐿𐑊𐐯𐑉𐐼 𐐮𐐻 𐐲𐑌𐐻𐐭 𐑄𐐯𐑋 𐐫𐑊, 𐐫𐑉 𐑅𐐯𐑌𐐻 𐐮𐐻 𐑁𐐬𐑉𐑃 𐐰𐑋𐐲𐑍 𐐫𐑊 𐑄 𐐹𐐨𐐹𐑊. 𐐈𐑌𐐼 𐐮𐐻 𐐿𐐩𐑋 𐐻𐐭 𐐹𐐰𐑅 𐑄𐐰𐐻 𐑄𐐩 𐐶𐐳𐐼 𐑌𐐱𐐻 𐐸𐐪𐑉𐐿𐑌 𐐲𐑌𐐻𐐭 𐐸𐐮𐑆 𐐶𐐲𐑉𐐼𐑆; 𐐰𐑌𐐼 𐑄𐐯𐑉 𐐺𐐨𐑀𐐰𐑌 𐐻𐐭 𐐺𐐨 𐐿𐐱𐑌𐐻𐐯𐑌𐑇𐐲𐑌𐑆, 𐐮𐑌𐑅𐐬𐑋𐐲𐐽 𐑄𐐰𐐻 𐑄𐐩 𐐶𐐲𐑉 𐐼𐐮𐑂𐐴𐐼𐐯𐐼 𐐰𐑀𐐯𐑌𐑅𐐻 𐑄𐐯𐑋𐑅𐐯𐑊𐑂𐑆, 𐐰𐑌𐐼 𐐺𐐨𐑀𐐰𐑌 𐐻𐐭 𐑅𐑊𐐩 𐐶𐐲𐑌 𐐰𐑌𐐲𐑄𐐲𐑉 𐐶𐐮𐑄 𐑄 𐑅𐐬𐑉𐐼. 𐐈𐑌𐐼 𐑄𐐲𐑅 𐐯𐑌𐐼𐐯𐐼 𐑄 𐑅𐐯𐑂𐑌𐐻𐐨 𐐰𐑌𐐼 𐑁𐐲𐑉𐑅𐐻 𐐷𐐨𐑉 𐐱𐑂 𐑄 𐑉𐐩𐑌 𐐱𐑂 𐑄 𐐾𐐲𐐾𐐯𐑆 𐐬𐑂𐐲𐑉 𐑄 𐐹𐐨𐐹𐑊 𐐱𐑂 𐐤𐐨𐑁𐐴.

𐐕𐐰𐐹𐐻𐐲𐑉 IV.

1. 𐐈𐑌𐐼 𐑌𐐵 𐐮𐐻 𐐿𐐩𐑋 𐐻𐐭 𐐹𐐰𐑅 𐐮𐑌 𐑄 𐑅𐐯𐑂𐑌𐐻𐐨 𐐰𐑌𐐼 𐑅𐐯𐐿𐐲𐑌𐐼 𐐷𐐨𐑉 𐐱𐑂 𐑄 𐑉𐐩𐑌 𐐱𐑂 𐑄 𐐾𐐲𐐾𐐯𐑆, 𐑄𐐰𐐻 𐑄 𐐿𐐱𐑌𐐻𐐯𐑌𐑇𐐲𐑌𐑆 𐐼𐐮𐐼 𐐮𐑌𐐿𐑉𐐨𐑅, 𐐮𐑌𐑅𐐬𐑋𐐲𐐽 𐑄𐐰𐐻 𐑄𐐯𐑉 𐐶𐐲𐑉 𐐶𐐫𐑉𐑆 𐑃𐑉𐐭𐐵𐐻 𐐫𐑊 𐑄 𐑊𐐰𐑌𐐼 𐐰𐑋𐐲𐑍 𐐫𐑊 𐑄 𐐹𐐨𐐹𐑊 𐐱𐑂 𐐤𐐨𐑁𐐴. 𐐈𐑌𐐼 𐐮𐐻 𐐶𐐱𐑆 𐑄𐐮𐑅 𐑅𐐨𐐿𐑉𐐯𐐻 𐐺𐐰𐑌𐐼 𐐱𐑂 𐑉𐐱𐐺𐐲𐑉𐑆 𐐸𐐭 𐐼𐐮𐐼 𐐿𐐰𐑉𐐨 𐐱𐑌 𐑄𐐮𐑅 𐐶𐐲𐑉𐐿 𐐱𐑂 𐐼𐐯𐑅𐐻𐑉𐐲𐐿𐑇𐐲𐑌 𐐰𐑌𐐼 𐐶𐐮𐐿𐐯𐐼𐑌𐐯𐑅. 𐐈𐑌𐐼 𐑄𐐮𐑅 𐐶𐐫𐑉 𐐼𐐮𐐼 𐑊𐐰𐑅𐐻 𐐫𐑊 𐑄𐐰𐐻 𐐷𐐨𐑉. 𐐈𐑌𐐼 𐐮𐑌 𐑄 𐑅𐐯𐑂𐑌𐐻𐐨 𐐰𐑌𐐼 𐑃𐐲𐑉𐐼 𐐷𐐨𐑉 𐐮𐐻 𐐼𐐮𐐼 𐐫𐑊𐑅𐐬 𐑊𐐰𐑅𐐻.

2. 𐐈𐑌𐐼 𐐮𐐻 𐐿𐐩𐑋 𐐻𐐭 𐐹𐐰𐑅 𐑄𐐰𐐻 𐐮𐑌 𐑄𐐮𐑅 𐐷𐐨𐑉, 𐐤𐐨𐑁𐐴 𐐼𐐮𐐼 𐐿𐑉𐐴 𐐲𐑌𐐻𐐭 𐑄 𐐢𐐫𐑉𐐼, 𐑅𐐩𐐮𐑍, 𐐄 𐐢𐐫𐑉𐐼 𐐼𐐭 𐑌𐐱𐐻 𐑅𐐲𐑁𐐲𐑉 𐑄𐐰𐐻 𐑄𐐮𐑅 𐐹𐐨𐐹𐑊 𐑇𐐰𐑊 𐐺𐐨 𐐼𐐯𐑅𐐻𐑉𐐦𐐼 𐐺𐐴 𐑄 𐑅𐐬𐑉𐐼; 𐐺𐐲𐐻 𐐄 𐐢𐐫𐑉𐐼, 𐑉𐐪𐑄𐐲𐑉 𐑊𐐯𐐻 𐑄𐐯𐑉 𐐺𐐨 𐐩 𐑁𐐰𐑋𐐮𐑌 𐐮𐑌 𐑄 𐑊𐐰𐑌𐐼, 𐐻𐐭 𐑅𐐻𐐲𐑉 𐑄𐐯𐑋 𐐲𐐹 𐐮𐑌 𐑉𐐨𐑋𐐯𐑋𐐺𐑉𐐲𐑌𐑅 𐐱𐑂 𐑄 𐐢𐐫𐑉𐐼 𐑄𐐯𐑉 𐐘𐐱𐐼, 𐐰𐑌𐐼 𐐹𐐲𐑉𐐸𐐰𐐹𐑅 𐑄𐐩 𐐶𐐮𐑊 𐑉𐐨𐐹𐐯𐑌𐐻 𐐰𐑌𐐼 𐐻𐐲𐑉𐑌 𐐲𐑌𐐻𐐭 𐑄𐐨; 𐐰𐑌𐐼 𐑅𐐬 𐐮𐐻 𐐶𐐱𐑆 𐐼𐐲𐑌, 𐐰𐐿𐐫𐑉𐐼𐐮𐑍 𐐻𐐭 𐑄 𐐶𐐲𐑉𐐼𐑆 𐐱𐑂 𐐤𐐨𐑁𐐴. 𐐈𐑌𐐼 𐑄𐐯𐑉 𐐶𐐱𐑆 𐐩 𐑀𐑉𐐩𐐻 𐑁𐐰𐑋𐐮𐑌 𐐲𐐹𐐱𐑌 𐑄 𐑊𐐰𐑌𐐼, 𐐰𐑋𐐲𐑍 𐐫𐑊 𐑄 𐐹𐐨𐐹𐑊 𐐱𐑂 𐐤𐐨𐑁𐐴. 𐐈𐑌𐐼 𐑄𐐲𐑅 𐐮𐑌 𐑄 𐑅𐐯𐑂𐑌𐐻𐐨 𐐰𐑌𐐼 𐑁𐐬𐑉𐑃 𐐷𐐨𐑉 𐑄 𐑁𐐰𐑋𐐮𐑌 𐐼𐐮𐐼 𐐿𐐱𐑌𐐻𐐮𐑌𐐷𐐭, 𐐰𐑌𐐼 𐑄 𐐶𐐲𐑉𐐿 𐐱𐑂 𐐼𐐯𐑅𐐻𐑉𐐲𐐿𐑇𐐲𐑌 𐐼𐐮𐐼 𐑅𐐨𐑅 𐐺𐐴 𐑄 𐑅𐐬𐑉𐐼, 𐐺𐐲𐐻 𐐺𐐨𐐿𐐩𐑋 𐑅𐐬𐑉 𐐺𐐴 𐑁𐐰𐑋𐐮𐑌.

𐐰𐑌𐐼 𐑄𐐮𐑅 𐐶𐐲𐑉𐐿 𐐱𐑂 𐐼𐐯𐑅𐐻𐑉𐐲𐐿𐑇𐐲𐑌 𐐼𐐮𐐼 𐐫𐑊𐑅𐐬 𐐿𐐱𐑌𐐻𐐮𐑌𐐷𐐭 𐐮𐑌 𐑄 𐑅𐐯𐑂𐐲𐑌𐐻𐐨 𐐰𐑌𐐼 𐑁𐐮𐑁𐑃 𐐷𐐨𐑉. 𐐙𐐫𐑉 𐑄 𐐲𐑉𐑃 𐐶𐐱𐑆 𐑅𐑋𐐮𐐻𐐲𐑌 𐑄𐐰𐐻 𐐮𐐻 𐐶𐐱𐑆 𐐼𐑉𐐴, 𐐰𐑌𐐼 𐐼𐐮𐐼 𐑌𐐱𐐻 𐐷𐐨𐑊𐐼 𐑁𐐫𐑉𐑃 𐑀𐑉𐐩𐑌 𐐮𐑌 𐑄 𐑅𐐨𐑆𐐲𐑌 𐐱𐑂 𐑀𐑉𐐩𐑌; 𐐰𐑌𐐼 𐑄 𐐸𐐬𐑊 𐐲𐑉𐑃 𐐶𐐱𐑆 𐑅𐑋𐐮𐐻𐐲𐑌, 𐐨𐑂𐐲𐑌 𐐲𐑋𐐲𐑍 𐑄 𐐢𐐰𐑋𐐲𐑌𐐴𐐻𐑅 𐐰𐑆 𐐶𐐯𐑊 𐐰𐑆 𐐲𐑋𐐲𐑍 𐑄 𐐤𐐨𐑁𐐴𐐻𐑅, 𐑅𐐬 𐑄𐐰𐐻 𐑄𐐩 𐐶𐐲𐑉 𐑅𐑋𐐮𐐻𐐲𐑌 𐑄𐐰𐐻 𐑄𐐩 𐐼𐐮𐐼 𐐹𐐯𐑉𐐮𐑇 𐐺𐐴 𐑃𐐵𐑆𐐲𐑌𐐼𐑆 𐐮𐑌 𐑄 𐑋𐐬𐑉 𐐶𐐮𐐿𐐲𐐼 𐐹𐐪𐑉𐐻𐑅 𐐱𐑂 𐑄 𐑊𐐰𐑌𐐼.

3. 𐐰𐑌𐐼 𐐮𐐻 𐐿𐐩𐑋 𐐻𐐭 𐐹𐐰𐑅 𐑄𐐰𐐻 𐑄 𐐹𐐨𐐹𐐲𐑊 𐑅𐐫 𐑄𐐰𐐻 𐑄𐐩 𐐶𐐲𐑉 𐐲𐐺𐐵𐐻 𐐻𐐭 𐐹𐐯𐑉𐐮𐑇 𐐺𐐴 𐑁𐐰𐑋𐐮𐑌, 𐐰𐑌𐐼 𐑄𐐩 𐐺𐐨𐑀𐐰𐑌 𐐻𐐭 𐑉𐐨𐑋𐐯𐑋𐐺𐐲𐑉 𐑄 𐐢𐐫𐑉𐐼 𐑄𐐯𐑉 𐐘𐐱𐐼; 𐐰𐑌𐐼 𐑄𐐩 𐐺𐐨𐑀𐐰𐑌 𐐻𐐭 𐑉𐐨𐑋𐐯𐑋𐐺𐐲𐑉 𐑄 𐐶𐐲𐑉𐐼𐑆 𐐱𐑂 𐐤𐐨𐑁𐐴. 𐐰𐑌𐐼 𐑄 𐐹𐐨𐐹𐐲𐑊 𐐺𐐨𐑀𐐰𐑌 𐐻𐐭 𐐹𐑊𐐨𐐼 𐐶𐐮𐑄 𐑄𐐯𐑉 𐐽𐐨𐑁 𐐾𐐲𐐾𐐲𐑆 𐐰𐑌𐐼 𐑄𐐯𐑉 𐑊𐐨𐐼𐐲𐑉𐑆, 𐑄𐐰𐐻 𐑄𐐩 𐐶𐐳𐐼 𐑅𐐩 𐐲𐑌𐐻𐐭 𐐤𐐨𐑁𐐴, 𐐒𐐨𐐸𐐬𐑊𐐼, 𐐶𐐨 𐑌𐐬 𐑄𐐰𐐻 𐑄𐐵 𐐪𐑉𐐻 𐐲 𐑋𐐰𐑌 𐐱𐑂 𐐘𐐱𐐼, 𐐰𐑌𐐼 𐑄𐐯𐑉𐑁𐐫𐑉 𐐿𐑉𐐴 𐐲𐑌𐐻𐐭 𐑄 𐐢𐐫𐑉𐐼 𐐵𐑉 𐐘𐐱𐐼 𐑄𐐰𐐻 𐐸𐐨 𐐻𐐲𐑉𐑌 𐐲𐐶𐐩 𐑁𐑉𐐱𐑋 𐐲𐑅 𐑄𐐮𐑅 𐑁𐐰𐑋𐐮𐑌, 𐑊𐐯𐑅𐐻 𐐫𐑊 𐑄 𐐶𐐲𐑉𐐼𐑆 𐐸𐐶𐐮𐐽 𐑄𐐵 𐐸𐐰𐑅𐐻 𐑅𐐹𐐬𐐿𐐲𐑌 𐐿𐐱𐑌𐑅𐐲𐑉𐑌𐐮𐑍 𐐵𐑉 𐐼𐐯𐑅𐐻𐑉𐐲𐐿𐑇𐐲𐑌 𐐺𐐨 𐑁𐐳𐑊𐑁𐐮𐑊𐐼. 𐐰𐑌𐐼 𐐮𐐻 𐐿𐐩𐑋 𐐻𐐭 𐐹𐐰𐑅 𐑄𐐰𐐻 𐑄 𐐾𐐲𐐾𐐲𐑆 𐐼𐐮𐐼 𐑅𐐩 𐐲𐑌𐐻𐐭 𐐤𐐨𐑁𐐴, 𐐰𐐿𐐫𐑉𐐼𐐮𐑍 𐐻𐐭 𐑄 𐐶𐐲𐑉𐐼𐑆 𐐸𐐶𐐮𐐽 𐐸𐐰𐐼 𐐺𐐨𐑌 𐐼𐐨𐑆𐐴𐑉𐐼. 𐐰𐑌𐐼 𐐮𐐻 𐐿𐐩𐑋 𐐻𐐭 𐐹𐐰𐑅 𐑄𐐰𐐻 𐐸𐐶𐐯𐑌 𐐤𐐨𐑁𐐴 𐑅𐐫 𐑄𐐰𐐻 𐑄 𐐹𐐨𐐹𐐲𐑊 𐐸𐐰𐐼 𐑉𐐨𐐹𐐯𐑌𐐻𐐲𐐼, 𐐰𐑌𐐼 𐐼𐐮𐐼 𐐸𐐲𐑋𐐺𐐲𐑊 𐑄𐐯𐑋𐑅𐐯𐑊𐑂𐑆 𐐮𐑌 𐑅𐐰𐐿𐐿𐑊𐐱𐑃, 𐐸𐐨 𐐿𐑉𐐴𐐼 𐐲𐑀𐐯𐑌 𐐲𐑌𐐻𐐭 𐑄 𐐢𐐫𐑉𐐼, 𐑅𐐩𐐮𐑍, 𐐄 𐐢𐐫𐑉𐐼, 𐐺𐐨𐐸𐐬𐑊𐐼 𐑄𐐮𐑅 𐐹𐐨𐐹𐐲𐑊 𐑉𐐨𐐹𐐯𐑌𐐻𐐯𐑃; 𐐰𐑌𐐼 𐑄𐐩 𐐸𐐰𐑂 𐑅𐐶𐐯𐐹𐐻 𐐲𐐶𐐩 𐑄 𐐺𐐰𐑌𐐼 𐐱𐑂 𐐘𐐰𐐼𐐨𐐰𐑌𐐻𐐲𐑌 𐑁𐑉𐐱𐑋 𐐲𐑋𐐲𐑍𐑅𐐻 𐑄𐐯𐑋, 𐐮𐑌𐑅𐐬𐑋𐐲𐐽 𐑄𐐰𐐻 𐑄𐐩 𐐸𐐰𐑂 𐐺𐐨𐐿𐐲𐑋 𐐯𐐿𐑅𐐻𐐮𐑍𐐿𐐻, 𐐰𐑌𐐼 𐑄𐐩 𐐸𐐰𐑂 𐐿𐐱𐑌𐑅𐐨𐑊𐐼 𐑄𐐯𐑉 𐑅𐐨𐐿𐑉𐐯𐐻 𐐹𐑊𐐰𐑌𐑆 𐐮𐑌 𐑄 𐐲𐑉𐑃. 𐐤𐐵, 𐐄 𐐢𐐫𐑉𐐼, 𐐺𐐨𐐿𐐱𐑆 𐐱𐑂 𐑄𐐮𐑅 𐑄𐐯𐑉 𐐸𐐷𐐭𐑋𐐮𐑊𐐮𐐻𐐨, 𐐶𐐮𐑊𐐻 𐑄𐐵 𐐻𐐲𐑉𐑌 𐐲𐐶𐐩 𐑄𐐴𐑌 𐐰𐑍𐑀𐐲𐑉, 𐐰𐑌𐐼 𐑊𐐯𐐻 𐑄𐐴𐑌 𐐰𐑍𐑀𐐲𐑉 𐐺𐐨 𐐰𐐹𐐨𐑆𐐼 𐐮𐑌 𐑄 𐐼𐐯𐑅𐐻𐑉𐐲𐐿𐑇𐐲𐑌 𐐱𐑂 𐑄𐐬𐑆 𐐶𐐮𐐿𐐲𐐼 𐑋𐐯𐑌 𐐸𐐭𐑋 𐑄𐐵 𐐸𐐰𐑅𐐻 𐐫𐑊𐑉𐐯𐐼𐐨 𐐼𐐯𐑅𐐻𐑉𐐶𐐮𐐼? 𐐄 𐐢𐐫𐑉𐐼, 𐐶𐐮𐑊𐐻 𐑄𐐵 𐐻𐐲𐑉𐑌 𐐲𐐶𐐩 𐑄𐐴𐑌 𐐰𐑍𐑀𐐲𐑉, 𐐷𐐩, 𐑄𐐴 𐑁𐐨𐑉𐑅 𐐰𐑍𐑀𐐲𐑉, 𐐰𐑌𐐼 𐐿𐐫𐑆 𐑄𐐰𐐻 𐑄𐐮𐑅 𐑁𐐰𐑋𐐮𐑌 𐑋𐐩 𐑅𐐨𐑅 𐐮𐑌 𐑄𐐮𐑅 𐑊𐐰𐑌𐐼? 𐐄 𐐢𐐫𐑉𐐼, 𐐶𐐮𐑊𐐻 𐑄𐐵 𐐸𐐪𐑉𐐿𐐲𐑌 𐐲𐑌𐐻𐐭 𐑋𐐨, 𐐰𐑌𐐼 𐐿𐐫𐑆 𐑄𐐰𐐻 𐐮𐐻 𐑋𐐩 𐐺𐐨 𐐼𐐲𐑌 𐐰𐐿𐐫𐑉𐐼𐐮𐑍 𐐻𐐭 𐑋𐐴 𐐶𐐲𐑉𐐼𐑆, 𐐰𐑌𐐼 𐑅𐐯𐑌𐐼 𐑁𐐫𐑉𐑃 𐑉𐐩𐑌 𐐲𐐹𐐱𐑌 𐑄 𐑁𐐩𐑅 𐐱𐑂 𐑄 𐐲𐑉𐑃, 𐑄𐐰𐐻 𐑇𐐨 𐑋𐐩 𐐺𐑉𐐮𐑍 𐑁𐐫𐑉𐑃 𐐸𐐲𐑉 𐑁𐑉𐐭𐐻, 𐐰𐑌𐐼 𐐸𐐲𐑉 𐑀𐑉𐐩𐑌 𐐮𐑌 𐑄 𐑅𐐨𐑆𐐲𐑌 𐐱𐑂 𐑀𐑉𐐩𐑌? 𐐄 𐐢𐐫𐑉𐐼, 𐑄𐐵 𐐼𐐮𐐼𐑅𐐻 𐐸𐐪𐑉𐐿𐐲𐑌 𐐲𐑌𐐻𐐭 𐑋𐐴 𐐶𐐲𐑉𐐼𐑆 𐐸𐐶𐐯𐑌 𐐌 𐑅𐐯𐐼, 𐐢𐐯𐐻 𐑄𐐯𐑉 𐐺𐐨 𐐲 𐑁𐐰𐑋𐐮𐑌, 𐑄𐐰𐐻 𐑄 𐐹𐐯𐑅𐐻𐐮𐑊𐐯𐑌𐑅 𐐱𐑂 𐑄 𐑅𐐫𐑉𐐼 𐑋𐐴𐐻 𐑅𐐨𐑅; 𐐰𐑌𐐼 𐐌 𐑌𐐬 𐑄𐐰𐐻 𐑄𐐵 𐐶𐐮𐑊𐐻, 𐐨𐑂𐐲𐑌 𐐰𐐻 𐑄𐐮𐑅 𐐻𐐴𐑋, 𐐸𐐪𐑉𐐿𐐲𐑌 𐐲𐑌𐐻𐐭 𐑋𐐴 𐐶𐐲𐑉𐐼𐑆, 𐑁𐐫𐑉 𐑄𐐵 𐑅𐐯𐐼𐑅𐐻 𐑄𐐰𐐻, 𐐆𐑁 𐑄𐐮𐑅 𐐹𐐨𐐹𐐲𐑊 𐑉𐐨𐐹𐐯𐑌𐐻 𐐌 𐐶𐐮𐑊 𐑅𐐹𐐩𐑉 𐑄𐐯𐑋; 𐐷𐐩, 𐐄 𐐢𐐫𐑉𐐼, 𐐰𐑌𐐼 𐑄𐐵 𐑅𐐨𐐯𐑅𐐻 𐑄𐐰𐐻 𐑄𐐩 𐐸𐐰𐑂 𐑉𐐨𐐹𐐯𐑌𐐻𐐲𐐼, 𐐺𐐨𐐿𐐱𐑆 𐐱𐑂 𐑄 𐑁𐐰𐑋𐐮𐑌 𐐰𐑌𐐼 𐑄 𐐹𐐯𐑅𐐻𐐮𐑊𐐯𐑌𐑅 𐐰𐑌𐐼 𐐼𐐯𐑅𐐻𐑉𐐲𐐿𐑇𐐲𐑌 𐐸𐐶𐐮𐐽 𐐸𐐰𐑆 𐐿𐐲𐑋 𐐲𐑌𐐻𐐭 𐑄𐐯𐑋. 𐐰𐑌𐐼 𐑌𐐵, 𐐄 𐐢𐐫𐑉𐐼, 𐐶𐐮𐑊𐐻 𐑄𐐵 𐐻𐐲𐑉𐑌 𐐲𐐶𐐩 𐑄𐐴𐑌 𐐰𐑍𐑀𐐲𐑉, 𐐰𐑌𐐼 𐐻𐑉𐐴 𐐲𐑀𐐯𐑌 𐐮𐑁 𐑄𐐩 𐐶𐐮𐑊 𐑅𐐲𐑉𐑂 𐑄𐐨? 𐐰𐑌𐐼 𐐮𐑁 𐑅𐐬, 𐐄 𐐢𐐫𐑉𐐼, 𐑄𐐵 𐐿𐐰𐑌𐑅𐐻 𐐺𐑊𐐯𐑅 𐑄𐐯𐑋 𐐰𐐿𐐫𐑉𐐼𐐮𐑍 𐐻𐐭 𐑄𐐴 𐐶𐐲𐑉𐐼𐑆 𐐸𐐶𐐮𐐽 𐑄𐐵 𐐸𐐰𐑅𐐻 𐑅𐐯𐐼.

4. 𐐰𐑌𐐼 𐐮𐐻 𐐿𐐩𐑋 𐐻𐐭 𐐹𐐰𐑅 𐑄𐐰𐐻 𐐮𐑌 𐑄 𐑅𐐯𐑂𐐲𐑌𐐻𐐨 𐐰𐑌𐐼 𐑅𐐮𐐿𐑅𐑃 𐐷𐐨𐑉, 𐑄 𐐢𐐫𐑉𐐼 𐐼𐐮𐐼 𐐻𐐲𐑉𐑌 𐐲𐐶𐐩 𐐸𐐮𐑆 𐐰𐑍𐑀𐐲𐑉 𐑁𐑉𐐱𐑋 𐑄 𐐹𐐨𐐹𐐲𐑊, 𐐰𐑌𐐼 𐐿𐐫𐑆𐐼 𐑄𐐰𐐻 𐑉𐐩𐑌 𐑇𐐳𐐼 𐑁𐐫𐑊 𐐲𐐹𐐱𐑌 𐑄 𐐲𐑉𐑃, 𐐮𐑌𐑅𐐬𐑋𐐲𐐽 𐑄𐐰𐐻 𐐮𐐻 𐐼𐐮𐐼 𐐺𐑉𐐮𐑍 𐑁𐐫𐑉𐑃 𐐸𐐲𐑉 𐑁𐑉𐐭𐐻 𐐮𐑌 𐑄 𐑅𐐨𐑆𐐲𐑌 𐐱𐑂 𐐸𐐲𐑉 𐑁𐑉𐐭𐐻. 𐐰𐑌𐐼 𐐮𐐻 𐐿𐐩𐑋 𐐻𐐭 𐐹𐐰𐑅 𐑄𐐰𐐻 𐐮𐐻 𐐼𐐮𐐼 𐐺𐑉𐐮𐑍 𐑁𐐫𐑉𐑃 𐐸𐐲𐑉 𐑀𐑉𐐩𐑌 𐐮𐑌 𐑄 𐑅𐐨𐑆𐐲𐑌 𐐱𐑂 𐐸𐐲𐑉 𐑀𐑉𐐩𐑌. 𐐰𐑌𐐼 𐐺𐐨𐐸𐐬𐑊𐐼, 𐑄 𐐹𐐨𐐹𐐲𐑊 𐐼𐐮𐐼 𐑉𐐨𐐾𐐱𐐮𐑅, 𐐰𐑌𐐼 𐑀𐑊𐐬𐑉𐐮𐑁𐐴 𐐘𐐱𐐼, 𐐰𐑌𐐼 𐑄 𐐸𐐬𐑊 𐑁𐐩𐑅 𐐱𐑂 𐑄 𐑊𐐰𐑌𐐼 𐐶𐐱𐑆 𐑁𐐮𐑊𐐼 𐐶𐐮𐑄 𐑉𐐨𐐾𐐱𐐮𐑅𐐮𐑍; 𐐰𐑌𐐼 𐑄𐐩 𐐼𐐮𐐼 𐑌𐐬 𐑋𐐬𐑉 𐑅𐐨𐐿 𐐻𐐭 𐐼𐐯𐑅𐐻𐑉𐐱𐐮 𐐤𐐨𐑁𐐴, 𐐺𐐲𐐻 𐑄𐐩 𐐼𐐮𐐼 𐐯𐑅𐐻𐐨𐑋 𐐸𐐮𐑋 𐐰𐑆 𐐲 𐑀𐑉𐐩𐐻 𐐹𐑉𐐱𐑁𐐯𐐻, 𐐰𐑌𐐼 𐐲 𐑋𐐰𐑌 𐐱𐑂 𐐘𐐱𐐼, 𐐸𐐰𐑂𐐮𐑍 𐑀𐑉𐐩𐐻 𐐹𐐵𐐲𐑉 𐐰𐑌𐐼 𐐫𐑃𐐱𐑉𐐮𐐻𐐨 𐑀𐐮𐑂𐐲𐑌 𐐲𐑌𐐻𐐭 𐐸𐐮𐑋 𐑁𐑉𐐱𐑋 𐐘𐐱𐐼. 𐐰𐑌𐐼 𐐺𐐨𐐸𐐬𐑊𐐼, 𐐢𐐨𐐸𐐴, 𐐸𐐮𐑆 𐐺𐑉𐐲𐑄𐐲𐑉, 𐐶𐐱𐑆 𐑌𐐱𐐻 𐐲 𐐸𐐶𐐮𐐻 𐐺𐐨𐐸𐐴𐑌𐐼 𐐸𐐮𐑋 𐐰𐑆 𐐻𐐭 𐑃𐐮𐑍𐑆 𐐹𐐲𐑉𐐻𐐩𐑌𐐮𐑍 𐐻𐐭 𐑉𐐴𐐽𐐲𐑅𐑌𐐯𐑅. 𐐰𐑌𐐼 𐑄𐐲𐑅 𐐮𐐻 𐐼𐐮𐐼 𐐿𐐲𐑋 𐐻𐐭 𐐹𐐰𐑅 𐑄𐐰𐐻 𐑄 𐐹𐐨𐐹𐐲𐑊 𐐱𐑂 𐐤𐐨𐑁𐐴 𐐺𐐨𐑀𐐰𐑌 𐐻𐐭 𐐹𐑉𐐱𐑅𐐹𐐲𐑉 𐐲𐑀𐐯𐑌 𐐮𐑌 𐑄 𐑊𐐰𐑌𐐼, 𐐰𐑌𐐼 𐐺𐐨𐑀𐐰𐑌 𐐻𐐭 𐐺𐐮𐑊𐐼 𐐲𐐹 𐑄𐐯𐑉 𐐶𐐩𐑅𐐻 𐐹𐑊𐐩𐑅𐐲𐑆, 𐐰𐑌𐐼 𐐺𐐨𐑀𐐰𐑌 𐐻𐐭 𐑋𐐲𐑊𐐻𐐮𐐹𐑊𐐴 𐐰𐑌𐐼 𐑅𐐹𐑉𐐯𐐼, 𐐨𐑂𐐲𐑌 𐐲𐑌𐐻𐐮𐑊 𐑄𐐩 𐐼𐐮𐐼 𐐿𐐲𐑂𐐲𐑉 𐑄 𐐸𐐬𐑊 𐑁𐐩𐑅 𐐱𐑂 𐑄 𐑊𐐰𐑌𐐼, 𐐺𐐬𐑃 𐐱𐑌 𐑄 𐑌𐐫𐑉𐑃𐐶𐐲𐑉𐐼 𐐰𐑌𐐼

𐐱𐑌 𐑄 𐑅𐐵𐑃𐐶𐐲𐑉𐐼, 𐑁𐑉𐐱𐑋 𐑄 𐑅𐐨 𐐶𐐯𐑅𐐻 𐐻𐐭 𐑄 𐑅𐐨 𐐨𐑅𐐻. 𐐈𐑌𐐼 𐐮𐐻 𐐿𐐩𐑋 𐐻𐐭 𐐹𐐰𐑅 𐑄𐐰𐐻 𐑄 𐑅𐐯𐑂𐐲𐑌𐐻𐐨 𐐰𐑌𐐼 𐑅𐐮𐐿𐑅𐑃 𐐷𐐨𐑉 𐐼𐐮𐐼 𐐯𐑌𐐼 𐐮𐑌 𐐹𐐨𐑅. 𐐈𐑌𐐼 𐑄 𐑅𐐯𐑂𐐲𐑌𐐻𐐨 𐐰𐑌𐐼 𐑅𐐯𐑂𐐲𐑌𐑃 𐐷𐐨𐑉 𐐺𐐨𐑀𐐰𐑌 𐐮𐑌 𐐹𐐨𐑅; 𐐰𐑌𐐼 𐑄 𐐽𐐲𐑉𐐽 𐐼𐐮𐐼 𐑅𐐹𐑉𐐯𐐼 𐑃𐑉𐐭𐐵𐐻 𐑄 𐑁𐐩𐑅 𐐱𐑂 𐐫𐑊 𐑄 𐑊𐐰𐑌𐐼; 𐐰𐑌𐐼 𐑄 𐑋𐐬𐑉 𐐹𐐪𐑉𐐻 𐐱𐑂 𐑄 𐐹𐐨𐐹𐐲𐑊, 𐐺𐐬𐑃 𐑄 𐐤𐐨𐑁𐐴𐐻𐑅 𐐰𐑌𐐼 𐑄 𐐢𐐩𐑋𐐲𐑌𐐴𐐻𐑅, 𐐼𐐮𐐼 𐐺𐐨𐑊𐐱𐑍 𐐻𐐭 𐑄 𐐽𐐲𐑉𐐽; 𐐰𐑌𐐼 𐑄𐐩 𐐼𐐮𐐼 𐐸𐐰𐑂 𐐯𐐿𐑅𐐨𐐼𐐮𐑍𐑊𐐨 𐑀𐑉𐐩𐐻 𐐹𐐨𐑅 𐐮𐑌 𐑄 𐑊𐐰𐑌𐐼; 𐐰𐑌𐐼 𐑄𐐲𐑅 𐐯𐑌𐐼𐐯𐐼 𐑄 𐑅𐐯𐑂𐐲𐑌𐐻𐐨 𐐰𐑌𐐼 𐑅𐐯𐑂𐐲𐑌𐑃 𐐷𐐨𐑉. 𐐈𐑌𐐼 𐐫𐑊𐑅𐐬 𐑄𐐩 𐐸𐐰𐐼 𐐹𐐨𐑅 𐐮𐑌 𐑄 𐑅𐐯𐑂𐐲𐑌𐐻𐐨 𐐰𐑌𐐼 𐐩𐐻𐑃 𐐷𐐨𐑉, 𐑅𐐩𐑂 𐐮𐐻 𐐶𐐲𐑉 𐐰 𐑁𐑏 𐐿𐐱𐑌𐐻𐐯𐑌𐑇𐐲𐑌𐑆 𐐿𐐱𐑌𐑅𐐲𐑉𐑌𐐮𐑍 𐑄 𐐹𐑎𐑌𐐻𐑅 𐐱𐑂 𐐼𐐱𐐿𐐻𐑉𐐮𐑌 𐐸𐐶𐐮𐐽 𐐸𐐰𐐼 𐐺𐐮𐑌 𐑊𐐩𐐼 𐐼𐐵𐑌 𐐺𐐴 𐑄 𐐹𐑉𐐱𐑁𐐯𐐻𐑅. 𐐈𐑌𐐼 𐐮𐑌 𐑄 𐑅𐐯𐑂𐐲𐑌𐐻𐐨 𐐰𐑌𐐼 𐑌𐐴𐑌𐑃 𐐷𐐨𐑉 𐑄𐐯𐑉 𐐺𐐨𐑀𐐰𐑌 𐐻𐐭 𐐺𐐨 𐑋𐐲𐐽 𐑅𐐻𐑉𐐴𐑁. 𐐒𐐲𐐻 𐐮𐐻 𐐿𐐩𐑋 𐐻𐐭 𐐹𐐰𐑅 𐑄𐐰𐐻 𐐤𐐨𐑁𐐴 𐐰𐑌𐐼 𐐢𐐨𐐸𐐴, 𐐰𐑌𐐼 𐑋𐐯𐑌𐐨 𐐱𐑂 𐑄𐐯𐑉 𐐺𐑉𐐯𐑄𐑉𐐯𐑌 𐐸𐐭 𐑌𐑏 𐐿𐐱𐑌𐑅𐐲𐑉𐑌𐐮𐑍 𐑄 𐐻𐑉𐐭 𐐹𐑎𐑌𐐻𐑅 𐐱𐑂 𐐼𐐱𐐿𐐻𐑉𐐮𐑌, 𐐸𐐰𐑂𐐮𐑍 𐑋𐐯𐑌𐐨 𐑉𐐯𐑂𐐯𐑊𐐩𐑇𐐲𐑌𐑆 𐐼𐐩𐑊𐐨, 𐑄𐐯𐑉𐑁𐐬𐑉 𐑄𐐩 𐐼𐐮𐐼 𐐹𐑉𐐨𐐽 𐐲𐑌𐐻𐐭 𐑄 𐐹𐐨𐐹𐐲𐑊, 𐐮𐑌𐑅𐐬𐑋𐐲𐐽 𐑄𐐰𐐻 𐑄𐐩 𐐼𐐮𐐼 𐐹𐐳𐐻 𐐰𐑌 𐐯𐑌𐐼 𐐻𐐭 𐑄𐐯𐑉 𐑅𐐻𐑉𐐴𐑁 𐐮𐑌 𐑄𐐰𐐻 𐑅𐐩𐑋 𐐷𐐨𐑉.

5. 𐐈𐑌𐐼 𐐮𐐻 𐐿𐐩𐑋 𐐻𐐭 𐐹𐐰𐑅 𐑄𐐰𐐻 𐐮𐑌 𐑄 𐐩𐐻𐐨𐐯𐑃 𐐷𐐨𐑉 𐐱𐑂 𐑄 𐑉𐐩𐑌 𐐱𐑂 𐑄 𐐾𐐲𐐾𐐯𐑆 𐐬𐑂𐐲𐑉 𐑄 𐐹𐐨𐐹𐐲𐑊 𐐱𐑂 𐐤𐐨𐑁𐐴, 𐑄𐐯𐑉 𐐶𐐲𐑉 𐐰 𐑅𐐲𐑉𐐻𐐯𐑌 𐑌𐐲𐑋𐐺𐐲𐑉 𐐱𐑂 𐑄 𐐼𐐮𐑅𐐯𐑌𐐻𐐲𐑉𐑆 𐑁𐑉𐐱𐑋 𐑄 𐐹𐐨𐐹𐐲𐑊 𐐱𐑂 𐐤𐐨𐑁𐐴, 𐐸𐐭 𐐸𐐰𐐼 𐑅𐐲𐑋 𐐷𐐨𐑉𐑆 𐐺𐐨𐑁𐐬𐑉 𐑀𐐱𐑌 𐐬𐑂𐐲𐑉 𐐲𐑌𐐻𐐭 𐑄 𐐢𐐩𐑋𐐲𐑌𐐴𐐻𐑅, 𐐰𐑌𐐼 𐐻𐐩𐐿𐐲𐑌 𐐲𐐹𐐱𐑌 𐑄𐐯𐑋𐑅𐐯𐑊𐑂𐑆 𐑄 𐑌𐐩𐑋 𐐱𐑂 𐐢𐐩𐑋𐐲𐑌𐐴𐐻𐑅; 𐐰𐑌𐐼 𐐫𐑊𐑅𐐬 𐐰 𐑅𐐲𐑉𐐻𐐯𐑌 𐑌𐐲𐑋𐐺𐐲𐑉 𐐸𐐭 𐐶𐐲𐑉 𐑉𐐨𐐲𐑊 𐐼𐐨𐑅𐐯𐑌𐐼𐐲𐑌𐐻𐑅 𐐱𐑂 𐑄 𐐢𐐩𐑋𐐲𐑌𐐴𐐻𐑅, 𐐺𐐨𐐮𐑍 𐑅𐐻𐐲𐑉𐐼 𐐲𐐹 𐐻𐐭 𐐰𐑍𐑀𐐲𐑉 𐐺𐐴 𐑄𐐯𐑋, 𐐫𐑉 𐐺𐐴 𐑄𐐬𐑆 𐐼𐐮𐑅𐐯𐑌𐐻𐐲𐑉𐑆, 𐑄𐐯𐑉𐑁𐐬𐑉 𐑄𐐩 𐐿𐐱𐑋𐐯𐑌𐑅𐐻 𐐰 𐐶𐐫𐑉 𐐶𐐮𐑄 𐑄𐐯𐑉 𐐺𐑉𐐯𐑄𐑉𐐯𐑌. 𐐈𐑌𐐼 𐑄𐐩 𐐼𐐮𐐼 𐐿𐐱𐑋𐐮𐐻 𐑋𐐲𐑉𐐼𐐲𐑉 𐐰𐑌𐐼 𐐹𐑊𐐲𐑌𐐼𐐲𐑉; 𐐰𐑌𐐼 𐑄𐐯𐑌 𐑄𐐩 𐐶𐐳𐐼 𐑉𐐨𐐻𐑉𐐨𐐻 𐐺𐐰𐐿 𐐮𐑌𐐻𐐭 𐑄 𐑋𐐵𐑌𐐻𐐩𐑌𐑆, 𐐰𐑌𐐼 𐐮𐑌𐐻𐐭 𐑄 𐐶𐐮𐑊𐐼𐐲𐑉𐑌𐐯𐑅 𐐰𐑌𐐼 𐑅𐐨𐐿𐑉𐐯𐐻 𐐹𐑊𐐩𐑅𐐯𐑆, 𐐸𐐴𐐼𐐮𐑍 𐑄𐐯𐑋𐑅𐐯𐑊𐑂𐑆 𐑄𐐰𐐻 𐑄𐐩 𐐿𐐳𐐼 𐑌𐐱𐐻 𐐺𐐨 𐐼𐐮𐑅𐐿𐐲𐑂𐐲𐑉𐐼, 𐑉𐐨𐑅𐐨𐑂𐐮𐑍 𐐼𐐩𐑊𐐨 𐐰𐑌 𐐰𐐼𐐮𐑇𐐲𐑌 𐐻𐐭 𐑄𐐯𐑉 𐑌𐐲𐑋𐐺𐐲𐑉𐑆, 𐐮𐑌𐐰𐑆𐑋𐐲𐐽 𐐰𐑆 𐑄𐐯𐑉 𐐶𐐲𐑉 𐐼𐐮𐑅𐐯𐑌𐐻𐐲𐑉𐑆 𐑄𐐰𐐻 𐐶𐐯𐑌𐐻 𐑁𐐬𐑉𐑃 𐐲𐑌𐐻𐐭 𐑄𐐯𐑋. 𐐈𐑌𐐼 𐑄𐐲𐑅 𐐮𐑌 𐐻𐐴𐑋, 𐐷𐐩, 𐐨𐑂𐐲𐑌 𐐮𐑌 𐑄 𐑅𐐹𐐩𐑅 𐐱𐑂 𐑌𐐱𐐻 𐑋𐐯𐑌𐐨 𐐷𐐨𐑉𐑆, 𐑄𐐩 𐐺𐐨𐐿𐐩𐑋 𐐰𐑌 𐐯𐐿𐑅𐐨𐐼𐐮𐑍𐑊𐐨 𐑀𐑉𐐩𐐻 𐐺𐐰𐑌𐐼 𐐱𐑂 𐑉𐐱𐐺𐐲𐑉𐑆; 𐐰𐑌𐐼 𐑄𐐩 𐐼𐐮𐐼 𐑅𐐲𐑉𐐽 𐐵𐐻 𐐫𐑊 𐑄 𐑅𐐨𐐿𐑉𐐯𐐻 𐐹𐑊𐐰𐑌𐑆 𐐱𐑂 𐐘𐐰𐐼𐐨𐐰𐑌𐐻𐐲𐑌; 𐐰𐑌𐐼 𐑄𐐲𐑅 𐑄𐐩 𐐺𐐨𐐿𐐩𐑋 𐑉𐐱𐐺𐐲𐑉𐑆 𐐱𐑂 𐐘𐐰𐐼𐐨𐐰𐑌𐐻𐐲𐑌. 𐐤𐐵 𐐺𐐨𐐸𐐬𐑊𐐼, 𐑄𐐨𐑆 𐑉𐐱𐐺𐐲𐑉𐑆 𐐼𐐮𐐼 𐑋𐐩𐐿 𐑀𐑉𐐩𐐻 𐐸𐐰𐑂𐐲𐐿, 𐐷𐐩, 𐐨𐑂𐐲𐑌 𐑀𐑉𐐩𐐻 𐐼𐐨𐑅𐐻𐑉𐐲𐐿𐑇𐐲𐑌 𐐰𐑋𐐲𐑍 𐑄 𐐹𐐨𐐹𐐲𐑊 𐐱𐑂 𐐤𐐨𐑁𐐴, 𐐰𐑌𐐼 𐐫𐑊𐑅𐐬 𐐰𐑋𐐲𐑍 𐑄 𐐹𐐨𐐹𐐲𐑊 𐐱𐑂 𐑄 𐐢𐐩𐑋𐐲𐑌𐐴𐐻𐑅.

6. 𐐈𐑌𐐼 𐐮𐐻 𐐿𐐩𐑋 𐐻𐐭 𐐹𐐰𐑅 𐑄𐐰𐐻 𐐮𐐻 𐐶𐐱𐑆 𐐯𐐿𐑅𐐹𐐨𐐼𐐨𐐯𐑌𐐻 𐑄𐐰𐐻 𐑄𐐯𐑉 𐑇𐐳𐐼 𐐺𐐨 𐐰 𐑅𐐻𐐱𐐹 𐐹𐐳𐐻 𐐻𐐭 𐑄𐐮𐑅 𐐶𐐲𐑉𐐿 𐐱𐑂 𐐼𐐨𐑅𐐻𐑉𐐲𐐿𐑇𐐲𐑌; 𐑄𐐯𐑉𐑁𐐬𐑉 𐑄𐐩 𐑅𐐯𐑌𐐻 𐐰𐑌 𐐪𐑉𐑋𐐨 𐐱𐑂 𐑅𐐻𐑉𐐱𐑍 𐑋𐐯𐑌 𐐮𐑌𐐻𐐭 𐑄 𐐶𐐮𐑊𐐼𐐲𐑉𐑌𐐯𐑅, 𐐰𐑌𐐼 𐐲𐐹𐐱𐑌 𐑄 𐑋𐐵𐑌𐐻𐐩𐑌𐑆 𐐻𐐭 𐑅𐐲𐑉𐐽 𐐵𐐻 𐑄𐐮𐑅 𐐺𐐰𐑌𐐼 𐐱𐑂 𐑉𐐱𐐺𐐲𐑉𐑆, 𐐰𐑌𐐼 𐐻𐐭 𐐼𐐨𐑅𐐻𐑉𐑎 𐑄𐐯𐑋. 𐐒𐐲𐐻 𐐺𐐨𐐸𐐬𐑊𐐼, 𐐮𐐻 𐐿𐐩𐑋 𐐻𐐭 𐐹𐐰𐑅 𐑄𐐰𐐻 𐐮𐑌 𐑄𐐰𐐻 𐑅𐐩𐑋 𐐷𐐨𐑉, 𐑄𐐩 𐐶𐐲𐑉 𐐼𐑉𐐮𐑂𐐲𐑌 𐐺𐐰𐐿 𐐨𐑂𐐲𐑌 𐐮𐑌𐐻𐐭 𐑄𐐯𐑉 𐐬𐑌 𐑊𐐰𐑌𐐼𐑆. 𐐈𐑌𐐼 𐑄𐐲𐑅 𐐯𐑌𐐼𐐯𐐼 𐑄 𐐩𐐻𐐨𐐯𐑃 𐐷𐐨𐑉 𐐱𐑂 𐑄 𐑉𐐩𐑌 𐐱𐑂 𐑄 𐐾𐐲𐐾𐐯𐑆 𐐬𐑂𐐲𐑉 𐑄 𐐹𐐨𐐹𐐲𐑊 𐐱𐑂 𐐤𐐨𐑁𐐴.

7. 𐐈𐑌𐐼 𐐮𐐻 𐐿𐐩𐑋 𐐻𐐭 𐐹𐐰𐑅 𐐮𐑌 𐑄 𐐿𐐱𐑋𐐯𐑌𐑅𐑋𐐯𐑌𐐻 𐐱𐑂 𐑄 𐐩𐐻𐐨 𐐰𐑌𐐼 𐑁𐐲𐑉𐑅𐐻 𐐷𐐨𐑉, 𐑄𐐩 𐐼𐐮𐐼 𐑀𐐬 𐑁𐐬𐑉𐑃 𐐰𐑀𐐯𐑌 𐐰𐑀𐐯𐑌𐑅𐐻 𐑄𐐮𐑅 𐐺𐐰𐑌𐐼 𐐱𐑂 𐑉𐐱𐐺𐐲𐑉𐑆, 𐐰𐑌𐐼 𐐼𐐮𐐼 𐐼𐐨𐑅𐐻𐑉𐑎 𐑋𐐯𐑌𐐨; 𐐰𐑌𐐼 𐑄𐐩 𐐶𐐲𐑉 𐐫𐑊𐑅𐐬 𐑂𐐮𐑆𐐮𐐻𐐯𐐼 𐐶𐐮𐑄 𐑋𐐲𐐽 𐐼𐐨𐑅𐐻𐑉𐐲𐐿𐑇𐐲𐑌; 𐐰𐑌𐐼 𐑄𐐩 𐐶𐐲𐑉 𐐰𐑀𐐯𐑌 𐐬𐐺𐑊𐐴𐐾𐐼 𐐻𐐭 𐑉𐐨𐐻𐐲𐑉𐑌 𐐵𐐻 𐐱𐑂 𐑄 𐐶𐐮𐑊𐐼𐐲𐑉𐑌𐐯𐑅, 𐐰𐑌𐐼 𐐵𐐻 𐐱𐑂 𐑄 𐑋𐐵𐑌𐐻𐐩𐑌𐑆 𐐲𐑌𐐻𐐭 𐑄𐐯𐑉 𐐬𐑌 𐑊𐐰𐑌𐐼𐑆, 𐐺𐐨𐐿𐐫𐑆 𐐱𐑂 𐑄 𐐯𐐿𐑅𐐨𐐼𐐮𐑍 𐑀𐑉𐐩𐐻𐑌𐐯𐑅 𐐱𐑂 𐑄 𐑌𐐲𐑋𐐺𐐲𐑉𐑆 𐐱𐑂 𐑄𐐬𐑆 𐑉𐐱𐐺𐐲𐑉𐑆 𐐸𐐭 𐐮𐑌𐑁𐐯𐑅𐐻𐐯𐐼 𐑄 𐑋𐐵𐑌𐐻𐐩𐑌𐑆 𐐰𐑌𐐼 𐑄 𐐶𐐮𐑊𐐼𐐲𐑉𐑌𐐯𐑅. 𐐈𐑌𐐼 𐐮𐐻 𐐿𐐩𐑋 𐐻𐐭 𐐹𐐰𐑅 𐑄𐐰𐐻 𐑄𐐲𐑅 𐐯𐑌𐐼𐐯𐐼 𐑄𐐮𐑅 𐐷𐐨𐑉. 𐐈𐑌𐐼 𐑄 𐑉𐐱𐐺𐐲𐑉𐑆 𐐼𐐮𐐼 𐑅𐐻𐐮𐑊 𐐮𐑌𐐿𐑉𐐨𐑅 𐐰𐑌𐐼 𐐶𐐰𐐿𐑅 𐑅𐐻𐑉𐐱𐑍, 𐐮𐑌𐑅𐐬𐑋𐐲𐐽 𐑄𐐰𐐻 𐑄𐐩 𐐼𐐮𐐼 𐐼𐐨𐑁𐐴 𐑄 𐐸𐐬𐑊 𐐪𐑉𐑋𐐨𐑆 𐐱𐑂 𐑄 𐐤𐐨𐑁𐐴𐐻𐑅, 𐐰𐑌𐐼 𐐫𐑊𐑅𐐬 𐐱𐑂 𐑄 𐐢𐐩𐑋𐐲𐑌𐐴𐐻𐑅; 𐐰𐑌𐐼 𐑄𐐩 𐐼𐐮𐐼 𐐿𐐫𐑆 𐑀𐑉𐐩𐐻 𐑁𐐨𐑉 𐐻𐐭 𐐿𐐲𐑋 𐐲𐑌𐐻𐐭 𐑄 𐐹𐐨𐐹𐐲𐑊 𐐲𐐹𐐱𐑌 𐐫𐑊 𐑄 𐑁𐐩𐑅 𐐱𐑂 𐑄 𐑊𐐰𐑌𐐼; 𐐷𐐩, 𐑁𐐫𐑉 𐑄𐐩 𐐼𐐮𐐼 𐑂𐐮𐑆𐐮𐐻 𐑋𐐯𐑌𐐨 𐐹𐐪𐑉𐐻𐑅 𐐱𐑂 𐑄 𐑊𐐰𐑌𐐼, 𐐰𐑌𐐼 𐐼𐐮𐐼 𐐼𐐭 𐑀𐑉𐐩𐐻 𐐼𐐨𐑅𐐻𐑉𐐲𐐿𐑇𐐲𐑌 𐐲𐑌𐐻𐐭 𐑄𐐯𐑋; 𐐷𐐩, 𐐼𐐮𐐼 𐐿𐐮𐑊 𐑋𐐯𐑌𐐨, 𐐰𐑌𐐼 𐐼𐐮𐐼 𐐿𐐰𐑉𐐨 𐐰𐐶𐐩 𐐲𐑄𐐲𐑉𐑆 𐐿𐐰𐐹𐐻𐐮𐑂 𐐮𐑌𐐻𐐭 𐑄 𐐶𐐮𐑊𐐼𐐲𐑉𐑌𐐯𐑅; 𐐷𐐩, 𐐰𐑌𐐼 𐑋𐐬𐑉 𐐯𐑅𐐹𐐯𐑇𐐲𐑊𐐨 𐑄𐐯𐑉 𐐶𐐮𐑋𐐯𐑌 𐐰𐑌𐐼 𐑄𐐯𐑉 𐐽𐐮𐑊𐐼𐑉𐐯𐑌. 𐐤𐐵 𐑄𐐮𐑅 𐑀𐑉𐐩𐐻 𐐨𐑂𐐲𐑊,

𐐸𐐶𐐮𐐽 𐐿𐐩𐑋 𐐲𐑌𐐻𐐭 𐑄 𐐹𐐨𐐹𐑊 𐐺𐐨𐐿𐐫𐑆 𐐱𐑂 𐑄𐐩𐑉 𐐮𐑌𐐮𐐿𐐶𐐮𐐻𐐨, 𐐼𐐮𐐼 𐑅𐐻𐐲𐑉 𐑄𐐯𐑋 𐐲𐐹 𐐲𐑀𐐯𐑌 𐐮𐑌 𐑉𐐨𐑋𐐯𐑋𐐺𐑉𐐰𐑌𐑅 𐐱𐑂 𐑄 𐐢𐐫𐑉𐐼 𐑄𐐩𐑉 𐐘𐐱𐐼. 𐐈𐑌𐐼 𐑄𐐲𐑅 𐐯𐑌𐐼𐐯𐐼 𐑄 𐐩𐐻𐐨 𐐰𐑌𐐼 𐑁𐐲𐑉𐑅𐐻 𐐷𐐨𐑉 𐐱𐑂 𐑄 𐑉𐐩𐑌 𐐱𐑂 𐑄 𐐾𐐲𐐾𐐯𐑆. 𐐈𐑌𐐼 𐐮𐑌 𐑄 𐐩𐐻𐐨 𐐰𐑌𐐼 𐑅𐐯𐐿𐐲𐑌𐐼 𐐷𐐨𐑉 𐑄𐐩 𐐺𐐨𐑀𐐰𐑌 𐐲𐑀𐐯𐑌 𐐻𐐭 𐑁𐐲𐑉𐑀𐐯𐐻 𐑄 𐐢𐐫𐑉𐐼 𐑄𐐩𐑉 𐐘𐐱𐐼. 𐐈𐑌𐐼 𐐮𐑌 𐑄 𐐩𐐻𐐨 𐐰𐑌𐐼 𐑃𐐲𐑉𐐼 𐐷𐐨𐑉 𐑄𐐩 𐐺𐐨𐑀𐐰𐑌 𐐻𐐭 𐐶𐐰𐐿𐑅 𐑅𐐻𐑉𐐱𐑍 𐐮𐑌 𐐮𐑌𐐮𐐿𐐶𐐮𐐻𐐨. 𐐈𐑌𐐼 𐐮𐑌 𐑄 𐐩𐐻𐐨 𐐰𐑌𐐼 𐑁𐐬𐑉𐑃 𐐷𐐨𐑉 𐑄𐐩 𐐼𐐮𐐼 𐑌𐐱𐐻 𐑋𐐯𐑌𐐼 𐑄𐐩𐑉 𐐶𐐩𐑆. 𐐈𐑌𐐼 𐐮𐐻 𐐿𐐩𐑋 𐐻𐐭 𐐹𐐰𐑅 𐐮𐑌 𐑄 𐐩𐐻𐐨 𐐰𐑌𐐼 𐑁𐐮𐑁𐑃 𐐷𐐨𐑉, 𐑄𐐩 𐐼𐐮𐐼 𐐶𐐰𐐿𐑅 𐑅𐐻𐑉𐐱𐑍𐑀𐐲𐑉 𐐰𐑌𐐼 𐑅𐐻𐑉𐐱𐑍𐑀𐐲𐑉 𐐮𐑌 𐑄𐐩𐑉 𐐹𐑉𐐴𐐼, 𐐰𐑌𐐼 𐐮𐑌 𐑄𐐩𐑉 𐐶𐐮𐐿𐐯𐐼𐑌𐐯𐑅; 𐐰𐑌𐐼 𐑄𐐲𐑅 𐑄𐐩 𐐶𐐯𐑉 𐑉𐐴𐐹𐑌𐐮𐑍 𐐲𐑀𐐯𐑌 𐑁𐐫𐑉 𐐼𐐮𐑅𐐻𐑉𐐲𐐿𐑇𐐲𐑌. 𐐈𐑌𐐼 𐑄𐐲𐑅 𐐯𐑌𐐼𐐯𐐼 𐑄 𐐩𐐻𐐨 𐐰𐑌𐐼 𐑁𐐮𐑁𐑃 𐐷𐐨𐑉.

8. 𐐈𐑌𐐼 𐑄𐐲𐑅 𐐶𐐨 𐐿𐐰𐑌 𐐺𐐨𐐸𐐬𐑊𐐼 𐐸𐐵 𐑁𐐫𐑊𐑅, 𐐰𐑌𐐼 𐐫𐑊𐑅𐐬 𐑄 𐐲𐑌𐑅𐐻𐐯𐐼𐐨𐑌𐐯𐑅 𐐱𐑂 𐑄 𐐸𐐪𐑉𐐻𐑅 𐐱𐑂 𐑄 𐐽𐐮𐑊𐐼𐑉𐐯𐑌 𐐱𐑂 𐑋𐐯𐑌; 𐐷𐐩, 𐐶𐐨 𐐿𐐰𐑌 𐑅𐐨 𐑄𐐰𐐻 𐑄 𐐢𐐫𐑉𐐼, 𐐮𐑌 𐐸𐐮𐑆 𐑀𐑉𐐩𐐻 𐐮𐑌𐑁𐐮𐑌𐐮𐐻 𐑀𐐳𐐼𐑌𐐯𐑅, 𐐼𐐲𐑃 𐐺𐑊𐐯𐑅 𐐰𐑌𐐼 𐐹𐑉𐐱𐑅𐐹𐐲𐑉 𐑄𐐬𐑆 𐐸𐐭 𐐹𐐳𐐻 𐑄𐐩𐑉 𐐻𐑉𐐲𐑅𐐻 𐐮𐑌 𐐸𐐮𐑋; 𐐷𐐩, 𐐰𐑌𐐼 𐐶𐐨 𐑋𐐩 𐑅𐐨 𐐰𐐻 𐑄 𐑂𐐯𐑉𐐨 𐐻𐐴𐑋 𐐸𐐶𐐯𐑌 𐐸𐐨 𐐼𐐲𐑃 𐐹𐑉𐐱𐑅𐐹𐐲𐑉 𐐸𐐮𐑆 𐐹𐐨𐐹𐑊; 𐐷𐐩, 𐐮𐑌 𐑄 𐐮𐑌𐐿𐑉𐐨𐑅 𐐱𐑂 𐑄𐐩𐑉 𐑁𐐨𐑊𐐼𐑆, 𐑄𐐩𐑉 𐑁𐑊𐐱𐐿𐑅, 𐐰𐑌𐐼 𐑄𐐩𐑉 𐐸𐐲𐑉𐐼𐑆, 𐐰𐑌𐐼 𐐮𐑌 𐑀𐐬𐑊𐐼, 𐐰𐑌𐐼 𐐮𐑌 𐑅𐐮𐑊𐑂𐐲𐑉, 𐐰𐑌𐐼 𐐮𐑌 𐐫𐑊 𐑋𐐰𐑌𐐲𐑉 𐐱𐑂 𐐹𐑉𐐯𐑇𐐲𐑅 𐑃𐐮𐑍𐑆 𐐱𐑂 𐐯𐑂𐐲𐑉𐐨 𐐿𐐴𐑌𐐼 𐐰𐑌𐐼 𐐪𐑉𐐻; 𐑅𐐹𐐩𐑉𐐮𐑍 𐑄𐐩𐑉 𐑊𐐴𐑂𐑆, 𐐰𐑌𐐼 𐐼𐐨𐑊𐐮𐑂𐐲𐑉𐐮𐑍 𐑄𐐯𐑋 𐐵𐐻 𐐱𐑂 𐑄 𐐸𐐰𐑌𐐼𐑆 𐐱𐑂 𐑄𐐩𐑉 𐐯𐑌𐐯𐑋𐐨𐑆; 𐑅𐐱𐑁𐐲𐑌𐐮𐑍 𐑄 𐐸𐐪𐑉𐐻𐑅 𐐱𐑂 𐑄𐐩𐑉 𐐯𐑌𐐯𐑋𐐨𐑆, 𐑄𐐰𐐻 𐑄𐐩 𐑇𐐳𐐼 𐑌𐐱𐐻 𐐼𐐨𐐿𐑊𐐩𐑉 𐐶𐐫𐑉𐑆 𐐲𐑀𐐯𐑌𐑅𐐻 𐑄𐐯𐑋; 𐐷𐐩, 𐐰𐑌𐐼 𐐮𐑌 𐑁𐐴𐑌, 𐐼𐐭𐐮𐑍 𐐫𐑊 𐑃𐐮𐑍𐑆 𐑁𐐫𐑉 𐑄 𐐶𐐯𐑊𐑁𐐩𐑉 𐐰𐑌𐐼 𐐸𐐰𐐹𐐨𐑌𐐯𐑅 𐐱𐑂 𐐸𐐮𐑆 𐐹𐐨𐐹𐑊; 𐐷𐐩, 𐑄𐐯𐑌 𐐮𐑆 𐑄 𐐻𐐴𐑋 𐑄𐐰𐐻 𐑄𐐩 𐐼𐐭 𐐸𐐪𐑉𐐼𐐯𐑌 𐑄𐐩𐑉 𐐸𐐪𐑉𐐻𐑅, 𐐰𐑌𐐼 𐐼𐐭 𐑁𐐲𐑉𐑀𐐯𐐻 𐑄 𐐢𐐫𐑉𐐼 𐑄𐐩𐑉 𐐘𐐱𐐼, 𐐰𐑌𐐼 𐐼𐐭 𐐻𐑉𐐰𐑋𐐹𐑊 𐐲𐑌𐐼𐐲𐑉 𐑄𐐩𐑉 𐑁𐐨𐐻 𐑄 𐐐𐐬𐑊𐐨 𐐎𐐲𐑌; 𐐷𐐩, 𐐰𐑌𐐼 𐑄𐐮𐑅 𐐺𐐨𐐿𐐫𐑆 𐐱𐑂 𐑄𐐩𐑉 𐐨𐑆, 𐐰𐑌𐐼 𐑄𐐩𐑉 𐐯𐐿𐑅𐐨𐐼𐐮𐑍 𐑀𐑉𐐩𐐻 𐐹𐑉𐐱𐑅𐐹𐐯𐑉𐐮𐐻𐐨. 𐐈𐑌𐐼 𐑄𐐲𐑅 𐐶𐐨 𐑅𐐨, 𐑄𐐰𐐻 𐐯𐐿𐑅𐐯𐐹𐐻 𐑄 𐐢𐐫𐑉𐐼 𐐼𐐲𐑃 𐐽𐐩𐑅𐐲𐑌 𐐸𐐮𐑆 𐐹𐐨𐐹𐑊 𐐶𐐮𐑄 𐑋𐐯𐑌𐐨 𐐰𐑁𐑊𐐮𐐿𐑇𐐲𐑌𐑆, 𐐷𐐩, 𐐯𐐿𐑅𐐯𐐹𐐻 𐐸𐐨 𐐼𐐲𐑃 𐑂𐐮𐑆𐐮𐐻 𐑄𐐯𐑋 𐐶𐐮𐑄 𐐼𐐯𐑃 𐐰𐑌𐐼 𐐶𐐮𐑄 𐐻𐐯𐑉𐐲𐑉, 𐐰𐑌𐐼 𐐶𐐮𐑄 𐑁𐐰𐑋𐐮𐑌, 𐐰𐑌𐐼 𐐶𐐮𐑄 𐐫𐑊 𐑋𐐰𐑌𐐲𐑉 𐐱𐑂 𐐹𐐯𐑅𐐻𐐮𐑊𐐯𐑌𐑅, 𐑄𐐩 𐐶𐐮𐑊 𐑌𐐱𐐻 𐑉𐐨𐑋𐐯𐑋𐐺𐐲𐑉 𐐸𐐮𐑋. 𐐄 𐐸𐐵 𐑁𐐭𐑊𐐮𐑇, 𐐰𐑌𐐼 𐐸𐐵 𐑂𐐩𐑌, 𐐰𐑌𐐼 𐐸𐐵 𐐨𐑂𐑊, 𐐰𐑌𐐼 𐐼𐐯𐑂𐐮𐑊𐐮𐑇, 𐐰𐑌𐐼 𐐸𐐵 𐐿𐐶𐐮𐐿 𐐻𐐭 𐐼𐐭 𐐮𐑌𐐮𐐿𐐶𐐮𐐻𐐨, 𐐰𐑌𐐼 𐐸𐐵 𐑅𐑊𐐬 𐐻𐐭 𐐼𐐭 𐑀𐐳𐐼, 𐐪𐑉 𐑄 𐐽𐐮𐑊𐐼𐑉𐐯𐑌 𐐱𐑂 𐑋𐐯𐑌; 𐐷𐐩, 𐐸𐐵 𐐿𐐶𐐮𐐿 𐐻𐐭 𐐸𐐪𐑉𐐿𐐲𐑌 𐐲𐑌𐐻𐐭 𐑄 𐐶𐐲𐑉𐐼𐑆 𐐱𐑂 𐑄 𐐨𐑂𐑊 𐐶𐐲𐑌, 𐐰𐑌𐐼 𐐻𐐭 𐑅𐐯𐐻 𐑄𐐩𐑉 𐐸𐐪𐑉𐐻𐑅 𐐲𐐹𐐱𐑌 𐑄 𐑂𐐩𐑌 𐑃𐐮𐑍𐑆 𐐱𐑂 𐑄 𐐶𐐲𐑉𐑊𐐼! 𐐏𐐩, 𐐸𐐵 𐐿𐐶𐐮𐐿 𐐻𐐭 𐐺𐐨 𐑊𐐮𐑁𐐻𐐯𐐼 𐐲𐐹 𐐮𐑌 𐐹𐑉𐐴𐐼; 𐐷𐐩, 𐐸𐐵 𐐿𐐶𐐮𐐿 𐐻𐐭 𐐺𐐬𐑅𐐻, 𐐰𐑌𐐼 𐐼𐐭 𐐫𐑊 𐑋𐐰𐑌𐐲𐑉 𐐱𐑂 𐑄𐐰𐐻 𐐸𐐶𐐮𐐽 𐐮𐑆 𐐮𐑌𐐮𐐿𐐶𐐮𐐻𐐨; 𐐰𐑌𐐼 𐐸𐐵 𐑅𐑊𐐬 𐐪𐑉 𐑄𐐩 𐐻𐐭 𐑉𐐨𐑋𐐯𐑋𐐺𐐲𐑉 𐑄 𐐢𐐫𐑉𐐼 𐑄𐐩𐑉 𐐘𐐱𐐼, 𐐰𐑌𐐼 𐐻𐐭 𐑀𐐮𐑂 𐐨𐑉 𐐲𐑌𐐻𐐭 𐐸𐐮𐑆 𐐿𐐵𐑌𐑅𐐯𐑊𐑆; 𐐷𐐩, 𐐸𐐵 𐑅𐑊𐐬 𐐻𐐭 𐐶𐐫𐐿 𐐮𐑌 𐐶𐐮𐑆𐐼𐐲𐑋'𐑆 𐐹𐐪𐑃𐑅! 𐐒𐐨𐐸𐐬𐑊𐐼, 𐑄𐐩 𐐼𐐭 𐑌𐐱𐐻 𐐼𐐨𐑆𐐴𐑉 𐑄𐐰𐐻 𐑄 𐐢𐐫𐑉𐐼 𐑄𐐩𐑉 𐐘𐐱𐐼, 𐐸𐐭 𐐸𐐰𐑃 𐐿𐑉𐐨𐐩𐐻𐐯𐐼 𐑄𐐯𐑋, 𐑇𐐳𐐼 𐑉𐐭𐑊 𐐰𐑌𐐼 𐑉𐐩𐑌 𐐬𐑂𐐲𐑉 𐑄𐐯𐑋; 𐑌𐐱𐐻𐐶𐐮𐑄𐑅𐐻𐐰𐑌𐐼𐐮𐑍 𐐸𐐮𐑆 𐑀𐑉𐐩𐐻 𐑀𐐳𐐼𐑌𐐯𐑅 𐐰𐑌𐐼 𐐸𐐮𐑆 𐑋𐐲𐑉𐑅𐐨 𐐻𐐫𐑉𐐼𐑆 𐑄𐐯𐑋, 𐑄𐐩 𐐼𐐭 𐑅𐐯𐐻 𐐰𐐻 𐑌𐐫𐐻 𐐸𐐮𐑆 𐐿𐐵𐑌𐑅𐐯𐑊𐑆, 𐐰𐑌𐐼 𐑄𐐩 𐐶𐐮𐑊 𐑌𐐱𐐻 𐑄𐐰𐐻 𐐸𐐨 𐑇𐐳𐐼 𐐺𐐨 𐑄𐐩𐑉 𐑀𐐴𐐼. 𐐄 𐐸𐐵 𐑀𐑉𐐩𐐻 𐐮𐑆 𐑄 𐑌𐐲𐑃𐐮𐑍𐑌𐐯𐑅 𐐱𐑂 𐑄 𐐽𐐮𐑊𐐼𐑉𐐯𐑌 𐐱𐑂 𐑋𐐯𐑌; 𐐷𐐩, 𐐨𐑂𐐯𐑌 𐑄𐐩 𐐪𐑉 𐑊𐐯𐑅 𐑄𐐰𐑌 𐑄 𐐼𐐲𐑅𐐻 𐐱𐑂 𐑄 𐐲𐑉𐑃. 𐐙𐐫𐑉 𐐺𐐨𐐸𐐬𐑊𐐼, 𐑄 𐐼𐐲𐑅𐐻 𐐱𐑂 𐑄 𐐲𐑉𐑃 𐑋𐐭𐑂𐐯𐑃 𐐸𐐮𐑄𐐲𐑉 𐐰𐑌𐐼 𐑄𐐮𐑄𐐲𐑉, 𐐻𐐭 𐑄 𐐼𐐨𐑂𐐴𐐼𐐮𐑍 𐐰𐑅𐐲𐑌𐐼𐐲𐑉, 𐐰𐐻 𐑄 𐐿𐐱𐑋𐐰𐑌𐐼 𐐱𐑂 𐐵𐑉 𐑀𐑉𐐩𐐻 𐐰𐑌𐐼 𐐯𐑂𐐲𐑉𐑊𐐰𐑅𐐻𐐮𐑍 𐐘𐐱𐐼; 𐐷𐐩, 𐐺𐐨𐐸𐐬𐑊𐐼 𐐰𐐻 𐐸𐐮𐑆 𐑂𐐱𐐮𐑅 𐐼𐐭 𐑄 𐐸𐐮𐑊𐑆 𐐰𐑌𐐼 𐑄 𐑋𐐵𐑌𐐻𐐩𐑌𐑆 𐐻𐑉𐐯𐑋𐐺𐑊 𐐰𐑌𐐼 𐐿𐐶𐐩𐐿; 𐐰𐑌𐐼 𐐺𐐴 𐑄 𐐹𐐵𐐲𐑉 𐐱𐑂 𐐸𐐮𐑆 𐑂𐐱𐐮𐑅 𐑄𐐩 𐐪𐑉 𐐺𐑉𐐬𐐿𐐲𐑌 𐐲𐐹, 𐐰𐑌𐐼 𐐺𐐨𐐿𐐲𐑋 𐑅𐑋𐐭𐑄, 𐐷𐐩, 𐐨𐑂𐐯𐑌 𐑊𐐴𐐿 𐐲𐑌𐐻𐐭 𐐩 𐑂𐐰𐑊𐐨; 𐐷𐐩, 𐐺𐐴 𐑄 𐐹𐐵𐐲𐑉 𐐱𐑂 𐐸𐐮𐑆 𐑂𐐱𐐮𐑅 𐐼𐐲𐑃 𐑄 𐐸𐐬𐑊 𐐲𐑉𐑃 𐑇𐐩𐐿; 𐐷𐐩, 𐐺𐐴 𐑄 𐐹𐐵𐐲𐑉 𐐱𐑂 𐐸𐐮𐑆 𐑂𐐱𐐮𐑅 𐐼𐐲𐑃 𐑄 𐑁𐐵𐑌𐐼𐐩𐑇𐐲𐑌𐑆 𐑉𐐱𐐿, 𐐨𐑂𐐯𐑌 𐐻𐐭 𐑄 𐑂𐐯𐑉𐐨 𐑅𐐯𐑌𐐻𐐲𐑉; 𐐷𐐩, 𐐰𐑌𐐼 𐐮𐑁 𐐸𐐨 𐑅𐐩 𐐲𐑌𐐻𐐭 𐑄 𐐲𐑉𐑃, 𐐣𐐭𐑂, 𐐮𐐻 𐐮𐑆 𐑋𐐭𐑂𐐼; 𐐷𐐩, 𐐮𐑁 𐐸𐐨 𐑅𐐩 𐐲𐑌𐐻𐐭 𐑄 𐐲𐑉𐑃, 𐐜𐐵 𐑇𐐰𐑊𐐻 𐑀𐐬 𐐺𐐰𐐿, 𐑄𐐰𐐻 𐐮𐐻 𐑊𐐯𐑍𐑃𐐲𐑌 𐐵𐐻 𐑄 𐐼𐐩 𐑁𐐫𐑉 𐑋𐐯𐑌𐐨 𐐵𐐲𐑉𐑆, 𐐮𐐻 𐐮𐑆 𐐼𐐲𐑌; 𐐰𐑌𐐼 𐑄𐐲𐑅, 𐐲𐐿𐐫𐑉𐐼𐐮𐑍 𐐻𐐭 𐐸𐐮𐑆 𐐶𐐲𐑉𐐼, 𐑄 𐐲𐑉𐑃 𐑀𐐬𐐯𐑃 𐐺𐐰𐐿, 𐐰𐑌𐐼 𐐮𐐻 𐐲𐐹𐐨𐑉𐐯𐑃 𐐲𐑌𐐻𐐭 𐑋𐐰𐑌 𐑄𐐰𐐻 𐑄 𐑅𐐲𐑌 𐑅𐐻𐐰𐑌𐐼𐐯𐑃 𐑅𐐻𐐮𐑊; 𐐷𐐩, 𐐰𐑌𐐼 𐐺𐐨𐐸𐐬𐑊𐐼, 𐑄𐐮𐑅 𐐮𐑆 𐑅𐐬; 𐑁𐐫𐑉 𐑇𐐳𐑉 𐐮𐐻 𐐮𐑆 𐑄 𐐲𐑉𐑃 𐑄𐐰𐐻 𐑋𐐭𐑂𐐯𐑃, 𐐰𐑌𐐼 𐑌𐐱𐐻 𐑄 𐑅𐐲𐑌.

9. 𐐈𐑌𐐼 𐐺𐐨𐐸𐐬𐑊𐐼, 𐐫𐑊𐑅𐐬, 𐐮𐑁 𐐸𐐨 𐑅𐐩 𐐲𐑌𐐻𐐭 𐑄 𐐶𐐫𐐻𐐲𐑉𐑆 𐐱𐑂 𐑄 𐑀𐑉𐐩𐐻 𐐼𐐨𐐹, 𐐒𐐨 𐑄𐐵 𐐼𐑉𐐴𐐼

𐐵𐑉𐑆, 𐐮𐐻 𐐮𐑆 𐐼𐐲𐑌. 𐐒𐐨𐐸𐐬𐑊𐐼, 𐐮𐑁 𐐸𐐨 𐑅𐐩 𐐲𐑌𐐻𐐭 𐑄𐐮𐑅 𐑋𐐵𐑌𐐻𐐩𐑌, 𐐒𐐨 𐑄𐐵 𐑉𐐩𐑆𐐼 𐐲𐐹, 𐐰𐑌𐐼 𐐿𐐲𐑋 𐐬𐑂𐐲𐑉 𐐰𐑌𐐼 𐑁𐐫𐑊 𐐲𐐹𐐱𐑌 𐑄𐐰𐐻 𐑅𐐮𐐻𐐨, 𐑄𐐰𐐻 𐐮𐐻 𐐺𐐨 𐐺𐐯𐑉𐐨𐐼 𐐲𐐹, 𐐺𐐨𐐸𐐬𐑊𐐼 𐐮𐐻 𐐮𐑆 𐐼𐐲𐑌. 𐐈𐑌𐐼 𐐺𐐨𐐸𐐬𐑊𐐼, 𐐮𐑁 𐐲 𐑋𐐰𐑌 𐐸𐐴𐐼 𐐲𐐹 𐐲 𐐻𐑉𐐯𐑈𐐲𐑉 𐐮𐑌 𐑄 𐐲𐑉𐑃, 𐐰𐑌𐐼 𐑄 𐐢𐐫𐑉𐐼 𐑇𐐰𐑊 𐑅𐐩, 𐐢𐐯𐐻 𐐮𐐻 𐐺𐐨 𐐰𐐿𐐲𐑉𐑅𐐯𐐼, 𐐺𐐨𐐿𐐫𐑆 𐐱𐑂 𐑄 𐐮𐑌𐐮𐐿𐐶𐐮𐐻𐐨 𐐱𐑂 𐐸𐐮𐑋 𐐸𐐭 𐐸𐐰𐑃 𐐸𐐮𐐼 𐐮𐐻 𐐲𐐹, 𐐺𐐨𐐸𐐬𐑊𐐼, 𐐮𐐻 𐑇𐐰𐑊 𐐺𐐨 𐐰𐐿𐐲𐑉𐑅𐐯𐐼; 𐐰𐑌𐐼 𐐮𐑁 𐑄 𐐢𐐫𐑉𐐼 𐑇𐐰𐑊 𐑅𐐩, 𐐒𐐨 𐑄𐐵 𐐰𐐿𐐲𐑉𐑅𐐯𐐼, 𐑄𐐰𐐻 𐑌𐐬 𐑋𐐰𐑌 𐑇𐐰𐑊 𐑁𐐴𐑌𐐼 𐑄𐐨 𐑁𐑉𐐱𐑋 𐑄𐐮𐑅 𐐻𐐴𐑋 𐐸𐐯𐑌𐑅𐑁𐐫𐑉𐑃 𐐰𐑌𐐼 𐑁𐐫𐑉𐐯𐑂𐐲𐑉, 𐐺𐐨𐐸𐐬𐑊𐐼, 𐑌𐐬 𐑋𐐰𐑌 𐑀𐐯𐐻𐐯𐑃 𐐮𐐻 𐐸𐐯𐑌𐑅𐑁𐐫𐑉𐑃 𐐰𐑌𐐼 𐑁𐐫𐑉𐐯𐑂𐐲𐑉. 𐐈𐑌𐐼 𐐺𐐨𐐸𐐬𐑊𐐼, 𐐮𐑁 𐑄 𐐢𐐫𐑉𐐼 𐑇𐐰𐑊 𐑅𐐩 𐐲𐑌𐐻𐐭 𐐲 𐑋𐐰𐑌, 𐐒𐐨𐐿𐐫𐑆 𐐱𐑂 𐑄𐐴𐑌 𐐮𐑌𐐮𐐿𐐶𐐮𐐻𐐨𐑆, 𐑄𐐵 𐑇𐐰𐑊𐐻 𐐺𐐨 𐐰𐐿𐐲𐑉𐑅𐐯𐐼 𐑁𐐫𐑉𐐯𐑂𐐲𐑉, 𐐮𐐻 𐑇𐐰𐑊 𐐺𐐨 𐐼𐐲𐑌. 𐐈𐑌𐐼 𐐮𐑁 𐑄 𐐢𐐫𐑉𐐼 𐑇𐐰𐑊 𐑅𐐩, 𐐒𐐨𐐿𐐫𐑆 𐐱𐑂 𐑄𐐴𐑌 𐐮𐑌𐐮𐐿𐐶𐐮𐐻𐐨𐑆, 𐑄𐐵 𐑇𐐰𐑊𐐻 𐐺𐐨 𐐿𐐲𐐻 𐐫𐑁 𐑁𐑉𐐱𐑋 𐑋𐐴 𐐹𐑉𐐯𐑆𐐯𐑌𐑅, 𐐸𐐨 𐐶𐐮𐑊 𐐿𐐫𐑆 𐑄𐐰𐐻 𐐮𐐻 𐑇𐐰𐑊 𐐺𐐨 𐑅𐐬. 𐐈𐑌𐐼 𐐶𐐬 𐐲𐑌𐐻𐐭 𐐸𐐮𐑋 𐐻𐐭 𐐸𐐭𐑋 𐐸𐐨 𐑇𐐰𐑊 𐑅𐐩 𐑄𐐮𐑅, 𐑁𐐫𐑉 𐐮𐐻 𐑇𐐰𐑊 𐐺𐐨 𐐲𐑌𐐻𐐭 𐐸𐐮𐑋 𐑄𐐰𐐻 𐐶𐐮𐑊 𐐼𐐭 𐐮𐑌𐐮𐐿𐐶𐐮𐐻𐐨, 𐐰𐑌𐐼 𐐸𐐨 𐐿𐐰𐑌𐐱𐐻 𐐺𐐨 𐑅𐐩𐑂𐐼; 𐑄𐐯𐑉𐑁𐐬𐑉, 𐑁𐐫𐑉 𐑄𐐮𐑅 𐐿𐐫𐑆, 𐑄𐐰𐐻 𐑋𐐯𐑌 𐑋𐐴𐐻 𐐺𐐨 𐑅𐐩𐑂𐐼, 𐐸𐐰𐑃 𐑉𐐨𐐹𐐯𐑌𐐻𐐰𐑌𐑅 𐐺𐐮𐑌 𐐼𐐨𐐿𐑊𐐩𐑉𐐼. 𐐜𐐯𐑉𐑁𐐬𐑉, 𐐺𐑊𐐯𐑅𐐯𐐼 𐐪𐑉 𐑄𐐩 𐐸𐐭 𐐶𐐮𐑊 𐑉𐐨𐐹𐐯𐑌𐐻 𐐰𐑌𐐼 𐐸𐐪𐑉𐐿𐐯𐑌 𐐲𐑌𐐻𐐭 𐑄 𐑂𐑎𐑅 𐐱𐑂 𐑄 𐐢𐐫𐑉𐐼 𐑄𐐩𐑉 𐐘𐐱𐐼; 𐑁𐐫𐑉 𐑄𐐨𐑆 𐐪𐑉 𐑄𐐩 𐑄𐐰𐐻 𐑇𐐰𐑊 𐐺𐐨 𐑅𐐩𐑂𐐼. 𐐈𐑌𐐼 𐑋𐐩 𐐘𐐱𐐼 𐑀𐑉𐐰𐑌𐐻, 𐐮𐑌 𐐸𐐮𐑆 𐑀𐑉𐐩𐐻 𐑁𐐳𐑊𐑌𐐯𐑅, 𐑄𐐰𐐻 𐑋𐐯𐑌 𐑋𐐴𐐻 𐐺𐐨 𐐺𐑉𐐫𐐻 𐐲𐑌𐐻𐐭 𐑉𐐨𐐹𐐯𐑌𐐻𐐰𐑌𐑅 𐐰𐑌𐐼 𐑀𐐳𐐼 𐐶𐐲𐑉𐐿𐑅, 𐑄𐐰𐐻 𐑄𐐩 𐑋𐐴𐐻 𐐺𐐨 𐑉𐐨𐑅𐐻𐐬𐑉𐐼 𐐲𐑌𐐻𐐭 𐑀𐑉𐐩𐑅 𐑁𐐫𐑉 𐑀𐑉𐐩𐑅, 𐐰𐐿𐐫𐑉𐐼𐐮𐑍 𐐻𐐭 𐑄𐐩𐑉 𐐶𐐲𐑉𐐿𐑅. 𐐈𐑌𐐼 𐐌 𐐶𐐳𐐼 𐑄𐐰𐐻 𐐫𐑊 𐑋𐐯𐑌 𐑋𐐴𐐻 𐐺𐐨 𐑅𐐩𐑂𐐼. 𐐒𐐲𐐻 𐐶𐐨 𐑉𐐨𐐼 𐑄𐐰𐐻 𐐮𐑌 𐑄 𐑀𐑉𐐩𐐻 𐐰𐑌𐐼 𐑊𐐰𐑅𐐻 𐐼𐐩, 𐑄𐐯𐑉 𐐪𐑉 𐑅𐐲𐑋 𐐸𐐭 𐑇𐐰𐑊 𐐺𐐨 𐐿𐐰𐑅𐐻 𐐵𐐻; 𐐷𐐩, 𐐸𐐭 𐑇𐐰𐑊 𐐺𐐨 𐐿𐐰𐑅𐐻 𐐫𐑁 𐑁𐑉𐐱𐑋 𐑄 𐐹𐑉𐐯𐑆𐐯𐑌𐑅 𐐱𐑂 𐑄 𐐢𐐫𐑉𐐼; 𐐷𐐩, 𐐸𐐭 𐑇𐐰𐑊 𐐺𐐨 𐐿𐐱𐑌𐑅𐐴𐑌𐐼 𐐻𐐭 𐐲 𐑅𐐻𐐩𐐻 𐐱𐑂 𐐯𐑌𐐼𐑊𐐯𐑅 𐑋𐐮𐑆𐐲𐑉𐐨, 𐑁𐐳𐑊𐑁𐐮𐑊𐐮𐑍 𐑄 𐐶𐐲𐑉𐐼𐑆 𐐸𐐶𐐮𐐽 𐑅𐐩, 𐐜𐐩 𐑄𐐰𐐻 𐐸𐐰𐑂 𐐼𐐲𐑌 𐑀𐐳𐐼 𐑇𐐰𐑊 𐐸𐐰𐑂 𐐯𐑂𐐲𐑉𐑊𐐰𐑅𐐻𐐮𐑍 𐑊𐐴𐑁; 𐐰𐑌𐐼 𐑄𐐩 𐑄𐐰𐐻 𐐸𐐰𐑂 𐐼𐐲𐑌 𐐨𐑂𐐮𐑊 𐑇𐐰𐑊 𐐸𐐰𐑂 𐐯𐑂𐐲𐑉𐑊𐐰𐑅𐐻𐐮𐑍 𐐼𐐰𐑋𐑌𐐩𐑇𐐲𐑌. 𐐈𐑌𐐼 𐑄𐐲𐑅 𐐮𐐻 𐐮𐑆. 𐐁𐑋𐐯𐑌.

𐐗𐐰𐐹𐐻𐐲𐑉 V.

𐐜 𐐹𐑉𐐱𐑁𐐯𐑅𐐨 𐐱𐑂 𐐝𐐰𐑋𐐷𐐭𐐯𐑊, 𐑄 𐐢𐐰𐑋𐐲𐑌𐐴𐐻, 𐐻𐐭 𐑄 𐐤𐐨𐑁𐐴𐐻𐑅.

1. 𐐈𐑌𐐼 𐑌𐐵 𐐮𐐻 𐐿𐐩𐑋 𐐻𐐭 𐐹𐐰𐑅 𐐮𐑌 𐑄 𐐩𐐻𐐨 𐐰𐑌𐐼 𐑅𐐮𐐿𐑅𐑃 𐐷𐐨𐑉, 𐑄 𐐤𐐨𐑁𐐴𐐻𐑅 𐐼𐐮𐐼 𐑅𐐻𐐮𐑊 𐑉𐐨𐑋𐐩𐑌 𐐮𐑌 𐐶𐐮𐐿𐐯𐐼𐑌𐐯𐑅, 𐐷𐐩, 𐐮𐑌 𐑀𐑉𐐩𐐻 𐐶𐐮𐐿𐐯𐐼𐑌𐐯𐑅, 𐐸𐐶𐐴𐑊 𐑄 𐐢𐐰𐑋𐐲𐑌𐐴𐐻𐑅 𐐼𐐮𐐼 𐐱𐐺𐑆𐐲𐑉𐑂 𐑅𐐻𐑉𐐮𐐿𐐻𐑊𐐨 𐐻𐐭 𐐿𐐨𐐹 𐑄 𐐿𐐱𐑋𐐰𐑌𐐼𐑋𐐯𐑌𐐻𐑅 𐐱𐑂 𐐘𐐱𐐼, 𐐰𐐿𐐫𐑉𐐼𐐮𐑍 𐐻𐐭 𐑄 𐑊𐐫 𐐱𐑂 𐐣𐐬𐑆𐐯𐑆. 𐐈𐑌𐐼 𐐮𐐻 𐐿𐐩𐑋 𐐻𐐭 𐐹𐐰𐑅 𐑄𐐰𐐻 𐐮𐑌 𐑄𐐮𐑅 𐐷𐐨𐑉 𐑄𐐯𐑉 𐐶𐐱𐑆 𐐶𐐲𐑌 𐐝𐐰𐑋𐐷𐐭𐐯𐑊, 𐐲 𐐢𐐰𐑋𐐲𐑌𐐴𐐻, 𐐿𐐩𐑋 𐐮𐑌𐐻𐐭 𐑄 𐑊𐐰𐑌𐐼 𐐱𐑂 𐐞𐐰𐑉𐐲𐐸𐐯𐑋𐑊𐐲, 𐐰𐑌𐐼 𐐺𐐨𐑀𐐰𐑌 𐐻𐐭 𐐹𐑉𐐨𐐽 𐐲𐑌𐐻𐐭 𐑄 𐐹𐐨𐐹𐑊. 𐐈𐑌𐐼 𐐮𐐻 𐐿𐐩𐑋 𐐻𐐭 𐐹𐐰𐑅 𐑄𐐰𐐻 𐐸𐐨 𐐼𐐮𐐼 𐐹𐑉𐐨𐐽 𐑋𐐯𐑌𐐨 𐐼𐐩𐑆, 𐑉𐐨𐐹𐐯𐑌𐐻𐐰𐑌𐑅 𐐲𐑌𐐻𐐭 𐑄 𐐹𐐨𐐹𐑊, 𐐰𐑌𐐼 𐑄𐐩 𐐼𐐮𐐼 𐐿𐐰𐑅𐐻 𐐸𐐮𐑋 𐐵𐐻, 𐐰𐑌𐐼 𐐸𐐨 𐐶𐐱𐑆 𐐰𐐺𐐵𐐻 𐐻𐐭 𐑉𐐨𐐻𐐲𐑉𐑌 𐐻𐐭 𐐸𐐮𐑆 𐐬𐑌 𐑊𐐰𐑌𐐼. 𐐒𐐲𐐻 𐐺𐐨𐐸𐐬𐑊𐐼, 𐑄 𐑂𐑎𐑅 𐐱𐑂 𐑄 𐐢𐐫𐑉𐐼 𐐿𐐩𐑋 𐐲𐑌𐐻𐐭 𐐸𐐮𐑋, 𐑄𐐰𐐻 𐐸𐐨 𐑇𐐳𐐼 𐑉𐐨𐐻𐐲𐑉𐑌 𐐰𐑀𐐯𐑌, 𐐰𐑌𐐼 𐐹𐑉𐐱𐑁𐐯𐑅𐐴 𐐲𐑌𐐻𐐭 𐑄 𐐹𐐨𐐹𐑊 𐐸𐐶𐐱𐐻𐑅𐐬𐐯𐑂𐐲𐑉 𐑃𐐮𐑍𐑆 𐑇𐐳𐐼 𐐿𐐲𐑋 𐐮𐑌𐐻𐐭 𐐸𐐮𐑆 𐐸𐐪𐑉𐐻.

2. 𐐈𐑌𐐼 𐐮𐐻 𐐿𐐩𐑋 𐐻𐐭 𐐹𐐰𐑅 𐑄𐐰𐐻 𐑄𐐩 𐐶𐐳𐐼 𐑌𐐱𐐻 𐑅𐐲𐑁𐐲𐑉 𐑄𐐰𐐻 𐐸𐐨 𐑇𐐳𐐼 𐐯𐑌𐐻𐐲𐑉 𐐮𐑌𐐻𐐭 𐑄 𐑅𐐮𐐻𐐨; 𐑄𐐯𐑉𐑁𐐬𐑉 𐐸𐐨 𐐶𐐯𐑌𐐻 𐐰𐑌𐐼 𐑀𐐱𐐻 𐐲𐐹𐐱𐑌 𐑄 𐐶𐐫𐑊 𐑄𐐯𐑉𐐱𐑂, 𐐰𐑌𐐼 𐑅𐐻𐑉𐐯𐐽𐐻 𐑁𐐬𐑉𐑃 𐐸𐐮𐑆 𐐸𐐰𐑌𐐼 𐐰𐑌𐐼 𐐿𐑉𐐴𐐼 𐐶𐐮𐑃 𐐲 𐑊𐐵𐐼 𐑂𐑎𐑅, 𐐰𐑌𐐼 𐐹𐑉𐐱𐑁𐐯𐑅𐐴𐐼 𐐲𐑌𐐻𐐭 𐑄 𐐹𐐨𐐹𐑊 𐐸𐐶𐐱𐐻𐑅𐐬𐐯𐑂𐐲𐑉 𐑃𐐮𐑍𐑆 𐑄 𐐢𐐫𐑉𐐼 𐐹𐐳𐐻 𐐮𐑌𐐻𐐭 𐐸𐐮𐑆 𐐸𐐪𐑉𐐻; 𐐰𐑌𐐼 𐐸𐐨 𐑅𐐯𐐼 𐐲𐑌𐐻𐐭 𐑄𐐯𐑋, 𐐒𐐨𐐸𐐬𐑊𐐼, 𐐌, 𐐝𐐰𐑋𐐷𐐭𐐯𐑊, 𐐲 𐐢𐐰𐑋𐐲𐑌𐐴𐐻, 𐐼𐐭 𐑅𐐹𐐨𐐿 𐑄 𐐶𐐲𐑉𐐼𐑆 𐐱𐑂 𐑄 𐐢𐐫𐑉𐐼 𐐸𐐶𐐮𐐽 𐐸𐐨 𐐼𐐲𐑃 𐐹𐐳𐐻 𐐮𐑌𐐻𐐭 𐑋𐐴 𐐸𐐪𐑉𐐻; 𐐰𐑌𐐼 𐐺𐐨𐐸𐐬𐑊𐐼 𐐸𐐨 𐐸𐐰𐑃 𐐹𐐳𐐻 𐐮𐐻 𐐮𐑌𐐻𐐭 𐑋𐐴 𐐸𐐪𐑉𐐻 𐐻𐐭 𐑅𐐩 𐐲𐑌𐐻𐐭 𐑄𐐮𐑅 𐐹𐐨𐐹𐑊, 𐑄𐐰𐐻 𐑄 𐑅𐐬𐑉𐐼 𐐱𐑂 𐐾𐐲𐑅𐐻𐐮𐑅 𐐸𐐰𐑍𐐯𐑃 𐐬𐑂𐐲𐑉 𐑄𐐮𐑅 𐐹𐐨𐐹𐑊;

𐐰𐑌𐐼 𐑁𐐬𐑉 𐐸𐐲𐑌𐐼𐑉𐐯𐐼 𐐷𐐨𐑉𐑆 𐐹𐐰𐑅 𐑌𐐱𐐻 𐐰𐐶𐐩 𐑅𐐩𐑂 𐑄 𐑅𐐬𐑉𐐼 𐐱𐑂 𐐾𐐲𐑅𐐻𐐮𐑅 𐑁𐐫𐑊𐐯𐑃 𐐲𐐹𐐱𐑌 𐑄𐐮𐑅 𐐹𐐨𐐹𐑊; 𐐷𐐩, 𐐸𐐯𐑂𐐨 𐐼𐐯𐑅𐐻𐑉𐐲𐐿𐑇𐐲𐑌 𐐰𐐶𐐩𐐻𐐯𐑃 𐑄𐐮𐑅 𐐹𐐨𐐹𐑊, 𐐰𐑌𐐼 𐐮𐐻 𐑇𐐭𐑉𐑊𐐨 𐐿𐐲𐑋𐐯𐑃 𐐲𐑌𐐻𐐭 𐑄𐐮𐑅 𐐹𐐨𐐹𐑊, 𐐰𐑌𐐼 𐑌𐐲𐑃𐐮𐑍 𐐿𐐰𐑌 𐑅𐐩𐑂 𐑄𐐮𐑅 𐐹𐐨𐐹𐑊, 𐑅𐐩𐑂 𐐮𐐻 𐐺𐐨 𐑉𐐨𐐹𐐯𐑌𐐻𐐰𐑌𐑅 𐐰𐑌𐐼 𐑁𐐩𐑃 𐐱𐑌 𐑄 𐐢𐐫𐑉𐐼 𐐖𐐨𐑆𐐲𐑅 𐐗𐑉𐐴𐑅𐐻, 𐐸𐐭 𐑇𐐭𐑉𐑊𐐨 𐑇𐐰𐑊 𐐿𐐲𐑋 𐐮𐑌𐐻𐐭 𐑄 𐐶𐐲𐑉𐑊𐐼, 𐐰𐑌𐐼 𐑇𐐰𐑊 𐑅𐐲𐑁𐐲𐑉 𐑋𐐯𐑌𐐨 𐑃𐐮𐑍𐑆, 𐐰𐑌𐐼 𐑇𐐰𐑊 𐐺𐐨 𐑅𐑊𐐩𐑌 𐑁𐐫𐑉 𐐸𐐮𐑆 𐐹𐐨𐐹𐑊. 𐐈𐑌𐐼 𐐺𐐨𐐸𐐬𐑊𐐼, 𐐰𐑌 𐐩𐑌𐐾𐐯𐑊 𐐱𐑂 𐑄 𐐢𐐫𐑉𐐼 𐐸𐐰𐑃 𐐼𐐨𐐿𐑊𐐩𐑉𐐼 𐐮𐐻 𐐲𐑌𐐻𐐭 𐑋𐐨, 𐐰𐑌𐐼 𐐸𐐨 𐐼𐐮𐐼 𐐺𐑉𐐮𐑍 𐑀𐑊𐐰𐐼 𐐻𐐴𐐼𐐮𐑍𐑆 𐐻𐐭 𐑋𐐴 𐑅𐐬𐑊. 𐐈𐑌𐐼 𐐺𐐨𐐸𐐬𐑊𐐼, 𐐌 𐐶𐐱𐑆 𐑅𐐯𐑌𐐻 𐐲𐑌𐐻𐐭 𐐷𐐭 𐐻𐐭 𐐼𐐨𐐿𐑊𐐩𐑉 𐐮𐐻 𐐲𐑌𐐻𐐭 𐐷𐐭 𐐫𐑊𐑅𐐬, 𐑄𐐰𐐻 𐐷𐐨 𐑋𐐴𐐻 𐐸𐐰𐑂 𐑀𐑊𐐰𐐼 𐐻𐐴𐐼𐐮𐑍𐑆; 𐐺𐐲𐐻 𐐺𐐨𐐸𐐬𐑊𐐼 𐐷𐐨 𐐶𐐳𐐼 𐑌𐐱𐐻 𐑉𐐨𐑅𐐨𐑂 𐑋𐐨, 𐑄𐐯𐑉𐑁𐐬𐑉 𐑄𐐲𐑅 𐑅𐐯𐑃 𐑄 𐐢𐐫𐑉𐐼, 𐐒𐐨𐐿𐐫𐑆 𐐱𐑂 𐑄 𐐸𐐪𐑉𐐼𐑌𐐯𐑅 𐐱𐑂 𐑄 𐐸𐐪𐑉𐐻𐑅 𐐱𐑂 𐑄 𐐹𐐨𐐹𐑊 𐐱𐑂 𐑄 𐐤𐐨𐑁𐐴𐐻𐑅, 𐐯𐐿𐑅𐐯𐐹𐐻 𐑄𐐩 𐑉𐐨𐐹𐐯𐑌𐐻 𐐌 𐐶𐐮𐑊 𐐻𐐩𐐿 𐐰𐐶𐐩 𐑋𐐴 𐐶𐐲𐑉𐐼 𐑁𐑉𐐱𐑋 𐑄𐐯𐑋, 𐐰𐑌𐐼 𐐌 𐐶𐐮𐑊 𐐶𐐮𐑄𐐼𐑉𐐫 𐑋𐐴 𐐝𐐹𐐮𐑉𐐮𐐻 𐑁𐑉𐐱𐑋 𐑄𐐯𐑋, 𐐰𐑌𐐼 𐐌 𐐶𐐮𐑊 𐑅𐐲𐑁𐐲𐑉 𐑄𐐯𐑋 𐑌𐐬 𐑊𐐱𐑍𐑀𐐲𐑉, 𐐰𐑌𐐼 𐐌 𐐶𐐮𐑊 𐐻𐐲𐑉𐑌 𐑄 𐐸𐐪𐑉𐐻𐑅 𐐱𐑂 𐑄𐐯𐑉 𐐺𐑉𐐯𐑄𐑉𐐯𐑌 𐐰𐑀𐐯𐑌𐑅𐐻 𐑄𐐯𐑋; 𐐰𐑌𐐼 𐑁𐐬𐑉 𐐸𐐲𐑌𐐼𐑉𐐯𐐼 𐐷𐐨𐑉𐑆 𐑇𐐰𐑊 𐑌𐐱𐐻 𐐹𐐰𐑅 𐐰𐐶𐐩, 𐐺𐐨𐑁𐐬𐑉 𐐌 𐐶𐐮𐑊 𐐿𐐫𐑆 𐑄𐐰𐐻 𐑄𐐩 𐑇𐐰𐑊 𐐺𐐨 𐑅𐑋𐐮𐐻𐐲𐑌; 𐐷𐐩, 𐐌 𐐶𐐮𐑊 𐑂𐐮𐑆𐐮𐐻 𐑄𐐯𐑋 𐐶𐐮𐑄 𐑄 𐑅𐐬𐑉𐐼, 𐐰𐑌𐐼 𐐶𐐮𐑄 𐑁𐐰𐑋𐐮𐑌, 𐐰𐑌𐐼 𐐶𐐮𐑄 𐐹𐐯𐑅𐐻𐐮𐑊𐐯𐑌𐑅; 𐐷𐐩, 𐐌 𐐶𐐮𐑊 𐑂𐐮𐑆𐐮𐐻 𐑄𐐯𐑋 𐐮𐑌 𐑋𐐴 𐑁𐐨𐑉𐑅 𐐰𐑍𐑀𐐲𐑉, 𐐰𐑌𐐼 𐑄𐐯𐑉 𐑇𐐰𐑊 𐐺𐐨 𐑄𐐬𐑆 𐐱𐑂 𐑄 𐑁𐐬𐑉𐑃 𐐾𐐯𐑌𐐲𐑉𐐩𐑇𐐲𐑌, 𐐸𐐭 𐑇𐐰𐑊 𐑊𐐮𐑂, 𐐱𐑂 𐐷𐐭𐑉 𐐯𐑌𐐯𐑋𐐨𐑆, 𐐻𐐭 𐐺𐐨𐐸𐐬𐑊𐐼 𐐷𐐭𐑉 𐐲𐐻𐐲𐑉 𐐼𐐯𐑅𐐻𐑉𐐲𐐿𐑇𐐲𐑌: 𐐰𐑌𐐼 𐑄𐐮𐑅 𐑇𐐰𐑊 𐑇𐐭𐑉𐑊𐐨 𐐿𐐲𐑋, 𐐯𐐿𐑅𐐯𐐹𐐻 𐐷𐐨 𐑉𐐨𐐹𐐯𐑌𐐻, 𐑅𐐯𐑃 𐑄 𐐢𐐫𐑉𐐼; 𐐰𐑌𐐼 𐑄𐐬𐑆 𐐱𐑂 𐑄 𐑁𐐬𐑉𐑃 𐐾𐐯𐑌𐐲𐑉𐐩𐑇𐐲𐑌 𐑇𐐰𐑊 𐑂𐐮𐑆𐐮𐐻 𐐷𐐭𐑉 𐐼𐐯𐑅𐐻𐑉𐐲𐐿𐑇𐐲𐑌. 𐐒𐐲𐐻 𐐮𐑁 𐐷𐐨 𐐶𐐮𐑊 𐑉𐐨𐐹𐐯𐑌𐐻 𐐰𐑌𐐼 𐑉𐐨𐐻𐐲𐑉𐑌 𐐲𐑌𐐻𐐭 𐑄 𐐢𐐫𐑉𐐼 𐐷𐐭𐑉 𐐘𐐱𐐼, 𐐌 𐐶𐐮𐑊 𐐻𐐲𐑉𐑌 𐐰𐐶𐐩 𐑋𐐴𐑌 𐐰𐑍𐑀𐐲𐑉, 𐑅𐐯𐑃 𐑄 𐐢𐐫𐑉𐐼; 𐐷𐐩, 𐑄𐐲𐑅 𐑅𐐯𐑃 𐑄 𐐢𐐫𐑉𐐼, 𐐒𐑊𐐯𐑅𐐯𐐼 𐐪𐑉 𐑄𐐩 𐐸𐐭 𐐶𐐮𐑊 𐑉𐐨𐐹𐐯𐑌𐐻 𐐰𐑌𐐼 𐐻𐐲𐑉𐑌 𐐲𐑌𐐻𐐭 𐑋𐐨, 𐐺𐐲𐐻 𐐶𐐬 𐐲𐑌𐐻𐐭 𐐸𐐮𐑋 𐑄𐐰𐐻 𐑉𐐨𐐹𐐯𐑌𐐻𐐯𐑃 𐑌𐐱𐐻; 𐐷𐐩, 𐐶𐐬 𐐲𐑌𐐻𐐭 𐑄𐐮𐑅 𐑀𐑉𐐩𐐻 𐑅𐐮𐐻𐐨 𐐱𐑂 𐐞𐐯𐑉𐐲𐐸𐐯𐑋𐑊𐐲; 𐑁𐐫𐑉 𐐺𐐨𐐸𐐬𐑊𐐼 𐐮𐐻 𐐮𐑆 𐐺𐐨𐐿𐐫𐑆 𐐱𐑂 𐑄𐐬𐑆 𐐸𐐭 𐐪𐑉 𐑉𐐴𐐽𐐲𐑅, 𐑄𐐰𐐻 𐐮𐐻 𐐮𐑆 𐑅𐐩𐑂𐐼; 𐐷𐐩, 𐐶𐐬 𐐲𐑌𐐻𐐭 𐑄𐐮𐑅 𐑀𐑉𐐩𐐻 𐑅𐐮𐐻𐐨, 𐑁𐐫𐑉 𐐌 𐐹𐐲𐑉𐑅𐐨𐑂, 𐑅𐐯𐑃 𐑄 𐐢𐐫𐑉𐐼, 𐑄𐐰𐐻 𐑄𐐯𐑉 𐐪𐑉 𐑋𐐯𐑌𐐨, 𐐷𐐩, 𐐨𐑂𐐲𐑌 𐑄 𐑋𐐬𐑉 𐐹𐐪𐑉𐐻 𐐱𐑂 𐑄𐐮𐑅 𐑀𐑉𐐩𐐻 𐑅𐐮𐐻𐐨 𐑄𐐰𐐻 𐐶𐐮𐑊 𐐸𐐪𐑉𐐼𐐲𐑌 𐑄𐐯𐑉 𐐸𐐪𐑉𐐻𐑅 𐐰𐑀𐐯𐑌𐑅𐐻 𐑋𐐨, 𐑅𐐯𐑃 𐑄 𐐢𐐫𐑉𐐼. 𐐒𐐲𐐻 𐐺𐑊𐐯𐑅𐐯𐐼 𐐪𐑉 𐑄𐐩 𐐸𐐭 𐐶𐐮𐑊 𐑉𐐨𐐹𐐯𐑌𐐻, 𐑁𐐫𐑉 𐑄𐐯𐑋 𐐶𐐮𐑊 𐐌 𐑅𐐹𐐩𐑉. 𐐒𐐲𐐻 𐐺𐐨𐐸𐐬𐑊𐐼 𐐮𐑁 𐐮𐐻 𐐶𐐲𐑉 𐑌𐐱𐐻 𐑁𐐫𐑉 𐑄 𐑉𐐴𐐽𐐲𐑅 𐐸𐐭 𐐪𐑉 𐐮𐑌 𐑄𐐮𐑅 𐑀𐑉𐐩𐐻 𐑅𐐮𐐻𐐨, 𐐺𐐨𐐸𐐬𐑊𐐼 𐐌 𐐶𐐳𐐼 𐐿𐐫𐑆 𐑄𐐰𐐻 𐑁𐐴𐑉 𐑇𐐳𐐼 𐐿𐐲𐑋 𐐼𐐵𐑌 𐐵𐐻 𐐱𐑂 𐐸𐐯𐑂𐐲𐑌, 𐐰𐑌𐐼 𐐼𐐯𐑅𐐻𐑉𐑎 𐐮𐐻. 𐐒𐐲𐐻 𐐺𐐨𐐸𐐬𐑊𐐼, 𐐮𐐻 𐐮𐑆 𐑁𐐫𐑉 𐑄 𐑉𐐴𐐽𐐲𐑅' 𐑅𐐩𐐿 𐑄𐐰𐐻 𐐮𐐻 𐐮𐑆 𐑅𐐹𐐩𐑉𐐼. 𐐒𐐲𐐻 𐐺𐐨𐐸𐐬𐑊𐐼, 𐑄 𐐻𐐴𐑋 𐐿𐐲𐑋𐐯𐑃, 𐑅𐐯𐑃 𐑄 𐐢𐐫𐑉𐐼, 𐑄𐐰𐐻 𐐸𐐶𐐯𐑌 𐐷𐐨 𐑇𐐰𐑊 𐐿𐐰𐑅𐐻 𐐵𐐻 𐑄 𐑉𐐴𐐽𐐲𐑅 𐑁𐑉𐐱𐑋 𐐰𐑋𐐲𐑍 𐐷𐐭, 𐑄𐐯𐑌 𐑇𐐰𐑊 𐐷𐐨 𐐺𐐨 𐑉𐐴𐐹 𐑁𐐫𐑉 𐐼𐐯𐑅𐐻𐑉𐐲𐐿𐑇𐐲𐑌; 𐐷𐐩, 𐐶𐐬 𐐺𐐨 𐐲𐑌𐐻𐐭 𐑄𐐮𐑅 𐑀𐑉𐐩𐐻 𐑅𐐮𐐻𐐨, 𐐺𐐨𐐿𐐫𐑆 𐐱𐑂 𐑄 𐐶𐐮𐐿𐐯𐐼𐑌𐐯𐑅 𐐰𐑌𐐼 𐐰𐐺𐐱𐑋𐐮𐑌𐐩𐑇𐐲𐑌𐑆 𐐸𐐶𐐮𐐽 𐐪𐑉 𐐮𐑌 𐐸𐐲𐑉; 𐐷𐐩, 𐐰𐑌𐐼 𐐶𐐬 𐐺𐐨 𐐲𐑌𐐻𐐭 𐑄 𐑅𐐮𐐻𐐨 𐐱𐑂 𐐘𐐮𐐼𐐨𐐲𐑌, 𐑁𐐫𐑉 𐑄 𐐶𐐮𐐿𐐯𐐼𐑌𐐯𐑅 𐐰𐑌𐐼 𐐰𐐺𐐱𐑋𐐮𐑌𐐩𐑇𐐲𐑌𐑆 𐐸𐐶𐐮𐐽 𐐪𐑉 𐐮𐑌 𐐸𐐲𐑉; 𐐷𐐩, 𐐰𐑌𐐼 𐐶𐐬 𐐺𐐨 𐐲𐑌𐐻𐐭 𐐫𐑊 𐑄 𐑅𐐮𐐻𐐨𐑆 𐐸𐐶𐐮𐐽 𐐪𐑉 𐐮𐑌 𐑄 𐑊𐐰𐑌𐐼 𐑉𐐵𐑌𐐼 𐐲𐐺𐐵𐐻, 𐐸𐐶𐐮𐐽 𐐪𐑉 𐐹𐐲𐑆𐐯𐑅𐐻 𐐺𐐴 𐑄 𐐤𐐨𐑁𐐴𐐻𐑅, 𐐺𐐨𐐿𐐫𐑆 𐐱𐑂 𐑄 𐐶𐐮𐐿𐐯𐐼𐑌𐐯𐑅 𐐰𐑌𐐼 𐐰𐐺𐐱𐑋𐐮𐑌𐐩𐑇𐐲𐑌𐑆 𐐸𐐶𐐮𐐽 𐐪𐑉 𐐮𐑌 𐑄𐐯𐑋; 𐐰𐑌𐐼 𐐺𐐨𐐸𐐬𐑊𐐼, 𐐲 𐐿𐐲𐑉𐑅 𐑇𐐰𐑊 𐐿𐐲𐑋 𐐲𐐹𐐱𐑌 𐑄 𐑊𐐰𐑌𐐼, 𐑅𐐯𐑃 𐑄 𐐢𐐫𐑉𐐼 𐐱𐑂 𐐐𐐬𐑅𐐻𐑅, 𐐺𐐨𐐿𐐫𐑆 𐐱𐑂 𐑄 𐐹𐐨𐐹𐑊𐑆 𐑅𐐩𐐿 𐐸𐐭 𐐪𐑉 𐐲𐐹𐐱𐑌 𐑄 𐑊𐐰𐑌𐐼; 𐐷𐐩, 𐐺𐐨𐐿𐐫𐑆 𐐱𐑂 𐑄𐐯𐑉 𐐶𐐮𐐿𐐯𐐼𐑌𐐯𐑅 𐐰𐑌𐐼 𐑄𐐯𐑉 𐐰𐐺𐐱𐑋𐐮𐑌𐐩𐑇𐐲𐑌𐑆.

3. 𐐈𐑌𐐼 𐐮𐐻 𐑇𐐰𐑊 𐐿𐐲𐑋 𐐻𐐭 𐐹𐐰𐑅, 𐑅𐐯𐑃 𐑄 𐐢𐐫𐑉𐐼 𐐱𐑂 𐐐𐐬𐑅𐐻𐑅, 𐐷𐐩, 𐐵𐑉 𐑀𐑉𐐩𐐻 𐐰𐑌𐐼 𐐻𐑉𐐭 𐐘𐐱𐐼, 𐑄𐐰𐐻 𐐸𐐭𐑅𐐬 𐑇𐐰𐑊 𐐸𐐴𐐼 𐐲𐐹 𐐻𐑉𐐯𐑈𐐲𐑉𐑆 𐐮𐑌 𐑄 𐐲𐑉𐑃, 𐑇𐐰𐑊 𐑁𐐴𐑌𐐼 𐑄𐐯𐑋 𐐰𐑀𐐯𐑌 𐑌𐐬 𐑋𐐬𐑉, 𐐺𐐨𐐿𐐫𐑆 𐐱𐑂 𐑄 𐑀𐑉𐐩𐐻 𐐿𐐲𐑉𐑅 𐐱𐑂 𐑄 𐑊𐐰𐑌𐐼, 𐑅𐐩𐑂 𐐸𐐨 𐐺𐐨 𐐲 𐑉𐐴𐐽𐐲𐑅 𐑋𐐰𐑌, 𐐰𐑌𐐼 𐑇𐐰𐑊 𐐸𐐴𐐼 𐐮𐐻 𐐲𐐹 𐐲𐑌𐐻𐐭 𐑄 𐐢𐐫𐑉𐐼, 𐐙𐐫𐑉 𐐌 𐐶𐐮𐑊, 𐑅𐐯𐑃 𐑄 𐐢𐐫𐑉𐐼, 𐑄𐐰𐐻 𐑄𐐩 𐑇𐐰𐑊 𐐸𐐴𐐼 𐐲𐐹 𐑄𐐯𐑉 𐐻𐑉𐐯𐑈𐐲𐑉𐑆 𐐲𐑌𐐻𐐭 𐑋𐐨; 𐐰𐑌𐐼 𐐿𐐲𐑉𐑅𐐯𐐼 𐐺𐐨 𐑄𐐩 𐐸𐐭 𐐸𐐴𐐼 𐑌𐐱𐐻 𐐲𐐹 𐑄𐐯𐑉 𐐻𐑉𐐯𐑈𐐲𐑉𐑆 𐐲𐑌𐐻𐐭 𐑋𐐨; 𐑁𐐫𐑉 𐑌𐐲𐑌 𐐸𐐴𐐼𐐯𐑃 𐐲𐐹 𐑄𐐯𐑉 𐐻𐑉𐐯𐑈𐐲𐑉𐑆 𐐲𐑌𐐻𐐭 𐑋𐐨, 𐑅𐐩𐑂 𐐮𐐻 𐐺𐐨 𐑄 𐑉𐐴𐐽𐐲𐑅; 𐐰𐑌𐐼 𐐸𐐨 𐑄𐐰𐐻 𐐸𐐴𐐼𐐯𐑃 𐑌𐐱𐐻 𐐲𐐹 𐐸𐐮𐑆 𐐻𐑉𐐯𐑈𐐲𐑉𐑆 𐐲𐑌𐐻𐐭 𐑋𐐨, 𐐿𐐲𐑉𐑅𐐯𐐼 𐐮𐑆 𐐸𐐨, 𐐰𐑌𐐼 𐐫𐑊𐑅𐐬 𐑄 𐐻𐑉𐐯𐑈𐐲𐑉, 𐐰𐑌𐐼 𐑌𐐲𐑌 𐑇𐐰𐑊 𐑉𐐨𐐼𐐨𐑋 𐐮𐐻, 𐐺𐐨𐐿𐐫𐑆 𐐱𐑂 𐑄 𐐿𐐲𐑉𐑅 𐐱𐑂 𐑄 𐑊𐐰𐑌𐐼. 𐐈𐑌𐐼 𐑄 𐐼𐐩 𐑇𐐰𐑊 𐐿𐐲𐑋 𐑄𐐰𐐻 𐑄𐐩 𐑇𐐰𐑊 𐐸𐐴𐐼 𐐲𐐹 𐑄𐐯𐑉 𐐻𐑉𐐯𐑈𐐲𐑉𐑆, 𐐺𐐨𐐿𐐫𐑆 𐑄𐐩 𐐸𐐰𐑂 𐑅𐐯𐐻 𐑄𐐯𐑉 𐐸𐐪𐑉𐐻𐑅

𐐲𐐹𐐪𐑌 𐑉𐐮𐐽𐐯𐑆; 𐐰𐑌𐐼 𐐺𐐨𐐿𐐫𐑆 𐑄𐐩 𐐸𐐰𐑂 𐑅𐐯𐐻 𐑄𐐩𐑉 𐐸𐐪𐑉𐐻𐑅 𐐲𐐹𐐪𐑌 𐑄𐐩𐑉 𐑉𐐮𐐽𐐯𐑆, & 𐐶𐐮𐑊 𐐸𐐴𐐼 𐐲𐐹 𐑄𐐩𐑉 𐐻𐑉𐐯𐑈𐐲𐑉𐑆 𐐸𐐶𐐯𐑌 𐑄𐐩 𐑇𐐰𐑊 𐑁𐑊𐐨 𐐺𐐨𐑁𐐬𐑉 𐑄𐐩𐑉 𐐯𐑌𐐯𐑋𐐨𐑆, 𐐺𐐨𐐿𐐫𐑆 𐑄𐐩 𐐶𐐮𐑊 𐑌𐐱𐐻 𐐸𐐴𐐼 𐑄𐐯𐑋 𐐲𐐹 𐐲𐑌𐐻𐐭 𐑋𐐨; 𐐿𐐲𐑉𐑅𐐯𐐼 𐐺 𐑄𐐩, 𐐰𐑌𐐼 𐐫𐑊𐑅𐐬 𐑄𐐩𐑉 𐐻𐑉𐐯𐑈𐐲𐑉𐑆; 𐐰𐑌𐐼 𐐮𐑌 𐑄𐐰𐐻 𐐼𐐩 𐑇𐐰𐑊 𐑄𐐩 𐐺 𐑅𐑋𐐮𐐻𐑌, 𐑅𐐯𐑃 𐑄 𐐢𐐫𐑉𐐼. 𐐒𐐨𐐸𐐬𐑊𐐼 𐐷, 𐑄 𐐹𐐨𐐹𐑊 𐐱𐑂 𐑄𐐮𐑅 𐑀𐑉𐐩𐐻 𐑅𐐮𐐻𐐨, 𐐰𐑌𐐼 𐐸𐐪𐑉𐐿𐑌 𐐲𐑌𐐻𐐭 𐑋𐐴 𐐶𐐲𐑉𐐼𐑆; 𐐷𐐩, 𐐸𐐪𐑉𐐿𐑌 𐐲𐑌𐐻𐐭 𐑄 𐐶𐐲𐑉𐐼𐑆 𐐸𐐶𐐮𐐽 𐑄 𐐢𐐫𐑉𐐼 𐑅𐐯𐑃; 𐑁𐐫𐑉 𐐺𐐨𐐸𐐬𐑊𐐼, 𐐸𐐨 𐑅𐐯𐑃 𐑄𐐰𐐻 𐐷 𐐪𐑉 𐐿𐐲𐑉𐑅𐐯𐐼 𐐺𐐨𐐿𐐫𐑆 𐐱𐑂 𐐷𐐫𐑉 𐑉𐐮𐐽𐐯𐑆, 𐐰𐑌𐐼 𐐫𐑊𐑅𐐬 𐐪𐑉 𐐷𐐫𐑉 𐑉𐐮𐐽𐐯𐑆 𐐿𐐲𐑉𐑅𐐯𐐼 𐐺𐐨𐐿𐐫𐑆 𐐷 𐐸𐐰𐑂 𐑅𐐯𐐻 𐐷𐐫𐑉 𐐸𐐪𐑉𐐻𐑅 𐐲𐐹𐐪𐑌 𐑄𐐯𐑋, 𐐰𐑌𐐼 𐐸𐐰𐑂 𐑌𐐱𐐻 𐐸𐐪𐑉𐐿𐑌𐐼 𐐲𐑌𐐻𐐭 𐑄 𐐶𐐲𐑉𐐼𐑆 𐐱𐑂 𐐸𐐮𐑋 𐐸𐐭 𐑀𐐩𐑂 𐑄𐐯𐑋 𐐲𐑌𐐻𐐭 𐐷𐐭. 𐐏 𐐼𐐭 𐑌𐐱𐐻 𐑉𐐨𐑋𐐯𐑋𐐺𐐲𐑉 𐑄 𐐢𐐫𐑉𐐼 𐐷𐐫𐑉 𐐘𐐱𐐼 𐐮𐑌 𐑄 𐑃𐐮𐑍𐑆 𐐶𐐮𐑄 𐐸𐐶𐐮𐐽 𐐸𐐨 𐐸𐐰𐑃 𐐺𐑊𐐯𐑅𐐯𐐼 𐐷𐐭, 𐐺𐐲𐐻 𐐷 𐐼𐐭 𐐫𐑊𐐶𐐩𐑆 𐑉𐐨𐑋𐐯𐑋𐐺𐐲𐑉 𐐷𐐫𐑉 𐑉𐐮𐐽𐐯𐑆, 𐑌𐐱𐐻 𐐻𐐭 𐑃𐐰𐑍𐐿 𐑄 𐐢𐐫𐑉𐐼 𐐷𐐫𐑉 𐐘𐐱𐐼 𐑁𐐫𐑉 𐑄𐐯𐑋; 𐐷𐐩, 𐐷𐐫𐑉 𐐸𐐪𐑉𐐻𐑅 𐐪𐑉 𐑌𐐱𐐻 𐐼𐑉𐐫𐑌 𐐵𐐻 𐐲𐑌𐐻𐐭 𐑄 𐐢𐐫𐑉𐐼, 𐐺𐐲𐐻 𐑄𐐩 𐐼𐐭 𐑅𐐶𐐯𐑊 𐐶𐐮𐑄 𐑀𐑉𐐩𐐻 𐐹𐑉𐐴𐐼, 𐐲𐑌𐐻𐐭 𐐺𐐬𐑅𐐻𐐮𐑍, 𐐰𐑌𐐼 𐐲𐑌𐐻𐐭 𐑀𐑉𐐩𐐻 𐑅𐐶𐐯𐑊𐐮𐑍, 𐐯𐑌𐑂𐐨𐐮𐑍𐑆, 𐑅𐐻𐑉𐐴𐑁𐑅, 𐑋𐐰𐑊𐐮𐑅, 𐐹𐐲𐑉𐑅𐐯𐐿𐐷𐐭𐑇𐐲𐑌𐑆, 𐐰𐑌𐐼 𐑋𐐲𐑉𐐼𐐲𐑉𐑆, 𐐰𐑌𐐼 𐐫𐑊 𐑋𐐰𐑌𐐲𐑉 𐐱𐑂 𐐮𐑌𐐮𐐿𐐶𐐮𐐻𐐨𐑆. 𐐙𐐫𐑉 𐑄𐐮𐑅 𐐿𐐫𐑆, 𐐸𐐰𐑃 𐑄 𐐢𐐫𐑉𐐼 𐐘𐐱𐐼 𐐿𐐫𐑆𐐼 𐑄𐐰𐐻 𐐩 𐐿𐐲𐑉𐑅 𐑇𐐳𐐼 𐐿𐐲𐑋 𐐲𐐹𐐪𐑌 𐑄 𐑊𐐰𐑌𐐼, 𐐰𐑌𐐼 𐐫𐑊𐑅𐐬 𐐲𐐹𐐪𐑌 𐐷𐐫𐑉 𐑉𐐮𐐽𐐯𐑆; 𐐰𐑌𐐼 𐑄𐐮𐑅 𐐺𐐨𐐿𐐫𐑆 𐐱𐑂 𐐷𐐫𐑉 𐐮𐑌𐐮𐐿𐐶𐐮𐐻𐐨𐑆; 𐐷𐐩, 𐐶𐐬 𐐲𐑌𐐻𐐭 𐑄𐐮𐑅 𐐹𐐨𐐹𐑊, 𐐺𐐨𐐿𐐫𐑆 𐐱𐑂 𐑄𐐮𐑅 𐐻𐐴𐑋 𐐸𐐶𐐮𐐽 𐐸𐐰𐑆 𐐲𐑉𐐴𐑂𐐼, 𐑄𐐰𐐻 𐐷 𐐼𐐭 𐐿𐐰𐑅𐐻 𐐵𐐻 𐑄 𐐹𐑉𐐱𐑁𐐯𐐻𐑅, 𐐰𐑌𐐼 𐐼𐐭 𐑋𐐱𐐿 𐑄𐐯𐑋, 𐐰𐑌𐐼 𐐿𐐰𐑅𐐻 𐑅𐐻𐐬𐑌𐑆 𐐰𐐻 𐑄𐐯𐑋, 𐐰𐑌𐐼 𐐼𐐭 𐑅𐑊𐐩 𐑄𐐯𐑋, 𐐰𐑌𐐼 𐐼𐐭 𐐫𐑊 𐑋𐐰𐑌𐐲𐑉 𐐱𐑂 𐐮𐑌𐐮𐐿𐐶𐐮𐐻𐐨 𐐲𐑌𐐻𐐭 𐑄𐐯𐑋, 𐐨𐑂𐑌 𐐰𐑆 𐑄𐐩 𐐼𐐮𐐼 𐐱𐑂 𐐬𐑊𐐼 𐐻𐐴𐑋. 𐐈𐑌𐐼 𐑌𐐵 𐐸𐐶𐐯𐑌 𐐷 𐐻𐐫𐐿, 𐐷 𐑅𐐩, 𐐆𐑁 𐐵𐑉 𐐼𐐩𐑆 𐐸𐐰𐐼 𐐺𐐮𐑌 𐐮𐑌 𐑄 𐐼𐐩𐑆 𐐱𐑂 𐐵𐑉 𐑁𐐪𐑄𐐲𐑉𐑆 𐐱𐑂 𐐬𐑊𐐼, 𐐶𐐨 𐐶𐐳𐐼 𐑌𐐱𐐻 𐐸𐐰𐑂 𐑅𐑊𐐩𐑌 𐑄 𐐹𐑉𐐱𐑁𐐯𐐻𐑅; 𐐶𐐨 𐐶𐐳𐐼 𐑌𐐱𐐻 𐐸𐐰𐑂 𐑅𐐻𐐬𐑌𐐼 𐑄𐐯𐑋, 𐐰𐑌𐐼 𐐿𐐰𐑅𐐻 𐑄𐐯𐑋 𐐵𐐻. 𐐒𐐨𐐸𐐬𐑊𐐼, 𐐷 𐐪𐑉 𐐶𐐲𐑉𐑅 𐑄𐐰𐑌 𐑄𐐩; 𐑁𐐫𐑉 𐐰𐑆 𐑄 𐐢𐐫𐑉𐐼 𐑊𐐮𐑂𐐯𐑃, 𐐮𐑁 𐐩 𐐹𐑉𐐱𐑁𐐯𐐻 𐐿𐐲𐑋 𐐲𐑋𐐲𐑍 𐐷𐐭, 𐐰𐑌𐐼 𐐼𐐨𐐿𐑊𐐩𐑉𐐯𐑃 𐐲𐑌𐐻𐐭 𐐷𐐭 𐑄 𐐶𐐲𐑉𐐼 𐐱𐑂 𐑄 𐐢𐐫𐑉𐐼, 𐐸𐐶𐐮𐐽 𐐻𐐯𐑅𐐻𐐮𐑁𐐴𐐯𐑃 𐐱𐑂 𐐷𐐫𐑉 𐑅𐐮𐑌𐑆 𐐰𐑌𐐼 𐐮𐑌𐐮𐐿𐐶𐐮𐐻𐐨𐑆, 𐐷 𐐪𐑉 𐐰𐑍𐑀𐑉𐐨 𐐶𐐮𐑄 𐐸𐐮𐑋, 𐐰𐑌𐐼 𐐿𐐰𐑅𐐻 𐐸𐐮𐑋 𐐵𐐻, 𐐰𐑌𐐼 𐑅𐐨𐐿 𐐫𐑊 𐑋𐐰𐑌𐐲𐑉 𐐱𐑂 𐐶𐐩𐑆 𐐻𐐭 𐐼𐐨𐑅𐐻𐑉𐑎 𐐸𐐮𐑋; 𐐷𐐩, 𐐷𐐭 𐐶𐐮𐑊 𐑅𐐩 𐑄𐐰𐐻 𐐸𐐨 𐐮𐑆 𐐩 𐑁𐐫𐑊𐑅 𐐹𐑉𐐱𐑁𐐯𐐻, 𐐰𐑌𐐼 𐑄𐐰𐐻 𐐸𐐨 𐐮𐑆 𐐩 𐑅𐐮𐑌𐐲𐑉, 𐐰𐑌𐐼 𐐱𐑂 𐑄 𐐼𐐯𐑂𐑊, 𐐺𐐨𐐿𐐫𐑆 𐐸𐐨 𐐻𐐯𐑅𐐻𐐮𐑁𐐴𐐯𐑃 𐑄𐐰𐐻 𐐷𐐫𐑉 𐐼𐐨𐐼𐑆 𐐪𐑉 𐐨𐑂𐑊. 𐐒𐐲𐐻 𐐺𐐨𐐸𐐬𐑊𐐼, 𐐮𐑁 𐐩 𐑋𐐰𐑌 𐑇𐐰𐑊 𐐿𐐲𐑋 𐐲𐑋𐐲𐑍 𐐷𐐭, 𐐰𐑌𐐼 𐑇𐐰𐑊 𐑅𐐩, 𐐔𐐭 𐑄𐐮𐑅, 𐐰𐑌𐐼 𐑄𐐩𐑉 𐐮𐑆 𐑌𐐬 𐐮𐑌𐐮𐐿𐐶𐐮𐐻𐐨; 𐐼𐐭 𐑄𐐰𐐻, 𐐰𐑌𐐼 𐐷 𐑇𐐰𐑊 𐑌𐐱𐐻 𐑅𐐲𐑁𐐲𐑉; 𐐷𐐩, 𐐸𐐨 𐐶𐐮𐑊 𐑅𐐩, 𐐎𐐫𐐿 𐐪𐑁𐐻𐐲𐑉 𐑄 𐐹𐑉𐐴𐐼 𐐱𐑂 𐐷𐐫𐑉 𐐬𐑌 𐐸𐐪𐑉𐐻𐑅; 𐐷𐐩, 𐐎𐐫𐐿 𐐪𐑁𐐻𐐲𐑉 𐑄 𐐹𐑉𐐴𐐼 𐐱𐑂 𐐷𐐫𐑉 𐐴𐑆, 𐐰𐑌𐐼 𐐼𐐭 𐐸𐐶𐐱𐐻𐑅𐐬𐐯𐑂𐐲𐑉 𐐷𐐫𐑉 𐐸𐐪𐑉𐐻 𐐼𐐨𐑆𐐴𐑉𐐯𐑃; 𐐰𐑌𐐼 𐐮𐑁 𐐩 𐑋𐐰𐑌 𐑇𐐰𐑊 𐐿𐐲𐑋 𐐲𐑋𐐲𐑍 𐐷𐐭 𐐰𐑌𐐼 𐑅𐐩 𐑄𐐮𐑅, 𐐷 𐐶𐐮𐑊 𐑉𐐨𐑅𐐨𐑂 𐐸𐐮𐑋, 𐐰𐑌𐐼 𐑅𐐩 𐑄𐐰𐐻 𐐸𐐨 𐐮𐑆 𐐩 𐐹𐑉𐐱𐑁𐐯𐐻; 𐐷𐐩, 𐐷 𐐶𐐮𐑊 𐑊𐐮𐑁𐐻 𐐸𐐮𐑋 𐐲𐐹, 𐐰𐑌𐐼 𐐷 𐐶𐐮𐑊 𐑀𐐮𐑂 𐐲𐑌𐐻𐐭 𐐸𐐮𐑋 𐐱𐑂 𐐷𐐫𐑉 𐑅𐐲𐐺𐑅𐐻𐐰𐑌𐑅; 𐐷 𐐶𐐮𐑊 𐑀𐐮𐑂 𐐲𐑌𐐻𐐭 𐐸𐐮𐑋 𐐱𐑂 𐐷𐐫𐑉 𐑀𐐬𐑊𐐼, 𐐰𐑌𐐼 𐐱𐑂 𐐷𐐫𐑉 𐑅𐐮𐑊𐑂𐐲𐑉, 𐐰𐑌𐐼 𐐷 𐐶𐐮𐑊 𐐿𐑊𐐬𐑄 𐐸𐐮𐑋 𐐶𐐮𐑄 𐐿𐐱𐑅𐐻𐑊𐐨 𐐰𐐹𐐰𐑉𐐯𐑊; 𐐰𐑌𐐼 𐐺𐐨𐐿𐐫𐑆 𐐸𐐨 𐑅𐐹𐐨𐐿𐐯𐑃 𐑁𐑊𐐰𐐻𐐲𐑉𐐮𐑍 𐐶𐐲𐑉𐐼𐑆 𐐲𐑌𐐻𐐭 𐐷𐐭, 𐐰𐑌𐐼 𐐸𐐨 𐑅𐐯𐑃 𐑄𐐰𐐻 𐐫𐑊 𐐮𐑆 𐐶𐐯𐑊, 𐑄𐐯𐑌 𐐷 𐐶𐐮𐑊 𐑌𐐱𐐻 𐑁𐐴𐑌𐐼 𐑁𐐫𐑊𐐻 𐐶𐐮𐑄 𐐸𐐮𐑋.

4. 𐐄 𐐷 𐐶𐐮𐐿𐐯𐐼 𐐰𐑌𐐼 𐐷 𐐹𐐲𐑉𐑂𐐲𐑉𐑅 𐐾𐐯𐑌𐐲𐑉𐐩𐑇𐐲𐑌; 𐐷 𐐸𐐪𐑉𐐼𐑌𐐼 𐐰𐑌𐐼 𐐷 𐑅𐐻𐐮𐑁𐑌𐐯𐐿𐐻 𐐹𐐨𐐹𐑊, 𐐸𐐵 𐑊𐐫𐑍 𐐶𐐮𐑊 𐐷 𐑅𐐲𐐹𐐬𐑆 𐑄𐐰𐐻 𐑄 𐐢𐐫𐑉𐐼 𐐶𐐮𐑊 𐑅𐐲𐑁𐐲𐑉 𐐷𐐭? 𐐏𐐩, 𐐸𐐵 𐑊𐐫𐑍 𐐶𐐮𐑊 𐐷 𐑅𐐲𐑁𐐲𐑉 𐐷𐐫𐑉𐑅𐐯𐑊𐑂𐑆 𐐻𐐭 𐐺 𐑊𐐯𐐼 𐐺𐐴 𐑁𐐭𐑊𐐮𐑇 𐐰𐑌𐐼 𐐺𐑊𐐴𐑌𐐼 𐑀𐐴𐐼𐑆? 𐐏𐐩, 𐐸𐐵 𐑊𐐫𐑍 𐐶𐐮𐑊 𐐷 𐐽𐐭𐑆 𐐼𐐪𐑉𐐿𐑌𐐯𐑅 𐑉𐐪𐑄𐐲𐑉 𐑄𐐰𐑌 𐑊𐐴𐐻? 𐐏𐐩, 𐐺𐐨𐐸𐐬𐑊𐐼 𐑄 𐐰𐑍𐑀𐐲𐑉 𐐱𐑂 𐑄 𐐢𐐫𐑉𐐼 𐐮𐑆 𐐫𐑊𐑉𐐯𐐼𐐨 𐐿𐐮𐑌𐐼𐑊𐐼 𐐲𐑀𐐯𐑌𐑅𐐻 𐐷𐐭; 𐐺𐐨𐐸𐐬𐑊𐐼, 𐐸𐐨 𐐸𐐰𐑃 𐐿𐐲𐑉𐑅𐐯𐐼 𐑄 𐑊𐐰𐑌𐐼, 𐐺𐐨𐐿𐐫𐑆 𐐱𐑂 𐐷𐐫𐑉 𐐮𐑌𐐮𐐿𐐶𐐮𐐻𐐨; 𐐰𐑌𐐼 𐐺𐐨𐐸𐐬𐑊𐐼, 𐑄 𐐻𐐴𐑋 𐐿𐐲𐑋𐐯𐑃 𐑄𐐰𐐻 𐐸𐐨 𐐿𐐲𐑉𐑅𐐯𐑃 𐐷𐐫𐑉 𐑉𐐮𐐽𐐯𐑆, 𐑄𐐰𐐻 𐑄𐐩 𐐺𐐨𐐿𐐲𐑋 𐑅𐑊𐐮𐐹𐐲𐑉𐐨, 𐑄𐐰𐐻 𐐷 𐐿𐐰𐑌𐐱𐐻 𐐸𐐬𐑊𐐼 𐑄𐐯𐑋; 𐐰𐑌𐐼 𐐮𐑌 𐑄 𐐼𐐩𐑆 𐐱𐑂 𐐷𐐫𐑉 𐐹𐐱𐑂𐐲𐑉𐐻𐐨 𐐷 𐐿𐐰𐑌𐐱𐐻 𐑉𐐨𐐻𐐩𐑌 𐑄𐐯𐑋; 𐐰𐑌𐐼 𐐮𐑌 𐑄 𐐼𐐩𐑆 𐐱𐑂 𐐷𐐫𐑉 𐐹𐐱𐑂𐐲𐑉𐐻𐐨 𐐷 𐑇𐐰𐑊 𐐿𐑉𐐴 𐐲𐑌𐐻𐐭 𐑄 𐐢𐐫𐑉𐐼; 𐐰𐑌𐐼 𐐮𐑌 𐑂𐐩𐑌 𐑇𐐰𐑊 𐐷 𐐿𐑉𐐴, 𐑁𐐫𐑉 𐐷𐐫𐑉 𐐼𐐯𐑅𐐬𐑊𐐩𐑇𐐲𐑌 𐐮𐑆 𐐫𐑊𐑉𐐯𐐼𐐨 𐐿𐐲𐑋 𐐲𐐹𐐪𐑌 𐐷𐐭, 𐐰𐑌𐐼 𐐷𐐫𐑉 𐐼𐐨𐑅𐐻𐑉𐐲𐐿𐑇𐐲𐑌 𐐮𐑆 𐑋𐐩𐐼 𐑇𐐳𐑉; 𐐰𐑌𐐼 𐑄𐐯𐑌 𐑇𐐰𐑊 𐐷 𐐶𐐨𐐹 𐐰𐑌𐐼 𐐸𐐵𐑊 𐐮𐑌 𐑄𐐰𐐻 𐐼𐐩, 𐑅𐐯𐑃 𐑄 𐐢𐐫𐑉𐐼 𐐱𐑂 𐐐𐐬𐑅𐐻𐑅. 𐐈𐑌𐐼 𐑄𐐯𐑌 𐑇𐐰𐑊 𐐷 𐑊𐐰𐑋𐐯𐑌𐐻, 𐐰𐑌𐐼 𐑅𐐩, 𐐄 𐑄𐐰𐐻

𐐌 𐐸𐐰𐐼 𐑉𐐨𐐹𐐯𐑌𐐻𐐯𐐼, 𐐰𐑌𐐼 𐐸𐐰𐐼 𐑌𐐱𐐻 𐐿𐐮𐑊𐐼 𐑄 𐐹𐑉𐐱𐑁𐐯𐐻𐑅, 𐐰𐑌𐐼 𐑅𐐻𐐬𐑌𐐼 𐑄𐐯𐑋, 𐐰𐑌𐐼 𐐿𐐰𐑅𐐻 𐑄𐐯𐑋 𐐵𐐻; 𐐏𐐩, 𐐮𐑌 𐑄𐐰𐐻 𐐼𐐩 𐐷 𐑇𐐰𐑊 𐑅𐐩, 𐐄 𐑄𐐰𐐻 𐐶𐐨 𐐸𐐰𐐼 𐑉𐐨𐑋𐐯𐑋𐐺𐐲𐑉𐐼 𐑄 𐐢𐐫𐑉𐐼 𐐵𐑉 𐐘𐐱𐐼, 𐐮𐑌 𐑄 𐐼𐐩 𐑄𐐰𐐻 𐐸𐐨 𐑀𐐩𐑂 𐐲𐑅 𐐵𐑉 𐑉𐐮𐐽𐐯𐑆, 𐐰𐑌𐐼 𐑄𐐯𐑌 𐑄𐐩 𐐶𐐳𐐼 𐑌𐐱𐐻 𐐸𐐰𐑂 𐐺𐐨𐐿𐐲𐑋 𐑅𐑊𐐮𐐹𐐲𐑉𐐨, 𐑄𐐰𐐻 𐐶𐐨 𐑇𐐳𐐼 𐑊𐐭𐑆 𐑄𐐯𐑋; 𐑁𐐫𐑉 𐐺𐐨𐐸𐐬𐑊𐐼, 𐐵𐑉 𐑉𐐮𐐽𐐯𐑆 𐐪𐑉 𐑀𐐫𐑌 𐑁𐑉𐐱𐑋 𐐲𐑅. 𐐒𐐨𐐸𐐬𐑊𐐼 𐐶𐐨 𐑊𐐩 𐐲 𐐻𐐭𐑊 𐐸𐐨𐑉, 𐐰𐑌𐐼 𐐱𐑌 𐑄 𐑋𐐱𐑉𐐬 𐐮𐐻 𐐮𐑆 𐑀𐐫𐑌; 𐐰𐑌𐐼 𐐺𐐨𐐸𐐬𐑊𐐼, 𐐵𐑉 𐑅𐐫𐑉𐐼𐑆 𐐪𐑉 𐐻𐐩𐐿𐑌 𐑁𐑉𐐱𐑋 𐐲𐑅 𐐮𐑌 𐑄 𐐼𐐩 𐐶𐐨 𐐸𐐰𐑂 𐑅𐐫𐐻 𐑄𐐯𐑋 𐑁𐐫𐑉 𐐺𐐰𐐻𐑊. 𐐏𐐩, 𐐶𐐨 𐐸𐐰𐑂 𐐸𐐮𐐼 𐐲𐐹 𐐵𐑉 𐐻𐑉𐐯𐑈𐐭𐑉𐑆, 𐐰𐑌𐐼 𐑄𐐩 𐐸𐐰𐑂 𐑅𐑊𐐮𐐹𐐻 𐐰𐐶𐐩 𐑁𐑉𐐱𐑋 𐐲𐑅, 𐐺𐐨𐐿𐐫𐑆 𐐱𐑂 𐑄 𐐿𐐲𐑉𐑅 𐐱𐑂 𐑄 𐑊𐐰𐑌𐐼. 𐐄 𐑄𐐰𐐻 𐐶𐐨 𐐸𐐰𐐼 𐑉𐐨𐐹𐐯𐑌𐐻𐐯𐐼 𐐮𐑌 𐑄 𐐼𐐩 𐑄𐐰𐐻 𐑄 𐐶𐐲𐑉𐐼 𐐱𐑂 𐑄 𐐢𐐫𐑉𐐼 𐐿𐐩𐑋 𐐲𐑌𐐻𐐭 𐐲𐑅; 𐑁𐐫𐑉 𐐺𐐨𐐸𐐬𐑊𐐼 𐑄 𐑊𐐰𐑌𐐼 𐐮𐑆 𐐿𐐲𐑉𐑅𐐻, 𐐰𐑌𐐼 𐐫𐑊 𐑃𐐮𐑍𐑆 𐐪𐑉 𐐺𐐨𐐿𐐲𐑋 𐑅𐑊𐐮𐐹𐐲𐑉𐐨, 𐐰𐑌𐐼 𐐶𐐨 𐐿𐐰𐑌𐐱𐐻 𐐸𐐬𐑊𐐼 𐑄𐐯𐑋. 𐐒𐐨𐐸𐐬𐑊𐐼 𐐶𐐨 𐐪𐑉 𐑅𐐲𐑉𐐵𐑌𐐼𐐯𐐼 𐐺𐐴 𐐼𐐨𐑋𐐲𐑌𐑆, 𐐷𐐩, 𐐶𐐨 𐐪𐑉 𐐯𐑌𐑅𐐲𐑉𐐿𐑊𐐼 𐐲𐐺𐐵𐐻 𐐺𐐴 𐑄 𐐩𐑌𐐾𐐯𐑊𐑆 𐐱𐑂 𐐸𐐮𐑋 𐐸𐐭 𐐸𐐰𐑃 𐑅𐐫𐐻 𐐻𐐭 𐐼𐐨𐑅𐐻𐑉𐑎 𐐵𐑉 𐑅𐐬𐑊𐑆. 𐐒𐐨𐐸𐐬𐑊𐐼, 𐐵𐑉 𐐮𐑌𐐮𐐿𐐶𐐮𐐻𐐮𐑆 𐐪𐑉 𐑀𐑉𐐩𐐻. 𐐄 𐐢𐐫𐑉𐐼, 𐐿𐐰𐑌𐑅𐐻 𐑄𐐵 𐑌𐐱𐐻 𐐻𐐲𐑉𐑌 𐐰𐐶𐐩 𐑄𐐴𐑌 𐐰𐑍𐑀𐐲𐑉 𐑁𐑉𐐱𐑋 𐐲𐑅? 𐐈𐑌𐐼 𐑄𐐮𐑅 𐑇𐐰𐑊 𐐺 𐐷𐐫𐑉 𐑊𐐰𐑍𐑀𐐶𐐩𐐾 𐐮𐑌 𐑄𐐬𐑆 𐐼𐐩𐑆. 𐐒𐐲𐐻 𐐺𐐨𐐸𐐬𐑊𐐼, 𐐷𐐫𐑉 𐐼𐐩𐑆 𐐱𐑂 𐐹𐑉𐐬𐐺𐐩𐑇𐐲𐑌 𐐪𐑉 𐐹𐐰𐑅𐐻; 𐐷 𐐸𐐰𐑂 𐐹𐑉𐐬𐐿𐑉𐐰𐑅𐐻𐐮𐑌𐐩𐐻𐐯𐐼 𐑄 𐐼𐐩 𐐱𐑂 𐐷𐐫𐑉 𐑅𐐰𐑊𐑂𐐩𐑇𐐲𐑌, 𐐲𐑌𐐻𐐮𐑊 𐐮𐐻 𐐮𐑆 𐐯𐑂𐐲𐑉𐑊𐐰𐑅𐐻𐐮𐑍𐑊𐐨 𐐻𐐭 𐑊𐐩𐐻, 𐐰𐑌𐐼 𐐷𐐫𐑉 𐐼𐐨𐑅𐐻𐑉𐐲𐐿𐑇𐐲𐑌 𐐮𐑆 𐑋𐐩𐐼 𐑇𐐳𐑉; 𐐷𐐩, 𐑁𐐫𐑉 𐐷 𐐸𐐰𐑂 𐑅𐐫𐐻 𐐫𐑊 𐑄 𐐼𐐩𐑆 𐐱𐑂 𐐷𐐫𐑉 𐑊𐐴𐑂𐑆 𐑁𐐫𐑉 𐑄𐐰𐐻 𐐸𐐶𐐮𐐽 𐐷 𐐿𐐳𐐼 𐑌𐐱𐐻 𐐱𐐺𐐻𐐩𐑌; 𐐰𐑌𐐼 𐐷 𐐸𐐰𐑂 𐑅𐐫𐐻 𐑁𐐫𐑉 𐐸𐐰𐐹𐐮𐑌𐐯𐑅 𐐮𐑌 𐐼𐐭𐐮𐑍 𐐮𐑌𐐮𐐿𐐶𐐮𐐻𐐨, 𐐸𐐶𐐮𐐽 𐑃𐐮𐑍 𐐮𐑆 𐐿𐐱𐑌𐐻𐑉𐐯𐑉𐐨 𐐻𐐭 𐑄 𐑌𐐩𐐻𐐷𐐭𐑉 𐐱𐑂 𐑄𐐰𐐻 𐑉𐐴𐐽𐐲𐑅𐑌𐐯𐑅 𐐸𐐶𐐮𐐽 𐐮𐑆 𐐮𐑌 𐐵𐑉 𐑀𐑉𐐩𐐻 𐐰𐑌𐐼 𐐨𐐻𐐲𐑉𐑌𐐰𐑊 𐐸𐐯𐐼. 𐐄 𐐷 𐐹𐐨𐐹𐐲𐑊 𐐱𐑂 𐑄 𐑊𐐰𐑌𐐼, 𐑄𐐰𐐻 𐐷 𐐶𐐳𐐼 𐐸𐐨𐑉 𐑋𐐴 𐐶𐐲𐑉𐐼𐑆. 𐐈𐑌𐐼 𐐌 𐐹𐑉𐐩 𐑄𐐰𐐻 𐑄 𐐰𐑍𐑀𐐲𐑉 𐐱𐑂 𐑄 𐐢𐐫𐑉𐐼 𐐺 𐐻𐐲𐑉𐑌𐐼 𐐰𐐶𐐩 𐑁𐑉𐐱𐑋 𐐷𐐭, 𐐰𐑌𐐼 𐑄𐐰𐐻 𐐷 𐐶𐐳𐐼 𐑉𐐨𐐹𐐯𐑌𐐻 𐐰𐑌𐐼 𐐺 𐑅𐐩𐑂𐐼.

5. 𐐈𐑌𐐼 𐑌𐐵 𐐮𐐻 𐐿𐐩𐑋 𐐻𐐭 𐐹𐐰𐑅 𐑄𐐰𐐻 𐐝𐐰𐑋𐐷𐐭𐐯𐑊, 𐑄 𐐢𐐰𐑋𐐲𐑌𐐴𐐻, 𐐼𐐮𐐼 𐐹𐑉𐐱𐑁𐐯𐑅𐐴 𐐲 𐑀𐑉𐐩𐐻 𐑋𐐯𐑌𐐨 𐑋𐐬𐑉 𐑃𐐮𐑍𐑆 𐐸𐐶𐐮𐐽 𐐿𐐰𐑌𐐱𐐻 𐐺 𐑉𐐮𐐻𐑌. 𐐈𐑌𐐼 𐐺𐐨𐐸𐐬𐑊𐐼, 𐐸𐐨 𐑅𐐯𐐼 𐐲𐑌𐐻𐐭 𐑄𐐯𐑋, 𐐒𐐨𐐸𐐬𐑊𐐼, 𐐌 𐑀𐐮𐑂 𐐲𐑌𐐻𐐭 𐐷𐐭 𐐲 𐑅𐐴𐑌; 𐑁𐐫𐑉 𐑁𐐴𐑂 𐐷𐐨𐑉𐑆 𐑋𐐬𐑉 𐐿𐐲𐑋𐐯𐑃, 𐐰𐑌𐐼 𐐺𐐨𐐸𐐬𐑊𐐼, 𐑄𐐯𐑌 𐐿𐐲𐑋𐐯𐑃 𐑄 𐐝𐐲𐑌 𐐱𐑂 𐐘𐐱𐐼 𐐻𐐭 𐑉𐐨𐐼𐐨𐑋 𐐫𐑊 𐑄𐐬𐑆 𐐸𐐭 𐑇𐐰𐑊 𐐺𐐨𐑊𐐨𐑂 𐐱𐑌 𐐸𐐮𐑆 𐑌𐐩𐑋. 𐐈𐑌𐐼 𐐺𐐨𐐸𐐬𐑊𐐼, 𐑄𐐮𐑅 𐐶𐐮𐑊 𐐌 𐑀𐐮𐑂 𐐲𐑌𐐻𐐭 𐐷𐐭 𐑁𐐫𐑉 𐐲 𐑅𐐴𐑌 𐐰𐐻 𐑄 𐐻𐐴𐑋 𐐱𐑂 𐐸𐐮𐑆 𐐿𐐲𐑋𐐮𐑍; 𐑁𐐫𐑉 𐐺𐐨𐐸𐐬𐑊𐐼, 𐑄𐐯𐑉 𐑇𐐰𐑊 𐐺 𐑀𐑉𐐩𐐻 𐑊𐐴𐐻𐑅 𐐮𐑌 𐐸𐐯𐑂𐐲𐑌, 𐐮𐑌𐑅𐐬𐑋𐐲𐐽 𐑄𐐰𐐻 𐑄 𐑌𐐴𐐻 𐐺𐐨𐑁𐐬𐑉 𐐸𐐨 𐐿𐐲𐑋𐐯𐑃 𐑄𐐯𐑉 𐑇𐐰𐑊 𐐺 𐑌𐐬 𐐼𐐪𐑉𐐿𐑌𐐯𐑅, 𐐮𐑌𐑅𐐬𐑋𐐲𐐽 𐑄𐐰𐐻 𐐮𐐻 𐑇𐐰𐑊 𐐰𐐹𐐨𐑉 𐐲𐑌𐐻𐐭 𐑋𐐰𐑌 𐐰𐑆 𐐮𐑁 𐐮𐐻 𐐶𐐱𐑆 𐐼𐐩, 𐑄𐐯𐑉𐑁𐐬𐑉 𐑄𐐯𐑉 𐑇𐐰𐑊 𐐺 𐐶𐐲𐑌 𐐼𐐩 𐐰𐑌𐐼 𐐲 𐑌𐐴𐐻, 𐐰𐑌𐐼 𐐲 𐐼𐐩, 𐐰𐑆 𐐮𐑁 𐐮𐐻 𐐶𐐲𐑉 𐐶𐐲𐑌 𐐼𐐩, 𐐰𐑌𐐼 𐑄𐐯𐑉 𐐶𐐲𐑉 𐑌𐐬 𐑌𐐴𐐻; 𐐰𐑌𐐼 𐑄𐐮𐑅 𐑇𐐰𐑊 𐐺 𐐲𐑌𐐻𐐭 𐐷𐐭 𐑁𐐫𐑉 𐐲 𐑅𐐴𐑌; 𐑁𐐫𐑉 𐐷 𐑇𐐰𐑊 𐑌𐐬 𐐱𐑂 𐑄 𐑉𐐴𐑆𐐮𐑍 𐐱𐑂 𐑄 𐑅𐐲𐑌, 𐐰𐑌𐐼 𐐫𐑊𐑅𐐬 𐐱𐑂 𐐮𐐻𐑅 𐑅𐐯𐐻𐐮𐑍; 𐑄𐐯𐑉𐑁𐐬𐑉 𐑄𐐩 𐑇𐐰𐑊 𐑌𐐬 𐐱𐑂 𐐲 𐑇𐐭𐑉𐐮𐐻𐐨 𐑄𐐰𐐻 𐑄𐐯𐑉 𐑇𐐰𐑊 𐐺 𐐻𐐭 𐐼𐐩𐑆 𐐰𐑌𐐼 𐐲 𐑌𐐴𐐻; 𐑌𐐯𐑂𐐲𐑉𐑄𐐲𐑊𐐯𐑅, 𐑄 𐑌𐐴𐐻 𐑇𐐰𐑊 𐑌𐐱𐐻 𐐺 𐐼𐐪𐑉𐐿𐐲𐑌𐐼; 𐐰𐑌𐐼 𐐮𐐻 𐑇𐐰𐑊 𐐺 𐑄 𐑌𐐴𐐻 𐐺𐐨𐑁𐐬𐑉 𐐸𐐨 𐐮𐑆 𐐺𐐫𐑉𐑌.

6. 𐐈𐑌𐐼 𐐺𐐨𐐸𐐬𐑊𐐼 𐑄𐐯𐑉 𐑇𐐰𐑊 𐐲 𐑌𐐭 𐑅𐐻𐐪𐑉 𐐲𐑉𐐴𐑆, 𐑅𐐲𐐽 𐐰𐑌 𐐶𐐲𐑌 𐐰𐑆 𐐷 𐑌𐐯𐑂𐐲𐑉 𐐸𐐰𐑂 𐐺𐐨𐐸𐐯𐑊𐐼; 𐐰𐑌𐐼 𐑄𐐮𐑅 𐐫𐑊𐑅𐐬 𐑇𐐰𐑊 𐐺 𐐲 𐑅𐐴𐑌 𐐲𐑌𐐻𐐭 𐐷𐐭. 𐐈𐑌𐐼 𐐺𐐨𐐸𐐬𐑊𐐼 𐑄𐐮𐑅 𐐮𐑆 𐑌𐐱𐐻 𐐫𐑊, 𐑄𐐯𐑉 𐑇𐐰𐑊 𐐺 𐑋𐐯𐑌𐐨 𐑅𐐴𐑌𐑆 𐐰𐑌𐐼 𐐶𐐲𐑌𐐼𐐲𐑉𐑆 𐐮𐑌 𐐸𐐯𐑂𐐲𐑌. 𐐈𐑌𐐼 𐐮𐐻 𐑇𐐰𐑊 𐐿𐐲𐑋 𐐻𐐭 𐐹𐐰𐑅 𐑄𐐰𐐻 𐐷 𐑇𐐰𐑊 𐐫𐑊 𐐺 𐐰𐑋𐐩𐑆𐐼, 𐐰𐑌𐐼 𐐶𐐲𐑌𐐼𐐲𐑉, 𐐮𐑌𐑅𐐬𐑋𐐲𐐽 𐑄𐐰𐐻 𐐷 𐑇𐐰𐑊 𐑁𐐫𐑊 𐐻𐐭 𐑄 𐐲𐑉𐑃. 𐐈𐑌𐐼 𐐮𐐻 𐑇𐐰𐑊 𐐿𐐲𐑋 𐐻𐐭 𐐹𐐰𐑅 𐑄𐐰𐐻 𐐸𐐭𐑅𐐬𐐯𐑂𐐲𐑉 𐑇𐐰𐑊 𐐺𐐨𐑊𐐨𐑂 𐐱𐑌 𐑄 𐐝𐐲𐑌 𐐱𐑂 𐐘𐐱𐐼, 𐑄 𐑅𐐩𐑋 𐑇𐐰𐑊 𐐸𐐰𐑂 𐐯𐑂𐐲𐑉𐑊𐐰𐑅𐐻𐐮𐑍 𐑊𐐴𐑁. 𐐈𐑌𐐼 𐐺𐐨𐐸𐐬𐑊𐐼, 𐑄𐐲𐑅 𐐸𐐰𐑃 𐑄 𐐢𐐫𐑉𐐼 𐐿𐐱𐑋𐐰𐑌𐐼𐐯𐐼 𐑋𐐨, 𐐺𐐴 𐐸𐐮𐑆 𐐩𐑌𐐾𐐯𐑊, 𐑄𐐰𐐻 𐐌 𐑇𐐳𐐼 𐐿𐐲𐑋 𐐰𐑌𐐼 𐐻𐐯𐑊 𐑄𐐮𐑅 𐑃𐐮𐑍 𐐲𐑌𐐻𐐭 𐐷𐐭; 𐐷𐐩, 𐐸𐐨 𐐸𐐰𐑃 𐐿𐐱𐑋𐐰𐑌𐐼𐐯𐐼 𐑄𐐰𐐻 𐐌 𐑇𐐳𐐼 𐐹𐑉𐐱𐑁𐐯𐑅𐐴 𐑄𐐨𐑆 𐑃𐐮𐑍𐑆 𐐲𐑌𐐻𐐭 𐐷𐐭; 𐐷𐐩, 𐐸𐐨 𐐸𐐰𐑃 𐑅𐐯𐐼 𐐲𐑌𐐻𐐭 𐑋𐐨, 𐐗𐑉𐐴 𐐲𐑌𐐻𐐭 𐑄𐐮𐑅 𐐹𐐨𐐹𐐲𐑊, 𐑉𐐨𐐹𐐯𐑌𐐻 𐐰𐑌𐐼 𐐹𐑉𐐨𐐹𐐩𐑉 𐑄 𐐶𐐩 𐐱𐑂 𐑄 𐐢𐐫𐑉𐐼. 𐐈𐑌𐐼 𐑌𐐵 𐐺𐐨𐐿𐐫𐑆 𐐌 𐐰𐑋 𐐲 𐐢𐐰𐑋𐐲𐑌𐐴𐐻, 𐐰𐑌𐐼 𐐸𐐰𐑂 𐑅𐐹𐐬𐐿𐑌 𐐲𐑌𐐻𐐭 𐐷𐐭 𐑄 𐐶𐐲𐑉𐐼𐑆 𐐸𐐶𐐮𐐽 𐑄 𐐢𐐫𐑉𐐼 𐐸𐐰𐑃 𐐿𐐱𐑋𐐰𐑌𐐼𐐯𐐼 𐑋𐐨, 𐐰𐑌𐐼 𐐺𐐨𐐿𐐫𐑆 𐐮𐐻 𐐶𐐱𐑆 𐐸𐐪𐑉𐐼 𐐲𐑀𐐯𐑌𐑅𐐻 𐐷𐐭, 𐐷 𐐪𐑉 𐐰𐑍𐑀𐑉𐐨 𐐶𐐮𐑄 𐑋𐐨, 𐐰𐑌𐐼 𐐼𐐭 𐑅𐐨𐐿 𐐻𐐭 𐐼𐐨𐑅𐐻𐑉𐑎 𐑋𐐨, 𐐰𐑌𐐼 𐐸𐐰𐑂 𐐿𐐰𐑅𐐻 𐑋𐐨 𐐵𐐻 𐑁𐑉𐐱𐑋 𐐲𐑋𐐲𐑍

𐐷𐐭. 𐐈𐑌𐐼 𐐷 𐑖𐐰𐑊 𐐸𐐨𐑉 𐑋𐐴 𐐶𐐲𐑉𐐼𐑆, 𐑁𐐫𐑉, 𐑁𐐫𐑉 𐑄𐐮𐑅 𐐮𐑌𐐻𐐯𐑌𐐻 𐐌 𐐸𐐰𐑂 𐐿𐐲𐑋 𐐲𐐹 𐐲𐐹𐐱𐑌 𐑄 𐐶𐐫𐑊𐑆 𐐱𐑂 𐑄𐐮𐑅 𐑅𐐮𐐻𐐨, 𐑄𐐰𐐻 𐐷 𐑋𐐴𐐻 𐐸𐐨𐑉 𐐰𐑌𐐼 𐑌𐐬 𐐱𐑂 𐑄 𐐾𐐲𐐾𐑋𐐯𐑌𐐻𐑅 𐐱𐑂 𐐘𐐱𐐼 𐐸𐐶𐐮𐐽 𐐼𐐭 𐐲𐐶𐐩𐐻 𐐷𐐭 𐐺𐐨𐐿𐐫𐑆 𐐱𐑂 𐐷𐐭𐑉 𐐮𐑌𐐮𐐿𐐶𐐮𐐻𐐨𐑆, 𐐰𐑌𐐼 𐐫𐑊𐑅𐐬 𐑄𐐰𐐻 𐐷 𐑋𐐴𐐻 𐑌𐐬 𐑄 𐐿𐐲𐑌𐐼𐐮𐑖𐐲𐑌𐑆 𐐱𐑂 𐑉𐐯𐐹𐐯𐑌𐐻𐐰𐑌𐑅; 𐐰𐑌𐐼 𐐫𐑊𐑅𐐬 𐑄𐐰𐐻 𐐷 𐑋𐐴𐐻 𐑌𐐬 𐐱𐑂 𐑄 𐐿𐐲𐑋𐐮𐑍 𐐱𐑂 𐐖𐐨𐑆𐐲𐑅 𐐗𐑉𐐴𐑅𐐻, 𐑄 𐐝𐐲𐑌 𐐱𐑂 𐐘𐐱𐐼, 𐑄 𐐙𐐪𐑄𐐲𐑉 𐐱𐑂 𐐸𐐯𐑂𐐲𐑌 𐐰𐑌𐐼 𐐱𐑂 𐐲𐑉𐑃, 𐑄 𐐗𐑉𐐨𐐩𐐻𐐲𐑉 𐐱𐑂 𐐫𐑊 𐑃𐐮𐑍𐑆, 𐑁𐑉𐐱𐑋 𐑄 𐐺𐐨𐑀𐐮𐑌𐐮𐑍; 𐐰𐑌𐐼 𐑄𐐰𐐻 𐐷 𐑋𐐴𐐻 𐑌𐐬 𐐱𐑂 𐑄 𐑅𐐴𐑌𐑆 𐐱𐑂 𐐸𐐮𐑆 𐐿𐐲𐑋𐐮𐑍, 𐐻𐐭 𐑄 𐐮𐑌𐐻𐐯𐑌𐐻, 𐑄𐐰𐐻 𐐷 𐑋𐐴𐐻 𐐺𐐨𐑊𐐨𐑂 𐐱𐑌 𐐸𐐮𐑆 𐑌𐐩𐑋. 𐐈𐑌𐐼 𐐮𐑁 𐐷 𐐺𐐨𐑊𐐨𐑂 𐐱𐑌 𐐸𐐮𐑆 𐑌𐐩𐑋, 𐐷 𐐶𐐮𐑊 𐑉𐐯𐐹𐐯𐑌𐐻 𐐱𐑂 𐐫𐑊 𐐷𐐭𐑉 𐑅𐐮𐑌𐑆, 𐑄𐐰𐐻 𐑄𐐯𐑉𐐺𐐴 𐐷 𐑋𐐩 𐐸𐐰𐑂 𐐰 𐑉𐐯𐑋𐐮𐑖𐐲𐑌 𐐱𐑂 𐑄𐐯𐑋 𐑃𐑉𐐭 𐐸𐐮𐑆 𐑋𐐯𐑉𐐮𐐻𐑅. 𐐈𐑌𐐼 𐐺𐐨𐐸𐐬𐑊𐐼, 𐐰𐑀𐐯𐑌 𐐰𐑌𐐲𐑄𐐲𐑉 𐑅𐐴𐑌 𐐌 𐑀𐐮𐑂 𐐲𐑌𐐻𐐭 𐐷𐐭; 𐐷𐐩, 𐐰 𐑅𐐴𐑌 𐐱𐑂 𐐸𐐮𐑆 𐐼𐐯𐑃; 𐑁𐐫𐑉 𐐺𐐨𐐸𐐬𐑊𐐼, 𐐸𐐨 𐑖𐐳𐑉𐑊𐐨 𐑋𐐲𐑅𐐻 𐐼𐐴, 𐑄𐐰𐐻 𐑅𐐰𐑊𐑂𐐩𐑖𐐲𐑌 𐑋𐐩 𐐿𐐲𐑋; 𐐷𐐩, 𐐮𐐻 𐐺𐐨𐐸𐐭𐑂𐐯𐑃 𐐸𐐮𐑋, 𐐰𐑌𐐼 𐐺𐐨𐐿𐐲𐑋𐐯𐑃 𐐯𐐿𐑅𐐹𐐨𐐼𐐨𐐯𐑌𐐻 𐑄𐐰𐐻 𐐸𐐨 𐐼𐐴𐐯𐑃, 𐐻𐐭 𐐺𐑉𐐮𐑍 𐐻𐐭 𐐹𐐰𐑅 𐑄 𐑉𐐯𐑆𐐲𐑉𐐯𐐿𐑖𐐲𐑌 𐐱𐑂 𐑄 𐐼𐐯𐐼, 𐑄𐐰𐐻 𐑄𐐯𐑉𐐺𐐴 𐑋𐐯𐑌 𐑋𐐩 𐐺 𐐺𐑉𐐫𐐻 𐐮𐑌𐐻𐐭 𐑄 𐐹𐑉𐐯𐑆𐐯𐑌𐑅 𐐱𐑂 𐑄 𐐢𐐫𐑉𐐼; 𐐷𐐩, 𐐺𐐨𐐸𐐬𐑊𐐼, 𐑄𐐮𐑅 𐐼𐐯𐑃 𐐺𐑉𐐮𐑍𐐯𐑃 𐐻𐐭 𐐹𐐰𐑅 𐑄 𐑉𐐯𐑆𐐲𐑉𐐯𐐿𐑖𐐲𐑌, 𐐰𐑌𐐼 𐑉𐐨𐐼𐐨𐑋𐐯𐑃 𐐫𐑊 𐑋𐐰𐑌𐐿𐐴𐑌𐐼 𐑁𐑉𐐱𐑋 𐑄 𐑁𐐲𐑉𐑅𐐻 𐐼𐐯𐑃, 𐑄𐐰𐐻 𐑅𐐹𐐮𐑉𐐮𐐻𐐷𐐭𐐰𐑊 𐐼𐐯𐑃; 𐑁𐐫𐑉 𐐫𐑊 𐑋𐐰𐑌𐐿𐐴𐑌𐐼, 𐐺𐐴 𐑄 𐑁𐐫𐑊 𐐱𐑂 𐐈𐐼𐐲𐑋, 𐐺𐐨𐐮𐑍 𐐿𐐲𐐻 𐐫𐑁 𐑁𐑉𐐱𐑋 𐑄 𐐹𐑉𐐯𐑆𐐯𐑌𐑅 𐐱𐑂 𐑄 𐐢𐐫𐑉𐐼, 𐐪𐑉 𐐿𐐲𐑌𐑅𐐮𐐼𐐲𐑉𐐼 𐐰𐑆 𐐼𐐯𐐼, 𐐺𐐬𐑃 𐐰𐑆 𐐻𐐭 𐑃𐐮𐑍𐑆 𐐻𐐯𐑋𐐹𐐬𐑉𐐲𐑊 𐐰𐑌𐐼 𐐻𐐭 𐑃𐐮𐑍𐑆 𐑅𐐹𐐮𐑉𐐮𐐻𐐷𐐭𐐰𐑊. 𐐒𐐲𐐻 𐐺𐐨𐐸𐐬𐑊𐐼, 𐑄 𐑉𐐯𐑆𐐲𐑉𐐯𐐿𐑖𐐲𐑌 𐐱𐑂 𐐗𐑉𐐴𐑅𐐻 𐑉𐐨𐐼𐐨𐑋𐐯𐑃 𐑋𐐰𐑌𐐿𐐴𐑌𐐼, 𐐷𐐩, 𐐨𐑂𐐲𐑌 𐐫𐑊 𐑋𐐰𐑌𐐿𐐴𐑌𐐼, 𐐰𐑌𐐼 𐐺𐑉𐐮𐑍𐐯𐑃 𐑄𐐯𐑋 𐐺𐐰𐐿 𐐮𐑌𐐻𐐭 𐑄 𐐹𐑉𐐯𐑆𐐯𐑌𐑅 𐐱𐑂 𐑄 𐐢𐐫𐑉𐐼; 𐐷𐐩, 𐐰𐑌𐐼 𐐮𐐻 𐐺𐑉𐐮𐑍𐐯𐑃 𐐻𐐭 𐐹𐐰𐑅 𐑄 𐐿𐐲𐑌𐐼𐐮𐑖𐐲𐑌 𐐱𐑂 𐑉𐐯𐐹𐐯𐑌𐐻𐐰𐑌𐑅, 𐑄𐐰𐐻 𐐸𐐭𐑅𐐬𐐯𐑂𐐲𐑉 𐑉𐐯𐐹𐐯𐑌𐐻𐐯𐑃, 𐑄 𐑅𐐩𐑋 𐐮𐑆 𐑌𐐱𐐻 𐐸𐐷𐐭𐑌 𐐼𐐵𐑌 𐐰𐑌𐐼 𐐿𐐰𐑅𐐻 𐐮𐑌𐐻𐐭 𐑄 𐑁𐐴𐑉; 𐐒𐐲𐐻 𐐸𐐭𐑅𐐬𐐯𐑂𐐲𐑉 𐑉𐐯𐐹𐐯𐑌𐐻𐐯𐑃 𐑌𐐱𐐻, 𐐮𐑆 𐐸𐐷𐐭𐑌 𐐼𐐵𐑌 𐐰𐑌𐐼 𐐿𐐰𐑅𐐻 𐐮𐑌𐐻𐐭 𐑄 𐑁𐐴𐑉, 𐐰𐑌𐐼 𐑄𐐯𐑉 𐐿𐐲𐑋𐐯𐑃 𐐲𐐹𐐱𐑌 𐑄𐐯𐑋 𐐰𐑀𐐯𐑌 𐐰 𐑅𐐹𐐮𐑉𐐮𐐻𐐷𐐭𐐰𐑊 𐐼𐐯𐑃, 𐐷𐐩, 𐐰 𐑅𐐯𐐿𐐲𐑌𐐼 𐐼𐐯𐑃, 𐑁𐐫𐑉 𐑄𐐩 𐐪𐑉 𐐿𐐲𐐻 𐐫𐑁 𐐰𐑀𐐯𐑌 𐐰𐑆 𐐻𐐭 𐑃𐐮𐑍𐑆 𐐹𐐲𐑉𐐻𐐩𐑌𐐮𐑍 𐐻𐐭 𐑉𐐴𐐽𐐲𐑅𐑌𐐯𐑅; 𐑄𐐯𐑉𐑁𐐬𐑉 𐑉𐐯𐐹𐐯𐑌𐐻 𐐷, 𐑉𐐯𐐹𐐯𐑌𐐻 𐐷, 𐑊𐐯𐑅𐐻 𐐺𐐴 𐑌𐐬𐐮𐑍 𐑄𐐨𐑆 𐑃𐐮𐑍𐑆 𐐰𐑌𐐼 𐑌𐐱𐐻 𐐼𐐭𐐮𐑍 𐑄𐐯𐑋, 𐐷 𐑖𐐰𐑊 𐑅𐐲𐑁𐐲𐑉 𐐷𐐭𐑉𐑅𐐯𐑊𐑂𐑆 𐐻𐐭 𐐿𐐲𐑋 𐐲𐑌𐐼𐐲𐑉 𐐿𐐱𐑌𐐼𐐯𐑋𐑌𐐩𐑖𐐲𐑌, 𐐰𐑌𐐼 𐐷 𐐪𐑉 𐐺𐑉𐐫𐐻 𐐼𐐵𐑌 𐐲𐑌𐐻𐐭 𐑄𐐮𐑅 𐑅𐐯𐐿𐐲𐑌𐐼 𐐼𐐯𐑃.

7. 𐐒𐐲𐐻 𐐺𐐨𐐸𐐬𐑊𐐼, 𐐰𐑆 𐐌 𐑅𐐯𐐼 𐐲𐑌𐐻𐐭 𐐷𐐭 𐐿𐐱𐑌𐑅𐐲𐑉𐑌𐐮𐑍 𐐰𐑌𐐲𐑄𐐲𐑉 𐑅𐐴𐑌, 𐐰 𐑅𐐴𐑌 𐐱𐑂 𐐸𐐮𐑆 𐐼𐐯𐑃, 𐐺𐐨𐐸𐐬𐑊𐐼, 𐐮𐑌 𐑄𐐰𐐻 𐐼𐐩 𐑄𐐰𐐻 𐐸𐐨 𐑖𐐰𐑊 𐑅𐐲𐑁𐐲𐑉 𐐼𐐯𐑃, 𐑄 𐑅𐐲𐑌 𐑖𐐰𐑊 𐐺 𐐼𐐪𐑉𐐿𐐲𐑌𐐼 𐐰𐑌𐐼 𐑉𐐨𐑁𐐷𐐭𐑆 𐐻𐐭 𐑀𐐮𐑂 𐐸𐐮𐑆 𐑊𐐴𐐻 𐐲𐑌𐐻𐐭 𐐷𐐭; 𐐰𐑌𐐼 𐐫𐑊𐑅𐐬 𐑄 𐑋𐐭𐑌, 𐐰𐑌𐐼 𐑄 𐑅𐐻𐐪𐑉𐑆; 𐐰𐑌𐐼 𐑄𐐯𐑉 𐑖𐐰𐑊 𐐺 𐑌𐐬 𐑊𐐴𐐻 𐐲𐐹𐐱𐑌 𐑄 𐑁𐐩𐑅 𐐱𐑂 𐑄𐐮𐑅 𐑊𐐰𐑌𐐼, 𐐨𐑂𐐲𐑌 𐑁𐑉𐐱𐑋 𐑄 𐐻𐐴𐑋 𐑄𐐰𐐻 𐐸𐐨 𐑖𐐰𐑊 𐑅𐐲𐑁𐐲𐑉 𐐼𐐯𐑃, 𐑁𐐫𐑉 𐑄 𐑅𐐹𐐩𐑅 𐐱𐑂 𐑃𐑉𐐨 𐐼𐐩𐑆, 𐐻𐐭 𐑄 𐐻𐐴𐑋 𐑄𐐰𐐻 𐐸𐐨 𐑖𐐰𐑊 𐑉𐐴𐑆 𐐰𐑀𐐯𐑌 𐑁𐑉𐐱𐑋 𐑄 𐐼𐐯𐐼; 𐐷𐐩, 𐐰𐐻 𐑄 𐐻𐐴𐑋 𐑄𐐰𐐻 𐐸𐐨 𐑖𐐰𐑊 𐐷𐐨𐑊𐐼 𐐲𐐹 𐑄 𐑀𐐬𐑅𐐻, 𐑄𐐯𐑉 𐑖𐐰𐑊 𐐺 𐑃𐐲𐑌𐐼𐐲𐑉𐐮𐑍𐑆 𐐰𐑌𐐼 𐑊𐐴𐐻𐑌𐐮𐑍𐑆 𐑁𐐫𐑉 𐑄 𐑅𐐹𐐩𐑅 𐐱𐑂 𐑋𐐯𐑌𐐨 𐐵𐐲𐑉𐑆, 𐐰𐑌𐐼 𐑄 𐐲𐑉𐑃 𐑖𐐰𐑊 𐑖𐐩𐐿 𐐰𐑌𐐼 𐐻𐑉𐐯𐑋𐐺𐐲𐑊, 𐐰𐑌𐐼 𐑄 𐑉𐐱𐐿𐑅 𐐸𐐶𐐮𐐽 𐐪𐑉 𐐲𐐹𐐱𐑌 𐑄 𐑁𐐩𐑅 𐐱𐑂 𐑄𐐮𐑅 𐐲𐑉𐑃; 𐐸𐐶𐐮𐐽 𐐪𐑉 𐐺𐐬𐑃 𐐲𐐺𐐲𐑂 𐑄 𐐲𐑉𐑃 𐐰𐑌𐐼 𐐺𐐨𐑌𐐨𐑃, 𐐸𐐶𐐮𐐽 𐐷 𐑌𐐬 𐐰𐐻 𐑄𐐮𐑅 𐐻𐐴𐑋 𐐪𐑉 𐑅𐐱𐑊𐐮𐐼, 𐐫𐑉 𐑄 𐑋𐐬𐑉 𐐹𐐪𐑉𐐻 𐐱𐑂 𐐮𐐻 𐐮𐑆 𐐶𐐲𐑌 𐑅𐐱𐑊𐐮𐐼 𐑋𐐰𐑅, 𐑖𐐰𐑊 𐐺 𐐺𐑉𐐬𐐿𐐲𐑌 𐐲𐐹; 𐐷𐐩, 𐑄𐐩 𐑖𐐰𐑊 𐐺 𐑉𐐯𐑌𐐻 𐐮𐑌 𐐻𐐶𐐩𐑌, 𐐰𐑌𐐼 𐑖𐐰𐑊 𐐯𐑂𐐲𐑉 𐐰𐑁𐐻𐐲𐑉 𐐺 𐑁𐐵𐑌𐐼 𐐮𐑌 𐑅𐐨𐑋𐑆 𐐰𐑌𐐼 𐐮𐑌 𐐿𐑉𐐰𐐿𐑅, 𐐰𐑌𐐼 𐐮𐑌 𐐺𐑉𐐬𐐿𐐲𐑌 𐑁𐑉𐐰𐑀𐑋𐐯𐑌𐐻𐑅 𐐲𐐹𐐱𐑌 𐑄 𐑁𐐩𐑅 𐐱𐑂 𐑄 𐐸𐐬𐑊 𐐲𐑉𐑃; 𐐷𐐩, 𐐺𐐬𐑃 𐐲𐐺𐐲𐑂 𐑄 𐐲𐑉𐑃 𐐰𐑌𐐼 𐐺𐐨𐑌𐐨𐑃. 𐐈𐑌𐐼 𐐺𐐨𐐸𐐬𐑊𐐼, 𐑄𐐯𐑉 𐑖𐐰𐑊 𐐺 𐑀𐑉𐐩𐐻 𐐻𐐯𐑋𐐹𐐯𐑅𐐻𐑅, 𐐰𐑌𐐼 𐑄𐐯𐑉 𐑖𐐰𐑊 𐐺 𐑋𐐯𐑌𐐨 𐑋𐐵𐑌𐐻𐐩𐑌𐑆 𐑊𐐩𐐼 𐑊𐐬, 𐑊𐐴𐐿 𐐲𐑌𐐻𐐭 𐐰 𐑂𐐰𐑊𐐨, 𐐰𐑌𐐼 𐑄𐐯𐑉 𐑖𐐰𐑊 𐐺 𐑋𐐯𐑌𐐨 𐐹𐑊𐐩𐑅𐐯𐑆, 𐐸𐐶𐐮𐐽 𐐪𐑉 𐑌𐐵 𐐿𐐫𐑊𐐼 𐑂𐐰𐑊𐐨𐑆, 𐐸𐐶𐐮𐐽 𐑖𐐰𐑊 𐐺𐐨𐐿𐐲𐑋 𐑋𐐵𐑌𐐻𐐩𐑌𐑆, 𐐸𐐭𐑆 𐐸𐐴𐐻 𐑄𐐯𐑉𐐱𐑂 𐐮𐑆 𐑀𐑉𐐩𐐻. 𐐈𐑌𐐼 𐑋𐐯𐑌𐐨 𐐸𐐴𐐶𐐩𐑆 𐑖𐐰𐑊 𐐺 𐐺𐑉𐐬𐐿𐐲𐑌 𐐲𐐹, 𐐰𐑌𐐼 𐑋𐐯𐑌𐐨 𐑅𐐮𐐻𐐨𐑆 𐑖𐐰𐑊 𐐺𐐨𐐿𐐲𐑋 𐐼𐐯𐑅𐐬𐑊𐐩𐐻, 𐐰𐑌𐐼 𐑋𐐯𐑌𐐨 𐑀𐑉𐐩𐑂𐑆 𐑖𐐰𐑊 𐐺 𐐬𐐹𐑌𐐼, 𐐰𐑌𐐼 𐑖𐐰𐑊 𐐷𐐨𐑊𐐼 𐐲𐐹 𐑋𐐯𐑌𐐨 𐐱𐑂 𐑄𐐩𐑉 𐐼𐐯𐐼; 𐐰𐑌𐐼 𐑋𐐯𐑌𐐨 𐑅𐐩𐑌𐐻𐑅 𐑖𐐰𐑊 𐐰𐐹𐐨𐑉 𐐲𐑌𐐻𐐭 𐑋𐐯𐑌𐐨. 𐐈𐑌𐐼 𐐺𐐨𐐸𐐬𐑊𐐼, 𐑄𐐲𐑅 𐐸𐐰𐑃 𐑄 𐐩𐑌𐐾𐐯𐑊 𐑅𐐹𐐬𐐿𐐲𐑌 𐐲𐑌𐐻𐐭 𐑋𐐨; 𐑁𐐫𐑉 𐐸𐐨 𐑅𐐯𐐼 𐐲𐑌𐐻𐐭 𐑋𐐨, 𐑄𐐰𐐻 𐑄𐐯𐑉 𐑖𐐳𐐼 𐐺 𐑃𐐲𐑌𐐼𐐲𐑉𐐮𐑍𐑆 𐐰𐑌𐐼 𐑊𐐴𐐻𐑌𐐮𐑍𐑆 𐑁𐐫𐑉 𐑄 𐑅𐐹𐐩𐑅 𐐱𐑂 𐑋𐐯𐑌𐐨 𐐵𐐲𐑉𐑆; 𐐰𐑌𐐼 𐐸𐐨 𐑅𐐯𐐼 𐐲𐑌𐐻𐐭 𐑋𐐨 𐑄𐐰𐐻 𐐸𐐶𐐴𐑊 𐑄 𐑃𐐲𐑌𐐼𐐲𐑉 𐐰𐑌𐐼 𐑄 𐑊𐐴𐐻𐑌𐐮𐑍 𐑊𐐰𐑅𐐻𐐯𐐼,

𐐰𐑌𐐼 𐑄 𐐻𐐯𐑋𐐹𐐯𐑅𐐻, 𐑄𐐰𐐻 𐑄𐐨𐑆 𐑃𐐮𐑍𐑆 𐑇𐐳𐐼 𐐺𐐨, 𐐰𐑌𐐼 𐑄𐐰𐐻 𐐼𐐪𐑉𐐿𐑌𐐯𐑅 𐑇𐐳𐐼 𐐿𐐲𐑂𐐲𐑉 𐑄 𐑁𐐩𐑅 𐐲𐑂 𐑄 𐐸𐐬𐑊 𐐲𐑉𐑃, 𐑁𐐫𐑉 𐑄 𐑅𐐹𐐩𐑅 𐐲𐑂 𐑃𐑉𐐨 𐐼𐐩𐑆. 𐐈𐑌𐐼 𐑄 𐐩𐑌𐐾𐐯𐑊 𐑅𐐯𐐼 𐐲𐑌𐐻𐐭 𐑋𐐨, 𐑄𐐰𐐻 𐑋𐐯𐑌𐐨 𐑇𐐰𐑊 𐑅𐐨 𐑀𐑉𐐩𐐻𐐲𐑉 𐑃𐐮𐑍𐑆 𐑄𐐰𐑌 𐑄𐐨𐑆, 𐐻𐐭 𐑄 𐐮𐑌𐐻𐐯𐑌𐐻 𐑄𐐰𐐻 𐑄𐐩 𐑋𐐴𐐻 𐐺𐐨𐑊𐐨𐑂 𐑄𐐰𐐻 𐑄𐐨𐑆 𐑅𐐴𐑌𐑆 𐐰𐑌𐐼 𐑄𐐨𐑆 𐐶𐐲𐑌𐐼𐐲𐑉𐑆 𐑇𐐳𐐼 𐐿𐐲𐑋 𐐻𐐭 𐐹𐐪𐑅, 𐐲𐐹𐐱𐑌 𐐫𐑊 𐑄 𐑁𐐩𐑅 𐐲𐑂 𐑄𐐮𐑅 𐑊𐐰𐑌𐐼; 𐐻𐐭 𐑄 𐐮𐑌𐐻𐐯𐑌𐐻 𐑄𐐰𐐻 𐑄𐐯𐑉 𐑇𐐳𐐼 𐐺𐐨 𐑌𐐬 𐐿𐐱𐑆 𐑁𐐫𐑉 𐐲𐑌𐐺𐐨𐑊𐐨𐑁 𐐲𐑋𐐲𐑍 𐑄 𐐽𐐮𐑊𐐼𐑉𐐯𐑌 𐐲𐑂 𐑋𐐯𐑌: 𐐰𐑌𐐼 𐑄𐐮𐑅 𐐻𐐭 𐑄 𐐮𐑌𐐻𐐯𐑌𐐻 𐑄𐐰𐐻 𐐸𐐭𐑅𐐬𐐯𐑂𐐲𐑉 𐐶𐐮𐑊 𐐺𐐨𐑊𐐨𐑂, 𐑋𐐴𐐻 𐐺𐐨 𐑅𐐩𐑂𐐼, 𐐰𐑌𐐼 𐑄𐐰𐐻 𐐸𐐭𐑅𐐬𐐯𐑂𐐲𐑉 𐐶𐐮𐑊 𐑌𐐱𐐻 𐐺𐐨𐑊𐐨𐑂, 𐐩 𐑉𐐴𐐽𐐲𐑅 𐐾𐐲𐐾𐑋𐐯𐑌𐐻 𐑋𐐴𐐻 𐐿𐐲𐑋 𐐲𐐹𐐱𐑌 𐑄𐐯𐑋; 𐐰𐑌𐐼 𐐫𐑊𐑅𐐬 𐐮𐑁 𐑄𐐩 𐐪𐑉 𐐿𐐲𐑌𐐼𐐯𐑋𐐼, 𐑄𐐩 𐐺𐑉𐐮𐑍 𐐲𐐹𐐱𐑌 𐑄𐐯𐑋𐑅𐐯𐑊𐑂𐑆 𐑄𐐯𐑉 𐐬𐑌 𐐿𐐱𐑌𐐼𐐯𐑋𐑌𐐩𐑇𐐲𐑌. 𐐈𐑌𐐼 𐑌𐐵, 𐑉𐐨𐑋𐐯𐑋𐐺𐐲𐑉, 𐑉𐐨𐑋𐐯𐑋𐐺𐐲𐑉, 𐑋𐐴 𐐺𐑉𐐯𐑄𐑉𐐯𐑌, 𐑄𐐰𐐻 𐐸𐐭𐑅𐐬𐐯𐑂𐐲𐑉 𐐹𐐯𐑉𐐮𐑇𐐯𐑃, 𐐹𐐯𐑉𐐮𐑇𐐯𐑃 𐐲𐑌𐐻𐐭 𐐸𐐮𐑋𐑅𐐯𐑊𐑁; 𐐰𐑌𐐼 𐐸𐐭𐑅𐐬𐐯𐑂𐐲𐑉 𐐼𐐭𐐯𐑃 𐐮𐑌𐐿𐐶𐐮𐐻𐐨, 𐐼𐐭𐐯𐑃 𐐮𐐻 𐐲𐑌𐐻𐐭 𐐸𐐮𐑋𐑅𐐯𐑊𐑁; 𐑁𐐫𐑉 𐐺𐐨𐐸𐐬𐑊𐐼, 𐐷𐐨 𐐪𐑉 𐑁𐑉𐐨; 𐐷𐐨 𐐪𐑉 𐐹𐐯𐑉𐑋𐐮𐐻𐐯𐐼 𐐻𐐭 𐐰𐐿𐐻 𐑁𐐫𐑉 𐐷𐐫𐑉𐑅𐐯𐑊𐑂𐑆; 𐑁𐐫𐑉 𐐺𐐨𐐸𐐬𐑊𐐼, 𐐘𐐱𐐼 𐐸𐐰𐑃 𐑀𐐮𐑂𐐲𐑌 𐐲𐑌𐐻𐐭 𐐷𐐭 𐐩 𐑌𐐱𐑊𐐲𐐾, 𐐰𐑌𐐼 𐐸𐐨 𐐸𐐰𐑃 𐑋𐐩𐐼 𐐷𐐭 𐑁𐑉𐐨; 𐐸𐐨 𐐸𐐰𐑃 𐑀𐐮𐑂𐐲𐑌 𐐲𐑌𐐻𐐭 𐐷𐐭 𐑄𐐰𐐻 𐐷𐐨 𐑋𐐴𐐻 𐑌𐐬 𐑀𐐳𐐼 𐑁𐑉𐐱𐑋 𐐨𐑂𐐲𐑊, 𐐰𐑌𐐼 𐐸𐐨 𐐸𐐰𐑃 𐑀𐐮𐑂𐐲𐑌 𐐲𐑌𐐻𐐭 𐐷𐐭 𐑄𐐰𐐻 𐐷𐐨 𐑋𐐴𐐻 𐐽𐐭𐑆 𐑊𐐴𐑁 𐐫𐑉 𐐼𐐯𐑃, 𐐰𐑌𐐼 𐐷𐐨 𐐿𐐰𐑌 𐐼𐐭 𐑀𐐳𐐼 𐐰𐑌𐐼 𐐺𐐨 𐑉𐐯𐑅𐐻𐐬𐑉𐐼 𐐲𐑌𐐻𐐭 𐑄𐐰𐐻 𐐸𐐶𐐮𐐽 𐐮𐑆 𐑀𐐳𐐼, 𐐫𐑉 𐐸𐐰𐑂 𐑄𐐰𐐻 𐐸𐐶𐐮𐐽 𐐮𐑆 𐑀𐐳𐐼 𐑉𐐨𐑅𐐻𐐬𐑉𐐼 𐐲𐑌𐐻𐐭 𐐷𐐭; 𐐫𐑉 𐐷𐐨 𐐿𐐰𐑌 𐐼𐐭 𐐨𐑂𐐲𐑊, 𐐰𐑌𐐼 𐐸𐐰𐑂 𐑄𐐰𐐻 𐐸𐐶𐐮𐐽 𐐮𐑆 𐐨𐑂𐐲𐑊 𐑉𐐨𐑅𐐻𐐬𐑉𐐼 𐐲𐑌𐐻𐐭 𐐷𐐭.

8. 𐐈𐑌𐐼 𐑌𐐵, 𐑋𐐴 𐐺𐐮𐑊𐐲𐑂𐐯𐐼 𐐺𐑉𐐯𐑄𐑉𐐯𐑌, 𐐺𐐨𐐸𐐬𐑊𐐼, 𐐴 𐐼𐐨𐐿𐑊𐐩𐑉 𐐲𐑌𐐻𐐭 𐐷𐐭, 𐑄𐐰𐐻 𐐯𐐿𐑅𐐯𐐹𐐻 𐐷𐐨 𐑇𐐰𐑊 𐑉𐐨𐐹𐐯𐑌𐐻, 𐐷𐐭𐑉 𐐸𐐵𐑆𐐯𐑆 𐑇𐐰𐑊 𐐺𐐨 𐑊𐐯𐑁𐐻 𐐲𐑌𐐻𐐭 𐐷𐐭 𐐼𐐯𐑅𐐬𐑊𐐩𐐻; 𐐷𐐨𐐩, 𐐯𐐿𐑅𐐯𐐹𐐻 𐐷𐐨 𐑉𐐨𐐹𐐯𐑌𐐻, 𐐷𐐭𐑉 𐐶𐐳𐑋𐐲𐑌 𐑇𐐰𐑊 𐐸𐐰𐑂 𐑀𐑉𐐩𐐻 𐐿𐐫𐑆 𐐻𐐭 𐑋𐐬𐑉𐑌 𐐮𐑌 𐑄 𐐼𐐩 𐑄𐐰𐐻 𐑄𐐩 𐑇𐐰𐑊 𐑀𐐮𐑂 𐑅𐐲𐐿, 𐑁𐐫𐑉 𐐷𐐨 𐑇𐐰𐑊 𐐰𐐻𐐯𐑋𐐹𐐻 𐐻𐐭 𐑁𐑊𐐨, 𐐰𐑌𐐼 𐑄𐐯𐑉 𐑇𐐰𐑊 𐐺𐐨 𐑌𐐬 𐐹𐑊𐐩𐑅 𐑁𐐫𐑉 𐑉𐐯𐑁𐐷𐐭𐐾; 𐐷𐐨𐐩, 𐐰𐑌𐐼 𐐶𐐬 𐐲𐑌𐐻𐐭 𐑄𐐯𐑋 𐐸𐐶𐐮𐐽 𐐪𐑉 𐐶𐐮𐑄 𐐽𐐴𐑊𐐼, 𐑁𐐫𐑉 𐑄𐐩 𐑇𐐰𐑊 𐐺𐐨 𐐸𐐯𐑂𐐨, 𐐰𐑌𐐼 𐐿𐐰𐑌𐐱𐐻 𐑁𐑊𐐨; 𐑄𐐯𐑉𐑁𐐫𐑉 𐑄𐐩 𐑇𐐰𐑊 𐐺𐐨 𐐻𐑉𐐱𐐼𐐲𐑌 𐐼𐐵𐑌, 𐐰𐑌𐐼 𐑇𐐰𐑊 𐐺𐐨 𐑊𐐯𐑁𐐻 𐐻𐐭 𐐹𐐯𐑉𐐮𐑇; 𐐷𐐨𐐩, 𐐶𐐬 𐐲𐑌𐐻𐐭 𐑄𐐮𐑅 𐐹𐐨𐐹𐐲𐑊 𐐸𐐶𐐮𐐽 𐐪𐑉 𐐿𐐱𐑊𐐼 𐑄 𐐹𐐨𐐹𐐲𐑊 𐐲𐑂 𐐤𐐨𐑁𐐴, 𐐯𐐿𐑅𐐯𐐹𐐻 𐑄𐐩 𐑇𐐰𐑊 𐑉𐐨𐐹𐐯𐑌𐐻 𐐸𐐶𐐯𐑌 𐑄𐐩 𐑇𐐰𐑊 𐑅𐐨 𐐫𐑊 𐑄𐐨𐑆 𐑅𐐴𐑌𐑆 𐐰𐑌𐐼 𐐶𐐲𐑌𐐼𐐲𐑉𐑆 𐐸𐐶𐐮𐐽 𐑇𐐰𐑊 𐐺𐐨 𐑇𐐬𐑌 𐐲𐑌𐐻𐐭 𐑄𐐯𐑋; 𐑁𐐫𐑉 𐐺𐐨𐐸𐐬𐑊𐐼, 𐑄𐐩 𐐸𐐰𐑂 𐐺𐐮𐑌 𐐩 𐐽𐐬𐑆𐐲𐑌 𐐹𐐨𐐹𐐲𐑊 𐐲𐑂 𐑄 𐐢𐐫𐑉𐐼; 𐐷𐐨𐐩, 𐑄 𐐹𐐨𐐹𐐲𐑊 𐐲𐑂 𐐤𐐨𐑁𐐴 𐐸𐐰𐑃 𐐸𐐨 𐑊𐐲𐑂𐐼, 𐐰𐑌𐐼 𐐫𐑊𐑅𐐬 𐐸𐐰𐑃 𐐸𐐨 𐐽𐐰𐑅𐑌𐐼 𐑄𐐯𐑋; 𐐷𐐨𐐩, 𐐮𐑌 𐑄 𐐼𐐩𐑆 𐐲𐑂 𐑄𐐯𐑉 𐐮𐑌𐐿𐐶𐐮𐐻𐐨𐑆 𐐸𐐰𐑃 𐐸𐐨 𐐽𐐰𐑅𐑌𐐼 𐑄𐐯𐑋, 𐐺𐐨𐐿𐐱𐑆 𐐸𐐨 𐑊𐐲𐑂𐐯𐑃 𐑄𐐯𐑋. 𐐒𐐲𐐻 𐐺𐐨𐐸𐐬𐑊𐐼, 𐑋𐐴 𐐺𐑉𐐯𐑄𐑉𐐯𐑌, 𐑄 𐐢𐐲𐑋𐐲𐑌𐐴𐐻𐑅, 𐐸𐐰𐑃 𐐸𐐨 𐐸𐐩𐐻𐐯𐐼, 𐐺𐐨𐐿𐐱𐑆 𐑄𐐯𐑉 𐐼𐐨𐐼𐑆 𐐸𐐰𐑂 𐐺𐐮𐑌 𐐨𐑂𐐲𐑊 𐐿𐐱𐑌𐐻𐐮𐑌𐐷𐐭𐐲𐑊𐐨; 𐐰𐑌𐐼 𐑄𐐮𐑅 𐐺𐐨𐐿𐐱𐑆 𐐲𐑂 𐑄 𐐮𐑌𐐿𐐶𐐮𐐻𐐨 𐐲𐑂 𐑄 𐐻𐑉𐐰𐐼𐐮𐑇𐐲𐑌 𐐲𐑂 𐑄𐐯𐑉 𐑁𐐲𐑄𐐲𐑉𐑆. 𐐒𐐲𐐻 𐐺𐐨𐐸𐐬𐑊𐐼, 𐑅𐐰𐑊𐑂𐐩𐑇𐐲𐑌 𐐸𐐰𐑃 𐐿𐐲𐑋 𐐲𐑌𐐻𐐭 𐑄𐐯𐑋, 𐑃𐑉𐐭 𐑄 𐐹𐑉𐐨𐐽𐐮𐑍 𐐲𐑂 𐑄 𐐤𐐨𐑁𐐴𐐻𐑅; 𐐰𐑌𐐼 𐑁𐐫𐑉 𐑄𐐮𐑅 𐐮𐑌𐐻𐐯𐑌𐐻 𐐸𐐰𐑃 𐑄 𐐢𐐫𐑉𐐼 𐐹𐑉𐐬𐑊𐐱𐑍𐐼 𐑄𐐯𐑉 𐐼𐐩𐑆. 𐐈𐑌𐐼 𐐴 𐐶𐐳𐐼 𐑄𐐰𐐻 𐐷𐐨 𐑇𐐳𐐼 𐐺𐐨𐐸𐐬𐑊𐐼 𐑄𐐰𐐻 𐑄 𐑋𐐬𐑉 𐐹𐐪𐑉𐐻 𐐲𐑂 𐑄𐐯𐑋 𐐪𐑉 𐐮𐑌 𐑄 𐐹𐐰𐑃 𐐲𐑂 𐑄𐐯𐑉 𐐼𐐷𐐭𐐻𐐨, 𐐰𐑌𐐼 𐑄𐐩 𐐼𐐭 𐐶𐐪𐐿 𐑅𐐲𐑉𐐿𐐲𐑋𐑅𐐹𐐯𐐿𐐻𐑊𐐨 𐐺𐐨𐑁𐐫𐑉 𐐘𐐱𐐼, 𐐰𐑌𐐼 𐑄𐐩 𐐼𐐭 𐐲𐐺𐑆𐐲𐑉𐑂 𐐻𐐭 𐐿𐐨𐐹 𐐸𐐮𐑆 𐐿𐐲𐑋𐐰𐑌𐐼𐑋𐐯𐑌𐐻𐑅, 𐐰𐑌𐐼 𐐸𐐮𐑆 𐑅𐐻𐐰𐐻𐐷𐐭𐐻𐑅, 𐐰𐑌𐐼 𐐸𐐮𐑆 𐐾𐐲𐐾𐑋𐐯𐑌𐐻𐑅 𐐰𐐿𐐫𐑉𐐼𐐮𐑍 𐐻𐐭 𐑄 𐑊𐐫 𐐲𐑂 𐐣𐐬𐑆𐐯𐑆. 𐐏𐐨𐐩, 𐐴 𐑅𐐩 𐐲𐑌𐐻𐐭 𐐷𐐭, 𐑄𐐰𐐻 𐑄 𐑋𐐬𐑉 𐐹𐐪𐑉𐐻 𐐲𐑂 𐑄𐐯𐑋 𐐪𐑉 𐐼𐐭𐐮𐑍 𐑄𐐮𐑅, 𐐰𐑌𐐼 𐑄𐐩 𐐪𐑉 𐑅𐐻𐑉𐐴𐑂𐐮𐑍 𐐶𐐮𐑄 𐐲𐑌𐐶𐐨𐑉𐐨𐐼 𐐼𐐮𐑊𐐮𐐾𐐯𐑌𐑅, 𐑄𐐰𐐻 𐑄𐐩 𐑋𐐩 𐐺𐑉𐐮𐑍 𐑄 𐑉𐐯𐑋𐐮𐑌𐐰𐑌𐐻 𐐲𐑂 𐑄𐐯𐑉 𐐺𐑉𐐯𐑄𐑉𐐯𐑌 𐐻𐐭 𐑄 𐑌𐐱𐑊𐐲𐐾 𐐲𐑂 𐑄 𐐻𐑉𐐭𐑃; 𐑄𐐯𐑉𐑁𐐫𐑉 𐑄𐐯𐑉 𐐪𐑉 𐑋𐐰𐑌𐐨 𐐸𐐭 𐐼𐐭 𐐰𐐼 𐐻𐐭 𐑄𐐯𐑉 𐑌𐐲𐑋𐐺𐐲𐑉 𐐼𐐩𐑊𐐨. 𐐈𐑌𐐼 𐐺𐐨𐐸𐐬𐑊𐐼, 𐐷𐐨 𐐼𐐭 𐑌𐐬 𐐲𐑂 𐐷𐐫𐑉𐑅𐐯𐑊𐑂𐑆, 𐑁𐐫𐑉 𐐷𐐨 𐐸𐐰𐑂 𐐶𐐮𐐻𐑌𐐯𐑅𐐻 𐐮𐐻, 𐑄𐐰𐐻 𐐰𐑆 𐑋𐐰𐑌𐐨 𐐲𐑂 𐑄𐐯𐑋 𐐰𐑆 𐐪𐑉 𐐺𐑉𐐫𐐻 𐐻𐐭 𐑄 𐑌𐐱𐑊𐐲𐐾 𐐲𐑂 𐑄 𐐻𐑉𐐭𐑃, 𐐰𐑌𐐼 𐐻𐐭 𐑌𐐬 𐐲𐑂 𐑄 𐐶𐐲𐐿𐐯𐐼 𐐰𐑌𐐼 𐐰𐐺𐐱𐑋𐐮𐑌𐐲𐐺𐑊 𐐻𐑉𐐰𐐼𐐮𐑇𐐲𐑌𐑆 𐐲𐑂 𐑄𐐯𐑉 𐑁𐐲𐑄𐐲𐑉𐑆, 𐐰𐑌𐐼 𐐪𐑉 𐑊𐐯𐐼 𐐻𐐭 𐐺𐐨𐑊𐐨𐑂 𐑄 𐐸𐐬𐑊𐐨 𐑅𐐿𐑉𐐮𐐹𐐽𐐲𐑉𐑆, 𐐷𐐨𐐩, 𐑄 𐐹𐑉𐐱𐑁𐐯𐑅𐐨𐑆 𐐲𐑂 𐑄 𐐸𐐬𐑊𐐨 𐐹𐑉𐐱𐑁𐐯𐐻𐑅, 𐐸𐐶𐐮𐐽 𐐪𐑉 𐑉𐐮𐐻𐑌, 𐐸𐐶𐐮𐐽 𐑊𐐨𐐼𐐯𐑃 𐑄𐐯𐑋 𐐻𐐭 𐑁𐐩𐑃 𐐱𐑌 𐑄 𐐢𐐫𐑉𐐼, 𐐰𐑌𐐼 𐐲𐑌𐐻𐐭 𐑉𐐨𐐹𐐯𐑌𐐻𐐲𐑌𐑅, 𐐸𐐶𐐮𐐽 𐑁𐐩𐑃 𐐰𐑌𐐼 𐑉𐐨𐐹𐐯𐑌𐐻𐐲𐑌𐑅 𐐺𐑉𐐮𐑍𐐯𐑃 𐐩 𐐽𐐩𐑌𐐾 𐐲𐑂 𐐸𐐪𐑉𐐻 𐐲𐑌𐐻𐐭 𐑄𐐯𐑋; 𐑄𐐯𐑉𐑁𐐫𐑉 𐐰𐑆 𐑋𐐰𐑌𐐨 𐐰𐑆 𐐸𐐰𐑂 𐐿𐐲𐑋 𐐻𐐭 𐑄𐐮𐑅, 𐐷𐐨 𐑌𐐬 𐐲𐑂 𐐷𐐫𐑉𐑅𐐯𐑊𐑂𐑆, 𐐪𐑉 𐑁𐐲𐑉𐑋 𐐰𐑌𐐼 𐑅𐐻𐐨𐐼𐑁𐐲𐑅𐐻 𐐮𐑌 𐑄 𐑁𐐩𐑃, 𐐰𐑌𐐼 𐐮𐑌 𐑄 𐑃𐐮𐑍 𐐸𐐶𐐯𐑉𐐶𐐮𐑄 𐑄𐐩 𐐸𐐰𐑂 𐐺𐐨𐑌 𐑋𐐩𐐼 𐑁𐑉𐐨. 𐐈𐑌𐐼 𐐷𐐨 𐑌𐐬 𐐫𐑊𐑅𐐬 𐑄𐐰𐐻 𐑄𐐩 𐐸𐐰𐑂 𐐺𐐲𐑉𐐨𐐼 𐑄𐐯𐑉 𐐶𐐯𐐹𐐲𐑌𐑆 𐐲𐑂 𐐶𐐫𐑉, 𐐰𐑌𐐼 𐑄𐐩 𐑁𐐨𐑉 𐐻𐐭 𐐻𐐩𐐿 𐑄𐐯𐑋 𐐲𐐹, 𐑊𐐯𐑅𐐻 𐐺𐐴 𐐯𐑌𐐨 𐑋𐐨𐑌𐑆 𐑄𐐩

𐑇𐐳𐐼 𐑅𐐮𐑌; 𐐷𐐩, 𐐷 𐐿𐐰𐑌 𐑅𐐨 𐑄𐐰𐐻 𐑄𐐩 𐑁𐐨𐑉 𐐻𐐭 𐑅𐐮𐑌; 𐑁𐐫𐑉 𐐺𐐨𐐸𐐬𐑊𐐼 𐑄𐐩 𐐶𐐮𐑊 𐑅𐐲𐑁𐐲𐑉 𐑄𐐯𐑋𐑅𐐯𐑊𐑂𐑆 𐑄𐐰𐐻 𐑄𐐩 𐐺 𐐻𐑉𐐱𐐼𐐲𐑌 𐐼𐐵𐑌 𐐰𐑌𐐼 𐑅𐑊𐐩𐑌 𐐺𐐴 𐑄𐐯𐑉 𐐯𐑌𐐯𐑋𐐮𐑆, 𐐰𐑌𐐼 𐐶𐐮𐑊 𐑌𐐱𐐻 𐑊𐐮𐑁𐐻 𐑄𐐯𐑉 𐑅𐐬𐑉𐐼𐑆 𐐰𐑀𐐯𐑌𐑅𐐻 𐑄𐐯𐑋; 𐐰𐑌𐐼 𐑄𐐮𐑅 𐐺𐐨𐐿𐐫𐑆 𐐱𐑂 𐑄𐐯𐑉 𐑁𐐩𐑃 𐐮𐑌 𐐗𐑉𐐴𐑅𐐻. 𐐈𐑌𐐼 𐑌𐐵 𐐺𐐨𐐿𐐫𐑆 𐐱𐑂 𐑄𐐯𐑉 𐑅𐐻𐐯𐐼𐑁𐐰𐑅𐐻𐑌𐐯𐑅 𐐸𐐶𐐯𐑌 𐑄𐐩 𐐼𐐭 𐐺𐐨𐑊𐐨𐑂 𐐮𐑌 𐑄𐐰𐐻 𐑃𐐮𐑍 𐐸𐐶𐐮𐐽 𐑄𐐩 𐐼𐐭 𐐺𐐨𐑊𐐨𐑂; 𐑁𐐫𐑉 𐐺𐐨𐐿𐐫𐑆 𐐱𐑂 𐑄𐐯𐑉 𐑁𐐲𐑉𐑋𐑌𐐯𐑅 𐐸𐐶𐐯𐑌 𐑄𐐩 𐐪𐑉 𐐶𐐲𐑌𐑅 𐐯𐑌𐑊𐐴𐐻𐐲𐑌𐐼, 𐐺𐐨𐐸𐐬𐑊𐐼 𐑄 𐐢𐐫𐑉𐐼 𐑇𐐰𐑊 𐐺𐑊𐐯𐑅 𐑄𐐯𐑋 𐐰𐑌𐐼 𐐹𐑉𐐬𐑊𐐱𐑍 𐑄𐐯𐑉 𐐼𐐩𐑆, 𐑌𐐱𐐻𐐶𐐮𐑄𐑅𐐻𐐰𐑌𐐼𐐮𐑍 𐑄𐐯𐑉 𐐮𐑌𐐮𐐿𐐶𐐮𐐻𐐨; 𐐷𐐩, 𐐨𐑂𐐯𐑌 𐐮𐑁 𐑄𐐩 𐑇𐐳𐐼 𐐼𐐶𐐮𐑌𐐼𐐲𐑊 𐐮𐑌 𐐲𐑌𐐺𐐨𐑊𐐨𐑁, 𐑄 𐐢𐐫𐑉𐐼 𐑇𐐰𐑊 𐐹𐑉𐐬𐑊𐐱𐑍 𐑄𐐯𐑉 𐐼𐐩𐑆 𐐲𐑌𐐻𐐮𐑊 𐑄 𐐻𐐴𐑋 𐑇𐐰𐑊 𐐿𐐲𐑋 𐐸𐐶𐐮𐐽 𐐸𐐰𐑃 𐐺𐐮𐑌 𐑅𐐹𐐬𐐿𐐲𐑌 𐐱𐑂 𐐺𐐴 𐐵𐑉 𐑁𐐪𐑄𐐲𐑉𐑆, 𐐰𐑌𐐼 𐐫𐑊𐑅𐐬 𐐺𐐴 𐑄 𐐹𐑉𐐱𐑁𐐯𐐻 𐐞𐐨𐑌𐐱𐑅, 𐐰𐑌𐐼 𐑋𐐯𐑌𐐨 𐐲𐑄𐐲𐑉 𐐹𐑉𐐱𐑁𐐯𐐻𐑅, 𐐿𐐱𐑌𐑅𐐲𐑉𐑌𐐮𐑍 𐑄 𐑉𐐯𐑅𐐻𐐬𐑉𐐩𐑇𐐲𐑌 𐐱𐑂 𐐵𐑉 𐐺𐑉𐐯𐑄𐑉𐐯𐑌, 𐑄 𐐢𐐰𐑋𐐲𐑌𐐴𐐻𐑅, 𐐰𐑀𐐯𐑌, 𐐻𐐭 𐑄 𐑌𐐱𐑊𐐯𐐾 𐐱𐑂 𐑄 𐐻𐑉𐐭𐑃; 𐐷𐐩, 𐐌 𐑅𐐩 𐐲𐑌𐐻𐐭 𐐷𐐭, 𐑄𐐰𐐻 𐐮𐑌 𐑄 𐑊𐐰𐐻𐐲𐑉 𐐻𐐴𐑋𐑆, 𐑄 𐐹𐑉𐐱𐑋𐐮𐑅𐐯𐑆 𐐱𐑂 𐑄 𐐢𐐫𐑉𐐼 𐐸𐐰𐑂 𐐺𐐮𐑌 𐐯𐐿𐑅𐐻𐐯𐑌𐐼𐐯𐐼 𐐻𐐭 𐐵𐑉 𐐺𐑉𐐯𐑄𐑉𐐯𐑌, 𐑄 𐐢𐐰𐑋𐐲𐑌𐐴𐐻𐑅; 𐐰𐑌𐐼 𐑌𐐱𐐻𐐶𐐮𐑄𐑅𐐻𐐰𐑌𐐼𐐮𐑍 𐑄 𐑋𐐯𐑌𐐨 𐐰𐑁𐑊𐐮𐐿𐑇𐐲𐑌𐑆 𐐸𐐶𐐮𐐽 𐑄𐐩 𐑇𐐰𐑊 𐐸𐐰𐑂, 𐐰𐑌𐐼 𐑌𐐱𐐻𐐶𐐮𐑄𐑅𐐻𐐰𐑌𐐼𐐮𐑍 𐑄𐐩 𐑇𐐰𐑊 𐐺 𐐼𐑉𐐮𐑂𐐲𐑌 𐐻𐐭 𐐰𐑌𐐼 𐑁𐑉𐐬 𐐲𐐹𐐱𐑌 𐑄 𐑁𐐩𐑅 𐐱𐑂 𐑄 𐐲𐑉𐑃, 𐐰𐑌𐐼 𐐺 𐐸𐐲𐑌𐐻𐐯𐐼, 𐐰𐑌𐐼 𐑇𐐰𐑊 𐐺 𐑅𐑋𐐮𐐻𐐲𐑌 𐐰𐑌𐐼 𐑅𐐿𐐰𐐻𐐲𐑉𐐼 𐐲𐐺𐑉𐐫𐐼, 𐐸𐐰𐑂𐐮𐑍 𐑌𐐬 𐐹𐑊𐐩𐑅 𐑁𐐫𐑉 𐑉𐐯𐑁𐐷𐐭𐐾, 𐑄 𐐢𐐫𐑉𐐼 𐑇𐐰𐑊 𐐺 𐑋𐐲𐑉𐑅𐐮𐑁𐐳𐑊 𐐲𐑌𐐻𐐭 𐑄𐐯𐑋; 𐐰𐑌𐐼 𐑄𐐮𐑅 𐐮𐑆 𐐰𐐿𐐫𐑉𐐼𐐮𐑍 𐐻𐐭 𐑄 𐐹𐑉𐐱𐑁𐐯𐑅𐐨, 𐑄𐐰𐐻 𐑄𐐩 𐑇𐐰𐑊 𐐺 𐐺𐑉𐐫𐐻 𐐻𐐭 𐑄 𐐻𐑉𐐭 𐑌𐐱𐑊𐐯𐐾, 𐐸𐐶𐐮𐐽 𐐮𐑆 𐑄 𐑌𐐱𐑊𐐯𐐾 𐐱𐑂 𐑄𐐯𐑉 𐐡𐐨𐐼𐐨𐑋𐐲𐑉, 𐐰𐑌𐐼 𐑄𐐯𐑉 𐑀𐑉𐐩𐐻 𐐰𐑌𐐼 𐐻𐑉𐐭 𐐟𐐯𐐹𐐲𐑉𐐼, 𐐰𐑌𐐼 𐐺 𐑌𐐲𐑋𐐺𐐲𐑉𐐼 𐐰𐑋𐐲𐑍 𐐸𐐮𐑆 𐑇𐐨𐐹. 𐐜𐐯𐑉𐑁𐐬𐑉 𐐌 𐑅𐐩 𐐲𐑌𐐻𐐭 𐐷𐐭, 𐐮𐐻 𐑇𐐰𐑊 𐐺 𐐺𐐯𐐻𐐲𐑉 𐑁𐐫𐑉 𐑄𐐯𐑋 𐑄𐐰𐑌 𐑁𐐫𐑉 𐐷𐐭, 𐐯𐐿𐑅𐐯𐐹𐐻 𐐷 𐑉𐐨𐐹𐐯𐑌𐐻. 𐐙𐐫𐑉 𐐺𐐨𐐸𐐬𐑊𐐼, 𐐸𐐰𐐼 𐑄 𐑋𐐴𐐻𐐨 𐐶𐐲𐑉𐐿𐑅 𐐺𐐮𐑌 𐑇𐐬𐑌 𐐲𐑌𐐻𐐭 𐑄𐐯𐑋 𐐸𐐶𐐮𐐽 𐐸𐐰𐑂 𐐺𐐮𐑌 𐑇𐐬𐑌 𐐲𐑌𐐻𐐭 𐐷𐐭; 𐐷𐐩, 𐐲𐑌𐐻𐐭 𐑄𐐯𐑋 𐐸𐐭 𐐸𐐰𐑂 𐐼𐐶𐐮𐑌𐐼𐐲𐑊𐐼 𐐮𐑌 𐐲𐑌𐐺𐐨𐑊𐐨𐑁 𐐺𐐨𐐿𐐫𐑆 𐐱𐑂 𐑄 𐐻𐑉𐐰𐐼𐐮𐑇𐐲𐑌𐑆 𐐱𐑂 𐑄𐐯𐑉 𐑁𐐪𐑄𐐲𐑉𐑆, 𐐷 𐐿𐐰𐑌 𐑅𐐨 𐐱𐑂 𐐷𐐭𐑉𐑅𐐯𐑊𐑂𐑆, 𐑄𐐰𐐻 𐑄𐐩 𐑌𐐯𐑂𐐲𐑉 𐐶𐐳𐐼 𐐰𐑀𐐯𐑌 𐐸𐐰𐑂 𐐼𐐶𐐮𐑌𐐼𐐲𐑊𐐼 𐐮𐑌 𐐲𐑌𐐺𐐨𐑊𐐨𐑁; 𐑄𐐯𐑉𐑁𐐬𐑉, 𐑅𐐯𐑃 𐑄 𐐢𐐫𐑉𐐼, 𐐌 𐐶𐐮𐑊 𐑌𐐱𐐻 𐐲𐐻𐐲𐑉𐑊𐐨 𐐼𐐯𐑅𐐻𐑉𐑎 𐑄𐐯𐑋, 𐐺𐐲𐐻 𐐌 𐐶𐐮𐑊 𐐿𐐫𐑆 𐑄𐐰𐐻 𐐮𐑌 𐑄 𐐼𐐩 𐐱𐑂 𐑋𐐴 𐐶𐐮𐑆𐐼𐐲𐑋, 𐑄𐐩 𐑇𐐰𐑊 𐑉𐐨𐐻𐐲𐑉𐑌 𐐰𐑀𐐯𐑌 𐐲𐑌𐐻𐐭 𐑋𐐨, 𐑅𐐯𐑃 𐑄 𐐢𐐫𐑉𐐼. 𐐈𐑌𐐼 𐑌𐐵 𐐺𐐨𐐸𐐬𐑊𐐼, 𐑅𐐯𐑃 𐑄 𐐢𐐫𐑉𐐼, 𐐿𐐱𐑌𐑅𐐲𐑉𐑌𐐮𐑍 𐑄 𐐹𐐨𐐹𐐲𐑊 𐐱𐑂 𐑄 𐐤𐐨𐑁𐐴𐐻𐑅, 𐐮𐑁 𐑄𐐩 𐐶𐐮𐑊 𐑌𐐱𐐻 𐑉𐐨𐐹𐐯𐑌𐐻, 𐐰𐑌𐐼 𐐱𐐺𐑆𐐲𐑉𐑂 𐐻𐐭 𐐼𐐭 𐑋𐐴 𐐶𐐮𐑊, 𐐌 𐐶𐐮𐑊 𐐲𐐻𐐲𐑉𐑊𐐨 𐐼𐐯𐑅𐐻𐑉𐑎 𐑄𐐯𐑋, 𐑅𐐯𐑃 𐑄 𐐢𐐫𐑉𐐼, 𐐺𐐨𐐿𐐫𐑆 𐐱𐑂 𐑄𐐯𐑉 𐐲𐑌𐐺𐐨𐑊𐐨𐑁, 𐑌𐐱𐐻𐐶𐐮𐑄𐑅𐐻𐐰𐑌𐐼𐐮𐑍 𐑄 𐑋𐐯𐑌𐐨 𐑋𐐴𐐻𐐨 𐐶𐐲𐑉𐐿𐑅 𐐸𐐶𐐮𐐽 𐐌 𐐸𐐰𐑂 𐐼𐐲𐑌 𐐰𐑋𐐲𐑍 𐑄𐐯𐑋; 𐐰𐑌𐐼 𐐰𐑆 𐑇𐐳𐑉𐑊𐐨 𐐰𐑆 𐑄 𐐢𐐫𐑉𐐼 𐑊𐐮𐑂𐐯𐑃, 𐑇𐐰𐑊 𐑄𐐨𐑆 𐑃𐐮𐑍𐑆 𐐺, 𐑅𐐯𐑃 𐑄 𐐢𐐫𐑉𐐼.

9. 𐐈𐑌𐐼 𐑌𐐵 𐐮𐐻 𐐿𐐩𐑋 𐐻𐐭 𐐹𐐰𐑅 𐑄𐐰𐐻 𐑄𐐩𐑉 𐐶𐐲𐑉 𐑋𐐯𐑌𐐨 𐐸𐐭 𐐸𐐲𐑉𐐼 𐑄 𐐶𐐲𐑉𐐼𐑆 𐐱𐑂 𐐝𐐰𐑋𐐷𐐭𐐯𐑊, 𐑄 𐐢𐐰𐑋𐐲𐑌𐐴𐐻, 𐐸𐐶𐐮𐐽 𐐸𐐨 𐑅𐐹𐐩𐐿 𐐲𐐹𐐱𐑌 𐑄 𐐶𐐫𐑊𐑆 𐐱𐑂 𐑄 𐑅𐐮𐐻𐐨. 𐐈𐑌𐐼 𐐰𐑆 𐑋𐐯𐑌𐐨 𐐰𐑆 𐐺𐐨𐑊𐐨𐑂𐐼 𐐱𐑌 𐐸𐐮𐑆 𐐶𐐲𐑉𐐼, 𐐶𐐯𐑌𐐻 𐑁𐐬𐑉𐑃 𐐰𐑌𐐼 𐑅𐐫𐐻 𐑁𐐫𐑉 𐐤𐐨𐑁𐐴; 𐐰𐑌𐐼 𐐸𐐶𐐯𐑌 𐑄𐐩 𐐸𐐰𐐼 𐐿𐐲𐑋 𐑁𐐬𐑉𐑃 𐐰𐑌𐐼 𐑁𐐵𐑌𐐼 𐐸𐐮𐑋, 𐑄𐐩 𐐿𐐱𐑌𐑁𐐯𐑅𐐻 𐐲𐑌𐐻𐐭 𐐸𐐮𐑋 𐑄𐐯𐑉 𐑅𐐮𐑌𐑆, 𐐰𐑌𐐼 𐐼𐐨𐑌𐐴𐐼 𐑌𐐱𐐻, 𐐼𐐨𐑆𐐴𐑉𐐮𐑍 𐑄𐐰𐐻 𐑄𐐩 𐑋𐐴𐐻 𐐺 𐐺𐐰𐐹𐐻𐐴𐑆𐐼 𐐲𐑌𐐻𐐭 𐑄 𐐢𐐫𐑉𐐼. 𐐒𐐲𐐻 𐐰𐑆 𐑋𐐯𐑌𐐨 𐐰𐑆 𐑄𐐩𐑉 𐐶𐐲𐑉 𐐸𐐭 𐐼𐐮𐐼 𐑌𐐱𐐻 𐐺𐐨𐑊𐐨𐑂 𐐮𐑌 𐑄 𐐶𐐲𐑉𐐼𐑆 𐐱𐑂 𐐝𐐰𐑋𐐷𐐭𐐯𐑊, 𐐶𐐲𐑉 𐐰𐑍𐑀𐑉𐐨 𐐶𐐮𐑄 𐐸𐐮𐑋; 𐐰𐑌𐐼 𐑄𐐩 𐐿𐐰𐑅𐐻 𐑅𐐻𐐬𐑌𐑆 𐐰𐐻 𐐸𐐮𐑋 𐐲𐐹𐐱𐑌 𐑄 𐐶𐐫𐑊, 𐐰𐑌𐐼 𐐫𐑊𐑅𐐬 𐑋𐐯𐑌𐐨 𐑇𐐱𐐻 𐐰𐑉𐐬𐑆 𐐰𐐻 𐐸𐐮𐑋, 𐐰𐑆 𐐸𐐨 𐑅𐐻𐐳𐐼 𐐲𐐹𐐱𐑌 𐑄 𐐶𐐫𐑊; 𐐺𐐲𐐻 𐑄 𐐝𐐹𐐮𐑉𐐮𐐻 𐐱𐑂 𐑄 𐐢𐐫𐑉𐐼 𐐶𐐱𐑆 𐐶𐐮𐑄 𐐸𐐮𐑋, 𐐮𐑌𐑅𐐬𐑋𐐲𐐽 𐑄𐐰𐐻 𐑄𐐩 𐐿𐐳𐐼 𐑌𐐱𐐻 𐐸𐐮𐐻 𐐸𐐮𐑋 𐐶𐐮𐑄 𐑄𐐯𐑉 𐑅𐐻𐐬𐑌𐑆, 𐑌𐐨𐑄𐐲𐑉 𐐶𐐮𐑄 𐑄𐐯𐑉 𐐰𐑉𐐬𐑆. 𐐤𐐵 𐐸𐐶𐐯𐑌 𐑄𐐩 𐑅𐐫 𐑄𐐮𐑅, 𐑄𐐰𐐻 𐑄𐐩 𐐿𐐳𐐼 𐑌𐐱𐐻 𐐸𐐮𐐻 𐐸𐐮𐑋, 𐑄𐐩𐑉 𐐶𐐲𐑉 𐑋𐐯𐑌𐐨 𐑋𐐬𐑉 𐐸𐐭 𐐼𐐮𐐼 𐐺𐐨𐑊𐐨𐑂 𐐱𐑌 𐐸𐐮𐑆 𐐶𐐲𐑉𐐼𐑆, 𐐮𐑌𐑅𐐬𐑋𐐲𐐽 𐑄𐐰𐐻 𐑄𐐩 𐐶𐐯𐑌𐐻 𐐰𐐶𐐩 𐐲𐑌𐐻𐐭 𐐤𐐨𐑁𐐴 𐐻𐐭 𐐺 𐐺𐐰𐐹𐐻𐐴𐑆𐐼. 𐐙𐐫𐑉 𐐺𐐨𐐸𐐬𐑊𐐼, 𐐤𐐨𐑁𐐴 𐐶𐐱𐑆 𐐺𐐰𐐹𐐻𐐴𐑆𐐮𐑍, 𐐰𐑌𐐼 𐐹𐑉𐐱𐑁𐐯𐑅𐐴𐐮𐑍, 𐐰𐑌𐐼 𐐹𐑉𐐨𐐽𐐮𐑍, 𐐿𐑉𐐴𐐮𐑍 𐑉𐐨𐐹𐐯𐑌𐐻𐐰𐑌𐑅 𐐲𐑌𐐻𐐭 𐑄 𐐹𐐨𐐹𐐲𐑊; 𐑇𐐬𐐮𐑍 𐑅𐐴𐑌𐑆 𐐰𐑌𐐼 𐐶𐐲𐑌𐐼𐐲𐑉𐑆; 𐐶𐐲𐑉𐐿𐐮𐑍 𐑋𐐮𐑉𐐲𐐿𐐲𐑊𐑆 𐐰𐑋𐐲𐑍 𐑄 𐐹𐐨𐐹𐐲𐑊, 𐑄𐐰𐐻 𐑄𐐩 𐑋𐐴𐐻 𐑌𐐬 𐑄𐐰𐐻 𐑄 𐐗𐑉𐐴𐑅𐐻 𐑋𐐲𐑅𐐻 𐑇𐐫𐑉𐐻𐑊𐐨 𐐿𐐲𐑋; 𐐻𐐯𐑊𐐮𐑍 𐑄𐐯𐑋 𐐱𐑂 𐑃𐐮𐑍𐑆 𐐸𐐶𐐮𐐽 𐑋𐐲𐑅𐐻 𐑇𐐫𐑉𐐻𐑊𐐨 𐐿𐐲𐑋, 𐑄𐐰𐐻 𐑄𐐩 𐑋𐐴𐐻 𐑌𐐬 𐐰𐑌𐐼 𐑉𐐨𐑋𐐯𐑋𐐺𐐲𐑉 𐐰𐐻 𐑄 𐐻𐐴𐑋 𐐱𐑂 𐑄𐐯𐑉 𐐿𐐲𐑋𐐮𐑍 𐑄𐐰𐐻 𐑄𐐩 𐐸𐐰𐐼 𐐺𐐮𐑌 𐑋𐐩𐐼 𐑌𐐬𐑌 𐐲𐑌𐐻𐐭 𐑄𐐯𐑋 𐐺𐐨𐑁𐐬𐑉𐐸𐐰𐑌𐐼, 𐐻𐐭 𐑄 𐐮𐑌𐐻𐐯𐑌𐐻 𐑄𐐰𐐻 𐑄𐐩 𐑋𐐴𐐻 𐐺𐐨𐑊𐐨𐑂; 𐑄𐐯𐑉𐑁𐐬𐑉 𐐰𐑆 𐑋𐐯𐑌𐐨 𐐰𐑆 𐐺𐐨𐑊𐐨𐑂𐐼 𐐱𐑌 𐑄 𐐶𐐲𐑉𐐼𐑆 𐐱𐑂 𐐝𐐰𐑋𐐷𐐭𐐯𐑊, 𐐶𐐯𐑌𐐻 𐑁𐐬𐑉𐑃 𐐲𐑌𐐻𐐭 𐐸𐐮𐑋 𐐻𐐭 𐐺 𐐺𐐰𐐹𐐻𐐴𐑆𐐼, 𐑁𐐫𐑉 𐑄𐐩

𐐿𐐩𐑋 𐑉𐐨𐐹𐐯𐑌𐐻𐐮𐑍 𐐰𐑌𐐼 𐐿𐐱𐑌𐑁𐐯𐑅𐐮𐑍 𐑄𐐩𐑉 𐑅𐐮𐑌𐑆. 𐐒𐐲𐐻 𐑄 𐑋𐐬𐑉 𐐹𐐪𐑉𐐻 𐐱𐑂 𐑄𐐯𐑋 𐐼𐐮𐐼 𐑌𐐱𐐻 𐐺𐐮𐑊𐐨𐑂 𐐮𐑌 𐑄 𐐶𐐲𐑉𐐼𐑆 𐐱𐑂 𐐝𐐰𐑋𐐷𐐭𐐯𐑊; 𐑄𐐩𐑉𐑁𐐬𐑉 𐐸𐐶𐐯𐑌 𐑄𐐩 𐑅𐐫 𐑄𐐰𐐻 𐑄𐐩 𐐿𐐳𐐼 𐑌𐐱𐐻 𐐸𐐮𐐻 𐐸𐐮𐑋 𐐶𐐮𐑃 𐑄𐐩𐑉 𐑅𐐻𐐬𐑌𐑆 𐐰𐑌𐐼 𐑄𐐩𐑉 𐐰𐑉𐐬𐑆, 𐑄𐐩 𐐿𐑉𐐴𐐼 𐐲𐑌𐐻𐐭 𐑄𐐩𐑉 𐐿𐐰𐐹𐐻𐐯𐑌𐑆, 𐑅𐐩𐐮𐑍, 𐐓𐐩𐐿 𐑄𐐮𐑅 𐑁𐐯𐑊𐐬 𐐰𐑌𐐼 𐐺𐐴𐑌𐐼 𐐸𐐮𐑋, 𐑁𐐫𐑉 𐐺𐐨𐐸𐐬𐑊𐐼 𐐸𐐨 𐐸𐐰𐑃 𐐲 𐐼𐐯𐑂𐐮𐑊; 𐐰𐑌𐐼 𐐺𐐨𐐿𐐫𐑆 𐐱𐑂 𐑄 𐐹𐐵𐐲𐑉 𐐱𐑂 𐑄 𐐼𐐯𐑂𐐮𐑊 𐐸𐐶𐐮𐐽 𐐮𐑆 𐐮𐑌 𐐸𐐮𐑋, 𐐶𐐨 𐐿𐐰𐑌𐐱𐐻 𐐸𐐮𐐻 𐐸𐐮𐑋 𐐶𐐮𐑃 𐐵𐐲𐑉 𐑅𐐻𐐬𐑌𐑆 𐐰𐑌𐐼 𐐵𐐲𐑉 𐐰𐑉𐐬𐑆; 𐑄𐐩𐑉𐑁𐐬𐑉 𐐻𐐩𐐿 𐐸𐐮𐑋 𐐰𐑌𐐼 𐐺𐐴𐑌𐐼 𐐸𐐮𐑋, 𐐰𐑌𐐼 𐐲𐐶𐐩 𐐶𐐮𐑃 𐐸𐐮𐑋. 𐐈𐑌𐐼 𐐰𐑆 𐑄𐐩 𐐶𐐯𐑌𐐻 𐑁𐐬𐑉𐑃 𐐻𐐭 𐑊𐐩 𐑄𐐩𐑉 𐐸𐐰𐑌𐐼𐑆 𐐱𐑌 𐐸𐐮𐑋, 𐐺𐐨𐐸𐐬𐑊𐐼 𐐸𐐨 𐐼𐐮𐐼 𐐿𐐰𐑅𐐻 𐐸𐐮𐑋𐑅𐐯𐑊𐑁 𐐼𐐵𐑌 𐑁𐑉𐐱𐑋 𐑄 𐐶𐐫𐑊, 𐐰𐑌𐐼 𐐼𐐮𐐼 𐑁𐑊𐐨 𐐵𐐻 𐐱𐑂 𐑄𐐩𐑉 𐑊𐐰𐑌𐐼𐑆, 𐐷𐐩, 𐐨𐑂𐐯𐑌 𐐲𐑌𐐻𐐭 𐐸𐐮𐑆 𐐬𐑌 𐐿𐐲𐑌𐐻𐑉𐐨, 𐐰𐑌𐐼 𐐺𐐨𐑀𐐰𐑌 𐐻𐐭 𐐹𐑉𐐨𐐽 𐐰𐑌𐐼 𐐻𐐭 𐐹𐑉𐐱𐑁𐐯𐑅𐐴 𐐰𐑋𐐲𐑍 𐐸𐐮𐑆 𐐬𐑌 𐐹𐐨𐐹𐐲𐑊. 𐐈𐑌𐐼 𐐺𐐨𐐸𐐬𐑊𐐼, 𐐸𐐨 𐐶𐐱𐑆 𐑌𐐯𐑂𐐲𐑉 𐐸𐐲𐑉𐐼 𐐱𐑂 𐑋𐐬𐑉 𐐰𐑋𐐲𐑍 𐑄 𐐤𐐨𐑁𐐴𐐻𐑅; 𐐰𐑌𐐼 𐑄𐐲𐑅 𐐶𐐲𐑉 𐑄 𐐰𐑁𐐩𐑉𐑆 𐐱𐑂 𐑄 𐐹𐐨𐐹𐐲𐑊. 𐐈𐑌𐐼 𐑄𐐲𐑅 𐐯𐑌𐐼𐐯𐐼 𐑄 𐐩𐐻𐐨 𐐰𐑌𐐼 𐑅𐐮𐐿𐑅𐑃 𐐷𐐨𐑉 𐐱𐑂 𐑄 𐑉𐐩𐑌 𐐱𐑂 𐑄 𐐾𐐲𐐾𐐯𐑆 𐐬𐑂𐐲𐑉 𐑄 𐐹𐐨𐐹𐐲𐑊 𐐱𐑂 𐐤𐐨𐑁𐐴. 𐐈𐑌𐐼 𐑄𐐲𐑅 𐐯𐑌𐐼𐐯𐐼, 𐐫𐑊𐑅𐐬, 𐑄 𐐩𐐻𐐨 𐐰𐑌𐐼 𐑅𐐯𐑂𐐯𐑌𐑃 𐐷𐐨𐑉 𐐱𐑂 𐑄 𐑉𐐩𐑌 𐐱𐑂 𐑄 𐐾𐐲𐐾𐐯𐑆, 𐑄 𐑋𐐬𐑉 𐐹𐐪𐑉𐐻 𐐱𐑂 𐑄 𐐹𐐨𐐹𐐲𐑊 𐑉𐐨𐑋𐐩𐑌𐐮𐑍 𐐮𐑌 𐑄𐐩𐑉 𐐹𐑉𐐴𐐼 𐐰𐑌𐐼 𐐶𐐮𐐿𐐯𐐼𐑌𐐯𐑅, 𐐰𐑌𐐼 𐑄 𐑊𐐯𐑅𐐲𐑉 𐐹𐐪𐑉𐐻 𐐶𐐫𐐿𐐮𐑍 𐑋𐐬𐑉 𐑅𐐲𐑉𐐿𐐲𐑋𐑅𐐹𐐯𐐿𐐻𐑊𐐨 𐐺𐐨𐑁𐐬𐑉 𐐘𐐱𐐼. 𐐈𐑌𐐼 𐑄𐐨𐑆 𐐶𐐲𐑉 𐑄 𐐿𐐱𐑌𐐼𐐮𐑇𐐲𐑌𐑆 𐐫𐑊𐑅𐐬 𐐮𐑌 𐑄 𐐩𐐻𐐨 𐐰𐑌𐐼 𐐩𐐻𐑃 𐐷𐐨𐑉 𐐱𐑂 𐑄 𐑉𐐩𐑌 𐐱𐑂 𐑄 𐐾𐐲𐐾𐐯𐑆. 𐐈𐑌𐐼 𐑄𐐩𐑉 𐐶𐐱𐑆 𐐺𐐲𐐻 𐑊𐐮𐐻𐑊 𐐫𐑊𐐻𐐲𐑉𐐩𐑇𐐲𐑌 𐐮𐑌 𐑄 𐐰𐑁𐐩𐑉𐑆 𐐱𐑂 𐑄 𐐹𐐨𐐹𐐲𐑊, 𐑅𐐩𐑂 𐐮𐐻 𐐶𐐲𐑉 𐑄 𐐹𐐨𐐹𐐲𐑊 𐐺𐐨𐑀𐐰𐑌 𐐻𐐭 𐐺𐐨 𐑋𐐬𐑉 𐐸𐐪𐑉𐐼𐐯𐑌𐐼 𐐮𐑌 𐐮𐑌𐐮𐐿𐐶𐐮𐐻𐐨, 𐐰𐑌𐐼 𐐼𐐭 𐑋𐐬𐑉 𐐰𐑌𐐼 𐑋𐐬𐑉 𐐱𐑂 𐑄𐐰𐐻 𐐸𐐶𐐮𐐽 𐐶𐐱𐑆 𐐿𐐱𐑌𐐻𐑉𐐩𐑉𐐨 𐐻𐐭 𐑄 𐐿𐐱𐑋𐐰𐑌𐐼𐑋𐐯𐑌𐐻𐑅 𐐱𐑂 𐐘𐐱𐐼, 𐐮𐑌 𐑄 𐐩𐐻𐐨 𐐰𐑌𐐼 𐑌𐐴𐑌𐑃 𐐷𐐨𐑉 𐐱𐑂 𐑄 𐑉𐐩𐑌 𐐱𐑂 𐑄 𐐾𐐲𐐾𐐯𐑆.

10. 𐐒𐐲𐐻 𐐮𐐻 𐐿𐐩𐑋 𐐻𐐭 𐐹𐐰𐑅 𐐮𐑌 𐑄 𐑌𐐴𐑌𐐻𐐨𐐯𐑃 𐐷𐐨𐑉 𐐱𐑂 𐑄 𐑉𐐩𐑌 𐐱𐑂 𐑄 𐐾𐐲𐐾𐐯𐑆, 𐑄𐐩𐑉 𐐶𐐲𐑉 𐑀𐑉𐐩𐐻 𐑅𐐴𐑌𐑆 𐑀𐐮𐑂𐐯𐑌 𐐲𐑌𐐻𐐭 𐑄 𐐹𐐨𐐹𐐲𐑊, 𐐰𐑌𐐼 𐐶𐐲𐑌𐐼𐐲𐑉𐑆; 𐐰𐑌𐐼 𐑄 𐐶𐐲𐑉𐐼𐑆 𐐱𐑂 𐑄 𐐹𐑉𐐱𐑁𐐯𐐻𐑅 𐐺𐐨𐑀𐐰𐑌 𐐻𐐭 𐐺𐐨 𐑁𐐳𐑊𐑁𐐮𐑊𐐼; 𐐰𐑌𐐼 𐐩𐑌𐐾𐐯𐑊𐑆 𐐼𐐮𐐼 𐐰𐐹𐐨𐑉 𐐲𐑌𐐻𐐭 𐑋𐐯𐑌, 𐐶𐐴𐑆 𐑋𐐯𐑌, 𐐰𐑌𐐼 𐐼𐐮𐐼 𐐼𐐨𐐿𐑊𐐩𐑉 𐐲𐑌𐐻𐐭 𐑄𐐯𐑋 𐑀𐑊𐐰𐐼 𐐻𐐴𐐼𐐮𐑍𐑆 𐐱𐑂 𐑀𐑉𐐩𐐻 𐐾𐑎; 𐑄𐐲𐑅 𐐮𐑌 𐑄𐐮𐑅 𐐷𐐨𐑉 𐑄 𐑅𐐿𐑉𐐮𐐹𐐽𐐲𐑉𐑆 𐐺𐐨𐑀𐐰𐑌 𐐻𐐭 𐐺𐐨 𐑁𐐳𐑊𐑁𐐮𐑊𐐼. 𐐤𐐯𐑂𐐲𐑉𐑄𐐯𐑊𐐯𐑅, 𐑄 𐐹𐐨𐐹𐐲𐑊 𐐺𐐨𐑀𐐰𐑌 𐐻𐐭 𐐸𐐪𐑉𐐼𐐯𐑌 𐑄𐐩𐑉 𐐸𐐪𐑉𐐻𐑅, 𐐫𐑊 𐑅𐐩𐑂 𐐮𐐻 𐐶𐐲𐑉 𐑄 𐑋𐐬𐑅𐐻 𐐺𐐮𐑊𐐨𐑂𐐮𐑍 𐐹𐐪𐑉𐐻 𐐱𐑂 𐑄𐐯𐑋, 𐐺𐐬𐑃 𐐱𐑂 𐑄 𐐤𐐨𐑁𐐴𐐻𐑅, 𐐰𐑌𐐼 𐐫𐑊𐑅𐐬 𐐱𐑂 𐑄 𐐢𐐩𐑋𐐲𐑌𐐴𐐻𐑅, 𐐰𐑌𐐼 𐐺𐐨𐑀𐐰𐑌 𐐻𐐭 𐐼𐐨𐐹𐐯𐑌𐐼 𐐲𐐹𐐱𐑌 𐑄𐐩𐑉 𐐬𐑌 𐑅𐐻𐑉𐐯𐑍𐑃 𐐰𐑌𐐼 𐐲𐐹𐐱𐑌 𐑄𐐩𐑉 𐐬𐑌 𐐶𐐮𐑆𐐼𐐲𐑋, 𐑅𐐩𐐮𐑍, 𐐝𐐲𐑋 𐑃𐐮𐑍𐑆 𐑄𐐩 𐑋𐐩 𐐸𐐰𐑂 𐑀𐐯𐑅𐐻 𐑉𐐴𐐻, 𐐰𐑋𐐲𐑍 𐑅𐐬 𐑋𐐯𐑌𐐨; 𐐺𐐲𐐻 𐐺𐐨𐐸𐐬𐑊𐐼, 𐐶𐐨 𐑌𐐬 𐑄𐐰𐐻 𐐫𐑊 𐑄𐐨𐑆 𐑀𐑉𐐩𐐻 𐐰𐑌𐐼 𐑋𐐪𐑉𐑂𐐯𐑊𐐲𐑅 𐐶𐐲𐑉𐐿𐑅 𐐿𐐰𐑌𐐱𐐻 𐐿𐐲𐑋 𐐻𐐭 𐐹𐐰𐑅, 𐐱𐑂 𐐸𐐶𐐮𐐽 𐐸𐐰𐑆 𐐺𐐮𐑌 𐑅𐐹𐐬𐐿𐐯𐑌. 𐐈𐑌𐐼 𐑄𐐩 𐐺𐐨𐑀𐐰𐑌 𐐻𐐭 𐑉𐐨𐑆𐐲𐑌 𐐰𐑌𐐼 𐐻𐐭 𐐿𐐱𐑌𐐻𐐯𐑌𐐼 𐐰𐑋𐐲𐑍 𐑄𐐯𐑋𐑅𐐯𐑊𐑂𐑆, 𐑅𐐩𐐮𐑍, 𐐜𐐰𐐻 𐐮𐐻 𐐮𐑆 𐑌𐐱𐐻 𐑉𐐨𐑆𐐲𐑌𐐲𐐺𐑊 𐑄𐐰𐐻 𐑅𐐲𐐽 𐐲 𐐺𐐨𐐮𐑍 𐐰𐑆 𐐲 𐐗𐑉𐐴𐑅𐐻 𐑇𐐰𐑊 𐐿𐐲𐑋; 𐐮𐑁 𐑅𐐬, 𐐰𐑌𐐼 𐐸𐐨 𐐺𐐨 𐑄 𐐝𐐲𐑌 𐐱𐑂 𐐘𐐱𐐼, 𐑄 𐐙𐐪𐑄𐐲𐑉 𐐱𐑂 𐐸𐐯𐑂𐐯𐑌 𐐰𐑌𐐼 𐐱𐑂 𐐲𐑉𐑃, 𐐰𐑆 𐐮𐐻 𐐸𐐰𐑆 𐐺𐐮𐑌 𐑅𐐹𐐬𐐿𐐯𐑌, 𐐸𐐶𐐴 𐐶𐐮𐑊 𐐸𐐨 𐑌𐐱𐐻 𐑇𐐬 𐐸𐐮𐑋𐑅𐐯𐑊𐑁 𐐲𐑌𐐻𐐭 𐐲𐑅 𐐰𐑆 𐐶𐐯𐑊 𐐰𐑆 𐐲𐑌𐐻𐐭 𐑄𐐯𐑋 𐐸𐐭 𐑇𐐰𐑊 𐐺𐐨 𐐰𐐻 𐐖𐐯𐑉𐐭𐑅𐐲𐑊𐐯𐑋? 𐐏𐐩, 𐐸𐐶𐐴 𐐶𐐮𐑊 𐐸𐐨 𐑌𐐱𐐻 𐑇𐐬 𐐸𐐮𐑋𐑅𐐯𐑊𐑁 𐐮𐑌 𐑄 𐑊𐐰𐑌𐐼 𐐱𐑂 𐐖𐐯𐑉𐐭𐑅𐐲𐑊𐐯𐑋? 𐐒𐐲𐐻 𐐺𐐨𐐸𐐬𐑊𐐼, 𐐶𐐨 𐑌𐐬 𐑄𐐰𐐻 𐑄𐐮𐑅 𐐮𐑆 𐐲 𐐶𐐮𐐿𐐯𐐼 𐐻𐑉𐐰𐐼𐐮𐑇𐐲𐑌, 𐐸𐐶𐐮𐐽 𐐸𐐰𐑆 𐐺𐐮𐑌 𐐸𐐰𐑌𐐼𐐯𐐼 𐐼𐐵𐑌 𐐲𐑌𐐻𐐭 𐐲𐑅 𐐺𐐴 𐐵𐐲𐑉 𐑁𐐪𐑄𐐲𐑉𐑆, 𐐻𐐭 𐐿𐐫𐑆 𐐲𐑅 𐑄𐐰𐐻 𐐶𐐨 𐑇𐐳𐐼 𐐺𐐮𐑊𐐨𐑂 𐐮𐑌 𐑅𐐲𐑋 𐑀𐑉𐐩𐐻 𐐰𐑌𐐼 𐑋𐐪𐑉𐑂𐐯𐑊𐐲𐑅 𐑃𐐮𐑍 𐐸𐐶𐐮𐐽 𐑇𐐳𐐼 𐐿𐐲𐑋 𐐻𐐭 𐐹𐐰𐑅, 𐐺𐐲𐐻 𐑌𐐱𐐻 𐐰𐑋𐐲𐑍 𐐲𐑅, 𐐺𐐲𐐻 𐐮𐑌 𐐲 𐑊𐐰𐑌𐐼 𐐸𐐶𐐮𐐽 𐐮𐑆 𐑁𐐪𐑉 𐐼𐐮𐑅𐐻𐐰𐑌𐐻, 𐐲 𐑊𐐰𐑌𐐼 𐐸𐐶𐐮𐐽 𐐶𐐨 𐑌𐐬 𐑌𐐱𐐻; 𐑄𐐩𐑉𐑁𐐬𐑉 𐑄𐐩 𐐿𐐰𐑌 𐐿𐐨𐐹 𐐲𐑅 𐐮𐑌 𐐮𐑀𐑌𐐬𐑉𐐰𐑌𐑅, 𐑁𐐫𐑉 𐐶𐐨 𐐿𐐰𐑌𐐱𐐻 𐐶𐐮𐐻𐑌𐐯𐑅 𐐶𐐮𐑃 𐐵𐐲𐑉 𐐬𐑌 𐐴𐑆 𐑄𐐰𐐻 𐑄𐐩 𐐪𐑉 𐐻𐑉𐐭. 𐐈𐑌𐐼 𐑄𐐩 𐐶𐐮𐑊, 𐐺𐐴 𐑄 𐐿𐐲𐑌𐐮𐑍 𐐰𐑌𐐼 𐑄 𐑋𐐮𐑅𐐻𐐨𐑉𐐨𐐲𐑅 𐐪𐑉𐐻𐑅 𐐱𐑂 𐑄 𐐨𐑂𐐮𐑊 𐐶𐐲𐑌, 𐐶𐐲𐑉𐐿 𐑅𐐲𐑋 𐑀𐑉𐐩𐐻 𐑋𐐮𐑅𐐻𐐲𐑉𐐨 𐐸𐐶𐐮𐐽 𐐶𐐨 𐐿𐐰𐑌𐐱𐐻 𐐲𐑌𐐼𐐲𐑉𐑅𐐻𐐰𐑌𐐼, 𐐸𐐶𐐮𐐽 𐐶𐐮𐑊 𐐿𐐨𐐹 𐐲𐑅 𐐼𐐵𐑌 𐐻𐐭 𐐺𐐨 𐑅𐐲𐑉𐑂𐐰𐑌𐐻𐑅 𐐻𐐭 𐑄𐐩𐑉 𐐶𐐲𐑉𐐼𐑆, 𐐰𐑌𐐼 𐐫𐑊𐑅𐐬 𐑅𐐲𐑉𐑂𐐰𐑌𐐻𐑅 𐐲𐑌𐐻𐐭 𐑄𐐯𐑋, 𐑁𐐫𐑉 𐐶𐐨 𐐼𐐨𐐹𐐯𐑌𐐼 𐐲𐐹𐐱𐑌 𐑄𐐯𐑋 𐐻𐐭 𐐻𐐨𐐽 𐐲𐑅 𐑄 𐐶𐐲𐑉𐐼; 𐐰𐑌𐐼 𐑄𐐲𐑅 𐐶𐐮𐑊 𐑄𐐩 𐐿𐐨𐐹 𐐲𐑅 𐐮𐑌 𐐮𐑀𐑌𐐬𐑉𐐰𐑌𐑅, 𐐮𐑁 𐐶𐐨 𐐶𐐮𐑊 𐐷𐐨𐑊𐐼 𐐵𐐲𐑉𐑅𐐯𐑊𐑂𐑆 𐐲𐑌𐐻𐐭 𐑄𐐯𐑋, 𐐫𐑊 𐑄 𐐼𐐩𐑆 𐐱𐑂 𐐵𐐲𐑉 𐑊𐐴𐑂𐑆. 𐐈𐑌𐐼 𐑋𐐯𐑌𐐨 𐑋𐐬𐑉 𐑃𐐮𐑍𐑆 𐐼𐐮𐐼 𐑄 𐐹𐐨𐐹𐐲𐑊 𐐮𐑋𐐰𐐾𐐮𐑌 𐐲𐐹 𐐮𐑌 𐑄𐐩𐑉 𐐸𐐪𐑉𐐻𐑅, 𐐸𐐶𐐮𐐽 𐐶𐐲𐑉 𐑁𐐭𐑊𐐮𐑇 𐐰𐑌𐐼 𐑂𐐩𐑌; 𐐰𐑌𐐼 𐑄𐐩 𐐶𐐲𐑉 𐑋𐐲𐐽 𐐼𐐮𐑅𐐻𐐲𐑉𐐺𐐼, 𐑁𐐫𐑉 𐐝𐐩𐐻𐐲𐑌 𐐼𐐮𐐼 𐑅𐐻𐐲𐑉 𐑄𐐯𐑋 𐐲𐐹 𐐻𐐭 𐐼𐐭 𐐮𐑌𐐮𐐿𐐶𐐮𐐻𐐨 𐐿𐐱𐑌𐐻𐐮𐑌𐐷𐐭-

𐐓𐐆𐐤𐐏𐐊𐐢𐐆; 𐐏𐐀, 𐐸𐐀 𐐔𐐆𐐔 𐐘𐐄 𐐊𐐒𐐍𐐓 𐐝𐐑𐐡𐐇𐐔𐐆𐐥 𐐡𐐅𐐣𐐊𐐡𐐞 𐐈𐐤𐐔 𐐗𐐊𐐤𐐓𐐇𐐤𐐟𐐊𐐤𐐞 𐐊𐐑𐐊𐐤 𐐃𐐢 𐐜 𐐙𐐁𐐝 𐐊𐐚 𐐜 𐐢𐐈𐐤𐐔, 𐐜𐐈𐐓 𐐸𐐀 𐐣𐐌𐐓 𐐐𐐂𐐡𐐔𐐤 𐐜 𐐐𐐂𐐡𐐓𐐝 𐐊𐐚 𐐜 𐐑𐐀𐐑𐐊𐐢 𐐊𐐘𐐇𐐤𐐝𐐓 𐐜𐐈𐐓 𐐐𐐎𐐆𐐗 𐐎𐐊𐐞 𐐘𐐋𐐔, 𐐈𐐤𐐔 𐐊𐐘𐐇𐐤𐐝𐐓 𐐜𐐈𐐓 𐐐𐐎𐐆𐐗 𐐟𐐋𐐔 𐐗𐐊𐐣; 𐐈𐐤𐐔 𐐤𐐊𐐓𐐎𐐆𐐜𐐝𐐓𐐈𐐤𐐔𐐆𐐥 𐐜 𐐝𐐌𐐤𐐞 𐐈𐐤𐐔 𐐜 𐐎𐐊𐐤𐐔𐐊𐐡𐐞 𐐐𐐎𐐆𐐗 𐐎𐐊𐐡 𐐡𐐃𐐓 𐐊𐐣𐐊𐐥 𐐜 𐐑𐐀𐐑𐐊𐐢 𐐊𐐚 𐐜 𐐢𐐃𐐡𐐔, 𐐈𐐤𐐔 𐐜 𐐣𐐇𐐤𐐆 𐐣𐐌𐐡𐐊𐐗𐐊𐐢𐐞 𐐐𐐎𐐆𐐗 𐐜𐐁 𐐔𐐆𐐔, 𐐝𐐁𐐓𐐊𐐤 𐐔𐐆𐐔 𐐘𐐇𐐓 𐐘𐐡𐐁𐐓 𐐐𐐄𐐢𐐔 𐐊𐐑𐐊𐐤 𐐜 𐐐𐐂𐐡𐐓𐐝 𐐊𐐚 𐐜 𐐑𐐀𐐑𐐊𐐢, 𐐊𐐑𐐊𐐤 𐐃𐐢 𐐜 𐐙𐐁𐐝 𐐊𐐚 𐐜 𐐢𐐈𐐤𐐔. 𐐈𐐤𐐔 𐐜𐐊𐐝 𐐇𐐤𐐔𐐇𐐔 𐐜 𐐤𐐌𐐤𐐓𐐀𐐇𐐛 𐐏𐐀𐐡 𐐊𐐚 𐐜 𐐡𐐁𐐤 𐐊𐐚 𐐜 𐐖𐐊𐐖𐐇𐐞 𐐄𐐚𐐊𐐡 𐐜 𐐑𐐀𐐑𐐊𐐢 𐐊𐐚 𐐤𐐀𐐙𐐌. 𐐈𐐤𐐔 𐐜𐐊𐐝 𐐇𐐤𐐔𐐇𐐔 𐐜 𐐒𐐋𐐗 𐐊𐐚 𐐐𐐇𐐢𐐊𐐣𐐊𐐤, 𐐊𐐗𐐃𐐡𐐔𐐆𐐥 𐐓𐐅 𐐜 𐐡𐐇𐐗𐐊𐐡𐐔 𐐊𐐚 𐐐𐐇𐐢𐐊𐐣𐐊𐐤 𐐈𐐤𐐔 𐐐𐐆𐐞 𐐝𐐊𐐤𐐞.

𐐜 𐐒𐐳𐐿 𐐱𐑂 𐐤𐐨𐑁𐐴,

𐐜 𐑅𐐲𐑌 𐐱𐑂 𐐤𐐨𐑁𐐴, 𐐸𐐭 𐐶𐐱𐑆 𐑄 𐑅𐐲𐑌 𐐱𐑂 𐐐𐐨𐑊𐐩𐑋𐐲𐑌.

𐐗𐐰𐐹𐐻𐐲𐑉 I.

𐐈𐑌𐐼 𐐐𐐨𐑊𐐩𐑋𐐲𐑌 𐐶𐐱𐑆 𐑄 𐑅𐐲𐑌 𐐱𐑂 𐐐𐐨𐑊𐐩𐑋𐐲𐑌, 𐐸𐐭 𐐶𐐱𐑆 𐑄 𐑅𐐲𐑌 𐐱𐑂 𐐈𐑊𐑋𐐰, 𐐸𐐭 𐐶𐐱𐑆 𐑄 𐑅𐐲𐑌 𐐱𐑂 𐐈𐑊𐑋𐐰, 𐐺𐐨𐐮𐑍 𐐲 𐐼𐐨𐑅𐐯𐑌𐐼𐐰𐑌𐐻 𐐱𐑂 𐐤𐐨𐑁𐐴 𐐸𐐭 𐐶𐐱𐑆 𐑄 𐑅𐐲𐑌 𐐱𐑂 𐐢𐐨𐐸𐐴, 𐐸𐐭 𐐿𐐩𐑋 𐐵𐐻 𐐱𐑂 𐐖𐐲𐑉𐐭𐑅𐐲𐑊𐐯𐑋 𐐮𐑌 𐑄 𐑁𐐲𐑉𐑅𐐻 𐐷𐐨𐑉 𐐱𐑂 𐑄 𐑉𐐩𐑌 𐐱𐑂 𐐞𐐯𐐼𐐯𐐿𐐴𐐲, 𐑄 𐐿𐐮𐑍 𐐱𐑂 𐐖𐐭𐐼𐐲.

1. 𐐤𐐵 𐐮𐐻 𐐿𐐩𐑋 𐐻𐐭 𐐹𐐰𐑅 𐑄𐐰𐐻 𐑄 𐑌𐐴𐑌𐐻𐐨 𐐰𐑌𐐼 𐑁𐐲𐑉𐑅𐐻 𐐷𐐨𐑉 𐐸𐐰𐐼 𐐹𐐰𐑅𐐻 𐐲𐐶𐐩, 𐐰𐑌𐐼 𐐮𐐻 𐐶𐐱𐑆 𐑅𐐮𐐿𐑅 𐐸𐐲𐑌𐐼𐑉𐐯𐐼 𐐷𐐨𐑉𐑆 𐑁𐑉𐐱𐑋 𐑄 𐐻𐐴𐑋 𐑄𐐰𐐻 𐐢𐐨𐐸𐐴 𐑊𐐯𐑁𐐻 𐐖𐐲𐑉𐐭𐑅𐐲𐑊𐐯𐑋; 𐐰𐑌𐐼 𐐮𐐻 𐐶𐐱𐑆 𐐮𐑌 𐑄 𐐷𐐨𐑉 𐑄𐐰𐐻 𐐢𐐰𐐿𐐬𐑌𐐨𐐲𐑅 𐐶𐐱𐑆 𐑄 𐐽𐐨𐑁 𐐖𐐲𐐾 𐐰𐑌𐐼 𐑄 𐑀𐐲𐑂𐐲𐑉𐑌𐐲𐑉 𐐬𐑂𐐲𐑉 𐑄 𐑊𐐰𐑌𐐼. 𐐈𐑌𐐼 𐐤𐐨𐑁𐐴, 𐑄 𐑅𐐲𐑌 𐐱𐑂 𐐐𐐨𐑊𐐩𐑋𐐲𐑌, 𐐸𐐰𐐼 𐐼𐐨𐐹𐐪𐑉𐐻𐐯𐐼 𐐵𐐻 𐐱𐑂 𐑄 𐑊𐐰𐑌𐐼 𐐱𐑂 𐐞𐐰𐑉𐐲𐐸𐐯𐑋𐑊𐐲, 𐑀𐐮𐑂𐐮𐑍 𐐽𐐪𐑉𐐾 𐐲𐑌𐐻𐐭 𐐸𐐮𐑆 𐑅𐐲𐑌 𐐤𐐨𐑁𐐴, 𐐸𐐭 𐐶𐐱𐑆 𐐸𐐮𐑆 𐐯𐑊𐐼𐐯𐑅𐐻 𐑅𐐲𐑌, 𐐿𐐱𐑌𐑅𐐲𐑉𐑌𐐮𐑍 𐑄 𐐹𐑊𐐩𐐻𐑅 𐐱𐑂 𐐺𐑉𐐰𐑅, 𐐰𐑌𐐼 𐐫𐑊 𐑄 𐑉𐐯𐐿𐐲𐑉𐐼𐑆 𐐸𐐶𐐮𐐽 𐐸𐐰𐐼 𐐺𐐨𐑌 𐐿𐐯𐐹𐐻, 𐐰𐑌𐐼 𐐫𐑊 𐑄𐐬𐑆 𐑃𐐮𐑍𐑆 𐐸𐐶𐐮𐐽 𐐸𐐰𐐼 𐐺𐐨𐑌 𐐿𐐯𐐹𐐻 𐑅𐐩𐐿𐑉𐐯𐐼 𐑁𐑉𐐱𐑋 𐑄 𐐼𐐨𐐹𐐪𐑉𐐽𐐲𐑉 𐐱𐑂 𐐢𐐨𐐸𐐴 𐐵𐐻 𐐱𐑂 𐐖𐐲𐑉𐐭𐑅𐐲𐑊𐐯𐑋; 𐑄𐐯𐑌 𐐸𐐨 𐐼𐐨𐐹𐐪𐑉𐐻𐐯𐐼 𐐵𐐻 𐐱𐑂 𐑄 𐑊𐐰𐑌𐐼, 𐐰𐑌𐐼 𐐸𐐶𐐮𐑄𐐲𐑉 𐐸𐐨 𐐶𐐯𐑌𐐻, 𐑌𐐬 𐑋𐐰𐑌 𐑌𐐬𐐯𐑃; 𐐰𐑌𐐼 𐐸𐐮𐑆 𐑅𐐲𐑌 𐐤𐐨𐑁𐐴 𐐼𐐮𐐼 𐐿𐐨𐐹 𐑄 𐑉𐐯𐐿𐐲𐑉𐐼𐑆 𐐮𐑌 𐐸𐐮𐑆 𐑅𐐻𐐯𐐼, 𐐷𐐩, 𐑄 𐑉𐐯𐐿𐐲𐑉𐐼 𐐱𐑂 𐑄𐐮𐑅 𐐹𐐨𐐹𐐲𐑊.

2. 𐐈𐑌𐐼 𐐮𐐻 𐐿𐐩𐑋 𐐻𐐭 𐐹𐐰𐑅 𐑄𐐰𐐻 𐐮𐑌 𐑄 𐐿𐐱𐑋𐐯𐑌𐑅𐑋𐐯𐑌𐐻 𐐱𐑂 𐑄 𐑌𐐴𐑌𐐻𐐨 𐐰𐑌𐐼 𐑅𐐯𐐿𐐲𐑌𐐼 𐐷𐐨𐑉, 𐐺𐐨𐐸𐐬𐑊𐐼, 𐑄 𐐹𐑉𐐱𐑁𐐯𐑅𐐨𐑆 𐐱𐑂 𐑄 𐐹𐑉𐐱𐑁𐐯𐐻𐑅 𐐺𐐨𐑀𐐰𐑌 𐐻𐐭 𐐺𐐨 𐑁𐐳𐑊𐑁𐐮𐑊𐐼 𐑋𐐬𐑉 𐑁𐐳𐑊𐐨; 𐑁𐐫𐑉 𐑄𐐯𐑉 𐐺𐐨𐑀𐐰𐑌 𐐻𐐭 𐐺𐐨 𐑀𐑉𐐩𐐻𐐲𐑉 𐑅𐐴𐑌𐑆 𐐰𐑌𐐼 𐑀𐑉𐐩𐐻𐐲𐑉 𐑋𐐮𐑉𐐲𐐿𐐲𐑊𐑆 𐑉𐐫𐐻 𐐲𐑋𐐲𐑍 𐑄 𐐹𐐨𐐹𐐲𐑊. 𐐒𐐲𐐻 𐑄𐐯𐑉 𐐶𐐲𐑉 𐑅𐐲𐑋 𐐸𐐭 𐐺𐐨𐑀𐐰𐑌 𐐻𐐭 𐑅𐐩 𐑄𐐰𐐻 𐑄 𐐻𐐴𐑋 𐐶𐐱𐑆 𐐹𐐰𐑅𐐻 𐑁𐐫𐑉 𐑄 𐐶𐐲𐑉𐐼𐑆 𐐻𐐭 𐐺𐐨 𐑁𐐳𐑊𐑁𐐮𐑊𐐼, 𐐸𐐶𐐮𐐽 𐐶𐐲𐑉 𐑅𐐹𐐬𐐿𐐲𐑌 𐐺𐐴 𐐝𐐰𐑋𐐷𐐲𐐰𐑊, 𐑄 𐐢𐐩𐑋𐐲𐑌𐐴𐐻. 𐐈𐑌𐐼 𐑄𐐩 𐐺𐐨𐑀𐐰𐑌 𐐻𐐭 𐑉𐐨𐐾𐐱𐐮𐑅 𐐬𐑂𐐲𐑉 𐑄𐐯𐑉 𐐺𐑉𐐯𐑄𐑉𐐯𐑌, 𐑅𐐩𐐮𐑍, 𐐒𐐨𐐸𐐬𐑊𐐼 𐑄 𐐻𐐴𐑋 𐐮𐑆 𐐹𐐰𐑅𐐻, 𐐰𐑌𐐼 𐑄 𐐶𐐲𐑉𐐼𐑆 𐐱𐑂 𐐝𐐰𐑋𐐷𐐲𐐰𐑊 𐐪𐑉 𐑌𐐱𐐻 𐑁𐐳𐑊𐑁𐐮𐑊𐐼: 𐑄𐐯𐑉𐑁𐐬𐑉, 𐐷𐐭𐑉 𐐾𐐱𐐮 𐐰𐑌𐐼 𐐷𐐭𐑉 𐑁𐐩𐑃 𐐿𐐱𐑌𐑅𐐲𐑉𐑌𐐮𐑍 𐑄𐐮𐑅 𐑃𐐮𐑍, 𐐸𐐰𐑃 𐐺𐐨𐑌 𐑂𐐩𐑌. 𐐈𐑌𐐼 𐐮𐐻 𐐿𐐩𐑋 𐐻𐐭 𐐹𐐰𐑅 𐑄𐐰𐐻 𐑄𐐩 𐐼𐐮𐐼 𐑋𐐩𐐿 𐐲 𐑀𐑉𐐩𐐻 𐐲𐐹𐑉𐐫𐑉 𐑃𐑉𐐭𐐵𐐻 𐑄 𐑊𐐰𐑌𐐼; 𐐰𐑌𐐼 𐑄 𐐹𐐨𐐹𐐲𐑊 𐐸𐐭 𐐺𐐨𐑊𐐨𐑂𐐼 𐐺𐐨𐑀𐐰𐑌 𐐻𐐭 𐐺𐐨 𐑂𐐯𐑉𐐨 𐑅𐐱𐑉𐐬𐑁𐐳𐑊, 𐑊𐐯𐑅𐐻 𐐺𐐴 𐐯𐑌𐐨 𐑋𐐨𐑌𐑆 𐑄𐐬𐑆 𐑃𐐮𐑍𐑆 𐐸𐐶𐐮𐐽 𐐸𐐰𐐼 𐐺𐐨𐑌 𐑅𐐹𐐬𐐿𐐲𐑌 𐑋𐐴𐐻 𐑌𐐱𐐻 𐐿𐐲𐑋 𐐻𐐭 𐐹𐐰𐑅. 𐐒𐐲𐐻 𐐺𐐨𐐸𐐬𐑊𐐼, 𐑄𐐩 𐐼𐐮𐐼 𐐶𐐱𐐽 𐑅𐐻𐐯𐐼𐑁𐐰𐑅𐐻𐑊𐐨 𐑁𐐫𐑉 𐑄𐐰𐐻 𐐼𐐩, 𐐰𐑌𐐼 𐑄𐐰𐐻 𐑌𐐴𐐻, 𐐰𐑌𐐼 𐑄𐐰𐐻 𐐼𐐩, 𐐸𐐶𐐮𐐽 𐑇𐐳𐐼 𐐺𐐨 𐐰𐑆 𐐶𐐲𐑌 𐐼𐐩, 𐐰𐑆 𐐮𐑁 𐑄𐐯𐑉 𐐶𐐲𐑉 𐑌𐐬 𐑌𐐴𐐻, 𐑄𐐰𐐻 𐑄𐐩 𐑋𐐴𐐻 𐑌𐐬 𐑄𐐰𐐻 𐑄𐐯𐑉 𐑁𐐩𐑃 𐐸𐐰𐐼 𐑌𐐱𐐻 𐐺𐐨𐑌 𐑂𐐩𐑌.

3. 𐐤𐐵 𐐮𐐻 𐐿𐐩𐑋 𐐻𐐭 𐐹𐐰𐑅 𐑄𐐰𐐻 𐑄𐐯𐑉 𐐶𐐱𐑆 𐐲 𐐼𐐩 𐑅𐐯𐐻 𐐲𐐹𐐪𐑉𐐻 𐐺𐐴 𐑄 𐐲𐑌𐐺𐐨𐑊𐐨𐑂𐐲𐑉𐑆, 𐑄𐐰𐐻 𐐫𐑊 𐑄𐐬𐑆 𐐸𐐭 𐐺𐐨𐑊𐐨𐑂𐐼 𐐮𐑌 𐑄𐐬𐑆 𐐻𐑉𐐲𐐼𐐮𐑇𐐲𐑌𐑆 𐑇𐐳𐐼 𐐺𐐨 𐐹𐐳𐐻 𐐻𐐭 𐐼𐐯𐑃 𐐯𐐿𐑅𐐯𐐹𐐻 𐑄 𐑅𐐴𐑌 𐑇𐐳𐐼 𐐿𐐲𐑋 𐐻𐐭 𐐹𐐰𐑅, 𐐸𐐶𐐮𐐽 𐐸𐐰𐐼 𐐺𐐨𐑌 𐑀𐐮𐑂𐐲𐑌 𐐺𐐴 𐐝𐐰𐑋𐐷𐐲𐐰𐑊 𐑄 𐐹𐑉𐐱𐑁𐐯𐐻. 𐐤𐐵 𐐮𐐻 𐐿𐐩𐑋 𐐻𐐭 𐐹𐐰𐑅 𐑄𐐰𐐻 𐐸𐐶𐐯𐑌 𐐤𐐨𐑁𐐴, 𐑄 𐑅𐐲𐑌 𐐱𐑂 𐐤𐐨𐑁𐐴, 𐑅𐐫 𐑄𐐮𐑅 𐐶𐐮𐐿𐐯𐐼𐑌𐐯𐑅 𐐱𐑂 𐐸𐐮𐑆 𐐹𐐨𐐹𐐲𐑊, 𐐸𐐮𐑆 𐐸𐐪𐑉𐐻 𐐶𐐱𐑆 𐐯𐐿𐑅𐐨𐐼𐐮𐑍𐑊𐐨

𐑅𐐱𐑉𐐬𐑁𐐳𐑊. 𐐈𐑌𐐼 𐐮𐐻 𐐿𐐩𐑋 𐐻𐐭 𐐹𐐪𐑅 𐑄𐐰𐐻 𐐸𐐨 𐐶𐐯𐑌𐐻 𐐵𐐻 𐐰𐑌𐐼 𐐺𐐵𐐼 𐐸𐐮𐑋𐑅𐐯𐑊𐑁 𐐼𐐵𐑌 𐐲𐐹𐐱𐑌 𐑄 𐐲𐑉𐑃, 𐐰𐑌𐐼 𐐿𐑉𐐴𐐼 𐑋𐐴𐐻𐐮𐑊𐐨 𐐻𐐭 𐐸𐐮𐑆 𐐘𐐱𐐼, 𐐮𐑌 𐐺𐐨𐐸𐐪𐑁 𐐱𐑂 𐐸𐐮𐑆 𐐹𐐨𐐹𐑊; 𐐷𐐩, 𐑄𐐬𐑆 𐐸𐐭 𐐶𐐲𐑉 𐐰𐐺𐐵𐐻 𐐻𐐭 𐐺 𐐼𐐲𐑅𐐻𐑉𐐱𐐮𐐼 𐐺𐐨𐐿𐐱𐑆 𐐱𐑂 𐑄𐐩𐑉 𐑁𐐩𐑃 𐐮𐑌 𐑄 𐐻𐑉𐐰𐐼𐐮𐑇𐐲𐑌 𐐱𐑂 𐑄𐐩𐑉 𐑁𐐪𐑄𐐲𐑉𐑆. 𐐈𐑌𐐼 𐐮𐐻 𐐿𐐩𐑋 𐐻𐐭 𐐹𐐪𐑅 𐑄𐐰𐐻 𐐸𐐨 𐐿𐑉𐐴𐐼 𐑋𐐴𐐻𐐮𐑊𐐨 𐐲𐑌𐐻𐐭 𐑄 𐐢𐐫𐑉𐐼, 𐐫𐑊 𐑄 𐐼𐐩; 𐐰𐑌𐐼 𐐺𐐨𐐸𐐬𐑊𐐼, 𐑄 𐑂𐐱𐐮𐑅 𐐱𐑂 𐑄 𐐢𐐫𐑉𐐼 𐐿𐐩𐑋 𐐲𐑌𐐻𐐭 𐐸𐐮𐑋, 𐑅𐐩𐐮𐑍, 𐐢𐐮𐑁𐐻 𐐲𐐹 𐐷𐐫𐑉 𐐸𐐯𐐼 𐐰𐑌𐐼 𐐺 𐐱𐑂 𐑀𐐳𐐼 𐐽𐐨𐑉, 𐑁𐐫𐑉 𐐺𐐨𐐸𐐬𐑊𐐼, 𐑄 𐐻𐐴𐑋 𐐮𐑆 𐐰𐐻 𐐸𐐰𐑌𐐼, 𐐰𐑌𐐼 𐐱𐑌 𐑄𐐮𐑅 𐑌𐐴𐐻 𐑇𐐰𐑊 𐑄 𐑅𐐴𐑌 𐐺 𐑀𐐮𐑂𐐲𐑌, 𐐰𐑌𐐼 𐐱𐑌 𐑄 𐑋𐐱𐑉𐐬 𐐿𐐲𐑋 𐐌 𐐮𐑌𐐻𐐭 𐑄 𐐶𐐲𐑉𐑊𐐼, 𐐻𐐭 𐑇𐐬 𐐲𐑌𐐻𐐭 𐑄 𐐶𐐲𐑉𐑊𐐼 𐑄𐐰𐐻 𐐌 𐐶𐐮𐑊 𐑁𐐳𐑊𐑁𐐮𐑊 𐐫𐑊 𐑄𐐰𐐻 𐐸𐐶𐐮𐐽 𐐌 𐐸𐐰𐑂 𐐿𐐫𐑆𐐼 𐐻𐐭 𐐺 𐑅𐐹𐐬𐐿𐐲𐑌 𐐺𐐴 𐑄 𐑋𐐵𐑃 𐐱𐑂 𐑋𐐴 𐐸𐐬𐑊𐐨 𐐹𐑉𐐱𐑁𐐯𐐻𐑅. 𐐒𐐨𐐸𐐬𐑊𐐼, 𐐌 𐐿𐐲𐑋 𐐲𐑌𐐻𐐭 𐑋𐐴 𐐬𐑌, 𐐻𐐭 𐑁𐐳𐑊𐑁𐐮𐑊 𐐫𐑊 𐑃𐐮𐑍𐑆 𐐸𐐶𐐮𐐽 𐐌 𐐸𐐰𐑂 𐑋𐐩𐐼 𐑌𐐬𐑌 𐐲𐑌𐐻𐐭 𐑄 𐐽𐐮𐑊𐐼𐑉𐐯𐑌 𐐱𐑂 𐑋𐐯𐑌, 𐑁𐑉𐐲𐑋 𐑄 𐑁𐐵𐑌𐐼𐐩𐑇𐐲𐑌 𐐱𐑂 𐑄 𐐶𐐲𐑉𐑊𐐼, 𐐰𐑌𐐼 𐐻𐐭 𐐼𐐭 𐑄 𐐶𐐮𐑊, 𐐺𐐬𐑃 𐐱𐑂 𐑄 𐐙𐐪𐑄𐐲𐑉, 𐐰𐑌𐐼 𐐱𐑂 𐑄 𐐝𐐲𐑌, 𐐱𐑂 𐑄 𐐙𐐪𐑄𐐲𐑉, 𐐺𐐨𐐿𐐱𐑆 𐐱𐑂 𐑋𐐨, 𐐰𐑌𐐼 𐐱𐑂 𐑄 𐐝𐐲𐑌, 𐐺𐐨𐐿𐐱𐑆 𐐱𐑂 𐑋𐐴 𐑁𐑊𐐯𐑇. 𐐈𐑌𐐼 𐐺𐐨𐐸𐐬𐑊𐐼, 𐑄 𐐻𐐴𐑋 𐐮𐑆 𐐰𐐻 𐐸𐐰𐑌𐐼, 𐐰𐑌𐐼 𐑄𐐮𐑅 𐑌𐐴𐐻 𐑇𐐰𐑊 𐑄 𐑅𐐴𐑌 𐐺 𐑀𐐮𐑂𐐲𐑌.

4. 𐐈𐑌𐐼 𐐮𐐻 𐐿𐐩𐑋 𐐻𐐭 𐐹𐐪𐑅 𐑄𐐰𐐻 𐑄 𐐶𐐲𐑉𐐼𐑆 𐐸𐐶𐐮𐐽 𐐿𐐩𐑋 𐐲𐑌𐐻𐐭 𐐤𐐨𐑁𐐴 𐐶𐐲𐑉 𐑁𐐳𐑊𐑁𐐮𐑊𐐼, 𐐰𐐿𐐫𐑉𐐼𐐮𐑍 𐐰𐑆 𐑄𐐩 𐐸𐐰𐐼 𐐺𐐮𐑌 𐑅𐐹𐐬𐐿𐐲𐑌; 𐑁𐐫𐑉 𐐺𐐨𐐸𐐬𐑊𐐼, 𐐰𐐻 𐑄 𐑀𐐬𐐮𐑍 𐐼𐐵𐑌 𐐱𐑂 𐑄 𐑅𐐲𐑌 𐑄𐐩𐑉 𐐶𐐱𐑆 𐑌𐐬 𐐼𐐪𐑉𐐿𐑌𐐯𐑅; 𐐰𐑌𐐼 𐑄 𐐹𐐨𐐹𐑊 𐐺𐐨𐑀𐐰𐑌 𐐻𐐭 𐐺 𐐰𐑅𐐻𐐱𐑌𐐮𐑇𐐻 𐐺𐐨𐐿𐐱𐑆 𐑄𐐩𐑉 𐐶𐐱𐑆 𐑌𐐬 𐐼𐐪𐑉𐐿𐑌𐐯𐑅 𐐸𐐶𐐯𐑌 𐑄 𐑌𐐴𐐻 𐐿𐐩𐑋. 𐐈𐑌𐐼 𐑄𐐩𐑉 𐐶𐐲𐑉 𐑋𐐯𐑌𐐨, 𐐸𐐭 𐐸𐐰𐐼 𐑌𐐱𐐻 𐐺𐐨𐑊𐐨𐑂𐐼 𐑄 𐐶𐐲𐑉𐐼𐑆 𐐱𐑂 𐑄 𐐹𐑉𐐱𐑁𐐯𐐻𐑅, 𐐸𐐭 𐑁𐐯𐑊 𐐻𐐭 𐑄 𐐲𐑉𐑃 𐐰𐑌𐐼 𐐺𐐨𐐿𐐩𐑋 𐐰𐑆 𐐮𐑁 𐑄𐐩 𐐶𐐲𐑉 𐐼𐐯𐐼, 𐑁𐐫𐑉 𐑄𐐩 𐑌𐐭 𐑄𐐰𐐻 𐑄 𐑀𐑉𐐩𐐻 𐐹𐑊𐐰𐑌 𐐱𐑂 𐐼𐐯𐑅𐐻𐑉𐐲𐐿𐑇𐐲𐑌 𐐸𐐶𐐮𐐽 𐑄𐐩 𐐸𐐰𐐼 𐑊𐐩𐐼 𐑁𐐫𐑉 𐑄𐐬𐑆 𐐸𐐭 𐐺𐐨𐑊𐐨𐑂𐐼 𐐮𐑌 𐑄 𐐶𐐲𐑉𐐼𐑆 𐐱𐑂 𐑄 𐐹𐑉𐐱𐑁𐐯𐐻𐑅, 𐐸𐐰𐐼 𐐺𐐮𐑌 𐑁𐑉𐐲𐑅𐐻𐑉𐐩𐐻𐐯𐐼; 𐑁𐐫𐑉 𐑄 𐑅𐐴𐑌 𐐸𐐶𐐮𐐽 𐐸𐐰𐐼 𐐺𐐮𐑌 𐑀𐐮𐑂𐐲𐑌 𐐶𐐱𐑆 𐐫𐑊𐑉𐐯𐐼𐐨 𐐰𐐻 𐐸𐐰𐑌𐐼; 𐐰𐑌𐐼 𐑄𐐩 𐐺𐐨𐑀𐐰𐑌 𐐻𐐭 𐑌𐐬 𐑄𐐰𐐻 𐑄 𐐝𐐲𐑌 𐐱𐑂 𐐘𐐱𐐼 𐑋𐐲𐑅𐐻 𐑇𐐫𐑉𐐻𐑊𐐨 𐐰𐐹𐐨𐑉; 𐐷𐐩, 𐐮𐑌 𐑁𐐴𐑌, 𐐫𐑊 𐑄 𐐹𐐨𐐹𐑊 𐐲𐐹𐐱𐑌 𐑄 𐑁𐐩𐑅 𐐱𐑂 𐑄 𐐸𐐬𐑊 𐐲𐑉𐑃 𐑁𐑉𐐲𐑋 𐑄 𐐶𐐯𐑅𐐻 𐐻𐐭 𐑄 𐐨𐑅𐐻, 𐐺𐐬𐑃 𐐮𐑌 𐑄 𐑊𐐰𐑌𐐼 𐑌𐐫𐑉𐑃 𐐰𐑌𐐼 𐐮𐑌 𐑄 𐑊𐐰𐑌𐐼 𐑅𐐵𐑃, 𐐶𐐲𐑉 𐑅𐐬 𐐯𐐿𐑅𐐨𐐼𐐮𐑍𐑊𐐨 𐐰𐑅𐐻𐐱𐑌𐐮𐑇𐐻 𐑄𐐰𐐻 𐑄𐐩 𐑁𐐯𐑊 𐐻𐐭 𐑄 𐐲𐑉𐑃; 𐑁𐐫𐑉 𐑄𐐩 𐑌𐐭 𐑄𐐰𐐻 𐑄 𐐹𐑉𐐱𐑁𐐯𐐻𐑅 𐐸𐐰𐐼 𐐻𐐯𐑅𐐻𐐮𐑁𐐴𐐼 𐐱𐑂 𐑄𐐨𐑆 𐑃𐐮𐑍𐑆 𐑁𐐫𐑉 𐑋𐐯𐑌𐐨 𐐷𐐨𐑉𐑆, 𐐰𐑌𐐼 𐑄𐐰𐐻 𐑄 𐑅𐐴𐑌 𐐸𐐶𐐮𐐽 𐐸𐐰𐐼 𐐺𐐮𐑌 𐑀𐐮𐑂𐐲𐑌 𐐶𐐱𐑆 𐐫𐑊𐑉𐐯𐐼𐐨 𐐰𐐻 𐐸𐐰𐑌𐐼; 𐐰𐑌𐐼 𐑄𐐩 𐐺𐐨𐑀𐐰𐑌 𐐻𐐭 𐑁𐐨𐑉 𐐺𐐨𐐿𐐱𐑆 𐐱𐑂 𐑄𐐩𐑉 𐐮𐑌𐐮𐐿𐐶𐐮𐐻𐐨 𐐰𐑌𐐼 𐑄𐐩𐑉 𐐲𐑌𐐺𐐨𐑊𐐨𐑁.

5. 𐐈𐑌𐐼 𐐮𐐻 𐐿𐐩𐑋 𐐻𐐭 𐐹𐐪𐑅 𐑄𐐰𐐻 𐑄𐐩𐑉 𐐶𐐱𐑆 𐑌𐐬 𐐼𐐪𐑉𐐿𐑌𐐯𐑅 𐐮𐑌 𐐫𐑊 𐑄𐐰𐐻 𐑌𐐴𐐻, 𐐺𐐲𐐻 𐐮𐐻 𐐶𐐱𐑆 𐐰𐑆 𐑊𐐴𐐻 𐐰𐑆 𐑄𐐬 𐐮𐐻 𐐶𐐱𐑆 𐑋𐐮𐐼-𐐼𐐩. 𐐈𐑌𐐼 𐐮𐐻 𐐿𐐩𐑋 𐐻𐐭 𐐹𐐪𐑅 𐑄𐐰𐐻 𐑄 𐑅𐐲𐑌 𐐼𐐮𐐼 𐑉𐐴𐑆 𐐮𐑌 𐑄 𐑋𐐫𐑉𐑌𐐮𐑍 𐐰𐑀𐐯𐑌, 𐐰𐐿𐐫𐑉𐐼𐐮𐑍 𐐻𐐭 𐐮𐐻𐑅 𐐹𐑉𐐱𐐹𐐲𐑉 𐐫𐑉𐐼𐐲𐑉; 𐐰𐑌𐐼 𐑄𐐩 𐑌𐐭 𐑄𐐰𐐻 𐐮𐐻 𐐶𐐱𐑆 𐑄 𐐼𐐩 𐑄𐐰𐐻 𐑄 𐐢𐐫𐑉𐐼 𐑇𐐳𐐼 𐐺 𐐺𐐫𐑉𐑌, 𐐺𐐨𐐿𐐱𐑆 𐐱𐑂 𐑄 𐑅𐐴𐑌 𐐸𐐶𐐮𐐽 𐐸𐐰𐐼 𐐺𐐮𐑌 𐑀𐐮𐑂𐐲𐑌. 𐐈𐑌𐐼 𐐮𐐻 𐐸𐐰𐐼 𐐿𐐲𐑋 𐐻𐐭 𐐹𐐪𐑅, 𐐷𐐩, 𐐫𐑊 𐑃𐐮𐑍𐑆, 𐐯𐑂𐐲𐑉𐐨 𐐸𐐶𐐮𐐻, 𐐰𐐿𐐫𐑉𐐼𐐮𐑍 𐐻𐐭 𐑄 𐐶𐐲𐑉𐐼𐑆 𐐱𐑂 𐑄 𐐹𐑉𐐱𐑁𐐯𐐻𐑅. 𐐈𐑌𐐼 𐐮𐐻 𐐿𐐩𐑋 𐐻𐐭 𐐹𐐪𐑅 𐐫𐑊𐑅𐐬, 𐑄𐐰𐐻 𐐰 𐑌𐐧 𐑅𐐻𐐪𐑉 𐐼𐐮𐐼 𐐰𐐹𐐨𐑉, 𐐰𐐿𐐫𐑉𐐼𐐮𐑍 𐐻𐐭 𐑄 𐐶𐐲𐑉𐐼. 𐐈𐑌𐐼 𐐮𐐻 𐐿𐐩𐑋 𐐻𐐭 𐐹𐐪𐑅 𐑄𐐰𐐻 𐑁𐑉𐐲𐑋 𐑄𐐮𐑅 𐐻𐐴𐑋 𐑁𐐬𐑉𐑃 𐑄𐐩𐑉 𐐺𐐨𐑀𐐰𐑌 𐐻𐐭 𐐺 𐑊𐐴𐐮𐑍𐑆 𐑅𐐯𐑌𐐻 𐑁𐐬𐑉𐑃 𐐰𐑋𐐲𐑍 𐑄 𐐹𐐨𐐹𐑊, 𐐺𐐴 𐐝𐐩𐐻𐐰𐑌, 𐐻𐐭 𐐸𐐪𐑉𐐼𐐯𐑌 𐑄𐐩𐑉 𐐸𐐪𐑉𐐻𐑅, 𐐻𐐭 𐑄 𐐮𐑌𐐻𐐯𐑌𐐻 𐑄𐐰𐐻 𐑄𐐩 𐑋𐐴𐐻 𐑌𐐱𐐻 𐐺𐐨𐑊𐐨𐑂 𐐮𐑌 𐑄𐐬𐑆 𐑅𐐴𐑌𐑆 𐐰𐑌𐐼 𐐶𐐲𐑌𐐼𐐲𐑉𐑆 𐐸𐐶𐐮𐐽 𐑄𐐩 𐐸𐐰𐐼 𐑅𐐨𐑌; 𐐺𐐲𐐻 𐑌𐐱𐐻𐐶𐐮𐑃𐑅𐐻𐐰𐑌𐐼𐐮𐑍 𐑄𐐨𐑆 𐑊𐐴𐐮𐑍𐑆 𐐰𐑌𐐼 𐐼𐐨𐑅𐐨𐑂𐐮𐑍𐑆, 𐑄 𐑋𐐬𐑉 𐐹𐐪𐑉𐐻 𐐱𐑂 𐑄 𐐹𐐨𐐹𐑊 𐐼𐐮𐐼 𐐺𐐨𐑊𐐨𐑂, 𐐰𐑌𐐼 𐐶𐐲𐑉 𐐿𐐱𐑌𐑂𐐲𐑉𐐻𐐯𐐼 𐐲𐑌𐐻𐐭 𐑄 𐐢𐐫𐑉𐐼. 𐐈𐑌𐐼 𐐮𐐻 𐐿𐐩𐑋 𐐻𐐭 𐐹𐐪𐑅 𐑄𐐰𐐻 𐐤𐐨𐑁𐐴 𐐶𐐯𐑌𐐻 𐑁𐐬𐑉𐑃 𐐰𐑋𐐲𐑍 𐑄 𐐹𐐨𐐹𐑊, 𐐰𐑌𐐼 𐐫𐑊𐑅𐐬 𐑋𐐯𐑌𐐨 𐐲𐑄𐐲𐑉𐑆, 𐐺𐐰𐐹𐐻𐐴𐑆𐐮𐑍 𐐲𐑌𐐻𐐭 𐑉𐐨𐐹𐐯𐑌𐐻𐐰𐑌𐑅, 𐐮𐑌 𐑄 𐐸𐐶𐐮𐐽 𐑄𐐩𐑉 𐐶𐐱𐑆 𐐰 𐑀𐑉𐐩𐐻 𐑉𐐨𐑋𐐮𐑇𐐲𐑌 𐐱𐑂 𐑅𐐮𐑌𐑆. 𐐈𐑌𐐼 𐑄𐐲𐑅 𐑄 𐐹𐐨𐐹𐑊 𐐺𐐨𐑀𐐰𐑌 𐐰𐑀𐐯𐑌 𐐻𐐭 𐐸𐐰𐑂 𐐹𐐨𐑅 𐐮𐑌 𐑄 𐑊𐐰𐑌𐐼. 𐐈𐑌𐐼 𐑄𐐩𐑉 𐐶𐐲𐑉 𐑌𐐬 𐐿𐐱𐑌𐐻𐐯𐑌𐑇𐐲𐑌𐑆, 𐑅𐐩𐑂 𐐮𐐻 𐐶𐐲𐑉 𐐰 𐑁𐐧 𐑄𐐰𐐻 𐐺𐐨𐑀𐐰𐑌 𐐻𐐭 𐐹𐑉𐐨𐐽, 𐐯𐑌𐐼𐐯𐑂𐐲𐑉𐐮𐑍 𐐻𐐭 𐐹𐑉𐐭𐑂 𐐺𐐴 𐑄 𐑅𐐿𐑉𐐮𐐹𐐽𐐲𐑉𐑆 𐑄𐐰𐐻 𐐮𐐻 𐐶𐐱𐑆 𐑌𐐬 𐑋𐐬𐑉 𐐯𐐿𐑅𐐹𐐨𐐼𐐷𐐯𐑌𐐻 𐐻𐐭 𐐱𐐺𐑆𐐲𐑉𐑂 𐑄 𐑊𐐫 𐐱𐑂 𐐣𐐬𐑆𐐯𐑆. 𐐤𐐵 𐐮𐑌 𐑄𐐮𐑅 𐑃𐐮𐑍 𐑄𐐩 𐐼𐐮𐐼 𐐲𐑉, 𐐸𐐰𐑂𐐮𐑍 𐑌𐐱𐐻 𐐲𐑌𐐼𐐲𐑉𐑅𐐻𐐳𐐼 𐑄 𐑅𐐿𐑉𐐮𐐹𐐽𐐲𐑉𐑆. 𐐒𐐲𐐻 𐐮𐐻 𐐿𐐩𐑋 𐐻𐐭 𐐹𐐪𐑅 𐑄𐐰𐐻 𐑄𐐩 𐑅𐐭𐑌 𐐺𐐨𐐿𐐩𐑋 𐐿𐐱𐑌𐑂𐐲𐑉𐐻𐐯𐐼, 𐐰𐑌𐐼

𐐶𐐲𐑉 𐐿𐐱𐑌𐑂𐐮𐑌𐑅𐐻 𐐱𐑂 𐑄 𐐯𐑉𐐲𐑉 𐐸𐐶𐐮𐐽 𐑄𐐩 𐐶𐐲𐑉 𐐮𐑌, 𐑁𐐫𐑉 𐐮𐐻 𐐶𐐱𐑆 𐑋𐐩𐐼 𐑌𐐬𐑌 𐐲𐑌𐐻𐐭 𐑄𐐯𐑋 𐑄𐐰𐐻 𐑄 𐑊𐐫 𐐶𐐱𐑆 𐑌𐐱𐐻 𐐷𐐯𐐻 𐑁𐐳𐑊𐑁𐐮𐑊𐐼, 𐐰𐑌𐐼 𐑄𐐰𐐻 𐐮𐐻 𐑋𐐲𐑅𐐻 𐐺 𐑁𐐳𐑊𐑁𐐮𐑊𐐼 𐐮𐑌 𐐯𐑂𐐲𐑉𐐨 𐐸𐐶𐐮𐐻; 𐐷𐐩 𐑄 𐐶𐐲𐑉𐐼 𐐿𐐩𐑋 𐐲𐑌𐐻𐐭 𐑄𐐯𐑋 𐑄𐐰𐐻 𐐮𐐻 𐑋𐐲𐑅𐐻 𐐺 𐑁𐐳𐑊𐑁𐐮𐑊𐐼; 𐐷𐐩, 𐑄𐐰𐐻 𐐶𐐲𐑌 𐐾𐐱𐐻 𐑌𐐫𐑉 𐐻𐐮𐐻𐐲𐑊 𐑇𐐳𐐼 𐑌𐐱𐐻 𐐹𐐰𐑅 𐐰𐐶𐐩 𐐻𐐮𐑊 𐐮𐐻 𐑇𐐳𐐼 𐐫𐑊 𐐺 𐑁𐐳𐑊𐑁𐐮𐑊𐐼: 𐑄𐐯𐑉𐑁𐐬𐑉 𐐮𐑌 𐑄𐐮𐑅 𐑅𐐩𐑋 𐐷𐐨𐑉, 𐐶𐐲𐑉 𐑄𐐩 𐐺𐑉𐐫𐐻 𐐻𐐭 𐐩 𐑌𐐱𐑊𐐯𐐾 𐐱𐑂 𐑄𐐩𐑉 𐐯𐑉𐐲𐑉, 𐐰𐑌𐐼 𐐼𐐮𐐼 𐐿𐐱𐑌𐑁𐐯𐑅 𐑄𐐩𐑉 𐑁𐐫𐑊𐐻𐑅. 𐐈𐑌𐐼 𐑄𐐲𐑅 𐑄 𐑌𐐴𐑌𐐻𐐨 𐐰𐑌𐐼 𐑅𐐯𐐿𐐲𐑌𐐼 𐐷𐐨𐑉 𐐼𐐮𐐼 𐐹𐐰𐑅 𐐰𐐶𐐩, 𐐺𐑉𐐮𐑍𐐮𐑍 𐑀𐑊𐐰𐐼 𐐻𐐴𐐼𐐮𐑍𐑆 𐐲𐑌𐐻𐐭 𐑄 𐐹𐐨𐐹𐐲𐑊, 𐐺𐐨𐐿𐐫𐑆 𐐱𐑂 𐑄 𐑅𐐴𐑌𐑆 𐐸𐐶𐐮𐐽 𐐼𐐮𐐼 𐐿𐐲𐑋 𐐻𐐭 𐐹𐐰𐑅, 𐐰𐐿𐐫𐑉𐐼𐐮𐑍 𐐻𐐭 𐑄 𐐶𐐲𐑉𐐼𐑆 𐐱𐑂 𐑄 𐐹𐑉𐐱𐑁𐐯𐑅𐐨 𐐱𐑂 𐐫𐑊 𐑄 𐐸𐐬𐑊𐐨 𐐹𐑉𐐱𐑁𐐯𐐻𐑅.

6. 𐐈𐑌𐐼 𐐮𐐻 𐐿𐐩𐑋 𐐻𐐭 𐐹𐐰𐑅 𐑄𐐰𐐻 𐑄 𐑌𐐴𐑌𐐻𐐨 𐐰𐑌𐐼 𐑃𐐲𐑉𐐼 𐐷𐐨𐑉 𐐼𐐮𐐼 𐐫𐑊𐑅𐐬 𐐹𐐰𐑅 𐐰𐐶𐐩 𐐮𐑌 𐐹𐐨𐑅, 𐑅𐐩𐑂 𐐮𐐻 𐐶𐐲𐑉 𐑁𐐫𐑉 𐑄 𐐘𐐩𐐼𐐨𐐰𐑌𐐻𐐲𐑌 𐑉𐐱𐐺𐐲𐑉𐑆, 𐐸𐐭 𐐼𐐶𐐯𐑊𐐻 𐐲𐐹𐐱𐑌 𐑄 𐑋𐐵𐑌𐐻𐐲𐑌𐑆, 𐐸𐐭 𐐼𐐮𐐼 𐐮𐑌𐑁𐐯𐑅𐐻 𐑄 𐑊𐐰𐑌𐐼; 𐑁𐐫𐑉 𐑅𐐬 𐑅𐐻𐑉𐐱𐑍 𐐶𐐲𐑉 𐑄𐐩𐑉 𐐸𐐬𐑊𐐼𐑆, 𐐰𐑌𐐼 𐑄𐐩𐑉 𐑅𐐨𐐿𐑉𐐯𐐻 𐐹𐑊𐐩𐑅𐐯𐑆, 𐑄𐐰𐐻 𐑄 𐐹𐐨𐐹𐐲𐑊 𐐿𐐳𐐼 𐑌𐐱𐐻 𐐬𐑂𐐲𐑉𐐹𐐵𐐲𐑉 𐑄𐐯𐑋; 𐑄𐐯𐑉𐑁𐐬𐑉 𐑄𐐩 𐐼𐐮𐐼 𐐿𐐱𐑋𐐮𐐻 𐑋𐐯𐑌𐐨 𐑋𐐲𐑉𐐼𐐲𐑉𐑆, 𐐰𐑌𐐼 𐐼𐐮𐐼 𐐼𐐭 𐑋𐐲𐐽 𐑅𐑊𐐫𐐻𐐲𐑉 𐐰𐑋𐐲𐑍 𐑄 𐐹𐐨𐐹𐐲𐑊. 𐐈𐑌𐐼 𐐮𐐻 𐐿𐐩𐑋 𐐻𐐭 𐐹𐐰𐑅 𐑄𐐰𐐻 𐐮𐑌 𐑄 𐑌𐐴𐑌𐐻𐐨 𐐰𐑌𐐼 𐑁𐐬𐑉𐑃 𐐷𐐨𐑉, 𐑄𐐩 𐐺𐐨𐑀𐐰𐑌 𐐻𐐭 𐐮𐑌𐐿𐑉𐐨𐑅 𐐮𐑌 𐐩 𐑀𐑉𐐩𐐻 𐐼𐐨𐑀𐑉𐐨, 𐐺𐐨𐐿𐐫𐑆 𐐱𐑂 𐑋𐐯𐑌𐐨 𐐼𐐮𐑅𐐯𐑌𐐻𐐲𐑉𐑆 𐐱𐑂 𐑄 𐐤𐐨𐑁𐐴𐐻𐑅 𐐸𐐭 𐐼𐐮𐐼 𐑁𐑊𐐨 𐐲𐑌𐐻𐐭 𐑄𐐯𐑋, 𐐸𐐶𐐮𐐽 𐐼𐐮𐐼 𐐿𐐫𐑆 𐑋𐐲𐐽 𐑅𐐱𐑉𐐬 𐐲𐑌𐐻𐐭 𐑄𐐬𐑆 𐐤𐐨𐑁𐐴𐐻𐑅 𐐸𐐭 𐐼𐐮𐐼 𐑉𐐨𐑋𐐩𐑌 𐐮𐑌 𐑄 𐑊𐐰𐑌𐐼; 𐐰𐑌𐐼 𐑄𐐩𐑉 𐐶𐐱𐑆 𐐫𐑊𐑅𐐬 𐐩 𐐿𐐫𐑆 𐐱𐑂 𐑋𐐲𐐽 𐑅𐐱𐑉𐐬 𐐰𐑋𐐲𐑍 𐑄 𐐢𐐰𐑋𐐲𐑌𐐴𐐻𐑅, 𐑁𐐫𐑉 𐐺𐐨𐐸𐐬𐑊𐐼, 𐑄𐐩 𐐸𐐰𐐼 𐑋𐐯𐑌𐐨 𐐽𐐮𐑊𐐼𐑉𐐯𐑌 𐐸𐐭 𐐼𐐮𐐼 𐑀𐑉𐐬 𐐲𐐹 𐐰𐑌𐐼 𐐺𐐨𐑀𐐰𐑌 𐐻𐐭 𐐶𐐰𐐿𐑅 𐑅𐐻𐑉𐐱𐑍 𐐮𐑌 𐐷𐐨𐑉𐑆, 𐑄𐐰𐐻 𐑄𐐩 𐐺𐐨𐐿𐐩𐑋 𐑁𐐫𐑉 𐑄𐐯𐑋𐑅𐐯𐑊𐑂𐑆, 𐐰𐑌𐐼 𐐶𐐲𐑉 𐑊𐐯𐐼 𐐰𐐶𐐩 𐐺𐐴 𐑅𐐲𐑋 𐐸𐐭 𐐶𐐲𐑉 𐐞𐐬𐑉𐐲𐑋𐐴𐐻𐑅, 𐐺𐐴 𐑄𐐩𐑉 𐑊𐐴𐐮𐑍𐑆 𐐰𐑌𐐼 𐑄𐐩𐑉 𐑁𐑊𐐰𐐻𐐲𐑉𐐮𐑍 𐐶𐐲𐑉𐐼𐑆, 𐐻𐐭 𐐾𐑎𐑌 𐑄𐐬𐑆 𐐘𐐩𐐼𐐨𐐰𐑌𐐻𐐲𐑌 𐑉𐐱𐐺𐐲𐑉𐑆; 𐐰𐑌𐐼 𐑄𐐲𐑅 𐐶𐐲𐑉 𐑄 𐐢𐐰𐑋𐐲𐑌𐐴𐐻𐑅 𐐰𐑁𐑊𐐮𐐿𐐻𐐯𐐼 𐐫𐑊𐑅𐐬, 𐐰𐑌𐐼 𐐺𐐨𐑀𐐰𐑌 𐐻𐐭 𐐼𐐨𐐿𐑉𐐨𐑅 𐐰𐑆 𐐻𐐭 𐑄𐐩𐑉 𐑁𐐩𐑃 𐐰𐑌𐐼 𐑉𐐴𐐽𐐲𐑅𐑌𐐯𐑅, 𐐺𐐨𐐿𐐫𐑆 𐐱𐑂 𐑄 𐐶𐐮𐐿𐐯𐐼𐑌𐐯𐑅 𐐱𐑂 𐑄 𐑉𐐴𐑆𐐮𐑍 𐐾𐐯𐑌𐐲𐑉𐐩𐑇𐐲𐑌.

7. 𐐈𐑌𐐼 𐐮𐐻 𐐿𐐩𐑋 𐐻𐐭 𐐹𐐰𐑅 𐑄𐐰𐐻 𐑄𐐲𐑅 𐐹𐐰𐑅𐐻 𐐰𐐶𐐩 𐑄 𐑌𐐴𐑌𐐻𐐨 𐐰𐑌𐐼 𐑁𐐮𐑁𐑃 𐐷𐐨𐑉 𐐫𐑊𐑅𐐬, 𐐰𐑌𐐼 𐑄 𐐹𐐨𐐹𐐲𐑊 𐐺𐐨𐑀𐐰𐑌 𐐻𐐭 𐑁𐐫𐑉𐑀𐐯𐐻 𐑄𐐬𐑆 𐑅𐐴𐑌𐑆 𐐰𐑌𐐼 𐐶𐐲𐑌𐐼𐐲𐑉𐑆 𐐸𐐶𐐮𐐽 𐑄𐐩 𐐸𐐰𐐼 𐐸𐐲𐑉𐐼, 𐐰𐑌𐐼 𐐺𐐨𐑀𐐰𐑌 𐐻𐐭 𐐺 𐑊𐐯𐑅 𐐰𐑌𐐼 𐑊𐐯𐑅 𐐰𐑅𐐻𐐱𐑌𐐮𐑇𐐻 𐐰𐐻 𐐩 𐑅𐐴𐑌 𐐫𐑉 𐐩 𐐶𐐲𐑌𐐼𐐲𐑉 𐑁𐑉𐐱𐑋 𐐸𐐯𐑂𐐲𐑌, 𐐮𐑌𐑅𐐬𐑋𐐲𐐽 𐑄𐐰𐐻 𐑄𐐩 𐐺𐐨𐑀𐐰𐑌 𐐻𐐭 𐐺 𐐸𐐪𐑉𐐼 𐐮𐑌 𐑄𐐩𐑉 𐐸𐐪𐑉𐐻𐑅, 𐐰𐑌𐐼 𐐺𐑊𐐴𐑌𐐼 𐐮𐑌 𐑄𐐩𐑉 𐑋𐐴𐑌𐐼𐑆, 𐐰𐑌𐐼 𐐺𐐨𐑀𐐰𐑌 𐐻𐐭 𐐼𐐮𐑅𐐺𐐨𐑊𐐨𐑂 𐐫𐑊 𐐸𐐶𐐮𐐽 𐑄𐐩 𐐸𐐰𐐼 𐐸𐐲𐑉𐐼 𐐰𐑌𐐼 𐑅𐐨𐑌, 𐐮𐑋𐐰𐐾𐐮𐑌𐐮𐑍 𐐲𐐹 𐑅𐐲𐑋 𐑂𐐩𐑌 𐑃𐐮𐑍 𐐮𐑌 𐑄𐐩𐑉 𐐸𐐪𐑉𐐻𐑅, 𐑄𐐰𐐻 𐐮𐐻 𐐶𐐱𐑆 𐑉𐐫𐐻 𐐺𐐴 𐑋𐐯𐑌, 𐐰𐑌𐐼 𐐺𐐴 𐑄 𐐹𐐵𐐲𐑉 𐐱𐑂 𐑄 𐐼𐐯𐑂𐐲𐑊, 𐐻𐐭 𐑊𐐨𐐼 𐐰𐐶𐐩 𐐰𐑌𐐼 𐐼𐐨𐑅𐐨𐑂 𐑄 𐐸𐐪𐑉𐐻𐑅 𐐱𐑂 𐑄 𐐹𐐨𐐹𐐲𐑊; 𐐰𐑌𐐼 𐑄𐐲𐑅 𐐼𐐮𐐼 𐐝𐐩𐐻𐐲𐑌 𐑀𐐯𐐻 𐐹𐐱𐑆𐐯𐑇𐐲𐑌 𐐱𐑂 𐑄 𐐸𐐪𐑉𐐻𐑅 𐐱𐑂 𐑄 𐐹𐐨𐐹𐐲𐑊 𐐰𐑀𐐯𐑌, 𐐮𐑌𐑅𐐬𐑋𐐲𐐽 𐑄𐐰𐐻 𐐸𐐨 𐐼𐐮𐐼 𐐺𐑊𐐴𐑌𐐼 𐑄𐐩𐑉 𐐴𐑆, 𐐰𐑌𐐼 𐑊𐐨𐐼 𐑄𐐯𐑋 𐐰𐐶𐐩 𐐻𐐭 𐐺𐐨𐑊𐐨𐑂 𐑄𐐰𐐻 𐑄 𐐼𐐱𐐿𐐻𐑉𐐮𐑌 𐐱𐑂 𐐗𐑉𐐴𐑅𐐻 𐐶𐐱𐑆 𐐩 𐑁𐐭𐑊𐐮𐑇 𐐰𐑌𐐼 𐐩 𐑂𐐩𐑌 𐑃𐐮𐑍.

8. 𐐈𐑌𐐼 𐐮𐐻 𐐿𐐩𐑋 𐐻𐐭 𐐹𐐰𐑅 𐑄𐐰𐐻 𐑄 𐐹𐐨𐐹𐐲𐑊 𐐺𐐨𐑀𐐰𐑌 𐐻𐐭 𐐶𐐰𐐿𐑅 𐑅𐐻𐑉𐐱𐑍 𐐮𐑌 𐐶𐐮𐐿𐐯𐐼𐑌𐐯𐑅 𐐰𐑌𐐼 𐐰𐐺𐐱𐑋𐐮𐑌𐐩𐑇𐐲𐑌𐑆; 𐐰𐑌𐐼 𐑄𐐩 𐐼𐐮𐐼 𐑌𐐱𐐻 𐐺𐐨𐑊𐐨𐑂 𐑄𐐰𐐻 𐑄𐐩𐑉 𐑇𐐳𐐼 𐐺 𐐯𐑌𐐨 𐑋𐐬𐑉 𐑅𐐴𐑌𐑆 𐐫𐑉 𐐶𐐲𐑌𐐼𐐲𐑉𐑆 𐑀𐐮𐑂𐐲𐑌; 𐐰𐑌𐐼 𐐝𐐩𐐻𐐲𐑌 𐐼𐐮𐐼 𐑀𐐬 𐐰𐐺𐐵𐐻, 𐑊𐐨𐐼𐐮𐑍 𐐰𐐶𐐩 𐑄 𐐸𐐪𐑉𐐻𐑅 𐐱𐑂 𐑄 𐐹𐐨𐐹𐐲𐑊, 𐐻𐐯𐑋𐐻𐐮𐑍 𐑄𐐯𐑋 𐐰𐑌𐐼 𐐿𐐫𐑆𐐮𐑍 𐑄𐐯𐑋 𐑄𐐰𐐻 𐑄𐐩 𐑇𐐳𐐼 𐐼𐐭 𐑀𐑉𐐩𐐻 𐐶𐐮𐐿𐐯𐐼𐑌𐐯𐑅 𐐮𐑌 𐑄 𐑊𐐰𐑌𐐼. 𐐈𐑌𐐼 𐑄𐐲𐑅 𐐼𐐮𐐼 𐐹𐐰𐑅 𐐰𐐶𐐩 𐑄 𐑌𐐴𐑌𐐻𐐨 𐐰𐑌𐐼 𐑅𐐮𐐿𐑅𐑃 𐐷𐐨𐑉; 𐐰𐑌𐐼 𐐫𐑊𐑅𐐬 𐑄 𐑌𐐴𐑌𐐻𐐨 𐐰𐑌𐐼 𐑅𐐯𐑂𐐲𐑌𐑃 𐐷𐐨𐑉; 𐐰𐑌𐐼 𐐫𐑊𐑅𐐬 𐑄 𐑌𐐴𐑌𐐻𐐨 𐐰𐑌𐐼 𐐩𐐻𐑃 𐐷𐐨𐑉; 𐐰𐑌𐐼 𐐫𐑊𐑅𐐬 𐑄 𐑌𐐴𐑌𐐻𐐨 𐐰𐑌𐐼 𐑌𐐴𐑌𐑃 𐐷𐐨𐑉; 𐐰𐑌𐐼 𐐫𐑊𐑅𐐬 𐐰𐑌 𐐸𐐲𐑌𐐼𐑉𐐯𐐼 𐐷𐐨𐑉𐑆 𐐸𐐰𐐼 𐐹𐐰𐑅𐐻 𐐰𐐶𐐩 𐑅𐐮𐑌𐑅 𐑄 𐐼𐐩𐑆 𐐱𐑂 𐐣𐐬𐑆𐐴𐐲, 𐐸𐐭 𐐶𐐱𐑆 𐐿𐐮𐑍 𐐬𐑂𐐲𐑉 𐑄 𐐤𐐨𐑁𐐴𐐻𐑅. 𐐈𐑌𐐼 𐑅𐐮𐐿𐑅 𐐸𐐲𐑌𐐼𐑉𐐯𐐼 𐐰𐑌𐐼 𐑌𐐴𐑌 𐐷𐐨𐑉𐑆 𐐸𐐰𐐼 𐐹𐐰𐑅𐐻 𐐰𐐶𐐩 𐑅𐐮𐑌𐑅 𐐢𐐨𐐸𐐴 𐑊𐐯𐑁𐐻 𐐖𐐲𐑉𐐭𐑅𐐲𐑊𐐯𐑋; 𐐰𐑌𐐼 𐑌𐐴𐑌 𐐷𐐨𐑉𐑆 𐐸𐐰𐐼 𐐹𐐰𐑅𐐻 𐐰𐐶𐐩 𐑁𐑉𐐱𐑋 𐑄 𐐻𐐴𐑋 𐐸𐐶𐐯𐑌 𐑄 𐑅𐐴𐑌 𐐶𐐱𐑆 𐑀𐐮𐑂𐐲𐑌, 𐐸𐐶𐐮𐐽 𐐶𐐱𐑆 𐑅𐐹𐐬𐐿𐐲𐑌 𐐱𐑂 𐐺𐐴 𐑄 𐐹𐑉𐐱𐑁𐐯𐐻𐑅, 𐑄𐐰𐐻 𐐗𐑉𐐴𐑅𐐻 𐑇𐐳𐐼 𐐿𐐲𐑋 𐐮𐑌𐐻𐐭 𐑄 𐐶𐐲𐑉𐑊𐐼. 𐐤𐐵 𐑄 𐐤𐐨𐑁𐐴𐐻𐑅 𐐺𐐨𐑀𐐰𐑌 𐐻𐐭 𐑉𐐯𐐿𐐲𐑌 𐑄𐐩𐑉 𐐻𐐴𐑋 𐑁𐑉𐐱𐑋 𐑄𐐮𐑅 𐐹𐐨𐑉𐐨𐐲𐐼 𐐸𐐶𐐯𐑌 𐑄 𐑅𐐴𐑌 𐐶𐐱𐑆 𐑀𐐮𐑂𐐲𐑌, 𐐫𐑉 𐑁𐑉𐐱𐑋 𐑄 𐐿𐐲𐑋𐐮𐑍 𐐱𐑂 𐐗𐑉𐐴𐑅𐐻: 𐑄𐐯𐑉𐑁𐐬𐑉, 𐑌𐐴𐑌 𐐷𐐨𐑉𐑆 𐐸𐐰𐐼 𐐹𐐰𐑅𐐻 𐐰𐐶𐐩, 𐐰𐑌𐐼 𐐤𐐨𐑁𐐴, 𐐸𐐭 𐐶𐐱𐑆 𐑄 𐑁𐐪𐑄𐐲𐑉 𐐱𐑂 𐐤𐐨𐑁𐐴, 𐐸𐐭 𐐸𐐰𐐼 𐑄

𐐽𐐪𐑉𐐾 𐐱𐑂 𐑄 𐑉𐐯𐐿𐐲𐑉𐐼𐑆, 𐐼𐐮𐐼 𐑌𐐱𐐻 𐑉𐐨𐐻𐐲𐑉𐑌 𐐻𐐭 𐑄 𐑊𐐰𐑌𐐼 𐐱𐑂 𐐞𐐩𐑉𐐲𐐸𐐯𐑋𐑊𐐲, 𐐰𐑌𐐼 𐐿𐐳𐐼 𐑌𐐬 𐐸𐐶𐐩𐑉 𐐺 𐑁𐐵𐑌𐐼 𐐮𐑌 𐐫𐑊 𐑄 𐑊𐐰𐑌𐐼.

9. 𐐈𐑌𐐼 𐐮𐐻 𐐿𐐩𐑋 𐐻𐐭 𐐹𐐪𐑅 𐑄𐐰𐐻 𐑄 𐐹𐐨𐐹𐑊 𐐼𐐮𐐼 𐑅𐐻𐐮𐑊 𐑉𐐨𐑋𐐩𐑌 𐐮𐑌 𐐶𐐮𐐿𐐯𐐼𐑌𐐯𐑅, 𐑌𐐱𐐻𐐶𐐮𐑄𐑅𐐻𐐰𐑌𐐼𐐮𐑍 𐑄 𐑋𐐲𐐽 𐐹𐑉𐐨𐐽𐐮𐑍 𐐰𐑌𐐼 𐐹𐑉𐐱𐑁𐐯𐑅𐐴𐐮𐑍 𐐸𐐶𐐮𐐽 𐐶𐐱𐑆 𐑅𐐯𐑌𐐻 𐐰𐑋𐐲𐑍 𐑄𐐯𐑋; 𐐰𐑌𐐼 𐑄𐐲𐑅 𐐹𐐪𐑅𐐻 𐐰𐐶𐐩 𐑄 𐐻𐐯𐑌𐑃 𐐷𐐨𐑉 𐐫𐑊𐑅𐐬; 𐐰𐑌𐐼 𐑄 𐐨𐑊𐐯𐑂𐐯𐑌𐑃 𐐷𐐨𐑉 𐐫𐑊𐑅𐐬 𐐹𐐪𐑅𐐻 𐐰𐐶𐐩 𐐮𐑌 𐐮𐑌𐐮𐐿𐐶𐐮𐐻𐐨. 𐐈𐑌𐐼 𐐮𐐻 𐐿𐐩𐑋 𐐻𐐭 𐐹𐐪𐑅 𐐮𐑌 𐑄 𐑃𐐲𐑉𐐻𐐨𐑌𐑃 𐐷𐐨𐑉 𐑄𐐩𐑉 𐐺𐐨𐑀𐐰𐑌 𐐻𐐭 𐐺 𐐶𐐫𐑉𐑆 𐐰𐑌𐐼 𐐿𐐱𐑌𐐻𐐯𐑌𐑇𐐲𐑌𐑆 𐑃𐑉𐐭𐐵𐐻 𐐫𐑊 𐑄 𐑊𐐰𐑌𐐼; 𐑁𐐫𐑉 𐑄 𐐘𐐰𐐼𐐨𐐰𐑌𐐻𐐲𐑌 𐑉𐐱𐐺𐐲𐑉𐑆 𐐸𐐰𐐼 𐐺𐐨𐐿𐐲𐑋 𐑅𐐬 𐑌𐐭𐑋𐐲𐑉𐐲𐑅, 𐐰𐑌𐐼 𐐼𐐮𐐼 𐑅𐑊𐐩 𐑅𐐬 𐑋𐐯𐑌𐐨 𐐱𐑂 𐑄 𐐹𐐨𐐹𐑊, 𐐰𐑌𐐼 𐐼𐐮𐐼 𐑊𐐩 𐐶𐐩𐑅𐐻 𐑅𐐬 𐑋𐐯𐑌𐐨 𐑅𐐮𐐻𐐨𐑆, 𐐰𐑌𐐼 𐐼𐐮𐐼 𐑅𐐹𐑉𐐯𐐼 𐑅𐐬 𐑋𐐲𐐽 𐐼𐐯𐑃 𐐰𐑌𐐼 𐐿𐐪𐑉𐑌𐐲𐐾 𐑃𐑉𐐭𐐵𐐻 𐑄 𐑊𐐰𐑌𐐼, 𐑄𐐰𐐻 𐐮𐐻 𐐺𐐨𐐿𐐩𐑋 𐐯𐐿𐑅𐐹𐐨𐐼𐐨𐐲𐑌𐐻 𐑄𐐰𐐻 𐐫𐑊 𐑄 𐐹𐐨𐐹𐑊, 𐐺𐐬𐑃 𐑄 𐐤𐐨𐑁𐐴𐐻𐑅 𐐰𐑌𐐼 𐑄 𐐢𐐩𐑋𐐲𐑌𐐴𐐻𐑅, 𐑇𐐳𐐼 𐐻𐐩𐐿 𐐲𐐹 𐐪𐑉𐑋𐑆 𐐰𐑀𐐯𐑌𐑅𐐻 𐑄𐐯𐑋; 𐑄𐐯𐑉𐑁𐐬𐑉 𐐫𐑊 𐑄 𐐢𐐩𐑋𐐲𐑌𐐴𐐻𐑅 𐐸𐐭 𐐸𐐰𐐼 𐐺𐐨𐐿𐐲𐑋 𐐿𐐱𐑌𐑂𐐲𐑉𐐻𐐯𐐼 𐐲𐑌𐐻𐐭 𐑄 𐐢𐐫𐑉𐐼, 𐐼𐐮𐐼 𐐷𐐭𐑌𐐴𐐻 𐐶𐐮𐑄 𐑄𐐩𐑉 𐐺𐑉𐐯𐑄𐑉𐐯𐑌, 𐑄 𐐤𐐨𐑁𐐴𐐻𐑅, 𐐰𐑌𐐼 𐐶𐐲𐑉 𐐿𐐲𐑋𐐹𐐯𐑊𐐼, 𐑁𐐫𐑉 𐑄 𐑅𐐩𐑁𐐻𐐨 𐐱𐑂 𐑄𐐩𐑉 𐑊𐐴𐑂𐑆, 𐐰𐑌𐐼 𐑄𐐩𐑉 𐐶𐐮𐑋𐐯𐑌 𐐰𐑌𐐼 𐑄𐐩𐑉 𐐽𐐮𐑊𐐼𐑉𐐯𐑌, 𐐻𐐭 𐐻𐐩𐐿 𐐲𐐹 𐐪𐑉𐑋𐑆 𐐰𐑀𐐯𐑌𐑅𐐻 𐑄𐐬𐑆 𐐘𐐰𐐼𐐨𐐰𐑌𐐻𐐲𐑌 𐑉𐐱𐐺𐐲𐑉𐑆; 𐐷𐐩, 𐐰𐑌𐐼 𐐫𐑊𐑅𐐬 𐐻𐐭 𐑋𐐩𐑌𐐻𐐩𐑌 𐑄𐐩𐑉 𐑉𐐴𐐻𐑅, 𐐰𐑌𐐼 𐑄𐐩𐑉 𐐹𐑉𐐮𐑂𐐮𐑊𐐯𐐾𐐯𐑆 𐐱𐑂 𐑄𐐩𐑉 𐐕𐐲𐑉𐐽, 𐐰𐑌𐐼 𐐱𐑂 𐑄𐐩𐑉 𐐶𐐲𐑉𐑇𐐮𐐹, 𐐰𐑌𐐼 𐑄𐐩𐑉 𐑁𐑉𐐨𐐼𐐲𐑋, 𐐰𐑌𐐼 𐑄𐐩𐑉 𐑊𐐮𐐺𐐲𐑉𐐻𐐨. 𐐈𐑌𐐼 𐐮𐐻 𐐿𐐩𐑋 𐐻𐐭 𐐹𐐪𐑅 𐑄𐐰𐐻 𐐺𐐨𐑁𐐬𐑉 𐑄𐐮𐑅 𐑃𐐲𐑉𐐻𐐨𐑌𐑃 𐐷𐐨𐑉 𐐸𐐰𐐼 𐐹𐐪𐑅𐐻 𐐰𐐶𐐩, 𐑄 𐐤𐐨𐑁𐐴𐐻𐑅 𐐶𐐲𐑉 𐑃𐑉𐐯𐐻𐐲𐑌𐐼 𐐶𐐮𐑄 𐐲𐐻𐐲𐑉 𐐼𐐯𐑅𐐻𐑉𐐲𐐿𐑇𐐲𐑌, 𐐺𐐨𐐿𐐫𐑆 𐐱𐑂 𐑄𐐮𐑅 𐐶𐐫𐑉, 𐐸𐐶𐐮𐐽 𐐸𐐰𐐼 𐐺𐐨𐐿𐐲𐑋 𐐯𐐿𐑅𐐨𐐼𐐮𐑍𐑊𐐨 𐑅𐐬𐑉. 𐐈𐑌𐐼 𐐮𐐻 𐐿𐐩𐑋 𐐻𐐭 𐐹𐐪𐑅 𐑄𐐰𐐻 𐑄𐐬𐑆 𐐢𐐩𐑋𐐲𐑌𐐴𐐻𐑅 𐐸𐐭 𐐸𐐰𐐼 𐐷𐐭𐑌𐐴𐐻𐐯𐐼 𐐶𐐮𐑄 𐑄 𐐤𐐨𐑁𐐴𐐻𐑅, 𐐶𐐲𐑉 𐑌𐐲𐑋𐐺𐐲𐑉𐐼 𐐰𐑋𐐲𐑍 𐑄 𐐤𐐨𐑁𐐴𐐻𐑅: 𐐰𐑌𐐼 𐑄𐐩𐑉 𐐿𐐲𐑉𐑅 𐐶𐐱𐑆 𐐻𐐩𐐿𐐯𐑌 𐑁𐑉𐐱𐑋 𐑄𐐯𐑋, 𐐰𐑌𐐼 𐑄𐐩𐑉 𐑅𐐿𐐮𐑌 𐐺𐐨𐐿𐐩𐑋 𐐸𐐶𐐴𐐻 𐑊𐐴𐐿 𐐲𐑌𐐻𐐭 𐑄 𐐤𐐨𐑁𐐴𐐻𐑅; 𐐰𐑌𐐼 𐑄𐐩𐑉 𐐷𐐲𐑍 𐑋𐐯𐑌 𐐰𐑌𐐼 𐑄𐐩𐑉 𐐼𐐫𐐻𐐲𐑉𐑆 𐐺𐐨𐐿𐐩𐑋 𐐯𐐿𐑅𐐨𐐼𐐮𐑍𐑊𐐨 𐑁𐐩𐑉, 𐐰𐑌𐐼 𐑄𐐩 𐐶𐐲𐑉 𐑌𐐲𐑋𐐺𐐲𐑉𐐼 𐐰𐑋𐐲𐑍 𐑄 𐐤𐐨𐑁𐐴𐐻𐑅, 𐐰𐑌𐐼 𐐶𐐲𐑉 𐐿𐐫𐑊𐐼 𐐤𐐨𐑁𐐴𐐻𐑅. 𐐈𐑌𐐼 𐑄𐐲𐑅 𐐯𐑌𐐼𐐯𐐼 𐑄 𐑃𐐲𐑉𐐻𐐨𐑌𐑃 𐐷𐐨𐑉.

10. 𐐈𐑌𐐼 𐐮𐐻 𐐿𐐩𐑋 𐐻𐐭 𐐹𐐪𐑅 𐐮𐑌 𐑄 𐐿𐐲𐑋𐐯𐑌𐑅𐑋𐐯𐑌𐐻 𐐱𐑂 𐑄 𐑁𐐬𐑉𐐻𐐨𐑌𐑃 𐐷𐐨𐑉, 𐑄 𐐶𐐫𐑉 𐐺𐐨𐐻𐐶𐐨𐑌 𐑄 𐑉𐐱𐐺𐐲𐑉𐑆 𐐰𐑌𐐼 𐑄 𐐹𐐨𐐹𐑊 𐐱𐑂 𐐤𐐨𐑁𐐴 𐐼𐐮𐐼 𐐿𐐲𐑌𐐻𐐮𐑌𐐷𐐭, 𐐰𐑌𐐼 𐐼𐐮𐐼 𐐺𐐨𐐿𐐲𐑋 𐐯𐐿𐑅𐐨𐐼𐐮𐑍𐑊𐐨 𐑅𐐬𐑉; 𐑌𐐯𐑂𐐲𐑉𐑄𐐲𐑊𐐯𐑅, 𐑄 𐐹𐐨𐐹𐑊 𐐱𐑂 𐐤𐐨𐑁𐐴 𐐼𐐮𐐼 𐑀𐐩𐑌 𐑅𐐲𐑋 𐐰𐐼𐑂𐐰𐑌𐐻𐐮𐐾 𐐱𐑂 𐑄 𐑉𐐱𐐺𐐲𐑉𐑆, 𐐮𐑌𐑅𐐬𐑋𐐲𐐽 𐑄𐐰𐐻 𐑄𐐩 𐐼𐐮𐐼 𐐼𐑉𐐴𐑂 𐑄𐐯𐑋 𐐺𐐰𐐿 𐐵𐐻 𐐱𐑂 𐑄𐐩𐑉 𐑊𐐰𐑌𐐼𐑆 𐐮𐑌𐐻𐐭 𐑄 𐑋𐐵𐑌𐐻𐐲𐑌𐑆, 𐐰𐑌𐐼 𐐮𐑌𐐻𐐭 𐑄𐐩𐑉 𐑅𐐨𐐿𐑉𐐯𐐻 𐐹𐑊𐐩𐑅𐐯𐑆. 𐐈𐑌𐐼 𐑄𐐲𐑅 𐐯𐑌𐐼𐐯𐐼 𐑄 𐑁𐐬𐑉𐐻𐐨𐑌𐑃 𐐷𐐨𐑉. 𐐈𐑌𐐼 𐐮𐑌 𐑄 𐑁𐐮𐑁𐐻𐐨𐑌𐑃 𐐷𐐨𐑉 𐑄𐐩 𐐼𐐮𐐼 𐐿𐐲𐑋 𐑁𐐬𐑉𐑃 𐐰𐑀𐐯𐑌𐑅𐐻 𐑄 𐐹𐐨𐐹𐑊 𐐱𐑂 𐐤𐐨𐑁𐐴; 𐐰𐑌𐐼 𐐺𐐨𐐿𐐫𐑆 𐐱𐑂 𐑄 𐐶𐐮𐐿𐐯𐐼𐑌𐐯𐑅 𐐱𐑂 𐑄 𐐹𐐨𐐹𐑊 𐐱𐑂 𐐤𐐨𐑁𐐴, 𐐰𐑌𐐼 𐑄𐐩𐑉 𐑋𐐯𐑌𐐨 𐐿𐐱𐑌𐐻𐐯𐑌𐑇𐐲𐑌𐑆 𐐰𐑌𐐼 𐐼𐐮𐑅𐐯𐑌𐑇𐐲𐑌𐑆, 𐑄 𐐘𐐰𐐼𐐨𐐰𐑌𐐻𐐲𐑌 𐑉𐐱𐐺𐐲𐑉𐑆 𐐼𐐮𐐼 𐑀𐐩𐑌 𐑋𐐯𐑌𐐨 𐐰𐐼𐑂𐐰𐑌𐐻𐐮𐐾𐐯𐑆 𐐬𐑂𐐲𐑉 𐑄𐐯𐑋. 𐐈𐑌𐐼 𐑄𐐲𐑅 𐐯𐑌𐐼𐐯𐐼 𐑄 𐑁𐐮𐑁𐐻𐐨𐑌𐑃 𐐷𐐨𐑉, 𐐰𐑌𐐼 𐑄𐐲𐑅 𐐶𐐲𐑉 𐑄 𐐹𐐨𐐹𐑊 𐐮𐑌 𐐰 𐑅𐐻𐐩𐐻 𐐱𐑂 𐑋𐐯𐑌𐐨 𐐰𐑁𐑊𐐮𐐿𐑇𐐲𐑌𐑆; 𐐰𐑌𐐼 𐑄 𐑅𐐬𐑉𐐼 𐐱𐑂 𐐼𐐯𐑅𐐻𐑉𐐲𐐿𐑇𐐲𐑌 𐐼𐐮𐐼 𐐸𐐰𐑍 𐐬𐑂𐐲𐑉 𐑄𐐯𐑋, 𐐮𐑌𐑅𐐬𐑋𐐲𐐽 𐑄𐐰𐐻 𐑄𐐩 𐐶𐐲𐑉 𐐰𐐺𐐵𐐻 𐐻𐐭 𐐺 𐑅𐑋𐐮𐐻𐐯𐑌 𐐼𐐵𐑌 𐐺𐐴 𐐮𐐻, 𐐰𐑌𐐼 𐑄𐐮𐑅 𐐺𐐨𐐿𐐫𐑆 𐐱𐑂 𐑄𐐩𐑉 𐐮𐑌𐐮𐐿𐐶𐐮𐐻𐐨.

𐐕𐐈𐐑𐐓𐐊𐐡 II.

1. 𐐈𐑌𐐼 𐑌𐐵 𐐮𐐻 𐐿𐐩𐑋 𐐻𐐭 𐐹𐐪𐑅 𐑄𐐰𐐻 𐐮𐑌 𐑄 𐑅𐐮𐐿𐑅𐐻𐐨𐑌𐑃 𐐷𐐨𐑉 𐑁𐑉𐐱𐑋 𐑄 𐐿𐐲𐑋𐐮𐑍 𐐱𐑂 𐐗𐑉𐐴𐑅𐐻, 𐐢𐐰𐐿𐐬𐑌𐐨𐐲𐑅, 𐑄 𐐘𐐲𐑂𐐲𐑉𐑌𐐲𐑉 𐐱𐑂 𐑄 𐑊𐐰𐑌𐐼, 𐑉𐐨𐑅𐐨𐑂𐐼 𐐰𐑌 𐐨𐐹𐐮𐑅𐑊 𐑁𐑉𐐱𐑋 𐑄 𐑊𐐨𐐼𐐲𐑉 𐐰𐑌𐐼 𐑄 𐑀𐐲𐑂𐐲𐑉𐑌𐐲𐑉 𐐱𐑂 𐑄𐐮𐑅 𐐺𐐰𐑌𐐼 𐐱𐑂 𐑉𐐱𐐺𐐲𐑉𐑆; 𐐰𐑌𐐼 𐑄𐐨𐑆 𐐶𐐲𐑉 𐑄 𐐶𐐲𐑉𐐼𐑆 𐐸𐐶𐐮𐐽 𐐶𐐲𐑉 𐑉𐐮𐐻𐑌, 𐑅𐐩𐐮𐑍, 𐐢𐐰𐐿𐐬𐑌𐐨𐐲𐑅, 𐑋𐐬𐑅𐐻 𐑌𐐬𐐺𐑊 𐐰𐑌𐐼 𐐽𐐨𐑁 𐐘𐐲𐑂𐐲𐑉𐑌𐐲𐑉 𐐱𐑂 𐑄 𐑊𐐰𐑌𐐼, 𐐺𐐨𐐸𐐬𐑊𐐼, 𐐌 𐑉𐐴𐐻 𐑄𐐮𐑅 𐐨𐐹𐐮𐑅𐑊 𐐲𐑌𐐻𐐭 𐐷𐐭, 𐐰𐑌𐐼 𐐼𐐭 𐑀𐐮𐑂 𐐲𐑌𐐻𐐭 𐐷𐐭 𐐯𐐿𐑅𐐨𐐼𐐮𐑍𐑊𐐨 𐑀𐑉𐐩𐐻 𐐹𐑉𐐩𐑆 𐐺𐐨𐐿𐐫𐑆 𐐱𐑂 𐐷𐐭𐑉 𐑁𐐲𐑉𐑋𐑌𐐯𐑅, 𐐰𐑌𐐼 𐐫𐑊𐑅𐐬 𐑄 𐑁𐐲𐑉𐑋𐑌𐐯𐑅 𐐱𐑂 𐐷𐐭𐑉 𐐹𐐨𐐹𐑊, 𐐮𐑌 𐑋𐐩𐑌𐐻𐐩𐑌𐐮𐑍 𐑄𐐰𐐻 𐐸𐐶𐐮𐐽 𐐷 𐑅𐐲𐐹𐐬𐑆 𐐻𐐭 𐐺 𐐷𐐭𐑉 𐑉𐐴𐐻 𐐰𐑌𐐼 𐑊𐐮𐐺𐐲𐑉𐐻𐐨;

𐐷𐐩, 𐐷 𐐼𐐭 𐑅𐐻𐐰𐑌𐐼 𐐶𐐯𐑊, 𐐰𐑆 𐐮𐑁 𐐷 𐐶𐐲𐑉 𐑅𐐲𐐹𐐬𐑉𐐻𐐯𐐼 𐐺𐐴 𐑄 𐐸𐐰𐑌𐐼 𐐱𐑂 𐐩 𐐘𐐱𐐼, 𐐮𐑌 𐑄 𐐼𐐨𐑁𐐯𐑌𐑅 𐐱𐑂 𐐷𐐬𐑉 𐑊𐐮𐐺𐐲𐑉𐐻𐐮, 𐐰𐑌𐐼 𐐷𐐬𐑉 𐐹𐑉𐐱𐐹𐐲𐑉𐐻𐐮, 𐐰𐑌𐐼 𐐷𐐬𐑉 𐐿𐐲𐑌𐐻𐑉𐐮, 𐐫𐑉 𐑄𐐰𐐻 𐐸𐐶𐐮𐐽 𐐷 𐐼𐐭 𐐿𐐫𐑊 𐑅𐐬. 𐐰𐑌𐐼 𐐮𐐻 𐑅𐐨𐑋𐐯𐑃 𐐩 𐐹𐐮𐐻𐐮 𐐲𐑌𐐻𐐭 𐑋𐐨, 𐑋𐐬𐑅𐐻 𐑌𐐬𐐺𐑊 𐐢𐐩𐐿𐐬𐑌𐐨𐐲𐑅, 𐑄𐐰𐐻 𐐷 𐑇𐐳𐐼 𐐺 𐑅𐐬 𐑁𐐭𐑊𐐮𐑇 𐐰𐑌𐐼 𐑂𐐩𐑌 𐐰𐑆 𐐻𐐭 𐑅𐐲𐐹𐐬𐑆 𐑄𐐰𐐻 𐐷 𐐿𐐰𐑌 𐑅𐐻𐐰𐑌𐐼 𐐰𐑀𐐯𐑌𐑅𐐻 𐑅𐐬 𐑋𐐯𐑌𐐮 𐐺𐑉𐐩𐑂 𐑋𐐯𐑌 𐐸𐐭 𐐪𐑉 𐐰𐐻 𐑋𐐴 𐐿𐐲𐑋𐑋𐐰𐑌𐐼, 𐐸𐐭 𐐼𐐭 𐑌𐐵 𐐰𐐻 𐑄𐐮𐑅 𐐻𐐴𐑋 𐑅𐐻𐐰𐑌𐐼 𐐮𐑌 𐑄𐐩𐑉 𐐪𐑉𐑋𐑆, 𐐰𐑌𐐼 𐐼𐐭 𐐰𐐶𐐩𐐻 𐐶𐐮𐑄 𐑀𐑉𐐩𐐻 𐐰𐑍𐑆𐐴𐐯𐐻𐐮 𐑁𐐫𐑉 𐑄 𐐶𐐲𐑉𐐼, 𐐘𐐬 𐐼𐐵𐑌 𐐲𐐹𐐱𐑌 𐑄 𐐤𐐨𐑁𐐴𐐻𐑅 𐐰𐑌𐐼 𐐼𐐯𐑅𐐻𐑉𐑎 𐑄𐐯𐑋. 𐐰𐑌𐐼 𐐌, 𐑌𐐬𐐮𐑍 𐐱𐑂 𐑄𐐩𐑉 𐐲𐑌𐐿𐐱𐑍𐐿𐐲𐑉𐐰𐐺𐑊 𐑅𐐹𐐮𐑉𐐮𐐻, 𐐸𐐰𐑂𐐮𐑍 𐐹𐑉𐐭𐑂𐐼 𐑄𐐯𐑋 𐐮𐑌 𐑄 𐑁𐐨𐑊𐐼 𐐱𐑂 𐐺𐐰𐐻𐑊, 𐐰𐑌𐐼 𐑌𐐬𐐮𐑍 𐐱𐑂 𐑄𐐩𐑉 𐐯𐑂𐐲𐑉𐑊𐐰𐑅𐐻𐐮𐑍 𐐸𐐩𐐻𐑉𐐯𐐼 𐐻𐐬𐑉𐐼𐑆 𐐷𐐭, 𐐺𐐨𐐿𐐫𐑆 𐐱𐑂 𐑄 𐑋𐐯𐑌𐐮 𐑉𐐱𐑍𐑆 𐐸𐐶𐐮𐐽 𐐷 𐐸𐐰𐑂 𐐼𐐲𐑌 𐐲𐑌𐐻𐐭 𐑄𐐯𐑋, 𐑄𐐯𐑉𐑁𐐬𐑉 𐐮𐑁 𐑄𐐩 𐑇𐐳𐐼 𐐿𐐲𐑋 𐐼𐐵𐑌 𐐰𐑀𐐯𐑌𐑅𐐻 𐐷𐐭, 𐑄𐐩 𐐶𐐳𐐼 𐑂𐐮𐑆𐐮𐐻 𐐷𐐭 𐐶𐐮𐑄 𐐲𐐻𐐲𐑉 𐐼𐐯𐑅𐐻𐑉𐐲𐐿𐑇𐐲𐑌; 𐑄𐐯𐑉𐑁𐐬𐑉, 𐐌 𐐸𐐰𐑂 𐑉𐐬𐐻 𐑄𐐮𐑅 𐐨𐐹𐐮𐑅𐑊, 𐑅𐐨𐑊𐐮𐑍 𐐮𐐻 𐐶𐐮𐑄 𐑋𐐴𐑌 𐐬𐑌 𐐸𐐰𐑌𐐼, 𐑁𐐨𐑊𐐮𐑍 𐑁𐐫𐑉 𐐷𐐬𐑉 𐐶𐐯𐑊𐑁𐐩𐑉. 𐐺𐐨𐐿𐐫𐑆 𐐱𐑂 𐐷𐐬𐑉 𐑁𐐲𐑉𐑋𐑌𐐯𐑅 𐐮𐑌 𐑄𐐰𐐻 𐐸𐐶𐐮𐐽 𐐷 𐐺𐐨𐑊𐐨𐑂 𐐻𐐭 𐐺 𐑉𐐴𐐻, 𐐰𐑌𐐼 𐐷𐐬𐑉 𐑌𐐬𐐺𐑊 𐑅𐐹𐐮𐑉𐐮𐐻 𐐮𐑌 𐑄 𐑁𐐨𐑊𐐼 𐐱𐑂 𐐺𐐰𐐻𐑊; 𐑄𐐯𐑉𐑁𐐬𐑉 𐐌 𐑉𐐴𐐻 𐐲𐑌𐐻𐐭 𐐷𐐭, 𐐼𐐨𐑆𐐴𐑉𐐮𐑍 𐑄𐐰𐐻 𐐷 𐐶𐐳𐐼 𐐷𐐨𐑊𐐼 𐐲𐐹 𐐲𐑌𐐻𐐭 𐑄𐐮𐑅 𐑋𐐴 𐐹𐐨𐐹𐑊, 𐐷𐐬𐑉 𐑅𐐮𐐻𐐮𐑆, 𐐷𐐬𐑉 𐑊𐐰𐑌𐐼𐑆; 𐐰𐑌𐐼 𐐷𐐬𐑉 𐐹𐐲𐑆𐐯𐑇𐐲𐑌𐑆, 𐑉𐐰𐑄𐐲𐑉 𐑄𐐰𐑌 𐑄𐐰𐐻 𐑄𐐩 𐑇𐐳𐐼 𐑂𐐮𐑆𐐮𐐻 𐐷𐐭 𐐶𐐮𐑄 𐑄 𐑅𐐬𐑉𐐼, 𐐰𐑌𐐼 𐑄𐐰𐐻 𐐼𐐯𐑅𐐻𐑉𐐲𐐿𐑇𐐲𐑌 𐑇𐐳𐐼 𐐿𐐲𐑋 𐐲𐐹𐐱𐑌 𐐷𐐭; 𐐫𐑉 𐐮𐑌 𐐲𐑄𐐲𐑉-𐐶𐐲𐑉𐐼𐑆, 𐐷𐐨𐑊𐐼 𐐷𐐬𐑉𐑅𐐯𐑊𐑂𐑆 𐐲𐐹 𐐲𐑌𐐻𐐭 𐐲𐑅, 𐐰𐑌𐐼 𐐷𐐭𐑌𐐴𐐻 𐐶𐐮𐑄 𐐲𐑅, 𐐰𐑌𐐼 𐐺𐐨𐐿𐐲𐑋 𐐰𐐿𐐶𐐩𐑌𐐻𐐯𐐼 𐐶𐐮𐑄 𐐵𐑉 𐑅𐐨𐐿𐑉𐐯𐐻 𐐶𐐲𐑉𐐿𐑅, 𐐰𐑌𐐼 𐐺𐐨𐐿𐐲𐑋 𐐵𐑉 𐐺𐑉𐐯𐑄𐑉𐐯𐑌, 𐑄𐐰𐐻 𐐷 𐑋𐐩 𐐺 𐑊𐐴𐐿 𐐲𐑌𐐻𐐭 𐐲𐑅; 𐑌𐐱𐐻 𐐵𐑉 𐑅𐑊𐐩𐑂𐑆, 𐐺𐐲𐐻 𐐵𐑉 𐐺𐑉𐐯𐑄𐑉𐐯𐑌, 𐐰𐑌𐐼 𐐹𐐪𐑉𐐻𐑌𐐲𐑉𐑆 𐐱𐑂 𐐫𐑊 𐐵𐑉 𐑅𐐲𐐺𐑅𐐻𐐲𐑌𐑅. 𐐰𐑌𐐼 𐐺𐐨𐐸𐐬𐑊𐐼, 𐐌 𐑅𐐶𐐩𐑉 𐐲𐑌𐐻𐐭 𐐷𐐭, 𐐮𐑁 𐐷 𐐶𐐮𐑊 𐐼𐐭 𐑄𐐮𐑅, 𐐶𐐮𐑄 𐐰𐑌 𐐬𐑃, 𐐷 𐑇𐐰𐑊 𐑌𐐱𐐻 𐐺 𐐼𐐯𐑅𐐻𐑉𐑎𐐼; 𐐺𐐲𐐻 𐐮𐑁 𐐷 𐐶𐐮𐑊 𐑌𐐱𐐻 𐐼𐐭 𐑄𐐮𐑅, 𐐌 𐑅𐐶𐐩𐑉 𐐲𐑌𐐻𐐭 𐐷𐐭, 𐐶𐐮𐑄 𐐰𐑌 𐐬𐑃, 𐑄𐐰𐐻 𐐱𐑌 𐑄 𐑋𐐱𐑉𐐬 𐑋𐐲𐑌𐑃, 𐐌 𐐶𐐮𐑊 𐐿𐐲𐑋𐐰𐑌𐐼 𐑄𐐰𐐻 𐑋𐐴 𐐪𐑉𐑋𐐨𐑆 𐑇𐐰𐑊 𐐿𐐲𐑋 𐐼𐐵𐑌 𐐰𐑀𐐯𐑌𐑅𐐻 𐐷𐐭, 𐐰𐑌𐐼 𐑄𐐩 𐑇𐐰𐑊 𐑌𐐱𐐻 𐑅𐐻𐐩 𐑄𐐩𐑉 𐐸𐐰𐑌𐐼, 𐐰𐑌𐐼 𐑇𐐰𐑊 𐑅𐐹𐐩𐑉 𐑌𐐱𐐻, 𐐺𐐲𐐻 𐑇𐐰𐑊 𐑅𐑊𐐩 𐐷𐐭, 𐐰𐑌𐐼 𐑇𐐰𐑊 𐑊𐐯𐐻 𐑁𐐫𐑊 𐑄 𐑅𐐬𐑉𐐼 𐐲𐐹𐐱𐑌 𐐷𐐭, 𐐨𐑂𐐯𐑌 𐐲𐑌𐐻𐐮𐑊 𐐷 𐑇𐐰𐑊 𐐺𐐨𐐿𐐲𐑋 𐐯𐐿𐑅𐐻𐐮𐑍𐐿𐐻. 𐐰𐑌𐐼 𐐺𐐨𐐸𐐬𐑊𐐼, 𐐌 𐐰𐑋 𐐘𐐮𐐼𐐨𐐰𐑌𐐸𐐴; 𐐰𐑌𐐼 𐐌 𐐰𐑋 𐑄 𐐘𐐲𐑂𐐲𐑉𐑌𐐲𐑉 𐐱𐑂 𐑄𐐮𐑅 𐑄 𐑅𐐨𐐿𐑉𐐯𐐻 𐑅𐐬𐑅𐐴𐐯𐐻𐐮 𐐱𐑂 𐐘𐐰𐐼𐐨𐐰𐑌𐐻𐐲𐑌; 𐐸𐐶𐐮𐐽 𐑅𐐬𐑅𐐴𐐯𐐻𐐮, 𐐰𐑌𐐼 𐑄 𐐶𐐲𐑉𐐿𐑅 𐑄𐐯𐑉𐐱𐑂, 𐐌 𐑌𐐬 𐐻𐐭 𐐺 𐑀𐐳𐐼: 𐐰𐑌𐐼 𐑄𐐩 𐐪𐑉 𐐱𐑂 𐐩𐑌𐑇𐐲𐑌𐐻 𐐼𐐩𐐻, 𐐰𐑌𐐼 𐑄𐐩 𐐸𐐰𐑂 𐐺𐐮𐑌 𐐸𐐰𐑌𐐼𐐯𐐼 𐐼𐐵𐑌 𐐲𐑌𐐻𐐭 𐐲𐑅. 𐐰𐑌𐐼 𐐌 𐑉𐐴𐐻 𐑄𐐮𐑅 𐐨𐐹𐐮𐑅𐑊 𐐲𐑌𐐻𐐭 𐐷𐐭, 𐐢𐐩𐐿𐐬𐑌𐐨𐐲𐑅, 𐐰𐑌𐐼 𐐌 𐐸𐐬𐐹 𐑄𐐰𐐻 𐐷 𐐶𐐮𐑊 𐐼𐐨𐑊𐐮𐑂𐐲𐑉 𐐲𐐹 𐐷𐐬𐑉 𐑊𐐰𐑌𐐼𐑆, 𐐰𐑌𐐼 𐐷𐐬𐑉 𐐹𐐲𐑆𐐯𐑇𐐲𐑌𐑆, 𐐶𐐮𐑄𐐵𐐻 𐑄 𐑇𐐯𐐼𐐮𐑍 𐐱𐑂 𐐺𐑊𐐲𐐼, 𐑄𐐰𐐻 𐑄𐐮𐑅 𐑋𐐴 𐐹𐐨𐐹𐑊 𐑋𐐩 𐑉𐐨𐐿𐐲𐑂𐐲𐑉 𐑄𐐩𐑉 𐑉𐐴𐐻𐑅 𐐰𐑌𐐼 𐑀𐐲𐑂𐐲𐑉𐑌𐑋𐐯𐑌𐐻, 𐐸𐐭 𐐸𐐰𐑂 𐐼𐐮𐑅𐐯𐑌𐐻𐐯𐐼 𐐰𐐶𐐩 𐑁𐑉𐐱𐑋 𐐷𐐭, 𐐺𐐨𐐿𐐫𐑆 𐐱𐑂 𐐷𐐬𐑉 𐐶𐐮𐐿𐐯𐐼𐑌𐐯𐑅 𐐮𐑌 𐑉𐐨𐐻𐐩𐑌𐐮𐑍 𐑁𐑉𐐱𐑋 𐑄𐐯𐑋 𐑄𐐩𐑉 𐑉𐐴𐐻𐑅 𐐱𐑂 𐑀𐐲𐑂𐐲𐑉𐑌𐑋𐐯𐑌𐐻, 𐐰𐑌𐐼 𐐯𐐿𐑅𐐯𐐹𐐻 𐐷 𐐼𐐭 𐑄𐐮𐑅, 𐐌 𐐶𐐮𐑊 𐐰𐑂𐐯𐑌𐐾 𐑄𐐩𐑉 𐑉𐐱𐑍𐑆. 𐐌 𐐰𐑋 𐐘𐐮𐐼𐐨𐐰𐑌𐐸𐐴.

2. 𐐰𐑌𐐼 𐑌𐐵 𐐮𐐻 𐐿𐐩𐑋 𐐻𐐭 𐐹𐐰𐑅 𐑄𐐰𐐻 𐐸𐐶𐐯𐑌 𐐢𐐩𐐿𐐬𐑌𐐨𐐲𐑅 𐑉𐐨𐑅𐐨𐑂𐐼 𐑄𐐮𐑅 𐐨𐐹𐐮𐑅𐑊, 𐐸𐐨 𐐶𐐱𐑆 𐐯𐐿𐑅𐐨𐐼𐐮𐑍𐑊𐐮 𐐰𐑅𐐻𐐱𐑌𐐮𐑇𐐻, 𐐺𐐨𐐿𐐫𐑆 𐐱𐑂 𐑄 𐐺𐐬𐑊𐐼𐑌𐐯𐑅 𐐱𐑂 𐐘𐐮𐐼𐐨𐐰𐑌𐐸𐐴 𐐼𐐨𐑋𐐰𐑌𐐼𐐮𐑍 𐑄 𐐹𐐲𐑆𐐯𐑇𐐲𐑌 𐐱𐑂 𐑄 𐑊𐐰𐑌𐐼 𐐱𐑂 𐑄 𐐤𐐨𐑁𐐴𐐻𐑅, 𐐰𐑌𐐼 𐐫𐑊𐑅𐐬 𐐱𐑂 𐑃𐑉𐐯𐐻𐑌𐐮𐑍 𐑄 𐐹𐐨𐐹𐑊 𐐰𐑌𐐼 𐐰𐑂𐐯𐑌𐐾𐐮𐑍 𐑄 𐑉𐐱𐑍𐑆 𐐱𐑂 𐑄𐐬𐑆 𐑄𐐰𐐻 𐐸𐐰𐐼 𐑉𐐨𐑅𐐨𐑂𐐼 𐑌𐐬 𐑉𐐱𐑍, 𐑅𐐩𐑂 𐐮𐐻 𐐶𐐲𐑉 𐑄𐐩 𐐸𐐰𐐼 𐑉𐐱𐑍𐐼 𐑄𐐯𐑋𐑅𐐯𐑊𐑂𐑆, 𐐺𐐴 𐐼𐐮𐑅𐐯𐑌𐐻𐐮𐑍 𐐰𐐶𐐩 𐐲𐑌𐐻𐐭 𐑄𐐬𐑆 𐐶𐐮𐐿𐐯𐐼 𐐰𐑌𐐼 𐐰𐐺𐐱𐑋𐐮𐑌𐐰𐐺𐑊 𐑉𐐱𐐺𐐲𐑉𐑆. 𐐤𐐵 𐐺𐐨𐐸𐐬𐑊𐐼, 𐑄𐐮𐑅 𐐢𐐩𐐿𐐬𐑌𐐨𐐲𐑅 𐑄 𐐘𐐲𐑂𐐲𐑉𐑌𐐲𐑉, 𐐶𐐱𐑆 𐐩 𐐾𐐲𐑅𐐻 𐑋𐐰𐑌, 𐐰𐑌𐐼 𐐿𐐳𐐼 𐑌𐐱𐐻 𐐺 𐑁𐑉𐐴𐐻𐐲𐑌𐐼 𐐺𐐴 𐑄 𐐼𐐨𐑋𐐰𐑌𐐼𐑆 𐐰𐑌𐐼 𐑄 𐑃𐑉𐐯𐐻𐑌𐐮𐑍𐑆 𐐱𐑂 𐐩 𐑉𐐱𐐺𐐲𐑉; 𐑄𐐯𐑉𐑁𐐬𐑉 𐐸𐐨 𐐼𐐮𐐼 𐑌𐐱𐐻 𐐸𐐲𐑉𐐿𐐲𐑌 𐐻𐐭 𐑄 𐐨𐐹𐐮𐑅𐑊 𐐱𐑂 𐐘𐐮𐐼𐐨𐐰𐑌𐐸𐐴, 𐑄 𐐘𐐲𐑂𐐲𐑉𐑌𐐲𐑉 𐐱𐑂 𐑄 𐑉𐐱𐐺𐐲𐑉𐑆, 𐐺𐐲𐐻 𐐸𐐨 𐐼𐐮𐐼 𐐿𐐫𐑆 𐑄𐐰𐐻 𐐸𐐮𐑆 𐐹𐐨𐐹𐑊 𐑇𐐳𐐼 𐐿𐑉𐐴 𐐲𐑌𐐻𐐭 𐑄 𐐢𐐫𐑉𐐼 𐑁𐐫𐑉 𐑅𐐻𐑉𐐯𐑍𐑃 𐐰𐑀𐐯𐑌𐑅𐐻 𐑄 𐐻𐐴𐑋 𐑄𐐰𐐻 𐑄 𐑉𐐱𐐺𐐲𐑉𐑆 𐑇𐐳𐐼 𐐿𐐲𐑋 𐐼𐐵𐑌 𐐰𐑀𐐯𐑌𐑅𐐻 𐑄𐐯𐑋; 𐐷𐐩, 𐐸𐐨 𐑅𐐯𐑌𐐻 𐐩 𐐹𐑉𐐱𐐿𐑊𐐲𐑋𐐩𐑇𐐲𐑌 𐐰𐑋𐐲𐑍 𐐫𐑊 𐑄 𐐹𐐨𐐹𐑊, 𐑄𐐰𐐻 𐑄𐐩 𐑇𐐳𐐼 𐑀𐐰𐑄𐐲𐑉 𐐻𐐭𐑀𐐯𐑄𐐲𐑉 𐑄𐐩𐑉 𐐶𐐮𐑋𐐯𐑌 𐐰𐑌𐐼 𐑄𐐩𐑉 𐐽𐐮𐑊𐐼𐑉𐐯𐑌, 𐑄𐐩𐑉 𐑁𐑊𐐱𐐿𐑅 𐐰𐑌𐐼 𐑄𐐩𐑉 𐐸𐐲𐑉𐐼𐑆, 𐐰𐑌𐐼 𐐫𐑊 𐑄𐐩𐑉 𐑅𐐲𐐺𐑅𐐻𐐲𐑌𐑅, 𐑅𐐩𐑂 𐐮𐐻 𐐶𐐲𐑉 𐑄𐐩𐑉 𐑊𐐰𐑌𐐼, 𐐲𐑌𐐻𐐭 𐐶𐐲𐑌 𐐹𐑊𐐩𐑅. 𐐰𐑌𐐼 𐐸𐐨 𐐿𐐫𐑆𐐼 𐑄𐐰𐐻 𐑁𐐫𐑉𐐻𐐮𐑁𐐮𐐿𐐩𐑇𐐲𐑌𐑆 𐑇𐐳𐐼 𐐺 𐐺𐐮𐑊𐐻 𐑉𐐵𐑌𐐼 𐐰𐐺𐐵𐐻 𐑄𐐯𐑋, 𐐰𐑌𐐼 𐑄

𐑅𐐻𐑉𐐯𐑍𐑃 𐑄𐐩𐑉𐐱𐑂 𐑇𐐳𐐼 𐐺 𐐯𐐿𐑅𐐨𐐼𐐮𐑍𐑊𐐨 𐑀𐑉𐐩𐐻. 𐐈𐑌𐐼 𐐸𐐨 𐐿𐐫𐑆𐐼 𐑄𐐰𐐻 𐑄𐐩𐑉 𐑇𐐳𐐼 𐐺 𐐪𐑉𐑋𐐨𐑆, 𐐺𐐬𐑃 𐐱𐑂 𐑄 𐐤𐐨𐑁𐐴𐐻𐑅 𐐰𐑌𐐼 𐐱𐑂 𐑄 𐐢𐐰𐑋𐐲𐑌𐐴𐐻𐑅, 𐐫𐑉 𐐱𐑂 𐐫𐑊 𐑄𐐯𐑋 𐐸𐐭 𐐶𐐲𐑉 𐑌𐐲𐑋𐐺𐐲𐑉𐐼 𐐲𐑋𐐲𐑍 𐑄 𐐤𐐨𐑁𐐴𐐻𐑅, 𐑇𐐳𐐼 𐐺 𐐹𐑊𐐩𐑅𐐻 𐐰𐑆 𐑀𐐪𐑉𐐼𐑆 𐑉𐐵𐑌𐐼 𐐲𐐺𐐵𐐻, 𐐻𐐭 𐐶𐐱𐐽 𐑄𐐯𐑋, 𐐰𐑌𐐼 𐐻𐐭 𐑀𐐪𐑉𐐼 𐑄𐐯𐑋 𐑁𐑉𐐱𐑋 𐑄 𐑉𐐱𐐺𐐲𐑉𐑆, 𐐼𐐩 𐐰𐑌𐐼 𐑌𐐴𐐻; 𐐏𐐩 𐐸𐐨 𐑅𐐯𐐼 𐐲𐑌𐐻𐐭 𐑄𐐯𐑋, 𐐈𐑆 𐑄 𐐢𐐫𐑉𐐼 𐑊𐐮𐑂𐐯𐑃, 𐐯𐐿𐑅𐐯𐐹𐐻 𐐷 𐑉𐐨𐐹𐐯𐑌𐐻 𐐱𐑂 𐐫𐑊 𐐷𐐫𐑉 𐐮𐑌𐐮𐐿𐐶𐐮𐐻𐐮𐑆, 𐐰𐑌𐐼 𐐿𐑉𐐴 𐐲𐑌𐐻𐐭 𐑄 𐐢𐐫𐑉𐐼, 𐑄𐐰𐐻 𐑄𐐩 𐐶𐐳𐐼 𐐮𐑌 𐑌𐐬 𐐶𐐴𐑆 𐐺 𐐼𐐯𐑊𐐮𐑂𐐲𐑉𐐼 𐐵𐐻 𐐱𐑂 𐑄 𐐸𐐰𐑌𐐼𐑆 𐐱𐑂 𐑄𐐬𐑆 𐐘𐐰𐐼𐐨𐐰𐑌𐐻𐐲𐑌 𐑉𐐱𐐺𐐲𐑉𐑆. 𐐈𐑌𐐼 𐑅𐐬 𐑀𐑉𐐩𐐻 𐐰𐑌𐐼 𐑋𐐪𐑉𐑂𐐯𐑊𐐲𐑅 𐐶𐐲𐑉 𐑄 𐐶𐐲𐑉𐐼𐑆 𐐰𐑌𐐼 𐐹𐑉𐐱𐑁𐐯𐑅𐐮𐑆 𐐱𐑂 𐐢𐐩𐐿𐐬𐑌𐐨𐐲𐑅, 𐑄𐐰𐐻 𐑄𐐩 𐐼𐐮𐐼 𐐿𐐫𐑆 𐑁𐐨𐑉 𐐻𐐭 𐐿𐐲𐑋 𐐲𐐹𐐱𐑌 𐐫𐑊 𐑄 𐐹𐐨𐐹𐐲𐑊, 𐐰𐑌𐐼 𐑄𐐩 𐐼𐐮𐐼 𐐯𐑀𐑆𐐲𐑉𐐻 𐑄𐐯𐑋𐑅𐐯𐑊𐑂𐑆 𐐮𐑌 𐑄𐐩𐑉 𐑋𐐴𐐻, 𐐻𐐭 𐐼𐐭 𐐰𐐿𐐫𐑉𐐼𐐮𐑍 𐐻𐐭 𐑄 𐐶𐐲𐑉𐐼𐑆 𐐱𐑂 𐐢𐐩𐐿𐐬𐑌𐐨𐐲𐑅.

3. 𐐈𐑌𐐼 𐐮𐐻 𐐿𐐩𐑋 𐐻𐐭 𐐹𐐰𐑅 𐑄𐐰𐐻 𐐢𐐩𐐿𐐬𐑌𐐨𐐲𐑅 𐐼𐐮𐐼 𐐰𐐹𐑎𐑌𐐻 𐐽𐐨𐑁 𐐿𐐰𐐹𐐻𐐮𐑌𐑆 𐐬𐑂𐐲𐑉 𐐫𐑊 𐑄 𐐪𐑉𐑋𐐨𐑆 𐐱𐑂 𐑄 𐐤𐐨𐑁𐐴𐐻𐑅, 𐐻𐐭 𐐿𐐲𐑋𐐰𐑌𐐼 𐑄𐐯𐑋 𐐰𐐻 𐑄 𐐻𐐴𐑋 𐑄𐐰𐐻 𐑄 𐑉𐐱𐐺𐐲𐑉𐑆 𐑇𐐳𐐼 𐐿𐐲𐑋 𐐼𐐵𐑌 𐐵𐐻 𐐱𐑂 𐑄 𐐶𐐮𐑊𐐼𐐲𐑉𐑌𐐯𐑅 𐐲𐑀𐐯𐑌𐑅𐐻 𐑄𐐯𐑋. 𐐤𐐵 𐑄 𐐽𐐨𐑁𐐯𐑅𐐻 𐐲𐑋𐐲𐑍 𐐫𐑊 𐑄 𐐽𐐨𐑁 𐐿𐐰𐐹𐐻𐐮𐑌𐑆, 𐐰𐑌𐐼 𐑄 𐑀𐑉𐐩𐐻 𐐿𐐲𐑋𐐰𐑌𐐼𐐲𐑉 𐐱𐑂 𐐫𐑊 𐑄 𐐪𐑉𐑋𐐨𐑆 𐐱𐑂 𐑄 𐐤𐐨𐑁𐐴𐐻𐑅, 𐐶𐐱𐑆 𐐰𐐹𐑎𐑌𐐻𐐯𐐼, 𐐰𐑌𐐼 𐐸𐐮𐑆 𐑌𐐩𐑋 𐐶𐐱𐑆 𐐘𐐮𐐼𐑀𐐮𐐼𐐬𐑌𐐴. 𐐤𐐵 𐐮𐐻 𐐶𐐱𐑆 𐑄 𐐿𐐲𐑅𐐻𐐲𐑋 𐐲𐑋𐐲𐑍 𐐫𐑊 𐑄 𐐤𐐨𐑁𐐴𐐻𐑅, 𐐻𐐭 𐐰𐐹𐑎𐑌𐐻 𐑁𐐫𐑉 𐑄𐐩𐑉 𐐽𐐨𐑁 𐐿𐐰𐐹𐐻𐐮𐑌𐑆, 𐑅𐐩𐑂 𐐮𐐻 𐐶𐐲𐑉 𐐮𐑌 𐑄𐐩𐑉 𐐻𐐴𐑋𐑆 𐐱𐑂 𐐶𐐮𐐿𐐯𐐼𐑌𐐯𐑅, 𐑅𐐲𐑋 𐐶𐐲𐑌 𐑄𐐰𐐻 𐐸𐐰𐐼 𐑄 𐑅𐐹𐐮𐑉𐐮𐐻 𐐱𐑂 𐑉𐐯𐑂𐐯𐑊𐐩𐑇𐐲𐑌, 𐐰𐑌𐐼 𐐫𐑊𐑅𐐬 𐐹𐑉𐐱𐑁𐐯𐑅𐐮; 𐑄𐐩𐑉𐑁𐐬𐑉 𐑄𐐮𐑅 𐐘𐐮𐐼𐑀𐐮𐐼𐐬𐑌𐐴 𐐶𐐱𐑆 𐐲 𐑀𐑉𐐩𐐻 𐐹𐑉𐐱𐑁𐐯𐐻 𐐲𐑋𐐲𐑍 𐑄𐐯𐑋, 𐐰𐑌𐐼 𐐫𐑊𐑅𐐬 𐐶𐐱𐑆 𐑄 𐐽𐐨𐑁 𐐖𐐲𐐾. 𐐤𐐵 𐑄 𐐹𐐨𐐹𐐲𐑊 𐑅𐐯𐐼 𐐲𐑌𐐻𐐭 𐐘𐐮𐐼𐑀𐐮𐐼𐐬𐑌𐐴, 𐐑𐑉𐐩 𐐲𐑌𐐻𐐭 𐑄 𐐢𐐫𐑉𐐼, 𐐰𐑌𐐼 𐑊𐐯𐐻 𐐲𐑅 𐑀𐐬 𐐲𐐹 𐐲𐐹𐐱𐑌 𐑄 𐑋𐐵𐑌𐐻𐐮𐑌𐑆, 𐐰𐑌𐐼 𐐮𐑌𐐻𐐭 𐑄 𐐶𐐮𐑊𐐼𐐲𐑉𐑌𐐯𐑅, 𐑄𐐰𐐻 𐐶𐐨 𐑋𐐩 𐑁𐐫𐑊 𐐲𐐹𐐱𐑌 𐑄 𐑉𐐱𐐺𐐲𐑉𐑆 𐐰𐑌𐐼 𐐼𐐨𐑅𐐻𐑉𐑎 𐑄𐐯𐑋 𐐮𐑌 𐑄𐐩𐑉 𐐬𐑌 𐑊𐐰𐑌𐐼𐑆. 𐐒𐐲𐐻 𐐘𐐮𐐼𐑀𐐮𐐼𐐬𐑌𐐴 𐑅𐐯𐑃 𐐲𐑌𐐻𐐭 𐑄𐐯𐑋, 𐑄 𐐢𐐫𐑉𐐼 𐑁𐐫𐑉𐐺𐐮𐐼; 𐑁𐐫𐑉 𐐮𐑁 𐐶𐐨 𐑇𐐳𐐼 𐑀𐐬 𐐲𐐹 𐐲𐑀𐐯𐑌𐑅𐐻 𐑄𐐯𐑋, 𐑄 𐐢𐐫𐑉𐐼 𐐶𐐳𐐼 𐐼𐐯𐑊𐐮𐑂𐐲𐑉 𐐲𐑅 𐐮𐑌𐐻𐐭 𐑄𐐩𐑉 𐐸𐐰𐑌𐐼𐑆; 𐑄𐐩𐑉𐑁𐐬𐑉 𐐶𐐨 𐐶𐐮𐑊 𐐹𐑉𐐨𐐹𐐩𐑉 𐐵𐑉𐑅𐐯𐑊𐑂𐑆 𐐮𐑌 𐑄 𐑅𐐯𐑌𐐻𐐲𐑉 𐐱𐑂 𐐵𐑉 𐑊𐐰𐑌𐐼𐑆, 𐐰𐑌𐐼 𐐶𐐨 𐐶𐐮𐑊 𐑀𐐰𐑄𐐲𐑉 𐐫𐑊 𐐵𐑉 𐐪𐑉𐑋𐐨𐑆 𐐻𐐭𐑀𐐯𐑄𐐲𐑉, 𐐰𐑌𐐼 𐐶𐐨 𐐶𐐮𐑊 𐑌𐐱𐐻 𐑀𐐬 𐐲𐑀𐐯𐑌𐑅𐐻 𐑄𐐯𐑋, 𐐺𐐲𐐻 𐐶𐐨 𐐶𐐮𐑊 𐐶𐐩𐐻 𐐻𐐮𐑊 𐑄𐐩 𐑇𐐰𐑊 𐐿𐐲𐑋 𐐲𐑀𐐯𐑌𐑅𐐻 𐐲𐑅; 𐑄𐐩𐑉𐑁𐐬𐑉 𐐰𐑆 𐑄 𐐢𐐫𐑉𐐼 𐑊𐐮𐑂𐐯𐑃, 𐐮𐑁 𐐶𐐨 𐐼𐐭 𐑄𐐮𐑅, 𐐸𐐨 𐐶𐐮𐑊 𐐼𐐯𐑊𐐮𐑂𐐲𐑉 𐑄𐐯𐑋 𐐮𐑌𐐻𐐭 𐐵𐑉 𐐸𐐰𐑌𐐼𐑆.

4. 𐐈𐑌𐐼 𐐮𐐻 𐐿𐐩𐑋 𐐻𐐭 𐐹𐐰𐑅 𐐮𐑌 𐑄 𐑅𐐯𐑂𐐲𐑌𐐻𐐨𐑌𐑃 𐐷𐐨𐑉, 𐐮𐑌 𐑄 𐑊𐐰𐐻𐐲𐑉 𐐯𐑌𐐼 𐐱𐑂 𐑄 𐐷𐐨𐑉, 𐑄 𐐹𐑉𐐱𐐿𐑊𐐲𐑋𐐩𐑇𐐲𐑌 𐐱𐑂 𐐢𐐩𐐿𐐬𐑌𐐨𐐲𐑅 𐐸𐐰𐐼 𐑀𐐱𐑌 𐑁𐐬𐑉𐑃 𐑃𐑉𐐭𐐵𐐻 𐐫𐑊 𐑄 𐑁𐐩𐑅 𐐱𐑂 𐑄 𐑊𐐰𐑌𐐼, 𐐰𐑌𐐼 𐑄𐐩 𐐸𐐰𐐼 𐐻𐐩𐐿𐐲𐑌 𐑄𐐩𐑉 𐐸𐐫𐑉𐑅𐐯𐑆, 𐐰𐑌𐐼 𐑄𐐩𐑉 𐐽𐐰𐑉𐐮𐐲𐐻𐑅, 𐐰𐑌𐐼 𐑄𐐩𐑉 𐐿𐐰𐐻𐐲𐑊, 𐐰𐑌𐐼 𐐫𐑊 𐑄𐐩𐑉 𐑁𐑊𐐱𐐿𐑅, 𐐰𐑌𐐼 𐑄𐐩𐑉 𐐸𐐲𐑉𐐼𐑆, 𐐰𐑌𐐼 𐑄𐐩𐑉 𐑀𐑉𐐩𐑌, 𐐰𐑌𐐼 𐐫𐑊 𐑄𐐩𐑉 𐑅𐐲𐐺𐑅𐐻𐐰𐑌𐑅, 𐐰𐑌𐐼 𐐼𐐮𐐼 𐑋𐐪𐑉𐐽 𐑁𐐬𐑉𐑃 𐐺𐐴 𐑃𐐵𐑆𐐲𐑌𐐼𐑆, 𐐰𐑌𐐼 𐐺𐐴 𐐻𐐯𐑌𐑆 𐐱𐑂 𐑃𐐵𐑆𐐲𐑌𐐼𐑆, 𐐲𐑌𐐻𐐮𐑊 𐑄𐐩 𐐸𐐰𐐼 𐐫𐑊 𐑀𐐱𐑌 𐑁𐐬𐑉𐑃 𐐻𐐭 𐑄 𐐹𐑊𐐩𐑅 𐐸𐐶𐐮𐐽 𐐸𐐰𐐼 𐐺𐐮𐑌 𐐰𐐹𐑎𐑌𐐻𐐯𐐼 𐑄𐐰𐐻 𐑄𐐩 𐑇𐐳𐐼 𐑀𐐰𐑄𐐲𐑉 𐑄𐐯𐑋𐑅𐐯𐑊𐑂𐑆 𐐻𐐭𐑀𐐯𐑄𐐲𐑉, 𐐻𐐭 𐐼𐐨𐑁𐐯𐑌𐐼 𐑄𐐯𐑋𐑅𐐯𐑊𐑂𐑆 𐐲𐑀𐐯𐑌𐑅𐐻 𐑄𐐩𐑉 𐐯𐑌𐐯𐑋𐐮𐑆. 𐐈𐑌𐐼 𐑄 𐑊𐐰𐑌𐐼 𐐸𐐶𐐮𐐽 𐐶𐐱𐑆 𐐰𐐹𐑎𐑌𐐻𐐯𐐼 𐐶𐐱𐑆 𐑄 𐑊𐐰𐑌𐐼 𐐱𐑂 𐐞𐐰𐑉𐐰𐐸𐐯𐑋𐑊𐐲, 𐐰𐑌𐐼 𐑄 𐑊𐐰𐑌𐐼 𐐸𐐶𐐮𐐽 𐐶𐐱𐑆 𐐺𐐨𐐻𐐶𐐨𐑌 𐑄 𐑊𐐰𐑌𐐼 𐐞𐐰𐑉𐐰𐐸𐐯𐑋𐑊𐐲 𐐰𐑌𐐼 𐑄 𐑊𐐰𐑌𐐼 𐐒𐐵𐑌𐐻𐐮𐑁𐐳𐑊; 𐐷𐐩, 𐐻𐐭 𐑄 𐑊𐐴𐑌 𐐸𐐶𐐮𐐽 𐐶𐐱𐑆 𐐺𐐨𐐻𐐶𐐨𐑌 𐑄 𐑊𐐰𐑌𐐼 𐐒𐐵𐑌𐐻𐐮𐑁𐐳𐑊 𐐰𐑌𐐼 𐑄 𐑊𐐰𐑌𐐼 𐐔𐐯𐑅𐐬𐑊𐐩𐑇𐐲𐑌; 𐐰𐑌𐐼 𐑄𐐩𐑉 𐐶𐐲𐑉 𐐲 𐑀𐑉𐐩𐐻 𐑋𐐯𐑌𐐮 𐑃𐐵𐑆𐐲𐑌𐐼 𐐹𐐨𐐹𐐲𐑊 𐐸𐐭 𐐶𐐲𐑉 𐐿𐐫𐑊𐐼 𐐤𐐨𐑁𐐴𐐻𐑅, 𐐸𐐭 𐐼𐐮𐐼 𐑀𐐰𐑄𐐲𐑉 𐑄𐐯𐑋𐑅𐐯𐑊𐑂𐑆 𐐻𐐭𐑀𐐯𐑄𐐲𐑉 𐐮𐑌 𐑄𐐮𐑅 𐑊𐐰𐑌𐐼. 𐐤𐐵 𐐢𐐩𐐿𐐬𐑌𐐨𐐲𐑅 𐐼𐐮𐐼 𐐿𐐫𐑆 𐑄𐐰𐐻 𐑄𐐩 𐑇𐐳𐐼 𐑀𐐰𐑄𐐲𐑉 𐑄𐐯𐑋𐑅𐐯𐑊𐑂𐑆 𐐻𐐭𐑀𐐯𐑄𐐲𐑉 𐐮𐑌 𐑄 𐑊𐐰𐑌𐐼 𐑅𐐵𐑃𐐶𐐲𐑉𐐼, 𐐺𐐨𐐿𐐫𐑆 𐐱𐑂 𐑄 𐑀𐑉𐐩𐐻 𐐿𐐲𐑉𐑅 𐐸𐐶𐐮𐐽 𐐶𐐱𐑆 𐐲𐐹𐐱𐑌 𐑄 𐑊𐐰𐑌𐐼 𐑌𐐫𐑉𐑃𐐶𐐲𐑉𐐼; 𐐰𐑌𐐼 𐑄𐐩 𐐼𐐮𐐼 𐑁𐐫𐑉𐐻𐐮𐑁𐐴 𐑄𐐯𐑋𐑅𐐯𐑊𐑂𐑆 𐐲𐑀𐐯𐑌𐑅𐐻 𐑄𐐩𐑉 𐐯𐑌𐐯𐑋𐐮𐑆; 𐐰𐑌𐐼 𐑄𐐩 𐐼𐐮𐐼 𐐼𐐶𐐯𐑊 𐐮𐑌 𐐶𐐲𐑌 𐑊𐐰𐑌𐐼, 𐐰𐑌𐐼 𐐮𐑌 𐐶𐐲𐑌 𐐺𐐱𐐼𐐮, 𐐰𐑌𐐼 𐑄𐐩 𐐼𐐮𐐼 𐑁𐐨𐑉 𐑄 𐐶𐐲𐑉𐐼𐑆 𐐸𐐶𐐮𐐽 𐐸𐐰𐐼 𐐺𐐮𐑌 𐑅𐐹𐐬𐐿𐐲𐑌 𐐺𐐴 𐐢𐐩𐐿𐐬𐑌𐐨𐐲𐑅, 𐐮𐑌𐑅𐐬𐑋𐐲𐐽 𐑄𐐰𐐻 𐑄𐐩 𐐼𐐮𐐼 𐑉𐐨𐐹𐐯𐑌𐐻 𐐱𐑂 𐐫𐑊 𐑄𐐩𐑉 𐑅𐐮𐑌𐑆; 𐐰𐑌𐐼 𐑄𐐩 𐐼𐐮𐐼 𐐹𐐳𐐻 𐐲𐐹 𐑄𐐩𐑉 𐐹𐑉𐐩𐐲𐑉𐑆 𐐲𐑌𐐻𐐭 𐑄 𐐢𐐫𐑉𐐼 𐑄𐐩𐑉 𐐘𐐱𐐼, 𐑄𐐰𐐻 𐐸𐐨 𐐶𐐳𐐼 𐐼𐐯𐑊𐐮𐑂𐐲𐑉 𐑄𐐯𐑋 𐐮𐑌 𐑄 𐐻𐐴𐑋 𐑄𐐰𐐻 𐑄𐐩𐑉 𐐯𐑌𐐯𐑋𐐮𐑆 𐑇𐐳𐐼 𐐿𐐲𐑋 𐐼𐐵𐑌 𐐲𐑀𐐯𐑌𐑅𐐻 𐑄𐐯𐑋 𐐻𐐭 𐐺𐐰𐐻𐐲𐑊. 𐐈𐑌𐐼 𐑄𐐩 𐐶𐐲𐑉 𐐯𐐿𐑅𐐨𐐼𐐮𐑍𐑊𐐨 𐑅𐐱𐑉𐐬𐑁𐐳𐑊 𐐺𐐨𐐿𐐫𐑆 𐐱𐑂 𐑄𐐩𐑉 𐐯𐑌𐐯𐑋𐐮𐑆. 𐐈𐑌𐐼 𐐘𐐮𐐼𐑀𐐮𐐼𐐬𐑌𐐴 𐐼𐐮𐐼 𐐿𐐫𐑆 𐑄𐐰𐐻 𐑄𐐩 𐑇𐐳𐐼 𐑋𐐩𐐿 𐐶𐐯𐐹𐐲𐑌𐑆 𐐱𐑂 𐐶𐐫𐑉 𐐱𐑂 𐐯𐑂𐐲𐑉𐐮 𐐿𐐴𐑌𐐼, 𐐰𐑌𐐼 𐑄𐐩 𐑇𐐳𐐼 𐐺 𐑅𐐻𐑉𐐱𐑍 𐐶𐐮𐑄 𐐪𐑉𐑋𐐲𐑉, 𐐰𐑌𐐼 𐐶𐐮𐑄 𐑇𐐨𐑊𐐼𐑆, 𐐰𐑌𐐼 𐐶𐐮𐑄 𐐺𐐲𐐿𐑊𐐲𐑉𐑆, 𐐰𐑁𐐻𐐲𐑉 𐑄 𐑋𐐰𐑌𐐲𐑉 𐐱𐑂 𐐸𐐮𐑆 𐐮𐑌𐑅𐐻𐑉𐐲𐐿𐑇𐐲𐑌.

5. 𐐈𐑌𐐼 𐐮𐐻 𐐿𐐩𐑋 𐐻𐐭 𐐹𐐰𐑅 𐑄𐐰𐐻 𐐮𐑌 𐑄 𐑊𐐰𐐻𐐲𐑉 𐐯𐑌𐐼 𐐱𐑂 𐑄 𐐩𐐻𐐨𐑌𐑃 𐐷𐐨𐑉, 𐑄𐐬𐑆 𐐪𐑉𐑋𐐨𐑆 𐐱𐑂 𐑉𐐱𐐺𐐲𐑉𐑆 𐐸𐐰𐐼 𐐹𐑉𐐨𐐹𐐩𐑉𐐼 𐑁𐐫𐑉 𐐺𐐰𐐻𐑊, 𐐰𐑌𐐼 𐐺𐐨𐑀𐐰𐑌 𐐻𐐭 𐐿𐐲𐑋 𐐼𐐵𐑌 𐐰𐑌𐐼 𐐻𐐭 𐑅𐐰𐑊𐐨 𐑁𐐬𐑉𐑃 𐑁𐑉𐐱𐑋 𐑄 𐐸𐐮𐑊𐑆, 𐐰𐑌𐐼 𐐵𐐻 𐐱𐑂 𐑄 𐑋𐐵𐑌𐐻𐐩𐑌𐑆, 𐐰𐑌𐐼 𐑄 𐐶𐐮𐑊𐐼𐐲𐑉𐑌𐐯𐑅, 𐐰𐑌𐐼 𐑄𐐩𐑉 𐑅𐐻𐑉𐐱𐑍𐐸𐐬𐑊𐐼𐑆, 𐐰𐑌𐐼 𐑄𐐩𐑉 𐑅𐐨𐐿𐑉𐐯𐐻 𐐹𐑊𐐩𐑅𐐯𐑆, 𐐰𐑌𐐼 𐐺𐐨𐑀𐐰𐑌 𐐻𐐭 𐐻𐐩𐐿 𐐹𐐱𐑆𐐯𐑇𐐲𐑌 𐐱𐑂 𐑄 𐑊𐐰𐑌𐐼𐑆, 𐐺𐐬𐑃 𐐸𐐶𐐮𐐽 𐐶𐐲𐑉 𐐮𐑌 𐑄 𐑊𐐰𐑌𐐼 𐑅𐐵𐑃, 𐐰𐑌𐐼 𐐸𐐶𐐮𐐽 𐐶𐐲𐑉 𐐮𐑌 𐑄 𐑊𐐰𐑌𐐼 𐑌𐐫𐑉𐑃, 𐐰𐑌𐐼 𐐺𐐨𐑀𐐰𐑌 𐐻𐐭 𐐻𐐩𐐿 𐐹𐐱𐑆𐐯𐑇𐐲𐑌 𐐱𐑂 𐐫𐑊 𐑄 𐑊𐐰𐑌𐐼𐑆 𐐸𐐶𐐮𐐽 𐐸𐐰𐐼 𐐺𐐨𐑌 𐐼𐐯𐑆𐐲𐑉𐐻𐐯𐐼 𐐺𐐴 𐑄 𐐤𐐨𐑁𐐴𐐻𐑅, 𐐰𐑌𐐼 𐑄 𐑅𐐮𐐻𐐨𐑆 𐐸𐐶𐐮𐐽 𐐸𐐰𐐼 𐐺𐐨𐑌 𐑊𐐯𐑁𐐻 𐐼𐐯𐑅𐐬𐑊𐐩𐐻. 𐐒𐐲𐐻 𐐺𐐨𐐸𐐬𐑊𐐼, 𐑄𐐩𐑉 𐐶𐐲𐑉 𐑌𐐬 𐐶𐐴𐑊𐐼 𐐺𐐨𐑅𐐻𐑅 𐑌𐐫𐑉 𐑀𐐩𐑋 𐐮𐑌 𐑄𐐬𐑆 𐑊𐐰𐑌𐐼𐑆 𐐸𐐶𐐮𐐽 𐐸𐐰𐐼 𐐺𐐨𐑌 𐐼𐐯𐑆𐐲𐑉𐐻𐐯𐐼 𐐺𐐴 𐑄 𐐤𐐨𐑁𐐴𐐻𐑅, 𐐰𐑌𐐼 𐑄𐐩𐑉 𐐶𐐱𐑆 𐑌𐐬 𐑀𐐩𐑋 𐑁𐐫𐑉 𐑄 𐑉𐐱𐐺𐐲𐑉𐑆 𐑅𐐩𐑂 𐐮𐐻 𐐶𐐲𐑉 𐐮𐑌 𐑄 𐐶𐐮𐑊𐐼𐐲𐑉𐑌𐐯𐑅; 𐐰𐑌𐐼 𐑄 𐑉𐐱𐐺𐐲𐑉𐑆 𐐿𐐳𐐼 𐑌𐐱𐐻 𐐯𐑀𐑆𐐮𐑅𐐻 𐑅𐐩𐑂 𐐮𐐻 𐐶𐐲𐑉 𐐮𐑌 𐑄 𐐶𐐮𐑊𐐼𐐲𐑉𐑌𐐯𐑅, 𐑁𐐫𐑉 𐑄 𐐶𐐱𐑌𐐻 𐐱𐑂 𐑁𐐭𐐼; 𐑁𐐫𐑉 𐑄 𐐤𐐨𐑁𐐴𐐻𐑅 𐐸𐐰𐐼 𐑊𐐯𐑁𐐻 𐑄𐐩𐑉 𐑊𐐰𐑌𐐼𐑆 𐐼𐐯𐑅𐐬𐑊𐐩𐐻, 𐐰𐑌𐐼 𐐸𐐰𐐼 𐑀𐐰𐑄𐐲𐑉𐐼 𐑄𐐩𐑉 𐑁𐑊𐐱𐐿𐑅, 𐐰𐑌𐐼 𐑄𐐩𐑉 𐐸𐐲𐑉𐐼𐑆, 𐐰𐑌𐐼 𐐫𐑊 𐑄𐐩𐑉 𐑅𐐲𐐺𐑅𐐻𐐰𐑌𐑅, 𐐰𐑌𐐼 𐑄𐐩 𐐶𐐲𐑉 𐐮𐑌 𐐶𐐲𐑌 𐐺𐐱𐐼𐐨; 𐑄𐐩𐑉𐑁𐐫𐑉 𐑄𐐩𐑉 𐐶𐐱𐑆 𐑌𐐬 𐐽𐐰𐑌𐑅 𐑁𐐫𐑉 𐑄 𐑉𐐱𐐺𐐲𐑉𐑆 𐐻𐐭 𐐹𐑊𐐲𐑌𐐼𐐲𐑉 𐐰𐑌𐐼 𐐻𐐭 𐐱𐐺𐐻𐐩𐑌 𐑁𐐭𐐼, 𐑅𐐩𐑂 𐐮𐐻 𐐶𐐲𐑉 𐐻𐐭 𐐿𐐲𐑋 𐐲𐐹 𐐮𐑌 𐐬𐐹𐐯𐑌 𐐺𐐰𐐻𐑊 𐐰𐑀𐐯𐑌𐑅𐐻 𐑄 𐐤𐐨𐑁𐐴𐐻𐑅; 𐐰𐑌𐐼 𐑄 𐐤𐐨𐑁𐐴𐐻𐑅 𐐺𐐨𐐮𐑍 𐐮𐑌 𐐶𐐲𐑌 𐐺𐐱𐐼𐐨, 𐐰𐑌𐐼 𐐸𐐰𐑂𐐮𐑍 𐑅𐐬 𐑀𐑉𐐩𐐻 𐐰 𐑌𐐲𐑋𐐺𐐲𐑉, 𐐰𐑌𐐼 𐐸𐐰𐑂𐐮𐑍 𐑉𐐨𐑆𐐲𐑉𐑂𐐼 𐑁𐐫𐑉 𐑄𐐯𐑋𐑅𐐯𐑊𐑂𐑆 𐐹𐑉𐐱𐑂𐐮𐑈𐐲𐑌𐑆, 𐐰𐑌𐐼 𐐸𐐫𐑉𐑅𐐯𐑆, 𐐰𐑌𐐼 𐐿𐐰𐐻𐑊, 𐐰𐑌𐐼 𐑁𐑊𐐱𐐿𐑅 𐐱𐑂 𐐯𐑂𐐲𐑉𐐨 𐐿𐐴𐑌𐐼, 𐑄𐐰𐐻 𐑄𐐩 𐑋𐐴𐐻 𐑅𐐲𐐺𐑅𐐮𐑅𐐻 𐑁𐐫𐑉 𐑄 𐑅𐐹𐐩𐑅 𐐱𐑂 𐑅𐐯𐑂𐐲𐑌 𐐷𐐨𐑉𐑆, 𐐮𐑌 𐑄 𐐸𐐶𐐮𐐽 𐐻𐐴𐑋 𐑄𐐩 𐐼𐐮𐐼 𐐸𐐬𐐹 𐐻𐐭 𐐼𐐯𐑅𐐻𐑉𐐫𐐶 𐑄 𐑉𐐱𐐺𐐲𐑉𐑆 𐑁𐑉𐐱𐑋 𐐱𐑁 𐑄 𐑁𐐩𐑅 𐐱𐑂 𐑄 𐑊𐐰𐑌𐐼. 𐐈𐑌𐐼 𐑄𐐲𐑅 𐑄 𐐩𐐻𐐨𐑌𐑃 𐐷𐐨𐑉 𐐼𐐮𐐼 𐐹𐐰𐑅 𐐰𐐶𐐩.

6. 𐐈𐑌𐐼 𐐮𐐻 𐐿𐐩𐑋 𐐻𐐭 𐐹𐐰𐑅 𐑄𐐰𐐻 𐐮𐑌 𐑄 𐑌𐐴𐑌𐐻𐐨𐑌𐑃 𐐷𐐨𐑉 𐐘𐐮𐐼𐐨𐐰𐑌𐐸𐐴 𐑁𐐵𐑌𐐼 𐑄𐐰𐐻 𐐮𐐻 𐐶𐐱𐑆 𐐯𐐿𐑅𐐹𐐨𐐼𐐨𐐲𐑌𐐻 𐑄𐐰𐐻 𐐸𐐨 𐑇𐐳𐐼 𐑀𐐬 𐐲𐐹 𐐻𐐭 𐐺𐐰𐐻𐑊 𐐰𐑀𐐯𐑌𐑅𐐻 𐑄 𐐤𐐨𐑁𐐴𐐻𐑅, 𐑁𐐫𐑉 𐑄𐐩𐑉 𐐶𐐱𐑆 𐑌𐐬 𐐶𐐩 𐑄𐐰𐐻 𐑄𐐩 𐐿𐐳𐐼 𐑅𐐲𐐺𐑅𐐮𐑅𐐻 𐑅𐐩𐑂 𐐮𐐻 𐐶𐐲𐑉 𐐻𐐭 𐐹𐑊𐐲𐑌𐐼𐐲𐑉, 𐐰𐑌𐐼 𐑉𐐱𐐺, 𐐰𐑌𐐼 𐑋𐐲𐑉𐐼𐐲𐑉. 𐐈𐑌𐐼 𐑄𐐩 𐐼𐐲𐑉𐑅𐐻 𐑌𐐱𐐻 𐑅𐐹𐑉𐐯𐐼 𐑄𐐯𐑋𐑅𐐯𐑊𐑂𐑆 𐐲𐐹𐐱𐑌 𐑄 𐑁𐐩𐑅 𐐱𐑂 𐑄 𐑊𐐰𐑌𐐼, 𐐮𐑌𐑅𐐬𐑋𐐲𐐽 𐑄𐐰𐐻 𐑄𐐩 𐐿𐐳𐐼 𐑉𐐩𐑆 𐑀𐑉𐐩𐑌, 𐑊𐐯𐑅𐐻 𐑄 𐐤𐐨𐑁𐐴𐐻𐑅 𐑇𐐳𐐼 𐐿𐐲𐑋 𐐲𐐹𐐱𐑌 𐑄𐐯𐑋 𐐰𐑌𐐼 𐑅𐑊𐐩 𐑄𐐯𐑋; 𐑄𐐩𐑉𐑁𐐫𐑉 𐐘𐐮𐐼𐐨𐐰𐑌𐐸𐐴 𐑀𐐩𐑂 𐐿𐐱𐑋𐐰𐑌𐐼𐑋𐐯𐑌𐐻 𐐲𐑌𐐻𐐭 𐐸𐐮𐑆 𐐪𐑉𐑋𐐨𐑆 𐑄𐐰𐐻 𐐮𐑌 𐑄𐐮𐑅 𐐷𐐨𐑉 𐑄𐐩 𐑇𐐳𐐼 𐑀𐐬 𐐲𐐹 𐐻𐐭 𐐺𐐰𐐻𐑊 𐐰𐑀𐐯𐑌𐑅𐐻 𐑄 𐐤𐐨𐑁𐐴𐐻𐑅.

7. 𐐈𐑌𐐼 𐐮𐐻 𐐿𐐩𐑋 𐐻𐐭 𐐹𐐰𐑅 𐑄𐐰𐐻 𐑄𐐩 𐐼𐐮𐐼 𐐿𐐲𐑋 𐐲𐐹 𐐻𐐭 𐐺𐐰𐐻𐑊; 𐐰𐑌𐐼 𐐮𐐻 𐐶𐐱𐑆 𐐮𐑌 𐑄 𐑅𐐮𐐿𐑅𐑃 𐑋𐐲𐑌𐑃; 𐐰𐑌𐐼 𐐺𐐨𐐸𐐬𐑊𐐼, 𐑀𐑉𐐩𐐻 𐐰𐑌𐐼 𐐻𐐯𐑉𐐮𐐺𐑊 𐐶𐐱𐑆 𐑄 𐐼𐐩 𐑄𐐰𐐻 𐑄𐐩 𐐼𐐮𐐼 𐐿𐐲𐑋 𐐲𐐹 𐐻𐐭 𐐺𐐰𐐻𐑊; 𐐰𐑌𐐼 𐑄𐐩 𐐶𐐲𐑉 𐑀𐐲𐑉𐐼𐐯𐐼 𐐰𐐺𐐵𐐻 𐐰𐑁𐐻𐐲𐑉 𐑄 𐑋𐐰𐑌𐐲𐑉 𐐱𐑂 𐑉𐐱𐐺𐐲𐑉𐑆; 𐐰𐑌𐐼 𐑄𐐩 𐐸𐐰𐐼 𐐰 𐑊𐐰𐑋-𐑅𐐿𐐮𐑌 𐐰𐐺𐐵𐐻 𐑄𐐩𐑉 𐑊𐐲𐐮𐑌𐑆, 𐐰𐑌𐐼 𐑄𐐩 𐐶𐐲𐑉 𐐼𐐴𐐼 𐐮𐑌 𐐺𐑊𐐲𐐼, 𐐰𐑌𐐼 𐑄𐐩𐑉 𐐸𐐯𐐼𐑆 𐐶𐐲𐑉 𐑇𐐬𐑉𐑌, 𐐰𐑌𐐼 𐑄𐐩 𐐸𐐰𐐼 𐐸𐐯𐐼-𐐹𐑊𐐩𐐻𐑅 𐐲𐐹𐐱𐑌 𐑄𐐯𐑋; 𐐰𐑌𐐼 𐑀𐑉𐐩𐐻 𐐰𐑌𐐼 𐐻𐐯𐑉𐐮𐐺𐑊 𐐶𐐱𐑆 𐑄 𐐰𐐹𐐨𐑉𐐲𐑌𐑅 𐐱𐑂 𐑄 𐐪𐑉𐑋𐐨𐑆 𐐱𐑂 𐐘𐐮𐐼𐐨𐐰𐑌𐐸𐐴, 𐐺𐐨𐐿𐐫𐑆 𐐱𐑂 𐑄𐐩𐑉 𐐪𐑉𐑋𐐲𐑉, 𐐰𐑌𐐼 𐐺𐐨𐐿𐐫𐑆 𐐱𐑂 𐑄𐐩𐑉 𐐺𐐨𐐮𐑍 𐐼𐐴𐐼 𐐮𐑌 𐐺𐑊𐐲𐐼. 𐐈𐑌𐐼 𐐮𐐻 𐐿𐐩𐑋 𐐻𐐭 𐐹𐐰𐑅 𐑄𐐰𐐻 𐑄 𐐪𐑉𐑋𐐨𐑆 𐐱𐑂 𐑄 𐐤𐐨𐑁𐐴𐐻𐑅, 𐐸𐐶𐐯𐑌 𐑄𐐩 𐑅𐐫 𐑄 𐐰𐐹𐐨𐑉𐐲𐑌𐑅 𐐱𐑂 𐑄 𐐪𐑉𐑋𐐨 𐐱𐑂 𐐘𐐮𐐼𐐨𐐰𐑌𐐸𐐴, 𐐸𐐰𐐼 𐐫𐑊 𐑁𐐫𐑊𐐲𐑌 𐐻𐐭 𐑄 𐐲𐑉𐑃, 𐐰𐑌𐐼 𐐼𐐮𐐼 𐑊𐐮𐑁𐐻 𐑄𐐩𐑉 𐐿𐑉𐐴𐑆 𐐻𐐭 𐑄 𐐢𐐫𐑉𐐼 𐑄𐐩𐑉 𐐘𐐱𐐼, 𐑄𐐰𐐻 𐐸𐐨 𐐶𐐳𐐼 𐑅𐐹𐐩𐑉 𐑄𐐯𐑋, 𐐰𐑌𐐼 𐐼𐐯𐑊𐐮𐑂𐐲𐑉 𐑄𐐯𐑋 𐐵𐐻 𐐱𐑂 𐑄 𐐸𐐰𐑌𐐼𐑆 𐐱𐑂 𐑄𐐩𐑉 𐐯𐑌𐐯𐑋𐐨𐑆. 𐐈𐑌𐐼 𐐮𐐻 𐐿𐐩𐑋 𐐻𐐭 𐐹𐐰𐑅 𐑄𐐰𐐻 𐐸𐐶𐐯𐑌 𐑄 𐐪𐑉𐑋𐐨𐑆 𐐱𐑂 𐐘𐐮𐐼𐐨𐐰𐑌𐐸𐐴 𐑅𐐫 𐑄𐐮𐑅, 𐑄𐐩 𐐺𐐨𐑀𐐰𐑌 𐐻𐐭 𐑇𐐵𐐻 𐐶𐐮𐑄 𐐰 𐑊𐐵𐐼 𐑂𐐦𐑅, 𐐺𐐨𐐿𐐫𐑆 𐐱𐑂 𐑄𐐩𐑉 𐐾𐐦, 𐑁𐐫𐑉 𐑄𐐩 𐐸𐐰𐐼 𐑅𐐲𐐹𐐬𐑆𐐼 𐑄𐐰𐐻 𐑄 𐐤𐐨𐑁𐐴𐐻𐑅 𐐸𐐰𐐼 𐑁𐐫𐑊𐐲𐑌 𐐶𐐮𐑄 𐑁𐐨𐑉, 𐐺𐐨𐐿𐐫𐑆 𐐱𐑂 𐑄 𐐻𐐯𐑉𐐲𐑉 𐐱𐑂 𐑄𐐩𐑉 𐐪𐑉𐑋𐐨𐑆; 𐐺𐐲𐐻 𐐮𐑌 𐑄𐐮𐑅 𐑃𐐮𐑍 𐑄𐐩 𐐶𐐲𐑉 𐐼𐐮𐑅𐐰𐐹𐐱𐐮𐑌𐐻𐐯𐐼, 𐑁𐐫𐑉 𐑄 𐐤𐐨𐑁𐐴𐐻𐑅 𐐼𐐮𐐼 𐑌𐐱𐐻 𐑁𐐨𐑉 𐑄𐐯𐑋, 𐐺𐐲𐐻 𐑄𐐩 𐐼𐐮𐐼 𐑁𐐨𐑉 𐑄𐐩𐑉 𐐘𐐱𐐼, 𐐰𐑌𐐼 𐐼𐐮𐐼 𐑅𐐲𐐹𐑊𐐮𐐿𐐩𐐻 𐐸𐐮𐑋 𐑁𐐫𐑉 𐐹𐑉𐐬𐐻𐐯𐐿𐑇𐐲𐑌; 𐑄𐐩𐑉𐑁𐐫𐑉 𐐸𐐶𐐯𐑌 𐑄 𐐪𐑉𐑋𐐨𐑆 𐐱𐑂 𐐘𐐮𐐼𐐨𐐰𐑌𐐸𐐴 𐐼𐐮𐐼 𐑉𐐲𐑇 𐐲𐐹𐐱𐑌 𐑄𐐯𐑋, 𐑄𐐩 𐐶𐐲𐑉 𐐹𐑉𐐨𐐹𐐩𐑉𐐼 𐐻𐐭 𐑋𐐨𐐻 𐑄𐐯𐑋; 𐐷𐐩, 𐐮𐑌 𐑄 𐑅𐐻𐑉𐐯𐑍𐑃 𐐱𐑂 𐑄 𐐢𐐫𐑉𐐼 𐑄𐐩 𐐼𐐮𐐼 𐑉𐐨𐑅𐐨𐑂 𐑄𐐯𐑋; 𐐰𐑌𐐼 𐑄 𐐺𐐰𐐻𐑊 𐐿𐐱𐑋𐐯𐑌𐑅𐐼 𐐮𐑌 𐑄𐐮𐑅 𐑄 𐑅𐐮𐐿𐑅𐑃 𐑋𐐲𐑌𐑃; 𐐰𐑌𐐼 𐑀𐑉𐐩𐐻 𐐰𐑌𐐼 𐐻𐐯𐑉𐐮𐐺𐑊 𐐶𐐱𐑆 𐑄 𐐺𐐰𐐻𐑊 𐑄𐐩𐑉𐐱𐑂, 𐐷𐐩, 𐑀𐑉𐐩𐐻 𐐰𐑌𐐼 𐐻𐐯𐑉𐐮𐐺𐑊 𐐶𐐱𐑆 𐑄 𐑅𐑊𐐫𐐻𐐲𐑉 𐑄𐐩𐑉𐐱𐑂, 𐐮𐑌𐑅𐐬𐑋𐐲𐐽 𐑄𐐰𐐻 𐑄𐐩𐑉 𐑌𐐯𐑂𐐲𐑉 𐐶𐐱𐑆 𐑌𐐬𐑌 𐑅𐐬 𐑀𐑉𐐩𐐻 𐐰 𐑅𐑊𐐫𐐻𐐲𐑉 𐐰𐑋𐐲𐑍 𐐫𐑊 𐑄 𐐹𐐨𐐹𐑊 𐐱𐑂 𐐢𐐨𐐸𐐴 𐑅𐐮𐑌𐑅 𐐸𐐨 𐑊𐐯𐑁𐐻 𐐖𐐲𐑉𐐭𐑅𐐲𐑊𐐯𐑋. 𐐈𐑌𐐼 𐑌𐐱𐐻𐐶𐐮𐑃𐑅𐐻𐐰𐑌𐐼𐐮𐑍 𐑄 𐑃𐑉𐐯𐐻𐑌𐐮𐑍𐑆 𐐰𐑌𐐼 𐑄

𐐬𐑃𐑅 𐐸𐐶𐐮𐐽 𐐘𐐮𐐼𐐨𐐰𐑌𐐸𐐴 𐐸𐐰𐐼 𐑋𐐩𐐼, 𐐺𐐨𐐸𐐬𐑊𐐼, 𐑄 𐐤𐐨𐑁𐐴𐐻𐑅 𐐼𐐮𐐼 𐐺𐐨𐐻 𐑄𐐯𐑋, 𐐮𐑌𐑅𐐬𐑋𐐲𐐽 𐑄𐐰𐐻 𐑄𐐩 𐐼𐐮𐐼 𐑁𐐫𐑊 𐐺𐐰𐐿 𐑁𐑉𐐱𐑋 𐐺𐐨𐑁𐐬𐑉 𐑄𐐯𐑋.

8. 𐐈𐑌𐐼 𐐮𐐻 𐐿𐐩𐑋 𐐻𐐭 𐐹𐐪𐑅 𐑄𐐰𐐻 𐐘𐐮𐐼𐑀𐐮𐐼𐐬𐑌𐐴 𐐿𐐱𐑋𐐰𐑌𐐼𐐯𐐼 𐑄𐐰𐐻 𐐸𐐮𐑆 𐐪𐑉𐑋𐐨𐑆 𐑇𐐳𐐼 𐐹𐐲𐑉𐑅𐐭 𐑄𐐯𐑋 𐐰𐑆 𐑁𐐪𐑉 𐐰𐑆 𐑄 𐐺𐐫𐑉𐐼𐐲𐑉𐑆 𐐱𐑂 𐑄 𐐶𐐮𐑊𐐼𐐲𐑉𐑌𐐯𐑅, 𐐰𐑌𐐼 𐑄𐐰𐐻 𐑄𐐩 𐑇𐐳𐐼 𐑌𐐱𐐻 𐑅𐐹𐐯𐑉 𐐯𐑌𐐨 𐑄𐐰𐐻 𐑇𐐳𐐼 𐑁𐐫𐑊 𐐮𐑌𐐻𐐭 𐑄𐐯𐑉 𐐸𐐰𐑌𐐼𐑆 𐐺𐐴 𐑄 𐐶𐐩; 𐐰𐑌𐐼 𐑄𐐲𐑅 𐑄𐐩 𐐼𐐮𐐼 𐐹𐐲𐑉𐑅𐐭 𐑄𐐯𐑋, 𐐰𐑌𐐼 𐐼𐐮𐐼 𐑅𐑊𐐩 𐑄𐐯𐑋, 𐐻𐐭 𐑄 𐐺𐐫𐑉𐐼𐐲𐑉𐑆 𐐱𐑂 𐑄 𐐶𐐮𐑊𐐼𐐲𐑉𐑌𐐯𐑅, 𐐨𐑂𐐲𐑌 𐐲𐑌𐐻𐐮𐑊 𐑄𐐩 𐐸𐐰𐐼 𐑁𐐳𐑊𐑁𐐮𐑊𐐼 𐑄 𐐿𐐱𐑋𐐰𐑌𐐼𐑋𐐯𐑌𐐻 𐐱𐑂 𐐘𐐮𐐼𐑀𐐮𐐼𐐬𐑌𐐴. 𐐈𐑌𐐼 𐐮𐐻 𐐿𐐩𐑋 𐐻𐐭 𐐹𐐪𐑅 𐑄𐐰𐐻 𐐘𐐮𐐼𐐨𐐰𐑌𐐸𐐴, 𐐸𐐭 𐐸𐐰𐐼 𐑅𐐻𐐳𐐼 𐐰𐑌𐐼 𐑁𐐫𐐻 𐐶𐐮𐑄 𐐺𐐬𐑊𐐼𐑌𐐯𐑅, 𐐶𐐱𐑆 𐐹𐐲𐑉𐑅𐐭𐐼 𐐰𐑆 𐐸𐐨 𐑁𐑊𐐯𐐼; 𐐰𐑌𐐼 𐐺𐐨𐐮𐑍 𐐶𐐨𐑉𐐨 𐐺𐐨𐐿𐐫𐑆 𐐱𐑂 𐐸𐐮𐑆 𐑋𐐲𐐽 𐑁𐐴𐐻𐐮𐑍, 𐐸𐐨 𐐶𐐱𐑆 𐐬𐑂𐐲𐑉𐐻𐐩𐐿𐐲𐑌 𐐰𐑌𐐼 𐑅𐑊𐐩𐑌. 𐐈𐑌𐐼 𐑄𐐲𐑅 𐐶𐐱𐑆 𐑄 𐐯𐑌𐐼 𐐱𐑂 𐐘𐐮𐐼𐐨𐐰𐑌𐐸𐐴 𐑄 𐑉𐐱𐐺𐐲𐑉.

9. 𐐈𐑌𐐼 𐐮𐐻 𐐿𐐩𐑋 𐐻𐐭 𐐹𐐪𐑅 𐑄𐐰𐐻 𐑄 𐐪𐑉𐑋𐐨𐑆 𐐱𐑂 𐑄 𐐤𐐨𐑁𐐴𐐻𐑅 𐐼𐐮𐐼 𐑉𐐨𐐻𐐲𐑉𐑌 𐐲𐑀𐐯𐑌 𐐻𐐭 𐑄𐐩𐑉 𐐹𐑊𐐩𐑅 𐐱𐑂 𐑅𐐨𐐿𐐷𐐭𐑉𐐮𐐻𐐨. 𐐈𐑌𐐼 𐐮𐐻 𐐿𐐩𐑋 𐐻𐐭 𐐹𐐪𐑅 𐑄𐐰𐐻 𐑄𐐮𐑅 𐑌𐐴𐑌𐐻𐐨𐑌𐑃 𐐷𐐨𐑉 𐐼𐐮𐐼 𐐹𐐪𐑅 𐐲𐐶𐐩, 𐐰𐑌𐐼 𐑄 𐑉𐐱𐐺𐐲𐑉𐑆 𐐼𐐮𐐼 𐑌𐐱𐐻 𐐿𐐲𐑋 𐐲𐑀𐐯𐑌 𐐻𐐭 𐐺𐐰𐐻𐑊; 𐑌𐐨𐑄𐐲𐑉 𐐼𐐮𐐼 𐑄𐐩 𐐿𐐲𐑋 𐐲𐑀𐐯𐑌 𐐮𐑌 𐑄 𐐻𐐶𐐯𐑌𐐻𐐨𐐯𐑃 𐐷𐐨𐑉; 𐐰𐑌𐐼 𐐮𐑌 𐑄 𐐻𐐶𐐯𐑌𐐻𐐨 𐐰𐑌𐐼 𐑁𐐲𐑉𐑅𐐻 𐐷𐐨𐑉 𐑄𐐩 𐐼𐐮𐐼 𐑌𐐱𐐻 𐐿𐐲𐑋 𐐲𐐹 𐐻𐐭 𐐺𐐰𐐻𐑊, 𐐺𐐲𐐻 𐑄𐐩 𐐿𐐩𐑋 𐐲𐐹 𐐱𐑌 𐐫𐑊 𐑅𐐴𐐼𐑆 𐐻𐐭 𐑊𐐩 𐑅𐐨𐐾 𐑉𐐵𐑌𐐼 𐐲𐐺𐐵𐐻 𐑄 𐐹𐐨𐐹𐑊 𐐱𐑂 𐐤𐐨𐑁𐐴; 𐑁𐐫𐑉 𐑄𐐩 𐐼𐐮𐐼 𐑅𐐲𐐹𐐬𐑆 𐑄𐐰𐐻 𐐮𐑁 𐑄𐐩 𐑇𐐳𐐼 𐐿𐐲𐐻 𐐫𐑁 𐑄 𐐹𐐨𐐹𐑊 𐐱𐑂 𐐤𐐨𐑁𐐴 𐑁𐑉𐐱𐑋 𐑄𐐩𐑉 𐑊𐐰𐑌𐐼𐑆, 𐐰𐑌𐐼 𐑇𐐳𐐼 𐐸𐐯𐑋 𐑄𐐯𐑋 𐐮𐑌 𐐱𐑌 𐐯𐑂𐐲𐑉𐐨 𐑅𐐴𐐼, 𐐰𐑌𐐼 𐐮𐑁 𐑄𐐩 𐑇𐐳𐐼 𐐿𐐲𐐻 𐑄𐐯𐑋 𐐫𐑁 𐑁𐑉𐐱𐑋 𐐫𐑊 𐑄𐐩𐑉 𐐵𐐻𐐶𐐲𐑉𐐼 𐐹𐑉𐐮𐑂𐐮𐑊𐐯𐐾𐐯𐑆, 𐑄𐐰𐐻 𐑄𐐩 𐐿𐐳𐐼 𐐿𐐫𐑆 𐑄𐐯𐑋 𐐻𐐭 𐐷𐐨𐑊𐐼 𐑄𐐯𐑋𐑅𐐯𐑊𐑂𐑆 𐐲𐐹 𐐰𐐿𐐫𐑉𐐼𐐮𐑍 𐐻𐐭 𐑄𐐩𐑉 𐐶𐐮𐑇𐐯𐑆. 𐐤𐐵 𐑄𐐩 𐐸𐐰𐐼 𐐰𐐹𐐱𐐮𐑌𐐻𐐯𐐼 𐐲𐑌𐐻𐐭 𐑄𐐯𐑋𐑅𐐯𐑊𐑂𐑆 𐐰𐑌𐐲𐑄𐐲𐑉 𐑊𐐨𐐼𐐲𐑉, 𐐸𐐭𐑆 𐑌𐐩𐑋 𐐶𐐱𐑆 𐐞𐐯𐑋𐑌𐐩𐑉𐐴𐐸𐐪; 𐑄𐐯𐑉𐑁𐐬𐑉 𐐮𐐻 𐐶𐐱𐑆 𐐞𐐯𐑋𐑌𐐩𐑉𐐴𐐸𐐪 𐑄𐐰𐐻 𐐼𐐮𐐼 𐐿𐐫𐑆 𐑄𐐰𐐻 𐑄𐐮𐑅 𐑅𐐨𐐾 𐑇𐐳𐐼 𐐻𐐩𐐿 𐐹𐑊𐐩𐑅. 𐐒𐐲𐐻 𐐺𐐨𐐸𐐬𐑊𐐼, 𐑄𐐮𐑅 𐐶𐐱𐑆 𐐰𐑌 𐐰𐐼𐑂𐐰𐑌𐐻𐐩𐐾 𐐻𐐭 𐑄 𐐤𐐨𐑁𐐴𐐻𐑅; 𐑁𐐫𐑉 𐐮𐐻 𐐶𐐱𐑆 𐐮𐑋𐐹𐐱𐑅𐐮𐐺𐑊 𐑁𐐫𐑉 𐑄 𐑉𐐱𐐺𐐲𐑉𐑆 𐐻𐐭 𐑊𐐩 𐑅𐐨𐐾 𐑅𐐲𐑁𐐮𐑇𐐲𐑌𐐻𐑊𐐨 𐑊𐐱𐑍 𐐻𐐭 𐐸𐐰𐑂 𐐯𐑌𐐨 𐐯𐑁𐐯𐐿𐐻 𐐲𐐹𐐱𐑌 𐑄 𐐤𐐨𐑁𐐴𐐻𐑅, 𐐺𐐨𐐿𐐫𐑆 𐐱𐑂 𐑄𐐩𐑉 𐑋𐐲𐐽 𐐹𐑉𐐬𐑂𐐮𐑆𐐲𐑌 𐐸𐐶𐐮𐐽 𐑄𐐩 𐐸𐐰𐐼 𐑊𐐩𐐼 𐐲𐐹 𐐮𐑌 𐑅𐐻𐐬𐑉, 𐐺𐐨𐐿𐐫𐑆 𐐱𐑂 𐑄 𐑅𐐿𐐰𐑌𐐻𐐨𐑌𐐯𐑅 𐐱𐑂 𐐹𐑉𐐬𐑂𐐮𐑆𐐲𐑌𐑆 𐐲𐑋𐐲𐑍 𐑄 𐑉𐐱𐐺𐐲𐑉𐑆; 𐑁𐐫𐑉 𐐺𐐨𐐸𐐬𐑊𐐼, 𐑄𐐩 𐐸𐐰𐐼 𐑌𐐲𐑃𐐮𐑍 𐑅𐐩𐑂 𐐮𐐻 𐐶𐐲𐑉 𐑋𐐨𐐻 𐑁𐐫𐑉 𐑄𐐩𐑉 𐑅𐐲𐐺𐑅𐐮𐑅𐐻𐐯𐑌𐑅, 𐐸𐐶𐐮𐐽 𐑋𐐨𐐻 𐑄𐐩 𐐼𐐮𐐼 𐐱𐐺𐐻𐐩𐑌 𐐮𐑌 𐑄 𐐶𐐮𐑊𐐼𐐲𐑉𐑌𐐯𐑅. 𐐈𐑌𐐼 𐐮𐐻 𐐿𐐩𐑋 𐐻𐐭 𐐹𐐪𐑅 𐑄𐐰𐐻 𐑄 𐐶𐐴𐑊𐐼 𐑀𐐩𐑋 𐐺𐐨𐐿𐐩𐑋 𐑅𐐿𐐩𐑉𐑅 𐐮𐑌 𐑄 𐐶𐐮𐑊𐐼𐐲𐑉𐑌𐐯𐑅, 𐐮𐑌𐑅𐐬𐑋𐐲𐐽 𐑄𐐰𐐻 𐑄 𐑉𐐱𐐺𐐲𐑉𐑆 𐐶𐐲𐑉 𐐲𐐺𐐵𐐻 𐐻𐐭 𐐹𐐯𐑉𐐮𐑇 𐐶𐐮𐑄 𐐸𐐲𐑍𐐲𐑉. 𐐈𐑌𐐼 𐑄 𐐤𐐨𐑁𐐴𐐻𐑅 𐐶𐐲𐑉 𐐿𐐱𐑌𐐻𐐮𐑌𐐷𐐭𐐰𐑊𐐨 𐑋𐐪𐑉𐐽𐐮𐑍 𐐵𐐻 𐐺𐐴 𐐼𐐩 𐐰𐑌𐐼 𐐺𐐴 𐑌𐐴𐐻, 𐐰𐑌𐐼 𐑁𐐫𐑊𐐮𐑍 𐐲𐐹𐐱𐑌 𐑄𐐩𐑉 𐐪𐑉𐑋𐐨𐑆, 𐐰𐑌𐐼 𐐿𐐲𐐻𐐮𐑍 𐑄𐐯𐑋 𐐫𐑁 𐐺𐐴 𐑃𐐵𐑆𐐰𐑌𐐼𐑆 𐐰𐑌𐐼 𐐺𐐴 𐐻𐐯𐑌𐑆 𐐱𐑂 𐑃𐐵𐑆𐐰𐑌𐐼𐑆. 𐐈𐑌𐐼 𐑄𐐲𐑅 𐐮𐐻 𐐺𐐨𐐿𐐩𐑋 𐑄 𐐼𐐨𐑆𐐴𐐲𐑉 𐐱𐑂 𐑄 𐐹𐐨𐐹𐑊 𐐱𐑂 𐐞𐐯𐑋𐑌𐐩𐑉𐐴𐐸𐐪 𐐻𐐭 𐐶𐐮𐑄𐐼𐑉𐐫 𐑁𐑉𐐱𐑋 𐑄𐐩𐑉 𐐼𐐨𐑆𐐴𐑌, 𐐺𐐨𐐿𐐫𐑆 𐐱𐑂 𐑄 𐑀𐑉𐐩𐐻 𐐼𐐨𐑅𐐻𐑉𐐲𐐿𐑇𐐲𐑌 𐐸𐐶𐐮𐐽 𐐿𐐩𐑋 𐐲𐐹𐐱𐑌 𐑄𐐯𐑋 𐐺𐐴 𐑌𐐴𐐻 𐐰𐑌𐐼 𐐺𐐴 𐐼𐐩.

10. 𐐈𐑌𐐼 𐐮𐐻 𐐿𐐩𐑋 𐐻𐐭 𐐹𐐪𐑅 𐑄𐐰𐐻 𐐞𐐯𐑋𐑌𐐩𐑉𐐴𐐸𐐪 𐐼𐐮𐐼 𐑀𐐮𐑂 𐐿𐐱𐑋𐐰𐑌𐐼 𐐲𐑌𐐻𐐭 𐑄 𐐹𐐨𐐹𐑊 𐑄𐐰𐐻 𐑄𐐩 𐑇𐐳𐐼 𐐶𐐮𐑄𐐼𐑉𐐫 𐑄𐐯𐑋𐑅𐐯𐑊𐑂𐑆 𐑁𐑉𐐱𐑋 𐑄 𐑅𐐨𐐾, 𐐰𐑌𐐼 𐑋𐐪𐑉𐐽 𐐮𐑌𐐻𐐭 𐑄 𐑁𐐲𐑉𐑄𐐲𐑉𐑋𐐬𐑅𐐻 𐐹𐐪𐑉𐐻𐑅 𐐱𐑂 𐑄 𐑊𐐰𐑌𐐼 𐑌𐐫𐑉𐑃𐐶𐐲𐑉𐐼. 𐐈𐑌𐐼 𐑌𐐵, 𐐘𐐮𐐼𐑀𐐮𐐼𐐬𐑌𐐴 𐐺𐐨𐐮𐑍 𐐲𐐶𐐯𐑉 𐐱𐑂 𐑄𐐩𐑉 𐐼𐐨𐑆𐐴𐑌, 𐐰𐑌𐐼 𐑌𐐬𐐮𐑍 𐐱𐑂 𐑄𐐩𐑉 𐐶𐐨𐐿𐑌𐐯𐑅 𐐺𐐨𐐿𐐫𐑆 𐐱𐑂 𐑄 𐐶𐐫𐑌𐐻 𐐱𐑂 𐑁𐐭𐐼, 𐐰𐑌𐐼 𐑄 𐑀𐑉𐐩𐐻 𐑅𐑊𐐫𐐻𐐲𐑉 𐐸𐐶𐐮𐐽 𐐸𐐰𐐼 𐐺𐐮𐑌 𐑋𐐩𐐼 𐐲𐑋𐐲𐑍 𐑄𐐯𐑋, 𐑄𐐯𐑉𐑁𐐬𐑉 𐐸𐐨 𐐼𐐮𐐼 𐑅𐐯𐑌𐐼 𐐵𐐻 𐐸𐐮𐑆 𐐪𐑉𐑋𐐨𐑆 𐐮𐑌 𐑄 𐑌𐐴𐐻 𐐻𐐴𐑋, 𐐰𐑌𐐼 𐐼𐐮𐐼 𐐿𐐲𐐻 𐐫𐑁 𐑄 𐐶𐐩 𐐱𐑂 𐑄𐐩𐑉 𐑉𐐨𐐻𐑉𐐨𐐻, 𐐰𐑌𐐼 𐐼𐐮𐐼 𐐹𐑊𐐩𐑅 𐐸𐐮𐑆 𐐪𐑉𐑋𐐨𐑆 𐐮𐑌 𐑄 𐐶𐐩 𐐱𐑂 𐑄𐐩𐑉 𐑉𐐨𐐻𐑉𐐨𐐻; 𐐰𐑌𐐼 𐑄𐐮𐑅 𐐼𐐮𐐼 𐑄𐐩 𐐼𐐭 𐐮𐑌 𐑄 𐑌𐐴𐐻 𐐻𐐴𐑋, 𐐰𐑌𐐼 𐑀𐐱𐐻 𐐱𐑌 𐑄𐐩𐑉 𐑋𐐪𐑉𐐽 𐐺𐐨𐐷𐐱𐑌𐐼 𐑄 𐑉𐐱𐐺𐐲𐑉𐑆, 𐑅𐐬 𐑄𐐰𐐻 𐐱𐑌 𐑄 𐑋𐐱𐑉𐐬, 𐐸𐐶𐐯𐑌 𐑄 𐑉𐐱𐐺𐐲𐑉𐑆 𐐺𐐨𐑀𐐰𐑌 𐑄𐐩𐑉 𐑋𐐪𐑉𐐽, 𐑄𐐩 𐐶𐐲𐑉 𐑋𐐯𐐻 𐐺𐐴 𐑄 𐐪𐑉𐑋𐐨𐑆 𐐱𐑂 𐑄 𐐤𐐨𐑁𐐴𐐻𐑅, 𐐺𐐬𐑃 𐐮𐑌 𐑄𐐩𐑉 𐑁𐑉𐐲𐑌𐐻 𐐰𐑌𐐼 𐐮𐑌 𐑄𐐩𐑉 𐑉𐐨𐑉. 𐐈𐑌𐐼 𐑄 𐑉𐐱𐐺𐐲𐑉𐑆 𐐸𐐭 𐐶𐐲𐑉 𐐱𐑌 𐑄 𐑅𐐵𐑃 𐐶𐐲𐑉 𐐫𐑊𐑅𐐬 𐐿𐐲𐐻 𐐫𐑁 𐐮𐑌 𐑄𐐩𐑉 𐐹𐑊𐐩𐑅𐐯𐑆 𐐱𐑂 𐑉𐐨𐐻𐑉𐐨𐐻. 𐐈𐑌𐐼 𐐫𐑊 𐑄𐐨𐑆 𐑃𐐮𐑍𐑆 𐐶𐐲𐑉 𐐼𐐲𐑌 𐐺𐐴 𐐿𐐱𐑋𐐰𐑌𐐼 𐐱𐑂 𐐘𐐮𐐼𐑀𐐮𐐼𐐬𐑌𐐴. 𐐈𐑌𐐼 𐑄𐐯𐑉 𐐶𐐲𐑉 𐑋𐐯𐑌𐐨 𐑃𐐵𐑆𐐰𐑌𐐼𐑆 𐐸𐐭 𐐼𐐮𐐼 𐐷𐐨𐑊𐐼 𐑄𐐯𐑋𐑅𐐯𐑊𐑂𐑆 𐐲𐐹 𐐹𐑉𐐮𐑆𐐲𐑌𐐲𐑉𐑆 𐐲𐑌𐐻𐐭 𐑄 𐐤𐐨𐑁𐐴𐐻𐑅, 𐐰𐑌𐐼 𐑄 𐑉𐐨𐑋𐐩𐑌𐐼𐐲𐑉 𐐱𐑂 𐑄𐐯𐑋 𐐶𐐲𐑉 𐑅𐑊𐐩𐑌; 𐐰𐑌𐐼 𐑄𐐩𐑉 𐑊𐐨𐐼𐐲𐑉, 𐐞𐐯𐑋𐑌𐐩𐑉𐐴𐐸𐐪, 𐐶𐐱𐑆 𐐻𐐩𐐿𐐲𐑌 𐐰𐑌𐐼 𐐸𐐰𐑍𐐼 𐐲𐐹𐐱𐑌 𐐩 𐐻𐑉𐐨, 𐐷𐐩,

𐐨𐑂𐑌 𐐲𐐹𐐱𐑌 𐑄 𐐻𐐱𐐹 𐑄𐐩𐑉𐐱𐑂 𐐲𐑌𐐻𐐮𐑊 𐐸𐐨 𐐶𐐱𐑆 𐐼𐐯𐐼. 𐐈𐑌𐐼 𐐸𐐶𐐯𐑌 𐑄𐐩 𐐸𐐰𐐼 𐐸𐐰𐑍𐐼 𐐸𐐮𐑋 𐐲𐑌𐐻𐐮𐑊 𐐸𐐨 𐐶𐐱𐑆 𐐼𐐯𐐼, 𐑄𐐩 𐐼𐐮𐐼 𐑁𐐯𐑊 𐑄 𐐻𐑉𐐨 𐐻𐐭 𐑄 𐐲𐑉𐑃, 𐐰𐑌𐐼 𐐼𐐮𐐼 𐐿𐑉𐐴 𐐶𐐮𐑄 𐐲 𐑊𐐵𐐼 𐑂𐑎𐑅, 𐑅𐐩𐐮𐑍, 𐐣𐐩 𐑄 𐐢𐐫𐑉𐐼 𐐹𐑉𐐨𐑆𐐲𐑉𐑂 𐐸𐐮𐑆 𐐹𐐨𐐹𐑊 𐐮𐑌 𐑉𐐴𐐽𐐲𐑅𐑌𐐯𐑅 𐐰𐑌𐐼 𐐮𐑌 𐐸𐐬𐑊𐐨𐑌𐐯𐑅 𐐱𐑂 𐐸𐐪𐑉𐐻, 𐑄𐐰𐐻 𐑄𐐩 𐑋𐐩 𐐿𐐫𐑆 𐐻𐐭 𐐺𐐨 𐑁𐐯𐑊𐐼 𐐻𐐭 𐑄 𐐲𐑉𐑃 𐐫𐑊 𐐸𐐭 𐑇𐐰𐑊 𐑅𐐨𐐿 𐐻𐐭 𐑅𐑊𐐩 𐑄𐐯𐑋 𐐺𐐨𐐿𐐫𐑆 𐐱𐑂 𐐹𐐵𐐲𐑉 𐐰𐑌𐐼 𐑅𐐨𐐿𐑉𐐯𐐻 𐐿𐐱𐑋𐐺𐐮𐑌𐐩𐑇𐐲𐑌𐑆, 𐐨𐑂𐑌 𐐰𐑆 𐑄𐐮𐑅 𐑋𐐰𐑌 𐐸𐐰𐑃 𐐺𐐮𐑌 𐑁𐐯𐑊𐐼 𐐻𐐭 𐑄 𐐲𐑉𐑃. 𐐈𐑌𐐼 𐑄𐐩 𐐼𐐮𐐼 𐑉𐐨𐐾𐑎𐑅 𐐰𐑌𐐼 𐐿𐑉𐐴 𐐲𐑀𐐯𐑌 𐐶𐐮𐑄 𐐶𐐲𐑌 𐑂𐑎𐑅, 𐑅𐐩𐐮𐑍, 𐐣𐐩 𐑄 𐐘𐐱𐐼 𐐱𐑂 𐐁𐐺𐑉𐐲𐐸𐐰𐑋, 𐐰𐑌𐐼 𐑄 𐐘𐐱𐐼 𐐱𐑂 𐐌𐑆𐐲𐐿, 𐐰𐑌𐐼 𐑄 𐐘𐐱𐐼 𐐱𐑂 𐐖𐐩𐐿𐐲𐐺, 𐐹𐑉𐐬𐐻𐐯𐐿𐐻 𐑄𐐮𐑅 𐐹𐐨𐐹𐑊 𐐮𐑌 𐑉𐐴𐐽𐐲𐑅𐑌𐐯𐑅, 𐑅𐐬 𐑊𐐱𐑍 𐐰𐑆 𐑄𐐩 𐑇𐐰𐑊 𐐿𐐫𐑊 𐐱𐑌 𐑄 𐑌𐐩𐑋 𐐱𐑂 𐑄𐐩𐑉 𐐘𐐱𐐼 𐑁𐐫𐑉 𐐹𐑉𐐬𐐻𐐯𐐿𐑇𐐲𐑌. 𐐈𐑌𐐼 𐐮𐐻 𐐿𐐩𐑋 𐐻𐐭 𐐹𐐰𐑅 𐑄𐐰𐐻 𐑄𐐩 𐐼𐐮𐐼 𐐺𐑉𐐩𐐿 𐑁𐐫𐑉𐑃, 𐐫𐑊 𐐰𐑆 𐐶𐐲𐑌, 𐐮𐑌 𐑅𐐮𐑍𐐮𐑍, 𐐰𐑌𐐼 𐐹𐑉𐐩𐑆𐐮𐑍 𐑄𐐩𐑉 𐐘𐐱𐐼 𐑁𐐫𐑉 𐑄 𐑀𐑉𐐩𐐻 𐑃𐐮𐑍 𐐸𐐶𐐮𐐽 𐐸𐐨 𐐸𐐰𐐼 𐐼𐐲𐑌 𐑁𐐫𐑉 𐑄𐐯𐑋, 𐐮𐑌 𐐹𐑉𐐨𐑆𐐲𐑉𐑂𐐮𐑍 𐑄𐐯𐑋 𐑁𐑉𐐱𐑋 𐑁𐐫𐑊𐐮𐑍 𐐮𐑌𐐻𐐭 𐑄 𐐸𐐰𐑌𐐼𐑆 𐐱𐑂 𐑄𐐩𐑉 𐐯𐑌𐐯𐑋𐐨𐑆; 𐐷𐐩, 𐑄𐐩 𐐼𐐮𐐼 𐐿𐑉𐐴, 𐐐𐐬𐑆𐐰𐑌𐐲 𐐻𐐭 𐑄 𐐣𐐬𐑅𐐻 𐐐𐐴 𐐘𐐱𐐼; 𐐰𐑌𐐼 𐑄𐐩 𐐼𐐮𐐼 𐐿𐑉𐐴, 𐐒𐑊𐐯𐑅𐐯𐐼 𐐺𐐨 𐑄 𐑌𐐩𐑋 𐐱𐑂 𐑄 𐐢𐐫𐑉𐐼 𐐘𐐱𐐼 𐐃𐑊𐑋𐐴𐐻𐐨, 𐑄 𐐣𐐬𐑅𐐻 𐐐𐐴 𐐘𐐱𐐼. 𐐈𐑌𐐼 𐑄𐐩𐑉 𐐸𐐪𐑉𐐻𐑅 𐐶𐐲𐑉 𐑅𐐶𐐬𐑊𐐲𐑌 𐐶𐐮𐑄 𐐾𐑎, 𐐲𐑌𐐻𐐭 𐑄 𐑀𐐲𐑇𐐮𐑍 𐐵𐐻 𐐱𐑂 𐑋𐐯𐑌𐐨 𐐻𐐨𐑉𐑆, 𐐺𐐨𐐿𐐫𐑆 𐐱𐑂 𐑄 𐑀𐑉𐐩𐐻 𐑀𐐳𐐼𐑌𐐯𐑅 𐐱𐑂 𐐘𐐱𐐼 𐐮𐑌 𐐼𐐯𐑊𐐮𐑂𐐲𐑉𐐮𐑍 𐑄𐐯𐑋 𐐵𐐻 𐐱𐑂 𐑄 𐐸𐐰𐑌𐐼𐑆 𐐱𐑂 𐑄𐐩𐑉 𐐯𐑌𐐯𐑋𐐨𐑆; 𐐰𐑌𐐼 𐑄𐐩 𐑌𐐭 𐐮𐐻 𐐶𐐱𐑆 𐐺𐐨𐐿𐐫𐑆 𐐱𐑂 𐑄𐐩𐑉 𐑉𐐨𐐹𐐯𐑌𐐻𐐲𐑌𐑅 𐐰𐑌𐐼 𐑄𐐩𐑉 𐐸𐐷𐐭𐑋𐐮𐑊𐐮𐐻𐐨 𐑄𐐰𐐻 𐑄𐐩 𐐸𐐰𐐼 𐐺𐐮𐑌 𐐼𐐯𐑊𐐮𐑂𐐲𐑉𐐼 𐑁𐑉𐐱𐑋 𐐰𐑌 𐐯𐑂𐐲𐑉𐑊𐐰𐑅𐐻𐐮𐑍 𐐼𐐯𐑅𐐻𐑉𐐲𐐿𐑇𐐲𐑌. 𐐈𐑌𐐼 𐑌𐐵 𐐺𐐨𐐸𐐬𐑊𐐼, 𐑄𐐩𐑉 𐐶𐐱𐑆 𐑌𐐱𐐻 𐐲 𐑊𐐮𐑂𐐮𐑍 𐑅𐐬𐑊 𐐲𐑋𐐲𐑍 𐐫𐑊 𐑄 𐐹𐐨𐐹𐑊 𐐱𐑂 𐑄 𐐤𐐀𐑁𐐴𐐻𐑅, 𐐸𐐭 𐐼𐐮𐐼 𐐼𐐵𐐻 𐐮𐑌 𐑄 𐑊𐐨𐑅𐐻 𐑄 𐐶𐐲𐑉𐐼𐑆 𐐱𐑂 𐑄 𐐸𐐬𐑊𐐨 𐐹𐑉𐐱𐑁𐐯𐐻𐑅 𐐸𐐭 𐐸𐐰𐐼 𐑅𐐹𐐬𐐿𐐲𐑌; 𐑁𐐫𐑉 𐑄𐐩 𐑌𐐭 𐑄𐐰𐐻 𐐮𐐻 𐑋𐐲𐑅𐐻 𐑌𐐨𐐼𐑆 𐐺𐐨 𐑄𐐰𐐻 𐑄𐐩 𐑋𐐲𐑅𐐻 𐐺𐐨 𐑁𐐳𐑊𐑁𐐮𐑊𐐼; 𐐰𐑌𐐼 𐑄𐐩 𐑌𐐭 𐑄𐐰𐐻 𐐮𐐻 𐑋𐐲𐑅𐐻 𐐺𐐨 𐐯𐐿𐑅𐐹𐐨𐐼𐐨𐐯𐑌𐐻 𐑄𐐰𐐻 𐐗𐑉𐐴𐑅𐐻 𐐸𐐰𐐼 𐐿𐐲𐑋, 𐐺𐐨𐐿𐐫𐑆 𐐱𐑂 𐑄 𐑋𐐯𐑌𐐨 𐑅𐐴𐑌𐑆 𐐸𐐶𐐮𐐽 𐐸𐐰𐐼 𐐺𐐮𐑌 𐑀𐐮𐑂𐐲𐑌, 𐐰𐐿𐐫𐑉𐐼𐐮𐑍 𐐻𐐭 𐑄 𐐶𐐲𐑉𐐼𐑆 𐐱𐑂 𐑄 𐐹𐑉𐐱𐑁𐐯𐐻𐑅; 𐐰𐑌𐐼 𐐺𐐨𐐿𐐫𐑆 𐐱𐑂 𐑄 𐑃𐐮𐑍𐑆 𐐸𐐶𐐮𐐽 𐐸𐐰𐐼 𐐿𐐲𐑋 𐐻𐐭 𐐹𐐰𐑅 𐐫𐑊𐑉𐐯𐐼𐐨, 𐑄𐐩 𐑌𐐭 𐑄𐐰𐐻 𐐮𐐻 𐑋𐐲𐑅𐐻 𐑌𐐨𐐼𐑆 𐐺𐐨 𐑄𐐰𐐻 𐐫𐑊 𐑃𐐮𐑍𐑆 𐑇𐐳𐐼 𐐿𐐲𐑋 𐐻𐐭 𐐹𐐰𐑅 𐐰𐐿𐐫𐑉𐐼𐐮𐑍 𐐻𐐭 𐑄𐐰𐐻 𐐸𐐶𐐮𐐽 𐐸𐐰𐐼 𐐺𐐮𐑌 𐑅𐐹𐐬𐐿𐐲𐑌; 𐑄𐐩𐑉𐑁𐐫𐑉 𐑄𐐩 𐐼𐐮𐐼 𐑁𐐫𐑉𐑅𐐩𐐿 𐐫𐑊 𐑄𐐩𐑉 𐑅𐐮𐑌𐑆, 𐐰𐑌𐐼 𐑄𐐩𐑉 𐐲𐐺𐐱𐑋𐐮𐑌𐐩𐑇𐐲𐑌𐑆, 𐐰𐑌𐐼 𐑄𐐩𐑉 𐐸𐐬𐑉𐐼𐐲𐑋𐑆, 𐐰𐑌𐐼 𐐼𐐮𐐼 𐑅𐐲𐑉𐑂 𐐘𐐱𐐼 𐐶𐐮𐑄 𐐫𐑊 𐐼𐐮𐑊𐐮𐐾𐐯𐑌𐑅 𐐼𐐩 𐐰𐑌𐐼 𐑌𐐴𐐻.

11. 𐐈𐑌𐐼 𐑌𐐵 𐐮𐐻 𐐿𐐩𐑋 𐐻𐐭 𐐹𐐰𐑅 𐑄𐐰𐐻 𐐸𐐶𐐯𐑌 𐑄𐐩 𐐸𐐰𐐼 𐐻𐐩𐐿𐐲𐑌 𐐫𐑊 𐑄 𐑉𐐱𐐺𐐲𐑉𐑆 𐐹𐑉𐐮𐑆𐐲𐑌𐐲𐑉𐑆, 𐐮𐑌𐑅𐐬𐑋𐐲𐐽 𐑄𐐰𐐻 𐑌𐐲𐑌 𐐼𐐮𐐼 𐐯𐑅𐐿𐐩𐐹 𐐸𐐭 𐐶𐐲𐑉 𐑌𐐱𐐻 𐑅𐑊𐐩𐑌, 𐑄𐐩 𐐼𐐮𐐼 𐐿𐐰𐑅𐐻 𐑄𐐩𐑉 𐐹𐑉𐐮𐑆𐐲𐑌𐐲𐑉𐑆 𐐮𐑌𐐻𐐭 𐐹𐑉𐐮𐑆𐐲𐑌, 𐐰𐑌𐐼 𐐼𐐮𐐼 𐐿𐐫𐑆 𐑄 𐐶𐐲𐑉𐐼 𐐱𐑂 𐐘𐐱𐐼 𐐻𐐭 𐐺𐐨 𐐹𐑉𐐨𐐽𐐻 𐐲𐑌𐐻𐐭 𐑄𐐯𐑋; 𐐰𐑌𐐼 𐐰𐑆 𐑋𐐯𐑌𐐨 𐐰𐑆 𐐶𐐳𐐼 𐑉𐐨𐐹𐐯𐑌𐐻 𐐱𐑂 𐑄𐐩𐑉 𐑅𐐮𐑌𐑆 𐐰𐑌𐐼 𐐯𐑌𐐻𐐲𐑉 𐐮𐑌𐐻𐐭 𐐲 𐐿𐐲𐑂𐐯𐑌𐐰𐑌𐐻 𐑄𐐰𐐻 𐑄𐐩 𐐶𐐳𐐼 𐑋𐐲𐑉𐐼𐐲𐑉 𐑌𐐬 𐑋𐐬𐑉, 𐐶𐐲𐑉 𐑅𐐯𐐻 𐐰𐐻 𐑊𐐮𐐺𐐲𐑉𐐻𐐨; 𐐺𐐲𐐻 𐐰𐑆 𐑋𐐯𐑌𐐨 𐐰𐑆 𐑄𐐩𐑉 𐐶𐐲𐑉 𐐸𐐭 𐐼𐐮𐐼 𐑌𐐱𐐻 𐐯𐑌𐐻𐐲𐑉 𐐮𐑌𐐻𐐭 𐐲 𐐿𐐲𐑂𐐯𐑌𐐰𐑌𐐻, 𐐰𐑌𐐼 𐐸𐐭 𐐼𐐮𐐼 𐑅𐐻𐐮𐑊 𐐿𐐱𐑌𐐻𐐮𐑌𐐷𐐭 𐐻𐐭 𐐸𐐰𐑂 𐑄𐐬𐑆 𐑅𐐨𐐿𐑉𐐯𐐻 𐑋𐐲𐑉𐐼𐐲𐑉𐑆 𐐮𐑌 𐑄𐐩𐑉 𐐸𐐪𐑉𐐻𐑅; 𐐷𐐩, 𐐰𐑆 𐑋𐐯𐑌𐐨 𐐰𐑆 𐐶𐐲𐑉 𐑁𐐵𐑌𐐼 𐐺𐑉𐐨𐑄𐐮𐑍 𐐵𐐻 𐑃𐑉𐐯𐐻𐐲𐑌𐐮𐑍𐑆 𐐲𐑀𐐯𐑌𐑅𐐻 𐑄𐐩𐑉 𐐺𐑉𐐯𐑄𐑉𐐯𐑌, 𐐶𐐲𐑉 𐐿𐐱𐑌𐐼𐐯𐑋𐐼 𐐰𐑌𐐼 𐐹𐐲𐑌𐐮𐑇𐐻 𐐰𐐿𐐫𐑉𐐼𐐮𐑍 𐐻𐐭 𐑄 𐑊𐐫. 𐐈𐑌𐐼 𐑄𐐲𐑅 𐑄𐐩 𐐼𐐮𐐼 𐐹𐐳𐐻 𐐰𐑌 𐐯𐑌𐐼 𐐻𐐭 𐐫𐑊 𐑄𐐬𐑆 𐐶𐐮𐐿𐐯𐐼, 𐐰𐑌𐐼 𐑅𐐨𐐿𐑉𐐯𐐻, 𐐰𐑌𐐼 𐐲𐐺𐐱𐑋𐐮𐑌𐐲𐐺𐑊 𐐿𐐱𐑋𐐺𐐮𐑌𐐩𐑇𐐲𐑌𐑆, 𐐮𐑌 𐑄 𐐸𐐶𐐮𐐽 𐑄𐐩𐑉 𐐶𐐱𐑆 𐑅𐐬 𐑋𐐲𐐽 𐐶𐐮𐐿𐐯𐐼𐑌𐐯𐑅, 𐐰𐑌𐐼 𐑅𐐬 𐑋𐐯𐑌𐐨 𐑋𐐲𐑉𐐼𐐲𐑉𐑆 𐐿𐐱𐑋𐐮𐐻𐐯𐐼. 𐐈𐑌𐐼 𐑄𐐲𐑅 𐐸𐐰𐐼 𐑄 𐐻𐐶𐐯𐑌𐐻𐐨 𐐰𐑌𐐼 𐑅𐐯𐐿𐐲𐑌𐐼 𐐷𐐨𐑉 𐐹𐐰𐑅𐐻 𐐲𐐶𐐩, 𐐰𐑌𐐼 𐑄 𐐻𐐶𐐯𐑌𐐻𐐨 𐐰𐑌𐐼 𐑃𐐲𐑉𐐼 𐐷𐐨𐑉 𐐫𐑊𐑅𐐬, 𐐰𐑌𐐼 𐑄 𐐻𐐶𐐯𐑌𐐻𐐨 𐐰𐑌𐐼 𐑁𐐬𐑉𐑃, 𐐰𐑌𐐼 𐑄 𐐻𐐶𐐯𐑌𐐻𐐨 𐐰𐑌𐐼 𐑁𐐮𐑁𐑃; 𐐰𐑌𐐼 𐑄𐐲𐑅 𐐸𐐰𐐼 𐐻𐐶𐐯𐑌𐐻𐐨 𐐰𐑌𐐼 𐑁𐐴𐑂 𐐷𐐨𐑉𐑆 𐐹𐐰𐑅𐐻 𐐲𐐶𐐩, 𐐰𐑌𐐼 𐑄𐐩𐑉 𐐸𐐰𐐼 𐑋𐐯𐑌𐐨 𐑃𐐮𐑍𐑆 𐐻𐑉𐐰𐑌𐑅𐐹𐐴𐑉𐐼 𐐸𐐶𐐮𐐽, 𐐮𐑌 𐑄 𐐴𐑆 𐐱𐑂 𐑅𐐲𐑋, 𐐶𐐳𐐼 𐐺𐐨 𐑀𐑉𐐩𐐻 𐐰𐑌𐐼 𐑋𐐪𐑉𐑂𐐯𐑊𐐲𐑅; 𐑌𐐯𐑂𐐲𐑉𐑄𐐯𐑊𐐯𐑅, 𐑄𐐩 𐐿𐐰𐑌𐐱𐐻 𐐫𐑊 𐐺𐐨 𐑉𐐮𐐻𐐲𐑌 𐐮𐑌 𐑄𐐮𐑅 𐐺𐐳𐐿; 𐐷𐐩, 𐑄𐐮𐑅 𐐺𐐳𐐿 𐐿𐐰𐑌𐐱𐐻 𐐿𐐱𐑌𐐻𐐩𐑌 𐐨𐑂𐑌 𐐲 𐐸𐐲𐑌𐐼𐑉𐐯𐐼𐑃 𐐹𐐪𐑉𐐻 𐐱𐑂 𐐸𐐶𐐱𐐻 𐐶𐐱𐑆 𐐼𐐲𐑌 𐐲𐑋𐐲𐑍 𐑅𐐬 𐑋𐐯𐑌𐐨 𐐹𐐨𐐹𐑊 𐐮𐑌 𐑄 𐑅𐐹𐐩𐑅 𐐱𐑂 𐐻𐐶𐐯𐑌𐐻𐐨 𐐰𐑌𐐼 𐑁𐐴𐑂 𐐷𐐨𐑉𐑆; 𐐺𐐲𐐻 𐐺𐐨𐐸𐐬𐑊𐐼 𐑄𐐩𐑉 𐐪𐑉 𐑉𐐯𐐿𐐲𐑉𐐼𐑆 𐐸𐐶𐐮𐐽 𐐼𐐭 𐐿𐐱𐑌𐐻𐐩𐑌 𐐫𐑊 𐑄 𐐹𐑉𐐬𐑅𐐨𐐼𐐮𐑍𐑆 𐐱𐑂 𐑄𐐮𐑅 𐐹𐐨𐐹𐑊; 𐐰𐑌𐐼 𐐲 𐑇𐐫𐑉𐐻𐐲𐑉 𐐺𐐲𐐻 𐐻𐑉𐐭 𐐲𐐿𐐵𐑌𐐻 𐐶𐐱𐑆 𐑀𐐮𐑂𐐲𐑌 𐐺𐐴 𐐤𐐀𐑁𐐴; 𐑄𐐩𐑉𐑁𐐫𐑉 𐐌 𐐸𐐰𐑂 𐑋𐐩𐐼 𐑋𐐴 𐑉𐐯𐐿𐐲𐑉𐐼 𐐱𐑂 𐑄𐐨𐑆 𐑃𐐮𐑍𐑆 𐐰𐐿𐐫𐑉𐐼𐐮𐑍 𐐻𐐭 𐑄 𐑉𐐯𐐿𐐲𐑉𐐼 𐐱𐑂 𐐤𐐀𐑁𐐴, 𐐸𐐶𐐮𐐽 𐐶𐐱𐑆 𐐯𐑌𐑀𐑉𐐩𐑂𐐲𐑌 𐐱𐑌 𐑄 𐐹𐑊𐐩𐐻𐑅 𐐸𐐶𐐮𐐽 𐐶𐐲𐑉 𐐿𐐫𐑊𐐼 𐑄 𐐹𐑊𐐩𐐻𐑅

𐐱𐑂 𐐤𐐨𐑁𐐴. 𐐈𐑌𐐼 𐐺𐐨𐐸𐐬𐑊𐐼 𐐌 𐐼𐐭 𐑋𐐩𐐿 𐑄 𐑉𐐯𐐿𐐫𐑉𐐼 𐐱𐑌 𐐹𐑊𐐩𐐻𐑅 𐐸𐐶𐐮𐐽 𐐌 𐐸𐐰𐑂 𐑋𐐩𐐼 𐐶𐐮𐑄 𐑋𐐴𐑌 𐐬𐑌 𐐸𐐰𐑌𐐼𐑆. 𐐈𐑌𐐼 𐐺𐐨𐐸𐐬𐑊𐐼, 𐐌 𐐰𐑋 𐐿𐐫𐑊𐐼 𐐣𐐫𐑉𐑋𐐲𐑌, 𐐺𐐨𐐮𐑍 𐐿𐐫𐑊𐐼 𐐰𐑁𐐻𐐲𐑉 𐑄 𐑊𐐰𐑌𐐼 𐐱𐑂 𐐣𐐫𐑉𐑋𐐲𐑌, 𐑄 𐑊𐐰𐑌𐐼 𐐮𐑌 𐑄 𐐸𐐶𐐮𐐽 𐐈𐑊𐑋𐐲 𐐼𐐮𐐼 𐐯𐑅𐐻𐐰𐐺𐑊𐐮𐑇 𐑄 𐐕𐐲𐑉𐐽 𐐲𐑋𐐲𐑍 𐑄 𐐹𐐨𐐹𐑊; 𐐷𐐩, 𐑄 𐑁𐐲𐑉𐑅𐐻 𐐕𐐲𐑉𐐽 𐐸𐐶𐐮𐐽 𐐶𐐱𐑆 𐐯𐑅𐐻𐐰𐐺𐑊𐐮𐑇𐐻 𐐲𐑋𐐲𐑍 𐑄𐐯𐑋 𐐰𐑁𐐻𐐲𐑉 𐑄𐐩𐑉 𐐻𐑉𐐰𐑌𐑆𐑀𐑉𐐯𐑇𐐲𐑌. 𐐒𐐨𐐸𐐬𐑊𐐼, 𐐌 𐐰𐑋 𐐲 𐐼𐐮𐑅𐐴𐐹𐑊 𐐱𐑂 𐐖𐐨𐑆𐐲𐑅 𐐗𐑉𐐴𐑅𐐻, 𐑄 𐐝𐐲𐑌 𐐱𐑂 𐐘𐐱𐐼. 𐐌 𐐸𐐰𐑂 𐐺𐐮𐑌 𐐿𐐫𐑊𐐼 𐐱𐑂 𐐸𐐮𐑋 𐐻𐐭 𐐼𐐨𐐿𐑊𐐩𐑉 𐐸𐐮𐑆 𐐶𐐲𐑉𐐼 𐐲𐑋𐐲𐑍 𐐸𐐮𐑆 𐐹𐐨𐐹𐑊, 𐑄𐐰𐐻 𐑄𐐩 𐑋𐐴𐐻 𐐸𐐰𐑂 𐐯𐑂𐐲𐑉𐑊𐐰𐑅𐐻𐐮𐑍 𐑊𐐴𐑁. 𐐈𐑌𐐼 𐐮𐐻 𐐸𐐰𐑃 𐐺𐐨𐐿𐐲𐑋 𐐯𐐿𐑅𐐹𐐨𐐼𐐨𐐲𐑌𐐻 𐑄𐐰𐐻 𐐌, 𐐰𐐿𐐫𐑉𐐼𐐮𐑍 𐐻𐐭 𐑄 𐐶𐐮𐑊 𐐱𐑂 𐐘𐐱𐐼, 𐑄𐐰𐐻 𐑄 𐐹𐑉𐐩𐑉𐑆 𐐱𐑂 𐑄𐐬𐑆 𐐸𐐭 𐐸𐐰𐑂 𐑀𐐫𐑌 𐐸𐐯𐑌𐑅, 𐐸𐐭 𐐶𐐲𐑉 𐑄 𐐸𐐬𐑊𐐨 𐐶𐐲𐑌𐑆, 𐑇𐐳𐐼 𐐺𐐨 𐑁𐐳𐑊𐑁𐐮𐑊𐐼 𐐰𐐿𐐫𐑉𐐼𐐮𐑍 𐐻𐐭 𐑄𐐩𐑉 𐑁𐐩𐑃, 𐑇𐐳𐐼 𐑋𐐩𐐿 𐐲 𐑉𐐯𐐿𐐫𐑉𐐼 𐐱𐑂 𐑄𐐨𐑆 𐑃𐐮𐑍𐑆 𐐸𐐶𐐮𐐽 𐐸𐐰𐑂 𐐺𐐮𐑌 𐐼𐐲𐑌; 𐐷𐐩, 𐐲 𐑅𐑋𐐫𐑊 𐑉𐐯𐐿𐐫𐑉𐐼 𐐱𐑂 𐑄𐐰𐐻 𐐸𐐶𐐮𐐽 𐐸𐐰𐑃 𐐻𐐩𐐿𐐲𐑌 𐐹𐑊𐐩𐑅 𐑁𐑉𐐱𐑋 𐑄 𐐻𐐴𐑋 𐑄𐐰𐐻 𐐢𐐨𐐸𐐴 𐑊𐐯𐑁𐐻 𐐖𐐯𐑉𐐭𐑅𐐲𐑊𐐯𐑋, 𐐨𐑂𐐲𐑌 𐐼𐐵𐑌 𐐲𐑌𐐻𐐮𐑊 𐑄 𐐹𐑉𐐯𐑆𐐲𐑌𐐻 𐐻𐐴𐑋. 𐐜𐐩𐑉𐑁𐐬𐑉 𐐌 𐐼𐐭 𐑋𐐩𐐿 𐑋𐐴 𐑉𐐯𐐿𐐫𐑉𐐼 𐑁𐑉𐐱𐑋 𐑄 𐐰𐐿𐐵𐑌𐐻𐑅 𐐸𐐶𐐮𐐽 𐐸𐐰𐑂 𐐺𐐮𐑌 𐑀𐐮𐑂𐐲𐑌 𐐺𐐴 𐑄𐐬𐑆 𐐸𐐭 𐐶𐐲𐑉 𐐺𐐨𐑁𐐬𐑉 𐑋𐐨, 𐐲𐑌𐐻𐐮𐑊 𐑄 𐐿𐐲𐑋𐐯𐑌𐑅𐑋𐐯𐑌𐐻 𐐱𐑂 𐑋𐐴 𐐼𐐩; 𐐰𐑌𐐼 𐑄𐐯𐑌 𐐌 𐐼𐐭 𐑋𐐩𐐿 𐐲 𐑉𐐯𐐿𐐫𐑉𐐼 𐐱𐑂 𐑄 𐑃𐐮𐑍𐑆 𐐸𐐶𐐮𐐽 𐐌 𐐸𐐰𐑂 𐑅𐐨𐑌 𐐶𐐮𐑄 𐑋𐐴𐑌 𐐬𐑌 𐐴𐑆. 𐐈𐑌𐐼 𐐌 𐑌𐐬 𐑄 𐑉𐐯𐐿𐐫𐑉𐐼 𐐸𐐶𐐮𐐽 𐐌 𐑋𐐩𐐿 𐐻𐐭 𐐺𐐨 𐐲 𐐾𐐲𐑅𐐻 𐐰𐑌𐐼 𐐲 𐐻𐑉𐐭 𐑉𐐯𐐿𐐫𐑉𐐼; 𐑌𐐯𐑂𐐲𐑉𐑄𐐲𐑊𐐯𐑅 𐑄𐐩𐑉 𐐪𐑉 𐑋𐐯𐑌𐐨 𐑃𐐮𐑍𐑆 𐐸𐐶𐐮𐐽, 𐐰𐐿𐐫𐑉𐐼𐐮𐑍 𐐻𐐭 𐐵𐑉 𐑊𐐰𐑍𐑀𐐶𐐩𐐾, 𐐶𐐨 𐐪𐑉 𐑌𐐱𐐻 𐐩𐐺𐑊 𐐻𐐭 𐑉𐐴𐐻.

12. 𐐈𐑌𐐼 𐑌𐐵 𐐌 𐑋𐐩𐐿 𐐰𐑌 𐐯𐑌𐐼 𐐱𐑂 𐑋𐐴 𐑅𐐩𐐮𐑍, 𐐸𐐶𐐮𐐽 𐐮𐑆 𐐱𐑂 𐑋𐐴𐑅𐐯𐑊𐑁, 𐐰𐑌𐐼 𐐹𐑉𐐬𐑅𐐨𐐼 𐐻𐐭 𐑀𐐮𐑂 𐑋𐐴 𐐰𐐿𐐵𐑌𐐻 𐐱𐑂 𐑄 𐑃𐐮𐑍𐑆 𐐸𐐶𐐮𐐽 𐐸𐐰𐑂 𐐺𐐮𐑌 𐐺𐐨𐑁𐐬𐑉 𐑋𐐨. 𐐌 𐐰𐑋 𐐣𐐫𐑉𐑋𐐲𐑌, 𐐰𐑌𐐼 𐐲 𐐹𐑏𐑉 𐐼𐐨𐑅𐐯𐑌𐐼𐐲𐑌𐐻 𐐱𐑂 𐐢𐐨𐐸𐐴. 𐐌 𐐸𐐰𐑂 𐑉𐐨𐑆𐐲𐑌 𐐻𐐭 𐐺𐑊𐐯𐑅 𐑋𐐴 𐐘𐐱𐐼 𐐰𐑌𐐼 𐑋𐐴 𐐝𐐩𐑂𐐷𐐲𐑉 𐐖𐐨𐑆𐐲𐑅 𐐗𐑉𐐴𐑅𐐻, 𐑄𐐰𐐻 𐐸𐐨 𐐺𐑉𐐫𐐻 𐐵𐑉 𐑁𐐪𐑄𐐲𐑉𐑆 𐐵𐐻 𐐱𐑂 𐑄 𐑊𐐰𐑌𐐼 𐐱𐑂 𐐖𐐯𐑉𐐭𐑅𐐲𐑊𐐯𐑋, (𐐰𐑌𐐼 𐑌𐐬 𐐶𐐲𐑌 𐑌𐑏 𐐮𐐻 𐑅𐐩𐑂 𐐮𐐻 𐐶𐐲𐑉 𐐸𐐮𐑋𐑅𐐯𐑊𐑁 𐐰𐑌𐐼 𐑄𐐬𐑆 𐐸𐐭𐑋 𐐸𐐨 𐐺𐑉𐐫𐐻 𐐵𐐻 𐐱𐑂 𐑄𐐰𐐻 𐑊𐐰𐑌𐐼,) 𐐰𐑌𐐼 𐑄𐐰𐐻 𐐸𐐨 𐐸𐐰𐑃 𐑀𐐮𐑂𐐲𐑌 𐑋𐐨 𐐰𐑌𐐼 𐑋𐐴 𐐹𐐨𐐹𐑊 𐑅𐐬 𐑋𐐲𐐽 𐑌𐐱𐑊𐐯𐐾 𐐲𐑌𐐻𐐭 𐑄 𐑅𐐰𐑊𐑂𐐩𐑇𐐲𐑌 𐐱𐑂 𐐵𐑉 𐑅𐐬𐑊𐑆. 𐐟𐐭𐑉𐑊𐐨 𐐸𐐨 𐐸𐐰𐑃 𐐺𐑊𐐯𐑅𐐻 𐑄 𐐸𐐵𐑅 𐐱𐑂 𐐖𐐩𐐿𐐲𐐺, 𐐰𐑌𐐼 𐐸𐐰𐑃 𐐺𐐮𐑌 𐑋𐐲𐑉𐑅𐐮𐑁𐐳𐑊 𐐲𐑌𐐻𐐭 𐑄 𐑅𐐨𐐼 𐐱𐑂 𐐖𐐬𐑆𐐯𐑁. 𐐈𐑌𐐼 𐐮𐑌𐑅𐐬𐑋𐐲𐐽 𐐰𐑆 𐑄 𐐽𐐮𐑊𐐼𐑉𐐯𐑌 𐐱𐑂 𐐢𐐨𐐸𐐴 𐐸𐐰𐑂 𐐿𐐯𐐹𐐻 𐐸𐐮𐑆 𐐿𐐲𐑋𐐰𐑌𐐼𐑋𐐯𐑌𐐻𐑅, 𐐸𐐨 𐐸𐐰𐑃 𐐺𐑊𐐯𐑅𐐻 𐑄𐐯𐑋 𐐰𐑌𐐼 𐐹𐑉𐐱𐑅𐐹𐐲𐑉𐐼 𐑄𐐯𐑋 𐐰𐐿𐐫𐑉𐐼𐐮𐑍 𐐻𐐭 𐐸𐐮𐑆 𐐶𐐲𐑉𐐼; 𐐷𐐩, 𐐰𐑌𐐼 𐑇𐐭𐑉𐑊𐐨 𐑇𐐰𐑊 𐐸𐐨 𐐲𐑀𐐯𐑌 𐐺𐑉𐐮𐑍 𐐲 𐑉𐐯𐑋𐑌𐐲𐑌𐐻 𐐱𐑂 𐑄 𐑅𐐨𐐼 𐐱𐑂 𐐖𐐬𐑆𐐯𐑁 𐐻𐐭 𐑄 𐑌𐐱𐑊𐐯𐐾 𐐱𐑂 𐑄 𐐢𐐫𐑉𐐼 𐑄𐐩𐑉 𐐘𐐱𐐼; 𐐰𐑌𐐼 𐐰𐑆 𐑇𐐭𐑉𐑊𐐨 𐐰𐑆 𐑄 𐐢𐐫𐑉𐐼 𐑊𐐮𐑂𐐯𐑃, 𐐶𐐮𐑊 𐐸𐐨 𐑀𐐰𐑄𐐲𐑉 𐐮𐑌 𐑁𐑉𐐱𐑋 𐑄 𐑁𐐬𐑉 𐐿𐐶𐐫𐑉𐐻𐐲𐑉𐑆 𐐱𐑂 𐑄 𐐲𐑉𐑃 𐐫𐑊 𐑄 𐑉𐐯𐑋𐑌𐐲𐑌𐐻 𐐱𐑂 𐑄 𐑅𐐨𐐼 𐐱𐑂 𐐖𐐩𐐿𐐲𐐺, 𐐸𐐭 𐐪𐑉 𐑅𐐿𐐰𐐻𐐲𐑉𐐼 𐐲𐐺𐑉𐐫𐐼 𐐲𐐹𐐱𐑌 𐐫𐑊 𐑄 𐑁𐐩𐑅 𐐱𐑂 𐑄 𐐲𐑉𐑃; 𐐰𐑌𐐼 𐐰𐑆 𐐸𐐨 𐐸𐐰𐑃 𐐿𐐲𐑂𐐯𐑌𐐰𐑌𐐻𐐯𐐼 𐐶𐐮𐑄 𐐫𐑊 𐑄 𐐸𐐵𐑅 𐐱𐑂 𐐖𐐩𐐿𐐲𐐺, 𐐨𐑂𐐲𐑌 𐑅𐐬 𐑇𐐰𐑊 𐑄 𐐿𐐲𐑂𐐯𐑌𐐰𐑌𐐻 𐐸𐐶𐐩𐑉𐐶𐐮𐑄 𐐸𐐨 𐐸𐐰𐑃 𐐿𐐲𐑂𐐯𐑌𐐰𐑌𐐻𐐯𐐼 𐐶𐐮𐑄 𐑄 𐐸𐐵𐑅 𐐱𐑂 𐐖𐐩𐐿𐐲𐐺, 𐐺𐐨 𐑁𐐳𐑊𐑁𐐮𐑊𐐼 𐐮𐑌 𐐸𐐮𐑆 𐐬𐑌 𐐼𐑏 𐐻𐐴𐑋, 𐐲𐑌𐐻𐐭 𐑄 𐑉𐐨𐑅𐐻𐐬𐑉𐐮𐑍 𐐫𐑊 𐑄 𐐸𐐵𐑅 𐐱𐑂 𐐖𐐩𐐿𐐲𐐺 𐐲𐑌𐐻𐐭 𐑄 𐑌𐐱𐑊𐐯𐐾 𐐱𐑂 𐑄 𐐿𐐲𐑂𐐯𐑌𐐰𐑌𐐻 𐑄𐐰𐐻 𐐸𐐨 𐐸𐐰𐑃 𐐿𐐲𐑂𐐯𐑌𐐰𐑌𐐻𐐯𐐼 𐐶𐐮𐑄 𐑄𐐯𐑋; 𐐰𐑌𐐼 𐑄𐐯𐑌 𐑇𐐰𐑊 𐑄𐐩 𐑌𐐬 𐑄𐐩𐑉 𐐡𐐨𐐼𐐨𐑋𐐲𐑉, 𐐸𐐭 𐐮𐑆 𐐖𐐨𐑆𐐲𐑅 𐐗𐑉𐐴𐑅𐐻, 𐑄 𐐝𐐲𐑌 𐐱𐑂 𐐘𐐱𐐼; 𐐰𐑌𐐼 𐑄𐐯𐑌 𐑇𐐰𐑊 𐑄𐐩 𐐺𐐨 𐑀𐐰𐑄𐐲𐑉𐐼 𐐮𐑌 𐑁𐑉𐐱𐑋 𐑄 𐑁𐐬𐑉 𐐿𐐶𐐫𐑉𐐻𐐲𐑉𐑆 𐐱𐑂 𐑄 𐐲𐑉𐑃 𐐲𐑌𐐻𐐭 𐑄𐐩𐑉 𐐬𐑌 𐑊𐐰𐑌𐐼𐑆, 𐑁𐑉𐐱𐑋 𐐸𐐶𐐯𐑌𐑅 𐑄𐐩 𐐸𐐰𐑂 𐐺𐐮𐑌 𐐼𐐮𐑅𐐹𐐲𐑉𐑅𐐻; 𐐷𐐩, 𐐰𐑆 𐑄 𐐢𐐫𐑉𐐼 𐑊𐐮𐑂𐐯𐑃, 𐑅𐐬 𐑇𐐰𐑊 𐐮𐐻 𐐺𐐨. 𐐁𐑋𐐯𐑌.

𐐕𐐈𐐑𐐓𐐊𐐡 III.

1. 𐐈𐑌𐐼 𐑌𐐵 𐐮𐐻 𐐿𐐩𐑋 𐐻𐐭 𐐹𐐰𐑅 𐑄𐐰𐐻 𐑄 𐐹𐐨𐐹𐑊 𐐱𐑂 𐑄 𐐤𐐨𐑁𐐴𐐻𐑅 𐐼𐐮𐐼 𐐫𐑊 𐑉𐐨𐐻𐐲𐑉𐑌 𐐻𐐭 𐑄𐐩𐑉 𐐬𐑌 𐑊𐐰𐑌𐐼𐑆, 𐐮𐑌 𐑄 𐐻𐐶𐐯𐑌𐐻𐐨 𐐰𐑌𐐼 𐑅𐐮𐐿𐑅𐑃 𐐷𐐨𐑉, 𐐯𐑂𐐲𐑉𐐨 𐑋𐐰𐑌, 𐐶𐐮𐑄 𐐸𐐮𐑆 𐑁𐐰𐑋𐐮𐑊𐐨, 𐐸𐐮𐑆 𐑁𐑊𐐱𐐿𐑅 𐐰𐑌𐐼 𐐸𐐮𐑆 𐐸𐐲𐑉𐐼𐑆, 𐐸𐐮𐑆 𐐸𐐫𐑉𐑅𐐯𐑆 𐐰𐑌𐐼 𐐸𐐮𐑆 𐐿𐐰𐐻𐑊, 𐐰𐑌𐐼 𐐫𐑊 𐑃𐐮𐑍𐑆 𐐸𐐶𐐱𐐻𐑅𐐬𐐯𐑂𐐲𐑉 𐐼𐐮𐐼 𐐺𐐨𐑊𐐱𐑍 𐐲𐑌𐐻𐐭 𐑄𐐯𐑋. 𐐈𐑌𐐼 𐐮𐐻 𐐿𐐩𐑋 𐐻𐐭 𐐹𐐰𐑅 𐑄𐐰𐐻 𐑄𐐩 𐐸𐐰𐐼 𐑌𐐱𐐻 𐐨𐐻𐐲𐑌 𐐲𐐹 𐐫𐑊 𐑄𐐩𐑉 𐐹𐑉𐐬𐑂𐐮𐑈𐐲𐑌𐑆; 𐑄𐐩𐑉𐑁𐐬𐑉 𐑄𐐩 𐐼𐐮𐐼 𐐻𐐩𐐿

𐐶𐐮𐑄 𐑄𐐯𐑋 𐐫𐑊 𐑄𐐩 𐐸𐐰𐐼 𐑌𐐱𐐻 𐐼𐐨𐑂𐐵𐑉𐐼, 𐐱𐑂 𐐫𐑊 𐑄𐐩𐑉 𐑀𐑉𐐩𐑌 𐐱𐑂 𐐯𐑂𐐯𐑉𐐨 𐐿𐐴𐑌𐐼, 𐐰𐑌𐐼 𐑄𐐩𐑉 𐑀𐐬𐑊𐐼, 𐐰𐑌𐐼 𐑄𐐩𐑉 𐑅𐐮𐑊𐑂𐐲𐑉, 𐐰𐑌𐐼 𐐫𐑊 𐑄𐐩𐑉 𐐹𐑉𐐯𐑇𐐲𐑅 𐑃𐐮𐑍𐑆, 𐐰𐑌𐐼 𐑄𐐩 𐐼𐐮𐐼 𐑉𐐨𐐻𐐲𐑉𐑌 𐐻𐐭 𐑄𐐩𐑉 𐐬𐑌 𐑊𐐰𐑌𐐼𐑆 𐐰𐑌𐐼 𐑄𐐩𐑉 𐐹𐐲𐑆𐐯𐑇𐐲𐑌𐑆, 𐐺𐐬𐑃 𐐱𐑌 𐑄 𐑌𐐫𐑉𐑃 𐐰𐑌𐐼 𐐱𐑌 𐑄 𐑅𐐵𐑃, 𐐺𐐬𐑃 𐐱𐑌 𐑄 𐑊𐐰𐑌𐐼 𐑌𐐫𐑉𐑃𐐶𐐲𐑉𐐼 𐐰𐑌𐐼 𐐱𐑌 𐑄 𐑊𐐰𐑌𐐼 𐑅𐐵𐑃𐐶𐐲𐑉𐐼. 𐐈𐑌𐐼 𐑄𐐩 𐑀𐑉𐐰𐑌𐐻𐐯𐐼 𐐲𐑌𐐻𐐭 𐑄𐐬𐑆 𐑉𐐱𐐺𐐲𐑉𐑆 𐐸𐐭 𐐸𐐰𐐼 𐐯𐑌𐐻𐐲𐑉𐐼 𐐮𐑌𐐻𐐭 𐐩 𐐿𐐲𐑂𐐨𐑌𐐲𐑌𐐻 𐐻𐐭 𐐿𐐨𐐹 𐑄 𐐹𐐨𐑅, 𐐱𐑂 𐑄 𐑊𐐰𐑌𐐼, 𐐸𐐭 𐐶𐐲𐑉 𐐼𐐨𐑆𐐴𐑉𐐲𐑅 𐐻𐐭 𐑉𐐨𐑋𐐩𐑌 𐐢𐐰𐑋𐐲𐑌𐐴𐐻𐑅, 𐑊𐐰𐑌𐐼𐑆, 𐐰𐐿𐐫𐑉𐐼𐐮𐑍 𐐻𐐭 𐑄𐐩𐑉 𐑌𐐲𐑋𐐺𐐲𐑉𐑆, 𐑄𐐰𐐻 𐑄𐐩 𐑋𐐴𐐻 𐐸𐐰𐑂, 𐐶𐐮𐑄 𐑄𐐩𐑉 𐑊𐐩𐐺𐐲𐑉𐑆, 𐐸𐐶𐐩𐑉𐐶𐐮𐑃 𐐻𐐭 𐑅𐐲𐐺𐑅𐐮𐑅𐐻 𐐲𐐹𐐱𐑌; 𐐰𐑌𐐼 𐑄𐐲𐑅 𐑄𐐩 𐐼𐐮𐐼 𐐯𐑅𐐻𐐰𐐺𐑊𐐮𐑇 𐐹𐐨𐑅 𐐮𐑌 𐐫𐑊 𐑄 𐑊𐐰𐑌𐐼. 𐐈𐑌𐐼 𐑄𐐩 𐐺𐐨𐑀𐐰𐑌 𐐰𐑀𐐯𐑌 𐐻𐐭 𐐹𐑉𐐱𐑅𐐹𐐲𐑉 𐐰𐑌𐐼 𐐻𐐭 𐐶𐐰𐐿𐑅 𐑀𐑉𐐩𐐻; 𐐰𐑌𐐼 𐑄 𐐻𐐶𐐯𐑌𐐻𐐨 𐐰𐑌𐐼 𐑅𐐮𐐿𐑅𐑃 𐐰𐑌𐐼 𐑅𐐯𐑂𐐯𐑌𐑃 𐐷𐐨𐑉𐑆 𐐹𐐰𐑅𐐻 𐐰𐐶𐐩, 𐐰𐑌𐐼 𐑄𐐩𐑉 𐐶𐐱𐑆 𐑀𐑉𐐩𐐻 𐐫𐑉𐐼𐐲𐑉 𐐮𐑌 𐑄 𐑊𐐰𐑌𐐼; 𐐰𐑌𐐼 𐑄𐐩 𐐸𐐰𐐼 𐑁𐐫𐑉𐑋𐐼 𐑄𐐩𐑉 𐑊𐐫𐑆 𐐰𐐿𐐫𐑉𐐼𐐮𐑍 𐐻𐐭 𐐯𐐿𐐶𐐮𐐻𐐨 𐐰𐑌𐐼 𐐾𐐲𐑅𐐻𐐮𐑅. 𐐈𐑌𐐼 𐑌𐐵 𐑄𐐩𐑉 𐐶𐐱𐑆 𐑌𐐲𐑃𐐮𐑍 𐐮𐑌 𐐫𐑊 𐑄 𐑊𐐰𐑌𐐼 𐐻𐐭 𐐸𐐮𐑌𐐼𐐲𐑉 𐑄 𐐹𐐨𐐹𐑊 𐑁𐑉𐐱𐑋 𐐹𐑉𐐱𐑅𐐹𐐲𐑉𐐮𐑍 𐐿𐐲𐑌𐐻𐐮𐑌𐐷𐐭𐐲𐑊𐐨, 𐐯𐐿𐑅𐐯𐐹𐐻 𐑄𐐩 𐑇𐐳𐐼 𐑁𐐫𐑊 𐐮𐑌𐐻𐐭 𐐻𐑉𐐰𐑌𐑆𐑀𐑉𐐯𐑇𐐲𐑌. 𐐈𐑌𐐼 𐑌𐐵 𐐮𐐻 𐐶𐐱𐑆 𐐘𐐮𐐼𐑀𐐮𐐼𐐬𐑌𐐴, 𐐰𐑌𐐼 𐑄 𐐾𐐲𐐾 𐐢𐐰𐐿𐐬𐑌𐐨𐐲𐑅, 𐐰𐑌𐐼 𐑄𐐬𐑆 𐐸𐐭 𐐸𐐰𐐼 𐐺𐐮𐑌 𐐲𐐹𐑎𐑌𐐻𐐯𐐼 𐑊𐐨𐐼𐐲𐑉𐑆, 𐐸𐐭 𐐸𐐰𐐼 𐐯𐑅𐐻𐐰𐐺𐑊𐐮𐑇𐐻 𐑄𐐮𐑅 𐑀𐑉𐐩𐐻 𐐹𐐨𐑅 𐐮𐑌 𐑄 𐑊𐐰𐑌𐐼.

2. 𐐈𐑌𐐼 𐐮𐐻 𐐿𐐩𐑋 𐐻𐐭 𐐹𐐰𐑅 𐑄𐐰𐐻 𐑄𐐩𐑉 𐐶𐐲𐑉 𐑋𐐯𐑌𐐨 𐑅𐐮𐐻𐐨𐑆 𐐺𐐮𐑊𐐻 𐐰𐑌𐑏, 𐐰𐑌𐐼 𐑄𐐩𐑉 𐐶𐐲𐑉 𐑋𐐯𐑌𐐨 𐐬𐑊𐐼 𐑅𐐮𐐻𐐨𐑆 𐑉𐐨𐐹𐐩𐑉𐐼; 𐐰𐑌𐐼 𐑄𐐩𐑉 𐐶𐐲𐑉 𐑋𐐯𐑌𐐨 𐐸𐐴𐐶𐐩𐑆 𐐿𐐰𐑅𐐻 𐐲𐐹, 𐐰𐑌𐐼 𐑋𐐯𐑌𐐨 𐑉𐐬𐐼𐑆 𐑋𐐩𐐼, 𐐸𐐶𐐮𐐽 𐑊𐐯𐐼 𐑁𐑉𐐱𐑋 𐑅𐐮𐐻𐐨 𐐻𐐭 𐑅𐐮𐐻𐐨, 𐐰𐑌𐐼 𐑁𐑉𐐱𐑋 𐑊𐐰𐑌𐐼 𐐻𐐭 𐑊𐐰𐑌𐐼, 𐐰𐑌𐐼 𐑁𐑉𐐱𐑋 𐐹𐑊𐐩𐑅 𐐻𐐭 𐐹𐑊𐐩𐑅. 𐐈𐑌𐐼 𐑄𐐲𐑅 𐐹𐐰𐑅𐐻 𐐰𐐶𐐩 𐑄 𐐻𐐶𐐯𐑌𐐻𐐨 𐐰𐑌𐐼 𐐩𐐻𐑃 𐐷𐐨𐑉, 𐐰𐑌𐐼 𐑄 𐐹𐐨𐐹𐑊 𐐸𐐰𐐼 𐐿𐐲𐑌𐐻𐐮𐑌𐐷𐐭𐐲𐑊 𐐹𐐨𐑅. 𐐒𐐲𐐻 𐐮𐐻 𐐿𐐩𐑋 𐐻𐐭 𐐹𐐰𐑅 𐐮𐑌 𐑄 𐐻𐐶𐐯𐑌𐐻𐐨 𐐰𐑌𐐼 𐑌𐐴𐑌𐑃 𐐷𐐨𐑉 𐑄𐐩𐑉 𐐺𐐨𐑀𐐰𐑌 𐐻𐐭 𐐺𐐨 𐑅𐐲𐑋 𐐼𐐮𐑅𐐹𐐷𐐭𐐻𐐮𐑍𐑆 𐐰𐑋𐐲𐑍 𐑄 𐐹𐐨𐐹𐑊; 𐐰𐑌𐐼 𐑅𐐲𐑋 𐐶𐐲𐑉 𐑊𐐮𐑁𐐻𐐯𐐼 𐐲𐐹 𐐲𐑌𐐻𐐭 𐐹𐑉𐐴𐐼 𐐰𐑌𐐼 𐐺𐐬𐑅𐐻𐐮𐑍𐑆, 𐐺𐐨𐐿𐐫𐑆 𐐱𐑂 𐑄𐐩𐑉 𐐯𐐿𐑅𐐨𐐼𐐮𐑍𐑊𐐨 𐑀𐑉𐐩𐐻 𐑉𐐮𐐽𐐯𐑆, 𐐷𐐩, 𐐨𐑂𐐯𐑌 𐐲𐑌𐐻𐐭 𐑀𐑉𐐩𐐻 𐐹𐐲𐑉𐑅𐐨𐐿𐐷𐐭𐑇𐐲𐑌𐑆; 𐑁𐐫𐑉 𐑄𐐩𐑉 𐐶𐐲𐑉 𐑋𐐯𐑌𐐨 𐑋𐐲𐑉𐐽𐐰𐑌𐐻𐑅 𐐮𐑌 𐑄 𐑊𐐰𐑌𐐼, 𐐰𐑌𐐼 𐐫𐑊𐑅𐐬 𐑋𐐯𐑌𐐨 𐑊𐐫𐐷𐐲𐑉𐑆, 𐐰𐑌𐐼 𐑋𐐯𐑌𐐨 𐐱𐑁𐐮𐑅𐐲𐑉𐑆. 𐐈𐑌𐐼 𐑄 𐐹𐐨𐐹𐑊 𐐺𐐨𐑀𐐰𐑌 𐐻𐐭 𐐺𐐨 𐐼𐐮𐑅𐐻𐐮𐑍𐑀𐐶𐐮𐑇𐐻 𐐺𐐴 𐑉𐐰𐑍𐐿𐑅; 𐐰𐐿𐐫𐑉𐐼𐐮𐑍 𐐻𐐭 𐑄𐐩𐑉 𐑉𐐮𐐽𐐯𐑆 𐐰𐑌𐐼 𐑄𐐩𐑉 𐐽𐐰𐑌𐑅𐐯𐑆 𐑁𐐫𐑉 𐑊𐐲𐑉𐑌𐐮𐑍; 𐐷𐐩, 𐑅𐐲𐑋 𐐶𐐲𐑉 𐐮𐑀𐑌𐐬𐑉𐐰𐑌𐐻 𐐺𐐨𐐿𐐫𐑆 𐐱𐑂 𐑄𐐩𐑉 𐐹𐐱𐑂𐐲𐑉𐐻𐐨, 𐐰𐑌𐐼 𐐲𐑄𐐲𐑉𐑆 𐐼𐐮𐐼 𐑉𐐨𐑅𐐨𐑂 𐑀𐑉𐐩𐐻 𐑊𐐲𐑉𐑌𐐮𐑍 𐐺𐐨𐐿𐐫𐑆 𐐱𐑂 𐑄𐐩𐑉 𐑉𐐮𐐽𐐯𐑆; 𐑅𐐲𐑋 𐐶𐐲𐑉 𐑊𐐮𐑁𐐻𐐯𐐼 𐐲𐐹 𐐮𐑌 𐐹𐑉𐐴𐐼, 𐐰𐑌𐐼 𐐲𐑄𐐲𐑉𐑆 𐐶𐐲𐑉 𐐯𐐿𐑅𐐨𐐼𐐮𐑍𐑊𐐨 𐐸𐐲𐑋𐐺𐑊; 𐑅𐐲𐑋 𐐼𐐮𐐼 𐑉𐐨𐐻𐐲𐑉𐑌 𐑉𐐩𐑊𐐮𐑍 𐑁𐐫𐑉 𐑉𐐩𐑊𐐮𐑍, 𐐸𐐶𐐴𐑊 𐐲𐑄𐐲𐑉𐑆 𐐶𐐳𐐼 𐑉𐐨𐑅𐐨𐑂 𐑉𐐩𐑊𐐮𐑍 𐐰𐑌𐐼 𐐹𐐲𐑉𐑅𐐨𐐿𐐷𐐭𐑇𐐲𐑌, 𐐰𐑌𐐼 𐐫𐑊 𐑋𐐰𐑌𐐲𐑉 𐐱𐑂 𐐰𐑁𐑊𐐮𐐿𐑇𐐲𐑌𐑆, 𐐰𐑌𐐼 𐐶𐐳𐐼 𐑌𐐱𐐻 𐐻𐐲𐑉𐑌 𐐰𐑌𐐼 𐑉𐐨𐑂𐐴𐑊 𐐰𐑀𐐯𐑌, 𐐺𐐲𐐻 𐐶𐐲𐑉 𐐸𐐲𐑋𐐺𐑊 𐐰𐑌𐐼 𐐹𐐯𐑌𐐮𐐻𐐯𐑌𐐻 𐐺𐐨𐑁𐐫𐑉 𐐘𐐱𐐼; 𐐰𐑌𐐼 𐑄𐐲𐑅 𐑄𐐩𐑉 𐐺𐐨𐐿𐐩𐑋 𐐩 𐑀𐑉𐐩𐐻 𐐮𐑌𐐨𐐿𐐶𐐱𐑊𐐮𐐻𐐨 𐐮𐑌 𐐫𐑊 𐑄 𐑊𐐰𐑌𐐼, 𐐮𐑌𐑅𐐬𐑋𐐲𐐽 𐑄𐐰𐐻 𐑄 𐐕𐐲𐑉𐐽 𐐺𐐨𐑀𐐰𐑌 𐐻𐐭 𐐺𐐨 𐐺𐑉𐐬𐐿𐐲𐑌 𐐲𐐹; 𐐷𐐩, 𐐮𐑌𐑅𐐬𐑋𐐲𐐽 𐑄𐐰𐐻 𐐮𐑌 𐑄 𐑃𐐲𐑉𐐻𐐨𐐯𐑃 𐐷𐐨𐑉 𐑄 𐐕𐐲𐑉𐐽 𐐶𐐱𐑆 𐐺𐑉𐐬𐐿𐐲𐑌 𐐲𐐹 𐐮𐑌 𐐫𐑊 𐑄 𐑊𐐰𐑌𐐼, 𐑅𐐩𐑂 𐐮𐐻 𐐶𐐲𐑉 𐐰𐑋𐐲𐑍 𐐩 𐑁𐑏 𐐱𐑂 𐑄 𐐢𐐰𐑋𐐲𐑌𐐴𐐻𐑅, 𐐸𐐭 𐐶𐐲𐑉 𐐿𐐲𐑌𐑂𐐲𐑉𐐻𐐯𐐼 𐐲𐑌𐐻𐐭 𐑄 𐐻𐑉𐐭 𐑁𐐩𐑃; 𐐰𐑌𐐼 𐑄𐐩 𐐶𐐳𐐼 𐑌𐐱𐐻 𐐼𐐨𐐹𐐪𐑉𐐻 𐑁𐑉𐐱𐑋 𐐮𐐻, 𐑁𐐫𐑉 𐑄𐐩 𐐶𐐲𐑉 𐑁𐐲𐑉𐑋, 𐐰𐑌𐐼 𐑅𐐻𐐯𐐼𐑁𐐰𐑅𐐻, 𐐰𐑌𐐼 𐐮𐑋𐐭𐑂𐐲𐐺𐑊, 𐐶𐐮𐑊𐐮𐑍 𐐶𐐮𐑄 𐐫𐑊 𐐼𐐮𐑊𐐮𐐾𐐯𐑌𐑅 𐐻𐐭 𐐿𐐨𐐹 𐑄 𐐿𐐱𐑋𐐰𐑌𐐼𐑋𐐯𐑌𐐻𐑅 𐐱𐑂 𐑄 𐐢𐐫𐑉𐐼. 𐐤𐐵 𐑄 𐐿𐐫𐑆 𐐱𐑂 𐑄𐐮𐑅 𐐮𐑌𐐮𐐿𐐶𐐮𐐻𐐨 𐐱𐑂 𐑄 𐐹𐐨𐐹𐑊 𐐶𐐱𐑆 𐑄𐐮𐑅, 𐐝𐐩𐐻𐐲𐑌 𐐸𐐰𐐼 𐑀𐑉𐐩𐐻 𐐹𐐵𐐲𐑉, 𐐲𐑌𐐻𐐭 𐑄 𐑅𐐻𐐲𐑉𐐮𐑍 𐐲𐐹 𐐱𐑂 𐑄 𐐹𐐨𐐹𐑊 𐐻𐐭 𐐼𐐭 𐐫𐑊 𐑋𐐰𐑌𐐲𐑉 𐐱𐑂 𐐮𐑌𐐮𐐿𐐶𐐮𐐻𐐨, 𐐰𐑌𐐼 𐐻𐐭 𐑄 𐐹𐐲𐑁𐐮𐑍 𐑄𐐯𐑋 𐐲𐐹 𐐶𐐮𐑄 𐐹𐑉𐐴𐐼, 𐐻𐐯𐑋𐐹𐐻𐐮𐑍 𐑄𐐯𐑋 𐐻𐐭 𐑅𐐨𐐿 𐑁𐐫𐑉 𐐹𐐵𐐲𐑉, 𐐰𐑌𐐼 𐐫𐑃𐐱𐑉𐐮𐐻𐐨, 𐐰𐑌𐐼 𐑉𐐮𐐽𐐯𐑆, 𐐰𐑌𐐼 𐑄 𐑂𐐩𐑌 𐑃𐐮𐑍𐑆 𐐱𐑂 𐑄 𐐶𐐲𐑉𐑊𐐼. 𐐈𐑌𐐼 𐑄𐐲𐑅 𐐝𐐩𐐻𐐲𐑌 𐐼𐐮𐐼 𐑊𐐨𐐼 𐐰𐐶𐐩 𐑄 𐐸𐐪𐑉𐐻𐑅 𐐱𐑂 𐑄 𐐹𐐨𐐹𐑊 𐐻𐐭 𐐼𐐭 𐐫𐑊 𐑋𐐰𐑌𐐲𐑉 𐐱𐑂 𐐮𐑌𐐮𐐿𐐶𐐮𐐻𐐨: 𐑄𐐩𐑉𐑁𐐫𐑉 𐑄𐐩 𐐸𐐰𐐼 𐐯𐑌𐐾𐑎𐐼 𐐹𐐨𐑅 𐐺𐐲𐐻 𐐩 𐑁𐑏 𐐷𐐨𐑉𐑆.

3. 𐐈𐑌𐐼 𐑄𐐲𐑅 𐐮𐑌 𐑄 𐐿𐐱𐑋𐐯𐑌𐑅𐑋𐐯𐑌𐐻 𐐱𐑂 𐑄 𐑃𐐲𐑉𐐻𐐨𐐯𐑃 𐐷𐐨𐑉, 𐑄 𐐹𐐨𐐹𐑊 𐐸𐐰𐑂𐐮𐑍 𐐺𐐮𐑌 𐐼𐐮𐑊𐐮𐑂𐐲𐑉𐐼 𐐲𐐹 𐑁𐐫𐑉 𐑄 𐑅𐐹𐐩𐑅 𐐱𐑂 𐐩 𐑊𐐫𐑍 𐐻𐐴𐑋 𐐻𐐭 𐐺𐐨 𐐿𐐰𐑉𐐨𐐼 𐐰𐐺𐐵𐐻 𐐺𐐴 𐑄 𐐻𐐯𐑋𐐹𐐻𐐩𐑇𐐲𐑌𐑆 𐐱𐑂 𐑄 𐐼𐐯𐑂𐐮𐑊 𐐸𐐶𐐮𐑄𐐲𐑉𐑅𐐬𐐯𐑂𐐲𐑉 𐐸𐐨 𐐼𐐨𐑆𐐴𐑉𐐼 𐐻𐐭 𐐿𐐰𐑉𐐨 𐑄𐐯𐑋, 𐐰𐑌𐐼 𐐻𐐭 𐐼𐐭 𐐸𐐶𐐱𐐻𐑅𐐬𐐯𐑂𐐲𐑉 𐐮𐑌𐐮𐐿𐐶𐐮𐐻𐐨 𐐸𐐨 𐐼𐐨𐑆𐐴𐑉𐐼 𐑄𐐩 𐑇𐐳𐐼; 𐐰𐑌𐐼 𐑄𐐲𐑅 𐐮𐑌 𐑄 𐐿𐐱𐑋𐐯𐑌𐑅𐑋𐐯𐑌𐐻 𐐱𐑂 𐑄𐐮𐑅, 𐑄 𐑃𐐲𐑉𐐻𐐨𐐯𐑃 𐐷𐐨𐑉, 𐑄𐐩 𐐶𐐲𐑉 𐐮𐑌 𐐩 𐑅𐐻𐐩𐐻 𐐱𐑂 𐐫𐑁𐐳𐑊 𐐶𐐮𐐿𐐯𐐼𐑌𐐯𐑅. 𐐤𐐵 𐑄𐐩 𐐼𐐮𐐼 𐑌𐐱𐐻 𐑅𐐮𐑌 𐐮𐑀𐑌𐐬𐑉𐐰𐑌𐐻𐑊𐐨, 𐑁𐐫𐑉 𐑄𐐩 𐑌𐑏 𐑄 𐐶𐐮𐑊 𐐱𐑂

𐐘𐐱𐐼 𐐿𐐱𐑌𐑅𐐲𐑉𐑌𐐮𐑍 𐑄𐐯𐑋, 𐑁𐐫𐑉 𐐮𐐻 𐐸𐐰𐐼 𐐺𐐮𐑌 𐐻𐐫𐐻 𐐲𐑌𐐻𐐭 𐑄𐐯𐑋; 𐑄𐐩𐑉𐑁𐐫𐑉 𐑄𐐩 𐐼𐐮𐐼 𐐶𐐮𐑊𐑁𐐳𐑊𐐮 𐑉𐐯𐐺𐐯𐑊 𐐰𐑀𐐯𐑌𐑅𐐻 𐐘𐐱𐐼. 𐐈𐑌𐐼 𐑌𐐵 𐐮𐐻 𐐶𐐱𐑆 𐐮𐑌 𐑄 𐐼𐐩𐑆 𐐱𐑂 𐐢𐐩𐐿𐐬𐑌𐐨𐐲𐑅, 𐑄 𐑅𐐲𐑌 𐐱𐑂 𐐢𐐩𐐿𐐬𐑌𐐨𐐲𐑅, 𐑁𐐫𐑉 𐐢𐐩𐐿𐐬𐑌𐐨𐐲𐑅 𐐼𐐮𐐼 𐑁𐐮𐑊 𐑄 𐑅𐐨𐐻 𐐱𐑂 𐐸𐐮𐑆 𐑁𐐪𐑄𐐲𐑉 𐐰𐑌𐐼 𐐼𐐮𐐼 𐑀𐐲𐑂𐐲𐑉𐑌 𐑄 𐐹𐐨𐐹𐐲𐑊 𐑄𐐰𐐻 𐐷𐐨𐑉. 𐐈𐑌𐐼 𐑄𐐩𐑉 𐐺𐐨𐑀𐐰𐑌 𐐻𐐭 𐐺𐐨 𐑋𐐯𐑌 𐐮𐑌𐑅𐐹𐐴𐑉𐐼 𐑁𐑉𐐱𐑋 𐐸𐐯𐑂𐐲𐑌, 𐐰𐑌𐐼 𐑅𐐯𐑌𐐻 𐑁𐐫𐑉𐑃, 𐑅𐐻𐐰𐑌𐐼𐐮𐑍 𐐲𐑋𐐲𐑍 𐑄 𐐹𐐨𐐹𐐲𐑊 𐐮𐑌 𐐫𐑊 𐑄 𐑊𐐰𐑌𐐼, 𐐹𐑉𐐨𐐽𐐮𐑍 𐐰𐑌𐐼 𐐻𐐯𐑅𐐻𐐮𐑁𐐴𐐮𐑍 𐐺𐐬𐑊𐐼𐑊𐐨 𐐱𐑂 𐑄 𐑅𐐮𐑌𐑆 𐐰𐑌𐐼 𐐮𐑌𐐮𐐿𐐶𐐮𐐻𐐨𐑆 𐐱𐑂 𐑄 𐐹𐐨𐐹𐐲𐑊, 𐐰𐑌𐐼 𐐻𐐯𐑅𐐻𐐮𐑁𐐴𐐮𐑍 𐐲𐑌𐐻𐐭 𐑄𐐯𐑋 𐐿𐐱𐑌𐑅𐐲𐑉𐑌𐐮𐑍 𐑄 𐑉𐐨𐐼𐐯𐑋𐐹𐑇𐐲𐑌 𐐸𐐶𐐮𐐽 𐑄 𐐢𐐫𐑉𐐼 𐐶𐐳𐐼 𐑋𐐩𐐿 𐑁𐐫𐑉 𐐸𐐮𐑆 𐐹𐐨𐐹𐐲𐑊; 𐐫𐑉 𐐮𐑌 𐐲𐑄𐐲𐑉 𐐶𐐲𐑉𐐼𐑆, 𐑄 𐑉𐐯𐑆𐐲𐑉𐐯𐐿𐑇𐐲𐑌 𐐱𐑂 𐐗𐑉𐐴𐑅𐐻; 𐐰𐑌𐐼 𐑄𐐩 𐐼𐐮𐐼 𐐻𐐯𐑅𐐻𐐮𐑁𐐴 𐐺𐐬𐑊𐐼𐑊𐐨 𐐱𐑂 𐐸𐐮𐑆 𐐼𐐯𐑃 𐐰𐑌𐐼 𐑅𐐲𐑁𐐲𐑉𐐮𐑍𐑆. 𐐤𐐵 𐑄𐐩𐑉 𐐶𐐲𐑉 𐑋𐐯𐑌𐐨 𐐱𐑂 𐑄 𐐹𐐨𐐹𐐲𐑊 𐐸𐐭 𐐶𐐲𐑉 𐐯𐐿𐑅𐐨𐐼𐐮𐑍𐑊𐐨 𐐰𐑍𐑀𐑉𐐨, 𐐺𐐨𐐿𐐫𐑆 𐐱𐑂 𐑄𐐬𐑆 𐐸𐐭 𐐻𐐯𐑅𐐻𐐮𐑁𐐴𐐼 𐐱𐑂 𐑄𐐨𐑆 𐑃𐐮𐑍𐑆; 𐐰𐑌𐐼 𐑄𐐬𐑆 𐐸𐐭 𐐶𐐲𐑉 𐐰𐑍𐑀𐑉𐐨 𐐶𐐲𐑉 𐐽𐐨𐑁𐑊𐐨 𐑄 𐐽𐐨𐑁 𐐾𐐲𐐾𐐯𐑆, 𐐰𐑌𐐼 𐑄𐐩 𐐸𐐭 𐐸𐐰𐐼 𐐺𐐮𐑌 𐐸𐐴 𐐹𐑉𐐨𐑅𐐻𐑅 𐐰𐑌𐐼 𐑊𐐫𐐷𐐲𐑉𐑆; 𐐷𐐩, 𐐫𐑊 𐑄𐐬𐑆 𐐸𐐭 𐐶𐐲𐑉 𐑊𐐫𐐷𐐲𐑉𐑆, 𐐶𐐲𐑉 𐐰𐑍𐑀𐑉𐐨 𐐶𐐮𐑄 𐑄𐐬𐑆 𐐸𐐭 𐐻𐐯𐑅𐐻𐐮𐑁𐐴𐐼 𐐱𐑂 𐑄𐐨𐑆 𐑃𐐮𐑍𐑆. 𐐤𐐵 𐑄𐐩𐑉 𐐶𐐱𐑆 𐑌𐐬 𐑊𐐫𐐷𐐲𐑉, 𐑌𐐫𐑉 𐐾𐐲𐐾, 𐑌𐐫𐑉 𐐸𐐴 𐐹𐑉𐐨𐑅𐐻, 𐑄𐐰𐐻 𐐿𐐳𐐼 𐐸𐐰𐑂 𐐹𐐵𐐲𐑉 𐐻𐐭 𐐿𐐲𐑌𐐼𐐯𐑋 𐐯𐑌𐐨 𐐶𐐲𐑌 𐐻𐐭 𐐼𐐯𐑃, 𐑅𐐩𐑂 𐑄𐐩𐑉 𐐿𐐱𐑌𐐼𐐯𐑋𐑌𐐩𐑇𐐲𐑌 𐐶𐐱𐑆 𐑅𐐴𐑌𐐼 𐐺𐐴 𐑄 𐑀𐐲𐑂𐐲𐑉𐑌𐐲𐑉 𐐱𐑂 𐑄 𐑊𐐰𐑌𐐼. 𐐤𐐵 𐑄𐐩𐑉 𐐶𐐲𐑉 𐑋𐐯𐑌𐐨 𐐱𐑂 𐑄𐐬𐑆 𐐸𐐭 𐐻𐐯𐑅𐐻𐐮𐑁𐐴𐐼 𐐱𐑂 𐑄 𐑃𐐮𐑍𐑆 𐐹𐐲𐑉𐐻𐐩𐑌𐐮𐑍 𐐻𐐭 𐐗𐑉𐐴𐑅𐐻, 𐐸𐐭 𐐻𐐯𐑅𐐻𐐮𐑁𐐴𐐼 𐐺𐐬𐑊𐐼𐑊𐐨, 𐐸𐐭 𐐶𐐲𐑉 𐐻𐐩𐐿𐐲𐑌 𐐰𐑌𐐼 𐐹𐐳𐐻 𐐻𐐭 𐐼𐐯𐑃 𐑅𐐨𐐿𐑉𐐯𐐻𐑊𐐨 𐐺𐐴 𐑄 𐐾𐐲𐐾𐐯𐑆, 𐑄𐐰𐐻 𐑄 𐑌𐐱𐑊𐐯𐐾 𐐱𐑂 𐑄𐐩𐑉 𐐼𐐯𐑃 𐐿𐐩𐑋 𐑌𐐱𐐻 𐐲𐑌𐐻𐐭 𐑄 𐑀𐐲𐑂𐐲𐑉𐑌𐐲𐑉 𐐱𐑂 𐑄 𐑊𐐰𐑌𐐼, 𐐲𐑌𐐻𐐮𐑊 𐐪𐑁𐐻𐐲𐑉 𐑄𐐩𐑉 𐐼𐐯𐑃. 𐐤𐐵 𐐺𐐨𐐸𐐬𐑊𐐼, 𐑄𐐮𐑅 𐐶𐐱𐑆 𐐿𐐱𐑌𐐻𐑉𐐩𐑉𐐨 𐐻𐐭 𐑄 𐑊𐐫𐑆 𐐱𐑂 𐑄 𐑊𐐰𐑌𐐼, 𐑄𐐰𐐻 𐐯𐑌𐐨 𐑋𐐰𐑌 𐑇𐐳𐐼 𐐺𐐨 𐐹𐐳𐐻 𐐻𐐭 𐐼𐐯𐑃, 𐐯𐐿𐑅𐐯𐐹𐐻 𐑄𐐩 𐐸𐐰𐐼 𐐹𐐵𐐲𐑉 𐑁𐑉𐐱𐑋 𐑄 𐑀𐐲𐑂𐐲𐑉𐑌𐐲𐑉 𐐱𐑂 𐑄 𐑊𐐰𐑌𐐼; 𐑄𐐩𐑉𐑁𐐫𐑉 𐐲 𐐿𐐱𐑋𐐹𐑊𐐩𐑌𐐻 𐐿𐐩𐑋 𐐲𐐹 𐐲𐑌𐐻𐐭 𐑄 𐑊𐐰𐑌𐐼 𐐱𐑂 𐐞𐐪𐑉𐐲𐐸𐐯𐑋𐑊𐐲, 𐐻𐐭 𐑄 𐑀𐐲𐑂𐐲𐑉𐑌𐐲𐑉 𐐱𐑂 𐑄 𐑊𐐰𐑌𐐼, 𐐰𐑀𐐯𐑌𐑅𐐻 𐑄𐐨𐑆 𐐾𐐲𐐾𐐯𐑆 𐐸𐐭 𐐸𐐰𐐼 𐐿𐐱𐑌𐐼𐐯𐑋𐐼 𐑄 𐐹𐑉𐐱𐑁𐐯𐐻𐑅 𐐱𐑂 𐑄 𐐢𐐫𐑉𐐼 𐐲𐑌𐐻𐐭 𐐼𐐯𐑃, 𐑌𐐱𐐻 𐐰𐐿𐐫𐑉𐐼𐐮𐑍 𐐻𐐭 𐑄 𐑊𐐫.

4. 𐐤𐐵 𐐮𐐻 𐐿𐐩𐑋 𐐻𐐭 𐐹𐐪𐑅 𐑄𐐰𐐻 𐑄𐐩 𐐶𐐲𐑉 𐐻𐐩𐐿𐐲𐑌 𐐰𐑌𐐼 𐐺𐑉𐐫𐐻 𐐲𐐹 𐐺𐐨𐑁𐐬𐑉 𐑄 𐐾𐐲𐐾, 𐐻𐐭 𐐺𐐨 𐐾𐐲𐐾𐐼 𐐱𐑂 𐑄 𐐿𐑉𐐴𐑋 𐐸𐐶𐐮𐐽 𐑄𐐩 𐐸𐐰𐐼 𐐼𐐲𐑌, 𐐰𐐿𐐫𐑉𐐼𐐮𐑍 𐐻𐐭 𐑄 𐑊𐐫 𐐸𐐶𐐮𐐽 𐐸𐐰𐐼 𐐺𐐮𐑌 𐑀𐐮𐑂𐐲𐑌 𐐺𐐴 𐑄 𐐹𐐨𐐹𐐲𐑊. 𐐤𐐵 𐐮𐐻 𐐿𐐩𐑋 𐐻𐐭 𐐹𐐪𐑅 𐑄𐐰𐐻 𐑄𐐬𐑆 𐐾𐐲𐐾𐐯𐑆 𐐸𐐰𐐼 𐑋𐐯𐑌𐐨 𐑁𐑉𐐯𐑌𐐼𐑆 𐐰𐑌𐐼 𐐿𐐮𐑌𐐼𐑉𐐯𐐼𐑆; 𐐰𐑌𐐼 𐑄 𐑉𐐨𐑋𐐩𐑌𐐼𐐲𐑉, 𐐷𐐩, 𐐨𐑂𐐲𐑌, 𐐫𐑊𐑋𐐬𐑅𐐻 𐐫𐑊 𐑄 𐑊𐐫𐐷𐐲𐑉𐑆 𐐰𐑌𐐼 𐑄 𐐸𐐴 𐐹𐑉𐐨𐑅𐐻𐑅, 𐐼𐐮𐐼 𐑀𐐰𐑄𐐲𐑉 𐑄𐐯𐑋𐑅𐐯𐑊𐑂𐑆 𐐻𐐳𐑀𐐯𐑄𐐲𐑉, 𐐰𐑌𐐼 𐐷𐐭𐑌𐐴𐐻 𐐶𐐮𐑄 𐑄 𐐿𐐮𐑌𐐼𐑉𐐯𐐼𐑆 𐐱𐑂 𐑄𐐬𐑆 𐐾𐐲𐐾𐐯𐑆 𐐸𐐭 𐐶𐐲𐑉 𐐻𐐭 𐐺𐐨 𐐻𐑉𐐴𐐼 𐐰𐐿𐐫𐑉𐐼𐐮𐑍 𐐻𐐭 𐑄 𐑊𐐫; 𐐰𐑌𐐼 𐑄𐐩 𐐼𐐮𐐼 𐐯𐑌𐐻𐐲𐑉 𐐮𐑌𐐻𐐭 𐐲 𐐿𐐲𐑂𐐯𐑌𐐰𐑌𐐻 𐐶𐐲𐑌 𐐶𐐮𐑄 𐐰𐑌𐐲𐑄𐐲𐑉, 𐐷𐐩, 𐐨𐑂𐐲𐑌 𐐮𐑌𐐻𐐭 𐑄𐐰𐐻 𐐿𐐲𐑂𐐯𐑌𐐰𐑌𐐻 𐐸𐐶𐐮𐐽 𐐶𐐱𐑆 𐑀𐐮𐑂𐐲𐑌 𐐺𐐴 𐑄𐐯𐑋 𐐱𐑂 𐐬𐑊𐐼, 𐐸𐐶𐐮𐐽 𐐿𐐲𐑂𐐯𐑌𐐰𐑌𐐻 𐐶𐐱𐑆 𐑀𐐮𐑂𐐲𐑌 𐐰𐑌𐐼 𐐰𐐼𐑋𐐮𐑌𐐮𐑅𐐻𐐲𐑉𐐼 𐐺𐐴 𐑄 𐐼𐐯𐑂𐐮𐑊, 𐐻𐐭 𐐿𐐱𐑋𐐺𐐴𐑌 𐐰𐑀𐐯𐑌𐑅𐐻 𐐫𐑊 𐑉𐐴𐐽𐐲𐑅𐑌𐐯𐑅; 𐑄𐐩𐑉𐑁𐐫𐑉 𐑄𐐩 𐐼𐐮𐐼 𐐿𐐱𐑋𐐺𐐴𐑌 𐐰𐑀𐐯𐑌𐑅𐐻 𐑄 𐐹𐐨𐐹𐐲𐑊 𐐱𐑂 𐑄 𐐢𐐫𐑉𐐼, 𐐰𐑌𐐼 𐐯𐑌𐐻𐐲𐑉 𐐮𐑌𐐻𐐭 𐐲 𐐿𐐲𐑂𐐯𐑌𐐰𐑌𐐻 𐐻𐐭 𐐼𐐯𐑅𐐻𐑉𐐦 𐑄𐐯𐑋, 𐐰𐑌𐐼 𐐻𐐭 𐐼𐐯𐑊𐐮𐑂𐐲𐑉 𐑄𐐬𐑆 𐐸𐐭 𐐶𐐲𐑉 𐑀𐐮𐑊𐐻𐐨 𐐱𐑂 𐑋𐐲𐑉𐐼𐐲𐑉 𐑁𐑉𐐱𐑋 𐑄 𐑀𐑉𐐪𐑅𐐹 𐐱𐑂 𐐾𐐲𐑅𐐻𐐮𐑅, 𐐸𐐶𐐮𐐽 𐐶𐐱𐑆 𐐲𐐺𐐵𐐻 𐐻𐐭 𐐺𐐨 𐐰𐐼𐑋𐐮𐑌𐐮𐑅𐐻𐐲𐑉𐐼 𐐰𐐿𐐫𐑉𐐼𐐮𐑍 𐐻𐐭 𐑄 𐑊𐐫. 𐐈𐑌𐐼 𐑄𐐩 𐐼𐐮𐐼 𐑅𐐯𐐻 𐐰𐐻 𐐼𐐯𐑁𐐴𐐲𐑌𐑅 𐑄 𐑊𐐫 𐐰𐑌𐐼 𐑄 𐑉𐐴𐐻𐑅 𐐱𐑂 𐑄𐐩𐑉 𐐿𐐲𐑌𐐻𐑉𐐨; 𐐰𐑌𐐼 𐑄𐐩 𐐼𐐮𐐼 𐐿𐐲𐑂𐐯𐑌𐐰𐑌𐐻 𐐶𐐲𐑌 𐐶𐐮𐑄 𐐰𐑌𐐲𐑄𐐲𐑉, 𐐻𐐭 𐐼𐐯𐑅𐐻𐑉𐐦 𐑄 𐑀𐐲𐑂𐐲𐑉𐑌𐐲𐑉, 𐐰𐑌𐐼 𐐻𐐭 𐐯𐑅𐐻𐐰𐐺𐑊𐐮𐑇 𐐲 𐐿𐐮𐑍 𐐬𐑂𐐲𐑉 𐑄 𐑊𐐰𐑌𐐼, 𐑄𐐰𐐻 𐑄 𐑊𐐰𐑌𐐼 𐑇𐐳𐐼 𐑌𐐬 𐑋𐐬𐑉 𐐺𐐨 𐐰𐐻 𐑊𐐮𐐺𐐲𐑉𐐻𐐨, 𐐺𐐲𐐻 𐑇𐐳𐐼 𐐺𐐨 𐑅𐐲𐐺𐐾𐐯𐐿𐐻 𐐲𐑌𐐻𐐭 𐐿𐐮𐑍𐑆. 𐐤𐐵, 𐐺𐐨𐐸𐐬𐑊𐐼, 𐐌 𐐶𐐮𐑊 𐑇𐐬 𐐲𐑌𐐻𐐭 𐐷𐐭 𐑄𐐰𐐻 𐑄𐐩 𐐼𐐮𐐼 𐑌𐐱𐐻 𐐯𐑅𐐻𐐰𐐺𐑊𐐮𐑇 𐐲 𐐿𐐮𐑍 𐐬𐑂𐐲𐑉 𐑄 𐑊𐐰𐑌𐐼; 𐐺𐐲𐐻 𐐮𐑌 𐑄𐐮𐑅 𐑅𐐩𐑋 𐐷𐐨𐑉, 𐐷𐐩, 𐑄 𐑃𐐲𐑉𐐻𐐨𐐯𐑃 𐐷𐐨𐑉, 𐑄𐐩 𐐼𐐮𐐼 𐐼𐐯𐑅𐐻𐑉𐐦 𐐲𐐹𐐱𐑌 𐑄 𐐾𐐲𐐾𐑋𐐯𐑌𐐻 𐑅𐐨𐐻, 𐐷𐐩, 𐐼𐐮𐐼 𐑋𐐲𐑉𐐼𐐲𐑉 𐑄 𐐽𐐨𐑁 𐐾𐐲𐐾 𐐱𐑂 𐑄 𐑊𐐰𐑌𐐼. 𐐈𐑌𐐼 𐑄 𐐹𐐨𐐹𐐲𐑊 𐐶𐐲𐑉 𐐼𐐮𐑂𐐴𐐼𐐲𐐼 𐐶𐐲𐑌 𐐰𐑀𐐯𐑌𐑅𐐻 𐐰𐑌𐐲𐑄𐐲𐑉; 𐐰𐑌𐐼 𐑄𐐩 𐐼𐐮𐐼 𐑅𐐯𐐹𐐲𐑉𐐩𐐻 𐐶𐐲𐑌 𐑁𐑉𐐱𐑋 𐐰𐑌𐐲𐑄𐐲𐑉, 𐐮𐑌𐐻𐐭 𐐻𐑉𐐴𐐺𐑆, 𐐯𐑂𐐲𐑉𐐨 𐑋𐐰𐑌 𐐰𐐿𐐫𐑉𐐼𐐮𐑍 𐐻𐐭 𐐸𐐮𐑆 𐑁𐐰𐑋𐐮𐑊𐐨, 𐐰𐑌𐐼 𐐸𐐮𐑆 𐐿𐐮𐑌𐐼𐑉𐐯𐐼, 𐐰𐑌𐐼 𐑁𐑉𐐯𐑌𐐼𐑆; 𐐰𐑌𐐼 𐑄𐐲𐑅 𐑄𐐩 𐐼𐐮𐐼 𐐼𐐯𐑅𐐻𐑉𐐦 𐑄 𐑀𐐲𐑂𐐲𐑉𐑌𐑋𐐯𐑌𐐻 𐐱𐑂 𐑄 𐑊𐐰𐑌𐐼. 𐐈𐑌𐐼 𐐯𐑂𐐲𐑉𐐨 𐐻𐑉𐐴𐐺 𐐼𐐮𐐼 𐐰𐐹𐐱𐐮𐑌𐐻 𐐲 𐐽𐐨𐑁, 𐐫𐑉 𐐲 𐑊𐐨𐐼𐐲𐑉 𐐬𐑂𐐲𐑉 𐑄𐐯𐑋; 𐐰𐑌𐐼 𐑄𐐲𐑅 𐑄𐐩 𐐺𐐨𐐿𐐩𐑋 𐐻𐑉𐐴𐐺𐑆 𐐰𐑌𐐼 𐑊𐐨𐐼𐐲𐑉𐑆 𐐱𐑂 𐐻𐑉𐐴𐐺𐑆. 𐐤𐐵 𐐺𐐨𐐸𐐬𐑊𐐼, 𐑄𐐩𐑉 𐐶𐐱𐑆 𐑌𐐬 𐑋𐐰𐑌 𐐲𐑋𐐲𐑍 𐑄𐐯𐑋, 𐑅𐐩𐑂 𐐸𐐨 𐐸𐐰𐐼 𐑋𐐲𐐽 𐑁𐐰𐑋𐐮𐑊𐐨 𐐰𐑌𐐼 𐑋𐐯𐑌𐐨 𐐿𐐮𐑌𐐼𐑉𐐯𐐼𐑆 𐐰𐑌𐐼 𐑁𐑉𐐯𐑌𐐼𐑆;

𐑄𐐯𐑉𐑁𐐬𐑉 𐑄𐐯𐑉 𐐻𐑉𐐴𐐺𐑆 𐐺𐐨𐐿𐐩𐑋 𐐯𐐿𐑅𐐨𐐼𐐮𐑍𐑊𐐨 𐑀𐑉𐐩𐐻. 𐐤𐐵 𐐫𐑊 𐑄𐐮𐑅 𐐶𐐱𐑆 𐐼𐐲𐑌 𐐰𐑌𐐼 𐑄𐐯𐑉 𐐶𐐲𐑉 𐑌𐐬 𐐶𐐬𐑉𐑆 𐐰𐑆 𐐷𐐯𐐻 𐐰𐑋𐐲𐑍 𐑄𐐯𐑋; 𐐰𐑌𐐼 𐐫𐑊 𐑄𐐮𐑅 𐐮𐑌𐐮𐐿𐐶𐐮𐐻𐐨 𐐸𐐰𐐼 𐐿𐐲𐑋 𐐲𐐹𐐱𐑌 𐑄 𐐹𐐨𐐹𐐲𐑊, 𐐺𐐨𐐿𐐫𐑆 𐑄𐐩 𐐼𐐮𐐼 𐐷𐐨𐑊𐐼 𐑄𐐯𐑋𐑅𐐯𐑊𐑂𐑆 𐐲𐑌𐐻𐐭 𐑄 𐐹𐐵𐑉 𐐱𐑂 𐐝𐐩𐐻𐐲𐑌; 𐐰𐑌𐐼 𐑄 𐑉𐐯𐑀𐐷𐐭𐑊𐐩𐑇𐐲𐑌𐑆 𐐱𐑂 𐑄 𐑀𐐲𐑂𐐲𐑉𐑌𐑋𐐯𐑌𐐻 𐐶𐐲𐑉 𐐼𐐨𐑅𐐻𐑉𐑎𐐼, 𐐺𐐨𐐿𐐫𐑆 𐐱𐑂 𐑄 𐑅𐐨𐐿𐑉𐐯𐐻 𐐿𐐱𐑋𐐺𐐮𐑌𐐩𐑇𐐲𐑌 𐐱𐑂 𐑄 𐑁𐑉𐐯𐑌𐐼𐑆 𐐰𐑌𐐼 𐐿𐐮𐑌𐐼𐑉𐐯𐐼𐑆 𐐱𐑂 𐑄𐐬𐑆 𐐸𐐭 𐑋𐐲𐑉𐐼𐐲𐑉𐐼 𐑄 𐐹𐑉𐐱𐑁𐐯𐐻𐑅. 𐐈𐑌𐐼 𐑄𐐩 𐐼𐐮𐐼 𐐿𐐫𐑆 𐐩 𐑀𐑉𐐩𐐻 𐐿𐐲𐑌𐐻𐐯𐑌𐑇𐐲𐑌 𐐮𐑌 𐑄 𐑊𐐰𐑌𐐼, 𐐮𐑌𐑅𐐬𐑋𐐲𐐽 𐑄𐐰𐐻 𐑄 𐑋𐐬𐑉 𐑉𐐴𐐽𐐲𐑅 𐐹𐐪𐑉𐐻 𐐱𐑂 𐑄 𐐹𐐨𐐹𐐲𐑊 𐐸𐐰𐐼 𐑌𐐨𐑉𐑊𐐨 𐐫𐑊 𐐺𐐨𐐿𐐲𐑋 𐐶𐐮𐐿𐐯𐐼; 𐐷𐐩, 𐑄𐐯𐑉 𐐶𐐲𐑉 𐐺𐐲𐐻 𐑁𐐷𐐭 𐑉𐐴𐐽𐐲𐑅 𐑋𐐯𐑌 𐐰𐑋𐐲𐑍 𐑄𐐯𐑋.

5. 𐐈𐑌𐐼 𐑄𐐲𐑅 𐑅𐐮𐐿𐑅 𐐷𐐨𐑉𐑆 𐐸𐐰𐐼 𐑌𐐱𐐻 𐐹𐐪𐑅𐐻 𐐰𐐶𐐩, 𐑅𐐮𐑌𐑅 𐑄 𐑋𐐬𐑉 𐐹𐐪𐑉𐐻 𐐱𐑂 𐑄 𐐹𐐨𐐹𐐲𐑊 𐐸𐐰𐐼 𐐻𐐲𐑉𐑌𐐼 𐑁𐑉𐐱𐑋 𐑄𐐯𐑉 𐑉𐐴𐐽𐐲𐑅𐑌𐐯𐑅, 𐑊𐐴𐐿 𐑄 𐐼𐐱𐑀 𐐻𐐭 𐐸𐐮𐑆 𐑂𐐱𐑋𐐮𐐻, 𐐫𐑉 𐑊𐐴𐐿 𐑄 𐑅𐐵 𐐻𐐭 𐐸𐐲𐑉 𐐶𐐱𐑊𐐬𐐮𐑍 𐐮𐑌 𐑄 𐑋𐐴𐑉. 𐐤𐐵 𐑄𐐮𐑅 𐑅𐐨𐐿𐑉𐐯𐐻 𐐿𐐱𐑋𐐺𐐮𐑌𐐩𐑇𐐲𐑌 𐐸𐐶𐐮𐐽 𐐸𐐰𐐼 𐐺𐑉𐐫𐐻 𐑅𐐬 𐑀𐑉𐐩𐐻 𐐮𐑌𐐮𐐿𐐶𐐮𐐻𐐨 𐐲𐐹𐐱𐑌 𐑄 𐐹𐐨𐐹𐐲𐑊, 𐐼𐐮𐐼 𐑀𐐰𐑄𐐲𐑉 𐑄𐐯𐑋𐑅𐐯𐑊𐑂𐑆 𐐻𐐭𐑀𐐯𐑄𐐲𐑉, 𐐰𐑌𐐼 𐐼𐐮𐐼 𐐹𐑊𐐩𐑅 𐐰𐐻 𐑄𐐯𐑉 𐐸𐐯𐐼 𐐩 𐑋𐐰𐑌 𐐸𐐭𐑋 𐑄𐐩 𐐼𐐮𐐼 𐐿𐐫𐑊 𐐖𐐩𐐿𐐲𐐺; 𐐰𐑌𐐼 𐑄𐐩 𐐼𐐮𐐼 𐐿𐐫𐑊 𐐸𐐮𐑋 𐑄𐐯𐑉 𐐿𐐮𐑍; 𐑄𐐯𐑉𐑁𐐬𐑉 𐐸𐐨 𐐺𐐨𐐿𐐩𐑋 𐐩 𐐿𐐮𐑍 𐐬𐑂𐐲𐑉 𐑄𐐮𐑅 𐐶𐐮𐐿𐐯𐐼 𐐺𐐰𐑌𐐼; 𐐰𐑌𐐼 𐐸𐐨 𐐶𐐱𐑆 𐐶𐐲𐑌 𐐱𐑂 𐑄 𐐽𐐨𐑁𐐯𐑅𐐻 𐐸𐐭 𐐸𐐰𐐼 𐑀𐐮𐑂𐐲𐑌 𐐸𐐮𐑆 𐑂𐑎𐑅 𐐰𐑀𐐯𐑌𐑅𐐻 𐑄 𐐹𐑉𐐱𐑁𐐯𐐻𐑅 𐐸𐐭 𐐻𐐯𐑅𐐻𐐮𐑁𐐴𐐼 𐐱𐑂 𐐖𐐨𐑆𐐲𐑅. 𐐈𐑌𐐼 𐐮𐐻 𐐿𐐩𐑋 𐐻𐐭 𐐹𐐪𐑅 𐑄𐐰𐐻 𐑄𐐩 𐐶𐐲𐑉 𐑌𐐱𐐻 𐑅𐐬 𐑅𐐻𐑉𐐱𐑍 𐐮𐑌 𐑌𐐲𐑋𐐺𐐲𐑉 𐐰𐑆 𐑄 𐐻𐑉𐐴𐐺𐑆 𐐱𐑂 𐑄 𐐹𐐨𐐹𐐲𐑊 𐐸𐐭 𐐶𐐲𐑉 𐐷𐐭𐑌𐐴𐐻𐐯𐐼 𐐻𐐲𐑀𐐯𐑄𐐲𐑉, 𐑅𐐩𐑂 𐐮𐐻 𐐶𐐲𐑉 𐑄𐐯𐑉 𐑊𐐨𐐼𐐲𐑉𐑆 𐐼𐐮𐐼 𐐯𐑅𐐻𐐰𐐺𐑊𐐮𐑇 𐑄𐐯𐑉 𐑊𐐫𐑆, 𐐯𐑂𐐲𐑉𐐨 𐐶𐐲𐑌 𐐰𐐿𐐫𐑉𐐼𐐮𐑍 𐐻𐐭 𐐸𐐮𐑆 𐐻𐑉𐐴𐐺; 𐑌𐐯𐑂𐐲𐑉𐑄𐐲𐑊𐐯𐑅 𐑄𐐩 𐐶𐐲𐑉 𐐯𐑌𐐯𐑋𐐨𐑆, 𐑌𐐱𐐻𐐶𐐮𐑄𐑅𐐻𐐰𐑌𐐼𐐮𐑍 𐑄𐐩 𐐶𐐲𐑉 𐑌𐐱𐐻 𐐩 𐑉𐐴𐐽𐐲𐑅 𐐹𐐨𐐹𐐲𐑊; 𐐷𐐯𐐻 𐑄𐐩 𐐶𐐲𐑉 𐐷𐐭𐑌𐐴𐐻𐐯𐐼 𐐮𐑌 𐑄 𐐸𐐩𐐻𐑉𐐯𐐼 𐐱𐑂 𐑄𐐬𐑆 𐐸𐐭 𐐸𐐰𐐼 𐐯𐑌𐐻𐐲𐑉𐐼 𐐮𐑌𐐻𐐭 𐐩 𐐿𐐲𐑂𐐯𐑌𐐲𐑌𐐻 𐐻𐐭 𐐼𐐨𐑅𐐻𐑉𐑎 𐑄 𐑀𐐲𐑂𐐲𐑉𐑌𐑋𐐯𐑌𐐻; 𐑄𐐯𐑉𐑁𐐬𐑉 𐐖𐐩𐐿𐐲𐐺 𐑅𐐨𐐮𐑍 𐑄𐐰𐐻 𐑄𐐯𐑉 𐐯𐑌𐐯𐑋𐐨𐑆 𐐶𐐲𐑉 𐑋𐐬𐑉 𐑌𐐷𐐭𐑋𐐲𐑉𐐲𐑅 𐑄𐐰𐑌 𐑄𐐩, 𐐸𐐨 𐐺𐐨𐐮𐑍 𐑄 𐐿𐐮𐑍 𐐱𐑂 𐑄 𐐺𐐰𐑌𐐼, 𐑄𐐯𐑉𐑁𐐬𐑉 𐐸𐐨 𐐿𐐲𐑋𐐰𐑌𐐼𐐯𐐼 𐐸𐐮𐑆 𐐹𐐨𐐹𐐲𐑊 𐑄𐐰𐐻 𐑄𐐩 𐑇𐐳𐐼 𐐻𐐩𐐿 𐑄𐐯𐑉 𐑁𐑊𐐴𐐻 𐐮𐑌𐐻𐐭 𐑄 𐑌𐐫𐑉𐑄𐐲𐑉𐑌𐑋𐐬𐑅𐐻 𐐹𐐪𐑉𐐻 𐐱𐑂 𐑄 𐑊𐐰𐑌𐐼, 𐐰𐑌𐐼 𐑄𐐯𐑉 𐐺𐐮𐑊𐐼 𐐲𐐹 𐐲𐑌𐐻𐐭 𐑄𐐯𐑋𐑅𐐯𐑊𐑂𐑆 𐐩 𐐿𐐮𐑍𐐼𐐲𐑋, 𐐲𐑌𐐻𐐮𐑊 𐑄𐐩 𐐶𐐲𐑉 𐐾𐑎𐑌𐐼 𐐺𐐴 𐐼𐐮𐑅𐐯𐑌𐐻𐐲𐑉𐑆, (𐑁𐐬𐑉 𐐸𐐨 𐑁𐑊𐐰𐐻𐐲𐑉𐐼 𐑄𐐯𐑋 𐑄𐐰𐐻 𐑄𐐯𐑉 𐐶𐐳𐐼 𐐺 𐑋𐐯𐑌𐐨 𐐼𐐮𐑅𐐯𐑌𐐻𐐲𐑉𐑆,) 𐐰𐑌𐐼 𐑄𐐩 𐐺𐐨𐐿𐐲𐑋 𐑅𐐲𐑁𐐮𐑇𐐲𐑌𐐻𐑊𐐨 𐑅𐐻𐑉𐐱𐑍 𐐻𐐭 𐐿𐐲𐑌𐐻𐐯𐑌𐐼 𐐶𐐮𐑄 𐑄 𐐻𐑉𐐴𐐺𐑆 𐐱𐑂 𐑄 𐐹𐐨𐐹𐐲𐑊, 𐐰𐑌𐐼 𐑄𐐩 𐐼𐐮𐐼 𐑅𐐬; 𐐰𐑌𐐼 𐑅𐐬 𐑅𐐹𐐨𐐼𐐨 𐐶𐐱𐑆 𐑄𐐯𐑉 𐑋𐐪𐑉𐐽, 𐑄𐐰𐐻 𐐮𐐻 𐐿𐐳𐐼 𐑌𐐱𐐻 𐐺 𐐮𐑋𐐹𐐨𐐼𐐯𐐼, 𐐲𐑌𐐻𐐮𐑊 𐑄𐐩 𐐸𐐰𐐼 𐑀𐐱𐑌 𐑁𐐬𐑉𐑃 𐐵𐐻 𐐱𐑂 𐑄 𐑉𐐨𐐽 𐐱𐑂 𐑄 𐐹𐐨𐐹𐐲𐑊. 𐐈𐑌𐐼 𐑄𐐲𐑅 𐐯𐑌𐐼𐐯𐐼 𐑄 𐑃𐐲𐑉𐐻𐐨𐐯𐑃 𐐷𐐨𐑉: 𐐰𐑌𐐼 𐑄𐐲𐑅 𐐶𐐲𐑉 𐑄 𐐰𐑁𐐩𐑉𐑆 𐐱𐑂 𐑄 𐐹𐐨𐐹𐐲𐑊 𐐱𐑂 𐐤𐐀𐑁𐐴.

6. 𐐈𐑌𐐼 𐐮𐐻 𐐿𐐩𐑋 𐐻𐐭 𐐹𐐪𐑅 𐐮𐑌 𐑄 𐑃𐐲𐑉𐐻𐐨 𐐰𐑌𐐼 𐑁𐐲𐑉𐑅𐐻 𐐷𐐨𐑉, 𐑄𐐰𐐻 𐑄𐐩 𐐶𐐲𐑉 𐐼𐐮𐑂𐐴𐐼𐐯𐐼 𐐮𐑌𐐻𐐭 𐐻𐑉𐐴𐐺𐑆, 𐐯𐑂𐐲𐑉𐐨 𐑋𐐰𐑌 𐐰𐐿𐐫𐑉𐐼𐐮𐑍 𐐻𐐭 𐐸𐐮𐑆 𐑁𐐰𐑋𐐮𐑊𐐨, 𐐿𐐮𐑌𐐼𐑉𐐯𐐼 𐐰𐑌𐐼 𐑁𐑉𐐯𐑌𐐼𐑆; 𐑌𐐯𐑂𐐲𐑉𐑄𐐲𐑊𐐯𐑅 𐑄𐐩 𐐸𐐰𐐼 𐐿𐐲𐑋 𐐻𐐭 𐐰𐑌 𐐰𐑀𐑉𐐨𐑋𐐯𐑌𐐻 𐑄𐐰𐐻 𐑄𐐩 𐐶𐐳𐐼 𐑌𐐱𐐻 𐑀𐐬 𐐻𐐭 𐐶𐐫𐑉 𐐶𐐲𐑌 𐐶𐐮𐑄 𐐰𐑌𐐲𐑄𐐲𐑉; 𐐺𐐲𐐻 𐑄𐐩 𐐶𐐲𐑉 𐑌𐐱𐐻 𐐷𐐭𐑌𐐴𐐻𐐯𐐼 𐐰𐑆 𐐻𐐭 𐑄𐐯𐑉 𐑊𐐫𐑆, 𐐰𐑌𐐼 𐑄𐐯𐑉 𐑋𐐰𐑌𐐲𐑉 𐐱𐑂 𐑀𐐲𐑂𐐲𐑉𐑌𐑋𐐯𐑌𐐻, 𐑁𐐬𐑉 𐑄𐐩 𐐶𐐲𐑉 𐐯𐑅𐐻𐐰𐐺𐑊𐐮𐑇𐐻 𐐰𐐿𐐫𐑉𐐼𐐮𐑍 𐐻𐐭 𐑄 𐑋𐐴𐑌𐐼𐑆 𐐱𐑂 𐑄𐐬𐑆 𐐸𐐭 𐐶𐐲𐑉 𐑄𐐯𐑉 𐐽𐐨𐑁𐑅 𐐰𐑌𐐼 𐑄𐐯𐑉 𐑊𐐨𐐼𐐲𐑉𐑆. 𐐒𐐲𐐻 𐑄𐐩 𐐼𐐮𐐼 𐐯𐑅𐐻𐐰𐐺𐑊𐐮𐑇 𐑂𐐯𐑉𐐨 𐑅𐐻𐑉𐐮𐐿𐐻 𐑊𐐫𐑆 𐑄𐐰𐐻 𐐶𐐲𐑌 𐐻𐑉𐐴𐐺 𐑇𐐳𐐼 𐑌𐐱𐐻 𐐻𐑉𐐯𐑅𐐹𐐰𐑅 𐐰𐑀𐐯𐑌𐑅𐐻 𐐰𐑌𐐲𐑄𐐲𐑉, 𐐮𐑌𐑅𐐬𐑋𐐲𐐽 𐑄𐐰𐐻 𐐮𐑌 𐑅𐐲𐑋 𐐼𐐨𐑀𐑉𐐨 𐑄𐐩 𐐸𐐰𐐼 𐐹𐐨𐑅 𐐮𐑌 𐑄 𐑊𐐰𐑌𐐼; 𐑌𐐯𐑂𐐲𐑉𐑄𐐲𐑊𐐯𐑅 𐑄𐐯𐑉 𐐸𐐪𐑉𐐻𐑅 𐐶𐐲𐑉 𐐻𐐲𐑉𐑌𐐼 𐑁𐑉𐐱𐑋 𐑄 𐐢𐐫𐑉𐐼 𐑄𐐯𐑉 𐐘𐐱𐐼, 𐐰𐑌𐐼 𐑄𐐩 𐐼𐐮𐐼 𐑅𐐻𐐬𐑌 𐑄 𐐹𐑉𐐱𐑁𐐯𐐻𐑅, 𐐰𐑌𐐼 𐐼𐐮𐐼 𐐿𐐰𐑅𐐻 𐑄𐐯𐑋 𐐵𐐻 𐑁𐑉𐐱𐑋 𐐰𐑋𐐲𐑍 𐑄𐐯𐑋.

7. 𐐈𐑌𐐼 𐐮𐐻 𐐿𐐩𐑋 𐐻𐐭 𐐹𐐪𐑅 𐑄𐐰𐐻 𐐤𐐀𐑁𐐴, 𐐸𐐰𐑂𐐮𐑍 𐐺𐐨𐑌 𐑂𐐮𐑆𐐮𐐻𐐯𐐼 𐐺𐐴 𐐩𐑌𐐾𐐯𐑊𐑆, 𐐰𐑌𐐼 𐐫𐑊𐑅𐐬 𐑄 𐑂𐑎𐑅 𐐱𐑂 𐑄 𐐢𐐫𐑉𐐼, 𐑄𐐯𐑉𐑁𐐬𐑉 𐐸𐐰𐑂𐐮𐑍 𐑅𐐨𐑌 𐐩𐑌𐐾𐐯𐑊𐑆, 𐐰𐑌𐐼 𐐺𐐨𐐮𐑍 𐐴 𐐶𐐮𐐻𐑌𐐯𐑅, 𐐰𐑌𐐼 𐐸𐐰𐑂𐐮𐑍 𐐸𐐰𐐼 𐐹𐐵𐑉 𐑀𐐮𐑂𐐲𐑌 𐐲𐑌𐐻𐐭 𐐸𐐮𐑋 𐑄𐐰𐐻 𐐸𐐨 𐑋𐐴𐐻 𐑌𐐬 𐐿𐐲𐑌𐑅𐐲𐑉𐑌𐐮𐑍 𐑄 𐑋𐐮𐑌𐐮𐑅𐐻𐑉𐐨 𐐱𐑂 𐐗𐑉𐐴𐑅𐐻, 𐐰𐑌𐐼 𐐫𐑊𐑅𐐬 𐐺𐐨𐐮𐑍 𐐴 𐐶𐐮𐐻𐑌𐐯𐑅 𐐻𐐭 𐑄𐐯𐑉 𐐿𐐶𐐮𐐿 𐑉𐐨𐐻𐐲𐑉𐑌 𐑁𐑉𐐱𐑋 𐑉𐐴𐐽𐐲𐑅𐑌𐐯𐑅 𐐲𐑌𐐻𐐭 𐑄𐐯𐑉 𐐶𐐮𐐿𐐯𐐼𐑌𐐯𐑅 𐐰𐑌𐐼 𐐰𐐺𐐱𐑋𐐮𐑌𐐩𐑇𐐲𐑌𐑆; 𐑄𐐯𐑉𐑁𐐬𐑉, 𐐺𐐨𐐮𐑍 𐑀𐑉𐐨𐑂𐐼 𐑁𐐬𐑉 𐑄 𐐸𐐪𐑉𐐼𐑌𐐯𐑅 𐐱𐑂 𐑄𐐯𐑉 𐐸𐐪𐑉𐐻𐑅, 𐐰𐑌𐐼 𐑄 𐐺𐑊𐐴𐑌𐐼𐑌𐐯𐑅 𐐱𐑂 𐑄𐐯𐑉 𐑋𐐴𐑌𐐼𐑆, 𐐶𐐯𐑌𐐻 𐑁𐐬𐑉𐑃 𐐰𐑋𐐲𐑍 𐑄𐐯𐑋 𐐮𐑌 𐑄𐐰𐐻 𐑅𐐩𐑋 𐐷𐐨𐑉, 𐐰𐑌𐐼 𐐺𐐨𐑀𐐰𐑌 𐐻𐐭 𐐻𐐯𐑅𐐻𐐮𐑁𐐴

𐐺𐐬𐑊𐐼𐑊𐐨, 𐑉𐐨𐐹𐐯𐑌𐐻𐐰𐑌𐑅 𐐰𐑌𐐼 𐑉𐐨𐑋𐐮𐑇𐐲𐑌 𐐱𐑂 𐑅𐐮𐑌𐑆 𐑃𐑉𐐭 𐑁𐐩𐑃 𐐱𐑌 𐑄 𐐢𐐫𐑉𐐼 𐐖𐐨𐑆𐐲𐑅 𐐗𐑉𐐴𐑅𐐻. 𐐈𐑌𐐼 𐐸𐐨 𐐼𐐮𐐼 𐑋𐐮𐑌𐐮𐑅𐐻𐐲𐑉 𐑋𐐯𐑌𐐨 𐑃𐐮𐑍𐑆 𐐲𐑌𐐻𐐭 𐑄𐐯𐑋; 𐐰𐑌𐐼 𐐫𐑊 𐐱𐑂 𐑄𐐯𐑋 𐐿𐐰𐑌𐐱𐐻 𐐺 𐑉𐐮𐐻𐑌, 𐐰𐑌𐐼 𐐲 𐐹𐐪𐑉𐐻 𐐱𐑂 𐑄𐐯𐑋 𐐶𐐳𐐼 𐑌𐐱𐐻 𐑅𐐲𐑁𐐴𐑅; 𐑄𐐯𐑉𐑁𐐫𐑉 𐑄𐐩 𐐪𐑉 𐑌𐐱𐐻 𐑉𐐮𐐻𐑌 𐐮𐑌 𐑄𐐮𐑅 𐐺𐐳𐐿. 𐐈𐑌𐐼 𐐤𐐨𐑁𐐴 𐐼𐐮𐐼 𐑋𐐮𐑌𐐮𐑅𐐻𐐲𐑉 𐐶𐐮𐑄 𐐹𐐵𐑉 𐐰𐑌𐐼 𐐶𐐮𐑄 𐑀𐑉𐐩𐐻 𐐫𐑃𐐱𐑉𐐮𐐻𐐨.

8. 𐐈𐑌𐐼 𐐮𐐻 𐐿𐐩𐑋 𐐻𐐭 𐐹𐐰𐑅 𐑄𐐰𐐻 𐑄𐐩 𐐶𐐲𐑉 𐐰𐑍𐑀𐑉𐐨 𐐶𐐮𐑄 𐐸𐐮𐑋, 𐐨𐑂𐑌 𐐺𐐨𐐿𐐫𐑆 𐐸𐐨 𐐸𐐰𐐼 𐑀𐑉𐐩𐐻𐐲𐑉 𐐹𐐵𐑉 𐑄𐐰𐑌 𐑄𐐩, 𐑁𐐫𐑉 𐐮𐐻 𐐶𐐲𐑉 𐑌𐐱𐐻 𐐹𐐱𐑅𐐮𐐺𐑊 𐑄𐐰𐐻 𐑄𐐩 𐐿𐐳𐐼 𐐼𐐮𐑅𐐺𐐨𐑊𐐨𐑂 𐐸𐐮𐑆 𐐶𐐲𐑉𐐼𐑆, 𐑁𐐫𐑉 𐑅𐐬 𐑀𐑉𐐩𐐻 𐐶𐐱𐑆 𐐸𐐮𐑆 𐑁𐐩𐑃 𐐱𐑌 𐑄 𐐢𐐫𐑉𐐼 𐐖𐐨𐑆𐐲𐑅 𐐗𐑉𐐴𐑅𐐻, 𐑄𐐰𐐻 𐐩𐑌𐐾𐐯𐑊𐑆 𐐼𐐮𐐼 𐑋𐐮𐑌𐐮𐑅𐐻𐐲𐑉 𐐲𐑌𐐻𐐭 𐐸𐐮𐑋 𐐼𐐩𐑊𐐨: 𐐰𐑌𐐼 𐐮𐑌 𐑄 𐑌𐐩𐑋 𐐱𐑂 𐐖𐐨𐑆𐐲𐑅 𐐼𐐮𐐼 𐐸𐐨 𐐿𐐰𐑅𐐻 𐐵𐐻 𐐼𐐯𐑂𐑊𐑆 𐐰𐑌𐐼 𐐲𐑌𐐿𐑊𐐨𐑌 𐑅𐐹𐐮𐑉𐐮𐐻𐑅; 𐐰𐑌𐐼 𐐨𐑂𐑌 𐐸𐐮𐑆 𐐺𐑉𐐲𐑄𐐲𐑉 𐐼𐐮𐐼 𐐸𐐨 𐑉𐐩𐑆 𐑁𐑉𐐱𐑋 𐑄 𐐼𐐯𐐼, 𐐰𐑁𐐻𐐲𐑉 𐐸𐐨 𐐸𐐰𐐼 𐐺𐐮𐑌 𐑅𐐻𐐬𐑌𐐼 𐐰𐑌𐐼 𐑅𐐲𐑁𐐲𐑉𐐼 𐐼𐐯𐑃 𐐺𐐴 𐑄 𐐹𐐨𐐹𐑊; 𐐰𐑌𐐼 𐑄 𐐹𐐨𐐹𐑊 𐑅𐐫 𐐮𐐻, 𐐰𐑌𐐼 𐐼𐐮𐐼 𐐶𐐮𐐻𐑌𐐯𐑅 𐐱𐑂 𐐮𐐻, 𐐰𐑌𐐼 𐐶𐐲𐑉 𐐰𐑍𐑀𐑉𐐨 𐐶𐐮𐑄 𐐸𐐮𐑋, 𐐺𐐨𐐿𐐫𐑆 𐐱𐑂 𐐸𐐮𐑆 𐐹𐐵𐑉; 𐐰𐑌𐐼 𐐸𐐨 𐐼𐐮𐐼 𐐫𐑊𐑅𐐬 𐐼𐐭 𐑋𐐯𐑌𐐨 𐑋𐐬𐑉 𐑋𐐮𐑉𐐲𐐿𐑊𐑆, 𐐮𐑌 𐑄 𐑅𐐴𐐻 𐐱𐑂 𐑄 𐐹𐐨𐐹𐑊, 𐐮𐑌 𐑄 𐑌𐐩𐑋 𐐱𐑂 𐐖𐐨𐑆𐐲𐑅.

9. 𐐈𐑌𐐼 𐐮𐐻 𐐿𐐩𐑋 𐐻𐐭 𐐹𐐰𐑅 𐑄𐐰𐐻 𐑄 𐑃𐐲𐑉𐐻𐐨 𐐰𐑌𐐼 𐑁𐐲𐑉𐑅𐐻 𐐷𐐨𐑉 𐐼𐐮𐐼 𐐹𐐰𐑅 𐐲𐐶𐐩, 𐐰𐑌𐐼 𐑄𐐯𐑉 𐐶𐐲𐑉 𐐺𐐲𐐻 𐑁𐑏 𐐸𐐭 𐐶𐐲𐑉 𐐿𐐱𐑌𐑂𐐲𐑉𐐻𐐯𐐼 𐐲𐑌𐐻𐐭 𐑄 𐐢𐐫𐑉𐐼; 𐐺𐐲𐐻 𐐰𐑆 𐑋𐐯𐑌𐐨 𐐰𐑆 𐐶𐐲𐑉 𐐿𐐱𐑌𐑂𐐲𐑉𐐻𐐯𐐼 𐐼𐐮𐐼 𐐻𐑉𐐭𐑊𐐨 𐑅𐐮𐑀𐑌𐐮𐑁𐐴 𐐲𐑌𐐻𐐭 𐑄 𐐹𐐨𐐹𐑊 𐑄𐐰𐐻 𐑄𐐩 𐐸𐐰𐐼 𐐺𐐮𐑌 𐑂𐐮𐑆𐐮𐐻𐐯𐐼 𐐺𐐴 𐑄 𐐹𐐵𐑉 𐐰𐑌𐐼 𐐝𐐹𐐮𐑉𐐮𐐻 𐐱𐑂 𐐘𐐱𐐼, 𐐸𐐶𐐮𐐽 𐐶𐐱𐑆 𐐮𐑌 𐐖𐐨𐑆𐐲𐑅 𐐗𐑉𐐴𐑅𐐻, 𐐮𐑌 𐐸𐐭𐑋 𐑄𐐩 𐐺𐐨𐑊𐐨𐑂𐐼. 𐐈𐑌𐐼 𐐰𐑆 𐑋𐐯𐑌𐐨 𐐰𐑆 𐐸𐐰𐐼 𐐼𐐯𐑂𐑊𐑆 𐐿𐐰𐑅𐐻 𐐵𐐻 𐑁𐑉𐐱𐑋 𐑄𐐯𐑋, 𐐰𐑌𐐼 𐐶𐐲𐑉 𐐸𐐨𐑊𐐼 𐐱𐑂 𐑄𐐯𐑉 𐑅𐐮𐐿𐑌𐐯𐑅𐐯𐑆 𐐰𐑌𐐼 𐑄𐐯𐑉 𐐮𐑌𐑁𐐲𐑉𐑋𐐮𐐻𐐨𐑆, 𐐼𐐮𐐼 𐐻𐑉𐐭𐑊𐐨 𐑋𐐰𐑌𐐮𐑁𐐯𐑅𐐻 𐐲𐑌𐐻𐐭 𐑄 𐐹𐐨𐐹𐑊 𐑄𐐰𐐻 𐑄𐐩 𐐸𐐰𐐼 𐐺𐐮𐑌 𐑉𐐫𐐻 𐐲𐐹𐐱𐑌 𐐺𐐴 𐑄 𐐝𐐹𐐮𐑉𐐮𐐻 𐐱𐑂 𐐘𐐱𐐼, 𐐰𐑌𐐼 𐐸𐐰𐐼 𐐺𐐮𐑌 𐐸𐐨𐑊𐐼; 𐐰𐑌𐐼 𐑄𐐩 𐐼𐐮𐐼 𐑇𐐬 𐑁𐐬𐑉𐑃 𐑅𐐴𐑌𐑆 𐐫𐑊𐑅𐐬, 𐐰𐑌𐐼 𐐼𐐮𐐼 𐐼𐐭 𐑅𐐲𐑋 𐑋𐐮𐑉𐐲𐐿𐑊𐑆 𐐲𐑋𐐲𐑍 𐑄 𐐹𐐨𐐹𐑊.

10. 𐐜𐐲𐑅 𐐹𐐰𐑅𐐻 𐐲𐐶𐐩 𐑄 𐑃𐐲𐑉𐐻𐐨 𐐰𐑌𐐼 𐑅𐐯𐐿𐐲𐑌𐐼 𐐷𐐨𐑉 𐐫𐑊𐑅𐐬. 𐐈𐑌𐐼 𐐤𐐨𐑁𐐴 𐐼𐐮𐐼 𐐿𐑉𐐴 𐐲𐑌𐐻𐐭 𐑄 𐐹𐐨𐐹𐑊 𐐮𐑌 𐑄 𐐿𐐱𐑋𐐯𐑌𐑅𐑋𐐯𐑌𐐻 𐐱𐑂 𐑄 𐑃𐐲𐑉𐐻𐐨 𐐰𐑌𐐼 𐑃𐐲𐑉𐐼 𐐷𐐨𐑉; 𐐰𐑌𐐼 𐐸𐐨 𐐼𐐮𐐼 𐐹𐑉𐐨𐐽 𐐲𐑌𐐻𐐭 𐑄𐐯𐑋 𐑉𐐨𐐹𐐯𐑌𐐻𐐰𐑌𐑅 𐐰𐑌𐐼 𐑉𐐨𐑋𐐮𐑇𐐲𐑌 𐐱𐑂 𐑅𐐮𐑌𐑆. 𐐤𐐵 𐐌 𐐶𐐳𐐼 𐐸𐐰𐑂 𐐷𐐭 𐐻𐐭 𐑉𐐨𐑋𐐯𐑋𐐺𐐲𐑉 𐐫𐑊𐑅𐐬, 𐑄𐐰𐐻 𐑄𐐯𐑉 𐐶𐐲𐑉 𐑌𐐲𐑌 𐐸𐐭 𐐶𐐲𐑉 𐐺𐑉𐐫𐐻 𐐲𐑌𐐻𐐭 𐑉𐐨𐐹𐐯𐑌𐐻𐐰𐑌𐑅, 𐐸𐐭 𐐶𐐲𐑉 𐑌𐐱𐐻 𐐺𐐰𐐹𐐻𐐴𐑆𐐼 𐐶𐐮𐑄 𐐶𐐫𐐻𐐲𐑉; 𐑄𐐯𐑉𐑁𐐫𐑉 𐑄𐐯𐑉 𐐶𐐲𐑉 𐐫𐑉𐐼𐐩𐑌𐐼 𐐱𐑂 𐐤𐐨𐑁𐐴, 𐑋𐐯𐑌 𐐲𐑌𐐻𐐭 𐑄𐐮𐑅 𐑋𐐮𐑌𐐮𐑅𐐻𐑉𐐨, 𐑄𐐰𐐻 𐐫𐑊 𐑅𐐲𐐽 𐐰𐑆 𐑇𐐳𐐼 𐐿𐐲𐑋 𐐲𐑌𐐻𐐭 𐑄𐐯𐑋, 𐑇𐐳𐐼 𐐺 𐐺𐐰𐐹𐐻𐐴𐑆𐐼 𐐶𐐮𐑄 𐐶𐐫𐐻𐐲𐑉, 𐐰𐑌𐐼 𐑄𐐮𐑅 𐐰𐑆 𐐲 𐐶𐐮𐐻𐑌𐐯𐑅 𐐰𐑌𐐼 𐐲 𐐻𐐯𐑅𐐻𐐮𐑋𐐬𐑌𐐨 𐐺𐐨𐑁𐐬𐑉 𐐘𐐱𐐼, 𐐰𐑌𐐼 𐐲𐑌𐐻𐐭 𐑄 𐐹𐐨𐐹𐑊, 𐑄𐐰𐐻 𐑄𐐩 𐐸𐐰𐐼 𐑉𐐨𐐹𐐯𐑌𐐻𐐯𐐼 𐐰𐑌𐐼 𐑉𐐨𐑅𐐨𐑂𐐼 𐐲 𐑉𐐨𐑋𐐮𐑇𐐲𐑌 𐐱𐑂 𐑄𐐯𐑉 𐑅𐐮𐑌𐑆. 𐐈𐑌𐐼 𐑄𐐯𐑉 𐐶𐐲𐑉 𐑋𐐯𐑌𐐨 𐐮𐑌 𐑄 𐐿𐐱𐑋𐐯𐑌𐑅𐑋𐐯𐑌𐐻 𐐱𐑂 𐑄𐐮𐑅 𐐷𐐨𐑉, 𐑄𐐰𐐻 𐐶𐐲𐑉 𐐺𐐰𐐹𐐻𐐴𐑆𐐼 𐐲𐑌𐐻𐐭 𐑉𐐨𐐹𐐯𐑌𐐻𐐰𐑌𐑅; 𐐰𐑌𐐼 𐑄𐐲𐑅 𐑄 𐑋𐐬𐑉 𐐹𐐪𐑉𐐻 𐐱𐑂 𐑄 𐐷𐐨𐑉 𐐼𐐮𐐼 𐐹𐐰𐑅 𐐲𐐶𐐩.

𐐕𐐰𐐹𐐻𐐲𐑉 IV.

1. 𐐈𐑌𐐼 𐑌𐐵 𐐮𐐻 𐐿𐐩𐑋 𐐻𐐭 𐐹𐐰𐑅 𐑄𐐰𐐻 𐐰𐐿𐐫𐑉𐐼𐐮𐑍 𐐻𐐭 𐐵𐑉 𐑉𐐯𐐿𐐫𐑉𐐼, 𐐰𐑌𐐼 𐐶𐐨 𐑌𐐬 𐐵𐑉 𐑉𐐯𐐿𐐫𐑉𐐼 𐐻𐐭 𐐺 𐐻𐑉𐐭, 𐑁𐐫𐑉 𐐺𐐨𐐸𐐬𐑊𐐼, 𐐮𐐻 𐐶𐐱𐑆 𐐲 𐐾𐐲𐑅𐐻 𐑋𐐰𐑌 𐐸𐐭 𐐼𐐮𐐼 𐐿𐐨𐐹 𐑄 𐑉𐐯𐐿𐐫𐑉𐐼; 𐑁𐐫𐑉 𐐸𐐨 𐐻𐑉𐐭𐑊𐐨 𐐼𐐮𐐼 𐑋𐐯𐑌𐐨 𐑋𐐮𐑉𐐲𐐿𐑊𐑆 𐐮𐑌 𐑄 𐑌𐐩𐑋 𐐱𐑂 𐐖𐐨𐑆𐐲𐑅; 𐐰𐑌𐐼 𐑄𐐯𐑉 𐐶𐐱𐑆 𐑌𐐱𐐻 𐐯𐑌𐐨 𐑋𐐰𐑌 𐐸𐐭 𐐿𐐳𐐼 𐐼𐐭 𐐲 𐑋𐐮𐑉𐐲𐐿𐑊 𐐮𐑌 𐑄 𐑌𐐩𐑋 𐐱𐑂 𐐖𐐨𐑆𐐲𐑅, 𐑅𐐩𐑂 𐐸𐐨 𐐶𐐲𐑉 𐐿𐑊𐐯𐑌𐑆𐐼 𐐯𐑂𐐲𐑉𐐨 𐐸𐐶𐐮𐐻 𐑁𐑉𐐱𐑋 𐐸𐐮𐑆 𐐮𐑌𐐮𐐿𐐶𐐮𐐻𐐨. 𐐈𐑌𐐼 𐑌𐐵 𐐮𐐻 𐐿𐐩𐑋 𐐻𐐭 𐐹𐐰𐑅, 𐐮𐑁 𐑄𐐯𐑉 𐐶𐐱𐑆 𐑌𐐬 𐑋𐐮𐑅𐐻𐐩𐐿 𐑋𐐩𐐼 𐐺𐐴 𐑄𐐮𐑅 𐑋𐐰𐑌 𐐮𐑌 𐑄 𐑉𐐯𐐿𐐲𐑌𐐮𐑍 𐐱𐑂 𐐵𐑉 𐐻𐐴𐑋, 𐑄 𐑃𐐲𐑉𐐻𐐨 𐐰𐑌𐐼 𐑃𐐲𐑉𐐼 𐐷𐐨𐑉 𐐸𐐰𐐼 𐐹𐐰𐑅𐐻 𐐲𐐶𐐩, 𐐰𐑌𐐼 𐑄 𐐹𐐨𐐹𐑊 𐐺𐐨𐑀𐐰𐑌 𐐻𐐭 𐑊𐐳𐐿 𐐶𐐮𐑄 𐑀𐑉𐐩𐐻 𐐲𐑉𐑌𐐯𐑅𐐻𐑌𐐯𐑅 𐑁𐐫𐑉 𐑄 𐑅𐐴𐑌 𐐸𐐶𐐮𐐽 𐐸𐐰𐐼 𐐺𐐮𐑌 𐑀𐐮𐑂𐑌 𐐺𐐴 𐑄 𐐹𐑉𐐱𐑁𐐯𐐻 𐐝𐐰𐑋𐐷𐐭𐐯𐑊, 𐑄 𐐢𐐰𐑋𐐲𐑌𐐴𐐻; 𐐷𐐩, 𐑁𐐫𐑉 𐑄 𐐻𐐴𐑋 𐑄𐐰𐐻 𐑄𐐯𐑉 𐑇𐐳𐐼 𐐺 𐐼𐐪𐑉𐐿𐑌𐐯𐑅 𐑁𐐫𐑉 𐑄 𐑅𐐹𐐩𐑅 𐐱𐑂 𐑃𐑉𐐨 𐐼𐐩𐑆 𐐬𐑂𐐲𐑉 𐑄 𐑁𐐩𐑅

𐐱𐑂 𐑄 𐑊𐐰𐑌𐐼. 𐐈𐑌𐐼 𐑄𐐩𐑉 𐐺𐐨𐑀𐐰𐑌 𐐻𐐭 𐐺𐐨 𐑀𐑉𐐩𐐻 𐐼𐐵𐐻𐐮𐑍𐑆 𐐰𐑌𐐼 𐐼𐐮𐑅𐐹𐐷𐐭𐐻𐐩𐑇𐐲𐑌𐑆 𐐲𐑋𐐲𐑍 𐑄 𐐹𐐨𐐹𐑊, 𐑌𐐱𐐻𐐶𐐮𐑄𐑅𐐻𐐰𐑌𐐼𐐮𐑍 𐑅𐐬 𐑋𐐯𐑌𐐨 𐑅𐐴𐑌𐑆 𐐸𐐰𐐼 𐐺𐐮𐑌 𐑀𐐮𐑂𐑌.

2. 𐐈𐑌𐐼 𐐮𐐻 𐐿𐐩𐑋 𐐻𐐭 𐐹𐐰𐑅 𐐮𐑌 𐑄 𐑃𐐲𐑉𐐻𐐨 𐐰𐑌𐐼 𐑁𐐬𐑉𐑃 𐐷𐐨𐑉, 𐐮𐑌 𐑄 𐑁𐐲𐑉𐑅𐐻 𐑋𐐲𐑌𐑃, 𐐮𐑌 𐑄 𐑁𐐬𐑉𐑃 𐐼𐐩 𐐱𐑂 𐑄 𐑋𐐲𐑌𐑃, 𐑄𐐩𐑉 𐐲𐑉𐐬𐑆 𐐩 𐑀𐑉𐐩𐐻 𐑅𐐻𐐫𐑉𐑋, 𐑅𐐲𐐽 𐐰𐑌 𐐶𐐲𐑌 𐐰𐑆 𐑌𐐯𐑂𐐲𐑉 𐐸𐐰𐐼 𐐺𐐮𐑌 𐑌𐐬𐑌 𐐮𐑌 𐐫𐑊 𐑄 𐑊𐐰𐑌𐐼; 𐐰𐑌𐐼 𐑄𐐩𐑉 𐐶𐐲𐑆 𐐫𐑊𐑅𐐬 𐐩 𐑀𐑉𐐩𐐻 𐐰𐑌𐐼 𐐻𐐯𐑉𐐮𐐺𐑊 𐐻𐐯𐑋𐐹𐐯𐑅𐐻; 𐐰𐑌𐐼 𐑄𐐩𐑉 𐐶𐐲𐑆 𐐻𐐯𐑉𐐮𐐺𐑊 𐑃𐐲𐑌𐐼𐐲𐑉, 𐐮𐑌𐑅𐐬𐑋𐐲𐐽 𐑄𐐰𐐻 𐐮𐐻 𐐼𐐮𐐼 𐑇𐐩𐐿 𐑄 𐐸𐐬𐑊 𐐲𐑉𐑃 𐐰𐑆 𐐮𐑁 𐐮𐐻 𐐶𐐲𐑆 𐐲𐐺𐐵𐐻 𐐻𐐭 𐐼𐐮𐑂𐐴𐐼 𐐲𐑅𐐲𐑌𐐼𐐲𐑉; 𐐰𐑌𐐼 𐑄𐐩𐑉 𐐶𐐲𐑉 𐐯𐐿𐑅𐐨𐐼𐐮𐑍𐑊𐐨 𐑇𐐪𐑉𐐹 𐑊𐐴𐐻𐑌𐐮𐑍𐑆, 𐑅𐐲𐐽 𐐰𐑆 𐑌𐐯𐑂𐐲𐑉 𐐸𐐰𐐼 𐐺𐐮𐑌 𐑌𐐬𐑌 𐐮𐑌 𐐫𐑊 𐑄 𐑊𐐰𐑌𐐼. 𐐈𐑌𐐼 𐑄 𐑅𐐮𐐻𐐨 𐐱𐑂 𐐞𐐯𐑉𐐲𐐸𐐯𐑋𐑊𐐲 𐐼𐐮𐐼 𐐻𐐩𐐿 𐑁𐐴𐑉; 𐐰𐑌𐐼 𐑄 𐑅𐐮𐐻𐐨 𐐱𐑂 𐐣𐐫𐑉𐐬𐑌𐐴 𐐼𐐮𐐼 𐑅𐐮𐑍𐐿 𐐮𐑌𐐻𐐭 𐑄 𐐼𐐯𐐹𐑃𐑅 𐐱𐑂 𐑄 𐑅𐐨, 𐐰𐑌𐐼 𐑄 𐐮𐑌𐐸𐐰𐐺𐐮𐐻𐐲𐑌𐐻𐑅 𐑄𐐩𐑉𐐲𐑂 𐐶𐐲𐑉 𐐼𐑉𐐵𐑌𐐼; 𐐰𐑌𐐼 𐑄 𐐲𐑉𐑃 𐐶𐐲𐑆 𐐿𐐰𐑉𐐨𐐼 𐐲𐐹 𐐲𐐹𐐱𐑌 𐑄 𐑅𐐮𐐻𐐨 𐐱𐑂 𐐣𐐫𐑉𐐬𐑌𐐴𐐸𐐪, 𐑄𐐰𐐻 𐐮𐑌 𐑄 𐐹𐑊𐐩𐑅 𐐱𐑂 𐑄 𐑅𐐮𐐻𐐨 𐑄𐐩𐑉𐐲𐑂, 𐑄𐐩𐑉 𐐺𐐨𐐿𐐩𐑋 𐐩 𐑀𐑉𐐩𐐻 𐑋𐐵𐑌𐐻𐐲𐑌; 𐐰𐑌𐐼 𐑄𐐩𐑉 𐐶𐐲𐑆 𐐩 𐑀𐑉𐐩𐐻 𐐰𐑌𐐼 𐐻𐐯𐑉𐐮𐐺𐑊 𐐼𐐯𐑅𐐻𐑉𐐲𐐿𐑇𐐲𐑌 𐐮𐑌 𐑄 𐑊𐐰𐑌𐐼 𐑅𐐵𐑃𐐶𐐲𐑉𐐼. 𐐒𐐲𐐻 𐐺𐐨𐐸𐐬𐑊𐐼, 𐑄𐐩𐑉 𐐶𐐲𐑆 𐐩 𐑋𐐬𐑉 𐑀𐑉𐐩𐐻 𐐰𐑌𐐼 𐐻𐐯𐑉𐐮𐐺𐑊 𐐼𐐯𐑅𐐻𐑉𐐲𐐿𐑇𐐲𐑌 𐐮𐑌 𐑄 𐑊𐐰𐑌𐐼 𐑌𐐫𐑉𐑃𐐶𐐲𐑉𐐼: 𐑁𐐫𐑉 𐐺𐐨𐐸𐐬𐑊𐐼, 𐑄 𐐸𐐬𐑊 𐑁𐐩𐑅 𐐱𐑂 𐑄 𐑊𐐰𐑌𐐼 𐐶𐐲𐑆 𐐽𐐩𐑌𐐾𐐼, 𐐺𐐨𐐿𐐫𐑆 𐐱𐑂 𐑄 𐐻𐐯𐑋𐐹𐐯𐑅𐐻, 𐐰𐑌𐐼 𐑄 𐐸𐐶𐐲𐑉𐑊𐐶𐐮𐑌𐐼𐑆, 𐐰𐑌𐐼 𐑄 𐑃𐐲𐑌𐐼𐐲𐑉𐐮𐑍𐑆, 𐐰𐑌𐐼 𐑄 𐑊𐐴𐐻𐑌𐐮𐑍𐑆, 𐐰𐑌𐐼 𐑄 𐐯𐐿𐑅𐐨𐐼𐐮𐑍𐑊𐐨 𐑀𐑉𐐩𐐻 𐐿𐐶𐐩𐐿𐐮𐑍 𐐱𐑂 𐑄 𐐸𐐬𐑊 𐐲𐑉𐑃; 𐐰𐑌𐐼 𐑄 𐐸𐐴𐐶𐐩𐑆 𐐶𐐲𐑉 𐐺𐑉𐐬𐐿𐐲𐑌 𐐲𐐹, 𐐰𐑌𐐼 𐑄 𐑊𐐯𐑂𐐲𐑊 𐑉𐐬𐐼𐑆 𐐶𐐲𐑉 𐑅𐐹𐐦𐑊𐐼, 𐐰𐑌𐐼 𐑋𐐯𐑌𐐨 𐑅𐑋𐐭𐑄 𐐹𐑊𐐩𐑅𐐲𐑆 𐐺𐐨𐐿𐐩𐑋 𐑉𐐲𐑁, 𐐰𐑌𐐼 𐑋𐐯𐑌𐐨 𐑀𐑉𐐩𐐻 𐐰𐑌𐐼 𐑌𐐬𐐻𐐲𐐺𐑊 𐑅𐐮𐐻𐐨𐑆 𐐶𐐲𐑉 𐑅𐐲𐑍𐐿, 𐐰𐑌𐐼 𐑋𐐯𐑌𐐨 𐐶𐐲𐑉 𐐺𐐲𐑉𐑌𐐼, 𐐰𐑌𐐼 𐑋𐐯𐑌𐐨 𐐶𐐲𐑉 𐑇𐐩𐐿𐑌 𐐻𐐮𐑊 𐑄 𐐺𐐮𐑊𐐼𐐮𐑍𐑆 𐑄𐐩𐑉𐐲𐑂 𐐸𐐰𐐼 𐑁𐐫𐑊𐑌 𐐻𐐭 𐑄 𐐲𐑉𐑃, 𐐰𐑌𐐼 𐑄 𐐮𐑌𐐸𐐰𐐺𐐮𐐻𐐲𐑌𐐻𐑅 𐑄𐐩𐑉𐐲𐑂 𐐶𐐲𐑉 𐑅𐑊𐐩𐑌, 𐐰𐑌𐐼 𐑄 𐐹𐑊𐐩𐑅𐐲𐑆 𐐶𐐲𐑉 𐑊𐐯𐑁𐐻 𐐼𐐯𐑅𐐬𐑊𐐩𐐻; 𐐰𐑌𐐼 𐑄𐐩𐑉 𐐶𐐲𐑉 𐑅𐐲𐑋 𐑅𐐮𐐻𐐨𐑆 𐐸𐐶𐐮𐐽 𐑉𐐨𐑋𐐩𐑌𐐼; 𐐺𐐲𐐻 𐑄 𐐼𐐰𐑋𐐲𐐾 𐑄𐐩𐑉𐐲𐑂 𐐶𐐲𐑆 𐐯𐐿𐑅𐐨𐐼𐐮𐑍𐑊𐐨 𐑀𐑉𐐩𐐻, 𐐰𐑌𐐼 𐑄𐐩𐑉 𐐶𐐲𐑉 𐑋𐐯𐑌𐐨 𐐮𐑌 𐑄𐐯𐑋 𐐸𐐭 𐐶𐐲𐑉 𐑅𐑊𐐩𐑌; 𐐰𐑌𐐼 𐑄𐐩𐑉 𐐶𐐲𐑉 𐑅𐐲𐑋 𐐸𐐭 𐐶𐐲𐑉 𐐿𐐰𐑉𐐨𐐼 𐐲𐐶𐐩 𐐮𐑌 𐑄 𐐸𐐶𐐲𐑉𐑊𐐶𐐮𐑌𐐼; 𐐰𐑌𐐼 𐐸𐐶𐐮𐑄𐐲𐑉 𐑄𐐩 𐐶𐐯𐑌𐐻, 𐑌𐐬 𐑋𐐰𐑌 𐑌𐐬𐐯𐑃, 𐑅𐐩𐑂 𐑄𐐩 𐑌𐐬 𐑄𐐰𐐻 𐑄𐐩 𐐶𐐲𐑉 𐐿𐐰𐑉𐐨𐐼 𐐲𐐶𐐩; 𐐰𐑌𐐼 𐑄𐐲𐑅 𐑄 𐑁𐐩𐑅 𐐱𐑂 𐑄 𐐸𐐬𐑊 𐐲𐑉𐑃 𐐺𐐨𐐿𐐩𐑋 𐐼𐐨𐑁𐐫𐑉𐑋𐐼, 𐐺𐐨𐐿𐐫𐑆 𐐱𐑂 𐑄 𐐻𐐯𐑋𐐹𐐯𐑅𐐻𐑅, 𐐰𐑌𐐼 𐑄 𐑃𐐲𐑌𐐼𐐲𐑉𐐮𐑍𐑆, 𐐰𐑌𐐼 𐑄 𐑊𐐴𐐻𐑌𐐮𐑍𐑆, 𐐰𐑌𐐼 𐑄 𐐿𐐶𐐩𐐿𐐮𐑍 𐐱𐑂 𐑄 𐐲𐑉𐑃. 𐐈𐑌𐐼 𐐺𐐨𐐸𐐬𐑊𐐼, 𐑄 𐑉𐐱𐐿𐑅 𐐶𐐲𐑉 𐑉𐐯𐑌𐐻 𐐮𐑌 𐐻𐐶𐐩𐑌; 𐑄𐐩 𐐶𐐲𐑉 𐐺𐑉𐐬𐐿𐐲𐑌 𐐲𐐹 𐐲𐐹𐐱𐑌 𐑄 𐑁𐐩𐑅 𐐱𐑂 𐑄 𐐸𐐬𐑊 𐐲𐑉𐑃, 𐐮𐑌𐑅𐐬𐑋𐐲𐐽 𐑄𐐰𐐻 𐑄𐐩 𐐶𐐲𐑉 𐑁𐐵𐑌𐐼 𐐮𐑌 𐐺𐑉𐐬𐐿𐐲𐑌 𐑁𐑉𐐰𐑀𐑋𐐲𐑌𐐻𐑅, 𐐰𐑌𐐼 𐐮𐑌 𐑅𐐨𐑋𐑆, 𐐰𐑌𐐼 𐐮𐑌 𐐿𐑉𐐰𐐿𐑅, 𐐲𐐹𐐱𐑌 𐐫𐑊 𐑄 𐑁𐐩𐑅 𐐱𐑂 𐑄 𐑊𐐰𐑌𐐼.

3. 𐐈𐑌𐐼 𐐮𐐻 𐐿𐐩𐑋 𐐻𐐭 𐐹𐐰𐑅 𐑄𐐰𐐻 𐐸𐐶𐐯𐑌 𐑄 𐑃𐐲𐑌𐐼𐐲𐑉𐐮𐑍𐑆, 𐐰𐑌𐐼 𐑄 𐑊𐐴𐐻𐑌𐐮𐑍𐑆, 𐐰𐑌𐐼 𐑄 𐑅𐐻𐐫𐑉𐑋, 𐐰𐑌𐐼 𐑄 𐐻𐐯𐑋𐐹𐐯𐑅𐐻, 𐐰𐑌𐐼 𐑄 𐐿𐐶𐐩𐐿𐐮𐑍𐑆 𐐱𐑂 𐑄 𐐲𐑉𐑃 𐐼𐐮𐐼 𐑅𐐨𐑅—𐑁𐐫𐑉 𐐺𐐨𐐸𐐬𐑊𐐼, 𐑄𐐩 𐐼𐐮𐐼 𐑊𐐰𐑅𐐻 𐑁𐐫𐑉 𐐲𐐺𐐵𐐻 𐑄 𐑅𐐹𐐩𐑅 𐐱𐑂 𐑃𐑉𐐨 𐐵𐐲𐑉𐑆; 𐐰𐑌𐐼 𐐮𐐻 𐐶𐐲𐑆 𐑅𐐯𐐼 𐐺𐐴 𐑅𐐲𐑋 𐑄𐐰𐐻 𐑄 𐐻𐐴𐑋 𐐶𐐲𐑆 𐑀𐑉𐐩𐐻𐐲𐑉; 𐑌𐐯𐑂𐐲𐑉𐑄𐐯𐑊𐐯𐑅, 𐐫𐑊 𐑄𐐨𐑆 𐑀𐑉𐐩𐐻 𐐰𐑌𐐼 𐐻𐐯𐑉𐐮𐐺𐑊 𐑃𐐮𐑍𐑆 𐐶𐐲𐑉 𐐼𐐲𐑌 𐐮𐑌 𐐲𐐺𐐵𐐻 𐑄 𐑅𐐹𐐩𐑅 𐐱𐑂 𐑃𐑉𐐨 𐐵𐐲𐑉𐑆; 𐐰𐑌𐐼 𐑄𐐯𐑌 𐐺𐐨𐐸𐐬𐑊𐐼, 𐑄𐐩𐑉 𐐶𐐲𐑆 𐐼𐐪𐑉𐐿𐑌𐐯𐑅 𐐲𐐹𐐱𐑌 𐑄 𐑁𐐩𐑅 𐐱𐑂 𐑄 𐑊𐐰𐑌𐐼.

4. 𐐈𐑌𐐼 𐐮𐐻 𐐿𐐩𐑋 𐐻𐐭 𐐹𐐰𐑅 𐑄𐐰𐐻 𐑄𐐩𐑉 𐐶𐐲𐑆 𐑃𐐮𐐿 𐐼𐐪𐑉𐐿𐑌𐐯𐑅 𐐲𐐹𐐱𐑌 𐐫𐑊 𐑄 𐑁𐐩𐑅 𐐱𐑂 𐑄 𐑊𐐰𐑌𐐼, 𐐮𐑌𐑅𐐬𐑋𐐲𐐽 𐑄𐐰𐐻 𐑄 𐐮𐑌𐐸𐐰𐐺𐐮𐐻𐐲𐑌𐐻𐑅 𐑄𐐩𐑉𐐲𐑂 𐐸𐐭 𐐸𐐰𐐼 𐑌𐐱𐐻 𐑁𐐫𐑊𐑌 𐐿𐐳𐐼 𐑁𐐨𐑊 𐑄 𐑂𐐩𐐹𐐲𐑉 𐐱𐑂 𐐼𐐪𐑉𐐿𐑌𐐯𐑅; 𐐰𐑌𐐼 𐑄𐐩𐑉 𐐿𐐳𐐼 𐐺𐐨 𐑌𐐬 𐑊𐐴𐐻, 𐐺𐐨𐐿𐐫𐑆 𐐱𐑂 𐑄 𐐼𐐪𐑉𐐿𐑌𐐯𐑅, 𐑌𐐨𐑄𐐲𐑉 𐐿𐐰𐑌𐐼𐑊𐑆, 𐑌𐐨𐑄𐐲𐑉 𐐻𐐫𐑉𐐽𐐯𐑆; 𐑌𐐨𐑄𐐲𐑉 𐐿𐐳𐐼 𐑄𐐩𐑉 𐐺𐐨 𐑁𐐴𐑉 𐐿𐐮𐑌𐐼𐑊𐐼 𐐶𐐮𐑄 𐑄𐐩𐑉 𐑁𐐴𐑌 𐐰𐑌𐐼 𐐯𐐿𐑅𐐨𐐼𐐮𐑍𐑊𐐨 𐐼𐑉𐐴 𐐶𐐳𐐼, 𐑅𐐬 𐑄𐐰𐐻 𐑄𐐩𐑉 𐐿𐐳𐐼 𐑌𐐱𐐻 𐐺𐐨 𐐯𐑌𐐨 𐑊𐐴𐐻 𐐰𐐻 𐐫𐑊; 𐐰𐑌𐐼 𐑄𐐩𐑉 𐐶𐐲𐑆 𐑌𐐱𐐻 𐐯𐑌𐐨 𐑊𐐴𐐻 𐑅𐐨𐑌, 𐑌𐐨𐑄𐐲𐑉 𐑁𐐴𐑉, 𐑌𐐫𐑉 𐑀𐑊𐐮𐑋𐐲𐑉, 𐑌𐐨𐑄𐐲𐑉 𐑄 𐑅𐐲𐑌, 𐑌𐐫𐑉 𐑄 𐑋𐐭𐑌, 𐑌𐐫𐑉 𐑄 𐑅𐐻𐐪𐑉𐑆, 𐑁𐐫𐑉 𐑅𐐬 𐑀𐑉𐐩𐐻 𐐶𐐲𐑉 𐑄 𐑋𐐮𐑅𐐻𐑅 𐐱𐑂 𐐼𐐪𐑉𐐿𐑌𐐯𐑅 𐐸𐐶𐐮𐐽 𐐶𐐲𐑉 𐐲𐐹𐐱𐑌 𐑄 𐑁𐐩𐑅 𐐱𐑂 𐑄 𐑊𐐰𐑌𐐼.

5. 𐐈𐑌𐐼 𐐮𐐻 𐐿𐐩𐑋 𐐻𐐭 𐐹𐐰𐑅 𐑄𐐰𐐻 𐐮𐐻 𐐼𐐮𐐼 𐑊𐐰𐑅𐐻 𐑁𐐫𐑉 𐑄 𐑅𐐹𐐩𐑅 𐐱𐑂 𐑃𐑉𐐨 𐐼𐐩𐑆, 𐑄𐐰𐐻 𐑄𐐩𐑉 𐐶𐐲𐑆 𐑌𐐬 𐑊𐐴𐐻 𐑅𐐨𐑌; 𐐰𐑌𐐼 𐑄𐐩𐑉 𐐶𐐲𐑆 𐑀𐑉𐐩𐐻 𐑋𐐬𐑉𐑌𐐮𐑍, 𐐰𐑌𐐼 𐐸𐐵𐑊𐐮𐑍, 𐐰𐑌𐐼 𐐶𐐨𐐹𐐮𐑍 𐐲𐑋𐐲𐑍 𐐫𐑊 𐑄 𐐹𐐨𐐹𐑊 𐐿𐐲𐑌𐐻𐐮𐑌𐐷𐐭𐐲𐑊𐐨; 𐐷𐐩, 𐑀𐑉𐐩𐐻 𐐶𐐲𐑉 𐑄 𐑀𐑉𐐬𐑌𐐮𐑍𐑆 𐐱𐑂 𐑄 𐐹𐐨𐐹𐑊, 𐐺𐐨𐐿𐐫𐑆 𐐱𐑂 𐑄 𐐼𐐪𐑉𐐿𐑌𐐯𐑅 𐐰𐑌𐐼 𐑄 𐑀𐑉𐐩𐐻 𐐼𐐯𐑅𐐻𐑉𐐲𐐿𐑇𐐲𐑌 𐐸𐐶𐐮𐐽 𐐸𐐰𐐼 𐐿𐐲𐑋 𐐲𐐹𐐱𐑌 𐑄𐐯𐑋. 𐐈𐑌𐐼 𐐮𐑌 𐐶𐐲𐑌 𐐹𐑊𐐩𐑅 𐑄𐐩 𐐶𐐲𐑉 𐐸𐐲𐑉𐐼 𐐻𐐭

𐐿𐑉𐐴, 𐑅𐐩𐐮𐑍, 𐐄 𐑄𐐰𐐻 𐐶𐐨 𐐸𐐰𐐼 𐑉𐐨𐐹𐐯𐑌𐐻𐐯𐐼 𐐺𐐨𐑁𐐫𐑉 𐑄𐐮𐑅 𐑀𐑉𐐩𐐻 𐐰𐑌𐐼 𐐻𐐯𐑉𐐮𐐺𐑊 𐐼𐐩, 𐐰𐑌𐐼 𐑄𐐯𐑌 𐐶𐐳𐐼 𐐵𐑉 𐐺𐑉𐐯𐑄𐑉𐐯𐑌 𐐸𐐰𐑂 𐐺𐐮𐑌 𐑅𐐹𐐩𐑉𐐼, 𐐰𐑌𐐼 𐑄𐐩 𐐶𐐳𐐼 𐑌𐐱𐐻 𐐸𐐰𐑂 𐐺𐐮𐑌 𐐺𐐲𐑉𐑌𐐼 𐐮𐑌 𐑄𐐰𐐻 𐑀𐑉𐐩𐐻 𐑅𐐮𐐻𐐨 𐐞𐐯𐑉𐐰𐐸𐐯𐑋𐑊𐐰. 𐐈𐑌𐐼 𐐮𐑌 𐐰𐑌𐐲𐑄𐐲𐑉 𐐹𐑊𐐩𐑅 𐑄𐐩 𐐶𐐲𐑉 𐐸𐐲𐑉𐐼 𐐻𐐭 𐐿𐑉𐐴 𐐰𐑌𐐼 𐑋𐐬𐑉𐑌, 𐑅𐐩𐐮𐑍, 𐐄 𐑄𐐰𐐻 𐐶𐐨 𐐸𐐰𐐼 𐑉𐐨𐐹𐐯𐑌𐐻𐐯𐐼 𐐺𐐨𐑁𐐫𐑉 𐑄𐐮𐑅 𐑀𐑉𐐩𐐻 𐐰𐑌𐐼 𐐻𐐯𐑉𐐮𐐺𐑊 𐐼𐐩, 𐐰𐑌𐐼 𐐸𐐰𐐼 𐑌𐐱𐐻 𐐿𐐮𐑊𐐼 𐐰𐑌𐐼 𐑅𐐻𐐬𐑌𐐼 𐑄 𐐹𐑉𐐱𐑁𐐯𐐻𐑅, 𐐰𐑌𐐼 𐐿𐐰𐑅𐐻 𐑄𐐯𐑋 𐐵𐐻; 𐑄𐐯𐑌 𐐶𐐳𐐼 𐐵𐑉 𐑋𐐲𐑄𐐲𐑉𐑆, 𐐰𐑌𐐼 𐐵𐑉 𐑁𐐩𐑉 𐐼𐐫𐐻𐐲𐑉𐑆, 𐐰𐑌𐐼 𐐵𐑉 𐐽𐐮𐑊𐐼𐑉𐐯𐑌 𐐸𐐰𐑂 𐐺𐐮𐑌 𐑅𐐹𐐩𐑉𐐼, 𐐰𐑌𐐼 𐑌𐐱𐐻 𐐸𐐰𐑂 𐐺𐐮𐑌 𐐺𐐯𐑉𐐨𐐼 𐐲𐐹 𐐮𐑌 𐑄𐐰𐐻 𐑀𐑉𐐩𐐻 𐑅𐐮𐐻𐐨 𐐣𐐬𐑉𐐱𐑌𐐴𐐸𐐪; 𐐰𐑌𐐼 𐑄𐐲𐑅 𐐶𐐲𐑉 𐑄 𐐸𐐵𐑊𐐮𐑍𐑆 𐐱𐑂 𐑄 𐐹𐐨𐐹𐑊 𐑀𐑉𐐩𐐻 𐐰𐑌𐐼 𐐻𐐯𐑉𐐮𐐺𐑊.

6. 𐐈𐑌𐐼 𐐮𐐻 𐐿𐐩𐑋 𐐻𐐭 𐐹𐐪𐑅 𐑄𐐰𐐻 𐑄𐐩𐑉 𐐶𐐱𐑆 𐐩 𐑂𐑎𐑅 𐐸𐐲𐑉𐐼 𐐲𐑋𐐲𐑍 𐐫𐑊 𐑄 𐐮𐑌𐐸𐐰𐐺𐐮𐐻𐐰𐑌𐐻𐑅 𐐱𐑂 𐑄 𐐲𐑉𐑃, 𐐲𐐹𐐱𐑌 𐐫𐑊 𐑄 𐑁𐐩𐑅 𐐱𐑂 𐑄𐐮𐑅 𐑊𐐰𐑌𐐼, 𐐿𐑉𐐴𐐮𐑍, 𐐎𐐬, 𐐶𐐬, 𐐶𐐬 𐐲𐑌𐐻𐐭 𐑄𐐮𐑅 𐐹𐐨𐐹𐑊; 𐐶𐐬 𐐲𐑌𐐻𐐭 𐑄 𐐮𐑌𐐸𐐰𐐺𐐮𐐻𐐰𐑌𐐻𐑅 𐐱𐑂 𐑄 𐐸𐐬𐑊 𐐲𐑉𐑃, 𐐯𐐿𐑅𐐯𐐹𐐻 𐑄𐐩 𐑇𐐰𐑊 𐑉𐐨𐐹𐐯𐑌𐐻, 𐑁𐐫𐑉 𐑄 𐐼𐐯𐑂𐐮𐑊 𐑊𐐪𐑁𐐯𐑃, 𐐰𐑌𐐼 𐐸𐐮𐑆 𐐩𐑌𐐾𐐯𐑊𐑆 𐑉𐐨𐐾𐑎𐑅, 𐐺𐐨𐐿𐐫𐑆 𐐱𐑂 𐑄 𐑅𐑊𐐩𐑌 𐐱𐑂 𐑄 𐑁𐐩𐑉 𐑅𐐲𐑌𐑆 𐐰𐑌𐐼 𐐼𐐫𐐻𐐲𐑉𐑆 𐐱𐑂 𐑋𐐴 𐐹𐐨𐐹𐑊; 𐐰𐑌𐐼 𐐮𐐻 𐐮𐑆 𐐺𐐨𐐿𐐫𐑆 𐐱𐑂 𐑄𐐩𐑉 𐐮𐑌𐐮𐐿𐐶𐐮𐐻𐐨 𐐰𐑌𐐼 𐐰𐐺𐐱𐑋𐐮𐑌𐐩𐑇𐐲𐑌𐑆 𐑄𐐰𐐻 𐑄𐐩 𐐪𐑉 𐑁𐐫𐑊𐐲𐑌. 𐐒𐐨𐐸𐐬𐑊𐐼, 𐑄𐐰𐐻 𐑀𐑉𐐩𐐻 𐑅𐐮𐐻𐐨 𐐞𐐯𐑉𐐰𐐸𐐯𐑋𐑊𐐰 𐐸𐐰𐑂 𐐌 𐐺𐐲𐑉𐑌𐐼 𐐶𐐮𐑄 𐑁𐐴𐑉, 𐐰𐑌𐐼 𐑄 𐐮𐑌𐐸𐐰𐐺𐐮𐐻𐐰𐑌𐐻𐑅 𐑄𐐩𐑉𐐱𐑂. 𐐈𐑌𐐼 𐐺𐐨-𐐸𐐬𐑊𐐼, 𐑄𐐰𐐻 𐑀𐑉𐐩𐐻 𐑅𐐮𐐻𐐨 𐐣𐐬𐑉𐐬𐑌𐐴 𐐸𐐰𐑂 𐐌 𐐿𐐫𐑆𐐼 𐐻𐐭 𐐺𐐨 𐑅𐐲𐑍𐐿 𐐮𐑌 𐑄 𐐼𐐯𐐹𐑃𐑅 𐐱𐑂 𐑄 𐑅𐐨, 𐐰𐑌𐐼 𐑄 𐐮𐑌𐐸𐐰𐐺𐐮𐐻𐐰𐑌𐐻𐑅 𐑄𐐩𐑉𐐱𐑂 𐐻𐐭 𐐺𐐨 𐐼𐑉𐐵𐑌𐐼. 𐐈𐑌𐐼 𐐺𐐨𐐸𐐬𐑊𐐼, 𐑄𐐰𐐻 𐑀𐑉𐐩𐐻 𐑅𐐮𐐻𐐨 𐐣𐐬𐑉𐐱𐑌𐐴𐐸𐐪 𐐸𐐰𐑂 𐐌 𐐿𐐲𐑂𐐲𐑉𐐼 𐐶𐐮𐑄 𐐲𐑉𐑃, 𐐰𐑌𐐼 𐑄 𐐮𐑌𐐸𐐰𐐺𐐮𐐻𐐰𐑌𐐻𐑅 𐑄𐐩𐑉𐐱𐑂, 𐐻𐐭 𐐸𐐴𐐼 𐑄𐐩𐑉 𐐮𐑌𐐮𐐿𐐶𐐮𐐻𐐨𐑆 𐐰𐑌𐐼 𐑄𐐩𐑉 𐐰𐐺𐐱𐑋𐐮-𐑌𐐩𐑇𐐲𐑌𐑆 𐑁𐑉𐐱𐑋 𐐺𐐨𐑁𐐫𐑉 𐑋𐐴 𐑁𐐩𐑅, 𐑄𐐰𐐻 𐑄 𐐺𐑊𐐲𐐼 𐐱𐑂 𐑄 𐐹𐑉𐐱𐑁𐐯𐐻𐑅 𐐰𐑌𐐼 𐑄 𐑅𐐩𐑌𐐻𐑅 𐑇𐐰𐑊 𐑌𐐱𐐻 𐐿𐐲𐑋 𐐯𐑌𐐨 𐑋𐐬𐑉 𐐲𐑌𐐻𐐭 𐑋𐐨 𐐰𐑀𐐯𐑌𐑅𐐻 𐑄𐐯𐑋. 𐐈𐑌𐐼 𐐺𐐨𐐸𐐬𐑊𐐼, 𐑄 𐑅𐐮𐐻𐐨 𐐱𐑂 𐐘𐐮𐑊𐑀𐐰𐑊 𐐸𐐰𐑂 𐐌 𐐿𐐫𐑆𐐼 𐐻𐐭 𐐺𐐨 𐑅𐐲𐑍𐐿, 𐐰𐑌𐐼 𐑄 𐐮𐑌𐐸𐐰𐐺𐐮𐐻𐐰𐑌𐐻𐑅 𐑄𐐩𐑉𐐱𐑂 𐐻𐐭 𐐺𐐨 𐐺𐐯𐑉𐐨𐐼 𐐲𐐹 𐐮𐑌 𐑄 𐐼𐐯𐐹𐑃𐑅 𐐱𐑂 𐑄 𐐲𐑉𐑃: 𐐷𐐩, 𐐰𐑌𐐼 𐑄 𐑅𐐮𐐻𐐨 𐐱𐑂 𐐄𐑌𐐴𐐸𐐪, 𐐰𐑌𐐼 𐑄 𐐮𐑌𐐸𐐰𐐺𐐮𐐻𐐰𐑌𐐻𐑅 𐑄𐐩𐑉𐐱𐑂, 𐐰𐑌𐐼 𐑄 𐑅𐐮𐐻𐐨 𐐱𐑂 𐐣𐐬𐐿𐐲𐑋, 𐐰𐑌𐐼 𐑄 𐐮𐑌-𐐸𐐰𐐺𐐮𐐻𐐰𐑌𐐻𐑅 𐑄𐐩𐑉𐐱𐑂, 𐐰𐑌𐐼 𐑄 𐑅𐐮𐐻𐐨 𐐱𐑂 𐐖𐐯𐑉𐐭𐑅𐐰𐑊𐐯𐑋, 𐐰𐑌𐐼 𐑄 𐐮𐑌𐐸𐐰𐐺𐐮𐐻𐐰𐑌𐐻𐑅 𐑄𐐩𐑉𐐱𐑂, 𐐰𐑌𐐼 𐐶𐐫-𐐻𐐲𐑉𐑆 𐐸𐐰𐑂 𐐌 𐐿𐐫𐑆𐐼 𐐻𐐭 𐐿𐐲𐑋 𐐲𐐹 𐐮𐑌 𐑄 𐑅𐐻𐐯𐐼 𐑄𐐩𐑉𐐱𐑂, 𐐻𐐭 𐐸𐐴𐐼 𐑄𐐩𐑉 𐐶𐐮𐐿𐐯𐐼𐑌𐐯𐑅 𐐰𐑌𐐼 𐐰𐐺𐐱𐑋𐐮-𐑌𐐩𐑇𐐲𐑌𐑆 𐑁𐑉𐐱𐑋 𐐺𐐨𐑁𐐫𐑉 𐑋𐐴 𐑁𐐩𐑅, 𐑄𐐰𐐻 𐑄 𐐺𐑊𐐲𐐼 𐐱𐑂 𐑄 𐐹𐑉𐐱𐑁𐐯𐐻𐑅 𐐰𐑌𐐼 𐑄 𐑅𐐩𐑌𐐻𐑅 𐑇𐐰𐑊 𐑌𐐱𐐻 𐐿𐐲𐑋 𐐲𐐹 𐐯𐑌𐐨 𐑋𐐬𐑉 𐐲𐑌𐐻𐐭 𐑋𐐨 𐐰𐑀𐐯𐑌𐑅𐐻 𐑄𐐯𐑋. 𐐈𐑌𐐼 𐐺𐐨𐐸𐐬𐑊𐐼, 𐑄 𐑅𐐮𐐻𐐨 𐐱𐑂 𐐘𐐰𐐼𐐨𐐰𐑌𐐼𐐴, 𐐰𐑌𐐼 𐑄 𐑅𐐮𐐻𐐨 𐐱𐑂 𐐘𐐰𐐼𐐨𐐱𐑋𐑌𐐪, 𐐰𐑌𐐼 𐑄 𐑅𐐮𐐻𐐨 𐐱𐑂 𐐖𐐩𐐿𐐲𐐺, 𐐰𐑌𐐼 𐑄 𐑅𐐮𐐻𐐨 𐐱𐑂 𐐘𐐮𐑋𐑀𐐮𐑋𐑌𐐬, 𐐫𐑊 𐑄𐐨𐑆 𐐸𐐰𐑂 𐐌 𐐿𐐫𐑆𐐼 𐐻𐐭 𐐺𐐨 𐑅𐐲𐑍𐐿, 𐐰𐑌𐐼 𐑋𐐩𐐼 𐐸𐐮𐑊𐑆 𐐰𐑌𐐼 𐑂𐐰𐑊𐐨𐑆 𐐮𐑌 𐑄 𐐹𐑊𐐩𐑅𐐯𐑆 𐑄𐐩𐑉𐐱𐑂, 𐐰𐑌𐐼 𐑄 𐐮𐑌𐐸𐐰𐐺𐐮𐐻𐐰𐑌𐐻𐑅 𐑄𐐩𐑉𐐱𐑂 𐐸𐐰𐑂 𐐌 𐐺𐐯𐑉𐐨𐐼 𐐲𐐹 𐐮𐑌 𐑄 𐐼𐐯𐐹𐑃𐑅 𐐱𐑂 𐑄 𐐲𐑉𐑃, 𐐻𐐭 𐐸𐐴𐐼 𐑄𐐩𐑉 𐐶𐐮𐐿𐐯𐐼-𐑌𐐯𐑅 𐐰𐑌𐐼 𐐰𐐺𐐱𐑋𐐮𐑌𐐩𐑇𐐲𐑌𐑆 𐑁𐑉𐐱𐑋 𐐺𐐨𐑁𐐫𐑉 𐑋𐐴 𐑁𐐩𐑅, 𐑄𐐰𐐻 𐑄 𐐺𐑊𐐲𐐼 𐐱𐑂 𐑄 𐐹𐑉𐐱𐑁𐐯𐐻𐑅 𐐰𐑌𐐼 𐑄 𐑅𐐩𐑌𐐻𐑅 𐑇𐐳𐐼 𐑌𐐱𐐻 𐐿𐐲𐑋 𐐲𐐹 𐐯𐑌𐐨 𐑋𐐬𐑉 𐐲𐑌𐐻𐐭 𐑋𐐨 𐐰𐑀𐐯𐑌𐑅𐐻 𐑄𐐯𐑋.

7. 𐐈𐑌𐐼 𐐺𐐨𐐸𐐬𐑊𐐼, 𐑄𐐰𐐻 𐑀𐑉𐐩𐐻 𐑅𐐮𐐻𐐨 𐐖𐐩𐐿𐐲𐐺𐐲𐑀𐐰𐑃, 𐐸𐐶𐐮𐐽 𐐶𐐱𐑆 𐐮𐑌𐐸𐐰𐐺𐐮𐐻𐐯𐐼 𐐺𐐴 𐑄 𐐹𐐨𐐹𐑊 𐐱𐑂 𐑄 𐐿𐐮𐑍 𐐱𐑂 𐐖𐐩𐐿𐐲𐐺, 𐐸𐐰𐑂 𐐌 𐐿𐐫𐑆𐐼 𐐻𐐭 𐐺𐐨 𐐺𐐲𐑉𐑌𐐼 𐐶𐐮𐑄 𐑁𐐴𐑉 𐐺𐐨𐐿𐐫𐑆 𐐱𐑂 𐑄𐐩𐑉 𐑅𐐮𐑌𐑆 𐐰𐑌𐐼 𐑄𐐩𐑉 𐐶𐐮𐐿𐐯𐐼𐑌𐐯𐑅, 𐐸𐐶𐐮𐐽 𐐶𐐱𐑆 𐐲𐐺𐐲𐑂 𐐫𐑊 𐑄 𐐶𐐮𐐿𐐯𐐼𐑌𐐯𐑅 𐐱𐑂 𐑄 𐐸𐐬𐑊 𐐲𐑉𐑃, 𐐺𐐨𐐿𐐫𐑆 𐐱𐑂 𐑄𐐩𐑉 𐑅𐐨𐐿𐑉𐐯𐐻 𐑋𐐲𐑉𐐼𐐲𐑉𐑆 𐐰𐑌𐐼 𐐿𐐱𐑋𐐺𐐮𐑌𐐩𐑇𐐲𐑌𐑆; 𐑁𐐫𐑉 𐐮𐐻 𐐶𐐱𐑆 𐑄𐐩 𐑄𐐰𐐻 𐐼𐐮𐐼 𐐼𐐯𐑅𐐻𐑉𐑎 𐑄 𐐹𐐨𐑅 𐐱𐑂 𐑋𐐴 𐐹𐐨𐐹𐑊 𐐰𐑌𐐼 𐑄 𐑀𐐲𐑂𐐲𐑉𐑌𐑋𐐯𐑌𐐻 𐐱𐑂 𐑄 𐑊𐐰𐑌𐐼: 𐑄𐐩𐑉𐑁𐐫𐑉 𐐌 𐐼𐐮𐐼 𐐿𐐫𐑆 𐑄𐐯𐑋 𐐻𐐭 𐐺𐐨 𐐺𐐲𐑉𐑌𐐼, 𐐻𐐭 𐐼𐐯-𐑅𐐻𐑉𐑎 𐑄𐐯𐑋 𐑁𐑉𐐱𐑋 𐐺𐐨𐑁𐐫𐑉 𐑋𐐴 𐑁𐐩𐑅, 𐑄𐐰𐐻 𐑄 𐐺𐑊𐐲𐐼 𐐱𐑂 𐑄 𐐹𐑉𐐱𐑁𐐯𐐻𐑅 𐐰𐑌𐐼 𐑄 𐑅𐐩𐑌𐐻𐑅 𐑇𐐳𐐼 𐑌𐐱𐐻 𐐿𐐲𐑋 𐐲𐐹 𐐲𐑌𐐻𐐭 𐑋𐐨 𐐯𐑌𐐨 𐑋𐐬𐑉 𐐰𐑀𐐯𐑌𐑅𐐻 𐑄𐐯𐑋. 𐐈𐑌𐐼 𐐺𐐨𐐸𐐬𐑊𐐼, 𐑄 𐑅𐐮𐐻𐐨 𐐱𐑂 𐐢𐐩𐑋𐐲𐑌, 𐐰𐑌𐐼 𐑄 𐑅𐐮𐐻𐐨 𐐱𐑂 𐐖𐐱𐑇, 𐐰𐑌𐐼 𐑄 𐑅𐐮𐐻𐐨 𐐱𐑂 𐐘𐐰𐐼, 𐐰𐑌𐐼 𐑄 𐑅𐐮𐐻𐐨 𐐱𐑂 𐐗𐐮𐑇𐐿𐐭𐑋𐐯𐑌, 𐐸𐐰𐑂 𐐌 𐐿𐐫𐑆𐐼 𐐻𐐭 𐐺𐐨 𐐺𐐲𐑉𐑌𐐼 𐐶𐐮𐑄 𐑁𐐴𐑉, 𐐰𐑌𐐼 𐑄 𐐮𐑌𐐸𐐰𐐺𐐮𐐻𐐰𐑌𐐻𐑅 𐑄𐐩𐑉𐐱𐑂, 𐐺𐐨𐐿𐐫𐑆 𐐱𐑂 𐑄𐐩𐑉 𐐶𐐮𐐿𐐯𐐼𐑌𐐯𐑅 𐐮𐑌 𐐿𐐪𐑅𐐻𐐮𐑍 𐐵𐐻 𐑄 𐐹𐑉𐐱𐑁𐐯𐐻𐑅, 𐐰𐑌𐐼 𐑅𐐻𐐬𐑌𐐮𐑍 𐑄𐐬𐑆 𐐸𐐭𐑋 𐐌 𐐼𐐮𐐼 𐑅𐐯𐑌𐐼 𐐻𐐭 𐐼𐐨𐐿𐑊𐐩𐑉 𐐲𐑌𐐻𐐭 𐑄𐐯𐑋 𐐿𐐱𐑌𐑅𐐲𐑉𐑌𐐮𐑍 𐑄𐐩𐑉 𐐶𐐮𐐿𐐯𐐼𐑌𐐯𐑅 𐐰𐑌𐐼 𐑄𐐩𐑉 𐐰𐐺𐐱𐑋𐐮𐑌𐐩𐑇𐐲𐑌𐑆; 𐐰𐑌𐐼 𐐺𐐨𐐿𐐫𐑆 𐑄𐐩 𐐼𐐮𐐼 𐐿𐐰𐑅𐐻 𐑄𐐯𐑋 𐐫𐑊 𐐵𐐻, 𐑄𐐰𐐻 𐑄𐐩𐑉 𐐶𐐲𐑉 𐑌𐐲𐑌 𐑉𐐴𐐽𐐲𐑅 𐐲𐑋𐐲𐑍 𐑄𐐯𐑋, 𐐌 𐐼𐐮𐐼 𐑅𐐯𐑌𐐼 𐐼𐐵𐑌 𐑁𐐴𐑉 𐐰𐑌𐐼 𐐼𐐯𐑅𐐻𐑉𐑎 𐑄𐐯𐑋, 𐑄𐐰𐐻 𐑄𐐩𐑉 𐐶𐐮𐐿𐐯𐐼-

𐑌𐐯𐑅 𐐰𐑌𐐼 𐐰𐐺𐐱𐑋𐐮𐑌𐐩𐑇𐐲𐑌𐑆 𐑋𐐴𐐻 𐐺 𐐸𐐮𐐼 𐑁𐑉𐐱𐑋 𐐺𐐨𐑁𐐬𐑉 𐑋𐐴 𐑁𐐩𐑅, 𐑄𐐰𐐻 𐑄 𐐺𐑊𐐲𐐼 𐐱𐑂 𐑄 𐐹𐑉𐐱𐑁𐐯𐐻𐑅 𐐰𐑌𐐼 𐑄 𐑅𐐩𐑌𐐻𐑅 𐐸𐐭𐑋 𐐌 𐑅𐐯𐑌𐐻 𐐰𐑋𐐲𐑍 𐑄𐐯𐑋, 𐑋𐐴𐐻 𐑌𐐱𐐻 𐐿𐑉𐐴 𐐲𐑌𐐻𐐭 𐑋𐐨 𐑁𐑉𐐱𐑋 𐑄 𐑀𐑉𐐵𐑌𐐼 𐐰𐑀𐐯𐑌𐑅𐐻 𐑄𐐯𐑋; 𐐰𐑌𐐼 𐑋𐐯𐑌𐐮 𐑀𐑉𐐩𐐻 𐐼𐐨𐑅𐐻𐑉𐐲𐐿𐑇𐐲𐑌𐑆 𐐸𐐰𐑂 𐐌 𐐿𐐫𐑆𐐼 𐐻𐐭 𐐿𐐲𐑋 𐐲𐐹𐐱𐑌 𐑄𐐮𐑅 𐑊𐐰𐑌𐐼, 𐐰𐑌𐐼 𐐲𐐹𐐱𐑌 𐑄𐐮𐑅 𐐹𐐨𐐹𐑊, 𐐺𐐨𐐿𐐫𐑆 𐐱𐑂 𐑄𐐩𐑉 𐐶𐐮𐐿𐐯𐐼𐑌𐐯𐑅 𐐰𐑌𐐼 𐑄𐐩𐑉 𐐰𐐺𐐱𐑋𐐮𐑌𐐩𐑇𐐲𐑌𐑆.

8. 𐐄 𐐫𐑊 𐐷 𐑄𐐰𐐻 𐐪𐑉 𐑅𐐹𐐩𐑉𐐼, 𐐺𐐨𐐿𐐫𐑆 𐐷 𐐶𐐲𐑉 𐑋𐐬𐑉 𐑉𐐴𐐽𐐲𐑅 𐑄𐐰𐑌 𐑄𐐩, 𐐶𐐮𐑊 𐐷 𐑌𐐱𐐻 𐑌𐐵 𐑉𐐨𐐻𐐲𐑉𐑌 𐐲𐑌𐐻𐐭 𐑋𐐨, 𐐰𐑌𐐼 𐑉𐐨𐐹𐐯𐑌𐐻 𐐱𐑂 𐐷𐐬𐑉 𐑅𐐮𐑌𐑆, 𐐰𐑌𐐼 𐐺 𐐿𐐲𐑌𐑂𐐲𐑉𐐻𐐯𐐼, 𐑄𐐰𐐻 𐐌 𐑋𐐩 𐐸𐐨𐑊 𐐷𐐭? 𐐏𐐩, 𐑂𐐯𐑉𐐮𐑊𐐮 𐐌 𐑅𐐩 𐐲𐑌𐐻𐐭 𐐷𐐭, 𐐮𐑁 𐐷 𐐶𐐮𐑊 𐐿𐐲𐑋 𐐲𐑌𐐻𐐭 𐑋𐐨, 𐐷 𐑇𐐰𐑊 𐐸𐐰𐑂 𐐨𐐻𐐲𐑉𐑌𐐲𐑊 𐑊𐐴𐑁. 𐐒𐐨𐐸𐐬𐑊𐐼, 𐑋𐐴𐑌 𐐪𐑉𐑋 𐐱𐑂 𐑋𐐲𐑉𐑅𐐮 𐐮𐑆 𐐯𐐿𐑅𐐻𐐯𐑌𐐼𐐯𐐼 𐐻𐐬𐑉𐐼𐑆 𐐷𐐭, 𐐰𐑌𐐼 𐐸𐐭𐑅𐐬𐐯𐑂𐐲𐑉 𐐶𐐮𐑊 𐐿𐐲𐑋, 𐐸𐐮𐑋 𐐶𐐮𐑊 𐐌 𐑉𐐨𐑅𐐨𐑂; 𐐰𐑌𐐼 𐐺𐑊𐐯𐑅𐐯𐐼 𐐪𐑉 𐑄𐐬𐑆 𐐸𐐭 𐐿𐐲𐑋 𐐲𐑌𐐻𐐭 𐑋𐐨. 𐐒𐐨𐐸𐐬𐑊𐐼, 𐐌 𐐰𐑋 𐐖𐐨𐑆𐐲𐑅 𐐗𐑉𐐴𐑅𐐻, 𐑄 𐐝𐐲𐑌 𐐱𐑂 𐐘𐐱𐐼. 𐐌 𐐿𐑉𐐨𐐩𐐻𐐯𐐼 𐑄 𐐸𐐯𐑂𐑌𐑆 𐐰𐑌𐐼 𐑄 𐐲𐑉𐑃, 𐐰𐑌𐐼 𐐫𐑊 𐑃𐐮𐑍𐑆 𐑄𐐰𐐻 𐐮𐑌 𐑄𐐯𐑋 𐐪𐑉. 𐐌 𐐶𐐱𐑆 𐐶𐐮𐑄 𐑄 𐐙𐐪𐑄𐐲𐑉 𐑁𐑉𐐱𐑋 𐑄 𐐺𐐨𐑀𐐮𐑌𐐮𐑍. 𐐌 𐐰𐑋 𐐮𐑌 𐑄 𐐙𐐪𐑄𐐲𐑉, 𐐰𐑌𐐼 𐑄 𐐙𐐪𐑄𐐲𐑉 𐐮𐑌 𐑋𐐨; 𐐰𐑌𐐼 𐐮𐑌 𐑋𐐨 𐐸𐐰𐑃 𐑄 𐐙𐐪𐑄𐐲𐑉 𐑀𐑊𐐬𐑉𐐮𐑁𐐴𐐼 𐐸𐐮𐑆 𐑌𐐩𐑋. 𐐌 𐐿𐐩𐑋 𐐲𐑌𐐻𐐭 𐑋𐐴 𐐬𐑌, 𐐰𐑌𐐼 𐑋𐐴 𐐬𐑌 𐑉𐐨𐑅𐐨𐑂𐐼 𐑋𐐨 𐑌𐐱𐐻. 𐐈𐑌𐐼 𐑄 𐑅𐐿𐑉𐐮𐐹𐐻𐐷𐐭𐑉𐑆 𐐿𐐲𐑌𐑅𐐲𐑉𐑌𐐮𐑍 𐑋𐐴 𐐿𐐲𐑋𐐮𐑍 𐐪𐑉 𐑁𐐳𐑊𐑁𐐮𐑊𐐼. 𐐈𐑌𐐼 𐐰𐑆 𐑋𐐯𐑌𐐮 𐐰𐑆 𐐸𐐰𐑂 𐑉𐐨𐑅𐐨𐑂𐐼 𐑋𐐨, 𐐻𐐭 𐑄𐐯𐑋 𐐸𐐰𐑂 𐐌 𐑀𐐮𐑂𐑌 𐐻𐐭 𐐺𐐨𐐿𐐲𐑋 𐑄 𐑅𐐲𐑌𐑆 𐐱𐑂 𐐘𐐱𐐼; 𐐰𐑌𐐼 𐐨𐑂𐑌 𐑅𐐬 𐐶𐐮𐑊 𐐌 𐐻𐐭 𐐰𐑆 𐑋𐐯𐑌𐐮 𐐰𐑆 𐑇𐐰𐑊 𐐺𐐨𐑊𐐨𐑂 𐐱𐑌 𐑋𐐴 𐑌𐐩𐑋, 𐑁𐐬𐑉 𐐺𐐨𐐸𐐬𐑊𐐼, 𐐺𐐴 𐑋𐐨 𐑉𐐨𐐼𐐯𐑋𐐹𐑇𐐲𐑌 𐐿𐐲𐑋𐐯𐑃, 𐐰𐑌𐐼 𐐮𐑌 𐑋𐐨 𐐮𐑆 𐑄 𐑊𐐫 𐐱𐑂 𐐣𐐬𐑆𐐯𐑆 𐑁𐐳𐑊𐑁𐐮𐑊𐐼. 𐐌 𐐰𐑋 𐑄 𐑊𐐴𐐻 𐐰𐑌𐐼 𐑄 𐑊𐐴𐑁 𐐱𐑂 𐑄 𐐶𐐲𐑉𐑊𐐼. 𐐌 𐐰𐑋 𐐈𐑊𐑁𐐪 𐐰𐑌𐐼 𐐄𐑋𐐨𐑀𐐪, 𐑄 𐐺𐐨𐑀𐐮𐑌𐐮𐑍 𐐰𐑌𐐼 𐑄 𐐯𐑌𐐼. 𐐈𐑌𐐼 𐐷 𐑇𐐰𐑊 𐐱𐑁𐐲𐑉 𐐲𐐹 𐐲𐑌𐐻𐐭 𐑋𐐨 𐑌𐐬 𐑋𐐬𐑉 𐑄 𐑇𐐯𐐼𐐮𐑍 𐐱𐑂 𐐺𐑊𐐲𐐼; 𐐷𐐩, 𐐷𐐬𐑉 𐑅𐐰𐐿𐑉𐐮𐑁𐐴𐑅𐐯𐑆 𐐰𐑌𐐼 𐐷𐐬𐑉 𐐺𐐲𐑉𐑌𐐻 𐐱𐑁𐐲𐑉𐐮𐑍𐑆 𐑇𐐰𐑊 𐐺 𐐼𐐲𐑌 𐐰𐐶𐐩, 𐑁𐐬𐑉 𐐌 𐐶𐐮𐑊 𐐰𐐿𐑅𐐯𐐹𐐻 𐑌𐐲𐑌 𐐱𐑂 𐐷𐐬𐑉 𐑅𐐰𐐿𐑉𐐮𐑁𐐴𐑅𐐯𐑆 𐐰𐑌𐐼 𐐷𐐬𐑉 𐐺𐐲𐑉𐑌𐐻 𐐱𐑁𐐲𐑉𐐮𐑍𐑆; 𐐰𐑌𐐼 𐐷 𐑇𐐰𐑊 𐐱𐑁𐐲𐑉 𐑁𐐬𐑉 𐐪 𐑅𐐰𐐿𐑉𐐮𐑁𐐴𐑅 𐐲𐑌𐐻𐐭 𐑋𐐨 𐐪 𐐺𐑉𐐬𐐿𐑌 𐐸𐐪𐑉𐐻 𐐰𐑌𐐼 𐐪 𐐿𐐱𐑌𐐻𐑉𐐴𐐻 𐑅𐐹𐐮𐑉𐐮𐐻. 𐐈𐑌𐐼 𐐸𐐭𐑅𐐬 𐐿𐐲𐑋𐐯𐑃 𐐲𐑌𐐻𐐭 𐑋𐐨 𐐶𐐮𐑄 𐐪 𐐺𐑉𐐬𐐿𐑌 𐐸𐐪𐑉𐐻 𐐰𐑌𐐼 𐐪 𐐿𐐱𐑌𐐻𐑉𐐴𐐻 𐑅𐐹𐐮𐑉𐐮𐐻, 𐐸𐐮𐑋 𐐶𐐮𐑊 𐐌 𐐺𐐰𐐹𐐻𐐴𐑆 𐐶𐐮𐑄 𐑁𐐴𐑉 𐐰𐑌𐐼 𐐶𐐮𐑄 𐑄 𐐐𐐬𐑊𐐮 𐐘𐐬𐑅𐐻, 𐐨𐑂𐑌 𐐰𐑆 𐑄 𐐢𐐩𐑋𐐰𐑌𐐴𐐻𐑅, 𐐺𐐨𐐿𐐫𐑆 𐐱𐑂 𐑄𐐩𐑉 𐑁𐐩𐑃 𐐮𐑌 𐑋𐐨 𐐰𐐻 𐑄 𐐻𐐴𐑋 𐐱𐑂 𐑄𐐩𐑉 𐐿𐐲𐑌𐑂𐐲𐑉𐑇𐐲𐑌, 𐐶𐐲𐑉 𐐺𐐰𐐹𐐻𐐴𐑆𐐼 𐐶𐐮𐑄 𐑁𐐴𐑉 𐐰𐑌𐐼 𐐶𐐮𐑄 𐑄 𐐐𐐬𐑊𐐮 𐐘𐐬𐑅𐐻, 𐐰𐑌𐐼 𐑄𐐩 𐑌𐐭 𐐮𐐻 𐑌𐐱𐐻. 𐐒𐐨𐐸𐐬𐑊𐐼, 𐐌 𐐸𐐰𐑂 𐐿𐐲𐑋 𐐲𐑌𐐻𐐭 𐑄 𐐶𐐲𐑉𐑊𐐼 𐐻𐐭 𐐺𐑉𐐮𐑍 𐑉𐐨𐐼𐐯𐑋𐐹𐑇𐐲𐑌 𐐲𐑌𐐻𐐭 𐑄 𐐶𐐲𐑉𐑊𐐼, 𐐻𐐭 𐑅𐐩𐑂 𐑄 𐐶𐐲𐑉𐑊𐐼 𐑁𐑉𐐱𐑋 𐑅𐐮𐑌: 𐑄𐐩𐑉𐑁𐐬𐑉 𐐸𐐭𐑅𐐬 𐑉𐐨𐐹𐐯𐑌𐐻𐐯𐑃 𐐰𐑌𐐼 𐐿𐐲𐑋𐐯𐑃 𐐲𐑌𐐻𐐭 𐑋𐐨 𐐰𐑆 𐐪 𐑊𐐮𐐻𐑊 𐐽𐐴𐑊𐐼, 𐐸𐐮𐑋 𐐶𐐮𐑊 𐐌 𐑉𐐨𐑅𐐨𐑂: 𐑁𐐬𐑉 𐐱𐑂 𐑅𐐲𐐽 𐐮𐑆 𐑄 𐐿𐐮𐑍𐐼𐐲𐑋 𐐱𐑂 𐐘𐐱𐐼. 𐐒𐐨𐐸𐐬𐑊𐐼, 𐑁𐐬𐑉 𐑅𐐲𐐽 𐐌 𐐸𐐰𐑂 𐑊𐐩𐐼 𐐼𐐵𐑌 𐑋𐐴 𐑊𐐴𐑁, 𐐰𐑌𐐼 𐐸𐐰𐑂 𐐻𐐩𐐿𐑌 𐐮𐐻 𐐲𐐹 𐐰𐑀𐐯𐑌; 𐑄𐐩𐑉𐑁𐐬𐑉 𐑉𐐨𐐹𐐯𐑌𐐻, 𐐰𐑌𐐼 𐐿𐐲𐑋 𐐲𐑌𐐻𐐭 𐑋𐐨, 𐐷 𐐯𐑌𐐼𐑆 𐐱𐑂 𐑄 𐐲𐑉𐑃, 𐐰𐑌𐐼 𐐺 𐑅𐐩𐑂𐐼.

9. 𐐈𐑌𐐼 𐑌𐐵 𐐺𐐨𐐸𐐬𐑊𐐼, 𐐮𐐻 𐐿𐐩𐑋 𐐻𐐭 𐐹𐐪𐑅 𐑄𐐰𐐻 𐐫𐑊 𐑄 𐐹𐐨𐐹𐑊 𐐱𐑂 𐑄 𐑊𐐰𐑌𐐼 𐐼𐐮𐐼 𐐸𐐨𐑉 𐑄𐐨𐑆 𐑅𐐩𐐮𐑍𐑆, 𐐰𐑌𐐼 𐐼𐐮𐐼 𐐶𐐮𐐻𐑌𐐯𐑅 𐐱𐑂 𐐮𐐻. 𐐈𐑌𐐼 𐐪𐑁𐐻𐐲𐑉 𐑄𐐨𐑆 𐑅𐐩𐐮𐑍𐑆 𐑄𐐩𐑉 𐐶𐐱𐑆 𐑅𐐴𐑊𐐯𐑌𐑅 𐐮𐑌 𐑄 𐑊𐐰𐑌𐐼 𐑁𐐬𐑉 𐑄 𐑅𐐹𐐩𐑅 𐐱𐑂 𐑋𐐯𐑌𐐮 𐐵𐑉𐑆; 𐑁𐐬𐑉 𐑅𐐬 𐑀𐑉𐐩𐐻 𐐶𐐱𐑆 𐑄 𐐰𐑅𐐻𐐱𐑌𐐮𐑇𐑋𐐯𐑌𐐻 𐐱𐑂 𐑄 𐐹𐐨𐐹𐑊 𐑄𐐰𐐻 𐑄𐐩 𐐼𐐮𐐼 𐑅𐐨𐑅 𐑊𐐰𐑋𐐯𐑌𐐻𐐮𐑍 𐐰𐑌𐐼 𐐸𐐵𐑊𐐮𐑍 𐑁𐐬𐑉 𐑄 𐑊𐐱𐑅 𐐱𐑂 𐑄𐐩𐑉 𐐿𐐮𐑌𐐼𐑉𐐯𐐼 𐐸𐐶𐐮𐐽 𐐸𐐰𐐼 𐐺𐐮𐑌 𐑅𐑊𐐩𐑌; 𐑄𐐩𐑉𐑁𐐬𐑉 𐑄𐐩𐑉 𐐶𐐱𐑆 𐑅𐐴𐑊𐐯𐑌𐑅 𐐮𐑌 𐐫𐑊 𐑄 𐑊𐐰𐑌𐐼 𐑁𐐬𐑉 𐑄 𐑅𐐹𐐩𐑅 𐐱𐑂 𐑋𐐯𐑌𐐮 𐐵𐑉𐑆.

10. 𐐈𐑌𐐼 𐐮𐐻 𐐿𐐩𐑋 𐐻𐐭 𐐹𐐪𐑅 𐑄𐐰𐐻 𐑄𐐩𐑉 𐐿𐐩𐑋 𐐪 𐑂𐐱𐐮𐑅 𐐰𐑀𐐯𐑌 𐐲𐑌𐐻𐐭 𐑄 𐐹𐐨𐐹𐑊, 𐐰𐑌𐐼 𐐫𐑊 𐑄 𐐹𐐨𐐹𐑊 𐐼𐐮𐐼 𐐸𐐨𐑉 𐐰𐑌𐐼 𐐶𐐮𐐻𐑌𐐯𐑅 𐐱𐑂 𐐮𐐻, 𐑅𐐩𐐮𐑍, 𐐄 𐐷 𐐹𐐨𐐹𐑊 𐐱𐑂 𐑄𐐨𐑆 𐑀𐑉𐐩𐐻 𐑅𐐮𐐻𐐮𐑆 𐐸𐐶𐐮𐐽 𐐸𐐰𐑂 𐑁𐐫𐑊𐑌, 𐐸𐐭 𐐪𐑉 𐐼𐐨𐑅𐐯𐑌𐐼𐐰𐑌𐐻𐑅 𐐱𐑂 𐐖𐐩𐐿𐐲𐐺, 𐐷𐐩, 𐐸𐐭 𐐪𐑉 𐐱𐑂 𐑄 𐐸𐐵𐑅 𐐱𐑂 𐐆𐑆𐑉𐐩𐐯𐑊, 𐐸𐐵 𐐱𐑁𐐻 𐐸𐐰𐑂 𐐌 𐑀𐐰𐑄𐐲𐑉𐐼 𐐷𐐭 𐐰𐑆 𐐪 𐐸𐐯𐑌 𐑀𐐰𐑄𐐲𐑉𐐯𐑃 𐐸𐐲𐑉 𐐽𐐮𐐿𐐯𐑌𐑆 𐐲𐑌𐐼𐐲𐑉 𐐸𐐲𐑉 𐐶𐐮𐑍𐑆, 𐐰𐑌𐐼 𐐸𐐰𐑂 𐑌𐐲𐑉𐐮𐑇𐐻 𐐷𐐭. 𐐈𐑌𐐼 𐐰𐑀𐐯𐑌, 𐐸𐐵 𐐱𐑁𐐻 𐐶𐐳𐐼 𐐌 𐐸𐐰𐑂 𐑀𐐰𐑄𐐲𐑉𐐼 𐐷𐐭 𐐰𐑆 𐐪 𐐸𐐯𐑌 𐑀𐐰𐑄𐐲𐑉𐐯𐑃 𐐸𐐲𐑉 𐐽𐐮𐐿𐐯𐑌𐑆 𐐲𐑌𐐼𐐲𐑉 𐐸𐐲𐑉 𐐶𐐮𐑍𐑆; 𐐷𐐩, 𐐄 𐐷 𐐹𐐨𐐹𐑊 𐐱𐑂 𐑄 𐐸𐐵𐑅 𐐱𐑂 𐐆𐑆𐑉𐐩𐐯𐑊, 𐐸𐐭 𐐸𐐰𐑂 𐑁𐐫𐑊𐑌; 𐐷𐐩, 𐐄 𐐷 𐐹𐐨𐐹𐑊 𐐱𐑂 𐑄 𐐸𐐵𐑅 𐐱𐑂 𐐆𐑆𐑉𐐩𐐯𐑊, 𐐷 𐑄𐐰𐐻 𐐼𐐶𐐯𐑊 𐐰𐐻 𐐖𐐨𐑉𐐭𐑅𐐲𐑊𐐯𐑋, 𐐰𐑆 𐐷 𐑄𐐰𐐻 𐐸𐐰𐑂 𐑁𐐫𐑊𐑌; 𐐷𐐩, 𐐸𐐵 𐐱𐑁𐐻 𐐶𐐳𐐼 𐐌 𐐸𐐰𐑂 𐑀𐐰𐑄𐐲𐑉𐐼 𐐷𐐭 𐐰𐑆 𐐪 𐐸𐐯𐑌 𐑀𐐰𐑄𐐲𐑉𐐯𐑃 𐐸𐐲𐑉 𐐽𐐮𐐿𐐯𐑌𐑆, 𐐰𐑌𐐼 𐐷 𐐶𐐳𐐼 𐑌𐐱𐐻. 𐐄 𐐷 𐐸𐐵𐑅 𐐱𐑂 𐐆𐑆𐑉𐐩𐐯𐑊

𐐸𐐭𐑋 𐐌 𐐸𐐰𐑂 𐑅𐐹𐐩𐑉𐐼, 𐐸𐐵 𐐱𐑁𐐻 𐐶𐐮𐑊 𐐌 𐑀𐐰𐑄𐐲𐑉 𐐷𐐭 𐐰𐑆 𐐲 𐐸𐐯𐑌 𐑀𐐰𐑄𐐲𐑉𐐯𐑄 𐐸𐐲𐑉 𐐽𐐮𐐿𐐲𐑌𐑆 𐐲𐑌𐐼𐐲𐑉 𐐸𐐲𐑉 𐐶𐐮𐑍𐑆, 𐐮𐑁 𐐷𐐨 𐐶𐐮𐑊 𐑉𐐨𐐹𐐯𐑌𐐻 𐐰𐑌𐐼 𐑉𐐨𐐻𐐲𐑉𐑌 𐐲𐑌𐐻𐐭 𐑋𐐨 𐐶𐐮𐑄 𐑁𐐳𐑊 𐐹𐐲𐑉𐐹𐐲𐑅 𐐱𐑂 𐐸𐐪𐑉𐐻. 𐐒𐐲𐐻 𐐮𐑁 𐑌𐐱𐐻, 𐐄 𐐸𐐵𐑅 𐐱𐑂 𐐆𐑆𐑉𐐨𐐲𐑊, 𐑄 𐐹𐑊𐐩𐑅𐐯𐑆 𐐱𐑂 𐐷𐐬𐑉 𐐼𐐶𐐯𐑊𐐮𐑍𐑆 𐑇𐐰𐑊 𐐺𐐨𐐿𐐲𐑋 𐐼𐐯𐑅𐐬𐑊𐐩𐐻 𐐲𐑌𐐻𐐮𐑊 𐑄 𐐻𐐴𐑋 𐐱𐑂 𐑄 𐑁𐐳𐑊𐑁𐐮𐑊𐐮𐑍 𐐱𐑂 𐑄 𐐿𐐲𐑂𐐯𐑌𐐲𐑌𐐻 𐐻𐐭 𐐷𐐬𐑉 𐑁𐐪𐑄𐐲𐑉𐑆.

11. 𐐈𐑌𐐼 𐑌𐐵 𐐮𐐻 𐐿𐐩𐑋 𐐻𐐭 𐐹𐐰𐑅 𐑄𐐰𐐻 𐐰𐑁𐐻𐐲𐑉 𐑄 𐐹𐐨𐐹𐑊 𐐸𐐰𐐼 𐐸𐐲𐑉𐐼 𐑄𐐨𐑆 𐐶𐐲𐑉𐐼𐑆, 𐐺𐐨𐐸𐐬𐑊𐐼 𐑄𐐩 𐐺𐐯𐑀𐐰𐑌 𐐻𐐭 𐐶𐐨𐐹 𐐰𐑌𐐼 𐐸𐐵𐑊 𐐲𐑀𐐯𐑌 𐐺𐐨𐐿𐐱𐑆 𐐱𐑂 𐑄 𐑊𐐱𐑅 𐐱𐑂 𐑄𐐯𐑉 𐐿𐐮𐑌𐑛𐑉𐐯𐐼 𐐰𐑌𐐼 𐑁𐑉𐐯𐑌𐐼𐑆. 𐐈𐑌𐐼 𐐮𐐻 𐐿𐐩𐑋 𐐻𐐭 𐐹𐐰𐑅 𐑄𐐰𐐻 𐑄𐐲𐑅 𐐼𐐮𐐼 𐑄 𐑄𐑉𐐨 𐐼𐐩𐑆 𐐹𐐰𐑅 𐐲𐐶𐐩. 𐐈𐑌𐐼 𐐮𐐻 𐐶𐐱𐑆 𐐮𐑌 𐑄 𐑋𐐫𐑉𐑌𐐮𐑍, 𐐰𐑌𐐼 𐑄 𐐼𐐪𐑉𐐿𐑌𐐯𐑅 𐐼𐐮𐑅𐐹𐐲𐑉𐑅𐐻 𐑁𐑉𐐱𐑋 𐐱𐑁 𐑄 𐑁𐐩𐑅 𐐱𐑂 𐑄 𐑊𐐰𐑌𐐼, 𐐰𐑌𐐼 𐑄 𐐲𐑉𐑄 𐐼𐐮𐐼 𐑅𐐨𐑅 𐐻𐐭 𐐻𐑉𐐯𐑋𐐺𐑊, 𐐰𐑌𐐼 𐑄 𐑉𐐱𐐿𐑅 𐐼𐐮𐐼 𐑅𐐨𐑅 𐐻𐐭 𐑉𐐯𐑌𐐼, 𐐰𐑌𐐼 𐑄 𐐼𐑉𐐯𐐼𐑁𐐳𐑊 𐑀𐑉𐐬𐑌𐐮𐑍𐑆 𐐼𐐮𐐼 𐑅𐐨𐑅, 𐐰𐑌𐐼 𐐫𐑊 𐑄 𐐻𐐭𐑋𐐲𐑊𐐽𐐭𐐲𐑅 𐑌𐐱𐐮𐑆𐐯𐑆 𐐼𐐮𐐼 𐐹𐐰𐑅 𐐲𐐶𐐩, 𐐰𐑌𐐼 𐑄 𐐲𐑉𐑄 𐐼𐐮𐐼 𐐿𐑊𐐨𐑂 𐐻𐐭𐑀𐐯𐑄𐐲𐑉 𐐲𐑀𐐯𐑌, 𐑄𐐰𐐻 𐐮𐐻 𐑅𐐻𐐳𐐼, 𐐰𐑌𐐼 𐑄 𐑋𐐫𐑉𐑌𐐮𐑍, 𐐰𐑌𐐼 𐑄 𐐶𐐨𐐹𐐮𐑍, 𐐰𐑌𐐼 𐑄 𐐶𐐩𐑊𐐮𐑍 𐐱𐑂 𐑄 𐐹𐐨𐐹𐑊 𐐸𐐭 𐐶𐐲𐑉 𐑅𐐹𐐩𐑉𐐼 𐐲𐑊𐐴𐑂, 𐐼𐐮𐐼 𐑅𐐨𐑅; 𐐰𐑌𐐼 𐑄𐐯𐑉 𐑋𐐫𐑉𐑌𐐮𐑍 𐐶𐐱𐑆 𐐻𐐲𐑉𐑌𐐼 𐐮𐑌𐐻𐐭 𐐾𐐱𐐮, 𐐰𐑌𐐼 𐑄𐐯𐑉 𐑊𐐰𐑋𐐯𐑌𐐻𐐩𐑇𐐲𐑌𐑆 𐐮𐑌𐐻𐐭 𐑄 𐐹𐑉𐐩𐑆 𐐰𐑌𐐼 𐑃𐐰𐑍𐐿𐑅𐑀𐐮𐑂𐐮𐑍 𐐲𐑌𐐻𐐭 𐑄 𐐢𐐫𐑉𐐼 𐐖𐐨𐑆𐐲𐑅 𐐗𐑉𐐴𐑅𐐻, 𐑄𐐯𐑉 𐐡𐐨𐐼𐐨𐑋𐐲𐑉. 𐐈𐑌𐐼 𐑄𐐲𐑅 𐑁𐐪𐑉 𐐶𐐲𐑉 𐑄 𐑅𐐿𐑉𐐮𐐹𐐽𐐲𐑉𐑆 𐑁𐐳𐑊𐑁𐐮𐑊𐐼 𐐸𐐶𐐮𐐽 𐐸𐐰𐐼 𐐺𐐨𐑌 𐑅𐐹𐐬𐐿𐐲𐑌 𐐺𐐴 𐑄 𐐹𐑉𐐱𐑁𐐯𐐻𐑅. 𐐈𐑌𐐼 𐐮𐐻 𐐶𐐱𐑆 𐑄 𐑋𐐬𐑉 𐑉𐐴𐐽𐐲𐑅 𐐹𐐪𐑉𐐻 𐐱𐑂 𐑄 𐐹𐐨𐐹𐑊 𐐸𐐭 𐐶𐐲𐑉 𐑅𐐩𐑂𐐼, 𐐰𐑌𐐼 𐐮𐐻 𐐶𐐱𐑆 𐑄𐐩 𐐸𐐭 𐑉𐐨𐑅𐐨𐑂𐐼 𐑄 𐐹𐑉𐐱𐑁𐐯𐐻𐑅 𐐰𐑌𐐼 𐑅𐐻𐐬𐑌𐐼 𐑄𐐯𐑋 𐑌𐐱𐐻; 𐐰𐑌𐐼 𐐮𐐻 𐐶𐐱𐑆 𐑄𐐩 𐐸𐐭 𐐸𐐰𐐼 𐑌𐐱𐐻 𐑇𐐯𐐼 𐑄 𐐺𐑊𐐲𐐼 𐐱𐑂 𐑄 𐑅𐐩𐑌𐐻𐑅, 𐐸𐐭 𐐶𐐲𐑉 𐑅𐐹𐐩𐑉𐐼; 𐐰𐑌𐐼 𐑄𐐩 𐐶𐐲𐑉 𐑅𐐹𐐩𐑉𐐼, 𐐰𐑌𐐼 𐐶𐐲𐑉 𐑌𐐱𐐻 𐑅𐐲𐑍𐐿 𐐰𐑌𐐼 𐐺𐐲𐑉𐐨𐐼 𐐲𐐹 𐐮𐑌 𐑄 𐐲𐑉𐑄; 𐐰𐑌𐐼 𐑄𐐩 𐐶𐐲𐑉 𐑌𐐱𐐻 𐐼𐑉𐐵𐑌𐐼 𐐮𐑌 𐑄 𐐼𐐯𐐹𐑃𐑅 𐐱𐑂 𐑄 𐑅𐐨; 𐐰𐑌𐐼 𐑄𐐩 𐐶𐐲𐑉 𐑌𐐱𐐻 𐐺𐐲𐑉𐑌𐐼 𐐺𐐴 𐑁𐐴𐑉; 𐑌𐐨𐑄𐐲𐑉 𐐶𐐲𐑉 𐑄𐐩 𐑁𐐫𐑊𐑌 𐐲𐐹𐐱𐑌 𐐰𐑌𐐼 𐐿𐑉𐐲𐑇𐐻 𐐻𐐭 𐐼𐐯𐑃; 𐐰𐑌𐐼 𐑄𐐩 𐐶𐐲𐑉 𐑌𐐱𐐻 𐐿𐐰𐑉𐐨𐐼 𐐲𐐶𐐩 𐐮𐑌 𐑄 𐐸𐐶𐐲𐑉𐑊𐐶𐐮𐑌𐐼; 𐑌𐐨𐑄𐐲𐑉 𐐶𐐲𐑉 𐑄𐐩 𐐬𐑂𐐲𐑉-𐐹𐐵𐐲𐑉𐐼 𐐺𐐴 𐑄 𐑂𐐩𐐹𐐲𐑉 𐐱𐑂 𐑅𐑋𐐬𐐿 𐐰𐑌𐐼 𐐱𐑂 𐐼𐐪𐑉𐐿𐑌𐐯𐑅. 𐐈𐑌𐐼 𐑌𐐵, 𐐸𐐭𐑆𐐬 𐑉𐐨𐐼𐐯𐑃, 𐑊𐐯𐐻 𐐸𐐮𐑋 𐐲𐑌-𐐼𐐲𐑉𐑅𐐻𐐰𐑌𐐼; 𐐸𐐨 𐑄𐐰𐐻 𐐸𐐰𐑃 𐑄 𐑅𐐿𐑉𐐮𐐹𐐽𐐲𐑉𐑆, 𐑊𐐯𐐻 𐐸𐐮𐑋 𐑅𐐲𐑉𐐽 𐑄𐐯𐑋, 𐐰𐑌𐐼 𐑅𐐨 𐐰𐑌𐐼 𐐺𐐨𐐸𐐬𐑊𐐼, 𐐮𐑁 𐐫𐑊 𐑄𐐨𐑆 𐐼𐐯𐑃𐑅 𐐰𐑌𐐼 𐐼𐐯𐑅𐐻𐑉𐐲𐐿𐑇𐐲𐑌𐑆 𐐺𐐴 𐑁𐐴𐑉, 𐐰𐑌𐐼 𐐺𐐴 𐑅𐑋𐐬𐐿, 𐐰𐑌𐐼 𐐺𐐴 𐐻𐐯𐑋𐐹𐐯𐑅𐐻𐑅, 𐐰𐑌𐐼 𐐺𐐴 𐐸𐐶𐐲𐑉𐑊𐐶𐐮𐑌𐐼𐑆, 𐐰𐑌𐐼 𐐺𐐴 𐑄 𐐬𐐹𐐲𐑌𐐮𐑍 𐐱𐑂 𐑄 𐐲𐑉𐑄 𐐻𐐭 𐑉𐐨𐑅𐐨𐑂 𐑄𐐯𐑋, 𐐰𐑌𐐼 𐐫𐑊 𐑄𐐨𐑆 𐑃𐐮𐑍𐑆 𐐪𐑉 𐑌𐐱𐐻 𐐲𐑌𐐻𐐭 𐑄 𐑁𐐳𐑊𐑁𐐮𐑊𐐮𐑍 𐐱𐑂 𐑄 𐐹𐑉𐐱𐑁𐐯𐑅𐐨𐑆 𐐱𐑂 𐑋𐐯𐑌𐐨 𐐱𐑂 𐑄 𐐸𐐬𐑊𐐨 𐐹𐑉𐐱𐑁𐐯𐐻𐑅. 𐐒𐐨𐐸𐐬𐑊𐐼, 𐐌 𐑅𐐩 𐐲𐑌𐐻𐐭 𐐷𐐭, 𐐏𐐯, 𐑋𐐯𐑌𐐨 𐐸𐐰𐑂 𐐻𐐯𐑅𐐻𐐮𐑁𐐴𐐼 𐐱𐑂 𐑄𐐨𐑆 𐑃𐐮𐑍𐑆 𐐰𐐻 𐑄 𐐿𐐲𐑋𐐮𐑍 𐐱𐑂 𐐗𐑉𐐴𐑅𐐻, 𐐰𐑌𐐼 𐐶𐐲𐑉 𐑅𐑊𐐩𐑌 𐐺𐐨𐐿𐐱𐑆 𐑄𐐩 𐐻𐐯𐑅𐐻𐐮𐑁𐐴𐐼 𐐱𐑂 𐑄𐐨𐑆 𐑃𐐮𐑍𐑆; 𐐏𐐯, 𐑄 𐐹𐑉𐐱𐑁𐐯𐐻 𐐞𐐨𐑌𐐬𐑅 𐐼𐐮𐐼 𐐻𐐯𐑅𐐻𐐮𐑁𐐴 𐐱𐑂 𐑄𐐨𐑆 𐑃𐐮𐑍𐑆, 𐐰𐑌𐐼 𐐫𐑊𐑅𐐬 𐐞𐐨𐑌𐐱𐐿 𐑅𐐹𐐩𐐿 𐐿𐐱𐑌𐑅𐐲𐑉𐑌𐐮𐑍 𐑄𐐨𐑆 𐑃𐐮𐑍𐑆, 𐐺𐐨𐐿𐐱𐑆 𐑄𐐩 𐐻𐐯𐑅𐐻𐐮𐑁𐐴𐐼 𐐹𐐲𐑉𐐻𐐮𐐿-𐐷𐐭𐑊𐐲𐑉𐑊𐐨 𐐿𐐱𐑌𐑅𐐲𐑉𐑌𐐮𐑍 𐐲𐑅, 𐐸𐐭 𐐪𐑉 𐑄 𐑉𐐯𐑋𐑌𐐲𐑌𐐻 𐐱𐑂 𐑄𐐯𐑉 𐑅𐐨𐐼. 𐐒𐐨𐐸𐐬𐑊𐐼 𐐵𐑉 𐑁𐐪𐑄𐐲𐑉 𐐖𐐩𐐿𐐲𐐺 𐐫𐑊𐑅𐐬 𐐻𐐯𐑅𐐻𐐮𐑁𐐴𐐼 𐐿𐐱𐑌𐑅𐐲𐑉𐑌𐐮𐑍 𐐲 𐑉𐐯𐑋𐑌𐐲𐑌𐐻 𐐱𐑂 𐑄 𐑅𐐨𐐼 𐐱𐑂 𐐖𐐬𐑆𐐯𐑁. 𐐈𐑌𐐼 𐐺𐐨𐐸𐐬𐑊𐐼, 𐐪𐑉 𐑌𐐱𐐻 𐐶𐐨 𐐲 𐑉𐐯𐑋𐑌𐐲𐑌𐐻 𐐱𐑂 𐑄 𐑅𐐨𐐼 𐐱𐑂 𐐖𐐬𐑆𐐯𐑁? 𐐈𐑌𐐼 𐑄𐐨𐑆 𐑃𐐮𐑍𐑆 𐐸𐐶𐐮𐐽 𐐻𐐯𐑅𐐻𐐮𐑁𐐴 𐐱𐑂 𐐲𐑅, 𐐪𐑉 𐑄𐐩 𐑌𐐱𐐻 𐑉𐐮𐐻𐑌 𐐲𐐹𐐱𐑌 𐑄 𐐹𐑊𐐩𐐻𐑅 𐐱𐑂 𐐺𐑉𐐰𐑅 𐐸𐐶𐐮𐐽 𐐵𐑉 𐑁𐐪𐑄𐐲𐑉 𐐢𐐨𐐸𐐴 𐐺𐑉𐐱𐐻 𐐵𐐻 𐐱𐑂 𐐖𐐨𐑉𐐭𐑅𐐲𐑊𐐯𐑋? 𐐈𐑌𐐼 𐐮𐐻 𐐿𐐩𐑋 𐐻𐐭 𐐹𐐰𐑅 𐑄𐐰𐐻 𐐮𐑌 𐑄 𐐯𐑌𐐼𐐮𐑍 𐐱𐑂 𐑄 𐑃𐐲𐑉𐐻𐐨 𐐰𐑌𐐼 𐑁𐐬𐑉𐑃 𐐷𐐨𐑉, 𐐺𐐨𐐸𐐬𐑊𐐼, 𐐌 𐐶𐐮𐑊 𐑇𐐬 𐐲𐑌𐐻𐐭 𐐷𐐭 𐑄𐐰𐐻 𐑄 𐐹𐐨𐐹𐑊 𐐱𐑂 𐐤𐐨𐑁𐐴 𐐸𐐭 𐐶𐐲𐑉 𐑅𐐹𐐩𐑉𐐼, 𐐰𐑌𐐼 𐐫𐑊𐑅𐐬 𐑄𐐬𐑆 𐐸𐐭 𐐸𐐰𐐼 𐐺𐐨𐑌 𐐿𐐫𐑊𐐼 𐐢𐐰𐑋𐐲𐑌𐐴𐐻𐑅, 𐐸𐐭 𐐸𐐰𐐼 𐐺𐐨𐑌 𐑅𐐹𐐩𐑉𐐼, 𐐼𐐮𐐼 𐐸𐐰𐑂 𐑀𐑉𐐩𐐻 𐑁𐐩𐑂𐐲𐑉𐑆 𐑇𐐬𐑌 𐐲𐑌𐐻𐐭 𐑄𐐯𐑋, 𐐰𐑌𐐼 𐑀𐑉𐐩𐐻 𐐺𐑊𐐯𐑅𐐮𐑍𐑆 𐐹𐐬𐑉𐐼 𐐵𐐻 𐐲𐐹𐐱𐑌 𐑄𐐯𐑉 𐐸𐐯𐐼𐑆, 𐐮𐑌𐑅𐐬𐑋𐐲𐐽 𐑄𐐰𐐻 𐑅𐐭𐑌 𐐰𐑁𐐻𐐲𐑉 𐑄 𐐰𐑅𐐯𐑌𐑇𐐲𐑌 𐐱𐑂 𐐗𐑉𐐴𐑅𐐻 𐐮𐑌𐐻𐐭 𐐸𐐯𐑂𐐲𐑌, 𐐸𐐨 𐐼𐐮𐐼 𐐻𐑉𐐭𐑊𐐨 𐑋𐐰𐑌𐐮𐑁𐐯𐑅𐐻 𐐸𐐮𐑋𐑅𐐯𐑊𐑁 𐐲𐑌𐐻𐐭 𐑄𐐯𐑋; 𐑇𐐬𐐮𐑍 𐐸𐐮𐑆 𐐺𐐱𐐼𐐨 𐐲𐑌𐐻𐐭 𐑄𐐯𐑋, 𐐰𐑌𐐼 𐑋𐐮𐑌𐐮𐑅𐐻𐐲𐑉𐐮𐑍 𐐲𐑌𐐻𐐭 𐑄𐐯𐑋; 𐐰𐑌𐐼 𐐰𐑌 𐐰𐐿𐐵𐑌𐐻 𐐱𐑂 𐐸𐐮𐑆 𐑋𐐮𐑌𐐮𐑅𐐻𐑉𐐨 𐑇𐐰𐑊 𐐺𐐨 𐑀𐐮𐑂𐑌 𐐸𐐨𐑉𐐰𐑁𐐻𐐲𐑉. 𐐜𐐯𐑉𐑁𐐬𐑉 𐑁𐐬𐑉 𐑄𐐮𐑅 𐐻𐐴𐑋 𐐌 𐑋𐐩𐐿 𐐰𐑌 𐐯𐑌𐐼 𐐱𐑂 𐑋𐐴 𐑅𐐩𐐮𐑍𐑆.

𐐕𐐈𐐑𐐓𐐊𐐡 V.

𐐖𐐨𐑆𐐲𐑅 𐐗𐑉𐐴𐑅𐐻 𐑇𐐬𐐯𐑃 𐐸𐐮𐑋𐑅𐐯𐑊𐑁 𐐲𐑌𐐻𐐭 𐑄 𐐹𐐨𐐹𐑊 𐐱𐑂 𐐤𐐨𐑁𐐴, 𐐰𐑆 𐑄 𐑋𐐲𐑊𐐻𐐮𐐻𐑏𐐼 𐐶𐐲𐑉 𐑀𐐰𐑄𐐲𐑉𐐼 𐐻𐐭𐑀𐐯𐑄𐐲𐑉 𐐮𐑌 𐑄 𐑊𐐰𐑌𐐼 𐐒𐐵𐑌𐐻𐐮𐑁𐐳𐑊, 𐐰𐑌𐐼 𐐼𐐮𐐼 𐑋𐐮𐑌𐐮𐑅𐐻𐐲𐑉 𐐲𐑌𐐻𐐭 𐑄𐐯𐑋; 𐐰𐑌𐐼 𐐱𐑌 𐑄𐐮𐑅 𐐶𐐴𐑆 𐐼𐐮𐐼 𐐸𐐨 𐑇𐐬 𐐸𐐮𐑋𐑅𐐯𐑊𐑁 𐐲𐑌𐐻𐐭 𐑄𐐯𐑋.

1. 𐐰𐑌𐐼 𐑌𐐵 𐐮𐐻 𐐿𐐩𐑋 𐐻𐐭 𐐹𐐪𐑅 𐑄𐐰𐐻 𐑄𐐩𐑉 𐐶𐐲𐑉 𐐩 𐑀𐑉𐐩𐐻 𐑋𐐲𐑊𐐻𐐮𐐻𐑏𐐼 𐑀𐐰𐑄𐐲𐑉𐐼 𐐻𐐭𐑀𐐯𐑄𐐲𐑉, 𐐱𐑂 𐑄 𐐹𐐨𐐹𐑊 𐐱𐑂 𐐤𐐨𐑁𐐴, 𐑉𐐵𐑌𐐼 𐐲𐐺𐐵𐐻 𐑄 𐐻𐐯𐑋𐐹𐑊 𐐸𐐶𐐮𐐽 𐐶𐐱𐑆 𐐮𐑌 𐑄 𐑊𐐰𐑌𐐼 𐐒𐐵𐑌𐐻𐐮𐑁𐐳𐑊; 𐐰𐑌𐐼 𐑄𐐩 𐐶𐐲𐑉 𐑋𐐪𐑉𐑂𐐯𐑊𐐮𐑍 𐐰𐑌𐐼 𐐶𐐲𐑌𐐼𐐲𐑉𐐮𐑍 𐐶𐐲𐑌 𐐶𐐮𐑄 𐐰𐑌𐐲𐑄𐐲𐑉, 𐐰𐑌𐐼 𐐶𐐲𐑉 𐑇𐐬𐐮𐑍 𐐶𐐲𐑌 𐐻𐐭 𐐰𐑌𐐲𐑄𐐲𐑉 𐑄 𐑀𐑉𐐩𐐻 𐐰𐑌𐐼 𐑋𐐪𐑉𐑂𐐯𐑊𐐲𐑅 𐐽𐐩𐑌𐐾 𐐸𐐶𐐮𐐽 𐐸𐐰𐐼 𐐻𐐩𐐿𐐲𐑌 𐐹𐑊𐐩𐑅; 𐐰𐑌𐐼 𐑄𐐩 𐐶𐐲𐑉 𐐫𐑊𐑅𐐬 𐐿𐐱𐑌𐑂𐐲𐑉𐑅𐐮𐑍 𐐲𐐺𐐵𐐻 𐑄𐐮𐑅 𐐖𐐨𐑆𐐲𐑅 𐐗𐑉𐐴𐑅𐐻, 𐐱𐑂 𐐸𐐭𐑋 𐑄 𐑅𐐴𐑌 𐐸𐐰𐐼 𐐺𐐮𐑌 𐑀𐐮𐑂𐐲𐑌 𐐿𐐱𐑌𐑅𐐲𐑉𐑌𐐮𐑍 𐐸𐐮𐑆 𐐼𐐯𐑃.

2. 𐐰𐑌𐐼 𐐮𐐻 𐐿𐐩𐑋 𐐻𐐭 𐐹𐐪𐑅 𐑄𐐰𐐻 𐐸𐐶𐐴𐑊 𐑄𐐩 𐐶𐐲𐑉 𐑄𐐲𐑅 𐐿𐐱𐑌𐑂𐐲𐑉𐑅𐐮𐑍 𐐶𐐲𐑌 𐐶𐐮𐑄 𐐰𐑌𐐲𐑄𐐲𐑉, 𐑄𐐩 𐐸𐐲𐑉𐐼 𐐩 𐑂𐐦𐑅 𐐰𐑆 𐐮𐑁 𐐮𐐻 𐐿𐐩𐑋 𐐵𐐻 𐐱𐑂 𐐸𐐯𐑂𐐲𐑌; 𐐰𐑌𐐼 𐑄𐐩 𐐿𐐪𐑅𐐻 𐑄𐐩𐑉 𐐴𐑆 𐑉𐐵𐑌𐐼 𐐲𐐺𐐵𐐻, 𐑁𐐫𐑉 𐑄𐐩 𐐲𐑌𐐼𐐲𐑉𐑅𐐻𐐳𐐼 𐑌𐐱𐐻 𐑄 𐑂𐐦𐑅 𐐸𐐶𐐮𐐽 𐑄𐐩 𐐸𐐲𐑉𐐼; 𐐰𐑌𐐼 𐐮𐐻 𐐶𐐱𐑆 𐑌𐐱𐐻 𐐩 𐐸𐐪𐑉𐑇 𐑂𐐦𐑅, 𐑌𐐨𐑄𐐲𐑉 𐐶𐐱𐑆 𐐮𐐻 𐐩 𐑊𐐵𐐼 𐑂𐐦𐑅; 𐑌𐐯𐑂𐐲𐑉𐑄𐐲𐑊𐐯𐑅, 𐐰𐑌𐐼 𐑌𐐱𐐻𐐶𐐮𐑃𐑅𐐻𐐰𐑌𐐼𐐮𐑍 𐐮𐐻 𐐺𐐨𐐮𐑍 𐐩 𐑅𐑋𐐫𐑊 𐑂𐐦𐑅 𐐮𐐻 𐐼𐐮𐐼 𐐹𐐨𐑉𐑅 𐑄𐐯𐑋 𐑄𐐰𐐻 𐐼𐐮𐐼 𐐸𐐨𐑉 𐐻𐐭 𐑄 𐑅𐐯𐑌𐐻𐐲𐑉, 𐐮𐑌𐑅𐐬𐑋𐐲𐐽 𐑄𐐰𐐻 𐑄𐐩𐑉 𐐶𐐱𐑆 𐑌𐐬 𐐹𐐪𐑉𐐻 𐐱𐑂 𐑄𐐩𐑉 𐑁𐑉𐐩𐑋 𐑄𐐰𐐻 𐐮𐐻 𐐼𐐮𐐼 𐑌𐐱𐐻 𐐿𐐫𐑆 𐐻𐐭 𐐿𐐶𐐩𐐿; 𐐷𐐩, 𐐮𐐻 𐐼𐐮𐐼 𐐹𐐨𐑉𐑅 𐑄𐐯𐑋 𐐻𐐭 𐑄 𐑂𐐯𐑉𐐨 𐑅𐐬𐑊, 𐐰𐑌𐐼 𐐼𐐮𐐼 𐐿𐐫𐑆 𐑄𐐩𐑉 𐐸𐐪𐑉𐐻𐑅 𐐻𐐭 𐐺𐐲𐑉𐑌. 𐐰𐑌𐐼 𐐮𐐻 𐐿𐐩𐑋 𐐻𐐭 𐐹𐐪𐑅 𐑄𐐰𐐻 𐐰𐑀𐐯𐑌 𐑄𐐩 𐐸𐐲𐑉𐐼 𐑄 𐑂𐐦𐑅, 𐐰𐑌𐐼 𐑄𐐩 𐐲𐑌𐐼𐐲𐑉𐑅𐐻𐐳𐐼 𐐮𐐻 𐑌𐐱𐐻; 𐐰𐑌𐐼 𐐰𐑀𐐯𐑌 𐑄 𐑃𐐲𐑉𐐼 𐐻𐐴𐑋 𐑄𐐩 𐐼𐐮𐐼 𐐸𐐨𐑉 𐑄 𐑂𐐦𐑅, 𐐰𐑌𐐼 𐐼𐐮𐐼 𐐬𐐹𐐲𐑌 𐑄𐐩𐑉 𐐨𐑉𐑆 𐐻𐐭 𐐸𐐨𐑉 𐐮𐐻; 𐐰𐑌𐐼 𐑄𐐩𐑉 𐐴𐑆 𐐶𐐲𐑉 𐐻𐐬𐐲𐑉𐐼𐑆 𐑄 𐑅𐐵𐑌𐐼 𐑄𐐩𐑉𐐱𐑂; 𐐰𐑌𐐼 𐑄𐐩 𐐼𐐮𐐼 𐑊𐐳𐐿 𐑅𐐻𐐯𐐼𐑁𐐪𐑅𐐻𐑊𐐨 𐐻𐐬𐐲𐑉𐐼𐑆 𐐸𐐯𐑂𐐲𐑌, 𐑁𐑉𐐱𐑋 𐐸𐐶𐐯𐑌𐑅 𐑄 𐑅𐐵𐑌𐐼 𐐿𐐩𐑋. 𐐰𐑌𐐼 𐐺𐐨𐐸𐐬𐑊𐐼, 𐑄 𐑃𐐲𐑉𐐼 𐐻𐐴𐑋 𐑄𐐩 𐐼𐐮𐐼 𐐲𐑌𐐼𐐲𐑉𐑅𐐻𐐰𐑌𐐼 𐑄 𐑂𐐦𐑅 𐐸𐐶𐐮𐐽 𐑄𐐩 𐐸𐐲𐑉𐐼; 𐐰𐑌𐐼 𐐮𐐻 𐑅𐐯𐐼 𐐲𐑌𐐻𐐭 𐑄𐐯𐑋, 𐐒𐐨𐐸𐐬𐑊𐐼 𐑋𐐴 𐐒𐐨𐑊𐐲𐑂𐐯𐐼 𐐝𐐲𐑌, 𐐮𐑌 𐐸𐐭𐑋 𐐌 𐐰𐑋 𐐶𐐯𐑊 𐐹𐑊𐐨𐑆𐐼, 𐐮𐑌 𐐸𐐭𐑋 𐐌 𐐸𐐰𐑂 𐑀𐑊𐐬𐑉𐐮𐑁𐐴𐐼 𐑋𐐴 𐑌𐐩𐑋: 𐐸𐐨𐑉 𐐷𐐨 𐐸𐐮𐑋.

3. 𐐰𐑌𐐼 𐐮𐐻 𐐿𐐩𐑋 𐐻𐐭 𐐹𐐪𐑅 𐐰𐑆 𐑄𐐩 𐐲𐑌𐐼𐐲𐑉𐑅𐐻𐐳𐐼, 𐑄𐐩 𐐿𐐪𐑅𐐻 𐑄𐐩𐑉 𐐴𐑆 𐐲𐐹 𐐰𐑀𐐯𐑌 𐐻𐐬𐐲𐑉𐐼𐑆 𐐸𐐯𐑂𐐲𐑌; 𐐰𐑌𐐼 𐐺𐐨𐐸𐐬𐑊𐐼, 𐑄𐐩 𐑅𐐫 𐐩 𐑋𐐰𐑌 𐐼𐐨𐑅𐐯𐑌𐐼𐐮𐑍 𐐵𐐻 𐐱𐑂 𐐸𐐯𐑂𐐲𐑌; 𐐰𐑌𐐼 𐐸𐐨 𐐶𐐱𐑆 𐐿𐑊𐐬𐑄𐐼 𐐮𐑌 𐐩 𐐸𐐶𐐴𐐻 𐑉𐐬𐐺, 𐐰𐑌𐐼 𐐸𐐨 𐐿𐐩𐑋 𐐼𐐵𐑌 𐐰𐑌𐐼 𐑅𐐻𐐳𐐼 𐐮𐑌 𐑄 𐑋𐐮𐐼𐑅𐐻 𐐱𐑂 𐑄𐐯𐑋; 𐐰𐑌𐐼 𐑄 𐐴𐑆 𐐱𐑂 𐑄 𐐸𐐬𐑊 𐑋𐐲𐑊𐐻𐐮𐐻𐑏𐐼 𐐶𐐲𐑉 𐐻𐐲𐑉𐑌𐐼 𐐲𐐹𐐱𐑌 𐐸𐐮𐑋, 𐐰𐑌𐐼 𐑄𐐩 𐐼𐐲𐑉𐑅𐐻 𐑌𐐱𐐻 𐐬𐐹𐐲𐑌 𐑄𐐩𐑉 𐑋𐐵𐑃𐑅, 𐐨𐑂𐐲𐑌 𐐶𐐲𐑌 𐐻𐐭 𐐰𐑌𐐲𐑄𐐲𐑉, 𐐰𐑌𐐼 𐐶𐐮𐑅𐐻 𐑌𐐱𐐻 𐐸𐐶𐐱𐐻 𐐮𐐻 𐑋𐐯𐑌𐐻, 𐑁𐐫𐑉 𐑄𐐩 𐑃𐐫𐐻 𐐮𐐻 𐐶𐐱𐑆 𐐰𐑌 𐐩𐑌𐐾𐐯𐑊 𐑄𐐰𐐻 𐐸𐐰𐐼 𐐰𐐹𐐨𐑉𐐼 𐐲𐑌𐐻𐐭 𐑄𐐯𐑋.

4. 𐐰𐑌𐐼 𐐮𐐻 𐐿𐐩𐑋 𐐻𐐭 𐐹𐐪𐑅 𐑄𐐰𐐻 𐐸𐐨 𐑅𐐻𐑉𐐯𐐽𐐻 𐑁𐐬𐑉𐑃 𐐸𐐮𐑆 𐐸𐐰𐑌𐐼 𐐰𐑌𐐼 𐑅𐐹𐐩𐐿 𐐲𐑌𐐻𐐭 𐑄 𐐹𐐨𐐹𐑊, 𐑅𐐩𐐮𐑍, 𐐒𐐨𐐸𐐬𐑊𐐼, 𐐌 𐐰𐑋 𐐖𐐨𐑆𐐲𐑅 𐐗𐑉𐐴𐑅𐐻, 𐐸𐐭𐑋 𐑄 𐐹𐑉𐐱𐑁𐐯𐐻𐑅 𐐻𐐯𐑅𐐻𐐮𐑁𐐴𐐼 𐑇𐐰𐑊 𐐿𐐲𐑋 𐐮𐑌𐐻𐐭 𐑄 𐐶𐐲𐑉𐑊𐐼; 𐐰𐑌𐐼 𐐺𐐨𐐸𐐬𐑊𐐼, 𐐌 𐐰𐑋 𐑄 𐑊𐐴𐐻 𐐰𐑌𐐼 𐑄 𐑊𐐴𐑁 𐐱𐑂 𐑄 𐐶𐐲𐑉𐑊𐐼; 𐐰𐑌𐐼 𐐌 𐐸𐐰𐑂 𐐼𐑉𐐲𐑍𐐿 𐐵𐐻 𐐱𐑂 𐑄𐐰𐐻 𐐺𐐮𐐻𐐲𐑉 𐐿𐐲𐐹 𐐸𐐶𐐮𐐽 𐑄 𐐙𐐪𐑄𐐲𐑉 𐐸𐐰𐑃 𐑀𐐮𐑂𐐲𐑌 𐑋𐐨, 𐐰𐑌𐐼 𐐸𐐰𐑂 𐑀𐑊𐐬𐑉𐐮𐑁𐐴𐐼 𐑄 𐐙𐐪𐑄𐐲𐑉 𐐮𐑌 𐐻𐐩𐐿𐐮𐑍 𐐲𐐹𐐱𐑌 𐑋𐐨 𐑄 𐑅𐐮𐑌𐑆 𐐱𐑂 𐑄 𐐶𐐲𐑉𐑊𐐼, 𐐮𐑌 𐑄 𐐸𐐶𐐮𐐽 𐐌 𐐸𐐰𐑂 𐑅𐐲𐑁𐐲𐑉𐐼 𐑄 𐐶𐐮𐑊 𐐱𐑂 𐑄 𐐙𐐪𐑄𐐲𐑉 𐐮𐑌 𐐫𐑊 𐑃𐐮𐑍𐑆 𐑁𐑉𐐱𐑋 𐑄 𐐺𐐨𐑀𐐮𐑌𐐮𐑍.

5. 𐐰𐑌𐐼 𐐮𐐻 𐐿𐐩𐑋 𐐻𐐭 𐐹𐐪𐑅 𐑄𐐰𐐻 𐐸𐐶𐐯𐑌 𐐖𐐨𐑆𐐲𐑅 𐐸𐐰𐐼 𐑅𐐹𐐬𐐿𐐲𐑌 𐑄𐐨𐑆 𐐶𐐲𐑉𐐼𐑆, 𐑄 𐐸𐐬𐑊 𐑋𐐲𐑊𐐻𐐮𐐻𐑏𐐼 𐑁𐐯𐑊 𐐻𐐭 𐑄 𐐲𐑉𐑃, 𐑁𐐫𐑉 𐑄𐐩 𐑉𐐨𐑋𐐯𐑋𐐺𐐲𐑉𐐼 𐑄𐐰𐐻 𐐮𐐻 𐐸𐐰𐐼 𐐺𐐮𐑌 𐐹𐑉𐐱𐑁𐐯𐑅𐐴𐐼 𐐲𐑋𐐲𐑍 𐑄𐐯𐑋 𐑄𐐰𐐻 𐐗𐑉𐐴𐑅𐐻 𐑇𐐳𐐼 𐑇𐐬 𐐸𐐮𐑋𐑅𐐯𐑊𐑁 𐐲𐑌𐐻𐐭 𐑄𐐯𐑋 𐐪𐑁𐐻𐐲𐑉 𐐸𐐮𐑆 𐐰𐑅𐐯𐑌𐑇𐐲𐑌 𐐮𐑌𐐻𐐭 𐐸𐐯𐑂𐐲𐑌.

6. 𐐰𐑌𐐼 𐐮𐐻 𐐿𐐩𐑋 𐐻𐐭 𐐹𐐪𐑅 𐑄𐐰𐐻 𐑄 𐐢𐐫𐑉𐐼 𐑅𐐹𐐩𐐿 𐐲𐑌𐐻𐐭 𐑄𐐯𐑋, 𐑅𐐩𐐮𐑍, 𐐊𐑉𐐴𐑆 𐐰𐑌𐐼 𐐿𐐲𐑋 𐑁𐐬𐑉𐑃 𐐲𐑌𐐻𐐭 𐑋𐐨, 𐑄𐐰𐐻 𐐷𐐨 𐑋𐐩 𐑃𐑉𐐲𐑅𐐻 𐐷𐐳𐑉 𐐸𐐰𐑌𐐼𐑆 𐐮𐑌𐐻𐐭 𐑋𐐴 𐑅𐐴𐐼, 𐐰𐑌𐐼 𐐫𐑊𐑅𐐬 𐑄𐐰𐐻 𐐷𐐨 𐑋𐐩 𐑁𐐨𐑊 𐑄

𐐹𐑉𐐮𐑌𐐻𐑅 𐐱𐑂 𐑄 𐑌𐐩𐑊𐑆 𐐮𐑌 𐑋𐐴 𐐸𐐰𐑌𐐼𐑆 𐐰𐑌𐐼 𐐮𐑌 𐑋𐐴 𐑁𐐨𐐻, 𐑄𐐰𐐻 𐐷𐐨 𐑋𐐩 𐑌𐐬 𐑄𐐰𐐻 𐐌 𐐰𐑋 𐑄 𐐘𐐪𐐼 𐐱𐑂 𐐆𐑆𐑉𐐩𐐯𐑊, 𐐰𐑌𐐼 𐑄 𐐘𐐪𐐼 𐐱𐑂 𐑄 𐐸𐐬𐑊 𐐲𐑉𐑃, 𐐰𐑌𐐼 𐐸𐐰𐑂 𐐺𐐨𐑌 𐑅𐑊𐐩𐑌 𐑁𐐫𐑉 𐑄 𐑅𐐮𐑌𐑆 𐐱𐑂 𐑄 𐐶𐐲𐑉𐑊𐐼.

7. 𐐈𐑌𐐼 𐐮𐐻 𐐿𐐩𐑋 𐐻𐐭 𐐹𐐪𐑅 𐑄𐐰𐐻 𐑄 𐑋𐐲𐑊𐐻𐐮𐐻𐐷𐐭𐐼 𐐶𐐯𐑌𐐻 𐑁𐐫𐑉𐑃, 𐐰𐑌𐐼 𐑃𐑉𐐲𐑅𐐻 𐑄𐐯𐑉 𐐸𐐰𐑌𐐼𐑆 𐐮𐑌𐐻𐐭 𐐸𐐮𐑆 𐑅𐐴𐐼, 𐐰𐑌𐐼 𐐼𐐮𐐼 𐑁𐐨𐑊 𐑄 𐐹𐑉𐐮𐑌𐐻𐑅 𐐱𐑂 𐑄 𐑌𐐩𐑊𐑆 𐐮𐑌 𐐸𐐮𐑆 𐐸𐐰𐑌𐐼𐑆 𐐰𐑌𐐼 𐐮𐑌 𐐸𐐮𐑆 𐑁𐐨𐐻; 𐐰𐑌𐐼 𐑄𐐮𐑅 𐑄𐐩 𐐼𐐮𐐼 𐐼𐐭, 𐑀𐐬𐐮𐑍 𐑁𐐫𐑉𐑃 𐐶𐐲𐑌 𐐺𐐴 𐐶𐐲𐑌, 𐐲𐑌𐐻𐐮𐑊 𐑄𐐩 𐐸𐐰𐐼 𐐫𐑊 𐑀𐐫𐑌 𐑁𐐫𐑉𐑃, 𐐰𐑌𐐼 𐐼𐐮𐐼 𐑅𐐨 𐐶𐐮𐑄 𐑄𐐯𐑉 𐐴𐑆, 𐐰𐑌𐐼 𐐼𐐮𐐼 𐑁𐐨𐑊 𐐶𐐮𐑄 𐑄𐐯𐑉 𐐸𐐰𐑌𐐼𐑆, 𐐰𐑌𐐼 𐐼𐐮𐐼 𐑌𐐬 𐐱𐑂 𐐰 𐑇𐐭𐑉𐐻𐐨, 𐐰𐑌𐐼 𐐼𐐮𐐼 𐐺𐐯𐑉 𐑉𐐯𐐿𐐫𐑉𐐼, 𐑄𐐰𐐻 𐐮𐐻 𐐶𐐱𐑆 𐐸𐐨 𐐱𐑂 𐐸𐐭𐑋 𐐮𐐻 𐐶𐐱𐑆 𐑉𐐮𐐻𐑌 𐐺𐐴 𐑄 𐐹𐑉𐐱𐑁𐐯𐐻𐑅, 𐑄𐐰𐐻 𐑇𐐳𐐼 𐐿𐐲𐑋. 𐐈𐑌𐐼 𐐸𐐶𐐯𐑌 𐑄𐐩 𐐸𐐰𐐼 𐐫𐑊 𐑀𐐫𐑌 𐑁𐐫𐑉𐑃 𐐰𐑌𐐼 𐐸𐐰𐐼 𐐶𐐮𐐻𐑌𐐯𐑅𐐻 𐑁𐐫𐑉 𐑄𐐯𐑋𐑅𐐯𐑊𐑂𐑆, 𐑄𐐩 𐐼𐐮𐐼 𐐿𐑉𐐴 𐐵𐐻 𐐶𐐮𐑄 𐐶𐐲𐑌 𐐰𐐿𐐫𐑉𐐼, 𐑅𐐩𐐮𐑍, 𐐐𐐬𐑆𐐰𐑌𐐰! 𐐒𐑊𐐯𐑅𐐯𐐼 𐐺𐐨 𐑄 𐑌𐐩𐑋 𐐱𐑂 𐑄 𐐣𐐬𐑅𐐻 𐐐𐐴 𐐘𐐪𐐼! 𐐈𐑌𐐼 𐑄𐐩 𐐼𐐮𐐼 𐑁𐐫𐑊 𐐼𐐵𐑌 𐐰𐐻 𐑄 𐑁𐐨𐐻 𐐱𐑂 𐐖𐐨𐑆𐐲𐑅, 𐐰𐑌𐐼 𐐼𐐮𐐼 𐐶𐐲𐑉𐑇𐐮𐐹 𐐸𐐮𐑋.

8. 𐐈𐑌𐐼 𐐮𐐻 𐐿𐐩𐑋 𐐻𐐭 𐐹𐐪𐑅 𐑄𐐰𐐻 𐐸𐐨 𐑅𐐹𐐩𐐿 𐐲𐑌𐐻𐐭 𐐤𐐨𐑁𐐴, (𐑁𐐫𐑉 𐐤𐐨𐑁𐐴 𐐶𐐱𐑆 𐐰𐑋𐐲𐑍 𐑄 𐑋𐐲𐑊𐐻𐐮𐐻𐐷𐐭𐐼,) 𐐰𐑌𐐼 𐐸𐐨 𐐿𐐱𐑋𐐰𐑌𐐼𐐯𐐼 𐐸𐐮𐑋 𐑄𐐰𐐻 𐐸𐐨 𐑇𐐳𐐼 𐐿𐐲𐑋 𐑁𐐫𐑉𐑃. 𐐈𐑌𐐼 𐐤𐐨𐑁𐐴 𐐰𐑉𐐬𐑆 𐐰𐑌𐐼 𐐶𐐯𐑌𐐻 𐑁𐐫𐑉𐑃 𐐰𐑌𐐼 𐐺𐐵𐐼 𐐸𐐮𐑋𐑅𐐯𐑊𐑁 𐐺𐐨𐑁𐐬𐑉 𐑄 𐐢𐐫𐑉𐐼, 𐐰𐑌𐐼 𐐸𐐨 𐐼𐐮𐐼 𐐿𐐮𐑅 𐐸𐐮𐑆 𐑁𐐨𐐻. 𐐈𐑌𐐼 𐑄 𐐢𐐫𐑉𐐼 𐐿𐐱𐑋𐐰𐑌𐐼𐐯𐐼 𐐸𐐮𐑋 𐑄𐐰𐐻 𐐸𐐨 𐑇𐐳𐐼 𐐰𐑉𐐴𐑆. 𐐈𐑌𐐼 𐐸𐐨 𐐰𐑉𐐬𐑆 𐐰𐑌𐐼 𐑅𐐻𐐳𐐼 𐐺𐐨𐑁𐐬𐑉 𐐸𐐮𐑋. 𐐈𐑌𐐼 𐑄 𐐢𐐫𐑉𐐼 𐑅𐐯𐐼 𐐲𐑌𐐻𐐭 𐐸𐐮𐑋, 𐐌 𐑀𐐮𐑂 𐐲𐑌𐐻𐐭 𐐷𐐭 𐐹𐐵𐐲𐑉 𐑄𐐰𐐻 𐐷𐐨 𐑇𐐰𐑊 𐐺𐐰𐐹𐐻𐐴𐑆 𐑄𐐮𐑅 𐐹𐐨𐐹𐑊 𐐸𐐶𐐯𐑌 𐐌 𐐰𐑋 𐐰𐑀𐐯𐑌 𐐰𐑅𐐯𐑌𐐼𐐯𐐼 𐐮𐑌𐐻𐐭 𐐸𐐯𐑂𐑌. 𐐈𐑌𐐼 𐐰𐑀𐐯𐑌 𐑄 𐐢𐐫𐑉𐐼 𐐿𐐫𐑊𐐼 𐐲𐑄𐐲𐑉𐑆, 𐐰𐑌𐐼 𐑅𐐯𐐼 𐐲𐑌𐐻𐐭 𐑄𐐯𐑋 𐑊𐐴𐐿𐐶𐐴𐑆; 𐐰𐑌𐐼 𐐸𐐨 𐑀𐐩𐑂 𐐲𐑌𐐻𐐭 𐑄𐐯𐑋 𐐹𐐵𐐲𐑉 𐐻𐐭 𐐺𐐰𐐹𐐻𐐴𐑆. 𐐈𐑌𐐼 𐐸𐐨 𐑅𐐯𐐼 𐐲𐑌𐐻𐐭 𐑄𐐯𐑋, 𐐉𐑌 𐑄𐐮𐑅 𐐶𐐴𐑆 𐑇𐐰𐑊 𐐷𐐨 𐐺𐐰𐐹𐐻𐐴𐑆; 𐐰𐑌𐐼 𐑄𐐯𐑉 𐑇𐐰𐑊 𐐺𐐨 𐑌𐐬 𐐼𐐮𐑅𐐹𐐷𐐭𐐻𐐩𐑇𐐲𐑌𐑆 𐐰𐑋𐐲𐑍 𐐷𐐭. 𐐚𐐯𐑉𐐮𐑊𐐨 𐐌 𐑅𐐩 𐐲𐑌𐐻𐐭 𐐷𐐭, 𐑄𐐰𐐻 𐐸𐐭𐑅𐐬 𐑉𐐨𐐹𐐯𐑌𐐻𐐯𐑃 𐐱𐑂 𐐸𐐮𐑆 𐑅𐐮𐑌𐑆 𐑃𐑉𐐭 𐐷𐐭𐑉 𐐶𐐲𐑉𐐼𐑆, 𐐰𐑌𐐼 𐐼𐐨𐑆𐐴𐑉𐐯𐑃 𐐻𐐭 𐐺𐐨 𐐺𐐰𐐹𐐻𐐴𐑆𐐼 𐐮𐑌 𐑋𐐴 𐑌𐐩𐑋, 𐐱𐑌 𐑄𐐮𐑅 𐐶𐐴𐑆 𐑇𐐰𐑊 𐐷𐐨 𐐺𐐰𐐹𐐻𐐴𐑆 𐑄𐐯𐑋: 𐐒𐐨𐐸𐐬𐑊𐐼, 𐐷𐐨 𐑇𐐰𐑊 𐑀𐐬 𐐼𐐵𐑌 𐐰𐑌𐐼 𐑅𐐻𐐰𐑌𐐼 𐐮𐑌 𐑄 𐐶𐐫𐐻𐐲𐑉, 𐐰𐑌𐐼 𐐮𐑌 𐑋𐐴 𐑌𐐩𐑋 𐑇𐐰𐑊 𐐷𐐨 𐐺𐐰𐐹𐐻𐐴𐑆 𐑄𐐯𐑋. 𐐈𐑌𐐼 𐑌𐐵 𐐺𐐨𐐸𐐬𐑊𐐼, 𐑄𐐨𐑆 𐐪𐑉 𐑄 𐐶𐐲𐑉𐐼𐑆 𐐸𐐶𐐮𐐽 𐐷𐐨 𐑇𐐰𐑊 𐑅𐐩, 𐐿𐐫𐑊𐐮𐑍 𐑄𐐯𐑋 𐐺𐐴 𐑌𐐩𐑋, 𐑅𐐩𐐮𐑍, 𐐐𐐰𐑂𐐮𐑍 𐐫𐑃𐐱𐑉𐐮𐐻𐐨 𐑀𐐮𐑂𐑌 𐑋𐐨 𐐱𐑂 𐐖𐐨𐑆𐐲𐑅 𐐗𐑉𐐴𐑅𐐻, 𐐌 𐐺𐐰𐐹𐐻𐐴𐑆 𐐷𐐭 𐐮𐑌 𐑄 𐑌𐐩𐑋 𐐱𐑂 𐑄 𐐙𐐪𐑄𐐲𐑉, 𐐰𐑌𐐼 𐐱𐑂 𐑄 𐐝𐐲𐑌, 𐐰𐑌𐐼 𐐱𐑂 𐑄 𐐐𐐬𐑊𐐨 𐐘𐐬𐑅𐐻. 𐐁𐑋𐐯𐑌. 𐐈𐑌𐐼 𐑄𐐯𐑌 𐑇𐐰𐑊 𐐷𐐨 𐐮𐑋𐐲𐑉𐑅 𐑄𐐯𐑋 𐐮𐑌 𐑄 𐐶𐐫𐐻𐐲𐑉, 𐐰𐑌𐐼 𐐿𐐲𐑋 𐑁𐐫𐑉𐑃 𐐰𐑀𐐯𐑌 𐐵𐐻 𐐱𐑂 𐑄 𐐶𐐫𐐻𐐲𐑉. 𐐈𐑌𐐼 𐐰𐑁𐐻𐐲𐑉 𐑄𐐮𐑅 𐑋𐐰𐑌𐐲𐑉 𐑇𐐰𐑊 𐐷𐐨 𐐺𐐰𐐹𐐻𐐴𐑆 𐐮𐑌 𐑋𐐴 𐑌𐐩𐑋, 𐑁𐐫𐑉 𐐺𐐨𐐸𐐬𐑊𐐼, 𐑂𐐯𐑉𐐮𐑊𐐨 𐐌 𐑅𐐩 𐐲𐑌𐐻𐐭 𐐷𐐭, 𐑄𐐰𐐻 𐑄 𐐙𐐪𐑄𐐲𐑉, 𐐰𐑌𐐼 𐑄 𐐝𐐲𐑌, 𐐰𐑌𐐼 𐑄 𐐐𐐬𐑊𐐨 𐐘𐐬𐑅𐐻 𐐪𐑉 𐐶𐐲𐑌; 𐐰𐑌𐐼 𐐌 𐐰𐑋 𐐮𐑌 𐑄 𐐙𐐪𐑄𐐲𐑉, 𐐰𐑌𐐼 𐑄 𐐙𐐪𐑄𐐲𐑉 𐐮𐑌 𐑋𐐨, 𐐰𐑌𐐼 𐑄 𐐙𐐪𐑄𐐲𐑉 𐐰𐑌𐐼 𐐌 𐐪𐑉 𐐶𐐲𐑌. 𐐈𐑌𐐼 𐐰𐐿𐐫𐑉𐐼𐐮𐑍 𐐰𐑆 𐐌 𐐸𐐰𐑂 𐐿𐐱𐑋𐐰𐑌𐐼𐐯𐐼 𐐷𐐭, 𐑄𐐲𐑅 𐑇𐐰𐑊 𐐷𐐨 𐐺𐐰𐐹𐐻𐐴𐑆. 𐐈𐑌𐐼 𐑄𐐯𐑉 𐑇𐐰𐑊 𐐺𐐨 𐑌𐐬 𐐼𐐮𐑅𐐹𐐷𐐭𐐻𐐩𐑇𐐲𐑌𐑆 𐐰𐑋𐐲𐑍 𐐷𐐭, 𐐰𐑆 𐑄𐐯𐑉 𐐸𐐰𐑃 𐐸𐐮𐑄𐐲𐑉𐐻𐐭 𐐺𐐨𐑌; 𐑌𐐨𐑄𐐲𐑉 𐑇𐐰𐑊 𐑄𐐯𐑉 𐐺𐐨 𐐼𐐮𐑅𐐹𐐷𐐭𐐻𐐩𐑇𐐲𐑌𐑆 𐐰𐑋𐐲𐑍 𐐷𐐭 𐐿𐐱𐑌𐑅𐐲𐑉𐑌𐐮𐑍 𐑄 𐐹𐑎𐑌𐐻𐑅 𐐱𐑂 𐑋𐐴 𐐼𐐱𐐿𐐻𐑉𐐮𐑌, 𐐰𐑆 𐑄𐐯𐑉 𐐸𐐰𐑃 𐐸𐐮𐑄𐐲𐑉𐐻𐐭 𐐺𐐨𐑌; 𐑁𐐫𐑉 𐑂𐐯𐑉𐐮𐑊𐐨, 𐑂𐐯𐑉𐐮𐑊𐐨 𐐌 𐑅𐐩 𐐲𐑌𐐻𐐭 𐐷𐐭, 𐐸𐐨 𐑄𐐰𐐻 𐐸𐐰𐑃 𐑄 𐑅𐐹𐐮𐑉𐐮𐐻 𐐱𐑂 𐐿𐐱𐑌𐐻𐐯𐑌𐑇𐐲𐑌 𐐮𐑆 𐑌𐐱𐐻 𐐱𐑂 𐑋𐐨, 𐐺𐐲𐐻 𐐮𐑆 𐐱𐑂 𐑄 𐐼𐐯𐑂𐑊, 𐐸𐐭 𐐮𐑆 𐑄 𐑁𐐪𐑄𐐲𐑉 𐐱𐑂 𐐿𐐱𐑌𐐻𐐯𐑌𐑇𐐲𐑌, 𐐰𐑌𐐼 𐐸𐐨 𐑅𐐻𐐲𐑉𐐯𐑃 𐐲𐐹 𐑄 𐐸𐐪𐑉𐐻𐑅 𐐱𐑂 𐑋𐐯𐑌 𐐻𐐭 𐐿𐐱𐑌𐐻𐐯𐑌𐐼 𐐶𐐮𐑄 𐐰𐑍𐑀𐐲𐑉 𐐶𐐲𐑌 𐐶𐐮𐑄 𐐰𐑌𐐲𐑄𐐲𐑉. 𐐒𐐨𐐸𐐬𐑊𐐼, 𐑄𐐮𐑅 𐐮𐑆 𐑌𐐱𐐻 𐑋𐐴 𐐼𐐱𐐿𐐻𐑉𐐮𐑌, 𐐻𐐭 𐑅𐐻𐐲𐑉 𐐲𐐹 𐑄 𐐸𐐪𐑉𐐻𐑅 𐐱𐑂 𐑋𐐯𐑌 𐐶𐐮𐑄 𐐰𐑍𐑀𐐲𐑉 𐐶𐐲𐑌 𐐰𐑀𐐯𐑌𐑅𐐻 𐐰𐑌𐐲𐑄𐐲𐑉; 𐐺𐐲𐐻 𐑄𐐮𐑅 𐐮𐑆 𐑋𐐴 𐐼𐐱𐐿𐐻𐑉𐐮𐑌, 𐑄𐐰𐐻 𐑅𐐲𐐽 𐑃𐐮𐑍𐑆 𐑇𐐳𐐼 𐐺𐐨 𐐼𐐲𐑌 𐐰𐐶𐐩. 𐐒𐐨𐐸𐐬𐑊𐐼, 𐑂𐐯𐑉𐐮𐑊𐐨, 𐑂𐐯𐑉𐐮𐑊𐐨, 𐐌 𐑅𐐩 𐐲𐑌𐐻𐐭 𐐷𐐭, 𐐌 𐐶𐐮𐑊 𐐼𐐯𐐿𐑊𐐩𐑉 𐐲𐑌𐐻𐐭 𐐷𐐭 𐑋𐐴 𐐼𐐱𐐿𐐻𐑉𐐮𐑌. 𐐈𐑌𐐼 𐑄𐐮𐑅 𐐮𐑆 𐑋𐐴 𐐼𐐱𐐿𐐻𐑉𐐮𐑌, 𐐰𐑌𐐼 𐐮𐐻 𐐮𐑆 𐑄 𐐼𐐱𐐿𐐻𐑉𐐮𐑌 𐐸𐐶𐐮𐐽 𐑄 𐐙𐐪𐑄𐐲𐑉 𐐸𐐰𐑃 𐑀𐐮𐑂𐑌 𐐲𐑌𐐻𐐭 𐑋𐐨; 𐐰𐑌𐐼 𐐌 𐐺𐐯𐑉 𐑉𐐯𐐿𐐫𐑉𐐼 𐐱𐑂 𐑄 𐐙𐐪𐑄𐐲𐑉, 𐐰𐑌𐐼 𐑄 𐐙𐐪𐑄𐐲𐑉 𐐺𐐯𐑉𐐯𐑃 𐑉𐐯𐐿𐐫𐑉𐐼 𐐱𐑂 𐑋𐐨, 𐐰𐑌𐐼 𐑄 𐐐𐐬𐑊𐐨 𐐘𐐬𐑅𐐻 𐐺𐐯𐑉𐐯𐑃 𐑉𐐯𐐿𐐫𐑉𐐼 𐐱𐑂 𐑄 𐐙𐐪𐑄𐐲𐑉 𐐰𐑌𐐼 𐑋𐐨; 𐐰𐑌𐐼 𐐌 𐐺𐐯𐑉 𐑉𐐯𐐿𐐫𐑉𐐼 𐑄𐐰𐐻 𐑄 𐐙𐐪𐑄𐐲𐑉 𐐿𐐱𐑋𐐰𐑌𐐼𐐯𐑃 𐐫𐑊 𐑋𐐯𐑌, 𐐯𐑂𐐲𐑉𐐨𐐸𐐶𐐯𐑉, 𐐻𐐭 𐑉𐐨𐐹𐐯𐑌𐐻 𐐰𐑌𐐼 𐐺𐐨𐑊𐐨𐑂 𐐮𐑌 𐑋𐐨; 𐐰𐑌𐐼 𐐸𐐭𐑅𐐬 𐐺𐐨𐑊𐐨𐑂𐐯𐑃 𐐮𐑌 𐑋𐐨, 𐐰𐑌𐐼 𐐮𐑆 𐐺𐐰𐐹𐐻𐐴𐑆𐐼, 𐑄 𐑅𐐩𐑋 𐑇𐐰𐑊 𐐺𐐨 𐑅𐐩𐑂𐐼; 𐐰𐑌𐐼 𐑄𐐩 𐐪𐑉 𐑄𐐩 𐐸𐐭 𐑇𐐰𐑊 𐐮𐑌𐐸𐐯𐑉𐐮𐐻 𐑄 𐐿𐐮𐑍𐐼𐐲𐑋 𐐱𐑂 𐐘𐐪𐐼. 𐐈𐑌𐐼 𐐸𐐭𐑅𐐬 𐐺𐐨𐑊𐐨𐑂𐐯𐑃 𐑌𐐱𐐻 𐐮𐑌 𐑋𐐨, 𐐰𐑌𐐼 𐐮𐑆 𐑌𐐱𐐻

𐐺𐐰𐐹𐐻𐐴𐑆𐐼, 𐑇𐐰𐑊 𐐺 𐐼𐐰𐑋𐐼. 𐐚𐐯𐑉𐐮𐑊𐐨, 𐑂𐐯𐑉𐐮𐑊𐐨, 𐐌 𐑅𐐩 𐐲𐑌𐐻𐐭 𐐷𐐭, 𐑄𐐰𐐻 𐑄𐐮𐑅 𐐮𐑆 𐑋𐐴 𐐼𐐪𐐿𐐻𐑉𐐮𐑌, 𐐰𐑌𐐼 𐐌 𐐺𐐯𐑉 𐑉𐐯𐐿𐐫𐑉𐐼 𐐲𐑂 𐐮𐐻 𐑁𐑉𐐲𐑋 𐑄 𐐙𐐪𐑄𐐲𐑉; 𐐰𐑌𐐼 𐐸𐐭𐑅𐐬 𐐺𐐨𐑊𐐨𐑂𐐯𐑃 𐐮𐑌 𐑋𐐨, 𐐺𐐨𐑊𐐨𐑂𐐯𐑃 𐐮𐑌 𐑄 𐐙𐐪𐑄𐐲𐑉 𐐫𐑊𐑅𐐬, 𐐰𐑌𐐼 𐐲𐑌𐐻𐐭 𐐸𐐮𐑋 𐐶𐐮𐑊 𐑄 𐐙𐐪𐑄𐐲𐑉 𐐺𐐯𐑉 𐑉𐐯𐐿𐐫𐑉𐐼 𐐲𐑂 𐑋𐐨; 𐑁𐐫𐑉 𐐸𐐨 𐐶𐐮𐑊 𐑂𐐮𐑆𐐮𐐻 𐐸𐐮𐑋 𐐶𐐮𐑄 𐑁𐐴𐑉, 𐐰𐑌𐐼 𐐶𐐮𐑄 𐑄 𐐐𐐬𐑊𐐨 𐐘𐐬𐑅𐐻. 𐐈𐑌𐐼 𐑄𐐲𐑅 𐐶𐐮𐑊 𐑄 𐐙𐐪𐑄𐐲𐑉 𐐺𐐯𐑉 𐑉𐐯𐐿𐐫𐑉𐐼 𐐲𐑂 𐑋𐐨, 𐐰𐑌𐐼 𐑄 𐐐𐐬𐑊𐐨 𐐘𐐬𐑅𐐻 𐐶𐐮𐑊 𐐺𐐯𐑉 𐑉𐐯𐐿𐐫𐑉𐐼 𐐲𐑌𐐻𐐭 𐐸𐐮𐑋 𐐲𐑂 𐑄 𐐙𐐪𐑄𐐲𐑉 𐐰𐑌𐐼 𐑋𐐨; 𐑁𐐫𐑉 𐑄 𐐙𐐪𐑄𐐲𐑉, 𐐰𐑌𐐼 𐐌, 𐐰𐑌𐐼 𐑄 𐐐𐐬𐑊𐐨 𐐘𐐬𐑅𐐻 𐐪𐑉 𐐶𐐲𐑌.

9. 𐐈𐑌𐐼 𐐰𐑀𐐯𐑌 𐐌 𐑅𐐩 𐐲𐑌𐐻𐐭 𐐷𐐭, 𐐷𐐨 𐑋𐐲𐑅𐐻 𐑉𐐨𐐹𐐯𐑌𐐻, 𐐰𐑌𐐼 𐐺𐐨𐐿𐐲𐑋 𐐰𐑆 𐐲 𐑊𐐮𐐻𐑊 𐐽𐐴𐑊𐐼, 𐐰𐑌𐐼 𐐺 𐐺𐐰𐐹𐐻𐐴𐑆𐐼 𐐮𐑌 𐑋𐐴 𐑌𐐩𐑋, 𐐫𐑉 𐐷𐐨 𐐿𐐰𐑌 𐐮𐑌 𐑌𐐬𐐶𐐴𐑆 𐑉𐐨𐑅𐐨𐑂 𐑄𐐨𐑆 𐑃𐐮𐑍𐑆. 𐐈𐑌𐐼 𐐰𐑀𐐯𐑌 𐐌 𐑅𐐩 𐐲𐑌𐐻𐐭 𐐷𐐭, 𐐷𐐨 𐑋𐐲𐑅𐐻 𐑉𐐨𐐹𐐯𐑌𐐻, 𐐰𐑌𐐼 𐐺 𐐺𐐰𐐹𐐻𐐴𐑆𐐼 𐐮𐑌 𐑋𐐴 𐑌𐐩𐑋, 𐐰𐑌𐐼 𐐺𐐨𐐿𐐲𐑋 𐐰𐑆 𐐲 𐑊𐐮𐐻𐑊 𐐽𐐴𐑊𐐼, 𐐫𐑉 𐐷𐐨 𐐿𐐰𐑌 𐐮𐑌 𐑌𐐬𐐶𐐴𐑆 𐐮𐑌𐐸𐐯𐑉𐐮𐐻 𐑄 𐐿𐐮𐑍𐐼𐐲𐑋 𐐲𐑂 𐐘𐐪𐐼. 𐐚𐐯𐑉𐐮𐑊𐐨, 𐑂𐐯𐑉𐐮𐑊𐐨 𐐌 𐑅𐐩 𐐲𐑌𐐻𐐭 𐐷𐐭, 𐑄𐐰𐐻 𐑄𐐮𐑅 𐐮𐑆 𐑋𐐴 𐐼𐐪𐐿𐐻𐑉𐐮𐑌, 𐐰𐑌𐐼 𐐸𐐭𐑅𐐬 𐐺𐐮𐑊𐐼𐐯𐑃 𐐲𐐹𐐪𐑌 𐑄𐐮𐑅, 𐐺𐐮𐑊𐐼𐐯𐑃 𐐲𐐹𐐪𐑌 𐑋𐐴 𐑉𐐪𐐿, 𐐰𐑌𐐼 𐑄 𐑀𐐩𐐻𐑅 𐐲𐑂 𐐸𐐯𐑊 𐑇𐐰𐑊 𐑌𐐪𐐻 𐐹𐑉𐐨𐑂𐐩𐑊 𐐰𐑀𐐯𐑌𐑅𐐻 𐑄𐐯𐑋. 𐐈𐑌𐐼 𐐸𐐭𐑅𐐬 𐑇𐐰𐑊 𐐼𐐨𐐿𐑊𐐩𐑉 𐑋𐐬𐑉 𐐫𐑉 𐑊𐐯𐑅 𐑄𐐰𐑌 𐑄𐐮𐑅, 𐐰𐑌𐐼 𐐯𐑅𐐻𐐰𐐺𐑊𐐮𐑇 𐐮𐐻 𐑁𐐫𐑉 𐑋𐐴 𐐼𐐪𐐿𐐻𐑉𐐮𐑌, 𐑄 𐑅𐐩𐑋 𐐿𐐲𐑋𐐯𐑃 𐐲𐑂 𐐨𐑂𐐮𐑊, 𐐰𐑌𐐼 𐐮𐑆 𐑌𐐪𐐻 𐐺𐐮𐑊𐐻 𐐲𐐹𐐪𐑌 𐑋𐐴 𐑉𐐪𐐿, 𐐺𐐲𐐻 𐐸𐐨 𐐺𐐮𐑊𐐼𐐯𐑃 𐐲𐐹𐐪𐑌 𐐲 𐑅𐐰𐑌𐐼𐐨 𐑁𐐵𐑌𐐼𐐩𐑇𐐲𐑌, 𐐰𐑌𐐼 𐑄 𐑀𐐩𐐻𐑅 𐐲𐑂 𐐸𐐯𐑊 𐑅𐐻𐐰𐑌𐐼 𐐬𐐹𐐲𐑌 𐐻𐐭 𐑉𐐨𐑅𐐨𐑂 𐑅𐐲𐐽, 𐐸𐐶𐐯𐑌 𐑄 𐑁𐑊𐐲𐐼𐑆 𐐿𐐲𐑋 𐐰𐑌𐐼 𐑄 𐐶𐐮𐑌𐐼𐑆 𐐺𐐨𐐻 𐐲𐐹𐐪𐑌 𐑄𐐯𐑋. 𐐜𐐯𐑉𐑁𐐬𐑉 𐑀𐐬 𐑁𐐬𐑉𐑃 𐐲𐑌𐐻𐐭 𐑄𐐮𐑅 𐐹𐐨𐐹𐑊, 𐐰𐑌𐐼 𐐼𐐨𐐿𐑊𐐩𐑉 𐑄 𐐶𐐲𐑉𐐼𐑆 𐐸𐐶𐐮𐐽 𐐌 𐐸𐐰𐑂 𐑅𐐹𐐬𐐿𐐲𐑌 𐐲𐑌𐐻𐐭 𐑄 𐐯𐑌𐐼𐑆 𐐲𐑂 𐑄 𐐲𐑉𐑃. 𐐈𐑌𐐼 𐐮𐐻 𐐿𐐩𐑋 𐐻𐐭 𐐹𐐰𐑅 𐑄𐐰𐐻 𐐸𐐶𐐯𐑌 𐐖𐐨𐑆𐐲𐑅 𐐸𐐰𐐼 𐑅𐐹𐐬𐐿𐐲𐑌 𐑄𐐨𐑆 𐐶𐐲𐑉𐐼𐑆 𐐲𐑌𐐻𐐭 𐐤𐐨𐑁𐐴, 𐐰𐑌𐐼 𐐻𐐭 𐑄𐐬𐑆 𐐸𐐭 𐐸𐐰𐐼 𐐺𐐮𐑌 𐐿𐐫𐑊𐐼, (𐑌𐐵 𐑄 𐑌𐐲𐑋𐐺𐐲𐑉 𐐲𐑂 𐑄𐐯𐑋 𐐸𐐭 𐐸𐐰𐐼 𐐺𐐮𐑌 𐐿𐐫𐑊𐐼 𐐰𐑌𐐼 𐑉𐐨𐑅𐐨𐑂𐐼 𐐹𐐵𐐲𐑉 𐐰𐑌𐐼 𐐫𐑃𐐪𐑉𐐮𐐻𐐨 𐐻𐐭 𐐺𐐰𐐹𐐻𐐴𐑆, 𐐶𐐪𐑆 𐐻𐐶𐐯𐑊𐑂,) 𐐰𐑌𐐼 𐐺𐐨𐐸𐐬𐑊𐐼 𐐸𐐨 𐑅𐐻𐑉𐐯𐐽𐐻 𐑁𐐬𐑉𐑃 𐐸𐐮𐑆 𐐸𐐰𐑌𐐼 𐐲𐑌𐐻𐐭 𐑄 𐑋𐐲𐑊𐐻𐐮𐐻𐐭𐐼, 𐐰𐑌𐐼 𐐿𐑉𐐴𐐼 𐐲𐑌𐐻𐐭 𐑄𐐯𐑋, 𐑅𐐩𐐮𐑍, 𐐒𐑊𐐯𐑅𐐯𐐼 𐐪𐑉 𐐷𐐨 𐐮𐑁 𐐷𐐨 𐑇𐐰𐑊 𐑀𐐮𐑂 𐐸𐐨𐐼 𐐲𐑌𐐻𐐭 𐑄 𐐶𐐲𐑉𐐼𐑆 𐐲𐑂 𐑄𐐨𐑆 𐐻𐐶𐐯𐑊𐑂 𐐸𐐭𐑋 𐐌 𐐸𐐰𐑂 𐐽𐐬𐑆𐐲𐑌 𐑁𐑉𐐲𐑋 𐐰𐑋𐐲𐑍 𐐷𐐭 𐐻𐐭 𐑋𐐮𐑌𐐮𐑅𐐻𐐲𐑉 𐐲𐑌𐐻𐐭 𐐷𐐭, 𐐰𐑌𐐼 𐐻𐐭 𐐺 𐐷𐐭𐑉 𐑅𐐲𐑉𐑂𐐲𐑌𐐻𐑅; 𐐰𐑌𐐼 𐐲𐑌𐐻𐐭 𐑄𐐯𐑋 𐐌 𐐸𐐰𐑂 𐑀𐐮𐑂𐐲𐑌 𐐹𐐵𐐲𐑉 𐑄𐐰𐐻 𐑄𐐩 𐑋𐐩 𐐺𐐰𐐹𐐻𐐴𐑆 𐐷𐐭 𐐶𐐮𐑄 𐐶𐐫𐐻𐐲𐑉; 𐐰𐑌𐐼 𐐰𐑁𐐻𐐲𐑉 𐑄𐐰𐐻 𐐷𐐨 𐐪𐑉 𐐺𐐰𐐹𐐻𐐴𐑆𐐼 𐐶𐐮𐑄 𐐶𐐫𐐻𐐲𐑉, 𐐺𐐨𐐸𐐬𐑊𐐼 𐐌 𐐶𐐮𐑊 𐐺𐐰𐐹𐐻𐐴𐑆 𐐷𐐭 𐐶𐐮𐑄 𐑁𐐴𐑉 𐐰𐑌𐐼 𐐶𐐮𐑄 𐑄 𐐐𐐬𐑊𐐨 𐐘𐐬𐑅𐐻; 𐑄𐐯𐑉𐑁𐐬𐑉 𐐺𐑊𐐯𐑅𐐯𐐼 𐐪𐑉 𐐷𐐨 𐐮𐑁 𐐷𐐨 𐑇𐐰𐑊 𐐺𐐨𐑊𐐨𐑂 𐐮𐑌 𐑋𐐨 𐐰𐑌𐐼 𐐺 𐐺𐐰𐐹𐐻𐐴𐑆𐐼, 𐐰𐑁𐐻𐐲𐑉 𐑄𐐰𐐻 𐐷𐐨 𐐸𐐰𐑂 𐑅𐐨𐑌 𐑋𐐨 𐐰𐑌𐐼 𐑌𐐬 𐑄𐐰𐐻 𐐌 𐐰𐑋. 𐐈𐑌𐐼 𐐰𐑀𐐯𐑌 𐑋𐐬𐑉 𐐺𐑊𐐯𐑅𐐯𐐼 𐐪𐑉 𐑄𐐩 𐐸𐐭 𐑇𐐰𐑊 𐐺𐐨𐑊𐐨𐑂 𐐮𐑌 𐐷𐐭𐑉 𐐶𐐲𐑉𐐼𐑆 𐐺𐐨𐐿𐐫𐑆 𐑄𐐰𐐻 𐐷𐐨 𐑇𐐰𐑊 𐐻𐐯𐑅𐐻𐐮𐑁𐐴 𐑄𐐰𐐻 𐐷𐐨 𐐸𐐰𐑂 𐑅𐐨𐑌 𐑋𐐨, 𐐰𐑌𐐼 𐑄𐐰𐐻 𐐷𐐨 𐑌𐐬 𐑄𐐰𐐻 𐐌 𐐰𐑋. 𐐏𐐩, 𐐺𐑊𐐯𐑅𐐯𐐼 𐐪𐑉 𐑄𐐩 𐐸𐐭 𐑇𐐰𐑊 𐐺𐐨𐑊𐐨𐑂 𐐮𐑌 𐐷𐐭𐑉 𐐶𐐲𐑉𐐼𐑆, 𐐰𐑌𐐼 𐐿𐐲𐑋 𐐼𐐵𐑌 𐐮𐑌𐐻𐐭 𐑄 𐐼𐐯𐐹𐑃𐑅 𐐲𐑂 𐐸𐐷𐐭𐑋𐐮𐑊𐐮𐐻𐐨 𐐰𐑌𐐼 𐐺 𐐺𐐰𐐹𐐻𐐴𐑆𐐼, 𐑁𐐫𐑉 𐑄𐐩 𐑇𐐰𐑊 𐐺 𐑂𐐮𐑆𐐮𐐻𐐯𐐼 𐐶𐐮𐑄 𐑁𐐴𐑉 𐐰𐑌𐐼 𐐶𐐮𐑄 𐑄 𐐐𐐬𐑊𐐨 𐐘𐐬𐑅𐐻, 𐐰𐑌𐐼 𐑇𐐰𐑊 𐑉𐐨𐑅𐐨𐑂 𐐲 𐑉𐐨𐑋𐐮𐑇𐐲𐑌 𐐲𐑂 𐑄𐐩𐑉 𐑅𐐮𐑌𐑆. 𐐏𐐩, 𐐺𐑊𐐯𐑅𐐯𐐼 𐐪𐑉 𐑄 𐐹𐐭𐑉 𐐮𐑌 𐑅𐐹𐐮𐑉𐐮𐐻 𐐸𐐭 𐐿𐐲𐑋 𐐲𐑌𐐻𐐭 𐑋𐐨, 𐑁𐐫𐑉 𐑄𐐩𐑉𐑆 𐐮𐑆 𐑄 𐐿𐐮𐑍𐐼𐐲𐑋 𐐲𐑂 𐐸𐐯𐑂𐐲𐑌. 𐐈𐑌𐐼 𐐰𐑀𐐯𐑌, 𐐺𐑊𐐯𐑅𐐯𐐼 𐐪𐑉 𐐫𐑊 𐑄𐐩 𐑄𐐰𐐻 𐑋𐐬𐑉𐑌, 𐑁𐐫𐑉 𐑄𐐩 𐑇𐐰𐑊 𐐺 𐐿𐐲𐑋𐑁𐐲𐑉𐐻𐐯𐐼. 𐐈𐑌𐐼 𐐺𐑊𐐯𐑅𐐯𐐼 𐐪𐑉 𐑄 𐑋𐐨𐐿, 𐑁𐐫𐑉 𐑄𐐩 𐑇𐐰𐑊 𐐮𐑌𐐸𐐯𐑉𐐮𐐻 𐑄 𐐲𐑉𐑃. 𐐈𐑌𐐼 𐐺𐑊𐐯𐑅𐐯𐐼 𐐪𐑉 𐐫𐑊 𐑄𐐩 𐐸𐐭 𐐼𐐭 𐐸𐐲𐑍𐑀𐐲𐑉 𐐰𐑌𐐼 𐑃𐐲𐑉𐑅𐐻 𐐰𐑁𐐻𐐲𐑉 𐑉𐐴𐐽𐐲𐑅𐑌𐐯𐑅, 𐑁𐐫𐑉 𐑄𐐩 𐑇𐐰𐑊 𐐺 𐑁𐐮𐑊𐐼 𐐶𐐮𐑄 𐑄 𐐐𐐬𐑊𐐨 𐐘𐐬𐑅𐐻. 𐐈𐑌𐐼 𐐺𐑊𐐯𐑅𐐯𐐼 𐐪𐑉 𐑄 𐑋𐐲𐑉𐑅𐐮𐑁𐐳𐑊, 𐑁𐐫𐑉 𐑄𐐩 𐑇𐐰𐑊 𐐪𐐺𐐻𐐩𐑌 𐑋𐐲𐑉𐑅𐐨. 𐐈𐑌𐐼 𐐺𐑊𐐯𐑅𐐯𐐼 𐐪𐑉 𐐫𐑊 𐑄 𐐹𐐷𐐭𐑉 𐐮𐑌 𐐸𐐪𐑉𐐻, 𐑁𐐫𐑉 𐑄𐐩 𐑇𐐰𐑊 𐑅𐐨 𐐘𐐪𐐼. 𐐈𐑌𐐼 𐐺𐑊𐐯𐑅𐐯𐐼 𐐪𐑉 𐐫𐑊 𐑄 𐐹𐐨𐑅-𐑋𐐩𐐿𐐲𐑉𐑆, 𐑁𐐫𐑉 𐑄𐐩 𐑇𐐰𐑊 𐐺 𐐿𐐫𐑊𐐼 𐑄 𐐽𐐮𐑊𐐼𐑉𐐯𐑌 𐐲𐑂 𐐘𐐪𐐼. 𐐈𐑌𐐼 𐐺𐑊𐐯𐑅𐐯𐐼 𐐪𐑉 𐐫𐑊 𐑄𐐩 𐐸𐐭 𐐪𐑉 𐐹𐐲𐑉𐑅𐐨𐐿𐐷𐐭𐐻𐐯𐐼 𐑁𐐫𐑉 𐑋𐐴 𐑌𐐩𐑋'𐑆 𐑅𐐩𐐿, 𐑁𐐫𐑉 𐑄𐐩𐑉𐑆 𐐮𐑆 𐑄 𐐿𐐮𐑍𐐼𐐲𐑋 𐐲𐑂 𐐸𐐯𐑂𐐲𐑌. 𐐈𐑌𐐼 𐐺𐑊𐐯𐑅𐐯𐐼 𐐪𐑉 𐐷𐐨 𐐸𐐶𐐯𐑌 𐑋𐐯𐑌 𐑇𐐰𐑊 𐑉𐐨𐑂𐐴𐑊 𐐷𐐭 𐐰𐑌𐐼 𐐹𐐲𐑉𐑅𐐨𐐿𐐷𐐭𐐻, 𐐰𐑌𐐼 𐑇𐐰𐑊 𐑅𐐩 𐐫𐑊 𐑋𐐰𐑌𐐲𐑉 𐐲𐑂 𐐨𐑂𐐮𐑊 𐐰𐑀𐐯𐑌𐑅𐐻 𐐷𐐭 𐑁𐐫𐑊𐑅𐑊𐐨, 𐑁𐐫𐑉 𐑋𐐴 𐑅𐐩𐐿; 𐑁𐐫𐑉 𐐷𐐨 𐑇𐐰𐑊 𐐸𐐰𐑂 𐑀𐑉𐐩𐐻 𐐾𐐦, 𐐰𐑌𐐼 𐐺 𐐯𐐿𐑅𐐨𐐼𐐮𐑍𐑊𐐨 𐑀𐑊𐐰𐐼, 𐑁𐐫𐑉 𐑀𐑉𐐩𐐻 𐑇𐐰𐑊 𐐺 𐐷𐐭𐑉 𐑉𐐨𐐶𐐫𐑉𐐼 𐐮𐑌 𐐸𐐯𐑂𐐲𐑌; 𐑁𐐫𐑉 𐑅𐐬 𐐹𐐲𐑉𐑅𐐨𐐿𐐷𐐭𐐻𐐯𐐼 𐑄𐐩 𐑄 𐐹𐑉𐐪𐑁𐐯𐐻𐑅 𐐸𐐭 𐐶𐐲𐑉 𐐺𐐨𐑁𐐬𐑉 𐐷𐐭. 𐐚𐐯𐑉𐐮𐑊𐐨, 𐑂𐐯𐑉𐐮𐑊𐐨, 𐐌 𐑅𐐩 𐐲𐑌𐐻𐐭 𐐷𐐭, 𐐌 𐑀𐐮𐑂 𐐲𐑌𐐻𐐭 𐐷𐐭 𐐻𐐭 𐐺 𐑄 𐑅𐐫𐑊𐐻 𐐲𐑂 𐑄 𐐲𐑉𐑃; 𐐺𐐲𐐻 𐐮𐑁 𐑄 𐑅𐐫𐑊𐐻 𐑇𐐰𐑊 𐑊𐐭𐑆 𐐮𐐻𐑅 𐑅𐐩𐑂𐐲𐑉, 𐐸𐐶𐐯𐑉-

𐐶𐐮𐑃 𐑇𐐰𐑊 𐑄 𐐲𐑉𐑃 𐐺 𐑅𐐫𐑊𐐻𐐯𐐼? 𐐜 𐑅𐐫𐑊𐐻 𐑇𐐰𐑊 𐐺 𐑄𐐯𐑌𐑅𐑁𐐫𐑉𐑃 𐑀𐐳𐐼 𐑁𐐫𐑉 𐑌𐐲𐑃𐐮𐑍, 𐐺𐐲𐐻 𐐻𐐭 𐐺
𐐿𐐰𐑅𐐻 𐐵𐐻, 𐐰𐑌𐐼 𐐻𐐭 𐐺 𐐻𐑉𐐱𐐼𐑌 𐐲𐑌𐐼𐐲𐑉 𐑁𐐳𐐻 𐐱𐑂 𐑋𐐯𐑌. 𐐚𐐯𐑉𐐮𐑊𐐨, 𐑂𐐯𐑉𐐮𐑊𐐨, 𐐌 𐑅𐐩 𐐲𐑌𐐻𐐭 𐐷𐐭, 𐐌 𐑀𐐮𐑂
𐐲𐑌𐐻𐐭 𐐷𐐭 𐐻𐐭 𐐺 𐑄 𐑊𐐴𐐻 𐐱𐑂 𐑄𐐮𐑅 𐐹𐐨𐐹𐑊. 𐐈 𐑅𐐮𐐻𐐨 𐑄𐐰𐐻 𐐮𐑆 𐑅𐐯𐐻 𐐱𐑌 𐐰 𐐸𐐮𐑊 𐐿𐐰𐑌𐐱𐐻 𐐺 𐐸𐐮𐐼.
𐐒𐐨𐐸𐐬𐑊𐐼, 𐐼𐐭 𐑋𐐯𐑌 𐑊𐐴𐐻 𐐰 𐐿𐐰𐑌𐐼𐑊 𐐰𐑌𐐼 𐐹𐐳𐐻 𐐮𐐻 𐐲𐑌𐐼𐐲𐑉 𐐰 𐐺𐐳𐑇𐐯𐑊? 𐐤𐐩, 𐐺𐐲𐐻 𐐱𐑌 𐐰 𐐿𐐰𐑌𐐼𐑊-
𐑅𐐻𐐮𐐿 𐐰𐑌𐐼 𐐮𐐻 𐑀𐐮𐑂𐐯𐑃 𐑊𐐴𐐻 𐐻𐐭 𐐫𐑊 𐑄𐐰𐐻 𐐪𐑉 𐐮𐑌 𐑄 𐐸𐐵𐑅; 𐑄𐐯𐑉𐑁𐐬𐑉 𐑊𐐯𐐻 𐐷𐐲𐑉 𐑊𐐴𐐻 𐑅𐐬 𐑇𐐴𐑌 𐐺𐐨𐑁𐐬𐑉 𐑄𐐮𐑅 𐐹𐐨𐐹𐑊, 𐑄𐐰𐐻 𐑄𐐩 𐑋𐐩 𐑅𐐨 𐐷𐐲𐑉 𐑀𐐳𐐼 𐐶𐐲𐑉𐐿𐑅 𐐰𐑌𐐼 𐑀𐑊𐐬𐑉𐐮𐑁𐐴 𐐷𐐲𐑉 𐐙𐐪𐑄𐐲𐑉 𐐸𐐭 𐐮𐑆 𐐮𐑌
𐐸𐐯𐑂𐐲𐑌. 𐐛𐐮𐑍𐐿 𐑌𐐱𐐻 𐑄𐐰𐐻 𐐌 𐐰𐑋 𐐿𐐲𐑋 𐐻𐐭 𐐼𐐯𐑅𐐻𐑉𐑎 𐑄 𐑊𐐫 𐐫𐑉 𐑄 𐐹𐑉𐐱𐑁𐐯𐐻𐑅. 𐐌 𐐰𐑋 𐑌𐐱𐐻 𐐿𐐲𐑋
𐐻𐐭 𐐼𐐯𐑅𐐻𐑉𐑎 𐐺𐐲𐐻 𐐻𐐭 𐑁𐐳𐑊𐑁𐐮𐑊; 𐑁𐐫𐑉 𐑂𐐯𐑉𐐮𐑊𐐨 𐐌 𐑅𐐩 𐐲𐑌𐐻𐐭 𐐷𐐭, 𐐶𐐲𐑌 𐐾𐐱𐐻 𐑌𐐫𐑉 𐐶𐐲𐑌 𐐻𐐮𐐻𐑊 𐐸𐐰𐑃 𐑌𐐱𐐻
𐐹𐐰𐑅𐐻 𐐲𐐶𐐩 𐑁𐑉𐐱𐑋 𐑄 𐑊𐐫, 𐐺𐐲𐐻 𐐮𐑌 𐑋𐐨 𐐮𐐻 𐐸𐐰𐑃 𐐫𐑊 𐐺𐐮𐑌 𐑁𐐳𐑊𐑁𐐮𐑊𐐼.

10. 𐐈𐑌𐐼 𐐺𐐨𐐸𐐬𐑊𐐼 𐐌 𐐸𐐰𐑂 𐑀𐐮𐑂𐑌 𐐷𐐭 𐑄 𐑊𐐫 𐐰𐑌𐐼 𐑄 𐐿𐐱𐑋𐐰𐑌𐐼𐑋𐐯𐑌𐐻𐑅 𐐱𐑂 𐑋𐐴 𐐙𐐪𐑄𐐲𐑉, 𐑄𐐰𐐻
𐐷 𐑇𐐰𐑊 𐐺𐐨𐑊𐐨𐑂 𐐮𐑌 𐑋𐐨, 𐐰𐑌𐐼 𐑄𐐰𐐻 𐐷 𐑇𐐰𐑊 𐑉𐐨𐐹𐐯𐑌𐐻 𐐱𐑂 𐐷𐐲𐑉 𐑅𐐮𐑌𐑆, 𐐰𐑌𐐼 𐐿𐐲𐑋 𐐲𐑌𐐻𐐭 𐑋𐐨 𐐶𐐮𐑄 𐐰
𐐺𐑉𐐬𐐿𐑌 𐐸𐐪𐑉𐐻 𐐰𐑌𐐼 𐐰 𐐿𐐱𐑌𐐻𐑉𐐴𐐻 𐑅𐐹𐐮𐑉𐐮𐐻. 𐐒𐐨𐐸𐐬𐑊𐐼, 𐐷 𐐸𐐰𐑂 𐑄 𐐿𐐱𐑋𐐰𐑌𐐼𐑋𐐯𐑌𐐻𐑅 𐐺𐐨𐑁𐐬𐑉 𐐷𐐭,
𐐰𐑌𐐼 𐑄 𐑊𐐫 𐐮𐑆 𐑁𐐳𐑊𐑁𐐮𐑊𐐼; 𐑄𐐯𐑉𐑁𐐬𐑉 𐐿𐐲𐑋 𐐲𐑌𐐻𐐭 𐑋𐐨 𐐰𐑌𐐼 𐐺 𐐷 𐑅𐐩𐑂𐐼; 𐑁𐐫𐑉 𐑂𐐯𐑉𐐮𐑊𐐨 𐐌 𐑅𐐩 𐐲𐑌𐐻𐐭
𐐷𐐭, 𐑄𐐰𐐻 𐐯𐐿𐑅𐐯𐐹𐐻 𐐷 𐑇𐐰𐑊 𐐿𐐨𐐹 𐑋𐐴 𐐿𐐱𐑋𐐰𐑌𐐼𐑋𐐯𐑌𐐻𐑅, 𐐸𐐶𐐮𐐽 𐐌 𐐸𐐰𐑂 𐐿𐐱𐑋𐐰𐑌𐐼𐐯𐐼 𐐷𐐭 𐐰𐐻 𐑄𐐮𐑅
𐐻𐐴𐑋, 𐐷 𐑇𐐰𐑊 𐐮𐑌 𐑌𐐬 𐐿𐐩𐑅 𐐯𐑌𐐻𐐲𐑉 𐐮𐑌𐐻𐐭 𐑄 𐐿𐐮𐑍𐐼𐐲𐑋 𐐱𐑂 𐐸𐐯𐑂𐐲𐑌. 𐐏 𐐸𐐰𐑂 𐐸𐐲𐑉𐐼 𐑄𐐰𐐻 𐐮𐐻 𐐸𐐰𐑃
𐐺𐐮𐑌 𐑅𐐯𐐼 𐐺𐐴 𐑄𐐯𐑋 𐐱𐑂 𐐬𐑊𐐼 𐐻𐐴𐑋, 𐐰𐑌𐐼 𐐮𐐻 𐐮𐑆 𐐫𐑊𐑅𐐬 𐑉𐐮𐐻𐑌 𐐺𐐨𐑁𐐬𐑉 𐐷𐐭, 𐑄𐐰𐐻 𐑄𐐵 𐑇𐐰𐑊𐐻 𐑌𐐱𐐻
𐐿𐐮𐑊; 𐐰𐑌𐐼 𐐸𐐭𐑅𐐬𐐯𐑂𐐲𐑉 𐑇𐐰𐑊 𐐿𐐮𐑊 𐑇𐐰𐑊 𐐺 𐐮𐑌 𐐼𐐩𐑌𐐾𐐲𐑉 𐐱𐑂 𐑄 𐐾𐐲𐐾𐑋𐐯𐑌𐐻 𐐱𐑂 𐐘𐐱𐐼. 𐐒𐐲𐐻 𐐌 𐑅𐐩
𐐲𐑌𐐻𐐭 𐐷𐐭, 𐑄𐐰𐐻 𐐸𐐭𐑅𐐬𐐯𐑂𐐲𐑉 𐐮𐑆 𐐰𐑍𐑀𐑉𐐨 𐐶𐐮𐑄 𐐸𐐮𐑆 𐐺𐑉𐐲𐑄𐐲𐑉, 𐑇𐐰𐑊 𐐺 𐐮𐑌 𐐼𐐩𐑌𐐾𐐲𐑉 𐐱𐑂 𐐸𐐮𐑆 𐐾𐐲𐐾𐑋𐐯𐑌𐐻. 𐐈𐑌𐐼 𐐸𐐭𐑅𐐬𐐯𐑂𐐲𐑉 𐑇𐐰𐑊 𐑅𐐩 𐐻𐐭 𐐸𐐮𐑆 𐐺𐑉𐐲𐑄𐐲𐑉, 𐐡𐐪𐐿𐐪, 𐑇𐐰𐑊 𐐺 𐐮𐑌 𐐼𐐩𐑌𐐾𐐲𐑉 𐐱𐑂 𐑄
𐐿𐐵𐑌𐑅𐐮𐑊; 𐐰𐑌𐐼 𐐸𐐭𐑅𐐬𐐯𐑂𐐲𐑉 𐑇𐐰𐑊 𐑅𐐩 𐐜𐐵 𐑁𐐭𐑊, 𐑇𐐰𐑊 𐐺 𐐮𐑌 𐐼𐐩𐑌𐐾𐐲𐑉 𐐱𐑂 𐐸𐐯𐑊 𐑁𐐴𐑉; 𐑄𐐯𐑉𐑁𐐬𐑉, 𐐮𐑁
𐐷 𐑇𐐰𐑊 𐐿𐐲𐑋 𐐲𐑌𐐻𐐭 𐑋𐐨, 𐐫𐑉 𐑇𐐰𐑊 𐐼𐐨𐑆𐐴𐑉 𐐻𐐭 𐐿𐐲𐑋 𐐲𐑌𐐻𐐭 𐑋𐐨, 𐐰𐑌𐐼 𐑉𐐨𐑋𐐯𐑋𐐺𐐲𐑉𐐯𐑅𐐻 𐑄𐐰𐐻 𐑄𐐴
𐐺𐑉𐐲𐑄𐐲𐑉 𐐸𐐰𐑃 𐐫𐐻 𐐲𐑀𐐯𐑌𐑅𐐻 𐑄𐐨, 𐑀𐐬 𐑄𐐴 𐐶𐐩 𐐲𐑌𐐻𐐭 𐑄𐐴 𐐺𐑉𐐲𐑄𐐲𐑉, 𐐰𐑌𐐼 𐑁𐐲𐑉𐑅𐐻 𐐺 𐑉𐐯𐐿𐐲𐑌𐑅𐐴𐑊𐐼 𐐻𐐭
𐑄𐐴 𐐺𐑉𐐲𐑄𐐲𐑉, 𐐰𐑌𐐼 𐑄𐐯𐑌 𐐿𐐲𐑋 𐐲𐑌𐐻𐐭 𐑋𐐨 𐐶𐐮𐑄 𐑁𐐳𐑊 𐐹𐐲𐑉𐐹𐐲𐑅 𐐱𐑂 𐐸𐐪𐑉𐐻, 𐐰𐑌𐐼 𐐌 𐐶𐐮𐑊 𐑉𐐨𐑅𐐨𐑂 𐐷𐐭.
𐐈𐑀𐑉𐐨 𐐶𐐮𐑄 𐑄𐐴𐑌 𐐰𐐼𐑂𐐲𐑉𐑅𐐯𐑉𐐨 𐐿𐐶𐐮𐐿𐑊𐐨 𐐸𐐶𐐴𐑊 𐑄𐐵 𐐪𐑉𐐻 𐐮𐑌 𐑄 𐐶𐐩 𐐶𐐮𐑄 𐐸𐐮𐑋, 𐑊𐐯𐑅𐐻 𐐰𐐻 𐐯𐑌𐐨 𐐻𐐴𐑋
𐐸𐐨 𐑇𐐰𐑊 𐑀𐐯𐐻 𐑄𐐨, 𐐰𐑌𐐼 𐑄𐐵 𐑇𐐰𐑊𐐻 𐐺 𐐿𐐰𐑅𐐻 𐐮𐑌𐐻𐐭 𐐹𐑉𐐮𐑆𐑌. 𐐚𐐯𐑉𐐮𐑊𐐨, 𐑂𐐯𐑉𐐮𐑊𐐨 𐐌 𐑅𐐩 𐐲𐑌𐐻𐐭 𐑄𐐨, 𐑄𐐵
𐑇𐐰𐑊𐐻 𐐺𐐴 𐑌𐐬 𐑋𐐨𐑌𐑆 𐐿𐐲𐑋 𐐵𐐻 𐑄𐐯𐑌𐑅 𐐲𐑌𐐻𐐮𐑊 𐑄𐐵 𐐸𐐰𐑅𐐻 𐐹𐐩𐐼 𐑄 𐐲𐐻𐐲𐑉𐑋𐐬𐑅𐐻 𐑅𐐨𐑌𐐴𐑌. 𐐈𐑌𐐼 𐐸𐐶𐐴𐑊
𐐷 𐐪𐑉 𐐮𐑌 𐐹𐑉𐐮𐑆𐑌, 𐐿𐐰𐑌 𐐷 𐐹𐐩 𐐨𐑂𐑌 𐐶𐐲𐑌 𐑅𐐨𐑌𐐴𐑌? 𐐚𐐯𐑉𐐮𐑊𐐨, 𐑂𐐯𐑉𐐮𐑊𐐨 𐐌 𐑅𐐩 𐐲𐑌𐐻𐐭 𐐷𐐭, 𐐤𐐩.
𐐒𐐨𐐸𐐬𐑊𐐼, 𐐮𐐻 𐐮𐑆 𐑉𐐮𐐻𐑌 𐐺𐐴 𐑄𐐯𐑋 𐐱𐑂 𐐬𐑊𐐼 𐐻𐐴𐑋, 𐑄𐐰𐐻 𐑄𐐵 𐑇𐐰𐑊𐐻 𐑌𐐱𐐻 𐐿𐐱𐑋𐐮𐐻 𐐰𐐼𐐲𐑊𐐻𐐲𐑉𐐨; 𐐺𐐲𐐻 𐐌
𐑅𐐩 𐐲𐑌𐐻𐐭 𐐷𐐭, 𐑄𐐰𐐻 𐐸𐐭𐑅𐐬𐐯𐑂𐐲𐑉 𐑊𐐳𐐿𐐯𐑃 𐐱𐑌 𐐰 𐐶𐐳𐑋𐐲𐑌, 𐐻𐐭 𐑊𐐲𐑅𐐻 𐐰𐑁𐐻𐐲𐑉 𐐸𐐲𐑉, 𐐸𐐰𐑃 𐐿𐐱𐑋𐐮𐐻𐐯𐐼
𐐰𐐼𐐲𐑊𐐻𐐲𐑉𐐨 𐐫𐑊𐑉𐐯𐐼𐐨 𐐮𐑌 𐐸𐐮𐑆 𐐸𐐪𐑉𐐻. 𐐒𐐨𐐸𐐬𐑊𐐼, 𐐌 𐑀𐐮𐑂 𐐲𐑌𐐻𐐭 𐐷𐐭 𐐰 𐐿𐐱𐑋𐐰𐑌𐐼𐑋𐐯𐑌𐐻, 𐑄𐐰𐐻 𐐷
𐑅𐐲𐑁𐐲𐑉 𐑌𐐲𐑌 𐐱𐑂 𐑄𐐨𐑆 𐑃𐐮𐑍𐑆 𐐻𐐭 𐐯𐑌𐐻𐐲𐑉 𐐮𐑌𐐻𐐭 𐐷𐐲𐑉 𐐸𐐪𐑉𐐻; 𐑁𐐫𐑉 𐐮𐐻 𐐮𐑆 𐐺𐐯𐐻𐐲𐑉 𐑄𐐰𐐻 𐐷 𐑇𐐳𐐼
𐐼𐐨𐑌𐐴 𐐷𐐲𐑉𐑅𐐯𐑊𐑂𐑆 𐐱𐑂 𐑄𐐨𐑆 𐑃𐐮𐑍𐑆, 𐐸𐐶𐐯𐑉𐐮𐑌 𐐷 𐐶𐐮𐑊 𐐻𐐩𐐿 𐐲𐐹 𐐷𐐲𐑉 𐐿𐑉𐐱𐑅, 𐑄𐐰𐑌 𐑄𐐰𐐻 𐐷 𐑇𐐳𐐼 𐐺
𐐿𐐰𐑅𐐻 𐐮𐑌𐐻𐐭 𐐸𐐯𐑊. 𐐆𐐻 𐐸𐐰𐑃 𐐺𐐮𐑌 𐑉𐐮𐐻𐑌, 𐑄𐐰𐐻 𐐸𐐭𐑅𐐬𐐯𐑂𐐲𐑉 𐑇𐐰𐑊 𐐹𐐳𐐻 𐐲𐐶𐐩 𐐸𐐮𐑆 𐐶𐐴𐑁, 𐑊𐐯𐐻 𐐸𐐮𐑋
𐑀𐐮𐑂 𐐸𐐲𐑉 𐐰 𐑉𐐴𐐻𐐮𐑍 𐐱𐑂 𐐼𐐮𐑂𐐬𐑉𐑅𐑋𐐯𐑌𐐻. 𐐚𐐯𐑉𐐮𐑊𐐨, 𐑂𐐯𐑉𐐮𐑊𐐨 𐐌 𐑅𐐩 𐐲𐑌𐐻𐐭 𐐷𐐭, 𐑄𐐰𐐻 𐐸𐐭𐑅𐐬𐐯𐑂𐐲𐑉
𐑇𐐰𐑊 𐐹𐐳𐐻 𐐲𐐶𐐩 𐐸𐐮𐑆 𐐶𐐴𐑁, 𐑅𐐩𐑂𐐮𐑍 𐑁𐐫𐑉 𐑄 𐐿𐐫𐑆 𐐱𐑂 𐑁𐐫𐑉𐑌𐐮𐐿𐐩𐑇𐐲𐑌, 𐐿𐐫𐑆𐐯𐑃 𐐸𐐲𐑉 𐐻𐐭 𐐿𐐱𐑋𐐮𐐻
𐐰𐐼𐐲𐑊𐐻𐐲𐑉𐐨; 𐐰𐑌𐐼 𐐸𐐭𐑅𐐬 𐑇𐐰𐑊 𐑋𐐰𐑉𐐨 𐐸𐐲𐑉 𐐸𐐭 𐐮𐑆 𐐼𐐮𐑂𐐬𐑉𐑅𐐯𐐼, 𐐿𐐱𐑋𐐮𐐻𐐯𐑃 𐐰𐐼𐐲𐑊𐐻𐐲𐑉𐐨.

11. 𐐈𐑌𐐼 𐐲𐑀𐐯𐑌 𐐮𐐻 𐐮𐑆 𐑉𐐮𐐻𐑌, 𐑄𐐵 𐑇𐐰𐑊𐐻 𐑌𐐱𐐻 𐑁𐐫𐑉𐑅𐐶𐐯𐑉 𐑄𐐴𐑅𐐯𐑊𐑁, 𐐺𐐲𐐻 𐑇𐐰𐑊𐐻 𐐹𐐲𐑉𐑁𐐫𐑉𐑋 𐐲𐑌𐐻𐐭
𐑄 𐐢𐐫𐑉𐐼 𐑄𐐴𐑌 𐐬𐑃𐑅. 𐐒𐐲𐐻 𐑂𐐯𐑉𐐮𐑊𐐨, 𐑂𐐯𐑉𐐮𐑊𐐨 𐐌 𐑅𐐩 𐐲𐑌𐐻𐐭 𐐷𐐭, 𐐝𐐶𐐯𐑉 𐑌𐐱𐐻 𐐰𐐻 𐐫𐑊; 𐑌𐐨𐑄𐐲𐑉 𐐺𐐴
𐐸𐐯𐑂𐐲𐑌, 𐑁𐐫𐑉 𐐮𐐻 𐐮𐑆 𐐘𐐱𐐼'𐑆 𐑃𐑉𐐬𐑌; 𐑌𐐫𐑉 𐐺𐐴 𐑄 𐐲𐑉𐑃, 𐑁𐐫𐑉 𐐮𐐻 𐐮𐑆 𐐸𐐮𐑆 𐑁𐐳𐐻𐑅𐐻𐐭𐑊; 𐑌𐐨𐑄𐐲𐑉 𐑇𐐰𐑊𐐻
𐑄𐐵 𐑅𐐶𐐯𐑉 𐐺𐐴 𐑄𐐴 𐐸𐐯𐐼, 𐐺𐐨𐐿𐐫𐑆 𐑄𐐵 𐐿𐐰𐑌𐑅𐐻 𐑌𐐱𐐻 𐑋𐐩𐐿 𐐶𐐲𐑌 𐐸𐐯𐑉 𐐺𐑊𐐰𐐿 𐐫𐑉 𐐸𐐶𐐴𐐻; 𐐺𐐲𐐻 𐑊𐐯𐐻
𐐷𐐲𐑉 𐐿𐐱𐑋𐐷𐐭𐑌𐐮𐐿𐐩𐑇𐐲𐑌 𐐺 𐐏𐐩, 𐐷𐐩; 𐐤𐐩, 𐑌𐐩; 𐑁𐐫𐑉 𐐸𐐶𐐱𐐻𐑅𐐬𐐯𐑂𐐲𐑉 𐐿𐐲𐑋𐐯𐑃 𐐱𐑂 𐑋𐐬𐑉 𐑄𐐰𐑌 𐑄𐐨𐑆 𐐮𐑆

𐐮𐑆 𐐨𐑂𐐮𐑊. 𐐈𐑌𐐼 𐐺𐐨𐐸𐐬𐑊𐐼, 𐐮𐐻 𐐮𐑆 𐑉𐐮𐐻𐑌, 𐐰𐑌 𐐴 𐑁𐐫𐑉 𐐰𐑌 𐐴, 𐐰𐑌𐐼 𐐲 𐐻𐐭𐑃 𐑁𐐫𐑉 𐐲 𐐻𐐭𐑃. 𐐒𐐲𐐻 𐐌 𐑅𐐩 𐐲𐑌𐐻𐐭 𐐷𐐭, 𐑄𐐰𐐻 𐐷𐐨 𐑇𐐰𐑊 𐑌𐐪𐐻 𐑉𐐨𐑆𐐮𐑅𐐻 𐐨𐑂𐐮𐑊, 𐐺𐐲𐐻 𐐸𐐭𐑅𐐬𐐯𐑂𐐯𐑉 𐑇𐐰𐑊 𐑅𐑋𐐴𐐻 𐑄𐐨 𐐪𐑌 𐑄𐐴 𐑉𐐴𐐻 𐐽𐐨𐐿, 𐐻𐐲𐑉𐑌 𐐻𐐭 𐐸𐐮𐑋 𐑄 𐐲𐑄𐐲𐑉 𐐫𐑊𐑅𐐬. 𐐈𐑌𐐼 𐐮𐑁 𐐯𐑌𐐨 𐑋𐐰𐑌 𐐶𐐮𐑊 𐑅𐐭 𐑄𐐨 𐐰𐐻 𐑄 𐑊𐐫, 𐐰𐑌𐐼 𐐻𐐩𐐿 𐐲𐐶𐐩 𐑄𐐴 𐐿𐐬𐐻, 𐑊𐐯𐐻 𐐸𐐮𐑋 𐐸𐐰𐑂 𐑄𐐴 𐐿𐑊𐐬𐐿 𐐫𐑊𐑅𐐬. 𐐈𐑌𐐼 𐐸𐐭𐑅𐐬𐐯𐑂𐐯𐑉 𐑇𐐰𐑊 𐐿𐐪𐑋𐐹𐐯𐑊 𐑄𐐨 𐐻𐐭 𐑀𐐬 𐐲 𐑋𐐴𐑊, 𐑀𐐬 𐐶𐐮𐑄 𐐸𐐮𐑋 𐐻𐐶𐐩𐑌. 𐐘𐐮𐑂 𐐻𐐭 𐐸𐐮𐑋 𐑄𐐰𐐻 𐐰𐑅𐐿𐐯𐑃 𐑄𐐨, 𐐰𐑌𐐼 𐐻𐐭 𐐸𐐮𐑋 𐑄𐐰𐐻 𐐶𐐳𐐼 𐐺𐐪𐑉𐐬 𐐱𐑂 𐑄𐐨 𐐻𐐲𐑉𐑌 𐑄𐐵 𐑌𐐪𐐻 𐐲𐐶𐐩. 𐐈𐑌𐐼 𐐺𐐨𐐸𐐬𐑊𐐼, 𐐮𐐻 𐐮𐑆 𐑉𐐮𐐻𐑌 𐐫𐑊𐑅𐐬, 𐑄𐐰𐐻 𐑄𐐵 𐑇𐐰𐑊𐐻 𐑊𐐲𐑂 𐑄𐐴 𐑌𐐩𐐺𐐲𐑉, 𐐰𐑌𐐼 𐐸𐐩𐐻 𐑄𐐴𐑌 𐐯𐑌𐐯𐑋𐐨; 𐐺𐐲𐐻 𐐺𐐨𐐸𐐬𐑊𐐼 𐐌 𐑅𐐩 𐐲𐑌𐐻𐐭 𐐷𐐭, 𐑊𐐲𐑂 𐐷𐐭𐑉 𐐯𐑌𐐯𐑋𐐨𐑆, 𐐺𐑊𐐯𐑅 𐑄𐐯𐑋 𐑄𐐰𐐻 𐐿𐐲𐑉𐑅 𐐷𐐭, 𐐼𐐭 𐑀𐐳𐐼 𐐻𐐭 𐑄𐐯𐑋 𐑄𐐰𐐻 𐐸𐐩𐐻 𐐷𐐭, 𐐰𐑌𐐼 𐐹𐑉𐐩 𐑁𐐫𐑉 𐑄𐐯𐑋 𐐸𐐭 𐐼𐐯𐑅𐐹𐐴𐐻𐑁𐐳𐑊𐐨 𐐷𐐭𐑆 𐐷𐐭 𐐰𐑌𐐼 𐐹𐐲𐑉𐑅𐐨𐐿𐐷𐐭𐐻 𐐷𐐭; 𐑄𐐰𐐻 𐐷𐐨 𐑋𐐩 𐐺𐐨 𐑄 𐐽𐐮𐑊𐐼𐑉𐐯𐑌 𐐱𐑂 𐐷𐐭𐑉 𐐙𐐪𐑄𐐲𐑉 𐐸𐐭 𐐮𐑆 𐐮𐑌 𐐸𐐯𐑂𐐲𐑌; 𐑁𐐫𐑉 𐐸𐐨 𐑋𐐩𐐿𐐯𐑃 𐐸𐐮𐑆 𐑅𐐲𐑌 𐐻𐐭 𐑉𐐴𐑆 𐐪𐑌 𐑄 𐐨𐑂𐐮𐑊 𐐰𐑌𐐼 𐐪𐑌 𐑄 𐑀𐐳𐐼; 𐑄𐐯𐑉𐑁𐐫𐑉 𐑄𐐬𐑆 𐑃𐐮𐑍𐑆 𐐸𐐶𐐮𐐽 𐐶𐐲𐑉 𐐱𐑂 𐐬𐑊𐐼 𐐻𐐴𐑋, 𐐸𐐶𐐮𐐽 𐐶𐐲𐑉 𐐲𐑌𐐼𐐲𐑉 𐑄 𐑊𐐫, 𐐮𐑌 𐑋𐐨 𐐪𐑉 𐐫𐑊 𐑁𐐳𐑊𐑁𐐮𐑊𐐼. 𐐄𐑊𐐼 𐑃𐐮𐑍𐑆 𐐪𐑉 𐐼𐐲𐑌 𐐲𐐶𐐩, 𐐰𐑌𐐼 𐐫𐑊 𐑃𐐮𐑍𐑆 𐐸𐐰𐑂 𐐺𐐨𐐿𐐲𐑋 𐑌𐐭; 𐑄𐐯𐑉𐑁𐐫𐑉 𐐌 𐐶𐐳𐐼 𐑄𐐰𐐻 𐐷𐐨 𐑇𐐳𐐼 𐐺𐐨 𐐹𐐲𐑉𐑁𐐯𐐿𐐻 𐐨𐑂𐐲𐑌 𐐰𐑆 𐐌, 𐐫𐑉 𐐷𐐭𐑉 𐐙𐐪𐑄𐐲𐑉 𐐸𐐭 𐐮𐑆 𐐮𐑌 𐐸𐐯𐑂𐐲𐑌 𐐮𐑆 𐐹𐐲𐑉𐑁𐐯𐐿𐐻. 𐐚𐐯𐑉𐐮𐑊𐐨, 𐑂𐐯𐑉𐐮𐑊𐐨, 𐐌 𐑅𐐩 𐑄𐐰𐐻 𐐌 𐐶𐐳𐐼 𐑄𐐰𐐻 𐐷𐐨 𐑇𐐳𐐼 𐐼𐐭 𐐪𐑋𐑆 𐐲𐑌𐐻𐐭 𐑄 𐐹𐐭𐑉; 𐐺𐐲𐐻 𐐻𐐩𐐿 𐐸𐐨𐐼 𐑄𐐰𐐻 𐐷𐐨 𐐼𐐭 𐑌𐐪𐐻 𐐷𐐭𐑉 𐐪𐑋𐑆 𐐺𐐨𐑁𐐬𐑉 𐑋𐐯𐑌 𐐻𐐭 𐐺𐐨 𐑅𐐨𐑌 𐐱𐑂 𐑄𐐯𐑋; 𐐲𐑄𐐲𐑉𐐶𐐴𐑆 𐐷𐐨 𐐸𐐰𐑂 𐑌𐐬 𐑉𐐨𐐶𐐫𐑉𐐼 𐐱𐑂 𐐷𐐭𐑉 𐐙𐐪𐑄𐐲𐑉 𐐸𐐭 𐐮𐑆 𐐮𐑌 𐐸𐐯𐑂𐐲𐑌. 𐐜𐐯𐑉𐑁𐐫𐑉, 𐐸𐐶𐐯𐑌 𐐷𐐨 𐑇𐐰𐑊 𐐼𐐭 𐐷𐐭𐑉 𐐪𐑋𐑆, 𐐼𐐭 𐑌𐐪𐐻 𐑅𐐵𐑌𐐼 𐐲 𐐻𐑉𐐲𐑋𐐹𐐯𐐻 𐐺𐐨𐑁𐐬𐑉 𐐷𐐭, 𐐰𐑆 𐐶𐐮𐑊 𐐸𐐮𐐹𐐬𐐿𐑉𐐮𐐻𐑅 𐐼𐐭 𐐮𐑌 𐑄 𐑅𐐮𐑌𐐲𐑀𐐪𐑀𐑆 𐐰𐑌𐐼 𐐮𐑌 𐑄 𐑅𐐻𐑉𐐨𐐻𐑅, 𐑄𐐰𐐻 𐑄𐐩 𐑋𐐩 𐐸𐐰𐑂 𐑀𐑊𐐬𐑉𐐨 𐐱𐑂 𐑋𐐯𐑌. 𐐚𐐯𐑉𐐮𐑊𐐨 𐐌 𐑅𐐩 𐐲𐑌𐐻𐐭 𐐷𐐭, 𐑄𐐩 𐐸𐐰𐑂 𐑄𐐯𐑉 𐑉𐐨𐐶𐐫𐑉𐐼. 𐐒𐐲𐐻 𐐸𐐶𐐯𐑌 𐑄𐐵 𐐼𐐭𐐯𐑅𐐻 𐐪𐑋𐑆, 𐑊𐐯𐐻 𐑌𐐪𐐻 𐑄𐐴 𐑊𐐯𐑁𐐻 𐐸𐐰𐑌𐐼 𐑌𐐬 𐐸𐐶𐐪𐐻 𐑄𐐴 𐑉𐐴𐐻 𐐸𐐰𐑌𐐼 𐐼𐐭𐐯𐑃; 𐑄𐐰𐐻 𐑄𐐴𐑌 𐐪𐑋𐑆 𐑋𐐩 𐐺𐐨 𐐮𐑌 𐑅𐐨𐐿𐑉𐐯𐐻; 𐐰𐑌𐐼 𐑄𐐴 𐐙𐐪𐑄𐐲𐑉 𐐸𐐭 𐑅𐐨𐐯𐑃 𐐮𐑌 𐑅𐐨𐐿𐑉𐐯𐐻, 𐐸𐐮𐑋𐑅𐐯𐑊𐑁 𐑇𐐰𐑊 𐑉𐐨𐐶𐐫𐑉𐐼 𐑄𐐨 𐐬𐐹𐐲𐑌𐑊𐐨.

12. 𐐈𐑌𐐼 𐐸𐐶𐐯𐑌 𐑄𐐵 𐐹𐑉𐐩𐐯𐑅𐐻, 𐑄𐐵 𐑇𐐰𐑊𐐻 𐑌𐐪𐐻 𐐼𐐭 𐐰𐑆 𐑄 𐐸𐐮𐐹𐐬𐐿𐑉𐐮𐐻𐑅, 𐑁𐐫𐑉 𐑄𐐩 𐑊𐐲𐑂 𐐻𐐭 𐐹𐑉𐐩, 𐑅𐐻𐐰𐑌𐐼𐐮𐑍 𐐮𐑌 𐑄 𐑅𐐮𐑌𐐲𐑀𐐪𐑀𐑆, 𐐰𐑌𐐼 𐐮𐑌 𐑄 𐐿𐐫𐑉𐑌𐐲𐑉𐑆 𐐱𐑂 𐑄 𐑅𐐻𐑉𐐨𐐻𐑅, 𐑄𐐰𐐻 𐑄𐐩 𐑋𐐩 𐐺𐐨 𐑅𐐨𐑌 𐐱𐑂 𐑋𐐯𐑌. 𐐚𐐯𐑉𐐮𐑊𐐨 𐐌 𐑅𐐩 𐐲𐑌𐐻𐐭 𐐷𐐭, 𐑄𐐩 𐐸𐐰𐑂 𐑄𐐯𐑉 𐑉𐐨𐐶𐐫𐑉𐐼. 𐐒𐐲𐐻 𐑄𐐵, 𐐸𐐶𐐯𐑌 𐑄𐐵 𐐹𐑉𐐩𐐯𐑅𐐻, 𐐯𐑌𐐻𐐲𐑉 𐐮𐑌𐐻𐐭 𐑄𐐴 𐐿𐑊𐐪𐑆𐐯𐐻, 𐐰𐑌𐐼 𐐸𐐶𐐯𐑌 𐑄𐐵 𐐸𐐰𐑅𐐻 𐑇𐐲𐐻 𐑄𐐴 𐐼𐐬𐑉, 𐐹𐑉𐐩 𐐻𐐭 𐑄𐐴 𐐙𐐪𐑄𐐲𐑉 𐐸𐐭 𐐮𐑆 𐐮𐑌 𐑅𐐨𐐿𐑉𐐯𐐻; 𐐰𐑌𐐼 𐑄𐐴 𐐙𐐪𐑄𐐲𐑉, 𐐸𐐭 𐑅𐐨𐐯𐑃 𐐮𐑌 𐑅𐐨𐐿𐑉𐐯𐐻, 𐑇𐐰𐑊 𐑉𐐨𐐶𐐫𐑉𐐼 𐑄𐐨 𐐬𐐹𐐲𐑌𐑊𐐨. 𐐒𐐲𐐻 𐐸𐐶𐐯𐑌 𐐷𐐨 𐐹𐑉𐐩, 𐐷𐐭𐑆 𐑌𐐪𐐻 𐑂𐐩𐑌 𐑉𐐯𐐹𐐯𐐻𐐮𐑇𐐲𐑌𐑆, 𐐰𐑆 𐑄 𐐸𐐨𐑄𐐲𐑌, 𐑁𐐫𐑉 𐑄𐐩 𐑃𐐮𐑍𐐿 𐑄𐐰𐐻 𐑄𐐩 𐑇𐐰𐑊 𐐺𐐨 𐐸𐐲𐑉𐐼 𐑁𐐫𐑉 𐑄𐐯𐑉 𐑋𐐲𐐽 𐑅𐐹𐐨𐐿𐐮𐑍. 𐐒𐐨 𐑌𐐪𐐻 𐐷𐐨 𐑄𐐯𐑉𐑁𐐫𐑉 𐑊𐐴𐐿 𐐲𐑌𐐻𐐭 𐑄𐐯𐑋, 𐑁𐐫𐑉 𐐷𐐭𐑉 𐐙𐐪𐑄𐐲𐑉 𐑌𐐬𐐯𐑃 𐐸𐐶𐐪𐐻 𐑃𐐮𐑍𐑆 𐐷𐐨 𐐸𐐰𐑂 𐑌𐐨𐐼 𐐱𐑂 𐐺𐐨𐑁𐐬𐑉 𐐷𐐨 𐐰𐑅𐐿 𐐸𐐮𐑋. 𐐂𐑁𐐻𐐲𐑉 𐑄𐐮𐑅 𐑋𐐰𐑌𐐲𐑉 𐑄𐐯𐑉𐑁𐐫𐑉 𐐹𐑉𐐩 𐐷𐐨: 𐐍𐐲𐑉 𐐙𐐪𐑄𐐲𐑉 𐐸𐐭 𐐪𐑉𐐻 𐐮𐑌 𐐸𐐯𐑂𐐲𐑌, 𐐸𐐰𐑊𐐬𐐲𐐼 𐐺𐐨 𐑄𐐴 𐑌𐐩𐑋. 𐐜𐐴 𐐶𐐮𐑊 𐐺𐐨 𐐼𐐲𐑌 𐐪𐑌 𐐲𐑉𐑃, 𐐰𐑆 𐐮𐐻 𐐮𐑆 𐐮𐑌 𐐸𐐯𐑂𐐲𐑌. 𐐈𐑌𐐼 𐑁𐐫𐑉𐑀𐐮𐑂 𐐲𐑅 𐐵𐑉 𐐼𐐯𐐻𐑅, 𐐰𐑆 𐐶𐐨 𐑁𐐫𐑉𐑀𐐮𐑂 𐐵𐑉 𐐼𐐯𐐻𐐲𐑉𐑆. 𐐈𐑌𐐼 𐑊𐐨𐐼 𐐲𐑅 𐑌𐐪𐐻 𐐮𐑌𐐻𐐭 𐐻𐐯𐑋𐐻𐐩𐑇𐐲𐑌, 𐐺𐐲𐐻 𐐼𐐯𐑊𐐮𐑂𐐲𐑉 𐐲𐑅 𐑁𐑉𐐲𐑋 𐐨𐑂𐐮𐑊. 𐐙𐐫𐑉 𐑄𐐴𐑌 𐐮𐑆 𐑄 𐐿𐐮𐑍𐐼𐐲𐑋, 𐐰𐑌𐐼 𐑄 𐐹𐐵𐐲𐑉, 𐐰𐑌𐐼 𐑄 𐑀𐑊𐐬𐑉𐐨, 𐑁𐐫𐑉 𐐯𐑂𐐲𐑉. 𐐁𐑋𐐯𐑌. 𐐙𐐫𐑉, 𐐮𐑁 𐐷𐐨 𐑁𐐫𐑉𐑀𐐮𐑂 𐑋𐐯𐑌 𐑄𐐯𐑉 𐐻𐑉𐐯𐑅𐐹𐐰𐑅𐐲𐑆, 𐐷𐐭𐑉 𐐸𐐯𐑂𐐲𐑌𐑊𐐨 𐐙𐐪𐑄𐐲𐑉 𐐶𐐮𐑊 𐐫𐑊𐑅𐐬 𐑁𐐫𐑉𐑀𐐮𐑂 𐐷𐐭; 𐐺𐐲𐐻 𐐮𐑁 𐐷𐐨 𐑁𐐫𐑉𐑀𐐮𐑂 𐑌𐐪𐐻 𐑋𐐯𐑌 𐑄𐐯𐑉 𐐻𐑉𐐯𐑅𐐹𐐰𐑅𐐲𐑆, 𐑌𐐨𐑄𐐲𐑉 𐐶𐐮𐑊 𐐷𐐭𐑉 𐐙𐐪𐑄𐐲𐑉 𐑁𐐫𐑉𐑀𐐮𐑂 𐐷𐐭𐑉 𐐻𐑉𐐯𐑅𐐹𐐰𐑅𐐲𐑆. 𐐣𐐫𐑉𐐬𐐲𐑂𐐲𐑉, 𐐸𐐶𐐯𐑌 𐐷𐐨 𐑁𐐰𐑅𐐻, 𐐺𐐨 𐑌𐐪𐐻 𐐰𐑆 𐑄 𐐸𐐮𐐹𐐬𐐿𐑉𐐮𐐻𐑅, 𐐱𐑂 𐐲 𐑅𐐰𐐼 𐐿𐐵𐑌𐐻𐐲𐑌𐐲𐑌𐑅, 𐑁𐐫𐑉 𐑄𐐩 𐐼𐐮𐑅𐑁𐐮𐑀𐐷𐐲𐑉 𐑄𐐯𐑉 𐑁𐐩𐑅𐐯𐑆, 𐑄𐐰𐐻 𐑄𐐩 𐑋𐐩 𐐲𐐹𐐨𐑉 𐐲𐑌𐐻𐐭 𐑋𐐯𐑌 𐐻𐐭 𐑁𐐰𐑅𐐻. 𐐚𐐯𐑉𐐮𐑊𐐨, 𐐌 𐑅𐐩 𐐲𐑌𐐻𐐭 𐐷𐐭, 𐑄𐐩 𐐸𐐰𐑂 𐑄𐐯𐑉 𐑉𐐨𐐶𐐫𐑉𐐼. 𐐒𐐲𐐻 𐑄𐐵, 𐐸𐐶𐐯𐑌 𐑄𐐵 𐑁𐐰𐑅𐐻𐐯𐑅𐐻, 𐐰𐑌𐐶𐐴𐑌𐐻 𐑄𐐴 𐐸𐐯𐐼, 𐐰𐑌𐐼 𐐶𐐪𐑇 𐑄𐐴 𐑁𐐩𐑅; 𐑄𐐰𐐻 𐑄𐐵 𐐲𐐹𐐨𐑉 𐑌𐐪𐐻 𐐲𐑌𐐻𐐭 𐑋𐐯𐑌 𐐻𐐭 𐑁𐐰𐑅𐐻, 𐐺𐐲𐐻 𐐲𐑌𐐻𐐭 𐑄𐐴 𐐙𐐪𐑄𐐲𐑉, 𐐸𐐭 𐐮𐑆 𐐮𐑌 𐑅𐐨𐐿𐑉𐐯𐐻; 𐐰𐑌𐐼 𐑄𐐴 𐐙𐐪𐑄𐐲𐑉, 𐐸𐐭 𐑅𐐨𐐯𐑃 𐐮𐑌 𐑅𐐨𐐿𐑉𐐯𐐻, 𐑇𐐰𐑊 𐑉𐐨𐐶𐐫𐑉𐐼 𐑄𐐨 𐐬𐐹𐐲𐑌𐑊𐐨.

13. 𐐢𐐩 𐑌𐐪𐐻 𐐲𐐹 𐑁𐐫𐑉 𐐷𐐭𐑉𐑅𐐯𐑊𐑂𐑆 𐐻𐑉𐐯𐑆𐐷𐐲𐑉𐑆 𐐲𐐹𐐪𐑌 𐐲𐑉𐑃, 𐐸𐐶𐐯𐑉 𐑋𐐫𐑃 𐐰𐑌𐐼 𐑉𐐲𐑅𐐻 𐐼𐐲𐑃 𐐿𐐫𐑉𐐲𐐹𐐻, 𐐰𐑌𐐼 𐑃𐐨𐑂𐑆 𐐺𐑉𐐩𐐿 𐑃𐑉𐐭 𐐰𐑌𐐼 𐑅𐐻𐐨𐑊, 𐐺𐐲𐐻 𐑊𐐩 𐐲𐐹 𐑁𐐫𐑉 𐐷𐐭𐑉𐑅𐐯𐑊𐑂𐑆 𐐻𐑉𐐯𐑆𐐷𐐲𐑉𐑆 𐐮𐑌 𐐸𐐯𐑂𐐲𐑌, 𐐸𐐶𐐯𐑉 𐑌𐐨𐑄𐐲𐑉 𐑋𐐫𐑃 𐑌𐐫𐑉 𐑉𐐲𐑅𐐻 𐐼𐐲𐑃 𐐿𐐫𐑉𐐲𐐹𐐻, 𐐰𐑌𐐼 𐐸𐐶𐐯𐑉 𐑃𐐨𐑂𐑆 𐐼𐐭 𐑌𐐪𐐻 𐐺𐑉𐐩𐐿 𐑃𐑉𐐭 𐑌𐐫𐑉

𐑅𐐻𐐨𐑊. 𐐙𐐫𐑉 𐐸𐐶𐐯𐑉 𐐷𐐭𐑉 𐐻𐑉𐐯𐑈𐐲𐑉 𐐮𐑆, 𐑄𐐯𐑉 𐐶𐐮𐑊 𐐷𐐭𐑉 𐐸𐐪𐑉𐐻 𐐺𐐨 𐐫𐑊𐑅𐐬. 𐐜 𐑊𐐴𐐻 𐐱𐑂 𐑄 𐐺𐐱𐐼𐐨 𐐮𐑆 𐑄 𐐴; 𐐮𐑁 𐑄𐐯𐑉𐑁𐐬𐑉 𐑄𐐴𐑌 𐐴 𐐺𐐨 𐑅𐐮𐑍𐑀𐑊, 𐑄𐐴 𐐸𐐬𐑊 𐐺𐐱𐐼𐐨 𐑇𐐰𐑊 𐐺𐐨 𐑁𐐳𐑊 𐐱𐑂 𐑊𐐴𐐻. 𐐒𐐲𐐻 𐐮𐑁 𐑄𐐴𐑌 𐐴 𐐺𐐨 𐐨𐑂𐐲𐑊, 𐑄𐐴 𐐸𐐬𐑊 𐐺𐐱𐐼𐐨 𐑇𐐰𐑊 𐐺𐐨 𐑁𐐳𐑊 𐐱𐑂 𐐼𐐪𐑉𐐿𐑌𐐯𐑅. 𐐆𐑁, 𐑄𐐯𐑉𐑁𐐬𐑉, 𐑄 𐑊𐐴𐐻 𐑄𐐰𐐻 𐐮𐑆 𐐮𐑌 𐑄𐐨 𐐺𐐨 𐐼𐐪𐑉𐐿𐑌𐐯𐑅, 𐐸𐐵 𐑀𐑉𐐩𐐻 𐐮𐑆 𐑄𐐰𐐻 𐐼𐐪𐑉𐐿𐑌𐐯𐑅! 𐐤𐐬 𐑋𐐰𐑌 𐐿𐐰𐑌 𐑅𐐲𐑉𐑂 𐐻𐐭 𐑋𐐰𐑅𐐻𐐲𐑉𐑆, 𐑁𐐫𐑉 𐐨𐑄𐐲𐑉 𐐸𐐨 𐐶𐐮𐑊 𐐸𐐩𐐻 𐑄 𐐶𐐲𐑌 𐐰𐑌𐐼 𐑊𐐲𐑂 𐑄 𐐲𐑄𐐲𐑉; 𐐫𐑉 𐐯𐑊𐑅 𐐸𐐨 𐐶𐐮𐑊 𐐸𐐬𐑊𐐼 𐐻𐐭 𐑄 𐐶𐐲𐑌 𐐰𐑌𐐼 𐐼𐐯𐑅𐐹𐐴𐑆 𐑄 𐐲𐑄𐐲𐑉. 𐐏 𐐿𐐰𐑌𐐱𐐻 𐑅𐐲𐑉𐑂 𐐘𐐱𐐼 𐐰𐑌𐐼 𐐣𐐰𐑋𐐲𐑌.

𐐕𐐰𐐹𐐻𐐲𐑉 VI.

1. 𐐈𐑌𐐼 𐑌𐐵 𐐮𐐻 𐐿𐐩𐑋 𐐻𐐭 𐐹𐐰𐑅 𐑄𐐰𐐻 𐐸𐐶𐐯𐑌 𐐖𐐨𐑆𐐲𐑅 𐐸𐐰𐐼 𐑅𐐹𐐬𐐿𐐲𐑌 𐑄𐐨𐑆 𐐶𐐲𐑉𐐼𐑆, 𐐸𐐨 𐑊𐐳𐐿𐐻 𐐲𐐹𐐱𐑌 𐑄 𐐻𐐶𐐯𐑊𐑂 𐐸𐐭𐑋 𐐸𐐨 𐐸𐐰𐐼 𐐽𐐬𐑆𐐲𐑌, 𐐰𐑌𐐼 𐑅𐐯𐐼 𐐲𐑌𐐻𐐭 𐑄𐐯𐑋, 𐐡𐐨𐑋𐐯𐑋𐐺𐐲𐑉 𐑄 𐐶𐐲𐑉𐐼𐑆 𐐸𐐶𐐮𐐽 𐐴 𐐸𐐰𐑂 𐑅𐐹𐐬𐐿𐐲𐑌. 𐐙𐐫𐑉 𐐺𐐨𐐸𐐬𐑊𐐼, 𐐷𐐨 𐐪𐑉 𐑄𐐩 𐐸𐐭𐑋 𐐴 𐐸𐐰𐑂 𐐽𐐬𐑆𐐲𐑌 𐐻𐐭 𐑋𐐮𐑌𐐮𐑅𐐻𐐲𐑉 𐐲𐑌𐐻𐐭 𐑄𐐮𐑅 𐐹𐐨𐐹𐑊. 𐐜𐐯𐑉𐑁𐐬𐑉 𐐴 𐑅𐐩 𐐲𐑌𐐻𐐭 𐐷𐐭, 𐐓𐐩𐐿 𐑌𐐬 𐑃𐐫𐐻 𐑁𐐫𐑉 𐐷𐐭𐑉 𐑊𐐴𐑁, 𐐸𐐶𐐱𐐻 𐐷𐐨 𐑇𐐰𐑊 𐐨𐐻, 𐐫𐑉 𐐸𐐶𐐱𐐻 𐐷𐐨 𐑇𐐰𐑊 𐐼𐑉𐐮𐑍𐐿; 𐑌𐐫𐑉 𐐷𐐯𐐻 𐑁𐐫𐑉 𐐷𐐭𐑉 𐐺𐐱𐐼𐐨, 𐐸𐐶𐐱𐐻 𐐷𐐨 𐑇𐐰𐑊 𐐹𐐳𐐻 𐐱𐑌. 𐐆𐑆 𐑌𐐱𐐻 𐑄 𐑊𐐴𐑁 𐑋𐐬𐑉 𐑄𐐰𐑌 𐑋𐐨𐐻, 𐐰𐑌𐐼 𐑄 𐐺𐐱𐐼𐐨 𐑄𐐰𐑌 𐑉𐐩𐑋𐐯𐑌𐐻? 𐐒𐐨𐐸𐐬𐑊𐐼 𐑄 𐑁𐐵𐑊𐑆 𐐱𐑂 𐑄 𐐩𐑉, 𐑁𐐫𐑉 𐑄𐐩 𐑅𐐬 𐑌𐐱𐐻, 𐑌𐐨𐑄𐐲𐑉 𐐼𐐭 𐑄𐐩 𐑉𐐨𐐹, 𐑌𐐫𐑉 𐑀𐐰𐑄𐐲𐑉 𐐮𐑌𐐻𐐭 𐐺𐐪𐑉𐑌𐑆; 𐐷𐐯𐐻 𐐷𐐭𐑉 𐐸𐐯𐑂𐐲𐑌𐑊𐐨 𐐙𐐪𐑄𐐲𐑉 𐑁𐐨𐐼𐐯𐑃 𐑄𐐯𐑋. 𐐂𐑉 𐐷𐐨 𐑌𐐱𐐻 𐑋𐐲𐐽 𐐺𐐯𐐻𐐲𐑉 𐑄𐐰𐑌 𐑄𐐩? 𐐐𐐶𐐮𐐽 𐐱𐑂 𐐷𐐭 𐐺𐐴 𐐻𐐩𐐿𐐮𐑍 𐑃𐐫𐐻 𐐿𐐰𐑌 𐐰𐐼 𐐶𐐲𐑌 𐐿𐐷𐐭𐐺𐐮𐐻 𐐲𐑌𐐻𐐭 𐐸𐐮𐑆 𐑅𐐻𐐰𐐽𐐲𐑉? 𐐈𐑌𐐼 𐐸𐐶𐐴 𐐻𐐩𐐿 𐐷𐐨 𐑃𐐫𐐻 𐑁𐐫𐑉 𐑉𐐩𐑋𐐯𐑌𐐻? 𐐗𐐱𐑌𐑅𐐮𐐼𐐲𐑉 𐑄 𐑊𐐮𐑊𐐮𐑆 𐐱𐑂 𐑄 𐑁𐐨𐑊𐐼, 𐐸𐐵 𐑄𐐩 𐑀𐑉𐐬; 𐑄𐐩 𐐻𐑎𐑊 𐑌𐐱𐐻, 𐑌𐐨𐑄𐐲𐑉 𐐼𐐭 𐑄𐐩 𐑅𐐹𐐮𐑌; 𐐰𐑌𐐼 𐐷𐐯𐐻 𐐴 𐑅𐐩 𐐲𐑌𐐻𐐭 𐐷𐐭, 𐑄𐐰𐐻 𐐨𐑂𐐲𐑌 𐐝𐐱𐑊𐐬𐑋𐐲𐑌, 𐐮𐑌 𐐫𐑊 𐐸𐐮𐑆 𐑀𐑊𐐬𐑉𐐨, 𐐶𐐱𐑆 𐑌𐐱𐐻 𐐲𐑉𐐩𐐼 𐑊𐐴𐐿 𐐶𐐲𐑌 𐐱𐑂 𐑄𐐨𐑆. 𐐐𐐶𐐯𐑉𐑁𐐬𐑉, 𐐮𐑁 𐐘𐐱𐐼 𐑅𐐬 𐐿𐑊𐐬𐑄 𐑄 𐑀𐑉𐐰𐑅 𐐱𐑂 𐑄 𐑁𐐨𐑊𐐼, 𐐸𐐶𐐮𐐽 𐐻𐐭-𐐼𐐩 𐐮𐑆, 𐐰𐑌𐐼 𐐻𐐭-𐑋𐐱𐑉𐐬 𐐮𐑆 𐐿𐐰𐑅𐐻 𐐮𐑌𐐻𐐭 𐑄 𐐲𐑂𐐲𐑌, 𐐨𐑂𐐲𐑌 𐑅𐐬 𐐶𐐮𐑊 𐐸𐐨 𐐿𐑊𐐬𐑄 𐐷𐐭, 𐐮𐑁 𐐷𐐨 𐐪𐑉 𐑌𐐱𐐻 𐐱𐑂 𐑊𐐮𐐻𐑊 𐑁𐐩𐑃. 𐐜𐐯𐑉𐑁𐐬𐑉 𐐻𐐩𐐿 𐑌𐐬 𐑃𐐫𐐻, 𐑅𐐩𐐮𐑍, 𐐐𐐶𐐱𐐻 𐑇𐐰𐑊 𐐶𐐨 𐐨𐐻? 𐐫𐑉 𐐸𐐶𐐱𐐻 𐑇𐐰𐑊 𐐶𐐨 𐐼𐑉𐐮𐑍𐐿? 𐐫𐑉 𐐸𐐶𐐯𐑉𐐶𐐮𐑄𐐫𐑊 𐑇𐐰𐑊 𐐶𐐨 𐐺𐐨 𐐿𐑊𐐬𐑄𐐼? 𐐙𐐫𐑉 𐐷𐐭𐑉 𐐸𐐯𐑂𐐲𐑌𐑊𐐨 𐐙𐐪𐑄𐐲𐑉 𐑌𐐬𐐯𐑃 𐑄𐐰𐐻 𐐷𐐨 𐐸𐐰𐑂 𐑌𐐨𐐼 𐐱𐑂 𐐫𐑊 𐑄𐐨𐑆 𐑃𐐮𐑍𐑆. 𐐒𐐲𐐻 𐑅𐐨𐐿 𐐷𐐨 𐑁𐐲𐑉𐑅𐐻 𐑄 𐐿𐐮𐑍𐐼𐐲𐑋 𐐱𐑂 𐐘𐐱𐐼 𐐰𐑌𐐼 𐐸𐐮𐑆 𐑉𐐴𐐽𐐲𐑅𐑌𐐯𐑅, 𐐰𐑌𐐼 𐐫𐑊 𐑄𐐨𐑆 𐑃𐐮𐑍𐑆 𐑇𐐰𐑊 𐐺𐐨 𐐰𐐼𐐯𐐼 𐐲𐑌𐐻𐐭 𐐷𐐭. 𐐓𐐩𐐿 𐑄𐐯𐑉𐑁𐐬𐑉 𐑌𐐬 𐑃𐐫𐐻 𐑁𐐫𐑉 𐑄 𐑋𐐱𐑉𐐬, 𐑁𐐫𐑉 𐑄 𐑋𐐱𐑉𐐬 𐑇𐐰𐑊 𐐻𐐩𐐿 𐑃𐐫𐐻 𐑁𐐫𐑉 𐑄 𐑃𐐮𐑍𐑆 𐐱𐑂 𐐮𐐻𐑅𐐯𐑊𐑁. 𐐝𐐲𐑁𐐮𐑇𐐲𐑌𐐻 𐐮𐑆 𐑄 𐐼𐐩 𐐲𐑌𐐻𐐭 𐑄 𐐨𐑂𐐲𐑊 𐑄𐐯𐑉𐐱𐑂.

2. 𐐈𐑌𐐼 𐑌𐐵 𐐮𐐻 𐐿𐐩𐑋 𐐻𐐭 𐐹𐐰𐑅 𐑄𐐰𐐻 𐐸𐐶𐐯𐑌 𐐖𐐨𐑆𐐲𐑅 𐐸𐐰𐐼 𐑅𐐹𐐬𐐿𐐲𐑌 𐑄𐐨𐑆 𐐶𐐲𐑉𐐼𐑆, 𐐸𐐨 𐐻𐐲𐑉𐑌𐐼 𐐲𐑀𐐯𐑌 𐐻𐐭 𐑄 𐑋𐐲𐑊𐐻𐐮𐐻𐐷𐐭𐐼, 𐐰𐑌𐐼 𐐼𐐮𐐼 𐐬𐐹𐐲𐑌 𐐸𐐮𐑆 𐑋𐐵𐑃 𐐲𐑌𐐻𐐭 𐑄𐐯𐑋 𐐲𐑀𐐯𐑌, 𐑅𐐩𐐮𐑍, 𐐚𐐯𐑉𐐮𐑊𐐨, 𐑂𐐯𐑉𐐮𐑊𐐨, 𐐴 𐑅𐐩 𐐲𐑌𐐻𐐭 𐐷𐐭, 𐐖𐐲𐐾 𐑌𐐱𐐻, 𐑄𐐰𐐻 𐐷𐐨 𐐺𐐨 𐑌𐐱𐐻 𐐾𐐲𐐾𐐼. 𐐙𐐫𐑉 𐐶𐐮𐑄 𐐸𐐶𐐱𐐻 𐐾𐐲𐐾𐑋𐐯𐑌𐐻 𐐷𐐨 𐐾𐐲𐐾, 𐐷𐐨 𐑇𐐰𐑊 𐐺𐐨 𐐾𐐲𐐾𐐼; 𐐰𐑌𐐼 𐐶𐐮𐑄 𐐸𐐶𐐱𐐻 𐑋𐐯𐑈𐐲𐑉 𐐷𐐨 𐑋𐐨𐐻, 𐐮𐐻 𐑇𐐰𐑊 𐐺𐐨 𐑋𐐯𐑈𐐲𐑉𐐼 𐐻𐐭 𐐷𐐭 𐐲𐑀𐐯𐑌. 𐐈𐑌𐐼 𐐸𐐶𐐴 𐐺𐐨𐐸𐐬𐑊𐐼𐐯𐑅𐐻 𐑄𐐵 𐑄 𐑋𐐬𐐻 𐑄𐐰𐐻 𐐮𐑆 𐐮𐑌 𐑄𐐴 𐐺𐑉𐐲𐑄𐐲𐑉'𐑆 𐐴, 𐐺𐐲𐐻 𐐿𐐱𐑌𐑅𐐮𐐼𐐲𐑉𐐯𐑅𐐻 𐑌𐐱𐐻 𐑄 𐐺𐐨𐑋 𐑄𐐰𐐻 𐐮𐑆 𐐮𐑌 𐑄𐐴𐑌 𐐬𐑌 𐐴? 𐐉𐑉 𐐸𐐵 𐐶𐐮𐑊𐐻 𐑄𐐵 𐑅𐐩 𐐻𐐭 𐑄𐐴 𐐺𐑉𐐲𐑄𐐲𐑉, 𐐢𐐯𐐻 𐑋𐐨 𐐹𐐳𐑊 𐑄 𐑋𐐬𐐻 𐐵𐐻 𐐱𐑂 𐑄𐐴𐑌 𐐴, 𐐰𐑌𐐼 𐐺𐐨𐐸𐐬𐑊𐐼, 𐐲 𐐺𐐨𐑋 𐐮𐑆 𐐮𐑌 𐑄𐐴𐑌 𐐬𐑌 𐐴? 𐐜𐐵 𐐸𐐮𐐹𐐬𐐿𐑉𐐮𐐻, 𐑁𐐲𐑉𐑅𐐻 𐐿𐐰𐑅𐐻 𐑄 𐐺𐐨𐑋 𐐵𐐻 𐐱𐑂 𐑄𐐴𐑌 𐐬𐑌 𐐴, 𐐰𐑌𐐼 𐑄𐐯𐑌 𐑇𐐰𐑊𐐻 𐑄𐐵 𐑅𐐨 𐐿𐑊𐐨𐑉𐑊𐐨 𐐻𐐭 𐐿𐐰𐑅𐐻 𐑄 𐑋𐐬𐐻 𐐵𐐻 𐐱𐑂 𐑄𐐴 𐐺𐑉𐐲𐑄𐐲𐑉'𐑆 𐐴. 𐐘𐐮𐑂 𐑌𐐱𐐻 𐑄𐐰𐐻 𐐸𐐶𐐮𐐽 𐐮𐑆 𐐸𐐬𐑊𐐨 𐐲𐑌𐐻𐐭 𐑄 𐐼𐐱𐑀𐑆, 𐑌𐐨𐑄𐐲𐑉 𐐿𐐰𐑅𐐻 𐐷𐐨 𐐷𐐭𐑉 𐐹𐐲𐑉𐑊𐑆 𐐺𐐨𐑁𐐬𐑉 𐑅𐐶𐐴𐑌, 𐑊𐐯𐑅𐐻 𐑄𐐩 𐐻𐑉𐐰𐑋𐐹𐑊 𐑄𐐯𐑋 𐐲𐑌𐐼𐐲𐑉 𐑄𐐩𐑉 𐑁𐐨𐐻, 𐐰𐑌𐐼 𐐻𐐲𐑉𐑌 𐐲𐑀𐐯𐑌 𐐰𐑌𐐼 𐑉𐐯𐑌𐐼 𐐷𐐭.

3. 𐐈𐑅𐐿, 𐐰𐑌𐐼 𐐮𐐻 𐑇𐐰𐑊 𐐺𐐨 𐑀𐐮𐑂𐐲𐑌 𐐲𐑌𐐻𐐭 𐐷𐐭; 𐑅𐐨𐐿, 𐐰𐑌𐐼 𐐷𐐨 𐑇𐐰𐑊 𐑁𐐴𐑌𐐼; 𐑌𐐱𐐿, 𐐰𐑌𐐼 𐐮𐐻 𐑇𐐰𐑊 𐐺𐐨 𐐬𐐹𐐲𐑌𐐼 𐐲𐑌𐐻𐐭 𐐷𐐭, 𐑁𐐫𐑉 𐐯𐑂𐐲𐑉𐐨 𐐶𐐲𐑌 𐑄𐐰𐐻 𐐰𐑅𐐿𐐯𐑃, 𐑉𐐨𐑅𐐨𐑂𐐯𐑃; 𐐰𐑌𐐼 𐐸𐐨 𐑄𐐰𐐻 𐑅𐐨𐐿𐐯𐑃, 𐑁𐐴𐑌𐐼𐐯𐑃; 𐐰𐑌𐐼 𐐻𐐭 𐐸𐐮𐑋 𐑄𐐰𐐻 𐑌𐐱𐐿𐐯𐑃, 𐐮𐐻 𐑇𐐰𐑊 𐐺𐐨 𐐬𐐹𐐲𐑌𐐼. 𐐉𐑉 𐐸𐐶𐐱𐐻 𐑋𐐰𐑌 𐐮𐑆 𐑄𐐯𐑉 𐐱𐑂 𐐷𐐭,

𐐸𐐭𐑋, 𐐮𐑁 𐐸𐐮𐑆 𐑅𐐲𐑌 𐐰𐑅𐐿 𐐺𐑉𐐯𐐼, 𐐶𐐮𐑊 𐐸𐐨 𐑀𐐮𐑂 𐐸𐐮𐑋 𐐲 𐑅𐐻𐐬𐑌? 𐐃𐑉 𐐮𐑁 𐐸𐐨 𐐰𐑅𐐿 𐐲 𐑁𐐮𐑇, 𐐶𐐮𐑊 𐐸𐐨 𐑀𐐮𐑂 𐐸𐐮𐑋 𐐲 𐑅𐐲𐑉𐐹𐐯𐑌𐐻? 𐐆𐑁 𐐷𐐨 𐑄𐐯𐑌, 𐐺𐐨𐐮𐑍 𐐨𐑂𐐮𐑊, 𐑌𐐬 𐐸𐐵 𐐻𐐭 𐑀𐐮𐑂 𐑀𐐳𐐼 𐑀𐐮𐑁𐐻𐑅 𐐲𐑌𐐻𐐭 𐐷𐐭𐑉 𐐽𐐮𐑊𐐼𐑉𐐯𐑌, 𐐸𐐵 𐑋𐐲𐐽 𐑋𐐬𐑉 𐑇𐐰𐑊 𐐷𐐭𐑉 𐐙𐐪𐑄𐐲𐑉 𐐸𐐭 𐐮𐑆 𐐮𐑌 𐐸𐐯𐑂𐐲𐑌 𐑀𐐮𐑂 𐑀𐐳𐐼 𐑃𐐮𐑍𐑆 𐐻𐐭 𐑄𐐯𐑋 𐑄𐐰𐐻 𐐰𐑅𐐿 𐐸𐐮𐑋? 𐐜𐐯𐑉𐑁𐐬𐑉 𐐫𐑊 𐑃𐐮𐑍𐑆 𐐸𐐶𐐱𐐻𐑅𐐬𐐯𐑂𐐲𐑉 𐐷𐐨 𐐶𐐳𐐼 𐑄𐐰𐐻 𐑋𐐯𐑌 𐑇𐐳𐐼 𐐼𐐭 𐐻𐐭 𐐷𐐭, 𐐼𐐭 𐐷𐐨 𐐨𐑂𐐲𐑌 𐑅𐐬 𐐻𐐭 𐑄𐐯𐑋, 𐑁𐐫𐑉 𐑄𐐮𐑅 𐐮𐑆 𐑄 𐑊𐐫 𐐰𐑌𐐼 𐑄 𐐹𐑉𐐱𐑁𐐯𐐻𐑅.

4. 𐐇𐑌𐐻𐐲𐑉 𐐷𐐨 𐐮𐑌 𐐰𐐻 𐑄 𐑅𐐻𐑉𐐩𐐻 𐑀𐐩𐐻: 𐑁𐐫𐑉 𐐶𐐴𐐼 𐐮𐑆 𐑄 𐑀𐐩𐐻, 𐐰𐑌𐐼 𐐺𐑉𐐫𐐼 𐐮𐑆 𐑄 𐐶𐐩, 𐐸𐐶𐐮𐐽 𐑊𐐨𐐼𐐯𐑃 𐐻𐐭 𐐼𐐯𐑅𐐻𐑉𐐲𐐿𐑇𐐲𐑌, 𐐰𐑌𐐼 𐑋𐐯𐑌𐐨 𐑄𐐯𐑉 𐐺𐐨 𐐸𐐭 𐑀𐐬 𐐮𐑌 𐑄𐐯𐑉𐐰𐐻; 𐐺𐐨𐐿𐐫𐑆 𐑅𐐻𐑉𐐩𐐻 𐐮𐑆 𐑄 𐑀𐐩𐐻, 𐐰𐑌𐐼 𐑌𐐰𐑉𐐬 𐐮𐑆 𐑄 𐐶𐐩, 𐐸𐐶𐐮𐐽 𐑊𐐨𐐼𐐯𐑃 𐐲𐑌𐐻𐐭 𐑊𐐴𐑁, 𐐰𐑌𐐼 𐑁𐐷𐐭 𐑄𐐯𐑉 𐐺𐐨 𐑄𐐰𐐻 𐑁𐐴𐑌𐐼 𐐮𐐻. 𐐒𐐨𐐶𐐯𐑉 𐐱𐑂 𐑁𐐫𐑊𐑅 𐐹𐑉𐐱𐑁𐐯𐐻𐑅, 𐐸𐐭 𐐿𐐲𐑋 𐐲𐑌𐐻𐐭 𐐷𐐭 𐐮𐑌 𐑇𐐨𐐹'𐑅 𐐿𐑊𐐬𐑄𐐮𐑍, 𐐺𐐲𐐻 𐐮𐑌𐐶𐐲𐑉𐐼𐑊𐐨 𐑄𐐩 𐐪𐑉 𐑉𐐰𐑂𐐲𐑌𐐮𐑍 𐐶𐐳𐑊𐑂𐑆. 𐐏 𐑇𐐰𐑊 𐑌𐐬 𐑄𐐯𐑋 𐐺𐐴 𐑄𐐯𐑉 𐑁𐑉𐐭𐐻𐑅: 𐐔𐐭 𐑋𐐯𐑌 𐑀𐐰𐑄𐐲𐑉 𐑀𐑉𐐩𐐹𐑅 𐐱𐑂 𐑃𐐫𐑉𐑌𐑆, 𐐫𐑉 𐑁𐐮𐑀𐑆 𐐱𐑂 𐑃𐐮𐑅𐐲𐑊𐑆? 𐐀𐑂𐐲𐑌 𐑅𐐬 𐐯𐑂𐐲𐑉𐐨 𐑀𐐳𐐼 𐐻𐑉𐐨 𐐺𐑉𐐮𐑍𐐯𐑃 𐑁𐐬𐑉𐑃 𐑀𐐳𐐼 𐑁𐑉𐐭𐐻; 𐐺𐐲𐐻 𐐲 𐐿𐐫𐑉𐐲𐐹𐐻 𐐻𐑉𐐨 𐐺𐑉𐐮𐑍𐐯𐑃 𐑁𐐬𐑉𐑃 𐐨𐑂𐐮𐑊 𐑁𐑉𐐭𐐻. 𐐈 𐑀𐐳𐐼 𐐻𐑉𐐨 𐐿𐐰𐑌𐐱𐐻 𐐺𐑉𐐮𐑍 𐑁𐐬𐑉𐑃 𐐨𐑂𐐮𐑊 𐑁𐑉𐐭𐐻, 𐑌𐐨𐑄𐐲𐑉 𐐲 𐐿𐐫𐑉𐐲𐐹𐐻 𐐻𐑉𐐨 𐐺𐑉𐐮𐑍 𐑁𐐬𐑉𐑃 𐑀𐐳𐐼 𐑁𐑉𐐭𐐻. 𐐇𐑂𐐲𐑉𐐨 𐐻𐑉𐐨 𐑄𐐰𐐻 𐐺𐑉𐐮𐑍𐐯𐑃 𐑌𐐱𐐻 𐑁𐐬𐑉𐑃 𐑀𐐳𐐼 𐑁𐑉𐐭𐐻 𐐮𐑆 𐐸𐐷𐐭𐑌 𐐼𐐵𐑌, 𐐰𐑌𐐼 𐐿𐐰𐑅𐐻 𐐮𐑌𐐻𐐭 𐑄 𐑁𐐴𐑉. 𐐐𐐶𐐯𐑉𐑁𐐬𐑉, 𐐺𐐴 𐑄𐐯𐑉 𐑁𐑉𐐭𐐻𐑅 𐐷𐐨 𐑇𐐰𐑊 𐑌𐐬 𐑄𐐯𐑋.

5. 𐐤𐐱𐐻 𐐯𐑂𐐲𐑉𐐨 𐐶𐐲𐑌 𐑄𐐰𐐻 𐑅𐐯𐑃 𐐲𐑌𐐻𐐭 𐑋𐐨, 𐐢𐐫𐑉𐐼, 𐐢𐐫𐑉𐐼, 𐑇𐐰𐑊 𐐯𐑌𐐻𐐲𐑉 𐐮𐑌𐐻𐐭 𐑄 𐐿𐐮𐑍𐐼𐐲𐑋 𐐱𐑂 𐐸𐐯𐑂𐐲𐑌; 𐐺𐐲𐐻 𐐸𐐨 𐑄𐐰𐐻 𐐼𐐭𐐯𐑃 𐑄 𐐶𐐮𐑊 𐐱𐑂 𐑋𐐴 𐐙𐐪𐑄𐐲𐑉 𐐸𐐭 𐐮𐑆 𐐮𐑌 𐐸𐐯𐑂𐐲𐑌. 𐐣𐐯𐑌𐐨 𐐶𐐮𐑊 𐑅𐐩 𐐻𐐭 𐑋𐐨 𐐮𐑌 𐑄𐐰𐐻 𐐼𐐩, 𐐢𐐫𐑉𐐼, 𐐢𐐫𐑉𐐼, 𐐸𐐰𐑂 𐐶𐐨 𐑌𐐱𐐻 𐐹𐑉𐐱𐑁𐐯𐑅𐐴𐐼 𐐮𐑌 𐑄𐐴 𐑌𐐩𐑋? 𐐰𐑌𐐼 𐐮𐑌 𐑄𐐴 𐑌𐐩𐑋 𐐸𐐰𐑂 𐐿𐐰𐑅𐐻 𐐵𐐻 𐐼𐐯𐑂𐐲𐑊𐑆? 𐐰𐑌𐐼 𐐮𐑌 𐑄𐐴 𐑌𐐩𐑋 𐐼𐐲𐑌 𐑋𐐯𐑌𐐨 𐐶𐐲𐑌𐐼𐐲𐑉𐑁𐐳𐑊 𐐶𐐲𐑉𐐿𐑅? 𐐈𐑌𐐼 𐑄𐐯𐑌 𐐶𐐮𐑊 𐐌 𐐹𐑉𐐬𐑁𐐯𐑅 𐐲𐑌𐐻𐐭 𐑄𐐯𐑋, 𐐌 𐑌𐐯𐑂𐐲𐑉 𐑌𐐭 𐐷𐐭; 𐐼𐐨𐐹𐐪𐑉𐐻 𐑁𐑉𐐱𐑋 𐑋𐐨, 𐐷𐐨 𐑄𐐰𐐻 𐐶𐐲𐑉𐐿 𐐮𐑌𐐮𐐿𐐶𐐮𐐻𐐨.

6. 𐐜𐐯𐑉𐑁𐐬𐑉, 𐐸𐐭𐑅𐐬 𐐸𐐨𐑉𐐯𐑃 𐑄𐐨𐑆 𐑅𐐩𐐮𐑍𐑆 𐐱𐑂 𐑋𐐴𐑌, 𐐰𐑌𐐼 𐐼𐐭𐐯𐑃 𐑄𐐯𐑋, 𐐌 𐐶𐐮𐑊 𐑊𐐴𐐿𐐲𐑌 𐐸𐐮𐑋 𐐲𐑌𐐻𐐭 𐐲 𐐶𐐴𐑆 𐑋𐐰𐑌, 𐐸𐐭 𐐺𐐮𐑊𐐻 𐐸𐐮𐑆 𐐸𐐵𐑅 𐐲𐐹𐐱𐑌 𐐲 𐑉𐐱𐐿, 𐐰𐑌𐐼 𐑄 𐑉𐐩𐑌 𐐼𐐨𐑅𐐯𐑌𐐼𐐯𐐼, 𐐰𐑌𐐼 𐑄 𐑁𐑊𐐲𐐼𐑆 𐐿𐐩𐑋, 𐐰𐑌𐐼 𐑄 𐐶𐐮𐑌𐐼𐑆 𐐺𐑊𐐭, 𐐰𐑌𐐼 𐐺𐐨𐐻 𐐲𐐹𐐱𐑌 𐑄𐐰𐐻 𐐸𐐵𐑅; 𐐰𐑌𐐼 𐐮𐐻 𐑁𐐯𐑊 𐑌𐐱𐐻; 𐑁𐐫𐑉 𐐮𐐻 𐐶𐐱𐑆 𐑁𐐵𐑌𐐼𐐯𐐼 𐐲𐐹𐐱𐑌 𐐲 𐑉𐐱𐐿. 𐐈𐑌𐐼 𐐯𐑂𐐲𐑉𐐨 𐐶𐐲𐑌 𐑄𐐰𐐻 𐐸𐐨𐑉𐐯𐑃 𐑄𐐨𐑆 𐑅𐐩𐐮𐑍𐑆 𐐱𐑂 𐑋𐐴𐑌, 𐐰𐑌𐐼 𐐼𐐭𐐯𐑃 𐑄𐐯𐑋 𐑌𐐱𐐻, 𐑇𐐰𐑊 𐐺𐐨 𐑊𐐴𐐿𐐲𐑌𐐼 𐐲𐑌𐐻𐐭 𐐲 𐑁𐐭𐑊𐐮𐑇 𐑋𐐰𐑌, 𐐸𐐭 𐐺𐐮𐑊𐐻 𐐸𐐮𐑆 𐐸𐐵𐑅 𐐲𐐹𐐱𐑌 𐑄 𐑅𐐰𐑌𐐼, 𐐰𐑌𐐼 𐑄 𐑉𐐩𐑌 𐐼𐐨𐑅𐐯𐑌𐐼𐐯𐐼, 𐐰𐑌𐐼 𐑄 𐑁𐑊𐐲𐐼𐑆 𐐿𐐩𐑋, 𐐰𐑌𐐼 𐑄 𐐶𐐮𐑌𐐼𐑆 𐐺𐑊𐐭, 𐐰𐑌𐐼 𐐺𐐨𐐻 𐐲𐐹𐐱𐑌 𐑄𐐰𐐻 𐐸𐐵𐑅; 𐐰𐑌𐐼 𐐮𐐻 𐑁𐐯𐑊, 𐐰𐑌𐐼 𐑀𐑉𐐩𐐻 𐐶𐐱𐑆 𐑄 𐑁𐐫𐑊 𐐱𐑂 𐐮𐐻.

𐐕𐐈𐐑𐐓𐐊𐐡 VII.

1. 𐐈𐑌𐐼 𐑌𐐵 𐐮𐐻 𐐿𐐩𐑋 𐐻𐐭 𐐹𐐰𐑅 𐑄𐐰𐐻 𐐸𐐶𐐯𐑌 𐐖𐐨𐑆𐐲𐑅 𐐸𐐰𐐼 𐐯𐑌𐐼𐐯𐐼 𐑄𐐨𐑆 𐑅𐐩𐐮𐑍𐑆, 𐐸𐐨 𐐿𐐰𐑅𐐻 𐐸𐐮𐑆 𐐴𐑆 𐑉𐐵𐑌𐐼 𐐲𐐺𐐵𐐻 𐐱𐑌 𐑄 𐑋𐐲𐑊𐐻𐐨𐐻𐐷𐐭𐐼, 𐐰𐑌𐐼 𐑅𐐯𐐼 𐐲𐑌𐐻𐐭 𐑄𐐯𐑋, 𐐒𐐨𐐸𐐬𐑊𐐼, 𐐷𐐨 𐐸𐐰𐑂 𐐸𐐲𐑉𐐼 𐑄 𐑃𐐮𐑍𐑆 𐐸𐐶𐐮𐐽 𐐌 𐐻𐐫𐐻 𐐺𐐨𐑁𐐬𐑉 𐐌 𐐰𐑅𐐯𐑌𐐼𐐯𐐼 𐐻𐐭 𐑋𐐴 𐐙𐐪𐑄𐐲𐑉; 𐑄𐐯𐑉𐑁𐐬𐑉, 𐐸𐐭𐑅𐐬 𐑉𐐨𐑋𐐯𐑋𐐺𐐲𐑉𐐯𐑃 𐑄𐐨𐑆 𐑅𐐩𐐮𐑍𐑆 𐐱𐑂 𐑋𐐴𐑌, 𐐰𐑌𐐼 𐐼𐐭𐐯𐑃 𐑄𐐯𐑋, 𐐸𐐮𐑋 𐐶𐐮𐑊 𐐌 𐑉𐐩𐑆 𐐲𐐹 𐐰𐐻 𐑄 𐑊𐐰𐑅𐐻 𐐼𐐩. 𐐈𐑌𐐼 𐐮𐐻 𐐿𐐩𐑋 𐐻𐐭 𐐹𐐰𐑅 𐑄𐐰𐐻 𐐸𐐶𐐯𐑌 𐐖𐐨𐑆𐐲𐑅 𐐸𐐰𐐼 𐑅𐐯𐐼 𐑄𐐨𐑆 𐐶𐐲𐑉𐐼𐑆, 𐐸𐐨 𐐹𐐲𐑉𐑅𐐨𐑂𐐼 𐑄𐐰𐐻 𐑄𐐯𐑉 𐐶𐐲𐑉 𐑅𐐲𐑋 𐐲𐑋𐐲𐑍 𐑄𐐯𐑋 𐐸𐐭 𐑋𐐪𐑉𐑂𐐯𐑊𐐼, 𐐰𐑌𐐼 𐐶𐐲𐑌𐐼𐐲𐑉𐐼 𐐸𐐶𐐱𐐻 𐐸𐐨 𐐶𐐳𐐼 𐐿𐐲𐑌𐑅𐐲𐑉𐑌𐐮𐑍 𐑄 𐑊𐐫 𐐱𐑂 𐐣𐐬𐑆𐐯𐑆; 𐑁𐐫𐑉 𐑄𐐩 𐐲𐑌𐐼𐐲𐑉𐑅𐐻𐐳𐐼 𐑌𐐱𐐻 𐑄 𐑅𐐩𐐮𐑍 𐑄𐐰𐐻 𐐬𐑊𐐼 𐑃𐐮𐑍𐑆 𐐸𐐰𐐼 𐐹𐐰𐑅𐐻 𐐲𐐶𐐩, 𐐰𐑌𐐼 𐑄𐐰𐐻 𐐫𐑊 𐑃𐐮𐑍𐑆 𐐸𐐰𐐼 𐐺𐐨𐐿𐐲𐑋 𐑌𐐷𐐭. 𐐈𐑌𐐼 𐐸𐐨 𐑅𐐯𐐼 𐐲𐑌𐐻𐐭 𐑄𐐯𐑋, 𐐣𐐪𐑉𐑂𐐯𐑊 𐑌𐐱𐐻 𐑄𐐰𐐻 𐐌 𐑅𐐯𐐼 𐐲𐑌𐐻𐐭 𐐷𐐭, 𐑄𐐰𐐻 𐐬𐑊𐐼 𐑃𐐮𐑍𐑆 𐐸𐐰𐐼 𐐹𐐰𐑅𐐻 𐐲𐐶𐐩, 𐐰𐑌𐐼 𐑄𐐰𐐻 𐐫𐑊 𐑃𐐮𐑍𐑆 𐐸𐐰𐐼 𐐺𐐨𐐿𐐲𐑋 𐑌𐐷𐐭. 𐐒𐐨𐐸𐐬𐑊𐐼, 𐐌 𐑅𐐩 𐐲𐑌𐐻𐐭 𐐷𐐭, 𐑄𐐰𐐻 𐑄 𐑊𐐫 𐐮𐑆 𐑁𐐳𐑊𐑁𐐮𐑊𐐼 𐑄𐐰𐐻 𐐶𐐱𐑆 𐑀𐐮𐑂𐐲𐑌 𐐲𐑌𐐻𐐭 𐐣𐐬𐑆𐐯𐑆. 𐐒𐐨𐐸𐐬𐑊𐐼, 𐐌 𐐰𐑋 𐐸𐐨 𐑄𐐰𐐻 𐑀𐐩𐑂 𐑄 𐑊𐐫, 𐐰𐑌𐐼 𐐌 𐐰𐑋 𐐸𐐨 𐐸𐐭 𐐿𐐲𐑂𐐯𐑌𐐰𐑌𐐻𐐯𐐼 𐐶𐐮𐑄 𐑋𐐴 𐐹𐐨𐐹𐐲𐑊 𐐆𐑆𐑉𐐩𐐯𐑊: 𐑄𐐯𐑉𐑁𐐬𐑉, 𐑄 𐑊𐐫 𐐮𐑌 𐑋𐐨 𐐮𐑆 𐑁𐐳𐑊𐑁𐐮𐑊𐐼, 𐑁𐐫𐑉 𐐌 𐐸𐐰𐑂 𐐿𐐲𐑋 𐐻𐐭 𐑁𐐳𐑊𐑁𐐮𐑊 𐑄 𐑊𐐫; 𐑄𐐯𐑉𐑁𐐬𐑉 𐐮𐐻

𐐸𐐰𐑃 𐐰𐑌 𐐯𐑌𐐼. 𐐒𐐨𐐸𐐬𐑊𐐼, 𐐌 𐐼𐐭 𐑌𐐱𐐻 𐐼𐐨𐑅𐐻𐑉𐑎 𐑄 𐐹𐑉𐐱𐑁𐐯𐐻𐑅, 𐑁𐐫𐑉 𐐰𐑆 𐑋𐐯𐑌𐐨 𐐰𐑆 𐐸𐐰𐑂 𐑌𐐱𐐻 𐐺𐐮𐑌 𐑁𐐳𐑊𐑁𐐮𐑊𐐼 𐐺𐐴 𐑋𐐨, 𐑂𐐯𐑉𐐮𐑊𐐨 𐐌 𐑅𐐩 𐐲𐑌𐐻𐐭 𐐷𐐭, 𐑇𐐰𐑊 𐐫𐑊 𐐺𐐨 𐑁𐐳𐑊𐑁𐐮𐑊𐐼. 𐐈𐑌𐐼 𐐺𐐨𐐿𐐫𐑆 𐐌 𐑅𐐯𐐼 𐐲𐑌𐐻𐐭 𐐷𐐭, 𐑄𐐰𐐻 𐐬𐑊𐐼 𐑃𐐮𐑍𐑆 𐐸𐐰𐑃 𐐹𐐰𐑅𐐻 𐐰𐐶𐐩, 𐐌 𐐼𐐭 𐑌𐐱𐐻 𐐼𐐨𐑅𐐻𐑉𐑎 𐑄𐐰𐐻 𐐸𐐶𐐮𐐽 𐐸𐐰𐑃 𐐺𐐮𐑌 𐑅𐐹𐐬𐐿𐑌 𐐿𐐱𐑌𐑅𐐲𐑉𐑌𐐮𐑍 𐑄 𐑃𐐮𐑍𐑆 𐐸𐐶𐐮𐐽 𐐪𐑉 𐐻𐐭 𐐿𐐲𐑋. 𐐙𐐫𐑉 𐐺𐐨𐐸𐐬𐑊𐐼, 𐑄 𐐿𐐲𐑂𐐯𐑌𐐰𐑌𐐻 𐐸𐐶𐐮𐐽 𐐌 𐐸𐐰𐑂 𐑋𐐩𐐼 𐐶𐐮𐑄 𐑋𐐴 𐐹𐐨𐐹𐑊 𐐮𐑆 𐑌𐐱𐐻 𐐫𐑊 𐑁𐐳𐑊𐑁𐐮𐑊𐐼; 𐐺𐐲𐐻 𐑄 𐑊𐐫 𐐸𐐶𐐮𐐽 𐐶𐐱𐑆 𐑀𐐮𐑂𐐯𐑌 𐐲𐑌𐐻𐐭 𐐣𐐬𐑆𐐯𐑆, 𐐸𐐰𐑃 𐐰𐑌 𐐯𐑌𐐼 𐐮𐑌 𐑋𐐨. 𐐒𐐨𐐸𐐬𐑊𐐼, 𐐌 𐐰𐑋 𐑄 𐑊𐐫, 𐐰𐑌𐐼 𐑄 𐑊𐐴𐐻; 𐑊𐐳𐐿 𐐲𐑌𐐻𐐭 𐑋𐐨, 𐐰𐑌𐐼 𐐯𐑌𐐼𐐧𐑉 𐐻𐐭 𐑄 𐐯𐑌𐐼, 𐐰𐑌𐐼 𐐷𐐨 𐑇𐐰𐑊 𐑊𐐮𐑂, 𐑁𐐫𐑉 𐐲𐑌𐐻𐐭 𐐸𐐮𐑋 𐑄𐐰𐐻 𐐯𐑌𐐼𐐧𐑉𐐯𐑃 𐐻𐐭 𐑄 𐐯𐑌𐐼, 𐐶𐐮𐑊 𐐌 𐑀𐐮𐑂 𐐨𐐻𐐲𐑉𐑌𐐲𐑊 𐑊𐐴𐑁. 𐐒𐐨𐐸𐐬𐑊𐐼, 𐐌 𐐸𐐰𐑂 𐑀𐐮𐑂𐐯𐑌 𐐲𐑌𐐻𐐭 𐐷𐐭 𐑄 𐐿𐐱𐑋𐐰𐑌𐐼𐑋𐐯𐑌𐐻𐑅; 𐑄𐐯𐑉𐑁𐐫𐑉 𐐿𐐨𐐹 𐑋𐐴 𐐿𐐱𐑋𐐰𐑌𐐼𐑋𐐯𐑌𐐻𐑅. 𐐈𐑌𐐼 𐑄𐐮𐑅 𐐮𐑆 𐑄 𐑊𐐫 𐐰𐑌𐐼 𐑄 𐐹𐑉𐐱𐑁𐐯𐐻𐑅, 𐑁𐐫𐑉 𐑄𐐩 𐐻𐑉𐐭𐑊𐐨 𐐻𐐯𐑅𐐻𐐮𐑁𐐴𐐼 𐐱𐑂 𐑋𐐨.

2. 𐐈𐑌𐐼 𐑌𐐵 𐐮𐐻 𐐿𐐩𐑋 𐐻𐐭 𐐹𐐰𐑅 𐑄𐐰𐐻 𐐸𐐶𐐯𐑌 𐐖𐐨𐑆𐐲𐑅 𐐸𐐰𐐼 𐑅𐐹𐐬𐐿𐑌 𐑄𐐨𐑆 𐐶𐐲𐑉𐐼𐑆, 𐐸𐐨 𐑅𐐯𐐼 𐐲𐑌𐐻𐐭 𐑄𐐬𐑆 𐐻𐐶𐐯𐑊𐑂 𐐸𐐭𐑋 𐐸𐐨 𐐸𐐰𐐼 𐐽𐐬𐑆𐐲𐑌, 𐐏𐐨 𐐪𐑉 𐑋𐐴 𐐼𐐮𐑅𐐴𐐹𐑊𐑆; 𐐰𐑌𐐼 𐐷𐐨 𐐪𐑉 𐐲 𐑊𐐴𐐻 𐐲𐑌𐐻𐐭 𐑄𐐮𐑅 𐐹𐐨𐐹𐑊, 𐐸𐐭 𐐪𐑉 𐐲 𐑉𐐯𐑋𐑌𐐰𐑌𐐻 𐐱𐑂 𐑄 𐐸𐐵𐑅 𐐱𐑂 𐐖𐐬𐑆𐐯𐑁. 𐐈𐑌𐐼 𐐺𐐨𐐸𐐬𐑊𐐼, 𐑄𐐮𐑅 𐐮𐑆 𐑄 𐑊𐐰𐑌𐐼 𐐱𐑂 𐐷𐐫𐑉 𐐮𐑌𐐸𐐯𐑉𐐮𐐻𐐰𐑌𐑅; 𐐰𐑌𐐼 𐑄 𐐙𐐪𐑄𐐲𐑉 𐐸𐐰𐑃 𐑀𐐮𐑂𐐯𐑌 𐐮𐐻 𐐲𐑌𐐻𐐭 𐐷𐐭. 𐐈𐑌𐐼 𐑌𐐱𐐻 𐐰𐐻 𐐯𐑌𐐨 𐐻𐐴𐑋 𐐸𐐰𐑃 𐑄 𐐙𐐪𐑄𐐲𐑉 𐑀𐐮𐑂𐐯𐑌 𐑋𐐨 𐐿𐐱𐑋𐐰𐑌𐐼𐑋𐐯𐑌𐐻 𐑄𐐰𐐻 𐐌 𐑇𐐳𐐼 𐐻𐐯𐑊 𐐮𐐻 𐐲𐑌𐐻𐐭 𐐷𐐫𐑉 𐐺𐑉𐐯𐑄𐑉𐐯𐑌 𐐰𐐻 𐐖𐐭𐑉𐐭𐑅𐐲𐑊𐐯𐑋; 𐑌𐐨𐑄𐐲𐑉 𐐰𐐻 𐐯𐑌𐐨 𐐻𐐴𐑋 𐐸𐐰𐑃 𐑄 𐐙𐐪𐑄𐐲𐑉 𐑀𐐮𐑂𐐯𐑌 𐑋𐐨 𐐿𐐱𐑋𐐰𐑌𐐼𐑋𐐯𐑌𐐻, 𐑄𐐰𐐻 𐐌 𐑇𐐳𐐼 𐐻𐐯𐑊 𐐲𐑌𐐻𐐭 𐑄𐐯𐑋 𐐿𐐱𐑌𐑅𐐲𐑉𐑌𐐮𐑍 𐑄 𐐲𐑄𐐲𐑉 𐐻𐑉𐐴𐐺𐑆 𐐱𐑂 𐑄 𐐸𐐵𐑅 𐐱𐑂 𐐆𐑆𐑉𐐩𐐯𐑊, 𐐸𐐭𐑋 𐑄 𐐙𐐪𐑄𐐲𐑉 𐐸𐐰𐑃 𐑊𐐯𐐼 𐐰𐐶𐐩 𐐵𐐻 𐐱𐑂 𐑄 𐑊𐐰𐑌𐐼. 𐐜𐐮𐑅 𐑋𐐲𐐽 𐐼𐐮𐐼 𐑄 𐐙𐐪𐑄𐐲𐑉 𐐿𐐱𐑋𐐰𐑌𐐼 𐑋𐐨, 𐑄𐐰𐐻 𐐌 𐑇𐐳𐐼 𐐻𐐯𐑊 𐐲𐑌𐐻𐐭 𐑄𐐯𐑋, 𐑄𐐰𐐻 𐐲𐑄𐐲𐑉 𐑇𐐨𐐹 𐐌 𐐸𐐰𐑂, 𐐸𐐶𐐮𐐽 𐐪𐑉 𐑌𐐱𐐻 𐐱𐑂 𐑄𐐮𐑅 𐑁𐐬𐑊𐐼; 𐑄𐐯𐑋 𐐫𐑊𐑅𐐬 𐐌 𐑋𐐲𐑅𐐻 𐐺𐑉𐐮𐑍, 𐐰𐑌𐐼 𐑄𐐩 𐑇𐐰𐑊 𐐸𐐨𐑉 𐑋𐐴 𐑂𐑎𐑅; 𐐰𐑌𐐼 𐑄𐐯𐑉 𐑇𐐰𐑊 𐐺𐐨 𐐶𐐲𐑌 𐑁𐐬𐑊𐐼, 𐐰𐑌𐐼 𐐶𐐲𐑌 𐑇𐐯𐐹𐐲𐑉𐐼. 𐐈𐑌𐐼 𐑌𐐵 𐐺𐐨𐐿𐐫𐑆 𐐱𐑂 𐑅𐐻𐐮𐑁𐑌𐐯𐐿𐐯𐐼𐑌𐐯𐑅 𐐰𐑌𐐼 𐐲𐑌𐐺𐐨𐑊𐐨𐑁, 𐑄𐐩 𐐲𐑌𐐼𐐲𐑉𐑅𐐻𐐳𐐼 𐑌𐐱𐐻 𐑋𐐴 𐐶𐐲𐑉𐐼: 𐑄𐐯𐑉𐑁𐐫𐑉 𐐌 𐐶𐐱𐑆 𐐿𐐱𐑋𐐰𐑌𐐼𐐯𐐼 𐐻𐐭 𐑅𐐩 𐑌𐐬 𐑋𐐬𐑉 𐐱𐑂 𐑄 𐐙𐐪𐑄𐐲𐑉 𐐿𐐱𐑌𐑅𐐲𐑉𐑌𐐮𐑍 𐑄𐐮𐑅 𐑃𐐮𐑍 𐐲𐑌𐐻𐐭 𐑄𐐯𐑋. 𐐒𐐲𐐻, 𐑂𐐯𐑉𐐮𐑊𐐨, 𐐌 𐑅𐐩 𐐲𐑌𐐻𐐭 𐐷𐐭, 𐑄𐐰𐐻 𐑄 𐐙𐐪𐑄𐐲𐑉 𐐸𐐰𐑃 𐐿𐐱𐑋𐐰𐑌𐐼𐐯𐐼 𐑋𐐨, 𐐰𐑌𐐼 𐐌 𐐻𐐯𐑊 𐐮𐐻 𐐲𐑌𐐻𐐭 𐐷𐐭, 𐑄𐐰𐐻 𐐷𐐨 𐐶𐐲𐑉 𐑅𐐯𐐹𐐲𐑉𐐩𐐻𐐯𐐼 𐑁𐑉𐐱𐑋 𐐲𐑋𐐲𐑍 𐑄𐐯𐑋 𐐺𐐨𐐿𐐫𐑆 𐐱𐑂 𐑄𐐯𐑉 𐐮𐑌𐐮𐐿𐐶𐐮𐐻𐐨; 𐑄𐐯𐑉𐑁𐐫𐑉 𐐮𐐻 𐐮𐑆 𐐺𐐨𐐿𐐫𐑆 𐐱𐑂 𐑄𐐯𐑉 𐐮𐑌𐐮𐐿𐐶𐐮𐐻𐐨, 𐑄𐐰𐐻 𐑄𐐩 𐑌𐐬 𐑌𐐱𐐻 𐐱𐑂 𐐷𐐭. 𐐈𐑌𐐼 𐑂𐐯𐑉𐐮𐑊𐐨, 𐐌 𐑅𐐩 𐐲𐑌𐐻𐐭 𐐷𐐭 𐐲𐑀𐐯𐑌, 𐑄𐐰𐐻 𐑄 𐐲𐑄𐐲𐑉 𐐻𐑉𐐴𐐺𐑆 𐐸𐐰𐑃 𐑄 𐐙𐐪𐑄𐐲𐑉 𐑅𐐯𐐹𐐲𐑉𐐩𐐻𐐯𐐼 𐑁𐑉𐐱𐑋 𐑄𐐯𐑋; 𐐰𐑌𐐼 𐐮𐐻 𐐮𐑆 𐐺𐐨𐐿𐐫𐑆 𐐱𐑂 𐑄𐐯𐑉 𐐮𐑌𐐮𐐿𐐶𐐮𐐻𐐨, 𐑄𐐰𐐻 𐑄𐐩 𐑌𐐬 𐑌𐐱𐐻 𐐱𐑂 𐑄𐐯𐑋. 𐐈𐑌𐐼 𐑂𐐯𐑉𐐮𐑊𐐨, 𐐌 𐑅𐐩 𐐲𐑌𐐻𐐭 𐐷𐐭, 𐑄𐐰𐐻 𐐷𐐨 𐐪𐑉 𐑄𐐩 𐐱𐑂 𐐸𐐭𐑋 𐐌 𐑅𐐯𐐼, 𐐊𐑄𐐲𐑉 𐑇𐐨𐐹 𐐌 𐐸𐐰𐑂 𐐸𐐶𐐮𐐽 𐐪𐑉 𐑌𐐱𐐻 𐐱𐑂 𐑄𐐮𐑅 𐑁𐐬𐑊𐐼; 𐑄𐐯𐑋 𐐫𐑊𐑅𐐬 𐐌 𐑋𐐲𐑅𐐻 𐐺𐑉𐐮𐑍, 𐐰𐑌𐐼 𐑄𐐩 𐑇𐐰𐑊 𐐸𐐨𐑉 𐑋𐐴 𐑂𐑎𐑅; 𐐰𐑌𐐼 𐑄𐐯𐑉 𐑇𐐰𐑊 𐐺𐐨 𐐶𐐲𐑌 𐑁𐐬𐑊𐐼, 𐐰𐑌𐐼 𐐶𐐲𐑌 𐑇𐐯𐐹𐐲𐑉𐐼. 𐐈𐑌𐐼 𐑄𐐩 𐐲𐑌𐐼𐐲𐑉𐑅𐐻𐐳𐐼 𐑋𐐨 𐑌𐐱𐐻, 𐑁𐐫𐑉 𐑄𐐩 𐑅𐐲𐐹𐐬𐑆𐐼 𐐮𐐻 𐐸𐐰𐐼 𐐺𐐮𐑌 𐑄 𐐖𐐯𐑌𐐻𐐴𐑊𐑆; 𐑁𐐫𐑉 𐑄𐐩 𐐲𐑌𐐼𐐲𐑉𐑅𐐻𐐳𐐼 𐑌𐐱𐐻 𐑄𐐰𐐻 𐑄 𐐖𐐯𐑌𐐻𐐴𐑊𐑆 𐑇𐐳𐐼 𐐺𐐨 𐐿𐐱𐑌𐑂𐐲𐑉𐐻𐐯𐐼 𐑃𐑉𐐭 𐑄𐐯𐑉 𐐹𐑉𐐨𐐽𐐮𐑍; 𐐰𐑌𐐼 𐑄𐐩 𐐲𐑌𐐼𐐲𐑉𐑅𐐻𐐳𐐼 𐑋𐐨 𐑌𐐱𐐻 𐑄𐐰𐐻 𐐌 𐑅𐐯𐐼 𐑄𐐩 𐑇𐐰𐑊 𐐸𐐨𐑉 𐑋𐐴 𐑂𐑎𐑅; 𐐰𐑌𐐼 𐑄𐐩 𐐲𐑌𐐼𐐲𐑉𐑅𐐻𐐳𐐼 𐑋𐐨 𐑌𐐱𐐻 𐑄𐐰𐐻 𐑄 𐐖𐐯𐑌𐐻𐐴𐑊𐑆 𐑇𐐳𐐼 𐑌𐐱𐐻 𐐰𐐻 𐐯𐑌𐐨 𐐻𐐴𐑋 𐐸𐐨𐑉 𐑋𐐴 𐑂𐑎𐑅; 𐑄𐐰𐐻 𐐌 𐑇𐐳𐐼 𐑌𐐱𐐻 𐑋𐐰𐑌𐐮𐑁𐐯𐑅𐐻 𐑋𐐴𐑅𐐯𐑊𐑁 𐐲𐑌𐐻𐐭 𐑄𐐯𐑋, 𐑅𐐩𐑂 𐐮𐐻 𐐶𐐲𐑉 𐐺𐐴 𐑄 𐐐𐐬𐑊𐐨 𐐘𐐬𐑅𐐻. 𐐒𐐲𐐻 𐐺𐐨𐐸𐐬𐑊𐐼, 𐐷𐐨 𐐸𐐰𐑂 𐐺𐐬𐑃 𐐸𐐲𐑉𐐼 𐑋𐐴 𐑂𐑎𐑅, 𐐰𐑌𐐼 𐑅𐐨𐑌 𐑋𐐨; 𐐰𐑌𐐼 𐐷𐐨 𐐪𐑉 𐑋𐐴 𐑇𐐨𐐹, 𐐰𐑌𐐼 𐐷𐐨 𐐪𐑉 𐑌𐐲𐑋𐐺𐐲𐑉𐐼 𐐲𐑋𐐲𐑍 𐑄𐐬𐑆 𐐸𐐭𐑋 𐑄 𐐙𐐪𐑄𐐲𐑉 𐐸𐐰𐑃 𐑀𐐮𐑂𐐯𐑌 𐑋𐐨.

3. 𐐈𐑌𐐼 𐑂𐐯𐑉𐐮𐑊𐐨, 𐑂𐐯𐑉𐐮𐑊𐐨, 𐐌 𐑅𐐩 𐐲𐑌𐐻𐐭 𐐷𐐭, 𐑄𐐰𐐻 𐐌 𐐸𐐰𐑂 𐐲𐑄𐐲𐑉 𐑇𐐨𐐹, 𐐸𐐶𐐮𐐽 𐐪𐑉 𐑌𐐱𐐻 𐐱𐑂 𐑄𐐮𐑅 𐑊𐐰𐑌𐐼; 𐑌𐐨𐑄𐐲𐑉 𐐱𐑂 𐑄 𐑊𐐰𐑌𐐼 𐐱𐑂 𐐖𐐭𐑉𐐭𐑅𐐲𐑊𐐯𐑋; 𐑌𐐨𐑄𐐲𐑉 𐐮𐑌 𐐯𐑌𐐨 𐐹𐐪𐑉𐐻𐑅 𐐱𐑂 𐑄𐐰𐐻 𐑊𐐰𐑌𐐼 𐑉𐐵𐑌𐐼 𐐲𐐺𐐵𐐻, 𐐸𐐶𐐮𐑄𐐲𐑉 𐐌 𐐸𐐰𐑂 𐐺𐐮𐑌 𐐻𐐭 𐑋𐐮𐑌𐐮𐑅𐐻𐐲𐑉. 𐐙𐐫𐑉 𐑄𐐩 𐐱𐑂 𐐸𐐭𐑋 𐐌 𐑅𐐹𐐨𐐿, 𐐪𐑉 𐑄𐐩 𐐸𐐭 𐐸𐐰𐑂 𐑌𐐱𐐻 𐐰𐑆 𐐷𐐯𐐻 𐐸𐐲𐑉𐐼 𐑋𐐴 𐑂𐑎𐑅; 𐑌𐐨𐑄𐐲𐑉 𐐸𐐰𐑂 𐐌 𐐰𐐻 𐐯𐑌𐐨 𐐻𐐴𐑋 𐑋𐐰𐑌𐐮𐑁𐐯𐑅𐐻𐐯𐐼 𐑋𐐴𐑅𐐯𐑊𐑁 𐐲𐑌𐐻𐐭 𐑄𐐯𐑋. 𐐒𐐲𐐻 𐐌 𐐸𐐰𐑂 𐑉𐐨𐑅𐐨𐑂𐐼 𐐲 𐐿𐐱𐑋𐐰𐑌𐐼𐑋𐐯𐑌𐐻 𐐱𐑂 𐑄 𐐙𐐪𐑄𐐲𐑉, 𐑄𐐰𐐻 𐐌 𐑇𐐰𐑊 𐑀𐐬 𐐲𐑌𐐻𐐭 𐑄𐐯𐑋, 𐐰𐑌𐐼 𐑄𐐰𐐻 𐑄𐐩 𐑇𐐰𐑊 𐐸𐐨𐑉 𐑋𐐴 𐑂𐑎𐑅, 𐐰𐑌𐐼 𐑇𐐰𐑊 𐐺𐐨 𐑌𐐲𐑋𐐺𐐲𐑉𐐼 𐐲𐑋𐐲𐑍 𐑋𐐴 𐑇𐐨𐐹, 𐑄𐐰𐐻 𐑄𐐯𐑉 𐑋𐐩 𐐺𐐨 𐐶𐐲𐑌 𐑁𐐬𐑊𐐼, 𐐰𐑌𐐼 𐐶𐐲𐑌 𐑇𐐯𐐹𐐲𐑉𐐼; 𐑄𐐯𐑉𐑁𐐫𐑉 𐐌 𐑀𐐬 𐐻𐐭 𐑇𐐬 𐑋𐐴𐑅𐐯𐑊𐑁 𐐲𐑌𐐻𐐭 𐑄𐐯𐑋. 𐐈𐑌𐐼 𐐌 𐐿𐐱𐑋𐐰𐑌𐐼

𐐷𐐭 𐑄𐐰𐐻 𐐷 𐑇𐐰𐑊 𐑉𐐴𐐻 𐑄𐐨𐑆 𐑅𐐩𐐮𐑍𐑆, 𐐰𐑁𐐻𐐲𐑉 𐐌 𐐰𐑋 𐑀𐐱𐑌, 𐑄𐐰𐐻 𐐮𐑁 𐐮𐐻 𐑅𐐬 𐐺 𐑄𐐰𐐻 𐑋𐐴 𐐹𐐨𐐹𐑊 𐐰𐐻 𐐖𐐨𐑉𐐭𐑅𐐲𐑊𐐯𐑋, 𐑄𐐩 𐐸𐐭 𐐸𐐰𐑂 𐑅𐐨𐑌 𐑋𐐨, 𐐰𐑌𐐼 𐐺𐐮𐑌 𐐶𐐮𐑄 𐑋𐐨 𐐮𐑌 𐑋𐐴 𐑋𐐮𐑌𐐮𐑅𐐻𐑉𐐨, 𐐼𐐭 𐑌𐐱𐐻 𐐰𐑅𐐿 𐑄 𐐙𐐪𐑄𐐲𐑉 𐐮𐑌 𐑋𐐴 𐑌𐐩𐑋, 𐑄𐐰𐐻 𐑄𐐩 𐑋𐐩 𐑉𐐨𐑅𐐨𐑂 𐐲 𐑌𐐱𐑊𐐲𐐾 𐐱𐑂 𐐷𐐭 𐐺𐐴 𐑄 𐐐𐐬𐑊𐐨 𐐘𐐬𐑅𐐻, 𐐰𐑌𐐼 𐐫𐑊𐑅𐐬 𐐱𐑂 𐑄 𐐲𐑄𐐲𐑉 𐐻𐑉𐐴𐐺𐑆 𐐸𐐭𐑋 𐑄𐐩 𐑌𐐬 𐑌𐐱𐐻 𐐱𐑂, 𐑄𐐰𐐻 𐑄𐐨𐑆 𐑅𐐩𐐮𐑍𐑆 𐐸𐐶𐐮𐐽 𐐷 𐑇𐐰𐑊 𐑉𐐴𐐻, 𐑇𐐰𐑊 𐐺 𐐿𐐯𐐹𐐻, 𐐰𐑌𐐼 𐑇𐐰𐑊 𐐺 𐑋𐐰𐑌𐐮𐑁𐐯𐑅𐐻𐐨𐐼 𐐲𐑌𐐻𐐭 𐑄 𐐖𐐯𐑌𐐻𐐴𐑊𐑆, 𐑄𐐰𐐻 𐑃𐑉𐐭 𐑄 𐑁𐐳𐑊𐑌𐐯𐑅 𐐱𐑂 𐑄 𐐖𐐯𐑌𐐻𐐴𐑊𐑆, 𐑄 𐑉𐐯𐑋𐑌𐐲𐑌𐐻 𐐱𐑂 𐑄𐐯𐑉 𐑅𐐨𐐼 𐐸𐐭 𐑇𐐰𐑊 𐐺 𐑅𐐿𐐰𐐻𐐲𐑉𐐲𐐼 𐑁𐐫𐑉𐑃 𐐲𐐹𐐱𐑌 𐑄 𐑁𐐩𐑅 𐐱𐑂 𐑄 𐐲𐑉𐑃, 𐐺𐐨𐐿𐐫𐑆 𐐱𐑂 𐑄𐐯𐑉 𐐲𐑌𐐺𐐨𐑊𐐨𐑁, 𐑋𐐩 𐐺 𐐺𐑉𐐫𐐻 𐐮𐑌, 𐐫𐑉 𐑋𐐩 𐐺 𐐺𐑉𐐫𐐻 𐐻𐐭 𐐲 𐑌𐐱𐑊𐐲𐐾 𐐱𐑂 𐑋𐐨, 𐑄𐐯𐑉 𐐡𐐨𐐼𐐨𐑋𐐲𐑉. 𐐈𐑌𐐼 𐑄𐐯𐑌 𐐶𐐮𐑊 𐐌 𐑀𐐰𐑄𐐲𐑉 𐑄𐐯𐑋 𐐮𐑌 𐑁𐑉𐐱𐑋 𐑄 𐑁𐐬𐑉 𐐿𐐶𐐫𐑉𐐻𐐲𐑉𐑆 𐐱𐑂 𐑄 𐐲𐑉𐑃; 𐐰𐑌𐐼 𐑄𐐯𐑌 𐐶𐐮𐑊 𐐌 𐑁𐐳𐑊𐑁𐐮𐑊 𐑄 𐐿𐐲𐑂𐐯𐑌𐐲𐑌𐐻 𐐸𐐶𐐮𐐽 𐑄 𐐙𐐪𐑄𐐲𐑉 𐐸𐐰𐑃 𐑋𐐩𐐼 𐐲𐑌𐐻𐐭 𐐫𐑊 𐑄 𐐹𐐨𐐹𐑊 𐐱𐑂 𐑄 𐐸𐐵𐑅 𐐱𐑂 𐐆𐑆𐑉𐐩𐐯𐑊.

4. 𐐈𐑌𐐼 𐐺𐑊𐐯𐑅𐐲𐐼 𐐪𐑉 𐑄 𐐖𐐯𐑌𐐻𐐴𐑊𐑆, 𐐺𐐨𐐿𐐫𐑆 𐐱𐑂 𐑄𐐯𐑉 𐐺𐐨𐑊𐐨𐑁 𐐮𐑌 𐑋𐐨, 𐐮𐑌 𐐰𐑌𐐼 𐐱𐑂 𐑄 𐐐𐐬𐑊𐐨 𐐘𐐬𐑅𐐻, 𐐸𐐶𐐮𐐽 𐐶𐐮𐐻𐑌𐐯𐑅𐐯𐑆 𐐲𐑌𐐻𐐭 𐑄𐐯𐑋 𐐱𐑂 𐑋𐐨 𐐰𐑌𐐼 𐐱𐑂 𐑄 𐐙𐐪𐑄𐐲𐑉. 𐐒𐐨𐐸𐐬𐑊𐐼, 𐐺𐐨𐐿𐐫𐑆 𐐱𐑂 𐑄𐐯𐑉 𐐺𐐨𐑊𐐨𐑁 𐐮𐑌 𐑋𐐨, 𐑅𐐯𐑃 𐑄 𐐙𐐪𐑄𐐲𐑉, 𐐰𐑌𐐼 𐐺𐐨𐐿𐐫𐑆 𐐱𐑂 𐑄 𐐲𐑌𐐺𐐨𐑊𐐨𐑁 𐐱𐑂 𐐷𐐭, 𐐄 𐐸𐐵𐑅 𐐱𐑂 𐐆𐑆𐑉𐐩𐐯𐑊, 𐐮𐑌 𐑄 𐑊𐐰𐐻𐐲𐑉 𐐼𐐩 𐑇𐐰𐑊 𐑄 𐐻𐑉𐐭𐑃 𐐿𐐲𐑋 𐐲𐑌𐐻𐐭 𐑄 𐐖𐐯𐑌𐐻𐐴𐑊𐑆, 𐑄𐐰𐐻 𐑄 𐑁𐐳𐑊𐑌𐐯𐑅 𐐱𐑂 𐑄𐐨𐑆 𐑃𐐮𐑍𐑆 𐑇𐐰𐑊 𐐺 𐑋𐐩𐐼 𐑌𐐬𐑌 𐐲𐑌𐐻𐐭 𐑄𐐯𐑋. 𐐒𐐲𐐻 𐐶𐐬, 𐑅𐐯𐑃 𐑄 𐐙𐐪𐑄𐐲𐑉, 𐐲𐑌𐐻𐐭 𐑄 𐐲𐑌𐐺𐐨𐑊𐐨𐑂𐐮𐑍 𐐱𐑂 𐑄 𐐖𐐯𐑌𐐻𐐴𐑊𐑆, 𐑁𐐫𐑉 𐑌𐐱𐐻𐐶𐐮𐑄𐑅𐐻𐐰𐑌𐐼𐐮𐑍 𐑄𐐩 𐐸𐐰𐑂 𐐿𐐲𐑋 𐑁𐐫𐑉𐑃 𐐲𐐹𐐱𐑌 𐑄 𐑁𐐩𐑅 𐐱𐑂 𐑄𐐮𐑅 𐑊𐐰𐑌𐐼, 𐐰𐑌𐐼 𐐸𐐰𐑂 𐑅𐐿𐐰𐐻𐐲𐑉𐐲𐐼 𐑋𐐴 𐐹𐐨𐐹𐑊, 𐐸𐐭 𐐪𐑉 𐐱𐑂 𐑄 𐐸𐐵𐑅 𐐱𐑂 𐐆𐑆𐑉𐐩𐐯𐑊; 𐐰𐑌𐐼 𐑋𐐴 𐐹𐐨𐐹𐑊 𐐸𐐭 𐐪𐑉 𐐱𐑂 𐑄 𐐸𐐵𐑅 𐐱𐑂 𐐆𐑆𐑉𐐩𐐯𐑊, 𐐸𐐰𐑂 𐐺𐐮𐑌 𐐿𐐰𐑅𐐻 𐐵𐐻 𐑁𐑉𐐱𐑋 𐐲𐑋𐐲𐑍 𐑄𐐯𐑋, 𐐰𐑌𐐼 𐐸𐐰𐑂 𐐺𐐮𐑌 𐐻𐑉𐐱𐐼𐑌 𐐲𐑌𐐼𐐲𐑉 𐑁𐐨𐐻 𐐺𐐴 𐑄𐐯𐑋; 𐐰𐑌𐐼 𐐺𐐨𐐿𐐫𐑆 𐐱𐑂 𐑄 𐑋𐐲𐑉𐑅𐐨𐑆 𐐱𐑂 𐑄 𐐙𐐪𐑄𐐲𐑉 𐐲𐑌𐐻𐐭 𐑄 𐐖𐐯𐑌𐐻𐐴𐑊𐑆, 𐐰𐑌𐐼 𐐫𐑊𐑅𐐬 𐑄 𐐾𐐲𐐾𐑋𐐯𐑌𐐻𐑅 𐐱𐑂 𐑄 𐐙𐐪𐑄𐐲𐑉 𐐲𐐹𐐱𐑌 𐑋𐐴 𐐹𐐨𐐹𐑊, 𐐸𐐭 𐐪𐑉 𐐱𐑂 𐑄 𐐸𐐵𐑅 𐐱𐑂 𐐆𐑆𐑉𐐩𐐯𐑊, 𐑂𐐯𐑉𐐮𐑊𐐨, 𐑂𐐯𐑉𐐮𐑊𐐨, 𐐌 𐑅𐐩 𐐲𐑌𐐻𐐭 𐐷𐐭, 𐑄𐐰𐐻 𐐰𐑁𐐻𐐲𐑉 𐐫𐑊 𐑄𐐮𐑅, 𐐰𐑌𐐼 𐐌 𐐸𐐰𐑂 𐐿𐐫𐑆𐐼 𐑋𐐴 𐐹𐐨𐐹𐑊, 𐐸𐐭 𐐪𐑉 𐐱𐑂 𐑄 𐐸𐐵𐑅 𐐱𐑂 𐐆𐑆𐑉𐐩𐐯𐑊, 𐐻𐐭 𐐺 𐑅𐑋𐐮𐐻𐑌, 𐐰𐑌𐐼 𐐻𐐭 𐐺 𐐰𐑁𐑊𐐮𐐿𐐻𐐲𐐼, 𐐰𐑌𐐼 𐐻𐐭 𐐺 𐑅𐑊𐐩𐑌, 𐐰𐑌𐐼 𐐻𐐭 𐐺 𐐿𐐰𐑅𐐻 𐐵𐐻 𐑁𐑉𐐱𐑋 𐐲𐑋𐐲𐑍 𐑄𐐯𐑋, 𐐰𐑌𐐼 𐐻𐐭 𐐺𐐨𐐿𐐲𐑋 𐐸𐐩𐐻𐐲𐐼 𐐺𐐴 𐑄𐐯𐑋, 𐐰𐑌𐐼 𐐻𐐭 𐐺𐐨𐐿𐐲𐑋 𐐲 𐐸𐐮𐑅 𐐰𐑌𐐼 𐐲 𐐺𐐴-𐐶𐐲𐑉𐐼 𐐲𐑋𐐲𐑍 𐑄𐐯𐑋. 𐐈𐑌𐐼 𐑄𐐲𐑅 𐐿𐐲𐑋𐐰𐑌𐐼𐐯𐑃 𐑄 𐐙𐐪𐑄𐐲𐑉 𐑄𐐰𐐻 𐐌 𐑇𐐳𐐼 𐑅𐐩 𐐲𐑌𐐻𐐭 𐐷𐐭: 𐐈𐐻 𐑄𐐰𐐻 𐐼𐐩 𐐸𐐶𐐯𐑌 𐑄 𐐖𐐯𐑌𐐻𐐴𐑊𐑆 𐑇𐐰𐑊 𐑅𐐮𐑌 𐐲𐑀𐐯𐑌𐑅𐐻 𐑋𐐴 𐑀𐐱𐑅𐐹𐐯𐑊, 𐐰𐑌𐐼 𐑇𐐰𐑊 𐐺 𐑊𐐮𐑁𐐻𐐲𐐼 𐐲𐐹 𐐮𐑌 𐑄 𐐹𐑉𐐴𐐼 𐐱𐑂 𐑄𐐯𐑉 𐐸𐐪𐑉𐐻𐑅 𐐲𐐺𐐲𐑂 𐐫𐑊 𐑌𐐩𐑇𐐲𐑌𐑆, 𐐰𐑌𐐼 𐐲𐐺𐐲𐑂 𐐫𐑊 𐑄 𐐹𐐨𐐹𐑊 𐐱𐑂 𐑄 𐐸𐐬𐑊 𐐲𐑉𐑃, 𐐰𐑌𐐼 𐑇𐐰𐑊 𐐺 𐑁𐐮𐑊𐐼 𐐶𐐮𐑄 𐐫𐑊 𐑋𐐰𐑌𐐲𐑉 𐐱𐑂 𐑊𐐴𐐮𐑍𐑆, 𐐰𐑌𐐼 𐐱𐑂 𐐼𐐨𐑅𐐨𐐻𐑅, 𐐰𐑌𐐼 𐐱𐑂 𐑋𐐮𐑅𐐽𐐮𐑁𐑅, 𐐰𐑌𐐼 𐐫𐑊 𐑋𐐰𐑌𐐲𐑉 𐐱𐑂 𐐸𐐮𐐹𐐱𐐿𐑉𐐮𐑅𐐨, 𐐰𐑌𐐼 𐑋𐐲𐑉𐐼𐐲𐑉𐑆, 𐐰𐑌𐐼 𐐹𐑉𐐨𐑅𐐻𐐿𐑉𐐰𐑁𐐻𐑅, 𐐰𐑌𐐼 𐐸𐐬𐑉𐐼𐐲𐑋𐑆, 𐐰𐑌𐐼 𐐱𐑂 𐑅𐐨𐐿𐑉𐐯𐐻 𐐲𐐺𐐱𐑋𐐮𐑌𐐩𐑇𐐲𐑌𐑆; 𐐰𐑌𐐼 𐐮𐑁 𐑄𐐩 𐑇𐐰𐑊 𐐼𐐭 𐐫𐑊 𐑄𐐬𐑆 𐑃𐐮𐑍𐑆, 𐐰𐑌𐐼 𐑇𐐰𐑊 𐑉𐐨𐐾𐐯𐐿𐐻 𐑄 𐑁𐐳𐑊𐑌𐐯𐑅 𐐱𐑂 𐑋𐐴 𐑀𐐱𐑅𐐹𐐯𐑊, 𐐺𐐨𐐸𐐬𐑊𐐼, 𐑅𐐯𐑃 𐑄 𐐙𐐪𐑄𐐲𐑉, 𐐌 𐐶𐐮𐑊 𐐺𐑉𐐮𐑍 𐑄 𐑁𐐳𐑊𐑌𐐯𐑅 𐐱𐑂 𐑋𐐴 𐑀𐐱𐑅𐐹𐐯𐑊 𐑁𐑉𐐱𐑋 𐐲𐑋𐐲𐑍 𐑄𐐯𐑋; 𐐰𐑌𐐼 𐑄𐐯𐑌 𐐌 𐐶𐐮𐑊 𐑉𐐨𐑋𐐯𐑋𐐺𐐲𐑉 𐑋𐐴 𐐿𐐲𐑂𐐯𐑌𐐲𐑌𐐻 𐐸𐐶𐐮𐐽 𐐌 𐐸𐐰𐑂 𐑋𐐩𐐼 𐐲𐑌𐐻𐐭 𐑋𐐴 𐐹𐐨𐐹𐑊, 𐐄 𐐸𐐵𐑅 𐐱𐑂 𐐆𐑆𐑉𐐩𐐯𐑊, 𐐰𐑌𐐼 𐐌 𐐶𐐮𐑊 𐐺𐑉𐐮𐑍 𐑋𐐴 𐑀𐐱𐑅𐐹𐐯𐑊 𐐲𐑌𐐻𐐭 𐑄𐐯𐑋; 𐐰𐑌𐐼 𐐌 𐐶𐐮𐑊 𐑇𐐬 𐐲𐑌𐐻𐐭 𐑄𐐨, 𐐄 𐐸𐐵𐑅 𐐱𐑂 𐐆𐑆𐑉𐐩𐐯𐑊, 𐑄𐐰𐐻 𐑄 𐐖𐐯𐑌𐐻𐐴𐑊𐑆 𐑇𐐰𐑊 𐑌𐐱𐐻 𐐸𐐰𐑂 𐐹𐐵𐐲𐑉 𐐬𐑂𐐲𐑉 𐐷𐐭, 𐐺𐐲𐐻 𐐌 𐐶𐐮𐑊 𐑉𐐨𐑋𐐯𐑋𐐺𐐲𐑉 𐑋𐐴 𐐿𐐲𐑂𐐯𐑌𐐲𐑌𐐻 𐐲𐑌𐐻𐐭 𐐷𐐭, 𐐄 𐐸𐐵𐑅 𐐱𐑂 𐐆𐑆𐑉𐐩𐐯𐑊, 𐐰𐑌𐐼 𐐷 𐑇𐐰𐑊 𐐿𐐲𐑋 𐐲𐑌𐐻𐐭 𐑄 𐑌𐐱𐑊𐐲𐐾 𐐱𐑂 𐑄 𐑁𐐳𐑊𐑌𐐯𐑅 𐐱𐑂 𐑋𐐴 𐑀𐐱𐑅𐐹𐐯𐑊. 𐐒𐐲𐐻 𐐮𐑁 𐑄 𐐖𐐯𐑌𐐻𐐴𐑊𐑆 𐐶𐐮𐑊 𐑉𐐨𐐹𐐯𐑌𐐻, 𐐰𐑌𐐼 𐑉𐐨𐐻𐐲𐑉𐑌 𐐲𐑌𐐻𐐭 𐑋𐐨, 𐑅𐐯𐑃 𐑄 𐐙𐐪𐑄𐐲𐑉, 𐐺𐐨𐐸𐐬𐑊𐐼 𐑄𐐩 𐑇𐐰𐑊 𐐺 𐑌𐐲𐑋𐐺𐐲𐑉𐐼 𐐲𐑋𐐲𐑍 𐑋𐐴 𐐹𐐨𐐹𐑊, 𐐄 𐐸𐐵𐑅 𐐱𐑂 𐐆𐑆𐑉𐐩𐐯𐑊; 𐐰𐑌𐐼 𐐌 𐐶𐐮𐑊 𐑌𐐱𐐻 𐑅𐐲𐑁𐐲𐑉 𐑋𐐴 𐐹𐐨𐐹𐑊, 𐐸𐐭 𐐪𐑉 𐐱𐑂 𐑄 𐐸𐐵𐑅 𐐱𐑂 𐐆𐑆𐑉𐐩𐐯𐑊, 𐐻𐐭 𐑀𐐬 𐑃𐑉𐐭 𐐲𐑋𐐲𐑍 𐑄𐐯𐑋, 𐐰𐑌𐐼 𐐻𐑉𐐯𐐼 𐑄𐐯𐑋 𐐼𐐵𐑌, 𐑅𐐯𐑃 𐑄 𐐙𐐪𐑄𐐲𐑉. 𐐒𐐲𐐻 𐐮𐑁 𐑄𐐩 𐐶𐐮𐑊 𐑌𐐱𐐻 𐐻𐐲𐑉𐑌 𐐲𐑌𐐻𐐭 𐑋𐐨, 𐐰𐑌𐐼 𐐸𐐪𐑉𐐿𐐲𐑌 𐐲𐑌𐐻𐐭 𐑋𐐴 𐑂𐐶𐐮𐑅, 𐐌 𐐶𐐮𐑊 𐑅𐐲𐑁𐐲𐑉 𐑄𐐯𐑋, 𐐷𐐩, 𐐌 𐐶𐐮𐑊 𐑅𐐲𐑁𐐲𐑉 𐑋𐐴 𐐹𐐨𐐹𐑊, 𐐄 𐐸𐐵𐑅 𐐱𐑂 𐐆𐑆𐑉𐐩𐐯𐑊, 𐑄𐐰𐐻 𐑄𐐩 𐑇𐐰𐑊 𐑀𐐬 𐑃𐑉𐐭 𐐲𐑋𐐲𐑍 𐑄𐐯𐑋, 𐐰𐑌𐐼 𐑇𐐰𐑊 𐐻𐑉𐐯𐐼 𐑄𐐯𐑋 𐐼𐐵𐑌, 𐐰𐑌𐐼 𐑄𐐩 𐑇𐐰𐑊 𐐺 𐐰𐑆 𐑅𐐫𐑊𐐻 𐑄𐐰𐐻 𐐸𐐰𐑃 𐑊𐐱𐑅𐐻 𐐮𐐻𐑅 𐑅𐐩𐑂𐐲𐑉, 𐐸𐐶𐐮𐐽 𐐮𐑆 𐑄𐐯𐑌𐑅𐑁𐐫𐑉𐑃 𐑀𐐳𐐼 𐑁𐐫𐑉 𐑌𐐲𐑃𐐮𐑍, 𐐺𐐲𐐻 𐐻𐐭 𐐺 𐐿𐐰𐑅𐐻 𐐵𐐻, 𐐰𐑌𐐼 𐐻𐐭 𐐺 𐐻𐑉𐐱𐐼𐑌 𐐲𐑌𐐼𐐲𐑉 𐑁𐐳𐐻 𐐱𐑂 𐑋𐐴 𐐹𐐨𐐹𐑊, 𐐄 𐐸𐐵𐑅 𐐱𐑂 𐐆𐑆𐑉𐐩𐐯𐑊. 𐐚𐐯𐑉𐐮𐑊𐐨, 𐑂𐐯𐑉𐐮𐑊𐐨, 𐐌 𐑅𐐩 𐐲𐑌𐐻𐐭 𐐷𐐭, 𐐜𐐲𐑅 𐐸𐐰𐑃 𐑄 𐐙𐐪𐑄𐐲𐑉 𐐿𐐲𐑋𐐰𐑌𐐼𐐲𐐼 𐑋𐐨, 𐑄𐐰𐐻

𐐌 𐑇𐐳𐐼 𐑀𐐮𐑂 𐐲𐑌𐐻𐐭 𐑄𐐮𐑅 𐐹𐐨𐐹𐑊 𐑄𐐮𐑅 𐑊𐐰𐑌𐐼 𐑁𐐫𐑉 𐑄𐐩𐑉 𐐮𐑌𐐸𐐯𐑉𐐮𐐻𐐲𐑌𐑅. 𐐈𐑌𐐼 𐑄𐐯𐑌 𐑄 𐐶𐐲𐑉𐐼𐑆 𐐱𐑂 𐑄 𐐹𐑉𐐱𐑁𐐯𐐻 𐐌𐑆𐐩𐐲 𐑇𐐰𐑊 𐐺𐐨 𐑁𐐳𐑊𐑁𐐮𐑊𐐼, 𐐸𐐶𐐮𐐽 𐑅𐐩, 𐐜𐐴 𐐶𐐱𐐽𐑋𐐯𐑌 𐑇𐐰𐑊 𐑊𐐮𐑁𐐻 𐐲𐐹 𐑄 𐑂𐑎𐑅; 𐐶𐐮𐑄 𐑄 𐑂𐑎𐑅 𐐻𐐭𐑀𐐯𐑄𐐲𐑉 𐑇𐐰𐑊 𐑄𐐩 𐑅𐐮𐑍, 𐑁𐐫𐑉 𐑄𐐩 𐑇𐐰𐑊 𐑅𐐨 𐐴 𐐻𐐭 𐐴, 𐐸𐐶𐐯𐑌 𐑄 𐐢𐐫𐑉𐐼 𐑇𐐰𐑊 𐐺𐑉𐐮𐑍 𐐲𐑀𐐯𐑌 𐐞𐐴𐐲𐑌. 𐐒𐑉𐐩𐐿 𐑁𐐬𐑉𐑃 𐐮𐑌𐐻𐐭 𐑎, 𐑅𐐮𐑍 𐐻𐐭𐑀𐐯𐑄𐐲𐑉, 𐐷𐐨 𐐶𐐩𐑅𐐻 𐐹𐑊𐐩𐑅𐐯𐑆 𐐱𐑂 𐐖𐐨𐑉𐐭𐑅𐐲𐑊𐐯𐑋, 𐑁𐐫𐑉 𐑄 𐐢𐐫𐑉𐐼 𐐸𐐰𐑃 𐐿𐐲𐑋𐑁𐐲𐑉𐐻𐐯𐐼 𐐸𐐮𐑆 𐐹𐐨𐐹𐑊, 𐐸𐐨 𐐸𐐰𐑃 𐑉𐐨𐐼𐐨𐑋𐐼 𐐖𐐨𐑉𐐭𐑅𐐲𐑊𐐯𐑋. 𐐜 𐐢𐐫𐑉𐐼 𐐸𐐰𐑃 𐑋𐐩𐐼 𐐺𐐩𐑉 𐐸𐐮𐑆 𐐸𐐬𐑊𐐨 𐐪𐑉𐑋 𐐮𐑌 𐑄 𐐴𐑆 𐐱𐑂 𐐫𐑊 𐑄 𐑌𐐩𐑇𐐲𐑌𐑆; 𐐰𐑌𐐼 𐐫𐑊 𐑄 𐐯𐑌𐐼𐑆 𐐱𐑂 𐑄 𐐲𐑉𐑃 𐑇𐐰𐑊 𐑅𐐨 𐑄 𐑅𐐰𐑊-𐑂𐐩𐑇𐐲𐑌 𐐱𐑂 𐐘𐐱𐐼.

𐐗𐐰𐐹𐐻𐐲𐑉 VIII.

1. 𐐒𐐨𐐸𐐬𐑊𐐼, 𐑌𐐵 𐐮𐐻 𐐿𐐩𐑋 𐐻𐐭 𐐹𐐪𐑅 𐑄𐐰𐐻 𐐸𐐶𐐯𐑌 𐐖𐐨𐑆𐐲𐑅 𐐸𐐰𐐼 𐑅𐐹𐐬𐐿𐑌 𐑄𐐨𐑆 𐐶𐐲𐑉𐐼𐑆, 𐐸𐐨 𐑊𐐳𐐿𐐻 𐑉𐐵𐑌𐐼 𐐲𐐺𐐵𐐻 𐐲𐑀𐐯𐑌 𐐱𐑌 𐑄 𐑋𐐲𐑊𐐻𐐮𐐻𐐷𐐭𐐼, 𐐰𐑌𐐼 𐐸𐐨 𐑅𐐯𐐼 𐐲𐑌𐐻𐐭 𐑄𐐯𐑋, 𐐒𐐨𐐸𐐬𐑊𐐼, 𐑋𐐴 𐐻𐐴𐑋 𐐮𐑆 𐐰𐐻 𐐸𐐰𐑌𐐼. 𐐌 𐐹𐐲𐑉𐑅𐐨𐑂 𐑄𐐰𐐻 𐐷𐐨 𐐪𐑉 𐐶𐐨𐐿, 𐑄𐐰𐐻 𐐷𐐨 𐐿𐐰𐑌𐐱𐐻 𐐲𐑌𐐼𐐲𐑉𐑅𐐻𐐰𐑌𐐼 𐐫𐑊 𐑋𐐴 𐐶𐐲𐑉𐐼𐑆 𐐸𐐶𐐮𐐽 𐐌 𐐰𐑋 𐐿𐐲𐑋𐐰𐑌𐐼𐐯𐐼 𐐱𐑂 𐑄 𐐙𐐪𐑄𐐲𐑉 𐐻𐐭 𐑅𐐹𐐨𐐿 𐐲𐑌𐐻𐐭 𐐷𐐭, 𐐰𐐻 𐑄𐐮𐑅 𐐻𐐴𐑋; 𐑄𐐯𐑉𐑁𐐬𐑉, 𐑀𐐬 𐐷𐐨 𐐲𐑌𐐻𐐭 𐐷𐐭𐑉 𐐸𐐬𐑋𐑆, 𐐰𐑌𐐼 𐐹𐐱𐑌𐐼𐐲𐑉 𐐲𐐹𐐱𐑌 𐑄 𐑃𐐮𐑍𐑆 𐐸𐐶𐐮𐐽 𐐌 𐐸𐐰𐑂 𐑅𐐯𐐼, 𐐰𐑌𐐼 𐐪𐑅𐐿 𐐱𐑂 𐑄 𐐙𐐪𐑄𐐲𐑉, 𐐮𐑌 𐑋𐐴 𐑌𐐩𐑋, 𐑄𐐰𐐻 𐐷𐐨 𐑋𐐩 𐐲𐑌𐐼𐐲𐑉𐑅𐐻𐐰𐑌𐐼 𐐰𐑌𐐼 𐐹𐑉𐐨𐐹𐐩𐑉 𐐷𐐭𐑉 𐑋𐐴𐑌𐐼𐑆 𐑁𐐫𐑉 𐑄 𐑋𐐱𐑉𐐬, 𐐰𐑌𐐼 𐐌 𐐿𐐲𐑋 𐐲𐑌𐐻𐐭 𐐷𐐭 𐐲𐑀𐐯𐑌. 𐐒𐐲𐐻 𐑌𐐵 𐐌 𐑀𐐬 𐐲𐑌𐐻𐐭 𐑄 𐐙𐐪𐑄𐐲𐑉, 𐐰𐑌𐐼 𐐫𐑊𐑅𐐬 𐐻𐐭 𐑇𐐬 𐑋𐐴𐑅𐐯𐑊𐑁 𐐲𐑌𐐻𐐭 𐑄 𐑊𐐱𐑅𐐻 𐐻𐑉𐐴𐐺𐑆 𐐱𐑂 𐐆𐑆𐑉𐐩𐐯𐑊, 𐑁𐐫𐑉 𐑄𐐩 𐐪𐑉 𐑌𐐱𐐻 𐑊𐐱𐑅𐐻 𐐲𐑌𐐻𐐭 𐑄 𐐙𐐪𐑄𐐲𐑉, 𐑁𐐫𐑉 𐐸𐐨 𐑌𐐬𐐯𐑃 𐐸𐐶𐐮𐑄𐐲𐑉 𐐸𐐨 𐐸𐐰𐑃 𐐻𐐩𐐿𐑌 𐑄𐐯𐑋.

2. 𐐈𐑌𐐼 𐐮𐐻 𐐿𐐩𐑋 𐐻𐐭 𐐹𐐪𐑅 𐑄𐐰𐐻 𐐸𐐶𐐯𐑌 𐐖𐐨𐑆𐐲𐑅 𐐸𐐰𐐼 𐑄𐐲𐑅 𐑅𐐹𐐬𐐿𐑌, 𐐸𐐨 𐐿𐐪𐑅𐐻 𐐸𐐮𐑆 𐐴𐑆 𐑉𐐵𐑌𐐼 𐐲𐐺𐐵𐐻 𐐲𐑀𐐯𐑌 𐐱𐑌 𐑄 𐑋𐐲𐑊𐐻𐐮𐐻𐐷𐐭𐐼, 𐐰𐑌𐐼 𐐺𐐨𐐸𐐯𐑊𐐼 𐑄𐐩 𐐶𐐲𐑉 𐐮𐑌 𐐻𐐨𐑉𐑆, 𐐰𐑌𐐼 𐐼𐐮𐐼 𐑊𐐳𐐿 𐑅𐐻𐐯𐐼𐑁𐐪𐑅𐐻𐑊𐐨 𐐲𐐹𐐱𐑌 𐐸𐐮𐑋, 𐐰𐑆 𐐮𐑁 𐑄𐐩 𐐶𐐳𐐼 𐐪𐑅𐐿 𐐸𐐮𐑋 𐐻𐐭 𐐻𐐰𐑉𐐨 𐐲 𐑊𐐮𐐻𐑊 𐑊𐐱𐑍𐑀𐐲𐑉 𐐶𐐮𐑄 𐑄𐐯𐑋. 𐐈𐑌𐐼 𐐸𐐨 𐑅𐐯𐐼 𐐲𐑌𐐻𐐭 𐑄𐐯𐑋, 𐐒𐐨𐐸𐐬𐑊𐐼, 𐑋𐐴 𐐺𐐵𐐯𐑊𐑆 𐐪𐑉 𐑁𐐮𐑊𐐼 𐐶𐐮𐑄 𐐿𐐲𐑋𐐹𐐰𐑇𐐲𐑌 𐐻𐐬𐐲𐑉𐐼𐑆 𐐷𐐭; 𐐸𐐰𐑂 𐐷𐐨 𐐯𐑌𐐨 𐑄𐐰𐐻 𐐪𐑉 𐑅𐐮𐐿 𐐲𐑋𐐲𐑍 𐐷𐐭, 𐐺𐑉𐐮𐑍 𐑄𐐯𐑋 𐐸𐐮𐑄𐐲𐑉. 𐐐𐐰𐑂 𐐷𐐨 𐐯𐑌𐐨 𐑄𐐰𐐻 𐐪𐑉 𐑊𐐩𐑋, 𐐫𐑉 𐐺𐑊𐐴𐑌𐐼, 𐐫𐑉 𐐸𐐫𐑊𐐻, 𐐫𐑉 𐑋𐐩𐑋𐐼, 𐐫𐑉 𐑊𐐯𐐹𐑉𐐲𐑅, 𐐫𐑉 𐑄𐐰𐐻 𐐪𐑉 𐐶𐐮𐑄𐐲𐑉𐐼, 𐐫𐑉 𐑄𐐰𐐻 𐐪𐑉 𐐼𐐯𐑁, 𐐫𐑉 𐑄𐐰𐐻 𐐪𐑉 𐐰𐑁𐑊𐐮𐐿𐐻𐐯𐐼 𐐮𐑌 𐐯𐑌𐐨 𐑋𐐰𐑌𐐲𐑉? 𐐒𐑉𐐮𐑍 𐑄𐐯𐑋 𐐸𐐮𐑄𐐲𐑉 𐐰𐑌𐐼 𐐌 𐐶𐐮𐑊 𐐸𐐨𐑊 𐑄𐐯𐑋, 𐑁𐐫𐑉 𐐌 𐐸𐐰𐑂 𐐿𐐲𐑋𐐹𐐰𐑇𐐲𐑌 𐐲𐐹𐐱𐑌 𐐷𐐭; 𐑋𐐴 𐐺𐐵𐐯𐑊𐑆 𐐪𐑉 𐑁𐐮𐑊𐐼 𐐶𐐮𐑄 𐑋𐐲𐑉𐑅𐐨, 𐑁𐐫𐑉 𐐌 𐐹𐐲𐑉𐑅𐐨𐑂 𐑄𐐰𐐻 𐐷𐐨 𐐼𐐨𐑆𐐴𐑉 𐑄𐐰𐐻 𐐌 𐑇𐐳𐐼 𐑇𐐬 𐐲𐑌𐐻𐐭 𐐷𐐭 𐐸𐐶𐐱𐐻 𐐌 𐐸𐐰𐑂 𐐼𐐲𐑌 𐐲𐑌𐐻𐐭 𐐷𐐭𐑉 𐐺𐑉𐐯𐑄𐑉𐐯𐑌 𐐰𐐻 𐐖𐐨𐑉𐐭𐑅𐐲𐑊𐐯𐑋, 𐑁𐐫𐑉 𐐌 𐑅𐐨 𐑄𐐰𐐻 𐐷𐐭𐑉 𐑁𐐩𐑃 𐐮𐑆 𐑅𐐲𐑁𐐮𐑇𐐯𐑌𐐻 𐑄𐐰𐐻 𐐌 𐑇𐐳𐐼 𐐸𐐨𐑊 𐐷𐐭.

3. 𐐈𐑌𐐼 𐐮𐐻 𐐿𐐩𐑋 𐐻𐐭 𐐹𐐪𐑅 𐑄𐐰𐐻 𐐸𐐶𐐯𐑌 𐐸𐐨 𐐸𐐰𐐼 𐑄𐐲𐑅 𐑅𐐹𐐬𐐿𐑌, 𐐫𐑊 𐑄 𐑋𐐲𐑊𐐻𐐮𐐻𐐷𐐭𐐼, 𐐶𐐮𐑄 𐐶𐐲𐑌 𐐰𐐿𐐫𐑉𐐼, 𐐼𐐮𐐼 𐑀𐐬 𐑁𐐬𐑉𐑃 𐐶𐐮𐑄 𐑄𐐩𐑉 𐑅𐐮𐐿, 𐐰𐑌𐐼 𐑄𐐩𐑉 𐐰𐑁𐑊𐐮𐐿𐐻𐐯𐐼, 𐐰𐑌𐐼 𐑄𐐩𐑉 𐑊𐐩𐑋, 𐐰𐑌𐐼 𐐶𐐮𐑄 𐑄𐐩𐑉 𐐺𐑊𐐴𐑌𐐼, 𐐰𐑌𐐼 𐐶𐐮𐑄 𐑄𐐩𐑉 𐐼𐐲𐑋, 𐐰𐑌𐐼 𐐶𐐮𐑄 𐐫𐑊 𐑄𐐯𐑋 𐑄𐐰𐐻 𐐶𐐲𐑉 𐐰𐑁𐑊𐐮𐐿𐐻𐐯𐐼 𐐮𐑌 𐐯𐑌𐐨 𐑋𐐰𐑌𐐲𐑉; 𐐰𐑌𐐼 𐐸𐐨 𐐼𐐮𐐼 𐐸𐐨𐑊 𐑄𐐯𐑋 𐐯𐑂𐐲𐑉𐐨 𐐶𐐲𐑌 𐐰𐑆 𐑄𐐩 𐐶𐐲𐑉 𐐺𐑉𐐫𐐻 𐑁𐐬𐑉𐑃 𐐲𐑌𐐻𐐭 𐐸𐐮𐑋, 𐐰𐑌𐐼 𐑄𐐩 𐐼𐐮𐐼 𐐫𐑊, 𐐺𐐬𐑃 𐑄𐐩 𐐸𐐭 𐐸𐐰𐐼 𐐺𐐮𐑌 𐐸𐐨𐑊𐐼 𐐰𐑌𐐼 𐑄𐐩 𐐸𐐭 𐐶𐐲𐑉 𐐸𐐬𐑊, 𐐺𐐵 𐐼𐐵𐑌 𐐰𐐻 𐐸𐐮𐑆 𐑁𐐨𐐻, 𐐰𐑌𐐼 𐐼𐐮𐐼 𐐶𐐲𐑉𐑇𐐮𐐹 𐐸𐐮𐑋; 𐐰𐑌𐐼 𐐰𐑆 𐑋𐐯𐑌𐐨 𐐰𐑆 𐐿𐐳𐐼 𐐿𐐲𐑋 𐑁𐐫𐑉 𐑄 𐑋𐐲𐑊𐐻𐐮𐐻𐐷𐐭𐐼 𐐼𐐮𐐼 𐐿𐐮𐑅 𐐸𐐮𐑆 𐑁𐐨𐐻, 𐐮𐑌𐑅𐐬-𐑋𐐲𐐽 𐑄𐐰𐐻 𐑄𐐩 𐐼𐐮𐐼 𐐺𐐩𐑄 𐐸𐐮𐑆 𐑁𐐨𐐻 𐐶𐐮𐑄 𐑄𐐩𐑉 𐐻𐐨𐑉𐑆.

4. 𐐈𐑌𐐼 𐐮𐐻 𐐿𐐩𐑋 𐐻𐐭 𐐹𐐪𐑅 𐑄𐐰𐐻 𐐸𐐨 𐐿𐐲𐑋𐐰𐑌𐐼𐐯𐐼 𐑄𐐰𐐻 𐑄𐐩𐑉 𐑊𐐮𐐻𐑊 𐐽𐐮𐑊𐐼𐑉𐐯𐑌 𐑇𐐳𐐼 𐐺𐐨 𐐺𐑉𐐫𐐻. 𐐝𐐬 𐑄𐐩 𐐺𐑉𐐫𐐻 𐑄𐐩𐑉 𐑊𐐮𐐻𐑊 𐐽𐐮𐑊𐐼𐑉𐐯𐑌, 𐐰𐑌𐐼 𐑅𐐯𐐻 𐑄𐐯𐑋 𐐼𐐵𐑌 𐐲𐐹𐐱𐑌 𐑄 𐑀𐑉𐐵𐑌𐐼 𐑉𐐵𐑌𐐼 𐐲𐐺𐐵𐐻 𐐸𐐮𐑋, 𐐰𐑌𐐼 𐐖𐐨𐑆𐐲𐑅 𐑅𐐻𐐳𐐼 𐐮𐑌 𐑄 𐑋𐐮𐐼𐑅𐐻; 𐐰𐑌𐐼 𐑄 𐑋𐐲𐑊𐐻𐐮𐐻𐐷𐐭𐐼 𐑀𐐩𐑂 𐐶𐐩 𐐻𐐮𐑊 𐑄𐐩 𐐸𐐰𐐼 𐐫𐑊 𐐺𐐮𐑌 𐐺𐑉𐐫𐐻 𐐲𐑌𐐻𐐭 𐐸𐐮𐑋. 𐐈𐑌𐐼 𐐮𐐻 𐐿𐐩𐑋 𐐻𐐭 𐐹𐐪𐑅 𐑄𐐰𐐻 𐐸𐐶𐐯𐑌 𐑄𐐩 𐐸𐐰𐐼 𐐫𐑊 𐐺𐐮𐑌 𐐺𐑉𐐫𐐻, 𐐰𐑌𐐼 𐐖𐐨𐑆𐐲𐑅 𐑅𐐻𐐳𐐼 𐐮𐑌 𐑄 𐑋𐐮𐐼𐑅𐐻, 𐐸𐐨 𐐿𐐲𐑋𐐰𐑌𐐼𐐯𐐼 𐑄 𐑋𐐲𐑊𐐻𐐮𐐻𐐷𐐭𐐼 𐑄𐐰𐐻 𐑄𐐩 𐑇𐐳𐐼 𐑌𐐨𐑊 𐐼𐐵𐑌 𐐲𐐹𐐱𐑌 𐑄 𐑀𐑉𐐵𐑌𐐼. 𐐈𐑌𐐼

𐐮𐐻 𐐿𐐩𐑋 𐐻𐐭 𐐹𐐪𐑅 𐑄𐐰𐐻 𐐸𐐶𐐯𐑌 𐑄𐐩 𐐸𐐰𐐼 𐑌𐐯𐑊𐐻 𐐲𐐹𐐱𐑌 𐑄 𐑀𐑉𐐵𐑌𐐼, 𐐖𐐨𐑆𐐲𐑅 𐑀𐑉𐐬𐑌𐐼 𐐶𐐮𐑄𐐮𐑌 𐐸𐐮𐑋𐑅𐐯𐑊𐑁, 𐐰𐑌𐐼 𐑅𐐯𐐼, 𐐙𐐪𐑄𐐲𐑉, 𐐌 𐐰𐑋 𐐻𐑉𐐲𐐺𐑊𐐼 𐐺𐐨𐐿𐐫𐑆 𐐱𐑂 𐑄 𐐶𐐮𐐿𐐯𐐼𐑌𐐯𐑅 𐐱𐑂 𐑄 𐐹𐐨𐐹𐑊 𐐱𐑂 𐑄 𐐸𐐵𐑅 𐐱𐑂 𐐆𐑆𐑉𐐩𐐯𐑊. 𐐈𐑌𐐼 𐐸𐐶𐐯𐑌 𐐸𐐨 𐐸𐐰𐐼 𐑅𐐯𐐼 𐑄𐐨𐑆 𐐶𐐲𐑉𐐼𐑆, 𐐸𐐨 𐐸𐐮𐑋𐑅𐐯𐑊𐑁 𐐫𐑊𐑅𐐬 𐑌𐐯𐑊𐐻 𐐲𐐹𐐱𐑌 𐑄 𐐲𐑉𐑃; 𐐰𐑌𐐼 𐐺𐐨𐐸𐐬𐑊𐐼, 𐐸𐐨 𐐹𐑉𐐩𐐼 𐐲𐑌𐐻𐐭 𐑄 𐐙𐐪𐑄𐐲𐑉, 𐐰𐑌𐐼 𐑄 𐑃𐐮𐑍𐑆 𐐸𐐶𐐮𐐽 𐐸𐐨 𐐹𐑉𐐩𐐼 𐐿𐐰𐑌𐐱𐐻 𐐺𐐨 𐑉𐐮𐐻𐑌, 𐐰𐑌𐐼 𐑄 𐑋𐐲𐑊𐐻𐐨𐐻𐐷𐐭𐐼 𐐼𐐮𐐼 𐐺𐐩𐑉 𐑉𐐯𐐿𐐲𐑉𐐼 𐐸𐐭 𐐸𐐲𐑉𐐼 𐐸𐐮𐑋. 𐐈𐑌𐐼 𐐰𐑁𐐻𐐲𐑉 𐑄𐐮𐑅 𐑋𐐰𐑌𐐲𐑉 𐐼𐐭 𐑄𐐩 𐐺𐐩𐑉 𐑉𐐯𐐿𐐲𐑉𐐼: 𐐜 𐐴 𐐸𐐰𐑃 𐑌𐐯𐑂𐐲𐑉 𐑅𐐨𐑌, 𐑌𐐨𐑄𐐲𐑉 𐐸𐐰𐑃 𐑄 𐐨𐑉 𐐸𐐲𐑉𐐼, 𐐺𐐨𐑁𐐬𐑉, 𐑅𐐬 𐑀𐑉𐐩𐐻 𐐰𐑌𐐼 𐑋𐐪𐑉𐑂𐐯𐑊𐐲𐑅 𐑃𐐮𐑍𐑆 𐐰𐑆 𐐶𐐨 𐑅𐐫 𐐰𐑌𐐼 𐐸𐐲𐑉𐐼 𐐖𐐨𐑆𐐲𐑅 𐑅𐐹𐐨𐐿 𐐲𐑌𐐻𐐭 𐑄 𐐙𐐪𐑄𐐲𐑉; 𐐰𐑌𐐼 𐑌𐐬 𐐻𐐲𐑍 𐐿𐐰𐑌 𐑅𐐹𐐨𐐿, 𐑌𐐨𐑄𐐲𐑉 𐐿𐐰𐑌 𐑄𐐯𐑉 𐐺𐐨 𐑉𐐮𐐻𐑌 𐐺𐐴 𐐯𐑌𐐨 𐑋𐐰𐑌, 𐑌𐐨𐑄𐐲𐑉 𐐿𐐰𐑌 𐑄 𐐸𐐪𐑉𐐻𐑅 𐐱𐑂 𐑋𐐯𐑌 𐐿𐐱𐑌𐑅𐐨𐑂 𐑅𐐬 𐑀𐑉𐐩𐐻 𐐰𐑌𐐼 𐑋𐐪𐑉𐑂𐐯𐑊𐐲𐑅 𐑃𐐮𐑍𐑆 𐐰𐑆 𐐶𐐨 𐐺𐐬𐑃 𐑅𐐫 𐐰𐑌𐐼 𐐸𐐲𐑉𐐼 𐐖𐐨𐑆𐐲𐑅 𐑅𐐹𐐨𐐿; 𐐰𐑌𐐼 𐑌𐐬 𐐶𐐲𐑌 𐐿𐐰𐑌 𐐿𐐱𐑌𐑅𐐨𐑂 𐐱𐑂 𐑄 𐐾𐑎 𐐸𐐶𐐮𐐽 𐑁𐐮𐑊𐐼 𐐵𐑉 𐑅𐐬𐑊𐑆 𐐰𐐻 𐑄 𐐻𐐴𐑋 𐐶𐐨 𐐸𐐲𐑉𐐼 𐐸𐐮𐑋 𐐹𐑉𐐩 𐑁𐐫𐑉 𐐲𐑅 𐐲𐑌𐐻𐐭 𐑄 𐐙𐐪𐑄𐐲𐑉.

5. 𐐈𐑌𐐼 𐐮𐐻 𐐿𐐩𐑋 𐐻𐐭 𐐹𐐪𐑅 𐑄𐐰𐐻 𐐸𐐶𐐯𐑌 𐐖𐐨𐑆𐐲𐑅 𐐸𐐰𐐼 𐑋𐐩𐐼 𐐰𐑌 𐐯𐑌𐐼 𐐱𐑂 𐐹𐑉𐐩𐐮𐑍 𐐲𐑌𐐻𐐭 𐑄 𐐙𐐪𐑄𐐲𐑉, 𐐸𐐨 𐐲𐑉𐐬𐑆; 𐐺𐐲𐐻 𐑅𐐬 𐑀𐑉𐐩𐐻 𐐶𐐱𐑆 𐑄 𐐾𐑎 𐐱𐑂 𐑄 𐑋𐐲𐑊𐐻𐐨𐐻𐐷𐐭𐐼 𐑄𐐰𐐻 𐑄𐐩 𐐶𐐲𐑉 𐐬𐑂𐐲𐑉𐐿𐐲𐑋. 𐐈𐑌𐐼 𐐮𐐻 𐐿𐐩𐑋 𐐻𐐭 𐐹𐐪𐑅 𐑄𐐰𐐻 𐐖𐐨𐑆𐐲𐑅 𐑅𐐹𐐩𐐿 𐐲𐑌𐐻𐐭 𐑄𐐯𐑋, 𐐰𐑌𐐼 𐐺𐐰𐐼 𐑄𐐯𐑋 𐐲𐑉𐐴𐑆. 𐐈𐑌𐐼 𐑄𐐩 𐐲𐑉𐐬𐑆 𐑁𐑉𐐱𐑋 𐑄 𐐲𐑉𐑃, 𐐰𐑌𐐼 𐐸𐐨 𐑅𐐯𐐼 𐐲𐑌𐐻𐐭 𐑄𐐯𐑋, 𐐒𐑊𐐯𐑅𐐯𐐼 𐐪𐑉 𐐷𐐨 𐐺𐐨𐐿𐐫𐑆 𐐱𐑂 𐐷𐐳𐑉 𐑁𐐩𐑃. 𐐈𐑌𐐼 𐑌𐐵 𐐺𐐨𐐸𐐬𐑊𐐼, 𐑋𐐴 𐐾𐑎 𐐮𐑆 𐑁𐐳𐑊. 𐐈𐑌𐐼 𐐸𐐶𐐯𐑌 𐐸𐐨 𐐸𐐰𐐼 𐑅𐐯𐐼 𐑄𐐨𐑆 𐐶𐐲𐑉𐐼𐑆, 𐐸𐐨 𐐶𐐯𐐹𐐻, 𐐰𐑌𐐼 𐑄 𐑋𐐲𐑊𐐻𐐨𐐻𐐷𐐭𐐼 𐐺𐐩𐑉 𐑉𐐯𐐿𐐲𐑉𐐼 𐐱𐑂 𐐮𐐻, 𐐰𐑌𐐼 𐐸𐐨 𐐻𐐳𐐿 𐑄𐐩𐑉 𐑊𐐮𐐻𐑊 𐐽𐐮𐑊𐐼𐑉𐐯𐑌, 𐐶𐐲𐑌 𐐺𐐴 𐐶𐐲𐑌, 𐐰𐑌𐐼 𐐺𐑊𐐯𐑅𐐯𐐼 𐑄𐐯𐑋, 𐐰𐑌𐐼 𐐹𐑉𐐩𐐼 𐐲𐑌𐐻𐐭 𐑄 𐐙𐐪𐑄𐐲𐑉 𐑁𐐫𐑉 𐑄𐐯𐑋. 𐐈𐑌𐐼 𐐸𐐶𐐯𐑌 𐐸𐐨 𐐸𐐰𐐼 𐐼𐐲𐑌 𐑄𐐮𐑅 𐐸𐐨 𐐶𐐯𐐹𐐻 𐐲𐑀𐐯𐑌; 𐐰𐑌𐐼 𐐸𐐨 𐑅𐐹𐐩𐐿 𐐲𐑌𐐻𐐭 𐑄 𐑋𐐲𐑊𐐻𐐨𐐻𐐷𐐭𐐼, 𐐰𐑌𐐼 𐑅𐐯𐐼 𐐲𐑌𐐻𐐭 𐑄𐐯𐑋, 𐐒𐐨𐐸𐐬𐑊𐐼 𐐷𐐳𐑉 𐑊𐐮𐐻𐑊 𐐶𐐲𐑌𐑆. 𐐈𐑌𐐼 𐐰𐑆 𐑄𐐩 𐑊𐐳𐐿𐐻 𐐻𐐭 𐐺𐐨𐐸𐐬𐑊𐐼, 𐑄𐐩 𐐿𐐰𐑅𐐻 𐑄𐐩𐑉 𐐴𐑆 𐐻𐐬𐐲𐑉𐐼𐑆 𐐸𐐯𐑂𐐲𐑌, 𐐰𐑌𐐼 𐑄𐐩 𐑅𐐫 𐑄 𐐸𐐯𐑂𐐲𐑌𐑆 𐐬𐐹𐐲𐑌, 𐐰𐑌𐐼 𐑄𐐩 𐑅𐐫 𐐩𐑌𐐾𐐯𐑊𐑆 𐐼𐐨𐑅𐐯𐑌𐐼𐐮𐑍 𐐵𐐻 𐐱𐑂 𐐸𐐯𐑂𐐲𐑌 𐐰𐑆 𐐮𐐻 𐐶𐐲𐑉 𐐮𐑌 𐑄 𐑋𐐮𐐼𐑅𐐻 𐐱𐑂 𐑁𐐴𐑉; 𐐰𐑌𐐼 𐑄𐐩 𐐿𐐩𐑋 𐐼𐐵𐑌 𐐰𐑌𐐼 𐐯𐑌𐑅𐐲𐑉𐐿𐑊𐐼 𐑄𐐬𐑆 𐑊𐐮𐐻𐑊 𐐶𐐲𐑌𐑆 𐐲𐐺𐐵𐐻, 𐐰𐑌𐐼 𐑄𐐩 𐐶𐐲𐑉 𐐯𐑌𐑅𐐲𐑉𐐿𐑊𐐼 𐐲𐐺𐐵𐐻 𐐶𐐮𐑄 𐑁𐐴𐑉; 𐐰𐑌𐐼 𐑄 𐐩𐑌𐐾𐐯𐑊𐑆 𐐼𐐮𐐼 𐑋𐐮𐑌𐐮𐑅𐐻𐐲𐑉 𐐲𐑌𐐻𐐭 𐑄𐐯𐑋; 𐐰𐑌𐐼 𐑄 𐑋𐐲𐑊𐐻𐐨𐐻𐐷𐐭𐐼 𐐼𐐮𐐼 𐑅𐐨 𐐰𐑌𐐼 𐐸𐐨𐑉 𐐰𐑌𐐼 𐐺𐐩𐑉 𐑉𐐯𐐿𐐲𐑉𐐼; 𐐰𐑌𐐼 𐑄𐐩 𐑌𐐬 𐑄𐐰𐐻 𐑄𐐩𐑉 𐑉𐐯𐐿𐐲𐑉𐐼 𐐮𐑆 𐐻𐑉𐐭, 𐑁𐐫𐑉 𐑄𐐩 𐐫𐑊 𐐱𐑂 𐑄𐐯𐑋 𐐼𐐮𐐼 𐑅𐐨 𐐰𐑌𐐼 𐐸𐐨𐑉, 𐐯𐑂𐑉𐐨 𐑋𐐰𐑌 𐑁𐐫𐑉 𐐸𐐮𐑋𐑅𐐯𐑊𐑁; 𐐰𐑌𐐼 𐑄𐐩 𐐶𐐲𐑉 𐐮𐑌 𐑌𐐲𐑋𐐺𐐲𐑉 𐐲𐐺𐐵𐐻 𐐻𐐭 𐑃𐐵𐑆𐐲𐑌𐐼 𐐰𐑌𐐼 𐑁𐐴𐑂 𐐸𐐲𐑌𐐼𐑉𐐯𐐼 𐑅𐐬𐑊𐑆; 𐐰𐑌𐐼 𐑄𐐩 𐐼𐐮𐐼 𐐿𐐱𐑌𐑅𐐮𐑅𐐻 𐐱𐑂 𐑋𐐯𐑌, 𐐶𐐮𐑋𐐯𐑌, 𐐰𐑌𐐼 𐐽𐐮𐑊𐐼𐑉𐐯𐑌.

6. 𐐈𐑌𐐼 𐐮𐐻 𐐿𐐩𐑋 𐐻𐐭 𐐹𐐪𐑅 𐑄𐐰𐐻 𐐖𐐨𐑆𐐲𐑅 𐐿𐐱𐑋𐐰𐑌𐐼𐐯𐐼 𐐸𐐮𐑆 𐐼𐐮𐑅𐐴𐐹𐑊𐑆 𐑄𐐰𐐻 𐑄𐐩 𐑇𐐳𐐼 𐐺𐑉𐐮𐑍 𐑁𐐬𐑉𐑃 𐑅𐐲𐑋 𐐺𐑉𐐯𐐼 𐐰𐑌𐐼 𐐶𐐴𐑌 𐐲𐑌𐐻𐐭 𐐸𐐮𐑋. 𐐈𐑌𐐼 𐐸𐐶𐐴𐑊 𐑄𐐩 𐐶𐐲𐑉 𐑀𐐱𐑌 𐑁𐐫𐑉 𐐺𐑉𐐯𐐼 𐐰𐑌𐐼 𐐶𐐴𐑌, 𐐸𐐨 𐐿𐐱𐑋𐐰𐑌𐐼𐐯𐐼 𐑄 𐑋𐐲𐑊𐐻𐐨𐐻𐐷𐐭𐐼 𐑄𐐰𐐻 𐑄𐐩 𐑇𐐳𐐼 𐑅𐐮𐐻 𐑄𐐯𐑋𐑅𐐯𐑊𐑂𐑆 𐐼𐐵𐑌 𐐲𐐹𐐱𐑌 𐑄 𐐲𐑉𐑃. 𐐈𐑌𐐼 𐐸𐐶𐐯𐑌 𐑄 𐐼𐐮𐑅𐐴𐐹𐑊𐑆 𐐸𐐰𐐼 𐐿𐐲𐑋 𐐶𐐮𐑄 𐐺𐑉𐐯𐐼 𐐰𐑌𐐼 𐐶𐐴𐑌, 𐐸𐐨 𐐻𐐳𐐿 𐐱𐑂 𐑄 𐐺𐑉𐐯𐐼 𐐰𐑌𐐼 𐐺𐑉𐐩𐐿 𐐰𐑌𐐼 𐐺𐑊𐐯𐑅𐐯𐐼 𐐮𐐻; 𐐰𐑌𐐼 𐐸𐐨 𐑀𐐩𐑂 𐐲𐑌𐐻𐐭 𐑄 𐐼𐐮𐑅𐐴𐐹𐑊𐑆 𐐰𐑌𐐼 𐐿𐐱𐑋𐐰𐑌𐐼𐐯𐐼 𐑄𐐰𐐻 𐑄𐐩 𐑇𐐳𐐼 𐐨𐐻. 𐐈𐑌𐐼 𐐸𐐶𐐯𐑌 𐑄𐐩 𐐸𐐰𐐼 𐐨𐐻𐑌 𐐰𐑌𐐼 𐐶𐐲𐑉 𐑁𐐮𐑊𐐼, 𐐸𐐨 𐐿𐐱𐑋𐐰𐑌𐐼𐐯𐐼 𐑄𐐰𐐻 𐑄𐐩 𐑇𐐳𐐼 𐑀𐐮𐑂 𐐲𐑌𐐻𐐭 𐑄 𐑋𐐲𐑊𐐻𐐨𐐻𐐷𐐭𐐼. 𐐈𐑌𐐼 𐐸𐐶𐐯𐑌 𐑄 𐑋𐐲𐑊𐐻𐐨𐐻𐐷𐐭𐐼 𐐸𐐰𐐼 𐐨𐐻𐑌 𐐰𐑌𐐼 𐐶𐐲𐑉 𐑁𐐮𐑊𐐼, 𐐸𐐨 𐑅𐐯𐐼 𐐲𐑌𐐻𐐭 𐑄 𐐼𐐮𐑅𐐴𐐹𐑊𐑆, 𐐒𐐨𐐸𐐬𐑊𐐼 𐑄𐐯𐑉 𐑇𐐰𐑊 𐐶𐐲𐑌 𐐺𐐨 𐐫𐑉𐐼𐐩𐑌𐐼 𐐲𐑋𐐲𐑍 𐐷𐐭, 𐐰𐑌𐐼 𐐻𐐭 𐐸𐐮𐑋 𐐶𐐮𐑊 𐐌 𐑀𐐮𐑂 𐐹𐐵𐐲𐑉 𐑄𐐰𐐻 𐐸𐐨 𐑇𐐰𐑊 𐐺𐑉𐐩𐐿 𐐺𐑉𐐯𐐼 𐐰𐑌𐐼 𐐺𐑊𐐯𐑅 𐐮𐐻, 𐐰𐑌𐐼 𐑀𐐮𐑂 𐐮𐐻 𐐲𐑌𐐻𐐭 𐑄 𐐹𐐨𐐹𐑊 𐐱𐑂 𐑋𐐴 𐐽𐐲𐑉𐐽, 𐐲𐑌𐐻𐐭 𐐫𐑊 𐑄𐐬𐑆 𐐸𐐭 𐑇𐐰𐑊 𐐺𐐨𐑊𐐨𐑂 𐐰𐑌𐐼 𐐺𐐨 𐐺𐐰𐐹𐐻𐐴𐑆𐐼 𐐮𐑌 𐑋𐐴 𐑌𐐩𐑋. 𐐈𐑌𐐼 𐑄𐐮𐑅 𐑇𐐰𐑊 𐐷𐐨 𐐫𐑊𐐶𐐩𐑆 𐐱𐐺𐑆𐐲𐑉𐑂 𐐻𐐭 𐐼𐐭, 𐐨𐑂𐐲𐑌 𐐰𐑆 𐐌 𐐸𐐰𐑂 𐐼𐐲𐑌, 𐐨𐑂𐐲𐑌 𐐰𐑆 𐐌 𐐸𐐰𐑂 𐐺𐑉𐐬𐐿𐑌 𐐺𐑉𐐯𐐼 𐐰𐑌𐐼 𐐺𐑊𐐯𐑅𐐯𐐼 𐐮𐐻, 𐐰𐑌𐐼 𐑀𐐮𐑂𐑌 𐐮𐐻 𐐲𐑌𐐻𐐭 𐐷𐐭. 𐐈𐑌𐐼 𐑄𐐮𐑅 𐑇𐐰𐑊 𐐷𐐨 𐐼𐐭 𐐮𐑌 𐑉𐐨𐑋𐐯𐑋𐐺𐑉𐐰𐑌𐑅 𐐱𐑂 𐑋𐐴 𐐺𐐱𐐼𐐨, 𐐸𐐶𐐮𐐽 𐐌 𐐸𐐰𐑂 𐑇𐐬𐑌 𐐲𐑌𐐻𐐭 𐐷𐐭. 𐐈𐑌𐐼 𐐮𐐻 𐑇𐐰𐑊 𐐺𐐨 𐐲 𐐻𐐯𐑅𐐻𐐮𐑋𐐬𐑌𐐨 𐐲𐑌𐐻𐐭 𐑄 𐐙𐐪𐑄𐐲𐑉 𐑄𐐰𐐻 𐐷𐐨 𐐼𐐭 𐐫𐑊𐐶𐐩𐑆 𐑉𐐨𐑋𐐯𐑋𐐺𐐲𐑉 𐑋𐐨. 𐐈𐑌𐐼 𐐮𐑁 𐐷𐐨 𐐼𐐭 𐐫𐑊𐐶𐐩𐑆 𐑉𐐨𐑋𐐯𐑋𐐺𐐲𐑉 𐑋𐐨, 𐐷𐐨 𐑇𐐰𐑊 𐐸𐐰𐑂 𐑋𐐴 𐐝𐐹𐐮𐑉𐐮𐐻 𐐻𐐭 𐐺𐐨 𐐶𐐮𐑄 𐐷𐐭.

7. 𐐈𐑌𐐼 𐐮𐐻 𐐿𐐩𐑋 𐐻𐐭 𐐹𐐪𐑅 𐑄𐐰𐐻 𐐸𐐶𐐯𐑌 𐐸𐐨 𐐸𐐰𐐼 𐑅𐐯𐐼 𐑄𐐨𐑆 𐐶𐐲𐑉𐐼𐑆, 𐐸𐐨 𐐿𐐱𐑋𐐰𐑌𐐼𐐯𐐼 𐐸𐐮𐑆 𐐼𐐮𐑅𐐴-

𐐹𐑊𐑆 𐑄𐐰𐐻 𐑄𐐩 𐑇𐐳𐐼 𐐻𐐩𐐿 𐐱𐑂 𐑄 𐐶𐐴𐑌 𐐱𐑂 𐑄 𐐿𐐲𐐹, 𐐰𐑌𐐼 𐐼𐑉𐐮𐑍𐐿 𐐱𐑂 𐐮𐐻, 𐐰𐑌𐐼 𐑄𐐰𐐻 𐑄𐐩 𐑇𐐳𐐼 𐐫𐑊𐑅𐐬 𐑀𐐮𐑂 𐐲𐑌𐐻𐐭 𐑄 𐑋𐐲𐑊𐐻𐐮𐐻𐐷𐐭𐐼, 𐑄𐐰𐐻 𐑄𐐩 𐑋𐐴𐐻 𐐼𐑉𐐮𐑍𐐿 𐐱𐑂 𐐮𐐻. 𐐈𐑌𐐼 𐐮𐐻 𐐿𐐩𐑋 𐐻𐐭 𐐹𐐰𐑅 𐑄𐐰𐐻 𐑄𐐩 𐐼𐐮𐐼 𐑅𐐬, 𐐰𐑌𐐼 𐐼𐐮𐐼 𐐼𐑉𐐮𐑍𐐿 𐐱𐑂 𐐮𐐻, 𐐰𐑌𐐼 𐐶𐐲𐑉 𐑁𐐮𐑊𐐼; 𐐰𐑌𐐼 𐑄𐐩 𐑀𐐩𐑂 𐐲𐑌𐐻𐐭 𐑄 𐑋𐐲𐑊𐐻𐐮𐐻𐐷𐐭𐐼, 𐐰𐑌𐐼 𐑄𐐩 𐐼𐐮𐐼 𐐼𐑉𐐮𐑍𐐿, 𐐰𐑌𐐼 𐑄𐐩 𐐶𐐲𐑉 𐑁𐐮𐑊𐐼. 𐐈𐑌𐐼 𐐸𐐶𐐯𐑌 𐑄 𐐼𐐮𐑅𐐴𐐹𐑊𐑆 𐐸𐐰𐐼 𐐼𐐲𐑌 𐑄𐐮𐑅, 𐐖𐐨𐑆𐐲𐑅 𐑅𐐯𐐼 𐐲𐑌𐐻𐐭 𐑄𐐯𐑋, 𐐒𐑊𐐯𐑅𐐯𐐼 𐐪𐑉 𐐷𐐨 𐑁𐐫𐑉 𐑄𐐮𐑅 𐑃𐐮𐑍 𐐸𐐶𐐮𐐽 𐐷𐐨 𐐸𐐰𐑂 𐐼𐐲𐑌, 𐑁𐐫𐑉 𐑄𐐮𐑅 𐐮𐑆 𐑁𐐳𐑊𐑁𐐮𐑊𐐮𐑍 𐑋𐐴 𐐿𐐱𐑋𐐰𐑌𐐼-𐑋𐐯𐑌𐐻𐑅, 𐐰𐑌𐐼 𐑄𐐮𐑅 𐐼𐐲𐑃 𐐶𐐮𐐻𐑌𐐯𐑅 𐐲𐑌𐐻𐐭 𐑄 𐐙𐐪𐑄𐐲𐑉 𐑄𐐰𐐻 𐐷𐐨 𐐪𐑉 𐐶𐐮𐑊𐐮𐑍 𐐻𐐭 𐐼𐐭 𐑄𐐰𐐻 𐐸𐐶𐐮𐐽 𐐌 𐐸𐐰𐑂 𐐿𐐱𐑋𐐰𐑌𐐼𐐯𐐼 𐐷𐐭. 𐐈𐑌𐐼 𐑄𐐮𐑅 𐑇𐐰𐑊 𐐷𐐨 𐐫𐑊𐐶𐐩𐑆 𐐼𐐭 𐐻𐐭 𐑄𐐬𐑆 𐐸𐐭 𐑉𐐨𐐹𐐯𐑌𐐻 𐐰𐑌𐐼 𐐪𐑉 𐐺𐐰𐐹𐐻𐐴𐑆𐐼 𐐮𐑌 𐑋𐐴 𐑌𐐩𐑋; 𐐰𐑌𐐼 𐐷𐐨 𐑇𐐰𐑊 𐐼𐐭 𐐮𐐻 𐐮𐑌 𐑉𐐨𐑋𐐯𐑋𐐺𐑉𐐰𐑌𐑅 𐐱𐑂 𐑋𐐴 𐐺𐑊𐐲𐐼, 𐐸𐐶𐐮𐐽 𐐌 𐐸𐐰𐑂 𐑇𐐯𐐼 𐑁𐐫𐑉 𐐷𐐭, 𐑄𐐰𐐻 𐐷𐐨 𐑋𐐩 𐐶𐐮𐐻𐑌𐐯𐑅 𐐲𐑌𐐻𐐭 𐑄 𐐙𐐪𐑄𐐲𐑉 𐑄𐐰𐐻 𐐷𐐨 𐐼𐐭 𐐫𐑊𐐶𐐩𐑆 𐑉𐐨𐑋𐐯𐑋𐐺𐐲𐑉 𐑋𐐨. 𐐈𐑌𐐼 𐐮𐑁 𐐷𐐨 𐐼𐐭 𐐫𐑊𐐶𐐩𐑆 𐑉𐐨𐑋𐐯𐑋𐐺𐐲𐑉 𐑋𐐨, 𐐷𐐨 𐑇𐐰𐑊 𐐸𐐰𐑂 𐑋𐐴 𐐝𐐹𐐮𐑉𐐮𐐻 𐐻𐐭 𐐺𐐨 𐐶𐐮𐑄 𐐷𐐭. 𐐈𐑌𐐼 𐐌 𐑀𐐮𐑂 𐐲𐑌𐐻𐐭 𐐷𐐭 𐐰 𐐿𐐱𐑋𐐰𐑌𐐼𐑋𐐯𐑌𐐻 𐑄𐐰𐐻 𐐷𐐨 𐑇𐐰𐑊 𐐼𐐭 𐑄𐐨𐑆 𐑃𐐮𐑍𐑆. 𐐈𐑌𐐼 𐐮𐑁 𐐷𐐨 𐑇𐐰𐑊 𐐫𐑊𐐶𐐩𐑆 𐐼𐐭 𐑄𐐨𐑆 𐑃𐐮𐑍𐑆, 𐐺𐑊𐐯𐑅-𐐯𐐼 𐐪𐑉 𐐷𐐨, 𐑁𐐫𐑉 𐐷𐐨 𐐪𐑉 𐐺𐐮𐑊𐐻 𐐲𐐹𐐱𐑌 𐑋𐐴 𐑉𐐱𐐿. 𐐒𐐲𐐻 𐐸𐐭𐑅𐐬 𐐰𐑋𐐲𐑍 𐐷𐐭 𐑇𐐰𐑊 𐐼𐐭 𐑋𐐬𐑉 𐐫𐑉 𐑊𐐯𐑅 𐑄𐐰𐑌 𐑄𐐨𐑆 𐐪𐑉 𐑌𐐱𐐻 𐐺𐐮𐑊𐐻 𐐲𐐹𐐱𐑌 𐑋𐐴 𐑉𐐱𐐿, 𐐺𐐲𐐻 𐐪𐑉 𐐺𐐮𐑊𐐻 𐐲𐐹𐐱𐑌 𐐰 𐑅𐐰𐑌𐐼𐐨 𐑁𐐵𐑌𐐼𐐩𐑇𐐲𐑌; 𐐰𐑌𐐼 𐐸𐐶𐐯𐑌 𐑄 𐑉𐐩𐑌 𐐼𐐨𐑅𐐯𐑌𐐼𐑆, 𐐰𐑌𐐼 𐑄 𐑁𐑊𐐲𐐼𐑆 𐐿𐐲𐑋, 𐐰𐑌𐐼 𐑄 𐐶𐐮𐑌𐐼𐑆 𐐺𐑊𐐬, 𐐰𐑌𐐼 𐐺𐐨𐐻 𐐲𐐹𐐱𐑌 𐑄𐐯𐑋, 𐑄𐐩 𐑇𐐰𐑊 𐑁𐐫𐑊, 𐐰𐑌𐐼 𐑄 𐑀𐐩𐐻𐑅 𐐱𐑂 𐐸𐐯𐑊 𐐪𐑉 𐑉𐐯𐐼𐐨 𐐬𐐹𐑌 𐐻𐐭 𐑉𐐨𐑅𐐨𐑂 𐑄𐐯𐑋. 𐐜𐐯𐑉𐑁𐐬𐑉 𐐺𐑊𐐯𐑅𐐯𐐼 𐐪𐑉 𐐷𐐨 𐐮𐑁 𐐷𐐨 𐑇𐐰𐑊 𐐿𐐨𐐹 𐑋𐐴 𐐿𐐱𐑋𐐰𐑌𐐼𐑋𐐯𐑌𐐻𐑅, 𐐸𐐶𐐮𐐽 𐑄 𐐙𐐪𐑄𐐲𐑉 𐐸𐐰𐑃 𐐿𐐱𐑋𐐰𐑌𐐼𐐯𐐼 𐑋𐐨 𐑄𐐰𐐻 𐐌 𐑇𐐳𐐼 𐑀𐐮𐑂 𐐲𐑌𐐻𐐭 𐐷𐐭. 𐐚𐐯𐑉𐐮𐑊𐐨, 𐑂𐐯𐑉𐐮𐑊𐐨 𐐌 𐑅𐐩 𐐲𐑌𐐻𐐭 𐐷𐐭, 𐐷𐐨 𐑋𐐲𐑅𐐻 𐐶𐐱𐐽 𐐰𐑌𐐼 𐐹𐑉𐐩 𐐫𐑊𐐶𐐩𐑆, 𐑊𐐯𐑅𐐻 𐐷𐐨 𐐺𐐨 𐐻𐐯𐑋𐐹𐐻𐐯𐐼 𐐺𐐴 𐑄 𐐼𐐯𐑂𐐮𐑊, 𐐰𐑌𐐼 𐐷𐐨 𐐺𐐨 𐑊𐐯𐐼 𐐰𐐶𐐩 𐐿𐐰𐐹𐐻𐐮𐑂 𐐺𐐴 𐐸𐐮𐑋. 𐐈𐑌𐐼 𐐰𐑆 𐐌 𐐸𐐰𐑂 𐐹𐑉𐐩𐐼 𐐰𐑋𐐲𐑍 𐐷𐐭, 𐐨𐑂𐐯𐑌 𐑅𐐬 𐑇𐐰𐑊 𐐷𐐨 𐐹𐑉𐐩 𐐮𐑌 𐑋𐐴 𐐽𐐲𐑉𐐽, 𐐰𐑋𐐲𐑍 𐑋𐐴 𐐹𐐨𐐹𐑊 𐐸𐐭 𐐼𐐭 𐑉𐐨𐐹𐐯𐑌𐐻 𐐰𐑌𐐼 𐐪𐑉 𐐺𐐰𐐹𐐻𐐴𐑆𐐼 𐐮𐑌 𐑋𐐴 𐑌𐐩𐑋. 𐐒𐐨𐐸𐐬𐑊𐐼, 𐐌 𐐰𐑋 𐑄 𐑊𐐴𐐻; 𐐌 𐐸𐐰𐑂 𐑅𐐯𐐻 𐐰𐑌 𐐯𐑀𐑆𐐰𐑋𐐹𐑊 𐑁𐐫𐑉 𐐷𐐭.

8. 𐐈𐑌𐐼 𐐮𐐻 𐐿𐐩𐑋 𐐻𐐭 𐐹𐐰𐑅 𐑄𐐰𐐻 𐐸𐐶𐐯𐑌 𐐖𐐨𐑆𐐲𐑅 𐐸𐐰𐐼 𐑅𐐹𐐬𐐿𐐲𐑌 𐑄𐐨𐑆 𐐶𐐲𐑉𐐼𐑆 𐐲𐑌𐐻𐐭 𐐸𐐮𐑆 𐐼𐐮𐑅𐐴-𐐹𐑊𐑆, 𐐸𐐨 𐐻𐐲𐑉𐑌𐐼 𐐰𐑀𐐯𐑌 𐐲𐑌𐐻𐐭 𐑄 𐑋𐐲𐑊𐐻𐐮𐐻𐐷𐐭𐐼, 𐐰𐑌𐐼 𐑅𐐯𐐼 𐐲𐑌𐐻𐐭 𐑄𐐯𐑋, 𐐒𐐨𐐸𐐬𐑊𐐼, 𐑂𐐯𐑉𐐮𐑊𐐨, 𐑂𐐯𐑉𐐮𐑊𐐨 𐐌 𐑅𐐩 𐐲𐑌𐐻𐐭 𐐷𐐭, 𐐷𐐨 𐑋𐐲𐑅𐐻 𐐶𐐱𐐽 𐐰𐑌𐐼 𐐹𐑉𐐩 𐐫𐑊𐐶𐐩𐑆, 𐑊𐐯𐑅𐐻 𐐷𐐨 𐐯𐑌𐐻𐐲𐑉 𐐮𐑌𐐻𐐭 𐐻𐐯𐑋𐐻𐐩𐑇𐐲𐑌; 𐑁𐐫𐑉 𐐝𐐩𐐻𐐲𐑌 𐐼𐐨𐑆𐐴𐑉𐐯𐑃 𐐻𐐭 𐐸𐐰𐑂 𐐷𐐭; 𐑄𐐰𐐻 𐐸𐐨 𐑋𐐩 𐑅𐐮𐑁𐐻 𐐷𐐭 𐐰𐑆 𐐸𐐶𐐨𐐻; 𐑄𐐯𐑉𐑁𐐬𐑉 𐐷𐐨 𐑋𐐲𐑅𐐻 𐐫𐑊𐐶𐐩𐑆 𐐹𐑉𐐩 𐐲𐑌𐐻𐐭 𐑄 𐐙𐐪𐑄𐐲𐑉 𐐮𐑌 𐑋𐐴 𐑌𐐩𐑋; 𐐰𐑌𐐼 𐐸𐐶𐐱𐐻𐑅𐐬𐐯𐑂𐐲𐑉 𐐷𐐨 𐑇𐐰𐑊 𐐰𐑅𐐿 𐑄 𐐙𐐪𐑄𐐲𐑉 𐐮𐑌 𐑋𐐴 𐑌𐐩𐑋, 𐐸𐐶𐐮𐐽 𐐮𐑆 𐑉𐐴𐐻, 𐐺𐐨𐑊𐐨𐑂𐐮𐑍 𐑄𐐰𐐻 𐐷𐐨 𐑇𐐰𐑊 𐑉𐐨𐑅𐐨𐑂, 𐐺𐐨𐐸𐐬𐑊𐐼 𐐮𐐻 𐑇𐐰𐑊 𐐺𐐨 𐑀𐐮𐑂𐐲𐑌 𐐲𐑌𐐻𐐭 𐐷𐐭. 𐐑𐑉𐐩 𐐮𐑌 𐐷𐐭𐑉 𐑁𐐰𐑋𐐮𐑊𐐨𐑆 𐐲𐑌𐐻𐐭 𐑄 𐐙𐐪𐑄𐐲𐑉, 𐐫𐑊𐐶𐐩𐑆 𐐮𐑌 𐑋𐐴 𐑌𐐩𐑋, 𐑄𐐰𐐻 𐐷𐐭𐑉 𐐶𐐴𐑂𐑆 𐐰𐑌𐐼 𐐷𐐭𐑉 𐐽𐐮𐑊-𐐼𐑉𐐯𐑌 𐑋𐐩 𐐺𐐨 𐐺𐑊𐐯𐑅𐐯𐐼. 𐐈𐑌𐐼 𐐺𐐨𐐸𐐬𐑊𐐼, 𐐷𐐨 𐑇𐐰𐑊 𐑋𐐨𐐻 𐐻𐐭𐑀𐐯𐑄𐐲𐑉 𐐫𐑁𐐻; 𐐰𐑌𐐼 𐐷𐐨 𐑇𐐰𐑊 𐑌𐐱𐐻 𐑁𐐫𐑉𐐺𐐮𐐼 𐐯𐑌𐐨 𐑋𐐰𐑌 𐑁𐑉𐐱𐑋 𐐿𐐲𐑋𐐮𐑍 𐐲𐑌𐐻𐐭 𐐷𐐭 𐐸𐐶𐐯𐑌 𐐷𐐨 𐑇𐐰𐑊 𐑋𐐨𐐻 𐐻𐐭𐑀𐐯𐑄𐐲𐑉, 𐐺𐐲𐐻 𐑅𐐲𐑁𐐲𐑉 𐑄𐐯𐑋 𐑄𐐰𐐻 𐑄𐐩 𐑋𐐩 𐐿𐐲𐑋 𐐲𐑌𐐻𐐭 𐐷𐐭, 𐐰𐑌𐐼 𐑁𐐫𐑉𐐺𐐮𐐼 𐑄𐐯𐑋 𐑌𐐱𐐻; 𐐺𐐲𐐻 𐐷𐐨 𐑇𐐰𐑊 𐐹𐑉𐐩 𐑁𐐫𐑉 𐑄𐐯𐑋, 𐐰𐑌𐐼 𐑇𐐰𐑊 𐑌𐐱𐐻 𐐿𐐰𐑅𐐻 𐑄𐐯𐑋 𐐵𐐻; 𐐰𐑌𐐼 𐐮𐑁 𐐮𐐻 𐑅𐐬 𐐺𐐨 𐑄𐐰𐐻 𐑄𐐩 𐐿𐐲𐑋 𐐲𐑌𐐻𐐭 𐐷𐐭 𐐫𐑁𐐻, 𐐷𐐨 𐑇𐐰𐑊 𐐹𐑉𐐩 𐑁𐐫𐑉 𐑄𐐯𐑋 𐐲𐑌𐐻𐐭 𐑄 𐐙𐐪𐑄𐐲𐑉, 𐐮𐑌 𐑋𐐴 𐑌𐐩𐑋; 𐑄𐐯𐑉𐑁𐐬𐑉 𐐸𐐬𐑊𐐼 𐐲𐐹 𐐷𐐭𐑉 𐑊𐐴𐐻 𐑄𐐰𐐻 𐐮𐐻 𐑋𐐩 𐑇𐐴𐑌 𐐲𐑌𐐻𐐭 𐑄 𐐶𐐲𐑉𐑊𐐼. 𐐒𐐨𐐸𐐬𐑊𐐼 𐐌 𐐰𐑋 𐑄 𐑊𐐴𐐻 𐐸𐐶𐐮𐐽 𐐷𐐨 𐑇𐐰𐑊 𐐸𐐬𐑊𐐼 𐐲𐐹—𐑄𐐰𐐻 𐐸𐐶𐐮𐐽 𐐷𐐨 𐐸𐐰𐑂 𐑅𐐨𐑌 𐑋𐐨 𐐼𐐭. 𐐒𐐨-𐐸𐐬𐑊𐐼 𐐷𐐨 𐑅𐐨 𐑄𐐰𐐻 𐐌 𐐸𐐰𐑂 𐐹𐑉𐐩𐐼 𐐲𐑌𐐻𐐭 𐑄 𐐙𐐪𐑄𐐲𐑉, 𐐰𐑌𐐼 𐐷𐐨 𐐫𐑊 𐐸𐐰𐑂 𐐶𐐮𐐻𐑌𐐯𐑅𐐻; 𐐰𐑌𐐼 𐐷𐐨 𐑅𐐨 𐑄𐐰𐐻 𐐌 𐐸𐐰𐑂 𐐿𐐱𐑋𐐰𐑌𐐼𐐯𐐼 𐑄𐐰𐐻 𐑌𐐲𐑌 𐐱𐑂 𐐷𐐭 𐑇𐐳𐐼 𐑀𐐬 𐐰𐐶𐐩, 𐐺𐐲𐐻 𐑉𐐰𐑄𐐲𐑉 𐐸𐐰𐑂 𐐿𐐱𐑋𐐰𐑌𐐼𐐯𐐼 𐑄𐐰𐐻 𐐷𐐨 𐑇𐐳𐐼 𐐿𐐲𐑋 𐐲𐑌𐐻𐐭 𐑋𐐨, 𐑄𐐰𐐻 𐐷𐐨 𐑋𐐴𐐻 𐑁𐐨𐑊 𐐰𐑌𐐼 𐑅𐐨; 𐐨𐑂𐐯𐑌 𐑅𐐬 𐑇𐐰𐑊 𐐷𐐨 𐐼𐐭 𐐲𐑌𐐻𐐭 𐑄 𐐶𐐲𐑉𐑊𐐼; 𐐰𐑌𐐼 𐐸𐐭𐑅𐐬𐐯𐑂𐐲𐑉 𐐺𐑉𐐩𐐿𐐯𐑃 𐑄𐐮𐑅 𐐿𐐱𐑋𐐰𐑌𐐼𐑋𐐯𐑌𐐻, 𐑅𐐲𐑁𐐲𐑉𐐯𐑃 𐐸𐐮𐑋𐑅𐐯𐑊𐑁 𐐻𐐭 𐐺𐐨 𐑊𐐯𐐼 𐐮𐑌𐐻𐐭 𐐻𐐯𐑋-𐐻𐐩𐑇𐐲𐑌.

9. 𐐈𐑌𐐼 𐑌𐐵 𐐮𐐻 𐐿𐐩𐑋 𐐻𐐭 𐐹𐐰𐑅 𐑄𐐰𐐻 𐐸𐐶𐐯𐑌 𐐖𐐨𐑆𐐲𐑅 𐐸𐐰𐐼 𐑅𐐹𐐬𐐿𐐲𐑌 𐑄𐐨𐑆 𐐶𐐲𐑉𐐼𐑆, 𐐸𐐨 𐐻𐐲𐑉𐑌𐐼 𐐸𐐮𐑆 𐐴𐑆 𐐰𐑀𐐯𐑌 𐐲𐐹𐐱𐑌 𐑄 𐐼𐐮𐑅𐐴𐐹𐑊𐑆 𐐸𐐭𐑋 𐐸𐐨 𐐸𐐰𐐼 𐐽𐐬𐑆𐐲𐑌, 𐐰𐑌𐐼 𐑅𐐯𐐼 𐐲𐑌𐐻𐐭 𐑄𐐯𐑋, 𐐒𐐨𐐸𐐬𐑊𐐼, 𐑂𐐯𐑉𐐮𐑊𐐨, 𐑂𐐯𐑉𐐮𐑊𐐨 𐐌 𐑅𐐩 𐐲𐑌𐐻𐐭 𐐷𐐭, 𐐌 𐑀𐐮𐑂 𐐲𐑌𐐻𐐭 𐐷𐐭 𐐰𐑌𐐲𐑄𐐲𐑉 𐐿𐐱𐑋𐐰𐑌𐐼𐑋𐐯𐑌𐐻, 𐐰𐑌𐐼 𐑄𐐯𐑌 𐐌

𐑋𐐲𐑅𐐻 𐑀𐐬 𐐲𐑌𐐻𐐭 𐑋𐐴 𐐙𐐪𐑄𐐯𐑉, 𐑄𐐰𐐻 𐐌 𐑋𐐩 𐑁𐐳𐑊𐑁𐐮𐑊 𐐲𐑄𐐯𐑉 𐐿𐐲𐑋𐐰𐑌𐐼𐑋𐐯𐑌𐐻𐑆 𐐸𐐶𐐮𐐽 𐐸𐐨 𐐸𐐰𐑃 𐑀𐐮𐑂𐑌 𐑋𐐨. 𐐈𐑌𐐼 𐑌𐐵 𐐺𐐨𐐸𐐬𐑊𐐼, 𐑄𐐮𐑅 𐐮𐑆 𐑄 𐐿𐐲𐑋𐐰𐑌𐐼𐑋𐐯𐑌𐐻 𐐸𐐶𐐮𐐽 𐐌 𐑀𐐮𐑂 𐐲𐑌𐐻𐐭 𐐷𐐭, 𐑄𐐰𐐻 𐐷 𐑇𐐰𐑊 𐑌𐐱𐐻 𐑅𐐲𐑁𐐯𐑉 𐐯𐑌𐐮 𐐶𐐲𐑌 𐑌𐐬𐐮𐑍𐑊𐐮, 𐐻𐐭 𐐹𐐪𐑉𐐻𐐩𐐿 𐐱𐑂 𐑋𐐴 𐑁𐑊𐐯𐑇 𐐰𐑌𐐼 𐐺𐑊𐐲𐐼 𐐲𐑌𐐶𐐲𐑉𐑄𐐮𐑊𐐮, 𐐸𐐶𐐯𐑌 𐐷 𐑇𐐰𐑊 𐑋𐐮𐑌𐐮𐑅𐐻𐐯𐑉 𐐮𐐻, 𐑁𐐬𐑉 𐐸𐐭𐑅𐐬 𐐨𐐻𐐯𐑃 𐐰𐑌𐐼 𐐼𐑉𐐮𐑍𐐿𐐯𐑃 𐑋𐐴 𐑁𐑊𐐯𐑇 𐐰𐑌𐐼 𐐺𐑊𐐲𐐼 𐐲𐑌𐐶𐐲𐑉𐑄𐐮𐑊𐐮, 𐐨𐐻𐐯𐑃 𐐰𐑌𐐼 𐐼𐑉𐐮𐑍𐐿𐐯𐑃 𐐼𐐰𐑋𐑌𐐩𐑇𐐲𐑌 𐐻𐐭 𐐸𐐮𐑆 𐑅𐐬𐑊; 𐑄𐐩𐑉𐑁𐐬𐑉 𐐮𐑁 𐐷 𐑌𐐬 𐑄𐐰𐐻 𐐩 𐑋𐐰𐑌 𐐮𐑆 𐐲𐑌𐐶𐐲𐑉𐑄𐐮 𐐻𐐭 𐐨𐐻 𐐰𐑌𐐼 𐐼𐑉𐐮𐑍𐐿 𐐱𐑂 𐑋𐐴 𐑁𐑊𐐯𐑇 𐐰𐑌𐐼 𐐺𐑊𐐲𐐼, 𐐷 𐑇𐐰𐑊 𐑁𐐲𐑉𐐺𐐮𐐼 𐐸𐐮𐑋; 𐑌𐐯𐑂𐐯𐑉𐑄𐐯𐑊𐐯𐑅 𐐷 𐑇𐐰𐑊 𐑌𐐱𐐻 𐐿𐐰𐑅𐐻 𐐸𐐮𐑋 𐐵𐐻 𐑁𐑉𐐱𐑋 𐐲𐑋𐐲𐑍 𐐷𐐭, 𐐺𐐲𐐻 𐐷 𐑇𐐰𐑊 𐑋𐐮𐑌𐐮𐑅𐐻𐐯𐑉 𐐲𐑌𐐻𐐭 𐐸𐐮𐑋, 𐐰𐑌𐐼 𐑇𐐰𐑊 𐐹𐑉𐐩 𐑁𐐬𐑉 𐐸𐐮𐑋 𐐲𐑌𐐻𐐭 𐑄 𐐙𐐪𐑄𐐯𐑉, 𐐮𐑌 𐑋𐐴 𐑌𐐩𐑋, 𐐰𐑌𐐼 𐐮𐑁 𐐮𐐻 𐑅𐐬 𐐺 𐑄𐐰𐐻 𐐸𐐨 𐑉𐐨𐐹𐐯𐑌𐐻𐐯𐑃, 𐐰𐑌𐐼 𐐮𐑆 𐐺𐐰𐐹𐐻𐐴𐑆𐐼 𐐮𐑌 𐑋𐐴 𐑌𐐩𐑋, 𐑄𐐯𐑌 𐑇𐐰𐑊 𐐷 𐑉𐐨𐑅𐐨𐑂 𐐸𐐮𐑋, 𐐰𐑌𐐼 𐑇𐐰𐑊 𐑋𐐮𐑌𐐮𐑅𐐻𐐯𐑉 𐐲𐑌𐐻𐐭 𐐸𐐮𐑋 𐐱𐑂 𐑋𐐴 𐑁𐑊𐐯𐑇 𐐰𐑌𐐼 𐐺𐑊𐐲𐐼; 𐐺𐐲𐐻 𐐮𐑁 𐐸𐐨 𐑉𐐨𐐹𐐯𐑌𐐻 𐑌𐐱𐐻, 𐐸𐐨 𐑇𐐰𐑊 𐑌𐐱𐐻 𐐺 𐑌𐐲𐑋𐐺𐐯𐑉𐐼 𐐲𐑋𐐲𐑍 𐑋𐐴 𐐹𐐨𐐹𐑊, 𐑄𐐰𐐻 𐐸𐐨 𐑋𐐩 𐑌𐐱𐐻 𐐼𐐨𐑅𐐻𐑉𐐫𐐮 𐑋𐐴 𐐹𐐨𐐹𐑊, 𐑁𐐬𐑉 𐐺𐐨𐐸𐐬𐑊𐐼, 𐐌 𐑌𐐬 𐑋𐐴 𐑇𐐨𐐹, 𐐰𐑌𐐼 𐑄𐐩 𐐪𐑉 𐑌𐐲𐑋𐐺𐐯𐑉𐐼; 𐑌𐐯𐑂𐐯𐑉𐑄𐐯𐑊𐐯𐑅 𐐷 𐑇𐐰𐑊 𐑌𐐱𐐻 𐐿𐐰𐑅𐐻 𐐸𐐮𐑋 𐐵𐐻 𐐱𐑂 𐐷𐐬𐑉 𐑅𐐮𐑌𐐰𐑀𐐱𐑀𐑆, 𐐬𐑉 𐐷𐐬𐑉 𐐹𐑊𐐩𐑅𐐯𐑆 𐐱𐑂 𐐶𐐲𐑉𐑇𐐮𐐹, 𐑁𐐬𐑉 𐐲𐑌𐐻𐐭 𐑅𐐲𐐽 𐑇𐐰𐑊 𐐷 𐐿𐐲𐑌𐐻𐐮𐑌𐐷𐐭 𐐻𐐭 𐑋𐐮𐑌𐐮𐑅𐐻𐐯𐑉; 𐑁𐐬𐑉 𐐷 𐑌𐐬 𐑌𐐱𐐻 𐐺𐐲𐐻 𐐸𐐶𐐱𐐻 𐑄𐐩 𐐶𐐮𐑊 𐑉𐐨𐐻𐐲𐑉𐑌 𐐰𐑌𐐼 𐑉𐐨𐐹𐐯𐑌𐐻, 𐐰𐑌𐐼 𐐿𐐲𐑋 𐐲𐑌𐐻𐐭 𐑋𐐨 𐐶𐐮𐑄 𐑁𐐳𐑊 𐐹𐐲𐑉𐐹𐐲𐑅 𐐱𐑂 𐐸𐐪𐑉𐐻, 𐐰𐑌𐐼 𐐌 𐑇𐐰𐑊 𐐸𐐨𐑊 𐑄𐐯𐑋, 𐐰𐑌𐐼 𐐷 𐑇𐐰𐑊 𐐺 𐑄 𐑋𐐨𐑌𐑆 𐐱𐑂 𐐺𐑉𐐮𐑍𐐮𐑍 𐑅𐐰𐑊𐑂𐐩𐑇𐐲𐑌 𐐲𐑌𐐻𐐭 𐑄𐐯𐑋. 𐐜𐐩𐑉𐑁𐐬𐑉 𐐿𐐨𐐹 𐑄𐐨𐑆 𐑅𐐩𐐮𐑍𐑆 𐐸𐐶𐐮𐐽 𐐌 𐐸𐐰𐑂 𐐿𐐲𐑋𐐰𐑌𐐼𐐯𐐼 𐐷𐐭, 𐑄𐐰𐐻 𐐷 𐐿𐐲𐑋 𐑌𐐱𐐻 𐐲𐑌𐐼𐐯𐑉 𐐿𐐱𐑌𐐼𐐯𐑋𐑌𐐩𐑇𐐲𐑌, 𐑁𐐬𐑉 𐐶𐐬 𐐲𐑌𐐻𐐭 𐐸𐐮𐑋 𐐸𐐭𐑋 𐑄 𐐙𐐪𐑄𐐯𐑉 𐐿𐐲𐑌𐐼𐐯𐑋𐑌𐐯𐑃. 𐐈𐑌𐐼 𐐌 𐑀𐐮𐑂 𐐷𐐭 𐑄𐐨𐑆 𐐿𐐲𐑋𐐰𐑌𐐼𐑋𐐯𐑌𐐻𐑅, 𐐺𐐨𐐿𐐫𐑆 𐐱𐑂 𐑄 𐐼𐐮𐑅𐐹𐐷𐐭𐐻𐐩𐑇𐐲𐑌𐑆 𐐸𐐶𐐮𐐽 𐐸𐐰𐑂 𐐺𐐮𐑌 𐐲𐑋𐐲𐑍 𐐷𐐭. 𐐈𐑌𐐼 𐐺𐑊𐐯𐑅𐐯𐐼 𐐪𐑉 𐐷 𐐮𐑁 𐐷 𐐸𐐰𐑂 𐑌𐐬 𐐼𐐮𐑅𐐹𐐷𐐭𐐻𐐩𐑇𐐲𐑌𐑆 𐐲𐑋𐐲𐑍 𐐷𐐭. 𐐈𐑌𐐼 𐑌𐐵 𐐌 𐑀𐐬 𐐲𐑌𐐻𐐭 𐑄 𐐙𐐪𐑄𐐯𐑉 𐐺𐐨𐐿𐐫𐑆 𐐮𐐻 𐐮𐑆 𐐯𐐿𐑅𐐹𐐨𐐼𐐨𐐯𐑌𐐻 𐑄𐐰𐐻 𐐌 𐑇𐐳𐐼 𐑀𐐬 𐐲𐑌𐐻𐐭 𐑄 𐐙𐐪𐑄𐐯𐑉, 𐑁𐐬𐑉 𐐷𐐬𐑉 𐑅𐐩𐐿𐑅.

10. 𐐈𐑌𐐼 𐐮𐐻 𐐿𐐩𐑋 𐐻𐐭 𐐹𐐰𐑅 𐑄𐐰𐐻 𐐸𐐶𐐯𐑌 𐐖𐐨𐑆𐐲𐑅 𐐸𐐰𐐼 𐑋𐐩𐐼 𐐰𐑌 𐐯𐑌𐐼 𐐱𐑂 𐑄𐐨𐑆 𐑅𐐩𐐮𐑍𐑆, 𐐸𐐨 𐐻𐐲𐐽𐐻 𐐶𐐮𐑄 𐐸𐐮𐑆 𐐸𐐰𐑌𐐼 𐑄 𐐼𐐮𐑅𐐴𐐹𐑊𐑆 𐐸𐐭𐑋 𐐸𐐨 𐐸𐐰𐐼 𐐽𐐬𐑆𐑌, 𐐶𐐲𐑌 𐐺𐐴 𐐶𐐲𐑌, 𐐨𐑂𐑌 𐐲𐑌𐐻𐐮𐑊 𐐸𐐨 𐐸𐐰𐐼 𐐻𐐲𐐽𐐻 𐑄𐐯𐑋 𐐫𐑊, 𐐰𐑌𐐼 𐑅𐐹𐐩𐐿 𐐲𐑌𐐻𐐭 𐑄𐐯𐑋 𐐰𐑆 𐐸𐐨 𐐻𐐲𐐽𐐻 𐑄𐐯𐑋; 𐐰𐑌𐐼 𐑄 𐑋𐐲𐑊𐐻𐐮𐐻𐐮𐐭𐐼 𐐸𐐲𐑉𐐼 𐑌𐐱𐐻 𐑄 𐐶𐐲𐑉𐐼𐑆 𐐸𐐶𐐮𐐽 𐐸𐐨 𐑅𐐹𐐩𐐿, 𐑄𐐩𐑉𐑁𐐬𐑉 𐑄𐐩 𐐼𐐮𐐼 𐑌𐐱𐐻 𐐺𐐩𐑉 𐑉𐐯𐐿𐐲𐑉𐐼; 𐐺𐐲𐐻 𐑄 𐐼𐐮𐑅𐐴𐐹𐑊𐑆 𐐺𐐩𐑉 𐑉𐐯𐐿𐐲𐑉𐐼 𐑄𐐰𐐻 𐐸𐐨 𐑀𐐩𐑂 𐑄𐐯𐑋 𐐹𐐵𐐯𐑉 𐐻𐐭 𐑀𐐮𐑂 𐑄 𐐐𐐬𐑊𐐮 𐐘𐐬𐑅𐐻. 𐐈𐑌𐐼 𐐌 𐐶𐐮𐑊 𐑇𐐬 𐐲𐑌𐐻𐐭 𐐷𐐭 𐐸𐐨𐑉𐐰𐑁𐐻𐐯𐑉 𐑄𐐰𐐻 𐑄𐐮𐑅 𐑉𐐯𐐿𐐲𐑉𐐼 𐐮𐑆 𐐻𐑉𐐭.

11. 𐐈𐑌𐐼 𐐮𐐻 𐐿𐐩𐑋 𐐻𐐭 𐐹𐐰𐑅 𐑄𐐰𐐻 𐐸𐐶𐐯𐑌 𐐖𐐨𐑆𐐲𐑅 𐐸𐐰𐐼 𐐻𐐲𐐽𐐻 𐑄𐐯𐑋 𐐫𐑊, 𐑄𐐩𐑉 𐐿𐐩𐑋 𐐩 𐐿𐑊𐐵𐐼 𐐰𐑌𐐼 𐐬𐑂𐐯𐑉𐑇𐐰𐐼𐐬𐐼 𐑄 𐑋𐐲𐑊𐐻𐐮𐐻𐐮𐐭𐐼, 𐑄𐐰𐐻 𐑄𐐩 𐐿𐐳𐐼 𐑌𐐱𐐻 𐑅𐐨 𐐖𐐨𐑆𐐲𐑅. 𐐈𐑌𐐼 𐐸𐐶𐐴𐑊 𐑄𐐩 𐐶𐐲𐑉 𐐬𐑂𐐯𐑉𐑇𐐰𐐼𐐬𐐼, 𐐸𐐨 𐐼𐐨𐐹𐐪𐑉𐐻𐐯𐐼 𐑁𐑉𐐱𐑋 𐑄𐐯𐑋, 𐐰𐑌𐐼 𐐰𐑅𐐯𐑌𐐼𐐯𐐼 𐐮𐑌𐐻𐐭 𐐸𐐯𐑂𐑌. 𐐈𐑌𐐼 𐑄 𐐼𐐮𐑅𐐴𐐹𐑊𐑆 𐑅𐐫 𐐰𐑌𐐼 𐐺𐐩𐑉 𐑉𐐯𐐿𐐲𐑉𐐼 𐑄𐐰𐐻 𐐸𐐨 𐐰𐑅𐐯𐑌𐐼𐐯𐐼 𐐰𐑀𐐯𐑌 𐐮𐑌𐐻𐐭 𐐸𐐯𐑂𐑌.

𐐕𐐰𐐹𐐻𐐯𐑉 IX.

1. 𐐈𐑌𐐼 𐑌𐐵 𐐮𐐻 𐐿𐐩𐑋 𐐻𐐭 𐐹𐐰𐑅 𐑄𐐰𐐻 𐐸𐐶𐐯𐑌 𐐖𐐨𐑆𐐲𐑅 𐐸𐐰𐐼 𐐰𐑅𐐯𐑌𐐼𐐯𐐼 𐐮𐑌𐐻𐐭 𐐸𐐯𐑂𐑌, 𐑄 𐑋𐐲𐑊𐐻𐐮𐐻𐐮𐐭𐐼 𐐼𐐮𐐼 𐐼𐐮𐑅𐐹𐐲𐑉𐑅, 𐐰𐑌𐐼 𐐯𐑂𐐯𐑉𐐨 𐑋𐐰𐑌 𐐼𐐮𐐼 𐐻𐐩𐐿 𐐸𐐮𐑆 𐐶𐐴𐑁 𐐰𐑌𐐼 𐐸𐐮𐑆 𐐽𐐮𐑊𐐼𐑉𐐯𐑌, 𐐰𐑌𐐼 𐐼𐐮𐐼 𐑉𐐨𐐻𐐲𐑉𐑌 𐐻𐐭 𐐸𐐮𐑆 𐐬𐑌 𐐸𐐬𐑋. 𐐈𐑌𐐼 𐐮𐐻 𐐶𐐱𐑆 𐑌𐐫𐐮𐑆𐐼 𐐲𐐺𐑉𐐫𐐼 𐐲𐑋𐐲𐑍 𐑄 𐐹𐐨𐐹𐑊 𐐮𐑋𐐨𐐼𐐨𐐯𐐻𐑊𐐮, 𐐺𐐨𐑁𐐬𐑉 𐐮𐐻 𐐶𐐱𐑆 𐐷𐐯𐐻 𐐼𐐪𐑉𐐿, 𐑄𐐰𐐻 𐑄 𐑋𐐲𐑊𐐻𐐮𐐻𐐮𐐭𐐼 𐐸𐐰𐐼 𐑅𐐨𐑌 𐐖𐐨𐑆𐐲𐑅, 𐐰𐑌𐐼 𐑄𐐰𐐻 𐐸𐐨 𐐸𐐰𐐼 𐑋𐐮𐑌𐐮𐑅𐐻𐐯𐑉𐐼 𐐲𐑌𐐻𐐭 𐑄𐐯𐑋, 𐐰𐑌𐐼 𐑄𐐰𐐻 𐐸𐐨 𐐶𐐳𐐼 𐐫𐑊𐑅𐐬 𐑇𐐬 𐐸𐐮𐑋𐑅𐐯𐑊𐑁 𐐱𐑌 𐑄 𐑋𐐱𐑉𐐬 𐐲𐑌𐐻𐐭 𐑄 𐑋𐐲𐑊𐐻𐐮𐐻𐐮𐐭𐐼; 𐐷𐐩, 𐐰𐑌𐐼 𐐨𐑂𐑌 𐐫𐑊 𐑄 𐑌𐐴𐐻 𐐮𐐻 𐐶𐐱𐑆 𐑌𐐫𐐮𐑆𐐼 𐐲𐐺𐑉𐐫𐐼 𐐿𐐲𐑌𐑅𐐲𐑉𐑌𐐮𐑍 𐐖𐐨𐑆𐐲𐑅; 𐐰𐑌𐐼 𐐮𐑌𐑅𐐬𐑋𐐲𐐽 𐐼𐐮𐐼 𐑄𐐩 𐑅𐐯𐑌𐐼 𐑁𐐬𐑉𐑃 𐐲𐑌𐐻𐐭 𐑄 𐐹𐐨𐐹𐑊, 𐑄𐐰𐐻 𐑄𐐩𐑉 𐐶𐐲𐑉 𐑋𐐯𐑌𐐮, 𐐷𐐩, 𐐰𐑌 𐐯𐐿𐑅𐐨𐐼𐐮𐑍 𐑀𐑉𐐩𐐻 𐑌𐐲𐑋𐐺𐐯𐑉 𐐼𐐮𐐼 𐑊𐐩𐐺𐐲𐑉

𐐯𐐿𐑅𐐨𐐼𐐮𐑍𐑊𐐨 𐐫𐐢 𐑄𐐰𐐻 𐑌𐐴𐐻, 𐑄𐐰𐐻 𐑄𐐩 𐑋𐐴𐐻 𐐺 𐐱𐑌 𐑄 𐑋𐐱𐑉𐐬 𐐮𐑌 𐑄 𐐹𐑊𐐩𐑅 𐐸𐐶𐐯𐑉 𐐖𐐨𐑆𐐲𐑅 𐑇𐐳𐐼 𐑇𐐬 𐐸𐐮𐑋𐑅𐐯𐑊𐑁 𐐲𐑌𐐻𐐭 𐑄 𐑋𐐲𐑊𐐻𐐮𐐻𐐷𐐭𐐼.

2. 𐐈𐑌𐐼 𐐮𐐻 𐐿𐐩𐑋 𐐻𐐭 𐐹𐐪𐑅 𐑄𐐰𐐻 𐐱𐑌 𐑄 𐑋𐐱𐑉𐐬, 𐐸𐐶𐐯𐑌 𐑄 𐑋𐐲𐑊𐐻𐐮𐐻𐐷𐐭𐐼 𐐶𐐱𐑆 𐑀𐐰𐑄𐐲𐑉𐐼 𐐻𐐭𐑀𐐯𐑄𐐲𐑉, 𐐺𐐨𐐸𐐬𐑊𐐼, 𐐤𐐀𐑁𐐴 𐐰𐑌𐐼 𐐸𐐮𐑆 𐐺𐑉𐐲𐑄𐐲𐑉 𐐸𐐭𐑋 𐐸𐐨 𐐸𐐰𐐼 𐑉𐐩𐑆𐐼 𐑁𐑉𐐱𐑋 𐑄 𐐼𐐯𐐼, 𐐸𐐭𐑆 𐑌𐐩𐑋 𐐶𐐱𐑆 𐐓𐐮𐑋𐐬𐑃𐐨, 𐐰𐑌𐐼 𐐫𐐢𐑅𐐬 𐐸𐐮𐑆 𐑅𐐲𐑌, 𐐸𐐭𐑆 𐑌𐐩𐑋 𐐶𐐱𐑆 𐐖𐐬𐑌𐐲𐑅, 𐐰𐑌𐐼 𐐫𐐢𐑅𐐬 𐐣𐐰𐑃𐐬𐑌𐐴, 𐐰𐑌𐐼 𐐣𐐰𐑃𐐬𐑌𐐴𐐸𐐪, 𐐸𐐮𐑆 𐐺𐑉𐐲𐑄𐐲𐑉, 𐐰𐑌𐐼 𐐗𐐷𐐭𐑋𐐯𐑌, 𐐰𐑌𐐼 𐐗𐐷𐐭𐑋𐐯𐑌𐐱𐑌𐐸𐐴, 𐐰𐑌𐐼 𐐖𐐯𐑉𐐨𐑋𐐴𐐲, 𐐰𐑌𐐼 𐐟𐐯𐑋𐑌𐐱𐑌, 𐐰𐑌𐐼 𐐖𐐬𐑌𐐲𐑅, 𐐰𐑌𐐼 𐐞𐐯𐐼𐐯𐐿𐐴𐐲, 𐐰𐑌𐐼 𐐌𐑆𐐩𐐲; 𐑌𐐵 𐑄𐐨𐑆 𐐶𐐲𐑉 𐑄 𐑌𐐩𐑋𐑆 𐐱𐑂 𐑄 𐐼𐐮𐑅𐐴𐐹𐑊𐑆 𐐸𐐭𐑋 𐐖𐐨𐑆𐐲𐑅 𐐸𐐰𐐼 𐐽𐐬𐑆𐑌. 𐐈𐑌𐐼 𐐮𐐻 𐐿𐐩𐑋 𐐻𐐭 𐐹𐐪𐑅 𐑄𐐰𐐻 𐑄𐐩 𐐶𐐯𐑌𐐻 𐑁𐐬𐑉𐑃 𐐰𐑌𐐼 𐑅𐐻𐐳𐐼 𐐮𐑌 𐑄 𐑋𐐮𐐼𐑅𐐻 𐐱𐑂 𐑄 𐑋𐐲𐑊𐐻𐐮𐐻𐐷𐐭𐐼. 𐐈𐑌𐐼 𐐺𐐨𐐸𐐬𐑊𐐼, 𐑄 𐑋𐐲𐑊𐐻𐐮𐐻𐐷𐐭𐐼 𐐶𐐱𐑆 𐑅𐐬 𐑀𐑉𐐩𐐻, 𐑄𐐰𐐻 𐑄𐐩 𐐼𐐮𐐼 𐐿𐐫𐑆 𐑄𐐰𐐻 𐑄𐐩 𐑇𐐳𐐼 𐐺 𐑅𐐯𐐹𐐲𐑉𐐩𐐻𐐯𐐼 𐐮𐑌𐐻𐐭 𐐻𐐶𐐯𐑊𐑂 𐐺𐐱𐐼𐐮𐑆. 𐐈𐑌𐐼 𐑄 𐐻𐐶𐐯𐑊𐑂 𐐼𐐮𐐼 𐐻𐐨𐐽 𐑄 𐑋𐐲𐑊𐐻𐐮𐐻𐐷𐐭𐐼; 𐐰𐑌𐐼 𐐺𐐨𐐸𐐬𐑊𐐼, 𐑄𐐩 𐐼𐐮𐐼 𐐿𐐫𐑆 𐑄𐐰𐐻 𐑄 𐑋𐐲𐑊𐐻𐐮𐐻𐐷𐐭𐐼 𐑇𐐳𐐼 𐑌𐐨𐑊 𐐼𐐵𐑌 𐐲𐐹𐐱𐑌 𐑄 𐑁𐐩𐑅 𐐱𐑂 𐑄 𐐲𐑉𐑃, 𐐰𐑌𐐼 𐑇𐐳𐐼 𐐹𐑉𐐩 𐐲𐑌𐐻𐐭 𐑄 𐐙𐐪𐑄𐐲𐑉 𐐮𐑌 𐑄 𐑌𐐩𐑋 𐐱𐑂 𐐖𐐨𐑆𐐲𐑅. 𐐈𐑌𐐼 𐑄 𐐼𐐮𐑅𐐴𐐹𐑊𐑆 𐐼𐐮𐐼 𐐹𐑉𐐩 𐐲𐑌𐐻𐐭 𐑄 𐐙𐐪𐑄𐐲𐑉 𐐫𐐢𐑅𐐬, 𐐮𐑌 𐑄 𐑌𐐩𐑋 𐐱𐑂 𐐖𐐨𐑆𐐲𐑅. 𐐈𐑌𐐼 𐐮𐐻 𐐿𐐩𐑋 𐐻𐐭 𐐹𐐪𐑅 𐑄𐐰𐐻 𐑄𐐩 𐐰𐑉𐐬𐑆 𐐰𐑌𐐼 𐑋𐐮𐑌𐐮𐑅𐐻𐐲𐑉𐐼 𐐲𐑌𐐻𐐭 𐑄 𐐹𐐨𐐹𐑊. 𐐈𐑌𐐼 𐐸𐐶𐐯𐑌 𐑄𐐩 𐐸𐐰𐐼 𐑋𐐮𐑌𐐮𐑅𐐻𐐲𐑉𐐼 𐑄𐐬𐑆 𐑅𐐩𐑋 𐐶𐐲𐑉𐐼𐑆 𐐸𐐶𐐮𐐽 𐐖𐐨𐑆𐐲𐑅 𐐸𐐰𐐼 𐑅𐐹𐐬𐐿𐑌—𐑌𐐲𐑃𐐮𐑍 𐑂𐐩𐑉𐐨𐐮𐑍 𐑁𐑉𐐱𐑋 𐑄 𐐶𐐲𐑉𐐼𐑆 𐐸𐐶𐐮𐐽 𐐖𐐨𐑆𐐲𐑅 𐐸𐐰𐐼 𐑅𐐹𐐬𐐿𐑌—𐐺𐐨𐐸𐐬𐑊𐐼, 𐑄𐐩 𐑌𐐯𐑊𐐻 𐐲𐑀𐐯𐑌, 𐐰𐑌𐐼 𐐹𐑉𐐩𐐼 𐐻𐐭 𐑄 𐐙𐐪𐑄𐐲𐑉 𐐮𐑌 𐑄 𐑌𐐩𐑋 𐐱𐑂 𐐖𐐨𐑆𐐲𐑅; 𐐰𐑌𐐼 𐑄𐐩 𐐼𐐮𐐼 𐐹𐑉𐐩 𐑁𐐬𐑉 𐑄𐐰𐐻 𐐸𐐶𐐮𐐽 𐑄𐐩 𐑋𐐬𐑅𐐻 𐐼𐐨𐑆𐐴𐑉𐐼; 𐐰𐑌𐐼 𐑄𐐩 𐐼𐐨𐑆𐐴𐑉𐐼 𐑄𐐰𐐻 𐑄 𐐐𐐬𐑊𐐨 𐐘𐐬𐑅𐐻 𐑇𐐳𐐼 𐐺 𐑀𐐮𐑂𐑌 𐐲𐑌𐐻𐐭 𐑄𐐯𐑋. 𐐈𐑌𐐼 𐐸𐐶𐐯𐑌 𐑄𐐩 𐐸𐐰𐐼 𐑄𐐲𐑅 𐐹𐑉𐐩𐐼, 𐑄𐐩 𐐶𐐯𐑌𐐻 𐐼𐐵𐑌 𐐲𐑌𐐻𐐭 𐑄 𐐶𐐫𐐻𐐲𐑉'𐑆 𐐯𐐾, 𐐰𐑌𐐼 𐑄 𐑋𐐲𐑊𐐻𐐮𐐻𐐷𐐭𐐼 𐑁𐐱𐑊𐐬𐐼 𐑄𐐯𐑋. 𐐈𐑌𐐼 𐐮𐐻 𐐿𐐩𐑋 𐐻𐐭 𐐹𐐪𐑅 𐑄𐐰𐐻 𐐤𐐀𐑁𐐴 𐐶𐐯𐑌𐐻 𐐼𐐵𐑌 𐐮𐑌𐐻𐐭 𐑄 𐐶𐐫𐐻𐐲𐑉, 𐐰𐑌𐐼 𐐶𐐱𐑆 𐐺𐐰𐐹𐐻𐐴𐑆𐐼. 𐐈𐑌𐐼 𐐸𐐨 𐐿𐐩𐑋 𐐲𐐹 𐐵𐐻 𐐱𐑂 𐑄 𐐶𐐫𐐻𐐲𐑉 𐐰𐑌𐐼 𐐺𐐨𐑀𐐰𐑌 𐐻𐐭 𐐺𐐰𐐹𐐻𐐴𐑆. 𐐈𐑌𐐼 𐐸𐐨 𐐺𐐰𐐹𐐻𐐴𐑆𐐼 𐐫𐐢 𐑄𐐬𐑆 𐐸𐐭𐑋 𐐖𐐨𐑆𐐲𐑅 𐐸𐐰𐐼 𐐽𐐬𐑆𐑌. 𐐈𐑌𐐼 𐐮𐐻 𐐿𐐩𐑋 𐐻𐐭 𐐹𐐪𐑅 𐐸𐐶𐐯𐑌 𐑄𐐩 𐐶𐐲𐑉 𐐫𐐢 𐐺𐐰𐐹𐐻𐐴𐑆𐐼, 𐐰𐑌𐐼 𐐸𐐰𐐼 𐐿𐐲𐑋 𐐲𐐹 𐐵𐐻 𐐱𐑂 𐑄 𐐶𐐫𐐻𐐲𐑉, 𐑄 𐐐𐐬𐑊𐐨 𐐘𐐬𐑅𐐻 𐐼𐐮𐐼 𐑁𐐫𐐢 𐐲𐐹𐐱𐑌 𐑄𐐯𐑋, 𐐰𐑌𐐼 𐑄𐐩 𐐶𐐲𐑉 𐑁𐐮𐑊𐐼 𐐶𐐮𐑄 𐑄 𐐐𐐬𐑊𐐨 𐐘𐐬𐑅𐐻, 𐐰𐑌𐐼 𐐶𐐮𐑄 𐑁𐐴𐑉. 𐐈𐑌𐐼 𐐺𐐨𐐸𐐬𐑊𐐼, 𐑄𐐩 𐐶𐐲𐑉 𐐯𐑌𐑅𐐲𐑉𐐿𐑊𐐼 𐐰𐐺𐐵𐐻 𐐰𐑆 𐐮𐑁 𐐮𐐻 𐐶𐐲𐑉 𐐺𐐴 𐑁𐐴𐑉; 𐐰𐑌𐐼 𐐮𐐻 𐐿𐐩𐑋 𐐼𐐵𐑌 𐑁𐑉𐐱𐑋 𐐸𐐯𐑂𐑌, 𐐰𐑌𐐼 𐑄 𐑋𐐲𐑊𐐻𐐮𐐻𐐷𐐭𐐼 𐐼𐐮𐐼 𐐶𐐮𐐻𐑌𐐯𐑅 𐐮𐐻, 𐐰𐑌𐐼 𐐼𐐮𐐼 𐐺𐐩𐑉 𐑉𐐯𐐿𐐲𐑉𐐼; 𐐰𐑌𐐼 𐐩𐑌𐐾𐐯𐑊𐑆 𐐼𐐮𐐼 𐐿𐐲𐑋 𐐼𐐵𐑌 𐐵𐐻 𐐱𐑂 𐐸𐐯𐑂𐑌, 𐐰𐑌𐐼 𐐼𐐮𐐼 𐑋𐐮𐑌𐐮𐑅𐐻𐐲𐑉 𐐲𐑌𐐻𐐭 𐑄𐐯𐑋. 𐐈𐑌𐐼 𐐮𐐻 𐐿𐐩𐑋 𐐻𐐭 𐐹𐐪𐑅 𐑄𐐰𐐻 𐐸𐐶𐐴𐑊 𐑄 𐐩𐑌𐐾𐐯𐑊𐑆 𐐶𐐲𐑉 𐑋𐐮𐑌𐐮𐑅𐐻𐐲𐑉𐐮𐑍 𐐲𐑌𐐻𐐭 𐑄 𐐼𐐮𐑅𐐴𐐹𐑊𐑆, 𐐺𐐨𐐸𐐬𐑊𐐼, 𐐖𐐨𐑆𐐲𐑅 𐐿𐐩𐑋 𐐰𐑌𐐼 𐑅𐐻𐐳𐐼 𐐮𐑌 𐑄 𐑋𐐮𐐼𐑅𐐻, 𐐰𐑌𐐼 𐑋𐐮𐑌𐐮𐑅𐐻𐐲𐑉𐐼 𐐲𐑌𐐻𐐭 𐑄𐐯𐑋. 𐐈𐑌𐐼 𐐮𐐻 𐐿𐐩𐑋 𐐻𐐭 𐐹𐐪𐑅 𐑄𐐰𐐻 𐐸𐐨 𐑅𐐹𐐩𐐿 𐐲𐑌𐐻𐐭 𐑄 𐑋𐐲𐑊𐐻𐐮𐐻𐐷𐐭𐐼, 𐐰𐑌𐐼 𐐿𐐱𐑋𐐰𐑌𐐼𐐯𐐼 𐑄𐐯𐑋 𐑄𐐰𐐻 𐑄𐐩 𐑇𐐳𐐼 𐑌𐐨𐑊 𐐼𐐵𐑌 𐐲𐑀𐐯𐑌 𐐲𐐹𐐱𐑌 𐑄 𐐲𐑉𐑃, 𐐰𐑌𐐼 𐐫𐐢𐑅𐐬 𐑄𐐰𐐻 𐐸𐐮𐑆 𐐼𐐮𐑅𐐴𐐹𐑊𐑆 𐑇𐐳𐐼 𐑌𐐨𐑊 𐐼𐐵𐑌 𐐲𐐹𐐱𐑌 𐑄 𐐲𐑉𐑃. 𐐈𐑌𐐼 𐐮𐐻 𐐿𐐩𐑋 𐐻𐐭 𐐹𐐪𐑅 𐑄𐐰𐐻 𐐸𐐶𐐯𐑌 𐑄𐐩 𐐸𐐰𐐼 𐐫𐐢 𐑌𐐯𐑊𐐻 𐐼𐐵𐑌 𐐲𐐹𐐱𐑌 𐑄 𐐲𐑉𐑃, 𐐸𐐨 𐐿𐐱𐑋𐐰𐑌𐐼𐐯𐐼 𐐸𐐮𐑆 𐐼𐐮𐑅𐐴𐐹𐑊𐑆 𐑄𐐰𐐻 𐑄𐐩 𐑇𐐳𐐼 𐐹𐑉𐐩. 𐐈𐑌𐐼 𐐺𐐨𐐸𐐬𐑊𐐼, 𐑄𐐩 𐐺𐐨𐑀𐐰𐑌 𐐻𐐭 𐐹𐑉𐐩; 𐐰𐑌𐐼 𐑄𐐩 𐐼𐐮𐐼 𐐹𐑉𐐩 𐐲𐑌𐐻𐐭 𐐖𐐨𐑆𐐲𐑅, 𐐿𐐫𐑊𐐮𐑍 𐐸𐐮𐑋 𐑄𐐩𐑉 𐐢𐐫𐑉𐐼 𐐰𐑌𐐼 𐑄𐐩𐑉 𐐘𐐱𐐼.

3. 𐐈𐑌𐐼 𐐮𐐻 𐐿𐐩𐑋 𐐻𐐭 𐐹𐐪𐑅 𐑄𐐰𐐻 𐐖𐐨𐑆𐐲𐑅 𐐼𐐨𐐹𐐪𐑉𐐻𐐯𐐼 𐐵𐐻 𐐱𐑂 𐑄 𐑋𐐮𐐼𐑅𐐻 𐐱𐑂 𐑄𐐯𐑋, 𐐰𐑌𐐼 𐐶𐐯𐑌𐐻 𐐲 𐑊𐐮𐐻𐑊 𐐶𐐩 𐐱𐑁 𐑁𐑉𐐱𐑋 𐑄𐐯𐑋 𐐰𐑌𐐼 𐐺𐐵𐐼 𐐸𐐮𐑋𐑅𐐯𐑊𐑁 𐐻𐐭 𐑄 𐐲𐑉𐑃, 𐐰𐑌𐐼 𐐸𐐨 𐑅𐐯𐐼, 𐐙𐐪𐑄𐐲𐑉, 𐐌 𐑃𐐰𐑍𐐿 𐑄 𐑄𐐰𐐻 𐑄𐐵 𐐸𐐰𐑅𐐻 𐑀𐐮𐑂𐑌 𐑄 𐐐𐐬𐑊𐐨 𐐘𐐬𐑅𐐻 𐐲𐑌𐐻𐐭 𐑄𐐨𐑆 𐐸𐐭𐑋 𐐌 𐐸𐐰𐑂 𐐽𐐬𐑆𐑌; 𐐰𐑌𐐼 𐐮𐐻 𐐮𐑆 𐐺𐐨𐐿𐐫𐑆 𐐱𐑂 𐑄𐐩𐑉 𐐺𐐨𐑊𐐨𐑁 𐐮𐑌 𐑋𐐨, 𐑄𐐰𐐻 𐐌 𐐸𐐰𐑂 𐐽𐐬𐑆𐑌 𐑄𐐯𐑋 𐐵𐐻 𐐱𐑂 𐑄 𐐶𐐲𐑉𐑊𐐼. 𐐙𐐪𐑄𐐲𐑉, 𐐌 𐐹𐑉𐐩 𐑄 𐑄𐐰𐐻 𐑄𐐵 𐐶𐐮𐑊𐐻 𐑀𐐮𐑂 𐑄 𐐐𐐬𐑊𐐨 𐐘𐐬𐑅𐐻 𐐲𐑌𐐻𐐭 𐐫𐐢 𐑄𐐯𐑋 𐑄𐐰𐐻 𐑇𐐰𐑊 𐐺𐐨𐑊𐐨𐑂 𐐮𐑌 𐑄𐐩𐑉 𐐶𐐲𐑉𐐼𐑆. 𐐙𐐪𐑄𐐲𐑉, 𐑄𐐵 𐐸𐐰𐑅𐐻 𐑀𐐮𐑂𐑌 𐑄𐐯𐑋 𐑄 𐐐𐐬𐑊𐐨 𐐘𐐬𐑅𐐻, 𐐺𐐨𐐿𐐫𐑆 𐑄𐐩 𐐺𐐨𐑊𐐨𐑂 𐐮𐑌 𐑋𐐨, 𐐰𐑌𐐼 𐑄𐐵 𐑅𐐨𐐯𐑅𐐻 𐑄𐐰𐐻 𐑄𐐩 𐐺𐐨𐑊𐐨𐑂 𐐮𐑌 𐑋𐐨, 𐐺𐐨𐐿𐐫𐑆 𐑄𐐵 𐐸𐐨𐑉𐐯𐑅𐐻 𐑄𐐯𐑋, 𐐰𐑌𐐼 𐑄𐐩 𐐹𐑉𐐩 𐐲𐑌𐐻𐐭 𐑋𐐨; 𐐰𐑌𐐼 𐑄𐐩 𐐹𐑉𐐩 𐐲𐑌𐐻𐐭 𐑋𐐨 𐐺𐐨𐐿𐐫𐑆 𐐌 𐐰𐑋 𐐶𐐮𐑄 𐑄𐐯𐑋. 𐐈𐑌𐐼 𐑌𐐵 𐐙𐐪𐑄𐐲𐑉, 𐐌 𐐹𐑉𐐩 𐐲𐑌𐐻𐐭 𐑄 𐑁𐐬𐑉 𐑄𐐯𐑋, 𐐰𐑌𐐼 𐐫𐐢𐑅𐐬 𐑁𐐬𐑉 𐐫𐐢 𐑄𐐬𐑆 𐐸𐐭 𐑇𐐰𐑊 𐐺𐐨𐑊𐐨𐑂 𐐱𐑌 𐑄𐐩𐑉 𐐶𐐲𐑉𐐼𐑆, 𐑄𐐰𐐻 𐑄𐐩 𐑋𐐩 𐐺𐐨𐑊𐐨𐑂 𐐮𐑌 𐑋𐐨, 𐑄𐐰𐐻 𐐌 𐑋𐐩 𐐺 𐐮𐑌 𐑄𐐯𐑋 𐐰𐑆 𐑄𐐵, 𐐙𐐪𐑄𐐲𐑉, 𐐪𐑉𐐻 𐐮𐑌 𐑋𐐨, 𐑄𐐰𐐻 𐐶𐐨 𐑋𐐩 𐐺 𐐶𐐲𐑌.

4. 𐐈𐑌𐐼 𐐮𐐻 𐐿𐐩𐑋 𐐻𐐭 𐐹𐐪𐑅, 𐑄𐐰𐐻 𐐸𐐶𐐯𐑌 𐐖𐐨𐑆𐐲𐑅 𐐸𐐰𐐼 𐑄𐐲𐑅 𐐹𐑉𐐩𐐼 𐐲𐑌𐐻𐐭 𐑄 𐐙𐐪𐑄𐐲𐑉, 𐐸𐐨 𐐿𐐩𐑋 𐐲𐑌𐐻𐐭 𐐸𐐮𐑆 𐐼𐐮𐑅𐐴𐐹𐑊𐑆, 𐐰𐑌𐐼 𐐺𐐨𐐸𐐬𐑊𐐼, 𐑄𐐩 𐐼𐐮𐐼 𐑅𐐻𐐮𐑊 𐐿𐐲𐑌𐐻𐐮𐑌𐐷𐐭, 𐐶𐐮𐑄𐐵𐐻 𐑅𐐨𐑅𐐮𐑍, 𐐻𐐭 𐐹𐑉𐐩 𐐲𐑌𐐻𐐭 𐐸𐐮𐑋; 𐐰𐑌𐐼 𐑄𐐩 𐐼𐐮𐐼 𐑌𐐱𐐻 𐑋𐐲𐑊𐐻𐐮𐐹𐑊𐐴 𐑋𐐯𐑌𐐮 𐐶𐐲𐑉𐐼𐑆, 𐑁𐐬𐑉 𐐮𐐻 𐐶𐐱𐑆 𐑀𐐮𐑂𐑌 𐐲𐑌𐐻𐐭 𐑄𐐯𐑋 𐐸𐐶𐐱𐐻 𐑄𐐩 𐑇𐐳𐐼 𐐹𐑉𐐩, 𐐰𐑌𐐼 𐑄𐐩 𐐶𐐲𐑉 𐑁𐐮𐑊𐐼 𐐶𐐮𐑄 𐐼𐐨𐑆𐐴𐑉. 𐐈𐑌𐐼 𐐮𐐻 𐐿𐐩𐑋 𐐻𐐭 𐐹𐐪𐑅 𐑄𐐰𐐻 𐐖𐐨𐑆𐐲𐑅 𐐺𐑊𐐯𐑅𐐻 𐑄𐐯𐑋, 𐐰𐑆 𐑄𐐩 𐐼𐐮𐐼 𐐹𐑉𐐩 𐐲𐑌𐐻𐐭 𐐸𐐮𐑋, 𐐰𐑌𐐼 𐐸𐐮𐑆 𐐿𐐵𐑌𐐻𐐯𐑌𐐲𐑌𐑅 𐐼𐐮𐐼 𐑅𐑋𐐴𐑊 𐐲𐐹𐐱𐑌 𐑄𐐯𐑋, 𐐰𐑌𐐼 𐑄 𐑊𐐴𐐻 𐐱𐑂 𐐸𐐮𐑆 𐐿𐐵𐑌𐐻𐐯𐑌𐐲𐑌𐑅 𐐼𐐮𐐼 𐑇𐐴𐑌 𐐲𐐹𐐱𐑌 𐑄𐐯𐑋, 𐐰𐑌𐐼 𐐺𐐨𐐸𐐬𐑊𐐼, 𐑄𐐩 𐐶𐐲𐑉 𐐰𐑆 𐐸𐐶𐐴𐐻 𐐰𐑆 𐑄 𐐿𐐵𐑌𐐻𐐯𐑌𐐲𐑌𐑅, 𐐰𐑌𐐼 𐐫𐑊𐑅𐐬 𐑄 𐑀𐐪𐑉𐑋𐐯𐑌𐐻𐑅 𐐱𐑂 𐐖𐐨𐑆𐐲𐑅; 𐐰𐑌𐐼 𐐺𐐨𐐸𐐬𐑊𐐼 𐑄 𐐸𐐶𐐴𐐻𐑌𐐯𐑅 𐑄𐐩𐑉𐐱𐑂 𐐼𐐮𐐼 𐐯𐐿𐑅𐐨𐐼 𐐫𐑊 𐑄 𐐸𐐶𐐴𐐻𐑌𐐯𐑅; 𐐷𐐩, 𐐨𐑂𐑌 𐑄𐐩𐑉 𐐿𐐳𐐼 𐐺 𐑌𐐲𐑃𐐮𐑍 𐐲𐐹𐐱𐑌 𐐲𐑉𐑃 𐑅𐐬 𐐸𐐶𐐴𐐻 𐐰𐑆 𐑄 𐐸𐐶𐐴𐐻𐑌𐐯𐑅 𐑄𐐩𐑉𐐱𐑂. 𐐈𐑌𐐼 𐐖𐐨𐑆𐐲𐑅 𐑅𐐯𐐼 𐐲𐑌𐐻𐐭 𐑄𐐯𐑋, 𐐑𐑉𐐩 𐐱𐑌, 𐑌𐐯𐑂𐐲𐑉𐑄𐐯𐑊𐐯𐑅 𐑄𐐩 𐐼𐐮𐐼 𐑌𐐱𐐻 𐑅𐐨𐑅 𐐻𐐭 𐐹𐑉𐐩. 𐐈𐑌𐐼 𐐸𐐨 𐐻𐐲𐑉𐑌𐐼 𐑁𐑉𐐱𐑋 𐑄𐐯𐑋 𐐰𐑀𐐯𐑌, 𐐰𐑌𐐼 𐐶𐐯𐑌𐐻 𐐪 𐑊𐐮𐐻𐑊 𐐶𐐩 𐐱𐑁, 𐐰𐑌𐐼 𐐺𐐵𐐼 𐐸𐐮𐑋𐑅𐐯𐑊𐑁 𐐻𐐭 𐑄 𐐲𐑉𐑃; 𐐰𐑌𐐼 𐐸𐐨 𐐹𐑉𐐩𐐼 𐐰𐑀𐐯𐑌 𐐲𐑌𐐻𐐭 𐑄 𐐙𐐪𐑄𐐲𐑉, 𐑅𐐩𐐮𐑍, 𐐙𐐪𐑄𐐲𐑉, 𐐌 𐑃𐐰𐑍𐐿 𐑄𐐨 𐑄𐐰𐐻 𐑄𐐵 𐐸𐐰𐑅𐐻 𐐹𐐷𐐭𐑉𐐮𐑁𐐴𐐼 𐑄𐐬𐑆 𐐸𐐭𐑋 𐐌 𐐸𐐰𐑂 𐐕𐐬𐑆𐑌, 𐐺𐐨𐐿𐐫𐑆 𐐱𐑂 𐑄𐐩𐑉 𐑁𐐩𐑃, 𐐰𐑌𐐼 𐐌 𐐹𐑉𐐩 𐑁𐐬𐑉 𐑄𐐯𐑋, 𐐰𐑌𐐼 𐐫𐑊𐑅𐐬 𐑁𐐬𐑉 𐑄𐐯𐑋 𐐸𐐭 𐑇𐐰𐑊 𐐺𐐨𐑊𐐨𐑂 𐐱𐑌 𐑄𐐩𐑉 𐐶𐐲𐑉𐐼𐑆, 𐑄𐐰𐐻 𐑄𐐩 𐑋𐐩 𐐺 𐐹𐐷𐐭𐑉𐐮𐑁𐐴𐐼 𐐮𐑌 𐑋𐐨, 𐑃𐑉𐐭 𐑁𐐩𐑃 𐐱𐑌 𐑄𐐩𐑉 𐐶𐐲𐑉𐐼𐑆, 𐐨𐑂𐑌 𐐰𐑆 𐑄𐐩 𐐪𐑉 𐐹𐐷𐐭𐑉𐐮𐑁𐐴𐐼 𐐮𐑌 𐑋𐐨. 𐐙𐐪𐑄𐐲𐑉, 𐐌 𐐹𐑉𐐩 𐑌𐐱𐐻 𐑁𐐬𐑉 𐑄 𐐶𐐲𐑉𐑊𐐼, 𐐺𐐲𐐻 𐑁𐐬𐑉 𐑄𐐬𐑆 𐐸𐐭𐑋 𐑄𐐵 𐐸𐐰𐑅𐐻 𐑀𐐮𐑂𐑌 𐑋𐐨 𐐵𐐻 𐐱𐑂 𐑄 𐐶𐐲𐑉𐑊𐐼, 𐐺𐐨𐐿𐐫𐑆 𐐱𐑂 𐑄𐐩𐑉 𐑁𐐩𐑃, 𐑄𐐰𐐻 𐑄𐐩 𐑋𐐩 𐐺 𐐹𐐷𐐭𐑉𐐮𐑁𐐴𐐼 𐐮𐑌 𐑋𐐨, 𐑄𐐰𐐻 𐐌 𐑋𐐩 𐐺 𐐮𐑌 𐑄𐐯𐑋 𐐰𐑆 𐑄𐐵, 𐐙𐐪𐑄𐐲𐑉, 𐐪𐑉𐐻 𐐮𐑌 𐑋𐐨, 𐑄𐐰𐐻 𐐶𐐨 𐑋𐐩 𐐺 𐐶𐐲𐑌, 𐑄𐐰𐐻 𐐌 𐑋𐐩 𐐺 𐑀𐑊𐐬𐑉𐐮𐑁𐐴𐐼 𐐮𐑌 𐑄𐐯𐑋.

5. 𐐈𐑌𐐼 𐐸𐐶𐐯𐑌 𐐖𐐨𐑆𐐲𐑅 𐐸𐐰𐐼 𐑅𐐹𐐬𐐿𐑌 𐑄𐐨𐑆 𐐶𐐲𐑉𐐼𐑆, 𐐸𐐨 𐐿𐐩𐑋 𐐰𐑀𐐯𐑌 𐐲𐑌𐐻𐐭 𐐸𐐮𐑆 𐐼𐐮𐑅𐐴𐐹𐑊𐑆, 𐐰𐑌𐐼 𐐺𐐨𐐸𐐬𐑊𐐼 𐑄𐐩 𐐼𐐮𐐼 𐐹𐑉𐐩 𐑅𐐻𐐯𐐼𐑁𐐰𐑅𐐻𐑊𐐮, 𐐶𐐮𐑄𐐵𐐻 𐑅𐐨𐑅𐐮𐑍 𐐲𐑌𐐻𐐭 𐐸𐐮𐑋; 𐐰𐑌𐐼 𐐸𐐨 𐐼𐐮𐐼 𐑅𐑋𐐴𐑊 𐐲𐐹𐐱𐑌 𐑄𐐯𐑋 𐐰𐑀𐐯𐑌; 𐐰𐑌𐐼 𐐺𐐨𐐸𐐬𐑊𐐼 𐑄𐐩 𐐶𐐲𐑉 𐐸𐐶𐐴𐐻, 𐐨𐑂𐑌 𐐰𐑆 𐐖𐐨𐑆𐐲𐑅. 𐐈𐑌𐐼 𐐮𐐻 𐐿𐐩𐑋 𐐻𐐭 𐐹𐐪𐑅 𐑄𐐰𐐻 𐐸𐐨 𐐶𐐯𐑌𐐻 𐐰𐑀𐐯𐑌 𐐪 𐑊𐐮𐐻𐑊 𐐶𐐩 𐐱𐑁, 𐐰𐑌𐐼 𐐹𐑉𐐩𐐼 𐐲𐑌𐐻𐐭 𐑄 𐐙𐐪𐑄𐐲𐑉; 𐐰𐑌𐐼 𐐻𐐲𐑍 𐐿𐐰𐑌𐐱𐐻 𐑅𐐹𐐨𐐿 𐑄 𐐶𐐲𐑉𐐼𐑆 𐐸𐐶𐐮𐐽 𐐸𐐨 𐐹𐑉𐐩𐐼, 𐑌𐐨𐑄𐐲𐑉 𐐿𐐰𐑌 𐐺 𐑉𐐮𐐻𐑌 𐐺𐐴 𐑋𐐰𐑌 𐑄 𐐶𐐲𐑉𐐼𐑆 𐐸𐐶𐐮𐐽 𐐸𐐨 𐐹𐑉𐐩𐐼. 𐐈𐑌𐐼 𐑄 𐑋𐐲𐑊𐐻𐐮𐐻𐐷𐐭𐐼 𐐼𐐮𐐼 𐐸𐐨𐑉, 𐐰𐑌𐐼 𐐼𐐭 𐐺𐐩𐑉 𐑉𐐯𐐿𐐲𐑉𐐼; 𐐰𐑌𐐼 𐑄𐐩𐑉 𐐸𐐪𐑉𐐻𐑅 𐐶𐐲𐑉 𐐬𐐹𐑌, 𐐰𐑌𐐼 𐑄𐐩 𐐼𐐮𐐼 𐐲𐑌𐐼𐐲𐑉𐑅𐐻𐐰𐑌𐐼 𐐮𐑌 𐑄𐐩𐑉 𐐸𐐪𐑉𐐻𐑅 𐑄 𐐶𐐲𐑉𐐼𐑆 𐐸𐐶𐐮𐐽 𐐸𐐨 𐐹𐑉𐐩𐐼. 𐐤𐐯𐑂𐐲𐑉𐑄𐐯𐑊𐐯𐑅, 𐑅𐐬 𐑀𐑉𐐩𐐻 𐐰𐑌𐐼 𐑋𐐪𐑉𐑂𐐯𐑊𐐲𐑅 𐐶𐐲𐑉 𐑄 𐐶𐐲𐑉𐐼𐑆 𐐸𐐶𐐮𐐽 𐐸𐐨 𐐹𐑉𐐩𐐼, 𐑄𐐰𐐻 𐑄𐐩 𐐿𐐰𐑌𐐱𐐻 𐐺 𐑉𐐮𐐻𐑌, 𐑌𐐨𐑄𐐲𐑉 𐐿𐐰𐑌 𐑄𐐩 𐐺 𐐲𐐻𐐲𐑉𐐼 𐐺𐐴 𐑋𐐰𐑌.

6. 𐐈𐑌𐐼 𐐮𐐻 𐐿𐐩𐑋 𐐻𐐭 𐐹𐐪𐑅 𐑄𐐰𐐻 𐐸𐐶𐐯𐑌 𐐖𐐨𐑆𐐲𐑅 𐐸𐐰𐐼 𐑋𐐩𐐼 𐐰𐑌 𐐯𐑌𐐼 𐐱𐑂 𐐹𐑉𐐩𐐮𐑍, 𐐸𐐨 𐐿𐐩𐑋 𐐰𐑀𐐯𐑌 𐐻𐐭 𐑄 𐐼𐐮𐑅𐐴𐐹𐑊𐑆, 𐐰𐑌𐐼 𐑅𐐯𐐼 𐐲𐑌𐐻𐐭 𐑄𐐯𐑋, 𐐝𐐬 𐑀𐑉𐐩𐐻 𐑁𐐩𐑃 𐐸𐐰𐑂 𐐌 𐑌𐐯𐑂𐐲𐑉 𐑅𐐨𐑌 𐐰𐑋𐐲𐑍 𐐫𐑊 𐑄 𐐖𐐭𐑆; 𐐸𐐶𐐯𐑉𐑁𐐬𐑉 𐐌 𐐿𐐳𐐼 𐑌𐐱𐐻 𐑇𐐬 𐐲𐑌𐐻𐐭 𐑄𐐯𐑋 𐑅𐐬 𐑀𐑉𐐩𐐻 𐑋𐐮𐑉𐐲𐐿𐑊𐑆, 𐐺𐐨𐐿𐐫𐑆 𐐱𐑂 𐑄𐐩𐑉 𐐲𐑌𐐺𐐨𐑊𐐨𐑁. 𐐚𐐯𐑉𐐮𐑊𐐮 𐐌 𐑅𐐩 𐐲𐑌𐐻𐐭 𐐷𐐭, 𐑄𐐩𐑉 𐐪𐑉 𐑌𐐲𐑌 𐐱𐑂 𐑄𐐯𐑋 𐑄𐐰𐐻 𐐸𐐰𐑂 𐑅𐐨𐑌 𐑅𐐬 𐑀𐑉𐐩𐐻 𐑃𐐮𐑍𐑆 𐐰𐑆 𐐷𐐨 𐐸𐐰𐑂 𐑅𐐨𐑌; 𐑌𐐨𐑄𐐲𐑉 𐐸𐐰𐑂 𐑄𐐩 𐐸𐐲𐑉𐐼 𐑅𐐬 𐑀𐑉𐐩𐐻 𐑃𐐮𐑍𐑆 𐐰𐑆 𐐷𐐨 𐐸𐐰𐑂 𐐸𐐲𐑉𐐼.

7. 𐐈𐑌𐐼 𐐮𐐻 𐐿𐐩𐑋 𐐻𐐭 𐐹𐐪𐑅 𐑄𐐰𐐻 𐐸𐐨 𐐿𐐲𐑋𐐰𐑌𐐼𐐯𐐼 𐑄 𐑋𐐲𐑊𐐻𐐮𐐻𐐷𐐭𐐼 𐑄𐐰𐐻 𐑄𐐩 𐑇𐐳𐐼 𐑅𐐨𐑅 𐐻𐐭 𐐹𐑉𐐩, 𐐰𐑌𐐼 𐐫𐑊𐑅𐐬 𐐸𐐮𐑆 𐐼𐐮𐑅𐐴𐐹𐑊𐑆. 𐐈𐑌𐐼 𐐸𐐨 𐐿𐐲𐑋𐐰𐑌𐐼𐐯𐐼 𐑄𐐯𐑋 𐑄𐐰𐐻 𐑄𐐩 𐑇𐐳𐐼 𐑌𐐱𐐻 𐑅𐐨𐑅 𐐻𐐭 𐐹𐑉𐐩 𐐮𐑌 𐑄𐐩𐑉 𐐸𐐪𐑉𐐻𐑅. 𐐈𐑌𐐼 𐐸𐐨 𐐿𐐲𐑋𐐰𐑌𐐼𐐯𐐼 𐑄𐐯𐑋 𐑄𐐰𐐻 𐑄𐐩 𐑇𐐳𐐼 𐐰𐑉𐐴𐑆 𐐰𐑌𐐼 𐑅𐐻𐐰𐑌𐐼 𐐲𐐹 𐐲𐐹𐐱𐑌 𐑄𐐩𐑉 𐑁𐐨𐐻. 𐐈𐑌𐐼 𐑄𐐩 𐐰𐑉𐐬𐑆 𐐲𐐹 𐐰𐑌𐐼 𐑅𐐻𐐳𐐼 𐐲𐐹𐐱𐑌 𐑄𐐩𐑉 𐑁𐐨𐐻. 𐐈𐑌𐐼 𐐮𐐻 𐐿𐐩𐑋 𐐻𐐭 𐐹𐐪𐑅 𐑄𐐰𐐻 𐐸𐐨 𐐺𐑉𐐩𐐿 𐐺𐑉𐐯𐐼 𐐰𐑀𐐯𐑌, 𐐰𐑌𐐼 𐐺𐑊𐐯𐑅𐐻 𐐮𐐻, 𐐰𐑌𐐼 𐑀𐐩𐑂 𐐻𐐭 𐑄 𐐼𐐮𐑅𐐴𐐹𐑊𐑆 𐐻𐐭 𐐨𐐻. 𐐈𐑌𐐼 𐐸𐐶𐐯𐑌 𐑄𐐩 𐐸𐐰𐐼 𐐨𐐻𐑌, 𐐸𐐨 𐐿𐐲𐑋𐐰𐑌𐐼𐐯𐐼 𐑄𐐯𐑋 𐑄𐐰𐐻 𐑄𐐩 𐑇𐐳𐐼 𐐺𐑉𐐩𐐿 𐐺𐑉𐐯𐐼, 𐐰𐑌𐐼 𐑀𐐮𐑂 𐐲𐑌𐐻𐐭 𐑄 𐑋𐐲𐑊𐐻𐐮𐐻𐐷𐐭𐐼. 𐐈𐑌𐐼 𐐸𐐶𐐯𐑌 𐑄𐐩 𐐸𐐰𐐼 𐑀𐐮𐑂𐑌 𐐲𐑌𐐻𐐭 𐑄 𐑋𐐲𐑊𐐻𐐮𐐻𐐷𐐭𐐼, 𐐸𐐨 𐐫𐑊𐑅𐐬 𐑀𐐩𐑂 𐑄𐐯𐑋 𐐶𐐴𐑌 𐐻𐐭 𐐼𐑉𐐮𐑍𐐿, 𐐰𐑌𐐼 𐐿𐐲𐑋𐐰𐑌𐐼𐐯𐐼 𐑄𐐯𐑋 𐑄𐐰𐐻 𐑄𐐩 𐑇𐐳𐐼 𐑀𐐮𐑂 𐐲𐑌𐐻𐐭 𐑄 𐑋𐐲𐑊𐐻𐐮𐐻𐐷𐐭𐐼. 𐐤𐐵 𐑄𐐩𐑉 𐐸𐐰𐐼 𐐺𐐮𐑌 𐑌𐐬 𐐺𐑉𐐯𐐼, 𐑌𐐨𐑄𐐲𐑉 𐐶𐐴𐑌, 𐐺𐑉𐐫𐐻 𐐺𐐴 𐑄 𐐼𐐮𐑅𐐴𐐹𐑊𐑆, 𐑌𐐨𐑄𐐲𐑉 𐐺𐐴 𐑄 𐑋𐐲𐑊𐐻𐐮𐐻𐐷𐐭𐐼; 𐐺𐐲𐐻 𐐸𐐨 𐐻𐑉𐐭𐑊𐐮 𐑀𐐩𐑂 𐐲𐑌𐐻𐐭 𐑄𐐯𐑋 𐐺𐑉𐐯𐐼 𐐻𐐭 𐐨𐐻, 𐐰𐑌𐐼 𐐫𐑊𐑅𐐬 𐐶𐐴𐑌 𐐻𐐭 𐐼𐑉𐐮𐑍𐐿; 𐐰𐑌𐐼 𐐸𐐨 𐑅𐐯𐐼 𐐲𐑌𐐻𐐭 𐑄𐐯𐑋, 𐐐𐐨 𐑄𐐰𐐻 𐐨𐐻𐐯𐑃 𐑄𐐮𐑅 𐐺𐑉𐐯𐐼, 𐐨𐐻𐐯𐑃 𐐱𐑂 𐑋𐐴 𐐺𐐱𐐼𐐮 𐐻𐐭 𐐸𐐮𐑆 𐑅𐐬𐑊, 𐐰𐑌𐐼 𐐸𐐨 𐑄𐐰𐐻 𐐼𐑉𐐮𐑍𐐿𐐯𐑃 𐐱𐑂 𐑄𐐮𐑅 𐐶𐐴𐑌, 𐐼𐑉𐐮𐑍𐐿𐐯𐑃 𐐱𐑂 𐑋𐐴

𐐺𐑊𐐲𐐼 𐐻𐐭 𐐸𐐮𐑆 𐑅𐐬𐑊, 𐐰𐑌𐐼 𐐸𐐮𐑆 𐑅𐐬𐑊 𐑇𐐰𐑊 𐑌𐐯𐑂𐐲𐑉 𐐸𐐲𐑍𐑀𐐲𐑉 𐑌𐐫𐑉 𐑃𐐲𐑉𐑅𐐻, 𐐺𐐲𐐻 𐑇𐐰𐑊 𐐺𐐨 𐑁𐐮𐑊𐐼. 𐐤𐐵 𐐸𐐶𐐯𐑌 𐑄 𐑋𐐲𐑊𐐻𐐮𐐻𐑏𐐼 𐐸𐐰𐐼 𐐫𐑊 𐐨𐐻𐑌 𐐰𐑌𐐼 𐐼𐑉𐐲𐑍𐐿, 𐐺𐐨𐐸𐐬𐑊𐐼 𐑄𐐩 𐐶𐐲𐑉 𐑁𐐮𐑊𐐼 𐐶𐐮𐑄 𐑄 𐐝𐐹𐐮𐑉𐐮𐐻, 𐐰𐑌𐐼 𐑄𐐩 𐐼𐐮𐐼 𐐿𐑉𐐴 𐐵𐐻 𐐶𐐮𐑄 𐐶𐐲𐑌 𐑂𐐦𐑅, 𐐰𐑌𐐼 𐑀𐐩𐑂 𐑀𐑊𐐬𐑉𐐨 𐐻𐐭 𐐖𐐨𐑆𐐲𐑅, 𐐸𐐭𐑋 𐑄𐐩 𐐺𐐬𐑃 𐑅𐐫 𐐰𐑌𐐼 𐐸𐐲𐑉𐐼.

8. 𐐈𐑌𐐼 𐐮𐐻 𐐿𐐩𐑋 𐐻𐐭 𐐹𐐪𐑅 𐑄𐐰𐐻 𐐸𐐶𐐯𐑌 𐑄𐐩 𐐸𐐰𐐼 𐐫𐑊 𐑀𐐮𐑂𐑌 𐑀𐑊𐐬𐑉𐐨 𐐲𐑌𐐻𐐭 𐐖𐐨𐑆𐐲𐑅, 𐐸𐐨 𐑅𐐯𐐼 𐐲𐑌𐐻𐐭 𐑄𐐯𐑋, 𐐒𐐨𐐸𐐬𐑊𐐼 𐑌𐐵 𐐌 𐑁𐐮𐑌𐐮𐑇 𐑄 𐐿𐐲𐑋𐐰𐑌𐐼𐑋𐐯𐑌𐐻 𐐸𐐶𐐮𐐽 𐑄 𐐙𐐪𐑄𐐲𐑉 𐐸𐐰𐑃 𐐿𐐲𐑋𐐰𐑌𐐼𐐯𐐼 𐑋𐐨 𐐿𐐲𐑌𐑅𐐲𐑉𐑌𐐮𐑍 𐑄𐐮𐑅 𐐹𐐨𐐹𐐲𐑊, 𐐸𐐭 𐐪𐑉 𐐩 𐑉𐐯𐑋𐑌𐐰𐑌𐐻 𐐱𐑂 𐑄 𐐸𐐵𐑅 𐐱𐑂 𐐆𐑆𐑉𐐩𐐯𐑊. 𐐏𐐨 𐑉𐐨𐑋𐐯𐑋𐐺𐐲𐑉 𐑄𐐰𐐻 𐐌 𐑅𐐹𐐩𐐿 𐐲𐑌𐐻𐐭 𐐷𐐭, 𐐰𐑌𐐼 𐑅𐐯𐐼 𐑄𐐰𐐻 𐐸𐐶𐐯𐑌 𐑄 𐐶𐐲𐑉𐐼𐑆 𐐱𐑂 𐐌𐑆𐐩𐐲 𐑇𐐳𐐼 𐐺𐐨 𐑁𐐳𐑊𐑁𐐮𐑊𐐼, 𐐺𐐨𐐸𐐬𐑊𐐼 𐑄𐐩 𐐪𐑉 𐑉𐐮𐐻𐑌, 𐐷𐐨 𐐸𐐰𐑂 𐑄𐐯𐑋 𐐺𐐨𐑁𐐬𐑉 𐐷𐐭, 𐑄𐐯𐑉𐑁𐐬𐑉 𐑅𐐲𐑉𐐽 𐑄𐐯𐑋. 𐐈𐑌𐐼 𐑂𐐯𐑉𐐮𐑊𐐨, 𐑂𐐯𐑉𐐮𐑊𐐨, 𐐌 𐑅𐐩 𐐲𐑌𐐻𐐭 𐐷𐐭, 𐑄𐐰𐐻 𐐸𐐶𐐯𐑌 𐑄𐐩 𐑇𐐰𐑊 𐐺𐐨 𐑁𐐳𐑊𐑁𐐮𐑊𐐼, 𐑄𐐯𐑌 𐐮𐑆 𐑄 𐑁𐐳𐑊𐑁𐐮𐑊𐐮𐑍 𐐱𐑂 𐑄 𐐿𐐲𐑂𐐯𐑌𐐰𐑌𐐻 𐐸𐐶𐐮𐐽 𐑄 𐐙𐐪𐑄𐐲𐑉 𐐸𐐰𐑃 𐑋𐐩𐐼 𐐲𐑌𐐻𐐭 𐐸𐐮𐑆 𐐹𐐨𐐹𐐲𐑊, 𐐄 𐐸𐐵𐑅 𐐱𐑂 𐐆𐑆𐑉𐐩𐐯𐑊. 𐐈𐑌𐐼 𐑄𐐯𐑌 𐑇𐐰𐑊 𐑄 𐑉𐐯𐑋𐑌𐐰𐑌𐐻𐑅, 𐐸𐐶𐐮𐐽 𐑇𐐰𐑊 𐐺𐐨 𐑅𐐿𐐰𐐻𐐲𐑉𐐼 𐐲𐐺𐑉𐐫𐐼 𐐲𐐹𐐱𐑌 𐑄 𐑁𐐩𐑅 𐐱𐑂 𐑄 𐐲𐑉𐑃, 𐐺𐐨 𐑀𐐰𐑄𐐲𐑉𐐼 𐐮𐑌 𐑁𐑉𐐱𐑋 𐑄 𐐨𐑅𐐻, 𐐰𐑌𐐼 𐑁𐑉𐐱𐑋 𐑄 𐐶𐐯𐑅𐐻, 𐐰𐑌𐐼 𐑁𐑉𐐱𐑋 𐑄 𐑅𐐵𐑃, 𐐰𐑌𐐼 𐑁𐑉𐐱𐑋 𐑄 𐑌𐐫𐑉𐑃; 𐐰𐑌𐐼 𐑄𐐩 𐑇𐐰𐑊 𐐺𐐨 𐐺𐑉𐐫𐐻 𐐻𐐭 𐑄 𐑌𐐱𐑊𐐯𐐾 𐐱𐑂 𐑄 𐐢𐐫𐑉𐐼 𐑄𐐩𐑉 𐐘𐐱𐐼, 𐐸𐐭 𐐸𐐰𐑃 𐑉𐐨𐐼𐐨𐑋𐐼 𐑄𐐯𐑋. 𐐈𐑌𐐼 𐑄 𐐙𐐪𐑄𐐲𐑉 𐐸𐐰𐑃 𐐿𐐲𐑋𐐰𐑌𐐼𐐯𐐼 𐑋𐐨 𐑄𐐰𐐻 𐐌 𐑇𐐳𐐼 𐑀𐐮𐑂 𐐲𐑌𐐻𐐭 𐐷𐐭 𐑄𐐮𐑅 𐑊𐐰𐑌𐐼, 𐑁𐐫𐑉 𐐷𐐭𐑉 𐐮𐑌𐐸𐐯𐑉𐐮𐐻𐐰𐑌𐑅. 𐐈𐑌𐐼 𐐌 𐑅𐐩 𐐲𐑌𐐻𐐭 𐐷𐐭, 𐑄𐐰𐐻 𐐮𐑁 𐑄 𐐖𐐯𐑌𐐻𐐴𐑊𐑆 𐐼𐐭 𐑌𐐱𐐻 𐑉𐐨𐐹𐐯𐑌𐐻 𐐰𐑁𐐻𐐲𐑉 𐑄 𐐺𐑊𐐯𐑅𐐮𐑍 𐐸𐐶𐐮𐐽 𐑄𐐩 𐑇𐐰𐑊 𐑉𐐨𐑅𐐨𐑂, 𐐰𐑁𐐻𐐲𐑉 𐑄𐐩 𐐸𐐰𐑂 𐑅𐐿𐐰𐐻𐐲𐑉𐐼 𐑋𐐴 𐐹𐐨𐐹𐐲𐑊, 𐑄𐐯𐑌 𐑇𐐰𐑊 𐐷𐐨, 𐐸𐐭 𐐪𐑉 𐐩 𐑉𐐯𐑋𐑌𐐰𐑌𐐻 𐐱𐑂 𐑄 𐐸𐐵𐑅 𐐱𐑂 𐐖𐐩𐐿𐐲𐐺, 𐑀𐐬 𐑁𐐬𐑉𐑃 𐐲𐑋𐐲𐑍 𐑄𐐯𐑋; 𐐰𐑌𐐼 𐐷𐐨 𐑇𐐰𐑊 𐐺𐐨 𐐮𐑌 𐑄 𐑋𐐮𐐼𐑅𐐻 𐐱𐑂 𐑄𐐯𐑋, 𐐸𐐭 𐑇𐐰𐑊 𐐺𐐨 𐑋𐐯𐑌𐐨; 𐐰𐑌𐐼 𐐷𐐨 𐑇𐐰𐑊 𐐺𐐨 𐐲𐑋𐐲𐑍 𐑄𐐯𐑋 𐐰𐑆 𐐩 𐑊𐐴𐐲𐑌 𐐲𐑋𐐲𐑍 𐑄 𐐺𐐨𐑅𐐻𐑅 𐐱𐑂 𐑄 𐑁𐐱𐑉𐐯𐑅𐐻, 𐐰𐑌𐐼 𐐰𐑆 𐐩 𐐷𐐲𐑍 𐑊𐐴𐐲𐑌 𐐲𐑋𐐲𐑍 𐑄 𐑁𐑊𐐱𐐿𐑅 𐐱𐑂 𐑇𐐨𐐹, 𐐸𐐭, 𐐮𐑁 𐐸𐐨 𐑀𐐬𐐯𐑃 𐑃𐑉𐐭, 𐐺𐐬𐑃 𐐻𐑉𐐯𐐼𐐯𐑃 𐐼𐐵𐑌 𐐰𐑌𐐼 𐐻𐐩𐑉𐐯𐑃 𐐮𐑌 𐐹𐐨𐑅𐐯𐑆, 𐐰𐑌𐐼 𐑌𐐲𐑌 𐐿𐐰𐑌 𐐼𐐨𐑊𐐮𐑂𐐲𐑉. 𐐜𐐴 𐐸𐐰𐑌𐐼 𐑇𐐰𐑊 𐐺𐐨 𐑊𐐮𐑁𐐻𐐯𐐼 𐐲𐐹 𐐲𐐹𐐱𐑌 𐑄𐐴𐑌 𐐰𐐼𐑂𐐲𐑉𐑅𐐯𐑉𐐨𐑆, 𐐰𐑌𐐼 𐐫𐑊 𐑄𐐴𐑌 𐐯𐑌𐐯𐑋𐐨𐑆 𐑇𐐰𐑊 𐐺𐐨 𐐿𐐲𐐻 𐐫𐑁. 𐐈𐑌𐐼 𐐌 𐐶𐐮𐑊 𐑀𐐰𐑄𐐲𐑉 𐑋𐐴 𐐹𐐨𐐹𐐲𐑊 𐐻𐐭𐑀𐐯𐑄𐐲𐑉 𐐰𐑆 𐐩 𐑋𐐰𐑌 𐑀𐐰𐑄𐐲𐑉𐐯𐑃 𐐸𐐮𐑆 𐑇𐐨𐑂𐑆 𐐮𐑌𐐻𐐭 𐑄 𐑁𐑊𐐬𐑉, 𐑁𐐫𐑉 𐐌 𐐶𐐮𐑊 𐑋𐐩𐐿 𐑋𐐴 𐐹𐐨𐐹𐐲𐑊 𐐶𐐮𐑄 𐐸𐐭𐑋 𐑄 𐐙𐐪𐑄𐐲𐑉 𐐸𐐰𐑃 𐐿𐐲𐑂𐐯𐑌𐐰𐑌𐐻𐐯𐐼, 𐐷𐐩, 𐐌 𐐶𐐮𐑊 𐑋𐐩𐐿 𐑄𐐴 𐐸𐐫𐑉𐑌 𐐴𐐲𐑉𐑌, 𐐰𐑌𐐼 𐐌 𐐶𐐮𐑊 𐑋𐐩𐐿 𐑄𐐴 𐐸𐐭𐑁𐑅 𐐺𐑉𐐪𐑅. 𐐈𐑌𐐼 𐑄𐐵 𐑇𐐰𐑊𐐻 𐐺𐐨𐐻 𐐮𐑌 𐐹𐐨𐑅𐐯𐑆 𐑋𐐯𐑌𐐨 𐐹𐐨𐐹𐐲𐑊; 𐐰𐑌𐐼 𐐌 𐐶𐐮𐑊 𐐿𐐱𐑌𐑅𐐯𐐿𐑉𐐩𐐻 𐑄𐐩𐑉 𐑀𐐩𐑌 𐐲𐑌𐐻𐐭 𐑄 𐐢𐐫𐑉𐐼, 𐐰𐑌𐐼 𐑄𐐩𐑉 𐑅𐐲𐐺𐑅𐐻𐐰𐑌𐑅 𐐲𐑌𐐻𐐭 𐑄 𐐢𐐫𐑉𐐼 𐐱𐑂 𐑄 𐐸𐐬𐑊 𐐲𐑉𐑃. 𐐈𐑌𐐼 𐐺𐐨𐐸𐐬𐑊𐐼, 𐐌 𐐰𐑋 𐐸𐐨 𐐸𐐭 𐐼𐐭𐐯𐑃 𐐮𐐻.

9. 𐐈𐑌𐐼 𐐮𐐻 𐑇𐐰𐑊 𐐿𐐲𐑋 𐐻𐐭 𐐹𐐪𐑅, 𐑅𐐯𐑃 𐑄 𐐙𐐪𐑄𐐲𐑉, 𐑄𐐰𐐻 𐑄 𐑅𐐬𐑉𐐼 𐐱𐑂 𐑋𐐴 𐐾𐐲𐑅𐐻𐐮𐑅 𐑇𐐰𐑊 𐐸𐐰𐑍 𐐬𐑂𐐲𐑉 𐑄𐐯𐑋 𐐰𐐻 𐑄𐐰𐐻 𐐼𐐩; 𐐰𐑌𐐼 𐐯𐐿𐑅𐐯𐐹𐐻 𐑄𐐩 𐑉𐐨𐐹𐐯𐑌𐐻, 𐐮𐐻 𐑇𐐰𐑊 𐑁𐐫𐑊 𐐲𐐹𐐱𐑌 𐑄𐐯𐑋, 𐑅𐐯𐑃 𐑄 𐐙𐐪𐑄𐐲𐑉, 𐐷𐐩, 𐐨𐑂𐑌 𐐲𐐹𐐱𐑌 𐐫𐑊 𐑄 𐑌𐐩𐑇𐐲𐑌𐑆 𐐱𐑂 𐑄 𐐖𐐯𐑌𐐻𐐴𐑊𐑆. 𐐈𐑌𐐼 𐐮𐐻 𐑇𐐰𐑊 𐐿𐐲𐑋 𐐻𐐭 𐐹𐐪𐑅 𐑄𐐰𐐻 𐐌 𐐶𐐮𐑊 𐐯𐑅𐐻𐐰𐐺𐑊𐐮𐑇 𐑋𐐴 𐐹𐐨𐐹𐐲𐑊, 𐐄 𐐸𐐵𐑅 𐐱𐑂 𐐆𐑆𐑉𐐩𐐯𐑊. 𐐈𐑌𐐼 𐐺𐐨𐐸𐐬𐑊𐐼, 𐑄𐐮𐑅 𐐹𐐨𐐹𐐲𐑊 𐐶𐐮𐑊 𐐌 𐐯𐑅𐐻𐐰𐐺𐑊𐐮𐑇 𐐮𐑌 𐑄𐐮𐑅 𐑊𐐰𐑌𐐼, 𐐲𐑌𐐻𐐭 𐑄 𐑁𐐳𐑊𐑁𐐮𐑊𐐮𐑍 𐐱𐑂 𐑄 𐐿𐐲𐑂𐐯𐑌𐐰𐑌𐐻 𐐸𐐶𐐮𐐽 𐐌 𐑋𐐩𐐼 𐐶𐐮𐑄 𐐷𐐭𐑉 𐑁𐐪𐑄𐐲𐑉 𐐖𐐩𐐿𐐲𐐺; 𐐰𐑌𐐼 𐐮𐐻 𐑇𐐰𐑊 𐐺𐐨 𐐩 𐐤𐑏 𐐖𐐲𐑉𐐭𐑅𐐲𐑊𐐯𐑋. 𐐈𐑌𐐼 𐑄 𐐹𐐵𐐲𐑉𐑆 𐐱𐑂 𐐸𐐯𐑂𐑌 𐑇𐐰𐑊 𐐺𐐨 𐐮𐑌 𐑄 𐑋𐐮𐐼𐑅𐐻 𐐱𐑂 𐑄𐐮𐑅 𐐹𐐨𐐹𐐲𐑊; 𐐷𐐩, 𐐨𐑂𐑌 𐐌 𐐶𐐮𐑊 𐐺𐐨 𐐮𐑌 𐑄 𐑋𐐮𐐼𐑅𐐻 𐐱𐑂 𐐷𐐭. 𐐒𐐨𐐸𐐬𐑊𐐼, 𐐌 𐐰𐑋 𐐸𐐨 𐐱𐑂 𐐸𐐭𐑋 𐐣𐐬𐑆𐐯𐑆 𐑅𐐹𐐩𐐿, 𐑅𐐩𐐮𐑍, 𐐈 𐐹𐑉𐐱𐑁𐐯𐐻 𐑇𐐰𐑊 𐑄 𐐢𐐫𐑉𐐼 𐐷𐐭𐑉 𐐘𐐱𐐼 𐑉𐐩𐑆 𐐲𐐹 𐐲𐑌𐐻𐐭 𐐷𐐭 𐐱𐑂 𐐷𐐭𐑉 𐐺𐑉𐐯𐑄𐑉𐐯𐑌, 𐑊𐐴𐐿 𐐲𐑌𐐻𐐭 𐑋𐐨; 𐐸𐐮𐑋 𐑇𐐰𐑊 𐐷𐐨 𐐸𐐨𐑉 𐐮𐑌 𐐫𐑊 𐑃𐐮𐑍𐑆 𐐸𐐶𐐱𐐻𐑅𐐬𐐯𐑂𐐲𐑉 𐐸𐐨 𐑇𐐰𐑊 𐑅𐐩 𐐲𐑌𐐻𐐭 𐐷𐐭. 𐐈𐑌𐐼 𐐮𐐻 𐑇𐐰𐑊 𐐿𐐲𐑋 𐐻𐐭 𐐹𐐪𐑅 𐑄𐐰𐐻 𐐯𐑂𐐲𐑉𐐨 𐑅𐐬𐑊 𐐸𐐭 𐐶𐐮𐑊 𐑌𐐱𐐻 𐐸𐐨𐑉 𐑄𐐰𐐻 𐐹𐑉𐐱𐑁𐐯𐐻, 𐑇𐐰𐑊 𐐺𐐨 𐐿𐐲𐐻 𐐫𐑁 𐑁𐑉𐐱𐑋 𐐲𐑋𐐲𐑍 𐑄 𐐹𐐨𐐹𐐲𐑊. 𐐚𐐯𐑉𐐮𐑊𐐨, 𐐌 𐑅𐐩 𐐲𐑌𐐻𐐭 𐐷𐐭, 𐐷𐐩: 𐐰𐑌𐐼 𐐫𐑊 𐑄 𐐹𐑉𐐱𐑁𐐯𐐻𐑅 𐑁𐑉𐐱𐑋 𐐝𐐰𐑋𐐷𐐭𐐯𐑊, 𐐰𐑌𐐼 𐑄𐐬𐑆 𐑄𐐰𐐻 𐑁𐐱𐑊𐐬 𐐰𐑁𐐻𐐲𐑉, 𐐰𐑆 𐑋𐐯𐑌𐐨 𐐰𐑆 𐐸𐐰𐑂 𐑅𐐹𐐬𐐿𐑌, 𐐸𐐰𐑂 𐐻𐐯𐑅𐐻𐐮𐑁𐐴𐐼 𐐱𐑂 𐑋𐐨. 𐐈𐑌𐐼 𐐺𐐨𐐸𐐬𐑊𐐼, 𐐷𐐨 𐐪𐑉 𐑄 𐐽𐐮𐑊𐐼𐑉𐐯𐑌 𐐱𐑂 𐑄 𐐹𐑉𐐱𐑁𐐯𐐻𐑅; 𐐰𐑌𐐼 𐐷𐐨 𐐪𐑉 𐐱𐑂 𐑄 𐐸𐐵𐑅 𐐱𐑂 𐐆𐑆𐑉𐐩𐐯𐑊; 𐐰𐑌𐐼 𐐷𐐨 𐐪𐑉 𐐱𐑂 𐑄 𐐿𐐲𐑂𐐯𐑌𐐰𐑌𐐻 𐐸𐐶𐐮𐐽 𐑄 𐐙𐐪𐑄𐐲𐑉 𐑋𐐩𐐼 𐐶𐐮𐑄 𐐷𐐭𐑉 𐑁𐐪𐑄𐐲𐑉𐑆, 𐑅𐐩𐐮𐑍 𐐲𐑌𐐻𐐭 𐐁𐐺𐑉𐐲𐐸𐐰𐑋, 𐐈𐑌𐐼 𐐮𐑌 𐑄𐐴 𐑅𐐨𐐼 𐑇𐐰𐑊 𐐫𐑊 𐑄 𐐿𐐮𐑌𐐼𐑉𐐯𐐼𐑆 𐐱𐑂 𐑄 𐐲𐑉𐑃 𐐺𐐨 𐐺𐑊𐐯𐑅𐐯𐐼; 𐑄 𐐙𐐪𐑄𐐲𐑉 𐐸𐐰𐑂𐐮𐑍 𐑉𐐩𐑆𐐼 𐑋𐐨 𐐲𐐹

𐐲𐑌𐐻𐐭 𐐷𐐭 𐑁𐐲𐑉𐑅𐐻, 𐐰𐑌𐐼 𐑅𐐯𐑌𐐻 𐑋𐐨 𐐻𐐭 𐐺𐑊𐐯𐑅 𐐷𐐭, 𐐮𐑌 𐐻𐐲𐑉𐑌𐐮𐑍 𐐲𐐶𐐩 𐐯𐑂𐐲𐑉𐐨 𐐶𐐲𐑌 𐐱𐑂 𐐷𐐭 𐑁𐑉𐐱𐑋 𐐸𐐮𐑆 𐐮𐑌𐐮𐐿𐐶𐐮𐐻𐐮𐑆; 𐐰𐑌𐐼 𐑄𐐮𐑅 𐐺𐐨𐐿𐐪𐑆 𐐷 𐐪𐑉 𐑄 𐐽𐐮𐑊𐐼𐑉𐐯𐑌 𐐱𐑂 𐑄 𐐿𐐲𐑂𐐯𐑌𐐰𐑌𐐻. 𐐈𐑌𐐼 𐐰𐑁𐐻𐐲𐑉 𐑄𐐰𐐻 𐐷 𐐶𐐲𐑉 𐐺𐑊𐐯𐑅𐐻, 𐑄𐐯𐑌 𐑁𐐳𐑊𐑁𐐮𐑊𐐯𐑃 𐑄 𐐙𐐪𐑄𐐲𐑉 𐑄 𐐿𐐲𐑂𐐯𐑌𐐰𐑌𐐻 𐐸𐐶𐐮𐐽 𐐸𐐨 𐑋𐐩𐐼 𐐶𐐮𐑄 𐐁𐐺𐑉𐐲𐐸𐐰𐑋, 𐑅𐐩𐐮𐑍, 𐐆𐑌 𐑄𐐴 𐑅𐐨𐐼 𐑇𐐰𐑊 𐐫𐑊 𐑄 𐐿𐐮𐑌𐐼𐑉𐐯𐐼𐑆 𐐱𐑂 𐑄 𐐲𐑉𐑃 𐐺 𐐺𐑊𐐯𐑅𐐻, 𐐲𐑌𐐻𐐭 𐑄 𐐹𐐬𐑉𐐮𐑍 𐐵𐐻 𐐱𐑂 𐑄 𐐐𐐬𐑊𐐨 𐐘𐐬𐑅𐐻 𐑃𐑉𐐭 𐑋𐐨 𐐲𐐹𐐱𐑌 𐑄 𐐖𐐯𐑌𐐻𐐴𐑊𐑆, 𐐸𐐶𐐮𐐽 𐐺𐑊𐐯𐑅𐐮𐑍 𐐲𐐹𐐱𐑌 𐑄 𐐖𐐯𐑌𐐻𐐴𐑊𐑆 𐑇𐐰𐑊 𐑋𐐩𐐿 𐑄𐐯𐑋 𐑋𐐴𐐻𐐨 𐐲𐐺𐐲𐑂 𐐫𐑊, 𐐲𐑌𐐻𐐭 𐑄 𐑅𐐿𐐰𐐻𐐲𐑉𐐮𐑍 𐐱𐑂 𐑋𐐴 𐐹𐐨𐐹𐑊, 𐐄 𐐸𐐵𐑅 𐐱𐑂 𐐆𐑆𐑉𐐩𐐯𐑊; 𐐰𐑌𐐼 𐑄𐐩 𐑇𐐰𐑊 𐐺 𐐲 𐑅𐐿𐐲𐑉𐐾 𐐲𐑌𐐻𐐭 𐑄 𐐹𐐨𐐹𐑊 𐐱𐑂 𐑄𐐮𐑅 𐑊𐐰𐑌𐐼. 𐐤𐐯𐑂𐐲𐑉𐑄𐐲𐑊𐐯𐑅, 𐐸𐐶𐐯𐑌 𐑄𐐩 𐑇𐐰𐑊 𐐸𐐰𐑂 𐑉𐐨𐑅𐐨𐑂𐐼 𐑄 𐑁𐐳𐑊𐑌𐐯𐑅 𐐱𐑂 𐑋𐐴 𐐘𐐱𐑅𐐹𐐯𐑊, 𐑄𐐯𐑌 𐐮𐑁 𐑄𐐩 𐑇𐐰𐑊 𐐸𐐪𐑉𐐼𐑌 𐑄𐐩𐑉 𐐸𐐪𐑉𐐻𐑅 𐐲𐑀𐐯𐑌𐑅𐐻 𐑋𐐨, 𐐌 𐐶𐐮𐑊 𐑉𐐨𐐻𐐲𐑉𐑌 𐑄𐐩𐑉 𐐮𐑌𐐮𐐿𐐶𐐮𐐻𐐮𐑆 𐐲𐐹𐐱𐑌 𐑄𐐩𐑉 𐐬𐑌 𐐸𐐯𐐼𐑆, 𐑅𐐯𐑃 𐑄 𐐙𐐪𐑄𐐲𐑉. 𐐈𐑌𐐼 𐐌 𐐶𐐮𐑊 𐑉𐐨𐑋𐐯𐑋𐐺𐐲𐑉 𐑄 𐐿𐐲𐑂𐐯𐑌𐐰𐑌𐐻 𐐸𐐶𐐮𐐽 𐐌 𐐸𐐰𐑂 𐑋𐐩𐐼 𐐶𐐮𐑄 𐑋𐐴 𐐹𐐨𐐹𐑊, 𐐰𐑌𐐼 𐐌 𐐸𐐰𐑂 𐐿𐐲𐑂𐐯𐑌𐐰𐑌𐐻𐐯𐐼 𐐶𐐮𐑄 𐑄𐐯𐑋, 𐑄𐐰𐐻 𐐌 𐐶𐐳𐐼 𐑀𐐰𐑄𐐲𐑉 𐑄𐐯𐑋 𐐻𐐭𐑀𐐯𐑄𐐲𐑉 𐐮𐑌 𐑋𐐴𐑌 𐐬𐑌 𐐼𐑏 𐐻𐐴𐑋; 𐑄𐐰𐐻 𐐌 𐐶𐐳𐐼 𐑀𐐮𐑂 𐐲𐑌𐐻𐐭 𐑄𐐯𐑋 𐐲𐑀𐐯𐑌 𐑄 𐑊𐐰𐑌𐐼 𐐱𐑂 𐑄𐐩𐑉 𐑁𐐪𐑄𐐲𐑉𐑆, 𐑁𐐫𐑉 𐑄𐐩𐑉 𐐮𐑌𐐸𐐯𐑉𐐮𐐻𐐰𐑌𐑅, 𐐸𐐶𐐮𐐽 𐐮𐑆 𐑄 𐑊𐐰𐑌𐐼 𐐱𐑂 𐐖𐐲𐑉𐐭𐑅𐐲𐑊𐐯𐑋, 𐐸𐐶𐐮𐐽 𐐮𐑆 𐑄 𐐹𐑉𐐱𐑋𐐮𐑅𐐻 𐑊𐐰𐑌𐐼 𐐲𐑌𐐻𐐭 𐑄𐐯𐑋 𐑁𐐫𐑉 𐐯𐑂𐐲𐑉, 𐑅𐐯𐑃 𐑄 𐐙𐐪𐑄𐐲𐑉.

10. 𐐈𐑌𐐼 𐐮𐐻 𐑇𐐰𐑊 𐐿𐐲𐑋 𐐻𐐭 𐐹𐐪𐑅 𐑄𐐰𐐻 𐑄 𐐻𐐴𐑋 𐐿𐐲𐑋𐐯𐑃, 𐐸𐐶𐐯𐑌 𐑄 𐑁𐐳𐑊𐑌𐐯𐑅 𐐱𐑂 𐑋𐐴 𐐘𐐱𐑅𐐹𐐯𐑊 𐑇𐐰𐑊 𐐺 𐐹𐑉𐐨𐐽𐐻 𐐲𐑌𐐻𐐭 𐑄𐐯𐑋, 𐐰𐑌𐐼 𐑄𐐩 𐑇𐐰𐑊 𐐺𐐨𐑊𐐨𐑂 𐐮𐑌 𐑋𐐨, 𐑄𐐰𐐻 𐐌 𐐰𐑋 𐐖𐐨𐑆𐐲𐑅 𐐗𐑉𐐴𐑅𐐻, 𐑄 𐐝𐐲𐑌 𐐱𐑂 𐐘𐐱𐐼, 𐐰𐑌𐐼 𐑇𐐰𐑊 𐐹𐑉𐐩 𐐲𐑌𐐻𐐭 𐑄 𐐙𐐪𐑄𐐲𐑉 𐐮𐑌 𐑋𐐴 𐑌𐐩𐑋. 𐐜𐐯𐑌 𐑇𐐰𐑊 𐑄𐐩𐑉 𐐶𐐱𐐽𐑋𐐯𐑌 𐑊𐐮𐑁𐐻 𐐲𐐹 𐑄𐐩𐑉 𐑂𐑎𐑅, 𐐰𐑌𐐼 𐐶𐐮𐑄 𐑄 𐑂𐑎𐑅 𐐻𐐭𐑀𐐯𐑄𐐲𐑉 𐑇𐐰𐑊 𐑄𐐩 𐑅𐐮𐑍; 𐑁𐐫𐑉 𐑄𐐩 𐑇𐐰𐑊 𐑅𐐨 𐐴 𐐻𐐭 𐐴. 𐐜𐐯𐑌 𐐶𐐮𐑊 𐑄 𐐙𐐪𐑄𐐲𐑉 𐑀𐐰𐑄𐐲𐑉 𐑄𐐯𐑋 𐐻𐐭𐑀𐐯𐑄𐐲𐑉 𐐲𐑀𐐯𐑌, 𐐰𐑌𐐼 𐑀𐐮𐑂 𐐲𐑌𐐻𐐭 𐑄𐐯𐑋 𐐖𐐲𐑉𐐭𐑅𐐲𐑊𐐯𐑋 𐑁𐐫𐑉 𐑄 𐑊𐐰𐑌𐐼 𐐱𐑂 𐑄𐐩𐑉 𐐮𐑌𐐸𐐯𐑉𐐮𐐻𐐰𐑌𐑅. 𐐜𐐯𐑌 𐑇𐐰𐑊 𐑄𐐩 𐐺𐑉𐐩𐐿 𐑁𐐬𐑉𐑃 𐐮𐑌𐐻𐐭 𐐾𐑎—𐐝𐐮𐑍 𐐻𐐭𐑀𐐯𐑄𐐲𐑉, 𐐷 𐐶𐐩𐑅𐐻 𐐹𐑊𐐩𐑅𐐯𐑆 𐐱𐑂 𐐖𐐲𐑉𐐭𐑅𐐲𐑊𐐯𐑋; 𐑁𐐫𐑉 𐑄 𐐙𐐪𐑄𐐲𐑉 𐐸𐐰𐑃 𐐿𐐲𐑋𐑁𐐲𐑉𐐻𐐯𐐼 𐐸𐐮𐑆 𐐹𐐨𐐹𐑊, 𐐸𐐨 𐐸𐐰𐑃 𐑉𐐨𐐼𐐨𐑋𐐼 𐐖𐐲𐑉𐐭𐑅𐐲𐑊𐐯𐑋. 𐐜 𐐙𐐪𐑄𐐲𐑉 𐐸𐐰𐑃 𐑋𐐩𐐼 𐐺𐐩𐑉 𐐸𐐮𐑆 𐐸𐐬𐑊𐐨 𐐪𐑉𐑋 𐐮𐑌 𐑄 𐐴𐑆 𐐱𐑂 𐐫𐑊 𐑄 𐑌𐐩𐑇𐐲𐑌𐑆; 𐐰𐑌𐐼 𐐫𐑊 𐑄 𐐯𐑌𐐼𐑆 𐐱𐑂 𐑄 𐐲𐑉𐑃 𐑇𐐰𐑊 𐑅𐐨 𐑄 𐑅𐐰𐑊𐑂𐐩𐑇𐐲𐑌 𐐱𐑂 𐑄 𐐙𐐪𐑄𐐲𐑉, 𐐰𐑌𐐼 𐑄 𐐙𐐪𐑄𐐲𐑉 𐐰𐑌𐐼 𐐌 𐐪𐑉 𐐶𐐲𐑌. 𐐈𐑌𐐼 𐑄𐐯𐑌 𐑇𐐰𐑊 𐐺 𐐺𐑉𐐫𐐻 𐐻𐐭 𐐹𐐪𐑅 𐑄𐐰𐐻 𐐸𐐶𐐮𐐽 𐐮𐑆 𐑉𐐮𐐻𐑌, 𐐊𐐶𐐩𐐿, 𐐲𐐶𐐩𐐿 𐐲𐑀𐐯𐑌, 𐐰𐑌𐐼 𐐹𐐳𐐻 𐐱𐑌 𐑄𐐴 𐑅𐐻𐑉𐐯𐑍𐑃, 𐐄 𐐞𐐴𐐲𐑌; 𐐹𐐳𐐻 𐐱𐑌 𐑄𐐴 𐐺𐑏𐐻𐐮𐑁𐐳𐑊 𐑀𐐪𐑉𐑋𐐯𐑌𐐻𐑅, 𐐄 𐐖𐐲𐑉𐐭𐑅𐐲𐑊𐐯𐑋, 𐑄 𐐸𐐬𐑊𐐨 𐑅𐐮𐐻𐐨, 𐑁𐐫𐑉 𐐸𐐯𐑌𐑅𐑁𐐬𐑉𐑃 𐑄𐐩𐑉 𐑇𐐰𐑊 𐑌𐐬 𐑋𐐬𐑉 𐐿𐐲𐑋 𐐮𐑌𐐻𐐭 𐑄 𐑄 𐐲𐑌𐑅𐐲𐑉𐐿𐐲𐑋𐑅𐐴𐑆𐐼 𐐰𐑌𐐼 𐑄 𐐲𐑌𐐿𐑊𐐨𐑌. 𐐟𐐩𐐿 𐑄𐐴𐑅𐐯𐑊𐑁 𐑁𐑉𐐱𐑋 𐑄 𐐼𐐲𐑅𐐻; 𐐲𐑉𐐴𐑆, 𐑅𐐮𐐻 𐐼𐐵𐑌, 𐐄 𐐖𐐲𐑉𐐭𐑅𐐲𐑊𐐯𐑋, 𐑊𐐭𐑅 𐑄𐐴𐑅𐐯𐑊𐑁 𐑁𐑉𐐱𐑋 𐑄 𐐺𐐰𐑌𐐼𐑆 𐐱𐑂 𐑄𐐴 𐑌𐐯𐐿, 𐐄 𐐿𐐰𐐹𐐻𐐮𐑂 𐐼𐐫𐐻𐐲𐑉 𐐱𐑂 𐐞𐐴𐐲𐑌. 𐐙𐐫𐑉 𐑄𐐲𐑅 𐑅𐐯𐑃 𐑄 𐐢𐐫𐑉𐐼, 𐐏 𐐸𐐰𐑂 𐑅𐐬𐑊𐐼 𐐷𐐭𐑉𐑅𐐯𐑊𐑂𐑆 𐑁𐐫𐑉 𐑌𐐫𐐻; 𐐰𐑌𐐼 𐐷 𐑇𐐰𐑊 𐐺 𐑉𐐨𐐼𐐨𐑋𐐼 𐐶𐐮𐑄𐐵𐐻 𐑋𐐲𐑌𐐨. 𐐚𐐯𐑉𐐮𐑊𐐨, 𐑂𐐯𐑉𐐮𐑊𐐨, 𐐌 𐑅𐐩 𐐲𐑌𐐻𐐭 𐐷𐐭, 𐑄𐐰𐐻 𐑋𐐴 𐐹𐐨𐐹𐑊 𐑇𐐰𐑊 𐑌𐐬 𐑋𐐴 𐑌𐐩𐑋; 𐐷𐐩, 𐐮𐑌 𐑄𐐰𐐻 𐐼𐐩 𐑄𐐩 𐑇𐐰𐑊 𐑌𐐬 𐑄𐐰𐐻 𐐌 𐐰𐑋 𐐸𐐨 𐑄𐐰𐐻 𐐼𐐲𐑃 𐑅𐐹𐐨𐐿.

11. 𐐈𐑌𐐼 𐑄𐐯𐑌 𐑇𐐰𐑊 𐑄𐐩 𐑅𐐩, 𐐐𐐵 𐐺𐑏𐐻𐐮𐑁𐐳𐑊 𐐲𐐹𐐱𐑌 𐑄 𐑋𐐵𐑌𐐻𐐯𐑌𐑆 𐐪𐑉 𐑄 𐑁𐐨𐐻 𐐱𐑂 𐐸𐐮𐑋 𐑄𐐰𐐻 𐐺𐑉𐐮𐑍𐐯𐑃 𐑀𐐳𐐼 𐐻𐐴𐐼𐐮𐑍𐑆 𐐲𐑌𐐻𐐭 𐑄𐐯𐑋, 𐑄𐐰𐐻 𐐹𐐲𐐺𐑊𐐮𐑇𐐯𐑃 𐐹𐐨𐑅; 𐑄𐐰𐐻 𐐺𐑉𐐮𐑍𐐯𐑃 𐑀𐐳𐐼 𐐻𐐴𐐼𐐮𐑍𐑆 𐐲𐑌𐐻𐐭 𐑄𐐯𐑋 𐐱𐑂 𐑀𐐳𐐼, 𐑄𐐰𐐻 𐐹𐐲𐐺𐑊𐐮𐑇𐐯𐑃 𐑅𐐰𐑊𐑂𐐩𐑇𐐲𐑌; 𐑄𐐰𐐻 𐑅𐐯𐑃 𐐲𐑌𐐻𐐭 𐐞𐐴𐐲𐑌, 𐐜𐐴 𐐘𐐱𐐼 𐑉𐐩𐑌𐐯𐑃! 𐐈𐑌𐐼 𐑄𐐯𐑌 𐑇𐐰𐑊 𐐲 𐐿𐑉𐐴 𐑀𐐬 𐑁𐐬𐑉𐑃, 𐐔𐐨𐐹𐐪𐑉𐐻 𐐷, 𐐼𐐨𐐹𐐪𐑉𐐻 𐐷, 𐑀𐐬 𐐷 𐐵𐐻 𐑁𐑉𐐱𐑋 𐑄𐐯𐑌𐑅, 𐐻𐐲𐐽 𐑌𐐱𐐻 𐑄𐐰𐐻 𐐸𐐶𐐮𐐽 𐐮𐑆 𐐲𐑌𐐿𐑊𐐨𐑌; 𐑀𐐬 𐐷 𐐵𐐻 𐐱𐑂 𐑄 𐑋𐐮𐐼𐑅𐐻 𐐱𐑂 𐐸𐐲𐑉; 𐐺 𐐷 𐐿𐑊𐐨𐑌 𐑄𐐰𐐻 𐐺𐐩𐑉 𐑄 𐑂𐐯𐑅𐐯𐑊𐑆 𐐱𐑂 𐑄 𐐢𐐫𐑉𐐼. 𐐙𐐫𐑉 𐐷 𐑇𐐰𐑊 𐑌𐐱𐐻 𐑀𐐬 𐐵𐐻 𐐶𐐮𐑄 𐐸𐐩𐑅𐐻, 𐑌𐐫𐑉 𐑀𐐬 𐐺𐐴 𐑁𐑊𐐴𐐻, 𐑁𐐫𐑉 𐑄 𐐢𐐫𐑉𐐼 𐐶𐐮𐑊 𐑀𐐬 𐐺𐐨𐑁𐐬𐑉 𐐷𐐭, 𐐰𐑌𐐼 𐑄 𐐘𐐱𐐼 𐐱𐑂 𐐆𐑆𐑉𐐩𐐯𐑊 𐑇𐐰𐑊 𐐺 𐐷𐐭𐑉 𐑉𐐨𐑉𐐶𐐫𐑉𐐼. 𐐒𐐨𐐸𐐬𐑊𐐼, 𐑋𐐴 𐑅𐐲𐑉𐑂𐐰𐑌𐐻 𐑇𐐰𐑊 𐐼𐐨𐑊 𐐹𐑉𐐭𐐼𐐯𐑌𐐻𐑊𐐨, 𐐸𐐨 𐑇𐐰𐑊 𐐺 𐐯𐑀𐑆𐐫𐑊𐐻𐐯𐐼 𐐰𐑌𐐼 𐐯𐐿𐑅𐐻𐐬𐑊𐐼, 𐐰𐑌𐐼 𐐺 𐑂𐐯𐑉𐐨 𐐸𐐴. 𐐈𐑆 𐑋𐐯𐑌𐐨 𐐶𐐲𐑉 𐐲𐑅𐐻𐐱𐑌𐐮𐑇𐐻 𐐰𐐻 𐑄; (𐐸𐐮𐑆 𐑂𐐮𐑆𐐩𐐾 𐐶𐐱𐑆 𐑅𐐬 𐑋𐐪𐑉𐐼, 𐑋𐐬𐑉 𐑄𐐰𐑌 𐐯𐑌𐐨 𐑋𐐰𐑌, 𐐰𐑌𐐼 𐐸𐐮𐑆 𐑁𐐫𐑉𐑋 𐑋𐐬𐑉 𐑄𐐰𐑌 𐑄 𐑅𐐲𐑌𐑆 𐐱𐑂 𐑋𐐯𐑌;) 𐑅𐐬 𐑇𐐰𐑊 𐐸𐐨 𐑅𐐹𐑉𐐮𐑍𐐿𐑊 𐑋𐐯𐑌𐐨 𐑌𐐩𐑇𐐲𐑌𐑆: 𐑄 𐐿𐐮𐑍𐑆 𐑇𐐰𐑊 𐑇𐐲𐐻 𐑄𐐩𐑉 𐑋𐐵𐑄𐑆 𐐰𐐻 𐐸𐐮𐑋, 𐑁𐐫𐑉 𐑄𐐰𐐻 𐐸𐐶𐐮𐐽 𐐸𐐰𐐼 𐑌𐐱𐐻 𐐺𐐮𐑌 𐐻𐐬𐑊𐐼 𐑄𐐯𐑋 𐑇𐐰𐑊 𐑄𐐩 𐑅𐐨; 𐐰𐑌𐐼 𐑄𐐰𐐻 𐐸𐐶𐐮𐐽 𐑄𐐩 𐐸𐐰𐐼 𐑌𐐱𐐻

𐐸𐐲𐑉𐐼 𐑇𐐰𐑊 𐑄𐐩 𐐿𐐲𐑌𐑅𐐮𐐼𐐲𐑉. 𐐚𐐯𐑉𐐮𐑊𐐨, 𐑂𐐯𐑉𐐮𐑊𐐨, 𐐌 𐑅𐐩 𐐲𐑌𐐻𐐭 𐐷𐐭, 𐐃𐑊 𐑄𐐨𐑆 𐑃𐐮𐑍𐑆 𐑇𐐰𐑊 𐑇𐐭𐑉𐑊𐐨 𐐿𐐲𐑋, 𐐨𐑂𐐲𐑌 𐐰𐑆 𐑄 𐐙𐐪𐑄𐐲𐑉 𐐸𐐰𐑃 𐐿𐐲𐑋𐐰𐑌𐐼𐐯𐐼 𐑋𐐨. 𐐜𐐯𐑌 𐑇𐐰𐑊 𐑄𐐮𐑅 𐐿𐐲𐑂𐐯𐑌𐐰𐑌𐐻 𐐸𐐶𐐮𐐽 𐑄 𐐙𐐪𐑄𐐲𐑉 𐐸𐐰𐑃 𐐿𐐲𐑂𐐯𐑌𐐰𐑌𐐻𐐯𐐼 𐐶𐐮𐑄 𐐸𐐮𐑆 𐐹𐐨𐐹𐐲𐑊 𐐺𐐨 𐑁𐐳𐑊𐑁𐐮𐑊𐐼; 𐐰𐑌𐐼 𐑄𐐯𐑌 𐑇𐐰𐑊 𐐖𐐯𐑉𐐭𐑅𐐲𐑊𐐯𐑋 𐐺𐐨 𐐮𐑌𐐸𐐰𐐺𐐮𐐻𐐯𐐼 𐐲𐑀𐐯𐑌 𐐶𐐮𐑄 𐑋𐐴 𐐹𐐨𐐹𐐲𐑊, 𐐰𐑌𐐼 𐐮𐐻 𐑇𐐰𐑊 𐐺𐐨 𐑄 𐑊𐐰𐑌𐐼 𐐱𐑂 𐑄𐐩𐑉 𐐮𐑌𐐸𐐯𐑉𐐮𐐻𐐰𐑌𐑅. 𐐈𐑌𐐼, 𐑂𐐯𐑉𐐮𐑊𐐨, 𐐌 𐑅𐐩 𐐲𐑌𐐻𐐭 𐐷𐐭, 𐐌 𐑀𐐮𐑂 𐐲𐑌𐐻𐐭 𐐷𐐭 𐐲 𐑅𐐴𐑌, 𐑄𐐰𐐻 𐐷𐐨 𐑋𐐩 𐑌𐐬 𐑄 𐐻𐐴𐑋 𐐸𐐶𐐯𐑌 𐑄𐐨𐑆 𐑃𐐮𐑍𐑆 𐑇𐐰𐑊 𐐺𐐨 𐐲𐐺𐐵𐐻 𐐻𐐭 𐐻𐐩𐐿 𐐹𐑊𐐩𐑅, 𐑄𐐰𐐻 𐐌 𐑇𐐰𐑊 𐑀𐐰𐑄𐐲𐑉 𐐮𐑌 𐑁𐑉𐐱𐑋 𐑄𐐩𐑉 𐑊𐐱𐑍 𐐼𐐮𐑅𐐹𐐲𐑉𐑇𐐲𐑌, 𐑋𐐴 𐐹𐐨𐐹𐐲𐑊, 𐐄 𐐸𐐵𐑅 𐐱𐑂 𐐆𐑆𐑉𐐩𐐯𐑊, 𐐰𐑌𐐼 𐑇𐐰𐑊 𐐯𐑅𐐻𐐰𐐺𐑊𐐮𐑇 𐐲𐑀𐐯𐑌 𐐲𐑋𐐲𐑍 𐑄𐐯𐑋 𐑋𐐴 𐐞𐐴𐐲𐑌. 𐐈𐑌𐐼 𐐺𐐨𐐸𐐬𐑊𐐼, 𐑄𐐮𐑅 𐐮𐑆 𐑄 𐑃𐐮𐑍 𐐸𐐶𐐮𐐽 𐐌 𐐶𐐮𐑊 𐑀𐐮𐑂 𐐲𐑌𐐻𐐭 𐐷𐐭 𐑁𐐫𐑉 𐐲 𐑅𐐴𐑌, 𐑁𐐫𐑉 𐑂𐐯𐑉𐐮𐑊𐐨 𐐌 𐑅𐐩 𐐲𐑌𐐻𐐭 𐐷𐐭, 𐑄𐐰𐐻 𐐸𐐶𐐯𐑌 𐑄𐐨𐑆 𐑃𐐮𐑍𐑆 𐐸𐐶𐐮𐐽 𐐌 𐐼𐐯𐐿𐑊𐐩𐑉 𐐲𐑌𐐻𐐭 𐐷𐐭, 𐐰𐑌𐐼 𐐸𐐶𐐮𐐽 𐐌 𐑇𐐰𐑊 𐐼𐐯𐐿𐑊𐐩𐑉 𐐲𐑌𐐻𐐭 𐐷𐐭 𐐸𐐨𐑉𐐰𐑁𐐻𐐲𐑉 𐐱𐑂 𐑋𐐴𐑅𐐯𐑊𐑁, 𐐰𐑌𐐼 𐐺𐐴 𐑄 𐐹𐐵𐐲𐑉 𐐱𐑂 𐑄 𐐐𐐬𐑊𐐨 𐐘𐐬𐑅𐐻, 𐐸𐐶𐐮𐐽 𐑇𐐰𐑊 𐐺𐐨 𐑀𐐮𐑂𐐲𐑌 𐐲𐑌𐐻𐐭 𐐷𐐭 𐐱𐑂 𐑄 𐐙𐐪𐑄𐐲𐑉, 𐑇𐐰𐑊 𐐺𐐨 𐑋𐐩𐐼 𐑌𐐬𐑌 𐐲𐑌𐐻𐐭 𐑄 𐐖𐐯𐑌𐐻𐐴𐑊𐑆, 𐑄𐐰𐐻 𐑄𐐩 𐑋𐐩 𐑌𐐬 𐐿𐐱𐑌𐑅𐐲𐑉𐑌𐐮𐑍 𐑄𐐮𐑅 𐐹𐐨𐐹𐐲𐑊 𐐸𐐭 𐐪𐑉 𐐲 𐑉𐐯𐑋𐑌𐐰𐑌𐐻 𐐱𐑂 𐑄 𐐸𐐵𐑅 𐐱𐑂 𐐖𐐩𐐿𐐲𐐺, 𐐰𐑌𐐼 𐐿𐐱𐑌𐑅𐐲𐑉𐑌𐐮𐑍 𐑄𐐮𐑅 𐑋𐐴 𐐹𐐨𐐹𐐲𐑊 𐐸𐐭 𐑇𐐰𐑊 𐐺𐐨 𐑅𐐿𐐰𐐻𐐲𐑉𐐼 𐐺𐐴 𐑄𐐯𐑋; 𐑂𐐯𐑉𐐮𐑊𐐨, 𐑂𐐯𐑉𐐮𐑊𐐨, 𐐌 𐑅𐐩 𐐲𐑌𐐻𐐭 𐐷𐐭, 𐐸𐐶𐐯𐑌 𐑄𐐨𐑆 𐑃𐐮𐑍𐑆 𐑇𐐰𐑊 𐐺𐐨 𐑋𐐩𐐼 𐑌𐐬𐑌 𐐲𐑌𐐻𐐭 𐑄𐐯𐑋 𐐱𐑂 𐑄 𐐙𐐪𐑄𐐲𐑉, 𐐰𐑌𐐼 𐑇𐐰𐑊 𐐿𐐲𐑋 𐑁𐐬𐑉𐑃 𐐱𐑂 𐑄 𐐙𐐪𐑄𐐲𐑉, 𐑁𐑉𐐱𐑋 𐑄𐐯𐑋 𐐲𐑌𐐻𐐭 𐐷𐐭, 𐑁𐐫𐑉 𐐮𐐻 𐐮𐑆 𐐶𐐮𐑆𐐼𐐲𐑋 𐐮𐑌 𐑄 𐐙𐐪𐑄𐐲𐑉 𐑄𐐰𐐻 𐑄𐐩 𐑇𐐳𐐼 𐐺𐐨 𐐯𐑅𐐻𐐰𐐺𐑊𐐮𐑇𐐻 𐐮𐑌 𐑄𐐮𐑅 𐑊𐐰𐑌𐐼, 𐐰𐑌𐐼 𐐺𐐨 𐑅𐐯𐐻 𐐲𐐹 𐐰𐑆 𐐲 𐑁𐑉𐐨 𐐹𐐨𐐹𐐲𐑊 𐐺𐐴 𐑄 𐐹𐐵𐐲𐑉 𐐱𐑂 𐑄 𐐙𐐪𐑄𐐲𐑉, 𐑄𐐰𐐻 𐑄𐐨𐑆 𐑃𐐮𐑍𐑆 𐑋𐐴𐐻 𐐿𐐲𐑋 𐑁𐐬𐑉𐑃 𐑁𐑉𐐱𐑋 𐑄𐐯𐑋 𐐲𐑌𐐻𐐭 𐐲 𐑉𐐯𐑋𐑌𐐰𐑌𐐻 𐐱𐑂 𐐷𐐭𐑉 𐑅𐐨𐐼, 𐑄𐐰𐐻 𐑄 𐐿𐐲𐑂𐐯𐑌𐐰𐑌𐐻 𐐱𐑂 𐑄 𐐙𐐪𐑄𐐲𐑉 𐑋𐐩 𐐺𐐨 𐑁𐐳𐑊𐑁𐐮𐑊𐐼 𐐸𐐶𐐮𐐽 𐐸𐐨 𐐸𐐰𐑃 𐐿𐐲𐑂𐐯𐑌𐐰𐑌𐐻𐐯𐐼 𐐶𐐮𐑄 𐐸𐐮𐑆 𐐹𐐨𐐹𐐲𐑊, 𐐄 𐐸𐐵𐑅 𐐱𐑂 𐐆𐑆𐑉𐐩𐐯𐑊; 𐑄𐐯𐑉𐑁𐐬𐑉, 𐐸𐐶𐐯𐑌 𐑄𐐨𐑆 𐐶𐐲𐑉𐐿𐑅, 𐐰𐑌𐐼 𐑄 𐐶𐐲𐑉𐐿𐑅 𐐸𐐶𐐮𐐽 𐑇𐐰𐑊 𐐺𐐨 𐑉𐐫𐐻 𐐲𐑋𐐲𐑍 𐐷𐐭 𐐸𐐨𐑉𐐰𐑁𐐻𐐲𐑉, 𐑇𐐰𐑊 𐐿𐐲𐑋 𐑁𐐬𐑉𐑃 𐑁𐑉𐐱𐑋 𐑄 𐐖𐐯𐑌𐐻𐐴𐑊𐑆, 𐐲𐑌𐐻𐐭 𐐷𐐭𐑉 𐑅𐐨𐐼, 𐐸𐐶𐐮𐐽 𐑇𐐰𐑊 𐐼𐐶𐐮𐑌𐐼𐐲𐑊 𐐮𐑌 𐐲𐑌𐐺𐐨𐑊𐐨𐑁 𐐺𐐨𐐿𐐫𐑆 𐐱𐑂 𐐮𐑌𐐮𐐿𐐶𐐮𐐻𐐨; 𐑁𐐫𐑉 𐑄𐐲𐑅 𐐮𐐻 𐐺𐐨𐐸𐐭𐑂𐐯𐑃 𐑄 𐐙𐐪𐑄𐐲𐑉 𐑄𐐰𐐻 𐐮𐐻 𐑇𐐳𐐼 𐐿𐐲𐑋 𐑁𐐬𐑉𐑃 𐑁𐑉𐐱𐑋 𐑄 𐐖𐐯𐑌𐐻𐐴𐑊𐑆, 𐑄𐐰𐐻 𐐸𐐨 𐑋𐐩 𐑇𐐬 𐑁𐐬𐑉𐑃 𐐸𐐮𐑆 𐐹𐐵𐐲𐑉 𐐲𐑌𐐻𐐭 𐑄 𐐖𐐯𐑌𐐻𐐴𐑊𐑆, 𐑁𐐫𐑉 𐑄𐐮𐑅 𐐿𐐫𐑆, 𐑄𐐰𐐻 𐑄 𐐖𐐯𐑌𐐻𐐴𐑊𐑆, 𐐮𐑁 𐑄𐐩 𐐶𐐮𐑊 𐑌𐐱𐐻 𐐸𐐪𐑉𐐼𐐲𐑌 𐑄𐐩𐑉 𐐸𐐪𐑉𐐻𐑅, 𐑄𐐰𐐻 𐑄𐐩 𐑋𐐩 𐑉𐐨𐐹𐐯𐑌𐐻 𐐰𐑌𐐼 𐐿𐐲𐑋 𐐲𐑌𐐻𐐭 𐑋𐐨, 𐐰𐑌𐐼 𐐺𐐨 𐐺𐐰𐐹𐐻𐐴𐑆𐐼 𐐮𐑌 𐑋𐐴 𐑌𐐩𐑋, 𐐰𐑌𐐼 𐑌𐐬 𐐱𐑂 𐑄 𐐻𐑉𐐭 𐐹𐑎𐑌𐐻𐑅 𐐱𐑂 𐑋𐐴 𐐼𐐱𐐿𐐻𐑉𐐮𐑌, 𐑄𐐰𐐻 𐑄𐐩 𐑋𐐩 𐐺𐐨 𐑌𐐲𐑋𐐺𐐲𐑉𐐼 𐐲𐑋𐐲𐑍 𐑋𐐴 𐐹𐐨𐐹𐐲𐑊, 𐐄 𐐸𐐵𐑅 𐐱𐑂 𐐆𐑆𐑉𐐩𐐯𐑊; 𐐰𐑌𐐼 𐐸𐐶𐐯𐑌 𐑄𐐨𐑆 𐑃𐐮𐑍𐑆 𐐿𐐲𐑋 𐐻𐐭 𐐹𐐰𐑅, 𐑄𐐰𐐻 𐑄𐐴 𐑅𐐨𐐼 𐑇𐐰𐑊 𐐺𐐨𐑀𐐮𐑌 𐐻𐐭 𐑌𐐬 𐑄𐐨𐑆 𐑃𐐮𐑍𐑆, 𐐮𐐻 𐑇𐐰𐑊 𐐺𐐨 𐐲 𐑅𐐴𐑌 𐐲𐑌𐐻𐐭 𐑄𐐯𐑋, 𐑄𐐰𐐻 𐑄𐐩 𐑋𐐩 𐑌𐐬 𐑄𐐰𐐻 𐑄 𐐶𐐲𐑉𐐿 𐐱𐑂 𐑄 𐐙𐐪𐑄𐐲𐑉 𐐸𐐰𐑃 𐐫𐑊𐑉𐐯𐐼𐐨 𐐿𐐱𐑋𐐯𐑌𐑅𐐻 𐐲𐑌𐐻𐐭 𐑄 𐑁𐐳𐑊𐑁𐐮𐑊𐐮𐑍 𐐱𐑂 𐑄 𐐿𐐲𐑂𐐯𐑌𐐰𐑌𐐻 𐐸𐐶𐐮𐐽 𐐸𐐨 𐐸𐐰𐑃 𐑋𐐩𐐼 𐐲𐑌𐐻𐐭 𐑄 𐐹𐐨𐐹𐐲𐑊 𐐸𐐭 𐐪𐑉 𐐱𐑂 𐑄 𐐸𐐵𐑅 𐐱𐑂 𐐆𐑆𐑉𐐩𐐯𐑊. 𐐈𐑌𐐼 𐐸𐐶𐐯𐑌 𐑄𐐰𐐻 𐐼𐐩 𐑇𐐰𐑊 𐐿𐐲𐑋, 𐐮𐐻 𐑇𐐰𐑊 𐐿𐐲𐑋 𐐻𐐭 𐐹𐐰𐑅 𐑄𐐰𐐻 𐐿𐐮𐑍𐑆 𐑇𐐰𐑊 𐑇𐐲𐐻 𐑄𐐩𐑉 𐑋𐐵𐑄𐑆; 𐑁𐐫𐑉 𐑄𐐰𐐻 𐐸𐐶𐐮𐐽 𐐸𐐰𐐼 𐑌𐐱𐐻 𐐺𐐮𐑌 𐐻𐐬𐑊𐐼 𐑄𐐯𐑋 𐑇𐐰𐑊 𐑄𐐩 𐑅𐐨; 𐐰𐑌𐐼 𐑄𐐰𐐻 𐐸𐐶𐐮𐐽 𐑄𐐩 𐐸𐐰𐐼 𐑌𐐱𐐻 𐐸𐐲𐑉𐐼 𐑇𐐰𐑊 𐑄𐐩 𐐿𐐲𐑌𐑅𐐮𐐼𐐲𐑉. 𐐙𐐫𐑉 𐐮𐑌 𐑄𐐰𐐻 𐐼𐐩, 𐑁𐐫𐑉 𐑋𐐴 𐑅𐐩𐐿 𐑇𐐰𐑊 𐑄 𐐙𐐪𐑄𐐲𐑉 𐐶𐐲𐑉𐐿 𐐲 𐐶𐐲𐑉𐐿, 𐐸𐐶𐐮𐐽 𐑇𐐰𐑊 𐐺𐐨 𐐲 𐑀𐑉𐐩𐐻 𐐰𐑌𐐼 𐑋𐐪𐑉𐑂𐐯𐑊𐐲𐑅 𐐶𐐲𐑉𐐿 𐐲𐑋𐐲𐑍 𐑄𐐯𐑋; 𐐰𐑌𐐼 𐑄𐐩𐑉 𐑇𐐰𐑊 𐐺𐐨 𐐲𐑋𐐲𐑍 𐑄𐐯𐑋 𐐸𐐭 𐐶𐐮𐑊 𐑌𐐱𐐻 𐐺𐐨𐑊𐐨𐑂 𐐮𐐻, 𐐫𐑊𐑄𐐬 𐐲 𐑋𐐰𐑌 𐑇𐐰𐑊 𐐼𐐯𐐿𐑊𐐩𐑉 𐐮𐐻 𐐲𐑌𐐻𐐭 𐑄𐐯𐑋. 𐐒𐐲𐐻 𐐺𐐨𐐸𐐬𐑊𐐼, 𐑄 𐑊𐐴𐑁 𐐱𐑂 𐑋𐐴 𐑅𐐲𐑉𐑂𐐰𐑌𐐻 𐑇𐐰𐑊 𐐺𐐨 𐐮𐑌 𐑋𐐴 𐐸𐐰𐑌𐐼; 𐑄𐐯𐑉𐑁𐐬𐑉 𐑄𐐩 𐑇𐐰𐑊 𐑌𐐱𐐻 𐐸𐐲𐑉𐐻 𐐸𐐮𐑋, 𐐫𐑊𐑄𐐬 𐐸𐐨 𐑇𐐰𐑊 𐐺𐐨 𐑋𐐪𐑉𐐼 𐐺𐐨𐐿𐐫𐑆 𐐱𐑂 𐑄𐐯𐑋. 𐐏𐐯𐐻 𐐌 𐐶𐐮𐑊 𐐸𐐨𐑊 𐐸𐐮𐑋, 𐑁𐐫𐑉 𐐌 𐐶𐐮𐑊 𐑇𐐬 𐐲𐑌𐐻𐐭 𐑄𐐯𐑋 𐑄𐐰𐐻 𐑋𐐴 𐐶𐐮𐑆𐐼𐐲𐑋 𐐮𐑆 𐑀𐑉𐐩𐐻𐐲𐑉 𐑄𐐰𐑌 𐑄 𐐿𐐲𐑌𐐮𐑍 𐐱𐑂 𐑄 𐐼𐐯𐑂𐐮𐑊.

12. 𐐜𐐯𐑉𐑁𐐬𐑉 𐐮𐐻 𐑇𐐰𐑊 𐐿𐐲𐑋 𐐻𐐭 𐐹𐐰𐑅, 𐑄𐐰𐐻 𐐸𐐭𐑅𐐬𐐯𐑂𐐲𐑉 𐐶𐐮𐑊 𐑌𐐱𐐻 𐐺𐐨𐑊𐐨𐑂 𐐮𐑌 𐑋𐐴 𐐶𐐲𐑉𐐼𐑆, 𐐸𐐭 𐐰𐑋 𐐖𐐨𐑆𐐲𐑅 𐐗𐑉𐐴𐑅𐐻, 𐐸𐐶𐐮𐐽 𐑄 𐐙𐐪𐑄𐐲𐑉 𐑇𐐰𐑊 𐐿𐐫𐑆 𐐸𐐮𐑋 𐐻𐐭 𐐺𐑉𐐮𐑍 𐑁𐐬𐑉𐑃 𐐲𐑌𐐻𐐭 𐑄 𐐖𐐯𐑌𐐻𐐴𐑊𐑆, 𐐰𐑌𐐼 𐑇𐐰𐑊 𐑀𐐮𐑂 𐐲𐑌𐐻𐐭 𐐸𐐮𐑋 𐐹𐐵𐐲𐑉 𐑄𐐰𐐻 𐐸𐐨 𐑇𐐰𐑊 𐐺𐑉𐐮𐑍 𐑄𐐯𐑋 𐑁𐐬𐑉𐑃 𐐲𐑌𐐻𐐭 𐑄 𐐖𐐯𐑌𐐻𐐴𐑊𐑆, (𐐮𐐻 𐑇𐐰𐑊 𐐺𐐨 𐐼𐐲𐑌 𐐨𐑂𐐲𐑌 𐐰𐑆 𐐣𐐬𐑆𐐯𐑆 𐑅𐐯𐐼,) 𐑄𐐩 𐑇𐐰𐑊 𐐺𐐨 𐐿𐐲𐐻 𐐫𐑁 𐑁𐑉𐐱𐑋 𐐲𐑋𐐲𐑍 𐑋𐐴 𐐹𐐨𐐹𐐲𐑊 𐐸𐐭 𐐪𐑉 𐐱𐑂 𐑄 𐐿𐐲𐑂𐐯𐑌𐐰𐑌𐐻; 𐐰𐑌𐐼 𐑋𐐴 𐐹𐐨𐐹𐐲𐑊 𐐸𐐭 𐐪𐑉 𐐲 𐑉𐐯𐑋𐑌𐐰𐑌𐐻 𐐱𐑂 𐐖𐐩𐐿𐐲𐐺, 𐑇𐐰𐑊 𐐺𐐨 𐐲𐑋𐐲𐑍 𐑄 𐐖𐐯𐑌𐐻𐐴𐑊𐑆, 𐐷𐐩, 𐐮𐑌 𐑄 𐑋𐐮𐐼𐑅𐐻 𐐱𐑂 𐑄𐐯𐑋, 𐐰𐑆 𐐲 𐑊𐐴𐐲𐑌 𐐲𐑋𐐲𐑍 𐑄 𐐺𐐨𐑅𐐻𐑅 𐐱𐑂 𐑄 𐑁𐐱𐑉𐐯𐑅𐐻, 𐐰𐑆 𐐲 𐐷𐐲𐑍 𐑊𐐴𐐲𐑌 𐐲𐑋𐐲𐑍 𐑄 𐑁𐑊𐐱𐐿𐑅 𐐱𐑂

𐑇𐐨𐐹, 𐐸𐐭, 𐐮𐑁 𐐸𐐨 𐑀𐐬 𐑃𐑉𐐭, 𐐺𐐬𐑃 𐐻𐑉𐐯𐐼𐐯𐑃 𐐼𐐵𐑌 𐐰𐑌𐐼 𐐻𐐩𐑉𐐯𐑃 𐐮𐑌 𐐹𐐨𐑅𐐯𐑆, 𐐰𐑌𐐼 𐑌𐐲𐑌 𐐿𐐰𐑌 𐐼𐐨𐑊𐐮𐑂𐐲𐑉. 𐐜𐐩𐑉 𐐸𐐰𐑌𐐼 𐑇𐐰𐑊 𐐺 𐑊𐐮𐑁𐐻𐐯𐐼 𐐲𐐹 𐐲𐐹𐐱𐑌 𐑄𐐩𐑉 𐐰𐐼𐑂𐐲𐑉𐑅𐐯𐑉𐐮𐑆, 𐐰𐑌𐐼 𐐫𐑊 𐑄𐐩𐑉 𐐯𐑌𐐯𐑋𐐮𐑆 𐑇𐐰𐑊 𐐺 𐐿𐐲𐐻 𐐱𐑁. 𐐏𐐩, 𐐶𐐬 𐐺 𐐲𐑌𐐻𐐭 𐑄 𐐖𐐯𐑌𐐻𐐴𐑊𐑆, 𐐯𐐿𐑅𐐯𐐹𐐻 𐑄𐐩 𐑉𐐨𐐹𐐯𐑌𐐻, 𐐙𐐫𐑉 𐐮𐐻 𐑇𐐰𐑊 𐐿𐐲𐑋 𐐻𐐭 𐐹𐐪𐑅 𐐮𐑌 𐑄𐐰𐐻 𐐼𐐩, 𐑅𐐯𐑃 𐑄 𐐙𐐪𐑄𐐲𐑉, 𐑄𐐰𐐻 𐐴 𐐶𐐮𐑊 𐐿𐐲𐐻 𐐱𐑁 𐑄𐐴 𐐸𐐫𐑉𐑅𐐯𐑆 𐐵𐐻 𐐱𐑂 𐑄 𐑋𐐮𐐼𐑅𐐻 𐐱𐑂 𐑄, 𐐰𐑌𐐼 𐐴 𐐶𐐮𐑊 𐐼𐐨𐑅𐐻𐑉𐐱𐐮 𐑄𐐴 𐐽𐐰𐑉𐐨𐐲𐐻𐑅, 𐐰𐑌𐐼 𐐴 𐐶𐐮𐑊 𐐿𐐲𐐻 𐐱𐑁 𐑄 𐑅𐐮𐐻𐐮𐑆 𐐱𐑂 𐑄𐐴 𐑊𐐰𐑌𐐼, 𐐰𐑌𐐼 𐑃𐑉𐐬 𐐼𐐵𐑌 𐐫𐑊 𐑄𐐴 𐑅𐐻𐑉𐐱𐑍𐐸𐐬𐑊𐐼𐑆; 𐐰𐑌𐐼 𐐴 𐐶𐐮𐑊 𐐿𐐲𐐻 𐐱𐑁 𐐶𐐮𐐽𐐿𐑉𐐪𐑁𐐻𐑅 𐐵𐐻 𐐱𐑂 𐑄𐐴 𐑊𐐰𐑌𐐼, 𐐰𐑌𐐼 𐑄𐐵 𐑇𐐰𐑊𐐻 𐐸𐐰𐑂 𐑌𐐬 𐑋𐐬𐑉 𐑅𐐭𐑄𐑅𐐩𐐲𐑉𐑆; 𐑄𐐴 𐑀𐑉𐐩𐑂𐑌 𐐮𐑋𐐯𐐾𐐯𐑆 𐐴 𐐶𐐮𐑊 𐐫𐑊𐑅𐐬 𐐿𐐲𐐻 𐐱𐑁, 𐐰𐑌𐐼 𐑄𐐴 𐑅𐐻𐐰𐑌𐐼𐐮𐑍 𐐮𐑋𐐯𐐾𐐯𐑆 𐐵𐐻 𐐱𐑂 𐑄 𐑋𐐮𐐼𐑅𐐻 𐐱𐑂 𐑄, 𐐰𐑌𐐼 𐑄𐐵 𐑇𐐰𐑊𐐻 𐑌𐐬 𐑋𐐬𐑉 𐐶𐐲𐑉𐑇𐐮𐐹 𐑄 𐐶𐐲𐑉𐐿𐑅 𐐱𐑂 𐑄𐐴 𐐸𐐰𐑌𐐼𐑆; 𐐰𐑌𐐼 𐐴 𐐶𐐮𐑊 𐐹𐑊𐐲𐐿 𐐲𐐹 𐑄𐐴 𐑀𐑉𐐬𐑂𐑆 𐐵𐐻 𐐱𐑂 𐑄 𐑋𐐮𐐼𐑅𐐻 𐐱𐑂 𐑄; 𐑅𐐬 𐐶𐐮𐑊 𐐴 𐐼𐐨𐑅𐐻𐑉𐐱𐐮 𐑄𐐴 𐑅𐐮𐐻𐐮𐑆. 𐐈𐑌𐐼 𐐮𐐻 𐑇𐐰𐑊 𐐿𐐲𐑋 𐐻𐐭 𐐹𐐪𐑅 𐑄𐐰𐐻 𐐫𐑊 𐑊𐐴𐐮𐑍𐑆, 𐐰𐑌𐐼 𐐼𐐨𐑅𐐨𐑂𐐮𐑍𐑆, 𐐰𐑌𐐼 𐐯𐑌𐑂𐐨𐐮𐑍𐑆, 𐐰𐑌𐐼 𐑅𐐻𐑉𐐴𐑁𐑅, 𐐰𐑌𐐼 𐐹𐑉𐐨𐑅𐐻𐐿𐑉𐐪𐑁𐐻𐑅, 𐐰𐑌𐐼 𐐸𐐬𐑉𐐼𐐲𐑋𐑆, 𐑇𐐰𐑊 𐐺 𐐼𐐲𐑌 𐐰𐐶𐐩. 𐐙𐐫𐑉 𐐮𐐻 𐑇𐐰𐑊 𐐿𐐲𐑋 𐐻𐐭 𐐹𐐪𐑅, 𐑅𐐯𐑃 𐑄 𐐙𐐪𐑄𐐲𐑉, 𐑄𐐰𐐻 𐐰𐐻 𐑄𐐰𐐻 𐐼𐐩 𐐸𐐭𐑅𐐬𐐯𐑂𐐲𐑉 𐐶𐐮𐑊 𐑌𐐱𐐻 𐑉𐐨𐐹𐐯𐑌𐐻 𐐰𐑌𐐼 𐐿𐐲𐑋 𐐲𐑌𐐻𐐭 𐑋𐐴 𐐒𐐨𐑊𐐲𐑂𐐯𐐼 𐐝𐐲𐑌, 𐑄𐐯𐑋 𐐶𐐮𐑊 𐐴 𐐿𐐲𐐻 𐐱𐑁 𐑁𐑉𐐱𐑋 𐐰𐑋𐐲𐑍 𐑋𐐴 𐐹𐐨𐐹𐑊, 𐐄 𐐸𐐵𐑅 𐐱𐑂 𐐆𐑆𐑉𐐩𐐯𐑊; 𐐰𐑌𐐼 𐐴 𐐶𐐮𐑊 𐐯𐐿𐑅𐐨𐐿𐐷𐐭𐐻 𐑂𐐯𐑌𐐾𐐲𐑌𐑅 𐐰𐑌𐐼 𐑁𐐷𐐭𐑉𐐨 𐐲𐐹𐐱𐑌 𐑄𐐯𐑋, 𐐨𐑂𐑌 𐐰𐑆 𐐲𐐹𐐱𐑌 𐑄 𐐸𐐨𐑄𐐯𐑌, 𐑅𐐲𐐽 𐐰𐑆 𐑄𐐩 𐐸𐐰𐑂 𐑌𐐱𐐻 𐐸𐐲𐑉𐐼.

𐐕𐐈𐐑𐐓𐐊𐐡 X.

1. 𐐒𐐲𐐻 𐐮𐑁 𐑄𐐩 𐐶𐐮𐑊 𐑉𐐨𐐹𐐯𐑌𐐻, 𐐰𐑌𐐼 𐐸𐐪𐑉𐐿𐑌 𐐲𐑌𐐻𐐭 𐑋𐐴 𐐶𐐲𐑉𐐼𐑆, 𐐰𐑌𐐼 𐐸𐐪𐑉𐐼𐑌 𐑌𐐱𐐻 𐑄𐐩𐑉 𐐸𐐪𐑉𐐻𐑅, 𐐴 𐐶𐐮𐑊 𐐯𐑅𐐻𐐰𐐺𐑊𐐮𐑇 𐑋𐐴 𐐽𐐲𐑉𐐽 𐐰𐑋𐐲𐑍 𐑄𐐯𐑋, 𐐰𐑌𐐼 𐑄𐐩 𐑇𐐰𐑊 𐐿𐐲𐑋 𐐮𐑌 𐐲𐑌𐐻𐐭 𐑄 𐐿𐐲𐑂𐐯𐑌𐐲𐑌𐐻, 𐐰𐑌𐐼 𐐺 𐑌𐐲𐑋𐐺𐐲𐑉𐐼 𐐰𐑋𐐲𐑍 𐑄𐐮𐑅 𐑄 𐑉𐐯𐑋𐑌𐐲𐑌𐐻 𐐱𐑂 𐐖𐐩𐐿𐐲𐐺, 𐐲𐑌𐐻𐐭 𐐸𐐭𐑋 𐐴 𐐸𐐰𐑂 𐑀𐐮𐑂𐑌 𐑄𐐮𐑅 𐑊𐐰𐑌𐐼 𐑁𐐫𐑉 𐑄𐐩𐑉 𐐮𐑌𐐸𐐯𐑉𐐮𐐻𐐲𐑌𐑅, 𐐰𐑌𐐼 𐑄𐐩 𐑇𐐰𐑊 𐐰𐑅𐐮𐑅𐐻 𐑋𐐴 𐐹𐐨𐐹𐑊, 𐑄 𐑉𐐯𐑋𐑌𐐲𐑌𐐻 𐐱𐑂 𐐖𐐩𐐿𐐲𐐺, 𐐰𐑌𐐼 𐐫𐑊𐑅𐐬, 𐐰𐑆 𐑋𐐯𐑌𐐨 𐐱𐑂 𐑄 𐐸𐐵𐑅 𐐱𐑂 𐐆𐑆𐑉𐐩𐐯𐑊 𐐰𐑆 𐑇𐐰𐑊 𐐿𐐲𐑋, 𐑄𐐰𐐻 𐑄𐐩 𐑋𐐩 𐐺𐐮𐑊𐐼 𐐪 𐑅𐐮𐐻𐐨, 𐐸𐐶𐐮𐐽 𐑇𐐰𐑊 𐐺 𐐿𐐫𐑊𐐼 𐑄 𐑌𐐷𐐭 𐐖𐐯𐑉𐐭𐑅𐐰𐑊𐐯𐑋; 𐐰𐑌𐐼 𐑄𐐯𐑌 𐑇𐐰𐑊 𐑄𐐩 𐐰𐑅𐐮𐑅𐐻 𐑋𐐴 𐐹𐐨𐐹𐑊 𐑄𐐰𐐻 𐑄𐐩 𐑋𐐩 𐐺 𐑀𐐰𐑄𐐲𐑉𐐼 𐐮𐑌, 𐐸𐐭 𐐪𐑉 𐑅𐐿𐐰𐐻𐐲𐑉𐐼 𐐲𐐹𐐱𐑌 𐐫𐑊 𐑄 𐑁𐐩𐑅 𐐱𐑂 𐑄 𐑊𐐰𐑌𐐼, 𐐮𐑌 𐐲𐑌𐐻𐐭 𐑄 𐑌𐐷𐐭 𐐖𐐯𐑉𐐭𐑅𐐰𐑊𐐯𐑋. 𐐈𐑌𐐼 𐑄𐐯𐑌 𐑇𐐰𐑊 𐑄 𐐹𐐵𐑉 𐐱𐑂 𐐸𐐯𐑂𐑌 𐐿𐐲𐑋 𐐼𐐵𐑌 𐐰𐑋𐐲𐑍 𐑄𐐯𐑋; 𐐰𐑌𐐼 𐐴 𐐫𐑊𐑅𐐬 𐐶𐐮𐑊 𐐺 𐐮𐑌 𐑄 𐑋𐐮𐐼𐑅𐐻; 𐐰𐑌𐐼 𐑄𐐯𐑌 𐑇𐐰𐑊 𐑄 𐐶𐐲𐑉𐐿 𐐱𐑂 𐑄 𐐙𐐪𐑄𐐲𐑉 𐐿𐐲𐑋𐐯𐑌𐑅 𐐰𐐻 𐑄𐐰𐐻 𐐼𐐩, 𐐨𐑂𐑌 𐐸𐐶𐐯𐑌 𐑄𐐮𐑅 𐑀𐐱𐑅𐐹𐐯𐑊 𐑇𐐰𐑊 𐐺 𐐹𐑉𐐨𐐽𐐻 𐐰𐑋𐐲𐑍 𐑄 𐑉𐐯𐑋𐑌𐐲𐑌𐐻 𐐱𐑂 𐑄𐐮𐑅 𐐹𐐨𐐹𐑊. 𐐚𐐯𐑉𐐮𐑊𐐨 𐐴 𐑅𐐩 𐐲𐑌𐐻𐐭 𐐷𐐭, 𐐰𐐻 𐑄𐐰𐐻 𐐼𐐩 𐑇𐐰𐑊 𐑄 𐐶𐐲𐑉𐐿 𐐱𐑂 𐑄 𐐙𐐪𐑄𐐲𐑉 𐐿𐐲𐑋𐐯𐑌𐑅 𐐰𐑋𐐲𐑍 𐐫𐑊 𐑄 𐐼𐐮𐑅𐐹𐐲𐑉𐑅𐐻 𐐱𐑂 𐑋𐐴 𐐹𐐨𐐹𐑊; 𐐏𐐩, 𐐨𐑂𐑌 𐑄 𐐻𐑉𐐴𐐺𐑆 𐐸𐐶𐐮𐐽 𐐸𐐰𐑂 𐐺𐐮𐑌 𐑊𐐱𐑅𐐻, 𐐸𐐶𐐮𐐽 𐑄 𐐙𐐪𐑄𐐲𐑉 𐐸𐐰𐑃 𐑊𐐯𐐼 𐐰𐐶𐐩 𐐵𐐻 𐐱𐑂 𐐖𐐯𐑉𐐭𐑅𐐰𐑊𐐯𐑋. 𐐏𐐩, 𐑄 𐐶𐐲𐑉𐐿 𐑇𐐰𐑊 𐐿𐐲𐑋𐐯𐑌𐑅 𐐰𐑋𐐲𐑍 𐐫𐑊 𐑄 𐐼𐐮𐑅𐐹𐐲𐑉𐑅𐐻 𐐱𐑂 𐑋𐐴 𐐹𐐨𐐹𐑊, 𐐶𐐮𐑄 𐑄 𐐙𐐪𐑄𐐲𐑉, 𐐻𐐭 𐐹𐑉𐐨𐐹𐐩𐑉 𐑄 𐐶𐐩 𐐸𐐶𐐩𐑉𐐺𐐴 𐑄𐐩 𐑋𐐩 𐐿𐐲𐑋 𐐲𐑌𐐻𐐭 𐑋𐐨, 𐑄𐐰𐐻 𐑄𐐩 𐑋𐐩 𐐿𐐫𐑊 𐐱𐑌 𐑄 𐐙𐐪𐑄𐐲𐑉 𐐮𐑌 𐑋𐐴 𐑌𐐩𐑋; 𐐏𐐩, 𐐰𐑌𐐼 𐑄𐐯𐑌 𐑇𐐰𐑊 𐑄 𐐶𐐲𐑉𐐿 𐐿𐐲𐑋𐐯𐑌𐑅, 𐐶𐐮𐑄 𐑄 𐐙𐐪𐑄𐐲𐑉, 𐐰𐑋𐐲𐑍 𐐫𐑊 𐑌𐐩𐑇𐐲𐑌𐑆, 𐐮𐑌 𐐹𐑉𐐨𐐹𐐩𐑉𐐮𐑍 𐑄 𐐶𐐩 𐐸𐐶𐐩𐑉𐐺𐐴 𐐸𐐮𐑆 𐐹𐐨𐐹𐑊 𐑋𐐩 𐐺 𐑀𐐰𐑄𐐲𐑉𐐼 𐐸𐐬𐑋 𐐻𐐭 𐑄 𐑊𐐰𐑌𐐼 𐐱𐑂 𐑄𐐩𐑉 𐐮𐑌𐐸𐐯𐑉𐐮𐐻𐐲𐑌𐑅. 𐐈𐑌𐐼 𐑄𐐩 𐑇𐐰𐑊 𐑀𐐬 𐐵𐐻 𐑁𐑉𐐱𐑋 𐐫𐑊 𐑌𐐩𐑇𐐲𐑌𐑆; 𐐰𐑌𐐼 𐑄𐐩 𐑇𐐰𐑊 𐑌𐐱𐐻 𐑀𐐬 𐐵𐐻 𐐮𐑌 𐐸𐐩𐑅𐐻, 𐑌𐐫𐑉 𐑀𐐬 𐐺𐐴 𐑁𐑊𐐴𐐻, 𐑁𐐫𐑉 𐐴 𐐶𐐮𐑊 𐑀𐐬 𐐺𐐨𐑁𐐫𐑉 𐑄𐐯𐑋, 𐑅𐐯𐑃 𐑄 𐐙𐐪𐑄𐐲𐑉, 𐐰𐑌𐐼 𐐴 𐐶𐐮𐑊 𐐺 𐑄𐐩𐑉 𐑉𐐨𐑉𐐶𐐫𐑉𐐼. 𐐈𐑌𐐼 𐑄𐐯𐑌 𐑇𐐰𐑊 𐑄𐐰𐐻 𐐸𐐶𐐮𐐽 𐐮𐑆 𐑉𐐮𐐻𐑌 𐐿𐐲𐑋 𐐻𐐭 𐐹𐐪𐑅. 𐐝𐐮𐑍, 𐐄 𐐺𐐰𐑉𐐯𐑌, 𐑄𐐵 𐑄𐐰𐐻 𐐼𐐮𐐼𐑅𐐻 𐑌𐐱𐐻 𐐺𐐩𐑉: 𐐺𐑉𐐩𐐿 𐑁𐐬𐑉𐑃 𐐮𐑌𐐻𐐭 𐑅𐐮𐑍𐐮𐑍, 𐐰𐑌𐐼 𐐿𐑉𐐴 𐐰𐑊𐐵𐐼, 𐑄𐐵 𐑄𐐰𐐻 𐐼𐐮𐐼𐑅𐐻 𐑌𐐱𐐻 𐐻𐑉𐐰𐑂𐐯𐑊 𐐶𐐮𐑄 𐐽𐐴𐑊𐐼; 𐑁𐐫𐑉 𐑋𐐬𐑉 𐐪𐑉 𐑄 𐐽𐐮𐑊𐐼𐑉𐐯𐑌 𐐱𐑂 𐑄 𐐼𐐯𐑅𐐬𐑊𐐩𐐻, 𐑄𐐰𐑌 𐑄 𐐽𐐮𐑊𐐼𐑉𐐯𐑌 𐐱𐑂 𐑄 𐑋𐐰𐑉𐐨𐐼 𐐶𐐴𐑁, 𐑅𐐯𐑃 𐑄 𐐢𐐫𐑉𐐼. 𐐇𐑌𐑊𐐪𐑉𐐾 𐑄 𐐹𐑊𐐩𐑅 𐐱𐑂 𐑄𐐴 𐐻𐐯𐑌𐐻, 𐐰𐑌𐐼 𐑊𐐯𐐻 𐑄𐐯𐑋 𐑅𐐻𐑉𐐯𐐽 𐑁𐐬𐑉𐑃 𐑄 𐐿𐐲𐑉𐐻𐐮𐑌𐑆 𐐱𐑂 𐑄𐐴 𐐸𐐰𐐺𐐮𐐻𐐩𐑇𐐲𐑌𐑆; 𐑅𐐹𐐩𐑉 𐑌𐐱𐐻, 𐑊𐐯𐑍𐑃𐑌 𐑄𐐴 𐐿𐐫𐑉𐐼𐑆 𐐰𐑌𐐼 𐑅𐐻𐑉𐐯𐑍𐑃𐑌

𐑄𐐴 𐑅𐐻𐐩𐐿𐑅; 𐑁𐐫𐑉 𐑄𐐵 𐑇𐐰𐑊𐐻 𐐺𐑉𐐩𐐿 𐑁𐐫𐑉𐑃 𐐱𐑌 𐑄 𐑉𐐴𐐻 𐐸𐐰𐑌𐐼 𐐰𐑌𐐼 𐐱𐑌 𐑄 𐑊𐐯𐑁𐐻, 𐐰𐑌𐐼 𐑄𐐴 𐑅𐐨𐐼 𐑇𐐰𐑊 𐐮𐑌𐐸𐐯𐑉𐐮𐐻 𐑄 𐐖𐐯𐑌𐐻𐐴𐑊𐑆, 𐐰𐑌𐐼 𐑋𐐩𐐿 𐑄 𐐼𐐯𐑅𐐬𐑊𐐩𐐻 𐑅𐐮𐐻𐐮𐑆 𐐻𐐭 𐐺𐐨 𐐮𐑌𐐸𐐰𐐺𐐮𐐻𐐯𐐼. 𐐙𐐨𐑉 𐑌𐐱𐐻, 𐑁𐐫𐑉 𐑄𐐵 𐑇𐐰𐑊𐐻 𐑌𐐱𐐻 𐐺𐐨 𐐰𐑇𐐩𐑋𐐼; 𐑌𐐨𐑄𐐲𐑉 𐐺𐐨 𐑄𐐵 𐐿𐐱𐑌𐑁𐐵𐑌𐐼𐐯𐐼, 𐑁𐐫𐑉 𐑄𐐵 𐑇𐐰𐑊𐐻 𐑌𐐱𐐻 𐐺𐐨 𐐹𐐳𐐻 𐐻𐐭 𐑇𐐩𐑋; 𐑁𐐫𐑉 𐑄𐐵 𐑇𐐰𐑊𐐻 𐑁𐐫𐑉𐑀𐐯𐐻 𐑄 𐑇𐐩𐑋 𐐱𐑂 𐑄𐐴 𐐷𐐭𐑃, 𐐰𐑌𐐼 𐑇𐐰𐑊𐐻 𐑌𐐱𐐻 𐑉𐐨𐑋𐐯𐑋𐐺𐐲𐑉 𐑄 𐑉𐐨𐐹𐑉𐐬𐐽 𐐱𐑂 𐑄𐐴 𐐶𐐮𐐼𐐬𐐸𐐳𐐼 𐐯𐑌𐐨 𐑋𐐬𐑉. 𐐙𐐫𐑉 𐑄𐐴 𐐣𐐩𐐿𐐲𐑉, 𐑄𐐴 𐐐𐐲𐑆𐐺𐐲𐑌𐐼, 𐑄 𐐢𐐫𐑉𐐼 𐐱𐑂 𐐐𐐬𐑅𐐻𐑅 𐐮𐑆 𐐸𐐮𐑆 𐑌𐐩𐑋; 𐐰𐑌𐐼 𐑄𐐴 𐐡𐐨𐐼𐐨𐑋𐐲𐑉, 𐑄 𐐐𐐬𐑊𐐨 𐐎𐐲𐑌 𐐱𐑂 𐐆𐑆𐑉𐐩𐐯𐑊; 𐑄 𐐘𐐱𐐼 𐐱𐑂 𐑄 𐐸𐐬𐑊 𐐲𐑉𐑃 𐑇𐐰𐑊 𐐸𐐨 𐐺𐐨 𐐿𐐫𐑊𐐼. 𐐙𐐫𐑉 𐑄 𐐢𐐫𐑉𐐼 𐐸𐐰𐑃 𐐿𐐫𐑊𐐼 𐑄𐐨 𐐰𐑆 𐐲 𐐶𐐳𐑋𐐲𐑌 𐑁𐐫𐑉𐑅𐐩𐐿𐐲𐑌 𐐰𐑌𐐼 𐑀𐑉𐐨𐑂𐐼 𐐮𐑌 𐑅𐐹𐐮𐑉𐐮𐐻, 𐐰𐑌𐐼 𐐲 𐐶𐐴𐑁 𐐱𐑂 𐐷𐐭𐑃, 𐐸𐐶𐐯𐑌 𐑄𐐵 𐐶𐐱𐑅𐐻 𐑉𐐯𐑁𐐷𐐭𐑆𐐼, 𐑅𐐯𐑃 𐑄𐐴 𐐘𐐱𐐼. 𐐙𐐫𐑉 𐐲 𐑅𐑋𐐫𐑊 𐑋𐐬𐑋𐐯𐑌𐐻 𐐸𐐰𐑂 𐐌 𐑁𐐫𐑉𐑅𐐩𐐿𐐲𐑌 𐑄𐐨, 𐐺𐐲𐐻 𐐶𐐮𐑄 𐑀𐑉𐐩𐐻 𐑋𐐲𐑉𐑅𐐮𐑆 𐐶𐐮𐑊 𐐌 𐑀𐐰𐑄𐐲𐑉 𐑄𐐨. 𐐆𐑌 𐐲 𐑊𐐮𐐻𐑊 𐑉𐐫𐑃 𐐌 𐐸𐐮𐐼 𐑋𐐴 𐑁𐐩𐑅 𐑁𐑉𐐱𐑋 𐑄𐐨 𐑁𐐫𐑉 𐐲 𐑋𐐬𐑋𐐯𐑌𐐻, 𐐺𐐲𐐻 𐐶𐐮𐑄 𐐯𐑂𐐲𐑉𐑊𐐰𐑅𐐻𐐮𐑍 𐐿𐐴𐑌𐐼𐑌𐐯𐑅 𐐶𐐮𐑊 𐐌 𐐸𐐰𐑂 𐑋𐐲𐑉𐑅𐐨 𐐱𐑌 𐑄𐐨, 𐑅𐐯𐑃 𐑄 𐐢𐐫𐑉𐐼 𐑄𐐴 𐐡𐐨𐐼𐐨𐑋𐐲𐑉. 𐐙𐐫𐑉 𐑄𐐮𐑅, 𐑄 𐐶𐐫𐐻𐐲𐑉𐑆 𐐱𐑂 𐐤𐐬𐐲 𐐲𐑌𐐻𐐭 𐑋𐐨, 𐑁𐐫𐑉 𐐰𐑆 𐐌 𐐸𐐰𐑂 𐑅𐐶𐐫𐑉𐑌 𐑄𐐰𐐻 𐑄 𐐶𐐫𐐻𐐲𐑉𐑆 𐐱𐑂 𐐤𐐬𐐲 𐑇𐐳𐐼 𐑌𐐬 𐑋𐐬𐑉 𐑀𐐬 𐐬𐑂𐐲𐑉 𐑄 𐐲𐑉𐑃, 𐑅𐐬 𐐸𐐰𐑂 𐐌 𐑅𐐶𐐫𐑉𐑌 𐑄𐐰𐐻 𐐌 𐐶𐐳𐐼 𐑌𐐱𐐻 𐐺𐐨 𐑉𐐫𐑃 𐐶𐐮𐑄 𐑄𐐨. 𐐙𐐫𐑉 𐑄 𐑋𐐵𐑌𐐻𐐩𐑌𐑆 𐑇𐐰𐑊 𐐼𐐨𐐹𐐪𐑉𐐻 𐐰𐑌𐐼 𐑄 𐐸𐐮𐑊𐑆 𐐺𐐨 𐑉𐐨𐑋𐐭𐑂𐐼, 𐐺𐐲𐐻 𐑋𐐴 𐐿𐐴𐑌𐐼𐑌𐐯𐑅 𐑇𐐰𐑊 𐑌𐐱𐐻 𐐼𐐨𐐹𐐪𐑉𐐻 𐑁𐑉𐐱𐑋 𐑄𐐨, 𐑌𐐨𐑄𐐲𐑉 𐑇𐐰𐑊 𐑄 𐐿𐐲𐑂𐐯𐑌𐐰𐑌𐐻 𐐱𐑂 𐑋𐐴 𐐹𐐨𐑅 𐐺𐐨 𐑉𐐨𐑋𐐭𐑂𐐼, 𐑅𐐯𐑃 𐑄 𐐢𐐫𐑉𐐼 𐑄𐐰𐐻 𐐸𐐰𐑃 𐑋𐐲𐑉𐑅𐐨 𐐱𐑌 𐑄𐐨.

2. 𐐄 𐑄𐐵 𐐰𐑁𐑊𐐮𐐿𐐻𐐯𐐼, 𐐻𐐫𐑅𐐻 𐐶𐐮𐑄 𐐻𐐯𐑋𐐹𐐯𐑅𐐻, 𐐰𐑌𐐼 𐑌𐐱𐐻 𐐿𐐲𐑋𐑁𐐲𐑉𐐻𐐯𐐼! 𐐒𐐨𐐸𐐬𐑊𐐼, 𐐌 𐐶𐐮𐑊 𐑊𐐩 𐑄𐐴 𐑅𐐻𐐬𐑌𐑆 𐐶𐐮𐑄 𐑁𐐩𐑉 𐐿𐐲𐑊𐐲𐑉𐑆, 𐐰𐑌𐐼 𐑊𐐩 𐑄𐐴 𐑁𐐵𐑌𐐼𐐩𐑇𐐲𐑌𐑆 𐐶𐐮𐑄 𐑅𐐰𐑁𐐴𐑉𐑆. 𐐈𐑌𐐼 𐐌 𐐶𐐮𐑊 𐑋𐐩𐐿 𐑄𐐴 𐐶𐐮𐑌𐐼𐐬𐑆 𐐱𐑂 𐐰𐑀𐐩𐐻𐑅, 𐐰𐑌𐐼 𐑄𐐴 𐑀𐐩𐐻𐑅 𐐱𐑂 𐐿𐐪𐑉𐐺𐐲𐑍𐐿𐑊𐑆, 𐐰𐑌𐐼 𐐫𐑊 𐑄𐐴 𐐺𐐫𐑉𐐼𐐲𐑉𐑆 𐐱𐑂 𐐹𐑊𐐯𐑆𐐲𐑌𐐻 𐑅𐐻𐐬𐑌𐑆. 𐐈𐑌𐐼 𐐫𐑊 𐑄𐐴 𐐽𐐮𐑊𐐼𐑉𐐯𐑌 𐑇𐐰𐑊 𐐺𐐨 𐐻𐐫𐐻 𐐱𐑂 𐑄 𐐢𐐫𐑉𐐼; 𐐰𐑌𐐼 𐑀𐑉𐐩𐐻 𐑇𐐰𐑊 𐐺𐐨 𐑄 𐐹𐐨𐑅 𐐱𐑂 𐑄𐐴 𐐽𐐮𐑊𐐼𐑉𐐯𐑌. 𐐆𐑌 𐑉𐐴𐐽𐐲𐑅𐑌𐐯𐑅 𐑇𐐰𐑊𐐻 𐑄𐐵 𐐺𐐨 𐐯𐑅𐐻𐐰𐐺𐑊𐐮𐑇𐐻; 𐑄𐐵 𐑇𐐰𐑊𐐻 𐐺𐐨 𐑁𐐪𐑉 𐑁𐑉𐐱𐑋 𐐱𐐹𐑉𐐯𐑇𐐲𐑌, 𐑁𐐫𐑉 𐑄𐐵 𐑇𐐰𐑊𐐻 𐑌𐐱𐐻 𐑁𐐨𐑉, 𐐰𐑌𐐼 𐑁𐑉𐐱𐑋 𐐻𐐯𐑉𐐲𐑉, 𐑁𐐫𐑉 𐐮𐐻 𐑇𐐰𐑊 𐑌𐐱𐐻 𐐿𐐲𐑋 𐑌𐐨𐑉 𐑄𐐨. 𐐒𐐨𐐸𐐬𐑊𐐼, 𐑄𐐩 𐑇𐐰𐑊 𐑇𐐳𐑉𐑊𐐨 𐑀𐐰𐑄𐐲𐑉 𐐻𐐳𐑀𐐯𐑄𐐲𐑉 𐐰𐑀𐐯𐑌𐑅𐐻 𐑄𐐨, 𐑌𐐱𐐻 𐐺𐐴 𐑋𐐨; 𐐸𐐭𐑅𐐬𐐯𐑂𐐲𐑉 𐑇𐐰𐑊 𐑀𐐰𐑄𐐲𐑉 𐐻𐐳𐑀𐐯𐑄𐐲𐑉 𐐰𐑀𐐯𐑌𐑅𐐻 𐑄𐐨 𐑇𐐰𐑊 𐑁𐐫𐑊 𐑁𐐫𐑉 𐑄𐐴 𐑅𐐩𐐿. 𐐒𐐨𐐸𐐬𐑊𐐼, 𐐌 𐐸𐐰𐑂 𐐿𐑉𐐨𐐩𐐻𐐯𐐼 𐑄 𐑅𐑋𐐮𐑃 𐑄𐐰𐐻 𐐺𐑊𐐬𐐯𐑃 𐑄 𐐿𐐬𐑊𐑆 𐐮𐑌 𐑄 𐑁𐐴𐑉, 𐐰𐑌𐐼 𐑄𐐰𐐻 𐐺𐑉𐐮𐑍𐐯𐑃 𐑁𐐫𐑉𐑃 𐐰𐑌 𐐮𐑌𐑅𐐻𐑉𐐭𐑋𐐯𐑌𐐻 𐑁𐐫𐑉 𐐸𐐮𐑆 𐐶𐐲𐑉𐐿; 𐐰𐑌𐐼 𐐌 𐐸𐐰𐑂 𐐿𐑉𐐨𐐩𐐻𐐯𐐼 𐑄 𐐶𐐩𐑅𐐻𐐲𐑉 𐐻𐐭 𐐼𐐯𐑅𐐻𐑉𐑎. 𐐤𐐬 𐐶𐐯𐐹𐐲𐑌 𐑄𐐰𐐻 𐐮𐑆 𐑁𐐫𐑉𐑋𐐼 𐐰𐑀𐐯𐑌𐑅𐐻 𐑄𐐨 𐑇𐐰𐑊 𐐹𐑉𐐱𐑅𐐹𐐲𐑉; 𐐰𐑌𐐼 𐐯𐑂𐑉𐐨 𐐻𐐲𐑍 𐑄𐐰𐐻 𐑇𐐰𐑊 𐑉𐐨𐑂𐐴𐑊 𐐰𐑀𐐯𐑌𐑅𐐻 𐑄𐐨 𐐮𐑌 𐐾𐐲𐐾𐑋𐐯𐑌𐐻 𐑄𐐵 𐑇𐐰𐑊𐐻 𐐿𐐱𐑌𐐼𐐯𐑋. 𐐜𐐮𐑅 𐐮𐑆 𐑄 𐐸𐐯𐑉𐐮𐐻𐐩𐐾 𐐱𐑂 𐑄 𐑅𐐲𐑉𐑂𐐲𐑌𐐻𐑅 𐐱𐑂 𐑄 𐐢𐐫𐑉𐐼, 𐐰𐑌𐐼 𐑄𐐩𐑉 𐑉𐐴𐐽𐐲𐑅𐑌𐐯𐑅 𐐮𐑆 𐐱𐑂 𐑋𐐨, 𐑅𐐯𐑃 𐑄 𐐢𐐫𐑉𐐼. 𐐈𐑌𐐼 𐑌𐐵 𐐺𐐨𐐸𐐬𐑊𐐼, 𐐌 𐑅𐐩 𐐲𐑌𐐻𐐭 𐐷𐐭, 𐑄𐐰𐐻 𐐷𐐨 𐐫𐐻 𐐻𐐭 𐑅𐐲𐑉𐐽 𐑄𐐨𐑆 𐑃𐐮𐑍𐑆. 𐐏𐐩, 𐐲 𐐿𐐱𐑋𐐰𐑌𐐼𐑋𐐯𐑌𐐻 𐐌 𐑀𐐮𐑂 𐐲𐑌𐐻𐐭 𐐷𐐭 𐑄𐐰𐐻 𐐷𐐨 𐑅𐐲𐑉𐐽 𐑄𐐨𐑆 𐑃𐐮𐑍𐑆 𐐼𐐮𐑊𐐮𐐾𐐯𐑌𐐻𐑊𐐨; 𐑁𐐫𐑉 𐑀𐑉𐐩𐐻 𐐪𐑉 𐑄 𐐶𐐲𐑉𐐼𐑆 𐐱𐑂 𐐌𐑆𐐩𐐲. 𐐙𐐫𐑉 𐑇𐐳𐑉𐑊𐐨 𐐸𐐨 𐑅𐐹𐐩𐐿 𐐰𐑆 𐐻𐐲𐐽𐐮𐑍 𐐫𐑊 𐑃𐐮𐑍𐑆 𐐿𐐱𐑌𐑅𐐲𐑉𐑌𐐮𐑍 𐑋𐐴 𐐹𐐨𐐹𐑊 𐐸𐐶𐐮𐐽 𐐪𐑉 𐐱𐑂 𐑄 𐐸𐐵𐑅 𐐱𐑂 𐐆𐑆𐑉𐐩𐐯𐑊; 𐑄𐐯𐑉𐑁𐐬𐑉 𐐮𐐻 𐑋𐐲𐑅𐐻 𐑌𐐨𐐼𐑆 𐐺𐐨 𐑄𐐰𐐻 𐐸𐐨 𐑋𐐲𐑅𐐻 𐑅𐐹𐐨𐐿 𐐫𐑊𐑅𐐬 𐐻𐐭 𐑄 𐐖𐐯𐑌𐐻𐐴𐑊𐑆. 𐐈𐑌𐐼 𐐫𐑊 𐑃𐐮𐑍𐑆 𐑄𐐰𐐻 𐐸𐐨 𐑅𐐹𐐩𐐿 𐐸𐐰𐑂 𐐺𐐮𐑌 𐐰𐑌𐐼 𐑇𐐰𐑊 𐐺𐐨, 𐐨𐑂𐐯𐑌 𐐰𐐿𐐫𐑉𐐼𐐮𐑍 𐐻𐐭 𐑄 𐐶𐐲𐑉𐐼𐑆 𐐸𐐶𐐮𐐽 𐐸𐐨 𐑅𐐹𐐩𐐿. 𐐜𐐯𐑉𐑁𐐬𐑉 𐑀𐐮𐑂 𐐸𐐨𐐼 𐐻𐐭 𐑋𐐴 𐐶𐐲𐑉𐐼𐑆; 𐑉𐐴𐐻 𐑄 𐑃𐐮𐑍𐑆 𐐸𐐶𐐮𐐽 𐐌 𐐸𐐰𐑂 𐐻𐐬𐑊𐐼 𐐷𐐭; 𐐰𐑌𐐼 𐐰𐐿𐐫𐑉𐐼𐐮𐑍 𐐻𐐭 𐑄 𐐻𐐴𐑋 𐐰𐑌𐐼 𐑄 𐐶𐐮𐑊 𐐱𐑂 𐑄 𐐙𐐪𐑄𐐲𐑉, 𐑄𐐩 𐑇𐐰𐑊 𐑀𐐬 𐑁𐐫𐑉𐑃 𐐲𐑌𐐻𐐭 𐑄 𐐖𐐯𐑌𐐻𐐴𐑊𐑆. 𐐈𐑌𐐼 𐐸𐐭𐑅𐐬𐐯𐑂𐐲𐑉 𐐶𐐮𐑊 𐐸𐐪𐑉𐐿𐐲𐑌 𐐲𐑌𐐻𐐭 𐑋𐐴 𐐶𐐲𐑉𐐼𐑆 𐐰𐑌𐐼 𐑉𐐨𐐹𐐯𐑌𐐻𐐯𐑃, 𐐰𐑌𐐼 𐐮𐑆 𐐺𐐰𐐹𐐻𐐴𐑆𐐼, 𐑄 𐑅𐐩𐑋 𐑇𐐰𐑊 𐐺𐐨 𐑅𐐩𐑂𐐼. 𐐝𐐲𐑉𐐽 𐑄 𐐹𐑉𐐱𐑁𐐯𐐻𐑅, 𐑁𐐫𐑉 𐑋𐐯𐑌𐐨 𐑄𐐯𐑉 𐐺𐐨 𐑄𐐰𐐻 𐐻𐐯𐑅𐐻𐐮𐑁𐐴 𐐱𐑂 𐑄𐐨𐑆 𐑃𐐮𐑍𐑆.

3. 𐐈𐑌𐐼 𐑌𐐵 𐐮𐐻 𐐿𐐩𐑋 𐐻𐐭 𐐹𐐰𐑅 𐑄𐐰𐐻 𐐸𐐶𐐯𐑌 𐐖𐐨𐑆𐐲𐑅 𐐸𐐰𐐼 𐑅𐐯𐐼 𐑄𐐨𐑆 𐐶𐐲𐑉𐐼𐑆, 𐐸𐐨 𐑅𐐯𐐼 𐐲𐑌𐐻𐐭 𐑄𐐯𐑋 𐐰𐑀𐐯𐑌, 𐐰𐑁𐐻𐐲𐑉 𐐸𐐨 𐐸𐐰𐐼 𐐯𐐿𐑅𐐹𐐵𐑌𐐼𐐯𐐼 𐐫𐑊 𐑄 𐑅𐐿𐑉𐐮𐐹𐐽𐐲𐑉𐑆 𐐲𐑌𐐻𐐭 𐑄𐐯𐑋 𐐸𐐶𐐮𐐽 𐑄𐐩 𐐸𐐰𐐼 𐑉𐐨𐑅𐐨𐑂𐐼, 𐐸𐐨 𐑅𐐯𐐼 𐐲𐑌𐐻𐐭 𐑄𐐯𐑋, 𐐒𐐨𐐸𐐬𐑊𐐼, 𐐲𐑄𐐲𐑉 𐑅𐐿𐑉𐐮𐐹𐐽𐐲𐑉𐑆 𐐌 𐐶𐐳𐐼 𐑄𐐰𐐻 𐐷𐐨 𐑇𐐳𐐼 𐑉𐐴𐐻, 𐑄𐐰𐐻 𐐷𐐨 𐐸𐐰𐑂 𐑌𐐱𐐻. 𐐈𐑌𐐼 𐐮𐐻 𐐿𐐩𐑋 𐐻𐐭 𐐹𐐰𐑅 𐑄𐐰𐐻 𐐸𐐨 𐑅𐐯𐐼 𐐲𐑌𐐻𐐭 𐐤𐐨𐑁𐐴, 𐐒𐑉𐐮𐑍 𐑁𐐫𐑉𐑃 𐑄 𐑉𐐯𐐿𐐫𐑉𐐼 𐐸𐐶𐐮𐐽 𐐷𐐨 𐐸𐐰𐑂 𐐿𐐯𐐹𐐻. 𐐈𐑌𐐼 𐐸𐐶𐐯𐑌 𐐤𐐨𐑁𐐴 𐐸𐐰𐐼 𐐺𐑉𐐫𐐻 𐑁𐐫𐑉𐑃 𐑄 𐑉𐐯𐐿𐐫𐑉𐐼𐑆, 𐐰𐑌𐐼 𐑊𐐩𐐼 𐑄𐐯𐑋 𐐺𐐨-

𐑁𐐬𐑉 𐐸𐐮𐑋, 𐐸𐐨 𐐿𐐰𐑅𐐻 𐐸𐐮𐑆 𐐴𐑆 𐐲𐐹𐐪𐑌 𐑄𐐯𐑋 𐐰𐑌𐐼 𐑅𐐯𐐼, 𐐚𐐯𐑉𐐮𐑊𐐨 𐐌 𐑅𐐩 𐐲𐑌𐐻𐐭 𐐷𐐭, 𐐌 𐐿𐐲𐑋𐐰𐑌𐐼𐐯𐐼 𐑋𐐴 𐑅𐐲𐑉𐑂𐐲𐑌𐐻 𐐝𐐰𐑋𐐷𐐭𐐯𐑊, 𐑄 𐐢𐐩𐑋𐐲𐑌𐐴𐐻, 𐑄𐐰𐐻 𐐸𐐨 𐑇𐐳𐐼 𐐻𐐯𐑅𐐻𐐮𐑁𐐴 𐐲𐑌𐐻𐐭 𐑄𐐮𐑅 𐐹𐐨𐐹𐑊, 𐑄𐐰𐐻 𐐰𐐻 𐑄 𐐼𐐩 𐑄𐐰𐐻 𐑄 𐐙𐐪𐑄𐐲𐑉 𐑇𐐳𐐼 𐑀𐑊𐐬𐑉𐐮𐑁𐐴 𐐸𐐮𐑆 𐑌𐐩𐑋 𐐮𐑌 𐑋𐐨, 𐑄𐐰𐐻 𐑄𐐩𐑉 𐐶𐐲𐑉 𐑋𐐯𐑌𐐮 𐑅𐐩𐑌𐐻𐑅 𐐸𐐭 𐑇𐐳𐐼 𐐲𐑉𐐴𐑆 𐑁𐑉𐐱𐑋 𐑄 𐐼𐐯𐐼, 𐐰𐑌𐐼 𐑇𐐳𐐼 𐐲𐐹𐐨𐑉 𐐲𐑌𐐻𐐭 𐑋𐐯𐑌𐐮, 𐐰𐑌𐐼 𐑇𐐳𐐼 𐑋𐐮𐑌𐐮𐑅𐐻𐐲𐑉 𐐲𐑌𐐻𐐭 𐑄𐐯𐑋. 𐐈𐑌𐐼 𐐸𐐨 𐑅𐐯𐐼 𐐲𐑌𐐻𐐭 𐑄𐐯𐑋, 𐐎𐐱𐑆 𐐮𐐻 𐑌𐐱𐐻 𐑅𐐬? 𐐈𐑌𐐼 𐐸𐐮𐑆 𐐼𐐮𐑅𐐴𐐹𐑊𐑆 𐐰𐑌𐑅𐐲𐑉𐐼 𐐸𐐮𐑋, 𐐰𐑌𐐼 𐑅𐐯𐐼, 𐐏𐐩, 𐐢𐐫𐑉𐐼, 𐐝𐐰𐑋𐐷𐐭𐐯𐑊 𐐼𐐮𐐼 𐐹𐑉𐐱𐑁𐐲𐑅𐐴 𐐲𐐿𐐫𐑉𐐼𐐮𐑍 𐐻𐐭 𐑄𐐴 𐐶𐐲𐑉𐐼𐑆, 𐐰𐑌𐐼 𐑄𐐩 𐐶𐐲𐑉 𐐫𐑊 𐑁𐐳𐑊𐑁𐐮𐑊𐐼. 𐐈𐑌𐐼 𐐖𐐨𐑆𐐲𐑅 𐑅𐐯𐐼 𐐲𐑌𐐻𐐭 𐑄𐐯𐑋, 𐐐𐐵 𐐺𐐨 𐐮𐐻 𐑄𐐰𐐻 𐐷𐐨 𐐸𐐰𐑂 𐑌𐐱𐐻 𐑉𐐮𐐻𐑌 𐑄𐐮𐑅 𐑃𐐮𐑍, 𐑄𐐰𐐻 𐑋𐐯𐑌𐐮 𐑅𐐩𐑌𐐻𐑅 𐐼𐐮𐐼 𐐲𐑉𐐴𐑆 𐐰𐑌𐐼 𐐲𐐹𐐨𐑉 𐐲𐑌𐐻𐐭 𐑋𐐯𐑌𐐮, 𐐰𐑌𐐼 𐐼𐐮𐐼 𐑋𐐮𐑌𐐮𐑅𐐻𐐲𐑉 𐐲𐑌𐐻𐐭 𐑄𐐯𐑋? 𐐈𐑌𐐼 𐐮𐐻 𐐿𐐩𐑋 𐐻𐐭 𐐹𐐰𐑅 𐑄𐐰𐐻 𐐤𐐨𐑁𐐴 𐑉𐐨𐑋𐐯𐑋𐐺𐐲𐑉𐐼 𐑄𐐰𐐻 𐑄𐐮𐑅 𐑃𐐮𐑍 𐐸𐐰𐐼 𐑌𐐱𐐻 𐐺𐐨𐑌 𐑉𐐮𐐻𐑌. 𐐈𐑌𐐼 𐐮𐐻 𐐿𐐩𐑋 𐐻𐐭 𐐹𐐰𐑅 𐑄𐐰𐐻 𐐖𐐨𐑆𐐲𐑅 𐐿𐐲𐑋𐐰𐑌𐐼𐐯𐐼 𐑄𐐰𐐻 𐐮𐐻 𐑇𐐳𐐼 𐐺𐐨 𐑉𐐮𐐻𐑌; 𐑄𐐯𐑉𐑁𐐬𐑉 𐐮𐐻 𐐶𐐱𐑆 𐑉𐐮𐐻𐑌 𐐲𐐿𐐫𐑉𐐼𐐮𐑍 𐐰𐑆 𐐸𐐨 𐐿𐐲𐑋𐐰𐑌𐐼𐐯𐐼.

𐐕𐐰𐐹𐐻𐐲𐑉 XI.

1. 𐐈𐑌𐐼 𐑌𐐵 𐐮𐐻 𐐿𐐩𐑋 𐐻𐐭 𐐹𐐰𐑅 𐑄𐐰𐐻 𐐸𐐶𐐯𐑌 𐐖𐐨𐑆𐐲𐑅 𐐸𐐰𐐼 𐐯𐐿𐑅𐐹𐐵𐑌𐐼𐐯𐐼 𐐫𐑊 𐑄 𐑅𐐿𐑉𐐮𐐹𐐽𐐲𐑉𐑆 𐐮𐑌 𐐶𐐲𐑌, 𐐸𐐶𐐮𐐽 𐑄𐐩 𐐸𐐰𐐼 𐑉𐐮𐐻𐑌, 𐐸𐐨 𐐿𐐲𐑋𐐰𐑌𐐼𐐯𐐼 𐑄𐐯𐑋 𐑄𐐰𐐻 𐑄𐐩 𐑇𐐳𐐼 𐐻𐐨𐐽 𐑄 𐑃𐐮𐑍𐑆 𐐸𐐶𐐮𐐽 𐐸𐐨 𐐸𐐰𐐼 𐐯𐐿𐑅𐐹𐐵𐑌𐐼𐐯𐐼 𐐲𐑌𐐻𐐭 𐑄𐐯𐑋. 𐐈𐑌𐐼 𐐮𐐻 𐐿𐐩𐑋 𐐻𐐭 𐐹𐐰𐑅 𐑄𐐰𐐻 𐐸𐐨 𐐿𐐲𐑋𐐰𐑌𐐼𐐯𐐼 𐑄𐐯𐑋 𐑄𐐰𐐻 𐑄𐐩 𐑇𐐳𐐼 𐑉𐐴𐐻 𐑄 𐐶𐐲𐑉𐐼𐑆 𐐸𐐶𐐮𐐽 𐑄 𐐙𐐪𐑄𐐲𐑉 𐐸𐐰𐐼 𐑀𐐮𐑂𐑌 𐐲𐑌𐐻𐐭 𐐣𐐰𐑊𐐲𐐿𐐴, 𐐸𐐶𐐮𐐽 𐐸𐐨 𐑇𐐳𐐼 𐐻𐐯𐑊 𐐲𐑌𐐻𐐭 𐑄𐐯𐑋. 𐐈𐑌𐐼 𐐮𐐻 𐐿𐐩𐑋 𐐻𐐭 𐐹𐐰𐑅 𐑄𐐰𐐻 𐐰𐑁𐐻𐐲𐑉 𐑄𐐩 𐐶𐐲𐑉 𐑉𐐮𐐻𐑌, 𐐸𐐨 𐐯𐐿𐑅𐐹𐐵𐑌𐐼𐐯𐐼 𐑄𐐯𐑋. 𐐈𐑌𐐼 𐑄𐐨𐑆 𐐪𐑉 𐑄 𐐶𐐲𐑉𐐼𐑆 𐐸𐐶𐐮𐐽 𐐸𐐨 𐐼𐐮𐐼 𐐻𐐯𐑊 𐐲𐑌𐐻𐐭 𐑄𐐯𐑋, 𐑅𐐩𐐮𐑍, 𐐜𐐲𐑅 𐑅𐐯𐐼 𐑄 𐐙𐐪𐑄𐐲𐑉 𐐲𐑌𐐻𐐭 𐐣𐐰𐑊𐐲𐐿𐐴, 𐐒𐐨𐐸𐐬𐑊𐐼, 𐐌 𐐶𐐮𐑊 𐑅𐐯𐑌𐐼 𐑋𐐴 𐑋𐐯𐑅𐐯𐑌𐐾𐐲𐑉, 𐐰𐑌𐐼 𐐸𐐨 𐑇𐐰𐑊 𐐹𐑉𐐨𐐹𐐩𐑉 𐑄 𐐶𐐩 𐐺𐐨𐑁𐐬𐑉 𐑋𐐨, 𐐰𐑌𐐼 𐑄 𐐢𐐫𐑉𐐼 𐐸𐐭𐑋 𐐷𐐨 𐑅𐐨𐐿 𐑇𐐰𐑊 𐑅𐐲𐐼𐐲𐑌𐑊𐐨 𐐿𐐲𐑋 𐐻𐐭 𐐸𐐮𐑆 𐐻𐐯𐑋𐐹𐑊, 𐐨𐑂𐑌 𐑄 𐑋𐐯𐑅𐐯𐑌𐐾𐐲𐑉 𐐱𐑂 𐑄 𐐿𐐲𐑂𐐲𐑌𐐲𐑌𐐻, 𐐸𐐭𐑋 𐐷𐐨 𐐼𐐨𐑊𐐴𐐻 𐐮𐑌; 𐐺𐐨𐐸𐐬𐑊𐐼, 𐐸𐐨 𐑇𐐰𐑊 𐐿𐐲𐑋, 𐑅𐐯𐑃 𐑄 𐐢𐐫𐑉𐐼 𐐱𐑂 𐐐𐐬𐑅𐐻𐑅. 𐐒𐐲𐐻 𐐸𐐭 𐑋𐐩 𐐲𐐺𐐴𐐼 𐑄 𐐼𐐩 𐐱𐑂 𐐸𐐮𐑆 𐐿𐐲𐑋𐐮𐑍? 𐐈𐑌𐐼 𐐸𐐭 𐑇𐐰𐑊 𐑅𐐻𐐰𐑌𐐼 𐐸𐐶𐐯𐑌 𐐸𐐨 𐐲𐐹𐐨𐑉𐐯𐑃? 𐐙𐐫𐑉 𐐸𐐨 𐐮𐑆 𐑊𐐴𐐿 𐐰 𐑉𐐨𐑁𐐴𐑌𐐲𐑉'𐑆 𐑁𐐴𐑉, 𐐰𐑌𐐼 𐑊𐐴𐐿 𐑁𐐳𐑊𐐲𐑉'𐑆 𐑅𐐬𐐹. 𐐈𐑌𐐼 𐐸𐐨 𐑇𐐰𐑊 𐑅𐐮𐐻 𐐰𐑆 𐐰 𐑉𐐨𐑁𐐴𐑌𐐲𐑉 𐐰𐑌𐐼 𐐹𐐷𐐭𐑉𐐮𐑁𐐴𐐲𐑉 𐐱𐑂 𐑅𐐮𐑊𐑂𐐲𐑉: 𐐰𐑌𐐼 𐐸𐐨 𐑇𐐰𐑊 𐐹𐐷𐐭𐑉𐐮𐑁𐐴 𐑄 𐑅𐐲𐑌𐑆 𐐱𐑂 𐐢𐐨𐑂𐐴, 𐐰𐑌𐐼 𐐹𐐲𐑉𐐾 𐑄𐐯𐑋 𐐰𐑆 𐑀𐐬𐑊𐐼 𐐰𐑌𐐼 𐑅𐐮𐑊𐑂𐐲𐑉, 𐑄𐐰𐐻 𐑄𐐩 𐑋𐐩 𐐱𐑁𐐲𐑉 𐐲𐑌𐐻𐐭 𐑄 𐐢𐐫𐑉𐐼 𐐲𐑌 𐐱𐑁𐐲𐑉𐐮𐑍 𐐮𐑌 𐑉𐐴𐐽𐐲𐑅𐑌𐐯𐑅. 𐐜𐐯𐑌 𐑇𐐰𐑊 𐑄 𐐱𐑁𐐲𐑉𐐮𐑍 𐐱𐑂 𐐖𐐭𐐼𐐲 𐐰𐑌𐐼 𐐖𐐯𐑉𐐭𐑅𐐲𐑊𐐯𐑋 𐐺𐐨 𐐹𐑊𐐯𐑆𐐲𐑌𐐻 𐐲𐑌𐐻𐐭 𐑄 𐐢𐐫𐑉𐐼, 𐐰𐑆 𐐮𐑌 𐑄 𐐼𐐩𐑆 𐐱𐑂 𐐬𐑊𐐼, 𐐰𐑌𐐼 𐐰𐑆 𐐮𐑌 𐑁𐐫𐑉𐑋𐐲𐑉 𐐷𐐨𐑉𐑆. 𐐈𐑌𐐼 𐐌 𐐶𐐮𐑊 𐐿𐐲𐑋 𐑌𐐨𐑉 𐐻𐐭 𐐷𐐭 𐐻𐐭 𐐾𐐲𐐾𐑋𐐯𐑌𐐻; 𐐰𐑌𐐼 𐐌 𐐶𐐮𐑊 𐐺𐐨 𐐰 𐑅𐐶𐐮𐑁𐐻 𐐶𐐮𐐻𐑌𐐯𐑅 𐐲𐑀𐐯𐑌𐑅𐐻 𐑄 𐑅𐐫𐑉𐑅𐐲𐑉𐐲𐑉𐑆, 𐐰𐑌𐐼 𐐲𐑀𐐯𐑌𐑅𐐻 𐑄 𐐲𐐼𐐲𐑊𐐻𐐲𐑉𐐲𐑉𐑆, 𐐰𐑌𐐼 𐐲𐑀𐐯𐑌𐑅𐐻 𐑁𐐫𐑊𐑅 𐑅𐐶𐐩𐑉𐐲𐑉𐑆, 𐐰𐑌𐐼 𐐲𐑀𐐯𐑌𐑅𐐻 𐑄𐐬𐑆 𐑄𐐰𐐻 𐐲𐐹𐑉𐐯𐑅 𐑄 𐐸𐐴𐑉𐑊𐐮𐑍 𐐮𐑌 𐐸𐐮𐑆 𐐶𐐩𐐾𐐲𐑆, 𐑄 𐐶𐐮𐐼𐐬 𐐰𐑌𐐼 𐑄 𐑁𐐪𐑄𐐲𐑉𐑊𐐯𐑅, 𐐰𐑌𐐼 𐑄𐐰𐐻 𐐻𐐲𐑉𐑌 𐐲𐑅𐐴𐐼 𐑄 𐑅𐐻𐑉𐐩𐑌𐐾𐐲𐑉, 𐐰𐑌𐐼 𐑁𐐨𐑉 𐑌𐐱𐐻 𐑋𐐨, 𐑅𐐯𐑃 𐑄 𐐢𐐫𐑉𐐼 𐐱𐑂 𐐐𐐬𐑅𐐻𐑅. 𐐙𐐫𐑉 𐐌 𐐰𐑋 𐑄 𐐢𐐫𐑉𐐼, 𐐌 𐐽𐐩𐑌𐐾 𐑌𐐱𐐻; 𐑄𐐯𐑉𐑁𐐬𐑉 𐐷𐐨 𐑅𐐲𐑌𐑆 𐐱𐑂 𐐖𐐩𐐿𐐲𐐺 𐐪𐑉 𐑌𐐱𐐻 𐐿𐐲𐑌𐑅𐐭𐑋𐐼.

2. 𐐀𐑂𐑌 𐑁𐑉𐐱𐑋 𐑄 𐐼𐐩𐑆 𐐱𐑂 𐐷𐐭𐑉 𐑁𐐪𐑄𐐲𐑉𐑆 𐐷𐐨 𐐪𐑉 𐑀𐐱𐑌 𐐲𐐶𐐩 𐑁𐑉𐐱𐑋 𐑋𐐴𐑌 𐐫𐑉𐐼𐐮𐑌𐐲𐑌𐑅𐐯𐑆, 𐐰𐑌𐐼 𐐸𐐰𐑂 𐑌𐐱𐐻 𐐿𐐯𐐹𐐻 𐑄𐐯𐑋. 𐐡𐐨𐐻𐐲𐑉𐑌 𐐲𐑌𐐻𐐭 𐑋𐐨 𐐰𐑌𐐼 𐐌 𐐶𐐮𐑊 𐑉𐐨𐐻𐐲𐑉𐑌 𐐲𐑌𐐻𐐭 𐐷𐐭, 𐑅𐐯𐑃 𐑄 𐐢𐐫𐑉𐐼 𐐱𐑂 𐐐𐐬𐑅𐐻𐑅. 𐐒𐐲𐐻 𐐷𐐨 𐑅𐐩, 𐐐𐐶𐐯𐑉𐐮𐑌 𐑇𐐰𐑊 𐐶𐐨 𐑉𐐨𐐻𐐲𐑉𐑌?

3. 𐐎𐐮𐑊 𐐰 𐑋𐐰𐑌 𐑉𐐱𐐺 𐐘𐐱𐐼? 𐐏𐐯𐐻 𐐷𐐨 𐐸𐐰𐑂 𐑉𐐱𐐺𐐼 𐑋𐐨. 𐐒𐐲𐐻 𐐷𐐨 𐑅𐐩, 𐐐𐐶𐐯𐑉𐐮𐑌 𐐸𐐰𐑂 𐐶𐐨 𐑉𐐱𐐺𐐼 𐑄𐐨? 𐐆𐑌 𐐻𐐴𐑄𐑆 𐐰𐑌𐐼 𐐱𐑁𐐲𐑉𐐮𐑍𐑆. 𐐏𐐨 𐐪𐑉 𐐿𐐲𐑉𐑅𐐻 𐐶𐐮𐑄 𐐰 𐐿𐐲𐑉𐑅, 𐑁𐐫𐑉 𐐷𐐨 𐐸𐐰𐑂 𐑉𐐱𐐺𐐼 𐑋𐐨, 𐐨𐑂𐑌 𐑄𐐮𐑅 𐐸𐐬𐑊 𐑌𐐩𐑇𐐲𐑌. 𐐒𐑉𐐮𐑍 𐐷𐐨 𐐫𐑊 𐑄 𐐻𐐴𐑄𐑆 𐐮𐑌𐐻𐐭 𐑄 𐑅𐐻𐐬𐑉𐐸𐐵𐑅, 𐑄𐐰𐐻 𐑄𐐩𐑉 𐑋𐐩 𐐺𐐨 𐑋𐐨𐐻 𐐮𐑌 𐑋𐐴 𐐸𐐵𐑅; 𐐰𐑌𐐼 𐐹𐑉𐐭𐑂 𐑋𐐨 𐑌𐐵 𐐸𐐨𐑉𐐶𐐮𐑄, 𐑅𐐯𐑃 𐑄 𐐢𐐫𐑉𐐼 𐐱𐑂 𐐐𐐬𐑅𐐻𐑅, 𐐮𐑁 𐐌 𐐶𐐮𐑊 𐑌𐐱𐐻 𐐬𐐹𐑌 𐐷𐐭

𐑄 𐐶𐐮𐑌𐐼𐐬𐑆 𐐱𐑂 𐐸𐐯𐑂𐐲𐑌, 𐐰𐑌𐐼 𐐹𐐫𐑉 𐐷𐐭 𐐵𐐻 𐐲 𐐺𐑊𐐯𐑅𐐮𐑍, 𐑄𐐰𐐻 𐑄𐐩𐑉 𐑇𐐰𐑊 𐑌𐐱𐐻 𐐺 𐑉𐐭𐑋 𐐨𐑌𐐲𐑁 𐐻𐐭
𐑉𐐨𐑅𐐨𐑂 𐐮𐐻. 𐐈𐑌𐐼 𐐌 𐐶𐐮𐑊 𐑉𐐨𐐺𐐷𐐭𐐿 𐑄 𐐼𐐨𐑂𐐵𐑉𐐲𐑉 𐑁𐐫𐑉 𐐷𐐭𐑉 𐑅𐐩𐐿𐑅, 𐐰𐑌𐐼 𐐸𐐨 𐑇𐐰𐑊 𐑌𐐱𐐻 𐐼𐐨𐑅𐐻𐑉𐐦
𐑄 𐑁𐑉𐐭𐐻𐑅 𐐱𐑂 𐐷𐐭𐑉 𐑀𐑉𐐵𐑌𐐼; 𐑌𐐨𐑄𐐲𐑉 𐑇𐐰𐑊 𐐷𐐭𐑉 𐑂𐐴𐑌 𐐿𐐪𐑅𐐻 𐐸𐐲𐑉 𐑁𐑉𐐭𐐻 𐐺𐐨𐑁𐐬𐑉 𐑄 𐐻𐐴𐑋 𐐮𐑌 𐑄
𐑁𐐨𐑊𐐼𐑆, 𐑅𐐯𐑃 𐑄 𐐢𐐫𐑉𐐼 𐐱𐑂 𐐐𐐬𐑅𐐻𐑅. 𐐈𐑌𐐼 𐐫𐑊 𐑌𐐩𐑇𐐲𐑌𐑆 𐑇𐐰𐑊 𐐿𐐫𐑊 𐐷𐐭 𐐺𐑊𐐯𐑅𐐯𐐼, 𐑁𐐫𐑉 𐐷 𐑇𐐰𐑊
𐐺 𐐲 𐐼𐐨𐑊𐐴𐐻𐑅𐐲𐑋 𐑊𐐰𐑌𐐼, 𐑅𐐯𐑃 𐑄 𐐢𐐫𐑉𐐼 𐐱𐑂 𐐐𐐬𐑅𐐻𐑅.

4. 𐐏𐐭𐑉 𐐶𐐲𐑉𐐼𐑆 𐐸𐐰𐑂 𐐺𐐮𐑌 𐑅𐐻𐐵𐐻 𐐰𐑀𐐯𐑌𐑅𐐻 𐑋𐐨, 𐑅𐐯𐑃 𐑄 𐐢𐐫𐑉𐐼. 𐐏𐐯𐐻 𐐷 𐑅𐐩, 𐐐𐐶𐐱𐐻 𐐸𐐰𐑂
𐐶𐐨 𐑅𐐹𐐬𐐿𐐲𐑌 𐐰𐑀𐐯𐑌𐑅𐐻 𐑄? 𐐏 𐐸𐐰𐑂 𐑅𐐯𐐼, 𐐆𐐻 𐐮𐑆 𐑂𐐩𐑌 𐐻𐐭 𐑅𐐲𐑉𐑂 𐐘𐐱𐐼, 𐐰𐑌𐐼 𐐸𐐶𐐱𐐻 𐐼𐐲𐑃 𐐮𐐻
𐐹𐑉𐐱𐑁𐐮𐐻 𐑄𐐰𐐻 𐐶𐐨 𐐸𐐰𐑂 𐐿𐐯𐐹𐐻 𐐸𐐮𐑆 𐐫𐑉𐐼𐐮𐑌𐐰𐑌𐑅𐐯𐑆, 𐐰𐑌𐐼 𐑄𐐰𐐻 𐐶𐐨 𐐸𐐰𐑂 𐐶𐐫𐐿𐐻 𐑋𐐬𐑉𐑌𐑁𐐳𐑊𐐨 𐐺𐐨𐑁𐐬𐑉 𐑄
𐐢𐐫𐑉𐐼 𐐱𐑂 𐐐𐐬𐑅𐐻𐑅? 𐐈𐑌𐐼 𐑌𐐵 𐐶𐐨 𐐿𐐫𐑊 𐑄 𐐹𐑉𐐵𐐼 𐐸𐐰𐐹𐐨; 𐐷𐐩, 𐑄𐐩 𐑄𐐰𐐻 𐐶𐐲𐑉𐐿 𐐶𐐮𐐿𐐯𐐼𐑌𐐯𐑅 𐐪𐑉
𐑅𐐯𐐻 𐐲𐐹; 𐐷𐐩, 𐑄𐐩 𐑄𐐰𐐻 𐐻𐐯𐑋𐐹𐐻 𐐘𐐱𐐼 𐐪𐑉 𐐨𐑂𐑌 𐐼𐐨𐑊𐐮𐑂𐐲𐑉𐐼.

5. 𐐜𐐯𐑌 𐑄𐐩 𐑄𐐰𐐻 𐑁𐐨𐑉𐐼 𐑄 𐐢𐐫𐑉𐐼 𐑅𐐹𐐩𐐿 𐐱𐑁𐑌 𐐶𐐲𐑌 𐐻𐐭 𐐰𐑌𐐲𐑄𐐲𐑉, 𐐰𐑌𐐼 𐑄 𐐢𐐫𐑉𐐼 𐐸𐐪𐑉𐐿𐐲𐑌𐐼
𐐰𐑌𐐼 𐐸𐐲𐑉𐐼; 𐐰𐑌𐐼 𐐲 𐐺𐐳𐐿 𐐱𐑂 𐑉𐐨𐑋𐐯𐑋𐐺𐑉𐐰𐑌𐑅 𐐶𐐱𐑆 𐑉𐐮𐐻𐑌 𐐺𐐨𐑁𐐬𐑉 𐐸𐐮𐑋 𐑁𐐫𐑉 𐑄𐐯𐑋 𐑄𐐰𐐻 𐑁𐐨𐑉𐐼 𐑄
𐐢𐐫𐑉𐐼, 𐐰𐑌𐐼 𐑄𐐰𐐻 𐑃𐐫𐐻 𐐲𐐹𐐱𐑌 𐐸𐐮𐑆 𐑌𐐩𐑋. 𐐈𐑌𐐼 𐑄𐐩 𐑇𐐰𐑊 𐐺 𐑋𐐴𐑌, 𐑅𐐯𐑃 𐑄 𐐢𐐫𐑉𐐼 𐐱𐑂 𐐐𐐬𐑅𐐻𐑅,
𐐮𐑌 𐑄𐐰𐐻 𐐼𐐩 𐐸𐐶𐐯𐑌 𐐌 𐑋𐐩𐐿 𐐲𐐹 𐑋𐐴 𐐾𐐭𐐯𐑊𐑆; 𐐰𐑌𐐼 𐐌 𐐶𐐮𐑊 𐑅𐐹𐐩𐑉 𐑄𐐯𐑋 𐐰𐑆 𐐲 𐑋𐐰𐑌 𐑅𐐹𐐩𐑉𐐯𐑃
𐐸𐐮𐑆 𐐬𐑌 𐑅𐐲𐑌 𐑄𐐰𐐻 𐑅𐐲𐑉𐑂𐐯𐑃 𐐸𐐮𐑋. 𐐜𐐯𐑌 𐑇𐐰𐑊 𐐷 𐑉𐐨𐐻𐐲𐑉𐑌 𐐰𐑌𐐼 𐐼𐐮𐑆𐐲𐑉𐑌 𐐺𐐨𐐻𐐶𐐨𐑌 𐑄 𐑉𐐴𐐽𐐲𐑅
𐐰𐑌𐐼 𐑄 𐐶𐐮𐐿𐐯𐐼, 𐐺𐐨𐐻𐐶𐐨𐑌 𐐸𐐮𐑋 𐑄𐐰𐐻 𐑅𐐲𐑉𐑂𐐯𐑃 𐐘𐐱𐐼, 𐐰𐑌𐐼 𐐸𐐮𐑋 𐑄𐐰𐐻 𐑅𐐲𐑉𐑂𐐯𐑃 𐐸𐐮𐑋 𐑌𐐱𐐻. 𐐙𐐫𐑉
𐐺𐐨𐐸𐐬𐑊𐐼, 𐑄 𐐼𐐩 𐐿𐐲𐑋𐐯𐑃 𐑄𐐰𐐻 𐑇𐐰𐑊 𐐺𐐲𐑉𐑌 𐐰𐑆 𐐰𐑌 𐐲𐑂𐑌; 𐐰𐑌𐐼 𐐫𐑊 𐑄 𐐹𐑉𐐵𐐼, 𐐷𐐩, 𐐰𐑌𐐼 𐐫𐑊 𐑄𐐰𐐻
𐐼𐐭 𐐶𐐮𐐿𐐯𐐼𐑊𐐨, 𐑇𐐰𐑊 𐐺 𐑅𐐻𐐲𐐺𐑊: 𐐰𐑌𐐼 𐑄 𐐼𐐩 𐑄𐐰𐐻 𐐿𐐲𐑋𐐯𐑃 𐑇𐐰𐑊 𐐺𐐲𐑉𐑌 𐑄𐐯𐑋 𐐲𐐹, 𐑅𐐯𐑃 𐑄 𐐢𐐫𐑉𐐼
𐐱𐑂 𐐐𐐬𐑅𐐻𐑅, 𐑄𐐰𐐻 𐐮𐐻 𐑇𐐰𐑊 𐑊𐐨𐑂 𐑄𐐯𐑋 𐑌𐐨𐑄𐐲𐑉 𐑉𐐭𐐻 𐑌𐐫𐑉 𐐺𐑉𐐰𐑌𐐽.

6. 𐐒𐐲𐐻 𐐲𐑌𐐻𐐭 𐐷𐐭 𐑄𐐰𐐻 𐑁𐐨𐑉 𐑋𐐴 𐑌𐐩𐑋, 𐑇𐐰𐑊 𐑄 𐐝𐐲𐑌 𐐱𐑂 𐐡𐐴𐐽𐐲𐑅𐑌𐐯𐑅 𐐰𐑉𐐴𐑆 𐐶𐐮𐑄 𐐸𐐨𐑊𐐮𐑍 𐐮𐑌
𐐸𐐮𐑆 𐐶𐐮𐑍𐑆; 𐐰𐑌𐐼 𐐷 𐑇𐐰𐑊 𐑀𐐬 𐑁𐐫𐑉𐑃 𐐰𐑌𐐼 𐑀𐑉𐐬 𐐲𐐹 𐐰𐑆 𐐿𐐪𐑂𐑆 𐐮𐑌 𐑄 𐑅𐐻𐐫𐑊. 𐐈𐑌𐐼 𐐷 𐑇𐐰𐑊 𐐻𐑉𐐯𐐼
𐐼𐐵𐑌 𐑄 𐐶𐐮𐐿𐐯𐐼; 𐑁𐐫𐑉 𐑄𐐩 𐑇𐐰𐑊 𐐺 𐐰𐑇𐐯𐑆 𐐲𐑌𐐼𐐲𐑉 𐑄 𐑅𐐬𐑊𐑆 𐐱𐑂 𐐷𐐭𐑉 𐑁𐐨𐐻 𐐮𐑌 𐑄 𐐼𐐩 𐑄𐐰𐐻 𐐌 𐑇𐐰𐑊
𐐼𐐭 𐑄𐐮𐑅, 𐑅𐐯𐑃 𐑄 𐐢𐐫𐑉𐐼 𐐱𐑂 𐐐𐐬𐑅𐐻𐑅. 𐐡𐐨𐑋𐐯𐑋𐐺𐐲𐑉 𐐷 𐑄 𐑊𐐫 𐐱𐑂 𐐣𐐬𐑆𐐯𐑆, 𐑋𐐴 𐑅𐐲𐑉𐑂𐐲𐑌𐐻, 𐐸𐐶𐐮𐐽
𐐌 𐐿𐐱𐑋𐐰𐑌𐐼𐐯𐐼 𐐲𐑌𐐻𐐭 𐐸𐐮𐑋 𐐮𐑌 𐐐𐐬𐑉𐐯𐐺 𐑁𐐫𐑉 𐐫𐑊 𐐆𐑆𐑉𐐩𐐯𐑊, 𐐶𐐮𐑄 𐑄 𐑅𐐻𐐰𐐽𐐭𐐻𐑅 𐐰𐑌𐐼 𐐾𐐲𐐾𐑋𐐯𐑌𐐻𐑅.
𐐒𐐨𐐸𐐬𐑊𐐼, 𐐌 𐐶𐐮𐑊 𐑅𐐯𐑌𐐼 𐐷𐐭 𐐀𐑊𐐴𐐾𐐲 𐑄 𐐹𐑉𐐱𐑁𐐯𐐻 𐐺𐐨𐑁𐐬𐑉 𐑄 𐐿𐐲𐑋𐐮𐑍 𐐱𐑂 𐑄 𐑀𐑉𐐩𐐻 𐐰𐑌𐐼 𐐼𐑉𐐯𐐼𐑁𐐳𐑊
𐐼𐐩 𐐱𐑂 𐑄 𐐢𐐫𐑉𐐼; 𐐰𐑌𐐼 𐐸𐐨 𐑇𐐰𐑊 𐐻𐐲𐑉𐑌 𐑄 𐐸𐐪𐑉𐐻 𐐱𐑂 𐑄 𐑁𐐪𐑄𐐲𐑉𐑆 𐐻𐐭 𐑄 𐐽𐐮𐑊𐐼𐑉𐐯𐑌, 𐐰𐑌𐐼 𐑄 𐐸𐐪𐑉𐐻
𐐱𐑂 𐑄 𐐽𐐮𐑊𐐼𐑉𐐯𐑌 𐐻𐐭 𐑄𐐩𐑉 𐑁𐐪𐑄𐐲𐑉𐑆, 𐑊𐐯𐑅𐐻 𐐌 𐐿𐐲𐑋 𐐰𐑌𐐼 𐑅𐑋𐐴𐐻 𐑄 𐐲𐑉𐑃 𐐶𐐮𐑄 𐐲 𐐿𐐲𐑉𐑅.

7. 𐐈𐑌𐐼 𐑌𐐵 𐐮𐐻 𐐿𐐩𐑋 𐐻𐐭 𐐹𐐰𐑅 𐑄𐐰𐐻 𐐸𐐶𐐯𐑌 𐐖𐐨𐑆𐐲𐑅 𐐸𐐰𐐼 𐐻𐐬𐑊𐐼 𐑄𐐨𐑆 𐑃𐐮𐑍𐑆, 𐐸𐐨 𐐯𐐿𐑅𐐹𐐵𐑌𐐼𐐯𐐼
𐑄𐐯𐑋 𐐲𐑌𐐻𐐭 𐑄 𐑋𐐲𐑊𐐻𐐮𐐻𐐷𐐭𐐼, 𐐰𐑌𐐼 𐐸𐐨 𐐼𐐮𐐼 𐐯𐐿𐑅𐐹𐐵𐑌𐐼 𐐫𐑊 𐑃𐐮𐑍𐑆 𐐲𐑌𐐻𐐭 𐑄𐐯𐑋, 𐐺𐐬𐑃 𐑀𐑉𐐩𐐻
𐐰𐑌𐐼 𐑅𐑋𐐫𐑊. 𐐈𐑌𐐼 𐐸𐐨 𐑅𐐯𐑃, 𐐜𐐨𐑆 𐑅𐐿𐑉𐐮𐐹𐐽𐐲𐑉𐑆 𐐸𐐶𐐮𐐽 𐐷 𐐸𐐰𐐼 𐑌𐐱𐐻 𐐶𐐮𐑄 𐐷𐐭, 𐑄 𐐙𐐪𐑄𐐲𐑉
𐐿𐐱𐑋𐐰𐑌𐐼𐐯𐐼 𐑄𐐰𐐻 𐐌 𐑇𐐳𐐼 𐑀𐐮𐑂 𐐲𐑌𐐻𐐭 𐐷𐐭, 𐑁𐐫𐑉 𐐮𐐻 𐐶𐐱𐑆 𐐶𐐮𐑆𐐼𐐲𐑋 𐐮𐑌 𐐸𐐮𐑋 𐑄𐐰𐐻 𐑄𐐩 𐑇𐐳𐐼 𐐺 𐑀𐐮𐑂𐑌
𐐲𐑌𐐻𐐭 𐑁𐐷𐐭𐐽𐐲𐑉 𐐾𐐯𐑌𐐲𐑉𐐩𐑇𐐲𐑌𐑆. 𐐈𐑌𐐼 𐐸𐐨 𐐼𐐮𐐼 𐐯𐐿𐑅𐐹𐐵𐑌𐐼 𐐫𐑊 𐑃𐐮𐑍𐑆, 𐐨𐑂𐑌 𐑁𐑉𐐱𐑋 𐑄 𐐺𐐨𐑀𐐮𐑌𐐮𐑍
𐐲𐑌𐐻𐐮𐑊 𐑄 𐐻𐐴𐑋 𐑄𐐰𐐻 𐐸𐐨 𐑇𐐳𐐼 𐐿𐐲𐑋 𐐮𐑌 𐐸𐐮𐑆 𐑀𐑊𐐬𐑉𐐨; 𐐷𐐩, 𐐨𐑂𐑌 𐐫𐑊 𐑃𐐮𐑍𐑆 𐐸𐐶𐐮𐐽 𐑇𐐳𐐼 𐐿𐐲𐑋 𐐲𐐹𐐱𐑌 𐑄
𐑁𐐩𐑅 𐐱𐑂 𐑄 𐐲𐑉𐑃, 𐐨𐑂𐑌 𐐲𐑌𐐻𐐮𐑊 𐑄 𐐯𐑊𐐯𐑋𐐯𐑌𐐻𐑅 𐑇𐐳𐐼 𐑋𐐯𐑊𐐻 𐐶𐐮𐑄 𐑁𐐲𐑉𐑂𐐯𐑌𐐻 𐐸𐐨𐐻, 𐐰𐑌𐐼 𐑄 𐐲𐑉𐑃 𐑇𐐳𐐼
𐐺 𐑉𐐰𐐹𐐻 𐐻𐐭𐑀𐐯𐑄𐐲𐑉 𐐰𐑆 𐐲 𐑅𐐿𐑉𐐬𐑊, 𐐰𐑌𐐼 𐑄 𐐸𐐯𐑂𐑌𐑆 𐐰𐑌𐐼 𐑄 𐐲𐑉𐑃 𐑇𐐳𐐼 𐐹𐐰𐑅 𐐰𐐶𐐩; 𐐰𐑌𐐼 𐐨𐑂𐑌 𐐲𐑌𐐻𐐭
𐑄 𐑀𐑉𐐩𐐻 𐐰𐑌𐐼 𐑊𐐰𐑅𐐻 𐐼𐐩, 𐐸𐐶𐐯𐑌 𐐫𐑊 𐐹𐐨𐐹𐑊, 𐐰𐑌𐐼 𐐫𐑊 𐐿𐐮𐑌𐐼𐑉𐐯𐐼𐑆, 𐐰𐑌𐐼 𐐫𐑊 𐑌𐐩𐑇𐐲𐑌𐑆 𐐰𐑌𐐼 𐐻𐐲𐑍𐑆
𐑇𐐰𐑊 𐑅𐐻𐐰𐑌𐐼 𐐺𐐨𐑁𐐬𐑉 𐐘𐐱𐐼, 𐐻𐐭 𐐺 𐐾𐐲𐐾𐐼 𐐱𐑂 𐑄𐐩𐑉 𐐶𐐲𐑉𐐿𐑅, 𐐸𐐶𐐯𐑄𐐲𐑉 𐑄𐐩 𐐺 𐑀𐐳𐐼, 𐐫𐑉 𐐸𐐶𐐯𐑄𐐲𐑉
𐑄𐐩 𐐺 𐐨𐑂𐐮𐑊; 𐐮𐑁 𐑄𐐩 𐐺 𐑀𐐳𐐼, 𐐻𐐭 𐑄 𐑉𐐯𐑆𐐲𐑉𐐯𐐿𐑇𐐲𐑌 𐐱𐑂 𐐯𐑂𐐲𐑉𐑊𐐰𐑅𐐻𐐮𐑍 𐑊𐐴𐑁; 𐐰𐑌𐐼 𐐮𐑁 𐑄𐐩 𐐺 𐐨𐑂𐐮𐑊,
𐐻𐐭 𐑄 𐑉𐐯𐑆𐐲𐑉𐐯𐐿𐑇𐐲𐑌 𐐱𐑂 𐐼𐐰𐑋𐑌𐐩𐑇𐐲𐑌, 𐐺𐐨𐐮𐑍 𐐱𐑌 𐐲 𐐹𐐰𐑉𐐰𐑊𐐯𐑊, 𐑄 𐐶𐐲𐑌 𐐱𐑌 𐑄 𐐶𐐲𐑌 𐐸𐐰𐑌𐐼, 𐐰𐑌𐐼 𐑄
𐐲𐑄𐐲𐑉 𐐱𐑌 𐑄 𐐲𐑄𐐲𐑉 𐐸𐐰𐑌𐐼, 𐐰𐐿𐐫𐑉𐐼𐐮𐑍 𐐻𐐭 𐑄 𐑋𐐲𐑉𐑅𐐨, 𐐰𐑌𐐼 𐑄 𐐾𐐲𐑅𐐻𐐮𐑅, 𐐰𐑌𐐼 𐑄 𐐸𐐬𐑊𐐮𐑌𐐯𐑅 𐐸𐐶𐐮𐐽 𐐮𐑆
𐐮𐑌 𐐗𐑉𐐴𐑅𐐻, 𐐸𐐭 𐐶𐐱𐑆 𐐺𐐨𐑁𐐬𐑉 𐑄 𐐶𐐲𐑉𐑊𐐼 𐐺𐐨𐑀𐐰𐑌.

𐐕𐐈𐐑𐐓𐐊𐐡 XII.

1. 𐐈𐑌𐐼 𐑌𐐵 𐑄𐐯𐑉 𐐿𐐰𐑌𐐱𐐻 𐐺𐐨 𐑉𐐮𐐻𐑌 𐐮𐑌 𐑄𐐮𐑅 𐐺𐐳𐐿, 𐐨𐑂𐑌 𐐲 𐐸𐐲𐑌𐐼𐑉𐐯𐐼𐑃 𐐹𐐪𐑉𐐻 𐐱𐑂 𐑄 𐑃𐐮𐑍𐑆 𐐸𐐶𐐮𐐽 𐐖𐐨𐑆𐐲𐑅 𐐼𐐮𐐼 𐐻𐑉𐐭𐑊𐐨 𐐻𐐨𐐽 𐐲𐑌𐐻𐐭 𐑄 𐐹𐐨𐐹𐑊; 𐐺𐐲𐐻 𐐺𐐨𐐸𐐬𐑊𐐼, 𐑄 𐐹𐑊𐐩𐐻𐑅 𐐱𐑂 𐐤𐐨𐑁𐐴 𐐼𐐭 𐐿𐐱𐑌-𐐻𐐩𐑌 𐑄 𐑋𐐬𐑉 𐐹𐐪𐑉𐐻 𐐱𐑂 𐑄 𐑃𐐮𐑍𐑆 𐐸𐐶𐐮𐐽 𐐸𐐨 𐐻𐐫𐐻 𐑄 𐐹𐐨𐐹𐑊; 𐐰𐑌𐐼 𐑄𐐨𐑆 𐑃𐐮𐑍𐑆 𐐸𐐰𐑂 𐐌 𐑉𐐮𐐻𐑌, 𐐸𐐶𐐮𐐽 𐐪𐑉 𐐲 𐑊𐐯𐑅𐐲𐑉 𐐹𐐪𐑉𐐻 𐐱𐑂 𐑄 𐑃𐐮𐑍𐑆 𐐸𐐶𐐮𐐽 𐐸𐐨 𐐻𐐫𐐻 𐑄 𐐹𐐨𐐹𐑊, 𐐰𐑌𐐼 𐐌 𐐸𐐰𐑂 𐑉𐐮𐐻𐑌 𐑄𐐯𐑋 𐐻𐐭 𐑄 𐐮𐑌𐐻𐐯𐑌𐐻 𐑄𐐰𐐻 𐑄𐐩 𐑋𐐩 𐐺𐐨 𐐺𐑉𐐫𐐻 𐐲𐑀𐐯𐑌 𐐲𐑌𐐻𐐭 𐑄𐐮𐑅 𐐹𐐨𐐹𐑊, 𐑁𐑉𐐱𐑋 𐑄 𐐘𐐯𐑌𐐻𐐴𐑊𐑆, 𐐰𐐿𐐫𐑉𐐼𐐮𐑍 𐐻𐐭 𐑄 𐐶𐐲𐑉𐐼𐑆 𐐸𐐶𐐮𐐽 𐐖𐐨𐑆𐐲𐑅 𐐸𐐰𐑃 𐑅𐐹𐐬𐐿𐑌. 𐐈𐑌𐐼 𐐸𐐶𐐯𐑌 𐑄𐐩 𐑇𐐰𐑊 𐐸𐐰𐑂 𐑉𐐨𐑅𐐨𐑂𐐼 𐑄𐐮𐑅, 𐐸𐐶𐐮𐐽 𐐮𐑆 𐐯𐐿𐑅𐐹𐐨𐐼𐐨𐐯𐑌𐐻 𐑄𐐰𐐻 𐑄𐐩 𐑇𐐳𐐼 𐐸𐐰𐑂 𐑁𐐲𐑉𐑅𐐻, 𐐻𐐭 𐐻𐑉𐐴 𐑄𐐩𐑉 𐑁𐐩𐑃, 𐐰𐑌𐐼 𐐮𐑁 𐐮𐐻 𐑇𐐰𐑊 𐑅𐐬 𐐺𐐨 𐑄𐐰𐐻 𐑄𐐩 𐑇𐐰𐑊 𐐺𐐨𐑊𐐨𐑂 𐑄𐐨𐑆 𐑃𐐮𐑍𐑆, 𐑄𐐯𐑌 𐑇𐐰𐑊 𐑄 𐑀𐑉𐐩𐐻𐐲𐑉 𐑃𐐮𐑍𐑆 𐐺𐐨 𐑋𐐩𐐼 𐑋𐐰𐑌𐐮𐑁𐐯𐑅𐐻 𐐲𐑌𐐻𐐭 𐑄𐐯𐑋. 𐐈𐑌𐐼 𐐮𐑁 𐐮𐐻 𐑅𐐬 𐐺𐐨 𐑄𐐰𐐻 𐑄𐐩 𐐶𐐮𐑊 𐑌𐐱𐐻 𐐺𐐨𐑊𐐨𐑂 𐑄𐐨𐑆 𐑃𐐮𐑍𐑆, 𐑄𐐯𐑌 𐑇𐐰𐑊 𐑄 𐑀𐑉𐐩𐐻𐐲𐑉 𐑃𐐮𐑍𐑆 𐐺𐐨 𐐶𐐮𐑄𐐸𐐯𐑊𐐼 𐑁𐑉𐐱𐑋 𐑄𐐯𐑋, 𐐲𐑌𐐻𐐭 𐑄𐐩𐑉 𐐿𐐱𐑌𐐼𐐯𐑋𐑌𐐩𐑇𐐲𐑌. 𐐒𐐨𐐸𐐬𐑊𐐼, 𐐌 𐐶𐐱𐑆 𐐲𐐺𐐵𐐻 𐐻𐐭 𐑉𐐴𐐻 𐑄𐐯𐑋 𐐫𐑊 𐐸𐐶𐐮𐐽 𐐶𐐲𐑉 𐐯𐑌𐑀𐑉𐐩𐑂𐑌 𐐲𐐹𐐱𐑌 𐑄 𐐹𐑊𐐩𐐻𐑅 𐐱𐑂 𐐤𐐨𐑁𐐴, 𐐺𐐲𐐻 𐑄 𐐢𐐫𐑉𐐼 𐑁𐐫𐑉𐐺𐐩𐐼 𐐮𐐻, 𐑅𐐩𐐮𐑍, 𐐌 𐐶𐐮𐑊 𐐻𐑉𐐴 𐑄 𐑁𐐩𐑃 𐐱𐑂 𐑋𐐴 𐐹𐐨𐐹𐑊; 𐑄𐐯𐑉𐑁𐐬𐑉 𐐌, 𐐣𐐫𐑉𐑋𐐲𐑌, 𐐼𐐭 𐑉𐐴𐐻 𐑄 𐑃𐐮𐑍𐑆 𐐸𐐶𐐮𐐽 𐐸𐐰𐑂 𐐺𐐮𐑌 𐐿𐐱𐑋𐐰𐑌𐐼𐐯𐐼 𐑋𐐨 𐐱𐑂 𐑄 𐐢𐐫𐑉𐐼. 𐐈𐑌𐐼 𐑌𐐵 𐐌, 𐐣𐐫𐑉𐑋𐐲𐑌, 𐑋𐐩𐐿 𐐰𐑌 𐐯𐑌𐐼 𐐱𐑂 𐑋𐐴 𐑅𐐩𐐮𐑍𐑆, 𐐰𐑌𐐼 𐐹𐑉𐐬𐑅𐐨𐐼 𐐻𐐭 𐑉𐐴𐐻 𐑄 𐑃𐐮𐑍𐑆 𐐸𐐶𐐮𐐽 𐐸𐐰𐑂 𐐺𐐮𐑌 𐐿𐐱𐑋-𐐰𐑌𐐼𐐯𐐼 𐑋𐐨; 𐑄𐐯𐑉𐑁𐐬𐑉 𐐌 𐐶𐐳𐐼 𐑄𐐰𐐻 𐐷𐐨 𐑇𐐳𐐼 𐐺𐐨𐐸𐐬𐑊𐐼 𐑄𐐰𐐻 𐑄 𐐢𐐫𐑉𐐼 𐐻𐑉𐐭𐑊𐐨 𐐼𐐮𐐼 𐐻𐐨𐐽 𐑄 𐐹𐐨𐐹𐑊, 𐑁𐐫𐑉 𐑄 𐑅𐐹𐐩𐑅 𐐱𐑂 𐑃𐑉𐐨 𐐼𐐩𐑆; 𐐰𐑌𐐼 𐐪𐑁𐐻𐐲𐑉 𐑄𐐰𐐻 𐐸𐐨 𐐼𐐮𐐼 𐑇𐐬 𐐸𐐮𐑋𐑅𐐯𐑊𐑁 𐐲𐑌𐐻𐐭 𐑄𐐯𐑋 𐐫𐑁𐐻, 𐐰𐑌𐐼 𐐼𐐮𐐼 𐐺𐑉𐐩𐐿 𐐺𐑉𐐯𐐼 𐐫𐑁𐐻, 𐐰𐑌𐐼 𐐺𐑊𐐯𐑅 𐐮𐐻, 𐐰𐑌𐐼 𐑀𐐮𐑂 𐐮𐐻 𐐲𐑌𐐻𐐭 𐑄𐐯𐑋.

2. 𐐈𐑌𐐼 𐐮𐐻 𐐿𐐩𐑋 𐐻𐐭 𐐹𐐪𐑅 𐑄𐐰𐐻 𐐸𐐨 𐐼𐐮𐐼 𐐻𐐨𐐽 𐐰𐑌𐐼 𐑋𐐮𐑌𐐮𐑅𐐻𐐲𐑉 𐐲𐑌𐐻𐐭 𐑄 𐐽𐐮𐑊𐐼𐑉𐐯𐑌 𐐱𐑂 𐑄 𐑋𐐲𐑊𐐻𐐮𐐻𐑏𐐼 𐐱𐑂 𐐸𐐭𐑋 𐐸𐐰𐑃 𐐺𐐮𐑌 𐑅𐐹𐐬𐐿𐑌, 𐐰𐑌𐐼 𐐸𐐨 𐐼𐐮𐐼 𐑊𐐭𐑅 𐑄𐐩𐑉 𐐻𐐲𐑍𐑆, 𐐰𐑌𐐼 𐑄𐐩 𐐼𐐮𐐼 𐑅𐐹𐐨𐐿 𐐲𐑌𐐻𐐭 𐑄𐐩𐑉 𐑁𐐪𐑄𐐲𐑉𐑆 𐑀𐑉𐐩𐐻 𐐰𐑌𐐼 𐑋𐐪𐑉𐑂𐐯𐑊𐐲𐑅 𐑃𐐮𐑍𐑆, 𐐨𐑂𐑌 𐑀𐑉𐐩𐐻𐐲𐑉 𐑄𐐰𐑌 𐐸𐐨 𐐸𐐰𐐼 𐑉𐐨𐑂𐐨𐑊𐐼 𐐲𐑌𐐻𐐭 𐑄 𐐹𐐨𐐹𐑊; 𐐰𐑌𐐼 𐐸𐐨 𐑊𐐭𐑅𐐻 𐑄𐐩𐑉 𐐻𐐲𐑍𐑆 𐑄𐐰𐐻 𐑄𐐩 𐐿𐐳𐐼 𐐲𐐻𐐲𐑉. 𐐈𐑌𐐼 𐐮𐐻 𐐿𐐩𐑋 𐐻𐐭 𐐹𐐪𐑅 𐑄𐐰𐐻 𐐪𐑁𐐻𐐲𐑉 𐐸𐐨 𐐸𐐰𐐼 𐐰𐑅𐐯𐑌𐐼𐐯𐐼 𐐮𐑌𐐻𐐭 𐐸𐐯𐑂𐑌 𐑄 𐑅𐐯𐐿𐐲𐑌𐐼 𐐻𐐴𐑋 𐑄𐐰𐐻 𐐸𐐨 𐑇𐐬𐐼 𐐸𐐮𐑋𐑅𐐯𐑊𐑁 𐐲𐑌𐐻𐐭 𐑄𐐯𐑋, 𐐰𐑌𐐼 𐐸𐐰𐐼 𐑀𐐱𐑌 𐐲𐑌𐐻𐐭 𐑄 𐐙𐐪𐑄𐐲𐑉, 𐐪𐑁𐐻𐐲𐑉 𐐸𐐰𐑂𐐮𐑍 𐐸𐐨𐑊𐐼 𐐫𐑊 𐑄𐐩𐑉 𐑅𐐮𐐿, 𐐰𐑌𐐼 𐑄𐐩𐑉 𐑊𐐩𐑋, 𐐰𐑌𐐼 𐐬𐐹𐑌𐐼 𐑄 𐐴𐑆 𐐱𐑂 𐑄𐐩𐑉 𐐺𐑊𐐴𐑌𐐼 𐐰𐑌𐐼 𐐲𐑌𐑅𐐻𐐱𐐹𐐻 𐑄 𐐨𐑉𐑆 𐐱𐑂 𐑄 𐐼𐐯𐑁, 𐐰𐑌𐐼 𐐨𐑂𐑌 𐐸𐐰𐐼 𐐼𐐲𐑌 𐐫𐑊 𐑋𐐰𐑌𐐲𐑉 𐐱𐑂 𐐿𐑏𐑉𐑆 𐐲𐑋𐐲𐑍 𐑄𐐯𐑋, 𐐰𐑌𐐼 𐑉𐐩𐑆𐐼 𐐲 𐑋𐐰𐑌 𐑁𐑉𐐱𐑋 𐑄 𐐼𐐯𐐼, 𐐰𐑌𐐼 𐐸𐐰𐐼 𐑇𐐬𐑌 𐑁𐐬𐑉𐑃 𐐸𐐮𐑆 𐐹𐐵𐐲𐑉 𐐲𐑌𐐻𐐭 𐑄𐐯𐑋, 𐐰𐑌𐐼 𐐸𐐰𐐼 𐐰𐑅𐐯𐑌𐐼𐐯𐐼 𐐲𐑌𐐻𐐭 𐑄 𐐙𐐪𐑄𐐲𐑉, 𐐺𐐨𐐸𐐬𐑊𐐼 𐐮𐐻 𐐿𐐩𐑋 𐐻𐐭 𐐹𐐪𐑅 𐐱𐑌 𐑄 𐑋𐐱𐑉𐐬, 𐑄𐐰𐐻 𐑄 𐑋𐐲𐑊𐐻𐐮𐐻𐑏𐐼 𐑀𐐰𐑄𐐲𐑉𐐼 𐑄𐐯𐑋𐑅𐐯𐑊𐑂𐑆 𐐻𐐭𐑀𐐯𐑄𐐲𐑉, 𐐰𐑌𐐼 𐑄𐐩 𐐺𐐬𐑃 𐑅𐐫 𐐰𐑌𐐼 𐐸𐐲𐑉𐐼 𐑄𐐨𐑆 𐐽𐐮𐑊𐐼𐑉𐐯𐑌; 𐐷𐐩, 𐐨𐑂𐑌 𐐺𐐩𐐺𐑆 𐐼𐐮𐐼 𐐬𐐹𐑌 𐑄𐐩𐑉 𐑋𐐵𐑄𐑆, 𐐰𐑌𐐼 𐐲𐐻𐐲𐑉 𐑋𐐪𐑉𐑂𐐯𐑊𐐲𐑅 𐑃𐐮𐑍𐑆; 𐐰𐑌𐐼 𐑄 𐑃𐐮𐑍𐑆 𐐸𐐶𐐮𐐽 𐑄𐐩 𐐼𐐮𐐼 𐐲𐐻𐐲𐑉 𐐶𐐲𐑉 𐑁𐐫𐑉𐐺𐐮𐐼𐑌, 𐑄𐐰𐐻 𐑄𐐯𐑉 𐑇𐐳𐐼 𐑌𐐱𐐻 𐐯𐑌𐐨 𐑋𐐰𐑌 𐑉𐐴𐐻 𐑄𐐯𐑋. 𐐈𐑌𐐼 𐐮𐐻 𐐿𐐩𐑋 𐐻𐐭 𐐹𐐪𐑅 𐑄𐐰𐐻 𐑄 𐐼𐐮𐑅𐐴𐐹𐑊𐑆 𐐸𐐭𐑋 𐐖𐐨𐑆𐐲𐑅 𐐸𐐰𐐼 𐐽𐐬𐑆𐑌, 𐐺𐐨𐑀𐐰𐑌 𐑁𐑉𐐱𐑋 𐑄𐐰𐐻 𐐻𐐴𐑋 𐑁𐐬𐑉𐑃 𐐻𐐭 𐐺𐐰𐐹𐐻𐐴𐑆 𐐰𐑌𐐼 𐐻𐐭 𐐻𐐨𐐽 𐐰𐑆 𐑋𐐯𐑌𐐨 𐐰𐑆 𐐼𐐮𐐼 𐐿𐐲𐑋 𐐲𐑌𐐻𐐭 𐑄𐐯𐑋; 𐐰𐑌𐐼 𐐰𐑆 𐑋𐐯𐑌𐐨 𐐰𐑆 𐐶𐐲𐑉 𐐺𐐰𐐹𐐻𐐴𐑆𐐼 𐐮𐑌 𐑄 𐑌𐐩𐑋 𐐱𐑂 𐐖𐐨𐑆𐐲𐑅, 𐐶𐐲𐑉 𐑁𐐮𐑊𐐼 𐐶𐐮𐑄 𐑄 𐐐𐐬𐑊𐐨 𐐘𐐬𐑅𐐻. 𐐈𐑌𐐼 𐑋𐐯𐑌𐐨 𐐱𐑂 𐑄𐐯𐑋 𐑅𐐫 𐐰𐑌𐐼 𐐸𐐲𐑉𐐼 𐐲𐑌𐑅𐐹𐐨𐐿𐐲𐐺𐑊 𐑃𐐮𐑍𐑆, 𐐸𐐶𐐮𐐽 𐐪𐑉 𐑌𐐱𐐻 𐑊𐐫𐑁𐐳𐑊 𐐻𐐭 𐐺𐐨 𐑉𐐮𐐻𐑌; 𐐰𐑌𐐼 𐑄𐐩 𐐻𐐫𐐻, 𐐰𐑌𐐼 𐐼𐐮𐐼 𐑋𐐮𐑌𐐮𐑅𐐻𐐲𐑉 𐐶𐐲𐑌 𐐻𐐭 𐐲𐑌𐐲𐑄𐐲𐑉; 𐐰𐑌𐐼 𐑄𐐩 𐐸𐐰𐐼 𐐫𐑊 𐑃𐐮𐑍𐑆 𐐿𐐱𐑋𐐲𐑌 𐐲𐑋𐐲𐑍 𐑄𐐯𐑋, 𐐯𐑂𐑉𐐨 𐑋𐐰𐑌 𐐼𐐨𐑊𐐮𐑍 𐐾𐐲𐑅𐐻𐑊𐐨 𐐶𐐲𐑌 𐐶𐐮𐑄 𐐲𐑌𐐲𐑄𐐲𐑉. 𐐈𐑌𐐼 𐐮𐐻 𐐿𐐩𐑋 𐐻𐐭 𐐹𐐪𐑅 𐑄𐐰𐐻 𐑄𐐩 𐐼𐐮𐐼 𐐼𐐭 𐐫𐑊 𐑃𐐮𐑍𐑆 𐐨𐑂𐑌 𐐰𐑆 𐐖𐐨𐑆𐐲𐑅 𐐸𐐰𐐼 𐐿𐐱𐑋𐐰𐑌𐐼𐐯𐐼 𐑄𐐯𐑋. 𐐈𐑌𐐼 𐑄𐐩 𐐸𐐭 𐐶𐐲𐑉 𐐺𐐰𐐹𐐻𐐴𐑆𐐼 𐐮𐑌 𐑄 𐑌𐐩𐑋 𐐱𐑂 𐐖𐐨𐑆𐐲𐑅, 𐐶𐐲𐑉 𐐿𐐫𐑊𐐼 𐑄 𐐕𐐲𐑉𐐽 𐐱𐑂 𐐗𐑉𐐴𐑅𐐻.

3. 𐐈𐑌𐐼 𐐮𐐻 𐐿𐐩𐑋 𐐻𐐭 𐐹𐐪𐑅 𐑄𐐰𐐻 𐐰𐑆 𐑄 𐐼𐐮𐑅𐐴𐐹𐑊𐑆 𐐱𐑂 𐐖𐐨𐑆𐐲𐑅 𐐶𐐲𐑉 𐐾𐐲𐑉𐑌𐐨𐐮𐑍 𐐰𐑌𐐼 𐐶𐐲𐑉 𐐹𐑉𐐨𐐽𐐮𐑍 𐑄 𐑃𐐮𐑍𐑆 𐐸𐐶𐐮𐐽 𐑄𐐩 𐐸𐐰𐐼 𐐺𐐬𐑃 𐐸𐐲𐑉𐐼 𐐰𐑌𐐼 𐑅𐐨𐑌, 𐐰𐑌𐐼 𐐶𐐲𐑉 𐐺𐐰𐐹𐐻𐐴𐑆𐐮𐑍 𐐮𐑌 𐑄

𐑌𐐩𐑋 𐐱𐑂 𐐖𐐨𐑆𐐲𐑅, 𐐮𐐻 𐐿𐐩𐑋 𐐻𐐭 𐐹𐐰𐑅 𐑄𐐰𐐻 𐑄 𐐼𐐮𐑅𐐴𐐹𐑊𐑆 𐐶𐐲𐑉 𐑀𐐰𐑄𐐲𐑉𐐼 𐐻𐐭𐑀𐐯𐑄𐐲𐑉, 𐐰𐑌𐐼 𐐶𐐲𐑉
𐐷𐐭𐑌𐐴𐐻𐐯𐐼 𐐮𐑌 𐑋𐐴𐐻𐐨 𐐹𐑉𐐩𐑉 𐐰𐑌𐐼 𐑁𐐰𐑅𐐻𐐮𐑍. 𐐈𐑌𐐼 𐐖𐐨𐑆𐐲𐑅 𐐲𐑀𐐯𐑌 𐑇𐐬𐐼 𐐸𐐮𐑋𐑅𐐯𐑊𐑁 𐐲𐑌𐐻𐐭
𐑄𐐯𐑋, 𐑁𐐫𐑉 𐑄𐐩 𐐶𐐲𐑉 𐐹𐑉𐐩𐐮𐑍 𐐲𐑌𐐻𐐭 𐑄 𐐙𐐪𐑄𐐲𐑉, 𐐮𐑌 𐐸𐐮𐑆 𐑌𐐩𐑋; 𐐰𐑌𐐼 𐐖𐐨𐑆𐐲𐑅 𐐿𐐩𐑋 𐐰𐑌𐐼 𐑅𐐻𐐳𐐼 𐐮𐑌 𐑄
𐑋𐐮𐐼𐑅𐐻 𐐱𐑂 𐑄𐐯𐑋, 𐐰𐑌𐐼 𐑅𐐯𐐼 𐐲𐑌𐐻𐐭 𐑄𐐯𐑋, 𐐸𐐶𐐱𐐻 𐐶𐐮𐑊 𐐷𐐨 𐑄𐐰𐐻 𐐴 𐑇𐐰𐑊 𐑀𐐮𐑂 𐐲𐑌𐐻𐐭 𐐷𐐭? 𐐈𐑌𐐼 𐑄𐐩
𐑅𐐯𐐼 𐐲𐑌𐐻𐐭 𐐸𐐮𐑋, 𐐢𐐫𐑉𐐼, 𐐶𐐨 𐐶𐐮𐑊 𐑄𐐰𐐻 𐑄𐐵 𐐶𐐳𐐼𐑅𐐻 𐐻𐐯𐑊 𐐲𐑅 𐑄 𐑌𐐩𐑋 𐐸𐐶𐐯𐑉𐐺𐐴 𐐶𐐨 𐑇𐐰𐑊 𐐿𐐫𐑊 𐑄𐐮𐑅
𐐽𐐲𐑉𐐽; 𐑁𐐫𐑉 𐑄𐐯𐑉 𐐪𐑉 𐐼𐐮𐑅𐐹𐐷𐐭𐐻𐐩𐑇𐐲𐑌𐑆 𐐲𐑋𐐲𐑍 𐑄 𐐹𐐨𐐹𐑊 𐐿𐐱𐑌𐑅𐐲𐑉𐑌𐐮𐑍 𐑄𐐮𐑅 𐑋𐐰𐐻𐐲𐑉. 𐐈𐑌𐐼 𐑄 𐐢𐐫𐑉𐐼
𐑅𐐯𐐼 𐐲𐑌𐐻𐐭 𐑄𐐯𐑋, 𐐚𐐯𐑉𐐮𐑊𐐨, 𐑂𐐯𐑉𐐮𐑊𐐨 𐐴 𐑅𐐩 𐐲𐑌𐐻𐐭 𐐷𐐭, 𐐐𐐶𐐴 𐐮𐑆 𐐮𐐻 𐑄𐐰𐐻 𐑄 𐐹𐐨𐐹𐑊 𐑇𐐳𐐼 𐑋𐐲𐑉𐑋𐐲𐑉
𐐰𐑌𐐼 𐐼𐐮𐑅𐐹𐐷𐐭𐐻 𐐺𐐨𐐿𐐫𐑆 𐐱𐑂 𐑄𐐮𐑅 𐑃𐐮𐑍? 𐐐𐐰𐑂 𐑄𐐩 𐑌𐐱𐐻 𐑉𐐯𐐼 𐑄 𐑅𐐿𐑉𐐮𐐹𐐽𐐲𐑉𐑆, 𐐸𐐶𐐮𐐽 𐑅𐐩 𐐷𐐨 𐑋𐐲𐑅𐐻
𐐻𐐩𐐿 𐐲𐐹𐐱𐑌 𐐷𐐭 𐑄 𐑌𐐩𐑋 𐐱𐑂 𐐗𐑉𐐴𐑅𐐻, 𐐸𐐶𐐮𐐽 𐐮𐑆 𐑋𐐴 𐑌𐐩𐑋? 𐐙𐐫𐑉 𐐺𐐴 𐑄𐐮𐑅 𐑌𐐩𐑋 𐑇𐐰𐑊 𐐷𐐨 𐐺𐐨 𐐿𐐫𐑊𐐼 𐐰𐐻
𐑄 𐑊𐐰𐑅𐐻 𐐼𐐩; 𐐰𐑌𐐼 𐐸𐐭𐑅𐐬 𐐻𐐩𐐿𐐯𐑃 𐐲𐐹𐐱𐑌 𐐸𐐮𐑋 𐑋𐐴 𐑌𐐩𐑋, 𐐰𐑌𐐼 𐐯𐑌𐐼𐐷𐐭𐑉𐐯𐑃 𐐻𐐭 𐑄 𐐯𐑌𐐼, 𐑄 𐑅𐐩𐑋 𐑇𐐰𐑊
𐐺𐐨 𐑅𐐩𐑂𐐼 𐐰𐐻 𐑄 𐑊𐐰𐑅𐐻 𐐼𐐩; 𐑄𐐯𐑉𐑁𐐫𐑉 𐐸𐐶𐐱𐐻𐑅𐐬𐐯𐑂𐐲𐑉 𐐷𐐨 𐑇𐐰𐑊 𐐼𐐭, 𐐷𐐨 𐑇𐐰𐑊 𐐼𐐭 𐐮𐐻 𐐮𐑌 𐑋𐐴 𐑌𐐩𐑋; 𐑄𐐯𐑉𐑁𐐫𐑉 𐐷𐐨 𐑇𐐰𐑊 𐐿𐐫𐑊 𐑄 𐐽𐐲𐑉𐐽 𐐮𐑌 𐑋𐐴 𐑌𐐩𐑋; 𐐰𐑌𐐼 𐐷𐐨 𐑇𐐰𐑊 𐐿𐐫𐑊 𐐲𐐹𐐱𐑌 𐑄 𐐙𐐪𐑄𐐲𐑉 𐐮𐑌 𐑋𐐴 𐑌𐐩𐑋, 𐑄𐐰𐐻 𐐸𐐨
𐐶𐐮𐑊 𐐺𐑊𐐯𐑅 𐑄 𐐽𐐲𐑉𐐽 𐑁𐐫𐑉 𐑋𐐴 𐑅𐐩𐐿; 𐐰𐑌𐐼 𐐸𐐵 𐐺𐐨 𐐮𐐻 𐑋𐐴 𐐽𐐲𐑉𐐽, 𐑅𐐩𐑂 𐐮𐐻 𐐺𐐨 𐐿𐐫𐑊𐐼 𐐮𐑌 𐑋𐐴 𐑌𐐩𐑋?
𐐙𐐫𐑉 𐐮𐑁 𐐲 𐐽𐐲𐑉𐐽 𐐺𐐨 𐐿𐐫𐑊𐐼 𐐮𐑌 𐐣𐐬𐑆𐐯𐑆' 𐑌𐐩𐑋, 𐑄𐐯𐑌 𐐮𐐻 𐐺𐐨 𐐣𐐬𐑆𐐯𐑆' 𐐽𐐲𐑉𐐽; 𐐫𐑉 𐐮𐑁 𐐮𐐻 𐐺𐐨 𐐿𐐫𐑊𐐼 𐐮𐑌
𐑄 𐑌𐐩𐑋 𐐱𐑂 𐐲 𐑋𐐰𐑌, 𐑄𐐯𐑌 𐐮𐐻 𐐺𐐨 𐑄 𐐽𐐲𐑉𐐽 𐐱𐑂 𐐲 𐑋𐐰𐑌; 𐐺𐐲𐐻 𐐮𐑁 𐐮𐐻 𐐺𐐨 𐐿𐐫𐑊𐐼 𐐮𐑌 𐑋𐐴 𐑌𐐩𐑋,
𐑄𐐯𐑌 𐐮𐐻 𐐮𐑆 𐑋𐐴 𐐽𐐲𐑉𐐽, 𐐮𐑁 𐐮𐐻 𐑅𐐬 𐐺𐐨 𐑄𐐰𐐻 𐑄𐐩 𐐪𐑉 𐐺𐐮𐑊𐐻 𐐲𐐹𐐱𐑌 𐑋𐐴 𐑀𐐱𐑅𐐹𐐯𐑊. 𐐚𐐯𐑉𐐮𐑊𐐨
𐐴 𐑅𐐩 𐐲𐑌𐐻𐐭 𐐷𐐭, 𐐜𐐰𐐻 𐐷𐐨 𐐪𐑉 𐐺𐐮𐑊𐐻 𐐲𐐹𐐱𐑌 𐑋𐐴 𐑀𐐱𐑅𐐹𐐯𐑊; 𐑄𐐯𐑉𐑁𐐫𐑉 𐐷𐐨 𐑇𐐰𐑊 𐐿𐐫𐑊 𐐸𐐶𐐱𐐻𐑅𐐬𐐯𐑂𐐲𐑉 𐑃𐐮𐑍𐑆 𐐷𐐨 𐐼𐐭 𐐿𐐫𐑊 𐐮𐑌 𐑋𐐴 𐑌𐐩𐑋; 𐑄𐐯𐑉𐑁𐐫𐑉 𐐮𐑁 𐐷𐐨 𐐿𐐫𐑊 𐐲𐐹𐐱𐑌 𐑄 𐐙𐐪𐑄𐐲𐑉, 𐑁𐐫𐑉 𐑄 𐐽𐐲𐑉𐐽,
𐐮𐑁 𐐮𐐻 𐐺𐐨 𐐮𐑌 𐑋𐐴 𐑌𐐩𐑋, 𐑄 𐐙𐐪𐑄𐐲𐑉 𐐶𐐮𐑊 𐐸𐐨𐑉 𐐷𐐭; 𐐰𐑌𐐼 𐐮𐑁 𐐮𐐻 𐑅𐐬 𐐺𐐨 𐑄𐐰𐐻 𐑄 𐐽𐐲𐑉𐐽 𐐮𐑆 𐐺𐐮𐑊𐐻 𐐲𐐹𐐱𐑌
𐑋𐐴 𐑀𐐱𐑅𐐹𐐯𐑊, 𐑄𐐯𐑌 𐐶𐐮𐑊 𐑄 𐐙𐐪𐑄𐐲𐑉 𐑇𐐬 𐑁𐐫𐑉𐑃 𐐸𐐮𐑆 𐐬𐑌 𐐶𐐲𐑉𐐿𐑅 𐐮𐑌 𐐮𐐻; 𐐺𐐲𐐻 𐐮𐑁 𐐮𐐻 𐐺𐐨 𐑌𐐱𐐻
𐐺𐐮𐑊𐐻 𐐲𐐹𐐱𐑌 𐑋𐐴 𐑀𐐱𐑅𐐹𐐯𐑊, 𐐰𐑌𐐼 𐐮𐑆 𐐺𐐮𐑊𐐻 𐐲𐐹𐐱𐑌 𐑄 𐐶𐐲𐑉𐐿𐑅 𐐱𐑂 𐑋𐐯𐑌, 𐐫𐑉 𐐲𐐹𐐱𐑌 𐑄 𐐶𐐲𐑉𐐿𐑅 𐐱𐑂
𐑄 𐐼𐐯𐑂𐐮𐑊, 𐑂𐐯𐑉𐐮𐑊𐐨 𐐴 𐑅𐐩 𐐲𐑌𐐻𐐭 𐐷𐐭, 𐐜𐐩 𐐸𐐰𐑂 𐐾𐐱𐐮 𐐮𐑌 𐑄𐐯𐑉 𐐶𐐲𐑉𐐿𐑅 𐑁𐐫𐑉 𐐲 𐑅𐐨𐑆𐐲𐑌, 𐐰𐑌𐐼 𐐺𐐴 𐐰𐑌𐐼
𐐺𐐴 𐑄 𐐯𐑌𐐼 𐐿𐐲𐑋𐐯𐑃, 𐐰𐑌𐐼 𐑄𐐩 𐐪𐑉 𐐸𐐷𐐭𐑌 𐐼𐐵𐑌 𐐰𐑌𐐼 𐐿𐐰𐑅𐐻 𐐮𐑌𐐻𐐭 𐑄 𐑁𐐴𐑉, 𐑁𐑉𐐱𐑋 𐐸𐐶𐐯𐑌𐑅 𐑄𐐯𐑉 𐐮𐑆
𐑌𐐬 𐑉𐐨𐐻𐐲𐑉𐑌; 𐑁𐐫𐑉 𐑄𐐯𐑉 𐐶𐐲𐑉𐐿𐑅 𐐼𐐭 𐑁𐐱𐑊𐐬 𐑄𐐯𐑋, 𐑁𐐫𐑉 𐐮𐐻 𐐮𐑆 𐐺𐐨𐐿𐐫𐑆 𐐱𐑂 𐑄𐐯𐑉 𐐶𐐲𐑉𐐿𐑅 𐑄𐐰𐐻 𐑄𐐩
𐐪𐑉 𐐸𐐷𐐭𐑌 𐐼𐐵𐑌; 𐑄𐐯𐑉𐑁𐐫𐑉 𐑉𐐨𐑋𐐯𐑋𐐺𐐲𐑉 𐑄 𐑃𐐮𐑍𐑆 𐑄𐐰𐐻 𐐴 𐐸𐐰𐑂 𐐻𐐬𐑊𐐼 𐐷𐐭. 𐐒𐐨𐐸𐐬𐑊𐐼 𐐴 𐐸𐐰𐑂
𐑀𐐮𐑂𐐲𐑌 𐐲𐑌𐐻𐐭 𐐷𐐭 𐑋𐐴 𐑀𐐱𐑅𐐹𐐯𐑊, 𐐰𐑌𐐼 𐑄𐐮𐑅 𐐮𐑆 𐑄 𐑀𐐱𐑅𐐹𐐯𐑊 𐐸𐐶𐐮𐐽 𐐴 𐐸𐐰𐑂 𐑀𐐮𐑂𐐲𐑌 𐐲𐑌𐐻𐐭 𐐷𐐭, 𐐜𐐰𐐻
𐐴 𐐿𐐩𐑋 𐐮𐑌𐐻𐐭 𐑄 𐐶𐐲𐑉𐑊𐐼 𐐻𐐭 𐐼𐐭 𐑄 𐐶𐐮𐑊 𐐱𐑂 𐑋𐐴 𐐙𐐪𐑄𐐲𐑉, 𐐺𐐨𐐿𐐫𐑆 𐑋𐐴 𐐙𐐪𐑄𐐲𐑉 𐑅𐐯𐑌𐐻 𐑋𐐨; 𐐰𐑌𐐼
𐑋𐐴 𐐙𐐪𐑄𐐲𐑉 𐑅𐐯𐑌𐐻 𐑋𐐨 𐑄𐐰𐐻 𐐴 𐑋𐐴𐐻 𐐺𐐨 𐑊𐐮𐑁𐐻𐐯𐐼 𐐲𐐹 𐐲𐐹𐐱𐑌 𐑄 𐐿𐑉𐐱𐑅; 𐐰𐑌𐐼 𐐰𐑁𐐻𐐲𐑉 𐑄𐐰𐐻 𐐴 𐐸𐐰𐐼
𐐺𐐮𐑌 𐑊𐐮𐑁𐐻𐐯𐐼 𐐲𐐹 𐐲𐐹𐐱𐑌 𐑄 𐐿𐑉𐐱𐑅, 𐑄𐐰𐐻 𐐴 𐑋𐐴𐐻 𐐼𐑉𐐫 𐐫𐑊 𐑋𐐯𐑌 𐐲𐑌𐐻𐐭 𐑋𐐨; 𐑄𐐰𐐻 𐐰𐑆 𐐴 𐐸𐐰𐑂 𐐺𐐮𐑌
𐑊𐐮𐑁𐐻𐐯𐐼 𐐲𐐹 𐐺𐐴 𐑋𐐯𐑌, 𐐀𐑂𐐲𐑌 𐑅𐐬 𐑇𐐳𐐼 𐑋𐐯𐑌 𐐺𐐨 𐑊𐐮𐑁𐐻𐐯𐐼 𐐲𐐹 𐐺𐐴 𐑄 𐐙𐐪𐑄𐐲𐑉, 𐐻𐐭 𐑅𐐻𐐰𐑌𐐼 𐐺𐐨𐑁𐐫𐑉 𐑋𐐨,
𐐻𐐭 𐐺𐐨 𐐾𐐲𐐾𐐼 𐐱𐑂 𐑄𐐯𐑉 𐐶𐐲𐑉𐐿𐑅, 𐐸𐐶𐐯𐑄𐐲𐑉 𐑄𐐩 𐐺𐐨 𐑀𐐳𐐼 𐐫𐑉 𐐸𐐶𐐯𐑄𐐲𐑉 𐑄𐐩 𐐺𐐨 𐐀𐑂𐐲𐑊; 𐐰𐑌𐐼 𐑁𐐫𐑉 𐑄𐐮𐑅
𐐿𐐫𐑆 𐐸𐐰𐑂 𐐴 𐐺𐐮𐑌 𐑊𐐮𐑁𐐻𐐯𐐼 𐐲𐐹; 𐑄𐐯𐑉𐑁𐐫𐑉, 𐐰𐐿𐐫𐑉𐐼𐐮𐑍 𐐻𐐭 𐑄 𐐹𐐵𐐲𐑉 𐐱𐑂 𐑄 𐐙𐐪𐑄𐐲𐑉, 𐐴 𐐶𐐮𐑊 𐐼𐑉𐐫 𐐫𐑊
𐑋𐐯𐑌 𐐲𐑌𐐻𐐭 𐑋𐐨, 𐑄𐐰𐐻 𐑄𐐩 𐑋𐐩 𐐺𐐨 𐐾𐐲𐐾𐐼 𐐰𐐿𐐫𐑉𐐼𐐮𐑍 𐐻𐐭 𐑄𐐯𐑉 𐐶𐐲𐑉𐐿𐑅.

4. 𐐈𐑌𐐼 𐐮𐐻 𐑇𐐰𐑊 𐐿𐐲𐑋 𐐻𐐭 𐐹𐐰𐑅 𐑄𐐰𐐻 𐐸𐐭𐑅𐐬 𐑉𐐯𐐹𐐯𐑌𐐻𐐯𐑃 𐐰𐑌𐐼 𐐮𐑆 𐐺𐐰𐐹𐐻𐐴𐑆𐐼 𐐮𐑌 𐑋𐐴 𐑌𐐩𐑋, 𐑇𐐰𐑊
𐐺𐐨 𐑁𐐮𐑊𐐼; 𐐰𐑌𐐼 𐐮𐑁 𐐸𐐨 𐐯𐑌𐐼𐐷𐐭𐑉𐐯𐑃 𐐻𐐭 𐑄 𐐯𐑌𐐼, 𐐺𐐨𐐸𐐬𐑊𐐼, 𐐸𐐮𐑋 𐐶𐐮𐑊 𐐴 𐐸𐐬𐑊𐐼 𐑀𐐮𐑊𐐻𐑊𐐯𐑅 𐐺𐐨𐑁𐐫𐑉 𐑋𐐴
𐐙𐐪𐑄𐐲𐑉, 𐐰𐐻 𐑄𐐰𐐻 𐐼𐐩 𐐸𐐶𐐯𐑌 𐐴 𐑇𐐰𐑊 𐑅𐐻𐐰𐑌𐐼 𐐻𐐭 𐐾𐐲𐐾 𐑄 𐐶𐐲𐑉𐑊𐐼. 𐐈𐑌𐐼 𐐸𐐨 𐑄𐐰𐐻 𐐯𐑌𐐼𐐷𐐭𐑉𐐯𐑃 𐑌𐐱𐐻
𐐲𐑌𐐻𐐭 𐑄 𐐯𐑌𐐼, 𐑄 𐑅𐐩𐑋 𐐮𐑆 𐐸𐐨 𐑄𐐰𐐻 𐐮𐑆 𐐫𐑊𐑅𐐬 𐐸𐐷𐐭𐑌 𐐼𐐵𐑌 𐐰𐑌𐐼 𐐿𐐰𐑅𐐻 𐐮𐑌𐐻𐐭 𐑄 𐑁𐐴𐑉, 𐑁𐑉𐐱𐑋
𐐸𐐶𐐯𐑌𐑅 𐑄𐐩 𐐿𐐰𐑌 𐑌𐐬 𐑋𐐫𐑉 𐑉𐐨𐐻𐐲𐑉𐑌, 𐐺𐐨𐐿𐐫𐑆 𐐱𐑂 𐑄 𐐾𐐲𐑅𐐻𐐮𐑅 𐐱𐑂 𐑄 𐐙𐐪𐑄𐐲𐑉; 𐐰𐑌𐐼 𐑄𐐮𐑅 𐐮𐑆 𐑄
𐐶𐐲𐑉𐐼 𐐸𐐶𐐮𐐽 𐐸𐐨 𐐸𐐰𐑃 𐑀𐐮𐑂𐐲𐑌 𐐲𐑌𐐻𐐭 𐑄 𐐽𐐮𐑊𐐼𐑉𐐯𐑌 𐐱𐑂 𐑋𐐯𐑌. 𐐈𐑌𐐼 𐑁𐐫𐑉 𐑄𐐮𐑅 𐐿𐐫𐑆 𐐸𐐨 𐑁𐐳𐑊𐑁𐐮𐑊𐐯𐑃 𐑄
𐐶𐐲𐑉𐐼𐑆 𐐸𐐶𐐮𐐽 𐐸𐐨 𐐸𐐰𐑃 𐑀𐐮𐑂𐐲𐑌, 𐐰𐑌𐐼 𐐸𐐨 𐑊𐐴𐐯𐑃 𐑌𐐱𐐻, 𐐺𐐲𐐻 𐑁𐐳𐑊𐑁𐐮𐑊𐐯𐑃 𐐫𐑊 𐐸𐐮𐑆 𐐶𐐲𐑉𐐼𐑆; 𐐰𐑌𐐼 𐑌𐐬
𐐲𐑌𐐿𐑊𐐨𐑌 𐑃𐐮𐑍 𐐿𐐰𐑌 𐐯𐑌𐐻𐐲𐑉 𐐮𐑌𐐻𐐭 𐐸𐐮𐑆 𐐿𐐮𐑍𐐼𐐲𐑋; 𐑄𐐯𐑉𐑁𐐫𐑉 𐑌𐐲𐑃𐐮𐑍 𐐯𐑌𐐻𐐲𐑉𐐯𐑃 𐐮𐑌𐐻𐐭 𐐸𐐮𐑆 𐑉𐐯𐑅𐐻, 𐑅𐐩𐑂

𐐮𐐻 𐐺 𐑄𐐬𐑆 𐐸𐐭 𐐸𐐰𐑂 𐐶𐐱𐑇𐐻 𐑄𐐯𐑉 𐑀𐐪𐑉𐑋𐐲𐑌𐐻𐑅 𐐮𐑌 𐑋𐐴 𐐺𐑊𐐲𐐼, 𐐺𐐨𐐿𐐫𐑆 𐐲𐑂 𐑄𐐯𐑉 𐑁𐐩𐑃, 𐐰𐑌𐐼 𐑄 𐑉𐐨𐐹𐐯𐑌𐐻𐐲𐑌𐑅 𐐲𐑂 𐐫𐑊 𐑄𐐯𐑉 𐑅𐐮𐑌𐑆, 𐐰𐑌𐐼 𐑄𐐯𐑉 𐑁𐐩𐑃𐑁𐐳𐑊𐑌𐐯𐑅 𐐲𐑌𐐻𐐭 𐑄 𐐯𐑌𐐼. 𐐤𐐵 𐑄𐐮𐑅 𐐮𐑆 𐑄 𐐿𐐱𐑋𐐰𐑌𐐼𐑋𐐯𐑌𐐻, 𐐡𐐨𐐹𐐯𐑌𐐻, 𐐫𐑊 𐐷 𐐯𐑌𐐼𐑆 𐐲𐑂 𐑄 𐐲𐑉𐑃, 𐐰𐑌𐐼 𐐿𐐲𐑋 𐐲𐑌𐐻𐐭 𐑋𐐨, 𐐰𐑌𐐼 𐐺 𐐺𐐰𐐹𐐻𐐴𐑆𐐼 𐐮𐑌 𐑋𐐴 𐑌𐐩𐑋, 𐑄𐐰𐐻 𐐷 𐑋𐐩 𐐺 𐑅𐐰𐑍𐐿𐐻𐐮𐑁𐐴𐐼 𐐺𐐴 𐑄 𐑉𐐨𐑅𐐯𐐹𐑇𐐲𐑌 𐐲𐑂 𐑄 𐐐𐐬𐑊𐐨 𐐘𐐬𐑅𐐻, 𐑄𐐰𐐻 𐐷 𐑋𐐩 𐑅𐐻𐐰𐑌𐐼 𐑅𐐹𐐱𐐻𐑊𐐯𐑅 𐐺𐐨𐑁𐐬𐑉 𐑋𐐨 𐐰𐐻 𐑄 𐑊𐐰𐑅𐐻 𐐼𐐩. 𐐚𐐯𐑉𐐮𐑊𐐨, 𐑂𐐯𐑉𐐮𐑊𐐨, 𐐌 𐑅𐐩 𐐲𐑌𐐻𐐭 𐐷𐐭, 𐑄𐐮𐑅 𐐮𐑆 𐑋𐐴 𐐘𐐱𐑅𐐹𐐯𐑊; 𐐰𐑌𐐼 𐐷 𐑌𐐬 𐑄 𐑃𐐮𐑍𐑆 𐑄𐐰𐐻 𐐷 𐑋𐐲𐑅𐐻 𐐼𐐭 𐐮𐑌 𐑋𐐴 𐐕𐐲𐑉𐐽; 𐑁𐐫𐑉 𐑄 𐐶𐐲𐑉𐐿𐑅 𐐸𐐶𐐮𐐽 𐐷 𐐸𐐰𐑂 𐑅𐐨𐑌 𐑋𐐨 𐐼𐐭 𐑄𐐰𐐻 𐑇𐐰𐑊 𐐷 𐐫𐑊𐑅𐐬 𐐼𐐭; 𐑁𐐫𐑉 𐑄𐐰𐐻 𐐸𐐶𐐮𐐽 𐐷 𐐸𐐰𐑂 𐑅𐐨𐑌 𐑋𐐨 𐐼𐐭, 𐐨𐑂𐐲𐑌 𐑄𐐰𐐻 𐑇𐐰𐑊 𐐷 𐐼𐐭; 𐑄𐐯𐑉𐑁𐐬𐑉 𐐮𐑁 𐐷 𐐼𐐭 𐑄𐐨𐑆 𐑃𐐮𐑍𐑆, 𐐺𐑊𐐯𐑅𐐯𐐼 𐐪𐑉 𐐷, 𐑁𐐫𐑉 𐐷 𐑇𐐰𐑊 𐐺 𐑊𐐮𐑁𐐻𐐯𐐼 𐐲𐐹 𐐰𐐻 𐑄 𐑊𐐰𐑅𐐻 𐐼𐐩.

𐐕𐐈𐐑𐐓𐐊𐐡 XIII.

1. 𐐡𐐴𐐻 𐑄 𐑃𐐮𐑍𐑆 𐐸𐐶𐐮𐐽 𐐷 𐐸𐐰𐑂 𐑅𐐨𐑌 𐐰𐑌𐐼 𐐸𐐲𐑉𐐼, 𐑅𐐩𐑂 𐐮𐐻 𐐺 𐑄𐐬𐑆 𐐸𐐶𐐮𐐽 𐐪𐑉 𐑁𐐫𐑉𐐺𐐮𐐼𐐲𐑌; 𐑉𐐴𐐻 𐑄 𐐶𐐲𐑉𐐿𐑅 𐐲𐑂 𐑄𐐮𐑅 𐐹𐐨𐐹𐑊, 𐐸𐐶𐐮𐐽 𐑇𐐰𐑊 𐐺, 𐐨𐑂𐐲𐑌 𐐰𐑆 𐐸𐐰𐑃 𐐺𐐮𐑌 𐑉𐐮𐐻𐑌 𐐲𐑂 𐑄𐐰𐐻 𐐸𐐶𐐮𐐽 𐐸𐐰𐑃 𐐺𐐮𐑌; 𐑁𐐫𐑉 𐐺𐐨𐐸𐐬𐑊𐐼, 𐐵𐐻 𐐲𐑂 𐑄 𐐺𐐳𐐿𐑅 𐐸𐐶𐐮𐐽 𐐸𐐰𐑂 𐐺𐐮𐑌 𐑉𐐮𐐻𐑌, 𐐰𐑌𐐼 𐐸𐐶𐐮𐐽 𐑇𐐰𐑊 𐐺 𐑉𐐮𐐻𐑌, 𐑇𐐰𐑊 𐑄𐐮𐑅 𐐹𐐨𐐹𐑊 𐐺 𐐾𐐲𐐾𐐼, 𐑁𐐫𐑉 𐐺𐐴 𐑄𐐯𐑋 𐑇𐐰𐑊 𐑄𐐯𐑉 𐐶𐐲𐑉𐐿𐑅 𐐺 𐑌𐐬𐑌 𐐲𐑌𐐻𐐭 𐑋𐐯𐑌. 𐐈𐑌𐐼 𐐺𐐨𐐸𐐬𐑊𐐼, 𐐫𐑊 𐑃𐐮𐑍𐑆 𐐪𐑉 𐑉𐐮𐐻𐑌 𐐺𐐴 𐑄 𐐙𐐪𐑄𐐲𐑉; 𐑄𐐯𐑉𐑁𐐬𐑉 𐐵𐐻 𐐲𐑂 𐑄 𐐺𐐳𐐿𐑅 𐐸𐐶𐐮𐐽 𐑇𐐰𐑊 𐐺 𐑉𐐮𐐻𐑌 𐑇𐐰𐑊 𐑄 𐐶𐐲𐑉𐑊𐐼 𐐺 𐐾𐐲𐐾𐐼. 𐐈𐑌𐐼 𐑌𐐬 𐐷 𐑄𐐰𐐻 𐐷 𐑇𐐰𐑊 𐐺 𐐾𐐲𐐾𐐯𐑆 𐐲𐑂 𐑄𐐮𐑅 𐐹𐐨𐐹𐑊, 𐐰𐐿𐐫𐑉𐐼𐐮𐑍 𐐻𐐭 𐑄 𐐾𐐲𐐾𐑋𐐯𐑌𐐻 𐐸𐐶𐐮𐐽 𐐌 𐑇𐐰𐑊 𐑀𐐮𐑂 𐐲𐑌𐐻𐐭 𐐷𐐭, 𐐸𐐶𐐮𐐽 𐑇𐐰𐑊 𐐺 𐐾𐐲𐑅𐐻; 𐑄𐐯𐑉𐑁𐐬𐑉 𐐸𐐶𐐱𐐻 𐑋𐐰𐑌𐐲𐑉 𐐲𐑂 𐑋𐐯𐑌 𐐫𐐻 𐐷 𐐻𐐭 𐐺? 𐐚𐐯𐑉𐐮𐑊𐐨, 𐐌 𐑅𐐩 𐐲𐑌𐐻𐐭 𐐷𐐭, 𐐨𐑂𐐲𐑌 𐐰𐑆 𐐌 𐐰𐑋. 𐐈𐑌𐐼 𐑌𐐵 𐐌 𐑀𐐬 𐐲𐑌𐐻𐐭 𐑄 𐐙𐐪𐑄𐐲𐑉. 𐐈𐑌𐐼 𐑂𐐯𐑉𐐮𐑊𐐨 𐐌 𐑅𐐩 𐐲𐑌𐐻𐐭 𐐷𐐭, 𐐸𐐶𐐱𐐻𐑅𐐬𐐯𐑂𐐲𐑉 𐑃𐐮𐑍𐑆 𐐷 𐑇𐐰𐑊 𐐰𐑅𐐿 𐑄 𐐙𐐪𐑄𐐲𐑉 𐐮𐑌 𐑋𐐴 𐑌𐐩𐑋, 𐐮𐐻 𐑇𐐰𐑊 𐐺 𐑀𐐮𐑂𐑌 𐐲𐑌𐐻𐐭 𐐷𐐭; 𐑄𐐯𐑉𐑁𐐬𐑉 𐐰𐑅𐐿, 𐐰𐑌𐐼 𐐷 𐑇𐐰𐑊 𐑉𐐨𐑅𐐨𐑂; 𐑌𐐱𐐿, 𐐰𐑌𐐼 𐐮𐐻 𐑇𐐰𐑊 𐐺 𐐬𐐹𐐲𐑌𐐼 𐐲𐑌𐐻𐐭 𐐷𐐭; 𐑁𐐫𐑉 𐐸𐐨 𐑄𐐰𐐻 𐐰𐑅𐐿𐐯𐑃, 𐑉𐐨𐑅𐐨𐑂𐐯𐑃; 𐐰𐑌𐐼 𐐲𐑌𐐻𐐭 𐐸𐐮𐑋 𐑄𐐰𐐻 𐑌𐐱𐐿𐐯𐑃, 𐐮𐐻 𐑇𐐰𐑊 𐐺 𐐬𐐹𐐲𐑌𐐼. 𐐈𐑌𐐼 𐑌𐐵, 𐐺𐐨𐐸𐐬𐑊𐐼, 𐑋𐐴 𐐾𐐱𐐮 𐐮𐑆 𐑀𐑉𐐩𐐻, 𐐨𐑂𐐲𐑌 𐐲𐑌𐐻𐐭 𐑁𐐳𐑊𐑌𐐯𐑅, 𐐺𐐨𐐿𐐫𐑆 𐐲𐑂 𐐷𐐭, 𐐰𐑌𐐼 𐐫𐑊𐑅𐐬 𐑄𐐮𐑅 𐐾𐐯𐑌𐐲𐑉𐐩𐑇𐐲𐑌; 𐐷𐐩, 𐐰𐑌𐐼 𐐨𐑂𐐲𐑌 𐑄 𐐙𐐪𐑄𐐲𐑉 𐑉𐐨𐐾𐐱𐐮𐑅𐐯𐑃, 𐐰𐑌𐐼 𐐫𐑊𐑅𐐬 𐐫𐑊 𐑄 𐐸𐐬𐑊𐐨 𐐩𐑌𐐾𐐯𐑊𐑆, 𐐺𐐨𐐿𐐫𐑆 𐐲𐑂 𐐷𐐭 𐐰𐑌𐐼 𐑄𐐮𐑅 𐐾𐐯𐑌𐐲𐑉𐐩𐑇𐐲𐑌; 𐑁𐐫𐑉 𐑌𐐲𐑌 𐐲𐑂 𐑄𐐯𐑋 𐐪𐑉 𐑊𐐱𐑅𐐻. 𐐒𐐨𐐸𐐬𐑊𐐼, 𐐌 𐐶𐐳𐐼 𐑄𐐰𐐻 𐐷 𐑇𐐳𐐼 𐐲𐑌𐐼𐐲𐑉𐑅𐐻𐐰𐑌𐐼; 𐑁𐐫𐑉 𐐌 𐑋𐐨𐑌 𐑄𐐯𐑋 𐐸𐐭 𐐪𐑉 𐑌𐐵 𐐲𐑊𐐴𐑂 𐐲𐑂 𐑄𐐮𐑅 𐐾𐐯𐑌𐐲𐑉𐐩𐑇𐐲𐑌; 𐐰𐑌𐐼 𐑌𐐲𐑌 𐐲𐑂 𐑄𐐯𐑋 𐐪𐑉 𐑊𐐱𐑅𐐻; 𐐰𐑌𐐼 𐐮𐑌 𐑄𐐯𐑋 𐐌 𐐸𐐰𐑂 𐑁𐐳𐑊𐑌𐐯𐑅 𐐲𐑂 𐐾𐐱𐐮. 𐐒𐐲𐐻 𐐺𐐨𐐸𐐬𐑊𐐼, 𐐮𐐻 𐑅𐐱𐑉𐐬𐐯𐑃 𐑋𐐨 𐐺𐐨𐐿𐐫𐑆 𐐲𐑂 𐑄 𐑁𐐬𐑉𐑃 𐐾𐐯𐑌𐐲𐑉𐐩𐑇𐐲𐑌 𐑁𐑉𐐱𐑋 𐑄𐐮𐑅 𐐾𐐯𐑌𐐲𐑉𐐩𐑇𐐲𐑌, 𐑁𐐫𐑉 𐑄𐐩 𐐪𐑉 𐑊𐐯𐐼 𐐲𐐶𐐩 𐐿𐐰𐐹𐐻𐐮𐑂 𐐺𐐴 𐐸𐐮𐑋 𐐨𐑂𐐲𐑌 𐐰𐑆 𐐶𐐱𐑆 𐑄 𐑅𐐲𐑌 𐐲𐑂 𐐹𐐲𐑉𐐼𐐮𐑇𐐲𐑌; 𐑁𐐫𐑉 𐑄𐐩 𐐶𐐮𐑊 𐑅𐐯𐑊 𐑋𐐨 𐑁𐐫𐑉 𐑅𐐮𐑊𐑂𐐲𐑉, 𐐰𐑌𐐼 𐑁𐐫𐑉 𐑀𐐬𐑊𐐼, 𐐰𐑌𐐼 𐑁𐐫𐑉 𐑄𐐰𐐻 𐐸𐐶𐐮𐐽 𐑋𐐱𐑃 𐐼𐐲𐑃 𐐿𐐲𐑉𐐲𐐹𐐻 𐐰𐑌𐐼 𐐸𐐶𐐮𐐽 𐑃𐐨𐑂𐑆 𐐿𐐰𐑌 𐐺𐑉𐐩𐐿 𐑃𐑉𐐭 𐐰𐑌𐐼 𐑅𐐻𐐨𐑊. 𐐈𐑌𐐼 𐐮𐑌 𐑄𐐰𐐻 𐐼𐐩 𐐶𐐮𐑊 𐐌 𐑂𐐮𐑆𐐮𐐻 𐑄𐐯𐑋, 𐐨𐑂𐐲𐑌 𐐮𐑌 𐐻𐐲𐑉𐑌𐐮𐑍 𐑄𐐯𐑉 𐐶𐐲𐑉𐐿𐑅 𐐲𐐹𐐱𐑌 𐑄𐐯𐑉 𐐬𐑌 𐐸𐐯𐐼𐑆.

2. 𐐈𐑌𐐼 𐐮𐐻 𐐿𐐩𐑋 𐐻𐐭 𐐹𐐰𐑅 𐑄𐐰𐐻 𐐸𐐶𐐯𐑌 𐐖𐐨𐑆𐐲𐑅 𐐸𐐰𐐼 𐐯𐑌𐐼𐐯𐐼 𐑄𐐨𐑆 𐑅𐐩𐐮𐑍𐑆, 𐐸𐐨 𐑅𐐯𐐼 𐐲𐑌𐐻𐐭 𐐸𐐮𐑆 𐐼𐐮𐑅𐐴𐐹𐑊𐑆, 𐐇𐑌𐐻𐐲𐑉 𐐷 𐐮𐑌 𐐰𐐻 𐑄 𐑅𐐻𐑉𐐩𐐻 𐑀𐐩𐐻; 𐑁𐐫𐑉 𐑅𐐻𐑉𐐩𐐻 𐐮𐑆 𐑄 𐑀𐐩𐐻, 𐐰𐑌𐐼 𐑌𐐰𐑉𐐬 𐐮𐑆 𐑄 𐐶𐐩 𐑄𐐰𐐻 𐑊𐐨𐐼𐑆 𐐻𐐭 𐑊𐐴𐑁, 𐐰𐑌𐐼 𐑁𐐷𐐭 𐑄𐐯𐑉 𐐺 𐑄𐐰𐐻 𐑁𐐴𐑌𐐼 𐐮𐐻; 𐐺𐐲𐐻 𐐶𐐴𐐼 𐐮𐑆 𐑄 𐑀𐐩𐐻, 𐐰𐑌𐐼 𐐺𐑉𐐫𐐼 𐑄 𐐶𐐩 𐐸𐐶𐐮𐐽 𐑊𐐨𐐼𐑆 𐐻𐐭 𐐼𐐯𐑃, 𐐰𐑌𐐼 𐑋𐐯𐑌𐐨 𐑄𐐯𐑉 𐐺 𐑄𐐰𐐻 𐐻𐑉𐐰𐑂𐐯𐑊 𐑄𐐯𐑉𐐮𐑌, 𐐲𐑌𐐻𐐮𐑊 𐑄 𐑌𐐴𐐻 𐐿𐐲𐑋𐐯𐑃, 𐐸𐐶𐐯𐑉𐐮𐑌 𐑌𐐬 𐑋𐐰𐑌 𐐿𐐰𐑌 𐐶𐐲𐑉𐐿.

3. 𐐈𐑌𐐼 𐐮𐐻 𐐿𐐩𐑋 𐐻𐐭 𐐹𐐰𐑅 𐐸𐐶𐐯𐑌 𐐖𐐨𐑆𐐲𐑅 𐐸𐐰𐐼 𐑅𐐯𐐼 𐑄𐐨𐑆 𐐶𐐲𐑉𐐼𐑆, 𐐸𐐨 𐑅𐐹𐐩𐐿 𐐲𐑌𐐻𐐭 𐐸𐐮𐑆 𐐼𐐮𐑅𐐴𐐹𐑊𐑆, 𐐶𐐲𐑌 𐐺𐐴 𐐶𐐲𐑌, 𐑅𐐩𐐮𐑍 𐐲𐑌𐐻𐐭 𐑄𐐯𐑋, 𐐐𐐶𐐱𐐻 𐐮𐑆 𐐮𐐻 𐑄𐐰𐐻 𐐷 𐐼𐐨𐑆𐐴𐑉 𐐲𐑂 𐑋𐐨, 𐐰𐑁𐐻𐐲𐑉 𐑄𐐰𐐻 𐐌 𐐰𐑋 𐑀𐐱𐑌 𐐻𐐭 𐑄 𐐙𐐪𐑄𐐲𐑉? 𐐈𐑌𐐼 𐑄𐐩 𐐫𐑊 𐑅𐐹𐐩𐐿, 𐑅𐐩𐑂 𐐮𐐻 𐐶𐐲𐑉 𐑃𐑉𐐨, 𐑅𐐩𐐮𐑍, 𐐎𐐨 𐐼𐐨𐑆𐐴𐑉 𐑄𐐰𐐻 𐐰𐑁𐐻𐐲𐑉 𐐶𐐨 𐐸𐐰𐑂 𐑊𐐮𐑂𐐼 𐐲𐑌𐐻𐐭 𐑄 𐐩𐐾 𐐲𐑂 𐑋𐐰𐑌, 𐑄𐐰𐐻 𐐵𐑉 𐑋𐐮𐑌𐐮𐑅𐐻𐑉𐐨, 𐐸𐐶𐐯𐑉𐐮𐑌 𐑄𐐵 𐐸𐐰𐑅𐐻 𐐿𐐫𐑊𐐼 𐐲𐑅, 𐑋𐐩 𐐸𐐰𐑂 𐐰𐑌

𐐰𐑌𐐼, 𐑄𐐰𐐻 𐐶𐐨 𐑋𐐩 𐑅𐐹𐐨𐐼𐐮𐑊𐐮 𐐿𐐲𐑋 𐐲𐑌𐐻𐐭 𐑄𐐨, 𐐮𐑌 𐑄𐐴 𐐿𐐮𐑍𐐼𐐲𐑋. 𐐈𐑌𐐼 𐐸𐐨 𐑅𐐯𐐼 𐐲𐑌𐐻𐐭 𐑄𐐯𐑋, 𐐒𐑊𐐯𐑅𐐯𐐼 𐐪𐑉 𐐷, 𐐺𐐨𐐿𐐪𐑆 𐐷 𐐼𐐨𐑆𐐴𐑉𐐼 𐑄𐐮𐑅 𐑃𐐮𐑍 𐐱𐑂 𐑋𐐨; 𐑄𐐯𐑉𐑁𐐬𐑉 𐐰𐑁𐐻𐐲𐑉 𐑄𐐰𐐻 𐐷 𐐪𐑉 𐑅𐐯𐑂𐐲𐑌𐐻𐐨 𐐰𐑌𐐼 𐐻𐐭 𐐷𐐨𐑉𐑆 𐐬𐑊𐐼, 𐐷 𐑇𐐰𐑊 𐐿𐐲𐑋 𐐲𐑌𐐻𐐭 𐑋𐐨 𐐮𐑌 𐑋𐐴 𐐿𐐮𐑍𐐼𐐲𐑋, 𐐰𐑌𐐼 𐐶𐐮𐑄 𐑋𐐨 𐐷 𐑇𐐰𐑊 𐑁𐐴𐑌𐐼 𐑉𐐯𐑅𐐻. 𐐈𐑌𐐼 𐐸𐐶𐐯𐑌 𐐸𐐨 𐐸𐐰𐐼 𐑅𐐹𐐬𐐿𐐲𐑌 𐐲𐑌𐐻𐐭 𐑄𐐯𐑋, 𐐸𐐨 𐐻𐐲𐑉𐑌𐐼 𐐸𐐮𐑋𐑅𐐯𐑊𐑁 𐐲𐑌𐐻𐐭 𐑄 𐑃𐑉𐐨, 𐐰𐑌𐐼 𐑅𐐯𐐼 𐐲𐑌𐐻𐐭 𐑄𐐯𐑋, 𐐐𐐶𐐪𐐻 𐐶𐐮𐑊 𐐷 𐑄𐐰𐐻 𐐌 𐑇𐐳𐐼 𐐼𐐭 𐐲𐑌𐐻𐐭 𐐷𐐭, 𐐸𐐶𐐯𐑌 𐐌 𐐰𐑋 𐑀𐐱𐑌 𐐲𐑌𐐻𐐭 𐑄 𐐙𐐪𐑄𐐲𐑉? 𐐈𐑌𐐼 𐑄𐐩 𐑅𐐪𐑉𐐬𐐼 𐐮𐑌 𐑄𐐯𐑉 𐐸𐐪𐑉𐐻𐑅, 𐑁𐐫𐑉 𐑄𐐩 𐐼𐐲𐑉𐑅𐐻 𐑌𐐱𐐻 𐑅𐐹𐐨𐐿 𐐲𐑌𐐻𐐭 𐐸𐐮𐑋 𐑄 𐑃𐐮𐑍 𐐸𐐶𐐮𐐽 𐑄𐐩 𐐼𐐨𐑆𐐴𐑉𐐼. 𐐈𐑌𐐼 𐐸𐐨 𐑅𐐯𐐼 𐐲𐑌𐐻𐐭 𐑄𐐯𐑋, 𐐒𐐨𐐸𐐬𐑊𐐼, 𐐌 𐑌𐐬 𐐷𐐭𐑉 𐑃𐐫𐐻𐑅, 𐐰𐑌𐐼 𐐷 𐐸𐐰𐑂 𐐼𐐨𐑆𐐴𐑉𐐼 𐑄 𐑃𐐮𐑍 𐐸𐐶𐐮𐐽 𐐖𐐱𐑌, 𐑋𐐴 𐐺𐐨𐑊𐐲𐑂𐐯𐐼, 𐐸𐐭 𐐶𐐱𐑆 𐐶𐐮𐑄 𐑋𐐨 𐐮𐑌 𐑋𐐴 𐑋𐐮𐑌𐐮𐑅𐐻𐑉𐐨, 𐐺𐐨𐑁𐐬𐑉 𐑄𐐰𐐻 𐐌 𐐶𐐱𐑆 𐑊𐐮𐑁𐐻𐐯𐐼 𐐲𐐹 𐐺𐐴 𐑄 𐐖𐐭𐑆, 𐐼𐐨𐑆𐐴𐑉𐐼 𐐱𐑂 𐑋𐐨; 𐑄𐐯𐑉𐑁𐐬𐑉 𐑋𐐬𐑉 𐐺𐑊𐐯𐑅𐐯𐐼 𐐪𐑉 𐐷, 𐑁𐐫𐑉 𐐷 𐑇𐐰𐑊 𐑌𐐯𐑂𐐲𐑉 𐐻𐐩𐑅𐐻 𐐱𐑂 𐐼𐐯𐑃, 𐐺𐐲𐐻 𐐷 𐑇𐐰𐑊 𐑊𐐮𐑂 𐐻𐐭 𐐺𐐨𐐸𐐬𐑊𐐼 𐐫𐑊 𐑄 𐐼𐐭𐐮𐑍𐑆 𐐱𐑂 𐑄 𐐙𐐪𐑄𐐲𐑉, 𐐲𐑌𐐻𐐭 𐑄 𐐽𐐮𐑊𐐼𐑉𐐯𐑌 𐐱𐑂 𐑋𐐯𐑌, 𐐨𐑂𐐲𐑌 𐐲𐑌𐐻𐐮𐑊 𐐫𐑊 𐑃𐐮𐑍𐑆 𐑇𐐰𐑊 𐐺𐐨 𐑁𐐳𐑊𐑁𐐮𐑊𐐼 𐐰𐐿𐐫𐑉𐐼𐐮𐑍 𐐻𐐭 𐑄 𐐶𐐮𐑊 𐐱𐑂 𐑄 𐐙𐐪𐑄𐐲𐑉, 𐐸𐐶𐐯𐑌 𐐌 𐑇𐐰𐑊 𐐿𐐲𐑋 𐐮𐑌 𐑋𐐴 𐑀𐑊𐐬𐑉𐐨 𐐶𐐮𐑄 𐑄 𐐹𐐵𐐲𐑉𐑆 𐐱𐑂 𐐸𐐯𐑂𐐲𐑌; 𐐰𐑌𐐼 𐐷 𐑇𐐰𐑊 𐑌𐐯𐑂𐐲𐑉 𐐯𐑌𐐼𐐷𐐭𐑉 𐑄 𐐹𐐩𐑌𐑆 𐐱𐑂 𐐼𐐯𐑃; 𐐺𐐲𐐻 𐐸𐐶𐐯𐑌 𐐌 𐑇𐐰𐑊 𐐿𐐲𐑋 𐐮𐑌 𐑋𐐴 𐑀𐑊𐐬𐑉𐐨, 𐐷 𐑇𐐰𐑊 𐐺𐐨 𐐽𐐩𐑌𐐾𐐼 𐐮𐑌 𐑄 𐐻𐐶𐐮𐑍𐐿𐑊𐐮𐑍 𐐱𐑂 𐐰𐑌 𐐴, 𐑁𐑉𐐱𐑋 𐑋𐐫𐑉𐐻𐐰𐑊𐐮𐐻𐐨 𐐻𐐭 𐐮𐑋𐐫𐑉𐐻𐐰𐑊𐐮𐐻𐐨; 𐐰𐑌𐐼 𐑄𐐯𐑌 𐑇𐐰𐑊 𐐷 𐐺𐐨 𐐺𐑊𐐯𐑅𐐯𐐼 𐐮𐑌 𐑄 𐐿𐐮𐑍𐐼𐐲𐑋 𐐱𐑂 𐑋𐐴 𐐙𐐪𐑄𐐲𐑉. 𐐈𐑌𐐼 𐐰𐑀𐐯𐑌, 𐐷 𐑇𐐰𐑊 𐑌𐐱𐐻 𐐸𐐰𐑂 𐐹𐐩𐑌 𐐸𐐶𐐴𐑊 𐐷 𐑇𐐰𐑊 𐐼𐐶𐐯𐑊 𐐮𐑌 𐑄 𐑁𐑊𐐯𐑇, 𐑌𐐨𐑄𐐲𐑉 𐑅𐐱𐑉𐐬 𐑅𐐩𐑂 𐐮𐐻 𐐺𐐨 𐑁𐐫𐑉 𐑄 𐑅𐐮𐑌𐑆 𐐱𐑂 𐑄 𐐶𐐲𐑉𐑊𐐼; 𐐰𐑌𐐼 𐐫𐑊 𐑄𐐮𐑅 𐐶𐐮𐑊 𐐌 𐐼𐐭 𐐺𐐨𐐿𐐪𐑆 𐐱𐑂 𐑄 𐑃𐐮𐑍 𐐸𐐶𐐮𐐽 𐐷 𐐸𐐰𐑂 𐐼𐐨𐑆𐐴𐑉𐐼 𐐱𐑂 𐑋𐐨, 𐑁𐐫𐑉 𐐷 𐐸𐐰𐑂 𐐼𐐨𐑆𐐴𐑉𐐼 𐑄𐐰𐐻 𐐷 𐑋𐐴𐐻 𐐺𐑉𐐮𐑍 𐑄 𐑅𐐬𐑊𐑆 𐐱𐑂 𐑋𐐯𐑌 𐐲𐑌𐐻𐐭 𐑋𐐨, 𐐸𐐶𐐴𐑊 𐑄 𐐶𐐲𐑉𐑊𐐼 𐑇𐐰𐑊 𐑅𐐻𐐰𐑌𐐼: 𐐰𐑌𐐼 𐑁𐐫𐑉 𐑄𐐮𐑅 𐐿𐐫𐑆 𐐷 𐑇𐐰𐑊 𐐸𐐰𐑂 𐑁𐐳𐑊𐑌𐐯𐑅 𐐱𐑂 𐐾𐐱𐐮; 𐐰𐑌𐐼 𐐷 𐑇𐐰𐑊 𐑅𐐮𐐻 𐐼𐐵𐑌 𐐮𐑌 𐑄 𐐿𐐮𐑍𐐼𐐲𐑋 𐐱𐑂 𐑋𐐴 𐐙𐐪𐑄𐐲𐑉; 𐐷𐐩, 𐐷𐐭𐑉 𐐾𐐱𐐮 𐑇𐐰𐑊 𐐺𐐨 𐑁𐐳𐑊, 𐐨𐑂𐐲𐑌 𐐰𐑆 𐑄 𐐙𐐪𐑄𐐲𐑉 𐐸𐐰𐑃 𐑀𐐮𐑂𐐲𐑌 𐑋𐐨 𐑁𐐳𐑊𐑌𐐯𐑅 𐐱𐑂 𐐾𐐱𐐮; 𐐰𐑌𐐼 𐐷 𐑇𐐰𐑊 𐐺𐐨 𐐨𐑂𐐲𐑌 𐐰𐑆 𐐌 𐐰𐑋, 𐐰𐑌𐐼 𐐌 𐐰𐑋 𐐨𐑂𐐲𐑌 𐐰𐑆 𐑄 𐐙𐐪𐑄𐐲𐑉; 𐐰𐑌𐐼 𐑄 𐐙𐐪𐑄𐐲𐑉 𐐰𐑌𐐼 𐐌 𐐪𐑉 𐐶𐐲𐑌; 𐐰𐑌𐐼 𐑄 𐐐𐐬𐑊𐐨 𐐘𐐬𐑅𐐻 𐐺𐐯𐑉𐐯𐑃 𐑉𐐯𐐿𐐲𐑉𐐼 𐐱𐑂 𐑄 𐐙𐐪𐑄𐐲𐑉 𐐰𐑌𐐼 𐑋𐐨; 𐐰𐑌𐐼 𐑄 𐐙𐐪𐑄𐐲𐑉 𐑀𐐮𐑂𐐯𐑃 𐑄 𐐐𐐬𐑊𐐨 𐐘𐐬𐑅𐐻 𐐲𐑌𐐻𐐭 𐑄 𐐽𐐮𐑊𐐼𐑉𐐯𐑌 𐐱𐑂 𐑋𐐯𐑌, 𐐺𐐨𐐿𐐪𐑆 𐐱𐑂 𐑋𐐨.

4. 𐐈𐑌𐐼 𐐮𐐻 𐐿𐐩𐑋 𐐻𐐭 𐐹𐐰𐑅 𐑄𐐰𐐻 𐐸𐐶𐐯𐑌 𐐖𐐨𐑆𐐲𐑅 𐐸𐐰𐐼 𐑅𐐹𐐬𐐿𐐲𐑌 𐑄𐐨𐑆 𐐶𐐲𐑉𐐼𐑆, 𐐸𐐨 𐐻𐐲𐐽𐐻 𐐯𐑂𐐲𐑉𐐨 𐐶𐐲𐑌 𐐱𐑂 𐑄𐐯𐑋 𐐶𐐮𐑄 𐐸𐐮𐑆 𐑁𐐮𐑍𐑀𐐲𐑉, 𐑅𐐩𐑂 𐐮𐐻 𐐶𐐲𐑉 𐑄 𐑃𐑉𐐨 𐐸𐐭 𐐶𐐲𐑉 𐐻𐐭 𐐻𐐰𐑉𐐨, 𐐰𐑌𐐼 𐑄𐐯𐑌 𐐸𐐨 𐐼𐐨𐐹𐐪𐑉𐐻𐐯𐐼. 𐐈𐑌𐐼 𐐺𐐨𐐸𐐬𐑊𐐼, 𐑄 𐐸𐐯𐑂𐐲𐑌𐑆 𐐶𐐲𐑉 𐐬𐐹𐐲𐑌𐐼, 𐐰𐑌𐐼 𐑄𐐩 𐐶𐐲𐑉 𐐿𐐫𐐻 𐐲𐐹 𐐮𐑌𐐻𐐭 𐐸𐐯𐑂𐐲𐑌, 𐐰𐑌𐐼 𐑅𐐫 𐐰𐑌𐐼 𐐸𐐲𐑉𐐼 𐐲𐑌𐑅𐐹𐐨𐐿𐐲𐐺𐑊 𐑃𐐮𐑍𐑆; 𐐰𐑌𐐼 𐐮𐐻 𐐶𐐱𐑆 𐑁𐐫𐑉𐐺𐐮𐐼𐐲𐑌 𐑄𐐯𐑋 𐑄𐐰𐐻 𐑄𐐩 𐑇𐐳𐐼 𐐲𐐻𐐲𐑉; 𐑌𐐨𐑄𐐲𐑉 𐐶𐐱𐑆 𐐮𐐻 𐑀𐐮𐑂𐐲𐑌 𐐲𐑌𐐻𐐭 𐑄𐐯𐑋 𐐹𐐵𐐲𐑉 𐑄𐐰𐐻 𐑄𐐩 𐐿𐐳𐐼 𐐲𐐻𐐲𐑉 𐑄 𐑃𐐮𐑍𐑆 𐐸𐐶𐐮𐐽 𐑄𐐩 𐑅𐐫 𐐰𐑌𐐼 𐐸𐐲𐑉𐐼; 𐐰𐑌𐐼 𐐸𐐶𐐯𐑄𐐲𐑉 𐑄𐐩 𐐶𐐲𐑉 𐐮𐑌 𐑄 𐐺𐐱𐐼𐐨 𐐱𐑉 𐐵𐐻 𐐱𐑂 𐑄 𐐺𐐱𐐼𐐨, 𐑄𐐩 𐐿𐐳𐐼 𐑌𐐱𐐻 𐐻𐐯𐑊; 𐑁𐐫𐑉 𐐮𐐻 𐐼𐐮𐐼 𐑅𐐨𐑋 𐐲𐑌𐐻𐐭 𐑄𐐯𐑋 𐑊𐐴𐐿 𐐩 𐐻𐑉𐐰𐑌𐑅𐑁𐐮𐑀𐐷𐐭𐑉𐐩𐑇𐐲𐑌 𐐱𐑂 𐑄𐐯𐑋, 𐑄𐐰𐐻 𐑄𐐩 𐐶𐐲𐑉 𐐽𐐩𐑌𐐾𐐼 𐑁𐑉𐐱𐑋 𐑄𐐮𐑅 𐐺𐐱𐐼𐐨 𐐱𐑂 𐑁𐑊𐐯𐑇 𐐮𐑌𐐻𐐭 𐐰𐑌 𐐮𐑋𐐫𐑉𐐻𐐰𐑊 𐑅𐐻𐐩𐐻, 𐑄𐐰𐐻 𐑄𐐩 𐐿𐐳𐐼 𐐺𐐨𐐸𐐬𐑊𐐼 𐑄 𐑃𐐮𐑍𐑆 𐐱𐑂 𐐘𐐱𐐼. 𐐒𐐲𐐻 𐐮𐐻 𐐿𐐩𐑋 𐐻𐐭 𐐹𐐰𐑅 𐑄𐐰𐐻 𐑄𐐩 𐐼𐐮𐐼 𐐰𐑀𐐯𐑌 𐑋𐐮𐑌𐐮𐑅𐐻𐐲𐑉 𐐲𐐹𐐱𐑌 𐑄 𐑁𐐩𐑅 𐐱𐑂 𐑄 𐐲𐑉𐑃; 𐑌𐐯𐑂𐐲𐑉𐑄𐐯𐑊𐐯𐑅 𐑄𐐩 𐐼𐐮𐐼 𐑌𐐱𐐻 𐑋𐐮𐑌𐐮𐑅𐐻𐐲𐑉 𐐱𐑂 𐑄 𐑃𐐮𐑍𐑆 𐐸𐐶𐐮𐐽 𐑄𐐩 𐐸𐐰𐐼 𐐸𐐲𐑉𐐼 𐐰𐑌𐐼 𐑅𐐨𐑌, 𐐺𐐨𐐿𐐪𐑆 𐐱𐑂 𐑄 𐐿𐐱𐑋𐐰𐑌𐐼𐑋𐐯𐑌𐐻 𐐸𐐶𐐮𐐽 𐐶𐐱𐑆 𐑀𐐮𐑂𐐲𐑌 𐑄𐐯𐑋 𐐮𐑌 𐐸𐐯𐑂𐐲𐑌. 𐐈𐑌𐐼 𐑌𐐵, 𐐸𐐶𐐯𐑄𐐲𐑉 𐑄𐐩 𐐶𐐲𐑉 𐑋𐐫𐑉𐐻𐐰𐑊 𐐱𐑉 𐐮𐑋𐐫𐑉𐐻𐐰𐑊, 𐑁𐑉𐐱𐑋 𐑄 𐐼𐐩 𐐱𐑂 𐑄𐐯𐑉 𐐻𐑉𐐰𐑌𐑅𐑁𐐮𐑀𐐷𐐭𐑉𐐩𐑇𐐲𐑌, 𐐌 𐑌𐐬 𐑌𐐱𐐻; 𐐺𐐲𐐻 𐑄𐐮𐑅 𐑋𐐲𐐽 𐐌 𐑌𐐬, 𐐰𐐿𐐫𐑉𐐼𐐮𐑍 𐐻𐐭 𐑄 𐑉𐐯𐐿𐐲𐑉𐐼 𐐸𐐶𐐮𐐽 𐐸𐐰𐑃 𐐺𐐨𐑌 𐑀𐐮𐑂𐐲𐑌, 𐑄𐐩 𐐼𐐮𐐼 𐑀𐐬 𐑁𐐬𐑉𐑃 𐐲𐐹𐐱𐑌 𐑄 𐑁𐐩𐑅 𐐱𐑂 𐑄 𐑊𐐰𐑌𐐼, 𐐰𐑌𐐼 𐐼𐐮𐐼 𐑋𐐮𐑌𐐮𐑅𐐻𐐲𐑉 𐐲𐑌𐐻𐐭 𐐫𐑊 𐑄 𐐹𐐨𐐹𐑊, 𐐷𐐭𐑌𐐴𐐻𐐮𐑍 𐐰𐑆 𐑋𐐯𐑌𐐨 𐐻𐐭 𐑄 𐐽𐐲𐑉𐐽 𐐰𐑆 𐐶𐐳𐐼 𐐺𐐨𐑊𐐨𐑂 𐐮𐑌 𐑄𐐯𐑉 𐐹𐑉𐐨𐐽𐐮𐑍; 𐐺𐐰𐐹𐐻𐐴𐑆𐐮𐑍 𐑄𐐯𐑋; 𐐰𐑌𐐼 𐐰𐑆 𐑋𐐯𐑌𐐨 𐐰𐑆 𐐶𐐲𐑉 𐐺𐐰𐐹𐐻𐐴𐑆𐐼 𐐼𐐮𐐼 𐑉𐐨𐑅𐐨𐑂 𐑄 𐐐𐐬𐑊𐐨 𐐘𐐬𐑅𐐻; 𐐰𐑌𐐼 𐑄𐐩 𐐶𐐲𐑉 𐐿𐐪𐑅𐐻 𐐮𐑌𐐻𐐭 𐐹𐑉𐐮𐑆𐐲𐑌 𐐺𐐴 𐑄𐐯𐑋 𐐸𐐭 𐐼𐐮𐐼 𐑌𐐱𐐻 𐐺𐐨𐑊𐐱𐑍 𐐻𐐭 𐑄 𐐽𐐲𐑉𐐽. 𐐈𐑌𐐼 𐑄 𐐹𐑉𐐮𐑆𐐲𐑌𐑆 𐐿𐐳𐐼 𐑌𐐱𐐻 𐐸𐐬𐑊𐐼 𐑄𐐯𐑋, 𐑁𐐫𐑉 𐑄𐐩 𐐶𐐲𐑉 𐑉𐐯𐑌𐐻 𐐮𐑌 𐐻𐐶𐐩𐑌. 𐐈𐑌𐐼 𐑄𐐩 𐐶𐐲𐑉 𐐿𐐪𐑅𐐻 𐐼𐐵𐑌 𐐮𐑌𐐻𐐭 𐑄 𐐲𐑉𐑃; 𐐺𐐲𐐻 𐑄𐐩 𐐼𐐮𐐼 𐑅𐑋𐐴𐐻 𐑄 𐐲𐑉𐑃 𐐶𐐮𐑄 𐑄 𐐶𐐲𐑉𐐼 𐐱𐑂 𐐘𐐱𐐼, 𐐮𐑌𐑅𐐲𐑋𐐲𐐽 𐑄𐐰𐐻 𐐺𐐴 𐐸𐐮𐑆 𐐹𐐵𐐲𐑉 𐑄𐐩 𐐶𐐲𐑉 𐐼𐐮𐑊𐐮𐑂𐐲𐑉𐐼 𐐵𐐻 𐐱𐑂 𐑄 𐐼𐐯𐐹𐑃𐑅 𐐱𐑂 𐑄 𐐲𐑉𐑃; 𐐰𐑌𐐼 𐑄𐐯𐑉𐑁𐐬𐑉 𐑄𐐩 𐐿𐐳𐐼 𐑌𐐱𐐻 𐐼𐐮𐑀 𐐹𐐮𐐻𐑅 𐑅𐐲𐑁𐐮𐑇𐐲𐑌𐐻 𐐻𐐭 𐐸𐐬𐑊𐐼 𐑄𐐯𐑋. 𐐈𐑌𐐼 𐑃𐑉𐐴𐑅 𐑄𐐩

𐐶𐐯𐑉 𐐗𐐰𐑅𐐻 𐐮𐑌𐐻𐐭 𐐩 𐑁𐐲𐑉𐑌𐐲𐑅, 𐐰𐑌𐐼 𐑉𐐨𐑅𐐨𐑂𐐼 𐑌𐐬 𐐸𐐪𐑉𐑋. 𐐈𐑌𐐼 𐑃𐑉𐐴𐑅 𐑄𐐩 𐐶𐐯𐑉 𐐗𐐰𐑅𐐻 𐐮𐑌𐐻𐐭 𐐩 𐐼𐐯𐑌 𐐲𐑂 𐐶𐐴𐑊𐐼 𐐺𐐨𐑅𐐻𐑅; 𐐰𐑌𐐼 𐐺𐐨𐐸𐐬𐑊𐐼 𐑄𐐩 𐐼𐐮𐐼 𐐹𐑊𐐩 𐐶𐐮𐑄 𐑄 𐐺𐐨𐑅𐐻𐑅, 𐐰𐑆 𐐩 𐐽𐐴𐑊𐐼 𐐶𐐮𐑄 𐐩 𐑅𐐲𐐿𐑊𐐮𐑍 𐑊𐐰𐑋, 𐐰𐑌𐐼 𐑉𐐨𐑅𐐨𐑂𐐼 𐑌𐐬 𐐸𐐪𐑉𐑋. 𐐈𐑌𐐼 𐐮𐐻 𐐗𐐩𐑋 𐐻𐐭 𐐑𐐰𐑅 𐑄𐐰𐐻 𐑄𐐲𐑅 𐑄𐐩 𐐼𐐮𐐼 𐑀𐐬 𐑁𐐫𐑉𐑃 𐐰𐑋𐐲𐑍 𐐫𐑊 𐑄 𐐹𐐨𐐹𐑊 𐐲𐑂 𐐤𐐨𐑁𐐴, 𐐰𐑌𐐼 𐐼𐐮𐐼 𐐹𐑉𐐨𐐽 𐑄 𐐘𐐱𐑅𐐹𐐯𐑊 𐐲𐑂 𐐗𐑉𐐴𐑅𐐻 𐐲𐑌𐐻𐐭 𐐫𐑊 𐐹𐐨𐐹𐑊 𐐲𐐹𐐱𐑌 𐑄 𐑁𐐩𐑅 𐐲𐑂 𐑄 𐑊𐐰𐑌𐐼; 𐐰𐑌𐐼 𐑄𐐩 𐐶𐐯𐑉 𐐿𐐱𐑌𐑂𐐲𐑉𐐻𐐯𐐼 𐐲𐑌𐐻𐐭 𐑄 𐐢𐐫𐑉𐐼, 𐐰𐑌𐐼 𐐶𐐯𐑉 𐐷𐐭𐑌𐐴𐐻𐐯𐐼 𐐲𐑌𐐻𐐭 𐑄 𐐕𐐲𐑉𐐽 𐐲𐑂 𐐗𐑉𐐴𐑅𐐻, 𐐰𐑌𐐼 𐑄𐐲𐑅 𐑄 𐐹𐐨𐐹𐑊 𐐲𐑂 𐑄𐐰𐐻 𐐖𐐯𐑌𐐲𐑉𐐩𐑇𐐲𐑌 𐐶𐐯𐑉 𐐺𐑊𐐯𐑅𐐻, 𐐰𐐿𐐫𐑉𐐼𐐮𐑍 𐐻𐐭 𐑄 𐐶𐐲𐑉𐐼 𐐲𐑂 𐐖𐐨𐑆𐐲𐑅. 𐐈𐑌𐐼 𐑌𐐵 𐐌, 𐐣𐐫𐑉𐑋𐐲𐑌, 𐑋𐐩𐐿 𐐰𐑌 𐐯𐑌𐐼 𐐲𐑂 𐑅𐐹𐐨𐐿𐐮𐑍 𐐿𐐱𐑌𐑅𐐲𐑉𐑌𐐮𐑍 𐑄𐐨𐑆 𐑃𐐮𐑍𐑆 𐑁𐐫𐑉 𐐩 𐐻𐐴𐑋. 𐐒𐐨𐐸𐐬𐑊𐐼, 𐐌 𐐶𐐱𐑆 𐐰𐐺𐐵𐐻 𐐻𐐭 𐑉𐐴𐐻 𐑄 𐑌𐐩𐑋𐑆 𐐲𐑂 𐑄𐐬𐑆 𐐸𐐭 𐐶𐐯𐑉 𐑌𐐯𐑂𐐲𐑉 𐐻𐐭 𐐻𐐩𐑅𐐻 𐐲𐑂 𐐼𐐯𐑃; 𐐺𐐲𐐻 𐑄 𐐢𐐫𐑉𐐼 𐑁𐐫𐑉𐐺𐐰𐐼, 𐑄𐐯𐑉𐑁𐐫𐑉 𐐌 𐑉𐐴𐐻 𐑄𐐯𐑋 𐑌𐐱𐐻, 𐑁𐐫𐑉 𐑄𐐩 𐐪𐑉 𐐸𐐮𐐼 𐑁𐑉𐐲𐑋 𐑄 𐐶𐐲𐑉𐑊𐐼. 𐐒𐐲𐐻 𐐺𐐨𐐸𐐬𐑊𐐼 𐐌 𐐸𐐰𐑂 𐑅𐐨𐑌 𐑄𐐯𐑋, 𐐰𐑌𐐼 𐑄𐐩 𐐸𐐰𐑂 𐑋𐐮𐑌𐐮𐑅𐐻𐐲𐑉𐐼 𐐲𐑌𐐻𐐭 𐑋𐐨; 𐐰𐑌𐐼 𐐺𐐨𐐸𐐬𐑊𐐼 𐑄𐐩 𐐶𐐮𐑊 𐐺𐐨 𐐰𐑋𐐲𐑍 𐑄 𐐖𐐯𐑌𐐻𐐴𐑊𐑆, 𐐰𐑌𐐼 𐑄 𐐖𐐯𐑌𐐻𐐴𐑊𐑆 𐑇𐐰𐑊 𐑌𐐬 𐑄𐐯𐑋 𐑌𐐱𐐻. 𐐜𐐩 𐐶𐐮𐑊 𐐫𐑊𐑅𐐬 𐐺𐐨 𐐰𐑋𐐲𐑍 𐑄 𐐖𐐭𐑆, 𐐰𐑌𐐼 𐑄 𐐖𐐭𐑆 𐑇𐐰𐑊 𐑌𐐬 𐑄𐐯𐑋 𐑌𐐱𐐻.

5. 𐐈𐑌𐐼 𐐮𐐻 𐑇𐐰𐑊 𐐗𐐲𐑋 𐐻𐐭 𐐑𐐰𐑅, 𐐸𐐶𐐯𐑌 𐑄 𐐢𐐫𐑉𐐼 𐑅𐐨𐐯𐑃 𐑁𐐮𐐻 𐐮𐑌 𐐸𐐮𐑆 𐐶𐐮𐑆𐐼𐐲𐑋, 𐑄𐐰𐐻 𐑄𐐩 𐑇𐐰𐑊 𐑋𐐮𐑌𐐮𐑅𐐻𐐲𐑉 𐐲𐑌𐐻𐐭 𐐫𐑊 𐑄 𐑅𐐿𐐰𐐻𐐲𐑉𐐯𐐼 𐐻𐑉𐐴𐐺𐑆 𐐲𐑂 𐐆𐑆𐑉𐐩𐐲𐑊, 𐐰𐑌𐐼 𐐲𐑌𐐻𐐭 𐐫𐑊 𐑌𐐩𐑇𐐲𐑌𐑆, 𐐿𐐮𐑌𐑛𐑉𐐯𐐼𐑆, 𐐻𐐲𐑍𐑆, 𐐰𐑌𐐼 𐐹𐐨𐐹𐑊, 𐐰𐑌𐐼 𐑇𐐰𐑊 𐐺𐑉𐐮𐑍 𐐵𐐻 𐐲𐑂 𐑄𐐯𐑋 𐐲𐑌𐐻𐐭 𐐖𐐨𐑆𐐲𐑅 𐑋𐐯𐑌𐐨 𐑅𐐬𐑊𐑆, 𐑄𐐰𐐻 𐑄𐐯𐑉 𐐼𐐨𐑆𐐴𐑉 𐑋𐐩 𐐺𐐨 𐑁𐐳𐑊𐑁𐐮𐑊𐐼, 𐐰𐑌𐐼 𐐫𐑊𐑅𐐬 𐐺𐐨𐐿𐐫𐑆 𐐲𐑂 𐑄 𐐿𐐱𐑌𐑂𐐮𐑌𐑅𐐮𐑍 𐐹𐐵𐐲𐑉 𐐲𐑂 𐐘𐐱𐐼 𐐸𐐶𐐮𐐽 𐐮𐑆 𐐮𐑌 𐑄𐐯𐑋; 𐐰𐑌𐐼 𐑄𐐩 𐐪𐑉 𐐰𐑆 𐑄 𐐩𐑌𐐾𐐯𐑊𐑆 𐐲𐑂 𐐘𐐱𐐼, 𐐰𐑌𐐼 𐐮𐑁 𐑄𐐩 𐑇𐐰𐑊 𐐹𐑉𐐩 𐐲𐑌𐐻𐐭 𐑄 𐐙𐐪𐑄𐐲𐑉 𐐮𐑌 𐑄 𐑌𐐩𐑋 𐐲𐑂 𐐖𐐨𐑆𐐲𐑅, 𐑄𐐩 𐐿𐐰𐑌 𐑇𐐬 𐑄𐐯𐑋𐑅𐐯𐑊𐑂𐑆 𐐲𐑌𐐻𐐭 𐐸𐐶𐐱𐐻𐑅𐐬𐐯𐑂𐐲𐑉 𐑋𐐰𐑌 𐐮𐐻 𐑅𐐨𐑋𐐯𐑃 𐑄𐐯𐑋 𐑀𐐳𐐼; 𐑄𐐯𐑉𐑁𐐫𐑉 𐑀𐑉𐐩𐐻 𐐰𐑌𐐼 𐑋𐐪𐑉𐑂𐐯𐑊𐐲𐑅 𐐶𐐲𐑉𐐿𐑅 𐑇𐐰𐑊 𐐺𐐨 𐑉𐐫𐐻 𐐺𐐴 𐑄𐐯𐑋, 𐐺𐐨𐑁𐐫𐑉 𐑄 𐑀𐑉𐐩𐐻 𐐰𐑌𐐼 𐐿𐐲𐑋𐐮𐑍 𐐼𐐩, 𐐸𐐶𐐯𐑌 𐐫𐑊 𐐹𐐨𐐹𐑊 𐑋𐐲𐑅𐐻 𐑇𐐳𐑉𐑊𐐨 𐑅𐐻𐐰𐑌𐐼 𐐺𐐨𐑁𐐫𐑉 𐑄 𐐾𐐲𐐾𐑋𐐯𐑌𐐻 𐑅𐐨𐐻 𐐲𐑂 𐐗𐑉𐐴𐑅𐐻; 𐐷𐐩, 𐐨𐑂𐐯𐑌 𐐰𐑋𐐲𐑍 𐑄 𐐖𐐯𐑌𐐻𐐴𐑊𐑆 𐑇𐐰𐑊 𐑄𐐯𐑉 𐐺𐐨 𐐩 𐑀𐑉𐐩𐐻 𐐰𐑌𐐼 𐑋𐐪𐑉𐑂𐐯𐑊𐐲𐑅 𐐶𐐲𐑉𐐿 𐑉𐐫𐐻 𐐺𐐴 𐑄𐐯𐑋, 𐐺𐐨𐑁𐐫𐑉 𐑄𐐰𐐻 𐐾𐐲𐐾𐑋𐐯𐑌𐐻 𐐼𐐩. 𐐈𐑌𐐼 𐐮𐑁 𐐷𐐨 𐐸𐐰𐐼 𐐫𐑊 𐑄 𐑅𐐿𐑉𐐮𐐹𐐽𐐲𐑉𐑆 𐐸𐐶𐐮𐐽 𐑀𐐮𐑂 𐐰𐑌 𐐰𐐿𐐵𐑌𐐻 𐐲𐑂 𐐫𐑊 𐑄 𐑋𐐪𐑉𐑂𐐯𐑊𐐲𐑅 𐐶𐐲𐑉𐐿𐑅 𐐲𐑂 𐐗𐑉𐐴𐑅𐐻, 𐐷𐐨 𐐶𐐳𐐼, 𐐰𐐿𐐫𐑉𐐼𐐮𐑍 𐐻𐐭 𐑄 𐐶𐐲𐑉𐐼𐑆 𐐲𐑂 𐐗𐑉𐐴𐑅𐐻, 𐑌𐐬 𐑄𐐰𐐻 𐑄𐐨𐑆 𐑃𐐮𐑍𐑆 𐑋𐐲𐑅𐐻 𐑇𐐳𐑉𐑊𐐨 𐐿𐐲𐑋. 𐐈𐑌𐐼 𐐶𐐬 𐐺𐐨 𐐲𐑌𐐻𐐭 𐐸𐐮𐑋 𐑄𐐰𐐻 𐐶𐐮𐑊 𐑌𐐱𐐻 𐐸𐐪𐑉𐐿𐐲𐑌 𐐲𐑌𐐻𐐭 𐑄 𐐶𐐲𐑉𐐼𐑆 𐐲𐑂 𐐖𐐨𐑆𐐲𐑅, 𐐰𐑌𐐼 𐐫𐑊𐑅𐐬 𐐻𐐭 𐑄𐐯𐑋 𐐸𐐭𐑋 𐐸𐐨 𐐸𐐰𐑃 𐐽𐐬𐑆𐐲𐑌 𐐰𐑌𐐼 𐑅𐐯𐑌𐐻 𐐰𐑋𐐲𐑍 𐑄𐐯𐑋; 𐑁𐐫𐑉 𐐸𐐭𐑅𐐬 𐑉𐐨𐑅𐐨𐑂𐐯𐑃 𐑌𐐱𐐻 𐑄 𐐶𐐲𐑉𐐼𐑆 𐐲𐑂 𐐖𐐨𐑆𐐲𐑅, 𐐰𐑌𐐼 𐑄 𐐶𐐲𐑉𐐼𐑆 𐐲𐑂 𐑄𐐬𐑆 𐐸𐐭𐑋 𐐸𐐨 𐐸𐐰𐑃 𐑅𐐯𐑌𐐻, 𐑉𐐨𐑅𐐨𐑂𐐯𐑃 𐑌𐐱𐐻 𐐸𐐮𐑋; 𐐰𐑌𐐼 𐑄𐐯𐑉𐑁𐐫𐑉 𐐸𐐨 𐐶𐐮𐑊 𐑌𐐱𐐻 𐑉𐐨𐑅𐐨𐑂 𐑄𐐯𐑋 𐐰𐐻 𐑄 𐑊𐐰𐑅𐐻 𐐼𐐩; 𐐰𐑌𐐼 𐐮𐐻 𐐶𐐳𐐼 𐐺𐐨 𐐺𐐯𐐻𐐲𐑉 𐑁𐐫𐑉 𐑄𐐯𐑋 𐐮𐑁 𐑄𐐩 𐐸𐐰𐐼 𐑌𐐱𐐻 𐐺𐐨𐑌 𐐺𐐫𐑉𐑌. 𐐙𐐫𐑉 𐐼𐐭 𐐷𐐨 𐑅𐐲𐐹𐐬𐑆 𐑄𐐰𐐻 𐐷𐐨 𐐿𐐰𐑌 𐑀𐐯𐐻 𐑉𐐮𐐼 𐐲𐑂 𐑄 𐐾𐐲𐑅𐐻𐐮𐑅 𐐲𐑂 𐐰𐑌 𐐱𐑁𐐯𐑌𐐼𐐯𐐼 𐐘𐐱𐐼, 𐐸𐐭 𐐸𐐰𐑃 𐐺𐐨𐑌 𐐻𐑉𐐰𐑋𐐹𐑊𐐼 𐐲𐑌𐐼𐐲𐑉 𐑁𐐨𐐻 𐐲𐑂 𐑋𐐯𐑌, 𐑄𐐰𐐻 𐑄𐐯𐑉𐐺𐐴 𐑅𐐰𐑊𐑂𐐩𐑇𐐲𐑌 𐑋𐐴𐐻 𐐿𐐲𐑋?

6. 𐐈𐑌𐐼 𐑌𐐵 𐐺𐐨𐐸𐐬𐑊𐐼, 𐐰𐑆 𐐌 𐑅𐐹𐐩𐐿 𐐿𐐱𐑌𐑅𐐲𐑉𐑌𐐮𐑍 𐑄𐐬𐑆 𐐸𐐭𐑋 𐑄 𐐢𐐫𐑉𐐼 𐐸𐐰𐑃 𐐽𐐬𐑆𐐲𐑌, 𐐷𐐩, 𐐨𐑂𐐯𐑌 𐑃𐑉𐐨 𐐸𐐭 𐐶𐐯𐑉 𐐿𐐫𐐻 𐐲𐐹 𐐮𐑌𐐻𐐭 𐑄 𐐸𐐯𐑂𐐲𐑌𐑆, 𐑄𐐰𐐻 𐐌 𐑌𐐭 𐑌𐐱𐐻 𐐸𐐶𐐯𐑄𐐲𐑉 𐑄𐐩 𐐶𐐯𐑉 𐐿𐑊𐐯𐑌𐑆𐐼 𐑁𐑉𐐱𐑋 𐑋𐐫𐑉𐐻𐐰𐑊𐐮𐐻𐐨 𐐻𐐭 𐐮𐑋𐐫𐑉𐐻𐐰𐑊𐐮𐐻𐐨. 𐐒𐐲𐐻 𐐺𐐨𐐸𐐬𐑊𐐼, 𐑅𐐮𐑌𐑅 𐐌 𐑉𐐬𐐻, 𐐌 𐐸𐐰𐑂 𐐮𐑌𐐿𐐶𐐴𐑉𐐼 𐐲𐑂 𐑄 𐐢𐐫𐑉𐐼, 𐐰𐑌𐐼 𐐸𐐨 𐐸𐐰𐑃 𐑋𐐩𐐼 𐐮𐐻 𐑋𐐰𐑌𐐮𐑁𐐯𐑅𐐻 𐐲𐑌𐐻𐐭 𐑋𐐨, 𐑄𐐰𐐻 𐑄𐐯𐑉 𐑋𐐲𐑅𐐻 𐑌𐐨𐐼𐑆 𐐺𐐨 𐐩 𐐽𐐩𐑌𐐾 𐑉𐐫𐐻 𐐲𐐹𐐱𐑌 𐑄𐐯𐑉 𐐺𐐱𐐼𐐨𐑆, 𐐫𐑉 𐐯𐑊𐑅 𐐮𐐻 𐑌𐐨𐐼𐑆 𐐺𐐨 𐑄𐐰𐐻 𐑄𐐩 𐑋𐐲𐑅𐐻 𐐻𐐩𐑅𐐻 𐐲𐑂 𐐼𐐯𐑃; 𐑄𐐯𐑉𐑁𐐫𐑉 𐑄𐐰𐐻 𐑄𐐩 𐑋𐐴𐐻 𐑌𐐱𐐻 𐐻𐐩𐑅𐐻 𐐲𐑂 𐐼𐐯𐑃, 𐑄𐐯𐑉 𐐶𐐱𐑆 𐐩 𐐽𐐩𐑌𐐾 𐑉𐐫𐐻 𐐲𐐹𐐱𐑌 𐑄𐐯𐑉 𐐺𐐱𐐼𐐨𐑆, 𐑄𐐰𐐻 𐑄𐐩 𐑋𐐴𐐻 𐑌𐐱𐐻 𐑅𐐲𐑁𐐲𐑉 𐐹𐐩𐑌 𐑌𐐫𐑉 𐑅𐐱𐑉𐐬, 𐑅𐐩𐑂 𐐮𐐻 𐐶𐐯𐑉 𐑁𐐫𐑉 𐑄 𐑅𐐮𐑌𐑆 𐐲𐑂 𐑄 𐐶𐐲𐑉𐑊𐐼. 𐐤𐐵 𐑄𐐮𐑅 𐐽𐐩𐑌𐐾 𐐶𐐱𐑆 𐑌𐐱𐐻 𐐨𐐿𐐶𐐲𐑊 𐐻𐐭 𐑄𐐰𐐻 𐐸𐐶𐐮𐐽 𐑇𐐰𐑊 𐐻𐐩𐐿 𐐹𐑊𐐩𐑅 𐐰𐐻 𐑄 𐑊𐐰𐑅𐐻 𐐼𐐩; 𐐺𐐲𐐻 𐑄𐐯𐑉 𐐶𐐱𐑆 𐐩 𐐽𐐩𐑌𐐾 𐑉𐐫𐐻 𐐲𐐹𐐱𐑌 𐑄𐐯𐑋, 𐐮𐑌𐑅𐐲𐑋𐐲𐐽 𐑄𐐰𐐻 𐐝𐐩𐐻𐐲𐑌 𐐿𐐳𐐼 𐐸𐐰𐑂 𐑌𐐬 𐐹𐐵𐐲𐑉 𐐬𐑂𐐲𐑉 𐑄𐐯𐑋, 𐑄𐐰𐐻 𐐸𐐨 𐐿𐐳𐐼 𐑌𐐱𐐻 𐐻𐐯𐑋𐐹𐐻 𐑄𐐯𐑋; 𐐰𐑌𐐼 𐑄𐐩 𐐶𐐯𐑉 𐑅𐐰𐑍𐐿𐐻𐐮𐑁𐐴𐐼 𐐮𐑌 𐑄 𐑁𐑊𐐯𐑇, 𐑄𐐰𐐻 𐑄𐐩 𐐶𐐯𐑉 𐐸𐐬𐑊𐐨, 𐐰𐑌𐐼 𐑄𐐰𐐻 𐑄 𐐹𐐵𐐲𐑉𐑆 𐐲𐑂 𐑄 𐐲𐑉𐑃 𐐿𐐳𐐼 𐑌𐐱𐐻 𐐸𐐬𐑊𐐼 𐑄𐐯𐑋; 𐐰𐑌𐐼 𐐮𐑌 𐑄𐐮𐑅 𐑅𐐻𐐩𐐻 𐑄𐐩 𐐶𐐯𐑉 𐐻𐐭 𐑉𐐨𐑋𐐩𐑌 𐐲𐑌𐐻𐐮𐑊 𐑄 𐐾𐐲𐐾𐑋𐐯𐑌𐐻 𐐼𐐩 𐐲𐑂 𐐗𐑉𐐴𐑅𐐻;

𐐰𐑌𐐼 𐐰𐐻 𐑄𐐰𐐻 𐐼𐐩 𐑄𐐩 𐐶𐐯𐑉 𐐻𐐭 𐑉𐐨𐑅𐐨𐑂 𐐩 𐑀𐑉𐐩𐐻𐐲𐑉 𐐽𐐩𐑌𐑈, 𐐰𐑌𐐼 𐐻𐐭 𐐺𐐨 𐑉𐐨𐑅𐐨𐑂𐐼 𐐮𐑌𐐻𐐭 𐑄 𐐿𐐮𐑍𐐼𐐲𐑋 𐐱𐑂 𐑄 𐐙𐐪𐑄𐐲𐑉 𐐻𐐭 𐑀𐐬 𐑌𐐬 𐑋𐐬𐑉 𐐵𐐻, 𐐺𐐲𐐻 𐐻𐐭 𐐼𐐶𐐯𐑊 𐐶𐐮𐑄 𐐘𐐱𐐼 𐐨𐐻𐐲𐑉𐑌𐐲𐑊𐐨 𐐮𐑌 𐑄 𐐸𐐯𐑂𐐲𐑌𐑆.

𐐰𐑌𐐼 𐑌𐐵 𐐺𐐨𐐸𐐬𐑊𐐼, 𐐌 𐑅𐐩 𐐲𐑌𐐻𐐭 𐐷𐐭, 𐑄𐐰𐐻 𐐸𐐶𐐯𐑌 𐑄 𐐢𐐫𐑉𐐼 𐑇𐐰𐑊 𐑅𐐨 𐑁𐐮𐐻, 𐐮𐑌 𐐸𐐮𐑆 𐐶𐐮𐑆𐐼𐐲𐑋, 𐑄𐐰𐐻 𐑄𐐨𐑆 𐑅𐐩𐐮𐑍𐑆 𐑇𐐰𐑊 𐐿𐐲𐑋 𐐲𐑌𐐻𐐭 𐑄 𐐖𐐯𐑌𐐻𐐴𐑊𐑆, 𐐰𐐿𐐫𐑉𐐼𐐮𐑍 𐐻𐐭 𐐸𐐮𐑆 𐐶𐐲𐑉𐐼, 𐑄𐐯𐑌 𐐷𐐨 𐑋𐐩 𐑌𐐬 𐑄𐐰𐐻 𐑄 𐐿𐐲𐑂𐐲𐑌𐐰𐑌𐐻 𐐸𐐶𐐮𐐽 𐑄 𐐙𐐪𐑄𐐲𐑉 𐐸𐐰𐑃 𐑋𐐩𐐼 𐐶𐐮𐑄 𐑄 𐐽𐐮𐑊𐐼𐑉𐐯𐑌 𐐱𐑂 𐐀𐑆𐑉𐐩𐐯𐑊, 𐐿𐐱𐑌𐑅𐐲𐑉𐑌𐐮𐑍 𐑄𐐩𐑉 𐑉𐐯𐑅𐐻𐐬𐑉𐐩𐑇𐐲𐑌 𐐻𐐭 𐑄 𐑊𐐰𐑌𐐼𐑆 𐐱𐑂 𐑄𐐩𐑉 𐐮𐑌𐐸𐐯𐑉𐐮𐐻𐐲𐑌𐑅, 𐐮𐑆 𐐫𐑊𐑉𐐯𐐼𐐨 𐐺𐐨𐑀𐐮𐑌𐐮𐑍 𐐻𐐭 𐐺𐐨 𐑁𐐳𐑊𐑁𐐮𐑊𐐼; 𐐰𐑌𐐼 𐐷𐐨 𐑋𐐩 𐑌𐐬 𐑄𐐰𐐻 𐑄 𐐶𐐲𐑉𐐼𐑆 𐐱𐑂 𐑄 𐐢𐐫𐑉𐐼, 𐐸𐐶𐐮𐐽 𐐸𐐰𐑂 𐐺𐐨𐑌 𐑅𐐹𐐬𐐿𐐲𐑌 𐐺𐐴 𐑄 𐐸𐐬𐑊𐐨 𐐹𐑉𐐱𐑁𐐯𐐻𐑅, 𐑇𐐰𐑊 𐐫𐑊 𐐺𐐨 𐑁𐐳𐑊𐑁𐐮𐑊𐐼; 𐐰𐑌𐐼 𐐷𐐨 𐑌𐐨𐐼 𐑌𐐱𐐻 𐑅𐐩 𐑄𐐰𐐻 𐑄 𐐢𐐫𐑉𐐼 𐐼𐐨𐑊𐐩𐑆 𐐸𐐮𐑆 𐐿𐐲𐑋𐐮𐑍 𐐲𐑌𐐻𐐭 𐑄 𐐽𐐮𐑊𐐼𐑉𐐯𐑌 𐐱𐑂 𐐀𐑆𐑉𐐩𐐯𐑊; 𐐰𐑌𐐼 𐐷𐐨 𐑌𐐨𐐼 𐑌𐐱𐐻 𐐮𐑋𐐰𐐾𐐮𐑌 𐐮𐑌 𐐷𐐬𐑉 𐐸𐐪𐑉𐐻𐑅 𐑄𐐰𐐻 𐑄 𐐶𐐲𐑉𐐼𐑆 𐐸𐐶𐐮𐐽 𐐸𐐰𐑂 𐐺𐐨𐑌 𐑅𐐹𐐬𐐿𐐲𐑌 𐐪𐑉 𐑂𐐩𐑌, 𐑁𐐫𐑉 𐐺𐐨𐐸𐐬𐑊𐐼, 𐑄 𐐢𐐫𐑉𐐼 𐐶𐐮𐑊 𐑉𐐨𐑋𐐯𐑋𐐺𐐲𐑉 𐐸𐐮𐑆 𐐿𐐲𐑂𐐲𐑌𐐰𐑌𐐻 𐐸𐐶𐐮𐐽 𐐸𐐨 𐐸𐐰𐑃 𐑋𐐩𐐼 𐐲𐑌𐐻𐐭 𐐸𐐮𐑆 𐐹𐐨𐐹𐐲𐑊 𐐱𐑂 𐑄 𐐸𐐵𐑅 𐐱𐑂 𐐀𐑆𐑉𐐩𐐯𐑊. 𐐰𐑌𐐼 𐐸𐐶𐐯𐑌 𐐷𐐨 𐑇𐐰𐑊 𐑅𐐨 𐑄𐐨𐑆 𐑅𐐩𐐮𐑍𐑆 𐐿𐐲𐑋𐐮𐑍 𐑁𐐫𐑉𐑃 𐐲𐑋𐐲𐑍 𐐷𐐭, 𐑄𐐯𐑌 𐐷𐐨 𐑌𐐨𐐼 𐑌𐐱𐐻 𐐯𐑌𐐨 𐑊𐐱𐑍𐑀𐐲𐑉 𐑅𐐹𐐲𐑉𐑌 𐐰𐐻 𐑄 𐐼𐐭𐐮𐑍𐑆 𐐱𐑂 𐑄 𐐢𐐫𐑉𐐼, 𐑁𐐫𐑉 𐑄 𐑅𐐬𐑉𐐼 𐐱𐑂 𐐸𐐮𐑆 𐐾𐐲𐑅𐐻𐐮𐑅 𐐮𐑆 𐐮𐑌 𐐸𐐮𐑆 𐑉𐐴𐐻 𐐸𐐰𐑌𐐼, 𐐰𐑌𐐼 𐐺𐐨𐐸𐐬𐑊𐐼 𐐰𐐻 𐑄𐐰𐐻 𐐼𐐩, 𐐮𐑁 𐐷𐐨 𐑇𐐰𐑊 𐑅𐐹𐐲𐑉𐑌 𐐰𐐻 𐐸𐐮𐑆 𐐼𐐭𐐮𐑍𐑆, 𐐸𐐨 𐐶𐐮𐑊 𐐿𐐫𐑆 𐑄𐐰𐐻 𐐮𐐻 𐑇𐐰𐑊 𐑅𐐭𐑌 𐐬𐑂𐐲𐑉𐐻𐐩𐐿 𐐷𐐭. 𐐎𐐬 𐐲𐑌𐐻𐐭 𐐸𐐮𐑋 𐑄𐐰𐐻 𐑅𐐹𐐲𐑉𐑌𐐯𐑃 𐐰𐐻 𐑄 𐐼𐐭𐐮𐑍𐑆 𐐱𐑂 𐑄 𐐢𐐫𐑉𐐼; 𐐷𐐩, 𐐶𐐬 𐐲𐑌𐐻𐐭 𐐸𐐮𐑋 𐑄𐐰𐐻 𐑇𐐰𐑊 𐐼𐐨𐑌𐐴 𐑄 𐐗𐑉𐐴𐑅𐐻 𐐰𐑌𐐼 𐐸𐐮𐑆 𐐶𐐲𐑉𐐿𐑅; 𐐷𐐩, 𐐶𐐬 𐐲𐑌𐐻𐐭 𐐸𐐮𐑋 𐑄𐐰𐐻 𐑇𐐰𐑊 𐐼𐐨𐑌𐐴 𐑄 𐑉𐐯𐑂𐐯𐑊𐐩𐑇𐐲𐑌𐑆 𐐱𐑂 𐑄 𐐢𐐫𐑉𐐼, 𐐰𐑌𐐼 𐑄𐐰𐐻 𐑇𐐰𐑊 𐑅𐐩 𐑄 𐐢𐐫𐑉𐐼 𐑌𐐬 𐑊𐐱𐑍𐑀𐐲𐑉 𐐶𐐲𐑉𐐿𐐯𐑃 𐐺𐐴 𐑉𐐯𐑂𐐯𐑊𐐩𐑇𐐲𐑌, 𐐫𐑉 𐐺𐐴 𐐹𐑉𐐱𐑁𐐯𐑅𐐨, 𐐫𐑉 𐐺𐐴 𐑀𐐮𐑁𐐻𐑅, 𐐫𐑉 𐐺𐐴 𐐻𐐲𐑍𐑆, 𐐫𐑉 𐐺𐐴 𐐸𐐨𐑊𐐮𐑍𐑆, 𐐫𐑉 𐐺𐐴 𐑄 𐐹𐐵𐐲𐑉 𐐱𐑂 𐑄 𐐐𐐬𐑊𐐨 𐐘𐐬𐑅𐐻; 𐐷𐐩, 𐐰𐑌𐐼 𐐶𐐬 𐐲𐑌𐐻𐐭 𐐸𐐮𐑋 𐑄𐐰𐐻 𐑇𐐰𐑊 𐑅𐐩 𐐰𐐻 𐑄𐐰𐐻 𐐼𐐩, 𐐻𐐭 𐑀𐐯𐐻 𐑀𐐩𐑌, 𐑄𐐰𐐻 𐑄𐐩𐑉 𐐿𐐰𐑌 𐐺𐐨 𐑌𐐬 𐑋𐐮𐑉𐐲𐐿𐐲𐑊 𐑉𐐫𐐻 𐐺𐐴 𐐖𐐨𐑆𐐲𐑅 𐐗𐑉𐐴𐑅𐐻, 𐑁𐐫𐑉 𐐸𐐨 𐑄𐐰𐐻 𐐼𐐭𐐯𐑃 𐑄𐐮𐑅 𐑇𐐰𐑊 𐐺𐐨𐐿𐐲𐑋 𐑊𐐴𐐿 𐐲𐑌𐐻𐐭 𐑄 𐑅𐐲𐑌 𐐱𐑂 𐐹𐐲𐑉𐐼𐐮𐑇𐐲𐑌, 𐑁𐐫𐑉 𐐸𐐭𐑋 𐑄𐐩𐑉 𐐶𐐱𐑆 𐑌𐐬 𐑋𐐲𐑉𐑅𐐨, 𐐰𐐿𐐫𐑉𐐼𐐮𐑍 𐐻𐐭 𐑄 𐐶𐐲𐑉𐐼 𐐱𐑂 𐐗𐑉𐐴𐑅𐐻. 𐐏𐐩, 𐐰𐑌𐐼 𐐷𐐨 𐑌𐐨𐐼 𐑌𐐱𐐻 𐐯𐑌𐐨 𐑊𐐱𐑍𐑀𐐲𐑉 𐐸𐐮𐑅, 𐑌𐐫𐑉 𐑅𐐹𐐲𐑉𐑌, 𐑌𐐫𐑉 𐑋𐐩𐐿 𐑀𐐩𐑋 𐐱𐑂 𐑄 𐐖𐐭𐑆, 𐑌𐐫𐑉 𐐯𐑌𐐨 𐐱𐑂 𐑄 𐑉𐐯𐑋𐑌𐐲𐑌𐐻 𐐱𐑂 𐑄 𐐸𐐵𐑅 𐐱𐑂 𐐀𐑆𐑉𐐩𐐯𐑊, 𐑁𐐫𐑉 𐐺𐐨𐐸𐐬𐑊𐐼 𐑄 𐐢𐐫𐑉𐐼 𐑉𐐨𐑋𐐯𐑋𐐺𐐲𐑉𐐯𐑃 𐐸𐐮𐑆 𐐿𐐲𐑂𐐲𐑌𐐰𐑌𐐻 𐐲𐑌𐐻𐐭 𐑄𐐯𐑋, 𐐰𐑌𐐼 𐐸𐐨 𐐶𐐮𐑊 𐐼𐐭 𐐲𐑌𐐻𐐭 𐑄𐐯𐑋 𐐰𐐿𐐫𐑉𐐼𐐮𐑍 𐐻𐐭 𐑄𐐰𐐻 𐐸𐐶𐐮𐐽 𐐸𐐨 𐐸𐐰𐑃 𐑅𐐶𐐬𐑉𐑌; 𐑄𐐩𐑉𐑁𐐫𐑉 𐐷𐐨 𐑌𐐨𐐼 𐑌𐐱𐐻 𐑅𐐲𐐹𐐬𐑆 𐑄𐐰𐐻 𐐷𐐨 𐐿𐐰𐑌 𐐻𐐲𐑉𐑌 𐑄 𐑉𐐴𐐻 𐐸𐐰𐑌𐐼 𐐱𐑂 𐑄 𐐢𐐫𐑉𐐼 𐐲𐑌𐐻𐐭 𐑄 𐑊𐐯𐑁𐐻, 𐑄𐐰𐐻 𐐸𐐨 𐑋𐐩 𐑌𐐱𐐻 𐐯𐐿𐑅𐐯𐐿𐐷𐐭𐐻 𐐾𐐲𐐾𐑋𐐯𐑌𐐻 𐐲𐑌𐐻𐐭 𐑄 𐑁𐐳𐑊𐑁𐐮𐑊𐐮𐑍 𐐱𐑂 𐑄 𐐿𐐲𐑂𐐲𐑌𐐰𐑌𐐻 𐐸𐐶𐐮𐐽 𐐸𐐨 𐐸𐐰𐑃 𐑋𐐩𐐼 𐐲𐑌𐐻𐐭 𐑄 𐐸𐐵𐑅 𐐱𐑂 𐐀𐑆𐑉𐐩𐐯𐑊.

𐐕𐐰𐐹𐐻𐐲𐑉 XIV.

1. 𐐐𐐪𐑉𐐿𐐲𐑌, 𐐄 𐐷𐐨 𐐖𐐯𐑌𐐻𐐴𐑊𐑆, 𐐰𐑌𐐼 𐐸𐐨𐑉 𐑄 𐐶𐐲𐑉𐐼𐑆 𐐱𐑂 𐐖𐐨𐑆𐐲𐑅 𐐗𐑉𐐴𐑅𐐻, 𐑄 𐐝𐐲𐑌 𐐱𐑂 𐑄 𐑊𐐮𐑂𐐮𐑍 𐐘𐐱𐐼, 𐐸𐐶𐐮𐐽 𐐸𐐨 𐐸𐐰𐑃 𐐿𐐲𐑋𐐰𐑌𐐼𐐯𐐼 𐑋𐐨 𐑄𐐰𐐻 𐐌 𐑇𐐳𐐼 𐑅𐐹𐐨𐐿 𐐿𐐱𐑌𐑅𐐲𐑉𐑌𐐮𐑍 𐐷𐐭, 𐑁𐐫𐑉 𐐺𐐨𐐸𐐬𐑊𐐼 𐐸𐐨 𐐿𐐲𐑋𐐰𐑌𐐼𐐯𐑃 𐑋𐐨 𐑄𐐰𐐻 𐐌 𐑇𐐳𐐼 𐑉𐐴𐐻, 𐑅𐐩𐐮𐑍, 𐐓𐐲𐑉𐑌, 𐐫𐑊 𐐷𐐨 𐐖𐐯𐑌𐐻𐐴𐑊𐑆, 𐑁𐑉𐐱𐑋 𐐷𐐬𐑉 𐐶𐐮𐐿𐐯𐐼 𐐶𐐩𐑆, 𐐰𐑌𐐼 𐑉𐐨𐐹𐐯𐑌𐐻 𐐱𐑂 𐐷𐐬𐑉 𐐨𐑂𐐲𐑊 𐐼𐐭𐐮𐑍𐑆, 𐐱𐑂 𐐷𐐬𐑉 𐑊𐐴𐐮𐑍𐑆 𐐰𐑌𐐼 𐐼𐐨𐑅𐐨𐑂𐐮𐑍𐑆, 𐐰𐑌𐐼 𐐱𐑂 𐐷𐐬𐑉 𐐸𐐬𐑉𐐼𐐲𐑋𐑆, 𐐰𐑌𐐼 𐐱𐑂 𐐷𐐬𐑉 𐑅𐐨𐐿𐑉𐐯𐐻 𐐲𐐺𐐱𐑋𐐮𐑌𐐩𐑇𐐲𐑌𐑆, 𐐰𐑌𐐼 𐐷𐐬𐑉 𐐴𐐼𐐱𐑊𐐲𐐻𐑉𐐨𐑆, 𐐰𐑌𐐼 𐐱𐑂 𐐷𐐬𐑉 𐑋𐐲𐑉𐐼𐐲𐑉𐑆, 𐐰𐑌𐐼 𐐷𐐬𐑉 𐐹𐑉𐐨𐑅𐐻𐐿𐑉𐐰𐑁𐐻𐑅, 𐐰𐑌𐐼 𐐷𐐬𐑉 𐐯𐑌𐑂𐐨𐐮𐑍𐑆, 𐐰𐑌𐐼 𐐷𐐬𐑉 𐑅𐐻𐑉𐐴𐑁𐑅, 𐐰𐑌𐐼 𐑁𐑉𐐱𐑋 𐐫𐑊 𐐷𐐬𐑉 𐐶𐐮𐐿𐐯𐐼𐑌𐐯𐑅 𐐰𐑌𐐼 𐐲𐐺𐐱𐑋𐐮𐑌𐐩𐑇𐐲𐑌𐑆, 𐐰𐑌𐐼 𐐿𐐲𐑋 𐐲𐑌𐐻𐐭 𐑋𐐨, 𐐰𐑌𐐼 𐐺𐐨 𐐺𐐰𐐹𐐻𐐴𐑆𐐼 𐐮𐑌 𐑋𐐴 𐑌𐐩𐑋, 𐑄𐐰𐐻 𐐷𐐨 𐑋𐐩 𐑉𐐨𐑅𐐨𐑂 𐐩 𐑉𐐨𐑋𐐮𐑇𐐲𐑌 𐐱𐑂 𐐷𐐬𐑉 𐑅𐐮𐑌𐑆, 𐐰𐑌𐐼 𐐺𐐨 𐑁𐐮𐑊𐐼 𐐶𐐮𐑄 𐑄 𐐐𐐬𐑊𐐨 𐐘𐐬𐑅𐐻, 𐑄𐐰𐐻 𐐷𐐨 𐑋𐐩 𐐺𐐨 𐑌𐐲𐑋𐐺𐐲𐑉𐐼 𐐶𐐮𐑄 𐑋𐐴 𐐹𐐨𐐹𐐲𐑊, 𐐸𐐭 𐐪𐑉 𐐱𐑂 𐑄 𐐸𐐵𐑅 𐐱𐑂 𐐀𐑆𐑉𐐩𐐯𐑊.

𐑄 𐐺𐐳𐐿 𐐱𐑂 𐑌𐐨𐑁𐐴,

𐐸𐐭 𐐮𐑆 𐑄 𐑅𐐲𐑌 𐐱𐑂 𐑌𐐨𐑁𐐴, 𐐶𐐲𐑌 𐐱𐑂 𐑄 𐐼𐐮𐑅𐐴𐐹𐑊𐑆 𐐱𐑂 𐐾𐐨𐑆𐐲𐑅 𐐿𐑉𐐴𐑅𐐻.

𐐽𐐰𐐹𐐻𐐲𐑉 I.

𐐰𐑌 𐐰𐐿𐐵𐑌𐐻 𐐱𐑂 𐑄 𐐹𐐨𐐹𐑊 𐐱𐑂 𐑌𐐨𐑁𐐴, 𐐰𐐿𐐫𐑉𐐼𐐮𐑍 𐐻𐐭 𐐸𐐮𐑆 𐑉𐐯𐐿𐐲𐑉𐐼.

1. 𐐰𐑌𐐼 𐐮𐐻 𐐿𐐩𐑋 𐐻𐐭 𐐹𐐰𐑅 𐑄𐐰𐐻 𐑄 𐑃𐐲𐑉𐐻𐐨 𐐰𐑌𐐼 𐑁𐐬𐑉𐑃 𐐷𐐨𐑉 𐐹𐐰𐑅𐐻 𐐲𐐶𐐩, 𐐰𐑌𐐼 𐐫𐑊𐑅𐐬 𐑄 𐑃𐐲𐑉𐐻𐐨
𐐰𐑌𐐼 𐑁𐐮𐑁𐑃, 𐐰𐑌𐐼 𐐺𐐨𐐸𐐬𐑊𐐼 𐑄 𐐼𐐮𐑅𐐴𐐹𐑊𐑆 𐐱𐑂 𐐾𐐨𐑆𐐲𐑅 𐐸𐐰𐐼 𐑁𐐫𐑉𐑋𐐼 𐐩 𐐽𐐲𐑉𐐽 𐐱𐑂 𐐿𐑉𐐴𐑅𐐻 𐐮𐑌 𐐫𐑊 𐑄
𐑊𐐰𐑌𐐼𐑆 𐑉𐐵𐑌𐐼 𐐲𐐺𐐵𐐻. 𐐰𐑌𐐼 𐐰𐑆 𐑋𐐯𐑌𐐨 𐐰𐑆 𐐼𐐮𐐼 𐐿𐐲𐑋 𐐲𐑌𐐻𐐭 𐑄𐐯𐑋, 𐐰𐑌𐐼 𐐼𐐮𐐼 𐐻𐑉𐐭𐑊𐐨 𐑉𐐨𐐹𐐯𐑌𐐻 𐐱𐑂
𐑄𐐩𐑉 𐑅𐐮𐑌𐑆, 𐐶𐐲𐑉 𐐺𐐰𐐹𐐻𐐴𐑆𐐼 𐐮𐑌 𐑄 𐑌𐐩𐑋 𐐱𐑂 𐐾𐐨𐑆𐐲𐑅; 𐐰𐑌𐐼 𐑄𐐩 𐐼𐐮𐐼 𐐫𐑊𐑅𐐬 𐑉𐐨𐑅𐐨𐑂 𐑄 𐐸𐐬𐑊𐐨
𐑀𐐬𐑅𐐻.

2. 𐐰𐑌𐐼 𐐮𐐻 𐐿𐐩𐑋 𐐻𐐭 𐐹𐐰𐑅 𐐮𐑌 𐑄 𐑃𐐲𐑉𐐻𐐨 𐐰𐑌𐐼 𐑅𐐮𐐿𐑅𐑃 𐐷𐐨𐑉 𐑄 𐐹𐐨𐐹𐑊 𐐶𐐲𐑉 𐐫𐑊 𐐿𐐱𐑌𐑂𐐲𐑉𐐻𐐯𐐼
𐐲𐑌𐐻𐐭 𐑄 𐑊𐐫𐑉𐐼, 𐐲𐐹𐐱𐑌 𐐫𐑊 𐑄 𐑁𐐩𐑅 𐐱𐑂 𐑄 𐑊𐐰𐑌𐐼, 𐐺𐐬𐑃 𐑌𐐨𐑁𐐴𐐻𐑅 𐐰𐑌𐐼 𐑊𐐰𐑋𐐲𐑌𐐴𐐻𐑅, 𐐰𐑌𐐼 𐑄𐐩𐑉 𐐶𐐲𐑉
𐑌𐐬 𐐿𐐱𐑌𐐻𐐯𐑌𐑇𐐲𐑌𐑆 𐐰𐑌𐐼 𐐼𐐮𐑅𐐹𐐷𐐭𐐻𐐩𐑇𐐲𐑌𐑆 𐐲𐑋𐐲𐑍 𐑄𐐯𐑋, 𐐰𐑌𐐼 𐐯𐑂𐐲𐑉𐐨 𐑋𐐰𐑌 𐐼𐐮𐐼 𐐼𐐨𐑊 𐐾𐐲𐑅𐐻𐑊𐐨 𐐶𐐲𐑌
𐐶𐐮𐑄 𐐰𐑌𐐲𐑄𐐲𐑉; 𐐰𐑌𐐼 𐑄𐐩 𐐸𐐰𐐼 𐐫𐑊 𐑃𐐮𐑍𐑆 𐐿𐐱𐑋𐐲𐑌 𐐲𐑋𐐲𐑍 𐑄𐐯𐑋, 𐑄𐐯𐑉𐑁𐐬𐑉 𐑄𐐩 𐐶𐐲𐑉 𐑌𐐱𐐻 𐑉𐐮𐐽 𐐰𐑌𐐼
𐐹𐐭𐑉, 𐐺𐐱𐑌𐐼 𐐰𐑌𐐼 𐑁𐑉𐐨, 𐐺𐐲𐐻 𐑄𐐩 𐐶𐐲𐑉 𐐫𐑊 𐑋𐐩𐐼 𐑁𐑉𐐨, 𐐰𐑌𐐼 𐐹𐐪𐑉𐐻𐐩𐐿𐐲𐑉𐑆 𐐱𐑂 𐑄 𐐸𐐯𐑂𐐲𐑌𐑊𐐨 𐑀𐐮𐑁𐐻.

3. 𐐰𐑌𐐼 𐐮𐐻 𐐿𐐩𐑋 𐐻𐐭 𐐹𐐰𐑅 𐑄𐐰𐐻 𐑄 𐑃𐐲𐑉𐐻𐐨 𐐰𐑌𐐼 𐑅𐐯𐑂𐐲𐑌𐑃 𐐷𐐨𐑉 𐐹𐐰𐑅𐐻 𐐲𐐶𐐩 𐐫𐑊𐑅𐐬, 𐐰𐑌𐐼 𐑄𐐩𐑉
𐑅𐐻𐐮𐑊 𐐿𐐲𐑌𐐻𐐮𐑌𐐷𐐭𐐼 𐐻𐐭 𐐺𐐨 𐐹𐐨𐑅 𐐮𐑌 𐑄 𐑊𐐰𐑌𐐼. 𐐰𐑌𐐼 𐑄𐐩𐑉 𐐶𐐲𐑉 𐑀𐑉𐐩𐐻 𐐰𐑌𐐼 𐑋𐐪𐑉𐑂𐐯𐑊𐐲𐑅 𐐶𐐲𐑉𐐿𐑅
𐑉𐐫𐐻 𐐺𐐴 𐑄 𐐼𐐮𐑅𐐴𐐹𐑊𐑆 𐐱𐑂 𐐾𐐨𐑆𐐲𐑅, 𐐮𐑌𐑅𐐬𐑋𐐲𐐽 𐑄𐐰𐐻 𐑄𐐩 𐐼𐐮𐐼 𐐸𐐨𐑊 𐑄 𐑅𐐮𐐿, 𐐰𐑌𐐼 𐑉𐐩𐑆 𐑄 𐐼𐐯𐐼, 𐐰𐑌𐐼
𐐿𐐫𐑆 𐑄 𐑊𐐩𐑋 𐐻𐐭 𐐶𐐫𐐿, 𐐰𐑌𐐼 𐑄 𐐺𐑊𐐴𐑌𐐼 𐐻𐐭 𐑉𐐨𐑅𐐨𐑂 𐑅𐐴𐐻, 𐐰𐑌𐐼 𐑄 𐐼𐐯𐑁 𐐻𐐭 𐐸𐐨𐑉; 𐐰𐑌𐐼 𐐫𐑊 𐑋𐐰𐑌𐐲𐑉
𐐱𐑂 𐑋𐐮𐑉𐐲𐐿𐑊𐑆 𐐼𐐮𐐼 𐑄𐐩 𐐶𐐲𐑉𐐿 𐐲𐑋𐐲𐑍 𐑄 𐐽𐐮𐑊𐐼𐑉𐐯𐑌 𐐱𐑂 𐑋𐐯𐑌; 𐐰𐑌𐐼 𐐮𐑌 𐑌𐐲𐑃𐐮𐑍 𐐼𐐮𐐼 𐑄𐐩 𐐶𐐲𐑉𐐿 𐑋𐐮𐑉𐐲𐐿𐑊𐑆 𐑅𐐩𐑂 𐐮𐐻 𐐶𐐲𐑉 𐐮𐑌 𐑄 𐑌𐐩𐑋 𐐱𐑂 𐐾𐐨𐑆𐐲𐑅. 𐐰𐑌𐐼 𐑄𐐲𐑅 𐐼𐐮𐐼 𐑄 𐑃𐐲𐑉𐐻𐐨 𐐰𐑌𐐼 𐐩𐐻𐑃 𐐷𐐨𐑉 𐐹𐐰𐑅
𐐲𐐶𐐩, 𐐰𐑌𐐼 𐐫𐑊𐑅𐐬 𐑄 𐑃𐐲𐑉𐐻𐐨 𐐰𐑌𐐼 𐑌𐐴𐑌𐑃, 𐐰𐑌𐐼 𐑁𐐫𐑉𐐻𐐨 𐐰𐑌𐐼 𐑁𐐲𐑉𐑅𐐻, 𐐰𐑌𐐼 𐑄 𐑁𐐫𐑉𐐻𐐨 𐐰𐑌𐐼 𐑅𐐯𐐿𐐲𐑌𐐼;
𐐷𐐩, 𐐨𐑂𐐲𐑌 𐐲𐑌𐐻𐐮𐑊 𐑁𐐫𐑉𐐻𐐨 𐐰𐑌𐐼 𐑌𐐴𐑌 𐐷𐐨𐑉𐑆 𐐸𐐰𐐼 𐐹𐐰𐑅𐐻 𐐲𐐶𐐩, 𐐰𐑌𐐼 𐐫𐑊𐑅𐐬 𐑄 𐑁𐐮𐑁𐐻𐐨 𐐰𐑌𐐼 𐑁𐐲𐑉𐑅𐐻,
𐐰𐑌𐐼 𐑄 𐑁𐐮𐑁𐐻𐐨 𐐰𐑌𐐼 𐑅𐐯𐐿𐐲𐑌𐐼; 𐐷𐐩, 𐐰𐑌𐐼 𐐨𐑂𐐲𐑌 𐐲𐑌𐐻𐐮𐑊 𐑁𐐮𐑁𐐻𐐨 𐐰𐑌𐐼 𐑌𐐴𐑌 𐐷𐐨𐑉𐑆 𐐸𐐰𐐼 𐐹𐐰𐑅𐐻 𐐲𐐶𐐩;
𐐰𐑌𐐼 𐑄 𐑊𐐫𐑉𐐼 𐐼𐐮𐐼 𐐹𐑉𐐱𐑅𐐹𐐲𐑉 𐑄𐐯𐑋 𐐯𐐿𐑅𐐨𐐼𐐮𐑍𐑊𐐨 𐐮𐑌 𐑄 𐑊𐐰𐑌𐐼; 𐐷𐐩, 𐐮𐑌𐑅𐐬𐑋𐐲𐐽 𐑄𐐰𐐻 𐑄𐐩 𐐼𐐮𐐼 𐐺𐐮𐑊𐐼
𐑅𐐮𐐻𐐨𐑆 𐐲𐑀𐐯𐑌 𐐸𐐶𐐩𐑉 𐑄𐐩𐑉 𐐸𐐰𐐼 𐐺𐐮𐑌 𐑅𐐮𐐻𐐨𐑆 𐐺𐐲𐑉𐑌𐐼; 𐐷𐐩, 𐐨𐑂𐐲𐑌 𐑄𐐰𐐻 𐑀𐑉𐐩𐐻 𐑅𐐮𐐻𐐨 𐑆𐐰𐑉𐐲𐐸𐐯𐑋𐑊𐐲 𐐼𐐮𐐼
𐑄𐐩 𐐿𐐫𐑆 𐐻𐐭 𐐺𐐨 𐐺𐐮𐑊𐐻 𐐲𐑀𐐯𐑌. 𐐺𐐲𐐻 𐑄𐐩𐑉 𐐶𐐲𐑉 𐑋𐐯𐑌𐐨 𐑅𐐮𐐻𐐨𐑆 𐐸𐐶𐐮𐐽 𐐸𐐰𐐼 𐐺𐐮𐑌 𐑅𐐲𐑍𐐿, 𐐰𐑌𐐼 𐐶𐐫𐐻𐐲𐑉𐑆 𐐿𐐩𐑋 𐐲𐐹 𐐮𐑌 𐑄 𐑅𐐻𐐯𐐼 𐑄𐐩𐑉𐐱𐑂; 𐑄𐐯𐑉𐑁𐐬𐑉 𐑄𐐨𐑆 𐑅𐐮𐐻𐐨𐑆 𐐿𐐳𐐼 𐑌𐐱𐐻 𐐺𐐨 𐑉𐐨𐑌𐐭𐐼.

4. 𐐰𐑌𐐼 𐑌𐐵 𐐺𐐨𐐸𐐬𐑊𐐼 𐐮𐐻 𐐿𐐩𐑋 𐐻𐐭 𐐹𐐰𐑅 𐑄𐐰𐐻 𐑄 𐐹𐐨𐐹𐑊 𐐱𐑂 𐑌𐐨𐑁𐐴 𐐼𐐮𐐼 𐐶𐐰𐐿𐑅 𐑅𐐻𐑉𐐱𐑍, 𐐰𐑌𐐼
𐐼𐐮𐐼 𐑋𐐲𐑊𐐻𐐮𐐹𐑊𐐴 𐐯𐐿𐑅𐐨𐐼𐐮𐑍𐑊𐐨 𐑁𐐰𐑅𐐻, 𐐰𐑌𐐼 𐐺𐐨𐐿𐐩𐑋 𐐰𐑌 𐐯𐐿𐑅𐐨𐐼𐐮𐑍𐑊𐐨 𐑁𐐩𐑉 𐐰𐑌𐐼 𐐼𐐨𐑊𐐴𐐻𐑅𐐲𐑋 𐐹𐐨𐐹𐑊.

𐐰𐑌𐐼 𐑄𐐩 𐐶𐐲𐑉 𐑋𐐰𐑉𐐮𐐼, 𐐰𐑌𐐼 𐑀𐐮𐑂𐐲𐑌 𐐮𐑌 𐑋𐐰𐑉𐐮𐐾, 𐐰𐑌𐐼 𐐶𐐲𐑉 𐐺𐑊𐐯𐑅𐐻, 𐐲𐐿𐐫𐑉𐐼𐐮𐑍 𐐻𐐭 𐑄 𐑋𐐲𐑊𐐻𐐮𐐻𐐭𐐼 𐐲𐑂 𐑄 𐐹𐑉𐐱𐑋𐐮𐑅𐐯𐑆 𐐸𐐶𐐮𐐽 𐑄 𐐢𐐫𐑉𐐼 𐐸𐐰𐐼 𐑋𐐩𐐼 𐐲𐑌𐐻𐐭 𐑄𐐯𐑋. 𐐈𐑌𐐼 𐑄𐐩 𐐼𐐮𐐼 𐑌𐐱𐐻 𐐶𐐫𐐿 𐐯𐑌𐐮 𐑋𐐬𐑉 𐐰𐑁𐐻𐐲𐑉 𐑄 𐐹𐐲𐑉𐑁𐐫𐑉𐑋𐐰𐑌𐑅𐐯𐑆 𐐰𐑌𐐼 𐐫𐑉𐐼𐐮𐑌𐐰𐑌𐑅𐐯𐑆 𐐲𐑂 𐑄 𐑊𐐫 𐐲𐑂 𐐣𐐬𐑆𐐯𐑆, 𐐺𐐲𐐻 𐑄𐐩 𐐼𐐮𐐼 𐐶𐐫𐐿 𐐰𐑁𐐻𐐲𐑉 𐑄 𐐿𐐱𐑋𐐰𐑌𐐼𐑋𐐯𐑌𐐻𐑅 𐐸𐐶𐐮𐐽 𐑄𐐩 𐐸𐐰𐐼 𐑉𐐨𐑅𐐨𐑂𐐼 𐑁𐑉𐐱𐑋 𐑄𐐩𐑉 𐐢𐐫𐑉𐐼 𐐰𐑌𐐼 𐑄𐐩𐑉 𐐘𐐱𐐼, 𐐿𐐱𐑌𐐻𐐮𐑌𐐷𐐭𐐮𐑍 𐐮𐑌 𐑁𐐰𐑅𐐻𐐮𐑍 𐐰𐑌𐐼 𐐹𐑉𐐩𐐲𐑉, 𐐰𐑌𐐼 𐐮𐑌 𐑋𐐨𐐻𐐮𐑍 𐐻𐐭𐑀𐐯𐑄𐐲𐑉 𐐱𐑁𐐻, 𐐺𐐬𐑃 𐐻𐐭 𐐹𐑉𐐩 𐐰𐑌𐐼 𐐻𐐭 𐐸𐐨𐑉 𐑄 𐐶𐐲𐑉𐐼 𐐲𐑂 𐑄 𐐢𐐫𐑉𐐼. 𐐈𐑌𐐼 𐐮𐐻 𐐿𐐩𐑋 𐐻𐐭 𐐹𐐰𐑅 𐑄𐐰𐐻 𐑄𐐩𐑉 𐐶𐐱𐑆 𐑌𐐬 𐐿𐐱𐑌𐐻𐐯𐑌𐑇𐐲𐑌 𐐲𐑋𐐲𐑍 𐐫𐑊 𐑄 𐐹𐐨𐐹𐑊, 𐐮𐑌 𐐫𐑊 𐑄 𐑊𐐰𐑌𐐼, 𐐺𐐲𐐻 𐑄𐐩𐑉 𐐶𐐲𐑉 𐑋𐐴𐐻𐐨 𐑋𐐮𐑉𐐲𐐿𐑊𐑆 𐑉𐐫𐐻 𐐲𐑋𐐲𐑍 𐑄 𐐼𐐮𐑅𐐴𐐹𐑊𐑆 𐐲𐑂 𐐖𐐨𐑆𐐲𐑅.

5. 𐐈𐑌𐐼 𐐮𐐻 𐐿𐐩𐑋 𐐻𐐭 𐐹𐐰𐑅 𐑄𐐰𐐻 𐑄 𐑅𐐯𐑂𐐲𐑌𐐻𐐨 𐐰𐑌𐐼 𐑁𐐲𐑉𐑅𐐻 𐐷𐐨𐑉 𐐹𐐰𐑅𐐻 𐐲𐐶𐐩, 𐐰𐑌𐐼 𐐫𐑊𐑅𐐬 𐑄 𐑅𐐯𐑂𐐲𐑌𐐻𐐨 𐐰𐑌𐐼 𐑅𐐯𐐿𐐲𐑌𐐼 𐐷𐐨𐑉; 𐐷𐐩, 𐐰𐑌𐐼 𐐮𐑌 𐑁𐐴𐑌, 𐐻𐐮𐑊 𐑄 𐑅𐐯𐑂𐐲𐑌𐐻𐐨 𐐰𐑌𐐼 𐑌𐐴𐑌𐑃 𐐷𐐨𐑉 𐐸𐐰𐐼 𐐹𐐰𐑅𐐻 𐐲𐐶𐐩; 𐐷𐐩, 𐐨𐑂𐐲𐑌 𐐰𐑌 𐐸𐐲𐑌𐐼𐑉𐐯𐐼 𐐷𐐨𐑉𐑆 𐐸𐐰𐐼 𐐹𐐰𐑅𐐻 𐐲𐐶𐐩, 𐐰𐑌𐐼 𐑄 𐐼𐐮𐑅𐐴𐐹𐑊𐑆 𐐲𐑂 𐐖𐐨𐑆𐐲𐑅, 𐐸𐐭𐑋 𐐸𐐨 𐐸𐐰𐐼 𐐽𐐬𐑆𐐲𐑌, 𐐸𐐰𐐼 𐐫𐑊 𐑀𐐱𐑌 𐐻𐐭 𐑄 𐐹𐐰𐑉𐐲𐐼𐐴𐑅 𐐲𐑂 𐐘𐐱𐐼, 𐑅𐐩𐑂 𐐮𐐻 𐐶𐐲𐑉 𐑄 𐑃𐑉𐐨 𐐸𐐭 𐑇𐐳𐐼 𐐻𐐰𐑉𐐮; 𐐰𐑌𐐼 𐑄𐐩𐑉 𐐶𐐲𐑉 𐐲𐑄𐐲𐑉 𐐼𐐮𐑅𐐴𐐹𐑊𐑆 𐐫𐑉𐐼𐐩𐑌𐐼 𐐮𐑌 𐑄𐐩𐑉 𐑅𐐻𐐯𐐼; 𐐰𐑌𐐼 𐐫𐑊𐑅𐐬 𐑋𐐯𐑌𐐮 𐐲𐑂 𐑄𐐰𐐻 𐐾𐐯𐑌𐐲𐑉𐐩𐑇𐐲𐑌 𐐸𐐰𐐼 𐐹𐐰𐑅𐐻 𐐲𐐶𐐩. 𐐈𐑌𐐼 𐐮𐐻 𐐿𐐩𐑋 𐐻𐐭 𐐹𐐰𐑅 𐑄𐐰𐐻 𐑄𐐩𐑉 𐐶𐐱𐑆 𐑌𐐬 𐐿𐐱𐑌𐐻𐐯𐑌𐑇𐐲𐑌 𐐮𐑌 𐑄 𐑊𐐰𐑌𐐼, 𐐺𐐨𐐿𐐫𐑆 𐐲𐑂 𐑄 𐑊𐐲𐑂 𐐲𐑂 𐐘𐐱𐐼 𐐸𐐶𐐮𐐽 𐐼𐐮𐐼 𐐼𐐶𐐯𐑊 𐐮𐑌 𐑄 𐐸𐐪𐑉𐐻𐑅 𐐲𐑂 𐑄 𐐹𐐨𐐹𐑊. 𐐈𐑌𐐼 𐑄𐐩𐑉 𐐶𐐲𐑉 𐑌𐐬 𐐯𐑌𐑂𐐨𐐮𐑍𐑆, 𐑌𐐫𐑉 𐑅𐐻𐑉𐐴𐑁𐑅, 𐑌𐐫𐑉 𐐻𐐭𐑋𐐲𐑊𐐻𐑅, 𐑌𐐫𐑉 𐐸𐐬𐑉𐐼𐐲𐑋𐑆, 𐑌𐐫𐑉 𐑊𐐴𐐮𐑍𐑆, 𐑌𐐫𐑉 𐑋𐐲𐑉𐐼𐐲𐑉𐑆, 𐑌𐐫𐑉 𐐯𐑌𐐮 𐑋𐐰𐑌𐐲𐑉 𐐲𐑂 𐑊𐐰𐑅𐐮𐑂𐐨𐐲𐑅𐑌𐐯𐑅; 𐐰𐑌𐐼 𐑇𐐭𐑉𐑊𐐨 𐑄𐐩𐑉 𐐿𐐳𐐼 𐑌𐐱𐐻 𐐺𐐨 𐐩 𐐸𐐰𐐹𐐨𐐲𐑉 𐐹𐐨𐐹𐑊 𐐲𐑋𐐲𐑍 𐐫𐑊 𐑄 𐐹𐐨𐐹𐑊 𐐸𐐭 𐐸𐐰𐐼 𐐺𐐮𐑌 𐐿𐑉𐐨𐐩𐐻𐐯𐐼 𐐺𐐴 𐑄 𐐸𐐰𐑌𐐼 𐐲𐑂 𐐘𐐱𐐼; 𐑄𐐩𐑉 𐐶𐐲𐑉 𐑌𐐬 𐑉𐐱𐐺𐐲𐑉𐑆, 𐑌𐐫𐑉 𐑋𐐲𐑉𐐼𐐲𐑉𐐲𐑉𐑆, 𐑌𐐨𐑄𐐲𐑉 𐐶𐐲𐑉 𐑄𐐩𐑉 𐐢𐐩𐑋𐐲𐑌𐐴𐐻𐑅, 𐑌𐐫𐑉 𐐯𐑌𐐮 𐑋𐐰𐑌𐐲𐑉 𐐲𐑂 𐐴𐐻𐑅; 𐐺𐐲𐐻 𐑄𐐩 𐐶𐐲𐑉 𐐮𐑌 𐐶𐐲𐑌, 𐑄 𐐽𐐮𐑊𐐼𐑉𐐯𐑌 𐐲𐑂 𐐗𐑉𐐴𐑅𐐻, 𐐰𐑌𐐼 𐐩𐑉𐑆 𐐻𐐭 𐑄 𐐿𐐮𐑍𐐼𐐲𐑋 𐐲𐑂 𐐘𐐱𐐼; 𐐰𐑌𐐼 𐐸𐐵 𐐺𐑊𐐯𐑅𐐯𐐼 𐐶𐐲𐑉 𐑄𐐩, 𐑁𐐫𐑉 𐑄 𐐢𐐫𐑉𐐼 𐐼𐐮𐐼 𐐺𐑊𐐯𐑅 𐑄𐐯𐑋 𐐮𐑌 𐐫𐑊 𐑄𐐩𐑉 𐐼𐐭𐐮𐑍𐑆; 𐐷𐐩, 𐐨𐑂𐐲𐑌 𐑄𐐩 𐐶𐐲𐑉 𐐺𐑊𐐯𐑅𐐻 𐐰𐑌𐐼 𐐹𐑉𐐱𐑅𐐹𐐲𐑉𐐼, 𐐲𐑌𐐻𐐮𐑊 𐐰𐑌 𐐸𐐲𐑌𐐼𐑉𐐯𐐼 𐐰𐑌𐐼 𐐻𐐯𐑌 𐐷𐐨𐑉𐑆 𐐸𐐰𐐼 𐐹𐐰𐑅𐐻 𐐲𐐶𐐩; 𐐰𐑌𐐼 𐑄 𐑁𐐲𐑉𐑅𐐻 𐐾𐐯𐑌𐐲𐑉𐐩𐑇𐐲𐑌 𐑁𐑉𐐱𐑋 𐐗𐑉𐐴𐑅𐐻 𐐸𐐰𐐼 𐐹𐐰𐑅𐐻 𐐲𐐶𐐩, 𐐰𐑌𐐼 𐑄𐐩𐑉 𐐶𐐱𐑆 𐑌𐐬 𐐿𐐱𐑌𐐻𐐯𐑌𐑇𐐲𐑌 𐐮𐑌 𐐫𐑊 𐑄 𐑊𐐰𐑌𐐼.

6. 𐐈𐑌𐐼 𐐮𐐻 𐐿𐐩𐑋 𐐻𐐭 𐐹𐐰𐑅 𐑄𐐰𐐻 𐐤𐐨𐑁𐐴, 𐐸𐐨 𐑄𐐰𐐻 𐐿𐐯𐐹𐐻 𐑄𐐮𐑅 𐑊𐐰𐑅𐐻 𐑉𐐯𐐿𐐲𐑉𐐼, (𐐰𐑌𐐼 𐐸𐐨 𐐿𐐯𐐹𐐻 𐐮𐐻 𐐲𐐹𐐱𐑌 𐑄 𐐹𐑊𐐩𐐻𐑅 𐐲𐑂 𐐤𐐨𐑁𐐴,) 𐐼𐐴𐐼, 𐐰𐑌𐐼 𐐸𐐮𐑆 𐑅𐐲𐑌 𐐁𐑋𐐲𐑅 𐐿𐐯𐐹𐐻 𐐮𐐻 𐐮𐑌 𐐸𐐮𐑆 𐑅𐐻𐐯𐐼; 𐐰𐑌𐐼 𐐸𐐨 𐐿𐐯𐐹𐐻 𐐮𐐻 𐐲𐐹𐐱𐑌 𐑄 𐐹𐑊𐐩𐐻𐑅 𐐲𐑂 𐐤𐐨𐑁𐐴 𐐫𐑊𐑅𐐬; 𐐰𐑌𐐼 𐐸𐐨 𐐿𐐯𐐹𐐻 𐐮𐐻 𐐩𐐻𐐨 𐐰𐑌𐐼 𐑁𐐬𐑉 𐐷𐐨𐑉𐑆, 𐐰𐑌𐐼 𐑄𐐩𐑉 𐐶𐐱𐑆 𐑅𐐻𐐮𐑊 𐐹𐐨𐑅 𐐮𐑌 𐑄 𐑊𐐰𐑌𐐼, 𐑅𐐩𐑂 𐐮𐐻 𐐶𐐲𐑉 𐐩 𐑅𐑋𐐫𐑊 𐐹𐐪𐑉𐐻 𐐲𐑂 𐑄 𐐹𐐨𐐹𐑊 𐐸𐐭 𐐸𐐰𐐼 𐑉𐐨𐑂𐐬𐑊𐐻𐐯𐐼 𐑁𐑉𐐱𐑋 𐑄 𐐽𐐲𐑉𐐽, 𐐰𐑌𐐼 𐐻𐐩𐐿𐐲𐑌 𐐲𐐹𐐱𐑌 𐑄𐐯𐑋 𐑄 𐑌𐐩𐑋 𐐲𐑂 𐐢𐐩𐑋𐐲𐑌𐐴𐐻𐑅; 𐑄𐐩𐑉𐑁𐐬𐑉 𐑄𐐩𐑉 𐐺𐐨𐑀𐐰𐑌 𐐻𐐭 𐐺𐐨 𐐢𐐩𐑋𐐲𐑌𐐴𐐻𐑅 𐐲𐑀𐐯𐑌 𐐮𐑌 𐑄 𐑊𐐰𐑌𐐼.

7. 𐐈𐑌𐐼 𐐮𐐻 𐐿𐐩𐑋 𐐻𐐭 𐐹𐐰𐑅 𐑄𐐰𐐻 𐐁𐑋𐐲𐑅 𐐼𐐴𐐼 𐐫𐑊𐑅𐐬, (𐐰𐑌𐐼 𐐮𐐻 𐐶𐐱𐑆 𐐰𐑌 𐐸𐐲𐑌𐐼𐑉𐐯𐐼 𐐰𐑌𐐼 𐑌𐐴𐑌𐐻𐐨 𐐰𐑌𐐼 𐑁𐐬𐑉 𐐷𐐨𐑉𐑆 𐑁𐑉𐐱𐑋 𐑄 𐐿𐐲𐑋𐐮𐑍 𐐲𐑂 𐐗𐑉𐐴𐑅𐐻,) 𐐰𐑌𐐼 𐐸𐐮𐑆 𐑅𐐲𐑌 𐐁𐑋𐐲𐑅 𐐿𐐯𐐹𐐻 𐑄 𐑉𐐯𐐿𐐲𐑉𐐼 𐐮𐑌 𐐸𐐮𐑆 𐑅𐐻𐐯𐐼; 𐐰𐑌𐐼 𐐸𐐨 𐐫𐑊𐑅𐐬 𐐿𐐯𐐹𐐻 𐐮𐐻 𐐲𐐹𐐱𐑌 𐑄 𐐹𐑊𐐩𐐻𐑅 𐐲𐑂 𐐤𐐨𐑁𐐴; 𐐰𐑌𐐼 𐐮𐐻 𐐶𐐱𐑆 𐐫𐑊𐑅𐐬 𐑉𐐮𐐻𐑌 𐐮𐑌 𐑄 𐐺𐐳𐐿 𐐲𐑂 𐐤𐐨𐑁𐐴, 𐐸𐐶𐐮𐐽 𐐮𐑆 𐑄𐐮𐑅 𐐺𐐳𐐿. 𐐈𐑌𐐼 𐐮𐐻 𐐿𐐩𐑋 𐐻𐐭 𐐹𐐰𐑅 𐑄𐐰𐐻 𐐻𐐭 𐐸𐐲𐑌𐐼𐑉𐐯𐐼 𐐷𐐨𐑉𐑆 𐐸𐐰𐐼 𐐹𐐰𐑅𐐻 𐐲𐐶𐐩, 𐐰𐑌𐐼 𐑄 𐑅𐐯𐐿𐐲𐑌𐐼 𐐾𐐯𐑌𐐲𐑉𐐩𐑇𐐲𐑌 𐐸𐐰𐐼 𐐫𐑊 𐐹𐐰𐑅𐐻 𐐲𐐶𐐩 𐑅𐐩𐑂 𐐮𐐻 𐐶𐐲𐑉 𐐩 𐑁𐐷𐐭. 𐐈𐑌𐐼 𐑌𐐵 𐐌, 𐐣𐐫𐑉𐑋𐐲𐑌, 𐐶𐐳𐐼 𐑄𐐰𐐻 𐐷𐐨 𐑇𐐳𐐼 𐑌𐐬 𐑄𐐰𐐻 𐑄 𐐹𐐨𐐹𐑊 𐐸𐐰𐐼 𐑋𐐲𐑊𐐻𐐮𐐹𐑊𐐴𐐼, 𐐮𐑌𐑅𐐬𐑋𐐲𐐽 𐑄𐐰𐐻 𐑄𐐩 𐐶𐐲𐑉 𐑅𐐹𐑉𐐯𐐼 𐐲𐐹𐐱𐑌 𐐫𐑊 𐑄 𐑁𐐩𐑅 𐐲𐑂 𐑄 𐑊𐐰𐑌𐐼, 𐐰𐑌𐐼 𐑄𐐰𐐻 𐑄𐐩 𐐸𐐰𐐼 𐐺𐐨𐐿𐐲𐑋 𐐯𐐿𐑅𐐨𐐼𐐮𐑍𐑊𐐨 𐑉𐐮𐐽, 𐐺𐐨𐐿𐐫𐑆 𐐲𐑂 𐑄𐐩𐑉 𐐹𐑉𐐱𐑅𐐹𐐯𐑉𐐮𐐻𐐨 𐐮𐑌 𐐗𐑉𐐴𐑅𐐻. 𐐈𐑌𐐼 𐑌𐐵 𐐮𐑌 𐑄𐐮𐑅 𐐻𐐭 𐐸𐐲𐑌𐐼𐑉𐐯𐐼 𐐰𐑌𐐼 𐑁𐐲𐑉𐑅𐐻 𐐷𐐨𐑉 𐑄𐐩𐑉 𐐺𐐨𐑀𐐰𐑌 𐐻𐐭 𐐺𐐨 𐐲𐑋𐐲𐑍 𐑄𐐯𐑋 𐑄𐐬𐑆 𐐸𐐭 𐐶𐐲𐑉 𐑊𐐮𐑁𐐻𐐯𐐼 𐐲𐐹 𐐮𐑌 𐐹𐑉𐐴𐐼, 𐑅𐐲𐐽 𐐰𐑆 𐑄 𐐶𐐩𐑉𐐮𐑍 𐐲𐑂 𐐿𐐱𐑅𐐻𐑊𐐨 𐐲𐐹𐐰𐑉𐐯𐑊, 𐐰𐑌𐐼 𐐫𐑊 𐑋𐐰𐑌𐐲𐑉 𐐲𐑂 𐑁𐐴𐑌 𐐹𐐲𐑉𐑊𐑆, 𐐰𐑌𐐼 𐐲𐑂 𐑄 𐑁𐐴𐑌 𐑃𐐮𐑍𐑆 𐐲𐑂 𐑄 𐐶𐐲𐑉𐑊𐐼. 𐐈𐑌𐐼 𐑁𐑉𐐱𐑋 𐑄𐐰𐐻 𐐻𐐴𐑋 𐑁𐐬𐑉𐑃 𐑄𐐩 𐐼𐐮𐐼 𐐸𐐰𐑂 𐑄𐐩𐑉 𐑀𐐳𐐼𐑆 𐐰𐑌𐐼 𐑄𐐩𐑉 𐑅𐐲𐐺𐑅𐐻𐐰𐑌𐑅 𐑌𐐬 𐑋𐐬𐑉 𐐿𐐱𐑋𐐲𐑌 𐐲𐑋𐐲𐑍 𐑄𐐯𐑋, 𐐰𐑌𐐼 𐑄𐐩 𐐺𐐨𐑀𐐰𐑌 𐐻𐐭 𐐺𐐨 𐐼𐐮𐑂𐐴𐐼𐐯𐐼 𐐮𐑌𐐻𐐭 𐐿𐑊𐐰𐑅𐐯𐑆, 𐐰𐑌𐐼 𐑄𐐩 𐐺𐐨𐑀𐐰𐑌 𐐻𐐭 𐐺𐐮𐑊𐐼 𐐲𐐹 𐐽𐐲𐑉𐐽𐐯𐑆 𐐲𐑌𐐻𐐭 𐑄𐐯𐑋𐑅𐐯𐑊𐑂𐑆, 𐐻𐐭 𐑀𐐯𐐻 𐑀𐐩𐑌, 𐐰𐑌𐐼 𐐺𐐨𐑀𐐰𐑌 𐐻𐐭 𐐼𐐨𐑌𐐴 𐑄 𐐻𐑉𐐭 𐐽𐐲𐑉𐐽 𐐲𐑂 𐐗𐑉𐐴𐑅𐐻.

8. 𐐈𐑌𐐼 𐐮𐐻 𐐿𐐩𐑋 𐐻𐐭 𐐹𐐪𐑅 𐑄𐐰𐐻 𐐸𐐶𐐯𐑌 𐐻𐐭 𐐸𐐲𐑌𐐼𐑉𐐯𐐼 𐐰𐑌𐐼 𐐻𐐯𐑌 𐐷𐐨𐑉𐑆 𐐸𐐰𐐼 𐐹𐐪𐑅𐐻 𐐰𐐶𐐩 𐑄𐐩𐑉 𐐶𐐲𐑉 𐑋𐐯𐑌𐐨 𐐽𐐲𐑉𐐽𐐯𐑆 𐐮𐑌 𐑄 𐑊𐐰𐑌𐐼; 𐐷𐐩, 𐑄𐐩𐑉 𐐶𐐲𐑉 𐑋𐐯𐑌𐐨 𐐽𐐲𐑉𐐽𐐯𐑆 𐐸𐐶𐐮𐐽 𐐹𐑉𐐬𐑁𐐯𐑅𐐻 𐐻𐐭 𐑌𐐬 𐑄 𐐗𐑉𐐴𐑅𐐻, 𐐰𐑌𐐼 𐐷𐐯𐐻 𐑄𐐩 𐐼𐐮𐐼 𐐼𐐨𐑌𐐴 𐑄 𐑋𐐬𐑉 𐐹𐐪𐑉𐐻𐑅 𐐱𐑂 𐐸𐐮𐑆 𐐘𐐱𐑅𐐹𐐯𐑊, 𐐮𐑌𐑅𐐬𐑋𐐲𐐽 𐑄𐐰𐐻 𐑄𐐩 𐐼𐐮𐐼 𐑉𐐨𐑅𐐨𐑂 𐐫𐑊 𐑋𐐰𐑌𐐲𐑉 𐐱𐑂 𐐶𐐮𐐿𐐯𐐼𐑌𐐯𐑅, 𐐰𐑌𐐼 𐐼𐐮𐐼 𐐰𐐼𐑋𐐮𐑌𐐮𐑅𐐻𐐲𐑉 𐑄𐐰𐐻 𐐸𐐶𐐮𐐽 𐐶𐐱𐑆 𐑅𐐩𐐿𐑉𐐯𐐼 𐐲𐑌𐐻𐐭 𐐸𐐮𐑋 𐐻𐐭 𐐸𐐭𐑋 𐐮𐐻 𐐸𐐰𐐼 𐐺𐐮𐑌 𐑁𐐫𐑉𐐺𐐮𐐼𐐲𐑌, 𐐺𐐨𐐿𐐫𐑆 𐐱𐑂 𐐲𐑌𐐶𐐲𐑉𐑄𐐨𐑌𐐯𐑅. 𐐈𐑌𐐼 𐑄𐐮𐑅 𐐽𐐲𐑉𐐽 𐐼𐐮𐐼 𐑋𐐲𐑊𐐻𐐮𐐹𐑊𐐴 𐐯𐐿𐑅𐐨𐐼𐐮𐑍𐑊𐐨, 𐐺𐐨𐐿𐐫𐑆 𐐱𐑂 𐐮𐑌𐐮𐐿𐐶𐐮𐐻𐐨, 𐐰𐑌𐐼 𐐺𐐨𐐿𐐫𐑆 𐐱𐑂 𐑄 𐐹𐐵𐐲𐑉 𐐱𐑂 𐐝𐐩𐐻𐐲𐑌 𐐸𐐭 𐐼𐐮𐐼 𐑀𐐯𐐻 𐐸𐐬𐑊𐐼 𐐲𐐹𐐱𐑌 𐑄𐐩𐑉 𐐸𐐪𐑉𐐻𐑅. 𐐈𐑌𐐼 𐐰𐑀𐐯𐑌, 𐑄𐐩𐑉 𐐶𐐱𐑆 𐐰𐑌𐐲𐑄𐐲𐑉 𐐽𐐲𐑉𐐽 𐐸𐐶𐐮𐐽 𐐼𐐨𐑌𐐴𐐼 𐑄 𐐗𐑉𐐴𐑅𐐻; 𐐰𐑌𐐼 𐑄𐐩 𐐼𐐮𐐼 𐐹𐐲𐑉𐑅𐐨𐐿𐐷𐐭𐐻 𐑄 𐐻𐑉𐐭 𐐽𐐲𐑉𐐽 𐐱𐑂 𐐗𐑉𐐴𐑅𐐻, 𐐺𐐨𐐿𐐫𐑆 𐐱𐑂 𐑄𐐩𐑉 𐐸𐐷𐐭𐑋𐐮𐑊𐐮𐐻𐐨, 𐐰𐑌𐐼 𐑄𐐩𐑉 𐐺𐐨𐑊𐐨𐑁 𐐮𐑌 𐐗𐑉𐐴𐑅𐐻; 𐐰𐑌𐐼 𐑄𐐩 𐐼𐐮𐐼 𐐼𐐨𐑅𐐹𐐴𐑆 𐑄𐐯𐑋, 𐐺𐐨𐐿𐐫𐑆 𐐱𐑂 𐑄 𐑋𐐯𐑌𐐨 𐑋𐐮𐑉𐐲𐐿𐑊𐑆 𐐸𐐶𐐮𐐽 𐐶𐐲𐑉 𐑉𐐫𐐻 𐐰𐑋𐐲𐑍 𐑄𐐯𐑋; 𐑄𐐩𐑉𐑁𐐬𐑉 𐑄𐐩 𐐼𐐮𐐼 𐐯𐐿𐑅𐐲𐑉𐑅𐐴𐑆 𐐹𐐵𐐲𐑉 𐐰𐑌𐐼 𐐫𐑃𐐱𐑉𐐮𐐻𐐨 𐐬𐑂𐐲𐑉 𐑄 𐐼𐐮𐑅𐐴𐐹𐑊𐑆 𐐱𐑂 𐐖𐐨𐑆𐐲𐑅 𐐸𐐭 𐐼𐐮𐐼 𐐻𐐰𐑉𐐨 𐐶𐐮𐑄 𐑄𐐯𐑋, 𐐰𐑌𐐼 𐑄𐐩 𐐼𐐮𐐼 𐐿𐐪𐑅𐐻 𐑄𐐯𐑋 𐐮𐑌𐐻𐐭 𐐹𐑉𐐮𐑆𐐲𐑌: 𐐺𐐲𐐻 𐐺𐐴 𐑄 𐐹𐐵𐐲𐑉 𐐱𐑂 𐑄 𐐶𐐲𐑉𐐼 𐐱𐑂 𐐘𐐱𐐼, 𐐸𐐶𐐮𐐽 𐐶𐐱𐑆 𐐮𐑌 𐑄𐐯𐑋, 𐑄 𐐹𐑉𐐮𐑆𐐲𐑌𐑆 𐐶𐐲𐑉 𐑉𐐯𐑌𐐻 𐐮𐑌 𐐻𐐶𐐩𐑌, 𐐰𐑌𐐼 𐑄𐐩 𐐶𐐯𐑌𐐻 𐑁𐐬𐑉𐑃 𐐼𐐭𐐮𐑍 𐑋𐐴𐐻𐐨 𐑋𐐮𐑉𐐲𐐿𐑊𐑆 𐐰𐑋𐐲𐑍 𐑄𐐯𐑋. 𐐤𐐯𐑂𐐲𐑉𐑄𐐲𐑊𐐯𐑅, 𐐰𐑌𐐼 𐑌𐐱𐐻𐐶𐐮𐑄𐑅𐐻𐐰𐑌𐐼𐐮𐑍 𐐫𐑊 𐑄𐐨𐑆 𐑋𐐮𐑉𐐲𐐿𐑊𐑆, 𐑄 𐐹𐐨𐐹𐑊 𐐼𐐮𐐼 𐐸𐐪𐑉𐐼𐐲𐑌 𐑄𐐩𐑉 𐐸𐐪𐑉𐐻𐑅, 𐐰𐑌𐐼 𐐼𐐮𐐼 𐑅𐐨𐐿 𐐻𐐭 𐐿𐐮𐑊 𐑄𐐯𐑋, 𐐨𐑂𐐲𐑌 𐐰𐑆 𐑄 𐐖𐐭𐑆 𐐰𐐻 𐐖𐐯𐑉𐐭-𐑅𐐰𐑊𐐯𐑋 𐑅𐐫𐐻 𐐻𐐭 𐐿𐐮𐑊 𐐖𐐨𐑆𐐲𐑅, 𐐰𐐿𐐫𐑉𐐼𐐮𐑍 𐐻𐐭 𐐸𐐮𐑆 𐐶𐐲𐑉𐐼, 𐐰𐑌𐐼 𐑄𐐩 𐐼𐐮𐐼 𐐿𐐪𐑅𐐻 𐑄𐐯𐑋 𐐮𐑌𐐻𐐭 𐑁𐐲𐑉-𐑌𐐩𐑅𐐯𐑆 𐐱𐑂 𐑁𐐴𐑉, 𐐰𐑌𐐼 𐑄𐐩 𐐿𐐩𐑋 𐑁𐐬𐑉𐑃 𐑉𐐨𐑅𐐨𐑂𐐮𐑍 𐑌𐐬 𐐸𐐪𐑉𐑋; 𐐰𐑌𐐼 𐑄𐐩 𐐫𐑊𐑅𐐬 𐐿𐐪𐑅𐐻 𐑄𐐯𐑋 𐐮𐑌𐐻𐐭 𐐼𐐯𐑌𐑆 𐐱𐑂 𐐶𐐴𐑊𐐼 𐐺𐐨𐑅𐐻𐑅, 𐐰𐑌𐐼 𐑄𐐩 𐐼𐐮𐐼 𐐹𐑊𐐩 𐐶𐐮𐑄 𐑄 𐐶𐐴𐑊𐐼 𐐺𐐨𐑅𐐻𐑅 𐐨𐑂𐐲𐑌 𐐰𐑆 𐐩 𐐽𐐴𐑊𐐼 𐐶𐐮𐑄 𐐩 𐑊𐐰𐑋; 𐐰𐑌𐐼 𐑄𐐩 𐐼𐐮𐐼 𐐿𐐲𐑋 𐑁𐐬𐑉𐑃 𐑁𐑉𐐱𐑋 𐐰𐑋𐐲𐑍 𐑄𐐯𐑋, 𐑉𐐨𐑅𐐨𐑂𐐮𐑍 𐑌𐐬 𐐸𐐪𐑉𐑋. 𐐤𐐯𐑂𐐲𐑉𐑄𐐲𐑊𐐯𐑅, 𐑄 𐐹𐐨𐐹𐑊 𐐼𐐮𐐼 𐐸𐐪𐑉𐐼𐐲𐑌 𐑄𐐩𐑉 𐐸𐐪𐑉𐐻𐑅, 𐑁𐐫𐑉 𐑄𐐩 𐐶𐐲𐑉 𐑊𐐯𐐼 𐐺𐐴 𐑋𐐯𐑌𐐨 𐐹𐑉𐐨𐑅𐐻𐑅 𐐰𐑌𐐼 𐑁𐐫𐑊𐑅 𐐹𐑉𐐱𐑁𐐯𐐻𐑅 𐐻𐐭 𐐺𐐮𐑊𐐼 𐐲𐐹 𐑋𐐯𐑌𐐨 𐐽𐐲𐑉𐐽𐐯𐑆, 𐐰𐑌𐐼 𐐻𐐭 𐐼𐐭 𐐫𐑊 𐑋𐐰𐑌𐐲𐑉 𐐱𐑂 𐐮𐑌𐐮𐐿𐐶𐐮𐐻𐐨. 𐐈𐑌𐐼 𐑄𐐩 𐐼𐐮𐐼 𐑅𐑋𐐴𐐻 𐐲𐐹𐐱𐑌 𐑄 𐐹𐐨𐐹𐑊 𐐱𐑂 𐐖𐐨𐑆𐐲𐑅; 𐐺𐐲𐐻 𐑄 𐐹𐐨𐐹𐑊 𐐱𐑂 𐐖𐐨𐑆𐐲𐑅 𐐼𐐮𐐼 𐑌𐐱𐐻 𐑅𐑋𐐴𐐻 𐐰𐑀𐐯𐑌. 𐐈𐑌𐐼 𐑄𐐲𐑅 𐑄𐐩 𐐼𐐮𐐼 𐐼𐐶𐐮𐑌𐐼𐑊 𐐮𐑌 𐐲𐑌𐐺𐐨𐑊𐐨𐑁 𐐰𐑌𐐼 𐐶𐐮𐐿𐐯𐐼𐑌𐐯𐑅, 𐑁𐑉𐐱𐑋 𐐷𐐨𐑉 𐐻𐐭 𐐷𐐨𐑉, 𐐨𐑂𐐲𐑌 𐐲𐑌𐐻𐐮𐑊 𐐻𐐭 𐐸𐐲𐑌-𐐼𐑉𐐯𐐼 𐐰𐑌𐐼 𐑃𐐲𐑉𐐻𐐨 𐐷𐐨𐑉𐑆 𐐸𐐰𐐼 𐐹𐐪𐑅𐐻 𐐰𐐶𐐩. 𐐈𐑌𐐼 𐑌𐐵 𐐮𐐻 𐐿𐐩𐑋 𐐻𐐭 𐐹𐐪𐑅 𐐮𐑌 𐑄𐐮𐑅 𐐷𐐨𐑉, 𐐷𐐩, 𐐮𐑌 𐑄 𐐻𐐭 𐐸𐐲𐑌𐐼𐑉𐐯𐐼 𐐰𐑌𐐼 𐑃𐐲𐑉𐐻𐐨 𐐰𐑌𐐼 𐑁𐐲𐑉𐑅𐐻 𐐷𐐨𐑉, 𐑄𐐩𐑉 𐐶𐐱𐑆 𐐩 𐑀𐑉𐐩𐐻 𐐼𐐮𐑂𐐮𐑈𐐲𐑌 𐐰𐑋𐐲𐑍 𐑄 𐐹𐐨𐐹𐑊. 𐐈𐑌𐐼 𐐮𐐻 𐐿𐐩𐑋 𐐻𐐭 𐐹𐐪𐑅 𐑄𐐰𐐻 𐐮𐑌 𐑄𐐮𐑅 𐐷𐐨𐑉 𐑄𐐩𐑉 𐐰𐑉𐐬𐑆 𐐩 𐐹𐐨𐐹𐑊 𐐸𐐭 𐐶𐐲𐑉 𐐿𐐫𐑊𐐼 𐑄 𐐤𐐨𐑁𐐴𐐻𐑅, 𐐰𐑌𐐼 𐑄𐐩 𐐶𐐲𐑉 𐐻𐑉𐐭 𐐺𐐨𐑊𐐨𐑂𐐲𐑉𐑆 𐐮𐑌 𐐗𐑉𐐴𐑅𐐻; 𐐰𐑌𐐼 𐐰𐑋𐐲𐑍 𐑄𐐯𐑋 𐑄𐐩𐑉 𐐶𐐲𐑉 𐑄𐐬𐑆 𐐸𐐭 𐐶𐐲𐑉 𐐿𐐫𐑊𐐼 𐐺𐐴 𐑄 𐐢𐐰𐑋𐐲𐑌𐐴𐐻𐑅, 𐐖𐐩𐐿𐐲𐐺𐐴𐐻𐑅, 𐐰𐑌𐐼 𐐖𐐬𐑆𐐯𐑁𐐴𐐻𐑅, 𐐰𐑌𐐼 𐐞𐐬𐑉𐐲𐑋𐐴𐐻𐑅; 𐑄𐐩𐑉𐑁𐐬𐑉 𐑄 𐐻𐑉𐐭 𐐺𐐨-𐑊𐐨𐑂𐐲𐑉𐑆 𐐮𐑌 𐐗𐑉𐐴𐑅𐐻, 𐐰𐑌𐐼 𐑄 𐐻𐑉𐐭 𐐶𐐲𐑉𐑇𐐮𐐹𐐲𐑉𐑆 𐐱𐑂 𐐗𐑉𐐴𐑅𐐻, (𐐰𐑋𐐲𐑍 𐐸𐐭𐑋 𐐶𐐲𐑉 𐑄 𐑃𐑉𐐨 𐐼𐐮𐑅𐐴𐐹𐑊𐑆 𐐱𐑂 𐐖𐐨𐑆𐐲𐑅 𐐸𐐭 𐑇𐐳𐐼 𐐻𐐰𐑉𐐨,) 𐐶𐐲𐑉 𐐿𐐫𐑊𐐼 𐐤𐐨𐑁𐐴𐐻𐑅, 𐐰𐑌𐐼 𐐖𐐩𐐿𐐲𐐺𐐴𐐻𐑅, 𐐰𐑌𐐼 𐐖𐐬𐑆𐐯𐑁𐐴𐐻𐑅, 𐐰𐑌𐐼 𐐞𐐬𐑉𐐲𐑋𐐴𐐻𐑅. 𐐈𐑌𐐼 𐐮𐐻 𐐿𐐩𐑋 𐐻𐐭 𐐹𐐪𐑅 𐑄𐐰𐐻 𐑄𐐩 𐐸𐐭 𐑉𐐨𐐾𐐯𐐿𐐻𐐯𐐼 𐑄 𐐘𐐱𐑅𐐹𐐯𐑊, 𐐶𐐲𐑉 𐐿𐐫𐑊𐐼 𐐢𐐰-𐑋𐐲𐑌𐐴𐐻𐑅, 𐐰𐑌𐐼 𐐢𐐯𐑋𐐷𐐭𐐯𐑊𐐴𐐻𐑅, 𐐰𐑌𐐼 𐐆𐑇𐑋𐐩𐐯𐑊𐐴𐐻𐑅; 𐐰𐑌𐐼 𐑄𐐩 𐐼𐐮𐐼 𐑌𐐱𐐻 𐐼𐐶𐐮𐑌𐐼𐑊 𐐮𐑌 𐐲𐑌𐐺𐐨𐑊𐐨𐑁, 𐐺𐐲𐐻 𐑄𐐩 𐐼𐐮𐐼 𐐶𐐮𐑊𐑁𐐳𐑊𐐨 𐑉𐐯𐐺𐐯𐑊 𐐰𐑀𐐯𐑌𐑅𐐻 𐑄 𐐘𐐱𐑅𐐹𐐯𐑊 𐐱𐑂 𐐗𐑉𐐴𐑅𐐻; 𐐰𐑌𐐼 𐑄𐐩 𐐼𐐮𐐼 𐐻𐐨𐐽 𐑄𐐩𐑉 𐐽𐐮𐑊-𐐼𐑉𐐯𐑌 𐑄𐐰𐐻 𐑄𐐩 𐑇𐐳𐐼 𐑌𐐱𐐻 𐐺𐐨𐑊𐐨𐑂, 𐐨𐑂𐐲𐑌 𐐰𐑆 𐑄𐐩𐑉 𐑁𐐪𐑄𐐲𐑉𐑆, 𐑁𐑉𐐱𐑋 𐑄 𐐺𐐨𐑀𐐮𐑌𐐮𐑍, 𐐼𐐮𐐼 𐐼𐐶𐐮𐑌𐐼𐑊. 𐐈𐑌𐐼 𐐮𐐻 𐐶𐐱𐑆 𐐺𐐨𐐿𐐫𐑆 𐐱𐑂 𐑄 𐐶𐐮𐐿𐐯𐐼𐑌𐐯𐑅 𐐰𐑌𐐼 𐐲𐐺𐐱𐑋𐐮𐑌𐐩𐑇𐐲𐑌 𐐱𐑂 𐑄𐐩𐑉 𐑁𐐪𐑄𐐲𐑉𐑆, 𐐨𐑂𐐲𐑌 𐐰𐑆 𐐮𐐻 𐐶𐐱𐑆 𐐮𐑌 𐑄 𐐺𐐨𐑀𐐮𐑌𐐮𐑍. 𐐈𐑌𐐼 𐑄𐐩 𐐶𐐲𐑉 𐐻𐐫𐐻 𐐻𐐭 𐐸𐐩𐐻 𐑄 𐐽𐐮𐑊𐐼𐑉𐐯𐑌 𐐱𐑂 𐐘𐐱𐐼, 𐐨𐑂𐐲𐑌 𐐰𐑆 𐑄 𐐢𐐰𐑋𐐲-𐑌𐐴𐐻𐑅 𐐶𐐲𐑉 𐐻𐐫𐐻 𐐻𐐭 𐐸𐐩𐐻 𐑄 𐐽𐐮𐑊𐐼𐑉𐐯𐑌 𐐱𐑂 𐐤𐐨𐑁𐐴, 𐑁𐑉𐐱𐑋 𐑄 𐐺𐐨𐑀𐐮𐑌𐐮𐑍.

9. 𐐈𐑌𐐼 𐐮𐐻 𐐿𐐩𐑋 𐐻𐐭 𐐹𐐪𐑅 𐑄𐐰𐐻 𐐻𐐭 𐐸𐐲𐑌𐐼𐑉𐐯𐐼 𐐰𐑌𐐼 𐑁𐐫𐑉𐐻𐐨 𐐰𐑌𐐼 𐑁𐐬𐑉 𐐷𐐨𐑉𐑆 𐐸𐐰𐐼 𐐹𐐪𐑅𐐻 𐐰𐐶𐐩, 𐐰𐑌𐐼 𐑄𐐲𐑅 𐐶𐐲𐑉 𐑄 𐐰𐑁𐐩𐑉𐑆 𐐱𐑂 𐑄 𐐹𐐨𐐹𐑊. 𐐈𐑌𐐼 𐑄 𐑋𐐬𐑉 𐐶𐐮𐐿𐐯𐐼 𐐹𐐪𐑉𐐻 𐐱𐑂 𐑄 𐐹𐐨𐐹𐑊 𐐼𐐮𐐼 𐐶𐐰𐐿𐑅 𐑅𐐻𐑉𐐱𐑍, 𐐰𐑌𐐼 𐐺𐐨𐐿𐐩𐑋 𐐯𐐿𐑅𐐨𐐼𐐮𐑍𐑊𐐨 𐑋𐐬𐑉 𐑌𐐷𐐭𐑋𐐲𐑉𐐲𐑅 𐑄𐐰𐑌 𐐶𐐲𐑉 𐑄 𐐹𐐨𐐹𐑊 𐐱𐑂 𐐘𐐱𐐼. 𐐈𐑌𐐼 𐑄𐐩 𐐼𐐮𐐼 𐑅𐐻𐐮𐑊 𐐿𐐱𐑌𐐻𐐮𐑌𐐷𐐭 𐐻𐐭 𐐺𐐮𐑊𐐼 𐐲𐐹 𐐽𐐲𐑉𐐽𐐯𐑆 𐐲𐑌𐐻𐐭 𐑄𐐯𐑋𐑅𐐯𐑊𐑂𐑆, 𐐰𐑌𐐼 𐐰𐐼𐐫𐑉𐑌 𐑄𐐯𐑋 𐐶𐐮𐑄 𐐫𐑊 𐑋𐐰𐑌𐐲𐑉 𐐱𐑂 𐐹𐑉𐐯𐑇𐐲𐑅 𐑃𐐮𐑍𐑆. 𐐈𐑌𐐼 𐑄𐐲𐑅 𐐼𐐮𐐼 𐐻𐐭 𐐸𐐲𐑌𐐼𐑉𐐯𐐼 𐐰𐑌𐐼 𐑁𐐮𐑁𐐻𐐨 𐐷𐐨𐑉𐑆 𐐹𐐪𐑅 𐐰𐐶𐐩, 𐐰𐑌𐐼

𐐫𐑊𐑅𐐬 𐐻𐐭 𐐸𐐲𐑌𐐼𐑉𐐯𐐼 𐐰𐑌𐐼 𐑅𐐮𐐿𐑅𐐻𐐨 𐐷𐐨𐑉𐑆. 𐐈𐑌𐐼 𐐮𐐻 𐐿𐐩𐑋 𐐻𐐭 𐐹𐐪𐑅 𐑄𐐰𐐻 𐑄 𐐶𐐮𐐿𐐯𐐼 𐐹𐐪𐑉𐐻 𐐱𐑂 𐑄 𐐹𐐨𐐹𐐲𐑊 𐐺𐐨𐑀𐐰𐑌 𐐲𐑀𐐯𐑌 𐐻𐐭 𐐺𐐮𐑊𐐼 𐐲𐐹 𐑄 𐑅𐐨𐐿𐑉𐐯𐐻 𐐬𐑃𐑅 𐐰𐑌𐐼 𐐿𐐱𐑋𐐺𐐮𐑌𐐩𐑇𐐲𐑌𐑆 𐐱𐑂 𐐘𐐩𐐼𐐨𐐰𐑌𐐻𐐲𐑌. 𐐈𐑌𐐼 𐐫𐑊𐑅𐐬 𐑄 𐐹𐐨𐐹𐐲𐑊 𐐸𐐭 𐐶𐐲𐑉 𐐿𐐫𐑊𐐼 𐑄 𐐹𐐨𐐹𐐲𐑊 𐐱𐑂 𐐤𐐨𐑁𐐴, 𐐺𐐨𐑀𐐰𐑌 𐐻𐐭 𐐺𐐨 𐐹𐑉𐐵𐐼 𐐮𐑌 𐑄𐐩𐑉 𐐸𐐪𐑉𐐻𐑅, 𐐺𐐨𐐿𐐫𐑆 𐐱𐑂 𐑄𐐩𐑉 𐐯𐐿𐑅𐐨𐐼𐐮𐑍 𐑉𐐮𐐽𐐯𐑆, 𐐰𐑌𐐼 𐐺𐐨𐐿𐐲𐑋 𐑂𐐩𐑌, 𐑊𐐴𐐿 𐐲𐑌𐐻𐐭 𐑄𐐩𐑉 𐐺𐑉𐐯𐑄𐑉𐐯𐑌, 𐑄 𐐢𐐩𐑋𐐲𐑌𐐴𐐻𐑅. 𐐈𐑌𐐼 𐑁𐑉𐐱𐑋 𐑄𐐮𐑅 𐐻𐐴𐑋, 𐑄 𐐼𐐮𐑅𐐴𐐹𐑊𐑆 𐐺𐐨𐑀𐐰𐑌 𐐻𐐭 𐑅𐐱𐑉𐐬 𐑁𐐫𐑉 𐑄 𐑅𐐮𐑌𐑆 𐐱𐑂 𐑄 𐐶𐐲𐑉𐑊𐐼.

10. 𐐈𐑌𐐼 𐐮𐐻 𐐿𐐩𐑋 𐐻𐐭 𐐹𐐪𐑅 𐑄𐐰𐐻 𐐸𐐶𐐯𐑌 𐑃𐑉𐐨 𐐸𐐲𐑌𐐼𐑉𐐯𐐼 𐐷𐐨𐑉𐑆 𐐸𐐰𐐼 𐐹𐐪𐑅𐐻 𐐲𐐶𐐩, 𐐺𐐬𐑃 𐑄 𐐹𐐨𐐹𐐲𐑊 𐐱𐑂 𐐤𐐨𐑁𐐴 𐐰𐑌𐐼 𐑄 𐐢𐐩𐑋𐐲𐑌𐐴𐐻𐑅 𐐸𐐰𐐼 𐐺𐐨𐐿𐐲𐑋 𐐯𐐿𐑅𐐨𐐼𐐮𐑍𐑊𐐨 𐐶𐐮𐐿𐐯𐐼 𐐶𐐲𐑌 𐑊𐐴𐐿 𐐲𐑌𐐻𐐭 𐐲𐑌𐐲𐑄𐐲𐑉. 𐐈𐑌𐐼 𐐮𐐻 𐐿𐐩𐑋 𐐻𐐭 𐐹𐐪𐑅 𐑄𐐰𐐻 𐑄 𐑉𐐱𐐺𐐲𐑉𐑆 𐐱𐑂 𐐘𐐩𐐼𐐨𐐰𐑌𐐻𐐲𐑌 𐐼𐐮𐐼 𐑅𐐹𐑉𐐯𐐼 𐐬𐑂𐐲𐑉 𐐫𐑊 𐑄 𐑁𐐩𐑅 𐐱𐑂 𐑄 𐑊𐐰𐑌𐐼; 𐐰𐑌𐐼 𐑄𐐩𐑉 𐐶𐐲𐑉 𐑌𐐲𐑌 𐑄𐐰𐐻 𐐶𐐲𐑉 𐑉𐐴𐐽𐐲𐑅, 𐑅𐐩𐑂 𐐮𐐻 𐐶𐐲𐑉 𐑄 𐐼𐐮𐑅𐐴𐐹𐑊𐑆 𐐱𐑂 𐐖𐐨𐑆𐐲𐑅. 𐐈𐑌𐐼 𐑀𐐬𐑊𐐼 𐐰𐑌𐐼 𐑅𐐮𐑊𐑂𐐲𐑉 𐐼𐐮𐐼 𐑄𐐩 𐑊𐐩 𐐲𐐹 𐐮𐑌 𐑅𐐻𐐬𐑉 𐐮𐑌 𐐲𐐺𐐲𐑌𐐼𐐲𐑌𐑅, 𐐰𐑌𐐼 𐐼𐐮𐐼 𐐻𐑉𐐰𐑁𐐮𐐿 𐐮𐑌 𐐫𐑊 𐑋𐐰𐑌𐐲𐑉 𐐱𐑂 𐐻𐑉𐐰𐑁𐐮𐐿.

11. 𐐈𐑌𐐼 𐐮𐐻 𐐿𐐩𐑋 𐐻𐐭 𐐹𐐪𐑅 𐑄𐐰𐐻 𐐪𐑁𐐻𐐲𐑉 𐑃𐑉𐐨 𐐸𐐲𐑌𐐼𐑉𐐯𐐼 𐐰𐑌𐐼 𐑁𐐴𐑂 𐐷𐐨𐑉𐑆 𐐸𐐰𐐼 𐐹𐐪𐑅𐐻 𐐲𐐶𐐩, (𐐰𐑌𐐼 𐑄 𐐹𐐨𐐹𐐲𐑊 𐐼𐐮𐐼 𐑅𐐻𐐮𐑊 𐑉𐐨𐑋𐐩𐑌 𐐮𐑌 𐐶𐐮𐐿𐐯𐐼𐑌𐐯𐑅,) 𐐁𐑋𐐱𐑅 𐐼𐐴𐐼, 𐐰𐑌𐐼 𐐸𐐮𐑆 𐐺𐑉𐐲𐑄𐐲𐑉 𐐈𐑋𐐲𐑉𐐱𐑌, 𐐼𐐮𐐼 𐐿𐐨𐐹 𐑄 𐑉𐐯𐐿𐐲𐑉𐐼 𐐮𐑌 𐐸𐐮𐑆 𐑅𐐻𐐯𐐼. 𐐈𐑌𐐼 𐐮𐐻 𐐿𐐩𐑋 𐐻𐐭 𐐹𐐪𐑅 𐑄𐐰𐐻 𐐸𐐶𐐯𐑌 𐑃𐑉𐐨 𐐸𐐲𐑌𐐼𐑉𐐯𐐼 𐐰𐑌𐐼 𐐻𐐶𐐯𐑌𐐻𐐨 𐐷𐐨𐑉𐑆 𐐸𐐰𐐼 𐐹𐐪𐑅𐐻 𐐲𐐶𐐩, 𐐈𐑋𐐲𐑉𐐱𐑌, 𐐺𐐨𐐮𐑍 𐐿𐐱𐑌𐑅𐐻𐑉𐐩𐑌𐐼 𐐺𐐴 𐑄 𐐐𐐬𐑊𐐨 𐐘𐐬𐑅𐐻, 𐐼𐐮𐐼 𐐸𐐴𐐼 𐐲𐐹 𐑄 𐑉𐐯𐐿𐐲𐑉𐐼𐑆 𐐸𐐶𐐮𐐽 𐐶𐐲𐑉 𐑅𐐩𐐿𐑉𐐯𐐼; 𐐷𐐩, 𐐨𐑂𐐲𐑌 𐐫𐑊 𐑄 𐑅𐐩𐐿𐑉𐐯𐐼 𐑉𐐯𐐿𐐲𐑉𐐼𐑆 𐐸𐐶𐐮𐐽 𐐸𐐰𐐼 𐐺𐐮𐑌 𐐸𐐰𐑌𐐼𐐯𐐼 𐐼𐐵𐑌 𐑁𐑉𐐱𐑋 𐐾𐐯𐑌𐐲𐑉𐐩𐑇𐐲𐑌 𐐻𐐭 𐐾𐐯𐑌𐐲𐑉𐐩𐑇𐐲𐑌, 𐐸𐐶𐐮𐐽 𐐶𐐲𐑉 𐑅𐐩𐐿𐑉𐐯𐐼, 𐐨𐑂𐐲𐑌 𐐲𐑌𐐻𐐮𐑊 𐑄 𐑃𐑉𐐨 𐐸𐐲𐑌𐐼𐑉𐐯𐐼 𐐰𐑌𐐼 𐐻𐐶𐐯𐑌𐐻𐐨𐐯𐑃 𐐷𐐨𐑉 𐑁𐑉𐐱𐑋 𐑄 𐐿𐐲𐑋𐐮𐑍 𐐱𐑂 𐐗𐑉𐐴𐑅𐐻. 𐐈𐑌𐐼 𐐸𐐨 𐐼𐐮𐐼 𐐸𐐴𐐼 𐑄𐐯𐑋 𐐲𐐹 𐐲𐑌𐐻𐐭 𐑄 𐐢𐐫𐑉𐐼, 𐑄𐐰𐐻 𐑄𐐩 𐑋𐐴𐐻 𐐿𐐲𐑋 𐐲𐑀𐐯𐑌 𐐲𐑌𐐻𐐭 𐑄 𐑉𐐯𐑋𐑌𐐲𐑌𐐻 𐐱𐑂 𐑄 𐐸𐐵𐑅 𐐱𐑂 𐐖𐐩𐐿𐐲𐐺, 𐐰𐐿𐐫𐑉𐐼𐐮𐑍 𐐻𐐭 𐑄 𐐹𐑉𐐱𐑁𐐯𐑅𐐨𐑆 𐐰𐑌𐐼 𐑄 𐐹𐑉𐐱𐑋𐐮𐑅𐐯𐑆 𐐱𐑂 𐑄 𐐢𐐫𐑉𐐼. 𐐈𐑌𐐼 𐑄𐐲𐑅 𐐮𐑆 𐑄 𐐯𐑌𐐼 𐐱𐑂 𐑄 𐑉𐐯𐐿𐐲𐑉𐐼 𐐱𐑂 𐐈𐑋𐐲𐑉𐐱𐑌.

𐐜 𐐒𐐳𐐿 𐐲𐑂 𐐣𐐬𐑉𐐣𐐲𐑌.

𐐕𐐰𐐹𐐻𐐲𐑉 I.

1. 𐐈𐑌𐐼 𐑌𐐵 𐐌, 𐐣𐐬𐑉𐐣𐐲𐑌, 𐑋𐐩𐐿 𐐩 𐑉𐐯𐐿𐐲𐑉𐐼 𐐲𐑂 𐑄 𐑃𐐮𐑍𐑆 𐐸𐐶𐐮𐐽 𐐌 𐐸𐐰𐑂 𐐺𐐬𐑃 𐑅𐐨𐑌 𐐰𐑌𐐼 𐐸𐐲𐑉𐐼, 𐐰𐑌𐐼 𐐿𐐫𐑊 𐐮𐐻 𐑄 𐐒𐐳𐐿 𐐲𐑂 𐐣𐐬𐑉𐐣𐐲𐑌. 𐐈𐑌𐐼 𐐲𐐺𐐵𐐻 𐑄 𐐻𐐴𐑋 𐑄𐐰𐐻 𐐈𐑋𐐰𐑉𐐲𐑌 𐐸𐐮𐐼 𐐲𐐹 𐑄 𐑉𐐯𐐿𐐲𐑉𐐼𐑆 𐐲𐑌𐐻𐐭 𐑄 𐐢𐐫𐑉𐐼, 𐐸𐐨 𐐿𐐩𐑋 𐐲𐑌𐐻𐐭 𐑋𐐨, (𐐌 𐐺𐐨𐐮𐑍 𐐲𐐺𐐵𐐻 𐐻𐐯𐑌 𐐷𐐨𐑉𐑆 𐐲𐑂 𐐩𐐾; 𐐰𐑌𐐼 𐐌 𐐺𐐨𐑀𐐰𐑌 𐐻𐐭 𐐺𐐨 𐑊𐐲𐑉𐑌𐐼 𐑅𐐲𐑋𐐸𐐶𐐲𐐻 𐐰𐑁𐐻𐐲𐑉 𐑄 𐑋𐐰𐑌𐐲𐑉 𐐲𐑂 𐑄 𐑊𐐲𐑉𐑌𐐮𐑍 𐐲𐑂 𐑋𐐴 𐐹𐐨𐐹𐐲𐑊,) 𐐰𐑌𐐼 𐐈𐑋𐐰𐑉𐐲𐑌 𐑅𐐯𐐼 𐐲𐑌𐐻𐐭 𐑋𐐨, 𐐌 𐐹𐐲𐑉𐑅𐐨𐑂 𐑄𐐰𐐻 𐑄𐐵 𐐪𐑉𐐻 𐐩 𐑅𐐬𐐺𐐲𐑉 𐐽𐐴𐑊𐐼, 𐐰𐑌𐐼 𐐪𐑉𐐻 𐐿𐐶𐐮𐐿 𐐻𐐭 𐐲𐐺𐑆𐐲𐑉𐑂; 𐑄𐐯𐑉𐑁𐐬𐑉 𐐸𐐶𐐯𐑌 𐐷𐐨 𐐪𐑉 𐐲𐐺𐐵𐐻 𐐻𐐶𐐯𐑌𐐻𐐨 𐐰𐑌𐐼 𐑁𐐬𐑉 𐐷𐐨𐑉𐑆 𐐬𐑊𐐼, 𐐌 𐐶𐐳𐐼 𐑄𐐰𐐻 𐐷𐐨 𐑇𐐳𐐼 𐑉𐐨𐑋𐐯𐑋𐐺𐐲𐑉 𐑄 𐑃𐐮𐑍𐑆 𐑄𐐰𐐻 𐐷𐐨 𐐸𐐰𐑂 𐐲𐐺𐑆𐐲𐑉𐑂𐐼 𐐿𐐲𐑌𐑅𐐲𐑉𐑌𐐮𐑍 𐑄𐐮𐑅 𐐹𐐨𐐹𐐲𐑊; 𐐰𐑌𐐼 𐐸𐐶𐐯𐑌 𐐷𐐨 𐐪𐑉 𐐲𐑂 𐑄𐐰𐐻 𐐩𐐾, 𐑀𐐬 𐐻𐐭 𐑄 𐑊𐐰𐑌𐐼 𐐈𐑌𐐻𐐲𐑋, 𐐲𐑌𐐻𐐭 𐐩 𐐸𐐮𐑊, 𐐸𐐶𐐮𐐽 𐑇𐐰𐑊 𐐺𐐨 𐐿𐐫𐑊𐐼 𐐟𐐮𐑋; 𐐰𐑌𐐼 𐑄𐐯𐑉 𐐸𐐰𐑂 𐐌 𐐼𐐯𐐹𐐱𐑆𐐮𐐻𐐯𐐼 𐐲𐑌𐐻𐐭 𐑄 𐐢𐐫𐑉𐐼, 𐐫𐑊 𐑄 𐑅𐐩𐐿𐑉𐐯𐐼 𐐯𐑌𐑀𐑉𐐩𐑂𐐮𐑍𐑆 𐐿𐐲𐑌𐑅𐐲𐑉𐑌𐐮𐑍 𐑄𐐮𐑅 𐐹𐐨𐐹𐐲𐑊. 𐐈𐑌𐐼 𐐺𐐨𐐸𐐬𐑊𐐼, 𐐷𐐨 𐑇𐐰𐑊 𐐻𐐩𐐿 𐑄 𐐹𐑊𐐩𐐻𐑅 𐐲𐑂 𐐤𐐨𐑁𐐴 𐐲𐑌𐐻𐐭 𐐷𐐭𐑉𐑅𐐯𐑊𐑁, 𐐰𐑌𐐼 𐑄 𐑉𐐨𐑋𐐩𐑌𐐼𐐲𐑉 𐑇𐐰𐑊 𐐷𐐨 𐑊𐐨𐑂 𐐮𐑌 𐑄 𐐹𐑊𐐩𐑅 𐐸𐐶𐐯𐑉 𐑄𐐩 𐐪𐑉; 𐐰𐑌𐐼 𐐷𐐨 𐑇𐐰𐑊 𐐯𐑌𐑀𐑉𐐩𐑂 𐐱𐑌 𐑄 𐐹𐑊𐐩𐐻𐑅 𐐲𐑂 𐐤𐐨𐑁𐐴, 𐐫𐑊 𐑄 𐑃𐐮𐑍𐑆 𐑄𐐰𐐻 𐐷𐐨 𐐸𐐰𐑂 𐐲𐐺𐑆𐐲𐑉𐑂𐐼 𐐿𐐲𐑌𐑅𐐲𐑉𐑌𐐮𐑍 𐑄𐐮𐑅 𐐹𐐨𐐹𐐲𐑊. 𐐈𐑌𐐼 𐐌, 𐐣𐐬𐑉𐐣𐐲𐑌, 𐐺𐐨𐐮𐑍 𐐩 𐐼𐐯𐑅𐐯𐑌𐐼𐐲𐑌𐐻 𐐲𐑂 𐐤𐐨𐑁𐐴, (𐐰𐑌𐐼 𐑋𐐴 𐑁𐐪𐑄𐐲𐑉'𐑆 𐑌𐐩𐑋 𐐶𐐱𐑆 𐐣𐐬𐑉𐐣𐐲𐑌,) 𐐌 𐑉𐐨𐑋𐐯𐑋𐐺𐐲𐑉𐐼 𐑄 𐑃𐐮𐑍𐑆 𐐸𐐶𐐮𐐽 𐐈𐑋𐐰𐑉𐐲𐑌 𐐿𐐲𐑋𐐰𐑌𐐼𐐯𐐼 𐑋𐐨. 𐐈𐑌𐐼 𐐮𐐻 𐐿𐐩𐑋 𐐻𐐭 𐐹𐐰𐑅 𐑄𐐰𐐻 𐐌, 𐐺𐐨𐐮𐑍 𐐨𐑊𐐯𐑂𐐲𐑌 𐐷𐐨𐑉𐑆 𐐬𐑊𐐼, 𐐶𐐱𐑆 𐐿𐐰𐑉𐐨𐐼 𐐺𐐴 𐑋𐐴 𐑁𐐪𐑄𐐲𐑉 𐐮𐑌𐐻𐐭 𐑄 𐑊𐐰𐑌𐐼 𐑅𐐵𐑃𐐶𐐲𐑉𐐼, 𐐨𐑂𐐲𐑌 𐐻𐐭 𐑄 𐑊𐐰𐑌𐐼 𐐲𐑂 𐐞𐐰𐑉𐐲𐐸𐐯𐑋𐑊𐐲; 𐑄 𐐸𐐬𐑊 𐑁𐐩𐑅 𐐲𐑂 𐑄 𐑊𐐰𐑌𐐼 𐐸𐐰𐑂𐐮𐑍 𐐺𐐨𐐿𐐲𐑋 𐐿𐐲𐑂𐐲𐑉𐐼 𐐶𐐮𐑃 𐐺𐐮𐑊𐐼𐐮𐑍𐑆, 𐐰𐑌𐐼 𐑄 𐐹𐐨𐐹𐐲𐑊 𐐶𐐲𐑉 𐐰𐑆 𐑌𐐭𐑋𐐲𐑉𐐲𐑅 𐐫𐑊𐑋𐐬𐑅𐐻, 𐐰𐑆 𐐮𐐻 𐐶𐐲𐑉 𐑄 𐑅𐐰𐑌𐐼 𐐲𐑂 𐑄 𐑅𐐨. 𐐈𐑌𐐼 𐐮𐐻 𐐿𐐩𐑋 𐐻𐐭 𐐹𐐰𐑅 𐐮𐑌 𐑄𐐮𐑅 𐐷𐐨𐑉, 𐑄𐐯𐑉 𐐺𐐨𐑀𐐰𐑌 𐐻𐐭 𐐺𐐨 𐐩 𐐶𐐫𐑉 𐐺𐐨𐐻𐐶𐐨𐑌 𐑄 𐐤𐐨𐑁𐐴𐐻𐑅, 𐐸𐐶𐐮𐐽 𐐿𐐲𐑌𐑅𐐮𐑅𐐻𐐯𐐼 𐐲𐑂 𐑄 𐐤𐐨𐑁𐐴𐐻𐑅, 𐐰𐑌𐐼 𐑄 𐐖𐐩𐐿𐐲𐐺𐐴𐐻𐑅, 𐐰𐑌𐐼 𐑄 𐐖𐐬𐑆𐐯𐑁𐐴𐐻𐑅, 𐐰𐑌𐐼 𐑄 𐐞𐐬𐑉𐐲𐑋𐐴𐐻𐑅; 𐐰𐑌𐐼 𐑄𐐮𐑅 𐐶𐐫𐑉 𐐶𐐱𐑆 𐐺𐐨𐐻𐐶𐐨𐑌 𐑄 𐐤𐐨𐑁𐐴𐐻𐑅 𐐰𐑌𐐼 𐑄 𐐢𐐰𐑋𐐲𐑌𐐴𐐻𐑅, 𐐰𐑌𐐼 𐑄 𐐢𐐯𐑋𐐷𐐭𐐯𐑊𐐴𐐻𐑅, 𐐰𐑌𐐼 𐑄 𐐆𐑇𐑋𐐩𐐯𐑊𐐴𐐻𐑅. 𐐤𐐵 𐑄 𐐢𐐰𐑋𐐲𐑌𐐴𐐻𐑅, 𐐰𐑌𐐼 𐑄 𐐢𐐯𐑋𐐷𐐭𐐯𐑊𐐴𐐻𐑅, 𐐰𐑌𐐼 𐑄 𐐆𐑇𐑋𐐩𐐯𐑊𐐴𐐻𐑅, 𐐶𐐲𐑉 𐐿𐐫𐑊𐐼 𐐢𐐰𐑋𐐲𐑌𐐴𐐻𐑅, 𐐰𐑌𐐼 𐑄 𐐻𐐭 𐐹𐐪𐑉𐐻𐐨𐑆 𐐶𐐲𐑉 𐐤𐐨𐑁𐐴𐐻𐑅 𐐰𐑌𐐼 𐐢𐐰𐑋𐐲𐑌𐐴𐐻𐑅. 𐐈𐑌𐐼 𐐮𐐻 𐐿𐐩𐑋 𐐻𐐭 𐐹𐐰𐑅 𐑄𐐰𐐻 𐑄 𐐶𐐫𐑉 𐐺𐐨𐑀𐐰𐑌 𐐻𐐭 𐐺𐐨 𐐲𐑋𐐲𐑍 𐑄𐐯𐑋 𐐮𐑌 𐑄 𐐺𐐫𐑉𐐼𐐲𐑉𐑆 𐐲𐑂 𐐞𐐰𐑉𐐲𐐸𐐯𐑋𐑊𐐲, 𐐺𐐴 𐑄 𐐶𐐫𐐻𐐲𐑉𐑆 𐐲𐑂 𐐝𐐴𐐼𐐲𐑌.

2. 𐐈𐑌𐐼 𐐮𐐻 𐐿𐐩𐑋 𐐻𐐭 𐐹𐐰𐑅 𐑄𐐰𐐻 𐑄 𐐤𐐨𐑁𐐴𐐻𐑅 𐐸𐐰𐐼 𐑀𐐰𐑄𐐲𐑉𐐼 𐐻𐐳𐑀𐐯𐑄𐐲𐑉 𐐩 𐑀𐑉𐐩𐐻 𐑌𐐲𐑋𐐺𐐲𐑉 𐐲𐑂 𐑋𐐯𐑌, 𐐨𐑂𐐲𐑌 𐐻𐐭 𐐯𐐿𐑅𐐨𐐼 𐑄 𐑌𐐲𐑋𐐺𐐲𐑉 𐐲𐑂 𐑃𐐲𐑉𐐻𐐨 𐑃𐐵𐑆𐐲𐑌𐐼. 𐐈𐑌𐐼 𐐮𐐻 𐐿𐐩𐑋 𐐻𐐭 𐐹𐐰𐑅 𐑄𐐰𐐻 𐑄𐐩 𐐼𐐮𐐼 𐐸𐐰𐑂 𐐮𐑌 𐑄𐐮𐑅 𐑅𐐩𐑋 𐐷𐐨𐑉 𐐩 𐑌𐐲𐑋𐐺𐐲𐑉 𐐲𐑂 𐐺𐐰𐐻𐐲𐑊𐑆, 𐐮𐑌 𐐸𐐶𐐮𐐽 𐑄 𐐤𐐨𐑁𐐴𐐻𐑅 𐐼𐐮𐐼 𐐺𐐨𐐻 𐑄 𐐢𐐰𐑋𐐲𐑌𐐴𐐻𐑅, 𐐰𐑌𐐼 𐐼𐐮𐐼 𐑅𐑊𐐩 𐑋𐐯𐑌𐐨 𐐲𐑂 𐑄𐐯𐑋. 𐐈𐑌𐐼 𐐮𐐻 𐐿𐐩𐑋 𐐻𐐭 𐐹𐐰𐑅 𐑄𐐰𐐻 𐑄 𐐢𐐰𐑋𐐲𐑌𐐴𐐻𐑅 𐐶𐐮𐑃𐐼𐑉𐐭 𐑄𐐩𐑉 𐐼𐐯𐑆𐐴𐑌, 𐐰𐑌𐐼 𐑄𐐯𐑉 𐐶𐐱𐑆 𐐹𐐨𐑅 𐑅𐐯𐐻𐐲𐑊𐐼 𐐮𐑌 𐑄 𐑊𐐰𐑌𐐼, 𐐰𐑌𐐼 𐐹𐐨𐑅 𐐼𐐮𐐼 𐑉𐐨𐑋𐐩𐑌 𐑁𐐫𐑉 𐑄 𐑅𐐹𐐩𐑅 𐐲𐑂 𐐲𐐺𐐵𐐻 𐑁𐐬𐑉 𐐷𐐨𐑉𐑆, 𐑄𐐰𐐻 𐑄𐐯𐑉 𐐶𐐱𐑆 𐑌𐐬 𐐺𐑊𐐲𐐼𐑇𐐯𐐼. 𐐒𐐲𐐻 𐐶𐐮𐐿𐐯𐐼𐑌𐐯𐑅 𐐼𐐮𐐼 𐐹𐑉𐐨𐑂𐐩𐑊 𐐲𐐹𐐱𐑌 𐑄 𐑁𐐩𐑅 𐐲𐑂 𐑄 𐐸𐐬𐑊 𐑊𐐰𐑌𐐼, 𐐮𐑌𐑅𐐬𐑋𐐲𐐽 𐑄𐐰𐐻 𐑄 𐐢𐐫𐑉𐐼 𐐼𐐮𐐼 𐐻𐐩𐐿 𐐲𐐶𐐩 𐐸𐐮𐑆 𐐺𐐨𐑊𐐲𐑂𐐯𐐼 𐐼𐐮𐑅𐐴𐐹𐐲𐑊𐑆, 𐐰𐑌𐐼 𐑄 𐐶𐐲𐑉𐐿 𐐲𐑂 𐑋𐐮𐑉𐐲𐐿𐐲𐑊𐑆 𐐰𐑌𐐼 𐐲𐑂 𐐸𐐨𐑊𐐮𐑍 𐐼𐐮𐐼 𐑅𐐨𐑅, 𐐺𐐨𐐿𐐫𐑆 𐐲𐑂 𐑄 𐐮𐑌𐐮𐐿𐐶𐐮𐐻𐐨 𐐲𐑂 𐑄 𐐹𐐨𐐹𐐲𐑊.

𐐰𐑌𐐼 𐑄𐐩𐑉 𐐶𐐲𐑉 𐑌𐐬 𐑀𐐮𐑁𐐻𐑅 𐑁𐑉𐐱𐑋 𐑄 𐐢𐐫𐑉𐐼, 𐐰𐑌𐐼 𐑄 𐐐𐐬𐑊𐐨 𐐘𐐬𐑅𐐻 𐐼𐐮𐐼 𐑌𐐱𐐻 𐐿𐐲𐑋 𐐲𐐹𐐱𐑌 𐐯𐑌𐐨, 𐐺𐐨𐐿𐐫𐑆 𐐱𐑂 𐑄𐐩𐑉 𐐶𐐮𐐿𐐯𐐼𐑌𐐯𐑅 𐐰𐑌𐐼 𐐲𐑌𐐺𐐨𐑊𐐨𐑁. 𐐈𐑌𐐼 𐐌 𐐺𐐨𐐮𐑍 𐑁𐐮𐑁𐐻𐐨𐑌 𐐷𐐨𐑉𐑆 𐐱𐑂 𐐩𐐾, 𐐰𐑌𐐼 𐐺𐐨𐐮𐑍 𐑅𐐲𐑋𐐸𐐶𐐱𐐻 𐐱𐑂 𐐲 𐑅𐐬𐐺𐐲𐑉 𐑋𐐴𐑌𐐼, 𐑄𐐯𐑉𐑁𐐬𐑉 𐐌 𐐶𐐱𐑆 𐑂𐐮𐑆𐐮𐐻𐐯𐐼 𐐱𐑂 𐑄 𐐢𐐫𐑉𐐼, 𐐰𐑌𐐼 𐐻𐐩𐑅𐐻𐐯𐐼, 𐐰𐑌𐐼 𐑌𐐭 𐐱𐑂 𐑄 𐑀𐐳𐐼𐑌𐐯𐑅 𐐱𐑂 𐐖𐐨𐑆𐐲𐑅. 𐐈𐑌𐐼 𐐌 𐐼𐐮𐐼 𐐯𐑌𐐼𐐯𐑂𐐲𐑉 𐐻𐐭 𐐹𐑉𐐨𐐽 𐐲𐑌𐐻𐐭 𐑄𐐮𐑅 𐐹𐐨𐐹𐑊, 𐐺𐐲𐐻 𐑋𐐴 𐑋𐐵𐑃 𐐶𐐱𐑆 𐑇𐐲𐐻, 𐐰𐑌𐐼 𐐌 𐐶𐐱𐑆 𐑁𐐫𐑉𐐺𐐮𐐼𐐲𐑌 𐑄𐐰𐐻 𐐌 𐑇𐐳𐐼 𐐹𐑉𐐨𐐽 𐐲𐑌𐐻𐐭 𐑄𐐯𐑋; 𐑁𐐫𐑉 𐐺𐐨𐐸𐐬𐑊𐐼 𐑄𐐩 𐐸𐐰𐐼 𐐶𐐮𐑊𐑁𐐳𐑊𐐨 𐑉𐐨𐐺𐐯𐑊𐐼 𐐰𐑀𐐯𐑌𐑅𐐻 𐑄𐐩𐑉 𐐘𐐱𐐼, 𐐰𐑌𐐼 𐑄 𐐺𐐨𐑊𐐲𐑂𐐯𐐼 𐐼𐐮𐑅𐐴𐐹𐑊𐑆 𐐶𐐲𐑉 𐐻𐐩𐐿𐑌 𐐰𐐶𐐩 𐐵𐐻 𐐱𐑂 𐑄 𐑊𐐰𐑌𐐼, 𐐺𐐨𐐿𐐫𐑆 𐐱𐑂 𐑄𐐩𐑉 𐐮𐑌𐐮𐐿𐐶𐐮𐐻𐐨. 𐐒𐐲𐐻 𐐌 𐐼𐐮𐐼 𐑉𐐨𐑋𐐩𐑌 𐐰𐑋𐐲𐑍 𐑄𐐯𐑋, 𐐺𐐲𐐻 𐐌 𐐶𐐱𐑆 𐑁𐐫𐑉𐐺𐐮𐐼𐐲𐑌 𐐻𐐭 𐐹𐑉𐐨𐐽 𐐲𐑌𐐻𐐭 𐑄𐐯𐑋, 𐐺𐐨𐐿𐐫𐑆 𐐱𐑂 𐑄 𐐸𐐪𐑉𐐼𐑌𐐯𐑅 𐐱𐑂 𐑄𐐩𐑉 𐐸𐐪𐑉𐐻𐑅; 𐐰𐑌𐐼 𐐺𐐨𐐿𐐫𐑆 𐐱𐑂 𐑄 𐐸𐐪𐑉𐐼𐑌𐐯𐑅 𐐱𐑂 𐑄𐐩𐑉 𐐸𐐪𐑉𐐻𐑅, 𐑄 𐑊𐐰𐑌𐐼 𐐶𐐱𐑆 𐐿𐐲𐑉𐑅𐐻 𐑁𐐫𐑉 𐑄𐐩𐑉 𐑅𐐩𐐿. 𐐈𐑌𐐼 𐑄𐐨𐑆 𐐘𐐰𐐼𐐨𐐰𐑌𐐻𐐲𐑌 𐑉𐐱𐐺𐐲𐑉𐑆, 𐐸𐐭 𐐶𐐲𐑉 𐐰𐑋𐐲𐑍 𐑄 𐐢𐐩𐑋𐐲𐑌𐐴𐐻𐑅, 𐐼𐐮𐐼 𐐮𐑌𐑁𐐯𐑅𐐻 𐑄 𐑊𐐰𐑌𐐼, 𐐮𐑌𐑅𐐬𐑋𐐲𐐽 𐑄𐐰𐐻 𐑄 𐐮𐑌𐐸𐐰𐐺𐐮𐐻𐐰𐑌𐐻𐑅 𐑄𐐯𐑉𐐱𐑂 𐐺𐐨𐑀𐐰𐑌 𐐻𐐭 𐐸𐐴𐐼 𐐲𐐹 𐑄𐐩𐑉 𐐻𐑉𐐯𐑆𐐲𐑉𐑆 𐐮𐑌 𐑄 𐐲𐑉𐑃; 𐐰𐑌𐐼 𐑄𐐩 𐐺𐐨𐐿𐐩𐑋 𐑅𐑊𐐮𐐹𐐲𐑉𐐨, 𐐺𐐨𐐿𐐫𐑆 𐑄 𐐢𐐫𐑉𐐼 𐐸𐐰𐐼 𐐿𐐲𐑉𐑅𐐻 𐑄 𐑊𐐰𐑌𐐼, 𐑄𐐰𐐻 𐑄𐐩 𐐿𐐳𐐼 𐑌𐐱𐐻 𐐸𐐬𐑊𐐼 𐑄𐐯𐑋, 𐑌𐐫𐑉 𐑉𐐨𐐻𐐩𐑌 𐑄𐐯𐑋 𐐰𐑀𐐯𐑌. 𐐈𐑌𐐼 𐐮𐐻 𐐿𐐩𐑋 𐐻𐐭 𐐹𐐩𐑅 𐑄𐐰𐐻 𐑄𐐩𐑉 𐐶𐐲𐑉 𐑅𐐫𐑉𐑅𐐲𐑉𐐨𐑆, 𐐰𐑌𐐼 𐐶𐐮𐐽𐐿𐑉𐐰𐑁𐐻𐑅, 𐐰𐑌𐐼 𐑋𐐰𐐾𐐮𐐿𐑅; 𐐰𐑌𐐼 𐑄 𐐹𐐵𐐲𐑉 𐐱𐑂 𐑄 𐐨𐑂𐐮𐑊 𐐶𐐲𐑌 𐐶𐐱𐑆 𐑉𐐫𐐻 𐐲𐐹𐐱𐑌 𐐫𐑊 𐑄 𐑁𐐩𐑅 𐐱𐑂 𐑄 𐑊𐐰𐑌𐐼, 𐐨𐑂𐐯𐑌 𐐲𐑌𐐻𐐭 𐑄 𐑁𐐳𐑊𐑁𐐮𐑊𐐮𐑍 𐐱𐑂 𐐫𐑊 𐑄 𐐶𐐲𐑉𐐼𐑆 𐐱𐑂 𐐈𐐺𐐮𐑌𐐰𐐼𐐴, 𐐰𐑌𐐼 𐐫𐑊𐑅𐐬 𐐝𐐰𐑋𐐷𐐭𐐯𐑊 𐑄 𐐢𐐩𐑋𐐲𐑌𐐴𐐻.

3. 𐐈𐑌𐐼 𐐮𐐻 𐐿𐐩𐑋 𐐻𐐭 𐐹𐐩𐑅 𐐮𐑌 𐑄𐐰𐐻 𐑅𐐩𐑋 𐐷𐐨𐑉, 𐑄𐐩𐑉 𐐺𐐨𐑀𐐰𐑌 𐐻𐐭 𐐺𐐨 𐐲 𐐶𐐫𐑉 𐐰𐑀𐐯𐑌 𐐺𐐨𐐻𐐶𐐨𐑌 𐑄 𐐤𐐨𐑁𐐴𐐻𐑅 𐐰𐑌𐐼 𐑄 𐐢𐐩𐑋𐐲𐑌𐐴𐐻𐑅. 𐐈𐑌𐐼 𐑌𐐱𐐻𐐶𐐮𐑄𐑅𐐻𐐰𐑌𐐼𐐮𐑍 𐐌 𐐺𐐨𐐮𐑍 𐐷𐐲𐑍, 𐐶𐐱𐑆 𐑊𐐪𐑉𐐾 𐐮𐑌 𐑅𐐻𐐰𐐽𐐭𐑉; 𐑄𐐯𐑉𐑁𐐬𐑉 𐑄 𐐹𐐨𐐹𐑊 𐐱𐑂 𐐤𐐨𐑁𐐴 𐐰𐐹𐐱𐐮𐑌𐐻𐐯𐐼 𐑋𐐨 𐑄𐐰𐐻 𐐌 𐑇𐐳𐐼 𐐺𐐨 𐑄𐐩𐑉 𐑊𐐨𐐼𐐲𐑉, 𐐫𐑉 𐑄 𐑊𐐨𐐼𐐲𐑉 𐐱𐑂 𐑄𐐩𐑉 𐐪𐑉𐑋𐐨𐑆. 𐐜𐐯𐑉𐑁𐐬𐑉 𐐮𐐻 𐐿𐐩𐑋 𐐻𐐭 𐐹𐐩𐑅 𐑄𐐰𐐻 𐐮𐑌 𐑋𐐴 𐑅𐐮𐐿𐑅𐐻𐐨𐑌𐑃 𐐷𐐨𐑉 𐐌 𐐼𐐮𐐼 𐑀𐐬 𐑁𐐬𐑉𐑃 𐐰𐐻 𐑄 𐐸𐐯𐐼 𐐱𐑂 𐐰𐑌 𐐪𐑉𐑋𐐨 𐐱𐑂 𐑄 𐐤𐐨𐑁𐐴𐐻𐑅, 𐐰𐑀𐐯𐑌𐑅𐐻 𐑄 𐐢𐐩𐑋𐐲𐑌𐐴𐐻𐑅; 𐑄𐐯𐑉𐑁𐐬𐑉 𐑃𐑉𐐨 𐐸𐐲𐑌𐐼𐑉𐐯𐐼 𐐰𐑌𐐼 𐐻𐐶𐐯𐑌𐐻𐐨 𐐰𐑌𐐼 𐑅𐐮𐐿𐑅 𐐷𐐨𐑉𐑆 𐐸𐐰𐐼 𐐹𐐩𐑅𐐻 𐐰𐐶𐐩. 𐐈𐑌𐐼 𐐮𐐻 𐐿𐐩𐑋 𐐻𐐭 𐐹𐐩𐑅 𐑄𐐰𐐻 𐐮𐑌 𐑄 𐑃𐑉𐐨 𐐸𐐲𐑌𐐼𐑉𐐯𐐼 𐐰𐑌𐐼 𐐻𐐶𐐯𐑌𐐻𐐨 𐐰𐑌𐐼 𐑅𐐯𐑂𐐯𐑌𐑃 𐐷𐐨𐑉 𐑄 𐐢𐐩𐑋𐐲𐑌𐐴𐐻𐑅 𐐼𐐮𐐼 𐐿𐐲𐑋 𐐲𐐹𐐱𐑌 𐐲𐑅 𐐶𐐮𐑄 𐐯𐐿𐑅𐐨𐐼𐐮𐑍 𐑀𐑉𐐩𐐻 𐐹𐐵𐐲𐑉, 𐐮𐑌𐑅𐐬𐑋𐐲𐐽 𐑄𐐰𐐻 𐑄𐐩 𐐼𐐮𐐼 𐑁𐑉𐐴𐐻𐑌 𐑋𐐴 𐐪𐑉𐑋𐐨𐑆; 𐑄𐐯𐑉𐑁𐐬𐑉 𐑄𐐩 𐐶𐐳𐐼 𐑌𐐱𐐻 𐑁𐐴𐐻, 𐐰𐑌𐐼 𐑄𐐩 𐐺𐐨𐑀𐐰𐑌 𐐻𐐭 𐑉𐐨𐐻𐑉𐐨𐐻 𐐻𐐬𐑉𐐼𐑆 𐑄 𐑌𐐫𐑉𐑃 𐐿𐐲𐑌𐐻𐑉𐐨𐑆. 𐐈𐑌𐐼 𐐮𐐻 𐐿𐐩𐑋 𐐻𐐭 𐐹𐐩𐑅 𐑄𐐰𐐻 𐐶𐐨 𐐼𐐮𐐼 𐐿𐐲𐑋 𐐻𐐭 𐑄 𐑅𐐮𐐻𐐨 𐐱𐑂 𐐈𐑍𐑀𐐬𐑊𐐲, 𐐰𐑌𐐼 𐐶𐐨 𐐼𐐮𐐼 𐐻𐐩𐐿 𐐹𐐱𐑆𐐯𐑇𐐲𐑌 𐐱𐑂 𐑄 𐑅𐐮𐐻𐐨, 𐐰𐑌𐐼 𐑋𐐩𐐿 𐐹𐑉𐐯𐐹𐐲𐑉𐐩𐑇𐐲𐑌𐑆 𐐻𐐭 𐐼𐐨𐑁𐐯𐑌𐐼 𐐵𐑉𐑅𐐯𐑊𐑂𐑆 𐐰𐑀𐐯𐑌𐑅𐐻 𐑄 𐐢𐐩𐑋𐐲𐑌𐐴𐐻𐑅. 𐐈𐑌𐐼 𐐮𐐻 𐐿𐐩𐑋 𐐻𐐭 𐐹𐐩𐑅 𐑄𐐰𐐻 𐐶𐐨 𐐼𐐮𐐼 𐑁𐐫𐑉𐐻𐐮𐑁𐐴 𐑄 𐑅𐐮𐐻𐐨 𐐶𐐮𐑄 𐐵𐑉 𐑋𐐴𐐻; 𐐺𐐲𐐻 𐑌𐐱𐐻𐐶𐐮𐑄𐑅𐐻𐐰𐑌𐐼𐐮𐑍 𐐫𐑊 𐐵𐑉 𐑁𐐫𐑉𐐻𐐮𐑁𐐮𐐿𐐩𐑇𐐲𐑌𐑆, 𐑄 𐐢𐐩𐑋𐐲𐑌𐐴𐐻𐑅 𐐼𐐮𐐼 𐐿𐐲𐑋 𐐲𐐹𐐱𐑌 𐐲𐑅, 𐐰𐑌𐐼 𐐼𐐮𐐼 𐐼𐑉𐐴𐑂 𐐲𐑅 𐐵𐐻 𐐱𐑂 𐑄 𐑅𐐮𐐻𐐨. 𐐈𐑌𐐼 𐑄𐐩 𐐼𐐮𐐼 𐐫𐑊𐑅𐐬 𐐼𐑉𐐴𐑂 𐐲𐑅 𐑁𐐬𐑉𐑃 𐐵𐐻 𐐱𐑂 𐑄 𐑊𐐰𐑌𐐼 𐐱𐑂 𐐔𐐩𐑂𐐮𐐼. 𐐈𐑌𐐼 𐐶𐐨 𐑋𐐪𐑉𐐽𐐻 𐑁𐐬𐑉𐑃 𐐰𐑌𐐼 𐐿𐐩𐑋 𐐻𐐭 𐑄 𐑊𐐰𐑌𐐼 𐐱𐑂 𐐖𐐱𐑇𐐭𐐲, 𐐸𐐶𐐮𐐽 𐐶𐐱𐑆 𐐮𐑌 𐑄 𐐺𐐫𐑉𐐼𐐲𐑉𐑆 𐐶𐐯𐑅𐐻, 𐐺𐐴 𐑄 𐑅𐐨 𐑇𐐬𐑉. 𐐈𐑌𐐼 𐐮𐐻 𐐿𐐩𐑋 𐐻𐐭 𐐹𐐩𐑅 𐑄𐐰𐐻 𐐶𐐨 𐐼𐐮𐐼 𐑀𐐰𐑄𐐲𐑉 𐐮𐑌 𐐵𐑉 𐐹𐐨𐐹𐑊 𐐰𐑆 𐑁𐐪𐑅𐐻 𐐰𐑆 𐐮𐐻 𐐶𐐲𐑉 𐐹𐐱𐑅𐐮𐐺𐑊, 𐑄𐐰𐐻 𐐶𐐨 𐑋𐐴𐐻 𐑀𐐯𐐻 𐑄𐐯𐑋 𐐻𐐭𐑀𐐯𐑄𐐲𐑉 𐐮𐑌 𐐶𐐲𐑌 𐐺𐐱𐐼𐐨. 𐐒𐐲𐐻 𐐺𐐨𐐸𐐬𐑊𐐼 𐑄 𐑊𐐰𐑌𐐼 𐐶𐐱𐑆 𐑁𐐮𐑊𐐼 𐐶𐐮𐑄 𐑉𐐱𐐺𐐲𐑉𐑆 𐐰𐑌𐐼 𐐶𐐮𐑄 𐐢𐐩𐑋𐐲𐑌𐐴𐐻𐑅; 𐐰𐑌𐐼 𐑌𐐱𐐻𐐶𐐮𐑄𐑅𐐻𐐰𐑌𐐼𐐮𐑍 𐑄 𐑀𐑉𐐩𐐻 𐐼𐐯𐑅𐐻𐑉𐐲𐐿𐑇𐐲𐑌 𐐸𐐶𐐮𐐽 𐐸𐐲𐑍 𐐬𐑂𐐲𐑉 𐑋𐐴 𐐹𐐨𐐹𐑊, 𐑄𐐩 𐐼𐐮𐐼 𐑌𐐱𐐻 𐑉𐐨𐐹𐐯𐑌𐐻 𐐱𐑂 𐑄𐐩𐑉 𐐨𐑂𐐮𐑊 𐐼𐐭𐐮𐑍𐑆; 𐑄𐐯𐑉𐑁𐐬𐑉 𐑄𐐩𐑉 𐐶𐐱𐑆 𐐺𐑊𐐲𐐼 𐐰𐑌𐐼 𐐿𐐪𐑉𐑌𐐩𐐾 𐑅𐐹𐑉𐐯𐐼 𐑃𐑉𐐭𐐵𐐻 𐐫𐑊 𐑄 𐑁𐐩𐑅 𐐱𐑂 𐑄 𐑊𐐰𐑌𐐼, 𐐺𐐬𐑃 𐐱𐑌 𐑄 𐐹𐐪𐑉𐐻 𐐱𐑂 𐑄 𐐤𐐨𐑁𐐴𐐻𐑅, 𐐰𐑌𐐼 𐐫𐑊𐑅𐐬 𐐱𐑌 𐑄 𐐹𐐪𐑉𐐻 𐐱𐑂 𐑄 𐐢𐐩𐑋𐐲𐑌𐐴𐐻𐑅; 𐐰𐑌𐐼 𐐮𐐻 𐐶𐐱𐑆 𐐶𐐲𐑌 𐐿𐐱𐑋𐐹𐑊𐐨𐐻 𐑉𐐯𐑂𐐬𐑊𐐭𐑇𐐲𐑌 𐑃𐑉𐐭𐐵𐐻 𐐫𐑊 𐑄 𐑁𐐩𐑅 𐐱𐑂 𐑄 𐑊𐐰𐑌𐐼. 𐐈𐑌𐐼 𐑌𐐵 𐑄 𐐢𐐩𐑋𐐲𐑌𐐴𐐻𐑅 𐐸𐐰𐐼 𐐲 𐐿𐐮𐑍, 𐐰𐑌𐐼 𐐸𐐮𐑆 𐑌𐐩𐑋 𐐶𐐱𐑆 𐐁𐑉𐐲𐑌; 𐐰𐑌𐐼 𐐸𐐨 𐐿𐐩𐑋 𐐰𐑀𐐯𐑌𐑅𐐻 𐐲𐑅 𐐶𐐮𐑄 𐐰𐑌 𐐪𐑉𐑋𐐨 𐐱𐑂 𐑁𐐫𐑉𐐻𐐨 𐐰𐑌𐐼 𐑁𐐬𐑉 𐑃𐐵𐑆𐐲𐑌𐐼. 𐐈𐑌𐐼 𐐺𐐨𐐸𐐬𐑊𐐼, 𐐌 𐐶𐐮𐑄𐑅𐐻𐐳𐐼 𐐸𐐮𐑋 𐐶𐐮𐑄 𐑁𐐫𐑉𐐻𐐨 𐐰𐑌𐐼 𐐻𐐭 𐑃𐐵𐑆𐐲𐑌𐐼. 𐐈𐑌𐐼 𐐮𐐻 𐐿𐐩𐑋 𐐻𐐭 𐐹𐐩𐑅 𐑄𐐰𐐻 𐐌 𐐺𐐨𐐻 𐐸𐐮𐑋 𐐶𐐮𐑄 𐑋𐐴 𐐪𐑉𐑋𐐨, 𐑄𐐰𐐻 𐐸𐐨 𐑁𐑊𐐯𐐼 𐐺𐐨𐑁𐐬𐑉 𐑋𐐨. 𐐈𐑌𐐼 𐐺𐐨𐐸𐐬𐑊𐐼, 𐐫𐑊 𐑄𐐮𐑅 𐐶𐐱𐑆 𐐼𐐲𐑌, 𐐰𐑌𐐼 𐑃𐑉𐐨 𐐸𐐲𐑌𐐼𐑉𐐯𐐼 𐐰𐑌𐐼 𐑃𐐲𐑉𐐻𐐨 𐐷𐐨𐑉𐑆 𐐸𐐰𐐼 𐐹𐐩𐑅𐐻 𐐰𐐶𐐩.

4. 𐐈𐑌𐐼 𐐮𐐻 𐐿𐐩𐑋 𐐻𐐭 𐐹𐐩𐑅 𐑄𐐰𐐻 𐑄 𐐤𐐨𐑁𐐴𐐻𐑅 𐐺𐐨𐑀𐐰𐑌 𐐻𐐭 𐑉𐐨𐐹𐐯𐑌𐐻 𐐱𐑂 𐑄𐐩𐑉 𐐮𐑌𐐮𐐿𐐶𐐮𐐻𐐨, 𐐰𐑌𐐼

𐐺𐐨𐑀𐐰𐑌 𐐻𐐭 𐐿𐑉𐐴, 𐐨𐑂𐑌 𐐰𐑆 𐐸𐐰𐐼 𐐺𐐮𐑌 𐐹𐑉𐐱𐑁𐐯𐑅𐐴𐐼 𐐺𐐴 𐐝𐐰𐑋𐐷𐐭𐐯𐑊 𐑄 𐐹𐑉𐐱𐑁𐐯𐐻; 𐑁𐐬𐑉 𐐺𐐨𐐸𐐬𐑊𐐼, 𐑌𐐬 𐑋𐐰𐑌 𐐿𐐳𐐼 𐐿𐐨𐐹 𐑄𐐰𐐻 𐐸𐐶𐐮𐐽 𐐶𐐱𐑆 𐐸𐐮𐑆 𐐬𐑌, 𐑁𐐬𐑉 𐑄 𐑃𐐨𐑂𐑆, 𐐰𐑌𐐼 𐑄 𐑉𐐱𐐺𐐲𐑉𐑆, 𐐰𐑌𐐼 𐑄 𐑋𐐲𐑉𐐼𐐲𐑉𐐲𐑉𐑆, 𐐰𐑌𐐼 𐑄 𐑋𐐰𐐾𐐮𐐿 𐐪𐑉𐐻, 𐐰𐑌𐐼 𐑄 𐐶𐐮𐐽𐐿𐑉𐐰𐑁𐐻 𐐸𐐶𐐮𐐽 𐐶𐐱𐑆 𐐮𐑌 𐑄 𐑊𐐰𐑌𐐼. 𐐜𐐲𐑅 𐑄𐐩𐑉 𐐺𐐨𐑀𐐰𐑌 𐐻𐐭 𐐺 𐐩 𐑋𐐬𐑉𐑌𐐮𐑍, 𐐰𐑌𐐼 𐐩 𐑊𐐰𐑋𐐯𐑌𐐻𐐩𐑇𐐲𐑌 𐐮𐑌 𐐫𐑊 𐑄 𐑊𐐰𐑌𐐼 𐐺𐐨𐐿𐐫𐑆 𐐱𐑂 𐑄𐐨𐑆 𐑃𐐮𐑍𐑆; 𐐰𐑌𐐼 𐑋𐐬𐑉 𐐯𐑅𐐹𐐯𐑇𐐲𐑊𐐮 𐐰𐑋𐐲𐑍 𐑄 𐐹𐐨𐐹𐑊 𐐱𐑂 𐐤𐐨𐑁𐐴. 𐐈𐑌𐐼 𐐮𐐻 𐐿𐐩𐑋 𐐻𐐭 𐐹𐐪𐑅 𐑄𐐰𐐻 𐐸𐐶𐐯𐑌 𐐴, 𐐣𐐬𐑉𐑋𐐲𐑌, 𐑅𐐫 𐑄𐐩𐑉 𐑊𐐰𐑋𐐯𐑌𐐻𐐩𐑇𐐲𐑌, 𐐰𐑌𐐼 𐑄𐐩𐑉 𐑋𐐬𐑉𐑌𐐮𐑍, 𐐰𐑌𐐼 𐑄𐐩𐑉 𐑅𐐱𐑉𐐬 𐐺𐐨𐑁𐐬𐑉 𐑄 𐐢𐐬𐑉𐐼, 𐑋𐐴 𐐸𐐪𐑉𐐻 𐐼𐐮𐐼 𐐺𐐨𐑀𐐮𐑌 𐐻𐐭 𐑉𐐨𐐾𐐬𐐮𐑅 𐐶𐐮𐑄𐐮𐑌 𐑋𐐨, 𐑌𐐬𐐮𐑍 𐑄 𐑋𐐲𐑉𐑅𐐨𐑆 𐐰𐑌𐐼 𐑄 𐑊𐐫𐑍-𐑅𐐲𐑁𐐲𐑉𐐮𐑍 𐐱𐑂 𐑄 𐐢𐐬𐑉𐐼, 𐑄𐐩𐑉𐑁𐐬𐑉 𐑅𐐲𐐹𐐬𐑆𐐮𐑍 𐑄𐐰𐐻 𐐸𐐨 𐐶𐐳𐐼 𐐺 𐑋𐐲𐑉𐑅𐐮𐑁𐐳𐑊 𐐲𐑌𐐻𐐭 𐑄𐐯𐑋, 𐑄𐐰𐐻 𐑄𐐩 𐐶𐐳𐐼 𐐰𐑀𐐯𐑌 𐐺𐐨𐐿𐐲𐑋 𐐩 𐑉𐐴𐐽𐐲𐑅 𐐹𐐨𐐹𐑊. 𐐒𐐲𐐻 𐐺𐐨𐐸𐐬𐑊𐐼, 𐑄𐐮𐑅 𐑋𐐴 𐐾𐐱𐐮 𐐶𐐱𐑆 𐑂𐐩𐑌, 𐑁𐐬𐑉 𐑄𐐩𐑉 𐑅𐐱𐑉𐐬𐐮𐑍 𐐶𐐱𐑆 𐑌𐐱𐐻 𐐲𐑌𐐻𐐭 𐑉𐐯𐐹𐐯𐑌𐐻𐐲𐑌𐑅, 𐐺𐐨𐐿𐐫𐑆 𐐱𐑂 𐑄 𐑀𐐳𐐼𐑌𐐯𐑅 𐐱𐑂 𐐘𐐱𐐼, 𐐺𐐲𐐻 𐐮𐐻 𐐶𐐱𐑆 𐑉𐐰𐑄𐐲𐑉 𐑄 𐑅𐐱𐑉𐐬𐐮𐑍 𐐱𐑂 𐑄 𐐼𐐰𐑋𐐼, 𐐺𐐨𐐿𐐫𐑆 𐑄 𐐢𐐬𐑉𐐼 𐐶𐐳𐐼 𐑌𐐱𐐻 𐐫𐑊𐐶𐐩𐑆 𐑅𐐲𐑁𐐲𐑉 𐑄𐐯𐑋 𐐻𐐭 𐐻𐐩𐐿 𐐸𐐰𐐹𐐮𐑌𐐯𐑅 𐐮𐑌 𐑅𐐮𐑌. 𐐈𐑌𐐼 𐑄𐐩 𐐼𐐮𐐼 𐑌𐐱𐐻 𐐿𐐲𐑋 𐐲𐑌𐐻𐐭 𐐖𐐨𐑆𐐲𐑅 𐐶𐐮𐑄 𐐺𐑉𐐬𐐿𐐲𐑌 𐐸𐐪𐑉𐐻𐑅 𐐰𐑌𐐼 𐐿𐐱𐑌𐐻𐑉𐐴𐐻 𐑅𐐹𐐮𐑉𐐮𐐻𐑅, 𐐺𐐲𐐻 𐑄𐐩 𐐼𐐮𐐼 𐐿𐐲𐑉𐑅 𐐘𐐱𐐼 𐐰𐑌𐐼 𐐶𐐮𐑇 𐐻𐐭 𐐼𐐴. 𐐤𐐯𐑂𐐲𐑉𐑄𐐲𐑊𐐯𐑅 𐑄𐐩 𐐶𐐳𐐼 𐑅𐐻𐑉𐐲𐑀𐑊 𐐶𐐮𐑄 𐑄 𐑅𐐬𐑉𐐼 𐑁𐐬𐑉 𐑄𐐩𐑉 𐑊𐐴𐑂𐑆. 𐐈𐑌𐐼 𐐮𐐻 𐐿𐐩𐑋 𐐻𐐭 𐐹𐐪𐑅 𐑄𐐰𐐻 𐑋𐐴 𐑅𐐱𐑉𐐬 𐐼𐐮𐐼 𐑉𐐨𐐻𐐲𐑉𐑌 𐐲𐑌𐐻𐐭 𐑋𐐨 𐐰𐑀𐐯𐑌, 𐐰𐑌𐐼 𐐴 𐑅𐐫 𐑄𐐰𐐻 𐑄 𐐼𐐩 𐐱𐑂 𐑀𐑉𐐩𐑅 𐐶𐐱𐑆 𐐹𐐪𐑅𐐻 𐐶𐐮𐑄 𐑄𐐯𐑋, 𐐺𐐬𐑃 𐐻𐐯𐑋𐐹𐐬𐑉𐐲𐑊𐐮 𐐰𐑌𐐼 𐑅𐐹𐐮𐑉𐐮𐐻𐐷𐐭𐐲𐑊𐐮; 𐑁𐐬𐑉 𐐴 𐑅𐐫 𐑃𐐵𐑆𐐲𐑌𐐼𐑆 𐐱𐑂 𐑄𐐯𐑋 𐐸𐐷𐐭𐑌 𐐼𐐵𐑌 𐐮𐑌 𐐬𐐹𐑌 𐑉𐐯𐐺𐐯𐑊𐐷𐐲𐑌 𐐰𐑀𐐯𐑌𐑅𐐻 𐑄𐐩𐑉 𐐘𐐱𐐼, 𐐰𐑌𐐼 𐐸𐐨𐐹𐐻 𐐲𐐹 𐐰𐑆 𐐼𐐲𐑍 𐐲𐐹𐐱𐑌 𐑄 𐑁𐐩𐑅 𐐱𐑂 𐑄 𐑊𐐰𐑌𐐼. 𐐈𐑌𐐼 𐑄𐐲𐑅 𐑃𐑉𐐨 𐐸𐐲𐑌𐐼𐑉𐐯𐐼 𐐰𐑌𐐼 𐑁𐐬𐑉𐐻𐐨 𐐰𐑌𐐼 𐑁𐐬𐑉 𐐷𐐨𐑉𐑆 𐐸𐐰𐐼 𐐹𐐪𐑅𐐻 𐐰𐐶𐐩.

5. 𐐈𐑌𐐼 𐐮𐐻 𐐿𐐩𐑋 𐐻𐐭 𐐹𐐪𐑅 𐑄𐐰𐐻 𐐮𐑌 𐑄 𐑃𐑉𐐨 𐐸𐐲𐑌𐐼𐑉𐐯𐐼 𐐰𐑌𐐼 𐑁𐐬𐑉𐐻𐐨 𐐰𐑌𐐼 𐑁𐐮𐑁𐑃 𐐷𐐨𐑉, 𐑄 𐐤𐐨𐑁𐐴𐐻𐑅 𐐼𐐮𐐼 𐐺𐐨𐑀𐐮𐑌 𐐻𐐭 𐑁𐑊𐐨 𐐺𐐨𐑁𐐬𐑉 𐑄 𐐢𐐩𐑋𐐲𐑌𐐴𐐻𐑅, 𐐰𐑌𐐼 𐑄𐐩 𐐶𐐲𐑉 𐐹𐐲𐑉𐑅𐐭𐐼 𐐲𐑌𐐻𐐮𐑊 𐑄𐐩 𐐿𐐩𐑋 𐐨𐑂𐑌 𐐻𐐭 𐑄 𐑊𐐰𐑌𐐼 𐐱𐑂 𐐖𐐩𐑇𐐲𐑌, 𐐺𐐨𐑁𐐬𐑉 𐐮𐐻 𐐶𐐱𐑆 𐐹𐐱𐑅𐐮𐐺𐑊 𐐻𐐭 𐑅𐐻𐐱𐐹 𐑄𐐯𐑋 𐐮𐑌 𐑄𐐩𐑉 𐑉𐐨𐐻𐑉𐐨𐐻. 𐐈𐑌𐐼 𐑌𐐵 𐑄 𐑅𐐮𐐻𐐮 𐐱𐑂 𐐖𐐩𐑇𐐲𐑌 𐐶𐐱𐑆 𐑌𐐨𐑉 𐑄 𐑊𐐰𐑌𐐼 𐐸𐐶𐐯𐑉 𐐈𐑋𐐰𐑉𐐲𐑌 𐐸𐐰𐐼 𐐼𐐨𐐹𐐱𐑆𐐮𐐻𐐯𐐼 𐑄 𐑉𐐯𐐿𐐫𐑉𐐼𐑆 𐐲𐑌𐐻𐐭 𐑄 𐐢𐐬𐑉𐐼, 𐑄𐐰𐐻 𐑄𐐩 𐑋𐐴𐐻 𐑌𐐱𐐻 𐐺 𐐼𐐨𐑅𐐻𐑉𐐱𐐮𐐼. 𐐈𐑌𐐼 𐐺𐐨𐐸𐐬𐑊𐐼 𐐴 𐐸𐐰𐐼 𐑀𐐱𐑌 𐐰𐐿𐐫𐑉𐐼𐐮𐑍 𐐻𐐭 𐑄 𐐶𐐲𐑉𐐼 𐐱𐑂 𐐈𐑋𐐰𐑉𐐲𐑌, 𐐰𐑌𐐼 𐐻𐐩𐐿𐐲𐑌 𐑄 𐐹𐑊𐐩𐐻𐑅 𐐱𐑂 𐐤𐐨𐑁𐐴, 𐐰𐑌𐐼 𐐼𐐮𐐼 𐑋𐐩𐐿 𐐩 𐑉𐐯𐐿𐐫𐑉𐐼 𐐰𐐿𐐫𐑉𐐼𐐮𐑍 𐐻𐐭 𐑄 𐐶𐐲𐑉𐐼𐑆 𐐱𐑂 𐐈𐑋𐐰𐑉𐐲𐑌. 𐐈𐑌𐐼 𐐲𐐹𐐱𐑌 𐑄 𐐹𐑊𐐩𐐻𐑅 𐐱𐑂 𐐤𐐨𐑁𐐴 𐐴 𐐼𐐮𐐼 𐑋𐐩𐐿 𐐩 𐑁𐐳𐑊 𐐰𐐿𐐵𐑌𐐻 𐐱𐑂 𐐫𐑊 𐑄 𐐶𐐮𐐿𐐯𐐼𐑌𐐯𐑅 𐐰𐑌𐐼 𐐰𐐺𐐱𐑋𐐮𐑌𐐩𐑇𐐲𐑌𐑆; 𐐺𐐲𐐻 𐐲𐐹𐐱𐑌 𐑄𐐨𐑆 𐐹𐑊𐐩𐐻𐑅 𐐴 𐐼𐐮𐐼 𐑁𐐬𐑉𐐺𐐩𐑉 𐐻𐐭 𐑋𐐩𐐿 𐐩 𐑁𐐳𐑊 𐐰𐐿𐐵𐑌𐐻 𐐱𐑂 𐑄𐐩𐑉 𐐶𐐮𐐿𐐯𐐼𐑌𐐯𐑅 𐐰𐑌𐐼 𐐰𐐺𐐱𐑋𐐮𐑌𐐩𐑇𐐲𐑌𐑆, 𐑁𐐬𐑉 𐐺𐐨𐐸𐐬𐑊𐐼, 𐐩 𐐿𐐲𐑌𐐻𐐮𐑌𐐷𐐭𐐲𐑊 𐑅𐐨𐑌 𐐱𐑂 𐐶𐐮𐐿𐐯𐐼𐑌𐐯𐑅 𐐰𐑌𐐼 𐐰𐐺𐐱𐑋𐐮𐑌𐐩𐑇𐐲𐑌𐑆 𐐸𐐰𐑆 𐐺𐐮𐑌 𐐺𐐨𐑁𐐬𐑉 𐑋𐐴𐑌 𐐴𐑆 𐐯𐑂𐐲𐑉 𐑅𐐮𐑌𐑅 𐐴 𐐸𐐰𐑂 𐐺𐐮𐑌 𐑅𐐲𐑁𐐮𐑇𐐲𐑌𐐻 𐐻𐐭 𐐺𐐨𐐸𐐬𐑊𐐼 𐑄 𐐶𐐩𐑆 𐐱𐑂 𐑋𐐰𐑌. 𐐈𐑌𐐼 𐐶𐐬 𐐮𐑆 𐑋𐐨, 𐐺𐐨𐐿𐐫𐑆 𐐱𐑂 𐑄𐐩𐑉 𐐶𐐮𐐿𐐯𐐼𐑌𐐯𐑅, 𐑁𐐬𐑉 𐑋𐐴 𐐸𐐪𐑉𐐻 𐐸𐐰𐑆 𐐺𐐮𐑌 𐑁𐐮𐑊𐐼 𐐶𐐮𐑄 𐑅𐐱𐑉𐐬 𐐺𐐨𐐿𐐫𐑆 𐐱𐑂 𐑄𐐩𐑉 𐐶𐐮𐐿𐐯𐐼𐑌𐐯𐑅, 𐐫𐑊 𐑋𐐴 𐐼𐐩𐑆; 𐑌𐐯𐑂𐐲𐑉𐑄𐐲𐑊𐐯𐑅 𐐴 𐑌𐐬 𐑄𐐰𐐻 𐐴 𐑇𐐰𐑊 𐐺 𐑊𐐮𐑁𐐻𐐯𐐼 𐐲𐐹 𐐰𐐻 𐑄 𐑊𐐪𐑅𐐻 𐐼𐐩.

6. 𐐈𐑌𐐼 𐐮𐐻 𐐿𐐩𐑋 𐐻𐐭 𐐹𐐪𐑅 𐑄𐐰𐐻 𐐮𐑌 𐑄𐐮𐑅 𐐷𐐨𐑉 𐑄 𐐹𐐨𐐹𐑊 𐐱𐑂 𐐤𐐨𐑁𐐴 𐐰𐑀𐐯𐑌 𐐶𐐲𐑉 𐐸𐐲𐑌𐐻𐐯𐐼 𐐰𐑌𐐼 𐐼𐑉𐐮𐑂𐑌. 𐐈𐑌𐐼 𐐮𐐻 𐐿𐐩𐑋 𐐻𐐭 𐐹𐐪𐑅 𐑄𐐰𐐻 𐐶𐐨 𐐶𐐲𐑉 𐐼𐑉𐐮𐑂𐑌 𐑁𐐬𐑉𐑃 𐐲𐑌𐐻𐐮𐑊 𐐶𐐨 𐐸𐐰𐐼 𐐿𐐲𐑋 𐑌𐐫𐑉𐑃𐐶𐐲𐑉𐐼 𐐻𐐭 𐑄 𐑊𐐰𐑌𐐼 𐐸𐐶𐐮𐐽 𐐶𐐱𐑆 𐐿𐐫𐑊𐐼 𐐟𐐯𐑋. 𐐈𐑌𐐼 𐐮𐐻 𐐿𐐩𐑋 𐐻𐐭 𐐹𐐪𐑅 𐑄𐐰𐐻 𐐶𐐨 𐐼𐐮𐐼 𐑁𐐬𐑉𐐻𐐮𐑁𐐴 𐑄 𐑅𐐮𐐻𐐮 𐐱𐑂 𐐟𐐯𐑋, 𐐰𐑌𐐼 𐐶𐐨 𐐼𐐮𐐼 𐑀𐐰𐑄𐐲𐑉 𐐮𐑌 𐐵𐑉 𐐹𐐨𐐹𐑊 𐐰𐑆 𐑋𐐲𐐽 𐐰𐑆 𐐮𐐻 𐐶𐐲𐑉 𐐹𐐱𐑅𐐮𐐺𐑊, 𐑄𐐰𐐻 𐐹𐐲𐑉𐐸𐐰𐐹𐑅 𐐶𐐨 𐑋𐐴𐐻 𐑅𐐩𐑂 𐑄𐐯𐑋 𐑁𐑉𐐱𐑋 𐐼𐐨𐑅𐐻𐑉𐐲𐐿𐑇𐐲𐑌. 𐐈𐑌𐐼 𐐮𐐻 𐐿𐐩𐑋 𐐻𐐭 𐐹𐐪𐑅 𐐮𐑌 𐑄 𐑃𐑉𐐨 𐐸𐐲𐑌𐐼𐑉𐐯𐐼 𐐰𐑌𐐼 𐑁𐐬𐑉𐐻𐐨 𐐰𐑌𐐼 𐑅𐐮𐐿𐑅𐑃 𐐷𐐨𐑉, 𐑄𐐩 𐐺𐐨𐑀𐐰𐑌 𐐻𐐭 𐐿𐐲𐑋 𐐲𐐹𐐱𐑌 𐐲𐑅 𐐰𐑀𐐯𐑌. 𐐈𐑌𐐼 𐐮𐐻 𐐿𐐩𐑋 𐐻𐐭 𐐹𐐪𐑅 𐑄𐐰𐐻 𐐴 𐐼𐐮𐐼 𐑅𐐹𐐨𐐿 𐐲𐑌𐐻𐐭 𐑋𐐴 𐐹𐐨𐐹𐑊, 𐐰𐑌𐐼 𐐼𐐮𐐼 𐐲𐑉𐐾 𐑄𐐯𐑋 𐐶𐐮𐑄 𐑀𐑉𐐩𐐻 𐐯𐑌𐐲𐑉𐐾𐐮, 𐑄𐐰𐐻 𐑄𐐩 𐐶𐐳𐐼 𐑅𐐻𐐰𐑌𐐼 𐐺𐐬𐑊𐐼𐑊𐐮 𐐺𐐨𐑁𐐬𐑉 𐑄 𐐢𐐩𐑋𐐲𐑌𐐴𐐻𐑅, 𐐰𐑌𐐼 𐑁𐐴𐐻 𐑁𐐬𐑉 𐑄𐐩𐑉 𐐶𐐴𐑂𐑆, 𐐰𐑌𐐼 𐑄𐐩𐑉 𐐽𐐮𐑊𐐼𐑉𐐯𐑌, 𐐰𐑌𐐼 𐑄𐐩𐑉 𐐸𐐵𐑆𐐯𐑆, 𐐰𐑌𐐼 𐑄𐐩𐑉 𐐸𐐬𐑋𐑆. 𐐈𐑌𐐼 𐑋𐐴 𐐶𐐲𐑉𐐼𐑆 𐐼𐐮𐐼 𐐲𐑉𐐵𐑆 𐑄𐐯𐑋 𐑅𐐲𐑋𐐸𐐶𐐱𐐻 𐐻𐐭 𐑂𐐮𐑀𐐲𐑉, 𐐮𐑌𐑅𐐬𐑋𐐲𐐽 𐑄𐐰𐐻 𐑄𐐩 𐐼𐐮𐐼 𐑌𐐱𐐻 𐑁𐑊𐐨 𐑁𐑉𐐱𐑋 𐐺𐐨𐑁𐐬𐑉 𐑄 𐐢𐐩𐑋𐐲𐑌𐐴𐐻𐑅, 𐐺𐐲𐐻 𐐼𐐮𐐼 𐑅𐐻𐐰𐑌𐐼 𐐶𐐮𐑄 𐐺𐐬𐑊𐐼𐑌𐐯𐑅 𐐰𐑀𐐯𐑌𐑅𐐻 𐑄𐐯𐑋. 𐐈𐑌𐐼 𐐮𐐻 𐐿𐐩𐑋 𐐻𐐭 𐐹𐐪𐑅 𐑄𐐰𐐻 𐐶𐐨 𐐼𐐮𐐼 𐐿𐐲𐑌𐐻𐐯𐑌𐐼 𐐶𐐮𐑄 𐐰𐑌 𐐪𐑉𐑋𐐨 𐐱𐑂 𐑃𐐲𐑉𐐻𐐨

𐑃𐐵𐑆𐐲𐑌𐐼, 𐐲𐑀𐐯𐑌𐑅𐐻 𐐰𐑌 𐐪𐑉𐑋𐐨 𐐱𐑂 𐑁𐐮𐑁𐐻𐐨 𐑃𐐵𐑆𐐲𐑌𐐼. 𐐈𐑌𐐼 𐐮𐐻 𐐿𐐩𐑋 𐐻𐐭 𐐹𐐰𐑅 𐑄𐐰𐐻 𐐶𐐨 𐐼𐐮𐐼 𐑅𐐻𐐰𐑌𐐼 𐐺𐐨𐑁𐐬𐑉 𐑄𐐯𐑋 𐐶𐐮𐑄 𐑅𐐲𐐽 𐑁𐐲𐑉𐑋𐑌𐐯𐑅, 𐑄𐐰𐐻 𐑄𐐩 𐐼𐐮𐐼 𐑁𐑊𐐨 𐑁𐑉𐐱𐑋 𐐺𐐨𐑁𐐬𐑉 𐐲𐑅. 𐐈𐑌𐐼 𐐮𐐻 𐐿𐐩𐑋 𐐻𐐭 𐐹𐐰𐑅 𐑄𐐰𐐻 𐐸𐐶𐐯𐑌 𐑄𐐩 𐐸𐐰𐐼 𐑁𐑊𐐯𐐼 𐐶𐐨 𐐼𐐮𐐼 𐐹𐐲𐑉𐑅𐐭 𐑄𐐯𐑋 𐐶𐐮𐑄 𐐵𐑉 𐐪𐑉𐑋𐐨𐑆, 𐐰𐑌𐐼 𐐼𐐮𐐼 𐑋𐐨𐐻 𐑄𐐯𐑋 𐐲𐑀𐐯𐑌, 𐐰𐑌𐐼 𐐼𐐮𐐼 𐐺𐐨𐐻 𐑄𐐯𐑋; 𐑌𐐯𐑂𐐲𐑉𐑄𐐯𐑊𐐯𐑅, 𐑄 𐑅𐐻𐑉𐐯𐑍𐑃 𐐱𐑂 𐑄 𐐢𐐫𐑉𐐼 𐐶𐐱𐑆 𐑌𐐱𐐻 𐐶𐐮𐑄 𐐲𐑅; 𐐷𐐩, 𐐶𐐨 𐐶𐐲𐑉 𐑊𐐯𐑁𐐻 𐐻𐐭 𐐵𐑉𐑅𐐯𐑊𐑂𐑆, 𐑄𐐰𐐻 𐑄 𐐝𐐹𐐮𐑉𐐮𐐻 𐐱𐑂 𐑄 𐐢𐐫𐑉𐐼 𐐼𐐮𐐼 𐑌𐐱𐐻 𐐲𐐺𐐴𐐼 𐐮𐑌 𐐲𐑅; 𐑄𐐯𐑉𐑁𐐬𐑉 𐐶𐐨 𐐸𐐰𐐼 𐐺𐐨𐐿𐐲𐑋 𐐶𐐨𐐿 𐑊𐐴𐐿 𐐲𐑌𐐻𐐭 𐐵𐑉 𐐺𐑉𐐯𐑄𐑉𐐯𐑌. 𐐈𐑌𐐼 𐑋𐐴 𐐸𐐪𐑉𐐻 𐐼𐐮𐐼 𐑅𐐱𐑉𐐬 𐐺𐐨𐐿𐐫𐑆 𐐱𐑂 𐑄𐐮𐑅 𐑄 𐑀𐑉𐐩𐐻 𐐿𐐲𐑊𐐰𐑋𐐮𐐻𐐨 𐐱𐑂 𐑋𐐴 𐐹𐐨𐐹𐑊; 𐐺𐐨𐐿𐐫𐑆 𐐱𐑂 𐑄𐐩𐑉 𐐶𐐮𐐿𐐯𐐼𐑌𐐯𐑅 𐐰𐑌𐐼 𐑄𐐩𐑉 𐐲𐐺𐐱𐑋𐐮𐑌𐐩𐑇𐐲𐑌𐑆. 𐐒𐐲𐐻 𐐺𐐨𐐸𐐬𐑊𐐼, 𐐶𐐨 𐐼𐐮𐐼 𐑀𐐬 𐑁𐐬𐑉𐑃 𐐲𐑀𐐯𐑌𐑅𐐻 𐑄 𐐢𐐩𐑋𐐲𐑌𐐴𐐻𐑅, 𐐰𐑌𐐼 𐑄 𐑉𐐱𐐺𐐲𐑉𐑆 𐐱𐑂 𐐘𐐰𐐼𐐨𐐰𐑌𐐻𐐲𐑌, 𐐲𐑌𐐻𐐮𐑊 𐐶𐐨 𐐸𐐰𐐼 𐐲𐑀𐐯𐑌 𐐻𐐩𐐿𐐯𐑌 𐐹𐐱𐑆𐐯𐑇𐐲𐑌 𐐱𐑂 𐑄 𐑊𐐰𐑌𐐼𐑆 𐐱𐑂 𐐵𐑉 𐐮𐑌𐐸𐐯𐑉𐐮𐐻𐐰𐑌𐑅. 𐐈𐑌𐐼 𐑄 𐑃𐑉𐐨 𐐸𐐲𐑌𐐼𐑉𐐯𐐼 𐐰𐑌𐐼 𐑁𐐫𐑉𐐻𐐨 𐐰𐑌𐐼 𐑌𐐴𐑌𐑃 𐐷𐐨𐑉 𐐸𐐰𐐼 𐐹𐐰𐑅𐐻 𐐲𐐶𐐩. 𐐈𐑌𐐼 𐐮𐑌 𐑄 𐑃𐑉𐐨 𐐸𐐲𐑌𐐼𐑉𐐯𐐼 𐐰𐑌𐐼 𐑁𐐮𐑁𐐻𐐨𐐯𐑃 𐐷𐐨𐑉, 𐐶𐐨 𐑋𐐩𐐼 𐐰 𐐻𐑉𐐨𐐻𐐨 𐐶𐐮𐑄 𐑄 𐐢𐐩𐑋𐐲𐑌𐐴𐐻𐑅 𐐰𐑌𐐼 𐑄 𐑉𐐱𐐺𐐲𐑉𐑆 𐐱𐑂 𐐘𐐰𐐼𐐨𐐰𐑌𐐻𐐲𐑌, 𐐮𐑌 𐐸𐐶𐐮𐐽 𐐶𐐨 𐐼𐐮𐐼 𐑀𐐯𐐻 𐑄 𐑊𐐰𐑌𐐼𐑆 𐐱𐑂 𐐵𐑉 𐐮𐑌𐐸𐐯𐑉𐐮𐐻𐐰𐑌𐑅 𐐼𐐮𐑂𐐴𐐼𐐯𐐼. 𐐈𐑌𐐼 𐑄 𐐢𐐩𐑋𐐲𐑌𐐴𐐻𐑅 𐐼𐐮𐐼 𐑀𐐮𐑂 𐐲𐑌𐐻𐐭 𐐲𐑅 𐑄 𐑊𐐰𐑌𐐼 𐑌𐐫𐑉𐑃𐐶𐐲𐑉𐐼; 𐐷𐐩, 𐐨𐑂𐐯𐑌 𐐻𐐭 𐑄 𐑌𐐰𐑉𐐬 𐐹𐐰𐑅𐐲𐐾 𐐸𐐶𐐮𐐽 𐑊𐐯𐐼 𐐮𐑌𐐻𐐭 𐑄 𐑊𐐰𐑌𐐼 𐑅𐐵𐑃𐐶𐐲𐑉𐐼. 𐐈𐑌𐐼 𐐶𐐨 𐐼𐐮𐐼 𐑀𐐮𐑂 𐐲𐑌𐐻𐐭 𐑄 𐐢𐐩𐑋𐐲𐑌𐐴𐐻𐑅 𐐫𐑊 𐑄 𐑊𐐰𐑌𐐼 𐑅𐐵𐑃𐐶𐐲𐑉𐐼.

7. 𐐈𐑌𐐼 𐐮𐐻 𐐿𐐩𐑋 𐐻𐐭 𐐹𐐰𐑅 𐑄𐐰𐐻 𐑄 𐐢𐐩𐑋𐐲𐑌𐐴𐐻𐑅 𐐼𐐮𐐼 𐑌𐐱𐐻 𐐿𐐲𐑋 𐐻𐐭 𐐺𐐰𐐻𐐲𐑊 𐐲𐑀𐐯𐑌 𐐲𐑌𐐻𐐮𐑊 𐐻𐐯𐑌 𐐷𐐨𐑉𐑆 𐑋𐐬𐑉 𐐸𐐰𐐼 𐐹𐐰𐑅𐐻 𐐲𐐶𐐩. 𐐈𐑌𐐼 𐐺𐐨𐐸𐐬𐑊𐐼 𐐌 𐐸𐐰𐐼 𐐯𐑋𐐹𐑊𐑎𐐼 𐑋𐐴 𐐹𐐨𐐹𐑊, 𐑄 𐐤𐐨𐑁𐐴𐐻𐑅, 𐐮𐑌 𐐹𐑉𐐨𐐹𐐩𐑉𐐮𐑍 𐑄𐐩𐑉 𐑊𐐰𐑌𐐼𐑆 𐐰𐑌𐐼 𐑄𐐩𐑉 𐐪𐑉𐑋𐑆 𐐲𐑀𐐯𐑌𐑅𐐻 𐑄 𐐻𐐴𐑋 𐐱𐑂 𐐺𐐰𐐻𐐲𐑊. 𐐈𐑌𐐼 𐐮𐐻 𐐿𐐩𐑋 𐐻𐐭 𐐹𐐰𐑅 𐑄𐐰𐐻 𐑄 𐐢𐐫𐑉𐐼 𐐼𐐮𐐼 𐑅𐐩 𐐲𐑌𐐻𐐭 𐑋𐐨, 𐐗𐑉𐐴 𐐲𐑌𐐻𐐭 𐑄𐐮𐑅 𐐹𐐨𐐹𐑊, 𐐡𐐨𐐹𐐯𐑌𐐻 𐐷𐐨, 𐐰𐑌𐐼 𐐿𐐲𐑋 𐐲𐑌𐐻𐐭 𐑋𐐨, 𐐰𐑌𐐼 𐐺𐐨 𐐷𐐨 𐐺𐐰𐐹𐐻𐐴𐑆𐐼, 𐐰𐑌𐐼 𐐺𐐮𐑊𐐼 𐐲𐐹 𐐲𐑀𐐯𐑌 𐑋𐐴 𐐕𐐲𐑉𐐽, 𐐰𐑌𐐼 𐐷𐐨 𐑇𐐰𐑊 𐐺𐐨 𐑅𐐹𐐩𐑉𐐼. 𐐈𐑌𐐼 𐐌 𐐼𐐮𐐼 𐐿𐑉𐐴 𐐲𐑌𐐻𐐭 𐑄𐐮𐑅 𐐹𐐨𐐹𐑊, 𐐺𐐲𐐻 𐐮𐐻 𐐶𐐱𐑆 𐐮𐑌 𐑂𐐩𐑌, 𐐰𐑌𐐼 𐑄𐐩 𐐼𐐮𐐼 𐑌𐐱𐐻 𐑉𐐨𐐲𐑊𐐴𐑆 𐑄𐐰𐐻 𐐮𐐻 𐐶𐐱𐑆 𐑄 𐐢𐐫𐑉𐐼 𐑄𐐰𐐻 𐐸𐐰𐐼 𐑅𐐹𐐩𐑉𐐼 𐑄𐐯𐑋, 𐐰𐑌𐐼 𐑀𐑉𐐰𐑌𐐻𐐯𐐼 𐐲𐑌𐐻𐐭 𐑄𐐯𐑋 𐐰 𐐽𐐰𐑌𐑅 𐑁𐐫𐑉 𐑉𐐨𐐹𐐯𐑌𐐻𐐰𐑌𐑅. 𐐈𐑌𐐼 𐐺𐐨𐐸𐐬𐑊𐐼, 𐑄𐐩 𐐼𐐮𐐼 𐐸𐐪𐑉𐐼𐐯𐑌 𐑄𐐩𐑉 𐐸𐐪𐑉𐐻𐑅 𐐲𐑀𐐯𐑌𐑅𐐻 𐑄 𐐢𐐫𐑉𐐼 𐑄𐐩𐑉 𐐘𐐱𐐼. 𐐈𐑌𐐼 𐐮𐐻 𐐿𐐩𐑋 𐐻𐐭 𐐹𐐰𐑅 𐑄𐐰𐐻 𐐰𐑁𐐻𐐲𐑉 𐑄𐐮𐑅 𐐻𐐯𐑌𐑃 𐐷𐐨𐑉 𐐸𐐰𐐼 𐐹𐐰𐑅𐐻 𐐲𐐶𐐩, 𐑋𐐩𐐿𐐮𐑍 𐐮𐑌 𐑄 𐐸𐐬𐑊 𐑃𐑉𐐨 𐐸𐐲𐑌𐐼𐑉𐐯𐐼 𐐰𐑌𐐼 𐑅𐐮𐐿𐑅𐐻𐐨 𐐷𐐨𐑉𐑆 𐑁𐑉𐐱𐑋 𐑄 𐐿𐐲𐑋𐐮𐑍 𐐱𐑂 𐐗𐑉𐐴𐑅𐐻, 𐑄 𐐿𐐮𐑍 𐐱𐑂 𐑄 𐐢𐐩𐑋𐐲𐑌𐐴𐐻𐑅 𐑅𐐯𐑌𐐻 𐐰𐑌 𐐨𐐹𐐮𐑅𐑊 𐐲𐑌𐐻𐐭 𐑋𐐨, 𐐸𐐶𐐮𐐽 𐑀𐐩𐑂 𐐲𐑌𐐻𐐭 𐑋𐐨 𐐻𐐭 𐑌𐐬 𐑄𐐰𐐻 𐑄𐐩 𐐶𐐲𐑉 𐐹𐑉𐐨𐐹𐐩𐑉𐐮𐑍 𐐻𐐭 𐐿𐐲𐑋 𐐲𐑀𐐯𐑌 𐐻𐐭 𐐺𐐰𐐻𐐲𐑊 𐐲𐑀𐐯𐑌𐑅𐐻 𐐲𐑅. 𐐈𐑌𐐼 𐐮𐐻 𐐿𐐩𐑋 𐐻𐐭 𐐹𐐰𐑅 𐑄𐐰𐐻 𐐌 𐐼𐐮𐐼 𐐿𐐫𐑆 𐑋𐐴 𐐹𐐨𐐹𐑊 𐑄𐐰𐐻 𐑄𐐩 𐑇𐐳𐐼 𐑀𐐰𐑄𐐲𐑉 𐑄𐐯𐑋𐑅𐐯𐑊𐑂𐑆 𐐻𐐭𐑀𐐯𐑄𐐲𐑉 𐐰𐐻 𐑄 𐑊𐐰𐑌𐐼 𐐔𐐯𐑅𐐬𐑊𐐩𐑇𐐲𐑌, 𐐻𐐭 𐐰 𐑅𐐮𐐻𐐨 𐐸𐐶𐐮𐐽 𐐶𐐱𐑆 𐐮𐑌 𐑄 𐐺𐐫𐑉𐐼𐐲𐑉𐑆, 𐐺𐐴 𐑄 𐑌𐐰𐑉𐐬 𐐹𐐰𐑅 𐐸𐐶𐐮𐐽 𐑊𐐯𐐼 𐐮𐑌𐐻𐐭 𐑄 𐑊𐐰𐑌𐐼 𐑅𐐵𐑃𐐶𐐲𐑉𐐼. 𐐈𐑌𐐼 𐑄𐐩𐑉 𐐶𐐨 𐐼𐐮𐐼 𐐹𐑊𐐩𐑅 𐐵𐑉 𐐪𐑉𐑋𐐨𐑆, 𐑄𐐰𐐻 𐐶𐐨 𐑋𐐴𐐻 𐑅𐐻𐐱𐐹 𐑄 𐐪𐑉𐑋𐐨𐑆 𐐱𐑂 𐑄 𐐢𐐩𐑋𐐲𐑌𐐴𐐻𐑅, 𐑄𐐰𐐻 𐑄𐐩 𐑋𐐴𐐻 𐑌𐐱𐐻 𐑀𐐯𐐻 𐐹𐐱𐑆𐐯𐑇𐐲𐑌 𐐱𐑂 𐐯𐑌𐐨 𐐱𐑂 𐐵𐑉 𐑊𐐰𐑌𐐼𐑆; 𐑄𐐯𐑉𐑁𐐬𐑉 𐐶𐐨 𐐼𐐮𐐼 𐑁𐐫𐑉𐐻𐐮𐑁𐐴 𐐲𐑀𐐯𐑌𐑅𐐻 𐑄𐐯𐑋 𐐶𐐮𐑄 𐐫𐑊 𐐵𐑉 𐑁𐐬𐑉𐑅.

8. 𐐈𐑌𐐼 𐐮𐐻 𐐿𐐩𐑋 𐐻𐐭 𐐹𐐰𐑅 𐑄𐐰𐐻 𐐮𐑌 𐑄 𐑃𐑉𐐨 𐐸𐐲𐑌𐐼𐑉𐐯𐐼 𐐰𐑌𐐼 𐑅𐐮𐐿𐑅𐐻𐐨 𐐰𐑌𐐼 𐑁𐐲𐑉𐑅𐐻 𐐷𐐨𐑉, 𐑄 𐐢𐐩𐑋𐐲𐑌𐐴𐐻𐑅 𐐼𐐮𐐼 𐐿𐐲𐑋 𐐼𐐵𐑌 𐐻𐐭 𐑄 𐑅𐐮𐐻𐐨 𐐱𐑂 𐐔𐐯𐑅𐐬𐑊𐐩𐑇𐐲𐑌 𐐻𐐭 𐐺𐐰𐐻𐐲𐑊 𐐲𐑀𐐯𐑌𐑅𐐻 𐐲𐑅; 𐐰𐑌𐐼 𐐮𐐻 𐐿𐐩𐑋 𐐻𐐭 𐐹𐐰𐑅 𐑄𐐰𐐻 𐐮𐑌 𐑄𐐰𐐻 𐐷𐐨𐑉, 𐐶𐐨 𐐼𐐮𐐼 𐐺𐐨𐐻 𐑄𐐯𐑋, 𐐮𐑌𐑅𐐬𐑋𐐲𐐽 𐑄𐐰𐐻 𐑄𐐩 𐐼𐐮𐐼 𐑉𐐨𐐻𐐲𐑉𐑌 𐐻𐐭 𐑄𐐩𐑉 𐐬𐑌 𐑊𐐰𐑌𐐼𐑆 𐐲𐑀𐐯𐑌. 𐐈𐑌𐐼 𐐮𐑌 𐑄 𐑃𐑉𐐨 𐐸𐐲𐑌𐐼𐑉𐐯𐐼 𐐰𐑌𐐼 𐑅𐐮𐐿𐑅𐐻𐐨 𐐰𐑌𐐼 𐑅𐐯𐐿𐐲𐑌𐐼 𐐷𐐨𐑉, 𐑄𐐩 𐐼𐐮𐐼 𐐿𐐲𐑋 𐐼𐐵𐑌 𐐲𐑀𐐯𐑌 𐐻𐐭 𐐺𐐰𐐻𐐲𐑊. 𐐈𐑌𐐼 𐐶𐐨 𐐼𐐮𐐼 𐐺𐐨𐐻 𐑄𐐯𐑋 𐐲𐑀𐐯𐑌, 𐐰𐑌𐐼 𐐼𐐮𐐼 𐑅𐑊𐐩 𐐰 𐑀𐑉𐐩𐐻 𐑌𐐲𐑋𐐺𐐲𐑉 𐐱𐑂 𐑄𐐯𐑋, 𐐰𐑌𐐼 𐑄𐐩𐑉 𐐼𐐯𐐼 𐐶𐐲𐑉 𐐿𐐰𐑅𐐻 𐐮𐑌𐐻𐐭 𐑄 𐑅𐐨. 𐐈𐑌𐐼 𐑌𐐵 𐐺𐐨𐐿𐐫𐑆 𐐱𐑂 𐑄𐐮𐑅 𐑀𐑉𐐩𐐻 𐑃𐐮𐑍 𐐸𐐶𐐮𐐽 𐑋𐐴 𐐹𐐨𐐹𐑊, 𐑄 𐐤𐐨𐑁𐐴𐐻𐑅, 𐐸𐐰𐐼 𐐼𐐲𐑌, 𐑄𐐩 𐐺𐐨𐑀𐐰𐑌 𐐻𐐭 𐐺𐐬𐑅𐐻 𐐮𐑌 𐑄𐐩𐑉 𐐬𐑌 𐑅𐐻𐑉𐐯𐑍𐑃, 𐐰𐑌𐐼 𐐺𐐨𐑀𐐰𐑌 𐐻𐐭 𐑅𐐶𐐩𐑉 𐐺𐐨𐑁𐐬𐑉 𐑄 𐐸𐐯𐑂𐐯𐑌𐑆 𐑄𐐰𐐻 𐑄𐐩 𐐶𐐳𐐼 𐐲𐑂𐐯𐑌𐐾 𐑄𐐯𐑋𐑅𐐯𐑊𐑂𐑆 𐐱𐑂 𐑄 𐐺𐑊𐐲𐐼 𐐱𐑂 𐑄𐐩𐑉 𐐺𐑉𐐯𐑄𐑉𐐯𐑌 𐐸𐐭 𐐸𐐰𐐼 𐐺𐐮𐑌 𐑅𐑊𐐩𐑌 𐐺𐐴 𐑄𐐩𐑉 𐐯𐑌𐐯𐑋𐐨𐑆. 𐐈𐑌𐐼 𐑄𐐩 𐐼𐐮𐐼 𐑅𐐶𐐩𐑉 𐐺𐐴 𐑄 𐐸𐐯𐑂𐐯𐑌𐑆, 𐐰𐑌𐐼 𐐫𐑊𐑅𐐬 𐐺𐐴 𐑄 𐑃𐑉𐐬𐑌 𐐱𐑂 𐐘𐐱𐐼, 𐑄𐐰𐐻 𐑄𐐩 𐐶𐐳𐐼 𐑀𐐬 𐐲𐐹 𐐻𐐭 𐐺𐐰𐐻𐐲𐑊 𐐲𐑀𐐯𐑌𐑅𐐻 𐑄𐐩𐑉 𐐯𐑌𐐯𐑋𐐨𐑆, 𐐰𐑌𐐼 𐐶𐐳𐐼 𐐿𐐲𐐻 𐑄𐐯𐑋 𐐱𐑁 𐑁𐑉𐐱𐑋 𐑄 𐑁𐐩𐑅 𐐱𐑂 𐑄 𐑊𐐰𐑌𐐼.

9. 𐐈𐑌𐐼 𐐮𐐻 𐐿𐐩𐑋 𐐻𐐭 𐐹𐐰𐑅 𐑄𐐰𐐻 𐐌, 𐐣𐐫𐑉𐑋𐐲𐑌, 𐐼𐐮𐐼 𐐲𐐻𐐲𐑉𐑊𐐨 𐑉𐐯𐑁𐐷𐐭𐑆 𐑁𐑉𐐱𐑋 𐑄𐐮𐑅 𐐻𐐴𐑋 𐑁𐐬𐑉𐑃, 𐐻𐐭 𐐺 𐐰 𐐿𐐱𐑋𐐰𐑌𐐼𐐲𐑉 𐐰𐑌𐐼 𐐰 𐑊𐐨𐐼𐐲𐑉 𐐱𐑂 𐑄𐐮𐑅 𐐹𐐨𐐹𐑊, 𐐺𐐨𐐿𐐫𐑆 𐐱𐑂 𐑄𐐩𐑉 𐐶𐐮𐐿𐐯𐐼𐑌𐐯𐑅 𐐰𐑌𐐼 𐐲𐐺𐐱𐑋𐐮𐑌𐐩𐑇𐐲𐑌. 𐐒𐐨𐐸𐐬𐑊𐐼, 𐐌 𐐸𐐰𐐼 𐑊𐐯𐐼 𐑄𐐯𐑋, 𐑌𐐱𐐻𐐶𐐮𐑃𐑅𐐻𐐰𐑌𐐼𐐮𐑍 𐑄𐐩𐑉 𐐶𐐮𐐿𐐯𐐼𐑌𐐯𐑅, 𐐌 𐐸𐐰𐐼 𐑊𐐯𐐼 𐑄𐐯𐑋 𐑋𐐯𐑌𐐨 𐐻𐐴𐑋𐑆 𐐻𐐭 𐐺𐐰𐐻𐑊, 𐐰𐑌𐐼 𐐸𐐰𐐼 𐑊𐐲𐑂𐐼 𐑄𐐯𐑋, 𐐰𐐿𐐫𐑉𐐼𐐮𐑍 𐐻𐐭 𐑄 𐑊𐐲𐑂 𐐱𐑂 𐐘𐐱𐐼 𐐸𐐶𐐮𐐽 𐐶𐐱𐑆 𐐮𐑌 𐑋𐐨, 𐐶𐐮𐑄 𐐫𐑊 𐑋𐐴 𐐸𐐪𐑉𐐻; 𐐰𐑌𐐼 𐑋𐐴 𐑅𐐬𐑊 𐐸𐐰𐐼 𐐺𐐨𐑌 𐐹𐐬𐑉𐐼 𐐵𐐻 𐐮𐑌 𐐹𐑉𐐩𐑉 𐐲𐑌𐐻𐐭 𐑋𐐴 𐐘𐐱𐐼 𐐫𐑊 𐑄 𐐼𐐩 𐑊𐐱𐑍 𐑁𐐫𐑉 𐑄𐐯𐑋; 𐑌𐐯𐑂𐐲𐑉𐑄𐐯𐑊𐐯𐑅, 𐐮𐐻 𐐶𐐱𐑆 𐐶𐐮𐑄𐐵𐐻 𐑁𐐩𐑃, 𐐺𐐨𐐿𐐫𐑆 𐐱𐑂 𐑄 𐐸𐐪𐑉𐐼𐑌𐐯𐑅 𐐱𐑂 𐑄𐐩𐑉 𐐸𐐪𐑉𐐻𐑅. 𐐈𐑌𐐼 𐑃𐑉𐐴𐑅 𐐸𐐰𐑂 𐐌 𐐼𐐯𐑊𐐮𐑂𐐲𐑉𐐼 𐑄𐐯𐑋 𐐵𐐻 𐐱𐑂 𐑄 𐐸𐐰𐑌𐐼𐑆 𐐱𐑂 𐑄𐐩𐑉 𐐯𐑌𐐯𐑋𐐨𐑆, 𐐰𐑌𐐼 𐑄𐐩 𐐸𐐰𐑂 𐑉𐐯𐐹𐐯𐑌𐐻𐐯𐐼 𐑌𐐱𐐻 𐐱𐑂 𐑄𐐩𐑉 𐑅𐐮𐑌𐑆. 𐐈𐑌𐐼 𐐸𐐶𐐯𐑌 𐑄𐐩 𐐸𐐰𐐼 𐑅𐐶𐐫𐑉𐑌 𐐺𐐴 𐐫𐑊 𐑄𐐰𐐻 𐐸𐐰𐐼 𐐺𐐨𐑌 𐑁𐐫𐑉𐐺𐐮𐐼𐑌 𐑄𐐯𐑋 𐐺𐐴 𐐵𐑉 𐐢𐐫𐑉𐐼 𐐰𐑌𐐼 𐐝𐐩𐑂𐐷𐐲𐑉 𐐖𐐨𐑆𐐲𐑅 𐐗𐑉𐐴𐑅𐐻, 𐑄𐐰𐐻 𐑄𐐩 𐐶𐐳𐐼 𐑀𐐬 𐐲𐐹 𐐲𐑌𐐻𐐭 𐑄𐐩𐑉 𐐯𐑌𐐯𐑋𐐨𐑆 𐐻𐐭 𐐺𐐰𐐻𐑊, 𐐰𐑌𐐼 𐐰𐑂𐐯𐑌𐐾 𐑄𐐯𐑋𐑅𐐯𐑊𐑂𐑆 𐐱𐑂 𐑄 𐐺𐑊𐐲𐐼 𐐱𐑂 𐑄𐐩𐑉 𐐺𐑉𐐯𐑄𐑉𐐯𐑌, 𐐺𐐨𐐸𐐬𐑊𐐼 𐑄 𐑂𐐱𐐮𐑅 𐐱𐑂 𐑄 𐐢𐐫𐑉𐐼 𐐿𐐩𐑋 𐐲𐑌𐐻𐐭 𐑋𐐨, 𐑅𐐩𐐮𐑍, 𐐚𐐯𐑌𐐾𐐲𐑌𐑅 𐐮𐑆 𐑋𐐴𐑌, 𐐰𐑌𐐼 𐐌 𐐶𐐮𐑊 𐑉𐐨𐐹𐐩; 𐐰𐑌𐐼 𐐺𐐨𐐿𐐫𐑆 𐑄𐐮𐑅 𐐹𐐨𐐹𐑊 𐑉𐐯𐐹𐐯𐑌𐐻𐐯𐐼 𐑌𐐱𐐻 𐐰𐑁𐐻𐐲𐑉 𐐌 𐐸𐐰𐐼 𐐼𐐯𐑊𐐮𐑂𐐲𐑉𐐼 𐑄𐐯𐑋, 𐐺𐐨𐐸𐐬𐑊𐐼, 𐑄𐐩 𐑇𐐰𐑊 𐐺 𐐿𐐲𐐻 𐐫𐑁 𐑁𐑉𐐱𐑋 𐑄 𐑁𐐩𐑅 𐐱𐑂 𐑄 𐐲𐑉𐑃. 𐐈𐑌𐐼 𐐮𐐻 𐐿𐐩𐑋 𐐻𐐭 𐐹𐐰𐑅 𐑄𐐰𐐻 𐐌 𐐲𐐻𐐲𐑉𐑊𐐨 𐑉𐐯𐑁𐐷𐐭𐑆𐐼 𐐻𐐭 𐑀𐐬 𐐲𐐹 𐐰𐑀𐐯𐑌𐑅𐐻 𐑋𐐴𐑌 𐐯𐑌𐐯𐑋𐐨𐑆; 𐐰𐑌𐐼 𐐌 𐐼𐐮𐐼 𐐨𐑂𐑌 𐐰𐑆 𐑄 𐐢𐐫𐑉𐐼 𐐸𐐰𐐼 𐐿𐐱𐑋𐐰𐑌𐐼𐐯𐐼 𐑋𐐨; 𐐰𐑌𐐼 𐐌 𐐼𐐮𐐼 𐑅𐐻𐐰𐑌𐐼 𐐰𐑆 𐐰𐑌 𐐴𐐼𐑊 𐐶𐐮𐐻𐑌𐐯𐑅 𐐻𐐭 𐑋𐐰𐑌𐐮𐑁𐐯𐑅𐐻 𐐲𐑌𐐻𐐭 𐑄 𐐶𐐲𐑉𐑊𐐼 𐑄 𐑃𐐮𐑍𐑆 𐐸𐐶𐐮𐐽 𐐌 𐑅𐐫 𐐰𐑌𐐼 𐐸𐐲𐑉𐐼, 𐐰𐐿𐐫𐑉𐐼𐐮𐑍 𐐻𐐭 𐑄 𐑋𐐰𐑌𐐮𐑁𐐯𐑅𐐻𐐩𐑇𐐲𐑌𐑆 𐐱𐑂 𐑄 𐐝𐐹𐐮𐑉𐐮𐐻 𐐸𐐶𐐮𐐽 𐐸𐐰𐐼 𐐻𐐯𐑅𐐻𐐮𐑁𐐴𐐼 𐐱𐑂 𐑃𐐮𐑍𐑆 𐐻𐐭 𐐿𐐲𐑋. 𐐛𐐯𐑉𐑁𐐬𐑉 𐐌 𐑉𐐴𐐻 𐐲𐑌𐐻𐐭 𐐷𐐭, 𐐖𐐯𐑌𐐻𐐴𐑊𐑆, 𐐰𐑌𐐼 𐐫𐑊𐑅𐐬 𐐲𐑌𐐻𐐭 𐐷𐐭, 𐐸𐐵𐑅 𐐱𐑂 𐐆𐑆𐑉𐐩𐐯𐑊, 𐐸𐐶𐐯𐑌 𐑄 𐐶𐐲𐑉𐐿 𐑇𐐰𐑊 𐐿𐐱𐑋𐐯𐑌𐑅, 𐑄𐐰𐐻 𐐷𐐨 𐑇𐐰𐑊 𐐺 𐐲𐐺𐐵𐐻 𐐻𐐭 𐐹𐑉𐐨𐐹𐐩𐑉 𐐻𐐭 𐑉𐐨𐐻𐐲𐑉𐑌 𐐻𐐭 𐑄 𐑊𐐰𐑌𐐼 𐐱𐑂 𐐷𐐬𐑉 𐐮𐑌𐐸𐐯𐑉𐐮𐐻𐐰𐑌𐑅; 𐐷𐐩, 𐐺𐐨𐐸𐐬𐑊𐐼, 𐐌 𐑉𐐴𐐻 𐐲𐑌𐐻𐐭 𐐫𐑊 𐑄 𐐯𐑌𐐼𐑆 𐐱𐑂 𐑄 𐐲𐑉𐑃; 𐐷𐐩, 𐐲𐑌𐐻𐐭 𐐷𐐭, 𐐻𐐶𐐯𐑊𐑂 𐐻𐑉𐐴𐐺𐑆 𐐱𐑂 𐐆𐑆𐑉𐐩𐐯𐑊, 𐐸𐐭 𐑇𐐰𐑊 𐐺 𐐾𐐲𐐾𐐼 𐐰𐐿𐐫𐑉𐐼𐐮𐑍 𐐻𐐭 𐐷𐐬𐑉 𐐶𐐲𐑉𐐿𐑅, 𐐺𐐴 𐑄 𐐻𐐶𐐯𐑊𐑂 𐐸𐐭𐑋 𐐖𐐨𐑆𐐲𐑅 𐐽𐐬𐑆 𐐻𐐭 𐐺 𐐸𐐮𐑆 𐐼𐐮𐑅𐐴𐐹𐑊𐑆 𐐮𐑌 𐑄 𐑊𐐰𐑌𐐼 𐐱𐑂 𐐖𐐯𐑉𐐭𐑅𐐲𐑊𐐯𐑋. 𐐈𐑌𐐼 𐐌 𐑉𐐴𐐻 𐐫𐑊𐑅𐐬 𐐲𐑌𐐻𐐭 𐑄 𐑉𐐯𐑋𐑌𐐰𐑌𐐻 𐐱𐑂 𐑄𐐮𐑅 𐐹𐐨𐐹𐑊, 𐐸𐐭 𐑇𐐰𐑊 𐐫𐑊𐑅𐐬 𐐺 𐐾𐐲𐐾𐐼 𐐺𐐴 𐑄 𐐻𐐶𐐯𐑊𐑂 𐐸𐐭𐑋 𐐖𐐨𐑆𐐲𐑅 𐐽𐐬𐑆 𐐮𐑌 𐑄𐐮𐑅 𐑊𐐰𐑌𐐼; 𐐰𐑌𐐼 𐑄𐐩 𐑇𐐰𐑊 𐐺 𐐾𐐲𐐾𐐼 𐐺𐐴 𐑄 𐐲𐑄𐐲𐑉 𐐻𐐶𐐯𐑊𐑂 𐐸𐐭𐑋 𐐖𐐨𐑆𐐲𐑅 𐐽𐐬𐑆 𐐮𐑌 𐑄 𐑊𐐰𐑌𐐼 𐐱𐑂 𐐖𐐯𐑉𐐭𐑅𐐲𐑊𐐯𐑋. 𐐈𐑌𐐼 𐑄𐐨𐑆 𐑃𐐮𐑍𐑆 𐐼𐐲𐑃 𐑄 𐐝𐐹𐐮𐑉𐐮𐐻 𐑋𐐰𐑌𐐮𐑁𐐯𐑅𐐻 𐐲𐑌𐐻𐐭 𐑋𐐨; 𐑄𐐯𐑉𐑁𐐬𐑉 𐐌 𐑉𐐴𐐻 𐐲𐑌𐐻𐐭 𐐷𐐭 𐐫𐑊. 𐐈𐑌𐐼 𐑁𐐫𐑉 𐑄𐐮𐑅 𐐿𐐫𐑆 𐐌 𐑉𐐴𐐻 𐐲𐑌𐐻𐐭 𐐷𐐭, 𐑄𐐰𐐻 𐐷𐐨 𐑋𐐩 𐑌𐐬 𐑄𐐰𐐻 𐐷𐐨 𐑋𐐲𐑅𐐻 𐐫𐑊 𐑅𐐻𐐰𐑌𐐼 𐐺𐐨𐑁𐐬𐑉 𐑄 𐐾𐐲𐐾𐑋𐐯𐑌𐐻 𐑅𐐨𐐻 𐐱𐑂 𐐗𐑉𐐴𐑅𐐻, 𐐷𐐩, 𐐯𐑂𐐲𐑉𐐨 𐑅𐐬𐑊 𐐸𐐭 𐐺𐐨𐑊𐐱𐑍𐑆 𐐻𐐭 𐑄 𐐸𐐬𐑊 𐐸𐐷𐐭𐑋𐐲𐑌 𐑁𐐰𐑋𐐮𐑊𐐨 𐐱𐑂 𐐁𐐼𐐲𐑋; 𐐰𐑌𐐼 𐐷𐐨 𐑋𐐲𐑅𐐻 𐑅𐐻𐐰𐑌𐐼 𐐻𐐭 𐐺 𐐾𐐲𐐾𐐼 𐐱𐑂 𐐷𐐬𐑉 𐐶𐐲𐑉𐐿𐑅, 𐐸𐐶𐐯𐑄𐐲𐑉 𐑄𐐩 𐐺 𐑀𐐳𐐼 𐐫𐑉 𐐨𐑂𐑊; 𐐰𐑌𐐼 𐐫𐑊𐑅𐐬 𐑄𐐰𐐻 𐐷𐐨 𐑋𐐩 𐐺𐐨𐑊𐐨𐑂 𐑄 𐑀𐐱𐑅𐐹𐐯𐑊 𐐱𐑂 𐐖𐐨𐑆𐐲𐑅 𐐗𐑉𐐴𐑅𐐻, 𐐸𐐶𐐮𐐽 𐐷𐐨 𐑇𐐰𐑊 𐐸𐐰𐑂 𐐲𐑋𐐲𐑍 𐐷𐐭; 𐐰𐑌𐐼 𐐫𐑊𐑅𐐬 𐑄𐐰𐐻 𐑄 𐐖𐐭𐑆, 𐑄 𐐿𐐲𐑂𐐯𐑌𐐲𐑌𐐻 𐐹𐐨𐐹𐑊 𐐱𐑂 𐑄 𐐢𐐫𐑉𐐼, 𐑇𐐰𐑊 𐐸𐐰𐑂 𐐲𐑄𐐲𐑉 𐐶𐐮𐐻𐑌𐐯𐑅, 𐐺𐐨𐑅𐐴𐐼𐑆 𐐸𐐮𐑋 𐐸𐐭𐑋 𐑄𐐩 𐑅𐐫 𐐰𐑌𐐼 𐐸𐐲𐑉𐐼, 𐑄𐐰𐐻 𐐖𐐨𐑆𐐲𐑅, 𐐸𐐭𐑋 𐑄𐐩 𐑅𐑊𐐭, 𐐶𐐱𐑆 𐑄 𐑂𐐯𐑉𐐨 𐐗𐑉𐐴𐑅𐐻, 𐐰𐑌𐐼 𐑄 𐑂𐐯𐑉𐐨 𐐘𐐱𐐼; 𐐰𐑌𐐼 𐐌 𐐶𐐳𐐼 𐑄𐐰𐐻 𐐌 𐐿𐐳𐐼 𐐹𐐲𐑉𐑅𐐶𐐩𐐼 𐐫𐑊 𐐷𐐨 𐐯𐑌𐐼𐑆 𐐱𐑂 𐑄 𐐲𐑉𐑃 𐐻𐐭 𐑉𐐨𐐹𐐯𐑌𐐻 𐐰𐑌𐐼 𐐹𐑉𐐨𐐹𐐩𐑉 𐐻𐐭 𐑅𐐻𐐰𐑌𐐼 𐐺𐐨𐑁𐐬𐑉 𐑄 𐐾𐐲𐐾𐑋𐐯𐑌𐐻 𐑅𐐨𐐻 𐐱𐑂 𐐗𐑉𐐴𐑅𐐻.

𐐕𐐰𐐹𐐻𐐲𐑉 II.

1. 𐐈𐑌𐐼 𐑌𐐵 𐐮𐐻 𐐿𐐩𐑋 𐐻𐐭 𐐹𐐰𐑅 𐑄𐐰𐐻 𐐮𐑌 𐑄 𐑃𐑉𐐨 𐐸𐐲𐑌𐐼𐑉𐐯𐐼 𐐰𐑌𐐼 𐑅𐐮𐐿𐑅𐐻𐐨 𐐰𐑌𐐼 𐑃𐐲𐑉𐐼 𐐷𐐨𐑉, 𐑄 𐐤𐐨𐑁𐐴𐐻𐑅 𐐼𐐮𐐼 𐑀𐐬 𐐲𐐹 𐐶𐐮𐑄 𐑄𐐩𐑉 𐐪𐑉𐑋𐐨𐑆 𐐻𐐭 𐐺𐐰𐐻𐑊 𐐰𐑀𐐯𐑌𐑅𐐻 𐑄 𐐢𐐩𐑋𐐲𐑌𐐴𐐻𐑅, 𐐵𐐻 𐐱𐑂 𐑄 𐑊𐐰𐑌𐐼 𐐔𐐯𐑅𐐬𐑊𐐩𐑇𐐲𐑌. 𐐈𐑌𐐼 𐐮𐐻 𐐿𐐩𐑋 𐐻𐐭 𐐹𐐰𐑅 𐑄𐐰𐐻 𐑄 𐐪𐑉𐑋𐐨𐑆 𐐱𐑂 𐑄 𐐤𐐨𐑁𐐴𐐻𐑅 𐐶𐐲𐑉 𐐼𐑉𐐮𐑂𐑌 𐐺𐐰𐐿 𐐰𐑀𐐯𐑌 𐐻𐐭 𐑄 𐑊𐐰𐑌𐐼 𐐱𐑂 𐐔𐐯𐑅𐐬𐑊𐐩𐑇𐐲𐑌. 𐐈𐑌𐐼 𐐸𐐶𐐴𐑊 𐑄𐐩 𐐶𐐲𐑉 𐐷𐐯𐐻 𐐶𐐨𐑉𐐨, 𐐰 𐑁𐑉𐐯𐑇 𐐪𐑉𐑋𐐨 𐐱𐑂 𐑄 𐐢𐐩𐑋𐐲𐑌𐐴𐐻𐑅 𐐼𐐮𐐼 𐐿𐐲𐑋 𐐲𐐹𐐱𐑌 𐑄𐐯𐑋; 𐐰𐑌𐐼 𐑄𐐩 𐐸𐐰𐐼 𐐰 𐑅𐐬𐑉 𐐺𐐰𐐻𐑊, 𐐮𐑌𐑅𐐬𐑋𐐲𐐽 𐑄𐐰𐐻 𐑄 𐐢𐐩𐑋𐐲𐑌𐐴𐐻𐑅

𐐼𐐮𐐼 𐐻𐐩𐐿 𐐹𐐲𐑆𐐯𐑇𐐲𐑌 𐐱𐑂 𐑄 𐑅𐐮𐐻𐐨 𐐔𐐯𐑅𐐬𐑊𐐩𐑇𐐲𐑌, 𐐰𐑌𐐼 𐐼𐐮𐐼 𐑅𐑊𐐩 𐑋𐐯𐑌𐐨 𐐱𐑂 𐑄 𐐤𐐨𐑁𐐴𐐻𐑅; 𐐰𐑌𐐼 𐐼𐐮𐐼 𐐻𐐩𐐿 𐑋𐐯𐑌𐐨 𐐹𐑉𐐮𐑆𐐲𐑌𐐲𐑉𐑆; 𐐰𐑌𐐼 𐑄 𐑉𐐨𐑋𐐩𐑌𐐼𐐲𐑉 𐐼𐐮𐐼 𐑁𐑊𐐨 𐐰𐑌𐐼 𐐾𐑎𐑌 𐑄 𐐮𐑌𐐸𐐰𐐺𐐮𐐻𐐲𐑌𐐻𐑅 𐐱𐑂 𐑄 𐑅𐐮𐐻𐐨 𐐓𐐨𐐰𐑌𐐿𐐲𐑋. 𐐤𐐵 𐑄 𐑅𐐮𐐻𐐨 𐐓𐐨𐐰𐑌𐐿𐐲𐑋 𐑊𐐩 𐐮𐑌 𐑄 𐐺𐐫𐑉𐐼𐐲𐑉𐑆 𐐺𐐴 𐑄 𐑅𐐨𐑇𐐬𐑉; 𐐰𐑌𐐼 𐐮𐐻 𐐶𐐱𐑆 𐐫𐑊𐑅𐐬 𐑌𐐨𐑉 𐑄 𐑅𐐮𐐻𐐨 𐐔𐐯𐑅𐐬𐑊𐐩𐑇𐐲𐑌. 𐐈𐑌𐐼 𐐮𐐻 𐐶𐐱𐑆 𐐺𐐨𐐿𐐫𐑆 𐑄 𐐪𐑉𐑋𐐨𐑆 𐐱𐑂 𐑄 𐐤𐐨𐑁𐐴𐐻𐑅 𐐶𐐯𐑌𐐻 𐐲𐐹 𐐲𐑌𐐻𐐭 𐑄 𐐢𐐰𐑋𐐲𐑌𐐴𐐻𐑅, 𐑄𐐰𐐻 𐑄𐐩 𐐺𐐨𐑀𐐰𐑌 𐐻𐐭 𐐺𐐨 𐑅𐑋𐐮𐐻𐐲𐑌; 𐑁𐐫𐑉 𐐶𐐲𐑉 𐐮𐐻 𐑌𐐱𐐻 𐑁𐐫𐑉 𐑄𐐰𐐻, 𐑄 𐐢𐐰𐑋𐐲𐑌𐐴𐐻𐑅 𐐿𐐳𐐼 𐐸𐐰𐑂 𐐸𐐰𐐼 𐑌𐐬 𐐹𐐵𐐲𐑉 𐐬𐑂𐐲𐑉 𐑄𐐯𐑋. 𐐒𐐲𐐻, 𐐺𐐨𐐸𐐬𐑊𐐼, 𐑄 𐐾𐐲𐐾𐑋𐐯𐑌𐐻𐑅 𐐱𐑂 𐐘𐐱𐐼 𐐶𐐮𐑊 𐐬𐑂𐐲𐑉𐐻𐐩𐐿 𐑄 𐐶𐐮𐐿𐐯𐐼; 𐐰𐑌𐐼 𐐮𐐻 𐐮𐑆 𐐺𐐴 𐑄 𐐶𐐮𐐿𐐯𐐼 𐑄𐐰𐐻 𐑄 𐐶𐐮𐐿𐐯𐐼 𐐪𐑉 𐐹𐐲𐑌𐐮𐑇𐐻: 𐑁𐐫𐑉 𐐮𐐻 𐐮𐑆 𐑄 𐐶𐐮𐐿𐐯𐐼 𐑄𐐰𐐻 𐑅𐐻𐐲𐑉 𐐲𐐹 𐑄 𐐸𐐪𐑉𐐻𐑅 𐐱𐑂 𐑄 𐐽𐐮𐑊𐐼𐑉𐐯𐑌 𐐱𐑂 𐑋𐐯𐑌 𐐲𐑌𐐻𐐭 𐐺𐑊𐐲𐐼𐑇𐐯𐐼. 𐐈𐑌𐐼 𐐮𐐻 𐐿𐐩𐑋 𐐻𐐭 𐐹𐐰𐑅 𐑄𐐰𐐻 𐑄 𐐢𐐰𐑋𐐲𐑌𐐴𐐻𐑅 𐐼𐐮𐐼 𐑋𐐩𐐿 𐐹𐑉𐐯𐐹𐐪𐑉𐐩𐑇𐐲𐑌𐑆 𐐻𐐭 𐐿𐐲𐑋 𐐲𐑀𐐯𐑌𐑅𐐻 𐑄 𐑅𐐮𐐻𐐨 𐐓𐐨𐐰𐑌𐐿𐐲𐑋.

2. 𐐈𐑌𐐼 𐐮𐐻 𐐿𐐩𐑋 𐐻𐐭 𐐹𐐰𐑅 𐐮𐑌 𐑄 𐑃𐑉𐐨 𐐸𐐲𐑌𐐼𐑉𐐯𐐼 𐐰𐑌𐐼 𐑅𐐮𐐿𐑅𐐻𐐨 𐐰𐑌𐐼 𐑁𐐬𐑉𐑃 𐐷𐐨𐑉, 𐑄 𐐢𐐰𐑋𐐲𐑌𐐴𐐻𐑅 𐐼𐐮𐐼 𐐿𐐲𐑋 𐐲𐑀𐐯𐑌𐑅𐐻 𐑄 𐑅𐐮𐐻𐐨 𐐓𐐨𐐰𐑌𐐿𐐲𐑋, 𐑄𐐰𐐻 𐑄𐐩 𐑋𐐴𐐻 𐐻𐐩𐐿 𐐹𐐲𐑆𐐯𐑇𐐲𐑌 𐐱𐑂 𐑄 𐑅𐐮𐐻𐐨 𐐓𐐨𐐰𐑌𐐿𐐲𐑋 𐐫𐑊𐑅𐐬. 𐐈𐑌𐐼 𐐮𐐻 𐐿𐐩𐑋 𐐻𐐭 𐐹𐐰𐑅 𐑄𐐰𐐻 𐑄𐐩 𐐶𐐲𐑉 𐑉𐐨𐐹𐐲𐑊𐑅𐐻 𐐰𐑌𐐼 𐐼𐑉𐐮𐑂𐐲𐑌 𐐺𐐰𐐿 𐐺𐐴 𐑄 𐐤𐐨𐑁𐐴𐐻𐑅. 𐐈𐑌𐐼 𐐸𐐶𐐯𐑌 𐑄 𐐤𐐨𐑁𐐴𐐻𐑅 𐑅𐐫 𐑄𐐰𐐻 𐑄𐐩 𐐸𐐰𐐼 𐐼𐑉𐐮𐑂𐐲𐑌 𐑄 𐐢𐐰𐑋𐐲𐑌𐐴𐐻𐑅, 𐑄𐐩 𐐼𐐮𐐼 𐐲𐑀𐐯𐑌 𐐺𐐬𐑅𐐻 𐐱𐑂 𐑄𐐩𐑉 𐑅𐐻𐑉𐐯𐑍𐑃; 𐐰𐑌𐐼 𐑄𐐩 𐐶𐐯𐑌𐐻 𐑁𐐬𐑉𐑃 𐐮𐑌 𐑄𐐩𐑉 𐐬𐑌 𐑋𐐴𐐻, 𐐰𐑌𐐼 𐐻𐐳𐐿 𐐹𐐲𐑆𐐯𐑇𐐲𐑌 𐐲𐑀𐐯𐑌 𐐱𐑂 𐑄 𐑅𐐮𐐻𐐨 𐐔𐐯𐑅𐐬𐑊𐐩𐑇𐐲𐑌. 𐐈𐑌𐐼 𐑌𐐵 𐐫𐑊 𐑄𐐨𐑆 𐑃𐐮𐑍𐑆 𐐸𐐰𐐼 𐐺𐐮𐑌 𐐼𐐲𐑌, 𐐰𐑌𐐼 𐑄𐐩𐑉 𐐸𐐰𐐼 𐐺𐐮𐑌 𐑃𐐵𐑆𐐲𐑌𐐼𐑆 𐑅𐑊𐐩𐑌 𐐱𐑌 𐐺𐐬𐑃 𐑅𐐴𐐼𐑆, 𐐺𐐬𐑃 𐑄 𐐤𐐨𐑁𐐴𐐻𐑅 𐐰𐑌𐐼 𐑄 𐐢𐐰𐑋𐐲𐑌𐐴𐐻𐑅. 𐐈𐑌𐐼 𐐮𐐻 𐐿𐐩𐑋 𐐻𐐭 𐐹𐐰𐑅 𐑄𐐰𐐻 𐑄 𐑃𐑉𐐨 𐐸𐐲𐑌𐐼𐑉𐐯𐐼 𐐰𐑌𐐼 𐑅𐐮𐐿𐑅𐐻𐐨 𐐰𐑌𐐼 𐑅𐐮𐐿𐑅𐑃 𐐷𐐨𐑉 𐐸𐐰𐐼 𐐹𐐰𐑅𐐻 𐐲𐐶𐐩, 𐐰𐑌𐐼 𐑄 𐐢𐐰𐑋𐐲𐑌𐐴𐐻𐑅 𐐿𐐩𐑋 𐐲𐑀𐐯𐑌 𐐲𐐹𐐱𐑌 𐑄 𐐤𐐨𐑁𐐴𐐻𐑅 𐐻𐐭 𐐺𐐰𐐻𐑊; 𐐰𐑌𐐼 𐐷𐐯𐐻 𐑄 𐐤𐐨𐑁𐐴𐐻𐑅 𐑉𐐨𐐹𐐯𐑌𐐻𐐯𐐼 𐑌𐐱𐐻 𐐱𐑂 𐑄 𐐨𐑂𐐲𐑊 𐑄𐐩 𐐸𐐰𐐼 𐐼𐐲𐑌, 𐐺𐐲𐐻 𐐹𐐲𐑉𐑅𐐮𐑅𐐻𐐯𐐼 𐐮𐑌 𐑄𐐩𐑉 𐐶𐐮𐐿𐐯𐐼𐑌𐐯𐑅 𐐿𐐱𐑌𐐻𐐮𐑌𐐷𐐭𐐲𐑊𐐨. 𐐈𐑌𐐼 𐐮𐐻 𐐮𐑆 𐐮𐑋𐐹𐐱𐑅𐐮𐐺𐑊 𐑁𐐫𐑉 𐑄 𐐻𐐲𐑍 𐐻𐐭 𐐼𐐨𐑅𐐿𐑉𐐴𐐺, 𐐫𐑉 𐑁𐐫𐑉 𐑋𐐰𐑌 𐐻𐐭 𐑉𐐴𐐻 𐐲 𐐹𐐲𐑉𐑁𐐯𐐿𐐻 𐐼𐐨𐑅𐐿𐑉𐐮𐐹𐑇𐐲𐑌 𐐱𐑂 𐑄 𐐸𐐱𐑉𐐮𐐺𐑊 𐑅𐐨𐑌 𐐱𐑂 𐑄 𐐺𐑊𐐲𐐼 𐐰𐑌𐐼 𐐿𐐪𐑉𐑌𐐩𐐾 𐐸𐐶𐐮𐐽 𐐶𐐱𐑆 𐐲𐑋𐐲𐑍 𐑄 𐐹𐐨𐐹𐑊, 𐐺𐐬𐑃 𐐱𐑂 𐑄 𐐤𐐨𐑁𐐴𐐻𐑅 𐐰𐑌𐐼 𐐱𐑂 𐑄 𐐢𐐰𐑋𐐲𐑌𐐴𐐻𐑅; 𐐰𐑌𐐼 𐐯𐑂𐐲𐑉𐐨 𐐸𐐪𐑉𐐻 𐐶𐐱𐑆 𐐸𐐪𐑉𐐼𐐲𐑌𐐼, 𐑅𐐬 𐑄𐐰𐐻 𐑄𐐩 𐐼𐐨𐑊𐐴𐐻𐐯𐐼 𐐮𐑌 𐑄 𐑇𐐯𐐼𐐮𐑍 𐐱𐑂 𐐺𐑊𐐲𐐼 𐐿𐐱𐑌𐐻𐐮𐑌𐐷𐐭𐐲𐑊𐐨. 𐐈𐑌𐐼 𐑄𐐩𐑉 𐑌𐐯𐑂𐐲𐑉 𐐸𐐰𐐼 𐐺𐐮𐑌 𐑅𐐬 𐑀𐑉𐐩𐐻 𐐶𐐮𐐿𐐯𐐼𐑌𐐯𐑅 𐐲𐑋𐐲𐑍 𐐫𐑊 𐑄 𐐽𐐮𐑊𐐼𐑉𐐯𐑌 𐐱𐑂 𐐢𐐨𐐸𐐴, 𐑌𐐫𐑉 𐐨𐑂𐐲𐑌 𐐲𐑋𐐲𐑍 𐐫𐑊 𐑄 𐐸𐐵𐑅 𐐱𐑂 𐐆𐑆𐑉𐐩𐐯𐑊, 𐐰𐐿𐐫𐑉𐐼𐐮𐑍 𐐻𐐭 𐑄 𐐶𐐲𐑉𐐼𐑆 𐐱𐑂 𐑄 𐐢𐐫𐑉𐐼, 𐐰𐑆 𐐶𐐱𐑆 𐐲𐑋𐐲𐑍 𐑄𐐮𐑅 𐐹𐐨𐐹𐑊.

3. 𐐈𐑌𐐼 𐐮𐐻 𐐿𐐩𐑋 𐐻𐐭 𐐹𐐰𐑅 𐑄𐐰𐐻 𐑄 𐐢𐐰𐑋𐐲𐑌𐐴𐐻𐑅 𐐼𐐮𐐼 𐐻𐐩𐐿 𐐹𐐲𐑆𐐯𐑇𐐲𐑌 𐐱𐑂 𐑄 𐑅𐐮𐐻𐐨 𐐔𐐯𐑅𐐬𐑊𐐩𐑇𐐲𐑌, 𐐰𐑌𐐼 𐑄𐐮𐑅 𐐺𐐨𐐿𐐫𐑆 𐑄𐐩𐑉 𐑌𐐲𐑋𐐺𐐲𐑉 𐐼𐐮𐐼 𐐯𐐿𐑅𐐨𐐼 𐑄 𐑌𐐲𐑋𐐺𐐲𐑉 𐐱𐑂 𐑄 𐐤𐐨𐑁𐐴𐐻𐑅. 𐐈𐑌𐐼 𐑄𐐩 𐐼𐐮𐐼 𐐫𐑊𐑅𐐬 𐑋𐐪𐑉𐐽 𐑁𐐫𐑉𐐶𐐲𐑉𐐼 𐐲𐑀𐐯𐑌𐑅𐐻 𐑄 𐑅𐐮𐐻𐐨 𐐓𐐨𐐰𐑌𐐿𐐲𐑋, 𐐰𐑌𐐼 𐐼𐐮𐐼 𐐼𐑉𐐴𐑂 𐑄 𐐮𐑌𐐸𐐰𐐺𐐮𐐻𐐲𐑌𐐻𐑅 𐑁𐐬𐑉𐑃 𐐵𐐻 𐐱𐑂 𐐸𐐲𐑉, 𐐰𐑌𐐼 𐐼𐐮𐐼 𐐻𐐩𐐿 𐑋𐐯𐑌𐐨 𐐹𐑉𐐮𐑆𐐲𐑌𐐲𐑉𐑆, 𐐺𐐬𐑃 𐐶𐐮𐑋𐐯𐑌 𐐰𐑌𐐼 𐐽𐐮𐑊𐐼𐑉𐐯𐑌, 𐐰𐑌𐐼 𐐼𐐮𐐼 𐐫𐑁𐐲𐑉 𐑄𐐯𐑋 𐐲𐐹 𐐰𐑆 𐑅𐐰𐐿𐑉𐐮𐑁𐐴𐑅𐐯𐑆 𐐲𐑌𐐻𐐭 𐑄𐐩𐑉 𐐴𐐼𐐲𐑊 𐑀𐐱𐐼𐑆. 𐐈𐑌𐐼 𐐮𐐻 𐐿𐐩𐑋 𐐻𐐭 𐐹𐐰𐑅 𐑄𐐰𐐻 𐐮𐑌 𐑄 𐑃𐑉𐐨 𐐸𐐲𐑌𐐼𐑉𐐯𐐼 𐐰𐑌𐐼 𐑅𐐮𐐿𐑅𐐻𐐨 𐐰𐑌𐐼 𐑅𐐯𐑂𐐲𐑌𐑃 𐐷𐐨𐑉, 𐑄 𐐤𐐨𐑁𐐴𐐻𐑅 𐐺𐐨𐐮𐑍 𐐰𐑍𐑀𐑉𐐨 𐐺𐐨𐐿𐐫𐑆 𐑄 𐐢𐐰𐑋𐐲𐑌𐐴𐐻𐑅 𐐸𐐰𐐼 𐑅𐐰𐐿𐑉𐐮𐑁𐐴𐑅𐐻 𐑄𐐩𐑉 𐐶𐐮𐑋𐐯𐑌 𐐰𐑌𐐼 𐑄𐐩𐑉 𐐽𐐮𐑊𐐼𐑉𐐯𐑌, 𐑄𐐰𐐻 𐑄𐐩 𐐼𐐮𐐼 𐑀𐐬 𐐲𐑀𐐯𐑌𐑅𐐻 𐑄 𐐢𐐰𐑋𐐲𐑌𐐴𐐻𐑅 𐐶𐐮𐑄 𐐯𐐿𐑅𐐨𐐼𐐮𐑍𐑊𐐨 𐑀𐑉𐐩𐐻 𐐰𐑍𐑀𐐲𐑉, 𐐮𐑌𐑅𐐬𐑋𐐲𐐽 𐑄𐐰𐐻 𐑄𐐩 𐐼𐐮𐐼 𐐺𐐨𐐻 𐐲𐑀𐐯𐑌 𐑄 𐐢𐐰𐑋𐐲𐑌𐐴𐐻𐑅, 𐐰𐑌𐐼 𐐼𐑉𐐴𐑂 𐑄𐐯𐑋 𐐵𐐻 𐐱𐑂 𐑄𐐩𐑉 𐑊𐐰𐑌𐐼𐑆; 𐐰𐑌𐐼 𐑄 𐐢𐐰𐑋𐐲𐑌𐐴𐐻𐑅 𐐼𐐮𐐼 𐑌𐐱𐐻 𐐿𐐲𐑋 𐐲𐑀𐐯𐑌 𐐲𐑀𐐯𐑌𐑅𐐻 𐑄 𐐤𐐨𐑁𐐴𐐻𐑅, 𐐲𐑌𐐻𐐮𐑊 𐑄 𐑃𐑉𐐨 𐐸𐐲𐑌𐐼𐑉𐐯𐐼 𐐰𐑌𐐼 𐑅𐐯𐑂𐐲𐑌𐐻𐐨 𐐰𐑌𐐼 𐑁𐐮𐑁𐑃 𐐷𐐨𐑉. 𐐈𐑌𐐼 𐐮𐑌 𐑄𐐮𐑅 𐐷𐐨𐑉 𐑄𐐩 𐐼𐐮𐐼 𐐿𐐲𐑋 𐐼𐐵𐑌 𐐲𐑀𐐯𐑌𐑅𐐻 𐑄 𐐤𐐨𐑁𐐴𐐻𐑅 𐐶𐐮𐑄 𐐫𐑊 𐑄𐐩𐑉 𐐹𐐵𐐲𐑉𐑆; 𐐰𐑌𐐼 𐑄𐐩 𐐶𐐲𐑉 𐑌𐐱𐐻 𐑌𐐲𐑋𐐺𐐲𐑉𐐼 𐐺𐐨𐐿𐐫𐑆 𐐱𐑂 𐑄 𐑀𐑉𐐩𐐻𐑌𐐯𐑅 𐐱𐑂 𐑄𐐩𐑉 𐑌𐐲𐑋𐐺𐐲𐑉. 𐐈𐑌𐐼 𐑁𐑉𐐱𐑋 𐑄𐐮𐑅 𐐻𐐴𐑋 𐑁𐐬𐑉𐑃 𐐼𐐮𐐼 𐑄 𐐤𐐨𐑁𐐴𐐻𐑅 𐑀𐐩𐑌 𐑌𐐬 𐐹𐐵𐐲𐑉 𐐬𐑂𐐲𐑉 𐑄 𐐢𐐰𐑋𐐲𐑌𐐴𐐻𐑅, 𐐺𐐲𐐻 𐐺𐐨𐑀𐐰𐑌 𐐻𐐭 𐐺𐐨 𐑅𐐶𐐯𐐹𐐻 𐐫𐑁 𐐺𐐴 𐑄𐐯𐑋 𐐨𐑂𐐲𐑌 𐐰𐑆 𐐲 𐐼𐑏 𐐺𐐨𐑁𐐬𐑉 𐑄 𐑅𐐲𐑌. 𐐈𐑌𐐼 𐐮𐐻 𐐿𐐩𐑋 𐐻𐐭 𐐹𐐰𐑅 𐑄𐐰𐐻 𐑄 𐐢𐐰𐑋𐐲𐑌𐐴𐐻𐑅 𐐼𐐮𐐼 𐐿𐐲𐑋 𐐼𐐵𐑌 𐐲𐑀𐐯𐑌𐑅𐐻 𐑄 𐑅𐐮𐐻𐐨 𐐔𐐯𐑅𐐬𐑊𐐩𐑇𐐲𐑌; 𐐰𐑌𐐼 𐑄𐐩𐑉 𐐶𐐱𐑆 𐐰𐑌 𐐯𐐿𐑅𐐨𐐼𐐮𐑍𐑊𐐨 𐑅𐐬𐑉 𐐺𐐰𐐻𐑊 𐑁𐐫𐐻 𐐮𐑌 𐑄 𐑊𐐰𐑌𐐼 𐐔𐐯𐑅𐐬𐑊𐐩𐑇𐐲𐑌, 𐐮𐑌 𐑄 𐐸𐐶𐐮𐐽 𐑄𐐩 𐐼𐐮𐐼 𐐺𐐨𐐻 𐑄 𐐤𐐨𐑁𐐴𐐻𐑅. 𐐈𐑌𐐼 𐑄𐐩 𐑁𐑊𐐯𐐼 𐐲𐑀𐐯𐑌 𐑁𐑉𐐱𐑋 𐐺𐐨𐑁𐐬𐑉 𐑄𐐯𐑋, 𐐰𐑌𐐼 𐑄𐐩 𐐿𐐩𐑋 𐐻𐐭 𐑄 𐑅𐐮𐐻𐐨 𐐒𐐬𐐰𐑆; 𐐰𐑌𐐼

𐑄𐐯𐑉 𐑄𐐩 𐐼𐐮𐐼 𐑅𐐻𐐰𐑌𐐼 𐐰𐑀𐐯𐑌𐑅𐐻 𐑄 𐐢𐐩𐑋𐐲𐑌𐐴𐐻𐑅 𐐶𐐮𐑄 𐐯𐐿𐑅𐐨𐐼𐐮𐑍 𐐺𐐬𐑊𐐼𐑌𐐯𐑅, 𐐮𐑌𐑅𐐬𐑋𐐲𐐽 𐑄𐐰𐐻 𐑄 𐐢𐐩𐑋𐐲𐑌𐐴𐐻𐑅 𐐼𐐮𐐼 𐑌𐐱𐐻 𐐺𐐨𐐻 𐑄𐐯𐑋 𐐲𐑌𐐻𐐮𐑊 𐑄𐐩 𐐸𐐰𐐼 𐐿𐐲𐑋 𐐰𐑀𐐯𐑌 𐑄 𐑅𐐯𐐿𐐲𐑌𐐼 𐐻𐐴𐑋. 𐐈𐑌𐐼 𐐸𐐶𐐯𐑌 𐑄𐐩 𐐸𐐰𐐼 𐐿𐐲𐑋 𐑄 𐑅𐐯𐐿𐐲𐑌𐐼 𐐻𐐴𐑋, 𐑄 𐐤𐐨𐑁𐐴𐐻𐑅 𐐶𐐲𐑉 𐐼𐑉𐐮𐑂𐑌 𐐰𐑌𐐼 𐑅𐑊𐐫𐐻𐐲𐑉𐐼 𐐶𐐮𐑄 𐐰𐑌 𐐯𐐿𐑅𐐨𐐼𐐮𐑍 𐑀𐑉𐐩𐐻 𐑅𐑊𐐫𐐻𐐲𐑉; 𐑄𐐯𐑉 𐐶𐐮𐑋𐐮𐑌 𐐰𐑌𐐼 𐑄𐐯𐑉 𐐽𐐮𐑊𐐼𐑉𐐯𐑌 𐐶𐐲𐑉 𐐰𐑀𐐯𐑌 𐑅𐐰𐐿𐑉𐐮𐑁𐐴𐑅𐐻 𐐲𐑌𐐻𐐭 𐐴𐐼𐐲𐑊𐑆. 𐐈𐑌𐐼 𐐮𐐻 𐐿𐐩𐑋 𐐻𐐭 𐐹𐐰𐑅 𐑄𐐰𐐻 𐑄 𐐤𐐨𐑁𐐴𐐻𐑅 𐐼𐐮𐐼 𐐰𐑀𐐯𐑌 𐑁𐑊𐐨 𐑁𐑉𐐱𐑋 𐐺𐐨𐑁𐐬𐑉 𐑄𐐯𐑋, 𐐻𐐩𐐿𐐮𐑍 𐐫𐑊 𐑄 𐐮𐑌𐐸𐐰𐐺𐐮𐐻𐐲𐑌𐐻𐑅 𐐶𐐮𐑄 𐑄𐐯𐑋, 𐐺𐐬𐑃 𐐮𐑌 𐐻𐐵𐑌𐑆 𐐰𐑌𐐼 𐑂𐐮𐑊𐐯𐐾𐐯𐑆. 𐐈𐑌𐐼 𐑌𐐵 𐐌, 𐐣𐐫𐑉𐑋𐐲𐑌, 𐑅𐐨𐐮𐑍 𐑄𐐰𐐻 𐑄 𐐢𐐩𐑋𐐲𐑌𐐴𐐻𐑅 𐐶𐐲𐑉 𐐰𐐺𐐵𐐻 𐐻𐐭 𐐬𐑂𐐲𐑉𐑃𐑉𐐬 𐑄 𐑊𐐰𐑌𐐼, 𐑄𐐯𐑉𐑁𐐬𐑉 𐐌 𐐼𐐮𐐼 𐑀𐐬 𐐻𐐭 𐑄 𐐸𐐮𐑊 𐐟𐐮𐑋, 𐐰𐑌𐐼 𐐼𐐮𐐼 𐐻𐐩𐐿 𐐲𐐹 𐐫𐑊 𐑄 𐑉𐐯𐐿𐐲𐑉𐐼𐑆 𐐸𐐶𐐮𐐽 𐐈𐑋𐐰𐑉𐐲𐑌 𐐸𐐰𐐼 𐐸𐐮𐐼 𐐲𐐹 𐐲𐑌𐐻𐐭 𐑄 𐐢𐐫𐑉𐐼.

4. 𐐈𐑌𐐼 𐐮𐐻 𐐿𐐩𐑋 𐐻𐐭 𐐹𐐰𐑅 𐑄𐐰𐐻 𐐌 𐐼𐐮𐐼 𐑀𐐬 𐑁𐐫𐑉𐑃 𐐰𐑋𐐲𐑍 𐑄 𐐤𐐨𐑁𐐴𐐻𐑅, 𐐰𐑌𐐼 𐐼𐐮𐐼 𐑉𐐨𐐹𐐯𐑌𐐻 𐐱𐑂 𐑄 𐐬𐑃 𐐸𐐶𐐮𐐽 𐐌 𐐸𐐰𐐼 𐑋𐐩𐐼 𐑄𐐰𐐻 𐐌 𐐶𐐳𐐼 𐑌𐐬 𐑋𐐫𐑉 𐐰𐑅𐐮𐑅𐐻 𐑄𐐯𐑋; 𐐰𐑌𐐼 𐑄𐐩 𐑀𐐩𐑂 𐑋𐐨 𐐿𐐲𐑋𐐰𐑌𐐼 𐐰𐑀𐐯𐑌 𐐱𐑂 𐑄𐐯𐑉 𐐪𐑉𐑋𐐨𐑆; 𐑁𐐫𐑉 𐑄𐐩 𐑊𐐳𐐿𐐻 𐐲𐐹𐐱𐑌 𐑋𐐨 𐐰𐑆 𐑄𐐬 𐐌 𐐿𐐳𐐼 𐐼𐐨𐑊𐐮𐑂𐐲𐑉 𐑄𐐯𐑋 𐑁𐑉𐐱𐑋 𐑄𐐯𐑉 𐐰𐑁𐑊𐐮𐐿𐑇𐐲𐑌𐑆. 𐐒𐐲𐐻 𐐺𐐨𐐸𐐬𐑊𐐼, 𐐌 𐐶𐐱𐑆 𐐶𐐮𐑄𐐵𐐻 𐐸𐐬𐐹, 𐑁𐐫𐑉 𐐌 𐑌𐐭 𐑄 𐐖𐐲𐐾𐑋𐐯𐑌𐐻𐑅 𐐱𐑂 𐑄 𐐢𐐫𐑉𐐼 𐐸𐐶𐐮𐐽 𐑇𐐳𐐼 𐐿𐐲𐑋 𐐲𐐹𐐱𐑌 𐑄𐐯𐑋; 𐑁𐐫𐑉 𐑄𐐩 𐑉𐐨𐐹𐐯𐑌𐐻𐐯𐐼 𐑌𐐱𐐻 𐐱𐑂 𐑄𐐯𐑉 𐐮𐑌𐐮𐐿𐐶𐐮𐐻𐐮𐑆, 𐐺𐐲𐐻 𐐼𐐮𐐼 𐑅𐐻𐑉𐐲𐑀𐑊 𐑁𐐫𐑉 𐑄𐐯𐑉 𐑊𐐴𐑂𐑆, 𐐶𐐮𐑄𐐵𐐻 𐐿𐐫𐑊𐐮𐑍 𐐲𐐹𐐱𐑌 𐑄𐐰𐐻 𐐒𐐨𐐮𐑍 𐐸𐐭 𐐿𐑉𐐨𐐩𐐻𐐯𐐼 𐑄𐐯𐑋. 𐐈𐑌𐐼 𐐮𐐻 𐐿𐐩𐑋 𐐻𐐭 𐐹𐐰𐑅 𐑄𐐰𐐻 𐑄 𐐢𐐩𐑋𐐲𐑌𐐴𐐻𐑅 𐐼𐐮𐐼 𐐿𐐲𐑋 𐐰𐑀𐐯𐑌𐑅𐐻 𐐲𐑅 𐐰𐑆 𐐶𐐨 𐐸𐐰𐐼 𐑁𐑊𐐯𐐼 𐐻𐐭 𐑄 𐑅𐐮𐐻𐐮 𐐱𐑂 𐐖𐐫𐑉𐐼𐐲𐑌; 𐐒𐐲𐐻 𐐺𐐨𐐸𐐬𐑊𐐼, 𐑄𐐩 𐐶𐐲𐑉 𐐼𐑉𐐮𐑂𐑌 𐐺𐐰𐐿 𐑄𐐰𐐻 𐑄𐐩 𐐼𐐮𐐼 𐑌𐐱𐐻 𐐻𐐩𐐿 𐑄 𐑅𐐮𐐻𐐮 𐐰𐐻 𐑄𐐰𐐻 𐐻𐐴𐑋. 𐐈𐑌𐐼 𐐮𐐻 𐐿𐐩𐑋 𐐻𐐭 𐐹𐐰𐑅 𐑄𐐰𐐻 𐑄𐐩 𐐿𐐩𐑋 𐐰𐑀𐐯𐑌𐑅𐐻 𐐲𐑅 𐐰𐑀𐐯𐑌, 𐐰𐑌𐐼 𐐶𐐨 𐐼𐐮𐐼 𐑋𐐩𐑌𐐻𐐩𐑌 𐑄 𐑅𐐮𐐻𐐮. 𐐈𐑌𐐼 𐑄𐐯𐑉 𐐶𐐲𐑉 𐐫𐑊𐑅𐐬 𐐲𐑄𐐲𐑉 𐑅𐐮𐐻𐐮𐑆 𐐸𐐶𐐮𐐽 𐐶𐐲𐑉 𐑋𐐩𐑌𐐻𐐩𐑌𐐼 𐐺𐐴 𐑄 𐐤𐐨𐑁𐐴𐐻𐑅, 𐐸𐐶𐐮𐐽 𐑅𐐻𐑉𐐱𐑍𐐸𐐬𐑊𐐼𐑆 𐐼𐐮𐐼 𐐿𐐲𐐻 𐑄𐐯𐑋 𐐱𐑁 𐑄𐐰𐐻 𐑄𐐩 𐐿𐐳𐐼 𐑌𐐱𐐻 𐑀𐐯𐐻 𐐮𐑌𐐻𐐭 𐑄 𐐿𐐲𐑌𐐻𐑉𐐮 𐐸𐐶𐐮𐐽 𐑊𐐩 𐐺𐐨𐑁𐐬𐑉 𐐲𐑅 𐐻𐐭 𐐼𐐯𐑅𐐻𐑉𐐱𐐮 𐑄 𐐮𐑌𐐸𐐰𐐺𐐮𐐻𐐲𐑌𐐻𐑅 𐐱𐑂 𐐵𐑉 𐑊𐐰𐑌𐐼. 𐐒𐐲𐐻 𐐮𐐻 𐐿𐐩𐑋 𐐻𐐭 𐐹𐐰𐑅 𐑄𐐰𐐻 𐐸𐐶𐐱𐐻𐑅𐐬𐐯𐑂𐐲𐑉 𐑊𐐰𐑌𐐼𐑆 𐐶𐐨 𐐸𐐰𐐼 𐐹𐐰𐑅𐐻 𐐺𐐴, 𐐰𐑌𐐼 𐑄 𐐮𐑌𐐸𐐰𐐺𐐮𐐻𐐲𐑌𐐻𐑅 𐑄𐐯𐑉𐐱𐑂 𐐶𐐲𐑉 𐑌𐐱𐐻 𐑀𐐰𐑄𐐲𐑉𐐼 𐐮𐑌, 𐐶𐐲𐑉 𐐼𐐯𐑅𐐻𐑉𐐱𐐮𐐼 𐐺𐐴 𐑄 𐐢𐐩𐑋𐐲𐑌𐐴𐐻𐑅, 𐐰𐑌𐐼 𐑄𐐯𐑉 𐐻𐐵𐑌𐑆, 𐐰𐑌𐐼 𐑂𐐮𐑊𐐯𐐾𐐯𐑆, 𐐰𐑌𐐼 𐑅𐐮𐐻𐐮𐑆 𐐶𐐲𐑉 𐐺𐐲𐑉𐑌𐐼 𐐶𐐮𐑄 𐑁𐐴𐑉; 𐐰𐑌𐐼 𐑄𐐲𐑅 𐑃𐑉𐐨 𐐸𐐲𐑌𐐼𐑉𐐯𐐼 𐐰𐑌𐐼 𐑅𐐯𐑂𐐲𐑌𐐻𐐮 𐐰𐑌𐐼 𐑌𐐴𐑌 𐐷𐐨𐑉𐑆 𐐹𐐰𐑅𐐻 𐐰𐐶𐐩.

5. 𐐈𐑌𐐼 𐐮𐐻 𐐿𐐩𐑋 𐐻𐐭 𐐹𐐰𐑅 𐑄𐐰𐐻 𐐮𐑌 𐑄 𐑃𐑉𐐨 𐐸𐐲𐑌𐐼𐑉𐐯𐐼 𐐰𐑌𐐼 𐐩𐐻𐐨𐐲𐑃 𐐷𐐨𐑉, 𐑄 𐐢𐐩𐑋𐐲𐑌𐐴𐐻𐑅 𐐼𐐮𐐼 𐐿𐐲𐑋 𐐰𐑀𐐯𐑌 𐐰𐑀𐐯𐑌𐑅𐐻 𐐲𐑅 𐐻𐐭 𐐺𐐰𐐻𐑊, 𐐰𐑌𐐼 𐐶𐐨 𐐼𐐮𐐼 𐑅𐐻𐐰𐑌𐐼 𐐰𐑀𐐯𐑌𐑅𐐻 𐑄𐐯𐑋 𐐺𐐬𐑊𐐼𐑊𐐮; 𐐒𐐲𐐻 𐐮𐐻 𐐶𐐱𐑆 𐐫𐑊 𐐮𐑌 𐑂𐐩𐑌, 𐑁𐐫𐑉 𐑅𐐬 𐑀𐑉𐐩𐐻 𐐶𐐲𐑉 𐑄𐐯𐑉 𐑌𐐲𐑋𐐺𐐲𐑉𐑆 𐑄𐐰𐐻 𐑄𐐩 𐐼𐐮𐐼 𐐻𐑉𐐯𐐼 𐑄 𐐹𐐨𐐹𐑊 𐐱𐑂 𐑄 𐐤𐐨𐑁𐐴𐐻𐑅 𐐲𐑌𐐼𐐲𐑉 𐑄𐐯𐑉 𐑁𐐨𐐻. 𐐈𐑌𐐼 𐐮𐐻 𐐿𐐩𐑋 𐐻𐐭 𐐹𐐰𐑅 𐑄𐐰𐐻 𐐶𐐨 𐐼𐐮𐐼 𐐰𐑀𐐯𐑌 𐐻𐐩𐐿 𐐻𐐭 𐑁𐑊𐐴𐐻, 𐐰𐑌𐐼 𐑄𐐬𐑆 𐐸𐐭𐑆 𐑁𐑊𐐴𐐻 𐐶𐐱𐑆 𐑅𐐶𐐮𐑁𐐻𐐲𐑉 𐑄𐐰𐑌 𐑄 𐐢𐐩𐑋𐐲𐑌𐐴𐐻𐑅' 𐐼𐐮𐐼 𐐯𐑅𐐿𐐩𐐹, 𐐰𐑌𐐼 𐑄𐐬𐑆 𐐸𐐭𐑆 𐑁𐑊𐐴𐐻 𐐼𐐮𐐼 𐑌𐐱𐐻 𐐯𐐿𐑅𐐨𐐼 𐑄 𐐢𐐩𐑋𐐲𐑌𐐴𐐻𐑅', 𐐶𐐲𐑉 𐑅𐐶𐐯𐐹𐐻 𐐼𐐵𐑌 𐐰𐑌𐐼 𐐼𐐯𐑅𐐻𐑉𐐱𐐮𐐼. 𐐈𐑌𐐼 𐑌𐐵 𐐺𐐨𐐸𐐬𐑊𐐼, 𐐌, 𐐣𐐫𐑉𐑋𐐲𐑌, 𐐼𐐭 𐑌𐐱𐐻 𐐼𐐯𐑆𐐴𐑉 𐐻𐐭 𐐸𐐰𐑉𐐬 𐐲𐐹 𐑄 𐑅𐐬𐑊𐑆 𐐱𐑂 𐑋𐐯𐑌 𐐮𐑌 𐐿𐐰𐑅𐐻𐐮𐑍 𐐺𐐨𐑁𐐬𐑉 𐑄𐐯𐑋 𐑅𐐲𐐽 𐐰𐑌 𐐫𐑁𐐳𐑊 𐑅𐐨𐑌 𐐱𐑂 𐐺𐑊𐐲𐐼 𐐰𐑌𐐼 𐐿𐐪𐑉𐑌𐐯𐐾 𐐰𐑆 𐐶𐐱𐑆 𐑊𐐩𐐼 𐐺𐐨𐑁𐐬𐑉 𐑋𐐴𐑌 𐐴𐑆, 𐐺𐐲𐐻 𐐌 𐑌𐐬𐐮𐑍 𐑄𐐰𐐻 𐑄𐐨𐑆 𐑃𐐮𐑍𐑆 𐑋𐐲𐑅𐐻 𐑇𐐭𐑉𐑊𐐨 𐐺𐐨 𐑋𐐩𐐼 𐑌𐐬𐑌, 𐐰𐑌𐐼 𐑄𐐰𐐻 𐐫𐑊 𐑃𐐮𐑍𐑆 𐐸𐐶𐐮𐐽 𐐪𐑉 𐐸𐐮𐐼 𐑋𐐲𐑅𐐻 𐐺𐐨 𐑉𐐨𐑂𐐨𐑊𐐼 𐐲𐐹𐐱𐑌 𐑄 𐐸𐐵𐑅 𐐻𐐱𐐹𐑅, 𐐰𐑌𐐼 𐐫𐑊𐑅𐐬 𐑄𐐰𐐻 𐐩 𐑌𐐱𐑊𐐯𐐾 𐐱𐑂 𐑄𐐨𐑆 𐑃𐐮𐑍𐑆 𐑋𐐲𐑅𐐻 𐐿𐐲𐑋 𐐲𐑌𐐻𐐭 𐑄 𐑉𐐯𐑋𐑌𐐰𐑌𐐻 𐐱𐑂 𐑄𐐨𐑆 𐐹𐐨𐐹𐑊, 𐐰𐑌𐐼 𐐫𐑊𐑅𐐬 𐐲𐑌𐐻𐐭 𐑄 𐐖𐐯𐑌𐐻𐐴𐑊𐑆, 𐐸𐐶𐐮𐐽 𐑄 𐐢𐐫𐑉𐐼 𐐸𐐰𐑃 𐑅𐐯𐐼 𐑇𐐳𐐼 𐑅𐐿𐐰𐐻𐐲𐑉 𐑄𐐮𐑅 𐐹𐐨𐐹𐑊, 𐐰𐑌𐐼 𐑄𐐮𐑅 𐐹𐐨𐐹𐑊 𐑇𐐳𐐼 𐐺𐐨 𐐿𐐵𐑌𐐻𐐯𐐼 𐐰𐑆 𐑌𐐫𐐻 𐐰𐑋𐐲𐑍 𐑄𐐯𐑋, 𐑄𐐯𐑉𐑁𐐬𐑉 𐐌 𐑉𐐴𐐻 𐐩 𐑅𐑋𐐫𐑊 𐐰𐐺𐑉𐐮𐐾𐑋𐐯𐑌𐐻, 𐐼𐐩𐑉𐐮𐑍 𐑌𐐱𐐻 𐐻𐐭 𐑀𐐮𐑂 𐐩 𐑁𐐳𐑊 𐐰𐐿𐐵𐑌𐐻 𐐱𐑂 𐑄 𐑃𐐮𐑍𐑆 𐐸𐐶𐐮𐐽 𐐌 𐐸𐐰𐑂 𐑅𐐨𐑌, 𐐺𐐨𐐿𐐫𐑆 𐐱𐑂 𐑄 𐐿𐐲𐑋𐐰𐑌𐐼𐑋𐐯𐑌𐐻 𐐸𐐶𐐮𐐽 𐐌 𐐸𐐰𐑂 𐑉𐐨𐑅𐐨𐑂𐐼, 𐐰𐑌𐐼 𐐫𐑊𐑅𐐬 𐑄𐐰𐐻 𐐷𐐨 𐑋𐐴𐐻 𐑌𐐱𐐻 𐐸𐐰𐑂 𐐻𐐭 𐑀𐑉𐐩𐐻 𐑅𐐱𐑉𐐬 𐐺𐐨𐐿𐐫𐑆 𐐱𐑂 𐑄 𐐶𐐮𐐿𐐯𐐼𐑌𐐯𐑅 𐐱𐑂 𐑄𐐮𐑅 𐐹𐐨𐐹𐑊.

6. 𐐈𐑌𐐼 𐑌𐐵 𐐺𐐨𐐸𐐬𐑊𐐼, 𐑄𐐮𐑅 𐐌 𐑅𐐹𐐨𐐿 𐐲𐑌𐐻𐐭 𐑄𐐯𐑉 𐑅𐐨𐐼, 𐐰𐑌𐐼 𐐫𐑊𐑅𐐬 𐐻𐐭 𐑄 𐐖𐐯𐑌𐐻𐐴𐑊𐑆, 𐐸𐐭 𐐸𐐰𐑂 𐐿𐐩𐑉 𐑁𐐫𐑉 𐑄 𐐸𐐵𐑅 𐐱𐑂 𐐀𐑆𐑉𐐩𐐯𐑊, 𐑄𐐰𐐻 𐑉𐐨𐐰𐑊𐐴𐑆 𐐰𐑌𐐼 𐑌𐐬 𐑁𐑉𐐱𐑋 𐐸𐐶𐐯𐑌𐑅 𐑄𐐯𐑉 𐐺𐑊𐐯𐑅𐐮𐑍𐑆 𐐿𐐲𐑋. 𐐙𐐫𐑉 𐐌 𐑌𐐬 𐑄𐐰𐐻 𐑅𐐲𐐽 𐐶𐐮𐑊 𐑅𐐱𐑉𐐬 𐑁𐐫𐑉 𐑄 𐐿𐐰𐑊𐐰𐑋𐐮𐐻𐐮 𐐱𐑂 𐑄 𐐸𐐵𐑅 𐐱𐑂 𐐀𐑆𐑉𐐩𐐯𐑊; 𐐷𐐩, 𐑄𐐩 𐐶𐐮𐑊

𐑅𐐪𐑉𐐬 𐑁𐐫𐑉 𐑄 𐐼𐐨𐑅𐐻𐑉𐐲𐐿𐑇𐐲𐑌 𐐱𐑂 𐑄𐐮𐑅 𐐹𐐨𐐹𐑊; 𐑄𐐩 𐐶𐐮𐑊 𐑅𐐪𐑉𐐬 𐑄𐐰𐐻 𐑄𐐮𐑅 𐐹𐐨𐐹𐑊 𐐸𐐰𐐼 𐑌𐐪𐐻 𐑉𐐨𐐹𐐯𐑌𐐻𐐯𐐼, 𐑄𐐰𐐻 𐑄𐐩 𐑋𐐴𐐻 𐐸𐐰𐑂 𐐺𐐮𐑌 𐐿𐑊𐐰𐑅𐐹𐐻 𐐮𐑌 𐑄 𐐪𐑉𐑋𐑆 𐐱𐑂 𐐖𐐨𐑆𐐲𐑅. 𐐤𐐵 𐑄𐐨𐑆 𐑃𐐮𐑍𐑆 𐐪𐑉 𐑉𐐮𐐻𐑌 𐐲𐑌𐐻𐐭 𐑄 𐑉𐐯𐑋𐑌𐐲𐑌𐐻 𐐱𐑂 𐑄 𐐸𐐵𐑅 𐐱𐑂 𐐖𐐩𐐿𐐲𐐺; 𐐰𐑌𐐼 𐑄𐐩 𐐪𐑉 𐑉𐐮𐐻𐑌 𐐰𐑁𐐻𐐲𐑉 𐑄𐐮𐑅 𐑋𐐰𐑌𐐲𐑉, 𐐺𐐨𐐿𐐫𐑆 𐐮𐐻 𐐮𐑆 𐑌𐐬𐑌 𐐱𐑂 𐐘𐐱𐐼 𐑄𐐰𐐻 𐐶𐐮𐐿𐐯𐐼𐑌𐐯𐑅 𐐶𐐮𐑊 𐑌𐐪𐐻 𐐺𐑉𐐮𐑍 𐑄𐐯𐑋 𐑁𐐫𐑉𐑃 𐐲𐑌𐐻𐐭 𐑄𐐯𐑋; 𐐰𐑌𐐼 𐑄𐐩 𐐪𐑉 𐐻𐐭 𐐺𐐨 𐐸𐐮𐐼 𐐲𐐹 𐐲𐑌𐐻𐐭 𐑄 𐐢𐐫𐑉𐐼, 𐑄𐐰𐐻 𐑄𐐩 𐑋𐐩 𐐿𐐲𐑋 𐑁𐐫𐑉𐑃 𐐮𐑌 𐐸𐐮𐑆 𐐬𐑌 𐐼𐐭 𐐻𐐴𐑋. 𐐈𐑌𐐼 𐑄𐐮𐑅 𐐮𐑆 𐑄 𐐿𐐲𐑋𐐰𐑌𐐼𐑋𐐯𐑌𐐻 𐐸𐐶𐐮𐐽 𐐌 𐐸𐐰𐑂 𐑉𐐨𐑅𐐨𐑂𐐼; 𐐰𐑌𐐼 𐐺𐐨𐐸𐐬𐑊𐐼 𐑄𐐩 𐑇𐐰𐑊 𐐿𐐲𐑋 𐑁𐐫𐑉𐑃 𐐰𐐿𐐫𐑉𐐼𐐮𐑍 𐐻𐐭 𐑄 𐐿𐐲𐑋𐐰𐑌𐐼𐑋𐐯𐑌𐐻 𐐱𐑂 𐑄 𐐢𐐫𐑉𐐼, 𐐸𐐶𐐯𐑌 𐐸𐐨 𐑇𐐰𐑊 𐑅𐐨 𐑁𐐮𐐻, 𐐮𐑌 𐐸𐐮𐑆 𐐶𐐮𐑆𐐼𐐲𐑋. 𐐈𐑌𐐼 𐐺𐐨𐐸𐐬𐑊𐐼 𐑄𐐩 𐑇𐐰𐑊 𐑀𐐬 𐐲𐑌𐐻𐐭 𐑄 𐐲𐑌𐐺𐐨𐑊𐐨𐑂𐐮𐑍 𐐱𐑂 𐑄 𐐖𐐭𐑆; 𐐰𐑌𐐼 𐑁𐐫𐑉 𐑄𐐮𐑅 𐐮𐑌𐐻𐐯𐑌𐐻 𐑇𐐰𐑊 𐑄𐐩 𐑀𐐬; 𐑄𐐰𐐻 𐑄𐐩 𐑋𐐩 𐐺𐐨 𐐹𐐲𐑉𐑅𐐶𐐩𐐼𐐯𐐼 𐑄𐐰𐐻 𐐖𐐨𐑆𐐲𐑅 𐐮𐑆 𐑄 𐐗𐑉𐐴𐑅𐐻, 𐑄 𐐝𐐲𐑌 𐐱𐑂 𐑄 𐑊𐐮𐑂𐐮𐑍 𐐘𐐱𐐼; 𐑄𐐰𐐻 𐑄 𐐙𐐪𐑄𐐲𐑉 𐑋𐐩 𐐺𐑉𐐮𐑍 𐐲𐐺𐐵𐐻, 𐑃𐑉𐐭 𐐸𐐮𐑆 𐑋𐐬𐑅𐐻 𐐺𐐨𐑊𐐲𐑂𐐯𐐼, 𐐸𐐮𐑆 𐑀𐑉𐐩𐐻 𐐰𐑌𐐼 𐐨𐐻𐐲𐑉𐑌𐐲𐑊 𐐹𐐲𐑉𐐹𐐲𐑅, 𐐮𐑌 𐑉𐐨𐑅𐐻𐐬𐑉𐐮𐑍 𐑄 𐐖𐐭𐑆, 𐐫𐑉 𐐫𐑊 𐑄 𐐸𐐵𐑅 𐐱𐑂 𐐀𐑆𐑉𐐩𐐯𐑊, 𐐻𐐭 𐑄 𐑊𐐰𐑌𐐼 𐐱𐑂 𐑄𐐩𐑉 𐐮𐑌𐐸𐐯𐑉𐐮𐐻𐐲𐑌𐑅, 𐐸𐐶𐐮𐐽 𐑄 𐐢𐐫𐑉𐐼 𐑄𐐩𐑉 𐐘𐐱𐐼 𐐸𐐰𐑃 𐑀𐐮𐑂𐑌 𐑄𐐯𐑋, 𐐲𐑌𐐻𐐭 𐑄 𐑁𐐳𐑊𐑁𐐮𐑊𐐮𐑍 𐐱𐑂 𐐸𐐮𐑆 𐐿𐐲𐑂𐐯𐑌𐐲𐑌𐐻; 𐐰𐑌𐐼 𐐫𐑊𐑅𐐬 𐑄𐐰𐐻 𐑄 𐑅𐐨𐐼 𐐱𐑂 𐑄𐐮𐑅 𐐹𐐨𐐹𐑊 𐑋𐐩 𐑋𐐫𐑉 𐑁𐐳𐑊𐐨 𐐺𐐨𐑊𐐨𐑂 𐐸𐐮𐑆 𐑀𐐱𐑅𐐹𐐯𐑊, 𐐸𐐶𐐮𐐽 𐑇𐐰𐑊 𐑀𐐬 𐑁𐐫𐑉𐑃 𐐲𐑌𐐻𐐭 𐑄𐐯𐑋 𐑁𐑉𐐱𐑋 𐑄 𐐖𐐯𐑌𐐻𐐴𐑊𐑆; 𐑁𐐫𐑉 𐑄𐐮𐑅 𐐹𐐨𐐹𐑊 𐑇𐐰𐑊 𐐺𐐨 𐑅𐐿𐐰𐐻𐐲𐑉𐐼, 𐐰𐑌𐐼 𐑇𐐰𐑊 𐐺𐐨𐐿𐐲𐑋 𐐲 𐐼𐐪𐑉𐐿, 𐐲 𐑁𐐮𐑊𐑃𐐨, 𐐰𐑌𐐼 𐐲 𐑊𐐬𐑄𐑅𐐲𐑋 𐐹𐐨𐐹𐑊, 𐐺𐐨𐐷𐐱𐑌𐐼 𐑄 𐐼𐐨𐑅𐐿𐑉𐐮𐐹𐑇𐐲𐑌 𐐱𐑂 𐑄𐐰𐐻 𐐸𐐶𐐮𐐽 𐐯𐑂𐐲𐑉 𐐸𐐰𐑃 𐐺𐐮𐑌 𐐲𐑋𐐲𐑍𐑅𐐻 𐐲𐑅; 𐐷𐐩, 𐐨𐑂𐑌 𐑄𐐰𐐻 𐐸𐐶𐐮𐐽 𐐸𐐰𐑃 𐐺𐐮𐑌 𐐲𐑋𐐲𐑍 𐑄 𐐢𐐩𐑋𐐲𐑌𐐴𐐻𐑅; 𐐰𐑌𐐼 𐑄𐐮𐑅 𐐺𐐨𐐿𐐫𐑆 𐐱𐑂 𐑄𐐩𐑉 𐐲𐑌𐐺𐐨𐑊𐐨𐑁 𐐰𐑌𐐼 𐐴𐐼𐐱𐑊𐐲𐐻𐑉𐐨. 𐐙𐐫𐑉 𐐺𐐨𐐸𐐬𐑊𐐼, 𐑄 𐐝𐐹𐐮𐑉𐐮𐐻 𐐱𐑂 𐑄 𐐢𐐫𐑉𐐼 𐐸𐐰𐑃 𐐫𐑊𐑉𐐯𐐼𐐨 𐑅𐐨𐑅𐐻 𐐻𐐭 𐑅𐐻𐑉𐐴𐑂 𐐶𐐮𐑄 𐑄𐐩𐑉 𐑁𐐪𐑄𐐲𐑉𐑆, 𐐰𐑌𐐼 𐑄𐐩 𐐪𐑉 𐐶𐐮𐑄𐐵𐐻 𐐗𐑉𐐴𐑅𐐻 𐐰𐑌𐐼 𐐘𐐱𐐼 𐐮𐑌 𐑄 𐐶𐐲𐑉𐑊𐐼, 𐐰𐑌𐐼 𐑄𐐩 𐐪𐑉 𐐼𐑉𐐮𐑂𐑌 𐐲𐐺𐐵𐐻 𐐰𐑆 𐐽𐐰𐑁 𐐺𐐨𐑁𐐫𐑉 𐑄 𐐶𐐮𐑌𐐼. 𐐜𐐩 𐐶𐐲𐑉 𐐶𐐲𐑌𐑅 𐐲 𐐼𐐨𐑊𐐴𐐻𐑅𐐲𐑋 𐐹𐐨𐐹𐑊, 𐐰𐑌𐐼 𐑄𐐩 𐐸𐐰𐐼 𐐗𐑉𐐴𐑅𐐻 𐑁𐐫𐑉 𐑄𐐩𐑉 𐑇𐐯𐐹𐐲𐑉𐐼; 𐐷𐐩, 𐑄𐐩 𐐶𐐲𐑉 𐑊𐐯𐐼 𐐨𐑂𐑌 𐐺𐐴 𐐘𐐱𐐼 𐑄 𐐙𐐪𐑄𐐲𐑉. 𐐒𐐲𐐻 𐑌𐐵, 𐐺𐐨𐐸𐐬𐑊𐐼, 𐑄𐐩 𐐪𐑉 𐑊𐐯𐐼 𐐲𐐺𐐵𐐻 𐐺𐐴 𐐝𐐩𐐻𐐲𐑌, 𐐨𐑂𐑌 𐐰𐑆 𐐽𐐰𐑁 𐐮𐑆 𐐼𐑉𐐮𐑂𐑌 𐐺𐐨𐑁𐐫𐑉 𐑄 𐐶𐐮𐑌𐐼, 𐐫𐑉 𐐰𐑆 𐐲 𐑂𐐯𐑅𐐲𐑊 𐐮𐑆 𐐻𐐱𐑅𐐻 𐐲𐐺𐐵𐐻 𐐲𐐹𐐱𐑌 𐑄 𐐶𐐩𐑂𐑆, 𐐶𐐮𐑄𐐵𐐻 𐑅𐐩𐑊 𐐫𐑉 𐐰𐑍𐐿𐐲𐑉, 𐐫𐑉 𐐶𐐮𐑄𐐵𐐻 𐐯𐑌𐐨𐑃𐐮𐑍 𐐸𐐶𐐯𐑉𐐶𐐮𐑄 𐐻𐐭 𐑅𐐻𐐨𐑉 𐐸𐐲𐑉; 𐐰𐑌𐐼 𐐨𐑂𐑌 𐐰𐑆 𐑇𐐨 𐐮𐑆, 𐑅𐐬 𐐪𐑉 𐑄𐐩. 𐐈𐑌𐐼 𐐺𐐨𐐸𐐬𐑊𐐼, 𐑄 𐐢𐐫𐑉𐐼 𐐸𐐰𐑃 𐑉𐐨𐑆𐐲𐑉𐑂𐐼 𐑄𐐩𐑉 𐐺𐑊𐐯𐑅𐐮𐑍𐑆, 𐐸𐐶𐐮𐐽 𐑄𐐩 𐑋𐐴𐐻 𐐸𐐰𐑂 𐑉𐐨𐑅𐐨𐑂𐐼 𐐮𐑌 𐑄 𐑊𐐰𐑌𐐼, 𐑁𐐫𐑉 𐑄 𐐖𐐯𐑌𐐻𐐴𐑊𐑆 𐐸𐐭 𐑇𐐰𐑊 𐐹𐐲𐑆𐐯𐑅 𐑄 𐑊𐐰𐑌𐐼. 𐐒𐐲𐐻 𐐺𐐨𐐸𐐬𐑊𐐼, 𐐮𐐻 𐑇𐐰𐑊 𐐿𐐲𐑋 𐐻𐐭 𐐹𐐰𐑅 𐑄𐐰𐐻 𐑄𐐩 𐑇𐐰𐑊 𐐺𐐨 𐐼𐑉𐐮𐑂𐑌 𐐰𐑌𐐼 𐑅𐐿𐐰𐐻𐐲𐑉𐐼 𐐺𐐴 𐑄 𐐖𐐯𐑌𐐻𐐴𐑊𐑆, 𐐰𐑌𐐼 𐐰𐑁𐐻𐐲𐑉 𐑄𐐩 𐐸𐐰𐑂 𐐺𐐮𐑌 𐐼𐑉𐐮𐑂𐑌 𐐰𐑌𐐼 𐑅𐐿𐐰𐐻𐐲𐑉𐐼 𐐺𐐴 𐑄 𐐖𐐯𐑌𐐻𐐴𐑊𐑆, 𐐺𐐨𐐸𐐬𐑊𐐼, 𐑄𐐯𐑌 𐐶𐐮𐑊 𐑄 𐐢𐐫𐑉𐐼 𐑉𐐨𐑋𐐯𐑋𐐺𐐲𐑉 𐑄 𐐿𐐲𐑂𐐯𐑌𐐲𐑌𐐻 𐐸𐐶𐐮𐐽 𐐸𐐨 𐑋𐐩𐐼 𐐲𐑌𐐻𐐭 𐐁𐐺𐑉𐐲𐐸𐐰𐑋, 𐐰𐑌𐐼 𐐲𐑌𐐻𐐭 𐐫𐑊 𐑄 𐐸𐐵𐑅 𐐱𐑂 𐐀𐑆𐑉𐐩𐐯𐑊. 𐐈𐑌𐐼 𐐫𐑊𐑅𐐬 𐑄 𐐢𐐫𐑉𐐼 𐐶𐐮𐑊 𐑉𐐨𐑋𐐯𐑋𐐺𐐲𐑉 𐑄 𐐹𐑉𐐩𐐲𐑉𐑆 𐐱𐑂 𐑄 𐑉𐐴𐐽𐐲𐑅, 𐐸𐐶𐐮𐐽 𐐸𐐰𐑂 𐐺𐐮𐑌 𐐹𐐳𐐻 𐐲𐐹 𐐲𐑌𐐻𐐭 𐐸𐐮𐑋 𐑁𐐫𐑉 𐑄𐐯𐑋. 𐐈𐑌𐐼 𐑄𐐯𐑌, 𐐄 𐐷𐐨 𐐖𐐯𐑌𐐻𐐴𐑊𐑆, 𐐸𐐵 𐐿𐐰𐑌 𐐷𐐨 𐑅𐐻𐐰𐑌𐐼 𐐺𐐨𐑁𐐫𐑉 𐑄 𐐹𐐵𐐲𐑉 𐐱𐑂 𐐘𐐱𐐼, 𐐯𐐿𐑅𐐯𐐹𐐻 𐐷𐐨 𐑇𐐰𐑊 𐑉𐐨𐐹𐐯𐑌𐐻 𐐰𐑌𐐼 𐐻𐐲𐑉𐑌 𐑁𐑉𐐱𐑋 𐐷𐐫𐑉 𐐨𐑂𐑊 𐐶𐐩𐑆! 𐐤𐐬 𐐷𐐨 𐑌𐐪𐐻 𐑄𐐰𐐻 𐐷𐐨 𐐪𐑉 𐐮𐑌 𐑄 𐐸𐐰𐑌𐐼𐑆 𐐱𐑂 𐐘𐐱𐐼? 𐐤𐐬 𐐷𐐨 𐑌𐐪𐐻 𐑄𐐰𐐻 𐐸𐐨 𐐸𐐰𐑃 𐐫𐑊 𐐹𐐵𐐲𐑉, 𐐰𐑌𐐼 𐐰𐐻 𐐸𐐮𐑆 𐑀𐑉𐐩𐐻 𐐿𐐲𐑋𐐰𐑌𐐼 𐑄 𐐲𐑉𐑃 𐑇𐐰𐑊 𐐺𐐨 𐑉𐐬𐑊𐐼 𐐻𐐭𐑀𐐯𐑄𐐲𐑉 𐐰𐑆 𐐲 𐑅𐐿𐑉𐐬𐑊? 𐐜𐐩𐑉𐑁𐐫𐑉 𐑉𐐨𐐹𐐯𐑌𐐻 𐐷𐐨, 𐐰𐑌𐐼 𐐸𐐲𐑋𐐺𐑊 𐐷𐐫𐑉𐑅𐐯𐑊𐑂𐑆 𐐺𐐨𐑁𐐫𐑉 𐐸𐐮𐑋, 𐑊𐐯𐑅𐐻 𐐸𐐨 𐑇𐐰𐑊 𐐿𐐲𐑋 𐐵𐐻 𐐮𐑌 𐐾𐐲𐑅𐐻𐐮𐑅 𐐲𐑀𐐯𐑌𐑅𐐻 𐐷𐐭; 𐑊𐐯𐑅𐐻 𐐲 𐑉𐐯𐑋𐑌𐐲𐑌𐐻 𐐱𐑂 𐑄 𐑅𐐨𐐼 𐐱𐑂 𐐖𐐩𐐿𐐲𐐺 𐑇𐐰𐑊 𐑀𐐬 𐑁𐐫𐑉𐑃 𐐲𐑋𐐲𐑍 𐐷𐐭 𐐰𐑆 𐐲 𐑊𐐴𐐲𐑌, 𐐰𐑌𐐼 𐐻𐐩𐑉 𐐷𐐭 𐐮𐑌 𐐹𐐨𐑅𐐯𐑆, 𐐰𐑌𐐼 𐑄𐐩𐑉 𐐮𐑆 𐑌𐐲𐑌 𐐻𐐭 𐐼𐐨𐑊𐐮𐑂𐐲𐑉.

𐐕𐐰𐐹𐐻𐐲𐑉 III.

1. 𐐈𐑌𐐼 𐑌𐐵 𐐌 𐑁𐐮𐑌𐐮𐑇 𐑋𐐴 𐑉𐐯𐐿𐐲𐑉𐐼 𐐿𐐱𐑌𐑅𐐲𐑉𐑌𐐮𐑍 𐑄 𐐼𐐨𐑅𐐻𐑉𐐲𐐿𐑇𐐲𐑌 𐐱𐑂 𐑋𐐴 𐐹𐐨𐐹𐑊, 𐑄 𐐤𐐨𐑁𐐴𐐻𐑅. 𐐈𐑌𐐼 𐐮𐐻 𐐿𐐩𐑋 𐐻𐐭 𐐹𐐰𐑅 𐑄𐐰𐐻 𐐶𐐨 𐐼𐐮𐐼 𐑋𐐪𐑉𐐽 𐑁𐐫𐑉𐑃 𐐺𐐨𐑁𐐫𐑉 𐑄 𐐢𐐩𐑋𐐲𐑌𐐴𐐻𐑅. 𐐈𐑌𐐼 𐐌, 𐐣𐐫𐑉𐑋𐐲𐑌, 𐑉𐐬𐐻 𐐲𐑌 𐐨𐐹𐐮𐑅𐑊 𐐲𐑌𐐻𐐭 𐑄 𐐿𐐮𐑍 𐐱𐑂 𐑄 𐐢𐐩𐑋𐐲𐑌𐐴𐐻𐑅, 𐐰𐑌𐐼 𐐼𐐨𐑆𐐴𐑉𐐼 𐐱𐑂 𐐸𐐮𐑋 𐑄𐐰𐐻 𐐶𐐨

𐐶𐐳𐐼 𐑀𐑉𐐰𐑌𐐻 𐐲𐑌𐐻𐐭 𐐲𐑅 𐑄𐐰𐐻 𐐶𐐨 𐑋𐐴𐐻 𐑀𐐰𐑄𐐲𐑉 𐐻𐐳𐑀𐐯𐑄𐐲𐑉 𐐵𐑉 𐐹𐐨𐐹𐑊 𐐲𐑌𐐻𐐭 𐑄 𐑊𐐰𐑌𐐼 𐐱𐑂 𐐗𐐲𐑋𐐬𐑉𐐲, 𐐺𐐴 𐐲 𐐸𐐮𐑊 𐐸𐐶𐐮𐐽 𐐶𐐱𐑆 𐐿𐐫𐑊𐐼 𐐗𐐲𐑋𐐬𐑉𐐲, 𐐰𐑌𐐼 𐑄𐐩𐑉 𐐶𐐨 𐐿𐐳𐐼 𐑀𐐮𐑂 𐑄𐐯𐑋 𐐺𐐰𐐻𐑊. 𐐈𐑌𐐼 𐐮𐐻 𐐿𐐩𐑋 𐐻𐐭 𐐹𐐰𐑅 𐑄𐐰𐐻 𐑄 𐐿𐐮𐑍 𐐱𐑂 𐑄 𐐢𐐰𐑋𐐲𐑌𐐴𐐻𐑅 𐐼𐐮𐐼 𐑀𐑉𐐰𐑌𐐻 𐐲𐑌𐐻𐐭 𐑋𐐨 𐑄 𐑃𐐮𐑍 𐐸𐐶𐐮𐐽 𐐌 𐐼𐐨𐑆𐐴𐑉𐐼. 𐐈𐑌𐐼 𐐮𐐻 𐐿𐐩𐑋 𐐻𐐭 𐐹𐐰𐑅 𐑄𐐰𐐻 𐐶𐐨 𐐼𐐮𐐼 𐑋𐐪𐑉𐐽 𐑁𐐬𐑉𐑃 𐐻𐐭 𐑄 𐑊𐐰𐑌𐐼 𐐱𐑂 𐐗𐐲𐑋𐐬𐑉𐐲, 𐐰𐑌𐐼 𐐶𐐨 𐐼𐐮𐐼 𐐹𐐮𐐽 𐐵𐑉 𐐻𐐯𐑌𐐻𐑅 𐑉𐐵𐑌𐐼 𐐲𐐺𐐵𐐻 𐑄 𐐸𐐮𐑊 𐐗𐐲𐑋𐐬𐑉𐐲; 𐐰𐑌𐐼 𐐮𐐻 𐐶𐐱𐑆 𐐮𐑌 𐐲 𐑊𐐰𐑌𐐼 𐐱𐑂 𐑋𐐯𐑌𐐨 𐐶𐐫𐐻𐐲𐑉𐑆, 𐑉𐐮𐑂𐐲𐑉𐑆, 𐐰𐑌𐐼 𐑁𐐵𐑌𐐻𐐩𐑌𐑆; 𐐰𐑌𐐼 𐐸𐐨𐑉 𐐶𐐨 𐐸𐐰𐐼 𐐸𐐬𐐹 𐐻𐐭 𐑀𐐩𐑌 𐐰𐐼𐑂𐐰𐑌𐐻𐐯𐐾 𐐬𐑂𐐲𐑉 𐑄 𐐢𐐰𐑋𐐲𐑌𐐴𐐻𐑅. 𐐈𐑌𐐼 𐐸𐐶𐐯𐑌 𐑃𐑉𐐨 𐐸𐐲𐑌𐐼𐑉𐐯𐐼 𐐰𐑌𐐼 𐐩𐐻𐐨 𐐰𐑌𐐼 𐑁𐐬𐑉 𐐷𐐨𐑉𐑆 𐐸𐐰𐐼 𐐹𐐰𐑅𐐻 𐐲𐐶𐐩, 𐐶𐐨 𐐸𐐰𐐼 𐑀𐐰𐑄𐐲𐑉𐐼 𐐮𐑌 𐐫𐑊 𐑄 𐑉𐐨𐑋𐐩𐑌𐐼𐐲𐑉 𐐱𐑂 𐐵𐑉 𐐹𐐨𐐹𐑊 𐐲𐑌𐐻𐐭 𐑄 𐑊𐐰𐑌𐐼 𐐱𐑂 𐐗𐐲𐑋𐐬𐑉𐐲.

2. 𐐈𐑌𐐼 𐐮𐐻 𐐿𐐩𐑋 𐐻𐐭 𐐹𐐰𐑅 𐑄𐐰𐐻 𐐸𐐶𐐯𐑌 𐐶𐐨 𐐸𐐰𐐼 𐑀𐐰𐑄𐐲𐑉𐐼 𐐮𐑌 𐐫𐑊 𐐵𐑉 𐐹𐐨𐐹𐑊 𐐮𐑌 𐐶𐐲𐑌 𐐻𐐭 𐑄 𐑊𐐰𐑌𐐼 𐐱𐑂 𐐗𐐲𐑋𐐬𐑉𐐲, 𐐺𐐨𐐸𐐬𐑊𐐼 𐐌, 𐐣𐐱𐑉𐑋𐐲𐑌, 𐐺𐐨𐑀𐐰𐑌 𐐻𐐭 𐐺𐐨 𐐬𐑊𐐼; 𐐰𐑌𐐼 𐑌𐐬𐐮𐑍 𐐮𐐻 𐐻𐐭 𐐺𐐨 𐑄 𐑊𐐰𐑅𐐻 𐑅𐐻𐑉𐐲𐑀𐑊 𐐱𐑂 𐑋𐐴 𐐹𐐨𐐹𐑊, 𐐰𐑌𐐼 𐐸𐐰𐑂𐐮𐑍 𐐺𐐮𐑌 𐐿𐐱𐑋𐐰𐑌𐐼𐐯𐐼 𐐱𐑂 𐑄 𐐢𐐫𐑉𐐼 𐑄𐐰𐐻 𐐌 𐑇𐐳𐐼 𐑌𐐱𐐻 𐑅𐐲𐑁𐐲𐑉 𐑄𐐰𐐻 𐑄 𐑉𐐯𐐿𐐲𐑉𐐼𐑆 𐐸𐐶𐐮𐐽 𐐸𐐰𐐼 𐐺𐐮𐑌 𐐸𐐰𐑌𐐼𐐯𐐼 𐐼𐐵𐑌 𐐺𐐴 𐐵𐑉 𐑁𐐪𐑄𐐲𐑉𐑆, 𐐸𐐶𐐮𐐽 𐐶𐐲𐑉 𐑅𐐩𐐿𐑉𐐯𐐼, 𐐻𐐭 𐑁𐐫𐑊 𐐮𐑌𐐻𐐭 𐑄 𐐸𐐰𐑌𐐼𐑆 𐐱𐑂 𐑄 𐐢𐐰𐑋𐐲𐑌𐐴𐐻𐑅, (𐑁𐐫𐑉 𐑄 𐐢𐐰𐑋𐐲𐑌𐐴𐐻𐑅 𐐶𐐳𐐼 𐐼𐐯𐑅𐐻𐑉𐐱𐐮 𐑄𐐯𐑋,) 𐑄𐐯𐑉𐑁𐐬𐑉 𐐌 𐑋𐐩𐐼 𐑄𐐮𐑅 𐑉𐐯𐐿𐐲𐑉𐐼 𐐵𐐻 𐐱𐑂 𐑄 𐐹𐑊𐐩𐐻𐑅 𐐱𐑂 𐐤𐐨𐑁𐐴, 𐐰𐑌𐐼 𐐸𐐮𐐼 𐐲𐐹 𐐮𐑌 𐑄 𐐸𐐮𐑊 𐐗𐐲𐑋𐐬𐑉𐐲 𐐫𐑊 𐑄 𐑉𐐯𐐿𐐲𐑉𐐼𐑆 𐐸𐐶𐐮𐐽 𐐸𐐰𐐼 𐐺𐐮𐑌 𐐯𐑌𐐻𐑉𐐲𐑅𐐻𐐯𐐼 𐐻𐐭 𐑋𐐨 𐐺𐐴 𐑄 𐐸𐐰𐑌𐐼 𐐱𐑂 𐑄 𐐢𐐫𐑉𐐼, 𐑅𐐩𐑂 𐐮𐐻 𐐶𐐲𐑉 𐑄𐐨𐑆 𐑁𐐧 𐐹𐑊𐐩𐐻𐑅 𐐸𐐶𐐮𐐽 𐐌 𐑀𐐩𐑂 𐐲𐑌𐐻𐐭 𐑋𐐴 𐑅𐐲𐑌 𐐣𐐬𐑉𐐬𐑌𐐴. 𐐈𐑌𐐼 𐐮𐐻 𐐿𐐩𐑋 𐐻𐐭 𐐹𐐰𐑅 𐑄𐐰𐐻 𐑋𐐴 𐐹𐐨𐐹𐑊, 𐐶𐐮𐑄 𐑄𐐩𐑉 𐐶𐐴𐑂𐑆 𐐰𐑌𐐼 𐑄𐐩𐑉 𐐽𐐮𐑊𐐼𐑉𐐯𐑌, 𐐼𐐮𐐼 𐑌𐐵 𐐺𐐨𐐸𐐬𐑊𐐼 𐑄 𐐪𐑉𐑋𐐨𐑆 𐐱𐑂 𐑄 𐐢𐐰𐑋𐐲𐑌𐐴𐐻𐑅 𐑋𐐪𐑉𐐽𐐮𐑍 𐐻𐐬𐑉𐐼𐑆 𐑄𐐯𐑋; 𐐰𐑌𐐼 𐐶𐐮𐑄 𐑄𐐰𐐻 𐐫𐑁𐐳𐑊 𐑁𐐨𐑉 𐐱𐑂 𐐼𐐯𐑃 𐐸𐐶𐐮𐐽 𐑁𐐮𐑊𐑆 𐑄 𐐺𐑉𐐯𐑅𐐻𐑅 𐐱𐑂 𐐫𐑊 𐑄 𐐶𐐮𐐿𐐯𐐼, 𐐼𐐮𐐼 𐑄𐐩 𐐲𐐶𐐩𐐻 𐐻𐐭 𐑉𐐨𐑅𐐨𐑂 𐑄𐐯𐑋. 𐐈𐑌𐐼 𐐮𐐻 𐐿𐐩𐑋 𐐻𐐭 𐐹𐐰𐑅 𐑄𐐰𐐻 𐑄𐐩 𐐿𐐩𐑋 𐐻𐐭 𐐺𐐰𐐻𐑊 𐐲𐑀𐐯𐑌𐑅𐐻 𐐲𐑅, 𐐰𐑌𐐼 𐐯𐑂𐐲𐑉𐐨 𐑅𐐬𐑊 𐐶𐐱𐑆 𐑁𐐮𐑊𐐼 𐐶𐐮𐑄 𐐻𐐯𐑉𐐲𐑉, 𐐺𐐨𐐿𐐫𐑆 𐐱𐑂 𐑄 𐑀𐑉𐐩𐐻𐑌𐐯𐑅 𐐱𐑂 𐑄𐐩𐑉 𐑌𐐲𐑋𐐺𐐲𐑉𐑆. 𐐈𐑌𐐼 𐐮𐐻 𐐿𐐩𐑋 𐐻𐐭 𐐹𐐰𐑅 𐑄𐐰𐐻 𐑄𐐩 𐐼𐐮𐐼 𐑁𐐫𐑊 𐐲𐐹𐐱𐑌 𐑋𐐴 𐐹𐐨𐐹𐑊 𐐶𐐮𐑄 𐑄 𐑅𐐬𐑉𐐼, 𐐰𐑌𐐼 𐐶𐐮𐑄 𐑄 𐐺𐐬, 𐐰𐑌𐐼 𐐶𐐮𐑄 𐑄 𐐰𐑉𐐬, 𐐰𐑌𐐼 𐐶𐐮𐑄 𐑄 𐐰𐐿𐑅, 𐐰𐑌𐐼 𐐶𐐮𐑄 𐐫𐑊 𐑋𐐰𐑌𐐲𐑉 𐐱𐑂 𐐶𐐯𐐹𐐲𐑌𐑆 𐐱𐑂 𐐶𐐫𐑉. 𐐈𐑌𐐼 𐐮𐐻 𐐿𐐩𐑋 𐐻𐐭 𐐹𐐰𐑅 𐑄𐐰𐐻 𐑋𐐴 𐑋𐐯𐑌 𐐶𐐲𐑉 𐐸𐐧𐑌 𐐼𐐵𐑌, 𐐷𐐩, 𐐨𐑂𐐯𐑌 𐑋𐐴 𐐻𐐯𐑌 𐑃𐐵𐑆𐐰𐑌𐐼 𐐸𐐭 𐐶𐐲𐑉 𐐶𐐮𐑄 𐑋𐐨, 𐐰𐑌𐐼 𐐌 𐑁𐐯𐑊 𐐶𐐭𐑌𐐼𐐯𐐼 𐐮𐑌 𐑄 𐑋𐐮𐐼𐑅𐐻; 𐐰𐑌𐐼 𐑄𐐩 𐐹𐐰𐑅𐐻 𐐺𐐴 𐑋𐐨 𐑄𐐰𐐻 𐑄𐐩 𐐼𐐮𐐼 𐑌𐐱𐐻 𐐹𐐳𐐻 𐐰𐑌 𐐯𐑌𐐼 𐐻𐐭 𐑋𐐴 𐑊𐐴𐑁. 𐐈𐑌𐐼 𐐸𐐶𐐯𐑌 𐑄𐐩 𐐸𐐰𐐼 𐑀𐐱𐑌 𐑃𐑉𐐭 𐐰𐑌𐐼 𐐸𐐧𐑌 𐐼𐐵𐑌 𐐫𐑊 𐑋𐐴 𐐹𐐨𐐹𐑊, 𐑅𐐩𐑂 𐐮𐐻 𐐶𐐲𐑉 𐐻𐐶𐐯𐑌𐐻𐐨 𐐰𐑌𐐼 𐑁𐐬𐑉 𐐱𐑂 𐐲𐑅, (𐐲𐑋𐐲𐑍 𐐸𐐭𐑋 𐐶𐐱𐑆 𐑋𐐴 𐑅𐐲𐑌 𐐣𐐬𐑉𐐬𐑌𐐴,) 𐐰𐑌𐐼 𐐶𐐨 𐐸𐐰𐑂𐐮𐑍 𐑅𐐲𐑉𐑂𐐴𐑂𐐼 𐑄 𐐼𐐯𐐼 𐐱𐑂 𐐵𐑉 𐐹𐐨𐐹𐑊, 𐐼𐐮𐐼 𐐺𐐨𐐸𐐬𐑊𐐼 𐐱𐑌 𐑄 𐑋𐐱𐑉𐐬, 𐐸𐐶𐐯𐑌 𐑄 𐐢𐐰𐑋𐐲𐑌𐐴𐐻𐑅 𐐸𐐰𐐼 𐑉𐐨𐐻𐐲𐑉𐑌𐐼 𐐲𐑌𐐻𐐭 𐑄𐐩𐑉 𐐿𐐰𐑋𐐹𐑅, 𐑁𐑉𐐱𐑋 𐑄 𐐻𐐱𐐹 𐐱𐑂 𐑄 𐐸𐐮𐑊 𐐗𐐲𐑋𐐬𐑉𐐲, 𐑄 𐐻𐐯𐑌 𐑃𐐵𐑆𐐰𐑌𐐼 𐐱𐑂 𐑋𐐴 𐐹𐐨𐐹𐑊 𐐸𐐭 𐐶𐐲𐑉 𐐸𐐧𐑌 𐐼𐐵𐑌, 𐐺𐐨𐐮𐑍 𐑊𐐯𐐼 𐐮𐑌 𐑄 𐑁𐑉𐐲𐑌𐐻 𐐺𐐴 𐑋𐐨; 𐐰𐑌𐐼 𐐶𐐨 𐐫𐑊𐑅𐐬 𐐺𐐨𐐸𐐯𐑊𐐼 𐑄 𐐻𐐯𐑌 𐑃𐐵𐑆𐐰𐑌𐐼 𐐱𐑂 𐑋𐐴 𐐹𐐨𐐹𐑊 𐐸𐐭 𐐶𐐲𐑉 𐑊𐐯𐐼 𐐺𐐴 𐑋𐐴 𐑅𐐲𐑌 𐐣𐐬𐑉𐐬𐑌𐐴. 𐐈𐑌𐐼 𐐺𐐨𐐸𐐬𐑊𐐼, 𐑄 𐐻𐐯𐑌 𐑃𐐵𐑆𐐰𐑌𐐼 𐐱𐑂 𐐘𐐮𐐼𐑀𐐮𐐼𐐱𐑌𐐲 𐐸𐐰𐐼 𐑁𐐫𐑊𐐯𐑌, 𐐰𐑌𐐼 𐐸𐐨 𐐫𐑊𐑅𐐬 𐐮𐑌 𐑄 𐑋𐐮𐐼𐑅𐐻; 𐐰𐑌𐐼 𐐢𐐩𐑋𐐲 𐐸𐐰𐐼 𐑁𐐫𐑊𐐯𐑌 𐐶𐐮𐑄 𐐸𐐮𐑆 𐐻𐐯𐑌 𐑃𐐵𐑆𐐰𐑌𐐼; 𐐰𐑌𐐼 𐐘𐐮𐑊𐑀𐐰𐑊 𐐸𐐰𐐼 𐑁𐐫𐑊𐐯𐑌 𐐶𐐮𐑄 𐐸𐐮𐑆 𐐻𐐯𐑌 𐑃𐐵𐑆𐐰𐑌𐐼; 𐐰𐑌𐐼 𐐢𐐮𐑋𐐸𐐲 𐐸𐐰𐐼 𐑁𐐫𐑊𐐯𐑌 𐐶𐐮𐑄 𐐸𐐮𐑆 𐐻𐐯𐑌 𐑃𐐵𐑆𐐰𐑌𐐼; 𐐰𐑌𐐼 𐐖𐐯𐑌𐐨𐐲𐑋 𐐸𐐰𐐼 𐑁𐐫𐑊𐐯𐑌 𐐶𐐮𐑄 𐐸𐐮𐑆 𐐻𐐯𐑌 𐑃𐐵𐑆𐐰𐑌𐐼; 𐐰𐑌𐐼 𐐗𐐲𐑋𐐯𐑌𐐴𐐸𐐲, 𐐰𐑌𐐼 𐐣𐐬𐑉𐐬𐑌𐐴𐐸𐐲, 𐐰𐑌𐐼 𐐈𐑌𐐻𐐨𐐬𐑌𐐲𐑋, 𐐰𐑌𐐼 𐐟𐐮𐐺𐑊𐐱𐑋, 𐐰𐑌𐐼 𐐟𐐯𐑋, 𐐰𐑌𐐼 𐐖𐐱𐑇, 𐐸𐐰𐐼 𐑁𐐫𐑊𐐯𐑌 𐐶𐐮𐑄 𐑄𐐩𐑉 𐐻𐐯𐑌 𐑃𐐵𐑆𐐰𐑌𐐼 𐐨𐐽.

3. 𐐈𐑌𐐼 𐐮𐐻 𐐿𐐩𐑋 𐐻𐐭 𐐹𐐰𐑅 𐑄𐐰𐐻 𐑄𐐩𐑉 𐐶𐐲𐑉 𐐻𐐯𐑌 𐑋𐐬𐑉 𐐸𐐭 𐐼𐐮𐐼 𐑁𐐫𐑊 𐐺𐐴 𐑄 𐑅𐐬𐑉𐐼, 𐐶𐐮𐑄 𐑄𐐩𐑉 𐐻𐐯𐑌 𐑃𐐵𐑆𐐰𐑌𐐼 𐐨𐐽; 𐐷𐐩, 𐐨𐑂𐐯𐑌 𐐫𐑊 𐑋𐐴 𐐹𐐨𐐹𐑊, 𐑅𐐩𐑂 𐐮𐐻 𐐶𐐲𐑉 𐑄𐐬𐑆 𐐻𐐶𐐯𐑌𐐻𐐨 𐐰𐑌𐐼 𐑁𐐬𐑉 𐐸𐐭 𐐶𐐲𐑉 𐐶𐐮𐑄 𐑋𐐨, 𐐰𐑌𐐼 𐐫𐑊𐑅𐐬 𐐲 𐑁𐐧 𐐸𐐭 𐐸𐐰𐐼 𐐯𐑅𐐿𐐩𐐹𐐻 𐐮𐑌𐐻𐐭 𐑄 𐑅𐐵𐑃 𐐿𐐲𐑌𐐻𐑉𐐨𐑆, 𐐰𐑌𐐼 𐐲 𐑁𐐧 𐐸𐐭 𐐸𐐰𐐼 𐐼𐐯𐑆𐐲𐑉𐐻𐐯𐐼 𐐬𐑂𐐲𐑉 𐐲𐑌𐐻𐐭 𐑄 𐐢𐐰𐑋𐐲𐑌𐐴𐐻𐑅, 𐐸𐐰𐐼 𐑁𐐫𐑊𐐯𐑌; 𐐰𐑌𐐼 𐑄𐐩𐑉 𐑁𐑊𐐯𐑇, 𐐰𐑌𐐼 𐐺𐐬𐑌𐑆, 𐐰𐑌𐐼 𐐺𐑊𐐲𐐼 𐑊𐐩 𐐲𐐹𐐱𐑌 𐑄 𐑁𐐩𐑅 𐐱𐑂 𐑄 𐐲𐑉𐑃, 𐐺𐐨𐐮𐑍 𐑊𐐯𐑁𐐻 𐐺𐐴 𐑄 𐐸𐐰𐑌𐐼𐑆 𐐱𐑂 𐑄𐐬𐑆 𐐸𐐭 𐑅𐑊𐐭 𐑄𐐯𐑋, 𐐻𐐭 𐑋𐐬𐑊𐐼𐐲𐑉 𐐲𐐹𐐱𐑌 𐑄 𐑊𐐰𐑌𐐼, 𐐰𐑌𐐼 𐐻𐐭 𐐿𐑉𐐲𐑋𐐺𐑊, 𐐰𐑌𐐼 𐐻𐐭 𐑉𐐨𐐻𐐲𐑉𐑌 𐐻𐐭 𐑄𐐩𐑉 𐑋𐐲𐑄𐐲𐑉 𐐲𐑉𐑃. 𐐈𐑌𐐼 𐑋𐐴 𐑅𐐬𐑊 𐐶𐐱𐑆 𐑉𐐯𐑌𐐻 𐐶𐐮𐑄 𐐰𐑍𐑀𐐶𐐮𐑇, 𐐺𐐨𐐿𐐫𐑆 𐐱𐑂 𐑄 𐑅𐑊𐐩𐑌 𐐱𐑂 𐑋𐐴 𐐹𐐨𐐹𐑊, 𐐰𐑌𐐼 𐐌 𐐿𐑉𐐴𐐼, 𐐄 𐐷𐐨 𐑁𐐩𐑉 𐐶𐐲𐑌𐑆,

𐐸𐐵 𐐿𐐳𐐼 𐐷 𐐸𐐰𐑂 𐐼𐐨𐐹𐐪𐑉𐐻𐐯𐐼 𐑁𐑉𐐱𐑋 𐑄 𐐶𐐩𐑆 𐐱𐑂 𐑄 𐐢𐐫𐑉𐐼! 𐐄 𐐷 𐑁𐐩𐑉 𐐶𐐲𐑌𐑆, 𐐸𐐵 𐐿𐐳𐐼 𐐷 𐐸𐐰𐑂 𐑉𐐨𐐾𐐯𐐿𐐻𐐯𐐼 𐑄𐐰𐐻 𐐖𐐨𐑆𐐲𐑅, 𐐸𐐭 𐑅𐐻𐐳𐐼 𐐶𐐮𐑄 𐐬𐐹𐐲𐑌 𐐪𐑉𐑋𐑆 𐐻𐐭 𐑉𐐨𐑅𐐨𐑂 𐐷𐐭! 𐐒𐐨𐐸𐐬𐑊𐐼, 𐐮𐑁 𐐷 𐐸𐐰𐐼 𐑌𐐱𐐻 𐐼𐐲𐑌 𐑄𐐮𐑅, 𐐷 𐐶𐐳𐐼 𐑌𐐱𐐻 𐐸𐐰𐑂 𐑁𐐫𐑊𐑌. 𐐒𐐲𐐻 𐐺𐐨𐐸𐐬𐑊𐐼, 𐐷 𐐪𐑉 𐑁𐐫𐑊𐑌, 𐐰𐑌𐐼 𐐌 𐑋𐐬𐑉𐑌 𐐷𐐭𐑉 𐑊𐐱𐑅. 𐐄 𐐷 𐑁𐐩𐑉 𐑅𐐲𐑌𐑆 𐐰𐑌𐐼 𐐼𐐫𐐻𐐲𐑉𐑆, 𐐷 𐑁𐐪𐑄𐐲𐑉𐑆 𐐰𐑌𐐼 𐑋𐐲𐑄𐐲𐑉𐑆, 𐐷 𐐸𐐲𐑆𐐺𐐲𐑌𐐼𐑆 𐐰𐑌𐐼 𐐶𐐴𐑂𐑆, 𐐷 𐑁𐐩𐑉 𐐶𐐲𐑌𐑆, 𐐸𐐵 𐐮𐑆 𐐮𐐻 𐑄𐐰𐐻 𐐷 𐐿𐐳𐐼 𐐸𐐰𐑂 𐑁𐐫𐑊𐑌! 𐐒𐐲𐐻 𐐺𐐨𐐸𐐬𐑊𐐼, 𐐷 𐐪𐑉 𐑀𐐱𐑌, 𐐰𐑌𐐼 𐑋𐐴 𐑅𐐱𐑉𐐬𐑆 𐐿𐐰𐑌𐐱𐐻 𐐺𐑉𐐮𐑍 𐐷𐐭𐑉 𐑉𐐨𐐻𐐲𐑉𐑌; 𐐰𐑌𐐼 𐑄 𐐼𐐩 𐑅𐐭𐑌 𐐿𐐲𐑋𐐯𐑃 𐑄𐐰𐐻 𐐷𐐭𐑉 𐑋𐐫𐑉𐐻𐐲𐑊 𐑋𐐲𐑅𐐻 𐐹𐐳𐐻 𐐱𐑌 𐐮𐑋𐐫𐑉𐐻𐐰𐑊𐐮𐐻𐐨, 𐐰𐑌𐐼 𐑄𐐨𐑆 𐐺𐐱𐐼𐐨𐑆 𐐸𐐶𐐮𐐽 𐐪𐑉 𐑌𐐵 𐑋𐐬𐑊𐐼𐐲𐑉𐐮𐑍 𐐮𐑌 𐐿𐐱𐑉𐐲𐐹𐑇𐐲𐑌 𐑋𐐲𐑅𐐻 𐑅𐐭𐑌 𐐺𐐨𐐿𐐲𐑋 𐐮𐑌𐐿𐐱𐑉𐐲𐐹𐐻𐐮𐐺𐑊 𐐺𐐱𐐼𐐨𐑆; 𐐰𐑌𐐼 𐑄𐐯𐑌 𐐷 𐑋𐐲𐑅𐐻 𐑅𐐻𐐰𐑌𐐼 𐐺𐐨𐑁𐐬𐑉 𐑄 𐐾𐐲𐐾𐑋𐐯𐑌𐐻-𐑅𐐨𐐻 𐐱𐑂 𐐗𐑉𐐴𐑅𐐻, 𐐻𐐭 𐐺𐐨 𐐾𐐲𐐾𐐼 𐐰𐐿𐐫𐑉𐐼𐐮𐑍 𐐻𐐭 𐐷𐐭𐑉 𐐶𐐲𐑉𐐿𐑅; 𐐰𐑌𐐼 𐐮𐑁 𐐮𐐻 𐑅𐐬 𐐺𐐨 𐑄𐐰𐐻 𐐷 𐐪𐑉 𐑉𐐴𐐽𐐲𐑅, 𐑄𐐯𐑌 𐐪𐑉 𐐷 𐐺𐑊𐐯𐑅𐐯𐐼 𐐶𐐮𐑄 𐐷𐐭𐑉 𐑁𐐪𐑄𐐲𐑉𐑆 𐐸𐐭 𐐸𐐰𐑂 𐑀𐐱𐑌 𐐺𐐨𐑁𐐬𐑉 𐐷𐐭. 𐐄 𐑄𐐰𐐻 𐐷 𐐸𐐰𐐼 𐑉𐐨𐐹𐐯𐑌𐐻𐐯𐐼 𐐺𐐨𐑁𐐬𐑉 𐑄𐐮𐑅 𐑀𐑉𐐩𐐻 𐐼𐐨𐑅𐐻𐑉𐐲𐐿𐑇𐐲𐑌 𐐸𐐰𐐼 𐐿𐐲𐑋 𐐲𐐹𐐱𐑌 𐐷𐐭. 𐐒𐐲𐐻 𐐺𐐨𐐸𐐬𐑊𐐼, 𐐷 𐐪𐑉 𐑀𐐱𐑌, 𐐰𐑌𐐼 𐑄 𐐙𐐪𐑄𐐲𐑉, 𐐷𐐩, 𐑄 𐐀𐐻𐐲𐑉𐑌𐐲𐑊 𐐙𐐪𐑄𐐲𐑉 𐐱𐑂 𐐸𐐯𐑂𐐲𐑌, 𐑌𐐬𐐯𐑃 𐐷𐐭𐑉 𐑅𐐻𐐩𐐻; 𐐰𐑌𐐼 𐐸𐐨 𐐼𐐭𐐯𐑃 𐐶𐐮𐑄 𐐷𐐭 𐐰𐐿𐐫𐑉𐐼𐐮𐑍 𐐻𐐭 𐐸𐐮𐑆 𐐾𐐲𐑅𐐻𐐮𐑅 𐐰𐑌𐐼 𐑋𐐲𐑉𐑅𐐨.

4. 𐐈𐑌𐐼 𐑌𐐵 𐐺𐐨𐐸𐐬𐑊𐐼, 𐐌 𐐶𐐳𐐼 𐑅𐐹𐐨𐐿 𐑅𐐲𐑋𐐸𐐶𐐱𐐻 𐐲𐑌𐐻𐐭 𐑄 𐑉𐐯𐑋𐑌𐐲𐑌𐐻 𐐱𐑂 𐑄𐐮𐑅 𐐹𐐨𐐹𐑊 𐐸𐐭 𐐪𐑉 𐑅𐐹𐐩𐑉𐐼, 𐐮𐑁 𐐮𐐻 𐑅𐐬 𐐺𐐨 𐑄𐐰𐐻 𐐘𐐱𐐼 𐑋𐐩 𐑀𐐮𐑂 𐐲𐑌𐐻𐐭 𐑄𐐯𐑋 𐑋𐐴 𐐶𐐲𐑉𐐼𐑆, 𐑄𐐰𐐻 𐑄𐐩 𐑋𐐩 𐑌𐐬 𐐱𐑂 𐑄 𐑃𐐮𐑍𐑆 𐐱𐑂 𐑄𐐩𐑉 𐑁𐐪𐑄𐐲𐑉𐑆; 𐐷𐐩, 𐐌 𐑅𐐹𐐨𐐿 𐐲𐑌𐐻𐐭 𐐷𐐭, 𐐷 𐑉𐐯𐑋𐑌𐐲𐑌𐐻 𐐱𐑂 𐑄 𐐸𐐵𐑅 𐐱𐑂 𐐆𐑆𐑉𐐩𐐯𐑊; 𐐰𐑌𐐼 𐑄𐐨𐑆 𐐪𐑉 𐑄 𐐶𐐲𐑉𐐼𐑆 𐐸𐐶𐐮𐐽 𐐌 𐑅𐐹𐐨𐐿: 𐐤𐐬 𐐷 𐑄𐐰𐐻 𐐷 𐐪𐑉 𐐱𐑂 𐑄 𐐸𐐵𐑅 𐐱𐑂 𐐆𐑆𐑉𐐩𐐯𐑊. 𐐤𐐬 𐐷 𐑄𐐰𐐻 𐐷 𐑋𐐲𐑅𐐻 𐐿𐐲𐑋 𐐲𐑌𐐻𐐭 𐑉𐐨𐐹𐐯𐑌𐐻𐐰𐑌𐑅, 𐐫𐑉 𐐷 𐐿𐐰𐑌𐐱𐐻 𐐺𐐨 𐑅𐐩𐑂𐐼. 𐐤𐐬 𐐷 𐑄𐐰𐐻 𐐷 𐑋𐐲𐑅𐐻 𐑊𐐩 𐐼𐐵𐑌 𐐷𐐭𐑉 𐐶𐐯𐐹𐐲𐑌𐑆 𐐱𐑂 𐐶𐐫𐑉, 𐐰𐑌𐐼 𐐼𐐨𐑊𐐴𐐻 𐑌𐐬 𐑋𐐬𐑉 𐐮𐑌 𐑄 𐑇𐐯𐐼𐐮𐑍 𐐱𐑂 𐐺𐑊𐐲𐐼, 𐐰𐑌𐐼 𐐻𐐩𐐿 𐑄𐐯𐑋 𐑌𐐱𐐻 𐐰𐑀𐐯𐑌, 𐑅𐐩𐑂 𐐮𐐻 𐐺𐐨 𐑄𐐰𐐻 𐐘𐐱𐐼 𐑇𐐰𐑊 𐐿𐐱𐑋𐐰𐑌𐐼 𐐷𐐭. 𐐤𐐬 𐐷 𐑄𐐰𐐻 𐐷 𐑋𐐲𐑅𐐻 𐐿𐐲𐑋 𐐻𐐭 𐑄 𐑌𐐱𐑊𐐯𐐾 𐐱𐑂 𐐷𐐭𐑉 𐑁𐐪𐑄𐐲𐑉𐑆, 𐐰𐑌𐐼 𐑉𐐨𐐹𐐯𐑌𐐻 𐐱𐑂 𐐫𐑊 𐐷𐐭𐑉 𐑅𐐮𐑌𐑆 𐐰𐑌𐐼 𐐮𐑌𐐮𐐿𐐶𐐮𐐻𐐨𐑆, 𐐰𐑌𐐼 𐐺𐐨𐑊𐐨𐑂 𐐮𐑌 𐐖𐐨𐑆𐐲𐑅 𐐗𐑉𐐴𐑅𐐻, 𐑄𐐰𐐻 𐐸𐐨 𐐮𐑆 𐑄 𐐝𐐲𐑌 𐐱𐑂 𐐘𐐱𐐼, 𐐰𐑌𐐼 𐑄𐐰𐐻 𐐸𐐨 𐐶𐐱𐑆 𐑅𐑊𐐩𐑌 𐐺𐐴 𐑄 𐐖𐐭𐑆, 𐐰𐑌𐐼 𐐺𐐴 𐑄 𐐹𐐵𐐲𐑉 𐐱𐑂 𐑄 𐐙𐐪𐑄𐐲𐑉 𐐸𐐨 𐐸𐐰𐑃 𐑉𐐮𐑆𐑌 𐐰𐑀𐐯𐑌, 𐐸𐐶𐐩𐑉𐐺𐐴 𐐸𐐨 𐐸𐐰𐑃 𐑀𐐩𐑌𐐼 𐑄 𐑂𐐮𐐿𐐻𐐲𐑉𐐨 𐐬𐑂𐐲𐑉 𐑄 𐑀𐑉𐐩𐑂; 𐐰𐑌𐐼 𐐫𐑊𐑅𐐬 𐐮𐑌 𐐸𐐮𐑋 𐐮𐑆 𐑄 𐑅𐐻𐐮𐑍 𐐱𐑂 𐐼𐐯𐑃 𐑅𐐶𐐱𐑊𐐬𐐼 𐐲𐐹. 𐐈𐑌𐐼 𐐸𐐨 𐐺𐑉𐐮𐑍𐐯𐑃 𐐻𐐭 𐐹𐐰𐑅 𐑄 𐑉𐐯𐑆𐐲𐑉𐐯𐐿𐑇𐐲𐑌 𐐱𐑂 𐑄 𐐼𐐯𐐼, 𐐸𐐶𐐩𐑉𐐺𐐴 𐑋𐐰𐑌 𐑋𐐲𐑅𐐻 𐐺𐐨 𐑉𐐩𐑆𐐼 𐐻𐐭 𐑅𐐻𐐰𐑌𐐼 𐐺𐐨𐑁𐐬𐑉 𐐸𐐮𐑆 𐐾𐐲𐐾𐑋𐐯𐑌𐐻-𐑅𐐨𐐻. 𐐈𐑌𐐼 𐐸𐐨 𐐸𐐰𐑃 𐐺𐑉𐐫𐐻 𐐻𐐭 𐐹𐐰𐑅 𐑄 𐑉𐐨𐐼𐐯𐑋𐑇𐐲𐑌 𐐱𐑂 𐑄 𐐶𐐲𐑉𐑊𐐼, 𐐸𐐶𐐩𐑉𐐺𐐴 𐐸𐐨 𐑄𐐰𐐻 𐐮𐑆 𐑁𐐵𐑌𐐼 𐑀𐐮𐑊𐐻𐑊𐐯𐑅 𐐺𐐨𐑁𐐬𐑉 𐐸𐐮𐑋 𐐰𐐻 𐑄 𐐾𐐲𐐾𐑋𐐯𐑌𐐻 𐐼𐐩 𐐸𐐰𐑃 𐐮𐐻 𐑀𐐮𐑂𐑌 𐐲𐑌𐐻𐐭 𐐸𐐮𐑋 𐐻𐐭 𐐼𐐶𐐯𐑊 𐐮𐑌 𐑄 𐐹𐑉𐐯𐑆𐐯𐑌𐑅 𐐱𐑂 𐐘𐐱𐐼 𐐮𐑌 𐐸𐐮𐑆 𐐿𐐮𐑍𐐼𐐲𐑋, 𐐻𐐭 𐑅𐐮𐑍 𐑅𐐨𐑅𐑊𐐯𐑅 𐐹𐑉𐐩𐑆𐐯𐑆 𐐶𐐮𐑄 𐑄 𐐿𐐶𐐴𐑉𐑆 𐐲𐐺𐐲𐑂, 𐐲𐑌𐐻𐐭 𐑄 𐐙𐐪𐑄𐐲𐑉, 𐐰𐑌𐐼 𐐲𐑌𐐻𐐭 𐑄 𐐝𐐲𐑌, 𐐰𐑌𐐼 𐐲𐑌𐐻𐐭 𐑄 𐐐𐐬𐑊𐐨 𐐘𐐬𐑅𐐻, 𐐸𐐶𐐮𐐽 𐐪𐑉 𐐶𐐲𐑌 𐐘𐐱𐐼, 𐐮𐑌 𐐲 𐑅𐐻𐐩𐐻 𐐱𐑂 𐐸𐐰𐐹𐐨𐑌𐐯𐑅 𐐸𐐶𐐮𐐽 𐐸𐐰𐑃 𐑌𐐬 𐐯𐑌𐐼. 𐐜𐐩𐑉𐑁𐐬𐑉 𐑉𐐨𐐹𐐯𐑌𐐻, 𐐰𐑌𐐼 𐐺𐐨 𐐺𐐰𐐹𐐻𐐴𐑆𐐼 𐐮𐑌 𐑄 𐑌𐐩𐑋 𐐱𐑂 𐐖𐐨𐑆𐐲𐑅, 𐐰𐑌𐐼 𐑊𐐩 𐐸𐐬𐑊𐐼 𐐲𐐹𐐱𐑌 𐑄 𐑀𐐱𐑅𐐹𐐯𐑊 𐐱𐑂 𐐗𐑉𐐴𐑅𐐻, 𐐸𐐶𐐮𐐽 𐑇𐐰𐑊 𐐺𐐨 𐑅𐐯𐐻 𐐺𐐨𐑁𐐬𐑉 𐐷𐐭, 𐑌𐐱𐐻 𐐬𐑌𐑊𐐨 𐐮𐑌 𐑄𐐮𐑅 𐑉𐐯𐐿𐐲𐑉𐐼, 𐐺𐐲𐐻 𐐫𐑊𐑅𐐬 𐐮𐑌 𐑄 𐑉𐐯𐐿𐐲𐑉𐐼 𐐸𐐶𐐮𐐽 𐑇𐐰𐑊 𐐿𐐲𐑋 𐐲𐑌𐐻𐐭 𐑄 𐐖𐐯𐑌𐐻𐐴𐑊𐑆 𐑁𐑉𐐱𐑋 𐑄 𐐖𐐭𐑆, 𐐸𐐶𐐮𐐽 𐑉𐐯𐐿𐐲𐑉𐐼 𐑇𐐰𐑊 𐐿𐐲𐑋 𐑁𐑉𐐱𐑋 𐑄 𐐖𐐯𐑌𐐻𐐴𐑊𐑆 𐐲𐑌𐐻𐐭 𐐷𐐭. 𐐙𐐫𐑉 𐐺𐐨𐐸𐐬𐑊𐐼, 𐑄𐐮𐑅 𐐮𐑆 𐑉𐐮𐐻𐑌 𐑁𐐫𐑉 𐑄 𐐮𐑌𐐻𐐯𐑌𐐻 𐑄𐐰𐐻 𐐷 𐑋𐐩 𐐺𐐨𐑊𐐨𐑂 𐑄𐐰𐐻; 𐐰𐑌𐐼 𐐮𐑁 𐐷 𐐺𐐨𐑊𐐨𐑂 𐑄𐐰𐐻, 𐐷 𐐶𐐮𐑊 𐐺𐐨𐑊𐐨𐑂 𐑄𐐮𐑅 𐐫𐑊𐑅𐐬; 𐐰𐑌𐐼 𐐮𐑁 𐐷 𐐺𐐨𐑊𐐨𐑂 𐑄𐐮𐑅, 𐐷 𐐶𐐮𐑊 𐑌𐐬 𐐿𐐱𐑌𐑅𐐲𐑉𐑌𐐮𐑍 𐐷𐐭𐑉 𐑁𐐪𐑄𐐲𐑉𐑆, 𐐰𐑌𐐼 𐐫𐑊𐑅𐐬 𐑄 𐑋𐐪𐑉𐑂𐐯𐑊𐐲𐑅 𐐶𐐲𐑉𐐿𐑅 𐐸𐐶𐐮𐐽 𐐶𐐲𐑉 𐑉𐐫𐐻 𐐺𐐴 𐑄 𐐹𐐵𐐲𐑉 𐐱𐑂 𐐘𐐱𐐼 𐐰𐑋𐐲𐑍 𐑄𐐯𐑋; 𐐰𐑌𐐼 𐐷 𐐶𐐮𐑊 𐐫𐑊𐑅𐐬 𐑌𐐬 𐑄𐐰𐐻 𐐷 𐐪𐑉 𐐲 𐑉𐐯𐑋𐑌𐐲𐑌𐐻 𐐱𐑂 𐑄 𐑅𐐨𐐼 𐐱𐑂 𐐖𐐩𐐿𐐲𐐺; 𐑄𐐩𐑉𐑁𐐬𐑉 𐐷 𐐪𐑉 𐑌𐐲𐑋𐐺𐐲𐑉𐐼 𐐰𐑋𐐲𐑍 𐑄 𐐹𐐨𐐹𐑊 𐐱𐑂 𐑄 𐑁𐐲𐑉𐑅𐐻 𐐿𐐲𐑂𐐯𐑌𐐲𐑌𐐻; 𐐰𐑌𐐼 𐐮𐑁 𐐮𐐻 𐑅𐐬 𐐺𐐨 𐑄𐐰𐐻 𐐷 𐐺𐐨𐑊𐐨𐑂 𐐮𐑌 𐐗𐑉𐐴𐑅𐐻, 𐐰𐑌𐐼 𐐪𐑉 𐐺𐐰𐐹𐐻𐐴𐑆𐐼, 𐑁𐐲𐑉𐑅𐐻 𐐶𐐮𐑄 𐐶𐐫𐐻𐐲𐑉, 𐑄𐐯𐑌 𐐶𐐮𐑄 𐑁𐐴𐑉 𐐰𐑌𐐼 𐐶𐐮𐑄 𐑄 𐐐𐐬𐑊𐐨 𐐘𐐬𐑅𐐻, 𐑁𐐱𐑊𐐬𐐮𐑍 𐑄 𐐯𐑀𐑆𐐰𐑋𐐹𐑊 𐐱𐑂 𐐵𐑉 𐐝𐐩𐑂𐐷𐐲𐑉, 𐐰𐐿𐐫𐑉𐐼𐐮𐑍 𐐻𐐭 𐑄𐐰𐐻 𐐸𐐶𐐮𐐽 𐐸𐐨 𐐸𐐰𐑃 𐐿𐐱𐑋𐐰𐑌𐐼𐐯𐐼 𐐲𐑅, 𐐮𐐻 𐑇𐐰𐑊 𐐺𐐨 𐐶𐐯𐑊 𐐶𐐮𐑄 𐐷𐐭 𐐮𐑌 𐑄 𐐼𐐩 𐐱𐑂 𐐾𐐲𐐾𐑋𐐯𐑌𐐻. 𐐁𐑋𐐯𐑌.

𐐕𐐈𐐑𐐓𐐊𐐡 IV.

1. 𐐒𐐨𐐸𐐬𐑊𐐼 𐐌, 𐐣𐐬𐑉𐐬𐑌𐐴, 𐐼𐐭 𐑁𐐮𐑌𐐮𐑇 𐑄 𐑉𐐯𐐿𐐫𐑉𐐼 𐐲𐑂 𐑋𐐴 𐑁𐐪𐑄𐐲𐑉, 𐐣𐐫𐑉𐑋𐐲𐑌. 𐐒𐐨𐐸𐐬𐑊𐐼, 𐐌 𐐸𐐰𐑂 𐐺𐐲𐐻 𐑁𐐷𐐭 𐑃𐐮𐑍𐑆 𐐻𐐭 𐑉𐐴𐐻, 𐐸𐐶𐐮𐐽 𐑃𐐮𐑍𐑆 𐐌 𐐸𐐰𐑂 𐐺𐐮𐑌 𐐿𐐲𐑋𐐰𐑌𐐼𐐯𐐼 𐐺𐐴 𐑋𐐴 𐑁𐐪𐑄𐐲𐑉. 𐐈𐑌𐐼 𐑌𐐵 𐐮𐐻 𐐿𐐩𐑋 𐐻𐐭 𐐹𐐰𐑅 𐑄𐐰𐐻 𐐰𐑁𐐻𐐲𐑉 𐑄 𐑀𐑉𐐩𐐻 𐐰𐑌𐐼 𐐻𐑉𐐯𐑋𐐯𐑌𐐼𐐲𐑅 𐐺𐐰𐐻𐐲𐑊 𐐰𐐻 𐐗𐐭𐑋𐐬𐑉𐐪, 𐐺𐐨𐐸𐐬𐑊𐐼, 𐑄 𐐤𐐨𐑁𐐴𐐻𐑅 𐐸𐐭 𐐸𐐰𐐼 𐐯𐑅𐐿𐐩𐐹𐐻 𐐮𐑌𐐻𐐭 𐑄 𐐿𐐲𐑌𐐻𐑉𐐨 𐑅𐐵𐑃𐐶𐐲𐑉𐐼, 𐐶𐐲𐑉 𐐸𐐲𐑌𐐻𐐯𐐼 𐐺𐐴 𐑄 𐐢𐐰𐑋𐐲𐑌𐐴𐐻𐑅, 𐐲𐑌𐐻𐐮𐑊 𐑄𐐩 𐐶𐐲𐑉 𐐫𐑊 𐐼𐐯𐑅𐐻𐑉𐑎𐐼; 𐐰𐑌𐐼 𐑋𐐴 𐑁𐐪𐑄𐐲𐑉 𐐫𐑊𐑅𐐬 𐐶𐐱𐑆 𐐿𐐮𐑊𐐼 𐐺𐐴 𐑄𐐯𐑋, 𐐰𐑌𐐼 𐐌 𐐨𐑂𐐲𐑌 𐑉𐐨𐑋𐐩𐑌 𐐲𐑊𐐬𐑌 𐐻𐐭 𐑉𐐴𐐻 𐑄 𐑅𐐰𐐼 𐐻𐐩𐑊 𐐲𐑂 𐑄 𐐼𐐯𐑅𐐻𐑉𐐲𐐿𐑇𐐲𐑌 𐐲𐑂 𐑋𐐴 𐐹𐐨𐐹𐐲𐑊. 𐐒𐐲𐐻 𐐺𐐨𐐸𐐬𐑊𐐼, 𐑄𐐩 𐐪𐑉 𐑀𐐱𐑌, 𐐰𐑌𐐼 𐐌 𐑁𐐳𐑊𐑁𐐮𐑊 𐑄 𐐿𐐲𐑋𐐰𐑌𐐼𐑋𐐯𐑌𐐻 𐐲𐑂 𐑋𐐴 𐑁𐐪𐑄𐐲𐑉. 𐐈𐑌𐐼 𐐸𐐶𐐯𐑄𐐲𐑉 𐑄𐐩 𐐶𐐮𐑊 𐑅𐑊𐐩 𐑋𐐨, 𐐌 𐑌𐐬 𐑌𐐱𐐻; 𐑄𐐯𐑉𐑁𐐬𐑉 𐐌 𐐶𐐮𐑊 𐑉𐐴𐐻 𐐰𐑌𐐼 𐐸𐐴𐐼 𐐲𐐹 𐑄 𐑉𐐯𐐿𐐫𐑉𐐼𐑆 𐐮𐑌 𐑄 𐐲𐑉𐑃, 𐐰𐑌𐐼 𐐸𐐶𐐮𐑄𐐲𐑉 𐐌 𐑀𐐬 𐐮𐐻 𐑋𐐰𐐻𐐲𐑉𐐯𐑃 𐑌𐐱𐐻. 𐐒𐐨𐐸𐐬𐑊𐐼, 𐑋𐐴 𐑁𐐪𐑄𐐲𐑉 𐐸𐐰𐑃 𐑋𐐩𐐼 𐑄𐐮𐑅 𐑉𐐯𐐿𐐫𐑉𐐼, 𐐰𐑌𐐼 𐐸𐐨 𐐸𐐰𐑃 𐑉𐐮𐐻𐐲𐑌 𐑄 𐐮𐑌𐐻𐐯𐑌𐐻 𐑄𐐯𐑉𐐱𐑂. 𐐈𐑌𐐼 𐐺𐐨𐐸𐐬𐑊𐐼, 𐐌 𐐶𐐳𐐼 𐑉𐐴𐐻 𐐮𐐻 𐐫𐑊𐑅𐐬, 𐐮𐑁 𐐌 𐐸𐐰𐐼 𐑉𐐭𐑋 𐐲𐐹𐐱𐑌 𐑄 𐐹𐑊𐐩𐐻𐑅; 𐐺𐐲𐐻 𐐌 𐐸𐐰𐑂 𐑌𐐱𐐻; 𐐰𐑌𐐼 𐐬𐑉 𐐌 𐐸𐐰𐑂 𐑌𐐲𐑌, 𐑁𐐫𐑉 𐐌 𐐰𐑋 𐐲𐑊𐐬𐑌; 𐑋𐐴 𐑁𐐪𐑄𐐲𐑉 𐐸𐐰𐑃 𐐺𐐮𐑌 𐑅𐑊𐐩𐑌 𐐮𐑌 𐐺𐐰𐐻𐐲𐑊, 𐐰𐑌𐐼 𐐫𐑊 𐑋𐐴 𐐿𐐮𐑌𐑆𐑁𐐬𐐿, 𐐰𐑌𐐼 𐐌 𐐸𐐰𐑂 𐑌𐐱𐐻 𐑁𐑉𐐯𐑌𐐼𐑆 𐑌𐐫𐑉 𐐸𐐶𐐮𐑄𐐲𐑉 𐐻𐐭 𐑀𐐬; 𐐰𐑌𐐼 𐐸𐐵 𐑊𐐱𐑍 𐑄 𐐢𐐫𐑉𐐼 𐐶𐐮𐑊 𐑅𐐲𐑁𐐲𐑉 𐑄𐐰𐐻 𐐌 𐑋𐐩 𐑊𐐮𐑂, 𐐌 𐑌𐐬 𐑌𐐱𐐻. 𐐒𐐨𐐸𐐬𐑊𐐼, 𐑁𐐬𐑉 𐐸𐐲𐑌𐐼𐑉𐐯𐐼 𐐷𐐨𐑉𐑆 𐐸𐐰𐑂 𐐹𐐰𐑅𐐻 𐐰𐐶𐐩 𐑅𐐮𐑌𐑅 𐑄 𐐿𐐲𐑋𐐮𐑍 𐐲𐑂 𐐵𐑉 𐐢𐐫𐑉𐐼 𐐰𐑌𐐼 𐐝𐐩𐑂𐐷𐐲𐑉. 𐐈𐑌𐐼 𐐺𐐨𐐸𐐬𐑊𐐼, 𐑄 𐐢𐐰𐑋𐐲𐑌𐐴𐐻𐑅 𐐸𐐰𐑂 𐐸𐐲𐑌𐐻𐐯𐐼 𐑋𐐴 𐐹𐐨𐐹𐐲𐑊, 𐑄 𐐤𐐨𐑁𐐴𐐻𐑅, 𐐼𐐵𐑌 𐑁𐑉𐐱𐑋 𐑅𐐮𐐻𐐨 𐐻𐐭 𐑅𐐮𐐻𐐨, 𐐰𐑌𐐼 𐑁𐑉𐐱𐑋 𐐹𐑊𐐩𐑅 𐐻𐐭 𐐹𐑊𐐩𐑅, 𐐨𐑂𐐲𐑌 𐐲𐑌𐐻𐐮𐑊 𐑄𐐩 𐐪𐑉 𐑌𐐬 𐑋𐐬𐑉; 𐐰𐑌𐐼 𐑀𐑉𐐩𐐻 𐐸𐐰𐑆 𐐺𐐮𐑌 𐑄𐐩𐑉 𐑁𐐫𐑊; 𐐷𐐩, 𐑀𐑉𐐩𐐻 𐐰𐑌𐐼 𐑋𐐪𐑉𐑂𐐯𐑊𐐲𐑅 𐐮𐑆 𐑄 𐐼𐐯𐑅𐐻𐑉𐐲𐐿𐑇𐐲𐑌 𐐲𐑂 𐑋𐐴 𐐹𐐨𐐹𐐲𐑊, 𐑄 𐐤𐐨𐑁𐐴𐐻𐑅. 𐐈𐑌𐐼 𐐺𐐨𐐸𐐬𐑊𐐼, 𐐮𐐻 𐐮𐑆 𐑄 𐐸𐐰𐑌𐐼 𐐲𐑂 𐑄 𐐢𐐫𐑉𐐼 𐐸𐐶𐐮𐐽 𐐸𐐰𐑃 𐐼𐐲𐑌 𐐮𐐻. 𐐈𐑌𐐼 𐐺𐐨𐐸𐐬𐑊𐐼 𐐫𐑊𐑅𐐬, 𐑄 𐐢𐐰𐑋𐐲𐑌𐐴𐐻𐑅 𐐪𐑉 𐐰𐐻 𐐶𐐫𐑉 𐐶𐐲𐑌 𐐶𐐮𐑄 𐐰𐑌𐐲𐑄𐐲𐑉; 𐐰𐑌𐐼 𐑄 𐐸𐐬𐑊 𐑁𐐩𐑅 𐐲𐑂 𐑄𐐮𐑅 𐑊𐐰𐑌𐐼 𐐮𐑆 𐐶𐐲𐑌 𐐿𐐲𐑌𐐻𐐮𐑌𐐷𐐭𐐲𐑊 𐑉𐐵𐑌𐐼 𐐲𐑂 𐑋𐐲𐑉𐐼𐐲𐑉 𐐰𐑌𐐼 𐐺𐑊𐐲𐐼𐑇𐐯𐐼; 𐐰𐑌𐐼 𐑌𐐬 𐐶𐐲𐑌 𐑌𐐬𐐯𐑃 𐑄 𐐯𐑌𐐼 𐐲𐑂 𐑄 𐐶𐐫𐑉. 𐐈𐑌𐐼 𐑌𐐵 𐐺𐐨𐐸𐐬𐑊𐐼, 𐐌 𐑅𐐩 𐑌𐐬 𐑋𐐬𐑉 𐐿𐐲𐑌𐑅𐐲𐑉𐑌𐐮𐑍 𐑄𐐯𐑋, 𐑁𐐫𐑉 𐑄𐐩𐑉 𐐪𐑉 𐑌𐐲𐑌, 𐑅𐐩𐑂 𐐮𐐻 𐐺𐐨 𐑄 𐐢𐐰𐑋𐐲𐑌𐐴𐐻𐑅 𐐰𐑌𐐼 𐑉𐐱𐐺𐐲𐑉𐑆, 𐑄𐐰𐐻 𐐼𐐭 𐐯𐑀𐑆𐐮𐑅𐐻 𐐲𐐹𐐱𐑌 𐑄 𐑁𐐩𐑅 𐐲𐑂 𐑄 𐑊𐐰𐑌𐐼; 𐐰𐑌𐐼 𐑄𐐩𐑉 𐐪𐑉 𐑌𐐲𐑌 𐑄𐐰𐐻 𐐼𐐭 𐑌𐐬 𐑄 𐐻𐑉𐐭 𐐘𐐱𐐼, 𐑅𐐩𐑂 𐐮𐐻 𐐺𐐨 𐑄 𐐼𐐮𐑅𐐴𐐹𐐲𐑊𐑆 𐐲𐑂 𐐖𐐨𐑆𐐲𐑅, 𐐸𐐭 𐐼𐐮𐐼 𐐻𐐰𐑉𐐨 𐐮𐑌 𐑄 𐑊𐐰𐑌𐐼 𐐲𐑌𐐻𐐮𐑊 𐑄 𐐶𐐮𐐿𐐯𐐼𐑌𐐯𐑅 𐐲𐑂 𐑄 𐐹𐐨𐐹𐐲𐑊 𐐶𐐱𐑆 𐑅𐐬 𐑀𐑉𐐩𐐻, 𐑄𐐰𐐻 𐑄 𐐢𐐫𐑉𐐼 𐐶𐐳𐐼 𐑌𐐱𐐻 𐑅𐐲𐑁𐐲𐑉 𐑄𐐯𐑋 𐐻𐐭 𐑉𐐨𐑋𐐩𐑌 𐐶𐐮𐑄 𐑄 𐐹𐐨𐐹𐐲𐑊; 𐐰𐑌𐐼 𐐸𐐶𐐯𐑄𐐲𐑉 𐑄𐐩 𐐺𐐨 𐐲𐐹𐐱𐑌 𐑄 𐑁𐐩𐑅 𐐲𐑂 𐑄 𐑊𐐰𐑌𐐼, 𐑌𐐬 𐑋𐐰𐑌 𐑌𐐬𐐯𐑃. 𐐒𐐲𐐻 𐐺𐐨𐐸𐐬𐑊𐐼, 𐑋𐐴 𐑁𐐪𐑄𐐲𐑉 𐐰𐑌𐐼 𐐌 𐐸𐐰𐑂 𐑅𐐨𐑌 𐑄𐐯𐑋, 𐐰𐑌𐐼 𐑄𐐩 𐐸𐐰𐑂 𐑋𐐮𐑌𐐮𐑅𐐻𐐲𐑉𐐼 𐐲𐑌𐐻𐐭 𐐲𐑅. 𐐈𐑌𐐼 𐐸𐐭𐑅𐐬 𐑉𐐨𐑅𐐨𐑂𐐯𐑃 𐑄𐐮𐑅 𐑉𐐯𐐿𐐫𐑉𐐼, 𐐰𐑌𐐼 𐑇𐐰𐑊 𐑌𐐱𐐻 𐐿𐐲𐑌𐐼𐐯𐑋 𐐮𐐻 𐐺𐐨𐐿𐐫𐑆 𐐲𐑂 𐑄 𐐮𐑋𐐹𐐲𐑉𐑁𐐯𐐿𐑇𐐲𐑌𐑆 𐐸𐐶𐐮𐐽 𐐪𐑉 𐐮𐑌 𐐮𐐻, 𐑄 𐑅𐐩𐑋 𐑇𐐰𐑊 𐑌𐐬 𐐲𐑂 𐑀𐑉𐐩𐐻𐐲𐑉 𐑃𐐮𐑍𐑆 𐑄𐐰𐑌 𐑄𐐨𐑆. 𐐒𐐨𐐸𐐬𐑊𐐼, 𐐌 𐐰𐑋 𐐣𐐬𐑉𐐬𐑌𐐴; 𐐰𐑌𐐼 𐐶𐐲𐑉 𐐮𐐻 𐐹𐐱𐑅𐐮𐐺𐐲𐑊, 𐐌 𐐶𐐳𐐼 𐑋𐐩𐐿 𐐫𐑊 𐑃𐐮𐑍𐑆 𐑌𐐬𐑌 𐐲𐑌𐐻𐐭 𐐷𐐭.

2. 𐐒𐐨𐐸𐐬𐑊𐐼, 𐐌 𐑋𐐩𐐿 𐐰𐑌 𐐯𐑌𐐼 𐐲𐑂 𐑅𐐹𐐨𐐿𐐮𐑍 𐐿𐐲𐑌𐑅𐐲𐑉𐑌𐐮𐑍 𐑄𐐮𐑅 𐐹𐐨𐐹𐐲𐑊. 𐐌 𐐰𐑋 𐑄 𐑅𐐲𐑌 𐐲𐑂 𐐣𐐫𐑉𐑋𐐲𐑌, 𐐰𐑌𐐼 𐑋𐐴 𐑁𐐪𐑄𐐲𐑉 𐐶𐐱𐑆 𐐰 𐐼𐐯𐑅𐐯𐑌𐐼𐐲𐑌𐐻 𐐲𐑂 𐐤𐐨𐑁𐐴; 𐐰𐑌𐐼 𐐌 𐐰𐑋 𐑄 𐑅𐐩𐑋 𐐸𐐭 𐐸𐐴𐐼𐐯𐑃 𐐲𐐹 𐑄𐐮𐑅 𐑉𐐯𐐿𐐫𐑉𐐼 𐐲𐑌𐐻𐐭 𐑄 𐐢𐐫𐑉𐐼; 𐑄 𐐹𐑊𐐩𐐻𐑅 𐑄𐐯𐑉𐐱𐑂 𐐪𐑉 𐐲𐑂 𐑌𐐬 𐐶𐐲𐑉𐑃, 𐐺𐐨𐐿𐐫𐑆 𐐲𐑂 𐑄 𐐿𐐲𐑋𐐰𐑌𐐼𐑋𐐯𐑌𐐻 𐐲𐑂 𐑄 𐐢𐐫𐑉𐐼. 𐐙𐐫𐑉 𐐸𐐨 𐐻𐑉𐐭𐑊𐐨 𐑅𐐯𐑃, 𐑄𐐰𐐻 𐑌𐐬 𐐶𐐲𐑌 𐑇𐐰𐑊 𐐸𐐰𐑂 𐑄𐐯𐑋 𐐻𐐭 𐑀𐐯𐐻 𐑀𐐩𐑌; 𐐺𐐲𐐻 𐑄 𐑉𐐯𐐿𐐫𐑉𐐼 𐑄𐐯𐑉𐐱𐑂 𐐮𐑆 𐐲𐑂 𐑀𐑉𐐩𐐻 𐐶𐐲𐑉𐑃; 𐐰𐑌𐐼 𐐸𐐭𐑅𐐬 𐑇𐐰𐑊 𐐺𐑉𐐮𐑍 𐐮𐐻 𐐻𐐭 𐑊𐐴𐐻, 𐐸𐐮𐑋 𐐶𐐮𐑊 𐑄 𐐢𐐫𐑉𐐼 𐐺𐑊𐐯𐑅. 𐐙𐐫𐑉 𐑌𐐲𐑌 𐐿𐐰𐑌 𐐸𐐰𐑂 𐐹𐐵𐐲𐑉 𐐻𐐭 𐐺𐑉𐐮𐑍 𐐮𐐻 𐐻𐐭 𐑊𐐴𐐻, 𐑅𐐩𐑂 𐐮𐐻 𐐺𐐨 𐑀𐐮𐑂𐐲𐑌 𐐸𐐮𐑋 𐐲𐑂 𐐘𐐱𐐼; 𐑁𐐫𐑉 𐐘𐐱𐐼 𐐶𐐮𐑊 𐑄𐐰𐐻 𐐮𐐻 𐑇𐐰𐑊 𐐺𐐨 𐐼𐐲𐑌 𐐶𐐮𐑄 𐐰𐑌 𐐴 𐑅𐐮𐑍𐑀𐐲𐑊 𐐻𐐭 𐐸𐐮𐑆 𐑀𐑊𐐬𐑉𐐨, 𐐫𐑉 𐑄 𐐶𐐯𐑊𐑁𐐩𐑉 𐐲𐑂 𐑄 𐐩𐑌𐑇𐐯𐑌𐐻 𐐰𐑌𐐼 𐑊𐐱𐑍 𐐼𐐮𐑅𐐹𐐲𐑉𐑅𐐻 𐐿𐐲𐑂𐐯𐑌𐐰𐑌𐐻 𐐹𐐨𐐹𐐲𐑊 𐐲𐑂 𐑄 𐐢𐐫𐑉𐐼. 𐐈𐑌𐐼 𐐺𐑊𐐯𐑅𐐯𐐼 𐐺𐐨 𐐸𐐨 𐑄𐐰𐐻 𐑇𐐰𐑊 𐐺𐑉𐐮𐑍 𐑄𐐮𐑅 𐑃𐐮𐑍 𐐻𐐭 𐑊𐐴𐐻; 𐑁𐐫𐑉 𐐮𐐻 𐑇𐐰𐑊 𐐺𐐨 𐐺𐑉𐐫𐐻 𐐵𐐻 𐐲𐑂 𐐼𐐪𐑉𐐿𐑌𐐯𐑅 𐐲𐑌𐐻𐐭 𐑊𐐴𐐻, 𐐰𐐿𐐫𐑉𐐼𐐮𐑍 𐐻𐐭 𐑄 𐐶𐐲𐑉𐐼 𐐲𐑂 𐐘𐐱𐐼; 𐐷𐐩, 𐐮𐐻 𐑇𐐰𐑊 𐐺𐐨 𐐺𐑉𐐫𐐻 𐐵𐐻 𐐲𐑂 𐑄 𐐲𐑉𐑃, 𐐰𐑌𐐼 𐐮𐐻 𐑇𐐰𐑊 𐑇𐐴𐑌

𐑁𐐫𐑉𐑃 𐐵𐐻 𐐱𐑂 𐐼𐐪𐑉𐐿𐑌𐐯𐑅, 𐐰𐑌𐐼 𐐿𐐲𐑋 𐐲𐑌𐐻𐐭 𐑄 𐑌𐐱𐑊𐐯𐐾 𐐱𐑂 𐑄 𐐹𐐨𐐹𐑊; 𐐰𐑌𐐼 𐐮𐐻 𐑇𐐰𐑊 𐐺𐐨 𐐼𐐲𐑌 𐐺𐐴 𐑄 𐐹𐐵𐐲𐑉 𐐱𐑂 𐐘𐐱𐐼; 𐐰𐑌𐐼 𐐮𐑁 𐑄𐐯𐑉 𐐺𐐨 𐑁𐐫𐑊𐐻𐑅, 𐑄𐐩 𐐺𐐨 𐑄 𐑁𐐫𐑊𐐻𐑅 𐐱𐑂 𐐰 𐑋𐐰𐑌. 𐐒𐐲𐐻 𐐺𐐨𐐸𐐬𐑊𐐼, 𐐶𐐨 𐑌𐐬 𐑌𐐬 𐑁𐐫𐑊𐐻. 𐐤𐐯𐑂𐐲𐑉𐑄𐐲𐑊𐐯𐑅, 𐐘𐐱𐐼 𐑌𐐬𐐯𐑃 𐐫𐑊 𐑃𐐮𐑍𐑆; 𐑄𐐯𐑉𐑁𐐫𐑉 𐐸𐐨 𐑄𐐰𐐻 𐐿𐐲𐑌𐐼𐐯𐑋𐑌𐐯𐑃, 𐑊𐐯𐐻 𐐸𐐮𐑋 𐐺𐐨 𐐰𐐶𐐯𐑉 𐑊𐐯𐑅𐐻 𐐸𐐨 𐑇𐐰𐑊 𐐺𐐨 𐐮𐑌 𐐼𐐩𐑌𐐾𐐲𐑉 𐐱𐑂 𐐸𐐯𐑊 𐑁𐐴𐐲𐑉. 𐐈𐑌𐐼 𐐸𐐨 𐑄𐐰𐐻 𐑅𐐯𐑃, 𐐞𐐬 𐐲𐑌𐐻𐐭 𐑋𐐨, 𐐫𐑉 𐐷𐐨 𐑇𐐰𐑊 𐐺𐐨 𐑅𐑋𐐮𐐻𐑌, 𐑊𐐯𐐻 𐐸𐐮𐑋 𐐺𐐨𐐶𐐯𐑉 𐑊𐐯𐑅𐐻 𐐸𐐨 𐐿𐐲𐑋𐐰𐑌𐐼𐐯𐑃 𐑄𐐰𐐻 𐐸𐐶𐐮𐐽 𐐮𐑆 𐑁𐐫𐑉𐐺𐐮𐐼𐑌 𐐱𐑂 𐑄 𐐢𐐫𐑉𐐼. 𐐙𐐫𐑉 𐐺𐐨𐐸𐐬𐑊𐐼, 𐑄 𐑅𐐩𐑋 𐑄𐐰𐐻 𐐾𐐲𐐾𐐯𐑃 𐑉𐐰𐑇𐑊𐐨, 𐑇𐐰𐑊 𐐺𐐨 𐐾𐐲𐐾𐐼 𐑉𐐰𐑇𐑊𐐨 𐐰𐑀𐐯𐑌; 𐑁𐐫𐑉 𐐰𐐿𐐫𐑉𐐼𐐮𐑍 𐐻𐐭 𐐸𐐮𐑆 𐐶𐐲𐑉𐐿𐑅 𐑇𐐰𐑊 𐐸𐐮𐑆 𐐶𐐩𐐾𐐯𐑆 𐐺𐐨; 𐑄𐐯𐑉𐑁𐐫𐑉, 𐐸𐐨 𐑄𐐰𐐻 𐑅𐑋𐐴𐐻𐐯𐑃, 𐑇𐐰𐑊 𐐺𐐨 𐑅𐑋𐐮𐐻𐑌 𐐰𐑀𐐯𐑌 𐐱𐑂 𐑄 𐐢𐐫𐑉𐐼. 𐐒𐐨𐐸𐐬𐑊𐐼 𐐸𐐶𐐱𐐻 𐑄 𐑅𐐿𐑉𐐮𐐹𐐽𐐲𐑉 𐑅𐐯𐑆, 𐐣𐐰𐑌 𐑇𐐰𐑊 𐑌𐐱𐐻 𐑅𐑋𐐴𐐻, 𐑌𐐨𐑄𐐲𐑉 𐑇𐐰𐑊 𐐸𐐨 𐐾𐐲𐐾; 𐑁𐐫𐑉 𐐾𐐲𐐾𐑋𐐯𐑌𐐻 𐐮𐑆 𐑋𐐴𐑌, 𐑅𐐯𐑆 𐑄 𐐢𐐫𐑉𐐼; 𐐰𐑌𐐼 𐑂𐐯𐑌𐐾𐐲𐑌𐑅 𐐮𐑆 𐑋𐐴𐑌 𐐫𐑊𐑅𐐬, 𐐰𐑌𐐼 𐐴 𐐶𐐮𐑊 𐑉𐐨𐐹𐐩. 𐐈𐑌𐐼 𐐸𐐨 𐑄𐐰𐐻 𐑇𐐰𐑊 𐐺𐑉𐐨𐑄 𐐵𐐻 𐑉𐐲𐑃 𐐰𐑌𐐼 𐑅𐐻𐑉𐐴𐑁𐑅 𐐰𐑀𐐯𐑌𐑅𐐻 𐑄 𐐶𐐲𐑉𐐿 𐐱𐑂 𐑄 𐐢𐐫𐑉𐐼, 𐐰𐑌𐐼 𐐰𐑀𐐯𐑌𐑅𐐻 𐑄 𐐿𐐲𐑂𐐯𐑌𐐰𐑌𐐻 𐐹𐐨𐐹𐑊 𐐱𐑂 𐑄 𐐢𐐫𐑉𐐼, 𐐸𐐭 𐐪𐑉 𐑄 𐐸𐐵𐑅 𐐱𐑂 𐐆𐑆𐑉𐐩𐐯𐑊, 𐐰𐑌𐐼 𐑇𐐰𐑊 𐑅𐐩, 𐐎𐐨 𐐶𐐮𐑊 𐐼𐐯𐑅𐐻𐑉𐐱𐐮 𐑄 𐐶𐐲𐑉𐐿 𐐱𐑂 𐑄 𐐢𐐫𐑉𐐼, 𐐰𐑌𐐼 𐑄 𐐢𐐫𐑉𐐼 𐐶𐐮𐑊 𐑌𐐱𐐻 𐑉𐐨𐑋𐐯𐑋𐐺𐐲𐑉 𐐸𐐮𐑆 𐐿𐐲𐑂𐐯𐑌𐐰𐑌𐐻 𐐸𐐶𐐮𐐽 𐐸𐐨 𐐸𐐰𐑃 𐑋𐐩𐐼 𐐲𐑌𐐻𐐭 𐑄 𐐸𐐵𐑅 𐐱𐑂 𐐆𐑆𐑉𐐩𐐯𐑊, 𐑄 𐑅𐐩𐑋 𐐮𐑆 𐐮𐑌 𐐼𐐩𐑌𐐾𐐲𐑉 𐐻𐐭 𐐺𐐨 𐐸𐐷𐐭𐑌 𐐼𐐵𐑌 𐐰𐑌𐐼 𐐿𐐰𐑅𐐻 𐐮𐑌𐐻𐐭 𐑄 𐑁𐐴𐐲𐑉; 𐑁𐐫𐑉 𐑄 𐐨𐐻𐐲𐑉𐑌𐐲𐑊 𐐹𐐲𐑉𐐹𐐲𐑅𐐯𐑆 𐐱𐑂 𐑄 𐐢𐐫𐑉𐐼 𐑇𐐰𐑊 𐑉𐐬𐑊 𐐱𐑌, 𐐲𐑌𐐻𐐮𐑊 𐐫𐑊 𐐸𐐮𐑆 𐐹𐑉𐐱𐑋𐐮𐑅𐐯𐑆 𐑇𐐰𐑊 𐐺𐐨 𐑁𐐳𐑊𐑁𐐮𐑊𐐼. 𐐝𐐲𐑉𐐽 𐑄 𐐹𐑉𐐱𐑁𐐯𐑅𐐨𐑆 𐐱𐑂 𐐌𐑆𐐩𐐲𐑄. 𐐒𐐨𐐸𐐬𐑊𐐼, 𐐴 𐐿𐐰𐑌𐑌𐐱𐐻 𐑉𐐴𐐻 𐑄𐐯𐑋. 𐐏𐐩, 𐐺𐐨𐐸𐐬𐑊𐐼 𐐴 𐑅𐐩 𐐲𐑌𐐻𐐭 𐐷𐐭, 𐑄𐐰𐐻 𐑄𐐬𐑆 𐑅𐐩𐑌𐐻𐑅 𐐸𐐭 𐐸𐐰𐑂 𐑀𐐱𐑌 𐐺𐐨𐑁𐐫𐑉 𐑋𐐨, 𐐸𐐭 𐐸𐐰𐑂 𐐹𐐲𐑆𐐯𐑅𐐻 𐑄𐐮𐑅 𐑊𐐰𐑌𐐼, 𐑇𐐰𐑊 𐐿𐑉𐐴; 𐐷𐐩, 𐐨𐑂𐐯𐑌 𐑁𐑉𐐱𐑋 𐑄 𐐼𐐲𐑅𐐻 𐐶𐐮𐑊 𐑄𐐩 𐐿𐑉𐐴 𐐲𐑌𐐻𐐭 𐑄 𐐢𐐫𐑉𐐼; 𐐰𐑌𐐼 𐐰𐑆 𐑄 𐐢𐐫𐑉𐐼 𐑊𐐮𐑂𐐯𐑃, 𐐸𐐨 𐐶𐐮𐑊 𐑉𐐨𐑋𐐯𐑋𐐺𐐲𐑉 𐑄 𐐿𐐲𐑂𐐯𐑌𐐰𐑌𐐻 𐐸𐐶𐐮𐐽 𐐸𐐨 𐐸𐐰𐑃 𐑋𐐩𐐼 𐐶𐐮𐑄 𐑄𐐯𐑋. 𐐈𐑌𐐼 𐐸𐐨 𐑌𐐬𐐯𐑃 𐑄𐐯𐑉 𐐹𐑉𐐩𐐲𐑉𐑆, 𐑄𐐰𐐻 𐑄𐐩 𐐶𐐲𐑉 𐐮𐑌 𐐺𐐨𐐸𐐪𐑁 𐐱𐑂 𐑄𐐯𐑉 𐐺𐑉𐐯𐑄𐑉𐐯𐑌. 𐐈𐑌𐐼 𐐸𐐨 𐑌𐐬𐐯𐑃 𐑄𐐯𐑉 𐑁𐐩𐑃; 𐑁𐐫𐑉 𐐮𐑌 𐐸𐐮𐑆 𐑌𐐩𐑋 𐐿𐐳𐐼 𐑄𐐩 𐑉𐐨𐑋𐐭𐑂 𐑋𐐵𐑌𐐻𐐯𐑌𐑆; 𐐰𐑌𐐼 𐐮𐑌 𐐸𐐮𐑆 𐑌𐐩𐑋 𐐿𐐳𐐼 𐑄𐐩 𐐿𐐫𐑆 𐑄 𐐲𐑉𐑃 𐐻𐐭 𐑇𐐩𐐿; 𐐰𐑌𐐼 𐐺𐐴 𐑄 𐐹𐐵𐐲𐑉 𐐱𐑂 𐐸𐐮𐑆 𐐶𐐲𐑉𐐼 𐐼𐐮𐐼 𐑄𐐩 𐐿𐐫𐑆 𐐹𐑉𐐮𐑆𐐲𐑌𐑆 𐐻𐐭 𐐻𐐲𐑋𐐺𐑊 𐐻𐐭 𐑄 𐐲𐑉𐑃; 𐐷𐐩, 𐐨𐑂𐐯𐑌 𐑄 𐑁𐐴𐐲𐑉𐐨 𐑁𐐲𐑉𐑌𐐯𐑅 𐐿𐐳𐐼 𐑌𐐱𐐻 𐐸𐐪𐑉𐑋 𐑄𐐯𐑋, 𐑌𐐨𐑄𐐲𐑉 𐐶𐐴𐑊𐐼 𐐺𐐨𐑅𐐻𐑅, 𐑌𐐫𐑉 𐐹𐐱𐐮𐑆𐐲𐑌𐐲𐑅 𐑅𐐲𐑉𐐹𐐯𐑌𐐻𐑅, 𐐺𐐨𐐿𐐫𐑆 𐐱𐑂 𐑄 𐐹𐐵𐐲𐑉 𐐱𐑂 𐐸𐐮𐑆 𐐶𐐲𐑉𐐼. 𐐈𐑌𐐼 𐐺𐐨𐐸𐐬𐑊𐐼, 𐑄𐐯𐑉 𐐹𐑉𐐩𐐲𐑉𐑆 𐐶𐐲𐑉 𐐫𐑊𐑅𐐬 𐐮𐑌 𐐺𐐨𐐸𐐪𐑁 𐐱𐑂 𐐸𐐮𐑋 𐑄𐐰𐐻 𐑄 𐐢𐐫𐑉𐐼 𐑇𐐳𐐼 𐑅𐐲𐑁𐐲𐑉 𐐻𐐭 𐐺𐑉𐐮𐑍 𐑄𐐨𐑆 𐑃𐐮𐑍𐑆 𐑁𐐫𐑉𐑃. 𐐈𐑌𐐼 𐑌𐐬 𐐶𐐲𐑌 𐑌𐐨𐐼 𐑅𐐩, 𐑄𐐩 𐑇𐐰𐑊 𐑌𐐱𐐻 𐐿𐐲𐑋, 𐑁𐐫𐑉 𐑄𐐩 𐑇𐐳𐑉𐑊𐐨 𐑇𐐰𐑊, 𐑁𐐫𐑉 𐑄 𐐢𐐫𐑉𐐼 𐐸𐐰𐑃 𐑅𐐹𐐬𐐿𐐲𐑌 𐐮𐐻; 𐑁𐐫𐑉 𐐵𐐻 𐐱𐑂 𐑄 𐐲𐑉𐑃 𐑇𐐰𐑊 𐑄𐐩 𐐿𐐲𐑋, 𐐺𐐴 𐑄 𐐸𐐰𐑌𐐼 𐐱𐑂 𐑄 𐐢𐐫𐑉𐐼, 𐐰𐑌𐐼 𐑌𐐲𐑌 𐐿𐐰𐑌 𐑅𐐻𐐩 𐐮𐐻; 𐐰𐑌𐐼 𐐮𐐻 𐑇𐐰𐑊 𐐿𐐲𐑋 𐐮𐑌 𐐰 𐐼𐐩 𐐸𐐶𐐯𐑌 𐐮𐐻 𐑇𐐰𐑊 𐐺𐐨 𐑅𐐯𐐼 𐑄𐐰𐐻 𐑋𐐮𐑉𐐲𐐿𐑊𐑆 𐐪𐑉 𐐼𐐲𐑌 𐐰𐐶𐐩; 𐐰𐑌𐐼 𐐮𐐻 𐑇𐐰𐑊 𐐿𐐲𐑋 𐐨𐑂𐐯𐑌 𐐰𐑆 𐐮𐑁 𐐶𐐲𐑌 𐑇𐐳𐐼 𐑅𐐹𐐨𐐿 𐑁𐑉𐐱𐑋 𐑄 𐐼𐐯𐐼.

3. 𐐈𐑌𐐼 𐐮𐐻 𐑇𐐰𐑊 𐐿𐐲𐑋 𐐮𐑌 𐐰 𐐼𐐩 𐐸𐐶𐐯𐑌 𐑄 𐐺𐑊𐐲𐐼 𐐱𐑂 𐑅𐐩𐑌𐐻𐑅 𐑇𐐰𐑊 𐐿𐑉𐐴 𐐲𐑌𐐻𐐭 𐑄 𐐢𐐫𐑉𐐼, 𐐺𐐨𐐿𐐫𐑆 𐐱𐑂 𐑅𐐨𐐿𐑉𐐯𐐻 𐐿𐐱𐑋𐐺𐐮𐑌𐐩𐑇𐐲𐑌𐑆 𐐰𐑌𐐼 𐑄 𐐶𐐲𐑉𐐿𐑅 𐐱𐑂 𐐼𐐪𐑉𐐿𐑌𐐯𐑅; 𐐷𐐩, 𐐮𐐻 𐑇𐐰𐑊 𐐿𐐲𐑋 𐐮𐑌 𐐰 𐐼𐐩 𐐸𐐶𐐯𐑌 𐑄 𐐹𐐵𐐲𐑉 𐐱𐑂 𐐘𐐱𐐼 𐑇𐐰𐑊 𐐺𐐨 𐐼𐐨𐑌𐐴𐐲𐐼, 𐐰𐑌𐐼 𐐽𐐲𐑉𐐽𐐯𐑆 𐐺𐐨𐐿𐐲𐑋 𐐼𐐨𐑁𐐴𐑊𐐼, 𐐰𐑌𐐼 𐑇𐐰𐑊 𐐺𐐨 𐑊𐐮𐑁𐐻𐐯𐐼 𐐲𐐹 𐐮𐑌 𐑄 𐐹𐑉𐐴𐐼 𐐱𐑂 𐑄𐐯𐑉 𐐸𐐪𐑉𐐻𐑅; 𐐷𐐩, 𐐨𐑂𐐯𐑌 𐐮𐑌 𐐰 𐐼𐐩 𐐸𐐶𐐯𐑌 𐑊𐐨𐐼𐐲𐑉𐑆 𐐱𐑂 𐐽𐐲𐑉𐐽𐐯𐑆 𐐰𐑌𐐼 𐐻𐐨𐐽𐐲𐑉𐑆 𐑇𐐰𐑊 𐑉𐐴𐑆 𐐮𐑌 𐑄 𐐹𐑉𐐴𐐼 𐐱𐑂 𐑄𐐯𐑉 𐐸𐐪𐑉𐐻𐑅, 𐐨𐑂𐐯𐑌 𐐻𐐭 𐑄 𐐯𐑌𐑂𐐨𐐮𐑍 𐐱𐑂 𐑄𐐯𐑋 𐐸𐐭 𐐺𐐨𐑊𐐱𐑍 𐐻𐐭 𐑄𐐯𐑉 𐐽𐐲𐑉𐐽𐐯𐑆; 𐐷𐐩, 𐐮𐐻 𐑇𐐰𐑊 𐐿𐐲𐑋 𐐮𐑌 𐐰 𐐼𐐩 𐐸𐐶𐐯𐑌 𐑄𐐯𐑉 𐑇𐐰𐑊 𐐺𐐨 𐐸𐐲𐑉𐐼 𐐱𐑂 𐑁𐐴𐐲𐑉𐑆, 𐐰𐑌𐐼 𐐻𐐯𐑋𐐹𐐯𐑅𐐻𐑅, 𐐰𐑌𐐼 𐑂𐐩𐐹𐐲𐑉𐑆 𐐱𐑂 𐑅𐑋𐐬𐐿 𐐮𐑌 𐑁𐐱𐑉𐐯𐑌 𐑊𐐰𐑌𐐼𐑆; 𐐰𐑌𐐼 𐑄𐐯𐑉 𐑇𐐰𐑊 𐐫𐑊𐑅𐐬 𐐺𐐨 𐐸𐐲𐑉𐐼 𐐱𐑂 𐐶𐐫𐑉𐑆, 𐑉𐐭𐑋𐐲𐑉𐑆 𐐱𐑂 𐐶𐐫𐑉𐑆, 𐐰𐑌𐐼 𐐲𐑉𐑃𐐿𐐶𐐩𐐿𐑅 𐐮𐑌 𐐼𐐴𐑂𐐲𐑉𐑆 𐐹𐑊𐐩𐑅𐐯𐑆; 𐐷𐐩, 𐐮𐐻 𐑇𐐰𐑊 𐐿𐐲𐑋 𐐮𐑌 𐐰 𐐼𐐩 𐐸𐐶𐐯𐑌 𐑄𐐯𐑉 𐑇𐐰𐑊 𐐺𐐨 𐑀𐑉𐐩𐐻 𐐹𐐱𐑊𐐭𐑇𐐲𐑌𐑆 𐐲𐐹𐐱𐑌 𐑄 𐑁𐐩𐑅 𐐱𐑂 𐑄 𐐲𐑉𐑃; 𐑄𐐯𐑉 𐑇𐐰𐑊 𐐺𐐨 𐑋𐐲𐑉𐐼𐐲𐑉𐑆, 𐐰𐑌𐐼 𐑉𐐱𐐺𐐮𐑍, 𐐰𐑌𐐼 𐑊𐐴𐐮𐑍, 𐐰𐑌𐐼 𐐼𐐨𐑅𐐨𐑂𐐮𐑍𐑆, 𐐰𐑌𐐼 𐐸𐐬𐑉𐐼𐐲𐑋𐑆, 𐐰𐑌𐐼 𐐫𐑊 𐑋𐐰𐑌𐐲𐑉 𐐱𐑂 𐐲𐐺𐐱𐑋𐐮𐑌𐐩𐑇𐐲𐑌𐑆; 𐐸𐐶𐐯𐑌 𐑄𐐯𐑉 𐑇𐐰𐑊 𐐺𐐨 𐑋𐐯𐑌𐐨 𐐸𐐭 𐐶𐐮𐑊 𐑅𐐩, 𐐔𐐭 𐑄𐐮𐑅, 𐐫𐑉 𐐼𐐭 𐑄𐐰𐐻, 𐐰𐑌𐐼 𐐮𐐻 𐑋𐐰𐐻𐐲𐑉𐐯𐑃 𐑌𐐱𐐻, 𐑁𐐫𐑉 𐑄 𐐢𐐫𐑉𐐼 𐐶𐐮𐑊 𐐲𐐹𐐸𐐬𐑊𐐼 𐑅𐐲𐐽 𐐰𐐻 𐑄 𐑊𐐰𐑅𐐻 𐐼𐐩. 𐐒𐐲𐐻 𐐶𐐬 𐐲𐑌𐐻𐐭 𐑅𐐲𐐽, 𐑁𐐫𐑉 𐑄𐐩 𐐪𐑉 𐐮𐑌 𐑄 𐑀𐐫𐑊 𐐱𐑂 𐐺𐐮𐐻𐐲𐑉𐑌𐐯𐑅, 𐐰𐑌𐐼 𐐮𐑌 𐑄 𐐺𐐱𐑌𐐼𐑆 𐐱𐑂 𐐮𐑌𐐮𐐿𐐶𐐮𐐻𐐨. 𐐏𐐩, 𐐮𐐻 𐑇𐐰𐑊 𐐿𐐲𐑋 𐐮𐑌 𐐰 𐐼𐐩 𐐸𐐶𐐯𐑌 𐑄𐐯𐑉 𐑇𐐰𐑊

𐐺 𐐽𐐲𐑉𐐽𐐯𐑆 𐐺𐐮𐑊𐐻 𐐲𐐹 𐑄𐐰𐐻 𐑇𐐰𐑊 𐑅𐐩, 𐐗𐐲𐑋 𐐲𐑌𐐻𐐭 𐑋𐐨, 𐐰𐑌𐐼 𐑁𐐫𐑉 𐐷𐐬𐑉 𐑋𐐲𐑌𐐨 𐐷𐐭 𐑇𐐰𐑊 𐐺 𐑁𐐫𐑉𐑀𐐮𐑂𐐲𐑌 𐐱𐑂 𐐷𐐬𐑉 𐑅𐐮𐑌𐑆. 𐐄 𐐷 𐐶𐐮𐐿𐐯𐐼 𐐰𐑌𐐼 𐐹𐐲𐑉𐑂𐐲𐑉𐑅, 𐐰𐑌𐐼 𐑅𐐻𐐮𐑁𐑌𐐯𐐿𐐻 𐐹𐐨𐐹𐑊, 𐐸𐐶𐐴 𐐸𐐰𐑂 𐐷 𐐺𐐮𐑊𐐻 𐐲𐐹 𐐽𐐲𐑉𐐽𐐯𐑆 𐐲𐑌𐐻𐐭 𐐷𐐬𐑉𐑅𐐯𐑊𐑂𐑆 𐐻𐐭 𐑀𐐯𐐻 𐑀𐐩𐑌? 𐐐𐐶𐐴 𐐸𐐰𐑂 𐐷 𐐻𐑉𐐰𐑌𐑅𐑁𐐮𐑀𐐷𐐲𐑉𐐼 𐑄 𐐸𐐬𐑊𐐨 𐐶𐐲𐑉𐐼 𐐱𐑂 𐐘𐐪𐐼, 𐑄𐐰𐐻 𐐷 𐑋𐐴𐐻 𐐺𐑉𐐮𐑍 𐐼𐐰𐑋𐑌𐐩𐑇𐐲𐑌 𐐲𐐹𐐱𐑌 𐐷𐐬𐑉 𐑅𐐬𐑊𐑆? 𐐒𐐨𐐸𐐬𐑊𐐼, 𐑊𐐳𐐿 𐐷 𐐲𐑌𐐻𐐭 𐑄 𐑉𐐯𐑂𐐯𐑊𐐩𐑇𐐲𐑌𐑆 𐐱𐑂 𐐘𐐪𐐼. 𐐙𐐫𐑉 𐐺𐐨𐐸𐐬𐑊𐐼, 𐑄 𐐻𐐴𐑋 𐐿𐐲𐑋𐐯𐑃 𐐰𐐻 𐑄𐐰𐐻 𐐼𐐩 𐐸𐐶𐐯𐑌 𐐫𐑊 𐑄𐐨𐑆 𐑃𐐮𐑍𐑆 𐑋𐐲𐑅𐐻 𐐺 𐑁𐐳𐑊𐑁𐐮𐑊𐐼.

4. 𐐒𐐨𐐸𐐬𐑊𐐼 𐑄 𐐢𐐫𐑉𐐼 𐐸𐐰𐑃 𐑇𐐬𐑌 𐐲𐑌𐐻𐐭 𐑋𐐨 𐑀𐑉𐐩𐐻 𐐰𐑌𐐼 𐑋𐐪𐑉𐑂𐐯𐑊𐐲𐑅 𐑃𐐮𐑍𐑆 𐐿𐐱𐑌𐑅𐐲𐑉𐑌𐐮𐑍 𐑄𐐰𐐻 𐐸𐐶𐐮𐐽 𐑋𐐲𐑅𐐻 𐑇𐐫𐑉𐐻𐑊𐐨 𐐿𐐲𐑋, 𐐰𐐻 𐑄𐐰𐐻 𐐼𐐩 𐐸𐐶𐐯𐑌 𐑄𐐨𐑆 𐑃𐐮𐑍𐑆 𐑇𐐰𐑊 𐐿𐐲𐑋 𐑁𐐬𐑉𐑃 𐐰𐑋𐐲𐑍 𐐷𐐭. 𐐒𐐨𐐸𐐬𐑊𐐼, 𐐴 𐑅𐐹𐐨𐐿 𐐲𐑌𐐻𐐭 𐐷𐐭 𐐰𐑆 𐐮𐑁 𐐷 𐐶𐐲𐑉 𐐹𐑉𐐯𐑆𐐯𐑌𐐻, 𐐰𐑌𐐼 𐐷𐐯𐐻 𐐷 𐐪𐑉 𐑌𐐱𐐻. 𐐒𐐲𐐻 𐐺𐐨𐐸𐐬𐑊𐐼, 𐐖𐐨𐑆𐐲𐑅 𐐗𐑉𐐴𐑅𐐻 𐐸𐐰𐑃 𐑇𐐬𐑌 𐐷𐐭 𐐲𐑌𐐻𐐭 𐑋𐐨, 𐐰𐑌𐐼 𐐴 𐑌𐐬 𐐷𐐬𐑉 𐐼𐐭𐐮𐑍; 𐐰𐑌𐐼 𐐴 𐑌𐐬 𐑄𐐰𐐻 𐐷 𐐼𐐭 𐐶𐐫𐐿 𐐮𐑌 𐑄 𐐹𐑉𐐴𐐼 𐐱𐑂 𐐷𐐬𐑉 𐐸𐐪𐑉𐐻𐑅; 𐐰𐑌𐐼 𐑄𐐯𐑉 𐐪𐑉 𐑌𐐲𐑌 𐑅𐐩𐑂 𐐩 𐑁𐐷𐐭 𐐬𐑌𐑊𐐨 𐐸𐐭 𐐼𐐭 𐑌𐐱𐐻 𐑊𐐮𐑁𐐻 𐑄𐐯𐑋𐑅𐐯𐑊𐑂𐑆 𐐲𐐹 𐐮𐑌 𐑄 𐐹𐑉𐐴𐐼 𐐱𐑂 𐑄𐐯𐑉 𐐸𐐪𐑉𐐻𐑅, 𐐲𐑌𐐻𐐭 𐑄 𐐶𐐯𐑉𐐮𐑍 𐐱𐑂 𐑂𐐯𐑉𐐨 𐑁𐐴𐑌 𐐰𐐹𐐰𐑉𐐯𐑊, 𐐲𐑌𐐻𐐭 𐐯𐑌𐑂𐐨𐐮𐑍, 𐐰𐑌𐐼 𐑅𐐻𐑉𐐴𐑁𐑅, 𐐰𐑌𐐼 𐑋𐐰𐑊𐐮𐑅, 𐐰𐑌𐐼 𐐹𐐲𐑉𐑅𐐨𐐿𐐷𐐭𐑇𐐲𐑌𐑆, 𐐰𐑌𐐼 𐐫𐑊 𐑋𐐰𐑌𐐲𐑉 𐐱𐑂 𐐮𐑌𐐮𐐿𐐶𐐮𐐻𐐨𐑆; 𐐰𐑌𐐼 𐐷𐐬𐑉 𐐽𐐲𐑉𐐽𐐯𐑆, 𐐷𐐩, 𐐨𐑂𐐲𐑌 𐐯𐑂𐐲𐑉𐐨 𐐶𐐲𐑌, 𐐸𐐰𐑂 𐐺𐐨𐐿𐐲𐑋 𐐹𐐱𐑊𐐭𐐻𐐯𐐼 𐐺𐐨𐐿𐐫𐑆 𐐱𐑂 𐑄 𐐹𐑉𐐴𐐼 𐐱𐑂 𐐷𐐬𐑉 𐐸𐐪𐑉𐐻𐑅. 𐐙𐐫𐑉 𐐺𐐨𐐸𐐬𐑊𐐼, 𐐷 𐐼𐐭 𐑊𐐲𐑂 𐑋𐐲𐑌𐐨, 𐐰𐑌𐐼 𐐷𐐬𐑉 𐑅𐐲𐐺𐑅𐐻𐐰𐑌𐑅𐐯𐑆, 𐐰𐑌𐐼 𐐷𐐬𐑉 𐑁𐐴𐑌 𐐰𐐹𐐰𐑉𐐯𐑊, 𐐰𐑌𐐼 𐑄 𐐰𐐼𐐫𐑉𐑌𐐮𐑍 𐐱𐑂 𐐷𐐬𐑉 𐐽𐐲𐑉𐐽𐐯𐑆, 𐑋𐐬𐑉 𐑄𐐰𐑌 𐐷 𐑊𐐲𐑂 𐑄 𐐹𐐭𐑉 𐐰𐑌𐐼 𐑄 𐑌𐐨𐐼𐐨, 𐑄 𐑅𐐮𐐿 𐐰𐑌𐐼 𐑄 𐐰𐑁𐑊𐐮𐐿𐐻𐐯𐐼. 𐐄 𐐷 𐐹𐐱𐑊𐐭𐑇𐐲𐑌𐑆, 𐐷 𐐸𐐮𐐹𐐬𐐿𐑉𐐮𐐻𐑅, 𐐷 𐐻𐐨𐐽𐐲𐑉𐑆, 𐐸𐐭 𐑅𐐯𐑊 𐐷𐐬𐑉𐑅𐐯𐑊𐑂𐑆 𐑁𐐫𐑉 𐑄𐐰𐐻 𐐸𐐶𐐮𐐽 𐐶𐐮𐑊 𐐿𐐰𐑍𐐿𐐲𐑉, 𐐸𐐶𐐴 𐐸𐐰𐑂 𐐷 𐐹𐐱𐑊𐐭𐐻𐐯𐐼 𐑄 𐐸𐐬𐑊𐐨 𐐕𐐲𐑉𐐽 𐐱𐑂 𐐘𐐪𐐼? 𐐐𐐶𐐴 𐐪𐑉 𐐷 𐐰𐑇𐐩𐑋𐐼 𐐻𐐭 𐐻𐐩𐐿 𐐲𐐹𐐱𐑌 𐐷𐐭 𐑄 𐑌𐐩𐑋 𐐱𐑂 𐐗𐑉𐐴𐑅𐐻? 𐐐𐐶𐐴 𐐼𐐭 𐐷 𐑌𐐱𐐻 𐑃𐐮𐑍𐐿 𐑄𐐰𐐻 𐑀𐑉𐐩𐐻𐐲𐑉 𐐮𐑆 𐑄 𐑂𐐰𐑊𐐷𐐭 𐐱𐑂 𐐰𐑌 𐐯𐑌𐐼𐑊𐐯𐑅 𐐸𐐰𐐹𐐨𐑌𐐯𐑅 𐑄𐐰𐑌 𐑄𐐰𐐻 𐑋𐐮𐑆𐐲𐑉𐐨 𐐸𐐶𐐮𐐽 𐑌𐐯𐑂𐐲𐑉 𐐼𐐴𐑆, 𐐺𐐨𐐿𐐫𐑆 𐐱𐑂 𐑄 𐐹𐑉𐐩𐑆 𐐱𐑂 𐑄 𐐶𐐲𐑉𐑊𐐼? 𐐐𐐶𐐴 𐐼𐐭 𐐷 𐐰𐐼𐐫𐑉𐑌 𐐷𐐬𐑉𐑅𐐯𐑊𐑂𐑆 𐐶𐐮𐑄 𐑄𐐰𐐻 𐐸𐐶𐐮𐐽 𐐸𐐰𐑃 𐑌𐐬 𐑊𐐴𐑁, 𐐰𐑌𐐼 𐐷𐐯𐐻 𐑅𐐲𐑁𐐲𐑉 𐑄 𐐸𐐲𐑍𐑀𐑉𐐨, 𐐰𐑌𐐼 𐑄 𐑌𐐨𐐼𐐨, 𐐰𐑌𐐼 𐑄 𐑌𐐩𐐿𐐯𐐼, 𐐰𐑌𐐼 𐑄 𐑅𐐮𐐿, 𐐰𐑌𐐼 𐑄 𐐰𐑁𐑊𐐮𐐿𐐻𐐯𐐼 𐐻𐐭 𐐹𐐰𐑅 𐐺𐐴 𐐷𐐭, 𐐰𐑌𐐼 𐑌𐐬𐐻𐐮𐑅 𐑄𐐯𐑋 𐑌𐐱𐐻? 𐐏𐐩, 𐐸𐐶𐐴 𐐼𐐭 𐐷 𐐺𐐮𐑊𐐼 𐐲𐐹 𐐷𐐬𐑉 𐑅𐐨𐐿𐑉𐐯𐐻 𐐰𐐺𐐱𐑋𐐮𐑌𐐩𐑇𐐲𐑌𐑆 𐐻𐐭 𐑀𐐯𐐻 𐑀𐐩𐑌, 𐐰𐑌𐐼 𐐿𐐫𐑆 𐑄𐐰𐐻 𐐶𐐮𐐼𐐬𐑆 𐑇𐐳𐐼 𐑋𐐬𐑉𐑌 𐐺𐐨𐑁𐐬𐑉 𐑄 𐐢𐐫𐑉𐐼, 𐐰𐑌𐐼 𐐫𐑊𐑅𐐬 𐐫𐑉𐑁𐐲𐑌𐑆 𐐻𐐭 𐑋𐐬𐑉𐑌 𐐺𐐨𐑁𐐬𐑉 𐑄 𐐢𐐫𐑉𐐼; 𐐰𐑌𐐼 𐐫𐑊𐑅𐐬 𐑄 𐐺𐑊𐐲𐐼 𐐱𐑂 𐑄𐐯𐑉 𐑁𐐪𐑄𐐲𐑉𐑆, 𐐰𐑌𐐼 𐑄𐐯𐑉 𐐸𐐲𐑆𐐺𐐲𐑌𐐼𐑆, 𐐻𐐭 𐐿𐑉𐐴 𐐲𐑌𐐻𐐭 𐑄 𐐢𐐫𐑉𐐼 𐑁𐑉𐐱𐑋 𐑄 𐑀𐑉𐐵𐑌𐐼, 𐑁𐐫𐑉 𐑂𐐯𐑌𐐾𐐲𐑌𐑅 𐐲𐐹𐐱𐑌 𐐷𐐬𐑉 𐐸𐐯𐐼𐑆? 𐐒𐐨𐐸𐐬𐑊𐐼, 𐑄 𐑅𐐬𐑉𐐼 𐐱𐑂 𐑂𐐯𐑌𐐾𐐲𐑌𐑅 𐐸𐐰𐑍𐐯𐑃 𐐬𐑂𐐲𐑉 𐐷𐐭; 𐐰𐑌𐐼 𐑄 𐐻𐐴𐑋 𐑅𐐭𐑌 𐐿𐐲𐑋𐐯𐑃 𐑄𐐰𐐻 𐐸𐐨 𐐰𐑂𐐯𐑌𐐾𐐯𐑃 𐑄 𐐺𐑊𐐲𐐼 𐐱𐑂 𐑄 𐑅𐐩𐑌𐐻𐑅 𐐲𐐹𐐱𐑌 𐐷𐐭, 𐑁𐐫𐑉 𐐸𐐨 𐐶𐐮𐑊 𐑌𐐱𐐻 𐑅𐐲𐑁𐐲𐑉 𐑄𐐯𐑉 𐐿𐑉𐐴𐑆 𐐯𐑌𐐨 𐑊𐐱𐑍𐐲𐑉.

5. 𐐈𐑌𐐼 𐑌𐐵, 𐐴 𐑅𐐹𐐨𐐿 𐐫𐑊𐑅𐐬 𐐿𐐱𐑌𐑅𐐲𐑉𐑌𐐮𐑍 𐑄𐐬𐑆 𐐸𐐭 𐐼𐐭 𐑌𐐱𐐻 𐐺𐐨𐑊𐐨𐑂 𐐮𐑌 𐐗𐑉𐐴𐑅𐐻. 𐐒𐐨𐐸𐐬𐑊𐐼, 𐐶𐐮𐑊 𐐷 𐐺𐐨𐑊𐐨𐑂 𐐮𐑌 𐑄 𐐼𐐩 𐐱𐑂 𐐷𐐬𐑉 𐑂𐐮𐑆𐐮𐐻𐐩𐑇𐐲𐑌, 𐐺𐐨𐐸𐐬𐑊𐐼, 𐐸𐐶𐐯𐑌 𐑄 𐐢𐐫𐑉𐐼 𐑇𐐰𐑊 𐐿𐐲𐑋; 𐐷𐐩, 𐐨𐑂𐐲𐑌 𐑄𐐰𐐻 𐑀𐑉𐐩𐐻 𐐼𐐩 𐐸𐐶𐐯𐑌 𐑄 𐐲𐑉𐑃 𐑇𐐰𐑊 𐐺 𐑉𐐬𐑊𐐼 𐐻𐐭𐑀𐐯𐑄𐐲𐑉 𐐰𐑆 𐐩 𐑅𐐿𐑉𐐬𐑊, 𐐰𐑌𐐼 𐑄 𐐯𐑊𐐯𐑋𐐯𐑌𐐻𐑅 𐑇𐐰𐑊 𐑋𐐯𐑊𐐻 𐐶𐐮𐑄 𐑁𐐲𐑉𐑂𐐯𐑌𐐻 𐐸𐐨𐐻; 𐐷𐐩, 𐐮𐑌 𐑄𐐰𐐻 𐑀𐑉𐐩𐐻 𐐼𐐩 𐐸𐐶𐐯𐑌 𐐷 𐑇𐐰𐑊 𐐺 𐐺𐑉𐐫𐐻 𐐻𐐭 𐑅𐐻𐐰𐑌𐐼 𐐺𐐨𐑁𐐬𐑉 𐑄 𐐢𐐰𐑋 𐐱𐑂 𐐘𐐪𐐼, 𐑄𐐯𐑌 𐐶𐐮𐑊 𐐷 𐑅𐐩 𐑄𐐰𐐻 𐑄𐐯𐑉 𐐮𐑆 𐑌𐐬 𐐘𐐪𐐼? 𐐜𐐯𐑌 𐐶𐐮𐑊 𐐷 𐑊𐐱𐑍𐐲𐑉 𐐼𐐨𐑌𐐴 𐑄 𐐗𐑉𐐴𐑅𐐻, 𐐫𐑉 𐐿𐐰𐑌 𐐷 𐐺𐐨𐐸𐐬𐑊𐐼 𐑄 𐐢𐐰𐑋 𐐱𐑂 𐐘𐐪𐐼? 𐐔𐐭 𐐷 𐑅𐐲𐐹𐐬𐑆 𐑄𐐰𐐻 𐐷 𐑇𐐰𐑊 𐐼𐐶𐐯𐑊 𐐶𐐮𐑄 𐐸𐐮𐑋 𐐲𐑌𐐼𐐲𐑉 𐐩 𐐿𐐱𐑌𐑇𐐲𐑅𐑌𐐯𐑅 𐐱𐑂 𐐷𐐬𐑉 𐑀𐐮𐑊𐐻? 𐐔𐐭 𐐷 𐑅𐐲𐐹𐐬𐑆 𐑄𐐰𐐻 𐐷 𐐿𐐳𐐼 𐐺 𐐸𐐰𐐹𐐨 𐐻𐐭 𐐼𐐶𐐯𐑊 𐐶𐐮𐑄 𐑄𐐰𐐻 𐐸𐐬𐑊𐐨 𐐒𐐨𐐮𐑍, 𐐸𐐶𐐯𐑌 𐐷𐐬𐑉 𐑅𐐬𐑊𐑆 𐐪𐑉 𐑉𐐰𐐿𐐻 𐐶𐐮𐑄 𐐩 𐐿𐐱𐑌𐑇𐐲𐑅𐑌𐐯𐑅 𐐱𐑂 𐑀𐐮𐑊𐐻 𐑄𐐰𐐻 𐐷 𐐸𐐰𐑂 𐐯𐑂𐐲𐑉 𐐰𐐺𐐷𐐭𐑆𐐼 𐐸𐐮𐑆 𐑊𐐫𐑆? 𐐒𐐨𐐸𐐬𐑊𐐼, 𐐴 𐑅𐐩 𐐲𐑌𐐻𐐭 𐐷𐐭, 𐑄𐐰𐐻 𐐷 𐐶𐐳𐐼 𐐺 𐑋𐐬𐑉 𐑋𐐮𐑆𐐲𐑉𐐲𐐺𐑊 𐐻𐐭 𐐼𐐶𐐯𐑊 𐐶𐐮𐑄 𐐩 𐐸𐐬𐑊𐐨 𐐰𐑌𐐼 𐐾𐐲𐑅𐐻 𐐘𐐪𐐼, 𐐲𐑌𐐼𐐲𐑉 𐐩 𐐿𐐱𐑌𐑇𐐲𐑅𐑌𐐯𐑅 𐐱𐑂 𐐷𐐬𐑉 𐑁𐐮𐑊𐑃𐐨𐑌𐐯𐑅 𐐺𐐨𐑁𐐬𐑉 𐐸𐐮𐑋, 𐑄𐐰𐑌 𐐷 𐐶𐐳𐐼 𐐻𐐭 𐐼𐐶𐐯𐑊 𐐶𐐮𐑄 𐑄 𐐼𐐰𐑋𐐼 𐑅𐐬𐑊𐑆 𐐮𐑌 𐐸𐐯𐑊! 𐐙𐐫𐑉 𐐺𐐨𐐸𐐬𐑊𐐼, 𐐸𐐶𐐯𐑌 𐐷 𐑇𐐰𐑊 𐐺 𐐺𐑉𐐫𐐻 𐐻𐐭 𐑅𐐨 𐐷𐐬𐑉 𐑌𐐩𐐿𐐯𐐼𐑌𐐯𐑅 𐐺𐐨𐑁𐐬𐑉 𐐘𐐪𐐼, 𐐰𐑌𐐼 𐐫𐑊𐑅𐐬, 𐑄 𐑀𐑊𐐬𐑉𐐨 𐐱𐑂 𐐘𐐪𐐼, 𐐰𐑌𐐼 𐑄 𐐸𐐬𐑊𐐨𐑌𐐯𐑅 𐐱𐑂 𐐖𐐨𐑆𐐲𐑅 𐐗𐑉𐐴𐑅𐐻, 𐐮𐐻 𐐶𐐮𐑊 𐐿𐐮𐑌𐐼𐑊 𐐩 𐑁𐑊𐐩𐑋 𐐱𐑂 𐐲𐑌𐐿𐐶𐐯𐑌𐐽𐐲𐐺𐑊 𐑁𐐴𐑉

𐐲𐐹𐐱𐑌 𐐷𐐭. 𐐄 𐑄𐐯𐑌 𐐷𐐨 𐐲𐑌𐐺𐐨𐑊𐐨𐑂𐐲𐑉𐑆, 𐐻𐐲𐑉𐑌 𐐷𐐨 𐐲𐑌𐐻𐐭 𐑄 𐐢𐐫𐑉𐐼; 𐐿𐑉𐐴 𐑋𐐴𐐻𐐮𐑊𐐨 𐐲𐑌𐐻𐐭 𐑄 𐐙𐐪𐑄𐐲𐑉 𐐮𐑌 𐑄 𐑌𐐩𐑋 𐐱𐑂 𐐖𐐨𐑆𐐲𐑅, 𐑄𐐰𐐻 𐐹𐐲𐑉𐐸𐐰𐐹𐑅 𐐷𐐨 𐑋𐐩 𐐺𐐨 𐑁𐐵𐑌𐐼 𐑅𐐹𐐱𐐻𐑊𐐯𐑅, 𐐹𐐷𐐭𐑉, 𐑁𐐩𐑉 𐐰𐑌𐐼 𐐸𐐶𐐴𐐻, 𐐸𐐰𐑂𐐮𐑍 𐐺𐐮𐑌 𐐿𐑊𐐯𐑌𐑆𐐼 𐐺𐐴 𐑄 𐐺𐑊𐐲𐐼 𐐱𐑂 𐑄 𐐢𐐰𐑋, 𐐰𐐻 𐑄𐐰𐐻 𐑀𐑉𐐩𐐻 𐐰𐑌𐐼 𐑊𐐰𐑅𐐻 𐐼𐐩.

6. 𐐈𐑌𐐼 𐐲𐑀𐐯𐑌 𐐌 𐑅𐐹𐐨𐐿 𐐲𐑌𐐻𐐭 𐐷𐐭, 𐐸𐐭 𐐼𐐨𐑌𐐴 𐑄 𐑉𐐯𐑂𐐯𐑊𐐩𐑇𐐲𐑌𐑆 𐐱𐑂 𐐘𐐱𐐼, 𐐰𐑌𐐼 𐑅𐐩 𐑄𐐰𐐻 𐑄𐐩 𐐪𐑉 𐐼𐐲𐑌 𐐲𐐶𐐩, 𐑄𐐰𐐻 𐑄𐐯𐑉 𐐪𐑉 𐑌𐐬 𐑉𐐯𐑂𐐯𐑊𐐩𐑇𐐲𐑌𐑆, 𐑌𐐫𐑉 𐐹𐑉𐐱𐑁𐐯𐑅𐐨𐑆, 𐑌𐐫𐑉 𐑀𐐮𐑁𐐻𐑅, 𐑌𐐫𐑉 𐐸𐐨𐑊𐐮𐑍, 𐑌𐐫𐑉 𐑅𐐹𐐨𐐿𐐮𐑍 𐐶𐐮𐑄 𐐻𐐲𐑍𐑆, 𐐰𐑌𐐼 𐑄 𐐮𐑌𐐻𐐲𐑉𐐹𐑉𐐯𐐻𐐩𐑇𐐲𐑌 𐐱𐑂 𐐻𐐲𐑍𐑆. 𐐒𐐨𐐸𐐬𐑊𐐼, 𐐌 𐑅𐐩 𐐲𐑌𐐻𐐭 𐐷𐐭, 𐐸𐐨 𐑄𐐰𐐻 𐐼𐐨𐑌𐐴𐐯𐑃 𐑄𐐨𐑆 𐑃𐐮𐑍𐑆, 𐑌𐐬𐐯𐑃 𐑌𐐱𐐻 𐑄 𐑀𐐱𐑅𐐹𐐯𐑊 𐐱𐑂 𐐗𐑉𐐴𐑅𐐻; 𐐷𐐩, 𐐸𐐨 𐐸𐐰𐑆 𐑌𐐱𐐻 𐑉𐐯𐐼 𐑄 𐑅𐐿𐑉𐐮𐐹𐐽𐐲𐑉𐑆; 𐐮𐑁 𐑅𐐬, 𐐸𐐨 𐐼𐐲𐑆 𐑌𐐱𐐻 𐐲𐑌𐐼𐐲𐑉𐑅𐐻𐐰𐑌𐐼 𐑄𐐯𐑋. 𐐙𐐫𐑉 𐐼𐐭 𐐶𐐨 𐑌𐐱𐐻 𐑉𐐨𐐼 𐑄𐐰𐐻 𐐘𐐱𐐼 𐐮𐑆 𐑄 𐑅𐐩𐑋 𐐷𐐯𐑅𐐻𐐲𐑉𐐼𐐩, 𐐻𐐭-𐐼𐐩, 𐐰𐑌𐐼 𐑁𐐫𐑉𐐯𐑂𐐲𐑉; 𐐰𐑌𐐼 𐐮𐑌 𐐸𐐮𐑋 𐑄𐐯𐑉 𐐮𐑆 𐑌𐐬 𐑂𐐩𐑉𐐨𐐲𐐺𐑊𐑌𐐯𐑅, 𐑌𐐨𐑄𐐲𐑉 𐑇𐐰𐐼𐐬 𐐱𐑂 𐐽𐐩𐑌𐐾𐐮𐑍? 𐐈𐑌𐐼 𐑌𐐵, 𐐮𐑁 𐐷𐐨 𐐸𐐰𐑂 𐐮𐑋𐐰𐐾𐐮𐑌𐐼 𐐲𐐹 𐐲𐑌𐐻𐐭 𐐷𐐭𐑉𐑅𐐯𐑊𐑂𐑆 𐐰 𐑀𐐱𐐼 𐐸𐐭 𐐼𐐲𐑃 𐑂𐐩𐑉𐐨, 𐐰𐑌𐐼 𐐮𐑌 𐐸𐐭𐑋 𐑄𐐯𐑉 𐐮𐑆 𐑇𐐰𐐼𐐬 𐐱𐑂 𐐽𐐩𐑌𐐾𐐮𐑍, 𐑄𐐯𐑌 𐐸𐐰𐑂 𐐷𐐨 𐐮𐑋𐐰𐐾𐐮𐑌𐐼 𐐲𐐹 𐐲𐑌𐐻𐐭 𐐷𐐭𐑉𐑅𐐯𐑊𐑂𐑆 𐐰 𐑀𐐱𐐼 𐐸𐐭 𐐮𐑆 𐑌𐐱𐐻 𐐰 𐐘𐐱𐐼 𐐱𐑂 𐑋𐐮𐑉𐐲𐐿𐑊𐑆. 𐐒𐐲𐐻 𐐺𐐨𐐸𐐬𐑊𐐼, 𐐌 𐐶𐐮𐑊 𐑇𐐬 𐐲𐑌𐐻𐐭 𐐷𐐭 𐐰 𐐘𐐱𐐼 𐐱𐑂 𐑋𐐮𐑉𐐲𐐿𐑊𐑆, 𐐨𐑂𐐯𐑌 𐑄 𐐘𐐱𐐼 𐐱𐑂 𐐈𐐺𐑉𐐲𐐸𐐰𐑋, 𐐰𐑌𐐼 𐑄 𐐘𐐱𐐼 𐐱𐑂 𐐌𐑆𐐲𐐿, 𐐰𐑌𐐼 𐑄 𐐘𐐱𐐼 𐐱𐑂 𐐖𐐩𐐿𐐲𐐺; 𐐰𐑌𐐼 𐐮𐐻 𐐮𐑆 𐑄𐐰𐐻 𐑅𐐩𐑋 𐐘𐐱𐐼 𐐸𐐭 𐐿𐑉𐐨𐐩𐐻𐐯𐐼 𐑄 𐐸𐐯𐑂𐐲𐑌𐑆 𐐰𐑌𐐼 𐑄 𐐲𐑉𐑃, 𐐰𐑌𐐼 𐐫𐑊 𐑃𐐮𐑍𐑆 𐑄𐐰𐐻 𐐮𐑌 𐑄𐐯𐑋 𐐪𐑉. 𐐒𐐨𐐸𐐬𐑊𐐼, 𐐸𐐨 𐐿𐑉𐐨𐐩𐐻𐐯𐐼 𐐁𐐼𐐲𐑋; 𐐰𐑌𐐼 𐐺𐐴 𐐁𐐼𐐲𐑋 𐐿𐐩𐑋 𐑄 𐑁𐐫𐑊 𐐱𐑂 𐑋𐐰𐑌. 𐐈𐑌𐐼 𐐺𐐨𐐿𐐫𐑆 𐐱𐑂 𐑄 𐑁𐐫𐑊 𐐱𐑂 𐑋𐐰𐑌, 𐐿𐐩𐑋 𐐖𐐨𐑆𐐲𐑅 𐐗𐑉𐐴𐑅𐐻, 𐐨𐑂𐐯𐑌 𐑄 𐐙𐐪𐑄𐐲𐑉 𐐰𐑌𐐼 𐑄 𐐝𐐲𐑌; 𐐰𐑌𐐼 𐐺𐐨𐐿𐐫𐑆 𐐱𐑂 𐐖𐐨𐑆𐐲𐑅 𐐗𐑉𐐴𐑅𐐻 𐐿𐐩𐑋 𐑄 𐑉𐐨𐐼𐐯𐑋𐐹𐑇𐐲𐑌 𐐱𐑂 𐑋𐐰𐑌. 𐐈𐑌𐐼 𐐺𐐨𐐿𐐫𐑆 𐐱𐑂 𐑄 𐑉𐐨𐐼𐐯𐑋𐐹𐑇𐐲𐑌 𐐱𐑂 𐑋𐐰𐑌, 𐐸𐐶𐐮𐐽 𐐿𐐩𐑋 𐐺𐐴 𐐖𐐨𐑆𐐲𐑅 𐐗𐑉𐐴𐑅𐐻, 𐑄𐐩 𐐪𐑉 𐐺𐑉𐐫𐐻 𐐺𐐰𐐿 𐐮𐑌𐐻𐐭 𐑄 𐐹𐑉𐐯𐑆𐐯𐑌𐑅 𐐱𐑂 𐑄 𐐢𐐫𐑉𐐼; 𐐷𐐩, 𐑄𐐮𐑅 𐐮𐑆 𐐸𐐶𐐯𐑉𐐮𐑌 𐐫𐑊 𐑋𐐯𐑌 𐐪𐑉 𐑉𐐨𐐼𐐨𐑋𐐼, 𐐺𐐨𐐿𐐫𐑆 𐑄 𐐼𐐯𐑃 𐐱𐑂 𐐗𐑉𐐴𐑅𐐻 𐐺𐑉𐐮𐑍𐐯𐑃 𐐻𐐭 𐐹𐐰𐑅 𐑄 𐑉𐐯𐑆𐐲𐑉𐐯𐐿𐑇𐐲𐑌, 𐐸𐐶𐐮𐐽 𐐺𐑉𐐮𐑍𐐯𐑃 𐐻𐐭 𐐹𐐰𐑅 𐐰 𐑉𐐨𐐼𐐯𐑋𐐹𐑇𐐲𐑌 𐑁𐑉𐐱𐑋 𐐰𐑌 𐐯𐑌𐐼𐑊𐐯𐑅 𐑅𐑊𐐨𐐹, 𐑁𐑉𐐱𐑋 𐐸𐐶𐐮𐐽 𐑅𐑊𐐨𐐹 𐐫𐑊 𐑋𐐯𐑌 𐑇𐐰𐑊 𐐺𐐨 𐐲𐐶𐐩𐐿𐐻 𐐺𐐴 𐑄 𐐹𐐵𐐲𐑉 𐐱𐑂 𐐘𐐱𐐼, 𐐸𐐶𐐯𐑌 𐑄 𐐻𐑉𐐲𐑋𐐹 𐑇𐐰𐑊 𐑅𐐵𐑌𐐼; 𐐰𐑌𐐼 𐑄𐐩 𐑇𐐰𐑊 𐐿𐐲𐑋 𐑁𐐬𐑉𐑃, 𐐺𐐬𐑃 𐑅𐑋𐐫𐑊 𐐰𐑌𐐼 𐑀𐑉𐐩𐐻, 𐐰𐑌𐐼 𐐫𐑊 𐑇𐐰𐑊 𐑅𐐻𐐰𐑌𐐼 𐐺𐐨𐑁𐐬𐑉 𐐸𐐮𐑆 𐐺𐐪𐑉, 𐐺𐐨𐐮𐑍 𐑉𐐨𐐼𐐨𐑋𐐼 𐐰𐑌𐐼 𐑊𐐭𐑅𐐻 𐑁𐑉𐐱𐑋 𐑄𐐮𐑅 𐐨𐐻𐐲𐑉𐑌𐐲𐑊 𐐺𐐰𐑌𐐼 𐐱𐑂 𐐼𐐯𐑃, 𐐸𐐶𐐮𐐽 𐐼𐐯𐑃 𐐮𐑆 𐐰 𐐻𐐯𐑋𐐹𐐬𐑉𐐲𐑊 𐐼𐐯𐑃; 𐐰𐑌𐐼 𐑄𐐯𐑌 𐐿𐐲𐑋𐐯𐑃 𐑄 𐐾𐐲𐐾𐑋𐐯𐑌𐐻 𐐱𐑂 𐑄 𐐐𐐬𐑊𐐨 𐐎𐐲𐑌 𐐲𐐹𐐱𐑌 𐑄𐐯𐑋; 𐐰𐑌𐐼 𐑄𐐯𐑌 𐐿𐐲𐑋𐐯𐑃 𐑄 𐐻𐐴𐑋 𐑄𐐰𐐻 𐐸𐐨 𐑄𐐰𐐻 𐐮𐑆 𐑁𐐮𐑊𐑃𐐨 𐑇𐐰𐑊 𐐺𐐨 𐑁𐐮𐑊𐑃𐐨 𐑅𐐻𐐮𐑊; 𐐰𐑌𐐼 𐐸𐐨 𐑄𐐰𐐻 𐐮𐑆 𐑉𐐴𐐽𐐲𐑅, 𐑇𐐰𐑊 𐐺𐐨 𐑉𐐴𐐽𐐲𐑅 𐑅𐐻𐐮𐑊; 𐐸𐐨 𐑄𐐰𐐻 𐐮𐑆 𐐸𐐰𐐹𐐨 𐑇𐐰𐑊 𐐺𐐨 𐐸𐐰𐐹𐐨 𐑅𐐻𐐮𐑊; 𐐰𐑌𐐼 𐐸𐐨 𐑄𐐰𐐻 𐐮𐑆 𐐲𐑌𐐸𐐰𐐹𐐨, 𐑇𐐰𐑊 𐐺𐐨 𐐲𐑌𐐸𐐰𐐹𐐨 𐑅𐐻𐐮𐑊.

7. 𐐈𐑌𐐼 𐑌𐐵, 𐐄 𐐫𐑊 𐐷𐐨 𐑄𐐰𐐻 𐐸𐐰𐑂 𐐮𐑋𐐰𐐾𐐮𐑌𐐼 𐐲𐐹 𐐲𐑌𐐻𐐭 𐐷𐐭𐑉𐑅𐐯𐑊𐑂𐑆 𐐰 𐑀𐐱𐐼 𐐸𐐭 𐐿𐐰𐑌 𐐼𐐭 𐑌𐐬 𐑋𐐮𐑉𐐲𐐿𐑊𐑆, 𐐌 𐐶𐐳𐐼 𐐰𐑅𐐿 𐐱𐑂 𐐷𐐭, 𐐐𐐰𐑂 𐐫𐑊 𐑄𐐨𐑆 𐑃𐐮𐑍𐑆 𐐹𐐰𐑅𐐻, 𐐱𐑂 𐐸𐐶𐐮𐐽 𐐌 𐐸𐐰𐑂 𐑅𐐹𐐬𐐿𐐲𐑌? 𐐐𐐰𐑆 𐑄 𐐯𐑌𐐼 𐐿𐐲𐑋 𐐷𐐯𐐻? 𐐒𐐨𐐸𐐬𐑊𐐼, 𐐌 𐑅𐐩 𐐲𐑌𐐻𐐭 𐐷𐐭, 𐐤𐐩; 𐐰𐑌𐐼 𐐘𐐱𐐼 𐐸𐐰𐑆 𐑌𐐱𐐻 𐑅𐐨𐑅𐐻 𐐻𐐭 𐐺𐐨 𐐰 𐐘𐐱𐐼 𐐱𐑂 𐑋𐐮𐑉𐐲𐐿𐑊𐑆. 𐐒𐐨𐐸𐐬𐑊𐐼, 𐐪𐑉 𐑌𐐱𐐻 𐑄 𐑃𐐮𐑍𐑆 𐑄𐐰𐐻 𐐘𐐱𐐼 𐐸𐐰𐑃 𐑉𐐫𐐻 𐑋𐐪𐑉𐑂𐐯𐑊𐐲𐑅 𐐮𐑌 𐐵𐑉 𐐴𐑆? 𐐏𐐩, 𐐰𐑌𐐼 𐐸𐐭 𐐿𐐰𐑌 𐐿𐐱𐑋𐐹𐑉𐐨𐐸𐐯𐑌𐐼 𐑄 𐑋𐐪𐑉𐑂𐐯𐑊𐐲𐑅 𐐶𐐲𐑉𐐿𐑅 𐐱𐑂 𐐘𐐱𐐼? 𐐐𐐭 𐑇𐐰𐑊 𐑅𐐩 𐑄𐐰𐐻 𐐮𐐻 𐐶𐐱𐑆 𐑌𐐱𐐻 𐐰 𐑋𐐮𐑉𐐲𐐿𐑊 𐑄𐐰𐐻 𐐺𐐴 𐐸𐐮𐑆 𐐶𐐲𐑉𐐼 𐑄 𐐸𐐯𐑂𐐲𐑌 𐐰𐑌𐐼 𐑄 𐐲𐑉𐑃 𐑇𐐳𐐼 𐐺𐐨; 𐐰𐑌𐐼 𐐺𐐴 𐑄 𐐹𐐵𐐲𐑉 𐐱𐑂 𐐸𐐮𐑆 𐐶𐐲𐑉𐐼, 𐑋𐐰𐑌 𐐶𐐱𐑆 𐐿𐑉𐐨𐐩𐐻𐐯𐐼 𐐱𐑂 𐑄 𐐼𐐲𐑅𐐻 𐐱𐑂 𐑄 𐐲𐑉𐑃; 𐐰𐑌𐐼 𐐺𐐴 𐑄 𐐹𐐵𐐲𐑉 𐐱𐑂 𐐸𐐮𐑆 𐐶𐐲𐑉𐐼, 𐐸𐐰𐑂 𐑋𐐮𐑉𐐲𐐿𐑊𐑆 𐐺𐐮𐑌 𐑉𐐫𐐻? 𐐈𐑌𐐼 𐐸𐐭 𐑇𐐰𐑊 𐑅𐐩 𐑄𐐰𐐻 𐐖𐐨𐑆𐐲𐑅 𐐗𐑉𐐴𐑅𐐻 𐐼𐐮𐐼 𐑌𐐱𐐻 𐐼𐐭 𐑋𐐯𐑌𐐨 𐑋𐐴𐐻𐐨 𐑋𐐮𐑉𐐲𐐿𐑊𐑆? 𐐈𐑌𐐼 𐑄𐐯𐑉 𐐶𐐲𐑉 𐑋𐐯𐑌𐐨 𐑋𐐴𐐻𐐨 𐑋𐐮𐑉𐐲𐐿𐑊𐑆 𐑉𐐫𐐻 𐐺𐐴 𐑄 𐐸𐐰𐑌𐐼𐑆 𐐱𐑂 𐑄 𐐰𐐹𐐱𐑅𐑊𐑆. 𐐈𐑌𐐼 𐐮𐑁 𐑄𐐯𐑉 𐐶𐐲𐑉 𐑋𐐮𐑉𐐲𐐿𐑊𐑆 𐑉𐐫𐐻 𐑄𐐯𐑌, 𐐸𐐶𐐴 𐐸𐐰𐑆 𐐘𐐱𐐼 𐑅𐐨𐑅𐐻 𐐻𐐭 𐐺𐐨 𐐰 𐐘𐐱𐐼 𐐱𐑂 𐑋𐐮𐑉𐐲𐐿𐑊𐑆, 𐐰𐑌𐐼 𐐷𐐯𐐻 𐐺𐐨 𐐰𐑌 𐐲𐑌𐐽𐐩𐑌𐐾𐐲𐐺𐑊 𐐒𐐨𐐮𐑍? 𐐈𐑌𐐼 𐐺𐐨𐐸𐐬𐑊𐐼, 𐐌 𐑅𐐩 𐐲𐑌𐐻𐐭 𐐷𐐭, 𐐸𐐨 𐐽𐐩𐑌𐐾𐐯𐑃 𐑌𐐱𐐻; 𐐮𐑁 𐑅𐐬, 𐐸𐐨 𐐶𐐳𐐼 𐑅𐐨𐑅 𐐻𐐭 𐐺𐐨 𐐘𐐱𐐼; 𐐰𐑌𐐼 𐐸𐐨 𐑅𐐨𐑅𐐯𐑃 𐑌𐐱𐐻 𐐻𐐭 𐐺𐐨 𐐘𐐱𐐼, 𐐰𐑌𐐼 𐐮𐑆 𐐰 𐐘𐐱𐐼 𐐱𐑂 𐑋𐐮𐑉𐐲𐐿𐑊𐑆. 𐐈𐑌𐐼 𐑄 𐑉𐐨𐑆𐐲𐑌 𐐸𐐶𐐴 𐐸𐐨 𐑅𐐨𐑅𐐯𐑃 𐐻𐐭 𐐼𐐭 𐑋𐐮𐑉𐐲𐐿𐑊𐑆 𐐲𐑋𐐲𐑍 𐑄 𐐽𐐮𐑊𐐼𐑉𐐯𐑌 𐐱𐑂 𐑋𐐯𐑌 𐐮𐑆 𐐺𐐨𐐿𐐫𐑆 𐑄𐐰𐐻 𐑄𐐩 𐐼𐐶𐐮𐑌𐐼𐑊 𐐮𐑌 𐐲𐑌𐐺𐐨𐑊𐐨𐑁, 𐐰𐑌𐐼 𐐼𐐨𐐹𐐪𐑉𐐻 𐑁𐑉𐐱𐑋 𐑄 𐑉𐐴𐐻 𐐶𐐩, 𐐰𐑌𐐼 𐑌𐐬 𐑌𐐱𐐻 𐑄 𐐘𐐱𐐼 𐐮𐑌 𐐸𐐭𐑋 𐑄𐐩 𐑇𐐳𐐼 𐐻𐑉𐐲𐑅𐐻. 𐐒𐐨𐐸𐐬𐑊𐐼, 𐐌 𐑅𐐩 𐐲𐑌𐐻𐐭 𐐷𐐭, 𐑄𐐰𐐻 𐐸𐐭𐑅𐐬 𐐺𐐨𐑊𐐨𐑂𐐯𐑃 𐐮𐑌 𐐗𐑉𐐴𐑅𐐻, 𐐼𐐵𐐻𐐮𐑍 𐑌𐐲𐑃𐐮𐑍, 𐐸𐐶𐐱𐐻𐑅𐐬𐐯𐑂𐐲𐑉 𐐸𐐨 𐑇𐐰𐑊 𐐰𐑅𐐿 𐑄 𐐙𐐪𐑄𐐲𐑉 𐐮𐑌 𐑄 𐑌𐐩𐑋 𐐱𐑂 𐐗𐑉𐐴𐑅𐐻 𐐮𐐻

𐑇𐐰𐑊 𐐺 𐑀𐑉𐐰𐑌𐐻𐐯𐐼 𐐸𐐮𐑋; 𐐰𐑌𐐼 𐑄𐐮𐑅 𐐹𐑉𐐱𐑋𐐮𐑅 𐐮𐑆 𐐲𐑌𐐻𐐭 𐐫𐑊, 𐐨𐑂𐐯𐑌 𐐲𐑌𐐻𐐭 𐑄 𐐯𐑌𐐼𐑆 𐐱𐑂 𐑄 𐐲𐑉𐑃. 𐐙𐐫𐑉 𐐺𐐨𐐸𐐬𐑊𐐼, 𐑄𐐲𐑅 𐑅𐐯𐐼 𐐖𐐨𐑆𐐲𐑅 𐐗𐑉𐐴𐑅𐐻, 𐑄 𐐝𐐲𐑌 𐐱𐑂 𐐘𐐱𐐼, 𐐲𐑌𐐻𐐭 𐐸𐐮𐑆 𐐼𐐮𐑅𐐴𐐹𐑊𐑆 𐐸𐐭 𐑇𐐳𐐼 𐐻𐐰𐑉𐐨; 𐐷𐐩, 𐐰𐑌𐐼 𐐫𐑊𐑅𐐬 𐐻𐐭 𐐫𐑊 𐐸𐐮𐑆 𐐼𐐮𐑅𐐴𐐹𐑊𐑆, 𐐮𐑌 𐑄 𐐸𐐨𐑉𐐮𐑍 𐐱𐑂 𐑄 𐑋𐐲𐑊𐐻𐐮𐐻𐐷𐐭𐐼, 𐐘𐐬 𐐷 𐐮𐑌𐐻𐐭 𐐫𐑊 𐑄 𐐶𐐲𐑉𐑊𐐼, 𐐰𐑌𐐼 𐐹𐑉𐐨𐐽 𐑄 𐐘𐐱𐑅𐐹𐐯𐑊 𐐻𐐭 𐐯𐑂𐐯𐑉𐐨 𐐿𐑉𐐨𐐻𐐷𐐭𐑉; 𐐰𐑌𐐼 𐐸𐐨 𐑄𐐰𐐻 𐐺𐐮𐑊𐐨𐑂𐐯𐑃, 𐐰𐑌𐐼 𐐮𐑆 𐐺𐐰𐐹𐐻𐐴𐑆𐐼, 𐑇𐐰𐑊 𐐺 𐑅𐐩𐑂𐐼, 𐐺𐐲𐐻 𐐸𐐨 𐑄𐐰𐐻 𐐺𐐮𐑊𐐨𐑂𐐯𐑃 𐑌𐐱𐐻, 𐑇𐐰𐑊 𐐺 𐐼𐐰𐑋𐐼. 𐐈𐑌𐐼 𐑄𐐨𐑆 𐑅𐐴𐑌𐑆 𐑇𐐰𐑊 𐑁𐐱𐑊𐐬 𐑄𐐯𐑋 𐑄𐐰𐐻 𐐺𐐮𐑊𐐨𐑂, 𐐮𐑌 𐑋𐐴 𐑌𐐩𐑋 𐑇𐐰𐑊 𐑄𐐩 𐐿𐐰𐑅𐐻 𐐵𐐻 𐐼𐐯𐑂𐑊𐑆; 𐑄𐐩 𐑇𐐰𐑊 𐑅𐐹𐐨𐐿 𐐶𐐮𐑄 𐑌𐐷𐐭 𐐻𐐲𐑍𐑆; 𐑄𐐩 𐑇𐐰𐑊 𐐻𐐩𐐿 𐐲𐐹 𐑅𐐲𐑉𐐹𐐯𐑌𐐻𐑅; 𐐰𐑌𐐼 𐐮𐑁 𐑄𐐩 𐐼𐑉𐐮𐑍𐐿 𐐯𐑌𐐨 𐐼𐐯𐐼𐑊𐐨 𐑃𐐮𐑍, 𐐮𐐻 𐑇𐐰𐑊 𐑌𐐱𐐻 𐐸𐐲𐑉𐐻 𐑄𐐯𐑋; 𐑄𐐩 𐑇𐐰𐑊 𐑊𐐩 𐐸𐐰𐑌𐐼𐑆 𐐱𐑌 𐑄 𐑅𐐮𐐿, 𐐰𐑌𐐼 𐑄𐐩 𐑇𐐰𐑊 𐑉𐐨𐐿𐐲𐑂𐐲𐑉; 𐐰𐑌𐐼 𐐸𐐭𐑅𐐬𐐯𐑂𐐲𐑉 𐑇𐐰𐑊 𐐺𐐮𐑊𐐨𐑂 𐐮𐑌 𐑋𐐴 𐑌𐐩𐑋, 𐐼𐐵𐐻𐐮𐑍 𐑌𐐲𐑃𐐮𐑍, 𐐲𐑌𐐻𐐭 𐐸𐐮𐑋 𐐶𐐮𐑊 𐐌 𐐿𐐱𐑌𐑁𐐲𐑉𐑋 𐐫𐑊 𐑋𐐴 𐐶𐐲𐑉𐐼𐑆, 𐐨𐑂𐐯𐑌 𐐲𐑌𐐻𐐭 𐑄 𐐯𐑌𐐼𐑆 𐐱𐑂 𐑄 𐐲𐑉𐑃. 𐐈𐑌𐐼 𐑌𐐵 𐐺𐐨𐐸𐐬𐑊𐐼, 𐐸𐐭 𐐿𐐰𐑌 𐑅𐐻𐐰𐑌𐐼 𐐰𐑀𐐯𐑌𐑅𐐻 𐑄 𐐶𐐲𐑉𐐿𐑅 𐐱𐑂 𐑄 𐐢𐐫𐑉𐐼? 𐐐𐐭 𐐿𐐰𐑌 𐐼𐐨𐑌𐐴 𐐸𐐮𐑆 𐑅𐐩𐐮𐑍𐑆? 𐐐𐐭 𐐶𐐮𐑊 𐑉𐐴𐑆 𐐲𐐹 𐐰𐑀𐐯𐑌𐑅𐐻 𐑄 𐐫𐑊𐑋𐐴𐐻𐐨 𐐹𐐵𐐲𐑉 𐐱𐑂 𐑄 𐐢𐐫𐑉𐐼? 𐐐𐐭 𐐶𐐮𐑊 𐐼𐐨𐑅𐐹𐐴𐑆 𐑄 𐐶𐐲𐑉𐐿𐑅 𐐱𐑂 𐑄 𐐢𐐫𐑉𐐼? 𐐐𐐭 𐐶𐐮𐑊 𐐼𐐨𐑅𐐹𐐴𐑆 𐑄 𐐽𐐮𐑊𐐼𐑉𐐯𐑌 𐐱𐑂 𐐗𐑉𐐴𐑅𐐻? 𐐒𐐨-𐐸𐐬𐑊𐐼, 𐐫𐑊 𐐷 𐐸𐐭 𐐪𐑉 𐐼𐐨𐑅𐐹𐐴𐑆𐐲𐑉𐑆 𐐱𐑂 𐑄 𐐶𐐲𐑉𐐿𐑅 𐐱𐑂 𐑄 𐐢𐐫𐑉𐐼, 𐑁𐐫𐑉 𐐷 𐑇𐐰𐑊 𐐶𐐲𐑌𐐼𐐲𐑉 𐐰𐑌𐐼 𐐹𐐯𐑉𐐮𐑇. 𐐄 𐑄𐐯𐑌 𐐼𐐨𐑅𐐹𐐴𐑆 𐑌𐐱𐐻, 𐐰𐑌𐐼 𐐶𐐲𐑌𐐼𐐲𐑉 𐑌𐐱𐐻, 𐐺𐐲𐐻 𐐸𐐪𐑉𐐿𐐯𐑌 𐐲𐑌𐐻𐐭 𐑄 𐐶𐐲𐑉𐐼𐑆 𐐱𐑂 𐑄 𐐢𐐫𐑉𐐼, 𐐰𐑌𐐼 𐐪𐑅𐐿 𐑄 𐐙𐐪𐑄𐐲𐑉 𐐮𐑌 𐑄 𐑌𐐩𐑋 𐐱𐑂 𐐖𐐨𐑆𐐲𐑅 𐑁𐐫𐑉 𐐸𐐶𐐱𐐻 𐑃𐐮𐑍𐑆 𐑅𐐬𐐯𐑂𐐲𐑉 𐐷 𐑇𐐰𐑊 𐑅𐐻𐐰𐑌𐐼 𐐮𐑌 𐑌𐐨𐐼. 𐐔𐐵𐐻 𐑌𐐱𐐻, 𐐺𐐲𐐻 𐐺 𐐺𐐮𐑊𐐨𐑂𐐮𐑍, 𐐰𐑌𐐼 𐐺𐐨𐑀𐐮𐑌 𐐰𐑆 𐐮𐑌 𐐻𐐴𐑋𐑆 𐐱𐑂 𐐬𐑊𐐼, 𐐰𐑌𐐼 𐐿𐐲𐑋 𐐲𐑌𐐻𐐭 𐑄 𐐢𐐫𐑉𐐼 𐐶𐐮𐑄 𐐫𐑊 𐐷𐐬𐑉 𐐸𐐪𐑉𐐻, 𐐰𐑌𐐼 𐐶𐐲𐑉𐐿 𐐵𐐻 𐐷𐐬𐑉 𐐬𐑌 𐑅𐐰𐑊𐑂𐐩𐑇𐐲𐑌 𐐶𐐮𐑄 𐑁𐐨𐑉 𐐰𐑌𐐼 𐐻𐑉𐐯𐑋𐐺𐑊𐐮𐑍 𐐺𐐨𐑁𐐬𐑉 𐐸𐐮𐑋. 𐐒 𐐶𐐴𐑆 𐐮𐑌 𐑄 𐐼𐐩𐑆 𐐱𐑂 𐐷𐐬𐑉 𐐹𐑉𐐬𐐺𐐩𐑇𐐲𐑌; 𐑅𐐻𐑉𐐮𐐹 𐐷𐐬𐑉𐑅𐐯𐑊𐑂𐑆 𐐱𐑂 𐐫𐑊 𐐲𐑌𐐿𐑊𐐨𐑌𐐯𐑅; 𐐪𐑅𐐿 𐑌𐐱𐐻, 𐑄𐐰𐐻 𐐷 𐑋𐐩 𐐿𐐱𐑌𐑅𐐭𐑋 𐐮𐐻 𐐱𐑌 𐐷𐐬𐑉 𐑊𐐲𐑅𐐻𐑅, 𐐺𐐲𐐻 𐐪𐑅𐐿 𐐶𐐮𐑄 𐐩 𐑁𐐲𐑉𐑋𐑌𐐯𐑅 𐐲𐑌𐑇𐐩𐐿𐑌, 𐑄𐐰𐐻 𐐷 𐐶𐐮𐑊 𐐷𐐨𐑊𐐼 𐐻𐐭 𐑌𐐬 𐐻𐐯𐑋𐐻𐐩𐑇𐐲𐑌, 𐐺𐐲𐐻 𐑄𐐰𐐻 𐐷 𐐶𐐮𐑊 𐑅𐐲𐑉𐑂 𐑄 𐐻𐑉𐐭 𐐰𐑌𐐼 𐑊𐐮𐑂𐐮𐑍 𐐘𐐱𐐼. 𐐝𐐨 𐑄𐐰𐐻 𐐷 𐐪𐑉 𐑌𐐱𐐻 𐐺𐐰𐐹𐐻𐐴𐑆𐐼 𐐲𐑌𐐶𐐲𐑉𐑄𐐮𐑊𐐨; 𐑅𐐨 𐑄𐐰𐐻 𐐷 𐐹𐐪𐑉𐐻𐐩𐐿 𐑌𐐱𐐻 𐐱𐑂 𐑄 𐑅𐐰𐐿𐑉𐐲𐑋𐐯𐑌𐐻 𐐱𐑂 𐐗𐑉𐐴𐑅𐐻 𐐲𐑌𐐶𐐲𐑉𐑄𐐮𐑊𐐨; 𐐺𐐲𐐻 𐑅𐐨 𐑄𐐰𐐻 𐐷 𐐼𐐭 𐐫𐑊 𐑃𐐮𐑍𐑆 𐐮𐑌 𐐶𐐲𐑉𐑄𐐨𐑌𐐯𐑅, 𐐰𐑌𐐼 𐐼𐐭 𐐮𐐻 𐐮𐑌 𐑄 𐑌𐐩𐑋 𐐱𐑂 𐐖𐐨𐑆𐐲𐑅 𐐗𐑉𐐴𐑅𐐻, 𐑄 𐐝𐐲𐑌 𐐱𐑂 𐑄 𐑊𐐮𐑂𐐮𐑍 𐐘𐐱𐐼: 𐐰𐑌𐐼 𐐮𐑁 𐐷 𐐼𐐭 𐑄𐐮𐑅, 𐐰𐑌𐐼 𐐯𐑌𐐼𐐷𐐭𐑉 𐐻𐐭 𐑄 𐐯𐑌𐐼, 𐐷 𐐶𐐮𐑊 𐐮𐑌 𐑌𐐬 𐐶𐐴𐑆 𐐺 𐐿𐐰𐑅𐐻 𐐵𐐻. 𐐒𐐨𐐸𐐬𐑊𐐼, 𐐌 𐑅𐐹𐐨𐐿 𐐲𐑌𐐻𐐭 𐐷𐐭 𐐰𐑆 𐑄𐐬 𐐌 𐑅𐐹𐐩𐐿 𐑁𐑉𐐱𐑋 𐑄 𐐼𐐯𐐼; 𐑁𐐫𐑉 𐐌 𐑌𐐬 𐑄𐐰𐐻 𐐷 𐑇𐐰𐑊 𐐸𐐰𐑂 𐑋𐐴 𐐶𐐲𐑉𐐼𐑆. 𐐗𐐱𐑌𐐼𐐯𐑋 𐑋𐐨 𐑌𐐱𐐻 𐐺𐐨𐐿𐐫𐑆 𐐱𐑂 𐑋𐐴𐑌 𐐮𐑋𐐹𐐲𐑉𐑁𐐯𐐿𐑇𐐲𐑌; 𐑌𐐨𐑄𐐲𐑉 𐑋𐐴 𐑁𐐪𐑄𐐲𐑉, 𐐺𐐨𐐿𐐫𐑆 𐐱𐑂 𐐸𐐮𐑆 𐐮𐑋𐐹𐐲𐑉𐑁𐐯𐐿𐑇𐐲𐑌; 𐑌𐐨𐑄𐐲𐑉 𐑄𐐯𐑋 𐐸𐐭 𐐸𐐰𐑂 𐑉𐐮𐐻𐑌 𐐺𐐨𐑁𐐬𐑉 𐐸𐐮𐑋; 𐐺𐐲𐐻 𐑉𐐰𐑄𐐲𐑉 𐑀𐐮𐑂 𐑃𐐰𐑍𐐿𐑅 𐐲𐑌𐐻𐐭 𐐘𐐱𐐼 𐑄𐐰𐐻 𐐸𐐨 𐐸𐐰𐑃 𐑋𐐩𐐼 𐑋𐐰𐑌𐐮𐑁𐐯𐑅𐐻 𐐲𐑌𐐻𐐭 𐐷𐐭 𐐵𐑉 𐐮𐑋𐐹𐐲𐑉𐑁𐐯𐐿𐑇𐐲𐑌𐑆, 𐑄𐐰𐐻 𐐷 𐑋𐐩 𐑊𐐲𐑉𐑌 𐐻𐐭 𐐺 𐑋𐐬𐑉 𐐶𐐴𐑆 𐑄𐐰𐑌 𐐶𐐨 𐐸𐐰𐑂 𐐺𐐮𐑌.

8. 𐐈𐑌𐐼 𐑌𐐵 𐐺𐐨𐐸𐐬𐑊𐐼, 𐐶𐐨 𐐸𐐰𐑂 𐑉𐐮𐐻𐑌 𐑄𐐮𐑅 𐑉𐐯𐐿𐐲𐑉𐐼 𐐰𐐿𐐫𐑉𐐼𐐮𐑍 𐐻𐐭 𐐵𐑉 𐑌𐐱𐑊𐐯𐐾, 𐐮𐑌 𐑄 𐐿𐐰𐑉𐐰𐐿𐐻𐐲𐑉𐑆 𐐸𐐶𐐮𐐽 𐐪𐑉 𐐿𐐫𐑊𐐼 𐐰𐑋𐐲𐑍 𐐲𐑅 𐑄 𐑉𐐨𐑁𐐫𐑉𐑋𐐼 𐐀𐐾𐐮𐐹𐑇𐐲𐑌, 𐐺𐐨𐐮𐑍 𐐸𐐰𐑌𐐼𐐯𐐼 𐐼𐐵𐑌 𐐰𐑌𐐼 𐐫𐑊𐐻𐐲𐑉𐐼 𐐺𐐴 𐐲𐑅, 𐐰𐐿𐐫𐑉𐐼𐐮𐑍 𐐻𐐭 𐐵𐑉 𐑋𐐰𐑌𐐲𐑉 𐐱𐑂 𐑅𐐹𐐨𐐽. 𐐈𐑌𐐼 𐐮𐑁 𐐵𐑉 𐐹𐑊𐐩𐐻𐑅 𐐸𐐰𐐼 𐐺𐐮𐑌 𐑅𐐲𐑁𐐮𐑇𐐯𐑌𐐻𐑊𐐨 𐑊𐐪𐑉𐐾, 𐐶𐐨 𐑇𐐳𐐼 𐐸𐐰𐑂 𐑉𐐮𐐻𐑌 𐐮𐑌 𐐐𐐨𐐺𐑉𐐭; 𐐺𐐲𐐻 𐑄 𐐐𐐨𐐺𐑉𐐭 𐐸𐐰𐑃 𐐺𐐮𐑌 𐐫𐑊𐐻𐐲𐑉𐐼 𐐺𐐴 𐐲𐑅 𐐫𐑊𐑅𐐬; 𐐰𐑌𐐼 𐐮𐑁 𐐶𐐨 𐐿𐐳𐐼 𐐸𐐰𐑂 𐑉𐐮𐐻𐑌 𐐮𐑌 𐐐𐐨𐐺𐑉𐐭, 𐐺𐐨𐐸𐐬𐑊𐐼, 𐐷 𐐶𐐳𐐼 𐐸𐐰𐑂 𐐸𐐰𐐼 𐑌𐐬 𐐮𐑋𐐹𐐲𐑉𐑁𐐯𐐿𐑇𐐲𐑌 𐐮𐑌 𐐵𐑉 𐑉𐐯𐐿𐐲𐑉𐐼. 𐐒𐐲𐐻 𐑄 𐐢𐐫𐑉𐐼 𐑌𐐬𐐯𐑃 𐑄 𐑃𐐮𐑍𐑆 𐐸𐐶𐐮𐐽 𐐶𐐨 𐐸𐐰𐑂 𐑉𐐮𐐻𐑌, 𐐰𐑌𐐼 𐐫𐑊𐑅𐐬 𐑄𐐰𐐻 𐑌𐐲𐑌 𐐲𐑄𐐲𐑉 𐐹𐐨𐐹𐑊 𐑌𐐬𐐯𐑃 𐐵𐑉 𐑊𐐰𐑍𐑀𐐶𐐯𐐾; 𐐰𐑌𐐼 𐐺𐐨𐐿𐐫𐑆 𐑄𐐰𐐻 𐑌𐐲𐑌 𐐲𐑄𐐲𐑉 𐐹𐐨𐐹𐑊 𐑌𐐬𐐯𐑃 𐐵𐑉 𐑊𐐰𐑍𐑀𐐶𐐯𐐾, 𐑄𐐯𐑉𐑁𐐬𐑉 𐐸𐐨 𐐸𐐰𐑃 𐐹𐑉𐐨𐐹𐐯𐑉𐐼 𐑋𐐨𐑌𐑆 𐑁𐐫𐑉 𐑄 𐐮𐑌𐐻𐐲𐑉𐐹𐑉𐐨𐐻𐐩𐑇𐐲𐑌 𐑄𐐯𐑉𐐱𐑂. 𐐈𐑌𐐼 𐑄𐐨𐑆 𐑃𐐮𐑍𐑆 𐐪𐑉 𐑉𐐮𐐻𐑌 𐑄𐐰𐐻 𐐶𐐨 𐑋𐐩 𐑉𐐮𐐼 𐐵𐑉 𐑀𐐪𐑉𐑋𐐯𐑌𐐻𐑅 𐐱𐑂 𐑄 𐐺𐑊𐐲𐐼 𐐱𐑂 𐐵𐑉 𐐺𐑉𐐯𐑄𐑉𐐯𐑌, 𐐸𐐭 𐐸𐐰𐑂 𐐼𐐶𐐮𐑌𐐼𐑊𐐼 𐐮𐑌 𐐲𐑌𐐺𐐨𐑊𐐨𐑁. 𐐈𐑌𐐼 𐐺𐐨𐐸𐐬𐑊𐐼, 𐑄𐐨𐑆 𐑃𐐮𐑍𐑆 𐐸𐐶𐐮𐐽 𐐶𐐨 𐐸𐐰𐑂 𐐼𐐨𐑆𐐴𐑉𐐼 𐐿𐐱𐑌𐑅𐐲𐑉𐑌𐐮𐑍 𐐵𐑉 𐐺𐑉𐐯𐑄𐑉𐐯𐑌, 𐐷𐐩, 𐐨𐑂𐐯𐑌 𐑄𐐯𐑉 𐑉𐐯𐑅𐐻𐐬𐑉𐐩𐑇𐐲𐑌 𐐻𐐭 𐑄 𐑌𐐱𐑊𐐯𐐾 𐐱𐑂 𐐗𐑉𐐴𐑅𐐻, 𐐪𐑉 𐐰𐐿𐐫𐑉𐐼𐐮𐑍 𐐻𐐭 𐑄 𐐹𐑉𐐯𐑉𐑆 𐐱𐑂 𐐫𐑊 𐑄 𐑅𐐩𐑌𐐻𐑅 𐐸𐐭 𐐸𐐰𐑂 𐐼𐐶𐐯𐑊𐐻 𐐮𐑌 𐑄 𐑊𐐰𐑌𐐼. 𐐈𐑌𐐼 𐑋𐐩 𐑄 𐐢𐐫𐑉𐐼 𐐖𐐨𐑆𐐲𐑅 𐐗𐑉𐐴𐑅𐐻 𐑀𐑉𐐰𐑌𐐻 𐑄𐐰𐐻 𐑄𐐯𐑉 𐐹𐑉𐐯𐑉𐑆 𐑋𐐩 𐐺 𐐪𐑌𐑅𐐲𐑉𐐼 𐐰𐐿𐐫𐑉𐐼𐐮𐑍 𐐻𐐭 𐑄𐐯𐑉 𐑁𐐩𐑃; 𐐰𐑌𐐼 𐑋𐐩 𐐘𐐱𐐼 𐑄 𐐙𐐪𐑄𐐲𐑉 𐑉𐐨𐑋𐐯𐑋𐐺𐐲𐑉 𐑄 𐐿𐐲𐑂𐐯𐑌𐐰𐑌𐐻 𐐸𐐶𐐮𐐽 𐐸𐐨 𐐸𐐰𐑃 𐑋𐐩𐐼 𐐶𐐮𐑄 𐑄 𐐸𐐵𐑅 𐐱𐑂 𐐆𐑆𐑉𐐩𐐯𐑊; 𐐰𐑌𐐼 𐑋𐐩 𐐸𐐨 𐐺𐑊𐐯𐑅 𐑄𐐯𐑋 𐑁𐐫𐑉𐐯𐑂𐐲𐑉, 𐑃𐑉𐐭 𐑁𐐩𐑃 𐐱𐑌 𐑄 𐑌𐐩𐑋 𐐱𐑂 𐐖𐐨𐑆𐐲𐑅 𐐗𐑉𐐴𐑅𐐻. 𐐁𐑋𐐯𐑌.

𐐜 𐐒𐐳𐐿 𐐱𐑂 𐐀𐑃𐐲𐑉.

𐐕𐐰𐐹𐐻𐐲𐑉 I.

1. 𐐈𐑌𐐼 𐑌𐐵 𐐌, 𐐣𐐬𐑉𐐬𐑌𐐴, 𐐹𐑉𐐬𐑅𐐨𐐼 𐐻𐐭 𐑀𐐮𐑂 𐐰𐑌 𐐰𐐿𐐵𐑌𐐻 𐐱𐑂 𐑄𐐬𐑆 𐐩𐑌𐑇𐐲𐑌𐐻 𐐮𐑌𐐸𐐰𐐺𐐮𐐻𐐰𐑌𐐻𐑅 𐐸𐐭 𐐶𐐲𐑉 𐐼𐐲𐑅𐐻𐑉𐐱𐐮𐐼 𐐺𐐴 𐑄 𐐸𐐰𐑌𐐼 𐐱𐑂 𐑄 𐐢𐐱𐑉𐐼 𐐲𐐹𐐱𐑌 𐑄 𐑁𐐩𐑅 𐐱𐑂 𐑄𐐮𐑅 𐑌𐐱𐑉𐑃 𐐿𐐲𐑌𐐻𐑉𐐨. 𐐈𐑌𐐼 𐐌 𐐻𐐩𐐿 𐑋𐐴𐑌 𐐰𐐿𐐵𐑌𐐻 𐑁𐑉𐐱𐑋 𐑄 𐐻𐐶𐐯𐑌𐐻𐐨 𐐰𐑌𐐼 𐑁𐐬𐑉 𐐹𐑊𐐩𐐻𐑅 𐐸𐐶𐐮𐐽 𐐶𐐲𐑉 𐑁𐐵𐑌𐐼 𐐺𐐴 𐑄 𐐹𐐨𐐹𐑊 𐐱𐑂 𐐢𐐮𐑋𐐸𐐴, 𐐸𐐶𐐮𐐽 𐐮𐑆 𐐿𐐫𐑊𐐼 𐑄 𐐒𐐳𐐿 𐐱𐑂 𐐀𐑃𐐲𐑉. 𐐈𐑌𐐼 𐐰𐑆 𐐌 𐑅𐐲𐐹𐐬𐑆 𐑄𐐰𐐻 𐑄 𐑁𐐲𐑉𐑅𐐻 𐐹𐐪𐑉𐐻 𐐱𐑂 𐑄𐐮𐑅 𐑉𐐯𐐿𐐲𐑉𐐼, 𐐸𐐶𐐮𐐽 𐑅𐐹𐐨𐐿𐑅 𐐿𐐱𐑌𐑅𐐲𐑉𐑌𐐮𐑍 𐑄 𐐿𐑉𐐨𐐩𐑇𐐲𐑌 𐐱𐑂 𐑄 𐐶𐐲𐑉𐑊𐐼, 𐐰𐑌𐐼 𐐫𐑊𐑅𐐬 𐐱𐑂 𐐈𐐼𐐲𐑋, 𐐰𐑌𐐼 𐐰𐑌 𐐰𐐿𐐵𐑌𐐻 𐑁𐑉𐐱𐑋 𐑄𐐰𐐻 𐐻𐐴𐑋 𐐨𐑂𐐲𐑌 𐐻𐐭 𐑄 𐑀𐑉𐐩𐐻 𐐻𐐵𐐲𐑉, 𐐰𐑌𐐼 𐐸𐐶𐐱𐐻𐑅𐐬𐐯𐑂𐐲𐑉 𐑃𐐮𐑍𐑆 𐐻𐑉𐐰𐑌𐑅𐐹𐐴𐑉𐐼 𐐲𐑋𐐲𐑍 𐑄 𐐽𐐮𐑊𐐼𐑉𐐯𐑌 𐐱𐑂 𐑋𐐯𐑌 𐐲𐑌𐐻𐐮𐑊 𐑄𐐰𐐻 𐐻𐐴𐑋, 𐐮𐑆 𐐸𐐰𐐼 𐐲𐑋𐐲𐑍 𐑄 𐐖𐐭𐑆, 𐑄𐐯𐑉𐑁𐐬𐑉 𐐌 𐐼𐐭 𐑌𐐱𐐻 𐑉𐐴𐐻 𐑄𐐬𐑆 𐑃𐐮𐑍𐑆 𐐸𐐶𐐮𐐽 𐐻𐑉𐐰𐑌𐑅𐐹𐐴𐑉𐐼 𐑁𐑉𐐱𐑋 𐑄 𐐼𐐩𐑆 𐐱𐑂 𐐈𐐼𐐲𐑋 𐐲𐑌𐐻𐐮𐑊 𐑄𐐰𐐻 𐐻𐐴𐑋; 𐐺𐐲𐐻 𐑄𐐩 𐐪𐑉 𐐸𐐰𐐼 𐐲𐐹𐐱𐑌 𐑄 𐐹𐑊𐐩𐐻𐑅; 𐐰𐑌𐐼 𐐸𐐭𐑅𐐬 𐑁𐐴𐑌𐐼𐐯𐑃 𐑄𐐯𐑋, 𐑄 𐑅𐐩𐑋 𐐶𐐮𐑊 𐐸𐐰𐑂 𐐹𐐵𐐲𐑉 𐑄𐐰𐐻 𐐸𐐨 𐑋𐐩 𐑀𐐯𐐻 𐑄 𐑁𐐳𐑊 𐐰𐐿𐐵𐑌𐐻. 𐐒𐐲𐐻 𐐺𐐨𐐸𐐬𐑊𐐼, 𐐌 𐑀𐐮𐑂 𐑌𐐱𐐻 𐑄 𐑁𐐳𐑊 𐐰𐐿𐐵𐑌𐐻, 𐐺𐐲𐐻 𐐩 𐐹𐐪𐑉𐐻 𐐱𐑂 𐑄 𐐰𐐿𐐵𐑌𐐻 𐐌 𐑀𐐮𐑂, 𐑁𐑉𐐱𐑋 𐑄 𐐻𐐵𐐲𐑉 𐐼𐐵𐑌 𐐲𐑌𐐻𐐮𐑊 𐑄𐐩 𐐶𐐲𐑉 𐐼𐐲𐑅𐐻𐑉𐐱𐐮𐐼. 𐐈𐑌𐐼 𐐱𐑌 𐑄𐐮𐑅 𐐶𐐴𐑆 𐐼𐐭 𐐌 𐑀𐐮𐑂 𐑄 𐐰𐐿𐐵𐑌𐐻. 𐐐𐐨 𐑄𐐰𐐻 𐑉𐐬𐐻 𐑄𐐮𐑅 𐑉𐐯𐐿𐐲𐑉𐐼 𐐶𐐱𐑆 𐐀𐑃𐐲𐑉, 𐐰𐑌𐐼 𐐸𐐨 𐐶𐐱𐑆 𐐩 𐐼𐐯𐑅𐐯𐑌𐐼𐐰𐑌𐐻 𐐱𐑂 𐐗𐐬𐑉𐐨𐐰𐑌𐐻𐐲𐑉: 𐐗𐐬𐑉𐐨𐐰𐑌𐐻𐐲𐑉 𐐶𐐱𐑆 𐑄 𐑅𐐲𐑌 𐐱𐑂 𐐣𐐬𐑉𐐱𐑌; 𐐰𐑌𐐼 𐐣𐐬𐑉𐐱𐑌 𐐶𐐱𐑆 𐑄 𐑅𐐲𐑌 𐐱𐑂 𐐀𐑃𐐯𐑋; 𐐰𐑌𐐼 𐐀𐑃𐐯𐑋 𐐶𐐱𐑆 𐑄 𐑅𐐲𐑌 𐐱𐑂 𐐈𐐸𐐪; 𐐰𐑌𐐼 𐐈𐐸𐐪 𐐶𐐱𐑆 𐑄 𐑅𐐲𐑌 𐐱𐑂 𐐝𐐯𐑃; 𐐰𐑌𐐼 𐐝𐐯𐑃 𐐶𐐱𐑆 𐑄 𐑅𐐲𐑌 𐐱𐑂 𐐟𐐮𐐺𐑊𐐱𐑌; 𐐰𐑌𐐼 𐐟𐐮𐐺𐑊𐐱𐑌 𐐶𐐱𐑆 𐑄 𐑅𐐲𐑌 𐐱𐑂 𐐗𐐱𐑋; 𐐰𐑌𐐼 𐐗𐐱𐑋 𐐶𐐱𐑆 𐑄 𐑅𐐲𐑌 𐐱𐑂 𐐗𐐬𐑉𐐨𐐰𐑌𐐻𐐲𐑋; 𐐰𐑌𐐼 𐐗𐐬𐑉𐐨𐐰𐑌𐐻𐐲𐑋 𐐶𐐱𐑆 𐑄 𐑅𐐲𐑌 𐐱𐑂 𐐈𐑋𐑌𐐮𐑀𐐰𐐼𐐪; 𐐰𐑌𐐼 𐐈𐑋𐑌𐐮𐑀𐐰𐐼𐐪 𐐶𐐱𐑆 𐑄 𐑅𐐲𐑌 𐐱𐑂 𐐁𐑉𐐲𐑌; 𐐰𐑌𐐼 𐐁𐑉𐐲𐑌 𐐶𐐱𐑆 𐐩 𐐼𐐯𐑅𐐯𐑌𐐼𐐰𐑌𐐻 𐐱𐑂 𐐐𐐯𐑃, 𐐸𐐭 𐐶𐐱𐑆 𐑄 𐑅𐐲𐑌 𐐱𐑂 𐐐𐐨𐐪𐑉𐑃𐐲𐑋; 𐐰𐑌𐐼 𐐐𐐨𐐪𐑉𐑃𐐲𐑋 𐐶𐐱𐑆 𐑄 𐑅𐐲𐑌 𐐱𐑂 𐐢𐐮𐐺; 𐐰𐑌𐐼 𐐢𐐮𐐺 𐐶𐐱𐑆 𐑄 𐑅𐐲𐑌 𐐱𐑂 𐐗𐐮𐑇; 𐐰𐑌𐐼 𐐗𐐮𐑇 𐐶𐐱𐑆 𐑄 𐑅𐐲𐑌 𐐱𐑂 𐐗𐐬𐑉𐐱𐑋; 𐐰𐑌𐐼 𐐗𐐬𐑉𐐱𐑋 𐐶𐐱𐑆 𐑄 𐑅𐐲𐑌 𐐱𐑂 𐐢𐐨𐑂𐐴; 𐐰𐑌𐐼 𐐢𐐨𐑂𐐴 𐐶𐐱𐑆 𐑄 𐑅𐐲𐑌 𐐱𐑂 𐐗𐐮𐑋; 𐐰𐑌𐐼 𐐗𐐮𐑋 𐐶𐐱𐑆 𐑄 𐑅𐐲𐑌 𐐱𐑂 𐐣𐐬𐑉𐐨𐐰𐑌𐐻𐐲𐑌; 𐐰𐑌𐐼 𐐣𐐬𐑉𐐨𐐰𐑌𐐻𐐲𐑌 𐐶𐐱𐑆 𐐩 𐐼𐐯𐑅𐐯𐑌𐐼𐐰𐑌𐐻 𐐱𐑂 𐐡𐐮𐐹𐑊𐐰𐐿𐐮𐑇; 𐐰𐑌𐐼 𐐡𐐮𐐹𐑊𐐰𐐿𐐮𐑇 𐐶𐐱𐑆 𐑄 𐑅𐐲𐑌 𐐱𐑂 𐐟𐐯𐑆; 𐐰𐑌𐐼 𐐟𐐯𐑆 𐐶𐐱𐑆 𐑄 𐑅𐐲𐑌 𐐱𐑂 𐐐𐐯𐑃; 𐐰𐑌𐐼 𐐐𐐯𐑃 𐐶𐐱𐑆 𐑄 𐑅𐐲𐑌 𐐱𐑂 𐐗𐐱𐑋; 𐐰𐑌𐐼 𐐗𐐱𐑋 𐐶𐐱𐑆 𐑄 𐑅𐐲𐑌 𐐱𐑂 𐐗𐐬𐑉𐐨𐐰𐑌𐐻𐐲𐑋; 𐐰𐑌𐐼 𐐗𐐬𐑉𐐨𐐰𐑌𐐻𐐲𐑋 𐐶𐐱𐑆 𐑄 𐑅𐐲𐑌 𐐱𐑂 𐐀𐑋𐐲𐑉; 𐐰𐑌𐐼 𐐀𐑋𐐲𐑉 𐐶𐐱𐑆 𐑄 𐑅𐐲𐑌 𐐱𐑂 𐐄𐑋𐐲𐑉; 𐐰𐑌𐐼 𐐄𐑋𐐲𐑉 𐐶𐐱𐑆 𐑄 𐑅𐐲𐑌 𐐱𐑂 𐐟𐐭𐑊; 𐐰𐑌𐐼 𐐟𐐭𐑊 𐐶𐐱𐑆 𐑄 𐑅𐐲𐑌 𐐱𐑂 𐐗𐐮𐐺; 𐐰𐑌𐐼 𐐗𐐮𐐺 𐐶𐐱𐑆 𐑄 𐑅𐐲𐑌 𐐱𐑂 𐐄𐑉𐐴𐐸𐐪, 𐐸𐐭 𐐶𐐱𐑆 𐑄 𐑅𐐲𐑌 𐐱𐑂 𐐖𐐩𐑉𐐯𐐼; 𐐸𐐶𐐮𐐽 𐐖𐐩𐑉𐐯𐐼 𐐿𐐩𐑋 𐑁𐐬𐑉𐑃 𐐶𐐮𐑄 𐐸𐐮𐑆 𐐺𐑉𐐲𐑄𐐲𐑉 𐐰𐑌𐐼 𐑄𐐩𐑉 𐑁𐐰𐑋𐐮𐑊𐐨𐑆, 𐐶𐐮𐑄 𐑅𐐲𐑋 𐐲𐑄𐐲𐑉𐑆 𐐰𐑌𐐼 𐑄𐐩𐑉 𐑁𐐰𐑋𐐮𐑊𐐨𐑆, 𐑁𐑉𐐱𐑋 𐑄 𐑀𐑉𐐩𐐻 𐐻𐐵𐐲𐑉, 𐐰𐐻 𐑄 𐐻𐐴𐑋 𐑄 𐐢𐐱𐑉𐐼 𐐿𐐱𐑌𐑁𐐵𐑌𐐼𐐯𐐼 𐑄 𐑊𐐰𐑍𐑀𐐶𐐩𐐾 𐐱𐑂 𐑄 𐐹𐐨𐐹𐑊, 𐐰𐑌𐐼 𐑅𐐶𐐬𐑉 𐐮𐑌 𐐸𐐮𐑆 𐑉𐐪𐑃 𐑄𐐰𐐻 𐑄𐐩 𐑇𐐳𐐼 𐐺𐐨 𐑅𐐿𐐰𐐻𐐲𐑉𐐼 𐐲𐐹𐐱𐑌 𐐫𐑊 𐑄 𐑁𐐩𐑅 𐐱𐑂 𐑄 𐐲𐑉𐑃; 𐐰𐑌𐐼 𐐰𐐿𐐬𐑉𐐼𐐮𐑍 𐐻𐐭 𐑄 𐐶𐐲𐑉𐐼 𐐱𐑂 𐑄 𐐢𐐱𐑉𐐼 𐑄 𐐹𐐨𐐹𐑊 𐐶𐐲𐑉 𐑅𐐿𐐰𐐻𐐲𐑉𐐼. 𐐈𐑌𐐼 𐑄 𐐺𐑉𐐲𐑄𐐲𐑉 𐐱𐑂 𐐖𐐩𐑉𐐯𐐼 𐐺𐐨𐐮𐑍 𐐩 𐑊𐐪𐑉𐐾 𐐰𐑌𐐼 𐑋𐐴𐐻𐐨 𐑋𐐰𐑌, 𐐰𐑌𐐼 𐐩 𐑋𐐰𐑌 𐐸𐐴𐑊𐐨 𐑁𐐩𐑂𐐲𐑉𐐼 𐐱𐑂 𐑄 𐐢𐐱𐑉𐐼; 𐑁𐐱𐑉 𐐖𐐩𐑉𐐯𐐼 𐐸𐐮𐑆 𐐺𐑉𐐲𐑄𐐲𐑉 𐑅𐐯𐐼 𐐲𐑌𐐻𐐭 𐐸𐐮𐑋, 𐐗𐑉𐐴 𐐲𐑌𐐻𐐭 𐑄 𐐢𐐱𐑉𐐼, 𐑄𐐰𐐻 𐐸𐐨 𐑋𐐩 𐑌𐐱𐐻 𐐿𐐱𐑌𐑁𐐵𐑌𐐼 𐐲𐑅 𐑄𐐰𐐻 𐐶𐐨 𐑋𐐩 𐑌𐐱𐐻 𐐲𐑌𐐼𐐲𐑉𐑅𐐻𐐰𐑌𐐼 𐐵𐐲𐑉 𐐶𐐲𐑉𐐼𐑆. 𐐈𐑌𐐼 𐐮𐐻 𐐿𐐩𐑋 𐐻𐐭 𐐹𐐰𐑅 𐑄𐐰𐐻 𐑄 𐐺𐑉𐐲𐑄𐐲𐑉 𐐱𐑂 𐐖𐐩𐑉𐐯𐐼 𐐼𐐮𐐼 𐐿𐑉𐐴 𐐲𐑌𐐻𐐭 𐑄 𐐢𐐱𐑉𐐼,

𐐰𐑌𐐼 𐑄 𐐢𐐫𐑉𐐼 𐐸𐐰𐐼 𐐿𐐲𐑋𐐹𐐰𐑇𐐲𐑌 𐐲𐐹𐐱𐑌 𐐖𐐯𐑉𐐲𐐼; 𐑄𐐯𐑉𐑁𐐫𐑉 𐐸𐐨 𐐼𐐮𐐼 𐑌𐐱𐐻 𐐿𐐱𐑌𐑁𐐵𐑌𐐼 𐑄 𐑊𐐰𐑍𐑀𐐶𐐩𐐾 𐐱𐑂 𐐖𐐯𐑉𐐲𐐼; 𐐰𐑌𐐼 𐐖𐐯𐑉𐐲𐐼 𐐰𐑌𐐼 𐐸𐐮𐑆 𐐺𐑉𐐲𐑄𐐲𐑉 𐐶𐐲𐑉 𐑌𐐱𐐻 𐐿𐐱𐑌𐑁𐐵𐑌𐐼𐐲𐐼. 𐐜𐐯𐑌 𐐖𐐯𐑉𐐲𐐼 𐑅𐐯𐐼 𐐲𐑌𐐻𐐭 𐐸𐐮𐑆 𐐺𐑉𐐲𐑄𐐲𐑉, 𐐗𐑉𐐴 𐐲𐑀𐐯𐑌 𐐲𐑌𐐻𐐭 𐑄 𐐢𐐫𐑉𐐼, 𐐰𐑌𐐼 𐐮𐐻 𐑋𐐩 𐐺 𐑄𐐰𐐻 𐐸𐐨 𐐶𐐮𐑊 𐐻𐐲𐑉𐑌 𐐲𐐶𐐩 𐐸𐐮𐑆 𐐰𐑍𐑀𐐲𐑉 𐑁𐑉𐐱𐑋 𐑄𐐯𐑋 𐐸𐐭 𐐪𐑉 𐐵𐑉 𐑁𐑉𐐯𐑌𐐼𐑆, 𐑄𐐰𐐻 𐐸𐐨 𐐿𐐱𐑌𐑁𐐵𐑌𐐼 𐑌𐐱𐐻 𐑄𐐩𐑉 𐑊𐐰𐑍𐑀𐐶𐐩𐐾. 𐐈𐑌𐐼 𐐮𐐻 𐐿𐐩𐑋 𐐻𐐭 𐐹𐐰𐑅 𐑄𐐰𐐻 𐑄 𐐺𐑉𐐲𐑄𐐲𐑉 𐐱𐑂 𐐖𐐯𐑉𐐲𐐼 𐐼𐐮𐐼 𐐿𐑉𐐴 𐐲𐑌𐐻𐐭 𐑄 𐐢𐐫𐑉𐐼, 𐐰𐑌𐐼 𐑄 𐐢𐐫𐑉𐐼 𐐸𐐰𐐼 𐐿𐐲𐑋𐐹𐐰𐑇𐐲𐑌 𐐲𐐹𐐱𐑌 𐑄𐐩𐑉 𐑁𐑉𐐯𐑌𐐼𐑆, 𐐰𐑌𐐼 𐑄𐐩𐑉 𐑁𐐰𐑋𐐮𐑊𐐮𐑆 𐐫𐑊𐑅𐐬, 𐑄𐐰𐐻 𐑄𐐩 𐐶𐐲𐑉 𐑌𐐱𐐻 𐐿𐐱𐑌𐑁𐐵𐑌𐐼𐐲𐐼. 𐐈𐑌𐐼 𐐮𐐻 𐐿𐐩𐑋 𐐻𐐭 𐐹𐐰𐑅 𐑄𐐰𐐻 𐐖𐐯𐑉𐐲𐐼 𐑅𐐹𐐩𐐿 𐐲𐑀𐐯𐑌 𐐲𐑌𐐻𐐭 𐐸𐐮𐑆 𐐺𐑉𐐲𐑄𐐲𐑉, 𐑅𐐩𐐮𐑍, 𐐘𐐬, 𐐰𐑌𐐼 𐐮𐑌𐐿𐐶𐐴𐑉 𐐱𐑂 𐑄 𐐢𐐫𐑉𐐼 𐐸𐐶𐐯𐑄𐐲𐑉 𐐸𐐨 𐐶𐐮𐑊 𐐼𐑉𐐴𐑂 𐐲𐑅 𐐵𐐻 𐐱𐑂 𐑄 𐑊𐐰𐑌𐐼, 𐐰𐑌𐐼 𐐮𐑁 𐐸𐐨 𐐶𐐮𐑊 𐐼𐑉𐐴𐑂 𐐲𐑅 𐐵𐐻 𐐱𐑂 𐑄 𐑊𐐰𐑌𐐼, 𐐿𐑉𐐴 𐐲𐑌𐐻𐐭 𐐸𐐮𐑋 𐐸𐐶𐐮𐑄𐐲𐑉 𐐶𐐨 𐑇𐐰𐑊 𐑀𐐬. 𐐈𐑌𐐼 𐐸𐐭 𐑌𐐬𐐯𐑃 𐐺𐐲𐐻 𐑄 𐐢𐐫𐑉𐐼 𐐶𐐮𐑊 𐐿𐐰𐑉𐐨 𐐲𐑅 𐑁𐐫𐑉𐑃 𐐮𐑌𐐻𐐭 𐐩 𐑊𐐰𐑌𐐼 𐐸𐐶𐐮𐐽 𐐮𐑆 𐐽𐐦𐑅 𐐲𐐺𐐲𐑂 𐐫𐑊 𐑄 𐐲𐑉𐑃? 𐐈𐑌𐐼 𐐮𐑁 𐐮𐐻 𐑅𐐬 𐐺, 𐑊𐐯𐐻 𐐲𐑅 𐐺 𐑁𐐩𐑃𐑁𐐳𐑊 𐐲𐑌𐐻𐐭 𐑄 𐐢𐐫𐑉𐐼, 𐑄𐐰𐐻 𐐶𐐨 𐑋𐐩 𐑉𐐨𐑅𐐨𐑂 𐐮𐐻 𐑁𐐫𐑉 𐐵𐑉 𐐮𐑌𐐸𐐯𐑉𐐮𐐻𐐲𐑌𐑅.

2. 𐐈𐑌𐐼 𐐮𐐻 𐐿𐐩𐑋 𐐻𐐭 𐐹𐐰𐑅 𐑄𐐰𐐻 𐑄 𐐺𐑉𐐲𐑄𐐲𐑉 𐐱𐑂 𐐖𐐯𐑉𐐲𐐼 𐐼𐐮𐐼 𐐿𐑉𐐴 𐐲𐑌𐐻𐐭 𐑄 𐐢𐐫𐑉𐐼 𐐰𐐿𐐫𐑉𐐼𐐮𐑍 𐐻𐐭 𐑄𐐰𐐻 𐐸𐐶𐐮𐐽 𐐸𐐰𐐼 𐐺𐐮𐑌 𐑅𐐹𐐬𐐿𐐲𐑌 𐐺𐐴 𐑄 𐑋𐐵𐑃 𐐱𐑂 𐐖𐐯𐑉𐐲𐐼. 𐐈𐑌𐐼 𐐮𐐻 𐐿𐐩𐑋 𐐻𐐭 𐐹𐐰𐑅 𐑄𐐰𐐻 𐑄 𐐢𐐫𐑉𐐼 𐐼𐐮𐐼 𐐸𐐨𐑉 𐑄 𐐺𐑉𐐲𐑄𐐲𐑉 𐐱𐑂 𐐖𐐯𐑉𐐲𐐼, 𐐰𐑌𐐼 𐐸𐐰𐐼 𐐿𐐲𐑋𐐹𐐰𐑇𐐲𐑌 𐐲𐐹𐐱𐑌 𐐸𐐮𐑋, 𐐰𐑌𐐼 𐑅𐐯𐐼 𐐲𐑌𐐻𐐭 𐐸𐐮𐑋, 𐐘𐐬 𐐻𐐭 𐐰𐑌𐐼 𐑀𐐰𐑄𐐲𐑉 𐐻𐐭𐑀𐐯𐑄𐐲𐑉 𐑄𐐴 𐑁𐑊𐐱𐐿𐑅, 𐐺𐐬𐑃 𐑋𐐩𐑊 𐐰𐑌𐐼 𐑁𐐨𐑋𐐩𐑊, 𐐱𐑂 𐐯𐑂𐐲𐑉𐐨 𐐿𐐴𐑌𐐼; 𐐰𐑌𐐼 𐐫𐑊𐑅𐐬 𐐱𐑂 𐑄 𐑅𐐨𐐼 𐐱𐑂 𐑄 𐐲𐑉𐑃 𐐱𐑂 𐐯𐑂𐐲𐑉𐐨 𐐿𐐴𐑌𐐼; 𐐰𐑌𐐼 𐑄𐐴 𐑁𐐰𐑋𐐮𐑊𐐮𐑆; 𐐰𐑌𐐼 𐐫𐑊𐑅𐐬 𐐖𐐯𐑉𐐲𐐼 𐑄𐐴 𐐺𐑉𐐲𐑄𐐲𐑉 𐐰𐑌𐐼 𐐸𐐮𐑆 𐑁𐐰𐑋𐐮𐑊𐐨; 𐐰𐑌𐐼 𐐫𐑊𐑅𐐬 𐑄𐐴 𐑁𐑉𐐯𐑌𐐼𐑆 𐐰𐑌𐐼 𐑄𐐩𐑉 𐑁𐐰𐑋𐐮𐑊𐐮𐑆, 𐐰𐑌𐐼 𐑄 𐑁𐑉𐐯𐑌𐐼𐑆 𐐱𐑂 𐐖𐐯𐑉𐐲𐐼 𐐰𐑌𐐼 𐑄𐐩𐑉 𐑁𐐰𐑋𐐮𐑊𐐮𐑆. 𐐈𐑌𐐼 𐐸𐐶𐐯𐑌 𐑄𐐵 𐐸𐐰𐑅𐐻 𐐼𐐲𐑌 𐑄𐐮𐑅 𐑄𐐵 𐑇𐐰𐑊𐐻 𐑀𐐬 𐐰𐐻 𐑄 𐐸𐐯𐐼 𐐱𐑂 𐑄𐐯𐑋 𐐼𐐵𐑌 𐐮𐑌𐐻𐐭 𐑄 𐑂𐐰𐑊𐐨 𐐸𐐶𐐮𐐽 𐐮𐑆 𐑌𐐫𐑉𐑃𐐶𐐲𐑉𐐼. 𐐈𐑌𐐼 𐑄𐐯𐑉 𐐶𐐮𐑊 𐐌 𐑋𐐨𐐻 𐑄𐐨, 𐐰𐑌𐐼 𐐌 𐐶𐐮𐑊 𐑀𐐬 𐐺𐐨𐑁𐐬𐑉 𐑄𐐨 𐐮𐑌𐐻𐐭 𐐩 𐑊𐐰𐑌𐐼 𐐸𐐶𐐮𐐽 𐐮𐑆 𐐽𐐦𐑅 𐐲𐐺𐐲𐑂 𐐫𐑊 𐑄 𐑊𐐰𐑌𐐼𐑆 𐐱𐑂 𐑄 𐐲𐑉𐑃. 𐐈𐑌𐐼 𐑄𐐯𐑉 𐐶𐐮𐑊 𐐌 𐐺𐑊𐐯𐑅 𐑄𐐨 𐐰𐑌𐐼 𐑄𐐴 𐑅𐐨𐐼, 𐐰𐑌𐐼 𐑉𐐩𐑆 𐐲𐐹 𐐲𐑌𐐻𐐭 𐑋𐐨 𐐱𐑂 𐑄𐐴 𐑅𐐨𐐼, 𐐰𐑌𐐼 𐐱𐑂 𐑄 𐑅𐐨𐐼 𐐱𐑂 𐑄𐐴 𐐺𐑉𐐲𐑄𐐲𐑉, 𐐰𐑌𐐼 𐑄𐐩 𐐸𐐭 𐑇𐐰𐑊 𐑀𐐬 𐐶𐐮𐑄 𐑄𐐨, 𐐩 𐑀𐑉𐐩𐐻 𐑌𐐩𐑇𐐲𐑌. 𐐈𐑌𐐼 𐑄𐐯𐑉 𐑇𐐰𐑊 𐐺 𐑌𐐲𐑌 𐑀𐑉𐐩𐐻𐐲𐑉 𐑄𐐰𐑌 𐑄 𐑌𐐩𐑇𐐲𐑌 𐐸𐐶𐐮𐐽 𐐌 𐐶𐐮𐑊 𐑉𐐩𐑆 𐐲𐐹 𐐲𐑌𐐻𐐭 𐑋𐐨 𐐱𐑂 𐑄𐐴 𐑅𐐨𐐼, 𐐲𐐹𐐱𐑌 𐐫𐑊 𐑄 𐑁𐐩𐑅 𐐱𐑂 𐑄 𐐲𐑉𐑃. 𐐈𐑌𐐼 𐑄𐐲𐑅 𐐌 𐐶𐐮𐑊 𐐼𐐭 𐐲𐑌𐐻𐐭 𐑄𐐨 𐐺𐐨𐐿𐐫𐑆 𐑄𐐮𐑅 𐑊𐐱𐑍 𐐻𐐴𐑋 𐐷𐐨 𐐸𐐰𐑂 𐐿𐑉𐐴𐐼 𐐲𐑌𐐻𐐭 𐑋𐐨.

3. 𐐈𐑌𐐼 𐐮𐐻 𐐿𐐩𐑋 𐐻𐐭 𐐹𐐰𐑅 𐑄𐐰𐐻 𐐖𐐯𐑉𐐲𐐼, 𐐰𐑌𐐼 𐐸𐐮𐑆 𐐺𐑉𐐲𐑄𐐲𐑉, 𐐰𐑌𐐼 𐑄𐐩𐑉 𐑁𐐰𐑋𐐮𐑊𐐮𐑆, 𐐰𐑌𐐼 𐐫𐑊𐑅𐐬 𐑄 𐑁𐑉𐐯𐑌𐐼𐑆 𐐱𐑂 𐐖𐐯𐑉𐐲𐐼 𐐰𐑌𐐼 𐐸𐐮𐑆 𐐺𐑉𐐲𐑄𐐲𐑉 𐐰𐑌𐐼 𐑄𐐩𐑉 𐑁𐐰𐑋𐐮𐑊𐐮𐑆 𐐶𐐯𐑌𐐻 𐐼𐐵𐑌 𐐮𐑌𐐻𐐭 𐑄 𐑂𐐰𐑊𐐨 𐐸𐐶𐐮𐐽 𐐶𐐱𐑆 𐑌𐐫𐑉𐑃𐐶𐐲𐑉𐐼, (𐐰𐑌𐐼 𐑄 𐑌𐐩𐑋 𐐱𐑂 𐑄 𐑂𐐰𐑊𐐨 𐐶𐐱𐑆 𐐤𐐮𐑋𐑉𐐱𐐼, 𐐺𐐨𐐮𐑍 𐐿𐐫𐑊𐐼 𐐰𐑁𐐻𐐲𐑉 𐑄 𐑋𐐴𐐻𐐨 𐐸𐐲𐑌𐐻𐐲𐑉,) 𐐶𐐮𐑄 𐑄𐐩𐑉 𐑁𐑊𐐱𐐿𐑅 𐐸𐐶𐐮𐐽 𐑄𐐩 𐐸𐐰𐐼 𐑀𐐰𐑄𐐲𐑉𐐼 𐐻𐐭𐑀𐐯𐑄𐐲𐑉, 𐑋𐐩𐑊 𐐰𐑌𐐼 𐑁𐐨𐑋𐐩𐑊, 𐐱𐑂 𐐯𐑂𐐲𐑉𐐨 𐐿𐐴𐑌𐐼. 𐐈𐑌𐐼 𐑄𐐩 𐐼𐐮𐐼 𐐫𐑊𐑅𐐬 𐑊𐐩 𐑅𐑌𐐩𐑉𐑆 𐐰𐑌𐐼 𐐿𐐰𐐽 𐑁𐐵𐑊𐑆 𐐱𐑂 𐑄 𐐩𐑉; 𐐰𐑌𐐼 𐑄𐐩 𐐼𐐮𐐼 𐐫𐑊𐑅𐐬 𐐹𐑉𐐨𐐹𐐩𐑉 𐐩 𐑂𐐯𐑅𐐲𐑊, 𐐮𐑌 𐐸𐐶𐐮𐐽 𐑄𐐩 𐐼𐐮𐐼 𐐿𐐰𐑉𐐨 𐐶𐐮𐑄 𐑄𐐯𐑋 𐑄 𐑁𐐮𐑇 𐐱𐑂 𐑄 𐐶𐐫𐐻𐐲𐑉𐑆; 𐐰𐑌𐐼 𐑄𐐩 𐐼𐐮𐐼 𐐫𐑊𐑅𐐬 𐐿𐐰𐑉𐐨 𐐶𐐮𐑄 𐑄𐐯𐑋 𐐼𐐯𐑆𐐲𐑉𐐯𐐻, 𐐸𐐶𐐮𐐽, 𐐺𐐴 𐐮𐑌𐐻𐐲𐑉𐐹𐑉𐐨𐐻𐐩𐑇𐐲𐑌, 𐐮𐑆 𐐩 𐐸𐐲𐑌𐐨 𐐺𐐨; 𐐰𐑌𐐼 𐑄𐐲𐑅 𐑄𐐩 𐐼𐐮𐐼 𐐿𐐰𐑉𐐨 𐐶𐐮𐑄 𐑄𐐯𐑋 𐑅𐐶𐐫𐑉𐑋𐑆 𐐱𐑂 𐐺𐐨𐑆, 𐐰𐑌𐐼 𐐫𐑊 𐑋𐐰𐑌𐐲𐑉 𐐱𐑂 𐑄𐐰𐐻 𐐸𐐶𐐮𐐽 𐐶𐐱𐑆 𐐲𐐹𐐱𐑌 𐑄 𐑁𐐩𐑅 𐐱𐑂 𐑄 𐑊𐐰𐑌𐐼, 𐑅𐐨𐐼𐑆 𐐱𐑂 𐐯𐑂𐐲𐑉𐐨 𐐿𐐴𐑌𐐼. 𐐈𐑌𐐼 𐐮𐐻 𐐿𐐩𐑋 𐐻𐐭 𐐹𐐰𐑅 𐑄𐐰𐐻 𐐸𐐶𐐯𐑌 𐑄𐐩 𐐸𐐰𐐼 𐐿𐐲𐑋 𐐼𐐵𐑌 𐐮𐑌𐐻𐐭 𐑄 𐑂𐐰𐑊𐐨 𐐱𐑂 𐐤𐐮𐑋𐑉𐐱𐐼, 𐑄 𐐢𐐫𐑉𐐼 𐐿𐐩𐑋 𐐼𐐵𐑌 𐐰𐑌𐐼 𐐻𐐫𐐿𐐻 𐐶𐐮𐑄 𐑄 𐐺𐑉𐐲𐑄𐐲𐑉 𐐱𐑂 𐐖𐐯𐑉𐐲𐐼; 𐐰𐑌𐐼 𐐸𐐨 𐐶𐐱𐑆 𐐮𐑌 𐐩 𐐿𐑊𐐵𐐼, 𐐰𐑌𐐼 𐑄 𐐺𐑉𐐲𐑄𐐲𐑉 𐐱𐑂 𐐖𐐯𐑉𐐲𐐼 𐑅𐐫 𐐸𐐮𐑋 𐑌𐐱𐐻. 𐐈𐑌𐐼 𐐮𐐻 𐐿𐐩𐑋 𐐻𐐭 𐐹𐐰𐑅 𐑄𐐰𐐻 𐑄 𐐢𐐫𐑉𐐼 𐐿𐐱𐑋𐐰𐑌𐐼𐐲𐐼 𐑄𐐯𐑋 𐑄𐐰𐐻 𐑄𐐩 𐑇𐐳𐐼 𐑀𐐬 𐑁𐐫𐑉𐑃 𐐮𐑌𐐻𐐭 𐑄 𐐶𐐮𐑊𐐼𐐲𐑉𐑌𐐯𐑅, 𐐷𐐩, 𐐮𐑌𐐻𐐭 𐑄𐐰𐐻 𐐿𐐶𐐫𐑉𐐻𐐲𐑉 𐐸𐐶𐐯𐑉 𐑄𐐯𐑉 𐑌𐐯𐑂𐐲𐑉 𐐸𐐰𐐼 𐑋𐐰𐑌 𐐺𐐮𐑌. 𐐈𐑌𐐼 𐐮𐐻 𐐿𐐩𐑋 𐐻𐐭 𐐹𐐰𐑅 𐑄𐐰𐐻 𐑄 𐐢𐐫𐑉𐐼 𐐼𐐮𐐼 𐑀𐐬 𐐺𐐨𐑁𐐬𐑉 𐑄𐐯𐑋, 𐐰𐑌𐐼 𐐼𐐮𐐼 𐐻𐐫𐐿 𐐶𐐮𐑄 𐑄𐐯𐑋 𐐰𐑆 𐐸𐐨 𐑅𐐻𐐳𐐼 𐐮𐑌 𐐩 𐐿𐑊𐐵𐐼, 𐐰𐑌𐐼 𐑀𐐩𐑂 𐐼𐐴𐑉𐐯𐐿𐑇𐐲𐑌𐑆 𐐸𐐶𐐮𐑄𐐲𐑉 𐑄𐐩 𐑇𐐳𐐼 𐐻𐑉𐐰𐑂𐐲𐑊.

4. 𐐈𐑌𐐼 𐐮𐐻 𐐿𐐩𐑋 𐐻𐐭 𐐹𐐰𐑅 𐑄𐐰𐐻 𐑄𐐩 𐐼𐐮𐐼 𐐻𐑉𐐰𐑂𐐲𐑊 𐐮𐑌 𐑄 𐐶𐐮𐑊𐐼𐐲𐑉𐑌𐐯𐑅, 𐐰𐑌𐐼 𐐼𐐮𐐼 𐐺𐐮𐑊𐐼 𐐺𐐪𐑉𐐾𐐯𐑆, 𐐮𐑌 𐐸𐐶𐐮𐐽 𐑄𐐩 𐐼𐐮𐐼 𐐿𐑉𐐱𐑅 𐑋𐐯𐑌𐐨 𐐶𐐫𐐻𐐲𐑉𐑆, 𐐺𐐨𐐮𐑍 𐐼𐐴𐑉𐐯𐐿𐐻𐐯𐐼 𐐿𐐱𐑌𐐻𐐮𐑌𐐷𐐭𐐲𐑊𐐨 𐐺𐐴 𐑄

𐐸𐐰𐑌𐐼 𐐱𐑂 𐑄 𐐢𐐫𐑉𐐼. 𐐈𐑌𐐼 𐑄 𐐢𐐫𐑉𐐼 𐐶𐐳𐐼 𐑌𐐱𐐻 𐑅𐐲𐑁𐐲𐑉 𐑄𐐰𐐻 𐑄𐐩 𐑇𐐳𐐼 𐑅𐐻𐐱𐐹 𐐺𐐨𐐷𐐱𐑌𐐼 𐑄 𐑅𐐨 𐐮𐑌 𐑄 𐐶𐐮𐑊𐐼𐐲𐑉𐑌𐐯𐑅, 𐐺𐐲𐐻 𐐸𐐨 𐐶𐐳𐐼 𐑄𐐰𐐻 𐑄𐐩 𐑇𐐳𐐼 𐐿𐐲𐑋 𐑁𐐫𐑉𐑃 𐐨𐑂𐑌 𐐲𐑌𐐻𐐭 𐑄 𐑊𐐰𐑌𐐼 𐐱𐑂 𐐹𐑉𐐱𐑋𐐮𐑅, 𐐸𐐶𐐮𐐽 𐐶𐐱𐑆 𐐽𐐱𐐮𐑅 𐐲𐐺𐐲𐑂 𐐫𐑊 𐐲𐑄𐐲𐑉 𐑊𐐰𐑌𐐼𐑆, 𐐸𐐶𐐮𐐽 𐑄 𐐢𐐫𐑉𐐼 𐐘𐐱𐐼 𐐸𐐰𐐼 𐐹𐑉𐐨𐑆𐐲𐑉𐑂𐐼 𐑁𐐫𐑉 𐐲 𐑉𐐴𐐽𐐲𐑅 𐐹𐐨𐐹𐑊, 𐐰𐑌𐐼 𐐸𐐨 𐐸𐐰𐐼 𐑅𐐶𐐫𐑉𐑌 𐐮𐑌 𐐸𐐮𐑆 𐑉𐐰𐑃 𐐲𐑌𐐻𐐭 𐑄 𐐺𐑉𐐲𐑄𐐲𐑉 𐐱𐑂 𐐖𐐯𐑉𐐲𐐼, 𐑄𐐰𐐻 𐐸𐐭𐑅𐐬 𐑇𐐳𐐼 𐐹𐐲𐑅𐐯𐑅 𐑄𐐮𐑅 𐑊𐐰𐑌𐐼 𐐱𐑂 𐐹𐑉𐐱𐑋𐐮𐑅, 𐑁𐑉𐐲𐑋 𐑄𐐰𐐻 𐐻𐐴𐑋 𐐸𐐯𐑌𐑅𐑁𐐫𐑉𐑃 𐐰𐑌𐐼 𐑁𐐫𐑉𐐯𐑂𐐲𐑉, 𐑇𐐳𐐼 𐑅𐐲𐑉𐑂 𐐸𐐮𐑋, 𐑄 𐐻𐑉𐐭 𐐰𐑌𐐼 𐐬𐑌𐑊𐐨 𐐘𐐱𐐼, 𐐫𐑉 𐑄𐐩 𐑇𐐳𐐼 𐐺 𐑅𐐶𐐯𐐹𐐻 𐐫𐑁 𐐸𐐶𐐯𐑌 𐑄 𐑁𐐳𐑊𐑌𐐯𐑅 𐐱𐑂 𐐸𐐮𐑆 𐑉𐐰𐑃 𐑇𐐳𐐼 𐐿𐐲𐑋 𐐲𐐹𐐱𐑌 𐑄𐐯𐑋. 𐐈𐑌𐐼 𐑌𐐵 𐐶𐐨 𐐿𐐰𐑌 𐐺𐐨𐐸𐐬𐑊𐐼 𐑄 𐐼𐐨𐐿𐑉𐐨𐑆 𐐱𐑂 𐐘𐐱𐐼 𐐿𐐱𐑌𐑅𐐲𐑉𐑌𐐮𐑍 𐑄𐐮𐑅 𐑊𐐰𐑌𐐼, 𐑄𐐰𐐻 𐐮𐐻 𐐮𐑆 𐐲 𐑊𐐰𐑌𐐼 𐐱𐑂 𐐹𐑉𐐱𐑋𐐮𐑅, 𐐰𐑌𐐼 𐐸𐐶𐐱𐐻𐑅𐐯𐑂𐐲𐑉 𐑌𐐩𐑇𐐲𐑌 𐑇𐐰𐑊 𐐹𐐲𐑅𐐯𐑅 𐐮𐐻, 𐑇𐐰𐑊 𐑅𐐲𐑉𐑂 𐐘𐐱𐐼, 𐐫𐑉 𐑄𐐩 𐑇𐐰𐑊 𐐺 𐑅𐐶𐐯𐐹𐐻 𐐫𐑁 𐐸𐐶𐐯𐑌 𐑄 𐑁𐐳𐑊𐑌𐐯𐑅 𐐱𐑂 𐐸𐐮𐑆 𐑉𐐰𐑃 𐑇𐐰𐑊 𐐿𐐲𐑋 𐐲𐐹𐐱𐑌 𐑄𐐯𐑋. 𐐈𐑌𐐼 𐑄 𐑁𐐳𐑊𐑌𐐯𐑅 𐐱𐑂 𐐸𐐮𐑆 𐑉𐐰𐑃 𐐿𐐲𐑋𐐯𐑃 𐐲𐐹𐐱𐑌 𐑄𐐯𐑋 𐐸𐐶𐐯𐑌 𐑄𐐩 𐐪𐑉 𐑉𐐴𐐹𐐯𐑌𐐼 𐐮𐑌 𐐮𐑌𐐮𐐿𐐶𐐮𐐻𐐨; 𐑁𐐫𐑉 𐐺𐐨𐐸𐐬𐑊𐐼, 𐑄𐐮𐑅 𐐮𐑆 𐐲 𐑊𐐰𐑌𐐼 𐐸𐐶𐐮𐐽 𐐮𐑆 𐐽𐐱𐐮𐑅 𐐲𐐺𐐲𐑂 𐐫𐑊 𐐲𐑄𐐲𐑉 𐑊𐐰𐑌𐐼𐑆; 𐐸𐐶𐐩𐑉𐑁𐐫𐑉 𐐸𐐨 𐑄𐐰𐐻 𐐼𐐲𐑃 𐐹𐐲𐑅𐐯𐑅 𐐮𐐻 𐑇𐐰𐑊 𐑅𐐲𐑉𐑂 𐐘𐐱𐐼, 𐐫𐑉 𐑇𐐰𐑊 𐐺 𐑅𐐶𐐯𐐹𐐻 𐐫𐑁; 𐑁𐐫𐑉 𐐮𐐻 𐐮𐑆 𐑄 𐐯𐑂𐐲𐑉𐑊𐐰𐑅𐐻𐐮𐑍 𐐼𐐨𐐿𐑉𐐨 𐐱𐑂 𐐘𐐱𐐼. 𐐈𐑌𐐼 𐐮𐐻 𐐮𐑆 𐑌𐐱𐐻 𐐲𐑌𐐻𐐮𐑊 𐑄 𐑁𐐳𐑊𐑌𐐯𐑅 𐐱𐑂 𐐮𐑌𐐮𐐿𐐶𐐮𐐻𐐨 𐐲𐑋𐐲𐑍 𐑄 𐐽𐐮𐑊𐐼𐑉𐐯𐑌 𐐱𐑂 𐑄 𐑊𐐰𐑌𐐼, 𐑄𐐰𐐻 𐑄𐐩 𐐪𐑉 𐑅𐐶𐐯𐐹𐐻 𐐫𐑁. 𐐈𐑌𐐼 𐑄𐐮𐑅 𐐿𐐲𐑋𐐯𐑃 𐐲𐑌𐐻𐐭 𐐷𐐭, 𐐄 𐐷𐐨 𐐖𐐯𐑌𐐻𐐴𐑊𐑆, 𐑄𐐰𐐻 𐐷𐐨 𐑋𐐩 𐑌𐐬 𐑄 𐐼𐐨𐐿𐑉𐐨𐑆 𐐱𐑂 𐐘𐐱𐐼, 𐑄𐐰𐐻 𐐷𐐨 𐑋𐐩 𐑉𐐨𐐹𐐯𐑌𐐻, 𐐰𐑌𐐼 𐑌𐐱𐐻 𐐿𐐲𐑌𐐻𐐮𐑌𐐷𐐭 𐐮𐑌 𐐷𐐭𐑉 𐐮𐑌𐐮𐐿𐐶𐐮𐐻𐐨𐑆 𐐲𐑌𐐻𐐮𐑊 𐑄 𐑁𐐳𐑊𐑌𐐯𐑅 𐐿𐐲𐑋, 𐑄𐐰𐐻 𐐷𐐨 𐑋𐐩 𐑌𐐱𐐻 𐐺𐑉𐐮𐑍 𐐼𐐵𐑌 𐑄 𐑁𐐳𐑊𐑌𐐯𐑅 𐐱𐑂 𐑄 𐑉𐐰𐑃 𐐱𐑂 𐐘𐐱𐐼 𐐲𐐹𐐱𐑌 𐐷𐐭, 𐐰𐑆 𐑄 𐐮𐑌𐐸𐐰𐐺𐐮𐐻𐐰𐑌𐐻𐑅 𐐱𐑂 𐑄 𐑊𐐰𐑌𐐼 𐐸𐐰𐑃 𐐸𐐮𐑄𐐲𐑉𐐻𐐭 𐐼𐐲𐑌. 𐐒𐐨𐐸𐐬𐑊𐐼, 𐑄𐐮𐑅 𐐮𐑆 𐐲 𐐽𐐱𐐮𐑅 𐑊𐐰𐑌𐐼, 𐐰𐑌𐐼 𐐸𐐶𐐱𐐻𐑅𐐯𐑂𐐲𐑉 𐑌𐐩𐑇𐐲𐑌 𐑇𐐰𐑊 𐐹𐐲𐑅𐐯𐑅 𐐮𐐻, 𐑇𐐰𐑊 𐐺 𐑁𐑉𐐨 𐑁𐑉𐐲𐑋 𐐺𐐱𐑌𐐼𐐩𐐖, 𐐰𐑌𐐼 𐑁𐑉𐐲𐑋 𐐿𐐰𐐹𐐻𐐮𐑂𐐮𐐻𐐨, 𐐰𐑌𐐼 𐑁𐑉𐐲𐑋 𐐫𐑊 𐐲𐑄𐐲𐑉 𐑌𐐩𐑇𐐲𐑌𐑆 𐐲𐑌𐐼𐐲𐑉 𐐸𐐯𐑂𐐯𐑌, 𐐮𐑁 𐑄𐐩 𐐶𐐮𐑊 𐐺𐐲𐐻 𐑅𐐲𐑉𐑂 𐑄 𐐘𐐱𐐼 𐐱𐑂 𐑄 𐑊𐐰𐑌𐐼, 𐐸𐐭 𐐮𐑆 𐐖𐐨𐑆𐐲𐑅 𐐗𐑉𐐴𐑅𐐻, 𐐸𐐭 𐐸𐐰𐑃 𐐺𐐮𐑌 𐑋𐐰𐑌𐐮𐑁𐐯𐑅𐐻𐐯𐐼 𐐺𐐴 𐑄 𐑃𐐮𐑍𐑆 𐐸𐐶𐐮𐐽 𐐶𐐨 𐐸𐐰𐑂 𐑉𐐮𐐻𐑌.

5. 𐐈𐑌𐐼 𐑌𐐵 𐐌 𐐹𐑉𐐬𐑅𐐨𐐼 𐐶𐐮𐑄 𐑋𐐴 𐑉𐐯𐐿𐐲𐑉𐐼; 𐑁𐐫𐑉 𐐺𐐨𐐸𐐬𐑊𐐼 𐐮𐐻 𐐿𐐩𐑋 𐐻𐐭 𐐹𐐰𐑅 𐑄𐐰𐐻 𐑄 𐐢𐐫𐑉𐐼 𐐼𐐮𐐼 𐐺𐑉𐐮𐑍 𐐖𐐯𐑉𐐲𐐼 𐐰𐑌𐐼 𐐸𐐮𐑆 𐐺𐑉𐐯𐑄𐑉𐐯𐑌 𐑁𐐫𐑉𐑃 𐐨𐑂𐑌 𐐻𐐭 𐑄𐐰𐐻 𐑀𐑉𐐩𐐻 𐑅𐐨 𐐸𐐶𐐮𐐽 𐐼𐐮𐑂𐐴𐐼𐐯𐑃 𐑄 𐑊𐐰𐑌𐐼𐑆. 𐐈𐑌𐐼 𐐰𐑆 𐑄𐐩 𐐿𐐩𐑋 𐐻𐐭 𐑄 𐑅𐐨, 𐑄𐐩 𐐹𐐮𐐽𐐻 𐑄𐐩𐑉 𐐻𐐯𐑌𐐻𐑅; 𐐰𐑌𐐼 𐑄𐐩 𐐿𐐫𐑊𐐼 𐑄 𐑌𐐩𐑋 𐐱𐑂 𐑄 𐐹𐑊𐐩𐑅 𐐣𐐫𐑉𐐨𐐰𐑌𐐿𐐭𐑋𐐲𐑉; 𐐰𐑌𐐼 𐑄𐐩 𐐼𐐶𐐯𐑊𐐻 𐐮𐑌 𐐻𐐯𐑌𐐻𐑅: 𐐰𐑌𐐼 𐐼𐐶𐐯𐑊𐐻 𐐮𐑌 𐐻𐐯𐑌𐐻𐑅 𐐲𐐹𐐱𐑌 𐑄 𐑅𐐨 𐑇𐐫𐑉 𐑁𐐫𐑉 𐑄 𐑅𐐹𐐩𐑅 𐐱𐑂 𐑁𐐫𐑉 𐐷𐐨𐑉𐑆. 𐐈𐑌𐐼 𐐮𐐻 𐐿𐐩𐑋 𐐻𐐭 𐐹𐐰𐑅 𐐰𐐻 𐑄 𐐯𐑌𐐼 𐐱𐑂 𐑁𐐫𐑉 𐐷𐐨𐑉𐑆 𐑄𐐰𐐻 𐑄 𐐢𐐫𐑉𐐼 𐐿𐐩𐑋 𐐲𐑀𐐯𐑌 𐐲𐑌𐐻𐐭 𐑄 𐐺𐑉𐐲𐑄𐐲𐑉 𐐱𐑂 𐐖𐐯𐑉𐐲𐐼, 𐐰𐑌𐐼 𐑅𐐻𐐳𐐼 𐐮𐑌 𐐲 𐐿𐑊𐐵𐐼 𐐰𐑌𐐼 𐐻𐐫𐐿𐐻 𐐶𐐮𐑄 𐐸𐐮𐑋. 𐐈𐑌𐐼 𐑁𐐫𐑉 𐑄 𐑅𐐹𐐩𐑅 𐐱𐑂 𐑃𐑉𐐨 𐐵𐑉𐑆 𐐼𐐮𐐼 𐑄 𐐢𐐫𐑉𐐼 𐐻𐐫𐐿 𐐶𐐮𐑄 𐑄 𐐺𐑉𐐲𐑄𐐲𐑉 𐐱𐑂 𐐖𐐯𐑉𐐲𐐼, 𐐰𐑌𐐼 𐐽𐐩𐑅𐑌𐐼 𐐸𐐮𐑋 𐐺𐐨𐐿𐐫𐑆 𐐸𐐨 𐑉𐐨𐑋𐐯𐑋𐐺𐐲𐑉𐐼 𐑌𐐱𐐻 𐐻𐐭 𐐿𐐫𐑊 𐐲𐐹𐐱𐑌 𐑄 𐑌𐐩𐑋 𐐱𐑂 𐑄 𐐢𐐫𐑉𐐼. 𐐈𐑌𐐼 𐑄 𐐺𐑉𐐲𐑄𐐲𐑉 𐐱𐑂 𐐖𐐯𐑉𐐲𐐼 𐑉𐐨𐐹𐐯𐑌𐐻𐐯𐐼 𐐱𐑂 𐑄 𐐨𐑂𐑊 𐐸𐐶𐐮𐐽 𐐸𐐨 𐐸𐐰𐐼 𐐼𐐲𐑌, 𐐰𐑌𐐼 𐐼𐐮𐐼 𐐿𐐫𐑊 𐐲𐐹𐐱𐑌 𐑄 𐑌𐐩𐑋 𐐱𐑂 𐑄 𐐢𐐫𐑉𐐼 𐑁𐐫𐑉 𐐸𐐮𐑆 𐐺𐑉𐐯𐑄𐑉𐐯𐑌 𐐸𐐭 𐐶𐐲𐑉 𐐶𐐮𐑄 𐐸𐐮𐑋. 𐐈𐑌𐐼 𐑄 𐐢𐐫𐑉𐐼 𐑅𐐯𐐼 𐐲𐑌𐐻𐐭 𐐸𐐮𐑋, 𐐌 𐐶𐐮𐑊 𐑁𐐲𐑉𐑀𐐮𐑂 𐑄𐐨 𐐰𐑌𐐼 𐑄𐐴 𐐺𐑉𐐯𐑄𐑉𐐯𐑌 𐐱𐑂 𐑄𐐩𐑉 𐑅𐐮𐑌𐑆; 𐐺𐐲𐐻 𐑄𐐵 𐑇𐐰𐑊𐐻 𐑌𐐱𐐻 𐑅𐐮𐑌 𐐯𐑌𐐨 𐑋𐐫𐑉, 𐑁𐐫𐑉 𐐷𐐨 𐑇𐐰𐑊 𐑉𐐨𐑋𐐯𐑋𐐺𐐲𐑉 𐑄𐐰𐐻 𐑋𐐴 𐐝𐐹𐐮𐑉𐐮𐐻 𐐶𐐮𐑊 𐑌𐐱𐐻 𐐫𐑊𐐶𐐩𐑆 𐑅𐐻𐑉𐐴𐑂 𐐶𐐮𐑄 𐑋𐐰𐑌; 𐐸𐐶𐐩𐑉𐑁𐐫𐑉, 𐐮𐑁 𐐷𐐨 𐐶𐐮𐑊 𐑅𐐮𐑌 𐐲𐑌𐐻𐐮𐑊 𐐷𐐨 𐐪𐑉 𐑁𐐳𐑊𐐨 𐑉𐐴𐐹, 𐐷𐐨 𐑇𐐰𐑊 𐐺 𐐿𐐲𐐻 𐐫𐑁 𐑁𐑉𐐲𐑋 𐑄 𐐹𐑉𐐯𐑆𐐯𐑌𐑅 𐐱𐑂 𐑄 𐐢𐐫𐑉𐐼. 𐐈𐑌𐐼 𐑄𐐨𐑆 𐐪𐑉 𐑋𐐴 𐑃𐐫𐐻𐑅 𐐲𐐹𐐱𐑌 𐑄 𐑊𐐰𐑌𐐼 𐐸𐐶𐐮𐐽 𐐌 𐑇𐐰𐑊 𐑀𐐮𐑂 𐐷𐐭 𐑁𐐫𐑉 𐐷𐐭𐑉 𐐮𐑌𐐸𐐯𐑉𐐮𐐻𐐰𐑌𐑅; 𐑁𐐫𐑉 𐐮𐐻 𐑇𐐰𐑊 𐐺 𐐲 𐑊𐐰𐑌𐐼 𐐽𐐱𐐮𐑅 𐐲𐐺𐐲𐑂 𐐫𐑊 𐐲𐑄𐐲𐑉 𐑊𐐰𐑌𐐼𐑆. 𐐈𐑌𐐼 𐑄 𐐢𐐫𐑉𐐼 𐑅𐐯𐐼, 𐐘𐐬 𐐻𐐭 𐐶𐐲𐑉𐐿 𐐰𐑌𐐼 𐐺𐐮𐑊𐐼, 𐐰𐑁𐐻𐐲𐑉 𐑄 𐑋𐐰𐑌𐐲𐑉 𐐱𐑂 𐐺𐐪𐑉𐐖𐐯𐑆 𐐸𐐶𐐮𐐽 𐐷𐐨 𐐸𐐰𐑂 𐐸𐐮𐑄𐐲𐑉𐐻𐐭 𐐺𐐮𐑊𐐻. 𐐈𐑌𐐼 𐐮𐐻 𐐿𐐩𐑋 𐐻𐐭 𐐹𐐰𐑅 𐑄𐐰𐐻 𐑄 𐐺𐑉𐐲𐑄𐐲𐑉 𐐱𐑂 𐐖𐐯𐑉𐐲𐐼 𐐼𐐮𐐼 𐑀𐐬 𐐻𐐭 𐐶𐐲𐑉𐐿, 𐐰𐑌𐐼 𐐫𐑊𐑅𐐬 𐐸𐐮𐑆 𐐺𐑉𐐯𐑄𐑉𐐯𐑌, 𐐰𐑌𐐼 𐐺𐐮𐑊𐐻 𐐺𐐪𐑉𐐖𐐯𐑆 𐐰𐑁𐐻𐐲𐑉 𐑄 𐑋𐐰𐑌𐐲𐑉 𐐸𐐶𐐮𐐽 𐑄𐐩 𐐸𐐰𐐼 𐐺𐐮𐑊𐐻, 𐐲𐐿𐐫𐑉𐐼𐐮𐑍 𐐻𐐭 𐑄 𐐮𐑌𐑅𐐻𐑉𐐲𐐿𐑇𐐲𐑌𐑆 𐐱𐑂 𐑄 𐐢𐐫𐑉𐐼. 𐐈𐑌𐐼 𐑄𐐩 𐐶𐐲𐑉 𐑅𐑋𐐫𐑊, 𐐰𐑌𐐼 𐑄𐐩 𐐶𐐲𐑉 𐑊𐐴𐐻 𐐲𐐹𐐱𐑌 𐑄 𐐶𐐫𐐻𐐲𐑉, 𐐨𐑂𐑌 𐐲𐑌𐐻𐐭 𐑄 𐑊𐐴𐐻𐑌𐐯𐑅 𐐱𐑂 𐐲 𐑁𐐵𐑊 𐐲𐐹𐐱𐑌 𐑄 𐐶𐐫𐐻𐐲𐑉; 𐐰𐑌𐐼 𐑄𐐩 𐐶𐐲𐑉 𐐺𐐮𐑊𐐻 𐐰𐑁𐐻𐐲𐑉 𐐲 𐑋𐐰𐑌𐐲𐑉 𐑄𐐰𐐻 𐑄𐐩 𐐶𐐲𐑉 𐐯𐐿𐑅𐐨𐐼𐐮𐑍 𐐻𐐴𐐻, 𐐨𐑂𐑌 𐑄𐐰𐐻 𐑄𐐩 𐐶𐐳𐐼 𐐸𐐬𐑊𐐼 𐐶𐐫𐐻𐐲𐑉 𐑊𐐴𐐿 𐐲𐑌𐐻𐐭 𐐲 𐐼𐐮𐑇; 𐐰𐑌𐐼 𐑄 𐐺𐐱𐐻𐐲𐑋 𐑄𐐩𐑉𐐱𐑂 𐐶𐐱𐑆 𐐻𐐴𐐻 𐑊𐐴𐐿 𐐲𐑌𐐻𐐭 𐐲 𐐼𐐮𐑇; 𐐰𐑌𐐼 𐑄 𐑅𐐴𐐼𐑆 𐑄𐐩𐑉𐐱𐑂

𐐶𐐲𐑉 𐐻𐐴𐐻 𐑊𐐴𐐿 𐐲𐑌𐐻𐐭 𐐩 𐐼𐐮𐑇; 𐐰𐑌𐐼 𐑄 𐐯𐑌𐐼𐑆 𐑄𐐯𐑉𐐱𐑂 𐐶𐐲𐑉 𐐹𐐨𐐿𐐯𐐼; 𐐰𐑌𐐼 𐑄 𐐻𐐱𐐹 𐑄𐐯𐑉𐐱𐑂 𐐶𐐱𐑆 𐐻𐐴𐐻 𐑊𐐴𐐿 𐐲𐑌𐐻𐐭 𐐩 𐐼𐐮𐑇; 𐐰𐑌𐐼 𐑄 𐑊𐐯𐑍𐑃 𐑄𐐯𐑉𐐱𐑂 𐐶𐐱𐑆 𐑄 𐑊𐐯𐑍𐑃 𐐱𐑂 𐐩 𐐻𐑉𐐨; 𐐰𐑌𐐼 𐑄 𐐼𐐬𐑉 𐑄𐐯𐑉𐐱𐑂, 𐐸𐐶𐐯𐑌 𐐮𐐻 𐐶𐐱𐑆 𐑇𐐲𐐻, 𐐶𐐱𐑆 𐐻𐐴𐐻, 𐑊𐐴𐐿 𐐲𐑌𐐻𐐭 𐐩 𐐼𐐮𐑇.

6. 𐐈𐑌𐐼 𐐮𐐻 𐐿𐐩𐑋 𐐻𐐭 𐐹𐐰𐑅 𐑄𐐰𐐻 𐑄 𐐺𐑉𐐲𐑄𐐲𐑉 𐐱𐑂 𐐖𐐯𐑉𐐯𐐼 𐐿𐑉𐐴𐐼 𐐲𐑌𐐻𐐭 𐑄 𐐢𐐫𐑉𐐼, 𐑅𐐩𐐮𐑍, 𐐄 𐐢𐐫𐑉𐐼 𐐌 𐐸𐐰𐑂 𐐹𐐲𐑉𐑁𐐫𐑉𐑋𐐼 𐑄 𐐶𐐲𐑉𐐿 𐐸𐐶𐐮𐐽 𐑄𐐵 𐐸𐐰𐑅𐐻 𐐿𐐱𐑋𐐰𐑌𐐼𐐯𐐼 𐑋𐐨, 𐐰𐑌𐐼 𐐌 𐐸𐐰𐑂 𐑋𐐩𐐼 𐑄 𐐺𐐪𐑉𐐾𐐯𐑆 𐐰𐐿𐐫𐑉𐐼𐐮𐑍 𐐰𐑆 𐑄𐐵 𐐸𐐰𐑅𐐻 𐐼𐐴𐑉𐐯𐐿𐐻𐐯𐐼 𐑋𐐨. 𐐈𐑌𐐼 𐐺𐐨𐐸𐐬𐑊𐐼, 𐐄 𐐢𐐫𐑉𐐼, 𐐮𐑌 𐑄𐐯𐑋 𐑄𐐯𐑉 𐐮𐑆 𐑌𐐬 𐑊𐐴𐐻, 𐐸𐐶𐐮𐑄𐐲𐑉 𐑇𐐰𐑊 𐐶𐐨 𐑅𐐻𐐨𐑉? 𐐈𐑌𐐼 𐐫𐑊𐑅𐐬 𐐶𐐨 𐑇𐐰𐑊 𐐹𐐯𐑉𐐮𐑇, 𐑁𐐫𐑉 𐐮𐑌 𐑄𐐯𐑋 𐐶𐐨 𐐿𐐰𐑌𐐱𐐻 𐐺𐑉𐐨𐑄, 𐑅𐐩𐑂 𐐮𐐻 𐐮𐑆 𐑄 𐐩𐑉 𐐸𐐶𐐮𐐽 𐐮𐑆 𐐮𐑌 𐑄𐐯𐑋; 𐑄𐐯𐑉𐑁𐐬𐑉 𐐶𐐨 𐑇𐐰𐑊 𐐹𐐯𐑉𐐮𐑇. 𐐈𐑌𐐼 𐑄 𐐢𐐫𐑉𐐼 𐑅𐐯𐐼 𐐲𐑌𐐻𐐭 𐑄 𐐺𐑉𐐲𐑄𐐲𐑉 𐐱𐑂 𐐖𐐯𐑉𐐯𐐼, 𐐒𐐨𐐸𐐬𐑊𐐼, 𐑄𐐵 𐑇𐐰𐑊𐐻 𐑋𐐩𐐿 𐐩 𐐸𐐬𐑊 𐐮𐑌 𐑄 𐐻𐐱𐐹 𐑄𐐯𐑉𐐱𐑂, 𐐰𐑌𐐼 𐐫𐑊𐑅𐐬 𐐮𐑌 𐑄 𐐺𐐱𐐻𐐲𐑋 𐑄𐐯𐑉𐐱𐑂; 𐐰𐑌𐐼 𐐸𐐶𐐯𐑌 𐑄𐐵 𐑇𐐰𐑊𐐻 𐑅𐐲𐑁𐐲𐑉 𐑁𐐫𐑉 𐐩𐑉, 𐑄𐐵 𐑇𐐰𐑊𐐻 𐐲𐑌𐑅𐐻𐐱𐐹 𐑄 𐐸𐐬𐑊 𐑄𐐯𐑉𐐱𐑂, 𐐰𐑌𐐼 𐑉𐐨𐑅𐐨𐑂 𐐩𐑉. 𐐈𐑌𐐼 𐐮𐑁 𐐮𐐻 𐑅𐐬 𐐺𐐨 𐑄𐐰𐐻 𐑄 𐐶𐐫𐐻𐐲𐑉 𐐿𐐲𐑋 𐐮𐑌 𐐲𐐹𐐱𐑌 𐑄𐐨, 𐐺𐐨𐐸𐐬𐑊𐐼 𐐷𐐨 𐑇𐐰𐑊 𐑅𐐻𐐱𐐹 𐑄 𐐸𐐬𐑊 𐑄𐐯𐑉𐐱𐑂, 𐑄𐐰𐐻 𐐷𐐨 𐑋𐐩 𐑌𐐱𐐻 𐐹𐐯𐑉𐐮𐑇 𐐮𐑌 𐑄 𐑁𐑊𐐲𐐼. 𐐈𐑌𐐼 𐐮𐐻 𐐿𐐩𐑋 𐐻𐐭 𐐹𐐰𐑅 𐑄𐐰𐐻 𐑄 𐐺𐑉𐐲𐑄𐐲𐑉 𐐱𐑂 𐐖𐐯𐑉𐐯𐐼 𐐼𐐮𐐼 𐑅𐐬, 𐐰𐐿𐐫𐑉𐐼𐐮𐑍 𐐰𐑆 𐑄 𐐢𐐫𐑉𐐼 𐐸𐐰𐐼 𐐿𐐱𐑋𐐰𐑌𐐼𐐯𐐼. 𐐈𐑌𐐼 𐐸𐐨 𐐿𐑉𐐴𐐼 𐐲𐑀𐐯𐑌 𐐲𐑌𐐻𐐭 𐑄 𐐢𐐫𐑉𐐼, 𐑅𐐩𐐮𐑍, 𐐄 𐐢𐐫𐑉𐐼, 𐐺𐐨𐐸𐐬𐑊𐐼 𐐌 𐐸𐐰𐑂 𐐼𐐲𐑌 𐐨𐑂𐐯𐑌 𐐰𐑆 𐑄𐐵 𐐸𐐰𐑅𐐻 𐐿𐐱𐑋𐐰𐑌𐐼𐐯𐐼 𐑋𐐨; 𐐰𐑌𐐼 𐐌 𐐸𐐰𐑂 𐐹𐑉𐐨𐐹𐐩𐑉𐐼 𐑄 𐑂𐐯𐑅𐐯𐑊𐑆 𐑁𐐫𐑉 𐑋𐐴 𐐹𐐨𐐹𐑊, 𐐰𐑌𐐼 𐐺𐐨𐐸𐐬𐑊𐐼 𐑄𐐯𐑉 𐐮𐑆 𐑌𐐬 𐑊𐐴𐐻 𐐮𐑌 𐑄𐐯𐑋. 𐐒𐐨𐐸𐐬𐑊𐐼, 𐐄 𐐢𐐫𐑉𐐼, 𐐶𐐮𐑊𐐻 𐑄𐐵 𐑅𐐲𐑁𐐲𐑉 𐑄𐐰𐐻 𐐶𐐨 𐑇𐐰𐑊 𐐿𐑉𐐫𐑅 𐑄𐐮𐑅 𐑀𐑉𐐩𐐻 𐐶𐐫𐐻𐐲𐑉 𐐮𐑌 𐐼𐐪𐑉𐐿𐑌𐐯𐑅? 𐐈𐑌𐐼 𐑄 𐐢𐐫𐑉𐐼 𐑅𐐯𐐼 𐐲𐑌𐐻𐐭 𐑄 𐐺𐑉𐐲𐑄𐐲𐑉 𐐱𐑂 𐐖𐐯𐑉𐐯𐐼, 𐐸𐐶𐐱𐐻 𐐶𐐮𐑊 𐐷𐐨 𐑄𐐰𐐻 𐐌 𐑇𐐳𐐼 𐐼𐐭 𐑄𐐰𐐻 𐐷𐐨 𐑋𐐩 𐐸𐐰𐑂 𐑊𐐴𐐻 𐐮𐑌 𐐷𐐭𐑉 𐑂𐐯𐑅𐐯𐑊𐑆? 𐐙𐐫𐑉 𐐺𐐨𐐸𐐬𐑊𐐼, 𐐷𐐨 𐐿𐐰𐑌𐐱𐐻 𐐸𐐰𐑂 𐐶𐐮𐑌𐐼𐐬𐑆, 𐑁𐐫𐑉 𐑄𐐩 𐐶𐐮𐑊 𐐺𐐨 𐐼𐐰𐑇𐐼 𐐮𐑌 𐐹𐐨𐑅𐐯𐑆; 𐑌𐐨𐑄𐐲𐑉 𐑇𐐰𐑊 𐐷𐐨 𐐻𐐩𐐿 𐑁𐐴𐑉 𐐶𐐮𐑄 𐐷𐐭, 𐑁𐐫𐑉 𐐷𐐨 𐑇𐐰𐑊 𐑌𐐱𐐻 𐑀𐐬 𐐺𐐴 𐑄 𐑊𐐴𐐻 𐐱𐑂 𐑁𐐴𐑉; 𐑁𐐫𐑉 𐐺𐐨𐐸𐐬𐑊𐐼, 𐐷𐐨 𐑇𐐰𐑊 𐐺𐐨 𐐰𐑆 𐐩 𐐸𐐶𐐩𐑊 𐐮𐑌 𐑄 𐑋𐐮𐐼𐑅𐐻 𐐱𐑂 𐑄 𐑅𐐨; 𐑁𐐫𐑉 𐑄 𐑋𐐵𐑌𐐻𐐩𐑌 𐐶𐐩𐑂𐑆 𐑇𐐰𐑊 𐐼𐐰𐑇 𐐲𐐹𐐱𐑌 𐐷𐐭. 𐐤𐐯𐑂𐐲𐑉𐑄𐐯𐑊𐐯𐑅, 𐐌 𐐶𐐮𐑊 𐐺𐑉𐐮𐑍 𐐷𐐭 𐐲𐐹 𐐲𐑀𐐯𐑌 𐐵𐐻 𐐱𐑂 𐑄 𐐼𐐯𐐹𐑃𐑅 𐐱𐑂 𐑄 𐑅𐐨; 𐑁𐐫𐑉 𐑄 𐐶𐐮𐑌𐐼𐑆 𐐸𐐰𐑂 𐑀𐐫𐑌 𐑁𐐬𐑉𐑃 𐐵𐐻 𐐱𐑂 𐑋𐐴 𐑋𐐵𐑃, 𐐰𐑌𐐼 𐐫𐑊𐑅𐐬 𐑄 𐑉𐐩𐑌𐑆 𐐰𐑌𐐼 𐑄 𐑁𐑊𐐲𐐼𐑆 𐐸𐐰𐑂 𐐌 𐑅𐐯𐑌𐐻 𐑁𐐬𐑉𐑃. 𐐈𐑌𐐼 𐐺𐐨𐐸𐐬𐑊𐐼, 𐐌 𐐹𐑉𐐨𐐹𐐩𐑉 𐐷𐐭 𐐲𐑀𐐯𐑌𐑅𐐻 𐑄𐐨𐑆 𐑃𐐮𐑍𐑆; 𐑁𐐫𐑉 𐐷𐐨 𐐿𐐰𐑌𐐱𐐻 𐐿𐑉𐐫𐑅 𐑄𐐮𐑅 𐑀𐑉𐐩𐐻 𐐼𐐨𐐹, 𐑅𐐩𐑂 𐐌 𐐹𐑉𐐨𐐹𐐩𐑉 𐐷𐐭 𐐲𐑀𐐯𐑌𐑅𐐻 𐑄 𐐶𐐩𐑂𐑆 𐐱𐑂 𐑄 𐑅𐐨, 𐐰𐑌𐐼 𐑄 𐐶𐐮𐑌𐐼𐑆 𐐸𐐶𐐮𐐽 𐐸𐐰𐑂 𐑀𐐫𐑌 𐑁𐐬𐑉𐑃, 𐐰𐑌𐐼 𐑄 𐑁𐑊𐐲𐐼𐑆 𐐸𐐶𐐮𐐽 𐑇𐐰𐑊 𐐿𐐲𐑋. 𐐜𐐯𐑉𐑁𐐬𐑉 𐐸𐐶𐐱𐐻 𐐶𐐮𐑊 𐐷𐐨 𐑄𐐰𐐻 𐐌 𐑇𐐳𐐼 𐐹𐑉𐐨𐐹𐐩𐑉 𐑁𐐫𐑉 𐐷𐐭 𐑄𐐰𐐻 𐐷𐐨 𐑋𐐩 𐐸𐐰𐑂 𐑊𐐴𐐻 𐐸𐐶𐐯𐑌 𐐷𐐨 𐐪𐑉 𐑅𐐶𐐱𐑊𐐬𐐼 𐐲𐐹 𐐮𐑌 𐑄 𐐼𐐯𐐹𐑃𐑅 𐐱𐑂 𐑄 𐑅𐐨?

7. 𐐈𐑌𐐼 𐐮𐐻 𐐿𐐩𐑋 𐐻𐐭 𐐹𐐰𐑅 𐑄𐐰𐐻 𐑄 𐐺𐑉𐐲𐑄𐐲𐑉 𐐱𐑂 𐐖𐐯𐑉𐐯𐐼, (𐑌𐐵 𐑄 𐑌𐐲𐑋𐐺𐐲𐑉 𐐱𐑂 𐑄 𐑂𐐯𐑅𐐯𐑊𐑆 𐐸𐐶𐐮𐐽 𐐸𐐰𐐼 𐐺𐐮𐑌 𐐹𐑉𐐨𐐹𐐩𐑉𐐼 𐐶𐐱𐑆 𐐩𐐻,) 𐐶𐐯𐑌𐐻 𐑁𐐬𐑉𐑃 𐐲𐑌𐐻𐐭 𐑄 𐑋𐐵𐑌𐐻, 𐐸𐐶𐐮𐐽 𐑄𐐩 𐐿𐐫𐑊𐐼 𐑄 𐑋𐐵𐑌𐐻 𐐟𐐯𐑊𐐯𐑋, 𐐺𐐨𐐿𐐫𐑆 𐐱𐑂 𐐮𐐻𐑅 𐐯𐐿𐑅𐐨𐐼𐐮𐑍 𐐸𐐴𐐻, 𐐰𐑌𐐼 𐐼𐐮𐐼 𐑋𐐬𐑊𐐻𐐯𐑌 𐐵𐐻 𐐱𐑂 𐐩 𐑉𐐱𐐿 𐑅𐐮𐐿𐑅𐐻𐐨𐑌 𐑅𐑋𐐫𐑊 𐑅𐐻𐐬𐑌𐑆; 𐐰𐑌𐐼 𐑄𐐩 𐐶𐐲𐑉 𐐸𐐶𐐴𐐻 𐐰𐑌𐐼 𐐿𐑊𐐨𐑉, 𐐨𐑂𐐯𐑌 𐐰𐑆 𐐻𐑉𐐰𐑌𐑅𐐹𐐩𐑉𐐯𐑌𐐻 𐑀𐑊𐐰𐑅; 𐐰𐑌𐐼 𐐸𐐨 𐐼𐐮𐐼 𐐿𐐰𐑉𐐨 𐑄𐐯𐑋 𐐮𐑌 𐐸𐐮𐑆 𐐸𐐰𐑌𐐼𐑆 𐐲𐐹𐐱𐑌 𐑄 𐐻𐐱𐐹 𐐱𐑂 𐑄 𐑋𐐵𐑌𐐻, 𐐰𐑌𐐼 𐐿𐑉𐐴𐐼 𐐲𐑀𐐯𐑌 𐐲𐑌𐐻𐐭 𐑄 𐐢𐐫𐑉𐐼, 𐑅𐐩𐐮𐑍, 𐐄 𐐢𐐫𐑉𐐼, 𐑄𐐵 𐐸𐐰𐑅𐐻 𐑅𐐯𐐼 𐑄𐐰𐐻 𐐶𐐨 𐑋𐐲𐑅𐐻 𐐺𐐨 𐐯𐑌𐐿𐐲𐑋𐐹𐐰𐑅𐐻 𐐲𐐺𐐵𐐻 𐐺𐐴 𐑄 𐑁𐑊𐐲𐐼𐑆. 𐐤𐐵 𐐺𐐨𐐸𐐬𐑊𐐼, 𐐄 𐐢𐐫𐑉𐐼, 𐐰𐑌𐐼 𐐼𐐭 𐑌𐐱𐐻 𐐺𐐨 𐐰𐑍𐑀𐑉𐐨 𐐶𐐮𐑄 𐑄𐐴 𐑅𐐲𐑉𐑂𐐰𐑌𐐻 𐐺𐐨𐐿𐐫𐑆 𐐱𐑂 𐐸𐐮𐑆 𐐶𐐨𐐿𐑌𐐯𐑅 𐐺𐐨𐑁𐐬𐑉 𐑄𐐨; 𐑁𐐫𐑉 𐐶𐐨 𐑌𐐬 𐑄𐐰𐐻 𐑄𐐵 𐐪𐑉𐐻 𐐸𐐬𐑊𐐨 𐐰𐑌𐐼 𐐼𐐶𐐯𐑊𐐯𐑅𐐻 𐐮𐑌 𐑄 𐐸𐐯𐑂𐐯𐑌𐑆; 𐐰𐑌𐐼 𐑄𐐰𐐻 𐐶𐐨 𐐪𐑉 𐐲𐑌𐐶𐐲𐑉𐑄𐐨 𐐺𐐨𐑁𐐬𐑉 𐑄𐐨; 𐐺𐐨𐐿𐐫𐑆 𐐱𐑂 𐑄 𐑁𐐫𐑊, 𐐵𐑉 𐑌𐐩𐐽𐐲𐑉𐑆 𐐸𐐰𐑂 𐐺𐐨𐐿𐐲𐑋 𐐨𐑂𐐮𐑊 𐐿𐐱𐑌𐐻𐐮𐑌𐐷𐐭𐐰𐑊𐐨; 𐑌𐐯𐑂𐐲𐑉𐑄𐐯𐑊𐐯𐑅, 𐐄 𐐢𐐫𐑉𐐼, 𐑄𐐵 𐐸𐐰𐑅𐐻 𐑀𐐮𐑂𐐯𐑌 𐐲𐑅 𐐩 𐐿𐐱𐑋𐐰𐑌𐐼𐑋𐐯𐑌𐐻 𐑄𐐰𐐻 𐐶𐐨 𐑋𐐲𐑅𐐻 𐐿𐐫𐑊 𐐲𐐹𐐱𐑌 𐑄𐐨, 𐑄𐐰𐐻 𐑁𐑉𐐱𐑋 𐑄𐐨 𐐶𐐨 𐑋𐐩 𐑉𐐨𐑅𐐨𐑂 𐐰𐐿𐐫𐑉𐐼𐐮𐑍 𐐻𐐭 𐐵𐑉 𐐼𐐨𐑆𐐴𐑉𐑆. 𐐒𐐨𐐸𐐬𐑊𐐼, 𐐄 𐐢𐐫𐑉𐐼, 𐑄𐐵 𐐸𐐰𐑅𐐻 𐑅𐑋𐐮𐐻𐐯𐑌 𐐲𐑅 𐐺𐐨𐐿𐐫𐑆 𐐱𐑂 𐐵𐑉 𐐮𐑌𐐮𐐿𐐶𐐮𐐻𐐨, 𐐰𐑌𐐼 𐐸𐐰𐑅𐐻 𐐼𐑉𐐮𐑂𐐯𐑌 𐐲𐑅 𐑁𐐬𐑉𐑃, 𐐰𐑌𐐼 𐑁𐐫𐑉 𐑄𐐨𐑆 𐑋𐐯𐑌𐐨 𐐷𐐨𐑉𐑆 𐐶𐐨 𐐸𐐰𐑂 𐐺𐐮𐑌 𐐮𐑌 𐑄 𐐶𐐮𐑊𐐼𐐲𐑉𐑌𐐯𐑅; 𐑌𐐯𐑂𐐲𐑉𐑄𐐯𐑊𐐯𐑅, 𐑄𐐵 𐐸𐐰𐑅𐐻 𐐺𐐮𐑌 𐑋𐐲𐑉𐑅𐐮𐑁𐐳𐑊 𐐲𐑌𐐻𐐭 𐐲𐑅. 𐐄 𐐢𐐫𐑉𐐼, 𐑊𐐳𐐿 𐐲𐐹𐐱𐑌 𐑋𐐨 𐐮𐑌 𐐹𐐮𐐻𐐨, 𐐰𐑌𐐼 𐐻𐐲𐑉𐑌 𐐲𐐶𐐩 𐑄𐐴𐑌 𐐰𐑍𐑀𐐲𐑉 𐑁𐑉𐐱𐑋 𐑄𐐮𐑅 𐑄𐐴 𐐹𐐨𐐹𐑊, 𐐰𐑌𐐼 𐑅𐐲𐑁𐐲𐑉 𐑌𐐱𐐻 𐑄𐐰𐐻 𐑄𐐩 𐑇𐐰𐑊 𐑀𐐬 𐑁𐐬𐑉𐑃 𐐲𐐿𐑉𐐫𐑅 𐑄𐐮𐑅 𐑉𐐩𐐾𐐮𐑍 𐐼𐐨𐐹 𐐮𐑌 𐐼𐐪𐑉𐐿𐑌𐐯𐑅, 𐐺𐐲𐐻 𐐺𐐨𐐸𐐬𐑊𐐼 𐑄𐐨𐑆 𐑃𐐮𐑍𐑆

𐐸𐐶𐐮𐐽 𐐴 𐐸𐐰𐑂 𐑋𐐬𐑊𐐻𐑌 𐐵𐐻 𐐱𐑂 𐑄 𐑉𐐪𐐿. 𐐈𐑌𐐼 𐐴 𐑌𐐬, 𐐄 𐐢𐐫𐑉𐐼, 𐑄𐐰𐐻 𐑄𐐵 𐐸𐐰𐑅𐐻 𐐫𐑊 𐐹𐐵𐐲𐑉, 𐐰𐑌𐐼 𐐿𐐰𐑌 𐐼𐐭 𐐸𐐶𐐱𐐻𐑅𐐬𐐯𐑂𐐲𐑉 𐑄𐐵 𐐶𐐮𐑊𐐻 𐑁𐐫𐑉 𐑄 𐐺𐐯𐑌𐐯𐑁𐐮𐐻 𐐱𐑂 𐑋𐐰𐑌; 𐑄𐐯𐑉𐑁𐐫𐑉 𐐻𐐲𐐽 𐑄𐐨𐑆 𐑅𐐻𐐬𐑌𐑆, 𐐄 𐐢𐐫𐑉𐐼, 𐐶𐐮𐑄 𐑄𐐴 𐑁𐐮𐑍𐑀𐐲𐑉, 𐐰𐑌𐐼 𐐹𐑉𐐨𐐹𐐩𐑉 𐑄𐐯𐑋 𐑄𐐰𐐻 𐑄𐐩 𐑋𐐩 𐑇𐐴𐑌 𐑁𐐫𐑉𐑃 𐐮𐑌 𐐼𐐪𐑉𐐿𐑌𐐯𐑅; 𐐰𐑌𐐼 𐑄𐐩 𐑇𐐰𐑊 𐑇𐐴𐑌 𐑁𐐫𐑉𐑃 𐐲𐑌𐐻𐐭 𐐲𐑅 𐐮𐑌 𐑄 𐑂𐐯𐑅𐐯𐑊𐑆 𐐸𐐶𐐮𐐽 𐐶𐐨 𐐸𐐰𐑂 𐐹𐑉𐐨𐐹𐐩𐑉𐐼, 𐑄𐐰𐐻 𐐶𐐨 𐑋𐐩 𐐸𐐰𐑂 𐑊𐐴𐐻 𐐸𐐶𐐴𐑊 𐐶𐐨 𐑇𐐰𐑊 𐐿𐑉𐐫𐑅 𐑄 𐑅𐐨. 𐐒𐐨𐐸𐐬𐑊𐐼, 𐐄 𐐢𐐫𐑉𐐼, 𐑄𐐵 𐐿𐐰𐑌𐑅𐐻 𐐼𐐭 𐑄𐐮𐑅. 𐐎𐐨 𐑌𐐬 𐑄𐐰𐐻 𐑄𐐵 𐐪𐑉𐐻 𐐩𐐺𐑊 𐐻𐐭 𐑇𐐬 𐑁𐐫𐑉𐑃 𐑀𐑉𐐩𐐻 𐐹𐐵𐐲𐑉, 𐐸𐐶𐐮𐐽 𐑊𐐳𐐿𐑅 𐑅𐑋𐐫𐑊 𐐲𐑌𐐻𐐭 𐑄 𐐲𐑌𐐼𐐲𐑉𐑅𐐻𐐰𐑌𐐼𐐮𐑍 𐐱𐑂 𐑋𐐯𐑌.

8. 𐐈𐑌𐐼 𐐮𐐻 𐐿𐐩𐑋 𐐻𐐭 𐐹𐐪𐑅 𐑄𐐰𐐻 𐐸𐐶𐐯𐑌 𐑄 𐐺𐑉𐐲𐑄𐐲𐑉 𐐱𐑂 𐐖𐐩𐑉𐐯𐐼 𐐸𐐰𐐼 𐑅𐐯𐐼 𐑄𐐨𐑆 𐐶𐐲𐑉𐐼𐑆, 𐐺𐐨𐐸𐐬𐑊𐐼, 𐑄 𐐢𐐫𐑉𐐼 𐑅𐐻𐑉𐐯𐐽𐐻 𐑁𐐫𐑉𐑃 𐐸𐐮𐑆 𐐸𐐰𐑌𐐼 𐐰𐑌𐐼 𐐻𐐲𐐽𐐻 𐑄 𐑅𐐻𐐬𐑌𐑆, 𐐶𐐲𐑌 𐐺𐐴 𐐶𐐲𐑌 𐐶𐐮𐑄 𐐸𐐮𐑆 𐑁𐐮𐑍𐑀𐐲𐑉; 𐐰𐑌𐐼 𐑄 𐑂𐐩𐑊 𐐶𐐱𐑆 𐐻𐐩𐐿𐑌 𐑁𐑉𐐱𐑋 𐐫𐑁 𐑄 𐐴𐑆 𐐱𐑂 𐑄 𐐺𐑉𐐲𐑄𐐲𐑉 𐐱𐑂 𐐖𐐩𐑉𐐯𐐼, 𐐰𐑌𐐼 𐐸𐐨 𐑅𐐫 𐑄 𐑁𐐮𐑍𐑀𐐲𐑉 𐐱𐑂 𐑄 𐐢𐐫𐑉𐐼; 𐐰𐑌𐐼 𐐮𐐻 𐐶𐐱𐑆 𐐰𐑆 𐑄 𐑁𐐮𐑍𐑀𐐲𐑉 𐐱𐑂 𐐩 𐑋𐐰𐑌, 𐑊𐐴𐐿 𐐲𐑌𐐻𐐭 𐑁𐑊𐐯𐑇 𐐰𐑌𐐼 𐐺𐑊𐐲𐐼; 𐐰𐑌𐐼 𐑄 𐐺𐑉𐐲𐑄𐐲𐑉 𐐱𐑂 𐐖𐐩𐑉𐐯𐐼 𐑁𐐯𐑊 𐐼𐐵𐑌 𐐺𐐨𐑁𐐬𐑉 𐑄 𐐢𐐫𐑉𐐼, 𐑁𐐫𐑉 𐐸𐐨 𐐶𐐱𐑆 𐑅𐐻𐑉𐐲𐐿 𐐶𐐮𐑄 𐑁𐐨𐑉. 𐐈𐑌𐐼 𐑄 𐐢𐐫𐑉𐐼 𐑅𐐫 𐑄𐐰𐐻 𐑄 𐐺𐑉𐐲𐑄𐐲𐑉 𐐱𐑂 𐐖𐐩𐑉𐐯𐐼 𐐸𐐰𐐼 𐑁𐐫𐑊𐑌 𐐻𐐭 𐑄 𐐲𐑉𐑃; 𐐰𐑌𐐼 𐑄 𐐢𐐫𐑉𐐼 𐑅𐐯𐐼 𐐲𐑌𐐻𐐭 𐐸𐐮𐑋, 𐐈𐑉𐐴𐑆, 𐐸𐐶𐐴 𐐸𐐰𐑅𐐻 𐑄𐐵 𐑁𐐫𐑊𐑌? 𐐈𐑌𐐼 𐐸𐐨 𐑅𐐩𐑃 𐐲𐑌𐐻𐐭 𐑄 𐐢𐐫𐑉𐐼, 𐐌 𐑅𐐫 𐑄 𐑁𐐮𐑍𐑀𐐲𐑉 𐐱𐑂 𐑄 𐐢𐐫𐑉𐐼, 𐐰𐑌𐐼 𐐴 𐑁𐐨𐑉𐐼 𐑊𐐯𐑅𐐻 𐐸𐐨 𐑇𐐳𐐼 𐑅𐑋𐐴𐐻 𐑋𐐨; 𐑁𐐫𐑉 𐐴 𐑌𐐭 𐑌𐐱𐐻 𐑄𐐰𐐻 𐑄 𐐢𐐫𐑉𐐼 𐐸𐐰𐐼 𐑁𐑊𐐯𐑇 𐐰𐑌𐐼 𐐺𐑊𐐲𐐼. 𐐈𐑌𐐼 𐑄 𐐢𐐫𐑉𐐼 𐑅𐐯𐐼 𐐲𐑌𐐻𐐭 𐐸𐐮𐑋, 𐐒𐐨𐐿𐐫𐑆 𐐱𐑂 𐑄𐐴 𐑁𐐩𐑃 𐑄𐐵 𐐸𐐰𐑅𐐻 𐑅𐐨𐑌 𐑄𐐰𐐻 𐐴 𐑇𐐰𐑊 𐐻𐐩𐐿 𐐲𐐹𐐱𐑌 𐑋𐐨 𐑁𐑊𐐯𐑇 𐐰𐑌𐐼 𐐺𐑊𐐲𐐼; 𐐰𐑌𐐼 𐑌𐐯𐑂𐐲𐑉 𐐸𐐰𐑆 𐑋𐐰𐑌 𐐿𐐲𐑋 𐐺𐐨𐑁𐐬𐑉 𐑋𐐨 𐐶𐐮𐑄 𐑅𐐲𐐽 𐐯𐐿𐑅𐐨𐐼𐐮𐑍 𐑁𐐩𐑃 𐐰𐑆 𐑄𐐵 𐐸𐐰𐑅𐐻; 𐑁𐐫𐑉 𐐶𐐲𐑉 𐐮𐐻 𐑌𐐱𐐻 𐑅𐐬, 𐐷𐐨 𐐿𐐳𐐼 𐑌𐐱𐐻 𐐸𐐰𐑂 𐑅𐐨𐑌 𐑋𐐴 𐑁𐐮𐑍𐑀𐐲𐑉. 𐐝𐐫𐐯𐑅𐐻 𐑄𐐵 𐑋𐐬𐑉 𐑄𐐰𐑌 𐑄𐐮𐑅? 𐐈𐑌𐐼 𐐸𐐨 𐐰𐑌𐑅𐐲𐑉𐐼, 𐐤𐐩: 𐐢𐐫𐑉𐐼, 𐑇𐐬 𐑄𐐴𐑅𐐯𐑊𐑁 𐐲𐑌𐐻𐐭 𐑋𐐨. 𐐈𐑌𐐼 𐑄 𐐢𐐫𐑉𐐼 𐑅𐐯𐐼 𐐲𐑌𐐻𐐭 𐐸𐐮𐑋, 𐐒𐐨𐑊𐐨𐑂𐐯𐑅𐐻 𐑄𐐵 𐑄 𐐶𐐲𐑉𐐼𐑆 𐐸𐐶𐐮𐐽 𐐴 𐑇𐐰𐑊 𐑅𐐹𐐨𐐿? 𐐈𐑌𐐼 𐐸𐐨 𐐰𐑌𐑅𐐲𐑉𐐼, 𐐏𐐩, 𐐢𐐫𐑉𐐼, 𐐴 𐑌𐐬 𐑄𐐰𐐻 𐑄𐐵 𐑅𐐹𐐨𐐿𐐯𐑅𐐻 𐑄 𐐻𐑉𐐭𐑃, 𐑁𐐫𐑉 𐑄𐐵 𐐪𐑉𐐻 𐐩 𐐘𐐱𐐼 𐐱𐑂 𐐻𐑉𐐭𐑃, 𐐰𐑌𐐼 𐐿𐐰𐑌𐑅𐐻 𐑌𐐱𐐻 𐑊𐐴. 𐐈𐑌𐐼 𐐸𐐶𐐯𐑌 𐐸𐐨 𐐸𐐰𐐼 𐑅𐐯𐐼 𐑄𐐨𐑆 𐐶𐐲𐑉𐐼𐑆, 𐐺𐐨𐐸𐐬𐑊𐐼, 𐑄 𐐢𐐫𐑉𐐼 𐑇𐐬𐐼 𐐸𐐮𐑋𐑅𐐯𐑊𐑁 𐐲𐑌𐐻𐐭 𐐸𐐮𐑋, 𐐰𐑌𐐼 𐑅𐐯𐐼, 𐐒𐐨𐐿𐐫𐑆 𐑄𐐵 𐑌𐐬𐐯𐑅𐐻 𐑄𐐨𐑆 𐑃𐐮𐑍𐑆, 𐐷𐐨 𐐪𐑉 𐑉𐐨𐐼𐐨𐑋𐐼 𐑁𐑉𐐱𐑋 𐑄 𐑁𐐫𐑊; 𐑄𐐯𐑉𐑁𐐫𐑉 𐐷𐐨 𐐪𐑉 𐐺𐑉𐐫𐐻 𐐺𐐰𐐿 𐐮𐑌𐐻𐐭 𐑋𐐴 𐐹𐑉𐐯𐑆𐐯𐑌𐑅; 𐑄𐐯𐑉𐑁𐐫𐑉 𐐴 𐑇𐐬 𐑋𐐴𐑅𐐯𐑊𐑁 𐐲𐑌𐐻𐐭 𐐷𐐭. 𐐒𐐨𐐸𐐬𐑊𐐼, 𐐴 𐐰𐑋 𐐸𐐨 𐐸𐐭 𐐶𐐱𐑆 𐐹𐑉𐐨𐐹𐐩𐑉𐐼 𐑁𐑉𐐱𐑋 𐑄 𐑁𐐵𐑌𐐼𐐩𐑇𐐲𐑌 𐐱𐑂 𐑄 𐐶𐐲𐑉𐑊𐐼 𐐻𐐭 𐑉𐐨𐐼𐐨𐑋 𐑋𐐴 𐐹𐐨𐐹𐑊. 𐐒𐐨𐐸𐐬𐑊𐐼, 𐐴 𐐰𐑋 𐐖𐐨𐑆𐐲𐑅 𐐗𐑉𐐴𐑅𐐻. 𐐌 𐐰𐑋 𐑄 𐐙𐐪𐑄𐐲𐑉 𐐰𐑌𐐼 𐑄 𐐝𐐲𐑌. 𐐆𐑌 𐑋𐐨 𐑇𐐰𐑊 𐐫𐑊 𐑋𐐰𐑌𐐿𐐴𐑌𐐼 𐐸𐐰𐑂 𐑊𐐴𐑁, 𐐰𐑌𐐼 𐑄𐐰𐐻 𐐨𐐻𐐲𐑉𐑌𐐰𐑊𐐨, 𐐨𐑂𐐯𐑌 𐑄𐐩 𐐸𐐭 𐑇𐐰𐑊 𐐺𐐨𐑊𐐨𐑂 𐐱𐑌 𐑋𐐴 𐑌𐐩𐑋; 𐐰𐑌𐐼 𐑄𐐩 𐑇𐐰𐑊 𐐺𐐨𐐿𐐲𐑋 𐑋𐐴 𐑅𐐲𐑌𐑆 𐐰𐑌𐐼 𐑋𐐴 𐐼𐐫𐐻𐐲𐑉𐑆. 𐐈𐑌𐐼 𐑌𐐯𐑂𐐲𐑉 𐐸𐐰𐑂 𐐴 𐑇𐐬𐐼 𐑋𐐴𐑅𐐯𐑊𐑁 𐐲𐑌𐐻𐐭 𐑋𐐰𐑌 𐐸𐐭𐑋 𐐴 𐐸𐐰𐑂 𐐿𐑉𐐨𐐩𐐻𐐯𐐼, 𐑁𐐫𐑉 𐑌𐐯𐑂𐐲𐑉 𐐸𐐰𐑆 𐑋𐐰𐑌 𐐺𐐨𐑊𐐨𐑂𐐼 𐐮𐑌 𐑋𐐨 𐐰𐑆 𐑄𐐵 𐐸𐐰𐑅𐐻. 𐐝𐐨𐐯𐑅𐐻 𐑄𐐵 𐑄𐐰𐐻 𐐷𐐨 𐐪𐑉 𐐿𐑉𐐨𐐩𐐻𐐯𐐼 𐐪𐑁𐐻𐐲𐑉 𐑋𐐴𐑌 𐐬𐑌 𐐮𐑋𐐯𐐾? 𐐏𐐩, 𐐨𐑂𐐯𐑌 𐐫𐑊 𐑋𐐯𐑌 𐐶𐐲𐑉 𐐿𐑉𐐨𐐩𐐻𐐯𐐼 𐐮𐑌 𐑄 𐐺𐐨𐑀𐐮𐑌𐐮𐑍 𐐪𐑁𐐻𐐲𐑉 𐑋𐐴𐑌 𐐬𐑌 𐐮𐑋𐐯𐐾. 𐐒𐐨𐐸𐐬𐑊𐐼, 𐑄𐐮𐑅 𐐺𐐱𐐼𐐨, 𐐸𐐶𐐮𐐽 𐐷𐐨 𐑌𐐵 𐐺𐐨𐐸𐐬𐑊𐐼, 𐐮𐑆 𐑄 𐐺𐐱𐐼𐐨 𐐱𐑂 𐑋𐐴 𐑅𐐹𐐮𐑉𐐮𐐻; 𐐰𐑌𐐼 𐑋𐐰𐑌 𐐸𐐰𐑂 𐐴 𐐿𐑉𐐨𐐩𐐻𐐯𐐼 𐐪𐑁𐐻𐐲𐑉 𐑄 𐐺𐐱𐐼𐐨 𐐱𐑂 𐑋𐐴 𐑅𐐹𐐮𐑉𐐮𐐻; 𐐰𐑌𐐼 𐐨𐑂𐐯𐑌 𐐰𐑆 𐐴 𐐰𐐹𐐨𐑉 𐐲𐑌𐐻𐐭 𐑄𐐨 𐐻𐐭 𐐺𐐨 𐐮𐑌 𐑄 𐑅𐐹𐐮𐑉𐐮𐐻 𐐶𐐮𐑊 𐐴 𐐰𐐹𐐨𐑉 𐐲𐑌𐐻𐐭 𐑋𐐴 𐐹𐐨𐐹𐑊 𐐮𐑌 𐑄 𐑁𐑊𐐯𐑇.

9. 𐐈𐑌𐐼 𐑌𐐵, 𐐰𐑆 𐐴, 𐐣𐐫𐑉𐐬𐑌𐐴, 𐑅𐐯𐐼 𐐴 𐐿𐐳𐐼 𐑌𐐱𐐻 𐑋𐐩𐐿 𐐩 𐑁𐐳𐑊 𐐰𐐿𐐵𐑌𐐻 𐐱𐑂 𐑄𐐨𐑆 𐑃𐐮𐑍𐑆 𐐸𐐶𐐮𐐽 𐐪𐑉 𐑉𐐮𐐻𐑌, 𐑄𐐯𐑉𐑁𐐫𐑉 𐐮𐐻 𐑅𐐲𐑁𐐴𐑅𐐯𐑃 𐑋𐐨 𐐻𐐭 𐑅𐐩, 𐑄𐐰𐐻 𐐖𐐨𐑆𐐲𐑅 𐑇𐐬𐐼 𐐸𐐮𐑋𐑅𐐯𐑊𐑁 𐐲𐑌𐐻𐐭 𐑄𐐮𐑅 𐑋𐐰𐑌 𐐮𐑌 𐑄 𐑅𐐹𐐮𐑉𐐮𐐻, 𐐨𐑂𐐯𐑌 𐐪𐑁𐐻𐐲𐑉 𐑄 𐑋𐐰𐑌𐐲𐑉 𐐰𐑌𐐼 𐐮𐑌 𐑄 𐑊𐐴𐐿𐑌𐐯𐑅 𐐱𐑂 𐑄 𐑅𐐩𐑋 𐐺𐐱𐐼𐐨, 𐐨𐑂𐐯𐑌 𐐰𐑆 𐐸𐐨 𐑇𐐬𐐼 𐐸𐐮𐑋𐑅𐐯𐑊𐑁 𐐲𐑌𐐻𐐭 𐑄 𐐤𐐨𐑁𐐴𐐻𐑅; 𐐰𐑌𐐼 𐐸𐐨 𐑋𐐮𐑌𐐮𐑅𐐻𐐲𐑉𐐼 𐐲𐑌𐐻𐐭 𐐸𐐮𐑋 𐐨𐑂𐐯𐑌 𐐰𐑆 𐐸𐐨 𐑋𐐮𐑌𐐮𐑅𐐻𐐲𐑉𐐼 𐐲𐑌𐐻𐐭 𐑄 𐐤𐐨𐑁𐐴𐐻𐑅; 𐐰𐑌𐐼 𐐫𐑊 𐑄𐐮𐑅, 𐑄𐐰𐐻 𐑄𐐮𐑅 𐑋𐐰𐑌 𐑋𐐴𐐻 𐑌𐐬 𐑄𐐰𐐻 𐐸𐐨 𐐶𐐱𐑆 𐐘𐐱𐐼, 𐐺𐐨𐐿𐐫𐑆 𐐱𐑂 𐑄 𐑋𐐯𐑌𐐨 𐑀𐑉𐐩𐐻 𐐶𐐲𐑉𐐿𐑅 𐐸𐐶𐐮𐐽 𐑄 𐐢𐐫𐑉𐐼 𐐸𐐰𐐼 𐑇𐐬𐐼 𐐲𐑌𐐻𐐭 𐐸𐐮𐑋. 𐐈𐑌𐐼 𐐺𐐨𐐿𐐫𐑆 𐐱𐑂 𐑄 𐑌𐐱𐑊𐐯𐐾 𐐱𐑂 𐑄𐐮𐑅 𐑋𐐰𐑌, 𐐸𐐨 𐐿𐐳𐐼 𐑌𐐱𐐻 𐐺𐐨 𐐿𐐯𐐹𐐻 𐑁𐑉𐐱𐑋 𐐺𐐨𐐸𐐬𐑊𐐼𐐮𐑍 𐐶𐐮𐑄𐐮𐑌 𐑄 𐑂𐐩𐑊; 𐐰𐑌𐐼 𐐸𐐨 𐑅𐐫 𐑄 𐑁𐐮𐑍𐑀𐐲𐑉 𐐱𐑂 𐐖𐐨𐑆𐐲𐑅, 𐐸𐐶𐐮𐐽, 𐐸𐐶𐐯𐑌 𐐸𐐨 𐑅𐐫, 𐐸𐐨 𐑁𐐯𐑊 𐐶𐐮𐑄 𐑁𐐨𐑉; 𐑁𐐫𐑉 𐐸𐐨 𐑌𐐭 𐑄𐐰𐐻 𐐮𐐻 𐐶𐐱𐑆 𐑄 𐑁𐐮𐑍𐑀𐐲𐑉 𐐱𐑂 𐑄 𐐢𐐫𐑉𐐼; 𐐰𐑌𐐼 𐐸𐐨 𐐸𐐰𐐼 𐑁𐐩𐑃 𐑌𐐬 𐑊𐐱𐑍𐑀𐐲𐑉, 𐑁𐐫𐑉 𐐸𐐨 𐑌𐐭, 𐑌𐐲𐑃𐐮𐑍 𐐼𐐵𐐻𐐮𐑍; 𐐸𐐶𐐯𐑉𐑁𐐫𐑉, 𐐸𐐰𐑂𐐮𐑍

𐑄𐐮𐑅 𐐹𐐲𐑉𐑁𐐯𐐿𐐻 𐑌𐐱𐑊𐐯𐐾 𐐱𐑂 𐐘𐐱𐐼, 𐐸𐐨 𐐿𐐳𐐼 𐑌𐐱𐐻 𐐺𐐨 𐐿𐐯𐐹𐐻 𐑁𐑉𐐱𐑋 𐐶𐐮𐑄𐐮𐑌 𐑄 𐑂𐐩𐑊; 𐑄𐐯𐑉𐑁𐐬𐑉 𐐸𐐨 𐑅𐐫 𐐖𐐨𐑆𐐲𐑅, 𐐰𐑌𐐼 𐐸𐐨 𐐼𐐮𐐼 𐑋𐐮𐑌𐐮𐑅𐐻𐐲𐑉 𐐲𐑌𐐻𐐭 𐐸𐐮𐑋.

10. 𐐈𐑌𐐼 𐐮𐐻 𐐿𐐩𐑋 𐐻𐐭 𐐹𐐰𐑅 𐑄𐐰𐐻 𐑄 𐐢𐐫𐑉𐐼 𐑅𐐯𐐼 𐐲𐑌𐐻𐐭 𐑄 𐐺𐑉𐐲𐑄𐐲𐑉 𐐱𐑂 𐐖𐐯𐑉𐐲𐐼, 𐐒𐐨𐐸𐐬𐑊𐐼, 𐑄𐐵 𐑇𐐰𐑊𐐻 𐑌𐐱𐐻 𐑅𐐲𐑁𐐲𐑉 𐑄𐐨𐑆 𐑃𐐮𐑍𐑆 𐐸𐐶𐐮𐐽 𐐷𐐨 𐐸𐐰𐑂 𐑅𐐨𐑌 𐐰𐑌𐐼 𐐸𐐲𐑉𐐼, 𐐻𐐭 𐑀𐐬 𐑁𐐫𐑉𐑃 𐐲𐑌𐐻𐐭 𐑄 𐐶𐐲𐑉𐑊𐐼, 𐐲𐑌𐐻𐐮𐑊 𐑄 𐐻𐐴𐑋 𐐿𐐲𐑋𐐯𐑃 𐑄𐐰𐐻 𐐌 𐑇𐐰𐑊 𐑀𐑊𐐫𐑉𐐮𐑁𐐴 𐑋𐐴 𐑌𐐩𐑋 𐐮𐑌 𐑄 𐑁𐑊𐐯𐑇; 𐐸𐐶𐐯𐑉𐑁𐐫𐑉, 𐐷𐐨 𐑇𐐰𐑊 𐐻𐑉𐐯𐑈𐐲𐑉 𐐲𐐹 𐑄 𐑃𐐮𐑍𐑆 𐐸𐐶𐐮𐐽 𐐷𐐨 𐐸𐐰𐑂 𐑅𐐨𐑌 𐐰𐑌𐐼 𐐸𐐲𐑉𐐼, 𐐰𐑌𐐼 𐑇𐐬 𐐮𐐻 𐐻𐐭 𐑌𐐬 𐑋𐐰𐑌. 𐐈𐑌𐐼 𐐺𐐨𐐸𐐬𐑊𐐼, 𐐸𐐶𐐯𐑌 𐐷𐐨 𐑇𐐰𐑊 𐐿𐐲𐑋 𐐲𐑌𐐻𐐭 𐑋𐐨, 𐐷𐐨 𐑇𐐰𐑊 𐑉𐐴𐐻 𐑄𐐯𐑋 𐐰𐑌𐐼 𐑇𐐰𐑊 𐑅𐐨𐑊 𐑄𐐯𐑋 𐐲𐐹, 𐑄𐐰𐐻 𐑌𐐬 𐐶𐐲𐑌 𐐿𐐰𐑌 𐐮𐑌𐐻𐐲𐑉𐐹𐑉𐐯𐐻 𐑄𐐯𐑋; 𐑁𐐫𐑉 𐐷𐐨 𐑇𐐰𐑊 𐑉𐐴𐐻 𐑄𐐯𐑋 𐐮𐑌 𐐲 𐑊𐐰𐑍𐑀𐐶𐐩𐐾 𐑄𐐰𐐻 𐑄𐐩 𐐿𐐰𐑌𐐱𐐻 𐐺𐐨 𐑉𐐯𐐼. 𐐈𐑌𐐼 𐐺𐐨𐐸𐐬𐑊𐐼, 𐑄𐐨𐑆 𐐻𐐭 𐑅𐐻𐐬𐑌𐑆 𐐶𐐮𐑊 𐐌 𐑀𐐮𐑂 𐐲𐑌𐐻𐐭 𐑄𐐨, 𐐰𐑌𐐼 𐐷𐐨 𐑇𐐰𐑊 𐑅𐐨𐑊 𐑄𐐯𐑋 𐐲𐐹 𐐫𐑊𐑅𐐬, 𐐶𐐮𐑃 𐑄 𐑃𐐮𐑍𐑆 𐐸𐐶𐐮𐐽 𐐷𐐨 𐑇𐐰𐑊 𐑉𐐴𐐻. 𐐙𐐫𐑉 𐐺𐐨𐐸𐐬𐑊𐐼, 𐑄 𐑊𐐰𐑍𐑀𐐶𐐩𐐾 𐐸𐐶𐐮𐐽 𐐷𐐨 𐑇𐐰𐑊 𐑉𐐴𐐻 𐐌 𐐸𐐰𐑂 𐐿𐐱𐑌𐑁𐐵𐑌𐐼𐐯𐐼; 𐐸𐐶𐐯𐑉𐑁𐐫𐑉 𐐌 𐐶𐐮𐑊 𐐿𐐫𐑆 𐐮𐑌 𐑋𐐴 𐐬𐑌 𐐼𐐭 𐐻𐐴𐑋 𐑄𐐰𐐻 𐑄𐐨𐑆 𐑅𐐻𐐬𐑌𐑆 𐑇𐐰𐑊 𐑋𐐰𐑀𐑌𐐮𐑁𐐴 𐐻𐐭 𐑄 𐐴𐑆 𐐱𐑂 𐑋𐐯𐑌, 𐑄𐐨𐑆 𐑃𐐮𐑍𐑆 𐐸𐐶𐐮𐐽 𐐷𐐨 𐑇𐐰𐑊 𐑉𐐴𐐻. 𐐈𐑌𐐼 𐐸𐐶𐐯𐑌 𐑄 𐐢𐐫𐑉𐐼 𐐸𐐰𐐼 𐑅𐐯𐐼 𐑄𐐨𐑆 𐐶𐐲𐑉𐐼𐑆, 𐐸𐐨 𐑇𐐬𐐼 𐐲𐑌𐐻𐐭 𐑄 𐐺𐑉𐐲𐑄𐐲𐑉 𐐱𐑂 𐐖𐐯𐑉𐐲𐐼 𐐫𐑊 𐑄 𐐮𐑌𐐸𐐰𐐺𐐮𐐻𐐲𐑌𐐻𐑅 𐐱𐑂 𐑄 𐐲𐑉𐑃 𐐸𐐶𐐮𐐽 𐐸𐐰𐐼 𐐺𐐮𐑌, 𐐰𐑌𐐼 𐐫𐑊𐑅𐐬 𐐫𐑊 𐑄𐐰𐐻 𐐶𐐳𐐼 𐐺𐐨; 𐐰𐑌𐐼 𐐸𐐨 𐐶𐐮𐑃𐐸𐐯𐑊𐐼 𐑄𐐯𐑋 𐑌𐐱𐐻 𐑁𐑉𐐱𐑋 𐐸𐐮𐑆 𐑅𐐴𐐻, 𐐨𐑂𐐯𐑌 𐐲𐑌𐐻𐐭 𐑄 𐐯𐑌𐐼𐑆 𐐱𐑂 𐑄 𐐲𐑉𐑃; 𐑁𐐫𐑉 𐐸𐐨 𐐸𐐰𐐼 𐑅𐐯𐐼 𐐲𐑌𐐻𐐭 𐐸𐐮𐑋 𐐮𐑌 𐐻𐐴𐑋𐑆 𐐺𐐨𐑁𐐬𐑉, 𐑄𐐰𐐻 𐐮𐑁 𐐸𐐨 𐐶𐐳𐐼 𐐺𐐨𐑊𐐨𐑂 𐐮𐑌 𐐸𐐮𐑋, 𐑄𐐰𐐻 𐐸𐐨 𐐿𐐳𐐼 𐑇𐐬 𐐲𐑌𐐻𐐭 𐐸𐐮𐑋 𐐫𐑊 𐑃𐐮𐑍𐑆—𐐮𐐻 𐑇𐐳𐐼 𐐺𐐨 𐑇𐐬𐑌 𐐲𐑌𐐻𐐭 𐐸𐐮𐑋; 𐑄𐐯𐑉𐑁𐐬𐑉 𐑄 𐐢𐐫𐑉𐐼 𐐿𐐳𐐼 𐑌𐐱𐐻 𐐶𐐮𐑃𐐸𐐬𐑊𐐼 𐐯𐑌𐐮𐑃𐐮𐑍 𐑁𐑉𐐱𐑋 𐐸𐐮𐑋, 𐑁𐐫𐑉 𐐸𐐨 𐑌𐐭 𐑄𐐰𐐻 𐑄 𐐢𐐫𐑉𐐼 𐐿𐐳𐐼 𐑇𐐬 𐐸𐐮𐑋 𐐫𐑊 𐑃𐐮𐑍𐑆. 𐐈𐑌𐐼 𐑄 𐐢𐐫𐑉𐐼 𐑅𐐯𐐼 𐐲𐑌𐐻𐐭 𐐸𐐮𐑋, 𐐡𐐴𐐻 𐑄𐐨𐑆 𐑃𐐮𐑍𐑆 𐐰𐑌𐐼 𐑅𐐨𐑊 𐑄𐐯𐑋 𐐲𐐹, 𐐰𐑌𐐼 𐐌 𐐶𐐮𐑊 𐑇𐐬 𐑄𐐯𐑋 𐐮𐑌 𐑋𐐴𐑌 𐐬𐑌 𐐼𐐭 𐐻𐐴𐑋 𐐲𐑌𐐻𐐭 𐑄 𐐽𐐮𐑊𐐼𐑉𐐯𐑌 𐐱𐑂 𐑋𐐯𐑌.

11. 𐐈𐑌𐐼 𐐮𐐻 𐐿𐐩𐑋 𐐻𐐭 𐐹𐐰𐑅 𐑄𐐰𐐻 𐑄 𐐢𐐫𐑉𐐼 𐐿𐐱𐑋𐐰𐑌𐐼𐐯𐐼 𐐸𐐮𐑋 𐑄𐐰𐐻 𐐸𐐨 𐑇𐐳𐐼 𐑅𐐨𐑊 𐐲𐐹 𐑄 𐐻𐐭 𐑅𐐻𐐬𐑌𐑆 𐐸𐐶𐐮𐐽 𐐸𐐨 𐐸𐐰𐐼 𐑉𐐨𐑅𐐨𐑂𐐼, 𐐰𐑌𐐼 𐑇𐐬 𐑄𐐯𐑋 𐑌𐐱𐐻, 𐐲𐑌𐐻𐐮𐑊 𐑄 𐐢𐐫𐑉𐐼 𐑇𐐳𐐼 𐑇𐐬 𐑄𐐯𐑋 𐐲𐑌𐐻𐐭 𐑄 𐐽𐐮𐑊𐐼𐑉𐐯𐑌 𐐱𐑂 𐑋𐐯𐑌. 𐐈𐑌𐐼 𐑄 𐐢𐐫𐑉𐐼 𐐿𐐱𐑋𐐰𐑌𐐼𐐯𐐼 𐑄 𐐺𐑉𐐲𐑄𐐲𐑉 𐐱𐑂 𐐖𐐯𐑉𐐲𐐼 𐐻𐐭 𐑀𐐬 𐐼𐐵𐑌 𐐵𐐻 𐐱𐑂 𐑄 𐑋𐐵𐑌𐐻 𐑁𐑉𐐱𐑋 𐑄 𐐹𐑉𐐯𐑆𐐯𐑌𐑅 𐐱𐑂 𐑄 𐐢𐐫𐑉𐐼, 𐐰𐑌𐐼 𐑉𐐴𐐻 𐑄 𐑃𐐮𐑍𐑆 𐐸𐐶𐐮𐐽 𐐸𐐨 𐐸𐐰𐐼 𐑅𐐨𐑌; 𐐰𐑌𐐼 𐑄𐐩 𐐪𐑉 𐑁𐐫𐑉𐐺𐐮𐐼𐑌 𐐻𐐭 𐐿𐐲𐑋 𐐲𐑌𐐻𐐭 𐑄 𐐽𐐮𐑊𐐼𐑉𐐯𐑌 𐐱𐑂 𐑋𐐯𐑌, 𐐲𐑌𐐻𐐮𐑊 𐐰𐑁𐐻𐐲𐑉 𐑄𐐰𐐻 𐐸𐐨 𐑇𐐳𐐼 𐐺𐐨 𐑊𐐮𐑁𐐻𐐯𐐼 𐐲𐐹 𐐲𐐹𐐱𐑌 𐑄 𐐿𐑉𐐱𐑅; 𐐰𐑌𐐼 𐑁𐐫𐑉 𐑄𐐮𐑅 𐐿𐐫𐑆 𐐼𐐮𐐼 𐐿𐐮𐑍 𐐣𐐬𐑆𐐴𐐲 𐐿𐐨𐐹 𐑄𐐯𐑋, 𐑄𐐰𐐻 𐑄𐐩 𐑇𐐳𐐼 𐑌𐐱𐐻 𐐿𐐲𐑋 𐐲𐑌𐐻𐐭 𐑄 𐐶𐐲𐑉𐑊𐐼 𐐲𐑌𐐻𐐮𐑊 𐐰𐑁𐐻𐐲𐑉 𐐗𐑉𐐴𐑅𐐻 𐑇𐐳𐐼 𐑇𐐬 𐐸𐐮𐑋𐑅𐐯𐑊𐑁 𐐲𐑌𐐻𐐭 𐐸𐐮𐑆 𐐹𐐨𐐹𐑊. 𐐈𐑌𐐼 𐐰𐑁𐐻𐐲𐑉 𐐗𐑉𐐴𐑅𐐻 𐐻𐑉𐐭𐑊𐐨 𐐸𐐰𐐼 𐑇𐐬𐐼 𐐸𐐮𐑋𐑅𐐯𐑊𐑁 𐐲𐑌𐐻𐐭 𐐸𐐮𐑆 𐐹𐐨𐐹𐑊, 𐐸𐐨 𐐿𐐱𐑋𐐰𐑌𐐼𐐯𐐼 𐑄𐐰𐐻 𐑄𐐩 𐑇𐐳𐐼 𐐺𐐨 𐑋𐐩𐐼 𐑋𐐰𐑌𐐮𐑁𐐯𐑅𐐻. 𐐈𐑌𐐼 𐑌𐐵, 𐐰𐑁𐐻𐐲𐑉 𐑄𐐰𐐻 𐑄𐐩 𐐸𐐰𐑂 𐐫𐑊 𐐼𐐶𐐮𐑌𐐼𐑊𐐼 𐐮𐑌 𐐲𐑌𐐺𐐨𐑊𐐨𐑁, 𐐰𐑌𐐼 𐑄𐐯𐑉 𐐮𐑆 𐑌𐐲𐑌 𐑅𐐩𐑂 𐐮𐐻 𐐺𐐨 𐑄 𐐢𐐩𐑋𐐲𐑌𐐴𐐻𐑅, 𐐰𐑌𐐼 𐑄𐐩 𐐸𐐰𐑂 𐑉𐐨𐐾𐐯𐐿𐐻𐐯𐐼 𐑄 𐑀𐐱𐑅𐐹𐐯𐑊 𐐱𐑂 𐐗𐑉𐐴𐑅𐐻; 𐑄𐐯𐑉𐑁𐐬𐑉, 𐐌 𐐰𐑋 𐐿𐐱𐑋𐐰𐑌𐐼𐐯𐐼 𐑄𐐰𐐻 𐐌 𐑇𐐳𐐼 𐐸𐐴𐐼 𐑄𐐯𐑋 𐐲𐐹 𐐲𐑀𐐯𐑌 𐐮𐑌 𐑄 𐐲𐑉𐑃. 𐐒𐐨𐐸𐐬𐑊𐐼, 𐐌 𐐸𐐰𐑂 𐑉𐐮𐐻𐑌 𐐲𐐹𐐱𐑌 𐑄𐐨𐑆 𐐹𐑊𐐩𐐻𐑅 𐑄 𐑂𐐯𐑉𐐨 𐑃𐐮𐑍𐑆 𐐸𐐶𐐮𐐽 𐑄 𐐺𐑉𐐲𐑄𐐲𐑉 𐐱𐑂 𐐖𐐯𐑉𐐲𐐼 𐑅𐐫; 𐐰𐑌𐐼 𐑄𐐯𐑉 𐑌𐐯𐑂𐐲𐑉 𐐶𐐲𐑉 𐑀𐑉𐐩𐐻𐐲𐑉 𐑃𐐮𐑍𐑆 𐑋𐐩𐐼 𐑋𐐰𐑌𐐮𐑁𐐯𐑅𐐻 𐑄𐐰𐑌 𐑄𐐰𐐻 𐐸𐐶𐐮𐐽 𐐶𐐲𐑉 𐑋𐐩𐐼 𐑋𐐰𐑌𐐮𐑁𐐯𐑅𐐻 𐐲𐑌𐐻𐐭 𐑄 𐐺𐑉𐐲𐑄𐐲𐑉 𐐱𐑂 𐐖𐐯𐑉𐐲𐐼; 𐐸𐐶𐐯𐑉𐑁𐐫𐑉 𐑄 𐐢𐐫𐑉𐐼 𐐸𐐰𐑃 𐐿𐐱𐑋𐐰𐑌𐐼𐐯𐐼 𐑋𐐨 𐐻𐐭 𐑉𐐴𐐻 𐑄𐐯𐑋; 𐐰𐑌𐐼 𐐌 𐐸𐐰𐑂 𐑉𐐮𐐻𐑌 𐑄𐐯𐑋. 𐐈𐑌𐐼 𐐸𐐨 𐐿𐐱𐑋𐐰𐑌𐐼𐐯𐐼 𐑋𐐨 𐑄𐐰𐐻 𐐌 𐑇𐐳𐐼 𐑅𐐨𐑊 𐑄𐐯𐑋 𐐲𐐹; 𐐰𐑌𐐼 𐐸𐐨 𐐫𐑊𐑅𐐬 𐐸𐐰𐑃 𐐿𐐱𐑋𐐰𐑌𐐼𐐯𐐼 𐑄𐐰𐐻 𐐌 𐑇𐐳𐐼 𐑅𐐨𐑊 𐐲𐐹 𐑄 𐐮𐑌𐐻𐐲𐑉𐐹𐑉𐐯𐐻𐐩𐑇𐐲𐑌 𐑄𐐯𐑉𐐱𐑂; 𐐸𐐶𐐯𐑉𐑁𐐫𐑉 𐐌 𐐸𐐰𐑂 𐑅𐐨𐑊𐐼 𐐲𐐹 𐑄 𐐮𐑌𐐻𐐲𐑉𐐹𐑉𐐯𐐻𐐲𐑉𐑆, 𐐰𐐿𐐫𐑉𐐼𐐮𐑍 𐐻𐐭 𐑄 𐐿𐐱𐑋𐐰𐑌𐐼𐑋𐐯𐑌𐐻 𐐱𐑂 𐑄 𐐢𐐫𐑉𐐼. 𐐙𐐫𐑉 𐑄 𐐢𐐫𐑉𐐼 𐑅𐐯𐐼 𐐲𐑌𐐻𐐭 𐑋𐐨, 𐐜𐐩 𐑇𐐰𐑊 𐑌𐐱𐐻 𐑀𐐬 𐑁𐐫𐑉𐑃 𐐲𐑌𐐻𐐭 𐑄 𐐖𐐯𐑌𐐻𐐴𐑊𐑆 𐐲𐑌𐐻𐐮𐑊 𐑄 𐐼𐐩 𐑄𐐰𐐻 𐑄𐐩 𐑇𐐰𐑊 𐑉𐐨𐐹𐐯𐑌𐐻 𐐱𐑂 𐑄𐐯𐑉 𐐮𐑌𐐮𐐿𐐶𐐮𐐻𐐨, 𐐰𐑌𐐼 𐐺𐐨𐐿𐐲𐑋 𐐿𐑊𐐨𐑌 𐐺𐐨𐑁𐐬𐑉 𐑄 𐐢𐐫𐑉𐐼; 𐐰𐑌𐐼 𐐮𐑌 𐑄𐐰𐐻 𐐼𐐩 𐑄𐐰𐐻 𐑄𐐩 𐑇𐐰𐑊 𐐯𐐿𐑅𐐲𐑉𐑅𐐴𐑆 𐑁𐐩𐑃 𐐮𐑌 𐑋𐐨, 𐑅𐐯𐑃 𐑄 𐐢𐐫𐑉𐐼, 𐐨𐑂𐐯𐑌 𐐰𐑆 𐑄 𐐺𐑉𐐲𐑄𐐲𐑉 𐐱𐑂 𐐖𐐯𐑉𐐲𐐼 𐐼𐐮𐐼, 𐑄𐐰𐐻 𐑄𐐩 𐑋𐐩 𐐺𐐨𐐿𐐲𐑋 𐑅𐐰𐑍𐐿𐐻𐐮𐑁𐐴𐐼 𐐮𐑌 𐑋𐐨, 𐑄𐐯𐑌 𐐶𐐮𐑊 𐐌 𐑋𐐰𐑌𐐮𐑁𐐯𐑅𐐻 𐐲𐑌𐐻𐐭 𐑄𐐯𐑋 𐑄 𐑃𐐮𐑍𐑆 𐐸𐐶𐐮𐐽 𐑄 𐐺𐑉𐐲𐑄𐐲𐑉 𐐱𐑂 𐐖𐐯𐑉𐐲𐐼 𐑅𐐫, 𐐨𐑂𐐯𐑌 𐐻𐐭 𐑄 𐐲𐑌𐑁𐐬𐑊𐐼𐐮𐑍 𐐲𐑌𐐻𐐭 𐑄𐐯𐑋 𐐫𐑊 𐑋𐐴 𐑉𐐯𐑂𐐯𐑊𐐩𐑇𐐲𐑌𐑆, 𐑅𐐯𐑃 𐐖𐐨𐑆𐐲𐑅 𐐗𐑉𐐴𐑅𐐻, 𐑄 𐐝𐐲𐑌 𐐱𐑂 𐐘𐐱𐐼, 𐑄 𐐙𐐪𐑄𐐲𐑉 𐐱𐑂 𐑄 𐐸𐐯𐑂𐑌𐑆 𐐰𐑌𐐼 𐐱𐑂 𐑄 𐐲𐑉𐑃, 𐐰𐑌𐐼 𐐫𐑊 𐑃𐐮𐑍𐑆 𐑄𐐰𐐻 𐐮𐑌 𐑄𐐯𐑋 𐐮𐑆. 𐐈𐑌𐐼 𐐸𐐨 𐑄𐐰𐐻 𐐶𐐮𐑊 𐐿𐐱𐑌𐐻𐐯𐑌𐐼 𐐲𐑀𐐯𐑌𐑅𐐻 𐑄 𐐶𐐲𐑉𐐼 𐐱𐑂 𐑄

𐐢𐐫𐑉𐐼, 𐑊𐐯𐐻 𐐸𐐮𐑋 𐐺 𐐰𐐿𐐲𐑉𐑅𐐻; 𐐰𐑌𐐼 𐐸𐐨 𐑄𐐰𐐻 𐑇𐐰𐑊 𐐼𐐨𐑌𐐴 𐑄𐐨𐑆 𐑃𐐮𐑍𐑆, 𐑊𐐯𐐻 𐐸𐐮𐑋 𐐺 𐐰𐐿𐐲𐑉𐑅𐐻: 𐑁𐐫𐑉 𐐲𐑌𐐻𐐭 𐑄𐐯𐑋 𐐶𐐮𐑊 𐐌 𐑇𐐬 𐑌𐐬 𐑀𐑉𐐩𐐻𐐲𐑉 𐑃𐐮𐑍𐑆, 𐑅𐐯𐑃 𐐖𐐨𐑆𐐲𐑅 𐐗𐑉𐐴𐑅𐐻, 𐑁𐐫𐑉 𐐌 𐐰𐑋 𐐸𐐨 𐐸𐐭 𐑅𐐹𐐨𐐿𐐯𐑃; 𐐰𐑌𐐼 𐐰𐐻 𐑋𐐴 𐐿𐐱𐑋𐐰𐑌𐐼 𐑄 𐐸𐐯𐑂𐐯𐑌𐑆 𐐪𐑉 𐐬𐐹𐐯𐑌𐐼 𐐰𐑌𐐼 𐐪𐑉 𐑇𐐲𐐻; 𐐰𐑌𐐼 𐐰𐐻 𐑋𐐴 𐐶𐐲𐑉𐐼, 𐑄 𐐲𐑉𐑃 𐑇𐐰𐑊 𐑇𐐩𐐿; 𐐰𐑌𐐼 𐐰𐐻 𐑋𐐴 𐐿𐐱𐑋𐐰𐑌𐐼, 𐑄 𐐮𐑌𐐸𐐰𐐺𐐮𐐻𐐰𐑌𐐻𐑅 𐑄𐐯𐑉𐐱𐑂 𐑇𐐰𐑊 𐐹𐐰𐑅 𐐰𐐶𐐩, 𐐨𐑂𐐯𐑌 𐑅𐐬 𐐰𐑆 𐐺𐐴 𐑁𐐴𐑉; 𐐰𐑌𐐼 𐐸𐐨 𐑄𐐰𐐻 𐐺𐐯𐑊𐐨𐑂𐐯𐑃 𐑌𐐪𐐻 𐑋𐐴 𐐶𐐲𐑉𐐼𐑆, 𐐺𐐯𐑊𐐨𐑂𐐯𐑃 𐑌𐐪𐐻 𐑋𐐴 𐐼𐐮𐑅𐐴𐐹𐑊𐑆; 𐐰𐑌𐐼 𐐮𐑁 𐐮𐐻 𐑅𐐬 𐐺 𐑄𐐰𐐻 𐐌 𐐼𐐭 𐑌𐐪𐐻 𐑅𐐹𐐨𐐿, 𐐾𐐲𐐾 𐐷; 𐑁𐐫𐑉 𐐷 𐑇𐐰𐑊 𐑌𐐬 𐑄𐐰𐐻 𐐮𐐻 𐐮𐑆 𐐌 𐑄𐐰𐐻 𐑅𐐹𐐨𐐿𐐯𐑃, 𐐰𐐻 𐑄 𐑊𐐰𐑅𐐻 𐐼𐐩.

12. 𐐒𐐲𐐻 𐐸𐐨 𐑄𐐰𐐻 𐐺𐐯𐑊𐐨𐑂𐐯𐑃 𐑄𐐨𐑆 𐑃𐐮𐑍𐑆 𐐸𐐶𐐮𐐽 𐐌 𐐸𐐰𐑂 𐑅𐐹𐐬𐐿𐐯𐑌, 𐐸𐐮𐑋 𐐶𐐮𐑊 𐐌 𐑂𐐮𐑆𐐮𐐻 𐐶𐐮𐑄 𐑄 𐑋𐐰𐑌𐐮𐑁𐐯𐑅𐐻𐐩𐑇𐐲𐑌𐑆 𐐱𐑂 𐑋𐐴 𐐝𐐹𐐮𐑉𐐮𐐻, 𐐰𐑌𐐼 𐐸𐐨 𐑇𐐰𐑊 𐑌𐐬 𐐰𐑌𐐼 𐐺𐐩𐑉 𐑉𐐯𐐿𐐲𐑉𐐼. 𐐙𐐫𐑉 𐐺𐐨𐐿𐐫𐑆 𐐱𐑂 𐑋𐐴 𐐝𐐹𐐮𐑉𐐮𐐻, 𐐸𐐨 𐑇𐐰𐑊 𐑌𐐬 𐑄𐐰𐐻 𐑄𐐨𐑆 𐑃𐐮𐑍𐑆 𐐪𐑉 𐐻𐑉𐐭; 𐑁𐐫𐑉 𐐮𐐻 𐐹𐐲𐑉𐑅𐐶𐐩𐐼𐐯𐑃 𐑋𐐯𐑌 𐐻𐐭 𐐼𐐭 𐑀𐐳𐐼; 𐐰𐑌𐐼 𐐸𐐶𐐱𐐻𐑅𐐬𐐯𐑂𐐲𐑉 𐑃𐐮𐑍 𐐹𐐲𐑉𐑅𐐶𐐩𐐼𐐯𐑃 𐑋𐐯𐑌 𐐻𐐭 𐐼𐐭 𐑀𐐳𐐼 𐐮𐑆 𐐱𐑂 𐑋𐐨; 𐑁𐐫𐑉 𐑀𐐳𐐼 𐐿𐐲𐑋𐐯𐑃 𐐱𐑂 𐑌𐐲𐑌 𐑅𐐩𐑂 𐐮𐐻 𐐺 𐐱𐑂 𐑋𐐨. 𐐌 𐐰𐑋 𐑄 𐑅𐐩𐑋 𐑄𐐰𐐻 𐑊𐐨𐐼𐐯𐑃 𐑋𐐯𐑌 𐐻𐐭 𐐫𐑊 𐑀𐐳𐐼; 𐐸𐐨 𐑄𐐰𐐻 𐐶𐐮𐑊 𐑌𐐪𐐻 𐐺𐐯𐑊𐐨𐑂 𐑋𐐴 𐐶𐐲𐑉𐐼𐑆, 𐐶𐐮𐑊 𐑌𐐪𐐻 𐐺𐐯𐑊𐐨𐑂 𐑋𐐨, 𐑄𐐰𐐻 𐐌 𐐰𐑋; 𐐰𐑌𐐼 𐐸𐐨 𐑄𐐰𐐻 𐐶𐐮𐑊 𐑌𐐪𐐻 𐐺𐐯𐑊𐐨𐑂 𐑋𐐨, 𐐶𐐮𐑊 𐑌𐐪𐐻 𐐺𐐯𐑊𐐨𐑂 𐑄 𐐙𐐪𐑄𐐲𐑉 𐐸𐐭 𐑅𐐯𐑌𐐻 𐑋𐐨. 𐐙𐐫𐑉 𐐺𐐨𐐸𐐬𐑊𐐼, 𐐌 𐐰𐑋 𐑄 𐐙𐐪𐑄𐐲𐑉; 𐐌 𐐰𐑋 𐑄 𐑊𐐴𐐻, 𐐰𐑌𐐼 𐑄 𐑊𐐴𐑁, 𐐰𐑌𐐼 𐑄 𐐻𐑉𐐭𐑃 𐐱𐑂 𐑄 𐐶𐐲𐑉𐑊𐐼. 𐐗𐐲𐑋 𐐲𐑌𐐻𐐭 𐑋𐐨, 𐐄 𐐷 𐐘𐐯𐑌𐐻𐐴𐑊𐑆, 𐐰𐑌𐐼 𐐌 𐐶𐐮𐑊 𐑇𐐬 𐐲𐑌𐐻𐐭 𐐷𐐭 𐑄 𐑀𐑉𐐩𐐻𐐲𐑉 𐑃𐐮𐑍𐑆, 𐑄 𐑌𐐱𐑊𐐯𐐾 𐐸𐐶𐐮𐐽 𐐮𐑆 𐐸𐐮𐐼 𐐲𐐹 𐐺𐐨𐐿𐐫𐑆 𐐱𐑂 𐐲𐑌𐐺𐐯𐑊𐐨𐑁. 𐐗𐐲𐑋 𐐲𐑌𐐻𐐭 𐑋𐐨, 𐐄 𐐷 𐐸𐐵𐑅 𐐱𐑂 𐐆𐑆𐑉𐐩𐐯𐑊, 𐐰𐑌𐐼 𐐮𐐻 𐑇𐐰𐑊 𐐺 𐑋𐐩𐐼 𐑋𐐰𐑌𐐮𐑁𐐯𐑅𐐻 𐐲𐑌𐐻𐐭 𐐷𐐭 𐐸𐐵 𐑀𐑉𐐩𐐻 𐑃𐐮𐑍𐑆 𐑄 𐐙𐐪𐑄𐐲𐑉 𐐸𐐰𐑃 𐑊𐐩𐐼 𐐲𐐹 𐑁𐐫𐑉 𐐷𐐭, 𐑁𐑉𐐱𐑋 𐑄 𐑁𐐵𐑌𐐼𐐩𐑇𐐲𐑌 𐐱𐑂 𐑄 𐐶𐐲𐑉𐑊𐐼; 𐐰𐑌𐐼 𐐮𐐻 𐐸𐐰𐑃 𐑌𐐪𐐻 𐐿𐐲𐑋 𐐲𐑌𐐻𐐭 𐐷𐐭, 𐐺𐐨𐐿𐐫𐑆 𐐱𐑂 𐐲𐑌𐐺𐐯𐑊𐐨𐑁. 𐐒𐐨𐐸𐐬𐑊𐐼, 𐐸𐐶𐐯𐑌 𐐷 𐑇𐐰𐑊 𐑉𐐯𐑌𐐼 𐑄𐐰𐐻 𐑂𐐩𐑊 𐐱𐑂 𐐲𐑌𐐺𐐯𐑊𐐨𐑁 𐐸𐐶𐐮𐐽 𐐼𐐲𐑃 𐐿𐐫𐑆 𐐷𐐭 𐐻𐐭 𐑉𐐯𐑋𐐩𐑌 𐐮𐑌 𐐷𐐭𐑉 𐐫𐑁𐐳𐑊 𐑅𐐻𐐩𐐻 𐐱𐑂 𐐶𐐮𐐿𐐯𐐼𐑌𐐯𐑅, 𐐰𐑌𐐼 𐐸𐐪𐑉𐐼𐑌𐐯𐑅 𐐱𐑂 𐐸𐐪𐑉𐐻, 𐐰𐑌𐐼 𐐺𐑊𐐴𐑌𐐼𐑌𐐯𐑅 𐐱𐑂 𐑋𐐴𐑌𐐼, 𐑄𐐯𐑌 𐑇𐐰𐑊 𐑄 𐑀𐑉𐐩𐐻 𐐰𐑌𐐼 𐑋𐐪𐑉𐑂𐐯𐑊𐐲𐑅 𐑃𐐮𐑍𐑆 𐐸𐐶𐐮𐐽 𐐸𐐰𐑂 𐐺𐐮𐑌 𐐸𐐮𐐼 𐐲𐐹 𐑁𐑉𐐱𐑋 𐑄 𐑁𐐵𐑌𐐼𐐩𐑇𐐲𐑌 𐐱𐑂 𐑄 𐐶𐐲𐑉𐑊𐐼 𐑁𐑉𐐱𐑋 𐐷𐐭: 𐐷𐐩, 𐐸𐐶𐐯𐑌 𐐷 𐑇𐐰𐑊 𐐿𐐫𐑊 𐐲𐐹𐐱𐑌 𐑄 𐐙𐐪𐑄𐐲𐑉 𐐮𐑌 𐑋𐐴 𐑌𐐩𐑋, 𐐶𐐮𐑄 𐐲 𐐺𐑉𐐬𐐿𐐯𐑌 𐐸𐐪𐑉𐐻 𐐰𐑌𐐼 𐐲 𐐿𐐱𐑌𐐻𐑉𐐴𐐻 𐑅𐐹𐐮𐑉𐐮𐐻, 𐑄𐐯𐑌 𐑇𐐰𐑊 𐐷 𐑌𐐬 𐑄𐐰𐐻 𐑄 𐐙𐐪𐑄𐐲𐑉 𐐸𐐰𐑃 𐑉𐐯𐑋𐐯𐑋𐐺𐐲𐑉𐐼 𐑄 𐐿𐐲𐑂𐐯𐑌𐐰𐑌𐐻 𐐸𐐶𐐮𐐽 𐐸𐐨 𐑋𐐩𐐼 𐐲𐑌𐐻𐐭 𐐷𐐭𐑉 𐑁𐐪𐑄𐐲𐑉𐑆, 𐐄 𐐸𐐵𐑅 𐐱𐑂 𐐆𐑆𐑉𐐩𐐯𐑊; 𐐰𐑌𐐼 𐑄𐐯𐑌 𐑇𐐰𐑊 𐑋𐐴 𐑉𐐯𐑂𐐯𐑊𐐩𐑇𐐲𐑌𐑆 𐐸𐐶𐐮𐐽 𐐌 𐐸𐐰𐑂 𐐿𐐫𐑆𐐼 𐐻𐐭 𐐺 𐑉𐐮𐐻𐐯𐑌 𐐺𐐴 𐑋𐐴 𐑅𐐲𐑉𐑂𐐰𐑌𐐻 𐐖𐐱𐑌, 𐐺 𐐲𐑌𐑁𐐬𐑊𐐼𐐯𐐼 𐐮𐑌 𐑄 𐐴𐑆 𐐱𐑂 𐐫𐑊 𐑄 𐐹𐐨𐐹𐑊. 𐐡𐐯𐑋𐐯𐑋𐐺𐐲𐑉, 𐐸𐐶𐐯𐑌 𐐷 𐑅𐐨 𐑄𐐨𐑆 𐑃𐐮𐑍𐑆, 𐐷 𐑇𐐰𐑊 𐑌𐐬 𐑄𐐰𐐻 𐑄 𐐻𐐴𐑋 𐐮𐑆 𐐰𐐻 𐐸𐐰𐑌𐐼 𐑄𐐰𐐻 𐑄𐐩 𐑇𐐰𐑊 𐐺 𐑋𐐩𐐼 𐑋𐐰𐑌𐐮𐑁𐐯𐑅𐐻 𐐮𐑌 𐑂𐐯𐑉𐐮 𐐼𐐨𐐼; 𐑄𐐯𐑉𐑁𐐫𐑉, 𐐸𐐶𐐯𐑌 𐐷 𐑇𐐰𐑊 𐑉𐐯𐑅𐐨𐑂 𐑄𐐮𐑅 𐑉𐐯𐐿𐐲𐑉𐐼, 𐐷 𐑋𐐩 𐑌𐐬 𐑄𐐰𐐻 𐑄 𐐶𐐲𐑉𐐿 𐐱𐑂 𐑄 𐐙𐐪𐑄𐐲𐑉 𐐸𐐰𐑆 𐐿𐐱𐑋𐐯𐑌𐑅𐐻 𐐲𐐹𐐱𐑌 𐐫𐑊 𐑄 𐑁𐐩𐑅 𐐱𐑂 𐑄 𐑊𐐰𐑌𐐼. 𐐜𐐯𐑉𐑁𐐫𐑉, 𐑉𐐯𐐹𐐯𐑌𐐻, 𐐫𐑊 𐐷 𐐯𐑌𐐼𐑆 𐐱𐑂 𐑄 𐐲𐑉𐑃, 𐐰𐑌𐐼 𐐿𐐲𐑋 𐐲𐑌𐐻𐐭 𐑋𐐨, 𐐰𐑌𐐼 𐐺𐐯𐑊𐐨𐑂 𐐮𐑌 𐑋𐐴 𐐘𐐱𐑅𐐹𐐯𐑊, 𐐰𐑌𐐼 𐐺 𐐺𐐰𐐹𐐻𐐴𐑆𐐼 𐐮𐑌 𐑋𐐴 𐑌𐐩𐑋; 𐑁𐐫𐑉 𐐸𐐨 𐑄𐐰𐐻 𐐺𐐯𐑊𐐨𐑂𐐯𐑃, 𐐰𐑌𐐼 𐐮𐑆 𐐺𐐰𐐹𐐻𐐴𐑆𐐼, 𐑇𐐰𐑊 𐐺 𐑅𐐩𐑂𐐼; 𐐺𐐲𐐻 𐐸𐐨 𐑄𐐰𐐻 𐐺𐐯𐑊𐐨𐑂𐐯𐑃 𐑌𐐪𐐻 𐑇𐐰𐑊 𐐺 𐐼𐐰𐑋𐐼; 𐐰𐑌𐐼 𐑅𐐴𐑌𐑆 𐑇𐐰𐑊 𐑁𐐱𐑊𐐬 𐑄𐐯𐑋 𐑄𐐰𐐻 𐐺𐐯𐑊𐐨𐑂 𐐮𐑌 𐑋𐐴 𐑌𐐩𐑋. 𐐈𐑌𐐼 𐐺𐑊𐐯𐑅𐐯𐐼 𐐮𐑆 𐐸𐐨 𐑄𐐰𐐻 𐐮𐑆 𐑁𐐵𐑌𐐼 𐑁𐐩𐑃𐑁𐐳𐑊 𐐲𐑌𐐻𐐭 𐑋𐐴 𐑌𐐩𐑋, 𐐰𐐻 𐑄 𐑊𐐰𐑅𐐻 𐐼𐐩, 𐑁𐐫𐑉 𐐸𐐨 𐑇𐐰𐑊 𐐺 𐑊𐐮𐑁𐐻𐐯𐐼 𐐲𐐹 𐐻𐐭 𐐼𐐶𐐯𐑊 𐐮𐑌 𐑄 𐐿𐐮𐑍𐐼𐐲𐑋 𐐹𐑉𐐨𐐹𐐩𐑉𐐼 𐑁𐐫𐑉 𐐸𐐮𐑋 𐑁𐑉𐐱𐑋 𐑄 𐑁𐐵𐑌𐐼𐐩𐑇𐐲𐑌 𐐱𐑂 𐑄 𐐶𐐲𐑉𐑊𐐼. 𐐈𐑌𐐼 𐐺𐐨𐐸𐐬𐑊𐐼 𐐮𐐻 𐐮𐑆 𐐌 𐑄𐐰𐐻 𐐸𐐰𐑃 𐑅𐐹𐐬𐐿𐐯𐑌 𐐮𐐻. 𐐁𐑋𐐯𐑌.

𐐗𐐰𐐹𐐻𐐲𐑉 II.

1. 𐐈𐑌𐐼 𐑌𐐵 𐐌, 𐐣𐐫𐑉𐐬𐑌𐐴, 𐐸𐐰𐑂 𐑉𐐮𐐻𐐯𐑌 𐑄 𐐶𐐲𐑉𐐼𐑆 𐐸𐐶𐐮𐐽 𐐶𐐲𐑉 𐐿𐐱𐑋𐐰𐑌𐐼𐐯𐐼 𐑋𐐨, 𐐰𐐿𐐫𐑉𐐼𐐮𐑍 𐐻𐐭 𐑋𐐴 𐑋𐐯𐑋𐐬𐑉𐐮; 𐐰𐑌𐐼 𐐌 𐐸𐐰𐑂 𐐻𐐬𐑊𐐼 𐐷𐐭 𐑄 𐑃𐐮𐑍𐑆 𐐸𐐶𐐮𐐽 𐐌 𐐸𐐰𐑂 𐑅𐐨𐑊𐐼 𐐲𐐹; 𐑄𐐯𐑉𐑁𐐫𐑉 𐐻𐐲𐐽 𐑄𐐯𐑋 𐑌𐐪𐐻, 𐐮𐑌 𐐫𐑉𐐼𐐲𐑉 𐑄𐐰𐐻 𐐷 𐑋𐐩 𐐻𐑉𐐰𐑌𐑅𐑊𐐩𐐻; 𐑁𐐫𐑉 𐑄𐐰𐐻 𐑃𐐮𐑍 𐐮𐑆 𐑁𐐫𐑉𐐺𐐮𐐼𐐯𐑌 𐐷𐐭, 𐐯𐐿𐑅𐐯𐐹𐐻 𐐺𐐴 𐐰𐑌𐐼 𐐺𐐴 𐐮𐐻 𐑇𐐰𐑊 𐐺 𐐶𐐮𐑆𐐼𐐲𐑋 𐐮𐑌 𐐘𐐱𐐼. 𐐈𐑌𐐼 𐐺𐐨𐐸𐐬𐑊𐐼, 𐐷 𐑋𐐩 𐐺 𐐹𐑉𐐮𐑂𐐮𐑊𐐯𐐾𐐼 𐑄𐐰𐐻 𐐷 𐑋𐐩 𐑇𐐬 𐑄

𐐲𐑌𐐻𐐭 𐑄𐐬𐑆 𐐸𐐭 𐑇𐐰𐑊 𐐰𐑅𐐮𐑅𐐻 𐐻𐐭 𐐺𐑉𐐮𐑍 𐑁𐐫𐑉𐑃 𐑄𐐮𐑅 𐐶𐐲𐑉𐐿; 𐐰𐑌𐐼 𐐲𐑌𐐻𐐭 𐑃𐑉𐐨 𐑇𐐰𐑊 𐑄𐐩 𐐺𐐨 𐑇𐐬𐑌 𐐺𐐴 𐑄 𐐹𐐵𐐲𐑉 𐐱𐑂 𐐘𐐱𐐼; 𐐸𐐶𐐯𐑉𐑁𐐫𐑉 𐑄𐐩 𐑇𐐰𐑊 𐑌𐐬 𐐱𐑂 𐐲 𐑇𐐳𐑉𐐮𐐻𐐨 𐑄𐐰𐐻 𐑄𐐨𐑆 𐑃𐐮𐑍𐑆 𐐪𐑉 𐐻𐑉𐐭. 𐐈𐑌𐐼 𐐮𐑌 𐑄 𐑋𐐵𐑃 𐐱𐑂 𐑃𐑉𐐨 𐐶𐐮𐐻𐑌𐐯𐑅𐐯𐑆 𐑇𐐰𐑊 𐑄𐐨𐑆 𐑃𐐮𐑍𐑆 𐐺𐐨 𐐯𐑅𐐻𐐰𐐺𐑊𐐮𐑇𐐻; 𐐰𐑌𐐼 𐑄 𐐻𐐯𐑅𐐻𐐮𐑋𐐬𐑌𐐨 𐐱𐑂 𐑃𐑉𐐨, 𐐰𐑌𐐼 𐑄𐐮𐑅 𐐶𐐲𐑉𐐿, 𐐮𐑌 𐑄 𐐸𐐶𐐮𐐽 𐑇𐐰𐑊 𐐺𐐨 𐑇𐐬𐑌 𐑁𐐫𐑉𐑃 𐑄 𐐹𐐵𐐲𐑉 𐐱𐑂 𐐘𐐱𐐼, 𐐰𐑌𐐼 𐐫𐑊𐑅𐐬 𐐸𐐮𐑆 𐐶𐐲𐑉𐐼, 𐐱𐑂 𐐸𐐶𐐮𐐽 𐑄 𐐙𐐪𐑄𐐲𐑉, 𐐰𐑌𐐼 𐑄 𐐝𐐲𐑌, 𐐰𐑌𐐼 𐑄 𐐐𐐬𐑊𐐨 𐐘𐐬𐑅𐐻 𐐺𐐯𐑉 𐑉𐐯𐐿𐐫𐑉𐐼; 𐐰𐑌𐐼 𐐫𐑊 𐑄𐐮𐑅 𐑇𐐰𐑊 𐑅𐐻𐐰𐑌𐐼 𐐰𐑆 𐐲 𐐻𐐯𐑅𐐻𐐮𐑋𐐬𐑌𐐨 𐐲𐑀𐐯𐑌𐑅𐐻 𐑄 𐐶𐐲𐑉𐑊𐐼 𐐰𐐻 𐑄 𐑊𐐪𐑅𐐻 𐐼𐐩. 𐐈𐑌𐐼 𐐮𐑁 𐐮𐐻 𐑅𐐬 𐐺𐐨 𐑄𐐰𐐻 𐑄𐐩 𐑉𐐨𐐹𐐯𐑌𐐻 𐐰𐑌𐐼 𐐿𐐲𐑋 𐐲𐑌𐐻𐐭 𐑄 𐐙𐐪𐑄𐐲𐑉 𐐮𐑌 𐑄 𐑌𐐩𐑋 𐐱𐑂 𐐖𐐨𐑆𐐲𐑅, 𐑄𐐩 𐑇𐐰𐑊 𐐺𐐨 𐑉𐐨𐑅𐐨𐑂𐐼 𐐮𐑌𐐻𐐭 𐑄 𐐿𐐮𐑍𐐼𐐲𐑋 𐐱𐑂 𐐘𐐱𐐼. 𐐈𐑌𐐼 𐑌𐐵, 𐐮𐑁 𐐌 𐐸𐐰𐑂 𐑌𐐬 𐐫𐑃𐐫𐑉𐐮𐐻𐐨 𐑁𐐫𐑉 𐑄𐐨𐑆 𐑃𐐮𐑍𐑆, 𐐾𐐲𐐾 𐐷𐐨; 𐑁𐐫𐑉 𐐷𐐨 𐑇𐐰𐑊 𐑌𐐬 𐑄𐐰𐐻 𐐌 𐐸𐐰𐑂 𐐫𐑃𐐫𐑉𐐮𐐻𐐨 𐐸𐐶𐐯𐑌 𐐷𐐨 𐑇𐐰𐑊 𐑅𐐨 𐑋𐐨, 𐐰𐑌𐐼 𐐶𐐨 𐑇𐐰𐑊 𐑅𐐻𐐰𐑌𐐼 𐐺𐐨𐑁𐐬𐑉 𐐘𐐱𐐼 𐐰𐐻 𐑄 𐑊𐐪𐑅𐐻 𐐼𐐩. 𐐁𐑋𐐯𐑌.

𐐕𐐰𐐹𐐻𐐲𐑉 III.

1. 𐐈𐑌𐐼 𐑌𐐵 𐐌, 𐐣𐐫𐑉𐐬𐑌𐐴, 𐐹𐑉𐐬𐑅𐐨𐐼 𐐻𐐭 𐑀𐐮𐑂 𐑄 𐑉𐐯𐐿𐐫𐑉𐐼 𐐱𐑂 𐐖𐐯𐑉𐐲𐐼 𐐰𐑌𐐼 𐐸𐐮𐑆 𐐺𐑉𐐲𐑄𐐲𐑉. 𐐙𐐫𐑉 𐐮𐐻 𐐿𐐩𐑋 𐐻𐐭 𐐹𐐪𐑅 𐐰𐑁𐐻𐐲𐑉 𐑄 𐐢𐐫𐑉𐐼 𐐸𐐰𐐼 𐐹𐑉𐐨𐐹𐐯𐑉𐐼 𐑄 𐑅𐐻𐐬𐑌𐑆 𐐸𐐶𐐮𐐽 𐑄 𐐺𐑉𐐲𐑄𐐲𐑉 𐐱𐑂 𐐖𐐯𐑉𐐲𐐼 𐐸𐐰𐐼 𐐿𐐰𐑉𐐨𐐼 𐐲𐐹 𐐮𐑌𐐻𐐭 𐑄 𐑋𐐵𐑌𐐻, 𐑄 𐐺𐑉𐐲𐑄𐐲𐑉 𐐱𐑂 𐐖𐐯𐑉𐐲𐐼 𐐿𐐩𐑋 𐐼𐐵𐑌 𐐵𐐻 𐐱𐑂 𐑄 𐑋𐐵𐑌𐐻, 𐐰𐑌𐐼 𐐸𐐨 𐐼𐐮𐐼 𐐹𐐳𐐻 𐑁𐐫𐑉𐑃 𐑄 𐑅𐐻𐐬𐑌𐑆 𐐮𐑌𐐻𐐭 𐑄 𐑂𐐯𐑅𐐯𐑊𐑆 𐐸𐐶𐐮𐐽 𐐶𐐲𐑉 𐐹𐑉𐐨𐐹𐐯𐑉𐐼, 𐐶𐐲𐑌 𐐮𐑌 𐐨𐐽 𐐯𐑌𐐼 𐑄𐐯𐑉𐐱𐑂; 𐐰𐑌𐐼 𐐺𐐨𐐸𐐬𐑊𐐼, 𐑄𐐩 𐐼𐐮𐐼 𐑀𐐮𐑂 𐑊𐐴𐐻 𐐲𐑌𐐻𐐭 𐑄 𐑂𐐯𐑅𐐯𐑊𐑆. 𐐈𐑌𐐼 𐑄𐐲𐑅 𐑄 𐐢𐐫𐑉𐐼 𐐿𐐫𐑆𐐼 𐑅𐐻𐐬𐑌𐑆 𐐻𐐭 𐑇𐐴𐑌 𐐮𐑌 𐐼𐐪𐑉𐐿𐑌𐐯𐑅, 𐐻𐐭 𐑀𐐮𐑂 𐑊𐐴𐐻 𐐲𐑌𐐻𐐭 𐑋𐐯𐑌, 𐐶𐐮𐑋𐐯𐑌, 𐐰𐑌𐐼 𐐽𐐮𐑊𐐼𐑉𐐯𐑌, 𐑄𐐰𐐻 𐑄𐐩 𐑋𐐴𐐻 𐑌𐐱𐐻 𐐿𐑉𐐫𐑅 𐑄 𐑀𐑉𐐩𐐻 𐐶𐐫𐐻𐐲𐑉𐑆 𐐮𐑌 𐐼𐐪𐑉𐐿𐑌𐐯𐑅.

2. 𐐈𐑌𐐼 𐐮𐐻 𐐿𐐩𐑋 𐐻𐐭 𐐹𐐪𐑅 𐑄𐐰𐐻 𐐸𐐶𐐯𐑌 𐑄𐐩 𐐸𐐰𐐼 𐐹𐑉𐐨𐐹𐐯𐑉𐐼 𐐫𐑊 𐑋𐐰𐑌𐐲𐑉 𐐱𐑂 𐑁𐐭𐐼, 𐑄𐐰𐐻 𐑄𐐯𐑉𐐺𐐴 𐑄𐐩 𐑋𐐴𐐻 𐑅𐐲𐐺𐑅𐐮𐑅𐐻 𐐲𐐹𐐱𐑌 𐑄 𐐶𐐫𐐻𐐲𐑉, 𐐰𐑌𐐼 𐐫𐑊𐑅𐐬 𐑁𐐭𐐼 𐑁𐐫𐑉 𐑄𐐯𐑉 𐑁𐑊𐐱𐐿𐑅 𐐰𐑌𐐼 𐐸𐐲𐑉𐐼𐑆, 𐐰𐑌𐐼 𐐸𐐶𐐱𐐻𐑅𐐬𐐯𐑂𐐲𐑉 𐐺𐐨𐑅𐐻, 𐐫𐑉 𐐰𐑌𐐮𐑋𐐲𐑊, 𐐫𐑉 𐑁𐐵𐐲𐑊 𐑄𐐰𐐻 𐑄𐐩 𐑇𐐳𐐼 𐐿𐐰𐑉𐐨 𐐶𐐮𐑄 𐑄𐐯𐑋. 𐐈𐑌𐐼 𐐮𐐻 𐐿𐐩𐑋 𐐻𐐭 𐐹𐐪𐑅 𐑄𐐰𐐻 𐐸𐐶𐐯𐑌 𐑄𐐩 𐐸𐐰𐐼 𐐼𐐲𐑌 𐐫𐑊 𐑄𐐨𐑆 𐑃𐐮𐑍𐑆, 𐑄𐐩 𐑀𐐱𐐻 𐐲𐐺𐐬𐑉𐐼 𐐱𐑂 𐑄𐐯𐑉 𐑂𐐯𐑅𐐯𐑊𐑆 𐐫𐑉 𐐺𐐪𐑉𐐾𐐯𐑆, 𐐰𐑌𐐼 𐑅𐐯𐐻 𐑁𐐫𐑉𐑃 𐐮𐑌𐐻𐐭 𐑄 𐑅𐐨, 𐐿𐐱𐑋𐐯𐑌𐐼𐐮𐑍 𐑄𐐯𐑋𐑅𐐯𐑊𐑂𐑆 𐐲𐑌𐐻𐐭 𐑄 𐐢𐐫𐑉𐐼 𐑄𐐯𐑉 𐐘𐐱𐐼. 𐐈𐑌𐐼 𐐮𐐻 𐐿𐐩𐑋 𐐻𐐭 𐐹𐐪𐑅 𐑄𐐰𐐻 𐑄 𐐢𐐫𐑉𐐼 𐐘𐐱𐐼 𐐿𐐫𐑆𐐼 𐑄𐐰𐐻 𐑄𐐯𐑉 𐑇𐐳𐐼 𐐺𐐨 𐐲 𐑁𐐷𐐭𐑉𐐨𐐲𐑅 𐐶𐐮𐑌𐐼 𐐺𐑊𐐬 𐐲𐐹𐐱𐑌 𐑄 𐑁𐐩𐑅 𐐱𐑂 𐑄 𐐶𐐫𐐻𐐲𐑉𐑆, 𐐻𐐫𐑉𐐼𐑆 𐑄 𐐹𐑉𐐱𐑋𐐮𐑅𐐻 𐑊𐐰𐑌𐐼; 𐐰𐑌𐐼 𐑄𐐲𐑅 𐑄𐐩 𐐶𐐲𐑉 𐐻𐐱𐑅𐐻 𐐲𐐹𐐱𐑌 𐑄 𐐶𐐩𐑂𐑆 𐐱𐑂 𐑄 𐑅𐐨 𐐺𐐨𐑁𐐬𐑉 𐑄 𐐶𐐮𐑌𐐼. 𐐈𐑌𐐼 𐐮𐐻 𐐿𐐩𐑋 𐐻𐐭 𐐹𐐪𐑅 𐑄𐐰𐐻 𐑄𐐩 𐐶𐐲𐑉 𐑋𐐯𐑌𐐨 𐐻𐐴𐑋𐑆 𐐺𐐯𐑉𐐨𐐼 𐐮𐑌 𐑄 𐐼𐐯𐐹𐑃𐑅 𐐱𐑂 𐑄 𐑅𐐨, 𐐺𐐨𐐿𐐫𐑆 𐐱𐑂 𐑄 𐑋𐐵𐑌𐐻𐐲𐑌 𐐶𐐩𐑂𐑆 𐐸𐐶𐐮𐐽 𐐺𐑉𐐬𐐿 𐐲𐐹𐐱𐑌 𐑄𐐯𐑋, 𐐰𐑌𐐼 𐐫𐑊𐑅𐐬 𐑄 𐑀𐑉𐐩𐐻 𐐰𐑌𐐼 𐐻𐐯𐑉𐐲𐐺𐑊 𐐻𐐯𐑋𐐹𐐯𐑅𐐻𐑅 𐐸𐐶𐐮𐐽 𐐶𐐲𐑉 𐐿𐐫𐑆𐐼 𐐺𐐴 𐑄 𐑁𐐨𐑉𐑅𐑌𐐯𐑅 𐐱𐑂 𐑄 𐐶𐐮𐑌𐐼.

3. 𐐈𐑌𐐼 𐐮𐐻 𐐿𐐩𐑋 𐐻𐐭 𐐹𐐪𐑅 𐑄𐐰𐐻 𐐸𐐶𐐯𐑌 𐑄𐐩 𐐶𐐲𐑉 𐐺𐐯𐑉𐐨𐐼 𐐮𐑌 𐑄 𐐼𐐨𐐹, 𐑄𐐯𐑉 𐐶𐐱𐑆 𐑌𐐬 𐐶𐐫𐐻𐐲𐑉 𐑄𐐰𐐻 𐐿𐐳𐐼 𐐸𐐲𐑉𐐻 𐑄𐐯𐑋, 𐑄𐐯𐑉 𐑂𐐯𐑅𐐯𐑊𐑆 𐐺𐐨𐐮𐑍 𐐻𐐴𐐻 𐑊𐐴𐐿 𐐲𐑌𐐻𐐭 𐐲 𐐼𐐮𐑇, 𐐰𐑌𐐼 𐐫𐑊𐑅𐐬 𐑄𐐩 𐐶𐐲𐑉 𐐻𐐴𐐻 𐑊𐐴𐐿 𐐲𐑌𐐻𐐭 𐑄 𐐪𐑉𐐿 𐐱𐑂 𐐤𐐬𐐰; 𐑄𐐯𐑉𐑁𐐫𐑉 𐐸𐐶𐐯𐑌 𐑄𐐩 𐐶𐐲𐑉 𐐯𐑌𐐿𐐲𐑋𐐹𐐰𐑅𐐻 𐐲𐐺𐐵𐐻 𐐺𐐴 𐑋𐐯𐑌𐐨 𐐶𐐫𐐻𐐲𐑉𐑆, 𐑄𐐩 𐐼𐐮𐐼 𐐿𐑉𐐴 𐐲𐑌𐐻𐐭 𐑄 𐐢𐐫𐑉𐐼, 𐐰𐑌𐐼 𐐸𐐨 𐐼𐐮𐐼 𐐺𐑉𐐮𐑍 𐑄𐐯𐑋 𐑁𐐫𐑉𐑃 𐐲𐑀𐐯𐑌 𐐲𐐹𐐱𐑌 𐑄 𐐻𐐱𐐹 𐐱𐑂 𐑄 𐐶𐐫𐐻𐐲𐑉𐑆. 𐐈𐑌𐐼 𐐮𐐻 𐐿𐐩𐑋 𐐻𐐭 𐐹𐐪𐑅 𐑄𐐰𐐻 𐑄 𐐶𐐮𐑌𐐼 𐐼𐐮𐐼 𐑌𐐯𐑂𐐲𐑉 𐑅𐐨𐑅 𐐻𐐭 𐐺𐑊𐐬 𐐻𐐫𐑉𐐼𐑆 𐑄 𐐹𐑉𐐱𐑋𐐮𐑅𐐻 𐑊𐐰𐑌𐐼 𐐸𐐶𐐴𐑊 𐑄𐐩 𐐶𐐲𐑉 𐐲𐐹𐐱𐑌 𐑄 𐐶𐐫𐐻𐐲𐑉𐑆; 𐐰𐑌𐐼 𐑄𐐲𐑅 𐑄𐐩 𐐶𐐲𐑉 𐐼𐑉𐐮𐑂𐐲𐑌 𐑁𐐫𐑉𐑃 𐐺𐐨𐑁𐐬𐑉 𐑄 𐐶𐐮𐑌𐐼. 𐐈𐑌𐐼 𐑄𐐩 𐐼𐐮𐐼 𐑅𐐮𐑍 𐐹𐑉𐐩𐑆𐐯𐑆 𐐲𐑌𐐻𐐭 𐑄 𐐢𐐫𐑉𐐼; 𐐷𐐩, 𐑄 𐐺𐑉𐐲𐑄𐐲𐑉 𐐱𐑂 𐐖𐐯𐑉𐐲𐐼 𐐼𐐮𐐼 𐑅𐐮𐑍 𐐹𐑉𐐩𐑆𐐯𐑆 𐐲𐑌𐐻𐐭 𐑄 𐐢𐐫𐑉𐐼, 𐐰𐑌𐐼 𐐸𐐨 𐐼𐐮𐐼 𐑃𐐰𐑍𐐿 𐐰𐑌𐐼 𐐹𐑉𐐩𐑆 𐑄 𐐢𐐫𐑉𐐼 𐐫𐑊 𐑄 𐐼𐐩 𐑊𐐱𐑍; 𐐰𐑌𐐼 𐐸𐐶𐐯𐑌 𐑄 𐑌𐐴𐐻 𐐿𐐩𐑋, 𐑄𐐩 𐐼𐐮𐐼 𐑌𐐱𐐻 𐑅𐐨𐑅 𐐻𐐭 𐐹𐑉𐐩𐑆 𐑄 𐐢𐐫𐑉𐐼. 𐐈𐑌𐐼 𐑄𐐲𐑅 𐑄𐐩 𐐶𐐲𐑉 𐐼𐑉𐐮𐑂𐐲𐑌 𐑁𐐫𐑉𐑃; 𐐰𐑌𐐼 𐑌𐐬 𐑋𐐱𐑌𐑅𐐻𐐲𐑉 𐐱𐑂 𐑄 𐑅𐐨 𐐿𐐳𐐼 𐐺𐑉𐐩𐐿 𐑄𐐯𐑋, 𐑌𐐨𐑄𐐲𐑉 𐐸𐐶𐐩𐑊 𐑄𐐰𐐻 𐐿𐐳𐐼 𐑋𐐪𐑉 𐑄𐐯𐑋; 𐐰𐑌𐐼 𐑄𐐩 𐐼𐐮𐐼 𐐸𐐰𐑂 𐑊𐐴𐐻 𐐿𐐲𐑌𐐻𐐮𐑌𐐷𐐭𐐰𐑊𐐨, 𐐸𐐶𐐯𐑄𐐲𐑉 𐐮𐐻 𐐶𐐱𐑆 𐐲𐐺𐐲𐑂 𐑄 𐐶𐐫𐐻𐐲𐑉 𐐫𐑉 𐐲𐑌𐐼𐐲𐑉 𐑄 𐐶𐐫𐐻𐐲𐑉. 𐐈𐑌𐐼 𐑄𐐲𐑅 𐑄𐐩 𐐶𐐲𐑉 𐐼𐑉𐐮𐑂𐐲𐑌 𐑁𐐫𐑉𐑃

𐑁𐐫𐑉𐑃, 𐑃𐑉𐐨 𐐸𐐲𐑌𐐼𐑉𐐯𐐼 𐐰𐑌𐐼 𐑁𐐫𐑉𐐻𐐨 𐐰𐑌𐐼 𐑁𐐬𐑉 𐐼𐐩𐑆 𐐲𐐹𐐱𐑌 𐑄 𐐶𐐫𐐻𐐲𐑉; 𐐰𐑌𐐼 𐑄𐐩 𐐼𐐮𐐼 𐑊𐐰𐑌𐐼 𐐲𐐹𐐱𐑌 𐑄 𐑇𐐬𐑉 𐐱𐑂 𐑄 𐐹𐑉𐐱𐑋𐐮𐑅𐐻 𐑊𐐰𐑌𐐼. 𐐈𐑌𐐼 𐐸𐐶𐐯𐑌 𐑄𐐩 𐐸𐐰𐐼 𐑅𐐯𐐻 𐑄𐐩𐑉 𐑁𐐨𐐻 𐐲𐐹𐐱𐑌 𐑄 𐑇𐐬𐑉𐑆 𐐱𐑂 𐑄 𐐹𐑉𐐱𐑋𐐮𐑅𐐻 𐑊𐐰𐑌𐐼, 𐑄𐐩 𐐺𐐵𐐼 𐑄𐐯𐑋𐑅𐐯𐑊𐑂𐑆 𐐼𐐵𐑌 𐐲𐐹𐐱𐑌 𐑄 𐑁𐐩𐑅 𐐱𐑂 𐑄 𐑊𐐰𐑌𐐼, 𐐰𐑌𐐼 𐐼𐐮𐐼 𐐸𐐲𐑋𐐺𐑊 𐑄𐐯𐑋𐑅𐐯𐑊𐑂𐑆 𐐺𐐨𐑁𐐬𐑉 𐑄 𐐢𐐫𐑉𐐼, 𐐰𐑌𐐼 𐐼𐐮𐐼 𐑇𐐯𐐼 𐐻𐐨𐑉𐑆 𐐱𐑂 𐐾𐐦 𐐺𐐨𐑁𐐬𐑉 𐑄 𐐢𐐫𐑉𐐼, 𐐺𐐨𐐿𐐫𐑆 𐐱𐑂 𐑄 𐑋𐐲𐑊𐐻𐐮𐐻𐐧𐐼 𐐱𐑂 𐐸𐐮𐑆 𐐻𐐯𐑌𐐼𐐲𐑉 𐑋𐐲𐑉𐑅𐐨𐑆 𐐬𐑂𐐲𐑉 𐑄𐐯𐑋.

4. 𐐈𐑌𐐼 𐐮𐐻 𐐿𐐩𐑋 𐐻𐐭 𐐹𐐰𐑅 𐑄𐐰𐐻 𐑄𐐩 𐐶𐐯𐑌𐐻 𐑁𐐫𐑉𐑃 𐐲𐐹𐐱𐑌 𐑄 𐑁𐐩𐑅 𐐱𐑂 𐑄 𐑊𐐰𐑌𐐼, 𐐰𐑌𐐼 𐐺𐐨𐑀𐐰𐑌 𐐻𐐭 𐐻𐐮𐑊 𐑄 𐐲𐑉𐑃. 𐐈𐑌𐐼 𐐖𐐩𐑉𐐯𐐼 𐐸𐐰𐐼 𐑁𐐬𐑉 𐑅𐐲𐑌𐑆; 𐐰𐑌𐐼 𐑄𐐩 𐐶𐐲𐑉 𐐿𐐫𐑊𐐼 𐐖𐐩𐐿𐐲𐑋, 𐐘𐐮𐑊𐑀𐐲, 𐐰𐑌𐐼 𐐣𐐩𐐸𐐲, 𐐰𐑌𐐼 𐐄𐑉𐐴𐐸𐐲. 𐐈𐑌𐐼 𐑄 𐐺𐑉𐐲𐑄𐐲𐑉 𐐱𐑂 𐐖𐐩𐑉𐐯𐐼 𐐫𐑊𐑅𐐬 𐐺𐐨𐑀𐐰𐐻 𐑅𐐲𐑌𐑆 𐐰𐑌𐐼 𐐼𐐫𐐻𐐲𐑉𐑆. 𐐈𐑌𐐼 𐑄 𐑁𐑉𐐯𐑌𐐼𐑆 𐐱𐑂 𐐖𐐩𐑉𐐯𐐼 𐐰𐑌𐐼 𐐸𐐮𐑆 𐐺𐑉𐐲𐑄𐐲𐑉 𐐶𐐲𐑉 𐐮𐑌 𐑌𐐲𐑋𐐺𐐲𐑉 𐐲𐐺𐐵𐐻 𐐻𐐶𐐯𐑌𐐻𐐨 𐐰𐑌𐐼 𐐻𐐭 𐑅𐐬𐑊𐑆; 𐐰𐑌𐐼 𐑄𐐩 𐐫𐑊𐑅𐐬 𐐺𐐨𐑀𐐰𐐻 𐑅𐐲𐑌𐑆 𐐰𐑌𐐼 𐐼𐐫𐐻𐐲𐑉𐑆, 𐐺𐐨𐑁𐐬𐑉 𐑄𐐩 𐐿𐐩𐑋 𐐻𐐭 𐑄 𐐹𐑉𐐱𐑋𐐮𐑅𐐻 𐑊𐐰𐑌𐐼; 𐐰𐑌𐐼 𐑄𐐯𐑉𐑁𐐬𐑉 𐑄𐐩 𐐺𐐨𐑀𐐰𐑌 𐐻𐐭 𐐺𐐨 𐑋𐐯𐑌𐐨. 𐐈𐑌𐐼 𐑄𐐩 𐐶𐐲𐑉 𐐻𐐫𐐻 𐐻𐐭 𐐶𐐫𐐿 𐐸𐐲𐑋𐐺𐑊𐐨 𐐺𐐨𐑁𐐬𐑉 𐑄 𐐢𐐫𐑉𐐼; 𐐰𐑌𐐼 𐑄𐐩 𐐶𐐲𐑉 𐐫𐑊𐑅𐐬 𐐻𐐫𐐻 𐑁𐑉𐐱𐑋 𐐱𐑌 𐐸𐐴.

5. 𐐈𐑌𐐼 𐐮𐐻 𐐿𐐩𐑋 𐐻𐐭 𐐹𐐰𐑅 𐑄𐐰𐐻 𐑄𐐩 𐐺𐐨𐑀𐐰𐑌 𐐻𐐭 𐑅𐐹𐑉𐐯𐐼 𐐲𐐹𐐱𐑌 𐑄 𐑁𐐩𐑅 𐐱𐑂 𐑄 𐑊𐐰𐑌𐐼, 𐐰𐑌𐐼 𐐻𐐭 𐑋𐐲𐑊𐐻𐐮𐐹𐑊𐐴 𐐰𐑌𐐼 𐐻𐐭 𐐻𐐮𐑊 𐑄 𐐲𐑉𐑃; 𐐰𐑌𐐼 𐑄𐐩 𐐼𐐮𐐼 𐐶𐐰𐐿𐑅 𐑅𐐻𐑉𐐱𐑍 𐐮𐑌 𐑄 𐑊𐐰𐑌𐐼. 𐐈𐑌𐐼 𐑄 𐐺𐑉𐐲𐑄𐐲𐑉 𐐱𐑂 𐐖𐐩𐑉𐐯𐐼 𐐺𐐨𐑀𐐰𐑌 𐐻𐐭 𐐺𐐨 𐐬𐑊𐐼, 𐐰𐑌𐐼 𐑅𐐫 𐑄𐐰𐐻 𐐸𐐨 𐑋𐐲𐑅𐐻 𐑅𐐭𐑌 𐑀𐐬 𐐼𐐵𐑌 𐐻𐐭 𐑄 𐑀𐑉𐐩𐑂; 𐐸𐐶𐐯𐑉𐑁𐐬𐑉 𐐸𐐨 𐑅𐐯𐐼 𐐲𐑌𐐻𐐭 𐐖𐐩𐑉𐐯𐐼, 𐐢𐐯𐐻 𐐲𐑅 𐑀𐐰𐑄𐐲𐑉 𐐻𐐭𐑀𐐯𐑄𐐲𐑉 𐐵𐑉 𐐹𐐨𐐹𐑊, 𐑄𐐰𐐻 𐐶𐐨 𐑋𐐩 𐑌𐐲𐑋𐐺𐐲𐑉 𐑄𐐯𐑋, 𐑄𐐰𐐻 𐐶𐐨 𐑋𐐩 𐑌𐐬 𐐱𐑂 𐑄𐐯𐑋 𐐸𐐶𐐱𐐻 𐑄𐐩 𐐶𐐮𐑊 𐐼𐐨𐑆𐐴𐑉 𐐱𐑂 𐐲𐑅 𐐺𐐨𐑁𐐬𐑉 𐐶𐐨 𐑀𐐬 𐐼𐐵𐑌 𐐻𐐭 𐐵𐑉 𐑀𐑉𐐩𐑂𐑆. 𐐈𐑌𐐼 𐐰𐐿𐐫𐑉𐐼𐐮𐑍𐑊𐐨 𐑄 𐐹𐐨𐐹𐑊 𐐶𐐲𐑉 𐑀𐐰𐑄𐐲𐑉𐐼 𐐻𐐭𐑀𐐯𐑄𐐲𐑉. 𐐤𐐵 𐑄 𐑌𐐲𐑋𐐺𐐲𐑉 𐐱𐑂 𐑄 𐑅𐐲𐑌𐑆 𐐰𐑌𐐼 𐑄 𐐼𐐫𐐻𐐲𐑉𐑆 𐐱𐑂 𐑄 𐐺𐑉𐐲𐑄𐐲𐑉 𐐱𐑂 𐐖𐐩𐑉𐐯𐐼 𐐶𐐲𐑉 𐐻𐐶𐐯𐑌𐐻𐐨 𐐰𐑌𐐼 𐐻𐐭 𐑅𐐬𐑊𐑆; 𐐰𐑌𐐼 𐑄 𐑌𐐲𐑋𐐺𐐲𐑉 𐐱𐑂 𐑅𐐲𐑌𐑆 𐐰𐑌𐐼 𐐼𐐫𐐻𐐲𐑉𐑆 𐐱𐑂 𐐖𐐩𐑉𐐯𐐼 𐐶𐐲𐑉 𐐻𐐶𐐯𐑊𐑂, 𐐸𐐨 𐐸𐐰𐑂𐐮𐑍 𐑁𐐬𐑉 𐑅𐐲𐑌𐑆. 𐐈𐑌𐐼 𐐮𐐻 𐐿𐐩𐑋 𐐻𐐭 𐐹𐐰𐑅 𐑄𐐰𐐻 𐑄𐐩 𐐼𐐮𐐼 𐑌𐐲𐑋𐐺𐐲𐑉 𐑄𐐩𐑉 𐐹𐐨𐐹𐑊; 𐐰𐑌𐐼 𐐰𐑁𐐻𐐲𐑉 𐑄𐐰𐐻 𐑄𐐩 𐐸𐐰𐐼 𐑌𐐲𐑋𐐺𐐲𐑉𐐼 𐑄𐐯𐑋, 𐑄𐐩 𐐼𐐮𐐼 𐐼𐐨𐑆𐐴𐑉 𐐱𐑂 𐑄𐐯𐑋 𐑄 𐑃𐐮𐑍𐑆 𐐸𐐶𐐮𐐽 𐑄𐐩 𐐶𐐳𐐼 𐑄𐐰𐐻 𐑄𐐩 𐑇𐐳𐐼 𐐼𐐭 𐐺𐐨𐑁𐐬𐑉 𐑄𐐩 𐐶𐐯𐑌𐐻 𐐼𐐵𐑌 𐐻𐐭 𐑄𐐩𐑉 𐑀𐑉𐐩𐑂𐑆. 𐐈𐑌𐐼 𐐮𐐻 𐐿𐐩𐑋 𐐻𐐭 𐐹𐐰𐑅 𐑄𐐰𐐻 𐑄 𐐹𐐨𐐹𐑊 𐐼𐐨𐑆𐐴𐑉𐐼 𐐱𐑂 𐑄𐐯𐑋 𐑄𐐰𐐻 𐑄𐐩 𐑇𐐳𐐼 𐐰𐑌𐐦𐑌𐐻 𐐶𐐲𐑌 𐐱𐑂 𐑄𐐩𐑉 𐑅𐐲𐑌𐑆 𐐻𐐭 𐐺𐐨 𐐩 𐐿𐐮𐑍 𐐬𐑂𐐲𐑉 𐑄𐐯𐑋. 𐐈𐑌𐐼 𐑌𐐵 𐐺𐐨𐐸𐐬𐑊𐐼, 𐑄𐐮𐑅 𐐶𐐱𐑆 𐑀𐑉𐐨𐑂𐐲𐑅 𐐲𐑌𐐻𐐭 𐑄𐐯𐑋. 𐐈𐑌𐐼 𐑄 𐐺𐑉𐐲𐑄𐐲𐑉 𐐱𐑂 𐐖𐐩𐑉𐐯𐐼 𐑅𐐯𐐼 𐐲𐑌𐐻𐐭 𐑄𐐯𐑋, 𐐟𐐭𐑉𐑊𐐨 𐑄𐐮𐑅 𐑃𐐮𐑍 𐑊𐐨𐐼𐐯𐑃 𐐮𐑌𐐻𐐭 𐐿𐐰𐐹𐐻𐐮𐑂𐐮𐐻𐐨. 𐐒𐐲𐐻 𐐖𐐩𐑉𐐯𐐼 𐑅𐐯𐐼 𐐲𐑌𐐻𐐭 𐐸𐐮𐑆 𐐺𐑉𐐲𐑄𐐲𐑉, 𐐝𐐲𐑁𐐲𐑉 𐑄𐐯𐑋 𐑄𐐰𐐻 𐑄𐐩 𐑋𐐩 𐐸𐐰𐑂 𐐩 𐐿𐐮𐑍; 𐐰𐑌𐐼 𐑄𐐯𐑉𐑁𐐬𐑉 𐐸𐐨 𐑅𐐯𐐼 𐐲𐑌𐐻𐐭 𐑄𐐯𐑋, 𐐕𐐭𐑆 𐐷𐐨 𐐵𐐻 𐑁𐑉𐐱𐑋 𐐲𐑋𐐲𐑍 𐐵𐑉 𐑅𐐲𐑌𐑆 𐐩 𐐿𐐮𐑍, 𐐨𐑂𐐲𐑌 𐐸𐐭𐑋 𐐷𐐨 𐐶𐐮𐑊.

6. 𐐈𐑌𐐼 𐐮𐐻 𐐿𐐩𐑋 𐐻𐐭 𐐹𐐰𐑅 𐑄𐐰𐐻 𐑄𐐩 𐐽𐐬𐑆 𐐨𐑂𐐲𐑌 𐑄 𐑁𐐲𐑉𐑅𐐻 𐐺𐐫𐑉𐑌 𐐱𐑂 𐑄 𐐺𐑉𐐲𐑄𐐲𐑉 𐐱𐑂 𐐖𐐩𐑉𐐯𐐼; 𐐰𐑌𐐼 𐐸𐐮𐑆 𐑌𐐩𐑋 𐐶𐐱𐑆 𐐑𐐩𐑀𐐰𐑀. 𐐈𐑌𐐼 𐐮𐐻 𐐿𐐩𐑋 𐐻𐐭 𐐹𐐰𐑅 𐑄𐐰𐐻 𐐸𐐨 𐑉𐐨𐑁𐐧𐑆𐐼 𐐰𐑌𐐼 𐐶𐐳𐐼 𐑌𐐱𐐻 𐐺𐐨 𐑄𐐩𐑉 𐐿𐐮𐑍. 𐐈𐑌𐐼 𐑄 𐐹𐐨𐐹𐑊 𐐶𐐳𐐼 𐑄𐐰𐐻 𐐸𐐮𐑆 𐑁𐐫𐑄𐐲𐑉 𐑇𐐳𐐼 𐐿𐐱𐑌𐑅𐐻𐑉𐐩𐑌 𐐸𐐮𐑋; 𐐒𐐲𐐻 𐐸𐐮𐑆 𐑁𐐫𐑄𐐲𐑉 𐐶𐐳𐐼 𐑌𐐱𐐻; 𐐰𐑌𐐼 𐐸𐐨 𐐿𐐲𐑋𐐰𐑌𐐼𐐯𐐼 𐑄𐐯𐑋 𐑄𐐰𐐻 𐑄𐐩 𐑇𐐳𐐼 𐐿𐐱𐑌𐑅𐐻𐑉𐐩𐑌 𐑌𐐬 𐑋𐐰𐑌 𐐻𐐭 𐐺𐐨 𐑄𐐩𐑉 𐐿𐐮𐑍. 𐐈𐑌𐐼 𐐮𐐻 𐐿𐐩𐑋 𐐻𐐭 𐐹𐐰𐑅 𐑄𐐰𐐻 𐑄𐐩 𐐽𐐬𐑆 𐐫𐑊 𐑄 𐐺𐑉𐐲𐑄𐐲𐑉𐑆 𐐱𐑂 𐐑𐐩𐑀𐐰𐑀, 𐐰𐑌𐐼 𐑄𐐩 𐐶𐐳𐐼 𐑌𐐱𐐻. 𐐈𐑌𐐼 𐐮𐐻 𐐿𐐩𐑋 𐐻𐐭 𐐹𐐰𐑅 𐑄𐐰𐐻 𐑌𐐨𐑄𐐲𐑉 𐐶𐐳𐐼 𐑄 𐑅𐐲𐑌𐑆 𐐱𐑂 𐐖𐐩𐑉𐐯𐐼, 𐐨𐑂𐐲𐑌 𐐫𐑊, 𐑅𐐩𐑂 𐐮𐐻 𐐶𐐲𐑉 𐐶𐐲𐑌; 𐐰𐑌𐐼 𐐄𐑉𐐴𐐸𐐲 𐐶𐐱𐑆 𐐰𐑌𐐦𐑌𐐻𐐯𐐼 𐐻𐐭 𐐺𐐨 𐐿𐐮𐑍 𐐬𐑂𐐲𐑉 𐑄 𐐹𐐨𐐹𐑊. 𐐈𐑌𐐼 𐐸𐐨 𐐺𐐨𐑀𐐰𐑌 𐐻𐐭 𐑉𐐩𐑌, 𐐰𐑌𐐼 𐑄 𐐹𐐨𐐹𐑊 𐐺𐐨𐑀𐐰𐑌 𐐻𐐭 𐐹𐑉𐐱𐑅𐐹𐐲𐑉; 𐐰𐑌𐐼 𐑄𐐩 𐐺𐐨𐐿𐐩𐑋 𐐯𐐿𐑅𐐨𐐼𐐮𐑍𐑊𐐨 𐑉𐐮𐐽. 𐐈𐑌𐐼 𐐮𐐻 𐐿𐐩𐑋 𐐻𐐭 𐐹𐐰𐑅 𐑄𐐰𐐻 𐐖𐐩𐑉𐐯𐐼 𐐼𐐴𐐼, 𐐰𐑌𐐼 𐐸𐐮𐑆 𐐺𐑉𐐲𐑄𐐲𐑉 𐐫𐑊𐑅𐐬. 𐐈𐑌𐐼 𐐮𐐻 𐐿𐐩𐑋 𐐻𐐭 𐐹𐐰𐑅 𐑄𐐰𐐻 𐐄𐑉𐐴𐐸𐐲 𐐼𐐮𐐼 𐐶𐐫𐐿 𐐸𐐲𐑋𐐺𐑊𐐨 𐐺𐐨𐑁𐐬𐑉 𐑄 𐐢𐐫𐑉𐐼, 𐐰𐑌𐐼 𐐼𐐮𐐼 𐑉𐐨𐑋𐐯𐑋𐐺𐐲𐑉 𐐸𐐵 𐑀𐑉𐐩𐐻 𐑃𐐮𐑍𐑆 𐑄 𐐢𐐫𐑉𐐼 𐐸𐐰𐐼 𐐼𐐲𐑌 𐑁𐐫𐑉 𐐸𐐮𐑆 𐑁𐐫𐑄𐐲𐑉, 𐐰𐑌𐐼 𐐫𐑊𐑅𐐬 𐐻𐐫𐐻 𐐸𐐮𐑆 𐐹𐐨𐐹𐑊 𐐸𐐵 𐑀𐑉𐐩𐐻 𐑃𐐮𐑍𐑆 𐑄 𐐢𐐫𐑉𐐼 𐐸𐐰𐐼 𐐼𐐲𐑌 𐑁𐐫𐑉 𐑄𐐩𐑉 𐑁𐐫𐑄𐐲𐑉𐑆.

7. 𐐈𐑌𐐼 𐐮𐐻 𐐿𐐩𐑋 𐐻𐐭 𐐹𐐰𐑅 𐑄𐐰𐐻 𐐄𐑉𐐴𐐸𐐲 𐐼𐐮𐐼 𐐯𐐿𐑅𐐨𐐿𐐧𐐻 𐐾𐐲𐐾𐑋𐐯𐑌𐐻 𐐲𐐹𐐱𐑌 𐑄 𐑊𐐰𐑌𐐼, 𐐮𐑌 𐑉𐐴𐐽𐐲𐑅𐑌𐐯𐑅 𐐫𐑊 𐐸𐐮𐑆 𐐼𐐩𐑆, 𐐸𐐭𐑆 𐐼𐐩𐑆 𐐶𐐲𐑉 𐐯𐐿𐑅𐐨𐐼𐐮𐑍𐑊𐐨 𐑋𐐯𐑌𐐨. 𐐈𐑌𐐼 𐐸𐐨 𐐺𐐨𐑀𐐰𐐻 𐑅𐐲𐑌𐑆 𐐰𐑌𐐼 𐐼𐐫𐐻𐐲𐑉𐑆; 𐐷𐐩, 𐐸𐐨 𐐺𐐨𐑀𐐰𐐻 𐑃𐐲𐑉𐐻𐐨 𐐰𐑌𐐼 𐐶𐐲𐑌, 𐐲𐑋𐐲𐑍 𐐸𐐭𐑋 𐐶𐐲𐑉 𐐻𐐶𐐯𐑌𐐻𐐨 𐐰𐑌𐐼 𐑃𐑉𐐨 𐑅𐐲𐑌𐑆. 𐐈𐑌𐐼

𐐮𐐻 𐐿𐐩𐑋 𐐻𐐭 𐐹𐐰𐑅 𐑄𐐰𐐻 𐐸𐐨 𐐫𐑊𐑅𐐬 𐐺𐐨𐑀𐐰𐐻 𐐗𐐮𐐺 𐐮𐑌 𐐸𐐮𐑆 𐐬𐑊𐐼 𐐩𐐾. 𐐈𐑌𐐼 𐐮𐐻 𐐿𐐩𐑋 𐐻𐐭 𐐹𐐰𐑅 𐑄𐐰𐐻 𐐗𐐮𐐺 𐑉𐐩𐑌𐐼 𐐮𐑌 𐐸𐐮𐑆 𐑅𐐻𐐯𐐼; 𐐰𐑌𐐼 𐐗𐐮𐐺 𐐺𐐨𐑀𐐰𐐻 𐐗𐐫𐑉𐐮𐐸𐐫𐑉. 𐐈𐑌𐐼 𐐸𐐶𐐯𐑌 𐐗𐐫𐑉𐐮𐐸𐐫𐑉 𐐶𐐱𐑆 𐑃𐐲𐑉𐐻𐐨 𐐰𐑌𐐼 𐐻𐐭 𐐷𐐨𐑉𐑆 𐐬𐑊𐐼 𐐸𐐨 𐑉𐐨𐐺𐐯𐑊𐐼 𐐰𐑀𐐯𐑌𐑅𐐻 𐐸𐐮𐑆 𐑁𐐪𐑄𐐲𐑉, 𐐰𐑌𐐼 𐐶𐐯𐑌𐐻 𐐬𐑂𐐲𐑉 𐐰𐑌𐐼 𐐼𐐶𐐯𐑊𐐻 𐐮𐑌 𐑄 𐑊𐐰𐑌𐐼 𐐱𐑂 𐐤𐐨𐐸𐐫𐑉; 𐐰𐑌𐐼 𐐸𐐨 𐐺𐐨𐑀𐐰𐐻 𐑅𐐲𐑌𐑆 𐐰𐑌𐐼 𐐼𐐫𐐻𐐲𐑉𐑆; 𐐰𐑌𐐼 𐑄𐐩 𐐺𐐨𐐿𐐩𐑋 𐐯𐐿𐑅𐐨𐐼𐐮𐑍𐑊𐐨 𐑁𐐯𐑉; 𐐸𐐶𐐯𐑉𐑁𐐫𐑉, 𐐗𐐫𐑉𐐮𐐸𐐫𐑉 𐐼𐑉𐐭 𐐰𐐶𐐩 𐑋𐐯𐑌𐐨 𐐹𐐨𐐹𐑊 𐐰𐑁𐐻𐐲𐑉 𐐸𐐮𐑋. 𐐈𐑌𐐼 𐐸𐐶𐐯𐑌 𐐸𐐨 𐐸𐐰𐐼 𐑀𐐰𐑄𐐲𐑉𐐼 𐐻𐐭𐑀𐐯𐑄𐐲𐑉 𐐰𐑌 𐐪𐑉𐑋𐐨, 𐐸𐐨 𐐿𐐩𐑋 𐐲𐐹 𐐲𐑌𐐻𐐭 𐑄 𐑊𐐰𐑌𐐼 𐐱𐑂 𐐣𐐫𐑉𐐱𐑌 𐐸𐐶𐐯𐑉 𐑄 𐐿𐐮𐑍 𐐼𐐶𐐯𐑊𐐻, 𐐰𐑌𐐼 𐐻𐐳𐐿 𐐸𐐮𐑋 𐐿𐐰𐐹𐐻𐐮𐑂, 𐐸𐐶𐐮𐐽 𐐺𐑉𐐫𐐻 𐐻𐐭 𐐹𐐰𐑅 𐑄 𐑅𐐩𐐮𐑍 𐐱𐑂 𐑄 𐐺𐑉𐐲𐑄𐐲𐑉 𐐱𐑂 𐐖𐐯𐑉𐐯𐐼, 𐑄𐐰𐐻 𐑄𐐩 𐐶𐐳𐐼 𐐺𐐨 𐐺𐑉𐐫𐐻 𐐮𐑌𐐻𐐭 𐐿𐐰𐐹𐐻𐐮𐑂𐐮𐐻𐐨. 𐐤𐐵 𐑄 𐑊𐐰𐑌𐐼 𐐱𐑂 𐐣𐐫𐑉𐐱𐑌, 𐐸𐐶𐐯𐑉 𐑄 𐐿𐐮𐑍 𐐼𐐶𐐯𐑊𐐻, 𐐶𐐱𐑆 𐑌𐐨𐑉 𐑄 𐑊𐐰𐑌𐐼 𐐸𐐶𐐮𐐽 𐐮𐑆 𐐿𐐫𐑊𐐼 𐐔𐐯𐑅𐐬𐑊𐐩𐑇𐐲𐑌 𐐺𐐴 𐑄 𐐤𐐨𐑁𐐴𐐻𐑅. 𐐈𐑌𐐼 𐐮𐐻 𐐿𐐩𐑋 𐐻𐐭 𐐹𐐰𐑅 𐑄𐐰𐐻 𐐗𐐮𐐺 𐐼𐐶𐐯𐑊𐐻 𐐮𐑌 𐐿𐐰𐐹𐐻𐐮𐑂𐐮𐐻𐐨, 𐐰𐑌𐐼 𐐸𐐮𐑆 𐐹𐐨𐐹𐑊 𐐲𐑌𐐼𐐲𐑉 𐐗𐐫𐑉𐐮𐐸𐐫𐑉 𐐸𐐮𐑆 𐑅𐐲𐑌, 𐐲𐑌𐐻𐐮𐑊 𐐸𐐨 𐐺𐐨𐐿𐐩𐑋 𐐯𐐿𐑅𐐨𐐼𐐮𐑍𐑊𐐨 𐐬𐑊𐐼; 𐑌𐐯𐑂𐐲𐑉𐑄𐐯𐑊𐐯𐑅 𐐗𐐮𐐺 𐐺𐐨𐑀𐐰𐐻 𐐟𐐮𐐭𐑊 𐐮𐑌 𐐸𐐮𐑆 𐐬𐑊𐐼 𐐩𐐾, 𐐸𐐶𐐴𐑊 𐐸𐐨 𐐶𐐱𐑆 𐐷𐐯𐐻 𐐮𐑌 𐐿𐐰𐐹𐐻𐐮𐑂𐐮𐐻𐐨.

8. 𐐈𐑌𐐼 𐐮𐐻 𐐿𐐩𐑋 𐐻𐐭 𐐹𐐰𐑅 𐑄𐐰𐐻 𐐟𐐮𐐭𐑊 𐐶𐐱𐑆 𐐰𐑍𐑀𐑉𐐨 𐐶𐐮𐑄 𐐸𐐮𐑆 𐐺𐑉𐐲𐑄𐐲𐑉; 𐐰𐑌𐐼 𐐟𐐮𐐭𐑊 𐐶𐐰𐐿𐑅𐐻 𐑅𐐻𐑉𐐱𐑍, 𐐰𐑌𐐼 𐐺𐐨𐐿𐐩𐑋 𐑋𐐴𐐻𐐨, 𐐰𐑆 𐐻𐐭 𐑄 𐑅𐐻𐑉𐐯𐑍𐑃 𐐱𐑂 𐐲 𐑋𐐰𐑌; 𐐰𐑌𐐼 𐐸𐐨 𐐶𐐱𐑆 𐐫𐑊𐑅𐐬 𐑋𐐴𐐻𐐨 𐐮𐑌 𐐾𐐲𐐾𐑋𐐲𐑌𐐻. 𐐐𐐶𐐯𐑉𐑁𐐫𐑉 𐐸𐐨 𐐿𐐩𐑋 𐐻𐐭 𐑄 𐐸𐐮𐑊 𐐀𐑁𐑉𐐨𐐰𐑋, 𐐰𐑌𐐼 𐐸𐐨 𐐼𐐮𐐼 𐑋𐐬𐑊𐐻𐑌 𐐵𐐻 𐐱𐑂 𐑄 𐐸𐐮𐑊, 𐐰𐑌𐐼 𐑋𐐩𐐼 𐑅𐐫𐑉𐐼𐑆 𐐵𐐻 𐐱𐑂 𐑅𐐻𐐨𐑊 𐑁𐐫𐑉 𐑄𐐬𐑆 𐐸𐐭𐑋 𐐸𐐨 𐐸𐐰𐐼 𐐼𐑉𐐫𐑌 𐐰𐐶𐐩 𐐶𐐮𐑄 𐐸𐐮𐑋; 𐐰𐑌𐐼 𐐰𐑁𐐻𐐲𐑉 𐐸𐐨 𐐸𐐰𐐼 𐐪𐑉𐑋𐐼 𐑄𐐯𐑋 𐐶𐐮𐑄 𐑅𐐫𐑉𐐼𐑆, 𐐸𐐨 𐑉𐐨𐐻𐐲𐑉𐑌𐐼 𐐻𐐭 𐑄 𐑅𐐮𐐻𐐨 𐐤𐐨𐐸𐐫𐑉, 𐐰𐑌𐐼 𐑀𐐩𐑂 𐐺𐐰𐐻𐑊 𐐲𐑌𐐻𐐭 𐐸𐐮𐑆 𐐺𐑉𐐲𐑄𐐲𐑉 𐐗𐐫𐑉𐐮𐐸𐐫𐑉, 𐐺𐐴 𐐸𐐶𐐮𐐽 𐑋𐐨𐑌𐑆 𐐸𐐨 𐐱𐐺𐐻𐐩𐑌𐐼 𐑄 𐐿𐐮𐑍𐐼𐐲𐑋, 𐐰𐑌𐐼 𐑉𐐨𐑅𐐻𐐫𐑉𐐼 𐐮𐐻 𐐲𐑌𐐻𐐭 𐐸𐐮𐑆 𐑁𐐪𐑄𐐲𐑉 𐐗𐐮𐐺. 𐐈𐑌𐐼 𐑌𐐵 𐐺𐐨𐐿𐐱𐑆 𐐱𐑂 𐑄 𐑃𐐮𐑍 𐐸𐐶𐐮𐐽 𐐟𐐮𐐭𐑊 𐐸𐐰𐐼 𐐼𐐲𐑌, 𐐸𐐮𐑆 𐑁𐐪𐑄𐐲𐑉 𐐺𐐨𐑅𐐻𐐬𐐼 𐐲𐐹𐐱𐑌 𐐸𐐮𐑋 𐑄 𐐿𐐮𐑍𐐼𐐲𐑋; 𐑄𐐯𐑉𐑁𐐫𐑉 𐐸𐐨 𐐺𐐨𐑀𐐰𐑌 𐐻𐐭 𐑉𐐩𐑌 𐐮𐑌 𐑄 𐑅𐐻𐐯𐐼 𐐱𐑂 𐐸𐐮𐑆 𐑁𐐪𐑄𐐲𐑉. 𐐈𐑌𐐼 𐐮𐐻 𐐿𐐩𐑋 𐐻𐐭 𐐹𐐰𐑅 𐑄𐐰𐐻 𐐸𐐨 𐐼𐐮𐐼 𐐯𐐿𐑅𐐨𐐿𐐷𐐭𐐻 𐐾𐐲𐐾𐑋𐐲𐑌𐐻 𐐮𐑌 𐑉𐐴𐐽𐐲𐑅𐑌𐐯𐑅; 𐐰𐑌𐐼 𐐸𐐨 𐐼𐐮𐐼 𐑅𐐹𐑉𐐯𐐼 𐐸𐐮𐑆 𐐿𐐮𐑍𐐼𐐲𐑋 𐐲𐐹𐐱𐑌 𐐫𐑊 𐑄 𐑁𐐩𐑅 𐐱𐑂 𐑄 𐑊𐐰𐑌𐐼, 𐑁𐐫𐑉 𐑄 𐐹𐐨𐐹𐑊 𐐸𐐰𐐼 𐐺𐐨𐐿𐐲𐑋 𐐯𐐿𐑅𐐨𐐼𐐮𐑍𐑊𐐨 𐑌𐐭𐑋𐐲𐑉𐐲𐑅. 𐐈𐑌𐐼 𐐮𐐻 𐐿𐐩𐑋 𐐻𐐭 𐐹𐐰𐑅 𐑄𐐰𐐻 𐐟𐐮𐐭𐑊 𐐫𐑊𐑅𐐬 𐐺𐐨𐑀𐐰𐐻 𐑋𐐯𐑌𐐨 𐑅𐐲𐑌𐑆 𐐰𐑌𐐼 𐐼𐐫𐐻𐐲𐑉𐑆. 𐐈𐑌𐐼 𐐗𐐫𐑉𐐮𐐸𐐫𐑉 𐑉𐐨𐐹𐐯𐑌𐐻𐐯𐐼 𐐱𐑂 𐑄 𐑋𐐯𐑌𐐨 𐐨𐑂𐐮𐑊𐑆 𐐸𐐶𐐮𐐽 𐐸𐐨 𐐸𐐰𐐼 𐐼𐐲𐑌; 𐐸𐐶𐐯𐑉𐑁𐐫𐑉 𐐟𐐮𐐭𐑊 𐑀𐐩𐑂 𐐸𐐮𐑋 𐐹𐐵𐐲𐑉 𐐮𐑌 𐐸𐐮𐑆 𐐿𐐮𐑍𐐼𐐲𐑋. 𐐈𐑌𐐼 𐐮𐐻 𐐿𐐩𐑋 𐐻𐐭 𐐹𐐰𐑅 𐑄𐐰𐐻 𐐗𐐫𐑉𐐮𐐸𐐫𐑉 𐐸𐐰𐐼 𐑋𐐯𐑌𐐨 𐑅𐐲𐑌𐑆 𐐰𐑌𐐼 𐐼𐐫𐐻𐐲𐑉𐑆. 𐐈𐑌𐐼 𐐰𐑋𐐲𐑍 𐑄 𐑅𐐲𐑌𐑆 𐐱𐑂 𐐗𐐫𐑉𐐮𐐸𐐫𐑉 𐑄𐐯𐑉 𐐶𐐱𐑆 𐐶𐐲𐑌 𐐸𐐭𐑆 𐑌𐐩𐑋 𐐶𐐱𐑆 𐐤𐐬𐐲.

9. 𐐈𐑌𐐼 𐐮𐐻 𐐿𐐩𐑋 𐐻𐐭 𐐹𐐰𐑅 𐑄𐐰𐐻 𐐤𐐬𐐲 𐑉𐐨𐐺𐐯𐑊𐐼 𐐰𐑀𐐯𐑌𐑅𐐻 𐐟𐐮𐐭𐑊, 𐑄 𐐿𐐮𐑍, 𐐰𐑌𐐼 𐐫𐑊𐑅𐐬 𐐸𐐮𐑆 𐑁𐐪𐑄𐐲𐑉 𐐗𐐫𐑉𐐮𐐸𐐫𐑉, 𐐰𐑌𐐼 𐐼𐑉𐐭 𐐰𐐶𐐩 𐐗𐐬𐐸𐐫𐑉 𐐸𐐮𐑆 𐐺𐑉𐐲𐑄𐐲𐑉, 𐐰𐑌𐐼 𐐫𐑊𐑅𐐬 𐐫𐑊 𐐸𐐮𐑆 𐐺𐑉𐐯𐑃𐑉𐐯𐑌 𐐰𐑌𐐼 𐑋𐐯𐑌𐐨 𐐱𐑂 𐑄 𐐹𐐨𐐹𐑊. 𐐈𐑌𐐼 𐐸𐐨 𐑀𐐩𐑂 𐐺𐐰𐐻𐑊 𐐲𐑌𐐻𐐭 𐐟𐐮𐐭𐑊, 𐑄 𐐿𐐮𐑍, 𐐮𐑌 𐐸𐐶𐐮𐐽 𐐸𐐨 𐐼𐐮𐐼 𐐱𐐺𐐻𐐩𐑌 𐑄 𐑊𐐰𐑌𐐼 𐐱𐑂 𐑄𐐯𐑉 𐑁𐐲𐑉𐑅𐐻 𐐮𐑌𐐸𐐯𐑉𐐮𐐻𐐲𐑌𐑅; 𐐰𐑌𐐼 𐐸𐐨 𐐺𐐨𐐿𐐩𐑋 𐐲 𐐿𐐮𐑍 𐐬𐑂𐐲𐑉 𐑄𐐰𐐻 𐐹𐐪𐑉𐐻 𐐱𐑂 𐑄 𐑊𐐰𐑌𐐼. 𐐈𐑌𐐼 𐐮𐐻 𐐿𐐩𐑋 𐐻𐐭 𐐹𐐰𐑅 𐑄𐐰𐐻 𐐸𐐨 𐑀𐐩𐑂 𐐺𐐰𐐻𐑊 𐐰𐑀𐐯𐑌 𐐲𐑌𐐻𐐭 𐐟𐐮𐐭𐑊, 𐑄 𐐿𐐮𐑍, 𐐰𐑌𐐼 𐐸𐐨 𐐻𐐳𐐿 𐐟𐐮𐐭𐑊, 𐑄 𐐿𐐮𐑍, 𐐰𐑌𐐼 𐐿𐐰𐑉𐐨𐐼 𐐸𐐮𐑋 𐐰𐐶𐐩 𐐿𐐰𐐹𐐻𐐮𐑂 𐐮𐑌𐐻𐐭 𐐣𐐫𐑉𐐱𐑌. 𐐈𐑌𐐼 𐐮𐐻 𐐿𐐩𐑋 𐐻𐐭 𐐹𐐰𐑅 𐐰𐑆 𐐸𐐨 𐐶𐐱𐑆 𐐰𐐺𐐵𐐻 𐐻𐐭 𐐹𐐳𐐻 𐐸𐐮𐑋 𐐻𐐭 𐐼𐐯𐑃, 𐑄 𐑅𐐲𐑌𐑆 𐐱𐑂 𐐟𐐮𐐭𐑊 𐐿𐑉𐐯𐐹𐐻 𐐮𐑌𐐻𐐭 𐑄 𐐸𐐵𐑅 𐐱𐑂 𐐤𐐬𐐲 𐐺𐐴 𐑌𐐴𐐻 𐐰𐑌𐐼 𐑅𐑊𐐭 𐐸𐐮𐑋, 𐐰𐑌𐐼 𐐺𐑉𐐬𐐿 𐐼𐐵𐑌 𐑄 𐐼𐐬𐑉 𐐱𐑂 𐑄 𐐹𐑉𐐮𐑆𐐲𐑌, 𐐰𐑌𐐼 𐐺𐑉𐐫𐐻 𐐵𐐻 𐑄𐐯𐑉 𐑁𐐪𐑄𐐲𐑉, 𐐰𐑌𐐼 𐐹𐑊𐐩𐑅𐐻 𐐸𐐮𐑋 𐐲𐐹𐐱𐑌 𐐸𐐮𐑆 𐑃𐑉𐐬𐑌 𐐮𐑌 𐐸𐐮𐑆 𐐬𐑌 𐐿𐐮𐑍𐐼𐐲𐑋; 𐐸𐐶𐐯𐑉𐑁𐐫𐑉 𐑄 𐑅𐐲𐑌 𐐱𐑂 𐐤𐐬𐐲 𐐼𐐮𐐼 𐐺𐐮𐑊𐐼 𐐲𐐹 𐐸𐐮𐑆 𐐿𐐮𐑍𐐼𐐲𐑋 𐐮𐑌 𐐸𐐮𐑆 𐑅𐐻𐐯𐐼; 𐑌𐐯𐑂𐐲𐑉𐑄𐐯𐑊𐐯𐑅 𐑄𐐩 𐐼𐐮𐐼 𐑌𐐱𐐻 𐑀𐐩𐑌 𐐹𐐵𐐲𐑉 𐐯𐑌𐐨 𐑋𐐬𐑉 𐐬𐑂𐐲𐑉 𐐟𐐮𐐭𐑊 𐑄 𐐿𐐮𐑍, 𐐰𐑌𐐼 𐑄 𐐹𐐨𐐹𐑊 𐐸𐐭 𐐶𐐲𐑉 𐐲𐑌𐐼𐐲𐑉 𐑄 𐑉𐐩𐑌 𐐱𐑂 𐐟𐐮𐐭𐑊 𐑄 𐐿𐐮𐑍, 𐐼𐐮𐐼 𐐹𐑉𐐱𐑅𐐹𐐲𐑉 𐐯𐐿𐑅𐐨𐐼𐐮𐑍𐑊𐐨 𐐰𐑌𐐼 𐐶𐐰𐐿𐑅 𐑀𐑉𐐩𐐻. 𐐈𐑌𐐼 𐑄 𐐿𐐲𐑌𐐻𐑉𐐨 𐐶𐐱𐑆 𐐼𐐨𐑂𐐴𐐼𐐯𐐼; 𐐰𐑌𐐼 𐑄𐐯𐑉 𐐶𐐲𐑉 𐐻𐐭 𐐿𐐮𐑍𐐼𐐲𐑋𐑆, 𐑄 𐐿𐐮𐑍𐐼𐐲𐑋 𐐱𐑂 𐐟𐐮𐐭𐑊, 𐐰𐑌𐐼 𐑄 𐐿𐐮𐑍𐐼𐐲𐑋 𐐱𐑂 𐐗𐐬𐐸𐐫𐑉, 𐑄 𐑅𐐲𐑌 𐐱𐑂 𐐤𐐬𐐲. 𐐈𐑌𐐼 𐐗𐐬𐐸𐐫𐑉, 𐑄 𐑅𐐲𐑌 𐐱𐑂 𐐤𐐬𐐲, 𐐿𐐫𐑆𐐼 𐑄𐐰𐐻 𐐸𐐮𐑆 𐐹𐐨𐐹𐑊 𐑇𐐳𐐼 𐑀𐐮𐑂 𐐺𐐰𐐻𐑊 𐐲𐑌𐐻𐐭 𐐟𐐮𐐭𐑊, 𐐮𐑌 𐐸𐐶𐐮𐐽 𐐟𐐮𐐭𐑊 𐐼𐐮𐐼 𐐺𐐨𐐻 𐑄𐐯𐑋 𐐰𐑌𐐼 𐐼𐐮𐐼 𐑅𐑊𐐩 𐐗𐐬𐐸𐐫𐑉. 𐐈𐑌𐐼 𐑌𐐵 𐐗𐐬𐐸𐐫𐑉 𐐸𐐰𐐼 𐐲 𐑅𐐲𐑌 𐐸𐐭 𐐶𐐱𐑆 𐐿𐐫𐑊𐐼 𐐤𐐮𐑋𐑉𐐱𐐼; 𐐰𐑌𐐼 𐐤𐐮𐑋𐑉𐐱𐐼 𐑀𐐩𐑂 𐐲𐐹 𐑄 𐐿𐐮𐑍𐐼𐐲𐑋 𐐱𐑂 𐐗𐐬𐐸𐐫𐑉 𐐲𐑌𐐻𐐭 𐐟𐐮𐐭𐑊, 𐐰𐑌𐐼 𐐸𐐨 𐐼𐐮𐐼 𐑀𐐩𐑌 𐑁𐐩𐑂𐐲𐑉 𐐮𐑌 𐑄 𐐴𐑆 𐐱𐑂 𐐟𐐮𐐭𐑊;

𐐸𐐶𐐯𐑉𐑁𐐫𐑉 𐐟𐐷𐐭𐑊 𐐼𐐮𐐼 𐐺𐐯𐑅𐐻𐐬 𐑀𐑉𐐩𐐻 𐑁𐐩𐑂𐐲𐑉𐑆 𐐲𐐹𐐱𐑌 𐐸𐐮𐑋, 𐐰𐑌𐐼 𐐸𐐨 𐐼𐐮𐐼 𐐼𐐭 𐐮𐑌 𐑄 𐐿𐐮𐑍𐐼𐐲𐑋 𐐱𐑂 𐐟𐐷𐐭𐑊 𐐰𐐿𐐫𐑉𐐼𐐮𐑍 𐐻𐐭 𐐸𐐮𐑆 𐐼𐐨𐑆𐐴𐑉𐑆; 𐐰𐑌𐐼 𐐫𐑊𐑅𐐬 𐐮𐑌 𐑄 𐑉𐐩𐑌 𐐱𐑂 𐐟𐐷𐐭𐑊 𐑄𐐯𐑉 𐐿𐐩𐑋 𐐹𐑉𐐱𐑁𐐯𐐻𐑅 𐐰𐑋𐐲𐑍 𐑄 𐐹𐐨𐐹𐑊, 𐐸𐐭 𐐶𐐲𐑉 𐑅𐐯𐑌𐐻 𐑁𐑉𐐱𐑋 𐑄 𐐢𐐫𐑉𐐼, 𐐹𐑉𐐱𐑁𐐯𐑅𐐴𐐮𐑍 𐑄𐐰𐐻 𐑄 𐐶𐐮𐐿𐐯𐐼𐑌𐐯𐑅 𐐰𐑌𐐼 𐐴𐐼𐐱𐑊𐐰𐐻𐑉𐐮 𐐱𐑂 𐑄 𐐹𐐨𐐹𐑊 𐐶𐐱𐑆 𐐺𐑉𐐮𐑍𐐮𐑍 𐐰 𐐿𐐲𐑉𐑅 𐐲𐐹𐐱𐑌 𐑄 𐑊𐐰𐑌𐐼, 𐐰𐑌𐐼 𐑄𐐩 𐑇𐐳𐐼 𐐺𐐨 𐐼𐐨𐑅𐐻𐑉𐑎𐐼, 𐐮𐑁 𐑄𐐩 𐐼𐐮𐐼 𐑌𐐱𐐻 𐑉𐐨𐐹𐐯𐑌𐐻.

10. 𐐰𐑌𐐼 𐐮𐐻 𐐿𐐩𐑋 𐐻𐐭 𐐹𐐰𐑅 𐑄𐐰𐐻 𐑄 𐐹𐐨𐐹𐑊 𐐼𐐮𐐼 𐑉𐐨𐑂𐐴𐑊 𐐰𐑀𐐯𐑌𐑅𐐻 𐑄 𐐹𐑉𐐱𐑁𐐯𐐻𐑅, 𐐰𐑌𐐼 𐐼𐐮𐐼 𐑋𐐱𐐿 𐑄𐐯𐑋. 𐐰𐑌𐐼 𐐮𐐻 𐐿𐐩𐑋 𐐻𐐭 𐐹𐐰𐑅 𐑄𐐰𐐻 𐐿𐐮𐑍 𐐟𐐷𐐭𐑊 𐐼𐐮𐐼 𐐯𐐿𐑅𐐯𐐿𐐷𐐭𐐻 𐐾𐐲𐐾𐑋𐐯𐑌𐐻 𐐰𐑀𐐯𐑌𐑅𐐻 𐐫𐑊 𐑄𐐬𐑆 𐐸𐐭 𐐼𐐮𐐼 𐑉𐐨𐑂𐐴𐑊 𐐰𐑀𐐯𐑌𐑅𐐻 𐑄 𐐹𐑉𐐱𐑁𐐯𐐻𐑅; 𐐰𐑌𐐼 𐐸𐐨 𐐼𐐮𐐼 𐐯𐐿𐑅𐐯𐐿𐐷𐐭𐐻 𐐰 𐑊𐐫 𐑃𐑉𐐭𐐵𐐻 𐐫𐑊 𐑄 𐑊𐐰𐑌𐐼, 𐐸𐐶𐐮𐐽 𐑀𐐩𐑂 𐐹𐐵𐑉 𐐲𐑌𐐻𐐭 𐑄 𐐹𐑉𐐱𐑁𐐯𐐻𐑅 𐑄𐐰𐐻 𐑄𐐩 𐑇𐐳𐐼 𐑀𐐬 𐐸𐐶𐐮𐑄𐐲𐑉𐑅𐐬𐐯𐑂𐐲𐑉 𐑄𐐩 𐐶𐐳𐐼; 𐐰𐑌𐐼 𐐺𐐴 𐑄𐐮𐑅 𐐿𐐫𐑆 𐑄 𐐹𐐨𐐹𐑊 𐐶𐐲𐑉 𐐺𐑉𐐫𐐻 𐐲𐑌𐐻𐐭 𐑉𐐨𐐹𐐯𐑌𐐻𐐰𐑌𐑅. 𐐰𐑌𐐼 𐐺𐐨𐐿𐐫𐑆 𐑄 𐐹𐐨𐐹𐑊 𐐼𐐮𐐼 𐑉𐐨𐐹𐐯𐑌𐐻 𐐱𐑂 𐑄𐐩𐑉 𐐮𐑌𐐮𐐿𐐶𐐮𐐻𐐮𐑆 𐐰𐑌𐐼 𐐴𐐼𐐱𐑊𐐰𐐻𐑉𐐮𐑆, 𐑄 𐐢𐐫𐑉𐐼 𐐼𐐮𐐼 𐑅𐐹𐐩𐑉 𐑄𐐯𐑋, 𐐰𐑌𐐼 𐑄𐐩 𐐺𐐨𐑀𐐰𐑌 𐐻𐐭 𐐹𐑉𐐱𐑅𐐹𐐲𐑉 𐐰𐑀𐐯𐑌 𐐮𐑌 𐑄 𐑊𐐰𐑌𐐼. 𐐰𐑌𐐼 𐐮𐐻 𐐿𐐩𐑋 𐐻𐐭 𐐹𐐰𐑅 𐑄𐐰𐐻 𐐟𐐷𐐭𐑊 𐐺𐐨𐑀𐐰𐐻 𐑅𐐲𐑌𐑆 𐐰𐑌𐐼 𐐼𐐫𐐻𐐲𐑉𐑆 𐐮𐑌 𐐸𐐮𐑆 𐐬𐑊𐐼 𐐩𐐾. 𐐰𐑌𐐼 𐑄𐐯𐑉 𐐶𐐲𐑉 𐑌𐐬 𐑋𐐬𐑉 𐐶𐐫𐑉𐑆 𐐮𐑌 𐑄 𐐼𐐩𐑆 𐐱𐑂 𐐟𐐷𐐭𐑊; 𐐰𐑌𐐼 𐐸𐐨 𐑉𐐨𐑋𐐯𐑋𐐺𐐲𐑉𐐼 𐑄 𐑀𐑉𐐩𐐻 𐑃𐐮𐑍𐑆 𐑄𐐰𐐻 𐑄 𐐢𐐫𐑉𐐼 𐐸𐐰𐐼 𐐼𐐲𐑌 𐑁𐐫𐑉 𐐸𐐮𐑆 𐑁𐐪𐑄𐐲𐑉𐑆 𐐮𐑌 𐐺𐑉𐐮𐑍𐐮𐑍 𐑄𐐯𐑋 𐐰𐐿𐑉𐐫𐑅 𐑄 𐑀𐑉𐐩𐐻 𐐼𐐨𐐹 𐐮𐑌𐐻𐐭 𐑄 𐐹𐑉𐐱𐑋𐐮𐑅𐐻 𐑊𐐰𐑌𐐼; 𐐸𐐶𐐯𐑉𐑁𐐫𐑉 𐐸𐐨 𐐼𐐮𐐼 𐐯𐐿𐑅𐐯𐐿𐐷𐐭𐐻 𐐾𐐲𐐾𐑋𐐯𐑌𐐻 𐐮𐑌 𐑉𐐴𐐽𐐲𐑅𐑌𐐯𐑅 𐐫𐑊 𐐸𐐮𐑆 𐐼𐐩𐑆.

11. 𐐰𐑌𐐼 𐐮𐐻 𐐿𐐩𐑋 𐐻𐐭 𐐹𐐰𐑅 𐑄𐐰𐐻 𐐸𐐨 𐐺𐐨𐑀𐐰𐐻 𐐄𐑋𐐲𐑉, 𐐰𐑌𐐼 𐐄𐑋𐐲𐑉 𐑉𐐩𐑌𐐼 𐐮𐑌 𐐸𐐮𐑆 𐑅𐐻𐐯𐐼. 𐐰𐑌𐐼 𐐄𐑋𐐲𐑉 𐐺𐐨𐑀𐐰𐐻 𐐖𐐯𐑉𐐯𐐼; 𐐰𐑌𐐼 𐐖𐐯𐑉𐐯𐐼 𐐺𐐨𐑀𐐰𐐻 𐑅𐐲𐑌𐑆 𐐰𐑌𐐼 𐐼𐐫𐐻𐐲𐑉𐑆. 𐐰𐑌𐐼 𐐖𐐯𐑉𐐯𐐼 𐑉𐐨𐐺𐐯𐑊𐐼 𐐰𐑀𐐯𐑌𐑅𐐻 𐐸𐐮𐑆 𐑁𐐪𐑄𐐲𐑉, 𐐰𐑌𐐼 𐐿𐐩𐑋 𐐰𐑌𐐼 𐐼𐐶𐐯𐑊𐐻 𐐮𐑌 𐑄 𐑊𐐰𐑌𐐼 𐐱𐑂 𐐐𐐯𐑃. 𐐰𐑌𐐼 𐐮𐐻 𐐿𐐩𐑋 𐐻𐐭 𐐹𐐰𐑅 𐑄𐐰𐐻 𐐸𐐨 𐐼𐐮𐐼 𐑁𐑊𐐰𐐻𐐲𐑉 𐑋𐐯𐑌𐐮 𐐹𐐨𐐹𐑊, 𐐺𐐨𐐿𐐫𐑆 𐐱𐑂 𐐸𐐮𐑆 𐐿𐐲𐑌𐐮𐑍 𐐶𐐲𐑉𐐼𐑆, 𐐲𐑌𐐻𐐮𐑊 𐐸𐐨 𐐸𐐰𐐼 𐑀𐐩𐑌𐐼 𐑄 𐐸𐐪𐑁 𐐱𐑂 𐑄 𐐿𐐮𐑍𐐼𐐲𐑋. 𐐰𐑌𐐼 𐐸𐐶𐐯𐑌 𐐸𐐨 𐐸𐐰𐐼 𐑀𐐩𐑌𐐼 𐑄 𐐸𐐪𐑁 𐐱𐑂 𐑄 𐐿𐐮𐑍𐐼𐐲𐑋, 𐐸𐐨 𐑀𐐩𐑂 𐐺𐐰𐐻𐑊 𐐲𐑌𐐻𐐭 𐐸𐐮𐑆 𐑁𐐪𐑄𐐲𐑉, 𐐰𐑌𐐼 𐐸𐐨 𐐼𐐮𐐼 𐐿𐐰𐑉𐐮 𐐰𐐶𐐩 𐐸𐐮𐑆 𐑁𐐪𐑄𐐲𐑉 𐐮𐑌𐐻𐐭 𐐿𐐰𐐹𐐻𐐮𐑂𐐮𐐻𐐮, 𐐰𐑌𐐼 𐐼𐐮𐐼 𐑋𐐩𐐿 𐐸𐐮𐑋 𐑅𐐲𐑉𐑂 𐐮𐑌 𐐿𐐰𐐹𐐻𐐮𐑂𐐮𐐻𐐮. 𐐰𐑌𐐼 𐑌𐐵 𐐮𐑌 𐑄 𐐼𐐩𐑆 𐐱𐑂 𐑄 𐑉𐐩𐑌 𐐱𐑂 𐐄𐑋𐐲𐑉, 𐐸𐐨 𐐶𐐱𐑆 𐐮𐑌 𐐿𐐰𐐹𐐻𐐮𐑂𐐮𐐻𐐮 𐑄 𐐸𐐪𐑁 𐐱𐑂 𐐸𐐮𐑆 𐐼𐐩𐑆. 𐐰𐑌𐐼 𐐮𐐻 𐐿𐐩𐑋 𐐻𐐭 𐐹𐐰𐑅 𐑄𐐰𐐻 𐐸𐐨 𐐺𐐨𐑀𐐰𐐻 𐑅𐐲𐑌𐑆 𐐰𐑌𐐼 𐐼𐐫𐐻𐐲𐑉𐑆, 𐐰𐑋𐐲𐑍 𐐸𐐭𐑋 𐐶𐐲𐑉 𐐇𐑆𐑉𐐲𐑋 𐐰𐑌𐐼 𐐗𐐫𐑉𐐨𐐰𐑌𐐻𐐲𐑋𐐲𐑉; 𐐰𐑌𐐼 𐑄𐐩 𐐶𐐲𐑉 𐐯𐐿𐑅𐐨𐐼𐐮𐑍 𐐰𐑍𐑀𐑉𐐮 𐐺𐐨𐐿𐐫𐑆 𐐱𐑂 𐑄 𐐼𐐭𐐮𐑍𐑆 𐐱𐑂 𐐖𐐯𐑉𐐯𐐼, 𐑄𐐩𐑉 𐐺𐑉𐐲𐑄𐐲𐑉, 𐐮𐑌𐑅𐐬𐑋𐐲𐐽 𐑄𐐰𐐻 𐑄𐐩 𐐼𐐮𐐼 𐑉𐐩𐑆 𐐰𐑌 𐐪𐑉𐑋𐐮, 𐐰𐑌𐐼 𐑀𐐩𐑂 𐐺𐐰𐐻𐑊 𐐲𐑌𐐻𐐭 𐐖𐐯𐑉𐐯𐐼. 𐐰𐑌𐐼 𐐮𐐻 𐐿𐐩𐑋 𐐻𐐭 𐐹𐐰𐑅 𐑄𐐰𐐻 𐑄𐐩 𐐼𐐮𐐼 𐑀𐐮𐑂 𐐺𐐰𐐻𐑊 𐐲𐑌𐐻𐐭 𐐸𐐮𐑋 𐐺𐐴 𐑌𐐴𐐻. 𐐰𐑌𐐼 𐐮𐐻 𐐿𐐩𐑋 𐐻𐐭 𐐹𐐰𐑅 𐑄𐐰𐐻 𐐸𐐶𐐯𐑌 𐑄𐐩 𐐸𐐰𐐼 𐑅𐑊𐐩𐑌 𐑄 𐐪𐑉𐑋𐐮 𐐱𐑂 𐐖𐐯𐑉𐐯𐐼, 𐑄𐐩 𐐶𐐲𐑉 𐐰𐐺𐐵𐐻 𐐻𐐭 𐑅𐑊𐐩 𐐸𐐮𐑋 𐐫𐑊𐑅𐐬; 𐐰𐑌𐐼 𐐸𐐨 𐐹𐑊𐐯𐐼 𐐶𐐮𐑄 𐑄𐐯𐑋 𐑄𐐰𐐻 𐑄𐐩 𐐶𐐳𐐼 𐑌𐐱𐐻 𐑅𐑊𐐩 𐐸𐐮𐑋, 𐐰𐑌𐐼 𐐸𐐨 𐐶𐐳𐐼 𐑀𐐮𐑂 𐐲𐐹 𐑄 𐐿𐐮𐑍𐐼𐐲𐑋 𐐲𐑌𐐻𐐭 𐐸𐐮𐑆 𐑁𐐪𐑄𐐲𐑉. 𐐰𐑌𐐼 𐐮𐐻 𐐿𐐩𐑋 𐐻𐐭 𐐹𐐰𐑅 𐑄𐐰𐐻 𐑄𐐩 𐐼𐐮𐐼 𐑀𐑉𐐰𐑌𐐻 𐐲𐑌𐐻𐐭 𐐸𐐮𐑋 𐐸𐐮𐑆 𐑊𐐴𐑁. 𐐰𐑌𐐼 𐑌𐐵 𐐖𐐯𐑉𐐯𐐼 𐐺𐐨𐐿𐐩𐑋 𐐯𐐿𐑅𐐨𐐼𐐮𐑍 𐑅𐐱𐑉𐐬𐑁𐐳𐑊 𐐺𐐨𐐿𐐫𐑆 𐐱𐑂 𐑄 𐑊𐐫𐑅 𐐱𐑂 𐑄 𐐿𐐮𐑍𐐼𐐲𐑋, 𐑁𐐫𐑉 𐐸𐐨 𐐸𐐰𐐼 𐑅𐐯𐐻 𐐸𐐮𐑆 𐐸𐐪𐑉𐐻 𐐲𐐹𐐱𐑌 𐑄 𐐿𐐮𐑍𐐼𐐲𐑋 𐐰𐑌𐐼 𐐲𐐹𐐱𐑌 𐑄 𐑀𐑊𐐬𐑉𐐮 𐐱𐑂 𐑄 𐐶𐐲𐑉𐑊𐐼. 𐑌𐐵 𐑄 𐐼𐐫𐐻𐐲𐑉 𐐱𐑂 𐐖𐐯𐑉𐐯𐐼 𐐺𐐨𐐮𐑍 𐐯𐐿𐑅𐐨𐐼𐐮𐑍 𐐯𐐿𐑅𐐹𐐲𐑉𐐻, 𐐰𐑌𐐼 𐑅𐐨𐐮𐑍 𐑄 𐑅𐐱𐑉𐐬𐑆 𐐱𐑂 𐐸𐐲𐑉 𐑁𐐪𐑄𐐲𐑉, 𐑃𐐫𐐻 𐐻𐐭 𐐼𐐨𐑂𐐴𐑆 𐐰 𐐹𐑊𐐰𐑌 𐐸𐐶𐐯𐑉𐐺𐐴 𐑇𐐨 𐐿𐐳𐐼 𐑉𐐨𐐼𐐨𐑋 𐑄 𐐿𐐮𐑍𐐼𐐲𐑋 𐐲𐑌𐐻𐐭 𐐸𐐲𐑉 𐑁𐐪𐑄𐐲𐑉. 𐑌𐐵 𐑄 𐐼𐐫𐐻𐐲𐑉 𐐱𐑂 𐐖𐐯𐑉𐐯𐐼 𐐶𐐱𐑆 𐐯𐐿𐑅𐐨𐐼𐐮𐑍 𐑁𐐩𐑉. 𐐰𐑌𐐼 𐐮𐐻 𐐿𐐩𐑋 𐐻𐐭 𐐹𐐰𐑅 𐑄𐐰𐐻 𐑇𐐨 𐐼𐐮𐐼 𐐻𐐫𐐿 𐐶𐐮𐑄 𐐸𐐲𐑉 𐑁𐐪𐑄𐐲𐑉, 𐐰𐑌𐐼 𐑅𐐯𐐼 𐐲𐑌𐐻𐐭 𐐸𐐮𐑋, 𐐎𐐯𐑉𐐺𐐴 𐐸𐐰𐑃 𐑋𐐴 𐑁𐐪𐑄𐐲𐑉 𐑅𐐬 𐑋𐐲𐐽 𐑅𐐱𐑉𐐬? 𐐐𐐰𐑃 𐐸𐐨 𐑌𐐱𐐻 𐑉𐐯𐐼 𐑄 𐑉𐐯𐐿𐐲𐑉𐐼 𐐸𐐶𐐮𐐽 𐐵𐑉 𐑁𐐪𐑄𐐲𐑉𐑆 𐐺𐑉𐐫𐐻 𐐰𐐿𐑉𐐫𐑅 𐑄 𐑀𐑉𐐩𐐻 𐐼𐐨𐐹? 𐐒𐐨𐐸𐐬𐑊𐐼, 𐐮𐑆 𐑄𐐯𐑉 𐑌𐐱𐐻 𐐰𐑌 𐐰𐐿𐐵𐑌𐐻 𐐿𐐱𐑌𐑅𐐲𐑉𐑌𐐮𐑍 𐑄𐐯𐑋 𐐱𐑂 𐐬𐑊𐐼, 𐑄𐐰𐐻 𐑄𐐩 𐐺𐐴 𐑄𐐩𐑉 𐑅𐐨𐐿𐑉𐐯𐐻 𐐹𐑊𐐰𐑌𐑆 𐐼𐐮𐐼 𐐱𐐺𐐻𐐩𐑌 𐐿𐐮𐑍𐐼𐐲𐑋𐑆 𐐰𐑌𐐼 𐑀𐑉𐐩𐐻 𐑀𐑊𐐬𐑉𐐮? 𐐰𐑌𐐼 𐑌𐐵, 𐑄𐐯𐑉𐑁𐐫𐑉, 𐑊𐐯𐐻 𐑋𐐴 𐑁𐐪𐑄𐐲𐑉 𐑅𐐯𐑌𐐼 𐑁𐐫𐑉 𐐁𐐿𐐮𐑇, 𐑄 𐑅𐐲𐑌 𐐱𐑂 𐐗𐐮𐑋𐑌𐐫𐑉; 𐐰𐑌𐐼 𐐺𐐨𐐸𐐬𐑊𐐼, 𐐌 𐐰𐑋 𐑁𐐩𐑉, 𐐰𐑌𐐼 𐐌 𐐶𐐮𐑊 𐐼𐐰𐑌𐑅 𐐺𐐨𐑁𐐬𐑉 𐐸𐐮𐑋, 𐐰𐑌𐐼 𐐌 𐐶𐐮𐑊 𐐹𐑊𐐨𐑆 𐐸𐐮𐑋, 𐑄𐐰𐐻 𐐸𐐨 𐐶𐐮𐑊 𐐼𐐨𐑆𐐴𐑉 𐑋𐐨 𐐻𐐭 𐐶𐐴𐑁; 𐐸𐐶𐐯𐑉𐑁𐐫𐑉 𐐮𐑁 𐐸𐐨 𐑇𐐰𐑊 𐐼𐐨𐑆𐐴𐑉 𐐱𐑂 𐑄𐐨 𐑄𐐰𐐻 𐐷𐐨 𐑇𐐰𐑊 𐑀𐐮𐑂 𐐲𐑌𐐻𐐭 𐐸𐐮𐑋 𐑋𐐨 𐐻𐐭 𐐶𐐴𐑁, 𐑄𐐯𐑌 𐑇𐐰𐑊 𐐷𐐨 𐑅𐐩, 𐐌 𐐶𐐮𐑊 𐑀𐐮𐑂 𐐸𐐲𐑉, 𐐮𐑁 𐐷𐐨 𐐶𐐮𐑊 𐐺𐑉𐐮𐑍 𐐲𐑌𐐻𐐭 𐑋𐐨 𐑄 𐐸𐐯𐐼 𐐱𐑂 𐑋𐐴 𐑁𐐪𐑄𐐲𐑉, 𐑄 𐐿𐐮𐑍.

12. 𐐈𐑌𐐼 𐑌𐐵 𐐄𐑋𐐲𐑉 𐐶𐐱𐑆 𐐲 𐑁𐑉𐐯𐑌𐐼 𐐻𐐭 𐐁𐐿𐐮𐑇, 𐐸𐐶𐐯𐑉𐑁𐐬𐑉 𐐸𐐶𐐯𐑌 𐐖𐐯𐑉𐐲𐐼 𐐸𐐰𐐼 𐑅𐐯𐑌𐐻 𐑁𐐬𐑉 𐐁𐐿𐐮𐑇, 𐑄 𐐼𐐫𐐻𐐲𐑉 𐐲𐑂 𐐖𐐯𐑉𐐲𐐼 𐐼𐐰𐑌𐑅𐐻 𐐺𐐨𐑁𐐬𐑉 𐐸𐐮𐑋, 𐑄𐐰𐐻 𐑇𐐨 𐐹𐑊𐐨𐑆𐐼 𐐸𐐮𐑋, 𐐮𐑌𐑅𐐬𐑋𐐲𐐽 𐑄𐐰𐐻 𐐸𐐨 𐐼𐐯𐑆𐐴𐑉𐐼 𐐸𐐲𐑉 𐐻𐐭 𐐶𐐴𐑁. 𐐈𐑌𐐼 𐐮𐐻 𐐿𐐩𐑋 𐐻𐐭 𐐹𐐰𐑅 𐑄𐐰𐐻 𐐸𐐨 𐑅𐐯𐐼 𐐲𐑌𐐻𐐭 𐐖𐐯𐑉𐐲𐐼, 𐐘𐐮𐑂 𐐸𐐲𐑉 𐐲𐑌𐐻𐐭 𐑋𐐨 𐐻𐐭 𐐶𐐴𐑁. 𐐈𐑌𐐼 𐐖𐐯𐑉𐐲𐐼 𐑅𐐯𐐼 𐐲𐑌𐐻𐐭 𐐸𐐮𐑋, 𐐌 𐐶𐐮𐑊 𐑀𐐮𐑂 𐐸𐐲𐑉 𐐲𐑌𐐻𐐭 𐐷𐐭, 𐐮𐑁 𐐷 𐐶𐐮𐑊 𐐺𐑉𐐮𐑍 𐐲𐑌𐐻𐐭 𐑋𐐨 𐑄 𐐸𐐯𐐼 𐐲𐑂 𐑋𐐴 𐑁𐐪𐑄𐐲𐑉, 𐑄 𐐿𐐮𐑍. 𐐈𐑌𐐼 𐐮𐐻 𐐿𐐩𐑋 𐐻𐐭 𐐹𐐰𐑅 𐑄𐐰𐐻 𐐁𐐿𐐮𐑇 𐑀𐐰𐑄𐐲𐑉𐐼 𐐮𐑌 𐐲𐑌𐐻𐐭 𐑄 𐐸𐐵𐑅 𐐲𐑂 𐐖𐐯𐑉𐐲𐐼 𐐫𐑊 𐐸𐐮𐑆 𐐿𐐮𐑌𐑆𐑁𐐬𐐿𐑅, 𐐰𐑌𐐼 𐑅𐐯𐐼 𐐲𐑌𐐻𐐭 𐑄𐐯𐑋, 𐐎𐐮𐑊 𐐷 𐑅𐐶𐐯𐑉 𐐲𐑌𐐻𐐭 𐑋𐐨 𐑄𐐰𐐻 𐐷 𐐶𐐮𐑊 𐐺 𐑁𐐩𐑃𐑁𐐳𐑊 𐐲𐑌𐐻𐐭 𐑋𐐨 𐐮𐑌 𐑄 𐑃𐐮𐑍 𐐸𐐶𐐮𐐽 𐐌 𐑇𐐰𐑊 𐐼𐐯𐑆𐐴𐑉 𐐲𐑂 𐐷𐐭? 𐐈𐑌𐐼 𐐮𐐻 𐐿𐐩𐑋 𐐻𐐭 𐐹𐐰𐑅 𐑄𐐰𐐻 𐑄𐐩 𐐫𐑊 𐑅𐐶𐐯𐑉 𐐲𐑌𐐻𐐭 𐐸𐐮𐑋, 𐐺𐐴 𐑄 𐐘𐐱𐐼 𐐲𐑂 𐐸𐐯𐑂𐑌, 𐐰𐑌𐐼 𐐫𐑊𐑅𐐬 𐐺𐐴 𐑄 𐐸𐐯𐑂𐑌𐑆, 𐐰𐑌𐐼 𐐫𐑊𐑅𐐬 𐐺𐐴 𐑄 𐐲𐑉𐑃, 𐐰𐑌𐐼 𐐺𐐴 𐑄𐐯𐑉 𐐸𐐯𐐼𐑆, 𐑄𐐰𐐻 𐐸𐐭𐑅𐐬 𐑇𐐳𐐼 𐑂𐐯𐑉𐐨 𐑁𐑉𐐲𐑋 𐑄 𐐲𐑅𐐮𐑅𐐻𐐲𐑌𐑅 𐐸𐐶𐐮𐐽 𐐁𐐿𐐮𐑇 𐐼𐐯𐑆𐐴𐑉𐐼, 𐑇𐐳𐐼 𐑊𐐭𐑆 𐐸𐐮𐑆 𐐸𐐯𐐼; 𐐰𐑌𐐼 𐐸𐐭𐑅𐐬 𐑇𐐳𐐼 𐐼𐐮𐑂𐐲𐑊𐐾 𐐸𐐶𐐱𐐻𐑅𐐬𐐯𐑂𐐲𐑉 𐑃𐐮𐑍 𐐁𐐿𐐮𐑇 𐑋𐐩𐐼 𐑌𐐬𐑌 𐐲𐑌𐐻𐐭 𐑄𐐯𐑋, 𐑄 𐑅𐐩𐑋 𐑇𐐳𐐼 𐑊𐐭𐑆 𐐸𐐮𐑆 𐑊𐐴𐑁. 𐐈𐑌𐐼 𐐮𐐻 𐐿𐐩𐑋 𐐻𐐭 𐐹𐐰𐑅 𐑄𐐰𐐻 𐑄𐐲𐑅 𐑄𐐩 𐐼𐐮𐐼 𐐲𐑀𐑉𐐨 𐐶𐐮𐑄 𐐁𐐿𐐮𐑇. 𐐈𐑌𐐼 𐐁𐐿𐐮𐑇 𐐼𐐮𐐼 𐐰𐐼𐑋𐐮𐑌𐐮𐑅𐐻𐐲𐑉 𐐲𐑌𐐻𐐭 𐑄𐐯𐑋 𐑄 𐐬𐑃𐑅 𐐸𐐶𐐮𐐽 𐐶𐐲𐑉 𐑀𐐮𐑂𐑌 𐐺𐐴 𐑄𐐯𐑋 𐐲𐑂 𐐬𐑊𐐼, 𐐸𐐭 𐐫𐑊𐑅𐐬 𐑅𐐫𐐻 𐐹𐐵𐑉, 𐐸𐐶𐐮𐐽 𐐸𐐰𐐼 𐐺𐐮𐑌 𐐸𐐰𐑌𐐼𐐯𐐼 𐐼𐐵𐑌 𐐨𐑂𐑌 𐑁𐑉𐐲𐑋 𐐗𐐩𐑌, 𐐸𐐭 𐐶𐐱𐑆 𐐲 𐑋𐐲𐑉𐐼𐐲𐑉𐐲𐑉 𐑁𐑉𐐲𐑋 𐑄 𐐺𐐨𐑀𐐮𐑌𐐮𐑍. 𐐈𐑌𐐼 𐑄𐐩 𐐶𐐲𐑉 𐐿𐐯𐐹𐐻 𐐲𐐹 𐐺𐐴 𐑄 𐐹𐐵𐑉 𐐲𐑂 𐑄 𐐼𐐯𐑂𐑊 𐐻𐐭 𐐰𐐼𐑋𐐮𐑌𐐮𐑅𐐻𐐲𐑉 𐑄𐐨𐑆 𐐬𐑃𐑅 𐐲𐑌𐐻𐐭 𐑄 𐐹𐐨𐐹𐑊, 𐐻𐐭 𐐿𐐨𐐹 𐑄𐐯𐑋 𐐮𐑌 𐐼𐐪𐑉𐐿𐑌𐐯𐑅, 𐐻𐐭 𐐸𐐯𐑊𐐹 𐑅𐐲𐐽 𐐰𐑆 𐑅𐐫𐐻 𐐹𐐵𐑉 𐐻𐐭 𐑀𐐩𐑌 𐐹𐐵𐑉, 𐐰𐑌𐐼 𐐻𐐭 𐑋𐐲𐑉𐐼𐐲𐑉, 𐐰𐑌𐐼 𐐻𐐭 𐐹𐑊𐐲𐑌𐐼𐐲𐑉, 𐐰𐑌𐐼 𐐻𐐭 𐑊𐐴, 𐐰𐑌𐐼 𐐻𐐭 𐐿𐐱𐑋𐐮𐐻 𐐫𐑊 𐑋𐐰𐑌𐐲𐑉 𐐲𐑂 𐐶𐐮𐐿𐐯𐐼𐑌𐐯𐑅 𐐰𐑌𐐼 𐐸𐐬𐑉𐐼𐐲𐑋𐑆. 𐐈𐑌𐐼 𐐮𐐻 𐐶𐐱𐑆 𐑄 𐐼𐐫𐐻𐐲𐑉 𐐲𐑂 𐐖𐐯𐑉𐐲𐐼 𐐸𐐭 𐐹𐐳𐐻 𐐮𐐻 𐐮𐑌𐐻𐐭 𐐸𐐮𐑆 𐐸𐐪𐑉𐐻 𐐻𐐭 𐑅𐐲𐑉𐐽 𐐲𐐹 𐑄𐐨𐑆 𐑃𐐮𐑍𐑆 𐐲𐑂 𐐬𐑊𐐼; 𐐰𐑌𐐼 𐐖𐐯𐑉𐐲𐐼 𐐹𐐳𐐻 𐐮𐐻 𐐮𐑌𐐻𐐭 𐑄 𐐸𐐪𐑉𐐻 𐐲𐑂 𐐁𐐿𐐮𐑇; 𐐸𐐶𐐯𐑉𐑁𐐬𐑉 𐐁𐐿𐐮𐑇 𐐰𐐼𐑋𐐮𐑌𐐮𐑅𐐻𐐲𐑉𐐼 𐐮𐐻 𐐲𐑌𐐻𐐭 𐐸𐐮𐑆 𐐿𐐮𐑌𐐼𐑉𐐯𐐼 𐐰𐑌𐐼 𐑁𐑉𐐯𐑌𐐼𐑆, 𐑊𐐨𐐼𐐮𐑍 𐑄𐐯𐑋 𐐲𐐶𐐩 𐐺𐐴 𐑁𐐯𐑉 𐐹𐑉𐐱𐑋𐐮𐑅𐐯𐑆 𐐻𐐭 𐐼𐐭 𐐸𐐶𐐱𐐻𐑅𐐬𐐯𐑂𐐲𐑉 𐑃𐐮𐑍 𐐸𐐨 𐐼𐐯𐑆𐐴𐑉𐐼. 𐐈𐑌𐐼 𐐮𐐻 𐐿𐐩𐑋 𐐻𐐭 𐐹𐐰𐑅 𐑄𐐰𐐻 𐑄𐐩 𐑁𐐬𐑉𐑋𐐼 𐐲 𐑅𐐨𐐿𐑉𐐯𐐻 𐐿𐐱𐑋𐐺𐐮𐑌𐐩𐑇𐐲𐑌, 𐐨𐑂𐑌 𐐰𐑆 𐑄𐐩 𐐲𐑂 𐐬𐑊𐐼; 𐐸𐐶𐐮𐐽 𐐿𐐱𐑋𐐺𐐮𐑌𐐩𐑇𐐲𐑌 𐐮𐑆 𐑋𐐬𐑅𐐻 𐐲𐐺𐐱𐑋𐐮𐑌𐐲𐐺𐑊 𐐰𐑌𐐼 𐐶𐐮𐐿𐐯𐐼 𐐲𐐺𐐲𐑂 𐐫𐑊, 𐐮𐑌 𐑄 𐑅𐐴𐐻 𐐲𐑂 𐐘𐐱𐐼; 𐑁𐐬𐑉 𐑄 𐐢𐐫𐑉𐐼 𐐶𐐲𐑉𐐿𐐯𐑃 𐑌𐐱𐐻 𐐮𐑌 𐑅𐐨𐐿𐑉𐐯𐐻 𐐿𐐱𐑋𐐺𐐮𐑌𐐩𐑇𐐲𐑌𐑆, 𐑌𐐨𐑄𐐲𐑉 𐐼𐐲𐑃 𐐸𐐨 𐐶𐐮𐑊 𐑄𐐰𐐻 𐑋𐐰𐑌 𐑇𐐳𐐼 𐑇𐐯𐐼 𐐺𐑊𐐲𐐼, 𐐺𐐲𐐻 𐐮𐑌 𐐫𐑊 𐑃𐐮𐑍𐑆 𐐸𐐰𐑃 𐑁𐐬𐑉𐐺𐐮𐐼𐐯𐑌 𐐮𐐻, 𐑁𐑉𐐲𐑋 𐑄 𐐺𐐨𐑀𐐮𐑌𐐮𐑍 𐐲𐑂 𐑋𐐰𐑌.

13. 𐐈𐑌𐐼 𐑌𐐵 𐐌, 𐐣𐐬𐑉𐐬𐑌𐐴, 𐐼𐐭 𐑌𐐱𐐻 𐑉𐐴𐐻 𐑄 𐑋𐐰𐑌𐐲𐑉 𐐲𐑂 𐑄𐐯𐑉 𐐬𐑃𐑅 𐐰𐑌𐐼 𐐿𐐱𐑋𐐺𐐮𐑌𐐩𐑇𐐲𐑌𐑆, 𐑁𐐬𐑉 𐐮𐐻 𐐸𐐰𐑃 𐐺𐐮𐑌 𐑋𐐩𐐼 𐑌𐐬𐑌 𐐲𐑌𐐻𐐭 𐑋𐐨 𐑄𐐰𐐻 𐑄𐐩 𐐪𐑉 𐐸𐐰𐐼 𐐲𐑋𐐲𐑍 𐐫𐑊 𐐹𐐨𐐹𐑊, 𐐰𐑌𐐼 𐑄𐐩 𐐪𐑉 𐐸𐐰𐐼 𐐲𐑋𐐲𐑍 𐑄 𐐢𐐰𐑋𐐲𐑌𐐴𐐻𐑅, 𐐰𐑌𐐼 𐑄𐐩 𐐸𐐰𐑂 𐐿𐐫𐑆𐐼 𐑄 𐐼𐐯𐑅𐐻𐑉𐐲𐐿𐑇𐐲𐑌 𐐲𐑂 𐑄𐐮𐑅 𐐹𐐨𐐹𐑊 𐐲𐑂 𐐸𐐭𐑋 𐐌 𐐰𐑋 𐑌𐐵 𐑅𐐹𐐨𐐿𐐮𐑍, 𐐰𐑌𐐼 𐐫𐑊𐑅𐐬 𐑄 𐐼𐐯𐑅𐐻𐑉𐐲𐐿𐑇𐐲𐑌 𐐲𐑂 𐑄 𐐹𐐨𐐹𐑊 𐐲𐑂 𐐤𐐨𐑁𐐴; 𐐰𐑌𐐼 𐐸𐐶𐐱𐐻𐑅𐐬𐐯𐑂𐐲𐑉 𐑌𐐩𐑇𐐲𐑌 𐑇𐐰𐑊 𐐲𐐹𐐸𐐬𐑊𐐼 𐑅𐐲𐐽 𐑅𐐨𐐿𐑉𐐯𐐻 𐐿𐐱𐑋𐐺𐐮𐑌𐐩𐑇𐐲𐑌𐑆, 𐐻𐐭 𐑀𐐯𐐻 𐐹𐐵𐑉 𐐰𐑌𐐼 𐑀𐐩𐑌, 𐐲𐑌𐐻𐐮𐑊 𐑄𐐩 𐑇𐐰𐑊 𐑅𐐹𐑉𐐯𐐼 𐐬𐑂𐐲𐑉 𐑄 𐑌𐐩𐑇𐐲𐑌, 𐐺𐐨𐐸𐐬𐑊𐐼, 𐑄𐐩 𐑇𐐰𐑊 𐐺 𐐼𐐯𐑅𐐻𐑉𐑎𐐼; 𐑁𐐬𐑉 𐑄 𐐢𐐫𐑉𐐼 𐐶𐐮𐑊 𐑌𐐱𐐻 𐑅𐐲𐑁𐐲𐑉 𐑄𐐰𐐻 𐑄 𐐺𐑊𐐲𐐼 𐐲𐑂 𐐸𐐮𐑆 𐑅𐐩𐑌𐐻𐑅, 𐐸𐐶𐐮𐐽 𐑇𐐰𐑊 𐐺 𐑇𐐯𐐼 𐐺𐐴 𐑄𐐯𐑋, 𐑇𐐰𐑊 𐐫𐑊𐐶𐐩𐑆 𐐿𐑉𐐴 𐐲𐑌𐐻𐐭 𐐸𐐮𐑋 𐑁𐑉𐐲𐑋 𐑄 𐑀𐑉𐐵𐑌𐐼 𐑁𐐬𐑉 𐑂𐐯𐑌𐐾𐐲𐑌𐑅 𐐲𐐹𐐱𐑌 𐑄𐐯𐑋, 𐐰𐑌𐐼 𐐷𐐯𐐻 𐐸𐐨 𐐲𐑂𐐯𐑌𐐾 𐑄𐐯𐑋 𐑌𐐱𐐻; 𐐸𐐶𐐯𐑉𐑁𐐬𐑉, 𐐄 𐐷 𐐖𐐯𐑌𐐻𐐴𐑊𐑆, 𐐮𐐻 𐐮𐑆 𐐶𐐮𐑆𐐼𐐲𐑋 𐐮𐑌 𐐘𐐱𐐼 𐑄𐐰𐐻 𐑄𐐨𐑆 𐑃𐐮𐑍𐑆 𐑇𐐳𐐼 𐐺 𐑇𐐬𐑌 𐐲𐑌𐐻𐐭 𐐷𐐭, 𐑄𐐰𐐻 𐑄𐐯𐑉𐐺𐐴 𐐷 𐑋𐐩 𐑉𐐨𐐹𐐯𐑌𐐻 𐐲𐑂 𐐷𐐭𐑉 𐑅𐐮𐑌𐑆, 𐐰𐑌𐐼 𐑅𐐲𐑁𐐲𐑉 𐑌𐐱𐐻 𐑄𐐰𐐻 𐑄𐐨𐑆 𐑋𐐲𐑉𐐼𐐲𐑉𐐲𐑅 𐐿𐐱𐑋𐐺𐐮𐑌𐐩𐑇𐐲𐑌𐑆 𐑇𐐰𐑊 𐑀𐐯𐐻 𐐲𐐺𐐲𐑂 𐐷𐐭, 𐐸𐐶𐐮𐐽 𐐪𐑉 𐐺𐐮𐑊𐐻 𐐲𐐹 𐐻𐐭 𐑀𐐯𐐻 𐐹𐐵𐑉 𐐰𐑌𐐼 𐑀𐐩𐑌, 𐐰𐑌𐐼 𐑄 𐐶𐐲𐑉𐐿, 𐐷𐐩, 𐐨𐑂𐑌 𐑄 𐐶𐐲𐑉𐐿 𐐲𐑂 𐐼𐐯𐑅𐐻𐑉𐐲𐐿𐑇𐐲𐑌 𐐿𐐲𐑋 𐐲𐐹𐐱𐑌 𐐷𐐭, 𐐷𐐩, 𐐨𐑂𐑌 𐑄 𐑅𐐬𐑉𐐼 𐐲𐑂 𐑄 𐐾𐐲𐑅𐐻𐐮𐑅 𐐲𐑂 𐑄 𐐀𐐻𐐲𐑉𐑌𐐲𐑊 𐐘𐐱𐐼 𐑇𐐰𐑊 𐑁𐐫𐑊 𐐲𐐹𐐱𐑌 𐐷𐐭, 𐐻𐐭 𐐷𐐭𐑉 𐐬𐑂𐐲𐑉𐑃𐑉𐐬 𐐰𐑌𐐼 𐐼𐐯𐑅𐐻𐑉𐐲𐐿𐑇𐐲𐑌, 𐐮𐑁 𐐷 𐑇𐐰𐑊 𐑅𐐲𐑁𐐲𐑉 𐑄𐐨𐑆 𐑃𐐮𐑍𐑆 𐐻𐐭 𐐺; 𐐸𐐶𐐯𐑉𐑁𐐬𐑉 𐑄 𐐢𐐫𐑉𐐼 𐐿𐐱𐑋𐐰𐑌𐐼𐐯𐑃 𐐷𐐭, 𐐸𐐶𐐯𐑌 𐐷 𐑇𐐰𐑊 𐑅𐐨 𐑄𐐨𐑆 𐑃𐐮𐑍𐑆 𐐿𐐲𐑋 𐐲𐑋𐐲𐑍 𐐷𐐭, 𐑄𐐰𐐻 𐐷 𐑇𐐰𐑊 𐐲𐐶𐐩𐐿 𐐻𐐭 𐐲 𐑅𐐯𐑌𐑅 𐐲𐑂 𐐷𐐭𐑉 𐐫𐑁𐐳𐑊 𐑅𐐮𐐻𐐷𐐭𐐩𐑇𐐲𐑌, 𐐺𐐨𐐿𐐫𐑆 𐐲𐑂 𐑄𐐮𐑅 𐑅𐐨𐐿𐑉𐐯𐐻 𐐿𐐱𐑋𐐺𐐮𐑌𐐩𐑇𐐲𐑌 𐐸𐐶𐐮𐐽 𐑇𐐰𐑊 𐐺 𐐲𐑋𐐲𐑍 𐐷𐐭; 𐐫𐑉 𐐶𐐬 𐐺 𐐲𐑌𐐻𐐭 𐐮𐐻, 𐐺𐐨𐐿𐐫𐑆 𐐲𐑂 𐑄 𐐺𐑊𐐲𐐼 𐐲𐑂 𐑄𐐯𐑋 𐐸𐐭 𐐸𐐰𐑂 𐐺𐐮𐑌 𐑅𐑊𐐩𐑌; 𐑁𐐬𐑉 𐑄𐐩 𐐿𐑉𐐴 𐑁𐑉𐐲𐑋 𐑄 𐐼𐐲𐑅𐐻 𐑁𐐬𐑉 𐑂𐐯𐑌𐐾𐐲𐑌𐑅 𐐲𐐹𐐱𐑌 𐐮𐐻, 𐐰𐑌𐐼 𐐫𐑊𐑅𐐬 𐐲𐐹𐐱𐑌 𐑄𐐬𐑆 𐐸𐐭 𐐺𐐮𐑊𐐻 𐐮𐐻

𐐲𐐹. 𐐙𐐫𐑉 𐐮𐐻 𐐿𐐲𐑋𐐯𐑃 𐐻𐐭 𐐹𐐰𐑅 𐑄𐐰𐐻 𐐸𐐭𐑆𐐬 𐐺𐐮𐑊𐐼𐐯𐑃 𐐮𐐻 𐐲𐐹, 𐑅𐐨𐐿𐐯𐑃 𐐻𐐭 𐐬𐑂𐐲𐑉𐑃𐑉𐐬 𐑄 𐑁𐑉𐐨𐐼𐐲𐑋 𐐱𐑂 𐐫𐑊 𐑊𐐰𐑌𐐼𐑆, 𐑌𐐩𐑇𐐲𐑌𐑆, 𐐰𐑌𐐼 𐐿𐐲𐑌𐐻𐑉𐐨𐑆; 𐐰𐑌𐐼 𐐮𐐻 𐐺𐑉𐐮𐑍𐐯𐑃 𐐻𐐭 𐐹𐐰𐑅 𐑄 𐐼𐐨𐑅𐐻𐑉𐐲𐐿𐑇𐐲𐑌 𐐱𐑂 𐐫𐑊 𐐹𐐨𐐹𐑊, 𐑁𐐫𐑉 𐐮𐐻 𐐮𐑆 𐐺𐐮𐑊𐐻 𐐲𐐹 𐐺𐐴 𐑄 𐐼𐐯𐑂𐑊, 𐐸𐐭 𐐮𐑆 𐑄 𐑁𐐪𐑄𐐲𐑉 𐐱𐑂 𐐫𐑊 𐑊𐐴𐑆; 𐐨𐑂𐑌 𐑄𐐰𐐻 𐑅𐐩𐑋 𐑊𐐴𐐲𐑉 𐐸𐐭 𐐺𐐨𐑀𐐴𐑊𐐼 𐐵𐑉 𐑁𐐲𐑉𐑅𐐻 𐐹𐐩𐑉𐐯𐑌𐐻𐑅; 𐐷𐐩, 𐐨𐑂𐑌 𐑄𐐰𐐻 𐑅𐐩𐑋 𐑊𐐴𐐲𐑉 𐐸𐐭 𐐸𐐰𐑃 𐐿𐐫𐑆𐐼 𐑋𐐰𐑌 𐐻𐐭 𐐿𐐲𐑋𐐮𐐻 𐑋𐐲𐑉𐐼𐐲𐑉 𐑁𐑉𐐱𐑋 𐑄 𐐺𐐨𐑀𐐮𐑌𐐮𐑍; 𐐸𐐭 𐐸𐐰𐑃 𐐸𐐪𐑉𐐼𐑌𐐼 𐑄 𐐸𐐪𐑉𐐻𐑅 𐐱𐑂 𐑋𐐯𐑌, 𐑄𐐰𐐻 𐑄𐐩 𐐸𐐰𐑂 𐑋𐐲𐑉𐐼𐐲𐑉𐐼 𐑄 𐐹𐑉𐐱𐑁𐐯𐐻𐑅, 𐐰𐑌𐐼 𐑅𐐻𐐬𐑌𐐼 𐑄𐐯𐑋, 𐐰𐑌𐐼 𐐿𐐰𐑅𐐻 𐑄𐐯𐑋 𐐵𐐻 𐑁𐑉𐐱𐑋 𐑄 𐐺𐐨𐑀𐐮𐑌𐐮𐑍. 𐐐𐐶𐐩𐑉𐑁𐐫𐑉, 𐐌, 𐐣𐐬-𐑉𐐬𐑌𐐴, 𐐰𐑋 𐐿𐐲𐑋𐐰𐑌𐐼𐐯𐐼 𐐻𐐭 𐑉𐐴𐐻 𐑄𐐨𐑆 𐑃𐐮𐑍𐑆, 𐑄𐐰𐐻 𐐨𐑂𐑊 𐑋𐐩 𐐺 𐐼𐐲𐑌 𐐲𐐶𐐩, 𐐰𐑌𐐼 𐑄𐐰𐐻 𐑄 𐐻𐐴𐑋 𐑋𐐩 𐐿𐐲𐑋 𐑄𐐰𐐻 𐐝𐐩𐐻𐐲𐑌 𐑋𐐩 𐐸𐐰𐑂 𐑌𐐬 𐐹𐐵𐑉 𐐲𐐹𐐱𐑌 𐑄 𐐸𐐪𐑉𐐻𐑅 𐐱𐑂 𐑄 𐐽𐐮𐑊𐐼𐑉𐐯𐑌 𐐱𐑂 𐑋𐐯𐑌, 𐐺𐐲𐐻 𐑄𐐰𐐻 𐑄𐐩 𐑋𐐩 𐐺 𐐹𐐲𐑉𐑅𐐶𐐩𐐼𐐯𐐼 𐐻𐐭 𐐼𐐭 𐑀𐐳𐐼 𐐿𐐲𐑌𐐻𐐮𐑌𐐷𐐭𐐲𐑊𐐮 𐑄𐐰𐐻 𐑄𐐩 𐑋𐐩 𐐿𐐲𐑋 𐐲𐑌𐐻𐐭 𐑄 𐑁𐐵𐑌𐐻𐐮𐑌 𐐱𐑂 𐐫𐑊 𐑉𐐴𐐽𐐲𐑅-𐑌𐐯𐑅 𐐰𐑌𐐼 𐐺 𐑅𐐩𐑂𐐼.

𐐕𐐰𐐹𐐻𐐲𐑉 IV.

1. 𐐈𐑌𐐼 𐑌𐐵 𐐌, 𐐣𐐬𐑉𐐬𐑌𐐴, 𐐹𐑉𐐬𐑅𐐨𐐼 𐐶𐐮𐑄 𐑋𐐴 𐑉𐐯𐐿𐐲𐑉𐐼. 𐐜𐐩𐑉𐑁𐐫𐑉 𐐺𐐨𐐸𐐬𐑊𐐼, 𐐮𐐻 𐐿𐐩𐑋 𐐻𐐭 𐐹𐐰𐑅 𐑄𐐰𐐻 𐐺𐐨𐐿𐐫𐑆 𐐱𐑂 𐑄 𐑅𐐨𐐿𐑉𐐯𐐻 𐐿𐐱𐑋𐐺𐐮𐑌𐐩𐑇𐐲𐑌𐑆 𐐱𐑂 𐐁𐐿𐐮𐑇 𐐰𐑌𐐼 𐐸𐐮𐑆 𐑁𐑉𐐯𐑌𐐼𐑆, 𐐺𐐨𐐸𐐬𐑊𐐼 𐑄𐐩 𐐼𐐮𐐼 𐐬𐑂𐐲𐑉𐑃𐑉𐐬 𐑄 𐐿𐐮𐑍𐐼𐐲𐑋 𐐱𐑂 𐐄𐑋𐐲𐑉; 𐑌𐐯𐑂𐐲𐑉𐑄𐐲𐑊𐐯𐑅 𐑄 𐐢𐐫𐑉𐐼 𐐶𐐱𐑆 𐑋𐐲𐑉𐑅𐐮𐑁𐐳𐑊 𐐲𐑌𐐻𐐭 𐐄𐑋𐐲𐑉, 𐐰𐑌𐐼 𐐫𐑊𐑅𐐬 𐐻𐐭 𐐸𐐮𐑆 𐑅𐐲𐑌𐑆 𐐰𐑌𐐼 𐐻𐐭 𐐸𐐮𐑆 𐐼𐐫𐐻𐐲𐑉𐑆, 𐐸𐐭 𐐼𐐮𐐼 𐑌𐐱𐐻 𐑅𐐨𐐿 𐐸𐐮𐑆 𐐼𐐨𐑅𐐻𐑉𐐲𐐿𐑇𐐲𐑌. 𐐈𐑌𐐼 𐑄 𐐢𐐫𐑉𐐼 𐐶𐐫𐑉𐑌𐐼 𐐄𐑋𐐲𐑉 𐐮𐑌 𐐩 𐐼𐑉𐐨𐑋 𐑄𐐰𐐻 𐐸𐐨 𐑇𐐳𐐼 𐐼𐐨𐐹𐐪𐑉𐐻 𐐵𐐻 𐐱𐑂 𐑄 𐑊𐐰𐑌𐐼; 𐐸𐐶𐐩𐑉𐑁𐐫𐑉 𐐄𐑋𐐲𐑉 𐐼𐐨𐐹𐐪𐑉𐐻𐐯𐐼 𐐵𐐻 𐐱𐑂 𐑄 𐑊𐐰𐑌𐐼 𐐶𐐮𐑄 𐐸𐐮𐑆 𐑁𐐰𐑋𐐮𐑊𐐮, 𐐰𐑌𐐼 𐐻𐑉𐐰𐑂𐐯𐑊𐐼 𐑋𐐯𐑌𐐮 𐐼𐐩𐑆, 𐐰𐑌𐐼 𐐿𐐩𐑋 𐐬𐑂𐐲𐑉 𐐰𐑌𐐼 𐐹𐐰𐑅𐐻, 𐐺𐐴 𐑄 𐐸𐐮𐑊 𐐱𐑂 𐐟𐐮𐑋, 𐐰𐑌𐐼 𐐿𐐩𐑋 𐐬𐑂𐐲𐑉 𐐺𐐴 𐑄 𐐹𐑊𐐩𐑅 𐐸𐐶𐐩𐑉 𐑄 𐐤𐐨𐑁𐐴𐐻𐑅 𐐶𐐲𐑉 𐐼𐐨𐑅𐐻𐑉𐐫𐐮𐐼, 𐐰𐑌𐐼 𐑁𐑉𐐱𐑋 𐑄𐐯𐑌𐑅 𐐨𐑅𐐻𐐶𐐲𐑉𐐼, 𐐰𐑌𐐼 𐐿𐐩𐑋 𐐻𐐭 𐐩 𐐹𐑊𐐩𐑅 𐐸𐐶𐐮𐐽 𐐶𐐱𐑆 𐐿𐐫𐑊𐐼 𐐈𐐺𐑊𐐲𐑋, 𐐺𐐴 𐑄 𐑅𐐨𐑇𐐬𐑉, 𐐰𐑌𐐼 𐑄𐐩𐑉 𐐸𐐨 𐐹𐐮𐐽𐐻 𐐸𐐮𐑆 𐐻𐐯𐑌𐐻, 𐐰𐑌𐐼 𐐫𐑊𐑅𐐬 𐐸𐐮𐑆 𐑅𐐲𐑌𐑆 𐐰𐑌𐐼 𐐸𐐮𐑆 𐐼𐐫𐐻𐐲𐑉𐑆, 𐐰𐑌𐐼 𐐫𐑊 𐐸𐐮𐑆 𐐸𐐵𐑅𐐸𐐬𐑊𐐼, 𐑅𐐩𐑂 𐐮𐐻 𐐶𐐲𐑉 𐐖𐐩𐑉𐐯𐐼 𐐰𐑌𐐼 𐐸𐐮𐑆 𐑁𐐰𐑋𐐮𐑊𐐮.

2. 𐐈𐑌𐐼 𐐮𐐻 𐐿𐐩𐑋 𐐻𐐭 𐐹𐐰𐑅 𐑄𐐰𐐻 𐐖𐐩𐑉𐐯𐐼 𐐶𐐱𐑆 𐐲𐑌𐐱𐐮𐑌𐐻𐐯𐐼 𐐿𐐮𐑍 𐐬𐑂𐐲𐑉 𐑄 𐐹𐐨𐐹𐑊, 𐐺𐐴 𐑄 𐐸𐐰𐑌𐐼 𐐱𐑂 𐐶𐐮𐐿𐐯𐐼𐑌𐐯𐑅; 𐐰𐑌𐐼 𐐸𐐨 𐑀𐐩𐑂 𐐲𐑌𐐻𐐭 𐐁𐐿𐐮𐑇 𐐸𐐮𐑆 𐐼𐐫𐐻𐐲𐑉 𐐻𐐭 𐐶𐐴𐑁. 𐐈𐑌𐐼 𐐮𐐻 𐐿𐐩𐑋 𐐻𐐭 𐐹𐐰𐑅 𐑄𐐰𐐻 𐐁𐐿𐐮𐑇 𐑅𐐫𐐻 𐑄 𐑊𐐴𐑁 𐐱𐑂 𐐸𐐮𐑆 𐑁𐐪𐑄𐐲𐑉-𐐮𐑌-𐑊𐐫; 𐐰𐑌𐐼 𐐸𐐨 𐐰𐐹𐑊𐐴𐐼 𐐲𐑌𐐻𐐭 𐑄𐐬𐑆 𐐸𐐭𐑋 𐐸𐐨 𐐸𐐰𐐼 𐑅𐐶𐐬𐑉𐑌 𐐺𐐴 𐑄 𐐬𐑃 𐐱𐑂 𐑄 𐐩𐑌𐑇𐐯𐑌𐐻𐑅, 𐐰𐑌𐐼 𐑄𐐩 𐐱𐐺𐐻𐐩𐑌𐐼 𐑄 𐐸𐐯𐐼 𐐱𐑂 𐐸𐐮𐑆 𐑁𐐪𐑄𐐲𐑉-𐐮𐑌-𐑊𐐫, 𐐰𐑆 𐐸𐐨 𐑅𐐰𐐻 𐐲𐐹𐐱𐑌 𐐸𐐮𐑆 𐑃𐑉𐐬𐑌, 𐑀𐐮𐑂𐐮𐑍 𐐫𐐼𐐨𐐯𐑌𐑅 𐐻𐐭 𐐸𐐮𐑆 𐐹𐐨𐐹𐑊; 𐑁𐐫𐑉 𐑅𐐬 𐑀𐑉𐐩𐐻 𐐸𐐰𐐼 𐐺𐐮𐑌 𐑄 𐑅𐐹𐑉𐐯𐐼𐐮𐑍 𐐱𐑂 𐑄𐐮𐑅 𐐶𐐮𐐿𐐯𐐼 𐐰𐑌𐐼 𐑅𐐨𐐿𐑉𐐯𐐻 𐑅𐐬𐑅𐐴𐐯𐐻𐐮, 𐑄𐐰𐐻 𐐮𐐻 𐐸𐐰𐐼 𐐿𐐲𐑉𐐲𐐹𐐻𐐯𐐼 𐑄 𐐸𐐪𐑉𐐻𐑅 𐐱𐑂 𐐫𐑊 𐑄 𐐹𐐨𐐹𐑊; 𐑄𐐩𐑉𐑁𐐫𐑉 𐐖𐐩𐑉𐐯𐐼 𐐶𐐱𐑆 𐑋𐐲𐑉𐐼𐐲𐑉𐐼 𐐲𐐹𐐱𐑌 𐐸𐐮𐑆 𐑃𐑉𐐬𐑌, 𐐰𐑌𐐼 𐐁𐐿𐐮𐑇 𐑉𐐩𐑌𐐼 𐐮𐑌 𐐸𐐮𐑆 𐑅𐐻𐐯𐐼. 𐐈𐑌𐐼 𐐮𐐻 𐐿𐐩𐑋 𐐻𐐭 𐐹𐐰𐑅 𐑄𐐰𐐻 𐐁𐐿𐐮𐑇 𐐺𐐨𐑀𐐰𐑌 𐐻𐐭 𐐺 𐐾𐐯𐑊𐐲𐑅 𐐱𐑂 𐐸𐐮𐑆 𐑅𐐲𐑌, 𐑄𐐩𐑉𐑁𐐫𐑉 𐐸𐐨 𐑇𐐲𐐻 𐐸𐐮𐑋 𐐲𐐹 𐐮𐑌 𐐹𐑉𐐮𐑆𐑌, 𐐰𐑌𐐼 𐐿𐐯𐐹𐐻 𐐸𐐮𐑋 𐐲𐐹𐐱𐑌 𐑊𐐮𐐻𐑊 𐐫𐑉 𐑌𐐬 𐑁𐐭𐐼 𐐲𐑌𐐻𐐮𐑊 𐐸𐐨 𐐸𐐰𐐼 𐑅𐐲𐑁𐐲𐑉𐐼 𐐼𐐯𐑃. 𐐈𐑌𐐼 𐑌𐐵 𐑄 𐐺𐑉𐐲𐑄𐐲𐑉 𐐱𐑂 𐐸𐐮𐑋 𐑄𐐰𐐻 𐑅𐐲𐑁𐐲𐑉𐐼 𐐼𐐯𐑃, (𐐰𐑌𐐼 𐐸𐐮𐑆 𐑌𐐩𐑋 𐐶𐐱𐑆 𐐤𐐮𐑋𐑉𐐲,) 𐐶𐐱𐑆 𐐰𐑍𐑀𐑉𐐮 𐐶𐐮𐑄 𐐸𐐮𐑆 𐑁𐐪𐑄𐐲𐑉, 𐐺𐐨𐐿𐐫𐑆 𐐱𐑂 𐑄𐐰𐐻 𐐸𐐶𐐮𐐽 𐐸𐐮𐑆 𐑁𐐪𐑄𐐲𐑉 𐐸𐐰𐐼 𐐼𐐲𐑌 𐐲𐑌𐐻𐐭 𐐸𐐮𐑆 𐐺𐑉𐐲𐑄𐐲𐑉. 𐐈𐑌𐐼 𐐮𐐻 𐐿𐐩𐑋 𐐻𐐭 𐐹𐐰𐑅 𐑄𐐰𐐻 𐐤𐐮𐑋𐑉𐐲 𐑀𐐰𐑄𐐲𐑉𐐼 𐐻𐐭𐑀𐐯𐑄𐐲𐑉 𐐩 𐑅𐑋𐐫𐑊 𐑌𐐲𐑋𐐺𐐲𐑉 𐐱𐑂 𐑋𐐯𐑌, 𐐰𐑌𐐼 𐑁𐑊𐐯𐐼 𐐵𐐻 𐐱𐑂 𐑄 𐑊𐐰𐑌𐐼, 𐐰𐑌𐐼 𐐿𐐩𐑋 𐐬𐑂𐐲𐑉 𐐰𐑌𐐼 𐐼𐐶𐐯𐑊𐐻 𐐶𐐮𐑄 𐐄𐑋𐐲𐑉. 𐐈𐑌𐐼 𐐮𐐻 𐐿𐐩𐑋 𐐻𐐭 𐐹𐐰𐑅 𐑄𐐰𐐻 𐐁𐐿𐐮𐑇 𐐺𐐨𐑀𐐰𐐻 𐐲𐑄𐐲𐑉 𐑅𐐲𐑌𐑆, 𐐰𐑌𐐼 𐑄𐐩 𐐶𐐲𐑌 𐑄 𐐸𐐪𐑉𐐻𐑅 𐐱𐑂 𐑄 𐐹𐐨𐐹𐑊, 𐑌𐐱𐐻𐐶𐐮𐑄𐑅𐐻𐐰𐑌𐐼𐐮𐑍 𐑄𐐩 𐐸𐐰𐐼 𐑅𐐶𐐬𐑉𐑌 𐐲𐑌𐐻𐐭 𐐸𐐮𐑋 𐐻𐐭 𐐼𐐭 𐐫𐑊 𐑋𐐰𐑌𐐲𐑉 𐐱𐑂 𐐮𐑌𐐮𐐿𐐶𐐮𐐻𐐮, 𐐲𐐿𐐫𐑉𐐼𐐮𐑍 𐐻𐐭 𐑄𐐰𐐻 𐐸𐐶𐐮𐐽 𐐸𐐨 𐐼𐐨𐑆𐐴𐑉𐐼. 𐐤𐐵 𐑄 𐐹𐐨𐐹𐑊 𐐱𐑂 𐐁𐐿𐐮𐑇 𐐶𐐲𐑉 𐐼𐐨𐑆𐐴𐑉𐐲𐑅 𐑁𐐫𐑉 𐑀𐐩𐑌, 𐐨𐑂𐑌 𐐰𐑆 𐐁𐐿𐐮𐑇 𐐶𐐱𐑆 𐐼𐐨𐑆𐐴𐑉𐐲𐑅 𐑁𐐫𐑉 𐐹𐐵𐑉; 𐐸𐐶𐐩𐑉𐑁𐐫𐑉 𐑄 𐑅𐐲𐑌𐑆 𐐱𐑂 𐐁𐐿𐐮𐑇 𐐼𐐮𐐼 𐐱𐑁𐐲𐑉 𐑄𐐯𐑋 𐑋𐐲𐑌𐐮, 𐐺𐐴 𐐸𐐶𐐮𐐽 𐑋𐐨𐑌𐑆 𐑄𐐩 𐐼𐑉𐐭 𐐲𐐶𐐩 𐑄 𐑋𐐬𐑉 𐐹𐐪𐑉𐐻 𐐱𐑂 𐑄 𐐹𐐨𐐹𐑊 𐐰𐑁𐐻𐐲𐑉 𐑄𐐯𐑋; 𐐰𐑌𐐼 𐑄𐐩𐑉 𐐺𐐨𐑀𐐰𐑌 𐐻𐐭 𐐺 𐐩 𐐶𐐫𐑉 𐐺𐐨𐐻𐐶𐐨𐑌 𐑄 𐑅𐐲𐑌𐑆 𐐱𐑂 𐐁𐐿𐐮𐑇

𐐰𐑌𐐼 𐐁𐐿𐐮𐑇, 𐐸𐐶𐐮𐐽 𐑊𐐰𐑅𐐻𐐯𐐼 𐑁𐐫𐑉 𐑄 𐑅𐐹𐐩𐑅 𐐲𐑂 𐑋𐐯𐑌𐐨 𐐷𐐨𐑉𐑆; 𐐷𐐩, 𐐲𐑌𐐻𐐭 𐑄 𐐼𐐯𐑅𐐻𐑉𐐲𐐿𐑇𐐲𐑌 𐐲𐑂 𐑌𐐨𐑉𐑊𐐨 𐐫𐑊 𐑄 𐐹𐐨𐐹𐑊 𐐲𐑂 𐑄 𐐿𐐮𐑍𐐼𐐲𐑋; 𐐷𐐩, 𐐨𐑂𐐲𐑌 𐐫𐑊, 𐑅𐐩𐑂 𐐮𐐻 𐐶𐐲𐑉 𐑃𐐲𐑉𐐻𐐨 𐑅𐐬𐑊𐑆, 𐐰𐑌𐐼 𐑄𐐩 𐐸𐐭 𐑁𐑊𐐯𐐼 𐐶𐐮𐑃 𐑄 𐐸𐐵𐑅 𐐲𐑂 𐐄𐑋𐐲𐑉; 𐐸𐐶𐐯𐑉𐑁𐐫𐑉 𐐄𐑋𐐲𐑉 𐐶𐐱𐑆 𐑉𐐨𐑅𐐻𐐬𐑉𐐼 𐐰𐑀𐐯𐑌 𐐻𐐭 𐑄 𐑊𐐰𐑌𐐼 𐐲𐑂 𐐸𐐮𐑆 𐐮𐑌𐐸𐐯𐑉𐐮𐐻𐐰𐑌𐑅. 𐐈𐑌𐐼 𐐮𐐻 𐐿𐐩𐑋 𐐻𐐭 𐐹𐐰𐑅 𐑄𐐰𐐻 𐐄𐑋𐐲𐑉 𐐺𐐨𐑀𐐰𐑌 𐐻𐐭 𐐺𐐨 𐐬𐑊𐐼, 𐑌𐐯𐑂𐐲𐑉𐑄𐐯𐑊𐐯𐑅, 𐐮𐑌 𐐸𐐮𐑆 𐐬𐑊𐐼 𐐩𐑂 𐐸𐐨 𐐺𐐨𐑀𐐰𐐻 𐐀𐑋𐐲𐑉; 𐐰𐑌𐐼 𐐸𐐨 𐐰𐑌𐐱𐐮𐑌𐐻𐐯𐐼 𐐀𐑋𐐲𐑉 𐐻𐐭 𐐺𐐨 𐐿𐐮𐑍 𐐻𐐭 𐑉𐐩𐑌 𐐮𐑌 𐐸𐐮𐑆 𐑅𐐻𐐯𐐼. 𐐈𐑌𐐼 𐐪𐑁𐐻𐐲𐑉 𐑄𐐰𐐻 𐐸𐐨 𐐸𐐰𐐼 𐐰𐑌𐐱𐐮𐑌𐐻𐐯𐐼 𐐀𐑋𐐲𐑉 𐐻𐐭 𐐺𐐨 𐐿𐐮𐑍, 𐐸𐐨 𐑅𐐫 𐐹𐐨𐑅 𐐮𐑌 𐑄 𐑊𐐰𐑌𐐼 𐑁𐐫𐑉 𐑄 𐑅𐐹𐐩𐑅 𐐲𐑂 𐐻𐐭 𐐷𐐨𐑉𐑆, 𐐰𐑌𐐼 𐐸𐐨 𐐼𐐴𐐼, 𐐸𐐰𐑂𐐮𐑍 𐑅𐐨𐑌 𐐯𐐿𐑅𐐨𐐼𐐮𐑍 𐑋𐐯𐑌𐐨 𐐼𐐩𐑆, 𐐸𐐶𐐮𐐽 𐐶𐐲𐑉 𐑁𐐳𐑊 𐐲𐑂 𐑅𐐱𐑉𐐬. 𐐈𐑌𐐼 𐐮𐐻 𐐿𐐩𐑋 𐐻𐐭 𐐹𐐰𐑅 𐑄𐐰𐐻 𐐀𐑋𐐲𐑉 𐐼𐐮𐐼 𐑉𐐩𐑌 𐐮𐑌 𐐸𐐮𐑆 𐑅𐐻𐐯𐐼, 𐐰𐑌𐐼 𐐼𐐮𐐼 𐑁𐐮𐑊 𐑄 𐑅𐐻𐐯𐐹𐑅 𐐲𐑂 𐐸𐐮𐑆 𐑁𐐪𐑄𐐲𐑉.

3. 𐐈𐑌𐐼 𐑄 𐐢𐐫𐑉𐐼 𐐺𐐨𐑀𐐰𐑌 𐐰𐑀𐐯𐑌 𐐻𐐭 𐐻𐐩𐐿 𐑄 𐐿𐐲𐑉𐑅 𐑁𐑉𐐱𐑋 𐐫𐑁 𐑄 𐑊𐐰𐑌𐐼, 𐐰𐑌𐐼 𐑄 𐐸𐐵𐑅 𐐲𐑂 𐐀𐑋𐐲𐑉 𐐼𐐮𐐼 𐐹𐑉𐐱𐑅𐐹𐐲𐑉 𐐯𐐿𐑅𐐨𐐼𐐮𐑍𐑊𐐨 𐐲𐑌𐐼𐐲𐑉 𐑄 𐑉𐐩𐑌 𐐲𐑂 𐐀𐑋𐐲𐑉; 𐐰𐑌𐐼 𐐮𐑌 𐑄 𐑅𐐹𐐩𐑅 𐐲𐑂 𐑅𐐮𐐿𐑅𐐻𐐨 𐐰𐑌𐐼 𐐻𐐭 𐐷𐐨𐑉𐑆, 𐑄𐐩 𐐸𐐰𐐼 𐐺𐐨𐐿𐐲𐑋 𐐯𐐿𐑅𐐨𐐼𐐮𐑍𐑊𐐨 𐑅𐐻𐑉𐐱𐑍, 𐐮𐑌𐑅𐐬𐑋𐐲𐐽 𐑄𐐰𐐻 𐑄𐐩 𐐺𐐨𐐿𐐩𐑋 𐐯𐐿𐑅𐐨𐐼𐐮𐑍𐑊𐐨 𐑉𐐮𐐽, 𐐸𐐰𐑂𐐮𐑍 𐐫𐑊 𐑋𐐰𐑌𐐲𐑉 𐐲𐑂 𐑁𐑉𐐭𐐻, 𐐰𐑌𐐼 𐐲𐑂 𐑀𐑉𐐩𐑌, 𐐰𐑌𐐼 𐐲𐑂 𐑅𐐮𐑊𐐿𐑅, 𐐰𐑌𐐼 𐐲𐑂 𐑁𐐴𐑌 𐑊𐐮𐑌𐐯𐑌, 𐐰𐑌𐐼 𐐲𐑂 𐑀𐐬𐑊𐐼, 𐐰𐑌𐐼 𐐲𐑂 𐑅𐐮𐑊𐑂𐐲𐑉, 𐐰𐑌𐐼 𐐲𐑂 𐐹𐑉𐐯𐑇𐐲𐑅 𐑃𐐮𐑍𐑆, 𐐰𐑌𐐼 𐐫𐑊𐑅𐐬 𐐫𐑊 𐑋𐐰𐑌𐐲𐑉 𐐲𐑂 𐐿𐐰𐐻𐑊, 𐐲𐑂 𐐱𐐿𐑅𐐯𐑌, 𐐰𐑌𐐼 𐐿𐐵𐑆, 𐐰𐑌𐐼 𐐲𐑂 𐑇𐐨𐐹, 𐐰𐑌𐐼 𐐲𐑂 𐑅𐐶𐐴𐑌, 𐐰𐑌𐐼 𐐲𐑂 𐑀𐐬𐐻𐑅, 𐐰𐑌𐐼 𐐫𐑊𐑅𐐬 𐑋𐐯𐑌𐐨 𐐲𐑄𐐲𐑉 𐐿𐐴𐑌𐐼𐑆 𐐲𐑂 𐐰𐑌𐐮𐑋𐐰𐑊𐑆 𐐸𐐶𐐮𐐽 𐐶𐐲𐑉 𐐷𐐭𐑆𐑁𐐳𐑊 𐑁𐐫𐑉 𐑄 𐑁𐐭𐐼 𐐲𐑂 𐑋𐐰𐑌; 𐐰𐑌𐐼 𐑄𐐩 𐐫𐑊𐑅𐐬 𐐸𐐰𐐼 𐐸𐐫𐑉𐑅𐐯𐑆, 𐐰𐑌𐐼 𐐰𐑅𐐯𐑆, 𐐰𐑌𐐼 𐑄𐐯𐑉 𐐶𐐲𐑉 𐐯𐑊𐐯𐑁𐐰𐑌𐐻𐑅, 𐐰𐑌𐐼 𐐿𐐷𐐭𐑉𐐯𐑊𐐱𐑋𐑆, 𐐰𐑌𐐼 𐐿𐐷𐐭𐑋𐐱𐑋𐑆; 𐐫𐑊 𐐲𐑂 𐐸𐐶𐐮𐐽 𐐶𐐲𐑉 𐐷𐐭𐑆𐑁𐐳𐑊 𐐲𐑌𐐻𐐭 𐑋𐐰𐑌, 𐐰𐑌𐐼 𐑋𐐬𐑉 𐐯𐑅𐐹𐐯𐑇𐐲𐑊𐐨 𐑄 𐐯𐑊𐐯𐑁𐐰𐑌𐐻𐑅, 𐐰𐑌𐐼 𐐿𐐷𐐭𐑉𐐯𐑊𐐱𐑋𐑆, 𐐰𐑌𐐼 𐐿𐐷𐐭𐑋𐐱𐑋𐑆. 𐐈𐑌𐐼 𐑄𐐲𐑅 𐑄 𐐢𐐫𐑉𐐼 𐐼𐐮𐐼 𐐹𐐬𐑉 𐐵𐐻 𐐸𐐮𐑆 𐐺𐑊𐐯𐑅𐐮𐑍𐑆 𐐲𐐹𐐱𐑌 𐑄𐐮𐑅 𐑊𐐰𐑌𐐼, 𐐸𐐶𐐮𐐽 𐐶𐐱𐑆 𐐽𐐱𐐮𐑅 𐐲𐐺𐐲𐑂 𐐫𐑊 𐐲𐑄𐐲𐑉 𐑊𐐰𐑌𐐼𐑆; 𐐰𐑌𐐼 𐐸𐐨 𐐿𐐱𐑋𐐰𐑌𐐼𐐯𐐼 𐑄𐐰𐐻 𐐸𐐭𐑅𐐬 𐑇𐐳𐐼 𐐹𐐱𐑆𐐯𐑅 𐑄 𐑊𐐰𐑌𐐼, 𐑇𐐳𐐼 𐐹𐐱𐑆𐐯𐑅 𐐮𐐻 𐐲𐑌𐐻𐐭 𐑄 𐐢𐐫𐑉𐐼, 𐐫𐑉 𐑄𐐩 𐑇𐐳𐐼 𐐺𐐨 𐐼𐐯𐑅𐐻𐑉𐐱𐐮𐐼 𐐸𐐶𐐯𐑌 𐑄𐐩 𐐶𐐲𐑉 𐑉𐐴𐐹𐐲𐑌𐐼 𐐮𐑌 𐐮𐑌𐐮𐐿𐐶𐐮𐐻𐐨; 𐑁𐐫𐑉 𐐲𐐹𐐱𐑌 𐑅𐐲𐐽, 𐑅𐐯𐑃 𐑄 𐐢𐐫𐑉𐐼, 𐐌 𐐶𐐮𐑊 𐐹𐐬𐑉 𐐵𐐻 𐑄 𐑁𐐳𐑊𐑌𐐯𐑅 𐐲𐑂 𐑋𐐴 𐑉𐐪𐑃. 𐐈𐑌𐐼 𐐀𐑋𐐲𐑉 𐐼𐐮𐐼 𐐯𐐿𐑅𐐯𐐿𐐷𐐭𐐻 𐐾𐐲𐐾𐑋𐐯𐑌𐐻 𐐮𐑌 𐑉𐐴𐐽𐐲𐑅𐑌𐐯𐑅 𐐫𐑊 𐐸𐐮𐑆 𐐼𐐩𐑆, 𐐰𐑌𐐼 𐐸𐐨 𐐺𐐨𐑀𐐰𐐻 𐑋𐐯𐑌𐐨 𐑅𐐲𐑌𐑆 𐐰𐑌𐐼 𐐼𐐫𐐻𐐲𐑉𐑆; 𐐰𐑌𐐼 𐐸𐐨 𐐺𐐨𐑀𐐰𐐻 𐐗𐐬𐑉𐐨𐐰𐑌𐐻𐐲𐑋, 𐐰𐑌𐐼 𐐸𐐨 𐐰𐑌𐐱𐐮𐑌𐐻𐐯𐐼 𐐗𐐬𐑉𐐨𐐰𐑌𐐻𐐲𐑋 𐐻𐐭 𐑉𐐩𐑌 𐐮𐑌 𐐸𐐮𐑆 𐑅𐐻𐐯𐐼. 𐐈𐑌𐐼 𐐪𐑁𐐻𐐲𐑉 𐑄𐐰𐐻 𐐸𐐨 𐐸𐐰𐐼 𐐰𐑌𐐱𐐮𐑌𐐻𐐯𐐼 𐐗𐐬𐑉𐐨𐐰𐑌𐐻𐐲𐑋 𐐻𐐭 𐑉𐐩𐑌 𐐮𐑌 𐐸𐐮𐑆 𐑅𐐻𐐯𐐼, 𐐸𐐨 𐑊𐐮𐑂𐐼 𐑁𐐬𐑉 𐐷𐐨𐑉𐑆, 𐐰𐑌𐐼 𐐸𐐨 𐑅𐐫 𐐹𐐨𐑅 𐐮𐑌 𐑄 𐑊𐐰𐑌𐐼; 𐐷𐐩, 𐐰𐑌𐐼 𐐸𐐨 𐐨𐑂𐐲𐑌 𐑅𐐫 𐑄 𐐝𐐲𐑌 𐐲𐑂 𐐡𐐴𐐽𐐲𐑅𐑌𐐯𐑅, 𐐰𐑌𐐼 𐐼𐐮𐐼 𐑉𐐨𐐾𐐱𐐮𐑅 𐐰𐑌𐐼 𐑀𐑊𐐬𐑉𐐨 𐐮𐑌 𐐸𐐮𐑆 𐐼𐐩; 𐐰𐑌𐐼 𐐸𐐨 𐐼𐐴𐐼 𐐮𐑌 𐐹𐐨𐑅. 𐐈𐑌𐐼 𐐮𐐻 𐐿𐐩𐑋 𐐻𐐭 𐐹𐐰𐑅 𐑄𐐰𐐻 𐐗𐐬𐑉𐐨𐐰𐑌𐐻𐐲𐑋 𐐼𐐮𐐼 𐐶𐐫𐐿 𐐮𐑌 𐑄 𐑅𐐻𐐯𐐹𐑅 𐐲𐑂 𐐸𐐮𐑆 𐑁𐐪𐑄𐐲𐑉, 𐐰𐑌𐐼 𐐼𐐮𐐼 𐐺𐐮𐑊𐐼 𐑋𐐯𐑌𐐨 𐑋𐐴𐐻𐐨 𐑅𐐮𐐻𐐨𐑆, 𐐰𐑌𐐼 𐐼𐐮𐐼 𐐰𐐼𐑋𐐮𐑌𐐮𐑅𐐻𐐲𐑉 𐑄𐐰𐐻 𐐸𐐶𐐮𐐽 𐐶𐐱𐑆 𐑀𐐳𐐼 𐐲𐑌𐐻𐐭 𐐸𐐮𐑆 𐐹𐐨𐐹𐑊, 𐐮𐑌 𐐫𐑊 𐐸𐐮𐑆 𐐼𐐩𐑆. 𐐈𐑌𐐼 𐐮𐐻 𐐿𐐩𐑋 𐐻𐐭 𐐹𐐰𐑅 𐑄𐐰𐐻 𐐸𐐨 𐐸𐐰𐐼 𐑌𐐬 𐐽𐐮𐑊𐐼𐑉𐐯𐑌, 𐐨𐑂𐐲𐑌 𐐲𐑌𐐻𐐮𐑊 𐐸𐐨 𐐶𐐱𐑆 𐐯𐐿𐑅𐐨𐐼𐐮𐑍 𐐬𐑊𐐼. 𐐈𐑌𐐼 𐐮𐐻 𐐿𐐩𐑋 𐐻𐐭 𐐹𐐰𐑅 𐑄𐐰𐐻 𐐸𐐮𐑆 𐐶𐐴𐑁 𐐼𐐴𐐼, 𐐺𐐨𐐮𐑍 𐐰𐑌 𐐸𐐲𐑌𐐼𐑉𐐯𐐼 𐐰𐑌𐐼 𐐻𐐭 𐐷𐐨𐑉𐑆 𐐬𐑊𐐼. 𐐈𐑌𐐼 𐐮𐐻 𐐿𐐩𐑋 𐐻𐐭 𐐹𐐰𐑅 𐑄𐐰𐐻 𐐗𐐬𐑉𐐨𐐰𐑌𐐻𐐲𐑋 𐐻𐐳𐐿 𐐻𐐭 𐐶𐐴𐑁, 𐐮𐑌 𐐸𐐮𐑆 𐐬𐑊𐐼 𐐩𐑂, 𐐰 𐐷𐐲𐑍 𐑋𐐩𐐼, 𐐰𐑌𐐼 𐐺𐐨𐑀𐐰𐐻 𐑅𐐲𐑌𐑆 𐐰𐑌𐐼 𐐼𐐫𐐻𐐲𐑉𐑆; 𐐸𐐶𐐯𐑉𐑁𐐫𐑉 𐐸𐐨 𐑊𐐮𐑂𐐼 𐐲𐑌𐐻𐐮𐑊 𐐸𐐨 𐐶𐐱𐑆 𐐰𐑌 𐐸𐐲𐑌𐐼𐑉𐐯𐐼 𐐰𐑌𐐼 𐑁𐐫𐑉𐐻𐐨 𐐰𐑌𐐼 𐐻𐐭 𐐷𐐨𐑉𐑆 𐐬𐑊𐐼. 𐐈𐑌𐐼 𐐮𐐻 𐐿𐐩𐑋 𐐻𐐭 𐐹𐐰𐑅 𐑄𐐰𐐻 𐐸𐐨 𐐺𐐨𐑀𐐰𐐻 𐐗𐐱𐑋, 𐐰𐑌𐐼 𐐗𐐱𐑋 𐑉𐐩𐑌𐐼 𐐮𐑌 𐐸𐐮𐑆 𐑅𐐻𐐯𐐼; 𐐰𐑌𐐼 𐐸𐐨 𐑉𐐩𐑌𐐼 𐑁𐐫𐑉𐐻𐐨 𐐰𐑌𐐼 𐑌𐐴𐑌 𐐷𐐨𐑉𐑆, 𐐰𐑌𐐼 𐐸𐐨 𐐺𐐨𐑀𐐰𐐻 𐐐𐐯𐑃; 𐐰𐑌𐐼 𐐸𐐨 𐐫𐑊𐑅𐐬 𐐺𐐨𐑀𐐰𐐻 𐐲𐑄𐐲𐑉 𐑅𐐲𐑌𐑆 𐐰𐑌𐐼 𐐼𐐫𐐻𐐲𐑉𐑆. 𐐈𐑌𐐼 𐑄 𐐹𐐨𐐹𐑊 𐐸𐐰𐐼 𐑅𐐹𐑉𐐯𐐼 𐐰𐑀𐐯𐑌 𐐬𐑂𐐲𐑉 𐐫𐑊 𐑄 𐑁𐐩𐑅 𐐲𐑂 𐑄 𐑊𐐰𐑌𐐼, 𐐰𐑌𐐼 𐑄𐐯𐑉 𐐺𐐨𐑀𐐰𐑌 𐐰𐑀𐐯𐑌 𐐻𐐭 𐐺𐐨 𐐰𐑌 𐐯𐐿𐑅𐐨𐐼𐐮𐑍 𐑀𐑉𐐩𐐻 𐐶𐐮𐐿𐐯𐐼𐑌𐐯𐑅 𐐲𐐹𐐱𐑌 𐑄 𐑁𐐩𐑅 𐐲𐑂 𐑄 𐑊𐐰𐑌𐐼, 𐐰𐑌𐐼 𐐐𐐯𐑃 𐐺𐐨𐑀𐐰𐑌 𐐻𐐭 𐐯𐑋𐐺𐑉𐐩𐑅 𐑄 𐑅𐐨𐐿𐑉𐐯𐐻 𐐹𐑊𐐰𐑌𐑆 𐐰𐑀𐐯𐑌 𐐲𐑂 𐐬𐑊𐐼, 𐐻𐐭 𐐼𐐯𐑅𐐻𐑉𐐱𐐮 𐐸𐐮𐑆 𐑁𐐪𐑄𐐲𐑉. 𐐈𐑌𐐼 𐐮𐐻 𐐿𐐩𐑋 𐐻𐐭 𐐹𐐰𐑅 𐑄𐐰𐐻 𐐸𐐨 𐐼𐐮𐐼 𐐼𐐨𐑃𐑉𐐬𐑌 𐐸𐐮𐑆 𐑁𐐪𐑄𐐲𐑉, 𐑁𐐫𐑉 𐐸𐐨 𐑅𐑊𐐭 𐐸𐐮𐑋 𐐶𐐮𐑃 𐐸𐐮𐑆 𐐬𐑌 𐑅𐐬𐑉𐐼; 𐐰𐑌𐐼 𐐸𐐨 𐐼𐐮𐐼 𐑉𐐩𐑌 𐐮𐑌 𐐸𐐮𐑆 𐑅𐐻𐐯𐐼. 𐐈𐑌𐐼 𐑄𐐯𐑉 𐐿𐐩𐑋 𐐹𐑉𐐱𐑁𐐯𐐻𐑅 𐐮𐑌 𐑄 𐑊𐐰𐑌𐐼 𐐰𐑀𐐯𐑌, 𐐿𐑉𐐴𐐮𐑍 𐑉𐐯𐐹𐐯𐑌𐐻𐐰𐑌𐑅 𐐲𐑌𐐻𐐭 𐑄𐐯𐑋; 𐑄𐐰𐐻 𐑄𐐩 𐑋𐐲𐑅𐐻 𐐹𐑉𐐨𐐹𐐩𐑉 𐑄 𐐶𐐩 𐐲𐑂 𐑄 𐐢𐐫𐑉𐐼, 𐐫𐑉 𐑄𐐯𐑉 𐑇𐐳𐐼 𐐿𐐲𐑋 𐐰

𐐿𐐲𐑉𐑅 𐐲𐐹𐐪𐑌 𐑄 𐑁𐐩𐑅 𐐱𐑂 𐑄 𐑊𐐰𐑌𐐼; 𐐷𐐩, 𐐨𐑂𐐲𐑌 𐑄𐐯𐑉 𐑇𐐳𐐼 𐐺𐐨 𐐩 𐑀𐑉𐐩𐐻 𐑁𐐰𐑋𐐮𐑌, 𐐮𐑌 𐐸𐐶𐐮𐐽 𐑄𐐩 𐑇𐐳𐐼 𐐺𐐨 𐐼𐐯𐑅𐐻𐑉𐑎𐐼, 𐐮𐑁 𐑄𐐩 𐐼𐐮𐐼 𐑌𐐱𐐻 𐑉𐐨𐐹𐐯𐑌𐐻. 𐐒𐐲𐐻 𐑄 𐐹𐐨𐐹𐑊 𐐺𐐨𐑊𐐨𐑂𐐼 𐑌𐐱𐐻 𐑄 𐐶𐐲𐑉𐐼𐑆 𐐱𐑂 𐑄 𐐹𐑉𐐱𐑁𐐯𐐻𐑅, 𐐺𐐲𐐻 𐑄𐐩 𐐿𐐪𐑅𐐻 𐑄𐐯𐑋 𐐵𐐻; 𐐰𐑌𐐼 𐑅𐐲𐑋 𐐱𐑂 𐑄𐐯𐑋 𐑄𐐩 𐐿𐐪𐑅𐐻 𐐮𐑌𐐻𐐭 𐐹𐐮𐐻𐑅, 𐐰𐑌𐐼 𐑊𐐯𐑁𐐻 𐑄𐐯𐑋 𐐻𐐭 𐐹𐐯𐑉𐐮𐑇. 𐐈𐑌𐐼 𐐮𐐻 𐐿𐐩𐑋 𐐻𐐭 𐐹𐐰𐑅 𐑄𐐰𐐻 𐑄𐐩 𐐼𐐮𐐼 𐐫𐑊 𐑄𐐨𐑆 𐑃𐐮𐑍𐑆 𐐰𐐿𐐫𐑉𐐼𐐮𐑍 𐐻𐐭 𐑄 𐐿𐐲𐑋𐐰𐑌𐐼𐑋𐐯𐑌𐐻 𐐱𐑂 𐑄 𐐿𐐮𐑍 𐐐𐐯𐑃.

4. 𐐈𐑌𐐼 𐐮𐐻 𐐿𐐩𐑋 𐐻𐐭 𐐹𐐰𐑅 𐑄𐐰𐐻 𐑄𐐯𐑉 𐐺𐐨𐑀𐐰𐑌 𐐻𐐭 𐐺𐐨 𐐩 𐑀𐑉𐐩𐐻 𐐼𐐲𐑉𐑃 𐐲𐐹𐐪𐑌 𐑄 𐑊𐐰𐑌𐐼, 𐐰𐑌𐐼 𐑄 𐐮𐑌𐐸𐐰𐐺𐐮𐐻𐐰𐑌𐐻𐑅 𐐺𐐨𐑀𐐰𐑌 𐐻𐐭 𐐺𐐨 𐐼𐐯𐑅𐐻𐑉𐑎𐐼 𐐯𐐿𐑅𐐨𐐼𐐮𐑍𐑊𐐨 𐑁𐐪𐑅𐐻, 𐐺𐐨𐐿𐐫𐑆 𐐱𐑂 𐑄 𐐼𐐲𐑉𐑃, 𐑁𐐫𐑉 𐑄𐐯𐑉 𐐶𐐱𐑆 𐑌𐐬 𐑉𐐩𐑌 𐐲𐐹𐐪𐑌 𐑄 𐑁𐐩𐑅 𐐱𐑂 𐑄 𐐲𐑉𐑃; 𐐰𐑌𐐼 𐑄𐐯𐑉 𐐿𐐩𐑋 𐑁𐐬𐑉𐑃 𐐹𐑎𐑆𐐲𐑌𐐲𐑅 𐑅𐐲𐑉𐐹𐐯𐑌𐐻𐑅 𐐫𐑊𐑅𐐬 𐐲𐐹𐐪𐑌 𐑄 𐑁𐐩𐑅 𐐱𐑂 𐑄 𐑊𐐰𐑌𐐼, 𐐰𐑌𐐼 𐐼𐐮𐐼 𐐹𐑎𐑆𐐲𐑌 𐑋𐐯𐑌𐐨 𐐹𐐨𐐹𐑊. 𐐈𐑌𐐼 𐐮𐐻 𐐿𐐩𐑋 𐐻𐐭 𐐹𐐰𐑅 𐑄𐐰𐐻 𐑄𐐯𐑉 𐑁𐑊𐐱𐐿𐑅 𐐺𐐨𐑀𐐰𐑌 𐐻𐐭 𐑁𐑊𐐨 𐐺𐐨𐑁𐐬𐑉 𐑄 𐐹𐑎𐑆𐐲𐑌𐐲𐑅 𐑅𐐲𐑉𐐹𐐯𐑌𐐻𐑅, 𐐻𐐬𐑉𐐼𐑆 𐑄 𐑊𐐰𐑌𐐼 𐑅𐐵𐑃𐐶𐐲𐑉𐐼, 𐐸𐐶𐐮𐐽 𐐶𐐱𐑆 𐐿𐐫𐑊𐐼 𐐺𐐴 𐑄 𐐤𐐨𐑁𐐴𐐻𐑅, 𐐞𐐯𐑉𐐲𐐸𐐯𐑋𐑊𐐲. 𐐈𐑌𐐼 𐐮𐐻 𐐿𐐩𐑋 𐐻𐐭 𐐹𐐰𐑅 𐑄𐐰𐐻 𐑄𐐯𐑉 𐐶𐐲𐑉 𐑋𐐯𐑌𐐨 𐐱𐑂 𐑄𐐯𐑋 𐐸𐐶𐐮𐐽 𐐼𐐮𐐼 𐐹𐐯𐑉𐐮𐑇 𐐺𐐴 𐑄 𐐶𐐩; 𐑌𐐯𐑂𐐲𐑉𐑄𐐯𐑊𐐯𐑅, 𐑄𐐯𐑉 𐐶𐐲𐑉 𐑅𐐲𐑋 𐐸𐐶𐐮𐐽 𐑁𐑊𐐯𐐼 𐐮𐑌𐐻𐐭 𐑄 𐑊𐐰𐑌𐐼 𐑅𐐵𐑃𐐶𐐲𐑉𐐼. 𐐈𐑌𐐼 𐐮𐐻 𐐿𐐩𐑋 𐐻𐐭 𐐹𐐰𐑅 𐑄𐐰𐐻 𐑄 𐐢𐐫𐑉𐐼 𐐼𐐮𐐼 𐐿𐐫𐑆 𐑄 𐑅𐐲𐑉𐐹𐐯𐑌𐐻𐑅 𐑄𐐰𐐻 𐑄𐐩 𐑇𐐳𐐼 𐐹𐐲𐑉𐑅𐐭 𐑄𐐯𐑋 𐑌𐐬 𐑋𐐬𐑉, 𐐺𐐲𐐻 𐑄𐐰𐐻 𐑄𐐩 𐑇𐐳𐐼 𐐸𐐯𐐾 𐐲𐐹 𐑄 𐐶𐐩 𐑄𐐰𐐻 𐑄 𐐹𐐨𐐹𐑊 𐐿𐐳𐐼 𐑌𐐱𐐻 𐐹𐐰𐑅, 𐑄𐐰𐐻 𐐸𐐭𐑅𐐬 𐑇𐐳𐐼 𐐰𐐻𐐯𐑋𐐹𐐻 𐐻𐐭 𐐹𐐰𐑅 𐑋𐐴𐐻 𐑁𐐫𐑊 𐐺𐐴 𐑄 𐐹𐑎𐑆𐐲𐑌𐐲𐑅 𐑅𐐲𐑉𐐹𐐯𐑌𐐻𐑅. 𐐈𐑌𐐼 𐐮𐐻 𐐿𐐩𐑋 𐐻𐐭 𐐹𐐰𐑅 𐑄𐐰𐐻 𐑄 𐐹𐐨𐐹𐑊 𐐼𐐮𐐼 𐑁𐐱𐑊𐐬 𐑄 𐐿𐐬𐑉𐑅 𐐱𐑂 𐑄 𐐺𐐨𐑅𐐻𐑅, 𐐰𐑌𐐼 𐐼𐐮𐐼 𐐼𐐨𐑂𐐵𐑉 𐑄 𐐿𐐪𐑉𐐿𐐰𐑅𐐯𐑆 𐐱𐑂 𐑄𐐯𐑋 𐐸𐐶𐐮𐐽 𐑁𐐯𐑊 𐐺𐐴 𐑄 𐐶𐐩, 𐐲𐑌𐐻𐐮𐑊 𐑄𐐩 𐐸𐐰𐐼 𐐼𐐨𐑂𐐵𐑉𐐼 𐑄𐐯𐑋 𐐫𐑊. 𐐤𐐵 𐐸𐐶𐐯𐑌 𐑄 𐐹𐐨𐐹𐑊 𐑅𐐫 𐑄𐐰𐐻 𐑄𐐩 𐑋𐐲𐑅𐐻 𐐹𐐯𐑉𐐮𐑇, 𐑄𐐩 𐐺𐐨𐑀𐐰𐑌 𐐻𐐭 𐑉𐐨𐐹𐐯𐑌𐐻 𐐱𐑂 𐑄𐐯𐑉 𐐮𐑌𐐮𐐿𐐶𐐮𐐻𐐨𐑆, 𐐰𐑌𐐼 𐐿𐑉𐐴 𐐲𐑌𐐻𐐭 𐑄 𐐢𐐫𐑉𐐼. 𐐈𐑌𐐼 𐐮𐐻 𐐿𐐩𐑋 𐐻𐐭 𐐹𐐰𐑅 𐑄𐐰𐐻 𐐸𐐶𐐯𐑌 𐑄𐐩 𐐸𐐰𐐼 𐐸𐐲𐑋𐐺𐑊𐐼 𐑄𐐯𐑋𐑅𐐯𐑊𐑂𐑆 𐑅𐐲𐑁𐐮𐑇𐐯𐑌𐐻𐑊𐐨 𐐺𐐨𐑁𐐬𐑉 𐑄 𐐢𐐫𐑉𐐼, 𐐸𐐨 𐐼𐐮𐐼 𐑅𐐯𐑌𐐼 𐑉𐐩𐑌 𐐲𐐹𐐪𐑌 𐑄 𐑁𐐩𐑅 𐐱𐑂 𐑄 𐐲𐑉𐑃; 𐐰𐑌𐐼 𐑄 𐐹𐐨𐐹𐑊 𐐺𐐨𐑀𐐰𐑌 𐐻𐐭 𐑉𐐨𐑂𐐴𐑂 𐐰𐑀𐐯𐑌, 𐐰𐑌𐐼 𐑄𐐯𐑉 𐐺𐐨𐑀𐐰𐑌 𐐻𐐭 𐐺𐐨 𐑁𐑉𐐭𐐻 𐐮𐑌 𐑄 𐑌𐐫𐑉𐑃 𐐿𐐲𐑌𐐻𐑉𐐨𐑆, 𐐰𐑌𐐼 𐐮𐑌 𐐫𐑊 𐑄 𐐿𐐲𐑌𐐻𐑉𐐨𐑆 𐑉𐐵𐑌𐐼 𐐰𐐺𐐵𐐻. 𐐈𐑌𐐼 𐑄 𐐢𐐫𐑉𐐼 𐐼𐐮𐐼 𐑇𐐬 𐑁𐐬𐑉𐑃 𐐸𐐮𐑆 𐐹𐐵𐐲𐑉 𐐲𐑌𐐻𐐭 𐑄𐐯𐑋 𐐮𐑌 𐐹𐑉𐐨𐑆𐐲𐑉𐑂𐐮𐑍 𐑄𐐯𐑋 𐑁𐑉𐐱𐑋 𐑁𐐰𐑋𐐮𐑌. 𐐈𐑌𐐼 𐐮𐐻 𐐿𐐩𐑋 𐐻𐐭 𐐹𐐰𐑅 𐑄𐐰𐐻 𐐟𐐯𐑆, 𐐸𐐭 𐐶𐐱𐑆 𐐩 𐐼𐐨𐑅𐐯𐑌𐐼𐐰𐑌𐐻 𐐱𐑂 𐐐𐐯𐑃, (𐑁𐐫𐑉 𐐐𐐯𐑃 𐐸𐐰𐐼 𐐹𐐯𐑉𐐮𐑇𐐻 𐐺𐐴 𐑄 𐑁𐐰𐑋𐐮𐑌, 𐐰𐑌𐐼 𐐫𐑊 𐐸𐐮𐑆 𐐸𐐵𐑅𐐸𐐬𐑊𐐼, 𐑅𐐩𐑂 𐐮𐐻 𐐶𐐲𐑉 𐐟𐐯𐑆;) 𐐸𐐶𐐯𐑉𐑁𐐬𐑉 𐐟𐐯𐑆 𐐺𐐨𐑀𐐰𐑌 𐐻𐐭 𐐺𐐮𐑊𐐼 𐐲𐐹 𐐰𐑀𐐯𐑌 𐐩 𐐺𐑉𐐬𐐿𐐲𐑌 𐐹𐐨𐐹𐑊. 𐐈𐑌𐐼 𐐮𐐻 𐐿𐐩𐑋 𐐻𐐭 𐐹𐐰𐑅 𐑄𐐰𐐻 𐐟𐐯𐑆 𐐼𐐮𐐼 𐑉𐐨𐑋𐐯𐑋𐐺𐐲𐑉 𐑄 𐐼𐐯𐑅𐐻𐑉𐐲𐐿𐑇𐐲𐑌 𐐱𐑂 𐐸𐐮𐑆 𐑁𐐪𐑄𐐲𐑉𐑆, 𐐰𐑌𐐼 𐐸𐐨 𐐼𐐮𐐼 𐐺𐐮𐑊𐐼 𐐲𐐹 𐐩 𐑉𐐴𐐽𐐲𐑅 𐐿𐐮𐑍𐐼𐐲𐑋; 𐑁𐐫𐑉 𐐸𐐨 𐑉𐐨𐑋𐐯𐑋𐐺𐐲𐑉𐐼 𐐸𐐶𐐱𐐻 𐑄 𐐢𐐫𐑉𐐼 𐐸𐐰𐐼 𐐼𐐲𐑌 𐐮𐑌 𐐺𐑉𐐮𐑍𐐮𐑍 𐐖𐐩𐑉𐐯𐐼 𐐰𐑌𐐼 𐐸𐐮𐑆 𐐺𐑉𐐲𐑄𐐲𐑉 𐐰𐐿𐑉𐐱𐑅 𐑄 𐐼𐐨𐐹; 𐐰𐑌𐐼 𐐸𐐨 𐐼𐐮𐐼 𐐶𐐫𐐿 𐐮𐑌 𐑄 𐐶𐐩𐑆 𐐱𐑂 𐑄 𐐢𐐫𐑉𐐼, 𐐰𐑌𐐼 𐐸𐐨 𐐺𐐨𐑀𐐰𐐻 𐑅𐐲𐑌𐑆 𐐰𐑌𐐼 𐐼𐐫𐐻𐐲𐑉𐑆. 𐐈𐑌𐐼 𐐸𐐮𐑆 𐐯𐑊𐐼𐐯𐑅𐐻 𐑅𐐲𐑌, 𐐸𐐭𐑆 𐑌𐐩𐑋 𐐶𐐱𐑆 𐐟𐐯𐑆, 𐐼𐐮𐐼 𐑉𐐨𐐺𐐯𐑊 𐐰𐑀𐐯𐑌𐑅𐐻 𐐸𐐮𐑋; 𐑌𐐯𐑂𐐲𐑉𐑄𐐯𐑊𐐯𐑅 𐐟𐐯𐑆 𐐶𐐱𐑆 𐑅𐑋𐐮𐐻𐑌 𐐺𐐴 𐑄 𐐸𐐰𐑌𐐼 𐐱𐑂 𐐩 𐑉𐐱𐐺𐐲𐑉, 𐐺𐐨𐐿𐐫𐑆 𐐱𐑂 𐐸𐐮𐑆 𐐯𐐿𐑅𐐨𐐼𐐮𐑍 𐑉𐐮𐐽𐐯𐑆, 𐐸𐐶𐐮𐐽 𐐺𐑉𐐫𐐻 𐐹𐐨𐑅 𐐰𐑀𐐯𐑌 𐐲𐑌𐐻𐐭 𐐸𐐮𐑆 𐑁𐐪𐑄𐐲𐑉. 𐐈𐑌𐐼 𐐮𐐻 𐐿𐐩𐑋 𐐻𐐭 𐐹𐐰𐑅 𐑄𐐰𐐻 𐐸𐐮𐑆 𐑁𐐪𐑄𐐲𐑉 𐐼𐐮𐐼 𐐺𐐮𐑊𐐼 𐐲𐐹 𐑋𐐯𐑌𐐨 𐑅𐐮𐐻𐐨𐑆 𐐲𐐹𐐪𐑌 𐑄 𐑁𐐩𐑅 𐐱𐑂 𐑄 𐑊𐐰𐑌𐐼, 𐐰𐑌𐐼 𐑄 𐐹𐐨𐐹𐑊 𐐺𐐨𐑀𐐰𐑌 𐐰𐑀𐐯𐑌 𐐻𐐭 𐑅𐐹𐑉𐐯𐐼 𐐬𐑂𐐲𐑉 𐐫𐑊 𐑄 𐑁𐐩𐑅 𐐱𐑂 𐑄 𐑊𐐰𐑌𐐼. 𐐈𐑌𐐼 𐐟𐐯𐑆 𐐼𐐮𐐼 𐑊𐐮𐑂 𐐻𐐭 𐐰𐑌 𐐯𐐿𐑅𐐨𐐼𐐮𐑍𐑊𐐨 𐐬𐑊𐐼 𐐩𐐾; 𐐰𐑌𐐼 𐐸𐐨 𐐺𐐨𐑀𐐰𐐻 𐐡𐐮𐐹𐑊𐐩𐐿𐐮𐑇, 𐐰𐑌𐐼 𐐸𐐨 𐐼𐐴𐐼. 𐐈𐑌𐐼 𐐡𐐮𐐹𐑊𐐩𐐿𐐮𐑇 𐑉𐐩𐑌𐐼 𐐮𐑌 𐐸𐐮𐑆 𐑅𐐻𐐯𐐼.

5. 𐐈𐑌𐐼 𐐮𐐻 𐐿𐐩𐑋 𐐻𐐭 𐐹𐐰𐑅 𐑄𐐰𐐻 𐐡𐐮𐐹𐑊𐐩𐐿𐐮𐑇 𐐼𐐮𐐼 𐑌𐐱𐐻 𐐼𐐭 𐑄𐐰𐐻 𐐸𐐶𐐮𐐽 𐐶𐐱𐑆 𐑉𐐴𐐻 𐐮𐑌 𐑄 𐑅𐐴𐐻 𐐱𐑂 𐑄 𐐢𐐫𐑉𐐼, 𐑁𐐫𐑉 𐐸𐐨 𐐼𐐮𐐼 𐐸𐐰𐑂 𐑋𐐯𐑌𐐨 𐐶𐐴𐑂𐑆 𐐰𐑌𐐼 𐐿𐐱𐑍𐐿𐐷𐐭𐐺𐐴𐑌𐑆, 𐐰𐑌𐐼 𐐼𐐮𐐼 𐑊𐐩 𐑄𐐰𐐻 𐐲𐐹𐐪𐑌 𐑋𐐯𐑌'𐑆 𐑇𐐬𐑊𐐼𐐲𐑉𐑆 𐐸𐐶𐐮𐐽 𐐶𐐱𐑆 𐑀𐑉𐐨𐑂𐐲𐑅 𐐻𐐭 𐐺𐐨 𐐺𐐬𐑉𐑌; 𐐷𐐩, 𐐸𐐨 𐐼𐐮𐐼 𐐻𐐰𐐿𐑅 𐑄𐐯𐑋 𐐶𐐮𐑃 𐐸𐐯𐑂𐐨 𐐻𐐰𐐿𐑅𐐯𐑆; 𐐰𐑌𐐼 𐐶𐐮𐑃 𐑄 𐐻𐐰𐐿𐑅𐐯𐑆 𐐸𐐨 𐐼𐐮𐐼 𐐺𐐮𐑊𐐼 𐑋𐐯𐑌𐐨 𐑅𐐹𐐩𐑇𐐲𐑅 𐐺𐐮𐑊𐐼𐐮𐑍𐑆. 𐐈𐑌𐐼 𐐸𐐨 𐐼𐐮𐐼 𐐨𐑉𐐯𐐿𐐻 𐐸𐐮𐑋 𐐰𐑌 𐐯𐐿𐑅𐐨𐐼𐐮𐑍𐑊𐐨 𐐺𐐷𐐭𐐻𐐨𐑁𐐳𐑊 𐑃𐑉𐐬𐑌; 𐐰𐑌𐐼 𐐸𐐨 𐐼𐐮𐐼 𐐺𐐮𐑊𐐼 𐑋𐐯𐑌𐐨 𐐹𐑉𐐮𐑆𐐲𐑌𐑆, 𐐰𐑌𐐼 𐐸𐐭𐑅𐐬 𐐶𐐳𐐼 𐑌𐐱𐐻 𐐺𐐨 𐑅𐐲𐐺𐐾𐐯𐐿𐐻 𐐲𐑌𐐻𐐭 𐐻𐐰𐐿𐑅𐐯𐑆, 𐐸𐐨 𐐼𐐮𐐼 𐐿𐐪𐑅𐐻 𐐮𐑌𐐻𐐭 𐐹𐑉𐐮𐑆𐐲𐑌; 𐐰𐑌𐐼 𐐸𐐭𐑅𐐬 𐐶𐐱𐑆 𐑌𐐱𐐻 𐐩𐐺𐑊 𐐻𐐭 𐐹𐐩 𐐻𐐰𐐿𐑅𐐯𐑆, 𐐸𐐨 𐐼𐐮𐐼 𐐿𐐪𐑅𐐻 𐐮𐑌𐐻𐐭 𐐹𐑉𐐮𐑆𐐲𐑌; 𐐰𐑌𐐼 𐐸𐐨 𐐼𐐮𐐼 𐐿𐐫𐑆 𐑄𐐰𐐻 𐑄𐐩 𐑇𐐳𐐼 𐑊𐐩𐐺𐐲𐑉

𐐿𐐲𐑌𐐻𐐮𐑌𐐷𐐭𐐲𐑊𐐨 𐑁𐐫𐑉 𐑄𐐯𐑉 𐑅𐐲𐐹𐐬𐑉𐐻; 𐐰𐑌𐐼 𐐸𐐭𐑅𐐬 𐑉𐐨𐑁𐐷𐐭𐑆𐐼 𐐻𐐭 𐑊𐐩𐐺𐐲𐑉, 𐐸𐐨 𐐼𐐮𐐼 𐐿𐐫𐑆 𐐻𐐭 𐐺 𐐹𐐳𐐻 𐐻𐐭 𐐼𐐯𐑃; 𐐸𐐶𐐯𐑉𐑁𐐫𐑉 𐐸𐐨 𐐼𐐮𐐼 𐐱𐐺𐐻𐐩𐑌 𐐫𐑊 𐐸𐐮𐑆 𐑁𐐴𐑌 𐐶𐐲𐑉𐐿; 𐐷𐐩, 𐐨𐑂𐐲𐑌 𐐸𐐮𐑆 𐑁𐐴𐑌 𐑀𐐬𐑊𐐼 𐐸𐐨 𐐼𐐮𐐼 𐐿𐐫𐑆 𐐻𐐭 𐐺 𐑉𐐨𐑁𐐴𐑌𐐼 𐐮𐑌 𐐹𐑉𐐮𐑆𐐲𐑌; 𐐰𐑌𐐼 𐐫𐑊 𐑋𐐰𐑌𐐲𐑉 𐐱𐑂 𐑁𐐴𐑌 𐐶𐐲𐑉𐐿𐑋𐐰𐑌𐑇𐐮𐐹 𐐸𐐨 𐐼𐐮𐐼 𐐿𐐫𐑆 𐐻𐐭 𐐺 𐑉𐐫𐐻 𐐮𐑌 𐐹𐑉𐐮𐑆𐐲𐑌. 𐐈𐑌𐐼 𐐮𐐻 𐐿𐐩𐑋 𐐻𐐭 𐐹𐐰𐑅 𐑄𐐰𐐻 𐐸𐐨 𐐼𐐮𐐼 𐐰𐑁𐑊𐐮𐐿𐐻 𐑄 𐐹𐐨𐐹𐑊 𐐶𐐮𐑄 𐐸𐐮𐑆 𐐸𐐬𐑉𐐼𐐲𐑋𐑆 𐐰𐑌𐐼 𐐰𐐺𐐱𐑋𐐮𐑌𐐩𐑇𐐲𐑌𐑆; 𐐰𐑌𐐼 𐐸𐐶𐐯𐑌 𐐸𐐨 𐐸𐐰𐐼 𐑉𐐩𐑌𐐼 𐑁𐐫𐑉 𐑄 𐑅𐐹𐐩𐑅 𐐱𐑂 𐑁𐐫𐑉𐐻𐐨 𐐰𐑌𐐼 𐐻𐐭 𐐷𐐨𐑉𐑆, 𐑄 𐐹𐐨𐐹𐑊 𐐼𐐮𐐼 𐑉𐐴𐑆 𐐲𐐹 𐐮𐑌 𐑉𐐨𐐺𐐯𐑊𐐷𐐲𐑌 𐐰𐑀𐐯𐑌𐑅𐐻 𐐸𐐮𐑋, 𐐰𐑌𐐼 𐑄𐐯𐑉 𐐺𐐨𐑀𐐰𐑌 𐐻𐐭 𐐺 𐐶𐐫𐑉 𐐰𐑀𐐯𐑌 𐐮𐑌 𐑄 𐑊𐐰𐑌𐐼, 𐐮𐑌𐑅𐐬𐑋𐐲𐐽 𐑄𐐰𐐻 𐐡𐐮𐐹𐑊𐐰𐐿𐐮𐑇 𐐶𐐱𐑆 𐐿𐐮𐑊𐐼, 𐐰𐑌𐐼 𐐸𐐮𐑆 𐐼𐐨𐑅𐐯𐑌𐐼𐐰𐑌𐐻𐑅 𐐶𐐲𐑉 𐐼𐑉𐐮𐑂𐐲𐑌 𐐵𐐻 𐐱𐑂 𐑄 𐑊𐐰𐑌𐐼.

6. 𐐈𐑌𐐼 𐐮𐐻 𐐿𐐩𐑋 𐐻𐐭 𐐹𐐰𐑅 𐐰𐑁𐐻𐐲𐑉 𐑄 𐑅𐐹𐐩𐑅 𐐱𐑂 𐑋𐐯𐑌𐐨 𐐷𐐨𐑉𐑆, 𐐣𐐬𐑉𐐴𐐰𐑌𐐻𐐲𐑌, (𐐸𐐨 𐐺𐐨𐐮𐑍 𐐲 𐐼𐐨𐑅𐐯𐑌𐐼𐐰𐑌𐐻 𐐱𐑂 𐐡𐐮𐐹𐑊𐐰𐐿𐐮𐑇,) 𐑀𐐰𐑄𐐲𐑉𐐼 𐐻𐐭𐑀𐐯𐑄𐐲𐑉 𐐰𐑌 𐐪𐑉𐑋𐐨 𐐱𐑂 𐐵𐐻𐐿𐐰𐑅𐐻𐑅, 𐐰𐑌𐐼 𐐶𐐯𐑌𐐻 𐑁𐐬𐑉𐑃 𐐰𐑌𐐼 𐑀𐐩𐑂 𐐺𐐰𐐻𐑊 𐐲𐑌𐐻𐐭 𐑄 𐐹𐐨𐐹𐑊; 𐐰𐑌𐐼 𐐸𐐨 𐑀𐐩𐑌𐐼 𐐹𐐵𐐲𐑉 𐐬𐑂𐐲𐑉 𐑋𐐯𐑌𐐨 𐑅𐐮𐐻𐐨𐑆; 𐐰𐑌𐐼 𐑄 𐐶𐐫𐑉 𐐺𐐨𐐿𐐩𐑋 𐐯𐐿𐑅𐐨𐐼𐐮𐑍𐑊𐐨 𐑅𐐬𐑉, 𐐰𐑌𐐼 𐐼𐐮𐐼 𐑊𐐪𐑅𐐻 𐑁𐐫𐑉 𐑄 𐑅𐐹𐐩𐑅 𐐱𐑂 𐑋𐐯𐑌𐐨 𐐷𐐨𐑉𐑆, 𐐰𐑌𐐼 𐐸𐐨 𐐼𐐮𐐼 𐑀𐐩𐑌 𐐹𐐵𐐲𐑉 𐐬𐑂𐐲𐑉 𐐫𐑊 𐑄 𐑊𐐰𐑌𐐼. 𐐈𐑌𐐼 𐐼𐐮𐐼 𐐯𐑅𐐻𐐰𐐺𐑊𐐮𐑇 𐐸𐐮𐑋𐑅𐐯𐑊𐑁 𐐿𐐮𐑍 𐐬𐑂𐐲𐑉 𐐫𐑊 𐑄 𐑊𐐰𐑌𐐼. 𐐈𐑌𐐼 𐐰𐑁𐐻𐐲𐑉 𐑄𐐰𐐻 𐐸𐐨 𐐸𐐰𐐼 𐐯𐑅𐐻𐐰𐐺𐑊𐐮𐑇𐐻 𐐸𐐮𐑋𐑅𐐯𐑊𐑁 𐐿𐐮𐑍, 𐐸𐐨 𐐼𐐮𐐼 𐐨𐑆 𐑄 𐐺𐐲𐑉𐐼𐐲𐑌 𐐱𐑂 𐑄 𐐹𐐨𐐹𐑊, 𐐺𐐴 𐐸𐐶𐐮𐐽 𐐸𐐨 𐐼𐐮𐐼 𐑀𐐩𐑌 𐑁𐐩𐑂𐐲𐑉 𐐮𐑌 𐑄 𐐴𐑆 𐐱𐑂 𐑄 𐐹𐐨𐐹𐑊, 𐐰𐑌𐐼 𐑄𐐩 𐐼𐐮𐐼 𐐲𐑌𐐱𐐮𐑌𐐻 𐐸𐐮𐑋 𐐻𐐭 𐐺 𐑄𐐯𐑉 𐐿𐐮𐑍. 𐐈𐑌𐐼 𐐸𐐨 𐐼𐐮𐐼 𐐼𐐭 𐐾𐐲𐑅𐐻𐐮𐑅 𐐲𐑌𐐻𐐭 𐑄 𐐹𐐨𐐹𐑊, 𐐺𐐲𐐻 𐑌𐐱𐐻 𐐲𐑌𐐻𐐭 𐐸𐐮𐑋𐑅𐐯𐑊𐑁, 𐐺𐐨𐐿𐐫𐑆 𐐱𐑂 𐐸𐐮𐑆 𐑋𐐯𐑌𐐨 𐐸𐐬𐑉𐐼𐐲𐑋𐑆; 𐐸𐐶𐐯𐑉𐑁𐐫𐑉 𐐸𐐨 𐐶𐐱𐑆 𐐿𐐲𐐻 𐐫𐑁 𐑁𐑉𐐱𐑋 𐑄 𐐹𐑉𐐯𐑆𐐯𐑌𐑅 𐐱𐑂 𐑄 𐐢𐐫𐑉𐐼. 𐐈𐑌𐐼 𐐮𐐻 𐐿𐐩𐑋 𐐻𐐭 𐐹𐐰𐑅 𐑄𐐰𐐻 𐐣𐐬𐑉𐐴𐐰𐑌𐐻𐐲𐑌 𐐺𐐮𐑊𐐻 𐐲𐐹 𐑋𐐯𐑌𐐨 𐑅𐐮𐐻𐐨𐑆, 𐐰𐑌𐐼 𐑄 𐐹𐐨𐐹𐑊 𐐺𐐨𐐿𐐩𐑋 𐐯𐐿𐑅𐐨𐐼𐐮𐑍𐑊𐐨 𐑉𐐮𐐽 𐐲𐑌𐐼𐐲𐑉 𐐸𐐮𐑆 𐑉𐐩𐑌, 𐐺𐐬𐑃 𐐮𐑌 𐐺𐐮𐑊𐐼𐐮𐑍𐑆, 𐐰𐑌𐐼 𐐮𐑌 𐑀𐐬𐑊𐐼 𐐰𐑌𐐼 𐑅𐐮𐑊𐑂𐐲𐑉, 𐐰𐑌𐐼 𐐮𐑌 𐑉𐐩𐑆𐐮𐑍 𐑀𐑉𐐩𐑌, 𐐰𐑌𐐼 𐐮𐑌 𐑁𐑊𐐱𐐿𐑅, 𐐰𐑌𐐼 𐐸𐐲𐑉𐐼𐑆, 𐐰𐑌𐐼 𐑅𐐲𐐽 𐑃𐐮𐑍𐑆 𐐸𐐶𐐮𐐽 𐐸𐐰𐐼 𐐺𐐮𐑌 𐑉𐐨𐑅𐐻𐐬𐑉𐐼 𐐲𐑌𐐻𐐭 𐑄𐐯𐑋. 𐐈𐑌𐐼 𐐣𐐬𐑉𐐴𐐰𐑌𐐻𐐲𐑌 𐐼𐐮𐐼 𐑊𐐮𐑂 𐐻𐐭 𐐰𐑌 𐐯𐐿𐑅𐐨𐐼𐐮𐑍𐑊𐐨 𐑀𐑉𐐩𐐻 𐐩𐐾, 𐐰𐑌𐐼 𐑄𐐯𐑌 𐐸𐐨 𐐺𐐨𐑀𐐰𐐻 𐐗𐐮𐑋; 𐐰𐑌𐐼 𐐗𐐮𐑋 𐐼𐐮𐐼 𐑉𐐩𐑌 𐐮𐑌 𐑄 𐑅𐐻𐐯𐐼 𐐱𐑂 𐐸𐐮𐑆 𐑁𐐪𐑄𐐲𐑉; 𐐰𐑌𐐼 𐐸𐐨 𐐼𐐮𐐼 𐑉𐐩𐑌 𐐩𐐻 𐐷𐐨𐑉𐑆, 𐐰𐑌𐐼 𐐸𐐮𐑆 𐑁𐐪𐑄𐐲𐑉 𐐼𐐴𐐼. 𐐈𐑌𐐼 𐐮𐐻 𐐿𐐩𐑋 𐐻𐐭 𐐹𐐰𐑅 𐑄𐐰𐐻 𐐗𐐮𐑋 𐐼𐐮𐐼 𐑌𐐱𐐻 𐑉𐐩𐑌 𐐮𐑌 𐑉𐐴𐐽𐐲𐑅𐑌𐐯𐑅, 𐐸𐐶𐐯𐑉𐑁𐐫𐑉 𐐸𐐨 𐐶𐐱𐑆 𐑌𐐱𐐻 𐑁𐐩𐑂𐐲𐑉𐐼 𐐱𐑂 𐑄 𐐢𐐫𐑉𐐼. 𐐈𐑌𐐼 𐐸𐐮𐑆 𐐺𐑉𐐲𐑄𐐲𐑉 𐐼𐐮𐐼 𐑉𐐴𐑆 𐐲𐐹 𐐮𐑌 𐑉𐐨𐐺𐐯𐑊𐐷𐐲𐑌 𐐰𐑀𐐯𐑌𐑅𐐻 𐐸𐐮𐑋, 𐐺𐐴 𐐸𐐶𐐮𐐽 𐐸𐐨 𐐼𐐮𐐼 𐐺𐑉𐐮𐑍 𐐸𐐮𐑋 𐐮𐑌𐐻𐐭 𐐿𐐰𐐹𐐻𐐮𐑂𐐮𐐻𐐨; 𐐰𐑌𐐼 𐐸𐐨 𐐼𐐮𐐼 𐑉𐐨𐑋𐐩𐑌 𐐮𐑌 𐐿𐐰𐐹𐐻𐐮𐑂𐐮𐐻𐐨 𐐫𐑊 𐐸𐐮𐑆 𐐼𐐩𐑆; 𐐰𐑌𐐼 𐐸𐐨 𐐺𐐨𐑀𐐰𐐻 𐑅𐐲𐑌𐑆 𐐰𐑌𐐼 𐐼𐐫𐐻𐐲𐑉𐑆 𐐮𐑌 𐐿𐐰𐐹𐐻𐐮𐑂𐐮𐐻𐐨; 𐐰𐑌𐐼 𐐮𐑌 𐐸𐐮𐑆 𐐬𐑊𐐼 𐐩𐐾 𐐸𐐨 𐐺𐐨𐑀𐐰𐐻 𐐢𐐨𐑂𐐴; 𐐰𐑌𐐼 𐐸𐐨 𐐼𐐴𐐼.

7. 𐐈𐑌𐐼 𐐮𐐻 𐐿𐐩𐑋 𐐻𐐭 𐐹𐐰𐑅 𐑄𐐰𐐻 𐐢𐐨𐑂𐐴 𐐼𐐮𐐼 𐑅𐐲𐑉𐑂 𐐮𐑌 𐐿𐐰𐐹𐐻𐐮𐑂𐐮𐐻𐐨 𐐰𐑁𐐻𐐲𐑉 𐑄 𐐼𐐯𐑃 𐐱𐑂 𐐸𐐮𐑆 𐑁𐐪𐑄𐐲𐑉, 𐑁𐐫𐑉 𐑄 𐑅𐐹𐐩𐑅 𐐱𐑂 𐑁𐐫𐑉𐐻𐐨 𐐰𐑌𐐼 𐐻𐐭 𐐷𐐨𐑉𐑆. 𐐈𐑌𐐼 𐐸𐐨 𐐼𐐮𐐼 𐑋𐐩𐐿 𐐶𐐫𐑉 𐐰𐑀𐐯𐑌𐑅𐐻 𐑄 𐐿𐐮𐑍 𐐱𐑂 𐑄 𐑊𐐰𐑌𐐼, 𐐺𐐴 𐐸𐐶𐐮𐐽 𐐸𐐨 𐐼𐐮𐐼 𐐱𐐺𐐻𐐩𐑌 𐐲𐑌𐐻𐐭 𐐸𐐮𐑋𐑅𐐯𐑊𐑁 𐑄 𐐿𐐮𐑍𐐼𐐲𐑋. 𐐈𐑌𐐼 𐐰𐑁𐐻𐐲𐑉 𐐸𐐨 𐐸𐐰𐐼 𐐱𐐺𐐻𐐩𐑌𐐼 𐐲𐑌𐐻𐐭 𐐸𐐮𐑋𐑅𐐯𐑊𐑁 𐑄 𐐿𐐮𐑍𐐼𐐲𐑋, 𐐸𐐨 𐐼𐐮𐐼 𐑄𐐰𐐻 𐐸𐐶𐐮𐐽 𐐶𐐱𐑆 𐑉𐐴𐐻 𐐮𐑌 𐑄 𐑅𐐴𐐻 𐐱𐑂 𐑄 𐐢𐐫𐑉𐐼; 𐐰𐑌𐐼 𐑄 𐐹𐐨𐐹𐑊 𐐼𐐮𐐼 𐐹𐑉𐐱𐑅𐐹𐐲𐑉 𐐮𐑌 𐑄 𐑊𐐰𐑌𐐼; 𐐰𐑌𐐼 𐐸𐐨 𐐼𐐮𐐼 𐑊𐐮𐑂 𐐻𐐭 𐐲 𐑀𐐳𐐼 𐐬𐑊𐐼 𐐩𐐾, 𐐰𐑌𐐼 𐐺𐐨𐑀𐐰𐐻 𐑅𐐲𐑌𐑆 𐐰𐑌𐐼 𐐼𐐫𐐻𐐲𐑉𐑆; 𐐰𐑌𐐼 𐐸𐐨 𐐫𐑊𐑅𐐬 𐐺𐐨𐑀𐐰𐐻 𐐗𐐬𐑉𐐲𐑋, 𐐸𐐭𐑋 𐐸𐐨 𐐲𐑌𐐱𐐮𐑌𐐻𐐲𐐼 𐐿𐐮𐑍 𐐮𐑌 𐐸𐐮𐑆 𐑅𐐻𐐯𐐼. 𐐈𐑌𐐼 𐐮𐐻 𐐿𐐩𐑋 𐐻𐐭 𐐹𐐰𐑅 𐑄𐐰𐐻 𐐗𐐬𐑉𐐲𐑋 𐐼𐐮𐐼 𐑄𐐰𐐻 𐐸𐐶𐐮𐐽 𐐶𐐱𐑆 𐑀𐐳𐐼 𐐮𐑌 𐑄 𐑅𐐴𐐻 𐐱𐑂 𐑄 𐐢𐐫𐑉𐐼, 𐐫𐑊 𐐸𐐮𐑆 𐐼𐐩𐑆; 𐐰𐑌𐐼 𐐸𐐨 𐐺𐐨𐑀𐐰𐐻 𐑋𐐯𐑌𐐨 𐑅𐐲𐑌𐑆 𐐰𐑌𐐼 𐐼𐐫𐐻𐐲𐑉𐑆; 𐐰𐑌𐐼 𐐰𐑁𐐻𐐲𐑉 𐐸𐐨 𐐸𐐰𐐼 𐑅𐐨𐑌 𐑋𐐯𐑌𐐨 𐐼𐐩𐑆, 𐐸𐐨 𐐼𐐮𐐼 𐐹𐐰𐑅 𐐲𐐶𐐩, 𐐨𐑂𐐲𐑌 𐑊𐐴𐐿 𐐲𐑌𐐻𐐭 𐑄 𐑉𐐯𐑅𐐻 𐐱𐑂 𐑄 𐐲𐑉𐑃; 𐐰𐑌𐐼 𐐗𐐮𐑇 𐑉𐐩𐑌𐐼 𐐮𐑌 𐐸𐐮𐑆 𐑅𐐻𐐯𐐼. 𐐈𐑌𐐼 𐐮𐐻 𐐿𐐩𐑋 𐐻𐐭 𐐹𐐰𐑅 𐑄𐐰𐐻 𐐗𐐮𐑇 𐐹𐐰𐑅𐐻 𐐲𐐶𐐩 𐐫𐑊𐑅𐐬, 𐐰𐑌𐐼 𐐢𐐮𐐺 𐑉𐐩𐑌𐐼 𐐮𐑌 𐐸𐐮𐑆 𐑅𐐻𐐯𐐼. 𐐈𐑌𐐼 𐐮𐐻 𐐿𐐩𐑋 𐐻𐐭 𐐹𐐰𐑅 𐑄𐐰𐐻 𐐢𐐮𐐺 𐐫𐑊𐑅𐐬 𐐼𐐮𐐼 𐑄𐐰𐐻 𐐸𐐶𐐮𐐽 𐐶𐐱𐑆 𐑀𐐳𐐼 𐐮𐑌 𐑄 𐑅𐐴𐐻 𐐱𐑂 𐑄 𐐢𐐫𐑉𐐼. 𐐈𐑌𐐼 𐐮𐑌 𐑄 𐐼𐐩𐑆 𐐱𐑂 𐐢𐐮𐐺 𐑄 𐐹𐐱𐐮𐑆𐐲𐑌𐐲𐑅 𐑅𐐲𐑉𐐹𐐲𐑌𐐻𐑅 𐐶𐐲𐑉 𐐼𐐯𐑅𐐻𐑉𐐱𐐮𐐼; 𐐸𐐶𐐯𐑉𐑁𐐫𐑉 𐑄𐐩 𐐼𐐮𐐼 𐑀𐐬 𐐮𐑌𐐻𐐭 𐑄 𐑊𐐰𐑌𐐼 𐑅𐐵𐑃𐐶𐐲𐑉𐐼, 𐐻𐐭 𐐸𐐲𐑌𐐻 𐑁𐐭𐐼 𐑁𐐫𐑉 𐑄 𐐹𐐨𐐹𐑊 𐐱𐑂 𐑄 𐑊𐐰𐑌𐐼, 𐑁𐐫𐑉 𐑄 𐑊𐐰𐑌𐐼 𐐶𐐱𐑆 𐐿𐐲𐑂𐐲𐑉𐐼 𐐶𐐮𐑄 𐐰𐑌𐐮𐑋𐐲𐑊𐑆 𐐱𐑂 𐑄 𐑁𐐱𐑉𐐯𐑅𐐻. 𐐈𐑌𐐼 𐐢𐐮𐐺 𐐫𐑊𐑅𐐬 𐐸𐐮𐑋𐑅𐐯𐑊𐑁 𐐺𐐨𐐿𐐩𐑋 𐐲 𐑀𐑉𐐩𐐻 𐐸𐐲𐑌𐐻𐐲𐑉. 𐐈𐑌𐐼 𐑄𐐩 𐐺𐐮𐑊𐐻 𐐲 𐑀𐑉𐐩𐐻 𐑅𐐮𐐻𐐨 𐐺𐐴 𐑄 𐑌𐐰𐑉𐐬 𐑌𐐯𐐿 𐐱𐑂 𐑊𐐰𐑌𐐼, 𐐺𐐴 𐑄 𐐹𐑊𐐩𐑅 𐐸𐐶𐐯𐑉 𐑄 𐑅𐐨 𐐼𐐨𐑂𐐴𐐼𐑆 𐑄 𐑊𐐰𐑌𐐼.

𐐰𐑌𐐼 𐑄𐐩 𐐼𐐮𐐼 𐐹𐑉𐐨𐑆𐐲𐑉𐑂 𐑄 𐑊𐐰𐑌𐐼 𐑅𐐵𐑃𐐶𐐲𐑉𐐼 𐑁𐐫𐑉 𐐲 𐐶𐐮𐑊𐐼𐐲𐑉𐑌𐐯𐑅, 𐐻𐐭 𐑀𐐯𐐻 𐑀𐐩𐑋. 𐐈𐑌𐐼 𐑄 𐐸𐐬𐑊 𐑁𐐩𐑅 𐐱𐑂 𐑄 𐑊𐐰𐑌𐐼 𐑌𐐫𐑉𐑃𐐶𐐲𐑉𐐼 𐐶𐐱𐑆 𐐿𐐲𐑂𐐲𐑉𐐼 𐐶𐐮𐑄 𐐮𐑌𐐸𐐰𐐺𐐮𐐻𐐲𐑌𐐻𐑅; 𐐰𐑌𐐼 𐑄𐐩 𐐶𐐲𐑉 𐐯𐐿𐑅𐐨𐐼𐐮𐑍𐑊𐐨 𐐮𐑌𐐼𐐲𐑅𐐻𐑉𐐨𐐲𐑅, 𐐰𐑌𐐼 𐑄𐐩 𐐼𐐮𐐼 𐐺𐐴 𐐰𐑌𐐼 𐑅𐐯𐑊, 𐐰𐑌𐐼 𐐻𐑉𐐰𐑁𐐮𐐿 𐐶𐐲𐑌 𐐶𐐮𐑄 𐐰𐑌𐐲𐑄𐐲𐑉, 𐑄𐐰𐐻 𐑄𐐩 𐑋𐐴𐐻 𐑀𐐯𐐻 𐑀𐐩𐑌. 𐐈𐑌𐐼 𐑄𐐩 𐐼𐐮𐐼 𐐶𐐲𐑉𐐿 𐐮𐑌 𐐫𐑊 𐑋𐐰𐑌𐐲𐑉 𐐱𐑂 𐐬𐑉, 𐐰𐑌𐐼 𐑄𐐩 𐐼𐐮𐐼 𐑋𐐩𐐿 𐑀𐐬𐑊𐐼, 𐐰𐑌𐐼 𐑅𐐮𐑊𐑂𐐲𐑉, 𐐰𐑌𐐼 𐐴𐐲𐑉𐑌, 𐐰𐑌𐐼 𐐺𐑉𐐰𐑅, 𐐰𐑌𐐼 𐐫𐑊 𐑋𐐰𐑌𐐲𐑉 𐐱𐑂 𐑋𐐯𐐻𐐲𐑊𐑆; 𐐰𐑌𐐼 𐑄𐐩 𐐼𐐮𐐼 𐐼𐐮𐑀 𐐮𐐻 𐐵𐐻 𐐱𐑂 𐑄 𐐲𐑉𐑃; 𐐸𐐶𐐯𐑉𐑁𐐬𐑉 𐑄𐐩 𐐼𐐮𐐼 𐐿𐐰𐑅𐐻 𐐲𐐹 𐑋𐐴𐐻𐐨 𐐸𐐨𐐹𐑅 𐐱𐑂 𐐲𐑉𐑃 𐐻𐐭 𐑀𐐯𐐻 𐐬𐑉, 𐐱𐑂 𐑀𐐬𐑊𐐼, 𐐰𐑌𐐼 𐐱𐑂 𐑅𐐮𐑊𐑂𐐲𐑉, 𐐰𐑌𐐼 𐐱𐑂 𐐴𐐲𐑉𐑌, 𐐰𐑌𐐼 𐐱𐑂 𐐿𐐱𐐹𐐲𐑉. 𐐈𐑌𐐼 𐑄𐐩 𐐼𐐮𐐼 𐐶𐐲𐑉𐐿 𐐫𐑊 𐑋𐐰𐑌𐐲𐑉 𐐱𐑂 𐑁𐐴𐑌 𐐶𐐲𐑉𐐿. 𐐈𐑌𐐼 𐑄𐐩 𐐼𐐮𐐼 𐐸𐐰𐑂 𐑅𐐮𐑊𐐿𐑅, 𐐰𐑌𐐼 𐑁𐐴𐑌 𐐻𐐶𐐴𐑌𐐼 𐑊𐐮𐑌𐐯𐑌; 𐐰𐑌𐐼 𐑄𐐩 𐐼𐐮𐐼 𐐶𐐲𐑉𐐿 𐐫𐑊 𐑋𐐰𐑌𐐲𐑉 𐐱𐑂 𐐿𐑊𐐫𐑃, 𐑄𐐰𐐻 𐑄𐐩 𐑋𐐴𐐻 𐐿𐑊𐐬𐑄 𐑄𐐯𐑋𐑅𐐯𐑊𐑂𐑆 𐑁𐑉𐐱𐑋 𐑄𐐩𐑉 𐑌𐐩𐐿𐐯𐐼𐑌𐐯𐑅. 𐐈𐑌𐐼 𐑄𐐩 𐐼𐐮𐐼 𐑋𐐩𐐿 𐐫𐑊 𐑋𐐰𐑌𐐲𐑉 𐐱𐑂 𐐻𐐭𐑊𐑆 𐐻𐐭 𐐻𐐮𐑊 𐑄 𐐲𐑉𐑃, 𐐺𐐬𐑃 𐐻𐐭 𐐹𐑊𐐵 𐐰𐑌𐐼 𐐻𐐭 𐑅𐐬, 𐐻𐐭 𐑉𐐨𐐹 𐐰𐑌𐐼 𐐻𐐭 𐐸𐐬, 𐐰𐑌𐐼 𐐫𐑊𐑅𐐬 𐐻𐐭 𐑃𐑉𐐰𐑇. 𐐈𐑌𐐼 𐑄𐐩 𐐼𐐮𐐼 𐑋𐐩𐐿 𐐫𐑊 𐑋𐐰𐑌𐐲𐑉 𐐱𐑂 𐐻𐐭𐑊𐑆 𐐶𐐮𐑄 𐐸𐐶𐐮𐐽 𐑄𐐩 𐐼𐐮𐐼 𐐶𐐲𐑉𐐿 𐑄𐐩𐑉 𐐺𐐨𐑅𐐻𐑅. 𐐈𐑌𐐼 𐑄𐐩 𐐼𐐮𐐼 𐑋𐐩𐐿 𐐫𐑊 𐑋𐐰𐑌𐐲𐑉 𐐱𐑂 𐐶𐐯𐐹𐐲𐑌𐑆 𐐱𐑂 𐐶𐐫𐑉. 𐐈𐑌𐐼 𐑄𐐩 𐐼𐐮𐐼 𐐶𐐲𐑉𐐿 𐐫𐑊 𐑋𐐰𐑌𐐲𐑉 𐐱𐑂 𐐶𐐲𐑉𐐿 𐐱𐑂 𐐯𐐿𐑅𐐨𐐼𐐮𐑍𐑊𐐨 𐐿𐐷𐐭𐑉𐐨𐐲𐑅 𐐶𐐲𐑉𐐿𐑋𐐰𐑌𐑇𐐮𐐹. 𐐈𐑌𐐼 𐑌𐐯𐑂𐐲𐑉 𐐿𐐳𐐼 𐐺𐐨 𐐲 𐐹𐐨𐐹𐑊 𐑋𐐬𐑉 𐐺𐑊𐐯𐑅𐐯𐐼 𐑄𐐰𐑌 𐐶𐐲𐑉 𐑄𐐩, 𐐰𐑌𐐼 𐑋𐐬𐑉 𐐹𐑉𐐱𐑅𐐹𐐲𐑉𐐼 𐐺𐐴 𐑄 𐐸𐐰𐑌𐐼 𐐱𐑂 𐑄 𐐢𐐫𐑉𐐼. 𐐈𐑌𐐼 𐑄𐐩 𐐶𐐲𐑉 𐐮𐑌 𐐲 𐑊𐐰𐑌𐐼 𐑄𐐰𐐻 𐐶𐐱𐑆 𐐽𐑎𐑅 𐐲𐐺𐐲𐑂 𐐫𐑊 𐑊𐐰𐑌𐐼𐑆, 𐑁𐐫𐑉 𐑄 𐐢𐐫𐑉𐐼 𐐸𐐰𐐼 𐑅𐐹𐐬𐐿𐐲𐑌 𐐮𐐻. 𐐈𐑌𐐼 𐐮𐐻 𐐿𐐩𐑋 𐐻𐐭 𐐹𐐰𐑅 𐑄𐐰𐐻 𐐢𐐮𐐺 𐐼𐐮𐐼 𐑊𐐮𐑂 𐑋𐐯𐑌𐐨 𐐷𐐨𐑉𐑆, 𐐰𐑌𐐼 𐐺𐐨𐑀𐐰𐐻 𐑅𐐲𐑌𐑆 𐐰𐑌𐐼 𐐼𐐫𐐻𐐲𐑉𐑆; 𐐰𐑌𐐼 𐐸𐐨 𐐫𐑊𐑅𐐬 𐐺𐐨𐑀𐐰𐐻 𐐐𐐨𐐲𐑉𐑃𐐲𐑋. 𐐈𐑌𐐼 𐐮𐐻 𐐿𐐩𐑋 𐐻𐐭 𐐹𐐰𐑅 𐑄𐐰𐐻 𐐐𐐨𐐲𐑉𐑃𐐲𐑋 𐑉𐐩𐑌𐐼 𐐮𐑌 𐑄 𐑅𐐻𐐯𐐼 𐐱𐑂 𐐸𐐮𐑆 𐑁𐐪𐑄𐐲𐑉. 𐐈𐑌𐐼 𐐸𐐶𐐯𐑌 𐐐𐐨𐐲𐑉𐑃𐐲𐑋 𐐸𐐰𐐼 𐑉𐐩𐑌𐐼 𐐻𐐶𐐯𐑌𐐻𐐨 𐐰𐑌𐐼 𐑁𐐬𐑉 𐐷𐐨𐑉𐑆, 𐐺𐐨𐐸𐐬𐑊𐐼, 𐑄 𐐿𐐮𐑍𐐼𐐲𐑋 𐐶𐐱𐑆 𐐻𐐩𐐿𐐲𐑌 𐐲𐐶𐐩 𐑁𐑉𐐱𐑋 𐐸𐐮𐑋. 𐐈𐑌𐐼 𐐸𐐨 𐑅𐐲𐑉𐑂𐐼 𐑋𐐯𐑌𐐨 𐐷𐐨𐑉𐑆 𐐮𐑌 𐐿𐐰𐐹𐐻𐐮𐑂𐐮𐐻𐐨; 𐐷𐐩, 𐐨𐑂𐐲𐑌 𐐫𐑊 𐑄 𐑉𐐨𐑋𐐩𐑌𐐼𐐲𐑉 𐐱𐑂 𐐸𐐮𐑆 𐐼𐐩𐑆. 𐐈𐑌𐐼 𐐸𐐨 𐐺𐐨𐑀𐐰𐐻 𐐐𐐯𐑃, 𐐰𐑌𐐼 𐐐𐐯𐑃 𐑊𐐮𐑂𐐼 𐐮𐑌 𐐿𐐰𐐹𐐻𐐮𐑂𐐮𐐻𐐨 𐐫𐑊 𐐸𐐮𐑆 𐐼𐐩𐑆. 𐐈𐑌𐐼 𐐐𐐯𐑃 𐐺𐐨𐑀𐐰𐐻 𐐁𐑉𐐲𐑌, 𐐰𐑌𐐼 𐐁𐑉𐐲𐑌 𐐼𐐶𐐯𐑊𐐻 𐐮𐑌 𐐿𐐰𐐹𐐻𐐮𐑂𐐮𐐻𐐨 𐐫𐑊 𐐸𐐮𐑆 𐐼𐐩𐑆; 𐐰𐑌𐐼 𐐸𐐨 𐐺𐐨𐑀𐐰𐐻 𐐈𐑋𐑌𐐮𐑀𐐰𐐼𐐪, 𐐰𐑌𐐼 𐐈𐑋𐑌𐐮𐑀𐐰𐐼𐐪 𐐫𐑊𐑅𐐬 𐐼𐐶𐐯𐑊𐐻 𐐮𐑌 𐐿𐐰𐐹𐐻𐐮𐑂𐐮𐐻𐐨 𐐫𐑊 𐐸𐐮𐑆 𐐼𐐩𐑆; 𐐰𐑌𐐼 𐐸𐐨 𐐺𐐨𐑀𐐰𐐻 𐐗𐐬𐑉𐐨𐐰𐑌𐐻𐐲𐑋, 𐐰𐑌𐐼 𐐗𐐬𐑉𐐨𐐰𐑌𐐻𐐲𐑋 𐐼𐐶𐐯𐑊𐐻 𐐮𐑌 𐐿𐐰𐐹𐐻𐐮𐑂𐐮𐐻𐐨 𐐫𐑊 𐐸𐐮𐑆 𐐼𐐩𐑆; 𐐰𐑌𐐼 𐐸𐐨 𐐺𐐨𐑀𐐰𐐻 𐐗𐐱𐑋. 𐐈𐑌𐐼 𐐮𐐻 𐐿𐐩𐑋 𐐻𐐭 𐐹𐐰𐑅 𐑄𐐰𐐻 𐐗𐐱𐑋 𐐼𐑉𐐭 𐐲𐐶𐐩 𐑄 𐐸𐐪𐑁 𐐱𐑂 𐑄 𐐿𐐮𐑍𐐼𐐲𐑋. 𐐈𐑌𐐼 𐐸𐐨 𐑉𐐩𐑌𐐼 𐐬𐑂𐐲𐑉 𐑄 𐐸𐐪𐑁 𐐱𐑂 𐑄 𐐿𐐮𐑍𐐼𐐲𐑋 𐑁𐐫𐑉𐐻𐐨 𐐰𐑌𐐼 𐐻𐐭 𐐷𐐨𐑉𐑆; 𐐰𐑌𐐼 𐐸𐐨 𐐶𐐯𐑌𐐻 𐐻𐐭 𐐺𐐰𐐻𐑊 𐐲𐑀𐐯𐑌𐑅𐐻 𐑄 𐐿𐐮𐑍, 𐐈𐑋𐑀𐐮𐐼, 𐐰𐑌𐐼 𐑄𐐩 𐑁𐐫𐐻 𐑁𐐫𐑉 𐑄 𐑅𐐹𐐩𐑅 𐐱𐑂 𐑋𐐯𐑌𐐨 𐐷𐐨𐑉𐑆, 𐐼𐐷𐐭𐑉𐐮𐑍 𐐸𐐶𐐮𐐽 𐐻𐐴𐑋 𐐗𐐱𐑋 𐑀𐐩𐑌𐐼 𐐹𐐵𐐲𐑉 𐐬𐑂𐐲𐑉 𐐈𐑋𐑀𐐮𐐼, 𐐰𐑌𐐼 𐐱𐐺𐐻𐐩𐑌𐐼 𐐹𐐵𐐲𐑉 𐐬𐑂𐐲𐑉 𐑄 𐑉𐐨𐑋𐐩𐑌𐐼𐐲𐑉 𐐱𐑂 𐑄 𐐿𐐮𐑍𐐼𐐲𐑋. 𐐈𐑌𐐼 𐐮𐑌 𐑄 𐐼𐐩𐑆 𐐱𐑂 𐐗𐐱𐑋 𐑄𐐯𐑉 𐐺𐐨𐑀𐐰𐑌 𐐻𐐭 𐐺𐐨 𐑉𐐱𐐺𐐲𐑉𐑆 𐐮𐑌 𐑄 𐑊𐐰𐑌𐐼: 𐐰𐑌𐐼 𐑄𐐩 𐐲𐐼𐐱𐐹𐐻𐐯𐐼 𐑄 𐐬𐑊𐐼 𐐹𐑊𐐰𐑌𐑆, 𐐰𐑌𐐼 𐐰𐐼𐑋𐐮𐑌𐐮𐑅𐐻𐐲𐑉𐐼 𐐬𐑃𐑅 𐐰𐑁𐐻𐐲𐑉 𐑄 𐑋𐐰𐑌𐐲𐑉 𐐱𐑂 𐑄 𐐩𐑌𐑇𐐯𐑌𐐻𐑅, 𐐰𐑌𐐼 𐑅𐐫𐐻 𐐲𐑀𐐯𐑌 𐐻𐐭 𐐼𐐯𐑅𐐻𐑉𐑎 𐑄 𐐿𐐮𐑍𐐼𐐲𐑋. 𐐤𐐵 𐐗𐐱𐑋 𐐼𐐮𐐼 𐑁𐐴𐐻 𐐲𐑀𐐯𐑌𐑅𐐻 𐑄𐐯𐑋 𐑋𐐲𐐽; 𐑌𐐯𐑂𐐲𐑉𐑄𐐯𐑊𐐯𐑅, 𐐸𐐨 𐐼𐐮𐐼 𐑌𐐱𐐻 𐐹𐑉𐐨𐑂𐐩𐑊 𐐲𐑀𐐯𐑌𐑅𐐻 𐑄𐐯𐑋. 𐐈𐑌𐐼 𐑄𐐯𐑉 𐐿𐐩𐑋 𐐫𐑊𐑅𐐬 𐐮𐑌 𐑄 𐐼𐐩𐑆 𐐱𐑂 𐐗𐐱𐑋 𐑋𐐯𐑌𐐨 𐐹𐑉𐐱𐑁𐐯𐐻𐑅, 𐐰𐑌𐐼 𐐹𐑉𐐱𐑁𐐯𐑅𐐴𐐼 𐐱𐑂 𐑄 𐐼𐐯𐑅𐐻𐑉𐐲𐐿𐑇𐐲𐑌 𐐱𐑂 𐑄𐐰𐐻 𐑀𐑉𐐩𐐻 𐐹𐐨𐐹𐑊, 𐐯𐐿𐑅𐐯𐐹𐐻 𐑄𐐩 𐑇𐐳𐐼 𐑉𐐨𐐹𐐯𐑌𐐻, 𐐰𐑌𐐼 𐐻𐐲𐑉𐑌 𐐲𐑌𐐻𐐭 𐑄 𐐢𐐫𐑉𐐼, 𐐰𐑌𐐼 𐑁𐐫𐑉𐑅𐐩𐐿 𐑄𐐩𐑉 𐑋𐐲𐑉𐐼𐐲𐑉𐑆 𐐰𐑌𐐼 𐐶𐐮𐐿𐐯𐐼𐑌𐐯𐑅.

8. 𐐈𐑌𐐼 𐐮𐐻 𐐿𐐩𐑋 𐐻𐐭 𐐹𐐰𐑅 𐑄𐐰𐐻 𐑄 𐐹𐑉𐐱𐑁𐐯𐐻𐑅 𐐶𐐲𐑉 𐑉𐐨𐐾𐐯𐐿𐐻𐐯𐐼 𐐺𐐴 𐑄 𐐹𐐨𐐹𐑊, 𐐰𐑌𐐼 𐑄𐐩 𐑁𐑊𐐯𐐼 𐐲𐑌𐐻𐐭 𐐗𐐱𐑋 𐑁𐐫𐑉 𐐹𐑉𐐬𐐻𐐯𐐿𐑇𐐲𐑌, 𐑁𐐫𐑉 𐑄 𐐹𐐨𐐹𐑊 𐑅𐐫𐐻 𐐻𐐭 𐐼𐐯𐑅𐐻𐑉𐑎 𐑄𐐯𐑋; 𐐰𐑌𐐼 𐑄𐐩 𐐹𐑉𐐱𐑁𐐯𐑅𐐴𐐼 𐐲𐑌𐐻𐐭 𐐗𐐱𐑋 𐑋𐐯𐑌𐐨 𐑃𐐮𐑍𐑆; 𐐰𐑌𐐼 𐐸𐐨 𐐶𐐱𐑆 𐐺𐑊𐐯𐑅𐐯𐐼 𐐮𐑌 𐐫𐑊 𐑄 𐑉𐐨𐑋𐐩𐑌𐐼𐐲𐑉 𐐱𐑂 𐐸𐐮𐑆 𐐼𐐩𐑆. 𐐈𐑌𐐼 𐐸𐐨 𐑊𐐮𐑂𐐼 𐐻𐐭 𐐲 𐑀𐐳𐐼 𐐬𐑊𐐼 𐐩𐐾, 𐐰𐑌𐐼 𐐺𐐨𐑀𐐰𐐻 𐐟𐐮𐐺𐑊𐐲𐑋; 𐐰𐑌𐐼 𐐟𐐮𐐺𐑊𐐲𐑋 𐑉𐐩𐑌𐐼 𐐮𐑌 𐐸𐐮𐑆 𐑅𐐻𐐯𐐼. 𐐈𐑌𐐼 𐑄 𐐺𐑉𐐲𐑄𐐲𐑉 𐐱𐑂 𐐟𐐮𐐺𐑊𐐲𐑋 𐑉𐐨𐐺𐐯𐑊𐐼 𐐲𐑀𐐯𐑌𐑅𐐻 𐐸𐐮𐑋, 𐐰𐑌𐐼 𐑄𐐯𐑉 𐐺𐐨𐑀𐐰𐑌 𐐻𐐭 𐐺𐐨 𐐰𐑌 𐐯𐐿𐑅𐐨𐐼𐐮𐑍 𐑀𐑉𐐩𐐻 𐐶𐐫𐑉 𐐮𐑌 𐐫𐑊 𐑄 𐑊𐐰𐑌𐐼.

9. 𐐈𐑌𐐼 𐐮𐐻 𐐿𐐩𐑋 𐐻𐐭 𐐹𐐰𐑅 𐑄𐐰𐐻 𐑄 𐐺𐑉𐐲𐑄𐐲𐑉 𐐱𐑂 𐐟𐐮𐐺𐑊𐐲𐑋 𐐿𐐫𐑆𐐼 𐑄𐐰𐐻 𐐫𐑊 𐑄 𐐹𐑉𐐱𐑁𐐯𐐻𐑅 𐐸𐐭 𐐹𐑉𐐱𐑁𐐯𐑅𐐴𐐼 𐐱𐑂 𐑄 𐐼𐐯𐑅𐐻𐑉𐐲𐐿𐑇𐐲𐑌 𐐱𐑂 𐑄 𐐹𐐨𐐹𐑊 𐑇𐐳𐐼 𐐺𐐨 𐐹𐐳𐐻 𐐻𐐭 𐐼𐐯𐑃; 𐐰𐑌𐐼 𐑄𐐯𐑉 𐐶𐐱𐑆 𐑀𐑉𐐩𐐻 𐐿𐐰𐑊𐐰𐑋𐐮𐐻𐐨 𐐮𐑌 𐐫𐑊 𐑄 𐑊𐐰𐑌𐐼, 𐑁𐐫𐑉 𐑄𐐩 𐐸𐐰𐐼 𐐻𐐯𐑅𐐻𐐮𐑁𐐴𐐼 𐑄𐐰𐐻 𐐲 𐑀𐑉𐐩𐐻 𐐿𐐲𐑉𐑅 𐑇𐐳𐐼 𐐿𐐲𐑋 𐐲𐐹𐐱𐑌 𐑄

𐑊𐐰𐑌𐐼, 𐐰𐑌𐐼 𐐫𐑊𐑅𐐬 𐐲𐐹𐐱𐑌 𐑄 𐐹𐐨𐐹𐑊, 𐐰𐑌𐐼 𐑄𐐰𐐻 𐑄𐐯𐑉 𐑇𐐳𐐼 𐐺𐐨 𐐲 𐑀𐑉𐐩𐐻 𐐼𐐯𐑅𐐻𐑉𐐲𐐿𐑇𐐲𐑌 𐐲𐑋𐐲𐑍 𐑄𐐯𐑋, 𐑅𐐲𐐽 𐐰𐑌 𐐶𐐲𐑌 𐐰𐑆 𐑌𐐯𐑂𐐲𐑉 𐐸𐐰𐐼 𐐺𐐮𐑌 𐐲𐐹𐐱𐑌 𐑄 𐑁𐐩𐑅 𐐱𐑂 𐑄 𐐲𐑉𐑃; 𐐰𐑌𐐼 𐑄𐐩𐑉 𐐺𐐬𐑌𐑆 𐑇𐐳𐐼 𐐺𐐨𐐿𐐲𐑋 𐐰𐑆 𐐸𐐨𐐹𐑅 𐐱𐑂 𐐲𐑉𐑃 𐐲𐐹𐐱𐑌 𐑄 𐑁𐐩𐑅 𐐱𐑂 𐑄 𐑊𐐰𐑌𐐼, 𐐯𐐿𐑅𐐯𐐹𐐻 𐑄𐐩 𐑇𐐳𐐼 𐑉𐐨𐐹𐐯𐑌𐐻 𐐱𐑂 𐑄𐐩𐑉 𐐶𐐮𐐿𐐯𐐼𐑌𐐯𐑅. 𐐈𐑌𐐼 𐑄𐐩 𐐸𐐪𐑉𐐿𐐲𐑌𐐼 𐑌𐐱𐐻 𐐲𐑌𐐻𐐭 𐑄 𐑂𐑎𐑅 𐐱𐑂 𐑄 𐐢𐐫𐑉𐐼, 𐐺𐐨𐐿𐐫𐑆 𐐱𐑂 𐑄𐐩𐑉 𐐶𐐮𐐿𐐯𐐼 𐐿𐐱𐑋𐐺𐐮𐑌𐐩𐑇𐐲𐑌𐑆; 𐐸𐐶𐐯𐑉𐑁𐐬𐑉 𐑄𐐯𐑉 𐐺𐐨𐑀𐐰𐑌 𐐻𐐭 𐐺𐐨 𐐶𐐫𐑉𐑆 𐐰𐑌𐐼 𐐿𐐱𐑌𐐻𐐯𐑌𐑇𐐲𐑌𐑆 𐐮𐑌 𐐫𐑊 𐑄 𐑊𐐰𐑌𐐼, 𐐰𐑌𐐼 𐐫𐑊𐑅𐐬 𐑋𐐯𐑌𐐨 𐑁𐐰𐑋𐐮𐑌𐑆 𐐰𐑌𐐼 𐐹𐐯𐑅𐐻𐐮𐑊𐐯𐑌𐑅𐐯𐑆, 𐐮𐑌𐑅𐐬𐑋𐐲𐐽 𐑄𐐰𐐻 𐑄𐐯𐑉 𐐶𐐱𐑆 𐐲 𐑀𐑉𐐩𐐻 𐐼𐐯𐑅𐐻𐑉𐐲𐐿𐑇𐐲𐑌, 𐑅𐐲𐐽 𐐰𐑌 𐐶𐐲𐑌 𐐰𐑆 𐑌𐐯𐑂𐐲𐑉 𐐸𐐰𐐼 𐐺𐐮𐑌 𐑌𐐬𐑌 𐐲𐐹𐐱𐑌 𐑄 𐑁𐐩𐑅 𐐱𐑂 𐑄 𐐲𐑉𐑃; 𐐰𐑌𐐼 𐐫𐑊 𐑄𐐮𐑅 𐐿𐐩𐑋 𐐻𐐭 𐐹𐐰𐑅 𐐮𐑌 𐑄 𐐼𐐩𐑆 𐐱𐑂 𐐟𐐮𐐺𐑊𐐲𐑋. 𐐈𐑌𐐼 𐑄 𐐹𐐨𐐹𐑊 𐐺𐐨𐑀𐐰𐑌 𐐻𐐭 𐑉𐐨𐐹𐐯𐑌𐐻 𐐱𐑂 𐑄𐐩𐑉 𐐮𐑌𐐮𐐿𐐶𐐮𐐻𐐨; 𐐰𐑌𐐼 𐐮𐑌𐐰𐑆𐑋𐐲𐐽 𐐰𐑆 𐑄𐐩 𐐼𐐮𐐼, 𐑄 𐐢𐐫𐑉𐐼 𐐼𐐮𐐼 𐐸𐐰𐑂 𐑋𐐲𐑉𐑅𐐨 𐐱𐑌 𐑄𐐯𐑋.

10. 𐐈𐑌𐐼 𐐮𐐻 𐐿𐐩𐑋 𐐻𐐭 𐐹𐐰𐑅 𐑄𐐰𐐻 𐐟𐐮𐐺𐑊𐐲𐑋 𐐶𐐱𐑆 𐑅𐑊𐐩𐑌, 𐐰𐑌𐐼 𐐝𐐯𐑃 𐐶𐐱𐑆 𐐺𐑉𐐫𐐻 𐐮𐑌𐐻𐐭 𐐿𐐰𐐹𐐻𐐮𐑂𐐮𐐻𐐨, 𐐰𐑌𐐼 𐐼𐐮𐐼 𐐼𐐶𐐯𐑊 𐐮𐑌 𐐿𐐰𐐹𐐻𐐮𐑂𐐮𐐻𐐨 𐐫𐑊 𐐸𐐮𐑆 𐐼𐐩𐑆. 𐐈𐑌𐐼 𐐮𐐻 𐐿𐐩𐑋 𐐻𐐭 𐐹𐐰𐑅 𐑄𐐰𐐻 𐐁𐐸𐐪, 𐐸𐐮𐑆 𐑅𐐲𐑌, 𐐼𐐮𐐼 𐐱𐐺𐐻𐐩𐑌 𐑄 𐐿𐐮𐑍𐐼𐐲𐑋; 𐐰𐑌𐐼 𐐸𐐨 𐐼𐐮𐐼 𐑉𐐩𐑌 𐐬𐑂𐐲𐑉 𐑄 𐐹𐐨𐐹𐑊 𐐫𐑊 𐐸𐐮𐑆 𐐼𐐩𐑆. 𐐈𐑌𐐼 𐐸𐐨 𐐼𐐮𐐼 𐐼𐐭 𐐫𐑊 𐑋𐐰𐑌𐐲𐑉 𐐱𐑂 𐐮𐑌𐐮𐐿𐐶𐐮𐐻𐐨 𐐮𐑌 𐐸𐐮𐑆 𐐼𐐩𐑆, 𐐺𐐴 𐐸𐐶𐐮𐐽 𐐸𐐨 𐐼𐐮𐐼 𐐿𐐫𐑆 𐑄 𐑇𐐯𐐼𐐮𐑍 𐐱𐑂 𐑋𐐲𐐽 𐐺𐑊𐐲𐐼; 𐐰𐑌𐐼 𐑁𐐧 𐐶𐐲𐑉 𐐸𐐮𐑆 𐐼𐐩𐑆. 𐐈𐑌𐐼 𐐀𐑃𐐲𐑋, 𐐺𐐨𐐮𐑍 𐐲 𐐼𐐯𐑅𐐯𐑌𐐼𐐰𐑌𐐻 𐐱𐑂 𐐁𐐸𐐪, 𐐼𐐮𐐼 𐐱𐐺𐐻𐐩𐑌 𐑄 𐐿𐐮𐑍𐐼𐐲𐑋; 𐐰𐑌𐐼 𐐸𐐨 𐐫𐑊𐑅𐐬 𐐼𐐮𐐼 𐐼𐐭 𐑄𐐰𐐻 𐐸𐐶𐐮𐐽 𐐶𐐱𐑆 𐐶𐐮𐐿𐐯𐐼 𐐮𐑌 𐐸𐐮𐑆 𐐼𐐩𐑆. 𐐈𐑌𐐼 𐐮𐐻 𐐿𐐩𐑋 𐐻𐐭 𐐹𐐰𐑅 𐑄𐐰𐐻 𐐮𐑌 𐑄 𐐼𐐩𐑆 𐐱𐑂 𐐀𐑃𐐲𐑋, 𐑄𐐯𐑉 𐐿𐐩𐑋 𐑋𐐯𐑌𐐨 𐐹𐑉𐐱𐑁𐐯𐐻𐑅, 𐐰𐑌𐐼 𐐹𐑉𐐱𐑁𐐯𐑅𐐴𐐼 𐐲𐑀𐐯𐑌 𐐲𐑌𐐻𐐭 𐑄 𐐹𐐨𐐹𐑊; 𐐷𐐩, 𐑄𐐩 𐐼𐐮𐐼 𐐹𐑉𐐱𐑁𐐯𐑅𐐴 𐑄𐐰𐐻 𐑄 𐐢𐐫𐑉𐐼 𐐶𐐳𐐼 𐐲𐐻𐐲𐑉𐑊𐐨 𐐼𐐯𐑅𐐻𐑉𐑎 𐑄𐐯𐑋 𐑁𐑉𐐱𐑋 𐐫𐑁 𐑄 𐑁𐐩𐑅 𐐱𐑂 𐑄 𐐲𐑉𐑃, 𐐯𐐿𐑅𐐯𐐹𐐻 𐑄𐐩 𐑉𐐨𐐹𐐯𐑌𐐻𐐯𐐼 𐐱𐑂 𐑄𐐩𐑉 𐐮𐑌𐐮𐐿𐐶𐐮𐐻𐐨𐑆. 𐐈𐑌𐐼 𐐮𐐻 𐐿𐐩𐑋 𐐻𐐭 𐐹𐐰𐑅 𐑄𐐰𐐻 𐑄 𐐹𐐨𐐹𐑊 𐐸𐐪𐑉𐐼𐐲𐑌𐐼 𐑄𐐩𐑉 𐐸𐐪𐑉𐐻𐑅, 𐐰𐑌𐐼 𐐶𐐳𐐼 𐑌𐐱𐐻 𐐸𐐪𐑉𐐿𐐲𐑌 𐐲𐑌𐐻𐐭 𐑄𐐩𐑉 𐐶𐐲𐑉𐐼𐑆; 𐐰𐑌𐐼 𐑄 𐐹𐑉𐐱𐑁𐐯𐐻𐑅 𐑋𐐬𐑉𐑌𐐼 𐐰𐑌𐐼 𐐶𐐮𐑃𐐼𐑉𐐭 𐑁𐑉𐐱𐑋 𐐲𐑋𐐲𐑍 𐑄 𐐹𐐨𐐹𐑊.

11. 𐐈𐑌𐐼 𐐮𐐻 𐐿𐐩𐑋 𐐻𐐭 𐐹𐐰𐑅 𐑄𐐰𐐻 𐐀𐑃𐐲𐑋 𐐼𐐮𐐼 𐐯𐐿𐑅𐐯𐐿𐐷𐐭𐐻 𐐾𐐲𐐾𐑋𐐯𐑌𐐻 𐐮𐑌 𐐶𐐮𐐿𐐯𐐼𐑌𐐯𐑅 𐐫𐑊 𐐸𐐮𐑆 𐐼𐐩𐑆; 𐐰𐑌𐐼 𐐸𐐨 𐐺𐐨𐑀𐐰𐐻 𐐣𐐬𐑉𐐱𐑌. 𐐈𐑌𐐼 𐐮𐐻 𐐿𐐩𐑋 𐐻𐐭 𐐹𐐰𐑅 𐑄𐐰𐐻 𐐣𐐬𐑉𐐱𐑌 𐐼𐐮𐐼 𐑉𐐩𐑌 𐐮𐑌 𐐸𐐮𐑆 𐑅𐐻𐐯𐐼: 𐐰𐑌𐐼 𐐣𐐬𐑉𐐱𐑌 𐐼𐐮𐐼 𐑄𐐰𐐻 𐐸𐐶𐐮𐐽 𐐶𐐱𐑆 𐐶𐐮𐐿𐐯𐐼 𐐺𐐨𐑁𐐬𐑉 𐑄 𐐢𐐫𐑉𐐼. 𐐈𐑌𐐼 𐐮𐐻 𐐿𐐩𐑋 𐐻𐐭 𐐹𐐰𐑅 𐑄𐐰𐐻 𐑄𐐯𐑉 𐐲𐑉𐐬𐑆 𐐲 𐑉𐐨𐐺𐐯𐑊𐐷𐐲𐑌 𐐲𐑋𐐲𐑍 𐑄 𐐹𐐨𐐹𐑊, 𐐺𐐨𐐿𐐫𐑆 𐐱𐑂 𐑄𐐰𐐻 𐑅𐐨𐐿𐑉𐐯𐐻 𐐿𐐱𐑋𐐺𐐮𐑌𐐩𐑇𐐲𐑌 𐐸𐐶𐐮𐐽 𐐶𐐱𐑆 𐐺𐐮𐑊𐐻 𐐲𐐹 𐐻𐐭 𐑀𐐯𐐻 𐐹𐐵𐐲𐑉 𐐰𐑌𐐼 𐑀𐐩𐑌; 𐐰𐑌𐐼 𐑄𐐯𐑉 𐐲𐑉𐐬𐑆 𐐲 𐑋𐐴𐐻𐐨 𐑋𐐰𐑌 𐐲𐑋𐐲𐑍 𐑄𐐯𐑋 𐐮𐑌 𐐮𐑌𐐮𐐿𐐶𐐮𐐻𐐨, 𐐰𐑌𐐼 𐑀𐐩𐑂 𐐺𐐰𐐻𐑊 𐐲𐑌𐐻𐐭 𐐣𐐬𐑉𐐱𐑌, 𐐮𐑌 𐐸𐐶𐐮𐐽 𐐸𐐨 𐐼𐐮𐐼 𐐬𐑂𐐲𐑉𐑃𐑉𐐬 𐑄 𐐸𐐪𐑁 𐐱𐑂 𐑄 𐐿𐐮𐑍𐐼𐐲𐑋; 𐐰𐑌𐐼 𐐸𐐨 𐐼𐐮𐐼 𐑋𐐩𐑌𐐻𐐩𐑌 𐑄 𐐸𐐪𐑁 𐐱𐑂 𐑄 𐐿𐐮𐑍𐐼𐐲𐑋 𐑁𐐫𐑉 𐑋𐐯𐑌𐐨 𐐷𐐨𐑉𐑆. 𐐈𐑌𐐼 𐐮𐐻 𐐿𐐩𐑋 𐐻𐐭 𐐹𐐰𐑅 𐑄𐐰𐐻 𐐣𐐬𐑉𐐱𐑌 𐐼𐐮𐐼 𐐬𐑂𐐲𐑉𐑃𐑉𐐬 𐐸𐐮𐑋, 𐐰𐑌𐐼 𐐼𐐮𐐼 𐐱𐐺𐐻𐐩𐑌 𐑄 𐐿𐐮𐑍𐐼𐐲𐑋 𐐲𐑀𐐯𐑌. 𐐈𐑌𐐼 𐐮𐐻 𐐿𐐩𐑋 𐐻𐐭 𐐹𐐰𐑅 𐑄𐐰𐐻 𐑄𐐯𐑉 𐐲𐑉𐐬𐑆 𐐲𐑌𐐲𐑄𐐲𐑉 𐑋𐐴𐐻𐐨 𐑋𐐰𐑌; 𐐰𐑌𐐼 𐐸𐐨 𐐶𐐱𐑆 𐐲 𐐼𐐯𐑅𐐯𐑌𐐼𐐰𐑌𐐻 𐐱𐑂 𐑄 𐐺𐑉𐐲𐑄𐐲𐑉 𐐱𐑂 𐐖𐐯𐑉𐐲𐐼. 𐐈𐑌𐐼 𐐮𐐻 𐐿𐐩𐑋 𐐻𐐭 𐐹𐐰𐑅 𐑄𐐰𐐻 𐐸𐐨 𐐼𐐮𐐼 𐐬𐑂𐐲𐑉𐑃𐑉𐐬 𐐣𐐬𐑉𐐱𐑌 𐐰𐑌𐐼 𐐱𐐺𐐻𐐩𐑌 𐑄 𐐿𐐮𐑍𐐼𐐲𐑋; 𐐸𐐶𐐯𐑉𐑁𐐬𐑉 𐐣𐐬𐑉𐐱𐑌 𐐼𐐶𐐯𐑊𐐻 𐐮𐑌 𐐿𐐰𐐹𐐻𐐮𐑂𐐮𐐻𐐨 𐐫𐑊 𐑄 𐑉𐐨𐑋𐐩𐑌𐐼𐐲𐑉 𐐱𐑂 𐐸𐐮𐑆 𐐼𐐩𐑆: 𐐰𐑌𐐼 𐐸𐐨 𐐺𐐨𐑀𐐰𐐻 𐐗𐐫𐑉𐐨𐐰𐑌𐐻𐐫𐑉.

12. 𐐈𐑌𐐼 𐐮𐐻 𐐿𐐩𐑋 𐐻𐐭 𐐹𐐰𐑅 𐑄𐐰𐐻 𐐗𐐫𐑉𐐨𐐰𐑌𐐻𐐫𐑉 𐐼𐐶𐐯𐑊𐐻 𐐮𐑌 𐐿𐐰𐐹𐐻𐐮𐑂𐐮𐐻𐐨 𐐫𐑊 𐐸𐐮𐑆 𐐼𐐩𐑆. 𐐈𐑌𐐼 𐐮𐑌 𐑄 𐐼𐐩𐑆 𐐱𐑂 𐐗𐐫𐑉𐐨𐐰𐑌𐐻𐐫𐑉 𐑄𐐯𐑉 𐐫𐑊𐑅𐐬 𐐿𐐩𐑋 𐑋𐐯𐑌𐐨 𐐹𐑉𐐱𐑁𐐯𐐻𐑅, 𐐰𐑌𐐼 𐐹𐑉𐐱𐑁𐐯𐑅𐐴𐐼 𐐱𐑂 𐑀𐑉𐐩𐐻 𐐰𐑌𐐼 𐑋𐐪𐑉𐑂𐐯𐑊𐐲𐑅 𐑃𐐮𐑍𐑆, 𐐰𐑌𐐼 𐐿𐑉𐐴𐐼 𐑉𐐨𐐹𐐯𐑌𐐻𐐲𐑌𐑅 𐐲𐑌𐐻𐐭 𐑄 𐐹𐐨𐐹𐑊, 𐐰𐑌𐐼 𐐯𐐿𐑅𐐯𐐹𐐻 𐑄𐐩 𐑇𐐳𐐼 𐑉𐐨𐐹𐐯𐑌𐐻, 𐑄 𐐢𐐫𐑉𐐼 𐐘𐐱𐐼 𐐶𐐳𐐼 𐐯𐐿𐑅𐐯𐐿𐐷𐐭𐐻 𐐾𐐲𐐾𐑋𐐯𐑌𐐻 𐐲𐑀𐐯𐑌𐑅𐐻 𐑄𐐯𐑋 𐐻𐐭 𐑄𐐩𐑉 𐐲𐐻𐐲𐑉 𐐼𐐯𐑅𐐻𐑉𐐲𐐿𐑇𐐲𐑌; 𐐰𐑌𐐼 𐑄𐐰𐐻 𐑄 𐐢𐐫𐑉𐐼 𐐘𐐱𐐼 𐐶𐐳𐐼 𐑅𐐯𐑌𐐼 𐐫𐑉 𐐺𐑉𐐮𐑍 𐑁𐐬𐑉𐑃 𐐲𐑌𐐲𐑄𐐲𐑉 𐐹𐐨𐐹𐑊 𐐻𐐭 𐐹𐐲𐑆𐐯𐑅 𐑄 𐑊𐐰𐑌𐐼, 𐐺𐐴 𐐸𐐮𐑆 𐐹𐐵𐐲𐑉, 𐐰𐑁𐐻𐐲𐑉 𐑄 𐑋𐐰𐑌𐐲𐑉 𐐺𐐴 𐐸𐐶𐐮𐐽 𐐸𐐨 𐐺𐑉𐐫𐐻 𐑄𐐩𐑉 𐑁𐐪𐑄𐐲𐑉𐑆. 𐐈𐑌𐐼 𐑄𐐩 𐐼𐐮𐐼 𐑉𐐨𐐾𐐯𐐿𐐻 𐐫𐑊 𐑄 𐐶𐐲𐑉𐐼𐑆 𐐱𐑂 𐑄 𐐹𐑉𐐱𐑁𐐯𐐻𐑅, 𐐺𐐨𐐿𐐫𐑆 𐐱𐑂 𐑄𐐩𐑉 𐑅𐐨𐐿𐑉𐐯𐐻 𐑅𐐬𐑅𐐴𐐯𐐻𐐨 𐐰𐑌𐐼 𐐶𐐮𐐿𐐯𐐼 𐐲𐐺𐐱𐑋𐐮𐑌𐐩𐑇𐐲𐑌𐑆. 𐐈𐑌𐐼 𐐮𐐻 𐐿𐐩𐑋 𐐻𐐭 𐐹𐐰𐑅 𐑄𐐰𐐻 𐐗𐐫𐑉𐐨𐐰𐑌𐐻𐐫𐑉 𐐺𐐨𐑀𐐰𐐻 𐐀𐑃𐐲𐑉, 𐐰𐑌𐐼 𐐸𐐨 𐐼𐐴𐐼, 𐐸𐐰𐑂𐐮𐑍 𐐼𐐶𐐯𐑊𐐻 𐐮𐑌 𐐿𐐰𐐹𐐻𐐮𐑂𐐮𐐻𐐨 𐐫𐑊 𐐸𐐮𐑆 𐐼𐐩𐑆.

𐐕𐐰𐐹𐐻𐐲𐑉 V.

1. 𐐈𐑌𐐼 𐐮𐐻 𐐿𐐩𐑋 𐐻𐐭 𐐹𐐰𐑅 𐑄𐐰𐐻 𐑄 𐐼𐐩𐑆 𐐱𐑂 𐐀𐑃𐐲𐑉 𐐶𐐲𐑉 𐐮𐑌 𐑄 𐐼𐐩𐑆 𐐱𐑂 𐐗𐐬𐑉𐐨𐐰𐑌𐐻𐐲𐑋𐑉; 𐐰𐑌𐐼 𐐗𐐬𐑉𐐨𐐰𐑌𐐻𐐲𐑋𐑉 𐐶𐐱𐑆 𐐿𐐮𐑍 𐐬𐑂𐐲𐑉 𐐫𐑊 𐑄 𐑊𐐰𐑌𐐼. 𐐈𐑌𐐼 𐐀𐑃𐐲𐑉 𐐶𐐱𐑆 𐐲 𐐹𐑉𐐱𐑁𐐯𐐻 𐐱𐑂 𐑄 𐐢𐐫𐑉𐐼; 𐐸𐐶𐐯𐑉𐑁𐐬𐑉 𐐀𐑃𐐲𐑉 𐐿𐐩𐑋 𐑁𐐬𐑉𐑃 𐐮𐑌 𐑄 𐐼𐐩𐑆 𐐱𐑂 𐐗𐐬𐑉𐐨𐐰𐑌𐐻𐐲𐑋𐑉, 𐐰𐑌𐐼 𐐺𐐮𐑀𐐰𐑌 𐐻𐐭 𐐹𐑉𐐱𐑁𐐯𐑅𐐴 𐐲𐑌𐐻𐐭 𐑄 𐐹𐐨𐐹𐑊, 𐑁𐐬𐑉 𐐸𐐨 𐐿𐐳𐐼 𐑌𐐱𐐻 𐐺 𐑉𐐨𐑅𐐻𐑉𐐩𐑌𐐼 𐐺𐐨𐐿𐐫𐑆 𐐱𐑂 𐑄 𐐝𐐹𐐮𐑉𐐮𐐻 𐐱𐑂 𐑄 𐐢𐐫𐑉𐐼 𐐸𐐶𐐮𐐽 𐐶𐐱𐑆 𐐮𐑌 𐐸𐐮𐑋; 𐑁𐐬𐑉 𐐸𐐨 𐐼𐐮𐐼 𐐿𐑉𐐴 𐑁𐑉𐐱𐑋 𐑄 𐑋𐐫𐑉𐑌𐐮𐑍 𐐨𐑂𐑌 𐐲𐑌𐐻𐐮𐑊 𐑄 𐑀𐐬𐐮𐑍 𐐼𐐵𐑌 𐐱𐑂 𐑄 𐑅𐐲𐑌, 𐐯𐑀𐑆𐐫𐑉𐐻𐐮𐑍 𐑄 𐐹𐐨𐐹𐑊 𐐻𐐭 𐐺𐐨𐑊𐐨𐑂 𐐮𐑌 𐐘𐐱𐐼 𐐲𐑌𐐻𐐭 𐑉𐐨𐐹𐐯𐑌𐐻𐐲𐑌𐑅, 𐑊𐐯𐑅𐐻 𐑄𐐩 𐑇𐐳𐐼 𐐺 𐐼𐐯𐑅𐐻𐑉𐐱𐐮𐐼, 𐑅𐐩𐐮𐑍 𐐲𐑌𐐻𐐭 𐑄𐐯𐑋 𐑄𐐰𐐻 𐐺𐐴 𐑁𐐩𐑃 𐐫𐑊 𐑃𐐮𐑍𐑆 𐐪𐑉 𐑁𐐳𐑊𐑁𐐮𐑊𐐼; 𐐸𐐶𐐯𐑉𐑁𐐬𐑉, 𐐸𐐭𐑅𐐬 𐐺𐐨𐑊𐐨𐑂𐐯𐑃 𐐮𐑌 𐐘𐐱𐐼 𐑋𐐴𐐻 𐐶𐐮𐑄 𐑇𐐳𐑉𐐯𐐻𐐨 𐐸𐐬𐐹 𐑁𐐬𐑉 𐐲 𐐺𐐯𐐻𐐲𐑉 𐐶𐐲𐑉𐑊𐐼, 𐐷𐐩, 𐐨𐑂𐑌 𐐲 𐐹𐑊𐐩𐑅 𐐰𐐻 𐑄 𐑉𐐴𐐻 𐐸𐐰𐑌𐐼 𐐱𐑂 𐐘𐐱𐐼; 𐐸𐐶𐐮𐐽 𐐸𐐬𐐹 𐐿𐐲𐑋𐐯𐑃 𐐱𐑂 𐑁𐐩𐑃, 𐑋𐐩𐐿𐐯𐑃 𐐰𐑌 𐐰𐑍𐐿𐐲𐑉 𐐻𐐭 𐑄 𐑅𐐬𐑊𐑆 𐐱𐑂 𐑋𐐯𐑌, 𐐸𐐶𐐮𐐽 𐐶𐐳𐐼 𐑋𐐩𐐿 𐑄𐐯𐑋 𐑇𐐳𐑉 𐐰𐑌𐐼 𐑅𐐻𐐯𐐼𐑁𐐰𐑅𐐻, 𐐫𐑊𐐶𐐩𐑆 𐐲𐐺𐐵𐑌𐐼𐐮𐑍 𐐮𐑌 𐑀𐐳𐐼 𐐶𐐲𐑉𐐿𐑅, 𐐺𐐨𐐮𐑍 𐑊𐐯𐐼 𐐻𐐭 𐑀𐑊𐐬𐑉𐐮𐑁𐐴 𐐘𐐱𐐼. 𐐈𐑌𐐼 𐐮𐐻 𐐿𐐩𐑋 𐐻𐐭 𐐹𐐰𐑅 𐑄𐐰𐐻 𐐀𐑃𐐲𐑉 𐐼𐐮𐐼 𐐹𐑉𐐱𐑁𐐯𐑅𐐴 𐑀𐑉𐐩𐐻 𐐰𐑌𐐼 𐑋𐐪𐑉𐑂𐐯𐑊𐐲𐑅 𐑃𐐮𐑍𐑆 𐐲𐑌𐐻𐐭 𐑄 𐐹𐐨𐐹𐑊, 𐐸𐐶𐐮𐐽 𐑄𐐩 𐐼𐐮𐐼 𐑌𐐱𐐻 𐐺𐐨𐑊𐐨𐑂, 𐐺𐐨𐐿𐐫𐑆 𐑄𐐩 𐑅𐐫 𐑄𐐯𐑋 𐑌𐐱𐐻. 𐐈𐑌𐐼 𐑌𐐵, 𐐌, 𐐣𐐬𐑉𐐬𐑌𐐴, 𐐶𐐳𐐼 𐑅𐐹𐐨𐐿 𐑅𐐲𐑋𐐸𐐶𐐱𐐻 𐐿𐐱𐑌𐑅𐐲𐑉𐑌𐐮𐑍 𐑄𐐨𐑆 𐑃𐐮𐑍𐑆; 𐐌 𐐶𐐳𐐼 𐑇𐐬 𐐲𐑌𐐻𐐭 𐑄 𐐶𐐲𐑉𐑊𐐼 𐑄𐐰𐐻 𐑁𐐩𐑃 𐐮𐑆 𐑃𐐮𐑍𐑆 𐐸𐐶𐐮𐐽 𐐪𐑉 𐐸𐐬𐐹𐐻 𐑁𐐬𐑉 𐐰𐑌𐐼 𐑌𐐱𐐻 𐑅𐐨𐑌; 𐐸𐐶𐐯𐑉𐑁𐐬𐑉, 𐐼𐐮𐑅𐐹𐐧𐐻 𐑌𐐱𐐻 𐐺𐐨𐐿𐐫𐑆 𐐷𐐨 𐑅𐐨 𐑌𐐱𐐻, 𐑁𐐬𐑉 𐐷𐐨 𐑉𐐨𐑅𐐨𐑂 𐑌𐐬 𐐶𐐮𐐻𐑌𐐯𐑅 𐐲𐑌𐐻𐐮𐑊 𐐰𐑁𐐻𐐲𐑉 𐑄 𐐻𐑉𐐴𐐲𐑊 𐐱𐑂 𐐷𐐳𐑉 𐑁𐐩𐑃; 𐑁𐐬𐑉 𐐮𐐻 𐐶𐐱𐑆 𐐺𐐴 𐑁𐐩𐑃 𐑄𐐰𐐻 𐐗𐑉𐐴𐑅𐐻 𐑇𐐬𐐼 𐐸𐐮𐑋𐑅𐐯𐑊𐑁 𐐲𐑌𐐻𐐭 𐐵𐑉 𐑁𐐪𐑄𐐲𐑉𐑆, 𐐰𐑁𐐻𐐲𐑉 𐐸𐐨 𐐸𐐰𐐼 𐑉𐐮𐑆𐐲𐑌 𐑁𐑉𐐱𐑋 𐑄 𐐼𐐯𐐼; 𐐰𐑌𐐼 𐐸𐐨 𐑇𐐬𐐼 𐑌𐐱𐐻 𐐸𐐮𐑋𐑅𐐯𐑊𐑁 𐐲𐑌𐐻𐐭 𐑄𐐯𐑋 𐐲𐑌𐐻𐐮𐑊 𐐰𐑁𐐻𐐲𐑉 𐑄𐐩 𐐸𐐰𐐼 𐑁𐐩𐑃 𐐮𐑌 𐐸𐐮𐑋; 𐐸𐐶𐐯𐑉𐑁𐐬𐑉, 𐐮𐐻 𐑋𐐲𐑅𐐻 𐑌𐐨𐐼𐑆 𐐺 𐑄𐐰𐐻 𐑅𐐲𐑋 𐐸𐐰𐐼 𐑁𐐩𐑃 𐐮𐑌 𐐸𐐮𐑋, 𐑁𐐬𐑉 𐐸𐐨 𐑇𐐬𐐼 𐐸𐐮𐑋𐑅𐐯𐑊𐑁 𐑌𐐱𐐻 𐐲𐑌𐐻𐐭 𐑄 𐐶𐐲𐑉𐑊𐐼. 𐐒𐐲𐐻 𐐺𐐨𐐿𐐫𐑆 𐐱𐑂 𐑄 𐑁𐐩𐑃 𐐱𐑂 𐑋𐐯𐑌, 𐐸𐐨 𐐸𐐰𐑆 𐑇𐐬𐑌 𐐸𐐮𐑋𐑅𐐯𐑊𐑁 𐐲𐑌𐐻𐐭 𐑄 𐐶𐐲𐑉𐑊𐐼, 𐐰𐑌𐐼 𐑀𐑊𐐬𐑉𐐮𐑁𐐴𐐼 𐑄 𐑌𐐩𐑋 𐐱𐑂 𐑄 𐐙𐐪𐑄𐐲𐑉, 𐐰𐑌𐐼 𐐹𐑉𐐨𐐹𐐩𐑉𐐼 𐐲 𐐶𐐩 𐑄𐐰𐐻 𐑄𐐯𐑉𐐺𐐴 𐐲𐑄𐐲𐑉𐑆 𐑋𐐴𐐻 𐐺 𐐹𐐪𐑉𐐻𐐩𐐿𐐲𐑉𐑆 𐐱𐑂 𐑄 𐐸𐐯𐑂𐐲𐑌𐑊𐐨 𐑀𐐮𐑁𐐻, 𐑄𐐰𐐻 𐑄𐐩 𐑋𐐴𐐻 𐐸𐐬𐐹 𐑁𐐬𐑉 𐑄𐐬𐑆 𐑃𐐮𐑍𐑆 𐐸𐐶𐐮𐐽 𐑄𐐩 𐐸𐐰𐑂 𐑌𐐱𐐻 𐑅𐐨𐑌; 𐐸𐐶𐐯𐑉𐑁𐐬𐑉 𐐷𐐨 𐑋𐐩 𐐫𐑊𐑅𐐬 𐐸𐐰𐑂 𐐸𐐬𐐹, 𐐰𐑌𐐼 𐐺 𐐹𐐪𐑉𐐻𐐩𐐿𐐲𐑉𐑆 𐐱𐑂 𐑄 𐑀𐐮𐑁𐐻, 𐐮𐑁 𐐷𐐨 𐐶𐐮𐑊 𐐺𐐲𐐻 𐐸𐐰𐑂 𐑁𐐩𐑃. 𐐒𐐨𐐸𐐬𐑊𐐼 𐐮𐐻 𐐶𐐱𐑆 𐐺𐐴 𐑁𐐩𐑃 𐑄𐐰𐐻 𐑄𐐩 𐐱𐑂 𐐬𐑊𐐼 𐐶𐐲𐑉 𐐿𐐫𐑊𐐼 𐐰𐑁𐐻𐐲𐑉 𐑄 𐐸𐐬𐑊𐐨 𐐫𐑉𐐼𐐲𐑉 𐐱𐑂 𐐘𐐱𐐼; 𐐸𐐶𐐯𐑉𐑁𐐬𐑉, 𐐺𐐴 𐑁𐐩𐑃 𐐶𐐱𐑆 𐑄 𐑊𐐫 𐐱𐑂 𐐣𐐬𐑆𐐯𐑆 𐑀𐐮𐑂𐐲𐑌. 𐐒𐐲𐐻 𐐮𐑌 𐑄 𐑀𐐮𐑁𐐻 𐐱𐑂 𐐸𐐮𐑆 𐐝𐐲𐑌, 𐐸𐐰𐑃 𐐘𐐱𐐼 𐐹𐑉𐐨𐐹𐐩𐑉𐐼 𐐲 𐑋𐐬𐑉 𐐯𐐿𐑅𐐯𐑊𐐯𐑌𐐻 𐐶𐐩; 𐐰𐑌𐐼 𐐮𐐻 𐐮𐑆 𐐺𐐴 𐑁𐐩𐑃 𐑄𐐰𐐻 𐐮𐐻 𐐸𐐰𐑃 𐐺𐐮𐑌 𐑁𐐳𐑊𐑁𐐮𐑊𐐼; 𐑁𐐬𐑉 𐐮𐑁 𐑄𐐯𐑉 𐐺 𐑌𐐬 𐑁𐐩𐑃 𐐲𐑋𐐲𐑍 𐑄 𐐽𐐮𐑊𐐼𐑉𐐯𐑌 𐐱𐑂 𐑋𐐯𐑌, 𐐘𐐱𐐼 𐐿𐐰𐑌 𐐼𐐭 𐑌𐐬 𐑋𐐮𐑉𐐲𐐿𐑊 𐐲𐑋𐐲𐑍 𐑄𐐯𐑋; 𐐸𐐶𐐯𐑉𐑁𐐬𐑉 𐐸𐐨 𐑇𐐬𐐼 𐑌𐐱𐐻 𐐸𐐮𐑋𐑅𐐯𐑊𐑁 𐐲𐑌𐐻𐐮𐑊 𐐰𐑁𐐻𐐲𐑉 𐑄𐐯𐑉 𐑁𐐩𐑃. 𐐒𐐨𐐸𐐬𐑊𐐼, 𐐮𐐻 𐐶𐐱𐑆 𐑄 𐑁𐐩𐑃 𐐱𐑂 𐐈𐑊𐑋𐐲 𐐰𐑌𐐼 𐐈𐑋𐐷𐐭𐑊𐐯𐐿 𐑄𐐰𐐻 𐐿𐐫𐑆𐐼 𐑄 𐐹𐑉𐐮𐑆𐐲𐑌 𐐻𐐭 𐐻𐐲𐑋𐐺𐑊 𐐻𐐭 𐑄 𐐲𐑉𐑃. 𐐒𐐨𐐸𐐬𐑊𐐼, 𐐮𐐻 𐐶𐐱𐑆 𐑄 𐑁𐐩𐑃 𐐱𐑂 𐐤𐐨𐑁𐐴 𐐰𐑌𐐼 𐐢𐐨𐐸𐐴, 𐑄𐐰𐐻 𐑉𐐫𐐻 𐑄 𐐽𐐩𐑌𐐾 𐐲𐐹𐐱𐑌 𐑄 𐐢𐐩𐑋𐐲𐑌𐐴𐐻𐑅, 𐑄𐐰𐐻 𐑄𐐩 𐐶𐐲𐑉 𐐺𐐰𐐹𐐻𐐴𐑆𐐼 𐐶𐐮𐑄 𐑁𐐴𐑉 𐐰𐑌𐐼 𐐶𐐮𐑄 𐑄 𐐐𐐬𐑊𐐨 𐐘𐐬𐑅𐐻. 𐐒𐐨𐐸𐐬𐑊𐐼, 𐐮𐐻 𐐶𐐱𐑆 𐑄 𐑁𐐩𐑃 𐐱𐑂 𐐈𐑋𐐲𐑌 𐐰𐑌𐐼 𐐸𐐮𐑆 𐐺𐑉𐐯𐑄𐑉𐐯𐑌, 𐐸𐐶𐐮𐐽 𐑉𐐫𐐻 𐑅𐐬 𐑀𐑉𐐩𐐻 𐐲 𐑋𐐮𐑉𐐲𐐿𐑊 𐐲𐑋𐐲𐑍 𐑄 𐐢𐐩𐑋𐐲𐑌𐐴𐐻𐑅; 𐐷𐐩, 𐐰𐑌𐐼 𐐨𐑂𐑌 𐐫𐑊 𐑄𐐩 𐐸𐐭 𐑉𐐫𐐻 𐑋𐐮𐑉𐐲𐐿𐑊𐑆, 𐑉𐐫𐐻 𐑄𐐯𐑋 𐐺𐐴 𐑁𐐩𐑃, 𐐨𐑂𐑌 𐑄𐐬𐑆 𐐸𐐭 𐐶𐐲𐑉 𐐺𐐨𐑁𐐬𐑉 𐐗𐑉𐐴𐑅𐐻, 𐐰𐑌𐐼 𐐫𐑊𐑅𐐬 𐑄𐐬𐑆 𐐸𐐭 𐐶𐐲𐑉 𐐰𐑁𐐻𐐲𐑉. 𐐈𐑌𐐼 𐐮𐐻 𐐶𐐱𐑆 𐐺𐐴 𐑁𐐩𐑃 𐑄𐐰𐐻 𐑄 𐑃𐑉𐐨 𐐼𐐮𐑅𐐴𐐹𐑊𐑆 𐐱𐐺𐐻𐐩𐑌𐐼 𐐲 𐐹𐑉𐐱𐑋𐐮𐑅 𐑄𐐰𐐻 𐑄𐐩 𐑇𐐳𐐼 𐑌𐐱𐐻 𐐻𐐩𐑅𐐻 𐐱𐑂 𐐼𐐯𐑃; 𐐰𐑌𐐼 𐑄𐐩 𐐱𐐺𐐻𐐩𐑌𐐼 𐑌𐐱𐐻 𐑄 𐐹𐑉𐐱𐑋𐐮𐑅 𐐲𐑌𐐻𐐮𐑊 𐐰𐑁𐐻𐐲𐑉 𐑄𐐯𐑉 𐑁𐐩𐑃. 𐐈𐑌𐐼 𐑌𐐨𐑄𐐲𐑉 𐐰𐐻 𐐯𐑌𐐨 𐐻𐐴𐑋 𐐸𐐰𐑃 𐐯𐑌𐐨 𐑉𐐫𐐻 𐑋𐐮𐑉𐐲𐐿𐑊𐑆 𐐲𐑌𐐻𐐮𐑊 𐐰𐑁𐐻𐐲𐑉 𐑄𐐯𐑉 𐑁𐐩𐑃; 𐐸𐐶𐐯𐑉𐑁𐐬𐑉 𐑄𐐩 𐑁𐐲𐑉𐑅𐐻 𐐺𐐨𐑊𐐨𐑂𐐼 𐐮𐑌 𐑄 𐐝𐐲𐑌 𐐱𐑂 𐐘𐐱𐐼.

2. 𐐈𐑌𐐼 𐑄𐐯𐑉 𐐶𐐲𐑉 𐑋𐐯𐑌𐐨 𐐸𐐭𐑆 𐑁𐐩𐑃 𐐶𐐱𐑆 𐑅𐐬 𐐯𐐿𐑅𐐨𐐼𐐮𐑍𐑊𐐨 𐑅𐐻𐑉𐐱𐑍 𐐨𐑂𐑌 𐐺𐐨𐑁𐐬𐑉 𐐗𐑉𐐴𐑅𐐻 𐐿𐐩𐑋

𐐸𐐭 𐐿𐐳𐐼 𐑌𐐱𐐻 𐐺 𐐿𐐯𐐹𐐻 𐑁𐑉𐐱𐑋 𐐶𐐮𐑄𐐮𐑌 𐑄 𐑂𐐩𐑊, 𐐺𐐲𐐻 𐐻𐑉𐐭𐑊𐐨 𐑅𐐫 𐐶𐐮𐑄 𐑄𐐩𐑉 𐐴𐑆 𐑄 𐑃𐐮𐑍𐑆 𐐸𐐶𐐮𐐽 𐑄𐐩 𐐸𐐰𐐼 𐐺𐐨𐐸𐐯𐑊𐐼 𐐶𐐮𐑄 𐐰𐑌 𐐴 𐐱𐑂 𐑁𐐩𐑃, 𐐰𐑌𐐼 𐑄𐐩 𐐶𐐲𐑉 𐑀𐑊𐐰𐐼. 𐐈𐑌𐐼 𐐺𐐨𐐸𐐬𐑊𐐼, 𐐶𐐨 𐐸𐐰𐑂 𐑅𐐨𐑌 𐐮𐑌 𐑄𐐮𐑅 𐑉𐐯𐐿𐐫𐑉𐐼, 𐑄𐐰𐐻 𐐶𐐲𐑌 𐐱𐑂 𐑄𐐨𐑆 𐐶𐐱𐑆 𐑄 𐐺𐑉𐐲𐑄𐐲𐑉 𐐱𐑂 𐐖𐐩𐑉𐐯𐐼: 𐑁𐐫𐑉 𐑅𐐬 𐑀𐑉𐐩𐐻 𐐶𐐱𐑆 𐐸𐐮𐑆 𐑁𐐩𐑃 𐐮𐑌 𐐘𐐱𐐼, 𐑄𐐰𐐻 𐐸𐐶𐐯𐑌 𐐘𐐱𐐼 𐐹𐐳𐐻 𐑁𐐬𐑉𐑃 𐐸𐐮𐑆 𐑁𐐮𐑍𐑀𐐲𐑉, 𐐸𐐨 𐐿𐐳𐐼 𐑌𐐱𐐻 𐐸𐐴𐐼 𐐮𐐻 𐑁𐑉𐐱𐑋 𐑄 𐑅𐐴𐐻 𐐱𐑂 𐑄 𐐺𐑉𐐲𐑄𐐲𐑉 𐐱𐑂 𐐖𐐩𐑉𐐯𐐼, 𐐺𐐨𐐿𐐫𐑆 𐐱𐑂 𐐸𐐮𐑆 𐐶𐐲𐑉𐐼 𐐸𐐶𐐮𐐽 𐐸𐐨 𐐸𐐰𐐼 𐑅𐐹𐐬𐐿𐐲𐑌 𐐲𐑌𐐻𐐭 𐐸𐐮𐑋, 𐐸𐐶𐐮𐐽 𐐶𐐲𐑉𐐼 𐐸𐐨 𐐸𐐰𐐼 𐐱𐐺𐐻𐐩𐑌𐐼 𐐺𐐴 𐑁𐐩𐑃. 𐐈𐑌𐐼 𐐰𐑁𐐻𐐲𐑉 𐑄 𐐺𐑉𐐲𐑄𐐲𐑉 𐐱𐑂 𐐖𐐩𐑉𐐯𐐼 𐐸𐐰𐐼 𐐺𐐨𐐸𐐯𐑊𐐼 𐑄 𐑁𐐮𐑍𐑀𐐲𐑉 𐐱𐑂 𐑄 𐐢𐐫𐑉𐐼, 𐐺𐐨𐐿𐐫𐑆 𐐱𐑂 𐑄 𐐹𐑉𐐱𐑋𐐮𐑅 𐐸𐐶𐐮𐐽 𐑄 𐐺𐑉𐐲𐑄𐐲𐑉 𐐱𐑂 𐐖𐐩𐑉𐐯𐐼 𐐸𐐰𐐼 𐐱𐐺𐐻𐐩𐑌𐐼 𐐺𐐴 𐑁𐐩𐑃, 𐑄 𐐢𐐫𐑉𐐼 𐐿𐐳𐐼 𐑌𐐱𐐻 𐐶𐐮𐑄𐐸𐐬𐑊𐐼 𐐯𐑌𐐨𐑃𐐮𐑍 𐑁𐑉𐐱𐑋 𐐸𐐮𐑆 𐑅𐐴𐐻; 𐐸𐐶𐐩𐑉𐑁𐐬𐑉 𐐸𐐨 𐑇𐐬𐐼 𐐸𐐮𐑋 𐐫𐑊 𐑃𐐮𐑍𐑆, 𐑁𐐫𐑉 𐐸𐐨 𐐿𐐳𐐼 𐑌𐐬 𐑊𐐱𐑍𐑀𐐲𐑉 𐐺 𐐿𐐯𐐹𐐻 𐐶𐐮𐑄𐐵𐐻 𐑄 𐑂𐐩𐑊. 𐐈𐑌𐐼 𐐮𐐻 𐐮𐑆 𐐺𐐴 𐑁𐐩𐑃 𐑄𐐰𐐻 𐑋𐐴 𐑁𐐪𐑄𐐲𐑉𐑆 𐐸𐐰𐑂 𐐱𐐺𐐻𐐩𐑌𐐼 𐑄 𐐹𐑉𐐱𐑋𐐮𐑅 𐑄𐐰𐐻 𐑄𐐨𐑆 𐑃𐐮𐑍𐑆 𐑇𐐳𐐼 𐐿𐐲𐑋 𐐲𐑌𐐻𐐭 𐑄𐐩𐑉 𐐺𐑉𐐯𐑄𐑉𐐯𐑌 𐑃𐑉𐐭 𐑄 𐐖𐐯𐑌𐐻𐐴𐑊𐑆; 𐑄𐐩𐑉𐑁𐐬𐑉 𐑄 𐐢𐐫𐑉𐐼 𐐸𐐰𐑃 𐐿𐐱𐑋𐐰𐑌𐐼𐐯𐐼 𐑋𐐨, 𐐷𐐩, 𐐨𐑂𐐲𐑌 𐐖𐐨𐑆𐐲𐑅 𐐗𐑉𐐴𐑅𐐻. 𐐈𐑌𐐼 𐐴 𐑅𐐯𐐼 𐐲𐑌𐐻𐐭 𐐸𐐮𐑋, 𐐢𐐫𐑉𐐼, 𐑄 𐐖𐐯𐑌𐐻𐐴𐑊𐑆 𐐶𐐮𐑊 𐑋𐐱𐐿 𐐰𐐻 𐑄𐐨𐑆 𐑃𐐮𐑍𐑆, 𐐺𐐨𐐿𐐫𐑆 𐐱𐑂 𐐵𐑉 𐐶𐐨𐐿𐑌𐐯𐑅 𐐮𐑌 𐑉𐐴𐐻𐐮𐑍; 𐑁𐐫𐑉 𐐢𐐫𐑉𐐼 𐑄𐐵 𐐸𐐰𐑅𐐻 𐑋𐐩𐐼 𐐲𐑅 𐑋𐐴𐐻𐐨 𐐮𐑌 𐐶𐐲𐑉𐐼 𐐺𐐴 𐑁𐐩𐑃, 𐐺𐐲𐐻 𐑄𐐵 𐐸𐐰𐑅𐐻 𐑌𐐱𐐻 𐑋𐐩𐐼 𐐲𐑅 𐑋𐐴𐐻𐐨 𐐮𐑌 𐑉𐐴𐐻𐐮𐑍; 𐑁𐐫𐑉 𐑄𐐵 𐐸𐐰𐑅𐐻 𐑋𐐩𐐼 𐐫𐑊 𐑄𐐮𐑅 𐐹𐐨𐐹𐐲𐑊 𐑄𐐰𐐻 𐑄𐐩 𐐿𐐳𐐼 𐑅𐐹𐐨𐐿 𐑋𐐲𐐽, 𐐺𐐨𐐿𐐫𐑆 𐐱𐑂 𐑄 𐐐𐐬𐑊𐐨 𐐘𐐬𐑅𐐻 𐐸𐐶𐐮𐐽 𐑄𐐵 𐐸𐐰𐑅𐐻 𐑀𐐮𐑂𐐲𐑌 𐑄𐐯𐑋; 𐐰𐑌𐐼 𐑄𐐵 𐐸𐐰𐑅𐐻 𐑋𐐩𐐼 𐐲𐑅 𐑄𐐰𐐻 𐐶𐐨 𐐿𐐳𐐼 𐑉𐐴𐐻 𐐺𐐲𐐻 𐑊𐐮𐐻𐑊, 𐐺𐐨𐐿𐐫𐑆 𐐱𐑂 𐑄 𐐫𐐿𐐶𐐲𐑉𐐼𐑌𐐯𐑅 𐐱𐑂 𐐵𐑉 𐐸𐐰𐑌𐐼𐑆. 𐐒𐐨𐐸𐐬𐑊𐐼, 𐑄𐐵 𐐸𐐰𐑅𐐻 𐑌𐐱𐐻 𐑋𐐩𐐼 𐐲𐑅 𐑋𐐴𐐻𐐨 𐐮𐑌 𐑉𐐴𐐻𐐮𐑍 𐑊𐐴𐐿 𐐲𐑌𐐻𐐭 𐑄 𐐺𐑉𐐲𐑄𐐲𐑉 𐐱𐑂 𐐖𐐩𐑉𐐯𐐼, 𐑁𐐫𐑉 𐑄𐐵 𐑋𐐩𐐼𐐯𐑅𐐻 𐐸𐐮𐑋 𐑄𐐰𐐻 𐑄 𐑃𐐮𐑍𐑆 𐐸𐐶𐐮𐐽 𐐸𐐨 𐑉𐐬𐐻 𐐶𐐲𐑉 𐑋𐐴𐐻𐐨 𐐨𐑂𐐲𐑌 𐐰𐑆 𐑄𐐵 𐐪𐑉𐐻, 𐐲𐑌𐐻𐐭 𐑄 𐐬𐑂𐐲𐑉𐐹𐐵𐐲𐑉𐐮𐑍 𐐱𐑂 𐑋𐐰𐑌 𐐻𐐭 𐑉𐐨𐐼 𐑄𐐯𐑋. 𐐜𐐵 𐐸𐐰𐑅𐐻 𐐫𐑊𐑅𐐬 𐑋𐐩𐐼 𐐵𐑉 𐐶𐐲𐑉𐐼𐑆 𐐹𐐵𐐲𐑉𐑁𐐳𐑊 𐐰𐑌𐐼 𐑀𐑉𐐩𐐻, 𐐨𐑂𐐲𐑌 𐑄𐐰𐐻 𐐶𐐨 𐐿𐐰𐑌𐐱𐐻 𐑉𐐴𐐻 𐑄𐐯𐑋; 𐐸𐐶𐐩𐑉𐑁𐐬𐑉, 𐐸𐐶𐐯𐑌 𐐶𐐨 𐑉𐐴𐐻 𐐶𐐨 𐐺𐐨𐐸𐐬𐑊𐐼 𐐵𐑉 𐐶𐐨𐐿𐑌𐐯𐑅, 𐐰𐑌𐐼 𐑅𐐻𐐲𐑋𐐺𐑊 𐐺𐐨𐐿𐐫𐑆 𐐱𐑂 𐑄 𐐹𐑊𐐩𐑅𐐮𐑍 𐐱𐑂 𐐵𐑉 𐐶𐐲𐑉𐐼𐑆; 𐐰𐑌𐐼 𐐴 𐑁𐐨𐑉 𐑊𐐯𐑅𐐻 𐑄 𐐖𐐯𐑌𐐻𐐴𐑊𐑆 𐑇𐐰𐑊 𐑋𐐱𐐿 𐐰𐐻 𐐵𐑉 𐐶𐐲𐑉𐐼𐑆. 𐐈𐑌𐐼 𐐸𐐶𐐯𐑌 𐐴 𐐸𐐰𐐼 𐑅𐐯𐐼 𐑄𐐮𐑅, 𐑄 𐐢𐐫𐑉𐐼 𐑅𐐹𐐩𐐿 𐐲𐑌𐐻𐐭 𐑋𐐨, 𐑅𐐩𐐮𐑍, 𐐙𐐭𐑊𐑆 𐑋𐐱𐐿, 𐐺𐐲𐐻 𐑄𐐩 𐑇𐐰𐑊 𐑋𐐬𐑉𐑌; 𐐰𐑌𐐼 𐑋𐐴 𐑀𐑉𐐩𐑅 𐐮𐑆 𐑅𐐲𐑁𐐮𐑇𐐯𐑌𐐻 𐑁𐐫𐑉 𐑄 𐑋𐐨𐐿, 𐑄𐐰𐐻 𐑄𐐩 𐑇𐐰𐑊 𐐻𐐩𐐿 𐑌𐐬 𐐰𐐼𐑂𐐰𐑌𐐻𐐩𐐾 𐐱𐑂 𐐷𐐭𐑉 𐐶𐐨𐐿𐑌𐐯𐑅; 𐐰𐑌𐐼 𐐮𐑁 𐑋𐐯𐑌 𐐿𐐲𐑋 𐐲𐑌𐐻𐐭 𐑋𐐨, 𐐴 𐐶𐐮𐑊 𐑇𐐬 𐐲𐑌𐐻𐐭 𐑄𐐯𐑋 𐑄𐐩𐑉 𐐶𐐨𐐿𐑌𐐯𐑅. 𐐌 𐑀𐐮𐑂 𐐲𐑌𐐻𐐭 𐑋𐐯𐑌 𐐶𐐨𐐿𐑌𐐯𐑅, 𐑄𐐰𐐻 𐑄𐐩 𐑋𐐩 𐐺 𐐸𐐲𐑋𐐺𐑊; 𐐰𐑌𐐼 𐑋𐐴 𐑀𐑉𐐩𐑅 𐐮𐑆 𐑅𐐲𐑁𐐮𐑇𐐯𐑌𐐻 𐑁𐐫𐑉 𐐫𐑊 𐑋𐐯𐑌 𐑄𐐰𐐻 𐐸𐐲𐑋𐐺𐑊 𐑄𐐯𐑋𐑅𐐯𐑊𐑂𐑆 𐐺𐐨𐑁𐐬𐑉 𐑋𐐨; 𐑁𐐫𐑉 𐐮𐑁 𐑄𐐩 𐐸𐐲𐑋𐐺𐑊 𐑄𐐯𐑋𐑅𐐯𐑊𐑂𐑆 𐐺𐐨𐑁𐐬𐑉 𐑋𐐨, 𐐰𐑌𐐼 𐐸𐐰𐑂 𐑁𐐩𐑃 𐐮𐑌 𐑋𐐨, 𐑄𐐯𐑌 𐐶𐐮𐑊 𐐴 𐑋𐐩𐐿 𐐶𐐨𐐿 𐑃𐐮𐑍𐑆 𐐺𐐨𐐿𐐲𐑋 𐑅𐐻𐑉𐐱𐑍 𐐲𐑌𐐻𐐭 𐑄𐐯𐑋. 𐐒𐐨𐐸𐐬𐑊𐐼, 𐐴 𐐶𐐮𐑊 𐑇𐐬 𐐲𐑌𐐻𐐭 𐑄 𐐖𐐯𐑌𐐻𐐴𐑊𐑆 𐑄𐐩𐑉 𐐶𐐨𐐿𐑌𐐯𐑅, 𐐰𐑌𐐼 𐐴 𐐶𐐮𐑊 𐑇𐐬 𐐲𐑌𐐻𐐭 𐑄𐐯𐑋 𐑄𐐰𐐻 𐑁𐐩𐑃, 𐐸𐐬𐐹, 𐐰𐑌𐐼 𐐽𐐰𐑉𐐮𐐻𐐨, 𐐺𐑉𐐮𐑍𐐯𐑃 𐐲𐑌𐐻𐐭 𐑋𐐨—𐑄 𐑁𐐵𐑌𐐻𐐩𐑌 𐐱𐑂 𐐫𐑊 𐑉𐐴𐐽𐐲𐑅𐑌𐐯𐑅.

3. 𐐈𐑌𐐼 𐐴, 𐐣𐐬𐑉𐐬𐑌𐐴, 𐐸𐐰𐑂𐐮𐑍 𐐸𐐲𐑉𐐼 𐑄𐐨𐑆 𐐶𐐲𐑉𐐼𐑆, 𐐶𐐱𐑆 𐐿𐐲𐑋𐑁𐐲𐑉𐐻𐐯𐐼, 𐐰𐑌𐐼 𐑅𐐯𐐼, 𐐄 𐐢𐐫𐑉𐐼, 𐑄𐐴 𐑉𐐴𐐽𐐲𐑅 𐐶𐐮𐑊 𐐺 𐐼𐐲𐑌, 𐑁𐐫𐑉 𐐴 𐑌𐐬 𐑄𐐰𐐻 𐑄𐐵 𐐶𐐲𐑉𐐿𐐯𐑅𐐻 𐐲𐑌𐐻𐐭 𐑄 𐐽𐐮𐑊𐐼𐑉𐐯𐑌 𐐱𐑂 𐑋𐐯𐑌 𐐰𐐿𐐫𐑉𐐼𐐮𐑍 𐐻𐐭 𐑄𐐩𐑉 𐑁𐐩𐑃; 𐑁𐐫𐑉 𐑄 𐐺𐑉𐐲𐑄𐐲𐑉 𐐱𐑂 𐐖𐐩𐑉𐐯𐐼 𐑅𐐯𐐼 𐐲𐑌𐐻𐐭 𐑄 𐑋𐐵𐑌𐐻𐐩𐑌 𐐞𐐨𐑉𐐮𐑌, 𐐡𐐨𐑋𐐭𐑂, 𐐰𐑌𐐼 𐐮𐐻 𐐶𐐱𐑆 𐑉𐐨𐑋𐐭𐑂𐐼. 𐐈𐑌𐐼 𐐮𐑁 𐐸𐐨 𐐸𐐰𐐼 𐑌𐐱𐐻 𐐸𐐰𐐼 𐑁𐐩𐑃, 𐐮𐐻 𐐶𐐳𐐼 𐑌𐐱𐐻 𐐸𐐰𐑂 𐑋𐐭𐑂𐐼; 𐐸𐐶𐐩𐑉𐑁𐐬𐑉 𐑄𐐵 𐐶𐐲𐑉𐐿𐐯𐑅𐐻 𐐰𐑁𐐻𐐲𐑉 𐑋𐐯𐑌 𐐸𐐰𐑂 𐑁𐐩𐑃; 𐑁𐐫𐑉 𐑄𐐲𐑅 𐐼𐐮𐐼𐑅𐐻 𐑄𐐵 𐑋𐐰𐑌𐐮𐑁𐐯𐑅𐐻 𐑄𐐴𐑅𐐯𐑊𐑁 𐐲𐑌𐐻𐐭 𐑄𐐴 𐐼𐐮𐑅𐐴𐐹𐑊𐑆. 𐐙𐐫𐑉 𐐰𐑁𐐻𐐲𐑉 𐑄𐐩 𐐸𐐰𐐼 𐑁𐐩𐑃, 𐐰𐑌𐐼 𐐼𐐮𐐼 𐑅𐐹𐐨𐐿 𐐮𐑌 𐑄𐐴 𐑌𐐩𐑋, 𐑄𐐵 𐐼𐐮𐐼𐑅𐐻 𐑇𐐬 𐑄𐐴𐑅𐐯𐑊𐑁 𐐲𐑌𐐻𐐭 𐑄𐐯𐑋 𐐮𐑌 𐑀𐑉𐐩𐐻 𐐹𐐵𐐲𐑉; 𐐰𐑌𐐼 𐐴 𐐫𐑊𐑅𐐬 𐑉𐐨𐑋𐐯𐑋𐐺𐐲𐑉 𐑄𐐰𐐻 𐑄𐐵 𐐸𐐰𐑅𐐻 𐑅𐐯𐐼 𐑄𐐰𐐻 𐑄𐐵 𐐸𐐰𐑅𐐻 𐐹𐑉𐐨𐐹𐐩𐑉𐐼 𐐩 𐐸𐐵𐑅 𐑁𐐫𐑉 𐑋𐐰𐑌; 𐐷𐐩, 𐐨𐑂𐐲𐑌 𐐲𐑋𐐲𐑍 𐑄 𐑋𐐰𐑌𐑇𐐲𐑌𐑆 𐐱𐑂 𐑄𐐴 𐐙𐐪𐑄𐐲𐑉, 𐐮𐑌 𐐸𐐶𐐮𐐽 𐑋𐐰𐑌 𐑋𐐴𐐻 𐐸𐐰𐑂 𐐩 𐑋𐐬𐑉 𐐯𐐿𐑅𐐯𐑊𐐯𐑌𐐻 𐐸𐐬𐐹; 𐐸𐐶𐐩𐑉𐑁𐐬𐑉 𐑋𐐰𐑌 𐑋𐐲𐑅𐐻 𐐸𐐬𐐹, 𐐫𐑉 𐐸𐐨 𐐿𐐰𐑌𐐱𐐻 𐑉𐐨𐑅𐐨𐑂 𐐰𐑌 𐐮𐑌𐐸𐐯𐑉𐐮𐐻𐐰𐑌𐑅 𐐮𐑌 𐑄 𐐹𐑊𐐩𐑅 𐐸𐐶𐐮𐐽 𐑄𐐵 𐐸𐐰𐑅𐐻 𐐹𐑉𐐨𐐹𐐩𐑉𐐼. 𐐈𐑌𐐼 𐐰𐑀𐐯𐑌, 𐐴 𐑉𐐨𐑋𐐯𐑋𐐺𐐲𐑉 𐑄𐐰𐐻 𐑄𐐵 𐐸𐐰𐑅𐐻 𐑅𐐯𐐼 𐑄𐐰𐐻 𐑄𐐵 𐐸𐐰𐑅𐐻 𐑊𐐲𐑂𐐼 𐑄 𐐶𐐲𐑉𐑊𐐼, 𐐨𐑂𐐲𐑌 𐐲𐑌𐐻𐐭 𐑄 𐑊𐐩𐐮𐑍 𐐼𐐵𐑌 𐐱𐑂 𐑄𐐴 𐑊𐐴𐑁 𐑁𐐫𐑉 𐑄 𐐶𐐲𐑉𐑊𐐼, 𐑄𐐰𐐻 𐑄𐐵 𐑋𐐴𐐻𐐯𐑅𐐻 𐐻𐐩𐐿 𐐮𐐻 𐐰𐑀𐐯𐑌 𐐻𐐭 𐐹𐑉𐐨𐐹𐐩𐑉 𐐩 𐐹𐑊𐐩𐑅 𐑁𐐫𐑉 𐑄 𐐽𐐮𐑊𐐼𐑉𐐯𐑌 𐐱𐑂 𐑋𐐯𐑌. 𐐈𐑌𐐼 𐑌𐐵 𐐴 𐑌𐐬 𐑄𐐰𐐻 𐑄𐐮𐑅 𐑊𐐲𐑂 𐐸𐐶𐐮𐐽 𐑄𐐵 𐐸𐐰𐑅𐐻 𐐸𐐰𐐼 𐑁𐐫𐑉 𐑄 𐐽𐐮𐑊𐐼𐑉𐐯𐑌 𐐱𐑂 𐑋𐐯𐑌 𐐮𐑆 𐐽𐐰𐑉𐐮𐐻𐐨; 𐐸𐐶𐐩𐑉𐑁𐐬𐑉, 𐐯𐐿𐑅𐐯𐐹𐐻 𐑋𐐯𐑌

𐑇𐐰𐑊 𐐸𐐰𐑂 𐐽𐐰𐑉𐐮𐐻𐐨, 𐑄𐐩 𐐿𐐰𐑌𐐱𐐻 𐐮𐑌𐐸𐐯𐑉𐐮𐐻 𐑄𐐰𐐻 𐐹𐑊𐐩𐑅 𐐸𐐶𐐮𐐽 𐑄𐐵 𐐸𐐰𐑅𐐻 𐐹𐑉𐐨𐐹𐐩𐑉𐐼 𐐮𐑌 𐑄 𐑋𐐰𐑌𐑇𐐲𐑌𐑆 𐐱𐑂 𐑄𐐴 𐐙𐐪𐑄𐐲𐑉. 𐐐𐐶𐐯𐑉𐑁𐐫𐑉, 𐐌 𐑌𐐬 𐐺𐐴 𐑄𐐮𐑅 𐑃𐐮𐑍 𐐸𐐶𐐮𐐽 𐑄𐐵 𐐸𐐰𐑅𐐻 𐑅𐐯𐐼, 𐑄𐐰𐐻 𐐮𐑁 𐑄 𐐖𐐯𐑌𐐻𐐴𐑊𐑆 𐐸𐐰𐑂 𐑌𐐱𐐻 𐐽𐐰𐑉𐐮𐐻𐐨, 𐐺𐐨𐐿𐐫𐑆 𐐱𐑂 𐐵𐑉 𐐶𐐨𐐿𐑌𐐯𐑅, 𐑄𐐰𐐻 𐑄𐐵 𐐶𐐮𐑊𐐻 𐐹𐑉𐐭𐑂 𐑄𐐯𐑋, 𐐰𐑌𐐼 𐐻𐐩𐐿 𐐰𐐶𐐩 𐑄𐐩𐑉 𐐻𐐰𐑊𐐯𐑌𐐻, 𐐷𐐩, 𐐨𐑂𐑌 𐑄𐐰𐐻 𐐸𐐶𐐮𐐽 𐑄𐐩 𐐸𐐰𐑂 𐑉𐐨𐑅𐐨𐑂𐐼, 𐐰𐑌𐐼 𐑀𐐮𐑂 𐐲𐑌𐐻𐐭 𐑄𐐯𐑋 𐐸𐐭 𐑇𐐰𐑊 𐐸𐐰𐑂 𐑋𐐬𐑉 𐐰𐐺𐐲𐑌𐐼𐐲𐑌𐐻𐑊𐐨.

4. 𐐈𐑌𐐼 𐐮𐐻 𐐿𐐩𐑋 𐐻𐐭 𐐹𐐰𐑅 𐑄𐐰𐐻 𐐌 𐐹𐑉𐐩𐐼 𐐲𐑌𐐻𐐭 𐑄 𐐢𐐫𐑉𐐼, 𐑄𐐰𐐻 𐐸𐐨 𐐶𐐳𐐼 𐑀𐐮𐑂 𐐲𐑌𐐻𐐭 𐑄 𐐖𐐯𐑌𐐻𐐴𐑊𐑆 𐑀𐑉𐐩𐑅, 𐑄𐐰𐐻 𐑄𐐩 𐑋𐐴𐐻 𐐸𐐰𐑂 𐐽𐐰𐑉𐐮𐐻𐐨. 𐐈𐑌𐐼 𐐮𐐻 𐐿𐐩𐑋 𐐻𐐭 𐐹𐐰𐑅 𐑄𐐰𐐻 𐑄 𐐢𐐫𐑉𐐼 𐑅𐐯𐐼 𐐲𐑌𐐻𐐭
𐑋𐐨, 𐐆𐑁 𐑄𐐩 𐐸𐐰𐑂 𐑌𐐱𐐻 𐐽𐐰𐑉𐐮𐐻𐐨, 𐐮𐐻 𐑋𐐰𐐻𐐲𐑉𐐯𐑃 𐑌𐐱𐐻 𐐲𐑌𐐻𐐭 𐑄, 𐑄𐐵 𐐸𐐰𐑅𐐻 𐐺𐐮𐑌 𐑁𐐩𐑃𐑁𐐳𐑊; 𐐸𐐶𐐯𐑉𐑁𐐫𐑉
𐑄𐐴 𐑀𐐪𐑉𐑋𐐯𐑌𐐻𐑅 𐑇𐐰𐑊 𐐺 𐑋𐐩𐐼 𐐿𐑊𐐨𐑌. 𐐈𐑌𐐼 𐐺𐐨𐐿𐐫𐑆 𐑄𐐵 𐐸𐐰𐑅𐐻 𐑅𐐨𐑌 𐑄𐐴 𐐶𐐨𐐿𐑌𐐯𐑅, 𐑄𐐵 𐑇𐐰𐑊𐐻
𐐺 𐑋𐐩𐐼 𐑅𐐻𐑉𐐱𐑍, 𐐨𐑂𐑌 𐐲𐑌𐐻𐐭 𐑄 𐑅𐐮𐐻𐐮𐑍 𐐼𐐵𐑌 𐐮𐑌 𐑄 𐐹𐑊𐐩𐑅 𐐸𐐶𐐮𐐽 𐐌 𐐸𐐰𐑂 𐐹𐑉𐐨𐐹𐐩𐑉𐐼 𐐮𐑌 𐑄 𐑋𐐰𐑌𐑇𐐲𐑌𐑆
𐐱𐑂 𐑋𐐴 𐐙𐐪𐑄𐐲𐑉. 𐐈𐑌𐐼 𐑌𐐵 𐐌, 𐐣𐐫𐑉𐐬𐑌𐐴, 𐐺𐐮𐐼 𐑁𐐩𐑉𐐶𐐯𐑊 𐐲𐑌𐐻𐐭 𐑄 𐐖𐐯𐑌𐐻𐐴𐑊𐑆, 𐐷𐐩, 𐐰𐑌𐐼 𐐫𐑊𐑅𐐬
𐐲𐑌𐐻𐐭 𐑋𐐴 𐐺𐑉𐐯𐑄𐑉𐐯𐑌 𐐸𐐭𐑋 𐐌 𐑊𐐲𐑂, 𐐲𐑌𐐻𐐮𐑊 𐐶𐐨 𐑇𐐰𐑊 𐑋𐐨𐐻 𐐺𐐨𐑁𐐬𐑉 𐑄 𐐾𐐲𐐾𐑋𐐯𐑌𐐻 𐑅𐐨𐐻 𐐱𐑂 𐐗𐑉𐐴𐑅𐐻,
𐐸𐐶𐐯𐑉 𐐫𐑊 𐑋𐐯𐑌 𐑇𐐰𐑊 𐑌𐐬 𐑄𐐰𐐻 𐑋𐐴 𐑀𐐪𐑉𐑋𐐯𐑌𐐻𐑅 𐐪𐑉 𐑌𐐱𐐻 𐑅𐐹𐐱𐐻𐐯𐐼 𐐶𐐮𐑄 𐐷𐐬𐑉 𐐺𐑊𐐲𐐼; 𐐰𐑌𐐼 𐑄𐐯𐑌
𐑇𐐰𐑊 𐐷 𐑌𐐬 𐑄𐐰𐐻 𐐌 𐐸𐐰𐑂 𐑅𐐨𐑌 𐐖𐐨𐑆𐐲𐑅, 𐐰𐑌𐐼 𐑄𐐰𐐻 𐐸𐐨 𐐸𐐰𐑃 𐐻𐐫𐐿𐐻 𐐶𐐮𐑄 𐑋𐐨 𐑁𐐩𐑅 𐐻𐐭 𐑁𐐩𐑅, 𐐰𐑌𐐼
𐑄𐐰𐐻 𐐸𐐨 𐐻𐐬𐑊𐐼 𐑋𐐨 𐐮𐑌 𐐹𐑊𐐩𐑌 𐐸𐐷𐐭𐑋𐐮𐑊𐐮𐐻𐐨, 𐐨𐑂𐑌 𐐰𐑆 𐐩 𐑋𐐰𐑌 𐐻𐐯𐑊𐐯𐑃 𐐰𐑌𐐲𐑄𐐲𐑉 𐐮𐑌 𐑋𐐴𐑌 𐐬𐑌 𐑊𐐰𐑍𐑀𐐶𐐯𐐾,
𐐿𐐱𐑌𐑅𐐲𐑉𐑌𐐮𐑍 𐑄𐐨𐑆 𐑃𐐮𐑍𐑆; 𐐰𐑌𐐼 𐐬𐑌𐑊𐐨 𐐩 𐑁𐐷𐐭 𐐸𐐰𐑂 𐐌 𐑉𐐮𐐻𐑌, 𐐺𐐨𐐿𐐫𐑆 𐐱𐑂 𐑋𐐴 𐐶𐐨𐐿𐑌𐐯𐑅 𐐮𐑌 𐑉𐐴𐐻𐐮𐑍.
𐐈𐑌𐐼 𐑌𐐵 𐐌 𐐶𐐳𐐼 𐐿𐐱𐑋𐐯𐑌𐐼 𐐷𐐭 𐐻𐐭 𐑅𐐨𐐿 𐑄𐐮𐑅 𐐖𐐨𐑆𐐲𐑅 𐐱𐑂 𐐸𐐭𐑋 𐑄 𐐹𐑉𐐱𐑁𐐯𐐻𐑅 𐐰𐑌𐐼 𐐰𐐹𐐱𐑅𐐲𐑊𐑆 𐐸𐐰𐑂
𐑉𐐮𐐻𐑌, 𐑄𐐰𐐻 𐑄 𐑀𐑉𐐩𐑅 𐐱𐑂 𐐘𐐱𐐼 𐑄 𐐙𐐪𐑄𐐲𐑉, 𐐰𐑌𐐼 𐐫𐑊𐑅𐐬 𐑄 𐐢𐐫𐑉𐐼 𐐖𐐨𐑆𐐲𐑅 𐐗𐑉𐐴𐑅𐐻, 𐐰𐑌𐐼 𐑄
𐐐𐐬𐑊𐐨 𐐘𐐬𐑅𐐻, 𐐸𐐶𐐮𐐽 𐐺𐐯𐑉𐐯𐑃 𐑉𐐯𐐿𐐲𐑉𐐼 𐐱𐑂 𐑄𐐯𐑋, 𐑋𐐩 𐐺, 𐐰𐑌𐐼 𐐰𐐺𐐴𐐼 𐐮𐑌 𐐷𐐭 𐑁𐐫𐑉 𐐯𐑂𐐲𐑉.
𐐁𐑋𐐯𐑌.

𐐕𐐰𐐹𐐻𐐲𐑉 VI.

1. 𐐈𐑌𐐼 𐑌𐐵 𐐌, 𐐣𐐫𐑉𐐬𐑌𐐴, 𐐹𐑉𐐬𐑅𐐨𐐼 𐐻𐐭 𐑁𐐮𐑌𐐮𐑇 𐑋𐐴 𐑉𐐯𐐿𐐲𐑉𐐼 𐐿𐐱𐑌𐑅𐐲𐑉𐑌𐐮𐑍 𐑄 𐐼𐐯𐑅𐐻𐑉𐐲𐐿𐑇𐐲𐑌
𐐱𐑂 𐑄 𐐹𐐨𐐹𐐲𐑊 𐐱𐑂 𐐸𐐭𐑋 𐐌 𐐸𐐰𐑂 𐐺𐐮𐑌 𐑉𐐴𐐻𐐮𐑍. 𐐙𐐫𐑉 𐐺𐐨𐐸𐐬𐑊𐐼, 𐑄𐐩 𐑉𐐨𐐾𐐯𐐿𐐻𐐯𐐼 𐐫𐑊 𐑄 𐐶𐐲𐑉𐐼𐑆 𐐱𐑂
𐐀𐑃𐐲𐑉; 𐑁𐐫𐑉 𐐸𐐨 𐐻𐑉𐐭𐑊𐐨 𐐻𐐬𐑊𐐼 𐑄𐐯𐑋 𐐱𐑂 𐐫𐑊 𐑃𐐮𐑍𐑆, 𐑁𐑉𐐱𐑋 𐑄 𐐺𐐨𐑀𐐮𐑌𐐮𐑍 𐐱𐑂 𐑋𐐰𐑌; 𐐰𐑌𐐼 𐑄𐐰𐐻
𐐰𐑁𐐻𐐲𐑉 𐑄 𐐶𐐫𐐻𐐲𐑉𐑆 𐐸𐐰𐐼 𐑉𐐨𐑅𐐨𐐼𐐯𐐼 𐑁𐑉𐐱𐑋 𐐫𐑁 𐑄 𐑁𐐩𐑅 𐐱𐑂 𐑄𐐮𐑅 𐑊𐐰𐑌𐐼, 𐐮𐐻 𐐺𐐨𐐿𐐩𐑋 𐐩 𐐽𐐦𐑅 𐑊𐐰𐑌𐐼
𐐰𐐺𐐲𐑂 𐐫𐑊 𐐲𐑄𐐲𐑉 𐑊𐐰𐑌𐐼𐑆, 𐐩 𐐽𐐬𐑆𐑌 𐑊𐐰𐑌𐐼 𐐱𐑂 𐑄 𐐢𐐫𐑉𐐼; 𐐸𐐶𐐯𐑉𐑁𐐫𐑉 𐑄 𐐢𐐫𐑉𐐼 𐐶𐐳𐐼 𐐸𐐰𐑂 𐑄𐐰𐐻 𐐫𐑊
𐑋𐐯𐑌 𐑇𐐳𐐼 𐑅𐐲𐑉𐑂 𐐸𐐮𐑋 𐐸𐐭 𐐼𐐶𐐯𐑊 𐐲𐐹𐐱𐑌 𐑄 𐑁𐐩𐑅 𐑄𐐯𐑉𐐱𐑂; 𐐰𐑌𐐼 𐑄𐐰𐐻 𐐮𐐻 𐐶𐐱𐑆 𐑄 𐐹𐑊𐐩𐑅 𐐱𐑂 𐑄 𐐤𐐷𐐭
𐐖𐐨𐑉𐐭𐑅𐐲𐑊𐐯𐑋, 𐐸𐐶𐐮𐐽 𐑇𐐳𐐼 𐐿𐐲𐑋 𐐼𐐵𐑌 𐐵𐐻 𐐱𐑂 𐐸𐐯𐑂𐑌, 𐐰𐑌𐐼 𐑄 𐐸𐐬𐑊𐐨 𐑅𐐰𐑍𐐿𐐽𐐭𐐯𐑉𐐨 𐐱𐑂 𐑄 𐐢𐐫𐑉𐐼.
𐐒𐐨𐐸𐐬𐑊𐐼, 𐐀𐑃𐐲𐑉 𐑅𐐫 𐑄 𐐼𐐩𐑆 𐐱𐑂 𐐗𐑉𐐴𐑅𐐻, 𐐰𐑌𐐼 𐐸𐐨 𐑅𐐹𐐩𐐿 𐐿𐐱𐑌𐑅𐐲𐑉𐑌𐐮𐑍 𐐩 𐐤𐐷𐐭 𐐖𐐨𐑉𐐭𐑅𐐲𐑊𐐯𐑋
𐐲𐐹𐐱𐑌 𐑄𐐮𐑅 𐑊𐐰𐑌𐐼; 𐐰𐑌𐐼 𐐸𐐨 𐑅𐐹𐐩𐐿 𐐫𐑊𐑅𐐬 𐐿𐐱𐑌𐑅𐐲𐑉𐑌𐐮𐑍 𐑄 𐐸𐐵𐑅 𐐱𐑂 𐐆𐑆𐑉𐐩𐐯𐑊, 𐐰𐑌𐐼 𐑄 𐐖𐐨𐑉𐐭𐑅𐐲𐑊𐐯𐑋 𐑁𐑉𐐱𐑋 𐐸𐐶𐐯𐑌𐑅 𐐢𐐨𐐸𐐴 𐑇𐐳𐐼 𐐿𐐲𐑋; 𐐰𐑁𐐻𐐲𐑉 𐐮𐐻 𐑇𐐳𐐼 𐐺 𐐼𐐯𐑅𐐻𐑉𐐦𐐼, 𐐮𐐻 𐑇𐐳𐐼 𐐺 𐐺𐐮𐑊𐐻 𐐲𐐹 𐐲𐑀𐐯𐑌
𐐩 𐐸𐐬𐑊𐐨 𐑅𐐮𐐻𐐨 𐐲𐑌𐐻𐐭 𐑄 𐐢𐐫𐑉𐐼; 𐐸𐐶𐐯𐑉𐑁𐐫𐑉 𐐮𐐻 𐐿𐐳𐐼 𐑌𐐱𐐻 𐐺 𐐩 𐐤𐐷𐐭 𐐖𐐨𐑉𐐭𐑅𐐲𐑊𐐯𐑋, 𐑁𐐫𐑉 𐐮𐐻 𐐸𐐰𐐼
𐐺𐐮𐑌 𐐮𐑌 𐐩 𐐻𐐴𐑋 𐐱𐑂 𐐬𐑊𐐼, 𐐺𐐲𐐻 𐐮𐐻 𐑇𐐳𐐼 𐐺 𐐺𐐮𐑊𐐻 𐐲𐐹 𐐲𐑀𐐯𐑌, 𐐰𐑌𐐼 𐐺𐐨𐐿𐐲𐑋 𐐩 𐐸𐐬𐑊𐐨 𐑅𐐮𐐻𐐨 𐐱𐑂 𐑄
𐐢𐐫𐑉𐐼; 𐐰𐑌𐐼 𐐮𐐻 𐑇𐐳𐐼 𐐺 𐐺𐐮𐑊𐐻 𐐲𐑌𐐻𐐭 𐑄 𐐸𐐵𐑅 𐐱𐑂 𐐆𐑆𐑉𐐩𐐯𐑊; 𐐰𐑌𐐼 𐑄𐐰𐐻 𐐩 𐐤𐐷𐐭 𐐖𐐨𐑉𐐭𐑅𐐲𐑊𐐯𐑋 𐑇𐐳𐐼 𐐺
𐐺𐐮𐑊𐐻 𐐲𐐹𐐱𐑌 𐑄𐐮𐑅 𐑊𐐰𐑌𐐼, 𐐲𐑌𐐻𐐭 𐑄 𐑉𐐯𐑋𐑌𐐰𐑌𐐻 𐐱𐑂 𐑄 𐑅𐐨𐐼 𐐱𐑂 𐐖𐐬𐑆𐐯𐑁, 𐑁𐐫𐑉 𐐸𐐶𐐮𐐽 𐑃𐐮𐑍𐑆 𐑄𐐯𐑉 𐐸𐐰𐑆
𐐺𐐮𐑌 𐐩 𐐻𐐴𐐹; 𐑁𐐫𐑉 𐐰𐑆 𐐖𐐬𐑆𐐯𐑁 𐐺𐑉𐐫𐐻 𐐸𐐮𐑆 𐑁𐐪𐑄𐐲𐑉 𐐼𐐵𐑌 𐐮𐑌𐐻𐐭 𐑄 𐑊𐐰𐑌𐐼 𐐱𐑂 𐐀𐐾𐐮𐐹𐐻, 𐐀𐑂𐑌
𐑅𐐬 𐐸𐐨 𐐼𐐴𐐼 𐑄𐐯𐑉; 𐐸𐐶𐐯𐑉𐑁𐐫𐑉 𐑄 𐐢𐐫𐑉𐐼 𐐺𐑉𐐫𐐻 𐐩 𐑉𐐯𐑋𐑌𐐰𐑌𐐻 𐐱𐑂 𐑄 𐑅𐐨𐐼 𐐱𐑂 𐐖𐐬𐑆𐐯𐑁 𐐵𐐻 𐐱𐑂 𐑄
𐑊𐐰𐑌𐐼 𐐱𐑂 𐐖𐐨𐑉𐐭𐑅𐐲𐑊𐐯𐑋, 𐑄𐐰𐐻 𐐸𐐨 𐑋𐐴𐐻 𐐺 𐑋𐐲𐑉𐑅𐐮𐑁𐐳𐑊 𐐲𐑌𐐻𐐭 𐑄 𐑅𐐨𐐼 𐐱𐑂 𐐖𐐬𐑆𐐯𐑁, 𐑄𐐰𐐻 𐑄𐐩 𐑇𐐳𐐼
𐐹𐐯𐑉𐐮𐑇 𐑌𐐱𐐻, 𐐨𐑂𐑌 𐐰𐑆 𐐸𐐨 𐐶𐐱𐑆 𐑋𐐲𐑉𐑅𐐮𐑁𐐳𐑊 𐐲𐑌𐐻𐐭 𐑄 𐑁𐐪𐑄𐐲𐑉 𐐱𐑂 𐐖𐐬𐑆𐐯𐑁, 𐑄𐐰𐐻 𐐸𐐨 𐑇𐐳𐐼 𐐹𐐯𐑉𐐮𐑇

𐑌𐐱𐐻; 𐐸𐐶𐐯𐑉𐑁𐐬𐑉 𐑄 𐑉𐐯𐑋𐑌𐐲𐑌𐐻 𐐱𐑂 𐑄 𐐸𐐵𐑅 𐐱𐑂 𐐖𐐬𐑆𐐯𐑁 𐑇𐐰𐑊 𐐺𐐨 𐐺𐐮𐑊𐐻 𐐲𐐹𐐱𐑌 𐑄𐐮𐑅 𐑊𐐰𐑌𐐼; 𐐰𐑌𐐼 𐐮𐐻 𐑇𐐰𐑊 𐐺𐐨 𐐩 𐑊𐐰𐑌𐐼 𐐱𐑂 𐑄𐐯𐑉 𐐮𐑌𐐸𐐯𐑉𐐮𐐻𐐲𐑌𐑅; 𐐰𐑌𐐼 𐑄𐐩 𐑇𐐰𐑊 𐐺𐐮𐑊𐐼 𐐲𐐹 𐐩 𐐸𐐬𐑊𐐨 𐑅𐐮𐐻𐐨 𐐲𐑌𐐻𐐭 𐑄 𐐢𐐫𐑉𐐼, 𐑊𐐴𐐿 𐐲𐑌𐐻𐐭 𐑄 𐐖𐐯𐑉𐐭𐑅𐐰𐑊𐐯𐑋 𐐱𐑂 𐐬𐑊𐐼; 𐐰𐑌𐐼 𐑄𐐩 𐑇𐐰𐑊 𐑌𐐬 𐑋𐐬𐑉 𐐺𐐨 𐐿𐐱𐑌𐑁𐐵𐑌𐐼𐐯𐐼, 𐐲𐑌𐐻𐐮𐑊 𐑄 𐐯𐑌𐐼 𐐿𐐲𐑋 𐐸𐐶𐐯𐑌 𐑄 𐐲𐑉𐑃 𐑇𐐰𐑊 𐐹𐐪𐑅 𐐰𐐶𐐩. 𐐰𐑌𐐼 𐑄𐐯𐑉 𐑇𐐰𐑊 𐐺𐐨 𐐩 𐑌𐐭 𐐸𐐯𐑂𐐲𐑌 𐐰𐑌𐐼 𐐩 𐑌𐐭 𐐲𐑉𐑃; 𐐰𐑌𐐼 𐑄𐐩 𐑇𐐰𐑊 𐐺𐐨 𐑊𐐴𐐿 𐐲𐑌𐐻𐐭 𐑄 𐐬𐑊𐐼, 𐑅𐐩𐑂 𐑄 𐐬𐑊𐐼 𐐸𐐰𐑂 𐐹𐐪𐑅𐐻 𐐰𐐶𐐩, 𐐰𐑌𐐼 𐐫𐑊 𐑃𐐮𐑍𐑆 𐐸𐐰𐑂 𐐺𐐨𐐿𐐲𐑋 𐑌𐐭. 𐐰𐑌𐐼 𐑄𐐯𐑌 𐐿𐐲𐑋𐐯𐑃 𐑄 𐑌𐐭 𐐖𐐯𐑉𐐭𐑅𐐰𐑊𐐯𐑋; 𐐰𐑌𐐼 𐐺𐑊𐐯𐑅𐐯𐐼 𐐪𐑉 𐑄𐐩 𐐸𐐭 𐐼𐐶𐐯𐑊 𐑄𐐯𐑉𐐮𐑌, 𐑁𐐫𐑉 𐐮𐐻 𐐮𐑆 𐑄𐐩 𐐸𐐭𐑆 𐑀𐐪𐑉𐑋𐐲𐑌𐐻𐑅 𐐪𐑉 𐐸𐐶𐐴𐐻 𐑃𐑉𐐭 𐑄 𐐺𐑊𐐲𐐼 𐐱𐑂 𐑄 𐐢𐐰𐑋; 𐐰𐑌𐐼 𐑄𐐩 𐐪𐑉 𐑄𐐩 𐐸𐐭 𐐪𐑉 𐑌𐐲𐑋𐐺𐐲𐑉𐐼 𐐲𐑋𐐲𐑍 𐑄 𐑉𐐯𐑋𐑌𐐲𐑌𐐻 𐐱𐑂 𐑄 𐑅𐐨𐐼 𐐱𐑂 𐐖𐐬𐑆𐐯𐑁, 𐐸𐐭 𐐶𐐲𐑉 𐐱𐑂 𐑄 𐐸𐐵𐑅 𐐱𐑂 𐐆𐑆𐑉𐐩𐐯𐑊. 𐐰𐑌𐐼 𐑄𐐯𐑌 𐐫𐑊𐑅𐐬 𐐿𐐲𐑋𐐯𐑃 𐑄 𐐖𐐯𐑉𐐭𐑅𐐰𐑊𐐯𐑋 𐐱𐑂 𐐬𐑊𐐼; 𐐰𐑌𐐼 𐑄 𐐮𐑌𐐸𐐰𐐺𐐮𐐻𐐲𐑌𐐻𐑅 𐑄𐐯𐑉𐐱𐑂, 𐐺𐑊𐐯𐑅𐐯𐐼 𐐪𐑉 𐑄𐐩, 𐑁𐐫𐑉 𐑄𐐩 𐐸𐐰𐑂 𐐺𐐮𐑌 𐐶𐐱𐑇𐐻 𐐮𐑌 𐑄 𐐺𐑊𐐲𐐼 𐐱𐑂 𐑄 𐐢𐐰𐑋; 𐐰𐑌𐐼 𐑄𐐩 𐐪𐑉 𐑄𐐩 𐐸𐐭 𐐶𐐲𐑉 𐑅𐐿𐐰𐐻𐐲𐑉𐐼 𐐰𐑌𐐼 𐑀𐐰𐑄𐐲𐑉𐐼 𐐮𐑌 𐑁𐑉𐐱𐑋 𐑄 𐑁𐐬𐑉 𐐿𐐶𐐫𐑉𐐻𐐲𐑉𐑆 𐐱𐑂 𐑄 𐐲𐑉𐑃, 𐐰𐑌𐐼 𐑁𐑉𐐱𐑋 𐑄 𐑌𐐫𐑉𐑃 𐐿𐐲𐑌𐐻𐑉𐐨𐑆, 𐐰𐑌𐐼 𐐪𐑉 𐐹𐐪𐑉𐐻𐐩𐐿𐐲𐑉𐑆 𐐱𐑂 𐑄 𐑁𐐳𐑊𐑁𐐮𐑊𐐮𐑍 𐐱𐑂 𐑄 𐐿𐐲𐑂𐐯𐑌𐐰𐑌𐐻 𐐸𐐶𐐮𐐽 𐐘𐐱𐐼 𐑋𐐩𐐼 𐐶𐐮𐑄 𐑄𐐯𐑉 𐑁𐐪𐑄𐐲𐑉 𐐁𐐺𐑉𐐰𐐸𐐰𐑋. 𐐰𐑌𐐼 𐐸𐐶𐐯𐑌 𐑄𐐨𐑆 𐑃𐐮𐑍𐑆 𐐿𐐲𐑋, 𐐺𐑉𐐮𐑍𐐯𐑃 𐐻𐐭 𐐹𐐪𐑅 𐑄 𐑅𐐿𐑉𐐮𐐹𐐽𐐲𐑉 𐐸𐐶𐐮𐐽 𐑅𐐯𐑃, 𐑄𐐯𐑉 𐐪𐑉 𐑄𐐩 𐐸𐐭 𐐶𐐲𐑉 𐑁𐐲𐑉𐑅𐐻, 𐐸𐐭 𐑇𐐰𐑊 𐐺𐐨 𐑊𐐪𐑅𐐻; 𐐰𐑌𐐼 𐑄𐐯𐑉 𐐪𐑉 𐑄𐐩 𐐸𐐭 𐐶𐐲𐑉 𐑊𐐪𐑅𐐻, 𐐸𐐭 𐑇𐐰𐑊 𐐺𐐨 𐑁𐐲𐑉𐑅𐐻.

2. 𐐰𐑌𐐼 𐐌 𐐶𐐱𐑆 𐐰𐐺𐐵𐐻 𐐻𐐭 𐑉𐐴𐐻 𐑋𐐬𐑉, 𐐺𐐲𐐻 𐐌 𐐰𐑋 𐑁𐐫𐑉𐐺𐐮𐐼𐐲𐑌; 𐐺𐐲𐐻 𐑀𐑉𐐩𐐻 𐐰𐑌𐐼 𐑋𐐪𐑉𐑂𐐯𐑊𐐲𐑅 𐐶𐐲𐑉 𐑄 𐐹𐑉𐐱𐑁𐐯𐑅𐐨𐑆 𐐱𐑂 𐐀𐑃𐐲𐑉, 𐐺𐐲𐐻 𐑄𐐩 𐐯𐑅𐐻𐐨𐑋𐐼 𐐸𐐮𐑋 𐐰𐑆 𐑌𐐫𐐻, 𐐰𐑌𐐼 𐐿𐐪𐑅𐐻 𐐸𐐮𐑋 𐐵𐐻; 𐐰𐑌𐐼 𐐸𐐨 𐐸𐐮𐐼 𐐸𐐮𐑋𐑅𐐯𐑊𐑁 𐐮𐑌 𐑄 𐐿𐐰𐑂𐐮𐐻𐐨 𐐱𐑂 𐐩 𐑉𐐱𐐿 𐐺𐐴 𐐼𐐩; 𐐰𐑌𐐼 𐐺𐐴 𐑌𐐴𐐻 𐐸𐐨 𐐶𐐯𐑌𐐻 𐑁𐐬𐑉𐑃 𐑂𐐷𐐭𐐮𐑍 𐑄 𐑃𐐮𐑍𐑆 𐐸𐐶𐐮𐐽 𐑇𐐳𐐼 𐐿𐐲𐑋 𐐲𐐹𐐱𐑌 𐑄 𐐹𐐨𐐹𐐲𐑊. 𐐰𐑌𐐼 𐐰𐑆 𐐸𐐨 𐐼𐐶𐐯𐑊𐐻 𐐮𐑌 𐑄 𐐿𐐰𐑂𐐮𐐻𐐨 𐐱𐑂 𐐩 𐑉𐐱𐐿, 𐐸𐐨 𐑋𐐩𐐼 𐑄 𐑉𐐨𐑋𐐩𐑌𐐼𐐲𐑉 𐐱𐑂 𐑄𐐮𐑅 𐑉𐐯𐐿𐐲𐑉𐐼, 𐑂𐐷𐐭𐐮𐑍 𐑄 𐐼𐐯𐑅𐐻𐑉𐐲𐐿𐑇𐐲𐑌𐑆 𐐸𐐶𐐮𐐽 𐐿𐐩𐑋 𐐲𐐹𐐱𐑌 𐑄 𐐹𐐨𐐹𐐲𐑊, 𐐺𐐴 𐑌𐐴𐐻. 𐐰𐑌𐐼 𐐮𐐻 𐐿𐐩𐑋 𐐻𐐭 𐐹𐐪𐑅 𐑄𐐰𐐻 𐐮𐑌 𐑄𐐰𐐻 𐑅𐐩𐑋 𐐷𐐨𐑉 𐐮𐑌 𐐸𐐶𐐮𐐽 𐐸𐐨 𐐶𐐱𐑆 𐐿𐐪𐑅𐐻 𐐵𐐻 𐑁𐑉𐐱𐑋 𐐲𐑋𐐲𐑍 𐑄 𐐹𐐨𐐹𐐲𐑊, 𐑄𐐯𐑉 𐐺𐐨𐑀𐐰𐑌 𐐻𐐭 𐐺𐐨 𐐩 𐑀𐑉𐐩𐐻 𐐶𐐫𐑉 𐐲𐑋𐐲𐑍 𐑄 𐐹𐐨𐐹𐐲𐑊, 𐑁𐐫𐑉 𐑄𐐯𐑉 𐐶𐐲𐑉 𐑋𐐯𐑌𐐨 𐐸𐐭 𐑉𐐬𐑆 𐐲𐐹, 𐐸𐐭 𐐶𐐲𐑉 𐑋𐐴𐐻𐐨 𐑋𐐯𐑌, 𐐰𐑌𐐼 𐑅𐐫𐐻 𐐻𐐭 𐐼𐐯𐑅𐐻𐑉𐐱𐐨 𐐗𐐬𐑉𐐨𐐰𐑌𐐻𐐲𐑋𐐲𐑉 𐐺𐐴 𐑄𐐯𐑉 𐑅𐐨𐐿𐑉𐐯𐐻 𐐹𐑊𐐰𐑌𐑆 𐐱𐑂 𐐶𐐮𐐿𐐯𐐼𐑌𐐯𐑅, 𐐱𐑂 𐐸𐐶𐐮𐐽 𐐸𐐰𐑃 𐐺𐐮𐑌 𐑅𐐹𐐬𐐿𐐲𐑌. 𐐰𐑌𐐼 𐑌𐐵 𐐗𐐬𐑉𐐨𐐰𐑌𐐻𐐲𐑋𐐲𐑉, 𐐸𐐰𐑂𐐮𐑍 𐑅𐐻𐐲𐐼𐐨𐐼, 𐐸𐐮𐑋𐑅𐐯𐑊𐑁, 𐐮𐑌 𐐫𐑊 𐑄 𐐪𐑉𐐻𐑅 𐐱𐑂 𐐶𐐫𐑉, 𐐰𐑌𐐼 𐐫𐑊 𐑄 𐐿𐐲𐑌𐐮𐑍 𐐱𐑂 𐑄 𐐶𐐲𐑉𐑊𐐼, 𐐸𐐶𐐯𐑉𐑁𐐬𐑉 𐐸𐐨 𐑀𐐩𐑂 𐐺𐐰𐐻𐐲𐑊 𐐲𐑌𐐻𐐭 𐑄𐐯𐑋 𐐸𐐭 𐑅𐐫𐐻 𐐻𐐭 𐐼𐐯𐑅𐐻𐑉𐐱𐐨 𐐸𐐮𐑋; 𐐺𐐲𐐻 𐐸𐐨 𐑉𐐯𐐹𐐯𐑌𐐻𐐯𐐼 𐑌𐐱𐐻, 𐑌𐐨𐑄𐐲𐑉 𐐸𐐮𐑆 𐑁𐐯𐑉 𐑅𐐲𐑌𐑆 𐑌𐐫𐑉 𐐼𐐫𐐻𐐲𐑉𐑆; 𐑌𐐨𐑄𐐲𐑉 𐑄 𐑁𐐯𐑉 𐑅𐐲𐑌𐑆 𐐰𐑌𐐼 𐐼𐐫𐐻𐐲𐑉𐑆 𐐱𐑂 𐐗𐐬𐐸𐐫𐑉; 𐑌𐐨𐑄𐐲𐑉 𐑄 𐑁𐐯𐑉 𐑅𐐲𐑌𐑆 𐐰𐑌𐐼 𐐼𐐫𐐻𐐲𐑉𐑆 𐐱𐑂 𐐗𐐬𐑉𐐴𐐸𐐫𐑉; 𐐰𐑌𐐼 𐐮𐑌 𐑁𐐴𐑌, 𐑄𐐯𐑉 𐐶𐐲𐑉 𐑌𐐲𐑌 𐐱𐑂 𐑄 𐑁𐐯𐑉 𐑅𐐲𐑌𐑆 𐐰𐑌𐐼 𐐼𐐫𐐻𐐲𐑉𐑆 𐐲𐐹𐐱𐑌 𐑄 𐑁𐐩𐑅 𐐱𐑂 𐑄 𐐸𐐬𐑊 𐐲𐑉𐑃, 𐐸𐐭 𐑉𐐯𐐹𐐯𐑌𐐻𐐯𐐼 𐐱𐑂 𐑄𐐯𐑉 𐑅𐐮𐑌𐑆; 𐐸𐐶𐐯𐑉𐑁𐐬𐑉 𐐮𐐻 𐐿𐐩𐑋 𐐻𐐭 𐐹𐐪𐑅 𐑄𐐰𐐻 𐐮𐑌 𐑄 𐑁𐐲𐑉𐑅𐐻 𐐷𐐨𐑉 𐑄𐐰𐐻 𐐀𐑃𐐲𐑉 𐐼𐐶𐐯𐑊𐐻 𐐮𐑌 𐑄 𐐿𐐰𐑂𐐮𐐻𐐨 𐐱𐑂 𐐩 𐑉𐐱𐐿, 𐑄𐐯𐑉 𐐶𐐲𐑉 𐑋𐐯𐑌𐐨 𐐹𐐨𐐹𐐲𐑊 𐐸𐐭 𐐶𐐲𐑉 𐑅𐑊𐐩𐑌 𐐺𐐴 𐑄 𐑅𐐬𐑉𐐼 𐐱𐑂 𐑄𐐬𐑆 𐑅𐐨𐐿𐑉𐐯𐐻 𐐿𐐱𐑋𐐺𐐮𐑌𐐩𐑇𐐲𐑌𐑆, 𐑁𐐴𐐻𐐮𐑍 𐐰𐑀𐐯𐑌𐑅𐐻 𐐗𐐬𐑉𐐨𐐰𐑌𐐻𐐲𐑋𐐲𐑉, 𐑄𐐰𐐻 𐑄𐐩 𐑋𐐴𐐻 𐐱𐐺𐐻𐐩𐑌 𐑄 𐐿𐐮𐑍𐐼𐐲𐑋. 𐐰𐑌𐐼 𐐮𐐻 𐐿𐐩𐑋 𐐻𐐭 𐐹𐐪𐑅 𐑄𐐰𐐻 𐑄 𐑅𐐲𐑌𐑆 𐐱𐑂 𐐗𐐬𐑉𐐨𐐰𐑌𐐻𐐲𐑋𐐲𐑉 𐑁𐐫𐐻 𐑋𐐲𐐽, 𐐰𐑌𐐼 𐐺𐑊𐐯𐐼 𐑋𐐲𐐽. 𐐰𐑌𐐼 𐐮𐑌 𐑄 𐑅𐐯𐐿𐐲𐑌𐐼 𐐷𐐨𐑉, 𐑄 𐐶𐐲𐑉𐐼 𐐱𐑂 𐑄 𐐢𐐫𐑉𐐼 𐐿𐐩𐑋 𐐻𐐭 𐐀𐑃𐐲𐑉, 𐑄𐐰𐐻 𐐸𐐨 𐑇𐐳𐐼 𐑀𐐬 𐐰𐑌𐐼 𐐹𐑉𐐱𐑁𐐯𐑅𐐴 𐐲𐑌𐐻𐐭 𐐗𐐬𐑉𐐨𐐰𐑌𐐻𐐲𐑋𐐲𐑉, 𐑄𐐰𐐻 𐐮𐑁 𐐸𐐨 𐐶𐐳𐐼 𐑉𐐯𐐹𐐯𐑌𐐻, 𐐰𐑌𐐼 𐐫𐑊 𐐸𐐮𐑆 𐐸𐐵𐑅𐐸𐐬𐑊𐐼, 𐑄 𐐢𐐫𐑉𐐼 𐐶𐐳𐐼 𐑀𐐮𐑂 𐐲𐑌𐐻𐐭 𐐸𐐮𐑋 𐐸𐐮𐑆 𐐿𐐮𐑍𐐼𐐲𐑋, 𐐰𐑌𐐼 𐑅𐐹𐐯𐑉 𐑄 𐐹𐐨𐐹𐐲𐑊, 𐐲𐑄𐐲𐑉𐐶𐐴𐑆 𐑄𐐩 𐑇𐐳𐐼 𐐺𐐨 𐐼𐐯𐑅𐐻𐑉𐐱𐐨𐐼, 𐐰𐑌𐐼 𐐫𐑊 𐐸𐐮𐑆 𐐸𐐵𐑅𐐸𐐬𐑊𐐼, 𐑅𐐩𐑂 𐐮𐐻 𐐶𐐲𐑉 𐐸𐐮𐑋𐑅𐐯𐑊𐑁, 𐐰𐑌𐐼 𐐸𐐨 𐑇𐐳𐐼 𐐬𐑌𐑊𐐨 𐑊𐐮𐑂 𐐻𐐭 𐑅𐐨 𐑄 𐑁𐐳𐑊𐑁𐐮𐑊𐐮𐑍 𐐱𐑂 𐑄 𐐹𐑉𐐱𐑁𐐯𐑅𐐨𐑆 𐐸𐐶𐐮𐐽 𐐸𐐰𐐼 𐐺𐐮𐑌 𐑅𐐹𐐬𐐿𐐲𐑌 𐐿𐐲𐑌𐑅𐐲𐑉𐑌𐐮𐑍 𐐰𐑌𐐲𐑄𐐲𐑉 𐐹𐐨𐐹𐐲𐑊 𐑉𐐨𐑅𐐨𐑂𐐮𐑍 𐑄 𐑊𐐰𐑌𐐼 𐑁𐐫𐑉 𐑄𐐯𐑉 𐐮𐑌𐐸𐐯𐑉𐐮𐐻𐐲𐑌𐑅; 𐐰𐑌𐐼 𐐗𐐬𐑉𐐨𐐰𐑌𐐻𐐲𐑋𐐲𐑉 𐑇𐐳𐐼 𐑉𐐨𐑅𐐨𐑂 𐐩 𐐺𐐯𐑉𐐨𐐲𐑊 𐐺𐐴 𐑄𐐯𐑋; 𐐰𐑌𐐼 𐐯𐑂𐐲𐑉𐐨 𐑅𐐬𐑊 𐑇𐐳𐐼 𐐺𐐨 𐐼𐐯𐑅𐐻𐑉𐐱𐐨𐐼 𐑅𐐩𐑂 𐐮𐐻 𐐶𐐲𐑉 𐐗𐐬𐑉𐐨𐐰𐑌𐐻𐐲𐑋𐐲𐑉.

3. 𐐰𐑌𐐼 𐐮𐐻 𐐿𐐩𐑋 𐐻𐐭 𐐹𐐪𐑅 𐑄𐐰𐐻 𐐗𐐬𐑉𐐨𐐰𐑌𐐻𐐲𐑋𐐲𐑉 𐑉𐐯𐐹𐐯𐑌𐐻𐐯𐐼 𐑌𐐱𐐻, 𐑌𐐨𐑄𐐲𐑉 𐐸𐐮𐑆 𐐸𐐵𐑅𐐸𐐬𐑊𐐼, 𐑌𐐨𐑄𐐲𐑉 𐑄 𐐹𐐨𐐹𐐲𐑊; 𐐰𐑌𐐼 𐑄 𐐶𐐫𐑉𐑆 𐑅𐐨𐑅𐐻 𐑌𐐱𐐻; 𐐰𐑌𐐼 𐑄𐐩 𐑅𐐫𐐻 𐐻𐐭 𐐿𐐮𐑊 𐐀𐑃𐐲𐑉, 𐐺𐐲𐐻 𐐸𐐨 𐑁𐑊𐐯𐐼 𐑁𐑉𐐱𐑋 𐐺𐐨𐑁𐐬𐑉 𐑄𐐯𐑋, 𐐰𐑌𐐼 𐐸𐐮𐐼 𐐰𐑀𐐯𐑌 𐐮𐑌 𐑄 𐐿𐐰𐑂𐐮𐐻𐐨 𐐱𐑂 𐑄 𐑉𐐱𐐿. 𐐰𐑌𐐼 𐐮𐐻 𐐿𐐩𐑋 𐐻𐐭 𐐹𐐪𐑅 𐑄𐐰𐐻

𐐜𐐯𐑉 𐐲𐑉𐐬𐑆 𐐲𐐹 𐐟𐐩𐑉𐐯𐐼, 𐐰𐑌𐐼 𐐸𐐨 𐐫𐑊𐑅𐐬 𐑀𐐩𐑂 𐐺𐐰𐐻𐑊 𐐲𐑌𐐻𐐭 𐐗𐐬𐑉𐐨𐐰𐑌𐐻𐐲𐑋𐐲𐑉; 𐐰𐑌𐐼 𐐸𐐨 𐐼𐐮𐐼 𐐺𐐨𐐻 𐐸𐐮𐑋, 𐐮𐑌𐑅𐐬𐑋𐐲𐐽 𐑄𐐰𐐻 𐐮𐑌 𐑄 𐑃𐐲𐑉𐐼 𐐷𐐨𐑉 𐐸𐐨 𐐼𐐮𐐼 𐐺𐑉𐐮𐑍 𐐸𐐮𐑋 𐐮𐑌𐐻𐐭 𐐿𐐰𐐹𐐻𐐮𐑂𐐮𐐻𐐨. 𐐈𐑌𐐼 𐑄 𐑅𐐲𐑌𐑆 𐐱𐑂 𐐗𐐬𐑉𐐨𐐰𐑌𐐻𐐲𐑋𐐲𐑉, 𐐮𐑌 𐑄 𐑁𐐬𐑉𐑃 𐐷𐐨𐑉, 𐐼𐐮𐐼 𐐺𐐨𐐻 𐐟𐐩𐑉𐐯𐐼, 𐐰𐑌𐐼 𐐼𐐮𐐼 𐐱𐐺𐐻𐐩𐑌 𐑄 𐐿𐐮𐑍𐐼𐐲𐑋 𐐲𐑀𐐯𐑌 𐐲𐑌𐐻𐐭 𐑄𐐯𐑉 𐑁𐐪𐑄𐐲𐑉. 𐐤𐐵 𐑄𐐯𐑉 𐐺𐐨𐑀𐐰𐑌 𐐻𐐭 𐐺𐐨 𐐲 𐐶𐐪𐑉 𐐲𐐹𐐱𐑌 𐐫𐑊 𐑄 𐑁𐐩𐑅 𐐱𐑂 𐑄 𐑊𐐰𐑌𐐼, 𐐯𐑂𐐲𐑉𐐨 𐑋𐐰𐑌 𐐶𐐮𐑄 𐐸𐐮𐑆 𐐺𐐰𐑌𐐼 𐑁𐐴𐐻𐐮𐑍 𐑁𐐬𐑉 𐑄𐐰𐐻 𐐸𐐶𐐮𐐽 𐐸𐐨 𐐼𐐮𐑆𐐴𐑉𐐼. 𐐈𐑌𐐼 𐑄𐐯𐑉 𐐶𐐲𐑉 𐑉𐐱𐐺𐐲𐑉𐑆, 𐐰𐑌𐐼 𐐮𐑌 𐑁𐐴𐑌, 𐐫𐑊 𐑋𐐰𐑌𐐲𐑉 𐐱𐑂 𐐶𐐮𐐿𐐯𐐼𐑌𐐯𐑅 𐐲𐐹𐐱𐑌 𐐫𐑊 𐑄 𐑁𐐩𐑅 𐐱𐑂 𐑄 𐑊𐐰𐑌𐐼. 𐐈𐑌𐐼 𐐮𐐻 𐐿𐐩𐑋 𐐻𐐭 𐐹𐐰𐑅 𐑄𐐰𐐻 𐐗𐐬𐑉𐐨𐐰𐑌𐐻𐐲𐑋𐐲𐑉 𐐶𐐱𐑆 𐐯𐐿𐑅𐐨𐐼𐐮𐑍𐑊𐐨 𐐰𐑍𐑀𐑉𐐨 𐐶𐐮𐑄 𐐟𐐩𐑉𐐯𐐼, 𐐰𐑌𐐼 𐐸𐐨 𐐶𐐯𐑌𐐻 𐐲𐑀𐐯𐑌𐑅𐐻 𐐸𐐮𐑋 𐐶𐐮𐑄 𐐸𐐮𐑆 𐐪𐑉𐑋𐐨𐑆 𐐻𐐭 𐐺𐐰𐐻𐑊; 𐐰𐑌𐐼 𐑄𐐩 𐐼𐐮𐐼 𐑋𐐨𐐻 𐐮𐑌 𐑀𐑉𐐩𐐻 𐐰𐑍𐑀𐐲𐑉, 𐐰𐑌𐐼 𐑄𐐩 𐐼𐐮𐐼 𐑋𐐨𐐻 𐐮𐑌 𐑄 𐑂𐐰𐑊𐐨 𐐱𐑂 𐐘𐐮𐑊𐑀𐐰𐑊; 𐐰𐑌𐐼 𐑄 𐐺𐐰𐐻𐑊 𐐺𐐨𐐿𐐩𐑋 𐐯𐐿𐑅𐐨𐐼𐐮𐑍𐑊𐐨 𐑅𐐬𐑉. 𐐈𐑌𐐼 𐐮𐐻 𐐿𐐩𐑋 𐐻𐐭 𐐹𐐰𐑅 𐑄𐐰𐐻 𐐟𐐩𐑉𐐯𐐼 𐑁𐐫𐐻 𐐲𐑀𐐯𐑌𐑅𐐻 𐐸𐐮𐑋 𐑁𐐬𐑉 𐑄 𐑅𐐹𐐩𐑅 𐐱𐑂 𐑃𐑉𐐨 𐐼𐐩𐑆. 𐐈𐑌𐐼 𐐮𐐻 𐐿𐐩𐑋 𐐻𐐭 𐐹𐐰𐑅 𐑄𐐰𐐻 𐐗𐐬𐑉𐐨𐐰𐑌𐐻𐐲𐑋𐐲𐑉 𐐺𐐨𐐻 𐐸𐐮𐑋, 𐐰𐑌𐐼 𐐼𐐮𐐼 𐐹𐐲𐑉𐑅𐐭 𐐸𐐮𐑋 𐐲𐑌𐐻𐐮𐑊 𐐸𐐨 𐐿𐐩𐑋 𐐻𐐭 𐑄 𐐹𐑊𐐩𐑌𐑆 𐐱𐑂 𐐐𐐯𐑇𐑊𐐱𐑌. 𐐈𐑌𐐼 𐐮𐐻 𐐿𐐩𐑋 𐐻𐐭 𐐹𐐰𐑅 𐑄𐐰𐐻 𐐟𐐩𐑉𐐯𐐼 𐑀𐐩𐑂 𐐸𐐮𐑋 𐐺𐐰𐐻𐑊 𐐲𐑀𐐯𐑌 𐐲𐐹𐐱𐑌 𐑄 𐐹𐑊𐐩𐑌𐑆; 𐐰𐑌𐐼 𐐺𐐨𐐸𐐬𐑊𐐼, 𐐸𐐨 𐐼𐐮𐐼 𐐺𐐨𐐻 𐐗𐐬𐑉𐐨𐐰𐑌𐐻𐐲𐑋𐐲𐑉, 𐐰𐑌𐐼 𐐼𐑉𐐬𐑂 𐐸𐐮𐑋 𐐺𐐰𐐿 𐐲𐑀𐐯𐑌 𐐻𐐭 𐑄 𐑂𐐰𐑊𐐨 𐐱𐑂 𐐘𐐮𐑊𐑀𐐰𐑊. 𐐈𐑌𐐼 𐐗𐐬𐑉𐐨𐐰𐑌𐐻𐐲𐑋𐐲𐑉 𐑀𐐩𐑂 𐐟𐐩𐑉𐐯𐐼 𐐺𐐰𐐻𐑊 𐐲𐑀𐐯𐑌 𐐮𐑌 𐑄 𐑂𐐰𐑊𐐨 𐐱𐑂 𐐘𐐮𐑊𐑀𐐰𐑊, 𐐮𐑌 𐐸𐐶𐐮𐐽 𐐸𐐨 𐐺𐐨𐐻 𐐟𐐩𐑉𐐯𐐼 𐐰𐑌𐐼 𐑅𐑊𐐭 𐐸𐐮𐑋. 𐐈𐑌𐐼 𐐟𐐩𐑉𐐯𐐼 𐐶𐐭𐑌𐐼𐐯𐐼 𐐗𐐬𐑉𐐨𐐰𐑌𐐻𐐲𐑋𐐲𐑉 𐐮𐑌 𐐸𐐮𐑆 𐑃𐐴, 𐑄𐐰𐐻 𐐸𐐨 𐐼𐐮𐐼 𐑌𐐱𐐻 𐑀𐐬 𐐻𐐭 𐐺𐐰𐐻𐑊 𐐲𐑀𐐯𐑌 𐑁𐐬𐑉 𐑄 𐑅𐐹𐐩𐑅 𐐱𐑂 𐐻𐐭 𐐷𐐨𐑉𐑆, 𐐮𐑌 𐐸𐐶𐐮𐐽 𐐻𐐴𐑋 𐐫𐑊 𐑄 𐐹𐐨𐐹𐑊 𐐲𐐹𐐱𐑌 𐑄 𐑁𐐩𐑅 𐐱𐑂 𐑄 𐑊𐐰𐑌𐐼 𐐶𐐲𐑉 𐑇𐐯𐐼𐐮𐑍 𐐺𐑊𐐲𐐼, 𐐰𐑌𐐼 𐑄𐐯𐑉 𐐶𐐱𐑆 𐑌𐐲𐑌 𐐻𐐭 𐑉𐐨𐑅𐐻𐑉𐐩𐑌 𐑄𐐯𐑋. 𐐈𐑌𐐼 𐑌𐐵 𐑄𐐯𐑉 𐐺𐐨𐑀𐐰𐑌 𐐻𐐭 𐐺𐐨 𐐲 𐑀𐑉𐐩𐐻 𐐿𐐲𐑉𐑅 𐐲𐐹𐐱𐑌 𐐫𐑊 𐑄 𐑊𐐰𐑌𐐼, 𐐺𐐨𐐿𐐫𐑆 𐐱𐑂 𐑄 𐐮𐑌𐐮𐐿𐐶𐐮𐐻𐐨 𐐱𐑂 𐑄 𐐹𐐨𐐹𐑊, 𐐮𐑌 𐐸𐐶𐐮𐐽, 𐐮𐑁 𐐲 𐑋𐐰𐑌 𐑇𐐳𐐼 𐑊𐐩 𐐸𐐮𐑆 𐐻𐐭𐑊 𐐫𐑉 𐐸𐐮𐑆 𐑅𐐬𐑉𐐼 𐐲𐐹𐐱𐑌 𐐸𐐮𐑆 𐑇𐐯𐑊𐑁, 𐐫𐑉 𐐲𐐹𐐱𐑌 𐑄 𐐹𐑊𐐩𐑅 𐐸𐐶𐐮𐑄𐐲𐑉 𐐸𐐨 𐐶𐐳𐐼 𐐿𐐨𐐹 𐐮𐐻, 𐐺𐐨𐐸𐐬𐑊𐐼, 𐐲𐐹𐐱𐑌 𐑄 𐑋𐐱𐑉𐐬, 𐐸𐐨 𐐿𐐳𐐼 𐑌𐐱𐐻 𐑁𐐴𐑌𐐼 𐐮𐐻, 𐑅𐐬 𐑀𐑉𐐩𐐻 𐐶𐐱𐑆 𐑄 𐐿𐐲𐑉𐑅 𐐲𐐹𐐱𐑌 𐑄 𐑊𐐰𐑌𐐼. 𐐐𐐶𐐯𐑉𐑁𐐬𐑉 𐐯𐑂𐐲𐑉𐐨 𐑋𐐰𐑌 𐐼𐐮𐐼 𐐿𐑊𐐨𐑂 𐐲𐑌𐐻𐐭 𐑄𐐰𐐻 𐐸𐐶𐐮𐐽 𐐶𐐱𐑆 𐐸𐐮𐑆 𐐬𐑌, 𐐶𐐮𐑄 𐐸𐐮𐑆 𐐸𐐰𐑌𐐼𐑆, 𐐰𐑌𐐼 𐐶𐐳𐐼 𐑌𐐱𐐻 𐐺𐐱𐑉𐐬, 𐑌𐐨𐑄𐐲𐑉 𐐶𐐳𐐼 𐐸𐐨 𐑊𐐯𐑌𐐼; 𐐰𐑌𐐼 𐐯𐑂𐐲𐑉𐐨 𐑋𐐰𐑌 𐐿𐐯𐐹𐐻 𐑄 𐐸𐐮𐑊𐐻 𐐱𐑂 𐐸𐐮𐑆 𐑅𐐬𐑉𐐼 𐐮𐑌 𐐸𐐮𐑆 𐑉𐐴𐐻 𐐸𐐰𐑌𐐼, 𐐮𐑌 𐑄 𐐼𐐨𐑁𐐯𐑌𐑅 𐐱𐑂 𐐸𐐮𐑆 𐐹𐑉𐐱𐐹𐐲𐑉𐐻𐐨 𐐰𐑌𐐼 𐐸𐐮𐑆 𐐬𐑌 𐑊𐐴𐑁, 𐐰𐑌𐐼 𐐱𐑂 𐐸𐐮𐑆 𐐶𐐴𐑂𐑆 𐐰𐑌𐐼 𐐽𐐮𐑊𐐼𐑉𐐯𐑌.

4. 𐐈𐑌𐐼 𐑌𐐵, 𐐰𐑁𐐻𐐲𐑉 𐑄 𐑅𐐹𐐩𐑅 𐐱𐑂 𐐻𐐭 𐐷𐐨𐑉𐑆, 𐐰𐑌𐐼 𐐰𐑁𐐻𐐲𐑉 𐑄 𐐼𐐯𐑃 𐐱𐑂 𐐟𐐩𐑉𐐯𐐼, 𐐺𐐨𐐸𐐬𐑊𐐼, 𐑄𐐯𐑉 𐐲𐑉𐐬𐑆 𐑄 𐐺𐑉𐐲𐑄𐐲𐑉 𐐱𐑂 𐐟𐐩𐑉𐐯𐐼, 𐐰𐑌𐐼 𐐸𐐨 𐑀𐐩𐑂 𐐺𐐰𐐻𐑊 𐐲𐑌𐐻𐐭 𐐗𐐬𐑉𐐨𐐰𐑌𐐻𐐲𐑋𐐲𐑉, 𐐮𐑌 𐐸𐐶𐐮𐐽 𐐗𐐬𐑉𐐨𐐰𐑌𐐻𐐲𐑋𐐲𐑉 𐐼𐐮𐐼 𐐺𐐨𐐻 𐐸𐐮𐑋, 𐐰𐑌𐐼 𐐼𐐮𐐼 𐐹𐐲𐑉𐑅𐐭 𐐸𐐮𐑋 𐐻𐐭 𐑄 𐐶𐐮𐑊𐐼𐐲𐑉𐑌𐐯𐑅 𐐱𐑂 𐐈𐐿𐐮𐑇. 𐐈𐑌𐐼 𐐮𐐻 𐐿𐐩𐑋 𐐻𐐭 𐐹𐐰𐑅 𐑄𐐰𐐻 𐑄 𐐺𐑉𐐲𐑄𐐲𐑉 𐐱𐑂 𐐟𐐩𐑉𐐯𐐼 𐐼𐐮𐐼 𐑀𐐮𐑂 𐐺𐐰𐐻𐑊 𐐲𐑌𐐻𐐭 𐐸𐐮𐑋 𐐮𐑌 𐑄 𐐶𐐮𐑊𐐼𐐲𐑉𐑌𐐯𐑅 𐐱𐑂 𐐈𐐿𐐮𐑇; 𐐰𐑌𐐼 𐑄 𐐺𐐰𐐻𐑊 𐐺𐐨𐐿𐐩𐑋 𐐯𐐿𐑅𐐨𐐼𐐮𐑍𐑊𐐨 𐑅𐐬𐑉, 𐐰𐑌𐐼 𐑋𐐯𐑌𐐨 𐑃𐐵𐑆𐐲𐑌𐐼𐑆 𐑁𐐯𐑊 𐐺𐐴 𐑄 𐑅𐐬𐑉𐐼. 𐐈𐑌𐐼 𐐮𐐻 𐐿𐐩𐑋 𐐻𐐭 𐐹𐐰𐑅 𐑄𐐰𐐻 𐐗𐐬𐑉𐐨𐐰𐑌𐐻𐐲𐑋𐐲𐑉 𐐼𐐮𐐼 𐑊𐐩 𐑅𐐨𐐾 𐐻𐐭 𐑄 𐐶𐐮𐑊𐐼𐐲𐑉𐑌𐐯𐑅; 𐐰𐑌𐐼 𐑄 𐐺𐑉𐐲𐑄𐐲𐑉 𐐱𐑂 𐐟𐐩𐑉𐐯𐐼 𐐼𐐮𐐼 𐑋𐐪𐑉𐐽 𐑁𐐬𐑉𐑃 𐐵𐐻 𐐱𐑂 𐑄 𐐶𐐮𐑊𐐼𐐲𐑉𐑌𐐯𐑅 𐐺𐐴 𐑌𐐴𐐻, 𐐰𐑌𐐼 𐑅𐑊𐐭 𐐲 𐐹𐐪𐑉𐐻 𐐱𐑂 𐑄 𐐪𐑉𐑋𐐨 𐐱𐑂 𐐗𐐬𐑉𐐨𐐰𐑌𐐻𐐲𐑋𐐲𐑉, 𐐰𐑆 𐑄𐐩 𐐶𐐲𐑉 𐐼𐑉𐐲𐑍𐐿𐐲𐑌. 𐐈𐑌𐐼 𐐸𐐨 𐐿𐐩𐑋 𐑁𐐬𐑉𐑃 𐐻𐐭 𐑄 𐑊𐐰𐑌𐐼 𐐱𐑂 𐐣𐐬𐑉𐐱𐑌, 𐐰𐑌𐐼 𐐹𐑊𐐩𐑅𐐻 𐐸𐐮𐑋𐑅𐐯𐑊𐑁 𐐲𐐹𐐱𐑌 𐑄 𐑃𐑉𐐬𐑌 𐐱𐑂 𐐗𐐬𐑉𐐨𐐰𐑌𐐻𐐲𐑋𐐲𐑉. 𐐈𐑌𐐼 𐐮𐐻 𐐿𐐩𐑋 𐐻𐐭 𐐹𐐰𐑅 𐑄𐐰𐐻 𐐗𐐬𐑉𐐨𐐰𐑌𐐻𐐲𐑋𐐲𐑉 𐐼𐐶𐐯𐑊𐐻 𐐶𐐮𐑄 𐐸𐐮𐑆 𐐪𐑉𐑋𐐨 𐐮𐑌 𐑄 𐐶𐐮𐑊𐐼𐐲𐑉𐑌𐐯𐑅 𐑁𐐬𐑉 𐑄 𐑅𐐹𐐩𐑅 𐐱𐑂 𐐻𐐭 𐐷𐐨𐑉𐑆, 𐐮𐑌 𐐸𐐶𐐮𐐽 𐐸𐐨 𐐼𐐮𐐼 𐑉𐐨𐑅𐐨𐑂 𐑀𐑉𐐩𐐻 𐑅𐐻𐑉𐐯𐑍𐑃 𐐻𐐭 𐐸𐐮𐑆 𐐪𐑉𐑋𐐨. 𐐤𐐵 𐑄 𐐺𐑉𐐲𐑄𐐲𐑉 𐐱𐑂 𐐟𐐩𐑉𐐯𐐼, 𐐸𐐭𐑆 𐑌𐐩𐑋 𐐶𐐱𐑆 𐐘𐐮𐑊𐐨𐐲𐐼, 𐐫𐑊𐑅𐐬 𐑉𐐨𐑅𐐨𐑂𐐼 𐑀𐑉𐐩𐐻 𐑅𐐻𐑉𐐯𐑍𐑃 𐐻𐐭 𐐸𐐮𐑆 𐐪𐑉𐑋𐐨, 𐐺𐐨𐐿𐐫𐑆 𐐱𐑂 𐑅𐐨𐐿𐑉𐐯𐐻 𐐿𐐱𐑋𐐺𐐮𐑌𐐩𐑇𐐲𐑌𐑆. 𐐈𐑌𐐼 𐐮𐐻 𐐿𐐩𐑋 𐐻𐐭 𐐹𐐰𐑅 𐑄𐐰𐐻 𐐸𐐮𐑆 𐐸𐐴 𐐹𐑉𐐨𐑅𐐻 𐑋𐐲𐑉𐐼𐐲𐑉𐐼 𐐸𐐮𐑋 𐐰𐑆 𐐸𐐨 𐑅𐐰𐐻 𐐲𐐹𐐱𐑌 𐐸𐐮𐑆 𐑃𐑉𐐬𐑌. 𐐈𐑌𐐼 𐐮𐐻 𐐿𐐩𐑋 𐐻𐐭 𐐹𐐰𐑅 𐑄𐐰𐐻 𐐶𐐲𐑌 𐐱𐑂 𐑄 𐑅𐐨𐐿𐑉𐐯𐐻 𐐿𐐱𐑋𐐺𐐮𐑌𐐩𐑇𐐲𐑌𐑆 𐑋𐐲𐑉𐐼𐐲𐑉𐐼 𐐸𐐮𐑋 𐐮𐑌 𐐲 𐑅𐐨𐐿𐑉𐐯𐐻 𐐹𐐰𐑅, 𐐰𐑌𐐼 𐐱𐐺𐐻𐐩𐑌𐐼 𐐲𐑌𐐻𐐭 𐐸𐐮𐑋𐑅𐐯𐑊𐑁 𐑄 𐐿𐐮𐑍𐐼𐐲𐑋; 𐐰𐑌𐐼 𐐸𐐮𐑆 𐑌𐐩𐑋 𐐶𐐱𐑆 𐐢𐐮𐐺; 𐐰𐑌𐐼 𐐢𐐮𐐺 𐐶𐐱𐑆 𐐲 𐑋𐐰𐑌 𐐱𐑂 𐑀𐑉𐐩𐐻 𐑅𐐻𐐰𐐽𐐲𐑉, 𐑋𐐬𐑉 𐑄𐐰𐑌 𐐯𐑌𐐨 𐐲𐑄𐐲𐑉 𐑋𐐰𐑌 𐐲𐑋𐐲𐑍 𐐫𐑊 𐑄 𐐹𐐨𐐹𐑊. 𐐈𐑌𐐼 𐐮𐐻 𐐿𐐩𐑋 𐐻𐐭 𐐹𐐰𐑅 𐑄𐐰𐐻 𐐮𐑌 𐑄 𐑁𐐲𐑉𐑅𐐻 𐐷𐐨𐑉 𐐱𐑂 𐐢𐐮𐐺 𐐗𐐬𐑉𐐨𐐰𐑌𐐻𐐲𐑋𐐲𐑉 𐐿𐐩𐑋 𐐲𐐹 𐐲𐑌𐐻𐐭 𐑄 𐑊𐐰𐑌𐐼 𐐱𐑂 𐐣𐐬𐑉𐐱𐑌, 𐐰𐑌𐐼 𐑀𐐩𐑂 𐐺𐐰𐐻𐑊

𐐲𐑌𐐻𐐭 𐐢𐐮𐐺. 𐐈𐑌𐐼 𐐮𐐻 𐐿𐐩𐑋 𐐻𐐭 𐐹𐐰𐑅 𐑄𐐰𐐻 𐐸𐐨 𐑁𐐫𐐻 𐐶𐐮𐑄 𐐢𐐮𐐺, 𐐮𐑌 𐐸𐐶𐐮𐐽 𐐢𐐮𐐺 𐐼𐐮𐐼 𐑅𐑋𐐴𐐻 𐐲𐐹𐐱𐑌 𐐸𐐮𐑆 𐐪𐑉𐑋 𐑄𐐰𐐻 𐐸𐐨 𐐶𐐱𐑆 𐐶𐐭𐑌𐐼𐐯𐐼; 𐑌𐐯𐑂𐐲𐑉𐑄𐐲𐑊𐐯𐑅, 𐑄 𐐪𐑉𐑋𐐨 𐐱𐑂 𐐗𐐬𐑉𐐨𐐰𐑌𐐻𐐲𐑋𐑉 𐐼𐐮𐐼 𐐹𐑉𐐯𐑅 𐑁𐐫𐑉𐐶𐐲𐑉𐐼 𐐲𐐹𐐱𐑌 𐐢𐐮𐐺, 𐑄𐐰𐐻 𐐸𐐨 𐑁𐑊𐐯𐐼 𐐻𐐭 𐑄 𐐺𐐫𐑉𐐼𐐲𐑉𐑆 𐐲𐐹𐐱𐑌 𐑄 𐑅𐐨 𐑇𐐬𐑉. 𐐈𐑌𐐼 𐐮𐐻 𐐿𐐩𐑋 𐐻𐐭 𐐹𐐰𐑅 𐑄𐐰𐐻 𐐗𐐬𐑉𐐨𐐰𐑌𐐻𐐲𐑋𐑉 𐐹𐐲𐑉𐑅𐐷𐐭𐐼 𐐸𐐮𐑋; 𐐰𐑌𐐼 𐐢𐐮𐐺 𐑀𐐩𐑂 𐐺𐐰𐐻𐐲𐑊 𐐲𐑌𐐻𐐭 𐐸𐐮𐑋 𐐲𐐹𐐱𐑌 𐑄 𐑅𐐨 𐑇𐐬𐑉. 𐐈𐑌𐐼 𐐮𐐻 𐐿𐐩𐑋 𐐻𐐭 𐐹𐐰𐑅 𐑄𐐰𐐻 𐐢𐐮𐐺 𐐼𐐮𐐼 𐑅𐑋𐐴𐐻 𐑄 𐐪𐑉𐑋𐐨 𐐱𐑂 𐐗𐐬𐑉𐐨𐐰𐑌𐐻𐐲𐑋𐑉, 𐑄𐐰𐐻 𐑄𐐩 𐑁𐑊𐐯𐐼 𐐲𐑀𐐯𐑌 𐐻𐐭 𐑄 𐐶𐐮𐑊𐐼𐐲𐑉𐑌𐐯𐑅 𐐱𐑂 𐐁𐐿𐐮𐑇. 𐐈𐑌𐐼 𐐮𐐻 𐐿𐐩𐑋 𐐻𐐭 𐐹𐐰𐑅 𐑄𐐰𐐻 𐐢𐐮𐐺 𐐼𐐮𐐼 𐐹𐐲𐑉𐑅𐐷𐐭 𐐸𐐮𐑋 𐐲𐑌𐐻𐐮𐑊 𐐸𐐨 𐐿𐐩𐑋 𐐻𐐭 𐑄 𐐹𐑊𐐩𐑌𐑆 𐐱𐑂 𐐁𐑀𐐱𐑇. 𐐈𐑌𐐼 𐐗𐐬𐑉𐐨𐐰𐑌𐐻𐐲𐑋𐑉 𐐸𐐰𐐼 𐐻𐐩𐐿𐐲𐑌 𐐫𐑊 𐑄 𐐹𐐨𐐹𐐲𐑊 𐐶𐐮𐑄 𐐸𐐮𐑋 𐐰𐑆 𐐸𐐨 𐑁𐑊𐐯𐐼 𐐺𐐨𐑁𐐬𐑉 𐐢𐐮𐐺 𐐮𐑌 𐑄𐐰𐐻 𐐿𐐶𐐫𐑉𐐻𐐲𐑉 𐐱𐑂 𐑄 𐑊𐐰𐑌𐐼 𐐸𐐶𐐮𐑄𐐲𐑉 𐐸𐐨 𐑁𐑊𐐯𐐼. 𐐈𐑌𐐼 𐐸𐐶𐐯𐑌 𐐸𐐨 𐐸𐐰𐐼 𐐿𐐲𐑋 𐐻𐐭 𐑄 𐐹𐑊𐐩𐑌𐑆 𐐱𐑂 𐐁𐑀𐐱𐑇, 𐐸𐐨 𐑀𐐩𐑂 𐐺𐐰𐐻𐐲𐑊 𐐲𐑌𐐻𐐭 𐐢𐐮𐐺, 𐐰𐑌𐐼 𐐸𐐨 𐑅𐑋𐐬𐐻 𐐲𐐹𐐱𐑌 𐐸𐐮𐑋 𐐲𐑌𐐻𐐮𐑊 𐐸𐐨 𐐼𐐴𐐼; 𐑌𐐯𐑂𐐲𐑉𐑄𐐲𐑊𐐯𐑅, 𐑄 𐐺𐑉𐐲𐑄𐐲𐑉 𐐱𐑂 𐐢𐐮𐐺 𐐼𐐮𐐼 𐐿𐐲𐑋 𐐲𐑀𐐯𐑌𐑅𐐻 𐐗𐐬𐑉𐐨𐐰𐑌𐐻𐐲𐑋𐑉 𐐮𐑌 𐑄 𐑅𐐻𐐯𐐼 𐑄𐐯𐑉𐐱𐑂, 𐐰𐑌𐐼 𐑄 𐐺𐐰𐐻𐐲𐑊 𐐺𐐨𐐿𐐩𐑋 𐐯𐐿𐑅𐐨𐐼𐐮𐑍 𐑅𐐬𐑉, 𐐮𐑌 𐑄 𐐸𐐶𐐮𐐽 𐐗𐐬𐑉𐐨𐐰𐑌𐐻𐐲𐑋𐑉 𐑁𐑊𐐯𐐼 𐐲𐑀𐐯𐑌 𐐺𐐨𐑁𐐬𐑉 𐑄 𐐪𐑉𐑋𐐨 𐐱𐑂 𐑄 𐐺𐑉𐐲𐑄𐐲𐑉 𐐱𐑂 𐐢𐐮𐐺.

5. 𐐤𐐵 𐑄 𐑌𐐩𐑋 𐐱𐑂 𐑄 𐐺𐑉𐐲𐑄𐐲𐑉 𐐱𐑂 𐐢𐐮𐐺 𐐶𐐱𐑆 𐐿𐐫𐑊𐐼 𐐟𐐮𐑆. 𐐈𐑌𐐼 𐐮𐐻 𐐿𐐩𐑋 𐐻𐐭 𐐹𐐰𐑅 𐑄𐐰𐐻 𐐟𐐮𐑆 𐐹𐐲𐑉𐑅𐐷𐐭𐐼 𐐰𐑁𐐻𐐲𐑉 𐐗𐐬𐑉𐐨𐐰𐑌𐐻𐐲𐑋𐑉, 𐐰𐑌𐐼 𐐸𐐨 𐐼𐐮𐐼 𐐬𐑂𐐲𐑉𐑃𐑉𐐬 𐑋𐐯𐑌𐐨 𐑅𐐮𐐻𐐨𐑆, 𐐰𐑌𐐼 𐐸𐐨 𐐼𐐮𐐼 𐑅𐑊𐐩 𐐺𐐬𐑃 𐐶𐐮𐑋𐐯𐑌 𐐰𐑌𐐼 𐐽𐐮𐑊𐐼𐑉𐐯𐑌, 𐐰𐑌𐐼 𐐸𐐨 𐐼𐐮𐐼 𐐺𐐲𐑉𐑌 𐑄 𐑅𐐮𐐻𐐨𐑆 𐑄𐐯𐑉𐐱𐑂. 𐐈𐑌𐐼 𐑄𐐯𐑉 𐐶𐐯𐑌𐐻 𐐲 𐑁𐐨𐑉 𐐱𐑂 𐐟𐐮𐑆 𐑃𐑉𐐭𐐵𐐻 𐐫𐑊 𐑄 𐑊𐐰𐑌𐐼; 𐐷𐐩, 𐐲 𐐿𐑉𐐴 𐐶𐐯𐑌𐐻 𐑁𐐬𐑉𐑃 𐑃𐑉𐐭𐐵𐐻 𐑄 𐑊𐐰𐑌𐐼, 𐐐𐐭 𐐿𐐰𐑌 𐑅𐐻𐐰𐑌𐐼 𐐺𐐨𐑁𐐬𐑉 𐑄 𐐪𐑉𐑋𐐨 𐐱𐑂 𐐟𐐮𐑆? 𐐒𐐨𐐸𐐬𐑊𐐼, 𐐸𐐨 𐑅𐐶𐐨𐐹𐐯𐑃 𐑄 𐐲𐑉𐑃 𐐺𐐨𐑁𐐬𐑉 𐐸𐐮𐑋! 𐐈𐑌𐐼 𐐮𐐻 𐐿𐐩𐑋 𐐻𐐭 𐐹𐐰𐑅 𐑄𐐰𐐻 𐑄 𐐹𐐨𐐹𐐲𐑊 𐐺𐐨𐑀𐐰𐑌 𐐻𐐭 𐑁𐑊𐐱𐐿 𐐻𐐭𐑀𐐯𐑄𐐲𐑉 𐐮𐑌 𐐪𐑉𐑋𐐨𐑆, 𐑃𐑉𐐭𐐵𐐻 𐐫𐑊 𐑄 𐑁𐐩𐑅 𐐱𐑂 𐑄 𐑊𐐰𐑌𐐼. 𐐈𐑌𐐼 𐑄𐐩 𐐶𐐲𐑉 𐐼𐐮𐑂𐐴𐐼𐐯𐐼; 𐐰𐑌𐐼 𐐲 𐐹𐐪𐑉𐐻 𐐱𐑂 𐑄𐐯𐑋 𐑁𐑊𐐯𐐼 𐐻𐐭 𐑄 𐐪𐑉𐑋𐐨 𐐱𐑂 𐐟𐐮𐑆, 𐐰𐑌𐐼 𐐲 𐐹𐐪𐑉𐐻 𐐱𐑂 𐑄𐐯𐑋 𐑁𐑊𐐯𐐼 𐐻𐐭 𐑄 𐐪𐑉𐑋𐐨 𐐱𐑂 𐐗𐐬𐑉𐐨𐐰𐑌𐐻𐐲𐑋𐑉. 𐐈𐑌𐐼 𐑅𐐬 𐑀𐑉𐐩𐐻 𐐰𐑌𐐼 𐑊𐐪𐑅𐐻𐐮𐑍 𐐸𐐰𐐼 𐐺𐐮𐑌 𐑄 𐐶𐐫𐑉, 𐐰𐑌𐐼 𐑅𐐬 𐑊𐐱𐑍 𐐸𐐰𐐼 𐐺𐐮𐑌 𐑄 𐑅𐐨𐑌 𐐱𐑂 𐐺𐑊𐐲𐐼𐑇𐐯𐐼 𐐰𐑌𐐼 𐐿𐐪𐑉𐑌𐐩𐐾, 𐑄𐐰𐐻 𐑄 𐐸𐐬𐑊 𐑁𐐩𐑅 𐐱𐑂 𐑄 𐑊𐐰𐑌𐐼 𐐶𐐱𐑆 𐐿𐐲𐑂𐐲𐑉𐐼 𐐶𐐮𐑄 𐑄 𐐺𐐱𐐼𐐨𐑆 𐐱𐑂 𐑄 𐐼𐐯𐐼. 𐐈𐑌𐐼 𐑅𐐬 𐑅𐐶𐐮𐑁𐐻 𐐰𐑌𐐼 𐑅𐐹𐐨𐐼𐐨 𐐶𐐱𐑆 𐑄 𐐶𐐫𐑉 𐑄𐐰𐐻 𐑄𐐯𐑉 𐐶𐐱𐑆 𐑌𐐲𐑌 𐑊𐐯𐑁𐐻 𐐻𐐭 𐐺𐐯𐑉𐐨 𐑄 𐐼𐐯𐐼, 𐐺𐐲𐐻 𐑄𐐩 𐐼𐐮𐐼 𐑋𐐪𐑉𐐽 𐑁𐐬𐑉𐑃 𐑁𐑉𐐱𐑋 𐑄 𐑇𐐯𐐼𐐮𐑍 𐐱𐑂 𐐺𐑊𐐲𐐼 𐐻𐐭 𐑄 𐑇𐐯𐐼𐐮𐑍 𐐱𐑂 𐐺𐑊𐐲𐐼, 𐑊𐐨𐑂𐐮𐑍 𐑄 𐐺𐐱𐐼𐐨𐑆 𐐱𐑂 𐐺𐐬𐑃 𐑋𐐯𐑌, 𐐶𐐮𐑋𐐯𐑌, 𐐰𐑌𐐼 𐐽𐐮𐑊𐐼𐑉𐐯𐑌 𐑅𐐻𐑉𐐭𐐼 𐐲𐐹𐐱𐑌 𐑄 𐑁𐐩𐑅 𐐱𐑂 𐑄 𐑊𐐰𐑌𐐼, 𐐻𐐭 𐐺𐐨𐐿𐐲𐑋 𐐲 𐐹𐑉𐐩 𐐻𐐭 𐑄 𐐶𐐲𐑉𐑋𐑆 𐐱𐑂 𐑄 𐑁𐑊𐐯𐑇. 𐐈𐑌𐐼 𐑄 𐑅𐐯𐑌𐐻 𐑄𐐯𐑉𐐱𐑂 𐐶𐐯𐑌𐐻 𐑁𐐬𐑉𐑃 𐐲𐐹𐐱𐑌 𐑄 𐑁𐐩𐑅 𐐱𐑂 𐑄 𐑊𐐰𐑌𐐼, 𐐨𐑂𐐯𐑌 𐐲𐐹𐐱𐑌 𐐫𐑊 𐑄 𐑁𐐩𐑅 𐐱𐑂 𐑄 𐑊𐐰𐑌𐐼; 𐐸𐐶𐐯𐑉𐑁𐐬𐑉 𐑄 𐐹𐐨𐐹𐐲𐑊 𐐺𐐨𐐿𐐩𐑋 𐐻𐑉𐐲𐐺𐐲𐑊𐐼 𐐺𐐴 𐐼𐐩 𐐰𐑌𐐼 𐐺𐐴 𐑌𐐴𐐻, 𐐺𐐨𐐿𐐫𐑆 𐐱𐑂 𐑄 𐑅𐐯𐑌𐐻 𐑄𐐯𐑉𐐱𐑂. 𐐤𐐯𐑂𐐲𐑉𐑄𐐲𐑊𐐯𐑅, 𐐟𐐮𐑆 𐐼𐐮𐐼 𐑌𐐱𐐻 𐑅𐐨𐑅 𐐻𐐭 𐐹𐐲𐑉𐑅𐐷𐐭 𐐗𐐬𐑉𐐨𐐰𐑌𐐻𐐲𐑋𐑉, 𐑁𐐫𐑉 𐐸𐐨 𐐸𐐰𐐼 𐑅𐐶𐐬𐑉𐑌 𐐻𐐭 𐐲𐑂𐐯𐑌𐐾 𐐸𐐮𐑋𐑅𐐯𐑊𐑁 𐐲𐐹𐐱𐑌 𐐗𐐬𐑉𐐨𐐰𐑌𐐻𐐲𐑋𐑉 𐐱𐑂 𐑄 𐐺𐑊𐐲𐐼 𐐱𐑂 𐐸𐐮𐑆 𐐺𐑉𐐲𐑄𐐲𐑉, 𐐸𐐭 𐐸𐐰𐐼 𐐺𐐮𐑌 𐑅𐑊𐐩𐑌, 𐐰𐑌𐐼 𐑄 𐐶𐐲𐑉𐐼 𐐱𐑂 𐑄 𐐢𐐫𐑉𐐼 𐐸𐐶𐐮𐐽 𐐿𐐩𐑋 𐐻𐐭 𐐀𐑃𐐲𐑉 𐑄𐐰𐐻 𐐗𐐬𐑉𐐨𐐰𐑌𐐻𐐲𐑋𐑉 𐑇𐐳𐐼 𐑌𐐱𐐻 𐑁𐐫𐑊 𐐺𐐴 𐑄 𐑅𐐬𐑉𐐼. 𐐈𐑌𐐼 𐑄𐐲𐑅 𐐶𐐨 𐑅𐐨 𐑄𐐰𐐻 𐑄 𐐢𐐫𐑉𐐼 𐐼𐐮𐐼 𐑂𐐮𐑆𐐮𐐻 𐑄𐐯𐑋 𐐮𐑌 𐑄 𐑁𐐳𐑊𐑌𐐯𐑅 𐐱𐑂 𐐸𐐮𐑆 𐑉𐐪𐑃, 𐐰𐑌𐐼 𐑄𐐯𐑉 𐐶𐐮𐐿𐐯𐐼𐑌𐐯𐑅 𐐰𐑌𐐼 𐐲𐐺𐐱𐑋𐐮𐑌𐐩𐑇𐐲𐑌𐑆 𐐸𐐰𐐼 𐐹𐑉𐐨𐐹𐐯𐑉𐐼 𐐲 𐐶𐐩 𐑁𐐫𐑉 𐑄𐐯𐑉 𐐯𐑂𐐲𐑉𐑊𐐪𐑅𐐻𐐮𐑍 𐐼𐐯𐑅𐐻𐑉𐐲𐐿𐑇𐐲𐑌. 𐐈𐑌𐐼 𐐮𐐻 𐐿𐐩𐑋 𐐻𐐭 𐐹𐐰𐑅 𐑄𐐰𐐻 𐐟𐐮𐑆 𐐼𐐮𐐼 𐐹𐐲𐑉𐑅𐐷𐐭 𐐗𐐬𐑉𐐨𐐰𐑌𐐻𐐲𐑋𐑉 𐐨𐑅𐐻𐐶𐐲𐑉𐐼, 𐐨𐑂𐐯𐑌 𐐻𐐭 𐑄 𐐺𐐫𐑉𐐼𐐲𐑉𐑆 𐐺𐐴 𐑄 𐑅𐐨 𐑇𐐬𐑉, 𐐰𐑌𐐼 𐑄𐐯𐑉 𐐸𐐨 𐑀𐐩𐑂 𐐺𐐰𐐻𐐲𐑊 𐐲𐑌𐐻𐐭 𐐟𐐮𐑆 𐑁𐐫𐑉 𐑄 𐑅𐐹𐐩𐑅 𐐱𐑂 𐑃𐑉𐐨 𐐼𐐩𐑆. 𐐈𐑌𐐼 𐑅𐐬 𐐻𐐯𐑉𐐮𐐺𐐲𐑊 𐐶𐐱𐑆 𐑄 𐐼𐐯𐑅𐐻𐑉𐐲𐐿𐑇𐐲𐑌 𐐲𐑋𐐲𐑍 𐑄 𐐪𐑉𐑋𐐨𐑆 𐐱𐑂 𐐟𐐮𐑆 𐑄𐐰𐐻 𐑄 𐐹𐐨𐐹𐐲𐑊 𐐺𐐨𐑀𐐰𐑌 𐐻𐐭 𐐺𐐨 𐑁𐑉𐐴𐐻𐐲𐑌𐐼, 𐐰𐑌𐐼 𐐺𐐨𐑀𐐰𐑌 𐐻𐐭 𐑁𐑊𐐨 𐐺𐐨𐑁𐐬𐑉 𐑄 𐐪𐑉𐑋𐐨𐑆 𐐱𐑂 𐐗𐐬𐑉𐐨𐐰𐑌𐐻𐐲𐑋𐑉; 𐐰𐑌𐐼 𐑄𐐩 𐑁𐑊𐐯𐐼 𐐻𐐭 𐑄 𐑊𐐰𐑌𐐼 𐐱𐑂 𐐗𐐬𐑉𐐮𐐸𐐬𐑉, 𐐰𐑌𐐼 𐑅𐐶𐐯𐐹𐐻 𐐫𐑁 𐑄 𐐮𐑌𐐸𐐰𐐺𐐮𐐻𐐰𐑌𐐻𐑅 𐐺𐐨𐑁𐐬𐑉 𐑄𐐯𐑋, 𐐫𐑊 𐑄𐐯𐑋 𐑄𐐰𐐻 𐐶𐐳𐐼 𐑌𐐱𐐻 𐐾𐑎𐑌 𐑄𐐯𐑋; 𐐰𐑌𐐼 𐑄𐐩 𐐹𐐮𐐽𐐻 𐑄𐐯𐑉 𐐻𐐯𐑌𐐻𐑅 𐐮𐑌 𐑄 𐑂𐐰𐑊𐐨 𐐱𐑂 𐐗𐐬𐑉𐐮𐐸𐐬𐑉. 𐐈𐑌𐐼 𐐗𐐬𐑉𐐨𐐰𐑌𐐻𐐲𐑋𐑉 𐐹𐐮𐐽𐐻 𐐸𐐮𐑆 𐐻𐐯𐑌𐐻𐑅 𐐮𐑌 𐑄 𐑂𐐰𐑊𐐨 𐐱𐑂 𐐟𐐲𐑉. 𐐤𐐵 𐑄 𐑂𐐰𐑊𐐨 𐐱𐑂 𐐟𐐲𐑉 𐐶𐐱𐑆 𐑌𐐨𐑉 𐑄 𐐸𐐮𐑊 𐐗𐐱𐑋𐑌𐐫𐑉; 𐐸𐐶𐐯𐑉𐑁𐐬𐑉 𐐗𐐬𐑉𐐨𐐰𐑌𐐻𐐲𐑋𐑉 𐐼𐐮𐐼 𐑀𐐰𐑄𐐲𐑉 𐐸𐐮𐑆 𐐪𐑉𐑋𐐨𐑆 𐐻𐐭𐑀𐐯𐑄𐐲𐑉 𐐲𐐹𐐱𐑌 𐑄 𐐸𐐮𐑊 𐐗𐐱𐑋𐑌𐐫𐑉, 𐐰𐑌𐐼 𐐼𐐮𐐼 𐑅𐐵𐑌𐐼 𐐲 𐐻𐑉𐐲𐑋𐐹𐐯𐐻 𐐲𐑌𐐻𐐭 𐑄 𐐪𐑉𐑋𐐨𐑆 𐐱𐑂 𐐟𐐮𐑆, 𐐻𐐭 𐐮𐑌𐑂𐐴𐐻 𐑄𐐯𐑋 𐑁𐐬𐑉𐑃 𐐻𐐭 𐐺𐐰𐐻𐐲𐑊. 𐐈𐑌𐐼 𐐮𐐻 𐐿𐐩𐑋 𐐻𐐭 𐐹𐐰𐑅 𐑄𐐰𐐻 𐑄𐐩 𐐿𐐩𐑋

𐑁𐐫𐑉𐑃, 𐐺𐐲𐐻 𐐶𐐲𐑉 𐐼𐑉𐐮𐑂𐑌 𐐰𐑀𐐯𐑌; 𐐰𐑌𐐼 𐑄𐐩 𐐿𐐩𐑋 𐑄 𐑅𐐯𐐿𐐲𐑌𐐼 𐐻𐐴𐑋, 𐐰𐑌𐐼 𐑄𐐩 𐐶𐐲𐑉 𐐼𐑉𐐮𐑂𐑌 𐐰𐑀𐐯𐑌 𐑄 𐑅𐐯𐐿𐐲𐑌𐐼 𐐻𐐴𐑋. 𐐈𐑌𐐼 𐐮𐐻 𐐿𐐩𐑋 𐐻𐐭 𐐹𐐰𐑅 𐑄𐐰𐐻 𐑄𐐩 𐐿𐐩𐑋 𐐰𐑀𐐯𐑌 𐑄 𐑃𐐲𐑉𐐼 𐐻𐐴𐑋, 𐐰𐑌𐐼 𐑄 𐐺𐐰𐐻𐑊 𐐺𐐨𐐿𐐩𐑋 𐐯𐐿𐑅𐐨𐐼𐐮𐑍𐑊𐐨 𐑅𐐬𐑉. 𐐈𐑌𐐼 𐐮𐐻 𐐿𐐩𐑋 𐐻𐐭 𐐹𐐰𐑅 𐑄𐐰𐐻 𐐟𐐮𐑆 𐑅𐑋𐐬𐐻 𐐲𐐹𐐱𐑌 𐐗𐐬𐑉𐐨𐐰𐑌𐐻𐐲𐑋𐑉 𐑄𐐰𐐻 𐐸𐐨 𐑀𐐩𐑂 𐐸𐐮𐑋 𐑋𐐯𐑌𐐨 𐐼𐐨𐐹 𐐶𐐭𐑌𐐼𐑆, 𐐰𐑌𐐼 𐐗𐐬𐑉𐐨𐐰𐑌𐐻𐐲𐑋𐑉 𐐸𐐰𐑂𐐮𐑍 𐑊𐐱𐑅𐐻 𐐸𐐮𐑆 𐐺𐑊𐐲𐐼, 𐑁𐐩𐑌𐐻𐐯𐐼, 𐐰𐑌𐐼 𐐶𐐱𐑆 𐐿𐐰𐑉𐐨𐐼 𐐰𐐶𐐩 𐐰𐑆 𐑄𐐬 𐐸𐐨 𐐶𐐲𐑉 𐐼𐐯𐐼. 𐐤𐐵 𐑄 𐑊𐐱𐑅 𐐱𐑂 𐑋𐐯𐑌, 𐐶𐐮𐑋𐐯𐑌, 𐐰𐑌𐐼 𐐽𐐮𐑊𐐼𐑉𐐯𐑌, 𐐱𐑌 𐐺𐐬𐑃 𐑅𐐴𐐼𐑆, 𐐶𐐱𐑆 𐑅𐐬 𐑀𐑉𐐩𐐻, 𐑄𐐰𐐻 𐐟𐐮𐑆 𐐿𐐱𐑋𐐰𐑌𐐼𐐯𐐼 𐐸𐐮𐑆 𐐹𐐨𐐹𐑊 𐑄𐐰𐐻 𐑄𐐩 𐑇𐐳𐐼 𐑌𐐱𐐻 𐐹𐐲𐑉𐑅𐐭 𐑄 𐐪𐑉𐑋𐐨𐑆 𐐱𐑂 𐐗𐐬𐑉𐐨𐐰𐑌𐐻𐐲𐑋𐑉; 𐐸𐐶𐐯𐑉𐑁𐐬𐑉 𐑄𐐩 𐑉𐐨𐐻𐐲𐑉𐑌𐐼 𐐻𐐭 𐑄𐐩𐑉 𐐿𐐰𐑋𐐹.

6. 𐐈𐑌𐐼 𐐮𐐻 𐐿𐐩𐑋 𐐻𐐭 𐐹𐐰𐑅 𐐸𐐶𐐯𐑌 𐐗𐐬𐑉𐐨𐐰𐑌𐐻𐐲𐑋𐑉 𐐸𐐰𐐼 𐑉𐐨𐐿𐐲𐑂𐐲𐑉𐐼 𐐱𐑂 𐐸𐐮𐑆 𐐶𐐭𐑌𐐼𐑆, 𐐸𐐨 𐐺𐐨𐑀𐐰𐑌 𐐻𐐭 𐑉𐐨𐑋𐐯𐑋𐐺𐐲𐑉 𐑄 𐐶𐐲𐑉𐐼𐑆 𐐸𐐶𐐮𐐽 𐐀𐑃𐐲𐑉 𐐸𐐰𐐼 𐑅𐐹𐐬𐐿𐑌 𐐲𐑌𐐻𐐭 𐐸𐐮𐑋; 𐐸𐐨 𐑅𐐫 𐑄𐐰𐐻 𐑄𐐯𐑉 𐐸𐐰𐐼 𐐺𐐮𐑌 𐑅𐑊𐐩𐑌 𐐺𐐴 𐑄 𐑅𐐬𐑉𐐼 𐐫𐑊𐑉𐐯𐐼𐐨 𐑌𐐨𐑉𐑊𐐨 𐐻𐐭 𐑋𐐮𐑊𐐷𐐲𐑌𐑆 𐐱𐑂 𐐸𐐮𐑆 𐐹𐐨𐐹𐑊, 𐐰𐑌𐐼 𐐸𐐨 𐐺𐐨𐑀𐐰𐑌 𐐻𐐭 𐑅𐐪𐑉𐐬 𐐮𐑌 𐐸𐐮𐑆 𐐸𐐪𐑉𐐻; 𐐷𐐩, 𐑄𐐯𐑉 𐐸𐐰𐐼 𐐺𐐮𐑌 𐑅𐑊𐐩𐑌 𐐻𐐭 𐑋𐐮𐑊𐐷𐐲𐑌𐑆 𐐱𐑂 𐑋𐐴𐐻𐐨 𐑋𐐯𐑌, 𐐰𐑌𐐼 𐐫𐑊𐑅𐐬 𐑄𐐩𐑉 𐐶𐐴𐑂𐑆 𐐰𐑌𐐼 𐑄𐐩𐑉 𐐽𐐮𐑊𐐼𐑉𐐯𐑌. 𐐐𐐨 𐐺𐐨𐑀𐐰𐑌 𐐻𐐭 𐑉𐐨𐐹𐐯𐑌𐐻 𐐱𐑂 𐑄 𐐨𐑂𐐮𐑊 𐐸𐐶𐐮𐐽 𐐸𐐨 𐐸𐐰𐐼 𐐼𐐲𐑌; 𐐸𐐨 𐐺𐐨𐑀𐐰𐑌 𐐻𐐭 𐑉𐐨𐑋𐐯𐑋𐐺𐐲𐑉 𐑄 𐐶𐐲𐑉𐐼𐑆 𐐸𐐶𐐮𐐽 𐐸𐐰𐐼 𐐺𐐮𐑌 𐑅𐐹𐐬𐐿𐑌 𐐺𐐴 𐑄 𐑋𐐵𐑃 𐐱𐑂 𐐫𐑊 𐑄 𐐹𐑉𐐱𐑁𐐯𐐻𐑅, 𐐰𐑌𐐼 𐐸𐐨 𐑅𐐫 𐑄𐐯𐑋 𐑄𐐰𐐻 𐑄𐐩 𐐶𐐲𐑉 𐑁𐐳𐑊𐑁𐐮𐑊𐐼 𐑄𐐲𐑅 𐑁𐐪𐑉, 𐐯𐑂𐑉𐐨 𐐸𐐶𐐮𐐻; 𐐰𐑌𐐼 𐐸𐐮𐑆 𐑅𐐬𐑊 𐑋𐐬𐑉𐑌𐐼, 𐐰𐑌𐐼 𐑉𐐨𐑁𐐷𐐭𐑆𐐼 𐐻𐐭 𐐺𐐨 𐐿𐐲𐑋𐑁𐐲𐑉𐐻𐐯𐐼. 𐐈𐑌𐐼 𐐮𐐻 𐐿𐐩𐑋 𐐻𐐭 𐐹𐐰𐑅 𐑄𐐰𐐻 𐐸𐐨 𐑉𐐬𐐻 𐐰𐑌 𐐨𐐹𐐮𐑅𐑊 𐐲𐑌𐐻𐐭 𐐟𐐮𐑆, 𐐼𐐨𐑆𐐴𐑉𐐮𐑍 𐐸𐐮𐑋 𐑄𐐰𐐻 𐐸𐐨 𐐶𐐳𐐼 𐑅𐐹𐐩𐑉 𐑄 𐐹𐐨𐐹𐑊, 𐐰𐑌𐐼 𐐸𐐨 𐐶𐐳𐐼 𐑀𐐮𐑂 𐐲𐐹 𐑄 𐐿𐐮𐑍𐐼𐐲𐑋 𐑁𐐫𐑉 𐑄 𐑅𐐩𐐿 𐐱𐑂 𐑄 𐑊𐐴𐑂𐑆 𐐱𐑂 𐑄 𐐹𐐨𐐹𐑊. 𐐈𐑌𐐼 𐐮𐐻 𐐿𐐩𐑋 𐐻𐐭 𐐹𐐰𐑅 𐑄𐐰𐐻 𐐸𐐶𐐯𐑌 𐐟𐐮𐑆 𐐸𐐰𐐼 𐑉𐐨𐑅𐐨𐑂𐐼 𐐸𐐮𐑆 𐐨𐐹𐐮𐑅𐑊, 𐐸𐐨 𐑉𐐬𐐻 𐐰𐑌 𐐨𐐹𐐮𐑅𐑊 𐐲𐑌𐐻𐐭 𐐗𐐬𐑉𐐨𐐰𐑌𐐻𐐲𐑋𐑉, 𐑄𐐰𐐻 𐐮𐑁 𐐸𐐨 𐐶𐐳𐐼 𐑀𐐮𐑂 𐐸𐐮𐑋𐑅𐐯𐑊𐑁 𐐲𐐹, 𐑄𐐰𐐻 𐐸𐐨 𐑋𐐴𐐻 𐑅𐑊𐐩 𐐸𐐮𐑋 𐐶𐐮𐑄 𐐸𐐮𐑆 𐐬𐑌 𐑅𐐬𐑉𐐼, 𐑄𐐰𐐻 𐐸𐐨 𐐶𐐳𐐼 𐑅𐐹𐐩𐑉 𐑄 𐑊𐐴𐑂𐑆 𐐱𐑂 𐑄 𐐹𐐨𐐹𐑊. 𐐈𐑌𐐼 𐐮𐐻 𐐿𐐩𐑋 𐐻𐐭 𐐹𐐰𐑅 𐑄𐐰𐐻 𐑄 𐐹𐐨𐐹𐑊 𐑉𐐨𐐹𐐯𐑌𐐻𐐯𐐼 𐑌𐐱𐐻 𐐱𐑂 𐑄𐐩𐑉 𐐮𐑌𐐮𐐿𐐶𐐮𐐻𐐨; 𐐰𐑌𐐼 𐑄 𐐹𐐨𐐹𐑊 𐐱𐑂 𐐗𐐬𐑉𐐨𐐰𐑌𐐻𐐲𐑋𐑉 𐐶𐐲𐑉 𐑅𐐻𐐲𐑉𐐼 𐐲𐐹 𐐻𐐭 𐐰𐑍𐑀𐐲𐑉 𐐰𐑀𐐯𐑌𐑅𐐻 𐑄 𐐹𐐨𐐹𐑊 𐐱𐑂 𐐟𐐮𐑆; 𐐰𐑌𐐼 𐑄 𐐹𐐨𐐹𐑊 𐐱𐑂 𐐟𐐮𐑆 𐐶𐐲𐑉 𐑅𐐻𐐲𐑉𐐼 𐐲𐐹 𐐻𐐭 𐐰𐑍𐑀𐐲𐑉 𐐰𐑀𐐯𐑌𐑅𐐻 𐑄 𐐹𐐨𐐹𐑊 𐐱𐑂 𐐗𐐬𐑉𐐨𐐰𐑌𐐻𐐲𐑋𐑉; 𐐸𐐶𐐯𐑉𐑁𐐬𐑉 𐑄 𐐹𐐨𐐹𐑊 𐐱𐑂 𐐟𐐮𐑆 𐐼𐐮𐐼 𐑀𐐮𐑂 𐐺𐐰𐐻𐑊 𐐲𐑌𐐻𐐭 𐑄 𐐹𐐨𐐹𐑊 𐐱𐑂 𐐗𐐬𐑉𐐨𐐰𐑌𐐻𐐲𐑋𐑉. 𐐈𐑌𐐼 𐐸𐐶𐐯𐑌 𐐗𐐬𐑉𐐨𐐰𐑌𐐻𐐲𐑋𐑉 𐑅𐐫 𐑄𐐰𐐻 𐐸𐐨 𐐶𐐱𐑆 𐐰𐐺𐐵𐐻 𐐻𐐭 𐑁𐐫𐑊, 𐐸𐐨 𐑁𐑊𐐯𐐼 𐐰𐑀𐐯𐑌 𐐺𐐨𐑁𐐬𐑉 𐑄 𐐹𐐨𐐹𐑊 𐐱𐑂 𐐟𐐮𐑆. 𐐈𐑌𐐼 𐐮𐐻 𐐿𐐩𐑋 𐐻𐐭 𐐹𐐰𐑅 𐑄𐐰𐐻 𐐸𐐨 𐐿𐐩𐑋 𐐻𐐭 𐑄 𐐶𐐫𐐻𐐲𐑉𐑆 𐐱𐑂 𐐡𐐮𐐹𐑊𐐨𐐰𐑌𐐿𐐲𐑋, 𐐸𐐶𐐮𐐽, 𐐺𐐴 𐐮𐑌𐐻𐐲𐑉𐐹𐑉𐐨𐐻𐐩𐑇𐐲𐑌, 𐐮𐑆 𐑊𐐪𐑉𐐾, 𐐫𐑉 𐐻𐐭 𐐯𐐿𐑅𐐨𐐼 𐐫𐑊; 𐐸𐐶𐐯𐑉𐑁𐐬𐑉, 𐐸𐐶𐐯𐑌 𐑄𐐩 𐐿𐐩𐑋 𐐻𐐭 𐑄𐐨𐑆 𐐶𐐫𐐻𐐲𐑉𐑆, 𐑄𐐩 𐐹𐐮𐐽𐐻 𐑄𐐩𐑉 𐐻𐐯𐑌𐐻𐑅; 𐐰𐑌𐐼 𐐟𐐮𐑆 𐐫𐑊𐑅𐐬 𐐹𐐮𐐽𐐻 𐐸𐐮𐑆 𐐻𐐯𐑌𐐻𐑅 𐑌𐐨𐑉 𐐲𐑌𐐻𐐭 𐑄𐐯𐑋; 𐐰𐑌𐐼 𐑄𐐯𐑉𐑁𐐬𐑉 𐐱𐑌 𐑄 𐑋𐐱𐑉𐐬 𐑄𐐩 𐐼𐐮𐐼 𐐿𐐲𐑋 𐐻𐐭 𐐺𐐰𐐻𐑊. 𐐈𐑌𐐼 𐐮𐐻 𐐿𐐩𐑋 𐐻𐐭 𐐹𐐰𐑅 𐑄𐐰𐐻 𐑄𐐩 𐑁𐐫𐐻 𐐰𐑌 𐐯𐐿𐑅𐐨𐐼𐐮𐑍𐑊𐐨 𐑅𐐬𐑉 𐐺𐐰𐐻𐑊, 𐐮𐑌 𐐸𐐶𐐮𐐽 𐐗𐐬𐑉𐐨𐐰𐑌𐐻𐐲𐑋𐑉 𐐶𐐱𐑆 𐐶𐐭𐑌𐐼𐐯𐐼 𐐰𐑀𐐯𐑌, 𐐰𐑌𐐼 𐐸𐐨 𐑁𐐩𐑌𐐻𐐯𐐼 𐐶𐐮𐑄 𐑄 𐑊𐐱𐑅 𐐱𐑂 𐐺𐑊𐐲𐐼. 𐐈𐑌𐐼 𐐮𐐻 𐐿𐐩𐑋 𐐻𐐭 𐐹𐐰𐑅 𐑄𐐰𐐻 𐑄 𐐪𐑉𐑋𐐨𐑆 𐐱𐑂 𐐗𐐬𐑉𐐨𐐰𐑌𐐻𐐲𐑋𐑉 𐐼𐐮𐐼 𐐹𐑉𐐯𐑅 𐐲𐐹𐐱𐑌 𐑄 𐐪𐑉𐑋𐐨𐑆 𐐱𐑂 𐐟𐐮𐑆, 𐑄𐐰𐐻 𐑄𐐩 𐐺𐐨𐐻 𐑄𐐯𐑋, 𐑄𐐰𐐻 𐑄𐐩 𐐿𐐫𐑆𐐼 𐑄𐐯𐑋 𐐻𐐭 𐑁𐑊𐐨 𐐺𐐨𐑁𐐬𐑉 𐑄𐐯𐑋; 𐐰𐑌𐐼 𐑄𐐩 𐐼𐐮𐐼 𐑁𐑊𐐨 𐑅𐐵𐑃𐐶𐐲𐑉𐐼, 𐐰𐑌𐐼 𐐼𐐮𐐼 𐐹𐐮𐐽 𐑄𐐩𐑉 𐐻𐐯𐑌𐐻𐑅 𐐮𐑌 𐐰 𐐹𐑊𐐩𐑅 𐐸𐐶𐐮𐐽 𐐶𐐱𐑆 𐐿𐐫𐑊𐐼 𐐄𐑀𐐰𐑃. 𐐈𐑌𐐼 𐐮𐐻 𐐿𐐩𐑋 𐐻𐐭 𐐹𐐰𐑅 𐑄𐐰𐐻 𐑄 𐐪𐑉𐑋𐐨 𐐱𐑂 𐐗𐐬𐑉𐐨𐐰𐑌𐐻𐐲𐑋𐑉 𐐼𐐮𐐼 𐐹𐐮𐐽 𐑄𐐩𐑉 𐐻𐐯𐑌𐐻𐑅 𐐺𐐴 𐑄 𐐸𐐮𐑊 𐐡𐐩𐑋𐐪; 𐐰𐑌𐐼 𐐮𐐻 𐐶𐐱𐑆 𐑄𐐰𐐻 𐑅𐐩𐑋 𐐸𐐮𐑊 𐐸𐐶𐐯𐑉 𐑋𐐴 𐑁𐐪𐑄𐐲𐑉 𐐣𐐬𐑉𐐬𐑌𐐴 𐐼𐐮𐐼 𐐸𐐮𐐼 𐐲𐐹 𐑄 𐑉𐐯𐐿𐐲𐑉𐐼𐑆 𐐲𐑌𐐻𐐭 𐑄 𐐢𐐫𐑉𐐼, 𐐸𐐶𐐮𐐽 𐐶𐐲𐑉 𐑅𐐩𐐿𐑉𐐯𐐼.

7. 𐐈𐑌𐐼 𐐮𐐻 𐐿𐐩𐑋 𐐻𐐭 𐐹𐐰𐑅 𐑄𐐰𐐻 𐑄𐐩 𐐼𐐮𐐼 𐑀𐐰𐑄𐐲𐑉 𐐻𐐭𐑀𐐯𐑄𐐲𐑉 𐐫𐑊 𐑄 𐐹𐐨𐐹𐑊, 𐐲𐐹𐐱𐑌 𐐫𐑊 𐑄 𐑁𐐩𐑅 𐐱𐑂 𐑄 𐑊𐐰𐑌𐐼, 𐐸𐐭 𐐸𐐰𐐼 𐑌𐐱𐐻 𐐺𐐮𐑌 𐑅𐑊𐐩𐑌, 𐑅𐐩𐑂 𐐮𐐻 𐐶𐐱𐑆 𐐀𐑃𐐲𐑉. 𐐈𐑌𐐼 𐐮𐐻 𐐿𐐩𐑋 𐐻𐐭 𐐹𐐰𐑅 𐑄𐐰𐐻 𐐀𐑃𐐲𐑉 𐐼𐐮𐐼 𐐺𐐨𐐸𐐬𐑊𐐼 𐐫𐑊 𐑄 𐐼𐐭𐐮𐑍𐑆 𐐱𐑂 𐑄 𐐹𐐨𐐹𐑊; 𐐰𐑌𐐼 𐐸𐐨 𐐺𐐨𐐸𐐯𐑊𐐼 𐑄𐐰𐐻 𐑄 𐐹𐐨𐐹𐑊 𐐸𐐭 𐐶𐐲𐑉 𐑁𐐫𐑉 𐐗𐐬𐑉𐐨𐐰𐑌𐐻𐐲𐑋𐑉, 𐐶𐐲𐑉 𐑀𐐰𐑄𐐲𐑉𐐼 𐐻𐐭𐑀𐐯𐑄𐐲𐑉 𐐻𐐭 𐑄 𐐪𐑉𐑋𐐨 𐐱𐑂 𐐗𐐬𐑉𐐨𐐰𐑌𐐻𐐲𐑋𐑉; 𐐰𐑌𐐼 𐑄 𐐹𐐨𐐹𐑊 𐐸𐐭 𐐶𐐲𐑉 𐑁𐐫𐑉 𐐟𐐮𐑆, 𐐶𐐲𐑉 𐑀𐐰𐑄𐐲𐑉𐐼 𐐻𐐭𐑀𐐯𐑄𐐲𐑉 𐐻𐐭 𐑄 𐐪𐑉𐑋𐐨 𐐱𐑂 𐐟𐐮𐑆; 𐐸𐐶𐐯𐑉𐑁𐐬𐑉 𐑄𐐩 𐐶𐐲𐑉 𐑁𐐫𐑉 𐑄 𐑅𐐹𐐩𐑅 𐐱𐑂 𐑁𐐬𐑉 𐐷𐐨𐑉𐑆 𐑀𐐰𐑄𐐲𐑉𐐮𐑍 𐐻𐐭𐑀𐐯𐑄𐐲𐑉 𐑄 𐐹𐐨𐐹𐑊, 𐑄𐐰𐐻 𐑄𐐩 𐑋𐐴𐐻 𐑀𐐯𐐻 𐐫𐑊 𐐸𐐭 𐐶𐐲𐑉 𐐲𐐹𐐱𐑌 𐑄 𐑁𐐩𐑅 𐐱𐑂 𐑄 𐑊𐐰𐑌𐐼, 𐐰𐑌𐐼 𐑄𐐰𐐻 𐑄𐐩 𐑋𐐴𐐻 𐑉𐐨𐑅𐐨𐑂 𐐫𐑊 𐑄 𐑅𐐻𐑉𐐯𐑍𐑃 𐐸𐐶𐐮𐐽 𐐮𐐻 𐐶𐐱𐑆 𐐹𐐱𐑅𐐮𐐺𐑊 𐑄𐐰𐐻 𐑄𐐩

𐐿𐐳𐐼 𐑉𐐨𐑅𐐨𐑂. 𐐈𐑌𐐼 𐐮𐐻 𐐿𐐩𐑋 𐐻𐐭 𐐹𐐰𐑅 𐑄𐐰𐐻 𐐸𐐶𐐯𐑌 𐑄𐐩 𐐶𐐲𐑉 𐐫𐑊 𐑀𐐰𐑄𐐲𐑉𐐼 𐐻𐐭𐑀𐐯𐑄𐐲𐑉, 𐐯𐑂𐐲𐑉𐐨 𐐶𐐲𐑌 𐐻𐐭 𐑄 𐐪𐑉𐑋𐐨 𐐸𐐶𐐮𐐽 𐐸𐐨 𐐶𐐳𐐼, 𐐶𐐮𐑄 𐑄𐐩𐑉 𐐶𐐴𐑂𐑆 𐐰𐑌𐐼 𐑄𐐩𐑉 𐐽𐐮𐑊𐐼𐑉𐐯𐑌; 𐐺𐐬𐑃 𐑋𐐯𐑌, 𐐶𐐮𐑋𐐯𐑌, 𐐰𐑌𐐼 𐐽𐐮𐑊𐐼𐑉𐐯𐑌 𐐺𐐨𐐮𐑍 𐐪𐑉𐑋𐐼 𐐶𐐮𐑄 𐐶𐐯𐐹𐐲𐑌𐑆 𐐱𐑂 𐐶𐐫𐑉, 𐐸𐐰𐑂𐐮𐑍 𐑇𐐨𐑊𐐼𐑆, 𐐰𐑌𐐼 𐐺𐑉𐐯𐑅𐐻-𐐹𐑊𐐩𐐻𐑅, 𐐰𐑌𐐼 𐐸𐐯𐐼-𐐹𐑊𐐩𐐻𐑅, 𐐰𐑌𐐼 𐐺𐐨𐐮𐑍 𐐿𐑊𐐬𐑄𐐼 𐐰𐑁𐐻𐐲𐑉 𐑄 𐑋𐐰𐑌𐐲𐑉 𐐱𐑂 𐐶𐐫𐑉, 𐑄𐐩 𐐼𐐮𐐼 𐑋𐐪𐑉𐐽 𐑁𐐬𐑉𐑃 𐐶𐐲𐑌 𐐲𐑀𐐯𐑌𐑅𐐻 𐐲𐑌𐐲𐑄𐐲𐑉, 𐐻𐐭 𐐺𐐰𐐻𐑊; 𐐰𐑌𐐼 𐑄𐐩 𐑁𐐫𐐻 𐐫𐑊 𐑄𐐰𐐻 𐐼𐐩, 𐐰𐑌𐐼 𐐿𐐱𐑍𐐿𐐲𐑉𐐼 𐑌𐐱𐐻. 𐐈𐑌𐐼 𐐮𐐻 𐐿𐐩𐑋 𐐻𐐭 𐐹𐐰𐑅 𐑄𐐰𐐻 𐐸𐐶𐐯𐑌 𐐮𐐻 𐐶𐐱𐑆 𐑌𐐴𐐻 𐑄𐐩 𐐶𐐲𐑉 𐐶𐐨𐑉𐐨, 𐐰𐑌𐐼 𐑉𐐨𐐻𐐴𐑉𐐼 𐐻𐐭 𐑄𐐩𐑉 𐐿𐐰𐑋𐐹𐑅; 𐐰𐑌𐐼 𐐰𐑁𐐻𐐲𐑉 𐑄𐐩 𐐸𐐰𐐼 𐑉𐐨𐐻𐐴𐑉𐐼 𐐻𐐭 𐑄𐐩𐑉 𐐿𐐰𐑋𐐹𐑅, 𐑄𐐩 𐐻𐐳𐐿 𐐲𐐹 𐐲 𐐸𐐵𐑊𐐮𐑍 𐐰𐑌𐐼 𐐲 𐑊𐐰𐑋𐐯𐑌𐐻𐐩𐑇𐐲𐑌 𐑁𐐫𐑉 𐑄 𐑊𐐱𐑅 𐐱𐑂 𐑄 𐑅𐑊𐐩𐑌 𐐱𐑂 𐑄𐐩𐑉 𐐹𐐨𐐹𐑊; 𐐰𐑌𐐼 𐑅𐐬 𐑀𐑉𐐩𐐻 𐐶𐐲𐑉 𐑄𐐩𐑉 𐐿𐑉𐐴𐑆, 𐑄𐐩𐑉 𐐸𐐵𐑊𐐮𐑍𐑆 𐐰𐑌𐐼 𐑊𐐰𐑋𐐯𐑌𐐻𐐩𐑇𐐲𐑌𐑆, 𐑄𐐰𐐻 𐑄𐐩 𐐼𐐮𐐼 𐑉𐐯𐑌𐐼 𐑄 𐐯𐑉 𐐯𐐿𐑅𐐨𐐼𐐮𐑍𐑊𐐨. 𐐈𐑌𐐼 𐐮𐐻 𐐿𐐩𐑋 𐐻𐐭 𐐹𐐰𐑅 𐑄𐐰𐐻 𐐱𐑌 𐑄 𐑋𐐱𐑉𐐬 𐑄𐐩 𐐼𐐮𐐼 𐑀𐐬 𐐲𐑀𐐯𐑌 𐐻𐐭 𐐺𐐰𐐻𐑊, 𐐰𐑌𐐼 𐑀𐑉𐐩𐐻 𐐰𐑌𐐼 𐐻𐐯𐑉𐐮𐐺𐑊 𐐶𐐱𐑆 𐑄𐐰𐐻 𐐼𐐩; 𐑌𐐯𐑂𐐲𐑉𐑄𐐲𐑊𐐯𐑅, 𐑄𐐩 𐐿𐐱𐑍𐐿𐐲𐑉𐐼 𐑌𐐱𐐻, 𐐰𐑌𐐼 𐐸𐐶𐐯𐑌 𐑄 𐑌𐐴𐐻 𐐿𐐩𐑋 𐐲𐑀𐐯𐑌 𐑄𐐩 𐐼𐐮𐐼 𐑉𐐯𐑌𐐼 𐑄 𐐯𐑉 𐐶𐐮𐑄 𐑄𐐩𐑉 𐐿𐑉𐐴𐑆, 𐐰𐑌𐐼 𐑄𐐩𐑉 𐐸𐐵𐑊𐐮𐑍𐑆, 𐐰𐑌𐐼 𐑄𐐩𐑉 𐑋𐐬𐑉𐑌𐐮𐑍𐑆, 𐑁𐐫𐑉 𐑄 𐑊𐐱𐑅 𐐱𐑂 𐑄 𐑅𐑊𐐩𐑌 𐐱𐑂 𐑄𐐩𐑉 𐐹𐐨𐐹𐑊.

8. 𐐈𐑌𐐼 𐐮𐐻 𐐿𐐩𐑋 𐐻𐐭 𐐹𐐰𐑅 𐑄𐐰𐐻 𐐗𐐫𐑉𐐨𐐰𐑌𐐻𐐲𐑋𐑉 𐑉𐐬𐐻 𐐲𐑀𐐯𐑌 𐐰𐑌 𐐨𐐹𐐮𐑅𐑊 𐐲𐑌𐐻𐐭 𐑇𐐮𐑆, 𐐼𐐨𐑆𐐴𐑉𐐮𐑍 𐑄𐐰𐐻 𐐸𐐨 𐐶𐐳𐐼 𐑌𐐱𐐻 𐐿𐐲𐑋 𐐲𐑀𐐯𐑌 𐐻𐐭 𐐺𐐰𐐻𐑊, 𐐺𐐲𐐻 𐑄𐐰𐐻 𐐸𐐨 𐐶𐐳𐐼 𐐻𐐩𐐿 𐑄 𐐿𐐮𐑍𐐼𐐲𐑋, 𐐰𐑌𐐼 𐑅𐐹𐐯𐑉 𐑄 𐑊𐐴𐑂𐑆 𐐱𐑂 𐑄 𐐹𐐨𐐹𐑊. 𐐒𐐲𐐻 𐐺𐐨𐐸𐐬𐑊𐐼, 𐑄 𐐝𐐹𐐮𐑉𐐮𐐻 𐐱𐑂 𐑄 𐐢𐐫𐑉𐐼 𐐸𐐰𐐼 𐑅𐐨𐑅𐐻 𐑅𐐻𐑉𐐴𐑂𐐮𐑍 𐐶𐐮𐑄 𐑄𐐯𐑋, 𐐰𐑌𐐼 𐐝𐐩𐐻𐐲𐑌 𐐸𐐰𐐼 𐑁𐐳𐑊 𐐹𐐵𐐲𐑉 𐐬𐑂𐐲𐑉 𐑄 𐐸𐐪𐑉𐐻𐑅 𐐱𐑂 𐑄 𐐹𐐨𐐹𐑊, 𐑁𐐫𐑉 𐑄𐐩 𐐶𐐲𐑉 𐑀𐐮𐑂𐑌 𐐲𐐹 𐐲𐑌𐐻𐐭 𐑄 𐐸𐐪𐑉𐐼𐑌𐐯𐑅 𐐱𐑂 𐑄𐐩𐑉 𐐸𐐪𐑉𐐻𐑅, 𐐰𐑌𐐼 𐑄 𐐺𐑊𐐴𐑌𐐼𐑌𐐯𐑅 𐐱𐑂 𐑄𐐩𐑉 𐑋𐐴𐑌𐐼𐑆, 𐑄𐐰𐐻 𐑄𐐩 𐑋𐐴𐐻 𐐺𐐨 𐐼𐐯𐑅𐐻𐑉𐐶𐐮𐐼; 𐐸𐐶𐐯𐑉𐑁𐐬𐑉 𐑄𐐩 𐐶𐐯𐑌𐐻 𐐲𐑀𐐯𐑌 𐐻𐐭 𐐺𐐰𐐻𐑊. 𐐈𐑌𐐼 𐐮𐐻 𐐿𐐩𐑋 𐐻𐐭 𐐹𐐰𐑅 𐑄𐐰𐐻 𐑄𐐩 𐑁𐐫𐐻 𐐫𐑊 𐑄𐐰𐐻 𐐼𐐩, 𐐰𐑌𐐼 𐐸𐐶𐐯𐑌 𐑄 𐑌𐐴𐐻 𐐿𐐩𐑋 𐑄𐐩 𐑅𐑊𐐯𐐹𐐻 𐐲𐐹𐐱𐑌 𐑄𐐩𐑉 𐑅𐐬𐑉𐐼𐑆; 𐐰𐑌𐐼 𐐱𐑌 𐑄 𐑋𐐱𐑉𐐬 𐑄𐐩 𐑁𐐫𐐻 𐐨𐑂𐑌 𐐲𐑌𐐻𐐮𐑊 𐑄 𐑌𐐴𐐻 𐐿𐐩𐑋; 𐐰𐑌𐐼 𐐸𐐶𐐯𐑌 𐑄 𐑌𐐴𐐻 𐐿𐐩𐑋 𐑄𐐩 𐐶𐐲𐑉 𐐼𐑉𐐲𐑍𐐿𐑌 𐐶𐐮𐑄 𐐰𐑍𐑀𐐲𐑉, 𐐨𐑂𐑌 𐐰𐑆 𐐲 𐑋𐐰𐑌 𐐸𐐭 𐐮𐑆 𐐼𐑉𐐲𐑍𐐿𐑌 𐐶𐐮𐑄 𐐶𐐴𐑌; 𐐰𐑌𐐼 𐑄𐐩 𐑅𐑊𐐯𐐹𐐻 𐐲𐑀𐐯𐑌 𐐲𐐹𐐱𐑌 𐑄𐐩𐑉 𐑅𐐬𐑉𐐼𐑆; 𐐰𐑌𐐼 𐐱𐑌 𐑄 𐑋𐐱𐑉𐐬 𐑄𐐩 𐑁𐐫𐐻 𐐲𐑀𐐯𐑌; 𐐰𐑌𐐼 𐐸𐐶𐐯𐑌 𐑄 𐑌𐐴𐐻 𐐿𐐩𐑋 𐑄𐐩 𐐸𐐰𐐼 𐐫𐑊 𐑁𐐫𐑊𐑌 𐐺𐐴 𐑄 𐑅𐐬𐑉𐐼 𐑅𐐩𐑂 𐐮𐐻 𐐶𐐲𐑉 𐑁𐐮𐑁𐐻𐐨 𐐰𐑌𐐼 𐐻𐐭 𐐱𐑂 𐑄 𐐹𐐨𐐹𐑊 𐐱𐑂 𐐗𐐫𐑉𐐨𐐰𐑌𐐻𐐲𐑋𐑉, 𐐰𐑌𐐼 𐑅𐐮𐐿𐑅𐐻𐐨 𐐰𐑌𐐼 𐑌𐐴𐑌 𐐱𐑂 𐑄 𐐹𐐨𐐹𐑊 𐐱𐑂 𐐞𐐮𐑆. 𐐈𐑌𐐼 𐐮𐐻 𐐿𐐩𐑋 𐐻𐐭 𐐹𐐰𐑅 𐑄𐐰𐐻 𐑄𐐩 𐑅𐑊𐐯𐐹𐐻 𐐲𐐹𐐱𐑌 𐑄𐐩𐑉 𐑅𐐬𐑉𐐼𐑆 𐑄𐐰𐐻 𐑌𐐴𐐻, 𐐰𐑌𐐼 𐐱𐑌 𐑄 𐑋𐐱𐑉𐐬 𐑄𐐩 𐑁𐐫𐐻 𐐲𐑀𐐯𐑌, 𐐰𐑌𐐼 𐑄𐐩 𐐿𐐱𐑌𐐻𐐯𐑌𐐼𐐯𐐼 𐐮𐑌 𐑄𐐩𐑉 𐑋𐐴𐐻 𐐶𐐮𐑄 𐑄𐐩𐑉 𐑅𐐬𐑉𐐼𐑆, 𐐰𐑌𐐼 𐐶𐐮𐑄 𐑄𐐩𐑉 𐑇𐐨𐑊𐐼𐑆, 𐐫𐑊 𐑄𐐰𐐻 𐐼𐐩; 𐐰𐑌𐐼 𐐸𐐶𐐯𐑌 𐑄 𐑌𐐴𐐻 𐐿𐐩𐑋 𐑄𐐯𐑉 𐐶𐐲𐑉 𐑃𐐲𐑉𐐻𐐨 𐐰𐑌𐐼 𐐻𐐭 𐐱𐑂 𐑄 𐐹𐐨𐐹𐑊 𐐱𐑂 𐐞𐐮𐑆, 𐐰𐑌𐐼 𐐻𐐶𐐯𐑌𐐻𐐨 𐐰𐑌𐐼 𐑅𐐯𐑂𐑌 𐐱𐑂 𐑄 𐐹𐐨𐐹𐑊 𐐱𐑂 𐐗𐐫𐑉𐐨𐐰𐑌𐐻𐐲𐑋𐑉.

9. 𐐈𐑌𐐼 𐐮𐐻 𐐿𐐩𐑋 𐐻𐐭 𐐹𐐰𐑅 𐑄𐐰𐐻 𐑄𐐩 𐐩𐐻 𐐰𐑌𐐼 𐑅𐑊𐐯𐐹𐐻 𐐰𐑌𐐼 𐐹𐑉𐐨𐐹𐐯𐑉𐐼 𐑁𐐫𐑉 𐐼𐐯𐑃 𐐱𐑌 𐑄 𐑋𐐱𐑉𐐬. 𐐈𐑌𐐼 𐑄𐐩 𐐶𐐲𐑉 𐑊𐐪𐑉𐐾 𐐰𐑌𐐼 𐑋𐐴𐐻𐐨 𐑋𐐯𐑌 𐐰𐑆 𐐻𐐭 𐑄 𐑅𐐻𐑉𐐯𐑍𐑃 𐐱𐑂 𐑋𐐯𐑌. 𐐈𐑌𐐼 𐐮𐐻 𐐿𐐩𐑋 𐐻𐐭 𐐹𐐰𐑅 𐑄𐐰𐐻 𐑄𐐩 𐑁𐐫𐐻 𐑁𐐫𐑉 𐑄 𐑅𐐹𐐩𐑅 𐐱𐑂 𐑃𐑉𐐨 𐐵𐑉𐑆, 𐐰𐑌𐐼 𐑄𐐩 𐑁𐐩𐑌𐐻𐐯𐐼 𐐶𐐮𐑄 𐑄 𐑊𐐱𐑅 𐐱𐑂 𐐺𐑊𐐲𐐼. 𐐈𐑌𐐼 𐐮𐐻 𐐿𐐩𐑋 𐐻𐐭 𐐹𐐰𐑅 𐑄𐐰𐐻 𐐸𐐶𐐯𐑌 𐑄 𐑋𐐯𐑌 𐐱𐑂 𐐗𐐫𐑉𐐨𐐰𐑌𐐻𐐲𐑋𐑉 𐐸𐐰𐐼 𐑉𐐨𐑅𐐨𐑂𐐼 𐑅𐐲𐑁𐐮𐑇𐐯𐑌𐐻 𐑅𐐻𐑉𐐯𐑍𐑃, 𐑄𐐰𐐻 𐑄𐐩 𐐿𐐳𐐼 𐐶𐐫𐐿, 𐑄𐐩 𐐶𐐲𐑉 𐐲𐐺𐐵𐐻 𐐻𐐭 𐑁𐑊𐐨 𐑁𐐫𐑉 𐑄𐐩𐑉 𐑊𐐴𐑂𐑆, 𐐺𐐲𐐻 𐐺𐐨𐐸𐐬𐑊𐐼, 𐐞𐐮𐑆 𐐲𐑉𐐬𐑆, 𐐰𐑌𐐼 𐐫𐑊𐑅𐐬 𐐸𐐮𐑆 𐑋𐐯𐑌, 𐐰𐑌𐐼 𐐸𐐨 𐑅𐐶𐐬𐑉 𐐮𐑌 𐐸𐐮𐑆 𐑉𐐪𐑃 𐑄𐐰𐐻 𐐸𐐨 𐐶𐐳𐐼 𐑅𐑊𐐩 𐐗𐐫𐑉𐐨𐐰𐑌𐐻𐐲𐑋𐑉, 𐐫𐑉 𐐸𐐨 𐐶𐐳𐐼 𐐹𐐯𐑉𐐮𐑇 𐐺𐐴 𐑄 𐑅𐐬𐑉𐐼; 𐐸𐐶𐐯𐑉𐑁𐐬𐑉 𐐸𐐨 𐐼𐐮𐐼 𐐹𐐲𐑉𐑅𐐷𐐭 𐑄𐐯𐑋, 𐐰𐑌𐐼 𐐱𐑌 𐑄 𐑋𐐱𐑉𐐬 𐐸𐐨 𐐼𐐮𐐼 𐐬𐑂𐐲𐑉𐐻𐐩𐐿 𐑄𐐯𐑋; 𐐰𐑌𐐼 𐑄𐐩 𐑁𐐫𐐻 𐐲𐑀𐐯𐑌 𐐶𐐮𐑄 𐑄 𐑅𐐬𐑉𐐼. 𐐈𐑌𐐼 𐐮𐐻 𐐿𐐩𐑋 𐐻𐐭 𐐹𐐰𐑅 𐑄𐐰𐐻 𐐸𐐶𐐯𐑌 𐑄𐐩 𐐸𐐰𐐼 𐐫𐑊 𐑁𐐫𐑊𐑌 𐐺𐐴 𐑄 𐑅𐐬𐑉𐐼, 𐑅𐐩𐑂 𐐮𐐻 𐐶𐐲𐑉 𐐗𐐫𐑉𐐨𐐰𐑌𐐻𐐲𐑋𐑉 𐐰𐑌𐐼 𐐞𐐮𐑆, 𐐺𐐨𐐸𐐬𐑊𐐼 𐐞𐐮𐑆 𐐸𐐰𐐼 𐑁𐐩𐑌𐐻𐐯𐐼 𐐶𐐮𐑄 𐑄 𐑊𐐱𐑅 𐐱𐑂 𐐺𐑊𐐲𐐼. 𐐈𐑌𐐼 𐐮𐐻 𐐿𐐩𐑋 𐐻𐐭 𐐹𐐰𐑅 𐑄𐐰𐐻 𐐸𐐶𐐯𐑌 𐐗𐐫𐑉𐐨𐐰𐑌𐐻𐐲𐑋𐑉 𐐸𐐰𐐼 𐑊𐐨𐑌𐐼 𐐲𐐹𐐱𐑌 𐐸𐐮𐑆 𐑅𐐬𐑉𐐼, 𐑄𐐰𐐻 𐐸𐐨 𐑉𐐯𐑅𐐻𐐯𐐼 𐐲 𐑊𐐮𐐻𐑊, 𐐸𐐨 𐑅𐑋𐐬𐐻 𐐱𐑁 𐑄 𐐸𐐯𐐼 𐐱𐑂 𐐞𐐮𐑆. 𐐈𐑌𐐼 𐐮𐐻 𐐿𐐩𐑋 𐐻𐐭 𐐹𐐰𐑅 𐑄𐐰𐐻 𐐰𐑁𐐻𐐲𐑉 𐐸𐐨 𐐸𐐰𐐼 𐑅𐑋𐐮𐐻𐑌 𐐱𐑁 𐑄 𐐸𐐯𐐼 𐐱𐑂 𐐞𐐮𐑆, 𐑄𐐰𐐻 𐐞𐐮𐑆 𐑉𐐩𐑆𐐼 𐐲𐐹𐐱𐑌 𐐸𐐮𐑆 𐐸𐐰𐑌𐐼𐑆 𐐰𐑌𐐼 𐑁𐐯𐑊; 𐐰𐑌𐐼 𐐰𐑁𐐻𐐲𐑉 𐑄𐐰𐐻 𐐸𐐨 𐐸𐐰𐐼 𐑅𐐻𐑉𐐲𐑀𐑊𐐼 𐑁𐐫𐑉 𐐺𐑉𐐯𐑃, 𐐸𐐨 𐐼𐐴𐐼. 𐐈𐑌𐐼 𐐮𐐻 𐐿𐐩𐑋 𐐻𐐭 𐐹𐐰𐑅 𐑄𐐰𐐻 𐐗𐐫𐑉𐐨𐐰𐑌𐐻𐐲𐑋𐑉 𐑁𐐯𐑊 𐐻𐐭 𐑄 𐐲𐑉𐑃, 𐐰𐑌𐐼 𐐺𐐨𐐿𐐩𐑋 𐐰𐑆 𐐮𐑁 𐐸𐐨 𐐸𐐰𐐼 𐑌𐐬 𐑊𐐴𐑁. 𐐈𐑌𐐼 𐑄 𐐢𐐫𐑉𐐼 𐑅𐐹𐐩𐐿 𐐲𐑌𐐻𐐭 𐐀𐑃𐐲𐑉, 𐐰𐑌𐐼

𐑅𐐯𐐼 𐐲𐑌𐐻𐐭 𐐸𐐮𐑋, 𐐘𐐬 𐑁𐐬𐑉𐑃. 𐐈𐑌𐐼 𐐸𐐨 𐐶𐐯𐑌𐐻 𐑁𐐬𐑉𐑃, 𐐰𐑌𐐼 𐐺𐐨𐐸𐐯𐑊𐐼 𐑄𐐰𐐻 𐑄 𐐶𐐲𐑉𐐼𐑆 𐐱𐑂 𐑄 𐐢𐐫𐑉𐐼 𐐸𐐰𐐼 𐐫𐑊 𐐺𐐮𐑌 𐑁𐐳𐑊𐑁𐐮𐑊𐐼; 𐐰𐑌𐐼 𐐸𐐨 𐑁𐐮𐑌𐐮𐑇𐐻 𐐸𐐮𐑆 𐑉𐐯𐐿𐐲𐑉𐐼; (𐐰𐑌𐐼 𐑄 𐐸𐐲𐑌𐐼𐑉𐐯𐐼𐑃 𐐹𐐪𐑉𐐻 𐐌 𐐸𐐰𐑂 𐑌𐐱𐐻 𐑉𐐮𐐻𐐲𐑌;) 𐐰𐑌𐐼 𐐸𐐨 𐐸𐐮𐐼 𐑄𐐯𐑋 𐐮𐑌 𐐪 𐑋𐐰𐑌𐐲𐑉 𐑄𐐰𐐻 𐑄 𐐹𐐨𐐹𐑊 𐐱𐑂 𐐢𐐮𐑋𐐸𐐴 𐐼𐐮𐐼 𐑁𐐴𐑌𐐼 𐑄𐐯𐑋. 𐐤𐐵 𐑄 𐑊𐐰𐑅𐐻 𐐶𐐲𐑉𐐼𐑆 𐐸𐐶𐐮𐐽 𐐪𐑉 𐑉𐐮𐐻𐐲𐑌 𐐺𐐴 𐐀𐑃𐐲𐑉, 𐐪𐑉 𐑄𐐨𐑆, 𐐐𐐶𐐯𐑄𐐲𐑉 𐑄 𐐢𐐫𐑉𐐼 𐐶𐐮𐑊 𐑄𐐰𐐻 𐐌 𐐺𐐨 𐐻𐑉𐐰𐑌𐑅𐑊𐐩𐐻𐐲𐐼, 𐐫𐑉 𐑄𐐰𐐻 𐐌 𐑅𐐲𐑁𐐲𐑉 𐑄 𐐶𐐮𐑊 𐐱𐑂 𐑄 𐐢𐐫𐑉𐐼 𐐮𐑌 𐑄 𐑁𐑊𐐯𐑇, 𐐮𐐻 𐑋𐐰𐐻𐐲𐑉𐐯𐑃 𐑌𐐱𐐻, 𐐮𐑁 𐐮𐐻 𐑅𐐬 𐐺𐐨 𐑄𐐰𐐻 𐐌 𐐰𐑋 𐑅𐐩𐑂𐐼 𐐮𐑌 𐑄 𐐿𐐮𐑍𐐼𐐲𐑋 𐐱𐑂 𐐘𐐱𐐼. 𐐁𐑋𐐯𐑌.

𐐜 𐐒𐐳𐐿 𐐱𐑂 𐐣𐐬𐑉𐐬𐑌𐐴.

𐐕𐐰𐐹𐐻𐐲𐑉 I.

1. 𐑌𐐵 𐐌, 𐐣𐐬𐑉𐐬𐑌𐐴, 𐐪𐑁𐐻𐐲𐑉 𐐸𐐰𐑂𐐮𐑍 𐑋𐐩𐐼 𐐰𐑌 𐐯𐑌𐐼 𐐱𐑂 𐐰𐐺𐑉𐐮𐐾𐐮𐑍 𐑄 𐐰𐐿𐐵𐑌𐐻 𐐱𐑂 𐑄 𐐹𐐨𐐹𐑊 𐐱𐑂 𐐖𐐯𐑉𐐲𐐼, 𐐌 𐐸𐐰𐐼 𐑅𐐲𐐹𐐬𐑆𐐼 𐑌𐐱𐐻 𐐻𐐭 𐐸𐐰𐑂 𐑉𐐮𐐻𐑌 𐑋𐐬𐑉, 𐐺𐐲𐐻 𐐌 𐐸𐐰𐑂 𐑌𐐱𐐻 𐐰𐑆 𐐷𐐯𐐻 𐐹𐐯𐑉𐐮𐑇𐐻; 𐐰𐑌𐐼 𐐌 𐑋𐐩𐐿 𐑌𐐱𐐻 𐑋𐐴𐑅𐐯𐑊𐑁 𐑌𐐬𐑌 𐐻𐐭 𐑄 𐐢𐐩𐑋𐐲𐑌𐐴𐐻𐑅, 𐑊𐐯𐑅𐐻 𐑄𐐩 𐑇𐐳𐐼 𐐼𐐨𐑅𐐻𐑉𐐱𐐮 𐑋𐐨. 𐐙𐐫𐑉 𐐺𐐨𐐸𐐬𐑊𐐼, 𐑄𐐩𐑉 𐐶𐐫𐑉𐑆 𐐪𐑉 𐐯𐐿𐑅𐐨𐐼𐐮𐑍𐑊𐐮 𐑁𐐨𐑉𐑅 𐐲𐑋𐐲𐑍 𐑄𐐯𐑋𐑅𐐯𐑊𐑂𐑆; 𐐰𐑌𐐼 𐐺𐐨𐐿𐐫𐑆 𐐱𐑂 𐑄𐐩𐑉 𐐸𐐩𐐻𐑉𐐯𐐼, 𐑄𐐩 𐐹𐐳𐐻 𐐻𐐭 𐐼𐐯𐑃 𐐯𐑂𐐲𐑉𐐮 𐑌𐐨𐑁𐐴𐐻 𐑄𐐰𐐻 𐐶𐐮𐑊 𐑌𐐱𐐻 𐐼𐐨𐑌𐐴 𐑄 𐐗𐑉𐐴𐑅𐐻. 𐐈𐑌𐐼 𐐌, 𐐣𐐬𐑉𐐬𐑌𐐴, 𐐶𐐮𐑊 𐑌𐐱𐐻 𐐼𐐨𐑌𐐴 𐑄 𐐗𐑉𐐴𐑅𐐻; 𐐸𐐶𐐯𐑉𐑁𐐫𐑉, 𐐌 𐐶𐐱𐑌𐐼𐐲𐑉 𐐸𐐶𐐮𐑄𐐲𐑉𐑅𐐬𐐯𐑂𐐲𐑉 𐐌 𐐿𐐰𐑌, 𐑁𐐫𐑉 𐑄 𐑅𐐩𐑁𐐻𐐮 𐐱𐑂 𐑋𐐴𐑌 𐐬𐑌 𐑊𐐴𐑁. 𐐐𐐶𐐯𐑉𐑁𐐫𐑉 𐐌 𐑉𐐴𐐻 𐐪 𐑁𐐷𐐭 𐑋𐐬𐑉 𐑃𐐮𐑍𐑆, 𐐿𐐱𐑌𐐻𐑉𐐯𐑉𐐮 𐐻𐐭 𐑄𐐰𐐻 𐐸𐐶𐐮𐐽 𐐌 𐐸𐐰𐑂 𐑅𐐲𐐹𐐬𐑆𐐼; 𐑁𐐫𐑉 𐐌 𐐸𐐰𐑂 𐑅𐐲𐐹𐐬𐑆𐐼 𐑌𐐱𐐻 𐐻𐐭 𐐸𐐰𐑂 𐑉𐐮𐐻𐑌 𐐯𐑌𐐮 𐑋𐐬𐑉; 𐐺𐐲𐐻 𐐌 𐑉𐐴𐐻 𐐪 𐑁𐐷𐐭 𐑋𐐬𐑉 𐑃𐐮𐑍𐑆, 𐑄𐐰𐐻 𐐹𐐲𐑉𐐸𐐰𐐹𐑅 𐑄𐐩 𐑋𐐩 𐐺 𐐱𐑂 𐐶𐐲𐑉𐑃 𐐲𐑌𐐻𐐭 𐑋𐐴 𐐺𐑉𐐯𐑄𐑉𐐯𐑌, 𐑄 𐐢𐐩𐑋𐐲𐑌𐐴𐐻𐑅, 𐐮𐑌 𐑅𐐲𐑋 𐑁𐐷𐐭𐐻𐐷𐐭𐑉 𐐼𐐩, 𐐰𐐿𐐫𐑉𐐼𐐮𐑍 𐐻𐐭 𐑄 𐐶𐐮𐑊 𐐱𐑂 𐑄 𐐢𐐫𐑉𐐼.

𐐕𐐰𐐹𐐻𐐲𐑉 II.

1. 𐑄 𐐶𐐲𐑉𐐼𐑆 𐐱𐑂 𐐗𐑉𐐴𐑅𐐻, 𐐸𐐶𐐮𐐽 𐐸𐐨 𐑅𐐹𐐩𐐿 𐐲𐑌𐐻𐐭 𐐸𐐮𐑆 𐐼𐐮𐑅𐐴𐐹𐑊𐑆, 𐑄 𐐻𐐶𐐯𐑊𐑂 𐐸𐐭𐑋 𐐸𐐨 𐐸𐐰𐐼 𐐽𐐬𐑆𐑌, 𐐰𐑆 𐐸𐐨 𐑊𐐩𐐼 𐐸𐐮𐑆 𐐸𐐰𐑌𐐼𐑆 𐐲𐐹𐐱𐑌 𐑄𐐯𐑋. 𐐈𐑌𐐼 𐐸𐐨 𐐿𐐫𐑊𐐼 𐑄𐐯𐑋 𐐺𐐴 𐑌𐐩𐑋, 𐑅𐐩𐐮𐑍, 𐐷𐐨 𐑇𐐰𐑊 𐐿𐐫𐑊 𐐱𐑌 𐑄 𐐙𐐪𐑄𐐲𐑉 𐐮𐑌 𐑋𐐴 𐑌𐐩𐑋, 𐐮𐑌 𐑋𐐴𐐻𐐮 𐐹𐑉𐐩𐑉; 𐐰𐑌𐐼 𐐪𐑁𐐻𐐲𐑉 𐐷𐐨 𐐸𐐰𐑂 𐐼𐐲𐑌 𐑄𐐮𐑅, 𐐷𐐨 𐑇𐐰𐑊 𐐸𐐰𐑂 𐐹𐐵𐑉 𐑄𐐰𐐻 𐐱𐑌 𐐸𐐮𐑋 𐐸𐐭𐑋 𐐷𐐨 𐑇𐐰𐑊 𐑊𐐩 𐐷𐐬𐑉 𐐸𐐰𐑌𐐼𐑆, 𐐷𐐨 𐑇𐐰𐑊- 𐑀𐐮𐑂 𐑄 𐐐𐐬𐑊𐐮 𐐘𐐬𐑅𐐻; 𐐰𐑌𐐼 𐐮𐑌 𐑋𐐴 𐑌𐐩𐑋 𐑇𐐰𐑊 𐐷𐐨 𐑀𐐮𐑂 𐐮𐐻, 𐑁𐐫𐑉 𐑄𐐲𐑅 𐐼𐐭 𐑋𐐴𐑌 𐐰𐐹𐐱𐑅𐑊𐑆. 𐐤𐐵 𐐗𐑉𐐴𐑅𐐻 𐑅𐐹𐐩𐐿 𐑄𐐨𐑆 𐐶𐐲𐑉𐐼𐑆 𐐲𐑌𐐻𐐭 𐑄𐐯𐑋 𐐰𐐻 𐑄 𐐻𐐴𐑋 𐐱𐑂 𐐸𐐮𐑆 𐑁𐐲𐑉𐑅𐐻 𐐲𐐹𐐨𐑉𐐮𐑍; 𐐰𐑌𐐼 𐑄 𐑋𐐲𐑊𐐻𐐮𐐻𐐷𐐭𐐼 𐐸𐐲𐑉𐐼 𐐮𐐻 𐑌𐐱𐐻, 𐐺𐐲𐐻 𐑄 𐐼𐐮𐑅𐐴𐐹𐑊𐑆 𐐸𐐲𐑉𐐼 𐐮𐐻; 𐐰𐑌𐐼 𐐱𐑌 𐐰𐑆 𐑋𐐯𐑌𐐮 𐐰𐑆 𐑄𐐩 𐑊𐐩𐐼 𐑄𐐩𐑉 𐐸𐐰𐑌𐐼𐑆, 𐑁𐐯𐑊 𐑄 𐐐𐐬𐑊𐐮 𐐘𐐬𐑅𐐻.

𐐕𐐰𐐹𐐻𐐲𐑉 III.

1. 𐑄 𐑋𐐰𐑌𐐲𐑉 𐐸𐐶𐐮𐐽 𐑄 𐐼𐐮𐑅𐐴𐐹𐑊𐑆, 𐐸𐐭 𐐶𐐲𐑉 𐐿𐐫𐑊𐐼 𐑄 𐐯𐑊𐐼𐐲𐑉𐑆 𐐱𐑂 𐑄 𐐽𐐲𐑉𐐽, 𐐫𐑉𐐼𐐩𐑌𐐼 𐐹𐑉𐐨𐑅𐐻𐑅 𐐰𐑌𐐼 𐐻𐐨𐐽𐐲𐑉𐑆. 𐐂𐑁𐐻𐐲𐑉 𐑄𐐩 𐐸𐐰𐐼 𐐹𐑉𐐩𐐼 𐐲𐑌𐐻𐐭 𐑄 𐐙𐐪𐑄𐐲𐑉 𐐮𐑌 𐑄 𐑌𐐩𐑋 𐐱𐑂 𐐗𐑉𐐴𐑅𐐻, 𐑄𐐩 𐑊𐐩𐐼 𐑄𐐩𐑉 𐐸𐐰𐑌𐐼𐑆 𐐲𐐹𐐱𐑌 𐑄𐐯𐑋, 𐐰𐑌𐐼 𐑅𐐯𐐼, 𐐆𐑌 𐑄 𐑌𐐩𐑋 𐐱𐑂 𐐖𐐨𐑆𐐲𐑅 𐐗𐑉𐐴𐑅𐐻 𐐌 𐐫𐑉𐐼𐐩𐑌 𐐷𐐭 𐐻𐐭 𐐺 𐐪 𐐹𐑉𐐨𐑅𐐻; (𐐫𐑉, 𐐮𐑁 𐐸𐐨 𐐺 𐐪 𐐻𐐨𐐽𐐲𐑉;) 𐐌 𐐫𐑉𐐼𐐩𐑌 𐐷𐐭 𐐻𐐭 𐐺 𐐪 𐐻𐐨𐐽𐐲𐑉, 𐐻𐐭 𐐹𐑉𐐨𐐽 𐑉𐐨𐐹𐐯𐑌𐐻𐐰𐑌𐑅 𐐰𐑌𐐼 𐑉𐐨𐑋𐐮𐑇𐐲𐑌 𐐱𐑂 𐑅𐐮𐑌𐑆 𐑃𐑉𐐭 𐐖𐐨𐑆𐐲𐑅 𐐗𐑉𐐴𐑅𐐻 𐐺𐐴 𐑄 𐐯𐑌𐐼𐐷𐐭𐑉𐐰𐑌𐑅 𐐱𐑂 𐑁𐐩𐑃 𐐱𐑌 𐐸𐐮𐑆 𐑌𐐩𐑋 𐐻𐐭

𐑄 𐐯𐑌𐐼. 𐐁𐑋𐐯𐑌. 𐐈𐑌𐐼 𐐰𐑁𐐻𐐲𐑉 𐑄𐐮𐑅 𐑋𐐰𐑌𐐲𐑉 𐐼𐐮𐐼 𐑄𐐩 𐐫𐑉𐐼𐐩𐑌 𐐑𐑉𐐨𐑅𐐻𐑅 𐐰𐑌𐐼 𐐓𐐨𐐽𐐲𐑉𐑆, 𐐰𐐿𐐫𐑉𐐼𐐮𐑍 𐐻𐐭 𐑄 𐑀𐐮𐑁𐐻𐑅 𐐰𐑌𐐼 𐐿𐐫𐑊𐐮𐑍𐑆 𐐱𐑂 𐐘𐐱𐐼 𐐲𐑌𐐻𐐭 𐑋𐐯𐑌; 𐐰𐑌𐐼 𐑄𐐩 𐐫𐑉𐐼𐐩𐑌𐐼 𐑄𐐯𐑋 𐐺𐐴 𐑄 𐐹𐐵𐐲𐑉 𐐱𐑂 𐑄 𐐐𐐬𐑊𐐮 𐐘𐐬𐑅𐐻, 𐐸𐐶𐐮𐐽 𐐶𐐱𐑆 𐐮𐑌 𐑄𐐯𐑋.

𐐕𐐰𐐹𐐻𐐲𐑉 IV.

1. 𐐜 𐑋𐐰𐑌𐐲𐑉 𐐱𐑂 𐑄𐐩𐑉 𐐇𐑊𐐼𐐲𐑉𐑆 𐐰𐑌𐐼 𐐑𐑉𐐨𐑅𐐻𐑅 𐐰𐐼𐑋𐐮𐑌𐐮𐑅𐐻𐐲𐑉𐐮𐑍 𐑄 𐑁𐑊𐐯𐑇 𐐰𐑌𐐼 𐐺𐑊𐐲𐐼 𐐱𐑂 𐐗𐑉𐐴𐑅𐐻 𐐲𐑌𐐻𐐭 𐑄 𐐕𐐲𐑉𐐽. 𐐈𐑌𐐼 𐑄𐐩 𐐰𐐼𐑋𐐮𐑌𐐮𐑅𐐻𐐲𐑉𐐼 𐐮𐐻 𐐰𐐿𐐫𐑉𐐼𐐮𐑍 𐐻𐐭 𐑄 𐐿𐐱𐑋𐐰𐑌𐐼𐑋𐐯𐑌𐐻𐑅 𐐱𐑂 𐐗𐑉𐐴𐑅𐐻; 𐐸𐐶𐐯𐑉𐑁𐐫𐑉 𐐶𐐨 𐑌𐐬 𐑄 𐑋𐐰𐑌𐐲𐑉 𐐻𐐭 𐐺𐐨 𐐻𐑉𐐭; 𐐰𐑌𐐼 𐑄 𐐇𐑊𐐼𐐲𐑉 𐐫𐑉 𐐑𐑉𐐨𐑅𐐻 𐐼𐐮𐐼 𐑋𐐮𐑌𐐮𐑅𐐻𐐲𐑉 𐐮𐐻. 𐐈𐑌𐐼 𐑄𐐩 𐐼𐐮𐐼 𐑌𐐨𐑊 𐐼𐐵𐑌 𐐶𐐮𐑄 𐑄 𐐕𐐲𐑉𐐽, 𐐰𐑌𐐼 𐐹𐑉𐐩 𐐻𐐭 𐑄 𐐙𐐪𐑄𐐲𐑉 𐐮𐑌 𐑄 𐑌𐐩𐑋 𐐱𐑂 𐐗𐑉𐐴𐑅𐐻, 𐑅𐐩𐐮𐑍, 𐐄 𐐘𐐱𐐼, 𐑄 𐐀𐐻𐐲𐑉𐑌𐐲𐑊 𐐙𐐪𐑄𐐲𐑉, 𐐶𐐨 𐐰𐑅𐐿 𐑄𐐨 𐐮𐑌 𐑄 𐑌𐐩𐑋 𐐱𐑂 𐑄𐐴 𐐝𐐲𐑌 𐐖𐐨𐑆𐐲𐑅 𐐗𐑉𐐴𐑅𐐻, 𐐻𐐭 𐐺𐑊𐐯𐑅 𐐰𐑌𐐼 𐑅𐐰𐑍𐐿𐐻𐐮𐑁𐐴 𐑄𐐮𐑅 𐐺𐑉𐐯𐐼 𐐻𐐭 𐑄 𐑅𐐬𐑊𐑆 𐐱𐑂 𐐫𐑊 𐑄𐐬𐑆 𐐸𐐭 𐐹𐐪𐑉𐐻𐐩𐐿 𐐱𐑂 𐐮𐐻, 𐑄𐐰𐐻 𐑄𐐩 𐑋𐐩 𐐨𐐻 𐐮𐑌 𐑉𐐨𐑋𐐯𐑋𐐺𐑉𐐰𐑌𐑅 𐐱𐑂 𐑄 𐐺𐐱𐐼𐐮 𐐱𐑂 𐑄𐐴 𐐝𐐲𐑌, 𐐰𐑌𐐼 𐐶𐐮𐐻𐑌𐐯𐑅 𐐲𐑌𐐻𐐭 𐑄𐐨, 𐐄 𐐘𐐱𐐼, 𐑄 𐐀𐐻𐐲𐑉𐑌𐐲𐑊 𐐙𐐪𐑄𐐲𐑉, 𐑄𐐰𐐻 𐑄𐐩 𐐪𐑉 𐐶𐐮𐑊𐐮𐑍 𐐻𐐭 𐐻𐐩𐐿 𐐲𐐹𐐱𐑌 𐑄𐐯𐑋 𐑄 𐑌𐐩𐑋 𐐱𐑂 𐑄𐐴 𐐝𐐲𐑌, 𐐰𐑌𐐼 𐐫𐑊𐐶𐐩𐑆 𐑉𐐨𐑋𐐯𐑋𐐺𐐲𐑉 𐐸𐐮𐑋, 𐐰𐑌𐐼 𐐿𐐨𐐹 𐐸𐐮𐑆 𐐿𐐱𐑋𐐰𐑌𐐼𐑋𐐯𐑌𐐻𐑅 𐐸𐐶𐐮𐐽 𐐸𐐨 𐐸𐐰𐑃 𐑀𐐮𐑂𐐲𐑌 𐑄𐐯𐑋, 𐑄𐐰𐐻 𐑄𐐩 𐑋𐐩 𐐫𐑊𐐶𐐩𐑆 𐐸𐐰𐑂 𐐸𐐮𐑆 𐐝𐐹𐐮𐑉𐐮𐐻 𐐻𐐭 𐐺𐐨 𐐶𐐮𐑄 𐑄𐐯𐑋. 𐐁𐑋𐐯𐑌.

𐐕𐐰𐐹𐐻𐐲𐑉 V.

1. 𐐜 𐑋𐐰𐑌𐐲𐑉 𐐱𐑂 𐐰𐐼𐑋𐐮𐑌𐐮𐑅𐐻𐐲𐑉𐐮𐑍 𐑄 𐐶𐐴𐑌. 𐐒𐐨𐐸𐐬𐑊𐐼, 𐑄𐐩 𐐻𐐳𐐿 𐑄 𐐿𐐲𐐹, 𐐰𐑌𐐼 𐑅𐐯𐐼, 𐐄 𐐘𐐱𐐼, 𐑄 𐐀𐐻𐐲𐑉𐑌𐐲𐑊 𐐙𐐪𐑄𐐲𐑉, 𐐶𐐨 𐐰𐑅𐐿 𐑄𐐨, 𐐮𐑌 𐑄 𐑌𐐩𐑋 𐐱𐑂 𐑄𐐴 𐐝𐐲𐑌 𐐖𐐨𐑆𐐲𐑅 𐐗𐑉𐐴𐑅𐐻, 𐐻𐐭 𐐺𐑊𐐯𐑅 𐐰𐑌𐐼 𐑅𐐰𐑍𐐿𐐻𐐮𐑁𐐴 𐑄𐐮𐑅 𐐶𐐴𐑌 𐐻𐐭 𐑄 𐑅𐐬𐑊𐑆 𐐱𐑂 𐐫𐑊 𐑄𐐬𐑆 𐐸𐐭 𐐼𐑉𐐮𐑍𐐿 𐐱𐑂 𐐮𐐻, 𐑄𐐰𐐻 𐑄𐐩 𐑋𐐩 𐐼𐐭 𐐮𐐻 𐐮𐑌 𐑉𐐨𐑋𐐯𐑋𐐺𐑉𐐰𐑌𐑅 𐐱𐑂 𐑄 𐐺𐑊𐐲𐐼 𐐱𐑂 𐑄𐐴 𐐝𐐲𐑌, 𐐸𐐶𐐮𐐽 𐐶𐐱𐑆 𐑇𐐯𐐼 𐑁𐐫𐑉 𐑄𐐯𐑋, 𐑄𐐰𐐻 𐑄𐐩 𐑋𐐩 𐐶𐐮𐐻𐑌𐐯𐑅 𐐲𐑌𐐻𐐭 𐑄𐐨, 𐐄 𐐘𐐱𐐼, 𐑄 𐐀𐐻𐐲𐑉𐑌𐐲𐑊 𐐙𐐪𐑄𐐲𐑉, 𐑄𐐰𐐻 𐑄𐐩 𐐼𐐭 𐐫𐑊𐐶𐐩𐑆 𐑉𐐨𐑋𐐯𐑋𐐺𐐲𐑉 𐐸𐐮𐑋, 𐑄𐐰𐐻 𐑄𐐩 𐑋𐐩 𐐸𐐰𐑂 𐐸𐐮𐑆 𐐝𐐹𐐮𐑉𐐮𐐻 𐐻𐐭 𐐺𐐨 𐐶𐐮𐑄 𐑄𐐯𐑋. 𐐁𐑋𐐯𐑌.

𐐕𐐰𐐹𐐻𐐲𐑉 VI.

1. 𐐈𐑌𐐼 𐑌𐐵 𐐌 𐑅𐐹𐐨𐐿 𐐿𐐱𐑌𐑅𐐲𐑉𐑌𐐮𐑍 𐐺𐐰𐐹𐐻𐐮𐑆𐐲𐑋. 𐐒𐐨𐐸𐐬𐑊𐐼, 𐐇𐑊𐐼𐐲𐑉𐑆, 𐐑𐑉𐐨𐑅𐐻𐑅, 𐐰𐑌𐐼 𐐓𐐨𐐽𐐲𐑉𐑆 𐐶𐐲𐑉 𐐺𐐰𐐹𐐻𐐴𐑆𐐼; 𐐰𐑌𐐼 𐑄𐐩 𐐶𐐲𐑉 𐑌𐐱𐐻 𐐺𐐰𐐹𐐻𐐴𐑆𐐼, 𐑅𐐩𐑂 𐑄𐐩 𐐺𐑉𐐫𐐻 𐑁𐐫𐑉𐑃 𐑁𐑉𐐭𐐻 𐑋𐐨𐐻 𐑄𐐰𐐻 𐑄𐐩 𐐶𐐲𐑉 𐐶𐐲𐑉𐑄𐐮 𐐱𐑂 𐐮𐐻; 𐑌𐐨𐑄𐐲𐑉 𐐼𐐮𐐼 𐑄𐐩 𐑉𐐨𐑅𐐨𐑂 𐐯𐑌𐐮 𐐲𐑌𐐻𐐭 𐐺𐐰𐐹𐐻𐐮𐑆𐐲𐑋, 𐑅𐐩𐑂 𐑄𐐩 𐐿𐐩𐑋 𐑁𐐫𐑉𐑃 𐐶𐐮𐑄 𐐩 𐐺𐑉𐐬𐐿𐐲𐑌 𐐸𐐪𐑉𐐻 𐐰𐑌𐐼 𐐩 𐐿𐐱𐑌𐐻𐑉𐐴𐐻 𐑅𐐹𐐮𐑉𐐮𐐻, 𐐰𐑌𐐼 𐐶𐐮𐐻𐑌𐐯𐑅𐐻 𐐲𐑌𐐻𐐭 𐑄 𐐕𐐲𐑉𐐽 𐑄𐐰𐐻 𐑄𐐩 𐐻𐑉𐐭𐑊𐐮 𐑉𐐨𐐹𐐯𐑌𐐻𐐯𐐼 𐐱𐑂 𐐫𐑊 𐑄𐐩𐑉 𐑅𐐮𐑌𐑆. 𐐈𐑌𐐼 𐑌𐐲𐑌 𐐶𐐲𐑉 𐑉𐐨𐑅𐐨𐑂𐐼 𐐲𐑌𐐻𐐭 𐐺𐐰𐐹𐐻𐐮𐑆𐐲𐑋, 𐑅𐐩𐑂 𐑄𐐩 𐐻𐐳𐐿 𐐲𐐹𐐱𐑌 𐑄𐐯𐑋 𐑄 𐑌𐐩𐑋 𐐱𐑂 𐐗𐑉𐐴𐑅𐐻, 𐐸𐐰𐑂𐐮𐑍 𐐩 𐐼𐐨𐐻𐐲𐑉𐑋𐐮𐑌𐐩𐑇𐐲𐑌 𐐻𐐭 𐑅𐐲𐑉𐑂 𐐸𐐮𐑋 𐐻𐐭 𐑄 𐐯𐑌𐐼. 𐐈𐑌𐐼 𐐰𐑁𐐻𐐲𐑉 𐑄𐐩 𐐸𐐰𐐼 𐐺𐐮𐑌 𐑉𐐨𐑅𐐨𐑂𐐼 𐐲𐑌𐐻𐐭 𐐺𐐰𐐹𐐻𐐮𐑆𐐲𐑋, 𐐰𐑌𐐼 𐐶𐐲𐑉 𐑉𐐫𐐻 𐐲𐐹𐐱𐑌 𐐰𐑌𐐼 𐐿𐑊𐐯𐑌𐑆𐐼 𐐺𐐴 𐑄 𐐹𐐵𐐲𐑉 𐐱𐑂 𐑄 𐐐𐐬𐑊𐐮 𐐘𐐬𐑅𐐻, 𐑄𐐩 𐐶𐐲𐑉 𐑌𐐲𐑋𐐺𐐲𐑉𐐼 𐐲𐑋𐐲𐑍 𐑄 𐐹𐐨𐐹𐑊 𐐱𐑂 𐑄 𐐕𐐲𐑉𐐽 𐐱𐑂 𐐗𐑉𐐴𐑅𐐻, 𐐰𐑌𐐼 𐑄𐐩𐑉 𐑌𐐩𐑋𐑆 𐐶𐐲𐑉 𐐻𐐩𐐿𐐲𐑌, 𐑄𐐰𐐻 𐑄𐐩 𐑋𐐴𐐻 𐐺𐐨 𐑉𐐨𐑋𐐯𐑋𐐺𐐲𐑉𐐼 𐐰𐑌𐐼 𐑌𐐲𐑉𐐮𐑇𐐻 𐐺𐐴 𐑄 𐑀𐐳𐐼 𐐶𐐲𐑉𐐼 𐐱𐑂 𐐘𐐱𐐼, 𐐻𐐭 𐐿𐐨𐐹 𐑄𐐯𐑋 𐐮𐑌 𐑄 𐑉𐐴𐐻 𐐶𐐩, 𐐻𐐭 𐐿𐐨𐐹 𐑄𐐯𐑋 𐐿𐐱𐑌𐐻𐐮𐑌𐐷𐐭𐐰𐑊𐐮 𐐶𐐱𐐽𐑁𐐳𐑊 𐐲𐑌𐐻𐐭 𐐹𐑉𐐩𐐲𐑉, 𐑉𐐨𐑊𐐴𐐮𐑍 𐐲𐑊𐐬𐑌 𐐲𐐹𐐱𐑌

𐑄 𐑋𐐯𐑉𐐮𐐻𐑅 𐐱𐑂 𐐗𐑉𐐴𐑅𐐻, 𐐸𐐭 𐐶𐐱𐑆 𐑄 𐐫𐑃𐐲𐑉 𐐰𐑌𐐼 𐑄 𐑁𐐮𐑌𐐮𐑇𐐲𐑉 𐐱𐑂 𐑄𐐩𐑉 𐑁𐐩𐑃. 𐐈𐑌𐐼 𐑄 𐐽𐐲𐑉𐐽 𐐼𐐮𐐼 𐑋𐐨𐐻 𐐻𐐳𐑀𐐯𐑄𐐲𐑉 𐐫𐑁𐐻, 𐐻𐐭 𐑁𐐰𐑅𐐻 𐐰𐑌𐐼 𐐻𐐭 𐐹𐑉𐐩, 𐐰𐑌𐐼 𐐻𐐭 𐑅𐐹𐐨𐐿 𐐶𐐲𐑌 𐐶𐐮𐑄 𐐰𐑌𐐲𐑄𐐲𐑉 𐐿𐐱𐑌𐑅𐐲𐑉𐑌𐐮𐑍 𐑄 𐐶𐐯𐑊𐑁𐐩𐑉 𐐱𐑂 𐑄𐐩𐑉 𐑅𐐬𐑊𐑆; 𐐰𐑌𐐼 𐑄𐐩 𐐼𐐮𐐼 𐑋𐐨𐐻 𐐻𐐳𐑀𐐯𐑄𐐲𐑉 𐐫𐑁𐐻 𐐻𐐭 𐐹𐐪𐑉𐐻𐐩𐐿 𐐱𐑂 𐐺𐑉𐐯𐐼 𐐰𐑌𐐼 𐐶𐐴𐑌, 𐐮𐑌 𐑉𐐨𐑋𐐯𐑋𐐺𐑉𐐰𐑌𐑅 𐐱𐑂 𐑄 𐐢𐐫𐑉𐐼 𐐖𐐨𐑆𐐲𐑅; 𐐰𐑌𐐼 𐑄𐐩 𐐶𐐲𐑉 𐑅𐐻𐑉𐐮𐐿𐐻 𐐻𐐭 𐐱𐐺𐑆𐐲𐑉𐑂 𐑄𐐰𐐻 𐑄𐐩𐑉 𐑇𐐳𐐼 𐐺𐐨 𐑌𐐬 𐐮𐑌𐐮𐐿𐐶𐐮𐐻𐐨 𐐰𐑋𐐲𐑍 𐑄𐐯𐑋; 𐐰𐑌𐐼 𐐸𐐭𐑅𐐬 𐐶𐐱𐑆 𐑁𐐵𐑌𐐼 𐐻𐐭 𐐿𐐱𐑋𐐮𐐻 𐐮𐑌𐐮𐐿𐐶𐐮𐐻𐐨, 𐐰𐑌𐐼 𐑃𐑉𐐨 𐐶𐐮𐐻𐑌𐐯𐑅𐐯𐑆 𐐱𐑂 𐑄 𐐽𐐲𐑉𐐽 𐐼𐐮𐐼 𐐿𐐱𐑌𐐼𐐯𐑋 𐑄𐐯𐑋 𐐺𐐨𐑁𐐬𐑉 𐑄 𐐯𐑊𐐼𐐲𐑉𐑆; 𐐰𐑌𐐼 𐐮𐑁 𐑄𐐩 𐑉𐐨𐐹𐐯𐑌𐐻𐐯𐐼 𐑌𐐱𐐻, 𐐰𐑌𐐼 𐐿𐐱𐑌𐑁𐐯𐑅𐐻 𐑌𐐱𐐻, 𐑄𐐩𐑉 𐑌𐐩𐑋𐑆 𐐶𐐲𐑉 𐐺𐑊𐐱𐐻𐐯𐐼 𐐵𐐻, 𐐰𐑌𐐼 𐑄𐐩 𐐶𐐲𐑉 𐑌𐐱𐐻 𐑌𐐲𐑋𐐺𐐲𐑉𐐼 𐐰𐑋𐐲𐑍 𐑄 𐐹𐐨𐐹𐑊 𐐱𐑂 𐐗𐑉𐐴𐑅𐐻; 𐐺𐐲𐐻 𐐮𐑁 𐑄𐐩 𐑉𐐨𐐹𐐯𐑌𐐻𐐯𐐼 𐐰𐑌𐐼 𐑅𐐫𐐻 𐑁𐐫𐑉𐑀𐐮𐑂𐑌𐐯𐑅, 𐐶𐐮𐑄 𐑉𐐨𐐰𐑊 𐐮𐑌𐐻𐐯𐑌𐐻, 𐑄𐐩 𐐶𐐲𐑉 𐑁𐐫𐑉𐑀𐐮𐑂𐐯𐑌. 𐐈𐑌𐐼 𐑄𐐩𐑉 𐑋𐐨𐐻𐐮𐑍𐑆 𐐶𐐲𐑉 𐐿𐐱𐑌𐐼𐐲𐐿𐐻𐐯𐐼 𐐺𐐴 𐑄 𐐽𐐲𐑉𐐽, 𐐰𐑁𐐻𐐲𐑉 𐑄 𐑋𐐰𐑌𐐲𐑉 𐐱𐑂 𐑄 𐐶𐐲𐑉𐐿𐐮𐑍𐑆 𐐱𐑂 𐑄 𐐝𐐹𐐮𐑉𐐮𐐻, 𐐰𐑌𐐼 𐐺𐐴 𐑄 𐐹𐐵𐐲𐑉 𐐱𐑂 𐑄 𐐐𐐬𐑊𐐨 𐐘𐐬𐑅𐐻; 𐑁𐐫𐑉 𐐰𐑆 𐑄 𐐹𐐵𐐲𐑉 𐐱𐑂 𐑄 𐐐𐐬𐑊𐐨 𐐘𐐬𐑅𐐻 𐑊𐐯𐐼 𐑄𐐯𐑋 𐐸𐐶𐐯𐑄𐐲𐑉 𐐻𐐭 𐐹𐑉𐐨𐐽, 𐐫𐑉 𐐻𐐭 𐐯𐑀𐑆𐐫𐑉𐐻, 𐐫𐑉 𐐻𐐭 𐐹𐑉𐐩, 𐐫𐑉 𐐻𐐭 𐑅𐐲𐐹𐑊𐐮𐐿𐐩𐐻, 𐐫𐑉 𐐻𐐭 𐑅𐐮𐑍, 𐐨𐑂𐐯𐑌 𐑅𐐬 𐐮𐐻 𐐶𐐱𐑆 𐐼𐐲𐑌.

𐐗𐐰𐐹𐐻𐐲𐑉 VII.

1. 𐐈𐑌𐐼 𐑌𐐵 𐐌, 𐐣𐐫𐑉𐐬𐑌𐐴, 𐑉𐐴𐐻 𐐰 𐑁𐐧 𐐱𐑂 𐑄 𐐶𐐲𐑉𐐼𐑆 𐐱𐑂 𐑋𐐴 𐑁𐐪𐑄𐐲𐑉 𐐣𐐫𐑉𐑋𐐲𐑌, 𐐸𐐶𐐮𐐽 𐐸𐐨 𐑅𐐹𐐩𐐿 𐐿𐐱𐑌𐑅𐐲𐑉𐑌𐐮𐑍 𐑁𐐩𐑃, 𐐸𐐬𐐹, 𐐰𐑌𐐼 𐐽𐐰𐑉𐐮𐐻𐐨; 𐑁𐐫𐑉 𐐰𐑁𐐻𐐲𐑉 𐑄𐐮𐑅 𐑋𐐰𐑌𐐲𐑉 𐐼𐐮𐐼 𐐸𐐨 𐑅𐐹𐐨𐐿 𐐲𐑌𐐻𐐭 𐑄 𐐹𐐨𐐹𐑊, 𐐰𐑆 𐐸𐐨 𐐻𐐫𐐻 𐑄𐐯𐑋 𐐮𐑌 𐑄 𐑅𐐮𐑌𐐰𐑀𐐱𐑀 𐐸𐐶𐐮𐐽 𐑄𐐩 𐐸𐐰𐐼 𐐺𐐮𐑊𐐻 𐑁𐐫𐑉 𐑄 𐐹𐑊𐐩𐑅 𐐱𐑂 𐐶𐐲𐑉𐑇𐐮𐐹. 𐐈𐑌𐐼 𐑌𐐵 𐐌, 𐐣𐐫𐑉𐑋𐐲𐑌, 𐑅𐐹𐐨𐐿 𐐲𐑌𐐻𐐭 𐐷𐐭, 𐑋𐐴 𐐺𐐨𐑊𐐲𐑂𐐯𐐼 𐐺𐑉𐐯𐑄𐑉𐐯𐑌; 𐐰𐑌𐐼 𐐮𐐻 𐐮𐑆 𐐺𐐴 𐑄 𐑀𐑉𐐩𐑅 𐐱𐑂 𐐘𐐱𐐼, 𐑄 𐐙𐐪𐑄𐐲𐑉, 𐐰𐑌𐐼 𐐵𐑉 𐐢𐐫𐑉𐐼 𐐖𐐨𐑆𐐲𐑅 𐐗𐑉𐐴𐑅𐐻, 𐐰𐑌𐐼 𐐸𐐮𐑆 𐐸𐐬𐑊𐐨 𐐶𐐮𐑊, 𐐺𐐨𐐿𐐫𐑆 𐐱𐑂 𐑄 𐑀𐐮𐑁𐐻 𐐱𐑂 𐐸𐐮𐑆 𐐿𐐫𐑊𐐮𐑍 𐐲𐑌𐐻𐐭 𐑋𐐨, 𐑄𐐰𐐻 𐐌 𐐰𐑋 𐐹𐐲𐑉𐑋𐐮𐐻𐐯𐐼 𐐻𐐭 𐑅𐐹𐐨𐐿 𐐲𐑌𐐻𐐭 𐐷𐐭 𐐰𐐻 𐑄𐐮𐑅 𐐻𐐴𐑋; 𐐸𐐶𐐩𐑉𐑁𐐬𐑉 𐐌 𐐶𐐳𐐼 𐑅𐐹𐐨𐐿 𐐲𐑌𐐻𐐭 𐐷𐐭 𐑄𐐰𐐻 𐐪𐑉 𐐱𐑂 𐑄 𐐽𐐲𐑉𐐽, 𐑄𐐰𐐻 𐐪𐑉 𐑄 𐐹𐐨𐑅𐐲𐐺𐑊 𐑁𐐱𐑊𐐬𐐲𐑉𐑆 𐐱𐑂 𐐗𐑉𐐴𐑅𐐻, 𐐰𐑌𐐼 𐑄𐐰𐐻 𐐸𐐰𐑂 𐐱𐐺𐐻𐐩𐑌𐐼 𐐰 𐑅𐐲𐑁𐐮𐑇𐐯𐑌𐐻 𐐸𐐬𐐹, 𐐺𐐴 𐐸𐐶𐐮𐐽 𐐷𐐨 𐐿𐐰𐑌 𐐯𐑌𐐻𐐲𐑉 𐐮𐑌𐐻𐐭 𐑄 𐑉𐐯𐑅𐐻 𐐱𐑂 𐑄 𐐢𐐫𐑉𐐼, 𐑁𐑉𐐱𐑋 𐑄𐐮𐑅 𐐻𐐴𐑋 𐐸𐐯𐑌𐑅𐑁𐐬𐑉𐑃, 𐐲𐑌𐐻𐐮𐑊 𐐷𐐨 𐑇𐐰𐑊 𐑉𐐯𐑅𐐻 𐐶𐐮𐑄 𐐸𐐮𐑋 𐐮𐑌 𐐸𐐯𐑂𐐯𐑌. 𐐈𐑌𐐼 𐑌𐐵, 𐑋𐐴 𐐺𐑉𐐯𐑄𐑉𐐯𐑌, 𐐌 𐐾𐐲𐐾 𐑄𐐨𐑆 𐑃𐐮𐑍𐑆 𐐱𐑂 𐐷𐐭 𐐺𐐨𐐿𐐫𐑆 𐐱𐑂 𐐷𐐬𐑉 𐐹𐐨𐑅𐐲𐐺𐑊 𐐶𐐫𐐿 𐐶𐐮𐑄 𐑄 𐐽𐐮𐑊𐐼𐑉𐐯𐑌 𐐱𐑂 𐑋𐐯𐑌; 𐑁𐐫𐑉 𐐌 𐑉𐐨𐑋𐐯𐑋𐐺𐐲𐑉 𐑄 𐐶𐐲𐑉𐐼 𐐱𐑂 𐐘𐐱𐐼, 𐐸𐐶𐐮𐐽 𐑅𐐯𐑃, 𐐒𐐴 𐑄𐐩𐑉 𐐶𐐲𐑉𐐿𐑅 𐐷𐐨 𐑇𐐰𐑊 𐑌𐐬 𐑄𐐯𐑋; 𐑁𐐫𐑉 𐐮𐑁 𐑄𐐩𐑉 𐐶𐐲𐑉𐐿𐑅 𐐺𐐨 𐑀𐐳𐐼, 𐑄𐐯𐑌 𐑄𐐩 𐐪𐑉 𐑀𐐳𐐼 𐐫𐑊𐑅𐐬. 𐐙𐐫𐑉 𐐺𐐨𐐸𐐬𐑊𐐼, 𐐘𐐱𐐼 𐐸𐐰𐑃 𐑅𐐯𐐼, 𐐈 𐑋𐐰𐑌 𐐺𐐨𐐮𐑍 𐐨𐑂𐐮𐑊 𐐿𐐰𐑌𐐱𐐻 𐐼𐐭 𐑄𐐰𐐻 𐐸𐐶𐐮𐐽 𐐮𐑆 𐑀𐐳𐐼; 𐑁𐐫𐑉 𐐮𐑁 𐐸𐐨 𐐱𐑁𐐲𐑉𐐯𐑃 𐐰 𐑀𐐮𐑁𐐻, 𐐫𐑉 𐐹𐑉𐐩𐐯𐑃 𐐲𐑌𐐻𐐭 𐐘𐐱𐐼, 𐐯𐐿𐑅𐐯𐐹𐐻 𐐸𐐨 𐑇𐐰𐑊 𐐼𐐭 𐐮𐐻 𐐶𐐮𐑄 𐑉𐐨𐐰𐑊 𐐮𐑌𐐻𐐯𐑌𐐻, 𐐮𐐻 𐐹𐑉𐐱𐑁𐐮𐐻𐐯𐑃 𐐸𐐮𐑋 𐑌𐐲𐑃𐐮𐑍. 𐐙𐐫𐑉 𐐺𐐨𐐸𐐬𐑊𐐼, 𐐮𐐻 𐐮𐑆 𐑌𐐱𐐻 𐐿𐐵𐑌𐐻𐐯𐐼 𐐲𐑌𐐻𐐭 𐐸𐐮𐑋 𐑁𐐫𐑉 𐑉𐐴𐐽𐐲𐑅𐑌𐐯𐑅. 𐐙𐐫𐑉 𐐺𐐨𐐸𐐬𐑊𐐼, 𐐮𐑁 𐐰 𐑋𐐰𐑌 𐐺𐐨𐐮𐑍 𐐨𐑂𐐮𐑊 𐑀𐐮𐑂𐐯𐑃 𐐰 𐑀𐐮𐑁𐐻, 𐐸𐐨 𐐼𐐭𐐯𐑃 𐐮𐐻 𐑀𐑉𐐲𐐾𐐮𐑍𐑊𐐨; 𐐸𐐶𐐩𐑉𐑁𐐬𐑉 𐐮𐐻 𐐮𐑆 𐐿𐐵𐑌𐐻𐐯𐐼 𐐲𐑌𐐻𐐭 𐐸𐐮𐑋 𐑄 𐑅𐐩𐑋 𐐰𐑆 𐐮𐑁 𐐸𐐨 𐐸𐐰𐐼 𐑉𐐨𐐻𐐩𐑌𐐼 𐑄 𐑀𐐮𐑁𐐻; 𐐸𐐶𐐩𐑉𐑁𐐬𐑉 𐐸𐐨 𐐮𐑆 𐐿𐐵𐑌𐐻𐐯𐐼 𐐨𐑂𐐮𐑊 𐐺𐐨𐑁𐐬𐑉 𐐘𐐱𐐼. 𐐈𐑌𐐼 𐑊𐐴𐐿𐐶𐐴𐑆 𐐫𐑊𐑅𐐬 𐐮𐑆 𐐮𐐻 𐐿𐐵𐑌𐐻𐐯𐐼 𐐨𐑂𐐮𐑊 𐐲𐑌𐐻𐐭 𐐰 𐑋𐐰𐑌, 𐐮𐑁 𐐸𐐨 𐑇𐐰𐑊 𐐹𐑉𐐩, 𐐰𐑌𐐼 𐑌𐐱𐐻 𐐶𐐮𐑄 𐑉𐐨𐐰𐑊 𐐮𐑌𐐻𐐯𐑌𐐻 𐐱𐑂 𐐸𐐪𐑉𐐻; 𐐷𐐩, 𐐰𐑌𐐼 𐐮𐐻 𐐹𐑉𐐱𐑁𐐮𐐻𐐯𐑃 𐐸𐐮𐑋 𐑌𐐲𐑃𐐮𐑍; 𐑁𐐫𐑉 𐐘𐐱𐐼 𐑉𐐨𐑅𐐨𐑂𐐯𐑃 𐑌𐐲𐑌 𐑅𐐲𐐽; 𐐸𐐶𐐩𐑉𐑁𐐬𐑉 𐐰 𐑋𐐰𐑌 𐐺𐐨𐐮𐑍 𐐨𐑂𐐮𐑊 𐐿𐐰𐑌𐐱𐐻 𐐼𐐭 𐑄𐐰𐐻 𐐸𐐶𐐮𐐽 𐐮𐑆 𐑀𐐳𐐼; 𐑌𐐨𐑄𐐲𐑉 𐐶𐐮𐑊 𐐸𐐨 𐑀𐐮𐑂 𐐰 𐑀𐐳𐐼 𐑀𐐮𐑁𐐻. 𐐙𐐫𐑉 𐐺𐐨𐐸𐐬𐑊𐐼, 𐐰 𐐺𐐮𐐻𐐲𐑉 𐑁𐐵𐑌𐐻𐐩𐑌 𐐿𐐰𐑌𐐱𐐻 𐐺𐑉𐐮𐑍 𐑁𐐬𐑉𐑃 𐑀𐐳𐐼 𐐶𐐫𐐻𐐲𐑉; 𐑌𐐨𐑄𐐲𐑉 𐐿𐐰𐑌 𐐰 𐑀𐐳𐐼 𐑁𐐵𐑌𐐻𐐩𐑌 𐐺𐑉𐐮𐑍 𐑁𐐬𐑉𐑃 𐐺𐐮𐐻𐐲𐑉 𐐶𐐫𐐻𐐲𐑉; 𐐸𐐶𐐩𐑉𐑁𐐬𐑉 𐐰 𐑋𐐰𐑌 𐐺𐐨𐐮𐑍 𐐰 𐑅𐐲𐑉𐑂𐐰𐑌𐐻 𐐱𐑂 𐑄 𐐼𐐯𐑂𐐮𐑊, 𐐿𐐰𐑌𐐱𐐻 𐑁𐐱𐑊𐐬 𐐗𐑉𐐴𐑅𐐻; 𐐰𐑌𐐼 𐐮𐑁 𐐸𐐨 𐑁𐐱𐑊𐐬 𐐗𐑉𐐴𐑅𐐻, 𐐸𐐨 𐐿𐐰𐑌𐐱𐐻 𐐺𐐨 𐐰 𐑅𐐲𐑉𐑂𐐰𐑌𐐻 𐐱𐑂 𐑄 𐐼𐐯𐑂𐐮𐑊.

2. 𐐐𐐶𐐩𐑉𐑁𐐬𐑉, 𐐫𐑊 𐑃𐐮𐑍𐑆 𐐸𐐶𐐮𐐽 𐐪𐑉 𐑀𐐳𐐼, 𐐿𐐲𐑋𐐯𐑃 𐐱𐑂 𐐘𐐱𐐼; 𐐰𐑌𐐼 𐑄𐐰𐐻 𐐸𐐶𐐮𐐽 𐐮𐑆 𐐨𐑂𐐮𐑊, 𐐿𐐲𐑋𐐯𐑃 𐐱𐑂 𐑄 𐐼𐐯𐑂𐐮𐑊; 𐑁𐐫𐑉 𐑄 𐐼𐐯𐑂𐐮𐑊 𐐮𐑆 𐐰𐑌 𐐯𐑌𐐯𐑋𐐨 𐐲𐑌𐐻𐐭 𐐘𐐱𐐼, 𐐰𐑌𐐼 𐑁𐐴𐐻𐐯𐑃 𐐰𐑀𐐯𐑌𐑅𐐻 𐐸𐐮𐑋 𐐿𐐱𐑌𐐻𐐮𐑌𐐧𐐰𐑊𐐨, 𐐰𐑌𐐼 𐐮𐑌𐑂𐐴𐐻𐐯𐑃 𐐰𐑌𐐼 𐐯𐑌𐐻𐐴𐑅𐐯𐑃 𐐻𐐭 𐑅𐐮𐑌, 𐐰𐑌𐐼 𐐻𐐭 𐐼𐐭 𐑄𐐰𐐻 𐐸𐐶𐐮𐐽 𐐮𐑆 𐐨𐑂𐐮𐑊 𐐿𐐱𐑌𐐻𐐮𐑌-

𐐿𐐲𐑌𐐻𐐮𐑌𐐷𐐭𐐲𐑊𐐨. 𐐒𐐲𐐻 𐐺𐐨𐐸𐐬𐑊𐐼, 𐑄𐐰𐐻 𐐸𐐶𐐮𐐽 𐐮𐑆 𐐱𐑂 𐐘𐐱𐐼, 𐐮𐑌𐑂𐐴𐐻𐐯𐑃 𐐰𐑌𐐼 𐐯𐑌𐐻𐐴𐑅𐐯𐑃 𐐻𐐭 𐐼𐐭 𐑀𐐳𐐼 𐐿𐐲𐑌𐐻𐐮𐑌𐐷𐐭𐐲𐑊𐐨; 𐐸𐐶𐐯𐑉𐑁𐐬𐑉 𐐯𐑂𐐯𐑉𐐨 𐑃𐐮𐑍 𐐸𐐶𐐮𐐽 𐐮𐑌𐑂𐐴𐐻𐐯𐑃 𐐰𐑌𐐼 𐐯𐑌𐐻𐐴𐑅𐐯𐑃 𐐻𐐭 𐐼𐐭 𐑀𐐳𐐼, 𐐰𐑌𐐼 𐐻𐐭 𐑊𐐲𐑂 𐐘𐐱𐐼, 𐐰𐑌𐐼 𐐻𐐭 𐑅𐐲𐑉𐑂 𐐸𐐮𐑋, 𐐮𐑆 𐐮𐑌𐑅𐐹𐐴𐑉𐐼 𐐱𐑂 𐐘𐐱𐐼. 𐐐𐐶𐐯𐑉𐑁𐐬𐑉, 𐐻𐐩𐐿 𐐸𐐨𐐼, 𐑋𐐴 𐐺𐐨𐑊𐐲𐑂𐐯𐐼 𐐺𐑉𐐯𐑄𐑉𐐯𐑌, 𐑄𐐰𐐻 𐐷 𐐼𐐭 𐑌𐐱𐐻 𐐾𐐲𐐾 𐑄𐐰𐐻 𐐸𐐶𐐮𐐽 𐐮𐑆 𐐨𐑂𐐮𐑊 𐐻𐐭 𐐺 𐐱𐑂 𐐘𐐱𐐼, 𐐫𐑉 𐑄𐐰𐐻 𐐸𐐶𐐮𐐽 𐐮𐑆 𐑀𐐳𐐼 𐐰𐑌𐐼 𐐱𐑂 𐐘𐐱𐐼, 𐐻𐐭 𐐺 𐐱𐑂 𐑄 𐐼𐐯𐑂𐐮𐑊. 𐐙𐐫𐑉 𐐺𐐨𐐸𐐬𐑊𐐼, 𐑋𐐴 𐐺𐑉𐐯𐑄𐑉𐐯𐑌, 𐐮𐐻 𐐮𐑆 𐑀𐐮𐑂𐐯𐑌 𐐲𐑌𐐻𐐭 𐐷𐐭 𐐻𐐭 𐐾𐐲𐐾, 𐑄𐐰𐐻 𐐷 𐑋𐐩 𐑌𐐬 𐑀𐐳𐐼 𐑁𐑉𐐱𐑋 𐐨𐑂𐐮𐑊; 𐐰𐑌𐐼 𐑄 𐐶𐐩 𐐻𐐭 𐐾𐐲𐐾 𐐮𐑆 𐐰𐑆 𐐹𐑊𐐩𐑌, 𐑄𐐰𐐻 𐐷 𐑋𐐩 𐑌𐐬 𐐶𐐮𐑄 𐐲 𐐹𐐲𐑉𐑁𐐯𐐿𐐻 𐑌𐐱𐑊𐐯𐐾, 𐐰𐑆 𐑄 𐐼𐐩-𐑊𐐴𐐻 𐐮𐑆 𐑁𐑉𐐱𐑋 𐑄 𐐼𐐪𐑉𐐿 𐑌𐐴𐐻. 𐐙𐐫𐑉 𐐺𐐨𐐸𐐬𐑊𐐼, 𐑄 𐐝𐐹𐐮𐑉𐐮𐐻 𐐱𐑂 𐐗𐑉𐐴𐑅𐐻 𐐮𐑆 𐑀𐐮𐑂𐐯𐑌 𐐻𐐭 𐐯𐑂𐐯𐑉𐐨 𐑋𐐰𐑌, 𐑄𐐰𐐻 𐐸𐐨 𐑋𐐩 𐑌𐐬 𐑀𐐳𐐼 𐑁𐑉𐐱𐑋 𐐨𐑂𐐮𐑊; 𐐸𐐶𐐯𐑉𐑁𐐬𐑉 𐐌 𐑇𐐬 𐐲𐑌𐐻𐐭 𐐷𐐭 𐑄 𐐶𐐩 𐐻𐐭 𐐾𐐲𐐾; 𐑁𐐫𐑉 𐐯𐑂𐐯𐑉𐐨 𐑃𐐮𐑍 𐐸𐐶𐐮𐐽 𐐮𐑌𐑂𐐴𐐻𐐯𐑃 𐐻𐐭 𐐼𐐭 𐑀𐐳𐐼, 𐐰𐑌𐐼 𐐻𐐭 𐐹𐐲𐑉𐑅𐐶𐐩𐐼 𐐻𐐭 𐐺𐐨𐑊𐐨𐑂 𐐮𐑌 𐐗𐑉𐐴𐑅𐐻, 𐐮𐑆 𐑅𐐯𐑌𐐻 𐑁𐐫𐑉𐑃 𐐺𐐴 𐑄 𐐹𐐵𐐲𐑉 𐐰𐑌𐐼 𐑀𐐮𐑁𐐻 𐐱𐑂 𐐗𐑉𐐴𐑅𐐻; 𐐸𐐶𐐯𐑉𐑁𐐬𐑉 𐐷 𐑋𐐩 𐑌𐐬 𐐶𐐮𐑄 𐐲 𐐹𐐲𐑉𐑁𐐯𐐿𐐻 𐑌𐐱𐑊𐐯𐐾 𐐮𐐻 𐐮𐑆 𐐱𐑂 𐐘𐐱𐐼. 𐐒𐐲𐐻 𐐸𐐶𐐱𐐻𐑅𐐬𐐯𐑂𐐲𐑉 𐑃𐐮𐑍 𐐹𐐲𐑉𐑅𐐶𐐩𐐼𐐯𐑃 𐑋𐐯𐑌 𐐻𐐭 𐐼𐐭 𐐨𐑂𐐮𐑊, 𐐰𐑌𐐼 𐐺𐐨𐑊𐐨𐑂 𐑌𐐱𐐻 𐐮𐑌 𐐗𐑉𐐴𐑅𐐻, 𐐰𐑌𐐼 𐐼𐐨𐑌𐐴 𐐸𐐮𐑋, 𐐰𐑌𐐼 𐑅𐐲𐑉𐑂 𐑌𐐱𐐻 𐐘𐐱𐐼, 𐑄𐐯𐑌 𐐷 𐑋𐐩 𐑌𐐬 𐐶𐐮𐑄 𐐲 𐐹𐐲𐑉𐑁𐐯𐐿𐐻 𐑌𐐱𐑊𐐯𐐾 𐐮𐐻 𐐮𐑆 𐐱𐑂 𐑄 𐐼𐐯𐑂𐐮𐑊, 𐑁𐐫𐑉 𐐰𐑁𐐻𐐲𐑉 𐑄𐐮𐑅 𐑋𐐰𐑌𐐲𐑉 𐐼𐐲𐑃 𐑄 𐐼𐐯𐑂𐐮𐑊 𐐶𐐲𐑉𐐿, 𐑁𐐫𐑉 𐐸𐐨 𐐹𐐲𐑉𐑅𐐶𐐩𐐼𐐯𐑃 𐑌𐐬 𐑋𐐰𐑌 𐐻𐐭 𐐼𐐭 𐑀𐐳𐐼, 𐑌𐐬 𐑌𐐱𐐻 𐐶𐐲𐑌; 𐑌𐐨𐑄𐐲𐑉 𐐸𐐮𐑆 𐐩𐑌𐐾𐐯𐑊𐑆; 𐑌𐐨𐑄𐐲𐑉 𐑄𐐩 𐐸𐐭 𐑅𐐲𐐺𐐾𐐯𐐿𐐻 𐑄𐐯𐑋𐑅𐐯𐑊𐑂𐑆 𐐲𐑌𐐻𐐭 𐐸𐐮𐑋.

3. 𐐈𐑌𐐼 𐑌𐐵, 𐑋𐐴 𐐺𐑉𐐯𐑄𐑉𐐯𐑌, 𐑅𐐨𐐮𐑍 𐑄𐐰𐐻 𐐷 𐑌𐐬 𐑄 𐑊𐐴𐐻 𐐺𐐴 𐐸𐐶𐐮𐐽 𐐷 𐑋𐐩 𐐾𐐲𐐾, 𐐸𐐶𐐮𐐽 𐑊𐐴𐐻 𐐮𐑆 𐑄 𐑊𐐴𐐻 𐐱𐑂 𐐗𐑉𐐴𐑅𐐻, 𐑅𐐨 𐑄𐐰𐐻 𐐷 𐐼𐐭 𐑌𐐱𐐻 𐐾𐐲𐐾 𐑉𐐱𐑍𐑁𐐳𐑊𐐨; 𐑁𐐫𐑉 𐐶𐐮𐑄 𐑄𐐰𐐻 𐑅𐐩𐑋 𐐾𐐲𐐾𐑋𐐯𐑌𐐻 𐐸𐐶𐐮𐐽 𐐷 𐐾𐐲𐐾, 𐐷 𐑇𐐰𐑊 𐐫𐑊𐑅𐐬 𐐺 𐐾𐐲𐐾𐐼. 𐐐𐐶𐐯𐑉𐑁𐐬𐑉 𐐌 𐐺𐐨𐑅𐐨𐐽 𐐱𐑂 𐐷𐐭, 𐐺𐑉𐐯𐑄𐑉𐐯𐑌, 𐑄𐐰𐐻 𐐷 𐑇𐐳𐐼 𐑅𐐲𐑉𐐽 𐐼𐐮𐑊𐐮𐐾𐐯𐑌𐐻𐑊𐐨 𐐮𐑌 𐑄 𐑊𐐴𐐻 𐐱𐑂 𐐗𐑉𐐴𐑅𐐻, 𐑄𐐰𐐻 𐐷 𐑋𐐩 𐑌𐐬 𐑀𐐳𐐼 𐑁𐑉𐐱𐑋 𐐨𐑂𐐮𐑊; 𐐰𐑌𐐼 𐐮𐑁 𐐷 𐐶𐐮𐑊 𐑊𐐩 𐐸𐐬𐑊𐐼 𐐲𐐹𐐱𐑌 𐐯𐑂𐐯𐑉𐐨 𐑀𐐳𐐼 𐑃𐐮𐑍, 𐐰𐑌𐐼 𐐿𐐱𐑌𐐼𐐯𐑋 𐐮𐐻 𐑌𐐱𐐻, 𐐷 𐑅𐐲𐑉𐐻𐐯𐑌𐑊𐐨 𐐶𐐮𐑊 𐐺 𐐲 𐐽𐐴𐑊𐐼 𐐱𐑂 𐐗𐑉𐐴𐑅𐐻. 𐐈𐑌𐐼 𐑌𐐵, 𐑋𐐴 𐐺𐑉𐐯𐑄𐑉𐐯𐑌, 𐐸𐐵 𐐮𐑆 𐐮𐐻 𐐹𐐱𐑅𐐮𐐺𐑊 𐑄𐐰𐐻 𐐷 𐐿𐐰𐑌 𐑊𐐩 𐐸𐐬𐑊𐐼 𐐲𐐹𐐱𐑌 𐐯𐑂𐐯𐑉𐐨 𐑀𐐳𐐼 𐑃𐐮𐑍? 𐐈𐑌𐐼 𐑌𐐵 𐐌 𐐿𐐲𐑋 𐐻𐐭 𐑄𐐰𐐻 𐑁𐐩𐑃, 𐐱𐑂 𐐸𐐶𐐮𐐽 𐐌 𐑅𐐯𐐼 𐐌 𐐶𐐳𐐼 𐑅𐐹𐐨𐐿; 𐐰𐑌𐐼 𐐌 𐐶𐐮𐑊 𐐻𐐯𐑊 𐐷𐐭 𐑄 𐐶𐐩 𐐸𐐶𐐯𐑉𐐺𐐴 𐐷 𐑋𐐩 𐑊𐐩 𐐸𐐬𐑊𐐼 𐐱𐑌 𐐯𐑂𐐯𐑉𐐨 𐑀𐐳𐐼 𐑃𐐮𐑍. 𐐙𐐫𐑉 𐐺𐐨𐐸𐐬𐑊𐐼, 𐐘𐐱𐐼 𐑌𐐬𐐮𐑍 𐐫𐑊 𐑃𐐮𐑍𐑆, 𐐺𐐨𐐮𐑍 𐑁𐑉𐐱𐑋 𐐯𐑂𐐲𐑉𐑊𐐰𐑅𐐻𐐮𐑍 𐐻𐐭 𐐯𐑂𐐲𐑉𐑊𐐰𐑅𐐻𐐮𐑍, 𐐺𐐨𐐸𐐬𐑊𐐼, 𐐸𐐨 𐑅𐐯𐑌𐐻 𐐩𐑌𐐾𐐯𐑊𐑆 𐐻𐐭 𐑋𐐮𐑌𐐮𐑅𐐻𐐲𐑉 𐐲𐑌𐐻𐐭 𐑄 𐐽𐐮𐑊𐐼𐑉𐐯𐑌 𐐱𐑂 𐑋𐐯𐑌, 𐐻𐐭 𐑋𐐩𐐿 𐑋𐐰𐑌𐐮𐑁𐐯𐑅𐐻 𐐿𐐱𐑌𐑅𐐲𐑉𐑌𐐮𐑍 𐑄 𐐿𐐲𐑋𐐮𐑍 𐐱𐑂 𐐗𐑉𐐴𐑅𐐻; 𐐰𐑌𐐼 𐐮𐑌 𐐗𐑉𐐴𐑅𐐻 𐑄𐐯𐑉 𐑇𐐳𐐼 𐐿𐐲𐑋 𐐯𐑂𐐯𐑉𐐨 𐑀𐐳𐐼 𐑃𐐮𐑍. 𐐈𐑌𐐼 𐐘𐐱𐐼 𐐫𐑊𐑅𐐬 𐐼𐐨𐐿𐑊𐐩𐑉𐐼 𐐲𐑌𐐻𐐭 𐐹𐑉𐐱𐑁𐐯𐐻𐑅, 𐐺𐐴 𐐸𐐮𐑆 𐐬𐑌 𐑋𐐵𐑃, 𐑄𐐰𐐻 𐐗𐑉𐐴𐑅𐐻 𐑇𐐳𐐼 𐐿𐐲𐑋. 𐐈𐑌𐐼 𐐺𐐨𐐸𐐬𐑊𐐼, 𐑄𐐯𐑉 𐐶𐐲𐑉 𐐼𐐴𐑂𐐲𐑉𐑆 𐐶𐐩𐑆 𐑄𐐰𐐻 𐐸𐐨 𐐼𐐮𐐼 𐑋𐐰𐑌𐐮𐑁𐐯𐑅𐐻 𐑃𐐮𐑍𐑆 𐐲𐑌𐐻𐐭 𐑄 𐐽𐐮𐑊𐐼𐑉𐐯𐑌 𐐱𐑂 𐑋𐐯𐑌, 𐐸𐐶𐐮𐐽 𐐶𐐲𐑉 𐑀𐐳𐐼; 𐐰𐑌𐐼 𐐫𐑊 𐑃𐐮𐑍𐑆 𐐸𐐶𐐮𐐽 𐐪𐑉 𐑀𐐳𐐼, 𐐿𐐲𐑋𐐯𐑃 𐐱𐑂 𐐗𐑉𐐴𐑅𐐻; 𐐲𐑄𐐲𐑉𐐶𐐴𐑆 𐑋𐐯𐑌 𐐶𐐲𐑉 𐑁𐐫𐑊𐐯𐑌, 𐐰𐑌𐐼 𐑄𐐯𐑉 𐐿𐐳𐐼 𐑌𐐬 𐑀𐐳𐐼 𐑃𐐮𐑍 𐐿𐐲𐑋 𐐲𐑌𐐻𐐭 𐑄𐐯𐑋. 𐐐𐐶𐐯𐑉𐑁𐐬𐑉, 𐐺𐐴 𐑄 𐑋𐐮𐑌𐐮𐑅𐐻𐐲𐑉𐐮𐑍 𐐱𐑂 𐐩𐑌𐐾𐐯𐑊𐑆, 𐐰𐑌𐐼 𐐺𐐴 𐐯𐑂𐐯𐑉𐐨 𐐶𐐲𐑉𐐼 𐐸𐐶𐐮𐐽 𐐹𐑉𐐬𐑅𐐨𐐼𐐯𐐼 𐑁𐐫𐑉𐑃 𐐵𐐻 𐐱𐑂 𐑄 𐑋𐐵𐑃 𐐱𐑂 𐐘𐐱𐐼, 𐑋𐐯𐑌 𐐺𐐨𐑀𐐰𐑌 𐐻𐐭 𐐯𐐿𐑅𐐲𐑉𐑅𐐴𐑆 𐑁𐐩𐑃 𐐮𐑌 𐐗𐑉𐐴𐑅𐐻; 𐐰𐑌𐐼 𐑄𐐲𐑅 𐐺𐐴 𐑁𐐩𐑃 𐑄𐐩 𐐼𐐮𐐼 𐑊𐐩 𐐸𐐬𐑊𐐼 𐐲𐐹𐐱𐑌 𐐯𐑂𐐯𐑉𐐨 𐑀𐐳𐐼 𐑃𐐮𐑍; 𐐰𐑌𐐼 𐑄𐐲𐑅 𐐮𐐻 𐐶𐐱𐑆 𐐲𐑌𐐻𐐮𐑊 𐑄 𐐿𐐲𐑋𐐮𐑍 𐐱𐑂 𐐗𐑉𐐴𐑅𐐻. 𐐈𐑌𐐼 𐐰𐑁𐐻𐐲𐑉 𐑄𐐰𐐻 𐐸𐐨 𐐿𐐩𐑋, 𐑋𐐯𐑌 𐐫𐑊𐑅𐐬 𐐶𐐲𐑉 𐑅𐐩𐑂𐐼 𐐺𐐴 𐑁𐐩𐑃 𐐮𐑌 𐐸𐐮𐑆 𐑌𐐩𐑋; 𐐰𐑌𐐼 𐐺𐐴 𐑁𐐩𐑃, 𐑄𐐩 𐐺𐐨𐐿𐐲𐑋 𐑄 𐑅𐐲𐑌𐑆 𐐱𐑂 𐐘𐐱𐐼. 𐐈𐑌𐐼 𐐰𐑆 𐑇𐐭𐑉𐑊𐐨 𐐰𐑆 𐐗𐑉𐐴𐑅𐐻 𐑊𐐮𐑂𐐯𐑃, 𐐸𐐨 𐑅𐐹𐐩𐐿 𐑄𐐨𐑆 𐐶𐐲𐑉𐐼𐑆 𐐲𐑌𐐻𐐭 𐐵𐐲𐑉 𐑁𐐪𐑄𐐲𐑉𐑆, 𐑅𐐩𐐮𐑍, 𐐐𐐶𐐱𐐻𐑅𐐬𐐯𐑂𐐲𐑉 𐑃𐐮𐑍 𐐷 𐑇𐐰𐑊 𐐰𐑅𐐿 𐑄 𐐙𐐪𐑄𐐲𐑉 𐐮𐑌 𐑋𐐴 𐑌𐐩𐑋, 𐐸𐐶𐐮𐐽 𐐮𐑆 𐑀𐐳𐐼, 𐐮𐑌 𐑁𐐩𐑃 𐐺𐐨𐑊𐐨𐑂𐐮𐑍 𐑄𐐰𐐻 𐐷 𐑇𐐰𐑊 𐑉𐐨𐑅𐐨𐑂, 𐐺𐐨𐐸𐐬𐑊𐐼 𐐮𐐻 𐑇𐐰𐑊 𐐺 𐐼𐐲𐑌 𐐲𐑌𐐻𐐭 𐐷𐐭. 𐐐𐐶𐐯𐑉𐑁𐐬𐑉, 𐑋𐐴 𐐺𐐨𐑊𐐲𐑂𐐯𐐼 𐐺𐑉𐐯𐑄𐑉𐐯𐑌, 𐐸𐐰𐑂 𐑋𐐮𐑉𐐲𐐿𐑊𐑆 𐑅𐐨𐑅𐐻, 𐐺𐐨𐐿𐐫𐑆 𐐗𐑉𐐴𐑅𐐻 𐐸𐐰𐑃 𐐰𐑅𐐯𐑌𐐼𐐯𐐼 𐐮𐑌𐐻𐐭 𐐸𐐯𐑂𐐯𐑌, 𐐰𐑌𐐼 𐐸𐐰𐑃 𐑅𐐰𐐻 𐐼𐐵𐑌 𐐱𐑌 𐑄 𐑉𐐴𐐻 𐐸𐐰𐑌𐐼 𐐱𐑂 𐐘𐐱𐐼, 𐐻𐐭 𐐿𐑊𐐩𐑋 𐐱𐑂 𐑄 𐐙𐐪𐑄𐐲𐑉 𐐸𐐮𐑆 𐑉𐐴𐐻𐑅 𐐱𐑂 𐑋𐐲𐑉𐑅𐐨 𐐸𐐶𐐮𐐽 𐐸𐐨 𐐸𐐰𐑃 𐐲𐐹𐐱𐑌 𐑄 𐐽𐐮𐑊𐐼𐑉𐐯𐑌 𐐱𐑂 𐑋𐐯𐑌; 𐑁𐐫𐑉 𐐸𐐨 𐐸𐐰𐑃 𐐰𐑌𐑅𐐲𐑉𐐼 𐑄 𐐯𐑌𐐼𐑆 𐐱𐑂 𐑄 𐑊𐐫, 𐐰𐑌𐐼 𐐸𐐨 𐐿𐑊𐐩𐑋𐐯𐑃 𐐫𐑊 𐑄𐐬𐑆 𐐸𐐭 𐐸𐐰𐑂 𐑁𐐩𐑃 𐐮𐑌 𐐸𐐮𐑋; 𐐰𐑌𐐼 𐑄𐐩 𐐸𐐭 𐐸𐐰𐑂 𐑁𐐩𐑃 𐐮𐑌 𐐸𐐮𐑋, 𐐶𐐮𐑊 𐐿𐑊𐐨𐑂 𐐲𐑌𐐻𐐭 𐐯𐑂𐐯𐑉𐐨 𐑀𐐳𐐼 𐑃𐐮𐑍; 𐐸𐐶𐐯𐑉𐑁𐐬𐑉 𐐸𐐨 𐐰𐐼𐑂𐐬𐐿𐐩𐐻𐐯𐑃 𐑄 𐐿𐐫𐑆 𐐱𐑂 𐑄 𐐽𐐮𐑊-

𐑉𐐯𐑌 𐐱𐑂 𐑋𐐯𐑌; 𐐰𐑌𐐼 𐐸𐐨 𐐼𐐶𐐯𐑊𐐯𐑃 𐐨𐐻𐐲𐑉𐑌𐐲𐑊𐐨 𐐮𐑌 𐑄 𐐸𐐯𐑂𐐲𐑌𐑆. 𐐈𐑌𐐼 𐐺𐐨𐐿𐐫𐑆 𐐸𐐨 𐐸𐐰𐑃 𐐼𐐲𐑌 𐑄𐐮𐑅, 𐑋𐐴 𐐺𐐨𐑊𐐲𐑂𐐯𐐼 𐐺𐑉𐐯𐑃𐑉𐐯𐑌, 𐐸𐐰𐑂 𐑋𐐮𐑉𐐲𐐿𐑊𐑆 𐑅𐐨𐑅𐐻? 𐐒𐐨𐐸𐐬𐑊𐐼 𐐌 𐑅𐐩 𐐲𐑌𐐻𐐭 𐐷𐐭, 𐐤𐐩; 𐑌𐐨𐑄𐐲𐑉 𐐸𐐰𐑂 𐐩𐑌𐐾𐐯𐑊𐑆 𐑅𐐨𐑅𐐻 𐐻𐐭 𐑋𐐮𐑌𐐮𐑅𐐻𐐲𐑉 𐐲𐑌𐐻𐐭 𐑄 𐐽𐐮𐑊𐐼𐑉𐐯𐑌 𐐱𐑂 𐑋𐐯𐑌. 𐐙𐐫𐑉 𐐺𐐨𐐸𐐬𐑊𐐼, 𐑄𐐩 𐐪𐑉 𐑅𐐲𐐺-𐐾𐐯𐐿𐐻 𐐲𐑌𐐻𐐭 𐐸𐐮𐑋, 𐐻𐐭 𐑋𐐮𐑌𐐮𐑅𐐻𐐲𐑉 𐐰𐐿𐐫𐑉𐐼𐐮𐑍 𐐻𐐭 𐑄 𐐶𐐲𐑉𐐼 𐐱𐑂 𐐸𐐮𐑆 𐐿𐐱𐑋𐐰𐑌𐐼, 𐑇𐐬𐐮𐑍 𐑄𐐯𐑋𐑅𐐯𐑊𐑂𐑆 𐐲𐑌𐐻𐐭 𐑄𐐯𐑋 𐐱𐑂 𐑅𐐻𐑉𐐱𐑍 𐑁𐐩𐑃 𐐰𐑌𐐼 𐐲 𐑁𐐲𐑉𐑋 𐑋𐐴𐑌𐐼 𐐮𐑌 𐐯𐑂𐐲𐑉𐐨 𐑁𐐫𐑉𐑋 𐐱𐑂 𐑀𐐱𐐼𐑊𐐨𐑌𐐯𐑅. 𐐈𐑌𐐼 𐑄 𐐱𐑁𐐮𐑅 𐐱𐑂 𐑄𐐩𐑉 𐑋𐐮𐑌𐐮𐑅𐐻𐑉𐐨 𐐮𐑆 𐐻𐐭 𐐿𐐫𐑊 𐑋𐐯𐑌 𐐲𐑌𐐻𐐭 𐑉𐐨𐐹𐐯𐑌𐐻𐐰𐑌𐑅, 𐐰𐑌𐐼 𐐻𐐭 𐑁𐐳𐑊𐑁𐐮𐑊 𐐰𐑌𐐼 𐐻𐐭 𐐼𐐭 𐑄 𐐶𐐲𐑉𐐿 𐐱𐑂 𐑄 𐐿𐐲𐑂𐐯𐑌𐐰𐑌𐐻𐑅 𐐱𐑂 𐑄 𐐙𐐪𐑄𐐲𐑉, 𐐸𐐶𐐮𐐽 𐐸𐐨 𐐸𐐰𐑃 𐑋𐐩𐐼 𐐲𐑌𐐻𐐭 𐑄 𐐽𐐮𐑊𐐼𐑉𐐯𐑌 𐐱𐑂 𐑋𐐯𐑌, 𐐻𐐭 𐐹𐑉𐐨𐐹𐐩𐑉 𐑄 𐐶𐐩 𐐰𐑋𐐲𐑍 𐑄 𐐽𐐮𐑊𐐼𐑉𐐯𐑌 𐐱𐑂 𐑋𐐯𐑌, 𐐺𐐴 𐐼𐐨𐐿𐑊𐐩𐑉𐐮𐑍 𐑄 𐐶𐐲𐑉𐐼 𐐱𐑂 𐐗𐑉𐐴𐑅𐐻 𐐲𐑌𐐻𐐭 𐑄 𐐽𐐬𐑆𐐲𐑌 𐑂𐐯𐑅𐐲𐑊𐑆 𐐱𐑂 𐑄 𐐢𐐫𐑉𐐼, 𐑄𐐰𐐻 𐑄𐐩 𐑋𐐩 𐐺𐐩𐑉 𐐻𐐯𐑅𐐻𐐮𐑋𐐬𐑌𐐨 𐐱𐑂 𐐸𐐮𐑋; 𐐰𐑌𐐼 𐐺𐐴 𐑅𐐬 𐐼𐐭𐐮𐑍, 𐑄 𐐢𐐫𐑉𐐼 𐐘𐐱𐐼 𐐹𐑉𐐨𐐹𐐩𐑉𐐯𐑃 𐑄 𐐶𐐩 𐑄𐐰𐐻 𐑄 𐑉𐐯𐑆𐐮𐐼𐐭 𐐱𐑂 𐑋𐐯𐑌 𐑋𐐩 𐐸𐐰𐑂 𐑁𐐩𐑃 𐐮𐑌 𐐗𐑉𐐴𐑅𐐻, 𐑄𐐰𐐻 𐑄 𐐐𐐬𐑊𐐨 𐐘𐐬𐑅𐐻 𐑋𐐩 𐐸𐐰𐑂 𐐹𐑊𐐩𐑅 𐐮𐑌 𐑄𐐩𐑉 𐐸𐐪𐑉𐐻𐑅, 𐐰𐐿𐐫𐑉𐐼𐐮𐑍 𐐻𐐭 𐑄 𐐹𐐵𐐲𐑉 𐑄𐐩𐑉𐐱𐑂; 𐐰𐑌𐐼 𐐰𐑁𐐻𐐲𐑉 𐑄𐐮𐑅 𐑋𐐰𐑌𐐲𐑉 𐐺𐑉𐐮𐑍𐐯𐑃 𐐻𐐭 𐐹𐐰𐑅 𐑄 𐐙𐐪𐑄𐐲𐑉, 𐑄 𐐿𐐲𐑂𐐯𐑌𐐰𐑌𐐻𐑅 𐐸𐐶𐐮𐐽 𐐸𐐨 𐐸𐐰𐑃 𐑋𐐩𐐼 𐐲𐑌𐐻𐐭 𐑄 𐐽𐐮𐑊𐐼𐑉𐐯𐑌 𐐱𐑂 𐑋𐐯𐑌. 𐐈𐑌𐐼 𐐗𐑉𐐴𐑅𐐻 𐐸𐐰𐑃 𐑅𐐯𐐼, 𐐆𐑁 𐐷𐐨 𐐶𐐮𐑊 𐐸𐐰𐑂 𐑁𐐩𐑃 𐐮𐑌 𐑋𐐨 𐐷𐐨 𐑇𐐰𐑊 𐐸𐐰𐑂 𐐹𐐵𐐲𐑉 𐐻𐐭 𐐼𐐭 𐐸𐐶𐐱𐐻𐑅𐐬-𐐯𐑂𐐲𐑉 𐑃𐐮𐑍 𐐮𐑆 𐐯𐐿𐑅𐐹𐐨𐐼𐐨𐐯𐑌𐐻 𐐮𐑌 𐑋𐐨. 𐐈𐑌𐐼 𐐸𐐨 𐐸𐐰𐑃 𐑅𐐯𐐼, 𐐡𐐨𐐹𐐯𐑌𐐻 𐐫𐑊 𐐷𐐨 𐐯𐑌𐐼𐑆 𐐱𐑂 𐑄 𐐲𐑉𐑃, 𐐰𐑌𐐼 𐐿𐐲𐑋 𐐲𐑌𐐻𐐭 𐑋𐐨, 𐐰𐑌𐐼 𐐺𐐨 𐐺𐐰𐐹𐐻𐐴𐑆𐐼 𐐮𐑌 𐑋𐐴 𐑌𐐩𐑋, 𐐰𐑌𐐼 𐐸𐐰𐑂 𐑁𐐩𐑃 𐐮𐑌 𐑋𐐨 𐑄𐐰𐐻 𐐷𐐨 𐑋𐐩 𐐺𐐨 𐑅𐐩𐑂𐐼.

4. 𐐈𐑌𐐼 𐑌𐐵 𐑋𐐴 𐐺𐐨𐑊𐐲𐑂𐐯𐐼 𐐺𐑉𐐯𐑃𐑉𐐯𐑌, 𐐮𐑁 𐑄𐐮𐑅 𐐺𐐨 𐑄 𐐿𐐩𐑅 𐑄𐐰𐐻 𐑄𐐨𐑆 𐑃𐐮𐑍𐑆 𐐪𐑉 𐐻𐑉𐐭 𐐸𐐶𐐮𐐽 𐐌 𐐸𐐰𐑂 𐑅𐐹𐐬𐐿𐐲𐑌 𐐲𐑌𐐻𐐭 𐐷𐐭, 𐐰𐑌𐐼 𐐘𐐱𐐼 𐐶𐐮𐑊 𐑇𐐬 𐐲𐑌𐐻𐐭 𐐷𐐭 𐐶𐐮𐑄 𐐹𐐵𐐲𐑉 𐐰𐑌𐐼 𐑀𐑉𐐩𐐻 𐑀𐑊𐐬𐑉𐐨 𐐰𐐻 𐑄 𐑊𐐰𐑅𐐻 𐐼𐐩, 𐑄𐐰𐐻 𐑄𐐩 𐐪𐑉 𐐻𐑉𐐭; 𐐰𐑌𐐼 𐐮𐑁 𐑄𐐩 𐐪𐑉 𐐻𐑉𐐭, 𐐸𐐰𐑆 𐑄 𐐼𐐩 𐐱𐑂 𐑋𐐮𐑉𐐲𐐿𐑊𐑆 𐑅𐐨𐑅𐐻? 𐐉𐑉 𐐸𐐰𐑆 𐐩𐑌𐐾𐐯𐑊𐑆 𐑅𐐨𐑅𐐻 𐐻𐐭 𐐲𐐹𐐨𐑉 𐐲𐑌𐐻𐐭 𐑄 𐐽𐐮𐑊𐐼𐑉𐐯𐑌 𐐱𐑂 𐑋𐐯𐑌? 𐐉𐑉 𐐸𐐰𐑆 𐐸𐐨 𐐶𐐮𐑄𐐸𐐯𐑊𐐼 𐑄 𐐹𐐵𐐲𐑉 𐐱𐑂 𐑄 𐐐𐐬𐑊𐐨 𐐘𐐬𐑅𐐻 𐑁𐑉𐐱𐑋 𐑄𐐯𐑋? 𐐉𐑉 𐐶𐐮𐑊 𐐸𐐨, 𐑅𐐬 𐑊𐐱𐑍 𐐰𐑆 𐐻𐐴𐑋 𐑇𐐰𐑊 𐑊𐐰𐑅𐐻, 𐐫𐑉 𐑄 𐐲𐑉𐑃 𐑇𐐰𐑊 𐑅𐐻𐐰𐑌𐐼, 𐐫𐑉 𐑄𐐩𐑉 𐑇𐐰𐑊 𐐺𐐨 𐐶𐐲𐑌 𐑋𐐰𐑌 𐐲𐐹𐐱𐑌 𐑄 𐑁𐐩𐑅 𐑄𐐩𐑉𐐱𐑂 𐐻𐐭 𐐺𐐨 𐑅𐐩𐑂𐐼? 𐐒𐐨𐐸𐐬𐑊𐐼 𐐌 𐑅𐐩 𐐲𐑌𐐻𐐭 𐐷𐐭, 𐐤𐐩, 𐑁𐐫𐑉 𐐮𐐻 𐐮𐑆 𐐺𐐴 𐑁𐐩𐑃 𐑄𐐰𐐻 𐑋𐐮𐑉𐐲𐐿𐑊𐑆 𐐪𐑉 𐑉𐐫𐐻; 𐐰𐑌𐐼 𐐮𐐻 𐐮𐑆 𐐺𐐴 𐑁𐐩𐑃 𐑄𐐰𐐻 𐐩𐑌𐐾𐐯𐑊𐑆 𐐲𐐹𐐨𐑉 𐐰𐑌𐐼 𐑋𐐮𐑌𐐮𐑅𐐻𐐲𐑉 𐐲𐑌𐐻𐐭 𐑋𐐯𐑌; 𐐸𐐶𐐯𐑉𐑁𐐫𐑉, 𐐮𐑁 𐑄𐐨𐑆 𐑃𐐮𐑍𐑆 𐐸𐐰𐑂 𐑅𐐨𐑅𐐻, 𐐶𐐬 𐐺𐐨 𐐲𐑌𐐻𐐭 𐑄 𐐽𐐮𐑊𐐼𐑉𐐯𐑌 𐐱𐑂 𐑋𐐯𐑌, 𐑁𐐫𐑉 𐐮𐐻 𐐮𐑆 𐐺𐐨𐐿𐐫𐑆 𐐱𐑂 𐐲𐑌𐐺𐐨𐑊𐐨𐑁, 𐐰𐑌𐐼 𐐫𐑊 𐐮𐑆 𐑂𐐩𐑌; 𐑁𐐫𐑉 𐑌𐐬 𐑋𐐰𐑌 𐐿𐐰𐑌 𐐺𐐨 𐑅𐐩𐑂𐐼, 𐐰𐐿𐐫𐑉𐐼𐐮𐑍 𐐻𐐭 𐑄 𐐶𐐲𐑉𐐼𐑆 𐐱𐑂 𐐗𐑉𐐴𐑅𐐻, 𐑅𐐩𐑂 𐑄𐐩 𐑇𐐰𐑊 𐐸𐐰𐑂 𐑁𐐩𐑃 𐐮𐑌 𐐸𐐮𐑆 𐑌𐐩𐑋; 𐐸𐐶𐐯𐑉𐑁𐐫𐑉, 𐐮𐑁 𐑄𐐨𐑆 𐑃𐐮𐑍𐑆 𐐸𐐰𐑂 𐑅𐐨𐑅𐐻, 𐑄𐐯𐑌 𐐸𐐰𐑆 𐑁𐐩𐑃 𐑅𐐨𐑅𐐻 𐐫𐑊𐑅𐐬; 𐐰𐑌𐐼 𐐫𐑁𐐳𐑊 𐐮𐑆 𐑄 𐑅𐐻𐐩𐐻 𐐱𐑂 𐑋𐐰𐑌; 𐑁𐐫𐑉 𐑄𐐩 𐐪𐑉 𐐰𐑆 𐑄𐐬 𐑄𐐩𐑉 𐐸𐐰𐐼 𐐺𐐨𐑌 𐑌𐐬 𐑉𐐨𐐼𐐯𐑋𐑇𐐲𐑌 𐑋𐐩𐐼. 𐐒𐐲𐐻 𐐺𐐨𐐸𐐬𐑊𐐼, 𐑋𐐴 𐐺𐐨𐑊𐐲𐑂𐐯𐐼 𐐺𐑉𐐯𐑃-𐑉𐐯𐑌, 𐐌 𐐾𐐲𐐾 𐐺𐐯𐐻𐐲𐑉 𐑃𐐮𐑍𐑆 𐐱𐑂 𐐷𐐭, 𐑁𐐫𐑉 𐐌 𐐾𐐲𐐾 𐑄𐐰𐐻 𐐷𐐨 𐐸𐐰𐑂 𐑁𐐩𐑃 𐐮𐑌 𐐗𐑉𐐴𐑅𐐻 𐐺𐐨𐐿𐐫𐑆 𐐱𐑂 𐐷𐐲𐑉 𐑋𐐨𐐿𐑌𐐯𐑅: 𐑁𐐫𐑉 𐐮𐑁 𐐷𐐨 𐐸𐐰𐑂 𐑌𐐱𐐻 𐑁𐐩𐑃 𐐮𐑌 𐐸𐐮𐑋, 𐑄𐐯𐑌 𐐷𐐨 𐐪𐑉 𐑌𐐱𐐻 𐑁𐐮𐐻 𐐻𐐭 𐐺𐐨 𐑌𐐲𐑋𐐺𐐲𐑉𐐼 𐐰𐑋𐐲𐑍 𐑄 𐐹𐐨𐐹𐑊 𐐱𐑂 𐐸𐐮𐑆 𐐕𐐲𐑉𐐽. 𐐈𐑌𐐼 𐐲𐑀𐐯𐑌 𐑋𐐴 𐐺𐐨𐑊𐐲𐑂𐐯𐐼 𐐺𐑉𐐯𐑃𐑉𐐯𐑌, 𐐌 𐐶𐐳𐐼 𐑅𐐹𐐨𐐿 𐐲𐑌𐐻𐐭 𐐷𐐭 𐐿𐐱𐑌𐑅𐐲𐑉𐑌𐐮𐑍 𐐸𐐬𐐹. 𐐐𐐵 𐐮𐑆 𐐮𐐻 𐑄𐐰𐐻 𐐷𐐨 𐐿𐐰𐑌 𐐰𐐻𐐩𐑌 𐐲𐑌𐐻𐐭 𐑁𐐩𐑃, 𐑅𐐩𐑂 𐐷𐐨 𐑇𐐰𐑊 𐐸𐐰𐑂 𐐸𐐬𐐹? 𐐈𐑌𐐼 𐐸𐐶𐐱𐐻 𐐮𐑆 𐐮𐐻 𐑄𐐰𐐻 𐐷𐐨 𐑇𐐰𐑊 𐐸𐐬𐐹 𐑁𐐫𐑉? 𐐒𐐨𐐸𐐬𐑊𐐼 𐐌 𐑅𐐩 𐐲𐑌𐐻𐐭 𐐷𐐭, 𐑄𐐰𐐻 𐐷𐐨 𐑇𐐰𐑊 𐐸𐐰𐑂 𐐸𐐬𐐹 𐑃𐑉𐐭 𐑄 𐐰𐐻𐐬𐑌𐑋𐐯𐑌𐐻 𐐱𐑂 𐐗𐑉𐐴𐑅𐐻, 𐐰𐑌𐐼 𐑄 𐐹𐐵𐐲𐑉 𐐱𐑂 𐐸𐐮𐑆 𐑉𐐯𐑆𐐲𐑉𐐯𐐿𐑇𐐲𐑌, 𐐻𐐭 𐐺𐐨 𐑉𐐩𐑆𐐼 𐐲𐑌𐐻𐐭 𐑊𐐴𐑁 𐐨𐐻𐐲𐑉𐑌𐐲𐑊; 𐐰𐑌𐐼 𐑄𐐮𐑅 𐐺𐐨𐐿𐐫𐑆 𐐱𐑂 𐐷𐐲𐑉 𐑁𐐩𐑃 𐐮𐑌 𐐸𐐮𐑋 𐐰𐐿𐐫𐑉𐐼𐐮𐑍 𐐻𐐭 𐑄 𐐹𐑉𐐱𐑋𐐮𐑅; 𐐸𐐶𐐯𐑉𐑁𐐫𐑉 𐐮𐑁 𐐲 𐑋𐐰𐑌 𐐸𐐰𐑂 𐑁𐐩𐑃, 𐐸𐐨 𐑋𐐲𐑅𐐻 𐑌𐐨𐐼𐑆 𐐸𐐰𐑂 𐐸𐐬𐐹; 𐑁𐐫𐑉 𐐶𐐮𐑄𐐵𐐻 𐑁𐐩𐑃 𐑄𐐩𐑉 𐐿𐐰𐑌𐐱𐐻 𐐺𐐨 𐐯𐑌𐐨 𐐸𐐬𐐹. 𐐈𐑌𐐼 𐐲𐑀𐐯𐑌, 𐐺𐐨𐐸𐐬𐑊𐐼 𐐌 𐑅𐐩 𐐲𐑌𐐻𐐭 𐐷𐐭, 𐑄𐐰𐐻 𐐸𐐨 𐐿𐐰𐑌𐐱𐐻 𐐸𐐰𐑂 𐑁𐐩𐑃 𐐰𐑌𐐼 𐐸𐐬𐐹, 𐑅𐐩𐑂 𐐸𐐨 𐑇𐐰𐑊 𐐺𐐨 𐑋𐐨𐐿, 𐐰𐑌𐐼 𐑊𐐬𐑊𐐨 𐐱𐑂 𐐸𐐪𐑉𐐻; 𐐮𐑁 𐑅𐐬, 𐐸𐐮𐑆 𐑁𐐩𐑃 𐐰𐑌𐐼 𐐸𐐬𐐹 𐐮𐑆 𐑂𐐩𐑌, 𐑁𐐫𐑉 𐑌𐐲𐑌 𐐮𐑆 𐐰𐐿𐑅𐐯𐐹𐐻𐐲𐐺𐑊 𐐺𐐨𐑁𐐬𐑉 𐐘𐐱𐐼, 𐑅𐐩𐑂 𐑄 𐑋𐐨𐐿 𐐰𐑌𐐼 𐑊𐐬𐑊𐐨 𐐮𐑌 𐐸𐐪𐑉𐐻; 𐐰𐑌𐐼 𐐮𐑁 𐐲 𐑋𐐰𐑌 𐐺𐐨 𐑋𐐨𐐿 𐐰𐑌𐐼 𐑊𐐬𐑊𐐨 𐐮𐑌 𐐸𐐪𐑉𐐻, 𐐰𐑌𐐼 𐐿𐐱𐑌𐑁𐐯𐑅𐐯𐑆 𐐺𐐴 𐑄 𐐹𐐵𐐲𐑉 𐐱𐑂 𐑄 𐐐𐐬𐑊𐐨 𐐘𐐬𐑅𐐻, 𐑄𐐰𐐻 𐐖𐐨𐑆𐐲𐑅 𐐮𐑆 𐑄 𐐗𐑉𐐴𐑅𐐻, 𐐸𐐨 𐑋𐐲𐑅𐐻 𐑌𐐨𐐼𐑆 𐐸𐐰𐑂 𐐽𐐯𐑉𐐮𐐻𐐨; 𐑁𐐫𐑉 𐐮𐑁 𐐸𐐨 𐐸𐐰𐑂 𐑌𐐱𐐻 𐐽𐐯𐑉𐐮𐐻𐐨 𐐸𐐨 𐐮𐑆 𐑌𐐲𐑃𐐮𐑍; 𐐸𐐶𐐯𐑉𐑁𐐫𐑉 𐐸𐐨 𐑋𐐲𐑅𐐻 𐑌𐐨𐐼𐑆 𐐸𐐰𐑂

𐐽𐐰𐑉𐐮𐐻𐐨. 𐐈𐑌𐐼 𐐽𐐰𐑉𐐮𐐻𐐨 𐑅𐐲𐑁𐐲𐑉𐐯𐑃 𐑊𐐱𐑍, 𐐰𐑌𐐼 𐐮𐑆 𐐿𐐴𐑌𐐼, 𐐰𐑌𐐼 𐐯𐑌𐑂𐐨𐐯𐑃 𐑌𐐱𐐻, 𐐰𐑌𐐼 𐐮𐑆 𐑌𐐱𐐻 𐐹𐐲𐑁𐐻 𐐲𐐹, 𐑅𐐨𐐿𐐯𐑃 𐑌𐐱𐐻 𐐸𐐲𐑉 𐐬𐑌, 𐐮𐑆 𐑌𐐱𐐻 𐐨𐑆𐐮𐑊𐐨 𐐹𐑉𐐬𐑂𐐬𐐿𐐻, 𐑃𐐮𐑍𐐿𐐯𐑃 𐑌𐐬 𐐨𐑂𐐮𐑊, 𐐰𐑌𐐼 𐑉𐐨𐐾𐑎𐑅𐐯𐑃 𐑌𐐱𐐻 𐐮𐑌 𐐮𐑌𐐮𐐿𐐶𐐮𐐻𐐨, 𐐺𐐲𐐻 𐑉𐐨𐐾𐑎𐑅𐐯𐑃 𐐮𐑌 𐑄 𐐻𐑉𐐭𐑃, 𐐺𐐩𐑉𐐯𐑃 𐐫𐑊 𐑃𐐮𐑍𐑆, 𐐺𐐨𐑊𐐨𐑂𐐯𐑃 𐐫𐑊 𐑃𐐮𐑍𐑆, 𐐸𐐬𐐹𐐯𐑃 𐐫𐑊 𐑃𐐮𐑍𐑆, 𐐯𐑌𐐼𐐷𐐭𐑉𐐯𐑃 𐐫𐑊 𐑃𐐮𐑍𐑆; 𐐸𐐶𐐩𐑉𐑁𐐬𐑉, 𐑋𐐴 𐐺𐐨𐑊𐐲𐑂𐐯𐐼 𐐺𐑉𐐯𐑄𐑉𐐯𐑌, 𐐮𐑁 𐐷𐐨 𐐸𐐰𐑂 𐑌𐐱𐐻 𐐽𐐰𐑉𐐮𐐻𐐨, 𐐷𐐨 𐐪𐑉 𐑌𐐲𐑃𐐮𐑍, 𐑁𐐫𐑉 𐐽𐐰𐑉𐐮𐐻𐐨 𐑌𐐯𐑂𐐲𐑉 𐑁𐐩𐑊𐐯𐑃. 𐐐𐐶𐐩𐑉𐑁𐐬𐑉, 𐐿𐑊𐐨𐑂 𐐲𐑌𐐻𐐭 𐐽𐐰𐑉𐐮𐐻𐐨, 𐐸𐐶𐐮𐐽 𐐮𐑆 𐑄 𐑀𐑉𐐩𐐻𐐯𐑅𐐻 𐐱𐑂 𐐫𐑊, 𐑁𐐫𐑉 𐐫𐑊 𐑃𐐮𐑍𐑆 𐑋𐐲𐑅𐐻 𐑁𐐩𐑊; 𐐺𐐲𐐻 𐐽𐐰𐑉𐐮𐐻𐐨 𐐮𐑆 𐑄 𐐹𐐷𐐭𐑉 𐑊𐐲𐑂 𐐱𐑂 𐐗𐑉𐐴𐑅𐐻, 𐐰𐑌𐐼 𐐮𐐻 𐐯𐑌𐐼𐐷𐐭𐑉𐐯𐑃 𐑁𐐫𐑉 𐐯𐑂𐐲𐑉; 𐐰𐑌𐐼 𐐸𐐭𐑅𐐬 𐐮𐑆 𐑁𐐵𐑌𐐼 𐐹𐐱𐑆𐐯𐑅𐐻 𐐱𐑂 𐐮𐐻 𐐰𐐻 𐑄 𐑊𐐰𐑅𐐻 𐐼𐐩, 𐐮𐐻 𐑇𐐰𐑊 𐐺𐐨 𐐶𐐯𐑊 𐐶𐐮𐑄 𐐸𐐮𐑋. 𐐐𐐶𐐩𐑉𐑁𐐬𐑉, 𐑋𐐴 𐐺𐐨𐑊𐐲𐑂𐐯𐐼 𐐺𐑉𐐯𐑄𐑉𐐯𐑌, 𐐹𐑉𐐩 𐐲𐑌𐐻𐐭 𐑄 𐐙𐐪𐑄𐐲𐑉 𐐶𐐮𐑄 𐐫𐑊 𐑄 𐐯𐑌𐐲𐑉𐐾𐐨 𐐱𐑂 𐐸𐐪𐑉𐐻, 𐑄𐐰𐐻 𐐷𐐨 𐑋𐐩 𐐺𐐨 𐑁𐐮𐑊𐐼 𐐶𐐮𐑄 𐑄𐐮𐑅 𐑊𐐲𐑂 𐐸𐐶𐐮𐐽 𐐸𐐨 𐐸𐐰𐑃 𐐺𐐨𐑅𐐻𐐬𐐼 𐐲𐐹𐐱𐑌 𐐫𐑊 𐐸𐐭 𐐪𐑉 𐐻𐑉𐐭 𐑁𐐱𐑊𐐬𐐲𐑉𐑆 𐐱𐑂 𐐸𐐮𐑆 𐐝𐐲𐑌 𐐖𐐨𐑆𐐲𐑅 𐐗𐑉𐐴𐑅𐐻, 𐑄𐐰𐐻 𐐷𐐨 𐑋𐐩 𐐺𐐨𐐿𐐲𐑋 𐑄 𐑅𐐲𐑌𐑆 𐐱𐑂 𐐘𐐱𐐼, 𐑄𐐰𐐻 𐐸𐐶𐐯𐑌 𐐸𐐨 𐑇𐐰𐑊 𐐰𐐹𐐨𐑉, 𐐶𐐨 𐑇𐐰𐑊 𐐺𐐨 𐑊𐐴𐐿 𐐸𐐮𐑋; 𐑁𐐫𐑉 𐐶𐐨 𐑇𐐰𐑊 𐑅𐐨 𐐸𐐮𐑋 𐐰𐑆 𐐸𐐨 𐐮𐑆, 𐑄𐐰𐐻 𐐶𐐨 𐑋𐐩 𐐸𐐰𐑂 𐑄𐐮𐑅 𐐸𐐬𐐹, 𐑄𐐰𐐻 𐐶𐐨 𐑋𐐩 𐐺𐐨 𐐹𐐷𐐭𐑉𐐮𐑁𐐴𐐼 𐐨𐑂𐐲𐑌 𐐰𐑆 𐐸𐐨 𐐮𐑆 𐐹𐐷𐐭𐑉. 𐐁𐑋𐐯𐑌.

𐐕𐐰𐐹𐐻𐐲𐑉 VIII.

1. 𐐈𐑌 𐐯𐐹𐐮𐑅𐐲𐑊 𐐱𐑂 𐑋𐐴 𐑁𐐪𐑄𐐲𐑉 𐐣𐐫𐑉𐑋𐐲𐑌, 𐑉𐐮𐐻𐑌 𐐻𐐭 𐑋𐐨 𐐣𐐫𐑉𐐬𐑌𐐴; 𐐰𐑌𐐼 𐐮𐐻 𐐶𐐱𐑆 𐑉𐐮𐐻𐑌 𐐲𐑌𐐻𐐭 𐑋𐐨 𐑅𐐭𐑌 𐐰𐑁𐐻𐐲𐑉 𐑋𐐴 𐐿𐐫𐑊𐐮𐑍 𐐻𐐭 𐑄 𐑋𐐮𐑌𐐮𐑅𐐻𐑉𐐨. 𐐈𐑌𐐼 𐐱𐑌 𐑄𐐮𐑅 𐐶𐐴𐑆 𐐼𐐮𐐼 𐐸𐐨 𐑉𐐴𐐻 𐐲𐑌𐐻𐐭 𐑋𐐨, 𐑅𐐩𐐮𐑍, 𐐣𐐴 𐐺𐐨𐑊𐐲𐑂𐐯𐐼 𐑅𐐲𐑌, 𐐣𐐫𐑉𐐬𐑌𐐴, 𐐌 𐑉𐐨𐐾𐑎𐑅 𐐯𐐿𐑅𐐨𐐼𐐮𐑍𐑊𐐨 𐑄𐐰𐐻 𐐷𐐭𐑉 𐐢𐐫𐑉𐐼 𐐖𐐨𐑆𐐲𐑅 𐐗𐑉𐐴𐑅𐐻 𐐸𐐰𐑃 𐐺𐐮𐑌 𐑋𐐴𐑌𐐼𐑁𐐳𐑊 𐐱𐑂 𐐷𐐭, 𐐰𐑌𐐼 𐐸𐐰𐑃 𐐿𐐫𐑊𐐼 𐐷𐐭 𐐻𐐭 𐐸𐐮𐑆 𐑋𐐮𐑌𐐮𐑅𐐻𐑉𐐨, 𐐰𐑌𐐼 𐐻𐐭 𐐸𐐮𐑆 𐐸𐐬𐑊𐐨 𐐶𐐲𐑉𐐿. 𐐌 𐐰𐑋 𐑋𐐴𐑌𐐼𐑁𐐳𐑊 𐐱𐑂 𐐷𐐭 𐐫𐑊𐐶𐐩𐑆 𐐮𐑌 𐑋𐐴 𐐹𐑉𐐩𐐲𐑉𐑆, 𐐿𐐱𐑌𐐻𐐮𐑌𐐷𐐭𐐰𐑊𐐨 𐐹𐑉𐐩𐐮𐑍 𐐲𐑌𐐻𐐭 𐐘𐐱𐐼 𐑄 𐐙𐐪𐑄𐐲𐑉 𐐮𐑌 𐑄 𐑌𐐩𐑋 𐐱𐑂 𐐸𐐮𐑆 𐐐𐐬𐑊𐐨 𐐕𐐴𐑊𐐼, 𐐖𐐨𐑆𐐲𐑅, 𐑄𐐰𐐻 𐐸𐐨, 𐑃𐑉𐐭 𐐸𐐮𐑆 𐐮𐑌𐑁𐐮𐑌𐐮𐐻 𐑀𐐳𐐼𐑌𐐯𐑅 𐐰𐑌𐐼 𐑀𐑉𐐩𐑅, 𐐶𐐮𐑊 𐐿𐐨𐐹 𐐷𐐭 𐑃𐑉𐐭 𐑄 𐐯𐑌𐐼𐐷𐐭𐑉𐐰𐑌𐑅 𐐱𐑂 𐑁𐐩𐑃 𐐱𐑌 𐐸𐐮𐑆 𐑌𐐩𐑋 𐐻𐐭 𐑄 𐐯𐑌𐐼.

2. 𐐈𐑌𐐼 𐑌𐐵 𐑋𐐴 𐑅𐐲𐑌 𐐌 𐑅𐐹𐐨𐐿 𐐲𐑌𐐻𐐭 𐐷𐐭 𐐿𐐱𐑌𐑅𐐲𐑉𐑌𐐮𐑍 𐑄𐐰𐐻 𐐸𐐶𐐮𐐽 𐑀𐑉𐐨𐑂𐐯𐑃 𐑋𐐨 𐐯𐐿𐑅𐐨𐐼𐐮𐑍𐑊𐐨; 𐑁𐐫𐑉 𐐮𐐻 𐑀𐑉𐐨𐑂𐐯𐑃 𐑋𐐨 𐑄𐐰𐐻 𐑄𐐩𐑉 𐑇𐐳𐐼 𐐼𐐮𐑅𐐹𐐷𐐭𐐻𐐩𐑇𐐲𐑌𐑆 𐑉𐐴𐑆 𐐰𐑋𐐲𐑍 𐐷𐐭. 𐐙𐐫𐑉 𐐮𐑁 𐐌 𐐸𐐰𐑂 𐑊𐐲𐑉𐑌𐐼 𐑄 𐐻𐑉𐐭𐑃, 𐑄𐐩𐑉 𐐸𐐰𐑂 𐐺𐐮𐑌 𐐼𐐮𐑅𐐹𐐷𐐭𐐻𐐩𐑇𐐲𐑌𐑆 𐐰𐑋𐐲𐑍 𐐷𐐭 𐐿𐐱𐑌𐑅𐐲𐑉𐑌𐐮𐑍 𐑄 𐐺𐐰𐐹𐐻𐐮𐑆𐑋 𐐱𐑂 𐐷𐐭𐑉 𐑊𐐮𐐻𐑊 𐐽𐐮𐑊𐐼𐑉𐐯𐑌. 𐐈𐑌𐐼 𐑌𐐵 𐑋𐐴 𐑅𐐲𐑌 𐐌 𐐼𐐨𐑆𐐴𐑉 𐑄𐐰𐐻 𐐷𐐨 𐑇𐐳𐐼 𐑊𐐩𐐺𐐲𐑉 𐐼𐐮𐑊𐐮𐐾𐐯𐑌𐐻𐑊𐐨 𐑄𐐰𐐻 𐑄𐐮𐑅 𐑀𐑉𐐬𐑅 𐐯𐑉𐐲𐑉 𐑇𐐳𐐼 𐐺𐐨 𐑉𐐨𐑋𐐭𐑂𐐼 𐑁𐑉𐐱𐑋 𐐰𐑋𐐲𐑍 𐐷𐐭; 𐑁𐐫𐑉, 𐑁𐐫𐑉 𐑄𐐮𐑅 𐐮𐑌𐐻𐐯𐑌𐐻 𐐌 𐐸𐐰𐑂 𐑉𐐮𐐻𐑌 𐑄𐐮𐑅 𐐯𐐹𐐮𐑅𐐲𐑊. 𐐙𐐫𐑉 𐐮𐑋𐐨𐐼𐐨𐐰𐐻𐑊𐐨 𐐰𐑁𐐻𐐲𐑉 𐐌 𐐸𐐰𐐼 𐑊𐐲𐑉𐑌𐐼 𐑄𐐨𐑆 𐑃𐐮𐑍𐑆 𐐱𐑂 𐐷𐐭 𐐌 𐐮𐑌𐐿𐐶𐐴𐑉𐐼 𐐱𐑂 𐑄 𐐢𐐫𐑉𐐼 𐐿𐐱𐑌𐑅𐐲𐑉𐑌𐐮𐑍 𐑄 𐑋𐐰𐐻𐐲𐑉. 𐐈𐑌𐐼 𐑄 𐐶𐐲𐑉𐐼 𐐱𐑂 𐑄 𐐢𐐫𐑉𐐼 𐐿𐐩𐑋 𐐻𐐭 𐑋𐐨 𐐺𐐴 𐑄 𐐹𐐵𐐲𐑉 𐐱𐑂 𐑄 𐐐𐐬𐑊𐐨 𐐘𐐬𐑅𐐻, 𐑅𐐩𐐮𐑍, 𐐢𐐮𐑅𐐲𐑌 𐐻𐐭 𐑄 𐐶𐐲𐑉𐐼𐑆 𐐱𐑂 𐐗𐑉𐐴𐑅𐐻, 𐐷𐐭𐑉 𐐡𐐨𐐼𐐨𐑋𐐲𐑉, 𐐷𐐭𐑉 𐐢𐐫𐑉𐐼 𐐰𐑌𐐼 𐐷𐐭𐑉 𐐘𐐱𐐼. 𐐒𐐨𐐸𐐬𐑊𐐼, 𐐌 𐐿𐐩𐑋 𐐮𐑌𐐻𐐭 𐑄 𐐶𐐲𐑉𐑊𐐼 𐑌𐐱𐐻 𐐻𐐭 𐐿𐐫𐑊 𐑄 𐑉𐐴𐐽𐐲𐑅, 𐐺𐐲𐐻 𐑅𐐮𐑌𐐲𐑉𐑆 𐐻𐐭 𐑉𐐨𐐹𐐯𐑌𐐻𐐰𐑌𐑅: 𐑄 𐐸𐐬𐑊 𐑌𐐨𐐼 𐑌𐐬 𐑁𐐮𐑆𐐮𐑇𐐲𐑌, 𐐺𐐲𐐻 𐑄𐐩 𐑄𐐰𐐻 𐐪𐑉 𐑅𐐮𐐿; 𐐸𐐶𐐩𐑉𐑁𐐬𐑉 𐑊𐐮𐐻𐑊 𐐽𐐮𐑊𐐼𐑉𐐯𐑌 𐐪𐑉 𐐸𐐬𐑊, 𐑁𐐫𐑉 𐑄𐐩 𐐪𐑉 𐑌𐐱𐐻 𐐿𐐩𐐹𐐲𐐺𐑊 𐐱𐑂 𐐿𐐱𐑋𐐮𐐻𐐮𐑍 𐑅𐐮𐑌; 𐐸𐐶𐐩𐑉𐑁𐐬𐑉 𐑄 𐐿𐐲𐑉𐑅 𐐱𐑂 𐐁𐐼𐐲𐑋 𐐮𐑆 𐐻𐐩𐐿𐑌 𐑁𐑉𐐱𐑋 𐑄𐐯𐑋 𐐮𐑌 𐑋𐐨, 𐑄𐐰𐐻 𐐮𐐻 𐐸𐐰𐑃 𐑌𐐬 𐐹𐐵𐐲𐑉 𐐬𐑂𐐲𐑉 𐑄𐐯𐑋; 𐐰𐑌𐐼 𐑄 𐑊𐐫 𐐱𐑂 𐑅𐐲𐑉𐐿𐐲𐑋𐑅𐐮𐑈𐐲𐑌 𐐮𐑆 𐐼𐐲𐑌 𐐰𐐶𐐩 𐐮𐑌 𐑋𐐨. 𐐈𐑌𐐼 𐐰𐑁𐐻𐐲𐑉 𐑄𐐮𐑅 𐑋𐐰𐑌𐐲𐑉 𐐼𐐮𐐼 𐑄 𐐐𐐬𐑊𐐨 𐐘𐐬𐑅𐐻 𐑋𐐰𐑌𐐮𐑁𐐯𐑅𐐻 𐑄 𐐶𐐲𐑉𐐼 𐐱𐑂 𐐘𐐱𐐼 𐐲𐑌𐐻𐐭 𐑋𐐨; 𐐸𐐶𐐩𐑉𐑁𐐬𐑉, 𐑋𐐴 𐐺𐐨𐑊𐐲𐑂𐐯𐐼 𐑅𐐲𐑌, 𐐌 𐑌𐐬 𐑄𐐰𐐻 𐐮𐐻 𐐮𐑆 𐑅𐐱𐑊𐐯𐑋 𐑋𐐱𐐿𐐲𐑉𐐨 𐐺𐐨𐑁𐐬𐑉 𐐘𐐱𐐼, 𐑄𐐰𐐻 𐐷𐐨 𐑇𐐳𐐼 𐐺𐐰𐐹𐐻𐐴𐑆 𐑊𐐮𐐻𐑊 𐐽𐐮𐑊𐐼𐑉𐐯𐑌. 𐐒𐐨𐐸𐐬𐑊𐐼 𐐌 𐑅𐐩 𐐲𐑌𐐻𐐭 𐐷𐐭, 𐑄𐐰𐐻 𐑄𐐮𐑅 𐑃𐐮𐑍 𐑇𐐰𐑊 𐐷𐐨 𐐻𐐨𐐽, 𐑉𐐨𐐹𐐯𐑌𐐻𐐰𐑌𐑅 𐐰𐑌𐐼 𐐺𐐰𐐹𐐻𐐮𐑆𐑋 𐐲𐑌𐐻𐐭 𐑄𐐬𐑆 𐐸𐐭 𐐪𐑉 𐐰𐐿𐐵𐑌𐐻𐐲𐐺𐑊 𐐰𐑌𐐼 𐐿𐐩𐐹𐐲𐐺𐑊 𐐱𐑂 𐐿𐐱𐑋𐐮𐐻𐐮𐑍 𐑅𐐮𐑌; 𐐷𐐩, 𐐻𐐨𐐽 𐐹𐐩𐑉𐐯𐑌𐐻𐑅 𐑄𐐰𐐻 𐑄𐐩 𐑋𐐲𐑅𐐻 𐑉𐐨𐐹𐐯𐑌𐐻 𐐰𐑌𐐼 𐐺𐐨 𐐺𐐰𐐹𐐻𐐴𐑆𐐼, 𐐰𐑌𐐼 𐐸𐐲𐑋𐐺𐑊 𐑄𐐯𐑋𐑅𐐯𐑊𐑂𐑆 𐐰𐑆 𐑄𐐩𐑉 𐑊𐐮𐐻𐑊 𐐽𐐮𐑊𐐼𐑉𐐯𐑌, 𐐰𐑌𐐼 𐑄𐐩 𐑇𐐰𐑊 𐐫𐑊 𐐺𐐨 𐑅𐐩𐑂𐐼 𐐶𐐮𐑄 𐑄𐐩𐑉 𐑊𐐮𐐻𐑊 𐐽𐐮𐑊𐐼𐑉𐐯𐑌; 𐐰𐑌𐐼 𐑄𐐩𐑉 𐑊𐐮𐐻𐑊 𐐽𐐮𐑊𐐼𐑉𐐯𐑌 𐑌𐐨𐐼 𐑌𐐬 𐑉𐐨-

𐑉𐐯𐐹𐐯𐑌𐐻𐐰𐑌𐑅, 𐐰𐑌𐐼 𐐺𐐰𐐹𐐻𐐮𐑆𐑋. 𐐒𐐨𐐸𐐬𐑊𐐼, 𐐺𐐰𐐹𐐻𐐮𐑆𐑋 𐐮𐑆 𐐲𐑌𐐻𐐭 𐑉𐐯𐐹𐐯𐑌𐐻𐐰𐑌𐑅 𐐻𐐭 𐑄 𐑁𐐳𐑊𐑁𐐮𐑊𐐮𐑍 𐑄 𐐿𐐱𐑋𐐰𐑌𐐼𐑋𐐯𐑌𐐻𐑅 𐐲𐑌𐐻𐐭 𐑄 𐑉𐐨𐑋𐐮𐑇𐐲𐑌 𐐲𐑂 𐑅𐐮𐑌𐑆. 𐐒𐐲𐐻 𐑊𐐮𐐻𐑊 𐐽𐐮𐑊𐐼𐑉𐐯𐑌 𐐪𐑉 𐐰𐑊𐐴𐑂 𐐮𐑌 𐐗𐑉𐐴𐑅𐐻, 𐐨𐑂𐐯𐑌 𐑁𐑉𐐱𐑋 𐑄 𐑁𐐵𐑌𐐼𐐩𐑇𐐲𐑌 𐐲𐑂 𐑄 𐐶𐐲𐑉𐑊𐐼; 𐐮𐑁 𐑌𐐱𐐻 𐑅𐐬, 𐐘𐐱𐐼 𐐮𐑆 𐐩 𐐹𐐪𐑉𐑇𐐲𐑊 𐐘𐐱𐐼, 𐐰𐑌𐐼 𐐫𐑊𐑅𐐬 𐐩 𐐽𐐩𐑌𐐾𐐲𐐺𐑊 𐐘𐐱𐐼, 𐐰𐑌𐐼 𐐩 𐑉𐐯𐑅𐐹𐐯𐐿𐐻𐐲𐑉 𐐻𐐭 𐐹𐐲𐑉𐑅𐐲𐑌𐑆; 𐑁𐐫𐑉 𐐸𐐵 𐑋𐐯𐑌𐐨 𐑊𐐮𐐻𐑊 𐐽𐐮𐑊𐐼𐑉𐐯𐑌 𐐸𐐰𐑂 𐐼𐐴𐐼 𐐶𐐮𐑄𐐵𐐻 𐐺𐐰𐐹𐐻𐐮𐑆𐑋. 𐐐𐐶𐐯𐑉𐑁𐐫𐑉, 𐐮𐑁 𐑊𐐮𐐻𐑊 𐐽𐐮𐑊𐐼𐑉𐐯𐑌 𐐿𐐳𐐼 𐑌𐐱𐐻 𐐺𐐨 𐑅𐐩𐑂𐐼 𐐶𐐮𐑄𐐵𐐻 𐐺𐐰𐐹𐐻𐐮𐑆𐑋, 𐑄𐐨𐑆 𐑋𐐲𐑅𐐻 𐐸𐐰𐑂 𐑀𐐫𐑌 𐐻𐐭 𐐰𐑌 𐐯𐑌𐐼𐑊𐐯𐑅 𐐸𐐯𐑊. 𐐒𐐨𐐸𐐬𐑊𐐼 𐐌 𐑅𐐩 𐐲𐑌𐐻𐐭 𐐷𐐭, 𐑄𐐰𐐻 𐐸𐐨 𐑄𐐰𐐻 𐑅𐐲𐐹𐐬𐑆𐐯𐑃 𐑄𐐰𐐻 𐑊𐐮𐐻𐑊 𐐽𐐮𐑊𐐼𐑉𐐯𐑌 𐑌𐐨𐐼 𐐺𐐰𐐹𐐻𐐮𐑆𐑋, 𐐮𐑆 𐐮𐑌 𐑄 𐑀𐐫𐑊 𐐲𐑂 𐐺𐐮𐐻𐐲𐑉𐑌𐐯𐑅, 𐐰𐑌𐐼 𐐮𐑌 𐑄 𐐺𐐱𐑌𐐼𐑆 𐐲𐑂 𐐮𐑌𐐮𐐿𐐶𐐮𐐻𐐨; 𐑁𐐫𐑉 𐐸𐐨 𐐸𐐰𐑃 𐑌𐐨𐑄𐐲𐑉 𐑁𐐩𐑃, 𐐸𐐬𐐹, 𐑌𐐫𐑉 𐐽𐐯𐑉𐐮𐐻𐐨; 𐐸𐐶𐐯𐑉𐑁𐐫𐑉, 𐑇𐐳𐐼 𐐸𐐨 𐐺𐐨 𐐿𐐲𐐻 𐐫𐑁 𐐸𐐶𐐴𐑊 𐐮𐑌 𐑄 𐑃𐐫𐐻, 𐐸𐐨 𐑋𐐲𐑅𐐻 𐑀𐐬 𐐼𐐵𐑌 𐐻𐐭 𐐸𐐯𐑊. 𐐙𐐫𐑉 𐐫𐑁𐐳𐑊 𐐮𐑆 𐑄 𐐶𐐮𐐿𐐯𐐼𐑌𐐯𐑅 𐐻𐐭 𐑅𐐲𐐹𐐬𐑆 𐑄𐐰𐐻 𐐘𐐱𐐼 𐑅𐐩𐑂𐐯𐑃 𐐶𐐲𐑌 𐐽𐐴𐑊𐐼 𐐺𐐨𐐿𐐫𐑆 𐐲𐑂 𐐺𐐰𐐹𐐻𐐮𐑆𐑋, 𐐰𐑌𐐼 𐑄 𐐲𐑄𐐲𐑉 𐑋𐐲𐑅𐐻 𐐹𐐯𐑉𐐮𐑇 𐐺𐐨𐐿𐐫𐑆 𐐸𐐨 𐐸𐐰𐑃 𐑌𐐬 𐐺𐐰𐐹𐐻𐐮𐑆𐑋. 𐐎𐐬 𐐺𐐨 𐐲𐑌𐐻𐐭 𐑄𐐯𐑋 𐑄𐐰𐐻 𐑇𐐰𐑊 𐐹𐐲𐑉𐑂𐐲𐑉𐐻 𐑄 𐐶𐐩𐑆 𐐲𐑂 𐑄 𐐢𐐫𐑉𐐼 𐐪𐑁𐐻𐐲𐑉 𐑄𐐮𐑅 𐑋𐐰𐑌𐐲𐑉, 𐑁𐐫𐑉 𐑄𐐩 𐑇𐐰𐑊 𐐹𐐯𐑉𐐮𐑇 𐐯𐐿𐑅𐐯𐐹𐐻 𐑄𐐩 𐑉𐐨𐐹𐐯𐑌𐐻. 𐐒𐐨𐐸𐐬𐑊𐐼, 𐐌 𐑅𐐹𐐨𐐿 𐐶𐐮𐑄 𐐺𐐬𐑊𐐼𐑌𐐯𐑅, 𐐸𐐰𐑂𐐮𐑍 𐐫𐑃𐐱𐑉𐐮𐐻𐐨 𐑁𐑉𐐱𐑋 𐐘𐐱𐐼, 𐐰𐑌𐐼 𐐌 𐑁𐐨𐑉 𐑌𐐱𐐻 𐐸𐐶𐐱𐐻 𐑋𐐰𐑌 𐐿𐐰𐑌 𐐼𐐭; 𐑁𐐫𐑉 𐐹𐐲𐑉𐑁𐐯𐐿𐐻 𐑊𐐲𐑂 𐐿𐐪𐑅𐐻𐐯𐑃 𐐵𐐻 𐐫𐑊 𐑁𐐨𐑉; 𐐰𐑌𐐼 𐐌 𐐰𐑋 𐑁𐐮𐑊𐐼 𐐶𐐮𐑄 𐐽𐐯𐑉𐐮𐐻𐐨, 𐐸𐐶𐐮𐐽 𐐮𐑆 𐐯𐑂𐐲𐑉𐑊𐐪𐑅𐐻𐐮𐑍 𐑊𐐲𐑂; 𐐸𐐶𐐯𐑉𐑁𐐫𐑉 𐐫𐑊 𐐽𐐮𐑊𐐼𐑉𐐯𐑌 𐐪𐑉 𐐲𐑊𐐴𐐿 𐐲𐑌𐐻𐐭 𐑋𐐨; 𐐸𐐶𐐯𐑉𐑁𐐫𐑉 𐐌 𐑊𐐲𐑂 𐑊𐐮𐐻𐑊 𐐽𐐮𐑊𐐼𐑉𐐯𐑌 𐐶𐐮𐑄 𐐩 𐐹𐐲𐑉𐑁𐐯𐐿𐐻 𐑊𐐲𐑂; 𐐰𐑌𐐼 𐑄𐐩 𐐪𐑉 𐐫𐑊 𐐲𐑊𐐴𐐿 𐐰𐑌𐐼 𐐹𐐪𐑉𐐻𐐩𐐿𐐲𐑉𐑆 𐐲𐑂 𐑅𐐰𐑊𐑂𐐩𐑇𐐲𐑌.

3. 𐐙𐐫𐑉 𐐌 𐑌𐐬 𐑄𐐰𐐻 𐐘𐐱𐐼 𐐮𐑆 𐑌𐐱𐐻 𐐩 𐐹𐐪𐑉𐑇𐐲𐑊 𐐘𐐱𐐼, 𐑌𐐨𐑄𐐲𐑉 𐐩 𐐽𐐩𐑌𐐾𐐲𐐺𐑊 𐐺𐐨𐐮𐑍; 𐐺𐐲𐐻 𐐸𐐨 𐐮𐑆 𐐲𐑌𐐽𐐩𐑌𐐾𐐲𐐺𐑊 𐑁𐑉𐐱𐑋 𐐫𐑊 𐐨𐐻𐐲𐑉𐑌𐐮𐐻𐐨 𐐻𐐭 𐐫𐑊 𐐨𐐻𐐲𐑉𐑌𐐮𐐻𐐨. 𐐢𐐮𐐻𐑊 𐐽𐐮𐑊𐐼𐑉𐐯𐑌 𐐿𐐰𐑌 𐑌𐐱𐐻 𐑉𐐨𐐹𐐯𐑌𐐻; 𐐸𐐶𐐯𐑉𐑁𐐫𐑉 𐐮𐐻 𐐮𐑆 𐐫𐑁𐐳𐑊 𐐶𐐮𐐿𐐯𐐼𐑌𐐯𐑅 𐐻𐐭 𐐼𐐨𐑌𐐴 𐑄 𐐹𐐷𐐭𐑉 𐑋𐐲𐑉𐑅𐐨𐑆 𐐲𐑂 𐐘𐐱𐐼 𐐲𐑌𐐻𐐭 𐑄𐐯𐑋, 𐑁𐐫𐑉 𐑄𐐩 𐐪𐑉 𐐫𐑊 𐐰𐑊𐐴𐑂 𐐮𐑌 𐐸𐐮𐑋 𐐺𐐨𐐿𐐫𐑆 𐐲𐑂 𐐸𐐮𐑆 𐑋𐐲𐑉𐑅𐐨. 𐐈𐑌𐐼 𐐸𐐨 𐑄𐐰𐐻 𐑅𐐯𐑃 𐑄𐐰𐐻 𐑊𐐮𐐻𐑊 𐐽𐐮𐑊𐐼𐑉𐐯𐑌 𐑌𐐨𐐼 𐐺𐐰𐐹𐐻𐐮𐑆𐑋, 𐐼𐐨𐑌𐐴𐐯𐑃 𐑄 𐑋𐐲𐑉𐑅𐐨𐑆 𐐲𐑂 𐐗𐑉𐐴𐑅𐐻, 𐐰𐑌𐐼 𐑅𐐯𐐻𐐯𐑃 𐐰𐐻 𐑌𐐫𐐻 𐑄 𐐰𐐻𐐬𐑌𐑋𐐯𐑌𐐻 𐐲𐑂 𐐸𐐮𐑋 𐐰𐑌𐐼 𐑄 𐐹𐐵𐐲𐑉 𐐲𐑂 𐐸𐐮𐑆 𐑉𐐨𐐼𐐯𐑋𐑇𐐲𐑌. 𐐎𐐬 𐐲𐑌𐐻𐐭 𐑅𐐲𐐽, 𐑁𐐫𐑉 𐑄𐐩 𐐪𐑉 𐐮𐑌 𐐼𐐩𐑌𐐾𐐲𐑉 𐐲𐑂 𐐼𐐯𐑃, 𐐸𐐯𐑊, 𐐰𐑌𐐼 𐐰𐑌 𐐯𐑌𐐼𐑊𐐯𐑅 𐐻𐐫𐑉𐑋𐐯𐑌𐐻. 𐐌 𐑅𐐹𐐨𐐿 𐐮𐐻 𐐺𐐬𐑊𐐼𐑊𐐨, 𐐘𐐱𐐼 𐐸𐐰𐑃 𐐿𐐱𐑋𐐰𐑌𐐼𐐯𐐼 𐑋𐐨. 𐐢𐐮𐑅𐐲𐑌 𐐲𐑌𐐻𐐭 𐑄𐐯𐑋 𐐰𐑌𐐼 𐑀𐐮𐑂 𐐸𐐨𐐼, 𐐫𐑉 𐑄𐐩 𐑅𐐻𐐰𐑌𐐼 𐐲𐑀𐐯𐑌𐑅𐐻 𐐷𐐭 𐐰𐐻 𐑄 𐐾𐐲𐐾𐑋𐐯𐑌𐐻-𐑅𐐨𐐻 𐐲𐑂 𐐗𐑉𐐴𐑅𐐻. 𐐙𐐫𐑉 𐐺𐐨𐐸𐐬𐑊𐐼 𐑄𐐰𐐻 𐐫𐑊 𐑊𐐮𐐻𐑊 𐐽𐐮𐑊𐐼𐑉𐐯𐑌 𐐪𐑉 𐐰𐑊𐐴𐑂 𐐮𐑌 𐐗𐑉𐐴𐑅𐐻, 𐐰𐑌𐐼 𐐫𐑊𐑅𐐬 𐐫𐑊 𐑄𐐩 𐑄𐐰𐐻 𐐪𐑉 𐐶𐐮𐑄𐐵𐐻 𐑄 𐑊𐐫. 𐐙𐐫𐑉 𐑄 𐐹𐐵𐐲𐑉 𐐲𐑂 𐑉𐐨𐐼𐐯𐑋𐑇𐐲𐑌 𐐿𐐲𐑋𐐯𐑃 𐐱𐑌 𐐫𐑊 𐑄𐐩 𐑄𐐰𐐻 𐐸𐐰𐑂 𐑌𐐬 𐑊𐐫. 𐐐𐐶𐐯𐑉𐑁𐐫𐑉, 𐐸𐐨 𐑄𐐰𐐻 𐐮𐑆 𐑌𐐱𐐻 𐐿𐐱𐑌𐐼𐐯𐑋𐐼, 𐐫𐑉 𐐸𐐨 𐑄𐐰𐐻 𐐮𐑆 𐐲𐑌𐐼𐐲𐑉 𐑌𐐬 𐐿𐐱𐑌𐐼𐐯𐑋𐑌𐐩𐑇𐐲𐑌, 𐐿𐐰𐑌 𐑌𐐱𐐻 𐑉𐐨𐐹𐐯𐑌𐐻; 𐐰𐑌𐐼 𐐲𐑌𐐻𐐭 𐑅𐐲𐐽 𐐺𐐰𐐹𐐻𐐮𐑆𐑋 𐐲𐑂𐐩𐑊𐐯𐑃 𐑌𐐲𐑃𐐮𐑍. 𐐒𐐲𐐻 𐐮𐐻 𐐮𐑆 𐑋𐐱𐐿𐐲𐑉𐐨 𐐺𐐨𐑁𐐬𐑉 𐐘𐐱𐐼, 𐐼𐐨𐑌𐐴𐐮𐑍 𐑄 𐑋𐐲𐑉𐑅𐐨𐑆 𐐲𐑂 𐐗𐑉𐐴𐑅𐐻, 𐐰𐑌𐐼 𐑄 𐐹𐐵𐐲𐑉 𐐲𐑂 𐐸𐐮𐑆 𐐐𐐬𐑊𐐨 𐐝𐐹𐐮𐑉𐐮𐐻, 𐐰𐑌𐐼 𐐹𐐳𐐻𐐮𐑍 𐐻𐑉𐐲𐑅𐐻 𐐮𐑌 𐐼𐐯𐐼 𐐶𐐲𐑉𐐿𐑅. 𐐒𐐨𐐸𐐬𐑊𐐼, 𐑋𐐴 𐑅𐐲𐑌, 𐑄𐐮𐑅 𐑃𐐮𐑍 𐐫𐐻 𐑌𐐱𐐻 𐐻𐐭 𐐺𐐨; 𐑁𐐫𐑉 𐑉𐐯𐐹𐐯𐑌𐐻𐐰𐑌𐑅 𐐮𐑆 𐐲𐑌𐐻𐐭 𐑄𐐯𐑋 𐑄𐐰𐐻 𐐪𐑉 𐐲𐑌𐐼𐐲𐑉 𐐿𐐱𐑌𐐼𐐯𐑋𐑌𐐩𐑇𐐲𐑌 𐐰𐑌𐐼 𐐲𐑌𐐼𐐲𐑉 𐑄 𐐿𐐲𐑉𐑅 𐐲𐑂 𐐩 𐐺𐑉𐐬𐐿𐐲𐑌 𐑊𐐫. 𐐈𐑌𐐼 𐑄 𐑁𐐲𐑉𐑅𐐻 𐑁𐑉𐐭𐐻𐑅 𐐲𐑂 𐑉𐐯𐐹𐐯𐑌𐐻𐐰𐑌𐑅 𐐮𐑆 𐐺𐐰𐐹𐐻𐐮𐑆𐑋; 𐐰𐑌𐐼 𐐺𐐰𐐹𐐻𐐮𐑆𐑋 𐐿𐐲𐑋𐐯𐑃 𐐺𐐴 𐑁𐐩𐑃, 𐐲𐑌𐐻𐐭 𐑄 𐑁𐐳𐑊𐑁𐐮𐑊𐐮𐑍 𐑄 𐐿𐐱𐑋𐐰𐑌𐐼𐑋𐐯𐑌𐐻𐑅; 𐐰𐑌𐐼 𐑄 𐑁𐐳𐑊𐑁𐐮𐑊𐐮𐑍 𐑄 𐐿𐐱𐑋𐐰𐑌𐐼𐑋𐐯𐑌𐐻𐑅 𐐺𐑉𐐮𐑍𐐯𐑃 𐑉𐐨𐑋𐐮𐑇𐐲𐑌 𐐲𐑂 𐑅𐐮𐑌𐑆; 𐐰𐑌𐐼 𐑄 𐑉𐐨𐑋𐐮𐑇𐐲𐑌 𐐲𐑂 𐑅𐐮𐑌𐑆 𐐺𐑉𐐮𐑍𐐯𐑃 𐑋𐐨𐐿𐑌𐐯𐑅, 𐐰𐑌𐐼 𐑊𐐬𐑊𐐨𐑌𐐯𐑅 𐐲𐑂 𐐸𐐪𐑉𐐻, 𐐰𐑌𐐼 𐐺𐐨𐐿𐐫𐑆 𐐲𐑂 𐑋𐐨𐐿𐑌𐐯𐑅 𐐰𐑌𐐼 𐑊𐐬𐑊𐐨𐑌𐐯𐑅 𐐲𐑂 𐐸𐐪𐑉𐐻, 𐐿𐐲𐑋𐐯𐑃 𐑄 𐑂𐐮𐑆𐐮𐐻𐐩𐑇𐐲𐑌 𐐲𐑂 𐑄 𐐐𐐬𐑊𐐨 𐐘𐐬𐑅𐐻, 𐐸𐐶𐐮𐐽 𐐗𐐲𐑋𐑁𐐲𐑉𐐻𐐲𐑉 𐑁𐐮𐑊𐐯𐑃 𐐶𐐮𐑄 𐐸𐐬𐐹 𐐰𐑌𐐼 𐐹𐐲𐑉𐑁𐐯𐐿𐐻 𐑊𐐲𐑂, 𐐸𐐶𐐮𐐽 𐑊𐐲𐑂 𐐯𐑌𐐼𐐷𐐭𐑉𐐯𐑃 𐐺𐐴 𐐼𐐮𐑊𐐮𐐾𐐯𐑌𐑅 𐐲𐑌𐐻𐐭 𐐹𐑉𐐯𐑉, 𐐲𐑌𐐻𐐮𐑊 𐑄 𐐯𐑌𐐼 𐑇𐐰𐑊 𐐿𐐲𐑋, 𐐸𐐶𐐯𐑌 𐐫𐑊 𐑄 𐑅𐐩𐑌𐐻𐑅 𐑇𐐰𐑊 𐐼𐐶𐐯𐑊 𐐶𐐮𐑄 𐐘𐐱𐐼. 𐐒𐐨𐐸𐐬𐑊𐐼, 𐑋𐐴 𐑅𐐲𐑌, 𐐌 𐐶𐐮𐑊 𐑉𐐴𐐻 𐐲𐑌𐐻𐐭 𐐷𐐭 𐐲𐑀𐐯𐑌, 𐐮𐑁 𐐌 𐑀𐐬 𐑌𐐱𐐻 𐐵𐐻 𐑅𐐭𐑌 𐐲𐑀𐐯𐑌𐑅𐐻 𐑄 𐐢𐐩𐑋𐐲𐑌𐐴𐐻𐑅. 𐐒𐐨𐐸𐐬𐑊𐐼, 𐑄 𐐹𐑉𐐴𐐼 𐐲𐑂 𐑄𐐮𐑅 𐑌𐐩𐑇𐐲𐑌, 𐐫𐑉 𐑄 𐐹𐐨𐐹𐑊 𐐲𐑂 𐑄 𐐤𐐨𐑁𐐴𐐻𐑅, 𐐸𐐰𐑃 𐐹𐑉𐐭𐑂𐐲𐑌 𐑄𐐯𐑉 𐐼𐐯𐑅𐐻𐑉𐐲𐐿𐑇𐐲𐑌, 𐐯𐐿𐑅𐐯𐐹𐐻 𐑄𐐩 𐑇𐐳𐐼 𐑉𐐨𐐹𐐯𐑌𐐻. 𐐑𐑉𐐩 𐑁𐐫𐑉 𐑄𐐯𐑋, 𐑋𐐴 𐑅𐐲𐑌, 𐑄𐐰𐐻 𐑉𐐯𐐹𐐯𐑌𐐻𐐰𐑌𐑅 𐑋𐐩 𐐿𐐲𐑋 𐐲𐑌𐐻𐐭 𐑄𐐯𐑋. 𐐒𐐲𐐻 𐐺𐐨𐐸𐐬𐑊𐐼, 𐐌 𐑁𐐨𐑉 𐑊𐐯𐑅𐐻 𐑄 𐐝𐐹𐐮𐑉𐐮𐐻 𐐸𐐰𐑃 𐑅𐐨𐑅𐐻 𐑅𐐻𐑉𐐴𐑂𐐮𐑍 𐐶𐐮𐑄 𐑄𐐯𐑋; 𐐰𐑌𐐼 𐐮𐑌 𐑄𐐮𐑅 𐐹𐐪𐑉𐐻 𐐲𐑂 𐑄 𐑊𐐰𐑌𐐼 𐑄𐐩 𐐪𐑉 𐐫𐑊𐑅𐐬 𐑅𐐨𐐿𐐮𐑍 𐐻𐐭

𐐹𐐳𐐻 𐐼𐐵𐑌 𐐫𐑊 𐐹𐐵𐑉 𐐰𐑌𐐼 𐐫𐑃𐐫𐑉𐐮𐐻𐐨 𐐸𐐶𐐮𐐽 𐐿𐐲𐑋𐐯𐑃 𐑁𐑉𐐲𐑋 𐐘𐐫𐐼; 𐐰𐑌𐐼 𐑄𐐩 𐐪𐑉 𐐼𐐨𐑌𐐴𐐮𐑍 𐑄 𐐐𐐬𐑊𐐨 𐐘𐐬𐑅𐐻. 𐐈𐑌𐐼 𐐪𐑁𐐻𐐲𐑉 𐑉𐐨𐐾𐐯𐐿𐐻𐐮𐑍 𐑅𐐬 𐑀𐑉𐐩𐐻 𐐰 𐑌𐐫𐑊𐐯𐐾, 𐑋𐐴 𐑅𐐲𐑌, 𐑄𐐩 𐑋𐐲𐑅𐐻 𐐹𐐯𐑉𐐮𐑇 𐑅𐐭𐑌, 𐐲𐑌𐐻𐐭 𐑄 𐑁𐐳𐑊𐑁𐐮𐑊𐐮𐑍 𐐲𐑂 𐑄 𐐹𐑉𐐱𐑁𐐯𐑅𐐨𐑆 𐐸𐐶𐐮𐐽 𐐶𐐲𐑉 𐑅𐐹𐐬𐐿𐐲𐑌 𐐺𐐴 𐑄 𐐹𐑉𐐱𐑁𐐯𐐻𐑅, 𐐰𐑆 𐐶𐐯𐑊 𐐰𐑆 𐑄 𐐶𐐲𐑉𐐼𐑆 𐐲𐑂 𐐪𐑉 𐐝𐐩𐑂𐐷𐐲𐑉 𐐸𐐮𐑋𐑅𐐯𐑊𐑁. 𐐙𐐩𐑉𐐶𐐯𐑊, 𐑋𐐴 𐑅𐐲𐑌, 𐐲𐑌𐐻𐐮𐑊 𐐌 𐑇𐐰𐑊 𐑉𐐴𐐻 𐐲𐑌𐐻𐐭 𐐷𐐭, 𐐫𐑉 𐑇𐐰𐑊 𐑋𐐨𐐻 𐐷𐐭 𐐲𐑀𐐯𐑌. 𐐁𐑋𐐯𐑌.

𐐕𐐰𐐹𐐻𐐲𐑉 IX.

𐐜 𐐝𐐯𐐿𐐲𐑌𐐼 𐐇𐐹𐐮𐑅𐐲𐑊 𐐲𐑂 𐐣𐐫𐑉𐑋𐐲𐑌 𐐻𐐭 𐐸𐐮𐑆 𐐝𐐲𐑌 𐐣𐐫𐑉𐐬𐑌𐐴.

1. 𐐣𐐴 𐐺𐐨𐑊𐐲𐑂𐐯𐐼 𐑅𐐲𐑌, 𐐌 𐑉𐐴𐐻 𐐲𐑌𐐻𐐭 𐐷𐐭 𐐲𐑀𐐯𐑌 𐑄𐐰𐐻 𐐷𐐨 𐑋𐐩 𐑌𐐬 𐑄𐐰𐐻 𐐌 𐐰𐑋 𐐷𐐯𐐻 𐐲𐑊𐐴𐑂; 𐐺𐐲𐐻 𐐌 𐑉𐐴𐐻 𐑅𐐲𐑋𐐸𐐶𐐱𐐻 𐐲𐑂 𐑄𐐰𐐻 𐐸𐐶𐐮𐐽 𐐮𐑆 𐑀𐑉𐐨𐑂𐐲𐑅. 𐐙𐐫𐑉 𐐺𐐨𐐸𐐬𐑊𐐼, 𐐌 𐐸𐐰𐑂 𐐸𐐰𐐼 𐐰 𐑅𐐬𐑉 𐐺𐐰𐐻𐐲𐑊 𐐶𐐮𐑄 𐑄 𐐢𐐩𐑋𐐲𐑌𐐴𐐻𐑅, 𐐮𐑌 𐐸𐐶𐐮𐐽 𐐶𐐨 𐐼𐐮𐐼 𐑌𐐱𐐻 𐐿𐐱𐑍𐐿𐐲𐑉; 𐐰𐑌𐐼 𐐂𐑉𐐿𐐨𐐰𐑌𐐻𐐲𐑅 𐐸𐐰𐑆 𐑁𐐫𐑊𐐲𐑌 𐐺𐐴 𐑄 𐑅𐐬𐑉𐐼, 𐐰𐑌𐐼 𐐫𐑊𐑅𐐬 𐐢𐐭𐑉𐐰𐑋 𐐰𐑌𐐼 𐐇𐑋𐑉𐐱𐑌; 𐐷𐐩, 𐐰𐑌𐐼 𐐶𐐨 𐐸𐐰𐑂 𐑊𐐱𐑅𐐻 𐐰 𐑀𐑉𐐩𐐻 𐑌𐐲𐑋𐐺𐐲𐑉 𐐲𐑂 𐐪𐑉 𐐽𐐬𐐮𐑅 𐑋𐐯𐑌. 𐐈𐑌𐐼 𐑌𐐵 𐐺𐐨𐐸𐐬𐑊𐐼, 𐑋𐐴 𐑅𐐲𐑌, 𐐌 𐑁𐐨𐑉 𐑊𐐯𐑅𐐻 𐑄 𐐢𐐩𐑋𐐲𐑌𐐴𐐻𐑅 𐑇𐐰𐑊 𐐼𐐨𐑅𐐻𐑉𐐱𐐮 𐑄𐐮𐑅 𐐹𐐨𐐹𐑊, 𐑁𐐫𐑉 𐑄𐐩 𐐼𐐭 𐑌𐐱𐐻 𐑉𐐨𐐹𐐯𐑌𐐻, 𐐰𐑌𐐼 𐐝𐐩𐐻𐐲𐑌 𐑅𐐻𐐲𐑉𐐯𐑃 𐑄𐐯𐑋 𐐲𐐹 𐐿𐐲𐑌𐐻𐐮𐑌𐐷𐐭𐐰𐑊𐐨 𐐻𐐭 𐐰𐑍𐑀𐐲𐑉 𐐶𐐲𐑌 𐐶𐐮𐑄 𐐰𐑌𐐲𐑄𐐲𐑉. 𐐒𐐨𐐸𐐬𐑊𐐼, 𐐌 𐐰𐑋 𐑊𐐩𐐺𐐲𐑉𐐮𐑍 𐐶𐐮𐑄 𐑄𐐯𐑋 𐐿𐐲𐑌𐐻𐐮𐑌𐐷𐐭𐐰𐑊𐐨; 𐐰𐑌𐐼 𐐸𐐶𐐯𐑌 𐐌 𐑅𐐹𐐨𐐿 𐑄 𐐶𐐲𐑉𐐼 𐐲𐑂 𐐘𐐱𐐼 𐐶𐐮𐑄 𐑇𐐪𐑉𐐹𐑌𐐯𐑅, 𐑄𐐩 𐐻𐑉𐐯𐑋𐐺𐐲𐑊 𐐰𐑌𐐼 𐐰𐑍𐑀𐐲𐑉 𐐲𐑀𐐯𐑌𐑅𐐻 𐑋𐐨; 𐐰𐑌𐐼 𐐸𐐶𐐯𐑌 𐐌 𐐷𐐭𐑆 𐑌𐐬 𐑇𐐪𐑉𐐹𐑌𐐯𐑅, 𐑄𐐩 𐐸𐐪𐑉𐐼𐐲𐑌 𐑄𐐯𐑉 𐐸𐐪𐑉𐐻𐑅 𐐲𐑀𐐯𐑌𐑅𐐻 𐐮𐐻; 𐐸𐐶𐐯𐑉𐑁𐐫𐑉 𐐌 𐑁𐐨𐑉 𐑊𐐯𐑅𐐻 𐑄 𐐝𐐹𐐮𐑉𐐮𐐻 𐐲𐑂 𐑄 𐐢𐐫𐑉𐐼 𐐸𐐰𐑃 𐑅𐐨𐑅𐐻 𐑅𐐻𐑉𐐴𐑂𐐮𐑍 𐐶𐐮𐑄 𐑄𐐯𐑋. 𐐙𐐫𐑉 𐑅𐐬 𐐯𐐿𐑅𐐨𐐼𐐮𐑍𐑊𐐨 𐐼𐐭 𐑄𐐩 𐐰𐑍𐑀𐐲𐑉 𐑄𐐰𐐻 𐐮𐐻 𐑅𐐨𐑋𐐯𐑃 𐐻𐐭 𐑋𐐨 𐑄𐐰𐐻 𐑄𐐩 𐐸𐐰𐐼 𐑌𐐬 𐑁𐐨𐑉 𐐲𐑂 𐐼𐐯𐑃; 𐐰𐑌𐐼 𐑄𐐩 𐐸𐐰𐑂 𐑊𐐱𐑅𐐻 𐑄𐐯𐑉 𐑊𐐲𐑂, 𐐶𐐲𐑌 𐐻𐐬𐑉𐐼𐑆 𐐰𐑌𐐲𐑄𐐲𐑉; 𐐰𐑌𐐼 𐑄𐐩 𐑃𐐲𐑉𐑅𐐻 𐐪𐑁𐐻𐐲𐑉 𐐺𐑊𐐲𐐼 𐐰𐑌𐐼 𐑉𐐨𐑂𐐯𐑌𐐾 𐐿𐐲𐑌𐐻𐐮𐑌𐐷𐐭𐐰𐑊𐐨. 𐐈𐑌𐐼 𐑌𐐵, 𐑋𐐴 𐐺𐐨𐑊𐐲𐑂𐐯𐐼 𐑅𐐲𐑌, 𐑌𐐱𐐻𐐶𐐮𐑃𐑅𐐻𐐰𐑌𐐼𐐮𐑍 𐑄𐐯𐑉 𐐸𐐪𐑉𐐼𐑌𐐯𐑅, 𐑊𐐯𐐻 𐐲𐑅 𐑊𐐩𐐺𐐲𐑉 𐐼𐐮𐑊𐐮𐐾𐐯𐑌𐐻𐑊𐐨; 𐑁𐐫𐑉 𐐮𐑁 𐐶𐐨 𐑇𐐳𐐼 𐑅𐐨𐑅 𐐻𐐭 𐑊𐐩𐐺𐐲𐑉, 𐐶𐐨 𐑇𐐳𐐼 𐐺𐐨 𐐺𐑉𐐫𐐻 𐐲𐑌𐐼𐐲𐑉 𐐿𐐱𐑌𐐼𐐯𐑋𐑌𐐩𐑇𐐲𐑌; 𐑁𐐫𐑉 𐐶𐐨 𐐸𐐰𐑂 𐐰 𐑊𐐩𐐺𐐲𐑉 𐐻𐐭 𐐹𐐲𐑉𐑁𐐫𐑉𐑋 𐐸𐐶𐐴𐑊𐑅𐐻 𐐮𐑌 𐑄𐐮𐑅 𐐻𐐰𐐺𐐲𐑉𐑌𐐰𐐿𐐲𐑊 𐐲𐑂 𐐿𐑊𐐩, 𐑄𐐰𐐻 𐐶𐐨 𐑋𐐩 𐐿𐐱𐑍𐐿𐐲𐑉 𐑄 𐐯𐑌𐐯𐑋𐐨 𐐲𐑂 𐐫𐑊 𐑉𐐴𐐽𐐲𐑅𐑌𐐯𐑅, 𐐰𐑌𐐼 𐑉𐐯𐑅𐐻 𐐪𐑉 𐑅𐐬𐑊𐑆 𐐮𐑌 𐑄 𐐿𐐮𐑍𐐼𐐲𐑋 𐐲𐑂 𐐘𐐱𐐼.

2. 𐐈𐑌𐐼 𐑌𐐵 𐐌 𐑉𐐴𐐻 𐑅𐐲𐑋𐐸𐐶𐐱𐐻 𐐿𐐱𐑌𐑅𐐲𐑉𐑌𐐮𐑍 𐑄 𐑅𐐲𐑁𐐲𐑉𐐮𐑍𐑆 𐐲𐑂 𐑄𐐮𐑅 𐐹𐐨𐐹𐑊. 𐐙𐐫𐑉 𐐰𐐿𐐫𐑉𐐼𐐮𐑍 𐐻𐐭 𐑄 𐑌𐐱𐑊𐐯𐐾 𐐸𐐶𐐮𐐽 𐐌 𐐸𐐰𐑂 𐑉𐐨𐑅𐐨𐑂𐐼 𐑁𐑉𐐲𐑋 𐐂𐑋𐐫𐑉𐐱𐑌, 𐐺𐐨𐐸𐐬𐑊𐐼, 𐑄 𐐢𐐩𐑋𐐲𐑌𐐴𐐻𐑅 𐐸𐐰𐑂 𐑋𐐯𐑌𐐨 𐐹𐑉𐐮𐑆𐐲𐑌𐐲𐑉𐑆, 𐐸𐐶𐐮𐐽 𐑄𐐩 𐐻𐐳𐐿 𐑁𐑉𐐲𐑋 𐑄 𐐻𐐵𐐲𐑉 𐐲𐑂 𐐟𐐯𐑉𐐮𐑆𐐪; 𐐰𐑌𐐼 𐑄𐐯𐑉 𐐶𐐲𐑉 𐑋𐐯𐑌, 𐐶𐐮𐑋𐐯𐑌, 𐐰𐑌𐐼 𐐽𐐮𐑊𐐼𐑉𐐯𐑌. 𐐈𐑌𐐼 𐑄 𐐸𐐲𐑆𐐺𐐲𐑌𐐼𐑆 𐐰𐑌𐐼 𐑁𐐪𐑄𐐲𐑉𐑆 𐐲𐑂 𐑄𐐬𐑆 𐐶𐐮𐑋𐐯𐑌 𐐰𐑌𐐼 𐐽𐐮𐑊𐐼𐑉𐐯𐑌 𐑄𐐩 𐐸𐐰𐑂 𐑅𐑊𐐩𐑌; 𐐰𐑌𐐼 𐑄𐐩 𐑁𐐨𐐼 𐑄 𐐶𐐮𐑋𐐯𐑌 𐐲𐐹𐐱𐑌 𐑄 𐑁𐑊𐐯𐑇 𐐲𐑂 𐑄𐐯𐑉 𐐸𐐲𐑆𐐺𐐲𐑌𐐼𐑆, 𐐰𐑌𐐼 𐑄 𐐽𐐮𐑊𐐼𐑉𐐯𐑌 𐐲𐐹𐐱𐑌 𐑄 𐑁𐑊𐐯𐑇 𐐲𐑂 𐑄𐐯𐑉 𐑁𐐪𐑄𐐲𐑉𐑆; 𐐰𐑌𐐼 𐑌𐐬 𐐶𐐫𐐻𐐲𐑉, 𐑅𐐩𐑂 𐐰 𐑊𐐮𐐻𐐲𐑊, 𐐼𐐭 𐑄𐐩 𐑀𐐮𐑂 𐐲𐑌𐐻𐐭 𐑄𐐯𐑋. 𐐈𐑌𐐼 𐑌𐐱𐐻𐐶𐐮𐑃𐑅𐐻𐐰𐑌𐐼𐐮𐑍 𐑄𐐮𐑅 𐑀𐑉𐐩𐐻 𐐲𐐺𐐱𐑋𐐮𐑌𐐩𐑇𐐲𐑌 𐐲𐑂 𐑄 𐐢𐐩𐑋𐐲𐑌𐐴𐐻𐑅, 𐐮𐐻 𐐼𐐲𐑃 𐑌𐐱𐐻 𐐯𐐿𐑅𐐨𐐼 𐑄𐐰𐐻 𐐲𐑂 𐐪𐑉 𐐹𐐨𐐹𐑊 𐐮𐑌 𐐣𐐫𐑉𐐨𐐰𐑌𐐻𐐲𐑋. 𐐙𐐫𐑉 𐐺𐐨𐐸𐐬𐑊𐐼, 𐑋𐐯𐑌𐐨 𐐲𐑂 𐑄 𐐼𐐫𐐻𐐲𐑉𐑆 𐐲𐑂 𐑄 𐐢𐐩𐑋𐐲𐑌𐐴𐐻𐑅 𐐸𐐰𐑂 𐑄𐐩 𐐻𐐩𐐿𐐲𐑌 𐐹𐑉𐐮𐑆𐐲𐑌𐐲𐑉𐑆; 𐐰𐑌𐐼 𐐪𐑁𐐻𐐲𐑉 𐐼𐐨𐐹𐑉𐐴𐑂𐐮𐑍 𐑄𐐯𐑋 𐐲𐑂 𐑄𐐰𐐻 𐐸𐐶𐐮𐐽 𐐶𐐱𐑆 𐑋𐐬𐑅𐐻 𐐼𐐨𐑉 𐐰𐑌𐐼 𐐹𐑉𐐯𐑇𐐲𐑅 𐐲𐐺𐐲𐑂 𐐫𐑊 𐑃𐐮𐑍𐑆, 𐐸𐐶𐐮𐐽 𐐮𐑆 𐐽𐐰𐑅𐐻𐐮𐐻𐐨 𐐰𐑌𐐼 𐑂𐐲𐑉𐐽𐐭; 𐐰𐑌𐐼 𐐪𐑁𐐻𐐲𐑉 𐑄𐐩 𐐸𐐰𐐼 𐐼𐐲𐑌 𐑄𐐮𐑅 𐑃𐐮𐑍, 𐑄𐐩 𐐼𐐮𐐼 𐑋𐐲𐑉𐐼𐐲𐑉 𐑄𐐯𐑋 𐐮𐑌 𐐰 𐑋𐐬𐑅𐐻 𐐿𐑉𐐭𐐯𐑊 𐑋𐐰𐑌𐐲𐑉, 𐐻𐐫𐑉𐐽𐐲𐑉𐐮𐑍 𐑄𐐯𐑉 𐐺𐐱𐐼𐐨𐑆 𐐨𐑂𐐲𐑌 𐐲𐑌𐐻𐐭 𐐼𐐯𐑃; 𐐰𐑌𐐼 𐐪𐑁𐐻𐐲𐑉 𐑄𐐩 𐐸𐐰𐑂 𐐼𐐲𐑌 𐑄𐐮𐑅, 𐑄𐐩 𐐼𐐨𐑂𐐵𐑉 𐑄𐐯𐑉 𐑁𐑊𐐯𐑇 𐑊𐐴𐐿 𐐲𐑌𐐻𐐭 𐐶𐐴𐑊𐐼 𐐺𐐨𐑅𐐻𐑅, 𐐺𐐨𐐿𐐫𐑆 𐐲𐑂 𐑄 𐐸𐐪𐑉𐐼𐑌𐐯𐑅 𐐲𐑂 𐑄𐐯𐑉 𐐸𐐪𐑉𐐻𐑅; 𐐰𐑌𐐼 𐑄𐐩 𐐼𐐭 𐐮𐐻 𐑁𐐫𐑉 𐐰 𐐻𐐬𐐿𐐲𐑌 𐐲𐑂 𐐺𐑉𐐩𐑂𐐲𐑉𐐨. 𐐄 𐑋𐐴 𐐺𐐨𐑊𐐲𐑂𐐯𐐼 𐑅𐐲𐑌, 𐐸𐐵 𐐿𐐰𐑌 𐐰 𐐹𐐨𐐹𐑊 𐑊𐐴𐐿 𐑄𐐮𐑅, 𐑄𐐰𐐻 𐐪𐑉 𐐶𐐮𐑄𐐵𐐻 𐑅𐐮𐑂𐐮𐑊𐐮𐑆𐐩𐑇𐐲𐑌; (𐐈𐑌𐐼 𐐬𐑌𐑊𐐨 𐐰 𐑁𐐷𐐭 𐐷𐐨𐑉𐑆 𐐸𐐰𐑂 𐐹𐐰𐑅𐐻

𐐲𐐶𐐩, 𐐰𐑌𐐼 𐑄𐐩 𐐶𐐲𐑉 𐐪 𐑅𐐮𐑂𐐮𐑊 𐐰𐑌𐐼 𐐪 𐐼𐐨𐑊𐐴𐐻𐑅𐐲𐑋 𐐹𐐨𐐹𐑊;) 𐐺𐐲𐐻 𐐄, 𐑋𐐴 𐑅𐐲𐑌, 𐐸𐐵 𐐿𐐰𐑌 𐐪 𐐹𐐨𐐹𐑊 𐑊𐐴𐐿 𐑄𐐮𐑅 𐐸𐐭𐑆 𐐼𐐨𐑊𐐴𐐻 𐐮𐑆 𐐮𐑌 𐑅𐐬 𐑋𐐲𐐽 𐐰𐐺𐐱𐑋𐐮𐑌𐐩𐑇𐐲𐑌, 𐐸𐐵 𐐿𐐰𐑌 𐐶𐐨 𐐯𐐿𐑅𐐹𐐯𐐿𐐻 𐑄𐐰𐐻 𐐘𐐱𐐼 𐐶𐐮𐑊 𐑅𐐻𐐩 𐐸𐐮𐑆 𐐸𐐰𐑌𐐼 𐐮𐑌 𐐾𐐲𐐾𐑋𐐯𐑌𐐻 𐐰𐑀𐐯𐑌𐑅𐐻 𐐲𐑅? 𐐒𐐨𐐸𐐬𐑊𐐼, 𐑋𐐴 𐐸𐐪𐑉𐐻 𐐿𐑉𐐴𐑆, 𐐎𐐬 𐐲𐑌𐐻𐐭 𐑄𐐮𐑅 𐐹𐐨𐐹𐑊. 𐐗𐐲𐑋 𐐵𐐻 𐐮𐑌 𐐾𐐲𐐾𐑋𐐯𐑌𐐻, 𐐄 𐐘𐐱𐐼, 𐐰𐑌𐐼 𐐸𐐴𐐼 𐑄𐐩𐑉 𐑅𐐮𐑌𐑆, 𐐰𐑌𐐼 𐐶𐐮𐐿𐐯𐐼𐑌𐐯𐑅, 𐐰𐑌𐐼 𐐰𐐺𐐱𐑋𐐮𐑌𐐩𐑇𐐲𐑌𐑆 𐑁𐑉𐐱𐑋 𐐺𐐨𐑁𐐬𐑉 𐑄𐐴 𐑁𐐩𐑅. 𐐈𐑌𐐼 𐐰𐑀𐐯𐑌, 𐑋𐐴 𐑅𐐲𐑌, 𐑄𐐩𐑉 𐐪𐑉 𐑋𐐯𐑌𐐨 𐐶𐐮𐐼𐐬𐑆 𐐰𐑌𐐼 𐑄𐐩𐑉 𐐼𐐫𐐻𐐲𐑉𐑆, 𐐸𐐭 𐑉𐐨𐑋𐐩𐑌 𐐮𐑌 𐐟𐐯𐑉𐐮𐑆𐐪; 𐐰𐑌𐐼 𐑄𐐰𐐻 𐐹𐐪𐑉𐐻 𐐱𐑂 𐑄 𐐹𐑉𐐬𐑂𐐮𐑈𐐲𐑌𐑆 𐐸𐐶𐐮𐐽 𐑄 𐐢𐐰𐑋𐐲𐑌𐐴𐐻𐑅 𐐼𐐮𐐼 𐑌𐐱𐐻 𐐿𐐰𐑉𐐨 𐐲𐐶𐐩, 𐐺𐐨𐐸𐐬𐑊𐐼, 𐑄 𐐪𐑉𐑋𐐨 𐐱𐑂 𐐞𐐯𐑌𐐨𐑁𐐴 𐐸𐐰𐑆 𐐿𐐰𐑉𐐨𐐼 𐐲𐐶𐐩, 𐐰𐑌𐐼 𐑊𐐯𐑁𐐻 𐑄𐐯𐑋 𐐻𐐭 𐐶𐐪𐑌𐐼𐐲𐑉 𐐸𐐶𐐮𐑄𐐲𐑉𐑅𐐬𐐯𐑂𐐲𐑉 𐑄𐐩 𐐿𐐰𐑌 𐑁𐐫𐑉 𐑁𐐭𐐼; 𐐰𐑌𐐼 𐑋𐐯𐑌𐐨 𐐬𐑊𐐼 𐐶𐐮𐑋𐐯𐑌 𐐼𐐭 𐑁𐐩𐑌𐐻 𐐺𐐴 𐑄 𐐶𐐩 𐐰𐑌𐐼 𐐼𐐴. 𐐈𐑌𐐼 𐑄 𐐪𐑉𐑋𐐨 𐐸𐐶𐐮𐐽 𐐮𐑆 𐐶𐐮𐑃 𐑋𐐨 𐐮𐑆 𐐶𐐨𐐿; 𐐰𐑌𐐼 𐑄 𐐪𐑉𐑋𐐨𐑆 𐐱𐑂 𐑄 𐐢𐐰𐑋𐐲𐑌𐐴𐐻𐑅 𐐪𐑉 𐐺𐐨𐐻𐐶𐐮𐐿𐑅𐐻 𐐟𐐯𐑉𐐮𐑆𐐪 𐐰𐑌𐐼 𐑋𐐨; 𐐰𐑌𐐼 𐐰𐑆 𐑋𐐯𐑌𐐨 𐐰𐑆 𐐸𐐰𐑂 𐑁𐑊𐐯𐐼 𐐻𐐭 𐑄 𐐪𐑉𐑋𐐨 𐐱𐑂 𐐁𐑉𐐲𐑌, 𐐸𐐰𐑂 𐑁𐐫𐑊𐑌 𐑂𐐮𐐿𐐻𐐮𐑋𐑆 𐐻𐐭 𐑄𐐩𐑉 𐐫𐑁𐐳𐑊 𐐺𐑉𐐭𐐻𐐰𐑊𐐮𐐻𐐨.

3. 𐐄 𐑄 𐐼𐐨𐐹𐑉𐐰𐑂𐐮𐐻𐐨 𐐱𐑂 𐑋𐐴 𐐹𐐨𐐹𐑊! 𐐜𐐩 𐐪𐑉 𐐶𐐮𐑄𐐵𐐻 𐐫𐑉𐐼𐐲𐑉 𐐰𐑌𐐼 𐐶𐐮𐑄𐐵𐐻 𐑋𐐲𐑉𐑅𐐨. 𐐒𐐨𐐸𐐬𐑊𐐼, 𐐌 𐐰𐑋 𐐺𐐲𐐻 𐐪 𐑋𐐰𐑌, 𐐰𐑌𐐼 𐐌 𐐸𐐰𐑂 𐐺𐐲𐐻 𐑄 𐑅𐐻𐑉𐐯𐑍𐑃 𐐱𐑂 𐐪 𐑋𐐰𐑌, 𐐰𐑌𐐼 𐐌 𐐿𐐰𐑌𐐱𐐻 𐐯𐑌𐐨 𐑊𐐱𐑍𐑀𐐲𐑉 𐐯𐑌𐑁𐐬𐑉𐑅 𐑋𐐴 𐐿𐐱𐑋𐐰𐑌𐐼𐑆; 𐐰𐑌𐐼 𐑄𐐩 𐐸𐐰𐑂 𐐺𐐨𐐿𐐲𐑋 𐑅𐐻𐑉𐐱𐑍 𐐮𐑌 𐑄𐐩𐑉 𐐹𐐲𐑉𐑂𐐲𐑉𐑇𐐲𐑌; 𐐰𐑌𐐼 𐑄𐐩 𐐪𐑉 𐐲𐑊𐐴𐐿 𐐺𐑉𐐭𐐻𐐲𐑊, 𐑅𐐹𐐩𐑉𐐮𐑍 𐑌𐐲𐑌, 𐑌𐐨𐑄𐐲𐑉 𐐬𐑊𐐼 𐑌𐐫𐑉 𐐷𐐲𐑍; 𐐰𐑌𐐼 𐑄𐐩 𐐼𐐨𐑊𐐴𐐻 𐐮𐑌 𐐯𐑂𐐲𐑉𐐨𐑃𐐮𐑍 𐑅𐐩𐑂 𐑄𐐰𐐻 𐐸𐐶𐐮𐐽 𐐮𐑆 𐑀𐐳𐐼; 𐐰𐑌𐐼 𐑄 𐑅𐐲𐑁𐐲𐑉𐐮𐑍 𐐱𐑂 𐐵𐑉 𐐶𐐮𐑋𐐯𐑌 𐐰𐑌𐐼 𐐵𐑉 𐐽𐐮𐑊𐐼𐑉𐐯𐑌 𐐲𐐹𐐱𐑌 𐐫𐑊 𐑄 𐑁𐐩𐑅 𐐱𐑂 𐑄𐐮𐑅 𐑊𐐰𐑌𐐼 𐐼𐐲𐑃 𐐯𐐿𐑅𐐨𐐼 𐐯𐑂𐐲𐑉𐐨𐑃𐐮𐑍; 𐐷𐐩, 𐐻𐐲𐑍 𐐿𐐰𐑌𐐱𐐻 𐐻𐐯𐑊, 𐑌𐐨𐑄𐐲𐑉 𐐿𐐰𐑌 𐐮𐐻 𐐺𐐨 𐑉𐐮𐐻𐑌. 𐐈𐑌𐐼 𐑌𐐵, 𐑋𐐴 𐑅𐐲𐑌, 𐐌 𐐼𐐶𐐯𐑊 𐑌𐐬 𐑊𐐱𐑍𐑀𐐲𐑉 𐐲𐐹𐐱𐑌 𐑄𐐮𐑅 𐐸𐐱𐑉𐐮𐐺𐑊 𐑅𐐨𐑌. 𐐒𐐨𐐸𐐬𐑊𐐼, 𐑄𐐵 𐑌𐐬𐐯𐑅𐐻 𐑄 𐐶𐐮𐐿𐐯𐐼𐑌𐐯𐑅 𐐱𐑂 𐑄𐐮𐑅 𐐹𐐨𐐹𐑊; 𐑄𐐵 𐑌𐐬𐐯𐑅𐐻 𐑄𐐰𐐻 𐑄𐐩 𐐪𐑉 𐐶𐐮𐑄𐐵𐐻 𐐹𐑉𐐮𐑌𐑅𐐮𐐹𐑊, 𐐰𐑌𐐼 𐐹𐐰𐑅𐐻 𐑁𐐨𐑊𐐮𐑍; 𐐰𐑌𐐼 𐑄𐐩𐑉 𐐶𐐮𐐿𐐯𐐼𐑌𐐯𐑅 𐐼𐐲𐑃 𐐯𐐿𐑅𐐨𐐼 𐑄𐐰𐐻 𐐱𐑂 𐑄 𐐢𐐰𐑋𐐲𐑌𐐴𐐻𐑅. 𐐒𐐨𐐸𐐬𐑊𐐼, 𐑋𐐴 𐑅𐐲𐑌, 𐐌 𐐿𐐰𐑌𐐱𐐻 𐑉𐐯𐐿𐐱𐑋𐐯𐑌𐐼 𐑄𐐯𐑋 𐐲𐑌𐐻𐐭 𐐘𐐱𐐼, 𐑊𐐯𐑅𐐻 𐐸𐐨 𐑇𐐳𐐼 𐑅𐑋𐐴𐐻 𐑋𐐨. 𐐒𐐲𐐻 𐐺𐐨𐐸𐐬𐑊𐐼, 𐑋𐐴 𐑅𐐲𐑌, 𐐌 𐑉𐐯𐐿𐐱𐑋𐐯𐑌𐐼 𐑄𐐨 𐐲𐑌𐐻𐐭 𐐘𐐱𐐼, 𐐰𐑌𐐼 𐐌 𐐻𐑉𐐲𐑅𐐻 𐐮𐑌 𐐗𐑉𐐴𐑅𐐻 𐑄𐐰𐐻 𐑄𐐵 𐐶𐐮𐑊𐐻 𐐺𐐨 𐑅𐐩𐑂𐐼; 𐐰𐑌𐐼 𐐌 𐐹𐑉𐐩 𐐲𐑌𐐻𐐭 𐐘𐐱𐐼 𐑄𐐰𐐻 𐐸𐐨 𐐶𐐮𐑊 𐑅𐐹𐐩𐑉 𐑄𐐴 𐑊𐐴𐑁, 𐐻𐐭 𐐶𐐮𐐻𐑌𐐯𐑅 𐑄 𐑉𐐨𐐻𐐲𐑉𐑌 𐐱𐑂 𐐸𐐮𐑆 𐐹𐐨𐐹𐑊 𐐲𐑌𐐻𐐭 𐐸𐐮𐑋, 𐐫𐑉 𐑄𐐩𐑉 𐐲𐐻𐐲𐑉 𐐼𐐨𐑅𐐻𐑉𐐲𐐿𐑇𐐲𐑌; 𐑁𐐫𐑉 𐐌 𐑌𐐬 𐑄𐐰𐐻 𐑄𐐩 𐑋𐐲𐑅𐐻 𐐹𐐯𐑉𐐮𐑇, 𐐯𐐿𐑅𐐯𐐹𐐻 𐑄𐐩 𐑉𐐨𐐹𐐯𐑌𐐻 𐐰𐑌𐐼 𐑉𐐨𐐻𐐲𐑉𐑌 𐐲𐑌𐐻𐐭 𐐸𐐮𐑋; 𐐰𐑌𐐼 𐐮𐑁 𐑄𐐩 𐐹𐐯𐑉𐐮𐑇, 𐐮𐐻 𐐶𐐮𐑊 𐐺𐐨 𐑊𐐴𐐿 𐐲𐑌𐐻𐐭 𐑄 𐐖𐐯𐑉𐐯𐐼𐐴𐐻𐑅, 𐐺𐐨𐐿𐐫𐑆 𐐱𐑂 𐑄 𐐶𐐮𐑊𐑁𐐳𐑊𐑌𐐯𐑅 𐐱𐑂 𐑄𐐩𐑉 𐐸𐐪𐑉𐐻𐑅, 𐑅𐐨𐐿𐐮𐑍 𐑁𐐫𐑉 𐐺𐑊𐐲𐐼 𐐰𐑌𐐼 𐑉𐐨𐑂𐐯𐑌𐐾. 𐐈𐑌𐐼 𐐮𐑁 𐐮𐐻 𐑅𐐬 𐐺𐐨 𐑄𐐰𐐻 𐑄𐐩 𐐹𐐯𐑉𐐮𐑇, 𐐶𐐨 𐑌𐐬 𐑄𐐰𐐻 𐑋𐐯𐑌𐐨 𐐱𐑂 𐐵𐑉 𐐺𐑉𐐯𐑄𐑉𐐯𐑌 𐐸𐐰𐑂 𐐼𐐨𐑆𐐲𐑉𐐻𐐯𐐼 𐐬𐑂𐐲𐑉 𐐲𐑌𐐻𐐭 𐑄 𐐢𐐰𐑋𐐲𐑌𐐴𐐻𐑅, 𐐰𐑌𐐼 𐑋𐐯𐑌𐐨 𐑋𐐬𐑉 𐐶𐐮𐑊 𐐫𐑊𐑅𐐬 𐐼𐐨𐑆𐐲𐑉𐐻 𐐬𐑂𐐲𐑉 𐐲𐑌𐐻𐐭 𐑄𐐯𐑋; 𐐸𐐶𐐩𐑉𐑁𐐬𐑉, 𐑉𐐴𐐻 𐑅𐐲𐑋𐐸𐐶𐐱𐐻 𐐪 𐑁𐑏 𐑃𐐮𐑍𐑆, 𐐮𐑁 𐑄𐐵 𐐪𐑉𐐻 𐑅𐐹𐐩𐑉𐐼, 𐐰𐑌𐐼 𐐌 𐑇𐐰𐑊 𐐹𐐯𐑉𐐮𐑇 𐐰𐑌𐐼 𐑌𐐱𐐻 𐑅𐐨 𐑄𐐨; 𐐺𐐲𐐻 𐐌 𐐻𐑉𐐲𐑅𐐻 𐑄𐐰𐐻 𐐌 𐑋𐐩 𐑅𐐨 𐑄𐐨 𐑅𐐭𐑌; 𐑁𐐫𐑉 𐐌 𐐸𐐰𐑂 𐑅𐐩𐐿𐑉𐐯𐐼 𐑉𐐯𐐿𐐫𐑉𐐼𐑆 𐑄𐐰𐐻 𐐌 𐐶𐐳𐐼 𐐼𐐨𐑊𐐮𐑂𐐲𐑉 𐐲𐐹 𐐲𐑌𐐻𐐭 𐑄𐐨. 𐐣𐐴 𐑅𐐲𐑌, 𐐺𐐨 𐑁𐐩𐑃𐑁𐐳𐑊 𐐮𐑌 𐐗𐑉𐐴𐑅𐐻; 𐐰𐑌𐐼 𐑋𐐩 𐑌𐐱𐐻 𐑄 𐑃𐐮𐑍𐑆 𐐸𐐶𐐮𐐽 𐐌 𐐸𐐰𐑂 𐑉𐐮𐐻𐑌 𐑀𐑉𐐨𐑂 𐑄𐐨, 𐐻𐐭 𐐶𐐩 𐑄𐐨 𐐼𐐵𐑌 𐐲𐑌𐐻𐐭 𐐼𐐯𐑃; 𐐺𐐲𐐻 𐑋𐐩 𐐗𐑉𐐴𐑅𐐻 𐑊𐐮𐑁𐐻 𐑄𐐨 𐐲𐐹, 𐐰𐑌𐐼 𐑋𐐩 𐐸𐐮𐑆 𐑅𐐲𐑁𐐲𐑉𐐮𐑍𐑆 𐐰𐑌𐐼 𐐼𐐯𐑃, 𐐰𐑌𐐼 𐑄 𐑇𐐬𐐮𐑍 𐐸𐐮𐑆 𐐺𐐱𐐼𐐨 𐐲𐑌𐐻𐐭 𐐵𐑉 𐑁𐐪𐑄𐐲𐑉𐑆, 𐐰𐑌𐐼 𐐸𐐮𐑆 𐑋𐐲𐑉𐑅𐐨 𐐰𐑌𐐼 𐑊𐐱𐑍-𐑅𐐲𐑁𐐲𐑉𐐮𐑍, 𐐰𐑌𐐼 𐑄 𐐸𐐬𐐹 𐐱𐑂 𐐸𐐮𐑆 𐑀𐑊𐐬𐑉𐐨 𐐰𐑌𐐼 𐐱𐑂 𐐨𐐻𐐲𐑉𐑌𐐲𐑊 𐑊𐐴𐑁, 𐑉𐐯𐑅𐐻 𐐮𐑌 𐐷𐐭𐑉 𐑋𐐴𐑌𐐼 𐑁𐐫𐑉𐐯𐑂𐐲𐑉. 𐐈𐑌𐐼 𐑋𐐩 𐑄 𐑀𐑉𐐩𐑅 𐐱𐑂 𐐘𐐱𐐼 𐑄 𐐙𐐪𐑄𐐲𐑉, 𐐸𐐭𐑆 𐑃𐑉𐐬𐑌 𐐮𐑆 𐐸𐐴 𐐮𐑌 𐑄 𐐸𐐯𐑂𐐲𐑌𐑆, 𐐰𐑌𐐼 𐐵𐑉 𐐢𐐫𐑉𐐼 𐐖𐐨𐑆𐐲𐑅 𐐗𐑉𐐴𐑅𐐻, 𐐸𐐭 𐑅𐐮𐐻𐐯𐑃 𐐱𐑌 𐑄 𐑉𐐴𐐻 𐐸𐐰𐑌𐐼 𐐱𐑂 𐐸𐐮𐑆 𐐹𐐵𐐲𐑉, 𐐲𐑌𐐻𐐮𐑊 𐐫𐑊 𐑃𐐮𐑍𐑆 𐑇𐐰𐑊 𐐺𐐨𐐿𐐲𐑋 𐑅𐐲𐐺𐐾𐐯𐐿𐐻 𐐲𐑌𐐻𐐭 𐐸𐐮𐑋, 𐐺𐐨, 𐐰𐑌𐐼 𐐰𐐺𐐴𐐼 𐐶𐐮𐑃 𐐷𐐭 𐑁𐐫𐑉𐐯𐑂𐐲𐑉. 𐐁𐑋𐐯𐑌.

𐐕𐐰𐐹𐐻𐐲𐑉 X.

1. 𐐤𐐵 𐐌, 𐐣𐐬𐑉𐐬𐑌𐐴, 𐑉𐐴𐐻 𐑅𐐲𐑋𐐸𐐶𐐱𐐻 𐐰𐑆 𐑅𐐨𐑋𐐯𐑃 𐑋𐐨 𐑀𐐳𐐼; 𐐰𐑌𐐼 𐐌 𐑉𐐴𐐻 𐐲𐑌𐐻𐐭 𐑋𐐴 𐐺𐑉𐐯𐑄𐑉𐐯𐑌, 𐑄 𐐢𐐰𐑋𐐲𐑌𐐴𐐻𐑅; 𐐰𐑌𐐼 𐐌 𐐶𐐳𐐼 𐑄𐐰𐐻 𐑄𐐩 𐑇𐐳𐐼 𐑌𐐬 𐑄𐐰𐐻 𐑋𐐬𐑉 𐑄𐐰𐑌 𐑁𐐬𐑉 𐐸𐐲𐑌𐐼𐑉𐐯𐐼 𐐰𐑌𐐼 𐐻𐐶𐐯𐑌𐐻𐐨 𐐷𐐨𐑉𐑆 𐐸𐐰𐑂 𐐹𐐰𐑅𐐻 𐐰𐐶𐐩 𐑅𐐮𐑌𐑅 𐑄 𐑅𐐴𐑌 𐐶𐐱𐑆 𐑀𐐮𐑂𐐯𐑌 𐐱𐑂 𐑄 𐐿𐐲𐑋𐐮𐑍 𐐱𐑂 𐐗𐑉𐐴𐑅𐐻. 𐐈𐑌𐐼 𐐌 𐑅𐐨𐑊 𐐲𐐹 𐑄𐐨𐑆 𐑉𐐯𐐿𐐫𐑉𐐼𐑆, 𐐪𐑁𐐻𐐲𐑉 𐐌 𐐸𐐰𐑂 𐑅𐐹𐐬𐐿𐐯𐑌 𐐲 𐑁𐑏 𐐶𐐲𐑉𐐼𐑆 𐐺𐐴 𐐶𐐩 𐐱𐑂 𐐯𐑀𐑆𐐫𐑉𐐻𐐩𐑇𐐲𐑌 𐐲𐑌𐐻𐐭 𐐷𐐭. 𐐒𐐨𐐸𐐬𐑊𐐼, 𐐌 𐐶𐐳𐐼 𐐯𐑀𐑆𐐫𐑉𐐻 𐐷𐐭, 𐑄𐐰𐐻 𐐸𐐶𐐯𐑌 𐐷 𐑇𐐰𐑊 𐑉𐐨𐐼 𐑄𐐨𐑆 𐑃𐐮𐑍𐑆, 𐐮𐑁 𐐮𐐻 𐐺 𐐶𐐮𐑆𐐼𐐲𐑋 𐐮𐑌 𐐘𐐱𐐼 𐑄𐐰𐐻 𐐷 𐑇𐐳𐐼 𐑉𐐨𐐼 𐑄𐐯𐑋, 𐑄𐐰𐐻 𐐷 𐐶𐐳𐐼 𐑉𐐨𐑋𐐯𐑋𐐺𐐲𐑉 𐐸𐐵 𐑋𐐲𐑉𐑅𐐮𐑁𐐳𐑊 𐑄 𐐢𐐫𐑉𐐼 𐐸𐐰𐑃 𐐺𐐮𐑌 𐐲𐑌𐐻𐐭 𐑄 𐐽𐐮𐑊𐐼𐑉𐐯𐑌 𐐱𐑂 𐑋𐐯𐑌, 𐑁𐑉𐐱𐑋 𐑄 𐐿𐑉𐐨𐐩𐑇𐐲𐑌 𐐱𐑂 𐐁𐐼𐐲𐑋 𐐨𐑂𐐯𐑌 𐐼𐐵𐑌 𐐲𐑌𐐻𐐮𐑊 𐑄 𐐻𐐴𐑋 𐑄𐐰𐐻 𐐷 𐑇𐐰𐑊 𐑉𐐨𐑅𐐨𐑂 𐑄𐐨𐑆 𐑃𐐮𐑍𐑆 𐐰𐑌𐐼 𐐹𐐱𐑌𐐼𐐲𐑉 𐐮𐐻 𐐮𐑌 𐐷𐐭𐑉 𐐸𐐪𐑉𐐻𐑅. 𐐈𐑌𐐼 𐐸𐐶𐐯𐑌 𐐷 𐑇𐐰𐑊 𐑉𐐨𐑅𐐨𐑂 𐑄𐐨𐑆 𐑃𐐮𐑍𐑆, 𐐌 𐐶𐐳𐐼 𐐯𐑀𐑆𐐫𐑉𐐻 𐐷𐐭 𐑄𐐰𐐻 𐐷 𐐶𐐳𐐼 𐐪𐑅𐐿 𐐘𐐱𐐼, 𐑄 𐐀𐐻𐐲𐑉𐑌𐐲𐑊 𐐙𐐪𐑄𐐲𐑉, 𐐮𐑌 𐑄 𐑌𐐩𐑋 𐐱𐑂 𐐗𐑉𐐴𐑅𐐻, 𐐮𐑁 𐑄𐐨𐑆 𐑃𐐮𐑍𐑆 𐐪𐑉 𐑌𐐱𐐻 𐐻𐑉𐐭; 𐐰𐑌𐐼 𐐮𐑁 𐐷 𐑇𐐰𐑊 𐐪𐑅𐐿 𐐶𐐮𐑄 𐐲 𐑅𐐮𐑌𐑅𐐨𐑉 𐐸𐐪𐑉𐐻, 𐐶𐐮𐑄 𐑉𐐨𐐲𐑊 𐐮𐑌𐐻𐐯𐑌𐐻, 𐐸𐐰𐑂𐐮𐑍 𐑁𐐩𐑃 𐐮𐑌 𐐗𐑉𐐴𐑅𐐻, 𐐸𐐨 𐐶𐐮𐑊 𐑋𐐰𐑌𐐮𐑁𐐯𐑅𐐻 𐑄 𐐻𐑉𐐭𐑃 𐐱𐑂 𐐮𐐻 𐐲𐑌𐐻𐐭 𐐷𐐭, 𐐺𐐴 𐑄 𐐹𐐵𐐲𐑉 𐐱𐑂 𐑄 𐐐𐐬𐑊𐐨 𐐘𐐬𐑅𐐻, 𐐰𐑌𐐼 𐐺𐐴 𐑄 𐐹𐐵𐐲𐑉 𐐱𐑂 𐑄 𐐐𐐬𐑊𐐨 𐐘𐐬𐑅𐐻 𐐷 𐑋𐐩 𐑌𐐬 𐑄 𐐻𐑉𐐭𐑃 𐐱𐑂 𐐫𐑊 𐑃𐐮𐑍𐑆. 𐐈𐑌𐐼 𐐸𐐶𐐱𐐻𐑅𐐬𐐯𐑂𐐲𐑉 𐑃𐐮𐑍 𐐮𐑆 𐑀𐐳𐐼 𐐮𐑆 𐐾𐐲𐑅𐐻 𐐰𐑌𐐼 𐐻𐑉𐐭; 𐐸𐐶𐐯𐑉𐑁𐐬𐑉, 𐑌𐐲𐑃𐐮𐑍 𐑄𐐰𐐻 𐐮𐑆 𐑀𐐳𐐼 𐐼𐐨𐑌𐐴𐐯𐑃 𐑄 𐐗𐑉𐐴𐑅𐐻, 𐐺𐐲𐐻 𐐰𐐿𐑌𐐱𐑊𐐯𐐾𐐯𐑃 𐑄𐐰𐐻 𐐸𐐨 𐐮𐑆. 𐐈𐑌𐐼 𐐷 𐑋𐐩 𐑌𐐬 𐑄𐐰𐐻 𐐸𐐨 𐐮𐑆, 𐐺𐐴 𐑄 𐐹𐐵𐐲𐑉 𐐱𐑂 𐑄 𐐐𐐬𐑊𐐨 𐐘𐐬𐑅𐐻; 𐐸𐐶𐐯𐑉𐑁𐐬𐑉 𐐌 𐐶𐐳𐐼 𐐯𐑀𐑆𐐫𐑉𐐻 𐐷𐐭, 𐑄𐐰𐐻 𐐷 𐐼𐐨𐑌𐐴 𐑌𐐱𐐻 𐑄 𐐹𐐵𐐲𐑉 𐐱𐑂 𐐘𐐱𐐼; 𐑁𐐫𐑉 𐐸𐐨 𐐶𐐲𐑉𐐿𐐯𐑃 𐐺𐐴 𐐹𐐵𐐲𐑉, 𐐰𐐿𐐫𐑉𐐼𐐮𐑍 𐐻𐐭 𐑄 𐑁𐐩𐑃 𐐱𐑂 𐑄 𐐽𐐮𐑊𐐼𐑉𐐯𐑌 𐐱𐑂 𐑋𐐯𐑌, 𐑄 𐑅𐐩𐑋 𐐻𐐭-𐐼𐐩, 𐐰𐑌𐐼 𐐻𐐭-𐑋𐐱𐑉𐐬, 𐐰𐑌𐐼 𐑁𐐫𐑉 𐐯𐑂𐐲𐑉. 𐐈𐑌𐐼 𐐰𐑀𐐯𐑌 𐐌 𐐯𐑀𐑆𐐫𐑉𐐻 𐐷𐐭, 𐑋𐐴 𐐺𐑉𐐯𐑄𐑉𐐯𐑌, 𐑄𐐰𐐻 𐐷 𐐼𐐨𐑌𐐴 𐑌𐐱𐐻 𐑄 𐑀𐐮𐑁𐐻𐑅 𐐱𐑂 𐐘𐐱𐐼, 𐑁𐐫𐑉 𐑄𐐩 𐐪𐑉 𐑋𐐯𐑌𐐨; 𐐰𐑌𐐼 𐑄𐐩 𐐿𐐲𐑋 𐑁𐑉𐐱𐑋 𐑄 𐑅𐐩𐑋 𐐘𐐱𐐼. 𐐈𐑌𐐼 𐑄𐐯𐑉 𐐪𐑉 𐐼𐐮𐑁𐐲𐑉𐐯𐑌𐐻 𐐶𐐩𐑆 𐑄𐐰𐐻 𐑄𐐨𐑆 𐑀𐐮𐑁𐐻𐑅 𐐪𐑉 𐐰𐐼𐑋𐐮𐑌𐐮𐑅𐐻𐐲𐑉𐐼; 𐐺𐐲𐐻 𐐮𐐻 𐐮𐑆 𐑄 𐑅𐐩𐑋 𐐘𐐱𐐼 𐐸𐐭 𐐶𐐲𐑉𐐿𐐯𐑃 𐐫𐑊 𐐮𐑌 𐐫𐑊; 𐐰𐑌𐐼 𐑄𐐩 𐐪𐑉 𐑀𐐮𐑂𐐯𐑌 𐐺𐐴 𐑄 𐑋𐐰𐑌𐐮𐑁𐐯𐑅𐐻𐐩𐑇𐐲𐑌𐑆 𐐱𐑂 𐑄 𐐝𐐹𐐮𐑉𐐮𐐻 𐐱𐑂 𐐘𐐱𐐼 𐐲𐑌𐐻𐐭 𐑋𐐯𐑌, 𐐻𐐭 𐐹𐑉𐐱𐑁𐐮𐐻 𐑄𐐯𐑋. 𐐙𐐫𐑉 𐐺𐐨𐐸𐐬𐑊𐐼, 𐐻𐐭 𐐶𐐲𐑌 𐐮𐑆 𐑀𐐮𐑂𐐯𐑌 𐐺𐐴 𐑄 𐐝𐐹𐐮𐑉𐐮𐐻 𐐱𐑂 𐐘𐐱𐐼, 𐑄𐐰𐐻 𐐸𐐨 𐑋𐐩 𐐻𐐨𐐽 𐑄 𐐶𐐲𐑉𐐼 𐐱𐑂 𐐶𐐮𐑆𐐼𐐲𐑋; 𐐰𐑌𐐼 𐐻𐐭 𐐰𐑌𐐲𐑄𐐲𐑉, 𐑄𐐰𐐻 𐐸𐐨 𐑋𐐩 𐐻𐐨𐐽 𐑄 𐐶𐐲𐑉𐐼 𐐱𐑂 𐑌𐐱𐑊𐐯𐐾 𐐺𐐴 𐑄 𐑅𐐩𐑋 𐐝𐐹𐐮𐑉𐐮𐐻; 𐐰𐑌𐐼 𐐻𐐭 𐐰𐑌𐐲𐑄𐐲𐑉, 𐐯𐐿𐑅𐐨𐐼𐐮𐑍𐑊𐐨 𐑀𐑉𐐩𐐻 𐑁𐐩𐑃; 𐐰𐑌𐐼 𐐻𐐭 𐐰𐑌𐐲𐑄𐐲𐑉, 𐑄 𐑀𐐮𐑁𐐻𐑅 𐐱𐑂 𐐸𐐨𐑊𐐮𐑍 𐐺𐐴 𐑄 𐑅𐐩𐑋 𐐝𐐹𐐮𐑉𐐮𐐻. 𐐈𐑌𐐼 𐐰𐑀𐐯𐑌, 𐐻𐐭 𐐰𐑌𐐲𐑄𐐲𐑉, 𐑄𐐰𐐻 𐐸𐐨 𐑋𐐩 𐐶𐐲𐑉𐐿 𐑋𐐴𐐻𐐨 𐑋𐐮𐑉𐐲𐐿𐑊𐑆; 𐐰𐑌𐐼 𐐰𐑀𐐯𐑌, 𐐻𐐭 𐐰𐑌𐐲𐑄𐐲𐑉, 𐑄𐐰𐐻 𐐸𐐨 𐑋𐐩 𐐹𐑉𐐱𐑁𐐯𐑅𐐴 𐐿𐐱𐑌𐑅𐐲𐑉𐑌𐐮𐑍 𐐫𐑊 𐑃𐐮𐑍𐑆; 𐐰𐑌𐐼 𐐰𐑀𐐯𐑌, 𐐻𐐭 𐐰𐑌𐐲𐑄𐐲𐑉, 𐑄 𐐺𐐨𐐸𐐬𐑊𐐼𐐮𐑍 𐐱𐑂 𐐩𐑌𐐾𐐯𐑊𐑆 𐐰𐑌𐐼 𐑋𐐮𐑌𐐮𐑅𐐻𐐲𐑉𐐮𐑍 𐑅𐐹𐐮𐑉𐐮𐐻𐑅; 𐐰𐑌𐐼 𐐰𐑀𐐯𐑌, 𐐻𐐭 𐐰𐑌𐐲𐑄𐐲𐑉, 𐐫𐑊 𐐿𐐴𐑌𐐼𐑆 𐐱𐑂 𐐻𐐲𐑍𐑆; 𐐰𐑌𐐼 𐐰𐑀𐐯𐑌, 𐐻𐐭 𐐰𐑌𐐲𐑄𐐲𐑉, 𐑄 𐐮𐑌𐐻𐐲𐑉𐐹𐑉𐐯𐐻𐐩𐑇𐐲𐑌 𐐱𐑂 𐑊𐐰𐑍𐑀𐐶𐐩𐐾𐐯𐑆 𐐰𐑌𐐼 𐐱𐑂 𐐼𐐴𐑂𐐲𐑉𐑆 𐐿𐐴𐑌𐐼𐑆 𐐱𐑂 𐐻𐐲𐑍𐑆. 𐐈𐑌𐐼 𐐫𐑊 𐑄𐐨𐑆 𐑀𐐮𐑁𐐻𐑅 𐐿𐐲𐑋 𐐺𐐴 𐑄 𐐝𐐹𐐮𐑉𐐮𐐻 𐐱𐑂 𐐗𐑉𐐴𐑅𐐻; 𐐰𐑌𐐼 𐑄𐐩 𐐿𐐲𐑋 𐐲𐑌𐐻𐐭 𐐯𐑂𐐲𐑉𐐨 𐑋𐐰𐑌 𐑅𐐯𐑂𐐲𐑉𐐲𐑊𐐨, 𐐰𐐿𐐫𐑉𐐼𐐮𐑍 𐐰𐑆 𐐸𐐨 𐐶𐐮𐑊. 𐐈𐑌𐐼 𐐌 𐐶𐐳𐐼 𐐯𐑀𐑆𐐫𐑉𐐻 𐐷𐐭, 𐑋𐐴 𐐺𐐨𐑊𐐲𐑂𐐯𐐼 𐐺𐑉𐐯𐑄𐑉𐐯𐑌, 𐑄𐐰𐐻 𐐷 𐑉𐐨𐑋𐐯𐑋𐐺𐐲𐑉 𐑄𐐰𐐻 𐐯𐑂𐐲𐑉𐐨 𐑀𐐳𐐼 𐑀𐐮𐑁𐐻 𐐿𐐲𐑋𐐯𐑃 𐐱𐑂 𐐗𐑉𐐴𐑅𐐻. 𐐈𐑌𐐼 𐐌 𐐶𐐳𐐼 𐐯𐑀𐑆𐐫𐑉𐐻 𐐷𐐭, 𐑋𐐴 𐐺𐐨𐑊𐐲𐑂𐐯𐐼 𐐺𐑉𐐯𐑄𐑉𐐯𐑌, 𐑄𐐰𐐻 𐐷 𐑉𐐨𐑋𐐯𐑋𐐺𐐲𐑉 𐑄𐐰𐐻 𐐸𐐨 𐐮𐑆 𐑄 𐑅𐐩𐑋 𐐷𐐯𐑅𐐻𐐲𐑉𐐼𐐩, 𐐻𐐭-𐐼𐐩, 𐐰𐑌𐐼 𐑁𐐫𐑉 𐐯𐑂𐐲𐑉, 𐐰𐑌𐐼 𐑄𐐰𐐻 𐐫𐑊 𐑄𐐨𐑆 𐑀𐐮𐑁𐐻𐑅 𐐱𐑂 𐐸𐐶𐐮𐐽 𐐌 𐐸𐐰𐑂 𐑅𐐹𐐬𐐿𐐯𐑌, 𐐸𐐶𐐮𐐽 𐐪𐑉 𐑅𐐹𐐮𐑉𐐮𐐻𐐷𐐭𐐲𐑊, 𐑌𐐯𐑂𐐲𐑉 𐐶𐐮𐑊 𐐺 𐐼𐐲𐑌 𐐰𐐶𐐩, 𐐨𐑂𐐯𐑌 𐐰𐑆 𐑊𐐱𐑍 𐐰𐑆 𐑄 𐐶𐐲𐑉𐑊𐐼 𐑇𐐰𐑊 𐑅𐐻𐐰𐑌𐐼, 𐐬𐑌𐑊𐐨 𐐰𐐿𐐫𐑉𐐼𐐮𐑍 𐐻𐐭 𐑄 𐐲𐑌𐐺𐐨𐑊𐐨𐑁 𐐱𐑂 𐑄 𐐽𐐮𐑊𐐼𐑉𐐯𐑌 𐐱𐑂 𐑋𐐯𐑌. 𐐎𐐸𐐯𐑉𐑁𐐬𐑉, 𐑄𐐯𐑉 𐑋𐐲𐑅𐐻 𐐺 𐑁𐐩𐑃; 𐐰𐑌𐐼 𐐮𐑁 𐑄𐐯𐑉 𐑋𐐲𐑅𐐻 𐐺 𐑁𐐩𐑃, 𐑄𐐯𐑉 𐑋𐐲𐑅𐐻 𐐫𐑊𐑅𐐬 𐐺 𐐸𐐬𐐹; 𐐰𐑌𐐼 𐐮𐑁 𐑄𐐯𐑉 𐑋𐐲𐑅𐐻 𐐺 𐐸𐐬𐐹, 𐑄𐐯𐑉 𐑋𐐲𐑅𐐻 𐐫𐑊𐑅𐐬 𐐺 𐐽𐐰𐑉𐐮𐐻𐐨; 𐐰𐑌𐐼 𐐯𐐿𐑅𐐯𐐹𐐻 𐐷 𐐸𐐰𐑂 𐐽𐐰𐑉𐐮𐐻𐐨, 𐐷 𐐿𐐰𐑌 𐐮𐑌 𐑌𐐬𐐶𐐴𐑆 𐐺 𐑅𐐩𐑂𐐼 𐐮𐑌 𐑄 𐐿𐐮𐑍𐐼𐐲𐑋 𐐱𐑂 𐐘𐐱𐐼; 𐑌𐐨𐑄𐐲𐑉 𐐿𐐰𐑌 𐐷 𐐺 𐑅𐐩𐑂𐐼 𐐮𐑌 𐑄 𐐿𐐮𐑍𐐼𐐲𐑋 𐐱𐑂 𐐘𐐱𐐼, 𐐮𐑁 𐐷 𐐸𐐰𐑂 𐑌𐐱𐐻 𐑁𐐩𐑃;

𐑌𐐨𐑄𐐲𐑉 𐐿𐐰𐑌 𐐷 𐐮𐑁 𐐷 𐐸𐐰𐑂 𐑌𐐬 𐐸𐐬𐐹; 𐐰𐑌𐐼 𐐮𐑁 𐐷 𐐸𐐰𐑂 𐑌𐐬 𐐸𐐬𐐹, 𐐷 𐑋𐐲𐑅𐐻 𐑌𐐨𐐼𐑆 𐐺 𐐮𐑌 𐐼𐐯𐑅𐐹𐐩𐑉; 𐐰𐑌𐐼 𐐼𐐯𐑅𐐹𐐩𐑉 𐐿𐐲𐑋𐐯𐑃 𐐺𐐨𐐿𐐫𐑆 𐐱𐑂 𐐮𐑌𐐮𐐿𐐶𐐮𐐻𐐨. 𐐈𐑌𐐼 𐐗𐑉𐐴𐑅𐐻 𐐻𐑉𐐭𐑊𐐨 𐑅𐐯𐐼 𐐲𐑌𐐻𐐭 𐐵𐑉 𐑁𐐪𐑄𐐲𐑉𐑆, 𐐮𐑁 𐐷 𐐸𐐰𐑂 𐑁𐐩𐑃, 𐐷 𐐿𐐰𐑌 𐐼𐐭 𐐫𐑊 𐑃𐐮𐑍𐑆 𐐸𐐶𐐮𐐽 𐐮𐑆 𐐯𐐿𐑅𐐹𐐨𐐼𐐨𐐯𐑌𐐻 𐐲𐑌𐐻𐐭 𐑋𐐨.

2. 𐐈𐑌𐐼 𐑌𐐵 𐐌 𐑅𐐹𐐨𐐿 𐐲𐑌𐐻𐐭 𐐫𐑊 𐑄 𐐯𐑌𐐼𐑆 𐐱𐑂 𐑄 𐐲𐑉𐑃, 𐑄𐐰𐐻 𐐮𐑁 𐑄 𐐼𐐩 𐐿𐐲𐑋𐐯𐑃 𐑄𐐰𐐻 𐑄 𐐹𐐵𐐲𐑉 𐐰𐑌𐐼 𐑀𐐮𐑁𐐻𐑅 𐐱𐑂 𐐘𐐱𐐼 𐑇𐐰𐑊 𐐺 𐐼𐐲𐑌 𐐰𐐶𐐩 𐐰𐑋𐐲𐑍 𐐷𐐭, 𐐮𐐻 𐑇𐐰𐑊 𐐺 𐐺𐐨𐐿𐐫𐑆 𐐱𐑂 𐐲𐑌𐐺𐐨𐑊𐐨𐑁. 𐐈𐑌𐐼 𐐶𐐬 𐐺 𐐲𐑌𐐻𐐭 𐑄 𐐽𐐮𐑊𐐼𐑉𐐯𐑌 𐐱𐑂 𐑋𐐯𐑌, 𐐮𐑁 𐑄𐐮𐑅 𐐺 𐑄 𐐿𐐩𐑅; 𐑁𐐫𐑉 𐑄𐐩𐑉 𐑇𐐰𐑊 𐐺 𐑌𐐲𐑌 𐑄𐐰𐐻 𐐼𐐭𐐯𐑃 𐑀𐐳𐐼 𐐰𐑋𐐲𐑍 𐐷𐐭, 𐑌𐐬 𐑌𐐱𐐻 𐐶𐐲𐑌. 𐐙𐐫𐑉 𐐮𐑁 𐑄𐐩𐑉 𐐺 𐐶𐐲𐑌 𐐰𐑋𐐲𐑍 𐐷𐐭 𐑄𐐰𐐻 𐐼𐐭𐐯𐑃 𐑀𐐳𐐼, 𐐸𐐨 𐑇𐐰𐑊 𐐶𐐲𐑉𐐿 𐐺𐐴 𐑄 𐐹𐐵𐐲𐑉 𐐰𐑌𐐼 𐑀𐐮𐑁𐐻𐑅 𐐱𐑂 𐐘𐐱𐐼. 𐐈𐑌𐐼 𐐶𐐬 𐐲𐑌𐐻𐐭 𐑄𐐯𐑋 𐐸𐐭 𐑇𐐰𐑊 𐐼𐐭 𐑄𐐨𐑆 𐑃𐐮𐑍𐑆 𐐰𐐶𐐩 𐐰𐑌𐐼 𐐼𐐴, 𐑁𐐫𐑉 𐑄𐐩 𐐼𐐴 𐐮𐑌 𐑄𐐩𐑉 𐑅𐐮𐑌𐑆, 𐐰𐑌𐐼 𐑄𐐩 𐐿𐐰𐑌𐐱𐐻 𐐺 𐑅𐐩𐑂𐐼 𐐮𐑌 𐑄 𐐿𐐮𐑍𐐼𐐲𐑋 𐐱𐑂 𐐘𐐱𐐼; 𐐰𐑌𐐼 𐐌 𐑅𐐹𐐨𐐿 𐐮𐐻 𐐰𐐿𐐫𐑉𐐼𐐮𐑍 𐐻𐐭 𐑄 𐐶𐐲𐑉𐐼𐑆 𐐱𐑂 𐐗𐑉𐐴𐑅𐐻, 𐐰𐑌𐐼 𐐌 𐑊𐐴 𐑌𐐱𐐻. 𐐈𐑌𐐼 𐐌 𐐯𐑀𐑆𐐫𐑉𐐻 𐐷𐐭 𐐻𐐭 𐑉𐐨𐑋𐐯𐑋𐐺𐐲𐑉 𐑄𐐨𐑆 𐑃𐐮𐑍𐑆; 𐑁𐐫𐑉 𐑄 𐐻𐐴𐑋 𐑅𐐹𐐨𐐼𐐮𐑊𐐨 𐐿𐐲𐑋𐐯𐑃 𐑄𐐰𐐻 𐐷 𐑇𐐰𐑊 𐑌𐐬 𐑄𐐰𐐻 𐐌 𐑊𐐴 𐑌𐐱𐐻, 𐑁𐐫𐑉 𐐷 𐑇𐐰𐑊 𐑅𐐨 𐑋𐐨 𐐰𐐻 𐑄 𐐺𐐪𐑉 𐐱𐑂 𐐘𐐱𐐼; 𐐰𐑌𐐼 𐑄 𐐢𐐫𐑉𐐼 𐐘𐐱𐐼 𐐶𐐮𐑊 𐑅𐐩 𐐲𐑌𐐻𐐭 𐐷𐐭, 𐐔𐐮𐐼 𐐌 𐑌𐐱𐐻 𐐼𐐯𐐿𐑊𐐩𐑉 𐑋𐐴 𐐶𐐲𐑉𐐼𐑆 𐐲𐑌𐐻𐐭 𐐷𐐭, 𐐸𐐶𐐮𐐽 𐐶𐐲𐑉 𐑉𐐮𐐻𐑌 𐐺𐐴 𐑄𐐮𐑅 𐑋𐐰𐑌, 𐑊𐐴𐐿 𐐰𐑆 𐐶𐐲𐑌 𐐿𐑉𐐴𐐮𐑍 𐑁𐑉𐐱𐑋 𐑄 𐐼𐐯𐐼? 𐐏𐐩, 𐐨𐑂𐐲𐑌 𐐰𐑆 𐐶𐐲𐑌 𐑅𐐹𐐨𐐿𐐮𐑍 𐐵𐐻 𐐱𐑂 𐑄 𐐼𐐲𐑅𐐻? 𐐌 𐐼𐐯𐐿𐑊𐐩𐑉 𐑄𐐨𐑆 𐑃𐐮𐑍𐑆 𐐲𐑌𐐻𐐭 𐑄 𐑁𐐳𐑊𐑁𐐮𐑊𐐮𐑍 𐐱𐑂 𐑄 𐐹𐑉𐐱𐑁𐐯𐑅𐐨𐑆. 𐐈𐑌𐐼 𐐺𐐨𐐸𐐬𐑊𐐼, 𐑄𐐩 𐑇𐐰𐑊 𐐹𐑉𐐬𐑅𐐨𐐼 𐑁𐐬𐑉𐑃 𐐵𐐻 𐐱𐑂 𐑄 𐑋𐐵𐑃 𐐱𐑂 𐑄 𐐯𐑂𐐲𐑉𐑊𐐰𐑅𐐻𐐮𐑍 𐐘𐐱𐐼; 𐐰𐑌𐐼 𐐸𐐮𐑆 𐐶𐐲𐑉𐐼 𐑇𐐰𐑊 𐐸𐐮𐑅 𐑁𐐬𐑉𐑃 𐑁𐑉𐐱𐑋 𐐾𐐯𐑌𐐲𐑉𐐩𐑇𐐲𐑌 𐐻𐐭 𐐾𐐯𐑌𐐲𐑉𐐩𐑇𐐲𐑌. 𐐈𐑌𐐼 𐐘𐐱𐐼 𐑇𐐰𐑊 𐑇𐐬 𐐲𐑌𐐻𐐭 𐐷𐐭, 𐑄𐐰𐐻 𐑄𐐰𐐻 𐐸𐐶𐐮𐐽 𐐌 𐐸𐐰𐑂 𐑉𐐮𐐻𐑌 𐐮𐑆 𐐻𐑉𐐭. 𐐈𐑌𐐼 𐐲𐑀𐐯𐑌 𐐌 𐐶𐐳𐐼 𐐯𐑀𐑆𐐫𐑉𐐻 𐐷𐐭, 𐑄𐐰𐐻 𐐷 𐐶𐐳𐐼 𐐿𐐲𐑋 𐐲𐑌𐐻𐐭 𐐗𐑉𐐴𐑅𐐻, 𐐰𐑌𐐼 𐑊𐐩 𐐸𐐬𐑊𐐼 𐐲𐐹𐐱𐑌 𐐯𐑂𐐲𐑉𐐨 𐑀𐐳𐐼 𐑀𐐮𐑁𐐻, 𐐰𐑌𐐼 𐐻𐐲𐐽 𐑌𐐱𐐻 𐑄 𐐨𐑂𐑊 𐑀𐐮𐑁𐐻, 𐑌𐐫𐑉 𐑄 𐐲𐑌𐐿𐑊𐐨𐑌 𐑃𐐮𐑍. 𐐈𐑌𐐼 𐐰𐐶𐐩𐐿, 𐐰𐑌𐐼 𐐰𐑉𐐴𐑆 𐑁𐑉𐐱𐑋 𐑄 𐐼𐐲𐑅𐐻, 𐐄 𐐖𐐭𐑉𐐭𐑅𐐲𐑊𐐯𐑋; 𐐷𐐩, 𐐰𐑌𐐼 𐐹𐐳𐐻 𐐱𐑌 𐑄𐐴 𐐺𐐷𐐭𐐻𐐨𐑁𐐳𐑊 𐑀𐐪𐑉𐑋𐐯𐑌𐐻𐑅, 𐐄 𐐼𐐫𐐻𐐲𐑉 𐐱𐑂 𐐞𐐴𐐲𐑌; 𐐰𐑌𐐼 𐑅𐐻𐑉𐐯𐑍𐑃𐐲𐑌 𐑄𐐴 𐑅𐐻𐐩𐐿𐑅 𐐰𐑌𐐼 𐐯𐑌𐑊𐐪𐑉𐐾 𐑄𐐴 𐐺𐐫𐑉𐐼𐐲𐑉𐑆 𐑁𐐫𐑉𐐯𐑂𐐲𐑉, 𐑄𐐰𐐻 𐑄𐐵 𐑋𐐩𐐯𐑅𐐻 𐑌𐐬 𐑋𐐬𐑉 𐐺 𐐿𐐱𐑌𐑁𐐵𐑌𐐼𐐯𐐼, 𐑄𐐰𐐻 𐑄 𐐿𐐲𐑂𐐯𐑌𐐰𐑌𐐻𐑅 𐐱𐑂 𐑄 𐐨𐐻𐐲𐑉𐑌𐐲𐑊 𐐙𐐪𐑄𐐲𐑉 𐐸𐐶𐐮𐐽 𐐸𐐨 𐐸𐐰𐑃 𐑋𐐩𐐼 𐐲𐑌𐐻𐐭 𐑄𐐨, 𐐄 𐐸𐐵𐑅 𐐱𐑂 𐐆𐑆𐑉𐐩𐐯𐑊, 𐑋𐐩 𐐺 𐑁𐐳𐑊𐑁𐐮𐑊𐐼. 𐐏𐐩, 𐐿𐐲𐑋 𐐲𐑌𐐻𐐭 𐐗𐑉𐐴𐑅𐐻, 𐐰𐑌𐐼 𐐺 𐐹𐐲𐑉𐑁𐐯𐐿𐐻𐐯𐐼 𐐮𐑌 𐐸𐐮𐑋, 𐐰𐑌𐐼 𐐼𐐨𐑌𐐴 𐐷𐐭𐑉𐑅𐐯𐑊𐑂𐑆 𐐱𐑂 𐐫𐑊 𐐲𐑌𐑀𐐱𐐼𐑊𐐨𐑌𐐯𐑅; 𐐰𐑌𐐼 𐐮𐑁 𐐷 𐑇𐐰𐑊 𐐼𐐨𐑌𐐴 𐐷𐐭𐑉𐑅𐐯𐑊𐑂𐑆 𐐱𐑂 𐐫𐑊 𐐲𐑌𐑀𐐱𐐼𐑊𐐨𐑌𐐯𐑅, 𐐰𐑌𐐼 𐑊𐐲𐑂 𐐘𐐱𐐼 𐐶𐐮𐑃 𐐫𐑊 𐐷𐐭𐑉 𐑋𐐴𐐻, 𐑋𐐴𐑌𐐼, 𐐰𐑌𐐼 𐑅𐐻𐑉𐐯𐑍𐑃, 𐑄𐐯𐑌 𐐮𐑆 𐐸𐐮𐑆 𐑀𐑉𐐩𐑅 𐑅𐐲𐑁𐐮𐑇𐐯𐑌𐐻 𐑁𐐫𐑉 𐐷𐐭, 𐑄𐐰𐐻 𐐺𐐴 𐐸𐐮𐑆 𐑀𐑉𐐩𐑅 𐐷 𐑋𐐩 𐐺 𐐹𐐲𐑉𐑁𐐯𐐿𐐻 𐐮𐑌 𐐗𐑉𐐴𐑅𐐻; 𐐰𐑌𐐼 𐐮𐑁 𐐺𐐴 𐑄 𐑀𐑉𐐩𐑅 𐐱𐑂 𐐘𐐱𐐼 𐐷 𐐪𐑉 𐐹𐐲𐑉𐑁𐐯𐐿𐐻 𐐮𐑌 𐐗𐑉𐐴𐑅𐐻, 𐐷 𐐿𐐰𐑌 𐐮𐑌 𐑌𐐬𐐶𐐴𐑆 𐐼𐐨𐑌𐐴 𐑄 𐐹𐐵𐐲𐑉 𐐱𐑂 𐐘𐐱𐐼. 𐐈𐑌𐐼 𐐲𐑀𐐯𐑌, 𐐮𐑁 𐐷 𐐺𐐴 𐑄 𐑀𐑉𐐩𐑅 𐐱𐑂 𐐘𐐱𐐼 𐐪𐑉 𐐹𐐲𐑉𐑁𐐯𐐿𐐻 𐐮𐑌 𐐗𐑉𐐴𐑅𐐻, 𐐰𐑌𐐼 𐐼𐐨𐑌𐐴 𐑌𐐱𐐻 𐐸𐐮𐑆 𐐹𐐵𐐲𐑉, 𐑄𐐯𐑌 𐐪𐑉 𐐷 𐑅𐐰𐑍𐐿𐐻𐐮𐑁𐐴𐐼 𐐮𐑌 𐐗𐑉𐐴𐑅𐐻 𐐺𐐴 𐑄 𐑀𐑉𐐩𐑅 𐐱𐑂 𐐘𐐱𐐼, 𐑃𐑉𐐭 𐑄 𐑇𐐯𐐼𐐮𐑍 𐐱𐑂 𐑄 𐐺𐑊𐐲𐐼 𐐱𐑂 𐐗𐑉𐐴𐑅𐐻, 𐐸𐐶𐐮𐐽 𐐮𐑆 𐐮𐑌 𐑄 𐐿𐐲𐑂𐐯𐑌𐐰𐑌𐐻 𐐱𐑂 𐑄 𐐙𐐪𐑄𐐲𐑉, 𐐲𐑌𐐻𐐭 𐑄 𐑉𐐨𐑋𐐮𐑇𐐲𐑌 𐐱𐑂 𐐷𐐭𐑉 𐑅𐐮𐑌𐑆, 𐑄𐐰𐐻 𐐷 𐐺𐐨𐐿𐐲𐑋 𐐸𐐬𐑊𐐨, 𐐶𐐮𐑄𐐵𐐻 𐑅𐐹𐐱𐐻. 𐐈𐑌𐐼 𐑌𐐵 𐐌 𐐺𐐮𐐼 𐐲𐑌𐐻𐐭 𐐫𐑊, 𐑁𐐯𐑉𐐶𐐯𐑊. 𐐌 𐑅𐐭𐑌 𐑀𐐬 𐐻𐐭 𐑉𐐯𐑅𐐻 𐐮𐑌 𐑄 𐐹𐐰𐑉𐐲𐐼𐐴𐑅 𐐱𐑂 𐐘𐐱𐐼, 𐐲𐑌𐐻𐐮𐑊 𐑋𐐴 𐑅𐐹𐐮𐑉𐐮𐐻 𐐰𐑌𐐼 𐐺𐐱𐐼𐐨 𐑇𐐰𐑊 𐐲𐑀𐐯𐑌 𐑉𐐨-𐐷𐐭𐑌𐐴𐐻, 𐐰𐑌𐐼 𐐌 𐐰𐑋 𐐺𐑉𐐫𐐻 𐑁𐐬𐑉𐑃 𐐻𐑉𐐴𐐲𐑋𐑁𐐰𐑌𐐻 𐑃𐑉𐐭 𐑄 𐐩𐑉, 𐐻𐐭 𐑋𐐨𐐻 𐐷𐐭 𐐺𐐨𐑁𐐬𐑉 𐑄 𐐹𐑊𐐨𐑆𐐮𐑍 𐐺𐐪𐑉 𐐱𐑂 𐑄 𐑀𐑉𐐩𐐻 𐐖𐐨𐐸𐐬𐑂𐐲, 𐑄 𐐨𐐻𐐲𐑉𐑌𐐲𐑊 𐐖𐐲𐐾 𐐱𐑂 𐐺𐐬𐑃 𐐿𐐶𐐮𐐿 𐐰𐑌𐐼 𐐼𐐯𐐼. 𐐁𐑋𐐯𐑌.

www.ingramcontent.com/pod-product-compliance
Lightning Source LLC
Chambersburg PA
CBHW022133300426
44115CB00006B/167
* 9 7 8 3 3 3 7 2 9 8 1 6 6 *